Baker's Biographical Dictionary of Musicians

SEVENTH EDITION

Baker's Biographical Dictionary of Musicians

SEVENTH EDITION

Revised by

Nicolas Slonimsky

SCHIRMER BOOKS
A Division of Macmillan, Inc.
NEW YORK

Collier Macmillan Publishers
LONDON

Schirmer Books
A Division of Macmillan, Inc.
866 Third Avenue, New York, N.Y. 10022

Collier Macmillan Canada, Inc.

Library of Congress Catalog Card Number: 84-5595

Printed in the United States of America

printing number
1 2 3 4 5 6 7 8 9 10

Library of Congress Cataloging in Publication Data

Baker, Theodore, 1851–1934.
  Baker's biographical dictionary of musicians.

  1. Music—Bio-bibliography. I. Slonimsky, Nicolas,
1894–   . II. Title. III. Title: Biographical
dictionary of musicians.
ML105.B16 1984 780′.92′2 [B] 84-5595
ISBN 0-02-870270-0

Preface to the Seventh Edition

This is the third time I preside over the changing fates of *Baker's Biographical Dictionary of Musicians:* the number would be five if I were to count the 1965 and 1971 Supplements between the regular 1958 and 1978 editions. Every time I approach my task I make a solemn vow to myself that this time over there will be no avoidable errors generated by a mysterious amblyopia, the cause of which may be hysteria, poisoning with ethyl or methyl alcohol, lead, arsenic, thallium, quinine, ergot, male fern, carbon disulfide, or *Cannabis indica* (the plant from which marijuana and hashish are derived). Green cucumbers! The cow jumped over the moon! I swore to myself in the paragraph on the Poltergeist in the preface to the 1978 edition of *Baker's* that I would exercise strict control over common dyslexia leading to the transposition of adjacent letters, such as occurs when "sacred music" is converted into "scared music." But lo and behold, there was "scared music" again on page 1866 in the 1978 edition on which I worked with such desperate dedication. Dyslexia is treacherous and elusive. I asked a couple of professional writers to read the sentence containing "scared music" and they sailed right through it, asking irrelevantly, "What's wrong? He did not compose any sacred music?"

In this edition I have determined to include a number of rock-'n'-roll musicians, crooners, songstresses, movie stars who occasionally sang, in fact, everyone with an operative larynx short of singing whales.

The most delicate part of my lexicographical pursuits is to determine who is alive and who has crossed the bar, to use Tennyson's poetic euphemism. I have in my possession a list of all the inmates of *Baker's Biographical Dictionary of Musicians* who were born in the nineteenth century (myself included) and who, according to actuarial tables, ought to be among the "stiffs," as I inelegantly call them. More than two hundred of them have already died on me since the 1978 publication of *Baker's*. The champion among the living as of the summer of 1984 is Paul Le Flem, who celebrated his 103rd anniversary on March 18, 1984. I hold my breath for his continued health out of grateful remembrance for his front-page write-ups in the Paris journal *Comoedia* of the concerts of American music I conducted in Paris in the summer of 1931. The trouble about the unknown dead is that not all of them rate an obituary in the public press. The only way the newspapers can be apprised of the demise of a notable musician (or artist, or writer, or actor) is for a relative or friend of the departed to inform a newspaper. The death of Hugo Leichtentritt, an estimable German-American scholar, is a case in point. He lectured at Harvard, and after his mandatory retirement lived in Cambridge with his nonagenarian mother. She kept a vigilant eye on his whereabouts. Once he ventured forth with a middle-aged woman student, who induced him to have dinner with her. His mother anxiously waited for him to return, and reprimanded him severely for going out unescorted. She soon died. One day Leichtentritt's sister, who also lived in Cambridge, phoned me and asked what to do with his manuscripts; I could not understand what she meant.

Preface to the Seventh Edition

"But Hugo is dead," she said. "I buried him on Tuesday. I have to get his belongings out of the apartment to avoid paying his rent next month." I said I would come right over. When I arrived at his place, his sister had already piled up his pitiful music manuscripts for further disposition. I noticed the score of his cello concerto, in which he had written, in German, "Herr Piatigorsky said he might perform it upon occasion." This *Gelegenheit* never came. Leichtentritt's sister grumbled something to the effect that he was not a composer but only a writer about other composers, and that his own compositions were of no importance. I said all manuscripts by scholarly musicians were of value, and volunteered to send them to the Library of Congress for safekeeping in perpetuity. They were gratefully accepted by Harold Spivacke, chairman of the Library's Music Division, who had studied with Leichtentritt in Berlin, and were deposited in a special collection in the Music Division, to be kept until the unlikely eventuality that some music historian would "discover" them. I notified the *Boston Herald* of Leichtentritt's death, and a belated obituary appeared under the caption "Noted Music Scholar Dies in Obscurity." I also sent a telegram to Olin Downes, the music editor of the *New York Times,* who knew and admired Leichtentritt. According to the rules of the obituary department of the *New York Times,* I had to submit some kind of official certification of his death or a statement from a member of the family, to avoid a possible error. (It had happened once that the *New York Times* published an obit of a living person.) In due time a compassionate notice appeared on the obituary page.

It is annoying to miss a ghost, but it is terrifying to bury someone who is still alive. The strangest case of such a premature burial is found in the 1928 edition of a memoir by Amy Fay, entitled *Music-Study in Germany.* In his preface to this edition, the eminent Oscar Sonneck remarked that almost all the people mentioned therein were dead, including the author herself. But Amy Fay was not dead at the time; she had only moved to a small town in Massachusetts, a locality that seemed to be the equivalent of a cemetery to people living in larger communities. She died on Feb. 28, 1928, and Sonneck himself died later that year, on Oct. 30, 1928. I inquired at the publisher whether she had collected any royalties in her incorporeal state, but was told that the information was restricted.

Shall I confess? In rushing into print my 1971 Supplement to *Baker's,* and eager to bring up to date the latest entombments, I caught sight of an obit in the *New York Times* of William John Mitchell, an American music pedagogue; he died in Binghamton, N.Y., on Aug. 17, 1971. I received the last page proofs of the 1971 Supplement in September of that year, and in haste jotted down the date under the entry on Donald Mitchell, a British musicologist who was just then transacting business with G. Schirmer, the publisher of *Baker's Dictionary,* and was commuting between London and New York. I could not believe my eyes when I received the published copy of the Supplement and saw that the date of death of W.J. Mitchell had got into the entry on Donald Mitchell. Trembling in fear, I tried to calm myself with the thought that it would be unlikely that Donald Mitchell himself would come across this item and discover himself dead. No balm in Gilead! Only days after the publication of the tainted little book, I received an anguished letter from Hans Heinsheimer, director of publications at

G. Schirmer, bristling with despairing question marks and exclamation points, addressed, "Not so dear Nicolas," and telling me that Donald Mitchell had just stormed into his office brandishing the dreadful book. He had never even been to Binghamton, he protested, so how could he have died there? This is one of those situations in which the more you try to explain the reasons for your predicament the deeper you sink into the ill-smelling mud of inconsistency. In desperation I wrote to the managing director of the firm telling him of what I had wrought, and begging him to eliminate the entire entry containing the hideous death notice, or else to blacken and cover utterly the single horripilating line. If the printer could not do it, would he hire a couple of menial helpers to ink out the mortuary reference manually? Only a couple of thousand copies of the 1971 Supplement were printed, and I volunteered to cover the expenses of the reparations. No, it could not be done; the books had already been sent out to retailers and music stores and could no longer be retrieved. Just as I was slowly recovering from my distress, a letter came from Donald Mitchell containing some up-to-date information about his newest publications, and mentioning ever so casually that he did not die in Binghamton, or any other place. A sense of gnawing guilt was instantly washed off the atrium and ventriculum of my heart, and I wrote Mitchell an impassioned letter hailing his spirit of Christian forgiveness. He replied that it was well worth it to endure a temporary (and, as it proved, a harmless) burial to have received such a "charming" letter from me.

The avenging Eumenides willed it that I myself became, retroactively, a victim of a premature entombment. Early in the 1960s the Philadelphia Orchestra program book quoted something I wrote on Shostakovich, prefixing my name with the adjective "late." Several of my friends were greatly alarmed and called me up to find out under what circumstances I had died. I immediately shot off a wire to the management of the Philadelphia Orchestra, protesting that I was late only in delivering my manuscripts to the publisher. In reply, I received a penitential letter from the orchestra's program book annotator, apologizing for his "stupid" mistake, but trying to deflect my discomfiture by saying that he was definitely under the impression that he had read about my demise in the papers. I wrote back, saying that he must have read about the actual decease of Lazare Saminsky, with whom I was often confused.

During recent years, a tendency has developed to add demeaning details to the lives of the great. To judge by some recently published scholia, it is essential for a composer of stature to have had syphilis. Of course, some of them did, but why should a respected music dictionary inject spirochetes and vibrions into Schubert's arteries? Even more fascinating for biographers is the discovery that a great composer was a victim of poison. The alleged murder of Mozart by Salieri still agitates playwrights and would-be Mozartologists. A variant of the Mozartocidal theories is that he was killed by the estranged husband of his alleged mistress. The tale is calculated to stir the blood of idle readers much more than a prosaic finding that Mozart had died of nephritis.

Suicides by famous musicians make equally attractive reading. In my preface to the 6th edition I covered the case of Tchaikovsky's Choleric Suicide, but now more is to be added. Rumors of Tchaikovsky's suicide sprouted in British and American journals almost immediately upon his death. Tchaikovsky was a notoriously melancholy genius, and once he really tried to end his difficult existence by walking into the cold waters of the Moskva River, but the chill was so unpleasant that he walked right back to shore. When he died of cholera in November of 1893, it was widely believed that he had deliberately drunk unboiled water in a restaurant during a raging cholera epidemic. Why would Tchaikovsky commit suicide? Imagination ran wild. Tchaikovsky had had a homosexual liaison with a member of the Romanov dynasty, it was said; Czar Alexander III found out about it and in his righteous wrath served notice on Tchaikovsky either to do away with himself or else stand trial, be disgraced, and undergo exile for life in Siberia. It is true that homosexuality was a statutory offense in old Russia, and it continued to be such under the Soviet regime. When subterranean gossip began to spread around the Moscow Conservatory, where Tchaikovsky was teaching, about some exotic sexual ways among faculty members, Tchaikovsky decided to end the nasty talk by marrying a rather stupid spinster. But on the wedding night she sat on his lap, and Tchaikovsky, repelled by such an unnatural (to him) contact, ran out of his apartment and walked the streets of Moscow in utter despair. He never faced his uncomprehending bride again, but he paid her substantial alimony from funds generously provided by his adoring but not very bright benefactress, Madame von Meck, whom Tchaikovsky was careful never to meet face to face. The first Russian mention of Tchaikovsky's pederasty appeared in the preface to the correspondence between Tchaikovsky and Madame von Meck, published in 1934; but Tchaikovsky was an idol of Russian musicians, and Soviet officials gave orders not to mention in print that he was what he was. A serial biography of Tchaikovsky that began publication in East Germany was quickly suppressed. But this Victorian prejudice did not apply to articles and books published outside Russia, and if anything, it whetted the appetite of writers in the West for more sensational stories. The most outrageous of them all, because it totally lacked any documentary evidence, was the one published in a small Russian periodical in America, authored by a Madame Orlova, who before emigration had worked in a music publishing house in Moscow. In her story, it was not a member of the Romanov dynasty who was involved with Tchaikovsky, but the nephew of a certain Russian nobleman. Outraged by the victimization of his young relative, the uncle threatened to report it to the Czar unless Tchaikovsky committed suicide. A court of honor was then set up by alumni of the law school which Tchaikovsky had attended as a youth, and he was sentenced to death by a unanimous decision of this incredible "court." A Czarist official gave Tchaikovsky some arsenic tablets, with instructions for use. Tchaikovsky's family doctor, Lev Bertenson, a highly esteemed physician, was also drawn into the conspiracy, according to the story. This was in striking contradiction to the known correspondence between Dr. Bertenson and Modest Tchaikovsky, Tchaikovsky's brother and biographer, detailing the course of Tchaikovsky's illness. But the crucial letter in which Dr. Bertenson offered his condolences to Modest Tchaikovsky had mysteriously disappeared from the archives at the Klin Museum, or so asserted one of the champions of Madame Orlova's theories. This was a surprise to me, for I had copied the letter in question during my visit at Klin in 1935, and published it, in an English translation, in Herbert Weinstock's biography of Tchaikovsky. Cholera epidemics in St. Petersburg were frequent and deadly. Tchaikovsky's mother had died of cholera. Tchaikovsky's body was allowed to lie in state, and friends reverentially kissed him on the mouth, as was the common Slavic custom. Had Tchaikovsky died of cholera, would they not have risked contamination? Not so; cholera could be transmitted only by the ingestion of contaminated food or water, not by contact with the body of one of the victims. Chekhov, the famous Russian writer who served as a medical inspector during the cholera epidemic that carried off Tchaikovsky, makes no mention in his reports of such a danger. The sources of Madame Orlova's story would hardly stand in court. A certain person told her in 1966 that he had heard it in 1913 from a woman who heard it in turn from her husband, who died in 1902. This is certainly an extraordinary way of building up the chain of evidence, without a single piece of paper to substantiate it.

Dealing with people and their inevitable frailties is often a problem of morality, compassion, and decent respect for personal privacy. But in retelling a person's life one cannot omit essential facts. So when Liberace's chauffeur and constant companion sued him for $379,000,000 for abandonment, and the story made the front page of that scrupulously informative publication, *The National Enquirer*, one could not ignore it simply because of its scabrous connotations. And what a strange sum to ask in payment for dissolution of employment! Why not a round sum, like $400,000,000? Anyway, the plaintiff lost his suit and was left to make do with just a house, a car, and some petty cash in five figures granted oh, so liberally by Liberace before the break.

A delicate problem confronted me in putting together a biographical sketch on the electronic composer Walter Carlos, who on St. Valentine's Day of 1971 had surgery performed in which his natural male organ was everted to form a respectable receptive vagina, and thereby became Wendy Carlos. He recounted his transformation in full anatomical detail in an interview with *Playboy* magazine. I listed him/her as Carlos, Wendy (née Walter). In my preface to the 6th edition of *Baker's* I had already cited other curious biological phenomena, such as the elopement of the castrato Tenducci with a young English girl who bore him a child (he was a triorchis).

Such human stories are always welcome to the prurient palate, but the fundamental duty of any self-doubting lexicographer is to make sure that hard facts are accurately reported, and this requirement applies especially to the dates of birth and death. Copying data from other dictionaries would be a case of *petitio principii*, considering that editors and publishers of supposedly immaculate lexica must know deep in their heart's ventricula and their brain's sulci, or wherever conscience resides in their mortal frames, that when these facts come ostensibly from the horse's mouth, they may in reality originate at the other end of the horse. For years, Riemann's *Musik-Lexikon* was my "freeman's music-lexicon"; I put total faith in its Supplements. When it said "nicht," canceling a date as it appeared in the basic volume, I accepted the negation absolutely. Thus, when the Riemann Supplement said "nicht" to Cherubini's date of death, March 15, 1842, and replaced it with March 13, I corrected my correct date as it appeared in *Baker 5*, and replaced it with the incorrect correction in *Baker 6*, only to be assailed by a chorus of private correctors telling me that the Riemann correction was all wet. Unbelieving, I wrote to the registry of deaths in Paris, asking for Cherubini's death certificate. Blessed be the Catholic countries and their public servants, who since Napoleonic times discharge their services free to anyone! By return airmail (they did not even charge me for the *timbres-poste*!) I got a photocopy of Cherubini's death certificate, stating that he expired on March 15, not March 13, 1842, thus confirming my *Baker 5* date, confounding my *Baker 6* date, and enabling me to restore the correct *Baker 5* date in the present *Baker 7*. Now that my faith in Riemann's Supplement has been so rudely shaken, I have begun questioning every "nichting" in it, which means more work. But, normal, intelligent people may ask, who the hell cares? Well, nobody except a small band of benighted chronologists who are determined to put things straight.

   Some facts, reports, or accepted interpretations of musical events that took place, or did not take place, according to the fancy of a particular historian, are obviously impossible to verify. What was the origin of the British custom of standing up when the strains of the Hallelujah Chorus ring out at the close of Part II of Handel's *Messiah*? Seems that George II was so moved when he heard it at the first London performance in Covent Garden Theatre on March 23, 1743, that he stood up; the audience followed suit, and by so doing established a British custom. Another interpretation, amounting to a *lèse majesté*, is that George II was seized with an irrepressible itch in his buttocks, and had to get up to put his hand inside his breeches to scratch.

   Beethoven specifically denied having said "Thus fate knocks at my door" with reference to the opening notes of the Fifth Symphony, but the quotation lingers in the corridors of music history. One of my favorite stories about Rossini deals with the project of his *concitoyens* of Pesaro to erect a statue for him while he was still living. They had raised enough money to build the pedestal but they needed 10,000 francs for the statue itself, so they put it up to Rossini. "Ten thousand francs!" Rossini was supposed to have exclaimed. "For 10,000 francs I will stand on the pedestal myself." *Se non è vero è ben trovato*.

   Historic facts are by necessity historians' facts, for we know about them from reports by historians. Did Caesar really exclaim "Et tu Brute" when he was stabbed by his friend? Shakespeare was right in his use of ungrammatical double superlatives, saying that it was "the most unkindest cut of all." Great men often quote themselves in their memoirs for self-aggrandizement. Did Napoleon really deliver that famous phrase, on seeing the Egyptian pyramids, that forty centuries looked down upon his soldiers? Goethe did say "mehr Licht" before he died, a phrase that has been elevated to a philosophical profundity, but some of those present thought he merely asked that the window blinds be raised to let more light into the room. The most famous words of recorded history may have never been uttered, or if they were, their meaning might have been unremarkable.

   Titles of famous musical compositions are often nicknames generated by popular usage or created by publishers for the sake of promotion. *Moonlight Sonata* was merely *Sonata quasi una fantasia*. God only knows who gave the name *Em-*

peror Concerto to Beethoven's Piano Concerto in E-flat. *Appassionata Sonata* fits the music but Beethoven never called it so. Chopin had a batch of unwarranted sobriquets for many of his works. The *Raindrop Prelude* may have been written while rain was falling rhythmically on the roof of the monastery of Valldemosa, but Chopin denied this connection. Then there is the *Minute Waltz*, which can be played in sixty seconds only by omitting repeats. Handel never heard any blacksmith whistle the tune he incorporated in one of his harpsichord suites, but the title *The Harmonious Blacksmith*, spontaneously generated more than a hundred years after its composition, can no longer be removed from hundreds of published editions of the piece. Haydn holds the record of nicknamed compositions. The most notorious is the *Farewell Symphony*, in which one player after another departs from the scene, leaving the conductor to wield his baton before a nonexistent orchestra. According to the common accounts in music dictionaries, Haydn's intention was to indicate to his employer, Prince Esterházy, that his musicians needed a vacation, but the more plausible explanation is that the Prince planned to disband the orchestra and that Haydn tried to move his heart by his clever stage play. At least a dozen of Haydn's string quartets have acquired a nickname. Of Mendelssohn's *Songs without Words*, only a couple or so have authentic titles. And whoever thought of calling Mozart's great C major Symphony the *Jupiter Symphony*? The name apparently first emerged in England. Spurious as many of these titles may be, it is the duty of a conscientious lexicographer to list them, in quotation marks or in italics, according to typographical preference.

In my preface to the 6th edition I sang paeans, dithyrambs, hosannahs, and hallelujahs to Steve Ellis, who corrected oodles of stupid errors that infested the previous edition of my ailing dictionary. And I paid tribute to the dogged determination of Samuel Sprince in tracking down solitary deaths of *Baker's* musicians who never made it into the public press. After the publication of the 6th edition of *Baker's*, Ellis continued to supply me with up-to-date lists of works by composers of so-called third-world countries, and whenever the sad occasion required it, their dates of death. I joyfully added all this information to the present edition.

A few months after the publication of the 6th edition of *Baker's* in 1978, I received a letter from one Dennis McIntire of Indianapolis, asking my forbearance for his intrusion upon my busy time. His justification for addressing me frontally was his concern about the omission in my tome of a number of reputable contemporary singers, conductors, violinists, and pianists. Would I have time to answer his queries? I jumped from my seat at the very thought that I might not be interested, and replied in an exclamatory affirmative. During one of my transcontinental travels I stopped over in Indianapolis to meet McIntire. Age: 35; glasses. Profession: college instructor in cultural history and literature. Avocation: voracious, ferocious reading. Passion: listening to recordings from his own immense collection of phonograph albums. Knowledge about composers and performers, dead and living: unbounded. We cemented a firm intellectual and personal friendship. I invited him to visit me in Los Angeles; he stayed with me for a week, and spent most of his time examining my card file that I had collected

Preface to the Seventh Edition

in anticipation of the birth of the 7th edition of *Baker's*, yet in limbo, picking up errors and pointing out inadequacies, right out of his head. Ever since, we maintained a voluminous correspondence, if that is the term to describe the constant flow of information arriving from him in a steady stream on neatly typed single-spaced sheets, while I could reciprocate only by acknowledging receipt in florid terms of wonderment at his erudition and his investigative skill in finding out things. Altogether he sent me 1,425 new articles, including many rewrites of the old entries.

It has ever been my notion that people who know most about composers and performers are not professional musicians, while venerable academics whose names stand for musicological greatness know their Mozart and Beethoven, their Handel and Haydn, their Brahms and Bruckner, their Schubert and Schumann, but are utterly ignorant of the lesser breed who populate biographical dictionaries of musicians. As if to confirm my contention, I found, to my absolute astonishment and delight, that Dennis McIntire did not compose music, could not even read music, and did not play an instrument. Yet he possessed a fine discrimination as to the absolute value of musical compositions and the relative artistry of performers, and is the author of numerous articles in music journals.

I must be lucky. On top of the galactic immensities of McIntire's contribution, I received a communication from Mike Keyton, a mathematician (a specialist in advanced calculus) from Dallas, Texas, who was also a reader of *Baker's*. He, too, scrutinized it carefully, weeding out discrepancies, logical hiatuses, vacuities, and various puzzlements. He, too, was a rabid record collector, and he had access to obscure newsletters and dealers' catalogues containing information not obtainable in general reference works. He was writing a doctoral dissertation on Euler, the famous mathematician who also was a musician of sorts, and whose name I had in *Baker's*. Sure enough, he found that the date of Euler's death in *Baker's* was a month off, which was a shame, since Euler had spent many years in Russia and died in the capital city of St. Petersburg where I was born 111 years later. Knowing my interest in mathematical puzzles, Mike sent me some good ones. We exchanged comments on such abstruse subjects as the sieve of Eratosthenes, the Greek who devised an early trick of fishing out prime numbers. Mike arranged for me to give a series of lectures, some of them on nonmusical subjects, in schools where he taught. Unafraid of tackling enormous tasks, he proceeded to systematically check *Baker's* dates vs. the dates in the formidable multivolume *New Grove*. The *New Grove* had me down on some British biographies, but I had some winning points too, which filled me with justifiable pride. Some time later Mike came to visit me in Los Angeles, and we had a wonderful time together. Contrary to all expectations, he not only could read music but could actually compose some, not without a measure of modernistic fioriture.

The number of people who seemed to take a masochistic pleasure in scanning the thousands of entries in *Baker 6* in search of inconsistencies, self-contradictions, imbecilities, inanities, and plain idiocies, was augmented by an accession from England, in the person of a schoolteacher named David Cummings. True to form among musicographical volunteers, he could not read music, but by God, he knew more about musicians than most editors of special dictionaries, myself included. The wonderful thing about him was that he was willing and able to collect detailed information on contemporary British composers, including the exact dates of first performance of their major works. He seemed to be surprised that I was so glad to receive his addenda atque corrigenda, and said that most music editors regarded him as a nuisance. I assured him that such was not the case with me. So herewith I extend to David Cummings my hand in lexicographical friendship across the sea.

In handling the materials which I received first from Ellis and then in an even greater abundance from McIntire, I faced a case of conscience: to what extent should I acknowledge their contributions? There was no problem about the lists of works that I received from them; there can be no individual authorship attached to such compilations. But what about the biographical sections? Well, in practically all cases, I revised them radically, imparting to the text, for better or for worse, my inimitable touch; whether I ruined their original by such wholesale substitution is beside the point. *Le style c'est l'homme*, and I surely injected my verbiage into the text without stint. No one, I hope, can dissect the final product so as to discover stylistic, grammatical, or syntactic elements existing before my intervention. *Dixi et animam levavi.*

The help I received from these friends and correspondents is not all. In addition, Ellis, McIntire, and myself were the recipients of priceless information from countless librarians, curators, orchestral managers, opera directors, and individual musicologists from all parts of the world. Russian musicians have been amazingly cooperative. I recall with sadness and gratitude the various bits of information I received from my dear late friend Gregory Schneerson; Boris Steinpress, the author of an invaluable book on operatic premieres, helped me enormously to establish exact dates of performances of works by Soviet composers. And the Union of Soviet Composers itself sent me all kinds of informative material. In Russia they publish monographs about their composers; my nephew Sergei Slonimsky already had a rather solid book on him published in Moscow long before he reached the status of bona fide celebrity (if he has reached it now).

All those wonderful contributions from far and wide would amount to naught if they were messed up by copyists and proofreaders. During the last year of my travail I had the extraordinary luck of securing the services of the sweetest 28-year-old lady who ever belied the common belief that good-looking girls are necessarily dumb. And to add to my lucky find, she is bilingual in English and German, unafraid of Umlauts, and attacking sesquipedalian compound Teutonic nouns with hardly a blink of the eye. She claims that she actually enjoys doing lexicographical work. But she has one serious defect: unwarranted shyness. So her name will have to be noted here in the form of a Krebsgang: M.M. Elk Anid. Here M.M. may stand for Music Major, which in fact she is.

Effusive credit is to be given to the splendiferous Laura Kuhn, who lent me spiritual succor in the lamentable state of my mental exhaustion by illuminating scholiums to adorn my rather sciolistic pages. Thanks, Laura.

Last but not least. I am perilously short of laudatory participles or exalting gerunds to describe the editorial assistance I received from Sylvia Juran,

Preface to the Seventh Edition

charged by my publishers to exercise vigilance over the factual contents of the multitudinous entries in the present volume, to watch over grammatical and syntactical propriety, and to weed out insidious solecisms. For these tasks she is admirably equipped. She is a linguist, with expertise not only in the "usual" Roman and Teutonic languages but also in Russian and Polish, and fully versed in the bewildering variety of diacritical signs occurring in the titles of musical works and bibliographic items in such exotic idioms. She sent me hundreds of queries, couched with a compassionate regard for my sensitivity, never correcting my recurring inanities and gross incongruities with blunt remonstrances but invariably using gentle question marks even in the most obvious cases of my embarrassing delinquencies. As Shakespeare said, and Schubert sang, "Who is Sylvia? what is she...that she might admired be."

The following individuals and institutions have lent their most valuable assistance in preparing the present edition of *Baker's:*

Steven Aechternacht, Artistic Director, Houston Symphony Orchestra
Dr. William W. Austin, Professor of Music, Cornell University, Ithaca, New York
Australia Music Centre, Sydney
Antony Beaumont, Cologne
Christopher Bishop, Managing Director, Philharmonic Orchestra, London
Stanislaw Bromilski, Head of the Music Department, Polska Agencja Artystyczna, Warsaw
Robert L. Brubaker, Curator of Special Collections, Chicago Historical Society
Canadian Music Centre, Toronto
Charles Collett, formerly of the British Broadcasting Corporation, London
Columbia Artists Management, Inc., New York
Christopher Dyment, London
John S. Edwards, General Manager, Chicago Symphony Orchestra
Richard D. Freed, Baltimore
Dr. Robert Freeman, Director, Eastman School of Music, Rochester, New York
Prof. Raymond Gallois-Montbrun, Director, Conservatoire National Supérieur de Musique, Paris
Dr. Karl Geiringer, Santa Barbara, California
Dr. Peter Girth, Intendant, Berlin Philharmonic Orchestra
Dr. phil. habil. Dieter Härtwig, Deputy Artistic Director, Dresden Philharmonic Orchestra
Vigdis Hauge, Norsk Musikkinformasjon, Oslo
Gisela Huwe, Press Office, Berlin Philharmonic Orchestra
Indianapolis–Marion County Public Library, Central Library Arts Division Staff: Dan Gann, Head; Virginia Andis, Sue Chapman, Claire Connor, Eileen Dolan-Heitlinger, Madge Engle, Nancy Norcross Gootee, Gwen Harden, Kathy Read, and Ophelia Georgiev Roop
Gunnar Arne Jensen, Artist and Concert Manager, Sveriges Riksradio, Stockholm

Arthur Kaplan, Public Relations Department, San Francisco Opera

Dr. János Kárpáti, Chief Librarian, Franz Liszt Academy of Music, Budapest

Koninklijke Nederlandse Toonkunstenaars-Vereniging, Amsterdam

Steven Ledbetter, Director of Publications, Boston Symphony Orchestra

Sir Anthony Lewis, formerly Principal, Royal Academy of Music, London

Per Olof Lundahl, STIMs Informationscentral för Svensk Musik, Stockholm

Dr. Hugh Macdonald, Gardiner Professor of Music, University of Glasgow

Dr. Vasco Mariz, Rio de Janeiro

Erich Mauermann, Bayerischer Rundfunk, Munich

Archives Office, Metropolitan Opera, New York

Inge Müller, Danmarks Radio, Copenhagen

Jack Murphy, Archives Office, New York Philharmonic Orchestra

Kären Nagy, Head Reference Librarian at Northwestern University and compiler of the "Index to Music Necrology" for *Notes*

Archie Newman, Head of Press and Public Relations, Royal Philharmonic Orchestra, London

Danny Newman, Lyric Opera of Chicago

Mimi O'Malley, Office of the Executive Director, Philadelphia Orchestra

Donald E. Osborne, Mariedi Anders Artists Management, Inc., San Francisco

Dr. Jiří Pauer, Head, Prague National Theater Opera

Prof. Samuel F. Pogue, College-Conservatory of Music, University of Cincinnati

Dr. Jack W. Porter, Executive Director, The Jussi Bjoerling Memorial Archive, Indianapolis

Ida Poulsen, Librarian, Det Kongelige Teater, Copenhagen

Harold Rosenthal, Editor, *Opera*, London

Klaus G. Roy, Director of Publications, Cleveland Orchestra

Royal Opera House, Covent Garden, London

Hans-Hubert Schönzeler, London

Desmond Shawe-Taylor, Music Critic, *Sunday Times*, London

Wayne D. Shirley, Reference Librarian, The Library of Congress, Washington, D.C.

Jeanne Siegel, Office of the President, The Juilliard School of Music, New York

Maynard Solomon, New York

Dr. Hella Somogyi, Hochschule für Musik und Darstellende Kunst, Vienna

Eberhard Steindorf, Konzertdramaturg, Dresden State Opera and Orchestra

Dr. H.H. Stuckenschmidt, Berlin

Dr. Benjamin Suchoff, New York Bartók Archive

Teatro alla Scala, Milan

Dr. Hans Tischler, Professor of Musicology, School of Music, Indiana University, Bloomington

Peter Tracton, Publicity Director, ICM Artists, Ltd., New York

Yvonne K. Unrath, Alumni Liaison Officer, The Curtis Institute of Music, Philadelphia

Sjoerd G.A.M. van den Berg, Public Relations Officer, Concertgebouw Orchestra, Amsterdam

Preface to the Seventh Edition

Leon Van Dyke, Maxim Gershunoff, Inc., New York

Anna Van Steenbergen, Secretary General, Centre Belge de Documentation Musicale, Brussels

Prof. Bálint Vázsonyi, School of Music, Indiana University, Bloomington

Paul Vetricek, Vienna State Opera

Willem Vos, Artistic Advisor, Rotterdam Philharmonic Orchestra

Dr. Charles H. Webb, Dean, School of Music, Indiana University, Bloomington

Dr. Joachim E. Wenzel, formerly Archivist, Hamburg State Opera

Special acknowledgment must be accorded the following individuals:

Dr. Stanley Sadie, editor in chief of *The New Grove Dictionary of Music and Musicians* and editor of the *Musical Times*. Dr. Sadie, as well as Susan Feder, editorial coordinator of the forthcoming *New Grove Dictionary of Music in the United States*, was most unselfish in allowing updated material in their files to be utilized in *Baker 7*. In return, corrections and revisions were duly sent to *The New Grove* editors in London and New York for their future use.

Dr. Kurt Oehl, professor of the Johannes Gutenberg University in Mainz and one of the editors of the Riemann *Musik-Lexikon*. Throughout the period *Baker 7* was in preparation, Dr. Oehl shared a vast amount of material in his files for use in the new edition.

Brigitta Grabner, secretary, Vienna Philharmonic Orchestra. Thanks to her, dates of tenure for the various conductors of the Vienna Philharmonic Orchestra have been verified, world premieres confirmed, etc. Her willingness to provide all the program lists of the subscription series from the founding of the orchestra in 1842 was extraordinary.

R. Michael Fling, reference librarian, The Music Library, Indiana University, Bloomington. A great debt is owed to Fling for his patience and perseverance in answering every query sent to him.

David Cummings, Wembley, Middlesex, England

Stephen W. Ellis, Glenview, Illinois

Nicolas Slonimsky
El Pueblo de Nuestra Señora la Reina
    de Los Angeles
September 1984

Preface to the Sixth Edition

If I were to write an autobiography (which God forbid!) I would call it *I am a footnote*, or *I am a parenthesis*. I am a footnote in the entry on Carl Maria von Weber in the Fifth Edition of *Grove's Dictionary* and a parenthesis in the article on Lully in *Die Musik in Geschichte und Gegenwart*. And I am a paragraph in the Fifteenth Edition of the *Encyclopaedia Britannica* under Pandiatonicism, which is my polysyllabic brainchild.

Dr. Samuel Johnson defines a lexicographer in his famous dictionary as "a harmless drudge." Harmless? Not necessarily. In fact, lexicography, when practiced in excess, may well be harmful to the lexicographer's psyche. Consider the melancholy case of John Wall Callcott (1766–1821) as related in *Baker's Biographical Dictionary of Musicians:* "His mind gave way from overwork on a projected biographical dictionary of musicians,... He recovered, but not sufficiently to continue his work." Callcott reached the letter Q, associated with such disturbing images as queer, quaquaversal, and quagmire, and then quit.

One of my predecessors in editing *Baker's* jotted down these words in the margin of the galley proofs: "I will go mad if I have to continue this for a long time." Another music editor, working on another dictionary, deliberately rented a room on the ground floor lest he should be tempted to jump out the window in despair over the contents of the book.

Although most of my friends regard me as an eccentric, I am not given to suicidal impulses while working on a dictionary. But I am rather paranoiac in my suspicions about melodrama, except in opera librettos. I never believed that Salieri poisoned Mozart, even though I memorized, as part of my school assignments in St. Petersburg, Salieri's monologue in Pushkin's play *Mozart and Salieri*, in which Salieri explains his reason for poisoning Mozart lest his blazing genius should eclipse the work of such humble votaries in the divine art of harmony as himself. In another tale of Mozart, I became suspicious of the reports in practically every reference work and every biography that a fierce snowstorm was raging in Vienna on the day of his funeral in December 1791, which made it impossible for his friends to follow his body to the cemetery (the snowballs were as large as tennis balls, the top Vienna Mozartologist, Erich Schenk, asserts). Why wasn't this meteorological phenomenon as much as mentioned in early Mozart biographies? It would have at least explained why Mozart's widow did not attend the funeral, if not her failure to pay dues for keeping Mozart's grave in perpetuity, which was the reason why he was eventually moved to the place of common burial. The snowstorm episode appears for the first time in Otto Jahn's monumental biography of Mozart, and the only source to substantiate it was an anonymous article published in a Vienna newspaper on the occasion of Mozart's centennial in 1856. Some Mozartologists identified the writer (who signed his report as "a man of the people") as the bartender of Mozart's favorite Vienna tavern, although by the time of Mozart's centennial he himself, if still living, would have been about a hundred years old. To resolve my puzzlement, I wrote to the Vienna Weather Bureau for a report on the climatic conditions on that December day in 1791. Great was my malicious sense of gratification when I received a report that the temperature on that day was well above freezing and that a gentle Zephyr wind blew from the West. No snowballs. No frigid weather which frightened away Mozart's friends. No melodrama, except the tragedy of Mozart's death so young. Encouraged by the prompt response of the Vienna Weather Bureau (which had kept records for more than two centuries), I inquired about another melodramatic episode: an electric storm on the afternoon of Beethoven's death. Yes, there was an electric storm, even though it was hardly likely that Beethoven in his debilitated physical condition could have lifted his clenched first toward heaven in a gesture of defiance of *Jupiter tonans*.

Not every melodramatic report is necessarily a pabulum for the gullible. I became incredulous of the tale told in *Baker's* about the French singer Alexandre Taskin, who reportedly displayed an untenorlike bravery during a conflagration at the Opéra-Comique in Paris on the night of May 25, 1887, when he sang in *Mignon*. The lives of hundreds of panic-stricken opera-goers were supposedly saved thanks to his *sang-froid*. Well, it turns out that there was a rather horrendous fire at the Opéra-Comique on that night, and that "le beau Taskin," as he was known to his admirers, did display courage in calming down the audience, and was commended for it by the French government.

I was smugly confident of the accuracy of the report that the Italian conductor Gino Marinuzzi was assassinated by the anti-Fascist partisans in Milan on August 17, 1945, as duly noted in *Baker's*, and also in *Grove*, in Riemann's *Musik-Lexikon* ("ermordet") and in the Italian encyclopedia *La Musica* ("mori assassinato"). But why did the anti-Fascist partisans wait so long after the end of the Mussolini regime to shoot him? True, he was the author of a triumphal ode on the occasion of the historic meeting between Hitler and Mussolini in an Alpine tunnel, but many other Italian composers expressed a similar lack of precognition in glorifying the Fascist regime. I received many letters from Italian composers during the Fascist years, dated E.F. XV, E.F. XVIII, etc., i.e., Era Fascista followed by the year, in Roman numerals, since Mussolini's march on Rome ("tough on Jesus Christ," a witty Bostonian remarked when I showed him these letters), and they remained unscathed. However that might be, the publishers of *Baker's* received an irate letter from a Milan lawyer, acting on behalf of the Marinuzzi family, protesting that the account of the assassination was false and demanding an immediate rectification. Gino Marinuzzi, the letter said, died peacefully in a Milan hospital on the date correctly given in *Baker's*, succumbing not to a bullet wound but to hepatic anemia. Fortunately, *Baker's* VI was still in a fluid state, and the publishers were able to pacify the Marinuzzi family lawyer, promising to make a correction. But why did the Marinuzzis wait all these years to fire their salvo, and why zero in on *Baker's* rather than on their own Italian dictionaries? And where did the original report of assassination come from? The *Corriere della Sera*, Milan's major newspaper, carried an *R.I.P.* notice of Marinuzzi's death, with no mention of the cause. The case was clinched eventually by the Servizio Mortuario of the city of Milan, stating that Marinuzzi had indeed died of acute atrophy of the liver. No bullets, no assassination, no melodrama.

Beware of false suspicions! Could two musicians with identical last names (except for a nobiliary particle), Victor Alessandro of Texas and Raffaele d'Allesandro of Switzerland, have died on their respective, albeit mutually different, birthdays? They could, and they did. Could Raselius have written a book on Roselius? He could, and he did. Could Gabriel Faure (no accent) have written a monograph on Gabriel Fauré (accent)? He could and he did. Was Schubart really the author of the words of *Die Forelle* by Schubert? Yes, he was. Could two composers, each named Victor Young, have been active in the movies in Hollywood during the same period? They were. Could I myself have had a classmate, in a St. Petersburg high school, called Nicolas Slonimsky? I had, and since I joined the class after him, my name was registered as Nicolas II, which was the official name of the then reigning Czar of all the Russians.

Among the many persistent errors plaguing musical biography is the belief that Wagner originated the term *Leitmotiv*. He did not; it was first proposed by Friedrich Wilhelm Jähns in the preface to his book on Weber published in 1871. Bizet did not write the famous *Habanera* in *Carmen*. He took it from a collection of Spanish songs by Sebastián Yradier, without any alteration of key, harmonization, tempo, rhythm, and dynamics.

The Russians have a marvelously expressive word for a story unsupported by evidence—"nyebylitsa," an "un-was-ity." Famous last words by historic personages are almost all such un-was-ities. Madame Roland's exclamation on her way to the guillotine, "Liberty, how many crimes are committed in thy name!" first appeared in print in Lamartine's *Histoire de la Révolution française*, or so it is cited in *Bartlett's Familiar Quotations*. But browsing through the 1793 volume of *The Annual Register* of London, I came upon a Paris dispatch quoting the famous phrase. Is one to suppose then the the British Paris correspondent actually followed the tumbril taking Madame Roland to the place of execution and actually heard her utter the famous apostrophe? Not bloody likely.

"Lexicographis secundus post Herculem labor" was the judgment pronounced by Joseph Justus Scaliger (1540–1609), himself a lexicographer of stature. The mythological reference is, of course, to the labor performed by Hercules in cleaning up the manure-filled stables of King Augeus, son of the sun god Helius. Hercules did the job in twenty-four hours; to clean up a clogged music dictionary takes a little longer. But sanitation must be done with circumspection; one never knows what shining gems, what bits of fascinating tektite, are embedded in rejected debris. Take the story of the Italian singer Giulio Rossi as related by *Baker's*. He started out as a tenor, but unintentionally plunged into the Tiber on a cold day and as a consequence became a *basso profondo*. Incredible? Yes, incredible, but what lexicographer would have the heart to throw it into the pile of refuse? I couldn't. So—*stet!*

There should be no such spirit of acceptance for the purple prose that some editors indulged in while describing the life and works of admired persons. I had to deflate somewhat the verbal effusions in the original *Baker's* entry on A.W. Thayer, biographer of Beethoven. Here is a sample: "Unhappily, his wonderful capacity for work was overtaxed, and volume IV of his nobly conceived Beethoven biography, executed with a painstaking thoroughness and scrupulous fidelity beyond praise, was left unfinished. Though he lived for years in straitened circumstances, he resolutely refused offers from firms like Novello & Co. and G. Schirmer, Inc., hoping to recast entirely the English version of his *Beethoven*." Suffocating! Give us air to breathe!

A biographical dictionary ought to be a democratic assembly of factual information. Great masters are by right to be given preferential treatment, but opaque luminaries, e.g., Bibl, Kittl, Lickl, or Titl, ought to be tendered hospitality, if not lavish accommodations. Ay, there's the rub! Proportionate representation is the ideal desideratum, but availability of information and productivity of work determine the space allowance. One would fain wish that there were more biographical information on Shakespeare than on Pepys, on Josquin Des Prez than on a whole gallery of later madrigalists, on Bach than on Reger. As it is, an unhappy editor must gather every bit of information on the great masters of the past and make a judicious selection of biographical data and a list of works of *dii minores* in the arts.

One must also beware of lexicographical zombies, typographical clones and monsters. The great Eitner, who spent a lifetime tabulating manuscripts in European libraries, was also a progenitor of such teratological creatures. Working on a pile of anonymous French songs, he apparently mistook the nouns in their titles for names of composers. Thus we learn from Eitner that "La Chanson d'un gai Berger" was a song by Ungay Berger, and that "La Chanson de l'Auberge Isolée" was composed by Mlle. Isolée L'Auberge. There must be a number of desperate music researchers trying to find out who Mr. Gay Shepherd and Miss Isolated Tavern were in life. *Cobbett's Cyclopedia of Chamber Music* is responsible for spawning D. Michaud (a misprint for D. Milhaud), Marcel Babey (for Marcel Labey), and, most intriguing, a famous violinist, Heinrich Wehtan, generated through the transliteration of the Russian spelling in Cyrillic letters of the name of Henri Vieuxtemps via a German translation of an article originally written in Russian by a contributor to *Cobbett*.

To exorcise such vampires and to drive a stake through their hideous hearts I myself decided to create a monster as the last entry of the 1958 edition of *Baker's*. Never fear: I killed it in page proofs. But here it is *à titre documentaire:*

Zyžík, Krsto, Czech composer; b. Pressburg, Feb. 29, 1900. [1900 was not a leap year in the West.] He traveled widely to Pozsony and Bratislava [Pozsony and Bratislava are respectively the Hungarian and Slovak names of Pressburg], and back to Pressburg. He attracted attention with his oratorio *Dieta Wormsová*, written for the quadricentennial of the Diet of Worms in a vermicular counterpoint [the Diet of Worms was an actual historic assembly, held in the city of Worms in 1521; it condemned Luther as a heretic]; then brought out a bel canto work, *Strč prst skrz krk* (a Czech tongue twister, meaning *put your finger on your throat*), using only consonants in consonant harmony. His works include *Pinč mj šuga* (*Pinch me, Sugar,* or *Pinch Meshuga* in phonetical transcription) for chorus and pinched strings; *Smyccový Kvartet* (string quartet) for woodwind quintet; *Sappho LXIX* for 2 female participants (Lesbos Festival, 1955); *Macho* for large secular organ (male player), etc. In 1979, after many years of aggravated floccillation and severe dyscrasia, he was committed to a dissident asylum. See Sol Mysnik [rather obvious anagram of Slonimsky], *A Czech Checkmate: The Story of Krsto Zyžik* (Los Angeles, 1979).

The most authentic sources of information ought to be diaries and autobiographies, correspondence, and reminiscences of friends and relatives. But much too frequently, at least in musical biography, accounts by musicians themselves are tainted by a desire for self-glorification hidden behind a mask of assumed modesty. "Look at me," they seem to tell the reader, "and marvel at my accomplishments; starting out in poverty, privations, and need, and by dint of faith in my destiny and hard work, rising to the top of the pyramid of fame, recognition, and even wealth." Wagner's autobiography abounds in trivia, including some tedious pages about his pet dogs, but he never mentions the episode of his incarceration at the Clichy prison in Paris from October 28 to November 17, 1840, for non-payment of debt. True, it was one of those permissive jailings, with easy family furloughs, but still the episode is a legitimate part of Wagner's biography. Naturally, Wagner never gave an account in his autobiography of his cavalier treatment of the women in his life, nor did he make clear the circumstances of the birth of his natural daughter Isolde, born to Cosima on April 10, 1865, while she was still married to Hans von Bülow. In 1914 Isolde petitioned the Bavarian Civil Court to grant her a share in Wagner's royalties; her claim was rejected on the ground that there was no evidence that Cosima had ceased all communication with her legitimate husband, Hans von Bülow, within the period of ten months before Isolde's birth, a legal maximum for the length of gestation. The court also overruled the evidence submitted by Isolde's lawyer husband, based on the phrenological and hemological similarities between Wagner and Isolde.

It was fashionable among artists of the nineteenth century to claim paternity from celebrated or titled persons. Was the French cellist François Servais actually a bastard child of Liszt, as was claimed for him in various sources, including *Baker's*? He was born in St. Petersburg, or so the dictionaries said, in 1846, a date that fits the chronology of Liszt's liaison with Princess Sayn-Wittgenstein. But nothing in the voluminous correspondence between her and Liszt during that period indicated that she was a prospective mother. My earnest inquiries in Russia brought no results. The verdict in this case, therefore, must remain unproven.

A more involved claim of desirable paternity concerns the once famous pianist Sigismond Thalberg, who apparently authorized the report that he was the son of a Prince Dietrichstein and a baroness. Further inquiries were discouraged by a footnote in the 1954 edition of *Grove's Dictionary* stating that Thalberg's birth certificate (he was born in Geneva) was unobtainable. Distrustful of this notice, I wrote to Geneva and obtained a copy of the certificate by airmail within a matter of days. I discovered later that the document had been previously published in a Belgian magazine on the occasion of Thalberg's centenary in 1912. The certificate stated that Thalberg was a legitimate son of Joseph Thalberg and Fortunee Stein, both of Frankfurt am Main, and that he was born in Geneva on January 8, 1812. The case was further complicated by the publication in various sources of a letter allegedly written by Thalberg's natural mother to Prince Die-trichstein at the time of Thalberg's birth, suggesting that he should be given the name Thalberg, so that he would grow as peacefully as a Thal (valley) and would tower over humanity as high as a Berg (mountain). Just who fabricated this let-ter and for what purpose remains unclear. The Supplement to Riemann's *Musik-Lexikon*, published in 1975, adds the intriguing bit of information that Thalberg was indeed adopted by Prince Dietrichstein later in life.

The strange lure of aristocratic birth seems to be undiminished even in our own century. An English singer who was active in recital and on the light-opera stage in the early 1900s under the name Louis Graveure declared in an interview published in the *New York Times* in 1947 that he was of royal or possibly imperi-al birth, and that it would be worth a fortune to him to find out who he really was. Well, for the modest sum of two shillings and sixpence I obtained from Lon-don a copy of his birth certificate which dispelled the mystery. His real name was Wilfrid Douthitt, and he used it in his early appearances in England as a bari-tone; later he changed to tenor and gave concerts as Louis Graveure, which was his mother's maiden name.

Much more honest was the search for true paternity undertaken by the Amer-ican folk songster and poet Rod McKuen. He knew he was illegitimate, and his mother never told him who his father was. He undertook a long quest, almost epic in its simple grandeur, and in the end established the identity of his father, a backwoods lumberjack.

The desire to recreate one's life according to one's fancy is universal, and ar-tists are particularly apt to imagine, and at times consciously to contrive, the tales of might-have-been. Was Liszt actually kissed on the brow by Beethoven at the concert he played in Vienna as a child? There is a charming lithograph of the supposed event, which is reproduced in several Liszt biographies. But the evi-dence of Beethoven's archives suggests that Beethoven was annoyed by Liszt's father's bringing the child Liszt to Beethoven's quarters, and that he never went to the concert, despite Schindler's efforts to persuade him to attend. Liszt did play for Beethoven in private, but whether he was kissed on the brow or not remains uncertain.

Working on a biographical dictionary of musicians, I have found myself in the uncomfortable position of private detective. Some years back I received a letter from a Russian woman living in Rome. She asked my help to find out whether her father, the Russian violinist Bezekirsky, who emigrated to America when she was a child, was still alive. Since Bezekirsky was in *Baker's*, I had to search for him anyway to bring him up to date, dead or alive. Tracking him down through several music schools where he taught violin, I finally reached him in a small locality in upstate New York. Delighted that I could restore a missing fa-ther to an anxious daughter, I wrote to both, giving their mutual addresses. Frankly, I expected letters full of emotional gratitude for my humanitarian en-deavor, but I got none from either father or daughter. I do not relish unfinished human symphonies, so I wrote to Bezekirsky again, asking him to let me know whether he had established contact with his long-lost offspring. Great was my shock when I received from him a postcard scribbled in English in a senile hand, saying as follows: "Your mission was successful, if you call several unpleasant and demanding letters from my daughter a success. I am in no position to help her in any way." I never heard from the daughter.

One of the sharpest rebukes I ever received for trying to obtain information was administered by the remarkable English composer Kaikhosru Sorabji. I made the terrible *faux pas* of describing him as an Indian composer. "Do not dare to call me an Indian," he thundered in reply. "We are Parsi, followers of Zarathustra." He flatly refused to supply biographical data about himself, but he sent me a signed copy of his formidable *Opus Clavicembalisticum*, and pointed out for my information that it is the greatest polyphonic work since Bach's *Kunst der Fuge*. For all I know, it may be exactly that, at least in the grandeur of conception and extraordinary skill of its structure. But his rebuke to me was mild in comparison with the eruption of invective he poured on Percy Scholes for what he deemed to be an undignified and inadequate entry on himself in the *Oxford Companion to Music*. Scholes sent the letter to me with the inscription "For your delectation." It is worth reproducing *in toto:*

Corfe Castle, Dorset, XXII.II.MCMLII A.D.
My Good Sir:

A valued friend draws my attention to a lucubration of yours under the entry of my name in a recently published book of reference. One is hard put to it at which to marvel the more, the exiguity of your sense of proportion or the poverty of your taste in devoting double the amount of space to cheap impertinences regarding the place and date of my birth (which is as little business of yours as of any other prying nosey busybody) to that which is devoted to my work, which is all that concerns anyone and which carefully conveys inaccurate and false information by leaving out material facts. Formerly I used to consider it enough when dealing with these stupid and impudent enquiries from lexicographical persons, deliberately to mislead them as to dates and places. This is a mistake: their enquiries should either be ignored or refused. And the sooner folk of their kidney grasp the fact that one is under no moral obligation to provide them with accurate, or indeed any information at all just because they choose to ask for it, the very much better for all concerned.

I have the honor to be, Sir, Yours very faithfully,
Kaikhosru Shapurji Sorabji

Sorabji is a unique figure in music, and his full biography would be fascinating. Erik Chisholm, who knew him personally, told me that the gate of Sorabji's castle in Dorset bears this legend: "Visitors Unwelcome. Roman Catholic Nuns in Full Habit May Enter Without An Appointment." In reckless disregard of Sorabji's demurrer at biographical information about himself, I wrote to the London registry of birth to find out at least when and where he was born. To my surprise the document stated that his real name was Leon Dudley Sorabji; Kaikhosru was apparently his Parsi name assumed later in life. I informed Eric Blom, who was then working on the Fifth Edition of *Grove*, of my findings. His response was prompt. "I knew right along," he wrote, "that Sorabji's name was Leon Dudley, but if you value your life I would not advise you to put it in print, for I fear that if you do he would take the next plane to America and assassinate you personally." And Samuel Johnson said that a lexicographer is a "harmless drudge"!

Once in a while in a beleaguered lexicographer's life the subject of an entry in a biographical dictionary voices his gratitude for the honor. A letter I received from Walter Stockhoff, an American composer whose music was praised by Busoni as "a fresh voice from the New World that could revitalize the tired art of Europe," certainly warmed the cockles of my heart. "As pure, cool, crystal-clear water," he wrote me, "revives one thirsting in the desert, so intelligence, understanding, sympathy and sense of values come to brighten one's pathway. There is a noble generosity in your giving thought to my work. Through the greatness of your nature you strengthen others."

Chronological memory is treacherous. Casals owned the manuscript of the B-flat major string quartet, op. 67, of Brahms, given to him by a Vienna collector. It was, he told me, mysteriously connected with his life, for he was conceived when Brahms began the composition of the quartet, and was born when Brahms completed it. Leaving aside the problem of knowing the date of one's conception, the chronology does not support this fancy. Brahms wrote the work during the summer and fall of 1875, and it was first performed in Berlin on October 30, 1876. Casals was born two months after its performance and could not have been conceived fourteen or fifteen months previously.

Lexicographical cross-pollination of inaccurate information in similar wording is a hazard. Philip Hale used to say that when several mutually independent reference works vouchsafe identical data, he deems the information reliable. Not necessarily so. If we consider the case of Mascagni, one comes upon a curious iteration of idiom that arouses suspicion. The 1906 edition of *Grove's* states that Mascagni was compelled to study music "by stealth" because his father, a baker, wanted him to be a lawyer. The *Oxford Companion to Music* paraphrases *Grove's*: "Mascagni was the son of a baker who took music lessons by stealth." The 1940 edition of *Baker's* echoes: "Mascagni's father (a baker) wished him to study jurisprudence, but he learned piano-playing by stealth." What is this obsession with the quaint locution "by stealth" in all these reference works? In point of fact, Mascagni's father was quite proud of his son's achievement as a musician and eagerly supported his studies at the Conservatory of Milan, as attested by their published correspondence.

If autobiographies are inevitably images of one's life as refracted through a prism resulting in an attractive and colorful spectrum, it is nevertheless strange that a composer would alter the history of the creation of a particular work. Berlioz did so paraleptically in his most famous score, *Symphonie fantastique*, by leaving out of its program the fact that one of the movements was taken from his early school work and that he implanted the unifying *idée fixe* surgically in a vacant measure containing a fermata, in order to justify its inclusion. And yet this manipulation creates the false impression of coherence. Of course, composers need not apologize to their biographers and analysts for revising their works in the light of later wisdom. Mahler denied the programmatic intent of several of his symphonies even though the descriptive titles appeared in the manuscripts. Beethoven carefully disavowed the pictorial nature of his *Pastoral Symphony* by stating that the music represented an impression rather than a description of a day in the country, and this despite the birdcalls and the electric storm in the score. Schoenberg, who was opposed to representational music, nevertheless yielded to the importunities of his publishers in authorising romantic titles for the individual movements of his *Five Orchestral Pieces*.

On the other hand, Stravinsky's latter-day denial that his early *Scherzo fantastique* was inspired by his reading of Maeterlinck's *La Vie des Abeilles* is puzzling. In Robert Craft's *Conversations with Igor Stravinsky*, in reply to the question about the subject matter of the work, Stravinsky replies unequivocally: "I wrote the *Scherzo* as a piece of pure symphonic music. The bees were a choreographer's idea . . . Some bad literature about bees was published on the fly-leaf of the score to satisfy my publisher who thought a 'story' would help to sell the music." This declaration was most unfair to the publisher and to the choreographer. In his own letters to Rimsky-Korsakov at the time of composition of the score (1907), published in Moscow in 1973, Stravinsky writes: "I intended to write a scherzo already in St. Petersburg, but I lacked subject matter. It so happens that I have been reading *La Vie des Abeilles* by Maeterlinck, a half-philosophical, half-poetic work, which captivated me completely. At first, I intended to use direct quotations so as to make the program of my piece quite clear, but then I realized that it would not do because in the book the scientific and poetic elements are closely interwoven. I decided therefore to guide myself by a definite programmatic design without actual quotations, and to entitle the work simply *The Bees*, after Maeterlinck, a fantastic scherzo."

In the nineteenth century America was, to all practical purposes, a German colony in instrumental music and an Italian colony in opera. Lillian Norton would never have made a singing career had she not changed her name to Nordica. Conductors had to be German or Austrian (Damrosch, Muck, Henschel, Nikisch, Mahler). Pianists prospered when their last names ended with "sky" or "ski." Paderewski was a shining example of grandeur and glory. (I myself profited peripherally when I entered the United States in 1923 exempt from the rigid quota imposed by the Immigration Office on Slavs and such, exception being made for "artists," particularly those whose names looked and sounded artistic.) Ethel Liggins, an Englishwoman intent on making an American career, was advised to change her name to Leginska ("ska" being the feminine counterpart of "ski"). She told me interesting stories about herself; among her many memories, she said that as a child she was bounced by Winston Churchill on his knee after his return as a hero from the Boer War. She volunteered her own date of birth, April 13, 1886, and I checked on it by securing her birth certificate; it was correct. Now, Churchill came home in glory in 1899, and since it is unlikely that he proceeded right away to bounce Liggins (not yet Leginska) on his knee, she must have reached a nubile adolescence at the time, and the whole episode assumed a totally different complexion. "Botheration!" she exclaimed when I pointed out the embarrassing chronology to her. "How do you know when Churchill returned to England from South Africa? You are not British!"

No greater splendor among contemporary orchestral conductors surrounded the career of Leopold Stokowski, who lived to be 95, working in music to the last days of his life. And his name ended in "ski"! Invidious rumors had it that his real name was Stokes, and that he polonized it as many other artists did. False! He was born in London, the son of a Polish cabinetmaker named Kopernik Joseph Boleslaw Stokowski and an Irishwoman, Annie Marion Moore-Stokowski, on April 18, 1882. Not satisfied with his true half-Polish origin, he for some reason chose to maintain that he was totally Polish, born in Cracow in 1887 (rather than 1882), and that his name was Leopold Boleslawowicz Stokowski. This bit of fantasy appears in the main volume of Riemann's *Musik-Lexikon*. When I sounded the alarm, pointing out that the patronymic ending on "which" or "wicz" or "witch" is possible in Russian, but not in Polish, the Riemann's editors sent me a photostat copy of the original questionnaire in Stokowski's own hand embodying all this fanciful information. By way of rebuttal, I forwarded to the Riemann's people a copy of Stokowski's birth certificate which I had obtained from London. The 1975 supplement to Riemann's carries a corresponding correction.

Among many fantastic tales that accompany musical biographies there is one concerning Werner Egk. The name sounded like a manufactured logogriph, or an acronym for "ein guter Künstler," and even more self-anointed, "ein genialer Künstler." I wrote to the director of the archives of the city of Augsburg where Egk was born, and elicited the information that his real name was Mayer. If so, whence Egk? The composer himself came forward with an explanation that was more puzzling than the original riddle: he changed his name from Mayer to Egk after his marriage to Elisabeth Karl; the initials of her first and last name formed the outer letters of Egk, and the middle "g" was added "for euphony." Guttural euphony?

No experience in my "harmless drudgery" equaled the Case of Walter Dahms, an obscure German author of musical biographies. According to musical lexica that listed his name, including *Baker's*, he went to Rome in 1922, and promptly vanished. I did not care to leave him dangling like an unshriven ghost, an elusive zombie. I used to mention Dahms to every musicologist I met as a disappearing act, and one of them told me that there was nothing mysterious about Dahms, that he went to Lisbon, adopted a Portuguese-sounding pseudonym, and continued publishing books on music. I inserted this seemingly innocuous bit of information in my 1965 Supplement to *Baker's*, but unbeknownst to myself it unleashed a fantastic chain of events. The editors of the Supplement to Riemann's *Musik-Lexikon*, who were also interested to bring Dahms up to date, seized upon my addendum and inquired through Santiago Kastner, a London-born German-educated music scholar resident in Lisbon, to find out facts about Dahms. But no one in the rather flourishing German colony in Lisbon, not even anyone at the German embassy, knew anything about Dahms. The Riemann editors would not be pacified. "Baker (really Slonimsky)," they wrote Kastner again, "is greatly valued here because of its reliability. Behind the bland statement that Dahms was still in Lisbon in 1960 must lie a lot of painstaking research." Kastner volunteered a guess that Dahms might be a German-speaking Portuguese citizen named Gualterio Armando, Gualterio being a Portuguese form of Walter, and Armando containing three letters of the name Dahms. He addressed the question directly to Dahms, whether he was or was not Dahms.

All hell broke loose thereafter. "I am not identical with anyone but myself," replied Gualterio Armando. "I have absolutely nothing to say about Herr W. D. mentioned in your letter because I know nothing about him. I hope that this will put an end to this whole business once and for all." Kastner reported his failure to the Riemann's editors, and announced that he was through with his investigation, but voiced his conviction that Dahms "must be identical with that asshole Gualterio Armando after all." Why was he so vehement in denying his real identity? He died on October 5, 1973, carrying the secret to his grave.

Among the unburied musical ghosts that haunted me through the years was Alois Minkus, an Austrian composer of operas and ballets who spent most of his career in Russia. For a hundred years, first under the Czars, then under the Soviets, his ballets never ceased to be the favorite numbers in the Russian ballet repertory. Not a year passed without my receiving an insistent inquiry from Russia and abroad as to the fate of Minkus after he left Russia in 1891. Some reference works have him dead in that year; others prolong his life until 1907, with the date accompanied by a parenthetical question mark. I must have written a dozen letters to various registries of vital statistics in Vienna on the supposition that Minkus returned to Vienna, where he was born, and died there. I did obtain his birth certificate ascertaining that he was born on March 23, 1826, rather than 1827 as most Russian and other music reference sources have it, but the Vienna archivists could tell me nothing as to his date of death. Then in the summer of 1976 I made one more half-hearted inquiry in Vienna. To my astonishment I got a clue that all death notices before 1939 were moved from the Stadtarchive, the Landesarchiv, and the Vienna Rathaus and its numerous subdivisions to the corresponding parochial registries. Hot on the scent, I wrote to the proper Lutheran parish, and to my absolute joy of discovery I received a document certifying that Alois Minkus died at Gentzgasse 92 in Vienna, on December 7, 1917, in the 92nd year of his life, from pneumonia, and that his mortal remains were deposed at the cemetery of Döbling. I immediately rushed this information and the pertinent documentation to the editors of the big Russian musical encyclopedia, which had just reached the letter M, and the date got in at the last moment before going to press, with an appropriate proud parenthetical clause testifying to its authenticity.

One of the most fantastic episodes in my hunt for missing musical persons was the search for Heinrich Hammer, a German conductor and composer who emigrated to the United States about the turn of the century, and then vanished from the musical scene. I appealed for help to William Lichtenwanger, who combines profound erudition with a detective flair that would have made him a rich man had he dedicated himself to the search for missing heirs and holders of unused bank accounts. Quick as a panther, he produced a clipping from the *Los Angeles Times* of October 25, 1953, which carried on its society page a photograph of Heinrich Hammer, 91, and his young bride Arlene, 22. Their address was given in the story, but when I wrote to him my letter came back with the notation "Deceased." But when and where? Lichtenwanger got on the telephone, and after a few inquiries got hold of Hammer's son, a repair worker of the California telephone company. Unbelievably, contact was established with him atop a telephone pole, and he gave Lichtenwanger the needed information.

Preface to the Sixth Edition

Hammer had moved to Phoenix, Arizona, where he died on October 28, 1954, just a year after his marriage.

How much of personal life ought to be reported in a dignified biographical dictionary? Volumes have been written speculating about the identity of Beethoven's "Immortal Beloved," even though the famous letter addressed to her was never sent off. Should a biographer be so bold as to doubt a great man's own confession of love? A conscientious biographer took exception to Goethe's declaration that he had never loved anyone as much as Lili Schönemann. "Here the great Goethe errs," he commented: "His greatest love was Frederike Brion." From the sublime to contemporary love lore. The formidable Hungarian pianist Nyiregyhazi was married nine times, and admitted to 65 extramarital liaisons. Is this proper information in a biographical dictionary? The marriages, perhaps; the liaisons, only famous ones, like Liszt's and Chopin's.

It was only recently that the known homosexuality of Tchaikovsky became a matter of open discussion in his biographies; the first inkling of it appeared in the preface to the 1934 edition of Tchaikovsky's correspondence with his benefactress, Madame von Meck. In 1940 a collection of his letters to the family, including those to his brother and biographer Modest, who was also a homosexual, was published in Russia, but it was soon withdrawn from publication and became a sort of bibliographical phantom; an expurgated edition was published later. In subsequent books on Tchaikovsky published in Russia the matter is unmentioned. But a strange mass of unfounded rumors began circulating both in Russia and abroad shortly after Tchaikovsky's death that he committed "suicide by cholera," that he deliberately drank unboiled water during a raging cholera epidemic in St. Petersburg, and this despite his fear of cholera, which had been the cause of his mother's death. The stories that I heard during my visit to Russia in 1962 were right out of Gothic horror tales. It seems that Tchaikovsky became involved in a homosexual affair with a young member of the Russian Imperial family, and that when Czar Alexander III got wind of it, he served the Tchaikovsky family an ultimatum: either have Tchaikovsky take poison, or have him tried for sodomy and sent to Siberia. Tchaikovsky accepted the verdict, and with the connivance of his personal physician, Dr. Bertenson, was given a poison that produced symptoms similar to those of cholera. As additional evidence that Tchaikovsky did not die of cholera, the proponents of this theory argue, is the fact that his body was allowed to lie in state and that several of his intimates kissed him on the mouth, as the Russian death ritual allows, whereas cholera victims were buried in zinc-lined sealed coffins to prevent contagion.

Dramatic deaths should rightly be noted in biographies, but grisly details had better be left out. It is not advisable to follow the type of reporting exemplified in an obituary of Sir Armine Woodhouse in *The Annual Register of London* for the year 1777, noting that his death "was occasioned by a fishbone in his throat."

Percy Scholes took credit for sending the British writer on music, Arthur Eaglefield Hull, to his death under the wheels of a train. He wrote me: "Hull's suicide was the result of my exposure of his thefts in his book *Music, Classical, Romantic and Modern.* He threw himself under a train."

A suicide directly connected with a musical composition was that of Rezsö

Seress, Hungarian author of the sad, sad song "Gloomy Sunday." At one time the playing of the tune was forbidden in Central Europe because it drove several impressionable people to suicide. Seress himself jumped out the window, on a Monday, not a gloomy Sunday.

Musical murders are surprisingly few; singers are occasionally murdered out of jealousy, but not famous singers. The most spectacular murder, never conclusively solved, was that of the French eighteenth-century musician Jean Marie Leclair, stabbed to death in his own house. Since nothing was taken, it could not have been a burglary. I proposed a theory that he was done to death by his estranged wife, who was a professional engraver and publisher of some of Leclair's music, and had sharp tools at her disposal, but my painstaking argumentation in favor of this theory was pooh-poohed by the foremost French music historian Marc Pincherle and others.

Dementia, insanity, and bodily disintegration are scourges that hit many composers, and in most cases they were caused by syphilis. Undoubtedly, the tragic illnesses of Schumann, Smetana, Hugo Wolf, and MacDowell were all caused by the lues, the *morbus gallicus*, as it was usually described in the past centuries. In his book on Delius, Sir Thomas Beecham remarks ruefully that the goddess Aphrodite Pandemos repaid Delius cruelly for his lifelong worship at her altar. Delius died blind and paralyzed.

In light of recent disclosures, free from displaced piety for a great man, it appears that Beethoven, too, was a victim of syphilis. His deafness was only a symptom (as in the case of Smetana) which does not necessarily indicate a venereal infection. But there are too many other circumstances that lead to this sad conclusion, recounted in the recent study by Dieter Kerner, *Krankheiten grosser Musiker*.

Even the worshipful speculation as to psychological causes of physical decline and death, so cherished in old-fashioned biography, has no place in a book of reference. I brushed aside such probings into a person's psyche as were found in an old entry on the eighteenth-century French composer Isouard, to the effect that he was so deeply "mortified" by his failure to be elected to the French Academy that "although a married man," he abandoned work, "plunged into dissipation, and died."

Triskaidecaphobia, an irrational fear of the number 13, demonstrably affected the state of mind of two great composers, Rossini and Schoenberg. In addition to his superstition about the malevolent character of 13, Rossini was also fearful of Friday. He died on November 13, 1868, which was a Friday. Numerologists could cite his case to prove predestination. Schoenberg's case is remarkable because there is so much recent evidence that his triskaidecaphobia was not a whimsical pose. He was born on the 13th of the month of September in 1874, and he regarded this as ominous in his personal destiny. He sometimes avoided using 13 in numbering the bars of his works. When he realized that the title of his work *Moses und Aaron* contained 13 letters, he crossed out the second "a" in Aaron, even though the spelling Aron cannot be substantiated either in German or in English. When someone thoughtlessly remarked to him on his 76th birthday that $7 + 6 = 13$, he seemed genuinely upset; he died at the age of 76. On his last day of life, July 13, 1951, he remarked to his wife that he would be all right if he would survive the ominous day, but he did not, and died.

Going over my list of *morituri*, centenarians or near-centenarians, I came upon the name of Victor Küzdö, a Hungarian-American violinist born, or so the old edition of *Baker's* said, in 1869. I wrote to Küzdö at his last known address, which I found in an old musical directory, in effect asking him whether he was living or dead. A few days later I received from him a dictated postcard saying that, although practically blind, he was still alive and well, in Glendale, California. Furthermore, he took the opportunity to correct his date of birth: he was born in 1863, not in 1869, and had shortly before celebrated his 100th anniversary! But this was not the end of the story; soon afterwards I got a letter from a real-estate man in Glendale notifying me that Küzdö was in the habit of diminishing his age, and that he was actually 103, not 100! How could he be sure? Simple: he was a numerologist. When the inevitable end came to Küzdö on February 24, 1966, his death certificate gave his age as 106. He was born in 1859, not in 1863, not in 1869.

The most remarkable woman centenarian on my list was Margaret Ruthven Lang, of the Boston musical dynasty of Lang, who died at the age of 104 in 1972. She was a regular symphony-goer since the early days of the Boston Symphony. On her 100th birthday the orchestra played the hymn *Old Hundred* in her honor. The Russian-French singer Marie Olénine d'Alheim lived to be 100. Among other recent centenarians was the French conductor and composer Henri-Paul Busser, who died in 1973 at the age of 101.

It would be most interesting to compile actuarial tables of the life expectancy of musicians according to their specialties. One thing appears certain: great musicians die young; consider Mozart, Schubert, Chopin, Mendelssohn, Scriabin. It is a fascinating speculation to project Mozart's life from 1756 into 1840, and Schubert's life to an even later date! One may indulge in a revery that very great musicians are summoned to Heaven because they would be more at home there.

Statistically speaking, organists live the longest lives, perhaps because their sedentary occupation keeps them from wasting their energy on idle pastimes. Scholars and pedagogues come next in longevity; conductors are fairly durable, too; among instrumentalists, those handling big instruments, like the double bass or trombone, live longer than violinists, who in turn live longer than flutists and oboe players, who are apt to be frail in physique. Among singers, tenors dissipate their vitality faster than bass singers. In all musical categories mediocrities outlive great artists by a large margin.

In addition to all the troubles involved in the compilation of a biographical dictionary, there are people who concoct sinister plots to further bamboozle the proverbial "harmless drudge." Mikhail Goldstein, a respectable Russian violinist, annoyed by his unfair treatment by the Soviet Music Publishing House in systematically rejecting his compositions, decided to take revenge on them. He invented a Russian composer named Ovsianiko-Kulikovsky, furnished him with a plausible biography, obtained a quantity of old manuscript paper, and composed a symphony in his name, pretending that he had found the score in the archives of the Odessa Conservatory, where he was librarian at the time. The Soviets swallowed the bait and published the score, proclaiming it to be a major discovery; it was also recorded, and greeted with enthusiastic reviews, not only in Russia but elsewhere. (Shall I confess, blushingly? I reviewed the recording for the *Musical Quarterly*, and announced with some reservations that if the work were genuine it would be the first Russian symphony ever written.) A doctoral dissertation was published on the work. When Goldstein admitted the hoax, he was accused of trying to appropriate an important piece of the national legacy. The situation degenerated into a farce, and Goldstein got out of Russia as soon as he could get an exit visa. But, as in Prokofiev's *Lieutenant Kije*, it was too late to kill off Ovsianiko-Kulikovsky, and his symphony is still listed in some record catalogues and is kept on the shelves of music libraries.

An even more dangerous mystification was perpetrated by the eminent Italian music scholar Alberto Cametti, who claimed discovery of an important biographical notebook of Palestrina, which established the elusive exact date of Palestrina's birth. He said he had purchased the document from one Telemaco Bratti, and even went to the trouble of reproducing, or rather forging, part of the manuscript in an article he wrote on the subject. Another Italian music scholar, Raffaele Casimiri, embraced the "discovery" as a gift of God to all true Palestrinologists. Then Alberto Cametti let it pass through various channels that the name of the alleged discoverer of the document, Telemaco Bratti, was an anagram of Alberto Cametti. A great inner storm ensued in the confined company of Italian music scholars, but in the meantime the hoax found its way into reputable bibliographies. (It was thanks to a knowledgeable friend that I myself did not fall into the trap in giving the exact date of Palestrina's birth in my edition of *Baker's;* this date remains unknown to this day.)

It is amazing that grown men and women would deliberately falsify their vital statistics, particularly their dates of birth, in order to appear younger in a reference work. The gambit is understandable among actresses and prima donnas; and it has been said that a woman has the privilege of improvising her age. It would also be understandable for men in their dotage who marry girls in their nonage, but both men and women of music rejuvenate themselves lexicographically even when they are not stage performers.

The Spanish composer Oscar Esplá produced his passport to prove to me that he was born in 1888 and not in 1886 as I had it in *Baker's*. But I had obtained a copy of his birth certificate which confirmed the accuracy of the earlier date.

Mabel Daniels, the Boston composer, once included in a piece a C-sharp against C, explaining that she "had to use a dissonance," since she was living in the same town with me. She petulantly accused me of being "no gentleman" in putting her down as born in 1878 rather than 1879, her own chosen year. She was born in November 1878, just a few weeks away from 1879, so why should I not accept the later year, she pleaded. Poor Mabel! She lived a full life until well into her tenth decade, dying in 1971.

A desire to appear young, if only on paper, is not a modern phenomenon. Since time immemorial, musicians, poets, painters, actors, even politicians, have exer-

Preface to the Sixth Edition

cised their unquestionable prerogative to fib about their age. Johann Jakob Froberger gave the date of May 18, 1620, as that of his birth to his physician, but his certificate of baptism reveals that he was baptized on May 19, 1616. It is a reasonable assumption that the day and the month of his birth, as given by himself, were correct, and that he was baptized on the next day, in 1616, not 1620.

In his handwritten autobiographical note for Mattheson's *Grundlage einer Ehrenpforte*, Telemann stated that he was born in 1682, whereas he was born a year earlier; as in many such cases, the day and the month of his birth, March 14, were given correctly.

The Italian composer and conductor Angelo Mariani, who was born on October 11, 1821, insisted in his communications to Francesco Regli, editor of an Italian biographical dictionary, that he was born on October 11, 1824. Mariani's birth certificate proves that he was born in 1821.

It was common practice in Catholic families to give identical Christian names to infants born after the death of a previous son, or a daughter, so as to perpetuate the memory of the lost child. This has led to a number of mistaken identities. The bicentennial of Giovanni Battista Viotti was widely celebrated in 1953, commemorating the birth in Fontanetto, Italy, of an infant of that name born on May 23, 1753, who died in the following year, on July 10, 1754. On May 12, 1755, another child was born to the Viottis and was given the names Giovanni Battista Guglielmo Domenico, retaining the first two names from those of their deceased son. This second similarly named child was the composer, whose bicentennial was celebrated two years early.

Biographical notices for Giacomo Insanguine found in old music dictionaries list his year of birth variously between 1712 and 1742. I applied for a copy of his birth certificate from the registries of his native town of Monopoli, and received a document purporting to show that he was born in 1712, a date that did not seem to agree with the known facts of his education and career. I pressed for a further search, which revealed that a Giacomo Insanguine who was born in 1712 died in 1726 at the age of 14. On March 22, 1728, a boy was born to the bereaved parents, and was given the names Giacomo Antonio Francesco Paolo Michele. This was the composer Insanguine.

Beethoven was eager to prove that he was born in 1772, not in 1770, and that he had an older brother who was born in 1770. It was discovered that a Ludwig Maria van Beethoven was born on April 1, 1769, but he died a few days later. The great Beethoven was born in the following year.

Next to birth certificates, the best sources of information are family Bibles, marriage certificates, and school registries. The date of birth of Kaspar Othmayr—March 12, 1515—is verified by his astrological chart, and one can be sure that in those remote times no one would hoodwink one's own astrologer. Even in modern times there are practicing astrologers among composers; of these, Dane Rudhyar is professionally the most successful.

In one famous event the correct age of the protagonist became a matter of life or death. On June 28, 1914, Gavrilo Princip, a young Serbian patriot, assassinated Crown Prince Franz Ferdinand of Austria. His act precipitated World War I, which precipitated the Russian Revolution, which precipitated the rise of

Hitler, which precipitated World War II, etc., etc., etc. According to the Austrian law of the time no person less than twenty years of age could be executed for a capital crime. Gavrilo Princip was born on July 25, 1894, according to the Gregorian calendar, and was not quite twenty when he turned the world upside down. This saved him from execution, and he died in prison of tuberculosis of the bone marrow on April 28, 1918.

Oscar Wilde was not so lucky in his own chronology. He had whittled two years off his true age, claiming that he was born in 1856, whereas his real year of birth was 1854. Owing to a peculiar twist of English law, persons under forty indicted for immorality were granted leniency. Oscar Wilde was arrested for sodomy in 1895, and would have benefited by the law had it not been for the prying investigation of the court clerk, who secured Wilde's birth certificate proving that he was over forty at the time of his offense. This precluded leniency, and Wilde got a severe sentence. Despite the availability of the correct date, the *Encyclopaedia Britannica* carried the 1856 date in its article on Oscar Wilde right through its thirteenth edition. The *Century Cyclopedia* still gives the wrong date.

Much confusion is created in musical biography by the discrepancy in dating past events according to the Russian and Western calendars. The Greek Orthodox Church refused to accept the Gregorian calendar, and continued to use the Julian calendar until 1918. The Julian calendar was also in force in Bulgaria and Rumania during the same period. As a result, the dating of Russian births and deaths lagged behind the Western calendar, by 11 days in the 18th century, 12 days in the 19th century and 13 days in the 20th century. (The increase in discrepancy was caused by the fact that the years 1800 and 1900 were leap years in Russia but not in the West.) Stravinsky was born on June 5, 1882, according to the Julian calendar, which corresponded to June 17 of the Western calendar. But after 1900, when the difference between the two calendars increased by a day, he began celebrating his birthday on June 18. As his 80th anniversary approached in June 1962, he let it be known that he was going to celebrate it on June 18, which gave occasion to the *New York Times* to say that the faces of some lexicographers would be red on June 18, Stravinsky's preferred date for his birth, seeing that most dictionaries, including two edited by me, gave this date as June 17. I sent a rebuttal explaining my reasons for sticking to the June 17 date, and the *New York Times* published it under the caption, "It Is All Clear Now." This aroused Stravinsky's anger, and he shot off a wire to the paper reasserting his prerogative to celebrate his birthday on any date he wished. He declared his intention to mark the date in the twenty-first century on June 19, assuming that the difference between the two calendars would continue to increase a day each century, but he overlooked the fact that the year 2000 will be a leap year according to both the Gregorian and Julian calendars, because Pope Gregory ruled, on the advice of learned astronomers, that a year divisible by 400 must be reckoned as a leap year.

Are trivia worth mentioning in a biographical dictionary? It all depends. If such trivia have significant bearing on the subject's life and career, they should be given consideration. The unique case of the male castrato Tenducci, who eloped with a young girl and subsequently married her, deserves comment to dispel incredulity. He was a triorchis, and was therefore capable of marriage even after he was two-thirds castrated. His wife wrote a book of memoirs on the affair.

There remain a few categories that ought to be dealt with in separate rubrics.

INCLUSION AND EXCLUSION. *Baker's Biographical Dictionary of Musicians* must necessarily include men and women active in music who were not professional musicians, such as aristocratic patrons and patronesses, wealthy promoters of musical events, impresarios, music publishers, ballet masters who played important roles in commissioning and performing works from composers, and of course music critics. A practical criterion for including names of little-known composers, performers, and pedagogues should be the degree of likelihood that a music student, or a concertgoer, or a person who wants to know who is who in music would look it up in a dictionary. Thousands of names hover in the periphery of the music world and many more populate the index pages of biographies of famous composers. Still more are modest members of world orchestras who have distinguished themselves in various ways. Hugo Leichtentritt told me that Riemann, with whom he studied, used to play chamber music with amateurs and professionals at his home in Leipzig, and after each session, would ask them to fill out questionnaires for inclusion in his *Musik-Lexikon*. Theodore Baker, the compiler of the original edition of the present dictionary, collected biographical data from his friends who played in the Boston Symphony Orchestra. As a result, the early editions of both lexica became overpopulated with individuals who were perfectly honorable practitioners of their art, but who failed to leave an indelible, or even delible, mark on the sands of music. Most of these long-dead servants of music, whether borrowed by Baker from Riemann and other collectors of musical flesh, or installed anew by Baker and his successors out of personal friendship, have been allowed in the present edition to remain under their individual lexicographical tombstones for humanitarian reasons, rather than relegated to the common graves of crumbling newspaper clippings in public libraries; still, the paragraphs devoted to them originally have been mercifully cut down to commensurate size. No more will the impatient user of the dictionary be offered long lines of printed matter dealing with this or that obscure orchestral player, church organist, or provincial music teacher, relating in stultifying detail the advancement of their dull careers. But musical, or even unmusical, figures that multidentally smile on us from huge posters or gold-rimmed record albums, the glamorized purveyors of popular subculture of whatever degree of vulgarity, the Beatles and other singing coleoptera, are welcomed to this edition of *Baker's* even more liberally than they were to the 1958 edition and to the 1965 and 1971 Supplements. When, overcoming a natural revulsion, I dictated to my California secretary a paragraph on Humperdinck, the pop singer whose manager had the supreme *chutzpah* to appropriate the honored name of the composer of *Hänsel und Gretel* because it sounded "funny" and would attract attention, she was genuinely surprised at my liberality, but revealed her complete ignorance as to the existence of an earlier musician of the same name as the glorified rock singer.

DATES OF PERFORMANCE. A determined effort has been made in the present edition to list as many exact dates as possible of first performances of major works, especially operas and symphonies, not only by celebrated masters but also by modern composers. Care had to be taken to avoid duplication, for many composers are, and have been, in the habit of changing the titles of their works and then presenting them as new compositions. For instance, Don Emilio Arrieta y Corera wrote an opera, *La Conquista de Granada*, which was produced in Madrid in 1850 and revived under the title *Isabel la Católica* in 1855. The opera got a double billing in the valuable compilation *Cronica de la Opera italiana en Madrid*, published in 1878, the index of which correctly lists the two titles interchangeably, but this precaution has failed to deter other publications from duplicating the work. Quite often, composers append an optional descriptive title to an earlier work, which is apt to be duplicated in the catalogue.

SPELLING OF NAMES. Variants of spelling of celebrated musical names cause uncertainty, and choice had to be made in the present edition of *Baker's* guided by common usage; alternative spellings are then cross-referenced. Spanish, Portuguese, and Latin American names commonly include both the paternal and maternal surname; a selection has to be made according to the preferred usage. Thus, Alejandro García Caturla is listed under Caturla, the name he used in his published works; Oscar Lorenzo Fernandez is listed under Fernandez. In some instances, a musician changes the form of his name in the middle of his career. In the earlier editions of this dictionary the main entry on Edmund Rubbra appeared under Duncan-Rubbra; Duncan was the name of his first wife, which he adopted in some of his works; later he reverted to the legal name Rubbra, which is therefore used in the present edition of *Baker's*. Philip Heseltine published most of his music under the witching surname Peter Warlock, but Heseltine would seem preferable for a biographical dictionary. Americanization has produced several changes in the spelling of names; Arnold Schoenberg changed the spelling of his last name from Schönberg to Schoenberg when he emigrated to the United States. Carlos Salzedo dropped the acute accent that marked the antepenultimate letter of his original name. Eugen Zádor dropped the accent and changed his first name to Eugene when he came to America. Aladár Szendrei made his career in Europe under his original Hungarian name and surname, but changed it phonetically to Sendrey when he emigrated to the United States; a cross-reference has been made in the present edition under Sendrey to his original name. Edgar Varèse was baptized as Edgard Varèse, but most of his works were published with the first name spelled Edgar; in 1940 or thereabouts he changed it back to his legal name, Edgard. However, the present edition of *Baker's* keeps the familiar form Edgar. The existence of the alternate spellings Carl and Karl in many German names creates considerable confusion. The 1958 edition of *Baker's* modernized virtually all Carls to Karls, with some curious results, such as the spelling Karl Philipp Emanuel Bach instead of the standard Carl; the traditional spelling has been restored in the present edition. A curious case is that of Carl Ruggles, the American composer, whose real first name was Charles. He changed it to Carl as a youth when he decided to devote himself to music; he hoped that the Germanic form of the name would give him a better chance to succeed in the highly German-minded musical world of early twentieth-century America.

NOBILIARY PARTICLES. Early in this century it was common in American and British usage to put the nobiliary particle "von" in front of German names, such as "Von Bülow" and the like. In the wake of World War I the "von" became unpopular among the Allied nations. The original full name of the English composer Gustav Holst, who was of Swedish ancestry, was Von Holst. During the war, at the suggestion of Percy Scholes, he dropped the objectionable "von" from his name. Anton von Webern eliminated the "von" after the fall of the Austro-Hungarian Empire in 1918; the present edition lists his name under Webern, Anton von, in appreciation of the fact that he used the full name in the titles of many of his early works. A more difficult problem is encountered in the Dutch and Flemish nobiliary particle Van. Beethoven was very proprietary about his own "van" and regarded it as a proof of his noble origin, an important claim at the time when he tried to assure the guardianship of his nephew. The French and Spanish "de" and the Italian "di" often become coalesced with the last name. Debussy was Bussy to friends in his youth; Madame von Meck, the patroness of Tchaikovsky, who employed Debussy as a house musician and teacher in Moscow, referred to him as Bussy. No book of reference would list Bussy as an alternative for Debussy, but in some other names, not necessarily French, this nobiliary particle retains its independent existence. De Koven is an example. But De Falla is improper; his name should be listed under Falla, Manuel de.

RUSSIAN NAMES. The Russian alphabet has two intractable letters: one is represented by the Cyrillic symbol "bI," the other by a fence of three sticks with a line underneath it, and a wriggle, or a cedilla, on the right of the protracted horizontal line. Only Turkish has the phonetic equivalent of "bI," represented by an undotted "i" in the new Turkish alphabet. As for the second Cyrillic symbol aforementioned, it can be very adequately represented by the coalescence of the sounds "sh" and "ch" in a compound word such as fish-chips. The Russian sound for "e" is palatalized into "yeh" as in the now accepted English spelling of Dostoyevsky. English and American music dictionaries have inherited the spelling of Russian names of composers and performers from German, which has no "ch" sound, and in which the Russian (and English) "v" sound is represented by "w." As a result, we had Tschaikowsky for at least half a century. British and American librarians, realizing that Tsch = Ch, began spelling Tchaikovsky as Chaikovsky. But if we follow phonetics, then why do we need the diphthong "ai"? Why not plain "i" as in China? Here we come to the antinomy of sound, sight, and audiovisual association: Chikovsky has an impossible look. A compromise is necessary: hence, Tchaikovsky in *Baker's*. "Ch" in Rachmaninoff has a guttural German sound that English does not possess. The spelling Rachmaninoff is part-German ("ch") and part-French ("ff"), but this is the way he signed his name, familiar from printed music and concert programs. Most British sources prefer Rakhmaninov.

Once we start on the road to phonetics we will be bound for disaster. The name of the poet Evtushenko is pronounced Yevtushenko, but the eye rebels against its aspect. Besides, an unpalatalized "e" in such an initial sound is not necessarily un-Russian; some people from the northern provinces or from Siberia would say Evtushenko, just as if it were written in English. Another thing: the final diphthong "iy," as it is often represented phonetically in names like Tchaikovsky (or for that matter in Slonimsky), is nearest to the French "ille" in "volaille," but it is not as emphatically articulated. There is no reason to add ugliness to a name like Tchaikovsky by spelling it Tchaikovskiy. Then there is the vexing problem of transliterating Russian names of French or German origin back into their original languages. Some music dictionaries transliterate Cui as Kyue, a visual monstrosity. Cui was the son of a Napoleonic soldier who remained in Russia after the campaign of 1812 and married a Russian woman. His French name Cui ought to stay. The Soviet composer Shnitke (spelled phonetically in English) was of German origin, and his father signed his name in German as Schnittke; this spelling ought to remain even in an English reference work. The same consideration holds for names like Schneerson (Jewish-German) or Steinpress (pronounced Shteinpress in Russian) and Steinberg (for Shteinberg). If we try to transliterate foreign names in Russian back and forth, we will arrive at mutations such as Betkhoven and (yes, unbelievable but true) Poochcheenee, used for a time in the bibliography of *Notes*. I am proud to say that I opened such a vigorous letter-writing campaign against this practice that it was stopped. To conclude, the transliteration of Russian names and Russian titles of works should be guided by ear and by sight. There are seasonal changes and fashions for some Russian names. It used to be Sergey, Bolshoy Theater, etc. Now it is Sergei, Bolshoi, etc. Both visually and phonetically, these altered spellings are fine. In this edition of *Baker's* the paternal names have been omitted in listings of Russian composers, except in that of Piotr Ilyich Tchaikovsky, which has become traditional. The pronunciation of Russian names has been indicated only when mispronunciation is common, as for instance in Balakirev (stress on the second syllable, not the third), Borodin (stress on the last syllable). The pronunciation of Khachaturian's name with the accent on the third syllable has become so common that it would be idle to try to change it to the proper pronunciation, with the accent on the last syllable; equally futile would it be to persuade people to compress the last two vowels into one: "yan." The doubling of "s" between vowels in Russian names such as Mussorgsky is admittedly Germanic in origin; but in seeking to avoid the vocalization of the middle "s" in Mussorgsky the doubling of "s" becomes essential. Thus it is Mussorgsky rather than Musorgsky; but in less familiar names like Stasov, a single "s" is postulated. Illogical? So is the language itself.

GEOGRAPHIC NAMES. Place names have been playing musical chairs during the wars and revolutions of the first half of the present century. I was born in St. Petersburg, left Petrograd in 1918, and revisited Leningrad in 1962. One can travel from Pressburg to Bratislava to Pozsony without budging an inch. A person born in Klausenburg finds himself nominally transferred to Kolozsvár and then to Cluj without moving from one's house. Sometimes a town renamed to honor a current revolutionary figure resumes its original name when the eponymous hero falls into disfavor. Perm was renamed Molotov after the Soviet Revolution, but became Perm once more when Molotov faded out in 1956. In Poland, Katowice was named Stalinogorod in 1953 but became Katowice once more in 1956 when Stalin was posthumously disfranchised. Then there is Liège. For over a century it bore an unnatural acute accent over its middle letter. In 1946 its Municipal Council resolved that the accent should be changed to the grave one. A Belgian musician born in a town with an acute accent may die there with a grave.

ABBREVIATIONS. All abbreviations except the obvious ones, like vol., prof., symph. orch., etc., and the names of the months (except March and April, which remain unabbreviated), have been eliminated from this edition. No more the impenetrable jungle of Ztsch., Vsch., vcs., mvt., or Kgl.

BIBLIOGRAPHY. In listing sources of information pertaining to the subject of an entry, a conscientious bibliographer ought to use common sense. It would serve no rational purpose to cite general histories of music for references to Bach, Mozart, or Beethoven in the bibliographical section; obviously each of such books will have extended chapters on great masters of music. But in bibliographies on modern composers, it is worthwhile to mention collections of articles containing informative material relating to such composers. The same consideration would apply to books on great conductors, great instrumentalists, or great singers; they ought to be listed if they contain useful biographical information. Magazine articles of extensive length are also proper bibliographical material. Title pages are sometimes deceptive. A brochure on Louis-Gilbert Duprez by A.A. Elwart bears the claim on its title page "avec une biographie authentique de son maître A. Choron." Upon examination, it turns out that it contains only a couple of pages on Choron. On the other hand, there are books modestly titled that provide a wealth of biographical information not available in special monographs on the subject. Since it is patently impractical to append an evaluation of each bibliographical item in a book of general reference, a reader's attention can be called to a particularly valuable publication by a word or two, such as "important," "of fundamental value," etc. Conversely, a warning should be given against worthless publications of a biographical nature that for some reason have become widely read. A famous, or infamous, example is a purported book of memoirs attributed to the nineteenth-century German prima donna Wilhelmina Schröder-Devrient and duly listed under her name in the bibliography of a number of respectable music dictionaries. It is a mildly pornographic (as pornography went at the time of its publication a hundred years ago) volume recounting her amours with famous people. It was made available in German and French; there is even a French edition in existence illustrated with erotic drawings. Less obvious in intent, but much more harmful in its effect, is the notorious correspondence between Chopin and Potocka manufactured by a Polish woman in 1945 and broadcast over Warsaw Radio during the first months after the liberation of Poland from Nazi occupation. Respectable music scholars and Chopinologists eagerly accepted these letters, which portrayed Chopin as a sex maniac given to verbal obscenities, as genuine. In one of Chopin's alleged letters he is made to use a sexual pun on a vulgar Polish word that was not in use until 1900; and there were other indecencies. The poor woman who concocted these letters committed suicide, but even then some people refused to give up their faith in the authenticity of this clumsy forgery.

Archaic spelling of the titles of old books is preserved in the present edition of *Baker's*. Martin Agricola's work *Ein kurtz deudsche Musica* retains its ancient title. Varieties of spelling in different editions of old English books are indicated, as in Christopher Simpson's *Practicall Musick*. Inordinately long book titles are abbreviated unless they contain some specific limiting clauses. For instance, Karl Grunsky's volume *Die Technik des Klavierauszuges entwickelt am dritten Akt von Wagners Tristan und Isolde* treats the problem of piano reduction only of the third act of *Tristan*, and it would be misleading to list it as *Die Technik des Klavierauszuges* plain and simple. In all such cases, practical sense rather than pedantic considerations should guide the compiler.

POLTERGEIST. Typographical errors are not just human failures of perception. They are acts of a malevolent mischievous spirit that lays its eggs in the linotype ribbon. Or else how are we to account for alterations that are obviously intended as mockery? Such fanciful conceits as "scared music," "pubic rectal," or "anals of music" cannot be accidents endemic to the typesetter. Avaunt! Avaunt! (Memo to proofreader: typos intentional to illustrate the dreadful dangers in writing books; do not change to "sacred music," "public recital" and "annals of music.")

I have a recurrent dream: I am in the dock facing a trio of stern judges vaguely resembling my schoolteachers of long ago, about to hear a sentence pronounced upon me for incompetence, negligence, dereliction of duty, fraudulent pretense at lexicographical expertise. The judges exhibit grotesquely enlarged entries from my edition of Baker's, engraved on huge slabs of granite, as evidence against me. In my anguish I plead extenuating circumstances. Yes, I was guilty of procrastination, sloth, accidie, pigritude (a lovely old word for laziness), stupidity perhaps, but did I not try? Did I not get from Naples the birth certificates of thirteen Enrico Carusos before giving up? Did I not locate Edward Maryon in England after his publisher told me he had been dead for years? Maryon bequeathed to me his manuscripts and other memorabilia, going back to the seventeenth century (he was of the nobility; his full name was Maryon d'Aulby), which were sent to me in a huge trunk by his executors after his death. I donated the materials to the Boston Public Library.

At least one living composer showed kindness to me in appreciation of my efforts to get his biography right (and failing), Ezra Sims of Massachusetts. I got his string quartets all mixed up in my 1971 Supplement to *Baker's*, and created a nonexistent String Quartet No. 2, composed, according to my mistaken impression, in 1962. In an unparalleled act of forgiveness, Sims composed a piece scored for a quintet of winds and strings, called it String Quartet No. 2, dated it 1962, although he wrote it in 1974, and dedicated it to me so that I "may be now less in error."

De minimis non curat lex, says an old legal maxim. But still there are minutiae that ought to be attended to in a reference work. The title of Leoncavallo's most famous opera is *Pagliacci*, without the definite article, not *I Pagliacci*. The original manuscript score is in the Library of Congress in Washington, D.C., and the title page can be examined by any doubting person. But the bronze plaque underneath the precious relic bears the wrong title *I Pagliacci*! Aaron Copland's best-known work, *Lincoln Portrait*, was listed in *Baker's* 1958 as *A Lincoln Portrait*, and Copland specifically pointed out to me that the score has no such indefinite article in its title. And yet the program of its very first performance carried an intrusive "A," and many symphony programs repeated the error.

My medulla oblongata, or whatever part of the brain controls lexicographical reflexes, overflows with gratitude to the many unselfish people who have helped me in putting together the 1958 edition of *Baker's*, its two Supplements, of 1965 and 1971, and, most importantly, the present swollen edition. First to be thanked are the multitudinous registrars, clerks, and keepers of city or state archives all over the habitable world who have provided me with copies of birth and death certificates that have made it possible to establish correct chronology in the lives of thousands of musicians represented in *Baker's*. The editors of the Riemann *Musik-Lexikon* have most generously let me have hundreds of documents pertaining to musical biography and copies of a number of birth and death certificates which I had not had in my possession—a most extraordinary example of scholarly cooperation. Boris Steinpress, editor of the Soviet musical encyclopedia, patiently collected for me dates of first performances of Russian operas and symphonies and corrected numerous errors encountered in the articles on Russian composers in the previous editions of *Baker's*. Grigori Schneerson of Moscow was a great lexicographical and personal friend during the many years of our correspondence. And there were many others in Russia and in other countries in Europe.

How can I thank William Lichtenwanger, that magus of musical, and not only musical, encyclopedias, the polynomial scholar who possesses in his head a cross-reference to all subjects biographical, historical, and lexicographical? A polymath, a polyglot at home in all European languages, an enlightened opsimath in Russian and a philological connoisseur of Turkish and Japanese, he was willing to read and to critically annotate the galley proofs of the entire bulk of the present edition of *Baker's*; he got for me precious biographical data on *Baker* inmates who dwelt in the lexicographical nirvana for decades. To quote from James Joyce's passage in *Finnegans Wake*, written in bird language, "Nobirdy aviar soar anywing to eagle it." Lichtenwanger is unique.

Much as I welcome people volunteering corrections in *Baker's* and other lexicographical publications of which I have been in charge, I admit that I was somewhat startled when in August 1972 I received a letter from Stephen W. Ellis of Glenview, Illinois, in which he tore to pieces my 1971 Supplement to *Baker's*, sideswiping also at the basic 1958 volume. "Grossly incomplete," "flagrantly inaccurate," "absurd," "shockingly out of date," "sadly inadequate," "ridiculous," "disgraceful," and even "criminal," were some of his expletives. The 1971 Supplement must have been a "one-man job," he correctly surmised. But who *was* Stephen W. Ellis? I had never heard of him, and I could not find his name in any index of articles on music. Yet the man exhibited such precise knowledge of so many obscure items of music history and musical biography that he could not have been just an amateur. My first impulse was to respond with lofty indignation: "Sirrah! Do you realize that you are addressing one whom the *Penguin Dictionary of Music* called 'a modern prince of musical lexicography,' and for whom Percy A. Scholes invoked, in a personal letter *(rubesco referens)*, the famous lines of Goldsmith, 'and still the wonder grew that one small head could carry all he knew'? One, who..." But I quickly cooled down, realizing how valuable Ellis could be for the completely new edition of *Baker's*. I wrote him with genuine curiosity, asking how on earth he could have collected such a mountain of information on music and musicians, which he dispensed with such certainty of his sources. I was sure he was not an academic person, I wrote him, but I guessed that he was a record collector, that he was about 42 years old, married, and had two children. I was right, as it turned out, that he was not a professional musicologist (no professional musicologist would possess such a variety of knowledge), that he was an ardent collector of records, and subscribed to bulletins issued by unions of composers all over the world. He was not 42, but only 30 years old at the time; yes, he was married, but had only one child (a second child came along soon). By profession, he was a copy reader for a small publishing house. A fortunate publishing house it was indeed! It did not take me long to persuade Ellis to help me in putting together the present edition of *Baker's;* in fact he was eager to help. His proofreading ability, I soon found out, was prodigious, but what was most remarkable, and what still astounds me, is his uncanny knack for digging up information about contemporary composers, in precise detail, and his perseverance in getting these data for *Baker's* from reluctant, recalcitrant, and unwilling musicians. The wealth of information about modern Finns, Swedes, Norwegians, and Danes which he was able to gather for me was truly comprehensive; he was comparably "teeming with the news," to borrow a phrase from Gilbert and Sullivan, about composers of Iceland, Japan, Belgium, Holland, Spain, and Portugal; he seemed to be able to get more information about the musicians of Rumania than I could after my trip to Rumania in 1963; he was equally successful with Poles, Yugoslavs, Czechs, and Bulgarians, not to mention Americans. His special contribution was information on hard-to-get Australians. All told, he sent me about 1,250 biographies, each having a very complete list of works. I could not use all this material, and I had to cut down drastically on some catalogues of works. Inevitably, I had to use my own verbiage for the introductory paragraphs of each entry, but the hard core of information on hundreds of these contemporary composers from all lands under the lexicographical sun was furnished by Ellis.

My effusive thanks are owed to Samuel Sprince of Boston, Massachusetts. Like the Canadian Royal Mounties, he never failed to get his man; in this context, the man (or the woman) was some obscure musician whose opaque name made an insignificant blur on a page in an old edition of *Baker's* and who somehow remained unnoticed by subsequent editors. Still, such unfortunates had to be taken care of, dead or alive, to preserve the continuity of the *Baker's* heritage. Sprince tracked down for me quite a number of such personages, most of them hovering between uncertain life and certain death in some wretched nursing home. Several of them met their Maker without the benefit of an obituary, and were lost until some relative could be found to supply the missing obit. It is

Preface to the Sixth Edition

unfortunate that so many musicians die out of alphabetical order, so that when a dictionary is already half-printed, a *revenant* from the early part of the alphabet is apt to make a belated appearance. The entries under the early letters of the alphabet in the present edition of *Baker's* already constitute a sizable mortuary.

The following individuals and institutions have lent their most valuable assistance in preparing the present edition of *Baker's:*

Patsy Felch, Head Reference Librarian, and Don Roberts, Head Music Librarian, Northwestern University Music Library, Evanston, Illinois

Centre Belge de Documentation Musicale, Brussels

Per Olof Lundahl, Executive Secretary, Swedish Music Information Center, Stockholm

Bálint András Varga, Head of Promotion, Editio Musica Budapest, Budapest

Jarmo Sermilä, former Executive Secretary, Finnish Music Information Center, Helsinki

Kimiko Shimbo, Secretary General, The Japan Federation of Composers, Tokyo

Rina Smits-Westhof, Librarian, Foundation Donemus, Amsterdam

Canadian Music Centre, Toronto

Timothy Rice, Faculty of Music, University of Toronto

Czechoslovak Music Information Center, Prague

Magnhild Stoveland, Society of Norwegian Composers, Oslo

Secretaria de Estado da Comunicação Social, Lisbon

Union of Rumanian Composers, Bucharest

Icelandic Music Information Center, Reykjavik

Dimiter Christoff, Secretary General of the UNESCO International Music Council in Sofia, Bulgaria

Teresa Mochtak, Head of the Music Department, Polskie Wydawnictwo Muzyczne Edition, Warsaw

James Murdoch, National Director, Australia Music Centre, Ltd., Sydney

Wilhelm Hansen Edition, Copenhagen

Esperanza Pulido, editor, *Heterofonía*, Mexico City

Hellenic Association for Contemporary Music, Athens

Instituto de Cultura Puertorriqueña, San Juan

Benjamin Bar-Am, Secretary, League of Composers in Israel, Tel Aviv

I conclude this rather inflated preface, as I did my 1971 Supplement to *Baker's*, with a cherished quotation from a letter I received from Alfred Einstein shortly before his death. In his characteristic mood of gentle humor, he wondered "ob wir, und natürlich vor allem Sie, im Himmel einmal dafür belohnt werden, dass wir einige Ungenauigkeiten aus der Welt geschafft haben...." Onward to a heavenly reward!

Nicolas Slonimsky
Los Angeles, California
September 1978

A

Aaltonen, Erkki, Finnish composer; b. Hämeenlinna (Tavastehus), Aug. 17, 1910. He studied violin at the Helsinki Cons. and composition privately with Väinö Raitio and Selim Palmgren. In 1966 he became music director for the city of Kemi. His music often reflects topical subjects.

WORKS: 5 symphs.: No. 1 (1947); No. 2, *Hiroshima* (1949); No. 3, *Popular* (1952); No. 4 (1959); No. 5 (1964); *Hämeenlinna,* rhapsody for Orch. (1945); 2 piano concertos (1948, 1954); *Folk Music* for Orch. (1953–60); 2 ballet suites from *Lapponia* (1956, 1959); Violin Concerto (1966); Piano Sonata (1932; revised 1972); Oboe Sonata (1945); 5 string quartets; piano pieces; songs.

Aarne, Elze, Estonian pianist and composer; b. Makeyevka, Ukraine, March 30, 1917. She studied piano with Lemba at the Tallinn Cons. in Estonia and composition with A. Kapp. She subsequently joined the faculty of the Tallinn Cons. as an instructor in piano and theory.

WORKS: For Orch.: Symph. No. 1 (1961); Symph. No. 2 (1966); *Baltic Sea, the Sea of Peace* for Wind Orch. (1958); Piano Concerto (1945); Horn Concerto (1958); Double-bass concerto (1968). Chamber music: Wind Quintet (1965); Nocturne for Cello and Piano (1970). Vocal works: *Fatherland,* cantata for Chorus and Orch. (1939); *Sing, Free People,* cantata (1949); numerous songs.

Aaron, abbot of the monasteries of St. Martin and St. Pantaleon at Cologne, where he died on Dec. 14, 1052. He was the author of 2 historically important treatises: *De utilitate cantus vocalis et de modo cantandi atque psallendi* and *De regulis tonorum et symphoniarum.* He is believed to be the first cleric to introduce the Gregorian evening service (*nocturns*) into Germany.

Aaron, Pietro, Italian theorist; b. Florence, 1489; d. Venice, 1545. He was cantor at the Cathedral of Imola in 1521; at the Rimini Cathedral in 1523. In 1525 he was "maestro di casa" in a Venetian house; in 1536 entered the Order of Jerusalem. He publ. *Libri tres de institutione harmonica* (Bologna, 1516); *Thoscanello de la musica* (Venice, 1523; 4 reprints, 1525–62); *Trattato della natura et cognitione di tutti gli tuoni di canto figurato* (Venice, 1525; reproduced in part, in an Eng. trans., in O. Strunk's *Source Readings in Music History,* N.Y., 1950); *Lucidario in musica di alcune opinione antiche e moderne* (Venice, 1545); *Compendiolo di molti dubbi, segreti, et sentenze intorno al canto fermo et figurato* (Milan, posthumous; title page bears the inscription: "In memoria eterna erit Aron").

BIBLIOGRAPHY: J.W. Link, Jr., *Theory and Tuning: Aaron's Mean Tone Temperament* (Boston, 1963); Peter Berquist, "Mode and Polyphony around 1500; Theory and Practice," *Music Forum,* I (1967).

Aav, Evald, Estonian composer; b. Reval, Feb. 22, 1900; d. there, March 21, 1939. He studied composition in Reval with Arthur Kapp; wrote mostly vocal music to words in the Estonian language. In 1928 he composed the first national Estonian opera, *The Vikings* (Tallinn, Sept. 8, 1928). In his style of composition he followed the model of Tchaikovsky.

Aavik, Juhan, Estonian composer; b. Reval, Jan. 29, 1884; d. Stockholm, Nov. 26, 1982. He studied at the St. Petersburg Cons.; was a conductor in Dorpat (1911–25); settled again in Reval (1928–44) as prof. and director of the Cons. there; in 1944 he went to Sweden; was conductor of the Estonian song festivals there from 1948–61 before retirement. A highly prolific composer, he wrote about 200 opus numbers, among them 2 symphs.; a Cello Concerto (1949); Double-bass Concerto (1950); Piano Trio (1957); Requiem (1959); and numerous choral works, songs, and pieces of chamber music. He publ. a history of Estonian music in 4 vols. (Stockholm, 1965–69). He died at the age of 98.

Abaco, Evaristo Felice dall', Italian composer; b. Verona, July 12, 1675; d. Munich, July 12, 1742. He came from a well-placed family in Verona, and studied violin and cello there. He was in Modena from 1696–1701. In 1704 he was at the Bavarian court in Munich; then he followed the Duke of Bavaria to Belgium and France, where he became acquainted with French music, which left some influence on his later works. In 1715 he returned to Munich, and was active as leader of the court orch. He wrote 12 violin sonatas, with Cello or Cembalo, op. 1 (1706); *Concerti da chiesa* for 4 String Instruments, op. 2 (1714); *6 Sonate da chiesa* and *6 Sonate da camera* for 3 String Instruments, op. 3 (1715); *12 Sonate da camera* for Violin and Cello, op. 4 (1716); arranged by Chédeville for Musette, Flute, Oboe, and Continuo); *6 Concerti* for 7 Instruments (4 Violins, Viola, Bassoon or Cello, and Bass), op. 5 (1717); Concerto for Violin Solo with Instruments, op. 6 (1730; his most important work). Sandberger publ. a biographical sketch and a selection from op. 1–4 in vol. 1 of Denkmäler der Tonkunst in Bayern, and a 2nd selection in vol. 16 (9.i); Riemann edited 3 trio sonatas.

BIBLIOGRAPHY: R. Brenzon, "Un grande musicista veronese, Ev. Fel. dall'Abaco," *Note d'Archivio,* XII (1935); K.G. Fellerer's article in *Die Musik in Geschichte und Gegenwart.*

Abaco, Joseph Marie Clément dall', Belgian violoncellist and composer, son of **Evaristo Felice dall'Abaco;** b. Brussels (baptized, March 27), 1710; d. at Arbizzano di Valpolicella, near Verona, Aug. 31, 1805. He received his musical training from his father, and as a youth of 19 entered the service of the Prince Elector at Bonn; played in the court orch.; in 1738 was appointed music director. He was in England in 1740; in 1753 he went to Verona; was given the title of baron by Prince Maximilian of Bavaria (1766). His works include more than 30 cello sonatas and other compositions.

Abbadia, Natale, Italian composer; b. Genoa, March 11, 1792; d. Milan, Dec. 25, 1861. He composed the opera *Giannina di Pontieu* (1812); the musical farce *L'imbroglione ed il castigamatti;* masses, motets, and other religious music.

Abbado, Claudio, outstanding Italian conductor, brother of **Marcello Abbado;** b. Milan, June 26, 1933. If the documentation of the genealogical record of his family is to be trusted, he was a direct descendant of a Moorish chieftain, Abdul Abbad, who was expelled from Spain in 1492. Abbado received his early training in music from his father, a professional violinist; then enrolled in the Milan Cons., graduating in 1955 in piano; later took piano lessons in Salzburg with Friedrich Gulda; from 1956 to 1958 he attended the conducting classes of Hans Swarowsky at the Vienna Academy of Music; also spent the summers of 1956 and 1957 working with Carlo Zecchi and Alceo Galliera at the Accademia Chigiana in Siena. In 1958 he won the Koussevitzky conducting prize at the Berkshire Music Center in Tanglewood; in 1963 he was one of the three winners of the Mitropoulos Competition in N.Y. He made his professional American debut as conductor with the N.Y. Phil. on April 7, 1963. In 1965 he appeared as a symph. conductor at La Scala in Milan; also in 1965 he began conducting the Vienna Phil., leading it in Salzburg, in Vienna, and on tour. He began to conduct opera at La Scala in 1967; became its principal conductor in 1968, its music director in 1972, and its artistic director in 1976. In 1972–73 he took the Vienna Phil. to Japan and China; in 1974 he conducted concerts in Russia with the La Scala company; in 1976 he led appearances in the U.S. with both the Vienna Phil. and the La Scala company, which had its American debut during the celebrations of the Bicentennial. In 1979 he was appointed principal conductor of the London Symph. In 1982 he was named principal guest conductor of the Chicago Symph. Orch. In all these varied positions he proved himself a leader of the finest distinction, as competent and congenial with operas by Verdi as with symphs. by Mahler.

BIBLIOGRAPHY: David Ewen, *Musicians since 1900* (N.Y., 1978); P. Harg, *Conductors: A New Generation* (N.Y., 1979; pp. 69–103).

Abbado, Marcello, Italian pianist and composer; brother of **Claudio Abbado;** b. Milan, Oct. 7, 1926. He studied at the Cons. in Milan with Gavazzeni (piano) and Ghedini (composition), graduating in 1947. In 1951 he was appointed instructor at the Cons. of Venice; from 1958 to 1966 he was director of the Liceo Musicale in Piacenza; in 1966 was appointed director of the Rossini Cons. in Pesaro; in

1972 became director of the Milan Cons. In 1979 he became principal conductor of the London Symph. Orch., and in 1983 was appointed its music director. He has written a cantata, *Ciapo* (1945); *Lento e Rondo* for Violin and Piano (1949); *Costruziono* for 5 Small Orchs. (1964); Double Concerto for Violin, Piano, and 2 Chamber Orchs. (1967); Quadruple Concerto for Piano, Violin, Viola, Cello, and Orch. (1969); 3 string quartets (1947, 1953, 1969); piano pieces.

Abbatini, Antonio Maria, Italian composer; b. Tiferno (Città di Castello), c.1597; d. there, c.1679. He served as maestro di cappella at the Lateran (1626–28) and other Roman churches; was at the church of Loreto from March to Oct. 1667. In 1672 he was employed at S. Maria Maggiore. He wrote 3 operas; the first, *Dal male al bene,* written in 1653, is of historical importance because it introduced a final ensemble; his other operas were *Ione* (Vienna, 1666) and *La comica del cielo* or *La Baltasara* (Rome, 1668); he also composed a dramatic cantata, *Il pianto di Rodomonte* (Orvieto, 1633). He publ. 3 books of masses, 4 books of psalms, various antiphons (1630, 1638, 1677), and 5 books of motets (1635).
BIBLIOGRAPHY: H. Goldschmidt, *Studien zur Geschichte der italienischen Oper im 17. Jahrhundert* (Leipzig, 1901–4); F. Coradini, *A.M. Abbatini* (Arezzo, 1922).

Abbey, John, noted English organ builder; b. Whilton, Northamptonshire, Dec. 22, 1785; d. Versailles, Feb. 19, 1859. He went to Paris in 1826 at the invitation of Sébastien Erard to construct an organ for the Paris Exposition. He remained in France and built organs for the cathedrals of many French cities. In 1831 he installed an organ at the Paris Opéra. His innovations in the English type of bellows were adopted by many French organ builders. His sons, **E.** and **J. Abbey,** inherited the business, situated at Versailles.

Abbiati, Franco, Italian writer on music; b. Verdello, Sept. 14, 1898; d. Bergamo, Jan. 22, 1981. He studied composition at the Turin Cons., graduating in 1929; also took courses in musicology with Gaetano Cesari; was music critic of Milan's *Secolo Sera* (1928–34); in 1934 he became music critic of *Corriere della Sera,* a position he held until his retirement in 1973. He founded the Journal *La Scala* in 1949, and edited it until it ceased publication in 1963. He edited *Gaetano Cesari: Scritti inediti* (Milan, 1937); his other publications were *Storia della musica* (5 vols., Milan, 1939–46; 2nd ed., revised in 4 vols., 1967–68; also in an abridged ed., 1955; 2nd ed., revised 1971); publ. *Giuseppe Verdi* (4 vols., Milan, 1959), a basic source, and *Alti e bassi del Simon Boccanegra* (Verona, 1973).

Abbott, Emma, American soprano; b. Chicago, Dec. 9, 1850; d. Salt Lake City, Jan. 5, 1891. Her father was a singer and her brother a violinist; as a young woman she filled engagements with them in

hotels and clubs. Her first regular employment was with Chapin's choir in N.Y. (1870–72) at a salary of $1,500 a year. In March 1872 she went to Europe, where she took voice lessons with Sangiovanni in Milan and with Marchesi, Wartel, and Delle Sedie in Paris. She made her professional debut as an opera singer in London on May 2, 1876, in the role of Maria in Donizetti's *La Fille du régiment;* returning to America, she sang the same role in N.Y. on Feb. 8, 1877. She was in many ways an American primitive, traveling with her own small opera company across the country; at her performances she was prone to interpolate her "specialties" in the opera scores, such as singing the hymn "Nearer My God to Thee" in *Faust.*
BIBLIOGRAPHY: Sadie E. Martin, *The Life and Professional Career of Emma Abbott* (Minneapolis, 1891).

Abe, Komei, Japanese composer; b. Hiroshima, Sept. 1, 1911. He studied cello at the Tokyo Academy of Music, graduating in 1933; took postgraduate composition courses there with Klaus Pringsheim (1933–36) and conducting with Joseph Rosenstock (1935–39); then became a prof. at the Elizabeth Music College at Kyoto; was from 1969–74 a prof. at Kyoto Municipal Univ. of Arts.
WORKS: *Theme and Variations* for Orch. (Tokyo, Feb. 8, 1936); *Kleine Suite* for Orch. (Tokyo, Feb. 27, 1937); Cello Concerto (Tokyo, March 31, 1942); Piano Concerto (1945; Tokyo, March 27, 1947); 2 symphs.: No. 1 (Tokyo, May 9, 1957) and No. 2 (Tokyo, Oct. 10, 1960); *Serenade* for Orch. (Tokyo, Oct. 7, 1963); Sinfonietta (Tokyo, Jan. 14, 1965); 9 string quartets (1935, 1937, 1939, 1943, 1946, 1948, 1950, 1952, 1955); 2 flute sonatas (1942, 1949); Clarinet Quintet (1942); *Divertimento* for Saxophone and Piano (1951; orchestrated 1953); *Divertimento* for 9 Instruments (1954); Sextet for Flute, Clarinet, Violin, Viola, Cello, and Piano (1964); *A Picture Book for Children* for Piano (1967); Piano Sonatina (1970); 3 piano sonatinas for children (1971); *Variation on a Subject by Grieg* for 4 Trumpets, 4 Horns, 3 Trombones, and Tuba (1972); choral music; songs; film music.

Abeille, Johann Christian Ludwig, German organist and composer; b. Bayreuth, Feb. 20, 1761; d. Stuttgart, March 2, 1838. He was educated at Stuttgart; in 1782 he joined the private orch. of the Duke of Württemberg; in 1802 he became Konzertmeister, serving in this capacity until 1832. He publ. several albums of songs which found their way into vocal anthologies; wrote 2 light operas, *Amor und Psyche* (1800) and *Peter und Annchen* (1809); also composed harpsichord pieces and concerted music for small groups.

Abejo, Rosalina, Filipino pianist and composer; b. Tagoloan, Oriental Misamis, Philippines, July 13, 1922. She studied at the Philippine Women's Univ., receiving her M.M. in 1957; then went to Cincinnati, where she studied composition with Felix Labunski; later took courses with Wayne Barlow at the

Eastman School of Music in Rochester, N.Y. She joined the Order of the Virgin Mary, and was the first nun to conduct a symph. orch. An exceptionally prolific composer, she wrote a number of sacred works, among them *Thanatopsis* for Orch. (1956) and *The Trilogy of Man* for Orch. (1971), and also several secular works on political themes, including a symph. poem entitled *Guerrilla,* dedicated to President Marcos of the Philippines (1971). Other works include a Guitar Concerto, a Marimba Concerto, divers chamber music pieces, piano compositions, and song cycles. She also publ. several teaching manuals.

Abel, Carl Friedrich, German viola da gamba player and composer; b. Cöthen, Dec. 22, 1723; d. London, June 20, 1787. He studied with his father, a player on the gamba; then moved to Leipzig, where he enrolled in the Thomasschule; then lived for many years in Dresden, where he joined the Court Orch. (1743–58). In 1759 he went to London, making it his permanent home; in 1764 became court musician to Queen Charlotte, a position he held until his death. He also became associated with Bach's son, the "London Bach," John (Johann) Christian, and with him organized a series of concerts, which gained renown as as the Bach-Abel Concerts (1765–81). Abel composed a number of instrumental works, among them several symphs., a *Sinfonia concertante,* several piano concertos, string quartets, trio sonatas, piano sonatas, violin sonatas, and pieces for the viola da gamba. In his style of composition he followed the Mannheim School, emphasizing symmetric instrumental forms and diversified dynamics. His Symph. in E-flat major was erroneously ascribed to Mozart and even listed as K. 18; A51, which testifies, however obliquely, to the intrinsic worth of his music. Abel was the last great virtuoso on the viola da gamba of the Classical period, until the revival of Baroque instruments in the 20th century by Dolmetsch and others. Abel's compositions have been publ. in a collected edition by W. Knape, *K.F. Abel: Kompositionen* (Cuxhaven, 1958–74); Knape also prepared a *Bibliographisch-thematisches Verzeichnis der Kompositionen von Karl Friedrich Abel* (Cuxhaven, 1971).
BIBLIOGRAPHY: S. Helm, *Carl F. Abel, Symphonist: A Biographical, Stylistic and Bibliographical Study* (Diss., Univ. of Michigan, 1953); P. Young, "Johann Christian, der englische Bach," in H. Wegener, ed., *Musa—Mens—Musici: Im Gedenken an Walther Vetter* (Leipzig, 1969); G. Beechey, "Carl Friedrich Abel's Six Symphonies, op. 14," *Music & Letters* (July 1970).

Abel, Ludwig, German violinist; b. Eckartsberg, Thuringia, Jan. 14, 1834; d. Neu-Pasing, Bavaria, Aug. 13, 1895. He studied with Ferdinand David; played in the Gewandhaus Orch. in Leipzig, and was later a violinist in Weimar and Munich. He publ. a method of violin playing.

Abell, Arthur M., American music critic; b. Norwich, Conn., April 6, 1868; d. Hastings-on-Hudson,

N.Y., Feb. 8, 1958. He studied in Weimar with Carl Halir (violin), Wilhelm Saal (piano), and Fritz Hartmann (theory); remained in Europe for 28 years (1890–1918) as a correspondent for the *Musical Courier* and other publications. He knew Brahms, and was a friend of Richard Strauss, Max Bruch, Joseph Joachim, and other celebrated musicians. Upon his return to the U.S., he lived in retirement in Hastings-on-Hudson. In 1955 he publ. a book of memoirs, *Talks with Great Composers.*

Abell, John, celebrated Scottish lute player; b. Aberdeenshire, 1652; d. Cambridge, 1724. He was a chorister in the Chapel Royal in London; in 1679 received a stipend from Charles II which enabled him to study in Italy. He returned to London in 1681; suspected of Roman Catholic adherence, he was compelled to seek employment on the Continent; served as Intendant of music at Kassel (1698–99); was back in London shortly afterward, able to resume his career (he was described in a contemporary report as "a harmonious vagabond"). He gave his last London concert in 1716. He publ. *A Collection of Songs in Several Languages, A Collection of Songs in English, A Choice Collection of Italian Ayres.*
BIBLIOGRAPHY: H.G. Farmer, "John Abell," in *Hinrichsen's Music Book,* VII (1952).

Abendroth, Hermann, notable German conductor; b. Frankfurt, Jan. 19, 1883; d. Jena, May 29, 1956. He studied music in Munich with Thuille and Mottl (1900–5); in 1907 he was named chief conductor of the Städtische Oper in Lübeck; in 1911 he became music director in Essen; in 1915 he assumed the post of director of the Cologne Cons. and conductor of the Gürzenich Orch.; in 1918 he became Generalmusikdirektor in Cologne; in 1922–23 he served as conductor of the symph. concerts of the Berlin State Opera Orch. Arriving at a tenuous modus vivendi with the Nazi regime, he was appointed Kapellmeister of the Gewandhaus Orch. of Leipzig in 1934; also served as director of the Leipzig Cons.; in 1945 he became music director of the National Theater in Weimar and its Generalmusikdirektor in 1946. Abendroth was regarded as a model interpreter of German music and a faithful keeper of its traditions.

Abendroth, Walter, noted German writer on music; b. Hannover, May 29, 1896. He studied music in Berlin and Munich; eventually established himself in Hamburg. He publ. valuable biographical monographs on Pfitzner (Munich, 1935), Brahms (Berlin, 1939), and Bruckner (Berlin, 1940); also *Kleine Geschichte der Musik* (Frankfurt, 1959) and an autobiographical pamphlet, *Ich warne Neugierige* (Munich, 1966). He was also a prolific composer; among his works are 5 symphs., a Viola Concerto, several violin sonatas, and numerous songs.

Aber, Adolf, German musicologist; b. Apolda, Germany, Jan. 28, 1893; d. London, May 21, 1960. He studied music with Kretzschmar, Stumpf, Wolf, and

Friedländer. From 1919 to 1933 he served as chief music critic for the *Leipziger neueste Nachrichten;* then left Germany and settled in London, where he became an editorial adviser with the Novello publishing firm.

WRITINGS: *Handbuch der Musikliteratur* (1922); *Die Musikinstrumente und ihre Sprache* (1924); *Die Musik im Schauspiel, Geschichtliches und Ästhetisches* (1926); *Verzeichnis der Werke von Brahms* (1928).

Abert, Anna Amalie, distinguished German musicologist, daughter of **Hermann Abert;** b. Halle, Sept. 19, 1906. She studied musicology with her father, with Blume, and with Sachs at the Univ. of Berlin (Ph.D., 1934, with the dissertation *Die stilistischen Voraussetzungen der "Cantiones sacrae" von Heinrich Schütz*); then joined the staff of the Univ. of Kiel; completed her Habilitation there in 1943 with *Claudio Monteverdi und das musikalische Drama* (publ. in Lippstadt, 1954); in 1950 she became a prof. there, and also a research fellow in 1962; she retired in 1971. From 1949 to 1958 she was an editor of *Die Musik in Geschichte und Gegenwart*. She contributed important articles to the *Mozart-Jahrbuch;* her writings include *Christoph Willibald Gluck* (Munich, 1959); *Die Opern Mozarts* (Wolfenbüttel, 1970; in Eng. in *The New Oxford History of Music*, vol. VII, London, 1973); *Richard Strauss: Die Opern* (Velber, 1972).

BIBLIOGRAPHY: K. Hortschansky, ed., *Opernstudien: Anna Amalie Abert zum 65. Geburtstag* (Tutzing, 1975).

Abert, Hermann, eminent German musicologist; b. Stuttgart, March 25, 1871; d. there, Aug. 13, 1927. He studied with his father, a noted musician; then with Bellermann, Fleischer, and Friedlaender in Berlin; he received his Ph.D. from the Univ. of Berlin in 1897 with the dissertation *Die Lehre vom Ethos in der griechischen Musik* (publ. in Leipzig, 1899); completed his Habilitation in 1902 at the Univ. of Halle with *Die ästhetischen Grundsätze der mittelalterlichen Melodiebildung* (publ. in Halle, 1902); was named honorary prof. there in 1909 and lecturer in 1911. In 1920 he became prof. at the Univ. of Leipzig (succeeding Hugo Riemann) and in 1923, at the Univ. of Berlin (succeeding August Kretzschmar). He was one of the outstanding scholars of his time, noted for his wide-ranging musicological interests. Among his important writings, his exhaustively rewritten and revised edition of Jahn's biography of Mozart is still valuable; it was publ. as *Wolfgang Amadeus Mozart: Neu bearbeitete und erweiterte Ausgabe von Otto Jahns "Mozart"* (2 vols., Leipzig, 1919–21; it was further revised by his daughter and publ. in 1955–56); other books include *Robert Schumann* (Berlin, 1903; 4th ed., 1920); *Die Musikanschauung des Mittelalters und ihre Grundlagen* (Halle, 1905); *Niccolo Jommelli als Opernkomponist* (Halle, 1908); *Goethe und die Musik* (Engelhorn, 1922); he also wrote a biography of his father (Leipzig, 1916). His collected writings were posthumously edited by F. Blume as *Gesammelte Schriften und Vorträge* (Halle, 1929).

BIBLIOGRAPHY: F. Blume, ed., *Gedenkschrift für Hermann Abert von seinen Schülern* (Halle, 1928); H. Brockhaus, *Hermann Aberts Konzeption der musikalischen Historiographie* (Habilitationsschrift, Humboldt Univ. of Berlin, 1966); A. Abert, "Hermann Aberts Weg zur Musikwissenschaft," in *Musa—Mens—Musici: Im Gedenken an Walther Vetter* (Leipzig, 1969).

Abert, Johann Joseph, German composer; b. Kochowitz, Sept. 20, 1832; d. Stuttgart, April 1, 1915. He studied double bass and composition at the Prague Cons. (1846–53); then played the double bass in the court orch. at Stuttgart; in 1867 became its conductor, and held this post until 1888. Abert's style, greatly influenced by Mendelssohn and Schumann, represents the German Romantic tradition at its most typical among worthy epigones. His composing technique was flawless, however.

WORKS: Operas: *Anna von Landskron* (1858); *König Enzio* (1862); *Astorga,* based on the life of the composer Emanuele d'Astorga (Stuttgart, May 27, 1866; quite successful at the time); *Ekkehard* (Berlin, Oct. 11, 1878). He also wrote *Columbus,* a "musical sea picture" in the form of a symph. (Stuttgart, Jan. 26, 1864), 6 symphs., several overtures, chamber music, and pieces for double bass. His son, **Hermann Abert,** wrote a detailed biography: *Johann Joseph Abert, Sein Leben und seine Werke* (Leipzig, 1916).

Abos, Girolamo (baptismal name, **Geronimo**), Maltese composer; b. Valetta, Nov. 16, 1715; d. Naples, Oct. 1760. He was a student of Francesco Durante and Gerolimo Ferraro in Naples; served as secondo maestro at the Cons. Poveri di Gesù Cristo (1742–43); was also secondo maestro at the Cons. della Pietà dei Turchini (1754–59). Among his pupils was Paisiello. Abos wrote 14 operas which were produced in Naples and Rome; of these, *Tito Manlio* (Naples, May 30, 1751) was successful. He also wrote 7 masses and other church music.

Abraham, Gerald, eminent English writer on music; b. Newport, Isle of Wight, March 9, 1904. He studied piano; became interested in philology; mastered the Russian language and made a profound study of Russian music. He further extended his knowledge to embrace the development of Romantic and national music in the 19th century, and the modern trends of the 20th century. From 1935 to 1947 he was connected with the BBC in London; from 1947 to 1962 was a prof. of music at Liverpool Univ. (1947–62); then returned to work with the BBC (1962–67). In 1974 he was made a Commander of the Order of the British Empire.

WRITINGS: *Borodin: The Composer and His Music* (1927; 2nd ed., 1935); *This Modern Stuff* (1933; revised ed. under the title *This Modern Music,* 1952; 3rd ed., 1955); *Studies in Russian Music* (London, 1935; 2nd ed., 1969); *Masters of Russian Music* (in collaboration with M.D. Calvocoressi, 1936; revised 1958); *A Hundred Years of Music* (1938; revised ed.,

1974); *On Russian Music* (1939); *Chopin's Musical Style* (1939); *Beethoven's Second-period Quartets* (1942); *Eight Soviet Composers* (1943); *Rimsky-Korsakov: A Short Biography* (1945). He also edited collections of articles on Tchaikovsky (1945), Schubert (1947), Sibelius (1947), Schumann (1952), and Handel (1954); *Slavonic and Romantic Music* (1968); *The Tradition of Western Music* (1974); and *The Concise Oxford History of Music* (1979). For *The New Oxford History of Music* he was co-editor with Dom Anselm Hughes of vol. III, *Ars Nova and the Renaissance 1300–1540* (London, 1960), and editor of vol. IV, *The Age of Humanism 1540–1630* (London, 1968), and vol. VIII, *The Age of Beethoven* (London, 1982).

Abraham, Max, German publisher; b. Danzig, June 3, 1831; d. Leipzig, Dec. 8, 1900. He became a partner in C.F. Peters's "Bureau de Musique" in 1863, and sole proprietor in 1880. On Jan. 1, 1894, his nephew, Heinrich Hinrichsen, of Hamburg, entered the firm; upon Abraham's death, he became its head. The famous "Edition Peters" was inaugurated by Abraham.

Abraham, Otto, German specialist in tone psychology; b. Berlin, May 30, 1872; d. there, Jan. 24, 1926. He studied medicine, and served as an assistant to Stumpf at the Berlin Psychological Inst.; also collaborated with Hornbostel in building up the Archive of Phonographic Recordings in Berlin. He publ. several valuable treatises on acoustics and primitive music, among them *Wahrnehmung kürzester Töne und Geräusche* (1898); "Studien über das Tonsystem und die Musik der Japaner," publ. in *Sammelbände der internationalen Musikgesellschaft* (1902–3); "Phonographierte Indianermelodien aus British Columbia," in the *Festschrift* for Franz Boaz (N.Y., 1906). He also wrote studies on recorded Turkish, Siamese, and Hindu melodies, and a paper on Chinese musical notation.

Abraham, Paul, Hungarian composer of light operas; b. Apatin, Nov. 2, 1892; d. Hamburg, May 6, 1960. He studied in Budapest and wrote chamber music before turning to light opera. His most successful operetta was *Viktoria und ihr Husar* (Vienna, Dec. 23, 1930); his other popular productions were *Die Blume von Hawaii* (Leipzig, July 24, 1931) and *Ball im Savoy* (Berlin, Dec. 23, 1932). In 1938 Abraham went to the U.S., but suffered a mental breakdown and in 1955 was committed to a sanatorium in Hamburg, where he died.

Abrahamsen, Hans, Danish composer; b. Copenhagen, Dec. 23, 1952. He studied horn, theory, and music history at the Royal Danish Cons. (1969–71); then studied composition at the Jutland Academy of Music in Aarhus with Gudmundsen-Holmgreen and Norgaard. His music presents an effective blend of folkloric Scandinavian elements and modernistic devices often veering off into atonal melos, viralized by polyrhythmic dynamic contrasts.
WORKS: FOR ORCH.: *Skum (Foam,* 1970); Symph.

in C (1972); 2 numbered symphonies: No. 1 (1974) and No. 2 (1982); *Stratifications* (1973–75); *Nacht und Trompeten* (1981; Berlin, March 25, 1982). CHAMBER MUSIC: *Fantasy Pieces After Hans-Jørgen Nielsen* for Flute, Horn, Cello, and Piano (1969; revised 1976); *October* for Piano left hand (1969; revised 1976); *Herbst* for Tenor, Flute, Guitar, and Cello (1970–72; revised 1977); *Round and In Between* for Brass Quintet (1972); 2 woodwind quintets; No. 1, *Landscapes* (1972); No. 2, *Walden* (1978); Nocturnes, 4 pieces for Flute and Piano (1972); *Flowersongs* for 3 Flutes (1973); *Scraps* for Cello and Piano (1973); 2 String Quartets: No. 1, *10 Preludes* (1973); No. 2 (1981); *Flush* for Solo Saxophone (1974; revised 1979); *Songs of Denmark* for Soprano and 5 Instruments (1974; revised 1976); *Double* for Flute and Guitar (1975); *Winternacht* for 7 Instruments (1976–79); *Canzone* for Solo Accordion (1978); *Aria* for Soprano and 4 Instruments (1979); *Geduldspiel* for 10 Instruments (1980). VOCAL: *Universe Birds* for 10 Sopranos (1973).

Abramsky, Alexander, Russian composer; b. Lutsk, Jan. 22, 1898. He studied with Miaskovsky at the Moscow Cons., graduating in 1926. Commissioned to do research work in Asian folklore, he traveled to Uzbekistan; wrote a music drama on native themes, *Laylikhon and Anarkhon* (Andizhan, Dec. 28, 1943). Other works: Piano Concerto (1941); *Laconic Sonata* for Piano Solo; cantata, *Land of the Silent Lake* (1971); many choruses.

Ábrányi, Cornelius, Hungarian pianist, composer, and writer on music; grandfather of **Emil Ábrányi;** b. Szentgyörgy-Ábrányi, Oct. 15, 1822; d. Budapest, Dec. 20, 1903. He came of an ancient Magyar family whose name was originally **Eördögh.** He was first destined to a legal profession, but in 1834 a meeting with the Hungarian national composer Erkel made him decide to study music. In 1843 Ábrányi went abroad; in Munich he met Liszt, and became his lifelong friend. He went to Paris and took lessons with Chopin and Kalkbrenner for a short time, returning to Hungary in 1845. He took a leading part in the formation and encouragement of the Hungarian national school of composition. His own compositions (130 opus numbers) emphasize the Hungarian national elements, the most ambitious of these works being his *Hungarian Millennial Sonata,* op. 103. His books (all in Hungarian) include: *Art and Revolution* (1867); *Biography of Franz Liszt and Survey of His Oratorio Christus* (1873); *General History of Music* (1886); *History of Hungarian Music in the Nineteenth Century* (1900). He also wrote an autobiography, *From My Life and Memories* (1897).

Ábrányi, Emil, Hungarian composer and conductor; b. Budapest, Sept. 22, 1882; d. there, Feb. 11, 1970. His father was Emil Ábrányi, the poet, and his grandfather was **Cornelius Ábrányi,** the composer and pianist. In 1902 Emil Ábrányi went to Germany, where he had instruction in conducting in Leipzig with Nikisch. He subsequently held posts as conductor at the Municipal Theater in Cologne (1904) and at Hannover (1907). Returning to Budapest in 1911, he became conductor at the Royal Opera House; was also director of the Budapest Municipal Theater (1921–26). As a composer, Ábrányi was a convinced Wagnerian, building his operas on a series of leading themes.

WORKS: Operas: *Monna Vanna* (Budapest, March 2, 1907); *Paolo e Francesca* (Budapest, Jan. 13, 1912); *Don Quixote* (Budapest, Nov. 30, 1917); *Singing Dervishes* (1935); *The Prince with the Lilies* (1938); *Byzantium* (1945); and *The Cantor of St. Thomas Church* (1947; the first opera written on the life of Bach).

Abravanel, Maurice, distinguished American conductor; b. Saloniki, Greece, Jan. 6, 1903, of Sephardic Jewish parents (an ancestor is reputed to have been chancellor to Ferdinand and Isabella of Spain). He was taken to Switzerland at the age of 6, and studied general subjects at the Univ. of Lausanne; in 1922 he went to Berlin, where he took composition lessons with Kurt Weill; with the advent of the Nazi regime in 1933, Abravanel moved to Paris, where he conducted ballet; in 1934–35 he toured Australia; in 1936 he received an offer to join the staff of the Metropolitan Opera in N.Y.; made his debut there on Dec. 26, 1936, conducting *Samson et Dalila;* generally adverse reviews compelled him to leave the Metropolitan in 1938. He turned to leading Broadway musicals; conducted a season with the Chicago Opera Co. (1940–41). In 1947 he became conductor of the Utah Symph. Orch. at Salt Lake City, and revealed a great talent for building up the orch.; in the 30 years of his conductorship it became one of the finest symph. orchs. in the U.S.; he also introduced many modern works into its repertoire. In 1976 he underwent open-heart surgery; in 1979 he retired as music director of the Utah Symph.

Abreu, José Antonio, Venezuelan composer; b. Valera, Venezuela, May 17, 1939. He studied with local teachers before going to Caracas, where he took courses with Vicente Emilio Sojo. His works follow the traditional line of tonal composition. They include *Sinfonieta Neoclásica;* 2 symphs.; symph. poem, *Sancta et Immaculata Virginitas; Tríptico* for 11 Instruments; Quintet for Wind Instruments; String Quartet; choruses.

Abreu (Rebello), Sergio (b. Rio de Janeiro, June 5, 1948) and **Eduardo** (b. Rio de Janeiro, Sept. 19, 1949), sibling Brazilian guitarists. They first studied with their grandfather, Antonio Rebello, and then with Adolfina Raitzin Távora; they began their career in 1963 with concerts throughout South America; they made their European debut in London in 1968, and their U.S. debut in N.Y. in 1970; later toured extensively all over the world.

Absil, Jean, eminent Belgian composer; b. Bonsecours, Oct. 23, 1893; d. Brussels, Feb. 2, 1974. He studied organ and composition at the Brussels Cons.; later took lessons in advanced composition

with Gilson. He won the Prix Agniez for his First Symph. (1921); in 1922 won a 2nd Prix de Rome for the cantata *La Guerre;* also received the Prix Rubens. His First Piano Concerto was commissioned by the 1938 Concours Ysaÿe in Brussels as the compulsory work for the 12 finalists in the contest eventually won by Emil Gilels. He was music director of the Academy of Etterbeek in Brussels (1922–64); taught at the Brussels Cons. (1930–59); was also one of the founders of the *Revue Internationale de Musique.* Absil evolved an individual style, characterized by rhythmic variety, free tonality, and compact counterpoint.

WORKS: FOR THE STAGE: *Peau d'âne,* lyrical poem in 3 acts (1937); *Ulysse et les sirènes,* radio play (1939); *Fansou ou Le Chapeau chinois,* musical comedy (1944); *Le Miracle de Pan,* ballet (1949); *Pierre Breughel l'Ancien,* radio play (1950); *Epouvantail,* ballet (1950); *Les Voix de la mer,* opera (1951; Brussels, March 26, 1954); *Les Météores,* ballet (1951). FOR ORCH.: 5 symphs. (1920, 1936, 1943, 1969, 1970); *La Mort de Tintagiles,* symph. poem (1923–26); *Rapsodie flamande* (1928; also for Wind Ensemble); *Berceuse* for Small Orch., and Cello or Saxophone (1932); 2 violin concertos (1933, 1964); *Petite suite* for Small Orch. (1935; also for Wind Ensemble); 3 piano concertos (1937, 1967, 1973); *Rapsodie No. 2* (1938); *Hommage à Lekeu* (1939); Cello Concertino (1940); *Sérénade* (1940); *Variations symphoniques* (1942); Viola Concerto (1942); *Rapsodie roumaine* for Violin and Orch. (1943); *Concerto Grosso* for Wind Quintet and Orch. (1944); *Jeanne d'Arc,* symph. poem (1945); *Rites,* triptych for Wind Ensemble (1952); *Rapsodie brésilienne* (1953); *Mythologie,* suite (1954); *Croquis sportifs* for Wind Ensemble (1954); *Divertimento* for Saxophone Quartet and Chamber Orch. (1955); *Introduction et Valses* (1955); *Legend* for Wind Ensemble (1956); *Suite,* after Rumanian folklore (1956); *Suite bucolique* for Strings (1957); *Fantaisie concertante* for Violin, and Orch. or Piano (1959); *Danses bulgares* (1959; also for Wind Quintet or Piano); *Rapsodie bulgare* (1960); 2 *Danses rituelles* for Small Orch. (1960); *Triptyque* for Small Orch. (1960); *Fantaisie-humoresque* for Clarinet, and Strings or Piano (1962); *Rapsodie No. 6* for Horn, and Orch. or Piano (1963); Viola Concertino (1964); *Nymphes et faunes* for Wind Orch. (1966); *Allegro brillante* for Piano and Orch. (1967); *Fantaisie-caprice* for Saxophone and Strings (1971); Guitar Concerto (1971); *Ballade* for Saxophone, Piano, and Small Orch. (1971); *Déités,* suite (1973). VOCAL MUSIC: *La Guerre,* cantata (1922); *Philatélie,* chamber cantata (1940); *Les Bénédictions,* cantata (1941); *Les Chants du mort,* cantata for Vocal Quartet and Small Orch., to texts from old Rumanian ritual chants lamenting the death of a person (1941); *Le Zodiaque,* symph. variations with Chorus and Piano Concertante (1949); *Phantasmes* for Contralto, Saxophone, Piano, and Percussion (1950); *Le Cirque volant,* cantata (1953); *Petites polyphonies* for 2 Voices and Orch. (1966); *Acloche-pied* for Children's Chorus and Orch. (1968). CHAMBER MUSIC: 4 string quartets (1929, 1934, 1935, 1941); 2 piano trios (1931, 1972); 2 string trios (1935, 1939); *Fantaisie rapsodique* for 4 Cellos

(1936); Cello Quartet (1937); Quartet for Saxophones (1937); Piano Quartet (1938); *Fantaisie* for Piano Quartet (1939); *Concert à cinq* for Flute, Violin, Viola, Cello, and Harp (1939); 2 suites for Cello and Piano (1942, 1968); *Chaconne* for Solo Violin (1949); 3 *Contes* for Trumpet and Piano (1951); Suite for Trombone and Piano (1952); *Sonatine en duo* for Violin and Viola (1962); Saxophone Sonata (1963); 3 *Pièces* for Organ (1965); Quartet for Clarinets (1967); Solo Violin Sonata (1967); *Croquis pour un carnaval* for 4 Clarinets and Harp (1968); *Suite mystique* for 4 Flutes (1969); Violin Sonata (1970); *Esquisses* for Wind Quartet (1971); *Images stellaires* for Violin and Cello (1973). PIANO MUSIC: 3 *Impromptus* (1932); 3 sonatinas (1937, 1939, 1965); 3 *Marines* (1939); Bagatelles (1944); 2 *Grand suites* (1944, 1962); *Sketches on the 7 Capital Sins* (1954); Variations (1956); *Chess Game,* suite (1957); *Passacaglia* (1959); *Rapsodie No. 5* for 2 pianos (1959); *Humoresques* (1965); Ballade (1966); *Asymétries* for 2 Pianos (1968); *Alternances* (1968); *Féeries* (1971); *Poésie et vélocité,* 20 pieces (1972); also numerous pieces for guitar, a cappella choral works, songs.

BIBLIOGRAPHY: J. Dopp, "Jean Absil," *La Revue Musicale* (Oct./Dec. 1937); R. de Guide, *Jean Absil* (Tournai, 1965).

Abt, Franz, German songwriter and conductor; b. Eilenburg, Dec. 22, 1819; d. Wiesbaden, March 31, 1885. His father, a clergyman, sent him to Leipzig Thomasschule to study theology; he later obtained an excellent musical education both there and at the Univ. He became a choral conductor in Zürich (1841). In 1852 he was appointed 2nd conductor at the Brunswick Court; in 1855 became first conductor. In 1869 he traveled, as a choral conductor, to Paris, London, and Russia; in 1872 he made a highly successful tour in America. He retired on a pension from Brunswick in 1882. Abt wrote over 600 works, comprising more than 3,000 numbers; the largest are the 7 secular cantatas. His popularity as a songwriter is due chiefly to the flowing, easy, and elegant style of his vocal melodies, some of which *(Wenn die Schwalben heimwärts zieh'n, Gute Nacht, du mein herziges Kind, So viele Tausend Blumen,* etc.) have become so well-known as to be mistaken for genuine folk songs.

BIBLIOGRAPHY: B. Rost, *Vom Meister des volkstümlichen deutschen Liedes, Franz Abt* (Chemnitz, 1924).

Accardo, Salvatore, Italian violinist; b. Turin, Sept. 26, 1941. In 1958 he won the prestigious Paganini Competition, then embarked upon a concert career. His playing is marked by a fidelity to the classical school of violin playing, in which virtuosity is subordinated to stylistic propriety.

Achron, Isidor, Russian-American pianist, brother of **Joseph Achron;** b. Warsaw, Nov. 24, 1892; d. New York, May 12, 1948. He studied at the St. Petersburg Cons. with Anna Essipoff (piano) and with Liadov (composition). In 1922 he settled in the U.S.; naturalized in 1928. From 1922–33 he was accompanist to Jascha Heifetz; was also active as a piano teacher in N.Y. He was also a composer; played his Piano Concerto with the N.Y. Phil. Orch. on Dec. 9, 1937; his *Suite Grotesque* for Orch. was first performed in St. Louis, Jan. 30, 1942. He also wrote a number of piano pieces, all in a moderate Romantic manner in the prevalent tradition of the time.

Achron, Joseph, Russian-American violinist and composer, brother of **Isidor Achron;** b. Losdseje, near Suwalki, Poland, May 13, 1886; d. Hollywood, April 29, 1943. In 1890 the family moved to Warsaw. He studied violin there, and gave his first public concert at the age of 7. In 1898 he entered the St. Petersburg Cons. as a student of Leopold Auer in violin and with Liadov in music theory. Graduating in 1904, he went to Berlin, where he appeared as a soloist with orchs. In 1907 he returned to St. Petersburg to continue his studies in theory and orchestration at the conservatory there. In 1911 he organized, along with several Jewish musicians, a society for Jewish folklore. One of the products of his research was the popular *Hebrew Melody* for Violin and Piano (1911), based on a Hasidic theme. During World War I he was a member of the music corps of the Russian army. In 1919–21 he was active as composer for the Hebrew Chamber Theater in Petrograd; in 1922 he went again to Berlin; in 1924 he was in Palestine, and in 1925 emigrated to the U.S.; became a naturalized American citizen in 1930. He lived in N.Y. until 1934; then went to Hollywood, where he earned his living as a violinist in film studios, and continued to compose energetically. His early compositions are marked by characteristic Russian harmonies with a distinctly Romantic aura, but under the impact of modern techniques he developed a strong idiom based on purely structural principles employing atonal and polytonal devices. Schoenberg wrote about him in the program book of a memorial concert of Achron's compositions given in Los Angeles in 1945: "Joseph Achron is one of the most underestimated of modern composers, but the originality and profound elaboration of his ideas guarantee that his works will last." Achron's major compositions include a suite for Chamber Orch., *Golem* (1932), the last section of which is the exact retrograde movement of the first section, to symbolize the undoing of the monster Golem; 3 violin concertos in which he appeared as soloist: No. 1 (Boston, Jan. 24, 1927); No. 2 (Los Angeles, Dec. 19, 1936); No. 3 (Los Angeles, March 31, 1939); *4 tableaux fantastiques* for Violin and Piano (1907); *Chromatic String Quartet* (1907); 2 violin sonatas (1910, 1918); *Hazan* for Cello and Orch. (1912); *2 Hebrew Pieces* for Violin and Piano (1912); *Suite bizarre* for Violin and Piano (1916); *Scher* for Violin and Piano (1916); *Elegy* for String Quartet (1927); *Statuettes* for Piano (1929); *Sextet* for Flute, Oboe, Clarinet, Bassoon, Horn, and Trumpet (1938); Piano Concerto (1941); *Evening Service for the Sabbath* (1930); songs and choruses.

BIBLIOGRAPHY: Ph. Moddel, *Joseph Achron* (Tel Aviv, 1966).

Achucarro, Joaquín, Spanish pianist; b. Bilbao, Nov. 1, 1936. He began to play the piano as a child; made his public debut in Bilbao at the age of 12. At 17 he won first prize in the Viotti Competition in Vercelli, Italy; subsequently continued his studies with Gieseking, Magaloff, Seidhofer, and Kabos. In 1959 he won first prize in the Liverpool International Pianoforte Competition, which marked the beginning of a successful career as a concert pianist.

Acker, Dieter, Rumanian-born German composer; b. Sibiu, Nov. 3, 1940. He studied piano and organ in Sibiu (1950–58); then composition with Toduța at the Cluj Cons. (1958–64); subsequently went to Germany; in 1972 he was appointed teacher of composition at the Hochschule für Musik in Munich. His most notable work is the string quartet entitled *Prager Frühling* (1966); he also composed for orch. and for piano.

Ackermann, Otto, Rumanian conductor; b. Bucharest, Oct. 18, 1909; d. Wabern, near Bern, March 9, 1960. He was educated at the Royal Academy of Music in Bucharest and at the Hochschule für Musik in Berlin; then held numerous posts as an opera conductor at Düsseldorf (1927–32), Brno (1932–35), Bern (1935–46), Zürich (1948–53), Cologne (1953–58) and again Zürich (1958–60). He was noted for his authoritative interpretations of the operatic repertoire, but was also successful as an operetta conductor.

Ackté (real name, **Achté**), **Aïno,** Finnish dramatic soprano; b. Helsinki, April 23, 1876; d. Nummela, Aug. 8, 1944. She studied at the Paris Cons. and made her debut at the Paris Opéra as Marguerite (Oct. 8, 1897). She sang the same role at her first appearance in the U.S. at the Metropolitan Opera (Feb. 20, 1904). Her performance of Salomé in Strauss's opera at Covent Garden (Dec. 8, 1910) led to an invitation from Richard Strauss to sing the part in Dresden and Paris. Her other roles were Juliette, Ophélie, Gilda, Nedda, Elsa, Elisabeth, and Sieglinde. Her memoirs are publ. in Finnish, Swedish, and German.

Acuff, Roy (Claxton), American country-music singer, guitarist, and songwriter; b. Maynardville, Tenn., Sept. 15, 1903. He learned to play the fiddle, and later appeared as a singer and guitarist with local musicians; in 1938 he and his Smoky Mountain Boys became featured artists on the "Grand Ole Opry" radio program in Nashville; he gained fame with his renditions of such songs as *The Great Speckled Bird, Wabash Cannonball,* and *Night Train to Memphis.* He also composed songs, including the very popular *Precious Jewel,* and was active as a music publisher (with Fred Rose).

Adachi, Motohiko, Japanese composer; b. Osaka, Jan. 3, 1940. He studied composition with Yori-Aki Matsudaira, Y. Shimaoka, and S. Yamagata.
WORKS: Concerto for 5 Violins, 4 Violas, and 5 Cellos (1962); Concerto Grosso for String Orch. (1966); *Air* for Solo Violin (1968); Toccata for 4 Japanese Instruments (1968); *Monodia* for Piano (1968–69); *Concertanto* for String Quintet (1969); *Carmina Burana,* trio for Male Voice, Piano, and Double Bass (1971); *Talking the Future Out* for Soprano, Baritone, Children's Chorus, and Instrumental Ensemble (1971); Chaconne for Japanese Instruments (1971); *Capriccio* for Cello and Dai-byoshi (1971); *Per pianoforte* (1972); *Chase the Pigeon* for 2 Folksingers, 4 Actors, Chorus, and Instrumental Ensemble (1972).

Adalid y Gurréa, Marcial del, Spanish composer; b. La Coruña, Aug. 24, 1826; d. Lóngora, near La Coruña, Oct. 16, 1881. He studied piano in London with Moscheles (1844–49); then settled in Lóngora, where he devoted himself to composition. He composed mostly for piano, but also wrote songs; his opera, *Inese e Bianca,* was never performed.
BIBLIOGRAPHY: R. de Santiago, *Marcial del Adalid: Síntesis biográfica* (La Coruña, 1965).

Adam, Adolphe (-Charles), celebrated French opera composer; b. Paris, July 24, 1803; d. there, May 3, 1856. He studied piano with his father, a professional pianist, and with Lemoine; then went to the Paris Cons., where he became a student of Benoist in organ playing, of Reicha in counterpoint, and of Boieldieu in composition. Boieldieu exercised the greatest influence on Adam's development as an opera composer; another powerful influence was that of Hérold. Adam devoted his entire career exclusively to the music of the theater; he obtained his first success with a short comic opera, *Le Châlet,* produced at the Opéra-Comique in Paris on Sept. 25, 1834, which held the stage for 1,400 performances through the years; a far greater success was the production of *Le Postillon de Longjumeau* at the Opéra-Comique on Oct. 13, 1836, an opera that achieved permanence in the operatic repertoire all over the world. There followed a long series of stage works; at times Adam produced two or more operas in a single season. In the process of inevitable triage, most of them went by the board, but a considerable number remained in the repertoire; among these was the comic opera *Si j'étais roi* (Paris, Sept. 4, 1852). Adam wrote 53 operas in all, an astonishing example of fecundity, since his entire life comprised not quite 53 years. Perhaps his most durable work was not an opera but a ballet, *Giselle* (Paris Opéra, June 28, 1841), a perennial in choreographic history which continues to be performed with no sign of decline in popularity. His song *Cantique de Noël* also became popular. Unfortunately, Adam was a poor businessman; in 1847 he ventured into the field of management with an operatic enterprise, the Opéra-National, which failed miserably and brought him to the brink of financial ruin. In 1849 he was appointed prof. at the Paris Cons.; he also traveled widely in Europe, visiting London, Berlin, and St. Petersburg. As one of the creators of French opera, Adam ranks with Auber and Boieldieu in the expressive power of his melodic materi-

Adam – Adam de la Halle

al and a sense of dramatic development. Adam's memoirs were published posthumously in 2 volumes, *Souvenirs d'un musicien* (1857) and *Derniers Souvenirs d'un musicien* (1859).

WORKS: Operas (all produced in Paris; most of them at the Opéra-Comique): *Le Mal du pays, ou La Batelière de Brientz* (Dec. 28, 1827); *Pierre et Catherine* (Feb. 9, 1829); *Danilowa* (April 23, 1830); *Trois jours en une heure* (Aug. 21, 1830); *Le Morceau d'ensemble* (March 10, 1831); *Le Grand Prix* (July 9, 1831); *Casimir* (Dec. 1, 1831); *Le Proscrit* (Sept. 18, 1833); *Une Bonne Fortune* (Jan. 23, 1834); *Le Châlet* (Sept. 25, 1834); *La Marquise* (Feb. 28, 1835); *Micheline* (June 29, 1835); *Le Postillon de Longjumeau* (Oct. 13, 1836); *Le Fidèle Berger* (Jan. 6, 1838); *Régine* (Jan. 17, 1839); *La Reine d'un jour* (Sept. 19, 1839); *Le Brasseur de Preston* (Oct. 31, 1839); *La Rose de Péronne* (Dec. 12, 1840); *La Main de fer* (Oct. 26, 1841); *Le Roi d'Yvetôt* (Oct. 13, 1842); *Richard en Palestine* (Oct. 7, 1844, and on the same bill, *Cagliostro*); *La Bouquetière* (May 31, 1847); *Le Toréador* (May 18, 1849); *Giralda* (July 20, 1850); *La Poupée de Nuremberg* (Feb. 21, 1852); *Le Farfalet* (March 19, 1852); *Si j'étais roi* (Sept. 4, 1852; extremely successful); *Le Sourd* (Feb. 2, 1853); *Le Roi des Halles* (April 11, 1853); *Le Bijou perdu* (Oct. 6, 1853); *Le Muletier de Tolède* (Dec. 16, 1854); *A Clichy* (Dec. 24, 1854); *Le Houzard de Berchiny* (Oct. 17, 1855); *Falstaff* (Jan. 18, 1856); *Les Pantins de Violette* (April 29, 1856).

BIBLIOGRAPHY: J. Halévy, *Notice sur la vie et les ouvrages de Adolphe Adam* (Paris, 1859); A. Pougin, *Adolphe Adam* (Paris, 1877); P. Hering, "L.J.P. Hérold, A. Adam, E. Waldteufel," in *La Musique en Alsace hier et aujourd'hui* (Paris, 1970).

Adam, Claus, American cellist and composer; b. on a kapok plantation in Central Sumatra, of Austrian parents, Nov. 5, 1917; d. New York, July 4, 1983. His father was an ethnologist; the family moved to Austria in 1923, and Adam received his early musical training at the Mozarteum in Salzburg. In 1929 they emigrated to the U.S., and settled in Brooklyn. Claus Adam studied cello with E. Stoffnegen, D.C. Dounis, and Emanuel Feuermann; also took lessons in conducting with Leon Barzin. In 1940 he was engaged as a cellist with the Minneapolis Symph. Orch. He served in the U.S. Air Force; returning to N.Y., he studied composition with Stefan Wolpe. From 1948 to 1955 he was a founding member of the New Music Quartet; from 1955 to 1974 he was the cellist of the prestigious Juilliard String Quartet; in 1975 he held a Guggenheim Foundation grant, and was composer-in-residence at the American Academy in Rome in 1976. During all that time he was engaged in serious composition. His works are marked by pragmatic modernism free from doctrinaire adherence to any particular technique. He wrote mostly chamber music. His Concerto-Variations for Orch. were performed in N.Y. on April 5, 1977. He suffered a stroke on June 8, 1983, and never recovered.

Ádám, Jenö, Hungarian conductor and educator; b. Szigetszentmiklós, Dec. 12, 1896; d. Budapest, May 15, 1982. He studied composition in Budapest with Kodály (1921–25) and conducting in Basel with Felix Weingartner (1933–35); subsequently was associated with Kodály in reorganizing the system of musical education in Hungary. He was on the faculty of the Academy of Music in Budapest (1939–59).

WORKS: 2 operas: *Magyar Karácsony* (*Hungarian Christmas;* Budapest, Dec. 22, 1931) and *Mária Veronika* (Budapest, Oct. 27, 1938); *Dominica Suite* for Orch. (1925; transcribed as *My Village,* 1963); *Lacrima Sonata* for Baritone and Orch. (1927); 2 string quartets (1924, 1930); Cello Sonata (1926); choral works; songs.

Adam, Louis, Alsatian pianist, teacher, and composer, father of **Adolphe-Charles Adam;** b. Müttersholz, Dec. 3, 1758; d. Paris, April 8, 1848. He went to Paris in 1775; was later a prof. of piano at the Paris Cons. (1797–1842). He was the teacher of Kalkbrenner and Hérold; was also known as a composer of virtuoso piano pieces, some of which (especially variations on *Le Roi Dagobert*) were very popular. He was the author of 2 standard manuals for Piano: *Méthode générale du doigté* (Paris, 1798) and *Méthode nouvelle pour le piano* (5 eds., 1802–32), which he wrote for his pupils at the Paris Cons.

Adam, Theo, German bass-baritone; b. Dresden, Aug. 1, 1926. As a boy, he sang in the Dresdner Kreuzchor; made his professional debut at the Dresden State Opera in 1949; from 1952 he sang at the Bayreuth Festivals, at the Berlin State Opera, at Covent Garden in London, and at the Vienna State Opera. On Feb. 7, 1969, he made his debut at the Metropolitan Opera in N.Y. as Hans Sachs in *Die Meistersinger von Nürnberg.* An artist of versatile abilities, he gave excellent performances of such disparate roles as Don Giovanni, Boris Godunov, and Wozzeck.

Adamberger, (Josef) Valentin, noted German tenor; b. Munich, July 6, 1743; d. Vienna, Aug. 24, 1804. He studied in Italy with Valesi; made appearances there using the name **Adamonti.** He went to Munich in 1772; sang in London in 1777; settled in Vienna in 1780. He created the role of Belmonte in *Die Entführung aus dem Serail* (July 16, 1782); also sang the part of Herr Vogelsang in *Der Schauspieldirektor* (Feb. 7, 1786). In 1789 he became a member of the Italian Opera in Vienna, and remained there until his retirement in 1793. He then devoted himself to teaching voice.

Adam (or **Adan**) **de la Halle** (or **Hale**), called "Le Bossu d'Arras" ("Hunchback of Arras"); b. Arras, c.1237; d. Naples, c.1287. A famous trouvère, many of whose works have been preserved; the most interesting is a dramatic pastoral, *Le Jeu de Robin et de Marion* (1285), written for the Anjou court at Naples and resembling an opéra comique in its plan. He was gifted in the dual capacity of poet and composer. Both monodic and polyphonic works of his survive. A facsimile reprint of one of the important MS sources of Adam's works is issued as *Le*

Chansonnier d'Arras, introduction by A. Jeanroy (Paris, 1925). For transcriptions of most of the extant music, see E. de Coussemaker, *Œuvres complètes du trouvère Adam de la Halle* (1872); F. Gennrich, *Rondeaux, Virelais und Balladen* (Dresden; I, 1921; II, 1927); J. Chailley, *Adam de la Halle: Rondeaux* (Paris, 1942); F. Gennrich, *Le Jeu de Robin et de Marion,* in *Musikwissenschaftliche Studienbibliothek* (Langen, 1962); N. Wilkins, *The Lyric Works of Adam de la Halle: Chansons, Jeux-Partis, Rondeaux, Motets* (Dallas, 1967). Transcriptions of the texts only: R. Berger, *Canchons und Partures des altfranzösischen Trouvère Adan de la Halle le Bochu d'Arras* (1900); L. Nicod, *Les Partures Adan: Les Jeux-partis d'Adam de la Halle* (Paris, 1917); E. Langlois, *Le Jeu de la Feuillée* (Paris, 1923); id., *Le Jeu de Robin et de Marion* (Paris, 1924); A. Langfors, *Recueil général des jeux-partis français* (2 vols., Paris, 1926). A new edition of the complete works, using all known music and text sources, including those never before transcribed, is being prepared by a consortium of music and language specialists at City Univ. of N.Y.
BIBLIOGRAPHY: H. Guy, *Essai sur la vie et les œuvres littéraires d'Adam de la Hale* (Paris, 1898); J. Tiersot, *Sur le Jeu de Robin et Marion* (1897).

Adam de St. Victor, French Augustine monk who developed the rhymed liturgical sequence; b. c.1110; d. (possibly) July 8, 1192. He was cantor at the St. Victor Cloister in Paris. His significance lies in his decisive introduction of rhymed "proses," or sequences, each consisting of 12 or more stanzas, in which the first half was given a new melody, while the 2nd half was set to the same melody. Adam de St. Victor wrote a great many such sequences, and influenced their further development.
BIBLIOGRAPHY: L. Gautier, *Œuvres poétiques d'Adam de St. Victor* (Paris, 1858); E. Misset and P. Aubry, *Les Proses d'Adam de St. Victor* (Paris, 1900); F. Wellner, *Adam de St. Victor, Sämtliche Sequenzen* (Vienna, 1937).

Adamis, Michael, Greek composer of ultramodern music; b. Piraeus, May 19, 1929. While studying theology at Athens Univ. (1948–54), he took music courses at the Athens Cons. (1947–51) and courses on Byzantine music and harmony at Piraeus Cons. (1951–56); studied composition with Papaioannou at the Hellikon Cons. in Athens (1956–59), followed by advanced studies in electronic music and Byzantine musical palaeography at Brandeis Univ. in Waltham, Massachusetts (1962–65). His works are derived from a universal spectrum of musical techniques and sonorous resources: dodecaphonic, electronic, liturgical, neo-Baroque, choreographic.
WORKS: *Liturgikon Concerto* for Oboe, Clarinet, Bassoon, and String Orch. (1955); *2 Pieces* for Violin and Piano (1958); Variations for String Orch. (1958); *Suite in ritmo antico* for Piano (1959); *Sinfonia da camera* for Flute, Clarinet, Horn, Trumpet, Percussion, Piano, and String Orch. (1960–61); Duo for Violin and Piano (1961); *3 Pieces* for Double Bass and Piano (1962); *Anakyklesis* for Flute, Oboe, Celesta, Violin, and Cello (1964); *Perspective* for Flute, Piccolo, and Percussion (1965); *Apocalypse (6th Seal)* for Chorus, Narrator, Piano, and Tape (1967); *Byzantine Passion* for 6 Soloists, Chorus, and Percussion (1967); *Genesis* for 3 Choirs, Narrator, Tape, Painting, Projection, and Dance (1968); *Lamentation* for 2 Chanters, 2 Drone Chanters, Percussion, and Tape (1970); *Tetelestai* for Narrator, 3 Choirs, Tape, and Bells (1971); *Iketirion* for Women's Choir, Percussion, and Tape (1971); *Kratima* for Narrator, Oboe, Tuba, and Tape (1971); *The Fiery Furnace* for Chanters' Choir and 3 Children (1972; based on a 15th-century MS that is the only extant specimen of Byzantine liturgical drama); *Orestes* for Baritone, Percussion, and Tape (1972); *Photonymon* for Narrator, Chorus, and Percussion (1973). He also has numerous pieces for tape alone, and tape and voice, and has produced electronic stage music for plays by Aeschylus, Euripides, Shakespeare, and others.

Adamowski, Joseph, American cellist, brother of **Timothée Adamowski;** b. Warsaw, July 4, 1862; d. Cambridge, Mass., May 8, 1930. He studied at the Warsaw Cons. (1873–77) with Goebelt; and at the Moscow Cons. with Fitzenhagen; also attended Tchaikovsky's classes there. He gave concerts from 1883–89 in Warsaw. From 1889–1907 he played in the Boston Symph. Orch. In 1896 he married the pianist **Antoinette Szumowska.** With his wife and his brother Timothée, he formed the Adamowski Trio.

Adamowski, Timothée, American violinist, brother of **Joseph Adamowski;** b. Warsaw, March 24, 1857; d. Boston, April 18, 1943. He studied in Warsaw and at the Paris Cons.; in 1879 gave concerts in the U.S. with Maurice Strakosch and Clara Louise Kellogg, and settled in Boston, where he taught at the New England Cons. (until 1933). In 1888 he organized the Adamowski String Quartet, which gave about 30 concerts annually; he also conducted several summer seasons of popular concerts given by the Boston Symph. Orch. (1890–94, 1900–7). He publ. songs and violin pieces (*Barcarolle, Polish Dance,* etc.).

Adams, Charles, American dramatic tenor; b. Charlestown, Mass., Feb. 9, 1834; d. West Harwich, Mass., July 4, 1900. He studied music in Boston; then went to Vienna, where he took voice lessons with Barbieri; was subsequently a member of the Royal Opera in Berlin and of the Imperial Opera in Vienna (1867–76). He also sang at La Scala, Milan; Covent Garden, London; and in the U.S. He settled in Boston as a vocal teacher in 1879.

Adams, Horst, German musicologist; b. Merzig, Saar, Jan. 29, 1937. He studied musicology with Müller-Blattau. In 1962 he joined the Schott publishing house and participated in the editorship of the supplement to *Riemann's Musik Lexikon* (2 vols.; 1972, 1975).

Adams, John, American composer; b. Worcester, Mass., Feb. 15, 1947. He spent the tender years of his life in the healthy atmosphere of Vermont and New Hampshire; his father taught him clarinet, and he later took clarinet lessons with Felix Visculgia, a member of the Boston Symph. Orch. He subsequently entered Harvard College, receiving his B.A. (magna cum laude) in 1969 and his M.A. in music composition in 1971. At Harvard his principal teacher was Leon Kirchner; he also worked in composition with David Del Tredici and had some sessions with Sessions. While still in college he conducted the Bach Society Orch. and was a substitute clarinetist with the Boston Symph. and the Boston Opera Co. In 1969 he played the solo part in Walter Piston's Clarinet Concerto at Carnegie Hall in N.Y. In 1971 he moved to San Francisco, where he found a congenial environment for his activities as a conductor and composer. He was appointed head of the composition dept. at the San Francisco Cons. (1971–81). In 1978 he began working with Edo de Waart, music director of the San Francisco Symph., as new music adviser and later as composer-in-residence. His own music covers a wide spectrum of media, including works for video, tape, and live electronics; he also wrote the musical film score for *Matter of Heart,* a psychological documentary dealing with the life and theories of Carl G. Jung. In 1982 he was awarded a Guggenheim fellowship. In his compositions he reveals himself as an apostle of the idea that a maximum effect can be achieved with a minimum of practical means, a notion usually described by the somewhat inaccurate term "minimalism," wherein a composer postulates harmonic and melodic austerity with audacious repetitiveness, withal electing to use the simplest time-honored units of the musical structure, to wit, major triads in the fundamental positions, with the tonic in the bass. John Adams is a modernist among minimalists, for he allows for a constant flow of divergent tonalities in his works, but he also succeeds in exploiting such elementary harmonic progressions as the serenely cadential alternations of the tonic and the dominant, achieving a desired effect. Typical of such works are his *Harmonium* for Chorus and Orch. and the grandiose popular score titled *Grand Pianola Music.*

WORKS: For Orch., *Common Tones in Simple Time* (1979); *Harmonium* for Chorus and Orch., to verses by John Donne and Emily Dickinson (San Francisco, April 15, 1981); *Grand Pianola Music* for 2 Pianos, 2 Sopranos, and Contralto (San Francisco, Feb. 20, 1982, composer conducting); *Bridge of Dreams* for Orch. (1982–83); *Shaker Loops* for Strings (1978); for Piano: *Ragamarole* (1973); *China Gates* (1977); *Phrygian Gates* (1977).

Adams, Suzanne, American soprano; b. Cambridge, Mass., Nov. 28, 1872; d. London, Feb. 5, 1953. She studied with Bouhy in N.Y.; in 1889 went to Paris, where she took lessons with Mathilde Marchesi. She made her professional debut at the Paris Opéra as Juliette in Gounod's opera on Jan. 9, 1895; continued to sing there for 3 more seasons; in 1898 she sang at Covent Garden, London. Returning to the U.S., she made her debut at the Metropolitan

Opera in N.Y. as Juliette on Jan. 4, 1899. After the death of her husband, the cellist Leo Stein, in 1904, she retired from the stage.

Adams, Thomas, eminent English organist; b. London, Sept. 5, 1785; d. there, Sept. 15, 1858. He studied with Dr. Busby; was organist at various London churches. His publ. organ works include fugues, voluntaries, 90 interludes, and variations on popular airs.

Adam von Fulda, important German theorist; b. Fulda, c.1440; d. (of the plague) Wittenberg, 1505. His tract on music theory is publ. in Gerbert's *Scriptores ecclesiastici.*

BIBLIOGRAPHY: Hugo Riemann in *Kirchenmusikalisches Jahrbuch* (1879); W. Gurlitt in *Luther-Jahrbuch* (1932); W. Ehmann, *Adam von Fulda als Vertreter der ersten deutschen Komponistengeneration* (Berlin, 1936).

Adaskin, Murray, Canadian violinist and composer; b. Toronto, March 28, 1906. He studied violin with his older brother Harry; then went to Paris, where he took lessons with Marcel Chailley. Returning to Toronto, he continued his lessons with Luigi von Kunits and Kathleen Parlow. He subsequently played violin in the Toronto Symph. Orch. (1923–36). He studied composition with John Weinzweig (1944–48); also took a course with Darius Milhaud (1949–50, 1953). In 1952 he was appointed head of the music dept. at the Univ. of Saskatchewan; in 1966–72 was composer-in-residence there. He writes music in a facile laissez-faire manner, enlivened by a rhythmic pulse.

WORKS: Chamber opera, *Grant, Warden of the Plains* (Winnipeg, July 18, 1967); *Ballet Symphony* (1950–51); Violin Concerto (1956); *Algonquin Symphony* (1957–58); *Saskatchewan Legend* for Orch. (1959); Bassoon Concerto (1960); *Qalala and Nilaula of the North,* symph. poem based on Eskimo tunes (1969); *Fanfare* for Orch. (1970); *There Is My People Sleeping,* symph. poem (1970); *Nootka Ritual* for Small Orch. (1972); *Adagio* for Cello and Orch. (1973–75); Violin Sonata (1946); Piano Sonata (1950); *Sonatine Baroque* for Solo Violin (1952); 4 divertimentos: No. 1 for 2 Violins and Piano (1961); No. 2 for Violin and Harp (1964); No. 3 for Violin, Horn, and Bassoon (1965); No. 4 for Trumpet and Orch. (1970); *Introduction and Rondo* for Piano Quartet (1957); String Quartet (1963); *Calisthenics* for Violin and Piano (1968); Trio for Flute, Cello, and Piano (1970); *2 Pieces* for Viola da Gamba (1972); *2 Portraits* for Violin and Piano (1973); Wind Quintet (1974); songs.

Adderley, Julian Edwin ("Cannonball"), American jazz alto saxophone player; b. Tampa, Fla., Sept. 15, 1928; d. Gary, Ind., Aug. 8, 1975. He began his career as a member of a jazz group at a Greenwich Village club in N.Y.; in 1956 he formed his own combo with his brother **Nat Adderley** (b. Tampa, Nov. 25, 1931), who plays the cornet. He achieved fame mainly through his recordings, beginning with *African Waltz* in 1961. He received an academic education, graduating from Florida A. & M. with a B.A. in music. For 8 years (1948–56) he was a band director at Dillard High School in Fort Lauderdale. After leaving his school position, he lectured frequently in colleges on the subject of his "black experience in music." He owes his nickname, "Cannonball," to the mispronunciation of *cannibal,* a slurring reference to his voracious eating habits. He suffered a stroke during a concert engagement in Gary, Ind. Among his most successful recordings were *Dis Here; Sermonette; Work Song; Jive Samba; Mercy, Mercy, Mercy; Walk Tall.* He also wrote *Suite Cannon,* its title alluding both to his academic background and to his popular nickname.

Addinsell, Richard, English composer of theater and film music; b. London, Jan. 13, 1904; d. there, Nov. 14, 1977. He studied law at Oxford Univ. and music at the Royal College of Music in London. His first theater score was for Clemence Dane's play *Come of Age* (1928). In 1929 he went to Berlin and Vienna for further musical study. In 1933, Eva Le Gallienne commissioned him to write the music for her production of *Alice in Wonderland.* He then wrote a series of successful film scores, among them *A Tale of Two Cities, Blithe Spirit, Fire over England,* and *Dark Journey.* During World War II he wrote film music for several patriotic documentaries, among them *Siege of Tobruk* and *We Sail at Midnight.* He achieved fame with a score for the film *Dangerous Moonlight* (released in the U.S. as *Suicide Squadron*), containing a movement for piano and orch. which became immensely popular under the title *Warsaw Concerto.* While the music is a feeble imitation of Rachmaninoff's Second Piano Concerto, it possesses a popular flair that made it a classic of pop music.

Addison, Adele, American soprano; b. New York, July 24, 1925. She studied at Westminster Choir College, Princeton, and the Berkshire Music Center at Tanglewood; also took lessons with Povla Frijsh. She made her N.Y. debut at Town Hall in 1952; then sang with the New England Opera and the N.Y. City Opera; she made numerous appearances with major American orchs. Her extensive repertoire included works from the Baroque era to the 20th century.

Addison, John, English composer; b. Cobham, Surrey, March 16, 1920. He was educated at Wellington College, and in 1938 entered the Royal College of Music. His studies were interrupted by World War II, during which he served in a cavalry regiment. After the war he continued his musical education with Gordon Jacob in composition, Leon Goossens in oboe, and Frederick Thurston in clarinet. In 1951 he joined the staff of the Royal College of Music; there until 1958, when he decided to devote himself mainly to composition for films. He wrote music for more than 60 motion pictures, both in England and the U.S., including such popular productions as

Tom Jones (1963), which won for him an Academy Award; *The Loved One* (1965); *Torn Curtain* (1966); *The Charge of the Light Brigade* (1968); *Sleuth* (1972); *The Seven Per Cent Solution,* a comedy involving Sherlock Holmes and Freud (1976). His film music is particularly effective in epical subjects with understated humor. Apart from film music, he wrote *Variations* for Piano and Orch. (1948); Concerto for Trumpet, Strings, and Percussion (1949); Woodwind Sextet (1949); Trio for Oboe, Clarinet, and Bassoon (1950); Trio for Flute, Oboe, and Piano; *Serenade and Conversation Piece* for 2 Soprano Voices, Harpsichord, Organ, and Harp. He also wrote music for television documentaries. Since 1975 Addison has divided his time between Los Angeles and a small village in the French Alps, where he does some skiing and mountaineering.

Adelburg, August Ritter von, violinist and composer; b. Constantinople, Nov. 1, 1830; d. Vienna, Oct. 20, 1873. He studied violin with Mayseder in Vienna (1850–54) and composition with Hoffmann; then toured Europe as a violinist. He wrote 3 operas: *Zrinyi* (Budapest, June 23, 1868; his most successful work); *Martinuzzi* (1870); *Wallenstein* (on Schiller's drama); an oratorio, *War and Peace;* 5 string quartets; *School of Velocity* for Violin.

Adeney, Richard, English flute player; b. London, Jan. 25, 1920. He studied at the Royal College of Music in London; in 1941–50 and again in 1960–69 was principal flutist of the London Phil. Orch. He was a founder-member of the Melos Ensemble and played in the English Chamber Orch.; also gave solo flute concerts in Europe and North America.

Adgate, Andrew, American church organist and choral conductor; b. Norwich, Conn., March 22, 1762; d. Philadelphia, of yellow fever, Sept. 30, 1793. In 1784 he organized, in Philadelphia, the Institution for the Encouragement of Church Music; in 1785 he founded there the Free School for Spreading the Knowledge of Vocal Music, reorganized in 1787 as The Uranian Academy, the purpose of which was to urge the incorporation of musical study with general education. On May 4, 1786, he presented in Philadelphia "A Grand Concert of Sacred Music," with a chorus of 230 voices and an orch. of 50, featuring works by Handel, Billings, and others. Adgate compiled several publications: *Lessons for the Uranian Society* (1785); *Select Psalms and Hymns* (1787); *Rudiments of Music* (1788); *Selection of Sacred Harmony* (1788).

Adkins, Cecil Dale, American musicologist; b. Red Oak, Iowa, Jan. 30, 1932. He studied music at the Univ. of Omaha (B.F.A., 1953), the Univ. of South Dakota (M.M., 1959), and the Univ. of Iowa (Ph.D., 1963). In 1963 he was appointed prof. of musicology at North Texas State Univ., Denton. There he established a series devoted to reviving performances of Renaissance works. His publications include an important edition and translation of Orazio Vecchi's *L'Amfiparnaso* (1977); numerous technical papers in American music magazines. He also contributed articles on old instruments and biographies of Renaissance composers to *The New Grove.*

Adler, Clarence, American pianist; b. Cincinnati, March 10, 1886; d. New York, Dec. 24, 1969. He studied at the Cincinnati College of Music (1898–1904); then in Berlin with Godowsky (1905–09). He toured in Europe as a pianist in the Hekking Trio. Returning to America in 1913, he settled in N.Y.; made his American debut with the N.Y. Symph. Orch. (Feb. 8, 1914). In 1941 he broadcast all of Mozart's 28 piano concertos. He publ. an album of piano pieces; also arrangements of works by Dvořák and Franck.

Adler, F. Charles, conductor; b. London, July 2, 1889; d. Vienna, Feb. 16, 1959. He studied piano with August Halm in Munich, theory with Beer-Walbrunn, and conducting with Mahler. He was assistant to Felix Mottl at the Royal Opera in Munich (1908–11); in 1913 he became first conductor of the Municipal Opera in Düsseldorf; conducted symph. concerts in Europe (1919–33). He was owner of Edition Adler in Berlin until 1933, when he came to America. In 1937 he founded the Saratoga Springs Music Festivals in N.Y.

Adler, Guido, eminent Austrian musicologist; b. Eibenschütz, Moravia, Nov. 1, 1855; d. Vienna, Feb. 15, 1941. He studied at the Vienna Cons. under Bruckner and Dessoff; entered Vienna Univ. in 1874 and founded, in cooperation with Felix Mottl and K. Wolf, the academical Wagner Society; took the degree of Dr.Jur. in 1878, and in 1880 that of Dr.Phil. (Dissertation, *Die historischen Grundklassen der christlich-abendländischen Musik bis 1600*), and in 1881 qualified as an instructor, lecturing on musical science (thesis, *Studie zur Geschichte der Harmonie*). With Chrysander and Spitta he founded, in 1884, the *Vierteljahrsschrift für Musikwissenschaft.* In 1885 he was appointed prof. of musicology at the German Univ. at Prague. In 1892 he was elected president of the Central Committee of the Internationale Ausstellung für Musik und Theater. In 1895 he succeeded Hanslick as prof. of music history at the Univ. of Vienna, retiring in 1927. Important books by Adler are *Methode der Musikgeschichte* (1919); *Der Stil in der Musik* (1911; 2nd ed., 1929); *Gustav Mahler* (1916); *Handbuch der Musikgeschichte* (one vol., 1924; 2nd ed. in 2 vols., 1930); *Wollen und Wirken,* memoirs (Vienna, 1935). He was also editor of the monumental collection Denkmäler der Tonkunst in Österreich from its inception (the first vol. appeared in 1894) until 1938 (83 vols. in all). He contributed many articles to music periodicals.
BIBLIOGRAPHY: C. Engel, "Guido Adler in Retrospect," *Musical Quarterly* (July 1941); R. Heinz, "Guido Adlers Musikhistorik als historistisches Dokument," in W. Wiora, ed. *Die Ausbreitung des Historismus über die Musik* (Regensburg, 1969); E. Reilly, *Gustav Mahler and Guido Adler* (Vienna, 1978).

Adler, Israel, German-born Israeli musicologist; b. Berlin, Jan. 17, 1925. He studied at the Paris Cons. (1949–53) and at the Ecole Pratique des Hautes Etudes (diploma, 1961); also took courses in musicology with Chailley at the Sorbonne, where he received his Ph.D. in 1963 with the dissertation *La Pratique musicale savante dans quelques communautés juives en Europe aux XVIIᵉ et XVIIIᵉ siècles* (publ. in Paris, 1966). He dedicated himself mainly to Jewish music; from 1950–63 he was head of the Hebraica-Judaica dept. of the Bibliothèque Nationale in Paris; then went to Israel, where he worked as director of the national sound archives at the Jewish National and Hebrew Univ. library in Jerusalem (1963–69). In 1964 he organized the Jewish music research center at Hebrew Univ. He publ. the book *Musical Life and Traditions of the Portuguese Jewish Community of Amsterdam* (Jerusalem, 1974); with J. Cohen, compiled *Catalogue of the A.Z. Idelsohn Archives at the Jewish National and Hebrew University Library* (Jerusalem, 1976).

Adler, Kurt, American pianist and conductor; b. Neuhaus, Bohemia, March 1, 1907; d. Butler, N.J., Sept. 21, 1977. He was educated in Vienna, where he studied musicology with Guido Adler and Robert Lach at Vienna Univ. He served as assistant conductor of the Berlin State Opera (1927–29) and at the German Opera in Prague (1929–32). In 1933, with the advent of the Nazi regime, he went to Russia, where he was principal conductor of the Kiev State Opera (1933–35); then organized and conducted the Phil. Orch. of Stalingrad (1935–37). In 1938 he came to the U.S., first appearing as a pianist; then conducted in Canada and Mexico. In 1943 he joined the staff at the Metropolitan Opera as choirmaster and assistant conductor; made his conducting debut at the Metropolitan in N.Y. on Jan. 12, 1951, in Mozart's *Die Zauberflöte,* and led about 20 different operas there until he resigned in 1973. He edited several collections of vocal works: *Operatic Anthology; The Prima Donna Album; Arias from Light Operas; Famous Operatic Choruses.* He also brought out *The Art of Accompanying and Coaching* (Minneapolis, 1965) and *Phonetics and Diction in Singing* (Minneapolis, 1967). He is no relation to Kurt Herbert Adler.

Adler, Kurt Herbert, noted Austrian-born American conductor and operatic administrator; b. Vienna, April 2, 1905. He studied at the Vienna Academy of Music and the Univ. of Vienna; made his debut as a conductor at the Max Reinhardt Theater there in 1925; subsequently conducted at the Volksoper, and also in Germany, Italy, and Czechoslovakia. He served as assistant to Toscanini at the Salzburg Festival in 1936. In 1938 he settled in the U.S.; from 1938–43 was guest conductor of the Chicago Opera. In 1943 he was appointed chorus master of the San Francisco Opera, and in 1953 became its artistic director; in 1956 he was named its general director. He retired in 1981 and was made its general director emeritus. Under his direction the San Francisco Opera prospered greatly, advancing to the foremost ranks of American opera theaters. In 1980 Adler was made an Honorary Knight Commander of the Order of the British Empire. He is not related to Kurt Adler.

BIBLIOGRAPHY: *The Adler Years,* issued by the San Francisco Opera in 1981.

Adler, Larry (Lawrence), harmonica player; b. Baltimore, Feb. 10, 1914. He won a harmonica contest at 13 for the best rendition of Beethoven's Minuet in G. He has appeared in numerous revues; also gave concerts as a soloist with piano and with orch., as well as command performances for King George VI, King Gustav of Sweden, and presidents Roosevelt and Truman. In 1940, determined to learn to read music, he took lessons with Ernst Toch. In 1949 he was viciously attacked by a wolf pack of right-wing agitators who accused him of communistic leanings and un-American thoughts. Unable to get any engagements from frightened American managers, he went to England. When the winds of national hysteria subsided, he returned to the U.S. and resumed his concert career.

Adler, Peter Herman, conductor; b. Jablonec, Czechoslovakia, Dec. 2, 1899. He studied in Prague with Fidelio Finke, Vítězslav Novák, and Alexander von Zemlinsky. In 1923 he was appointed opera conductor in Brno; from 1929 to 1932 he conducted at the Bremen State Theater. In 1932 he went to Russia, where he served as the chief conductor of the Ukrainian State Orch. in Kiev; in 1937 he returned to Prague. With the occupation of Czechoslovakia by Nazi troops, he went to the U.S.; made his American debut as conductor at a concert for Czech relief in N.Y., Jan. 24, 1940; later filled guest engagements with several American orchs. From 1959 to 1967 he was music director of the Baltimore Symph. Orch. In 1972 he made his first conducting appearance at the Metropolitan Opera in N.Y.; then retired.

Adler, Richard, American composer of popular music; b. New York, Aug. 3, 1921. He was educated at the Univ. of North Carolina; served in the U.S. Navy (1942–46); then became a producer; staged shows at the White House during the Kennedy and Johnson administrations. He wrote his own musicals in collaboration with Jerry Ross. Of these the most popular were *The Pajama Game,* with its striking hit song *Hernando's Hideaway,* and *Damn Yankees* (1955).

Adler, Samuel, German-born American composer; b. Mannheim, March 4, 1928. His father was cantor in the Mannheim Synagogue, and his mother was an amateur pianist. Adler began to study the violin as a child with Albert Levy; in 1939 the family left Germany and settled in Worcester, Mass., where his father was appointed music director of the local temple. He took lessons with Herbert Fromm in Boston (1941–45); later attended Boston Univ. (1946–48), where his teachers were Hugo Norden, Karl Geiringer, and Paul Pisk; after receiving a B.A. in

1949 he entered Harvard Univ., where he attended the classes of Walter Piston, Randall Thompson, and Irving Fine (1948–50); he also took summer courses at the Berkshire Music Center at Tanglewood, where he studied composition with Aaron Copland and conducting with Serge Koussevitzky. He earned his master's degree in music from Harvard in 1950; then joined the U.S. Army, and served as conductor of the 7th Army Symph. in Germany. Returning to the U.S., he held the post of music director of Temple Emanu-El in Dallas (1953–56); then was prof. of composition at North Texas State Univ. at Denton (1957–66). In 1966 he was appointed prof. of composition at the Eastman School of Music in Rochester, N.Y., and in 1973 was named chairman of the music dept. there. His idiom of composition may be described as midstream modernism, in which densely interwoven contrapuntal lines support the basically tonal harmonic complex, with a frequent incidence of tangential atonal episodes. Much of his music is inspired by the liturgical cantilena of traditional Jewish music; oriental inflections also occur.

WORKS: OPERAS: One-act opera, *The Outcasts of Poker Flat,* after Bret Harte (1959; Denton, Tex., June 8, 1962); sacred opera, *The Wrestler* (Dallas, June 22, 1972); *The Lodge of Shadows,* a music drama for Baritone Solo, Dancers, and Orch. (1973); *The Disappointment,* a reconstruction of an early American ballad opera of 1767 (Washington, D.C., April 7, 1976). FOR ORCH.: Symph. No. 1 (Dallas, Dec. 7, 1953); Symph. No. 2 (Dallas, Feb. 12, 1958); Symph. No. 3, *Diptych* for Wind Orch. (1960); Symph. No. 4, *Geometrics* (1967); Symph. No. 5, *We Are the Echoes,* for Mezzo-soprano and Orch. (Fort Worth, Texas, Nov. 10, 1975); *Toccata* (1954); *Rhapsody* for Violin and Orch. (1961); *Song and Dance* for Viola and Orch. (1965); *City by the Lake,* "a portrait of Rochester, N.Y." (1968); Organ Concerto (1970); *Sinfonietta* (1970); Concerto for Orch. (1971); Flute Concerto (1977). SMALL ENSEMBLES AND CHAMBER MUSIC: *Five Vignettes* for 12 Trombones (1968); Concerto for Winds, Brass, and Percussion (1968); *Brass Fragments* for 20 Brass Instruments (1970); *Histrionics* for Brass and Percussion (1971); *Déjà Vu* for 6 Recorders (1975); 6 string quartets (1945–75), the last one with Mezzo-soprano; Piano Trio (1964); 3 violin sonatas (1948, 1956, 1965); Sonata for Horn and Piano (1948); Sonata for Cello Unaccompanied (1966); *7 Epigrams* for Woodwind Quintet (1966); *Intrada* for Woodwind (1967); 10 pieces, each titled *Canto,* most of them for a single unaccompanied instrument (trumpet, bass trombone, violin, saxophone, double bass, tuba, piano, cello), composed between 1970 and 1979; also one for Soprano, Flute, Cello, and Percussion; *Four Dialogues* for Euphonium and Marimba (1974); also 2 concertinos for String Orch. (1975–76); *Line Drawings* for Saxophone Quartet (1978); *Aeolus* for Clarinet and Piano Trio (1977); *A Little Night and Day Music* for Wind Ensemble (1978); *Trumpet Triptych* (1979). SACRED VOCAL WORKS: *From Out of Bondage,* biblical cantata (Temple Sinai, Brookline, Mass., April 4, 1969); *The Vision of Isaiah* for Bass, Chorus, and Orch. (1963); *The Binding* (1968); an untold number of vocal pieces with organ, songs, and piano pieces. He publ. *Anthology for the Teaching of Choral Conducting* (1971).

BIBLIOGRAPHY: David Ewen, *American Composers* (N.Y., 1982).

Adlgasser, Anton Cajetan, German organist and composer; b. Inzell, Bavaria, Oct. 1, 1729; d. Salzburg, Dec. 22, 1777. He studied with Johann Eberlin in Salzburg; on Dec. 11, 1750, was appointed organist at Salzburg Cathedral and held this post until his death (he died of a stroke while playing the organ). Adlgasser enjoyed a great reputation as a musical scholar and was admired by the young Mozart. He wrote an opera, *La Nitteti* (Salzburg, 1766); several oratorios and sacred dramas; 7 symphs.; piano sonatas and church works.

BIBLIOGRAPHY: C. Schneider, *Die Oratorien und Schuldramen A.C. Adlgassers* (Vienna, 1923); id., *Musikgeschichte von Salzburg* (1936).

Adlung, Jakob, German music scholar; b. Bindersleben, near Erfurt, Jan. 14, 1699; d. Erfurt, July 5, 1762. He studied with Christian Reichardt; in 1727 became organist at the Erfurt Lutheran Church; in 1741 was named prof. at the town school. A man of wide erudition, Adlung gave language lessons as well as musical instruction. He built 16 clavichords with his own hands. Of his writings, 3 have historical value: *Anleitung zu der musikalischen Gelehrtheit* (Erfurt, 1758; 2nd ed., revised by J.A. Hiller, 1783; facsimile ed. by H.J. Moser, Kassel, 1953); *Musica mechanica organoedi* (1768; facsimile ed. by Chr. Mahrenholz, Kassel, 1931); *Musikalisches Siebengestirn* (1768). His autobiographical sketch was publ. by Marpurg (*Kritische Briefe,* II).

BIBLIOGRAPHY: E. Valentin, s.v., *Die Musik in Geschichte und Gegenwart.*

Adni, Daniel, Israeli pianist; b. Haifa, Dec. 6, 1951. He received his musical education in Haifa; made his debut there at the age of 12; continued his studies with Vlado Perlemuter at the Paris Cons.; then with Geza Anda in Zürich. After making his London debut in a recital in 1970, he made many appearances in Europe and America.

Adolphus, Milton, productive American composer; b. New York, Jan. 27, 1913. In 1935 he moved to Philadelphia, where he took composition lessons with Rosario Scalero; in 1938 he relocated to Harrisburg, where he took a job in the Department of Labor and Industry of the Commonwealth of Pennsylvania. Although he never practiced music vocationally, he became extremely prolific; wrote 13 symphs. and 31 string quartets, in addition to other forms. Some of his works show a measure of sophisticated humor, exemplified by *Bitter Suite* for Oboe, 4 Clarinets, and Strings (1955) and *Petits fours* for Cello and Piano (1960), or his op. 147 for Violin, Horn, and Piano, entitled *Trio prosaico*. In 1980 he wrote a Concerto for Percussion and Orch.

Adomián, Lan, American composer; b. near Mogilyov, Russia, April 29, 1905; d. Mexico City, May 9, 1979. He studied violin; emigrated to the U.S. in 1923, and studied at the Peabody Cons. of Music in Baltimore (1924–26) and at the Curtis Inst. of Music in Philadelphia (1926–28), where his teachers were Bailly (viola) and R.O. Morris (composition). He moved to N.Y. in 1928; conducted working-class choruses and bands; in 1936 he joined the Abraham Lincoln Brigade and went to Spain to fight on the Republican side during the Spanish Civil War. Upon his return to America, he wrote music for documentary films. In 1952, his radical politics made it prudent for him to leave the U.S. He moved to Mexico and became a Mexican citizen. Adomián was uncommonly prolific as a composer. He wrote 8 symphs.; an opera, *La Macherata* (1969–72); a dramatic scene, *Auschwitz,* for Baritone and Instruments (1970); and numerous choruses and songs.

BIBLIOGRAPHY: *La voluntad de Crear* (2 vols., Mexico City, 1980, 1981; vol. 2 contains a complete list of works).

Adorno (real name, **Wiesengrund**), **Theodor,** significant German musician and philosopher; b. Frankfurt, Sept. 11, 1903; d. Visp, Switzerland, Aug. 6, 1969. He studied music with Sekles in Frankfurt and with Alban Berg in Vienna; was for several years prof. at the Univ. of Frankfurt. Devoting himself mainly to music criticism, he was editor of the progressive music journal *Anbruch* in Vienna (1928–31). In 1934 he went to Oxford, and later emigrated to the U.S., where he became connected with radio research at Princeton Univ. (1938–41); subsequently lived in California. He returned to Germany in 1949 and became director of the Institut für Sozialforschung in Frankfurt. He publ. numerous essays dealing with the sociology of music, among them *Philosophie der neuen Musik* (Tübingen, 1949); *Dissonanzen: Musik in der verwalteten Welt* (Göttingen, 1956); *Arnold Schönberg* (Berlin, 1957); *Klangfiguren* (Berlin, 1959); *Einleitung in die Musiksoziologie* (Frankfurt, 1962); *Moments musicaux* (Frankfurt, 1964); *Form in der Neuen Musik* (Mainz, 1966); *Impromptus* (Frankfurt, 1968); *Alban Berg, der Meister des kleinsten Übergangs* (Vienna, 1968). Adorno advised Thomas Mann in the musical parts of his novel *Doktor Faustus*. He exercised a deep influence on the trends in musical philosophy and general esthetics, applying the sociological tenets of Karl Marx and the psychoanalytic techniques of Freud. In his speculative writings he introduced the concept of "cultural industry," embracing all types of musical techniques, from dodecaphony to jazz. A Festschrift was publ. in honor of his 60th birthday under the title *Zeugnisse* (Frankfurt, 1963). Numerous articles in several languages have been publ. on Adorno's theories in various music journals. In his early writings he used the hyphenated name **Wiesengrund-Adorno.**

BIBLIOGRAPHY: R. Stephan, "Theodor W. Adorno (1903–1969)," *Die Musikforschung* (July/Sept. 1969); E. Werner, "Zu Theodor W. Adornos *Impromptus,*" *Die Musikforschung* (April/June 1970); R. Weitzman, "An Introduction to Adorno's Music and Social Criticism," *Music & Letters* (July 1971); C. Rittelmeyer, "Dogmatismus, Intoleranz und die Beurteilung moderner Kunstwerk," *Kölner Zeitschrift für Soziologie und Sozialpsychologie,* XXX/1 (1969); H. Sabbe, "Philosophie der neuesten Musik: Ein Versuch zur Extrapolation von Adornos *Philosophie der neuen Musik,*" *Philosophica Gandensia,* 9 (1972); F.C. Reininghaus and J.H. Traber, "Musik als Ware—Musik als Wahre. Zur politischen Hintergrund des musiksoziologischen Ansatzes von Theodor W. Adorno," *Zeitschrift für Musiktheorie,* IV/1 (1973); W. Gramer, *Musik und Verstehen: Eine Studie zur Musikästhetik Theodor W. Adorno* (Mainz, 1976).

Adriaensen (Adriaenssen, Hadrianus), Emanuel (Emmanuel), Flemish lutenist; b. Antwerp, in the 16th century; d. Antwerp (buried, Feb. 27, 1604). In 1584 he publ. *Pratum musicum,* a collection of songs and dances for 2, 3, and 4 Lutes; in 1592 he brought out another collection, entitled *Novum pratum musicum,* containing canzonets, dances, fantasias, madrigals, motets, and preludes by Cipriano de Rore, Orlando di Lasso, J. de Berchem, H. Waelrant, and others, freely arranged by him for lute in tablature.

Adrio, Adam, German musicologist; b. Essen, April 4, 1901; d. Schlüchtern, Sept. 18, 1973. He studied at the Univ. of Berlin (1923–25; 1927–31; Ph.D., 1934); served as a lecturer at the Univ. of Berlin from 1932 to 1945. In 1951 he joined the faculty of the Free Univ. of Berlin; was prof. of musicology there from 1953 to 1967. He was regarded as a foremost authority on Protestant church music. Among his publications of importance is the dissertation *Die Anfänge des geistlichen Konzerts* (Berlin, 1935).

Aerts, Egide, Belgian flutist; b. Boom, near Antwerp, March 1, 1822; d. Brussels, June 9, 1853. A precocious musician, he studied as a child at the Brussels Cons.; gave a concert in Paris at the age of 15. In 1847 he was appointed a teacher of flute at the Brussels Cons. He wrote numerous works for flute, most of which remain in MS.

Aeschbacher, Adrian, Swiss pianist; b. Langenthal, May 10, 1912. He studied at the Zürich Cons. with Emil Frey and Andreae; later took lessons with Schnabel in Berlin; subsequently engaged in a concert career. In 1965 he was appointed prof. of piano at the Hochschule für Musik in Saarbrücken.

Aeschbacher, Niklaus, Swiss conductor; b. Trogen, April 30, 1917. He studied in Zürich and Berlin. In 1942 he went to Bern; from 1949 was music director of the Bern Stadttheater. From 1954 to 1956 he was principal conductor of the NHK Symph. Orch. in Tokyo; returning to Germany, he was Generalmusikdirektor in Kiel; in 1964 he went to Detmold, where he led performances at the local opera theater.

Aeschbacher, Walther, Swiss conductor and composer; b. Bern, Oct. 2, 1901; d. Bern, Dec. 6, 1969. He studied music theory with Ernst Kurth, and conducting in Munich; then settled in Basel. He wrote much choral music and several orch. pieces in old forms.

Afanasiev, Nicolai, Russian composer; b. Tobolsk, Jan. 12, 1821; d. St. Petersburg, June 3, 1898. He studied violin with his father, an amateur musician, and joined the orch. of the Moscow Opera at the age of 17. Later he conducted Italian opera in Moscow and St. Petersburg. He traveled in Europe in 1857. Afanassiev was regarded as the first Russian composer to write a string quartet (1860), but this is refuted by the discovery of 3 string quartets by Aliabiev. He further wrote a cantata, *The Feast of Peter the Great;* 4 operas: *Ammalat-Bek,* which was produced at the Imperial Opera in St. Petersburg on Dec. 5, 1870; and 3 others, *Stenka Razin, Vakula the Smith,* and *Taras Bulba,* which were never performed. He also wrote some children's songs.

Afranio de Pavia (family name, **Albonese**), Italian theologian, reputed inventor of the bassoon; b. Pavia, 1480; d. Ferrara, c.1560, as canon of Ferrara. His claim to the invention of the bassoon is based on the attribution to him of the instrument Phagotus, in the book by his nephew Teseo Albonese *Introductio in chaldaicam linguam* (Pavia, 1539).

Agay, Dénes, Hungarian-American pianist, composer, and arranger; b. Budapest, June 10, 1911. He studied at the Budapest Academy of Music, graduating in 1933. In 1939 he went to the U.S. and settled in N.Y. as a piano teacher. Since 1950 he has been active mainly as an editor of educational material for piano students; he compiled several collections of piano music adapted for beginners (*Easy Classics to Moderns, The Young Pianist's Library,* etc.).

Agazzari, Agostino, Italian composer; b. Siena, Dec. 2, 1578; d. there, April 10, 1640. He was maestro di cappella at the German College in Rome (1602–3), then at the church of St. Apollinaris and the "seminario romano"; he adopted Viadana's innovations in sacred vocal music (writing church concertos for one or 2 voices with instrumental harmonic support). In 1613–14 he was organist at the Siena Cathedral. His works, variously reprinted in Germany and the Netherlands, were in great favor and very numerous (madrigals, Psalms, motets, and other church music). His treatise *La musica ecclesiastica* (Siena, 1638) is a theoretical endeavor to bring the practice of church music into accord with the Resolution of the Council of Trent; he was also among the first to give written instructions for performing the basso continuo, presented in the tract *Del sonare sopra il basso con tutti gli strumenti e del loro uso nel concerto* (Siena, 1607; in Eng., O. Strunk, *Source Readings in Music History,* N.Y., 1950). His pastoral drama *Eumelio* (1606) is one of the earliest operas.

Ager – Agostini

BIBLIOGRAPHY: A. Adrio, s.v., *Die Musik Geschichte und Gegenwart;* M.F. Johnson, "Agazzari's *Eumelio,* a 'Dramma pastorale,' " *Musical Quarterly* (July 1971).

Ager, Milton, American composer of popular music; b. Chicago, Oct. 6, 1893; d. Inglewood, Calif., May 6, 1979. He began his career as a pianist in silent film theaters and accompanist to singers in vaudeville. He served in the U.S. Army Morale Division during World War I. His song *Happy Days Are Here Again* was selected by Franklin D. Roosevelt as his campaign song in 1932, and became an anthem of the Democratic Party in subsequent election campaigns. Ager also wrote the greatly popular ballads *Ain't She Sweet, Crazy Words, Crazy Tune,* and *Hard-Hearted Hannah.*

AgghÁzy, KÁroly, Hungarian pianist, composer, and teacher; b. Pest, Oct. 30, 1855; d. Budapest, Oct. 8, 1918. He studied at the National Cons. in Pest (1867–70) and at the Vienna Cons. (1870–73); then had piano lessons with Liszt and took a course in composition with Volkmann at the Budapest Academy of Music (1875–78). From 1878–81 he toured in duo recitals with the violinist Jenö Hubay. From 1881–83 he was a prof. of piano at the National Cons. in Pest; from 1883–89 taught at the Stern and Kullak conservatories in Berlin; in 1889 returned to Pest and resumed his post at the National Cons. He composed some 100 piano pieces in a prevalent salon manner; also wrote 2 operas, choral pieces, and songs.

Agnesi, Maria Teresa, Italian harpsichordist, singer, and composer; b. Milan, Oct. 17, 1720; d. there, Jan. 19, 1795. She made appearances in Milan as a harpsichordist and singer; wrote a successful pastorale, *Il ristoro d'Arcadia,* which was produced in Milan at the Teatro Ducale in 1747, and an opera, *Ciro in Armenia,* to her own libretto (Milan, Dec. 26, 1753). Her other stage works were *Sofonisba* (Naples, 1765); *Insubria consolata* (Milan, 1766); and *Nitocri* (Venice, 1771). She also composed pieces for the keyboard.

Agnew, Roy, Australian composer and pianist; b. Sydney, Aug. 23, 1893; d. there, Nov. 12, 1944. He went to London and studied with Gerrard Williams (1923–28); gave concerts in England (1931–34). He then returned to Australia; was appointed director of Australian Radio (1938–43) and taught at the Sydney Cons.
WORKS: *Breaking of the Drought* for Mezzo-soprano and Orch. (1928); many piano works, including *Dance of the Wild Men* (1920); *Fantasia Sonata* (1927); *Sonata Poem* (1935); *Sonata Ballade* (1936); *Sonata Legend "Capricornia"* (1940).

Agosti, Guido, Italian pianist and teacher; b. Forlì, Aug. 11, 1901. He studied piano at the Bologna Cons. with Busoni, Mugellini, and Ivaldi; also took private lessons in composition with Benvenuti. He com-

menced his professional career as a pianist in 1921, and subsequently made several tours of Europe. He taught piano at the Venice Cons. (1933–40) and at the Rome Cons. (1941–45). In 1947 he was appointed prof. of piano at the Accademia Chigiana in Siena; in 1963 he joined the faculty of the Franz Liszt Hochschule für Musik in Weimar, and in 1970 was appointed prof. at the Sibelius Academy in Helsinki. He wrote a number of pieces for piano.

Agostini, Lodovico, Italian composer; b. Ferrara, 1534; d. there, Sept. 20, 1590. He served as maestro di cappella to Duke Alfonso II of Este of Ferrara. A number of his sacred and secular vocal works were published in Milan, Ferrara, and Venice between 1567 and 1586.

Agostini, Mezio, Italian composer; b. Fano, Aug. 12, 1875; d. there, April 22, 1944. He studied with his father and with Carlo Pedrotti at the Liceo Rossini in Pesaro (1885–92). He was a prof. of harmony there from 1900–9, when he was appointed as successor to Wolf-Ferrari in the position of director of the Liceo Benedetto Marcello in Venice (1909–40). He was active as an opera conductor in Venice and other Italian cities; also gave chamber music concerts as a pianist. His *Trio* won first prize at the international competition in Paris in 1904. He wrote the *Iovo e Maria* (1896); *Il Cavaliere del Sogno* (Fano, Feb. 24, 1897); *La penna d'Airone* (1896); *Alcibiade* (1902); *America* (also entitled *Hail Columbia,* after Longfellow, 1904); *L'ombra* (1907); *L'agnello del sogno* (1928); *La figlio del navarca* (Fano, Sept. 3, 1938). He also wrote a symph., 4 orch. suites, a piano concerto, 2 string quartets, 2 piano trios, a cello sonata, a violin sonata, the cantata *A Rossini,* numerous piano pieces and songs.

Agostini, Paolo, Italian organist and composer; b. Vallerano, 1583; d. Rome, Oct. 3, 1629. He studied with Giovanni Bernardino Nanino in Rome; was organist at S. Maria in Trastevere, in Rome, and at S. Lorenzo in Damaso. He succeeded Vincenzo Ugolini as maestro di cappella at the Vatican in 1626. Agostini's publ. works—7 books of Psalms (1619), 2 books of Magnificats and antiphons (1620), and 5 books of masses (1624–28)—are only a small portion of his total output. Most of his MSS are preserved in various Roman libraries. His music displays great ingenuity of contrapuntal structure; some of his choral works are written for 48 independent parts.

Agostini, Pietro Simone, Italian composer; b. Forlì, near Pesaro, in the first half of the 17th century; d. Parma, Oct. 1, 1680. He was in the service of the Duke of Parma as maestro di cappella during the last year of his life. He wrote 6 operas, some of which were written in collaboration with Busca, Ziani, and others: *Argia principessa di Negroponte* (probably Milan, 1669); *La Regina Floridea* (Milan, 1669); *Eliogabalo,* to his own libretto (Genoa, Jan. 28, 1670); *Ippolita regina delle Amazzoni* (Milan, 1670); *La Costanza di Rosmonda* (Genoa, 1670); *Gli inganni innocenti,* or *L'Adalinda* (Ariccia, near

Rome, 1673); *Il ratto delle Sabine* (Venice, 1680); he also wrote oratorios, motets, and secular cantatas.

Agrell, Johan Joachim, Swedish composer; b. Löth, Feb. 1, 1701; d. Nuremberg, Jan. 19, 1765. He studied at Uppsala Univ.; later was active in Kassel (1723–46) and in Nuremberg (from 1746). Among his publ. works are 5 concertos for Cembalo and Strings, 2 sonatas for Violin and Cembalo, 6 sonatas for Cembalo Solo, and pieces for Cembalo in dance forms. His symphs. and cantatas are preserved in various European libraries (Stockholm, Uppsala, Brussels, Berlin, Königsberg, Munich, and Darmstadt).

Agricola, Alexander, composer of the Netherlands school, sometimes said to have been of German extraction, but referred to as a Belgian in his epitaph; b. Flanders, c.1446; d. Valladolid, Spain, 1506. He entered the service of the Duke of Milan in 1471; then went to Cambrai; in 1476 he is mentioned as "petit vicaire" at Cambrai Cathedral. He later traveled in Italy; entered the service of Philip I of Burgundy in 1500 and followed him to Spain in 1502, returning to Belgium in 1505. He went to Spain again in January 1506 and died shortly afterward. Thirty-one of Agricola's songs and motets were printed by Petrucci (Venice, 1501–3), who also publ. a vol. of 5 masses based on chanson material: *Le Serviteur, Je ne demande, Malheur me bat, Primi toni, Secundi toni* (Venice, 1503).

Agricola (née **Molteni**), **Benedella Emilia,** Italian soprano; b. Modena, 1772; d. Berlin, 1780. She studied with Porpora, Hasse, and Salimbeni; made her operatic debut at the Berlin Opera in 1743 in C.H. Graun's *Cesare e Cleopatra.* She was married to Johann Friedrich Agricola, director of the Royal Chapel in Berlin; her connection with the court ceased upon his death in 1774, and she disappeared from the music scene.

Agricola, Johann Friedrich, German organist and composer; b. Dobitzschen, near Altenburg, Jan. 4, 1720; d. Berlin, Dec. 2, 1774. He entered the Univ. of Leipzig as a law student in 1738, studying music meanwhile with J.S. Bach, and later (1741) with Johann Quantz in Berlin. In 1751 Agricola was appointed court composer to Frederick the Great; in 1759 he succeeded Karl Graun as director of the Royal Chapel. Agricola wrote 11 operas (produced between 1750 and 1772 at Berlin and Potsdam) and church music; he also made arrangements of the King's compositions. He taught singing and in 1757 translated Pier Tosi's *Opinioni de' cantori.* Under the pseudonym **Flavio Amicio Olibrio** Agricola printed some polemical pamphlets directed against the theorist Friedrich Marpurg; he was also a collaborator with Jakob Adlung in the latter's *Musica mechanica organoedi* (1768).

Agricola, Martin, important German music theorist and writer; b. Schwiebus (Brandenburg), Jan. 6,

1486; d. Magdeburg, June 10, 1556. His real name was **Sore,** but he adopted the Latin name Agricola to indicate his peasant origin. Mattheson says that he was the first to abandon the old tablature for modern notation, but this is not quite accurate; Agricola merely proposed an improved system for lute tablature. From 1519 he was a private music teacher in Magdeburg; in 1525 was cantor at the first Lutheran church there. His friend and patron, Rhaw of Wittenberg, publ. most of Agricola's works, the magnum opus being *Musica instrumentalis deudsch* (i.e., "Set in German"; first ed., Wittenberg, 1529; 4th ed., considerably revised, 1545; modern reprint, Leipzig, 1896). This work, although derived from Virdung's *Musica getutscht,* contains much new material and is set in couplet verse in the German vernacular. Further works are: *Ein kurtz deudsche Musica* (1529; 3rd ed. as *Musica choralis deudsch,* 1533); *Musica figuralis deudsch,* with the supplement *Büchlein von den proportionibus* (1532); *Scholia in musicam planam Venceslai Philomatis* (1538); *Rudimenta musices* (1539); *Quaestiones vulgatiores in musicam* (1543); *Duo libri musices* (posthumous; Wittenberg, 1561; includes reprints of *Musica choralis* and *Musica figuralis;* and 54 *Instrumentelle Gesänge* as a supplement). Compositions: *Ein Sangbüchlein aller Sonntags-Evangelien* (1541); *Neue deutsche geistliche Gesänge* (1544); *Hymni aliquot sacri* (1552); *Melodiae scholasticae* (1557).
BIBLIOGRAPHY: Heinz Funck, *Martin Agricola* (Wolfenbüttel, 1933).

Aguado, Dionisio, Spanish guitar virtuoso and composer; b. Madrid, April 8, 1784; d. there, Dec. 29, 1849. He became a proficient player on the guitar; went to Paris in 1825, and attracted the attention of Rossini and Paganini by his virtuosity. Returning to Madrid in 1838, he was active as a teacher of guitar playing. He wrote *Estudio para la guitarra* (Madrid, 1820); *Escuela o método de guitarra* (Madrid, 1825); also 45 waltzes, 6 minuets, and other minor pieces.

Aguilar, Emanuel Abraham, English pianist and composer of Spanish descent; b. London, Aug. 23, 1824; d. there, Feb. 18, 1904. He wrote a collection of canons and fugues as preparatory exercises for the playing of Bach; also composed 3 symphs., 2 overtures, much chamber music, and the operas *Wave King* (1855) and *The Bridal Wreath* (1863).

Aguilar-Ahumada, Miguel, Chilean composer; b. Huara, April 12, 1931. He studied composition with Domingo Santa Cruz and Orrego-Salas in Santiago and later took a course in conducting in Cologne. Returning to Chile, he occupied various posts as a teacher, also giving piano recitals. Under the influence of the German avant-garde, he adopted an advanced atonal idiom.
WORKS: *Obertura al Teatro Integral* for Orch. (1954); Septet for Wind Instruments and Double Bass (1954); *Sonatina concertante* for Clarinet and Piano (1956); *Simetrias* for Piano (1958); an orch.

work entitled *Música aleatoria* (1969). In one of his electronic pieces he introduced tape recordings of a mooing cow, exploding balloons, and the sounds of an orch. tuning up before a rehearsal. He wrote several vocal works to texts by the Chilean poet Vicente Huidobro, among them *Torre Eifel* (1967).

Aguilera de Heredia, Sebastian, b. Aragon, c.1565; d. Saragossa, Dec. 16, 1627. He was organist at Huesca (1585–1603) and then maestro de musica at Saragossa Cathedral. He publ. there his collection *Canticum Beatissimae Virginis Deiparae Mariae octo modis seu tonis compositum, quaternisque vocibus, quinis, senis et octonis concionandum* (1618). It contains sacred choruses in 4, 5, 6, and 8 parts, derived from 8 church modes. His music is notable for skillful use of dissonances ("falsas").

BIBLIOGRAPHY: H. Anglès, "Orgelmusik der Schola Hispanica von XV–XVII. Jahrhunderte," in *Peter Wagner-Festschrift* (Leipzig, 1926).

Aguirre, Julián, Argentine composer; b. Buenos Aires, Jan. 28, 1868; d. there, Aug. 13, 1924. He was taken to Spain as a child; studied at the Madrid Cons., returning to Buenos Aires in 1887. His works are mostly miniatures for Piano in the form of stylized Argentine dances and songs. He wrote 61 opus numbers; *Gato* and *Huella* (op. 49), his most popular pieces, were orchestrated by Ansermet, who performed them in Buenos Aires (April 6, 1930); the *Huella* was also arranged for Violin and Piano by Jascha Heifetz. Other notable works are *Aires nacionales argentinos* (op. 17) and *Zamba* (op. 40).

BIBLIOGRAPHY: J.F. Giacobbe, *Julián Aguirre* (Buenos Aires, 1945); C. García Muñoz, *Julián Aguirre* (Buenos Aires, 1970).

Agujari, Lucrezia (known as **La Bastardina,** or **Bastardella**), being the natural daughter of a nobleman), a brilliant Italian singer; b. Ferrara, 1743; d. Parma, May 18, 1783. Her father entrusted her instruction to P. Lambertini; in 1764 she made a triumphant debut at Florence, followed by a succession of brilliant appearances in Milan and other Italian cities; also in London. Mozart wrote of her that she had "a lovely voice, a flexible throat, and an incredibly high range." In 1780 she married the Italian composer **Giuseppe Colla,** whose songs she constantly performed at her concerts. Her compass was phenomenal, embracing 3 octaves (C^1–C^4).

Ahern, David, Australian composer; b. Sydney, Nov. 2, 1947. He played piano and violin as a child; studied composition with Butterley and Meale; then went to Germany and took courses with Stockhausen in Cologne; also was in London, where he became a disciple of Cardew, exploring the outer regions of the art of hypermusical speculations. Returning to Australia, he formed an avant-garde performing group called Teletopa Improvisation in Sydney (1970). His early works are rigidly serial, but after 1965 he began employing random theatrical effects. His works include a Sonata for Solo Violin (1963);

After Mallarmé for Orch. (1966); *Annunciations* for Orch. (1966); *Auriga* for Wind Quartet (1966); *Arabesques* for 48 Solo Strings (1967); *Music for 9* (Piano, Flute, Clarinet, String Quartet, and 2 Percussionists, 1967); *Ned Kelly Music* for Orch. (1967); *Journal* for 6 Actors and Actresses, Didjeridu, Electric Bass, Violin, and Ring Modulator (1968); a symbolic score, *Stereo/Mono* (1971); *Cinemusic* (1972); *Hilo* for 6 Trumpets, 4 Tubas, 4 Percussionists, Harp, Piano, 16 Violins, and 8 Double Basses (1975).

Ahle, Johann Georg, German organist and composer (son of **Johann Rudolf Ahle**); b. Mühlhausen, June (baptized, June 12) 1651; d. there, Dec. 2, 1706. He succeeded his father as organist in Mühlhausen, and was made poet laureate by Emperor Leopold I. Among Ahle's works publ. during his lifetime are *Musikalische Frühlings-, Sommer-, Herbst-, und Wintergespräche* (1695–1701); written to illustrate his method of composition; *Instrumentalische Frühlingsmusik* (1676; publ. in 2 vols., 1675–76); *Anmuthige zehn vierstimmige Viol-di-gamba Spiele* (1681); many vols. of dances, sacred and secular songs.

Ahle, Johann Rudolf, German composer; b. Mühlhausen, Dec. 24, 1625; d. there, July 9, 1673. From 1646 he was cantor in Erfurt. He was organist of St. Blasius, Mühlhausen, in 1654, and in 1661 was elected burgomaster of the town. Ahle was a diligent composer of church music and writer of theoretical works. His *Compendium pro tonellis* (1648) ran through 4 editions, 2nd as *Brevis et perspicua introductio in artem musicum* (1673), 3rd and 4th as *Kurze und deutliche Anleitung* (1690 and 1704). His principal compositions include: *Geistlich Dialoge,* songs in several parts (1648); *Thüringischer Lustgarten* (1657); *Geistliche Fest- und Communionandachten* (posthumous). Many of his songs are still popular in Thuringia. A selection from his works was publ. by J. Wolf in Denkmäler Deutscher Tonkunst (vol. V).

BIBLIOGRAPHY: J. Wolf, "Johann Rudolph Ahle: Eine bio-bibliographische Skizze," *Sammelbände der Internationalen Musik-Gesellschaft,* II (1900–1); A. Adrio, s.v., *Die Musik in Geschichte und Gegenwart.*

Ahlersmeyer, Mathieu, German baritone; b. Cologne, June 29, 1896; d. Garmisch-Partenkirchen, July 23, 1979. He studied voice in Cologne; made his debut in Mönchen as Wolfram in *Tannhäuser* (1929); then sang with the Kroll Opera in Berlin (1930–31) and at the Hamburg State Opera (1931–33). He was subsequently on the staff of the Dresden State Opera, and again with the Hamburg State Opera (1946–61); also sang in Berlin, Vienna, Milan, and London until his retirement in 1973. He created the role of the Barber in Strauss's *Die schweigsame Frau* (Dresden, June 24, 1935).

Ahlgrimm, Isolde, Austrian harpsichordist; b. Vienna, July 31, 1914. She studied piano at the Vienna Academy of Music with Viktor Ebenstein, Franz

Schmidt, and Emil von Sauer; then turned her attention to the harpsichord, and toured as a soloist in Europe and the U.S. In 1945 she joined the faculty of the Vienna Hochschule für Musik; also taught at the Salzburg Mozarteum (1958–62).

Ahlstrom, David, American composer; b. Lancaster, N.Y., Feb. 22, 1927. He studied composition with Henry Cowell and Bernard Rogers; became interested in Asian philosophy and took lessons with Haridas Chaudhuri. He obtained a Ph.D. in composition from the Eastman School of Music in Rochester, N.Y., in 1961; then taught music theory at Northwestern Univ. (1961–62), Southern Methodist Univ. in Dallas (1962–67), and Eastern Illinois Univ. in Charleston (1967–76). In 1976 he moved to San Francisco, and became active in the production of new American stage music. Among his own works, the most significant is his opera *America, I Love You,* to a libretto by e.e. cummings, first produced in its entirety, composer conducting, in San Francisco on June 25, 1983; other operas are *Doctor Faustus Lights the Lights,* after Gertrude Stein (San Francisco, Oct. 29, 1982), and *Three Sisters Who Are Not Sisters,* also derived from Gertrude Stein's text, produced under Ahlstrom's direction in San Francisco, Sept. 17, 1982). He also wrote several symphs. and clarinet sonatas, and a number of theater works employing electronic sound and dance.

Ahna, Heinrich Karl Herman de. See **De Ahna, Heinrich Karl Herman.**

Aho, Kalevi, Finnish composer; b. Forssa, March 9, 1949. He studied composition with Rautavaara at the Sibelius Academy in Helsinki, graduating in 1971; then went to Berlin and took lessons in composition with Boris Blacher. In 1974 he was appointed to the music faculty at Helsinki Univ. His early music was influenced by Prokofiev and Shostakovich; later he diverged from his Russian antecedents and adopted a free-flowing cosmopolitan style, neoclassical in form and atonal in melodic structure. WORKS: A scenic monologue, *Avain (The Key),* for Baritone and Chamber Orch. (1978–79); 6 symphs.: No. 1 (1969); No. 2 (1970); No. 3, *Sinfonia concertante,* for Violin and Orch. (1973); No. 4 (1973); No. 5 (1976); No. 6 (1980); Chamber Symph. for Strings (1976); Violin Concerto (1981); *Hiljaisuus (Silence)* for Orch. (1982); 3 string quartets: No. 1 (suppressed); No. 2 (1970); No. 3 (1971); Sonata for Solo Violin (1974); Quintet for Oboe and String Quartet (1974); *Tumultos* for Solo Violin (1974); *Preludium, Toccata e Postludium* for Cello and Piano (1974); Quintet for Bassoon and String Quartet (1977); Quintet for Flute, Oboe, Violin, Viola, and Cello (1977); *Ludus solemnis* for Organ (1978); *In memoriam* for Organ (1980); Piano Sonata (1980); Quartet for Flute, Saxophone, Guitar, and Piano (1982); songs.

Ahrens, Joseph Johannes Clemens, eminent German organist and composer; b. Sommersell, Westphalia, April 17, 1904. He displayed an early talent for improvisation on the organ; after studying with Wilhelm Middelschulte, he was appointed an organist at St. Hedwigs-Kathedrale in Berlin; later was prof. of Catholic church music at the Berlin Hochschule für Musik. In 1968 he received a silver pontifical medal from the Vatican in appreciation of his accomplishments in sacred music. He composed almost exclusively for organ and chorus, maintaining the strict form of the Gregorian chorale within the framework of complex polyphony, and applying advanced melodic and harmonic formulas, including the 12-tone technique. His compositions, couched in a modern Baroque style, were highly esteemed by professional organists. WORKS: Several masses: *Missa choralis* (1945); *Missa dorica* (1946); *Missa gotica* (1948); *Missa hymnica* (1948); *Missa Salvatoris* (1949); *Missa pro unitate* (1963); *Missa dodekaphonica* (1966, in which Gregorian chant is combined with 12-tone melodic patterns); *Passion of St. Matthew* (1950); *Passion of St. John* (1961); *Fantasie und Ricercare* for Organ (1967).

Ahronovich, Yuri, Russian conductor; b. Leningrad, May 13, 1932. He studied conducting with Kurt Sanderling and Nathan Rachlin. He then appeared with leading opera houses and orchs. in the Soviet Union. In 1974 he conducted at the Cologne Opera and at Covent Garden in London. In 1975 he became chief conductor of the Gürzenich Orch. in Cologne; in 1982 he assumed the post of chief conductor of the Stockholm Phil., while retaining his position in Cologne.

Aibl, Joseph, founder of a music publishing house, established in Munich in 1824; his successors were **Eduard Spitzweg** (from 1836) and his sons, **Eugen** and **Otto.** In 1904 Universal Edition bought the firm.

Aiblinger, Johann Kaspar, German conductor and composer; b. Wasserburg, Bavaria, Feb. 23, 1779; d. Munich, May 6, 1867. He studied music in Munich, then at Bergamo under Simon Mayr (1802); lived at Vicenza (1803–11), then became 2nd maestro di cappella to the viceroy at Milan; founded the Odeon (a society for the cultivation of Classical vocal music) at Venice, in collaboration with Abbé Trentino; was engaged (1819) for the Italian opera in Munich as maestro al cembalo; returned in 1833 to Bergamo, and amassed a fine collection of ancient classical music, now in the Staatsbibliothek at Munich. He wrote many sacred compositions (masses, Requiems, liturgies, Psalms, etc.), which were very popular. He also wrote an opera, *Rodrigo e Ximene* (Munich, 1821), and 3 ballets.

Aichinger, Gregor, important German church composer; b. Regensburg, 1564; d. Augsburg, Jan. 21, 1628. At the age of 13 he went to Munich, where he was under the tutelage of Orlando Lasso; then entered the Univ. of Ingolstadt. He made 2 journeys to Rome; visited Venice, where he mastered the art of Venetian polyphony. He eventually settled in Augsburg as choirmaster and vicar of the Cathedral. He wrote almost exclusively for voices, to Latin texts; his sacred works are remarkable for their practical value and for the excellence of their musical content. Among his many publ. works are 3 books of *Sacrae cantiones* (Venice, 1590; Augsburg, 1595; Nuremberg, 1597); *Tricinia Mariana* (Innsbruck, 1598); *Divinae laudes* (Augsburg, 1602); etc. His publication *Cantiones ecclesiaticae cum basso generali et continuo* (Dillingen, 1607) is noteworthy as one of the earliest works in which the term "basso continuo" appears in the title. A selection of Aichinger's works is included in vol. 18 (formerly 10.i) of Denkmäler der Tonkunst in Bayern, prefaced with a biographical article by the editor, Th. Kroyer.

Aigner, Engelbert, Austrian composer and conductor; b. Vienna, Feb. 3, 1798; d. there, Aug. 27, 1866. He studied with Stadler, from whom he received a thorough training in church music; also wrote for the stage. Among his works are operettas: *Die Wunderlilie* (Vienna, 1827); *Das Hochzeitskonzert* (Vienna, 1829); *Der Angriffsplan* (Vienna, 1829); *Das geheime Fenster* (Vienna, 1829); several ballets; a canonic mass (1823); a cantata, *Lob der Musik;* *Kontrapunktischer Scherz* for Piano; Quintet for Piano, Flute, Violin, Viola, and Cello; some orch. pieces. He also participated in a society for the propagation of church music.

Aitken, Hugh, American composer; b. New York, Sept. 7, 1924. He received his primary training at home; his father was an accomplished violinist, and his paternal grandmother was a pianist. He took lessons in clarinet playing and also enrolled in a chemistry class at N.Y. Univ. In 1943–45 he served as a navigator in the U.S. Army Air Corps. Returning from the war, he entered the Juilliard School of Music in N.Y. as a student in composition of Bernard Wagenaar, Vincent Persichetti, and Robert Ward (M.S., 1950); in 1960 he joined the faculty there; in 1970 became a prof. of music at William Paterson College in Wayne, N.J. In his music he professes a moral dedication to the Classical ideals and regards any deviation from the natural melodic flow and harmonic euphony as unjustifiable tonicide.

WORKS: FOR THE STAGE: *Fables,* chamber opera after La Fontaine (1975); *Felipe,* opera after Cervantes (1981). FOR ORCH.: Chamber Concerto for Piano, Winds, Brass, and String Quintet (1947; revised 1977); *Toccata* (1950); Piano Concerto (1953); *Short Suite* for String Orch. (1954); *Partita I* (1957); *7 Pieces* for Chamber Orch. (1957); *Serenade* for Chamber Orch. (1958); *Partita II* (1959); *Partita* for String Orch. and Piano (1960); *Partita III* and *IV* (1964); *Partita* for String Quartet and Orch. (1964); *Rameau Remembered* for Flute, 2 Oboes, Bassoon, and Strings (1980); *In Praise of Ockeghem* for String Orch. (1981); Violin Concerto (1984). CHAMBER MUSIC: *Short Suite* for Wind Quintet and Piano (1948); String Trio (1951); *Suite* for Clarinet (1955); *Partita* for 6 Instruments (1956); Quintet for Oboe and Strings (1957); *8 Studies* for Wind Quintet (1958); *Partita* for Violin (1958); Quartet for Clarinet and

Strings (1959); *Trombone Music* (1961); *Suite* for Solo Bass (1961); *Montages* for Bassoon (1962); *Serenade* for Oboe and String Trio (1965); Trios for 11 Players (1970); *Trumpet!* (1974); *Oboe Music* (1975); *Tromba* for Trumpet and String Quartet (1976); *Johannes* for 5 Renaissance Instruments (N.Y., Oct. 27, 1977); *For the Violin* (1978); *For the Cello* (1980); *Op. 95 Revisited* for String Quartet (1980); *Flute Music* (1981); *5 Short Pieces* for 3 Clarinets (1982). VOCAL MUSIC: 6 cantatas (1958–81); oratorio, *The Revelation of St. John the Divine, Part I* for Soloists, Chorus, and Orch. (1965); choruses; songs. Also piano and organ pieces; band music.

Aitken, Robert, noted Canadian flutist and composer; b. Kentville, Nova Scotia, Aug. 28, 1939. He studied flute with Marcel Moyse, Julius Baker, and Jean-Pierre Rampal; took courses in composition with Barbara Pentland at the Univ. of British Columbia in Vancouver and with John Weinzweig at the Univ. of Toronto; also received instruction in electronic music from Myron Schaeffer. He then was principal flutist of several Canadian orchs. and taught flute playing at the Royal Cons. in Toronto; he held the degrees of B.M. in composition (1961) and M.M. (1964). In 1971 he organized the New Music Concerts in Toronto; in 1972 he was appointed to the faculty of the Univ. of Toronto. In his music he explores unusual instrumental combinations and spatial concepts of antiphonal groupings.

WORKS: *Rhapsody* for Orch. (1961); Quartet for Flute, Oboe, Viola, and Double Bass (1961); *Music for Flute and Electronic Tape* (1963); *Noēsis* for Electronic Tape (1963); Concerto for 12 Solo Instruments (1964); *Spectra* for 4 Chamber Groups (1969); *Kebyar* for Flute, Clarinet, 2 Double Basses, Percussion, and Tape (1971); *Shadows I: Nekuia* for Orch. (1971); *Shadows II: Lalitá* for Flute, 3 Cellos, 2 Percussionists, and 2 Harps (1972); *Shadows III: Nira* for Solo Violin, Flute, Oboe, Viola, Double Bass, Piano, and Harpsichord (1974–76); *Spiral* for Orch., with Amplified Flute, Oboe, Clarinet, and Bassoon (1975); *Icicle* for Solo Flute (1977); *Plainsong* for Solo Flute (1977); *Folia* for Woodwind Quintet (1980).

Aitken, Webster, American pianist; b. Los Angeles, June 17, 1908; d. Santa Fe, N.Mex., May 11, 1981. He studied piano in Europe with Artur Schnabel and Emil von Sauer; in 1929 he made his professional debut in Vienna. Returning to America, he gave a concert in N.Y. (Nov. 17, 1935); in 1938 he presented a series of recitals in N.Y. in programs featuring all of Schubert's piano works. He subsequently devoted himself mainly to teaching.

Ajmone-Marsan, Guido, Italian-born American conductor; b. Turin, March 24, 1947. He was brought to the U.S. as a child; became an American citizen in 1962. He studied clarinet and piano; continued his studies in Salzburg, Venice, and Siena. He took a course in conducting with Franco Ferrara at the Santa Cecilia Academy in Rome. His conducting career received its decisive impetus in 1973, when he won first prize in the Solti Competition in Chicago; subsequently he appeared as a guest conductor with the Chicago, Philadelphia, and Cleveland orchs.

Akeroyde, Samuel, English composer of songs; b. Yorkshire, c.1650; d. London, after 1706. He was in the service of James II in 1687 as Musician in Ordinary, and wrote songs for at least 8 plays produced in London between 1685 and 1706. His songs were printed in several contemporary collections: Durfey's *Third Collection of Songs* (1685); *The Theatre of Musick* (1685–87); *Vinculum Societatis* (1687); *Comes Amoris* (1687–94); *The Banquet of Musick* (1688); *Thesaurus Musicus* (1693–96).

Akimenko (real name, **Yakimenko**), **Fyodor,** Russian composer; b. Kharkov, Feb. 20, 1876; d. Paris, Jan. 3, 1945. He studied with Balakirev at the Court Chapel in St. Petersburg (1886–90), then with Liadov and Rimsky-Korsakov at the St. Petersburg Cons. (1895–1900). He was the first composition teacher of Stravinsky, whom he taught privately. After the Russian Revolution he emigrated to Paris, where he remained until his death. He wrote mostly for piano in the manner of the Russian lyric school, and had the good fortune of having his pieces and songs publ. by Belaiev; some of them were included in anthologies of Russian music. He wrote an opera, *The Fairy of the Snows* (1914); a concert overture, which was conducted by Rimsky-Korsakov in St. Petersburg on Nov. 20, 1899; an orch. fantasy, conducted by Glazunov in St. Petersburg on Oct. 28, 1900; *Petite ballade* for Clarinet and Piano; *Pastorale* for Oboe and Piano; Piano Trio; Violin Sonata; Cello Sonata; 2 *Sonata-Fantasias* for Piano; numerous character pieces for piano, and songs.

Akiyama, Kazuyoshi, brilliant Japanese conductor; b. Tokyo, Jan. 2, 1941. He attended the Toho School of Music, studying conducting with Hideo Saito. In 1964 he became conductor of the Tokyo Symph. Orch. His other posts include: principal guest conductor, New Japan Phil., Tokyo; principal conductor, Osaka Phil.; resident conductor and music director, Vancouver Symph. Orch.; music director, American Symph. Orch., N.Y. (1973–78).

Akiyama, Kuniharu, Japanese composer; b. Tokyo, May 22, 1929. After taking lessons in academic musical subjects, he dedicated himself to a thorough study of advanced trends in music, surrealist literature, and abstract expressionist painting. In 1967 he was one of the chief organizers of a modern series of performing arts in Tokyo, called Cross-Talk, with the participation of Japanese and American avant-garde artists and musicians. His own compositions make use of both electronic and primitive Japanese instruments; in this respect a characteristic item is *Music for Meals* (1964) for Tape and Stone Instruments, which he prepared for a cafeteria at the Olympic Games in Tokyo in 1964; even more physiologically specific is his *Onara no uta* (*Music for Farting and Belching;* 1971).

Akses, Necil Kâzim, Turkish composer; b. Istanbul, May 6, 1908. He studied at the Istanbul Cons.; in 1926 went to Vienna, where he had instruction with Joseph Marx; subsequently moved to Prague and took lessons with Alois Hába and Josef Suk (1931–34). Returning to Turkey in 1935, he was appointed to the Teachers College in Ankara; he also attended classes of Paul Hindemith, who was teaching in Ankara at the time. In 1936, Akses was appointed prof. of composition at the Ankara State Cons. His music incorporates elements of Turkish folk songs, but the contrapuntal and harmonic formulation is entirely modern.
WORKS: *Mete,* one-act opera (1933); *Bayönder,* opera (Ankara, Dec. 27, 1934); *Ankara Castle,* tone poem (Ankara, Oct. 22, 1942); *Poem* for Cello and Orch. (Ankara, June 29, 1946); *Ballade* for Orch. (Ankara, April 14, 1948); *Allegro feroce* for Saxophone and Piano (1931); Flute Sonata (1939); Symph. (1966); piano pieces.

Akutagawa, Yasushi, Japanese composer; b. Tokyo, July 12, 1925. He is the 3rd son of the famous writer Ryunosuke Akutagawa, author of *Rashomon.* Yasushi studied composition (with Hashimoto and Ifukube), conducting, and piano at the Tokyo Academy of Music (1943–49); was active in Tokyo as a conductor and organizer of groups promoting the cause of Japanese music.
WORKS: 2 operas: *Kurai Kagami* (*Dark Mirror;* Tokyo, 1960) and *L'Orphée in Hiroshima* (1967; Tokyo Television, Aug. 27, 1967); 4 ballets, all produced in Tokyo: *The Dream of the Lake* (Nov. 6, 1950); *Paradise Lost* (March 17, 1951); *Kappa* (July 21, 1957); and *Spider's Web* (March 17, 1969); *Prelude* for Orch. (1947); *3 Symphonic Movements* (Tokyo, Sept. 26, 1948); *Music for Orchestra* (1950); *Triptyque* for String Orch. (1953); *Sinfonia* (1953); Divertimento for Orch. (1955); *Symphony for Children* (*"Twin Stars"*) for Narrator and Orch. (1957); *Ellora Symphony* (1958); *Music for Strings* No. 1 for Double String Quartet and Double Bass (1962); *Gengaku no tame, no inga* (*Negative Picture*) for String Orch. (1966); *Ostinato Sinfonica* (Tokyo, May 25, 1967); *Concerto Ostinato* for Cello and Orch. (Tokyo, Dec. 16, 1969); *Ballata Ostinata* for Orch. (1970); *Rhapsody* for Orch. (Tokyo, Oct. 4, 1971); *Ballata* for Violin and Piano (1951); film music, including the prizewinning *Gate of Hell.*

Alain, Jehan, French organist and composer; b. St. Germain-en-Laye, Feb. 3, 1911; killed in action at Petits-Puis, near Saumur, June 20, 1940. He received his earliest instruction in music from his father; composed a piece entitled *Etude sur un thème de quatre notes* at the age of 8; then studied organ with Marcel Dupré and composition with Paul Dukas and Roger-Ducasse. Altogether he wrote 127 opus numbers, most of them for organ. His death at the age of 29, while he was leading a motorcycle patrol during the last days of hostilities in France, was a great loss to French music.
BIBLIOGRAPHY: B. Gavoty, *Jehan Alain, Musicien français* (Paris, 1945); F. Sabatier, "A propos

Alain – Albanese

de l'œuvre d'orgue de Jehan Alain," *Jeunesse et Orgue* (1973).

Alain, Marie-Claire, noted French organist, sister of **Jehan Alain;** b. St. Germain-en-Laye, Aug. 10, 1926. She was educated at the Paris Cons., studying harmony with Duruflé, counterpoint and fugue with Plé-Caussade, and organ with Dupré. She made her debut in Paris in 1950; later gave successful organ recitals in Europe and the U.S.; she became particularly noted for her authoritative renditions of the organ music of the Baroque period.

Alain, Olivier, French pianist, musicologist, and composer, brother of **Jehan** and **Marie-Claire Alain;** b. St. Germain-en-Laye, Aug. 3, 1918. He studied organ and piano in his youth; then took courses in composition with Aubin and Messiaen at the Paris Cons. From 1950–64 he served as director of the Cons. in St. Germain-en-Laye; in 1961 he was appointed to the faculty of the Ecole César Franck in Paris. He composed an oratorio, *Chant funèbre sur les morts en montagne* (1950); also wrote motets and pieces for organ and piano. He publ. the manual *L'Harmoni* (Paris, 1965) and the monograph *Bach* (Paris, 1970).

Alaleona, Domenico, Italian theorist and composer; b. Montegiorgio, Nov. 16, 1881; d. there, Dec. 28, 1928. He studied organ and clarinet in his native town; in 1901 went to Rome, where he studied piano with Sgambati, organ with Renzi, and theory with De Sanctis at Santa Cecilia Academy; was then active as a choral conductor in Leghorn and Rome; in 1911 obtained the post of prof. of musical esthetics at Santa Cecilia. He wrote an opera, *Mirra* (1912; produced in Rome, March 31, 1920, with critical acclaim, but not revived); a Requiem; *Sinfonia italiana;* 12 *Canzoni italiane;* and 4 *Laudi italiane* for various Instrumental Groups; a cycle of 18 songs, *Melodie Pascoliane;* etc. However, his importance lies in his theoretical writings. His valuable book *Studi sulla storia dell' oratorio musicale in Italia* (Turin, 1908) was reprinted in Milan (1945) as *Storia dell'oratorio musicale in Italia* and is now a standard work. A believer in musical progress, he contributed several original ideas to the theory of modern music, notably in his article "L'armonia modernissima," *Rivista Musicale Italiana* (1911), and originated the term "dodecafonia." He also contributed articles on Italian composers to Eaglefield-Hull's *Dictionary of Modern Music and Musicians* (London, 1924). The entry on Alaleona in that dictionary contains a detailed list of his works and bibliography.

Alard, Jean-Delphin, a distinguished violinist of the French school; b. Bayonne, March 8, 1815; d. Paris, Feb. 22, 1888. He was a student of Habeneck at the Paris Cons. He succeeded Baillot as a violin teacher there in 1843, and as leader of the royal orch. teaching in the Cons. till 1875. A fine instructor (Sarasate was his pupil), he publ. *Violin School,* a manual of high merit; *Les Maîtres classiques du*

violon, a selection from 18th-century classics; and numerous brilliant and popular pieces for violin (concertos, études, fantasias, etc.).

Alarie, Pierrette, Canadian soprano; b. Montreal, Nov. 9, 1921. She studied in Montreal and later with Elisabeth Schumann in Philadelphia; made her debut in Montreal in 1940; after winning the Metropolitan Opera Auditions of the Air, she made her debut with the company on Dec. 8, 1945, as Oscar in *Un ballo in maschera;* remained on its roster until 1948; made her Paris Opéra debut in 1949; also sang at La Scala in Milan, the Vienna State Opera, the Aix-en-Provence Festival, and the Salzburg Festival; in addition, she made concert appearances. She was married to the Canadian tenor **Léopold Simoneau.**

Alary, Jules (Giulio) Eugène Abraham, Italian-French composer; b. Mantua, March 16, 1814; d. Paris, April 17, 1891. He studied at the Cons. of Milan; then played the flute at La Scala. In 1838 he settled in Paris as a successful voice teacher and composer. He wrote numerous operas, among them *Rosamunda* (Florence, June 10, 1840); *Le tre nozze* (Paris, March 29, 1851; a polka-duet from it, sung by Henrietta Sontag and Lablache, was highly popular); and *Sardanapalo* (St. Petersburg, Feb. 16, 1852). His opera *La Voix humaine* had the curious distinction of being staged at the Paris Opéra (Dec. 30, 1861) with the sole purpose of making use of the scenery left over after the fiasco of *Tannhäuser* (the action of Alary's opera takes place in Wartburg, as does that of *Tannhäuser*). It held the stage for 13 performances (*Tannhäuser* had 3). Alary also wrote a mystery play, *Redemption* (Paris, April 14, 1850), much sacred music, and some chamber works.

Albanese, Licia, noted Italian-American soprano; b. Bari, July 22, 1913. She studied with Emanuel De Rosa in Bari and with Giuseppina Baldassare-Tedeschi in Milan. She made her operatic debut under unusual circumstances at the Teatro Lirico in Milan when she was urgently summoned to sing the second part of *Madama Butterfly* as Cio-Cio-San to substitute for a soprano who was taken ill during the first act. In 1935 she won first prize for best singing in a national Italian contest, and made her official debut in Parma on Dec. 10, 1935, again as Cio-Cio-San. Her success was so great that she was offered a contract with the San Carlo Opera in Naples, and subsequently became a member of La Scala in Milan. She received a number of high honors, among them the Order of Merit in Italy and the award of the Lady Grand Cross of the Equestrian Order of the Holy Sepulchre, which was given to her by Pope Pius XI. On Feb. 9, 1940, she made a brilliant debut at the Metropolitan Opera in N.Y. in her favorite role as Cio-Cio-San; she continued to sing with the Metropolitan for 26 years; altogether she sang there 286 times in N.Y. and 115 times on tour, in 17 roles; besides Cio-Cio-San, which she performed 72 times, she sang Mimi in *La Bohème,* Marguerite in *Faust,* Violetta in *La Traviata,* Desdemona in *Otello*, and Tosca. She gave her final performance at the Metropolitan on April 16, 1966. She returned to the stage for a recital at Carnegie Hall on Feb. 22, 1970, in a program of operatic arias; she sang again at a benefit of the Puccini Foundation in Town Hall, N.Y., on Feb. 5, 1975. She married in 1945 an Italian-American businessman, Joseph Gimma.

BIBLIOGRAPHY: David Ewen, *Musicians since 1900* (N.Y., 1978).

Albani, Dame Emma (stage name of **Marie Louise Cécile Emma Lajeunesse**), Canadian dramatic soprano; b. Chambly, near Montreal, Nov. 1, 1847; d. London, April 3, 1930. She sang in a Catholic church in Albany, N.Y., in 1864; was then sent to Europe for study, first in Paris with Duprez, and then in Milan with Lamperti, who dedicated to her his treatise on the trill). She made her debut as Amina in *La Sonnambula* in Messina in 1870, under the name of Albani, taken from an old Italian family. After further appearances in Italy, she made her London debut, again as Amina (Covent Garden, April 2, 1872). In 1873 she sang in Moscow and St. Petersburg. Her American operatic debut was in the same role at the N.Y. Academy of Music, in Max Strakosch's company (Oct. 21, 1874). It paved the way for later successes with the Metropolitan Opera, where she made her first appearance as Gilda (Dec. 23, 1891). Her last important operatic engagement was as Isolde at Covent Garden (June 26, 1896). She sang in concerts, however, for several years longer. Her farewell concert took place at the Royal Albert Hall in London on Oct. 14, 1911. Her repertoire included the roles of Marguerite, Mignon, Elsa, Elisabeth, Lucia, and Desdemona. Albani married Ernest Gye, the lessee of Covent Garden, in 1878. In her singing, she combined high technical skill with profound feeling. She was equally successful on the operatic stage and in oratorio. In appreciation of her services to British art, she was made a Dame of the British Empire (1925). She publ. her memoirs, *Forty Years of Song* (London, 1911).

Albani, Mattia (real name, **Mathias Alban**), violin maker; b. S. Niccolo di Kaltern (Alto Adige), March (baptized, March 28) 1621; d. Bolzano, Feb. 7, 1712. He was a pupil of Jakob Stainer. Violins of Albani's are extant dating from as early as the end of 1644. His best examples date from 1680 onward. The great vogue his violins enjoyed spawned many forgeries; false Albani labels have been discovered on violins dating from as early as 1640; the original labels appeared from 1690. A son, **Giuseppe,** his pupil, worked from 1680–1722 at Bolzano, and another son, **Michele** (1677–1730), at Graz. Other violin makers named Albani, or at least using the name on their instruments (perhaps for its commercial value), are the following, none appearing to have been connected with the family of the original Mattia: Mattia (Rome, c.1650–1715); Nicola (worked at Mantua, c.1763); Filippo (active c.1773); Francesco (active at Graz, c.1724); Michele (at Palermo,

18th century); and Paolo (at Palermo and Cremona, 1630–70).

Albéniz, Isaac, eminent Spanish composer; b. Camprodón, May 29, 1860; d. Cambo-les-Bains (Pyrénées), May 18, 1909. Endowed with exceptionally precocious musical gifts, he was exhibited as a child pianist at a tender age; soon he began taking formal piano lessons with Narciso Oliveros in Barcelona. His sister **Clementine Albéniz** was also a precocious pianist, and they gave concerts together. When he was seven, his mother took him to Paris, where he was accepted as a private pupil by the famous prof. Marmontel, the teacher of Bizet and Debussy. Returning to Spain, he studied with Mendizábal at the Madrid Cons., but possessed by the spirit of adventure, he stowed away on a ship bound for Puerto Rico; from there he made his way to the southern states of the U.S., where he earned a living by playing at places of entertainment. He finally returned to Spain and, having acquired a considerable technique as a serious pianist, he traveled to Europe, and enrolled at the Leipzig Cons. as a student of Jadassohn and Reinecke. Once again in Spain, he was befriended by Count Guillermo Morphy, who sent him to the Brussels Cons., where he studied piano with Brassin and composition with Gevaert and Dupont; he won first prize in 1879; in 1880 he met Liszt in Budapest. After a trip to South America he settled in Barcelona in 1883; there he married Rosina Jordana; one of their daughters, Laura Albéniz, became a well-known painter. A meeting with the eminent musicologist and folk song collector Felipe Pedrell influenced Albéniz in the direction of national Spanish music. Still anxious to perfect his technique of composition, he went to Paris for studies with Paul Dukas and Vincent d'Indy. Abandoning his career as concert pianist, he spent several years in London (1890–93), and in 1893 settled in Paris; there he taught piano at the Schola Cantorum; from 1900 to 1902 he was in Barcelona, and then returned once more to Paris; in 1903 he moved to Nice; later he went to Cambo-les-Bains in the Pyrénées, where he died shortly before his 49th birthday.

Almost all of the works of Albéniz are written for piano, and all without exception are inspired by Spanish folklore. He thus established the modern school of Spanish piano literature, derived from original rhythms and melodic patterns, rather than imitating the imitations of national Spanish music by French and Russian composers. His piano suite *Iberia*, composed between 1906 and 1909, is a brilliant display of piano virtuosity.

WORKS: FOR PIANO: *Iberia,* suite of 12 pieces (1906–09): *Evocación, El puerto, Fête-Dieu à Séville, Rondeña, Almería, Triana, El Albaicín, El polo, Lavapiés, Málaga, Jérez, Eritaña;* other piano works are *Suite española; La vega; Cantos de España;* several sonatas; two pieces left unfinished: *Azulejos* (completed by Granados); *Navarra* (completed by de Sévérac). Fernández Arbós made effective orchestral transcriptions of *Evocación, Triana,* and *Fête-Dieu à Séville* (also orchestrated by Leopold Stokowski). Among other piano pieces, the *Seguidillas, Córdova,* and the *Tango in D* have attained great popularity. FOR ORCH.: *Catalonia; Rapsodia española;* Piano Concerto. OPERAS: *The Magic Opal* (London, Jan. 19, 1893); *Enrico Clifford* (Barcelona, May 8, 1895); Pepita Jiménez (Barcelona, Jan. 5, 1896); *San Antonio de la Florida* (Madrid, Oct. 26, 1894); *Merlin,* first part of an uncompleted operatic trilogy on the legend of King Arthur.

BIBLIOGRAPHY: F. Pedrell, "Isaac Albéniz," *Revista musical catalana,* VI (1909); J. de Marliave, "Isaac Albéniz," *Etudes musicales* (Paris, 1917); G. Jean-Aubry, "Isaac Albéniz (1860–1909)," *Musical Times* (Dec. 1917); H. Klein, "Albéniz's Opera, *Pepita Jiménez,*" *Musical Times* (March 1918); G. Jean-Aubry, *La Musique et les nations* (Paris, 1922; Eng. trans., London, 1923); H. Collet, *Albéniz et Granados* (Paris, 1926; 2nd ed., 1948); E. Istel, "Isaac Albéniz," *Musical Quarterly* (Jan. 1929); R. Moragas, "Epistolario inédito de Isaac Albéniz," *Música,* I (1938); A. de las Heras, *Vida de Albéniz* (Barcelona and Madrid, 1940); V. Ruiz Albéniz, *Isaac Albéniz* (Madrid, 1948); M. Raux Deledicque, *Albéniz, su vida inquieta y ardorosa* (Buenos Aires, 1950); A. Sagardia, *Isaac Albéniz* (Madrid, 1951); G. Laplane, *Albéniz: Sa vie, son œuvre* (Paris, 1956).

Albéniz, Mateo (Antonio Perez de), Spanish composer; date of birth unknown; d. St. Sebastian, June 23, 1831. He was a church organist; publ. *Instrucción melódica especulativa y practica para enseñar a cantar y a tañer la música antigua* (St. Sebastian, 1802). His Sonata for Piano was publ. by Joaquín Nín in *16 Sonates anciennes d'auteurs espagnols* (Paris, 1925).

Albéniz, Pedro, Spanish organist and composer, son of **Mateo Albéniz;** b. Logroño, April 14, 1795; d. Madrid, April 12, 1855. He studied with his father; from his early youth, played the organ in various Spanish towns; later studied piano in Paris with Kalkbrenner and Henri Herz. In 1830 he was appointed prof. of piano at the Madrid Cons.; in 1834, became court organist. He was an energetic promoter of modern methods of piano playing in Spain. He publ. a manual (1840), which was adopted at the Madrid Cons.; also wrote some 70 piano pieces in a highly developed technical style (rondos, variations, medleys, etc.).

Albergati, Pirro Capacelli, Conte d', Italian composer; b. Bologna, Sept. 20, 1663; d. there, June 22, 1735. He wrote 2 operas, *Gli amici* (Bologna, Aug. 16, 1699) and *Il principe selvaggio* (Bologna, 1712), and numerous oratorios, which were regularly performed at various churches in Bologna (1686–1732): *Nabuccodonosor; Giobbe; S. Orsola; Il convito di Baldassare; L'innocenza di S. Eufemia; S. Catarina; S. Eustachio; Maria annunciata dall'angelo; La morte di Cristo;* etc. Besides these works, Albergati publ. during his lifetime 15 opus numbers, consisting of vocal and instrumental music, among them *Balletti; Correnti; Cantate morali; Cantate spirituali; Messa e salmi; Cantate da camera;* *Motetti et antifone; Capricci;* 12 sonatas for 2 Violins and Bass; etc.

Alberghetti, Anna Maria, Italian soprano; b. Rodi, May 5, 1936. She first sang in public at the age of 6; gave recitals in Milan at 9. She came to America in 1950; made her debut in Carnegie Hall; then became a film vedette.

Alberghi, Paolo Tommaso, Italian violinist, composer, and teacher; b. Faenza (baptized, Dec. 31), 1716; d. there, Oct. 11, 1785. He studied violin with Tartini; then was a violinist at the Faenza Cathedral, where his brother Don Francesco Alberghi was maestro di cappella; was named first violinist in 1755; upon the death of his brother in 1760, he was appointed maestro di cappella. He was highly esteemed as a violinist and a teacher; among his pupils was Giuseppe Sarti. He composed mostly instrumental works; wrote some 20 violin concertos, which are notable for their late Baroque virtuosity; also composed sonatas and trios; his sacred works include a Magnificat and a Mass.

Albersheim, Gerhard, German pianist and musicologist; b. Cologne, Nov. 17, 1902. After preliminary studies in Cologne, he went to Vienna, where he took courses at the Univ. of Vienna (1933–38). In 1940 he emigrated to America; was on the staff of the Univ. of Calif. at Los Angeles (1953–56) and later of the Calif. State College in Los Angeles (1956–70). He began his career as a piano accompanist, playing for Lotte Lehmann, Elisabeth Schumann, Ezio Pinza, and other eminent artists. His main interests were related to the psychology of tonal perception; he published *Zur Psychologie der Ton- und Klangeigenschaften* (Strasbourg, 1939; revised ed., 1975). He contributed numerous articles on musical sociology to various German and American journals.

Albert, Prince Consort of Queen Victoria; b. Rosenau, Coburg, Aug. 26, 1819; d. Windsor, Dec. 14, 1861. He married Queen Victoria on Feb. 10, 1840; lent energetic support to musical activities in England, sponsoring orchs. and choral societies. He studied organ and theory, and acquired an estimable technique of composition; wrote *Invocazione alla armonia* for Chorus and Orch. His songs were publ. in 1881 under the title *The Collected Compositions of His Royal Highness the Prince Consort.* They reveal a Romantic musical temper, influenced by Mendelssohn.

d'Albert, Eugène (Francis Charles), British-born German pianist and composer; b. Glasgow, April 10, 1864; d. Riga, March 3, 1932. His father, **Charles Louis Napoléon d'Albert** (b. Nienstetten, near Hamburg, Feb. 25, 1809; d. London, May 26, 1886), was a dancing master who wrote popular music; it was from him that d'Albert received his early instruction in music. At the age of 10 he entered the New Music School in London, where he studied piano with Pauer and theory with Stainer, Prout, and Sir Arthur

Sullivan. He made extraordinary progress as both a pianist and a composer, and after several appearances at the Popular Concerts, was the soloist in Schumann's concerto at the Crystal Palace in London (Feb. 5, 1881). On Oct. 24, 1881, when only 17, he played his own piano concerto at one of Hans Richter's concerts, arousing great enthusiasm; the press compared him to Mozart and Mendelssohn. He received a Mendelssohn fellowship and went to Vienna; later he studied with Liszt, who was greatly impressed by his technique and often referred to him as "the young Tausig." In 1895, d'Albert was appointed conductor at Weimar; in 1907, became director of the Hochschule für Musik in Berlin. In the wake of his success, he repudiated his English birth, adopting German citizenship, and made repeated statements derogatory to English culture and even to his former English teachers; he further changed his first name to a German form, **Eugen.** During the First World War, he was vocal in his enmity toward England, which led in turn to an understandable repugnance among British musicians to accept his music. Despite a brilliant beginning, Eugène d'Albert did not justify his early promise, and his operas and other works are rarely revived. His musical idiom oscillates between the Italian melodic style and German contrapuntal writing, and fails to achieve originality. A considerable corpus of his autograph music MSS, including 11 of his operas (though not *Tiefland*), was acquired in 1963 by the Library of Congress. Eugène d'Albert's personal life was a stormy one. He was married 6 times; his first wife (1892–95) was Teresa Carreño; his 2nd was the singer Hermine Finck.

WORKS: D'Albert composed industriously. He publ. 2 piano concertos (in B minor and E); Cello Concerto in C; 2 overtures: *Hyperion* and *Esther*; Symph. in F; Orch. Suite in 5 movements (1924); Piano Sonata; Piano Suite in 5 movements; 2 string quartets; *Der Mensch und das Leben* for 6-part Chorus and Orch. (op. 14); 4 piano pieces, op. 16 (Waltz, Scherzo, Intermezzo, Ballade); minor piano pieces and songs. However, his main interest was in the field of opera. Of his 20 operas, the most successful were *Tiefland*, first staged at the German opera in Prague (Nov. 15, 1903), and *Die toten Augen* (Dresden, March 5, 1916). His other operas include: *Der Rubin* (Karlsruhe, Oct. 12, 1893); *Ghismonda* (Dresden, Nov. 28, 1895); *Gernot* (Mannheim, April 11, 1897); *Die Abreise* (Frankfurt, Oct. 20, 1898); *Kain* (Berlin, Feb. 17, 1900); *Der Improvisator* (Berlin, Feb. 20, 1902); *Flauto solo* (Prague, Nov. 12, 1905); *Tragaldabas,* or *Der geborgte Ehemann* (Hamburg, Dec. 3, 1907); *Izeÿl* (Hamburg, Nov. 6, 1909); *Die verschenkte Frau* (Vienna, Feb. 6, 1912); *Liebesketten* (Vienna, Nov. 12, 1912); *Der Stier von Olivera* (Leipzig, March 10, 1918); *Revolutionshochzeit* (Leipzig, Oct. 26, 1919); *Scirocco* (Darmstadt, May 18, 1921); *Mareike von Nymwegen* (Hamburg, Oct. 31, 1923); *Der Golem* (Frankfurt, Nov. 14, 1926); *Die schwarze Orchidee* (Leipzig, Dec. 1, 1928); *Mister Wu* (unfinished; completed by Leo Blech; Dresden, Sept. 29, 1932).

BIBLIOGRAPHY: W. Raupp, *Eugen d'Albert: Ein Künstler- und Menschenschicksal* (Leipzig, 1930).

Albert, Heinrich, German composer; b. Lobenstein, Saxony, July 8, 1604; d. Königsberg, Oct. 6, 1651. In 1622 he went to Dresden to study music with his cousin Heinrich Schütz; then studied law at the Univ. of Leipzig; traveled to Warsaw with a peace delegation in 1627, but was seized as a prisoner of war by the Swedes; upon his release in 1628, he settled in Königsberg; was appointed cathedral organist in 1631; took courses with Johann Stobäus. He publ. in Königsberg 8 books of arias (1638–50); a cantata, *Musikalische Kürbs-Hütte* (1645), consisting of a cycle of 12 terzets to Albert's own texts (a modern reprint was issued by J.M. Müller-Blattau in 1932). A selection of his songs is found in the *Neudrucke deutscher Litteraturwerke* (Halle, 1883); the arias in vols. XII and XIII of Denkmäler Deutscher Tonkunst.
BIBLIOGRAPHY: L.H. Fischer, *Gedichte des Königsberger Dichterkreises* (Halle, 1883); G. Kraft, ed., *Festschrift zur Ehrung von Heinrich Albert (1604–1651)* (Weimar, 1954).

Albert, Herbert, German conductor; b. Lausick, Dec. 26, 1903; d. Bad Reichenhall, Sept. 15, 1973. He studied with Karl Muck in Hamburg; then with Grebner and Teichmüller in Leipzig. He began his career as a pianist; subsequently was a conductor in Rudolstadt, Kaiserslautern, and Wiesbaden. He was Generalmusikdirektor in Baden-Baden (1934–37); then of the Stuttgart Opera (1937–44); finally of the Mannheim National Theater (1952–63).

Albert, Karel, Belgian composer; b. Antwerp, April 16, 1901. He studied with Marinus de Jong at the Royal Flemish Cons. in Antwerp; in 1933 became associated with the music service of the NIR, predecessor to the Belgian Radio and Television, until his retirement in 1961.
WORKS: Opera buffa, *Europa ontvoerd* (1950); 2 ballets: *De toverlantaarn* (*The Magic Lantern*, 1942) and *Tornooi* (1953); 4 symphs. (1941, 1943, 1945, 1966); Sinfonietta (1968); *Pietà* (1933); *Wilde jacht* (1933); overture, *Ananke* (1934); *Lentewandeling* (1935); *Humoresque* (1936); *Het Land* (1937); *Impulsions* (1939); *Suite flamande* (1947); *De Nacht* (1956); Suite (1958); *Dansende beeldekens* (1959); *3 Constructions* for Strings (1959); *In the Beginning Was the Word* for Baritone and Orch. (1962); Chamber Symph. (1932); 2 string quartets (1929, 1941); Trio for Oboe, Clarinet, and Bassoon (1930); Quintet for Flute, Oboe, Violin, Viola, and Cello (1954); *Etude* for Alto and Wind Quintet (1958); Quartet for 4 Saxophones (1960); Brass Quintet (1962); Wind Quintet (1963); Brass Quartet (1964). He publ. *De evolutie van de muziek van de Oudheid tot aan Beethoven aan de hand van fonoplaten* (Brussels, 1947).

Albert, Stephen, American composer; b. New York, Feb. 6, 1941. He played trumpet, French horn, and piano in the school band in Great Neck, N.Y.; also took private lessons in composition with Elie Siegmeister, who made his home there. In 1958 he enrolled in the Eastman School of Music in Rochester, N.Y., in the class of Bernard Rogers. In 1960 he went to Stockholm to study with Karl-Birger Blomdahl; returning to the U.S., he took courses at the Philadelphia Musical Academy with Roy Harris and Joseph Castaldo. In 1962 he studied counterpoint with George Rochberg at the Univ. of Pennsylvania in Philadelphia. In 1965–67 he lived in Rome on an American Prix de Rome grant. In 1968–69 he held a Guggenheim fellowship; in 1970–71 he was a lecturer at Stanford Univ.; in 1974–76 was on the faculty at Smith College in Northampton, Mass. Albert's style of composition reflects his geographical wanderings and intellectual wonderings, resulting in a pragmatic and unprejudiced selection of fitting idioms. Thus, while refusing to renounce tonality, he espouses the quaquaversality of modern moods and modes without blundering into the crepuscular regions of serialistic glossolalia. *Musicus sum; musicae nil a me alienum puto,* seems to be his motto: nothing that is of music is alien to him.

WORKS: *Illuminations* for Brass, Pianos, Harps, and Percussion (1962); *Supernatural Songs* for Soprano and Chamber Orch. (1963); *Imitations* for String Quartet (1964); *Winter Songs* for Tenor and Orch. (1965); *Wedding Songs* for Soprano and Piano (1965); *Bacchae* for Narrator, Chorus, and Orch. (1967–68); *Wolf Time* for Soprano and Chamber Orch. (1968); *Letters from the Golden Notebook* for Orch. (1971); *Cathedral Music* for amplified Flutes, amplified Cellos, amplified Guitar, amplified Harpsichord, Brass, Percussion, Electronic Piano, Electronic Organ, and 2 Grand Pianos (1972); *Voices Within* for a Concertino Ensemble encased in an Orch. (1975); *To Wake the Dead* for Soprano, Flute, Clarinet, Violin, Cello, and Piano, to a text from James Joyce's *Finnegans Wake* (N.Y., March 21, 1979); *Winterfire* for 7 Players (1979); *Music from the Stone Harp* for 8 Players (1980).

BIBLIOGRAPHY: David Ewen, *American Composers* (N.Y., 1982).

Alberth, Rudolf, German conductor; b. Frankfurt, March 28, 1918. He studied in Frankfurt; then was a conductor with the Hessischen Radio there and with the Sudwestfunk in Baden-Baden; from 1949 to 1964 he was a conductor with the Bavarian Radio in Munich; also appeared as a conductor at the Bavarian State Opera; in later years he conducted in Hannover.

Alberti, Domenico, Venetian composer; b. Venice, 1710; d. Formio (or Rome), c.1740. He studied with Lotti, and won considerable renown as a singer and harpsichord player; wrote 3 operas, *Endimione, Galatea,* and *Olimpiade.* In 1737 he was a member of the Venetian Embassy in Rome, and made several appearances there as a singer and player. His fame in music history rests on his reputed invention of the arpeggio style of keyboard accompaniment, which became known as the "Alberti Bass." His set of 8 sonatas, publ. by Walsh in London, gives many illustrations of this device.

Alberti, Gasparo, Italian composer; b. Padua, c.1480; d. Bergamo, c.1560. He became a singer at Santa Maria Maggiore in Bergamo in 1508; periodically he served as its maestro di cappella (until 1554). He is regarded as one of the most significant composers of sacred polyphonic vocal music in Italy in the early Renaissance. His works include 2 8-voice Magnificat settings; Psalms; 5 masses; Lamentations; canticles.

BIBLIOGRAPHY: G. d'Alessi, "Precursors of Adriano Willaert in the Practice of Coro spezzato," *Journal of the American Musicological Society,* V (1952); K. Jeppesen, "A Forgotten Master of the Early 16th Century: Gasparo de Albertis," *Musical Quarterly,* XLIV (1958); K. Jeppesen, ed., *Italia sacra musica* (Copenhagen, 1962); A. Carver, "The Psalms of Willaert and His North Italian Contemporaries," *Acta Musicologica,* XLVII (1975).

Alberti, Giuseppe Matteo, Italian violinist and composer; b. Bologna, Sept. 20, 1685; d. there, 1751. He studied violin with C. Manzolini and P.M. Minelli, and took lessons in counterpoint with F. Arresti; then played violin in the orch. of S. Petronio in Bologna; he was also a member of the Accademia Filarmonica there, and was its president from 1721. He composed violin concertos, sonatas, sinfonias, and vocal works, several of which were publ. in his lifetime.

BIBLIOGRAPHY: M. Talbot, "A Thematic Catalogue of the Orchestral Works of Giuseppe Matteo Alberti (1685–1751)," *RMA Research Chronicle,* XIII (1976).

Alberti, Johann Friedrich, German organist and composer; b. Tönning, Schleswig, Jan. 11, 1642; d. Merseburg, June 14, 1710. He studied theology in Rostock, and jurisprudence at the Univ. of Leipzig; also took courses in music with Werner Fabricius and Vincenzo Albrici. He spent most of his life as cathedral organist in Merseburg. Some of his chorales, publ. in modern editions, testify to his aptitude.

Albertsen, Per Hjort, Norwegian composer; b. Trondheim, July 27, 1919. He studied organ at the Oslo Cons., graduating in 1946; took lessons in composition with Sven Erik Tarp in Copenhagen, Ralph Dawnes in London, and Hanns Jelinek in Vienna. He was an organist in Trondheim (1947–68); then lectured in the music department of the univ. there (1968–72). Much of his music has been written for performance in schools.

WORKS: A school opera, *Russicola* (1956); Flute Concertino (1948); *Villemann og Magnill,* folk ballad for Soprano, Baritone, Male Chorus, and Orch. (1951); *Symphonic Prelude* (1951); *Gunnerus Suite* for String Orch. (1952); *Little Suite* for String Orch. (1955); *Presentation,* overture (1958); *Notturno e Danza* for Orch. (1960); *Concerto Piccolo* for Violin or Clarinet, and Amateur String Orch. (1961); Concerto for Piano and School Orch. (1969); *Tordenskioldiana* for Orch. (1972); *Bendik og Årolilja,* folk ballad for Tenor, Chorus, and Piano (1943; orchestrated 1979); *Slåttesonata* for Piano (1946); Clarinet

Sonatina (1950); *4 Religious Folksongs* for Violin, Cello, and Organ (1974); *Toccata, Chaconne and Fugue* for Organ (1976); numerous choral works.

Albicastro, Henricus (real name, **Heinrich Weissenburg**), Swiss violinist and composer; b. Switzerland at an uncertain date; d. c.1738 in the Netherlands, where he was a court musician. His works for string instruments were publ. in Amsterdam between 1700 and 1706; of these, 12 concertos *a* 4, a trio sonata, and several violin sonatas with basso continuo are available in modern editions.

BIBLIOGRAPHY: W.S. Newman, *The Sonata in the Baroque Era* (Chapel Hill, 1959; pp. 343–44); M. Talbot, "The Concerto Allegro in the Early Eighteenth Century," *Music & Letters* (Jan., April 1971).

Albini, Srecko, Croatian composer and conductor; b. Zupanja, Dec. 10, 1869; d. Zagreb, April 18, 1933. He studied music in Vienna; then was a theater conductor in Graz and Zagreb. He composed an opera, *Maricon;* a ballet, *The Lake of Plotvice;* the operettas *Nabob, Madame Troubadour,* and *Baron Trenk* (1908; achieved considerable popularity); piano pieces and songs.

Albinoni, Tomaso, Italian violinist and composer; b. Venice, June 8, 1671; d. there, Jan. 17, 1750. Between 1694 and 1740 he produced 53 operas, most of them in Venice. He rarely absented himself from Venice, but it is known that he attended the premiere of his opera *Griselda* in Florence (1703), serving as concertmaster in the orch.; in 1722 he was in Munich, where he presented his festive opera *I veri amici*. It is, however, as a composer of instrumental music that he is significant. Bach, his close contemporary, admired Albinoni's music; made arrangements of 2 fugues from Albinoni's trio sonatas.

BIBLIOGRAPHY: A detailed catalogue of Albinoni's works and a thematic analysis are given by R. Giazotto in his exhaustive monograph *Tomaso Albinoni* (Milan, 1945); see also M. Talbot, "Albinoni: The Professional Dilettante," *Musical Times* (June 1971); id., "Vivaldi and Albinoni," *Informations de la Société Int. Antonio Vivaldi* (1972); id., "Albinoni's Oboe Concertos," *Consort* (July 1973); W. Kolneder, ed., *T.G. Albinoni: Gesamtausgabe der Instrumentalmusik* (1974).

Alboni, Marietta (real name, **Maria Anna Marzia Alboni**), famous Italian contralto; b. Città di Castello, March 6, 1823; d. Ville d'Avray, France, June 23, 1894. She studied in Bologna with Mombelli; in 1841 was introduced to Rossini, who agreed to give her lessons. She made her debut in Bologna, in Pacini's opera *Saffo* (Oct. 3, 1842); shortly afterward sang at La Scala in Rossini's *Assedio de Corinto* (*Le Siège de Corinthe;* Dec. 30, 1842). She then sang in Russia and obtained great success during the season of 1844–45 in St. Petersburg, appearing at the Italian opera with Tamburini, Rubini, and Mme. Viardot. After appearances in Prague, Berlin, and Hamburg, she appeared in the spring of 1847 in Rome and at Covent Garden, where she became a rival of Jenny Lind with the public. So successful were her London appearances that her fees were increased to 2,000 pounds a season. She gave 4 "concerts-spectacles" in Paris in Oct. 1847; made her Paris opera debut in Rossini's *Semiramide* (Dec. 2, 1847). Auber wrote the opera *Zéline ou La Corbeille d'oranges* for her and she sang at its premiere (May 16, 1851). She made an American tour from June 1852 till May 1853 in concert and opera, appearing in N.Y., Boston, and other cities. On July 21, 1853, Alboni married Count Pepoli, who died on Oct. 10, 1867; on Jan. 22, 1877, she married Charles Ziéger, a French officer, and settled in France. Suffering from excessive obesity, she gradually retired from the stage, but continued to appear occasionally in concert, singing while sitting in a large chair. Her vocal range was exceptional, from the contralto G to high soprano C, enabling her to sing soprano parts. She bequeathed a large sum of money to the city of Paris. In appreciation, the City Council, on Oct. 15, 1895, named a street in Passy after her. Arthur Pougin's monograph *Marietta Alboni* (Paris, 1912) quotes many of her autobiographical notes and presents a documented outline of her career.

Alborea, Francesco, Italian cellist; b. Naples, March 7, 1691; d. Vienna, July 20, 1739. He studied at the Cons. di Loreto in Naples; was a student of Gian Carlo Cailò; subsequently established himself as a concert artist in Naples and Rome. In 1726 he became chamber virtuoso to Count Uhlenfeld in Vienna, remaining there until his death.

Albrecht, Alexander, Slovak composer; b. Arad, Rumania, Aug. 12, 1885; d. Bratislava, July 30, 1958. He studied piano with Thomán and Bartók and composition with Koessler at the Budapest Academy of Music; after graduation, he settled in Bratislava. He wrote a number of orch. works for chamber ensemble, including *Šipková ružička* (*Sleeping Beauty;* 1919); a symph. poem, *Spomienky a túžby* (*Memories and Desires;* 1932); *Symphonic Variations* for Trumpet and Orch. (1947); chamber music, cantatas, and choruses.

BIBLIOGRAPHY: F. Klinda, *Alexander Albrecht* (Bratislava, 1959).

Albrecht, Evgeny, Russian violinist, son of **Karl Albrecht** and brother of **Konstantin Albrecht;** b. St. Petersburg, July 16, 1842; d. there, Feb. 9, 1894. He studied violin with Ferdinand David at the Leipzig Cons. (1857–60). Upon his return to Russia, he conducted the Italian opera in St. Petersburg (1860–77); was also music director of military schools there (1872–77). In 1877 he became inspector of the Imperial Orchs.; in 1892 was music librarian of the Imperial Theaters. He publ. 3 albums of Russian folk songs and a book of 128 children's songs.

Albrecht, George Alexander, German conductor; b. Bremen, Feb. 15, 1935. He studied conducting with Paul van Kempen and Kurt Eichhorn. In 1960 he joined the Hannover Opera, becoming its Generalmusikdirektor in 1965. He has also appeared as a guest conductor with a number of the leading German opera houses.

Albrecht, Gerd, German conductor; b. Essen, July 19, 1935. He studied at the univs. of Kiel and Hamburg. He then conducted opera in Stuttgart (1958–61), Mainz (1961–63), Lübeck (1963–66), and Kassel (1966–72). From 1972 to 1979 he held the post of chief conductor of the German Opera in West Berlin; concurrently he also served, from 1975 on, as conductor of the Tonhalle Orch. in Zürich.

Albrecht, Hans, German music scholar; b. Magdeburg, March 31, 1902; d. Kiel, Jan. 20, 1961. He studied music at the Essen Cons. and later at the Univ. of Münster; then went to the Univ. of Berlin (1921–25); in 1925 he joined the faculty of the Essen Cons., and taught there until 1937. During World War II he was prof. at the State Inst. in Berlin. In 1947 he became director of the Landesinstitut für Musikforschung in Kiel; also was on the faculty of the Univ. of Kiel; appointed prof. there in 1955. He edited several music journals; publ. a valuable monograph, *Caspar Othmayr, Leben und Werke* (Kassel, 1943).
BIBLIOGRAPHY: W. Brennecke and H. Haase, eds., *Hans Albrecht in Memoriam* (Kassel, 1962).

Albrecht, Johann Lorenz, German music scholar; b. Görmar (Thuringia), Jan. 8, 1732; d. Mühlhausen, Nov. 29, 1768. He studied at Leipzig; edited Adlung's *Musica mechanica* and *Siebengestirn* (Berlin, 1768); wrote the essay *Abhandlung über die Frage: Ob die Musik beim Gottesdienst zu dulden sei oder nicht* (1764), the manual *Gründliche Einleitung in die Anfangslehren der Tonkunst* (1761), and the treatise *Vom Hasse der Musik* (1765); contributed articles to Marpurg's *Kritische Beiträge,* etc. He also composed several cantatas.

Albrecht, Karl, German-Russian conductor, father of **Konstantin** and **Evgeni Albrecht;** b. Posen, Aug. 27, 1807; d. Gatchina, near St. Petersburg, March 8, 1863. He studied harmony and counterpoint with Josef Schnabel in Breslau; also learned to play on string and wind instruments. In 1825 he joined the Breslau Theater Orch. as first violinist; in 1835 he went to Düsseldorf, where he was engaged as répétiteur in the opera theater. In 1838 he went to St. Petersburg, where he conducted a German opera troupe; from 1840 to 1850 he conducted the Russian Opera there. In 1842 he conducted the first performance of Glinka's opera *Ruslan and Ludmila.*

Albrecht, Konstantin, Russian cellist, son of **Karl Albrecht** and brother of **Evgeny Albrecht;** b. Elberfeld, Oct. 4, 1835; d. Moscow, June 26, 1893. He was brought to Moscow by his father at the age of 2 and received his musical education from him. In 1854 he became a member of the orch. of the Moscow Opera. In 1860 he collaborated with Nicholas Rubinstein in organizing the Moscow Cons.; in 1866 he was appointed inspector there; also taught elementary theory. He was an intimate friend of Tchaikovsky and was a notable figure in the Moscow music world. He publ. a manual on solfeggio and compiled several collections of choral works.

Albrecht, Max, German composer and conductor; b. Chemnitz, March 14, 1890; d. Dresden, Feb. 13, 1945. He studied in Leipzig with Reger; conducted opera in Chemnitz (1911–13) and in Neisse (1914–15); then lived in Dresden. He wrote operas: *Neros Ende* (1927); *Rama und Sita* (1929); *Amosa* (1930); *Die Brücke* (1932); a cantata, *Marathon;* 2 symph. poems; a number of songs.

Albrecht, Otto Edwin, eminent American musicologist; b. Philadelphia, July 8, 1899; d. there, July 6, 1984. studied at the Univ. Pa. (A.B.,M.A., 1921; M.A., 1925; Ph.D., 1931, with the dissertation *Fore Latin Plays of St. Nicholas from the 12th Century Fleury Play-book,* Philadelphia and London, 1935); was an instructor in French at his alma mater (1935–38); in 1937 he became curator of the Music Library there; from 1938 was also a lecturer in the music dept.; retired in 1970 and was made emeritus prof. of music.
WRITINGS: "Microfilm Archives and Musicology," *American Musicological Society Papers, 1938; A Census of Autograph Music Manuscripts of European Composers in American Libraries* (Philadelphia, 1953); *The Mary Flagler Cary Music Collection* (N.Y., 1970).
BIBLIOGRAPHY: J. Hill, ed., *Studies in Musicology in Honor of Otto E. Albrecht* (Kassel, 1977; Clifton, N.J., 1980).

Albrechtsberger, Johann Georg, famous Austrian theoretical writer, composer, and teacher; b. Klosterneuburg, near Vienna, Feb. 3, 1736; d. Vienna, March 7, 1809. After holding positions as organist and music master in smaller towns, especially in Melk (1759–65), where his fine playing attracted the Emperor Joseph's notice, in 1772 he was engaged in Vienna as regens chori to the Carmelites; was appointed court organist in the same year, and, in 1792, music director at St. Stephen's Cathedral. His important theoretical writings (complete ed. publ. by Seyfried) are: *Gründliche Anweisung zur Composition* (1790 and 1818; French ed., 1814); *Kurzgefasste Methode, den Generalbass zu erlernen* (1792; also in French); *Clavierschule für Anfänger* (1808); and some lesser essays. A selection from his instrumental works is publ. in Denkmäler der Tonkunst in Österreich, vol. 33 (formerly 16.ii); the MS scores (in the possession of Prince Esterhazy-Galantha) comprise 26 masses, 43 graduals, 34 offertories, 6 oratorios; 28 trios, 42 quartets, and 38 quintets for strings; besides a great variety of church music. He had many celebrated pupils, among whom was Beethoven (from Jan. 1794 to March 1795). Scholars regard the quality of instruction he gave to Beethoven as of a very high order.
BIBLIOGRAPHY: G. Nottebohm, *Beethovens Unterricht bei J. Haydn, Albrechtsberger und Salieri* (Leipzig, 1873); R. Oppell, "Albrechtsberger

als Bindeglied zwischen Bach und Beethoven," *Neue Zeitschrift für Musik* (May 18, 1911); A. Weissenbäck, "J.G. Albrechtsberger als Kirchenkomponist," *Studien zur Musikwissenschaft* (1927); F. Brodsky and O. Biba, "J.G. Albrechtsberger: Instrumentalwerke," *Documenta Musicologica* (1968–75); E. Paul, *Johann Georg Albrechtsberger: Ein Klosterneuberger Meister der Musik und seine Schule* (Klosterneuberg, 1976).

Albrici (or **Alberici**), **Vincenzo,** Italian organist, harpsichordist, and composer; b. Rome, June 26, 1631; d. Prague, Aug. 8, 1696. He was born into a musical family; his father, Domenico, was an alto singer; his brother, Bartolomeo, was also a musician. Vincenzo Albrici was a boy soprano at the German College in Rome, where he studied with Carissimi (1641–46); he then accompanied his father and brother to Lombardy, Germany, Flanders, and Sweden; was in the service of Queen Christina of Sweden (1652–53); in 1654 he became a Kapellmeister at the Dresden court, where he served with Schütz and Bontempi; in 1660 he was once more in the service of Queen Christina; in 1662–63 he was again in Dresden. He subsequently went to England, where he entered the service of King Charles II. He returned to Dresden about 1668; was named director of the Italian musicians at the court in 1676; after the Italian musicians were dismissed in 1680, he became organist at the Thomaskirche in Leipzig in 1681 (he was briefly converted to the Protestant faith). In 1682 he became organist at St. Augustus in Prague, a post he held until his death. He composed about 40 Latin motets, Italian solo cantatas, and some other vocal works.
BIBLIOGRAPHY: C.-A. Moberg, "Vincenzo Albrici (1631–1696): Eine biographische Skizze mit besonderer Berücksichtigung seiner schwedischen Zeit," in *Festschrift Friedrich Blume zum 70. Geburtstag* (Kassel, 1963).

Albright, William (Hugh), American composer, pianist, and organist; b. Gary, Ind., Oct. 20, 1944. He studied piano with Rosetta Goodkind and music theory with Hugh Aitken at the Juilliard Preparatory Dept. in N.Y. (1959–62); then took courses in composition with Ross Lee Finney and Leslie Bassett at the Univ. of Michigan; also studied organ with Marilyn Mason there (1963–70). In 1968 he went to France and studied composition with Olivier Messiaen at the Paris Cons.; also took private lessons with Max Deutsch. In 1970 he joined the faculty of the Univ. of Michigan to teach composition; also served as associate director of its Electronic Music Studio. He received a Guggenheim fellowship in 1976; was composer-in-residence at the American Academy in Rome in 1979. In his compositions he pursues quaquaversal methods of experimental music, using varied techniques according to need. He has also made a concert career as a pianist in programs of ragtime and jazz.
WORKS: Multimedia pieces: *Tic* for Soloist, 2 Jazz-rock Improvisation Ensembles, Film, and Tape (1967); *Beulahland Rag* for Narrator, Jazz Quartet,

Improvisation Ensemble, Tape, Film, and Slide Projections (1967–69); *Cross of Gold* for Actors, Chorus, and Instruments (1975). Chamber music: *Foils* for Wind Instruments and Percussion (1963–64); 2 pieces for 9 Instruments (1966); *Caroms* for 7 Instruments (1966); *Marginal Worlds* for Winds, Strings, Piano, and Percussion (1970); *Alliance,* symph. suite (1967–70); *Night Procession* for Chamber Orch. (1972); *Take That* for Percussion (1972); *Gothic Suite* for Organ, Percussion, and Strings (1973); *Introduction, Passacaglia and Rondo Capriccioso* for Piano and Winds (1974); *7 Deadly Sins* for Flute, Clarinet, String Quartet, Piano, and Optional Narrator (1974). For Piano: *Pianoàgogo* (1965–66); *Grand Sonata in Rag* (1968); *5 Chromatic Dances* (1976). For Organ: *Chorale Partita in Old Style* (1963); *Juba* (1965); *Pneuma* (1966); 3 organ collections (1967, 1971, 1978); *Stipendium Peccati,* with Piano and Percussion (1973); *Jericho Battle Music,* with Trumpet (1976); *Halo,* with Metal Instruments (1978); *King of Instruments,* with Narrator (1978). Choral music: *An Alleluia Super-Round* (1973); *Mass* in D major (1974); *The Chichester Mass* (1974).

Alcaide, Tomáz, Portuguese tenor; b. Estremoz, Feb. 16, 1901; d. Lisbon, Nov. 9, 1967. He studied at the Univ. of Coimbra; took voice lessons in Lisbon, and later in Milan; in 1925 he made his debut at the Teatro Carcano in Milan as Wilhelm Meister in *Mignon;* subsequently sang principal roles in Italian and French operas at La Scala in Milan, at the Paris Opéra, at the Vienna State Opera, at the Salzburg Festival, and at the Rome Opera; also made concert tours of Europe and the U.S. After his retirement from the stage in 1948, he settled in Lisbon. He wrote an autobiography, *Um cantor no palco e na vida* (Lisbon, 1961).

Alcantara, Theo, Spanish conductor; b. Cuenca, April 16, 1941. He studied at the Madrid Cons.; then took courses in conducting at the Mozarteum in Salzburg. He began his career as a conductor with the Frankfurt Opera Orch. (1964–66); then came to the U.S., where he served as director of orchs. at the Univ. of Michigan in Ann Arbor (1968–73), and then music director of the Grand Rapids Symph. Orch. (1973–78). In 1978 he became music director and principal conductor of the Phoenix Symph. Orch.; also artistic director of the Music Academy of the West in Santa Barbara, in 1981. He appeared as a conductor with the Metropolitan Opera, N.Y. City Opera, Washington, D.C., Opera, San Diego Opera, and others; also conducted the orchs. of Philadelphia, Pittsburgh, and Detroit, and in Europe.

Alcock, John, Sr., English organist; b. London, April 11, 1715; d. Lichfield, Feb. 23, 1806. He served as a chorister at St. Paul's Cathedral and took lessons with the blind organist, Stanley; subsequently he held positions as organist at St. Andrew's Church in Plymouth (1737), at St. Laurence's Church in Reading (1742), and at Lichfield Cathedral (1750). In 1766 he took his degree of D.Mus. at Oxford. He published several suites for harpsichord, collec-

Alcock – Aldrovandini

tions of anthems, and sacred choral works; also wrote numerous glees, for which he obtained prizes from the Catch Club. His son, **John Alcock, Jr.** (baptized in Plymouth, Jan. 28, 1740; d. Walsall, Staffordshire, in March 1791; buried March 27, 1791), was organist at various churches and composer of anthems.

Alcock, Sir Walter (Galpin), English organist; b. Edenbridge, Dec. 29, 1861; d. Salisbury, Sept. 11, 1947. He studied with Sullivan and Stainer; in 1917 he became organist at Salisbury Cathedral, a post he held until his death; he also taught at the Royal College of Music. He officiated at the organ of Westminster Abbey for the coronations of King Edward VII, King George V, and King George VI. He was knighted in 1933.

Alda, Frances (real name, **Frances Davies**), lyric soprano; b. Christchurch, New Zealand, May 31, 1883; d. Venice, Sept. 18, 1952. She studied with Marchesi in Paris, and made her debut as Manon at the Opéra-Comique (April 15, 1904). She later sang in Brussels, London, Milan, Warsaw, and Buenos Aires. Her debut at the Metropolitan Opera was on Dec. 7, 1908 (opposite Caruso in *Rigoletto*); her farewell appearance there, on Dec. 28, 1929, in *Manon Lescaut*. She also made numerous recital tours in the U.S. Her principal roles included Louise, Mimi, Manon, Marguerite, Juliette, Gilda, Violetta, and Aida. She married Giulio Gatti-Casazza, manager of the Metropolitan Opera, on April 3, 1910; divorced, 1928; married Ray Vir Den in 1941. In 1939 she became an American citizen. She wrote an autobiography, *Men, Women and Tenors* (Boston, 1937).

Alden, John Carver, American pianist and teacher; b. Boston, Sept. 11, 1852; d. Cambridge, Mass., Oct. 20, 1935. He studied with Carl Faelten and was later associated with him at the New England Cons.; also took lessons with Plaidy at the Leipzig Cons. He wrote a piano concerto and several songs to German texts.

Alderighi, Dante, Italian composer and pianist; b. Taranto, July 7, 1898; d. Rome, Dec. 12, 1968. He went to Rome as a child and studied with Giovanni Sgambati; from 1911–14 he was in Leipzig, studying piano with Teichmüller and theory with Krehl. Returning to Italy, he took lessons in composition with Malipiero; gave many recitals and began to write music criticism. In 1936 he was appointed prof. of piano at Santa Cecilia Academy in Rome.
WORKS: 2 piano concertos; *Fantasia* for Piano and Chamber Orch. (1932); *Rococo Suite* for Band (1932; revised 1952); oratorio, *Maria a Nazareth* (1949); *Divertimento* for Piano and Strings (1952); many choral works.

Aldrich, Henry, English music scholar; b. Westminster, Jan. 1648; d. Oxford, Dec. 14, 1710. A man of versatile talents, excelling in music, he was also distinguished as an architect, theologian, linguist, and logician. He was educated at Christ Church, Oxford, receiving the degree of M.A. in 1669; in 1681 he became a canon, and in 1689, dean of Christ Church, and exercised decisive influence on the teaching of music and other arts. He wrote the learned works *On the Commencement of Greek Music, Theory of Organ-building,* and *Theory of Modern Instruments;* composed several services (one of which, in G, is still sung); in a lighter vein, glees and catches (among them the popular *Catches on Tobacco*). The collections of Boyce, Arnold, and Page contain numerous pieces by Aldrich.
BIBLIOGRAPHY: W.G. Hiscock, *Henry Aldrich of Christ Church* (Oxford, 1960).

Aldrich, Perley Dunn, American vocal teacher; b. Blackstone, Mass., Nov. 6, 1863; d. Philadelphia, Nov. 20, 1933. He studied at the New England Cons. (1883–86); then took singing lessons with William Shakespeare in London (1892–95) and with Sbriglia in Paris (1903); acted as Sbriglia's assistant in the summer classes in 1904 and 1908. He settled as a vocal teacher in Philadelphia; was the first head of the vocal dept. at the Curtis Inst. He publ. *Vocal Economy* (1895); composed several choruses, among them *The Sleeping Wood Nymph* for Mixed Voices (1896).

Aldrich, Putnam (Calder), American harpsichord player and music scholar; b. South Swansea, Mass., July 14, 1904; d. Cannes, France, April 18, 1975. He studied at Yale Univ. (B.A., 1926); then went to Europe and took piano lessons with Tobias Matthay in London (1926–27) and harpsichord with Wanda Landowska in Paris (1929–33); later took his Ph.D. at Harvard Univ. (1942). From 1950 to 1969 he was on the faculty at Stanford Univ. in California. He publ. an important treatise, *Ornamentation in J.S. Bach's Organ Works* (N.Y., 1950), as part of a much larger and very valuable work on Baroque ornamentation, originally submitted as his doctoral dissertation at Harvard; the work still awaits publication. He also publ. *Rhythm in 17th-century Italian Monody* (London, 1965).

Aldrich, Richard, American music critic; b. Providence, July 31, 1863; d. Rome, June 2, 1937. He studied with Paine at Harvard Univ., graduating in 1885. He then was music critic of the *Providence Journal* (1885–89) and the *Evening Star* (1889–91). From 1891–1901 he was assistant to H.E. Krehbiel on the *New York Tribune*, then became music editor of the *New York Times* (1902–23). A selection of his articles from the *Times* was publ. in *Musical Discourse* (1928) and, posthumously, in *Concert Life in New York, 1902–1923* (1941). He also wrote *Guide to Parsifal* (1904) and *Guide to the Ring of the Nibelung* (1905). His critical writings were urbane and witty; while liberal-minded in regard to milder types of modern music, he vehemently opposed its extreme trends.

Aldrovandini, Giuseppe (Antonio Vincenzo),

Italian composer; b. Bologna, 1665; d. there, Feb. 9, 1707, when, under the influence of alcohol, he fell into a canal and was drowned. He studied with Giacomo Perti at the Bologna Phil. Academy. In 1695 he was appointed to teach at his alma mater, and in 1702 became its head. He wrote about 15 operas; among them the following were produced in Bologna: *Gli inganni amorosi* (Jan. 28, 1696); *Dafne* (Aug. 10, 1696); *Le due Auguste* (Aug. 16, 1700); *I tre rivali in soglio* (posthumously, Jan. 2, 1711). He also wrote some instrumental music and a great many sacred works, among them 6 oratorios; some of these were published during his lifetime.

d'Alembert, Jean-le-Rond, French philosopher and encyclopedist; b. Paris, Nov. 16, 1717; d. there, Oct. 29, 1783. He was the illegitimate child of one Mme. de Tencin and an artillery officer named Destouches; his mother abandoned him on the steps of the church of St. Jean-le-Rond, which name was subsequently attached to him. Later his father acknowledged him, and enabled him to study. He was sent to the Mazarin College, and progressed rapidly in mathematics. He also was interested in theoretical musical subjects, and publ. several treatises on acoustics and on the theory of music: *Recherches sur la courbe, que forme une corde tendue mise en vibration* (1749); *Recherches sur les vibrations des cordes sonores* and *Recherches sur la vitesse du son* (both in *Opuscules mathématiques*, Paris, 1761–80); *Reflexions sur la musique en général et sur la musique française en particulier* (1754); *Reflexions sur la théorie de la musique* (1777). His best-known work on music was *Eléments de musique, théorique et pratique, suivant les principes de M. Rameau* (1752), which went into 6 editions. He contributed several articles on music to the famous *Encyclopédie*, which he edited with Diderot.
BIBLIOGRAPHY: J. Bertrand, *d'Alembert* (Paris, 1889).

Alemshah, Kourkene M., Armenian composer; b. Erevan, May 22, 1907; d. Detroit, Dec. 14, 1947. He studied in Milan with Pizzetti (1924–30); in 1931 he settled in Paris. He died during an American tour, which he undertook as a choral conductor. His music is strongly permeated with Armenian melos, and the settings are impressionistic. A memorial festival of his music was presented in Paris on Feb. 19, 1950.
WORKS: Symph. poems: *Légende* (Paris, June 19, 1932) and *La Bataille d'Avarayr* (Paris, June 2, 1934); *Danses populaires arméniennes* for Orch. (Paris, June 2, 1934).

Aler, John, American tenor; b. Baltimore, Oct. 4, 1949. He studied voice at the Catholic Univ. of America (M.M., 1972); also took courses at the Berkshire Music Center at Tanglewood; in 1977 he won first prize for men at the Concours International de Chant in Paris, and also first prize for interpretation of French art songs. As an opera singer he appeared with the N.Y. City Opera, the Glyndebourne Festival, the Netherlands Opera, and the Vienna State Opera.

Alessandrescu, Alfred, eminent Rumanian composer and conductor; b. Bucharest, Aug. 14, 1893; d. there, Feb. 18, 1959. He studied piano and theory at the Bucharest Cons. with Kiriac and Castaldi (1903–11); then went to Paris, where he took composition courses with Vincent d'Indy at the Schola Cantorum and with Paul Vidal at the Paris Cons. (1913–14). Returning to Bucharest, he was active as a pianist. In 1921 he was appointed conductor of the Rumanian Opera in Bucharest, retaining this post until his death; also conducted the Budapest Phil. Orch. (1926–40) and was artistic director of the Bucharest Radio (1933–59); appeared as a conductor in Germany and France; was piano accompanist to Georges Enesco, Jacques Thibaud, and others.
WORKS: *Amurg de toamnă (The Twilight of Autumn)* for String Orch. (1910); *Didona,* symph. poem (1911); *Fantezie română* for Orch. (1913); Violin Sonata (1914); *Acteon,* symph. poem (Bucharest, Dec. 20, 1915); *Pièce pour quatuor à cordes* (1921); songs; also orchestrated many works by Rumanian composers, as well as classical compositions; translated into Rumanian the libretti of *Parsifal, La Traviata, Aida,* etc.
BIBLIOGRAPHY: V. Tomescu, *Alfred Alessandrescu* (Bucharest, 1962).

Alessandri, Felice, Italian opera composer; b. Rome, Nov. 24, 1747; d. Casinalbo, Aug. 15, 1798. He studied music in Naples; then lived in Paris (1765–68) and in London (1768). From 1784–89 he was in Russia; then in Berlin as 2nd conductor at the Royal Opera (1789–92); finally returned to Italy. Alessandri wrote about 30 operas in all; 2 were produced in London: *La moglie fedele* (1768) and *Il re alla caccia* (1769); and 2 at La Scala in Milan: *Calliroe* (Dec. 26, 1778) and *Ezio* (first given in Verona for Carnevale, 1767; staged at La Scala Feb. 1, 1782). In Potsdam he produced *Il ritorno di Ulisse* (Jan. 25, 1790); *Dario* (1791); and the comic opera *La compagnia d'opera a Nanchino* (1790), which exhibited the colorful effects of pseudo-Chinese music. His opera *Virginia* was given in Venice (Dec. 26, 1793). He also wrote an oratorio, *Betulia liberata* (1781); *6 sinfonie* in 8 parts; 6 trio sonatas for 2 Violins and Basso Continuo; etc.; all in the then-prevalent Italian manner.
BIBLIOGRAPHY: L. Valdrighi, *Felice Alessandri* (Modena, 1896).

d'Alessandro, Raffaele, Swiss composer; b. Gallen, March 17, 1911; d. Lausanne, March 17, 1959 (on his 48th birthday). He studied music with Victor Schlatter and Willi Schuh in Zürich; then went to Paris, where he studied composition with Nadia Boulanger and organ with Marcel Dupré. In 1940 he returned to Switzerland and settled in Lausanne, where he became active as a pianist, organist, and composer.
WORKS: BALLET: *Isla persa* (1952). FOR ORCH.: *Rumba sinfonica* (1940); *Conga contrapuntique* (1941); *Thème et Variations* (1944); Symph. No. 1

Alessandro – Alexandrov

(1948); Symph. No. 2 (1953); *Tema variato* (1957); Piano Concerto No. 1 (1939); Violin Concerto (1941); Flute Concerto (1943); Piano Concerto No. 2 (1945); Piano Concerto No. 3 (1951); Bassoon Concerto (1955); Oboe Concerto with String Orch. (1958). CHAMBER MUSIC: 2 violin sonatas (1936, 1953); Cello Sonata (1937); Piano Trio (1940); Flute Sonata (1943); 2 string quartets (1947, 1952); Oboe Sonata (1949); Sonatina for Oboe Solo (1953); Sonatina for Clarinet and Piano (1953); Bassoon Sonata (1957); Sonata for Flute, Viola, and Piano (1958). FOR PIANO: Sonatina for left hand alone (1939); 24 Preludes (1940); Sonatina for 2 Pianos (1943); 12 études (1952); *Contes drolatiques* (1952); *6 Klavierstücke* for left hand alone (1958); many pieces for organ; choruses; several songs with orch., organ, or piano. A catalogue of his works is obtainable from the Association des Amis de Raffaele d'Alessandro in Lausanne.

Alessandro, Victor, American conductor; b. Waco, Texas, Nov. 27, 1915; d. San Antonio, Nov. 27, 1976 (on his 61st birthday). He studied French horn with his father; then took composition courses with Howard Hanson and Bernard Rogers at the Eastman School of Music in Rochester, N.Y.; subsequently attended classes at the Santa Cecilia Academy in Rome; returning to the U.S., he was conductor of the Oklahoma Symph. Orch. (1938–51); in 1951 was appointed conductor of the San Antonio Orch., a position which he held until his death.

Alexander, Haim, German-born Israeli composer; b. Berlin, Aug. 9, 1915. He studied piano at the Stern Cons.; emigrated to Palestine in 1936; then studied piano and composition with Irma and Stefan Wolpe at the Palestine Cons. and Academy of Music; subsequently was active as a teacher. His compositions encompass both traditional and avant-garde idioms. His *6 Israeli Dances* (1950) acquired considerable popularity; he also composed chamber works, cantatas, and many piano pieces, including *Patterns* (1973).

Alexander, John, American tenor; b. Meridian, Miss., Oct. 21, 1923. He received his musical training at the Cincinnati Cons. of Music; made his operatic debut in Cincinnati in 1952; in 1957 he sang at the N.Y. City Opera; he made his Metropolitan Opera debut as Ferrando in *Cosi fan tutte* on Dec. 19, 1961; also made appearances with the Vienna State Opera (1968) and the Royal Opera at Covent Garden in London (1970). He became particularly adept in lyric tenor roles; he also gained success as a concert artist.

Alexander, Josef, American composer; b. Boston, May 15, 1907. The only musical connection in his family was the fact that the paternal grandfather of his paternal grandfather played the clarinet in the Russian military band during the Crimean War (which ended inconclusively). He studied piano at the New England Cons. in Boston, graduating in 1925; then entered Harvard Univ., where he took a

course in composition with Walter Piston and in orchestration with Edward B. Hill; received his B.A. in 1938 and his M.A. in 1941. In 1939 he went to Paris, where he studied with Nadia Boulanger; returning to the U.S., he attended a class in composition with Aaron Copland at the Berkshire Music Center in Tanglewood in 1940. In 1943 he was appointed to the music faculty at Brooklyn College; retired in 1977 as prof. emeritus. In his compositions he adopted, from the very first, a facile laissez-faire idiom marked by a pleasurable admixture of euphonious dissonances.

WORKS: Symph. poem, *The Ancient Mariner* (Boston, June 8, 1940); 4 symphs.: No. 1, subtitled *Clockwork* (N.Y., Nov. 28, 1949); No. 2 (1954); No. 3 (1961; N.Y., April 27, 1970); No. 4 (1968); Piano Concerto (1938; Boston, June 8, 1940); *A New England Overture* (St. Louis, Feb. 12, 1943); *Williamsburg Suite* for Orch. (N.Y., Aug. 19, 1944); *Epitaphs* for Orch. (1947; N.Y., March 8, 1951); *Andante and Allegro* for String Orch. (1952; St. Louis, Feb. 20, 1953); *Concertino* for Trumpet and Strings (1959); *Celebrations* for Orch. (1960); *Quiet Music* for Strings (1966); String Quartet (1940); Piano Quintet (1942); Piano Trio (1944); Wind Quintet (1949); Piano Quartet (1952); Violin Sonata (1953); Cello Sonata (1953); Flute Sonata (1954); Clarinet Sonata (1957); *Songs for Eve,* a cycle of 15 songs for Soprano and Instruments (1957); 4 Movements for Brass (1958); Trombone Sonata (1959); *Nocturne and Scherzo* for Violin and Piano (1963); *3 Pieces* for 8 Instruments (1965); *Triptych* for Cornet, Marimba, and Guitar (1968); *Playthings of the Wind* for Voices, Brass, and Piano (1970); Brass Trio (1971); *Gitanjali* for Soprano, Harpsichord, and Percussion, based on texts from Rabindranath Tagore (N.Y., Nov. 14, 1975); *Symphonic Odes* for Male Chorus and Orch. (1975); Horn Sonata (1979); *Dyad* for 4 Tubas (1979).

BIBLIOGRAPHY: David Ewen, *American Composers* (N.Y., 1982).

Alexandre, Jacob, French organ builder; b. Paris, 1804; d. there, June 11, 1876. In 1829 he established a firm of harmonium manufacturers, which introduced the "Alexandre organ," a development of the so-called "American organ" (1874).

Alexandrov, Alexander, Russian composer; b. Plakhino (Riazan dist.), April 1, 1883; d. Berlin, July 8, 1946, during a concert tour. He studied with Rimsky-Korsakov and Glazunov at the St. Petersburg Cons. (1899–1901) and later at the Moscow Cons. with Vasilenko (1909–13). In 1928 he organized the Red Army Ensemble and conducted it on numerous tours in Russia and abroad. His song *Hymn of the Bolshevik Party,* with a new set of words, was proclaimed the Soviet national anthem on March 15, 1944.

Alexandrov, Anatoli, eminent Russian pianist and composer; b. Moscow, May 25, 1888; d. there, April 16, 1982. He studied with Taneyev at the Moscow Cons. (1907–10); also studied composition there with Vasilenko and piano with Igumnov, graduating in 1916. In 1923 he became a prof. at the Moscow Cons. He composed mainly for piano; wrote 14 piano sonatas (1914–71); in his style of composition he followed the main lines of Rachmaninoff and Scriabin. His other works include 2 operas, *Bela* (Moscow, Dec. 10, 1946) and *Wild Bara* (Moscow, March 2, 1957); 4 string quartets (1914–53); *Classical Suite* for Orch. (1926); *Dithyramb* for Double Bass and Piano (1959); several song cycles; and incidental music for theatrical plays.

Alfano, Franco, eminent Italian composer; b. Posilippo (Naples), March 8, 1875; d. San Remo, Oct. 27, 1954. He studied composition with Paolo Serrao in Naples, and with Jadassohn and Hans Sitt in Leipzig. From the beginning of his musical career, Alfano was interested in opera. His first stage work, *Miranda,* was produced in Leipzig when he was barely 20; another opera, *La fonte di Enchir,* followed (Breslau, Nov. 8, 1898). In 1899 he went to Paris and became fascinated by light theater music. While in Paris he wrote *Napoli,* a ballet in the folk manner, which was staged at the Folies-Bergères (Jan. 28, 1901), proving so successful that it ran for 160 successive performances. Returning to Italy, he began work on an opera based on Tolstoy's novel *Resurrection.* It was produced as *Risurrezione* in Turin (Nov. 4, 1904) with sensational acclaim; the American premiere (Chicago, Dec. 31, 1925) was equally successful; there were also numerous performances in Germany and France. The opera was widely praised for its dramatic power and melodic richness in the best tradition of realistic Italian opera. Alfano continued to compose industriously for another half-century, but his later operas failed to equal the success of *Risurrezione.* They are: *Il Principe Zilah* (Genoa, Feb. 3, 1909); *L'ombra di Don Giovanni* (La Scala, April 3, 1914); *La leggenda di Sakuntala* (Bologna, Dec. 10, 1921); *Madonna Imperia,* lyric comedy (Turin, May 5, 1927; Metropolitan Opera, N.Y., Feb. 8, 1928); *L'Ultimo Lord* (Naples, April 19, 1930); *Cyrano de Bergerac* (Rome, Jan. 22, 1936); *Il Dottor Antonio* (Rome, April 30, 1949). Alfano also wrote 3 symphs. (1909, 1932, 1934), 3 string quartets, a violin sonata, a cello sonata, and a ballet, *Vesuvius* (1938; a symph. poem was drawn from it in 1946). One of Alfano's signal achievements was that he completed Puccini's last opera, *Turandot,* adding the last scene. His *Hymn to Bolivar* for Chorus and Orch., written for the centennial of Bolivar's death, was performed in Caracas, Venezuela, on Dec. 22, 1930. He was also active in the field of musical education; was successively director of the Liceo Musicale in Bologna (1918–23); director of the Turin Cons. (1923–39); superintendent of the Teatro Massimo in Palermo (1940–42); and (1947–50) acting director of the Rossini Cons. in Pesaro.
BIBLIOGRAPHY: G.M. Gatti, "Franco Alfano," *Musicisti moderni d'Italia e di fuori* (Bologna, 1920; also in the *Musical Times,* March 1921); G. Cesàri, "La leggenda di Sakuntala di Franco Alfano," *Rivista Musicale Italiana* (1921); Andrea della Corte, *Ritratto di Franco Alfano* (Turin,

1935). Ettore Desderi publ. a list of Alfano's works in *Bolletino Bibliografico Musicale* (Milan, 1931).

Alfarabi (or **Alpharabius,** properly **Al Farabi**), **Abu Nasr,** so named from his birthplace, Farab (now transoxine Othrâx), Arabian music theorist; b. c.870; d. Damascus, c.950. Of Turkish descent, he was a Greek scholar and attempted unsuccessfully to introduce the Greek musical system into his country. He was renowned for his writings on philosophy, political science, and the arts; his principal work is *Kitab al-Musiqi al-Kabir* (*Greater Book about Music;* reprint with commentary, Cairo, 1967), dealing with acoustics, intervals, scales, instruments, and rhythm. The 2nd vol. of this work was lost. Excerpts from this book are contained in Kosegarten's *Alii Ispahanis Liber Cantilenarum Magnus* (1840) and in J. Land's *Recherches sur l'histoire de la gamme arabe* (Leyden, 1884). Another treatise, *Kitab al-Iqua'at,* was trans. into German by E. Neubauer in *Oriens* (1968/69).
BIBLIOGRAPHY: M. Steinschneider, *Al-Farabi* (St. Petersburg, 1869); Baron d'Erlanger, *La Musique arabe,* vol. I (Paris, 1930); E.A. Beichert, *Die Wissenschaft der Musik bei Al-Farabi* (Regensburg, 1931); H.G. Farmer, *Al-Farabi's Arabic-Latin Writings on Music* (Glasgow, 1934).

Alferaki, Achilles, Russian composer of Greek extraction; b. Kharkov, July 3, 1846; d. Petrograd, Dec. 27, 1919. He studied philology at the Univ. of Moscow; simultaneously he took lessons in piano and music theory. He joined the group of composers whose works were publ. by Belaiev, and wrote numerous songs and piano pieces in the manner of the Russian national school, many of them also publ. by Belaiev. He furthermore wrote an opera, *St. John's Eve,* which remains in MS.

Alfieri, Pietro, Italian music scholar; b. Rome, June 29, 1801; d. there, June 12, 1863. He was a member of the Camaldolese Order; taught Gregorian music at the English College in Rome. His major work is *Raccolta di musica sacra* (1841–46), a collection of 16th-century church music in 7 vols., which includes virtually all representative works of Palestrina; other collections are *Excerpta ex celebrioribus de musica viris* (Rome, 1840), containing works by Palestrina, Victoria, and Allegri; *Raccolta di motetti* (1841); etc. His essays on Gregorian chant are very valuable: *Ristabilimento del canto e della musica ecclesiastica* (1843); *Saggio storico del canto gregoriano* (1855); *Prodromo sulla restaurazione de' libri di canto ecclesiastico detto gregoriano* (1857); etc. He also publ. a biography of N. Jommelli (1845) and contributed articles on musical subjects to Italian periodicals.

Alfvén, Hugo, outstanding Swedish composer; b. Stockholm, May 1, 1872; d. Falun, May 8, 1960. He studied violin at the Stockholm Cons. (1887–91); continued these studies with Lars Zetterquist until 1896 while taking composition lessons from Johan Lindegren. He was then sent by the government to

Brussels to complete his violin studies with César Thomson (1896–99). Government scholarships in 1896, 1897, and 1899, as well as the Jenny Lind stipend (1900–03), enabled him to study composition in many European countries. In 1910 he became music director at the Univ. of Uppsala and conductor of the student chorus until his retirement in 1939; continued to conduct various mixed choruses.

WORKS: His best-known work is *Midsommarvaka* (*Midsummer Vigil;* Stockholm, May 10, 1904), the first of his 3 Swedish rhapsodies for Orch. It was produced as a ballet, *La Nuit de Saint-Jean,* by the Ballets Suédois in Paris, Oct. 25, 1920, and had over 250 perfs. in 4 years. His other works include the 2nd and 3rd Swedish rhapsodies: *Uppsala* (1907) and *Dalecarlian* (1937); 5 symphs.: No. 1 (1896–97; Stockholm, Feb. 9, 1897); No. 2 (1898–99; Stockholm, May 2, 1899); No. 3 (1905–06; Göteborg, Dec. 5, 1906); No. 4, with Soprano and Tenor (1918–19; Stockholm, Nov. 4, 1919); No. 5 (1942–52; first complete perf., Stockholm, April 30, 1952; Alfvén withdrew the work except for the first movement, which subsequently had frequent perfs. as a separate piece); 2 ballet pantomimes: *Bergakungen* (*The Mountain King;* 1923) and *Den förlorade sonen* (*The Prodigal Son;* 1957); *En skärgårdssägen* (*A Tale of the Skerries*), symph. poem (1905); *Festspiel (Festival Music)* for Orch. (1907); suite of incidental music to the play *Gustaf II Adolf* (1932); *Synnöve Solbakken,* suite for Small Orch. (1934); 10 cantatas, many contributed for various occasions, such as patriotic anniversaries, among them one celebrating the 450th year since the founding of Uppsala Univ. (1927) and another on the 500th jubilee of the Swedish Parliament (1935); Violin Sonata (1896); *Elegie* for Horn and Organ (1897); *Skärgårdsbilder (Pictures from the Skerries)* for Piano (1902); a ballad on Gustaf Vasa for Soloists, Mixed Chorus, and Organ (1920); numerous male choruses and folk-song arrangements. The music of Alfvén represents the best traits of Scandinavian national art, along the lines of Grieg and Sibelius. He publ. 4 vols. of memoirs: *Första satsen* (Stockholm, 1946); *Tempo furioso* (1948); *I dur och moll* (1949); *Finale* (1952).

BIBLIOGRAPHY: S.E. Svensson, *Hugo Alfvén, Som människa och konstnär* (Uppsala, 1946); J.O. Rudén, *Hugo Alfvéns kompositioner. Käll- och verkförteckning* (thematic index; Stockholm, 1972).

Algarotti, Francesco, Italian musician and scholar; b. Venice, Dec. 11, 1712; d. Pisa, May 3, 1764. The fame of his great knowledge reached Frederick the Great, who invited him to Berlin in 1740 and gave him the title of Count, and, in 1747, that of "Chevalier de l'ordre pour le mérite." In 1753 Algarotti returned to Italy. His musical monument is the *Saggio sopra l'opera in musica,* publ. in 1755; also in many later eds., including German and French translations. The English text of the *Saggio . . .* is reproduced in part in O. Strunk's *Source Readings in Music History* (N.Y., 1950).

BIBLIOGRAPHY: D. Michelessi, *Memorie intorno alla vita ed agli scritti del Francesco Algarotti* (Venice, 1770); R. Northcott, *Francesco Algarotti, A Reprint of His "Saggio . . ." and a Sketch of His Life* (London, 1917).

Aliabiev, Alexander, Russian song composer; b. Tobolsk, Siberia, Aug. 15, 1787; d. Moscow, March 6, 1851. His father was the governor of Tobolsk, and Aliabiev spent his childhood there. The family went to St. Petersburg in 1796, and in 1804 settled in Moscow. He studied music in Moscow and had his first songs publ. in 1810. During the War of 1812, he served in the Russian army, and participated in the entry of the Russian army into Dresden and Paris. Returning to Russia, he lived in St. Petersburg, in Voronezh, and in Moscow. In 1825 he was arrested on suspicion of murder after a card game, was sentenced to prison, and in 1828 was deported to his birthplace in Siberia. There he organized concerts of popular music and also composed. In 1831 he was allowed to return to European Russia and lived in the Caucasus and in Orenburg. In 1843 he returned to Moscow, but was still under police surveillance. He wrote more than 100 songs, of which *The Nightingale* became extremely popular; it is often used in the music lesson scene in Russian productions of Rossini's opera *The Barber of Seville;* Glinka and Liszt made piano arrangements of it. He also wrote a symph., 3 string quartets, 2 piano trios, a piano quintet, a violin sonata, a Quartet for 4 Flutes, a Quintet for Wind Instruments, a piano sonata, choruses. Among his works for the theater are scores of incidental music to *The Prisoner of the Caucasus* and to Shakespeare's plays; also stage ballads: *The Village Philosopher, The Moon Night,* and *Theatrical Combat* (with Verstovsky and Mauer).

BIBLIOGRAPHY: Igor Ilyin, "Aliabiev in Siberia" (with a facsimile reproduction of the registry of Aliabiev's birth), *Sovietskaya Muzyka* (Aug. 1952); Boris Steinpress, *Aliabiev in Exile* (Moscow, 1959); B. Dobrohotov, *Alexander Aliabiev* (Moscow, 1966).

Ali Akbar Khan, Indian instrumentalist; b. Shibpore, Bengal, April 14, 1922. He studied dhrupad, dhamar, khayal, and sarod with his father; pakhawaj and tabla with his uncle. He founded the Ali Akbar College of Music in Calcutta in 1956; toured widely in Europe, America, and Japan as a virtuoso; held the post of court musician in Jodhpur. He has written a number of new ragas. Several of his students achieved prominence as Indian instrumentalists in their own right.

Alió, Francisco, Spanish composer; b. Barcelona, March 21, 1862; d. there, March 31, 1908. He studied piano with Vidiella and composition with Anselmo Barba. He subsequently was active as a music critic in Catalan newspapers. A determined believer in the importance of folk songs, he traversed Catalonia, notating folk songs and dance tunes; these he later incorporated in his collections, among them *Cansons populars catalanas* (Barcelona, 1891). He also publ. his own piano pieces and songs based on Catalan melodies.

Aliprandi, Bernardo, Italian cellist and composer;

b. Milan, c.1710; d. Frankfurt, c.1792. On Oct. 1, 1731, he became a member of the Court Orch. in Munich, retiring in 1778. He wrote 3 theatrical works with music: *Apollo tra le Muse in Parnasso* (Munich, Aug. 6, 1737); *Mitridate* (Munich, 1738); *Semiramide riconosciuta* (Munich, 1740); and a *Stabat Mater* (1749).

Alkan (real name, **Morhange**), **Charles-Henri Valentin,** French pianist and composer of Jewish extraction; b. Paris, Nov. 30, 1813; d. there, March 29, 1888. His 4 brothers were also musicians; his father was the founder of a school for Jewish children. Alkan's talent was precocious; he was accepted at the Paris Cons. at the age of 6 and studied piano with Zimmermann. In 1833 he visited London, then returned to Paris, where his main activities were playing concerts in the fashionable salons and teaching piano. He entered the brilliant circle of musicians and littérateurs, among whom were Chopin, George Sand, Hugo, and Liszt.

WORKS: Like Chopin, Alkan wrote almost exclusively for piano; the list of his works includes 76 opus numbers, in addition to many pieces not numbered by opus. His pieces are programmatic, bearing such titles as *Désir;* a set of variations, *Les Omnibus; Le Vent* (op. 15); *Le Tambour bat aux champs* (op. 50); he was the first composer to write a piece descriptive of the railroad (*Le Chemin de fer,* op. 27). His 2 sets of études, in all major and minor keys (op. 35 and 39), of transcendent difficulty, present great interest as examples of modern piano technique. Other works are *3 études de bravoure* (op. 16); *Le Preux, Etude de concert* (op. 17); *3 pièces poétiques* (op. 18); *Bourrée d'Auvergne* (op. 29); Sonata (op. 33, subtitled *Les 4 Ages*); *Les Mois* (opp. 8, 74), comprising 12 pieces; etc. He also wrote 2 piano concertos, a Piano Trio, a Cello Sonata, and vocal music. César Franck arranged several of his pieces for organ. For a long time Alkan's music was completely forgotten, but his significance as an inventive composer became more evident in the 20th century.

BIBLIOGRAPHY: K. Sorabji, *Around Music* (London, 1932); Bernard van Dieren, *Down among the Dead Men and Other Essays* (London, 1935); Ronald Smith, *Alkan,* vol. 1, *The Enigma* (London, 1976).

Allanbrook, Douglas, American composer; b. Melrose, Mass., April 1, 1921. He studied with Nadia Boulanger at the Longy School of Music in Cambridge, with Walter Piston at Harvard College (B.A., magna cum laude, 1948), and again with Boulanger in Paris. During World War II he served in the infantry in Italy, receiving a Bronze Star Medal. In 1950 he received a Fulbright fellowship to study harpsichord and early keyboard music with Ruggero Gerlin in Naples; returning to the U.S. in 1952, he taught at St. John's College in Annapolis.

WORKS: 2 operas: *Ethan Frome* (1952); *Nightmare Abbey* (1960); Symph. No. 1 (1958); Symph. No. 2, *An Elegy;* Symph. No. 3, *Orchestral Landscapes* (1966); Symph. No. 4; Symph. No. 5 for Brass Quintet and Orch. (1977); Symph. No. 6, *5 Heroic Attitudes;* Symph. No. 7, *Music from the Country* (1979); Concerto for Harpsichord and Small Orch. (1957); Violin Concerto (1959); Serenade for Piano and Orch. (1982); Songs to Shakespeare Sonnets for Medium Voice and Orch. (1951); *3 Noble Love Songs* for Baritone and Orch. (1960); *The 7 Last Words* for Mezzosoprano, Baritone, Chorus, and Orch. (1970); *Te Deum* (1948); *Ash Wednesday* for Soprano, Chorus, and Orch. (1947); 2 piano sonatas (1948, 1949); 4 string quartets; Quintet for Oboe, Clarinet, Violin, Viola, and Cello; other chamber works.

Alldahl, Per-Gunnar, Swedish composer; b. Solna, Oct. 11, 1943. He studied organ and composition at the Royal College of Music in Stockholm (1968–71); later joined its staff as an instructor. In his music, he pursues the twin goals of total freedom of realization and strict observance of minuscule tonal data.

WORKS: *Nulla ars . . .* for String Orch. (1966; Helsinki, Feb. 24, 1967); *Biceps* for Chamber Orch. and Tape (1968–69; Swedish Radio, Dec. 7, 1969); *Music for Solo Cello* (1968); *Light Music* for 5 Flutes, Hammond Organ, and Vibraphone (1968); *Play* for Orch. (Bollnäs, April 4, 1970); *Ad lib* for Any Instruments, though originally for Bass Clarinet, Trombone, and Cello (1971); *Bruspolska* for Nyckelharps (1972); *Stämma blod* for Chorus and Percussion (1972); *Unisona* for Alto Voice, Flute, Trombone, Double Bass, and Vibraphone (1972); *Från när och fjärran* for Jazz Quartet (1973); *Mot värk* for Chorus and Percussion (1973; a sequel to *Stämma blod*); *Knaver-lik* for Nyckelharp and String Orch. (1974); *. . . ljudens dikt sjunger i venden . . .* for Narrator, Chorus, and Small Orch. (1974).

Alldis, John, English choral conductor; b. London, Aug. 10, 1929. He was educated at King's College, Cambridge. In 1962 he joined the faculty of the Guildhall School of Music in London; founded the John Alldis Choir, which soon achieved prominence. Later he conducted the London Symph. Orch. Chorus (1966–69), the London Phil. Orch. Chorus (until 1982), and, from 1972, the Danish Radio Chorus in Copenhagen.

Allegri, Domenico, Italian composer; b. Rome, 1585; d. there, Sept. 5, 1629. He was maestro di cappella at Santa Maria Maggiore from 1610–29, and was one of the first to provide vocal music with an independent instrumental accompaniment. A few of his motets are extant (a soprano solo, a tenor duet, and a bass solo, each accompanied by 2 violins).

Allegri, Gregorio, Italian composer; b. Rome, c.1582; d. there, Feb. 7, 1652. He was a choirboy in Rome from 1591–96; then studied with Giovanni Maria Nanino (1600–1607). He entered the Papal Chapel in 1630 after serving for some years as chorister and composer for the Cathedral at Fermo. He is chiefly known as the composer of the celebrated *Miserere* in 9 parts (i.e., for 2 Choirs, one singing 4 parts and one 5), regularly sung during Holy Week at the Sistine Chapel; Mozart wrote this out after hearing it twice, though surreptitiously, since its publication was forbidden on pain of excommunication; since then it has been frequently published. Many other works by Allegri are preserved in MS; one book of *concertini* and 2 books of *mottetti* have been printed; also a 4-part Sonata for Strings, which might be regarded as the prototype of the string quartet.

BIBLIOGRAPHY: A. Cametti, "La scuola dei pueri cantus di S. Luigi dei Francesi in Roma," *Rivista Musicale Italiana* (1915); J. Amann, *Allegris Miserere und die Aufführungspraxis in der Sixtina* (Regensburg, 1935); A. Eaglefield-Hull, "The Earliest Known String Quartet," *Musical Quarterly* (Jan. 1929).

Allegri, Lorenzo, Italian lutenist and composer; b. c.1573; d. Florence, July 15, 1648. He became a lutenist at the Medici court in Florence in 1604; remained at the court until his death. He publ. *Primo libro delle musiche* (Venice, 1618), a collection which contains mostly instrumental music.

BIBLIOGRAPHY: H. Bellermann, "Lorenzo Allegri," *Allgemeine Musikalische Zeitung,* IV (1869).

Allen, Betty, black American mezzo-soprano; b. Campbell, Ohio, March 17, 1930. She attended Wilberforce Univ. (1944–46); then studied at the Hartford School of Music (1950–53); among her teachers were Paul Ulanowsky and Zinka Milanov. She sang at the N.Y. City Opera in 1954; also sang opera in San Francisco, Houston, Boston, and Santa Fe. On Feb. 20, 1973, she made her Metropolitan Opera debut in N.Y. She taught at the Manhattan School of Music and the North Carolina School of the Arts. In 1979 she became executive director of the Harlem School of the Arts.

Allen, Creighton, American pianist and composer; b. Macon, Miss., March 26, 1900; d. New York, July 18, 1969. He studied piano and composition; then settled in N.Y. as a teacher and composer. Among his works are a Piano Concerto, a Violin Concerto, 17 settings to the poems of Edgar Allan Poe, piano pieces, and many songs.

Allen, George Benjamin, English singer and composer; b. London, April 21, 1822; d. Brisbane, Australia, Nov. 30, 1897. He was active successively as a chorister, conductor, and organist in England, Ireland, and Australia; managed a light opera company, producing several of Sullivan's operas. He composed the operas *Castle Grim* (London, 1865), *The Viking* (not performed), and *The Wicklow Rose* (Manchester, 1882); 3 cantatas; songs.

Allen, Henry James ("Red"), black American jazz trumpeter; b. New Orleans, Jan. 7, 1908; d. New York, April 17, 1967. His father, **Henry Allen** (1877–1952), was director of the New Orleans Brass Band; after studying the violin and alto horn, he turned to the trumpet; gained experience in his father's band; then played with King Oliver, Fletcher Henderson, and later Louis Armstrong (1937–40). In 1940 he formed his own group, Red's Sextet, and toured with it; also made solo appearances in the U.S. and Europe.

Allen, Sir Hugh Percy, eminent English organist and educator; b. Reading, Dec. 23, 1869; d. Oxford, Feb. 20, 1946. He studied with Dr. F. Read in Reading, and at Oxford Univ. (Mus.Doc., 1898). At the age of 11 he acted as church organist in Reading. Thereafter he was an organist at various churches and cathedrals until the turn of the century. He was appointed organist at New College, Oxford (1901–18), and later (1908–18) director of music at Univ. College in Reading. In 1918 he succeeded Sir Walter Parratt as prof. of music at Oxford, and in the same year became director of the Royal College of Music in London, from which he resigned in 1937 (succeeded by George Dyson). He was knighted in 1920. For many years he conducted the London and the Oxford Bach Choirs; he was an ardent promoter of British music.

BIBLIOGRAPHY: C. Bailey, *Hugh Percy Allen* (London, 1948).

Allen, Nathan H., American organist and choral conductor; b. Marion, Mass., April 14, 1848; d. Hartford, Conn., May 9, 1925. He studied organ in Berlin; was active as a church organist and teacher in Hartford, Conn. From 1906–11 he was an organist in Worcester, Mass., then returned to Hartford. He wrote church music (including a cantata, *The Apotheosis of St. Dorothy*), and concert pieces for organ, violin, and piano.

Allen, Paul Hastings, American composer; b. Hyde Park, Mass., Nov. 28, 1883; d. Boston, Sept. 28, 1952. He studied at Harvard Univ. (A.B., 1903); then went to Italy. During World War I he was in the American diplomatic service in Italy; returning to the U.S. in 1920, he settled in Boston. He learned to play virtually all the orch. instruments as well as piano, and acquired fluent knowledge in Italian, German, and French, as well as a smattering of Russian. His music reflected the Italian techniques in operatic composition, while his instrumental works were written largely in a Romantic manner. He wrote much chamber music for unusual combinations, such as a Quartet for 2 Clarinets, Basset Horn, and Bass Clarinet.

WORKS: Operas: *Il filtro* (Genoa, Oct. 26, 1912); *Milda* (Venice, June 14, 1913); *L'ultimo dei Mohicani* (Florence, Feb. 24, 1916); *Cleopatra* (1921); *La piccola Figaro* (1931); *Pilgrim Symphony* (1910; received the Paderewski prize); piano pieces; choral works; songs.

Allen, Thomas, English baritone; b. Seaham, Sept. 10, 1944. He was educated at the Royal College of Music in London; after singing in the Glyndebourne Chorus, he made his debut with the Welsh National Opera in 1969; from 1971 he sang at Covent Garden;

also at the Aldeburgh and Glyndebourne festivals, and in Paris, Florence, and Buenos Aires. He is generally regarded as one of the best European baritones, praised for both his lyric and dramatic abilities.

Allen, Warren D., American musicologist; b. San Jose, Calif., Aug. 3, 1885; d. Olympia, Wash., June 21, 1964. He studied at the Univ. of Calif., Berkeley; later took theory lessons with Fielitz in Berlin and with Widor in Paris. Returning to America, he was dean of music at the College of the Pacific in San Jose (1913–18). In 1918 he was appointed choral director at Stanford Univ.; from 1940–49 was on the faculty there, and from 1949–55 was a prof. at Florida State Univ.; after retirement in 1955 he lived in Seattle. He publ. the books *Philosophies of Music History* (1939) and *Our Marching Civilization* (1943).

Allende (-Sarón), (Pedro) Humberto, eminent Chilean composer; b. Santiago, June 29, 1885; d. there, Aug. 16, 1959. He studied violin and music theory at the National Cons. in Santiago (1889–1908); then taught in public schools there. In 1918 he visited France and Spain; in 1928 served as Chilean delegate to the Congress of Popular Arts in Prague, under the auspices of the League of Nations; in 1929 he took part in the Festival of Ibero-American Music in Barcelona. Returning to Santiago, he taught composition at the National Cons. (1930–50). He received the National Arts Prize in appreciation of his work in musical ethnology. His music is marked with an exquisite sense of authentic Chilean folk song, while the purely formal structure follows the impressionistic manner akin to that of Debussy, Ravel, and Granados.
WORKS: Symphony (1910; awarded Chilean Centennial Prize); *Escenas campesinas chilenas* for Orch. (1913); Cello Concerto (1915); *La voz de las calles,* symph. poem utilizing street cries of Chilean cities (Santiago, May 20, 1921); *La despedida* for 2 Sopranos, Contralto, and Orch. (Santiago, May 7, 1934); Violin Concerto (Santiago, Dec. 4, 1942); Piano Concerto (1945); String Quartet (1945); 3 piano sonatas (1906–15); *12 tonadas de carácter popular chileno* for Piano (1918–22); his most distinctive work in a national style; also arranged for Orch.); songs; a teaching manual, *Método original de iniciación musical* (Santiago, 1937).
BIBLIOGRAPHY: Special issue of *Revista Musical Chilena* (Sept. 1945); Nicolas Slonimsky, "Humberto Allende, First Modernist of Chile," *Musical America* (Aug. 1942); V.S. Viu, *La creación musical en Chile,* pp. 115–29 (Santiago, 1952).

Allers, Franz, Czech conductor; b. Karlovy Vary, Aug. 6, 1905. He studied violin; went to Berlin in 1926 and conducted theater orchs. He left Germany at the advent of the Nazis and held engagements conducting ballet performances in London, South America, and Canada. Eventually he settled in the U.S. He made his debut at the Metropolitan Opera in N.Y. as conductor on Nov. 30, 1963. From 1973 to

1976 he served as chief conductor of the Gärtnerplatz State Theater in Munich.

Allihn, Heinrich (Max), German music scholar; b. Halle an de Saale, Aug. 31, 1841; d. there, Nov. 15, 1910. From 1885 he was a pastor and school inspector at Allenstedt; edited the 2nd edition (1888) of Töpfer's *Lehrbuch der Orgelbaukunst (Theorie und Praxis des Orgelbaues)*; publ. *Die Hausinstrumente Klavier und Harmonium* (1892) and *Die Pflege des musikalisches Teils des Gottesdienstes* (1906); contributed many essays to De Wit's *Zeitschrift für Instrumentenbau.*

Allin, Norman, English operatic bass; b. Ashton-under-Lyne, Nov. 19, 1884; d. Hereford, Oct. 27, 1973. He studied at the Royal Manchester College of Music (1906–10); made his operatic debut with the Beecham Opera Co. in London in 1916. In 1922 he became a director and leading bass of the British National Opera Co. in London, remaining with it until 1929; from 1942 to 1949 he was a member of the Carl Rosa Opera Co. Later he became active as a teacher; led vocal classes at the Royal Academy of Music in London (1935–60) and the Royal Manchester College of Music (1938–42).

Allorto, Riccardo, Italian musicologist; b. Mosso, S. Maria, Vercelli, Jan. 31, 1921. He studied piano at the Parma Cons. and choral music at the Turin Cons.; subsequently took courses in music history with Della Corte at the Univ. of Turin, where he graduated in 1946. He taught music history at the Bolzano Cons. (1950–51) and the Parma Cons. (1951–55); in 1954 joined the faculty of the Milan Cons. In 1969 he became artistic director of La Scala in Milan. He compiled the valuable text *Storia della musica* (Milan, 1955; 10th ed., 1969); also edited *Nuovo dizionario Ricordi della musica e dei musicisti* (Milan, 1976).

Almeida, Antonio de, conductor and music editor; b. Paris, Jan. 1, 1928. The son of a Portuguese diplomat and an American mother, he was taken by the family to Buenos Aires, where he studied with Alberto Ginastera. He also took an interest in science and applied for a scholarship at the Massachusetts Inst. of Technology; there he attended courses in nuclear chemistry, and also conducted the student orch. He subsequently enrolled in the class of Paul Hindemith in advanced music theory at Yale Univ.; during the summers he attended the Berkshire Music Center in Tanglewood, where he received training as a conductor with Koussevitzky and Bernstein. He then went to England, where he became associated with Sir Thomas Beecham, who gave him an opportunity to conduct the Royal Phil. He made his American debut in N.Y. on Nov. 1, 1960, conducting Gluck's *Orfeo ed Euridice* with the American Opera Society; on Feb. 24, 1982, he gave a concert performance in N.Y. of Wagner's early opera *Die Feen.* His other engagements included several seasons in Lisbon (beginning in 1956), along with the posts of principal conductor of the Stuttgart Phil.

(1960–64), and guest conductor at the Paris Opéra (1964–68), of the Houston Symph. Orch. (1969–71), and of the Municipal Orch. in Nice (1976–78). While thus preoccupied, he devoted a great deal of eager attention to rescuing from oblivion little-known operas and operettas of Offenbach; from contacts with Offenbach's descendants he was able to recover the original uncut version of *The Tales of Hoffmann;* another find was the original score of Offenbach's comic opera *La Belle Hélène.* On April 15, 1982, he conducted at the N.Y. City Opera a newly restored version of Offenbach's operetta *La Grande Duchesse de Gérolstein.* In 1980 he assumed the general editorship of the multivolume edition of Offenbach's collected works, including his instrumental music, along with the publication of a catalogue raisonné of the entire Offenbach oeuvre.

d'Almeida, Fernando, Portuguese composer; b. Lisbon, c.1600; d. Thomar, March 21, 1660. He was a distinguished pupil of Duarte Lobo; in 1638, entered the Order of Christ at Thomar. Of his many church compositions, only one folio vol. in MS is known: *Lamentacões, Responsorias e Misereres das tres officias da Quarta, Quinta e Sexta-feria da Semana Santa.*

Almeida, Laurindo, Brazilian guitarist; b. São Paulo, Sept. 2, 1917. After mastering the guitar, he settled in Rio de Janeiro and made appearances on the radio; also led his own orch. at the Casino da Urca. In 1947 he moved to the U.S.; was a soloist with Stan Kenton's jazz band; subsequently gave numerous recitals and was a soloist with symph. orchs.; also appeared in recital with his wife, the soprano **Deltra Eamon.**

Almeida, Renato, Brazilian music historian; b. St. Antonio de Jesus, Bahia, Dec. 6, 1895; d. Rio de Janeiro, Jan. 24, 1981. He studied law; worked as a journalist in Rio de Janeiro. He is the author of the standard work on Brazilian music, *Historia da musica brasileira* (1926; new enlarged ed., 1942); *Danses africaines en Amerique Latine* (Rio de Janeiro, 1969); *Vivência e projeção do folclore* (Rio de Janeiro, 1971).

Almenräder, Karl, German bassoon virtuoso; b. Ronsdorf, near Düsseldorf, Oct. 3, 1786; d. Biebrich, Sept. 14, 1843. He was a prof. of bassoon at Cologne, a theater conductor in Frankfurt, and a regimental bandmaster; started a factory for wind instruments (1820) at Cologne, but gave it up in 2 years, entering the Nassau Court Orch. at Biebrich. He materially improved the bassoon, wrote a treatise on it (Mainz, 1824) and a method for it. He also publ. a Bassoon Concerto; Variations for Bassoon and Quartet; duettinos for 2 Bassoons; etc.; and the popular ballad *Des Hauses letzte Stunde.*

Almquist, Carl Jonas Love, Swedish composer; b. Stockholm, Nov. 28, 1793; d. Bremen, Nov. 26, 1866. He studied at Uppsala Univ., and composed songs to

his own words, but refused to study music theory for fear that his instinct for simple melodic writing might be destroyed by learning. His life was an adventurous one; he was forced to leave Sweden after an accusation of murder was leveled against him. From 1851 to 1865 he lived in America; then went to Germany, where he died. His publications included the song collection *Törnrosens bok* (Stockholm, 1832–42); he also publ. *Fria Fantasier* for Piano (1847–49).

Alnaes, Eyvind, Norwegian composer; b. Fredriksstad, April 29, 1872; d. Oslo, Dec. 24, 1932. He studied in Oslo with Ivar Holter (1889–92) and in Leipzig with Carl Reinecke (1892–95). From 1895 he occupied various positions as a church organist in Norway.
    WORKS: 2 symphs. (1898, 1923); *Variations symphoniques* (1898); Piano Concerto (Oslo, Feb. 7, 1914); *Marche symphonique* for 2 Pianos; several choruses and songs. He also publ. a collection of Norwegian folk songs (1922).

Alnar, Hasan Ferit, Turkish composer; b. Istanbul, March 11, 1906. As a child he played authentic Turkish instruments; at 16 composed an operetta in oriental style. In 1927 he went to Vienna, where he studied with Joseph Marx (composition) and Oswald Kabasta (conducting). Returning to Istanbul in 1932, he taught at the Municipal Cons. He was associate conductor of the Presidential Phil. Orch. in Ankara from 1936–49, and its director from 1949–52. He also taught composition at the Ankara Cons. (1937–46). Alnar's music reflects Turkish melodic and rhythmic patterns.
    WORKS: *Prelude and 2 Dances* for Orch. (1935); *Istanbul Suite* for Orch. (1938); Cello Concerto (Ankara, Feb. 15, 1943); Concerto for Kanun (Turkish psaltery) and Orch. (1951); Piano Trio (1967); etc.

Alpaerts, Flor, Belgian composer; b. Antwerp, Sept. 12, 1876; d. there, Oct. 5, 1954. He studied composition with Benoit and Blockx and violin at the Flemish Cons. in Antwerp; in 1903 he joined its staff; was its director from 1934–41. He conducted the local orch. at the Zoological Gardens (1919–51); was in charge of the edition of works by Peter Benoit. His own music is marked by an intense feeling for the modalities of Flemish folk songs.
    WORKS: Opera, *Shylock,* after Shakespeare (Antwerp, Nov. 22, 1913); *Symphonie du printemps* (1906); symph. poems: *Psyche* (1900); *Herleving* (1903); *Cyrus* (1905); *Pallieter* (1921); *Thijl Uilenspiegel* (1927); *Avondindruk* (1928); *Zomeridyll* (1928). Other symph. works include *Poème symphonique* for Flute and Orch. (1903); *Karakterstuk* for Trumpet and Strings (1904); *Bosspeling* (1904); *Salomé danse,* theme and variations (1907; based on incidental music to the Wilde play); *Vlaamse Idylle* (1920); *Romanza* for Violin and Small Orch. (1928); *James Ensor Suite* for Orch. (1932); *Humor* (1936); *Serenade* for Cello and Orch. (1936); *Small Suite* for Strings (1947); Violin Concerto (1948); *Capriccio* (1953). He also

wrote *Kolonos* for Soloists, Chorus, and Orch. (1901); a cantata, *Het schoner vaderland* (1912); *2 Pieces* for Piano Trio (1906); *Avondmuziek* for 8 Woodwinds (1915); 4 string quartets (1943, 1944, 1945, 1950); *3 Petite Pieces* for Violin and Piano (1944); *4 Bagatelles* for String Quartet (1953); incidental music to 6 plays; *Kinderleideren*, in 4 sets (1915–16). His 5-vol. treatise *Muzieklezen en Zingen* was adopted as the official textbook in all Flemish music institutions.

Alpaerts, Jef, Belgian conductor and pianist, son of **Flor Alpaerts;** b. Antwerp, July 17, 1904; d. there, Jan. 15, 1973. He received his primary education at the Royal Flemish Cons. in Antwerp; then went to Paris, where he studied piano with Isidor Philipp and with Cortot, and composition with Vincent d'Indy at the Schola Cantorum. Returning to Belgium in 1936, he was appointed to the faculty of the Antwerp Cons.; retired in 1969. In 1938 he inaugurated the Collegium Musicum Antverpiense for performances of old music.

Alpenheim, Ilse von, Austrian pianist; b. Innsbruck, Feb. 11, 1927. She studied with Franz Ledwinka and Winfried Wolf at the Salzburg Mozarteum; then appeared in recital and chamber music concerts; toured Europe, Japan, Australia, and the U.S. as a soloist; played with the Cleveland Orch., Philadelphia Orch., National Symph. of Washington, D.C., Detroit Symph., and Boston Symph. She was a sensitive interpreter of the Haydn and Mozart piano works. She was married to the conductor **Antal Dorati.**

Alsen, Elsa, Polish-American opera singer; b. Obra, Poland, April 7, 1880; d. New York, Jan. 31, 1975. She received her vocal training as a contralto in Breslau; made her operatic debut in Heidelberg in 1902 as Azucena in *Il Trovatore.* In 1912 she appeared for the first time as a soprano in Braunschweig. She made her American debut in Baltimore on Feb. 1, 1923, as Isolde, appearing with the German Opera Co. In her later years she taught voice in N.Y.

Alsina, Carlos Roqué, Argentine composer; b. Buenos Aires, Feb. 19, 1941. He studied music theory with various local teachers; in 1951 joined the modern society Agrupación de Nueva Música in Buenos Aires (1959–64); from 1964 to 1966 he worked in Berlin on a Ford Foundation grant; there he took instruction with Luciano Berio, who inculcated him in the arcana of ultramodern compositional techniques. From 1966 to 1968 he lived in Buffalo, where he taught at the State Univ. of N.Y.; in 1969 he founded, along with Vinko Globokar, Jean-Pierre Drouet, and Michel Portal, the improvisatory group "New Phonic Art," which toured Europe. He subsequently spent several years in Berlin, and eventually settled in Paris. His music is of a functional nature, peculiar to the cosmopolitan avant-garde; it presents a colorful synthesis of quaquaversal idioms, ranging from stark, cloistered dissonance to overt, triadic formalism. Aleatory techniques are in evidence in his improvisatory performances.

WORKS: FOR THE STAGE: *Texts 1967,* theater piece for Soprano, Flute, Trombone, Violin, Cello, Double Bass, Percussion, and Piano (1967); *Fusion,* choreographic music for Dancer, 2 Pianos, and 2 Percussionists (1974); *Encore,* musical spectacle to a text by Arie Dzierlatka (1976). FOR ORCH.: *3 Pieces* for String Orch. (1964); *Symptom* (1969); *Dispersion 1969* for Chamber Orch. (1969); *Überwindung (Conquest)* for 4 Instrumental Soloists and Orch. (1970; Donaueschingen, Oct. 18, 1970; "New Phonic Art" group soloists); *Omnipotenz* for Chamber Orch. (1971); *Schichten I (Layers)* for Chamber Orch. (1971) and *Schichten II* for Chamber Ensemble (1972); *Approach* for Piano, Percussion, and Orch. (1972; West Berlin, March 14, 1973); *Thema II* for Solo Percussion and String Orch. (1974–75; Royan, France, March 26, 1975); *Stücke* (1977; Royan, April 4, 1977); *Señales* for Piano and Chamber Orch. (1977; La Rochelle, July 3, 1977); *Decisions* for Chamber Orch. (1977); *Études* for Orch. and Tape (1979; Metz, Nov. 17, 1979). CHAMBER MUSIC: *Quinteto de Maderas* for Wind Quintet (1961); *Funktionen* for Flute, Clarinet, Bassoon, Trumpet, Violin, Cello, Piano, and 2 Percussionists (1965); *Consecuenza* for Solo Trombone (1966); *Auftrag* for 9 Players (1966); *Trio 1967* for Cello, Trombone, and Percussion (1967); *Rendez-vous* for 4 Players (1970); *Unity* for Clarinet and Cello (1973); *A Letter* for Wind Quintet (1973); *Etude* for Solo Zarb (1973); *Thema* for Percussion (1974). VOCAL: *Requiem y aleluya* for Soprano, 5 Instruments, and Percussion (1960); *Oratorio* for 3 Soloists, 4 Actors, and 3 Small Instrumental Ensembles (1964); *Text,* scene for Trombone, 3 Percussion Instruments, and Chorus (1966); *Consecuenza II* for Solo Voice (1971); Cantata for Tenor, Chorus, and Orch. (Radio France, April 22, 1977); *Harmonies* for Children's Chorus, 2 Lectors, Narrator, 4 Soloists, Tape, and Orch. (1979; Paris Radio, Dec. 22, 1979).

Alsleben, Julius, German pianist and pedagogue; b. Berlin, March 24, 1832; d. there, Dec. 8, 1894. He studied piano with Zech, and theory with S. Dehn. In 1865 he became president of the Berlin Tonkünstlerverein; in 1879 he was president of the Musiklehrerverein, of which he was also a founder. From 1874 he edited the periodical *Harmonie.* Alsleben publ. 12 *Vorlesungen über Musikgeschichte* (1862); *Über die Entwickelung des Klavierspiels* (1870); *Licht- und Wendepunkte in der Entwickelung der Musik* (1880). He wrote a Requiem, a liturgy, choral pieces, and some orch. overtures.

Alsted, Johann Heinrich, German music scholar; b. Ballersbach, Nassau, in March 1588; d. Weissenburg, Transylvania, Nov. 8, 1638. He taught philosophy and theology in Weissenburg. His articles on music are found in his *Encyclopädie der gesammten Wissenschaften* (1610) and in his *Elementale mathematicum* (1611; Eng. trans. by Birchensha, 1644).

Alt, Hansi, American pianist and composer; b.

Vienna, Feb. 25, 1911. She studied music at the Univ. of Vienna. In 1941 she went to the U.S.; taught at several private schools in N.Y. before moving to Washington, D.C. She publ. a number of piano pieces pleasingly adapted to popular tastes, among them *Parade, Sleepyhead, Splashing.*

Altar, Cevat Memduh, Turkish writer on music; b. Constantinople, Sept. 14, 1902. He studied in Leipzig (1922–27); taught music theory in Ankara (1927–35), and was a founder of the Ankara State Cons. (1936). In 1951 he was appointed director of Turkish theaters; in 1954 he visited the U.S. under the Educational Exchange Program. He translated several German books into Turkish, wrote several essays on Beethoven's use of so-called Turkish music, and initiated a 6-vol. musical biography.

Altenburg, Johann Ernst, German trumpet player and composer; b. Weissenfels, June 15, 1734; d. Bitterfeld, May 14, 1801. He served as a field trumpeter during the Seven Years' War; returning to civilian life, he became an organist at Bitterfeld. He wrote the first specialized manual on playing the trumpet and kettledrums, *Versuch einer Anleitung zur heroisch-musikalischen Trompeter- und Paukerkunst* (Halle, 1795; reprinted, Dresden, 1911); also pieces for 2, 4, 6, and 8 trumpets, and a Concerto for 7 Trumpets and Kettledrums.
BIBLIOGRAPHY: A. Werner, "Johann Ernst Altenburg: Der letzte Vertreter der heroischen Trompeter- und Paukerkunst," *Zeitschrift für Musikwissenschaft* (1932–33).

Altenburg, Michael, German church musician; b. Alach, near Erfurt, May 27, 1584; d. Erfurt, Feb. 12, 1640. He studied theology in Erfurt (1598–1603); in 1610 he moved to Tröchtelborn, where he was a pastor; then went to Gröss-Sommerda in 1621, and finally to Erfurt in 1637, remaining there until his death. He publ. a Wedding Motet in 7 parts; a collection of songs "for Church and Home" in 6, 7, 8, and 9 voices (3 vols.; Erfurt, 1620–21); 16 instrumental *Intraden* in 6 parts (Erfurt, 1620); and numerous church anthems, some of which have been permanently incorporated in the Lutheran service.
BIBLIOGRAPHY: K. Ameln, "Michael Altenburg," *Jahrbuch für Liturgik und Hymnologie* (1963).

Altenburger, Christian, German violinist; b. Heidelberg, Sept. 5, 1957. He began to study violin with his father; at the age of 7 he made his first public appearance; he subsequently enrolled at the Vienna Academy of Music, graduating at 16; then went to the U.S. as a scholarship student at the Juilliard School of Music in N.Y., where he studied with Dorothy DeLay; graduated in 1978. In 1976 he made his professional debut in a recital at the Musikverein in Vienna; then appeared as soloist with the Berlin Phil., Vienna Phil., Concertgebouw Orch. of Amsterdam, London Symph., Chicago Symph., and other orchs.

Altès, Ernest-Eugène, French violinist and conductor, brother of **Joseph-Henri Altès;** b. Paris, March 28, 1830; d. St.-Dyé, near Blois, July 8, 1899. He studied with Habeneck at the Paris Cons., where he won first prize for violin playing in 1848. In 1871 he joined the staff of the Paris Opéra as conductor, retiring in 1887. He composed a symph., chamber music, and an orchestral *Divertissement* on ballet airs by Auber on the occasion of Auber's centennial (1882).

Altès, Joseph-Henri, French flutist, brother of **Ernest-Eugène Altès;** b. Rouen, Jan. 18, 1826; d. Paris, July 24, 1895. He studied at the Paris Cons.; then became a flutist at the Paris Opéra. He was appointed prof. of flute at the Paris Cons. in 1868, holding this post to the end of his life. He published a number of flute pieces.

Altglass, Max, Polish lyric tenor; b. Warsaw, Feb. 16, 1880; d. New York, Feb. 13, 1952. He studied in Berlin; made his operatic debut in Frankfurt in 1913; then went to the U.S.; appeared with the Metropolitan Opera in N.Y. on Nov. 6, 1924, remaining on its roster until 1940. Subsequently he was active as a vocal teacher.

Althouse, Paul, American tenor; b. Reading, Pa., Dec. 2, 1889; d. New York, Feb. 6, 1954. He studied with Oscar Saenger; made his debut as Dimitri in the American premiere of *Boris Godunov* at the Metropolitan Opera on March 19, 1913; continued on its roster until 1920, and joined it again in 1923; sang Wagnerian roles as a Heldentenor at the Metropolitan from 1934 to 1940; was a soloist with Toscanini and the N.Y. Philharmonic in Beethoven's Ninth Symph.; also toured in Europe, Australia, and New Zealand as a concert singer; subsequently was chiefly active as a vocal teacher in N.Y. Among his most prominent students were Eleanor Steber and Richard Tucker.

Altman, Ludwig, German-American organist and composer; b. Breslau, Sept. 2, 1910. He studied at the Univ. of Breslau with Arnold Schmitz and Peter Epstein; in 1929–33 attended courses of Hans Joachim Moser, Arnold Schering, Johannes Wolf, and Friedrich Blume at the State Academy for Sacred Music in Berlin; also took private lessons in organ playing with Arthur Zubke. He remained in Berlin for three years after Hitler's advent to power, serving as organist at the Neue Synagoge, the largest Jewish synagogue still in operation (1933–36). In 1936 he emigrated to America; settled in San Francisco; in 1937 became organist and choral director at Temple Emanu-El; from 1940 to 1973 was organist of the San Francisco Symph. Orch.; from 1948 to 1965 he was also organist of the Bach Festivals in Carmel, Calif.; in 1952 he became Municipal Organist of San Francisco. In 1982 he received a doctorate *honoris causa* from the Univ. of San Francisco. He composed numerous scores of sacred music, among them *Sabbath Music* for Cantor, Choir, and Organ (1963); *The Blessing of Moses* for Baritone Solo,

Choir, and Organ (1977); several psalms for Voices and Organ; and works for organ solo. He furthermore edited Beethoven's organ works, Telemann's *Suite Baroque,* pieces by Ph.E. Bach for Organ Clock, and some organ compositions by Mendelssohn. As a concert organist he appeared in solo recitals in London, Berlin, Hamburg, Munich, Stuttgart, Frankfurt, Bern, Lausanne, and Zürich, as well as in San Francisco, in programs of Baroque and Classical music with a generous inclusion of ultramodern works by contemporary composers, receiving undiluted praise in the press.

Altmann, Wilhelm, German music bibliographer; b. Adelnau, near Posen, April 4, 1862; d. Hildesheim, March 25, 1951. He studied philology and government in Marburg and Berlin, and in 1885 received his Dr.Phil. He served as librarian in Greifswald (1889–1900). In 1900 he was appointed a librarian of the Prussian State Library in Berlin; in 1915 he became director of the music dept., retiring in 1927. In 1906 he founded, in cooperation with Breitkopf & Härtel, the Deutsche Musiksammlung at the Berlin library. From 1945 he lived in Hildesheim. Altmann compiled a number of valuable bibliographical works, among them *Chronik des Berliner Phil. Orchesters* (1902); *Richard Wagners Briefe* (1905; a list of 3,143 letters with brief synopses); *Brahms Briefwechsel* (1908); *Wagners Briefwechsel mit seinen Verlegern* (2 vols., 1911); *Kammermusik-Literatur-Verzeichnis,* a list of chamber music publ. since 1841 (1910; 6 revisions up to 1945); *Max-Reger-Katalog* (1917, 1923); a catalogue of music for viola and viola d'amore (1937) and a catalogue of music for piano, 4- and 6-hands, and for 2 pianos (1943). He also edited Paul Frank's *Tonkünstler-Lexikon* (1926, 1927, 1936, 1949). Furthermore, he publ. bibliographies of books on instruments and made arrangements of classical works.

Altmeyer, Theo, German tenor; b. Eschweiler, March 16, 1931. He was educated in Cologne; in 1956 he joined the Berlin City Opera, remaining on its roster until 1960; then became a member of the Hannover Opera; later appeared at the Stuttgart Opera and the Vienna State Opera; also toured North America. In 1974 he joined the faculty of the Hochschule für Musik in Hannover; continued to appear in opera and concerts.

Altnikol, Johann Christoph, German organist and composer; b. Berna, Silesia, Dec. 1719 (baptized, Jan. 1, 1720); d. Naumburg, July 25, 1759. He was a pupil of Bach during the period of 1744–48; then served as an organist at St. Wenzel's Church in Naumburg. On Jan. 20, 1749, Altnikol married Bach's daughter Elisabeth. In a letter of recommendation Bach described him as "quite skillful in composition." Furthermore, Altnikol acted as Bach's copyist and was instrumental in establishing authentic texts of several of Bach's works.
BIBLIOGRAPHY: H. David and A. Mendel, eds., *The Bach Reader* (N.Y., 1945; revised ed., 1966).

Altschuler, Modest, Russian cellist and conductor; b. Mogilev, Feb. 15, 1873; d. Los Angeles, Sept. 12, 1963. He studied cello at the Warsaw Cons. as a child; then went to Moscow, where he took courses in composition with Arensky and Taneyev and in piano and conducting with Safonov at the Moscow Cons., graduating in 1890. After touring Russia as a cellist, he emigrated to America, and in 1903 organized in N.Y. the Russian Symph. Society. He conducted its first concert on Jan. 7, 1904; for some 12 years the concerts of this organization became an important cultural medium for performances of Russian music in America. One of Altschuler's signal accomplishments was the world premiere of Scriabin's *Le Poème de l'extase,* which he gave in N.Y. on Dec. 10, 1908, in advance of its Russian performance. At the same concert Mischa Elman made his American debut as a concert violinist. Altschuler also conducted the first American performance of Scriabin's *Prométhée,* in N.Y. on March 20, 1915, at which he made an unsuccessful attempt to include the part of *Luce* (a color organ), prescribed by Scriabin in the score. Among other Russian composers whose works Altschuler presented for the first time in America were Rachmaninoff, Liadov, Vasilenko, and Ippolitov-Ivanov. Altschuler eventually retired to Los Angeles; he wrote an autobiography which remains unpublished.

Alva, Luigi, Peruvian tenor; b. Lima, April 10, 1927. He studied voice in Lima; made his operatic debut there in 1950; then continued his vocal studies in Milan. In 1954 he embarked on a European tour; sang at La Scala in Milan, at Edinburgh, at Salzburg, and at the Vienna State Opera; in 1960 he made his debut at Covent Garden in London; on March 6, 1964, he appeared at the Metropolitan Opera as Fenton in Verdi's *Falstaff.* As a leading lyric tenor, he excelled primarily in the Italian repertoire.

Alvarado, Alberto, Mexican composer; b. Durango, Dec. 10, 1864; d. there, June 18, 1939. He wrote nearly 1,000 pieces of various types, ranging from waltzes to symph. works, mostly of a descriptive nature (*El principe de Asturias; Angel mujer; Almas destrozadas; La fiesta encantadora; Suite tropical, Corazón latino*).

Alvarez (real name, **Gourron**), **Albert Raymond,** French tenor; b. Cenon, near Bordeaux, May 16, 1861; d. Nice, Feb. 1, 1933. He started his musical career as the leader of a military band in France; then began his vocal studies in Paris; made his debut at the Paris Opéra in 1892. He made successful appearances at Covent Garden in London; made his American debut at the Metropolitan Opera in N.Y. on Dec. 18, 1899, remaining with the company until 1903, when he returned to Paris to become a singing teacher. His repertoire included about 60 roles.

Alvary, Lorenzo, Hungarian tenor; b. Debrecen, Hungary, Feb. 20, 1909. He studied law at the Univ.

of Budapest and in Geneva; then took voice lessons in Milan and Berlin. In 1937 he made his first appearance at the Vienna State Opera; in 1939 he came to the U.S., where he sang with the San Francisco Opera. He made his Metropolitan Opera debut in N.Y. on Nov. 26, 1942, as Zuñiga in *Carmen;* subsequently became a regular member of the company; also gave solo recitals.

Alvary (real name, **Achenbach**), **Max,** German tenor; b. Düsseldorf, May 3, 1856; d. near Gross-Tabarz, Thuringia, Nov. 7, 1898. His father was a noted painter. Alvary studied with Julius Stockhausen in Frankfurt; later took voice lessons with Lamperti in Milan. He made his debut in Weimar in 1879, and lived in Weimar until 1885. On Nov. 25, 1885, he made his American debut at the Metropolitan Opera in N.Y. as Don José in *Carmen,* singing the role in German; he remained with the Metropolitan until 1889; then made guest appearances in Munich, Hamburg, and Bayreuth. He was particularly noted for his Wagnerian roles.

Alwin, Karl (original name, **Alwin Oskar Pinkus**), German conductor; b. Königsberg, April 15, 1891; d. Mexico City, Oct. 15, 1945. He studied composition in Berlin with Humperdinck and Hugo Kaun; later he dedicated himself mainly to conducting. He was Kapellmeister in Halle (1913), Posen (1914), Düsseldorf (1915–17), and Hamburg (1917–20). From 1920–38 he served as conductor of the Vienna Staatsoper. He left Austria in 1938, after the Anschluss, and went to Mexico, where he conducted opera from 1941 until his death. He was married to the singer **Elisabeth Schumann** (1920–36).

Alwyn, Kenneth, English conductor; b. Croydon, July 28, 1925. He received his musical training at the Royal Academy of Music in London; then conducted ballet at the Sadler's Wells Theatre; was an assistant conductor at the Royal Ballet (1957–61) and from 1961 a conductor at the Western Theatre Ballet; served as its music director in 1967–69. He was also active in broadcasting and films; was a conductor with the BBC Concert Orch. from 1968; in 1969 he became principal conductor of the BBC Northern Ireland Orch.

Alwyn, William, English composer; b. Northampton, Nov. 7, 1905. He studied with McEwen at the Royal Academy of Music in London (1920–23) but failed to graduate; non obstante he was appointed to the faculty of the Royal Academy in 1927, and taught there for 28 years. In 1949 he organized the Composers' Guild of Great Britain. In 1978 he was made a Commander of the Order of the British Empire. As a composer he acquired a knack for writing effective film music; between 1936 and 1963 he wrote background scores for more than 60 films, including *Desert Victory* (1943), *Odd Man Out* (1947), *Fallen Idol* (1949), *The Magic Box* (1951), *The Silent Enemy* (1958), *Swiss Family Robinson* (1960), *The Naked Edge* (1961), *In Search of the Castaways* (1961), and *The Running Man* (1963). He

also composed a great deal of instrumental and choral music; his early works were written in a straightforward neo-Classical manner, but eventually he began experimenting with continental atonality.
WORKS: 2 OPERAS: *Juan, or The Libertine* (1965–71) and *Miss Julie* (1970–73; BBC Radio, July 16, 1977). FOR ORCH.: *5 Orchestral Pieces* (London Proms, 1927); Piano Concerto (1930); Violin Concerto (1938); *Overture; Masquerade* (1940); 3 concerti grossi: No. 1 for Small Orch. (1942); No. 2 for String Orch. (1950); and No. 3, *Tribute to Sir Henry Wood* (1964); Concerto for Oboe, Harp, and Strings (1944); *Scottish Dances* for Small Orch. (1946); *Fanfare for a Joyful Occasion* (1948); 5 symphs.: No. 1 (1949); No. 2 (1953); No. 3 (1956); No. 4 (1959); and No. 5, *Hydriotaphia* (1973), based on the meditation on death by Thomas Browne; *Festival March* (1951); *The Magic Island,* symph. prelude (1952); *Lyra Angelica* for Harp and Strings (1954); *Autumn Legend* for English Horn and Strings (1955); *6 Elizabethan Dances* (1957); *Derby Day,* overture (1960); Sinfonietta for Strings (1970). VOCAL WORKS: Oratorio, *The Marriage of Heaven and Hell,* after Blake (1936); *Slum Song,* 3 songs after MacNeice (1947); *Mirages,* to Alwyn's own poems, for Baritone and Piano (1970); *A Leave-Taking* for Tenor and Piano (1979); *Invocation* for Soprano and Piano (1979); *Seascapes* for Soprano, Treble Recorder, and Piano (1980). CHAMBER MUSIC: *Rhapsody* for Piano Quartet (1939); *Divertimento* for Solo Flute (1939); *Sonata-Impromptu* for Violin and Viola (1939); *3 Winter Poems* for String Quartet (1948); 2 string quartets: No. 1 in D (1955) and No. 2, *Spring Waters* (1976); *Crépuscule* for Harp (1955); String Trio (1962); Clarinet Sonata (1963); *Moto Perpetuo* for Recorders (1970); *Naiades,* Fantasy-Sonata for Flute and Harp (1971); Concerto for Flute and 8 Wind Instruments (1980). FOR PIANO: *Sonata alla Toccata* (1942); *Fantasy-Waltzes* (1955); *12 Preludes* (1957); *Movements* (1963).

Alypios, Greek musical theorist, who flourished in the middle of the 4th century. His *Introduction to Music* is the chief source of specific information regarding ancient Greek notation; it contains a summary of Greek scales in all their transpositions, for both voices and instruments. This treatise was publ. by Meursius (Leyden, 1616); by Meibom in his *Antiquae musicae auctores septem* (Amsterdam, 1652); and reprinted by F. Bellermann in *Die Tonleitern und Musiknoten der Griechen* (Berlin, 1847). A new critical edition is found in Jan's *Musici scriptores graeci* (1895). A graphic explanation of the notation of Alypios is presented by A. Samoiloff in his article "Die Alypiusschen Reihen der altgriechischen Tonbezeichnung," *Archiv für Musikwissenschaft* (1924; pp. 383–400).

Åm, Magnar, Norwegian composer; b. Trondheim, April 9, 1952. He studied composition, organ, and singing at the Bergen Cons. (1968–71); then took a course in advanced composition in Stockholm with Lidholm (1971–72); later joined the music faculty of the Bergen Cons. His music expands classical forms and conventional harmony to conceptual grandiosity.

WORKS: *2 Movements* for String Quartet (1970); *Lydar i løynd (Sounds in Secret),* 7 poems for Piano (1971); *Poem* for 2 Horns and Hardanger Fiddle (1971); *Bøn (Prayer)* for Soprano, Chorus, and String Orch. (1972); *Mot dag (Dawn Is Breaking)* for Chorus and Orch. (1972); *Song* for Brass and Percussion (1974); *Intermezzo* for 3 Woodwinds (1976); *Dance* for Harp, Guitar, and Harpsichord (1977); *Octet* (1977); *Punkt null (Zero),* version A for Soprano, Alto, Chorus, Children's Chorus, and Amateur Orch. (1979); version B for Chorus (1978; revised 1983); version C for Solo Voice, Chorus, Audience, and Organ (1982); *Du, bli her! (You Stay Here!)* for Viola and Cello (1979); *Farewell, Limits* for Piano (1980); *Agamemnon,* Choral Drama for 5 Dancers, 8 Actors, Solo Voice, Women's Chorus, and 2 Clarinets (1981); *Veinje* for Mixed Chorus, Women's Chorus, Men's Chorus, 3 Clarinets, Bass Clarinet, and Cello (1981); *På Glytt...(Ajar...),* Double-bass concerto (1981); *Burfugls Draum (Dream of a Caged Bird),* multimedia score (1982); *Utenkjelege Far (Inconceivable Father)* for Child Soprano, Children's Chorus, Bass Clarinet, Tympani, Double Bass, and Organ (1982); *Min klode, mi sjel (My Planet, My Soul),* a symph. (1982).

Amadei, Filippo, Italian opera composer; b. Reggio, c.1670; d. probably in Rome, c.1729. His claim to attention is that under the name of **Signor Pippo** (diminutive of Filippo) he wrote the first act of the opera *Muzio Scevola,* for which Bononcini wrote the 2nd act and Handel the 3rd, and which was produced at the Royal Academy of Music in London on April 15, 1721. His other works are the opera *Teodosio il Giovane* (Rome, 1711), the oratorio *Il trionfo di Tito* (Rome, 1709), and the cantata *Il pensiero* (Rome, 1709). Amadei's name was erroneously converted into **Filippo Mattei** by Mattheson in his *Critica musica,* and the mistake was carried into reference works and Handel's biographies.

Amaducci, Bruno, Italian conductor; b. Lugano-Viganello, Jan. 5, 1925. He studied at the Ecole Normale de Musique in Paris and at the Verdi Cons. of Music in Milan; then began his conducting career. He appeared with many of the leading opera houses of Europe; also conducted at the Metropolitan Opera and the N.Y. City Opera.

Amalia Catharina, Countess of Erbach; b. Arolsen, Aug. 8, 1640; d. Cuylenburg, the Netherlands, Jan. 4, 1697. She was the daughter of Count von Waldeck; in 1664 she married Count Georg Ludwig von Erbach; of her 16 children only a few survived perilous infancy. She merits attention of musical biographers as one of the few women of the German nobility who actually composed all by herself a number of singable religious anthems.

Amalia Friederike, Princess of Saxony who wrote comedies under the name of **Amalie Heiter;** b. Dresden, Aug. 10, 1794; d. there, Sept. 18, 1870. She composed several light operas (*Una donna, Le tre cinture, Die Siegesfahne, Der Kanonenschuss,* etc.) and church music.

Amani, Nicolai, Russian composer; b. St. Petersburg, April 4, 1872; d. Yalta, Oct. 17, 1904. He studied piano with Anne Essipova and composition with Rimsky-Korsakov and Liadov at the St. Petersburg Cons. (1890–1900); then went to Italy and played a concert of his piano works at Naples (July 29, 1900); in 1901–2 he traveled in Germany. Tuberculosis forced him to stop working; he lived his last 2 years in the Crimea. Amani's music is close in style to Tchaikovsky's, but he wrote only in small forms. He composed a string trio (1900) and a number of harmonious piano pieces and songs, many of them published. A memoir of his short life was publ. in Italian by S. Gentile, *Breve ricordo della vita e opere di Nicolas Amani, musicista russo* (Palermo, 1911).

Amar, Licco, Hungarian violinist; b. Budapest, Dec. 4, 1891; d. Freiburg im Breisgau, July 19, 1959. He studied with Henri Marteau in Berlin and in 1912 joined the Marteau Quartet as 2nd violinist. He subsequently was appointed concertmaster of the Berlin Phil. (1915–20) and at the National Theater in Mannheim (1920–23). In 1921 he organized the Amar Quartet, with Paul Hindemith as the violist, Walter Caspar as 2nd violinist, and Maurits Frank as cellist. In 1933 he was compelled to leave Germany; in 1935 he was engaged as a prof. at the Cons. of Ankara in Turkey. In 1957 he returned to Germany and taught at the Hochschule für Musik in Freiburg im Breisgau.

Amara (real name, **Armaganian**), **Lucine,** American soprano; b. Hartford, Conn., March 1, 1927, of Armenian parentage. She studied violin; began her vocal training in San Francisco after her parents moved West. She made her operatic debut at the Metropolitan Opera in N.Y. on Nov. 6, 1950, as the Heavenly Voice in Verdi's *Don Carlos;* although criticized for the lack of celestial quality in that part, she made progress in her career; in 1954 she sang at the Glyndebourne Festival, and at the Vienna State Opera in 1960. She made a world tour in 1968, which included several appearances in Russia. She also made a cameo appearance in a movie, as the female interest in *The Great Caruso,* opposite Mario Lanza.

Amat, Juan Carlos, Spanish physician and writer on guitar playing; b. Monistrol, 1572; d. there, Feb. 10, 1642. His book *Guitarra Española en cinco ordenes* (Barcelona, 1596) has been reprinted many times.

BIBLIOGRAPHY: E. Pujol, "Significación de Juan Carlos Amat (1572–1642) en la historia de la guitarra," *Anuario Musical,* vol. V (Barcelona, 1950).

Amati, a renowned Italian family of violin makers working at Cremona. (1) **Andrea** (b. between 1500 and 1505; d. before 1580) was the first violin maker of the family. He established the prototype of Italian instruments, with characteristics found in modern violins. His sons were (2) **Antonio** (b. c.1538; d. c.1595), who built violins of varying sizes; and (3) **Girolamo** (b. c.1561; d. Nov. 2, 1630), who continued the tradition established by his father, and worked together with his brother, Antonio. (4) **Nicola,** or **Niccolò** (b. Dec. 3, 1596; d. April 12, 1684) was the most illustrious of the Amati family. He was the son of Girolamo Amati, and signed his labels "Nicolaus Amati Cremonens, Hieronimi filius Antonii nepos." He built some of the "grand Amatis," large violins of powerful tone surpassing in clarity and purity those made by his father and his grandfather, Andrea. In Nicola's workshop both Andrea Guarneri and Antonio Stradivari received their training. (5) **Girolamo** (b. Feb. 26, 1649; d. Feb. 21, 1740), son of Nicola and the last of the family, produced violins inferior to those of his father, his grandfather, and his great-grandfather. In his work he departed from the family tradition in many respects and seemed to be influenced by Stradivari's method without equaling his superb workmanship.

BIBLIOGRAPHY: G. de Picolellis, *Genealogia degli Amati e dei Guarneri* (Florence, 1886); W.L. von Lütgendorff, *Die Geigen- und Lautenmacher vom Mittelalter bis zur Gegenwart* (2 vols., in dictionary form; Frankfurt, 1904; 4th ed., 1922); D.D. Boyden, *The History of Violin Playing from Its Origins to 1761* (London, 1965).

Amato, Pasquale, Italian baritone; b. Naples, March 21, 1878; d. New York, Aug. 12, 1942. He studied at the Cons. of Naples (1896–99); made his debut in *La Traviata* in Naples in 1900. He later sang at leading European opera houses, and in Russia, England, Egypt, and Argentina. He made his American debut at the Metropolitan Opera in *La Traviata* (Nov. 20, 1908) with Sembrich and Caruso; remained a member of the Metropolitan until 1918, then again from 1919–21; eventually settled in N.Y. as a voice teacher.

Ambros, August Wilhelm, eminent musical historiographer; b. Mauth, near Prague, Nov. 17, 1816; d. Vienna, June 28, 1876. He studied law and music; rapidly rose in the legal profession; was appointed public prosecutor in Prague (1850), but continued to devote much time to music; publ. his *Die Grenzen der Musik und Poesie* (Leipzig, 1856; Eng. trans., N.Y., 1893) as a reply to Hanslick's views on esthetics; followed by a brilliant collection of essays under the title *Culturhistorische Bilder aus dem Musikleben der Gegenwart* (Leipzig, 1860); also publ. 2 collections of articles, *Bunte Blätter* (1872–74; 2nd ed. by E. Vogel, 1896). In 1869 Ambros was appointed prof. of music at Prague Univ. and Prague Cons.; in 1872 received a post in the Ministry of Justice in Vienna; he also taught at the Vienna Cons. His major work was the monumental *Geschichte der Musik* commissioned by the publisher Leuckart in 1860. Ambros spent many years of research in the libraries of Munich, Vienna, and several Italian cities for this work, but died before completing the 4th vol., which was edited from his notes by C.F. Becker and G. Nottebohm; a 5th vol. was publ. in 1882 by O. Kade from newly collected materials. W. Langhans wrote a sequel in a more popular style under the title *Die Geschichte der Musik des 17., 18. und 19. Jahrhunderts,* bringing the work up to date (2 vols., 1882–86). A list of names and a general index were issued by W. Bäumker (1882). A 2nd edition of the original 4 vols. (Leipzig, 1880) contains the following: Vol. I, *The Beginnings of Music;* Vol. II, *From the Christian Era to the First Flemish School;* Vol. III, *From the Netherlands Masters to Palestrina;* Vol. IV, *Palestrina, His Contemporaries and Immediate Successors.* Vol. I has been rewritten, not always for the better, by B. Sokolovsky; vol. II was reprinted in a new revision by Riemann (1892); vol. IV by Leichtentritt (1909); Vol. V was revised and enlarged by O. Kade (1911). Ambros was also an excellent practical musician, a proficient pianist, and a composer. He wrote an opera in Czech, *Bretislaw a Jitka;* overtures to *Othello* and *Magico prodigioso;* numerous songs; and religious music.

BIBLIOGRAPHY: Guido Adler, "August Wilhelm Ambros," *Musical Quarterly* (July 1931).

Ambrose (Ambrosius), Christian saint and creator of "Ambrosian Chant"; b. Trier (Trèves), c.333; d. Milan, April 4, 397. He was elected Bishop of Milan in 374; canonized after his death. In 384 he became responsible for the regulation and development of singing in the Western Church by the introduction and cultivation of ritual song (antiphonal and congregational) as practiced at the time in the Eastern Church. His indisputable authorship of several sacred songs has earned him the title of "Father of Christian Hymnology," but his reputed composition of the Ambrosian Chant *Te Deum laudamus* (said to have been sung by St. Ambrose and St. Augustine at the baptism of the latter) is mythical.

BIBLIOGRAPHY: Biraghi, *Inni sinceri e carmi di S. Ambrogio* (Milan, 1862); G.M. Dreves, *Aurelius Ambrosius, der Vater des Kirchengesanges* (Freiburg, 1893); A. Mocquereau, *Notes sur l'influence de l'accent et du cursus tonique latins dans le chant ambrosien* (Paris, 1897); A. Steier, *Untersuchungen über die Echtheit der Hymnen des Ambrosius* (Leipzig, 1903); P. Wagner, *Introduction to the Gregorian Melodies,* part 1, *Origin and Development of the Forms of Liturgical Chant* (London, 1907); E. Garbagnati, *Riviste sull'antica salmodia ambrosiana* (Rome, 1912); A.S. Parodi, *S. Ambrogio e la sua età* (Milan, 1941).

d'Ambrosio, Alfredo, Italian violinist and composer; b. Naples, June 13, 1871; d. Nice, Dec. 29, 1914. He studied composition with Enrico Bossi at the Cons. of Naples; then went to Madrid, where he took violin lessons with Sarasate; later continued his violin study with Willhelmj in London. He then went to Nice, where he was active mainly as a violin teacher. He wrote an opera, *Pia de Tolomei;* a ballet, *Ersilia;* a String Quintet; a String Quartet; and 2 violin concertos (1904, 1913); also numerous concert numbers for violin (*Romanza, Canzonetta,* etc.).

Ambrosius, Hermann, German composer; b. Hamburg, July 25, 1897. He studied at the Univ. of Leipzig; later took private lessons in composition with Pfitzner. In 1925 he joined the faculty of the Leipzig Cons.; eventually settled in Engen. A prolific composer, he wrote 12 symphs. (1920–63); 3 piano concertos (1926–52); 2 cello concertos (1928–38); 2 guitar concertos (1953–62); an orch. suite entitled *Iskusstvo* (the Russian word for "art"), inspired by Russian paintings; and an astonishing number of pieces for accordion; not to mention pieces for the electronic instrument Trautonium. His fecundity was noted in an admiring Festschrift, edited by F. Hirtler, publ. on his 70th birthday.

Ameling, Elly, Dutch soprano; b. Rotterdam, Feb. 8, 1934. She studied in Rotterdam, The Hague, and Paris; then began a most successful career as a concert singer; won great acclaim for her appearances with the Concertgebouw Orch. and the Rotterdam Phil. In 1973 she made her operatic debut at the Netherlands Opera, but continued to concentrate upon the concert literature. As a recitalist, she sang in many of the major European music centers; also in N.Y.

Ameller, André (Charles Gabriel), French composer; b. Arnaville, Jan. 2, 1912. He studied composition with Roger-Ducasse and Gaubert at the Paris Cons.; also violin and double bass. He was taken prisoner of war in Germany in 1940; after the end of the war he returned to France, and in 1953 was appointed director of the Cons. in Dijon. He wrote operas: *La Lance de Fingal* (1947); *Sampiero Corso, Monsieur Personne* (1957); *Cyrnos* (Nancy, April 8, 1962); ballets: *La Coupe de sang* (1950) and *Oiseaux du vieux Paris* (1967); Cello Concerto (1946); *Jeux de table* for Saxophone and Piano (1955); *Terre secrète,* 6 poems for Voice and Orch. (1956); *Airs hétérogènes* for Wind Ensemble (1966); *Hétérodoxes* for 2 Flutes, 2 Trumpets, String Quartet, and String Orch. (1969).

Ameln, Konrad, German musicologist and choral conductor; b. Neuss, Rhineland, July 6, 1899. He studied musicology at the Univ. of Göttingen (1919–21); then took courses with Gurlitt at the Univ. of Freiburg, where he received his Ph.D. in 1924 with the dissertation *Beiträge zur Geschichte der Melodien "Innsbruck, ich muss dich lassen" und "Ach Gott, vom Himmel sieh darein."* From 1926–28 he served as a music consultant to the Central Office for General Librarianship in Leipzig; then taught Protestant church music at the Univ. of Münster (1930–39); subsequently joined the staff of the Landeskirchenmusikschulen in Hannover (1947–48) and the Rhineland (1949–57). He founded the Lüdenscheider Musikvereinigung in 1935, serving as its director until 1973. He founded the Internationale Arbeitsgemeinschaft für Hymnologie in 1959. With C. Mahrenholz and others, he served as editor of the valuable *Handbuch der deutschen evangelischen Kirchenmusik* (Göttingen, 1935—).
WRITINGS: *Leonhard Lechner* (Lüdenscheid, 1957); *The Roots of German Hymnody of the Reformation Era* (St. Louis, 1964).
BIBLIOGRAPHY: G. Schuhmacher, ed., *Traditionen und Reformen in der Kirchenmusik: Festschrift für Konrad Ameln zum 75. Geburtstag* (Kassel, 1974).

Amengual, René, Chilean composer; b. Santiago, Sept. 2, 1911; d. there, Aug. 2, 1954. He studied with Humberto Allende at the National Cons. in Santiago. His compositions are few, and mostly in small forms; their style shows influences of the modern French school. He wrote: Piano Sonatina (1938); *Introduction and Allegro* for 2 Pianos (1939); Piano Concerto (Santiago, June 30, 1942); *El Vaso* for Voice and Chamber Orch. (Santiago, Aug. 25, 1944); etc. His *Burlesca* for Piano is included in the album *Latin American Art Music for the Piano* (N.Y., 1942).

Amfiteatrov, Daniele, Russian composer and conductor; b. St. Petersburg, Oct. 29, 1901. His father was a famous journalist. He studied composition with Wihtol in St. Petersburg and with Křička in Prague; later took lessons with Respighi in Rome. During the season of 1937–38 he was associate conductor of the Minneapolis Symph.; in 1941 he went to Hollywood and wrote film music; he became an American citizen in 1944. He eventually made his home in Venice. He composed *Poema del mare* for Orch. (1925); *American Panorama,* a symph. suite (1934); a Requiem (1960); and some chamber music.

Amfiteatrov, Massimo, cellist, brother of **Daniele Amfiteatrov;** b. Paris, Feb. 27, 1907. He studied in St. Petersburg, in Paris, and at the Cons. in Milan; then was first cellist in the orchs. of the Turin Radio (1936–37) and the Rome Radio (1938–47); subsequently pursued a career as a soloist, touring extensively throughout Europe, the U.S., and the Far East; also played in various chamber music ensembles.

Anievas, Augustin, talented American pianist; b. New York, June 11, 1934. He studied piano with his mother and later with Eduard Steuermann, Olga Samaroff, and Adele Marcus at the Juilliard School of Music. In 1961 he won the Mitropoulos Competition; made numerous appearances in the U.S., Europe, and the Far East; also taught piano at Brooklyn College (from 1974). He has been particularly commended for his performances of Romantic music.

Amiot, Père Jean Joseph Marie, French ecclesiastic; b. Toulon, Feb. 8, 1718; d. Peking, Oct. 9, 1793. He was a Jesuit missionary to China; while there, he translated Li Koang Ti's work on Chinese music: *Commentaire sur le livre classique touchant la* *musique des anciens;* also wrote *Mémoires sur la musique des Chinois, tant anciens que modernes* (vol. VI of *Mémoires concernant l'histoire, les sciences, les arts . . . des Chinois;* Paris, 1780, ed. by Abbé Roussier).

Amirkhanian, Charles, American avant-garde composer of Armenian extraction; b. Fresno, Calif., Jan. 19, 1945. He began experimenting in composition without outside help, probing the potentialities of sound phenomena independently of traditional musical content. His *Composition No. 1* was a solo for an acoustically amplified Ratchet (1965). His *Symphony I* (1965) is scored for 12 Players and 200-odd nonmusical objects, ranging from pitchpipes to pitchforks. In collaboration with the painter Ted Greer, Amirkhanian developed a radical system of notation in which visual images are transduced by performers into sound events. Representative of this intermedia genre are *Micah, the Prophet,* a cantata for 4 Intoning Males, 2 Accordions, 2 Drummers, and 2 Painters (1965); and particularly *Mooga Pook,* a tetraphallic action for Dancers, realistically notated on graph paper, which was produced in San Francisco, Dec. 12, 1967. He also evolved the art of "text-sound composition" for magnetic tape; to this category belong such pieces as *Words* (1969); *Oratora Konkurso Rezulto: Autoro de la Jaro,* an Esperanto recitation (1970); *If In Is* (1971); *Spoffy Nene* (1971); *Just* (1972); *Heavy Aspirations* (1973); *Seatbelt Seatbelt* (1973); MUGIC (1973); *Muchrooms* (1974); *Beemsterboer* (1975); *Mahogany Ballpark* (1976); *Dutiful Ducks* (1977). In 1969 Amirkhanian became "sound sensitivity information director" of radio station KPFA in Berkeley, Calif.; produced "Ode to Gravity," a weekly program of avant-garde music. In 1975 he organized, with the visual artists Carol Law and Jim Petrillo and poet Betsy Davids, a group called, with a deliberate letter substitution, Mugicians Union. In 1977 he was appointed to the faculty of the interdisciplinary creative arts dept. of San Francisco State Univ.

Amirov, Fikret Dzhamil, Azerbaijani composer; b. Kirovabad, Nov. 22, 1922; d. Baku, Feb. 20, 1984. He received his early musical instruction from his father, who was a singer and guitarist; he then studied composition at the Cons. of Azerbaijan, graduating in 1948. His compositions reflect the melorhythmic patterns of popular Azerbaijani music, marked by characteristic oriental inflections, while retaining a classical format and development, particularly in variation form. Among his works are a symph. poem, *To the Memory of the Heroes of the Great National War* (1944); Double Concerto for Violin, Piano, and Orch. (1948); *The Pledge of the Korean Guerrilla Fighter* for Voice and Orch. (1951); several symph. suites based on the national modes ("mugamas"), of which *Shur* is the best known; and the opera *Sevil* (Baku, Dec. 25, 1953). He also wrote a piano concerto on Arab themes (1957; in collaboration with Nazirova). In 1959 he visited the U.S. as a member of the Soviet delegation of composers under the auspices of the State Dept.

BIBLIOGRAPHY: D. Danilov, *Fikret Amirov* (Moscow, 1958).

Ammann, Benno, Swiss composer and conductor; b. Gersau, June 14, 1904. He studied composition with Karg-Elert at the Leipzig Cons.; later went to Paris, where he took private lessons with Honegger, Milhaud, and Albert Roussel. Returning to Switzerland, he served as chorus leader in Basel (1936–39); then was active as theater conductor at the Teatro Real in Rome (1939–42). He was also connected with various international festivals of modern music. His works include a mass, *Defensor pacis* (Rome, 1947); *Vision pastorale* for Orch. (1954); Wind Quintet (1956); a cantata, *Flucht aus der Tiefe,* for Baritone, Chorus, and a Battery of Percussion (1961); *Successions* for Flute Solo (1966); *Excursions* for Bass Clarinet and 2 Guitars; and numerous pieces for miscellaneous instruments, such as *Dialogues et Décisions* for 2 Guitars; *Composition en mouvement* for Double Bass Solo; *Remove* for Oboe Solo; etc.

Ammerbach, Elias Nikolaus, German organist; b. Naumburg, c.1530; d. Leipzig, Jan. (buried; Jan. 29) 1597. On Jan. 1, 1561, he became organist of the Thomaskirche in Leipzig, remaining at that post until 1595. He publ. *Orgel oder Instrument Tabulatur* (Leipzig, 1571; reprinted 1583), a work of importance detailing the practice of tuning, the fingering of keyboard instruments, execution of ornaments, etc. (described by Becker in *Die Hausmusik in Deutschland,* Leipzig, 1840); and *Ein neu künstlich Tabulaturbuch* (1575; 2nd ed., 1582). He further publ. several volumes of keyboard music.

Ammon, Blasius, contrapuntist; b. Hall, Tirol, 1558; d. Vienna, June 1590. He was a choirboy in the service of Archduke Ferdinand of Austria, who sent him to Venice for his musical education. In 1578 he returned to Innsbruck and joined the Franciscan order. In 1587 he went to the Franciscan monastery in Vienna, where he entered the priesthood. He printed a book of 5-part introits (Vienna, 1582); a book of 4-part masses (Vienna, 1588); 2 books of 4-, 5-, and 6-part motets (Munich, 1590). A number of works in MS are in the libraries of Munich and Vienna. A vol. containing his church music was publ. by Caecilianus Huigens in Denkmäler der Tonkunst in Österreich, 73 (38.i).

Ammons, Albert, black American jazz pianist; b. Chicago, 1907; d. there, Dec. 2, 1949. After playing in various Chicago clubs, he went to N.Y. in 1938, where he worked as a duo-pianist with Pete Johnson; eventually returned to Chicago. He excelled in the boogie-woogie style.

Amner, John, English organist and composer; b. Ely (baptized, Aug. 24), 1579; d. there (buried, July 28), 1641. He studied music in Oxford; in 1610 he became "informator choristarum" at Ely Cathedral; subsequently was ordained to the diaconate;

later was made "vicarius" (minor canon), and thus received remuneration as both organist and prebendary; obtained his B.Mus. from Cambridge in 1640. He publ. *Sacred Hymnes of 3. 4. 5 and 6 parts for Voyces and Vyols* (London, 1615).

Amon, Johann (Andreas), German musician; b. Bamberg, 1763; d. Wallerstein, Bavaria, March 29, 1825. He studied horn with Giovanni Punto and traveled with him on tours in France and Germany. From 1789–1817 he was music director at Heilbronn; then became court conductor to the Prince of Öttingen-Wallerstein. He wrote 2 operas, 3 Requiems (one of which he intended for performance at his funeral), and many pieces of chamber music.

Amorevoli, Angelo (Maria), Italian tenor; b. Venice, Sept. 16, 1716; d. Dresden, Nov. 15, 1798. He began his career in Rome in 1730; sang in Venice (1730), in Milan (1731–35), in Naples (1736–40), and in Florence (1741); he then went to London, where he was on the staff of the King's Theatre (1741–43). In 1745 he settled in Dresden, where he served as a chamber and church singer at the court.

Amoyal, Pierre, French violinist; b. Paris, June 22, 1949. He studied at the Paris Cons.; won the Ginette Neveu prize in 1963, the Paganini prize in 1964, and the Enesco prize in 1970; took sporadic lessons with Jascha Heifetz in Los Angeles (1966–71). He subsequently played concertos with the Orchestre de Paris, the BBC Symph. of London, the Hallé Orch. of Manchester, and the Berlin Phil.; also toured in Russia, Japan, and South Africa. In the U.S. he was a soloist with the Boston Symph., the Cleveland Orch., the Detroit Symph., and the Houston Symph. In 1977 he was appointed to the faculty of the Paris Cons.

Amram, David, American composer; b. Philadelphia, Nov. 17, 1930, of Jewish parents. He played a bugle in school; then studied trumpet at the Music Settlement School, and also played piano. When he was 12, the family moved to Washington, D.C.; soon he played trumpet in school bands; later switched to the French horn. In 1948 he enrolled at the Oberlin (Ohio) College Cons., and continued his practicing on the French horn; later shifted to George Washington Univ., graduating in 1952. He then enlisted in the U.S. Army, and played the French horn in the Seventh Army Symph. Orch., which was stationed in Germany. In 1955 he returned to the U.S. and studied composition with Vittorio Giannini at the Manhattan School of Music. He also studied privately with Charles Mills. Very soon he found his way into the inviting world of public theater. He wrote incidental music for off-Broadway productions of Shakespeare's plays, and finally landed lucrative jobs in the films; he composed sound tracks for such hits as *Splendor in the Grass* (1961), *The Manchurian Candidate* (1962), and *The Arrangement* (1969). He also wrote jazz music, sacred services for the Park Avenue Synagogue in N.Y., and straight concert pieces, braving somehow the danger of cross-pollination of these quaquaversal activities. On May 8, 1960, he gave an evening of his works in N.Y., among them a *Shakespearean Concerto,* and presented another pan-Amram concert in N.Y. on Feb. 20, 1962. There followed a cornucopia of cantatas, and in 1965, a radio opera, *The Final Ingredient.* In 1966–67 he received an exclusive appointment as composer-in-residence of the N.Y. Phil. As a sign of public recognition of his music, the National Education Television network broadcast on April 17, 1969, a documentary, proudly entitled "The World of David Amram." Amram was also the recipient of several grants by the State Dept. and U.S. Information Agency for travel abroad. He visited some 25 countries; he also joined a jazz group to play in Cuba in 1977. He eagerly absorbed the varicolored ethnic materials, which he used, in metamorphosis, in some of his own compositions. In 1979 he received an honorary doctorate from Moravian College, Bethlehem, Pa.

WORKS: FOR THE STAGE AND SCREEN: Opera, *The Final Ingredient,* to a story set in a Nazi concentration camp (ABC-TV network, April 11, 1965, composer conducting); *Twelfth Night,* after Shakespeare (Lake George Opera Festival, Aug. 1, 1968); incidental music for 28 off-Broadway productions. FOR FILMS: *The Young Savages* (1961); *Splendor in the Grass* (1961); *The Manchurian Candidate* (1962); *The Arrangement* (1969). FOR ORCH.: *Autobiography for Strings* (1959); *Shakespearean Concerto* for Oboe, 2 Horns, and Strings (N.Y., May 8, 1960); *King Lear Variations* for Woodwinds, Brass, Percussion, and Piano (N.Y. Philharmonic, March 23, 1967); *Elegy* for Violin and Orch. (1970); Horn Concerto (1968); Concerto for Jazz Quintet and Orch. (N.Y., Jan. 10, 1971); Bassoon Concerto (Washington, D.C., March 21, 1972); *The Trail of Beauty* for Mezzo-soprano, Oboe, and Orch. (Philadelphia, March 4, 1977); Violin Concerto (1980). CHAMBER MUSIC: Trio for Saxophone, Horn, and Bassoon (1958); *Overture and Allegro* for Solo Flute (1959); Violin Sonata (1960); *Three Songs for Marlboro* for Horn and Cello (1961); *Discussion* for Flute, Cello, Piano, and Percussion (1961); String Quartet (1961); *Dirge and Variations* for Piano Trio (1962); *The Wind and the Rain* for Viola and Piano (1963); Sonata for Solo Violin (1964); *Three Dances* for Oboe and Strings (1966); Wind Quintet (1968); *Triptych* for Solo Viola (1969); *Native American Portraits* for Violin, Piano, and Percussion (1976); *Zohar* for Flute Solo (1978). VOCAL WORKS: *Sacred Service for Sabbath Eve* for Tenor, Chorus, and Organ (1961); *The American Bell,* cantata (Philadelphia, July 4, 1962); *A Year in Our Land,* cantata (N.Y., May 13, 1964); *Let Us Remember,* cantata (San Francisco, Nov. 15, 1965); *By the Rivers of Babylon* for Soprano and Female Choir (1966); *Songs from Shakespeare* for Voice and Piano (1968); *Three Songs for America* for Baritone and String Quintet (1969). He also wrote a Piano Sonata and minor piano pieces. He publ. an autobiography, *Vibrations: The Adventures and Musical Times of David Amram* (N.Y., 1968).

BIBLIOGRAPHY: David Ewen, *American Composers* (N.Y., 1982).

Amy, Gilbert, French composer and conductor; b. Paris, Aug. 29, 1936. He studied composition with Darius Milhaud and Olivier Messiaen at the Paris Cons., and counterpoint and fugue with Plé-Caussade. In 1962 he began making appearances as a conductor; served as director of Domaine Musical from 1967 to 1973. In his music he followed the Baroque precepts of antiphony and concertante, combining these forms with serialist procedures.

WORKS: *Œil de fumée* for Soprano and Piano (1955); *Variations* for 4 Instruments (1956); *Cantate brève* to words by García Lorca (1957); *Mouvements* for 17 Instruments (1958); *Antiphonies* for 2 Orchs. (1963); *Triade* for Orch. (1964); *Trajectoires* for Violin and Orch. (1966); *Cycle* for 6 Percussion Players (1967); *Chant* for Orch. (Donaueschingen, Oct. 20, 1968); *Relais* for 5 Brass Instruments (1969); *Refrains* for Orch. (1972); *D'un espace déployé* for Solo Soprano, 2 Pianos, and 2 Orchs. (Paris, March 10, 1973); *Sonata pian' e forte* for 2 Voices and 12 Players (1974); *7 Sites* for 14 Players (1975).

Anacker, August Ferdinand, German cantor and composer; b. Freiberg, Saxony, Oct. 17, 1790; d. there, Aug. 21, 1854. He studied at the Univ. of Leipzig; returned to Freiberg in 1821 and served as cantor at the Cathedral; in 1823 he founded the Singakademie of Freiberg. He was closely acquainted with Beethoven, Mendelssohn, and Wagner. His oratorio, *Bergmannsgruss* (1831–32), was widely performed in his lifetime; but his music sank irretrievably into the bottomless pit of oblivion after his death.

Ančerl, Karel, Czech conductor; b. Tučapy, April 11, 1908; d. Toronto, Canada, July 3, 1973. He studied at the Prague Cons., taking courses in composition with Alois Hába and Křička and percussion playing with Šourek; at the same time he practiced conducting. He devoted himself mainly to the modern repertoire, and conducted several concerts at the festivals of the International Society for Contemporary Music. He held the post of music director of the Prague Radio; but as a Jew, was removed from this position when Czechoslovakia was occupied by the Nazis in 1939. In 1942 he was deported to the Jewish ghetto camp in Theresienstadt, and was later transported to Auschwitz; his entire family was put to death there but, providentially, he was spared. After the war he resumed his activities as a conductor; was at the Prague Opera from 1945–47; then with the Radio Orch. (1947–50), and from 1950–68 was conductor of the Czech Phil., with which he traveled through Europe, Canada, the U.S., Australia, and Japan. In 1970 he was appointed conductor of the Toronto Symph. Orch., and lived in Toronto until his death. He was distinguished mainly for his congenial interpretation of music by Czech composers; in appreciation of his service he was named a People's Artist in 1966.

BIBLIOGRAPHY: K. Šrom, *Karel Ančerl* (Prague, 1968).

Anchieta, Juan de, Spanish composer; b. probably in Urrestilla, near Azpeitia, 1462; d. Azpeitia, July 30, 1523. In 1489 he entered the service of Queen Isabella as a singer in the court chapel; upon the Queen's death in 1504, he entered the service of her daughter, Joanna, consort of Philip the Fair; he accompanied them to Flanders and England. In addition to his duties as Joanna's chaplain and singer, he was made a benefice-holder (in absentia) at Villarino in 1499; was also named rector of the parish church of S. Sebastian de Soreasu in Azpeitia in 1500; became Abbot of Arbos in 1518. He was pensioned by the court of Charles V in 1519. Anchieta composed sacred and secular vocal works, most of them for large choirs; several of these were publ. in modern editions in *Monumentos de la música española*, vols. I (1941), V (1947), and X (1951).

BIBLIOGRAPHY: A. Cohen, *The Vocal Polyphonic Style of Juan de Anchieta* (Diss., N.Y. Univ., 1953); R. Stevenson, *Spanish Music in the Age of Columbus* (The Hague, 1960).

Ancina, Giovanni Giovenale, Italian composer of sacred music; b. Fossano, Oct. 19, 1545; d. Saluzzo, Aug. 31, 1604. He was a student of medicine and theology, but became deeply interested in sacred services in music after he met Filippo Neri, the creator of the oratorio. On Oct. 1, 1580, he joined the Congregazione dei Preti dell'Oratorio, founded by Neri. He began writing music for the church; publ. *Tempio armonico della beata Vergine* (Rome, 1599).

BIBLIOGRAPHY: P.I. Bacci, *Vita del servo di Dio Giovenale Ancina* (Rome, 1671); Pietro Damilano, *G.G. Ancina e la lauda cinquecentesca* (Milan, 1953).

Ancona, Mario, Italian baritone; b. Livorno, Feb. 28, 1860; d. Florence, Feb. 22, 1931. He studied jurisprudence and was briefly engaged in a diplomatic career; then began to study voice; made his professional debut in Trieste in 1889. On May 19, 1893, he sang the part of Tonio in *Pagliacci* at Covent Garden, London; made regular appearances there during the period 1895–1905. He made his debut as Tonio at the Metropolitan Opera in N.Y. on Dec. 11, 1893, and remained on the roster of the Metropolitan until 1897; from 1906 to 1908 he was a member of the Manhattan Opera House; was also on the roster of the Chicago Opera (1915–16). He appeared as a guest artist in Spain, Portugal, Argentina, and Russia. After retiring from the stage he was active as a vocal teacher in Florence.

Ancot, a family of musicians at Bruges. (1) **Jean,** *père* (b. Bruges, Oct. 22, 1779; d. there, July 12, 1848), violin virtuoso, pianist, and composer. He studied (1799–1804) in Paris under Baillot, Kreutzer, and Catel; then settled in Bruges as a teacher; publ. 4 violin concertos, overtures, marches, sacred music, etc.; most of his works are still in MS. He taught his sons, Jean and Louis. (2) **Jean,** *fils* (b. Bruges, July 6, 1799; d. Boulogne, June 5, 1829). He finished his education at the Paris Cons. under Pradher and Berton; an accomplished pianist, he was successful in London

(1823–25); eventually settled in Boulogne. Considering that he died short of his 30th birthday, he was an astonishingly prolific composer (225 works, among them a piano concerto, sonatas, études, 4-hand fantasias, and violin concertos). (3) **Louis** (b. Bruges, June 3, 1803; d. there, 1836). For a time, he was pianist to the Duke of Sussex in London; made extended continental tours, taught at Boulogne and Tours, and finally returned to Bruges. He wrote piano music in salon style.

Anda, Géza, eminent Hungarian pianist; b. Budapest, Nov. 19, 1921; d. Zürich, June 13, 1976. He studied with Dohnányi at the Royal Academy of Music in Budapest; won the Liszt Prize. During World War II he went to Switzerland; became a Swiss citizen in 1955. He made his American debut with the Philadelphia Orch. on Oct. 21, 1955. He was an ardent champion of the music of Béla Bartók, and performed all of Bartók's 3 piano concertos numerous times; he also was a congenial interpreter of the music of Brahms. Later on he made a specialty of Mozart, acting both as soloist and conductor in all of Mozart's piano concertos. He publ. a vol. of Mozart cadenzas (Berlin and Wiesbaden, 1973). Apart from his concerts he also held seminars in Switzerland.

Anderberg, Carl-Olof, Swedish composer; b. Stockholm, March 13, 1914; d. Malmö, Jan. 4, 1972. He studied composition with Broman in Stockholm, piano in Copenhagen, and conducting with Weingartner in Salzburg. His early compositions are permeated with a romantic "Scandinavian" idiom; among them was an opera, *Hilde.* In the 1950s he joined various avant-garde groups active in Sweden. These associations led to a radical change in his style of composition toward advanced forms of musical expression.
WORKS: *Music I* and *II* for Chamber Orch. (1947, 1948); Symph. (1948); *Cyclus Stellarum I* and *II* for Strings (1949, 1957); *Episode,* chamber opera (1952); 3 piano sonatas (1950, 1952, 1956); *3 estampies* for Piano, Percussion, and Violins (1953); 2 string quartets (1955, 1957); Cello Sonata (1956); *4 Serious Caprices* for Clarinet and Piano (1956); *Fyra legeringar (4 Alloys)* for Soprano and 5 Instruments (1958); Duo I for Flute and Piano (1958); *Teater,* suite for Orch. (1958); *Höstens Hökar,* metamorphoses for Narrator and 5 Instruments (1959); *Triad* for Solo Violin (1959); *Variationer över Variationer* for Clarinet, Bassoon, Violin, Cello, and Harp (1959); *Transfers* for Symph. Groups (1960); *Di Mi Se Mai* for Soprano, Narrator, and Orch. (1963); *Hexafoni* for 6 Instruments (1963); *Execution I* for Clarinet, Piano, and Percussion (1963); *Strändernas svall (The Surge of the Seaside),* cantata for Soprano, Baritone, Narrator, and Instrumental Ensemble (1963–64); *Acroama I* and *II* for Orch. (1965–66); Duo II and III for Violin and Piano (1968); *Klangskap I (Soundscape)* for Piano (1968); Piano Concerto (Malmö, March 18, 1969); *Concerto for a Ballet* for Piano, Winds, Percussion, and Double Basses (1969–70; Swedish Radio perf., March 4, 1972); *Orkesterspel I* and *II* (*Orchestral Game;* 1969–70); *Music* for

Piano, Winds, and Tape (1970); *Dubbelspel (Double Play)* for Soprano, Baritone, Clarinet, Cello, Piano, and Tape (1971); piano pieces, songs.

Anders, Peter, German tenor; b. Essen, July 1, 1908; d. Hamburg, Sept. 10, 1954 (as a result of injuries sustained in an automobile accident). He studied at the Berlin Hochschule für Musik; began his professional appearances as an opera singer in 1932; from 1939 to 1948 was a member of the Berlin Staatsoper. On Nov. 29, 1936, he appeared with the Hamburg State Opera in the role of Tamino in Mozart's opera *Die Zauberflöte;* another appearance with the Hamburg Opera took place on Dec. 19, 1937. Anders was a distinguished interpreter of Wagnerian roles as well.

Andersen, (Carl) Joachim, Danish flute player and composer, son and pupil of the flutist **Christian Joachim Andersen;** b. Copenhagen, April 29, 1847; d. there, May 7, 1909. From 1869–77, he was a member of the Royal Orch.; in 1881 he was in Berlin, where he was co-founder and, for 10 years, first flutist and assistant conductor of the Phil. Orch.; from 1893, was conductor of the Palace Orch. at Copenhagen. He wrote solo works for Flute; also pieces with Orch.: *Hungarian Fantasia; Ballade; Dance of the Sylphs;* 24 easy and 24 difficult études, etc. His brother, **Vigo** (b. Copenhagen, April 21, 1852; d. by suicide in Chicago, Jan. 28, 1895), was an eminent flute player; he was first flutist in the Thomas Orch. in Chicago.

Andersen, Karl August, Norwegian composer and cellist; b. Oslo, Sept. 29, 1903; d. there, Aug. 15, 1970. He studied cello and composition in Oslo and later cello with Hugo Becker in Berlin (1921–22); then became a cellist in the Oslo Phil. Orch. (1924). From 1946–62 he was a member of the governing board of the Society of Norwegian Composers.
WORKS: 3 string quartets (No. 1, 1934; No. 3, 1961–67); Symph. for Chamber Orch. (1936); Suite for Orch. (1937); Trio for Flute, Clarinet, and Cello (1939); *Vårdagen* for Male Chorus (1942); *Allegro festivo e solenne Norwegese (Festforspill)* for Orch. (1950); *Variations over Theme and Rhythm* for Wind Quintet (1966).

Andersen, Karsten, Norwegian conductor; b. Oslo, Feb. 16, 1920. He began his career as a violinist. In 1945 he was named music director in Stavanger. In 1964 he became music director of the Bergen Harmonien Society, leading the concerts of the Bergen Symph. Orch. He was a founder of the noted Bergen Music Festival. In 1973 he also became chief conductor of the Iceland Symph. Orch. in Reykjavik.

Anderson, Arthur, American bass; b. Harvey, Ill., Aug. 16, 1898. He went to Italy for vocal study, and made his operatic debut in Malta. Returning to America, he appeared at the Metropolitan Opera in N.Y. as Donner in *Das Rheingold* (Feb. 26, 1932); he continued on the roster of the Metropolitan Opera until 1935; then was active as a vocal teacher.

Anderson, Beth, inventive American composer, performance artist, and astrologer; b. Lexington, Ky., Jan. 3, 1950. She moved to California and joined a group of the extreme avant-garde musicians at various places and in various points in time. She took advice in composition from John Cage, Robert Ashley, Larry Austin, Terry Riley, Helen Lipscomb, Richard Swift, Kenneth Wright, John B. Chance, and Nathan Rubin, but went on a diagonal tangent in her own original practices. Her resources were manifold, passing through the entire spectrum of sound, sight, and motion in specially designed multimedia productions. She espoused the method of composition known as text-sound as propounded by Charles Amirkhanian, which allows total freedom of improvisation while observing a minimum of controlling serialism of sounds, rhythms, and harmonic combinations. As a professional astrologer, she made an earnest attempt to connect ideas of harmony with cosmic consciousness, extrasensory perception, and numerology. She also applied the techniques of collage and cut-ups. An ardent feminist, she took part in organizing a women's group of composers under the suggestive name Hysteresis ("of the womb"); she also became co-editor of *Ear Magazine,* which explored the nature of sound from the psychological and surreal standpoints. She publ. poetry as well. Among her ascertainable works are an opera, *Queen Christina,* produced at Mills College in Oakland, Calif., on Dec. 1, 1973; an oratorio, *Joan,* performed at the Cabrillo Festival on Aug. 22, 1974; numerous multimedia works and ensembles with electronic sound. She also contributed to sculpture music and other spatial forms of video and audio arts.

Anderson, Emily, English musicologist; b. Galway, Ireland, March 17, 1891; d. London, Oct. 26, 1962. She went to Germany for her education, and attended the univs. of Berlin and Marburg. Returning to England, she was employed in the British Foreign Office while pursuing her interest in music history and biography as an avocation. Of value are her translations of the correspondence of Mozart and Beethoven: *Letters of Mozart and His Family* (3 vols., London, 1938; 2nd ed., revised by A. Hyatt King and M. Carolan, 1966); *The Letters of Beethoven* (3 vols., London, 1961).

Anderson, Laurie, seeded American composer of avant-garde persuasion; b. Chicago, June 5, 1947. Renouncing the tradition of conventional modernism, she set for herself a goal of uniting all arts as they were in ancient music, but co-opted the various techniques of new arts, from topical pop to electronics, playbacking with herself on magnetic tape and projecting images on a screen. In her performing techniques she combined speech, song, and facial mesmerization of the audience. The generic category of these exertions became known as "performance art." She uses a variety of instruments in her stage productions, including a homemade violin activated by a luminous bow made of electronic tape. She also changed her voice electronically, producing weird otherworldly effects. Her satirical piece *New York Social Life* was scored for voices and tamboura; another piece, *Time to Go,* for guitar, violin, and organ, repeated exhortations of a museum guard to visitors to leave at the closing time. Amazingly enough, her arcane art found enthusiastic response among young audiences commonly addicted to less subtle exhibitions, and she became a popular entertainer during her tours in the U.S. and in Europe. Her song *O, Superman* became a hit. In 1976 she gave a successful exhibition of her psychomusicurgy at the Berlin Akademie der Kunst. In 1983 she produced her multimedia epic, *United States,* on the themes of transportation, politics, money, and love.

Anderson, Leroy, American composer of light instrumental music; b. Cambridge, Mass., June 29, 1908; d. Woodbury, Conn., May 18, 1975. He received his first musical training from his mother, an organist, and studied double bass with Gaston Dufresne in Boston. He then took courses in theory of composition with Walter Spalding, Edward Ballantine, and Walter Piston at Harvard Univ., obtaining his B.A. magna cum laude in 1929 and his M.A. in 1930. From 1932–35 he was conductor of the Harvard Univ. Band. In 1935 he became an arranger for the Boston Pops. In 1942 he entered the U.S. Army and was stationed in Iceland. A linguist, he acted as translator, particularly in Scandinavian languages (Anderson was of Swedish extraction). In 1939 he wrote a piece for String Orch. called *Jazz Pizzicato,* which was played at the Boston Pops and became an immediate hit. This was followed by a number of similar inventive instrumental novelties, among them *Jazz Legato, The Syncopated Clock* (1950), *Fiddle Faddle, Sleigh Ride* (1950), *Serenata, A Trumpeter's Lullaby, China Doll, A Bugler's Holiday, Blue Tango* (his greatest success, 1952), *The Typewriter.* He also wrote a musical, *Goldilocks* (N.Y., Oct. 11, 1958).

Anderson (née **Philpot**), **Lucy,** English pianist; b. Bath, Dec. 12, 1797; d. London, Dec. 24, 1878. Her father, John Philpot, was a prof. of music; she settled in London; was the first woman to be engaged as piano soloist by the Phil. Society. She married George Frederick Anderson in 1820; he became Master of the Queen's Musick (1848–70); Lucy Anderson taught piano to Queen Victoria and her children.

Anderson, Marian, celebrated black American contralto; b. South Philadelphia, Feb. 17, 1902, into a poor family; her father sold ice and coal; her mother helped eke out the family income by taking in laundry. Marian Anderson sang in a choir at the Union Baptist Church in South Philadelphia. Funds were raised for her to study voice with Giuseppe Boghetti; in 1923 she won first prize at a singing contest in Philadelphia, and in 1925 she received first prize at a contest held by the N.Y. Phil. at Lewisohn Stadium, appearing as a soloist there on Aug. 27, 1925. In 1929 she gave a recital at Carnegie Hall. In 1930 she made her first European appearance in London; she soon extended her European tours to include Sweden, Norway, and Finland; she also gave successful concerts in Paris, Vienna, Brussels, Geneva, and Salzburg; also made a tour of Russia. Her singing of Negro spirituals produced a sensation wherever she sang in Europe. Returning to the U.S., she gave a concert in Town Hall, N.Y. (Nov. 30, 1935), and in Carnegie Hall (Jan. 30, 1936). In Feb. 1939, she became a center of national attention when the Daughters of the American Revolution refused to let her appear at Constitution Hall in Washington, D.C., citing the organization's rules of racial segregation. The resulting publicity only contributed to her success; Eleanor Roosevelt sent her resignation to the DAR, and the Secretary of the Interior, Harold L. Ickes, invited Marian Anderson to sing at the Lincoln Memorial on Easter Sunday, April 9, 1939: a huge audience attended; the concert was broadcast. She was given the prestigious Spingarn Award for the "highest and noblest achievement by an American Negro" during the year. Another landmark in the history of freedom was established when she sang the role of Ulrica in *Un ballo in maschera* at the Metropolitan Opera on Jan. 7, 1955, breaking the unspoken prohibition against black artists' singing there. In 1957 and 1958 she was designated by President Eisenhower to be a delegate to the General Assembly of the United Nations. Honors piled upon honors in her life. She was awarded honorary degrees from Princeton Univ. and N.Y. Univ., and received medals from the governments of Sweden, Finland, Japan, and other countries. President Johnson awarded her the American Freedom Medal. She sang at the inaugural ball for President Kennedy in 1961. On the occasion of her 75th birthday, a resolution was passed by the U.S. Congress to strike a gold medal in her honor. She publ. her autobiography, *My Lord, What a Morning* (N.Y., 1956).

BIBLIOGRAPHY: Kosti Vehanen, *Marian Anderson* (N.Y., 1941).

Anderson, Ruth, American composer of the avant-garde; b. Kalispell, Mont., March 21, 1928. She studied flute with Jean-Pierre Rampal; received her M.A. from the Univ. of Washington in Seattle; did postgraduate work at Columbia Univ. and Princeton; also took private lessons with Darius Milhaud; was an associate prof. at Hunter College in N.Y., where she designed and installed the Hunter College Electronic Music Studio in 1970; also organized meditation workshops and taught listening techniques; made use of human and artificial electronic sound for healing ailments. Her most successful composition in these fields is *Points* (1974) for multichannel electronic sound built entirely on sine waves. She utilizes the collage technique in her work *SUM* (State of the Union Message), incorporating television commercials in a presidential address.

Anderson, Thomas, English organist; b. Birmingham, April 15, 1836; d. there, Sept. 18, 1903. He served as an organist in churches in Birmingham; was also a music critic there. He composed several cantatas: *The Song of Deborah and Barak; The Wise and Foolish Virgins; The Wreck of the Hesperus; John Gilpin; The 3 Jovial Huntsmen; The Norman Baron; Yuletide; English Requiem;* and instrumental music.

Anderson, T.J. (Thomas Jefferson), black American composer; b. Coatesville, Pa., Aug. 17, 1928, a son of schoolteachers. He attended classes in Washington, D.C., and Cincinnati; played in a school orch.; then entered West Virginia State College; received his bachelor of music degree at Pa. State Univ.; then taught music at High Point, N.C. (1951–54). In 1954 he attended composition classes with Scott Huston at the Cincinnati Cons. of Music and with Philip Bezanson and Richard Hervig at the Univ. of Iowa in Iowa City, obtaining his Ph.D. in 1958. In 1964 he took a summer course in composition with Darius Milhaud at Aspen, Colorado. From 1958 to 1963 he was prof. of music at Langston Univ., Oklahoma; from 1963 to 1969 he taught at the Tennessee State Univ., Nashville; and from 1968 to 1971 he was composer-in-residence with the Atlanta Symph. Orch.; then taught at Morehouse College in Atlanta (1971–72), and in 1972 was appointed chairman of the Tufts Univ. music dept. in Medford, Mass., serving until 1980; and continued to teach there. He served as chairman of the Advisory Board of the Black Music Center at the Univ. of Indiana (1969–71). In 1976 he went to Brazil under the aegis of the Office of Cultural Relations of the U.S. Dept. of State. He played a major role in the revival of interest in the music of Scott Joplin, and arranged Joplin's opera *Treemonisha* for its production in Atlanta (Jan. 28, 1972). His own style of composition is audaciously modern, while preserving a deeply felt lyricism in melodic patterns; his harmonies are taut and intense without abandoning the basic tonal frame; his contrapuntal usages suggest folklike ensembles, but he freely varies his techniques according to the character of each particular piece. His resources are quaquaversal, and he excludes none in his creative process.

WORKS: FOR THE STAGE: Opera, *Soldier Boy, Soldier,* to a story of a Vietnam veteran (Bloomington, Oct. 23, 1982); operetta, *The Shell Fairy* (1977). FOR ORCH.: *Pyknon* (1958); *Introduction and Allegro* (1959); *New Dances* (1960); *Classical Symphony* (1961); *Symphony in Three Movements,* in memory of John F. Kennedy (1964; Oklahoma City, April 10, 1964); *Squares* (Chickasha, Oklahoma, Feb. 25, 1966); *Rotations* for Symphonic Band (1967); Chamber Symph. (Nashville, Nov. 24, 1969); *Transitions* for Chamber Orch. (Tanglewood Festival, Berkshire Music Center, Aug. 2, 1971); *Intervals,* 7 orch. sets (1970–71). FOR VOICES AND ORCH.: *Personals,* cantata in commemoration of the centennial of Fisk Univ. (Nashville, April 28, 1966); *Beyond Silence* for Tenor and Instruments (1973); *In Memoriam Malcolm X* (N.Y., April 7, 1974); *Horizons '76* for Soprano and Orch., a U.S. Bicentennial commission, for 3 Speakers, Dancer, and Instruments (Chicago, June 11, 1978); *Messages, a Creole Fantasy* for Voices and Orch. (1979). FOR CHAMBER GROUPS: *Pieces for Clarinet and Chamber Orchestra* (Oklahoma City, March 25, 1962); *5 Bagatelles* for Oboe, Violin, and Harpsichord (1963); *5 Etudes and a Fancy* for Woodwind Quintet (1964); *Connections* for String Quintet (1966); *Swing Set,* duo for Clarinet and Piano (1973); *5 Easy Pieces* for Violin, Piano, and Jew's Harp (1974); *Variations on a Theme by Alban Berg* for Viola and Piano (1977); also piano pieces, among them *5 Portraitures of 2 People* for Piano, 4-hands (1965), and *Watermelon* (1971).

BIBLIOGRAPHY: David Ewen, *American Composers* (N.Y., 1982).

Anderssén, Alfred, Finnish composer; b. Pietarsaari rural communal, Aug. 4, 1887; d. Turku (Åbo), Sept. 10, 1940. He studied in Helsinki and in Munich; settled in Turku as a music critic and was a conductor of the Swedish Theater there (1927–40). In 1926 he married the singer Karin Limnell. He wrote an opera, *Kohtalo (Destiny on Board)* (1928–32); 2 symphs. (1927, 1938); 15 cantatas; many choral works.

d'Andrade, Francesco, Portuguese baritone; b. Lisbon, Jan. 11, 1859; d. Berlin, Feb. 8, 1921. He studied in Italy; made his debut in San Remo (1882); then lived in Berlin. He was well-known as a successful singer in Europe; his most famous role was that of Don Giovanni.

Andrade, Mário de, significant Brazilian poet and writer on music; b. São Paulo, Oct. 9, 1893; d. there, Feb. 15, 1945. He studied at São Paulo Cons.; in 1935 he was appointed director of the São Paulo Dept. of Culture. Andrade spent much time on special research and reconstruction of Brazilian folk songs and dances; he was also active as a music critic. Among his publications are *Pequeña historica da musica* (1929; revised 1942); *Carlos Gomes* (1939); *Musica de feiticaria no Brasil* (1941).

BIBLIOGRAPHY: B. Kiefer, "Mário de Andrade e o modernismo na música brasileira," *R. Bimestra Cubana* (Jan./March 1971).

André, (Johann) Anton, 3rd son of **Johann André;** b. Offenbach, Oct. 6, 1775; d. there, April 6, 1842. A precocious talent, he studied with Karl Vollweiler in Mannheim (1792–93); was a fine pianist, violinist, and composer before entering the Univ. of Jena; after completing his studies, he made extensive travels; on his father's death, took charge of the business, adding particular luster to its good name by the purchase, in 1799, of Mozart's entire musical remains. He publ. Mozart's autograph thematic catalogue, and supplemented it by a list of the works so acquired. By accepting the application of the lithographic process to music engraving (1799), he took another long stride toward placing his firm in the front rank. He was also a composer (2 operas, symphs., songs, etc.), a successful teacher, and a

noteworthy theorist. He wrote 2 vols. on harmony, counterpoint, canon, and fugue (1832–42; new revised ed., abridged, 1974–78); and *Anleitung zum Violinspiele.* His sons were: (1) **Carl August** (b. Offenbach, June 15, 1806; d. Frankfurt, Feb. 15, 1887), head (from 1835) of the Frankfurt branch opened in 1828, and founder of a piano factory ("Mozartflügel"); author of *Der Klavierbau und seine Geschichte* (1855). (2) **Julius** (b. Offenbach, June 4, 1808; d. there, April 17, 1880), a fine organist and pianist, pupil of Aloys Schmitt (his grandfather's pupil), author of a *Praktische Orgelschule,* composer of several interesting organ compositions, and arranger of Mozart's works for piano, 4-hands. (3) **Johann August** (b. Offenbach, March 2, 1817; d. there, Oct. 29, 1887), his father's successor (1839) in the publishing establishment. His 2 sons, **Karl** (b. Aug. 24, 1853; d. June 29, 1914) and **Adolf** (b. April 10, 1855; d. Sept 10, 1910), succeeded to the business. (4) **Jean Baptiste (de St.-Gilles;** b. Offenbach, March 7, 1823; d. Frankfurt, Dec. 9, 1882), pianist and composer of various pieces for piano and voice, a pupil of A. Schmitt, Taubert (piano), and Kessler and Dehn (harmony); lived for years in Berlin; had the honorary title of "Herzoglich Bernbergischer Hofkapellmeister."

André, Franz, Belgian conductor; b. Brussels, June 10, 1893; d. there, Jan. 20, 1975. He studied violin with César Thomson at the Brussels Cons., and conducting with Weingartner in Berlin. He was mobilized at the advent of World War I, and spent the years 1914–18 on the crucial front in the trenches at Ypres. After the war he began teaching violin; was on the faculty of the Brussels Cons. from 1920 to 1944. In 1935 he organized the Belgian Radio Symph. Orch. and led it until 1958. He trained the orch. in difficult modern works which he insisted on reading *à livre ouvert* at rehearsals; he cultivated the works of modern French and Belgian composers, and conducted several orch. scores by Schoenberg.

André, Johann, German composer, publisher, and father of a musical family; b. Offenbach, March 28, 1741; d. there, June 18, 1799. He founded (Sept. 1, 1774) at Offenbach a music publishing house under his name and had publ. 1,200 compositions by the time of his death. For 7 years (1777–84) he was Kapellmeister of Döbbelin's Theater in Berlin. He was a prolific composer, author of 19 singspiels and 14 miscellaneous scores for the stage, among them *Der Töpfer* (Hanau, Jan. 22, 1773) and *Der Liebhaber als Automat* (Berlin, Sept. 11, 1782). Bretzner wrote the libretto of *Die Entführung aus dem Serail,* or *Belmont und Constanze,* for him; the opera was produced in Berlin, May 25, 1781. The same text was used the following year by Mozart for his celebrated work, which elicited Bretzner's haughty protest against "a certain man named Mozart" for the unauthorized use of his libretto. Among André's songs, the *Rheinweinlied* ("Bekränzt mit Laub") was widely performed. André is credited with being the composer of the first "durchkomponierte Ballade," *Die Weiber von Weinsberg* (1783).

André, Maurice, French trumpet virtuoso; b. Alès, near Nîmes, May 24, 1933. He was apprenticed as a coal miner, the trade he plied from his 14th through his 18th year; his father was also a coal miner, but he played the trumpet in his free hours; André practiced on the trumpet, too, and enrolled in the class of Barthélémy; received the Prix d'Honneur and joined the Paris Radio Orch.; was later the first trumpet in the Lamoureux Orch.; also played in jazz groups. In 1956 he won an international competition in Geneva, and in 1963 won the International Music Competition of the German Radio; then played in chamber orchs. In 1974 he made his American debut as a soloist with the Württemberg Chamber Orch. on tour. Soon he became well-known as a proponent of the Baroque repertoire; he also performed modern trumpet concertos, some written especially for him; he made some 260 recordings, including 30 different trumpet concertos. An ardent collector, he owns 80 trumpets of different types and national origins; as a trumpet virtuoso, he tours all over the world; in 1983 he made one of his frequent visits to America.

Andreae, Marc, Swiss conductor and composer, grandson of **Volkmar Andreae;** b. Zürich, Nov. 8, 1939. He studied piano and conducting at the Zürich Cons.; then went to Paris for studies in composition with Nadia Boulanger. Subsequently he took lessons in conducting with Franco Ferrara at the Santa Cecilia Academy in Rome. Eventually he became conductor of the Orch. del Radio della Svizzera Italiana in Lugano.

Andreae, Volkmar, eminent Swiss conductor and accomplished composer; b. Bern, July 5, 1879; d. Zürich, June 18, 1962. He studied music with Karl Munzinger in Bern and later with Wüllner at the Cologne Cons.; was then répétiteur at the Royal Opera in Munich; in 1902 he became conductor of the municipal chorus of Zürich, and in 1904 of the male chorus there; in 1906 was appointed to lead the Tonhalle Orch. of Zürich, a post he held until 1949; during his long tenure there, he championed the music of Bruckner, Strauss, Mahler, and Debussy. From 1914 until 1941 he served as director of the Zürich Cons. In his own compositions, Andreae reflected the post-Romantic tendencies of German music.
WORKS: 2 operas: *Ratcliff* (Duisburg, May 25, 1914) and *Abenteuer des Casanova* (Dresden, June 17, 1924); *Das Göttliche* for Tenor, Chorus, and Orch., to Goethe's poem (1902); *Charons Nachen* for Soloists, Chorus, and Orch. (1903); *Symphonic Fantasy* for Tenor Solo, Tenor Chorus, Organ, and Orch. (1904); *Vater unser* for Mezzo-soprano, Female Chorus, Mixed Chorus, and Organ (1911); *Li-tai-pe,* 8 Chinese songs for Tenor and Orch. (1931); *La Cité sur la montagne* for Tenor, Male Chorus, and Orch. (1942); *Little Suite* for Orch. (1916); Symph. in F major; *Notturno and Scherzo* for Orch. (1919); Symph. in C major (Zürich, Nov. 3, 1919); *Rhapsody* for Violin and Orch. (1920); *Music for Orch.* (Zürich, Nov. 12, 1929); Violin Concerto (1940); Oboe Concertino (1942); 2 piano trios (1901, 1908); Violin Sonata (1903); 2 string quartets (1905, 1922); String Trio (1919); Divertimento for Flute and String Trio (1945); *6 Piano Pieces* (1912); choruses; songs.
BIBLIOGRAPHY: F. Seiler, *Dr. Volkmar Andreae ... zum Jubiläum seiner 25-jährigen Tätigkeit* (Zürich, 1931); R. Schoch, *Hundert Jahre Tonhalle Zürich* (Zürich, 1968).

Andrée, Elfrida, Swedish organist and composer; b. Visby, Feb. 19, 1841; d. Göteborg, Jan. 11, 1929. She studied at the Stockholm Cons., and later took lessons with Niels Gade in Copenhagen; at the same time she also studied telegraphy and was the first woman telegraph operator in Sweden. In 1867 she was appointed organist at the Göteborg Cathedral. She established a series of popular concerts and presented about 800 programs. In consideration of her achievements, she was elected a member of the Swedish Academy of Music. She was a pioneer among Swedish women as an organist and composer. She wrote 4 symphs., and a Swedish Mass, which had frequent performances.

Andreis, Josip, eminent Croatian musicographer; b. Split, March 19, 1909; d. Zagreb, Jan. 16, 1982. He studied philology in Zagreb and Rome; also took courses in composition. In 1945 he was appointed to the faculty of the Music Academy in Zagreb, retiring in 1972. He publ. an encyclopedia of music in the Croatian language, issued in Zagreb in 2 vols. (1958, 1963); another work of importance was a 3-vol. edition, also in the Croatian language, on music history (Zagreb, 1951–54; 2nd ed., 1966). Other publications were *Yugoslav Music* (in English; Belgrade, 1959) and a monograph on the Yugoslav composer Gotovac (Split, 1957).

Andreoli, Carlo, Italian pianist, conductor, and composer; b. Mirandola, Jan. 8, 1840; d. Reggio Emilia, Jan. 22, 1908. He studied with his father, Evangelista Andreoli; then was a student of Antonio Angeleri at the Milan Cons. (1852–58). He made his debut as a pianist in Milan in 1858; subsequently appeared as a virtuoso throughout Italy and Europe. With his brother **Guglielmo Andreoli** (1862–1932), he organized the Società dei Concerti Sinfonica Popolari of Milan, serving as its conductor from 1877–87. He became insane in 1891, and lingered in this condition for many years until his death.
BIBLIOGRAPHY: G. Tebaldini, *In memoria di Carlo Andreoli* (Milan and Mirandola, 1910).

Andreoli, Evangelista, Italian pianist and organist; b. Disvetro, Modena, June 27, 1810; d. Mirandola, Modena, June 16, 1875. He spent his entire career as a teacher at the music school in Mirandola; his 2 sons were also musicians.

Andreoli, Guglielmo, Italian pianist, conductor, and composer; b. Mirandola, Jan. 9, 1862; d. Modena, April 26, 1932. He studied with his father, **Evangelista Andreoli;** then took organ lessons with Fuma-

Andrésen – Andriessen

galli, violin lessons with Rampazzini, and composition with Bazzini at the Milan Cons. With his brother **Carlo Andreoli**, he was active as a conductor of the Società dei Concerti Sinfonici Popolari in Milan (1877–87); he also taught harmony, counterpoint, and piano at the Milan Cons. He composed pieces for orch. and piano, and many songs.

Andrésen, Ivar, noted Norwegian bass; b. Oslo, July 27, 1896; d. Stockholm, Nov. 25, 1940. He studied at the Royal Opera School in Stockholm; made his debut there in 1919; in 1925 he joined the Dresden State Opera; then sang with the Berlin State Opera (1934–36), and concurrently at the Bayreuth Festivals (1927–36). On Nov. 1, 1930, he made his Metropolitan Opera debut in N.Y. as Daland in *Der Fliegende Holländer;* continued on its roster until 1932. He was particularly distinguished in Wagnerian roles.

Andrevi, Francisco, prominent Spanish church music composer; b. Sanahuja, near Lérida, Nov. 16, 1786; d. Barcelona, Nov. 23, 1853. He started as a choirboy, and from his earliest years devoted himself to the study of church music. At the age of 22 he became music director at the Cathedral of Segorbe; then held similar posts at the churches at Barcelona, Valencia, and Seville. During the civil war in Spain he was in Bordeaux (1832–42); later (1845–49) in Paris, where he publ. his *Traité d'Harmonie et de Composition* (1848; in the same year it was also publ. in Spanish). Andrevi returned to Barcelona in 1849. He wrote a sacred drama, *Juicio universal;* also much choral music, most of which is in MS; 2 of his sacred choruses (*Nunc dimittis* and *Salve regina*) are included in Eslava's *Lira Sacra-Hispana.*

Andricu, Mihail, Rumanian composer; b. Bucharest, Jan. 3, 1895; d. there, Feb. 4, 1974. He studied at the Bucharest Cons. (1903–9); later became a teacher there (1926–59). For many years he was an accompanist for Georges Enesco.
WORKS: Ballets: *Cenuşăreasa* (*Cinderella;* 1929); *Taina* (*The Secret;* 1933; Bucharest, Feb. 8, 1936); *Luceafărul* (*The Morning Star;* Bucharest, Sept. 24, 1951). For Orch.: 11 symphs. (1944, 1947, 1950, 1954, 1955, 1957, 1958, 1960, 1962, 1968; No. 11, *In Memoriam,* 1970); 3 chamber symphs. (1927, 1961, 1965); 11 sinfoniettas (1945–71); 9 suites (1924–58); *Poem* for Piano and Orch. (1923); *3 Symphonic Pictures* (1925); *Serenade* (1928); 2 sets of *3 Symphonic Sketches* (1936, 1951); *Fantezie* for Piano and Orch. (1940); *3 Symphonic Pieces* (1950); *Rapsodie* (1952); Violin Concerto (1960); Cello Concerto (1961); *6 Portraits* (1969); *Evocation* (1971); *Miniatures and Images* (1971). For Piano: *4 Novelettes* for Piano Quartet (1925); Octet (1928); Sextet (1932); 2 quintets (1938, 1956); Sonata for Piano, 4-hands (1946); Sonata (1949); *3 Pieces* for Piano and Winds (1964). Also wrote String Quartet (1931); Violin Sonata (1941); choral pieces and songs. A detailed list of his works, with exact dates of their first performances, is given in Viorel Cosma's *Muzicieni Români Lexicon*

(Bucharest, 1970).

Andries, Jean, Belgian musician; b. Ghent, April 25, 1798; d. there, Jan. 21, 1872. He played violin in a local theater orch. from 1817 to 1852; from 1835 he also taught at the Ghent Cons.; in 1851 he became its director; retired in 1859. He published several valuable treatises, among them *Aperçu historique de tous les instruments de musique actuellement en usage* (1856); *Précis de l'histoire de la musique depuis les temps les plus reculés* (1862); *Instruments à vent: La Flûte* (1866); *Remarques sur les cloches et les carillons* (1868).

Andriessen, Hendrik, eminent Dutch organist and composer, brother of **Willem Andriessen;** b. Haarlem, Sept. 17, 1892; d. Heemstede, April 12, 1981. He studied music with his brother; then took piano and organ lessons with Louis Robert and J.B. de Pauw; studied composition with Bernard Zweers at the Amsterdam Cons. (1914–16); subsequently taught harmony there (1928–34). He succeeded his father as organist at St. Joseph's Church in Haarlem (1916–34); was then organist at Utrecht Cathedral (1934–49). He was director of the Royal Cons. in The Hague (1949–57) and special prof. at the Catholic Univ. in Nijmegen (1952–63). His own music is Romantically inspired; some of his instrumental works make use of modern devices, including melodic atonality and triadic polytonality. He was particularly esteemed for his ability to revive the authentic modalities of Gregorian chant; his choral works present a remarkable confluence of old usages with modern technical procedures.
WORKS: OPERAS: *Philomela* (Holland Festival, June 23, 1950) and *De Spiegel uit Venetië* (*The Mirror from Venice;* 1964; Dutch Television, Oct. 5, 1967). FOR ORCH.: 4 symphs. (1930, 1937, 1946, 1954); *Variations and Fugue on a Theme of Kuhnau* for String Orch. (1935); *Capriccio* (1941); *Variations on a Theme of Couperin* for Flute, Harp, and Strings (1944); *Ballet Suite* (1947); *Ricercare* (1949); *Wilhemus van Nassouwe,* rhapsody (1950); Organ Concerto (1950); *Symphonic Etude* (1952; The Hague, Oct. 15, 1952); *Libertas venit,* rhapsody (1954); *Mascherata,* fantasy (1962); *Symphonie concertante* (1962); Violin Concerto (1968–69); Concertino for Oboe and String Orch. (1969–70); Concertino for Cello and Orch. (1970); *Chromatic Variations* for Flute, Oboe, Violin, Cello, and Strings (1970); *Canzone* (1971); *Chantecler,* overture (1972). CHAMBER MUSIC: Cello Sonata (1926); Violin Sonata (1932); *3 Inventions* for Violin and Cello (1937); Piano Trio (1939); Suite for Violin and Piano (1950); Solo Cello Sonata (1951); Suite for Brass Quintet (1951); Wind Quintet (1951); Ballade for Oboe and Piano (1952); Theme and Variations for Flute, Oboe, and Piano (1953); *Quartetto in stile antico,* String Quartet (1957); *Il peniero,* string quartet (1961); *Pezzo festoso* for Organ, 2 Trumpets, and 2 Trombones (1962); *Canzonetta* for Harpsichord (1963); *Canzone,* Trio No. 2 for Flute, Oboe, and Piano (1965); Viola Sonata (1967); *Concert spirituelle* for Flute, Oboe, Violin, and Cello (1967); *Haydn Variations* for English

Horn and Piano (1968); *L'Indifférent,* string quartet (1969); Clarinet Sonata (1971); *Choral varié* for 3 Trumpets and 3 Trombones (1973). SOLO SONG CYCLES (most with Organ or Orch.): *L'Aube spirituelle* (1916); *L'Invitation au voyage* (1918); *Magna res est amor* (1919); *L'Attente mystique* (1920); *Miroir de peine* (1923); *Cantique spirituel* (1924); *La Vièrge à midi* (1966). CHORAL WORKS: *Missa Simplex,* a cappella (1927); *Missa Sponsa Christi* for Male Chorus with Organ (1933); *Missa Christus Rex* for Double Chorus and Organ (1938); 2 Madrigals, with Strings (1940); *Te Deum Laudamus I,* with Organ or Orch. (1943–46), and *II,* with Orch. (1968); *De Zee en het land (Declamatorium),* with Speaker and Orch. (1953); *Veni Creator,* with Orch. (1960); *Psalm IX,* with Tenor and Orch. (1968); *Lux Jocunda,* with Tenor or Orch. (1968); *Carmen Saeculare (Horatius),* with Soprano, Tenor, Winds, Harpsichord, and Double Bass (1968). FOR ORGAN: 4 chorales (1913, c.1918, 1920, 1952); Toccata (1917); *Fête-Dieu* (1918); *Sonata de Chiesa* (1927); Passacaglia (1929); *Sinfonia* (1940); *Intermezzi* (1943); Theme and Variations (1949); 4 Studies (1953). FOR PIANO: 2 sonatas (1934, 1966); Pavane (1937); Serenade (1950).

BIBLIOGRAPHY: J. Wouters, *Negen portretten van Nederlandse componisten* (Amsterdam, 1971).

Andriessen, Jurriaan, Dutch composer, son of **Hendrik Andriessen;** b. Haarlem, Nov. 15, 1925. He studied theory with his father; took lessons in conducting with Willem van Otterloo at the Utrecht Cons. After graduating in 1947, he went to Paris to study film music; a Rockefeller Foundation fellowship enabled him to come to the U.S., where he studied composition with Copland at the Berkshire Music Center in Tanglewood during the summers of 1949 and 1950. Returning to the Netherlands, he was active mainly as a music consultant to the national radio and television. WORKS: He wrote the first television opera to be produced in Holland, *Kalchas* (June 28, 1959); an opera buffa, *Het Zwarte Blondje (The Black Blonde)* (1964); Piano Concertino (1943); Concerto for 2 Pianos Alone (1944); *Hommage à Milhaud* for 11 Instruments (1945; also for Flute and String Quartet, 1948); Violin Sonata (1946); *Symphonietta Concertante* for 4 Trumpets and Orch. (1947); Piano Concerto (1948); *Het wonderlijk uur (The Strange Hour),* suite No. 1 for Orch. (1948); *Octet Divertissement* for Winds (1948); 5 symphs.: No. 1, *Berkshire Symphonies* (1949; produced as a ballet under the title *Jones Beach,* N.Y., March 12, 1950); No. 2 for Wind Orch. (1962); No. 3, *Symphonyen fan Fryslàn* (1963); No. 4, *Aves (The Birds),* after Aristophanes, with Chorus (1963); No. 5, *Time Spirit,* after M.C. Escher's prints, for Clarinet, Orch., Pop Group, and 6 Dancers (Rotterdam, Nov. 19, 1970); *Magnificat* for Soprano, Chorus, and Orch. (1950); Flute Concerto (1951); *Les Otaries (The Seals),* classic ballet fantasy (1951); *Cymbeline,* overture (1954); *Rouw past Electra (Mourning Becomes Electra),* suite for 11 Winds and Percussion (1954); 2 piano sonatas; 5 trios: No. 1 for Flute, Oboe, and Piano (1955); No. 2 for Flute, Viola, and Piano (1955); No. 3 for 3 Record-

ers (1957); No. 4 for Flute, Oboe, and Bassoon (1957); No. 5, *Sonata da Camera,* for Flute, Viola, and Guitar (1959); *L'incontro di Cesare e Cleopatra,* sextet for Winds and Piano (1956); *Astrazione* for Piano (1957); *Inno della Tecnica,* introduction and scherzo for Orch. (1957); *Ritratto di una città (Ouverture Den Haag)* (1957); *Duo* for 2 Violins (1958); *Balocco* for Solo Oboe (1960); *Thai,* symph. rhapsody based on jazz tunes by King Phumiphon Aduldet of Thailand, written for a special perf. during the King's visit in the Netherlands (The Hague, Oct. 25, 1960); Concertino for Bassoon and Winds (1962); *Fantasy* for Piano, 4-hands (1962); *Respiration,* suite for Double Wind Quintet (1962); *Sciarada Spagnuola* for Wind Quintet (1962); *Movimenti I* for Trumpet, Horn, Trombone, Strings, and Timpani (1965), *II* for Oboe, Clarinet, Bassoon, Strings, and Percussion (1972), and *III* for Violin, Viola, Cello, Winds, and Percussion (1974); Trio for Clarinet, Cello, and Piano (1965); *Concerto Rotterdam* for Jazz Combo and Orch. (Rotterdam, June 20, 1966); *Entrata festiva* for Brass and Timpani (1966); *Antifono e Fusione* for Wind Quintet, Brass Quartet, and Timpani (1966); *In Pompa Magna* for Brass and Percussion (1966); *Summer-Dances* for 7 Percussionists, Harp, and Guitar (1966); *Les Bransles érotiques,* pantomime of the 16th century for 8 Performers (1967); *Contra-Bande,* a "rapsodia interrotta" for Sousaphone and Orch. (1967); *Il divorcio di Figaro,* variations for Amateur Orch. (1967); *Omaggio à Sweelinck* for Harpsichord and 24 Strings (1968); *Trelleborg Concerto* for Harpsichord and 3 Orch. Groups (Amsterdam, Sept. 27, 1969); *Antifona dell'Aja* for Orch. (1969); *Beestenkwartet (Animal Quartet)* for Amateur Orch. (1972); *Een Prince van Oraengien (Wilhelmus-Phantasy)* for Chorus and Orch. (1973); *Pasticcio-Finale* for Orch., Dixieland Band, and Tape (1974); *Quartetto Buffo* for Clarinet and String Trio (1974); *The Cave* for Solo Cello, 12 Winds, 4 Keyboard Instruments, and Electronics (1976); incidental music for more than 60 plays.

BIBLIOGRAPHY: W. Paap, "Jurriaan Andriessen and Incidental Music," *Sonorum Speculum* (Autumn 1969).

Andriessen, Louis, Dutch composer, son of **Hendrik Andriessen;** b. Utrecht, June 6, 1939. He first studied with his father and with Kees van Baaren at the Royal Cons. in The Hague (1957–62); also took lessons with Luciano Berio in Milan (1962–63). He was a co-founder of a Charles Ives Society in Amsterdam. His works are conceived in an advanced idiom. WORKS: Flute Sonata (1956); *Séries* for 2 Pianos (1958); *Percosse* for Flute, Trumpet, Bassoon, and Percussion (1958); Nocturnes for Soprano and Chamber Orch. (1959); *Aanloop en spiongen* for Flute, Oboe, and Clarinet (1961); *Ittrospezione I* for 2 Pianos (1961), *II* for Orch. (1963), and *III* for 2 Pianos, and Chamber Ensemble or Saxophone (1964); *A Flower Song I* for Solo Violin (1963), *II* for Solo Oboe (1963), and *III* for Solo Cello (1964); *Sweet* for Recorder or Flute (1964); *Double* for Clarinet and Piano (1965); *Paintings* for Recorder or Flute, and Piano (1965); *Souvenirs d'enfance* for Piano and Tape (1966); *Anachronie,* to the memory of Charles Ives, *I* for Orch. (1965–66; Rotterdam, Jan. 18, 1968) and *II* for Solo Oboe, 4 Horns, Piano, Harp, and String Orch. (1969); *Contra-tempus* for 23 Musicians (1968); the anti-imperialist collective opera *Reconstructie* (1968–69; Holland Festival, June 29, 1969; in collaboration with Reinbert de Leeuw, Misha Mengelberg, Peter Schat, and Jan van Vlijmen); *Hoe het is (What It's Like)* for Live-Electronic Improvisers and 52 Strings (Rotterdam, Sept. 14, 1970); *Spektakel (Uproar)* for 16 Winds, 6 Percussionists, and Electronic Instruments (1970); *The 9 Symphonies of Beethoven* for Promenade Orch. and Ice Cream Bell (1970); *De Volharding (The Persistence)* for Piano and Winds (1972); *On Jimmy Yancey* for Chamber Ensemble (1973); *II Principe,* after Machiavelli, for 2 Choirs, Winds, Piano, and Bass Guitar (1974); *Symphonieën der Nederlanden* for Brass Band (1974); *De Statt (The State)* for 4 Women's Voices and 27 Instruments (1972–76); *Workers' Union,* symph. movement for any loud-speaking group of Instruments (1975); *Hoketus* for 2 Panpipes, 2 Pianos, and Electronics (1977); *Orpheus,* for theater (1977); Symph. for Open Strings (1978).

Andriessen, Willem, Dutch pianist and composer, brother of **Hendrik Andriessen;** b. Haarlem, Oct. 25, 1887; d. Amsterdam, March 29, 1964. He studied piano and composition at the Amsterdam Cons. (1903–8); taught piano at The Hague Cons. (1910–17) and at the Rotterdam Cons.; from 1937–53 was director of the Amsterdam Cons. He was a professional pianist of a high caliber. He wrote a Piano Concerto (1908); *3 Songs* for Voice and Orch. (1911); *Hei, 't was de Mei,* scherzo for Orch. (1912); Piano Sonata (1938); Piano Sonatina (1945).

Anerio, Felice, Italian composer, brother of **Giovanni Francesco Anerio;** b. Rome, c.1560; d. there, Sept. 27, 1614. He studied with G.M. Manni; was a chorister at Santa Maria Maggiore in Rome (1568–75); then sang at St. Peter's under Palestrina (from May 1575 to March 1579). In 1584 he became maestro di cappella of the English College in Rome. After Palestrina's death, Anerio was appointed by Clement VIII to succeed him as composer to the Papal Chapel (April 3, 1594). His eminence as a composer is best attested by the fact that several of his compositions were for a long time supposed to be Palestrina's own. Besides MSS in Roman libraries, many of Anerio's works are extant in printed collections. They include: *Madrigali spirituali a 5* (1585; reprinted 1598); *Canzonette a 4* (1586; reprinted 1603, 1607); *Madrigali a 5* (1587); *Madrigali a 6,* book I (1590; reprinted 1599); *Concerti spirituali a 4* (1593); *Sacri hymni e cantica a 8,* book I (1596); *Madrigali a 3* (1598); *Madrigali a 6,* book II (1602); *Responsorii per la Settimana Santa a 4* (1602); *Sacri hymni e cantica a 8,* book II (1602); *Responsoria a 4* (1606).
BIBLIOGRAPHY: L. Torri, "Nei parentali di Felice Anerio," *Rivista Musicale Italiana* (1914); A.

Cametti, "Nuovi contributi alle biografie de Felice Anerio," *Rivista Musicale Italiana* (1915).

Anerio, Giovanni Francesco, Italian composer, younger brother of **Felice Anerio;** b. Rome, c.1567; d. on his way from Poland to Italy in June 1630 (buried in Graz, June 12, 1630). He served as a chorister at St. Peter's from 1575 to 1579, and sang, with his brother, under Palestrina. From 1600 to 1603 he was maestro di cappella at the Lateran church. In 1607 he was at the court of King Sigismund III of Poland in Cracow; in 1608 he returned to Rome; then became choirmaster at the Cathedral of Verona, and later held similar positions at the Seminario Romano (1611–12) and at the Jesuit Church of S. Maria dei Monti in Rome (1613–20). In 1616 he was ordained a priest. In 1624 he visited Treviso, near Venice; then became choirmaster at the Polish Court in Warsaw. He was a prolific composer; several of his works were printed in Italy. He also arranged Palestrina's 6-part *Missa Papae Marcelli* for 4 voices (Rome, 1600).
BIBLIOGRAPHY: G. Liberali, "G.F. Anerio," *Note d'Archivio* (Dec. 1940); G. Dixon, "G.F. Anerio (1567–1630) and the Roman School," *Musical Times* (June 1980).

Anet, Baptiste, (actually **Jean-Baptiste**), French violinist, son of **Jean-Baptiste Anet,** *père;* b. Paris, and was baptized on Jan. 2, 1676; d. Lunéville, Aug. 14, 1755. He was a pupil of Corelli in Rome; upon returning to France, he was a member of the Royal Chapel in Paris; in 1737 he went to Lunéville as a court musician to the former Polish King Stanislas Leszczynski. He publ. 3 sets of sonatas for violin with basso continuo (1729) and 3 collections of duets for musettes (1726, 1730, 1734).
BIBLIOGRAPHY: L. de La Laurencie, *L'Ecole française de violon de Lully à Viotti* (vol. 1, Paris, 1922).

Anet, Jean-Baptiste, père, French violinist; b. Paris, June 20, 1650; d. there, April 28, 1710. He was active as a teacher in Paris; in 1699 he became a member of the 24 Violons du Roi. He was the father of another **Jean-Baptiste Anet,** who was known simply as Baptiste Anet.

Anfossi, Pasquale, Italian opera composer; b. Taggia, near Naples, April 5, 1727; d. Rome, Feb. 1797. He studied composition with Piccinni, and began writing operas in the prevalent Italian manner. His third opera, *L'Incognita perseguitata,* produced in Rome in 1773, won popular approval; its subject was the same as Piccinni's previously staged opera, but if contemporary reports are to be trusted, Anfossi's opera was more successful than that of his erstwhile master. Encouraged by his success, Anfossi proceeded to write one opera after another; according to some accounts, he wrote 76 operas; a more plausible computation credits him with no fewer than 60, but no more than 70 operas. In 1779 he was in Paris; from Dec. 1782 to 1786 he was at the King's Theater in London as director of the Italian opera there. He then traveled in Germany; returning to Italy, he was appointed maestro di cappella at the Lateran church in 1791, and turned his attention to sacred compositions; he composed at least 12 oratorios, and a number of masses and Psalms. Mozart wrote two arias for use in Anfossi's opera *Il Curioso indiscreto* (Vienna, 1783) and for *Le Gelosie fortunate* (Vienna, 1788).

Angeles, Victoria de Los (real name, **Victoria Gómez Cima**), famous Spanish soprano; b. Barcelona, Nov. 1, 1923. She studied at the Barcelona Cons., and made her concert debut there in 1944. In 1946 she made her first operatic appearance at the Teatro Lírico in Barcelona. In 1947 she won first prize at the International Singing Contest in Geneva. Returning to Barcelona, she sang Elsa in *Lohengrin*, Marguerite in *Faust*, and other important roles. In 1949 she performed at the Paris Opéra as Marguerite; in 1950 she appeared at Covent Garden in London as Mimi in *La Bohème*. Her American debut took place in a recital at Carnegie Hall in N.Y., on Oct. 24, 1950. On March 17, 1951, she appeared at the Metropolitan Opera in N.Y. as Marguerite in *Faust*. She continued to sing at the Metropolitan during the years 1955–59 and in 1961. In 1953 she gave concerts in South Africa, and in 1956, in Australia. In 1957 she sang at the Vienna State Opera; in 1961–62 she was a guest artist at the Bayreuth Festival. She retired from the stage in 1969 but continued to give occasional recitals; she excelled particularly in Spanish and French songs. On Nov. 28, 1948, she married Enrique Magriñá Mir; they lived mostly in Barcelona.

d'Angeli, Andrea, Italian composer and writer on music; b. Padua, Nov. 9, 1868; d. S. Michele, near Verona, Oct. 28, 1940. He studied at the Univ. of Padua; then was an instructor at the Liceo Rossini in Pesaro. He wrote several operas: *L'Innocente; Il Negromante; Al Ridotto di Venezia; Fiori e Colombi; Maurizio e Lazzaro;* also a number of libretti. He publ. monographs on Verdi (Milan, 1924) and Benedetto Marcello (Milan, 1930), and numerous essays on music in *La Cronaca Musicale,* of which he was editor (1907–14).

Angelini, Bontempi Giovanni Andrea. See **Bontempi, Giovanni Andrea.**

d'Angelo, Louis, Italian baritone; b. Naples, May 6, 1888; d. Jersey City, N.J., Aug. 9, 1958. He was brought to the U.S. as a child, and was first apprenticed as a glove cutter in Gloversville, N.Y.; then sang in a local church choir. He went to N.Y. City at the age of 18 and appeared in vaudeville; in 1917 he joined the staff of the Metropolitan Opera, retiring in 1946. He had more than 300 operatic roles in his repertoire and was particularly successful in his interpretation of Bartolo in *The Barber of Seville.*

Angeloni, Carlo, Italian composer; b. Lucca, July 16, 1834; d. there, Jan. 13, 1901. He wrote a number

of operas, several of which were performed in Lucca: *Carlo di Viana* (1855); *Asraele degli Abenceragi* (1871); *Dramma in montagna* (posthumous, 1902).
BIBLIOGRAPHY: L. Landucci, *Carlo Angeloni* (Lucca, 1905).

Angeloni, Luigi, Italian writer on music; b. Frosione, Papal States, 1759; d. London, Feb. 5, 1842. He wrote a valuable monograph, *Sopra la vita, le opera ed il sapere di Guido d'Arezzo, restauratore della scienza e dell'arte musica* (Paris, 1811).

Angerer, Paul, Austrian conductor and composer; b. Vienna, May 16, 1927. He studied violin, piano, and music theory in Vienna; played viola in the Vienna Symph. Orch. (1953–56); then served as conductor of the Vienna Chamber Orch. (1956–63); subsequently held positions as city theater conductor in Bonn (1964–66) and Ulm (1966–68); from 1968 to 1972 he was opera conductor at the Landestheater in Salzburg. In 1971 he was appointed conductor of the South West German Chamber Orch. in Pforzheim. His music is marked by a theatrical quality, with frequent humorous allusions in the titles.
WORKS: *Passkontrolle,* television opera (1959); *Hotel Comédie,* a musical (1970); Quartet for Oboe, Horn, Viola, and Cello (1951); Trio for Recorder, Viola d'Amore, and Lute (1953); *Musica examinata* for Cello and Piano (1953); *Musica ad impulsum et pulsum* for Strings and Percussion (1955); *Musica fera* for Orch. (1956); *Concerto pour la jeunesse* for Orch. (1956); *Gloriatio* for Double Bass and Chamber Orch. (1957); Concerto for Piano and String Orch. (1962); Viola Concerto (1962); *Chanson gaillarde* for Oboe, Cello, and Harpsichord (1963); *Cogitatio* for Wind Quintet and Strings (1964).

Angermüller, Rudolph, German musicologist and editor; b. Gadderbaum, Bielefeld, Sept. 2, 1940. He studied musicology in Mainz and Münster; received his Ph.D. in 1970 from the Univ. of Salzburg with the dissertation *Antonio Salieri: Sein Leben und seine weltlichen Werke* (publ. in Munich, 1971). In 1968 he joined the faculty of the Univ. of Salzburg. In 1973 he was named editor in chief of the Neue Mozart-Ausgabe.

d'Anglebert, Jean-Henri, French clavecin player; b. Paris, probably in 1628; d. there, April 23, 1691. He studied with Champion de Chambonnières; in 1662 he succeeded his teacher as clavecinist to Louis XIV. In 1689 he publ. a collection, *Pièces de clavecin avec la manière de les jouer,* containing original suites, arrangements of airs from Lully's operas, and 22 variations on *Folies d'Espagne* (the theme later used by Corelli); the same vol. contains instruction on figured bass. D'Anglebert contributed greatly to the establishment of the French method of performance on the clavecin. His extant compositions were publ. in 1934 by Marguerite Roesgen-Champion in *Publications de la Société Française de Musicologie,* also containing biographical information. His son **Jean-Baptiste Henri d'Anglebert** (b. Paris, Sept. 5, 1661; d. there, Nov.

1735) succeeded him as court musician.

BIBLIOGRAPHY: Ch. Bouvet, "Les Deux d'Angleberts," *La Revue de Musicologie* (May 1928).

Anglès, Higini (Catalan form; in Spanish, **Higinio Anglès**), distinguished musicologist; b. Maspujols, Catalonia, Jan. 1, 1888; d. Rome, Dec. 8, 1969. He studied philosophy at Tarragona (1900–13); musicology with Felipe Pedrell and composition with V.M. Gibert in Barcelona (1913–19). In 1917 he became head of the music dept. of the Barcelona library. In 1923 he went to Germany and studied with W. Gurlitt at Freiburg and F. Ludwig at Göttingen. In 1924 he returned to Barcelona, and in 1927 became prof. of music history at the Cons. With the outbreak of the Spanish Civil War in 1936, he went to Munich; returned to Barcelona in 1939. In 1943 he was appointed director of the Instituto Español de Musicologia; in 1947 he became director of the Pontifical Inst. of Sacred Music in Rome. His most important publication is *El Códex Musical de Las Huelgas* (3 vols., 1928–31), containing facsimiles and transcriptions of Spanish music of the 13th and 14th centuries. Part of the text of this edition was publ. in the *Musical Quarterly* (Oct. 1940). He publ. the following books: *Cantigas del Rei N'Anfos el Savi* (Barcelona, 1927); *Historia de la música española* (Barcelona, 1935); *La música a Catalunya fins al segle XIII* (Barcelona, 1935); *La mú sica española desde la edad media hasta nuestros dias* (Barcelona, 1941); and many smaller works. He edited the collected works of J. Pujol (1925); the organ works of Cabanilles (1926); *La música en la corte de los reyes católicos* (2 vols.; Madrid, 1941; Barcelona, 1947); *Recopilación de sonetos*, etc. by Juan Vásquez (Barcelona, 1946); *El cancionero musical de Palacio* (Barcelona, 1947). Anglès contributed to many music journals and wrote articles on Spanish music for *Die Musik in Geschichte und Gegenwart.* He was regarded as an outstanding expert on Spanish music of the Middle Ages.

Anglès, Rafael, Spanish organist and composer; b. Rafales (Teruel), 1731; d. Valencia, Feb. 19, 1816. He was organist at Valencia Cathedral from 1762 until his death. He devoted his life to liturgical music; also wrote keyboard pieces, 4 of which are printed by J. Nín in his collection *17 Sonates et pièces anciennes d'auteurs espagnols* (Paris, 1929).

Anhalt, István, Hungarian-born Canadian composer; b. Budapest, April 12, 1919. He studied with Kodály at the Budapest Academy (1937–41); took lessons in Paris with Nadia Boulanger (1946–48). He came to Canada in 1949, settling in Montreal; was appointed to the faculty of music at McGill Univ., where he founded the electronic music studio in 1963. In 1971 he became head of the music dept. of Queen's Univ. at Kingston, Ontario. His music reflects serial procedures; in his works of a later period he applies electronic techniques and speech-sounds.

WORKS: *Concerto in stilo di Handel* for 2 Oboes, 2 Horns, and Strings (1946); *Interludium* for Strings, Piano, and Timpani (1950); *Arc en Ciel,* ballet for 2 Pianos (1951); Piano Sonata (1951); *Funeral Music* for Chamber Ensemble (1951); Piano Trio (1953); *Fantasia* for Piano (1954); Violin Sonata (1954); *Comments* for Alto and Piano Trio (1954); *3 Songs of Death* for a cappella Chorus (1954); *Chansons d'Aurore* for Soprano, Flute, and Piano (1955); Symph. (1954–58); 4 *Electronic Compositions* (1959, 1959, 1960, 1962); *Symphony of Modules* for Chorus, Orch., and Tape (1967); *Cento (Cantata Urbana)* for 12-part Chorus and Tape (1967); *Foci* for Soprano, 10 Instrumentalists, off-stage Percussionist, and Tape (1969); *La Tourangelle* for 3 Sopranos, Tenor, Bass, Chamber Ensemble, and Tape (1972–74; Toronto, July 17, 1975).

Animuccia, Giovanni, Italian composer of sacred music; b. Florence, c.1514; d. Rome, March 25, 1571. In 1555 he was appointed maestro di cappella at St. Peter's as successor to Palestrina (who returned to that post after Animuccia's death in 1571). He worked with Filippo Neri, for whom he composed his *Laudi spirituali* (2 vols.; 1563 and 1570), which were performed by Neri in his "oratorium." These are contrapuntal hymnlike songs of praise, rather than forerunners of true oratorio. Other publ. works are 4 books of madrigals (1547, 1551, 1554, 1565), a book of masses (1567), and a book of Magnificats (1568). Animuccia's compositions mark a gradual emancipation from the involved formalism of the Flemish School in the direction of a more practical style, which approached that of Palestrina. Animuccia possessed a great skill in polyphony, demonstrated especially in his ingenious canonic writing.

BIBLIOGRAPHY: L. Cervelli, "Le Laudi spirituali di Giovanni Animuccia," *Rassegna Musicale* (1950); Gustave Reese, *Music in the Renaissance* (N.Y., 1954; pp. 453–55).

Anka, Paul, popular Canadian singer and composer; b. Ottawa, July 30, 1941, of Syrian parentage. He began improvising songs as a child; at the age of 15 he recorded his song *Diana,* to his own lyrics, and it became a substantial hit. He then embarked on a highly successful career as a ballad singer; acquired considerable musical ability, and wrote some 300 songs. In 1962 he incorporated himself to manage his growing fortune. He had his nose remodeled in 1958 for television appearances.

Anna Amalia, Princess of Prussia, sister of Frederick the Great; b. Berlin, Nov. 9, 1723; d. there, Sept. 30, 1787. She received her general musical training from her brother; then studied with the cathedral organist Gottlieb Hayne, and with Johann Philipp Kirnberger. She wrote music to Ramler's *Tod Jesu* which was later set also by Graun; she also composed some instrumental works and many chorales. Her Sonata for Flute, a Trio Sonata, and 4 military marches have been publ. She assembled a great library of MSS, including some of Bach's; a catalogue was publ. by Eitner (Berlin, 1884).

Anna Amalia, Duchess of Saxe-Weimar; b. Wolfenbüttel, Oct. 24, 1739; d. Weimar, April 10, 1807. She was the mother of the Grand Duke Charles Augustus, who was Goethe's protector. Goethe supplied her with a libretto for *Erwin und Elmire,* a singspiel; first performed at the Weimar Court (May 24, 1776), it had numerous revivals. Max Friedländer publ. its vocal score in 1921. She also wrote some instrumental music (*Divertimento* for Piano, Clarinet, Viola, and Cello; etc.).
BIBLIOGRAPHY: W. Bode, *Amalie, Herzogin von Weimar* (3 vols.; Berlin, 1908); O. Heuschele, *Herzogin Anna Amalia* (Munich, 1947).

Annibale (Il Padovano, from his birthplace, Padua), Italian organist and composer; b. Padua, c.1527; d. Graz, March 15, 1575. He was organist at San Marco (1552–64); in 1567 was appointed "Obrister Musicus" to the Archduke Carl at Graz; in 1570 named Kapellmeister.
WORKS: A book of *ricercari a* 4 (1556; modern ed. by N. Pierront and J.P. Hennebains, 1934); a book of madrigals *a* 5 (1564); a book of motets *a* 5–6 (1567); a book of masses *a* 5 (1573); a book of *Toccate e Ricercari* for Organ (1604). Two ricercari for Organ are reprinted in vol. III of Torchi's *L'Arte musicale in Italia.*
BIBLIOGRAPHY: G. del Valle de Paz, *Annibale Il Padovano, Nella storia della musica del cinquecento* (Turin, 1933; contains complete bibliography and musical examples).

Anrooy (properly, **Anrooij**), **Peter van,** Dutch conductor and composer; b. Zalt-Boomel, Oct. 13, 1879; d. The Hague, Dec. 31, 1954. He studied with Johan Wagenaar in Utrecht; in 1899 he went to Moscow, where he studied violin and conducting with Willem Kes and Taneyev. He played the violin in the orchs. of Glasgow and Zürich (1902); then was active as a conductor in Groningen (1905) and Arnhem (1910); in 1917 became conductor of the Residentie Orch. in The Hague, retiring in 1935. He wrote an orch. rhapsody on Dutch themes, *Piet Hein* (1901); Ballade for Violin and Orch. (1902); several pieces of chamber music.

Anschütz, Johann Andreas, German musician, father of **Karl Anschütz;** b. Koblenz, March 19, 1772; d. there, Dec. 26, 1856. In 1808 he founded a school for vocal music at Koblenz. He was a lawyer by profession, but was also a pianist and conductor, and composed numerous vocal works.

Anshütz, Karl, German conductor, son of **Johann Andreas Anschütz;** b. Koblenz, Feb. 1815; d. New York, Dec. 30, 1870. He studied with Friedrich Schneider. In 1844 he assumed the directorship of the music school founded by his father; in 1848 went to London, where he conducted the Wednesday Concerts for a time. In 1857 he went to America and settled in N.Y. as an opera conductor. He was a cultivated musician; apart from his activity as a conductor, he publ. several piano pieces.

Anselmi, Giuseppe, noted Italian tenor; b. Catania, Nov. 16, 1876; d. Zoagli, May 27, 1929. He studied voice with Luigi Mancinelli; made his operatic debut in Athens in 1896; then sang in Naples, London, Buenos Aires, St. Petersburg, Warsaw, and Madrid; he retired in 1917. Anselmi was particularly successful in Spain, and as a token of his appreciation he bequeathed his heart to the Madrid Cons.; the rest of his body was deposed in the Cathedral of Catania. Apart from that he was immortalized in scratchy early records (1907).

Ansermet, Ernest, celebrated Swiss conductor; b. Vevey, Nov. 11, 1883; d. Geneva, Feb. 20, 1969. He studied mathematics with his father, who was a schoolteacher, and received his musical training from his mother. He became himself a mathematics teacher, and taught school in Lausanne (1906–10). At the same time he took courses in music with Denéréaz, Barblan, and Ernest Bloch; he also studied conducting with Mottl in Munich and with Nikisch in Berlin. From then on he devoted himself mainly to conducting. He led the summer concerts in Montreux (1912–14), and from 1915–18 was conductor of the regular symph. concerts in Geneva. In 1918 he organized the prestigious Orchestre de la Suisse Romande in Geneva, at which he performed a great deal of modern French and Russian music; he retired from conducting in 1967. He met Stravinsky, who introduced him to Diaghilev, and subsequently conducted Diaghilev's Ballets Russes. On Sept. 28, 1918, he presented in Lausanne the first performance of Stravinsky's *L'Histoire du soldat.* He made numerous guest appearances as conductor with the Ballets Russes in Paris, London, Italy, Spain, South America, and the U.S., and also conducted performances with major American symph. orchs., attaining the reputation of a scholarly and progressive musician capable of fine interpretations of both Classical and modern works. He himself composed a symph. poem, *Feuilles de printemps;* orchestrated Debussy's *6 épigraphes antiques,* and 2 Argentinian dances by Julian Aguirre. He publ. *Le Geste du chef d'orchestre* (Lausanne, 1943) and *Les Fondements de la musique dans la conscience humaine* (2 vols.; Neuchâtel, 1961), making use of mathematical formulations to demonstrate the lack of validity in 12-tone technique and other advanced methods of composition.

Ansorge, Conrad (Eduard Reinhold), German pianist; b. Buchwald, near Löbau, Silesia, Oct. 15, 1862; d. Berlin, Feb. 13, 1930. He studied at the Leipzig Cons. (1880–82) and was one of the last pupils of Liszt in Weimar (1885). He toured in Russia and America; then lived in Weimar (1893–95) and in Berlin (from 1895). From 1898 he taught at the Klindworth-Scharwenka Cons. In 1920 he gave courses at the German Cons. in Prague. Ansorge excelled as an interpreter of Romantic compositions; he was called "a metaphysician among pianists" for his insight into the inner meaning of the music of Beethoven, Schubert, and Schumann. He wrote a piano concerto, a string sextet, 2 string quartets, and a cello sonata; *Ballade, Traumbilder, Polish Dances,* and 3 sonatas for piano; and a Requiem.

Antegnati, Costanzo, Italian organist and composer; b. Brescia (baptized, Dec. 9), 1549; d. there, Nov. 14, 1624. He was descended from a family of organ builders, and served as an apprentice to his father. In 1584 he became organist at Brescia Cathedral. His madrigals and sacred compositions (masses, motets, Psalms, and canzoni) were publ. in Venice (1571–1608) with pieces in organ tablature; he also publ. an important treatise, *L'arte organica* (Brescia, 1608; new ed. by Renato Lunelli, Mainz, 1938). His *3 ricercari* for organ are reprinted in vol. III of Luigi Torchi's *L'arte musicale in Italia.*
BIBLIOGRAPHY: D. Muoni, *Gli Antegnati* (Milan, 1883).

Antes, John, American Moravian (*Unitas Fratrum*) minister; b. Frederickstownship, Pa., March 24, 1740; d. Bristol, England, Dec. 17, 1811. He left America in 1764, and was a missionary in Egypt, where he was beaten and crippled by order of a bey who tried to extort money from him. He spent the rest of his life in England. A watchmaker by trade, he was an inventive artisan. He constructed several string instruments; one violin made by him in Bethlehem, Pa., in 1759 is preserved in the Museum of the Moravian Historical Society at Nazareth, Pa. A contribution by Antes to the *Allgemeine musikalische Zeitung* in 1806 describes a device for better violin tuning, as well as improvements of the violin bow and of the keyboard hammer. Antes also invented a machine with which one could turn pages while playing. He wrote about 25 melodious short anthems to German or English words for Chorus, Winds, Strings, and Organ. All of his MS compositions are in the Archives of the Moravian Church at Bethlehem, and at Winston-Salem, N.C.; compositions in MS are also found in the Archiv der Brüder-Unität in Herrnhut, Germany. His 3 string trios were discovered in 1949. They are the earliest known chamber works by a native American. His interesting autobiography was publ. in *Nachrichten aus der Brüder-Gemeine* (1845).
BIBLIOGRAPHY: D.M. McCorkle, "John Antes, 'American Dilettante,'" *Musical Quarterly* (Oct. 1956; reprinted as No. 2 in the series Moravian Music Foundation Publications, Winston-Salem, N.C.).

Antheil, George, remarkable American composer who cut a powerful swath in the world of modern music by composing dissonant and loud pieces glorifying the age of the machine; b. Trenton, N.J., July 8, 1900; d. New York, Feb. 12, 1959. He studied music theory with Constantine von Sternberg in Philadelphia; then went to N.Y. to take lessons in composition with Ernest Bloch. Defying the norms of flickering musical conservatism, Antheil wrote piano pieces under such provocative titles as *Sonate sauvage, Mechanisms,* and *Airplane Sonata.* In 1922 he went to Europe and gave a number of concerts featuring his own compositions as well as some impressionist music. He spent a year in Berlin and then went to Paris, which had become his domicile for several years; he was one of the first American students of the legendary Nadia Boulanger, who was to be the *nourrice* of a whole generation of modernistically minded Americans. In Paris he also made contact with such great literary figures as James Joyce and Ezra Pound; in the natural course of events, Antheil became the self-styled *enfant terrible* of modern music. Naively infatuated with the new world of the modern machine, he composed a *Ballet mécanique* with the avowed intention to "épater les bourgeois." The culmination of Antheil's Paris period was marked by the performance of an orchestral suite from his *Ballet mécanique* (June 19, 1926), with musical material taken from a score he wrote for a film by Fernand Léger. He then returned to America as a sort of conquering hero of modern music, and staged a spectacular production of the *Ballet mécanique* at Carnegie Hall in N.Y. on April 10, 1927, employing a set of airplane propellers, 8 pianos, and a large battery of drums, creating an uproar in the audience and much publicity in the newspapers. A revival of the *Ballet mécanique* took place in N.Y. on Feb. 20, 1954, with a recording of the noise of a jet plane replacing the obsolescent propellers, but the piece was received by the public and press as merely a curiosity of the past.
Abandoning all attempts to shock the public by extravaganza, Antheil turned to composition of operas. His first complete opera, *Transatlantic,* to his own libretto, portraying the turmoil attendant on the presidential election, and employing jazz rhythms, was staged on May 25, 1930, in Frankfurt, Germany, arousing a modicum of interest. Another opera, *Mr. Bloom and the Cyclops,* based on James Joyce's novel *Ulysses,* never progressed beyond fragmentary sketches. A second opera, *Helen Retires,* with a libretto by John Erskine, was produced in N.Y. on Feb. 28, 1934. In 1936, Antheil moved to Hollywood, where he wrote some film music and ran a syndicated column of advice to perplexed lovers; another of his whimsical diversions was working on a torpedo device, in collaboration with the motion picture actress Hedy Lamarr; they actually filed a patent, No. 2,292,387, dated June 10, 1941, for an invention relating to a "secret communication system involving the use of carrier waves of different frequencies, especially useful in the remote control of dirigible craft, such as torpedoes." It is not known whether the Antheil-Lamarr device was ever used in naval warfare. He continued to write symphs., operas, and other works, but in the spirit of the times, reduced his musical idiom to accessible masses of sound. These works were rarely performed, and in the light of musical history, Antheil remains a herald of the avant-garde of yesterday. He publ. an autobiography, *Bad Boy of Music* (N.Y., 1945). He was married to Elizabeth ("Böski") Markus, a niece of the Austrian novelist Arthur Schnitzler; she died in 1978. Antheil was the subject of a monograph by Ezra Pound entitled *Antheil and the Treatise on Harmony, with Supplementary Notes* (Chicago, 1927), which, however, had little bearing on Antheil and even less on harmony.

WORKS: OPERAS: *Transatlantic* (Frankfurt, May 25, 1930); *Helen Retires* (N.Y., Feb. 28, 1934); *Volpone,* after Ben Jonson (Los Angeles, Jan. 9, 1953); *The Brothers* (Denver, July 28, 1954); *The Wish* (Louisville, Ky., April 2, 1955); *Cabeza de vaca,* opera cantata (produced posthumously on CBS Television, June 10, 1962). BALLETS: *Ballet mécanique* (Paris, June 19, 1926; N.Y., April 10, 1927); *The Capital of the World* (N.Y., Dec. 27, 1953). FOR ORCH.: *Zingareska* (Berlin, Nov. 21, 1922); a "symphony" for 5 Instruments, also referred to as "Quintet" (1923); Symph. No. 1, in F major (1926; N.Y., April 10, 1927; a finale from it was originally labeled *Jazz Symphonietta,* and later rescored and renamed *Jazz Symphony*); Symph. No. 2, subtitled *American Symphony* (1937); Symph. No. 3 (1942); Symph. No. 4 (NBC Symph. Orch., N.Y., Stokowski conducting, Feb. 13, 1944); Symph. No. 5, subtitled *The Joyous* (Philadelphia, Dec. 21, 1948); Symph. No. 6 (San Francisco, Feb. 10, 1949); Piano Concerto (1926); *McKonkey's Ferry,* orchestral overture (1948); *Over the Plains* (1948); *Serenade* for String Orch. (1948); *Tom Sawyer: A Mark Twain Overture* (1950). CHAMBER MUSIC: 3 string quartets (1924, 1928, 1948); 4 violin sonatas (1923–48); Piano Trio (1950); 5 piano sonatas (1922–50); a group of pieces for Piano Solo under the title *La Femme: 100 têtes,* inspired by Max Ernst's book of collages of that title (1933); *Eight Fragments* from Shelley, for Chorus (1951); *Songs of Experience* for Voice and Piano (1948). FOR FILMS: *The Plainsman* (1937); *Specter of the Rose* (1946); *Knock on Any Door* (1949); *The Juggler* (1953); *Not as a Stranger* (1955); *The Pride and the Passion* (1957).

BIBLIOGRAPHY: David Ewen, *American Composers* (N.Y., 1982).

Anthony, Charles, American tenor; b. New Orleans, July 15, 1929. He studied voice with Dorothy Hulse at Loyola Univ., and then continued his studies in N.Y. and Italy. He made his Metropolitan Opera debut in N.Y. as the Simpleton in *Boris Godunov* on March 6, 1954; subsequently sang a number of lyrical roles; also appeared as a concert artist.

Anthony, Ray (real name, **Raymond Antonini**), American trumpeter and bandleader; b. Bentleyville, Pa., Jan. 20, 1922. He studied trumpet with his father; then played in the Glenn Miller orch. (1940–41); subsequently served in the U.S. Navy during World War II, leading a band in the Pacific; after the war, formed his own band and toured widely with it in the U.S.

Antier, Marie, French soprano; b. Lyons, 1687; d. Paris, Dec. 3, 1747. She made her operatic debut at the Paris Opéra in 1711 in Michel de la Barre's *La Vénitienne;* was subsequently a leading soprano there until the 1720s; also sang at the Concert Spirituel and at court performances. She retired in 1741.

Antill, John Henry, Australian composer; b. Sydney, April 8, 1904. He studied with Alfred Hill at the Sydney Cons.; also worked as a mechanical drafts-

man and designed a steam whistle capable of producing a major ninth-chord, to be used by the New South Wales Government Railways; later sang in a local opera; from 1949 to 1969 he served as federal music editor for the Australian Broadcasting Commission (later Corp.); in 1971 he received the Order of the British Empire. He was greatly interested in indigenous Australian music and attended the rural festivals of the aborigines, the corroborees; many of these primitive songs he incorporated into his compositions.

WORKS: *Corroboree,* ballet (Sydney, July 3, 1950; revised 1960); 3 operas: *Endymion* (Sydney, July 22, 1953); *The Music Critic* (1953); *The First Christmas* (Australian Broadcasting Corp., Dec. 25, 1969); 5 chamber ballets: *G'Day Digger* (1953); *Sentimental Bloke* (1955); *Wakooka* (1957); *Black Opal* (1961); *Snowy* (1961); oratorio, *The Song of Hagar* (1958). For Orch.: *Variations* (1953); *Momentous Occasion Overture* (1957); *Symphony for a City* (1959); *Music for a Royal Pageant* (1962); Harmonica Concerto (1964); *Paean to the Spirit of Man* (1968); *The Unknown Land* (1968); songs on Australian themes; film scores.

BIBLIOGRAPHY: James Murdoch, *Australia's Contemporary Composers* (Melbourne, 1972; pp. 9–15).

Antiquus, Andreas (also known as **A. de Antiquiis Venetus,** or **Andrea Antico**), Italian music printer and composer; b. Montona (Istria) in the latter half of the 15th century. He printed music in Rome and in Venice and was possibly a trade competitor to Petrucci. His printed music dates from 1510 to 1518 under the imprint of Rome; and from 1510 to 1521, of Venice. He was apparently a competent composer. His collection of *Canzoni, sonetti, strambotti e frottole, libro tertio,* was brought out by Alfred Einstein (Northampton, Mass., 1941).

Antoine, Georges, Belgian composer; b. Liège, April 28, 1892; d. Bruges, Nov. 15, 1918 (of an ailment acquired during World War I). He studied at the Cons. of Liège (1902–13) with Sylvain Dupuis; joined the Belgian army in 1914. He wrote: Piano Concerto (1914); *Vendanges* for Voice and Orch. (1914); *Veillée d'Armes,* symph. poem (1918); Piano Quartet (1916); Violin Sonata (1912–15); songs.

BIBLIOGRAPHY: M. Paquot, *Georges Antoine* (Brussels, 1935).

Anton, Karl, German musicologist; b. Worms, June 2, 1887; d. Weinheim/Bergstrasse, Feb. 21, 1956. He studied music, history, and theology; received his Ph.D. in 1912; in 1919 he was appointed to the faculty of the Hochschule für Musik in Mannheim. Most of his publications deal with church music; among them are *Luther und die Musik* (1917), *Angewandte Liturgik* (1918), and *Erneuerung der Kirchenmusik* (1932).

Anton, Max, German conductor and pedagogue; b. Bornstedt, Aug. 2, 1877; d. Bonn, Aug. 18, 1939. He studied with Stavenhagen in Munich and James

Kwast in Frankfurt; then taught at Gladbach and Detmold; from 1922 until his retirement in 1934, was active in Bonn as a choral conductor. A prolific composer, he wrote an opera, *Die Getreuen;* an oratorio, *Ekkehard;* several instrumental concertos, piano pieces, and songs. He publ. *Versuch einer Kunstanschauung* (1922).

Antonini, Alfredo, Italian-American conductor; b. Milan, May 31, 1901; d. Clearwater, Fla., during heart surgery, Nov. 3, 1983. He studied at the Milan Cons.; then served as organist and pianist at La Scala under Toscanini. In 1929 he went to N.Y.; in 1941 he joined CBS as music director; supplied background scores for numerous television films; also composed semi-classical music, e.g., *Sicilian Rhapsody* and *The U.S. circa 1790.* In 1957 he became conductor of the Tampa Phil.

Antoniou, Theodore, Greek-American avant-garde composer; b. Athens, Feb. 10, 1935. He studied violin, voice, and music theory at the National Cons. in Athens, where his teachers were Manolis Kalomiris and Yannis Papaioannou (1947–61). In 1961 he went to Germany, where he studied composition with Günther Bialas at the Hochschule für Musik in Munich (1961–65); also attended summer seminars on new music in Darmstadt (1963–65). In 1966 he traveled in the U.S. on a State Dept. grant. Returning to Greece, he served as director of the Orch. of the City of Athens (1967); in 1968 took part in organizing the Hellenic Week of Contemporary Music. In 1969 he emigrated to America and was engaged as composer-in-residence at Stanford Univ. in Palo Alto, Calif., and at the Berkshire Center in Tanglewood; in the summers of 1970 and 1972 held a similar post at the Univ. of Utah in Salt Lake City. In 1970 he was appointed prof. of composition at the Philadelphia College of Performing Arts, and concurrently was engaged as conductor of the Symph. Orch. at the Philadelphia Musical Academy. In 1979 he was appointed prof. of composition at Boston Univ. Also in 1979 he received a Guggenheim fellowship. His music is remarkably compendious in its integration of quaquaversal layers of sound; folk elements in Greek modalities are also in evidence, and many titles have Greek philosophic or literary connotations. WORKS: FOR THE STAGE: *Riders without Horses* (Athens, April 26, 1961); *Rhinoceros,* after Ionesco's play (Athens, May 4, 1962); *Philoctet,* after Sophocles (Epidaurus, June 25, 1967); *Juno and the Peacock,* after O'Casey (Athens, Oct. 16, 1969); *Birds,* after Aristophanes (Nuremberg, Feb. 8, 1970); *Autopsy,* after G. Michaelidis (Athens, Dec. 14, 1970); *Midsummer Night's Dream,* after Shakespeare (Athens, Oct. 15, 1971); *Romeo and Juliet* (Athens, March 17, 1971); *Wozzeck,* after Büchner (Athens, July 30, 1972); *Sunday Walk,* after G. Michel (Athens, Sept. 29, 1972); *Oedipus at Colonus,* after Sophocles (Epidaurus, July 6, 1975); *Seven against Thebes,* after Aeschylus (Athens, July 25, 1975); *Oresteia,* after Aeschylus (Stanford Univ., Feb. 24, 1976); *Medea,* after Euripides (Saloniki,

Aug. 16, 1976); *Bacchae,* after Euripides (Comédie Française, Paris, April 14, 1976); *News from the New World Discovered in the Moon,* after Ben Jonson (Athens, Nov. 30, 1978); *Periander,* mixed-media opera (1979).
MULTIMEDIA PRODUCTIONS: *Clytemnestra,* sound-action for Actress, Dancers, Instruments, and Tape (Kassel, June 4, 1968); *Katharsis* for Flute, Orch., Tape, and Projections (Athens, Dec. 22, 1968); *Cassandra,* sound-action for Dancers, Actors, Chorus, Orch., Tapes, Lights, and Projections (Barcelona, Nov. 14, 1970); *Cheironomiai (Gestures),* improvisation by conductor and any combination of instruments and voices (Kassel, Oct. 31, 1971); *Chorochronos I* (Philadelphia, May 11, 1973); *Chorochronos II* (Reitlingenwest, Germany, Oct. 29, 1973); *Chorochronos III* (Berlin, Jan. 26, 1975).
VOCAL MUSIC: *Greek Folk Songs* for Mixed Choir (1961); *Epilogue,* after *The Odyssey,* for Voice and Orch. (Munich, March 10, 1964); *Kontakion* for Voices, Chorus, and String Orch. (Berlin, May 7, 1965); *Melos,* cantata after Sappho for Medium Voice and Orch. (Athens, April 2, 1967); *Climate of Absence* for Voice and Orch. (Munich, Nov. 12, 1968); *Die weisse Rose,* cantata (Philadelphia, April 25, 1976); *Circle of Thanatos and Genesis,* cantata (Boston, Jan. 23, 1981).
FOR ORCH.: Triple Concerto for Violin, Trumpet, Clarinet, and Orch. (1959); *Concertino* for Piano, String Orch., and Percussion (Athens, Dec. 16, 1962); *Antithesis* for Orch. (Hannover, Jan. 20, 1966); *Concertino* for Piano, 9 Wind Instruments, and Percussion (Philadelphia, Dec. 4, 1973); *Jeux* for Cello and String Orch. (March 4, 1968); Violin Concerto (Athens, Aug. 16, 1965); *Kinesis ABCD* for 2 Groups of Strings (Athens, July 13, 1966); *Op Overture* for Orch. and Tape (1966); *Micrographies* (Kassel, April 3, 1968); *Events I* for Violin, Piano, and Orch. (Hagen, June 10, 1968); *Events II* for Orch. (Tanglewood, Aug. 30, 1969); *Events III* for Orch. with Tape (Barcelona, Oct. 8, 1969); *Synthesis* for Oboe, Organ, Percussion, Double Bass, and 4 Synthesizers (1971); *Threnos* for Wind Orch. (Tanglewood, Aug. 7, 1974); *Fluxus I* (Basel, Dec. 18, 1979); *Fluxus II* (Philadelphia, April 4, 1976); *Circle of Accusation* (Lemesos, Cyprus, Aug. 8, 1977); *Parastasis I* for Percussion and Tape (1977); *Parastasis II* for Percussion and Instruments (1978); Double Concerto for Percussion and Orch. (Philadelphia, April 26, 1978).
CHAMBER MUSIC: Trio for Flute, Viola, and Cello (1961); *Dialogues* for Flute and Guitar (1962); *Quartetto giocoso* for Oboe, Violin, Cello, and Piano (West Berlin, June 8, 1968); *Six Likes* for Solo Tuba (1967); *Lyrics* for Violin and Piano (1967); *Five Likes* for Solo Oboe (1969); *Four Likes* for Solo Violin (1972); *Three Likes* for Solo Clarinet (1973); *Two Likes* for Solo Double Bass (1976); *Stichomythia II* for Solo Guitar (1977); *The Do Quintet* for 2 Trumpets, Horn, Trombone, and Tuba (1978).
FOR PIANO: *Aquarelle* (1958); *Syllables* (1965).

Antony, Franz Joseph, German organist and writer on music; b. Münster, Westphalia, Feb. 1, 1790; d. there, Jan. 7, 1837. He was appointed music director at Münster Cathedral in 1819; in 1832 succeeded his father, Joseph Antony (1758–1836), as organist. He publ. *Archäologisch-liturgisches Gesangbuch des Gregorianischen Kirchengesangs* (1829) and *Geschichtliche Darstellung der Entstehung und Vervollkommnung der Orgel* (1832).

Anzaghi, Davide, Italian composer; b. Milan, Nov. 29, 1936. He studied piano, conducting, and composition at the G. Verdi Cons. in Milan, graduating in 1957; then took courses in composition with Ghedini and Donatoni in Venice. He subsequently joined the faculty of his alma mater at the G. Verdi Cons.
WORKS: For Orch.: *Riturgia* (Venice, Sept. 14, 1972); *Limbale* (Bologna, Nov. 10, 1973); *Ausa* (La Rochelle, France, July 5, 1974); *Egophonie* (1974; Milan, Feb. 3, 1975); *Aur'ore* for Chorus and Orch. (1974–76; Milan, Feb. 4, 1977); *Ermosonio* (1978; Milan, Nov. 30, 1979). Chamber music: *Limine* for String Trio (1971); *Aulografia* for Solo Flute (1975); *In-Chiostro* for 2 Violins and Viola (1975); *Alena* for 10 Wind Instruments (1976); *Remota* for 7 Players (1977); *Alia* for Bass Clarinet and Piano (1980); *Oiseau triste* for Piccolo and Piano (1980); *Soavodia* for Clarinet and Piano (1980). For Piano: *Segni* (1968); *Ritografia* (1971).

Apel, Johann August, German scholar; b. Leipzig, Sept. 17, 1771; d. there, Aug. 9, 1816. He is important in music history for his collection *Gespensterbuch* (1810–14), dealing with supernatural tales, which was the inspiration for Weber's *Der Freischütz*. He also publ. several treatises on music, among them a series of articles on rhythm, in *Allgemeine Musikalische Zeitung* (1807–8), and a large work in 2 vols., *Metrik* (1814–16).

Apel, Willi, eminent music scholar; b. Konitz, Germany, Oct. 10, 1893. He studied mathematics at the univs. of Bonn (1912), Munich (1913), and Berlin (1918–21). He received his Ph.D. from the Univ. of Berlin in 1932; concurrently he studied music and took piano lessons. He taught mathematics and music in Germany until 1936, when he emigrated to the U.S. He gave lecture courses at Harvard Univ. (1938–42); in 1950 was engaged as prof. of musicology at Indiana Univ., Bloomington; retired in 1964 as prof. emeritus. While in Germany, he edited 2 volumes of early piano music, *Musik aus früher Zeit für Klavier* (Mainz, 1934). His other German publications were *Die Fuge* (1932) and his doctoral dissertation, *Accidentien und Tonalität in den Musikdenkmälern des 15. und 16. Jahrhunderts;* it was publ. as vol. 24 in the *Collection d'études musicologiques* (Strasbourg, 1937); a second augmented ed. appeared in Baden-Baden in 1972. In America he publ. the extremely valuable treatises and compilations *The Notation of Polyphonic Music, 900–1600* (Cambridge, Mass., 1942; 5th revised ed., 1961); *The Harvard Dictionary of Music,* a prime reference work of musical terminology (Cambridge, Mass., 1944; 2nd ed., revised and enlarged, Cambridge, 1969); *Historical Anthology of Music,* 2 vols. (with A.T. Davison; Cambridge, Mass.,

1946 and 1949); *Masters of the Keyboard* (Cambridge, Mass., 1947); *Gregorian Chant* (Bloomington, Ind., 1958). A Festschrift in Apel's honor, *Essays in Musicology,* ed. by H. Tischler (Bloomington, Ind., 1968), contains a bibliography of his writings.

Aperghis, Georges, avant-garde Greek composer; b. Athens, Dec. 23, 1945. He studied music privately with Yannis Papaioannou in Athens; in 1963 went to Paris and became a student of Xenakis, who initiated him into the mysteries of ultramodern techniques involving such arcana as musical indeterminacy and audiovisual coordinates in spatial projection.
WORKS: *Bis, spectacle musical* for 10 Actors and 10 Instruments (1968); *The Tragic Story of the Necromancer Hieronimo and His Mirror* for Puppets, Voice, Guitar, and Piano (1971); *Funeral Oration* (1971); *Concerto Grosso* (Paris, May 29, 1972); *Ouverture* (1973); *Pandaemonium* (1973); *Jacques le Fataliste* (1973). He also wrote *2 Movements* for String Quartet (1964); *Dialogues* for Flute, Harpsichord, and Xylophone (1965); *Antistixis A* for 3 String Quartets (1964–65), *B* for 4 Flutes, 4 Percussionists, Celesta, Harp, Ondes Martenot, and Double Bass (1965), and *C* for Orch. (1966); *Contrepoint* for Orch. (1967); *Libretto* for Orch. in 4 groups (1968); *Anacrusis* for Chamber Ensemble (1967); *Eluding Game* for Instrumental Ensemble (1968); *Freak Map* for 6 Instruments and 3 Percussionists (1968); *Contrepoint* for 3 String Quartets, Piano, Trombone, and Percussion (1968); *Plastic Piece* for 2 Orchs. (1968); *Music for an Orange Girl* for Chamber Ensemble and Tape (1968); *Color Music* for 19 Instruments (1966–69); *Musique automatique,* suite of 6 pieces for Female Voice and Chamber Ensemble (1969); *Boogie-Woogie* for Chamber Ensemble (1969); *Variations* for 10 Musicians (1969); *B.A.C.H.* for Chorus and Orch. (1969); *4 pièces superposables* for Conductor, Percussion, Voice, and Strings (1969); *La Création* for Speaker and Instrumental Ensemble (1969); *Variations sur un portrait de Bach* for Any Instrument (1970); *Le Fil d'Ariane* for Ondes Martenot (1970); *Variations 1 and 2* for 5 Percussionists and 5 Xylophones (1970); *Variations 3 and 4 (Awake)* for 6 Oboes (1970); *Music Box* for Harpsichord (1970); *Vesper,* oratorio (1970); *Quartet for 4 Double Basses* (1970); *Quartet for 4 Percussionists* (1970); *Symplexis* for 22 Jazz Soloists and Orch. (Paris, Nov. 3, 1970); *Puzzles* for 5 Woodwinds, 5 Brass, and Percussion (1971); *Die Wände haben Ohren (The Walls Have Ears)* for Orch. (Metz, France, Nov. 26, 1972); *BWV* for 6 Singers and Instrumental Ensemble (1973); *Sports et rebondissements* for 6 Voices, Actors, 2 Trombones, Tuba, Percussion, and Tape (1974); *Les Lauriers sont coupés* for Voice and Chamber Ensemble (1975); *Mouvement* for Violin, Viola, Cello, Clarinet, and Piano (1975).

Aplvor, Denis, Irish-born English composer; b. Collinstown, West Meath, April 14, 1916. He studied music theory privately in London with Patrick Hadley and Alan Rawsthorne (1937–39); adopted a fairly advanced technique of composition while adhering to tradition in formal design; his pieces are quite playable, and the associations he brings out with extramusical elements (painting, etc.) are most ingenious.

WORKS: 4 operas: opera-buffa, *She Stoops to Conquer,* after Goldsmith's play (1943–47; revised 1976–77); *Yerma,* after García Lorca's play (1955–58); *Ubu Roi,* after Alfred Jarry's play (1965–66); *Bouvard and Pecuchet,* after Flaubert (1970); 5 ballets: *The Goodman of Paris* (1951); *A Mirror for Witches* (1951); *Blood Wedding,* after Lorca (1953); *Saudades* (1954); *Corporal Jan* (1967); cantata, *The Hollow Men,* after T.S. Eliot's poem (1939; BBC Radio, London, Feb. 21, 1950); *Cantata,* to poems by Dylan Thomas (1960); Piano Concerto (1948); Concerto for Violin and 15 Instruments (1950); 2 symphs. (1952, 1963); Guitar Concertino (1953); *Overtones,* 9 short pieces for Orch., based on Paul Klee's paintings (1961–62); *String Abstract,* concerto for String Trio and Orch. (1967); *Tarot,* variations for Chamber Orch. (1968); *Neumes,* variations for Orch. (1969); *The Tremulous Silence* for Guitar and Chamber Orch. (1972); *Exotics Theater,* 10 pieces for Chamber Ensemble (1972; Klee pieces: iii); *Resonance of the Southern Flora* for wordless Chorus and Orch. (1972; Klee pieces: iv); *Fern Hill,* after Thomas, for Tenor and 11 Instruments (1973); Violin Concerto (1975); Violin Sonata (1944–45); *Concertante* for Clarinet, Piano, and Percussion (1944–45); *Variations* for Solo Guitar (1958); Wind Quintet (1960); *Mutations* for Cello and Piano (1962); 2 String Quartets (1964, 1976); *Crystals* for Percussion, Hammond Organ, Guitar, and Double Bass (1964–65); *Harp, Piano, Piano-Harp* (1966); *10 String Design* for Violin and Guitar (1967); *Discanti,* 5 pieces for Solo Guitar (1970); *Saeta* for Solo Guitar (1972); *Psycho-pieces,* 8 pieces for Clarinet and Piano (1973; Klee pieces: v); *Studies for Wind,* 7 pieces, one each for Flute, Oboe, Clarinet, Bassoon, Horn, Trumpet, and Trombone (1974); Clarinet Quintet (1975); *Liaison,* duo for Guitar and Keyboard (1976); *Animalcules,* 12 piano pieces (1962); *5 Piano Pieces* (1968); *Orgelberg* for Organ (1971; Klee pieces: ii); songs.

Aponte-Ledée, Rafael,
Puerto Rican composer; b. Guayama, Oct. 15, 1938. He studied composition with Cristóbal Halffter at the Madrid Cons. (1957–64); then took courses with Ginastera at the Latin American Center of Advanced Musical Studies at the Di Tella Inst. in Buenos Aires (1965–66). Returning to Puerto Rico, he founded in San Juan, with the collaboration of Francis Schwartz, the Fluxus group for the promotion of new music (1967); taught composition and theory at the Univ. of Puerto Rico (1968–74). His music is highly advanced, employing nearly every conceivable technique of the cosmopolitan avant-garde.

WORKS: *Tema y 6 Diferencias* for Piano (1963); *Dialogantes 1* for Flute and Violin (1965); *Elejía* for 13 Strings (1965; version for 50 Strings, 1967); *Presagio de Pájaros muertos* for Narrator and Tape (1966); *Epíthasis* for 3 Oboes, 2 Trombones, Double Bass, and 3 Percussionists (1967); *Dialogantes 2* for 3 Flutes, 3 Trombones, and 3 Clarinets (1968); *La ventana abierta* for 3 Mezzo-sopranos, 3 Flutes, Clarinet, Trumpet, 2 Percussionists, Celesta, Piano, Violin, Cello, and Double Bass (1968); version for 3 Mezzo-sopranos, Flutes, Clarinet, 2 Trumpets, Horn, 2 Percussionists, Guitar, Piano, and 2 String Quartets, 1969); *Streptomicyne* for Soprano, Flute, Clarinet, Trumpet, and Piano (1970); *SSSSSS²* for Double-bass Solo, 3 Flutes, Trumpet, and Percussion (1971); *Volúmenes* for Piano (1971); *Elvira en sombras* for Piano and Orch. (1973); *Estravagario, In memoriam Salvador Allende* for Orch. and Tape (1973); *Cuídese de los angeles que caen,* musique concrète (1974); *Los huevos de pandora* for Clarinet and Tape (1974); *El palacio en sombras* for Orch. without Violins and Cellos (1977).

Apostel, Hans Erich,
Austrian composer; b. Karlsruhe, Jan. 22, 1901; d. Vienna, Nov. 30, 1972. After early studies in Karlsruhe he went to Vienna in 1921, and became a pupil in composition of Schoenberg and Alban Berg. He served as an editor at Universal Edition and in that capacity prepared for publication the posthumous works of Berg. He was also active as a teacher. Apostel received numerous prizes for his own works, among them the Grand Prize of the City of Vienna (1948) and the Grand Prize of the Republic of Austria (1957). In 1951 he adopted the method of composition with 12 tones according to Schoenberg's precepts, without, however, avoiding tonal combinations. He experimented in Klangfarben effects, and applied audible overtones in his piano pieces by holding down the keys without striking them. His music was often performed at international festivals, but it never penetrated beyond the confines of Central Europe.

WORKS: Piano Sonata (1929); *Requiem,* to Rilke's words, for Chorus and Orch. (1933; Vienna Radio, May 3, 1958); *Sonatina ritmica* for Piano (1934); 2 string quartets (1935, 1956); *Adagio* for String Orch., 2 Harps, Celesta, and Piano (1937); *5 Songs,* after Hölderlin, for Low Voice and Orch. (1939–40); *Kubiniana,* 10 piano pieces (1945–50); Quartet for Flute, Clarinet, Horn, and Bassoon (1947–49); *Variations on a Theme of Joseph Haydn* for Orch. (1949; Zürich, May 10, 1951); *3 Songs,* after Trakl, for Low Female Voice, 4 Violins, 2 Cellos, and Double Bass (1951); Solo Flute Sonatina (1951); Solo Clarinet Sonatina (1951); Solo Bassoon Sonatina (1951); *5 Bagatelles* for Flute, Clarinet, and Bassoon (1952); *Intrada* for Brass and Percussion (1954); *Ballade* for Orch. (1955); *Suite concise,* 7 pieces for Piano (1955); *Variations on 3 Folk Songs* for Small Orch. (1956); *Rondo ritmico* for Orch. (1957); Piano Concerto (1958; Venice, Sept. 24, 1959); *Fantasie* for Piano (1959); *5 Austrian Miniatures* for Orch. (1959); *6 Epigrammes* for String Quartet (1962); Cello Sonata (1962); *Ode* for High Voice and Orch. (1961–62); *Kleine Kammerkonzert* for Flute, Viola, and Guitar (1964); Solo Oboe Sonatina (1964); Solo Horn Sonatina (1964); *Kammersymphonie* (1965–67; Vienna, June 4, 1968); *Epitaph* for String Orch. (1969); *Paralipomena dodekaphonika (Haydn*

Variations, Part II) for Orch. (1969–70; Donawitz, Oct. 29, 1970); *Fischerhaus-Serenade* for 4 Woodwinds, 3 Brasses, and String Quartet (1971); *Passacaglia* for Orch. (2nd movement of an uncompleted Concerto for Orch., 1972; posthumous, London, BBC, July 10, 1974).

Apostolescu, Nicu, Rumanian tenor; b. Brăila, July 31, 1896. He studied in Bucharest; made his debut as a baritone in 1921 in Cluj; then sang mostly tenor roles; was a prinicipal member of the Bucharest Opera (1926–44).

Appel, Richard Gilmore, American music librarian and organist; b. Lancaster, Pa., April 25, 1889; d. Cambridge, Mass., Nov. 18, 1975. He studied organ with Wallace Goodrich in Boston and Karl Straube in Germany; received his M.A. from Harvard Univ. in 1912; was church organist in Boston and vicinity; composed various pieces for organ. From 1922–54 he was head of the music dept. of the Boston Public Library. In 1975 he publ. *The Music of the Bay Psalm Book: 9th Edition (1698)* (No. 5, I.S.A.M. Monograph Series).

Appeldoorn, Dina, Dutch composer; b. Rotterdam, Feb. 26, 1884; d. The Hague, Dec. 4, 1938. She was the composer of several works in the Romantic style, including 2 symph. poems, *Noordzee* and *Volkfeest;* she also wrote chamber music and songs, and taught piano in The Hague.

Appenzeller (Appencellers, Appenzelder, Appenzelders), Benedictus, Franco-Flemish composer of the first half of the 16th century. Possibly a pupil of Josquin, he served Mary of Hungary as court musician and master of choirboys at her chapel in Brussels (1537–c.1554) and probably accompanied her on her visit to Germany (1551). Appenzeller's works were formerly attributed to Benedictus Ducis, a German composer whose identity was confused with his. Among Appenzeller's extant compositions are a book of chansons (1542; 2 of the chansons from this collection had been publ. by Attaingnant in 1529 without being ascribed to Appenzeller); a lament on the death of Josquin (1521), which uses half of the *Musae Jovis* text; and a double canon on *Sancta Maria* embroidered on a tablecloth for Mary of Hungary (1548). Pieces by him are included in the 2nd *Musyckboexken* of Susato; the *Hortus Musarum,* part I (1552), publ. by Phalese, contains a transcription for 2 lutes of a piece by Appenzeller.
BIBLIOGRAPHY: E. van der Straeten, *La Musique aux Pays-Bas* (Brussels, 1867–68; vols. 3, 7, and 8); D. Bartha, *Benedictus Ducis und Appenzeller* (Wolfenbüttel, 1930); G. Reese, *Music in the Renaissance* (N.Y., 1954).

Appia, Edmond, Italian-Swiss violinist and conductor; b. Turin, May 7, 1894; d. Geneva, Feb. 12, 1961. He studied violin with Henri Marteau at the Cons. of Geneva, in Paris with Lucien Capet, and at the Brussels Cons., obtaining the Premier Prix in 1920; toured Europe (1920–35); taught violin in Geneva and Lausanne. In 1935 he became a conductor of Radiodiffusion Suisse in Lausanne; in 1938 vas appointed conductor of the Geneva Radio Orch. He also wrote articles on Swiss music for the *Musical Quarterly* and many European publications.

Applebaum, Edward, American composer; b. Los Angeles, Sept. 28, 1937. He studied piano as a youth; later studied with Henri Lazarof and Lukas Foss at the Univ. of Calif. at Los Angeles (Ph.D., 1966). In 1969 he was composer-in-residence of the Oakland Symph. Orch.; in 1971 became a prof. of theory and composition at the Univ. of Calif. at Santa Barbara.
WORKS: Piano Sonata (1965); String Trio (1966); Variations for Orch. (1966); Concerto for Viola and Chamber Orch. (1967); *Montages* for Clarinet, Cello, and Piano (1968); *Shantih* for Cello and Piano (1969); Symph. No. 1 (1970); *Foci* for Viola and Piano (1971); *... When Dreams Do Show Thee Me ...* , triple concerto for Clarinet, Cello, Piano, Chamber Orch., and 9 Vocal Soloists (1972); Piano Trio (1972); *Reflections for Piano Trio* (1972); *The Face in the Cameo* for Clarinet and Piano (1973); *The Frieze of Life,* one-act chamber opera (1974); *To Remember,* trio for Clarinet, Cello, and Piano (1976); *The Garden* for Soprano, Chamber Ensemble, and Tape (1979); Piano Sonata No. 2 (1980); Symph. No. 2 (St. Louis, Oct. 6, 1983).

Applebaum, Louis, Canadian composer; b. Toronto, April 3, 1918. He studied with Healy Willan, Leo Smith, and Sir Ernest MacMillan at the Toronto Cons., graduating in 1940; then with Bernard Wagenaar and Roy Harris in N.Y. (1940–41). He returned to Canada in 1941 and was a member of the board of directors of the Composers, Authors and Publishers Association of Canada (1956–68) and then its music executive (1968–71).
WORKS: Musical comedy, *Ride a Pink Horse* (1960); 3 ballets: *Dark of the Moon* (1953; revised as *Barbara Allen,* 1960; concert suite, 1965); *Legend of the North* (1957); *Homage* (1969); for Orch., *East by North* (1947); *Variations on a Theme from a Film Score* for Oboe, Piano, and String Trio (1948; revised 1953); *Christmas Overture* (1951); *Suite of Miniature Dances* for Orch. (1958; arranged for Band, 1964); *3 Greek Dances* for Orch. (1958); *Moments from "Romeo and Juliet"* for Wind Quintet, Cello, Harp, and Percussion (1961); *Action Stations* for Orch. (1962); *Concertante* for Small Orch. (1967); *Fanfare and Anthem* for Orch. (1969); incidental music for plays and more than 100 films; piano pieces; songs.

Appledorn, Mary Jeanne van, American pianist and teacher; b. Holland, Mich., Oct. 2, 1927. She studied piano at the Eastman School of Music in Rochester, N.Y.; also received her M.M. in theory (1950) and Ph.D. in composition (1966) there. Among her works are *Burlesca* for Piano, Brass, and Percussion (1951); Piano Concerto (1954); Trumpet Concerto (1960); Passacaglia for Chamber Orch. (1958); and a number of piano pieces in a facile Western manner, such as *Apache Echoes, Indian Trail, Boots 'n' Saddles,* and *Wagon Train.* She publ. *Keyboard, Singing and Dictation Manual* (Dubuque, Iowa, 1968). In 1975 she was chairman of the music literature and theory division at Texas Tech. Univ. in Lubbock, Texas.

Aprile, Giuseppe, Italian male contralto; b. Martina Franca, Apulia, Oct. 28, 1731; d. there, Jan. 11, 1813. He studied voice with his father, and since he showed signs of excellence, his father had him evirated at the age of 11. He then studied singing in Naples and appeared as a soprano at the Naples Royal Chapel in 1751. He made his professional debut as a singer at the Teatro San Carlo in Naples in 1753; he subsequently sang at the Court of Württemberg in Stuttgart (1756), and remained in that service for 10 years. He later was active as a teacher in Naples; among his pupils was Cimarosa. Aprile's vocal treatise *The Modern Italian Method of Singing, with 36 Solfeggi* was publ. by Broderip in London in 1791 and was reprinted in several editions and translated into several languages.

Apthorp, William Foster, American music critic; b. Boston, Mass., Oct. 24, 1848; d. Vevey, Switzerland, Feb. 19, 1913. A graduate of Harvard Univ. (1869), he studied music with Paine. He taught music at the New England Cons. and lectured on music history at Boston Univ. He wrote music criticism for the *Atlantic Monthly* (1872–77); was music and drama critic on the *Boston Evening Transcript* (1881–1903). In his criticisms Apthorp violently opposed new Russian, French, and German music (his intemperate attacks on Tchaikovsky elicited protests from his readers). Apthorp was also the annotator of the Boston Symph. programs (1892–1901). He publ. several books: *Musicians and Music Lovers* (N.Y., 1894); *By the Way,* a collection of short essays in 2 vols.: I, *About Music,* and II, *About Musicians* (Boston, 1898); *The Opera, Past and Present* (N.Y., 1901). He was co-editor of *Scribner's Cyclopedia of Music and Musicians* (N.Y., 1888–90).

Ara, Ugo, Italian violinist and member of the Flonzaley Quartet; b. Venice, July 19, 1876; d. Lausanne, Switzerland, Dec. 10, 1936. He studied violin with Tirindelli in Venice; at the age of 13 played in theater orchs. In 1894 he went to Liège, where he studied with César Thomson; he then took lessons in composition with R. Fuchs at the Vienna Cons. When the Flonzaley Quartet was established, he joined it as a viola player (1903–17); later returned to Italy.

Aragall, Giacomo (Jaime), Spanish tenor; b. Barcelona, June 6, 1939. He won the Bussetto singing competition in 1963; then sang the role of Gastone in Verdi's *Gerusalemme* in Venice; during the 1963–64 season he appeared at La Scala in Milan; in 1965 sang at the Holland Festival and in Edinburgh. In 1966 he made his London debut at Covent Garden as the Duke of Mantua; in the 1982–83 season he attracted favorable publicity when he replaced Luciano Pavarotti as Cavaradossi on short notice. He made his Metropolitan Opera debut in N.Y. in 1968 as the Duke in *Rigoletto;* from 1973–77 he sang opera in Chicago and San Francisco.

Aragón, Prudencio, Argentine composer of tangos and other popular dances; b. Belgrano, April 28, 1886; d. Montevideo, Nov. 2, 1963. He worked as a pianist in Madame Blanche's establishment (bordello); his most signal success was *El talar* (1895).

Araiza, Francisco, Mexican tenor; b. Mexico City, Oct. 4, 1950. He studied at the Univ. of Mexico City, where he sang in the Univ. choir; made his concert debut in Mexico City in 1969, and subsequently sang in opera there; then went to Europe, where he joined the Karlsruhe Opera in 1974; also took lessons in Munich with Richard Holm and Erik Werba. He subsequently made appearances with opera houses in Zürich, Düsseldorf, Stuttgart, and Munich; also sang at the Bayreuth Festival. He received praise for his performances in Mozart's operas.

Araja, Francesco, Italian composer; b. Naples, June 25, 1709; d. Bologna, 1770. He produced his first opera, *Lo matremmonejo pe' mennetta,* in the Neapolitan dialect (Naples, 1729); his subsequent operas were *Berenice* (Florence, 1730); *La forza dell'amore e dell'odio* (Milan, 1734); *Lucio Vero* (Venice, Jan. 4, 1735). In 1735 he was engaged as music director and court composer in St. Petersburg. There he wrote annual pieces for court occasions, beginning with the cantata *La gara dell'amore e del zelo* (April 28, 1736). Among his operas given at the Russian court were *La Semiramide riconosciuta* (Feb. 9, 1737); *Artaserse* (1738); *Seleuco* (1744); *Scipione* (1745); *Mitridate* (1747); *L'asilo della pace* (1748); *Bellerofonte* (1750); *Eudossa incoronata* (1751). He wrote 17 operas; *La clemenza di Tito,* attributed to him by some, was the work of Hasse. On Feb. 27, 1755, Araja presented in St. Petersburg the first opera ever composed to a libretto in the Russian language, on the story of Cephalus and Procris, written by the famous Russian dramatist Sumarokov. Araja was in Italy from 1740–42, and again from 1759–62; in 1762 he revisited Russia briefly at the summons of Peter III, his great admirer, returning to Italy after the Czar's death. Nothing is known of Araja's last years.

BIBLIOGRAPHY: A. Mooser, *Annales de la musique et des musiciens en Russie au XVIII siècle,* vol. I, pp. 121–31 (Geneva, 1951).

Arakishvili, Dmitri, Georgian composer; b. Vladikavkaz, Feb. 23, 1873; d. Tiflis, Aug. 13, 1953. He studied composition at the Moscow Phil. Inst. with Ilyinsky and also took private lessons with Gretchaninov. At the same time he studied archaeology and ethnic sciences; in 1901 he became a member of the Musical Ethnographic Commission at the Univ. of Moscow. In 1906 he took part in the organization of the Moscow People's Cons., which offered free music lessons to impecunious students. He was editor of the Moscow publication *Music and Life* (1908–12). In 1918 he moved to Tiflis, where he was active as a teacher and conductor. He composed one of the earliest national Georgian operas, *The Legend of Shota Rustaveli* (Tiflis, Feb. 5, 1919); a comic opera, *Dinara* (1926); 3 symphs. (1934, 1942, 1951); *Hymn of the New East* for Orch. (1933); and film music. But his best compositions are some 80 art songs in a lyrico-dramatic manner reflecting the Georgian modalities.

Arámbarri (y Garate), Jesús, Spanish conductor; b. Bilbao, April 13, 1902; d. Madrid, July 11, 1960. He studied at the Vizcaino Cons. in Bilbao; then took courses in composition with Paul Le Flem and Paul Dukas, and conducting with Golschmann in Paris; later attended the conducting classes of Weingartner in Basel. In 1933 he was engaged as conductor of the Bilbao Municipal Orch. In 1953 he settled in Madrid. He composed vocal works, chamber music, and piano pieces.

Arangi-Lombardi, Giannina, Italian soprano; b. Marigliano, near Naples, June 20, 1891; d. Milan, July 9, 1951. She studied at the Naples Cons.; made her debut as a mezzo-soprano in 1920 at the Teatro Costanzi in Rome; sang soprano roles from 1923; appeared at La Scala in Milan (1924–30). In 1928 she accompanied Melba on an Australian tour; also sang in South America. After retiring from the stage she taught voice at the Milan Cons. (1938–47) and later at Ankara, Turkey. She was at her best in the lyrico-dramatic roles of the Italian repertoire.

Aranyi, Francis, Hungarian violinist; b. Budapest, March 21, 1893; d. Seattle, May 5, 1966. He studied at the Royal Academy of Music in Budapest, and later took violin lessons in Berlin with Willy Hess and Henri Marteau. His career as a violinist took him to Vienna, Stockholm, and Zagreb. In 1935 he emigrated to America; taught at Duquesne Univ. in Pittsburgh (1935–40) and at Michigan State College (1940–41); was concertmaster at the Seattle Symph. Orch. during the season 1941–42. In 1942 he organized the Youth Symph. Orch. of the Pacific Northwest in Seattle, where he remained until his death.

d'Aranyi, Jelly, Hungarian violinist, grandniece of **Joachim** and sister of the violinist **Adila Fachiri;** b. Budapest, May 30, 1893; d. Florence, March 30, 1966. She studied violin with Hubay in Budapest; after some concerts in Europe, she went to America and made her debut in a solo recital in N.Y. on Nov. 26, 1927; made her 2nd American tour in 1932. She frequently appeared in joint recitals with Myra Hess. A pioneer in modern music, she gave first performances of many new works. Béla Bartók's First Violin Sonata, Ravel's *Tzigane*, and the *Concerto Accademico* for Violin and Orch. by Vaughan Williams are dedicated to her. She attracted considerable attention in 1937 when she proclaimed that Schumann's spirit appeared to her during a séance and revealed the secret of his unpublished Violin

Concerto; but Schumann's ghost spoke ungrammatical German, which aroused suspicion concerning the authenticity of the phenomenon; besides, it had long been known that the MS of the concerto was preserved at the Berlin State Library; the first performance of the piece was eventually given in Germany by another violinist. Jelly d'Aranyi was given a chance, however, to perform it with the BBC Orch. in London on Feb. 16, 1938.

BIBLIOGRAPHY: J. Macleod, *The Sisters d'Aranyi* (London, 1969).

Arapov, Boris, eminent Russian composer and pedagogue; b. St. Petersburg, Sept. 12, 1905. He was a scion of an intellectual family; his grandfather was a lawyer; his father was a naturalist. He spent his childhood in Poltava, where he received his early musical training; in 1921 the family returned to St. Petersburg (now renamed Petrograd); he studied composition with Shcherbachev at the Cons. there, graduating in 1930; was then appointed to its faculty as an instructor (1930) and later prof. (1940). Among his pupils were many Soviet composers of stature, including Dmitri Tolstoy, Falik, Uspensky, Banshchikov, Knaifel, and Sergei Slonimsky. The years 1941–44 Arapov spent in Tashkent, in Uzbekistan, where the entire faculty of the Leningrad Cons. was evacuated during the siege of Leningrad. There he studied indigenous folklore, and wrote an Uzbeki opera, *Khodji Nasreddin*. After the siege was lifted, Arapov returned to Leningrad, resumed his pedagogical duties, and continued to compose. In 1955–56 he was in China, where he wrote several works on Chinese themes. In 1959 he visited Korea, and composed a symph. using the pentatonic Korean modes. During the years 1950–73 he also traveled in Europe. Arapov's compositions represent to perfection the evolutionary character of Soviet music, taking their source in the Russian traditions of the previous centuries, making ample use of ethnic materials of the constituent regions of the immense territory of the U.S.S.R., and integrating the native homophonic melorhythms in an increasingly complex tapestry of colorful fabrics, richly ornamented with occasional application of such modern devices as dodecaphonic melodic structures. But Arapov was also able to produce a virtuoso display of instrumental techniques for piano and other instruments.

WORKS: OPERAS: *Khodja Nasreddin*, on Uzbeki motifs (Tashkent, 1944); *Frigate Victory,* after Pushkin's novella *The Moor of Peter the Great* (radio premiere, Leningrad, Oct. 12, 1959); *Rain,* after Somerset Maugham's short story (Leningrad, April 25, 1968); ballet, *The Picture of Dorian Gray* (Leningrad, April 20, 1973). FOR ORCH.: *Fugato* (Leningrad, Feb. 2, 1928); *Tadzhikistan Suite* (Leningrad, Feb. 13, 1939); Symph. No. 1 (1947; unperformed); *Russian Suite* (Leningrad, March 11, 1950); Symph. No. 2 (Leningrad, Oct. 2, 1959); Symph. No. 3 (Leningrad, March 28, 1963); Symph. No. 4 for Mezzo-soprano, Baritone, Narrator, 2 Mixed Choirs, and Orch. (Leningrad, July 29, 1977); Violin Concerto (Leningrad, April 18, 1965); Concerto for Orch. (Leningrad, Dec. 29, 1969); Concerto for Violin, Piano, Percussion,

Arauxo – Arcadelt

and Chamber Orch., in memory of Stravinsky (Copenhagen, Feb. 21, 1974). VOCAL WORKS: Vocal symph. cycle to Pushkin's texts (Leningrad, Dec. 27, 1940); *Dzhelal Eddin,* oratorio (Tashkent, Dec. 26, 1944); *Songs of Protest,* suite for Bass Singer and Jazz Orch. (radio premiere, Feb. 12, 1940); *4 Songs* to texts by Alexander Blok (1948); *Monologue* for Voice, Piano, Trumpet, and Percussion (1969); *Sonnets of Petrarca,* song cycle for Mezzo-soprano and Piano (1975); *Four Seasons,* song cycle for Soprano, Tenor, and 9 Instruments, to text from Japanese haiku (1977); *Two Monologues* for Voice and Piano, to texts by Boris Pasternak (1979). CHAMBER MUSIC: Sonata for Solo Violin (1930); Trio on Mongol themes (1943); Violin Sonata No. 2 (1978); Quintet for Oboe, Horn, Harp, Viola, and Cello (1979). PIANO MUSIC: *Variations* (1929); *Humoresque* (1938); 6 Pieces on Chinese themes (1955); *Etude-Scherzo* (1969); 2 piano sonatas (1971, 1978); 3 Pieces (1976). He also composed film scores.
BIBLIOGRAPHY: L. Danke, *Boris Arapov* (Leningrad, 1980).

Arauxo (or **Araujo**), (**Francisco**). See **Correa de Araujo, (Francisco).**

Arban, (Joseph) Jean-Baptiste (Laurent), renowned French cornet player and pedagogue; b. Lyons, Feb. 28, 1825; d. Paris, April 9, 1889. He studied trumpet at the Paris Cons. with Dauverné (1841–45); then was engaged as a leader of Parisian salon orchs. In 1857 he became a prof. of saxhorn at the Ecole Militaire in Paris; in 1869 he joined the faculty of the Paris Cons. as a teacher of cornet; then traveled to Russia as a conductor; returning to Paris in 1880, he resumed his post as a teacher. Arban is acknowledged as the founder of the modern school of trumpet playing. He publ. the standard manual *Grande méthode complète pour cornet à pistons et de saxhorn* (Paris, 1864); also made arrangements for cornet.
BIBLIOGRAPHY: J.-P. Mathez, *Joseph Jean-Baptiste Laurent Arban (1825–1889)* (Moudon, 1977).

Arbatsky, Yuri, Russian music scholar; b. Moscow, April 15, 1911; d. New Hartford, N.Y., Sept. 3, 1963. His family left Russia in 1919, and proceeded to Dresden, where Arbatsky began to study music; later he enrolled at the Cons. of Leipzig, studying composition with Grabner. In 1932 he went to Yugoslavia, where he was active as a choral conductor and cathedral organist in Belgrade. In 1942 he went to Prague and studied at the German Univ. there, receiving his doctorate in 1944. After the war he emigrated to the U.S.; was active as a church musician in Chicago (1950–53); later was a consultant with the Newberry Library. He publ. several valuable tracts on folk music, among them *Beating the Tupan in the Central Balkans* (Chicago, 1953); also essays on *The History of Russian Music* (publ. in Russian, N.Y., 1956). He was also a composer; he wrote at least 8 symphs. and much choral music. See "The Arbatsky Collection," *Bulletin of the Newberry Library* (July 1954).

Arbeau, Thoinot (anagram of real name, **Jehan Tabourot**), French writer; b. Dijon, March 17, 1520; d. Langres, July 23, 1595. He owes his fame to his didactic treatise in dialogue form, *Orchésographie, et traité en forme de dialogue par lequel toutes personnes peuvent facilement apprendre et pratiquer l'honnête exercice des danses* (Langres, 1588; 2nd ed., 1589), which contains not only instructions for dancing (indicating dance steps by a simple system of initial letters), but also valuable observations on the dance music of his time. It was publ. in Eng. trans. by C.W. Beaumont (London, 1925) and M. Evans (N.Y., 1948).

Arbo, Jens, Norwegian music critic; b. Kristiansand, Aug. 20, 1885; d. Oslo, Jan. 8, 1944. He studied in Oslo; then in Germany (1911–14). He was a music critic for *Musikbladet* (1917–24) and *Morgenbladet* (1924–43).

Arbós, Enrique Fernández, Spanish violinist and conductor; b. Madrid, Dec. 24, 1863; d. San Sebastian, June 2, 1939. He studied violin with Monasterio in Madrid, with Vieuxtemps in Brussels, and with Joachim in Berlin. After successful tours in Europe, he returned to Spain in 1888; taught violin at the Madrid Cons. In 1889 he was concertmaster of the Glasgow Symph. Orch.; from 1894–1916 he held the post of honorary prof. at the Royal College of Music in London. He was appointed conductor of the new Madrid Symph. Orch. in 1904; conducted in the U.S. (1928–31), then in Europe. At the outbreak of the Spanish Civil War in 1936 he retired to San Sebastian. Arbós was the author of a comic opera, *El centro de la tierra* (Madrid, Dec. 22, 1895). He was a brilliant orchestrator; his arrangement of the music from *Iberia* by Albéniz is very popular.
BIBLIOGRAPHY: V. Espinós Moltó, *El Maestro Arbós* (Madrid, 1942).

Arbuckle, Matthew, American cornet player and bandmaster; b. 1828; d. New York, May 23, 1883. He publ. a manual, *Complete Cornet Method.*

Arbuthnot, John, British physician and musical amateur; b. Arbuthnot, Scotland, in 1667; d. London, Feb. 27, 1735. He was one of the founders of the Scriblerus Club in London (1714), and was friendly with Handel during the composer's difficulties with his opera company. Arbuthnot's publication *Miscellaneous Works* throws sharp sidelights on various persons of interest at the time. He wrote several anthems, glees, etc.

Arcadelt, Jacob (or **Jachet Arkadelt, Archadet, Arcadet, Harcadelt**), great Flemish composer; b. probably in Liège, c.1505; d. Paris, Oct. 14, 1568. He was "magister puerorum" to the Papal Chapel (1539), and choirmaster (1540). In 1544 he held the office of "camerlingo." He went to France in 1546; returned to Rome in May 1547. In 1555 he again went to

France, this time with the Duc de Guise. Arcadelt is mentioned in Paris as "Regis musicus" in 1557. In the domain of secular music, his Roman period was, in the main, devoted to the madrigal; his Paris period, to the French chanson.

WORKS: He wrote 20 motets, about 120 French chansons, and 200 madrigals. Of his extant works, the most important are 6 books of 5-part madrigals (Venice, 1538–56); his finest and most characteristic compositions) and 3 books of masses in 3–7 parts (Paris, 1557).

BIBLIOGRAPHY: W. Klefisch, *Arcadelt als Madrigalist* (Cologne, 1938); A. Einstein, *The Italian Madrigal* (Princeton, 1949); F. Lesure, "Notes et Documents," *Revue de Musicologie* (Dec. 1961).

d'Archambeau, Iwan, Belgian cellist and member of the Flonzaley Quartet; b. Hervé, Sept. 28, 1879; d. Villefranche-sur-Mer, France, Dec. 29, 1955. He studied music at home; played in a family quartet with his father and 2 brothers. He then studied cello with A. Massau in Verviers and with Hugo Becker in Frankfurt. In 1903 he became a member of the Flonzaley Quartet, until it disbanded in 1929; in 1935 he joined the Stradivarius Quartet in N.Y. From 1939–50 he lived in Cambridge, Mass.; then returned to Belgium.

Archangelsky, Alexander, Russian choral conductor; b. near Penza, Oct. 23, 1846; d. Prague, Nov. 16, 1924. He studied singing and music theory at the Court Chapel in St. Petersburg; in 1880 organized a chorus there, toured Russia with it in 1899–1900, presenting 110 concerts; also gave concerts with his chorus in Western Europe (1907 and 1912). He was the first choir leader in Russia to include women's voices in performances of sacred works. He supported (with Gretchaninov) the reform movement in Russian church music; wrote a number of choral pieces for his organization and made transcriptions of Russian church hymns. In 1923 he went to Prague as conductor of a students' choir, and died there the following year.

Archer, Frederick, English-American organist, conductor, and composer; b. Oxford, June 16, 1838; d. Pittsburgh, Oct. 22, 1901. He studied organ in Leipzig, and in 1873 was appointed organist of Alexandra Palace in London; then became conductor of a Glasgow choir (1878–80). In 1881 he came to America; was active as a church organist in Brooklyn and, from 1895, at Carnegie Inst. in Pittsburgh. He was the first conductor of the Pittsburgh Symph. Orch., from Feb. 27, 1896, until 1898, when he was succeeded by Victor Herbert. A prolific composer, he publ. a cantata, *King Witlaf's Drinking-horn*; also organ and piano pieces and songs. The bulk of his music remains in MS. He was the author of the manuals *The Organ* (1875) and *A Complete Method for the American Reed Organ* (1899), and founder and editor of the music magazine *Keynote* (1883).

Archer, Violet, prolific Canadian pianist and composer; b. Montreal, April 24, 1913. She studied composition with Champagne, and piano at the McGill Cons. in Montreal (1932–36); took private lessons with Bartók in N.Y. (1942) and attended courses in composition with Hindemith at Yale Univ. (1948–49). She taught at McGill (1944–47), at North Texas State College (1950–53), and at the Univ. of Oklahoma (1953–61), and served, since 1962, as chairman of the composition dept. at the Univ. of Alberta, Edmonton. Her music is structurally strong, polyphonically disciplined, and generally kept within organized tonality, with occasional dodecaphonic episodes.

WORKS: COMIC OPERA: *Sganarelle* (Edmonton, Feb. 5, 1974). FOR ORCH.: Timpani Concerto (1939); *Scherzo Sinfonico* (1940); *Poem* (1940); *Fantasia concertante* for Flute, Oboe, Clarinet, and Strings (1941); *Britannia, a Joyful Overture* (1941); Fantasy for Clarinet and Strings (1942); Clarinet Concertino (1946); Symph. (1946); *Fantasy on a Ground* (1946); *Fanfare and Passacaglia* (1949); Piano Concerto (1956); Divertimento (1957); Violin Concerto (1959); *3 Sketches* (1961); *Prelude-Incantation* (1964); *Sinfonietta* (1968); *Sinfonia* (1969; Edmonton, Oct. 24, 1970); Clarinet Concerto (1971); *Prairie Profiles* for Baritone, Horn, and Piano (1981). VOCAL MUSIC: *Choruses from "The Bacchae"* for Chorus and Orch. (1938); *Leaves of Grass,* after Whitman, for Chorus and Orch. (1940); *Lamentations of Jeremy* for Chorus and Orch. (1947); *The Bell,* cantata (1949); *Apocalypse* for Soprano, Chorus, Brass, and Timpani (1958); *Cantata Sacra* for 5 Soloists and Small Orch. (1966); songs, choruses, anthems. CHAMBER MUSIC: *6 Pieces* for Piano and Timpani (1939); 2 string quartets (1940, 1948–49); Theme and Variations for String Quartet (1942); Sonata for Flute, Clarinet, and Piano (1944); Quartet for Wind Instruments (1945); Divertimento No. 1 for Oboe, Clarinet, and Bassoon (1949); *Fugue Fantasy* for String Quartet (1949); 2 string trios (1953, 1961); 2 piano trios (1954, 1957); *Prelude and Allegro* for Violin and Piano (1954); Cello Sonata (1956); Violin Sonata (1956); Divertimento No. 2 for Oboe, Violin, and Cello (1957); Divertimento for Brass Quintet (1963); Horn Sonata (1965); Clarinet Sonata (1970); Suite for 4 Violins (1971); Fantasy for Violin and Piano (1971); Saxophone Sonata (1972); Oboe Sonata (1973). FOR PIANO: 3 sonatinas (1945, 1946, 1973); Sonata (1945); *3 Sketches* for 2 Pianos (1947); 6 preludes (1947); Fantasy (1947); Suite (1947); *11 Short Pieces* (1960); Theme and Variations (1963); *Improvisations* (1968); *Lydian Mood* (1971).

Ardévol, José, Cuban composer; b. Barcelona, March 13, 1911; d. Havana, Jan. 7, 1981. He studied with his father, conductor of an orch. in Barcelona; at the age of 19 he went to Havana, where he organized a chamber group; he also edited the magazine *La Música.* He became active in musical politics after the revolution of 1959, and served in various capacities in Cuba and elsewhere; was appointed national director for music, a post which he held until 1965. Several of his works have distinct revolutionary connotations.

WORKS: *Cantos de la revolución* (1962); *Por*

Arditi – Aretz

Viet-Nam, to words by Fidel Castro (1966); *Cantata Ché comandante* (glorifying the revolutionary role of Ché Guevara, 1968); *Cantata Lenin* (1970); Concerto for 3 Pianos and Orch. (1938); 3 symphs. (1943, 1945, 1946); several string quartets; numerous piano pieces and songs; *Música para pequeña orquestra* (Washington, D.C., April 19, 1958); *Triptico de Santiago* for Orch. (Cologne, May 25, 1953).

Arditi, Luigi, Italian composer and conductor; b. Crescentino, Piedmont, July 16, 1822; d. Hove, near Brighton, England, May 1, 1903. He studied violin, piano, and composition at the Milan Cons., where he also produced his first opera, *I Briganti* (1841). He then embarked on a career as an operatic conductor. From 1846 he traveled in Cuba, where he produced his opera *Il Corsaro* (Havana, 1846); also visited N.Y. and Philadelphia. In N.Y. he produced his opera *La Spia* (March 24, 1856). He finally settled in London (1858) as a conductor and vocal teacher, while making annual tours with the Italian Opera in Germany and Austria. He conducted in St. Petersburg in 1871 and 1873. His operas and other works were never revived, but he created a perennial success with his vocal waltz *Il bacio.* He wrote his autobiography, *My Reminiscences* (N.Y., 1896).

Arel, Bülent, Turkish composer and musicologist; b. Constantinople, April 23, 1918. He studied composition with Necil Kâzim Akses at the Ankara State Cons.; from 1951 to 1959 he was employed as sound engineer at Ankara Radio. In 1959 he went to the U.S.; gave instruction in electronic music at Yale Univ. in 1961–62 and 1965–70; also was on the faculty at Columbia Univ. from 1959 to 1963. His own compositions make use of a variety of modern techniques; a typical score is *Impressions of Wall Street* on Tape (1961); he also wrote 2 symphs. (1951, 1952); *Mimiana I* for Tape, Dance, and Film (1968); *Mimiana II* for Tape (1969); other electronic music.

Arens, Franz Xavier, German-American composer; b. Neef (Rhenish Prussia), Oct. 28, 1856; d. Los Angeles, Jan. 28, 1932. His family came to the U.S. and settled in Milwaukee when he was very young; he studied with his father and later in Germany with Rheinberger. Upon his return to America, he was active as a conductor of various choral and instrumental groups. He led the Gesangverein in Cleveland (1885–88); from 1890–92 he was again in Europe; he was the first to present complete programs of orch. works by American composers in Germany. He was president of the Indianapolis College of Music (1892–96), and later settled in N.Y. as a vocal teacher. In 1900 he established a series of People's Symph. Concerts, with low admission prices (from 5 to 50 cents). He wrote orch. music, a string quartet, and numerous songs.

Arensky, Anton, Russian composer; b. Novgorod, July 12, 1861; d. Terijoki, Finland, Feb. 25, 1906. He studied at the St. Petersburg Cons. with Johanssen and Rimsky-Korsakov (1879–82); then taught harmony at the Moscow Cons. (1882–94). Returning to St. Petersburg, he conducted the choir of the Imperial Chapel (1895–1901); a victim of tuberculosis, he spent his last years in a sanatorium in Finland. In his music he followed Tchaikovsky's lyric style.

WORKS: 3 operas: *A Dream on the Volga* (Moscow, Jan. 2, 1891); *Raphael* (Moscow, May 6, 1894); *Nal and Damayanti* (Moscow, Jan. 22, 1904); 2 symphs. (he conducted the first perfs. of both in Moscow, Nov. 24, 1883, and Dec. 21, 1889). He was more successful in his works for smaller forms; his *Variations* for String Orch. on Tchaikovsky's song *The Christ Child Had a Garden* (originally the *Variations* formed the slow movement of Arensky's Quartet, op. 35, in A minor for Violin, Viola, and 2 Cellos) became a standard work. His Piano Trio also retains its popularity. His 4 suites for 2 pianos, expertly written, are often heard; he also arranged these suites for orch. Some of his songs are included in vocal anthologies. Other works are: music to Pushkin's poem *The Fountain of Bakhtchissaray;* ballet, *Egyptian Nights* (St. Petersburg, 1900); *The Diver,* ballad for Voices and Orch.; *Coronation Cantata; Marche solennelle* for Orch.; *Intermezzo* for String Orch.; Piano Concerto; Violin Concerto in A minor; a Fantasy on epic Russian songs, for Piano and Orch.; Piano Quintet in D; String Quartet in G, op. 11; pieces for cello; works for violin; many pieces for piano solo. He publ. *Manual of Harmony* (translated into German) and *Handbook of Musical Forms.*

BIBLIOGRAPHY: G. Tzypin, *Arensky* (Moscow, 1966).

Aretz (de Ramón y Rivera), Isabel, Argentine-born Venezuelan folklorist and composer; b. Buenos Aires, April 13, 1909. She studied piano and composition at the National Cons. of Music in Buenos Aires; subsequently dedicated herself to research in Argentine folklore at the Museo de Ciencias Naturales de Buenos Aires (1938–44); she received her Ph.D. in musicology in 1967 at the Argentine Catholic Univ. in Buenos Aires with the dissertation *Música tradicional argentina: La Rioja.* She served as an associate member of the Instituto Argentino de Musicología (1938–50); then was the first prof. of ethnomusicology at the Escuela Nacional de Danzas de Argentina (1950–52). In 1953 she settled in Caracas, Venezuela, as a research fellow in ethnomusicology and folklore at the Instituto Nacional de Folklore de Venezuela; in 1965 she became director of the folklore dept. of the Instituto Nacional de Cultura y Bellas Artes; in 1970 she became director of the Instituto Interamericano de Etnomusicología y Folklore. As a composer, her music reflects her interest in folk music and contemporary European trends.

WRITINGS: *Música tradicional argentina: Tucumán, historia y folklore* (Buenos Aires, 1946); *El folklore musical argentino* (Buenos Aires, 1953); *Manual de folklore venezolano* (Caracas, 1957; 3rd ed., 1972); *Cantos navideños en el folklore venezolano* (Caracas, 1962); *Instrumentos musicales de Venezuela* (Cumaná, 1967); *La artesania en Venezuela* (Caracas, 1967); *El traje en Venezuela*

(Caracas, 1972); *El tamunangue* (Barquisimeto, 1976).

d'Arezzo, Guido. See **Guido d'Arezzo.**

Argenta, Ataulfo, Spanish conductor; b. Castro Urdiales, Santander, Nov. 19, 1913; d. in an automobile accident at Los Molinos, near Madrid, Jan. 21, 1958. He studied at the Madrid Cons.; then went to Germany, where he took lessons in conducting with Carl Schuricht. Returning to Spain in 1939, he conducted various small groups; in 1945 he was appointed director of the National Orch. in Madrid.
BIBLIOGRAPHY: A. Fernandez-Cid, *Ataulfo Argenta* (Madrid, 1958).

Argento, Dominick, greatly talented American composer excelling especially in opera; b. York, Pa., Oct. 27, 1927. He played the piano, but had no formal instruction in music theory; after high school he enlisted in the U.S. Army as a cryptographer (1945–47). In 1947 he enrolled at the Peabody Cons. of Music in Baltimore, where he took courses with Nicolas Nabokov and Hugo Weisgall, graduating in 1951 with a B.A. degree. He then went to Italy on a Fulbright fellowship and studied piano with Pietro Scarpini and composition with Luigi Dallapiccola at the Conservatorio Cherubini in Florence. Upon returning to the U.S., he attended classes of Henry Cowell in composition at the Peabody Cons. in Baltimore; eager to pursue his studies further, he entered the Eastman School of Music in Rochester, N.Y., where his teachers were Howard Hanson and Bernard Rogers; in 1957 he received his doctorate in music there. In 1957 he was awarded a Guggenheim fellowship, which enabled him to go once more to Florence and work on his opera *Colonel Jonathan the Saint;* in 1964 he obtained his second Guggenheim fellowship. In 1958 he was appointed to the music faculty of the Univ. of Minnesota in Minneapolis; also in 1964 he became a founder of the Center Opera in Minnesota, later renamed the Minnesota Opera. The connection gave Argento an opportunity to present his operas under his own supervision. In 1980 he was elected a member of the American Academy and Institute of Arts and Letters. In the pantheon of American composers Argento occupies a distinct individual category, outside any certifiable modernistic trend or technical idiom. He writes melodious music in a harmonious treatment, so deliberate in intent that even its apologists profess embarrassment at its unimpeded flow; there is also a perceptible ancestral strain in the bel canto style of his Italianate opera scores; most important, audiences, and an increasing number of sophisticated critics, profess their admiration for his unusual songfulness. Yet an analysis of Argento's productions reveals the presence of acerb harmonies and artfully acidulated melismas.
WORKS: OPERAS: *Sicilian Limes* (N.Y., Oct. 1, 1954); *The Boor,* after Chekhov's short comedy (Rochester, May 6, 1957); *Colonel Jonathan the Saint* (1958–61; Denver, Dec. 31, 1971); *Christopher*

Sly, a scene from Shakespeare's play *The Taming of the Shrew* (Minneapolis, May 31, 1963); *The Masque of Angels* (Minneapolis, Jan. 9, 1964); *Shoemaker's Holiday* (Minneapolis, June 1, 1967); *Postcard from Morocco* (Minneapolis, Oct. 14, 1971); *The Voyage of Edgar Allan Poe* (Minneapolis, April 24, 1976; achieved great critical acclaim); *Miss Havisham's Fire* (1978). OTHER VOCAL WORKS: Oratorio, *Jonah and the Whale* (Minneapolis, March 9, 1974); *Song about Spring,* song cycle for Soprano and Orch. (1950; revised in 1954 and 1960); *Ode to the West Wind,* Concerto for Soprano and Orch. (1956); *6 Elizabethan Songs* for Voice and Piano (1962); *The Revelation of St. John the Divine,* rhapsody for Tenor, Men's Chorus, Brass, and Percussion (1966); *A Nation of Cowslips* for Chorus (1968); *Letters from Composers,* song cycle for Tenor and Guitar (1968); *Tria Carmina Paschalia,* 3 songs to Latin verses for Women's Voices, Harp, and Guitar (1970); *To Be Sung upon the Water* for Voice, Clarinet, and Piano (1973); *A Waterbird Talks,* monodrama (1974); *From the Diary of Virginia Woolf* for Voice and Piano (1974; awarded the Pulitzer Prize); *In Praise of Music,* 7 songs for Orch. (1977). BALLET: *Resurrection of Don Juan* (Rochester, May 5, 1936). CHAMBER MUSIC: *Divertimento* for Piano and Strings (Rochester, July 2, 1958); String Quartet (1956); *Royal Invitation (or Homage to the Queen of Tonga)* for Chamber Orch. (St. Paul, Minn., March 22, 1964); *Variations (The Mask of Night)* for Orch. with Soprano Solo in the final variations (Minneapolis, Jan. 26, 1966); *Bravo Mozart!,* concerto for Oboe, Violin, Horn, and Orch. (1969); *A Ring of Time,* preludes and pageants for Instruments (1972).
BIBLIOGRAPHY: *Current Biography* (May 1977); David Ewen, *American Composers* (N.Y., 1982).

Argento, Pietro, Italian conductor; b. Gioia del Colle, March 7, 1909. He received his early musical training from his father; then entered the San Pietro a Majella Cons. of Naples, where he studied piano, oboe, organ, composition, and conducting. He subsequently became a student in conducting of Bernardino Molinari at Santa Cecilia Academy in Rome. He conducted orchs. in Germany, Austria, France, and Czechoslovakia; made 7 tours in Russia. Since 1953 he has been a conductor of the Orch. of Italian Radio-Television.

Argerich, Martha, pianist; b. Buenos Aires, June 5, 1941. She studied with Gulda, Magaloff, and Madeleine Lipatti; made her debut in Buenos Aires in 1949. After taking part in several piano competitions, she became successful as a soloist, both in Europe and America. She was married for some years to the Swiss conductor **Charles Dutoit.**
BIBLIOGRAPHY: J. Kaiser, *Grosse Pianisten in unserer Zeit* (Munich, 1965).

Aria, Cesare, Italian singing teacher; b. Bologna, Sept. 21, 1820; d. there, Jan. 30, 1894. He studied at the Bologna Cons. with Mattei. Rossini helped him in his career. For a number of years he was a voice teacher in France and England. He composed some church music; his *Dies irae* is particularly noteworthy.

Aribon (Aribo Scholasticus, Aribon de Liège, Aribon de Freising, and **Aribon d'Orléans),** medieval scholar; b. probably in Liège, c.1000; d. Orléans, c.1078. In 1024 he was chancellor to the Bishop of Liège; after a short period of service he went to Italy, where he acquired a knowledge of the methods of Guido d'Arezzo. From 1060–70 he was again in Liège as preceptor at the Cathedral school; then went to Orléans. Aribon was the author of the important treatise *De musica,* written in Liège c.1065. It is reproduced in Gerbert's *Scriptores* (vol. II, pp. 197–230) and in J. Smits van Waesberghe's *Corpus scriptorum de musica* (vol. II, Rome, 1951).
BIBLIOGRAPHY: J. Smits van Waesberghe, *Muziekgeschiedenis der Middeleeuwen* (Tilburg, 1936).

d'Arienzo, Nicola, Italian composer; b. Naples, Dec. 22, 1842; d. there, April 25, 1915. He composed an opera in the Neapolitan dialect at the age of 18; a series of Italian operas followed: *I due mariti* (Naples, Feb. 1, 1866); *Il cacciatore delle Alpi* (Naples, June 23, 1870); *Il cuoco* (Naples, June 11, 1873); *I Viaggi* (Milan, June 28, 1875); *La figlia del diavolo* (Naples, Nov. 16, 1879; his most successful opera, which aroused considerable controversy for its realistic tendencies); *I tre coscritti* (Naples, Feb. 10, 1880); etc. He also wrote 2 symphs. and much choral music. He publ. a treatise, *Introduzione del sistema tetacordale nella moderna musica,* favoring pure intonation; a historical essay, *Dell' opera comica dalle origini a Pergolesi* (1887; German trans., 1902); several monographs on Italian composers and numerous articles in periodicals.

Ariosti, Attilio, Italian opera composer; b. Bologna, Nov. 5, 1666; d. c.1729. He joined the Servite Order in 1688, but later abandoned it. He served as organist in Bologna in 1693; in 1697 he was in Berlin as court musician. From 1703–11 he was in Vienna, then returned to Bologna. He was in London in 1716 and again from 1723–27. A vol. of his cantatas and "lessons" for viola d'amore, on which he was an accomplished performer, was publ. in London in 1724. Ariosti then disappeared, the most probable conjecture being that he returned to Italy and died there in obscurity. Burney's attribution to Ariosti of one act of the opera *Muzio Scevola* (produced in London on April 15, 1721) is an anachronism, for Ariosti was not in London at the time.
WORKS: A list of his known operas includes the following: *Tirsi* (erroneously named *Dafne* by many music historians; Venice, 1696, in collaboration with Lotti and Caldara); *Mars und Irene* (Berlin, July 12, 1703); *Marte placato* (Vienna, March 19, 1707); *Artaserse* (London, Dec. 1, 1724); *Dario* (London, April 10, 1725); *Lucio Vero, Imperator di Roma* (London, Jan. 7, 1727). He also wrote 5 oratorios, some instrumental works, and numerous cantatas (many of which are preserved in various European libraries).
BIBLIOGRAPHY: G. Weiss, "57 unbekannte Instrumentalstücke (15 Sonaten) von Attilio Ariosti . . . ," *Die Musikforschung* (April–June 1970).

Aristakesian, Emon, Armenian composer; b. Erevan, Nov. 19, 1936. He studied composition with Yegiazarian at the Erevan Cons., graduating in 1961; then taught in various Armenian institutes. Much of his music is, in its melorhythmic structure, derived from Armenian folk songs.
WORKS: Ballet, *Prometheus* (Erevan, 1967); *Armenia,* oratorio (1961); 2 symphs. (1962, 1975); Viola Concerto (1963); Sinfonietta for Strings, Piano, and Xylophone (1969); *Suite* for String Quintet (1955); *Poem* for Piano Quintet (1959); *Polyphonic Variations* for String Quartet (1960); *Fantastic Variations* for Piano (1964); *Capriccio* for Piano (1965); *Poem about Lenin* for Chorus and Piano (1970); Piano Sonata (1971); *5 Sharageans of Saak Parteva* for Voice and Piano (1972); other songs.

Aristides Quintilianus, Greek writer on music; lived A.D. c.200 in Smyrna. His treatise *De musica libri VII* was printed in Meibom's *Antiquae musicae auctores septem* (1652) and by A. Jahn (1882); R. Schäfke publ. it in German (1937) with a commentary. Despite the dubious authenticity of some of his descriptions of Greek scales, the work is one of the basic sources of our knowledge of ancient Greek music.

Aristotle, famous Greek philosopher, pupil of Plato; b. Stagira, 384 B.C.; d. Chalcis, 322 B.C. The 19th section of the *Problems,* once ascribed to him, is the product of a much later follower of his theories; the English translation, by E.S. Forster, is found in *The Works of Aristotle,* vol. 7 (Oxford, 1927); the Greek text with French translation and commentary by F.A. Gevaert and C. Vollgraff is publ. in *Les Problèmes musicaux d'Aristote* (3 vols., 1899–1902). Aristotle's actual writings on music are reproduced by K. von Jan in his *Musici scriptores Graeci* (1895). The name Aristotle was also used by a writer on mensurable music of the 12th–13th centuries, whose treatise is publ. by E. de Coussemaker in his *Scriptores,* vol. I.

Aristoxenos, one of the earliest Greek writers on music; b. Tarentum, 354 B.C. His *Harmonic Elements* (complete) and *Rhythmical Elements* (fragmentary) are among the most important treatises on Greek music theory that have come down to us. They have been publ. by R. Westphal and F. Saran (2 vols.; 1883, 1893); also by H.S. Macran, with English and Greek text and a commentary (1902). The *Harmonic Elements* are included, in an English translation, in O. Strunk's *Source Readings in Music History* (N.Y., 1950). See also L. Laloy, *Aristoxène de Tarente* (1904); C.F.A. Williams, *The Aristoxenian Theory of Musical Rhythm* (Cambridge, 1911).

Arizaga, Rodolfo, Argentinian composer; b. Buenos Aires, July 11, 1926. He studied philosophy at the Univ. of Buenos Aires and composition with Luis Gianneo; then went to Paris, where he took lessons with Nadia Boulanger and Messiaen. Beginning with folkloric composition of the traditional Latin American type, he traversed the entire gamut of modern techniques, including 12-tone structures and aleatory composition, and applied these diverse methods liberally according to need and intention.
WORKS: Cantatas: *Martirio de Santa Olalla* (1952) and *Delires* (1957; revised 1970); *Prometeo 45,* opera (1958); Piano Concerto (1963); *Tientos para Santa Maria* for Orch. (1965); *Música para Christóbal Colón* for Orch. (1966); *Sonata breve* for Ondes Martenot and Piano (1958); *Diferenzas del tercer tiento* for Organ (1966); 2 string quartets (1968, 1969); various vocal works and piano pieces. Arizaga also publ. the monographs *Manuel de Falla* (Buenos Aires, 1961) and *Juan José Castro* (Buenos Aires, 1963) and edited *Enciclopedia de la música argentina* (Buenos Aires, 1971).

Arkhipova, Irina, outstanding Soviet mezzo-soprano; b. Moscow, Dec. 2, 1925. She studied architecture at the Moscow Architectural Inst., graduating in 1948; at the same time took private vocal lessons. In 1953 she entered the Moscow Cons., and in 1956 made her debut as Carmen at the Bolshoi Theater; this role became one of her best operatic interpretations. She gave recitals in Europe and in the U.S., receiving considerable acclaim.

Arkor, André d', Belgian tenor; b. Tilleur, near Liège, Feb. 23, 1901; d. Brussels, Dec. 19, 1971. He studied at the Liège Cons.; made his operatic debut in 1925 in *Lakmé* at the Liège Théâtre Royal; then sang in Ghent and Lyons; in 1930 he joined the Théâtre de la Monnaie in Brussels, where he remained as a leading tenor until 1945; from 1945–65 he was director of the Liège Théâtre Royal.

Arkwright, Godfrey Edward Pellew, English music editor; b. Norwich, April 10, 1864; d. Highclere, near Newbury, Aug. 16, 1944. He studied at Eton and at Oxford. His most important publication is *The Old English Edition,* in 25 vols. (1889–1902), containing masques, ballets, motets, and madrigals by English composers of the 17th and 18th centuries. He also edited Purcell's church music publ. by the Purcell Society. He was the editor of *Musical Antiquary* from 1909–13.

Arlen, Harold (real name, **Hyman Arluck**), American composer of popular music; b. Buffalo, Feb. 15, 1905. He studied music privately with Simon Bucharoff. As a small child he joined the choir of a synagogue where his father was cantor. At 15 he began to earn a living as a pianist on lake steamboats and in nightclubs. Then he went to N.Y., where he became engaged in a variety of professions, as a singer with jazz bands, a pianist, an arranger, and finally a composer. Possessing a natural gift for melody, he created numerous song hits, of

which *Stormy Weather* (1932) became a classic of American popular music. He wrote several successful musicals for Broadway, among them *Bloomer Girl* (1944); *St. Louis Woman* (1946); *House of Flowers* (1954); *Jamaica* (1957). He also wrote music for films, among them the score for *The Wizard of Oz* (1939).
BIBLIOGRAPHY: Edward Jablonski, *Harold Arlen: Happy with the Blues* (Garden City, 1961); A. Wilder, *American Popular Song* (N.Y., 1972).

Arlt, Wulf (Friedrich), German musicologist; b. Breslau, March 5, 1938. He studied musicology at the Univ. of Cologne; then received his Ph.D. in 1966 from the Univ. of Basel with the dissertation *Ein Festoffizium des Mittelalters aus Beauvais in seiner liturgischen Bedeutung* (publ. in Cologne, 1970); subsequently completed his Habilitation there in 1970 with his *Praxis und Lehre der "Ars subtilor": Studien zur Geschichte der Notation im Spätmittelalter.* He joined the faculty of the Univ. of Basel as a lecturer in 1965; became a prof. there in 1972. In 1971 he also became director of the Schola Cantorum Basiliensis. Arlt further devoted his critical capacities to elucidating the problems of music in the Middle Ages, and contributed important articles on the subject to music journals.

Arma, Paul (real name, **Imre Weisshaus**), cosmopolitan composer and theorist; b. Budapest, Oct. 22, 1904. He attended classes of Béla Bartók at the Budapest Academy of Music (1921–24), then went to N.Y., where he became associated with modern music groups and contributed compositions to Henry Cowell's *New Music Quarterly.* A composer of empiric music, he explored quaquaversal paths of musical techniques and contrasting sonorities. In 1930 he settled in Paris and worked under the pseudonym Paul Arma; publ. a *Nouveau dictionnaire de musique* (Paris, 1947).
WORKS: Concerto for String Quartet and Orch. (1947); Violin Sonata (1949); *31 instantanés* for Woodwind, Percussion, Celesta, Xylophone, and Piano (1951); *Polydiaphonie* for Orch. (1962); *Structures variées* for Orch. (1964); *Prismes sonores* for Orch. (1966); *Six transparences* for Oboe and String Orch. (1968); *Résonances* for Orch. (1971); numerous experimental pieces for various instrumental combinations.

Armbruster, Karl, conductor; b. Andernach-am-Rhein, Germany, July 13, 1846; d. London, June 10, 1917. He studied piano in Cologne; at the age of 17 settled in London, where he made propaganda for Wagner by means of numerous lectures. He was Hans Richter's assistant at the Wagner concerts in London in 1884; later conducted operas at London theaters. He was also one of the conductors of the Wagner cycles at Bayreuth (1884–94).

Armes, Philip, English organist and composer; b. Norwich, Aug. 15, 1836; d. Durham, Feb. 10, 1908. He received his early musical education from his father, a singer; was chorister at the cathedrals of

Norwich (1846) and Rochester (1848); for his work as a boy soloist he received the gift of a grand piano. He subsequently was an organist in London, Chichester, and Durham, retiring shortly before his death. He wrote the oratorios *Hezekiah* (1877), *St. John the Evangelist* (1881), and *Barnabas* (1891). His madrigal *Victoria* won the first prize of the Madrigal Society in 1897.

Armin, Georg (real name, **Herrmann**), German singer and pedagogue; b. Braunschweig, Nov. 10, 1871; d. Karlslunde Strand, Denmark, Feb. 16, 1963. He studied architecture; then turned to singing. He settled in Berlin as a voice teacher; from 1925–42 he edited the periodical *Der Stimmwart*. His home in Berlin was destroyed in an air raid during World War II; in 1949 he settled in Denmark. He publ. several papers on voice production, among them *Das Stauprinzip* (1905) and *Von der Urkraft der Stimme* (1921).

BIBLIOGRAPHY: J. Berntsen, *Ein Meister der Stimmbildungskunst* (Leipzig, 1936).

Armingaud, Jules, French violinist; b. Bayonne, May 3, 1820; d. Paris, Feb. 27, 1900. He began his career as a member of the orch. at the Paris Opéra. In 1855 he organized a string quartet, which he later enlarged by adding wind instruments and named the Société Classique. He publ. some violin pieces and 2 musico-philosophical books of essays: *Consonances et dissonances* and *Modulations*.

Armstrong, Karan, American soprano; b. Horne, Mont., Dec. 14, 1941. She studied at Concordia College in Moorhead, Minn. (B.A., 1963). In 1969 she won both the San Francisco Opera and Metropolitan Opera auditions; then appeared with the N.Y. City Opera, Baltimore Opera, Houston Opera, Seattle Opera, and others. In 1976 she made her European debut as Salome with the Strasbourg Opera; in 1979 she sang Elsa at the Bayreuth Festival, and returned there in subsequent seasons. She made her debut at Covent Garden in London as Lulu in Alban Berg's opera in 1981. She also appeared with the Vienna State Opera, Bavarian State Opera, Paris Opéra, and Hamburg State Opera. Her finest roles include Violetta, Tosca, Mimi, Alice Ford, Countess Almaviva, and Eva.

Armstrong, Louis, famous black American jazz trumpeter, familiarly known as "Satchmo" (for "Satchel Mouth," with reference to his spacious and resonant oral cavity); b. New Orleans, July 4, 1900; d. New York, July 6, 1971. At age 13 he was arrested for firing his stepfather's gun during a New Year's Eve celebration, and was placed in the black Waifs Home for Boys; there he learned to read music and play several instruments, excelling on the cornet. After his release he worked as a musician, mostly in Storyville, the red-light district of New Orleans; in 1921 he went to Chicago, where he played cornet in King Oliver's Creole Jazz Band until 1924; in 1925 he organized his own band—the Hot 5, later the Hot 7— and rapidly earned fame; set an endurance rec-

ord when he sounded high C on the trumpet 280 times in succession. His style of improvisation revolutionized jazz performance in the 1920s, and he won admirers all over the world; some critics hailed him as "the Einstein of Jazz." He continued to play at jazz festivals in the 1960s, and his recording of the song *Hello Dolly* was a best-seller in 1964. His wife during the years 1924–31 was **Lil(lian) Hardin** (b. Memphis, Tenn., Feb. 3, 1898; d. Chicago, Aug. 7, 1971), who served as pianist for King Oliver's group from 1920–23, and then with the Hot 5 and Hot 7 combos; they were divorced in 1938. Armstrong wrote an autobiography, *Satchmo, My Life in New Orleans* (N.Y., 1954).

BIBLIOGRAPHY: R. Goffin, *Horn of Plenty, The Story of Louis Armstrong* (N.Y., 1947); H. Panassié, *Louis Armstrong* (Paris, 1947; N.Y., 1971); A. McCarthy, *Louis Armstrong* (London, 1960); G. Schuller, *Early Jazz* (N.Y., 1968); M. Jones et al., *Salute to Satchmo* (London, 1970); R. Merryman, *Louis Armstrong—A Self-Portrait* (N.Y., 1971); M. Jones and J. Chilton, *Louis: The Louis Armstrong Story, 1900–1971* (Boston and Toronto, 1971); J.G. Jepsen, *Louis Armstrong Discography, 1923–1971* (Rugsted Vyst, Denmark, 1973); J.L. Collier, *Louis Armstrong, An American Genius* (N.Y., 1983).

Armstrong, Richard, English conductor; b. Leicester, Jan. 7, 1943. He studied at Corpus Christi College, Cambridge. In 1966 he joined the staff of the Royal Opera House, Covent Garden; in 1968 he became assistant conductor of the Welsh National Opera, Cardiff; in 1973 he became its music director. He also appeared as a guest conductor of various operatic and symph. units.

Armstrong, Sheila, English soprano; b. Ashington, Northumberland, Aug. 13, 1942. She was educated at the Royal Academy of Music in London, winning the 1965 Kathleen Ferrier Memorial Scholarship; made her operatic debut as Despina at the Sadler's Wells Theatre in 1965; then sang at the Glyndebourne Festival from 1966 and at the Royal Opera House, Covent Garden, from 1973. She was also active as an oratorio singer.

Armstrong, William Dawson, American organist and composer; b. Alton, Ill., Feb. 11, 1868; d. there, July 9, 1936. He studied with Clarence Eddy; occupied posts at various churches in Alton and St. Louis from 1890–1908; established a music school at Alton. He was active in local pedagogical groups. He wrote an opera, *The Specter Bridegroom* (St. Louis, 1899); publ. some church music, many pieces for Organ, and songs. He was the author of *The Romantic World of Music* (N.Y., 1922) and *Rudiments of Musical Notation, An Elementary Handbook*.

BIBLIOGRAPHY: W.T. Norton, *W.D. Armstrong* (N.Y., 1916).

Arndt, Günther, German choral conductor; b. Berlin-Charlottenburg, April 1, 1907; d. Berlin, Dec. 25, 1976. He was educated at the Academy for School and Church Music in Berlin; also studied musicology at the Univ. of Berlin; then was engaged as lecturer at the Volkshochschule in Berlin (1932–40). After the war he headed the chamber music department of the Berlin Radio RIAS; also conducted the Berlin Motet Choir (1950–60) and the RIAS Chamber Choir (1955–72); served as deputy head of music for the RIAS (1964–72). He gained distinction as a conductor of modern choral music.

Arne, Michael, English opera composer; b. London, 1741; d. there, Jan. 14, 1786. He was a natural son of **Thomas Augustine Arne.** He was trained as an actor and a singer, and made his debut in a concert in London on Feb. 20, 1750. He also acquired considerable skill as a harpsichord player. In 1771–72 he traveled in Germany as a conductor of stage music; from 1776 he was in Dublin; at some time prior to 1784 he returned to London. He was known for his eccentricities; among his vagaries was an earnest preoccupation with alchemy in search of the philosopher's stone to convert base metals into gold, a quest which proved a disappointment.
WORKS: 9 operas (all perf. in London), including *Hymen* (Jan. 23, 1764); *Cymon* (Jan. 2, 1767); *The Artifice* (April 14, 1780); *The Choice of Harlequin* (Dec. 26, 1781); *Vertumnus and Pomona* (Feb. 21, 1782); also collaborations with other composers in about 14 productions.
BIBLIOGRAPHY: J.A. Parkinson, *An Index to the Vocal Works of Thomas Augustine Arne and Michael Arne* (Detroit, 1972).

Arne, Thomas Augustine, famous English dramatic composer; b. London, March 12, 1710; d. there, March 5, 1778. His father, an upholsterer, sent him to Eton; he then spent 3 years in a solicitor's office. He studied music on the side, much against his father's wishes, and acquired considerable skill on the violin. He soon began to write musical settings, "after the Italian manner," to various plays. His first production was Addison's *Rosamond* (March 7, 1733). He renamed Fielding's *Tragedy of Tragedies* as *Opera of Operas,* and produced it at the Haymarket Theatre (Oct. 29, 1733); a masque, *Dido and Aeneas,* followed (Jan. 12, 1734). His most important work was the score of *Comus* (Drury Lane, March 4, 1738). On Aug. 1, 1740, he produced at Clivedon, Buckinghamshire, the masque *Alfred,* the finale of which contains the celebrated song *Rule Britannia,* which became a national patriotic song of Great Britain. In the meantime, on March 15, 1737, Arne married Cecilia Young, daughter of the organist Charles Young, and herself a fine singer. In 1742 he went with her to Dublin, where he also stayed in 1755 and 1758. Of his many dramatic productions the following were performed at Drury Lane in London: *The Temple of Dullness* (Jan. 17, 1745); *Harlequin Incendiary* (March 3, 1746); *The Triumph of Peace* (Feb. 21, 1748); *Britannia* (May 9, 1755); *Beauty and Virtue* (Feb. 26, 1762); *The Rose* (Dec. 2, 1772). The following were staged at Covent Garden: *Harlequin Sorcerer* (Feb. 11, 1752); *The Prophetess* (Feb. 1, 1758); *Thomas and Sally* (Nov. 28, 1760); *Love in a Village* (Dec. 8, 1762); *The Fairy Prince* (Nov. 12, 1771). He further contributed separate numbers to 28 theatrical productions, among them songs to Shakespeare's *As You Like It;* "Where the Bee Sucks" in *The Tempest;* etc. He wrote 2 oratorios: *The Death of Abel* (Dublin, Feb. 18, 1744) and *Judith* (Drury Lane, Feb. 27, 1761), the latter remarkable for the introduction of female voices into the choral parts. He also wrote numerous glees and catches, and miscellaneous instrumental music. He received the honorary degree of D.Mus. from Oxford Univ. (July 6, 1759), which accounts for his familiar appellation of "Dr. Arne."
BIBLIOGRAPHY: J.F. Parkinson, *An Index to the Vocal Works of Thomas Augustine Arne and Michael Arne* (Detroit, 1971).

d'Arneiro, (José Augusto) Ferreira Veiga, Viscount, distinguished Portuguese composer; b. Macao, China, Nov. 22, 1838; d. San Remo, July 7, 1903. He studied with Botelho, Schira, and Soares in Lisbon. The production of his ballet *Gina* (Lisbon, 1866) attracted attention; he then produced an opera, *L'Elisire di Giovinezza* (Lisbon, March 31, 1876), followed by *La Derelitta* (Lisbon, 1885). *Te Deum,* performed in Lisbon and in London in 1871, was very successful; it was later given in Paris under the somewhat affected title of "Symphonie-Cantate."

Arnell, Richard, English composer; b. London, Sept. 15, 1917. He studied with John Ireland at the Royal College of Music in London (1935–38). In 1939 he went to America; when Winston Churchill had a reception at Columbia Univ. in 1946, Arnell wrote *Prelude and Flourish* for Brass Instruments, performed at the occasion. In 1948 Arnell returned to London. His music may be described as festive without pomposity, and very English.
WORKS: Operas: *Love in Transit* (London, Feb. 27, 1958); *The Petrified Princess* (London, May 5, 1959); *Moonflowers* (Kent, July 23, 1959); *Combat Zone* (Hempstead, N.Y., Hofstra College, April 27, 1969). Ballets: *Harlequin in April,* suggested by T.S. Eliot's *The Waste Land* (London, May 8, 1951); *The Great Detective,* about Sherlock Holmes (1953). Also 5 symphs. (1941–68); Overture, *The New Age* (N.Y., Jan. 13, 1941); *Quasi variazioni* (N.Y., March 15, 1942); Violin Concerto (N.Y., April 22, 1946); 2 piano concertos (1946; 1966); *Abstract Forms,* Suite for Strings (Bath, June 2, 1951); *Lord Byron,* a symph. portrait (London, Nov. 19, 1952); 5 string quartets; other chamber music; piano pieces.

Arnestad, Finn, Norwegian composer; b. Oslo, Sept. 23, 1915. He studied violin and piano in Oslo and, briefly, composition with Bjarne Brustad; in 1952 he studied African and oriental folk music in Paris; after returning to Oslo he was active as a music critic. His music is influenced by French Impressionism, with tangential use of dodecaphony.
WORKS: FOR ORCH.: *Constellation,* intermezzo (1948); *Conversation,* concert intermezzo for Piano and Orch. (1950); *Meditation,* intermezzo (1952); *I.N.R.I.,* 2 concert suites from a symph. mystery

play (1952–55); Violin Concerto (1957); *Aria Appassionata* (1962); *Cavatina Cambiata* (1965; originally titled *Dopplersonance*); *Overture* (1970); *Væsletjennet* for Norwegian Recorder and Orch. (1970; based on a 1938 piano piece); *Toccata* (1972); *Arabesque* (1975); Piano Concerto (1976); *Mouvement Concertant*, Concert for Double Bass and Orch. (1978). CHAMBER MUSIC: String Quartet (1947); Sextet for Flute, Clarinet, Bassoon, Violin, Cello, and Piano (1959); Quintet for Flute and Strings (1962); *Suite in Old Dance Rhythms* for Flute, Oboe, Harpsichord, and Strings (1966); Trombone Sonata (1971); Solo Violin Sonata (1980); Solo Double-bass Sonata (1980). FOR PIANO: 2 sonatas: No. 1 (1967) and No. 2, *Ritagliata* (1967); *Tango*, 3-part canon (1981). VOCAL: *Missa Brevis* for Chorus and 6 Instruments (1951); *Amen* for Chorus a cappella (1959); *Smeden og Bageren* (*The Blacksmith and the Baker*) for Baritone, Flute, Oboe, Harpsichord, and Strings (1966).

Arnič, Blaž, Slovenian composer; b. Luče, Jan. 31, 1901; d. Ljubljana, Feb. 1, 1970. He studied organ and music theory at the Cons. of Ljubljana (1925–29) and at the New Vienna Cons. (1929–32). In 1945 he was appointed prof. at the Music Academy of Ljubljana. Most of his music is of programmatic content; all of his symphs. bear descriptive titles; the melodic and rhythmic material of his music reflects the folk motifs of Slovenia.

WORKS: *Symphonic Rhapsody* (1933); symphs.: *Resurrection* (1935); *Reverie* (1940); *The Whirlwind of War* (1941); *Pioneer* (1948); *Symphony of Labor* (1950); *In the Fatherland's Soul* (1951); *War and Peace* (1960); symph. poems, *Memento mori* (1934); *Witch Dance* (1951); Organ Concerto (1931); Cello Concerto (1960); Clarinet Concerto (1963); 3 violin concertos (1953, 1953, 1966); Viola Concerto (1967); chamber music; piano pieces; songs.

Arnold, Byron, American composer; b. Vancouver, Wash., Aug. 15, 1901. He studied at Willamette Univ. (B.A., 1924) and later at the Eastman School of Music in Rochester, N.Y., with Bernard Rogers and Howard Hanson. From 1938–48 he was on the faculty of the Univ. of Alabama. One of his most original pieces is a symph. suite entitled *5 Incapacitated Preludes*, each portraying a serious incapacitation (deafness, blindness, paralysis, etc.; the deaf prelude instructs the players to pretend they are playing music, but without producing any sounds); it was performed in Rochester on April 19, 1937. He also wrote *3 Fantasticisms* for Orch.; piano pieces; songs. He publ. *Folk Songs of Alabama* (1950).

Arnold, Denis, English musicologist; b. Sheffield, Dec. 15, 1926. He was educated at Sheffield Univ. (B.A., 1947; B.Mus., 1948; M.A., 1950). In 1951 he became a lecturer at Queen's Univ., Belfast; in 1964 he was made senior lecturer at the Univ. of Hull; in 1969 became a prof. of music at the Univ. of Nottingham; from 1975 was a prof. of music at Oxford Univ. In 1976 he became joint editor of *Music & Letters*. He is regarded as one of the foremost authorities on Italian music of the Renaissance and the early Baroque period.

WRITINGS: *Monteverdi* (London, 1963); *Marenzio* (London, 1965); *Monteverdi Madrigals* (London, 1967); *The Monteverdi Companion*, with N. Fortune (London, 1968); *Giovanni Gabrieli* (London, 1974); *Giovanni Gabrieli and the Music of the Venetian High Renaissance* (Oxford, 1979).

Arnold, Eddy (Richard Edward Arnold), American singer of country-western music; b. Henderson, Tenn., May 15, 1918. He took up the guitar and had some lessons with a traveling musician, but did not learn to read music; played in night spots; then became a favorite singer on the "Grand Ole Opry" radio program in Nashville, billing himself as the "Tennessee Plowboy." He gained fame with such songs as *That's How Much I Love You, Bouquet of Roses,* and *Anytime.* After the first wave of rock 'n' roll had subsided, he became a leading figure in the movement toward the urbanized country-music genre (country pop or Nashville sound); in 1966 he was the first country-western musician to lead a concert at Carnegie Hall in N.Y.; that earned him election to the Country Music Hall of Fame. His later successes included his renditions of *What's He Doing in My World, Make the World Go Away, Misty Blue, Turn the World Around, Here Comes Heaven,* etc. His autobiography, *It's a Long Way from Chester County,* was publ. in 1969.

Arnold, Frank Thomas, English music scholar; b. Rugby, Sept. 6, 1861; d. Bath, Sept. 24, 1940. He studied at Trinity College in Cambridge, and was lecturer in German literature at the Univ. College of South Wales at Cardiff (1886–1926). He wrote a valuable book, *The Art of Accompaniment from a Thorough-Bass, as Practiced in the 17th and 18th Centuries* (London, 1931), and contributed numerous papers on Bach, Viadana, Corelli, etc. to various music journals. He was also a collector of rare editions.

BIBLIOGRAPHY: D.R. Wakeling, "An Interesting Music Collection," *Music & Letters* (July 1945).

Arnold, Gustav, Swiss organist and composer; b. Altdorf, Uri, Sept. 1, 1831; d. Lucerne, Sept. 28, 1900. He studied at Innsbruck; in 1850 he went to England, where he was choirmaster and organist at various churches. He returned to Switzerland in 1865 and settled in Lucerne as an organizer of choral festivals and a conductor. He wrote some sacred music and piano pieces.

Arnold, Gyorgy, Hungarian composer; b. Paks, June 5, 1781; d. Subotica, Oct. 25, 1848. He studied with his father. In 1800 he became music director in Subotica, and also regens chori at St. Theresa's, holding both posts until his death. Adopting an operatic method in his treatment of religious music, he created some unusual stylistic hybrids. He wrote several operas which were never performed and the manuscripts of which seemed to be lost, but his church music is extant. In 1826 Arnold completed a music dictionary, which was never published. His songs, in a characteristic Hungarian manner, were once very popular.

BIBLIOGRAPHY: K. Isoz, *Gyorgy Arnold* (Budapest, 1908).

Arnold, Johann Gottfried, German violoncellist and composer; b. Niedernhall, near Öhringen, Feb. 1, 1773; d. Frankfurt, July 26, 1806. He studied with Willmann and Bernhard Romberg; after a brief concert career he became a theater cellist in Frankfurt. He wrote *Symphonie concertante* for 2 Flutes and Orch.; several cello concertos; 6 sets of variations for cello; and various pieces for the guitar and other instruments.

Arnold, Karl, German organist and conductor, son of **Johann Gottfried Arnold;** b. Neukirchen, near Mergentheim, Württemberg, May 6, 1794; d. Christiania (Oslo), Norway, Nov. 11, 1877. He studied with J.A. André and Vollweiler; then occupied various positions in St. Petersburg, Russia (1818), in Berlin (1824), and in Münster (1835). In 1847 he went to Norway, where he became conductor of the Phil. Society in Christiania, and also was a church organist there. He wrote an opera, *Irene* (Berlin, 1832), a piano sextet, and numerous works for piano solo.

Arnold, Malcolm, prolific and versatile British composer; b. Northampton, Oct. 21, 1921. He studied trumpet, conducting, and composition at the Royal College of Music in London (1938–40); played first trumpet with the London Phil. (1942–44, 1946–48). He then devoted himself chiefly to composition, developing a melodious and harmonious style of writing that possessed the quality of immediate appeal to the general public while avoiding obvious banality; many of his works reveal modalities common to English folk songs, often invested in acridly pleasing harmonies. His experience as a trumpeter and conductor of popular concerts provided a secure feeling for propulsive rhythms and brilliant sonorities. He had a knack for composing effective background music for films. In his sound track for *The Bridge on the River Kwai* he popularized the rollicking march *Colonel Bogey*, originally composed by Kenneth Alford in 1914. In 1970 Arnold was made a Commander of the Order of the British Empire.

WORKS: OPERAS: *The Dancing Master* (1951) and *The Open Window* (London, Dec. 14, 1956). BALLETS: *Homage to the Queen* (produced at Covent Garden, London, in the presence of Queen Elizabeth II, on June 2, 1953); *Rinaldo and Armida* (1954); *Sweeney Todd* (1958); and *Electra* (1963). OTHER STAGE WORKS: Nativity play, *Song of Simeon* (1958); a children's spectacle, *The Turtle Drum* (1967). FOR ORCH.: Symph. for Strings (1946); 8 numbered symphs.: No. 1 (Cheltenham Festival, July 6, 1951); No. 2 (Bournemouth, May 25, 1953); No. 3 (1954–57; London, Dec. 2, 1957); No. 4 (London, Nov. 2, 1960); No. 5 (Cheltenham Festival, 1961); No. 6 (Sheffield, June 28, 1968, Arnold conducting); No. 7 (London, May 1974, Arnold conducting); No. 8 (N.Y., May 5, 1979);

15 solo concertos: 2 for Horn (1945, 1956); 2 for Clarinet (1948, 1974); one for Piano Duet (1951); one for Oboe (1952); 2 for Flute (1954, 1972); one for Harmonica (1954; London, Aug. 14, 1954, Larry Adler, soloist); one for Organ (1954); one for Guitar (1958); one for 2 Violins (1962); one for 2 Pianos, 3-hands (1969); one for Viola (1970); one for Trumpet (1981); 10 overtures: *Beckus the Dandipratt* (1943); *Festival Overture* (1946); *The Smoke* (1948); *A Sussex Overture* (1951); *Tam O'Shanter* (1955); *A Grand, Grand Overture* for 3 Vacuum Cleaners, One Floor Polisher, 4 Rifles, and Orch. (1956; London, Nov. 13, 1956); *Commonwealth Christmas Overture* (1957); *Peterloo* (1968); *Anniversary Overture* (1968); *The Fair Field* (1972); tone poem, *Larch Trees* (1943); Serenade for Small Orch. (1950); *8 English Dances* in 2 sets (1950–51); *The Sound Barrier*, rhapsody (1952); 3 sinfoniettas (1954, 1958, 1964); *2 Little Suites* (1955, 1962); Serenade for Guitar and Strings (1955); *4 Scottish Dances* (1957); *4 Cornish Dances* (1966); Concerto for 28 Players (1970); *Fantasy for Audience and Orch.* (1970); *A Flourish for Orchestra* (1973); *Fantasy* for Brass Band (1974); *Philharmonic Concerto* (1977); Symph. for Brass Instruments (1979). CHAMBER MUSIC: Trio for Flute, Viola, and Bassoon (1943); *3 Shanties* for Wind Quintet (1944); Duo for Flute and Viola (1945); 2 violin sonatas (1947, 1953); Viola Sonata (1947); Flute Sonatina (1948); 2 string quartets (1949, 1976); Oboe Sonatina (1951); Clarinet Sonatina (1951); Recorder Sonatina (1953); Piano Trio (1955); Oboe Quartet (1957); *Toy Symphony* for 12 Toy Instruments, Piano, and String Quartet (1957); Brass Quintet (1961); 5 pieces for Violin and Piano (1965); 9 solo fantasies: for Bassoon, Clarinet, Horn, Flute, Oboe, Trumpet, Trombone, Tuba, and Guitar (1966–70); *Trevelyan Suite* for Wind Instruments (1968); piano pieces; songs. FOR FILMS: *The Captain's Paradise* (1953); *I Am a Camera* (1955); *Trapeze* (1956); *Island in the Sun* (1957); *The Bridge on the River Kwai* (1957); *Inn of the Sixth Happiness* (1958); *Roots of Heaven* (1958); *Nine Hours to Rama* (1962).

BIBLIOGRAPHY: Alan Poulton, *Malcolm Arnold: A Catalogue of His Music* (London, 1983).

Arnold, Maurice (real name, **Maurice Arnold Strothotte**), American violinist and composer; b. St. Louis, Jan. 19, 1865; d. New York, Oct. 23, 1937. He studied in Cincinnati; then in Germany with several teachers, including Max Bruch. The performance of his orch. work *American Plantation Dances* (N.Y., 1894) aroused the interest of Dvořák, because of the Negro melodies used in it, and he engaged Arnold to teach at the National Cons., of which Dvořák was then head. Arnold subsequently was active as a conductor of light opera, and as a violin teacher. He wrote a comic opera, *The Merry Benedicts* (Brooklyn, 1896); a grand opera, *Cleopatra;* a Symph.; a cantata, *The Wild Chase; Minstrel Serenade* for Violin and Piano; and a Fugue for Piano, 8-hands.

Arnold, Richard, German-American violinist; b. Eilenberg, Prussia, Jan. 10, 1845; d. New York, June

21, 1918. He emigrated to the U.S. in 1853, but returned to Germany in 1864 to study with Ferdinand David in Leipzig. He was a violinist in the Theodore Thomas Orch. (1869–76), and concertmaster of the N.Y. Phil. Orch. (1880–1909); then lived in N.Y., teaching violin.

Arnold, Samuel, celebrated English composer, organist, and music scholar; b. London, Aug. 10, 1740; d. there, Oct. 22, 1802. He received his musical training from Gates and Nares as a chorister of the Chapel Royal. He showed a gift for composition early on, and was commissioned to arrange the music for the play *The Maid of the Mill;* for this he selected songs by some 20 composers, including Bach, and added several numbers of his own; the resulting pasticcio was produced with success at Covent Garden (Jan. 31, 1765). This was the first of his annual productions for Covent Garden and other theaters in London, of which the following were composed mainly by Arnold: *Harlequin Dr. Faustus* (Nov. 18, 1766); *The Royal Garland* (Oct. 10, 1768); *The Magnet* (June 27, 1771); *A Beggar on Horseback* (June 16, 1785); *The Gnome* (Aug. 5, 1788); *New Spain, or Love in Mexico* (July 16, 1790); *The Surrender of Calais* (July 30, 1791); *The Enchanted Wood* (July 25, 1792); *The 63rd Letter* (July 18, 1802). He also wrote several oratorios, among them *The Cure of Saul* (1767); *Abimelech; The Resurrection; The Prodigal Son;* and *Elisha* (1795; his last oratorio). On the occasion of a performance of *The Prodigal Son* at Oxford Univ. in 1773, Arnold was given the degree of D.Mus. In 1783, he became the successor of Nares as composer to the Chapel Royal, for which he wrote several odes and anthems. In 1789 Arnold was engaged as conductor of the Academy of Ancient Music; in 1793 he became organist of Westminster Abbey. He was buried in Westminster Abbey, near Purcell and Blow. Arnold's edition of Handel's works, begun in 1786, was carried out by him in 36 vols., embracing about 180 numbers; it is, however, incomplete and inaccurate in many respects. His principal work is *Cathedral Music* (4 vols.; 1790); its subtitle describes its contents: "A collection in score of the most valuable and useful compositions for that Service by the several English Masters of the last 200 years." It forms a sequel to Boyce's work of the same name. A new edition of Arnold's *Cathedral Music* was issued by Rimbault (1847).

Arnold, Yuri, Russian opera composer and theorist; b. St. Petersburg, Nov. 13, 1811; d. Karakash, Crimea, July 20, 1898. He was of German extraction; studied at the German Univ. of Dorpat, Estonia; from 1863–71 he lived in Leipzig; then returned to Russia; he lived in Moscow until 1894, when he moved to St. Petersburg. He wrote a comic opera, *Treasure Trove* (St. Petersburg, Feb. 1, 1853), the MS of which was lost in a fire at the St. Petersburg Opera Theater in 1859, together with the MS of his other opera, *St. John's Eve.* He further composed an overture, *Boris Godunov.* Arnold was the author of the first book in the Russian language dealing with the theory of composition (1841); also publ. *Theory*

of Old Russian Religious Dance (Moscow, 1880) and many articles on Russian music for German periodicals. Among his publications in German was *Der Einfluss des Zeitgeistes auf die Entwickelung der Tonkunst* (Leipzig, 1867). He translated into German the librettos of operas by Tchaikovsky and Glinka, and publ. historically valuable memoirs (3 vols.; Moscow, 1893).

Arnoldson, Sigrid, Swedish dramatic soprano; b. Stockholm, March 20, 1861; d. there, Feb. 7, 1943. She was the daughter of the celebrated tenor **Oscar Arnoldson** (1830–81). She studied voice with Maurice Strakosch and Désirée Artôt; made her professional debut in Prague in 1885; in 1886 she was a guest artist in Moscow, and in 1887 appeared in London; subsequently sang in Paris, Nice, and Rome. In 1888 she was engaged as a regular member at Covent Garden in London. On Nov. 29, 1893, she made her debut at the Metropolitan Opera in N.Y., but remained on its roster for only one season. In 1910 she was elected a member of the Stockholm Academy; in 1922 she was in Vienna as a singing teacher; later also taught voice in Berlin. On June 16, 1888, she married the Austrian impresario Alfred Fischhof, a nephew of Maurice Strakosch.

Arnould, (Madeleine) Sophie, French operatic soprano; b. Paris, Feb. 13, 1740; d. there, Oct. 22, 1802. She studied singing with Mme. Fel and acting with Mlle. Clairon; made her debut at the Paris Opéra on Dec. 15, 1757. She created the title role in Gluck's *Iphigénie en Aulide* (April 19, 1774), and after a highly successful career, retired in 1778 with a pension of 2,000 livres. Gabriel Pierné wrote a one-act "lyric comedy," *Sophie Arnould* (1926), based on incidents of her life.
    BIBLIOGRAPHY: *Arnouldiana,* a large collection of anecdotes, publ. anonymously (Paris, 1813; real author, A. Deville); E. and J. de Goncourt, *Sophie Arnould d'après sa correspondance et ses mémoires* (Paris, 1857); R.B. Douglas, *Sophie Arnould, Actress and Wit* (Paris, 1898).

Aronowitz, Cecil, English violist; b. King William's Town, South Africa, March 4, 1916; d. Ipswich, Sept. 7, 1978. He was of Russian descent. He studied at the Royal College of Music in London, where his principal teachers were Vaughan Williams and Jacob (composition) and Rivarde (violin). He turned to viola playing later in life, and served as first violist in the Boyd Neel Orch., in the Goldsborough (later English) Chamber Orch., and in the London Mozart Players; also was a member of the Melos Ensemble and the Pro Arte Piano Quartet. From 1950–75 he taught viola and chamber music at the Royal College of Music in London.

Arquier, Joseph, French opera composer; b. Toulon, 1763; d. Bordeaux, Oct. 1816. He played the cello in a theater at Lyons; then lived in Marseilles and Paris. After 1800 he went to New Orleans as director of an opera troupe, but failed and returned to France in 1804, holding various positions in Paris,

Toulouse, Marseilles, and Perpignan; he died in poverty. Arquier wrote about 16 comic operas.

Arrau, Claudio, eminent Chilean pianist; b. Chillán, Feb. 6, 1903. He received his early training from his mother, an amateur pianist, and as a child played a program of pieces by Mozart, Beethoven, and Chopin at a public performance in Santiago. In 1911 he was sent by the Chilean government to Berlin, where he took lessons with Martin Krause. In 1914–15 he gave piano recitals in Germany and Scandinavia, attracting attention by his precocious talent. In 1921 he returned to Chile, making his first professional appearances there and elsewhere in South America. In 1924 he made his first American tour as a soloist with the Boston Symph. Orch. and the Chicago Symph. In 1925 he was appointed to the faculty of the Stern Cons. in Berlin. He won the Grand Prix International des Pianistes at Geneva in 1927; in 1929 he made a tour of Russia, returning for a 2nd tour the following year. During the season 1935–36 he presented in Berlin the complete keyboard works of Bach in 12 recitals; in 1936 he performed all keyboard works of Mozart in 5 recitals in Berlin. In 1938 he played all 32 piano sonatas and all 5 piano concertos of Beethoven in Mexico City, and in 1939 repeated this series in Buenos Aires and Santiago. In 1941 he settled permanently in N.Y., devoting himself to concert appearances and teaching. In 1947 he made a tour of Australia, and in 1949 gave a series of concerts in South Africa; in 1951 toured in Israel; in 1956 played in India; in 1958 gave concerts in Prague and Bucharest; in 1965 made his first tour in Japan. In 1962–69 he made a complete recording of Beethoven's sonatas. He also supervised the edition of the Urtext of Beethoven's piano sonatas. In his playing, Arrau combines a Classical purity and precision of style with a rhapsodic éclat.

Arregui Garay, Vicente, Spanish composer; b. Madrid, July 3, 1871; d. there, Dec. 1, 1925. He studied in Paris and Rome; was active in Madrid as a music critic; wrote a symph. poem, *Historia de una madre* (after H.C. Andersen, 1910); *Sinfonia vasca* for Orch.; the operas *Yolanda, La Maya,* and *El Cuento de Barba Azul;* a cantata, *El Lobo ciego;* chamber music and choral works. His music follows the Romantic school of programmatic writing.

Arriaga, Juan Crisóstomo, precocious Spanish composer; b. Rigoitia, near Bilbao, Jan. 27, 1806; d. Paris, Jan. 17, 1826 (10 days before his 20th birthday). At the age of 11, he wrote an Octet for French Horn, Strings, Guitar, and Piano, subtitled *Nada y mucho;* at 13, a 2-act opera, *Los esclavos felices.* On the strength of these works he was accepted at the Paris. Cons., where he studied with Baillot and Fétis. In Paris he wrote a Symph.; a biblical scene, *Agar;* 3 string quartets; several fugues; piano pieces; songs. On Aug. 13, 1933, a memorial to him was unveiled in Bilbao and a Comisión Permanente Arriaga was formed to publish his works. Under its auspices, the vocal score of the opera and the full scores of his Symph. and Octet were printed. A bibliographical pamphlet, *Resurgimiento de las obras de Arriaga,* by Juan de Eresalde was also publ. (Bilbao, 1953).

Arrieta y Corera, Pascual Juan Emilio, Spanish composer; b. Puente la Reina, Oct. 21, 1823; d. Madrid, Feb. 11, 1894. He studied at the Milan Cons. (1839–45) with Vaccai; returned to Spain in 1846; was a prof. at the Madrid Cons. in 1857; became its director in 1868. He wrote more than 50 zarzuelas and several grand operas in Italian. Of these productions the most important is *La conquista de Granada,* produced in Madrid (Oct. 10, 1850) with Arrieta himself conducting, and revived 5 years later under the title *Isabel la Católica* (Madrid, Dec. 18, 1855). Other successful zarzuelas and operas are *Ildegonda* (Milan, Feb. 28, 1845); *El Domino Azul* (Madrid, Feb. 19, 1853); *El Grumete* (Madrid, June 17, 1853; its sequel, *La Vuelta del Corsario,* was perf. in Madrid, Feb. 18, 1863); *Marina* (Madrid, Sept. 21, 1855; revised and produced as a grand opera, Madrid, Oct. 4, 1871); *S. Francesco da Siena* (Madrid, Oct. 27, 1883).

Arrieu, Claude, French pianist and composer; b. Paris, Nov. 30, 1903. She studied piano with Marguerite Lond, and took courses in composition at the Paris Cons. with Roger-Ducasse and Noël Gallon, graduating with Premier Prix in 1932. She achieved her best successes writing for the theater.
WORKS: *Noë,* music drama (Strasbourg, Jan. 29, 1950); *Cadet Roussel,* comic opera (Marseilles, Oct. 2, 1953); *La Cabine téléphonique,* radio sketch (Paris, March 15, 1959); *La Princesse de Babylone,* comic opera (Reims, March 4, 1960); *The Love of Don Perlimplin and Belisa in His Garden,* opera enlarged from incidental music to Lorca's play (Tours, March 1, 1980).

Arrigo, Girolamo, Italian composer; b. Palermo, April 2, 1930. He studied at the Palermo Cons., and later in Rome and Paris. His works are mostly in small forms, and virtually all with programmatic connotations. The most important among them are *3 occasione* for Soprano and 32 Instruments (1958); *4 occasione* for 7 Voices, Horn, Viola, Mandolin, Guitar, and Celesta (1959); *Fluxus* for 9 Instruments (1959); *Episodi* for Soprano and Flute, to texts by ancient Greek poets (1963); *Shadows* for Orch. (1965); and *Infrarosso (Infrared)* for 16 Instruments (1967). He also wrote a "collage opera" entitled *Orden* (1969), consisting of several not necessarily related numbers, to texts in French, Italian, and Spanish.

Arrigoni, Carlo, Italian composer; b. Florence, Dec. 5, 1697; d. there, Aug. 19, 1744. He left Italy as a young man; in 1728 he was in Brussels. In 1732 he was invited to London by a group favorable to Italian composers in opposition to Handel; there he produced an opera, *Fernando* (London, Feb. 5, 1734). Arrigoni then went back to Italy through Vienna, where he produced an oratorio, *Esther* (1738); returning to Florence, he staged his new operas *Sir-*

bace and *Scipione nelle Spagne* (1739). His 10 *Cantate da camera* were publ. in London (1732). Several airs from his opera *Fernando* are preserved in the British Museum; Burney mistakenly attributed the music of this opera to Porpora.

Arro, Elmar, Estonian musicologist; b. Riga, July 2, 1899. He studied musicology at the Univ. of Vienna, where he received his Ph.D. in 1928 with the dissertation *Über das Musikleben in Estland im 19. Jahrhundert;* in 1933 he joined the faculty of the German Luther Academy in Dorpat; in 1939 he went to Germany; taught at the Univ. of Heidelberg (from 1955) and the Univ. of Kiel (from 1968). He was instrumental in helping to found the Ost-Europa Institut (now the J.G. Herder Forschungsstelle für Musikgeschichte). He subsequently made his home in Vienna. He contributed valuable articles on the music of Russia and Eastern Europe to various music journals; he also founded and served as editor of the first 4 vols. of *Musik des Ostens* (1962–67).

l'Arronge, Adolf, German conductor and composer; b. Hamburg, March 8, 1838; d. Berlin, Dec. 25, 1908. He studied at the Leipzig Cons.; then conducted opera in Cologne, Danzig, Berlin, Breslau, and Budapest. He wrote a number of light operas which, however, failed to obtain any degree of success.

Arroyo, João Marcellino, eminent Portuguese composer, writer, and statesman; b. Oporto, Oct. 4, 1861; d. Colares, near Lisbon, May 18, 1930. A member of a musical family, he first took lessons with his father; at the same time he studied law. From 1884–1904 he was a member of the Portuguese parliament; in 1900–1 he held the posts of minister of foreign affairs and minister of public education. A royalist, he abandoned politics after the revolution of 1910, and received a professorship of law at the Univ. of Coimbra.
WORKS: 2 operas: *Amor de Perdição* (Lisbon, March 2, 1907; Hamburg, Jan. 25, 1910), regarded as the first modern Portuguese opera, and *Leonor Teles;* 2 symph. poems; several choral works and songs; also compiled a manual of solfeggio for primary schools.
BIBLIOGRAPHY: E. Amorim, *Dicionário biográfico de músicos do Norte de Portugal* (Oporto, 1941); C.A. Dos Santos, *João Arroyo* (Lisbon, 1941).

Arroyo, Martina, American soprano; b. Harlem, N.Y., Feb. 2, 1936. She is of partly Hispanic, partly black origin. Her voice teacher was Marinka Gurewich, who remained her principal mentor throughout her professional career. After graduation from Hunter College (B.A., 1956), she sang in the American premiere of Pizzetti's *Assassinio nella cattedrale* at Carnegie Hall in N.Y., on Sept. 17, 1958. In 1959 she married an Italian viola player, Emilio Poggioni, but their marriage ended in divorce. On March 14, 1959, she made her debut with the Metropolitan Opera as the Celestial Voice in *Don Carlos;* then sang incidental parts in Wagner's tetralogy. In 1963 she toured Europe; made appearances with the Vienna State Opera, at the Berlin State Opera, and in Zürich. Returning to the U.S., she was a soloist with the N.Y. Phil. and other orchs. She demonstrated her professional mettle when on Feb. 6, 1965, she was suddenly called to substitute for Birgit Nilsson as Aida at the Metropolitan Opera, a challenge she carried off brilliantly; after that she was given major roles at the Metropolitan; she sang Elvira in *Ernani,* Leonora in *Il Trovatore,* Elsa in *Lohengrin,* Donna Anna in *Don Giovanni,* and Aida, all with excellent success. What is even more remarkable, she proved herself technically equal to the complex soprano parts in the works of such avant-garde composers as Varèse, Dallapiccola, and Stockhausen, which she selflessly performed at special concerts.

Artaria, music publishing house in Vienna, founded by the cousins **Carlo** (1747–1808) and **Francesco Artaria** (1744–1808). They opened a music shop on Kohlmarkt in 1769, and in 1778 began printing music; they introduced the method of zinc plating for the first time in Vienna. In 1779 the firm acquired some of Haydn's works, which brought them fame; music of Clementi, Salieri, and Boccherini was publ. later. Artaria publ. Mozart's 6 violin sonatas (K. 296, 376–80), the *Haffner-Sinfonie,* and 6 string quartets dedicated to Haydn, among other works, thus becoming Mozart's most important publisher in his lifetime. Other first editions in Artaria's catalogue were several songs by Schubert; Beethoven's C major Quintet, op. 29, and string quartets, opp. 130 and 133. The last owners were **Carl August** (d. 1919), **Dominik** (d. 1936), and **Franz Artaria** (d. 1942). After 1932, the old house became an art gallery and an auction bureau, preserving the name Artaria.
BIBLIOGRAPHY: F. Artaria and Hugo Botstiber, *Joseph Haydn und das Verlagshaus Artaria* (Vienna, 1909); D. MacArdle, "Beethoven, Artaria, and the C major Quintet," *Musical Quarterly* (Oct. 1948); A. Weinmann, *Vollständiges Verlagsverzeichnis, Artaria & Comp.* (Vienna, 1952).

Arteaga, Esteban de, Spanish writer on music; b. Moraleja de Coca, Segovia, Dec. 26, 1747; d. Paris, Oct. 30, 1799. He joined the Jesuit Order at 16, and was banished to Corsica when the Jesuits were proscribed in Spain. He left the Order in 1769; from 1773–78 he studied philosophy at the Univ. of Bologna; there he formed a friendship with Padre Martini, and at his behest undertook a history of musical theater in Italy. The resulting work, *Le rivoluzioni del teatro musicale italiano dalla sua origine fino al presente,* was publ. in 3 vols. in Bologna and Venice (1783–86; the materials in the Bologna ed. partly supplement those in the Venice ed.); it was brought out in German by J. Forkel (2 vols., Leipzig, 1789); a summary was publ. in French (1802). Arteaga's strong and often critical opinions expressed in this work antagonized many Italian writers who resented the intrusion of a foreigner into their own field. A polemical exchange of considerable acrimony followed; Arteaga's views were attacked by Matteo Borsa in the tract *Del gusto presente in letteratura italiana . . .* and by Vincenzo Manfredini in *Difesa della musica moderna . . .* (Bologna, 1786). After a sojourn in Venice (1785), Arteaga lived in Rome (1786–87); in 1796 he went to Florence and later to Paris. In addition to his magnum opus, he publ. a book on esthetics, *Investigaciones filosóficas sobre la belleza ideal . . .* (Madrid, 1789; new ed., Madrid, 1943). A book of essays, *Lettere musico-filologiche,* and the treatise *Del ritmo sonoro e del ritmo muto nella musica degli antichi* (long regarded as lost) were publ. in Madrid in 1944, with an extensive biographical account by the editor Miguel Batllori, who also gives the bibliographical synopsis of the Bologna and Venice editions of *Rivoluzioni.*

Arthur, Alfred, American composer and choral conductor; b. Pittsburgh, Oct. 8, 1844; d. Lakewood, Ohio, Nov. 20, 1918. He studied with Eichberg at the Boston Cons.; sang at Boston churches; then moved to Cleveland, where he was conductor of the Vocal Society (from 1873) and director of the Cleveland School of Music. He wrote 3 operas which remain unperformed and unpubl.: *The Water-carrier* (1876); *The Roundheads and Cavaliers* (1878); *Adaline* (1879). He also brought out *Progressive Vocal Studies* (1887) and other manuals on singing.

Artôt, Alexandre-Joseph Montagney, Belgian violinist; b. Brussels, Jan. 25, 1815; d. Ville-d'Avray, July 20, 1845. He studied with his father, **Maurice Artôt,** and with Snel; then took lessons from Rodolphe and Auguste Kreutzer at the Paris Cons., obtaining first prize (1828). He then played concerts on the Continent; made his debut in London (June 3, 1839) in his own *Fantaisie* for Violin and Orch. In 1843 he embarked on an American concert tour. He wrote a violin concerto, several sets of variations for violin, and some chamber music.

Artôt, Désirée (baptismal name, **Marguerite-Joséphine Désirée Montagney**), Belgian mezzo-soprano, daughter of **Jean-Désiré Artôt**; b. Paris, July 21, 1835; d. Berlin, April 3, 1907. She studied with Mme. Viardot-Garcia; sang in Belgium, the Netherlands, and England (1857). Meyerbeer engaged her to sing in *Le Prophète* at the Paris Opéra (Feb. 5, 1858); she was greatly praised by Berlioz and other Paris musicians and critics. In 1858 she went to Italy; then made appearances in London. In 1868 she was in Russia, where she was briefly engaged to Tchaikovsky; however, this engagement was quickly disrupted by her marriage (on Sept. 15, 1869) to the Spanish singer **Padilla y Ramos** (1842–1906). Their daughter was **Lola Artôt de Padilla.**

Artôt, Jean-Désiré, Belgian horn player and composer; b. Paris, Sept. 23, 1803; d. Brussels, March 25, 1887. He was a pupil and successor of his father, **Maurice Artôt.** From 1843 he taught at the Brussels Cons.; also played in the court orch. He publ. fantasias and études for horn, and quartets for cornets à pistons.

Artôt, Maurice Montagney, ancestor of a celebrated line of musicians (the true family name being Montagney); b. Gray (Haute-Saône), Feb. 3, 1772; d. Brussels, Jan. 8, 1829. He was a bandmaster in the French army; then went to Brussels, where he became first horn player at the Théâtre de la Monnaie. A versatile musician, he also played the guitar and taught singing.

Artusi, Giovanni Maria, Italian contrapuntist and writer on music; b. Bologna, c.1540; d. there, Aug. 18, 1613. He became canon-in-ordinary at S. Salvatore in Bologna in Feb. 1562. A capable musician and writer who studied with Zarlino, Artusi was reactionary in his musical philosophy. His first publication, *L'arte del contrappunto* (in 2 parts; Venice, 1586 and 1598), has considerable theoretical value. He then publ. several polemical essays directed mainly against the innovations of Monteverdi and others: the characteristically named vol. *L'Artusi, ovvero Delle imperfettioni della moderna musica* (Venice, 1600; reproduced in part in Eng. by O. Strunk in *Source Readings in Music History,* N.Y., 1950); a posthumous attack on his teacher Zarlino in *Impresa del R.P. Gioseffo Zarlino* (Bologna, 1604); *Considerazioni musicali* (1603; as part II of *L'Artusi,* etc.); *Discorso musicale . . .* (1606) and *Discorso secondo musicale* (both attacking Monteverdi), and further polemical essays against Bottrigari and Vincenzo Galileo. Monteverdi replied to Artusi in a leaflet entitled *Ottuso accademico* and in the preface to his 5th book of madrigals; this reply is reproduced in Strunk's *Source Readings in Music History.* Bottrigari replied in a pamphlet entitled *Ant' Artusi.* As a composer, Artusi followed the old school; he publ. a set of 4-part *Canzonette* (1598) and an 8-part motet, *Cantate Domino* (1599).

BIBLIOGRAPHY: H. Redlich, *Claudio Monteverdi, Life and Works* (London, 1952).

Artyomov, Vyacheslav, Russian composer; b. Moscow, June 29, 1940. He studied composition with Pirumov and then at the Moscow Cons. with Sidelnikov, graduating in 1968. Together with Gubaidulina and Suslin, he formed the folk-instrument improvisatory group Astrea in 1975. In his compositions he applies euphonious dissonances over the basic lines of simulated Russian folk modalities, with asymmetrical rhythms in spasmodically lyric melos. WORKS: *String Quartet* (1960); 3 pieces for String Quartet (1960); Piano Concerto (1961); *Chamber Suite* for Wind Quintet (1966); 2 clarinet sonatas (1966, 1971); *Northern Songs* for Mezzo-soprano, Percussion, and Piano (1966); *Jubilee Overture* (1967); *Concerto 13* for instrumental and vocal ensemble (1967); Violin Concerto (1968); *Tempo constante* for Orch. (1970); Accordion Concerto (1971); *Variations* for Flute and Piano (1974); *Capriccio for 1975* for Soprano Saxophone, Baritone Saxophone, and Vibraphone (1975); *Totem* for Percussion Ensemble (1976); *Elegiac Symphony* for 2 Violins, Percussion, and Strings (1977); *Awakening* for 2 Violins

(1978); *The Road to Olympus* for Orch. (1978; Moscow, Oct. 11, 1979); *Invocations* for Soprano and Percussion (1979–80); *Recitations* for Various Solo Instruments (1976–80); songs.

Artzibushev, Nicolai, Russian composer, music editor, and pedagogue; b. Tsarskoe-Selo, March 7, 1858; d. Paris, April 15, 1937. He studied with Rimsky-Korsakov and Soloviev; in 1908 was elected president of the St. Petersburg Royal Music Society. After the Revolution he went to Paris, where he was in charge of the Belaiev publishing house. As a composer, he is chiefly known for his melodious piano pieces and songs in a distinct style of the Russian national school; he also wrote a *Valse Fantasia* for Orch. and was one of the group of composers who contributed to the collection *Variations on a Russian Theme* for String Quartet; other variations were by Rimsky-Korsakov, Glazunov, Liadov, and Scriabin.

Arundell, Dennis, English opera producer and writer on music; b. London, July 22, 1898. He studied at St. John's College, Cambridge, where his music teachers were C.B. Rootham, Henry Moule, and Stanford. He also pursued a career as an actor and singer. He was a regular producer with the Sadler's Wells Opera in London. His books include *Henry Purcell* (London, 1927); *The Critic at the Opera* (London, 1957); *The Story of Sadler's Wells* (London, 1965); *Introduction to Le nozze di Figaro and Così fan tutte* (London, 1971).

Arutiunian, Alexander, Armenian composer; b. Erevan, Sept. 23, 1920. He studied piano and composition at the local conservatory; later went to Moscow, where he took a course in composition with Litinsky. Returning to Armenia, he was appointed music director of the Armenian Phil. Society. In his works he utilizes authentic folk-song inflections of Armenian popular music; his *Cantata of the Fatherland* on native themes (1948) achieved considerable success. His other important works are Piano Concerto (1941); Trumpet Concerto (1950); Piano Concertino (1951); Symph. (1957); *Chronicle of the Armenian People,* symph. poem (1961); Horn Concerto (1962); Concerto for 5 Wind Instruments and Orch. (1964); opera, *Sayat-Nova* (1967); *Ode to Lenin* (1967); *Hymn to Brotherhood* (1970); cycle for Chorus a cappella, *My Armenia* (1971); chamber music. A monograph on him was publ. in the Armenian language in Erevan (1962).

Asafiev, Boris, Russian composer and writer on music; b. St. Petersburg, July 29, 1884; d. Moscow, Jan. 27, 1949. He studied with Kalafati and Liadov at the St. Petersburg Cons., graduating in 1910; at the same time he studied philology and history at St. Petersburg Univ. He then became a ballet coach at the Opera. In 1914 he began writing music criticism under the pseudonym **Igor Glebov.** Subsequently he publ. his literary writings under that name, sometimes indicating his real name as well. He always signed his musical works, however, with the name

Asafiev. In 1920 he was appointed dean of the dept. of music of the Inst. of History of Arts in Petrograd. He was also an editor of the journal *Novaya Muzyka* (1924–28); within a few years he publ. brief monographs on Mussorgsky, Scriabin, Rimsky-Korsakov, Liszt, Chopin, etc.; translated articles from German, French, and Italian. He was a prof. of history, theory, and composition at the Leningrad Cons. (1925–43); then was director of the research section at the Moscow Cons.; at the same time he continued to compose, mostly for the stage. The following ballets by him were performed in Leningrad: *Flames of Paris* (Nov. 7, 1932); *The Fountain of Bakhtchisaray,* after Pushkin (Sept. 28, 1934; very popular); *The Partisan Days* (May 16, 1937); *The Prisoner of the Caucasus* (April 14, 1938). Altogether he wrote 9 operas, 27 ballets, works for orch., and chamber music. But it was as a historian of Russian music that Asafiev-Glebov was especially important. He continued the tradition of Vladimir Stasov in his ardent advocacy of the national Russian style. He publ. *The Russian Poets in Russian Music* (with a valuable catalogue of Russian vocal works; 1921); *Symphonic Etudes,* an account of the evolution of the Russian operatic style (1922); *Stravinsky,* a comprehensive analysis of Stravinsky's works (Leningrad, 1929; later he repudiated the favorable view of Stravinsky expressed in this book); *Russian Music from the Beginning of the Nineteenth Century* (1930; Eng. trans. by A. Swan; American Council of Learned Societies, 1953); *Musical Form as a Process* (2 vols.; 1930 and 1947); *Glinka* (Moscow, 1947; the only book on music to receive the Stalin Prize). A 7-vol. edition of Asafiev's collected writings was begun in Moscow in 1952.

Aschaffenburg, Walter, German-born American composer; b. Essen, May 20, 1927. He came to America when he was 11; served in the U.S. Army in Germany in 1947; upon returning to America, he studied music at Oberlin College (B.A., 1951) and at the Eastman School of Music in Rochester, N.Y. (M.A., 1952). In 1952 he was appointed to the faculty of the Oberlin Cons.; in 1968 became chairman of the dept. of composition there.
WORKS: Opera, *Bartleby* (Oberlin, Nov. 12, 1964); *Ozymandias,* "symphonic reflections after Shelley" (Rochester, N.Y., April 22, 1952); *Oedipus Rex,* overture (1952); Piano Trio (1951); *Divertimento* for Trumpet, Horn, and Trombone (1951); Cello Sonata (1954); Sonata for Solo Violin (1954); String Quartet (1955); Woodwind Quintet (1967).

Aschenbrenner, Christian Heinrich, German violinist and composer; b. Altstettin, Dec. 29, 1654; d. Jena, Dec. 13, 1732. He studied music with his father; then took composition lessons with Johann Theile; went to Vienna and had some further studies with J.H. Schmelzer. He was active as a violinist at Zeitz (1677–82) and Merseburg (1683–90); served as music director to the Duke of Zeitz (1695–1713) and later to the Duke of Merseburg (1713–19); finally retired on a pension to Jena. His only known work is *Gast- und Hochzeitsfreude, bestehend in Sonaten, Präludien, Allemanden, Couranten, Balletten, Arien, Sarabanden mit 3, 4 und 5 Stimmen, nebst dem Basso continuo* (1673).

Ascher, Joseph, Dutch pianist and composer; b. Groningen, June 4, 1829; d. London, June 20, 1869. He studied with Moscheles; went to Paris in 1849 and was court pianist to the Empress Eugénie. He wrote numerous pieces of salon music (études, nocturnes, galops, etc.).

Ascher, Leo, Austrian composer of light operas; b. Vienna, Aug. 17, 1880; d. New York, Feb. 25, 1942. His first successful operetta was *Vergeltsgott* (Vienna, Oct. 14, 1905); *Soldat der Marie* and *Hoheit tanzt Walzer* followed. Altogether he composed some 50 stage works, and film music. In 1938 he left Austria to live in N.Y.

Asciolla, Dino, Italian violist; b. Rome, June 9, 1920. He studied both violin and viola at the Rome Cons.; then attended master classes at the Santa Cecilia Academy in Rome and the Accademia Chigiana in Siena; won the Vivaldi Competition as a violinist in 1950; later turned to the viola, and played in various chamber music ensembles.

Ascone, Vicente, Uruguayan composer of Italian extraction; b. Siderno, Aug. 16, 1897; d. Montevideo, March 5, 1979. He was brought to Uruguay as a child; studied trumpet and composition. Most of his music is rooted in Uruguayan folk songs, while stylistically he followed the traditional Italian formulas. He wrote 5 operas, of which *Paraná Gauzú,* based on an Indian subject, was produced in Montevideo on July 25, 1931. He further wrote 3 symphs. (1945, 1955, 1959); *Politonal* for Piano and Orch. (1967); a Trumpet Concerto (1969); a Violin Concerto (1970); a symph. poem, *Sobre el Río Uruguay* (1946); and numerous songs.

Ashbrook, William (Sinclair), American humanities scholar and writer on music; b. Philadelphia, Jan. 28, 1922. He studied at the Univ. of Pa. (B.A., 1946) and Harvard Univ. (M.A., 1947); in 1955 he joined the faculty of Indiana State Univ. at Terre Haute; was appointed prof. of English and the humanities there in 1963, and chairman of its humanities dept. in 1972. He devoted his musical interests mainly to Italian opera, and publ. the useful books *Donizetti* (London, 1965); *The Operas of Puccini* (N.Y., 1968); *Donizetti and His Operas* (Cambridge, 1982).

Ashdown, Edwin, London music publisher; successor (1884) of Ashdown & Parry, who were the successors (1860) to Wessel & Co. (founded 1825). Two grandsons of Edwin Ashdown inherited the company, and incorporated into it the catalogue of Enoch & Co., and also of J.H. Larway & Co. (1936), the official name of the enlarged business remaining Edwin Ashdown, Ltd. Their list of publications contains mostly pedagogical works.

Ashkenazy, Vladimir, greatly gifted Russian pianist and conductor; b. Gorkey, July 6, 1937. His parents were professional pianists and taught him to play at an early age; subsequently he took regular lessons with Anaida Sumbatian at the Central Music School in Moscow, and in 1955 entered the class of Lev Oborin at the Moscow Cons. In 1955 he won 2nd prize at the International Chopin Competition in Warsaw. A great turning point in his career was reached when in 1956, at the age of 19, he won first prize in the Queen Elisabeth of Belgium International Competition in Brussels; in 1958 he made his first tour of the U.S.; in 1962 he and John Ogdon were both awarded first prizes in the Tchaikovsky International Competition in Moscow. In 1961 he married a young pianist, Sofia Johannsdottir of Iceland, who was studying in Moscow at the time. In 1963 they went to England while retaining their common Soviet citizenship. In 1968 they moved to Reykjavik, and in 1972 Ashkenazy became a citizen of Iceland; their 4 children speak English and Icelandic. As a pianist, he proved himself a statistical maximalist with a desire for completeness; thus he played all of Beethoven's 5 piano concertos and all of Rachmaninoff's 4 piano concertos; he also performed works by Scriabin and other early modern composers. Like the best of prizewinning Russians, he possesses a formidable but well-controlled and intelligent virtuoso technique. He was also drawn into conducting, and in 1981 was appointed principal guest conductor of the Phil. Orch. of London.

Ashley, Robert, American composer; b. Ann Arbor, Mich., March 28, 1930. He studied music at the Univ. of Michigan (B.Mus., 1952) and The Manhattan School of Music (M.Mus., 1954); took postgraduate courses in psychoacoustics at the Univ. of Michigan (1957–60). In his independent composition he pursues the ideal of "total musical events," which absorbs gesticulation, natural human noises, and the entire planetary environment. In 1961 he became co-founder of the ONCE group, dedicated to such actions, in Ann Arbor; from 1958–66 he operated an electronic music studio in association with the composer Gordon Mumma; in 1970 was appointed co-director of the Center of Contemporary Music at Mills College in Oakland, California. WORKS: Most of his works utilize electronic sounds; of these the following are notable for the totality of their envergure: *The 4th of July* (1960); *Something* for Clarinet, Piano, and Tape (1961); *Detroit Divided* (1962); *Complete with Heat* (1962); *Kitty Hawk,* an "anti-gravity piece" (1964); *Untitled Mixes* (1965); *Night Train* (1966); *The Trial of Anne Opie Wehrer and Unknown Accomplices for Crimes against Humanity* (1968); *Purposeful Lady Slow Afternoon* (1968); *Illusion Models* for Hypothetical Computer (1970); *In Memoriam Crazy Horse,* symph. (1964); the episodic operas *Perfect Lives* (1977–81) and *Atalanta* (1982); several film scores: *The Image in Time* (1957); *The Bottleman* (1960); *Jenny and the Poet* (1964); *My May* (1965);

Overdrive (1968); *Portraits, Self-portraits and Still Lifes* (1969); *Battery Davis* (1970). He also composes music performable on traditional instruments, among them *Maneuvers for Small Hands* for Piano (1961), Quartet for any number of Instruments (1965), and organ pieces.

Ashrafi, Mukhtar, Soviet composer; b. Bukhara, June 11, 1912. He studied composition at Samarkand and later at the Moscow Cons. (1934–37) with Vasilenko, and at the Leningrad Cons. (1941–43) with Maximilian Steinberg. In 1944 he settled in Tashkent, and taught at the Cons. there. His music is dedicated mainly to heroic subjects of Central Asia.
WORKS: Opera, *Buran* (orchestrated and otherwise organized by Vasilenko; Tashkent, June 12, 1939); *The Grand Canal* (also greatly helped by Vasilenko; Tashkent, Jan. 12, 1941); ballets: *Love's Amulet* (1969) and *Love and the Sword* (1972); cantata, *Song of Happiness* (1951); 2 symphs.: *Heroic Symphony* (1942) and *Glory to the Victors* (1944); 5 symph. suites on native themes; songs; film scores.

Ashton, Algernon (Bennet Langton), English composer; b. Durham, Dec. 9, 1859; d. London, April 10, 1937. His family moved to Leipzig, and he studied at the Leipzig Cons. with Reinecke and Jadassohn (1875–79); later took lessons with Raff in Frankfurt (1880). Returning to England, he obtained the post of piano teacher at the Royal College of Music (1885–1910). He was a prolific composer, having written more than 160 opus numbers, mostly in a conventional German style: 5 symphs.; 3 overtures; a piano concerto; a violin concerto; 3 piano quintets; 3 piano quartets; 3 piano trios; Trio for Clarinet, Viola, and Bassoon; Trio for Piano, Horn, and Viola; 5 violin sonatas; 5 cello sonatas; a viola sonata; and more than 200 piano works (among them a sonata, 3 fantasias, and various picturesque pieces such as *Idyls* and *Roses and Thorns*); also more than 200 songs, choral pieces, and organ works. Many of his chamber music compositions were publ., but he was never given recognition as a composer; however, he acquired notoriety by his curious letters in the English press dealing with a variety of subjects. Many of these letters he collected in his vols. *Truth, Wit and Wisdom* (London, 1904) and *More Truth, Wit and Wisdom* (London, 1905).

Asioli, Bonifazio, Italian composer; b. Correggio, Aug. 30, 1769; d. there, May 18, 1832. He began writing music at a very early age. He studied with Angelo Morighi in Parma (1780–82); then lived in Bologna and Venice as a harpsichord player. His first opera, *La Volubile,* was produced in Correggio (1785) with marked success; it was followed by *Le nozze in villa* (Correggio, 1786); *Cinna* (Milan, 1793); and *Gustavo al Malabar* (Turin, 1802). In 1787 he was private maestro to the Marquis Gherardini in Turin; then in Venice (1796–99); subsequently he went to Milan and taught at the Cons. (1808–14). Asioli wrote 7 operas; an oratorio, *Giacobbe in Galaad;* many cantatas; instrumental music; sacred choral works; etc. He was the author of several textbooks: *Principi elementari di musica* (Milan, 1809; also in English, German, and French); *Trattato d'armonia e d'accompagnamento* (1813); also manuals for Harpsichord, Voice, and Double Bass. His theoretical book *Il maestro di composizione* was publ. posthumously (1836).
BIBLIOGRAPHY: A. Coli, *Vita di Bonifazio Asioli* (Milan, 1834); O.S. Ancarani, *Sopra alcune parole di Carlo Botta intorno al metodo musicale di Bonifazio Asioli* (1836); A. Amadei, *Intorno allo stile della moderna musica di chiesa* (1841).

Askenase, Stefan, Polish pianist; b. Lwow, July 10, 1896. He studied in his native city with Theodor Pollak and at the Vienna Academy of Music with Emil von Sauer; also took courses in composition with Joseph Marx. He made his debut in Vienna in 1919; in subsequent years he gave recitals; appeared with leading orchs. throughout the world; then taught at the Rotterdam Cons. (1937–40) and at the Brussels Cons. (1954–61). He adopted Belgian citizenship in 1950.

Asola, Giammateo, Italian composer; b. Verona, c. 1532; d. Venice, Oct. 1, 1609. He entered the congregation of secular canons at S. Giorgio in Alga in 1546; held benefices at S. Stefano in Verona from 1566; subsequently served as a secular priest. He became maestro di cappella at Treviso Cathedral in 1577; then served in a similar capacity at Vicenza Cathedral in 1578. In 1588 he became one of the chaplains at S. Severo in Venice. He was active as a teacher; among his pupils was Leone Leoni. He wrote much sacred music in the style of Palestrina. The *Opera omnia,* edited by G. Vecchi, began to appear in 1963.
BIBLIOGRAPHY: F. Caffi, *Della vita e delle opere Giammateo Asola* (Padua, 1862); D. Fouse, *The Sacred Music of Giammateo Asola* (Diss., Univ. of North Carolina, 1960).

Asow, Erich H. Müller von. See **Mueller von Asow, Erich H.**

Aspa, Mario, Italian opera composer; b. Messina, 1799; d. there, Dec. 14, 1868. He studied with Zingarelli in Naples. He produced 42 operas, of which the most successful were *Paolo e Virginia* (Rome, April 29, 1843) and *Il muratore di Napoli* (Naples, Oct. 16, 1850). His last opera, *Piero di Calais,* was produced posthumously in his native town (Messina, March 6, 1872).

Aspestrand, Sigwart, Norwegian opera composer; b. Fredrikshald, Nov. 13, 1856; d. Oslo, Dec. 31, 1941. He studied at Leipzig and Berlin and spent 30 years of his life (1885–1915) in Germany. Of his 7 operas, *Die Seemansbraut,* produced in Gotha (March 29, 1894) and later in Oslo (March 18, 1907), was the most successful. His other operas, all in German, are: *Der Recke von Lyrskovsheid, Freyas Alter, Die Wette, Der Kuss auf Sicht, Robin Hood,* and *Per-*

vonte.

Asplmayr, Franz, Austrian composer; b. Linz (baptized, April 2) 1728; d. Vienna, July 29, 1786. He studied violin with his father; wrote ballets for the Austrian court. Historically, Asplmayr was important as one of the earliest Austrian composers to adopt the instrumental style, rich in dynamics, as established by the Mannheim school.

WORKS: Ballets: *Agamemnon, Iphigenie en Tauride, Acis et Galathée;* a Singspiel, *Die Kinder der Natur;* music for Shakespeare's *Macbeth* (1777) and *The Tempest* (1781); chamber music: *6 Serenate,* op. 1; *6 Quatuors concertants,* op. 2; *6 Trios,* op. 5; *6 Quatours,* op. 6.

Asriel, André, Austrian composer; b. Vienna, Feb. 22, 1922. He enrolled in the Vienna Academy of Music at the age of 13; in 1938 he went to England, where he took courses at the Royal College of Music in London. In 1946 he went to East Berlin and studied piano and composition at the Hochschule für Musik in Berlin-Charlottenburg; he also took lessons with Hans Eisler at the Academy of the Arts. In 1951 he was appointed instructor at the newly founded Deutsche Hochschule für Musik; in 1968 was named prof. there. He wrote a number of songs on socialist themes, among them *Freundschaft, Einheit, Frieden, Das neue Deutschland;* he further composed music for film documentaries; also became interested in jazz as a type of American folk music. He wrote a cycle of choral pieces a cappella to the texts of Aesop's fables. Among his purely instrumental works are *Four Inventions* for Trumpet, Trombone, and Orch. (1963) and *Serenade* for 9 Instruments (1969). He publ. a book, *Jazz Analysen und Aspekte* (Berlin, 1966).

BIBLIOGRAPHY: H.A. Brockhaus and K. Niemann, eds., *Musikgeschichte der Deutschen Demokratischen Republik 1945–1976* (East Berlin, 1979).

Assmayer, Ignaz, Austrian composer; b. Salzburg, Feb. 11, 1790; d. Vienna, Aug. 31, 1862. He studied piano, organ, and theory with A. Brunmayrs in Salzburg and later with T. Gerls. In 1815 he moved to Vienna, where he took lessons with Salieri. In 1846 he was appointed first Kapellmeister in Vienna, succeeding Eybler. He wrote several oratorios, among them *Saul und David, Sauls Tod,* and *Das Gelübde,* which he performed with the Vienna Tonkünstler Society. He further wrote 21 masses, 2 requiems, and other sacred works, as well as some 60 instrumental compositions, many of which were publ.

Aston, Hugh, English composer; b. c.1480; d. York, Dec. 9, 1522. These dates apply to the son of a certain Richard Aston of Mawdesley in Lancashire. After obtaining his B.A. (1505–6) and M.A. (Oct. 30, 1507) from Oxford, he moved to Cambridge to study canon law; he was throughout his life associated with St. John's College, Cambridge. On May 27, 1509, he became Prebend of St. Stephen's, Westmin-

ster, and in 1515, Archdeacon of York. Among Aston's authentic works are 2 masses (*Te Deum* for 5 Voices and *Videte manus meas* for 6 Voices); 2 other vocal works for 5 Voices (*Gaude Virgo Mater Christi* and *Te Deum laudamus*); and 3 fragments publ. in *Tudor Church Music* (vol. X). More unusual for the time is Aston's *Hornpipe* for Virginal, which is preserved in a MS at the British Museum; it is the earliest-known piece for the instrument. Of the 10 other dances in this MS, some, notably *My Lady Carey's Dompe,* may also be Aston's work.

BIBLIOGRAPHY: W.H. Grattan Flood, *Early Tudor Composers* (London, 1925, pp. 30–33).

d'Astorga, Emanuele (Gioacchino Cesare Rincón), Italian composer of operas; b. Augusta, Sicily, March 20, 1680; d. probably in Madrid, after 1757. Of a noble Spanish family which had settled in Augusta early in the 17th century, he was a baron in his own right, from his estate Ogliastro, nearby. Later in life he moved to Palermo; during the revolution of 1708 he was an officer in the municipal guard. In 1712 he went to Vienna, and was in Znaim in 1713; he left Vienna in 1714 and returned to Palermo, where he became a senator. It is known that he sold his Sicilian estate in 1744 and went to Spain, where he was in the service of the king. D'Astorga was widely known as a versatile and highly educated person; he was also adept as a singer and a cembalo player, but never regarded music as his primary profession. He composed at least 3 operas: the first, *La moglie nemica,* was produced at Palermo in 1698; the 2nd and most notable, *Dafni,* was staged at Genoa on April 21, 1709, and was probably also heard in Barcelona (1709) and in Breslau (1726); the 3rd, *Amor tirannico,* was given in Venice in 1710. He also wrote numerous chamber cantatas and himself publ. 12 of them in one vol. (Lisbon, 1726). His best-known work is *Stabat Mater* for 4 Voices; it was first heard in Oxford in 1752; a new edition of it was publ. by R. Franz in 1878. In his 2-vol. biography of d'Astorga (Leipzig, 1911 and 1919), Hans Volkmann refutes the unsupported statement of R. Pohl in the first edition of *Grove's Dictionary* that d'Astorga died at Raudnitz on Aug. 21, 1736; Volkmann also exposes the romantic account of d'Astorga's life publ. by Rochlitz in vol. II of *Für Freunde der Tonkunst* (1825) as a fanciful invention. *Astorga,* an opera based on his life, was written by J.J. Abert (1866). See also O. Tiby, "E. D'Astorga," *Acta Musicologica* (1953).

Asuar, José Vicente, Chilean composer; b. Santiago, July 20, 1933. He studied electrical engineering and music, first in Santiago and later in Berlin. From 1963 to 1965 he was prof. of acoustics and contemporary music at the Santiago National Cons.; from 1965 to 1968 he led a studio for electronic music in Caracas; he composed and performed there a multimedia work, *Imagen de Caracas,* employing synchronized projectors of 8 films plus chorus and orch.; from 1968 to 1972 he directed a course in sound technology at the Univ. of Chile. He composed mostly for electronic tape; his *Estudio* *aleatorio* (1962) makes use of random devices. Among his purely instrumental works are *Heterophonías* for Orch. (1965), *Octet* for 4 Flutes and 4 Percussion Players (1966), and *Guararia repano* for Indigenous Indian Instruments (1968).

Atanasov, Georgi, Bulgarian composer; b. Plovdiv, May 18, 1881; d. Fasano, Italy, Nov. 17, 1931. He went to Italy in 1901, and took lessons in composition with Mascagni at the Pesaro Cons. Returning to Bulgaria, he became active as a military bandleader, as well as a composer. He wrote two of the earliest operas on national Bulgarian subjects, *Borislav* (Sofia, March 4, 1911) and *Gergana* (Stara Zagora, July 1, 1925); other operas were *Zapustialata vodenitza (The Abandoned Mill), Altzek,* and *Tzveta;* he also wrote two children's operas, *The Sick Teacher* and *About Birds.*
BIBLIOGRAPHY: I. Sagaev, *Maestro Georgi Atanasov* (Sofia, 1961).

Atherton, David, English conductor; b. Blackpool, Jan. 3, 1944. He studied at Cambridge Univ. In 1967 he founded the London Sinfonietta, serving as its music director until 1973. In 1968 he became a conductor at the Royal Opera House, Covent Garden. In 1978 he had several engagements at the San Francisco Opera. In 1980 he became principal conductor of the Royal Liverpool Phil. Orch.; in 1981 he was appointed music director of the San Diego Symph. Orch., but continued his association with the Liverpool Phil. as a principal guest conductor.

Atherton, Percy Lee, American composer; b. Boston, Sept. 25, 1871; d. Atlantic City, N.J., March 8, 1944. He studied music at Harvard Univ.; then with Rheinberger in Munich, Sgambati in Rome, and Widor in Paris. Returning to America, he served on various advisory boards in Boston. He wrote 2 operas, *The Heir Apparent* (1890) and *Maharajah* (1900); a symph. poem, *Noon in the Forest;* numerous songs.

Atkins, Chet (Chester Burton Atkins), American guitarist of country-western and popular music; b. Luttrell, Tenn., June 20, 1924. He began to play the guitar as a child, mastering it without formal instruction; from 1941 appeared on various radio programs, including the "Grand Ole Opry" in Nashville. In 1957 he became an executive with RCA Victor, managing its recording studio in Nashville; as such he became the leader in the movement toward popular country-western music (country pop or Nashville sound), emphasizing electronic instruments and techniques. A versatile guitarist, he felt at ease in the performance of many popular genres; he also played jazz and made successful tours to Europe, the Far East, and Africa. He was elected to the Country Music Hall of Fame in 1973. His autobiography, *Country Gentleman,* was publ. in 1974.

Atlantov, Vladimir, Russian tenor; b. Leningrad, Feb. 19, 1939. He was brought up in a musical atmosphere; his father was a professional singer. He studied voice at the Leningrad Cons., graduating in 1973; continued his vocal studies at the La Scala Opera School in Milan (1963–65). In 1967 he became a regular member of the Bolshoi Theater in Moscow; also gave concert recitals in Italy, Austria, Hungary, France, and Japan. He is especially effective in lyrico-dramatic parts; his interpretation of Don José in *Carmen,* Alfredo in *La Traviata,* Cavaradossi in *Tosca,* and Lensky in *Eugene Onegin* are especially fine. Later on he extended his repertoire to include baritone roles.

Attaignant (also **Attaingnant, Atteignant**), **Pierre,** French printer of music who lived during the first half of the 16th century; d. Paris, 1552. He was probably the earliest printer in France to employ movable type in music printing. His first publication was a *Breviarium Noviomense* (1525). He continued to publ. a great many works, including 18 dances in tablature for the Lute (1529); 25 pavans (1530); a folio edition of 7 books of masses (1532); 13 books of motets (1534–35); and a series of 35 books of chansons (1539–49) containing 927 part-songs by French and Flemish composers. Reprints: E. Bernoulli, facsimile edition of 4 books under the title *Chansons und Tänze* (Munich, 1914); 31 chansons in Henry Expert's *Les Maîtres Musiciens de la Renaissance française* (1894–1908); D. Heartz, *Preludes, Chansons, Dances for Lute (1529–30)* (1964); *Danseries à 4 parties,* in Le Pupitre, 9 (Paris, 1969).
BIBLIOGRAPHY: Yvonne Rihouet (Rokseth), "Note bibliographique sur Attaignant," *Revue de Musicologie* (1924); F. Lesure, "Pierre Attaignant, Notes et documents," *Musica Disciplina* (1949); D. Heartz, *Pierre Attaingnant, Royal Printer of Music* (Berkeley, Calif., 1969).

Attenhofer, Karl, Swiss conductor and composer; b. Wettingen, May 5, 1837; d. Zürich, May 22, 1914. He studied at the Leipzig Cons. with Richter and Dreyschock: went to Zürich in 1866, and in 1870 was appointed director of music at the Univ. of Zürich; also held the post of second director of the Zürich Cons. (the post of first director was held by Friedrich Hegar). Attenhofer wrote mainly for chorus; his cantatas *Hegelingenfahrt* (1890), *Frühlingsfeier,* and *Der deutsche Michel* for men's voices have achieved considerable popularity. For women's voices he wrote *Beim Rattenfänger im Zauberberg, Das Kind der Wüste, Prinzessin Wunderhold,* and *Rütlifahrt;* he also compiled a manual, *Liederbuch für Männergesang* (1882).
BIBLIOGRAPHY: Ernst Isler, *Karl Attenhofer* (Zürich, 1915).

Atterberg, Kurt, eminent Swedish composer; b. Göteborg, Dec. 12, 1887; d. Stockholm, Feb. 15, 1974. He studied engineering and was employed in the wireless service; then took courses in composition at the Stockholm Cons. with Hallén, and in Berlin with Schillings (1910–12). In 1913 he was appointed conductor at the Drama Theater in Stockholm, holding this post until 1922; in 1919 he began writing music criticism and continued to contribute to Stockholm newspapers until 1957; concurrently he was also employed at the Swedish patent office (1912–68) and served as secretary of the Royal Academy of Music in Stockholm (1940–53). He was one of the founders of the Society of Swedish Composers in 1924, and was on its board until 1947. During all this time he continued to compose with inexhaustible energy, producing works in all genres: operas, ballets, symphs., concertos, choruses, and chamber music, all with preordained precision of form and technique. It is ironic that his music remained hermetically sealed within the confines of Sweden, rarely if ever performed beyond its borders. Atterberg's name attracted unexpected attention when he was declared winner of the ill-conceived Schubert Centennial Contest organized in 1928 by the Columbia Phonograph Co., with the declared intention to finish Schubert's Unfinished Symphony. The entire venture was severely criticized in musical circles as an attempt to derive commercial advantage under the guise of an homage to a great composer. Rumors spread that Atterberg had deliberately imitated the style of composition of some members of the jury (Glazunov, Alfano, Nielsen) in order to ingratiate himself with them so as to secure the prize, but Atterberg denied any such suggestion, pointing out that he knew the names only of those in the jury from the Nordic zone, whereas the international membership comprised 10 national zones. Furthermore, the symph. he had submitted was written in a far more advanced style than Atterberg's previous symph. works and was certainly much more modern than any music by the jury members, using as it did such procedures as polytonality. There can be no doubt, however, that Atterberg was a master technician of his craft, and that his music had a powerful appeal. That it never gained a wider audience can be ascribed only to an unfathomable accident of world culture.

WORKS: OPERAS (all produced in Stockholm): *Härvard Harpolekare* (*Harvard the Potter,* 1915–17; Sept. 29, 1919; revised as *Härvard der Harfner* and produced in German at Chemnitz, 1936; a later version with new 3rd act produced in Linz, Austria, June 14, 1952); *Bäckahästen* (1923–24; Jan. 23, 1925); *Fanal* (1929–32; Jan. 27, 1934); *Aladdin* (1936–41; March 18, 1941); *Stormen,* after Shakespeare's *Tempest* (1946–47; Sept. 19, 1948). BALLETS: *Per Svinaherde* (*Peter the Swineherd,* 1914–15); ballet-pantomime, *De fåvitska jungfrurna* (*The Wise and Foolish Virgins,* 1920; Paris, Nov. 18, 1920). SYMPHS.: No. 1 (1909–11; Stockholm, Jan. 10, 1912); No. 2 (1911–13; Stockholm, Feb. 11, 1912); No. 3 (1914–16; Stockholm, Nov. 28, 1916); No. 4, *Sinfonia piccola* (1918; Stockholm, March 27, 1919); No. 5, Sinfonia funèbre (1919–22; Stockholm, Jan. 6, 1923); No. 6 (1927–28; won the Schubert Centennial Prize; Stockholm, Oct. 15, 1928); No. 7, *Sinfonia romantica* (1942; Frankfurt, Feb. 14, 1943); No. 8 (1944; Helsinki, Feb. 9, 1945); No. 9, *Sinfonia visionaria,* with Mezzo-soprano, Baritone, and Chorus (1955–56; Helsinki, Feb. 26, 1957); also a *Sinfonia* for Strings (1952–53); *Varmlandsrhapsodi* on northern Swed-

ish folk tunes, written in honor of Selma Lagerlöf's 75th birthday (broadcast over the Swedish radio Nov. 20, 1933). OTHER ORCH. WORKS: 9 suites, among them No. 3, for Violin, Viola, and Strings (1917); No. 4, *Turandot* (1921); No. 5, *Suite Barocco* (1922); and No. 8, *Suite Pastorale* (1931); Rhapsody for Piano and Orch. (1909); Violin Concerto (1913; Göteborg, Feb. 11, 1914); Cello Concerto (1917–22; Berlin, Jan. 6, 1923); 2 Suites for the play *Stormen,* after Shakespeare's *Tempest:* No. 1 (1921, revised 1962–63); No. 2 (1964–65); *Rondeau rétrospectif* for Orch. (1926); Horn Concerto (1926; Stockholm, March 20, 1927); *Älven (The River),* symph. poem (1929–30); Piano Concerto (1927–35; Stockholm, Jan. 12, 1936); *Ballad and Passacaglia* for Orch. (1936); *Rondeau caractéristique* (1939–40); *Indian Tunes* for Orch. (1950); *Ballad utan ord (Ballad without Words)* for Orch. (1957–58); Concerto for Violin, Cello or Viola, and Orch. (1959–60; version with String Orch., 1963); *Vittorioso* for Orch. (1962); *Adagio Amoroso* for Flute and Strings (1967); a *Requiem* (1913); a cantata, *Järnbäraland* (1919). CHAMBER MUSIC: 2 string quartets (1915, 1937); Cello Sonata (1925); Piano Quintet (1927); *Variations and Fugue* for String Quartet (1943); *Trio Concertante* for Violin, Cello, and Harp (1959–60; revised 1965).

Attwood, Thomas, English organist and composer; b. London, Nov. 23, 1765; d. there, March 24, 1838. He was a chorister at the Chapel Royal under Nares and Ayrton from the age of 9. Following a performance before the Prince of Wales (afterward George IV), he was sent to Italy for further study; there he received instruction in Naples from Filippo Cinque and Gaetano Latilla. He then went to Vienna, where Mozart accepted him as a pupil; his notes from these theory and composition lessons are printed in the *Neue Mozart Ausgabe,* X/30/1. In 1787 he returned to London and held various posts as an organist. He was also music tutor to the Duchess of York (1791) and to the Princess of Wales (1795). A founder of the London Phil. Society (1813), he conducted some of its concerts. He occupied an important position in the English music world; when Mendelssohn came to London as a young man, Attwood lent him enthusiastic support. Attwood was a prolific composer of operas, of which many were produced in London, including *The Prisoner* (Oct. 18, 1792); *The Mariners* (May 10, 1793); *The Packet Boat* (May 13, 1794); *The Smugglers* (April 13, 1796); *The Fairy Festival* (May 13, 1797); *The Irish Tar* (Aug. 24, 1797); *The Devil of a Lover* (March 17, 1798); *The Magic Oak* (Jan. 29, 1799); *True Friends* (Feb. 19, 1800); *The Sea-Side Story* (May 12, 1801). In all, Attwood wrote 28 operas, in some of which he used material from other composers (he included music by Mozart in *The Prisoner* and *The Mariners*). He also wrote church music, piano sonatas, songs, and glees.

BIBLIOGRAPHY: C. Oldman, "Thomas Attwood, 1765–1838," *Musical Times* (Nov. 1965).

Atzmon, Moshe, Israeli conductor; b. Budapest, July 30, 1931. He was educated in Tel Aviv. In 1969 he was named chief conductor of the Sydney (Australia) Symph. Orch. Other appointments were as chief conductor of the North German Radio Symph. Orch. (1972–76) and, concurrently, chief conductor of the Basel Symph. Orch. (from 1972).

Auber, Daniel-François-Esprit, prolific French composer of comic operas; b. Caen (Normandy), Jan. 29, 1782; d. Paris, May 12, 1871. His father, an art dealer in Paris, sent him to London to acquire knowledge of business. Auber learned music as well as trade and wrote several songs for social entertainment in London. Political tension between France and England, however, forced him to return to Paris in 1803; there he devoted himself exclusively to music. His pasticcio *L'Erreur d'un moment,* a resetting of an old libretto, was produced by an amateur group in Paris in 1806; his next theatrical work was *Julie,* performed privately, with an accompaniment of 6 string instruments, in 1811. Cherubini, who was in the audience, was attracted by Auber's talent and subsequently gave him some professional advice. Auber's first opera to be given publicly in Paris was *Le Séjour militaire* (1813); 6 years later the Opéra-Comique produced his new work *Le Testament et les billets-doux* (1819). These operas passed without favorable notice, but his next production, *La Bergère châtelaine* (1820), was a definite success. From that time until nearly the end of his life, hardly a year elapsed without the production of a new opera. Not counting amateur performances, 45 operas from Auber's pen were staged in Paris between 1813 and 1869. He was fortunate in having the collaboration of the best librettist of the time, Scribe, who wrote (alone, or with other writers) no fewer than 37 libretti for Auber's operas. Auber's fame reached its height with *Masaniello, ou La Muette de Portici,* produced at the Opéra, Feb. 29, 1828. Its success was enormous. Historically, it laid the foundation of French grand opera with Meyerbeer's *Robert le Diable* and Rossini's *Guillaume Tell.* Its vivid portrayal of popular fury stirred French and Belgian audiences; revolutionary riots followed its performance in Brussels (Aug. 25, 1830). Another popular success was achieved by him with his Romantic opera *Fra Diavolo* (Opéra-Comique, Jan. 28, 1830), which became a standard work. Despite these successes with grand opera, Auber may be rightfully regarded as a founder of the French comic opera, a worthy successor of Boieldieu and at least an equal of Adam and Hérold. The influence of Rossini was noted by contemporary critics, but on the whole, Auber's music preserves a distinctive quality of its own. Rossini himself remarked that although Auber's music is light, his art is profound. Auber was greatly appreciated by the successive regimes in France; in 1829 he succeeded Gossec at the Academy; in 1842 he was appointed director of the Paris Cons. by Louis Philippe, and retained this post until his death. In 1852 Napoleon III made him imperial maître de chapelle. At the age of 87 he produced his last opera, *Rêve d'amour.* Auber lived virtually all his life in Paris, remaining there even during the siege by the Germans. He died, during the days of the Paris Commune, at the age of 89. His memory was honored by the Academy. Among his operas (most of which were produced at the Opéra-Comique) are also the following: *Le Cheval de bronze* (March 23, 1835); *Le Domino noir* (Dec. 2, 1837); *Les Diamants de la couronne* (March 6, 1841); *Manon Lescaut* (Feb. 23, 1856); *Le Premier Jour de bonheur* (Feb. 15, 1868).

BIBLIOGRAPHY: A. Pougin, *Auber* (Paris, 1873); A. Kohut, *Auber* (Leipzig, 1895); Ch. Malherbe, *Auber* (Paris, 1911); J. Klein, "Daniel-François Auber (1782–1871)," *Opera* (Aug. 1971).

Auberson, Jean-Marie, Swiss conductor; b. Chavornay, May 2, 1920. He studied at the Lausanne Cons. and the Cologne Hochschule für Musik; he played in the Lausanne Chamber Orch. and the Orch. de la Suisse Romande in Geneva; subsequently studied conducting with Paul van Kempen in Siena and Gunter Wand in Cologne. From 1956 he appeared as a conductor with Radio Beromünster in Zürich, Radio Geneva, and others; also conducted opera and ballet.

Aubert, Jacques (called **"le vieux"**), celebrated French violinist; b. Paris, Sept. 30, 1689; d. Belleville, near Paris, May (buried, May 19) 1753. He was a pupil of Senaillé; in 1719 he became bandleader to the Duke of Bourbon; in 1727 was one of the King's 24 violinists; he played in the orch. of the Grand Opéra as first violinist from 1728–52, and took part in the Concert Spirituel (1729–40). He publ. 33 separate instrumental works; was also the first in France to write instrumental concertos (scored for 4 violins and a bass). His music, distinguished by elegance, contributed to the formation of the French "style galant."

BIBLIOGRAPHY: L. La Laurencie, *L'Ecole française de violon de Lully à Viotti* (Paris, 1922–23).

Aubert, Louis-François-Marie, French composer; b. Paramé, Ille-et-Vilaine, Feb. 19, 1877; d. Paris, Jan. 9, 1968. Of precocious talent, he entered the Paris Cons. as a child, and studied piano with Diémer, theory with Lavignac, and advanced composition with Gabriel Fauré; he also sang in church choirs. His song *Rimes tendres* was publ. when he was 19. His *Fantaisie* for Piano and Orch. was performed in Paris by the Colonne Orch. with his teacher Diémer as soloist (Nov. 17, 1901). His *Suite brève* for 2 Pianos was presented at the Paris Exposition in 1900; an orch. version of it was performed for the first time in Paris on April 27, 1916. Aubert's major work is an operatic fairy tale, *La Forêt bleue* (Geneva, Jan. 7, 1913); an American production was staged in Boston on March 8, 1913, attracting considerable attention. The Paris production of *La Forêt bleue,* delayed by the war, took place on June 10, 1924, at the Opéra-Comique. Aubert's style is largely determined by the impressionistic currents of the early 20th century; like Debussy and Ravel, he was attracted by the music of Spain and wrote several pieces in the Spanish idiom, of which the symph.

poem *Habanera* (Paris, March 22, 1919) was particularly successful.

WORKS: The list of Aubert's works further includes: *La Légende du sang* for Narrator, Chorus, and Orch. (1902); 3 ballets: *La Momie* (1903); *Chrysothémis* (1904); *La Nuit ensorcélée* (1922); *6 poèmes arabes* for Voice and Orch. (1907); a song cycle, *Crépuscules d'automne* (Paris, Feb. 20, 1909); *Nuit mauresque* for Voice and Orch. (1911); *Dryade* for Orch. (1921); *Caprice* for Violin and Orch. (1925); *Feuilles d'images,* symph. suite (Paris, March 7, 1931); *Saisons* for Chorus and Orch. (1937); *Offrande aux victimes de la guerre* for Orch. (1947); *Le Tombeau de Châteaubriand* for Orch. (1948); *Cinéma,* ballet (1953); *Improvisation* for 2 Guitars (1960); a set of 3 piano pieces, *Sillages* (1913); a piano quintet; songs; etc.

BIBLIOGRAPHY: L. Vuillemin, *Louis Aubert et son œuvre* (Paris, 1921); Marcel Landowski and Guy Morançon, *Louis Aubert* (Paris, 1967).

Aubéry du Boulley, Prudent-Louis, French composer; b. Verneuil, Eure, Dec. 9, 1796; d. there, Jan. 28, 1870. He studied at the Paris Cons. with Momigny, Méhul, and Cherubini. He wrote much chamber music, in which he used the guitar; publ. a guitar method and a textbook, *Grammaire musicale* (Paris, 1830). He was an active teacher in his native province, and contributed much to the cultivation of music there.

BIBLIOGRAPHY: J. de L'Avre, *Aubéry du Boulley* (Paris, 1896).

Aubin, Tony, French composer and pedagogue; b. Paris, Dec. 8, 1907; d. there, Sept. 21, 1981. He studied at the Paris Cons. with Samuel-Rousseau, Noël Gallon, and Paul Dukas; in 1930 he won the first Grand Prix de Rome. Upon return to Paris from Rome, he studied conducting with Philippe Gaubert, and later was in charge of the music division at the Paris Radio until the collapse of France in 1940; from 1945 to 1960 he served as conductor with the French Radio; concurrently he taught at the Paris Cons. In 1968 he was elected member of the Académie des Beaux-Arts. A pragmatic composer, Aubin cultivated an eclectic idiom calculated to impress professionals and please common music-lovers.

WORKS: *Symphonie romantique* (1937); *Suite éolienne* for Clarinet, Flute, and Strings (1958); *Concertinetto dell'amicizia* for Flute and Piano (1964); *Concertinetto* for Violin and Piano (1964); *Brughiera* for Bassoon and Piano (1966); and an opera, *Goya* (1970).

Aubry, Pierre, French music scholar; b. Paris, Feb. 14, 1874; d. (following a fencing accident) Dieppe, Aug. 31, 1910. He began his education as a philologist; studied oriental languages, and traveled to Turkestan on a research project. He then became interested in medieval music; was, for a time, lecturer on music history at the Ecole des Hautes Etudes Sociales. His theories of notation are based on a plausible interpretation of medieval writers.

WRITINGS: His many publications, distinguished by profound scholarship, include: *8 chants héroïques de l'ancienne France* (1896); *Mélanges de musicologie critique,* in 4 vols.: I, *La Musicologie médiévale* (1899); II, *Les Proses d'Adam de Saint-Victor* (1900, with Abbé Misset); III, *Lais et Descorts français du XIIIᵉ siècle* (1901, with Jeanroy and Brandin); IV, *Les Plus Anciens Monuments de la musique française* (1903, with 24 facsimiles); *Essais de musicologie comparée,* 2 vols.: I, *Le Rhythme tonique dans la poésie liturgique et dans le chant des églises chrétiennes au Moyen-Age* (1903); II, *Esquisse d'une bibliographie de la chanson populaire en Europe* (1905); *Les Caractères de la danse: Histoire d'un divertissement pendant la première moitié du XVIIIᵉ siècle* (1905); *Au Turkestan: Notes sur quelques habitudes musicales chez les Tadjikes et chez les Sartes* (1905); *La Musique et les musiciens d'église en Normandie au XIIIᵉ siècle* (1906); *Estampies et Danses royales: Les Plus Anciens Textes de musique instrumentale au Moyen-Age* (1907); *Recherches sur les ténors français dans les motets du XIIIᵉ siècle* (1907); *Recherches sur les ténors latins dans les motets du XIIIᵉ siècle* (1907; facsimile ed. of the Parisian MS, with index and editorial explanations); *Cent motets du XIIIᵉ siècle* (1908; 3 vols.; photographic facsimile of Bamberg Codex E. d. IV. 6, with annotations; a most important work); *Refrains et Rondeaux du XIIIᵉ siècle* (1909, in the Riemann Festschrift); *Trouvères et troubadours* (1909; Eng. ed., N.Y., 1914); and a number of essays on kindred topics, publ. in *Mercure Musical* (1903–8).

Auda, Antoine, French-Belgian organist and music scholar; b. St. Julien-en-Jarez (Loire), Oct. 28, 1879; d. Brussels, Aug. 19, 1964. He studied music at Marseilles; then established himself at Liège as an organist; publ. important studies on the musical history of the city: *Etienne de Liège* (1923); *La Musique et les musiciens de l'ancien pays de Liège* (1930); and valuable theoretical works: *Les Modes et les tons* (1931) and *Les Gammes musicales* (1947). A complete bibliography of his writings appears in *Archiefen Bibliotheckwezen in Belgie* (1967).

Audran, Edmond, French composer of light opera, son of **Marius-Pierre Audran;** b. Lyons, April 12, 1840; d. Tierceville, Aug. 17, 1901. He studied at the Ecole Niedermayer in Paris (graduated in 1859). In 1861 he was appointed organist at St. Joseph's Church in Marseilles, where he produced his first operetta, *L'Ours et le Pacha* (1862). He wrote a funeral march on Meyerbeer's death (1864). After the production of *Le Grand Mogol* (Marseilles, Feb. 24, 1877), he returned to Paris, and staged *Les Noces d'Olivette* (Nov. 13, 1879). With the production of *La Mascotte* (Bouffes-Parisiens, Dec. 28, 1880), Audran achieved fame; this operetta became immensely popular; thousands of performances were given in Paris and all over the world. He continued to produce new operettas almost annually; of these, the following were successful: *Gillette de Narbonne* (1882); *La Cigale et la fourmi* (1886); *Miss Hélyett* (1890); *Sainte Freya* (1892); *Madame Suzette* (1893);

Mon Prince (1893); *La Duchesse de Ferrare* (1895); *Photis* (1896); *La Poupée* (1896); *Monsieur Lohengrin* (1896); *Les Petites Femmes* (1897).

Audran, Marius-Pierre, French operatic tenor and composer of songs, father of **Edmond Audran;** b. Aix, Provence, Sept. 26, 1816; d. Marseilles, Jan. 9, 1887. He began his career in the provinces (Marseilles, Bordeaux, Lyons); then became first tenor at the Opéra-Comique in Paris. After a period of travel (1852–61), he settled in Marseilles and in 1863 became a prof. of voice and director of the Marseilles Cons.

Auer, Leopold, celebrated Hungarian violinist and pedagogue; b. Veszprém, June 7, 1845; d. Loschwitz, near Dresden, July 15, 1930. He studied with Ridley Kohné in Budapest and with Dont in Vienna; later took lessons with Joachim. From 1964–66 he was in Düsseldorf as concertmaster of the orch.; in 1866 in Hamburg. In 1868 he was called to St. Petersburg as soloist in the Imperial Orch., and prof. of violin at the newly founded Cons. He became one of the most famous violin teachers in Russia; among his pupils were Elman, Zimbalist, Heifetz, and many other virtuosos. Tchaikovsky originally dedicated his Violin Concerto to him, but was offended when Auer suggested some revisions, and changed the dedication to Brodsky. Nevertheless, the Concerto became Auer's favorite work, and he made it a *pièce de résistance* for all his pupils. After the Revolution he left Russia. On March 23, 1918, he played a concert in N.Y.; settling permanently in America, he devoted himself exclusively to teaching. He publ. the manuals *Violin Playing as I Teach It* (N.Y., 1921) and *Violin Master Works and Their Interpretation* (1925); and an autobiography, *My Long Life in Music* (1923).

Auer, Max, Austrian writer on music; b. Vöcklabruck, May 6, 1880; d. Vienna, Sept. 24, 1962. He studied in Vienna; later taught in provincial public schools in Austria. He was one of the foremost authorities on Bruckner. He publ. *Anton Bruckner, Sein Leben und Werk* (Vienna, 1923); *Anton Bruckner als Kirchenmusiker* (Regensburg, 1927); completed vols. 2–4 (1928, 1932, 1937) of Göllerich's monumental biography, *Anton Bruckner, Ein Lebens- und Schaffensbild.*

Augener, George, English publisher, founder of Augener & Co.; b. Germany, 1830; d. London, Aug. 25, 1915. He organized the firm in 1853 (incorporated Oct. 11, 1904), and was its head until he retired in 1910. In 1870 Augener started publishing the music periodical *Monthly Musical Record.* In 1896 the firm purchased the catalogue of Robert Cocks & Co.

Auger, Arleen, American soprano; b. Los Angeles, Sept. 13, 1939. She was educated at Calif. State Univ. in Long Beach; also studied with Ralph Errolle in Chicago; then went to Europe, where she made her debut in 1967 as the Queen of the Night in Mozart's *Die Zauberflöte* at the Vienna State Opera; was a member there until 1974; in 1969 she sang at the N.Y. City Opera; also sang in Munich, Hamburg, London, Paris, and other cities; in addition, made numerous concert appearances and gave lieder recitals. She made her Metropolitan Opera debut on Oct. 2, 1978, as Marzelline in *Fidelio.*

Augustine (Augustinus), Aurelius (known as **St. Augustine**), b. Tagaste, Numidia, Nov. 13, 354; d. as bishop, at Hippo (Annaba), Algeria, Aug. 28, 430. St. Augustine was one of the 4 great fathers of the Latin Church. He was educated at Madaura and Carthage. He became a Christian in 387, receiving his baptism from St. Ambrose. His writings contain valuable information concerning Ambrosian song; the book entitled *De musica* treats largely of meter. It is printed in Migne, *Patrologiae cursus* (vol. 32); German trans. by C.J. Perl (Strasbourg, 1937); Eng. trans. by R. Catesby Taliaferro in *The Classics of the St. John's Program* (1939). A synopsis of *De musica* in Eng. (with commentaries and trans. by W.F. Jackson Knight) was publ. by the Orthological Inst. (London, 1949).
  BIBLIOGRAPHY: J. Huré, *Saint Augustin Musicien* (1924); H. Edelstein, *Die Musikanschauung Augustins* (Freiburg, 1928); W. Hoffmann, *Philosophische Interpretation der Augustin-Schrift De Musica* (Freiburg, 1930); H. Davenson, *Traité de la musique selon l'esprit de Saint Augustin* (Neuchâtel, 1944).

Auletta, Pietro, Italian composer; b. S. Angelo, Avellino, c.1698; d. Naples, Sept. 1771. He studied at the Cons. of St. Onofrio in Naples; gained renown with his comic opera *Orazio* (Naples, Carnival 1737). Only a few of his stage works are extant, but *La locandiera* (Naples, July 10, 1738) survives as a testimony to his abilities as a dramatic composer.

Aulin, Tor, Swedish violinist and composer; b. Stockholm, Sept. 10, 1866; d. Saltsjobaden, March 1, 1914. He studied with C.J. Lindberg in Stockholm (1877–83) and with Sauret and P. Scharwenka in Berlin (1884–86). In 1887 he established the Aulin String Quartet, and traveled with it in Germany and Russia. He was concertmaster at the Stockholm Opera from 1889–1902, but continued his concert career, and was considered the greatest Scandinavian violinist since Ole Bull. Aulin was appointed conductor of the Stockholm Phil. Society in 1902; was leader of the Göteborg Orch. from 1909–12. As a conductor and violinist, he made determined propaganda for Swedish composers. He wrote incidental music to Strindberg's *Mäster Olof,* 3 violin concertos, several suites of Swedish dances for Orch., a violin sonata, a violin method, and songs. His sister, **Laura Aulin** (b. Gävle, Jan. 9, 1860; d. Orebro, Jan. 11, 1928), was a well-known pianist; she also composed chamber and piano music.

Aurelianus Reomensis (Aurelian of Réomé), French scholar; monk at Réomé in the 9th century. His treatise *Musica disciplina* (publ. by Gerbert in

Scriptores, I) contains the earliest information on the melodic character of the church modes.

BIBLIOGRAPHY: H. Riemann, *Handbuch der Musikgeschichte*, I (Leipzig, 1919).

Auriacombe, Louis, French conductor; b. Paris, Feb. 22, 1917. He received his musical training at the Toulouse Cons.; then studied conducting with Igor Markevitch in Salzburg. In 1953 he founded the Toulouse Chamber Orch., with which he made many tours; he was particularly noted for his performances of Baroque and 20th-century music.

Auric, Georges, notable French composer; b. Lodève (Hérault), Feb. 15, 1899; d. Paris, July 23, 1983. He first studied music at the Cons. of Montpellier; then went to Paris, where he was a student of Caussade at the Paris Cons. and of Vincent d'Indy and Albert Roussel at the Schola Cantorum. While still in his early youth (1911–15) he wrote something like 300 songs and piano pieces; at 18 he composed a ballet, *Les Noces de Gamache*. At 20 he completed a comic opera, *La Reine de cœur;* however, he was dissatisfied with this early effort and destroyed the manuscript. In the aftermath of continental disillusion following World War I he became a proponent of the anti-Romantic movement in France, with the apostles of this age of disenchantment, Erik Satie and Jean Cocteau, preaching the new values of urban culture, with modern America as a model. Satie urged young composers to produce "auditory pleasure without demanding disproportionate attention from the listener," while Cocteau elevated artistic ugliness to an aesthetic ideal. Under Satie's aegis, Auric joined several French composers of his generation in a group described as "Les Nouveaux Jeunes," which later became known as "Les Six" (the other five were Milhaud, Honegger, Poulenc, Durey, and Germaine Tailleferre). Auric soon established an important connection with the impresario Serge Diaghilev, who commissioned him to write a number of ballets for his Paris company; Auric's facile yet felicitous manner of composing, with mock-romantic connotations, fitted perfectly into Diaghilev's scheme; particularly successful were Auric's early ballets, *Les Fâcheux* (1924) and *Les Matelots* (1925). He also wrote music for the movies, of which *A nous la liberté* (1932) achieved popular success as a symph. suite. Auric's familiarity with the theater earned him important administrative posts; from 1962 to 1968 he acted as general administrator of both the Grand Opéra and Opéra-Comique in Paris. From 1954 to 1977 he served as president of the French Union of Composers and Authors. In 1962 he was elected to the membership of the Académie des Beaux-Arts.

WORKS: BALLETS: *Les Fâcheux* (Monte Carlo, Jan. 19, 1924); *Les Matelots* (Paris, June 17, 1925); *La Pastorale* (Paris, May 26, 1926); *Les Enchantements d'Alcine* (Paris, May 21, 1929); *Les Imaginaires* (Paris, May 31, 1934); *Le Peintre et son modèle* (Paris, Nov. 16, 1949); *Phèdre* (Paris, May 23, 1950); *La Pierre enchantée* (Paris, June 23, 1950); *Chemin de lumière* (Munich, March 27, 1952); *Coup de feu*

(Paris, May 7, 1952); *La Chambre* (Paris, 1955); *Le Bal des voleurs* (Paris, 1960); also (in collaboration with Milhaud and others), *Les Mariés de la Tour Eiffel,* to the scenario of Jean Cocteau (Paris, June 15, 1921). FILM MUSIC: *Le Sang d'un poète* (1930); *A nous la liberté* (1932); *Les Mystères de Paris* (1936); *La Belle et la bête* (1946); *Symphonie pastorale* (1946); *Les Parents terribles* (1949); *Orphée* (1950); *Moulin Rouge* (1952); *Gervaise* (1956); *Bonjour, tristesse* (1957). INSTRUMENTAL MUSIC: Piano Sonata (1932); Violin Sonata (1937); Partita for 2 Pianos (1958); *Suite Symphonique* (1960); Flute Sonata (1964).

BIBLIOGRAPHY: A. Goléa, *Georges Auric* (Paris, 1958).

Aus der Ohe, Adele, German pianist; b. Hannover, Dec. 11, 1864; d. Berlin, Dec. 7, 1937. She studied as a child with Kullak in Berlin; at the age of 12 became a pupil of Liszt for 7 years. She then played concerts in Europe; made her American debut with Liszt's First Piano Concerto in N.Y. (Dec. 23, 1886) and continued her American tours for 17 consecutive years. She played 51 times with the Boston Symph. Orch. between 1887 and 1906. One of the highlights of her career was her appearance as soloist in Tchaikovsky's First Piano Concerto under Tchaikovsky's own direction at his last concert (St. Petersburg, Oct. 28, 1893). Because of a crippling illness, she was forced to abandon her concert career; she lost her accumulated earnings in the German currency inflation in the 1920s, and from 1928 till her death, subsisted on a pension from the Bagby Music Lovers Foundation of N.Y.

Austin, Ernest, English composer, brother of **Frederick Austin**; b. London, Dec. 31, 1874; d. Wallington, Surrey, July 24, 1947. He had no formal musical education; began to compose at the age of 33 after a business career. His compositions, therefore, acquired an experimental air; he was particularly interested in a modern treatment of old English tunes.

WORKS: *The Vicar of Bray* for String Orch. (1910); *Hymn of Apollo* for Chorus and Orch. (Leeds, 1918); *Stella Mary Dances* (London, 1918); *Ode on a Grecian Urn,* after Keats (1922); 14 sonatinas on English folk songs for children; a cycle of organ works in 12 parts (inspired by Bunyan's *Pilgrim's Progress*); chamber music and songs. He publ. a book, *The Fairyland of Music* (1922).

Austin, Florence, American violinist; b. Galesburg, Mich., March 11, 1884; d. (in a railroad accident) Fairchild, Wis., Aug. 1926. She studied with Schradieck in N.Y., and with Musin at the Liège Cons., winning first prize (for the first time by an American). Upon her return to N.Y. (1901), she appeared in recitals, then settled in Newark, N.J., as a violin teacher.

Austin, Frederic, English baritone and composer, brother of **Ernest Austin**; b. London, March 30, 1872; d. there, April 10, 1952. He studied with his uncle,

Austin – Austral

Dr. W.H. Hunt; was employed as an organist in Liverpool; in 1902 he appeared as a singer in London; also became known in England as a composer; wrote a symph. and an overture. His most successful contribution was, however, not an original composition but a practical arrangement of *The Beggar's Opera* for its revival in London in 1920; he also wrote a modern version of its sequel, *Polly,* produced in London, Dec. 30, 1922.

Austin, Henry Richter, English-American organist, music publisher, and editor; b. London, May 17, 1882; d. Marblehead, Mass., May 13, 1961. He was organist at the English Royal Church in Berlin (1904–6); then settled in the U.S., occupying positions as a church organist in and around Boston until 1948. He conducted experiments with the acoustical characteristics of non–tempered scales and devised a keyboard, *Novaton,* of 16 keys (8 white, 8 black) providing the true 7th partial tone. Became president of the Arthur P. Schmidt Co. in 1954, after many years with the firm; after his death the firm was bought out by Summy-Birchard, Inc., of Evanston, Ill.

Austin, John Turnell, English-American organist; b. Podington, Bedfordshire, May 16, 1869; d. Hartford, Conn., Sept. 17, 1948. He came to the U.S. in 1889 and worked for various organ building firms. On March 3, 1899, he founded an organ company under his own name in Hartford, retiring in 1937. He patented the Austin Universal Air Chest. The Austin Organ Co. supplied organs for many concert halls in the U.S.

Austin, Larry, American avant-garde composer; b. Duncan, Okla., Sept. 12, 1930. He studied music with Violet Archer at the North Texas State Univ., Denton (B.M., 1951; M.M., 1952); with Darius Milhaud at Mills College; and with Andrew Imbrie and Seymour Shifrin at the Univ. of Calif., Berkeley (1955–58). In 1969 he took a special course in computer-generated music systems at Stanford Univ. From 1958 to 1972 he served as prof. of music at the Univ. of Calif., Davis; this sojourn was especially significant, since it was on the Davis campus that Austin became a co-founder of a unique modern music unperiodical, *Source,* which counted among its contributors the *crème de la crème* of the world's most intransigent modernists, who were given total freedom to express their innermost personalities in graphic notation and in verbal annotations. (Alas, *Source* dried out at its 13th issue, and became a collector's item.) In 1963, Austin and his colleagues at Davis formed the New Music Ensemble, exploring free group improvisation. This period was followed by further experimentation in synthetic arts in so-called "event/complexes," combining a quadrasterophonic tape with various instruments and voices. In the meantime, Austin was active as a lecturer and conductor. He made 3 European concert and lecture tours (1964–65, 1967, 1973), 2 in South America (1969, 1973), and several in the U.S. and Canada. In 1972 he was appointed chairman of the

dept. of music, Univ. of South Florida, Tampa; also served as director of systems complex for the Studio of Performing Arts at the univ. there. In 1978 he received a professorship at his alma mater, North Texas State Univ. He was a recipient of numerous grants and several commissions from various prestigious organizations. Most of Austin's compositions are cast for mixed media, in which theatrical, acoustical, and dynamic elements are integrated into manifestations of universal vitality. In order to attain a maximum impact with a minimum of anarchy, he introduced the concept of coordinated improvisation, which he termed "open styles." His research projects include the development of software for hybrid computer systems for electronic music.

WORKS: Woodwind Quartet (1948); Woodwind Quintet (1949); Brass Quintet (1949); String Trio (1952); Concertino for Flute, Trumpet, and Strings (1952); *Prosody* for Orch. (1953); *Improvisations for Orchestra and Jazz Soloists* (1961); *Collage* for Assorted Instruments (1963); *Continuum* for 2, 3, 4, 5, 6, or 7 Instruments (1964); *In Memoriam J.F. Kennedy* for Band (1964); Piano Variations (1964); *A Broken Consort* for 7 Instruments (1964); *Open Style* for Orch. and Piano Soloists (1965); *The Maze,* a theater piece in Open Style (1967); *Catharsis,* in Open Style, for 2 Improvisation Ensembles, Tapes, and Conductor (1967; Oakland, Nov. 11, 1969); *Accidents* for Electronically Prepared Piano, Magnetic Tape, Mirrors, Actions and Counteractions, and Black Light (1967); *Piano Set,* in Open Style (1968); *Current* for Clarinet and Piano (1968); *Transmission One,* a video-audio electronic composition for Color Television (1969); *Agape,* a celebration for Priests, Musicians, Dancers, a Rock Band, Actors, and Poets (Buffalo, Feb. 25, 1970); *Plastic Surgery* for Electric Piano, Percussion, Magnetic Tape, and Film (N.Y., March 1, 1970); *Heaven Music* for a Condominium of Flutes (Tampa, Fla., June 3, 1975); *Phoenix* for Tape (1976); *Catalogo sonoro* for Viola and Tape (1979); *Phantasmagoria,* a conjectural construction and fantasies on Ives's *Universe Symphony* for Narrator, Digital Synthesizer, Tape, and Orch. (Denton, Texas, Feb. 18, 1982).

Austin, William, American musicologist; b. Lawton, Okla., Jan. 18, 1920. He studied at Harvard Univ., obtaining his Ph.D. in 1951. In 1947, he was appointed to the faculty of Cornell Univ. In 1961–62 he was the recipient of a Guggenheim fellowship.

WRITINGS: *Music in the 20th Century from Debussy through Stravinsky* (N.Y., 1966); *Susanna, Jeanie and The Old Folks at Home: The Songs of Stephen Foster from His Time to Ours* (N.Y., 1975); ed. *New Looks at Italian Opera* (Ithaca, N.Y., 1968); transl. *Musikästhetik* by Carl Dahlhaus into Eng. as *Esthetics of Music* (Cambridge, 1982).

Austral (real name, **Wilson**), **Florence,** Australian soprano; b. Richmond, near Melbourne, April 26, 1892; d. Newcastle, New South Wales, May 15, 1968. She studied at the Melbourne Cons. (1914–18); made her operatic debut as Brünnhilde at Covent Garden

94

in London, under the auspices of the newly formed British National Opera Co. (May 16, 1922); later she sang the roles of Isolde and Aida. She toured the U.S. between 1925 and 1931 with her husband, the flutist **John Amadeo;** eventually returned to Australia.

Auteri Manzocchi, Salvatore, Italian opera composer; b. Palermo, Dec. 26, 1845; d. Parma, Feb. 21, 1924. He studied in Palermo with Platania, and with Mabellini in Florence. His first opera, *Marcellina,* was never performed; his 2nd, *Dolores* (Florence, Feb. 23, 1875), enjoyed considerable success, as did *Stella* (Piacenza, May 22, 1880). His other operas are *Il Negriero* (Milan, 1878); *Il Conte de Gleichen* (Milan, 1887); *Graziella* (Milan, Oct. 23, 1894); and *Severo Torelli* (Bologna, April 25, 1903).

Autori, Franco, Italian-American conductor; b. Naples, Nov. 29, 1903. After study in Italy, he emigrated to America in 1928. He conducted the Chicago Civic Opera Co. (1928–32) and the summer series of the Dallas Symph. Orch. (1932–34); was staff conductor of the Federal Music Project in N.Y. (1934–36); then held the post of conductor and music director of the Buffalo Phil. (1936–45); subsequently was active as guest conductor in Poland and Argentina; from 1949–59 served as associate conductor of the N.Y. Phil. From 1961–71 he was conductor of the Tulsa (Okla.) Phil.

Avdeyeva, Larissa, Russian mezzo-soprano; b. Moscow, June 21, 1925. She studied at the Stanislavsky Opera Studio in Moscow; in 1947 she joined the Stanislavsky Music Theater; in 1952 she became a member of the Bolshoi Theater, where she distinguished herself as an outstanding interpreter in operas by Tchaikovsky, Borodin, Mussorgsky, and Rimsky-Korsakov; she also made tours of Europe, the U.S., and Japan. She was made a People's Artist of the R.S.F.S.R. in 1964. She married the Russian conductor **Evgeny Svetlanov.**

Avenary, Hanoch (real name, **Herbert Loewenstein**), Israeli musicologist; b. Danzig, May 25, 1908. He studied musicology and other subjects at the univs. of Leipzig, Munich, and Frankfurt; then received his Ph.D. in 1931 from the Univ. of Königsberg with the dissertation *Wort und Ton bei Oswald von Wolkenstein* (publ. in Königsberg, 1932). He went to Palestine in 1936; there he was active as a publisher of Jewish art books. He also served in the Israeli air force; in 1965 he joined the faculty of Hebrew Univ., where he remained until 1972; from 1966 he was also a lecturer at the Univ. of Tel Aviv. His books include *Studies in the Hebrew, Syrian and Greek Liturgical Recitative* (Tel Aviv, 1963); *Hebrew Hymn Tunes: The Rise and Development of a Musical Tradition* (Tel Aviv, 1971); *The Ashkenazi Tradition of Biblical Chant between 1500 and 1900* (Tel Aviv, 1976).

Aventinus (real name, **Turmair**), **Johannes,** German theorist; b. Abensberg (whence Aventinus), July 4, 1477; d. Regensburg, Jan. 9, 1534. His treatise *Annales Boiorum* (1554) contains considerable information (not always trustworthy) about musical matters. He also edited Nicolaus Faber's *Musica rudimenta admodum brevia* (1516).

Averkamp, Anton, Dutch choral conductor and composer; b. Willige Langerak, Feb. 18, 1861; d. Bussum, June 1, 1934. He studied with Daniel de Lange in Amsterdam, with Friedrich Kiel in Berlin, and with Rheinberger in Munich. In 1890 he founded the famous chorus Amsterdam A Cappella Coor, with which he traveled in Europe, presenting programs of early polyphonic music. He wrote an opera, *De Heidebloem* (not produced); a symph. poem, *Elaine and Lancelot;* 2 choral works with Orch., *Decora Lux* and *Die versunkene Burg;* a symph.; a *Te Deum;* a violin sonata; and songs. He contributed numerous historical articles to music periodicals, and publ. a manual for singers, *Uit mijn practijk* (Groningen, 1916).

Avidom (original name, **Mahler-Kalkstein**), **Menahem,** Polish-born Israeli composer; b. Stanislawow, Jan. 6, 1908. He studied at the American Univ. in Beirut (1926–28) and at the Paris Cons. (1928–31). In 1935 he settled in Tel Aviv, teaching music theory at the Cons. there until 1946. From 1955 to 1970 he was the chairman of the Israeli Composers' League. His early works reflect the influences of Expressionism; in several of them he made explicit use of dodecaphonic techniques. After settling in Israel, he turned to the exploration of authentic Israeli folkways.
WORKS: For the Stage: *Alexander,* opera (Tel Aviv, Aug. 15, 1959); *In Every Generation,* opera (Ein-Gev Passover Festival, 1955); *The Crook,* comic opera (Tel Aviv, April 22, 1967); *The Farewell,* radiophonic opera (1969; broadcast perf., Nov. 1971); *The Pearl and the Coral,* ballet for 12 Instruments (1972); *The Emperor's New Clothes,* comic opera (Israel Festival, 1976); *Yodfat's Cave,* musical drama (1977); *The End of King Og,* children's opera (1979); *The First Sin,* satirical opera (1980). For Orch.: 10 symphs.: No. 1, *A Folk Symphony* (Prague Spring Festival, 1946); No. 2, *David Symphony* (Tel Aviv, Dec. 1, 1949); No. 3, *Mediterranean Sinfonietta* (1951); No. 4 (1955); No. 5, *The Song of Eilät,* for Voice and Orch. (1956–57); No. 6 (1960); No. 7, *Philharmonic* (1961); No. 8, *Festival Sinfonietta* (Jerusalem, July 27, 1966); No. 9, *Symphonie variée,* for Chamber Orch. (1968); No. 10, *Sinfonia brevis* (1980); Concerto for Flute and Strings (1946); *Music for Strings* (1949); *Jubilee Suite* (1959); *Triptyque symphonique* (1966); *Spring,* overture (Jerusalem, Dec. 13, 1973); *Movements* for String Orch. or String Quartet (1979). Chamber music: Concertino for Violin and Piano (1950; also with Chamber Orch., 1972); *Concertino for Piatigorsky* for Cello and Piano (1952); String Quartet No. 1 (1953); String Quartet No. 2, *Metamorphoses* (1960); *Adagio* for Harp (1962); *Enigma* for 5 Wind Instruments, Percussion, and Piano (1962); *Reflexions* for 2 Flutes (1963);

Brass Quartet (1963); *B-A-C-H,* suite for Woodwinds, Strings, Piano, and Percussion (1964); *Triptyque* for Solo Violin (1967); *Monothema,* sonatina for String Quartet (1982). For Piano: 2 sonatinas (1939, 1945); *12 Changing Preludes* (1965); *6 Inventions on the Name of Artur Rubinstein* (1973); *Yemenite Wedding Suite* (1973); *Piece on the Name of SCHoEnBerG* (1974). For Voice: *12 Hills,* cantata (1976); *Beyond,* cantata for Voice and 13 Instruments (1977).

Avison, Charles, English organist and composer; b. Newcastle-upon-Tyne, 1709 (old style; baptized, Feb. 16); d. there, May 9, 1770. He acquired the rudiments of music at home; was appointed organist at St. John's church in Newcastle on Oct. 13, 1735; took up his post in 1736. An enterprising musician, he organized in Newcastle a series of subscription concerts, one of the earliest musical presentations of its kind in Great Britain; was music director of the Newcastle Musical Society in 1738; held this post until his death. He wrote a large number of concertos employing various combinations of strings with harpsichord continuo, and sonatas in which the keyboard instrument is given a predominant function. These works were publ. between 1740 and 1769; in 1758 Avison collected 26 concertos in 4 books, arranged in score, for strings *a* 7 (4 violins, viola, cello, bass), with harpsichord; other works were 12 keyboard concertos with string quartet, 18 quartets for keyboard with 2 violins and cello, and 3 vols. of trio sonatas for keyboard with 2 violins. His *Essay on Musical Expression* (London, 1752) is historically important as an early exposition of relative musical values by an English musician. His views were opposed by an anonymous pamphlet, *Remarks on Mr. Avison's Essay . . . in a Letter from a Gentleman in London,* which was probably written by Prof. William Hayes of Oxford (London, 1753). Not to be thus thwarted, Avison publ. a rebuttal that same year, reinforced by a statement of worth contributed by a Dr. Jortin. He renewed his demurrer by publishing in 1775 another edition of the polemical exchange. Among his scholarly publications is Marcello's *Psalm-Paraphrases* with an English text, containing a biography of Marcello (jointly with John Garth, 1757).

BIBLIOGRAPHY: A. Milner, "Charles Avison," *Musical Times* (Jan. 1954); Ch. Cudworth, "Avison of Newcastle," *Musical Times* (May 1970); L. Lipking, "Charles Avison and the Founding of English Criticism of Music," chapter 8 of *The Ordering of the Arts in Eighteenth-Century England* (Princeton, 1970); O. Edwards, "Charles Avison: English Concerto-Writer Extraordinary," *Musical Quarterly* (July 1973).

Avni, Tzvi, German-born Israeli composer; b. Saarbrücken, Sept. 2, 1927. He emigrated to Palestine in 1935; studied composition with Seter, Ehrlich, and Ben-Haim in Tel Aviv (1954–56); then attended the courses of Aaron Copland and Lukas Foss at the Berkshire Music Center in Tanglewood, Massachusetts (1963), and the classes in electronics with Ussachevsky at Columbia Univ. (1963-64) and with Myron Schaeffer at the Univ. of Toronto. Returning to Tel Aviv, he became director of the Central Music Library; in 1971 was appointed an instructor in electronic music at the Rubin Music Academy in Jerusalem; also acted as music adviser to the Bat-Dor Ballet Co., for which he wrote special scores. In his music he makes use of Middle Eastern folk motifs, in ultramodern coloristic arrangements.

WORKS: *Songs* for Soprano and Orch. (1957); Wind Quintet (1959); *Prayer* for Strings (1961); 2 string quartets (1962, 1969); *2 Pieces for 4 Clarinets* (1965); *Meditations on a Drama,* metamorphoses for Chamber Orch. (1965–66); *Elegy* for Solo Cello (1967); *Collage* for Voice, Flute, Percussion, and Tape (1967); *5 Pantomimes* for 8 Players (1968); *Churban Habayit (Destruction of the Temple)* for Chorus and Orch. (1968); *Akeda (Sacrifice)* for 4 Chamber Groups and Narrator (1969); *Requiem for Sounds,* ballet music (1969); *Holiday Metaphors* for Orch. (1970); *All the King's Women,* ballet music (1971); *By the Waters of Babylon,* prelude for Chamber Orch. (1971); *From the Valley of Shadows I Shall Sing Thee a Song of Love,* ballet music for 10 Players (1971); *De Profundis* for Strings (1972); *Lyric Episodes,* ballet music for Oboe and Tape (1972); *Gilgulim (Reincarnations),* radiophonic poem for Narrator and Tape (1973); *On That Cape of Death* for Chamber Orch. (1974); *Frames,* ballet music (1974); *Retrospections* for Cello, Percussion, and Tape (1975); *Michtam for David* for Harp and String Quartet (1975); 2 Psalms for Oboe and Strings (1975); *Synchromotrask,* musical theater for a Woman, Tape, and a Door (1976); *He and She,* ballet music for 7 Instruments (1976); *Leda and the Swan* for Voice without text, and Clarinet (1976); numerous a cappella choruses; songs.

d'Avossa, Giuseppe, Italian composer; b. Paola, Calabria, 1708; d. Naples, Jan. 9, 1796. He studied with Gaetano Greco and Francesco Durante in Naples; later held the position of maestro di cappella at S. Maria Verticelli, Naples, and at Pesaro. He wrote 4 comic operas and much sacred music.

Avramov, Eugenii, Bulgarian composer; b. Svishtov, Sept. 13, 1929. He graduated in political science from Sofia Univ. in 1952; then studied composition with Vladigerov and Raichev at the Bulgarian State Cons., graduating in 1958; then taught harmony there.

WORKS: Piano Sonata (1960); Piano Trio (1963); Clarinet Concerto (1964); Symph. (1969); *Inventions* for Oboe, Clarinet, and Bassoon (1972); *A Mummer's Dance* for Piano (1974).

Avshalomov, Aaron, Russian-American composer; b. Nikolayevsk, Siberia, Nov. 11, 1894; d. New York, April 26, 1965. He studied at the Zürich Cons.; in 1914 he went to China, where he wrote a number of works on Chinese subjects, making use of authentic Chinese themes. On April 24, 1925, he conducted the first performance in Peking of his first opera on a Chinese subject, *Kuan Yin;* his 2nd opera, also on a Chinese subject, *The Great Wall,* was staged in Shanghai on Nov. 26, 1945, and also was presented in Nanking under the sponsorship of Madame Chiang Kai-Shek, the wife of the powerful generalissimo. His other works composed in China were also performed for the first time in Shanghai, among them: *Peiping Hutungs,* symph. sketch (Feb. 7, 1933; also given by Stokowski with the Philadelphia Orch., Nov. 8, 1935); *The Soul of the Ch'in,* ballet (May 21, 1933); *Incense Shadows,* pantomime (March 13, 1935); Piano Concerto (Jan. 19, 1936); Violin Concerto (Jan. 16, 1938); First Symph. (March 17, 1940, composer conducting); *Buddha and the 5 Planetary Deities,* choreographic tableau (April 18, 1942). In 1947 Avshalomov came to America, where he continued to compose works in large forms, among them his 2nd Symph. (Cincinnati, Dec. 30, 1949); 3rd Symph. (1950); 4th Symph. (1951).

Avshalomov, Jacob, American composer, son of **Aaron Avshalomov;** b. Tsingtao, China, March 28, 1919. His mother was American; his father, Russian. He studied music in Peking; in 1936 he was in Shanghai, where material circumstances forced him to work for a time in a slaughterhouse. In 1937 he came to the U.S.; studied with Ernst Toch in Los Angeles; then with Bernard Rogers in Rochester, N.Y. From 1943–45 he was in the U.S. Army as an interpreter. From 1947–54 he was an instructor at Columbia Univ.; received a Guggenheim fellowship in 1952; in 1954 he was appointed permanent conductor of the Portland (Oreg.) Junior Symph. His music reflects the many cultures with which he was in contact; while the form is cohesive, the materials are multifarious, with tense chromatic harmonies and quasi-oriental inflections.
    WORKS: *Sinfonietta* (1946; N.Y., Nov. 29, 1949); *Evocations* for Clarinet and Chamber Orch. (1947; Saratoga Springs, N.Y., Aug. 17, 1950); Sonatina for Viola and Piano (1947); *Prophecy* for Chorus, Tenor, and Organ (1948); *Taking of T'ung Kuan* for Orch. (1948; Detroit, Nov. 20, 1953); *Tom o' Bedlam* for Chorus (N.Y., Dec. 15, 1953; received the N.Y. Music Critics Award); *The Plywood Age* for Orch., commissioned for the 50th anniversary of the Fir Plywood Corp. (Portland, June 20, 1955); *Psalm 100* for Chorus and Wind Instruments (1956); *Inscriptions at the City of Brass* for Chorus, Narrator, and Large Orch., to a text from the *Arabian Nights* (1956); *Quodlibet Montagna* for Brass Sextet (1975).

Ax, Emanuel, outstanding Polish-born American pianist; b. Lwow, June 8, 1949. He began to play the violin at age 6; soon took up the piano and studied with his father, who was a coach at the Lwow Opera House. The family moved to Warsaw when he was 8, and then to Winnipeg, Canada, when he was 10; in 1961 settled in N.Y., where he enrolled at the Juilliard School of Music as a student of Mieczyslaw Munz; he also received a bachelor's degree in French from Columbia Univ., in 1970. He made a concert tour of South America in 1969; became a U.S. citizen in 1970. He competed at the Chopin (1970) and Queen Elisabeth (1972) competitions; in

both placed only 7th; in 1971 won 3rd place in the Vianna da Motta Competition in Lisbon; then made his N.Y. debut at Alice Tully Hall on March 12, 1973. A long-awaited victory came in 1974, when he won first place in the Artur Rubinstein International Piano Master Competition in Tel Aviv; among its awards was a contract for an American concert tour; there followed numerous appearances throughout the U.S. and Europe. He was awarded the Avery Fisher Prize in 1979. In addition to his fine interpretations of the standard repertoire, he has also distinguished himself as a champion of contemporary music.
    BIBLIOGRAPHY: *Current Biography* (March 1984).

Axman, Emil, Czech composer; b. Rataje, June 3, 1887; d. Prague, Jan. 25, 1949. Of a musical family, he began to compose at an early age. He studied musicology with Nejedlý at Prague Univ., obtaining his Ph.D. in 1912; took private composition lessons with Novák (1908–10) and Ostrčil (1920). In 1913 he was appointed keeper of the musical archives at the National Museum in Prague. He participated in the modern musical movement typified by Janáček but was not attracted to any spirit of experimentation, his music remaining highly lyrical.
    WORKS: 6 symphs.: No. 1, *Tragic* (1925–26); No. 2, *Giocosa* (1926–27; International Society for Contemporary Music Festival, Frankfurt, July 3, 1927); No. 3, *Spring* (1928); No. 4, *Eroica* (1932); No. 5, *Dithyrambic* (1936); No. 6, *Patriotic* (1942); symph. poems: *Sorrows and Hopes* (1919–20) and *A Bright Sky* (1921–22); 5 cantatas: *My Mother* (1926); *A Ballad on the Eyes of a Stoker* (1927); *Ilonka Beniačová* (1930); *The Cemetery of Sobotka* (1933); *Stabat Mater* (1938); *From the Beskids* for Chamber Orch. (1934); Violin Concerto (1936); Piano Concerto (1939); Cello Concerto (1940); Double Concerto for Violin, Cello, and Orch. (1944); Suite in the Form of Variations for Orch. (1943); Violin Sonata (1923); Cello Sonata (1924); 4 string quartets (1924, 1925, 1929, 1946); Piano Trio (1924–25); Wind Quintet (1938); Suite for String Quartet (1940); *Divertimento* for Nonet (1944); *3 Moravian Dances* for Nonet (1944); Variations for String Quartet (1944); 3 piano sonatas: No. 1, *Appassionata* (1922); No. 2, *To the Memory of a Great Man* (1922); No. 3 (1924); *Sonatina charakeristicka* for Piano (1922); *Moravia Sings* for Piano (1924; orchestrated 1935); several choruses and song cycles. His musicological writings include *Moravian Operas of the 18th Century* (1912) and *Moravia in Czech Music of the 19th Century* (1920).
    BIBLIOGRAPHY: F. Pala, *Emil Axman. Židot a dílo* (Prague, 1966).

Ayala, Daniel, Mexican (Indian) composer; b. Abalá, Yucatán, July 21, 1906; d. Veracruz, June 20, 1975. He went to Mérida, Yucatán, to study music; entered the National Cons. in Mexico City in 1927; studied violin with Ezequiel Sierra and Revueltas; composition with Ponce, Huízar, and Carrillo. He played in nightclubs in Mexico City; in 1931 became a violinist with the Orquesta Sinfónica de México; in 1934, together with Moncayo, Contreras, and Galindo, formed the Grupo de los Cuatro (Group of the 4). He became conductor of the Banda de Policía in Mérida in 1940 and in 1942 founded the Yucatán Orch. His music, inspired by ancestral melos of the Mayan civilization and legends, is cast in pentatonic modes and possesses a vigorous rhythmic pulse.

WORKS: 2 ballets: *El Hombre Maya* (as a symph. suite, Mexico City, Nov. 21, 1940) and *La gruta Diabólica* for Chamber Orch. (1940); symph. poems: *Tribú* (Mexico City, Oct. 18, 1935); *Paisaje (Landscape,* 1935; Mexico City, June 2, 1936); *Panoramas de México* (1936; Dallas, Dec. 1, 1940); *Mi viaje a Norte America* (1947). For Voice: *4 Canciones,* with Piano (1932); *Uchben X'Coholte (Ancient Cemetery)* for Soprano and Chamber Orch. (Mexico City, Oct. 13, 1933; ballet version, 1936; Mexico City, March 6, 1936); *El grillo (Cricket)* for Soprano, Clarinet, Violin, Timbrel, and Piano (1933); *U Kayil Chaac,* an incantation for rain, for Soprano, Mexican Percussion Instruments, and Chamber Orch. (1934); *Brigadier de Choque* for Chorus and Percussion (1935); *Suite infantil* for Soprano and Chamber Orch. (1937); *Los Yaquis y los Seris,* 2 suites for Voice, Chamber Ensemble, and Mexican Percussion Instruments (1938; Mérida, July 31, 1942); *Radiograma* for Piano, imitating radio code signals (1931).

Ayestarán, Lauro, Uruguayan musicologist; b. Montevideo, July 9, 1913; d. there, July 22, 1966. He studied voice and music history; became an instructor of choral music in municipal schools in Montevideo. He is the author of the important monograph *Domenico Zipoli, El gran compositor y organista romano en el Rio de la Plata* (Montevideo, 1941); *El folklore musical Uruguayo* (Montevideo, 1967).

Ayler, Albert, black American jazz saxophonist; b. Cleveland, July 13, 1936; d. (body found in the East River) New York, Nov. 25, 1970. He began playing the alto saxophone in his father's band; took up the tenor saxophone, and subsequently became a leading figure in avant-garde jazz circles in N.Y.; he also toured in Europe. He was highly regarded as an innovative jazz musician. His accidental death remained unexplained.

Ayo, Felix, Spanish-born Italian violinist; b. Sestao, July 1, 1933. He studied at the Bilbao Cons.; then went to Italy, and took courses at the Santa Cecilia Academy in Rome. In 1952 he became concertmaster of the newly formed ensemble I Musici, with which he toured in Europe and America. In 1968 he left the group to form his own piano quartet, which gave performances as the Quartetto Beethoven. In 1972 he was appointed to the faculty of the Rome Cons.

Ayres, Frederic (real name, **Frederick Ayres Johnson**), American composer; b. Binghamton, N.Y., March 17, 1876; d. Colorado Springs, Nov. 23, 1926. He studied with Edgar S. Kelley (1897–1901) and Arthur Foote (1899). His works include an overture, *From the Plains;* 2 string quartets; 2 piano trios; 2 violin sonatas; a cello sonata; and numerous songs. In his later music he showed a tendency toward Impressionism and used moderately complex harmonic combinations.

BIBLIOGRAPHY: William. T. Upton, "Frederick Ayres," *Musical Quarterly* (1932).

Ayrton, Edmund, English organist and composer, father of **William Ayrton;** b. Ripon, Yorkshire, baptized on Nov. 19, 1734, probably born the day before; d. London, May 22, 1808. He studied organ with Nares; from 1755 was organist in various churches; in 1764 was appointed Gentleman of the Chapel Royal, and in 1780 was appointed lay vicar at Westminster Abbey. He was in charge of the Chapel Royal from 1780–1805. In 1784, he was given the degree of D.Mus. at Trinity College in Cambridge, and in 1788, D.Mus. at Oxford. He wrote a number of anthems, of which *Begin unto My God with Timbrels,* scored for 4 vocal soloists, mixed choir, 2 oboes, 2 bassoons, 2 trumpets, timpani, and strings, obtained great success at its performance on June 29, 1784, in St. Paul's Cathedral in London. His glee *An Ode to Harmony* (1799) was also popular. He was admittedly a faithful imitator of Handel, but the judgment of Wesley, who described Ayrton as "one of the most egregious blockheads under the sun," seems unduly severe.

Ayrton, William, English organist, son of **Edmund Ayrton;** b. London, Feb. 24, 1777; d. there, March 8, 1858. He received a fine education; was one of the original founders of the London Phil. Society in 1813; wrote music criticism for the *Morning Chronicle* (1813–26) and for the *Examiner* (1837–51). In 1823 he started the publication of the historically important London music periodical *Harmonicon,* and was its editor; from 1834–37 edited *The Musical Library,* which publ. vocal and instrumental music. He also compiled a practical collection, *Sacred Minstrelsy* (2 vols.; 1835).

Azantchevsky, Mikhail, Russian music educator and composer; b. Moscow, April 5, 1839; d. there, Jan. 24, 1881. He studied composition with Richter and Hauptmann at the Leipzig Cons. (1861–64), and piano with Liszt in Rome. After a sojourn in Paris (1866–70) he returned to Russia, where he became an executive director of the St. Petersburg Cons. (1871–76). A disciplinarian by nature, he raised the minimal requirements for acceptance of new pupils and engaged important teachers, among them Rimsky-Korsakov. In Paris he purchased the important music library of Anders, which he later presented, together with other acquisitions, to the St. Petersburg Cons. He composed a concert overture, 2 string quartets, 2 piano trios, a cello sonata, a *Festival polonais* for 2 Pianos, and numerous piano solo pieces and songs.

Azevedo, Alexis-Jacob, French writer on music; b. Bordeaux, March 18, 1813; d. Paris, Dec. 21, 1875.

He was a prolific contributor to *Le Ménestrel* and other French music magazines; publ. monographs on Félicien David (1863) and Rossini (1864); a pamphlet, *La Verité sur Rouget de Lisle et la Marseillaise* (Dieppe, 1864); *La Transposition par les nombres* (Paris, 1874); a collection of articles, *Les Doubles-croches malades* (1874); etc.

Azkué, Resurrección María, Spanish composer and musicologist; b. Lequeitio, Aug. 5, 1864; d. Bilbao, Nov. 9, 1951. He studied theology in Spain, then went to Paris and studied music at the Schola Cantorum. He wrote 2 operas to Basque texts: *Ortzuri* (Bilbao, 1911) and *Urlo* (Bilbao, 1913); an oratorio, *Daniel;* a *Te Deum;* several zarzuelas. He publ. a valuable collection, *Cancionero Vasco* (11 vols.), and *Literatura popular del país Vasco* (4 vols., the last containing musical examples).

Azmayparashvili, Shalva, Georgian conductor and composer; b. Tiflis, Jan. 7, 1903. He studied trumpet and kettledrum at the Tiflis Cons.; from 1938–54 was conductor of the Tiflis Opera Theater.
    WORKS: Opera, *The Village Elder* (Tiflis, Jan. 21, 1951); musical comedy, *Times Are Different* (Tiflis, Feb. 12, 1952); symph. suite, *Pictures of Old Tiflis* (1941); a group of mass songs.

Aznavour (real name, **Aznavurian**), **Charles,** French chansonnier; b. Paris, May 22, 1924. A son of an Armenian baritone from Tiflis, he received his early musical training at home; acted in Paris variety shows at the age of 5; learned to play the guitar. He made several American tours as a nightclub entertainer with a valuable French accent; also acted in films. He composed a great number of songs, of the genre of "tristesse chansons" and frustration ballads, among them the popular tunes *On ne sait jamais, Comme des étrangers,* and *Ce jour tant attendu.* His operetta *Monsieur Carnaval* was produced in Paris on Dec. 17, 1965. He wrote an autobiography, entitled *Aznavour par Aznavour* (Paris, 1970).

Azzopardi, Francesco, Italian (Maltese) music theorist and composer; b. Rabat, Malta, May 5, 1748; d. there, Feb. 6, 1809. His fame rests on the school manual *Il musico prattico* (1760), published by Framéry in French translation (Paris, 1786) and quoted by Cherubini in his course on counterpoint and fugue, and by Grétry. He also composed sacred music, including an oratorio, *La Passione di Cristo.*
    BIBLIOGRAPHY: P. Pullicino, *Notizia biografica di Francesco Azzopardi* (1876).

B

Baaren, Kees van, Dutch composer; b. Enschede, Oct. 22, 1906; d. Oegstgeest, Sept. 2, 1970. He studied at the Hochschule für Musik in Berlin and later for 4 years with Willem Pijper in Rotterdam. His early works are in the lyric tradition of Grieg. However, he destroyed his early works in 1933 and started afresh in the direction of structural techniques, following the precepts of Schoenberg and Anton von Webern. His Trio (1936) shows traces of serialism, and his Septet (1952) is the first work by a Dutch composer written in an integral serial style, in which not only the 12 tones of the chromatic scale, but durations, dynamics, and meters, are organized according to a unifying thematic set. Baaren was director of the Amsterdam Music Academy (1948–53), the Cons. of Utrecht (1953–57), and the Royal Cons. of The Hague (1957–70).

WORKS: Piano Concertino (1934); cantata, *The Hollow Men,* after T.S. Eliot (1948); *Sinfonia* (1956–57); 5 *Variazioni* for Orch. (1959); Piano Concerto (1964); *Musica* for Orch. (Rotterdam, May 18, 1966); 2 string quartets (1932–33; *Sovraposizioni I,* 1962); Trio for Flute, Clarinet, and Bassoon (1936); Piano Sonatina (1948); Septet for Concertante Violin, Wind Quintet, and Double Bass (1952); *Sovraposizioni II,* wind quintet (1963); *Musica* for Solo Flute (1965); *Musica* for 72 Carillons (1964–68; alternate version for 47 Carillons, 1964–69); *Musica* for Organ (1968–69).

Babadzhanian, Arno, Armenian pianist and composer; b. Erevan, Jan. 22, 1921; d. Moscow, Nov. 15, 1983. He studied at the Erevan Cons.; after graduation in 1947, he went to Moscow, where he took courses in piano with Igumnov at the Moscow Cons. and in composition with Litinsky at the Armenian Culture Center in Moscow; graduated from both in 1948. In 1950 he returned to Armenia and joined the piano faculty at the Erevan Cons. His music is derived from the folk-song patterns of Armenia, continuing the line cultivated by Khachaturian, with emphasis on rhythmic coloration in a characteristic quasi-oriental manner. His most ambitious works are a Violin Concerto (1949) and a Cello Concerto (1962); he also wrote *Heroic Ballad* for Piano and Orch. (1950), 2 string quartets (1942, 1947), Piano Trio (1952), Violin Sonata (1959), and a number of popular ballads under such appealing titles as *The Song of First Love* and *Make a Wish.* A monograph on Babadzhanian by A. Grigorian was publ. in Moscow in 1961.

Babayev, Andrei, Soviet composer; b. Azerbaijan, Dec. 27, 1923; d. Moscow, Oct. 21, 1964. He studied in

Baku; played native instruments; then entered the Baku Cons., where he was a student in composition of Khadzhibekov and Karayev, graduating in 1950; later took advanced courses with Shaporin at the Moscow Cons. His music is inspired mainly by Armenian folk melodies; he also arranged songs of Central Asia and India; some of his original songs (*I Met a Girl, Lovely Eyes*, etc.) acquired popularity.

WORKS: *Eagles' Bastion*, opera (1957); *October*, cantata (1947); Symph. (1950); *Indian Fantasy* for Orch. (1958); pieces for native instruments.

Babbi, (Pietro Giovanni) Cristoforo (Bartolomeo Gasparre), Italian violinist and composer, son of **Gregorio Babbi**; b. Cesena, May 6, 1745; d. Dresden, Nov. 19, 1814. He studied violin, counterpoint, and composition with Paolo Alberghi in Faenza; subsequently was primo violino at the festas there (1766, 1769, 1770, 1772); also played in the orch. of the Rimini Opera (1773). In 1774 he was elected a member of the Accademia Filarmonica of Bologna; then was maestro di cappella at the Teatro Comunale there (1775–78); in 1779 he became primo violino and direttore d'orchestra in Forlì. He was called to Dresden in 1781 as provisional Konzertmeister; received a permanent appointment in 1782, and proceeded to reorganize the Kapelle; he held an equal place with J.G. Naumann, the Dresden Kapellmeister. He composed symphs., operas, concertos, and other works.

Babbi, Gregorio (Lorenzo), famous Italian tenor, father of **Cristoforo Babbi**; b. Cesena, Nov. 16, 1708; d. there, Jan. 2, 1768. He made his operatic debut in Florence in 1730; in 1741 he entered the service of Charles III, King of Naples; in 1748 he was engaged by the Teatro San Carlo of Naples, where his wife, **Giovanna Guaetta,** was also a singer; he was pensioned in 1759.

Babbitt, Milton Byron, American composer and theorist; b. Philadelphia, May 10, 1916. He received his early musical training in Jackson, Mississippi; at the same time he revealed an acute flair for mathematical reasoning; this double faculty determined the formulation of his musical theories, in which he promulgated a system of melodic and rhythmic sets ultimately leading to integral serialism. His academic studies included courses with Philip James and Marion Bauer at N.Y.Univ. (B.A. 1935) and at Princeton Univ. (M.A. 1942); he also had private sessions with Sessions. From 1943 to 1945 he taught both music theory and mathematics at Princeton Univ.; in 1960 was named prof. of music there. He held a Guggenheim grant in 1961; was elected a member of the National Institute of Arts and Letters in 1965. At Princeton and Columbia univs. he inaugurated an experimental program of electronic music, with the aid of a newly constructed synthesizer. Taking as the point of departure the Schoenbergian method of composition with 12 different tones, Babbitt extended the serial principle to embrace 12 different note values, 12 different time intervals between instrumental entries, 12 different dynamic levels, and 12 different instrumental timbres. In order to describe the potential combinations of the basic 4 aspects of the tone-row, he introduced the term "combinatoriality," with symmetric parts of a tone-row designated as "derivations." His paper "Twelve-Tone Invariants as Compositional Determinants," published in *The Musical Quarterly* of April 1960, gives a résumé of his system of total serialism. The serial application of rhythmic values is expounded in Babbitt's paper "Twelve-Tone Rhythmic Structure and the Electronic Medium," published in *Perspectives of New Music* (Fall 1962).

Babbitt's scientific-sounding theories have profoundly influenced the musical thinking of young American composers; a considerable literature, both intelligible and unintelligible, arose in special publications to penetrate and, if at all possible, to illuminate Babbitt's mind-boggling speculations. His original music, some of it aurallly beguiling, can be fully understood only after a preliminary study of its underlying compositional plan. In 1982 he won a special citation of the Pulitzer Committee for "his life's work as a distinguished and seminal American composer."

WORKS: *Three Compositions for Piano* (1947); *Composition for 4 Instruments* (1948); *Composition* for 12 Instruments (1948); *Composition* for Viola and Piano (1950); *The Widow's Lament in Springtime* for Voice and Piano (1950); *Du,* a song cycle (1951); Quartet for Flute, Oboe, Clarinet, and Bassoon (1953); String Quartet No. 1 (1954); String Quartet No. 2 (1954); *Two Sonnets* for Voice and 3 Instruments (1955); *Semisimple Variations* for Piano (1956); *All Set* for Jazz Ensemble (1957); *Sounds and Words,* to a text of disparate syllables for Voice and Piano (1958); *Composition* for Voice and 6 Instruments (1960); *Composition* for Synthesizer (1961); *Vision and Prayer,* song for Soprano and Synthesized Magnetic Tape (1961); *Philomel* for Voice and Magnetic Tape (1964); *Ensemble* for Synthesizer (1964); *Relata I* for Orch. (1965); *Post-Partitions* for Piano (1966); *Sextets* for Violin and Piano (the title refers to the sextuple parameters of the work, 1966); *Correspondences* for String Orch. and Synthesized Magnetic Tape (1967); *Relata II* for Orch. (1968); *Occasional Variations,* a compost collated by Synthesizer (1969); String Quartet No. 3 (1970); *Phonemena* for Soprano and Piano (1970); *Arie da Capo* for 5 Players, "models of similar, interval-preserving, registrally uninterpreted pitch-class and metrically-durationally uninterpreted time-point aggregate arrays" (1974); *Reflections* for Piano and Synthesized Tape (1975); Concerti for Violin, Small Orch., and Synthesized Tape (N.Y., March 13, 1976); *Paraphrases* for 9 Wind Instruments and Piano (1979); *A Solo Requiem* for Soprano and 2 Pianists (N.Y., Feb. 10, 1979); *Dual* for Cello and Piano (1980); *Elizabethan Sextette,* 6 poems for 6 Unaccompanied Voices (1981).

Babell, William, English harpsichordist, violinist, organist, and composer; b. probably in London, c.1690; d. there, Sept. 23, 1723. He studied music with his father and with Pepusch; was then active in London concert life as an instrumentalist; was also organist of All Hallows. He composed a number of works for the harpsichord; also concertos for violin and for flute.

Babić, Konstantin, Serbian composer; b. Belgrade, Feb. 10, 1927. He studied in Belgrade; wrote a number of symph. pieces in a neo-Classical vein; of these, *Konzertna Intrada* (Belgrade, Sept. 30, 1955) is the most effective. His *Levačka Svita (Suite from Levač)* for Mixed Choir (1966), in 3 classical sections, *Passacaglia, Fuga,* and *Toccata,* uses folkloric texts.

Babin, Victor, Russian pianist and composer; b. Moscow, Dec. 13, 1908; d. Cleveland, March 1, 1972. He studied at the Cons. of Riga, Latvia, graduating in 1927; in 1928 went to Berlin, where he took lessons in piano with Artur Schnabel and in composition with Franz Schreker at the Berlin Hochschule für Musik. On Aug. 31, 1933, he married the pianist **Vitya Vronsky;** they emigrated to the U.S. in 1937. From 1943 to 1946, Babin served in the U.S. Army; became a naturalized American citizen. From 1951 to 1954 he taught at the Aspen Music School in Colorado. In 1961 he was appointed director of the Cleveland Inst. of Music, a post he held until his death. He composed 2 piano concertos for 2 pianos and orch. and several pieces for duo-pianos, which he performed with his wife.

Babini, Matteo, famous Italian tenor; b. Bologna, Feb. 19, 1754; d. there, Sept. 22, 1816. He studied with Cortoni; made his debut in 1780; then toured England, Russia, Germany, and Austria with great acclaim. He settled in Paris as a court favorite until the Revolution forced him to leave France; he was in Berlin in 1792 and in Trieste in 1796. Brighenti publ. an "Elogio" in his memory (Bologna, 1821).

Babitz, Sol, American violinist; b. Brooklyn, Oct. 11, 1911; d. Los Angeles, Feb. 18, 1982. In 1932 he went to Berlin, where he studied violin with Carl Flesch and composition with Paul Juon; also took a course in musicology with Curt Sachs. In 1933 he proceeded to Paris and continued violin instruction with Marcel Chailley. Shortly afterwards he returned to the U.S., and became a violinist in the Los Angeles Phil. Orch. (1933–37). From 1942 to 1961 he played violin in studio orchs. in Hollywood. He publ. a manual of modern violin playing, *Principles of Extensions in Violin Fingering* (N.Y., 1947); also edited for publication violin works by contemporary composers. His autobiographical entry in the supplement to *Die Musik in Geschichte und Gegenwart* gives further details on his activities.

Bacarisse, Salvador, Spanish composer; b. Madrid, Sept. 12, 1898; d. Paris, Aug. 7, 1963. He studied at the Cons. of Madrid with Conrado del Campo; received the Premio Nacional de Música 3 times, in 1923, 1930, and 1934. During the Spanish Civil War he was active in the music section of the loyalist army, and after its defeat in 1939 went to Paris, where he remained until his death. He wrote music in all genres; among his works are an opera, *Charlot* (1933); the symph. poem *La tragedia de Doña Ajada* (1929); *Corrida de feria,* a ballet (1930); Piano Concerto (1933); *Tres movimientos concertantes* for String Trio and Orch. (1934); a cantata, *Por la paz y felicidad de las naciones* (1950); Concerto for Guitar and Orch. (Paris, Oct. 22, 1953); 2 string quartets; piano pieces; songs.

Baccaloni, Salvatore, Italian bass; b. Rome, April 4, 1900; d. New York, Dec. 31, 1969. He sang as a child in the Sistine Chapel at the Vatican; for some years studied architecture; then began his career as an opera singer. He made his debut in Rome in 1922; in 1926 he appeared at La Scala in Milan. In 1930 he went to the U.S.; was on the roster of the Chicago Civic Opera (1930–32); made his debut with the Metropolitan Opera in N.Y. on Dec. 7, 1940, as Bartolo in *Le nozze di Figaro;* remained on its staff until his final appearance there on Feb. 14, 1962. He specialized in buffo roles; his repertoire consisted of some 150 roles in several languages.

Bacchius, Greek theorist who flourished A.D. c.350. His treatise, *Isagoge musicae artis,* was publ. by Mersenne (1623); with Latin trans. and commentary by Morellus (1623); also by Meibom (1652) and Carl von Jan (with German trans. and analysis in the Program of the Strasbourg Lyceum, 1890; Greek text alone in Jan's "Scriptores," 1895). French translations were publ. by Mersenne (in Book I of his *Harmonie universelle,* 1627) and Ruelle (1896). The work is a musical catechism in dialogue form. Another treatise, having no dialogue, attributed to Bacchius and edited by Bellermann (in German, 1841) and Vincent (in French, 1847) is not by Bacchius but by his contemporary Dionysios.

Baccusi, Ippolito, Italian composer; b. Mantua, 1530; d. Verona, Sept. 2, 1608. He served as maestro di cappella at San Marco in Venice. In 1570 he was in Ravenna as an organist and in 1572 in Verona; from 1584 to 1587 he was maestro di cappella in Mantua; in 1591 went to Verona. He publ. 5 books of masses (1570–96); 7 books of madrigals (1570–1605); also numerous other choral works. His music shows the influence of the Venetian school; his motets have considerable expressive power.

Bacewicz, Grażyna, significant Polish composer; b. Lodz, Feb. 5, 1909; d. Warsaw, Jan. 17, 1969. She studied composition and violin at the Warsaw Cons., graduating in 1932; continued her study of composition with Nadia Boulanger in Paris (1933–34); upon her return to Poland, she taught at the Lodz Cons.; in 1966 she was appointed prof. at the State Academy of Music in Warsaw. A prolific composer, she adopted a neo-Classical style, characterized by a firm rhythmic pulse and crisp dissonant harmonies.

WORKS: Comic radio opera, *Przygody króla Ar-*

tura (*The Adventures of King Arthur,* 1959); 3 ballets: *Z chłopa Król* (*A Peasant Becomes King,* 1953); *Esik in Ostende* (1964); *Pożądanie* (*Desire,* 1968); Sinfonietta (1937); 7 violin concertos (1938, 1946, 1948, 1952, 1954, 1957, 1965); Overture (1943); 4 numbered symphs. (1942–45, 1950, 1952, 1953); an unnumbered Symph. for String Orch. (1943–46); *Olympic Cantata* (1948); Concerto for String Orch. (1948); Piano Concerto (1949); 2 cello concertos (1951, 1963); *Polish Overture* (1954); Partita for Orch. (1955); Variations for Orch. (1957); *Muzyka* for Strings, 5 Trumpets, and Percussion (Warsaw, Sept. 14, 1959); *Pensieri notturni* for Chamber Orch. (1961); Concerto for Orch. (1962); *Cantata,* after Wyspiański's "Acropolis" (1964); *Musica Sinfonica* (1965); Divertimento for String Orch. (1965); *Incrustations* for Horn and Chamber Ensemble (1965); *Contradizione* for Chamber Orch. (1966; Dartmouth College, Hanover, N.H., Aug. 2, 1967); 2-Piano Concerto (1966); *In una parte* for Orch. (1967); Viola Concerto (1967–68); Wind Quintet (1932); Trio for Oboe, Violin, and Cello (1935); 7 string quartets (1938, 1942, 1947, 1950, 1955, 1960, 1965); 5 violin sonatas (1945, 1946, 1947, 1951, 1955); Quartet for 4 Violins (1949); 2 piano quintets (1952, 1965); solo Violin Sonata (1958); Quartet for 4 Cellos (1964); Trio for Oboe, Harp, and Percussion (1965); *4 Caprices* for Solo Violin (1968); 3 piano sonatas (1935, 1949, 1952); *10 Concert Studies* for Piano (1957); *Esquisse* for Organ (1966).

Bach is the name of the illustrious family which, during 2 centuries, gave to the world a number of musicians and composers of distinction. History possesses few records of such remarkable examples of hereditary art, which culminated in the genius of Johann Sebastian Bach. In the Bach genealogy, the primal member was Johannes or Hans Bach, who is mentioned in 1561 as a guardian of the municipality of Wechmar, a town near Gotha. Also residing in Wechmar was his relative **Veit Bach;** a baker by trade, he was also skillful in playing on a small cittern. Another relative, **Caspar Bach,** who lived from 1570 to 1640, was a Stadtpfeifer in Gotha who later served as a town musician in Arnstadt. His 5 sons, **Caspar, Johannes, Melchior, Nicolaus,** and **Heinrich,** were all town musicians. Another Bach, **Johannes Bach** (1550–1626), was known as "der Spielmann," that is, "minstrel," and thus was definitely described as primarily a musician by vocation. His 3 sons, **Johannes, Christoph,** and **Heinrich,** were also musicians. J.S. Bach took great interest in his family history, and in 1735 prepared a genealogy under the title *Ursprung der musicalisch-Bachischen Familie. The Bach Reader,* compiled by H. David and A. Mendel (N.Y., 1945; revised ed., 1966), contains extensive quotations from this compendium. Karl Geiringer's books *The Bach Family: Seven Generations of Creative Genius* (N.Y., 1954) and *Music of the Bach Family: An Anthology* (Cambridge, Mass., 1955) give useful genealogical tables of Bach's family. Bach's father, **Johann Ambrosius,** was a twin brother of Bach's uncle; the twins bore such an extraordinary physical resemblance that, according to the testimony of Carl Philipp Emanuel Bach, their own wives had difficulty telling them apart after dark. To avoid confusion, they had them wear vests of different colors. A vulgar suggestion that because of this similarity Bach may have been begotten by his uncle is too gross to require a refutation.

When the family became numerous and widely dispersed, its members agreed to assemble on a fixed date each year. Erfurt, Eisenach, and Arnstadt were the places chosen for these meetings, which are said to have continued until the middle of the 18th century, as many as 120 persons of the name of Bach then assembling. At these meetings, a cherished pastime was the singing of "quodlibets," comic polyphonic potpourris of popular songs. An amusing example attributed to J.S. Bach is publ. in *Veröffentlichungen der Neuen Bach-Gesellschaft* (vol. XXXII, 2).

Bach, Carl Philipp Emanuel (the "Berlin" or "Hamburg" Bach), 3rd (and 2nd surviving) son of **Johann Sebastian;** b. Weimar, March 8, 1714; d. Hamburg, Dec. 14, 1788. He was educated under his father's tuition at the Thomasschule in Leipzig; then studied jurisprudence at the Univ. of Leipzig and at the Univ. of Frankfurt-an-der-Oder. Turning to music as his chief vocation, he went to Berlin in 1738; in 1740 he was confirmed as chamber musician to Frederick the Great of Prussia. In that capacity he arranged his father's visit to Potsdam. In March 1768 he assumed the post of cantor at the Johanneum (the Lateinschule) in Hamburg, and also served as music director for the 5 major churches. He held these posts until his death. Abandoning the strict polyphonic style of composition of his great father, he became an adept of the new school of piano writing, a master of "Empfindsamkeit" ("intimate expressiveness"), the North German counterpart of the French Rococo. His *Versuch über die wahre Art das Clavier zu spielen . . .* (2 parts, 1753–62; re-edited by Schelling in 1857; new, but incomplete, ed. by W. Niemann, 1906) became a very influential work which yielded much authentic information about musical practices of the 2nd half of the 18th century. An Eng. trans. of the *Versuch . . . ,* entitled *Essay on the True Art of Playing Keyboard Instruments,* was publ. by W. Mitchell (N.Y., 1949). His autobiography was reprinted by W. Kahl in *Selbstbiographien deutscher Musiker des XVIII. Jahrhunderts* (Cologne, 1948); an Eng. trans. was made by W. Newman, "Emanuel Bach's Autobiography," *Musical Quarterly* (April 1965). His compositions are voluminous (a complete catalogue by E. Helm, *A New Thematic Catalog of the Works of Carl Philipp Emanuel Bach,* is in preparation). WORKS: For clavier, numerous solo pieces, concertos with orch.; quartets; trios; duets; 20 orch. symphs.; many miscellaneous pieces for wind instruments; trios for flute, violin, and double bass; flute, oboe, and cello concertos; soli for flute, viola da gamba, oboe, cello, and harp; duets for flute and violin and for 2 violins; also pieces for clarinet. Vocal music: 2 oratorios: *Die Israeliten in der Wüste* and *Die Auferstehung und Himmelfahrt Jesu;* 22 Passions; cantatas; about 300 songs; etc. Editions of his various works include the following: C. Krebs, ed., *Die Sechs Sammlungen von Sonaten, freien Fantasien und Rondos für Kenner und Liebhaber* (Leipzig, 1895; revised ed. by L. Hoffmann, Erbrecht, 1953); O. Vrieslander, *Kleine Stücke für Klavier* (Hannover, 1930); O. Vrieslander, *Vier leichte Sonaten* (Hannover, 1932); K. Herrman, ed., *Sonaten und Stücke* (Leipzig, 1938); V. Luithlen and H. Kraus, eds., *Klavierstücke* (Vienna, 1938); K. Herrman, ed., *Leichte Tänze und Stücke für Klavier* (Hamburg, 1949); P. Friedheim, ed., *Six Sonatas for Keyboard* (N.Y., 1967); H. Ferguson, ed., *Keyboard Works of C.P.E. Bach* (4 vols., London, 1983).

BIBLIOGRAPHY: C. Bitter, *Carl Philipp Emanuel Bach und Wilhelm Friedemann Bach und deren Brüder* (2 vols., Berlin, 1868); M. Fleuler, *Die norddeutsche Symphonie zur Zeit Friedrichs des Grossen, und besonders die Werke Ph.E. Bachs* (Berlin, 1908); H. Schenker, *Ein Beitrag zur Ornamentik; Als Einführung zu P.E. Bachs Klavierwerke* (Vienna, 1908); O. Vrieslander, *Carl Philipp Emanuel Bach* (Munich, 1923); H. Wien-Claudi, *Zum Liedschaffen C.P.E. Bachs* (Reichenberg, 1928); H. Miesner, *Philipp Emanuel Bach in Hamburg* (Leipzig, 1929); E. Schmid, *Carl Philipp Emanuel Bach und seine Kammermusik* (Kassel, 1931); A.-E. Cherbuliez, *Carl Philipp Emanuel Bach 1714–1788* (Zürich and Leipzig, 1940); D. Plamenac, "New Light on the Last Years of Carl Philipp Emanuel Bach," *Musical Quarterly* (Oct. 1949); E. Beurmann, *Die Klaviersonaten Carl Philipp Emanuel Bachs* (Diss., Univ. of Göttingen, 1952); K. Geiringer, *The Bach Family: Seven Generations of Creative Genius* (N.Y., 1954); C. Haag, *The Keyboard Concertos of Karl Philipp Emanuel Bach* (Diss., Univ. of Calif., Los Angeles, 1956); G. Busch, *C.Ph.E. Bach und seine Lieder* (Regensburg, 1957); P. Barford, *The Keyboard Music of C.P.E. Bach* (London, 1965); E. Suchalla, *Die Orchestersinfonien Carl Philipp Emanuel Bachs nebst einem thematischen Verzeichnis seiner Orchesterwerke* (Augsburg, 1968); M.-G. Ottenberg, *Carl Philipp Emanuel Bach* (Leipzig, 1982).

Bach, Christoph, 2nd son of **Johann(es Hans)** "der Spielmann" and grandfather of **Johann Sebastian;** b. Wechmar, April 19, 1613; d. Arnstadt, Sept. 12, 1661. He was a court musician in Weimar; from 1642 he was a town musician in Erfurt; from 1654, court and town musician in Arnstadt. The only known musical item by him is publ. in the *Bach-Jahrbuch* (1928).

Bach, Georg Christoph, eldest son of **Christoph;** b. Erfurt, Sept. 6, 1642; d. Schweinfurt, April 24, 1697. He was cantor in Themar from 1668; in Schweinfurt from 1684. A cantata of his is publ. in *Das Erbe deutscher Musik* (vol. II, Leipzig, 1935).

Bach, Heinrich, 3rd son of **Johann(es Hans)** "der Spielmann"; b. Wechmar, Sept. 16, 1615; d. Arnstadt, July 10, 1692. He was a town musician in Schwein-

furt from 1629, in Erfurt fron 1635, and in Arnstadt from 1641; from 1641, was also organist at the Liebfrauenkirche in Arnstadt, a post he held for 51 years, until his death. M. Schneider publ. a thematic index of his works in the *Bach-Jahrbuch* (1907, pp. 105–9). A cantata of his is found in *Das Erbe deutscher Musik* (vol. II, Leipzig, 1935); also 3 organ chorales in D. Hellmann, ed., *Orgelwerke der Familie Bach* (Leipzig, 1967).

Bach, Johann Aegidius, 2nd son of **Johann(es Hans);** b. Erfurt, Feb. 9, 1645; d. there (buried, Nov. 22), 1716. He succeeded his father as municipal music director in Erfurt in 1682; was also organist at the Michaeliskirche there from 1690, succeeding Pachelbel.

Bach, Johann Ambrosius, 2nd son of **Christoph,** twin brother of **Johann Christoph,** and father of **Johann Sebastian;** b. Erfurt, Feb. 22, 1645; d. Eisenach, Feb. 20, 1695. As a boy, he went to Arnstadt; was trained as a Stadtpfeifer. In 1667 he became a member of the town band in Erfurt; from 1671 was court trumpeter and director of the town band in Eisenach. He was married twice: on April 8, 1668, to Maria Elisabeth Lämmerhirt (b. Erfurt, Feb. 24, 1644; d. Eisenach, May 3, 1694), the mother of Johann Sebastian; and on Nov. 27, 1694, to the widow of his cousin Johann Günther Bach.

BIBLIOGRAPHY: F. Rollberg, "Johann Ambrosius Bach, Stadtpfeifer zu Eisenach von 1671–1695," *Bach-Jahrbuch* (1927).

Bach, Johann Bernhard, son of **Johann Aegidius,** one of the best organists and composers of his generation; b. Erfurt, Nov. 23, 1676; d. Eisenach, June 11, 1749. He was an organist at Erfurt and Magdeburg, and the successor to **Johann Christoph** as organist at Eisenach (1703); also served the Duke of Saxe-Eisenach. He wrote harpsichord pieces; also a number of organ chorales: 2 of these have been publ. in *Das Erbe deutscher Musik* (vol. IX, Leipzig, 1937); 2 more in D. Hellmann, ed., *Orgelwerke der Familie Bach* (Leipzig, 1967). He also wrote 4 orch. suites; one was publ. by A. Fareanu (Leipzig, 1920); another by K. Geiringer, *Music of the Bach Family: An Anthology* (Cambridge, Mass., 1955).

BIBLIOGRAPHY: S. Orth, "Zu den Erfurter Jahren Johann Bernhard Bachs (1676–1749)," *Bach-Jahrbuch* (1971).

Bach, Johann (John) Christian (the "London" Bach), 11th and youngest surviving son of **Johann Sebastian Bach;** b. Leipzig, Sept. 5, 1735; d. London, Jan. 1, 1782. He received early instruction in music from his father, after whose death in 1750 he went to Berlin to study with his brother **Carl Philipp Emanuel.** In 1754 he went to Italy, where he continued his studies with Padre Martini; he also found a patron in Count Agostino Litta of Milan. He converted to the Roman Catholic faith in order to be able to obtain work, and became one of the organists at the Cathedral in Milan (1760–62); he also traveled throughout the country and composed several successful operas during his stay in Italy. In 1762 he went to England; his highly acclaimed opera *Orione* was given its premiere in London on Feb. 19, 1763; in 1764 he was appointed music master to the Queen. From 1764 to 1781 he gave, together with C.F. Abel, a series of London concerts. When child Mozart was taken to London in 1764, J.C. Bach took great interest in him and improvised with him at the keyboard; Mozart retained a lifelong affection for him; he used 3 of J.C. Bach's piano sonatas as thematic material for his piano concertos. J.C. Bach was a highly prolific composer; he wrote about 90 symphs., several piano concertos, 6 quintets, a Piano Sextet, violin sonatas, and numerous piano sonatas. In his music he adopted the *style galant* of the 2nd half of the 18th century, with an emphasis on expressive "affects" and brilliance of instrumental display. He thus totally departed from the ideals of his father, and became historically a precursor of the Classical era as exemplified by the works of Mozart.

WORKS: Although he was known mainly as an instrumental composer, J.C. Bach also wrote successful operas, most of them to Italian librettos, for production in London; among them were: *Artaserse* (Turin, Dec. 26, 1760); *Catone in Utica* (Naples, Nov. 4, 1761); *Alessandro nell' Indie* (Naples, Jan. 20, 1762); *Orione, ossia Diana vendicata* (London, Feb. 19, 1763); *Zanaida* (London, May 7, 1763); *Adriano in Siria* (London, Jan. 26, 1765); *Carattaco* (London, Feb. 14, 1767); *Temistocle* (Mannheim, Nov. 4, 1772); *Lucio Silla* (Mannheim, Nov. 4, 1774); *La clemenza di Scipione* (London, April 4, 1778); *Amadis de Gaule* (Paris, Dec. 14, 1779).

BIBLIOGRAPHY: M. Schwarz, "Johann Christian Bach," *Sammelbände der Internationalen Musik-Gesellschaft* (1900–1); idem, *J. Christian Bach: Sein Leben und seine Werke* (Leipzig, 1901); G. de Saint-Foix, "A propos de Jean-Crétien Bach," *Revue de Musicologie* (1926); H. Schökel, *J. Christian Bach und die Instrumentalmusik seiner Zeit* (Wolfenbüttel, 1926); F. Tutenberg, *Die Sinfonik Johann Christian Bach* (Wolfenbüttel, 1928); C. Terry, *John Christian Bach* (London, 1929; 2nd ed. by H.C. Robbins Landon, 1967); A. Wenk, *Beiträge zur Kenntnis des Opernschaffens von J. Christian Bach* (Diss., Univ. of Frankfurt am Main, 1932); E. Resser, *De zonen van Bach* (Amsterdam, 1941; in Eng., 1949); K. Geiringer, *The Bach Family: Seven Generations of Creative Genius* (N.Y., 1954); R. Seebandt, *Arientypen Johann Christian Bachs* (Diss., Humboldt Univ., Berlin, 1956); E. Downes, *The Operas of Johann Christian Bach as a Reflection of the Dominant Trends in Opera Seria 1750–1780* (Diss., Harvard Univ., 1958); J. White, Jr., *The Concerted Symphonies of John Christian Bach* (Diss., Univ. of Michigan, 1958); W. Haacke, *Die Söhne Bachs* (Königstein im Taunus, 1962); B. Mekota, *The Solo and Ensemble Keyboard Works of Johann Christian Bach* (Diss., Univ. of Michigan, 1969); M. Vos, *The Liturgical Choral Works of Johann Christian Bach* (Diss., Washington Univ., St. Louis, 1969); E. Warburton, *A Study of Johann Christian Bach's Operas* (Diss., Oxford Univ., 1969); I. Baierle, *Die Klavierwerke von Johann Christian Bach* (Diss.,

Univ. of Graz, 1974); S. Roe, "J.C. Bach, 1735–1782: Towards a New Biography," *Musical Times* (Jan. 1982); R. Maunder, "J.C. Bach's Endimione," *Musical Times* (July 1982); E. Warburton, "J.C. Bach's Latin Church Music," *Musical Times* (Nov. 1982); S. Roe, "J.C. Bach's Vauxhall Songs: A New Discovery," *Musical Times* (Nov. 1983).

Bach, Johann Christoph, eldest son of **Heinrich,** organist and composer of the highest distinction among the earlier Bachs; b. Arnstadt, Dec. 3, 1642; d. Eisenach, March 31, 1703. From 1663 to 1665 he was an organist in Arnstadt; from 1665, in Eisenach; from 1700, was court musician there. A thematic catalogue of his compositions was publ. by M. Schneider in the *Bach-Jahrbuch* (1907, pp. 132–77). C.P.E. Bach described him as a "great and expressive composer"; his works are printed in *Das Erbe deutscher Musik* (vols. I and II, Leipzig, 1935); several of his motets were publ. by V. Junk (Leipzig, 1922); 44 chorales with preludes for Organ were edited by M. Fischer (Kassel, 1936); his *Praeludium und Fuge* for Organ is in D. Hellman, ed., *Orgelwerke der Familie Bach* (Leipzig, 1967).

BIBLIOGRAPHY: M. Fischer, "Die organistische Improvisation bei Johann Christoph Bach," *Königsberger Studien zur Musikwissenschaft,* V (1928); F. Rollberg, "Johann Christoph Bach: Organist zu Eisenach 1665–1703," *Zeitschrift für Musikwissenschaft,* XI (1929); C. Freyse, "Johann Christoph Bach," *Bach-Jahrbuch* (1956).

Bach, Johann Christoph, twin brother of **Johann Ambrosius;** b. Erfurt, Feb. 22, 1645; d. Arnstadt, Aug. 25, 1693. He was a Stadtpfeifer in Erfurt from 1666; in Arnstadt, from 1671. The physical resemblance between him and his twin brother (father of **Johann Sebastian**) was such that, according to the testimony of C.P.E. Bach, even their wives had difficulty distinguishing between them.

Bach, Johann Christoph, brother of **Johann Sebastian** and eldest son of **Johann Ambrosius;** b. Erfurt, June 16, 1671; d. Ohrdruf, Feb. 22, 1721. He was a pupil of Pachelbel; served as organist at the Thomaskirche in Erfurt and for a short time at Arnstadt; from 1690 he was organist at the Michaeliskirche in Ohrdruf, where Johann Sebastian stayed with him for almost 5 years.

BIBLIOGRAPHY: C. Freyse, *Die Ohrdrufer Bache in der Silhouette: J.S. Bachs ältester Bruder Johann Christoph und seine Nachkommen* (Eisenach, 1957).

Bach, Johann Christoph Friedrich (the "Bückeburg" Bach), 9th son of **Johann Sebastian;** b. Leipzig, June 21, 1732; d. Bückeburg, Jan. 26, 1795. He studied music with his father; then attended the Univ. of Leipzig, where he took courses in jurisprudence. Adopting music as his principal vocation, he became a chamber musician in Bückeburg, a post he held until his death. Although less known as a composer than his brothers, he was a fine musician. A selected edition of his works was edited by G.

Schünemann and sponsored by the Fürstliches Institut für Musikwissenschaftliche Forschung (1920–22). Schünemann also edited several oratorios in the Denkmäler deutscher Tonkunst (vol. 56, 1917). G. Walter edited the cantata *Die Amerikanerin* (Berlin, 1919), and L. Duttenhofer, a set of 6 quartets (Paris, 1922); several other chamber works may be found in K. Geiringer, *Music of the Bach Family: An Anthology* (Cambridge, Mass., 1955); 3 symphs. have been edited in facsimile by H. Wohlfarth (Bückeburg, 1966).

BIBLIOGRAPHY: G. Schünemann, "Johann Christoph Friedrich Bach," *Bach-Jahrbuch* (1914); H. Wohlfarth, *Johann Christoph Friedrich Bach* (Bern, 1971; includes a catalogue of his works).

Bach, Johann Ernst, only son of **Johann Bernhard;** b. Eisenach, Jan. 28, 1722; d. there, Sept. 1, 1777. He was a pupil of his uncle, **Johann Sebastian.** After studying law at the Univ. of Leipzig, he returned to Eisenach and practiced as an advocate. In 1748 he became assistant organist to his father at the Georgenkirche; succeeded him as organist in 1749. In 1756 he became Court Kapellmeister to the fused courts of Weimar, Gotha, and Eisenach. When this arrangement was dissolved in 1758, he retained his position and worked in the administration of the ducal finances in Eisenach. He publ. *Sammlung auserlesener Fabeln mit Melodeyen* (ed. by H. Kretzschmar in Denkmäler Deutscher Tonkunst, vol. 42, 1910) and other works. Only a small part of his works has been publ.; his Passion oratorio, *O Seele, deren Sehen,* is in Denkmäler Deutscher Tonkunst, vol. 48, 1914. A sonata is in K. Geiringer, *Music of the Bach Family: An Anthology* (Cambridge, Mass., 1955). Two fantasies and fugues for organ are found in D. Hellmann, ed., *Orgelwerke der Familie Bach* (Leipzig, 1967).

Bach, Johann(es Hans), eldest son of **Johann(es Hans)** "der Spielmann"; b. Wechmar, Nov. 26, 1604; d. Erfurt, May 13, 1673. He was apprenticed to Christoph Hoffman, Stadtpfeifer in Suhl; was a town musician in Erfurt; from 1636, was organist at the Predigerkirche there. Several of his compositions are extant.

Bach, Johann Ludwig, son of **Johann Jacob** and a great-grandson of Lips Bach (d. Oct. 10, 1620); b. Thal, Feb. 4, 1677; d. Meiningen (buried, March 1), 1731. In 1699 he became a court musician in Meiningen; was appointed cantor in 1703, and Court Kapellmeister in 1711. He wrote numerous vocal compositions; also orch. works, but few have been preserved.

BIBLIOGRAPHY: A. Jaffé, *The Cantatas of Johann Ludwig Bach* (Diss., Boston Univ., 1957); W. Scheide, "Johann Sebastian Bachs Sammlung von Kantaten seines Vetters Johann Ludwig Bach," *Bach-Jahrbuch* (1959, 1961, 1962).

Bach, Johann Michael, brother of **Johann Christoph** and father of Maria Barbara, first wife of **Johann Sebastian;** b. Arnstadt, Aug. 9, 1648; d. Gehren,

May 17, 1694. From 1673 he was organist and town clerk of Gehren; also worked as a maker of instruments. His works are listed in the *Bach-Jahrbuch* (1907, pp. 109–32); many of them are included in *Das Erbe deutscher Musik* (vol. I, Leipzig, 1935); motets of his are publ. in Denkmäler Deutscher Tonkunst (vols. 49 and 50, 1915). Some of his organ compositions are found in *Das Erbe deutscher Musik* (vol. IX, Leipzig, 1937); 72 organ chorales are included in D. Hellman, ed., *Orgelwerke der Familie Bach* (Leipzig, 1967).

Bach, Johann Nicolaus, eldest son of **Johann Christoph;** b. Eisenach, Oct. 10, 1669; d. Jena, Nov. 4, 1753. He was educated at the Univ. of Jena; in 1694 he became organist at Jena, and in 1719 was also at the Univ. He was an expert on organ building and also made keyboard instruments. He wrote a fine *Missa* (Kyrie and Gloria; ed. by A. Fareanu and V. Junk, Leipzig, 1920); a comic cantata, *Der Jenaische Wein- und Bierrufer,* a scene from Jena Univ. life (ed. by F. Stein, Leipzig, 1921); suites for keyboard, which are not preserved, and organ chorales, of which only one is known.

BIBLIOGRAPHY: H. Koch, "Johann Nicolaus, der 'Jenaer' Bach," *Die Musikforschung,* XXI (1968).

Bach, Johann Sebastian, supreme arbiter and lawgiver of music, a master comparable in greatness of stature with Aristotle in philosophy and Leonardo da Vinci in art; b. Eisenach, March 21 (baptized, March 23), 1685; d. Leipzig, July 28, 1750. He was a member of an illustrious family of musicians who were active in various capacities as performing artists, composers, and teachers. That so many Bachs were musicians lends support to the notion that music is a hereditary faculty, that some subliminal cellular unit may be the nucleus of musicality. The word "Bach" itself means "stream" in the German language; the rhetorical phrase that Johann Sebastian Bach was not a mere stream but a whole ocean of music ("Nicht Bach aber Meer haben wir hier") epitomizes Bach's encompassing magnitude. Yet despite the grandeur of the phenomenon of Bach, he was not an isolated figure dwelling in the splendor of his genius apart from the zeitgeist, the spirit of his time. Just as Aristotle was not only an abstract philosopher but also an educator (Alexander the Great was his pupil), just as Leonardo da Vinci was not only a painter of portraits but also a practical man of useful inventions, so Bach was a mentor to young students, a master organist and instructor who spent his life within the confines of his native Thuringia as a teacher and composer of works designed for immediate performance in church and in the schoolroom. Indeed, the text of the dedication of his epoch-making work *Das wohltemperierte Clavier oder Praeludia und Fugen* emphasizes its pedagogical aspect: "The Well-tempered Clavier, or Preludes and Fugues in all tones and semitones, both with the major third of Ut Re Mi, and the minor third of Re Mi Fa, composed and notated for the benefit and exercise of musical young people eager to learn, as well as for a special practice for those who have already achieved proficiency and skill in this study." The MS is dated 1722. Bach's system of "equal temperament" (which is the meaning of "well-tempered" in the title *Well-tempered Clavier*) postulated the division of the octave into 12 equal semitones, making it possible to transpose and to effect a modulation into any key, a process unworkable in the chaotic tuning of keyboard instruments before Bach's time. Bach was not the first to attempt the tempered division, however. J.K.F. Fischer anticipated him in his collection *Ariadne musica* (with the allusion to the thread of Ariadne that allowed Theseus to find his way out of the Cretan labyrinth); publ. in 1700, it contained 20 preludes and fugues in 19 different keys. Undoubtedly Bach was aware of this edition; actually, the subjects of several of Bach's preludes and fugues are similar to the point of identity to the themes of Fischer's work. These coincidences do not detract from the significance of Bach's accomplishment, for it is the beauty and totality of development that makes Bach's work vastly superior to those of any of his putative predecessors.

It is interesting to note that Bach shared the belief in numerical symbolism held by many poets and artists of his time. By summing up the cardinal numbers corresponding to the alphabetical order of the letters of his last name, he arrived at the conclusion that the number 14 had a special significance in his life (B = 2, A = 1, C = 3, H = 8; 2 + 1 + 3 + 8 = 14). That the number of buttons on his waistcoat in one of his portraits is 14 may be an indication of the significance he attached to this number. The theme of Bach's chorale *Von deinen Thron tret' ich hiermit,* which he wrote shortly before his death, contains 14 notes, while the notes in the entire melody number 43, comprising the sum total of the alphabetical index of letters in J.S. Bach (10 + 19 + 2 + 1 + 3 + 8 = 43). In Bach's chorale prelude *Wenn wir in Höchsten Nöten sein,* the principal melody contains 166 notes, which represents the alphabetical sum of the full name JOHANN SEBASTIAN BACH (10 + 15 + 8 + 1 + 14 + 14 + 19 + 5 + 2 + 1 + 19 + 20 + 9 + 1 + 14 + 2 + 1 + 3 + 8 = 166). The symbolism of melodies and harmonies in Baroque music, expressing various states of mind, joy or sadness has been accepted as a valid "doctrine of affects" by musical philosophers, among them Albert Schweitzer. Indeed, there seems to be little doubt that a natural connection exists between such a line as "Geh' auf! Geh' auf!" and an ascending major arpeggio in a Bach cantata, or that, generally speaking, major modes represent joy and exhilaration, and minor keys suggest melancholy and sadness. We find numerous instances in the choral works of Baroque composers of the use of a broken diminished-seventh-chord in a precipitous downward movement to depict the fall from grace and regression to Hell. The chromatic weaving around a thematic tone often represents in Bach's cantatas and Passions the thorny crown around the head of Jesus Christ. An ascending scale of several octaves, sung by basses, tenors, altos, and sopranos in succession, is found to accompany the words "We follow you." A hypothesis may be advanced that such tonal patterns were used by Baroque composers to facilitate the comprehension of the meaning of the text by the congregation in church performances. Indeed, such word painting has become an accepted procedure in the last 2 or 3 centuries; composers equated major keys with joy and virtue, and minor keys with melancholy and sin. Similarly, fast tempos and duple time are commonly used by composers to express joy, while slow movements are reserved for scenes of sadness.

The term "Baroque" had a humble origin; it was probably derived from *barroco,* the Portuguese word for a deformed pearl; originally it had a decidedly negative meaning, and was often applied in the 17th century to describe a corrupt style of Renaissance architecture. Through the centuries the word underwent a change of meaning toward lofty excellence. In this elevated sense, "Baroque" came to designate an artistic development between the years 1600 and 1800. The advent of Bach marked the greatest flowering of Baroque music; his name became a synonym of perfection. Max Reger was told by Hugo Riemann that he could be the 2nd Bach, and his skill in composition almost justified his aspiration; Ferruccio Busoni was described by his admirers as the Bach of the modern era; a similar honor was claimed for Hindemith by his disciples. Yet the art of Bach remains unconquerable. Although he wrote most of his contrapuntal works as a didactic exercise, there are in his music extraordinary visions into the remote future; consider, for instance, the A minor Fugue of the first book of the *Well-tempered Clavier,* in which the inversion of the subject seems to violate all the rules of proper voice-leading in its bold leap from the tonic upward to the 7th of the scale and then up a third. The answer to the subject of the F minor Fugue of the first book suggests the chromatic usages of later centuries. In the art of variations, Bach was supreme. A suberp example is his set of keyboard pieces known as the *Goldberg Variations,* so named because it was commissioned by the Russian diplomat Kayserling through the mediation of Bach's pupil Johann Gottlieb Goldberg, who was in Kayserling's service as a harpsichord player. These variations are listed by Bach as the 4th part of the *Clavier-Übung;* the didactic title of this division is characteristic of Bach's intention to write music for utilitarian purposes, be it for keyboard exercises, for church services, or for chamber music. A different type of Bach's great musical projections is exemplified by his *Concerts à plusieurs instruments,* known popularly as the *Brandenburg Concertos,* for they were written for Christian Ludwig, margrave of Brandenburg. They represent the crowning achievement of the Baroque; each concerto is set in a balanced form of 3 movements, with the fast sections in the outer movements and the slow movement in the middle. Nos. 2, 4, and 5 of the *Brandenburg Concertos* are essentially concerti grossi, in which a group of solo instruments—the concertino —is contrasted with the accompanying string orch. Finally, *Die Kunst der Fuge,* Bach's last composition, which he wrote in 1749, represents an encyclopedia of fugues, canons, and various counterpoints based on the same theme. Here Bach's art of purely technical devices, such as inversion, canon, augmentation, diminution, double fugue, triple fugue, at times appearing in fantastic optical symmetry so that the written music itself forms a balanced design, is calculated to instruct the musical mind as well as delight the aural sense. Of these constructions, the most extraordinary is represented by *Das Musikalisches Opfer (A Musical Offering)*, composed by Bach for Frederick the Great of Prussia. Bach's 2nd son, **Carl Philipp Emanuel,** who served as chamber musician to the court of Prussia, arranged for Bach to visit Frederick's palace in Potsdam; Bach arrived there, accompanied by his son **Wilhelm Friedemann,** on May 7, 1747. The ostensible purpose of Bach's visit was to test the Silbermann pianos installed in the palace. The King, who liked to flaunt his love for the arts and sciences, gave Bach a musical theme of his own invention and asked him to compose a fugue upon it. Bach also presented an organ recital at the Heiliggeistkirche in Potsdam and attended a chamber music concert held by the King; on that occasion he improvised a fugue in 6 parts on a theme of his own. Upon his return to Leipzig, Bach set to work on the King's theme. Gallantly, elegantly, he inscribed the work, in scholastic Latin, "Regis Iussu Cantio et Reliqua Canonica Arte Resoluta" ("At the King's command, the cantus and supplements are in a canonic manner resolved"). The initials of the Latin words form the acronym RICECAR, a technical term etymologically related to the word "research" and applied to any study that is instructive in nature. The work is subdivided into 13 sections; it includes a puzzle canon in 2 parts, marked "quaerendo invenietis" ("you will find it by seeking"). Bach had the score engraved, and sent it to the King on July 7, 1747. Intellectually independent as Bach was, he never questioned the immanent rights of established authority. He was proud of the title Royal Polish and Electoral Saxon Court Composer to the King of Poland and Elector of Saxony, bestowed upon him in 1736 while he was in the service of Duke Christian of Weissenfels, and he even regarded the position of cantor of the Thomasschule in Leipzig as inferior to it. In his dedications to royal personages he adhered to the customary humble sytle, which was extended even to the typography of his dedicatory prefaces. In such dedications the name of the exalted commissioner was usually printed in large letters, with conspicuous indentation, while Bach's own signature, preceded by elaborate verbal genuflection, appeared in the smallest type of the typographer's box.

Bach's biography is singularly lacking in dramatic events. He attended the Latin school in Eisenach, and apparently was a good student, as demonstrated by his skill in the Latin language. When he was 9 years old, his mother died. His father remarried, and died when Bach was 20. Bach's school years were passed at the Lyceum in the town of Ohrdruf; his older brother **Johann Christoph** lived there; he helped Bach in his musical studies; stories that he treated Bach cruelly must be dismissed as melodramatic inventions. Through the good offices of Elias Herda, cantor of the Ohrdruf school, Bach received an opportunity to move, for further education, to Lüneburg; there he was admitted to the Mettenchor of the Michaeliskirche. In March of 1703 he obtained employment as an attendant to Johann Ernst, Duke of Weimar; he was commissioned to make tests on the new organ of the Neukirche in Arnstadt; on Aug. 9, 1703, he was appointed organist there. In Oct. 1705 he obtained a leave of absence to travel to Lübeck to hear the famous organist Dietrich Buxtehude. The physical mode of Bach's travel there leaves much to be explained. The common versions found in most biographies tell that Bach made that journey on foot. But the distance between Arnstadt and Lübeck is 212 miles (335 km) and the route lies through the forbidding Harz Mountain chain, with its legendary peak Brocken, which, according to common superstition, was the site of the midnight gathering of a coven of witches. Assuming that Bach had about a month to spend in Lübeck to attend Buxtehude's concerts (or else the journey would not have been worthwhile), he had about 45 days to cover 424 miles (670 km) for a round trip: he would have had to travel on the average of 20 miles a day. The actual travel time between Arnstadt and Lübeck, considering the absence of good roads, must have been much longer. Not only would it have been exhausting in the extreme, even for a young man of 19 (Bach's age at the time), but it would have necessitated a change of 3 or 4 pairs of heavy boots that would wear out in the generally inclement weather during the months of Nov. and Dec. A query for information from the office of the Oberbürgermeister of Arnstadt elicited the suggestion that Bach (and Handel, who made a similar journey before) must have hired himself out as a valet to a coach passenger, a not uncommon practice among young men of the time. The impetus of Bach's trip was presumably the hope of obtaining Buxtehude's position as organist upon his retirement, but there was a peculiar clause attached to the contract for such a candidate: Buxtehude had 5 unmarried daughters; his successor was expected to marry the eldest of them. Buxtehude himself obtained his post through such an expedient, but Bach apparently was not prepared for matrimony under such circumstances.

On June 15, 1707, Bach became organist at the Blasiuskirche in Mühlhausen. On Oct. 17, 1707, he married his cousin Maria Barbara Bach, who was the daughter of **Johann Michael Bach.** On Feb. 4, 1708, Bach composed his cantata *Gott ist mein König* for the ocassion of the installation of a new Mühlhausen town council. This was the first work of Bach's that was publ. Although the circumstances of his employment in Mühlhausen were seemingly favorable, Bach resigned his position on June 25, 1708, and accepted the post of court organist to Duke Wilhelm Ernst of Weimar. In Dec. 1713 Bach visited Halle, the birthplace of Handel; despite its proximity to Bach's own place of birth in Eisenach, the 2 great composers never met. On March 2, 1714, Duke Wilhelm Ernst offered Bach the position of Konzertmeister. In Sept. 1717 Bach went to Dresden to hear the famous French organist Louis Marchand, who resided there at the time. It was arranged that Bach and Marchand would hold a contest as virtuosos, but Marchand left Dresden before the scheduled event. This anecdote should not be interpreted frivolously as Marchand's fear of competing; other factors may have intervened to prevent the meeting. Johann Samuel Drese, the Weimar music director, died on Dec. 1, 1716; Bach expected to succeed him in that prestigious position, but the Duke gave the post to Drese's son. Again, this episode should not be interpreted as the Duke's lack of appreciation for Bach's superior abilities; the appointment may have merely followed the custom of letting such administrative posts remain in the family. In 1717 Bach accepted the position of Kapellmeister and music director to Prince Leopold of Anhalt in Cöthen, but a curious contretemps developed when the Duke of Weimar refused to release Bach from his obligation, and even had him held under arrest from Nov. 6 to Dec. 2, 1717, before Bach was finally allowed to proceed to Cöthen. The Cöthen period was one of the most productive in Bach's life; there he wrote his great set of *Brandenburg Concertos,* the *Clavierbüchlein für Wilhelm Friedemann Bach,* and the first book of *Das Wohltemperierte Clavier.* In Oct. 1719 Bach was in Halle once more, but again missed meeting Handel, who had already gone to England. In 1720 Bach accompanied Prince Leopold to Karlsbad. A tragedy supervened when Bach's devoted wife was taken ill and died before Bach could be called to her side; she was buried on July 7, 1720, leaving Bach to take care of their 7 children. In 1720 Bach made a long journey to Hamburg, where he again met the aged Reinken, who was then 97 years old. It is a part of the Bach legend that Reinken was greatly impressed with Bach's virtuosity and exclaimed, "I believed that the art of organ playing was dead, but it lives in you!" Bach remained a widower for nearly a year and a half before he married his 2nd wife, Anna Magdalena Wilcken, a daughter of a court trumpeter at Weissenfels, on Dec. 3, 1721. They had 13 children during their happy marital life. New avenues were opened to Bach when Johann Kuhnau, the cantor of Leipzig, died, on June 5, 1722. Although Bach applied for his post, the Leipzig authorities offered it first to Telemann of Hamburg, and when he declined, to Christoph Graupner of Darmstadt; only when Graupner was unable to obtain a release from his current position was Bach given the post. He traveled to Leipzig on Feb. 7, 1723, for a trial performance, earning a favorable reception. On April 22, 1723, Bach was elected to the post of cantor of the city of Leipzig and was officially installed on May 31, 1723. As director of church music, Bach's duties included the care of musicians for the Thomaskirche, Nicolaikirche, Matthaeikirche, and Petrikirche, and he was also responsible for the provision of the music to be performed at the Thomaskirche and Nicolaikirche. There were more mundane obligations that Bach was expected to discharge, such as gathering firewood for the Thomasschule, about which Bach had recurrent disputes with the rector; eventually he sought the interven-

tion of the Elector of Saxony in the affair. It was in Leipzig that Bach created his greatest sacred works: the *St. John Passion,* the Mass in B minor, and the *Christmas Oratorio.* In 1729 he organized at the Thomasschule the famous Collegium Musicum, composed of professional musicians and univ. students with whom he gave regular weekly concerts; he led this group until 1737, and again from 1739 to 1741. He made several visits to Dresden, where his eldest son, Wilhelm Friedemann, served as organist at the Sophienkirche. In June 1747 Bach joined the Societät der Musikalischen Wissenschaften, a scholarly organization founded by a former member of the Collegium Musicum, Lorenz C. Mizler, a learned musician, Latinist, and mathematician who spent his life confounding his contemporaries and denouncing them as charlatans and ignorant pretenders to knowledge. The rules of the society required an applicant to submit a sample of his works; Bach contributed a triple canon in 6 parts and presented it, along with the canonic variations *Vom Himmel hoch da komm' ich her.* This was one of Bach's last works. He suffered from a cataract that was gradually darkening his vision. A British optician named John Taylor, who plied his trade in Saxony, operated on Bach's eyes in the spring of 1749; the operation, performed with the crude instruments of the time, left Bach almost totally blind. The same specialist operated also on Handel, with no better results. The etiology of Bach's last illness is unclear. It is said that on July 18, 1750, his vision suddenly returned (possibly when the cataract receded spontaneously), but a cerebral hemorrhage supervened, and a few days later Bach was dead. Bach's great contrapuntal work, *Die Kunst der Fuge,* remained unfinished. The final page bears this inscription by C.P.E. Bach: "Upon this Fugue, in which the name B-A-C-H is applied as a countersubject, the author died." Bach's widow, Anna Magdalena, survived him by nearly 10 years; she died on Feb. 27, 1760. In 1895 Wilhelm His, an anatomy prof. at the Univ. of Leipzig, performed an exhumation of Bach's body, made necessary because of the deterioration of the wooden coffin, and took remarkable photographs of Bach's skeleton, which he publ. under the title *J.S. Bach, Forschungen über dessen Grabstätte, Gebeine und Antlitz* (Leipzig, 1895). On July 28, 1949, on the 199th anniversary of Bach's death, his coffin was transferred to the choir room of the Thomaskirche.

Of Bach's 20 children, 10 reached maturity. His sons Wilhelm Friedemann, Carl Philipp Emanuel, **Johann Christoph Friedrich,** and **Johann (John) Christian** (the "London" Bach) made their mark as independent composers. Among Bach's notable pupils were Johann Friedrich Agricola, Johann Christoph Altnikol, Heinrich Nilolaus Gerber, Johann Theophilus Goldberg, Gottfried August Homilius, Johann Philipp Kirnberger, Johann Christian Kettel, Johann Tobias Krebs, and Johann Ludwig Krebs. It is historically incorrect to maintain that Bach was not appreciated by his contemporaries; Bach's sons Carl Philipp Emanuel and the "London" Bach kept his legacy alive for a generation after Bach's death. True, they parted from

Bach's art of contrapuntal writing; Carl Philipp Emanuel turned to the fashionable *style galant,* and wrote keyboard works of purely harmonic content. The first important biography of Bach was publ. in 1802, by J.N. Forkel.

Dramatic accounts of music history are often inflated. It is conventional to say that Bach's music was rescued from oblivion by Mendelssohn, who conducted the *St. Matthew Passion* in Berlin in 1829, but Mozart and Beethoven had practiced Bach's preludes and fugues. Bach's genius was never dimmed; he was never a prophet without a world. The centennial of Bach's death in 1850 was observed by the inception of the Leipzig Bach-Gesellschaft, a society founded by Carl Becker, Moritz Hauptmann, Otto Jahn, and Robert Schumann. Concurrently, the publishing firm of Breitkopf & Härtel inaugurated the publication of the complete edition of Bach's works; a Neue Bach-Gesellschaft was founded in 1900; it supervised the publication of the important *Bach-Jahrbuch,* a scholarly journal begun in 1904. The bicentennial of Bach's death, in 1950, brought about a new series of memorials and celebrations. With the development of the electric phonograph record, and later of the digital method of recording with high fidelity, Bach's works were made available to large masses of the public. Modern composers, even those who champion the total abandonment of all conventional methods of composition and the abolition of musical notation, are irresistibly drawn to Bach as a precursor; suffice it to mention Alban Berg's use of Bach's chorale *Es ist genug* in the concluding section of his Violin Concerto dedicated to the memory of Alma Mahler's young daughter. It is interesting to note also that Bach's famous acronym B-A-C-H consists of 4 different notes in a chromatic alternation, thus making it possible to use it as an element of a 12-tone row. Bach's images have been imblazoned on popular T-shirts; postage stamps with his portrait have been issued by a number of nations in Europe, Asia, and Africa. The slogan "Back to Bach," adopted by composers of the early 20th century, seems to hold true for every musical era.

In the list of Bach's works given below, each composition is identified by the BWV (Bach-Werke-Verzeichnis) number established by W. Schmieder in his *Thematisch-systematisches Verzeichnis der musikalischen Werke von Johann Sebastian Bach. Bach-Werke-Verzeichnis* (Leipzig, 1950; 3rd ed., 1961).

WORKS: CHURCH CANTATAS: About 200 are extant. The following list gives the BWV number, title, and date of first performance: 1, *Wie schön leuchtet der Morgenstern* (March 25, 1725); 2, *Ach Gott, vom Himmel sieh darein* (June 18, 1724); 3, *Ach Gott, wie manches, Herzeleid* (Jan. 14, 1725); 4, *Christ lag in Todesbanden* (c.1707–8); 5, *Wo soll ich fliehen hin* (Oct. 15, 1724); 6, *Bleib bei uns, denn es will Abend werden* (April 2, 1725); 7, *Christ unser Herr zum Jordan kam* (June 24, 1724); 8, *Liebster Gott, wann werd ich sterben?* (Sept. 24, 1724); 9, *Es ist das Heil uns kommen her* (c.1732–35); 10, *Meine Seel erhebt den Herren* (July 2, 1724); 11, *Lobet Gott in seinen Reichen* (Ascension oratorio; May 19, 1735);

12, *Weinen, Klagen, Sorgen, Zagen* (April 22, 1714); 13, *Meine Seufzer, meine Tränen* (Jan. 20, 1726); 14, *Wär Gott nicht mit uns diese Zeit* (Jan. 30, 1735); 16, *Herr Gott, dich Loben wir* (Jan. 1, 1726); 17, *Wer Dank opfert, der preiset mich* (Sept. 22, 1726); 18, *Gleichwie der Regen und Schnee vom Himmel fällt* (c.1714); 19, *Es erhub sich ein Streit* (Sept. 29, 1726); 20, *O Ewigkeit, du Donnerwort* (June 11, 1724); 21, *Ich hatte viel Bekummernis* (c.1714); 22, *Jesus nahm zu sich die Zwölfe* (Feb. 7, 1723); 23, *Du wahrer Gott und Davids Sohn* (Feb. 7, 1723); 24, *Ein ungefärbt Gemüte* (June 20, 1723); 25, *Es ist nicht Gesundes an meinem Leibe* (Aug. 29, 1723); 26, *Ach wie flüchtig, ach wie nichtig* (Nov. 19, 1724); 27, *Wer weiss, wie nahe mir mein Ende!* (Oct. 6, 1726); 28, *Gottlob! nun geht das Jahr zu Ende* (Dec. 30, 1725); 29, *Wir danken dir, Gott, wir danken dir* (Aug. 27, 1731); 30, *Freue dich, erlöste Schar* (c.1738); 31, *Der Himmel lacht! die Erde jubilieret* (April 21, 1715); 32, *Liebster Jesu, mein Verlangen* (Jan. 13, 1726); 33, *Allein zu dir, Herr Jesu Christ* (Sept. 3, 1724); 34, *O ewiges Feuer, O Ursprung der Liebe* (based upon 34a; early 1740s); 34a, *O ewiges Feuer, O Ursprung der Liebe* (part of score not extant; 1726); 35, *Geist und Seele wird verwirret* (Sept. 8, 1726); 36, *Schwingt freudig euch empor* (based upon secular cantata 36c; Dec. 2, 1731); 37, *Wer da gläubet und getauft wird* (May 18, 1724); 38, *Aus tiefer Not schrei ich zu dir* (Oct. 29, 1724); 39, *Brich dem Hungrigen dein Brot* (June 23, 1726); 40, *Dazu ist erschienen der Sohn Gottes* (Dec. 26, 1723); 41, *Jesu, nun sei gepreiset* (Jan. 1, 1725); 42, *Am Abend aber desselbigen Sabbats* (April 8, 1725); 43, *Gott fähret auf mit Jauchzen* (May 30, 1726); 44, *Sie werden euch in den Bann tun* (May 21, 1724); 45, *Es ist dir gesagt, Mensch, was gut ist* (Aug. 11, 1726); 46, *Schauet doch und sehet* (Aug. 1, 1723); 47, *Wer sich selbst erhöhet* (Oct. 13, 1726); 48, *Ich elender Mensch, wer wird mich erlösen* (Oct. 3, 1723); 49, *Ich geh und suche mit Verlangen* (Nov. 3, 1726); 50, *Nun ist das Heil und die Kraft* (date unknown); 51, *Jauchzet Gott in allen Landen!* (Sept. 17, 1730); 52, *Falsche Welt, dir trau ich nicht* (Nov. 24, 1726); 54, *Widerstehe doch der Sünde* (July 15, 1714); 55, *Ich armer Mensch, ich Sündenknecht* (Nov. 17, 1726); 56, *Ich will den Kreuzstab gerne tragen* (Oct. 27, 1726); 57, *Selig ist der Mann* (Dec. 26, 1725); 58, *Ach Gott, wie manches Herzeleid* (Jan. 5, 1727); 59, *Wer mich liebet, der wird mein Wort halten* (c.1723–24); 60, *O Ewigkeit, du Donnerwort* (Nov. 7, 1723); 61, *Nun komm, der Heiden Heiland* (1714); 62, *Nun komm, der Heiden Heiland* (Dec. 3, 1724); 63, *Christen, ätzet diesen Tag* (c.1716); 64, *Sehet, welch eine Liebe* (Dec. 27, 1723); 65, *Sie werden aus Saba alle kommen* (Jan. 6, 1724); 66, *Erfreut euch, ihr Herzen* (based upon lost secular cantata 66a; April 10, 1724); 67, *Halt im Gedächtnis Jesum Christ* (April 16, 1724); 68, *Also hat Gott die Welt geliebt* (May 21, 1725); 69, *Lobe den Herrn, meine Seele* (based upon 69a; 1740s); 69a, *Lobe den Herrn, meine Seele* (Aug. 15, 1723); 70, *Wachet! betet! betet! wachet!* (based upon 70a; Nov. 21, 1723); 70a, *Wachet! betet! betet! wachet!* (music not extant; Dec. 6, 1716); 71, *Gott ist mein König* (Feb. 4, 1708); 72, *Alles nur nach Gottes Willen* (Jan. 27, 1726); 73, *Herr, wie du willt, so* schicks mit mir (Jan. 23, 1724); 74, *Wer mich liebet, der wird mein Wort halten* (based partly upon 59; May 20, 1725); 75, *Die Elenden sollen essen* (May 30, 1723); 76, *Die Himmel erzählen die Ehre Gottes* (June 6, 1723); 77, *Du sollt Gott, deinen Herren, lieben* (Aug. 22, 1723); 78, *Jesu, der du meine Seele* (Sept. 10. 1724); 79, *Gott der Herr ist Sonn und Schild* (Oct. 31, 1725); 80, *Ein feste Burg ist unser Gott* (based upon 80a; Oct. 31, 1724); 80a, *Alles, was von Gott geboren* (music not extant; 1715); 80b, *Ein feste Burg ist unser Gott* (Oct. 31, 1723); 81, *Jesus schläft, was soll ich hoffen?* (Jan. 30, 1724); 82, *Ich habe genug* (Feb. 2, 1727); 83, *Erfreute Zeit im neuen Bunde* (Feb. 2, 1724); 84, *Ich bin vergnügt mit meinem Glücke* (Feb. 9, 1727); 85, *Ich bin ein guter Hirt* (April 15, 1725); 86, *Wahrlich, wahrlich, ich sage euch* (May 14, 1724); 87, *Bisher habt ihr nichts gebeten* (May 6, 1725); 88, *Siehe, ich will viel Fischer aussenden* (July 21, 1726); 89, *Was soll ich aus dir machen, Ephraim?* (Oct. 24, 1723); 90, *Es reisset euch ein schrecklich Ende* (Nov. 14, 1723); 91, *Gelobet seist du, Jesu Christ* (Dec. 25, 1724); 92, *Ich hab in Gottes Herz und Sinn* (Jan. 28, 1725); 93, *Wer nur den lieben Gott lässt walten* (July 9, 1724); 94, *Was frag ich nach der Welt* (Aug. 6, 1724); 95, *Christus, der ist mein Leben* (Sept. 12, 1723); 96, *Herr Christ, der einge Gottessohn* (Oct. 8, 1724); 97, *In allen meinen Taten* (1734); 98, *Was Gott tut, das ist wohlgetan* (Nov. 10, 1726); 99, *Was Gott tut, das ist wohlgetan* (Sept. 17, 1724); 100, *Was Gott tut, das ist wohlgetan* (c.1732–35); 101, *Nimm von uns, Herr, du treuer Gott* (Aug. 13, 1724); 102, *Herr, deine Augen sehen nach dem Glauben* (Aug. 25, 1726); 103, *Ihr werdet weinen und heulen* (April 22, 1725); 104, *Du Hirte Israel* (April 23, 1724); 105, *Herr, gehe nicht ins Gericht* (July 25, 1723); 106, *Gottes Ziet ist die allerbeste Zeit* (c.1707); 107, *Was willst du dich betrüben* (July 23, 1724); 108, *Es ist euch gut, dass ich hingehe* (April 29, 1725); 109, *Ich glaube, lieber Herr, hilf meinem Unglauben!* (Oct. 17, 1723); 110, *Unser Mund sei voll Lachens* (Dec. 25, 1725); 111, *Was mein Gott will, das g'schen allzeit* (Jan. 21, 1725); 112, *Der Herr ist mein getreuer Hirt* (April 8, 1731); 113, *Herr Jesu Christ, du höchstes Gut* (Aug. 20, 1724); 114, *Ach, lieben Christen, seid getrost* (Oct. 1, 1724); 115, *Mache dich, mein Geist, bereit* (Nov. 5, 1724); 116, *Du Friedefürst, Herr Jesu Christ* (Nov. 26, 1724); 117, *Sei Lob und Ehr dem höchsten Gut* (c.1728–31); 119, *Preise, Jerusalem, den Herrn* (Aug. 30, 1723); 120, *Gott, man lobet dich in der Stille* (c.1728–29); 120a, *Herr Gott, Beherrscher aller Dinge* (based upon 120; part of score not extant; c.1729); 120b, *Gott, man lobet dich in der Stille* (based upon 120; music not extant; 1730); 121, *Christum wir sollen loben schon* (Dec. 26, 1724); 122, *Das neugeborne Kindelein* (Dec. 31, 1724); 123, *Liebster Immanuel, Herzog der Frommen* (Jan. 6, 1725); 124, *Meinen Jesum lass ich nicht* (Jan. 7, 1725); 125, *Mit Fried und Freud ich fahr dahin* (Feb. 2, 1725); 126, *Erhalt uns, Herr, bei deinem Wort* (Feb. 4, 1725); 127, *Herr Jesu Christ, wahr' Mensch und Gott* (Feb. 11, 1725); 128, *Auf Christi Himmelfahrt allein* (May 10, 1725); 129, *Gelobet sei der Herr, mein Gott* (c.1726–27); 130, *Herr Gott, dich loben alle wir* (Sept. 29, 1724); 131, *Aus der Tiefen rufe ich, Herr,* zu dir (1707); 132, *Bereitet die Wege, bereitet die Bahn!* (1715); 133, *Ich freue mich in dir* (Dec. 27, 1724); 134, *Ein Herz, das seinen Jesum lebend weiss* (based upon secular contata 134a; April 11, 1724); 135, *Ach Herr, mich armen Sünder* (June 25, 1724); 136, *Erforsche mich, Gott, und erfahre mein Herz* (July 18, 1723); 137, *Lobe den Herren, den mächtigen König der Ehren* (Aug. 19, 1725); 138, *Warum betrübst du dich, mein Herz?* (Sept. 5, 1723); 139, *Wohl dem, der sich auf seinen Gott* (Nov. 12, 1724); 140, *Wachet auf, ruft uns die Stimme* (Nov. 25, 1731); 144, *Nimm, was dein ist, und gehe hin* (Feb. 6, 1724); 145, *Ich lebe, mein Herze, zu deinem Ergötzen* (c. 1729); 146, *Wir müssen durch viel Trübsal* (c.1726–28); 147, *Herz und Mund und Tat und Leben* (based upon 147a; July 2, 1723); 147a, *Herz und Mund und Tat und Leben* (not extant; Dec. 20, 1716); 148, *Bringet dem Herrn Ehre seines Namens* (Sept. 19, 1723); 149, *Man singet mit Freuden vom Sieg* (c.1728–29); 150, *Nach dir, Herr, verlanget mich* (c.1708–9); 151, *Süsser Trost, mein Jesus kommt* (Dec. 27, 1725); 152, *Tritt auf die Glaubensbahn* (Dec. 30, 1714); 153, *Schau, lieber Gott, wie meine Feind* (Jan. 2, 1724); 154, *Mein liebster Jesus ist verloren* (Jan. 9, 1724); 155, *Mein Gott, wie lang, ach lange* (Jan. 19, 1716); 156, *Ich steh mit einem Fuss im Grabe* (Jan. 23, 1729); 157, *Ich lasse dich nicht, du segnest mich denn* (Feb. 6, 1727); 158, *Der Friede sei mit dir* (date unknown); 159, *Sehet, wir gehn hinauf gen Jerusalem* (Feb. 27, 1729); 161, *Komm, du süsse Todesstunde* (Oct. 6, 1715); 162, *Ach! ich sehe, jetzt, da ich zur Hochzeit gehe* (Nov. 3, 1715); 163, *Nur jedem das Seine* (Nov. 24, 1715); 164, *Ihr, die ihr euch von Christo nennet* (Aug. 26, 1725); 165, *O heilges Geist- und Wasserbad* (June 16, 1715); 166, *Wo gehest du hin?* (May 7, 1724); 167, *Ihr Menschen, rühmet Gottes Liebe* (June 24, 1723); 168, *Tue Rechnung! Donnerwort* (July 29, 1725); 169, *Gott soll allein mein Herze haben* (Oct. 20, 1726); 170, *Vergnügte Ruh', beliebte Seelenlust* (July 28, 1726); 171, *Gott, wie dein Name, so ist auch dein Ruhm* (c.1729); 172, *Erschallet, ihr Lieder* (May 20, 1714); 173, *Erhöhtes Fleisch und Blut* (based upon secular contata 173a; May 29, 1724); 174, *Ich liebe den Höchsten von ganzem Gemüte* (June 6, 1729); 175, *Er rufet seinen Schafen mit Namen* (May 22, 1725); 176, *Es ist ein trotzig, und versagt Ding* (May 27, 1725); 177, *Ich ruf zu dir, Herr Jesu Christ* (July 6, 1732); 178, *Wo Gott der Herr nicht bei uns hält* (July 30, 1724); 179, *Siehe zu, dass deine Gottesfurcht* (Aug. 8, 1723); 180, *Schmücke dich, o liebe Seele* (Oct. 22, 1724); 181, *Leichtgesinnte Flattergeister* (Feb. 13, 1724); 182, *Himmelskönig, sei willkommen* (1714); 183, *Sie werden euch in den Bann tun* (May 13, 1725); 184, *Erwünschtes Freudenlicht* (based upon lost secular cantata 184a; May 30, 1724); 185, *Barmherziges Herze der ewigen Liebe* (July 14, 1715); 186, *Ärgre dich, o Seele, nicht* (based upon 186a; July 11, 1723); 186a, *Ärgre dich, o Seele, nicht* (not extant; Dec. 13, 1716); 187, *Es wartet alles auf dich* (Aug. 4, 1726); 188, *Ich habe meine Zuversicht* (c.1728); 190, *Singet dem Herrn ein neues Lied!* (part of score not extant; Jan. 1, 1724); 190a, *Singet dem Herrn ein neues Lied!* (based upon 190; not extant; 1730); 191, *Gloria in excelsis Deo* (based upon 232, Mass in B minor; c.1740); 192, *Nun danket alle Gott* (part of score not extant; 1730); 193, *Ihr Tore zu Zion* (c.1727); 194, *Höchsterwünschtes Freudenfest* (based upon lost secular cantata 194a; Nov. 2, 1723); 195, *Dem Gerechten muss das Licht* (c.1737); 196, *Der Herr denket an uns* (c.1708); 197, *Gott ist unsre Zuversicht* (c.1742); 197a, *Ehre sie Gott in der Höhe* (part of score not extant, c.1728); 199, *Mein Herze schwimmt im Blut* (Aug. 12, 1714); 200, *Bekennen will ich seinen Namen* (fragment only extant; c.1742). BWV numbers have been assigned to the following lost or incomplete cantatas: 223, *Meine Seele soll Gott loben* (not extant; date unknown); 224a, *Klagt, Kinder, klagt es aller Welt* (music not extant; March 24, 1729); Anh., 1, *Gesegnet ist die Zuversicht* (not extant; date unknown); Anh. 2, fragment only; Anh. 3, *Gott, gib dein Gerichte dem Könige* (music not extant; 1730) Anh. 4, *Wünschet Jerusalem Glück* (music not extant; c.1727); Anh. 4a, *Wünschet Jerusalem Glück* (music not extant; 1730); Anh. 5, *Lobet den Herrn, alle seine Heerscharen* (music not extant; Dec. 10, 1718); Anh. 14, *Sein Segen fliesst daher wie ein Strom* (music not extant; Feb. 12, 1725); Anh. 15, *Siehe, der Hüter Israel* (not extant; April 27, 1724); Anh. 17, *Mein Gott, nimm die gerechte Seele* (not extant; date unknown); 1,045, title unknown (autograph fragment only extant; c.1742); also the following without BWV numbers: *Herrscher des Himmels, König der Ehren* (final chorus only, based upon secular cantata 208, extant; Aug. 29, 1740); *Ich bin ein Pilgrim auf der Welt* (fragment of 4th movement only extant; April 18, 1729); *Ihr wallenden Wolken* (not extant; date unknown); *Leb ich oder leb ich nicht* (music not extant; May 19, 1715); *Sie werden euch in den Bann tun* (6-bar sketch only); etc. BWV numbers have been assigned to the following doubtful and spurious cantatas: 15, *Denn du wirst meine Seele* (by J.L. Bach); 53, *Schlage doch, gewünschte Stunde* (by G.M. Hoffmann); 141, *Das ist je gewisslich wahr* (by Telemann); 142, *Uns ist ein Kind geboren* (doubtful); 143, *Lobe den Herrn, meine Seele* (doubtful); 160, *Ich weiss, dass mein Erlöser lebt* (by Telemann); 189, *Meine Seele rühmt und preist* (doubtful); 217, *Gedenke, Herr, wie es uns gehet* (spurious); 218, *Gott der Hoffnung erfülle euch* (by Telemann); 219, *Siehe, es hat überwunden der Löwe* (by Telemann); 220, *Lobt ihn mit Herz und Munde* (spurious); 221, *Wer sucht die Pracht, wer wünscht den Glanz* (spurious); 222, *Mein Odem ist schwach* (by J.E. Bach); Anh. 16, *Schliesset die Gruft! ihr Trauerglocken* (not extant; doubtful); also without BWV number, *Siehe, eine Jungfrau ist schwanger* (doubtful).

SECULAR CANTATAS: 22 are extant in full: 30a, *Angenehmes Wiederau, freue dich* (Sept. 28, 1737); 36b, *Die Freude reget sich* (c.1735); 36c, *Schwingt freudig euch empor* (1725); 134a, *Die Zeit, die Tag und Jahre macht* (Jan. 1, 1719); 173a, Durchlauchster Leopold (c.1722); 198, *Trauer Ode: Lass, Fürstin, lass noch einen Strahl* (Oct. 17, 1727); 201, *Der Streit zwischen Phoebus und Pan: Geschwinde, ihr wirbeln die Winde* (c.1729); 202, *Weichet nur, betrübte Schatten* (c.1718–23); 203, *Amore traditore* (date unknown); 204, *Ich bin in mir vergnügt*

(c.1726–27); 205, *Der zufriedengestellte Äolus: Zerreisset, zersprenget, zertrümmert die Gruft* (Aug. 3, 1725); 206, *Schleicht, spielende Wellen* (Oct. 7, 1736); 207, *Vereinigte Zwietracht der wechselnden Saiten* (Dec. 11, 1726); 207a, *Auf, schmetternde Töne* (Aug. 3, 1735); 208, *Was mir behagt, ist nur die muntre Jagd!* (c.1713); 209, *Non sa che sia dolore* (c.1734); 210, *O holder Tag, erwünschte Zeit* (c.1740); 211, *Schweigt stille, plaudert nicht* (*Coffee Cantata*; c.1734–35); 212, *Mer hahn en neue Oberkeet* (*Peasant Cantata*; Aug. 30, 1742); 213, *Hercules auf dem Scheidewege: Lasst uns sorgen, lasst uns wachen* (Sept. 5, 1733); 214, *Tönet, ihr Pauken! Erschallet, Trompeten!* (Dec. 8, 1733); 215, *Preise dein Glücke, gesegnetes Sachsen* (Oct. 5, 1734). BWV numbers have been assigned to the following lost or incomplete cantatas: 36a, *Steigt freudig in die Luft* (music not extant; Nov. 30, 1726); 66a, *Der Himmel dacht auf Anhalts Ruhm und Glück* (music not extant; Dec. 10, 1718); 184a, title unknown (not extant); 193a, *Ihr Häuser des Himmels, ihr scheinenden Lichter* (music not extant; Aug. 3, 1727); 194a, title unknown (not extant); 205a, *Blast Lärmen, ihr Feinde!* (based upon 205; music not extant; Feb. 19, 1734); 208a, *Was mir behagt, ist nur die muntre Jagd!* (music not extant; c.1740–42); 210a, *O angenehme Melodei!* (music not extant; c.1738–40); 216, *Vergnügte Pleissenstadt* (only partially extant; Feb. 5, 1728); 216a, *Erwählte Pleissenstadt* (music not extant; c.1728); 249a, *Entfliehet, verschwindet, entweichet, ihr Sorgen* (music not extant; Feb. 23, 1725); 249b, *Die Feier des Genius: Verjaget, zerstreuet, zerrüttet, ihr Sterne* (music not extant; Aug. 25, 1726); Anh. 6, *Dich loben die lieblichen Strahlen* (music not extant; Jan. 1, 1720); Anh. 7, *Heut ist gewiss ein guter Tag* (music not extant; Dec. 10, 1720); Anh. 8, title unknown (not extant); Anh. 9, *Entfernet euch, ihr heitern Sterne* (music not extant; May 12, 1727); Anh. 10, *So kämpfet nur, ihr muntern Töne* (music not extant; Aug. 25, 1731); Anh. 11, *Es lebe der König, der Vater im Lande* (music not extant; Aug. 3, 1732); Anh. 12, *Frohes Volk, vergnügte Sachsen* (based upon Anh. 18; music not extant; Aug. 3, 1733); Anh. 13, *Willkommen! Ihr herrschenden Götter* (music not extant; April 28, 1738); Anh. 18, *Froher Tag, verlangte Stunden* (music not extant; June 5, 1732); Anh. 19, *Thomana sass annoch betrübt* (music not extant; Nov. 21, 1734); Anh. 20, title unknown (not extant); also, without BWV number, *Auf! süss entzückende Gewalt* (music not extant; Nov. 27, 1725).

OTHER CHURCH MUSIC: 232, Mass in B minor (assembled c.1747–49 from music previously composed by Bach); 233, 233a, 234–36, 4 *missae breves:* F major (Kyrie in F major), A major, G minor, G major (late 1730s); 237–41, 5 settings of the Sanctus: C major, D major, D minor, G major, D major (although preserved in Bach's own hand, these appear to be arrangements of works by other composers, 238 excepted); 243a, Magnificat in E-flat major (including 4 Christmas texts: *Vom Himmel hoch, Freut euch und jubiliert, Gloria in excelsis, Virga Jesse floruit;* Dec. 25, 1723); 243, a revision of the preceding, without Christmas texts, as Magnificat in D major (c.1728–31); 244, *Matthäuspassion* (St. Matthew

Passion; first perf. April 11, 1727, or April 15, 1729); 245, *Johannespassion (St. John Passion;* April 7, 1724; later revised); 248, *Weihnachtsoratorium (Christmas Oratorio),* 6 cantatas for Christmas to Epiphany: *Jauchzet, frohlocket, auf preiset die Tage* (Dec. 25, 1734), *Und es waren Hirten in derselben Gegend* (Dec. 26, 1734), *Herrscher des Himmels, erhöre das Lallen* (Dec. 27, 1734), *Fallt mit Danken, fallt mit Loben* (Jan. 1, 1735), *Ehre sei dir, Gott, gesungen* (Jan. 2, 1735), *Herr, wenn die stolzen Feinde schnauben* (Jan. 6, 1735); 249, *Easter Oratorio* (first perf. as a cantata, April 1, 1725; revised as an oratorio 1732–35); motets, including 225, *Singet dem Herrn ein Neues Lied* (May 12, 1727), 226, *Der Geist hilft unser Schwachheit auf* (Oct. 24, 1729), 227, *Jesu, meine Freude* (July 18, 1723), 228, *Fürchte dich nicht* (Feb. 4, 1726), 229, *Komm, Jesu, komm!* (March 26, 1730), 230, *Lobet den Herrn alle Heiden* (date unknown). Also 247, *St. Mark Passion* (score and parts not extant; March 23, 1731; partial reconstruction from other works made by D. Hellmann, Stuttgart, 1964); 246, *St. Luke Passion* (spurious).

CHORALES: 3 wedding chorales for 4 Voices: 250, *Was Gott tut das ist wohlgetan;* 251, *Sei Lob und Ehr' dem höchsten Gut;* 252, *Nun danket alle Gott.* Also, 186 arrangements for 4 Voices: 253, *Ach bleib bei uns, Herr Jesu Christ;* 254, *Ach Gott, erhör' mein Seufzen;* 255, *Ach Gott und Herr;* 256, *Ach lieben Christen, seid getrost;* 259, *Ach, was soll ich Sünder machen;* 260, *Allein Gott in der Höh' sei Ehr';* 261, *Allein zu dir, Herr Jesu Christ;* 262, *Alle Menschen müssen sterben;* 263, *Alles ist an Gottes Segen;* 264, *Als der gütige Gott;* 265, *Als Jesus Christus in der Nacht;* 266, *Als vierzig Tag nach Ostern;* 267, *An Wasserflüssen Babylon;* 268, *Auf, auf, mein Herz, und du mein ganzer Sinn;* 269, *Aus meines Herzens Grunde;* 270, *Befiehl du deine Wege;* 271, *Befiehl du deine Wege;* 273, *Christ, der du bist der helle Tag;* 274, *Christe, der du bist Tag und Licht;* 275, *Christe, du Beistand deiner Kreuzgemeinde;* 276, *Christ ist erstanden;* 277, *Christ lag in Todesbanden;* 278, *Christ lag in Todesbanden;* 279, *Christ lag in Todesbanden;* 280, *Christ, unser Herr, zum Jordan kam;* 281, *Christus, der ist mein Leben;* 282, *Christus, der ist mein Leben;* 283, *Christus, der uns selig macht;* 284, *Christus ist erstanden, hat überwunden;* 285, *Da der Herr Christ zu Tische sass;* 286, *Danket dem Herren;* 287, *Dank sei Gott in der Höhe;* 288, *Das alte Jahr vergangen ist;* 289, *Das alte Jahr vergangen ist;* 290, *Das walt' Gott Vater und Gott Sohn;* 291, *Das walt' mein Gott, Vater, Sohn und heiliger Geist;* 292, *Den Vater dort oben;* 293, *Der du bist drei in Einigkeit;* 294, *Der Tag, der ist so freudenreich;* 295, *Das heil'gen Geistes reiche Gnad';* 296, *Die Nacht ist kommen;* 297, *Die Sonn' hat sich mit ihrem Glanz;* 298, *Dies sind die heil'gen zehn Gebot';* 299, *Dir, dir, Jehova, will ich singen;* 300, *Du grosser Schmerzensmann;* 301, *Du, o schönes Weltgebäude;* 302, *Ein' feste Burg ist unser Gott;* 303, *Ein' feste Burg ist unser Gott;* 304, *Eins ist Not! ach Herr, dies Eine;* 305, *Erbarm' dich mein, o, Herre Gott;* 306, *Erstanden ist der heil'ge Christ;* 307, *Es ist gewisslich an der Zeit;* 308, *Es spricht der Unweisen*

Mund wohl; 309, *Es stehn vor Gottes Throne;* 310, *Es wird schier der letzte Tag herkommen;* 311, *Es woll' uns Gott genädig sein;* 312, *Es woll' uns Gott genädig sein;* 327, *Für deinen Thron tret' ich hiermit;* 313, *Für Freuden lasst uns springen;* 314, *Gelobet seist du, Jesu Christ;* 315, *Gib dich zufrieden und sei stille;* 316, *Gott, der du selber bist das Licht;* 317, *Gott, der Vater, wohn' uns bei;* 318, *Gottes Sohn ist kommen;* 319, *Gott hat das Evangelium;* 320, *Gott lebet noch;* 321, *Gottlob, es geht nunmehr zu Ende;* 322, *Gott sei gelobet und gebenedeiet;* 323, *Gott sei uns gnädig;* 325, *Heilig, heilig;* 326, *Herr Gott, dich loben alle wir;* 328, *Herr Gott, dich loben wir;* 329, *Herr, ich denk' an jene Zeit;* 330, *Herr, ich habe missgehandelt;* 331, *Herr, ich habe missgehandelt;* 332, *Herr Jesu Christ, dich zu uns wend';* 333, *Herr Jesu Christ, du hast bereit't;* 334, *Herr Jesu Christ, du höchstes Gut;* 335, *Herr Jesu Christ, mein's Lebens Licht;* 336, *Herr Jesu Christ, wahr'r Mensch und Gott;* 337, *Herr, nun lass in Frieden;* 338, *Herr, straf mich nicht in deinem Zorn;* 339, *Herr, wie du willst, so schick's mit mir;* 340, *Herzlich lieb hab ich dich, o Herr;* 341, *Heut' ist, o Mensch, ein grosser Trauertag;* 342, *Heut' triumphieret Gottes Sohn;* 343, *Hilf, Gott, dass mir's gelinge;* 344, *Hilf, Herr Jesu, lass gelingen;* 345, *Ich bin ja, Herr, in deiner Macht;* 346, *Ich dank' dir, Gott, für all' Wohltat;* 347, *Ich dank' dir, lieber Herre;* 348, *Ich dank' dir, lieber Herre;* 349, *Ich dank' dis schon durch deinen Sohn;* 350, *Ich danke dir, o Gott, in deinem Throne;* 351, *Ich hab' mein' Sach' Gott heimgestellt;* 352, *Jesu, der du meine Seele;* 353, *Jesu, der du meine Seele;* 354, *Jesu, der du meine Seele;* 355, *Jesu, der du selbsten wohl;* 356, *Jesu, du mein liebstes Leben;* 357, *Jesu, du mein bein;* 358, *Jesu, meine Freude;* 359, *Jesu meiner Seelen Wonne;* 360, *Jesu meiner Seelen Wonne;* 361, *Jesu, meines Herzens Freud';* 362, *Jesu, nun sei gepreiset;* 363, *Jesus Christus, unser Heiland;* 364, *Jesus Christus, unser Heiland;* 365, *Jesus, meine Zuversicht;* 366, *Ihr Gestirn', ihr hohlen Lüfte;* 367, *In allen meinen Taten;* 368, *In dulci jubilo;* 369, *Keinen hat Gott verlassen;* 370, *Komm, Gott Schöpfer, heiliger Geist;* 371, *Kyrie, Gott Vater in Ewigkeit;* 372, *Lass, o Herr, dein Ohr sich neigen;* 373, *Liebster Jesu, wir sind hier;* 374, *Lobet den Herren, denn er ist freundlich;* 375, *Lobt Gott, ihr Christen, allzugleich;* 376, *Lobt Gott, ihr Christen, allzugleich;* 377, *Mach's mit mir, Gott, nach deiner Güt';* 378, *Meine Augen schliess' ich jetzt;* 379, *Meinen Jesum lass' ich nicht, Jesus;* 380, *Meinen Jesum lass' ich nicht, weil;* 322, *Meine Seele erhebt den Herrn;* 381, *Meines Lebens letzte Zeit;* 382, *Mit Fried' und Freud' ich fahr' dahin;* 383, *Mitten wir im Leben sind;* 384, *Nicht so traurig, nicht so sehr;* 385, *Nun bitten wir den heiligen Geist;* 386, *Nun danket alle Gott;* 387, *Nun freut euch, Gottes Kinder all';* 388, *Nun freut euch, lieben Christen, g'mein;* 389, *Nun lob', mein' Seel', den Herren;* 390, *Nun lob', mein' Seel', den Herren;* 391, *Nun preiset alle Gottes Barmherzigkeit;* 392, *Nun ruhen alle Wälder;* 393, *O Welt, sieh hier dein Leben;* 394, *O Welt, sieh hier dein Leben;* 395, *O Welt, sieh hier dein Leben;* 396, *Nun sich der Tag geendet hat;* 397, *O Ewigkeit, du Donnerwort;* 398, *O Gott, du frommer Gott;* 399, *O Gott, du frommer Gott;* 400, *O*

Bach

Herzensangst, o Bangigkeit; 401, *O Lamm Gottes, unschuldig;* 402, *O Mensch, bewein' dein' Sünde gross;* 403, *O Mensch, schau Jesum Christum an;* 404, *O Traurigkeit, o Herzeleid;* 393, *O Welt, sieh hier dein Leben;* 394, *O Welt, sieh hier dein Leben;* 395, *O Welt, sieh hier dein Leben;* 405, *O wie selig seid ihr doch, ihr Frommen;* 406, *O wie selig seid ihr doch, ihr Frommen;* 407, *O wir armen Sünder;* 408, *Schaut, ihr Sünder;* 409, *Seelen-Bräutigam;* 410, *Sei gegrüsset, Jesu gütig;* 411, *Singet dem Herrn ein neues Lied;* 412, *So gibst du nun, mein Jesu, gute Nacht;* 413, *Sollt' ich meinem Gott nicht singen;* 414, *Uns ist ein Kindlein heut' gebor'n;* 415, *Valet will ich dir geben;* 416, *Vater unser im Himmelreich;* 417, *Von Gott will ich nicht lassen;* 418, *Von Gott will ich nicht lassen;* 419, *Von Gott will ich nicht lassen;* 257, *Wär' Gott nicht mit uns diese Zeit;* 420, *Warum betrübst du dich, mein Herz;* 421, *Warum betrübst du dich, mein Herz;* 422, *Warum sollt' ich mich denn grämen;* 423, *Was betrübst du dich, mein Herze;* 424, *Was bist du doch, o Seele, so betrübet;* 425, *Was willst du dich, o meine Seele;* 426, *Weltlich Ehr' und zeitlich Gut;* 427, *Wenn ich in Angst und Not;* 428, *Wenn mein Stündlein vorhanden ist;* 429, *Wenn mein Stündlein vorhanden ist;* 430, *Wenn mein Stündlein vorhanden ist;* 431, *Wenn wir in höchsten Nöten sein;* 432, *Wenn wir in höchsten Nöten sein;* 433, *Wer Gott vertraut, hat wohl gebaut;* 434, *Wer nur den lieben Gott lässt walten;* 435, *Wie bist du, Seele, in mir so gar betrübt;* 436, *Wie schön leuchtet der Morgenstern;* 437, *Wir glauben all' an einen Gott;* 258, *Wo Gott der Herr nicht bei uns hält;* 438, *Wo Gott zum Haus nicht gibt sein' Gunst.*

SACRED SONGS: 69 for One Voice with Basso Continuo only: 439, *Ach, dass nicht die letzte Stunde;* 440, *Auf, auf! die rechte Zeit ist hier;* 441, *Auf, auf! mein Herz, mit Freuden;* 422, *Beglückter Stand getreuer Seelen;* 443, *Beschränkt, ihr Weisen dieser Welt;* 444, *Brich entzwei, mein armes Herze;* 445, *Brunnquell aller Güter;* 446, *Der lieben Sonnen Licht und Pracht;* 447, *Der Tag ist hin, die Sonne gehet nieder;* 448, *Der Tag mit seinem Lichte;* 449, *Dich bet' ich an, mein höchster Gott;* 450, *Die bittre Leidenszeit beginnet abermal;* 451, *Die goldne Sonne, voll Freud' und Wonne;* 452, *Dir, dir Jehovah, will ich singen* (melody by Bach); 453, *Eins ist Not! ach Herr, dies Eine;* 454, *Ermuntre dich, mein schwacher Geist;* 455, *Erwürgtes Lamm, das die verwahrten Siegel;* 456, *Es glänzet der Christen;* 457, *Es ist nun aus mit meinem Leben;* 458, *Es ist vollbracht! vergiss ja nicht;* 459, *Es kostet viel, ein Christ zu sein;* 460, *Gieb dich zufrieden und sei stille;* 461, *Gott lebet noch; Seele, was verzagst du doch?;* 462, *Gott, wie gross ist deine Güte;* 463, *Herr, nicht schicke deine Rache;* 464, *Ich bin ja, Herr, in deiner Macht;* 465, *Ich freue mich in der;* 466, *Ich halte treulich still und liebe;* 467, *Ich lass' dich nicht;* 468, *Ich liebe Jesum alle Stund';* 469, *Ich steh' an deiner Krippen hier;* 476, *Ihr Gestirn', ihr hohen Lüfte;* 471, *Jesu, deine Liebeswunden;* 470, *Jesu, Jesu, du bist mein;* 472, *Jesu, meines Glaubens Zier;* 473, *Jesu, meines Herzens Freud';* 474, *Jesus ist das schönste Licht;* 475, *Jesus, unser Trost und Leben;* 477, *Kein Stündlein geht dahin;* 478, *Komm, süsser*

Tod, komm, sel'ge Ruh'! (melody by Bach); 479, *Kommt, Seelen, dieser Tag;* 480, *Kommt wieder aus der finstern Gruft;* 481, *Lasset uns mit Jesu ziehen;* 482, *Liebes Herz, bedenke doch;* 483, *Liebster Gott, wann werd' ich sterben?;* 484, *Liebster Herr Jesu! wo bleibest du so lange?;* 485, *Liebster Immanuel, Herzog der Frommen;* 488, *Meines Lebens letzte Zeit;* 486, *Mein Jesu, dem die Seraphinen;* 487, *Mein Jesu! was für Seelenweh;* 489, *Nicht so traurig, nicht so sehr;* 490, *Nur mein Jesus ist mein Leben;* 491, *O du Liebe meine Liebe;* 492, *O finstre Nacht;* 493, *O Jesulein süss, o Jesulein mild;* 494, *O liebe Seele, zieh' die Sinnen;* 495, *O wie selig seid ihr doch, ihr Frommen;* 496, *Sellen-Bräutigam, Jesu, Gottes Lamm!;* 497, *Seelenweide, meine Freude;* 499, *Sei gegrüsset, Jesu gütig;* 498, *Selig, wer an Jesum denkt;* 500, *So gehst du nun, mein Jesu, hin;* 501, *So giebst du nun, mein Jesu, gute Nacht;* 502, *So wünsch' ich mir zu guter Letzt;* 503, *Steh' ich bei meinem Gott;* 504, *Vergiss mein nicht, dass ich dein nicht;* 505, *Vergiss mein nicht, vergiss mein nicht* (melody by Bach); 506, *Was bist du doch, o Seele, so betrübet;* 507, *Wo ist mein Schäflein, das ich liebe.* BWV numbers have been assigned to the following sacred songs, which are most likely spurious: 519, *Hier lieg' ich nun;* 520, *Das walt' mein Gott;* 521, *Gott mein Herz dir Dank;* 522, *Meine Seele, lass es gehen;* 523, *Ich gnüge mich an meinem Stande.*

FOR ORGAN: 525-30, 6 trio sonatas: E-flat major, C minor, D minor, E minor, G major; 531, Prelude and Fugue in C major; 532, Prelude and Fugue in D major; 533, Prelude and Fugue in E minor; 534, Prelude and Fugue in F minor; 535, Prelude and Fugue in G minor; 536, Prelude and Fugue in A major; 537, Fantasia and Fugue in C minor; 538, Toccata and Fugue in D minor, "Dorian"; 539, Prelude and Fugue in D minor; 540, Toccata and Fugue in F major; 541, Prelude and Fugue in G major; 542, Fantasia and Fugue in G minor; 543, Prelude and Fugue in A minor; 544, Prelude and Fugue in B minor; 545, Prelude and Fugue in C major; 546, Prelude and Fugue in C minor; 547, Prelude and Fugue in C major; 548, Prelude and Fugue in E minor; 549, Prelude and Fugue in C minor; 550, Prelude and Fugue in G major; 551, Prelude and Fugue in A minor; 552, Prelude and Fugue in E-flat major, "St. Anne"; 562, Fantasia and Fugue in C minor; 563, Fantasia in B minor; 564, Toccata, Adagio, and Fugue in C major; 565, Toccata and Fugue in D minor; 566, Prelude and Fugue in E major; 568, Prelude in G major; 569, Prelude in A minor; 570, Fantasia in C major; 572, Fantasia in G major; 573, Fantasia in C major; 574, Fugue in C minor (on a theme by Legrenzi); 575, Fugue in C minor; 578, Fugue in G minor; 579, Fugue in B minor (on a theme by Corelli); 582, Passacaglia in C minor; 583, Trio in D minor; 586, Trio in G major (Bach's organ transcription of a work by Telemann); 587, Aria in F major (transcription from Couperin); 588, Canzona in D minor; 590, Pastorale in F major; 592–97, 6 concertos: G major (arrangement of a concerto by Duke Johann Ernst of Saxe-Weimar), A minor (arrangement of Vivaldi's op. 3, no. 8), C major (arrangement of Vivaldi's op. 7, no. 5), C major (arrangement of a concerto by

Duke Johann Ernst of Saxe-Weimar), D minor (arrangement of Vivaldi's op. 3, no. 11), E-flat major (arrangement of a concerto by an unknown composer); 598, Pedal-Exercitium; 802–5, 4 duettos: E minor, F major, G major, A minor; 1,027a, Trio in G major (transcription from final movement of sonata 1,027). BWV numbers have been assigned to the following doubtful and spurious works: 131a, Fugue in G minor (spurious); 561, Fantasia and Fugue in A minor (spurious); 567, Prelude in C major (spurious); 571 Fantasia in G major (spurious); 576, Fugue in G major (spurious); 577, Fugue in G major (spurious); 580, Fugue in D major (spurious); 581, Fugue in G major (spurious); 584, Trio in G minor (doubtful); 585, Trio in C minor (by J.F. Fasch); 589, Allabreve in D major (doubtful); 591, Kleines harmonisches Labyrinth (doubtful); also 8 brief preludes and fugues: C major, D minor, E minor, F major, G major, G minor, A minor, B-flat major (doubtful).

OTHER ORGAN MUSIC: 45 Chorales in Das Orgel-Büchlein: 599, *Nun komm, der Heiden Heiland;* 600, *Gott, durch deine Güte;* 601, *Herr Christ, der ein'ge Gottes-Sohn;* 602, *Lob sei dem allmächtigen Gott;* 603, *Puer natus in Bethlehem;* 604, *Gelobet seist du, Jesu Christ;* 605, *Der Tag, der ist so freudenreich;* 606, *Vom Himmel hoch, da komm' ich her;* 607, *Vom Himmel kam der Engel Schar;* 608, *In dulci jubilo;* 609, *Lobt Gott, ihr Christen, allzugleich;* 610, *Jesu, meine Freude;* 611, *Christum wir sollen loben schon;* 612, *Wir Christenleut';* 613, *Helft mir Gottes Güte preisen;* 614, *Das alte Jahr vergangen ist;* 615, *In dir ist Freude;* 616, *Mit Fried' und Freud' ich fahr dahin;* 617, *Herr Gott, nun schleuss den Himmel auf;* 618, *O Lamm Gottes unschuldig;* 619, *Christe, du Lamm Gottes;* 620, *Christus, der uns selig macht;* 621, *Da Jesus an dem Kreuze stund;* 622, *O Mensch, bewein' dein' Sünde gross;* 623, *Wir danken dir, Herr Jesu Christ;* 624, *Hilf Gott, dass mir's gelinge;* 625, *Christ lag in Todesbanden;* 626, *Jesus Christus, unser Heiland;* 627, *Christ ist erstanden;* 628, *Erstanden ist der heil'ge Christ;* 629, *Erschienen ist der herrliche Tag;* 630, *Heut' triumphieret Gottes Sohn;* 631, *Komm, Gott Schöpfer, heiliger Geist;* 632, *Herr Jesu Christ, dich zu uns wend';* 633, *Liebster Jesu, wir sind hier;* 635, *Dies sind die heil'gen zehn Gebot';* 636, *Vater unser im Himmelreich;* 637, *Durch Adam's Fall ist ganz verderbt;* 638, *Es ist dos Heil uns Kommen her;* 639, *Ich ruf' zu dir, Herr Jesu Christ;* 640, *In dich hab' ich gehoffet, Herr;* 641, *Wenn wir in höchsten Nöten sein;* 642, *Wer nur den lieben Gott lässt walten;* 643, *Alle Menschen müssen sterben;* 644, *Ach wie nichtig, ach wie flüchtig;* 6 chorales publ. by J.G. Schübler, hence the name Schübler-Chorales: 645, *Wachet auf, ruft uns die Stimme* (based upon Cantata 140, 4th movement), 646, *Wo soll ich fliehen hin* (source unknown), 647, *Wer nur den lieben Gott lässt walten* (based upon Cantata 93, 4th movement), 648, *Meine Seele erhebet den Herren* (based upon Cantata 10, 5th movement), 649, *Ach bleib' bei uns, Herr Jesu Christ* (based upon Cantata 6, 3rd movement), 650, *Kommst du nun, Jesu, vom Himmel herunter* (based upon Cantata 137, 2nd movement); 651, *Fantasia super Komm, Heiliger Geist;* 652, *Komm, Hei-*

liger Geist; 653, *An Wasserflüssen Babylon;* 654, *Schmücke, dich, o liebe Seele;* 655, *Trio super Herr Jesu Christ, dich zu uns wend;* 656, *O Lamm Gottes, unschuldig;* 657, *Nun danket alle Gott;* 658, *Von Gott will ich nicht lassen;* 659, *Nun komm, der Heiden Heiland;* 660, *Trio super Nun komm, der Heiden Heiland;* 661, *Nun komm, der Heiden Heiland;* 662, *Allein Gott in der Höh sei Ehr;* 663, *Allein Gott in der Höh sei Ehr;* 664, *Trio super Allein Gott in der Höh sei Ehr;* 665, *Jesus Christus, unser Heiland;* 666, *Jesus Christus, unser Heiland;* 667, *Komm, Gott Schöpfer, Heiliger Geist;* 668, *Wenn wir in höchsten Nöten sein (Vor deinen Thron tret ich).* Chorale preludes in the 3rd part of the *Clavier-Übung:* 669, *Kyrie, Gott Vater in Ewigkeit;* 670, *Christe, aller Welt Trost;* 671, *Kyrie, Gott heiliger Geist;* 672, *Kyrie, Gott Vater in Ewigkeit;* 673, *Christe, aller Welt Trost;* 674, *Kyrie, Gott heiliger Geist;* 675, *Allein Gott in der Höh sei Ehr;* 676, *Allein Gott in der Höh sei Ehr;* 677, *Fughetta super Allein Gott in der Höh sei Ehr;* 678, *Dies sind die heiligen zehen Gebot;* 679, *Fughetta super Dies sind die heiligen zehen Gebot;* 680, *Wir glauben all an einen Gott;* 681, *Fughetta super Wir glauben all an einen Gott;* 682, *Vater unser im Himmelreich;* 683, *Vater unser im Himmelreich;* 684, *Christ, unser Herr, zum Jordan kam;* 685, *Christ, unser Herr, zum Jordan kam;* 686, *Aus tiefer Not schrei ich zu dir;* 687, *Aus tiefer Not schrei ich zu dir;* 688, *Jesus Christus, unser Heiland, der von uns den Zorn Gottes wandt;* 689, *Fuga super Jesus Christus unser Heiland.* Further chorales: 690, *Wer nur den lieben Gott lässt walten;* 691, *Wer nur den lieben Gott lässt walten;* 694, *Wo soll ich fliehen hin;* 695, *Fantasia super Christ lag in Todesbanden;* 696, *Christum wir sollen loben schon;* 697, *Gelobet seist du, Jesu Christ;* 698, *Herr Christ, der einig Gottes Sohn;* 699, *Nun komm, der Heiden Heiland;* 700, *Vom Himmel hoch, da komm ich her;* 701, *Vom Himmel hoch, da komm ich her;* 703, *Gottes Sohn ist kommen;* 704, *Lob sei dem allmächtigen Gott;* 706, *Liebster Jesu, wir sind hier;* 709, *Herr Jesu Christ, dich zu uns wend;* 710, *Wir Christenleut' haben jetzt Freud;* 711, *Allein Gott in der Höh sei Ehr;* 712, *In dich hab ich gehoffet, Herr;* 713, *Fantasia super Jesu, meine Freude;* 714, *Ach Gott und Herr;* 715, *Allein Gott in der Höh sei Ehr;* 717, *Allein Gott in der Höh sei Ehr;* 718, *Christ lag in Todesbanden;* 720, *Ein feste Burg ist unser Gott;* 721, *Erbarm dich mein, o Herre Gott;* 722, *Gelobet seist du, Jesu Christ;* 724, *Gott, durch deine Güte (Gottes Sohn ist kommen);* 725, *Herr Gott, dich loben wir;* 726, *Herr Jesu Christ, dich zu uns wend;* 727, *Herzlich tut mich verlangen;* 728, *Jesus, meine Zuversicht;* 729, *In dulci jubilo;* 730, *Liebster Jesu, wir sind hier;* 731, *Liebster Jesu, wir sind hier;* 732, *Lobt Gott, ihr Christen, allzugleich;* 733, *Meine Seele erhebet den Herren (Fuge über das Magnificat);* 734a, *Nun freut euch, lieben Christen gmein;* O Lamm Gottes, unschuldig; 735, *Fantasia super Valet will ich dir geben;* 736, *Valet will ich dir geben;* 737, *Vater unser im Himmelreich;* 738, *Vom Himmel hoch, da komm ich her;* 739, *Wie schön leucht't uns der Morgenstern;* 741, *Ach Gott vom Himmel sieh darein;* 753, *Jesu, meine Freude;* 764, *Wie schön leuchtet uns der Morgenstern;* 766, *Christ, der du bist der helle Tag;* 767, *O Gott, du frommer Gott;* 768, *Sei gegrüsset, Jesu gütig.* BWV numbers have been assigned to the following doubtful and spurious works: 691a, *Wer nur den lieben Gott lässt walten* (doubtful); 692, *Ach Gott und Herr* (by J.G. Walther); 693, *Ach Gott und Herr* (by J.G. Walther); 695a, *Fantasia super Christ lag in Todesbanden* (doubtful); 702, *Das Jesulein soll doch mein Trost* (doubtful); 705, *Durch Adam's Fall ist ganz verderbt* (doubtful); 707, *Ich hab' mein' Sach' Gott heimgestellt* (doubtful); 708, *Ich hab' mein' Sach' Gott heimgestellt* (doubtful); 713a, *Fantasia super Jesu, meine Freude* (doubtful); 716, *Fuga super Allein Gott in der Höh sei Ehr* (doubtful); 719, *Der Tag, der ist so freudenreich* (doubtful); 723, *Gelobet seist du, Jesu Christ* (doubtful); 734, *Nun freut euch, lieben Christen gmein* (doubtful); 740, *Wir glauben all' an einen Gott, Vater* (doubtful); 742, *Ach Herr, mich armen Sünder* (spurious); 743, *Ach, was ist doch unser Leben* (spurious); 744, *Auf meinen lieben Gott* (doubtful); 745, *Aus der Tiefe rufe ich* (doubtful); 746, *Christ ist erstanden* (doubtful); 747, *Christus, der uns selig macht* (spurious); 748, *Gott der Vater wohn' uns bei* (doubtful); 749, *Herr Jesu Christ, dich zu uns wend'* (spurious); 750, *Herr Jesu Christ, mein's Lebens Licht* (spurious); 751, *In dulci jubilo* (spurious); 752, *Jesu, der du meine Seele* (spurious); 754, *Liebster Jesu, wir sind hier* (spurious); 755, *Nun freut euch, lieben Christen* (spurious); 756, *Nun ruhen alle Wälder* (spurious); 757, *O Herre Gott, dein göttlich' Wort* (spurious); 758, *O Vater, allmächtiger Gott* (doubtful); 759, *Schmücke dich, o liebe Seele* (by G.A. Homilius); 760, *Vater unser im Himmelreich* (doubtful); 761, *Vater unser im Himmelreich* (doubtful); 762, *Vater user im Himmelreich* (spurious); 763, *Wie schön leuchtet der Morgenstern* (spurious); 765, *Wir glauben all' an einen Gott* (spurious); 770, *Ach, was soll ich Sünder machen?* (doubtful); 771, *Allein Gott in der Höh sei Ehr'* (nos. 3 and 8 by A.N. Vetter).

OTHER KEYBOARD MUSIC: 772–86, 15 2-part inventions in the *Clavier-Büchlein für Wilhelm Friedemann Bach:* C major, C minor, D major, D minor, E-flat major, E major, E minor, F major, F minor, G major, G minor, A major, A minor, B-flat major, B minor; 787–801, 15 3-part inventions, called sinfonias, in the *Clavier-Büchlein für Wilhelm Friedemann Bach:* C major, C minor, D major, D minor, E-flat major, E major, E minor, F major, F minor, G major, G minor, A major, A minor, B-flat major, B minor; 806–11, 6 English Suites: A major, A minor, G minor, F major, E minor, D minor; 812–17, 6 French Suites: D minor, C minor, B minor, E-flat major, G major, E major; 825–30, 6 partitas in part one of the *Clavier- Übung:* B-flat major, C minor, A minor, D major, G major, E minor; 831, *Ouvertüre nach französischer Art,* a partita in B minor in part 2 of the *Clavier-Übung;* 846–93, *Das wohltemperierte Clavier (The Well-Tempered Clavier),* in 2 parts: 24 Preludes and Fugues in each part in all the major and minor keys; 971, *Concerto nach Italiänischen Gusto (Concerto in the Italian Style)* in part 2 of the *Clavier-Übung;* 988, *Aria mit verschiedenen Veraenderungen* (the so-called *Gold-*

berg Variations), part 4 of the *Clavier-Übung.* Further keyboard works: 818, Suite in A minor; 819, Suite in E-flat major; 820, Ouverture in F major; 821, Suite in B-flat major; 822, Suite in G minor; 823, Suite in F minor; 832, Partie in A major; 833, Prelude and Partita in F major; 836 and 837, 2 allemandes in G minor (one unfinished); 841–43, 3 minuets: G major, G minor, G major; 894, Prelude and Fugue in A minor; 896, Prelude and Fugue in A major; 900, Prelude and Fughetta in E minor; 901, Prelude and Fughetta in F major; 902, Prelude and Fughetta in G major; 903, Chromatic Fantasia and Fugue in D minor; 904, Fantasia and Fugue in A minor; 906, Fantasia and Fugue in C minor; 910, Toccata in F-sharp minor; 911, Toccata in C minor; 912, Toccata in D major; 913, Toccata in D minor; 914, Toccata in E minor; 915, Toccata in G minor; 916, Toccata in G major; 944, Fugue in A minor; 946, Fugue in C major; 950, Fugue in A major (on a theme by Albinoni); 951, Fugue in B minor (on a theme by Albinoni); 953, Fugue in C major; 954, Fugue in B-flat major; 955, Fugue in B-flat major; 958, Fugue in A minor; 959, Fugue in A minor; 963, Sonata in D major; 965, Sonata in A minor (based upon a sonata by J.A. Reinken); 966, Sonata in C major (based upon part of a sonata by J.A. Reinken); 967, Sonata in A minor (based upon the first movement of a sonata by an unknown source); 989, Aria variata in A minor, 991, Air with variations in C minor (fragment); 992, *Capriccio sopra la lontananza del suo fratello dilettissimo (Capriccio on the Departure of His Most Beloved Brother),* in B-flat major; 993, Capriccio in E major; also 924–30, 6 works from the *Clavier-Büchlein für Wilhelm Friedemann Bach:* Praeambulum in C major, Prelude in D minor, Praeambulum in F major, Prelude in F major, Trio in G minor, Praeambulum in G minor; 933–38, 6 preludes: C major, C minor, D minor, D major, E major, E minor; 939-43, 5 Preludes: C major, D minor, E minor, A minor, C major; 994, Applicatio in C major, the first piece in the *Clavier-Büchlein für Wilhelm Friedemann Bach;* several pieces in the 2 parts of the *Clavier-Büchlein für Anna Magdalena Bach;* and 972–87, 16 concertos: D major (arrangement of Vivaldi's op. 3, no. 9), G major (arrangement of Vivaldi's op. 8/II, no. 2), D minor (arrangement of Oboe Concerto by A. Marcello), G minor (arrangement of Vivaldi's op. 4, no. 6), C major (arrangement of Vivaldi's op. 3, no. 12), C major (source unknown), F major (arrangement of Vivaldi's op. 3, no. 3), B minor (source unknown), G major (arrangement of Vivaldi's op. 4, no. 1), C minor (source unknown), B-flat major (arrangement of a concerto by Duke Johann Ernst of Saxe-Weimar), G minor (source unknown), C major (arrangement of a concerto by Duke Johann Ernst of Saxe-Weimar), G minor (arrangement of Violin Concerto by Telemann), G major (source unknown), D minor (arrangement of a concerto by Duke Johann Ernst of Saxe-Weimar). BWV numbers have been assigned to the following doubtful and spurious works: 824, Suite in A major (fragment; by Telemann); Allemande in C minor (spurious); 835, Allemande in A minor (by Kirnberger); 838, Allemande and Courante in A major (by C. Graupner); 839, Sarabande in G minor (spurious); 840, Courante in G major (by Telemann); 844, Scherzo in D minor (by W.F. Bach); 845, Gigue in F minor (spurious); 895, Prelude and Fugue in A minor (doubtful); 897, Prelude and Fugue in A minor (partly doubtful; prelude by C.H. Dretzel); 898, Prelude and Fugue in B-flat major (doubtful); 899, Prelude and Fughetta in D minor (doubtful); 905, Fantasia and Fugue in D minor (doubtful); 907, Fantasia and Fughetta in B-flat major (doubtful); 908, Fantasia and Fughetta in D major (doubtful); 909, Concerto and Fugue in C minor (doubtful); 917, Fantasia in G minor (doubtful); 918, Fantasia a on a rondo in C minor (doubtful); 919, Fantasia in C minor (doubtful); 920, Fantasia in G minor (doubtful); 921, Prelude in C minor (doubtful); 922, Prelude in A minor (doubtful); 923, Prelude in B minor (doubtful); 945, Fugue in E minor (spurious); 947, Fugue in A minor (doubtful); 948, Fugue in D minor (doubtful); 949, Fugue in A major (doubtful); 952, Fugue in C major (doubtful); 956, Fugue in E minor (doubtful); 957, Fugue in G major (doubtful); 960, Fugue in E minor (unfinished; spurious); 961, Fughetta in C minor (doubtful); 962, Fugato in E minor (by Albrechtsberger); 964; Sonata in D minor (doubtful; arrangement of Violin Sonata 1,003); 968, Adagio in G major (doubtful; arrangement of first movement of Violin Sonata 1,005); 969, Andante in G minor (spurious); 970, Presto in D minor (by W.F. Bach); 990, Sarabande con partite in C major (spurious); etc.

FOR LUTE: 995, Suite in G minor; 996, Suite in E minor; 997, Partita in C minor; 998, Prelude, Fugue, and Allegro in E-flat major; 999, Prelude in C minor; 1,000, Fugue in G minor; 1,006a, Partita in E major (arrangement of 1,006).

CHAMBER MUSIC: 1,001–6, sonatas and partitas for Solo Violin: Sonata No. 1 in G minor, Partita No. 1 in B minor, Sonata No. 2 in A minor, Partita No. 2 in D minor, Sonata No. 3 in C minor, Partita No. 3 in E major; 1,007–12, 6 suites for Solo Cello: G major, D minor, C major, E-flat major, C minor, D major; 1,013, Partita in A minor for flute; 1,014–19, 6 sonatas for Violin and Harpsichord: No. 1 in B minor, No. 2 in A major, No. 3 in E major, No. 4 in C minor, No. 5 in F minor, No. 6 in G major; 1,021, Sonata in G major for Violin and Basso Continuo; 1,023, Sonata in E minor for Violin and Basso Continuo; 1,027–29, 3 sonatas for Harpsichord and Viola da Gamba: G major, D major, G minor; 1,030, Sonata in B minor for Flute and Harpsichord; 1,032, Sonata in A major for Flute and Harpsichord; 1,034, Sonata in E minor for Flute and Basso Continuo; 1,035, Sonata in E major for Flute and Basso Continuo; 1,039, Sonata in G major for 2 Flutes and Basso Continuo; 1,040, Trio in F major for Violin, Oboe, and Basso Continuo. BWV numbers have been assigned to the following doubtful and spurious works: 1,020, Sonata in G minor for Violin and Harpsichord (doubtful); 1,022, Sonata in F major for Violin and Harpsichord (most likely spurious); 1,024, Sonata in C minor for Violin and Basso Continuo (doubtful); 1,025, Suite in A major for Violin and Harpsichord (doubtful); 1,026, Fugue in G minor for Violin and Harpsichord (doubtful); 1,037, Sonata in C major for 2 Violins and Harpsichord (most likely spurious); 1,031, Sonata in E-flat major for Flute and Harpsichord (doubtful);

1,033, Sonata in C major for Flute and Basso Continuo (doubtful); 1,036, Sonata in D minor for 2 Violins and Harpsichord (most likely spurious); 1,038, Sonata in G major for Flute, Violin, and Basso Continuo (most likely spurious).

FOR ORCH.: 1,041, Concerto in A minor for Violin; 1,042, Concerto in E major for Violin; 1,043, Concerto in D minor for 2 Violins; 1,044, Concerto in A minor for Flute, Violin, and Harpsichord; 1,046–51, 6 Brandenburg Concertos: No. 1 in F major, No. 2 in F major, No. 3 in G major, No. 4 in G major, No. 5 in D major, No. 6 in B-flat major; 1,052, Concerto in D minor for Harpsichord; 1053, Concerto in E major for Harpsichord; 1,054, Concerto in D major for Harpsichord; 1,055, Concerto in A major for Harpsichord; 1,056, Concerto in F minor for Harpsichord; 1,057, Concerto in F major for Harpsichord; 1,058, Concerto in G minor for Harpsichord; 1,059, Concerto in D minor for Harpsichord; 1,060, Concerto in C minor for 2 Harpsichords; 1,061, Concerto in C major for 2 Harpsichords; 1,062, Concerto in C minor for 2 Harpsichords; 1,063, Concerto in D minor for 3 Harpsichords; 1,064, Concerto in C major for 3 Harpsichords; 1,065, Concerto in A minor for 4 Harpsichords (arrangement of Vivaldi's op. 3, no. 10); 1,066–69, 4 suites or ouvertures: No. 1 in C major, No. 2 in B minor, No. 3 in D major, No. 4 in D major. Also 1,045, concerto movement in D major for Violin (fragment); 1,046a, Sinfonia in F major (early version of 1,046); 1,070, Overture in G minor (most likely spurious).

OTHER WORKS: 769, Einige canonische Veränderungen über das Weynacht Lied, Vom Himmel hoch da komm' ich her for Organ (composed for his membership in the Societät der Musikalischen Wissenschaften); 1,079, Musikalisches Opfer (Musical Offering); 1,080, Die Kunst der Fuge (The Art of the Fugue).

BIBLIOGRAPHY: COLLECTED EDITIONS, SOURCE MATERIAL: Johann Sebastian Bach's Werke, the first major ed. of his collected works, was publ. by the Bach-Gesellschaft (46 vols., Leipzig, 1851-99; vol. 47, supplement, 1932). The Johann-Sebastian-Bach-Inst. of Göttingen and the Bach-Archiv of Leipzig are now preparing a completely new ed., the Neue Ausgabe sämtlicher Werke (the Neue Bach-Ausgabe, or NBA). It began publication in 1954; a Kritischer Bericht accompanies each vol.; in addition, facsimile reproductions of Bach's original MSS and documents may be found in the Faksimile-Reihe Bachser Werke und Schriftstücke. When this monumental ed. is completed, it will contain over 80 vols. There are also innumerable reprints of many of Bach's compositions.

The standard thematic catalogue of Bach's works is to be found in W. Schmieder, Thematisch-systematisches Verzeichnis der musikalischen Werke von Johann Sebastian Bach. Bach-Werke-Verzeichnis (Leipzig, 1950; 3rd ed., 1961); it includes bibliographical information on each composition. See also M. McAll, Melodic Index to the Works of Johann Sebastian Bach (N.Y., 1962).

Other important sources are as follows: J. Schreyer, Beiträge zur B.-Kritik (vol. 1, Dresden, 1910; vol. 2, Leipzig, 1912); E. Müller von Asow, ed., J.S. B.,

Bach

Gesammelte Briefe (Regensburg, 1938; 2nd ed., with H. Müller von Asow, as *J.S. B., Briefe, Gesamtausgabe,* Regensburg, 1950); H. David and A. Mendel, eds., *The B. Reader: A Life of J.S. B. in Letters and Documents* (N.Y., 1945; revised ed., 1966); K. Matthaei, ed., *B.-Gedenkschrift* (Zürich, 1950); P. Kast, *Die B.-Handschriften der Berliner Staatsbibliothek,* Tübinger Bach-Studien, II–III (Trossingen, 1958); G. von Dadelsen, "Originale Daten auf den Handschriften J.S. B.s," *Hans Albrecht in Memoriam* (Kassel, 1962); W. Neumann and H.-J. Schulze, eds., *Schriftstücke von der Hand J.S. B.s,* Bach-Dokumente, I (Leipzig, 1963); P. Krause, ed., *Handschriften der Werke J.S. B.s. in der Musikbibliothek der Stadt Leipzig* (Leipzig, 1964); M. Geck, ed., *B.-Interpretationen* (Göttingen, 1969); H.-J. Schulze, ed., *Fremdschriftliche und gedruckte Dokument zur Lebensgeschichte J.S. B.s. 1685–1750,* Bach-Dokumente, II (Leipzig, 1969); P. Krause, ed., *Originalausgaben und ältere Drucke der Werke J.S. B.s in der Musikbibliothek der Stadt Leipzig* (Leipzig, 1970); H.-J. Schulze, ed., *Dokumente zum Nachwirken J.S. B.s 1750–1800,* Bach-Dokumente, III (Leipzig, 1972); K.-H. Köhler, "Die B.-Sammlung der Deutschen Staatsbibliothek— Überlieferung und Bedeutung," *Bach-Studien,* V (1975); W. Neumann, ed., *Bilddokumente zur Lebensgeschichte J.S. B.s,* Bach-Dokumente, IV (Leipzig, 1978).

BIOGRAPHICAL: C.P.E. Bach and J. Agricola publ. an obituary (*Nekrolog*) in L. Mizler's *Neu eröffnete musikalische Bibliothek* (Leipzig, 1754; reprint ed. by B. Richter in the *Bach-Jahrbuch,* 1920; Eng. trans. in H. David and A. Mendel, eds., *The B. Reader: A Life of J.S. B. in Letters and Documents,* N.Y., 1945; revised ed., 1966, pp. 213–24); Bach's first biographer was J. Forkel, *Über J.S. B.s Leben, Kunst und Kunstwerke* (an invaluable source based on information provided by C.P.E. Bach; Leipzig, 1802; Eng. trans., London, 1820; new Eng. trans. with notes by C. Terry, London, 1920); C. Hilgenfeldt, *J.S. B.'s Leben, Wirken und Werke; Ein Beitrag zur Kunstgeschichte des achtzehnten Jahrhunderts* (Leipzig, 1850); C. Bitter, *J.S. B.* (2 vols., Berlin, 1865; 2nd ed., 4 vols., Dresden, 1880); P. Spitta, *J.S. B.* (the standard source on Bach's life and work; although in error concerning some details, it remains an essential study; 2 vols., Leipzig, 1873–80; Eng. trans by C. Bell and J. Fuller-Maitland, with many additions, 3 vols., London, 1884–85; 2nd ed., 1899; reprint, 2 vols., N.Y., 1951); A. Schweitzer, *J.S. B., Le Musicien-poète* (an important biography which places special emphasis on esthetic problems; Paris, 1905; augmented German eds., 1908, 1915; Eng. trans. by E. Newman, 2 vols., London, 1911); C. Abdy Williams, *B.* (London, 1900; revised ed., 1934); A. Pirro, *J.-S. B.* (Paris, 1906; Eng. trans., N.Y., 1957); P. Wolfrum, *J.S. B.* (vol. 1, Berlin, 1906; 2nd ed., 1910; vol. 2, Leipzig, 1910); C. Parry, *J.S. B.: The Story of the Development of a Great Personality* (N.Y. and London, 1909; revised ed., 1934); J. Tiersot, *J.-S. B.* (Paris, 1912; 2nd ed., 1934); H. Kretzschmar, *B.-Kolleg* (Leipzig, 1922); W. Dahms, *J.S. B., Ein Bild seines Lebens* (Munich, 1924); T. Gérold, *J.-S. B.* (Paris, 1925); C. Terry, *B.: A Biography* (a major study based on extensive research; London, 1928; revised ed., 1933); R. Boughton, *B., the Master: A New Interpretation of His Genius* (N.Y. and London, 1930); H. Besseler, "J.S. B.," *Die grossen Deutschen* (Berlin, 1935; new ed., 1956); T. Scott Buhrmann, *B.'s Life Chronologically as He Lived It* (illustrated chronological tables; N.Y. 1935); H. Moser, *J.S. B.* (Berlin, 1935; 2nd ed., 1943); J. Müller-Blattau, *J.S. B.* (Leipzig, 1935; 2nd ed., Stuttgart, 1950); H. Preuss, *B., der Lutheraner* (Erlangen, 1935); R. Steglich, *J.S. B.* (richly illustrated; Potsdam, 1935); P. Collaer, *J.S. B.* (Brussels, 1936); W. Gurlitt, *J.S. B.: Der Meister und sein Werk* (an important study; Berlin, 1936; 3rd ed., 1949; Eng. trans., St. Louis, 1957); W. Vetter, *J.S. B.* (Leipzig, 1938; 2nd ed., 1943); K. Hasse, *J.S. B.* (Cologne and Krefeld, 1941; 2nd ed., 1948); R. Pitrou, *J.-S. B.* (Paris, 1941; 2nd ed., 1949); W. Cart, *J.S. B.: 1685–1750* (Lausanne, 1946); A.-E. Cherbuliez, *J.S. B.: sein Leben und sein Werk* (Olten, 1946; 2nd ed., 1947); H. Gadamer, *B. und Weimar* (Weimar, 1946); E. and S. Grew, *B.* (London, 1947); H. Keller, *J.S. B.* (Lorch, 1947); E. Fischer, *J.S. B.* (Bern, 1948); H. Engel, *J.S. B.* (Berlin, 1950); G. Fock, *Der junge B. in Lüneburg* (Hamburg, 1950); B. Paumgartner, *J.S. B.: Leben und Werk* (vol. I, Zürich, 1950); R. Petzoldt, *J.S. B., Sein Leben in Bildern* (Leipzig, 1950); F. Wiegand, *J.S. B. und seine Verwandten in Arnstadt* (Arnstadt, 1950); F. Smend, *B. in Köthen* (Berlin, 1951); H. Löffler, "Die Schüler J.S. B.s," *Bach-Jahrbuch* (1953); W. Neumann, *Auf den Lebenswegen J.S. B.s* (Berlin, 1953; 4th ed., 1962) K. Geiringer, *The B. Family: Seven Generations of Creative Genius* (N.Y., 1954); H. Franck, *J.S. B.: Die Geschichte seines Lebens* (Berlin, 1960); A. Mendel, "Recent Developments in B. Chronology," *Musical Quarterly* (July 1960); W. Neumann, *B.: Eine Bildbiographie* (Munich, 1960; Eng. trans. as *B.: A Pictorial Biography,* N.Y., 1961; revised ed. as *B. and His World,* N.Y., 1970); R. Miles, *J.S. B.* (Englewood Cliffs, N.J., 1962); F. Blume, "Outlines of a New Picture of B.," *Music & Letters* (July 1963); E. Buchet, *J.-S. B., L'Œuvre et la vie* (Paris, 1963); I. Holst, *B.* (London, 1965); K. Geiringer, *J.S. B.: The Culmination of an Era* (an important one-vol. study of Bach's life and works, especially valuable for its critical survey of his compositions; N.Y., 1966); F. Blume, *Der junge B.* (Wolfenbüttel, 1967; Eng. trans. as "J.S. B.'s Youth," *Musical Quarterly* [Jan. 1968]); E. Buchet, *J.-S. B., Apres deux siècles d'études et de témoignages* (Paris, 1968); B. Schwendowius and W. Dömling, eds., *J.S. B.: Zeit, Leben, Wirken* (Kassel, 1976; trans. as *J.S. B.: Life, Times, Influence,* London, 1978); M. Boyd, *B.* (London, 1983); Denis Arnold, *B.* (London, 1984).

CRITICAL, ANALYTICAL: In addition to the following writings, numerous articles of importance may be found in the *Bach-Jahrbuch* (1904—). F. Rochlitz, *Wege zu B.* (extracted from *Für Freunde der Tonkunst,* Leipzig, 1824–37, by J. Müller-Blattau, Augsburg, 1926); M. Hauptmann, *Erläuterungen zu J.S. B.s Kunst der Fuge* (Leipzig, 1841; 2nd ed., 1861); H. Riemann, *Handbuch der Fugenkomposition* (vols. I and II [analysis of *Das Wohltemperierte Klavier;* Berlin 1890–91; 3rd ed., 1914; Eng. trans. by J. Shedlock, 2 vols., London, 1893]; vol. III [analysis of the *Kunst der Fuge;* Berlin, 1894; 3rd ed., 1921]); A. Pirro,

L'Orgue de J.-S. B. (Paris, 1895; Eng. trans., London, 1902); F. Iliff, *The 48 Preludes and Fugues of J.S. B.* (London, 1897); A. Pirro, *L'Esthétique de J.-S. B.* (Paris, 1907); A. Heuss, *J.S. B.s Matthäuspassion* (Leipzig, 1909); R. Wustmann, *J.S. B.s Kantatentexte* (Leipzig, 1913; 2nd ed., 1967); J. Fuller-Maitland, "The Toccatas of B.," *Sammelbände der Internationalen Musik-Gesellschaft* (1915); C. Terry, *B.'s Chorals* (3 vols., Cambridge, 1915, 1917, 1921); idem, *B.'s Mass in B Minor: A Study* (Glasgow, 1915); E. Kurth, *Grundlagen des linearen Kontrapunkts. Einführung in Stil und Technik von B.s melodischer Polyphonie* (Bern, 1917; 5th ed., 1956); H. Grace, *The Organ Works of B.* (London, 1922); C. Terry, *J.S. B.'s Original Hymn-Tunes for Congregational Use* (London, 1922); W. Werker, *Studien über die Symmetrie im Bau der Fugen und die motivische Zusammengehörigkeit der Präludien und Fugen des Wohltemperierten Klaviers von J.S. B.* (Leipzig, 1922); C. Terry, *A B. Hymn Book for the Church's Seasons* (London, 1923); W. Werker, *Die Matthäus-Passion* (Leipzig, 1923); C. Terry, *B.: The Mass in B Minor* (London, 1924; revised ed., 1931); W. Whittaker, *Fugitive Notes on Certain Cantatas and the Motets of J.S. B.* (London, 1924); F. Franke, *B.s Kirchen-Kantaten* (Leipzig, 1925); J. Fuller-Maitland, *The "48": B.'s Wohltemperiertes Clavier* (London, 1925); idem, *The Keyboard Suites of J.S. B.* (London, 1925); C. Terry, *B.: The Cantatas and Oratorios* (2 vols., London, 1925); idem, *J.S. B.: Cantata Texts, Sacred and Secular, with a Reconstruction of the Leipzig Liturgy of His Period* (London, 1926); M. Zulauf, *Die Harmonik of J.S. B.s* (Bern, 1927; 2nd ed., 1937); H. David, "Zu B.'s Kunst der Fuge," *Peters-Jahrbuch* (1928); C. Terry, *B.: The Passions* (London, 1926; 2nd ed., 1935); P. Wackernagel, *B.s Brandenburgische Konzerte* (Berlin, 1928); H. Abert, *B.'s Matthäuspassion* (Halle, 1929); F. Atkins, *B.'s Passions* (London,1929); H. David, "Zur Gesamtgestalt von B.s H-moll Messe," *Festschrift für Johannes Wolf* (1929); J. Fuller-Maitland, *B.'s "Brandenburg" Concertos* (London, 1929; 2nd ed., 1945); A. Hull, *B.'s Organ Works* (London, 1929); C. Terry, *The Four-Part Chorales of J.S. B.* (5 vols., London, 1929); idem, *The Magnificat, Lutheran Masses and Motets* (London, 1929); idem, *B.: The Historical Approach* (London, 1930); K. Ziebler, *Das Symbol in der Kirchenmusik J.S. B.s* (Kassel, 1930); E. Schwebsch, *J.S. B. und die Kunst der Fuge* (Stuttgart, 1931; 2nd ed., 1955); D. Tovey, *A Companion to the Art of Fugue* (London, 1931); C. Terry, *B.'s Orchestra* (London, 1932; 2nd ed., 1958); C. Freyse, *Eisenacher Dokumente um J.S. B.* (Leipzig, 1933); L. Landshoff, *Revisionsbericht zur Urtextausgabe von J.S. B.s Inventionen und Sinfonien* (Leipzig, 1933); C. Terry, *The Music of B.: An Introduction* (London, 1933); C. Terry, "The Spurious B. 'Lukas-Passion,'" *Music & Letters* (July 1933); H. Huggler, *J.S. B.s Orgelbüchlein* (Bern, 1935); A. Dickinson, *The Art of J.S. B.* (London, 1936; revised ed., 1950); G. Herz, *J.S. B. im Zeitalter des Rationalismus und der Frühromantik* (Bern, 1936); L. Landshoff, *Musikalisches Opfer* (Leipzig, 1936); A. Schering, *J.S. B.s Leipziger Kirchenmusik* (Leipzig, 1936; 2nd ed., 1954); E. Thiele, *Die Chorfugen J.S. B.s* (Bern and Leipzig, 1936); H. Besch, *J.S. B., Frömmigkeit und Glaube* (Gütersloh, 1938; 2nd ed., Kassel, 1950); C. Gray, *The 48 Preludes and Fugues of J.S. B.* (London, 1938); W. Neumann, *J.S. B.'s Chorfuge* (Leipzig, 1938); C. Freyse, "Das Bach-Haus zu Eisenach," *Bach-Jahrbuch* (1939; 1940–48); G. Frotscher, *J.S. B. und die Musik des 17. Jahrhunderts* (Wadenswil, 1939); W. Korte, *Musik und Weltbild* (Leipzig, 1940); A. Schering, *Das Zeitalter J.S. B.s und Johann Adam Hillers* (Leipzig, 1940); B. Martin, *Untersuchungen zur Struktur der Kunst der Fuge* (Regensburg, 1941); H. Rutters, *J.S. B. en onze tijd* (Amsterdam, 1941); A. Schering, *Das Symbol in der Musik* (Leipzig, 1941); idem, *J.S. B. und das Musikleben Leipzigs im 18. Jahrhundert* (Leipzig, 1941); H. Boetticher, "B.s Kunst der Bearbeitung," *Festschrift zu Peter Raabes 70. Geburtstag* (Leipzig, 1942); H. Drinker, *Texts of the Choral Works of J.S. B. in English Translation* (4 vols., N.Y., 1942–43); A. Schering, *Über Kantaten J.S. B.s* (Leipzig, 1942; 3rd ed., 1950); F. Smend, "Neue B.-Funde," *Archiv Für Musikforschung* (1942); S. Taylor, *The Chorale Preludes of J.S. B.* (London, 1942); H. David *J.S. B's Musical Offering: History, Interpretation and Analysis* (N.Y., 1945); G. Herz, "B.'s Religion," *Journal of Renaissance and Baroque Music* (June 1946); M. Mayer, *J.-P. Rameau: J.S. B.* (Chambery, 1946); L. Schrade, "B.: The Conflict between the Sacred and Secular," *Journal of the History of Ideas* (April 1946); J. Barbour, "B. and 'The Art of Temperament,'" *Musical Quarterly* (Jan. 1947); F. Blume, *J.S. B. im Wandel der Geschichte* (Kassel, 1947; Eng. trans., 1950); F. Florand, *J.S. B.: L'Œuvre d'orgue* (Paris, 1947); W. Neumann, *Handbuch der Kantaten J.S. B.s* (Leipzig, 1947; 4th ed., 1971); F. Smend, *J.S. B.: Kirchen-Kantaten* (6 vols., Berlin, 1947–49; 3rd ed., 1966); idem, *Luther und B.* (Berlin, 1947); M. Dehnert, *Das Weltbild J.S. B.s* (Leipzig, 1948; 2nd ed., 1949); N. Dufourcq, *J.S. B., Le Maître de l'orgue* (Paris, 1948); H. Keller, *Die Orgelwerke B.s: Ein Beitrag zu ihrer Geschichte, Form, Deutung und Wiedergabe* (Leipzig, 1948; Eng. trans., 1967); W. Emery, "B.'s Symbolic Language," *Music & Letters* (Oct. 1949); R. Steglich, *Wege zu B.* (Regensburg, 1949); H. Besseler and G. Kraft, *J.S. B. in Thüringen* (Weimar, 1950); W. Blankenburg, *Einführung in B.s h-moll Messe* (Kassel and Basel, 1950; 3rd ed., 1973); H. Dräger and K. Laux., eds., *B.-Probleme* (Leipzig, 1950); I. Finlay, "B.'s Secular Cantata Texts," *Music & Letters* (July 1950); K. Geiringer, "Artistic Interrelations of the B.s," *Musical Quarterly* (July 1950); H. Keller, *Die Klavierwerke B.s* (Leipzig, 1950); C. Mahrenholz, *J.S. B. und der Gottesdienst seiner Zeit* (Kassel and Basel, 1950); R. Petzoldt and L. Weinhold, eds., *J.S. B.: Das Schaffen des Meisters im Spiegel einer Stadt* (Leipzig, 1950); A. Schmitz, *Die Bildlichkeit der wortgebundenen Musik J.S. B.s* (Mainz, 1950); W. Vetter, *Der Kapellmeister B.: Versuch einer Deutung* (Potsdam, 1950); P. Aldrich, *Ornamentation in J.S. B.'s Organ Works* (N.Y., 1951); W. David, *J.S. B.s Orgeln* (Berlin, 1951); A. Davison, *B. and Handel: the Consummation of the Baroque in Music* (Cambridge, Mass., 1951); A. Dürr, *Studien über die frühen Kantaten J.S. B.s* (Leipzig, 1951; revised ed., Wiesbaden, 1977); R. Gerber, *B.s Brandenburgische Konzerte* (Kassel and Basel, 1951); F.

Bach

Hamel *J.S. B.: Geistige Welt* (Göttingen, 1951); P. Hindemith, *J.S. B.: Heritage and Obligation* (New Haven, 1952); W. Scheide, *J.S. B. as a Biblical Interpreter* (Princeton, 1952); W. Emery, *B.'s Ornaments* (London, 1953; 2nd ed., 1961); idem, *Notes on B.'s Organ Works: A Companion to the Revised Edition* (London, 1953–57); F. Rothschild, *The Lost Tradition in Music: Rhythm and Tempo in J.S. B.'s Time* (N.Y., 1953); K. Geiringer, *Symbolism in the Music of B.* (Washington, D.C., 1955); L. Czaczkes, *Analyse des Wohltemperierten Klaviers* (Vienna, 1956–65); A. Dickinson, *B.'s Fugal Works* (London, 1956); H. Engel, *J.S. B.s Violinkonzerte* (Leipzig, 1956); J. Krey, *B.s Orgelmusik in der Weimarer Periode* (Diss., Univ. of Jena, 1956); W. Neumann, ed., *J.S. B.: Sämtliche Kantatentexte* (Leipzig, 1956; 2nd ed., 1967); L. Tagliavini, *Studi sui testi delle cantate sacre di J.S. B.* (Padua, 1956); G. von Dadelsen, *Bemerkungen zur Handschrift J.S. B.s, seiner Familie und seines Kreises,* Tübinger Bach-Studien, I (Trossingen, 1957); J. David, *Die zweistimmigen Inventionen von J.S. B.* (Göttingen, 1957); A. Dürr, "Zur Chronologie der Leipziger Vokalwerke J.S. B.s," *Bach-Jahrbuch* (1957; revised and publ. separately, Kassel, 1976); W. Reiche, ed., *J.S. B., Leben und Schaffen* (Zürich, 1957); G. von Dadelsen, *Beiträge zur Chronologie der Werke J.S. B.s,* Tübinger Bach-Studien, IV–V (Trossingen, 1958); J. David, *Die dreistimmigen Inventionen von J.S. B.* (Göttingen, 1959); W. Whittaker, *The Cantatas of J.S. B., Sacred and Secular* (2 vols., London, 1959; 2nd ed., 1964); E. Bodky, *The Interpretation of B.'s Keyboard Works* (Cambridge, Mass., 1960); R. Donington, *Tempo and Rhythm in B.'s Organ Music* (London, 1960); W. Neumann, "Das 'Bachische Collegium Musicum,'" *Bach-Jahrbuch* (1960); J. Day, *The Literary Background to B.'s Cantatas* (London, 1961); J. David, *Das wohltemperierte Klavier* (Göttingen, 1962); R. Davis, *Self Parody among the Cantatas of J.S. B.* (Diss., Boston Univ., 1962); R. Steglich, *Tanzrhythmen in der Musik J.S. B.s* (Wolfenbüttel, 1962); P. Aldrich, "On the Interpretation of B.'s Trills," *Musical Quarterly* (July 1963); N. Carrell, *B.'s Brandenburg Concertos* (London, 1963); J. Chailley, *Les Passions de J.-S. B.* (Paris, 1963); D. Johnston, "B. and the Bible," *Proceedings of the Renaissance Music Association,* XC (1963–64); H. Keller, *Das Wohltemperierte Klavier von J.S. B.: Werk und Wiedergabe* (Kassel, 1965); F. Neumann, "A New Look at B.'s Ornamentation," *Music & Letters* (April 1965); W. Siegmund-Schultze, "B. und Händel," *Händel-Jahrbuch* (1966); J. Westrup, *B. Cantatas* (London, 1966); N. Carrell, *B. The Borrower* (London, 1967); M. Geck, *Die Wiederentdeckung der Matthäuspassion im 19. Jahrhundert* (Regensburg, 1967); G. Kraft, *B. in Eisenach* (Jena, 1967); C. Wolff, *Der stile antico in der Musik J.S. B.s* (Wiesbaden, 1968); P. Brainard, "B.'s Parody Procedure and the St. Matthew Passion," *Journal of the American Musicological Society,* XXII (1969); A. Dürr, *Die Kantaten von J.S. B.* (Kassel and Munich, 1971; revised ed., 1975); C. Wolff, "New Research on B.'s Musical Offering," *Musical Quarterly* (July 1971); J. Chailley, *L'Art de la fugue de J.-S. B.* (Paris, 1971–72); R. Marshall, *The Compositional Process of J.S. B.: A Study of the Autograph Scores of the Vocal Works* (Princeton, 1972); A. Robertson, *The Church Cantatas of J.S. B.* (London, 1972); J. Rifkin, "The Chronology of B.'s Saint Matthew Passion," *Musical Quarterly* (July 1975); C. Wolff et al., "B.'s 'Art of Fugue'; An Examination of the Sources," *Current Musicology,* 19 (1975); N. Kenyon, "A Newly Discovered Group of Canons by B.," *Musical Times* (May 1976); R. Marshall, "B. the Progressive: Observations on His Later Works," *Musical Quarterly* (July 1976); W. Kolneder, *Die Kunst der Fuge: Mythen des 20. Jahrhunderts* (Wilhelmshaven, 1977); P. Williams, *The Organ Music of J.S. B.* (vol. I, Cambridge, 1979); W.H. Mellers, *B. and the Dance of God* (N.Y., 1980); S. Daw, *The Music of J.S. B.: The Choral Works* (East Brunswick, N.J., 1981); H. Klotz, *Streifzüge durch die Bachsche Orgelwelt* (Wiesbaden, 1981); R. Azeskus, *J.S. B. und die Aufklärung* (Leipzig, 1982); J. Rifkin, "B.'s 'Choruses,' The Record Cleared," *High Fidelity* (Dec. 1982); A. Heinich, *B.'s Die Kunst der Fuge: A Living Compendium of Fugal Procedures* (Washington, D.C., 1983). ICONOGRAPHY: M. Schneider, "Verzeichnis von Bildnissen B.s," *Bach-Jahrbuch* (1905); A. Kurzwelly, "Neues über das Bachbildnis der Thomasschule und andere Bildnisse J.S. B.s," *Bach-Jahrbuch* (1914); J. Müller, "B. Portraits," *Musical Quarterly* (April 1935); G. Herz, "A 'New' B. Portrait," *Musical Quarterly* (April 1943); K. Geiringer, *The Lost Portrait of J.S. B.* (N.Y., 1950); H. Raupach, *Das wahre Bildnis J.S. B.s* (Wolfenbüttel, 1950); F. Smend, *J.S. B. bei seinem Namen gerufen* (Kassel, 1950); H. Besseler, *Fünf echte Bildnisse J.S. B.s* (Kassel, 1956); H.O.R. van Tuyll van Serooskerken, *Probleme des Bachporträts* (Bilthoven, 1956); C. Freyse, *B.s Antilz. Betrachtungen und Erkenntnisse zur B.-Ikonographie* (Eisenach, 1964); W. His, *J.S. B., Forschungen über dessen Grabstätte, Gebeine und Antlitz* (dealing with the state of Bach's skull and bones at the time of his exhumation and reinterment; Leipzig, 1895).

Bach, Wilhelm Friedemann (the "Halle" Bach), eldest son of **Johann Sebastian;** b. Weimar, Nov. 22, 1710; d. Berlin, July 1, 1784. He was a pupil of his father; studied at the Thomasschule in Leipzig (1723–29); also studied violin with J.G. Graun in Merseburg (1726); in 1729 he enrolled at the Univ. of Leipzig, where he took courses in in mathematics, philosophy, and law. In 1733 he became organist of the Sophienkirche in Dresden; in 1746 he was appointed organist of the Liebfrauenkirche in Halle, a post he held until 1764. In 1774 he went to Berlin. As a composer, he was highly gifted; his music reflects the influences of the Baroque and Rococo styles. An edition of his selected works was begun by the Abteilung für Musik Preussischen Akademie der Kunste; vol. I contains 4 trios (Leipzig, 1935). His Sinfonias opp. 64 and 65 have been edited by W. Lebermann (Mainz, 1971); opp. 67–71 by M. Schneider (Leipzig, 1914); his piano compositions have been edited by W. Rehberg in *Die Söhne Bachs* (1933); 3 excerpts are in K. Geiringer, *Music of the Bach Family: An Anthology* (Cambridge, Mass., 1955).

His organ works are printed in E. Power Biggs and G. Weston, eds., *W.F. Bach: Complete Works for Organ* (N.Y., 1947).

BIBLIOGRAPHY: C. Bitter, *Carl Philip Emanuel und Wilhelm Friedemann Bach und deren Brüder* (2 vols., Berlin, 1868); M. Falck, *Wilhelm Friedemann Bach: Sein Leben und seine Werke* (Leipzig, 1913); K. Stabenow, *J.S. Bachs Sohn* (Leipzig, 1935); K. Geiringer, *The Bach Family: Seven Generations of Creative Genius* (N.Y., 1954); H. Franck, *Friedemann, der Sohn J.S. Bachs* (Berlin, 1963).

Bach, Wilhelm Friedrich Ernst, son of **Johann Christoph Friedrich,** and grandson and last male descendant of **Johann Sebastian;** b. Bückeburg, May 23, 1759; d. Berlin, Dec. 25, 1845. He studied with his father and with his uncle **Johann Christoph** in London. In 1787 he became music director at Minden; in 1788 he was named Kapellmeister and harpsichordist to Queen Friedrike of Prussia; in 1797 he was appointed to a similar position to Queen Luise; also served as music master to the royal princes. He attended the dedication of the J.S. Bach monument in Leipzig on April 23, 1843. See K. Geiringer, *Music of the Bach Family: An Anthology* (Cambridge, Mass., 1955).

Bach (real name, **Bak**), **Albert,** Hungarian singer; b. Gyula, March 24, 1844; d. Edinburgh, Nov. 19, 1912. He studied at the Vienna Cons.; gave his first concert there in 1871; continued his studies in Italy. He sang opera in Italy, Russia, Germany, and England. In his recitals he always performed Loewe's songs. He was a member of the Loewe-Verein in Berlin and edited 3 vols. of Loewe's ballades with English translations; also publ. several papers on music.

Bach, August Wilhelm, German organist; b. Berlin, Oct. 4, 1796; d. there, April 15, 1869. After a period of organ playing in churches and in concert, he became a teacher at and later director (1832) of the Royal Inst. for Church Music in Berlin. Mendelssohn was his pupil in organ playing.

Bach, Leonhard Emil, German pianist and composer; b. Posen, March 11, 1849; d. London, Feb. 15, 1902. He studied with Th. Kullak (piano) and with Kiel (theory); in 1869 became a teacher at Kullak's Academy in Berlin. He settled in London; from 1882 taught at the Guildhall School of Music. He wrote several short operas: *Irmengard* (London, 1892); *The Lady of Longford* (London, 1894); *Des Königs Garde* (Cologne, 1895); these were fairly successful at their first productions.

Bacharach, Burt, American composer of popular songs; b. Kansas City, May 12, 1928. He was raised in a cultural atmosphere (his father was a newspaper columnist). He played jazz piano in nightclubs; then studied music seriously at McGill Univ. in Montreal; also attended courses of Darius Milhaud and Henry Cowell at the New School for Social Research in N.Y. From 1958 to 1961 he traveled with Marlene Dietrich as her accompanist. In 1962 he joined forces with the lyricist Hal David with felicitous results; together they produced such fine songs as *Reach Out for Me, Trains and Boats and Planes, Make It Easy on Yourself, Blue on Blue, Walk on By, Always Something There to Remind Me, What the World Needs Now Is Love, Do You Know the Way to San Jose?, Raindrops Keep Fallin' on My Head, The Look of Love, I'll Never Fall in Love Again, Our Little Secret, She Likes Baseball.* He wrote the title songs for the films *What's New Pussycat?, Wives and Lovers, Alfie, Send Me No Flowers, Promise Her Anything,* and *Butch Cassidy and the Sundance Kid.* With Hal David again as his lyricist, he produced the highly successful Broadway musical *Promises, Promises* (1968).

Bachauer, Gina, eminent Greek pianist; b. Athens, May 21, 1913; d. there, Aug. 22, 1976. Her father was of Austrian descent; her mother, Italian. She showed her aptitude as a pianist at the age of 5; entered the Athens Cons., where her teacher was Waldemar Freeman. She then went to Paris, where she took lessons with Alfred Cortot at the Ecole Normale de Musique. In 1933 she won the Medal of Honor at the International Contest for Pianists in Vienna; between 1933 and 1935 she received occasional instructions from Rachmaninoff in France and Switzerland; in 1935 she made her professional début with the Athens Symph. Orch. under the direction of Mitropoulos; she was also piano soloist in Paris in 1937 with Monteux. During World War II she lived in Alexandria, Egypt, and played several hundred concerts for the Allied Forces in the Middle East. On Jan. 21, 1946, she made her London debut with the New London Orch. under the direction of Alec Sherman, who became her second husband. Her first American appearance took place in N.Y. on Oct. 15, 1950. Only 35 people attended this concert, but she received unanimous acclaim from the critics, and her career was assured. The uncommon vigor of her technique suggested comparisons with Teresa Carreño; her repertoire ranged from Mozart to Stravinsky; in both classical and modern works she displayed impeccable taste. She died suddenly of a heart attack in Athens on the day she was to appear as soloist with the National Symph. Orch. of Washington at the Athens Festival.

Bache, Constance, English writer and musician; b. Birmingham, March 11, 1846; d. Montreux, Switzerland, June 28, 1903. She was the sister of the English pianists **Francis Edward Bache** (1833–58) and **Walter Bache** (1842–88). She studied at the Munich Cons. and later with Klindworth; planned a piano career, but was forced to abandon it owing to an accident to her hand. In 1883 she settled in London. She publ. a vivid book of memoirs, *Brother Musicians* (London, 1901), describing the lives of her brothers; translated the letters of Hans von Bülow and Franz Liszt, and Heintz's analyses of Wagner's operas; also translated the libretto of Humperdinck's *Hänsel und Gretel.*

Bachelet, Alfred, French composer; b. Paris, Feb. 26, 1864; d. Nancy, Feb. 10, 1944. He studied at the Paris Cons.; received the Grand Prix de Rome for his cantata, *Cléopatre* (1890). From his earliest works, Bachelet devoted himself mainly to opera. In his youth, he was influenced by Wagnerian ideas, but later adopted a more national French style. During World War I he conducted at the Paris Opéra; in 1919 became director of the Nancy Cons.; in 1939 was elected a member of the Académie des Beaux Arts.

WORKS: Lyric dramas: *Scémo* (Paris Opéra, May 6, 1914) and *Un jardin sur l'Oronte* (Paris Opéra, Nov. 3, 1932); *Quand la cloche sonnera,* one-act music drama, his most successful work (Opéra-Comique, Nov.6, 1922); ballets: *La Fête chez la Pouplinière* and *Castor et Pollux* by Rameau (adapted and rewritten); orchestral works with voices: *L'Amour des Ondines, Joie, Le Songe de la Sulamith, Noël; Surya* for Tenor, Chorus, and Orch. (1940); *Ballade* for Violin and Orch.; songs.

Bachmann, Alberto Abraham, violinist and composer; b. Geneva, March 20, 1875; d. Neuilly-sur-Seine, Nov. 24, 1963. He studied violin at the Cons. of Lille, then took courses in succession with Ysaÿe, César, Thomson, Hubay, and Adolf Brodsky. He was in the U.S. from 1916 to 1926; then lived near Paris. He composed 3 violin concertos (the last of which is called *American Concerto*); 12 improvisations for solo violin; about 250 various pieces and as many transcriptions for violin. He publ. *Le Violon* (1906); *Les Grands Violonistes du passé* (1913); *Gymnastique à l'usage des violonistes* (1914); *L'Ecole du violoniste* (in 4 parts); and *Encyclopedia of the Violin* (N.Y., 1925).

Bachofen, Johann Caspar, Swiss composer; b. Zürich, Dec. 26, 1695; d. there, June 23, 1755. He studied in Zürich at the Cathedral school; received the title of V.D.M. (verbi divine minister) in 1720; in 1742 he was named cantor at the Grossmünster Cathedral there; concurrently served as Kapellmeister at the German School there (from 1739). He is best known for his popular collection of sacred songs for home use, publ. as *Musicalisches Hallelujah* (1727; many subsequent reprints).

BIBLIOGRAPHY: B. Arnold, *The Life and Works of J.C. Bachofen* (Diss., Univ. of Southern Calif., 1956).

Bachrich, Sigismund (Sigmund), Hungarian violist and composer; b. Zsambokreth, Jan. 23, 1841; d. Vienna, July 16, 1913. He studied violin in Vienna; spent several years in Paris, where he was viola player with the Hellmesberger and Rosé quartets. From 1869 to 1899 he was a member of the viola section in the Vienna Phil. He wrote several operas, among them *Muzzedin* (1883), *Heini von Steier* (1884), and *Der Fuchs-Major* (1889), as well as a ballet, *Sakuntala.* His memoirs were publ. posthumously under the title *Aus verklungenen Zeiten* (Vienna, 1914). In his professional activities he adopted Sigmund as his first name.

Bachschmidt, (Johann) Anton (Adam), Austrian-born German violinist and composer; b. Melk, Feb. 11, 1728; d. Eichstätt, Dec. 29, 1797. He was of a musical family; was director of instrumental music at Melk (1751–53); then settled in Eichstätt as a member of the court orch.; was made Konzertmeister there in 1768; then was promoted to Kapellmeister in 1773. He composed many sacred works, several operas, symphs., and 3 violin concertos.

Bacilly, Bénigne de, French composer and teacher; b. c.1625; d. Paris, Sept. 27, 1690. He composed a number of sacred and secular vocal works; however, he is best known for an important vocal treatise, *Remarques curieuses sur l'art de bien chanter* (Paris, 1668; Eng. ed., 1968).

Bäck, Knut, Swedish pianist and composer; b. Stockholm, April 22, 1868; d. Göteborg, Oct. 27, 1953. He studied music in Stockholm; later took lessons with Max Bruch in Berlin. He eventually settled in Göteborg as a music critic and teacher. Among his works are songs and piano pieces.

Bäck, Sven-Erik, significant Swedish composer; b. Stockholm, Sept. 16, 1919. He studied violin at the Royal Academy of Music in Stockholm (1938–43); composition with Hilding Rosenberg (1940–45); then went to Switzerland and took courses in medieval music at the Schola Cantorum in Basel (1948–50); later studied advanced composition with Petrassi in Rome (1951). Returning to Sweden, he played violin and also viola in two local string quartets and conducted the "Chamber Orchestra 1953" until 1957. In 1959 he was appointed director of the Swedish Radio music school at Edsberg Castle outside Stockholm. As a composer, he at first embraced the Scandinavian romantic manner, but soon began experimentation in serial procedures, later annexing electronic sound.

WORKS: His first important work which attracted merited praise was the radio opera *Tranfjädrarna (The Crane Feathers),* a symbolist subject from Japanese Noh drama (1956; Swedish Radio, Feb. 28, 1957; first stage performance, Stockholm, Feb. 19, 1958). His other works are: a scenic oratorio, *Ett spel om Maria, Jesu Moder (A Play about Mary, Mother of Jesus;* Swedish Radio, April 4, 1958); a chamber opera, *Gästabudet (The Feast;* Stockholm, Nov. 12, 1958); a radio opera, *Fågeln (The Birds;* Swedish Radio, Feb. 14, 1961; later versions for stage and commercial recording, 1969); a ballet, *Ikaros* (Stockholm, May, 1963); a television ballet, *Movements* (Swedish Television, Feb. 27, 1966); a ballet, *Kattresan (Cat's Journey;* 1969; original version was a "concerto per bambini" for Children's Chorus, 2 Recorders, Violin, and Percussion, 1952); 2 electronic ballets, *Mur och port (Wall and Gate;* Stockholm, Jan. 17, 1971) and *Genom Jorden genom havet (Through the Earth, Through the Sea;* 1971; Stockholm, June 1972); also, 3 string quartets (1945, 1947, 1962); string quintet, *Exercises* (1948); Solo Flute Sonata (1949); *Expansive Preludes* for Piano (1949); *Sonata alla ricercare* for Piano (1950); *Sinfonia per archi* (1951); *Sinfonia Sacra* for Chorus and Orch. (1953); Trio for Viola, Cello, and Double Bass (1953); *Sinfonia da camera* (1954); Sonata for 2 Cellos (1957); Violin Concerto (1957); *Impromptu* for Piano (1957); *A Game around a Game* for Strings and Percussion (Donaueschingen, Oct. 17, 1959); *Arkitektur* for 2 Wind Orchs. and Percussion (1960); *Favola* for Clarinet and Percussion (1962); *Intrada* for Orch. (Stockholm, April 26, 1964); Cello Concerto (1965); *O Altitudo I* for Organ (1966); orch. version, *O Altitudo II,* 1966); *5 Preludes* for Clarinet and Percussion (1966); *Humlan* for Chorus, Cello, Piano, and Percussion (1968); . . . *in principio* . . . for Tape (1969); String Trio (1970); *For Eliza* for Organ or Tape ad lib. (1971); *Aperio* for 3 Orch. Groups, each including Electronic Sound (1973); *Decet* for Wind Quintet, String Quartet, and Double Bass (1973); *Där fanns en brunn* for Chorus, Flute, Clarinet, Cello, Percussion, and Piano or Organ (1973); *Just da de langsta skuggorna* . . . for 4 Singers and 10 Instruments (1974); *Tollo I* for Piano Duet (1974) and *II* for 2 Pianos and Microphones (1975); *Time Present* for 2 Violins, Echo Filter, and Feedback Systems (1975); many motets and religious cantatas; short electronic pieces. A list of works is printed in "Verkerförteckning 1945–1966," *Nutida Musik* (1966/67).

Backer-Grøndahl, Agathe, Norwegian composer and pianist; b. Holmestrand, Dec. 1, 1847; d. Ormöen, near Oslo, June 16, 1907. She studied in Norway with Kjerulf and Lindemann, in Florence with Hans von Bülow, and in Weimar with Liszt; married the singing teacher Grøndahl (1875). Among her piano works, *Etudes de Concert, Romantische Stücke,* and *Trois Morceaux* became well known and have been frequently reprinted. She also wrote a song cycle, *Des Kindes Frühlingstag.*
BIBLIOGRAPHY: O. M. Sandvik, *Agathe Backer-Grøndahl* (Oslo, 1948), a centennial biography.

Backers, Cor, Dutch music historian and composer; b. Rotterdam, June 5, 1910. He studied piano with Dirk Schäfer and composition at the Rotterdam Cons. He gave piano recitals in the Netherlands; also traveled through Europe and East Africa; conducted the chamber choir Haags Kamerkoor (1950–60), specializing in the forgotten masterpieces of the past. He publ. a valuable compendium, *Nederlandse Componisten van 1400 tot op onze Tijd* (The Hague, 1941; 2nd enlarged ed., 1948), which details the evolution of music in the Netherlands, with particular emphasis on modern Dutch music; he also publ. monographs on Handel, Puccini, Gershwin, and others. He composes mostly for voices and organ; among his works are a "declamatorio," *Joost de Decker,* for Narrator and Piano; Piano Sonata (1935); *6 Goethe-Lieder* for Chorus a cappella (1969); *Missa Sancta* for Soloists, Chorus, and Organ (1973–74); *Te Deum Laudamus* for Chorus, and Organ or Orch. (1973–75).

Backhaus, Wilhelm, eminent German-born Swiss pianist and pedagogue; b. Leipzig, March 26, 1884; d. Villach, Austria, July 5, 1969. He studied with Reckendorf in Leipzig (1891–99); made his debut at the age of 8. After studying briefly with Eugène d'Albert in Frankfurt (1899), he began his career with a major tour in 1900; soon acquired a fine reputation in Europe as both a pianist and a teacher. He made his U.S. debut on Jan. 5, 1912, as soloist in Beethoven's 5th Piano Concerto with Walter Damrosch and the N.Y. Symph. Orch. In 1930 he settled in Lugano, where he continued to teach, and became a Swiss citizen. Following World War II, he resumed his concert tours; made his last appearance in the U.S. at a recital in N.Y. at the age of 78, displaying undiminished vigor as a virtuoso. He died while visiting Austria for a concert engagement. He was particularly distinguished in his interpretations of the works of Beethoven and Brahms.
BIBLIOGRAPHY: F. Herzog, *Wilhelm Backhaus* (Berlin, 1935); A.H. Eichmann, *Wilhelm Backhaus* (Ghent, 1957; Eng. trans., 1958).

Bacon, Ernst, remarkable American composer; b. Chicago, May 26, 1898. He studied music theory at Northwestern Univ. with P.C. Lutkin (1915–18), and later at the Univ. of Chicago with Arne Oldberg and T. Otterstroem; also took private piano lessons in Chicago with Alexander Raab (1916–21). In 1924 he went to Vienna, where he took private composition lessons with Karl Weigl and Franz Schmidt. Returning to America, he studied composition with Ernest Bloch in San Francisco, and conducting with Eugene Goossens in Rochester, N.Y. From 1934 to 1937 he was supervisor of the Federal Music Project in San Francisco; simultaneously deployed numerous related activities, as a conductor and a music critic. He was on the faculty of Converse College in South Carolina (1938–45) and Syracuse Univ. (1945–63). He also engaged in literary pursuits—wrote poetry and publ. a book of aphorisms—and espoused radical politics. A musician of exceptional inventive powers, he published a brochure, *Our Musical Idiom* (Chicago, 1917), when he was 19; in it he outlines the new resources of musical composition. In some of his piano works he evolved a beguiling technique of mirror reflection between the right and the left hand, exact as to the intervals, with white and black keys in one hand reflected respectively by white and black keys in the other hand. However, Ernst Bacon is generally regarded as primarily a composer of lyric songs. In 1963 he went to California and lived in Orinda, near San Francisco.
WORKS: Symph. No. 1 for Piano and Orch. (1932); Symph. No. 2 (1937; Chicago, Feb. 5, 1940); Symph. No. 3, *Great River,* for Narrator and Orch. (1956); Symph. No. 4 (1963); a musical play, *A Tree on the Plains* (Spartanburg, S.C., May 2, 1942); a folk opera, *A Drumlin Legend* (N.Y., May 4, 1949); *By Blue Ontario,* oratorio to words by Walt Whitman (1958); *The Last Invocation,* a Requiem, to poems by Walt Whitman, Emily Dickinson, and others (1968–71); *Nature,* a cantata cycle (1968); ballets: *Jehovah and the Ark* (1968–70) and *The Parliament of Fowls* (1975); songs to words by Emily Dickinson and Walt

Bacon – Badia

Whitman: *From Emily's Diary* for Soprano, Alto, Women's Chorus, and Orch. (1945); *The Lord Star,* cantata (1950); *Songs of Eternity* (1932); *Black and White Songs* for Baritone and Orch. (1932); *Twilight,* 3 songs for Voice and Orch. (1932); *Midnight Special,* 4 songs for Voice and Orch. (1932); Piano Quintet (1946); Cello Sonata (1946); String Quintet (1951); *Riolama* for Piano and Orch., in 10 short movements (1964); *Spirits and Places,* a cycle with geographical connotations for Organ (1966); *Saws,* a suite of canons for Chorus and Piano (1971); *Dr. Franklin,* music play for the bicentennial (1976), to text by Cornel Lengyel. Among Bacon's publ. books are *Words on Music* (1960) and *Notes on the Piano* (1963). A collection of his songs, *Grass Roots* for Soprano, Alto, and Piano, was publ. in 2 vols. in 1976.

Bacon, Richard Mackenzie, English writer on music; b. Norwich, May 1, 1776; d. Cossey, Nov. 27, 1844. He published *Elements of Vocal Science* (London, 1824) and *Art of Improving the Voice and Ear* (London, 1825); was the founder and editor of the *Quarterly Musical Magazine and Review* (1818–30), the first music periodical in England. He was also instrumental in organizing the triennial Music Festivals at Norwich.

Bacquier, Gabriel, French baritone; b. Béziers, May 17, 1924. He studied at the Paris Cons. His first notable success came in 1953, when he sang the role of Figaro in Rossini's *The Barber of Seville* in Brussels. On Oct. 17, 1964, he made his appearance at the Metropolitan Opera House in N.Y. A fine singing artist, he was especially notable in dramatic roles.

Badarzewska, Thekla, Polish composer of salon music; b. Warsaw, 1834; d. there, Sept. 29, 1861. At the age of 17 she publ. in Warsaw a piano piece, *Molitwa dziewicy (A Maiden's Prayer),* which was republ. as a supplement to the Paris *Revue et Gazette Musicale* in 1859, and unaccountably seized the imagination not only of inhibited virgins, but of sentimental amateur pianists all over the world. More than 100 editions of this unique piece of salon pianism, dripping maudlin arpeggios, were publ. in the 19th century, and the thing was still widely sold even in the 20th century. Badarzewska wrote 34 more piano pieces in the salon style, but none of them matched *A Maiden's Prayer.* An ungentlemanly German critic opined in an obituary that "Badarzewska's early death saved the musical world from a veritable inundation of intolerable lachrymosity."

Badea, Christian, Rumanian-born American conductor; b. Bucharest, Dec. 10, 1947. He studied violin and composition at the Bucharest Cons.; subsequently took courses in Brussels, in Salzburg, and at the Juilliard School of Music in N.Y. He conducted at the Spoleto Festival of Two Worlds in Charleston, S.C., and Spoleto, Italy; also served as conductor of the Savannah (Ga.) Symph. Orch. and the Columbus (Ohio) Symph. Orch. He had guest engagements with the Pittsburgh Symph., National Symph. of Washington, D.C., Detroit Symph., American Symph. of N.Y., BBC Symph. of London, and Amsterdam Phil.

Baden, Conrad, Norwegian composer, organist, and music critic; b. Drammen, Aug. 31, 1908. After studies in his hometown, he took advanced training in Leipzig (1931–32) and later in Paris with Honegger and Rivier (1951–52). He was organist in Drammen from 1943 and in Oslo from 1961; also taught at the Oslo Cons. (1948–73). He writes in a neo-Classical idiom.
WORKS: Mass for Soloists, Chorus, and Orch. (1949); Divertimento for Orch. (1950); *Overtura Gioia* (1951); 3 symphs. (1952, 1957, 1970); Concertino for Clarinet and Strings (1953); *Pastorale and Fugue* for Chamber Orch. (1957); 3 anniversary cantatas: for the city of Skien's 600th (1958), for Strömsö Church's 300th (1966–67), and for Dröbak Church's 200th (1973); *Eventyr-Suite (Fairytale Suite)* for Orch. (1960); *Fantasia Brevis* for Orch. (1965); *Concerto for Orchestra* (1968); *Intrada Sinfonica* for Orch. (1969); *Mennesket (The Human Being),* cantata for Chorus and Orch. (1971); Violin Sonata (c.1942); 3 string quartets (1944, 1946, 1961); 2 trios for Flute, Oboe, and Clarinet (1957, 1964); Sonata for Solo Flute (1958); Divertimento for Flute, Oboe, and Clarinet (1964); *Hymnus* for Alto Voice, Flute, Oboe, and Viola (1966); Wind Quintet; Piano Trio; piano pieces; *Sonata Sacra* for Organ (1974); choral works.
BIBLIOGRAPHY: B. Kortsen, *Contemporary Norwegian Orchestral Music* (Bergen, Norway, 1969); idem, *Contemporary Norwegian Chamber Music* (Bergen, 1971); H. Herresthal, "Kirckemusikeren og komponisten Conrad Baden," *Norsk musiktidsskrift* (1971/72).

Badescu, Dinu, Rumanian tenor; b. Craiova, Oct. 17, 1904. He studied in Bucharest; made his debut as a baritone in 1931 in Cluj; later began singing tenor roles. He was a leading member of the Bucharest Opera (1936–41); also sang at the Vienna Volksoper (1941–44) and made appearances at the Vienna State Opera (from 1948); was highly successful as a guest artist with the Bolshoi Theater in Moscow, in Leningrad, Budapest, Prague, etc. He made a specialty of lyrico-dramatic roles in Verdi's operas.

Badia, Carlo Agostino, Italian composer; b. probably in Venice, 1672; d. Vienna, Sept. 23, 1738. His first known work was his oratorio *La sete di Cristo in croce* (Innsbruck, 1691); soon thereafter he was made a court composer at Innsbruck. In 1694 he was called to Vienna, where he became Musik-Compositeur of the Imperial Court; he held that post for the rest of his life. His first wife was **Anna Maria Elisabetta Nonetti,** a prominent singer at the Viennese court (d. 1726). Badia was an important composer in his day, producing some 25 works for the stage, about 40 oratorios, and over 50 chamber cantatas and duets.
WORKS: FOR THE STAGE: *La ninfa Apollo* (1692); *Amor che vince lo sdegno, ovvero Olimpia placata*

124

(Rome, Carnival 1692); *La Rosaura ovvero Amore figlio della gratitudine* (Innsbruck, 1692); *L'Amazone corsara, ovvero L'Alvilda, regina de' Goti* (Innsbruck, 1692); *Bacco, vincitore dell'India* (Vienna, Carnival 1697); *La pace tra i numi discordi nella rovina di Troia* (Vienna, May 21, 1697); *L'idea del felice governo* (Vienna, June 9, 1698); *Lo squittinio dell'eroe* (Vienna, July 26, 1698); *Imeneo trionfante* (Vienna, Feb. 28, 1699); *Il Narciso* (Vienna, June 9, 1699); *Il commun giubilo del mondo* (Vienna, July 26, 1699); *Cupido fuggitivo da Venere e ritrovato a' piedi della Sacra Reale Maestà d'Amalia* (Vienna, Carnival 1700); *Le gare dei beni* (Vienna, Feb. 21, 1700); *Diana rappacificata con Venere e con Amore* (Vienna, April 21, 1700); *La costanza d'Ulisse* (Vienna, June 9, 1700); *L'amore vuol somiglianza* (Vienna, Jan. 7, 1702); *L'Arianna* (Vienna, Feb. 21, 1702); *Il Telemacco, ovvero Il valore coronato* (Vienna, March 19, 1702); *La concordia della Virtù e della Fortuna* (Vienna, April 21, 1702); *Enea negli Elisi* (Vienna, July 26, 1702); *La Psiche* (Vienna, Feb. 21, 1703); *Napoli ritornata ai Romani* (Vienna, Oct. 1, 1707); *Ercole, vincitore di Gerione* (Vienna, Nov. 4, 1708); *Gli amori di Circe con Ulisse* (Dresden, June 20, 1709); *Il bel genio dell'Austria ed il Fato* (Vienna, Nov. 1723).

BIBLIOGRAPHY: C. Nemeth, "Zur Lebensgeschichte von Carlo Agostino Badia (1672–1738)," *Anzeiger der phil.-hist. Klasse der Österreichischen Akademie der Wissenschaften* (1955).

Badia, Conchita (Conxita), noted Spanish soprano; b. Barcelona, Nov. 14, 1897; d. there, May 2, 1975. She studied piano and voice with Granados; also had lessons with Casals and Manuel de Falla. She made her debut in Barcelona as a concert singer in 1913 in the first performance of *Canciónes amatorias* by Granados, with the composer as piano accompanist. She subsequently devoted herself to concert appearances, excelling as an interpreter of Spanish and Latin American music; often appeared in performances with Casals and his orch. in Barcelona. In later years she taught voice in Barcelona, where her most famous pupil was Montserrat Caballé.

BIBLIOGRAPHY: J. Alavedra, *Conxita Badia: Una vida d'artista* (Barcelona, 1975).

Badings, Henk, eminent Dutch composer; b. Bandung, Indonesia, Jan. 17, 1907, of Dutch parents. He was orphaned at an early age and came to the Netherlands. He first studied mining engineering at the Delft Polytechnic Univ.; then began to compose without any formal study and produced a symph. which was performed in Amsterdam by Mengelberg with the Concertgebouw Orch. on July 6, 1930; however, he discarded the work, and wrote another symph. 2 years later to replace it. At the same time he began taking lessons in composition with Willem Pijper (1930–31); afterward taught music at the Rotterdam Cons. (1934–37), at the Lyceum in Amsterdam (1937–41), and at the Cons. of The Hague (1941–45). He was temporarily barred from professional activities after the end of World War II on charges

of cultural collaboration with the Germans during the Netherlands' occupation, but regained his status in 1947. In 1961 he was appointed prof. of acoustics at the Univ. of Utrecht. In 1962 he was guest lecturer at the Univ. of Adelaide in Australia. From 1966 to 1972 he was prof. of composition at the Staatliche Hochschule für Musik in Stuttgart. His style of composition may be described as romantic modernism marked by intense dynamism. In melodic progressions he often employs the scale of alternating major and minor seconds known in the Netherlands as the "Pijper scale." After 1950 he began experimenting with electronic sound and microtonal divisions, especially the 31-tone scale devised by the Dutch physicist Adriaan Fokker.

WORKS: 6 operas: *De Nachtwacht* (*The Night Watch,* 1942; Antwerp, May 13, 1950); *Liebesränke* (*Love's Ruses,* 1944–45; Hilversum, Jan. 6, 1948); *Orestes,* radio opera (Florence, Sept. 24, 1954); *Asterion,* radio opera (Johannesburg, April 11, 1958); *Salto mortale,* chamber opera, for television (Netherlands Television, Eindhoven, June 19, 1959; first opera to be accompanied solely by electronic sound); *Martin Korda, D.P.* (Amsterdam, June 15, 1960; includes electronic sound). Ballets for instruments: *Balletto Grottesco* for 2 Pianos (1939); *Orpheus und Eurydike* for Soloists, Chorus, and Orch. (1941; Amsterdam, April 17, 1941); *Balletto Serioso* for Orch. or 2 Pianos (1955); *Balletto Notturno* for 2 Pianos (1975). Ballets for electronic sound: *Cain and Abel* (The Hague, June 21, 1956; first all-electronic sound ballet); *Variations électroniques* (1957; originally film music, perf. as a ballet, *Marionetten,* Salzburg, 1961); *Évolutions* (Hannover, Sept. 28, 1958); *Genèse* for 5 Audio-frequency Oscillators in quadraphonic sound placement (Brussels, Oct. 7, 1958; produced as a ballet under the title *Der sechste Tag* at Innsbruck, Nov. 7, 1959; with new choreography produced as *Mikrobiologisches,* Linz, Feb. 22, 1960); *Jungle* (Amsterdam, 1959); *The Woman of Andras,* with Voices (Hannover, April 14, 1960). Oratorios: *Apocalypse* (1948; Rotterdam, Nov. 25, 1959) and *Jonah* (Adelaide, Australia, Sept. 30, 1963; includes electronic sound); *St. Mark Passion* for Soloists, Male Chorus, Orch., and Tape (1971; Rotterdam, May 18, 1972); 8 cantatas (1936–73); 14 symphs.: No. 1 for 16 Solo Instruments (1932; Hilversum, March 19, 1959); No. 2 (1932; Amsterdam, Oct. 5, 1932); No. 3 (1934; Amsterdam, May 2, 1935); No. 4 (1943; Rotterdam, Oct. 13, 1947); No. 5 (1949; Amsterdam, Dec. 7, 1949); No. 6, *Psalm,* with Chorus (1953; Holland Festival, Haarlem, June 25, 1953); No. 7, *Louisville* (1954; Louisville, Ky., Feb. 26, 1955); No. 8, *Hannover* (1956; Hannover, Jan. 11, 1957); No. 9 for String Orch. (1959; Amsterdam, Dec. 17, 1960); No. 10 (1961; Rotterdam, Jan. 29, 1962); No. 11, *Sinfonia Giocosa* (Eindhoven, Oct. 26, 1964); No. 12, *Symphonische klangfiguren* (The Hague, Nov. 20, 1964); No. 13 for Wind Orch. (Pittsburgh, June 29, 1967); No. 14, *Symphonische Triptiek* (Ghent, Sept. 4, 1968); Sinfonietta for Small Orch. (1971); 4 violin concertos (1928, 1933–35, 1944, 1947); 2 cello concertos: No. 1 (1930) and No. 2 (1939); *Symphonic Variations* (1936–37); 6 overtures, including *Tragic* (1937), *Heroic* (1937), *Symphonic Prologue* (1942), and

Irish (1961); 2 piano concertos (1939; *Atlantic Dances,* 1955); Concertino for Violin, Cello, Piano, and Chamber Orch. (1942); Divertimento (1949); Ballad, symph. variations (1950); Saxophone Concerto (1951–52); 2 organ concertos (1952, 1966); Serenade (1953); *Symphonic Scherzo* (1953); 2 Concertos for 2 Violins (1954; 1969, in the 31-tone temperament); *Dance Variations* (1956); 2 flute concertos (1956, 1963); *Mars* for Small Orch. (1957); *Nederlandse dansen* for Orch. (1957); Partita for Wind Orch. (1960); *Symphonic Variations on a South African Theme* (1960); Concerto for Bassoon, Double Bassoon, and Wind Orch. (1964); 2-Piano Concerto (1964); Concerto for Viola and String Orch. (1965); *Pittsburgh Concerto* for Solo Clarinet, Brass, Percussion, and Tape (1965); Concerto for Violin, Viola, and Orch. (1965); Concerto for Harp and Small Orch. (1967); *Tower Music* for Wind Orch. and Tape (1969); Concerto for 3 Horns, Wind Orch., and Tape (1970); *Variations on Green Sleeves* for Wind Orch. (1970); *Transitions* for Wind Orch. (1972); Concerto *(American Folk Song Suite)* for English Horn and Wind Orch. (1975); *Nederlandse dansen* for Small Orch. (1975); *Lieshout and Its Windmills,* suite for Wind Orch. (1976). For Voice and Orch.: *The West Wind* for Narrator and Orch. (1936); *Songs of Life and Death* for Tenor and Orch. (1940); *Psalm 147* for Chorus, Children's Chorus, and Orch. (1959); *Te Deum* for Male Chorus and Orch. (1961); *Hymnus, Ave Maris Stella* for Female Chorus and Orch. (1965); *Genesis* for Baritone, Tenor, Male Chorus, Tape, and 4 Percussionists (1967); *Armageddon* for Soprano, Wind Orch., and Tape (1968); Chamber and solo works in the 31-tone temperament: *Contrasts* for a cappella Chorus (1952); *Series of Small Pieces* for Organ (1954); 2-Violin Sonatas Nos. 2 and 3 (1963, 1967); String Quartet No. 4 (1966); *Variations on Seikilos Skolion* for 2 Violins (1975); *Archifonica* for Organ (1976). Other chamber and solo works: 3 sonatas for Solo Violin (1940, 1951, 1951); 2 sonatas for Solo Cello (1941, 1951); Sonata for Solo Harp (1944); Toccata for Solo Marimbaphone (1973); *Capriccio* for Violin and Tape (1959); Chaconne for Trumpet and Tape (1965); Sonata for Violin and Cello (1927); Sonata for Violin and Viola (1928); Sonata No. 1 for 2 Violins (1928); 2 cello sonatas (1929, 1934); 4 violin sonatas (1933; 1939; 1952; originally 1931, rescored 1966); *Capriccio* for Flute and Piano (1936); Ballade for Harp and Flute (1950); Viola Sonata (1951); Passacaglia for Timpani and Organ (1958); Canzona for Horn and Organ (1967); *It Is Dawning in the East,* balladic variations for Guitar and Organ (1967); 9 trios for varying instrumental combinations (1934–62); Nocturne for 3 Horns and Tape (1970); 4 string quartets (1931; 1936; 1944; 1966, in the 31-tone temperament); Piano Quartet (1973); Brass Quartet (1947); 5 quintets: No. 1 for Flute, Piano, and String Trio (1928); No. 2 for Wind Quintet (1929); No. 3 for Harp, Flute, and String Trio (1936); No. 4 for Wind Quintet (1948); No. 5 for Piano Quintet (1952); Sextet for Wind Quintet and Piano (1952); Octet (1952); *Twentse Suite* for 4 Soloists and 4 groups of Accordions (1976); 6 piano sonatas (1934, 1941, 1944, 1945, 1945, 1947); 3 piano sonatinas (1936, 1945, 1950); Suite for Piano (1930); Theme with

Variations for Piano (1938); *Arcadia,* little piano pieces for beginners, in 7 vols. (1945–67); *5 Small Pieces* for Piano (1967); Concertino for Piano and Tape (1967); *Kontrapunkte* for Piano and Tape (1970); Preludes for Piano (1976); *Preludium and Fuga I–IV* for Organ (1952, 1952, 1953, 1956); Toccata for Organ (1929); *Ricercare* for Organ (1973). Many songs and choruses; pieces for tape alone; piano pieces. Badings is the author of a book on contemporary Dutch music, *De Hedendaagsche Nederlandsche Muziek* (Amsterdam, 1936), and of *Elektronische Muziek* (Amsterdam, 1958).

BIBLIOGRAPHY: Cor Backers, *Nederlandse Componisten* (Amsterdam, 1949); Jos Wouters, "Henk Badings," *Sonorum Speculum,* 32 (1967, pp. 1–23). A complete catalogue of his works, in German and English, was issued in 1965, listing all publishers and recordings (supplement, 1965–70).

Badini, Ernesto, Italian baritone; b. San Colombano al Lambro, Sept. 14, 1876; d. Milan, July 6, 1937. He studied at the Cons. in Milan; made his debut in 1895; sang in many of the regional opera houses of Italy. In 1913 Toscanini chose him for the Verdi centennial celebrations in Parma; then invited him to La Scala; Badini remained on its roster until 1931. In addition to buffo roles, Badini also sang in a number of contemporary operas.

Badinski, Nicolai, Bulgarian composer; b. Sofia, Dec. 19, 1937. From 1963 to 1976 he lived in East Berlin; then moved to West Berlin, obtaining his German citizenship in 1980. After a study at the Sofia Academy of Music, he took courses at the Accademia Musicale in Siena; in Germany worked with Ligeti, Stockhausen, Xenakis, and Kagel at the Darmstadt International Courses for New Music. Besides composition, he was active as a concert violinist. In his music he follows practical modernistic trends, avoiding extreme applications of experimental techniques.

WORKS: 3 symphs. (1967, 1978, 1981); 3 violin concertos (1971, 1972, 1972); Viola Concerto (1975); Harpsichord Concerto (1977); *Klavieriada* for Piano and Orch. (1981); *Homage to Stravinsky* for String Orch. (1979); *The Ruins under Sofia,* octet (1972); *Silenzio disturbato* for Sextet (1976); 3 string quartets (1965, 1973, 1978); Wind Quintet (1969); *Imaginable Trio* for Computer (1980); numerous pieces of electronic music: *Rotation,* in memory of a Soviet cosmonaut, for Electronic Sound (1974); *Musik mit Papier* and *Luftmusik* for Electronics (1980–81); *Traumvisionen* for Electronic Sound (1982).

Badura-Skoda, Paul, eminent Austrian pianist, music editor, and pedagogue; b. Vienna, Oct. 6, 1927. He was brought up by his stepfather, Skoda, whose name he adopted professionally. He studied science as well as music; graduated from the Vienna Cons. in 1948. A scholarly musician, he won several prizes for excellence. He had a successful career as a concert pianist; gave recitals in Europe; made his N.Y. debut on Jan. 10, 1953. From 1966 until 1971 he was artist-in-residence at the Univ. of Wisconsin. On

Sept. 19, 1951, he married **Eva Halfar** (b. Munich, Jan. 15, 1929), who collaborated with him on his various editions. He publ. *Mozart-Interpretation* (Vienna, 1957; in collaboration with Eva Badura-Skoda; in Eng. as *Interpreting Mozart on the Keyboard,* N.Y., 1962; also in Japanese, Tokyo, 1963) and *Die Klaviersonaten von Ludwig van Beethoven* (with J. Demus, Wiesbaden, 1970); also contributed valuable articles on Chopin, Schubert, and others to German music journals.

Baervoets, Raymond, Belgian composer; b. Brussels, Nov. 6, 1930. He studied composition with Absil, Bourguignon, and Barbier, and conducting with Defossez at the Brussels Cons.; later took a course with Petrassi at the Santa Cecilia Academy in Rome (1961–62). His music follows the classical forms, while its content evolves in an ultra-chromatic coloristic idiom, including the use of quarter-tones.
WORKS: 2 ballets, *Metamorphose* (1963) and *La Chasse fantastique* (Antwerp, Sept. 28, 1968); *Concerto da Camera* for Violin and Chamber Orch. (1955); *Mouvement symphonique* (1955); *Petite suite* for Chamber Orch. (1955); *Elégie et Passacaille* for Orch. (1956); *Rhapsodie* for Viola and Chamber Orch. (1957); Concerto for Guitar and Chamber Orch. (1958); Fantasia for String Orch. (1958); Sinfonietta for String Orch. (1959); Violin Concerto (1961); *Improvvisazioni concertanti* for Cello and 19 Instruments (1962); *Musica* for 14 Instruments (1962); *Composizione* for Orch. (1962); *Espressioni* for Orch. (1966); *Constellations* for Orch. (1966); *Notturno* for Chamber Orch. (1971; performed as a ballet, Antwerp, Nov. 10, 1973); *Musica 1972* for Chamber Orch.; *Magnificat* for Soprano and Orch. (1964); *Erosions I* for Alto and 6 Performers, and *II* for Female Chorus and Orch. (both 1965); *Les Dents de la terre* for Narrator, Soloists, Chorus, and 2 Orchs. (1968); *Impromptu* for Trombone and Piano (1958); Etude for String Quartet (1961); *Musica Notturna* for Harpsichord, Violin, Cello, and Flute (1969); *Figures* for 4 Trombones, 4 Horns, and 4 Trumpets (1973); Quartet for Flute, Clarinet, Violin, and Piano (1974); *Scherzo* for 2 Pianos (1957); *Hommage à Serge Prokofieff* for Piano (1958); *Inventions* for Piano (1964); *Immagini* for Chamber Orch. (1976).

Baeyens, August, Belgian composer; b. Antwerp, June 5, 1895; d. there, July 17, 1966. He studied at the Royal Flemish Cons. in Antwerp; beginning in 1911, he was a viola player in Belgian orchs. In 1932 he became secretary of the Royal Flemish Opera, later serving as director (1944–48 and 1953–58). Despite his intimate association with the Flemish currents in the music of Belgium, he turned away from the dominant national direction and wrote music of a distinctly expressionistic type, rooted in a quasi-atonal chromaticism.
WORKS: 2 operas, *De Ring van Gyges* (1943) and *De Triomferende Min* (1948); a radio opera, *Coriolanus,* after Shakespeare (1941); a ballet, *De Dode Dichter* (*The Dead Poet,* 1920); *De Liefde en de*

Kakatoes (Love and the Cockatoos), a "grotesque" in one act (1928); 8 symphs. (1923, 1939, 1949, 1952, 1954, 1955, 1958, 1961); a *Sinfonia Breve* (1928); *Arkadia,* chamber symph. for 19 Soloists (1951); 6 orch. scores: *Entrata* (1917); *Niobé* (1918); *4 Small Pieces* (1923); *Arlequin* (1924); *Cyclops* (1925); *Notturno* (1953); Viola Concerto (1956); Trumpet Concerto (1959); Horn Concerto (1960); *Rhapsodie* for Clarinet and Orch. (1966); *Lofzang aan de haven (Hymn of Praise for the Port),* cantata (1929); *Barabbas* for Narrator and Orch. (1949); 6 string quartets (1922, 1925, 1927, 1949, 1951, 1962); Wind Quintet (1950); Concertino for Oboe, Clarinet, and Bassoon (1951); *Piranesi Suite* for Flute and Cello (1951); Violin Sonata (1952); Piano Sonata (1930); songs.

Baez, Joan, politically active American folksinger of English, Irish, and Mexican descent; b. Staten Island, N.Y., Jan. 9, 1941. She played the guitar by ear; then studied drama at Boston Univ. She made her first impact on American mass consciousness in 1959 when she appeared at the Newport Folk Festival. In 1965 she founded the Institute for the Study of Non-Violence; joined the struggle against the Vietnam War and supported the organizing fight of the United Farm Workers' Union. Accompanying herself on the guitar, she appeared at numerous concerts promoting topical humanitarian causes.

Bagby, Albert Morris, American pianist and concert manager; b. Rushville, Ill., April 29, 1859; d. New York, Feb. 26, 1941. He studied in Berlin, and with Liszt in Weimar. Returning to America in 1891, he organized in N.Y. the Bagby Morning Musicales, presenting 428 concerts; directed them until a few weeks before his death.

Bagge, Selmar, German composer and music pedagogue; b. Coburg, June 30, 1823; d. Basel, July 16, 1896. He studied in Vienna; from 1851 to 1855 was on the faculty of the Vienna Cons.; then went to Germany, and became the editor of the *Allgemeine Musikzeitung* in Leipzig (1863–68). In 1868 he was appointed director of the Basel Music School, retaining this post until his death. He composed 4 symphs., piano pieces, and other works; he publ. *Lehrbuch der Tonkunst* (1873); *Die geschichtliche Entwickelung der Sonate* (1880); *Die Symphonie in ihrer historischen Entwickelung* (1884). A biographical sketch of Bagge was publ. by Eglinger (Basel, 1897).

Baggiani, Guido, Italian composer; b. Naples, March 4, 1932. He studied composition at the Santa Cecilia Academy in Rome; then attended courses given by Stockhausen in Cologne, which were crucial for his further development. In Rome he organized a group for the propaganda of contemporary music with the meaningful name of Nuova Consonanza. In 1970 he was appointed prof. of composition at the Cons. of Pesaro. In 1972 he formed a group with the curious Italian-American name Gruppo Team Roma for performances of electronic music. His principal works are *Mimesi* for Strings and Woodwinds (1967); *Metafora* for Solo Strings (1968); *UBU-ng* for Soprano, Piano, Vibraphone, Electric Guitar, and 6 Chinese Gongs (of indeterminate duration; 1970); *Twins* for Piano and Magnetic Tape (1971); *Memoria* for Chamber Orch. and 2 Magnetic Tapes (1972); *Accordo Presunto* for 2 Instrumental Groups and Electronic Media (1973).

Bagier, Guido, German musicologist; b. Berlin, June 20, 1888; d. Düsseldorf, April 3, 1968. He studied at the Univ. of Leipzig with Max Reger and Riemann; taught at the State Academy of Arts in Düsseldorf; settled in Berlin, where he was connected with a motion picture company. He publ. a biography of Max Reger (Stuttgart, 1923).

Baguer, Carlos, Spanish organist and composer; b. Barcelona, 1768; d. there, Feb. 29, 1808. He served as the organist of the Cathedral in Barcelona throughout his entire career. He composed a large amount of organ music which reflects the influence of the Italian and German masters of his day.

Bahner, Gert, German conductor; b. Neuwiese, March 26, 1930. He was educated at the Leipzig Hochschule für Musik. In 1957 he made his debut at the Berlin Komische Opera; from 1958 to 1962 he was music director in Potsdam; then Generalmusikdirektor of Karl-Marx-Stadt (1962–65). In 1965 he became first conductor of the Berlin Komische Opera; in 1969 its music director. In 1973 he became music director of the Leipzig Opera.

Bähr, (Franz) Josef, noted Austrian clarinetist; b. Feb. 19, 1770; d. Vienna, Aug. 7, 1819. He was in the service of Prince Kraft Ernst of Oettingen-Wallerstein (1787–94); he settled in Vienna in 1797, and then became a court musician in the service of Count Johann Joseph Liechtenstein. Beethoven was impressed by his talent, and during the period 1796–1802 wrote his major solo clarinet parts with Bähr in mind.
BIBLIOGRAPHY: P. Weston, *Clarinet Virtuosi of the Past* (London, 1971).

Bai, Tommaso, Italian musician; b. Crevalcuore, near Bologna, c.1650; d. Rome, Dec. 22, 1714. He was a tenor at the Vatican, where he became maestro di cappella on Nov. 19, 1713. The best-known composition by Bai, follower of Palestrina, is a 5-part *Miserere* sung during Holy Week in the Papal Chapel alternately with those by Allegri and Baini. It is reprinted in various collections (Choron, Burney, Peters); other works of Bai are included in C. Proske's *Musica Divina* (1853–63).

Baïf, Jean-Antoine de, French composer and poet; b. Venice, Feb. 19, 1532; d. Paris, Sept. 19, 1589. He was brought to Paris as a child, and formed a friendship with Ronsard and other eminent poets. In 1570 he founded the Académie de Poésie et de Musique, with the aim of reviving the music and poetry of ancient Greece. He developed a system of "musique

mesurée," which he believed would possess a moral force similar to the Greek ideas of "ethos." Settings of his poems were composed by Jacques Maudit in *26 Chansonettes mesurées* (1586) for 4 Voices; and by Claude Le Jeune, in *Le Printemps* (1603). Both of these collections have been reprinted in Henri Expert's *Maîtres musiciens* (1899–1901; vols. X, XII, XIII, and XIV). Baïf's musical works comprise 12 sacred songs and several works in lute tablature.
BIBLIOGRAPHY: M. Auge-Chiquet, *La Vie, les idées et l'œuvre de Jean-Antoine de Baïf* (Paris, 1909); W. Müller-Blattau, "Chanson, Vaudeville, und Air de cour," *Volks- und Hochkunst in Dichtung und Musik* (Saarbrücken, 1968).

Bailey, Lilian, American soprano; b. Columbus, Ohio, Jan. 18, 1860; d. London, Nov. 4, 1901. She went to Boston as a young girl, and appeared in concert with **George Henschel,** the first conductor of the Boston Symph. Orch.; she married him in 1881, and after the end of his tenure in Boston, followed him to London, where they settled and became British subjects. Henschel, who himself began his career as a singer, often performed with Lilian Bailey some popular duets, such as "Oh that we two were maying," as interpolated numbers at Boston Symph. concerts.

Bailey, Mildred, American blues singer; b. Tekoa, Wash., Feb. 27, 1907; d. Poughkeepsie, N.Y., Dec. 12, 1951. After appearing on radio programs, she joined Paul Whiteman in 1929, remaining with his orch. until 1933; subsequently appeared with the bands of Red Norvo, Benny Goodman, and others. She married Red Norvo in 1933 and divorced him in 1945.

Bailey, Norman, English baritone; b. Birmingham, March 23, 1933. He received a B.Mus. degree from Rhodes Univ. in South Africa; then studied at the Vienna Academy of Music; his principal teachers there were Julius Patzak, Adolf Vogel, and Josef Witt. He made his operatic debut with the Vienna Chamber Opera in 1959; was then a member of the Linz Landestheater (1960–63), the Wuppertal Opera (1963–64), the Deutsche Oper am Rhein in Düsseldorf (1964–67), and the Sadler's Wells Opera Co. in London (1967–71). On Oct. 23, 1976, he made his Metropolitan Opera debut as Hans Sachs in *Die Meistersinger von Nürnberg.* In 1977 he was made a Commander of the Order of the British Empire. He was particularly noted for his performances in Wagner's operas.

Bailey, Pearl (Mae), black American singer of popular music; b. Newport News, Va., March 29, 1918. After winning an amateur contest in Philadelphia at 15, she quit school to pursue a career as an entertainer; worked as a dancer and a singer in various nightclubs in Washington, D.C., Baltimore, and N.Y. She made her Broadway debut in 1946 in *St. Louis Woman* and subsequently appeared in *Arms and the Girl* (1950), *Bless You All* (1950), and *House of Flowers* (1954); her greatest success came in 1967, when she starred in the all-black version of the hit musical *Hello, Dolly!* She also appeared in films, including *Carmen Jones* (1954), *St. Louis Blues* (1958), and *Porgy and Bess* (1959), and had her own television show (1970–71). She gained fame with her renditions of *Birth of the Blues; Toot Toot Tootsie, Goodbye; Takes Two to Tango,* and *Row, Row, Row.* She publ. 2 entertaining accounts of her life and career, *The Raw Pearl* (N.Y., 1968) and *Talking to Myself* (N.Y., 1971).

Baillie, Dame Isobel, Scottish soprano; b. Hawick, Roxburghshire, March 9, 1895; d. Manchester, Sept. 24, 1983. She was educated in Manchester; then went to Italy and began to take voice lessons in Milan. She made her concert debut in London in 1923, and through the years established herself as a successful singer, particularly in oratorio. It is said that she sang the *Messiah* more than 1,000 times. In 1978 Queen Elizabeth II made her a Dame Commander of the Order of the British Empire.

Baillot, Pierre-Marie-François de Sales, celebrated French violinist; b. Passy, near Paris, Oct. 1, 1771; d. Paris, Sept. 15, 1842. The son of a schoolmaster, he received an excellent education; at the age of 9 he became a pupil of the French violinist Sainte-Marie; he later was sent to Rome, where he studied under Pollani; returned to Paris in 1791. He met Viotti, who obtained for him a position in the orch. of the Théâtre Feydeau; later he served as a clerk in the Ministry of Finance. In 1795 he received the important appointment as violin teacher at the newly opened Paris Cons.; but continued to study composition with Cherubini, Reicha, and Catel. In 1802 he joined Napoleon's private instrumental ensemble; toured Russia with the cellist Lamarre (1805–8). Upon his return to Paris, he organized chamber music concerts, which enjoyed excellent success; also gave concerts in Belgium, the Netherlands, and England. In 1821 he became first violinist at the Paris Opéra; from 1825 he was also solo violinist in the Royal Orch. Baillot's musical compositions, rarely performed, comprise 9 violin concertos, 3 string quartets, 15 trios, a Symph. Concertante for 2 Violins with Orch., 6 violin duos, etc. Baillot's name is chiefly remembered through his manual *L'Art du violon* (1834); with Rode and Kreutzer he wrote a *Méthode de Violon,* adopted by the Paris Cons. and republished in numerous editions and languages; he also edited the *Méthode de violoncelle* by Levasseur, Catel, and Baudiot.

Bailly, Louis, French viola player; b. Valenciennes, June 13, 1882; d. Cowansville, Quebec, Nov. 21, 1974. He studied violin and viola at the Paris Cons., graduating with first prize in 1899; was subsequently the violist in the Capet, Flonzaley (1917–24), Elman, and Curtis quartets; served as head of the viola and chamber music dept. at the Curtis Inst. of Music in Philadelphia; in 1954 went to Canada and taught in Montreal.

Bain, Wilfred, American music educator and administrator; b. Shawville, Quebec, Jan. 20, 1908. He was educated at Houghton College (A.B., 1929) and York Univ. (M.A., 1936; Ed.D., 1938). He was head of the music dept. at Central College, S.C. (1929–30); then of voice and choral music at Houghton College (1931–38). He was dean of music at North Texas State Univ. (1938–47). In 1947 he was appointed dean of the Indiana Univ. School of Music; he retired in 1973.

Bainbridge, Katharine, American composer; b. Basingstoke, England, June 30, 1863; d. Hollywood, Feb. 12, 1967 (at the age of 103!). She settled in the U.S. in 1898 and became active as a poetess and composer. She wrote the lyrics of numerous songs, with music by Charles Wakefield Chadman, Rudolf Friml, and others. One of her songs won the First Prize of the Women's International Assoc. of Aeronautics.

Baines, Anthony, English music scholar; b. London, Oct. 6, 1912. He studied at the Royal College of Music in London; for several seasons (1935–39 and 1946–48) played the bassoon in the London Phil. Orch. In 1949 he became associate conductor of the International Ballet Co., and in 1970 was appointed curator of the Bate Collection of Historical Wind Instruments of the Faculty of Music at Oxford Univ. He publ. several valuable monographs dealing with musical instruments: *Woodwind Instruments and Their History* (London, 1957); *Bagpipes* (Oxford, 1960); *European and American Musical Instruments* (London, 1966); edited *Musical Instruments through the Ages* (Baltimore, 1961; revised ed., 1976).

Baini, Giuseppe (also known as **Abbate Baini**), Italian writer on music and composer; b. Rome, Oct. 21, 1775; d. there, May 21, 1844. He received rudimentary training from his uncle, Lorenzo Baini; then entered the Seminario Romano, where his instructor, Stefano Silveyra, indoctrinated him with the spirit of Palestrina's music. In 1795 he became a member of the papal choir at St. Peter's; he continued his studies there with Bianchini; in 1802 he took courses with Jannaconi, whom he succeeded as maestro di cappella at St. Peter's (1818). In 1821 he wrote his masterpiece, a 10-part *Miserere,* which was accepted for singing at the Sistine Chapel during Holy Week, in alternation with the *Misereres* of Allegri and Bai. He also wrote many Psalms, hymns, masses, and motets. His great ambition was to publ. a complete edition of Palestrina's works, but he was able to prepare only two vols. for publication. The monument of his devotion to Palestrina was his exhaustive biography, *Memorie storico-critiche della vita e delle opere di Giovanni Pierluigi da Palestrina* (Rome, 1828; German trans. by Kandler, with notes by Kiesewetter, 1834), which remains extremely valuable despite its occasional inaccuracies. He also wrote a *Saggio sopra l'identità de' ritmi musicali e poetici* (1820). Haberl publ. an essay on Baini in the *Kirchenmusikalisches Jahrbuch* (1894).

Bainton – Bajoras

Bainton, Edgar Leslie, English composer; b. London, Feb. 14, 1880; d. Sydney, Australia, Dec. 8, 1956. He studied piano and composition at the Royal College of Music with Walford Davies and Charles Stanford. He taught piano and composition at the Cons. of Newcastle upon Tyne from 1901 until 1914. The outbreak of World War I found him in Berlin, and he was interned as an enemy alien. After the end of the war he resumed his pedagogical activities as director of the Newcastle Cons. In 1934 he went to Australia and was director of the State Cons. at Sydney until 1947. WORKS: 3 symphs. (1903–56); *Before Sunrise* for Voice, Chorus, and Orch. (1917); symph. poem, *Paracelsus* (1921); *Concerto-Fantasia* for Piano and Orch. (Carnegie Award, 1917; London, Jan. 26, 1922); 2 operas: *Oithona,* after Ossian (Glastonbury, Aug. 11, 1915), and *The Pearl Tree* (Sydney, May 20, 1944); chamber music; and songs. In his style he followed the tenets of the British national school, writing in broad diatonic expanses with a Romantic élan.
BIBLIOGRAPHY: H. Bainton, *Remembered on Waking: E.L. Bainton* (Sydney, 1960).

Baird, Martha, American pianist and music patroness; b. Madera, Calif., March 15, 1895; d. New York, Jan. 24, 1971. She studied at the New England Cons. and with Artur Schnabel in Berlin; appeared as soloist with Sir Thomas Beecham in London and Koussevitzky in Boston. In 1957 she married John D. Rockefeller, Jr., and became a benefactress of opera and concert music.

Baird, Tadeusz, prominent Polish composer; b. Grodzisk Mazowiecki, July 26, 1928; d. Warsaw, Sept. 2, 1981. He studied music privately in Lodz with Sikorski and Woytowicz during the war years (1943–44); after the war he enrolled at the Warsaw Cons. and took courses with Rytel and Perkowski (1947–51); had piano lessons with Wituski (1948–51). He further studied musicology with Zofia Lissa at the Univ. of Warsaw (1948–52). In 1949, together with Jan Krenz and Kazimierz Serocki, he founded a progressive society of composers under the name Group 49. In 1956 he became active in initiating the First International Festival of Contemporary Music, during the "Warsaw Autumn." In 1977 he was appointed prof. of composition at the Chopin Academy of Music in Warsaw. As a composer, Baird won numerous awards, among them the Fitelberg Competition of 1958, 3 prizes of the Tribune Internationale des Compositeurs in Paris (1959, 1963, 1966), and the Polish State Awards for his 3 symphs. (1951, 1964, 1969). He also was awarded the Commander's Cross of the Order of Poland's Revival (1964) and the Order of the Banner of Labor, Second and First Class (1974, 1981). His early music followed the neo-Romantic modalities characteristic of Polish music; further evolution was marked by complex structures in the manner of dynamic expressionism, with occasional applications of serialism. WORKS: One-act opera, *Jutro (Tomorrow),* after a short story by Conrad (1964–66). FOR ORCH.: Sinfonietta (1949); 3 symphs. (1950; *Sinfonia quasi una fantasia,* 1952; 1969); *Overture in Old Style* (1950); *Colas Breugnon,* suite for Flute and String Orch. (1951); *Overture giocosa* (1952); *Concerto for Orchestra* (1953); *Cassazione* (1956); *4 Essays* (1958); *Espressioni varianti* for Violin and Orch. (1958–59); *Variations without a Theme* (1961–62); *Epiphany Music* (1963); *4 Dialogues* for Oboe and Chamber Orch (1966); *4 Novelettes* for Chamber Orch. (1967; Dartmouth College, Hanover, N.H., July 16, 1967); *Sinfonia breve* (1968); *Psychodrama* (1971–72); Concerto for Oboe and Orch. (1973; Warsaw, Sept. 23, 1973); *Elegy* (1973); *Concerto lugubre* for Viola and Orch. (1974–75; Nuremberg, May 21, 1976); Double Concerto for Cello, Harp, and Orch. (1976). CHAMBER MUSIC: *4 Preludes* for Bassoon and Piano (1954); *Divertimento* for Flute, Oboe, Clarinet, and Bassoon (1956); String Quartet (1957); *Play* for String Quartet (1971). FOR VOICES: *Lyrical Suite,* 4 songs for Soprano and Orch. (1953); *4 Love Sonnets,* after Shakespeare, for Baritone and Chamber Ensemble (1956; 2nd version with Strings and Harpsichord, 1969); *Exhortations* on old Hebrew texts, for Narrator, Chorus, and Orch. (1959–60) *Erotyki (Love Songs),* cycle of 6 songs for Soprano and Orch. (1961); *Study for 28 Mixed Voices, 6 Percussion Players, and Piano* (1967); *4 songs* for Mezzo-soprano and Chamber Orch. (1966); *5 Songs* for Mezzo-soprano and Chamber Orch. (1968); *Goethe-Briefe,* cantata (1970; Dresden, June 6, 1971).
BIBLIOGRAPHY: T. Zielinski, *Tadeusz Baird* (Cracow, 1966).

Bairstow, Sir Edward Cuthbert, English organist and composer; b. Huddersfield, Aug. 22, 1874; d. York, May 1, 1946. He studied organ and music theory at Durham Univ. (Mus.D., 1901); was organist at Wigan (1899–1906), Leeds (1906–13), and at the York Minster. He composed church music, anthems, part-songs, and an organ sonata (1937); he publ. *Counterpoint and Harmony* (1937) and *The Evolution of Musical Form* (1943).
BIBLIOGRAPHY: E. Bradbury, "Sir Edward Bairstow: A Birthday Tribute," *The Musical Times* (Aug. 1944).

Bajoras, Feliksas, Lithuanian composer; b. Alytus, Oct. 7, 1934. He studied violin and composition at the State Cons. in Vilnius (1957–63); in 1965 was appointed musical director of the Lithuanian State Youth Theater. In his compositions he employs melorhythmic features of Lithuanian folklore in a modern harmonic dressing. WORKS: FOR ORCH.: 3 symphs.: No. 1 (1964, revised 1968–70); No. 2, *Stalactites,* for String Orch. (1970); No. 3 (1972, revised 1976); *Intermezzo and Postlude* for Chamber Orch. (1964); *Suite of Verbs* for Chamber Orch. (1966); *Prelude and Toccata* for Strings (1966); *Legends,* symph. poem (1969); *Mourning Music* for Wind Orch. (1972); *Rondo* (1976). CHAMBER MUSIC: Violin Sonatina (1961); Variations for Double Bass and String Quartet (1968); *4 Pieces* for String Quartet (1968); *Cycle of 15 Pieces* for Violin and Piano (1973); 2 string quartets

(1974, 1975); Suite for Septet (1975); Violin Sonata (1979). FOR PIANO: *3 Pieces* (1958); Variations (1959); *Variations on a Folk Theme* (1971).

Bakala, Břetislav, Czech organist and conductor; b. Fryšták, Feb. 12, 1897; d. Brno, April 1, 1958. He studied organ in Brno (1912–15); then entered the Brno Cons., studying with Vilem Kurz (piano) and with Neumann (conducting); also attended the master class of Janáček there. In 1920–25 he was a répétiteur and chorus director at the Brno City Theater. He was also, for a season, an organist in Philadelphia (1925–26). Returning to Czechoslovakia, he served as pianist and conductor at the State Radio (1926–36) and later conductor of the Radio Orch. (1937–55). In 1956 he was appointed conductor-in-chief and music director of the State Phil. in Brno; also taught a conducting class at the Janáček Academy in Brno. He wrote a Scherzo for Orch. (1923), a *Fantasie* for String Quartet, and numerous choruses and songs. His chief merit was editing works by old Czech composers and arranging vocal scores of several operas by Janáček.

Bakaleinikov, Vladimir, Russian-American viola player and conductor; b. Moscow, Oct. 12, 1885; d. Pittsburgh, Nov. 5, 1953. He studied violin with Michael Press; graduated from the Moscow Cons. in 1907; subsequently played the viola in the Grand Duke of Mecklenburg Quartet (1910–20); taught at the Cons. of St. Petersburg (1913–20); conducted opera at the Musicalnaya Drama in St. Petersburg (1914–16). Returning to Moscow, he taught at the Moscow Cons. (1920–24); was in charge of the opera branch of the Moscow Art Theater (1920–27). He came to America in 1927; was associate conductor of the Cincinnati Symph. Orch.; eventually settled in Pittsburgh as a conductor and teacher; among his pupils was Lorin Maazel. He wrote a Viola Concerto (1937) and a suite of oriental dances for Orch.; publ. several arrangements of works by Bach and Beethoven; also *Elementary Rules of Conducting* (1937); *The Instruments of the Band and Orchestra* (with M. Rosen, N.Y., 1940); and an autobiography, *A Musician's Notes* (N.Y., 1943; in Russian).

Bake, Arnold Adriaan, Dutch music scholar; b. Hilversum, May 19, 1899; d. London, Oct. 8, 1963. He studied oriental languages at the Univ. of Leiden; received his Ph.D. in 1930 from the Univ. of Utrecht with the dissertation *Bytrage tot de Kennis der Voor-Indische musiek* (publ. in Paris, 1930). He subsequently went to India, where he studied Indian music and languages at Tagore's school in Santiniketan; he also served as music adviser to the All India Radio in Delhi and as director of European music of the Calcutta Radio. In 1948 he went to London, where he became a lecturer on Sanskrit and Indian music at the School of Oriental and African Studies. His interests also included Indian Philosophy, tribal music, and dance.

Baker, Benjamin Franklin, American music pedagogue; b. Wenham, Mass., July 10, 1811; d. Boston, March 11, 1889. He was a singer in various churches in Salem, Boston, and Portland; in 1841 he succeeded Lowell Mason as teacher of music in the public schools; sang with the Handel and Haydn Society. He founded the Boston Music School (1851–68) and edited the *Boston Musical Journal;* composed 3 cantatas: *The Storm King, The Burning Ship,* and *Camillus;* publ. a textbook, *Thorough-Bass and Harmony* (1870).

Baker, David, American composer and jazz musician; b. Indianapolis, Dec. 21, 1931. He graduated from Indiana Univ. in 1953; also studied music theory privately with Heiden, Schuller, Orrego-Salas, William Russo, and George Russell. He subsequently taught music in small colleges and public school; in 1966 became chairman of the dept. of jazz studies at Indiana Univ. As a jazz performer, he played the trombone with Stan Kenton, Lionel Hampton, and Quincy Jones. His own compositions fuse jazz improvisation with ultramodern devices, including serial procedures.

WORKS: FOR ORCH.: *Reflections* for Orch. and Jazz Ensemble (1969); Concerto for Violin and Jazz Band (1969; Indiana Univ., April 5, 1970); Concerto for Flute, Jazz Ensemble, and String Quartet (1971); Concerto for Double Bass, Jazz Ensemble, String Quartet, and Solo Violin (1972); Concerto for Trombone, Jazz Band, and Chamber Orch. (1972); *Kosbro* (1973; revised 1975); *Levels,* concerto for Double Bass, Jazz Band, Flute Quartet, Horn Quartet, and String Quartet (1973); *Le Chat qui pêche* for Orch., Jazz Quartet, and Soprano (1974); *2 Improvisations* for Orch. and Jazz Combo (1974); Concerto for Tuba, Jazz Band, Percussion, Chorus, Dancers, Slide Projections, and Tape Recorders (1975); Concerto for Cello and Chamber Orch. (1975–76); Concerto for 2 Pianos, Jazz Band, Chamber Orch., and Percussion (1976).

FOR VOICE: *Psalm 22,* jazz oratorio (1966); *Lutheran Mass* for Chorus and Jazz Septet (1967); *The Beatitudes* for Chorus, Soloists, Narrator, Jazz Ensemble, String Orch., and Dancers (1968); *Black America: To the Memory of Martin Luther King,* jazz cantata (1968); *Catholic Mass for Peace* for Chorus and Jazz Ensemble (1969); *A Song of Mankind* for Chorus, Orch., Jazz Ensemble, Rock Band, Lights, and Sound Effects (1970); *Songs of the Night* for Soprano, String Quartet, and Piano (1972); *Give and Take* for Soprano and Chamber Ensemble (1975).

CHAMBER MUSIC: String Quartet No. 1 (1962); Viola Sonata (1966); *Ballade* for Horn, Saxophone, and Cello (1967); Violin Sonata (1967); *Salute to Beethoven* for Piccolo, Wind Quintet, Flute Choir, Jazz Ensemble, and Tape (1970); Sonata for Brass Quintet and Piano (1970); Sonata for Piano and String Quintet (1971); Sonata for Tuba and String Quartet (1971); Sonata for Viola, Guitar, and Double Bass (1973); Cello Sonata (1973); Sonata for Violin and Cello (1974); Suite for Solo Violin (1975); *Contrasts* for Piano Trio (1976); *Ethnic Variations on a Theme of Paganini* for Violin and Piano (1976); *Roots* for Piano Trio (1976); numerous works for jazz ensembles of various instrumentations; also Piano Sonata (1968) and a 2-piano Sonata (1971).

Baker, George, English organist; b. Exeter, 1768; d. Rugeley, Feb. 19, 1847. He studied in Exeter with William Jackson; was organist at Stafford (1795), Derby (1810), and Rugeley, Staffordshire (1824). The opera *The Caffres, or Buried Alive* (produced at Covent Garden in London, June 2, 1802) is often listed as a work by Baker but was really written by John Davy. Among Baker's own works are numerous anthems and glees.

Baker, Israel, American violinist; b. Chicago, Feb. 11, 1921. He studied at the Chicago Cons.; then took lessons with Louis Persinger at the Juilliard School of Music in N.Y.; his other teachers included Jacques Gordon and Bronislaw Huberman. After settling in California, he became active as a chamber music player; was 2nd violinist in the Heifetz-Piatigorsky Concerts; later was a member of the Pacific Art Trio; also made solo appearances.

Baker, Dame Janet, celebrated English mezzo-soprano; b. Hatfield, Yorkshire, Aug. 21, 1933. Her parents were music-lovers and she grew up in an artistic atmosphere from her early childhood. She took academic courses at the College for Girls in York, and also began to take singing lessons in London, where her teachers were Helene Isepp and Meriel St. Clair. She won a prize in 1956 which made it possible for her to travel to Salzburg and attend singing classes at the Mozarteum there. Later she enrolled in a master class of Lotte Lehmann in London. She sang in the chorus at the Glyndebourne Festival (1956) and also filled engagements in opera productions in Oxford and London. In 1960 she gave a recital at the Edinburgh Festival. In 1961 she had a part in Bach's *St. John Passion* in Copenhagen, and later sang in Bach's B minor Mass in Zürich. A decisive turn in her career came with her membership in the English Opera Group directed by Benjamin Britten; on May 16, 1971, she appeared in the leading role in Britten's opera *Owen Wingrave* on television. She made her first American appearance in 1966 as soloist with the San Francisco Symph. in Mahler's *Das Lied von der Erde.* On Dec. 2, 1966, she presented a solo recital in N.Y., with excellent reviews. Her subsequent engagements took her all over Europe; her fame as an artist of intellectual brilliance grew. In 1970 she was named a Commander of the Order of the British Empire, and in 1976 Queen Elizabeth II made her a Dame of the British Empire. She gave her last operatic appearance in 1982. An account of her final operatic season was publ. in her book *Full Circle* (London, 1982).
BIBLIOGRAPHY: A. Blyth, *Janet Baker* (London, 1973); David Ewen, *Musicians since 1900* (N.Y., 1978).

Baker, Julius, distinguished American flutist; b. Cleveland, Sept. 23, 1915. He studied at the Eastman School of Music in Rochester and at the Curtis Inst.

of Music in Philadelphia. In 1937 he joined the Cleveland Orch.; then was principal flutist of the Pittsburgh Symph. (1941–43), of the CBS Symph. (1943–51), and of the Chicago Symph. (1951–53). In 1954 he was appointed to the faculty of the Juilliard School of Music. From 1947 to 1965 he was a member of the Bach Aria Group, with which he made several concert tours. In 1965 he became principal flutist of the N.Y. Phil.; retired in 1983.

Baker, Michael, American-born Canadian composer; b. West Palm Beach, Fla., March 13, 1942. He moved to Canada in 1958; studied composition with J. Coulthard and E. Weisgarber at the Univ. of British Columbia in Vancouver (1962–66); later took private lessons with Lennox Berkeley during a year in London (1974–75). Returning to Vancouver, he devoted himself to pedagogical work as well as composition.
WORKS: Ballet, *The Letter* (1974). FOR ORCH.: *Dialogues* for Orch., Chorus, and Solo Baritone (1971); *Counterplay* for Viola and String Orch. (1971; also for Viola and Piano); *Okanagan Landscapes* for Piano and Orch. (1972); *Contours* for Double Bass, Harpsichord, and String Orch. (1973); Concerto for Flute and String Orch. (1974); *Point No Point* for Viola and String Orch. (1975); Concerto for Piano and Chamber Orch. (1976); *Duo Concertante* for Violin, Viola, and String Orch. (London, Aug. 19, 1976); *A Struggle for Dominion* for Piano and Orch. (Vancouver, Sept. 26, 1976); *Baroque Diversions* for Chamber Orch. (Mannheim, Oct. 18, 1981); *Evocations* for Orch. (Winnipeg, Feb. 3, 1982). CHAMBER MUSIC: *Ballade* for Cello and Piano (1961); Flute Sonata (1963); *5 Epigrams* for Woodwind Trio (1965); Wind Quintet (1965); Piano Quartet (1966); Scherzo for Trumpet and Organ (1976); String Quartet (1969); *Concert Piece* for Organ, Piano, and Timpani (1969–70); Piano Trio (1972); *Elegy* for Flute and Organ (1972); *Music for 6 Players* for Flute, Oboe, Harpsichord, and String Trio (1973); *Combinations* for Double Bass and Harpsichord (1974); *En Rapport* for 2 Guitars (1974); *4 Views from a Nursery Tune* for Violin, Horn, and Piano (1975); *Dance Sequences* for Solo Cello (1975); *Capriccio* for 2 Pianos (1964); *Mirage* for Trumpet, Horn, and Organ (1981); *Red on White* for Flute and String Trio (1981).

Baker, Robert S(tevens), American organist and pedagogue; b. Pontiac, Ill., July 7, 1916. He studied at Illinois Wesleyan Univ. and at the Union Theological Seminary School of Sacred Music in N.Y., where he joined the faculty in 1946; he made his recital debut in St. Louis in 1947. In 1961 he was appointed dean of the School of Sacred Music at the Union Theological Seminary; when it became the Yale Inst. of Sacred Music at Yale Univ. in 1973, he was named its first dean.

Baker, Theodore, American writer on music, and the compiler of the original edition of the present dictionary bearing his name; b. New York, June 3, 1851; d. Dresden, Germany, Oct. 13, 1934. As a young man, he was trained for business pursuits; in 1874 he decided to devote himself to musical studies; he went to Leipzig, where he took courses with Oskar Paul; he received his Dr.Phil. there in 1882 for his dissertation *Über die Musik der nordamerikanischen Wilden,* the first serious study of American Indian music. He lived in Germany until 1890; then returned to the U.S., and became literary editor and translator for the publishing house of G. Schirmer, Inc. (1892); he retired in 1926 and went back to Germany. In 1895 he publ. *A Dictionary of Musical Terms,* which went through more than 25 printings and sold over a million copies; another valuable work was *A Pronouncing Pocket Manual of Musical Terms* (1905). He also issued *The Musician's Calendar and Birthday Book* (1915–17). In 1900 G. Schirmer, Inc., publ. *Baker's Biographical Dictionary of Musicians,* which became Baker's imperishable monument. The first edition included the names of many American musicians not represented in musical reference works at the time; a 2nd edition was publ. in 1905; the 3rd edition, revised and enlarged by Alfred Remy, was issued in 1919; the 4th edition appeared in 1940 under the general editorship of Carl Engel. A Supplement in 1949 was compiled by Nicolas Slonimsky, who undertook in 1958 a completely revised 5th edition of the Dictionary and compiled the Supplements of 1965 and 1971. In 1978 Slonimsky edited the 6th edition of *Baker's Biographical Dictionary of Musicians.* The present edition is also edited by him.

Bakfark, Valentin, celebrated Hungarian lutenist; b. Kronstadt, 1507; d. Padua, Aug. 15, 1576. He was brought up by the family of his brother's wife, **Greff** (or **Graew**), and used that name in conjunction with his own; the spelling **Bacfarc** or **Bekwark** is also encountered. As a youth he was in the service of the King of Hungary (1526–40) in Buda, where he studied lute. He was later attached to the court of Sigismund Augustus of Poland in Wilna (1549–66). He subsequently traveled in Germany, France, and Italy, eventually settling in Padua, where he died of the plague. He published works for the lute in tablature: *Intabulatura* (Lyons, 1552; reprinted as *Premier Livre de Tablature de Luth,* Paris, 1564). A 2nd book, *Harmonicarum Musicarum ... tomus primus,* appeared in Cracow in 1564, and was reprinted in Antwerp in 1569. Some of his works are included in Denkmäler der Tonkunst in Österreich (vol. XVIII, 2).
BIBLIOGRAPHY: H. Opienski, *Bekwark lutinista* (Warsaw, 1906; also in German as *Valentin Greff-Bekwark,* Leipzig, 1914); Otto Gombosi, *Der Lautenist Valentin Bekfark, Leben und Werke* (Budapest, 1935; in Hungarian and German).

Baklanov, George, Russian baritone; b. Riga, Jan. 4, 1881; d. Basel, Dec. 6, 1938. His real name was **Bakkis,** but he changed it to create the necessary euphony for professional appearances. He studied voice at the Kiev Cons.; also went to Milan for advanced voice lessons. He made his operatic debut with the Kiev Opera in 1903 as Amonasro; subsequently sang at the Bolshoi Theater in Moscow (1905–9). He made several tours in Europe and America; sang at Covent Garden, London (1910), with the Boston Opera (1911–14), and with the Chicago Opera (1917–26). He was particularly successful in dramatic roles, such as Rigoletto and Boris Godunov.

Balada, Leonardo, Spanish composer; b. Barcelona, Sept. 22, 1933. He was apprenticed to his father's tailoring shop in Barcelona, and also took piano at the Conservatorio del Liceo there. In 1956 he went to the U.S.; studied at the N.Y. College of Music (1956–57); then enrolled in the Juilliard School of Music (1958–60) to study composition; later attended classes at the Mannes College of Music (1961–62). His principal instructors in composition were Aaron Copland and Vincent Persichetti. He also studied conducting in Paris with Igor Markevitch. He eked out a living by working at odd jobs in the garment district in N.Y.; subsequently he obtained musical employment as teacher at the United Nations International School; then was composer-in-residence at the Aspen Inst. In 1970 he was appointed to the faculty of Carnegie-Mellon Univ. in Pittsburgh. His music retains much of his Spanish heritage, while its formal elements are Classical in structure.
WORKS: FOR THE STAGE: *Hangman, Hangman!,* chamber opera, based on a traditional cowboy song (Barcelona, Oct. 1982); *Zapata!,* based on the story of the famous Mexican revolutionary leader (1983). FOR ORCH.: *Musica Tranquila* for String Orch. (1960); Piano Concerto (1964); Guitar Concerto (1965); *Guernica* (1966; New Orleans, April 25, 1967); *Sinfonia en Negro* in homage to Martin Luther King (1968); Concerto for Bandoneon and Orch. (1970); Sinfonia Concertante for Guitar and Orch. (1972); *Sinfonia de Acero (Steel Symphony;* Pittsburgh, Jan. 12, 1973); *Auroris* (1973); *Ponce de Leon* for Narrator and Orch. (New Orleans, Oct. 9, 1973); Concerto for Piano, Winds, and Percussion (1974); *Homage to Casals* (Pittsburgh, May 7, 1976); *Homage to Sarasate* (Pittsburgh, May 7, 1976); Concerto for 4 Guitars and Orch. (Barcelona, Dec. 17, 1977); *Three Anecdotes,* Concertino for Castanets and Chamber Orch. (Pittsburgh, Nov. 8, 1978); *Sardana* (1979; Pittsburgh, Oct. 21, 1982); Violin Concerto (1982; Pittsburgh, Nov. 11, 1982); *Quasi un Pasodoble* (N.Y., Nov. 24, 1982). CHAMBER MUSIC: Violin Sonata (1960); Concerto for Cello and 9 Players (1962); *Geometrias No. 1* for Flute, Oboe, Clarinet, Bassoon, Trumpet, and Percussion (1966); *Geometrias No. 2* for String Quartet (1967); *Cuatris* for Instrumental Ensemble (1969); *Mosaico* for Brass Quintet (1970); *Tresis* for Flute, Guitar, and Cello (1973); *Apuntes* for Guitar Quartet (1974); Sonata for 10 Winds (1980); numerous pieces for Guitar Solo and Piano Solo; also *End and Beginning* for Rock Music Ensemble (1970). CHORAL WORKS: *Maria Sabina* for Narrators, Chorus, and Orch. (1969); *Las Moradas* for Mixed Chorus and Instrumental Ensemble (1970); *No-Res,* cantata (1974); *Torquemada,* cantata (1980).

Balakauskas, Osvaldas, Lithuanian composer; b. Ukmerge, Dec. 19, 1937. He graduated from the Vilna State Pedagogical Inst. in 1961; in 1969 took composition courses from Liatoshinsky at the Kiev Cons. In his music he adopts a colorful manner, often sharply modernistic in melodic curvature, rhythmic angularity, and harmonic heterophony, while retaining the generic classical definitions of form.

WORKS: FOR ORCH.: Piano Concertino (1966); *Rhapsody* (1967); *Ludus modorum,* cello concerto (1972); Symph. (1973); Suite for Strings (1973); *The Mountain Sonata,* a symphony for Piano and Orch. (1975); *Ad astra* (1976). CHAMBER MUSIC: *Dance Suite* for Violin and Piano (1964); Variations for Flute, Oboe, and Bassoon (1965); Suite for Cello and Violin (1965); *Auletika* for Flute and Oboe (1966); *Extrema* for Piccolo, English Horn, Bass Clarinet, Double Bassoon, Trumpet, Xylophone, and Harp (1966); *Aerophonia* for Wind Quintet (1968); Violin Sonata (1969); *Quartetto concertante* for Flute, Violin, Cello, and Piano (1970); 2 String Quartets (1971, 1971); *Les Musiques* for Cello and Wind Quintet (1972); Violin Sonatina (1972); *Impresonata* for Flute and Piano (1974); *Suite of the Globe* for Violin and Piano (1974); *Retrospectives* for Cello and Piano (1974); *9 Sources* for Oboe and Harpsichord (1974); *Like a Touch of a Sea Wave,* 3 pieces for Violin and Piano (1975); *A Tree and a Bird,* Viola Sonata (1976). FOR PIANO: *3 Caprices* (1964); *Cascades* (1967); *Studi sonori* for 2 Pianos (1971); also Organ Sonata (1973).

Balakirev, Mily (pronounced "Balákirev," with the stress on the second syllable, not the third), greatly significant Russian composer, protagonist of the Russian national school of composition; b. Nizhny-Novgorod, Jan. 2, 1837 (new style; Dec. 21, 1836, old style); d. St. Petersburg, May 29, 1910. His mother gave him his first piano lessons; he was then sent to Moscow, where he took piano lessons with Alexandre Dubuque, and studied music theory with a German musician named Karl Eisrich; he put Balakirev in touch with Oulibishev, author of a book on Mozart who owned an estate in Nizhny-Novgorod. Balakirev often took part in private musical evenings at Oulibishev's estate, playing piano. In 1853–54 he attended classes in mathematics at the Univ. of Kazan. In 1855 he went to St. Petersburg, where he was introduced to Glinka, who encouraged him to continue his musical studies. On Feb. 24, 1856, Balakirev made his first appearance as a composer in St. Petersburg, playing the solo part in the first movement of his Piano Concerto; his *Overture on the Theme of Three Russian Songs* was performed in Moscow on Jan. 2, 1859, and his overture *King Lear,* at a concert of the Univ. of St. Petersburg on Nov. 27, 1859. In 1860 he took a boat ride down the Volga River from his birthplace at Nizhny-Novgorod to the delta at the Caspian Sea; during this trip he collected, notated, and harmonized a number of Russian songs; his collection included the universally popular *Song of the Volga Boatmen,* also known as *Song of the Burlaks* (peasants who pulled large boats loaded with grain

upstream on the Volga). In 1863 Balakirev organized in St. Petersburg a musical group which became known as the Balakirev Circle. Its avowed aim was to make national propaganda of Russian music to oppose the passive imitation of classical German compositions, which at the time exercised a commanding influence in Russia. Simultaneously, he founded the Free Music School in St. Petersburg, and gave concerts which included works by Russian musicians as well as those of recognized German masters. These activities coincided with the rise of a Slavophile movement among patriotic Russian writers and artists, based on the realization of a kinship of blood and the similarity of the Slavic languages (Czech, Serbian, Polish, Bulgarian) and further stimulated by a series of wars against Turkey, aimed at the liberation of Bulgaria; a dream of uniting all Slavic nations under the loving domination of Mother Russia animated Balakirev and other musicians. In 1866 he went to Prague with the intention of conducting Glinka's operas there, but the outbreak of the Austro-Prussian War forced the cancellation of these plans. He repeated his visit to Prague in 1867 and was able to conduct *Ruslan and Ludmila* there on Feb. 16, 17, and 19, 1867; then he conducted *A Life for the Czar,* on Feb. 22, 1867. He took this opportunity to invite several Czech musicians to take part in a concert of music by Russian and Czech composers conducted by Balakirev at his Free Music School on May 24, 1867; the program included, besides the works by the Czech guests, compositions by Borodin, Cui, Mussorgsky, Rimsky-Korsakov, and Balakirev himself. The occasion proved to be of historical importance, for it moved the critic Vladimir Stasov to write an article in which he proudly declared that Russia, too, had its "mighty little company" (*moguchaya kuchka*) of fine musicians; the phrase became a catchword of Russian musical nationalism; in general music histories it came to be known as "The Mighty Five." But the spiritual drive toward the union with the Western Slavic nations was not the only animating force in the music of "The Mighty Five." It combines, somehow, with the historical drive toward the exotic Moslem lands through the Caucasus to Persia in the South and to Central Asia in the East. Balakirev became fascinated with the quasi-oriental melodies and rhythms of the Caucasus during his several trips there. In 1869 he wrote a brilliant oriental fantasy for piano entitled *Islamey;* its technical difficulties rival the transcendental studies of Liszt. His associates, especially Rimsky-Korsakov and Borodin, also paid tribute to the colorful glories of the East, the first in his *Scheherazade,* and the second in his symphonic movement *In the Steppes of Central Asia.* Among his comrades, Balakirev was always a leader; when Rimsky-Korsakov went on a prolonged cruise as a midshipman in the Russian Imperial Navy, he maintained a remarkable correspondence with Balakirev, who gave him specific advice in composition. Unaccountably, Balakirev slackened the tempo of his work as a composer, conductor, and teacher; he seems to have had trouble completing his scores. In 1872 he discontinued his concerts at the Free Music School, and took a clerical job in the railroad transport administration; in 1873 he became music inspector in a women's educational inst. in St. Petersburg; in 1875 he took another administrative job in a women's school. In 1881 he returned to musical activities, and on March 29, 1882, he conducted at the Free Music School the premiere of the first symph. by the 16-year-old Glazunov; he also began to work on the revision of his early scores. His *Second Overture on Russian Themes,* originally performed in St. Petersburg on April 18, 1864, and retitled *One Thousand Years* to commemorate the millennium of Russia observed in 1862, was revised by Balakirev in 1882 and renamed *Russia.* It took Balakirev many years to complete his symph. poem *Tamara,* which he conducted in St. Petersburg on March 19, 1883; the score, inspired by Lermontov's poem and permeated by Caucasian melodic inflections, was dedicated to Liszt. Balakirev spent 33 years (1864–97) working intermittently on his Symph. in C, which he conducted at a concert at the Free Music School on April 23, 1898; this was his last appearance as a conductor. He completed his 2nd Symph. in D minor between 1900 and 1908; it was performed in St. Petersburg on April 23, 1909. He worked on his First Piano Concerto in 1855 and began the composition of his 2nd Piano Concerto in 1861, but laid it aside until 1909; it was completed after his death by Liapunov. In 1883 he became director of music of the Imperial Chapel, resigning from this post in 1894. During his last years, Balakirev was increasingly unsociable and morose; he became estranged from Rimsky-Korsakov when the latter became chief adviser to Belayev, the wealthy publisher who ceased to support the Free School headed by Balakirev and instead sponsored a series of Russian Symphony Concerts in 1886, attracting a number of younger Russian composers, among them Glazunov, Liadov, Arensky, and Ippolitov-Ivanov. Their quarrel reached such lamentable extremes that they did not even greet each other at public places or at concerts. Still, Rimsky-Korsakov continued to perform Balakirev's music at his concerts. Balakirev made a tremendous impact on the destinies of Russian music, particularly because of his patriotic convictions that Russia could rival Germany and other nations in the art of music. But he left fewer works than his long life would have justified, and they are rarely performed. Among his lesser compositions are *Spanish Overture* (1886); *Czech Overture* (1867); Octet for Flute, Oboe, French Horn, Violin, Viola, Cello, Double Bass, and Piano (1850–56); 2 Piano Sonatas (1857, 1905); and a Piano Sonatina (1909). He made an effective piano transcription of Glinka's song *The Lark* and wrote about 35 original songs; he further publ. an important collection of Russian folk songs (1865). A complete edition of Balakirev's piano works was publ. in Moscow in 1952; a collection of all of his songs was publ. in Moscow in 1937.

BIBLIOGRAPHY: Balakirev's *Autobiography* was publ. in *Russkaya Musykalnaya Gazeta* in 1910. See also M.D. Calvocoressi, ed., "M. B.: Lettres inédites à M.D. Calvocoressi," *Revue Musicale Mensuelle,* VII (1911); S. Lyapunov, ed., *M.A. B.'s Correspondence with P.I. Tchaikovsky* (St. Petersburg, 1912); M.D. Calvocoressi and G. Abraham, "M. B.," *Masters of Russian Music* (London, 1936; revised ed., 1958); G. Kiselev, *B.* (Moscow, 1938); V. Muzalevsky, *M.A. B.: Critical-biographical Essay* (Leningrad, 1938); G. Abraham, *On Russian Music* (London, 1939); J. Leyda and S. Bertensson, *The Mussorgsky Reader* (N.Y., 1947); A. Kandinsky, *Symphonic Works of M. B.* (Moscow and Leningrad, 1950); G. Fedorova, *B.* (Moscow, 1951); V. Kiselyov, *M.A. B.: Correspondence with N.G. Rubinstein and M.P. Belaiev* (Moscow, 1956); V. Kiselyov and S. Lyapunova, eds., *M.A. B.'s Correspondence with P. Jurgenson's Publishing House* (Moscow, 1958); M. Gordeyeva, *The Mighty Company* (Moscow, 1960); E. Fried, ed., *M.A. B.: Essays and Articles* (Leningrad, 1961); E. Fried, general ed., *M.A. B.: Reminiscences and Letters* (Leningrad, 1962); A. Lyapunova, ed., *N. Rimsky-Korsakov: Complete Works* (vol. 5 includes the complete correspondence between Balakirev and Rimsky-Korsakov; Moscow, 1963); E. Garden, *B.: A Critical Study of His Life and Works* (the most detailed work in Eng.; London, 1967); I. Kunin, *M.A. B.: Life and Works in Letters and Documents* (Moscow, 1967); A. Lyapunova and E. Yazovitskaya, *M.A. B.: Chronicle of His Life and Works* (Leningrad, 1967); E. Garden, "B.'s Personality," *Proceedings of the Royal Musical Association,* XCVI (1969–70); A. Lyapunova, ed., *M.A. B.–V.V. Stasov: Correspondence* (2 vols., Moscow, 1970–71).

Balanchine, George, celebrated Russian-American choreographer; b. St. Petersburg, Jan. 22, 1904; d. New York, April 30, 1983. He was a son of the Georgian composer **Meliton Balanchivadze** and brother of the Soviet composer **Andrei Balanchivadze,** but reduced the number of syllables in his name for professional convenience. He attended the Imperial Theater School in St. Petersburg, where he learned the rudiments of classical dance. He also took piano lessons at the Petrograd Cons., and acquired a certain ability to read scores. In 1924 he undertook a tour through Germany and England; then joined Diaghilev's Ballets Russes in Paris and created a number of works for it. In 1933, at the invitation of the American dance specialist Lincoln Kirstein, he went to N.Y.; together they formed the School of American Ballet, which opened in Manhattan on Jan. 2, 1934. In 1935 it was incorporated as the American Ballet; Balanchine was the chief choreographer. The group was renamed Ballet Society in 1946, and in 1948 it was reorganized as the N.Y. City Ballet, and became part of the City Center. In 1962 Balanchine made a tour of Russia with this company. He was distinguished for his modern productions, with music by Stravinsky, Ives, and other contemporary composers. In 1983 he received the Presidential Medal of Freedom. Early in that year he was hospitalized with an ailment diagnosed as "progressive cerebral disintegration." As a gesture of devotion, he was named director emeritus of the N.Y. City Ballet, but had to abandon all active work, and soon died of pneumonia. Balanchine adored women; he used to say, "Ballet is woman."

He was married five times; all of his brides were dancers: the first was Tamara Geva, whom he married in Russia when he was 18 and she was 15; his second wife was Alexandra Danilova, whom he married in 1927; his third, and most famous one, was Vera Zorina, whom he married in 1938; then followed Maria Tallchief and finally Tanaquil Le-Clerq, from whom he was divorced in 1969. In his long life as a choreographer he created nearly 200 ballets to musical scores ranging from the Baroque to the avant-garde; he said once: "Music must be seen, and dance must be heard."

BIBLIOGRAPHY: George Balanchine and Francis Mason, *Balanchine's Complete Stories of the Great Ballets* (Garden City, N.Y., 1954); Bernard Taper, *Balanchine* (N.Y. 1963); Horst Koegler, *Balanchine und das moderne Ballet* (Hannover, 1964); Lincoln Kirstein, *The New York City Ballet* (N.Y., 1973); *Choreography by George Balanchine: A Catalogue of Works* (N.Y., 1983).

Balanchivadze, Andrei, Georgian composer (brother of the choreographer **George Balanchine**); b. St. Petersburg, June 1, 1906. He studied with his father, the composer **Meliton Balanchivadze;** then entered the Tiflis Cons., where he took courses in piano, and in composition with Ippolitov-Ivanov. In 1935 he joined the staff of the Tiflis Cons., and in 1962 became chairman of the composition dept.; numerous Georgian composers are his students. In his music he makes use of Georgian folk motifs in a tasteful harmonic framework characteristic of the national Russian school of composition. Among his works is the first Georgian ballet, *The Heart of the Mountains* (1936); another ballet, *Mtsyri*, after Lermontov, was produced in Tiflis in 1964. His other works include 2 symphs. (1944, 1959); symph. poem, *The Ocean* (1952); 4 piano concertos (1944, 1946, 1952, 1968); choruses and songs.

BIBLIOGRAPHY: G. Ordzhonikidze, *Andrei Balanchivadze* (Tiflis, 1967).

Balanchivadze, Meliton, noted Russian composer; b. in the village of Banodzha, Dec. 24, 1862; d. Kutaisi, Nov. 21, 1937. He was educated in the ecclesiastical seminary in Tiflis, where he sang in a chorus. In 1880 he became a member of the local opera theater; in 1882 he organized a chorus and arranged Georgian folk songs. In 1889 he went to St. Petersburg, where he took vocal lessons, and in 1891 entered Rimsky-Korsakov's class in composition. In 1895 he organized a series of choral concerts of Georgian music. After the Revolution he returned to Georgia, where he continued his work of ethnic research. He composed a national Georgian opera, *Tamara the Treacherous* (1897), and a number of songs in the manner of Georgian folk music.

BIBLIOGRAPHY: P. Khuchua, *Meliton Balanchivadze* (Tiflis, 1964).

Balart, Gabriel, Spanish composer; b. Barcelona, June 8, 1824; d. there, July 5, 1893. He studied at the Paris Cons.; composed various pieces of salon music, which enjoyed some success. In 1849 he went to Milan as a theater conductor; in 1853 was appointed musical director of the Teatro del Liceo in Barcelona. He wrote 5 symphs. in a romantic vein, which he conducted in Spain; for a time his light opera *Amore y Arte* enjoyed considerable success.

Balasanian, Sergei, Tadzhik composer; b. Ashkhabad, Aug. 26, 1902; d. Moscow, June 3, 1982. He studied at the Moscow Cons., graduating in music history in 1935. From 1936 to 1943 he was mainly active in Tadzhikistan; then was in charge of radio programming there. In 1948 he joined the faculty of the Moscow Cons.; in 1962–71 was chairman of the composition dept. He was one of the founders of the national school of composition in Tadzhikistan; in his works he made use of native folk motifs, in ingenious harmonic coloration.

WORKS: OPERAS: *The Revolt of Vose* (1939; revised 1959); *The Blacksmith Kova* (1941); *Bakhtyor and Nisso* (1954). BALLETS: *Leyly and Medzhnun* (1947) and *Shakuntala* (1963). FOR ORCH.: 4 symph. suites on Central Asian folk motifs; *Armenian Rhapsody* (1944); *The Islands of Indonesia* (1960); numerous choruses, songs, and various instrumental pieces.

Balassa, Sándor, Hungarian composer; b. Budapest, Jan. 20, 1935. He studied at the Budapest Cons. (1952–56), then with Endre Szervánszky at the Budapest Academy of Music (1960–65). Upon graduation he joined the staff of Hungarian Radio. His music is pragmatic in its structure and effect, with a fine veneer of impressionistic colors.

WORKS: *Bagatelles and Sequences* for Piano (1957); *Locks,* monologue for Soprano and Chamber Ensemble (1963); Violin Concerto (1964); Septet for Brass (1965); *Golden Age,* Cantata (1965); *3 Songs for Soprano and String Trio* (1965); *Dimensioni* for Flute and Viola (1966); Wind Quintet (1966); *Zenith* for Soprano and Orch. (1967); *Antinomia* for Soprano, Clarinet, and Cello (1968); Quartet for Percussion (1969); Trio for Violin, Viola, and Harp (1970); *Xénia,* Nonet (1970); *Iris* for Orch. (1971); *Lupercalia,* Concerto in memory of Stravinsky, for Woodwinds and Brass (1972); *Tabulae* for Chamber Ensemble (1972); opera, *Az ajtón Kivül* (*Beyond the Threshold,* 1973–76); *Calls and Cries* for Orch. (Boston, Oct. 21, 1982); songs and motets.

Balatka, Hans, Czech conductor and composer; b. Hoffnungsthal, Moravia, Feb. 26, 1825; d. Chicago, April 17, 1899. After studying music in Vienna, he emigrated to America in 1849; settled in Milwaukee, where he organized the German Musikverein, and in 1860 became conductor of the Chicago Phil. Society, which was the nucleus of the Theodore Thomas Symph. Orch. (later Chicago Symph. Orch.). He was an important figure in carrying German musical culture to the American Midwest. He also composed some insignificant choral works.

Balbastre (Balbâtre), Claude, French organist and composer; b. Dijon, Jan. 22, 1727; d. Paris, May 9, 1799. In about 1750 he began studying with Jean-

Philippe Rameau. Between 1755 and 1782 he served as organist in concerts held by the Concert Spirituel. In 1756 he was named organist at St. Roche in Paris; in 1760 he was organist at Notre-Dame de Paris, serving there 3 months a year. He wrote several piano suites based on the motifs of French Christmas songs; also composed numerous organ pieces.

Balbi (Balbus), Lodovico, Italian composer; b. Venice, 1545; d. there, Dec. 15, 1604. He was a pupil of Costanzo Porta; sang in the choir of San Marco in Venice (1570); then was maestro di cappella at the Franciscan monastery there (1578), and at San Antonio in Padua (1585–91); later returned to Venice. He publ. masses, motets, canzoni, madrigals, sacred songs, etc.; compiled a collection of graduals and antiphons by celebrated Italian masters, publ. by Gardano (Venice, 1591).

Balbi, Melchiore, Italian theorist and composer; b. Venice, June 4, 1796; d. Padua, June 21, 1879. He was a pupil of Nini, Valeri, and Calegari in Padua; was theater conductor there (1818–53); from 1854 was maestro di cappella at the Basilica San Antonio. He wrote 3 operas, all produced in Padua: *La notte perigliosa* (1820); *L'abitator del bosco* (1821); *L'alloggio militare* (1825); a Requiem (for Rossini, 1868); masses; Psalms; edited Calegari's *Trattato del sistema armonico* (Padua, 1829); and wrote *Grammatica ragionata della musica considerata sotto l'aspetto di lingua* (Milan, 1845) and *Nuova scuola basata sul sistema semitonato equabile* (1872).

Baldi, João José, Portuguese composer; b. Lisbon, 1770; d. there, May 18, 1816. He studied at the Seminário Patriarcal in Lisbon; in 1789 he became mestre de capela at Guarda Cathedral; in 1794 he went to Faro Cathedral in a similar capacity, and then returned to Lisbon in 1800 to become 2nd mestre de capela at the Royal Chapel of Bemposta; he was made first mestre de capela there and at the Lisbon Cathedral in 1806, holding these posts until his death. He composed mostly sacred works; also wrote some piano music.

Baldwin, Samuel Atkinson, American organist and composer; b. Lake City, Minn., Jan. 25, 1862; d. New York, Sept. 15, 1949. He studied organ playing in Dresden; upon returning to America, was church organist in Chicago, N.Y., and Brooklyn. He was one of the founders of the American Guild of Organists, and gave approximately 1,500 organ recitals. He also wrote symphs. and overtures, but is remembered chiefly, if at all, for an innocuous anthem, *Tarry with Me.*

Bales, Richard, American conductor and composer; b. Alexandria, Va., Feb. 3, 1915. He studied at the Eastman School of Music in Rochester, N.Y., and took a course in conducting under Koussevitzky at the Berkshire Music Center in Tanglewood. In 1943 he was appointed conductor of the National Gallery Orch. in Washington; at this post he introduced numerous works by American composers, both old and new. His ingenious potpourri of Southern songs, *The Confederacy* (1954), became very popular. Other works include 2 orch. suites inspired by watercolors in the National Gallery in Washington, *American Design* (Washington, May 26, 1957) and *American Chronicle* (Washington, May 23, 1965).

Balfe, Michael William, notable Irish composer; b. Dublin, May 15, 1808; d. Rowney Abbey, Hertfordshire, Oct. 20, 1870. He was the son of a dancing master, and as a small child played the violin for his father's dancing classes. He subsequently took violin lessons with O'Rourke. After his father's death on Jan. 6, 1823, Balfe went to London, where he studied violin with Charles Edward Horn and composition with Carl Friedrich Horn. In 1824 he was engaged as a violinist at the Drury Lane Theatre; also sang in London and in the provinces. His patron, Count Mazzara, took him to Italy in 1825; there he took composition lessons with Federici in Milan and voice lessons with Pilippo Galli; there he produced his first ballet, *La Pérouse* (1826). He met Rossini, who advised him to continue singing lessons with Bordogni; in 1828 he was engaged as principal baritone at the Italian Opera in Paris. In Italy he married the Hungarian vocalist **Lina Rosa** (b. 1808; d. London, June 8, 1888). Returning to England in 1833, he devoted himself to the management of opera houses and to composition. He was manager of the Lyceum Theatre during the 1841–42 season. He made London his principal residence, with occasional visits to Vienna (1846), Berlin (1848), St. Petersburg, and Trieste (1852–56). Apart from his administrative duties, he displayed great energy in composing operas, most of them to English librettos; of these, *The Bohemian Girl,* produced at the Drury Lane Theatre in London on Nov. 27, 1843, obtained an extraordinary success and became a perennial favorite on the English stage; it was also translated into French, German, and Italian. In 1864 he retired to his country seat at Rowney Abbey. His daughter, Victoire, made her debut as a singer at the Lyceum Theatre in London in 1857.
WORKS: OPERAS: 3 early operas in Italian, *I rivali di se stessi* (Palermo, 1829), *Un avertimento ai gelosi* (Pavia, 1830), *Enrico IV al Passo della Marna* (Milan, Feb. 19, 1833); in French, *L'Etoile de Séville* (Paris Opéra, Dec. 17, 1845). The following operas were produced in English at Drury Lane and Covent Garden in London and other theaters: *The Siege of Rochelle* (Drury Lane, London, Oct. 29, 1835); *The Maid of Artois* (May 27, 1836); *Catherine Grey* (May 27, 1837); *Joan of Arc* (Nov. 30, 1837); *Diadeste, or The Veiled Lady* (May 17, 1838); *Falstaff* (in Italian, July 19, 1838); *Këolanthe, or The Unearthly Bride* (March 9, 1841); *Le Puits d'amour* (Opéra-Comique, Paris, April 20, 1843; in Eng. as *Geraldine,* Princess's Theatre, London, Aug. 14, 1843); *The Bohemian Girl,* Balfe's most famous work (Drury Lane Theatre, London, Nov. 27, 1843); *Les Quatre Fils Aymon* (Opéra-Comique, Paris, July 29, 1844; in En-

glish as *The Castle of Aymon,* Princess's Theatre, London, Nov. 20, 1844); *The Daughter of St. Mark* (Nov. 27, 1844); *The Enchantress* (May 14, 1845); *The Bondman* (Dec. 11, 1846); *The Maid of Honour* (Dec. 20, 1847); *The Sicilian Bride* (March 6, 1852); *The Devil's in It* (July 26, 1852); *Moro, the Painter of Antwerp* (Jan. 28, 1882; originally produced as *Pittore e duca,* Trieste, Nov. 21, 1844); *The Rose of Castille* (Oct. 29, 1857); *Satanella, or The Power of Love* (Dec. 20, 1858); *Bianca, or The Bravo's Bride* (Dec. 6, 1860); *The Puritan's Daughter* (Nov. 30, 1861); *Blanche de Nevers* (Nov. 21, 1862); *The Armourer of Nantes* (Feb. 12, 1863); *The Sleeping Queen,* operetta (Aug. 31, 1864); *The Knight of the Leopard* (Liverpool, Jan. 15, 1891; originally produced in London as *Il Talismano,* June 11, 1874). FOR VOICE: *Mazeppa,* a cantata, and 2 other cantatas; ballads, glees, songs.

BIBLIOGRAPHY: Charles Lamb Kenney, *A Memoir of Michael William Balfe* (London, 1875); W.A. Barrett, *Balfe: His Life and Work* (London, 1882).

Balfoort, Dirk Jacobus, Dutch musicologist; b. Utrecht, July 19, 1886; d. The Hague, Nov. 11, 1964. He studied with Evert Cornelis; played violin in various German orchs.; then held teaching posts in the Netherlands; also organized concerts of old music by Dutch composers. He publ. valuable books (in Dutch) on music making in the Netherlands: *De Hollandsche vioolmakers* (Amsterdam, 1931); *Het Muziekleven in Nederland in de 17e en 18e eeuw* (Amsterdam, 1938); a monograph on Stradivarius (Amsterdam, 1945; also in German and Eng.); etc.

Balfour, Henry Lucas, English organist; b. London, Oct. 28, 1859; d. Croydon, Surrey, Dec. 27, 1946. He studied music in London with Arthur Sullivan; later in Leipzig; was organist at Croydon (1872–1902). In 1902 he became organist at the Church of the Holy Trinity.

Baliani, Carlo, Italian composer; b. probably in Milan, c.1680; d. there, Feb. 16, 1747. He was maestro di cappella at the church of Santa Maria della Passione in Milan before being named to the same post at the Milan Cathedral in 1714; he continued to serve as maestro di cappella there for the rest of his life. He wrote a great many sacred works, including masses, hymns, Psalms, and motets.

Balin, Marty, American pop musician, singer, and songwriter; b. Cincinnati, Jan. 30, 1942. His real name was **Martyn Jerel Buchwald.** He materialized in San Francisco, performing with a folk group; then formed a band under a puzzling name, The Jefferson Airplane, which specialized in a fusion of hard rock and soft folk music. Other members of the band were the guitarists **Paul Kantner** and Jorma Kaukonen, the vocalist Singe Toly, the string-bass player Bob Harvey, and the drummer Jerry Pelequin. The group gave its first performance in San Francisco on Aug. 13, 1965. There were inevitable changes in personnel, and the vocalist **Grace**

Slick joined the group. Their first album, under the proud name *Jefferson Airplane Takes Off,* inaugurated the so-called San Francisco sound. There followed the highly successful albums *Surrealistic Pillow, After Bathing at Baxter's, Volunteers,* and *Bless Its Pointed Head.* The Jefferson Airplane cultivated calculated absurdity in the titles of its songs and a total stylistic heterogeneity, covering the spectrum from the beatnik era through the hippie period and ending in psychedelic abstraction. Among Balin's contributions were a romantic ballad, *Comin' Back to Me;* a kinetic, frenetic, psychedelic song, *3/5 of a Mile in 10 Seconds;* and the surreal *Plastic Fantastic Lover.* In 1968 The Jefferson Airplane made a successful European tour, but soon personal discords and political divergencies in their common social radicalism led to a gradual dissolution of the group. They got together again in 1975 with the successful *Red Octopus,* which included Balin's hit *Miracles,* disbanded again, and reassembled for another psychedelic flight in 1980 with the self-denigrating collection *The Worst of The Jefferson Airplane.*

Balius y Vila, Jaime, Spanish composer; place and date of birth unknown; d. Córdoba, Nov. 3, 1822. He served as maestro de capella at Urgel Cathedral in 1780; held similar posts in Gerona (from 1781), in Córdoba (from 1785), and at the Convento de la Encarnación in Madrid (from 1787). He returned to his Córdoba post in 1789. He wrote mostly sacred music, and also popular villancicos.

Balkwill, Bryan, English conductor; b. London, July 2, 1922. After private studies, he won a scholarship to the Royal Academy of Music. He then was a conductor with the New London Opera. In 1950 he conducted at Glyndebourne, eventually becoming associate conductor. He also served as music director of the Festival Ballet (London). From 1959 to 1965 he was a resident conductor at the Royal Opera House, Covent Garden. He then was music director of the Welsh National Opera (1963–67) and music director of the Sadler's Wells Opera (1966–69). He then conducted widely in both opera and symph. In 1978 he was appointed a prof. of music at the Indiana Univ. School of Music.

Ball, Ernest R., American composer of popular songs; b. Cleveland, July 21, 1878; d. Santa Ana, Calif., May 3, 1927. He studied at Cleveland Cons.; moved to N.Y., where he earned his living as a vaudeville pianist. His first success came with the song *Will You Love Me in December as You Do in May?* to the words of James J. Walker (later, mayor of N.Y.). No less successful were his sentimental songs *Mother Machree, When Irish Eyes Are Smiling, Little Bit of Heaven, Dear Little Boy of Mine, Till the Sands of the Desert Grow Cold, Love Me and the World Is Mine,* etc., sung by John McCormack and other famous artists. Ball was a charter member of ASCAP (1914).

BIBLIOGRAPHY: I. Witmark and I. Goldberg, *The Story of the House of Witmark: From Ragtime to Swingtime* (N.Y., 1939; 1976).

Ballantine, Edward, American composer; b. Oberlin, Ohio, August 6, 1886; d. Oak Bluffs, Mass., July 2, 1971. He studied with Walter Spalding at Harvard Univ.; graduated with highest honors in 1907; took piano courses with Artur Schnabel and Rudolph Ganz in Berlin (1907–9). In 1912 he was appointed instructor at Harvard; became assistant prof. in 1926; associate prof. in 1932; retired in 1947. His first publ. work was a musical play, *The Lotos Eaters* (1907); 3 of his orch. pieces were performed by the Boston Symph. Orch.: *From the Garden of Hellas* (Feb. 9, 1923); *Prelude to The Delectable Forest* (Dec. 10, 1914); *The Eve of St. Agnes* (Jan. 19, 1917); and one, *By a Lake in Russia,* by the Boston Pops (June 27, 1922). He also wrote a Violin Sonata and songs. His most striking work is a set of piano variations on *Mary Had a Little Lamb* (1924) in the styles of 10 composers; a 2nd series of variations on the same tune (1943) includes stylizations of Stravinsky, Gershwin, and others.

Ballard, a family of French music printers. The establishment was founded on Aug. 14, 1551, by Robert Ballard, whose patent from Henri II made him "Seul imprimeur de la musique de la chambre, chapelle, et menus plaisirs du roy"; the patent was renewed to various members of the family until 1776, when it expired. The firm enjoyed a virtual monopoly on French music printing, and continued under the management of the Ballard family until 1788. Until c.1750, the movable types invented in 1540 by Guillaume le Bé were used; the Ballards printed Lully's operas in this style (from 1700); later printings were from engraved copper-plates.

Ballard, Louis W., American Indian composer of Quapaw-Cherokee extraction (his Indian name is **Hunka-No-Zhe,** which means Grand Eagle); b. Miami, Okla., July 8, 1931. He studied piano and composition at Oklahoma Univ. and Tulsa Univ.; obtained his B.A. in music in 1954, and M.M. in composition in 1962. He subsequently took private lessons with Darius Milhaud, Castelnuovo-Tedesco, and Carlos Surinach. In 1964 he traveled in Europe under the auspices of the State Dept.; was awarded a Ford Foundation grant in 1971. He was subsequently appointed program director at the Bureau of Indian Affairs in Washington, D.C. (1971–79). Virtually all his compositions are musical realizations of authentic Indian melodies and rhythms. WORKS: *Koshare,* ballet, on Hopi themes (Barcelona, May 16, 1966); *The God Will Hear,* cantata (1966); *The Four Moons,* ballet, commemorating the 60th anniversary of the statehood of Oklahoma (Tulsa, Oct. 28, 1967); *Devil's Promenade* for Orch. (Tulsa, May 20, 1973); *Incident at Wounded Knee* for Orch. in 4 sections, dramatizing the rebellion of the Sioux Indians at the locality known as Wounded Knee in S.Dak. (partial perf., St. Paul, Minn., April 16, 1974); *Ritmo Indio* for Woodwind Quintet and a Sioux Flute (1968); *Katcina Dances* for Cello and Piano (1970); *Desert Trilogy* for Winds, Strings, and

Percussion (1971); *Cacega Ayuwipi (The Decorative Drums)* for Percussion Ensemble of 35 instruments and Standard Drums (Washington, D.C., July 27, 1973). He publ. a collection of percussion pieces, *Pan-Indian Rhythms.*

Ballif, Claude, French composer; b. Paris, May 22, 1924. He studied composition at the Paris Cons. with Tony Aubin, Noël Gallon, and Messiaen, and later in Berlin with Blacher and Rufer. For several years he was connected with various pedagogical institutes in Paris; in 1964 he was appointed to the staff of the Cons. of Reims. He has also written articles on subjects dealing with modern musical techniques. WORKS: Several of his works bear surrealist titles, e.g., *Airs comprimés* for Piano (1953); *Voyage de mon oreille* for Orch. (1957); *Ceci et cela* for Orch. (1959); *A cor et à cri* for Orch. (1962); and several pieces under the generic title *Imaginaire* for Various Ensembles; also Quintet for Flute, Oboe, and String Trio (1958); and Double Trio for Flute, Oboe, Cello, Violin, Clarinet, and Horn (1961). Ballif has also written several books and many articles: *Introduction à la méta-tonalité* (Paris, 1956); *Berlioz* (Paris, 1968); "Claude Ballif: Essais, études, documents," *Revue Musicale, numéro spécial 263* (1968).

Balling, Michael, German conductor; b. Heidingsfeld, near Würzburg, Aug. 27, 1866; d. Darmstadt, Sept. 1, 1925. He began his career as an orchestral viola player. In 1892 he went to Nelson, New Zealand, where he organized a music school and a choral society. Returning to Europe, he conducted Wagner's operas in Bayreuth, Hamburg, and Lübeck. In 1912 he succeeded Hans Richter as conductor of the renowned Hallé Orch. in Manchester, leading it until 1914. In 1919 he went to Darmstadt, where he remained until his death.

Ballista, Antonio, Italian pianist; b. Milan, March 30, 1936. He studied piano and composition at the Milan Cons., graduating in 1955; subsequently pursued a successful career as a soloist; is particularly noted for his discerning performances of avant-garde music; he also appeared in duo recitals with the pianist Bruno Canino.

Ballou, Esther Williamson, American composer; b. Elmira, N.Y., July 17, 1915; d. Chichester, England, March 12, 1973. She studied at Bennington College in Vermont and at Mills College in Oakland, Calif.; subsequently obtained a graduate degree in composition at the Juilliard School of Music in N.Y. as a student of Bernard Wagenaar. She also took private lessons with Otto Luening and Wallingford Riegger. From 1959 to 1973 she was on the faculty of the American Univ. in Washington, D.C. WORKS: FOR ORCH.: Piano Concerto (1964); *Konzertstücke* for Viola and Orch. (1969); *Beguine* for Percussion and Strings; also arranged for 2 Pianos, 4-hands, and for 4 Pianos, for 8-hands; alternate title, *Forty-Finger Beguine* (1960). CHAMBER MUSIC: *Suite* for Double Wind Quintet (1957); *Sextette* for

Balmer – Bal y Gay

Brass and Piano (1962); Piano Trio (1956); *Prism* for String Trio (1969); *Capriccio* for Violin and Piano (1963); *A Plaintive Note* for Cello and Piano (1951); *A Cheerful Note* for Cello and Piano (1962); *Suite* for Cello and Piano (1952); 2 piano sonatas; *Street Scenes* for Piano (1960); a number of choruses and solo songs.

Balmer, Luc, Swiss conductor and composer; b. Munich, July 13, 1898. He studied piano and composition with Hans Huber, Egon Petri, and Ernst Levy at the Cons. of Basel, and took a course with Busoni in Berlin in 1922. Returning to Switzerland, he devoted himself to conducting; from 1941 to 1964 he conducted the Musical Society of Bern. He composed symphonic and chamber music in a healthy romantic manner; a Piano Concerto; a Violin Concerto; and a comic opera, after Tirso de Molina, *Die drei gefoppten Ehemänner* (1969).

Balogh, Ernö, Hungarian pianist and composer; b. Budapest, April 4, 1897. A precocious musician, he played in public literally as an infant, and at 7 entered the Royal Academy of Music in Budapest, where he studied piano with Bartók and composition with Kodály. He further studied piano with Leonid Kreutzer in Berlin. In 1924 he emigrated to America. His violin pieces *Caprice antique* and *Arabesque* were played by Kreisler; his piano pieces were performed by himself. He also wrote some symphonic miniatures.

Baloković, Zlatko, eminent Yugoslav violinist; b. Zagreb, March 21, 1895; d. Venice, March 29, 1965. He studied at the Zagreb Cons. as a child; then in Vienna with Ševčik. He appeared as a soloist all over the world, including Australia, where he received a state prize. He gave the first performance of John Alden Carpenter's Violin Concerto with the Chicago Symph. Orch. on Nov. 18, 1937. From that time on he divided his activities between America and Europe.

Balsam, Artur, Polish-born American pianist and pedagogue; b. Warsaw, Feb. 8, 1906. He studied in Lodz; made his debut there at the age of 12; then went to Berlin and enrolled at the Berlin Hochschule für Musik; in 1930 obtained the prestigious Mendelssohn Prize; in 1932 he made a U.S. tour with Yehudi Menuhin. With the advent of the anti-Semitic Nazi regime in 1933, he settled in America, where he became a superlative accompanist to celebrated artists; also played much chamber music and gave occasional solo recitals. He served on the faculties of the Eastman School of Music, Boston Univ., and the Manhattan School of Music; also composed cadenzas for several piano concertos of Mozart.

Balsis, Eduardas, Lithuanian composer; b. Nikolayev, Dec. 20, 1919. He studied composition with Račiunas at the Vilnius Cons., graduating in 1950; then took music courses at the Leningrad Cons. (1953). In 1953 he joined the faculty of the Vilnius Cons.; in 1960 was appointed chairman of the composition department. In his music he adheres to classical forms but makes experimental use of modern techniques, including dodecaphonic progressions.
WORKS: FOR THE STAGE: *Eglė žalčiu karalienė (Egle, Queen of Grass Snakes),* ballet (Vilna, 1960; orch. suite, 1961; 4 fragments for Violin and Piano, 1963). FOR ORCH.: *Vilnius,* a symph. (1950); *Heroic Poem* (1953); 2 violin concertos (1954, 1958); *Folk Dance Suite* (1958); *Dramatic Frescoes* for Violin, Piano, and Orch. (1965); *Symphony-Concerto* for Organ, Percussion, and Orch. (1977). VOCAL: 3 cantatas: *Song for My Land,* for Chorus and Orch. (1962), *Saulę nešantis (He Who Carries the Sun)* for High Voice, Chorus, Organ, and Percussion (1972); *Glory to Lenin* for Mixed Chorus, Male Chorus, and Children's Chorus (1976); an oratorio, *Nelieskite mėlyno gaublio (Don't Touch the Blue Globe)* for Soloists, Children's Chorus, 2 Pianos, Double Bass, and Percussion (1969). CHAMBER MUSIC: Piano Sonata (1947); *Variations* for Piano (1948); String Quartet (1953).

Baltsa, Agnes, Greek mezzo-soprano; b. Lefkas, Nov. 19, 1944. She was educated in Athens, Munich, and Frankfurt. In 1968 she made her debut at the Frankfurt State Opera, remaining there until 1972; also sang at the Deutsche Oper in West Berlin. In 1976 she made her debut at the Vienna State Opera; in 1977 she sang at Salzburg. On Dec. 13, 1979, she made her debut with the Metropolitan Opera in N.Y. as Octavian in *Der Rosenkavalier.*

Baltzar, Thomas, German violinist and composer; b. Lübeck, c.1630; d. London (buried, July 27), 1663. He was a member of a family of German musicians; in 1653 he was made a chamber violinist to Queen Christina of Sweden; about 1655 he went to England, where he established himself as a soloist at private musical gatherings. In 1661 he was named a musician-in-ordinary for the violin in the King's Private Musick. He also composed several works for violin.
BIBLIOGRAPHY: C. Stiehl, "Thomas Baltzar, Ein Paganini seiner Zeit," *Monatshefte für Musikgeschichte,* XX (1888); D. Boyden, *The History of Violin Playing* (London, 1965).

Baltzell, Winton James, American music editor; b. Shiremanstown, Pa., Dec. 18, 1864; d. New York, Jan. 10, 1928. He studied at the New England Cons. and in 1890 went to London, where he took lessons in singing with William Shakespeare and composition with Frederick Bridge. Returning to America, he devoted himself chiefly to editing school manuals; publ. *A Complete History of Music for Schools* (1905) and a *Dictionary of Musicians* (1912). He also composed some choral works and songs.

Bal y Gay, Jesús, Spanish composer and musicologist; b. Lugo, June 23, 1905. He studied in Madrid. After the outbreak of the Spanish Civil War he went to England, and eventually to Mexico, where he was appointed to the staff of the Instituto Nacional de Bellas Artes. He publ. a number of valuable essays on Spanish music, among them *Tientos* (Mexico City, 1960), which traces the development of the Ricercare in Spain. He composed some symph. and chamber music.

Bamberger, Carl, Austrian conductor; b. Vienna, Feb. 21, 1902. He studied at the Univ. of Vienna; conducted opera in Germany and in Russia. In 1937 he emigrated to the U.S., and conducted sporadically various symphonic and choral groups in N.Y.; later dedicated himself mainly to teaching. From 1938 to 1975 he was on the staff of Mannes College of Music in N.Y.; was also lecturer on music at Louisiana State Univ. in Baton Rouge (1975–76). From 1957 to 1974 he was guest conductor of the Stuttgart Radio Orch. He publ. a useful manual, *The Conductor's Art* (N.Y., 1965).

Bamboschek, Giuseppe, Italian conductor; b. Trieste, June 12, 1890; d. New York, June 24, 1969. He studied at the Trieste Cons., graduating in 1907. In 1913 he went to the U.S. as accompanist for Pasquale Amato; in 1919 he joined the staff at the Metropolitan Opera in N.Y., specializing in the Italian repertoire. After 1929 he was active mainly as conductor for radio and motion pictures.

Bamert, Matthias, Swiss composer and conductor; b. Ersigen, July 5, 1942. He studied in Bern, Zürich, Darmstadt, Salzburg, and Paris. His principal teachers in composition were Jean Rivier and Pierre Boulez. He was first oboist of the Salzburg Mozarteum Orch. (1965–69); then became assistant conductor to Leopold Stokowski with the American Symph. Orch. of N.Y. (1970–71). He received the first George Szell Memorial Award, joining the conducting staff of the Cleveland Orch. in 1971. In 1977 he was appointed music director of the Swiss Radio Orch. in Basel.

Bampton, Rose, American operatic soprano; b. Lakewood, Ohio, Nov. 28, 1908. She studied with Queena Mario at the Curtis Inst. of Music in Philadelphia; then took academic courses at Drake Univ. in Des Moines, Iowa, where she obtained a doctorate of fine arts. She sang as contralto with the Philadelphia Opera (1929–32), then changed to mezzosoprano and finally to soprano, so that she could sing the roles of both Amneris (mezzo-soprano) and Aida (soprano). She made her debut at the Metropolitan Opera in N.Y. on Nov. 28, 1932, as Laura in *La Gioconda,* and continued on its staff until 1945; she was again with the Metropolitan Opera from 1947 to 1950. She made annual appearances at the Teatro Colón in Buenos Aires from 1942 to 1948; then returned to N.Y. She was married to the conductor **Wilfrid Pelletier.**

Banchieri, Adriano, Italian organist and composer; b. Bologna, Sept. 3, 1568; d. there, 1634. He studied

with Lucio Barbieri and Giuseppe Guami. On Sept. 8, 1589, he took Holy Orders and entered the monastery of Monte Oliveto. In 1592 he was at the monastery of S. Bartolomeo in Lucca; 1593, in Siena; was organist at Santa Maria in Regola di Imola in 1600. In 1608 he returned to Bologna, remaining there until his death. Despite his clerical rank (he became abbot in 1620), Banchieri never abandoned music, and was active at the Accademia Filarmonica in Bologna (where he was known as "Il dissonante"). He wrote numerous stage works, historically important in the evolution of early opera. Among these dramatic works were *La pazzia senile* (1598); *Il zabaione musicale* (1604); *La barca da Venezia per Padova* (1605); *La prudenza giovanile* (1607); *Tirsi, Filli e Clori* (1614). He wrote a number of masses for 3 to 8 Voices, and other sacred vocal works; also several groups of instrumental works: *I canzoni alla francese a 4 voci per sonar* (1595); *Dialoghi, concentus e sinfonie* (1625); *Il virtuoso ritrovato accademico* (1626); etc. As a theorist, he advocated the extension of the hexachord and proposed to name the 7th degree of the scale by the syllables *ba* and *bi* (corresponding to B-flat and B). Banchieri's theoretical work *L'organo suonarino* (Venice, 1605) gives instructions for accompaniment with figured bass; his *Moderna prattica musicale* (Venice, 1613) contains further elaborations of the subject. Banchieri was the first to use the signs *f* and *p* for loudness and softness (in his *Libro III di nuovi pensieri ecclesiastici,* 1613). He also wrote dramatic plays under the name of **Camillo Scaligeri della Fratta.** A reprint of his *Sinfonia d'istromenti* (1607) is found in A. Schering's *Geschichte der Musik in Beispielen* (No. 151); the organ pieces from *L'organo suonarino* are reprinted in Torchi's *Arte musicale in Italia* (vol. III). Banchieri further publ. the treatises *Cartella musicale del canto figurato, fermo e contrappunto* (Venice, 1614); *Direttorio monastico di canto fermo* (Bologna, 1615); and *Lettere armoniche* (Bologna, 1628). BIBLIOGRAPHY: Max Schneider, *Die Anfänge des Basso continuo* (1918); F. Vatielli, "Il madrigale drammatico e Adriano Banchieri," in *Arte e vita musicale a Bologna* (1927); F.T. Arnold, *The Art of Accompaniment from a Thorough Bass* (London, 1931); Gustave Reese, *Music in the Renaissance* (N.Y., 1954); E. Capaccioli, "Precisazioni biografiche su Adriano Banchieri," *Rivista Musicale* (Oct.–Dec. 1954); H.J. Wilbert, *Die Messen des Adriano Banchieri* (Mainz, 1969); O. Mischiati, *Adriano Banchieri* (Bologna, 1972).

Band, Erich, German conductor; b. Berlin, May 10, 1876; d. Waidhofen, May 13, 1945. He studied at the Hochschule für Musik in Berlin; then was employed as conductor in Stuttgart (1905) and in Halle (1924–32). He published a manual, *Zur Entwicklungsgeschichte des modernen Orchesters* (1910); composed chamber music and songs.

Bandrowska-Turska, Eva, Polish soprano; b. Cracow, May 20, 1897. She studied with her uncle, **Aleksander Bandrowski-Sas;** then took further instruction with Helena Zboinska-Ruszkowska. She made her debut as a concert singer in 1919, and subsequently appeared in opera; in later years she gained distinction as a solo singer; she excelled as a congenial interpreter of the songs of Debussy, Ravel, Roussel, and Szymanowski.

Bandrowski-Sas, Aleksander, noted Polish tenor; b. Lubaczów, April 22, 1860; d. Cracow, May 28, 1913. He made his stage debut as a baritone in an operetta production in Lwow in 1881, using the name **Barski;** then studied voice with Sangiovanni in Milan and Salvi in Vienna; subsequently pursued a successful career as a tenor, using the name **Brandt;** sang in Vienna (1890), in Berlin (1896, 1898), and in Dresden and Munich, and at La Scala in Milan (1896, 1899); was a member of the Frankfurt Opera (1889–1901); also filled engagements in N.Y., Philadelphia, Chicago, and Boston. He retired from the stage in 1904, and then taught voice in Cracow.

Banevich, Sergei, Soviet composer; b. Okhansk, near Perm, Dec. 2, 1941. He studied composition at the Leningrad Cons., graduating in 1966. As a composer he devoted himself mainly to the musical theater; also wrote children's pieces for various instruments.
  WORKS: *White Is the Lonely Sail,* opera (1972); *Ferdinand the Magnificent,* opera (1974); *Goodbye, Arbat!,* operetta (1976); *The Cat That Walked by Himself,* musical play after Kipling (1977); songs.

Bang, Maia (Mrs. Charles Hohn), Norwegian-American violinist and teacher; b. Tromsö, April 24, 1879; d. New York, Jan. 3, 1940. She graduated from the Leipzig Cons. (1897); then studied with Leopold Auer in St. Petersburg. She came to the U.S. in 1919 and became Auer's assistant in N.Y. She was the author of several violin methods; at the time of her death, she was engaged in writing a biography of Paganini. Her collection of Paganini materials was given to the Library of Congress.

Banister, Henry Charles, English music theorist and teacher: b. London, June 13, 1831; d. Streatham, near London, Nov. 20, 1897. He studied music with his father, a cellist; then with Cipriani Potter at the Royal Academy of Music, where he twice gained the King's scholarship (1846 and 1848); was appointed assistant prof. (1853) of harmony and composition at the Royal Academy; taught harmony at Guildhall School (from 1880) and at the Royal Normal College for the Blind (from 1881). He publ. *Textbook of Music* (London, 1872; 15 eds. since); *Some Musical Ethics and Analogies* (1884); *Lectures on Musical Analysis* (1887); *Musical Art and Study* (1888); *George Alexander Macfarren* (1892); *Helpful Papers for Harmony Students* (1895); *The Harmonising of Melodies* (1897); and *The Art of Modulating* (1901). A collection of his lectures, *Interludes,* ed. by Macpherson, appeared in 1898. Banister composed 4 symphs. and 5 overtures, chamber music, cantatas, piano pieces, and songs.

Banister, Henry Joshua, English cellist; b. London, 1803; d. there, 1847. He was a skilled performer, and the author of several books on cello technique. His father, **Charles William Banister** (1768–1831), was a composer who published a *Collection of Vocal Music* (London, 1803).

Banister, John, English violinist and composer; b. London, 1630; d. there, Oct. 3, 1679. After he had received some musical instruction from his father, his skill earned him the patronage of King Charles II, who sent him to France for further study; was later a member of Charles's band, until an outspoken preference for the English over the French musicians playing in it caused his expulsion. Banister was director of a music school, and established the first public concerts not associated with taverns or other gathering places in which music was of only incidental importance, in London (1672–78); was a prominent figure in the English musical life of his day. He wrote music for Davenant's *Circe* and Shakespeare's *The Tempest* (both 1676); composed *New Ayres and Dialogues* for Voices and Viols (London, 1678); contributed to Playford's *Courtly Masquing Ayres* (1662), and to Lock's *Melothesia* (1673); also wrote music for plays by Dryden, Shadwell, and Wycherley.

Banister, John, Jr., English violinist, son of **John Banister;** b. London, c.1663; d. there, c.1725. He studied violin with his father; served as concertmaster at the Italian Opera in London. He composed mostly for the theater; contributed to Playford's *Division Violin* (1685), the first violin manual publ. in England.

Bank, Jacques, Dutch composer; b. Borne, April 18, 1943. He studied with Jos Kunst and Ton de Leeuw at the Amsterdam Cons., graduating in 1974. Apart from his musical activities, he taught English in Amsterdam schools.
  WORKS: *Blind Boy Fuller I* for Recorder, Piano, and optional Voice, being a recording of *Thousand Women Blues,* sung by Blind Boy Fuller in 1940 in Chicago (1966); *The Memoirs of a Cyclist* for 2 Recorders (1967–70); *Emcée* for Voices (1969); *Put Me on My Bike I* for Solo Baritone, Recorder, and Chorus (1971); *Fan It* for Orch. (1973); *Song of Sitting Bull* for Recorder Player possessing a Baritone Voice, and Organ (1974); *Monk's Blues* for Piano, 14 Voices, and 12 Winds (1974); *Blue Mosque* for Bass Recorder (1974); *Die Ouwe (The Old One)* for Bass Recorder, Bass Clarinet, and Piano (1975); *Hitch* for Piano (1975); *Last Post* for Bass Clarinet and Piano (1975); *Thomas* for the recorded Voice of poet Dylan Thomas reading his "Lament," and 19 Instruments (1975).

Banks, Don, Australian composer; b. Melbourne, Oct. 25, 1923; d. Sydney, Sept. 5, 1980. He took piano lessons as a child; played in dance bands as a youth; served in the Australian Army (1941–46). After World War II, he studied composition with Le Gallienne at the Melbourne Cons. (1947–49); went to

England, where he studied composition privately in London with Mátyás Seiber (1950–52), then in Florence with Luigi Dallapiccola (1953). He remained in England and worked as an arranger and composer of film and television music; was music director of Goldsmith's College of the Univ. of London (1969–71). In 1972 he went back to Australia and became head of the dept. of composition and electronic music at the Canberra School of Music. In some of his works he applied serial methods, modified so as not to destroy the sense of tonality; he also made effective use of electronics.

WORKS: FOR ORCH.: *4 Pieces* for Orch. (1953; London, June 1, 1954); *Episode* for Chamber Orch. (1958); *Elizabethan Miniatures* for Lute, Viola da Gamba, and Strings (1962); *Divisions* for Orch. (Cheltenham Festival, July 12, 1965); Horn Concerto (1965; London, Feb. 27, 1966; Barry Tuckwell, soloist); *Assemblies* for Orch. (1966; Melbourne, Dec. 3, 1966); Violin Concerto (1966; London, Aug. 12, 1966); *Dramatic Music* for Young Orch. (1969); *Fanfare* for Orch. (1969); *Intersections* for Orch. and Tape (1969; London, Jan. 1970); *Meeting Place* for Chamber Orch., Jazz Group, and 2 Synthesizers (1970; London, June 15, 1970); *Nexus* for Jazz Quintet and Orch. (1970; Kassel, April 8, 1971); *Music for Wind Band* (1971); *Prospects* (1974); *Trilogy* (1977).

CHAMBER MUSIC: *Duo* for Violin and Cello (1951–52); *Divertimento* for Flute and String Trio (1951–52); Violin Sonata (1953); *3 Studies* for Cello and Piano (1955); *Sonata da Camera,* in memory of Seiber, for 8 Instruments (1961); *Equation I* for 12 Players (1963), *II* for 12 Players (1969), and *III* for Chamber Group, Jazz Quartet, and Synthesizers (1972); Trio for Violin, Horn, and Piano (1962); *3 Episodes* for Flute and Piano (1964); *Sequence* for Solo Cello (1967); *Prelude, Night Piece and Blues for Two* for Clarinet and Piano (1968); *4 Pieces* for String Quartet (1971); *Take Eight* for String Quartet and Jazz Quartet (1973); String Quartet (1976); *One for Murray* for Solo Clarinet (1977); *4 × 2* for Clarinet(s) and Tape (1977).

FOR VOICE: *Psalm 70* for Voice and Chamber Orch. (1954); *5 North Country Folk Songs* for Voice, and String Orch. or Piano (1953–54); *3 North Country Folk Songs* for Soprano and Piano (1955); *Settings from Roget* for Voice and Jazz Quartet (1966); *Tirade,* triptych for Soprano, Harp, Piano, and 3 Percussionists (1968); *Findings Keepings* for Chorus and Percussion (1969); *3 Short Songs* for Voice and Jazz Quartet (1971); *Limbo,* cantata for 3 Singers, 8 Instruments, and 2-channel Tape (1971); Aria from *Limbo* for Voice, Chamber Ensemble, and Tape (1972); *Walkabout* for Children's Voices and Percussion (1972); *Benedictus* for Voices, Jazz Quartet, 5 Synthesizers, Fender Electric Piano, and Tape (1976).

FOR PIANO: *Pezzo Dramatico* (1956); *Commentary* for Piano and Tape (1971). He also composed 3 pieces for Solo Tape, as well as sound tracks for 19 films and 3 English television series.

BIBLIOGRAPHY: Roger Covell, *Australia's Music: Themes of a New Society* (Melbourne, 1967; pp. 178–82); William Mann, "The Music of Don Banks," *Musical Times* (August 1968); James Murdoch, *Aus-*tralia's *Contemporary Composers* (Sydney, 1972); Francis Routh, *Contemporary British Music* (London, 1972); Frank Callaway and David Tunley, *Australian Composition in the Twentieth Century* (Melbourne, 1978).

Bannister, Rev. Henry Marriott, English music editor and bibliographer; b. Oxford, March 18, 1854; d. there, Feb. 16, 1919. He studied theology; was ordained priest in 1878; publ. the valuable editions *Monumenti Vaticani di paleografia musicale latina* (Leipzig, 1913; also in Italian trans. by R. Baralli), a catalogue of the music MSS in the Vatican Library, including 141 plates; *Anglo-French Sequelae* (ed. by Dom Anselm Hughes and publ. by The Plainsong and Medieval Music Society in 1934); co-editor of vols. 47, 49, 53, and 54 of *Analecta Hymnica Medii Aevi* (1886–1922); also publ. some MSS of the Abbey of Coupar-Angus in Scotland, with a brief description (Rome, 1910); ed. a Gallican sacramentary, *Missale Gothicum,* with introduction and liturgical notes (London, 1917–19). He was for many years librarian of the Bodleian Library at Oxford.

Banshchikov, Gennadi, Soviet composer; b. Kazan, Nov. 9, 1943. He studied composition with Balasanian at the Moscow Cons. (1961–64) and with Arapov at the Leningrad Cons. (1965–66); in 1973 he was appointed to the faculty of the Leningrad Cons. In his works he adopts a fairly progressive, even aggressive, modern idiom, making an occasional use of serial techniques.

WORKS: FOR THE STAGE: *The Legend Remained,* radio opera for children (1967); *Lyubov and Silin,* chamber opera (1968); *The Stolen Sun,* television opera (1969); *Vestris,* ballet (1969); *Opera about How Ivan Ivanovich Quarreled with Ivan Nikiforovich,* comic opera after the Gogol tale (1971); *The Death of Cornet Klauzov,* one-act opera after Chekhov's "The Brimstone Match" (1976). FOR ORCH.: *Triade* (1962); 5 cello concertos: No. 1 (1962); No. 2 (1963); No. 3 for Cello Solo (1965); No. 4, *Duodecimet,* for Cello and 11 Instruments (1966); No. 5 (1970); Piano Concerto (1963; revised 1978); Trumpet Concertino (1963); 2 symphs.: No. 1 (1967) and No. 2 for Strings (1977). VOCAL MUSIC: Song cycle for Soprano and Piano, to poems by García Lorca (1962); 3 cantatas: *Architects* for Bass, Male Chorus, and Orch. (1964); *To the Memory of García Lorca* for Chorus and Chamber Orch. (1965); *Ashes in the Palms,* chamber cantata to poems by César Vallejo (1978). CHAMBER MUSIC: *4 Impressions* for Cello and Piano (1963; revised 1978); *Small Duet* for Violin and Piano (1965); *4 Pieces* for Clarinet and Piano (1968); Cello Sonata (1970); *Trio-Sonata* for Violin, Viola, and Cello (1972); Clarinet Sonata (1972); Flute Sonata (1975); Accordion Sonata (1977). FOR PIANO: *Concert Allegro* (1963); *Syllogisms* (1964); 3 sonatas (1968, 1973, 1974).

Banti-Giorgi, Brigida, famous Italian soprano; b. Monticelli d'Ongina (Piacenza), 1759; d. Bologna, Feb. 18, 1806. She sang in Paris cafés, where she attracted the attention of de Vismes, director of the

Paris Opéra, who engaged her to sing there. She made her debut on Nov. 1, 1776, singing a song during the intermission. She then studied with Sacchini. In 1779 she went to London for a season; then sang in Vienna (1780), Venice (1782–83), Warsaw (1789), and Madrid (1793–94). Paisiello wrote for her his opera *Giuochi di Agrigento,* and she sang at its premiere (Venice, May 16, 1792). From 1794 to 1802 she sang at King's Theatre in London; then retired. She married the dancer Zaccaria Banti; her son wrote her biography.

BIBLIOGRAPHY: Giuseppe Banti, *Vita de B. Banti-Giorgi* (Bologna, 1969); Carlo Lozzi, "Brigida Banti," *Rivista Musicale Italiana* (1904), pp. 64–76.

Bantock, Sir Granville, eminent English composer; b. London, Aug. 7, 1868; d. there, Oct. 16, 1946. He studied at the Royal Academy of Music, graduating in 1892; was the first holder of the Macfarren Scholarship. His earliest works were presented at the Academy concerts: an Egyptian ballet suite, *Rameses II;* overture, *The Fire Worshippers;* and a short opera, *Caedmar,* which was later presented at the Crystal Palace (Oct. 18, 1893). He then developed varied activities; he was founder and editor of *New Quarterly Musical Review* (1893–96); toured as a musical comedy conductor (1894–95); organized and conducted concerts devoted to works by young British composers; conducted a military band and later a full orch. at New Brighton (1897–1901). At the same time he was engaged in teaching activities; in 1907 he succeeded Sir Edward Elgar as prof. of music at Birmingham Univ., a post he retained until 1934, when he became chairman of the board of Trinity College of Music. In 1938, at the age of 70, he undertook a journey to India and Australia, returning to England on the eve of World War II. He was married in 1898 to Helen von Schweitzer, daughter of the poet Hermann von Schweitzer. Bantock was knighted in 1930. As a composer, he was attracted to exotic subjects with mystical overtones; his interests were cosmopolitan and embraced all civilizations, with a particular predilection for the Celtic and oriental cultures; however, his music was set in Western terms. He was a strong believer in the programmatic significance of musical images, and most of his works bear titles relating to literature, mythology, or legend. Yet he was a typically British composer in the treatment of his materials. His works are brilliantly scored and effective in performance, but few of them have been retained in the repertoire of musical organizations.

WORKS: 3 Celtic operas: *Caedmar* (1892); *The Pearl of Iran* (1894); and *The Seal-Woman* (Birmingham, Sept. 27, 1924); ballets: *Egypt* (1892); *Lalla Rookh* (1902); *The Great God Pan* (1902); 5 tone poems: *Thalaba the Destroyer* (1900); *Dante* (1901; revised 1910); *Fifine at the Fair* (1901); *Hudibras* (1902); *The Witch of Atlas* (1902); overture, *The Pierrot of the Minute* (1908); *Hebridean Symphony* (Glasgow, Jan. 17, 1916); *Pagan Symphony* (1923–28); *Celtic Symphony* for Strings and 6 Harps (1940); *2 Heroic Ballads* (1944); *The Funeral* (1946);

choral works with Orch.: *The Time Spirit* (1902); *Sea Wanderers* (1906); *Omar Khayyám* (in 3 parts; 1906–9; Bantock's most ambitious work); *The Pilgrim's Progress* (1928); *Prometheus Unbound* (1936); numerous works for Unaccompanied Chorus, among them 3 "choral symphonies": *Atalanta in Calydon* (1911); *Vanity of Vanities* (1913); *A Pageant of Human Life* (1913); also *The Golden Journey to Samarkand* (1922); choral suites to words from the Chinese; children's songs to the poems of Helen Bantock; works for brass band, cello, and orch. and for voice and orch.; 2 string quartets; 3 violin sonatas; viola sonatas; cello sonatas; several sets of piano pieces; *Songs of the East* (6 cycles of 6 songs each); several sets of *Songs from the Chinese Poets;* sets of Celtic songs; etc. Bantock also edited albums of keyboard pieces by Byrd.

BIBLIOGRAPHY: H.O. Anderton, *Granville Bantock* (London, 1915); H. Antcliffe, "A Brief Survey of the Works of Granville Bantock," *Musical Quarterly* (July 1918); P.J. Pirie, "Bantock and His Generation," *Musical Times* (Aug. 1968); M. Bantock, *Granville Bantock: A Personal Portrait* (London, 1972).

Banwart, Jakob, German composer; b. Sigmaringen, May 19, 1609; d. Konstanz, c.1657. He studied with Daniel Bollius, the court organist in Sigmaringen; then (1629–31) continued his education at Dillingen Univ., where he received a master's degree; he was ordained in Konstanz in 1632, and subsequently was active as a musician at the court there; in 1641 he became Kapellmeister of the Cathedral. He composed mostly music for the church, but also took time off to write a collection of humorous dialogues, quodlibets, and other pieces which were publ. in his lifetime.

Bar-Illan, David, Israeli pianist; b. Haifa, Feb. 7, 1930. He first studied piano in his native city; then continued his studies at the Juilliard School of Music and the Mannes College of Music in N.Y. After playing in his native Israel, he made his first appearance with the N.Y. Phil. in 1960; in subsequent seasons he appeared with all of the major orchs. of the U.S.; also played with many orchs. of Europe.

Baranović, Krešimir, eminent Croatian composer; b. Šibenik, July 25, 1894; d. Belgrade, Sept. 17, 1975. He studied piano and theory in Zagreb and in Vienna. He was subsequently a theater conductor in Zagreb (1915–27); then traveled with Anna Pavlova's ballet group (1927–28). Returning to Yugoslavia, he was music director of the Zagreb Opera (1929–40); then served as a prof. at the Belgrade Academy (1946–61); was also conductor of the Belgrade Phil. (1952–61). He retired in 1963. A prolific composer, he was successful mostly in music for the theater.

WORKS: 2 COMIC OPERAS: *Striženo-Košeno* (*Clipped and Mowed;* Zagreb, May 4, 1932, composer conducting) and *Nevjesta od Cetingrada* (*The Bride from Cetingrad;* Belgrade, May 12, 1951, composer conducting). BALLETS: *Kineska priča* (*Chinese Tale*), in which he made use of the pentatonic scale for local color (Belgrade, April 30, 1955); *The Gin-*

gerbread Heart (Edinburgh Festival, 1951). For
ORCH.: Pjesma guslara (Song of the Minstrel; Za-
greb, Jan. 25, 1947); Pan for Narrator, Voices, and
Orch. (Belgrade, March 10, 1958); Oblaci (The
Clouds) for Mezzo-soprano and Orch. (Belgrade,
Oct. 31, 1964).
BIBLIOGRAPHY: V. Peričić, Muzički Stvaraoci
u Srbiji (Belgrade, 1970).

Barati, George, eminent Hungarian-American
cellist, composer, and conductor; b. Györ, April 3,
1913. He studied cello and theory at the Budapest
Cons., and was first cellist at the Budapest Opera
(1936–38). In 1939 he emigrated to America; attended courses of Roger Sessions at Princeton Univ.
(1939–43); served as bandleader with the U.S. Army
(1943–46); from 1946 to 1950 he played cello with the
San Francisco Symph. Orch. In 1950 he was appointed conductor of the Honolulu Symph. Orch. in Hawaii, a post he held until 1968; then was executive
director of the Montalvo Center for the Arts in
Saratoga, Calif. (1968–78); concurrently served as
music director of the Santa Cruz County Symph.
(1971–80). As a composer, he wrote fine music in a
modern European tradition; during his stay in Hawaii he studied native melodic and rhythmic patterns of exotic South Sea islands, which found a
reflection in some of his works of the period.
WORKS: 2 operas, The Feather Cloak (1970) and
Noelani (1971); Cello Concerto (1957); Configurations for Orch. (1957); The Dragon and the Phoenix
for Orch. (1960); Quartet for Flute, Oboe, Double
Bass, and Harp (1964); Symph. (1964); Polarization
for Orch. (1965); The Waters of Kane, festival ode
for Chorus and Orch. (Honolulu, Sept. 23, 1966); Octet for Harpsichord, Flute, Oboe, Bassoon, and
String Quartet (1966); Festival Hula, symph. dance
(1969); South Seas Suite for Guitar and Orch. (1971);
Piano Concerto (1973); Cities of the Interior for Soprano and Chamber Orch. (1976); Branches of Time
for 2 Pianos and Orch. (1981; first performance,
Santa Cruz, Calif., March 21, 1981); Night Spectrum
for Piano (1981); Confluence for Orch. (Aptos,
Calif., Cabrillo Festival, Aug. 20, 1982); chamber
music.

Barbaja, Domenico, successful Italian impresario;
b. Milan, c.1775; d. Posillipo, near Naples, Oct. 19,
1841. Early in life he exhibited a talent for making
money by concocting and selling food and sweets
that satisfied popular tastes; he was reputed to be
the inventor of whipped cream with coffee or
chocolate, which became known as barbajata, or
granita di caffè. In 1808 he obtained the lease of the
gambling tables in Naples. On Oct. 7, 1809, he was
appointed manager of all of the royal opera houses
in Naples; so powerful did he become that he was
nicknamed "Viceroy of Naples." Upon the advice of
his mistress, the well-known singer Isabella Colbran, he entered the theatrical business, and in 1826
was appointed manager of La Scala in Milan; simultaneously he was impresario of San Carlo in Naples
(1809–24) and two theaters in Vienna (1821–28). He
continued the management of La Scala until 1832.

A convivial character, he easily formed friendships
with Rossini, Bellini, and Donizetti, and induced
them to write operas for the theaters under his
management. Emil Lucka wrote a novel, Der Impresario (Vienna, 1937), based on his life.
BIBLIOGRAPHY: G. Monaldi, Impresari celebri
del Secolo XIX (Milan, 1918).

Barbe, Helmut, organist and German composer; b.
Halle, Dec. 28, 1927. He studied music theory in Berlin with Ernst Pepping and choral conducting with
Gottfried Grote; was active as church organist and
conductor in Berlin. In 1952 he became Kantor at St.
Nikolai Church in Spandau; in 1955 was appointed
member of the faculty of the Berlin Kirchenmusikschule. In 1973 he was named Landeskirchenmusik-
direktor. In his own works he adopted a modified
dodecaphony. He composed mostly sacred choral
works and various organ pieces; also wrote a Violin
Concerto (1966) and Hovs Hallar for Organ, 12 Solo
Strings, and Percussion (1970). In his works he
adopted a median modernistic technique with polytonal and atonal elements applied when necessary.

Barbeau, Marius, eminent French-Canadian musician and folklorist; b. Ste. Marie de Beauce, Quebec, March 5, 1883; d. Ottawa, Feb. 27, 1969. He studied at Oxford Univ., obtaining his diploma in anthropology as a Rhodes scholar in 1910; later took
courses at the Sorbonne in Paris. In 1911 he was
appointed anthropologist at the Victoria Memorial
Museum in Ottawa; was pensioned in 1948. His
main study was devoted to the codification of folkloric materials of Canadian Indians and the French
population of Quebec. He collected more than 6,000
melodies and 13,000 texts of French-Canadian folk
songs and many thousands of Indian melodies,
making use of phonograph recordings. From 1927 to
1930 he was in charge of folk music festivals in
Quebec. In 1956 he organized the Canadian Folk
Music Society. He published 30 books and 10 anthologies of songs in collaboration with other
Canadian folklorists. Among his most important
publications are "Chants populaires du Canada,"
Journal of American Folklore (1919); Folksongs of
French Canada (with E. Sapir; New Haven, 1925);
Jongleur Songs of Old Quebec (Toronto, 1962). For
a bibliography of Barbeau's writings, almost 100
books and 600 articles, see Israel Katz, "Marius Bar-
beau, 1883–1969," Ethnomusicology (Jan. 1970).

Barber, Samuel, American composer of superlative gifts; b. West Chester, Pa., March 9, 1910; d. New
York, Jan. 23, 1981. His mother was a good pianist;
her sister was the famous opera contralto **Louise
Homer.** Barber began taking piano lessons as a child
with William Hatton Green; he also improvised,
and composed a piano piece, entitled Sadness. At
the age of 10 he attempted to write an opera, The
Rose Tree. He played piano at school functions, and
had an occasional job as organist in a local church.
At the age of 14 he enrolled at the newly founded
Curtis Inst. of Music in Philadelphia; there he studied piano with Isabelle Vengerova, composition

with Rosario Scalero, and conducting with Fritz Reiner. He also took singing lessons with Emilio de Gogorza. So successful was he as a voice student that he ventured to appear in public as a mellow baritone. However, it was free composition that became his absorbing labor. At the time when most American composers exerted their ingenuity writing sophisticated music laced with unresolvable dissonances, Barber kept aloof from facile and fashionable modernism. He adopted an idiom, lyrical and romantic in nature, which had a distinct originality in its melodic and harmonic aspects. His *Overture to the School for Scandal*, after Sheridan (1933), attracted favorable attention. It was closely followed by *Music for a Scene from Shelley*, which had numerous performances. In 1935 Barber received a Pulitzer traveling scholarship and the American Prix de Rome. His *Symphony No. 1*, in one movement, which he composed in Rome, became the first American work to be presented at the Salzburg Festival of Contemporary Music (July 25, 1937). On Nov. 5, 1938, Toscanini conducted the NBC Symph. Orch. in Barber's *Essay for Orchestra No. 1* and *Adagio for Strings* (arranged from Barber's String Quartet); the *Adagio* was destined to become one of the most popular American works of serious music, and through some lurid aberration of circumstance, it also became a favorite selection at state funerals. It formed the background music at Roosevelt's commemorative service in 1945; the passionate serenity of its modal strains moved the family and friends of Princess Grace of Monaco to tears when it was played at her funeral on Sept. 18, 1982. From 1939 to 1942, Barber intermittently taught orchestration at the Curtis Inst. In the autumn of 1942 he joined the Army Air Force, which commissioned him to write a symph., his second. The original score included an electronic instrument producing sound in imitation of radio signals; it was successfully performed by Koussevitzky with the Boston Symph. Orch. in 1944; but after the war Barber decided to eliminate such incidental intercalations; this demilitarized version was performed by the Philadelphia Orch. in 1949. Still dissatisfied with the resultant product, he discarded the work except for the 2nd movement, which he retitled as *Night Flight*, and had it performed in Cleveland in 1964. Barber was discharged from the air force in 1945 and settled in Mt. Kisco, N.Y., in a house (named "Capricorn") that he had purchased jointly with Gian Carlo Menotti in 1943. Barber was always devoted to the art of the theater. He wrote a ballet, *The Serpent Heart*, for Martha Graham (1946), which was later revised and produced by her group under the title *Cave of the Heart;* from it he drew an orchestral suite, *Medea;* a further version of the music was *Medea's Meditation and Dance of Vengeance.* In his *Prayers of Kierkegaard* for Soprano, Chorus, and Orch. (1954), Barber essayed the style of modern oratorio. But it was not until 1958 that he wrote his first opera, *Vanessa*, with a romantic libretto by his lifelong friend Gian Carlo Menotti; it was produced by the Metropolitan Opera in N.Y. on Jan. 15, 1958, and earned Barber his first of two Pulitzer Prizes in music; a revised version was pro-

duced in 1978 at the Spoleto Festival U.S.A. in Charleston, S.C., on May 27, 1978. A much more ambitious opera, commissioned by the Metropolitan Opera, was *Antony and Cleopatra*, in 3 acts, after Shakespeare, produced with a grand display of expectations at the opening of the new Metropolitan Opera House in N.Y. on Sept. 16, 1966. Unfortunately, the production was haunted by mechanical mishaps. A specially constructed revolving stage did not rotate properly, the acoustics were faulty, and the annoyed newspaper critics damned the music along with the staging. Barber attempted to recoup the work with a libretto revamped by Menotti, but the new version, performed at the Juilliard School of Music (1975), failed to justify his hopes. Disillusioned in his capacity to create a modern grand opera, Barber produced a light operatic sketch, *A Hand of Bridge,* to a libretto by Menotti (1959), but it passed without much notice. However, Barber was gloriously vindicated as an important composer by a succession of fine works of instrumental music; particularly notable was his Piano Concerto (1962), a striking work in an original modern idiom, spontaneously acclaimed in repeated performances in America and Europe, which won him his second Pulitzer Prize. No less remarkable was his Piano Sonata, introduced by Vladimir Horowitz in 1949; in it Barber made ample use of modernistic resources, including incidental applications of 12-tone writing. Another example of Barber's brilliant use of pianistic resources was his witty piano suite *Excursions* (1945). Barber excelled in new American music primarily as a melodist; perhaps the circumstance that he studied singing as a youth had contributed to his sensitive handling of vocally shaped patterns. Although the harmonic structures of his music remained fundamentally tonal, he made free use of chromatic techniques, verging on atonality and polytonality, while his mastery of modern counterpoint enabled him to write canons and fugues in effective neo-Baroque sequences. His orchestration was opulent without being turgid; his treatment of solo instruments was unfailingly congenial to their nature even though requiring a virtuoso technique. Barber held three Guggenheim fellowships (1945, 1947, 1949). In 1959 Harvard Univ. conferred upon him an honorary degree of Doctor of Fine Arts.

WORKS: OPERAS: *Vanessa,* to a libretto by Menotti (Metropolitan Opera, N.Y., Jan. 15, 1958; revised version, Spoleto Festival U.S.A., Charleston, S.C., May 27, 1978); *Antony and Cleopatra,* after Shakespeare (N.Y., Sept. 16, 1966; revised and produced in a new version at the Juilliard School of Music, N.Y., Feb. 6, 1975); *A Hand of Bridge,* one-act opera, to a libretto by Menotti, for 4 Solo Voices and Chamber Orch. (1958; Festival of Two Worlds, Spoleto, Italy, June 17, 1959).

BALLETS: *The Serpent Heart* (performed by Martha Graham and her dance group, N.Y., May 10, 1946; revised and produced under the title *Cave of the Heart,* N.Y., Feb. 27, 1947).

FOR ORCH.: *Overture to the School for Scandal,* after Sheridan (Philadelphia, Aug. 30, 1933); *Music for a Scene from Shelley* (N.Y., March 24, 1935);

Symphony No. 1, in one movement (Rome, Dec. 13, 1936); *Adagio for Strings,* arranged from the slow movement of the String Quartet (N.Y., NBC Symph. Orch., conducted by Toscanini, Nov. 5, 1938; *Barber's Essay No. 1* was performed at the same concert); *Essay No. 2* (N.Y. Philharmonic, Bruno Walter conducting, April 16, 1942); *Commando March,* originally for military band (performed in its symphonic form, Boston Symph., Koussevitzky conducting, Oct. 29, 1943); *Symphony No. 2* (Boston, March 3, 1944; conducted by Koussevitzky; an antiseptic version, radically cleansed of instrumental irrelevancies, was performed by the Philadelphia Orch., Ormandy conducting, Jan. 21, 1949; in another surgical operation, the second movement was reworked, retitled *Night Flight,* and first performed in Cleveland, Oct. 8, 1964); *Capricorn Concerto* for Flute, Oboe, Trumpet, and Strings (N.Y., Oct. 8, 1944); *Medea,* suite from the ballet *The Serpent Heart* (Philadelphia, Dec. 5, 1947); *Souvenirs,* ballet suite, originally for Piano, 4-hands; for Orch. (Chicago, Nov. 13, 1953; stage production, N.Y., Nov. 15, 1955); *Medea's Meditation and Dance of Vengeance,* a revised version of the symph. suite *Medea* (N.Y., Feb. 2, 1956); *Toccata Festiva* for Organ and Orch. (Philadelphia, Sept. 30, 1960); *Die Natali,* choral prelude for Christmas (Boston Symph. Orch., Lincoln Center, N.Y., Dec. 22, 1960); *Fadograph from a Yestern Scene,* after a line in James Joyce's *Finnegans Wake* (Pittsburgh, Sept. 10, 1971); *Essay No. 3* for Orch. (N.Y., Sept. 14, 1978); *Canzonetta* for Oboe and String Orch. (1980; incomplete; orchestrated by Charles Turner, and first perf. by the N.Y. Phil., Dec. 17, 1981).

CONCERTOS: Violin Concerto (Philadelphia, Feb. 7, 1941, Albert Spalding, soloist; Ormandy conducting); Cello Concerto (Boston Symph., Raya Garbuzova, soloist; Koussevitzky conducting, April 5, 1946); Piano Concerto (Boston Symph., Lincoln Center, N.Y., Sept. 24, 1962, John Browning, soloist; Erich Leinsdorf conducting).

VOCAL WORKS: *Dover Beach,* after a poem by Matthew Arnold, for Voice and String Quartet (1931; N.Y., March 5, 1933); *A Stopwatch and an Ordnance Map* for Male Chorus, Brass, and Timpani (Philadelphia, April 23, 1940); *Sure on This Shining Night,* to words by James Agee, for Voice and Orch. (1938); *Knoxville: Summer of 1915* for Voice and Orch., to a text of James Agee from his novel *A Death in the Family* (Boston Symph., Koussevitzky conducting, April 9, 1948); *Prayers of Kierkegaard* for Soprano, Chorus, and Orch. (Boston Symph., Dec. 3, 1954); *Andromache's Farewell* for Voice and Orch. (N.Y., April 4, 1963); *The Lovers* for Baritone, Chorus, and Orch., to words by Pablo Neruda (Philadelphia, Sept. 22, 1971).

CHAMBER MUSIC: *Serenade* for String Quartet, or String Orch. (Philadelphia, May 5, 1930); Cello Sonata (1932); String Quartet (1936; 2nd movement, *Adagio,* extracted from it and arranged for String Orch., was widely perf.); *Summer Music* for Woodwind Quintet (Detroit, March 20, 1956); *Canzone* for Flute and Piano (1962; arranged from the 2nd movement of the Piano Concerto); *Mutations from Bach* for Brass and Timpani (1968).

SONGS: *The Daisies,* to words by James Stephens (1927); *With Rue My Heart Is Laden,* to words by A.E. Housman (1928); 3 Songs to poems from *Chamber Music* by James Joyce (1936); *A Nun Takes the Veil,* to words by G.M. Hopkins (1937); *The Secrets of the Old,* to words by W.B. Yeats (1938); *The Queen's Face on the Summery Coin,* to words by Robert Horan (1942); *Monks and Raisins,* to words by J.G. Villa (1943); *Nuvoletta,* to words by James Joyce (1947); *Mélodies passagères,* 5 songs, to words by Rilke (1951); *Hermit Songs,* 10 songs after old Irish texts (Washington, D.C., Oct. 30, 1953, Leontyne Price, soloist); *Despite and Still,* 5 songs to words by Graves, Roethke, and Joyce (1969); *3 Songs* for Baritone and Piano (N.Y., April 30, 1974, Fischer-Dieskau, soloist).

FOR CHORUS: *The Virgin Martyrs* (1935); *Let Down the Bars, O Death* (1936); *Reincarnation,* 3 songs after poems by Stephens, for Mixed Chorus a cappella (1940).

FOR PIANO SOLO: *Excursions* (1944); Piano Sonata in E-flat minor (Havana, Cuba, Dec. 9, 1949, Horowitz, soloist; N.Y. performance, also by Horowitz, Jan. 23, 1950); *Souvenirs* for Piano, 4-hands, also for Orch. (1953); *Nocturne: Homage to John Field* (1959); *Ballade* (1977); also *Wonderous Love,* variations on a shape-note hymn, for Organ (1958).

BIBLIOGRAPHY: Nathan Broder, *Samuel Barber* (N.Y., 1954); Allan Kozinn, "Samuel Barber: The Last Interview and the Legacy" (*High Fidelity,* June and July 1981); David Ewen, *American Composers* (N.Y., 1982).

Barberá, José, Catalan music theorist; b. Barcelona, Jan. 27, 1874; d. there, Feb. 19, 1947. He studied in Barcelona with Pedrell; in 1924 he was appointed instructor in composition at the Conservatorio del Liceo, and from 1931 until 1938 was its director. He publ. an important manual, *Curso deo Melódica,* in which he derives all rules of music theory from the melodic structure. His *Cuatro lecciones del alta teoría musical* was issued posthumously (1948). He composed a Symph. (1928) and some piano pieces and songs.

Barbi, Alice, Italian mezzo-soprano; b. Modena, June 1, 1862; d. Rome, Sept. 4, 1948. She made her debut in Milan on April 2, 1882; sang recitals in England, Germany, and Russia. At her concert in Vienna on Dec. 21, 1893, Brahms played the accompaniments to his songs. She was married to Pietro della Torretta in 1920, and spent her last years in Rome.

Barbier, Jules Paul, French librettist and dramatist; b. Paris, March 8, 1822; d. there, Jan. 16, 1901. He was joint author (with Carré) of several librettos for famous operas, among them Gounod's *Faust* and *Roméo et Juliette,* and *Hamlet* by Ambroise Thomas.

Barbier, René (Auguste-Ernest), Belgian composer; b. Namur, July 12, 1890; d. Brussels, Dec. 24, 1981. He studied with Paul Gilson at the Brussels Cons. and with Sylvain Dupuis at the Liège Cons.;

taught at the Liège Cons. (from 1920 to 1949) and at the Brussels Cons. (from 1949); concurrently served as director of the Cons. of Namur (1923–63). He received the Belgian Royal Academy Prize for his symph. poem *Les Genies du sommeil* (1923).

WORKS: 2 operas: *Yvette* (1910) and *La Fête du vieux Tilleul* (1912); an operetta, *La Sultane de Paris;* 3 oratorios: *La Tour de Babel* (1932); *Le Chemin de la Croix (The Way of the Cross),* 14 commentaries for Narrator, Orch., and Organ (1952); *Lamentation de la 9ᵉ heure* (1961); a "pièce radiophonique," *La Mort de Prométhée* (1933); a ballet, *Les Pierres magiques* (1957); *Pièce symphonique* for Trumpet and Orch. (1918); 2 piano concertos (1922, 1934); *Les Eléments (Suite Platonicienne,* 1935); *Poème* for Cello and Orch. (1936); *Fantaisie concertante* for Violin and Orch. (1937); Cello Concerto (1938); *La Voix humaine* for Small Orch. (1940); *Poco Adagio et Allegro Brillante* for Clarinet and Orch. (1940); *Diptyque* for Orch., with Organ (1941); *La Musique de perdition,* symph. poem (1947); *Petite suite* for Orch. (1955); *Introduction (Fanfare) et 3 Esquisses symphoniques* for Orch. (1956); *Pièce concertante* for Violin or Saxophone, and Orch. (1958); Guitar Concerto (1960); *Te Deum laudamus* for Chorus, Brass, and Organ (1962); *3 mouvements symphoniques* for String Orch. (1962); *Tableau symphonique* (1963); Horn Concerto (1964); Concertino for Woodwind Quartet or 4 Clarinets, and String Orch. (1964); Sinfonietta for Small Orch. (1966); *Introduction et Allegro symphonique* (1967); Concerto for Organ, Strings, and Percussion (1967); *Ouverture concertante* (1969); Concertino for 2 Guitars and String Orch. (1971); Violin Sonata (1914); Piano Quintet (1915); Viola Sonata (1916); Piano Trio (1919); String Quartet (1939); Quartet for 4 Horns (1956); Quartet for 4 Saxophones (1961); *Divertissement* for 4 Clarinets (1962); *Petite suite* for Woodwind Quartet (1964); 2 *Petites suites* for 2 Guitars (1965, 1969); Trio for Flute, Cello, and Piano (1971).

Barbieri, Carlo Emmanuele, Italian conductor and composer; b. Genoa, Oct. 22, 1822; d. Budapest, Sept. 28, 1867. He was educated at the Naples Cons., where he studied voice with Crescenti and composition with Mercadante. In 1845 he embarked on a career as an opera conductor; eventually settled in Buda, where he conducted at the National Theater from 1862 until his death. He wrote 5 operas: *Cristoforo Colombo* (Berlin, 1848); *Nisida, la perla di Procida* (1851); *Carlo und Carlin* (1859); *Arabella* (Budapest, 1862); and *Perdita, Ein Wintermärchen* (Leipzig, 1865); church music, German and Italian songs.

Barbieri, Fedora, Italian mezzo-soprano; b. Trieste, June 4, 1920. She studied with local teachers; then moved to Milan, where her teacher was Giulia Tess. She made her professional debut at the Florence Opera in 1940; then filled engagements, in the midst of a raging war, in Germany, Belgium, and the Netherlands. After the end of hostilities she sang at La Scala in Milan, in Paris, and in London. She made her American debut in San Francisco; then sang in Chicago; from 1950 to 1953 and again in 1967 she appeared with the Metropolitan Opera in N.Y. Her best roles were Azucena in *Il Trovatore* and Amneris in *Aida;* she also sang the title role in *Carmen.*

Barbieri, Francisco Asenjo, Spanish composer; b. Madrid, Aug. 3, 1823; d. there, Feb. 19, 1894. He studied clarinet, voice, and composition at the Madrid Cons., then engaged in multifarious activities as a café pianist, music copyist, and choral conductor. He found his true vocation in writing zarzuelas, and composed 78 of them. The following, all produced in Madrid, were particularly successful: *Gloria y peluca* (March 9, 1850); *Jugar con fuego* (Oct. 6, 1851); *Los diamantes de la corona* (Sept. 15, 1854); *Pan y Toros* (Dec. 22, 1864); *El Barberillo de Lavapiés* (Dec. 18, 1874). Barbieri edited a valuable collection, *Cancionero musical de los siglos XV y XVI,* and publ. a number of essays on Spanish music.

BIBLIOGRAPHY: J. Subirá, *Manuscritos de Barbieri, existentes en la Biblioteca Nacional* (Madrid, 1936); Gilbert Chase, "Barbieri and the Spanish Zarzuela," *Music & Letters* (Jan. 1939); A. Martínez Olmedilla, *El maestro Barbieri y su tiempo* (Madrid, 1950).

Barbieri-Nini, Marianna, Italian soprano; b. Florence, c.1820; d. there, Nov. 27, 1887. She studied with Luigi Barbieri, Pasta, and Vaccai; made her operatic debut in 1840 at La Scala in Milan in Donizetti's *Belisario;* unfortunately her peculiarly asymmetrical facial features and an ill-constructed bodily frame produced such a vociferous outburst of revulsion on the part of the notoriously unrestrained Italian opera audiences that she was advised to wear a mask and a bodice to conceal her repellent physique. However, she astutely selected the part of Lucrezia Borgia, a historically celebrated poisoner, in Donizetti's eponymous opera at her next appearance in Florence, and there her ugly countenance fitted the role to a high C. She was also very successful in other bloody roles, among them that of Lady Macbeth in Verdi's opera and of the sympathetic but murderous Gulnara in Verdi's *Il Corsaro.* Still, she had to retire at menopause.

Barbion, Eustachius, Flemish composer; place and date of birth unknown; d. before July 9, 1556. In 1543 he was appointed maître de chapelle at Notre Dame in Courtrai. Among his extant works are 14 motets for 4 to 6 voices and 3 chansons for 4 to 5 voices, which testify to his ability.

Barbireau (or **Barbirau, Barbarieu, Barbyrianus, Barberau, Barbacola**), **Jacques (Jacobus),** Flemish composer; b. Mons, c.1408; d. Antwerp, Aug. 8, 1491. He was appointed Maître de Chapelle at Notre Dame Cathedral in Antwerp in 1448, and served there until his death. Okeghem was one of his pupils. Barbireau was greatly esteemed by his contemporaries; his opinions were copiously cited by Tinctoris. He wrote exclusively for the church; composed a Mass for 5 Voices, *Virgo parens Christi;*

Missa Pascale for 4 Voices; antiphons; Psalms; anthems.

BIBLIOGRAPHY: H. du Saar, *Het Leven en de composities van Jacobus Barbireau* (Utrecht, 1946); G. Reese, *Music in the Renaissance* (N.Y., 1954); B. Meier, ed., *J. Barbireau: Opera omnia corpus mensurabilis musicae* (1954–57).

Barbirolli, Sir John, eminent English conductor; b. London, Dec. 2, 1899, of Italian-French parentage; d. there, July 29, 1970. His baptismal names were Giovanni Battista, given by his father, a professional violinist. He studied cello; received a scholarship to the Trinity College of Music in 1910 and another scholarship to the Royal Academy of Music, graduating in 1916; he made his first appearance as a cellist at the age of 12, on Dec. 16, 1911, at the Queen's Hall. In 1916 he became a member of the Queen's Hall Orch. In 1918–19 he served in the British Army; afterwards resumed his musical career. In 1923 he joined the International String Quartet and toured with it. In 1925 he organized a chamber orch. in Chelsea, which he conducted for several years; later was a conductor with the British National Opera Co. (1926–29). He gained recognition when on Dec. 12, 1927, he successfully substituted for Beecham at a concert of the London Symph. Orch. In 1928 he was a guest conductor at Covent Garden, and a regular conductor there from 1929 to 1933; in 1933 he was named conductor of the Scottish Orch., Glasgow, and the Leeds Symph. Orch. He made his American debut with the N.Y. Phil. on Nov. 5, 1936, and was engaged as its permanent conductor in 1937. However, he failed to impress the N.Y. critics, and in 1943 he returned to England, where he was named conductor of the Hallé Orch. of Manchester. In 1958 he was appointed its conductor-in-chief. Renewing his American career, he served as conductor of the Houston Symph. (1961–67), while continuing his tenancy of the Hallé Orch., from which he finally retired in 1968 with the title of Conductor Laureate for Life. He was knighted in 1949 and made a Companion of Honour in 1969. A commemorative postage stamp with his portrait was issued by the Post Office of Great Britain on Sept. 1, 1980. Barbirolli was distinguished primarily in the Romantic repertoire; his interpretations were marked by nobility, expressive power, and brilliance. He had a fine pragmatic sense of shaping the music according to its inward style, without projecting his own personality upon it. However, this very objectivity tempered his success with American audiences, accustomed to charismatic flamboyance in music-making. He had a special affinity for English music, and performed many works of Elgar, Delius, and Britten. He conducted the first performances of the 7th and 8th symphs. by Vaughan Williams; also made transcriptions for string orch. and French horns of 5 pieces from the Fitzwilliam Virginal Book (perf. by him under the title *Elizabethan Suite* in Los Angeles, Dec. 4, 1941). He composed for his 2nd wife, the oboist Evelyn Rothwell, an Oboe Concerto on themes by Pergolesi.

BIBLIOGRAPHY: C. Rigby, *John Barbirolli* (Altrincham, 1948); M. Kennedy, *Hallé Orchestra* (Manchester, 1968; revised ed., 1976); M. Kennedy, *Barbirolli, Conductor Laureate* (London, 1971); C. Reid, *John Barbirolli* (London, 1971).

Barblan, Guglielmo, eminent Italian musicologist; b. Siena, May 27, 1906; d. Milan, March 24, 1978. He first studied jurisprudence; then entered the Rome Cons. as a cello student of Forino and Becker; also took courses in music theory at the Bolzano Cons. and attended lectures on musicology by Liuzzi in Rome and Sandberger in Munich. He served as a music critic for *La Provincia di Bolzano* (1932–50), and concurrently lectured on music history at the Bolzano Cons. (1932–49). In 1949 he became head librarian of the Milan Cons.; in 1965 was appointed prof. of music history there; also taught at the Univ. of Milan from 1961. Barblan's principal contribution as a music scholar was in the field of Italian music history. In addition to his books, he also edited works by Bonporti and Cambini.

WRITINGS: *Un musicista trentino: F.A. Bonporti* (Florence, 1940); *Musiche e strumenti musicali dell'Africa orientale italiana* (Naples, 1941); *L'opera di Donizetti nell'età romantica* (Bergamo, 1948); edited *Mozart in Italia: I viaggi e le lettere* (with A. Della Corte; Milan, 1956); *Guida al "Clavicembalo ben temperato" di J.S. Bach* (Milan, 1961); *Claudio Monteverdi nel quarto centenario della nascita* (with C. Gallico and G. Pannain; Turin, 1967); edited *Conservatorio di musica G. Verdi, Milano: Catalogo della biblioteca* (Florence, 1972).

Barblan, Otto, Swiss organist and composer; b. Scanfs, Switzerland, March 22, 1860; d. Geneva, Dec. 19, 1943. He studied at the Stuttgart Cons. (1878–84); made his debut as an organist at Augsburg (1885); taught at Chur (1885–87); then became organist at the Cathedral of Geneva, prof. at the Cons., and conductor of the "Société de Chant Sacré" (1887). He wrote an *Ode Patriotique* (1896); a *Festspiel* (Chur, May 28, 1899) commemorating the 400th anniversary of the battle of Calven, and containing the chorus *Terre des monts,* which has attained great popularity, placing it next to the national anthem as a patriotic song; *Post tenebras lux,* cantata for the Calvin jubilee (1909); String Quartet; Variations and Triple Fugue on B-A-C-H; Passion according to St. Luke (Geneva, April 9, 1919).

BIBLIOGRAPHY: A.-E. Cherbuliez in the *Schweizerische Musikzeitung* (1925, and on Barblan's 70th birthday, 1930); E. Perini, *Otto Barblan* (Zürich, 1960).

Barbosa-Lima, Carlos, Brazilian guitarist; b. São Paulo, Dec. 17, 1944. He began to study the guitar when he was 7; made his debut in São Paulo at 12. His principal teachers were Isaias Savio in Brazil and Andrés Segovia in Spain. In 1967 he made his first tour of the U.S.; also gave concerts in South America, Europe, and Israel, with notable success. He commissioned works for guitar from Ginastera, Balada, and Mignone; also made effective transcriptions of works by Bach, Handel, and other classical composers. He combined his concert career with teaching; was a member of the faculty at the Manhattan School of Music.

Barbot, Joseph-Théodore-Désiré, French tenor; b. Toulouse, April 12, 1824; d. Paris, Jan. 1, 1897. He studied with Garcia at the Paris Cons.; was engaged to sing at the Paris Opéra in 1848; sang Faust at the premiere of Gounod's opera (March 19, 1859). In 1875 he became a prof. at the Paris Cons., succeeding Mme. Viardot.

Barbour, Florence Newell, American composer and pianist; b. Providence, Aug. 4, 1866; d. there, July 24, 1946. She received her education in the U.S., then traveled through Europe and the Far East. Her works include the piano suites *Holland, Venice, Forest Sketches, A Day in Arcady, At Chamonix;* children's piano pieces and songs. She wrote *Childland in Song and Rhythm* (1921).

Barbour, J. Murray, American musicologist; b. Chambersburg, Pa., March 31, 1897; d. Homestead, a corporate entity surrounded by, but separate from, Pittsburgh, Jan. 4, 1970. He studied with Otto Kinkeldey at Cornell Univ.; in 1932 received there the first doctorate in musicology awarded by an American univ.; received a second Ph.D. in music from the Univ. of Toronto in 1936. He taught English at Ithaca College (1932–39) before receiving an appointment as prof. of musicology at Michigan State College; retired in 1964. He publ. *Tuning and Temperament: A Historical Survey* (East Lansing, 1960); *Trumpets, Horns and Music* (East Lansing, 1964).
BIBLIOGRAPHY: F. Kuttner, "J. Murray Barbour (1897–1970)," *Journal of the American Musicological Society,* XXIII (1970).

Barce, Ramón, Spanish composer; b. Madrid, March 16, 1928. He studied languages at the Univ. of Madrid; in music he was largely autodidact. In 1958 he organized the group Nueva Música in Madrid; in 1964 he founded the Zaj group for action music; as a music critic, he supported modern tendencies in Spanish music. The titles of many of his works indicate his trend toward absolute music in abstract modern forms: *Estudio de sonoridades* for Piano (1962); *Parábola* for Wind Quintet (1963); *Objetos sonoros* for Chamber Orch. and Percussion (1964); *Las cuatro estaciones* for Orch. (1966); *Estudio de densidades* for Piano (1965); *Obertura fonética* for Wind Sextet (1968); also a theater piece, *Abgrund Hintergrund* (1964).

Barcewicz, Stanislaw, Polish violinist and conductor; b. Warsaw, April 16, 1858; d. there, Sept. 1, 1929. He studied at the Warsaw Inst. of Music and the Moscow Cons., where he graduated with a gold medal for violin in 1876; he subsequently toured extensively in Europe. In 1886 he was engaged as a conductor at the Warsaw Opera; from 1886–1918 he also taught violin and viola at the Warsaw Inst. of Music.

Barclay, Arthur (original name, **Arthur Barclay Jones**), English choral conductor; b. London, Dec. 16, 1869; d. Purley, Surrey, Oct. 12, 1943. He studied at the Guildhall School of Music, where he later taught piano; served as music director of the Brompton Oratory Choir (1893–1935). He changed his name from Arthur Barclay Jones to Arthur Barclay about 1900. He wrote a Symph. (1896); Violin Sonata; hymns for children; and miscellaneous pieces for organ.

Bardi, Giovanni de', Count of Vernio, Italian nobleman, patron of music and art, and composer; b. Florence, Feb. 5, 1534; d. Rome, 1612. He was the founder of the Florentine Camerata, a group of musicians who met at his home (1576–c.1582) to discuss the music of Greek antiquity; this led to the beginnings of opera. Count Bardi was descended from an old Guelph banking family; he was a philologist, mathematician, neo-Platonic philosopher, and lover of Dante. He was a member of the Crusca Academy, a literary group founded in 1583 whose ideas had great influence on the Camerata. Bardi is known to have been in Rome in 1567; he lent support to Vincenzo Galilei, a member of the Camerata. In 1580 Bardi married Lucrezia Salvati. The masques of 1589, commemorating the marriage of Grand Duke Ferdinand, were conceived largely by Bardi. In 1592 he left for Rome to become chamberlain at the court of Pope Clement VIII. Caccini was his secretary in 1592. Bardi's writings are: *Discorso sopra il giuoco del calzio fiorentino* (Florence, 1580); *Ristretto delle grandezze di Roma* (Rome, 1600); *Discorso mandato a Caccini sopra la musica antica* in Doni's *Lyra Barberina* (Florence, 1763). Among his compositions are a madrigal in 4 Voices, *Misere habitator* in Malvezzi's *Intermedi e concerti* (Venice, 1591); the madrigal *Lauro ohime Lauro* in *Il Lauro secco, lib.* I (Ferrara, 1582). Among contemporary documents which refer to him are Vincenzo Galilei's *Dialogo della musica antica e della moderna* (translated in part in O. Strunk's *Source Readings in Music History,* N.Y., 1951; also included is a letter from Bardi's son to G.B. Doni commenting on Bardi's ideas).
BIBLIOGRAPHY: G. Gasperini, *Intorno alle origini del melodramma* (Rome, 1902); Henriette Martin, "La Camerata du comte Bardi et la musique florentine du XVIᵉ siècle," *Revue de Musicologie* (Nov. 1932); Nino Pirrotta, "Temperaments and Tendencies in the Florentine Camerata," *Musical Quarterly* (April 1954).

Bárdos, Lajos, Hungarian choral conductor, composer, and musicologist; b. Budapest, Oct. 1, 1899. He studied violin and viola; in 1919 entered the Budapest Academy of Music, where he took courses in composition with Siklós and Kodály. In 1928 he joined the faculty of the Academy and broadened the curriculum to include courses in church-music history and prosody; he retired in 1967. He was concurrently active as a choral conductor: he led the Cecilia Chorus (1926–41), the Palestrina Chorus (1929–33), the Budapest Chorus (1941–47), and the Choir of St. Mátyás in Budapest (1942–62). In the field of critical biography, he contributed valuable publications on Hungarian composers. He composed a considerable amount of choral and chamber music.

WRITINGS (all publ. in Budapest): *Modalis harmoniak* (1961); *Liszt Ferenc nepi' hangsorai* (1968); *Harmine irás* (1969); *Bartók dallamvilágából* (1970); *A Bartók-zene stiluselemsi a gyermekkarokban és a Mikrokozmoszban* (1971); *Stravinsky Zsoltárszimfóniájáról* (1971); Kodály-gyermekkarairól (1972); *Organika* (1972); *Tiz ujabb irás* (1974); *Liszt Ferenc, a jövo zenésze* (1976).

Barenboim, Daniel, greatly talented pianist and conductor; b. Buenos Aires, Argentina, Nov. 15, 1942. He studied music with his parents; appeared in public as a child pianist in Buenos Aires at the age of 7; in 1952 the family settled in Israel. During the summers of 1954 and 1955 he was in Salzburg, where he studied piano with Edwin Fischer and took lessons in conducting with Igor Markevitch, and chamber music playing with Enrico Mainardi. In 1954–56 he studied music theory with Nadia Boulanger in Paris; also enrolled at the Santa Cecilia Academy in Rome, where he became one of the youngest students to receive a diploma in 1956. He also studied conducting with Carlo Zecchi at the Chigiana Academy in Siena. He gave piano recitals in Paris in 1955 and in London in 1956. On Jan. 20, 1957, he made his American debut at Carnegie Hall, N.Y., playing Prokofiev's First Piano Concerto with Leopold Stokowski conducting the Symph. of the Air. He gave his first U.S. solo recital in N.Y. on Jan. 17, 1958. He made his debut as a conductor in Haifa in 1957; in 1960 he played all 32 Beethoven sonatas in a series of concerts in Tel Aviv; he repeated this cycle in N.Y. As a pianist, he subordinated Romantic passion to Classical balance of form and thematic content. As a conductor he gave congenial performances of the masterpieces of Romantic music; became particularly engrossed in the music of Anton Bruckner, and was awarded the Bruckner Medal of the Bruckner Society of America. In 1967 he conducted the Israel Phil. on its tour of the U.S.; in 1968 he led the London Symph. Orch. at its appearance in N.Y.; he subsequently filled engagements with the Boston Symph., Chicago Symph., Philadelphia Orch., and N.Y. Phil. He made his first appearance as an opera conductor at the Edinburgh Festival in 1973. In 1975 he was named music director of the Orch. de Paris. On June 15, 1967, he married, in Jerusalem, the English cellist **Jacqueline DuPré,** who became converted to Judaism. They appeared in numerous sonata programs until, tragically, she was stricken in 1972 with multiple sclerosis and had to abandon her career.

BIBLIOGRAPHY: David Ewen, *Musicians since 1900* (N.Y., 1978); P. Hart, *Conductors: A New Generation* (N.Y., 1979; pp. 3–44).

Barere, Simon, Russian virtuoso pianist; b. Odessa, Sept. 1, 1896; d. suddenly, while performing Grieg's Piano Concerto in Carnegie Hall, N.Y., April 2, 1951. He studied with Anna Essipoff at the St. Petersburg Cons. and, after her death, with Felix Blumenfeld. After graduation, concertized in Germany, Sweden, and the U.S. He was praised for his extraordinary virtuosity, and was once described in the *New York Times* as "truly a giant of the keyboard." His death came to him unexpectedly during a concert of the Philadelphia Orch. in Carnegie Hall; he suddenly collapsed, fell on the floor, and died backstage; the rest of the program was cancelled.

Bareva, Lilyana, Bulgarian soprano; b. Sofia, June 15, 1922. She studied at the Sofia Academy of Music; in 1946 made her debut as Violetta at the Sofia National Opera; she continued to sing there, where her reputation was secured by her fine performances of lyric soprano roles in the operas of Mozart, Tchaikovsky, Verdi, and Puccini; she also made appearances at opera houses elsewhere in Europe.

Barge, (Johann Heinrich) Wilhelm, German flute player and composer; b. Wulfsahl, Nov. 23, 1836; d. Hannover, July 16, 1925. He played in military bands; in 1867 was appointed as first flutist in the Gewandhaus Orch. in Leipzig; he was retired on a pension in 1895. He publ. a method for flute, 4 sets of orch. flute studies based on passages in classical symph. scores; also publ. flute arrangements of various popular pieces under the title *Sammlung beliebter Stücke;* edited the flute concertos of Frederick the Great.

Bargiel, Woldemar, German composer; b. Berlin, Oct. 3, 1828; d. there, Feb. 23, 1897. He was a half brother of **Clara Schumann.** As a boy he sang at the Berlin Cathedral and studied counterpoint with Dehn, and at the Leipzig Cons. (1846–50) with Hauptmann, Moscheles, Gade, and Rietz; became prof. at the Cologne Cons. in 1859. He was a teacher and conductor in Rotterdam (1865–75); in 1874 became prof. of composition at the Berlin Hochschule für Musik. He was greatly admired by Schumann and Brahms, and his works, in a Romantic vein, were frequently performed; almost all of his music was publ. during his lifetime. He wrote a Symph.; 3 overtures; String Octet; 4 string quartets; 3 piano trios; violin sonatas; numerous piano pieces and songs.

BIBLIOGRAPHY: E. Rudorff, *Aus den Tagen der Romantik; Bildnis einer deutschen Familie* (Leipzig, 1938).

Bargielski, Zbigniew, Polish composer; b. Lomza, Jan. 21, 1937. He studied composition with Szeligowski at the State College of Music in Warsaw; musicology with Szabelski at the State College in Katowice; completed his studies with Nadia Boulanger in Paris.

WORKS: *Danton, or Some Pictures from the History of the Great French Revolution,* surrealistic historical opera (1968–69); *Le Petit Prince,* after

Barili – Barkauskas

Saint-Exupéry (1970); a children's opera, *Alice in Wonderland* (1971–72); opera, *Phantoms Do Not Lie* (1971–72); *Parades* for Orch. (1965); *Espace attrapé* for Orch. (1973); Percussion Concerto (1975); Violin Concerto (1975); *Ballad* for Winds and Percussion (1976); *3 Sonnet-Capriccios* for Solo Clarinet (1976); *Impromptu* for Solo Percussion (1976); String Quartet (1976).

Barili, Alfredo, Italian-American pianist, composer, and pedagogue; b. Florence, Aug. 2, 1854; d. Atlanta, Ga., Nov. 17, 1935, in an accident when he took a walk and was struck by a bus. He was a scion of an illustrious musical family; his father, **Ettore Barili,** an excellent musician in his own right, was a half-brother of the operatic diva **Adelina Patti.** Alfredo Barili was taken to America in his infancy and was taught piano by his father, making his public debut as a pianist in N.Y. on April 7, 1865. In 1868 the family relocated to Philadelphia, where he studied with Carl Wolfsohn, a German musician who claimed to be the first to perform all 32 piano sonatas of Beethoven in a series of concerts. In 1872 Barili went to Germany and enrolled at the Cologne Cons., studying piano with Friedrich Gernsheim and James Kwast, and composition with Ferdinand Hiller. Returning to the U.S. in 1880, he settled in Atlanta, taught for 6 years at the Atlanta Female Inst., and in 1886 founded his own "music academy," teaching piano at a fee of $1.50 per lesson. He maintained a cordial relationship with his famous aunt, Adelina Patti, and acted as her piano accompanist at a London concert in 1911. He also composed some perishable salon music in the approved manner of the time. His piano piece *Cradle Song* went into 26 editions; also popular among his pupils were his *Danse caprice, Miniature Gavotte,* and *Spanish Serenade.*
BIBLIOGRAPHY: N. Lee Orr, "Alfredo Barili: Atlanta Musician," *American Music* (Spring 1984).

Barilli, Bruno, Italian writer on music; b. Fano, Dec. 14, 1880; d. Rome, April 15, 1952. He studied in Parma and later in Munich; his collections of essays were publ. under the titles *Il sorcio nel violino* and *Il paese del melodramma,* in Milan (1926) and in Lanciano (1929), respectively. He wrote 2 operas, *Medusa* (1910; first performed, Bergamo, Sept. 11, 1938) and *Emiral* (Rome, March 11, 1924).
BIBLIOGRAPHY: E. Falqui, ed., *Opere di Bruno Barilli* (Florence, 1963).

Barini, Giorgio, Italian musicologist; b. Turin, Aug. 3, 1864; d. Rome, Sept. 21, 1944. He is primarily noted for his authentic editions of operas by Paisiello and Cimarosa. He publ. *La donna e l'artista: Musicisti innamorati* (Rome, 1927) and several essays on Wagner's operas.

Bark, Jan, Swedish composer; b. Härnösand, April 19, 1934. He was first a jazz trombonist; then studied at the Royal Academy of Music in Stockholm, taking courses in composition with Lars-Erik Larsson and Karl-Birger Blomdahl; was initiated into ultra-modern music by György Ligeti in Stockholm; made an American trip in 1962 and worked with avant-garde groups at the Tape Music Center in San Francisco; in 1964 he traveled to the Far East to study oriental music. Returning to Sweden, he joined the radio and television center of the Swedish Broadcasting Service. He was co-founder with Folke Rabe of the Culture Quartet of 4 trombones, which explores the potentialities of modern trombone playing. Many of his pieces are of a theatrical, almost exhibitionistic, nature, often with a healthy radical tinge.
WORKS: Piano Sonata (1957); 2 string quartets (1959, 1962); *Metakronismer* for Orch. (1960; Oslo, March 4, 1961); 2 works for the Culture Quartet, composed in collaboration with Folke Rabe: *Bolos,* in an anarcho-Dadaistic manner (1962) and *Polonaise* (1965); *Lamento* for Percussion, Piano, and Double Basses (1962); *Boca Chica* for Chamber Ensemble (1962); *Pyknos* for Orch. (1962); *Eko* for News Broadcaster and 5 Tape Recorders (1962); *Missa Bassa* for Small Orch. with 7 Conductors, 6 of whom also sing (1964; Swedish Radio, April 1, 1967); *Nota* for "choreographic" Mixed Chorus (1964); *Ost-Funk* for 8 Jazz Musicians (1964); *Mansbot* for Male Chorus and 12 Guitars (1964); *Tredjedels Signeri* for 3 Hammond Organs (1967); *Bar,* electronic music (1967); *Light Music* for Chorus a cappella (1968); *Lyndon Bunk Johnson,* a "poster" work, composed collectively (1968); *Irk-Ork 1970* for Chamber Ensemble (1970); *Het Jacht von het vliegende Joachim* for Trombone, Cello, and Piano (1971).

Barkauskas, Vytautas, outstanding Lithuanian composer; b. Kaunas, March 25, 1931. He studied music at the Tallat-Kelpša Music College in Vilna while also studying physics and mathematics at the State Pedagogical Inst. there (1949–53); then took composition with Račiunas and orchestration with Balsis at the Lithuanian State Cons. (1953–59); in 1961 joined its faculty. He wrote several cantatas in the style of socialist realism; in his instrumental compositions he makes use of advanced cosmopolitan techniques, including serialism and aleatory improvisation.
WORKS: FOR THE STAGE: *Conflict,* a "choreographic scene" for 3 Performers (1965); *Legend about Love,* an opera (Vilna, March 29, 1975). FOR ORCH.: *Poem* for Piano and Orch. (1960); 3 symphs. (1962–63, 1971, 1979); *Choreographic Miniatures* (1965); Concertino for 4 Chamber Groups (1966); *Expressivistic Structures* for Chamber Orch. (1967); *Paraphrase* for Chamber Orch. (1967); *Three Aspects* (1969); *Overture a priori* (1976). VOCAL MUSIC: *Pathetic Thoughts* for Chorus a cappella (1962); *Word about Revolution,* cantata-poem for Narrator, Male Chorus, and Orch. (1967); *La vostra nominanza e color d'erba,* musical mirage, after Dante, for Chamber Chorus and String Quintet (1971); *Prelude and Fugue* for Chorus a cappella (1974); *Salute Your Land,* oratorio-mystery for 4 Soloists, Female Chorus, and Orch. (1976); *Open Window,* 5 sketches for Mezzo-soprano and 5 Instruments (1978). CHAMBER MUSIC: Piano Trio (1958); Partita for Solo Violin

(1967); *Intimate Composition* for Oboe and 12 Instruments (1968); *Contrast Music* for Flute, Cello, and Percussion (1969); *Pro memoria,* 3 movements for Flute, Bass Clarinet, Piano, Celesta, and 5 Percussion Instruments (1970); *Monologue* for Solo Oboe (1970); String Quartet (1972); *Sonata subita* for Violin and Piano (1976). FOR PIANO: *Poetry,* a cycle (1964); Variations for 2 Pianos (1967); *Sonate pathétique* (1969); *5 Pictures of Vytukas* for Piano, 4-hands (1971); *Legend about Čiurlionis* (1972); *Elegy and Fantastical Toccata* (1972); *Prelude and Fugue* for 2 Pianos (1974). FOR ORGAN: *Gloria Urbi* (1972).

Barkel, Charles, Swedish violinist and conductor; b. Stugun, Feb. 6, 1898; d. Stockholm, March 7, 1973. He studied at the Stockholm Cons. and the Copenhagen Cons.; then took lessons in Berlin with Carl Flesch; concurrently played in several Swedish orchs. In 1921 he joined the Stockholm Concert Society Orch. He founded his own string quartet in 1928; from 1942–54 he was conductor of the Uppsala Concert Society Orch. From 1926–65 he taught violin in Stockholm.

Barlow, Fred, French composer; b. Mulhouse, Oct. 2, 1881; d. Boulogne, Seine, Jan. 3, 1951. He was of British parentage; moved to Paris, where he took composition lessons with Jean Huré and Charles Koechlin. Not a prolific composer, he wrote a comic opera, *Sylvie* (Paris, March 2, 1923), and a ballet, *La Grande Jatte* (Paris, July 12, 1950); another ballet, *Gladys,* was performed posthumously at Mulhouse on Jan. 7, 1956. Other works included some chamber music, piano pieces, and songs.

Barlow, Harold, American composer of popular songs, bandleader, and musical lexicographer; b. Boston, May 15, 1915. He studied violin at Boston Univ., and later played in various orchs.; also led a U.S. Army band. He has compiled two valuable reference works for which he designed an original method of indexing melodic themes by letters plus accidentals: *A Dictionary of Musical Themes* (with Sam Morgenstern; N.Y., 1948) and *A Dictionary of Vocal Themes* (N.Y., 1950).

Barlow, Howard, American conductor; b. Plain City, Ohio, May 1, 1892; d. Bethel, Conn., Jan. 31, 1972. He studied at the Univ. of Colorado and at Columbia Univ. He conducted the American National Orch., N.Y. (1923–25) and at the Neighborhood Playhouse (1925–27); was conductor of the CBS Symph. Orch. (1927–43), with which he presented numerous new works.

Barlow, Samuel (Latham Mitchill), American composer; b. New York, June 1, 1892; d. Wyndmoor, Pa., Sept. 19, 1982. He studied at the Groton School (1904–10) and at Harvard Univ. (1910–14); went to Paris, where he took piano lessons with Isidor Philipp; then traveled to Rome to study orchestration with Respighi. He served as first lieutenant with the American Expeditionary Force in 1917; was decorated with the French Legion of Honor. He was active in various liberal causes; was a member of the Democratic Club Union in N.Y. and president of the Citizens Committee for Government Art Projects; also was moderator of the Forum for Democracy. In his compositions he endeavored to approach the taste of democratic audiences without sacrificing the inner meaning of the music. He presented his philosophical and artistic views in a book, *The Astonished Muse* (N.Y., 1961). His one-act opera *Mon ami Pierrot* was the first by an American composer to be given at the Opéra-Comique in Paris (Jan. 11, 1935). He also wrote 2 more operas, *Eugénie* and *Amanda.* His symph. concerto *Babar* (1935) employs magic lantern slides. He further wrote a Piano Concerto (Rochester, N.Y., Jan. 23, 1931, with himself as soloist); a symph. suite, *Biedermeier Waltzes* (Rome, 1935); *Circus Overture* (1930); choruses; and piano pieces.

Barlow, Wayne (Brewster), American composer; b. Elyria, Ohio, Sept. 6, 1912. He studied with Bernard Rogers and Howard Hanson at the Eastman School of Music in Rochester, N.Y. (B.M., 1934; M.M., 1935; Ph.D., 1937); also took courses from Schoenberg at the Univ. of Southern Calif. in Los Angeles (1935). In 1937 he was appointed to the faculty of the Eastman School of Music; in 1968 became chairman of its composition dept. and director of its electronic music studio; retired in 1973 from the former post and continued to hold the latter until his retirement in 1978. He publ. *Foundations of Music* (N.Y., 1963).
WORKS: *De Profundis* for Orch. (1934); *False Faces,* ballet suite (1935); Sinfonietta No. 1 (1936); *Zion in Exile,* cantata (1937); *The Winter's Passed* for Oboe and Strings (Rochester, Oct. 18, 1938); *Songs from the Silence of Amor* for Soprano and Orch. (1939); *3 Moods for Dancing,* ballet (1940); *Lyrical Pieces* for Clarinet and Strings (1943); *The 23rd Psalm* for Chorus and Orch. (1944); *Nocturne* for 18 Instruments (1946); *Rondo Overture* (1947); Piano Sonata (1948); *Prelude, Air, and Variations* for Bassoon, Piano, and String Quartet (1949); Sinfonietta No. 2 (1950); Piano Quintet (1951); Mass in G (1953); *Tryptych* for String Quartet (1953); *Lento and Allegro* for Orch. (1955); *Night Song* for Orch. (1958); *Poems for Music* for Soprano and Orch. (1958); *Rota* for Chamber Ensemble (1959); *Missa Sancti Thomae* for Chorus and Organ (1959); *Intrada, Fugue, and Postlude* for Brass (1959); *Images* for Harp and Orch. (1961); *Sinfonia da camera* for Orch. (1962); *Vistas* for Orch. (1963); Trio for Oboe, Viola, and Piano (1964); *We All Believe in One God* for Chorus, Brass Quartet, and Organ (1965); *Study in Electronic Sound* for Prerecorded Tape (1965); *Dynamisms* for 2 Pianos (1967); *Wait for the Promise of the Father,* cantata (1968); *Elegy* for Viola and Piano (1968); *Duo* for Harp and Tape (1969); Concerto for Saxophone and Band (1970); *Moonflight* for Prerecorded Tape (1970); *Overture: Hampton Beach* (1971); *Soundscapes* for Tape and Orch. (1972); *Soundprints in Concrete* for Prerecorded Tape (1975); *Voices of Faith,* secular cantata (1976);

Bärmann – Barnes

Vocalise and Canon for Tuba and Piano (1976); *Out of the Cradle Endlessly Rocking* for Tenor, Chorus, Clarinet, Viola, Piano, and Tape (1978); *Divertissement* for Flute and Chamber Orch. (1980).

Bärmann, Heinrich (Joseph), renowned German clarinetist; b. Potsdam, Feb. 14, 1784; d. Munich, June 11, 1847. He studied oboe at the School of Military Music in Potsdam, and as a youth served as bandmaster in the Prussian Life Guards; then studied clarinet with Beer and Tausch. He was in the Prussian army at Jena, and was captured by the French, but made his escape and traveled to Munich, where he obtained the post of a court musician. Weber became his friend, and wrote a Clarinet Concertino and the 2 Clarinet Concertos for him; they appeared together at concerts in Prague and in Germany (1811–12); later Bärmann gave concerts in France, England, and Russia. He wrote a number of works for the clarinet, including concertos, fantasias, quintets, quartets, and sonatas; he also prepared teaching pieces and technical exercises for the clarinet, which are still in use in Germany. The Adagio from his Quintet No. 3 in E-flat major, op. 23, which he wrote in 1821, has been unaccountably attributed to Wagner, and so listed in numerous collections of clarinet pieces. It was republ. in 1971 by Breitkopf und Härtel under Bärmann's name.
BIBLIOGRAPHY: P. Weston, *Clarinet Virtuosi of the Past* (London, 1971).

Bärmann, Karl, German clarinetist, son of **Heinrich Joseph Bärmann;** b. Munich, Oct. 24, 1811; d. there, May 23, 1885. He was a pupil of his father, whom he accompanied on his tours; later succeeded him at the Munich court orch. He wrote a method for clarinet, with a supplement entitled *Materalien zur weiteren technischen Ausbildung.*

Bärmann (Baermann), Karl, Jr., pianist and music pedagogue, son of the preceding; b. Munich, July 9, 1839; d. Boston, Jan. 17, 1913. He studied piano with Wanner, Wahlmuth, and Liszt, and composition with Franz Lachner; was appointed a teacher at the Munich Cons., but emigrated to the U.S. in 1881. He settled in Boston.

Barmas, Issaye, Russian violinist and pedagogue; b. Odessa, May 1, 1872; d. London, July 3, 1946. He studied in Moscow and with Joachim in Berlin; toured in Europe; settled in London. Among his publications are *Die Lösung des Geigentechnischen Problems* (1913); *Tonleiter-Spezialstudien; Doppelgriff Spezialstudien;* and many editions of classical works.

Barnard, Charlotte (Mrs. Charles Barnard), English songwriter; b. Louth, Dec. 23, 1830; d. Dover, Jan. 30, 1869. In 1866 she publ. under the pen name of **Claribel** the ballad *Come Back to Erin,* which attained great popularity. She also wrote poetry.

Barnby, Sir Joseph, English organist, conductor, and composer; b. York, Aug. 12, 1838; d. London, Jan. 28, 1896. He received his early training as a choirboy; then studied with Cipriani Potter at the Royal Academy of Music in London. In 1863 he was appointed organist at St. Andrew's Church in London, and soon presented sacred concerts there. In 1867 he founded Mr. Joseph Barnby's Choir. Subsequently he served as organist at St. Anne's, Soho (1871–76). In 1872 his own choir was merged with the Royal Albert Hall Choral Society, which he led until his death. He also served as precentor at Eton College (1875–92), and was principal of the Guildhall School of Music from 1892 until his death. He was knighted in 1892. Barnby composed numerous pieces of sacred music, including *246 Hymn Tunes,* publ. in 1897.

Barnekow, Christian, Danish composer; b. St. Sauveur, France, July 28, 1837; d. Copenhagen, March 20, 1913. He studied in Copenhagen; from 1871 to 1887 he directed the Society for Publication of Danish Music. He wrote numerous sacred choral works and also lieder in a folklike manner, as well as some estimable chamber music.

Barnes, Edward Shippen, American organist and composer; b. Seabright, N.J., Sept. 14, 1887; d. Idyllwild, Calif., Feb. 14, 1958. He was a student of Horatio Parker and David Stanley Smith at Yale Univ., and studied organ with Harry B. Jepson there. He was organist at St. Stephen's Episcopal Church in Philadelphia and later at the First Presbyterian Church in Santa Monica, Calif., retiring in 1954. He wrote 2 organ symphonies, much sacred music, and several books of organ arrangements for schools, among them *Bach for Beginners in Organ Playing.*

Barnes, Milton, Canadian conductor and composer; b. Toronto, Dec. 16, 1931. He studied music theory with Weinzweig at the Cons. of Toronto and conducting at the Berkshire Music Center, Tanglewood, Mass. (1958–61); also took a course in conducting with Swarowsky at the Vienna Academy (1959–61). Returning to Canada, he held positions as conductor of the Univ. of Toronto Orch. (1962–63), Toronto Repertory Ensemble (1964–70) and St. Catharines (Ontario) Symph. and Chorus (1964–73); concurrently conducted the Niagara Falls (N.Y.) Phil. In 1968 he was appointed director of the Toronto Dance Theater.
WORKS: Ballet scores: *Masque of the Red Death* (1971); *Three-Sided Room* (1972); and *Amber Garden* (1972); *Invocations* for Orch. (1962); Symph. No. 1 (1964); *Children's Suite* for Orch. (1966); *Pinocchio,* symph. poem (1966); Variations for Clarinet and Orch. (1968); *Classical Concerto* for Piano and Orch. (1973); *Psalms of David,* cantata (1972–73); *Shebetim,* tableau for String Orch. (1974); Concerto for Saxophone and Strings (1975); Concerto for Violin and Strings (1975); *3 Folk Dances* for Violin and Piano (1953); *Thespis,* scenic cantata (1956; revised 1973); *Burletta* for String Quartet (1957–58); *Lamentations of Jeremiah* for Solo Viola (1959);

Flute Sonata (1965); *Rhapsody on a Late Afternoon* for String Quartet (1971); Variations for Solo Violin (1972); Concerto Grosso for Flute, Clarinet, Violin, Cello, and 2 Pianos (1973); Serenade for Accordion and Guitar (1973); *Spiral Stairs,* dance septet (1973); *Madrigals* for Female Chorus, 2 Trumpets, and 2 Trombones (1975); Fantasy for Solo Guitar (1975); Symph. for Strings (1976); Chamber Concerto for Wind Quintet and Strings (1976).

Barnett, Alice, American song composer; b. Lewiston, Ill., May 26, 1886; d. San Diego, Aug. 28, 1975. She studied piano with Felix Borowski and Rudolph Ganz in Chicago; then went to Berlin and took lessons with Hugo Kaun. Returning to the U.S. in 1917, she settled in San Diego. She wrote a number of agreeable songs in a romantic vein.
BIBLIOGRAPHY: W.T. Upton, *Art-Song in America* (N.Y., 1930; pp. 214–24).

Barnett, John, English composer; b. Bedford, July 15, 1802; d. Leckhampton, April 17, 1890. He was the son of a German jeweler named Bernhard Beer, but Anglicized his name when he moved to England. He wrote operettas and various other pieces of light music before producing his first full-fledged opera, *The Mountain Sylph* (London, Aug. 25, 1834); this was followed by 2 more operas, *Fair Rosamond* (London, Feb. 28, 1837) and *Farinelli* (London, Feb. 8, 1839). In 1841 he settled in Cheltenham as a voice teacher, but about 1870 moved to a country residence, Cotteswold in Leckhampton, where he remained until his death. Among his works are a symph., 3 string quartets, and songs numbering in the thousands. He also publ. two singing methods, *Systems and Singing Masters* (1842) and *School for the Voice* (1844).

Barnett, John (Manley), American conductor; b. New York, Sept. 3, 1917. He studied piano, violin, and trumpet; took courses in conducting with Leon Barzin in New York and with Bruno Walter, Weingartner, Enesco, and Malko in Europe. From 1946 to 1956 he was associate conductor of the Los Angeles Phil., and from 1956 to 1958 its associate music director. In 1947 he organized the Phoenix (Arizona) Symph. Orch., conducting it until 1949. He later served as music director of the Hollywood Bowl (1953–57) and of the Los Angeles Guild Opera Co. (1954–79). From 1958 to 1972 he was music director of the National Orch. Association in N.Y.; from 1961 to 1971 he held the post of music director of the Phil. Symph. Orch. of Westchester, N.Y. From 1972 to 1978 he served as artistic consultant to the National Endowment for the Arts. In 1979 he was appointed music director of the Puerto Rico Symph. Orch. in San Juan.

Barnett, John Francis, English composer; nephew of **John Barnett;** b. London, Oct. 16, 1837; d. there, Nov. 24, 1916. He studied piano in London and in Leipzig. In 1883 he was appointed to the staff of the Royal College of Music in London. He wrote a Symph. (1864), several playable symphonic overtures and singable cantatas, several of them inspired by literary works. Among his oratorios, *The Raising of Lazarus,* first performed in London on June 18, 1873, was much performed in churches. He publ. an engaging vol., *Musical Reminiscences and Impressions* (London, 1906).

Barns, Ethel, English violinist and composer; b. London, 1880; d. Maidenhead, Dec. 31, 1948. She studied at the Royal Academy in London; made her debut at the Crystal Palace (1896); toured England (1897) and America (1913). Her compositions include a *Concertstück* for Violin and Orch.; 2 trios; *Phantasy* for 2 Violins and Piano; 5 violin sonatas.

Barolsky, Michael, Lithuanian-born German-Israeli composer; b. Vilnius, July 19, 1947. He studied piano, music theory, and ethnology; in 1965 took lessons in composition with Lutoslawski in Warsaw; in 1968 went to Moscow and studied privately with Denisov and Schnittke. In 1969–71 he was music adviser at the Lithuanian Radio. In 1971 he emigrated to Germany. In 1972 he attended seminars with Ligeti, Kagel, and Stockhausen in Darmstadt; in 1974 went to Israel, and taught at the Pedagogic Inst. in Tel Aviv. In 1977 he settled in Cologne on a stipend of the Deutsche Akademie; also worked on electronic music with Humpert. In his own compositions he devotes himself totally to the modern theater, astutely applying the full resources of electronic music.
WORKS: Violin Sonata (1964); String Trio (1964); Woodwind Quartet (1965); *Recitative and Melody* for Flute, Cello, and Piano (1966); Concertino for Violin, Trumpet, Trombone, Piano, and Percussion (1967); *Basso Ostinato* for Cello Solo (1967); *Telefonoballade,* cantata for Baritone, 6 Narrators, and Chamber Ensemble (1969); *Exodus* for Orch. (1970); *Scriptus,* after Kafka's letters, for Baritone, Mime, and Chamber Ensemble (1972); *Dakar* for Percussion, Piano, and Electronics (1972); *Photogenesis I, II, III,* and *IV,* respectively for Harpsichord, Brass Quintet, Bass Flute, and Solo Percussion (1973); *Melos* for Mezzo-soprano, Cello, Piano, Electric Organ, Percussion, and Synthesizer (1975); *Sublimatio* for Flute, Cello, 2 Pianos, Percussion, and Tape (1975); *Cries and Whispers* for Chamber Ensemble and Electronics (1975; Univ. of Chicago, Jan. 24, 1976); *Blue Eye, Brown Eye,* one-act opera (Tel Aviv, July 29, 1976); *Apocalypse,* song cycle with Electronic Tape (1976); *Iris* for Flute, Oboe, Clarinet, Violin, Cello, and Piano (1976); *Pranah* for Violin Solo and Electronic Tape (1976); *Sternengesang* for Chamber Orch. (1977); *The Book of Emanations* for Orch. (1978); *Ein Stück aus der Nacht* for Actor and Electronics (1978); *Tonus* for Quadraphonic Synthesizer (1979); *Cinderella* for Cello and Piano (1981); *Seelenkalender* for Mezzo-soprano and Piano (1982); *The Book of Changes* for Piano (1983); *Stück-Mund-Stück* for Trombone, Computer Sounds, and Video Tape (1983); *Piccolostück* for Piccolo and Computer Sounds (1983); *Rainbow Music* for 6 Recorders (Bonn, Feb. 12, 1984); *Trioirtrio* for Violin, Cello, and Piano (1984).

Baron, Ernst Gottlieb, German lutenist; b. Breslau, Feb. 17, 1696; d. Berlin, April 12, 1760. He studied lute playing with Kohott; later attended courses in philosophy and jurisprudence at the Univ. of Leipzig; then served as a court musician in various localities (1719–28); in 1728 he became court musician in Gotha, a post he held for 4 years; in 1737 he was appointed theorbist to Crown Prince Friedrich. He publ. a valuable manual, *Historisch-theoretische und praktische Untersuchung des Instruments der Laute* (1727), which was reprinted in English in 1976.

Baron, Maurice, American composer and conductor; b. Lille, France, Jan. 1, 1889; d. Oyster Bay, Long Island, N.Y., Sept. 5, 1964. He studied music in France; emigrated to America, where he became a theater conductor. He publ. several hundred pieces of light music under his own name and the whimsical noms de plume **Francis Delille** (i.e., "de Lille," a native of Lille); **Morris Aborn** (anagram of Baron); also used the name of his wife, **Alice Tremblay.** Among his more ambitious works was *Ode to Democracy* for Narrator, Chorus, and Orch. (N.Y., Jan. 23, 1949).

Baron, Samuel, American flutist and conductor; b. New York, April 27, 1925. He studied at Brooklyn College and the Juilliard School of Music; his flute teachers were Georges Barrère and Arthur Lora; he also took lessons in conducting with Edgar Schenkman; then played flute in several orchs. In 1949 he helped to found the N.Y. Woodwind Quintet, with which he played for 20 years; in 1948 he organized the N.Y. Brass Ensemble. He was also active as a teacher, serving on the faculties of the Mannes, Juilliard, and Yale schools of music; in 1966 he joined the faculty of the State Univ. of N.Y. at Stony Brook. He publ. *Chamber Music for Winds* (N.Y., 1969).

Baroni, Leonora, Italian singer, known as **"L'Adrianella"** and **"L'Adrianetta";** b. Mantua, Dec. 1611; d. Rome, April 6, 1670. She studied with her mother, the famous singer **Andreana Basile.** In 1633 she went to Rome; in 1644 she proceeded to Paris and appeared at the court of the Queen Regent of France, Anne of Austria. In 1645 she returned to Italy.

Barraine, Elsa, French composer; b. Paris, Feb. 13, 1910. Her father was a cellist, her mother a singer. She studied at the Paris Cons. with Paul Dukas, Jean Gallon, and Caussade; received the second Prix de Rome in 1928. She composed 3 symphs. (1931, 1938, 1947) and a curiously realistic symph. poem, *Pogromes* (*Pogroms;* referring to the Nazi persecutions of Jews; performed in Paris, March 11, 1939). Other works include *Suite astrologique* for Orch. (1947); *Atmosphère* for Oboe and 10 Instruments, on Hindu rhythms (1967); *Musique rituelle* for Organ, Gongs, and Xylorimba (1968).

Barraqué, Jean, French composer of advanced modern tendencies; b. Paris, Jan. 17, 1928; d. there, Aug. 17, 1973. He studied with Jean Langlais at the Paris Cons. and privately with Olivier Messiaen. From his early works, he devoted himself to experimentation, absorbing all resources of modern music, including dodecaphony and electronics. His most celebrated work is the Piano Sonata No. 1 (1950–52); another major work is *Séquence* (1950–55), scored for Soprano, Piano, Harp, Violin, Cello, and Assorted Percussion; other works are *Le temps restitué* for Voices and Orch. (1957); *Au-delà du hasard* for Voices and 4 Instrumental Groups (Paris, Jan. 26, 1960); *Chant après chant* for Voice, Percussion, and Piano (1966); Concerto for 6 Instrumental Groups, Vibraphone, and Clarinet (1968); and Piano Sonata No. 2 (1976). Barraqué planned the composition of an immense work in 13 parts which was to be the expression of his world philosophy, but the work remained in fragments at his death. A listing of his works is contained in "Propos impromptu. Jean Barraqué," *Courier Musical de France* 26 (1969). Despite the scarcity of his completed works, Barraqué impressed musicians as a potential genius. André Hodeir devotes an enthusiastic chapter to Barraqué in his book *La Musique depuis Debussy* (Paris, 1961; Eng. trans., *Since Debussy;* N.Y. and London, 1961).
WRITINGS: *Debussy* (Paris, 1962).

Barraud, Henry, French composer; b. Bordeaux, April 23, 1900. He studied music without a teacher, while engaged in the family wine business in Bordeaux. In 1926 he entered the Paris Cons. and studied with Louis Aubert; also studied composition with Dukas and fugue with Caussade. In 1937 Barraud was appointed director of music for the International Exposition in Paris. He served in the French army during World War II; after the demobilization he lived in Marseilles. After the liberation of Paris in 1944 he was appointed music director of Radiodiffusion Française; he retired in 1965. In 1969 he received the Grand Prix National de la Musique.
WORKS: *Finale dans le mode rustique* (Paris, 1932); *Poème* for Orch. (1934); *Concerto de camera* for 30 Instruments (1936); *Le Mystère des Saints Innocents,* oratorio (1942–44); *Le Diable à la Kermesse,* ballet (1943; a symph. suite from it was broadcast by Paris Radio, April 26, 1945); Piano Concerto (N.Y. Phil., Dec. 5, 1946); *Offrande à une ombre* (in memory of a brother killed by the Germans as a member of the Resistance; first U.S. performance, St. Louis, Jan. 10, 1947); *La Farce du Maître Pathelin* (Paris, June 24, 1948); *Symphonie de Numance* (Baden-Baden, Dec. 3, 1950); Concertino for Piano and 4 Winds (1953); *Numance,* opera (Paris, April 15, 1955); *Te Deum* for Chorus and 6 Instruments (1955); Symph. for String Orch. (1955); Symph. No. 3 (Boston, March 7, 1958); *Rapsodie cartésienne* for Orch. (1959); *Rapsodie dionysienne* for Orch. (1961); *Lavinia,* opera-buffa (Aix-en-Provence, July 20, 1961); Divertimento for Orch. (1962); Concerto for Flute and Strings (1963); *Symphonie concertante* for Trumpet and Orch. (1965); *3 études*

for Orch.; *Une Saison en enfer,* symph. suite after Rimbaud (1969). Barraud also publ. books on Berlioz (Paris, 1955; 2nd ed., 1966), on the problems of modern music, *Pour comprendre les musiques d'aujourd'hui* (Paris, 1968), and on the analysis of selected operas, *Les Cinq Grands Opéras* (Paris, 1972).

Barrera Gómez, Enrique, Spanish composer; b. Valladolid, April 26, 1844; d. there, July 3, 1922. He studied piano in Vienna; subsequently entered the Madrid Cons. in the classes of José Miró (piano) and Hilarión Eslava (composition). In 1867 he became choirmaster of Burgos Cathedral, a position he retained until his death. He composed several operas and numerous sacred and secular choruses.

Barrère, Georges, French flute virtuoso; b. Bordeaux, Oct. 31, 1876; d. Kingston, N.Y., June 14, 1944. He studied at the Paris Cons. (1889–95), graduating with first prize; was solo flutist at Colonne Concerts and at the Paris Opéra (1897–1905). He came to America in 1905; played flute with the N.Y. Symph. Orch. (1905–28); taught at the Inst. of Musical Art, N.Y., and at the Juilliard School of Music. He was the founder of the Barrère Little Symph. (1914); composed a *Nocturne* for Flute; *Chanson d'automne* for Voice; also edited classical works for flute.

Barret, Apollon (Marie-Rose), French oboist; b. Paris, c.1803; d. London, March 8, 1879. He studied at the Paris Cons.; played in the orchs. at opera houses; in 1874 went to London with the Italian Opera. Barret is the author of a standard manual, *Complete Method for the Oboe Comprising All The New Fingerings, New Tables of Shakes, Scales, Exercises.*

Barrett, Emma, black American jazz pianist, nicknamed "Sweet Emma, the Bell Gal"; b. New Orleans, March 25, 1898; d. there, Jan. 28, 1983. Her entire career was connected with traditional jazz in New Orleans; beginning in 1961 she was associated with Preservation Hall in New Orleans. She played with most of the leading bands, among them those headed by Oscar Celestin, William Ridgley, George McCullum, Sidney Desvigne, and Armand Piron; also formed her own bands. She suffered a stroke in 1967 which paralyzed her left side, but continued to perform, playing the right-hand part and beating time vigorously. At most public functions she used a wheelchair. She played her last engagement on Jan. 18, 1983, only a few days before her death.

Barrett, Reginald, English organist; b. London, Jan. 12, 1861; d. St. Petersburg, Florida, Feb. 7, 1940. He studied at the Guildhall School of Music and the Darmstadt Cons.; came to the U.S. in 1888; was an organist in Kansas City until 1898, when he settled in N.Y. as organist at St. James Church, Fordham. From 1917 until 1925 he played the organ in motion picture theaters. He composed some 100 preludes and interludes for organ, sacred songs, choruses, etc.

Barrett, "Syd" Roger, psychedelic British rock guitarist and lyricist; b. Cambridge, Jan. 6, 1946. He played guitar in a folk duo with his schoolmate Dave Gilmour (b. Cambridge, March 6, 1944); then teamed with Roger Waters (b. Great Bookham, Sept. 6, 1944), Nick Mason (b. Birmingham, Jan. 27, 1945), and Rick Wright (b. London, July 28, 1945) and played rhythm-and-blues type of music, with Barrett playing the lead guitar, Wright handling the keyboard instruments, Waters on the string bass, and Mason on the drums. All of them did vocals. They adopted the collective name Pink Floyd, the origin of which is obscure, and plunged into the murky waters of contemporary alienation and lugubrious mysticism. Barrett's first single record, *Arnold Layne,* dealt with a perverted transvestite, so strange in its slimy contortions that even a London underground radio station refused to put it on the air. Barrett's next release, *See Emily Play,* became a hit, however; he then put out *The Piper at the Gates of Dawn,* released in America in 1967 under the name Pink Floyd, which became a top attraction. But Barrett began to fall apart psychologically, with bizarre behavior and drug abuse; paradoxically, it was just this eccentricity that exercised irresistible fascination to the similarly disoriented youth on both sides of the Atlantic. Barrett departed the group in 1969, but Pink Floyd continued to function, perpetuating Barrett's surrealist visions and cultivating outer-space fantasies, as exemplified by the album *The Dark Side of the Moon* (written by Roger Waters), which included the megasmash *Money.* Among their other successful albums were *Meddle,* with the extraordinary *Echoes* and *Atom Heart Mother,* which featured a smattering of electronic sounds. In 1979 Pink Floyd produced a highly successful film, *The Wall,* dealing with lunacy.

Barrett, William Alexander, English writer on music; b. London, Oct. 15, 1834; d. there, Oct. 17, 1891. He was a choirboy in St. Paul's Cathedral; then studied at Oxford. From 1867 he was active mainly as music critic and editor. He publ. *English Glee and Madrigal Writers* (1877), *English Church Composers* (1882), and other books of reference. His son, **Francis Barrett,** was also a writer on music; he was born in London, Nov. 14, 1869, and died there, Jan. 19, 1925.

Barrientos, Maria, Spanish coloratura soprano; b. Barcelona, March 10, 1884; d. Ciboure, France, Aug. 8, 1946. She studied at the Barcelona Cons.; made her operatic debut at the age of 15 in Barcelona, on March 4, 1899, and while still at a very young age made a successful tour of Europe. She made her American debut at the Metropolitan Opera House in N.Y. as Lucia on Jan. 31, 1916, and remained with it until 1920; then returned to Europe.

Barrière, Jean, French cellist and composer; b. c.1705; d. Paris, June 6, 1747. In 1730 he was appointed as a musician-in-ordinary at the Royal Academy of Music in Paris; then went to Rome, where he studied cello with Alborea; returned to Paris in 1739, and made a fine career as a virtuoso cellist at the Concert Spirituel. He publ. 6 books of cello sonatas (Paris, 1733–39).

Barrington, Daines, English lawyer and music amateur; b. London, 1727; d. there, March 14, 1800. He was the author of the famous account of Mozart as a child prodigy publ. in *Philosophical Transactions of the Royal Society* in 1770. He also publ. an interesting volume, *Experiments and Observations on the Singing of Birds* (London, 1773), and a description of the ancient Welsh crwth and pibcorn, also in *Philosophical Transcriptions of the Royal Society.*

Barrios Fernandez, Angel, Spanish composer; b. Granada, Jan. 4, 1882; d. Madrid, Nov. 27, 1964. Of a musical family (his father was a famous guitarist), he studied violin and played in bands as a child. He later studied theory with Conrado del Campo in Madrid and with Gédalge in Paris. At the same time, he perfected his guitar playing; formed a trio, Iberia, and traveled in Europe playing Spanish popular music. He spent his declining years in Madrid. In collaboration with his teacher Conrado del Campo, he wrote a successful operetta, *El Avapiés* (Madrid, 1919) and several zarzuelas: *La Suerte, La Romería, Seguidilla gitana, Castigo de Dios, En Nombre del Rey,* and *Lola se va a los puertos;* also numerous overtures and other orchestral pieces based on popular Spanish motifs.

Barrows, John, American horn player; b. Glendale, Calif., Feb. 12, 1913; d. Madison, Wis., Jan. 11, 1974. His first instrument was the euphonium; he studied horn playing at the Eastman School in Rochester, N.Y. (1930–32), theory and orchestration at San Diego State Teachers College (1933–34), and composition (with Donovan and Smith) and cello at Yale Univ. (1934–38). He played horn with the Minneapolis Symph. (1938–42); with the N.Y. City Opera (1946–49) and N.Y. City Ballet orchs. (1952–55); and in San Juan with the Casals Festival orch. (1958–61). Barrows was a member of the N.Y. Woodwind Quintet (1952–61); toured Europe with the Marlboro Festival Orch. He taught horn at Yale Univ. (1957–61), at N.Y. Univ. (1958–61) and at the Univ. of Wisconsin (1961–74). He composed 2 string quartets, a String Trio, and a Wind Quintet, and made arrangements for band.

Barrozo Netto, Joaquim Antonio, Brazilian composer; b. Rio de Janeiro, Jan. 30, 1881; d. there, Sept. 1, 1941. He studied with Braga, Nepomuceno, and others; appeared as a pianist in public at an early age; his compositions, in a mildly romantic manner, are mostly for piano. He enjoyed a fine reputation in Brazil as a teacher.
BIBLIOGRAPHY: T. Gomes, *Barroso Neto* (Rio de Janeiro, 1939).

Barry, Charles Ainslie, English organist and mu-

sic editor; b. London, June 10, 1830; d. there, March 21, 1915. He studied with Walmisley; later at the Cologne Cons.; also with Moscheles, Plaidy, and Richter at the Leipzig Cons. Returning to England, he wrote for various music magazines; was editor of the *Monthly Musical Record* (1875–79); also served as an annotator for orch. programs conducted by Hans Richter in England.

Barry, Jerome, American baritone; b. Boston, Nov. 16, 1939. He studied voice and linguistics; in 1963 received his master's degree in languages from Tufts Univ., and acquired fluency in 8 European languages and in Hebrew. He studied voice privately with Pierre Bernac, Jennie Tourel, and Luigi Ricci; began his professional career in Italy; gave a great many concerts in Israel; returning to the U.S., he developed activities in many fields, as a lecturer and a singer; settled in Washington, D.C., where he organized the Washington Music Ensemble.

Barsanti, Francesco, Italian flutist and composer; b. Lucca, c.1690; d. London, 1772. He studied at the Univ. of Padua; served as a flutist and oboist in the Italian opera in London; then spent some time in Scotland, returning to London in 1743. He wrote 9 overtures; 12 violin concertos; 6 flute solos with Bass; 6 sonatas for 12 Violins with Bass; 6 antiphons in Palestrina style; numerous pieces for various instruments. He publ. *A Collection of Old Scots Tunes* (Edinburgh, 1742).
BIBLIOGRAPHY: Henry Farmer, *A History of Music in Scotland* (London, 1947); W. Bergmann, "Francesco Barsanti," *The Consort,* XVIII (1961).

Barshai, Rudolf, Russian conductor; b. Labinskaya, near Krasnodar, Sept. 28, 1924. He studied violin at the Moscow Cons. with Lev Zeitlin and viola with Borisovsky, graduating in 1948; also studied conducting with Ilya Musin in Leningrad; in 1955 he organized the Moscow Chamber Orch., which became extremely successful; many Soviet composers wrote works for it. In 1976 he emigrated to Israel, and led the Israel Chamber Orch. in Tel Aviv until 1981. He also appeared as a guest conductor in Europe, the U.S., and Japan. In 1982 he was named principal conductor and artistic adviser of the Bournemouth Symph. Orch.

Barsotti, Tommaso Gasparo Fortunato, Italian music teacher; b. Florence, Sept. 4, 1786; d. Marseilles, April 1868. He founded the Free School of Music in Marseilles (1821), and was its director until 1852; wrote a number of pieces for piano and voice; publ. *Méthode de musique* (1828).

Barsova, Valeria, Russian soprano; b. Astrakhan, June 13, 1892; d. Sochi, Dec. 13, 1967. Her real name was **Vladimirova.** She studied voice with Umberto Mazetti at the Moscow Cons., graduating in 1919; from 1920 to 1948 she was on the staff of the Bolshoi Theater in Moscow. She distinguished herself mainly in the Russian repertoire, but also sang Violetta and Gilda. Her silvery coloratura enabled her to sing such demanding roles as Lakmé. In 1950–53 she taught voice at the Moscow Cons. She gave solo recitals in Russia and abroad, including England and Germany.

BIBLIOGRAPHY: G. Polyanovsky, *V. V. Barsova* (Moscow and Leningrad, 1941).

Barstow, Josephine, English soprano; b. Sheffield, Sept. 27, 1940. She studied at the Univ. of Birmingham; then joined Opera for All in 1964; later studied at the London Opera Centre; was a member of the Sadler's Wells Opera (1967–68); from 1968 sang with the Welsh National Opera; from 1969 made many appearances at Covent Garden. She made her Metropolitan Opera debut on March 28, 1977, as Musetta in *La Bohème.* A versatile singer, her repertoire ranges from traditional to contemporary roles.

Bárta, Josef, Bohemian composer; b. Prague, c.1746; d. Vienna, June 13, 1787. After serving as an organist in Prague, he settled in Vienna; he composed his opera *La Diavolessa* for the Burgtheater (July 18, 1772); he wrote several other operas, as well as 13 symphs., 6 string quartets, 6 keyboard sonatas, and other works.

BIBLIOGRAPHY: J. Havlík, *Symfonie Antonína Laubeho a Josefa Bárty* (Diss., Univ. of Prague, 1974).

Bárta, Lubor, Czech composer; b. Lubná, Aug. 8, 1928; d. Prague, Nov. 5, 1972. He studied with Řídký at the Prague Academy of Musical Arts (1948–52). His music presents an effective amalgam of modernistic procedures, influenced by Bartók in its rhythm, by Stravinsky in its meters, and by Hindemith in its neo-Classical harmony.

WORKS: 2 violin concertos (1952, 1970); 3 symphonies (1955; *The Bitter Summer,* 1969; 1972); Concerto for Chamber Orch. (1956); Viola Concerto (1957); *Dramatic Suite* for Orch. (1958); Piano Concerto (1958–59); *From East Bohemia,* symph. suite (1961); *Concertante Overture* (1964); *Ludi* for 8 Winds and String Orch. (1964); *Musica Romantica* for Strings (1971); 2 cantatas: *Komsomol* (1951) and *Song of the New Age,* inspired by space flight (1962); 2 violin sonatas (1949, 1959); 2 wind quintets (Divertimento, 1949; 1969); 3 string quartets (1950, 1957, 1967); Piano Trio (1955); Trombone Sonatina (1956); Clarinet Sonata (1958); *Ballad and Burlesque* for Cello and Piano (1963); Concertino for Trombone and Piano (1964); Solo Guitar Sonata (1965); *4 Pieces* for Violin and Guitar (1966); Flute Sonata (1966); *Fragments* for Clarinet and Piano (1967); *Amoroso* for Horn and Piano (1970); Cello Sonata (1971); Variations for Piano (1948); 3 piano sonatas (1956, 1961, 1971); Harpsichord Sonata (1967); songs.

Bartalus, István, Hungarian musicologist; b. Bálványos-Váralja, Nov. 23, 1821; d. Budapest, Feb. 9, 1899. He received his musical training at the Kolozsvar Cons.; in 1851 went to Pest, where he was active as a teacher, pianist, musicologist, and journalist. He was one of the founders of Hungarian musicol-

ogy; his edition of *Magyar népdalok egyetemes gyüjteménye (Universal Collection of Hungarian Folksongs;* 7 vols., Budapest, 1873–96) sustains validity even at the present time.

Bartay, Andreas, Hungarian composer; b. Széplak, April 7, 1799; d. Mainz, Oct. 4, 1854. He began his career as a civil servant. At the same time he was engaged in collecting Hungarian folk songs and became interested in music in general. In 1829 he became a director of the first Pest singing academy; in 1834 he publ. one of the earliest collections of Hungarian folk songs and also a Hungarian book on music theory, *Magyar Apollo* (1834). A militant patriot, he participated in the Hungarian struggle for independence of 1848; after its defeat he emigrated to France and eventually to Germany. He wrote three operas: *Aurelia, oder Das Weib am Konradstein* (Pest, Dec. 16, 1837); *Csel (The Ruse:* Pest, April 29, 1839); *A magyarok Nápolyban (The Hungarians in Naples;* unperformed).

Bartay, Ede, Hungarian folk-song collector; son of **Andreas Bartay;** b. Budapest, Oct. 6, 1825; d. there, Aug. 31, 1901. He studied law and music and was for many years a practicing piano teacher. In 1876 he was appointed director of the National Cons. in Budapest, a post which he held until his death. In 1863 he founded the Hungarian Pension Fund for Musicians. Like his father, he was a Hungarian patriot. After the defeat of the Hungarian Revolution of 1848 he remained in Budapest, dedicating himself to collecting authentic Hungarian folk songs and dances. He also wrote a Symph., an overture, *Pericles,* and many piano pieces.

Bartels, Wolfgang von, German composer; b. Hamburg, July 21, 1883; d. Munich, April 19, 1938. He studied with Beer-Walbrunn in Munich and with Gédalge in Paris; then became a music critic in Munich. His early works show impressionist influences; later he adopted an eclectic style.

WORKS: Melodramas: *The Little Dream,* after Galsworthy (Manchester, 1911); *Li-I-Lan* (Kassel, 1918); song cycles *(Li-Tai-Pe, Baltic Songs, Minnesänge);* Violin Concerto; Viola Concerto.

Barth, Christian Samuel, German oboist; b. Glauchau, Jan. 11, 1735; d. Copenhagen, July 8, 1809. He studied at the Thomasschule in Leipzig at the time of Bach; played the oboe in various court orchs. in Rudolstadt (1753), Weimar (1762), Hannover (1768), and Kassel (1769). In 1786 he joined the court chapel at Copenhagen, where he remained until his death.

Barth, Hans, pianist and composer; b. Leipzig, June 25, 1897; d. Jacksonville, Fla., Dec. 9, 1956. When a small child, he won a scholarship at the Leipzig Cons. and studied under Carl Reinecke; came to the U.S. in 1907, but made frequent trips to Germany. His meeting with Busoni inspired him to experiment with new scales; with the aid of George L. Weitz, he perfected a portable quarter-tone piano

(1928), on which he played in Carnegie Hall (Feb. 3, 1930); composed a Piano Concerto for this instrument, with a string orch. also tuned in quarter-tones (played by him with Stokowski and the Philadelphia Orch., March 28, 1930). Other works using quarter-tones: Suite for Strings, Brass, and Kettledrums; Piano Quintet; also a Piano Concerto for normal tuning (1928) and two piano sonatas; operetta, *Miragia* (1938); a piano manual, *Technic* (1935); various essays, etc.

Barth, Karl Heinrich, German pianist and teacher; b. Pillau, near Königsberg, July 12, 1847; d. Berlin, Dec. 23, 1922. He was a pupil of Hans von Bülow in Berlin; also studied with Bronsart and Tausig. He became a teacher at the Stern Cons., Berlin, in 1868; then at the Hochschule für Musik (1871); established, with De Ahna and Hausmann, the Barth Trio, which enjoyed considerable success.

Barth, Richard, German violin virtuoso; b. Grosswanzleben, June 5, 1850; d. Marburg, Dec. 25, 1923. He studied with Joachim in Hannover; attracted considerable attention because he was left-handed, using his left hand for bowing and his right hand for fingering. He was also a professional conductor; he led the Phil. concerts in Hamburg from 1894 to 1904. In 1908 he became director of the Hamburg Cons. He wrote chamber music in the manner of Brahms and was the author of a biography, *Johannes Brahms und seine Musik* (1904).
BIBLIOGRAPHY: E. Deggeler-Engelke, *Richard Barth* (Marburg, 1949).

Bartha, Dénes, Hungarian musicologist; b. Budapest, Oct. 2, 1908. He attended courses in musicology at the Univ. of Berlin with Blume, Sachs, Hornbostel, and Schering (1926–30); received his doctorate with the thesis *Benedictus Ducis und Appenzeller* (Wolfenbüttel, 1930). Returning to Budapest, he was a lecturer at the Franz Liszt Academy of Music and Privatdozent at the Univ. of Budapest. In 1964 he was a visiting prof. at Smith College; in 1966–67 he was on the faculty of Carnegie-Mellon Univ. in Pittsburgh, and in 1969–78 was Andrew W. Mellon Prof. there. He also lectured at Harvard Univ. (1964–65) and Cornell Univ. (1965–66). He publ. *Das Musiklehrbuch einer ungarischen Klosterschule aus 1490* (Budapest, 1934); *Lehrbuch der Musikgeschichte* (Budapest, 1935); *Franz Liszt* (Leipzig, 1936); *Beethoven* (Budapest, 1939); *Die ungarische Musik* (with Kodály; Budapest, 1943); *Anthologie der Musikgeschichte* (Budapest, 1948); *J.S. Bach* (Budapest, 1956); *Beethoven kilenc szimfóniája* (Budapest, 1956; 5th ed., revised, 1975); *Haydn als Opernkapellmeister* (with L. Somfai; Budapest-Mainz, 1960); edited *J. Haydn: Gesammelte Briefe und Aifzeichnungen* (Kassel, 1965); also was on the editorial board of *Zénei Lexikon* (3 vols., Budapest, 1965).

Barthe, Grat-Norbert, French composer; b. Bayonne, June 7, 1828; d. Asnières (Seine), Aug. 13, 1898. He was a pupil of Leborne at the Paris Cons.;

won the Grand Prix de Rome (1854) with the cantata *Francesca da Rimini;* wrote the operas *Don Carlos* and *La Fiancée d'Abydos;* an oratorio, *Judith;* etc.

Barthélémon, François-Hippolyte, French violinist and composer; b. Bordeaux, July 27, 1741; d. London, July 20, 1808. His father was French and his mother Irish. He held posts as violinist in various theater orchs. in London; became intimately acquainted with Haydn during Haydn's London visit in 1792. He was greatly praised as a violinist; Burney speaks of his tone as being "truly vocal." Barthélémon wrote mostly for the stage; among his operas, the most notable are *Pelopida* (London, May 24, 1766); *The Judgement of Paris* (London, Aug. 24, 1768); *Le Fleuve Scamandre* (Paris, Dec. 22, 1768); *The Maid of the Oaks* (The Oaks, near Epsom, June 1774); *Belphegor* (London, March 16, 1778). In addition, he wrote a Violin Concerto; 2 sets of duos for violins; 6 string quartets; catches and glees to English words (many of them publ.). He was married to Mary Young, a noted singer descended from Anthony Young; his daughter contributed a biographical edition (London, 1827) of selections from Barthélémon's oratorio *Jefte in Masfa.*

Bartholomée, Pierre, Belgian composer; b. Brussels, Aug. 5, 1937. He studied with Louel, Souffrian, and Stekke at the Royal Cons. in Brussels (1952–57) and privately with Pousseur and Boulez. In 1962 he founded in Brussels an instrumental ensemble, Groupe Musiques Nouvelles. In 1972 he became a prof. at the Brussels Cons.
WORKS: *Chanson* for Solo Cello (1964); *Cantate aux Alentours* for Voices, Instruments, and Live Electronics (1966); *La Ténèbre souveraine* for Soloists, Double Chorus, and Orch. (1967); *Tombeau de Marin* for Violin, 2 Viole da Gamba, and Harpsichord (1967); *Premier alentour* for Flute and 2 Viole da Gamba (1967); *Catalogue* for 4 Harps (1968); *Deuxième alentour: "Cueillir"* for Mezzo-soprano, Piano, and Percussion (1969); *Harmonique* for Orch. (1970); *Fancy I* for Solo Harp and *Fancy II* for Instrumental Group (1974–75; can be played together under the title *Sonata quasi una fantasia*).

Bartholomew, Marshall, American choral conductor; b. Belleville, Ill., March 3, 1885; d. Guilford, Conn. April 16, 1978. He studied at Yale Univ. (B.A., 1907) with Horatio Parker and David Stanley Smith, and later in Berlin. Returning to America, he devoted himself mainly to choral conducting and arranging. In 1921 he founded the Yale Glee Club, which he conducted until 1928, and again in 1939–48. He publ. choral arrangements of American folk music; the *Yale Glee Club Series* for male voices (32 nos.); *The Yale Song Book 250th Anniversary Ed.* (N.Y., 1953); *Mountain Songs of North Carolina;* various songs for solo voice and piano; *100 Original Songs for Young Voices* (educational).

Bartholomew, William, English violinist, writer, and painter; b. London, 1793; d. there, Aug. 18, 1867.

A versatile artisan, he was proficient in chemistry, painting, and languages. He was a friend of Mendelssohn and trans. the texts of his oratorios (including *Elijah*) into Eng.; also wrote the Eng. text for Spohr's *Jessonda,* etc. During the last years of his life he was incapacitated by paralysis.

Bartlett, Ethel, English pianist; b. Epping Forest, June 6, 1896; d. Los Angeles, April 17, 1978. She studied with Matthay; specialized as a piano duet player with her husband, **Rae Robertson;** made annual tours in Europe and the U.S.

Bartlett, Homer Newton, American pianist, organist, and composer; b. Olive, N.Y., Dec. 28, 1845; d. Hoboken, N.J., April 3, 1920. He studied with Max Braun and Jacobsen; was organist at the Madison Avenue Baptist Church, N.Y., for 31 years. He was one of the founders of the American Guild of Organists. His publ. works include a cantata, *The Last Chieftain* (Boston, Jan. 29, 1891); a Sextet for Flute and Strings; quartets, anthems, carols, etc.; about 80 songs and piano pieces. The following are in manuscript: opera, *La Vallière;* unfinished Japanese opera, *Hinotito;* oratorio, *Samuel;* symph. poem, *Apollo;* Violin Concerto; Cello Concerto; etc. His first opus number, a *Grand Polka de Concert,* was very popular.

Bartmuss, Richard, German organist and composer; b. Schleesen, Dec. 23, 1859; d. Dessau, Dec. 25, 1910. He studied with Grell and Löschhorn; in 1885 became court organist in Dessau. He wrote numerous organ works that enjoyed considerable popularity, among them 2 concertos, 4 sonatas, and 2 chorale-fantasias; also an oratorio, *Der Tag der Pfingsten;* a cantata, *Die Apostel in Philippi;* motets; and songs. His sacred work *Liturgische Vespern* represents a partial formulation of his attempt to modernize the Lutheran musical service.

Bartók, Béla, great Hungarian composer; b. Nagyszentmiklós (now Sînnicolau Mare, Rumania), March 25, 1881; d. New York, Sept. 26, 1945. His father was a school headmaster; his mother was a proficient pianist, and he received his first piano lessons from her. He began playing the piano in public at the age of 11. In 1894 the family moved to Pressburg (Bratislava), where he took piano lessons with László Erkel, son of the famous Hungarian opera composer; he also studied harmony with Anton Hyrtl. In 1899 he enrolled at the Royal Academy of Music in Budapest, where he studied piano with István Thomán and composition with Hans Koessler; he graduated in 1903. His earliest compositions reveal the combined influence of Liszt, Brahms, and Richard Strauss; however, he soon became interested in exploring the resources of national folk music, which included not only Hungarian melorhythms but also elements of other ethnic strains in his native Transylvania , including Rumanian and Slovak. He formed a cultural friendship with Zoltán Kodály, and together they traveled through the land collecting folk songs, which they publ. in 1906. In

1907 Bartók succeeded István Thomán as professor of piano at the Royal Academy of Music. His interest in folk-song research led him to tour North Africa in 1913. In 1919 he served as a member of the musical directorate of the short-lived Hungarian Democratic Republic with Dohnányi and Kodály; was also deputy director of the Academy of Music. Although a brilliant pianist, he limited his concert programs mainly to his own compositions; he also gave concerts playing works for 2 pianos with his second wife, **Ditta Pásztory** (d. Budapest, Nov. 21, 1982, at the age of 80). In his own compositions he soon began to feel the fascination of tonal colors and impressionistic harmonies as cultivated by Debussy and other modern French composers. The basic texture of his music remained true to tonality, which he expanded to chromatic polymodal structures and unremittingly dissonant chordal combinations; in his piano works he exploited the extreme registers of the keyboard, often in the form of tone clusters to simulate pitchless drumbeats. He made use of strong asymmetrical rhythmic figures suggesting the modalities of Slavic folk music, a usage that imparted a somewhat acrid coloring to his music. The melodic line of his works sometimes veered toward atonality in its chromatic involutions; in some instances he employed melodic figures comprising the 12 different notes of the chromatic scale; however, he never adopted the integral techniques of the 12-tone method.

Bartók toured the U.S. as a pianist from Dec. 1927 to Feb. 1928; also gave concerts in the Soviet Union in 1929. He resigned his position at the Budapest Academy of Music in 1934, but continued his research work in ethnomusicology as a member of the Hungarian Academy of Sciences, where he was engaged in the preparation of the monumental *Corpus Musicae Popularis Hungaricae.* With the outbreak of World War II, Bartók decided to leave Europe; in the fall of 1940 he went to the U.S., where he remained until his death from polycythemia. In 1940 he received an honorary Ph.D. from Columbia Univ.; he also did folk-song research there as a visiting assistant in music (1941–42). His last completed score, the *Concerto for Orchestra,* commissioned by Koussevitzky, proved to be his most popular work. His Third Piano Concerto was virtually completed at the time of his death, except for the last 17 bars, which were arranged and orchestrated by his pupil Tibor Serly.

Throughout his life, and particularly during his last years in the U.S., Bartók experienced constant financial difficulties, and complained bitterly of his inability to support himself and his family. Actually, he was apt to exaggerate his pecuniary troubles, which were largely due to his uncompromising character. He arrived in America in favorable circumstances; his traveling expenses were paid by the American patroness Elizabeth Sprague Coolidge, who also engaged him to play at her festival at the Library of Congress for a generous fee. Bartók was offered the opportunity to give a summer course in composition at a midwestern college on advantageous terms, when he was still well enough to undertake such a task, but he proposed to teach

Bartók

piano instead, and the deal collapsed. Ironically, performances and recordings of his music increased enormously after his death, and the value of his estate reached a great sum of money. Posthumous honors were not lacking: Hungary issued a series of stamps with Bartók's image; a street in Budapest was named Bartók Street; the centenary of his birth (1981) was celebrated throughout the world by concerts and festivals devoted to his works.

Far from being a cerebral purveyor of abstract musical designs, Bartók was an ardent student of folkways, seeking the roots of meters, rhythms, and modalities in the spontaneous songs and dances of the people. Indeed, he regarded his analytical studies of popular melodies as his most important contribution to music. Even during the last years of his life, already weakened by illness, he applied himself assiduously to the arrangement of Serbo-Croatian folk melodies of Yugoslavia from recordings placed in his possession. He was similarly interested in the natural musical expression of children; he firmly believed that children are capable of absorbing modalities and asymmetrical rhythmic structures with greater ease than adults trained in the rigid disciplines of established music schools. His remarkable collection of piano pieces entitled, significantly, *Mikrokosmos* was intended as a method to initiate beginners into the world of unfamiliar tonal and rhythmic combinations; in this he provided a parallel means of instruction to the Kodály method of schooling.

WORKS: FOR THE STAGE: *A kékszakállú herceg vará (Duke Bluebeard's Castle)*, opera in one act, op. 11 (1911; revised 1912, 1918; Budapest, May 24, 1918, Egisto Tango conducting; U.S. premiere, N.Y. City Opera, Oct. 2, 1952); *A fából faragott királyfi (The Wooden Prince)*, ballet in one act, op. 13 (1914–16; Budapest, May 12, 1917, Egisto Tango conducting; orch. suite, 1924; Budapest, Nov. 23, 1931; revised, 1932); *A czodálatos mandarin (The Miraculous Mandarin)*, pantomime in one act, op. 19 (1918–19; Cologne, Nov. 27, 1926; orch. suite, 1924; revised, 1927; Budapest, Oct. 15, 1928, Ernst von Dohnányi conducting).

FOR ORCH.: *Scherzo* (only scored movement of a projected symph. in E-flat major, 1902; Budapest, Feb. 29, 1904); *Kossuth*, symph. poem (1903; Budapest, Jan. 13, 1904); *Rhapsody* for Piano and Orch., op. 1 (1904; Paris, Aug. 1905, Bartók, soloist); Scherzo for Piano and Orch., op. 2 (1904; posthumous, Budapest, Sept. 28, 1961); Suite No. 1, op. 3 (1905; movements 1, 3–5 performed in Vienna, Nov. 29, 1905; first complete performance, Budapest, March 1, 1909; revised, 1920); Suite No. 2, for Small Orch., op. 4 (1905–7; first performance of 2nd movement, Scherzo, only; Berlin, Jan. 2, 1909; first complete performance, Budapest, Nov. 22, 1909; revised, 1920, 1943; transcribed for 2 Pianos, 1941); *Two Portraits*, op. 5 (No. 1, 1907–8; No. 2, 1911; No. 1, Budapest, Feb. 12, 1911; first complete performance, Budapest, April 20, 1916); Violin Concerto No. 1 (1907–8; score discovered in 1958; posthumous, Basel, May 30, 1958, Schneeberger, soloist; Paul Sacher conducting); *Two Pictures (Deux Images)*, op. 10 (1910; Budapest,

Feb. 25, 1913); *Four Pieces*, op. 12 (1912, orchestrated, 1921; Budapest, Jan. 9, 1921; Budapest, Jan. 9, 1922); *Dance Suite* for Orch. (1923; Budapest, Nov. 19, 1923); 3 piano concertos: No. 1 (1926; Frankfurt, July 1, 1927, Bartók, soloist; Furtwängler conducting), No. 2 (1930–31; Frankfurt, Jan. 23, 1933, Bartók, soloist; Rosbaud conducting), and No. 3 (1945; last 17 measures composed by Tibor Serly; posthumous, Philadelphia, Feb. 8, 1946, Sándor, soloist; Ormandy conducting); *Rhapsody* No. 1 for Violin and Orch. (1928; also versions for Violin or Cello and Piano; Königsberg, Nov. 1, 1929, Szigeti, soloist; Scherchen conducting); *Rhapsody* No. 2 for Violin and Orch. (1928; also for Violin and Piano; Budapest, Nov. 25, 1929, Székely, soloist; E. Dohnányi conducting); *Music for Strings, Percussion, and Celesta*, one of Bartók's most often played works (1936; Basel, Jan. 21, 1937, Paul Sacher conducting); Violin Concerto No. 2 (1937–38; Amsterdam, March 23, 1939, Székely, soloist; Mengelberg conducting); *Divertimento* for String Orch. (1939; Basel, June 11, 1940); Concerto for 2 Pianos and Orch. (orchestration of Sonata for 2 Pianos and Percussion; London, Nov. 14, 1942); Concerto for Orch. (commissioned by Koussevitzky; 1943; performed under his direction, Boston, Dec. 1, 1944); Concerto (1945; left unfinished in sketches; reconstructed and orchestrated by Tibor Serly, 1947–49; posthumous, Minneapolis, Dec. 2, 1949, Primrose, soloist; Dorati conducting; also arranged by Serly for Cello and Orch.); various orch. transcriptions of Rumanian and Hungarian folk and peasant dances, originally for piano.

CHAMBER MUSIC: 3 youthful, unnumbered violin sonatas: C minor, Op. 5 (1895), A major, Op. 17 (1897), and E minor (1903); Piano Quartet in C minor, op. 20 (1898); an unnumbered String Quartet in F major (1898); Duo for 2 Violins (1902); *Albumblatt* for Violin and Piano (1902); Piano Quintet (1904; Vienna, Nov. 21, 1904); 6 numbered string quartets: No. 1, op. 7 (1908; Budapest, March 19, 1910), No. 2, op. 17 (1915–17; Budapest, March 3, 1918), No. 3 (1927; London, Feb. 19, 1929), No. 4 (1928; Budapest, March 20, 1929), No. 5 (1934; Washington, D.C., April 8, 1935), No. 6 (1939; N.Y., Jan. 20, 1941); 2 numbered violin sonatas: No. 1 (1921; London, March 24, 1922), No. 2 (1922; London, May 7, 1923); *Rhapsody* No. 1 for Violin and Piano (1928; Budapest, Nov. 22, 1929, Szigeti, violinist; Bartók, pianist; also versions for Cello and Piano, and Violin and Orch.); *Rhapsody* No. 2 for Violin and Piano (1928; Amsterdam, Nov. 19, 1928; revised, 1944; also a version for Violin and Orch.); *44 Duos* for 2 Violins (1931); Sonata for 2 Pianos and Percussion (1937; Basel, Jan. 16, 1938, Bartók and his wife, Ditta Bartók, soloists; also for Orch. as Concerto for 2 Pianos and Orch.); *Contrasts* for Violin, Clarinet, and Piano (1938; N.Y., Jan. 9, 1939; a ballet, *Caprichos*, based on the music of *Contrasts* (N.Y., Jan. 29, 1950); Sonata for Solo Violin (1944; N.Y., Nov. 26, 1944, Menuhin, soloist).

FOR PIANO: *Rhapsody*, op. 1 (1904; Pressburg, Nov. 4, 1906, Bartók, soloist); *14 Bagatelles*, op. 6 (1908; Berlin, June 29, 1908); *10 Easy Pieces* (1908); *2 Elegies*, op. 8b (1908–9; Budapest, April 21, 1919, Bartók, soloist); *For Children* (originally 85 easy pieces in 4 vols., 1908–9; revised, 1945, reducing the number to

79, divided into 2 vols.); *7 Sketches,* op. 9 (1908–10; revised, 1945); *4 Dirges* (1910); *3 Burlesques* (1908–11); *Allegro barbaro* (1911); *6 Rumanian Folk Dances* (1909–15); *Rumanian Christmas Carols,* or *Colinde* (1915); Sonatina (1915); *Suite,* op. 14 (1916; Budapest, April 21, 1919, Bartók, soloist); *15 Hungarian Peasant Songs* (1914–18); *3 Etudes,* op. 18 (1918); *8 Improvisations on Hungarian Peasant Songs* (1920; Budapest, Feb. 27, 1921, Bartók, soloist); Sonata (1926; Budapest, Dec. 8, 1926, Bartók, soloist); *Out of Doors* (1926); *9 Little Pieces* (1926; Budapest, Dec. 8, 1926, Bartók, soloist); *3 Rondos on Folk Tunes* (No. 1, 1916, Nos. 2 and 3, 1927); *Petite Suite* (1936); *Mikrokosmos* (1926–39), 153 progressive pieces publ. in 6 vols.; a unique attempt to write a piano method in a modern idiom with varying meters, modes, and dissonant counterpoint; *7 Pieces from Mikrokosmos* for 2 Pianos (c.1939); Suite for 2 Pianos (1941; transcription from Suite No. 2, for Small Orch., Op. 4).

For voice: *20 Hungarian Folksongs* for Voice and Piano (first 10 by Bartók, second 10 by Kodály; 1906; revised, 1938); *8 Hungarian Folksongs* for Voice and Piano (1907–17); *3 Village Scenes* for Female Voices and Chamber Orch. (1926; N.Y., Feb. 1, 1927; this is a transcription of 3 of *5 Village Scenes* for Voice and Piano, 1924; Budapest, Dec. 8, 1926); *20 Hungarian Folksongs* for Voice and Piano (4 vols., 1929); *Cantata Profana* for Tenor, Baritone, Chorus, and Orch. (1930; BBC, London, May 25, 1934); 27 Choruses for Women's or Children's Voices a cappella (1935); numerous settings of various folk songs.

WRITINGS: *Cântece poporale româneşti din comitatul Bihor (Ungaria)/Chansons populaires roumaines du département Bihar (Hongrie)* (Bucharest, 1913; revised ed. in Eng. as incorporated in B. Suchoff, ed., *Rumanian Folk Music,* The Hague, vols. I–III, 1967); *Erdélyi magyarság népdalok* (Transylvanian Folk Songs; Budapest, 1923; with Kodály); "Die Volksmusik der Rumänen von Maramureş," *Sammelbände für vergleichende Musikwissenschaft,* IV (Munich, 1923; in Eng. as incorporated in B. Suchoff, ed., *Rumanian Folk Music,* The Hague, vol. V, 1975); *A magyar népdal* (Budapest, 1924; in German as *Das ungarische Volkslied,* Berlin, 1925; in Eng. as *Hungarian Folk Music,* London, 1931; enlarged ed., with valuable addenda, as *The Hungarian Folk Song,* ed. by B. Suchoff, Albany, N.Y., 1981); *Népzenénk és a szomszéd népek népzenéje* (Our Folk Music and the Folk Music of Neighboring Peoples; Budapest, 1934; in German as *Die Volksmusik der Magyaren und der benachbarten Völker,* Berlin, 1935; in French as "La Musique populaire des Hongrois et des peuples voisins," *Archivum Europae Centro Orientalis,* II; Budapest, 1936); *Die Melodien der rumänischen Colinde (Weihnachtslieder)* (Vienna, 1935; in Eng. in B. Suchoff, ed., *Rumanian Folk Music,* The Hague, vol. IV, 1975); *Miért és hogyan gyüjtsünk népzenét* (Why and How Do We Collect Folk Music? Budapest, 1936; in French as *Pourquoi et comment recueille-t-on la musique populaire?,* Geneva, 1948); *Serbo-Croatian Folk Songs* (N.Y., 1951; with A. Lord; reprinted in B. Suchoff, ed., *Yugoslav Folk Music,* vol. I, Albany, N.Y., 1978); also articles in

various musical magazines, among them "Hungarian Peasant Music," *Musical Quarterly* (July 1933).

The New York Bartók Archive is publishing an edition of Bartók's writings in English translations in its Studies in Musicology series. The following vols., under the editorship of Benjamin Suchoff, have been publ.: *Rumanian Folk Music* (The Hague, vols. I–III, 1967; vols. IV–V, 1975); *Turkish Folk Music from Asia Minor* (Princeton, 1976); *Béla Bartók's Essays* (selected essays; London and N.Y., 1976); *Yugoslav Folk Music* (4 vols., Albany, N.Y., 1978); *The Hungarian Folk Song* (Albany, N.Y., 1981).

BIBLIOGRAPHY: An extensive literature in many languages exists concerning various aspects of Bartók's life and music; in addition to the writings listed below, see the journal *Documenta Bartókiana* (Budapest, 1964–70; 1977—). *Musikblätter des Anbruch,* III/5 (Vienna, 1921); *Zenei Szemle,* VIII (Budapest, 1928); A. Révész, *Bartók Béla utja* (Budapest, 1936); D. Dille, *Béla Bartók* (Antwerp, 1939); H. Pleasants and T. Serly, "Bartók's Historic Contribution," *Modern Music,* XVII (1940); G. Abraham, "The Bartók of the Quartets," *Music and Letters* (Oct. 1945); M. Seiber, *The String Quartets of Béla Bartók* (London, 1945); J. Demény, *Bartók* (Budapest, 1946); B. Kiss, *Bartók Béla müvészete* (Cluj, 1946); D. Dille, *Béla Bartók* (Brussels, 1947); G. Láng, *Bartók élete és müvei* (Budapest, 1947); J. Deményi, ed., *Bartók Béla levelei* (Budapest, 1948–71; 2nd ed., 1976; in German, 1960; 2nd ed., 1973; in Eng., 1971); J. Demény, *Bartók élete és müvei* (Budapest, 1948); A. Molnár, *Bartók müvészete* (Budapest, 1948); M. Babbitt, "The String Quartets of Bartok," *The Musical Quarterly* (July 1949); "Béla Bartók, A Memorial Review," *Tempo,* 13–14 (1949–50); S. Moreux, *Béla Bartók, Sa vie, ses œuvres, son langage* (Paris, 1949; in German, Zürich, 1950; in Eng., London, 1953); C. Mason, "Béla Bartók and Folksong," *Music Review,* XI (1950); B. Rondi, *Bartók* (Rome, 1950); *Uj Zenei Szemle,* I/4 (Budapest, 1950); *Musik der Zeit,* III (Bonn, 1953); H. Stevens, *The Life and Music of Béla Bartók* (a basic study in Eng.; N.Y., 1953; revised ed., 1964); *Revue Musicale,* 244 (1955); P. Csobádi, *Bartók* (Budapest, 1955); E. Lendvai, *Bartók stilusa* (Budapest, 1955); F. Bónis, *Bartók élete képekben* (Budapest, 1956; 4th ed. for the Bartók centenary, 1980; in German, 1964; in French, 1964; in Eng. as *Béla Bartók: His Life in Pictures,* 1964); B. Suchoff, *Guide to Bartók's Mikrokosmos* (London, 1957; 3rd ed., N.Y., 1982); B. Szabolcsi, ed., *Bartók, Sa vie et son œuvre* (Budapest, 1956; 2nd ed., 1968; in German, 1957; enlarged ed., 1972); J. Szegö, *Bartók Béla a népdalkutató* (Bucharest, 1956); R. Traimer, *Béla Bartóks Kompositionstechnik, dargestellt an seinen sechs Streichquartetten* (Regensburg, 1956); K. Kristóf, *Beszélgetések Bartók Bélaval* (Budapest, 1957); A. Fassett, *The Naked Face of Genius; Béla Bartók's American Years* (Boston, 1958; reprint as *Béla Bartók; The American Years,* N.Y., 1970); R. Petzoldt, *Béla Bartók, Sein Leben in Bildern* (Leipzig, 1958); W. Reich, *Béla Bartók; Eigene Schriften und Erinnerungen der Freunde* (Basel and Stuttgart, 1958); J. Ujfalussy, ed., *Bartók breviárium; Levelek, írasok, dokumentumok*

Bartoletti – Bartolozzi

(Budapest, 1958; 2nd ed., revised, 1974); J. Uhde, *Béla Bartók* (Berlin, 1959); J. Demény, ed., *Ausgewählte Briefe* (Budapest, 1960; in Eng., London, 1971); A. Forte, "Bartók's 'Serial' Composition," *The Musical Quarterly* (April 1960); L. Lesznai, *Béla Bartók: Sein Leben, seine Werke* (Leipzig, 1961; in Eng. as *Bartók*, London, 1973); B. Szabolcsi, *Béla Bartók: Leben und Werk* (Leipzig, 1961; 2nd ed., 1968); G. Kroó, *Bartók szinpadi müvei* (Budapest, 1962); V. Bator, *The Béla Bartók Archives: History and Catalogue* (N.Y., 1963); P. Citron, *Bartók* (Paris, 1963); Z. Pálová-Vrbova, *Béla Bartók: Zivot a dilo* (Prague, 1963); E. Lendvai, *Bartók dramaturgiája* (Budapest, 1964); W. Rudziński, *Warsztat kompozytorski Béli Bartóka* (Cracow, 1964); E. Helm, *Béla Bartók in Selbstzeugnissen und Bilddokumenten* (Hamburg, 1965); J. Ujfalussy, *Bartók Béla* (Budapest, 1965; 3rd ed., 1976; in Eng., Boston, 1972; in Russian, 1971; in German, 1973); J. Kárpáti, *Bartók vonósnégyesei* (Budapest, 1967; revised ed. as *Bartók kamarazenéje*, 1976; in Eng., 1975); A. Szöllösy, ed., *Bartók összegyüjtött irásai I* (Budapest, 1967); Sessja Bartókowska* (Warsaw, 1967); J. Demény, *Bartók Béla a zongoramüvész* (Budapest, 1968; 2nd ed., 1973); H. Heinsheimer, *Best Regards to Aida* (includes material on Bartók's American travels; N.Y., 1968); I. Martynov, *Béla Bartók* (Moscow, 1968); I. Nestyev, *Béla Bartók* (Moscow, 1969); J. Szegö, *Bartók Béla élete* (Budapest, 1969); F. Weselowski, ed., *Sesja Bartókowska* (Lodz, 1969); T. Zieliński, *Bartók* (Cracow, 1969; in German, Zürich, 1973); *Béla Bartók: A Complete Catalogue of His Published Works* (London, 1970); V. Čižik, *Bartóks Briefe in die Slowakei* (Bratislava, 1971); E. Kraus, "Bibliographie und Diskographie: Béla Bartók," *Musik und Bildung* (Oct. 1971); G. Kroó, *Bartók kalauz* (Budapest, 1971; Eng., 1974; in German, 1974); T. Hundt, *Bartók's Satztechnik in den Klavierwerken* (Regensburg, 1971); E. Lendvai, *Bartók költöi világa* (Budapest, 1971); E. Lendvai, *Béla Bartók: An Analysis of His Music* (London, 1971); *International Musicological Conference in Commemoration of Béla Bartók: Budapest 1971;* P. Petersen, *Die Tonalität im Instrumentalschaffen von Béla Bartók* (Hamburg, 1971); F. Bónis, *Bartók Béla élete képekben és dokumentumokban* (Budapest, 1972; in German, 1972; in Eng. as *Béla Bartók: His Life in Pictures and Documents*, 1972); D. Dille, *Thematisches Verzeichnis der Jugendwerke Béla Bartóks 1890–1904* (Budapest, 1974); H. Fladt, *Zur Problematik traditioneller Formtypen dargestellt an Sonatensätzen in den Streichquartetten Béla Bartóks* (Munich, 1974); F. László, ed., *Bartók-dolgozatok* (Bucharest, 1974); J. McCabe, *Bartók Orchestral Music* (London, 1974); T. Crow, ed., *Bartók Studies* (Detroit, 1976); B. Suchoff, "Bartók in America," *Musical Times* (Feb. 1976); G. Perle, "The String Quartets of Béla Bartók," in *A Musical Offering: Essays in Honor of Martin Bernstein* (N.Y., 1977); E. Lendvai, *Bartók and Kodály* (4 vols., Budapest, 1978–80); E. Antokoletz, "The Musical Language of Bartók's 14 Bagatelles for Piano," *Tempo*, 137 (1981); I. Kecskeméti, "A Chopin-Kodály-Bartók Analogy," *Musical Times* (March 1981); B. Suchoff, "The New York Bartók Archive," *Musical Times* (March 1981); A. Wight-man, "Szymanowski, Bartók and the Violin," *Musical Times* (March 1981); Yann Queffèlec, *Béla Bartók* (Paris, 1981); E. Antokoletz, *The Works of Béla Bartók: A Study in Tonality and Progression in Twentieth-century Music* (Berkeley, Calif., 1982); H. Milne, *Bartók: His Life and Times* (Tunbridge Wells, 1982); S. Walsh, *Bartók's Chamber Music* (London, 1982).

Bartoletti, Bruno, noted Italian conductor; b. Sesto Fiorentino, June 10, 1926. He studied flute at the Florence Cons.; then played flute at the Teatro Comunale in Florence; in 1949 he became an assistant conductor at the Teatro Comunale; later conducted at the Maggio Musicale Fiorentino and the Royal Theater in Copenhagen. In 1956 he made his U.S. debut with the Lyric Opera of Chicago; in 1964 became its co-artistic Director with Pino Donati, and sole artistic director in 1975; was also musical director of the Rome Opera (1965–69); made many guest appearances in Milan, Buenos Aires, San Francisco, and N.Y. In addition to his thorough knowledge of the Italian operatic repertoire, he also conducted French and Russian operas.

Bartolino da Padova (Magister **Frater Bartolinus** de Padua; **Frater carmelitus**), Italian composer; flourished in the 2nd half of the 14th century. He was a member of the Carmelite Order, active in Padua. Some 38 works have been attributed to him, consisting of ballads and madrigals in the style of Jacopo da Bologna. See J. Wolf, ed., *Der Squarcialupi-Codex Pal. 87 der Biblioteca Medicea Laurenziana zu Florenz* (Lippstadt, 1955); W. Marrocco, ed., *Italian Secular Music,* in *Polyphonic Music of the Fourteenth Century,* IX (1974).
BIBLIOGRAPHY: N. Goldine, "Fra Bartolino da Padova, Musicien de Court," *Acta Musicologica,* XXXIV (1962); P. Petrobelli, "Some Dates for Bartolino da Padova," in *Studies in Music History: Essays for Oliver Strunk* (Princeton, N.J., 1968).

Bartolomeo degli Organi (Baccio Fiorentino), Italian organist and composer; b. Florence, Dec. 24, 1474; d. there, Dec. 12, 1539. At the age of 13 he became a singer at Ss. Annunziata in Florence; subsequently served as organist at several Florentine churches; also was a singer in the service of Lorenzo de' Medici, Duke of Urbino. In 1509 he was appointed principal organist at the Cathedral in Florence. Among his extant compositions are 10 Italian secular pieces and several instrumental works. See F. D'Accone, ed., *Music of the Florentine Renaissance,* in Corpus Mensurabilis Musicae, XXXII/2 (1967).
BIBLIOGRAPHY: F. D'Accone, "Alessandro Coppini and Bartolomeo degli Organi: Two Florentine Composers of the Renaissance," *Analecta Musicologica,* no. 4 (1967).

Bartolozzi, Bruno, Italian violinist and composer; b. Florence, June 8, 1911; d. Fiesole, Dec. 12, 1980. After studying violin at the Cherubini Cons. in Florence (1926–30) he was active as a violinist from 1941 to 1969; turned to composition quite late in life; took courses with Fragapane at the Cherubini Cons. (1946–49); in 1964 was appointed to its faculty. In his own music he followed the modified dodecaphonic techniques as promulgated by Dallapiccola, including triadic constructions. He wrote a book, *New Sounds for Woodwind* (in Eng.; London, 1967; 2nd revised ed., 1982), demonstrating the possibility of producing simultaneously several pitches on a single woodwind instrument. WORKS: FOR ORCH.: Concerto for Orch. (1952; Rome, Jan. 18, 1956); Divertimento for Chamber Orch. (1953); 2 violin concertos: No. 1 for Violin, Strings, and Harpsichord (1957; San Francisco, Dec. 2, 1957) and No. 2 (1979); *Concertazioni* for Bassoon, Strings, and Percussion (1963; Rome, March 6, 1965); *Memorie* for 3 Guitars and Orch. (1975; Florence, Oct. 7, 1977); *Risonanze* for 18 Instruments and Percussion (1978). CHAMBER MUSIC: *Serenata* for Violin and Guitar (1952); *3 Pieces* for Guitar (1952); *Musica a 5* for Bassoon, Trumpet, Guitar, Violin, and Viola (1953); *Variazioni* for Solo Violin (1957); 2 string quartets (1960, 1979); *Concertazioni* for Solo Oboe, Viola, Guitar, Double Bass, and Percussion (1965); *Andamenti* for Solo Viola (1967); *Collage* for Solo Oboe (1968); *The Hollow Man* for Any Woodwind (1968); *Concertazioni a Quattro* for Flute, Oboe, Clarinet, and Bassoon (1969); *Collage* for Solo Bassoon (1969); *Sinaulodia* for 4 Flutes (1969); *Cantilena* for Solo Flute (1970); *Musica per Piero* for 2 Violas (1971); *Auser* for Oboe and Guitar (1973); *Collage* for Solo Bassoon (1973); *Concertazioni* for Solo Clarinet, Horn, Trumpet, Trombone, Guitar, Viola, Cello, Double Bass, and Percussion (1973); *Repitu* for Flute, Viola, Guitar, and Percussion (1975); *Per Olga* for Solo Flute (1976); *The Solitary* for English Horn and Percussion (1976); *Adles* for Guitar (1977); *Atma* for 3 groups of Solo Instruments (1978). FOR VOICE: *Sentimento del sogno* for Soprano and Orch. (1952); *Immagine,* after Rilke, for Soprano and 17 Instruments (1959); *Tres recuerdos del cielo* for Soprano and 10 Instruments (1967; Vienna Festival, Sept. 11, 1968).

Bartoš, František, Czech music critic, editor, and composer; b. Brněnec, June 13, 1905; d. Prague, May 21, 1973. He studied composition with Jirák and Křička at the Prague Cons. (1921–25), and later with J.B. Foerster (1925–28); wrote music criticism; was co-editor of *Tempo* (1935–38; 1946–48); took part in the founding of the annual Prague Spring Festival; was chairman of the editorial committee that arranged for the publication of Dvořák's complete works. He brought out *Mozart in Letters* (Prague, 1937, 1956); *Smetana in Memories and Letters* (Prague, 1939; in English, 1955); *Gustav Mahler's Correspondences* (Prague, 1962). WORKS: Melodrama, *Jaro* (*Spring,* 1925); String Sextet (1926); 2 string quartets (1928, 1935); *Scherzo* for Wind Quintet (1932); *Rozhlasová hudba (Radio Music)* for Chamber Orch. (1936); *Škola žen (The School for Women),* after Molière, for Wind Quartet or Orch. (1936); Duo for Violin and Viola (1937);

Polka rusticana for Wind Trio (1952); several song cycles.

Bartoš, František, Moravian music editor; b. Mlatcová, March 16, 1837; d. there, June 11, 1906. He was a schoolteacher; publ. important collections of Moravian folk songs between 1873 and 1901. His correspondence with Janáček was publ. in 1957.

Bartoš, Jan Zdeněk, Czech composer; b. Dvůr Králové nad-Labem, June 4, 1908; d. Prague, June 1, 1981. He played the violin as a youth; then took composition lessons with Otakar Šín and with Jaroslav Křička at the Prague Cons., graduating in 1943. He earned his living playing in dance orchs.; from 1945 to 1956 he was a member of the Music Section of the Ministry of Education and Culture; in 1958 was appointed teacher of composition at the Prague Cons. In his music he followed the national traditions of the Czech school. WORKS: FOR THE STAGE: Operas: *Rýparka (Ripar's Wife,* 1949); *Prokletý zámek (The Accursed Castle,* 1949); *Útok na nebe (The Attack of Heaven,* 1953–54); operetta, *Je libo ananas? (Do You Like Pineapples?* 1956); 3 ballets: *Hanuman* (1941); *Mirella* (1956); *Král manéže (King of the Manège,* 1963). CANTATAS: *Běžec miru (Peace Runner,* 1948); *Krásná země (Beautiful Land,* 1949); *Poselství (The Message,* 1960); *Country of Comenius* (1961); *Tractatus pacis* (1973); *Lidice* (1976); *The Most Beautiful Book* (1979). FOR ORCH.: *2 Feuilletons* (1935); *Dvůr Králové* for String Orch. (1941); Concertino for Bassoon and Orch. (1943); *Song of St. Matthias,* symph. poem (1945); 7 symphonies: No. 1 (1949–52); No. 2, *da camera* (1956); No. 3, *Giocosa,* for Strings (1964–65); No. 4, *Concertante,* for Oboe d'Amore and String Orch. (1968); No. 5 for Wind Orch. (1973–74); No. 6 for Wind Quartet and String Orch. (1977); No. 7, *Brevis* (1978); *Fronta (The Front),* suite (1950); *Capriccio* for Cello and Orch. (1956); *Events of a Single Day* (1957); *Intermezzo* (1961); *Concerto da camera* for Oboe and Strings (1963); 2 viola concertos (1963, 1970); *Fantasy* for Flute and Orch. (1964); *Rhapsody* for Wind Orch. (1966); *Inventions* for Bass Clarinet and String Orch. (1966); *Sonnets of Prague* for Narrator, Tenor, Harp, and String Orch. (1966); Concerto for Accordion and String Orch. (1966); Horn Concerto (1967); *Lyrical Scenes* for String Orch. (1969); Concerto for Violin and String Orch. (1970); Concerto-Symphony for Violin and String Orch. (1973); Concerto Grosso for Chamber Orch. (1974); *Fantasy* for Organ and String Orch. (1975); *Concerto per due Boemi* for Bass Clarinet, Piano, and String Orch. (1975); Concerto for Violin, Viola, and String Orch. (1976); *Music* for String Quartet and Orch. (1976); *Rhapsody* for Cello and String Orch. (1979). CHAMBER MUSIC: Cello Sonata (1938); 2 nonets (1939, 1974); 11 string quartets (1940, 1946, 1948, 1951, 1952, 1956, 1960, 1963, 1970, 1971, 1973); *Partita* for Solo Viola (1944); 3 wind quintets (1946–63); Quintet for Flute, Harp, Viola, Cello, and Guitar (1947); Viola Sonatina (1947); *Elegy and Rondino* for Horn and Piano (1947–48); 17 divertimentos for various combinations of instruments (1956–79); Trio for Violin, Viola, and Harp (1961); Double-bass Sonata (1962); Preludes for Flute and Piano (1963); *Suite Concertante* for Viola, Double Bass, and 9 Wind Instruments (1964); String Trio (1967); *Fantasy* for Violin and Piano (1967); 4 piano trios (1968, 1969, 1971, 1979); Sextet for 2 Oboes, English Horn, 2 Bassoons, and Harp (1976); Trombone Sonata (1978); Trumpet Sonatina (1979); Trio for Viola, Clarinet, and Piano (1980); *Fantasy* for Solo Viola (1980); *Tercattino* for Oboe, Clarinet, and Piano (1981); Suite for Brass (1981); also 2 piano sonatas (1953, 1959); choruses; songs.

Bartoš, Josef, Czech writer on music; b. Vysoké Myto, March 4, 1887; d. Prague, Oct. 27, 1952. He studied with Stecker at the Prague Cons.; also with Hostinský and Nejedlý at the Univ. of Prague (1905–9); was active as a teacher and music critic. He publ. valuable monographs on Dvořák (1913), Fibich (1914; new ed., 1941), and Otakar Ostrčil (1936); also an important work on the National Opera of Prague (1938).

Barvík, Miroslav, Czech composer; b. Luzice, Sept. 14, 1919. He studied with Kaprál at the Brno Cons. and with Novák in Prague. In 1948 he was appointed director of the Prague Cons.; in 1966 he was named director of the state theater in Brno. In his works he followed the prescriptions of socialist realism, advocating immediate accessibility and clear national reference. In this manner he wrote his politico-patriotic cantatas *Song of the Fatherland* (1944) and *Thanks to the Soviet Union* (1946). His choral work *Hands Off Korea* was directed against the participation of U.S. forces or other non-Korean combatants in the conflict. He publ. 3 books: *Music of the Revolutionaries* (Prague, 1964), *Jak poslouchat hudbu* (Prague, 1961; 2nd ed., 1962), and *Hovory o hudbe* (Prague, 1961).

Barwahser, Hubert, distinguished German flutist and teacher; b. Herzogenrath, Sept. 28, 1906. He began to play the flute at an early age; studied flute with Emil Delling at the Aachen Cons. (1924–28). He was the first flutist of the Hamburg Phil. and later of the orch. of the North German Radio. In 1936 he became principal flutist of the Concertgebouw Orch. of Amsterdam, a position he held until 1971; he also taught at several conservatories in the Netherlands.

Bary, Alfred Erwin von, opera singer; b. La Valetta, Malta, Jan. 18, 1873; d. Munich, Sept. 13, 1926. He studied medicine at Munich Univ. (M.D., 1898); later developed a dramatic tenor voice, and was engaged at the Dresden Court Opera (1902–12); then at the Court Opera in Munich; sang the roles of Parsifal, Siegmund, and Tristan at Bayreuth.

Baryphonus, Henricus (real name, **Heinrich Pipegrop**), German music theorist and composer; b.

Wernigerode, Harz, Sept. 17, 1581; d. Quedlinburg, Saxe-Anhalt, Jan. 13, 1655. He studied at the Lateinschule in his native town; continued his education at the Univ. of Helmstedt. In 1605 he went to Quedlinburg, where he became cantor at St. Benedicti and a teacher at the Gymnasium; from 1606 was Subkonrector there. He wrote some 17 treatises on music, but only his *Pleiades musicae, quae in certas sectiones distributae praecipuas quaestiones musicas discutiunt* (Halberstadt, 1615) is extant, and only 2 of his compositions survive.

Barzin, Leon, Belgian-American conductor; b. Brussels, Nov. 27, 1900. He was brought to the U.S. in 1902; his father played viola in the orch. of the Metropolitan Opera; his mother was a ballerina. He studied violin with his father and later in Belgium with Eugène Ysaÿe. In 1925 he was appointed first viola player of the N.Y. Phil., retaining his post until 1929, when he was engaged as assistant conductor of the American Orch. Society, which was reorganized in 1930 as the National Orch. Assoc., with Barzin as principal conductor and music director; he continued in this capacity until 1959, and again from 1970 till 1976. He was also music director of the Ballet Society and N.Y. City Ballet (1948–58); from 1958 until 1960 he conducted concerts of the Association des Concerts Pasdeloup in Paris, France; and was at the same time instructor at the Schola Cantorum there. He received the Order of the Légion d'Honneur in 1960. Barzin was particularly successful in training semi-professional and student orchs.; especially with the National Orch. Assoc., he attained remarkable results.

Barzun, Jacques, eminent French-American historian, educator, and author of books on music; b. Créteil (Seine), Nov. 30, 1907. He came to America in 1919; was educated at Columbia Univ. (A.B., 1927; Ph.D., 1932); became a lecturer in history there in 1927, and a full prof. in 1945; he became an American citizen in 1933. In 1955 he was made dean of the Columbia graduate faculties, then dean of faculties and provost in 1958; he also assumed the chair of Seth Low Prof. of History in 1960; he resigned these posts in 1967; continued to lecture there until 1975. He exercised considerable influence on American higher education by advocating broad reading in various fields rather than narrow specialization. His books concerned with music include *Darwin, Marx, Wagner; Critique of a Heritage* (Boston, 1941; revised ed., 1958); *Berlioz and the Romantic Century* (the outstanding modern study of his life and works, based upon exhaustive documentation; 2 vols., Boston, 1950; 3rd ed., revised, 1969); ed. *Pleasures of Music* (N.Y., 1951); ed. and trans. *Nouvelles lettres de Berlioz, 1830–1868; New Letters of Berlioz, 1830–1868* (N.Y., 1954); publ. a new trans. of Berlioz's *Evenings with the Orchestra* (N.Y., 1956; 2nd ed., 1973); also wrote a survey, *Music in American Life* (N.Y., 1956).

BIBLIOGRAPHY: D. Weiner and W. Keylor, eds., *From Parnassus: Essays in Honor of Jacques Barzun* (N.Y., 1976).

Bas, Giulio, Italian organist and music editor; b. Venice, April 21, 1874; d. Vobbia, near Genoa, July 27, 1929. He studied in Munich with Rheinberger and in Venice with Bossi; was organist in the churches of Venice and Rome; in 1915 became prof. of theory and history at the Milan Cons. He wrote several textbooks on music theory; was a department editor of *Musica d'oggi.* Among his textbooks are *Metodo per l'accompagnamento del canto gregoriano* (Turin, 1920); and *Manuale di canto gregoriano* (Dusseldorf, 1910).

Baselt, Fritz (Friedrich Gustav Otto), composer; b. Öls, Silesìa, May 26, 1863; d. Frankfurt, Nov. 11, 1931. He studied with Emil Kohler in Breslau and with Ludwig Bussler in Berlin; was a musician, music dealer, composer, teacher, and conductor in Breslau, Essen, and Nuremberg; after 1894 he settled in Frankfurt am Main, where he conducted the Philharmonischer Verein and the Frankfurt Sängervereinigung. He wrote many light operas: *Der Fürst von Sevilla* (Nuremberg, 1888); *Don Alvaro* (Ansbach, 1892); *Der Sohn des Peliden* (Kassel, 1893); *Die Annaliese* (Kassel, 1896); *Die Musketiere im Damenstift* (Kassel, 1896); *Die Circusfee* (Berlin, 1897); also 2 ballets: *Die Altweibermühle* (Frankfurt, 1906), and *Rokoko* (Frankfurt, 1907); some 100 male choruses; many instrumental pieces; songs.

Basevi, Abramo, Italian composer and writer on music; b. Livorno, Nov. 29, 1818; d. Florence, Nov. 25, 1885. He studied music with Pietro Romani, and also took courses in medicine at the Univ. of Pisa. He founded and edited the periodical *Harmonia* (1856–59) and the journal *Boccherini* (1862–82). He published *Studio sulle opere di G. Verdi* (1859), *Studi sul armonia* (1865), and *Compendio della storia della musica* (1866). His 2 operas, *Romilda ed Ezzelino* (Florence, Aug. 11, 1840) and *Enrico Odoardo* (Florence, 1847), were not successful.

Bashkirov, Dmitri, Russian pianist and pedagogue; b. Tiflis, Nov. 1, 1931. He studied in Moscow with Alexander Goldenweiser. In 1955 he won 2nd prize in the Marguerite Long–Jacques Thibaud Competition in Paris; in 1970 he won the International Schumann Competition in Zwickau. In 1957 he became a member of the faculty of the Moscow Cons.; also taught at the Kiev Cons. from 1968. His repertoire is a comprehensive one, ranging from classical music to contemporary Soviet compositions.

Bashmakov, Leonid, Finnish composer of Russian extraction; b. Terijoki, April 4, 1927. He studied composition and conducting at the Sibelius Academy (1947–54). In 1960 he became a theater conductor in Tampere.
WORKS: Suite for Marimba and String Quartet (1951); *Fantastic Pictures* for Orch. (1953); 6 symphs. (1963; 1965; Sinfonietta, 1971; 1977; 1979; 1982); Violin Concerto (1966); 2 violin sonatinas (1968–69); *Canzona I* for Chorus and Orch. (1969; Helsinki, Nov. 23, 1971); Octet for Piano, Winds, and Brass (1970); Sonata for Percussion (1970); *4 Bagatelles* for Flute and Percussion (1971); *Dialogues* for Organ and Percussion (1971); *Canzona II* for Soprano and Orch. (1971); Overture for Wind Orch. (1971); Divertimento for Oboe and Strings (1971); Sonata for Viola, Cello, and Piano (1971); String Quartet (1972); Fantasia for 3 Different Flutes, One Player (1972); Cello Concerto (1972); Flute Concerto (1973); Organ Concerto (1975); a ballet, *Tumma* (1976); *Conversazioni per 2* for Soprano and Violin Soloists, and Small Orch. (1978); Wind Quintet (1978); *Crescendo* for Wind Orch. (1980); music for plays and films.

Basie, Count (real name, **William**), topmost American jazz pianist, exponent of the Big Band era of jazzification; b. Red Bank, N.J., Aug. 21, 1904; d. Hollywood, Fla., April 26, 1984. He received his early musical training from his mother, a professional pianist; then played with Bennie Moten's orch. After various peripeteia he became stranded in Kansas City in 1935, playing in a small band in a nightclub; it was there that he acquired the derisively nobiliary appellation Count. In 1936 he took his band to Chicago and then to N.Y. He attracted attention by his peculiar piano technique, emphasizing passages played by a single finger while directing his band with a glance, or a movement of the eyebrow. He met Fats Waller in Harlem and was fascinated by his discursive brilliance on the keys; he adopted Waller's manner but altered it in the direction of rich economy of means. He conducted big band engagements, but in 1950 decided to give up the large sound and formed an octet; however, in 1951 he organized a new big band, with which he made a highly successful tour of Europe; he played a command performance for the Queen of England during his British tour in 1957. In 1976 he suffered a heart attack, but after a period of recuperation, returned to an active career. In 1981 he received the Kennedy Center honors for achievement in the performing arts; at a White House reception that followed, President Ronald Reagan said that Count Basie had revolutionized jazz. Among his greatest hits were *One O'Clock Jump,* which became his theme song; *Jumpin' at the Woodside; Goin' to Chicago; Lester Leaps In; Broadway; April in Paris;* and *L'il Darlin'.* Roulette Records released a 2-record set, *The Count Basie Story* (1961), which includes a biographical booklet by Leonard Feather.
BIBLIOGRAPHY: Raymond Horricks, *Count Basie and His Orchestra* (N.Y., 1957; reprint, London, 1971); S. Dance, *The World of Count Basie* (N.Y., 1980).

Basile, Andreana, famous Italian contralto and instrumentalist; b. Posillipo, c.1580; d. Rome, c.1640. She attracted the public by her extraordinary beauty and became known as "la bella Adriana." She often accompanied herself on the harp and guitar; in Naples she married Muzio Baroni, a Calabrian nobleman. In 1610 she was engaged by the court of Vincenzo Gonzaga, the Duke of Mantua; she remained a principal singer at his court until 1624, and was praised by Monteverdi for her musicianship. In 1633 she settled in Rome. Her daughter was **Leonora Baroni,** who became a famous singer in her own right.

BIBLIOGRAPHY: A. Ademollo, *La bell' Adriana ed altre virtuose del suo tempo alla corte di Mantova* (Città di Castello, 1888); U. Prota-Giurleo, "Adriana Basile Baronessa di Piancerreto," *Nostro tempo,* IV/2–3 (1955).

Basili, Francesco, Italian composer; b. Loreto, Jan. 31, 1767; d. Rome, March 25, 1850. He studied with his father, **Andrea Basili,** and later with Giovanni Battista Borghi; then entered the Santa Cecilia Academy in Rome, where he took courses with Jannaconi. He served as conductor in various provincial Italian theaters; from 1827 to 1837 he was director of the Milan Cons. He wrote 13 operas and a number of dramatic oratorios. In 1837 he became conductor at St. Peter's Cathedral in Rome.

Basilides, Mária, Hungarian contralto; b. Jolsva, Nov. 11, 1886; d. Budapest, Sept. 26, 1946. She was educated at the Royal Academy of Music in Budapest; in 1915 she became a member of the Budapest Opera, remaining on its roster until her death; she also made appearances with the Berlin State Opera, the Dresden State Opera, and the Bavarian State Opera of Munich. She championed the music of Bartók and Kodály as a soloist in recital and with symph. orchs.

BIBLIOGRAPHY: J. Molnár, *Basilides Mária* (Budapest, 1967).

Basil (Saint) the Great, b. 329 at Caesarea, Cappadocia; d. there in 379. He was a bishop in Caesarea; is reputed to have introduced congregational (antiphonal) singing into the Eastern Church, thus being the forerunner of St. Ambrose in the Western Church.

Bašinskas, Justinas, Lithuanian composer; b. Mariampol, Jan. 22, 1923. He studied composition with Juzeliunas at the Vilna Cons., graduating in 1955; then joined its faculty. A prolific composer, he dedicated himself to optimistic themes, glorifying nature and extolling human friendship in his vocal music, while building tense tonal structures in his instrumental compositions.

WORKS: FOR ORCH.: 6 symphs.: No. 1 (1953), No. 2 (1960), No. 3 (1970), No. 4, *Symphony of the Bells* (1973), No. 5, *Reality* (1976), No. 6, *Crying Symphony* (1979); *3 Symphonic Dances* (1967); Concerto for Flute, Strings, and Percussion (1971). CHAMBER MUSIC: Violin Sonata (1979). FOR PIANO: *Variations* (1951); Sonata (1952). Vocal music: Oratorio, *Oak* (1957); Requiem (1969). SONG CYCLES FOR VOICE AND PIANO: *After the Storm* (1958); *Running Flame* (1970); *Feral Animals in the Winter* (1971); children's songs; arrangements of Lithuanian folk songs.

Basiola, Mario, Italian baritone; b. Annico, July 12, 1892; d. there, Jan. 3, 1965. He studied in Rome; was engaged at the Metropolitan Opera in N.Y. (1925–32); at La Scala in Milan, and in Rome (1933–38); also sang at Covent Garden in London (1939) and in Australia (1949); then returned to Italy and was active there as a teacher.

Basner, Veniamin, Soviet composer; b. Yaroslavl, Jan. 1, 1925. He studied violin at the Leningrad Cons. Upon graduation in 1949, he devoted himself to concert activities and composition. Among his works are *Three Musketeers,* ballet (1964); *The Polar Star,* musical comedy (1966); *The Southern Cross,* musical comedy (1970); *Spring Floods,* opera (1975); *Poem of the Besieged Leningrad,* symph. poem (1957); Symph. No. 1 (1958); Violin Concerto (1966); *Eternal Fire,* for Voices and Orch. (1971); 5 string quartets; *Goya,* monologue for Bass, English Horn, Bassoon, and Piano; film music.

Bassani, Geronimo, Italian singer and composer; b. Padua, late 17th century. He studied with Lotti; was a fine contrapuntist, singer, and singing teacher; produced 2 operas at Venice: *Bertoldo* (1718) and *Amor per forza* (1721); also wrote masses, motets, and vespers.

Bassani (Bassano), Giovanni, Italian composer, singer, and violinist; b. c.1558; d. Venice, 1617. He was a singer at San Marco in Venice in 1585; then served as singing teacher at the seminary there in 1595; in 1615 he was first violin soloist at the Chapel of the Basilica; remained there until his death. The following instrumental works by him are extant: *Fantasie a tre voci per cantar e sonar* (1585); *Il fiore dei capricci musicali a 4 voci* (1588); *Motetti, madrigali e canzioni francesi di diversi auttori ... diminuiti per sonar con ogni sorti de stromenti* (1591; reprinted in 1602 in an arrangement for one voice with organ ad lib.; containing works of Clemens non Papa, Créquillon, Palestrina, and others; the term *diminuiti* refers to ornamentation of the original vocal compositions); 2 vols. of *Motetti per concerti ecclesiastici* for 5–12 voices (1598–99); a vol. of *Canzonette* for 4 voices (1587), etc.

Bassani (Bassano, Bassiani), Giovanni Battista, Italian composer, organist, and violinist; b. Padua, c.1647; d. Bergamo, Oct. 1, 1716. He studied with Legrenzi and Castrovillari; in 1667 he became a member of the funereally named Accademia della Morte in Ferrara, serving as organist. On July 3, 1677, he became a member of the more cheerful Accademia Filarmonica in Bologna; also served as maestro di cappella and organist of the apocalyptic Confraternità del Finale in Modena. In 1680 he became maestro di cappella to the Duke of Mirandola; in 1682 he was appointed principe of the Accademia Filarmonica; in 1683 and 1684 he was maestro di cappella of the Accademia della Morte. In 1687 he was named maestro di cappella of the Ferrara Cathedral, and in 1712, maestro di cappella at S. Maria Maggiore in Bergamo; also taught at the music school of the Congregazione di Carità there.

His extant works include the following: Operas, *Amorosa Preda di Paride* (Bologna, 1683); *Falaride tiranno d'Agrigento* (Venice, 1683); *Alarico re de Goti* (Ferrara, 1685); *Vitige* (Ferrara, 1686); *Il trionfo di Venere in Ida* (Ferrara, 1688); *Gli amori alla moda* (Ferrara, 1688); *Ginevra, infante di Scozia* (Ferrara, 1690); *Il coceio Nerva* (Ferrara, 1691); *Gli amori tra gl'odii* (Verona, 1693). Oratorios: *La morte delusa* (1686); *Giona* (1689); *Nella luna celestiale* (1687); *Il Conte de Bacheville* (1696); *Mose risorto dalle acque* (1698); *Gl'Impegni del divino amore* (1703); *Il trionfo della fede* (1707). He also wrote numerous masses, and other sacred music. Of his instrumental works, several suites and trio sonatas are reprinted in Torchi's *L'arte musicale in Italia* (vol. VII) and in J.W. Wasielewski's *Instrumentalsätze vom Ende des XVI. bis Ende des XVII. Jahrhunderts* (1874). A cantata is included in Riemann's *Kantaten-Frühling* (vol. II); some vocal works are publ. by G.F. Malipiero in *Classici della musica italiana*.

BIBLIOGRAPHY: J.W. Wasielewski, *Die Violine und ihre Meister* (1883); A. Moser, *Geschichte des Violinspiels* (1923); A. Schering, *Geschichte des Oratoriums* (1911); F. Pasini, "Notes sur la vie de G.B. Bassani," *Sammelbände der Internationalen Musik-Gesellschaft 7* (1906); R. Haselbach, *G.B. Bassani* (Kassel, 1955).

Bassett, Leslie, American composer; b. Hanford, Calif., Jan. 22, 1923. He studied piano; played the trombone in jazz combos; was a trombonist during his military service, playing in the 13th Armored Division Band. He then enrolled in Fresno (Calif.) State College (B.A., 1947); later studied composition with Ross Lee Finney at the Univ. of Michigan (M.M., 1949; D.M., 1956); also took private lessons with Arthur Honegger and Nadia Boulanger in Paris in 1950. In 1952 he was appointed to the faculty of the Univ. of Michigan; was made a prof. there in 1965 and became chairman of the composition dept. in 1970; in 1977 he became the Albert A. Stanley Distinguished Univ. Prof. of Music there. He held the American Prix de Rome in 1961–63, and received the National Inst. of Arts and Letters Award in 1964. In 1966 he received the Pulitzer Prize in music for his *Variations for Orchestra*. He held a Guggenheim fellowship in 1973–74 and again in 1980–81; in 1981 became a member of the American Academy and Inst. of Arts and Letters. In his music he pursues the ideal of structural logic within the judicial limits of the modern school of composition, with some serial elements discernible in his use of thematic rhythms and motivic periodicity.
WORKS: FOR ORCH.: Suite in G (Fresno, Dec. 3, 1946); *5 Movements* (1961; Rome, July 5, 1962); *Variations for Orchestra* (Rome, July 6, 1963; Philadelphia, Oct. 22, 1965; received the Pulitzer Prize in 1966); *Colloquy* (Fresno, May 23, 1969); *Forces* (1972; Des Moines, Iowa, May 1, 1973); *Echoes from an Invisible World* (1974–75; Philadelphia, Feb. 27, 1976); Concerto for 2 Pianos and Orch. (1976; Midland, Mich., April 30, 1977); *Concerto lirico* for Trombone and Orch. (1983; Toledo, Ohio, April 6, 1984). FOR BAND AND WIND ENSEMBLES: *Designs, Images, and Textures* (1964; Ithaca, N.Y., April 28, 1965); *Sounds, Shapes, and Symbols* (1977; Ann Arbor, Mich., March 17, 1978); *Concerto Grosso* (1982; Ann Arbor, Feb. 4, 1983); *Colors and Contours* (1984). CHAMBER MUSIC: 4 string quartets: No. 1 (1951); No. 2 (1957); No. 3 (1962); No. 4 (1978); Sonata for Horn and Piano (1952); Trio for Viola, Clarinet, and Piano (1953); Quintet for 2 Violins, Viola, Cello, and Double Bass (1954); Sonata for Viola and Piano (1956); *5 Pieces* for String Quartet (1957); Woodwind Quintet (1958); Sonata for Violin and Piano (1959); Quintet for 2 Violins, Viola, Cello, and Piano (1962); Nonet (1967); *Music* for Alto Saxophone and Piano (1968); Sextet for 2 Violins, 2 Violas, Cello, and Piano (1971); *Sounds Remembered* for Violin and Piano (1972); *Wind Music* for Wind Sextet (1975); Sextet for Flutes, Clarinets, and Strings (1979); Trio for Violin, Clarinet, and Piano (1980); *Concerto da camera* for Trumpet and Chamber Ensemble (1981); many choral works; songs; pieces for organ and for piano; electronic music.

Bassevi, Giacomo. See **Cervetto, Giacomo.**

Bassford, William Kipp, American pianist; b. New York, April 23, 1839; d. there, Dec. 22, 1902. He was a church organist in N.Y.; also gave piano concerts; composed an opera, *Cassilda*. He completed Vincent Wallace's unfinished opera, *Estrella*.

Bassi, Amadeo (Vittorio), Italian operatic tenor; b. Florence, July 20, 1874; d. there, Jan. 14, 1949. He studied with Pavese Negri in Florence, and made his operatic debut there in 1899. He subsequently toured South America (1902–7); sang at the Manhattan Opera House, N.Y. (1906–8) and at the Chicago Opera Co. (1910–12). His repertoire included more than 50 operas, mostly Italian.

Bassi, Luigi, Italian opera baritone; b. Pesaro, Sept. 4, 1766; d. Dresden, Sept. 13, 1825. He studied with Pietro Morandi of Bologna; made his debut in Pesaro at the age of thirteen; he then sang in Florence; went to Prague in 1784, where he soon became greatly appreciated. Mozart wrote the part of Don Giovanni for him and heeded his advice in matters of detail. Bassi was in Vienna from 1806–14; then briefly in Prague; in 1815 he joined an Italian opera company in Dresden.

Bastiaans, Johannes Gijsbertus, Dutch organist and composer; b. Wilp, Oct. 31, 1812; d. Haarlem, Feb. 16, 1875. He studied organ in Dessau with F. Rümpler and Schneider; then went to Leipzig, where he took organ lessons with C.F. Becker and composition with Mendelssohn. He subsequently occupied various posts as an organist: in Deventer (1838–40), then at Amsterdam's Zuiderkerk (1840–58); in 1858 he was appointed municipal organist at St. Bavo's in Haarlem. He composed mainly for organ and chorus; publ. several books of chorales. He was succeeded at St. Bavo's by his son, **Johann**

Bastianini – Bateson

Bastiaans (1854–85).

Bastianini, Ettore, Italian baritone; b. Siena, Sept. 24, 1922; d. Sirmione, Jan. 25, 1967. He made his debut as a bass in Ravenna in 1945; then sang baritone roles. In 1953 he made his American debut as Germont in *La Traviata,* at the Metropolitan Opera in N.Y. on Dec. 5, 1953, remaining with the company until 1965; among his best roles were Rigoletto, Amonasro, Don Carlo, Escamillo, and Scarpia.

Bastin, Jules, Belgian bass; b. Pont, Aug. 18, 1933. He studied at the Brussels Cons.; in 1960 became a member of the Théâtre de la Monnaie in Brussels; also appeared in London, Chicago, N.Y., and Toronto. He is best known for his appearances in such French operas as *Le Prophète, Benvenuto Cellini, Pelléas et Mélisande,* and Massenet's *Cendrillon.* In 1979 he took part in the Paris premiere of the 3-act version of Berg's *Lulu.*

Baston, Josquin, Flemish composer of the mid-16th century. It is known that from May 1552 to Oct. 1553 he was at the Polish Court of Sigismund Augustus at Cracow. Motets and chansons by Baston appeared between 1542 and 1559 in various collections: Susato's *Het ierste musyck boexken* (Antwerp, 1551); Salbinger's *Concertus* (Augsburg, 1545); also in Louvain (published by Phalèse). His *Lament* has 2 middle voices singing the *Requiem aeternam* in canon 6 times while the other voices have fresh parts. See R. van Maldeghem (ed.), *Trésor musical* (1865–93; vol. XII).

Bate, Philip, English music scholar; b. Glasgow, March 26, 1909. He studied clarinet in Aberdeen; then attended classes in general science at the Univ. of Aberdeen (B.Sc., 1932). In 1934 he joined the staff of the BBC in London, and subsequently held various positions there (until 1968). He gathered a valuable collection of wind instruments, which he donated to the Univ. of Oxford. In 1946 he founded the Galpin Society, serving as its first chairman; in 1977 became its president.
WRITINGS: *The Oboe* (London, 1956; 3rd ed., 1975); *The Trumpet and Trombone* (London, 1966); *The Flute: A Study of Its History, Development and Construction* (London, 1969; 2nd ed., 1975).

Bate, Stanley Richard, English composer; b. Plymouth, Dec. 12, 1911; d. London, Oct. 19, 1959. He studied composition with Vaughan Williams and piano with Arthur Benjamin at the Royal College of Music in London (1931–35); then took courses with Nadia Boulanger in Paris and with Hindemith in Berlin. During World War II he was in Australia; in 1942 he went to the U.S.; in 1945 he was in Brazil and in 1950 he returned to London. On Nov. 7, 1938, he married the Australian-born composer **Peggy Glanville-Hicks** (divorced 1948). He wrote music in a finely structured cosmopolitan manner, making use of modern devices but observing the classical forms and shunning doctrinaire systems. He wrote several ballets, among them *Goyescas* (1937), *Perseus* (1938), and *Cap over Mill* (1938). He composed 4 symphs.; of these, the 3rd (1940) was performed 14 years after its composition, at the Cheltenham Festival, July 14, 1954, with remarkable success. His 4th Symph. was given in London on Nov. 20, 1955. Other works are 3 piano concertos (he was the soloist in his 2nd Piano Concerto, which he performed with the N.Y. Phil., conducted by Thomas Beecham, on Feb. 8, 1942), 2 sinfoniettas, 3 violin concertos, Viola Concerto, Cello Concerto, Harpsichord Concerto, 2 string quartets, Sonata for Recorder and Piano, Violin Sonata, Flute Sonata, Oboe Sonata, 9 piano sonatinas, and other piano pieces.

Bates, Joah, British organist; b. Halifax (England), March (baptized, March 8) 1741; d. London, June 8, 1799. He studied organ with Hartley in Rochdale and Wainwright in Manchester; then went to Eton and Cambridge for further education. In 1760 became a tutor of King's College in Cambridge; received his B.A. in 1764 and M.A. in 1767. He then went to London, where he organized the series known as Concerts of Antient Music (1776); also acted as conductor of the famous Handel Commemoration Festivals (1784–87; 1791).

Bates (née **Harrop**), **Sarah,** English singer; b. c.1755; d. London, 1811. She was born into a poor family; worked in a Halifax factory to support herself; finally she made her way to London and studied with **Joah Bates,** whom she married in 1780; she also took lessons with Antonio Sacchini. She made her formal debut at Covent Garden in *Judas Maccabaeus* on Feb. 14, 1777. She made regular appearances at her husband's Concerts of Antient Music series.

Bates, William, English composer who flourished in the second half of the 18th century. He wrote popular English operas in the ballad-opera style. His most popular work was *Flora or Hob in the Well,* which he wrote and arranged in 1760 (Covent Garden, April 25, 1770), using 7 of John Hippisley's songs from the 1729 *Flora or Hob's Opera,* together with 8 new songs of his own and a new overture. Neither of his works is to be confused with Thomas Doggett's 1711 farce with songs, a forerunner of the true ballad opera, variously titled *The Country Wake or Hob* or *The Country Wake.* His other stage works are *The Jovial Crew* (1760, altered to *The Ladies Frolick* in 1770); *The Theatrical Candidates* (1775); *The Device, or The Marriage Officer* (1777); *Second Thought Is Best* (1778); also a grand opera, *Pharnaces* (London, Feb. 15, 1765).

Bateson, Thomas, English composer; b. Cheshire County; d. probably in Dublin, March 1630. He was organist at Chester Cathedral in 1599–1609. In 1609 he became vicar choral and organist of the Cathedral of the Holy Trinity in Dublin. He is said to have been the first music graduate of Trinity College, earning his Mus.B. in 1612 and his M.A. in 1622. As a composer, Bateson is especially noted for his madrigals, although they are regarded as inferior to those by Morley or Weelkes. In 1604 he publ. a collection of 29 madrigals for 3 to 6 voices; it included the madrigal *When Oriana walked to take the ayre,* originally intended for publication in Morley's *Triumphs of Oriana.* A second set of 30 madrigals was publ. in 1618. Both sets are reprinted in *The English Madrigal School* (vols. 21–22), edited by E.H. Fellowes.

Bath, Hubert, English composer; b. Barnstaple, Nov. 6, 1883; d. Harefield, April 24, 1945. He studied at the Royal Academy of Music in London; conducted Thomas Quinlan's opera troupe on its world tour in 1913–14. Returning to England, he conducted classes in opera at the Guildhall School of Music in London. As a composer he showed natural flare for light operas, of which *Bubbles* (Belfast, Nov. 26, 1923) was quite successful. He also wrote a grand opera, *Trilby.* He furthermore composed a number of symph. sketches, several of them on exotic subjects, such as *African Suite;* also 6 cantatas, more than 150 songs, and various pieces of chamber music.

Bathe, William, Irish writer on musical subjects; b. Dublin, April 2, 1564; d. Madrid, June 17, 1614. He studied at Oxford Univ.; instructed Queen Elizabeth in mnemonics and presented her with an Irish harp of his own design. In 1591 he went to Spain; then was in Flanders, where he entered the Jesuit order in 1596; was ordained in Padua in 1599; returned to Spain in 1601; held the post of spiritual director of the Irish College in Lisbon in 1604; eventually went to Madrid, where he remained until his death. His chief merit as a music theorist lay in fixing definite rules for the placing of accidentals and in changing the system of hexachordal modes to scales based on the octave. He was the author of one of the earliest theoretical works on music, *A Brief Introduction to the True Art of Musicke* (London, 1584); also publ. *A Brief Introduction to the Skill of Song* (London, c.1587).
BIBLIOGRAPHY: J. Pulver, "William Bathe," *Musical Times* (Oct. 1934); B. Rainbow, "Bathe and His Introduction to Music," ibid. (April 1982); P. Nixon, "William Bathe and His Times," ibid. (Feb. 1983).

Bathori, Jane, French mezzo-soprano; b. Paris, June 14, 1877; d. there, Jan 21, 1970. She was educated at the Paris Cons. and made her operatic debut at Nantes in 1900. She subsequently devoted herself to the cultivation of modern vocal music by French composers; sang first performances of songs by Debussy, Ravel, Satie, and Milhaud. After 1926 she gave regular concerts in Argentina, and lived mostly in Buenos Aires. Returning to Paris, she was active mainly as a singing teacher. She publ. *Conseils sur le chant* (Paris, 1929) and *Sur l'interprétation des mélodies de Claude Debussy* (Paris, 1953).

Báthy, Anna, Hungarian soprano; b. Beregszász, June 13, 1901; d. Budapest, May 20, 1962. She studied voice at the Academy of Music in Budapest; made her operatic debut at the Municipal Theater there in 1928 as Elisabeth in *Tannhäuser;* in 1929 she joined the Budapest Opera, where she sang mostly in the Wagnerian repertoire.
BIBLIOGRAPHY: V. Somogyi and I. Molnár, *Báthy Anna* (Budapest, 1969).

Batiste, Antoine-Edouard, French organist; b. Paris, March 28, 1820; d. there, Nov. 9, 1876. He studied at the Paris Cons. with Halévy; won 2nd Grand Prix de Rome with the cantata *Héloïse de Montfort* (1840); subsequently was organist of St.-Nicolas-des-Champs (1842–54), then of St. Eustache. He composed organ music, piano pieces, and songs; also edited the official *Solfèges du Conservatoire* (12 vols.), and publ. a *Petit solfège harmonique.*

Batistin. See **Stuck, Johann Baptist.**

Batiz, Enrique, Mexican conductor; b. Mexico City, May 4, 1942. He first studied piano; later went to the Juilliard School of Music in N.Y., and the Warsaw Cons. He then decided upon a conducting career. In 1971 he founded the Orquesta Sinfónica del Estado de Mexico, which developed into a leading Mexican orch.; he toured with it in Mexico and the U.S.

Batka, Richard, Czech music editor and critic; b. Prague, Dec. 14, 1868; d. Vienna, April 24, 1922. He was educated at the German Univ. in Prague; then went to Vienna, where he became active as a music critic. He published a number of valuable monographs on German composers, and historical essays, of which *Geschichte der Musik in Böhmen* (Prague, 1906) is of documentary importance. He also wrote *Allgemeine Geschichte der Musik* (3 vols., Stuttgart, 1909–15).

Batta, Alexandre, cellist; b. Maastricht, the Netherlands, July 9, 1816; d. Versailles, Oct. 8, 1902. He was a pupil of Platel at the Brussels Cons.; settled in Paris (1835); made successful concert tours on the Continent; wrote many melodious pieces and transcriptions for cello with piano accompaniment.

Battaille, Charles-Aimable, French bass; b. Nantes, Sept. 30, 1822; d. Paris, May 2, 1872. He was originally a medical student; then turned to music and studied voice at the Paris Cons. He made his debut at the Opéra-Comique in *La Fille du régiment* (June 22, 1848). He created several roles in operas by Thomas, Adam, Halévy, and Meyerbeer. A throat disorder ended his stage career; he retired in 1863. He was on the staff of the Paris Cons. from 1861. He publ. an extensive method of singing in 2 vols.: 1. *Nouvelles recherches sur la phonation* (1861); 2. *De la physiologie appliquée au mécanisme du chant* (1863).

Battanchon, Félix, French cellist and composer; b. Paris, April 9, 1814; d. there, July 1893. He studied with Vaslin and Norblin at the Paris Cons.; was a member of the Grand Opera Orch. (1840). In 1846 he invented, and vainly tried to popularize, a small type of cello called a baryton.

Batten, Adrian, English organist and composer; b. Salisbury (baptized, March 1), 1591; d. London, 1637. He studied at Winchester with the Cathedral organist John Holmes; in 1614 went to London as vicar choral of Westminster Abbey. In 1626 he became vicar choral and organist at St. Paul's Cathedral. A prolific composer, he left 15 services and 47 anthems in manuscript. Some of his pieces are included in Boyce's *Cathedral Music.* A modern reprint of one of his services is included in *The Choir;* several anthems have been publ. by Novello. Batten also transcribed into organ score numerous sacred choral works, some of which have come down to us only through his transcriptions. His organ book is described in *Tudor Church Music* (1922, vol. II).
BIBLIOGRAPHY: J.B. Clark, "Adrian Batten and John Barnard: Colleagues and Collaborators," *Musica Disciplina* (1968); J.B. Clark and M. Bevan, "New Biographical Facts about Adrian Batten," *Journal of the American Musicological Society* (Summer 1970).

Battishill, Jonathan, English organist and composer; b. London, May 1738; d. Islington, Dec. 10, 1801. He was a chorister in St. Paul's (1747); later apprenticed to William Savage; was deputy organist under Boyce at the Chapel Royal; then harpsichordist at Covent Garden and organist in several London parishes. He wrote an opera with Michael Arne: *Almena* (Drury Lane Theatre, Nov. 2, 1764); a pantomime, *The Rites of Hecate* (Drury Lane Theatre, Dec. 26, 1763); and many popular anthems, glees, and songs.
BIBLIOGRAPHY: J.B. Trend, "Jonathan Battishill," *Music & Letters* (July 1932).

Battista, Vincenzo, Italian composer; b. Naples, Oct. 5, 1823; d. there, Nov. 14, 1873. He studied at the Naples Cons.; wrote 13 operas, 11 of which were produced at Naples (1844–69).

Battistini, Gaudenzio, Italian composer, grandson of **Giacomo Battistini;** b. Novara, June 30, 1722; d. there, Feb. 25, 1800. He succeeded his father, Giuseppe Battistini, in 1747 as organist of the chapel of San Gaudenzio in Novara, and served for more than 50 years until his death. He wrote numerous church works in a highly developed polyphonic style. A biographical sketch and examples of his music are found in Vito Fedeli, *Le cappelle musicali di Novara* in vol. III of *Istituzioni e monumenti dell' arte musicale italiana* (Milan, 1933).

Battistini, Giacomo, Italian composer; b. 1665; d. Novara, Feb. 5, 1719. He was organist at the Novara Cathedral (1694–1706); then at the church of San Gaudenzio. He is reputed to have been the first to introduce the violoncello into instrumental accompaniment. He composed several masses, motets, organ works; also contributed music to the third act of the drama *Antemio in Roma* (1695; with A. Besozzi and D. Erba). See Vito Fedeli, *Le cappelle musicali di Novara* in vol. III of *Istituzioni e monumenti dell' arte musicale italiana* (Milan, 1933), containing musical illustrations from Battistini's works.

Battistini, Mattia, celebrated Italian baritone; b. Rome, Feb. 27, 1856; d. Collebaccaro, near Rome, Nov. 7, 1928. He first studied medicine at the Univ. of Rome; then began taking singing lessons. He made his debut at the Teatro Argentino in Rome on Dec. 11, 1878, as Alfonso XI in Donizetti's *La Favorita;* subsequently appeared at Covent Garden in London (1883), at the San Carlo Opera in Naples (1886), at Drury Lane in London (1887), and at La Scala in Milan (1888). He then embarked on a worldwide tour, and acquired great popularity in South America, Spain, and Russia, and continued his active career until the last months of his life. He was a master of bel canto, with a remarkably expressive high register; was particularly successful in the parts of Rigoletto, Figaro in Rossini's *Barber of Seville,* and Valentin in Gounod's *Faust.*
BIBLIOGRAPHY: G. Fracassini, *Mattia Battistini, profilo artistico* (Milan, 1915); G. Monaldi, *Cantanti celebri* (Rome, 1929); F. Palmegiani, *Mattia Battistini* (Milan, 1948).

Battke, Max, German teacher and writer; b. Schiffuss, near Wandlacken, Sept. 15, 1863; d. Berlin, Oct. 4, 1916. He studied at Königsberg and Berlin, where he later taught at various conservatories. He founded a music seminary in Berlin (1900), which became in 1910 the famous "Seminar für Schulgesang." He wrote numerous textbooks on music and methods for voice production; edited (with Humperdinck) collections of folk songs and piano pieces.

Battle, Kathleen, black American soprano; b. Portsmouth, Ohio, Aug. 13, 1948. She studied voice with Franklin Bens at the Univ. of Cincinnati College-Conservatory of Music (B.Mus., 1970; M.Mus., 1971); then made her debut at the Spoleto Festival in 1972 in the Brahms *Requiem;* subsequently sang with the N.Y. Phil., the Cleveland Orch., the Los Angeles Phil., and other leading American orchs. She made her Metropolitan Opera debut in N.Y. as the Shepherd in *Tannhäuser* on Sept. 18, 1978, and soon acquired a fine reputation among American singers. In 1983 she was awarded an honorary doctorate from her alma mater.

Battmann, Jacques-Louis, organist and composer; b. Maasmünster, Alsace, Aug. 25, 1818; d. Dijon, July 7, 1886. He wrote a great quantity of music for the organ and several school manuals on music theory.

Batton, Désiré-Alexandre, French composer; b. Paris, Jan. 2, 1798; d. Versailles, Oct. 15, 1855. He was a pupil of Cherubini at the Paris Cons.; won the Prix de Rome in 1817 for his cantata, *La Mort d'Adonis.* In 1851 he was appointed inspector of the branch schools of the cons.; also taught singing there. His most successful opera was *La Marquise de Brinvilliers*, written in collaboration with Auber, Hérold, and others, and produced in Paris on Oct. 31, 1831; other operas were *La Fenêtre secrète* (Paris, Nov. 17, 1818); *Velleda* (1820); *Ethelvina* (1827); *Le Prisonnier d'état* (1828); *Le Camp du drap d'or* (1828); and *Le Remplaçant* (1837).

Battu, Pantaléon, French violinist; b. Paris, 1799; d. there, Jan. 17, 1870. He studied with R. Kreutzer at the Paris Cons.; was a member of the orch. of the Opéra and the court until his retirement in 1859. He wrote 3 violin concertos; 3 violin duos; etc.

Bätz, Karl, German music editor; b. Sömmerda, March 17, 1851; d. Berlin, 1902. He lived in America (1871–86); then settled in Berlin, where he founded the *Musikinstrumenten-Zeitung* in 1890; published *Die Musikinstrumente der Indianer* (1876); also various pamphlets on instrument making.

Baudiot, Charles-Nicolas, French cellist; b. Nancy, March 29, 1773; d. Paris, Sept. 26, 1849. He was a pupil of the elder Janson, whom he succeeded as cello prof. at the Paris Cons. (1795–1802; 1805–27); from 1816 was first cellist in the royal orch.; retired in 1832. With Levasseur and Baillot he wrote a cello method which for a time was used at the Paris Cons.; also *Instruction pour les compositeurs* (a guide to composers for cello); composed 2 cello concertos; 2 cello concertinos; a great variety of chamber music for cello.

Baudo, Serge, French conductor; b. Marseilles, July 16, 1927. He studied at the Paris Cons., conducting with Louis Fourestier, and theory with Jean Gallon and Noël Gallon; received a Premier Prix as drummer (1948) and as conductor (1949). He was engaged as pianist and percussion player in the orch. of the Concerts Lamoureux; then toured as an opera conductor. In 1967 he was appointed music director and conductor of the Orch. de Paris.

Baudrier, Yves, French composer; b. Paris, Feb. 11, 1906. He was primarily a law student; was mainly autodidact in music. In 1936 he, jointly with Messiaen, Jolivet, and Daniel-Lesur, formed the group La Jeune France, dedicated to the promotion of purely national French music, whether modern or traditional. In 1946 he made a lecture tour in the U.S. He wrote a symph. poem, *Eleonora*, after Edgar Allan Poe (1938); a symph. poem, *Le Grand Voiler* (1939); a Symphony (1945); and Suite for Trumpet (1966).

Bauer, Harold, distinguished pianist; b. Kingston on Thames, near London, of an English mother and a German father, April 28, 1873; d. Miami, March 12, 1951. He studied violin with his father and Adolf Politzer; made his debut as a violinist in London; in 1892 he went to Paris and studied piano for a year with Paderewski; in 1893 made his first tour as a pianist in Russia; gave piano recitals throughout Europe; in 1900 made his U.S. debut with the Boston Symph. Orch.; appeared as soloist with other U.S. orchs., with eminent chamber music groups, and as a recitalist. He founded the Beethoven Assoc. in N.Y. (1918); was president of the Friends of Music in the Library of Congress, Washington, D.C. Among his writings are: "Self-Portrait of the Artist as a Young Man," *Musical Quarterly* (April 1943); *Harold Bauer, His Book* (N.Y., 1948). He edited works by Schubert and Brahms, and Mussorgsky's *Pictures at an Exhibition*. A considerable corpus of his papers was acquired by the Music Division of the Library of Congress.

Bauer, Marion Eugenie, American composer and writer; b. Walla Walla, Wash., Aug. 15, 1887; d. South Hadley, Mass., Aug. 9, 1955. Her parents were of French extraction; she received her early education from her father, who was an amateur musician. She then went to Paris, where she took piano lessons with Pugno, and theory with André Gédalge and Nadia Boulanger; also took some lessons with Jean Paul Ertel in Berlin. Returning to America, she continued her studies with Henry Holden Huss and others. She taught at N.Y. Univ. (1926–51); was associate prof. there (1930–51); was annual lecturer at the summer Chautauqua Institute in 1928 and 1929; from 1933 through 1952 gave lecture recitals each summer; in 1940 joined the faculty at the Inst. of Musical Arts in N.Y.; taught at the Juilliard School of Music from 1940 to 1944. She was a member of the executive board of the League of Composers in N.Y., and had an active teaching career in music history and composition. Her own music oscillates pleasurably between Germanic Romanticism and Gallic Impressionism. Prudently, she wrote mostly in small forms, and was at her best in her piano pieces; among them were *From New Hampshire Woods* (1921); *Indian Pipes* (1928); *Sun Splendor* (1926; later orchestrated and performed by Stokowski with the N.Y. Phil., Oct. 25, 1947); *Dance Sonata* (1932). Her choral works include *Three Noëls* (1929); *A Garden Is a Lovesome Thing* (1938); *The Thinker* (1938); and *China* for Chorus with Orch. (Worcester Festival, Oct. 12, 1945). She also wrote quite a few pieces of chamber music: String Quartet (1928); *Fantasia quasi una sonata* for Violin and Piano (1928); Suite for Oboe and Clarinet (1932); Viola Sonata (1936); *Pan,* choreographic sketch for 7 Instruments and Piano (1937); Concertino for Oboe, Clarinet, and String Quartet (1940); Sonatina for Oboe and Piano (1940); Trio Sonata for Flute, Cello, and Piano; and *American Youth Concerto* for Piano and Orch. (1943). She was a successful popularizer of music history. Her publications include *How Music Grew* (1925; with Ethel Peyser), which had several printings; *Music through the Ages* (1932; also with Ethel Peyser; revised ed., 1967); *Twentieth Century Music* (1933, and still of use); and *How Opera Grew* (1955; once more with Ethel Peyser), which had, despite the clumsy title, several reprints.

Bauer, Moritz, German teacher and writer on music; b. Hamburg, April 8, 1875; d. Frankfurt, Dec. 31, 1932. He first studied medicine; then turned to music (Mus.Doc., Zürich, 1904). He published *Die Lieder Franz Schuberts* (1915); *Iwan Knorr* (1916); *Formprobleme des späten Beethoven* (1927); also edited songs by Zelter.

BIBLIOGRAPHY: F. Szymickowski, "Moritz Bauer," *Zeitschrift für Musikwissenschaft* (1933).

Bauer-Theussl, Franz, Austrian conductor; b. Zillingdorf, Sept. 25, 1928. He received his musical training in Frankfurt; also studied conducting with Clemens Krauss in Vienna. He then conducted opera in the Austrian resort of Baden, near Vienna (1950–52); subsequently conducted at Salzburg, at the Volksoper in Vienna, and at the Netherlands Opera in Amsterdam.

Bäuerle, Hermann, German music editor; b. Ebersberg, Oct. 24, 1869; d. Ulm, May 21, 1936. He studied theology and music in Tübingen; in 1895 took holy orders; in 1906 he became papal privy chamberlain. In 1921 he founded the Ulm Cons., of which he remained music director. He publ. several valuable papers on sacred music, among them *Der Vatikanische Choral in Reformnotation* (1907), *Liturgie*, a manual of the Roman Catholic liturgy (1908), and several school manuals on elementary music theory. His most important work, however, was the series Bibliothek Altklassischer Kirchenmusik in Moderner Notation, which he edited beginning in 1903.

Bauermeister, Mathilde, German soprano; b. Hamburg, 1849; d. Herne Bay, in Kent, England, Oct. 15, 1926. She studied at the Royal Academy of Music in London; gave recitals in Dublin in 1866; then joined the company of the Covent Garden Opera in London and sang there each season from 1887 to 1905. On Dec. 14, 1891, she made her first appearance at the Metropolitan Opera in N.Y., as Gertrude in *Romeo et Juliette;* she was on its roster again from 1893 to 1897 and from 1898 to 1906. Her repertoire was exceptionally large; it numbered nearly 100 roles.

Baugé, André, French baritone, son of Alphonse Baugé and Anne Tariol-Baugé; b. Toulouse, Jan. 4, 1893; d. Paris, May 25, 1966. He made his debut at the Opéra-Comique in Paris in 1917; for many years was a prof. of phonology at the Paris Cons. (until 1965).

Bauldewijn, Noël, also known as **Baudoin, Bauldewyn, Bauldeweyn, Balduin, Bauldoin,** or in Latin as **Natalis Balduinus;** Flemish composer; b. c.1480; d. Antwerp, 1529. From Aug. 31, 1509, to July 29, 1513, he served as choir director at the Church of St. Rombaut at Mechelen. On Nov. 16, 1513, he was appointed choir director at Notre Dame in Antwerp, where he remained until his death. His 2 motets were included by Petrucci in his collection *Motetti della Corona* (1519); 3 motets were publ. by Proske; a Chanson was included in Tylman Susato's *Le Sixième Livre contenant 31 chansons* (Antwerp, 1545); in addition, 10 motets and 6 masses by him are also known.

BIBLIOGRAPHY: E. Sparks, *The Music of Noël Bauldeweyn* (N.Y., 1972).

Baumann, Hermann, noted German horn player and pedagogue; b. Hamburg, Aug. 1, 1934. He studied in Hamburg; then played first horn in Dortmund (1957–61) and with the Stuttgart Radio Symph. Orch. (1961–67); won the International Music Competition in Munich in 1964, and made tours in Germany and abroad. In 1969 he was appointed a prof. at the Staatliche Folkwang Hochschule in Essen.

Baumann, Max Georg, German composer; b. Kronach, Nov. 20, 1917. In 1939–43 he studied composition and conducting at the Berlin Hochschule für Musik, where his teachers included Blacher and Distler; he became a lecturer there in 1946, and a prof. in 1953; was named director of its school music dept. in 1963; also made appearances as a conductor with the Berlin Collegium Musicum. He composed much sacred vocal music, including masses, motets, a cantata, and an oratorio; also a ballet, *Pelleas und Melisande* (1954).

Baumbach, Friedrich August, German composer and conductor; b. Gotha (baptized, Sept. 12), 1753; d. Leipzig, Nov. 30, 1813. He was active in various capacities as a singer, violinist, and conductor; conducted the Hamburg Opera (1777–89); then went to Leipzig. He wrote numerous pieces for different ensembles; also contributed musical articles to the *Kurzgefasstes Handwörterbuch über die schönen Künste* (Leipzig, 1794).

Baumfelder, Friedrich, German pianist and composer; b. Dresden, May 28, 1836; d. there, Aug. 8, 1916. He studied at the Leipzig Cons. with Moscheles, Wenzel, and Hauptmann; was conductor of the Schumann Singakademie at Dresden. He wrote a cantata, *Der Geiger zu Gmünd;* a collection of piano studies, *Tirocinium musicae;* and a great number of piano pieces in the salon style (totaling more than 300 opus numbers).

Baumgarten, Gotthilf von, German composer; b. Berlin, Jan. 12, 1741; d. Gross-Strehlitz, Silesia, Oct. 1, 1813. He wrote 3 operas, produced in Breslau: *Zemire und Azor* (1775), *Andromeda* (1776), and *Das Grab des Mufti* (1778).

Baumgarten, Karl Friedrich, German composer; b. Lübeck, 1740; d. London, 1824. He studied music in Lübeck; then went to London, where he served as concertmaster at Covent Garden. He composed an overture to W. Shield's opera *Robin Hood* (London, 1784) and a pantomime, *Bluebeard, or The Flight of Harlequin* (1792).

Baumgartner, August, German composer and writer on music; b. Munich, Nov. 9, 1814; d. there, Sept. 29, 1862. He was choirmaster at the Church of St. Anna in Munich; wrote articles on "musical short-hand" for the *Stenographische Zeitschrift* (1852); published a *Kurzgefasste Anleitung zur musikalischen Stenographie oder Tonzeichenkunst* (1853), and a *Kurzgefasste Geschichte der musikalischen Notation* (1856); composed an instrumental Mass; a Requiem; Psalms; many choruses and piano pieces.

Baumgartner, Paul, Swiss pianist; b. Altstätten, July 21, 1903; d. Locarno, Oct. 19, 1976. He studied in St. Gall, Munich, and Cologne; was a piano teacher in Cologne (1927–35). In 1937 he became director of the piano dept. of the Basel Cons.; he continued to give concerts and play chamber music in Switzerland and elsewhere.

Baumgartner, Rudolf, Swiss violinist and conductor; b. Zürich, Sept. 14, 1917. He was educated at the Univ. of Zürich, and later went to Vienna and Paris for further study. He then began to appear as a violinist, both as a soloist and in chamber music ensembles. After World War II, he turned his energies to conducting. In 1956 he helped organize the Festival Strings at the Lucerne Music Festival, becoming its first music director. In 1960 he was appointed director of the Lucerne Cons.

Baumgartner, Wilhelm, Swiss pianist and composer, author of the popular Swiss song *O mein Heimatland;* b. Rorschach, Nov. 15, 1820; d. Zürich, March 17, 1867. He attended the Gymnasium in Zürich and the Univ. of Zürich; studied piano and music theory with Alexander Müller. In 1842 he moved to St. Gall; in 1844 he went to Berlin, where he continued his musical studies with Taubert. In 1845 he returned to Switzerland, where he taught piano and conducted choruses. He became greatly honored in Switzerland, when, in 1846, he wrote a patriotic male chorus in 4 parts, *O mein Heimatland,* which in time achieved the status of an unofficial national anthem.
BIBLIOGRAPHY: C. Widmer, *Wilhelm Baumgartner, Ein Lebensbild* (Zürich, 1868); L. Gross, *Wilhelm Baumgartner, Sein Leben und sein Schaffen* (Munich, 1930).

Bäumker, Wilhelm, German writer on music; b. Elberfeld, Oct. 25, 1842; d. Rurich, March 3, 1905. He studied theology and philology at Münster and Bonn; from 1892 was a priest at Rurich. His most important work is *Das katholische deutsche Kirchenlied in seinen Singweisen von den frühesten Zeiten bis gegen Ende des 17. Jahrhunderts* (4 vols., Freiburg, 1883–1911). Vol. II (1883) and vol. III (1891) appeared originally as continuation of the work begun by K.S. Meister, who publ. vol. I in 1862; Bäumker revised this vol. in 1886; vol. IV (1911) was edited by J. Gotzen from Bäumker's notes, and also contains supplements to the preceding vols. Other works by Bäumker are: *Palestrina, ein Beitrag*

(1877); *Orlandus de Lassus, ein historisches Bildniss* (1878); *Zur Geschichte der Tonkunst in Deutschland* (1881); *Der Todtentanz* (1881); *Niederländische geistliche Lieder nebst ihren Singweisen aus Handschriften des 15. Jahrhunderts* (1888); and *Ein deutsches geistliches Liederbuch,* melodies from the 15th century (Leipzig, 1896).

Baur, Jürg, German composer, pianist, and choral conductor; b. Düsseldorf, Nov. 11, 1918. He studied at the Cologne Hochschule für Musik; then studied theory at the Cons. of Cologne with Philipp Jarnach, and musicology at the Univ. of Cologne with Fellerer. In 1946 he joined the faculty of the Düsseldorf Cons.; was its director from 1965 to 1976. In 1971 he succeeded Zimmermann as chairman of the composition department at the Hochschule für Musik in Cologne. The idiom of his works evolved from Lutheran neo-Classicism in the manner of Reger and Hindemith, later adopting Schoenberg's method of composition with 12 tones and eventually total serialism.
WORKS: Viola Concerto (1952); *Sinfonia montana* (1953); Concerto for Trautonium and String Quartet (1955); Concerto for Strings (1957); *Quintetto sereno* for 5 Wind Instruments (1958); *Concerto romano* for Oboe and Orch. (1960); Divertimento for Harpsichord and Percussion (1962); *Romeo and Juliet* for Orch. (1963); *Piccolo mondo* for Orch. (1963); *Dialogue* for Cello and Piano (1963); *Lo specchio* for Orch. (1966); *Pentagram* for Wind Quintet and Orch. (1966); *Abbreviations* for 13 String Instruments (1969); Piano Concerto (1970); also 3 string quartets; a song cycle to words by García Lorca; *Metamorphosen* for Piano Trio; and many choruses.

Bausch, Ludwig Christian August, celebrated violin maker; b. Naumburg, Jan. 15, 1805; d. Leipzig, May 26, 1871. He established shops for making and repairing violins in Dresden (1826), Dessau (1828), Leipzig (1839), and Wiesbaden (1862). His son **Ludwig** (b. Dessau, Nov. 10, 1829; d. Leipzig, April 7, 1871) first lived in N.Y. and later established his own violin shop in Leipzig. **Otto,** a younger son (b. Leipzig, Aug. 6, 1841; d. there, Dec. 30, 1875), inherited the business, which then passed to A. Paulus at Markneukirchen.

Bausznern, Waldemar von, German composer; b. Berlin, Nov. 29, 1866; d. Potsdam, Aug. 20, 1931. He studied music with Kiel and Bargiel in Berlin; subsequently was active mainly as a choral conductor; also taught at the Cons. of Cologne (1903–8), at the Musikhochschule in Weimar (1908–16), where he also served as director, and at the Hoch Cons. in Frankfurt, where he was a teacher and director (1916–23). He also taught at the Academy of Arts and the Academy for Church and School Music in Berlin. He was a prolific composer; wrote the operas *Dichter und Welt* (Weimar, 1897); *Dürer in Venedig* (Weimar, 1901); *Herbort und Hilde* (Mannheim, 1902); *Der Bundschuh* (Frankfurt, 1904); 8 symphs., of which the 3rd and the 5th have choral finales;

numerous sacred choral works; 4 string quartets; 2 piano quintets; 2 piano trios; 2 violin sonatas. He edited the score of the opera *Der Barbier von Bagdad* by Peter Cornelius and completed his unfinished opera *Gunlöd,* which was produced in this version in Cologne in 1906. His symphs., academically Romantic in their high-flown idiom, still retain a spark of vitality, to judge by their infrequent performances in Germany.

BIBLIOGRAPHY: G. Wehle, "Waldemar von Bausznerns sinfonisches Schaffen." *Zeitschrift fur Musikwissenschaft,* XCVIII (1931); G. Wehle, "Zum 100. Geburtstag Waldemar von Bausznern," *Musica,* XX (1966).

Bautista, Julián, Spanish composer; b. Madrid, April 21, 1901; d. Buenos Aires, July 8, 1961. He studied violin with Julio Francés, piano with Pilar Fernández de la Mora, and composition with Conrado del Campo at the Madrid Cons.; then taught there during the Spanish Civil War. After Madrid fell, Bautista fled to Argentina, where he was on the faculty of the National Cons. of Buenos Aires. His music, delicately colored and rhythmically robust, invariably reflected Spanish folk melodies.

WORKS: *Juerga,* ballet (1921); *Colores,* 6 piano pieces (1922); Sonatina for String Trio (1924); *Obertura para una ópera grotesca* for Orch. (1932); *Tres ciudades* for Voice and Orch. (1937); *4 poemas gallegos* for Voice, Flute, Oboe, Clarinet, Viola, Cello, and Harp (1946); *Sinfonia breve* (1956); Symph. No. 2 (1957); 3 string quartets; songs.

Bavicchi, John, American composer; b. Boston, April 25, 1922. He studied at the New England Cons. of Music in Boston with Carl McKinley and Francis Judd Cooke (B.M., 1952); then attended Harvard Univ. Graduate School, taking courses in theory with Archibald T. Davison, composition with Walter Piston, and musicology with Otto Gombosi (1953–56). He served in the U.S. Navy; saw action in Guadalcanal, Okinawa, and Japan (1943–45). Returning to Boston after the war, he devoted himself to teaching, composing, and conducting; led the Arlington-Belmont Chorale; lectured on music history at the Cambridge Center for Adult Education (1960–73). His music is neo-Baroque, couched in Classical forms, while presenting a variegated texture of decidedly modernistic invention.

WORKS: *Festival Symphony* for Concert Band (Massachusetts Inst. of Technology, Cambridge, Mass., Nov. 6, 1965); Symph. No. 2 for Brass Ensemble (ibid., May 28, 1976); Concert for Clarinet and String Orch. (Boston, May 14, 1958); 3 suites: No. 1, for Orch. (Cambridge, Mass., April 16, 1961); No. 2, for Wind Ensemble (Eugene, Oreg., Nov. 15, 1966); No. 3, for Concert Band (Atlanta, Georgia, Feb. 3, 1970); *Concert Overture* (Boston, Dec. 5, 1957); *Fantasy* for Harp and Chamber Orch. (New York, March 18, 1960); *Concertante No. 1* for Oboe, Bassoon, and String Orch. (Erie, Pa., Nov. 12, 1974); *Concertante No. 2* for Flute, Clarinet, and Wind Ensemble (Boston, May 5, 1976); *Summer Incident* for Chamber Orch. (Boston, Nov. 17, 1959); *Music for*

Mallets and Percussion (Warwick, R.I., Feb. 3, 1969); *Fantasia on Korean Folk Tunes* for Orch. (Brookline, Mass., June 10, 1969); 3 string quartets (1950, 1952, 1960); Quartet for 2 Trumpets and 2 Trombones (1956); 2 saxophone quartets (1965, 1969); 2 woodwind quintets (1961, 1973); 9 trios: No. 1, for Clarinet, Trombone, and Violin (1950); No. 2, for Piano, Clarinet, and Viola (1951); No. 3, for Piano, Clarinet, and Cello (1954); No. 4, for Violin, Viola, and Cello (1955); No. 5, for Piano, Clarinet, and Violin (1958); No. 6, for Flute, Viola, and Cello (1962); No. 7, for Piano and 2 Percussionists (1970); No. 8 for Piano, Violin, and Cello (1980); No. 9, for Flute, Oboe, and Cello (1980); *4 Miniatures* for Flute, Oboe, Clarinet, and Bassoon (1976); 4 violin sonatas (1956, 1958, 1960, 1971); 2 cello sonatas (1953, 1956); 2 sonatas for Clarinet Solo (1956, 1959); Sonata for Clarinet and Piano (1969); *Toccata* for Piano (1956); Piano Sonata (1959); Sonata for 2 Pianos (1953); Sonatina for Oboe and Piano (1958); Theme and Variations for Flute Solo (1979); numerous choral works; songs.

Bax, Sir Arnold (Edward Trevor), outstanding English composer; b. London, Nov. 8, 1883; d. Cork, Ireland, Oct. 3, 1953. He entered the Royal Academy of Music in 1900; studied piano with Matthay and composition with Corder there; won its Gold Medal as a pianist in 1905, the year in which he completed his studies. After a visit to Dresden in 1905, he went to Ireland. Although not ethnically Irish, he became interested in ancient Irish folklore; wrote poetry and prose under the name of Dermot O'Byrne; also found inspiration in Celtic legends for his work as a composer. In 1910 he returned to England; that same year he visited Russia, and composed a series of piano pieces in a pseudo-Russian style: *May Night in the Ukraine; Gopak; In a Vodka Shop;* etc.; also wrote music to James M. Barrie's skit *The Truth about the Russian Dancers.* In 1931 he received the Gold Medal of the Royal Phil. Society of London; was awarded honorary degrees from the Univ. of Oxford in 1934 and Durham Univ. in 1935; was knighted at the Coronation of King George VI in 1937; was made Master of the King's Musick in 1941. He was an excellent pianist, but was reluctant to play in public; he never appeared as a conductor of his own works. Bax was an extremely prolific composer; his style is rooted in neo-Romanticism, but impressionistic elements are much in evidence in his instrumental compositions; his harmony is elaborate and rich in chromatic progressions; his contrapuntal fabric is free and emphasizes complete independence of component melodies. In his many settings of folk songs, he succeeded in adapting simple melodies to effective accompaniments in modern harmonies; in his adaptations of old English songs, he successfully re-created the archaic style of the epoch. He recorded the story of his life and travels in his candid autobiography, *Farewell, My Youth* (London, 1943).

WORKS: 7 symphs.: No. 1 (1921; London, Dec. 4, 1922); No. 2 (1924–25; Boston, Dec. 13, 1929); No. 3 (1929; London, March 14, 1930); No. 4 (1930; San

Francisco, March 16, 1932); No. 5 (dedicated to Sibelius; 1931; London, Jan. 15, 1934); No. 6 (1934; London, Nov. 21, 1935); No. 7 (dedicated to the American people; 1939; N.Y., June 9, 1939).

BALLETS: *Between Dusk and Dawn* (1917); *The Truth about the Russian Dancers* (1920).

SYMPH. POEMS: *In the Faery Hills* (1909); *Christmas Eve on the Mountains* (1911–12); *Nympholept* (1912); *The Garden of Fand* (1913); *The Happy Forest* (1914; orchestrated 1921); *November Woods* (1917); *Tintagel* (1917); *Summer Music* (1920); *Mediterranean* (1920 version for Piano; orchestrated 1921).

OTHER ORCH. WORKS: 4 pieces: *Pensive Twilight; Dance in the Sun; From the Mountains of Home; Dance of Wild Irravel* (1912–13); *Scherzo sinfonico* (1913); *Romantic Overture* (1926); *Two Northern Ballads* (1927; 1933); *Overture to a Picaresque Comedy* (1930); *The Tale the Pine Trees Knew* (1931); *Overture to Adventure* (1935–36); *Rogue's Comedy Overture* (1935–36); *London Pageant* (1937–38); *A Legend* (1944); *Coronation March* (1953).

INSTRUMENTAL WORKS WITH ORCH.: *Symphonic Variations* for Piano and Orch. (1917); *Phantasy* for Viola and Orch. (1920); Cello Concerto (1932); Violin Concerto (1937–38); Concertante for Piano, left-hand (1948–49).

VOCAL MUSIC: *Fatherland* for Tenor, Chorus, and Orch. (1906–7); *Enchanted Summer* (from Shelley's *Prometheus Unbound*) for 2 Sopranos, Chorus, and Orch. (1910); *The Bard of the Dimbovitza*, 6 poems for Voice and Orch. (1914); *Mater Ora Filium*, motet (1921); *Of a Rose I Sing a Song* for Small Chorus, Harp, Cello, and Double Bass (1921); *Now Is the Time of Christymas* for Male Voices, Flute, and Piano (1921); *This Worlde's Joie*, motet (1922); *To the Name above Every Name* for Chorus and Orch. (1923); *The Boar's Head*, carol for Male Voices (1923); *St. Patrick's Breastplate* for Chorus and Orch. (1923); *Walsinghame* for Tenor, Chorus, and Orch. (1926); *I Sing of a Maiden* for 5-part Small Chorus (1928); *The Morning Watch* for Chorus and Orch. (1935–36); also many solo songs.

CHAMBER MUSIC: 3 string quartets (1916; 1924–25; 1935–36); Piano Quintet (1915); Quintet for Strings and Harp (1919); Quintet for Oboe and Strings (1922); String Quintet (1930); also Trio for Flute, Viola, and Harp (1916); *An Irish Elegy* for English Horn, Harp, and String Quartet (1916); Nonet for Flute, Oboe, Clarinet, Harp, and String Quintet (1930); Octet for Horn, Piano, and String Sextet (1934); Concerto for Flute, Oboe, Harp, and String Quartet (1934); Threnody and Scherzo for Bassoon, Harp, and String Sextet (1935–36); additional works include 3 violin sonatas (1910; 1915; 1927); 2 viola sonatas (1922; 2nd with Harp, known as the *Fantasy* sonata, 1924–25); Cello Sonata (1923); *Legend Sonata* for Cello and Piano (1943); also 6 piano sonatas: No. 1 (1897–98); No. 2 (1910); No. 3 (2 movements only, 1913); No. 4 (1919); No. 5 (1926); No. 6 (1932); Clarinet Sonata (1934); works for 2 pianos, etc.

BIBLIOGRAPHY: E. Evans, "Arnold Bax," *The Musical Quarterly* (April 1923); R. Hull, *A Handbook on Arnold Bax's Symphonies* (London, 1932); A. Fleischmann, "Arnold Bax," *Recorded Sound* (Jan./April 1968); R. Foreman, "Bibliography of Writings on Arnold Bax," *Current Musicology* 10 (1970); R. Foreman, "The Musical Development of Arnold Bax," *Music and Letters* (Jan. 1971); C. Scott-Sutherland, *Arnold Bax* (London, 1973).

Bay, Emmanuel, Russian pianist; b. Simferopol, Crimea, Jan. 20, 1891; d. Jerusalem, Dec. 2, 1967. His father was cantor in the Lodz synagogue in Poland; in 1908 Bay enrolled at the St. Petersburg Cons., studying piano with Drosdov; graduated in 1913 with first prize. He subsequently took a master class in piano with Leopold Godowsky in Vienna. He became mainly known as an excellent accompanist; toured in that capacity with Efrem Zimbalist (1922–29) and with Jascha Heifetz (1931–51); also was accompanist to Mischa Elman, Nathan Milstein, Zino Francescatti, Joseph Szigeti, Gregor Piatigorsky, Jan Peerce, and Helen Traubel. He died of a heart attack on a trip to Israel.

Bayer, Josef, Austrian composer and conductor; b. Vienna, March 6, 1852; d. there, March 12, 1913. He studied at the Vienna Cons. (1859–70) with Georg and Josef Hellmesberger (violin), Dachs (piano), and Bruckner (theory). He wrote a great number of operettas and ballets which were quite popular owing to his facility for melodic writing and piquant rhythms. He traveled a great deal through Europe as a conductor; visited N.Y. in 1881, and conducted there the first performance of his operetta *Chevalier von San Marco* on Feb. 4, 1881. Other operettas successfully produced in Vienna were *Menelaus* (1892), *Fräulein Hexe* (1898), *Der Polizeichef* (1904); he also wrote 2 exotic comic operas: *Alien Fata*, on a Bosnian subject, and *Der Goldasoka*, on a Hindu theme. The list of his ballets includes the following, produced in Vienna: *Wiener Waltzer* (1886); *Die Puppenfee* (1888); *Sonne und Erde* (1889); *Ein Tanzmärchen* (1890); *Rouge et Noir* (1892); *Die Donaunixe* (1892); *Eine Hochzeit in Bosnien* (1893, with Bosnian folk melodies); *Burschenliebe* (1894); *Rund um Wien* (1894); *Die Braut von Korea* (1896); *Die kleine Welt* (1904); ballets produced at Berlin: *Deutsche Märsche* (1887); *Die Welt in Bild und Tanz* (1892); *Die Engelsjäger* (1896); *Columbia* (1893).

Bayle, François, French composer; b. Tamatabe, Madagascar, April 27, 1932. He studied academic sciences and music in France; was a student in composition of Olivier Messiaen, and with Pierre Schaeffer, whose Groupe de Recherches Musicales he joined in 1966. His works are mostly montages, collages, and acoustical barrages. He constructed the following musical compositions: *Points critiques* for Horn, Piano, Cello, and Percussion (1960); *Pluriel* for 19 Instruments and Loudspeakers (1963); *L'Oiseau chanteur,* musique concrète (1963); *Espaces inevitables,* musique concrète (1967); *L'Experience acoustique,* musique concrète (1970–77).

Bayoras, Feliksas, Lithuanian composer; b. Alitus, Oct. 7, 1934. He studied at the Lithuanian Cons. in

Vilna; in 1965 he was appointed music director of the Youth Theater there. He composed 3 symphs. (1969, 1970, 1972); a Symph. for Strings (1970); *Green March* for Military Band (1968); some chamber music; and a number of piano pieces and songs, mostly inspired by Lithuanian subjects.

Bazelaire, Paul, French cellist and composer; b. Sedan, March 4, 1886; d. Paris, Dec. 11, 1958. He graduated from the Paris Cons. as a cellist at the age of 11, with the Premier Prix; after a concert career became prof. of cello at the Paris Cons. (1918–56); founded a unique ensemble of 50 cellos.
WORKS: *Suite française sur des chants populaires* for Orch.; symph. poem, *Cléopâtre* (Paris, Jan. 23, 1908); *Suite grecque* for Small Orch. (1910); *Rapsodie dans le style russe* for Cello and Orch. (Paris, Feb. 2, 1941). He orchestrated Bach's 6 Cello Suites; publ. a teaching manual, *Pédagogie du violoncelle.*

Bazelon, Irwin (Allen), American composer; b. Evanston, Ill., June 4, 1922. He took piano lessons with Irving Harris and Magdalen Messmann; studied composition with Leon Stein. He received his B.A. degree from De Paul Univ. in Chicago in 1945 and his M.A. degree in 1946; then took composition lessons with Hindemith at Yale Univ., with Darius Milhaud at Mills College in Oakland, Calif. (1946–48), and with Ernest Bloch at the Univ. of Calif. in Berkeley (1947). In 1948 he settled in N.Y. and earned a living by writing commercial jingles; also contributed incidental music for Shakespeare plays produced at the American Shakespeare Theater in Stratford, Conn. In his compositions he makes use of quaquaversal techniques, ranging from rudimentary triadic progressions to complex dodecaphonic structures; rhythmically, he likes to inject jazz syncopation. He publ. *Knowing the Score: Notes on Film Music* in 1975.
WORKS: 7 symphs.: No. 1 (1960; Kansas City, Nov. 29, 1963); No. 2, subtitled *Short Symphony* (Washington, D.C., Dec. 4, 1962); No. 3 for Brass, Percussion, Piano, and String Sextet (1963); No. 4 (1965; first movement perf. under the title *Dramatic Movement for Orch.,* Seattle, Feb. 21, 1966); No. 5 (1966; Indianapolis, May 9, 1970); No. 6 (Kansas City, Nov. 17, 1970); No. 7, subtitled *Ballet for Orch.* (1980); *Suite* for Clarinet, Cello, and Piano (1947); *Ballet Suite* for Chamber Ensemble (1949); *Concert Overture* (1952; revised 1960); *Adagio and Fugue* for String Orch. (1952); *Movimento da camera* for Flute, Bassoon, Horn, and Harpsichord (1954); *Chamber Symphony* for 7 Instruments (1957); *Suite* from *The Merry Wives of Windsor* (1958); *Overture to The Taming of the Shrew* (1960); *Ballet Centauri 17* for Orch. (1960); *Symphonie concertante* for Clarinet, Trumpet, Marimba, and Orch. (1963); Brass Quintet (1963); *Early American Suite* for Flute, Oboe, Clarinet, Bassoon, Horn, and Harpsichord or Piano (1965–75); *Excursion* for Orch. (Kansas City, March 5, 1966); *Churchill Downs* (Chamber Concerto No. 2; 1970); *Dramatic Fanfare* for Orch. (Cleveland, June 23, 1970); *Duo* for Viola and Piano (1970); *Concerto for 14 Players* (N.Y., May 16, 1971); *Propulsions,* concerto for 7 Percussionists 1974); Woodwind Quintet (N.Y., May 22, 1975); *A Quiet Piece for a Violent Time* for Chamber Orch. (New Orleans, Oct. 28, 1975); *Spirits of the Night* for Orch. (1976); *Concatenations* for Percussion Quartet and Viola (1976); *Double-Crossings* for Trumpet and Percussion (Boston, Dec. 5, 1976); *Triple Play* for 2 Trombones and Solo Percussion (1977); *Sound Dreams* for 6 Instruments (Boston, Nov. 13., 1977); *Cross-Currents* for Brass Quintet and Percussion (1978); *Imprints* for Piano (1978); *Junctures* for Orch. (1979); *De-Tonations* for Brass Quintet and Orch. (N.Y., April 3, 1979); *3 Men on a Discourse* for Clarinet, Cello, and Solo Percussion (1979; N.Y., April 9, 1980); *Partnership* for 5 Timpani and Marimba (N.Y., May 19, 1980); *Memories of a Winter Childhood* for an Instrumental Group (1981); *Spires* for Trumpet and Orch. (1981); *Tides* for Clarinet and Orch. (1982); *Re-Percussions* for 2 Pianos (1982); *Fusions* (Chamber Concerto No. 3; 1983; Washington, D.C., Oct. 22, 1984); Piano Concerto (1983–84); 2 string quartets; 3 piano sonatas; chamber music.
BIBLIOGRAPHY: David Ewen, *American Composers* (N.Y., 1982).

Bazin, François-Emmanuel-Joseph, French composer; b. Marseilles, Sept. 4, 1816; d. Paris, July 2, 1878. He studied with Berton and Halévy at the Paris Cons.; was awarded the Prix de Rome in 1840; in 1844 he was appointed to the faculty of the Paris Cons. He wrote 8 comic operas, none of which was retained in the repertoire, although *Le Voyage en Chine,* produced in 1865, was temporarily acclaimed. He also publ. a manual, *Cours d'harmonie théorique et pratique,* which was adopted at the Paris Cons.

Bázlik, Miroslav, Slovak composer and pianist; b. Partizánská Lupča, April 12, 1931. He studied piano at the Bratislava Cons., and became an accomplished concert pianist; then took a course in composition with Cikker at the Bratislava Academy of Musical Arts, graduating in 1961. His musical idiom evolved along modern Romantic lines; in his later compositions he resorts to serial techniques.
WORKS: Opera, after Rolland, *Petr a Lucie* (1962–66; Bratislava, 1967); *Dvanást' (The Twelve),* oratorio after the poem of Alexander Blok (1967; Bratislava, Nov. 4, 1976); *Baroque Suite* for Small Orch. (1958); *5 Songs on Chinese Poetry* for Contralto, Flute, Piano, and Cello (1960); *Music for Violin and Orch.* (1961); *3 Pieces* for 14 Instruments (1964); *Music for Poetry* for Nonet, Harp, and Vibraphone (1966); *Bagatelles* for String Orch. or String Quartet (1972); *Pastorale* for Woodwinds and Harpsichord (1972); *Cantata without Words* for Mezzo-soprano, Madrigal Ensemble, and Chamber Orch. (1972); String Quartet (1974); Piano Sonata (1954); *Palette,* 5 bagatelles for Piano (1956).

Bazzini, Antonio, Italian violinist and composer; b. Brescia, March 11, 1818; d. Milan, Feb. 10, 1897.

Encouraged by Paganini, before whom he played in 1836, Bazzini embarked upon a series of successful tours through Italy, France, Spain, Belgium, Poland, England, and Germany (1837–63); taught at the Milan Cons. from 1873, and in 1882 became its director.

WORKS: *Turanda,* opera after Gozzi's *Turandot* (La Scala, Milan, Jan. 13, 1867); *Francesca da Rimini,* symph. poem (1890); symph. overtures to Alfieri's *Saul* (1866) and to Shakespeare's *King Lear* (1868); numerous violin pieces, of which *Ronde des lutins* became extremely popular.

Beach, Mrs. H.H.A. (maiden name, **Amy Marcy Cheney**), American composer; b. Henniker, N.H., Sept. 5, 1867; d. New York, Dec. 27, 1944. She was descended of early New England colonists, and was a scion of a cultural family. She entered a private school in Boston; studied piano with Ernest Perabo and Carl Baermann; received instruction in harmony from Junius W. Hill. She made her debut as a pianist in Boston on Oct. 24, 1883, playing a piano concerto by Moscheles with an orchestra. On Dec. 3, 1885, at the age of 18, she married Dr. H.H.A. Beach, a Boston surgeon, a quarter of a century older than she was. The marriage was a happy one, and as a token of her loyalty to her husband, see used as her professional name Mrs. H.H.A. Beach. She began to compose modestly, mostly for piano, but soon embarked on an ambitious project, a Mass, which was performed by the Handel and Haydn Society in Boston on Feb. 18, 1892; she was the first woman to have a composition performed by that organization. On Oct. 30, 1896, her *Gaelic Symphony,* based on Irish folk tunes, was performed by the Boston Symph. with exceptional success. In 1897 she played her Violin Sonata with Franz Kneisel. On April 6, 1900, she appeared as the soloist with the Boston Symph. in the first performance of her Piano Concerto. She also wrote a great many songs in an endearing Romantic manner. Her husband died in 1910, and Mrs. Beach decided to go to Europe; she played her works in Berlin, Leipzig, and Hamburg, attracting considerable attention as the first of her sex and national origin to be able to compose music of a European quality of excellence. She returned to the U.S. in 1914 and lived in N.Y. Her music, unpretentious in its idiom and epigonic in its historical aspect, retained its importance as the work of a pioneer woman composer in America.

WORKS: Mass in E flat (Boston, Feb. 18, 1892); *Gaelic Symphony* (Boston, Oct. 30, 1896); Piano Concerto (Boston, April 6, 1900). Cantatas: *The Minstrel and the King; Festival Jubilate; The Chambered Nautilus; Canticles of the Sun; Christ in the Universe; The Rose of Avontown, Sylvania; The Sea Fairies.* Chamber music: Violin Sonata (1896); Piano Quintet (1908); String Quartet (1929); Piano Trio (1938). For Piano: *Valse-Caprice; Ballad; 4 Sketches; Hermit Thrush at Morn; Nocturne; 5 Improvisations; Variations on Balkan Themes* for 2 Pianos.

BIBLIOGRAPHY: Percy Goetschius, *Mrs. H.H.A. Beach, Analytical Sketch* (Boston, 1906; contains contemporary reviews and a catalog); David Ewen, *American Composers* (N.Y., 1982).

Beach, John Parsons, American composer; b. Gloversville, N.Y., Oct. 11, 1877; d. Pasadena, Calif., Nov. 6, 1953. He studied piano at the New England Cons. in Boston; then went to Europe, where he took lessons with Gédalge in Paris and Malipiero in Venice. Returning to Boston, he took additional lessons with Loeffler. He held various teaching jobs; finally settled in Pasadena. His opera *Pippa's Holiday* was performed in Paris in 1915, and his ballet *Phantom Satyr* was given in Asolo, Italy, July 6, 1925; another ballet, *Mardi Gras,* was staged in New Orleans (Feb. 15, 1926). His orch. works include *New Orleans Street Cries* (Philadelphia, April 22, 1927; Stokowski conducting); *Asolani* (Minneapolis, Nov. 12, 1926); *Angelo's Letter* for Tenor and Chamber Orch. (N.Y., Feb. 27, 1929). He also composed *Naïve Landscapes* for Piano, Flute, Oboe, and Clarinet (1917); *Poem* for String Quartet (1920); *Concert* for Violin, Viola, Cello, Flute, Oboe, and Clarinet (1929); many songs.

Beale, Frederic Fleming, American organist and composer; b. Troy, Kans., July 13, 1876; d. Caldwell, Idaho, Feb. 16, 1948. He studied in Chicago with Adolf Weidig and Wilhelm Middelschulte; was a church organist in Chicago; taught piano at the Univ. of Washington, Seattle; in 1939 was appointed director of music at the College of Idaho at Caldwell. He wrote 3 operettas: *The Magic Wheel, Fatima,* and *Poor Richard; Dance-Caprice* for Orch.; numerous songs.

Beale, William, English organist and composer; b. Landrake, Cornwall, Jan. 1, 1784; d. London, May 3, 1854. His early training was as a chorister in Westminster Abbey; he then studied with Dr. Arnold and Robert Cooke. In 1813 his madrigal *Awake, sweet Muse* was awarded first prize by the London Madrigal Society; collections of his glees and madrigals were published in 1815 and 1820. From 1816–20 Beale was one of the Gentlemen of the Chapel Royal; served as organist of Trinity College, Cambridge (1820), Wandsworth Parish Church (1821), and St. John's, Clapham Rise.

Bean, Hugh, English violinist; b. Beckenham, Sept. 22, 1929. He began to study violin with his father; then took formal lessons with Albert Sammons; subsequently enrolled in the Royal College of Music in London and in the Brussels Cons., where he received prizes for both solo violin and chamber music playing. In 1953 he became a prof. of violin at the Royal College of Music; concurrently played in orchs.; joined the Philharmonia Orch. in 1956, becoming its concertmaster in 1957; then served as 2nd concertmaster of the BBC Symph. Orch. (1967–69). He was made a Commander of the Order of the British Empire in 1970.

Beard, John, renowned English tenor; b. c.1717; d. Hampton, Feb. 5, 1791. He studied with Bernard Gates at the Chapel Royal; while still a youth, he sang in Handel's *Esther* in London (1732). He left the Chapel Royal in 1734; on Nov. 9, 1734, he made his debut as Silvio in Handel's *Il Pastor fido* at Covent Garden; he subsequently appeared in about 10 operas, many oratorios, masques, and odes by Handel. In 1761 he became manager of Covent Garden, but continued to make appearances as a singer; he retired in 1767 owing to increasing deafness.

Beardslee, Bethany, American soprano; b. Lansing, Mich., Dec. 25, 1927. She studied at Michigan State Univ.; then received a scholarship to the Juilliard School of Music in N.Y.; she soon became known as a specialist in modern music, evolving an extraordinary technique with a flutelike ability to sound impeccably precise intonation; she mastered the art of *Sprechstimme,* which enabled her to give fine renditions of such works as Schoenberg's *Pierrot Lunaire;* she also was a brilliant performer of vocal parts in scores by Alban Berg, Anton von Webern, and Stravinsky. In 1976 she joined the faculty of Westminster Choir College; in 1981–82 was a prof. of music at the Univ. of Texas in Austin. She married the composer **Godfrey Winham** in 1960.

Beaton, Isabella, American pianist; b. Grinnell, Iowa, May 20, 1870; d. Mt. Pleasant, Henry County, Iowa, Jan. 19, 1929. She studied in Berlin with Moszkowski (1894–99); received her M.A. and Ph.B. from Western Reserve Univ. (1902); taught many private pupils in Cleveland (1910–19); also gave recitals. She wrote an opera, *Anacoana;* a Symph.; a Scherzo and piano pieces.

Beattie, Herbert, American bass; b. Chicago, Aug. 25, 1926. He studied voice at the American Cons. of Music in Chicago; made his operatic debut with the N.Y. City Opera in 1958 as Baron Douphol in *La Traviata;* also sang in Baltimore, San Francisco, Boston, and New Orleans. For several years he taught voice at Hofstra Univ.

Beaulieu (real name, **Martin-Beaulieu**), **Marie-Désiré,** French composer and author; b. Paris, April 11, 1791; d. Niort, Dec. 21, 1863. He studied violin with Kreutzer, composition with Benincori and Abbé Roze; then studied with Méhul at the Paris Cons.; won the Prix de Rome in 1810; wrote the operas *Anacréon* and *Philadelphie;* the oratorios *L'Hymne du matin, L'Hymne de la nuit,* etc.; also other sacred music, as well as secular songs. He publ. the essays: *Du rythme, des effets qu'il produit et de leurs causes* (1852); *Mémoire sur ce qui reste de la musique de l'ancienne Grèce dans les premiers chants de l'Eglise* (1852); *Mémoire sur le caractère que doit avoir la musique de l'Eglise* (1858); *Mémoire sur l'origine de la musique* (1859). His main contribution to French musical culture was his organizing of annual music festivals in provincial towns; founded the Association Musicale de l'Ouest in 1835, and the Societé des Concerts de Chant Classique in 1860, to which he bequeathed 100,000 francs.

Beauvarlet-Charpentier, Jean-Jacques, famous French organist; b. Abbeville, June 28, 1734; d. Paris, May 6, 1794. His father was organist of the Hospice de la Charité in Lyons; his mother was the singer **Marie Birol,** who appeared on the stage under the name Marie Beauvarlet-Charpentier. He succeeded his father as organist in Lyons; from 1763–71 he made appearances there at the Académie des Beaux Arts. He first played in Paris at a Concert Spirituel in 1759; in 1771 he was called to Paris as organist of the Royal Abbey of St. Victor; in 1772 he became organist at St. Paul, and also at St. Eloi des Orfèvres (from 1777) and Notre Dame (from 1783; with 3 other organists). He was also a composer, but his music attracted little notice. His son, **Jacques-Marie Beauvarlet-Charpentier** (b. Lyons, July 3, 1766; d. Paris, Sept. 7, 1834), was also an organist and composer.

Bécaud, Gilbert, French composer of popular songs; b. Toulon, Oct. 24, 1927. His real name was François Silly (sic; pronounced with the stress on the second syllable, and so not necessarily silly). He studied at Toulon and Nice; began to write his chansons at 19. On Dec. 20, 1952, he made his debut as a chansonnier in Versailles, where he was featured as "Monsieur 100,000 Volts." With this electric sobriquet and a moderately winning smile he launched a highly lucrative career, singing his own songs with his own piano accompaniments; in 1953 he produced his first big hit, *Quand tu danses;* other successful songs were *Le Jour où la pluie viendra, Viens danser, Plein soleil,* and *L'Orange.* He was piano accompanist to Edith Piaf on her American tours. Apart from his popular songs, he tried his hand at serious music; composed a cantata, *L'Enfant à l'Étoile* (Paris, Jan. 7, 1962), and *Opéra d'Aran* (Paris, Oct. 22, 1962).

Becerra Schmidt, Gustavo, Chilean composer; b. Temuco, Aug. 26, 1925. He studied at the Santiago Cons., first with Pedro Allende, and then with Domingo Santa Cruz; from 1953 to 1956 he traveled in Europe; from 1968 to 1970 he served as cultural attaché to the Chilean embassy in Bonn. In 1971 he received the Premio Nacional de Arte in music. His early works are set in the traditional manner of neo-Classical composition, but soon he adopted an extremely radical modern idiom, incorporating dodecaphonic and aleatory procedures and outlining a graphic system of notation, following the pictorial representation of musical sounds of the European avant-garde, but introducing some new elements, such as indication of relative loudness by increasing the size of the notes on a music staff with lines far apart. His works include the opera *La muerte de Don Rodrigo* (1958); 3 symphonies (1955, 1958, 1960); oratorios, *La Araucana* (1965) and *Lord Cochrane de Chile* (1967); Violin Concerto (1950); Flute Concerto (1957); Piano Concerto (1958); 4 guitar concertos (1964–70); Concerto for Oboe, Clarinet, and Bassoon, with String Orch. (1970); 7 string quartets; Saxophone Quartet; 3 violin sonatas; Viola Sonata; 3 cello sonatas; Sonata for Double Bass and

Piano; pieces for solo oboe and solo trombone; numerous choral works. A special issue of *Revista Musical Chilena* (1972), dedicated to Becerra Schmidt, contains a complete catalogue of his works.

Becher, Alfred Julius, English composer and music critic, who became a martyr of the revolutionary movement in 1848; b. Manchester, April 27, 1803; d. Vienna (executed), Nov. 23, 1848. He studied in Germany; in 1841 went to Vienna; in 1848 he began issuing the revolutionary paper *Der Radikale,* and that same year was arrested for treason and shot. He published a monograph on Jenny Lind, in German (Vienna, 1846); he also wrote a Symph., some chamber music, and songs.
BIBLIOGRAPHY: H. Ullrich, "Alfred Julius Becher (1803–1848) als Komponist," *Beiträge zur Musikwissenschaft,* XIII/3 (1971).

Becher, Josef, German composer; b. Neukirchen, Bavaria, Aug. 1, 1821; d. Mintraching, Sept. 23, 1888. He was a pastor in Mintraching; wrote 60 masses and other sacred music.

Bechet, Sidney, famous black American jazz clarinetist and soprano saxophonist; b. New Orleans, May 14, 1897; d. Garches, France, May 14, 1959. He took up the clarinet when he was 6 years old; learned to play blues and rags in black honky-tonks in Storyville, the brothel district of New Orleans; after playing with many of the leading jazz musicians in New Orleans and on tour, he went to Chicago in 1917; settled in N.Y. in 1919. He made tours to London and Paris; then led his own band in N.Y.; later worked with Noble Sissle, Duke Ellington, Tommy Ladnier, and Zutty Singleton. During the 1940s he led his own jazz groups in N.Y.; in 1947 he settled in Paris. He was one of the most important jazz musicians of his era, highly acclaimed as the master of the soprano saxophone. He publ. an autobiography, *Treat It Gentle* (N.Y., 1960).
BIBLIOGRAPHY: R. Mouly, *Sidney Bechet* (Paris, 1959).

Bechgaard, Julius, Danish composer; b. Copenhagen, Dec. 19, 1843; d. there, March 4, 1917. He studied at the Leipzig Cons. and with Gade in Copenhagen; lived in Germany, Italy, and Paris; then settled in Copenhagen. He wrote 2 operas: *Frode* (Copenhagen, May 11, 1893) and *Frau Inge* (Prague, 1894); many piano pieces and songs.

Bechi, Gino, Italian baritone; b. Florence, Oct. 16, 1913. He was educated at the Florence Cons.; then sang at the Rome Opera (1937) and at La Scala in Milan. He soon established himself as one of the leading Italian baritones of the day. After World War II, he appeared in many European music centers; also was well known in South America. He retired in 1965; then taught voice; also produced opera.

Bechler, Johann Christian, composer; b. island of Oesel, in the Baltic Sea, Jan. 7, 1784; d. Herrnhut, Saxony, April 15, 1857. He came to the U.S. in 1806 and became a prof. of theology at the seminary in Nazareth, Pa.; served as deacon, principal, and pastor in Philadelphia; returned to Europe in 1836 as a bishop, and was for some years active in Sarepta and Astrakhan, Russia. Bechler was one of the Moravians active in Pennsylvania. His works, which include anthems, hymns, and ariettas, are interesting more from a historical than a musical standpoint.
BIBLIOGRAPHY: A.G. Rau and H.T. David, *A Catalogue of Music by American Moravians, 1742–1842* (Bethlehem, Pa., 1938).

Bechstein, (Friedrich Wilhelm) Carl, German piano manufacturer; b. Gotha, June 1, 1826; d. Berlin, March 6, 1900. He worked in German factories; also in London; in 1853 set up a modest shop in Berlin; constructed his first grand piano in 1856; established branches in France, Russia, and England. After World War I, the London branch continued under the direction of C. Bechstein, grandson of the founder; after his death (1931), it became an independent British firm, Bechstein Piano Co., Ltd. The Bechstein piano possesses a particularly harmonious tone, capable of producing a mellifluous cantilena; for many years it was a favorite instrument of pianists of the Romantic school.
BIBLIOGRAPHY: *Bechstein-Chronik* (Berlin, 1926); Count du Moulin-Eckart, *Neue Briefe Hans von Bülow* (containing correspondence with Bechstein; Munich, 1927; Eng. trans., 1931); W. Huschke, "Zur Herkunft des Klavierbauers Carl Bechstein," *Genealogie* (1969), pp. 709–14.

Beck, Conrad, distinguished Swiss composer; b. Lohn, near Schaffhausen, June 16, 1901. He studied at the Zürich Cons. with Andreae, and in Paris with Ernst Lévy; lived in Paris and Berlin; settled in Basel in 1932 and became a radio conductor there. In 1939 he was appointed director of the music section of Radio Basel; resigned in 1966. A prolific composer, Beck adopted a neo-Classical style, rich in contrapuntal texture. Several of his works were featured at the festivals of the International Society for Contemporary Music, among them the overture *Innominata* (Vienna, June 16, 1932) and Chamber Cantata (Warsaw, April 15, 1939). He wrote 7 symphs. (1925–58; Symph. No. 7, subtitled *Aeneas-Silvius,* was first performed in Zürich, Feb. 25, 1958); *Lyric Cantata* (Munich, May 22, 1931); Piano Concerto (1933); *Konzertmusik* for Oboe and String Orch. (Basel, April 30, 1933); Chamber Concerto for Cembalo and String Orch. (Basel, Nov. 27, 1942); Viola Concerto (1949); oratorio *Der Tod zu Basel* (Basel, May 22, 1953); Concertino for Clarinet, Bassoon, and Orch. (1954); Christmas motet, *Es kommt ein Schiff geladen; Die Sonnenfinsternis,* cantata (Lucerne, Aug. 25, 1967); Clarinet Concerto (1968); *Fantasie* for Orch. (1969); *Sonata a quattro* for Violin, Flute, Oboe, and Bassoon (1970); 4 string quartets; 2 violin sonatas; 2 cello sonatas; 2 string trios;

piano music; choral works.

BIBLIOGRAPHY: Willi Schuh, *Schweizer Musik der Gegenwart* (Zürich, 1948); W. Schuh and D. Larese, *Conrad Beck: Eine Lebensskizze: Der Komponist und sein Werk* (Amriswil, 1972).

Beck, Franz, German violinist and composer; b. Mannheim, Feb. 20, 1734; d. Bordeaux, Dec. 31, 1809. He studied violin with his father and also had some instruction from Johann Stamitz. About 1750 he went to Italy; in 1761 he settled in Bordeaux, where he conducted at the Grand Théâtre. In 1783 he visited Paris to hear the first performance of his *Stabat Mater*. His works include 24 symphs.; several string quartets; piano sonatas; and church music; also 3 operas: *La Belle Jardinière* (Bordeaux, Aug. 24, 1767); *Pandora* (Paris, July 2, 1789); and *L'Ile déserte* (not produced).

BIBLIOGRAPHY: R. Sondheimer, "Die Sinfonien Franz Becks," *Zeitschrift für Musikwissenschaft*, IV (1922).

Beck, Hermann, German musicologist; b. Munich, July 20, 1929; d. Regensburg, Oct. 7, 1980. He studied at the univs. of Erlangen, Freiburg im Breisgau, and Basel; obtained his Ph.D. with the dissertation *Studien über das Tempoproblem bei Beethoven* (1954). From 1954 to 1968 he was on the faculty at the Univ. of Würzburg; in 1968 became prof. at Regensburg Univ. He publ. *Die Suite* (Cologne, 1964; Eng. ed., 1968) and *Die venezianische Musikerschule im 16. Jahrhundert* (Wilhelmshaven, 1968); contributed numerous investigative articles to German music magazines.

Beck, Jean-Baptiste, Alsatian-American musicologist; b. Gebweiler, Aug. 14, 1881; d. Philadelphia, June 23, 1943. He studied organ; received his Dr.Phil. at Strasbourg Univ. with the thesis *Die Melodien der Troubadours und Trouvères* (1908); later publ. a somewhat popularized edition of it in French, *La Musique des Troubadours* (Paris, 1910). Beck taught at the Univ. of Illinois from 1911 to 1914; then at Bryn Mawr College from 1914 to 1920. He settled in Philadelphia, where he taught at the Univ. of Pa., and from 1920 he taught at the Curtis Inst. In 1927 he initiated a project of publishing a *Corpus Cantilenarum Medii Aevi*, in 52 vols., but was able to bring out only 4 vols., under the subtitle *Les Chansonniers des troubadours et des trouvères* (all in French), containing phototype reproductions of medieval manuscripts, transcriptions in modern notation, and commentary: *Le Chansonnier cangé* (2 vols.; Philadelphia, 1927); *Le Manuscrit du roi* (2 vols.; Philadelphia, 1938). Among his other important writings is an essay, "Der Takt in den Musikaufzeichnungen des XII. und XIII. Jahrhunderts," *Riemann Festschrift* (1909). Beck was an outstanding scholar of medieval vocal music; his application of the modal rhythm of the polyphony of that time to the troubadour melodies was an important contribution to the problem of proper transcription into modern notation.

Beck, Johann Heinrich, American conductor and composer; b. Cleveland, Sept. 12, 1856; d. there, May 26, 1924. He was a pupil of Reinecke and Jadassohn at the Leipzig Cons. (1879–82), subsequently returning to America. In 1895 he was appointed conductor of the Detroit Symph. Orch., and from 1901–12 was conductor of the Cleveland Pops Orch.

WORKS: *Moorish Serenade* for Orch. (1889); a cantata, *Deukalion;* String Quartet; String Sextet; Overture to Byron's *Lara; Aus meinem Leben,* symph. poem; miscellaneous pieces for various instruments.

Beck, Johann Nepomuk, Hungarian singer; b. Budapest, May 5, 1827; d. Pressburg, April 9, 1904. His dramatic baritone voice was "discovered" in Budapest, where he made his professional debut; he then sang in Vienna, Frankfurt, and many other German cities; was a member of the court opera in Vienna from 1853; retired in 1885; died insane.

Beck, John Ness, American composer; b. Warren, Ohio, Nov. 11, 1930. He studied composition at Ohio State Univ. and subsequently taught harmony and theory there, resigning later to assume the management of a retail sheet music business in Columbus, Ohio. He has written mainly sacred choral works, among them *Upon This Rock, Hymn for Our Time, Canticle of Praise, Hymn for Easter Day, Litany of Thanksgiving,* and *Exhortation.* Other compositions include *5 Carol Fantasies* for Piano (1970); Sonata for Flute and Piano; pieces for concert band.

Beck, Karl, Austrian tenor; b. 1814; d. Vienna, March 3, 1879. He was the first to sing the role of Lohengrin (Weimar, Aug. 28, 1850).

Beck, Karl, German-American conductor; b. Ilmenau, Thuringia, April 26, 1850; d. San Antonio, Texas, Oct. 2, 1920. He came to the U.S. in 1875; toured with an opera company; in 1884 he moved to San Antonio, where he was appointed conductor of the Beethoven Society, a male chorus; he also organized an excellent military band. He was a confirmed Wagnerite, and conducted the first Texas performances of several Wagner works.

Beck, Martha, American composer; b. Sodaville, Oreg., Jan. 19, 1900. She studied at the American Cons. in Chicago; eventually she settled in Troy, N.Y., as a piano teacher. She publ. a number of piano pieces with exotic titles such as *Chinese Holiday* and *In Old Japan.*

Beck, Sydney, American music librarian; b. New York, Sept. 2, 1906. He studied at the College of the City Univ. of N.Y., at N.Y. Univ., at the Inst. of Musical Art, and at the Mannes College of Music; during this period he took courses in violin and composition with Wagenaar and Weisse, and in musicology with Sachs and Reese. In 1931 he became head of the Rare Book and Manuscript Collections of the N.Y. Public Library, holding this post until 1968. He also taught at the Mannes College of Music (1950–68). In 1968 he was appointed director of libraries at the New England Cons. of Music in Boston. He prepared editions of works by F. Geminiani and J.M. Leclair.

Beck, Thomas Ludvigsen, Norwegian composer; b. Horten, Dec. 5, 1899; d. Olso, Sept. 9, 1963. He studied piano, organ, and composition at the Oslo Cons.; also took a course of music theory in Leipzig. From 1930 until his death he was active as organist, choral conductor, and music teacher in Oslo; was a member of the board of the Society of Norwegian Composers (1938–46). He wrote many cantatas, among which are *Arnljot Gjelline* (1937), *Höifjell* (*In the Mountains;* 1945; Oslo, 1946), and *Heilag framtid* (*Holy Future;* Oslo, 1954); *Ballad on a Norwegian Folk Tune* for Orch. (Oslo, 1940); *3 Dances from Gudbrandsdal* for Orch. (Oslo, April 28, 1946); *Andante* for String Orch.; *Intrada* for Orch. or Piano; choruses; songs; film music.

Becker, Albert (Ernst Anton), German composer; b. Quedlinburg, June 13, 1834; d. Berlin, Jan. 10, 1899. He was a pupil of Dehn in Berlin (1853–56); was appointed teacher of composition at the Scharwenka Cons. (1881), and became the conductor of the Berlin Cathedral Choir (1891). His Symph. in G minor was awarded the prize of the Gesellschaft der Musikfreunde in Vienna (1861); he also wrote an opera, *Loreley* (1898), cantatas, and a number of sacred works.

Becker, Carl Ferdinand, German organist and bibliographer; b. Leipzig, July 17, 1804; d. there, Oct. 26, 1877. He studied at the Thomasschule in Leipzig; then played violin in the Gewandhaus Orch. there (1820–33); subsequently was organist at the Peterskirche and the Nikolaikirche. In 1843 he became the first prof. of organ at the new Leipzig Cons. under Mendelssohn's directorship; he held this post until 1851. He was a founding member of the Bach-Gesellschaft in 1850. He compiled a large collection of early printed music and books on music, which he gave to the city library of Leipzig in 1853. He further prepared a valuable list of old publications under the title *Systematisch-chronologische Darstellung der musikalischen Literatur* (Leipzig, 1836–39).

Becker, Carl Ferdinand, German organist and writer; b. Leipzig, July 17, 1804; d. there, Oct. 26, 1877. He was educated at the Thomasschule; played violin in the Gewandhaus Orch. (1820–33). He was organist at the Peterskirche and Nikolaikirche; then was a church organist at Leipzig. He was the first organ prof. at the new Leipzig Cons. from 1843. Among his publ. writings are: *Systematisch-chronologische Darstellung der Musikliteratur* (1836; Supplement, 1839); *Die Hausmusik in Deutschland im 16., 17., und 18. Jahrhundert* (1840); *Die Tonwerke des 16. und 17. Jahrhundert,* etc. He composed piano and organ pieces, and wrote a chorale book. He gave his library, containing valuable theoretical works, to the city of Leipzig.

Becker, Constantin Julius, German composer and author; b. Freiberg, Saxony, Feb. 3, 1811; d. Oberlössnitz, Feb. 26, 1859. He studied singing with Anacker and composition with Karl Becker; from 1837–46 edited the *Neue Zeitschrift für Musik,* in association with Schumann; in 1843 settled in Dresden; taught singing, composed, and wrote novels on musical subjects. In 1846 he went to Oberlössnitz, where he spent the remainder of his life. He wrote an opera, *Die Erstürmung von Belgrad* (Leipzig, May 21, 1848); a Symph.; various vocal works. However, he is best known for his manuals: *Männergesangschule* (1845), *Harmonielehre für Dilettanten* (1842), and *Kleine Harmonielehre* (1844). He also publ. the novel *Die Neuromantiker* (1840); trans. *Voyage musical* by Berlioz into German (1843).

Becker, Dietrich, German violinist, organist, and composer; b. Hamburg, 1623; d. there, 1679. He began his career as an organist in Ahrensburg, Holstein (1645); subsequently was active as a violinist in Hamburg. In 1658 he became violinist at the court chapel in Celle. In 1662 he was appointed court violinist in Hamburg; was named director of the court orch. in 1667 and was appointed director of music at the Hamburg Cathedral in 1674. As a composer, he wrote a number of works of chamber music.

WORKS: *Musicalische Frühlings-Früchte* for 3 to 5 Instruments and Basso Continuo (Hamburg, 1668; 2nd ed., 1673); *Erster Theil . . . Sonaten und Suiten* for 2 Violins and Basso Continuo (Hamburg, 1674); *Trauer- und Begrabnüss-Musik* for Soprano, Alto, Tenor, Bass, Violin, Bassoon, 3 Viole da Braccio, and Basso Continuo (Glückstadt, 1678); *Ander Theil . . . Sonaten und Suiten* for 2 Violins and Basso Continuo (Hamburg, 1679); also sacred choral music and songs.

Becker, Georges, Swiss music editor; b. Frankenthal, Palatinate, July 24, 1834; d. Lancy, near Geneva, July 18, 1928. He was a pupil of Prudent; lived in Geneva most of his life; published *La Musique en Suisse* (Geneva, 1874; reprinted, 1923); *Aperçu sur la chanson française* (from the 11th to 17th centuries); *Pygmalion de Jean-Jacques Rousseau; Les Projets de notation musicale du XIXe siècle; La Musique à Genève depuis 50 ans; Eustorg de Beaulieu; Guillaume de Guéroult; Notice sur Claude Goudimel; Jean Caulery et ses chansons spirituelles; H. Waelrant et ses psaumes* (1881); *De l'instrumentation du XVe au XVIIe siècle* (1844); edited the "Questionnaire de l'Association Internationale des Musiciens-Ecrivains"; contributed to the *Monatshefte für Musikgeschichte.*

Becker, Gustave Louis, American pianist and teacher; b. Richmond, Texas, May 22, 1861; d. Epsom, Surrey, England, Feb. 25, 1959. He made his public debut at the age of 11; studied in N.Y. with Constantin von Sternberg and at the Hochschule für Musik, Berlin (1888–91). Returning to N.Y., he became Rafael Joseffy's assistant at the National Cons. He continued his teaching activities privately. On May 23, 1952, the 80th anniversary of his public appearance as a child prodigy, he gave a piano recital in Steinway Hall; on his 94th birthday, May 22, 1955, played at a concert in N.Y., arranged by his friends. He wrote 2 suites for String Quartet; *Herald of Freedom* for Chorus (1925); many vocal and piano pieces, about 200 numbers in all. He publ. several pedagogic works: *Exercise for Accuracy; Superior Graded Course for the Piano; Musical Syllable System for Vocal Sight Reading;* and many magazine articles.

Becker, Heinz, German musicologist; b. Berlin, June 26, 1922. He studied at the Berlin Hochschule für Musik, taking courses in clarinet, piano, conducting, and composition; he then enrolled at Humboldt Univ. in Berlin; received his Ph.D. in 1951 with the dissertation *Zur Problematik und Technik der musikalischen Schlussgestaltung;* in 1956 he joined the musicological inst. of the Univ. of Hamburg as an assistant lecturer; he completed his Habilitation there with his *Studien zur Entwicklungsgeschichte der antiken und mittelalterlichen Rohrblattinstrumente* (1961; publ. in Hamburg, 1966). In 1966 he became a prof. of musicology at the Ruhr Univ. in Bochum. Apart from his professional duties, he wrote music for the clarinet.
WRITINGS: *Der Fall Heine-Meyerbeer* (Berlin, 1958); *Geschichte der Instrumentation,* in the Das Musikwerk series, XXIV (1964); ed., *Giacomo Meyerbeer: Briefwechsel und Tagebücher* (Berlin, 1960–75), *Beiträge zur Geschichte der Musikkritik* (Regensburg, 1965), *Beiträge zur Geschichte der Oper* (Regensburg, 1969), *Das Lokalkolorit in der Oper des 19. Jahrhunderts* (Regensburg, 1976).

Becker, Hugo, famous German cellist, son of **Jean Becker;** b. Strasbourg, Feb. 13, 1863; d. Geiselgasteig, July 30, 1941. He first studied with his father; later with Grützmacher, Kündinger, de Swert, and Piatti; was a cellist in the Frankfurt Opera orch. (1884–86); was a member of the Heermann quartet (1890–1906); taught at the Königliche Hochschule in Berlin (1909–29). He was not only one of the finest soloists, but also a remarkable ensemble player; was for many years a member of the Marteau-Dohnányi-Becker trio; also played with Ysaÿe and Busoni. Among his compositions are a Cello Concerto and smaller cello pieces. He publ. *Mechanik und Ästhetik des Violoncellspiels* (Vienna, 1929).

Becker, Jean, German violinist; b. Mannheim, May 11, 1833; d. there, Oct. 10, 1884. He studied with his father; then with Vincenz Lachner and Hugo Hildebrandt; his principal teacher was Aloys Kettenus. He was concertmaster of the Mannheim Orch. from 1855 to 1865. In 1865 he settled in Florence, and established the renowned Florentine Quartet (dissolved in 1880). The remaining years of his life were spent touring with his children: **Jeanne,** pianist, pupil of Reinecke and Bargiel (b. Mannheim, June 9, 1859; d. there, April 6, 1893); **Hans,** violist (b. Strasbourg, May 12, 1860; d. Leipzig, May 1, 1917); and the cellist **Hugo Becker.**

Becker, John J., remarkable American composer; b. Henderson, Ky., Jan. 22, 1886; d. Wilmette, Ill., Jan. 21, 1961. He studied at the Cincinnati Cons., then was at the Wisconsin Cons. in Milwaukee, where he was a pupil of Alexander von Fielitz, Carl Busch, and Wilhelm Middleschulte (Ph.D., 1923). From 1917 to 1927 he served as director of music at Notre Dame Univ.; was chairman of the fine arts dept. at the College of St. Thomas in St. Paul from 1929 to 1933. He was subsequently Minnesota State Director for the Federal Music Project (1935–41) and prof. of music at Barat College of the Sacred Heart at Lake Forest, Ill. (1943–57), and taught sporadically at the Chicago Musical College. His early works are characterized by romantic moods in a somewhat Germanic manner. About 1930 he was drawn into the circle of modern American music; was on the editorial board of *New Music Quarterly,* founded by Cowell, and became associated with Charles Ives. He conducted modern American works with various groups in St. Paul. Striving to form a style that would be both modern and recognizably American, he wrote a number of pieces for various instrumental groups under the title *Soundpiece.* He also developed a type of dramatic work connecting theatrical action with music. Becker's music is marked by sparse sonorities of an incisive rhythmic character contrasted with dissonant conglomerates of massive harmonies.
WORKS: FOR THE STAGE: *Dance Figure* for Singer, Dance Group, and Orch., on a poem by Ezra Pound (1932); *The Life of Man,* incidental music to the play by Leonid Andreyev (1932–43; unfinished); *Abongo: Dance Primitive* for 2 Solo Dancers, Dance Group, and Percussion (1933; N.Y., May 16, 1963); *A Marriage with Space,* "a drama in color, light, and sound" for Solo and Mass Recitation, Solo Dancer and Dance Group, and Large Orch., to a poem by Mark Turbyfill (1933–35); *Nostalgic Songs of Earth,* 3 dances for Solo Dancer and Piano (Northfield, Minn., Dec. 12, 1938); *Vigilante 1938* for Solo Dancer, Piano, and Percussion (Northfield, Minn., Dec. 12, 1938); *Rain Down Death,* incidental music for the play by Alfred Kreymborg (1939); *When the Willow Nods,* incidental music for the play by Kreymborg (1939); *Privilege and Privation,* "a playful affair with music," with libretto by Kreymborg (1940); *Antigone,* incidental music (1940); *Dierdre of the Sorrows,* lyric drama in one act, based on the play by John Synge (1945); *Faust,* monodrama (1951); *Madeleine et Judas,* incidental music for the play by Raymond Bruckberger (1958; radio perf., Paris, March 25, 1959). FOR ORCH.: *The Cossacks,* 3 sketches (1912); 7 symphonies: No. 1, *Etude Primitive* (1912–15); No. 2, *Fantasia Tragica* (1920); No. 3, *Symphonia Brevis* (1929; first complete perf., Minneapolis, May 20, 1937, composer conducting); No. 4, *Dramatic Episodes* (1938; uses material from *A Marriage with Space*); No. 5, *Homage to Mozart* (1942); No. 6, *Symphony of Democracy,* with Narrator and Chorus (1942); No. 7, based on the *Sermon on the Mount,* with Narrator and Singing and Speaking Chorus (1953–54; unfinished); *Concerto Arabesque* for Piano and Orch. (1930; St. Paul, Minn., Dec. 7, 1931, composer conducting); *Concertino Pas-*

torale, "A Forest Rhapsodie" for 2 Flutes and Orch. (1933; Cincinnati, Jan. 13, 1976); Concerto for Horn and Small Orch. (1933; N.Y., Feb. 8, 1953); *Mockery,* scherzo for Piano and Dance or Chamber Orch. (1933; first concert perf., N.Y., March 17, 1974); Viola Concerto (1937); 2nd Piano Concerto, *Satirico* (1938; St. Paul, Minn., March 28, 1939); *Rain Down Death,* first orch. suite (1939); *When the Willow Nods,* 2nd orch. suite (1940; Albert Lea, Minn., Jan. 9, 1941); *Antigone,* symph. dances (1940); *Victory March* (1942; last movement of 6th Symph.); *The Snow Goose: A Legend of World War II* (1944); Violin Concerto (1948). VOCAL WORKS: *Rouge Bouquet* for Male Chorus, with Trumpet and Piano (1917); *Out of the Cradle Endlessly Rocking,* cantata for Speaker, Soprano, Tenor, Chorus, and Orch. (1929; St. Cloud, Minn., July 19, 1931, composer conducting); *Missa Symphonica* for Male Chorus (1933); *Lincoln's Gettysburg Address* for Speaker, Chorus, and Orch. (1941); *Mass in Honor of the Sacred Heart* for Female Chorus (1944); *Moments from the Passion* for Solo Voice, Male and Female Voices, and Piano (1945); *Moments from the Liturgy* for Speaker, Women's Voices, Vocal Soloist, and Singing and Speaking Choruses (1948). CHAMBER MUSIC: *An American Sonata* for Violin and Piano (South Bend, Ind., July 28, 1926, composer at the piano); 8 *Soundpieces:* No. 1, for Piano Quintet (1932; N.Y., Nov. 13, 1933) or for Piano and String Orch. (1935); No. 2, *Homage to Haydn* (String Quartet No. 1, 1936), also for String Orch. (1937); No. 3 (Sonata for Violin and Piano, 1936; St. Paul, Minn., April 1, 1940); No. 4 (String Quartet No. 2, 1937; Lake Forest, Ill., Oct. 19, 1947); No. 5 (Sonata for Piano, 1938; St. Paul, Minn., April 13, 1943, Ernst Krenek performing); No. 6 for Flute and Clarinet (1940; Chapel Hill, N.C., April 26, 1970); No. 7, for 2 Pianos (1949); No. 8 (String Quartet No. 3, 1959; unfinished). FOR ORGAN: *Fantasia Tragica* (1920); *Improvisation* (1960). FOR FILM: Incidental music for *Julius Caesar,* a film by David Bradley (1949). In 1934 he scored Ives's song *General William Booth's Entrance into Heaven* for Chamber Orch.

BIBLIOGRAPHY: Don Gillespie, "John Becker, Musical Crusader from Saint Paul," *Musical Quarterly* (April 1976); idem, "John Becker's Correspondence with Ezra Pound," *Bulletin of Research in the Humanities* (Spring 1980).

Becker, Reinhold, German composer; b. Adorf, Aug. 11, 1842; d. Dresden, Dec. 4, 1924. He was originally a violinist, but because of a muscular disorder was obliged in 1870 to give up his playing; then lived in Dresden as a composer; from 1884–94 was conductor of the Dresdener Liedertafel, for which he wrote numerous choruses.
WORKS: *Frauenlob,* opera (Dresden, 1892); *Ratbold,* opera (Mainz, 1896); *Der Prinz von Homburg,* symph. poem; 2 violin concertos; String Quartet; Violin Sonata.

Becker, René Louis, organist and composer; b. Bischheim, Alsace, Nov. 7, 1882; d. Detroit, Mich., Jan. 28, 1956. He studied in Strasbourg at the Municipal Cons.; settled in the U.S.; taught piano at St. Louis Univ. (1905–11); was organist at the Blessed Sacrament Cathedral, Detroit (1930–42); then at St. Alphonsus Church in Dearborn; retired in 1952.
WORKS: 6 masses; 4 sonatas for Organ; motets; numerous compositions for piano and organ.

Becker, Valentin Eduard, German composer; b. Würzburg, Nov. 20, 1814; d. there, Jan. 25, 1890. He wrote 2 operas: *Die Bergknappen* and *Der Deserteur;* masses; males choruses.

Beckett, Wheeler, American conductor; b. San Francisco, March 7, 1898. He studied at Columbia Univ. and the Univ. of Calif.; took a course in conducting with Felix Weingartner in Basel (1928–30); served as organist and choirmaster at Grace Cathedral, San Francisco (1921–25); conducted Young People's Concerts with the San Francisco Symph. Orch. (1927–30); was conductor of the Richmond Symph. Orch. (1932–36); Boston Symph. Youth Concerts (1938–48); in 1957 organized the N.Y. Youth Concerts; under the auspices of the State Dept., conducted in the Far East (1959–62). He composed an opera, *Snow White;* an Organ Concerto; a Symph.; church music; songs.

Beckhelm, Paul, American composer; b. Kankakee, Ill., July 3, 1906; d. Mt. Vernon, Iowa, Nov. 6, 1966. He studied at the Eastman School of Music in Rochester, N.Y., obtaining his Ph.D. there in 1949. He publ. a number of teaching pieces for piano with romantically fanciful titles and contents, such as *Melancholy, Sunday Bells,* and *Sidewalk Games.*

Becking, Gustav, German musicologist; b. Bremen, March 4, 1894; lost his life in Prague, May 8, 1945, during street fighting. He studied in Berlin with J. Wolf and in Leipzig with Riemann; received his doctorate for a paper on Beethoven (Leipzig, 1921); in 1922 he was appointed a lecturer at Univ. of Erlangen; in 1929 he became a member of the faculty at the Univ. of Utrecht. In 1930 he became a prof. at the German Univ. in Prague. He publ. *Der Musikalische Rhythmus als Erkenntnisquelle* (Augsburg, 1928); also edited the collected works of E.T.A. Hoffmann (2 vols.; Leipzig, 1922–23).

Beckmann, Gustav, German musicologist; b. Berlin, Feb. 28, 1883; d. there, Nov. 14, 1948. He studied philology; served as a librarian at the Berlin State Library (1906–11); from 1934 to his death was councillor of the univ. library. He wrote some instrumental and vocal music; publ. the valuable paper *Das Violinspiel in Deutschland vor 1700* (Leipzig, 1918) and an essay on Leopold Mozart (1937); edited various bibliographical publications.

Beckmann, Johann Friedrich Gottlieb, German composer and organist; b. Celle, Sept. 6, 1737; d. there, April 25, 1792. He was one of the finest players and improvisers on the organ of his time; was for many years active in Celle. He wrote an opera, *Lukas und Hännchen* (Braunschweig, 1768); 6 harpsichord concertos; 12 keyboard sonatas; miscellaneous piano pieces.

Beckwith, John, Canadian composer; b. Victoria, British Columbia, March 9, 1927. He studied music with Alberto Guerrero at the Univ. of Toronto (Mus.B., 1947); then went to Paris to study with Nadia Boulanger (1950–52). Returning to Toronto, he served as music critic of the Toronto *Star* (1959–65); in 1952 he was appointed to the music faculty of the Univ. of Toronto; served as its dean in 1970–77. His music is marked by pragmatic modernism, with ingenious application of urban folk tunes, occasionally venturing into the hazardous regions of structural collage.
WORKS: Opera, *The Shivaree* (Toronto, April 3, 1982); chamber opera, *Night Blooming Cereus* (1953–58; Toronto Radio, March 4, 1959; first stage production, Toronto, April 5, 1960); *Montage* for Orch. (1953); *Fall Scene and Fair Dance* for Violin, Clarinet, and String Orch. (1956); *Music for Dancing* for Small Orch. (1959); *Concerto Fantasy* for Piano and Orch. (1958–59); *Flower Variations and Wheels* for Orch. (1962); Horn Concertino (1963); *Jonah*, chamber cantata (1963); *The Trumpets of Summer* for Narrator, Soloists, Chorus, and Instruments (1964); *Place of Meeting* for Narrator, Tenor, and Blues Singer, with Guitar, Chorus, and Orch. (Toronto, Nov. 15, 1967); *Circle, with Tangents* for Harpsichord and 13 Solo Strings (1967); *The Sun Dance* for Narrator, 6 Soloists, Chorus, Organ, and Percussion (1968); *All the Bees and All the Keys* for Narrator and Orch. (1973); *4 Conceits* for Piano (1945–48); *The Great Lakes Suite* for Soprano, Baritone, Clarinet, Cello, and Piano (1949); *5 Pieces* for Brass Trio (1951); *5 Pieces* for 2 Flutes (1951); Woodwind Quartet (1951); *3 Studies* for String Trio (1956); 4 "collages" for radio: *A Message to Winnipeg* for 4 Narrators, Violin, Cello, Piano, and Percussion (1960); *12 Letters to a Small Town* for 4 Narrators, Flute, Oboe, Guitar, and Piano (1961); *Wednesday's Child* for 3 Narrators, Soprano, Tenor, Flute, Viola, Piano, and Percussion (1962); and *Canada Dash, Canada Dot* for 8 Narrators and Singers, and Chamber Group (1965–67); *Gas!* for 20 Speakers (1969; text derives from Ontario street signs); *New Mobiles* for Piano (1971); *Taking a Stand* for 5 Players, 8 Brass Instruments, 14 Music Stands, and One Platform (1972); *Musical Chairs,* string quintet (1973); songs.

Beckwith, John Christmas, English organist; b. Norwich, Dec. 25, 1750; d. there, June 3, 1809. He studied at Oxford; became organist of St. Peter Mancroft (1794); was awarded the degrees Mus.Bac. and Mus.Doc., Oxon. (1803); became organist of Norwich Cathedral (1808). Beckwith's proficiency as an organist was coupled with fine musical scholarship. His collection of chants, *The First Verse of Every Psalm of David, with an Ancient or Modern Chant in Score, adapted as much as possible to the Sentiment of each Psalm* (London, 1808), includes a valuable preface, "A short history of chanting." He also publ. numerous pieces for chorus and organ.

Becquié, A., French flutist; b. Toulouse, 1800; d. Paris, Nov. 10, 1825. He was a pupil of Tulou and Guillou at the Paris Cons.; became first flutist at the Opéra-Comique; wrote many compositions for flute, including *Grande fantaisie et variations* (concerto); *Les Regrets* (sonata); rondos; airs; etc. His brilliant career was cut short by his untimely death at the age of 25.

Becquié ("de Peyreville"), Jean-Marie, French violinist, brother of **A. Becquié;** b. Toulouse, April 28, 1795; d. Paris, Jan. 1876. He studied with R. and A. Kreutzer at the Paris Cons.; wrote chamber music and many pieces for violin.

Bečvařovský, Antonin František, Bohemian organist; b. Mladá Boleslav, April 9, 1754; d. Berlin, May 15, 1823. He received his primary education in music at the Piarist College of Kosmonosy (1767–74); then had instruction in Prague with Kuchař; subsequently occupied various posts as organist: in Prague; in Braunschweig (1779–96), and finally in Berlin. He composed 5 keyboard concertos and several piano sonatas, as well as choral works.

Bédard, Jean-Baptiste, French violinist and harpist; b. Rennes, c.1765; d. Paris, c.1815. He lived in Paris after 1796; wrote 2 *Symphonies périodiques,* and numerous works for the harp.

Bedford, David, English composer; b. London, Aug. 4, 1937. He studied at the Royal Academy of Music in London with Lennox Berkeley (1958–61); then went to Italy, where he took lessons with Luigi Nono in Venice; also worked in the electronic music studios in Milan. Returning to England, he taught at Queen's College in London and played the organ in pop groups.
WORKS: *Concerto for 24 Instruments* (1960); *Piece II* for Electronic Instruments (1962); *+2, −2,* for Orch. (1963); *Piece for Mo* for Percussion, Vibraphone, Accordion, and Strings (1963); *Music for Albion Moonlight* for Soprano and Chamber Ensemble (1964); *The Great Birds* for 30-part Chorus (1964); *Octet for 9* (1964); *A Dream of the Seven Lost Stars* for Chorus and Instruments (1965); *This One for You* for Chamber Orch. (1965); *Gastrula* for Orch. (1968); *The Tentacles of the Dark Nebula* for Tenor and Solo Strings (London, Sept. 22, 1969); *The Sword for Orion* for Flute, Clarinet, Violin, Cello, 4 Metronomes, and 32 Percussion Instruments (1970); *Holy Thursday with Squeakers* for Soprano and Instruments (1972); *When I Heard the Learn'd Astronomer* for Tenor and Wind Ensemble (1972); *Jack of Shadows* for Viola and Chamber Ensemble (1973); *Pancakes with Butter, Maple Syrup, and Bacon and the TV Weatherman* for Horn, 2 Trumpets, Trombone, and Tuba (1973); *A Horse, His Name Was Henry Fencewaver Walkins* for Guitar and Chamber Ensemble (1973); *Twelve Hours of Sunset* for

Chorus and Orch. (1974); *Star's End* for 3 Rock Instruments and Orch. (1974); *Star's End* for Guitar and Orch. (London, Nov. 5, 1974); *The Rime of the Ancient Mariner,* children's opera (1975–76).

Bedford, Herbert, English composer; b. London, Jan. 23, 1867; d. there, March 13, 1945. He studied at the Guildhall School of Music; at the same time was active as a painter. He wrote an opera, *Kit Marlowe; The Optimist* for Orch.; Nocturne, for Alto Voice and Orch.; *Sowing the Wind,* symph. poem; *Over the Hills and Far Away,* symph. interlude; *Queen Mab,* suite for Orch.; *Ode to Music* and other songs. He publ. an *Essay on Unaccompanied Song* (1923) and *Robert Schumann* (London and N.Y., 1925; 2nd ed., 1933).

Bedford, Stuart, English conductor; b. London, July 31, 1939. He was educated at the Royal Academy of Music; also studied organ at Worcester College, Oxford. He made his conducting debut with the English Opera Group in London in 1967; toured with this group in England, Europe, and North America; was also a conductor at Covent Garden in London, and at the Aldeburgh Festival; in 1973 he became artistic director of the Aldeburgh Festival; in 1975 he was appointed co-artistic director of the English Music Theatre Co. (formerly the English Opera Group).

Bedos de Celles, Dom François, French organ theorist; b. Caux, near Béziers, Jan. 24, 1709; d. Saint-Denis, Nov. 25, 1779. He became a Benedictine monk at Toulouse in 1726; wrote an important treatise, *L'Art du facteur d'orgues* (3 vols.; Paris, 1766–78); a 4th volume, containing historical notes on the organ, appeared in German (1793); a modern edition was publ. in Kassel (1934–36; Eng. trans., 1977). He also wrote an account of a new organ at St. Martin de Tours in the *Mercure de France* (Jan. 1762; a German trans. is included in Adlung's *Musica mechanica organoedi*).
BIBLIOGRAPHY: Félix Raugel, "Dom Bedos de Celles," *Bulletin de la Société Française de Musicologie* (1917); E. Leipp, "La Régale," *Bulletin du Groupe d'Acoustique Musicale* (Dec. 1968); P. Hardoin, "L'Orgue de référence de Dom Bédos aux Jésuits de Paris," *Renaissance de l'Orgue* (Nov. 1969); D. Chailley, "Autour de l'édition originale de *L'Art du facteur d'orgues.*" *Renaissance de l'Orgue* (Nov. 1969).

Beecham, Sir Thomas, celebrated English conductor; b. St. Helens, near Liverpool, April 29, 1879; d. London, March 8, 1961. His father, Sir Joseph Beecham, was a man of great wealth derived from the manufacture of the once-famous Beecham pills, which worked wonders on anemic people; thanks to them, young Beecham could engage in life's pleasures and the arts without troublesome regard for economic limitations. He had his first music lessons from a rural organist; from 1892 to 1897 he attended the Rossall School at Lancashire, and later went to Wadham College, Oxford. In 1899 he organized,

mainly for his own delectation, an amateur ensemble, the St. Helen's Orch. Society; also in 1899 he had a chance to conduct a performance with the prestigious Hallé Orch. in Manchester. In 1902 he got a job as conductor of K. Trueman's traveling opera company, which gave him valuable practical experience in dealing with theater music. In 1905 he gave his first professional symph. concert in London, with members of the Queen's Hall Orch.; in 1906 he assembled the New Symph. Orch., which he led until 1908; then formed a group in his own name, the Beecham Symph. Orch., which presented its first concert in London on Feb. 22, 1909. In 1910, Beecham appeared in a new role, that of operatic impresario; from then until 1913 he worked at Covent Garden and at His Majesty's Theatre. During this period he made bold to invite Richard Strauss to Covent Garden to conduct his own operas. Next, Beecham conducted opera at the Theatre Royal at Drury Lane. In 1916 he became conductor of the Royal Phil. Society concerts; then gave operatic productions with the Beecham Opera Company. By that time his reputation as a forceful and charismatic conductor was securely established in England. His audiences grew; the critics, impressed by his imperious ways and his unquestioned ability to bring out spectacular operatic productions, sang his praise; however, some commentators found much to criticize in his somewhat cavalier treatment of the classics. In appreciation of his services to British music, Beecham was knighted in 1916; at the death of his father, he succeeded to the title of baronet. But all of his inherited money was not enough to pay for Beecham's exorbitant financial disbursements in his ambitious enterprises, and in 1919 he was declared bankrupt. He rebounded a few years later and continued his extraordinary career. In 1928 he made his American debut conducting the N.Y. Phil. In 1929 he organized and conducted the Delius Festival in London, to which Delius himself, racked by tertiary syphilitic affliction, paralyzed and blind, was brought from his residence in France to attend Beecham's musical homage to him. In 1932, Beecham organized the London Phil. Orch.; contemptuous of general distaste for the Nazi regime in Germany, he took the London Phil. to Berlin in 1936 for a concert which was attended by the Führer in person. Returning to England, he continued his activities, conducting opera and symphony. As the war situation deteriorated on the Continent, Beecham went to the U.S. in May 1940, and also toured Australia. In 1941 he was engaged as music director and conductor of the Seattle Symph. Orch., retaining this post until 1943; he also filled guest engagements at the Metropolitan Opera in N.Y. from 1942 to 1944. In America he was not exempt from sharp criticism, which he haughtily dismissed as philistine complaints. On his part, he was outspoken in his snobbish disdain for the cultural inferiority of England's wartime allies, often spicing his comments with mild obscenities, usually of a scatological nature. Returning to England, he founded, in 1946, still another orch., the Royal Phil.; in 1951 he resumed his post as conductor at Covent Garden. In 1957 Queen Elizabeth II made him a Companion of Honour. Beecham was married three times: to Utica Celestia Wells, in 1903 (divorced in 1942); Betty Hamby (in 1943), who died in 1957; and to his young secretary, Shirley Hudson, in 1959. In 1960 he suffered a series of massive heart attacks and died. He publ. an autobiography, *A Mingled Chime* (London, 1943), and also an extensive biography of Delius (London, 1959). To mark his centennial, a commemorative postage stamp with Beecham's portrait was issued by the Post Office of Great Britain on Sept. 1, 1980.

BIBLIOGRAPHY: Ethel Symth, *Beecham and Pharaoh* (London, 1935); Charles Reid, *Thomas Beecham: An Independent Biography* (London, 1961); Sir Neville Cardus, *Sir Thomas Beecham: A Memoir* (London, 1961); H. Procter-Gregg, ed., *Sir Thomas Beecham, Conductor and Impresario; As Remembered by His Friends and Colleagues* (London, 1975); H. Atkins and A. Newman, *Beecham Stories* (1978); J.D. Gilmour, *Sir Thomas Beecham: The Seattle Years 1941–1943* (1978) and *Sir Thomas Beecham: The North American Tour 1950* (1979); A. Jefferson, *Sir Thomas Beecham: A Centenary Tribute* (London, 1979). In 1964 the Sir Thomas Beecham Society, which is dedicated to preserving his memory, was organized with chapters in America and England. The Society publishes an official journal, *Le Grand Baton*, devoted to Beecham and the art of conducting; the Beecham Centenary Edition appeared in March–June 1979.

Beecher, Carl Milton, American composer; b. Lafayette, Ind., Oct. 22, 1883; d. Portland, Oreg., Nov. 21, 1968. He graduated from Northwestern Univ. in 1908; then went to Berlin, where he took lessons in piano with Josef Lhévinne. Returning to America, he was on the faculty of his alma mater (1913–36); then spent 11 years in Tahiti. Returning finally to America in 1947, he became prof. at the Portland (Oreg.) School of Music. He wrote mainly for piano in miniature forms; among his piano pieces is a suite, *Remembrances of Times Past;* 9 *Musical Profiles;* and 5 *Aquatints.*

Beecke, Ignaz von, German clavier performer and composer; b. Wimpfen, Oct. 28, 1733; d. Wallerstein, Jan. 2, 1803. He studied with Gluck; was a captain of dragoons; later became Musikintendant to the prince of Öttingen-Wallerstein. A highly accomplished pianist, he was a friend of Jommelli, Gluck, and Mozart. Among his compositions are 8 operas; an oratorio, *Die Auferstehung Jesu;* cantatas; symphonies; quartets; 4 harpsichord trios; 6 harpsichord sonatas; string quartets

BIBLIOGRAPHY: L. Schiedermair, "Die Blütezeit der Öttingen-Wallerstein'schen Hofkapelle," *Sammelbände der Internationalen Musik-Gesellschaft* (Oct. 1907).

Beecroft, Norma, Canadian composer; b. Oshawa, Ontario, April 11, 1934. She studied composition with John Weinzweig at the Toronto Cons. (1950–58); took summer composition courses at Tanglewood (1958; with Copland and Foss), at Darmstadt (1960; with Maderna), and in Rome (1960–61; with Petrassi). She then attended seminars in electronic music with Myron Schaeffer at the Univ. of Toronto (1962–63) and with Mario Davidovsky at Columbia Univ. (1964). She was subsequently engaged in various organizing activities in Toronto (1965–73) and since 1971 was a member of the board of the New Music Concerts. Her own music takes a modernistic direction without doctrinaire affiliations.

WORKS: Fantasy for Orch. (1958); *3 Pezzi brevi* for Flute, and Harp or Guitar or Piano (1960–61); 3 *Improvvisazioni concertanti: I* for Flute and Small Orch. (1961), *II* for Orch. (1971), and *III* for Flute, 2 Timpanists, and Orch. (1973); *Contrasts for 6 Performers* for Oboe, Viola, Xylophone, Vibraphone, Percussion, and Harp (1962); *From Dreams of Brass* for Narrator, Soprano, Chorus, Orch., and Tape (1963–64); *Pièce concertante* No. 1 for Orch. (1966); *Elegy* and *Two Went to Sleep* for Soprano, Flute, Percussion or Piano, and Tape (1967); 3 *Rasas: I* for Flute, Harp, Violin, Viola, Cello, Percussion, and Piano (1968), *II* for Contralto, Flute, Guitar, Piano or Organ, Horn, 2 Percussionists, and Tape (1972–73), and *III* for Soprano, Flute, Trombone, Piano, Percussion, and Tape (1974); *3 Impressions* for Chorus, Piano, and/or Percussion (1973); *11 and 7 for 5 Plus* for Brass Quintet and Tape (1975).

Beellaerts, Jean. See **Bellère, Jean.**

Beer, Jacob Liebmann. Original name of **Giacomo Meyerbeer.**

Beer, Johann, Austrian-born German music theorist and polemicist; b. St. Georg, Upper Austria, Feb. 28, 1655; d. (accidentally shot while watching a shooting contest) Weissenfels, Aug. 6, 1700. He studied music at the Benedictine monastery in Lambach; then attended classes at Reichersberg, Passau, and the Gymnasium Poeticum in Regensburg; in 1676 he became a student in theology at the Univ. of Leipzig; in 1685 he was appointed Konzertmeister of the court orch. in Weissenfels. His writings are of interest as a curiosity reflecting the musical mores of his time; he publ. polemical pamphlets directed against contemporary writers who deprecated music as dangerous for morals. In such pamphlets he used the pseudonym **Ursus,** Latin for the German *Bär,* which is a homonym of his real name, Beer, i.e., Bear, the ursine animal. One such publication opens with the words "Ursus murmurat" ("The Bear growls"), and another, "Ursus vulpinatur," i.e., "Bear leads a fox hunt." Both assail a certain Gottfried Vockerodt, who claimed that the depravity of Nero and Caligula was the result of their immoderate love of music. Beer also publ. *Bellum musicum (Musical War;* Nuremberg, 1719).

BIBLIOGRAPHY: R. Alewyn, *Johann Beer: Studien zum Roman des 17. Jahrhundert* (Leipzig, 1932); H. Krause, *Johann Beer: Zur Musikauffassung im 17. Jahrhundert* (Diss., Univ. of Leipzig, 1935); A. Schmiedecke, "Johann Beer und die Musik," *Die Musikforschung,* XVIII (1965).

Beer, Joseph, Bohemian clarinetist; b. Grünwald,

May 18, 1744; d. Berlin, Oct. 28, 1812. He was first a trumpet player; served in the Austro-Hungarian army, and later was in the service of France. He learned to play the clarinet in Paris; from 1780 to 1792 he was a chamber musician in St. Petersburg; upon his return he was attached to the court chapel in Potsdam. Beer's principal improvement of the clarinet was the attachment of a fifth key. He wrote many compositions for his instrument.

Beer, Max Josef, Austrian pianist and composer; b. Vienna, Aug. 25, 1851; d. there, Nov. 25, 1908. He was a pupil of Dessoff; wrote the comic operas *Friedel mit der leeren Tasche* (Prague, 1892); *Der Streik der Schmiede* (Augsburg, 1897); *Das Stelldichein auf der Pfahlbrücke;* a cantata, *Der wilde Jäger;* many songs and piano pieces.

Beer-Walbrunn, Anton, German composer; b. Kohlberg, Bavaria, June 29, 1864; d. Munich, March 22, 1929. He was a pupil of Rheinberger, Bussmeyer, and Abel at the Akademie der Tonkunst in Munich; from 1901 was an instructor there; made prof. in 1908. He wrote the operas: *Die Sühne* (Lübeck, 1894); *Don Quixote* (Munich, 1908); *Das Ungeheuer* (Karlsruhe, 1914); *Der Sturm* (1914; after Shakespeare); incidental music to *Hamlet* (1909); 2 symphs.; *Mahomet's Gesang* for Chorus and Orch.; *Lustspielouvertüre;* Violin Concerto; Piano Quintet; church music; many compositions for various instruments. He also supervised new editions of works of Wilhelm Friedemann Bach.
BIBLIOGRAPHY: O.G. Sonneck, *Suum cuique: Essays in Music* (N.Y., 1916).

Beeson, Jack Hamilton, American composer; b. Muncie, Ind., July 15, 1921. He studied at the Eastman School of Music in Rochester, N.Y., with Burrill Phillips, Bernard Rogers, and Howard Hanson; received his M.M. in 1943; later studied at Columbia Univ., and took private lessons with Béla Bartók during Bartók's stay in N.Y. in his last year of life. In 1945 Beeson joined the staff of Columbia Univ.; was made a prof. there in 1965; served as chairman of the music dept. from 1968 to 1972; was named MacDowell Prof. of Music in 1967. He held the American Prix de Rome in 1948–50; in 1958–59 received a Guggenheim fellowship; in 1976 was made a member of the American Academy and Inst. of Arts and Letters. His music is marked by enlightened utilitarianism; particularly forceful are his operatic compositions.
WORKS: Operas: *Jonah* (1950); *Hello, Out There* (N.Y., May 27, 1954); *The Sweet Bye and Bye* (N.Y., Nov. 21, 1957); *Lizzie Borden,* based on a story of the famous murder trial in Fall River, Mass., in 1892 (N.Y., March 25, 1965; his most successful opera); *Dr. Heidegger's Fountain of Youth,* based on the story by Hawthorne (N.Y., Nov. 17, 1978); musical comedy, *Captain Jinks of the Horse Marines* (Kansas City, Sept. 20, 1975); Symph. in A (1959); *Transformations* for Orch. (1959); *Commemoration* for Band (1960); 5 piano sonatas; Viola Sonata (1953); many vocal works; also a television opera, *My*

Heart's in the Highlands, after a play by William Saroyan (National Educational Television Theater, March 17, 1970).

Beeth, Lola, dramatic soprano; b. Cracow, Nov. 23, 1862; d. Berlin, March 18, 1940. She studied with Mme. Viardot-Garcia and Désirée Artôt; made her debut as Elsa in *Lohengrin* at the Berlin Court Opera (1882); sang there from 1882 to 1888 and at the Vienna Court Theater from 1888 to 1895. After appearances in Paris and N.Y., she settled in Berlin as a teacher.

Beethoven, Ludwig van, the great German composer whose unsurpassed genius, expressed with supreme mastery in his symphs., chamber music, concertos, and piano sonatas, revealing an extraordinary power of invention, marked a historic turn in the art of composition; b. Bonn, Dec. 15 or 16 (baptized, Dec. 17), 1770; d. Vienna, March 26, 1827. (Beethoven himself maintained, against all evidence, that he was born in 1772, and that the 1770 date referred to his older brother, deceased in infancy, whose forename was also Ludwig.) The family was of Dutch extraction (the surname Beethoven meant "beet garden" in Dutch). Beethoven's grandfather, **Ludwig van Beethoven** (b. Malines, Belgium, Jan. 5, 1712; d. Bonn, Dec. 24, 1773), served as choir director of the church of St. Pierre in Louvain in 1731; in 1732 he went to Liège, where he sang bass in the cathedral choir of St. Lambert; in 1733 he became a member of the choir in Bonn; there he married Maria Poll. Prevalent infant mortality took its statistically predictable tribute; the couple's only surviving child was Johann van Beethoven; he married a young widow, Maria Magdalena Leym (born Keverich), daughter of the chief overseer of the kitchen at the palace in Ehrenbreitstein; they were the composer's parents. Beethoven firmly believed that the nobiliary particle "van" in the family name betokened a nobility; in his demeaning litigation with his brother's widow over the guardianship of Beethoven's nephew Karl, he argued before the Vienna magistrate that as a nobleman he should be given preference over his sister-in-law, a commoner, but the court rejected his contention on the ground that "van" lacked the elevated connotation of its German counterpart, "von." Beethoven could never provide a weightier claim of noble descent. In private, he even tolerated without forceful denial the fantastic rumor that he was a natural son of royalty, a love child of Friedrich Wilhelm II, or even of Frederick the Great.
Beethoven's father gave him rudimentary instruction in music; he learned to play both the violin and the piano; Tobias Friedrich Pfeiffer, a local musician, gave him formal piano lessons; the court organist in Bonn, Gilles van Eeden, instructed him in keyboard playing and in music theory; Franz Rovantini gave him violin lessons; another violinist who taught Beethoven was Franz Reis. Beethoven also learned to play the French horn, under the guidance of the professional musician Nikolaus Simrock. Beethoven's academic training was mea-

Beethoven

ger; he was, however, briefly enrolled at the Univ. of Bonn in 1789. His first important teacher of composition was Christian Gottlob Neefe, a thorough musician who seemed to understand his pupil's great potential even in his early youth. He guided Beethoven in the study of Bach and encouraged him in keyboard improvisation. At the age of 12, in 1782, Beethoven composed *9 Variations for Piano on a March of Dressler,* his first work to be publ. In 1783 he played the cembalo in the court orch. in Bonn; in 1784 the Elector Maximilian Franz officially appointed him to the post of deputy court organist, a position he retained until 1792; from 1788–92 Beethoven also served as a violist in theater orchs. In 1787 the Elector sent Beethoven to Vienna, where he stayed for a short time; the report that he played for Mozart and that Mozart pronounced him a future great composer seems to be a figment of somebody's eager imagination. After a few weeks in Vienna Beethoven went to Bonn when he received news that his mother was gravely ill; she died on July 17, 1787. Beethoven was obliged to provide sustenance for his 2 younger brothers; his father, who took to drink in excess, could not meet his obligations. Beethoven earned some money by giving piano lessons to the children of Helene von Breuning, the widow of a court councillor. He also met important wealthy admirers, among them Count Ferdinand von Waldstein, who was to be immortalized by Beethoven's dedication to him of a piano sonata bearing his name. Beethoven continued to compose; some of his works of the period were written in homage to royalty, as a cantata on the death of the Emperor Joseph II and a cantata on the accession of Emperor Leopold II; other pieces were designed for performance at aristocratic gatherings.

In 1790 an event of importance took place in Beethoven's life when Haydn was honored in Bonn by the Elector on his way to London; it is likely that Beethoven was introduced to him, and that Haydn encouraged him to come to Vienna to study with him. However that might be, Beethoven went to Vienna in November 1792, and began his studies with Haydn. Not very prudently, Beethoven approached the notable teacher Johann Schenk to help him write the mandatory exercises prior to delivering them to Haydn for final appraisal. In the meantime, Haydn had to go to London again, and Beethoven's lessons with him were discontinued. Instead, Beethoven began a formal study of counterpoint with Johann Georg Albrechtsberger, a learned musician and knowledgeable pedagogue; these studies continued for about a year, until 1795. Furthermore, Beethoven took lessons in vocal composition with the illustrious Italian composer Salieri, who served as Imperial Kappelmeister at the Austrian Court. Beethoven was fortunate to find a generous benefactor in Prince Karl Lichnowsky, who awarded him, beginning about 1800, an annual stipend of 600 florins; he was amply repaid for this bounty by entering the pantheon of music history through Beethoven's dedication to him of the *Sonate pathétique* and other works, as well as his first opus number, a piano trio. Among other aristocrats of Vienna who were introduced into the gates of permanence through Beethoven's dedications was Prince Franz Joseph Lobkowitz, whose name adorns the title pages of the 6 String Quartets, op. 18; the Eroica Symph. (after Beethoven unsuccessfully tried to dedicate it to Napoleon); the Triple Concerto, op. 56; and (in conjunction with Prince Razumovsky) the 5th and 6th symphs.—a glorious florilegium of great music. Prince Razumovsky, the Russian ambassador to Vienna, played an important role in Beethoven's life. From 1808–16 he maintained in his residence a string quartet in which he himself played the 2nd violin (the leader was Beethoven's friend Schuppanzigh). It was to Razumovsky that Beethoven dedicated his 3 string quartets that became known as the Razumovsky quartets, in which Beethoven made use of authentic Russian folk themes. Razumovsky also shared with Lobkowitz the dedications of Beethoven's 5th and 6th symphs. Another Russian patron was Prince Golitzyn, for whom Beethoven wrote his great string quartets opp. 127, 130, and 132.

Beethoven made his first public appearance in Vienna on March 29, 1795, as soloist in one of his piano concertos (probably the B-flat major Concerto, op. 19). In 1796 he played in Prague, Dresden, Leipzig, and Berlin. He also participated in "competitions," fashionable at the time, with other pianists, which were usually held in aristocratic salons. In 1799 he competed with Joseph Wölffl and in 1800 with Daniel Steibelt. On April 2, 1800, he presented a concert of his works in the Burgtheater in Vienna, at which his First Symph. in C major and the Septet in E-flat major were performed for the first time. Other compositions at the threshold of the century were the Piano Sonata in C minor, op. 13, the *Pathétique;* the C-major Piano Concerto, op. 15; "sonata quasi una fantasia" for Piano in C-sharp minor, op. 27, celebrated under the nickname *Moonlight Sonata* (so described by a romantically inclined critic but not specifically accepted by Beethoven); the D major Piano Sonata known as *Pastoral;* 8 violin sonatas; 4 piano trios; 4 string trios; 6 string quartets; Septet for Wind Instruments and Strings; several sets of variations; and a number of songs.

Wilhelm von Lenz, a Russian musician of German extraction who wrote books in the French language, publ. in St. Petersburg in 1852 a 2-vol. essay, *Beethoven et ses trois styles,* in which he separated Beethoven's list of compositions into 3 periods. Despite this arbitrary chronological division, the work became firmly established in Beethoven literature. According to Lenz, the first period embraced Beethoven's works from his early years to the end of the 18th century, marked by a style closely related to the formal methods of Haydn. The 2nd period, covering the years 1801–14, was signaled by a more personal, quasi-Romantic mood, beginning with the *Moonlight Sonata;* the last period, extending from 1814 to Beethoven's death in 1827, comprised the most individual, the most unconventional, the most innovative works, such as his last string quartets and the 9th Symph., with its extraordinary choral finale.

Beethoven's early career in Vienna was marked

by fine success; he was popular not only as a virtuoso pianist and a composer, but also as a social figure who was welcome in the aristocratic circles of Vienna; Beethoven's students included society ladies and even royal personages, such as Archduke Rudolf of Austria, to whom Beethoven dedicated the so-called Archduke Trio, op. 97. But Beethoven's progress was fatefully affected by a mysteriously growing deafness, which reached a crisis in 1802. On Oct. 8 and 10, 1802, Beethoven wrote a poignant document known as the "Heiligenstadt Testament," for it was drawn in the village of Heiligenstadt, where Beethoven resided at the time. The document, not discovered until after Beethoven's death, voiced Beethoven's despair at the realization that the most important sense of his being, the sense of hearing, was inexorably failing. He implored his brothers, in case of his early death, to consult his physician, Dr. Schmidt, who knew the secret of his "lasting malady" contracted 6 years before he wrote the Testament, i.e., in 1796. The etiology of his illness leaves little doubt that the malady was the dreaded "lues," with symptoms including painful intestinal disturbances, enormous enlargement of the pancreas, cirrhosis of the liver, and, most ominously, the porous degeneration of the roof of the cranium, observable in the life mask of 1812 and clearly shown in the photograph of Beethoven's skull taken when his body was exhumed in 1863. However, the impairment of his hearing may have had an independent cause, an otosclerosis, resulting in the shriveling of the auditory nerves and concomitant dilation of the accompanying arteries. Externally, there were signs of tinnitus, a constant buzzing in the ears, about which Beethoven complained. Beethoven's reverential biographer A.W. Thayer states plainly in a letter dated Oct. 29, 1880, that it was known to several friends of Beethoven that the cause of his combined ailments was syphilis. A full account of Beethoven's illness is found in Dr. Dieter Kerner's book *Krankheiten grosser Musiker* (Stuttgart, 1973; vol. 1, pp. 89–140).

To the end of his life Beethoven hoped to find a remedy for his deafness among the latest "scientific" medications. His Konversationshefte bear a pathetic testimony to these hopes; in one, dated 1819, he notes down the address of a Dr. Mayer, who treated deafness by "sulphur vapor" and a vibrations machine. By tragic irony, Beethoven's deafness greatly contributed to the study of his personality, thanks to the existence of the "conversation books" in which his interlocutors wrote down their questions and Beethoven replied, also usually in writing, a method of communication which became a rule in Beethoven's life after 1818. Unfortunately, Beethoven's friend and amanuensis, Anton Schindler, altered or deleted many of these; it seems also likely that he destroyed Beethoven's correspondence with his doctors, as well as the recipes which apparently contained indications of treatment by mercury, the universal medication against venereal and other diseases at the time.

It is remarkable that under these conditions Beethoven was able to continue his creative work with his usual energy; there seem to be no periods of interruption in the chronology of his list of works, and similarly there is no apparent influence of his moods of depression on the content of his music; tragic and joyful musical passages had equal shares in his inexhaustible flow of varied works. On April 5, 1803, Beethoven presented a concert of his compositions in Vienna at which he was soloist in his 3rd Piano Concerto; the program also contained performances of his 2nd Symph. and of the oratorio *Christus am Oelberge*. On May 24, 1803, he played in Vienna the piano part of his Violin Sonata, op. 47, known as the *Kreutzer Sonata,* although Kreutzer himself did not introduce it; in his place the violin part was taken over by the mulatto artist George Bridgetower. During the years of 1803 and 1804 Beethoven composed his great Symph. No. 3 in E-flat major, op. 55, the *Eroica.* It has an interesting history. Beethoven's disciple Ferdinand Ries relates that Beethoven tore off the title page of the MS of the score originally dedicated to Napoleon, after learning of his proclamation as Emperor of France in 1804, and supposedly exclaimed, "So he is a tyrant like all the others after all!" Ries reported this story shortly before his death, some 34 years after the composition of the *Eroica,* which throws great doubt on its credibility. Indeed, in a letter to the publishing firm of Breitkopf & Härtel, dated Aug. 26, 1804, long after Napoleon's proclamation of Empire, Beethoven still refers to the title of the work as "really Bonaparte." His own copy of the score shows that he crossed out the designation "Intitulata Bonaparte," but allowed the words written in pencil, in German, "Geschrieben auf Bonaparte" to stand. In October 1806, when the first edition of the orch. parts was publ. in Vienna, the symph. received the title "Sinfonia eroica composta per festeggiare il sovvenire d'un grand' uomo" ("heroic symphony, composed to celebrate the memory of a great man"). But who was the great man whose memory was being celebrated in Beethoven's masterpiece? Napoleon was very much alive and was still leading his Grand Armée to new conquests, so the title would not apply. Yet, the famous funeral march in the score expressed a sense of loss and mourning. The mystery remains. There is evidence that Beethoven continued to have admiration for Napoleon. He once remarked that had he been a military man he could have matched Napoleon's greatness on the battlefield. Beethoven and Napoleon were close contemporaries; Napoleon was a little more than a year older than Beethoven.

In 1803 Emanuel Schikaneder, manager of the Theater an der Wien, asked Beethoven to compose an opera to a libretto he had prepared under the title *Vestas Feuer (The Vestal Flame),* but Beethoven showed no interest in such a project; instead he began work on another opera, based on J.N. Bouilly's *Léonore, ou L'Amour conjugal.* The completed opera was named *Fidelio,* which was the heroine's assumed name in her successful efforts to save her imprisoned husband. The opera was given at the Theater an der Wien on Nov. 20, 1805, under difficult circumstances, a few days after the French army entered Vienna. There were only 3 performances before the opera was rescheduled for March 29 and

Beethoven

April 10, 1806; after another long hiatus a greatly revised version of *Fidelio* was produced on May 23, 1814. Beethoven wrote 3 versions of the Overture for *Léonore;* for another performance, on May 26, 1814, he revised the Overture once more, and this time it was performed under the title *Fidelio Overture.*

An extraordinary profusion of creative masterpieces marked the years 1802–8 in Beethoven's life. During these years he brought out the 3 String Quartets, op. 59, dedicated to Count Razumovsky; the 4th, 5th, and 6th symphs.; the Violin Concerto; the 4th Piano Concerto; the Triple Concerto; the *Coriolan* Overture; and a number of piano sonatas, including the D minor, op. 31; No. 2, the *Tempest;* the C major, op. 53, the *Waldstein;* and the F minor, op. 57, the *Appassionata.* On Dec. 22, 1808, Beethoven played in Vienna the solo part of his 4th Piano Concerto, and in the same concert the 5th and 6th symphs. were heard for the first time; the concert lasted some 4 hours. Still, financial difficulties beset Beethoven. The various annuities from patrons were uncertain, and the devaluation of the Austrian currency played havoc with his calculations. In Oct. 1808, King Jerome Bonaparte of Westphalia offered Beethoven the post of Kapellmeister of Kassel at a substantial salary, but Beethoven decided to remain in Vienna. Between 1809 and 1812, Beethoven wrote his 5th Piano Concerto; the String Quartet in E-flat major, op. 74; the incidental music to Goethe's drama *Egmont;* the 7th and 8th symphs.; and his Piano Sonata in E-flat major, op. 81a, whimsically subtitled "Das Lebewohl, Abwesenheit und Wiedersehn," also known by its French subtitle, "Les Adieux, l'absence, et le retour." He also added a specific description to the work, "Sonate caractéristique." This explicit characterization was rare with Beethoven; he usually avoided programmatic descriptions, preferring to have his music stand by itself. Even in his 6th Symph., the *Pastorale,* which bore specific subtitles for each movement and had the famous imitations of birds singing and the realistic portrayal of a storm, Beethoven decided to append a cautionary phrase: "More as an expression of one's feelings than a picture." Beethoven specifically denied that the famous introductory call in the 5th Symph. represented the knock of Fate at his door, but the symbolic association was too powerful to be removed from the legend; yet the characteristic iambic tetrameter was anticipated in several of Beethoven's works, among them the *Appassionata* and the 4th Piano Concerto. Czerny, who was close to Beethoven in Vienna, claimed that the theme was derived by Beethoven from the cry of the songbird Emberiza, or Emmerling, a species to which the common European goldfinch belongs, which Beethoven may have heard during his walks in the Vienna woods, a cry that is piercing enough to compensate for Beethoven's loss of aural acuity. However that may be, the 4-note motif became inexorably connected with the voice of doom for enemies and the exultation of the victor in battle. It was used as a victory call by the Allies in World War II; the circumstance that 3 short beats followed by one long beat spelled V for Victory in Morse code reinforced its effectiveness. The Germans could not very well jail people for whistling a Beethoven tune, so they took it over themselves as the first letter of the archaic German word Viktoria, and trumpeted it blithely over their radios. Another famous nicknamed work by Beethoven was the *Emperor Concerto,* a label attached to the 5th Piano Concerto, op. 73. Beethoven wrote it in 1809, when Napoleon's star was still high in the European firmament, and some publicist decided that the martial strains of the music, with its sonorous fanfares, must have been a tribute to the Emperor of the French. Patriotic reasons seemed to underlie Beethoven's designation of his Piano Sonata, op. 106, as the *Hammerklavier Sonata,* that is, a work written for a hammer keyboard, or fortepiano, as distinct from harpsichord. But all of Beethoven's piano sonatas were for fortepiano; moreover, Beethoven assigned the title *Hammerklavier* to each of the 4 sonatas, namely opp. 101, 106, 109, and 110, using the old German word for fortepiano; by so doing, Beethoven desired to express his patriotic consciousness of being a German.

Like many professional musicians, Beethoven was occasionally called upon to write a work glorifying an important event or a famous personage. Pieces of this kind seldom achieve validity, and usually produce bombast. Such a work was Beethoven's *Wellingtons Sieg oder Die Schlacht bei Vittoria,* celebrating the British victory over Joseph Bonaparte, Napoleon's brother who temporarily sat on the Spanish throne. In 1814, Beethoven wrote a cantata entitled *Der glorreiche Augenblick,* intended to mark the "glorious moment" of the fall of Beethoven's erstwhile idol, Napoleon.

Personal misfortunes, chronic ailments, and intermittent quarrels with friends and relatives preoccupied Beethoven's entire life. He ardently called for peace among men, but he never achieved peace with himself. Yet he could afford to disdain the attacks in the press; on the margin of a critical but justified review of Beethoven's *Wellington's Victory,* he wrote, addressing the writer: "You wretched scoundrel! What I excrete [he used the vulgar German word *scheisse*] is better than anything you could ever think up!"

Beethoven was overly suspicious; he even accused the faithful Schindler of dishonestly mishandling the receipts from the sale of tickets at the first performance of the 9th Symph. He exaggerated his poverty; he possessed some shares and bonds which he kept in a secret drawer. He was untidy in personal habits: he often used preliminary drafts of his compositions to cover the soup and even the chamber pot, leaving telltale circles on the MS. He was strangely naive; he studiously examined the winning numbers of the Austrian government lottery, hoping to find a numerological clue to a fortune for himself. His handwriting was all but indecipherable. An earnest Beethoveniac spent time with a microscope trying to figure out what kind of soap Beethoven wanted his housekeeper to purchase for him; the scholar's efforts were crowned with triumphant success: the indecipherable word was *gelbe*— Beethoven wanted a piece of yellow soap. Q.E.D.

The copying of his MSS presented difficulties; not only were the notes smudged, but sometimes Beethoven even failed to mark a crucial accidental. A copyist said that he would rather copy 20 pages of Rossini than a single page of Beethoven. On the other hand, Beethoven's sketchbooks, containing many alternative drafts, are extremely valuable, for they introduce a scholar into the inner sanctum of Beethoven's creative process.

Beethoven had many devoted friends and admirers in Vienna, but he spent most of his life in solitude. Carl Czerny reports in his diary that Beethoven once asked him to let him lodge in his house, but Czerny declined, explaining that his aged parents lived with him and he had no room for Beethoven. Deprived of the pleasures and comforts of family life, Beethoven sought to find a surrogate in his nephew Karl, son of Caspar Carl Beethoven, who died in 1815. Beethoven regarded his sister-in-law as an unfit mother; he went to court to gain sole guardianship over the boy; in his private letters, and even in his legal depositions, he poured torrents of vilification upon the woman, implying even that she was engaged in prostitution. In his letters to Karl he often signed himself as the true father of the boy. In 1826 Karl attempted suicide; it would be unfair to ascribe this act to Beethoven's stifling avuncular affection; Karl later went into the army and enjoyed a normal life.

Gallons of ink have been unnecessarily expended on the crucial question of Beethoven's relationship with women. That Beethoven dreamed of an ideal life companion is clear from his numerous utterances and candid letters to friends, in some of which he asked them to find a suitable bride for him. But there is no inkling that he kept company with any particular woman in Vienna. Beethoven lacked social graces; he could not dance; he was unable to carry on a light conversation about trivia; and behind it all there was the dreadful reality of his deafness. He could speak, but could not always understand when he was spoken to. With close friends he used an unwieldy ear trumpet; but such contrivances were obviously unsuitable in a social gathering. There were several objects of his secret passions, among his pupils or the society ladies to whom he dedicated his works. But somehow he never actually proposed marriage, and they usually married less hesitant suitors. It was inevitable that Beethoven should seek escape in fantasies. The greatest of these fantasies was the famous letter addressed to an "unsterbliche Geliebte," the "Immortal Beloved," couched in exuberant emotional tones characteristic of the sentimental romances of the time, and strangely reminiscent of Goethe's novel *The Sorrows of Young Werther*. The letter was never mailed; it was discovered in the secret compartment of Beethoven's writing desk after his death. The clues to the identity of the object of his passion were maddeningly few. He voiced his fervid anticipation of an impending meeting at some place indicated only by the initial letter "K."; he dated his letter as Monday, the 6th of July, without specifying the year. Eager Beethoveniacs readily established that the most likely year was 1812,

when July 6 fell on a Monday. A complete inventory of ladies of Beethoven's acquaintance from 14 to 40 years of age was laid out, and the lengthy charade unfolded, lasting one and a half centuries. The most likely "Immortal Beloved" seemed to be Antoine Brentano, the wife of a merchant. But Beethoven was a frequent visitor at their house; his letters to her (sent by ordinary city post) and her replies expressed mutual devotion, but they could not be stylistically reconciled with the torrid protestation of undying love in the unmailed letter. And if indeed Frau Brentano was the "Immortal Beloved," why could not a tryst have been arranged in Vienna when her husband was away on business? There were other candidates; one researcher established, from consulting the town records of arrivals and departures, that Beethoven and a certain lady of his Vienna circle were in Prague on the same day, and that about 9 months later she bore a child who seemed to bear a remarkable resemblance to Beethoven. Another researcher, exploring the limits of the incredible, concluded that Beethoven had sexual relations with his sister-in-law and that his execration of her stemmed from this relationship. It was asserted also that a certain musician conversant with the lowlife of Vienna supplied Beethoven with *filles de joie* for pay. The nadir of monstrous speculation was reached by a pseudo-Freudian investigator who advanced the notion that Beethoven nurtured incestuous desires toward his nephew and that his demands drove the boy to his suicide attempt.

The so-called 3rd style of Beethoven was assigned by biographers to the last 10 or 15 years of his life. It included the composition of his monumental 9th Symph., completed in 1824 and first performed in Vienna on May 7, 1824; the program also included excerpts from the *Missa Solemnis* and *Die Weihe des Hauses (The Consecration of the House)*. It was reported, on scant evidence, that Caroline Unger, the contralto soloist in the *Missa Solemnis,* had to pull Beethoven by the sleeve at the end of the performance so that he would acknowledge the applause he could not hear. With the 9th Symph., Beethoven completed the evolution of the symph. form as he envisioned it. Its choral finale was Beethoven's manifesto addressed to the world at large, to the text from Schiller's ode *An die Freude (To Joy)*. In it, Beethoven, through Schiller, appealed to all humanity to unite in universal love. Here a musical work, for the first time, served a political ideal. Rumors that Beethoven was planning to compose still another symph. were not substantiated; indeed, the number 9 became symbolic for future composers as the point of musical infinity; Mahler and Bruckner recoiled from exceeding the magic number. Beethoven's last string quartets, opp. 127, 130, 131, and 132, served as counterparts of Beethoven's last symph. in their striking innovations, dramatic pauses, and novel instrumental tone colors.

In Dec. 1826, on his way back to Vienna from a visit in Gneixendorf, Beethoven was stricken with a fever that developed into a mortal pleurisy; dropsy and jaundice supervened to this condition; surgery to relieve the accumulated fluid in his or-

Beethoven

ganism was unsuccessful, and he died on the afternoon of March 26, 1827. It was widely reported that an electric storm struck Vienna as Beethoven lay dying; its occurrence was indeed confirmed by the contemporary records in the Vienna weather bureau, but the story that Beethoven raised his clenched fist aloft as a gesture of defiance to an overbearing Heaven must be relegated to fantasy; he was far too feeble either to clench his fist or to raise his arm. The funeral of Beethoven was held in all solemnity.

Beethoven was memorialized in festive observations of the centennial and bicentennial of his birth, and of the centennial and sesquicentennial of his death. The house where he was born in Bonn was declared a museum. Monuments were erected to him in many cities. Commemorative postage stamps bearing his image were issued not only in Germany and Austria, but in Russia and other countries. Streets were named after him in many cities of the civilized world, including even Los Angeles.

Beethoven's music marks a division between the Classical period of the 18th century, exemplified by the great names of Mozart and Haydn, and the new spirit of Romantic music that characterized the entire course of the 19th century. There are certain purely external factors that distinguish these 2 periods of musical evolution; one of them pertains to sartorial matters. Music before Beethoven was *Zopfmusik,* pigtail music. Haydn and Mozart are familiar to us by portraits in which their heads are crowned by elaborate wigs; Beethoven's hair was by contrast luxuriant in its unkempt splendor. The music of the 18th century possessed the magnitude of mass production. The accepted number of Haydn's symphs., according to his own count, is 104, but even in his own catalogue Haydn allowed a duplication of one of his symph. works. Mozart wrote about 40 symphs. during his short lifetime. Haydn's symphs. were constructed according to an easily defined formal structure; while Mozart's last symphs. show greater depth of penetration, they do not depart from the Classical convention. Besides, both Haydn and Mozart wrote instrumental works variously entitled cassations, serenades, divertimentos, and suites, which were basically synonymous with symphs. But Beethoven did not write serenades or other works in quasi-symph. form. And his symphs. were few in number and mutually different. The first and 2nd symphs. may still be classified as *Zopfmusik,* but with the 3rd Symph. he entered a new world of music. No symph. written before had contained a clearly defined funeral march. Although the 5th Symph. had no designated program, it lent itself easily to programmatic interpretation. Wagner attached a bombastic label, "Apotheosis of the Dance," to Beethoven's 7th Symph. The 8th escaped a sobriquet, and the 9th is usually known as the *Choral* symph. With the advent of Beethoven, the manufacture of symphs. en masse had ceased; Schumann, Brahms, Tchaikovsky, and their contemporaries wrote but a few symphs. each, and each had a distinctive physiognomy. Beethoven had forever destroyed *Zopfmusik,* and opened the floodgates of the Romantic era. Bee-

thoven's music was individual; it was emotionally charged; his Kreutzer Sonata served as a symbol for Tolstoy's celebrated moralistic tale of that name, in which the last movement of the sonata leads the woman pianist into the receptive arms of the concupiscent violinist. But technically the sonata is very difficult for amateurs to master, and Tolstoy's sinners were an ordinary couple in old Russia.

Similarly novel were Beethoven's string quartets; a musical abyss separated his last string quartets from his early essays in the same form. Trios, violin sonatas, cello sonatas, and the 32 great piano sonatas also represent evolutionary concepts. Yet Beethoven's melody and harmony did not diverge from the sacrosanct laws of euphony and tonality. The famous dissonant chord introducing the last movement of the 9th Symph. resolves naturally into the tonic, giving only a moment's pause to the ear. Beethoven's favorite device of pairing the melody in the high treble with triadic chords in close harmony in the deep bass was a peculiarity of his style but not necessarily an infringement of the Classical rules. Yet contemporary critics found some of these practices repugnant and described Beethoven as an eccentric bent on creating unconventional sonorities. Equally strange to the untutored ear were pregnant pauses and sudden modulations in his instrumental works. Beethoven was not a contrapuntist by taste or skill. With the exception of his monumental *Grosse Fuge,* composed as the finale of the String Quartet, op. 133, his fugal movements were usually free canonic imitations. There is only a single instance in Beethoven's music of the crab movement, a variation achieved by running the theme in reverse. But Beethoven was a master of instrumental variation, deriving extraordinary transformations through melodic and rhythmic alterations of a given theme. Beethoven's op. 120, 33 variations for piano on a waltz theme by the Viennese publisher Diabelli, represents one of the greatest achievements in the art.

When Hans von Bülow was asked which was his favorite key signature, he replied that it was E-flat major, the tonality of the *Eroica,* for it had 3 flats: one for Bach, one for Beethoven, and one for Brahms. Beethoven became forever the 2nd B in popular music books.

The literature on Beethoven is immense. The basic catalogues are those by G. Kinsky and H. Halm, *Das Werk Beethovens. Thematisch-Bibliographisches Verzeichnis seiner sämtlichen vollendenten Kompositionen,* publ. in Munich and Duisburg in 1955, and by W. Hess, *Verzeichnis der Gesamtausgabe veröffentlichen Werke Ludwig van Beethovens,* publ. in Wiesbaden in 1957. Beethoven attached opus numbers to most of his works, and they are essential in a catalogue of his works.

WORKS: FOR ORCH.: 9 symphs.: No. 1, in C major, op. 21 (1800; Vienna, April 2, 1800); No. 2, in D major, op. 36 (1801–2; Vienna, April 5, 1803); No. 3, in E-flat major, op. 55, *Eroica* (1803–4; Vienna, April 7, 1805); No. 4, in B-flat major, op. 60 (1806; Vienna, March 5, 1807); No. 5, in C minor, op. 67 (sketches from 1803; 1807–8; Vienna, Dec. 22, 1808); No. 6, in F major, op. 68, *Pastoral* (sketches from 1803; 1808; Vienna, Dec.

22, 1808); No. 7, in A major, op. 92 (1811–12; Vienna, Dec. 8, 1813); No. 8, in F major, op. 93 (1812; Vienna, Feb. 27, 1814); No. 9, in D minor, op. 125, *Choral* (sketches from 1815–18; 1822–24; Vienna, May 7, 1824); also a fragment of a Symph. in C minor, Hess 298 from the Bonn period.—Incidental music: Overture to Collin's *Coriolan*, in C minor, op. 62 (1807; Vienna, March 1807); *Egmont*, op. 84, to Goethe's drama (with overture; 1809–10; Vienna, June 15, 1810); *Die Ruinen von Athen (The Ruins of Athens)*, op. 113, to Kotzebue's drama (with overture; 1811; Pest, Feb. 10, 1812); *König Stephan (King Stephen)*, op. 117, to Kotzebue's drama (with overture; 1811; Pest, Feb. 10, 1812); Triumphal March in C major for Kuffner's *Tarpeja* (1813; March 26, 1813); music to Duncker's drama *Leonore Prohaska* (1815); Overture in C major, op. 124, to Meisl's drama *Die Weihe des Hauses (The Consecration of the House;* 1822; Vienna, Oct. 3, 1822).—Further overtures: 4 overtures written for the opera *Leonore,* later named *Fidelio: Leonore* No. 1, in C major, op. 138 (1806–7; Feb. 7, 1828); *Leonore* No. 2, op. 72a (1804–5; Vienna, Nov. 20, 1805); *Leonore* No. 3, op. 72b (1805–6; Vienna, March 29, 1806); *Fidelio,* op. 72c (1814; Vienna, May 27, 1814); *Namensfeier (Nameday)* in C major, op. 115 (1814–15; Vienna, Dec. 25, 1815).—Other works for Orch. or Wind Band: 12 Minuets, WoO 7 (1795); 12 German Dances (1795); 12 Contredanses (1802?); March "für die bohmische Landwehr" in F major (1809); March in F major (1810); Polonaise in D major, WoO 21 (1810); Ecossaise in D major (1810); Ecossaise in G major (1810); *Wellingtons Sieg oder Die Schlacht bei Vittoria (Wellington's Victory or The Battle of Vittoria;* also known as the *Battle* symph.), op. 91 (1813; Vienna, Dec. 8, 1813); March in D major (1816); *Gratulations-Menuet* in E-flat major, WoO 3 (1822; Nov. 3, 1822); March with Trio in C major (1822?).—Ballets: *Ritterballett (Knight's Ballet;* 1790–91; Bonn, March 6, 1791); *Die Geschöpfe des Prometheus (The Creatures of Prometheus),* op. 43 (overture, introduction, and 16 numbers; 1800–1; Vienna, March 28, 1801).—Works for Solo Instruments and Orch.: Piano Concerto in E-flat major (1784); *Romance* in E minor for Piano, Flute, Bassoon, and Orch., Hess 13 (1786; only a fragment extant); Violin Concerto in C major (1790–92; only a portion of the first movement is extant); Oboe Concerto in F major, Hess 12 (1792?–93?; not extant; only a few sketches survive); Rondo in B-flat major for Piano and Orch. (1793; solo part finished by Czerny); Piano Concerto No. 2, in B-flat major, op. 19 (probably begun during the Bonn period, perhaps as early as 1785; revised 1794–95 and 1798; Vienna, March 29, 1795; when publ. in Leipzig in 1801, it was listed as "No. 2"); Piano Concerto No. 1, in C major, op. 15 (1795; revised 1800; Vienna, Dec. 18, 1795; when publ. in Vienna in 1801, it was listed as "No. 1"); *Romance* in F major for Violin and Orch., op. 50 (1798?; Nov. 1798?); Piano Concerto No. 3, in C minor, op. 37 (1800?; Vienna, April 5, 1803); *Romance* in G major for Violin and Orch., op. 40 (1801?–2); Triple Concerto in C major for Piano, Violin, Cello, and Orch., op. 56 (1803–4; Vienna, May 1808); Piano Concerto No. 4, in G major, op. 58 (1805–6; Vienna,

March 1807); Violin Concerto in D major, op. 61 (1806; Vienna, Dec. 23, 1806; cadenza for the first movement and 3 cadenzas for the finale; also arranged as a piano concerto in 1807); Fantasia in C minor for Piano, Chorus, and Orch., op. 80, *Choral Fantasy* (1808; Vienna, Dec. 22, 1808); Piano Concerto No. 5, in E-flat major, op. 73, *Emperor* (1809; Leipzig, 1810; first Vienna perf., Nov. 28, 1811); also 11 cadenzas for piano concertos nos. 1–4, and 2 for Mozart's Piano Concerto No. 20, in D minor, K. 466.

CHAMBER MUSIC: 3 String Quartets: E-flat major, D major, and C major (1785); Trio in G major for Piano, Flute, and Bassoon, WoO 37 (1786); Minuet in A-flat major for String Quartet, Hess 33 (1790); Piano Trio in E-flat major (1791); *Allegretto* in E-flat major for Piano Trio, Hess 48 (1790–92); Violin Sonata in A major, Hess 46 (1790–92; only a fragment is extant); *Allegro and Minuet* in G major for 2 Flutes (1792); Octet in E-flat major for 2 Oboes, 2 Clarinets, 2 Horns, and 2 Bassoons, op. 103 (1792–93); Variations in F major on Mozart's "Se vuol ballare" from *Le nozze di Figaro* for Piano and Violin (1792–93); *Rondino* in E-flat major for 2 Oboes, 2 Clarinets, 2 Horns, and 2 Bassoons (1793); Quintet in E-flat major for Oboe, 3 Horns, and Bassoon, Hess 19 (1793); *Rondo* in G major for Piano and Violin (1793–94); String Trio in E-flat major, op. 3 (1793); 3 Piano Trios: E-flat major, G major, and C minor, op. 1 (1794–95); Trio in C major for 2 Oboes and English Horn, op. 87 (1795); String Quintet in E-flat major, op. 4 (1795); Variations in C major on Mozart's "La ci darem la mano" from *Don Giovanni* for 2 Oboes and English Horn (1795); Sextet in E-flat major for 2 Horns, 2 Violins, Viola, and Cello, op. 81b (1795); Sextet in E-flat major for 2 Clarinets, 2 Horns, and 2 Bassoons, op. 71 (1796); Sonatina in C minor for Piano and Mandolin (1796); *Adagio* in E-flat major for Piano and Mandolin (1796); Sonatina in C major for Piano and Mandolin (1796); *Andante and Variations* in D major for Piano and Mandolin (1796); 6 German Dances for Piano and Violin (1796); 2 Cello Sonatas: F major and G minor, op. 5 (1796); Variations in G major on Handel's "See the Conquering Hero Comes" from *Judas Maccabaeus* for Piano and Cello (1796); Variations in F major on Mozart's "Ein Mädchen oder Weibchen" from *Die Zauberflöte* for Piano and Cello, op. 66 (1796); Quintet in E-flat major for Piano, Oboe, Clarinet, Horn, and Bassoon, op. 16 (1796–97); Duet in E-flat major for Viola and Cello (1796–97); Serenade in D major for String Trio, op. 8 (1796–97); Trio in B-flat major for Piano, Clarinet or Violin, and Cello, op. 11 (1797); 3 String Trios: G major, D major, and C minor, op. 9 (1797–98); 3 Violin Sonatas: D major, A major, and E-flat major, op. 12 (1797–98); March in B-flat major for 2 Clarinets, 2 Horns, and 2 Bassoons (1798); 6 String Quartets: F major, G major, D major, C minor, A major, and B-flat major, op. 18 (1798–1800); Septet in E-flat major for Clarinet, Horn, Bassoon, Violin, Viola, Cello, and Double Bass, op. 20 (1799–1800); Horn (or Cello) Sonata in F major, op. 17 (1800; Vienna, April 18, 1800); Violin Sonata in A minor, op. 23 (1800–1); Violin Sonata in F major, op. 24, *Spring* (1800–1); Variations in E-flat major on Mozart's "Bei Männern, welche Liebe fühlen" from

Beethoven

Die Zauberflöte for Piano and Cello (1801); Serenade in D major for Flute, Violin, and Viola, op. 25 (1801); String Quintet in C major, op. 29 (1801); String Quartet in F major, Hess 34 (an arrangement of the Piano Sonata No. 9, in E-flat major, op. 14, No. 1; 1801–2); 3 Violin Sonatas: A major, C minor, and G major, op. 30 (1801–2); 14 Variations in E-flat major for Piano, Violin, and Cello, op. 44 (sketches from 1792; 1802?); Violin Sonata in A minor, op. 47, *Kreutzer* (1802–3; Vienna, May 24, 1803); Trio in E-flat major for Piano, Clarinet or Violin, and Cello, op. 38 (an arrangement of the Septet, op. 20; 1803); Variations in G major on Müller's "Ich bin der Schneider Kakadu" for Piano, Violin, and Cello, op. 121a (1803?; revised 1816); Serenade in D major for Piano, and Flute or Violin, op. 41 (an arrangement of the Serenade in D major, op. 25; 1803); *Notturno* in D major for Piano and Viola, op. 42 (an arrangement of the Serenade in D major, op. 8; 1803); 3 String Quartets: F major, E minor, and C major, op. 59, *Razumovsky* (1805–6); Cello Sonata in A major, op. 69 (1807–8); 2 Piano Trios: D major and E-flat major, op. 70 (1808); String Quartet in E-flat major, op. 74, *Harp* (1809); String Quartet in F minor, op. 95, *Serioso* (1810); Piano Trio in B-flat major, op. 97, *Archduke* (1810–11); Violin Sonata in G major, op. 96 (1812); *Allegretto* in B-flat major for Piano Trio (1812); *3 equali* for 4 Trombones: D minor, D major, and B-flat major (1812); 2 Cello Sonatas: C major and D major, op. 102 (1815); String Quintet in C minor, op. 104 (an arrangement of the Piano Trio, op. 1, No. 3; 1817); Prelude in D minor for String Quintet, Hess 40 (1817?); Fugue in D major for String Quintet, op. 137 (1817); 6 National Airs with Variations for Piano, and Flute or Violin, op. 105 (1818?); 10 National Airs with Variations for Piano, and Flute or Violin, op. 107 (1818); Duet in A major for 2 Violins (1822); String Quartet in E-flat major, op. 127 (1824–25); String Quartet in A minor, op. 132 (1825); String Quartet in B-flat major, op. 130 (with the *Grosse Fuge* as the finale, 1825; *Rondo finale*, 1826); *Grosse Fuge* in B-flat major for String Quartet, op. 133 (1825); String Quartet in C-sharp minor, op. 131 (1825–26); String Quartet in F major, op. 135 (1826); String Quintet in C major, Hess 41 (1826; extant in piano transcription only).

PIANO SONATAS: Three: in E-flat major, F minor, and D major, *Kurfürstensonaten* (1783); F major (1792); No. 1, in F minor, op. 2, No. 1 (1793–95); No. 2, in A major, op. 2, No. 2 (1794–95); No. 3, in C major, op. 2, No. 3 (1794–95); No. 19, in G minor, op. 49, No. 1 (1797); No. 20, in G major, op. 49, No. 2 (1795–96); No. 4, in E-flat major, op. 7 (1796–97); No. 5, in C minor, op. 10, No. 1 (1795–97); No. 6, in F major, op. 10, No. 2 (1796–97); No. 7, in D major, op. 10, No. 3 (1797–98); C major, WoO 51 (fragment; 1797–98); No. 8, in C minor, op. 13, *Pathétique* (1798–99); No. 9, in E major, op. 14, No. 1 (1798); No. 10, in G major, op. 14, No. 2 (1799); No. 11, in B-flat major, op. 22 (1800); No. 12, in A-flat major, op. 26, *Funeral March* (1800–1); No. 13, in E-flat major, op. 27, No. 1, "quasi una fantasia" (1800–1); No. 14, in C-sharp minor, op. 27, No. 2, "quasi una fantasia," *Moonlight* (1801); No. 15, in D major, op. 28, *Pastoral* (1801); No. 16, in G major, op. 31, No. 1 (1801–2); No. 17, in D minor, op.

31, No. 2, *Tempest* (1801–2); No. 18, in E-flat major, op. 31, No. 3 (1801–2); No. 21, in C major, op. 53, *Waldstein* (1803–4); No. 22, in F major, op. 54 (1803–4); No. 23, in F minor, op. 57, *Appassionata* (1804–5); No. 24, in F-sharp minor, op. 78 (1809); No. 25, in G major, op. 79 (1809); No. 26, in E-flat major, op. 81a, "Das Lebewohl, Abwesenheit und Wiedersehn"; also known by its French subtitle, "Les Adieux, l'absence, et le retour" (1809); No. 27, in E minor, op. 90 (1814); No. 28, in A major, op. 101 (1816); No. 29, in B-flat major, op. 106, *Hammerklavier* (1817–18); No. 30, in E major, op. 109 (1820); No. 31, in A-flat major, op. 110 (1821); No. 31, in C minor, op. 111 (1821–22).

VARIATIONS FOR PIANO: 9 Variations in C minor on a March by Dressler (1782); 24 Variations in D major on Righini's Arietta "Venni amore" (1790–91); 13 Variations in A major on the Arietta "Es war einmal ein alter Mann" from Dittersdorf's *Das rote Käppchen* (1792); 6 Variations in F major on a Swiss Song (1792?; also for Harp); 12 Variations on the "Menuet à la Viganò" from Haibel's *Le nozze disturbate* in C major (1795); 9 Variations in A major on the Aria "Quant' è più bello" from Paisiello's *La molinara* (1795); 6 Variations in G major on the Duet "Nel cor più non mi sento" from Paisiello's *Le molinara* (1795); 8 Variations in C major on the Romance "Un Fièvre brûlante" from Grétry's *Richard Cœur de Lion* (1795?); 12 Variations in A major on a Russian Dance from Wranitzky's *Das Waldmädchen* (1796–97); 10 Variations in B-flat major on the Duet "La stessa, le stessissima" from Salieri's *Falstaff* (1799); 7 Variations in F major on the Quartet "Kind, willst du ruhig schlafen" from Winter's *Das unterbrochene Opferfest* (1799); 6 Variations in F major on the Trio "Tändeln und Scherzen" from Süssmayr's *Soliman II* (1799); 6 Variations in G major on an Original Theme (1800); 6 Variations in F major on an Original Theme, op. 34 (1802); 15 Variations and a Fugue in E-flat major on an Original Theme, op. 35, *Eroica* (1802); 7 Variations in C major on "God Save the King" (1803); 5 Variations in D major on "Rule Britannia" (1803); 32 Variations in C minor on an Original Theme (1806); 6 Variations in D major on an Original Theme, op. 76 (1809); 33 Variations in C major on a Waltz by Diabelli, op. 120 (1819; 1823).

OTHER WORKS FOR PIANO: Rondo in C major (1783); Rondo in A major (1783); 2 Preludes through All 12 Major Keys, op. 39 (1789; also for Organ); *Allemande* in A major (1793); *Rondo a capriccio* in G major, op. 129, "Rage over a Lost Penny" (1795); Fugue in C major, Hess 64 (1795); *Presto* in C minor (1795?); *Allegretto* in C minor (1796–97); *Allegretto* in C minor, Hess 69 (1796–97); Rondo in C major, op. 51, No. 1 (1796?–97?); Rondo in G major, op. 51, No. 2 (1798?); 7 Bagatelles: E-flat major, C major, F major, A major, C major, D major, and A-flat major, op. 33 (1801–2); Bagatelle "Lustig-Traurig" in C major, WoO 54 (1802); *Allegretto* in C major (1803); Andante in F major, "Andante favori" (1803); Prelude in F minor (1804); Minuet in E-flat major (1804); Fantasia in G minor/B-flat major, op. 77 (1809); Bagatelle "Für Elise" in A minor (1810); Polonaise in C major, op. 89 (1814); Bagatelle in B-flat major

(1818); Concert Finale in C major, Hess 65 (1820–21); Allegretto in B minor (1821); 11 Bagatelles: G minor, C major, D major, A major, C minor, G major, C major, C major, A minor, A major, and B-flat major, op. 119 (1820–22); 6 Bagatelles: G major, G minor, E-flat major, B minor, G major, and E-flat major, op. 126 (1823–24); Waltz in E-flat major (1824); *Allegretto quasi andante* in G minor (1825); Waltz in D major (1825); Ecossaise in E-flat major (1825).—For Piano, 4-hands: 8 Variations in C major on a Theme by Count Waldstein (1792); Sonata in D major, op. 6 (1796–97); 6 Variations in D major on "Ich denke dein" (by Beethoven) (1799–1803); 3 Marches: C major, E-flat major, and D major, op. 45 (1803?); an arrangement of the *Grosse Fuge*, op. 133, as op. 134 (1826).

VOCAL MUSIC: Operas: *Fidelio*, op. 72 (first version, 1804–5; Theater an der Wien, Vienna, Nov. 20, 1805; 2nd version, 1805–6; Theater an der Wien, March 29, 1806; final version, 1814; Kärnthnertortheater, Vienna, May 23, 1814); also a fragment from the unfinished opera *Vestas Feuer (The Vestal Flame)*, Hess 115 (1803); singspiels: "Germania," the finale of the pasticcio *Die gute Nachricht* (1814; Kärnthnertortheater, April 11, 1814), and "Es ist vollbracht," the finale of the pasticcio *Die Ehrenpforten* (1815; Kärnthnertortheater, July 15, 1815).—Choral works with Orch.: *Cantate auf den Tod Kaiser Joseph des Zweiten (Cantata on the Death of the Emperor Joseph II;* 1790); *Cantate auf die Erhebung Leopold des Zweiten zur Kaiserwürde (Cantata on the Accession of Emperor Leopold II;* 1790); oratorio, *Christus am Oelberge (Christ on the Mount of Olives),* op. 85 (1803; Vienna, April 5, 1803; revised 1804 and 1811); Mass in C major, op. 86 (1807; Eisenstadt, Sept. 13, 1807); *Chor auf die verbündeten Fürsten "Ihr weisen Gründer"* (1814); cantata, *Der glorreiche Augenblick (The Glorious Moment),* op. 136 (1814; Vienna, Nov. 29, 1814); *Meeresstille und glückliche Fahrt (Calm Seas and Prosperous Voyage),* op. 112, after Goethe (1814–15; Vienna, Dec. 25, 1815); Mass in D major, op. 123, *Missa Solemnis* (1819–23; Kyrie, Credo, and Agnus Dei only, Vienna, May 7, 1824); Opferlied, "Die Flamme lodert" (1822; 2nd version, op. 121b, 1823–24); Bundeslied, "In allen guten Stunden," op. 122, after Goethe (1823–24).—Additional choral works: Abschiedsgesang, "Die Stunde schlägt" (1814); Cantata campestre, "Un lieto brindisi" (1814); Gesang der Mönche, "Rasch tritt der Tod," from Schiller's *Wilhelm Tell* (1817); Hochzeitslied, "Auf Freunde, singt dem Gott der Ehen" (2 versions; 1819); Birthday Cantata for Prince Lobkowitz, "Es lebe unser theurer Fürst" (1823).—Works for Solo Voices and Orch.: Prüfung des Küssens "Meine weise Mutter spricht" for Bass (1790–92); "Mit Mädeln sich vertragen" from Goethe's *Claudine von Villa Bella* for Bass (1790?–92); *Primo amore,* scena and aria for Soprano (1790–92); 2 arias: "O welch' ein Leben" for Tenor and "Soll ein Schuh nicht drücken" for Soprano, for Umlauf's singspiel *Die schöne Schusterin* (1795–96); *Ah, perfido!,* scena and aria for Soprano from Metastasio's *Achille in Sciro,* op. 65 (1795–96); *No, non turbarti,* scena and aria for Soprano from Metastasio's *La tempesta* (1801–2); "Ne' giorni tuoi felici,"

duet for Soprano and Tenor from Metastasio's *Olimpiade* (1802–3); *Tremate, empi, tremate* for Soprano, Tenor, and Bass, op. 116 (1801–2; 1814); *Elegischer Gesang:* "Sanft wie du lebtest" for Soprano, Alto, Tenor, Bass, and String Quartet or Piano, op. 118 (1814).—Songs: More than 80, including the following: *O care selve* (1794); *Opferlied* (1794; revised 1801–2); *Adelaide,* op. 46 (1794–95); 6 Songs, op. 48, after Gellert (1802); 8 Songs, op. 52 (1790–96); *An die Hoffnung,* op. 32 (1805); 6 Songs, op. 75 (1809); 4 Ariettas and a Duet for Soprano and Tenor, op. 82 (1809); 3 Songs, op. 83, after Goethe (1810); *Merkenstein,* op. 100 (1814–15); *An die Hoffnung,* op. 94 (1815); 6 Songs: *An die ferne Geliebte,* op. 98 (1815–16); *Der Mann von Wort,* op. 99 (1816); *Der Kuss,* op. 128 (1822); arrangements of English, Scottish, Irish, Welsh, Italian, and other folk songs for voice, piano, violin, and cello; numerous canons; etc.

BIBLIOGRAPHY: COLLECTED EDITIONS, SOURCE MATERIAL: *Ludwig van Beethoven's Werke: Vollständige kritisch durchgesehene überall berechtigte Ausgabe,* the first major ed. of his works, was publ. by Breitkopf & Härtel (series 1–24, Leipzig, 1862–65; 25 [supplement], Leipzig, 1888). An extensive supplement was ed. by W. Hess, *Ludwig van Beethoven: Sämtliche Werke: Supplemente zur Gesamtausgabe* (14 vols., Wiesbaden, 1959–71). A new critical ed., *Ludwig van Beethoven: Werke; neue Ausgabe sämtlicher Werke* (Munich and Duisburg, 1961–), is being publ. by the Beethoven-Archiv of Bonn.

The standard thematic and bibliographic index of all of Beethoven's completed publ. works is to be found in G. Kinsky and H. Halm, *Das Werk Beethovens. Thematisch-Bibliographisches Verzeichnis seiner sämtlichen vollendeten Kompositionen* (Munich and Duisburg, 1955). An important supplement to this source is K. Dorfmüller, ed., *Beiträge zur Beethoven-Bibliographie: Studien und Materialien zum Werkverzeichnis von Kinsky-Halm* (Munich, 1978). See also W. Hess, ed., *Verzeichnis der nicht in der Gesamtausgabe veröffentlichen Werke Ludwig van Beethovens* (Wiesbaden, 1957), which lists missing works in the old Leipzig ed.

Other sources include the following: The first valuable thematic catalogue, *Thematisches Verzeichniss sämmtlicher im Druck erschienen Werke von L. van B.,* was publ. by Breitkopf & Härtel (Leipzig, 1851); it was thoroughly revised and enlarged by G. Nottebohm and publ. as *Thematisches Verzeichniss der im Druck erschienenen Werke von L. van B.* (Leipzig, 1868; new ed., together with *Bibliotheca Beethoveniana,* by E. Kastner, Leipzig, 1913; 2nd ed. by T. von Frimmel, Leipzig, 1925); A. Thayer, *Chronologisches Verzeichniss der Werke L. van B.'s* (Berlin, 1865); G. Adler, *Verzeichniss der musikalischen Autographe von L. van B. ... im Besitze von A. Artaria in Wien* (Vienna, 1890); A. Artaria, *Verzeichnis von musikalischen Autographen ... vornehmlich der reichen Bestände aus dem Nachlasse ... L. van B.'s ...* (Vienna, 1893); A. Kalischer, "Die B.-Autographe der Königlichen Bibliothek zu Berlin," *Monatshefte für Musikgeschichte,* XXVII (1895) and XXVIII (1896); W. Haas, *Systematische Ordnung Beethovenscher*

Beethoven

Melodien (Leipzig, 1932); J. Schmidt-Görg, *Katalog der Handschriften des B.-Hauses und B.-Archivs Bonn* (Bonn, 1935); A. Tyson, *The Authentic English Editions of B.* (London, 1963); G. Biamonti, *Catalogo cronologico e tematico delle opere di B., comprese quelle inedite e gli abbozzi non utilizzati* (Turin, 1968); P. Willets, *B. and England: An Account of Sources in the British Museum* (London, 1970); D. MacArdle, *B. Abstracts* (Detroit, 1973).

SKETCHES AND AUTOGRAPHS: G. Nottebohm, *Ein Skizzenbuch von B.* (Leipzig, 1865) and *Ein Skizzenbuch von B. aus dem Jahre 1803* (Leipzig, 1880). P. Mies republ. 2 of Nottebohm's eds. as *Zwei Skizzenbücher von B. aus den Jahren 1801 bis 1803* (Leipzig, 1924; Eng. trans. as *Two B. Sketchbooks*, London, 1979). W. Engelmann, ed., *B.s eigenhändiges Skizzenbuch zur 9. Symphonie* (facsimile; Leipzig, 1913); H. Mersmann, *B.s Skizzen* (Basel, 1924); P. Mies, *Die Bedeutung der Skizzen B.s zur Erkenntnis seines Stiles* (Leipzig, 1925; Eng. trans. as *B.'s Sketches* by D. Mackinnon, London, 1929); K. Mikulicz, *Ein Notierungsbuch von B. aus dem Besitze der Preussischen Staatsbibliothek zu Berlin* (transcription of the sketchbook of 1800–1; Leipzig, 1927); J. Schmidt-Görg, *B.: Drei Skizzenbücher zur Missa Solemnis* (facsimile and transcription; Bonn, vol. I, *Ein Skizzenbuch aus den Jahren 1819/20* [1952]; vol. II, *Ein Skizzenbuch zum Credo* [1970]; and vol. III, *Ein Skizzenbuch zum Benedictus* [1970]; P. Mies, *Textkritische Untersuchungen bei B.* (Bonn, 1957); D. Weise, *B.: Ein Skizzenbuch zur Chorfantasie op. 80 und zu anderen Werken* (transcription; Bonn, 1957); H. Unverricht, *Die Eigenschriften und die Originalausgaben von Werken B.s in ihrer Bedeutung für die moderne Textkritik* (Kassel, 1960); D. Weise, *B.: Ein Skizzenbuch zur Pastoralsymphonie op. 68 und zu den Trios op. 70, 1 und 2* (transcription; Bonn, 1961); J. Schmidt-Görg, *B.: Ein Skizzenbuch zu den Diabelli-Variationen und zur Missa Solemnis, SV 154* (facsimile and transcription; 2 vols., Bonn, 1968 and 1972); H. Schmidt, "Verzeichnis der Skizzen B.s," *Beethoven-Jahrbuch, 1965–68* (Bonn, 1969); J. Kerman, "B.'s Early Sketches," *Musical Quarterly* (Oct. 1970); idem, *L. van B.: Autograph Miscellany from circa 1786 to 1799* (facsimile and transcription; London, 1970); L. Lockwood, "On B.'s Sketches and Autographs: Some Problems of Definition and Interpretation," *Acta Musicologica*, 42 (1970); A. Tyson and D. Johnson, "Reconstructing B.'s Sketchbooks," *Journal of the American Musicological Society,* 25 (1972); R. Wade, "B.'s Eroica Sketchbook," *Fontes Artis Musicae*, XXIV (1977); D. Johnson, "B. Scholars and B.'s Sketches," *19th Century Music,* 2 (1978–79).

CONVERSATION BOOKS: G. Schünemann, ed., *L. van B.s Konversationshefte* (not complete; 3 vols., Berlin, 1941–43); J.-G. Prod'homme, ed. and translator, *Les Cahiers de conversation, 1819–1827* (excerpts; Paris, 1946); D. MacArdle, *An Index to B.'s Conversation Books* (Detroit, 1962); K.-H. Köhler et al., eds., *L. van B.s Konversationshefte* (a complete ed., with annotations; 6 vols. to date: Leipzig, vol. 1, 1972; vol. 2, 1976; vol. 4, 1968; vol. 5, 1970; vol. 6, 1974; vol. 7, 1978); D. Beck and G. Herre, "Einige Zweifel an der

Überlieferung der Konversationshefte," *Internationaler Beethoven-Kongress: Berlin 1977;* P. Stadlen, "Schindler's B. Forgeries," *Musical Times* (July 1977); D. Beck and G. Herre, "Anton Schindlers fingierte Eintragungen in den Konversationsheften," in H. Goldschmidt, ed., *Zu B.: Aufsätze und Annotationen* (Berlin, 1979).

CORRESPONDENCE, NOTEBOOKS, AND OTHER DOCUMENTS: L. Nohl, *Briefe B.s* (Stuttgart, 1865); idem, *Neue Briefe B.s* (Stuttgart, 1867); idem, *B.'s Brevier* (Leipzig, 1870; 2nd ed., 1901); idem, *Die B.-Feier und die Kunst der Gegenwart* (Vienna, 1871); A. Kalischer, ed., *B.s sämtliche Briefe* (5 vols., Berlin and Leipzig, 1906–8; partial Eng. trans. by J. Shedlock, 2 vols., London and N.Y., 1909; T. von Frimmel edited a 2nd ed. of the German original, Berlin, 1908–11); F. Prelinger, ed., *L. van B.s sämtliche Briefe und Aufzeichnungen* (5 vols., Vienna and Leipzig, 1907–11); E. Kastner, ed., *L. van B.s sämtliche Briefe* (the standard German ed.; Leipzig, 1910; 2nd ed. prepared by J. Kapp, Leipzig, 1923); A. Leitzmann, ed., *B.s Persönlichkeit* (2 vols., Leipzig, 1914; 2nd ed. as *L. van B., Berichte der Zeitgenossen*, 2 vols., Leipzig, 1921); M. Unger, *L. van B. und seine Verleger, S. A. Steiner und Tobias Haslinger in Wien, Ad. Mart. Schlesinger in Berlin, ihr Verkehr und Briefwechsel* (Berlin and Vienna, 1921); idem, *B.s Handschrift* (Bonn, 1926); O. Sonneck, *B. Letters in America* (N.Y., 1927); G. Kinsky, *Die Handschriften zu B.s Egmont-Musik* (Vienna, 1933); A. Klarer, ed., *Briefe B.s und das Heiligenstädter Testament* (Zürich, 1944); H. Freiberger, *L. van B., Ein Bekenntnis, mit Briefen und Zeitdokumenten* (Berlin, 1951); H. Müller von Asow, *Heiligenstädter Testament (Faksimile)* (Hamburg, 1952; several later eds.); E. Anderson, "The Text of B.'s Letters," *Music & Letters* (July 1953); D. Weise, ed., *B.: Entwurf einer Denkschrift an das Apellationsgericht in Wien vom 18. Februar 1820* (Bonn, 1953); D. MacArdle and L. Misch, eds. and translators, *New B. Letters* (annotated; Norman, Okla., 1857); J. Schmidt-Görg, *B. Dreizehn unbekannte Briefe an Josephine Gräfin Deym geb. v. Brunsvik* (facsimile; Bonn, 1957); E. Anderson, ed. and translator, *The Letters of B.* (the finest modern ed.; 3 vols., London, 1961); D. von Busch-Weise, ed., "B.s Jugendtagebuch," *Studien zur Musikwissenschaft*, 25 (Graz, 1962); J. Schmidt-Görg, "Wasserzeichen in B.-Briefen," *Beethoven-Jahrbuch* (Bonn, 1966); M. Braubach, ed., *Die Stammbücher B.s und der Babette Koch. Faksimile* (Bonn, 1970); K.-H. Köhler and G. Herre, eds., *L. van B.: Neun ausgewählte Briefe an Anton Schindler* (facsimile and transcription; Leipzig, 1971); H. Goldschmidt, "B. in neuen Brunsvik-Briefen," *Beethoven-Jahrbuch* (Bonn, 1977).

YEARBOOKS, HANDBOOKS, STUDIES: G. Nottebohm, *B.'s Studien* (Leipzig and Winterthur, 1873); T. von Frimmel, *Neue Beethoveniana* (Vienna, 1888; 2nd ed., 1890); idem, *B.-Studien* (2 vols., Munich and Leipzig, 1905–6); T. von Frimmel, ed., *Beethoven-jahrbuch* (2 vols., Munich and Leipzig, 1908–9); T. von Frimmel, ed., *B.-Forschung, Lose Blätter* (10 issues, Vienna and Mödling, 1911–25); L. Schiedermair, ed., *Veröffentlichungen des B.-Hauses in Bonn* (10 vols., Bonn, 1920–34); A. Sandberger, ed.,

Neues B.-Jahrbuch (10 vols., Augsburg and Braunschweig, 1924–42); T. von Frimmel, *B.-Handbuch* (2 vols., Leipzig, 1926); P. Mies and J. Schmidt-Görg, eds., B.-Jahrbuch (this important series began publ. with the 1953–54 yearbook; Bonn, 1954—); P. Nettl, *B. Encyclopedia* (N.Y., 1956; 2nd ed. as *B. Handbook,* N.Y., 1967); L. Misch, *Neue B.-Studien* (Bonn, 1967); E. Schenk, ed., *B.-Studien* (Vienna, 1970); A. Tyson, ed., *B. Studies* (N.Y., 1973, and London, 1974); A. Tyson, ed., *B. Studies 2* (London, 1977); H. Goldschmidt, ed., *Zu B.: Aufsätze und Annotationen* (Berlin, 1979); R. Winter and B. Carr, *B., Performers, and Critics* (Detroit, 1980); A. Tyson, ed., *B. Studies 3* (London, 1982).

BIOGRAPHICAL: J. Schlosser, *L. van B.* (Prague, 1828); F. Wegeler and F. Ries, *Biographische Notizen über L. van B.* (Coblenz, 1838; Nachtrag by Wegeler, Coblenz, 1845; new ed. by A. Kalischer, Berlin and Leipzig, 1906); A. Schindler, *Biographie von L. van B.* (Münster, 1840; new ed. by A. Kalischer, Berlin, 1909; Eng. trans. by I. Moscheles as *The Life of B.,* London, 1841, and Boston, n.d. [1841]. The 1860 German ed., publ. in Münster, was trans. and ed. by D. MacArdle under the title *B. As I Knew Him,* (London and Chapel Hill, N.C., 1966); W. von Lenz, *B.: Eine Kunststudie* (2 vols., Kassel, 1855; 2nd ed., Hamburg, 1860; new ed. by A. Kalischer, Berlin and Leipzig, 1908); A. Oulibicheff, *B., Ses critiques et ses glossateurs* (Leipzig and Paris, 1857); A. Marx, *L. van B. Leben und Schaffen* (2 vols., Berlin, 1859; many subsequent eds.); A. Thayer, *L. van B.s Leben* (still the standard and most extensive biography; publ. in a German trans. from the Eng. MS by H. Deiters, 3 vols., Berlin, 1866, 1872, and 1877. After the author's death, Deiters completed vols. IV and V from Thayer's material, but also died before their publication. He had also revised and enlarged vol. I, Leipzig, 1901. Deiters's MS was revised and ed. by H. Riemann, vol. IV, Leipzig, 1907; vol. V, Leipzig, 1908. Vols. II and III were then revised and enlarged by Riemann and publ. in Leipzig, 1910–11. He completed his task by reediting vol. I, Leipzig, 1917. Thayer's original Eng. MS was completed by H. Krehbiel and publ. as *The Life of L. van B.,* 3 vols., N.Y., 1921. It was in turn revised by E. Forbes and publ. as *Thayer's Life of B.,* 2 vols., Princeton, N.J., 1964; revised ed., 1967); L. Nohl, *B.s Leben* (a major work based upon original sources; publ. in various eds. and formats, Vienna and Leipzig, 1864–77; new ed. by P. Sakolowski, 3 vols., Berlin, 1909–13, omits valuable material); G. von Breuning, *Aus dem Schwarzspanierhause...* (Vienna, 1874; revised ed. by A. Kalischer, Berlin and Leipzig, 1907); L. Nohl, *Eine stille Liebe zu B.* (Leipzig, 1875; Eng. trans. as *An Unrequited Love,* London, 1876; 2nd German ed., Leipzig, 1902); idem, *B.: Nach den Schilderungen seiner Zeitgenossen* (Stuttgart, 1877; Eng. trans. as *B. as Depicted by His Contemporaries,* London, 1880); V. Wilder, *B., Sa vie et son œuvre* (Paris, 1883); W. von Wasielewski, *L. van B.* (2 vols., Berlin, 1888; 2nd ed., 1895); T. von Frimmel, "B." in Riemann's *Berühmte Meister* (Berlin, 1901; 6th ed., 1922); R. Rolland, *B.* (Paris, 1903); G. Fischer, *B., A Character Study* (N.Y., 1905); F. Kerst, *B. im eigenen Wort* (Berlin and Leipzig, 1904; Eng. trans. by H. Krehbiel

as *B., The Man and the Artist, as Revealed in His Own Words,* N.Y., 1905); E. Walker, *B.* (London, 1905; 3rd ed., 1920); A. Kalischer, *B. und seine Zeitgenossen* (4 vols., Leipzig, n.d. [1908–10]); A. de Hevesy, *Petites amies de B.* (Paris, 1910); P. Bekker, *B.* (Berlin and Leipzig, 1911; Eng. trans. and adaptation by M. Bosman, London, 1925; new German ed., 1927); M. Belpaire, *B., Een kunsten levensbeeld* (Antwerp, 1911); V. d'Indy, *B.: Biographie critique* (Paris, 1911; Eng. trans. by T. Baker, Boston, 1913; 2nd French ed., 1927); F. Kerst, ed., *Die Erinnerungen an B.* (2 vols., Stuttgart, 1913; 2nd ed., 1925); W. Thomas-San-Galli, *L. van B.* (Berlin, 1913; many subsequent eds.); A. Hensel, *B. Der Versuch einer musikphilosophischen Darstellung* (Berlin, 1918); La Mara, *B. und die Brunsviks* (Leipzig, 1920); G. Bilancioni, *La sordità di B.* (Rome, 1921); J.-G. Prod'homme, *La Jeunesse de B. ...* (Paris, 1921; new ed., 1927); W. Schweisheimer, *B.s Leiden: Ihr Einfluss auf sein Leben und Schaffen* (Munich, 1922); T. von Frimmel, *B. im zeitgenössischen Bildnis* (Vienna, 1923); A. Albertini, *B., L'Uomo* (Turin, 1924; 4th ed., Milan, 1944); W. Krug, *B.s Vollendung* (Munich, 1924); M. Reinitz, *B. im Kampf mit dem Schicksal* (Vienna, 1924); S. Ley, *B.s Leben in authentischen Bildern und Texten* (Berlin, 1925; 2nd ed., 1970); L. Schiedermair, *Der junge B.* (Leipzig, 1925; 3rd ed., Wilhelmshaven, 1970); K. Kobald, *B.: Seine Beziehungen zu Wiens Kunst und Kultur, Gesellschaft und Landschaft* (Vienna, 1926; latest ed., 1953); O. Sonneck, ed., *B.: Impressions of Contemporaries* (N.Y., 1926); G. Adler, *B.s Charakter* (Regensburg, 1927); B. Bartels, *B.* (Hildesheim, 1927); L. Bertrán, *Anecdotario completo de B.* (Buenos Aires, 1927); A. de Hevesy, *B.: Vie intime* (Paris, 1926; Eng. trans. as *B. the Man,* London, 1927); S. Ley, *B. als Freund der Familie der Familie Wegeler-von Breuning* (Bonn, 1927); E. Newman, *The Unconscious B.: An Essay in Musical Psychology* (N.Y. and London, 1927; 2nd ed., 1969); A. Orel, *B.* (Vienna, 1927); J.-G. Prod'homme, *B. raconté par ceux qui l'ont vu* (Paris, 1927); idem, "B.'s Intellectual Education," *Musical Quarterly* (April 1927); A. Schmitz, *Das romantische Beethovenbild* (Berlin and Bonn, 1927); W. Turner, *B., The Search for Reality* (London, 1927; 2nd ed., 1933); R. van Aerde, *Les Ancêtres flamands de B.* (Malines, 1927); E. Closson, *L'Elément flamand dans B.* (Brussels, 1928; Eng. trans., London, 1934; 2nd Brussels ed., 1946); R. Rolland, *B.: Les Grandes Epoques créatrices* (5 vols. in 7; Paris, 1928–57; in one vol. as Edition définitive, Paris, 1966; Eng. trans. of first 2 vols. by E. Newman as *B. the Creator,* N.Y., 1929, and *Goethe and B.,* N.Y., 1931); R. Schauffler, *B., The Man Who Freed Music* (N.Y. and London, 1929); E. Herriot, *La Vie de B.* (Paris, 1929; Eng. trans. as *The Life of B.,* N.Y., 1935); A. Boschot, *B., La Musique et la vie* (Paris, 1931); R. Specht, *Bildnis B.s* (Hellerau, 1931; Eng. trans., London, 1933); E. Brümmer, *B., Im Spiegel der zeitgenössischen rheinischen Presse* (Würzburg, 1932); J. Heer, *Der Graf von Waldstein und sein Verhältnis zu B.* (Leipzig, 1933); F. Howes, *B.* (London, 1933); M. Scott, *B.* (London, 1934; revised ed. by J. Westrup, 1974); E. Bücken, *L. van B.* (Potsdam, 1935); C. Carpenter, *French Factors in B.'s Life* (N.Y., 1935); F. von Reinhöl, "Neues zu B.s Lehrjahr bei Haydn," *Neues Beethoven-Jahrbuch* (1935); E. Buenzod, *Pouvoirs de B.* (Paris, 1936); W. Riezler, *B.* (Berlin and Zürich, 1936; 9th ed., 1966; Eng. trans., London, 1938); H. Schultz, *L. van B., Sein Leben in Bildern* (Leipzig, 1936); H. Kesser, *B. der Europäer* (Zürich, 1937); A. Schmitz, ed., *B. und die Gegenwart: . . . Ludwig Schiedermair zum 60. Geburtstag* (Berlin and Bonn, 1937); H. von Hofmannsthal, *B.* (Vienna, 1938); R. Petzoldt, *L. van B., Leben und Werk* (Leipzig, 1938); R. van Aerde, "A la recherche des ascendants de B.," *Revue Belge Archeologique*, 2 (1939); C. Brandt, *B., Su vida, su obra, y el sentido de su música* (Caracas, 1940); A. Orel, *Grillparzer und B.* (Vienna, 1941); H. Volkmann, *B. in seinen Beziehungen zu Dresden* (Dresden, 1942); J. Burk, *The Life and Works of B.* (N.Y., 1943); E. Corti, *B.-Anekdoten* (Berlin, 1943); W. Schweisheimer, "B.'s Physicians," *Musical Quarterly* (July 1945); S. Ley, *Aus B.s Erdentagen* (Bonn, 1948); A. Pryce-Jones, *B.* (London, 1948); D. MacArdle, "The Family van B.," *Musical Quarterly* (Oct. 1949); R. Petzoldt, *L. van B.: Sein Leben in Bildern* (Leipzig, 1952; 7th ed., 1968); B. Bartels, *B. und Bonn* (Dinkelsbühl, 1954); S. Ley, *B.: Sein Leben in Selbstzeugnissen, Briefen und Berichten* (Vienna, 1954; 2nd ed., 1970); E. and R. Sterba, *B. and His Nephew, A Psychoanalytical Study of Their Relationship* (N.Y., 1954); W. Forster, *B.s Krankheiten und ihre Beurteilung* (Wiesbaden, 1955); S. Ley, *Wahrheit, Zweifel und Irrtum in der Kunde von B.s Leben* (Wiesbaden, 1955); W. Hess, *B.* (Zürich, 1956; 2nd ed., 1976); D. MacArdle, "B. and George Thomson," *Music & Letters* (Jan. 1956); idem, "B. and the Bach Family," ibid. (Oct. 1957); idem, "B. and the Czernys," *Monthly Musical Record*, 88 (1958); idem, "The Brentano Family in Its Relations with B.," *Music Review*, XIX (1958); idem, "B. and Grillparzer," *Music & Letters* (Jan. 1959); R. Bory, *La Vie et l'œuvre de L. van B.* (Paris, 1960; Eng. trans. as *L. van B.: His Life and His Work in Pictures*, Zürich and N.Y., 1960); D. MacArdle, "B. and the Archduke Rudolph," *Beethoven-Jahrbuch, 1959–60* (Bonn, 1962); idem, "B. and the Philharmonic Society of London," *Music Review*, XXI (1960); idem, "Anton Felix Schindler, Friend of B.," ibid., XXIV (1963); J. Schmidt-Görg, *B.: Die Geschichte seiner Familie* (Bonn, 1964); D. MacArdle, "B. and Ferdinand Ries," *Music & Letters* (Jan. 1965); idem, "B. and Schuppanzigh," *Music Review*, XXVI (1965); idem, "B. und Karl Holz," *Die Musikforschung*, XX (1967); J. and B. Massin, *L. van B.* (Paris, 1967); M. Solomon, "B. and Bonaparte," *Music Review*, XXIX (1968); G. Marek, *B.: Biography of a Genius* (N.Y., 1969); J. Schmidt-Görg and H. Schmidt, eds., *L. van B.* (pictorial ed. with commentaries; Bonn, 1969; Eng. trans., N.Y., 1970); M. Cooper, *B.: The Last Decade, 1817–27* (with a medical appendix by E. Larkin; London, 1970); H.C. Robbins Landon, *B.: A Documentary Study* (N.Y. and London, 1970); A. Mann, "B.'s Contrapuntal Studies with Haydn," *Musical Quarterly* (Oct. 1970); M. Solomon, "B. and the Enlightenment," *Telos* (Spring 1970); J. Schmidt-Görg, ed., *Des Bonner Bäckermeisters Gottfried Fischer Aufzeichnung über B.s Jugend* (Bonn and Munich, 1971); F. Knight, *B. and the Age of Revolution* (London, 1973); R. Kramer, "Notes to

B.'s Education," *Journal of the American Musicological Society*, 28 (1975); M. Solomon, "B.: The Nobility Pretense," *Musical Quarterly* (April 1975); idem, *B.* (a provocative study which offers a psychoanalytic profile of the composer; N.Y., 1977); R.M. James, *B.* (London, 1983).

THE IMMORTAL BELOVED: La Mara, *B.s Unsterbliche Geliebte: Das Geheimnis der Gräfin Brunsvik und ihre Memoiren* (Leipzig, 1909); W. Thomas-San-Galli, *Die unsterbliche Geliebte B.s: Lösung eines vielumstrittenen Problems* (Halle, 1909); idem, *B. und die unsterbliche Geliebte: Amalie Sebald/Goethe/Therese Brunsvik und Anderes* (Munich, 1909); M. Unger, *Auf Spuren von B.s "Unsterblicher Geliebten"* (Langensalza, 1911); La Mara, *B. und die Brunsviks* (Leipzig, 1920); O. Sonneck, *The Riddle of the Immortal Beloved* (N.Y., 1927); K. Smolle, *B.s unsterbliche Geliebte* (Vienna, 1947); S. Kaznelson, *B.s ferne und unsterbliche Geliebte* (Zürich, 1954); M. Solomon, "New Light on B.'s Letter to an Unknown Woman," *Musical Quarterly* (Oct. 1972); H. Goldschmidt, *B.-Studien, 2: Um die unsterbliche Geliebte* (Leipzig, 1977); M. Solomon, "Antoine Brentano and B.," *Music & Letters* (April 1977).

CRITICAL, ANALYTICAL: GENERAL: I. von Seyfried, ed., *L. van B.'s Studien im Generalbass, Contrapunct, und in der Compositionslehre* (Vienna, 1832; Eng. trans. by H. Pierson, Leipzig, 1853; new German eds. by G. Nottebohm, Leipzig, 1873, and L. Köhler, Leipzig, 1880); W. von Lenz, *B. et ses trois styles* (2 vols. in one, St. Petersburg, 1852; new ed. by M.D. Calvocoressi, Paris, 1909); H. Berlioz, *A travers chant: Etudes musicales, adorations, boutades, et critiques* (Paris, 1862); R. Wagner, *B.* (Leipzig, 1870; Eng. trans. by A. Parsons, N.Y., 1872; 3rd ed., 1883); G. Nottebohm, *Beethoveniana* (Leipzig and Winterthur, 1872; 2nd ed., 1925); L. Nohl, *B., Liszt, Wagner* (Vienna, 1874); E. Mandyczewski, ed., *Zweite Beethoveniana* (Leipzig, 1887; 2nd ed., 1925); T. de Wyzewa, *B. et Wagner* (Paris, 1898; 4th ed., 1914); D. Mason, *B. and His Forerunners* (N.Y., 1904; 2nd ed., 1930); H. Volkmann, *Neues über B.* (Berlin and Leipzig, 1904); F. Volbach, *B.* (Munich, 1905); R. Rolland, *B.* (trans. by B. Constance Hull, with brief analyses of the symphs., sonatas, and quartets by A. Eaglefield Hull, N.Y., 1917; 6th ed., 1927); G. Becking, *Studien zu B.s Personalstil: Das Scherzothema* (Leipzig, 1921); H. Mersmann, *B., Die Synthese der Stile* (Berlin, n.d. [1922]); A. Schmitz, *B.s "zwei Prinzipe"* (Berlin and Bonn, 1923); F. Cassirer, *B. und die Gestalt: Ein Kommentar* (Stuttgart, 1925); A. Halm, *B.* (Berlin, 1926); J.W.N. Sullivan, *B.: His Spiritual Development* (London, 1927; 2nd ed., 1936); T. Veidl, *Der musikalische Humor bei B.* (Leipzig, 1929); H. Naumann, *Strukturkadenzen bei B.* (Meissen, 1931); A. Schering, *B. in neuer Deutung* (Leipzig, 1934); D. Tovey, *Essays in Musical Analysis* (7 vols., London, 1935–44); A. Schering, *B. und die Dichtung* (Berlin, 1936); W. Broel, *Die Durchführungsgestaltung in B.s Sonatensätzen* (Braunschweig, 1937); A. Schering, *Zur Erkenntnis B.s; Neue Beiträge zur Deutung seiner Werke* (Würzburg, 1938); K. Storck and M. Wiemann, *Wege zu B.* (Regensburg, 1938); J. Boyer, *Le "Romantisme" de B.* (Paris, 1939); L. Schrade, *B. in France:*

The Growth of an Idea (New Haven, 1942); D. Tovey, *B.* (London, 1944); K. von Fischer, *Die Beziehung von Form und Motiv in B.s Instrumentalwerken* (Strasbourg and Zürich, 1948; 2nd ed., 1977); L. Misch, *B.-Studien* (Berlin, 1950; Eng. trans. as *B. Studies*, Norman, Okla., 1953); K. Schönewolf, *B. in der Zeitenwende* (2 vols., Halle, 1953); L. Ronga, *Bach, Mozart, B.: Tre problemi critici* (Venice, 1956); S. Ley, *Aus B.s Erdentagen* (Siegburg, 1957); L. Misch, *Die Faktoren der Einheit in der Mehrsätzigkeit der Werke B.s* (Munich and Duisburg, 1958); P. Nettl, *B. und seine Zeit* (Hamburg, 1958); A. Tyson, "B.'s Heroic Phase," *Musical Times* (Feb. 1969); D. Arnold and N. Fortune, eds., *The B. Reader* (N.Y., 1971); M. Solomon, "B., Sonata, and Utopia," *Telos* (Fall 1971); T. Scherman and L. Biancolli, eds., *The B. Companion* (Garden City, N.Y., 1972); M. Solomon, "The Creative Periods of B.," *Music Review*, XXXIV (1973); H. Goldschmidt, *Die Erscheinung B.* (Leipzig, 1974); idem, *B.: Werkeinfuhrungen* (Leipzig, 1975); I. Kolodin, *The Interior B.: A Biography of the Music* (N.Y., 1975); M. Solomon, "The Dreams of B.," *American Imago*, 32 (1975); M. Chan, *B. in the United States to 1865* (Diss., Univ. of North Carolina, 1976); W. Drabkin, "Some Recent B. Research," *Musical Times* (Oct. 1981); Gerald Abraham, ed., "The Age of B., 1790–1830," in vol. VIII of *The New Oxford History of Music* (London, 1982); J. Crabbe, *B.'s Empire of the Mind* (Newbury, 1982); W. Mellers, *B. and the Voice of God* (London, 1983).

ORCHESTRAL: G. Erlanger et al., *B.s Symphonien erläutert* (Frankfurt, 1896); G. Grove, *B.'s Nine Symphonies* (London, 1884; enlarged ed. as *B. and His Nine Symphonies*, London, 1896; 3rd ed., 1898); A. Colombani, *Le nove sinfonie di B.* (Turin, 1897); J. Hartog, *L. van B. en zijne negen symphonieën* (Amsterdam, 1904); J.-G. Prod'homme, *Les Symphonies de B.* (Paris, 1906; 5th ed., 1949); F. Weingartner, *Ratschläge für Aüffuhrungen der Symphonien B.s* (Leipzig, 1906; 2nd ed., 1916; Eng. trans., N.Y., n.d. [1907]); M. Barroso, *La IX sinfonía de B.* (Madrid, 1912); H. Schenker, *B.s neunte Sinfonie* (Vienna and Leipzig, 1912; 2nd ed., 1969); E. Evans, Sr., *B's Nine Symphonies, fully described and analyzed* (2 vols., London, 1923–24); H. Schenker, *B.s Fünfte Sinfonie* (Vienna, n.d. [1925]; 2nd ed., Vienna, 1970); E. de la Guardia, *Las sinfonías de B.* (Buenos Aires, 1927); D. Berg, *B. and the Romantic Symphony* (N.Y., 1927); J. Braunstein, *B.s Leonore-Ouvertüren* (Leipzig, 1927); W. Hutschenruijter, *De symphonieën van B. geänalyseerd* (The Hague, 1928); K. Nef, *Die neun Sinfonien B.s* (Leipzig, 1928); O. Baensch, *Aufbau und Sinn des Chorfinales in B.s neunter Symphonie* (Berlin and Leipzig, 1930); H. Schenker, "B.s Dritte Sonfonie zum erstenmal in ihrem wahren Inhalt dargestellt," *Das Meisterwerk in der Musik*, 3 (Munich, 1930); J. Chantavoine, *Les Symphonies de B.* (Paris, 1932); E. Magni Dufflocq, *Le sinfonie di B.* (Milan, 1935); W. Osthoff, *L. van B.: Klavierkonzert Nr. 3, C-moll op. 37* (Munich, 1965); A. Tyson, "The Textual Problems of B.'s Violin Concerto," *Musical Quarterly* (Oct. 1967); F. Kirby, "B.'s Pastoral Symphony as a *Sinfonia caracteristica*," *Musical Quarterly* (Oct. 1970); E. Forbes, ed., *Symphony no. 5 in C Minor: L. van B.* (Norton Critical Score; N.Y., 1971); P. Gossett, "B.'s Sixth Symphony: Sketches for the First Movement," *Journal of the American Musicological Society*, 27 (1974); A. Tyson, "The Problem of B.'s 'First' *Leonore* Overture," *Journal of the American Musicological Society*, 28 (1975); A. Hopkins, *The Nine Symphonies of B.* (London, 1981); L. Lockwood, "B.'s Earliest Sketches for the *Eroica* Symphony," *Musical Quarterly* (Oct. 1981).

CHAMBER MUSIC: T. Helm, *B.s Streichquartette: Versuch einer technischen Analyse im Zusammenhang mit ihrem geistigen Gehalt* (Leipzig, 1885; 3rd ed., 1921); J. Matthews, *The Violin Music of B.* (London, 1902); H. Riemann, "B.s Streichquartette," *Musikführer* (Leipzig, 1901–7); idem, *B.s Streichquartette erläutert* (Berlin, 1910); S. Midgley, *Handbook to B.'s Sonatas for Violin and Pianoforte* (London, 1911); O. Rupertus, *Erläuterunger zu B.s Violinsonaten* (Cologne, 1915); H. Wedig, *B.s Streichquartett op. 18, 1 und seine erste Fassung* (Bonn, 1922); E. Albini, *B. e le sue cinque sonate per violoncello* (Turin, 1923); J. Wetzel, *B.s Violinsonaten, nebst den Romanzen und dem Konzert* (Berlin, 1924); J. de Marliave, *Les Quatuors de B.* (Paris, 1925; Eng. trans. by H. Andrews, London, 1928); M. Herwegh, *Technique d'interprétation sous forme d'essai d'analyse psychologique expérimentale appliqué aux sonates pour piano et violon de B.* (Paris, 1926); W. Hadow, *B.'s Op. 18 Quartets* (London, 1926); H. Mersmann, *Die Kammermusik. Vol. II, B.* (Leipzig, 1930); W. Engelsmann, *B.s Kompositionspläne dargestellt in den Sonaten für Klavier und Violine* (Augsburg, 1931); S. Grew, "B.'s 'Grosse Fuge,'" *Musical Quarterly* (Oct. 1931); R. Giraldi, *Analisi formale ed estetica dei primi tempi Quartetti Op. 18* (Rome, 1933); S. Kjellstrom, *B.'s strakkvartetter, en orientering* (Stockholm, 1936); G. Abraham, *B.'s Second-Period Quartets* (London, 1942); D. Mason, *The Quartets of B.* (N.Y., 1947); D. Cooke, "The Unity of B.'s Late Quartets," *Music Review*, XXIV (1963); W. Kirkendale, "The 'Great Fugue' Op. 133: B.'s 'Art of Fugue,'" *Acta Musicologica*, XXXV (1963); I. Mahaim, *B.: Naissance et renaissance des derniers quatuors* (an original and informative investigation, including valuable biographical documentation on 19th-century performances of Beethoven's late quartets; 2 vols., Paris, 1964); J. Szigeti, *The Ten B. Sonatas for Piano and Violin* (Urbana, Ill., 1965); P. Radcliffe, *B.'s String Quartets* (London, 1965, and N.Y., 1968); J. Kerman, *The B. Quartets* (an important study; N.Y., 1967); H. Truscott, *B.'s Late String Quartets* (London, 1968); R. Stephan, "Zu B.s letzten Quartetten," *Die Musikforschung*, XXIII (1970); C. Wolff, ed., *The String Quartets of Haydn, Mozart, and B.: Studies of the Autograph Manuscripts* (a valuable investigation; Cambridge, Mass., 1980).

PIANO MUSIC: E. von Elterlein, *B.s Klaviersonaten* (Leipzig, 1856; 5th ed., 1895; Eng. trans., London, 1898); A. Marx, *Anleitung zum Vortrag Beethovensche Klavierwerke* (Berlin, 1863; 4th ed., 1912); C. Reinecke, *Die Beethovenschen Klaviersonaten* (Leipzig, 1873; many subsequent printings; Eng. trans., London, 1898); W. Nagel, *B. und seine Klaviersonaten* (2 vols., Langensalza, 1903–5; 2nd ed.,

1923–24); R. Nesieht, *Das goldene Zeitalter der Klaviersonate* (Cologne, 1910); H. Schenker, ed., *Die letzten fünf Sonaten von B.: Kritische Ausgabe mit Einführung und Erläuterung* (4 vols., Vienna, 1913–21; new ed., abridged, 1971–72); H. Riemann, *L. van B.s sämtliche Klavier-Solosonaten* (3 vols., Berlin, 1919–20); S. Leoni, *Le sonate per pianoforte di B.* (Turin, 1922); W. Behrend, *L. van B.s klaversonater* . . . (Copenhagen, 1923; Eng. trans. as *L. van B.'s Pianoforte Sonatas,* London, 1927); F. Volbach, *Erläuterungen zu den Klaviersonaten B.s* (3rd ed., Cologne, 1924); A. Milne, *B., The Pianoforte Sonatas* (London, 1925–28); I. Peters, *B.s Klaviermusik* (Berlin, 1925); J. Johnstone, *Notes on the Interpretation of 24 Famous Pianoforte Sonatas by B.* (London, 1927); D. Tovey, *A Companion to B.'s Pianoforte Sonatas (Bar-to-Bar Analysis)* (London, 1931); H. Westerby, *B. and His Piano Works* (London, 1931); A. Coviello, *Difficulties of B.'s Pianoforte Sonatas* (London, 1935); R. Kastner, *B.'s Pianoforte Sonatas; A Descriptive Commentary on the Sonatas in the Light of Schnabel's Interpretations* (London, 1935); H. Leichtentritt, *The Complete Pianoforte Sonatas of B.* (N.Y., 1936); J.-G. Prod'homme, *Les Sonates pour piano de B. (1782–1823)* (Paris, 1937; 2nd ed., 1950); E. Blom, *B.'s Pianoforte Sonatas Discussed* (London, 1938); E. Fischer, *L. van B.'s Klaviersonaten* (Wiesbaden, 1956; 2nd ed., 1966; Eng. trans., 1959); R. Rosenberg, *Die Klaviersonaten L. van B.s* (Olten, 1957); J. Cockshoot, *The Fugue in B.'s Piano Music* (London, 1959); R. Réti *Thematic Patterns in the Sonatas of B.* (London, 1965); W. Newman, *Performance Practices in B.'s Piano Sonatas: An Introduction* (N.Y., 1971); A. Leicher-Olbrich, *Untersuchungen zu Originalausgaben Beethovenscher Klavierwerke* (Wiesbaden, 1976); A. Münster, *Studien zu B.'s Diabelli-Variationen* (Munich, 1982).

VOCAL AND CHORAL MUSIC: M. Bouchor, *La Messe en ré de B.* (Paris, 1886); M. Remy, *Missa solemnis* (Brussels, 1897); R. Sternfeld, *Zur Einführung in L. van B.s Missa solemnis* (Berlin, 1900); H. de Curzon, *Les Lieder et airs détachés de B.* (Paris, 1905); W. Weber, *B.s Missa solemnis* (Leipzig, 1908); R. Hohenemser-Halensee, "B. als Bearbeiter schottischer und anderen Volksweisen," *Die Musik,* X (1910); M. Kufferath, *Fidelio de L. van B.* (Paris, 1913); M. Chop, *L. van B.: Missa solemnis geschichtlich und musikalisch analysiert* (Leipzig, 1921); H. Böttcher, *B.s Lieder* (Berlin, 1927); idem, *B. als Liederkomponist* (Augsburg, 1928); J. Schmidt, *Unbekannte Manuskripte zu B.s weltlichen und geistlichen Gesangmusik* (Leipzig, 1928); F. Lederer, *B.s Bearbeitungen schottischer und anderer Volkslieder* (Bonn, 1934); A. Schering, *B. und die Dichtung* (Berlin, 1936); W. Hess, *B.s Oper Fidelio und ihre drei Fassungen* (Zürich, 1953); W. Hess, *B.s Bühnenwerke* (Göttingen, 1962); M. Ruhnke, "Die Librettisten des *Fidelio,*" *Opernstudien: Anna Amalie Abert zum 65. Geburtstag* (Tutzing, 1975).

MISCELLANEOUS: A. Orel, ed., *Ein Wiener B. Buch* (Vienna, 1921); *B.-Zentenarfeier internationaler musikhistorischer Kongress* (Vienna, 1927); G. Bosse, ed., *B.-Almanach der deutschen Musikbücherei* (Regensburg, 1927); J. Levien, *B. and the Royal Philharmonic Society* (London, 1927); *Musical Quarterly* (April 1927); *Music & Letters* (April 1927); *La Revue Musicale* (April 1927); A. Schmitz, ed., *B. und die Gegenwart* (Berlin and Bonn, 1937); L. Bachmann, *B. contra B.; Geschichte eines berühmten Rechtsfalles* (Munich, 1963); S. Kross and H. Schmidt, eds., *Colloquium Amicorum: Joseph Schmidt-Görg zum 70. Geburtstag* (Bonn, 1967); *Journal of the American Musicological Society* (Fall 1970); R. Klein, *Beethovenstätten in Österreich* (Vienna, 1970); H. Sittner, ed., *B-Almanach 1970* (Vienna, 1970); *Musical Quarterly* (Oct. 1970; publ. separately as *The Creative World of B.,* ed. by P. Lang, N.Y., 1971); K. Smolle, *Wohnstätten L. van B.s von 1792 bis zu seinem Tod* (Munich and Duisburg, 1970); H. Brockhaus and K. Niemann, eds., *Bericht über den internationalen B.-Kongress 10.–12. Dezember 1970 in Berlin* (Berlin, 1971); C. Dahlhaus et al., eds., *Bericht über den internationalen musikwissenschaftlichen Kongress Bonn 1970* (Kassel, 1971); E. Schenk, ed., *B.-Symposion Wien 1970* (Vienna, 1971); D. Kerner, *Krankheiten grosser Musiker* (Stuttgart, 1973; vol. I, pp. 89–140, attempts to prove that Beethoven was a victim of syphilis).

Beffara, Louis-François, French writer on music; b. Nonancourt, Eure, Aug. 23, 1751; d. Paris, Feb. 2, 1838. He was Commissaire de Police in Paris from 1792 to 1816; left his rare collection of books and MSS to the city of Paris. Practically all of these were burned during the Commune in 1871, but a few are preserved in the Opéra library and at the Bibliothèque Nationale. He wrote a *Dictionnaire de l'Académie royale de Musique* (7 vols.) and 7 vols. of rules and regulations of the Académie (Grand Opéra); also a *Dictionnaire alphabétique des acteurs,* etc. (3 vols.); *Tableau chronologique des représentations journalières,* etc. (from 1671); *Dictionnaire alphabétique des tragédies lyriques . . . non représentées à l'Académie,* etc. (5 vols.); and *Dramaturgie lyrique étrangère* (17 vols.).

Beglarian, Grant, American composer and pedagogue; b. Tiflis, Georgia (Russian Caucasus), Dec. 1, 1927. His family moved to Teheran, Persia; he emigrated to the U.S. in 1947; studied viola with Paul Doktor; then enrolled at the Univ. of Michigan, where he was a student of composition with Ross Lee Finney and musicology with Hans T. David, obtaining his doctorate in music in 1957. He was subsequently on the faculty of the Army School of Music in Munich. In 1969 he was appointed dean of the School of Performing Arts at the Univ. of Southern Calif. in Los Angeles; he left this post in 1982. His compositions include: String Quartet (1948); Violin Sonata (1949); *Symphony in 2 Movements* (1950); Cello Sonata (1951); Divertimento for Orch. (1957); *Sinfonia* for Winds (1960); Woodwind Quintet (1966); *Diversions* for Viola, Cello, and Orch. (1972).

Begnis, Giuseppe de, Italian bass; b. Lugo, 1793; d. New York, Aug. 1849. He made his debut in Modena in 1813; subsequently specialized in buffo roles. He created the role of Dandini in Rossini's *La Cenerentola* (Rome, Jan. 25, 1817). In 1816 he married the soprano **Giuseppina Ronzi;** they sang in Paris in 1819; they also appeared in London at the King's Theatre in 1821. He continued to sing at the King's Theatre until 1827, and then was active as an opera manager in England and Ireland. He eventually went to the U.S., and settled in N.Y.

Begrez, Pierre, French tenor; b. Namur, Dec. 23, 1787; d. London, Dec. 19, 1863. He made his debut at the Paris Opéra in 1815, and then went to London, where he made his first appearance on Jan. 13, 1816, in Paer's *Griselda* at the King's Theatre; he also sang in operas of Mozart and Rossini.

Béhague, Gerard (Henri), French-born American musicologist; b. Montpellier, Nov. 2, 1937. He studied piano and composition at the National School of Music at the Univ. of Brazil, and at the Brazilian Cons. of Music in Rio de Janeiro; subsequently took courses in musicology at the Institut de Musicologie at the Univ. of Paris with Chailley; moving to the U.S., he continued his musicological studies with Gilbert Chase at Tulane Univ. (Ph.D., 1966). In 1974 he became a prof. of music at the Univ. of Texas in Austin. He made a specialty of American and Latin American music; in 1974 he became editor of the periodical *Ethnomusicology.* He publ. *The Beginnings of Musical Nationalism in Brazil* (Detroit, 1971) and *Music in Latin America: An Introduction* (Englewood Cliffs, N.J., 1977). He contributed a number of articles to *The New Grove Dictionary of Music and Musicians* (London, 1980).

Beheim, Michel, German minnesinger; b. Sülzbach, near Weinsberg, Sept. 27, 1416; d. there (murdered), 1474. He was active as a soldier and singer in the service of various German, Danish, and Hungarian princes; was one of the earliest of the Meistersingers who still retained some of the characteristics of the Minnesinger; finally settled in Sülzbach as village mayor or magistrate. He composed many songs; 11 are preserved at Heidelberg and Munich.
BIBLIOGRAPHY: Alfred Kühn, *Rhythmik und Melodik Michel Beheims* (1907); C. Petzsch, "Text-Form-Korrespondenzen im mittelalterlichen Strophenlied. Zur Hofweise Michel Beheims," *Deutsches Vierteljahrsschrift für Literatur- und Geistesgeschichte* (1967); idem, "Frühlingsteien als Vertrags-form und seine Bedeutung im Bîspel," *Deutsches Vierteljahrsschrift für Literaturwissenschaft und Geistesgeschichte* (March 1971).

Behm, Eduard, German composer; b. Stettin, April 8, 1862; d. Bad Harzburg, Feb. 6, 1946. He studied at the Leipzig Cons.; taught at the Erfurt Academy of Music; became director of the Scharwenka Cons. in Berlin (until 1901), and prof. in 1917. He was awarded the Mendelssohn prize for a symph. and the Bösendorfer prize for a piano concerto. He wrote the operas *Der Schelm von Bergen* (Dresden, 1899), *Marienkind* (1902), *Das Gelöbnis* (1914); a String

Sextet, using the Stelzner Violotta; a Piano Trio; a Clarinet Quintet; 3 violin sonatas; a Violin Concerto; *Frühlingsidylle* for Violin and Orch.; male choruses, songs, etc. Behm wrote a short autobiography in *Musik in Pommern* (1932).

Behr, Franz, German composer; b. Lübtheen, Mecklenburg, July 22, 1837; d. Dresden, Feb. 15, 1898. He published many salon pieces for the piano, some under the pseudonyms **Georges Bachmann, William Cooper, Charles Morley,** and **Francesco d'Orso.** His waltz *Les Sylphes* became very popular.

Behrend, Jeanne, American pianist and teacher; b. Philadelphia, May 11, 1911. She studied piano with Josef Hofmann and composition with Rosario Scalero at the Curtis Inst. of Music in Philadelphia; subsequently taught piano at various institutions, including her alma mater and the Juilliard School of Music in N.Y. She particularly distinguished herself as a proponent of American music. She edited songs of Stephen Foster, piano music of Gottschalk, and early American choral music.

Behrend, Siegfried, German guitarist; b. Berlin, Nov. 19, 1933. His father, a guitar virtuoso, guided his early interest in that instrument. At the age of 16 he entered the Klindworth-Scharwenka Cons. in Berlin, where he studied piano, composition, and conducting; made his debut as a guitarist in Berlin in 1952; then toured Europe. He is particularly known for his performances of contemporary music, and has commissioned many works for the guitar.

Behrend, William, Danish musicologist; b. Copenhagen, May 16, 1861; d. there, April 23, 1940. He studied law; held various government positions. At the same time he took courses in music theory; from 1917 taught music history at the Royal Danish Cons. He was one of the founders of the Wagner Society of Denmark. Under the influence of Niels Gade he turned to music criticism, and became critic of *Politiken.* Among his writings are biographies of J.P.E. Hartmann (1895) and of Gade (1917). He contributed to the Danish *Illustreret Musikhistorie* (1905; vol. II, from Gluck to modern times); and to Salmonsen's *Konversationslexikon.*

Behrens, Hildegard, noted German soprano; b. Varel, Oldenburg, Feb. 9, 1937. Of an intellectual bent, she entered the Univ. of Freiburg in the faculty of jurisprudence, astoundingly graduating as a junior barrister. Making a sudden decision to exploit her natural vocal talents, she began to study voice with Ines Leuwen at the Freiburg Academy of Music. In 1971 she became a member of the Opera Studio of the Deutsche Oper am Rhein in Düsseldorf; in 1972 became a member of the Deutsche Oper; also made guest appearances with the Frankfurt Opera, Zürich Opera, Vienna State Opera, Salzburg Festival, Bavarian State Opera in Munich, and Paris Opéra. She was particularly impressive in dramatic roles in modern operas, as *Salome* and *Fidelio*, as Marie in *Wozzeck*, and Kát'a Kabanová in Janáček's opera. On Oct. 15, 1976, she made her American debut at the Metropolitan Opera, N.Y., as Giorgetta in *Il Tabarro*.

Behrens, Jack, American composer; b. Lancaster, Pa., March 25, 1935. He studied composition at the Juilliard School of Music, N.Y., with Bergsma, Persichetti, and Mennin, graduating in 1959; then took courses at Harvard Univ. with Leon Kirchner and Roger Sessions, obtaining his Ph.D. in composition in 1973. He was subsequently on the faculty of the Univ. of Saskatchewan, Canada (1962–66), and of Calif. State College, Bakersfield (1970–76); in 1976 he was appointed chairman of the dept. of theory and composition at the Univ. of Western Ontario, London, Canada. In his music he adopts a sophisticated modern idiom without transgressing into the musically unfeasible.
WORKS: *Introspection* for Strings (1956); *Quarter-Tone Quartet* (1960); Concertino for Trombone and 8 Instruments (1961); Passacaglia for Piano (1963); *Declaration 1964* for Orch. (1964); *Pentad* for Vibraphone and Piano (1965); *The Lay of Thrym,* opera (Regina, Saskatchewan, April 13, 1968); *The Sound of Milo* for Orch. (1970); *Triple Concerto* for Clarinet, Violin, Piano, and Orch. (1971); *The Feast of Life* for Piano (1975); Fantasia on Francis Hopkinson's tune "My Days Have Been So Wondrous Free" for Orch. (Fresno, Calif., March 20, 1976).

Behrens, Johan Diderik, Norwegian choral conductor; b. Bergen, Feb. 26, 1820; d. Christiania, Jan. 29, 1890. He studied theology; then decided upon a career in music; in 1846 he became a singing teacher at the Latinskole in Christiania. He organized various choral groups in Norway and led performances at choral festivals. He also compiled valuable editions of songs for men's choral groups.

Beiderbecke, Bix (real name, **Leon Bismarck Beiderbecke**), American jazz cornet player; b. Davenport, Iowa, March 10, 1903; d. New York, Aug. 6, 1931. His parents, German immigrants, were amateur musicians, and he began to play as a small child. As he grew he developed a flair for ragtime and jazz. He played cornet in various jazz groups in Chicago and St. Louis, and developed his distinctive style of rhythmic lyricism. In 1927 he joined the Paul Whiteman band. Although lacking a formal musical education, he wrote a number of beguilingly attractive piano pieces of which one, *In a Mist,* shows a curious impressionistic coloring. Addicted to alcohol, he succumbed at the age of 28. His musical legacy was preserved in recordings, and soon a cult was formed around his name, which was greatly enhanced by the publication of Dorothy Baker's semi-fictional biography, *Young Man with a Horn* (N.Y., 1938). Two factual biographies were publ. in 1974: R. Berton, *Remembering Bix: A Memoir of the Jazz Age,* and R. Sudhalter and P. Evans, *Bix: Man and Legend.*

Beilschmidt, Curt, German composer; b. Magdeburg, March 20, 1886; d. Leipzig, March 7, 1962. He studied in Magdeburg with Fritz Kauffmann; then in Leipzig (1905–9) with Stephan Krehl (theory), Adolf Ruthardt (piano), and Hans Sitt (violin). He served in the German army in World War I; returned to Leipzig in 1923 and founded a choral-symph. group which he continued to lead until 1954; also taught at the Leipzig Hochschule für Musik (1946–56). His catalogue comprises 141 opus numbers, among them the dance opera *Das Abenteuer im Walde* (Leipzig, 1918); the opera buffa *Meister Innocenz;* the pastoral play *Der schlaue Amor* (Leipzig, 1921); the musical divertimento *Der Tugendwächter* (Halle, 1927); and numerous works for orch. and chamber groups.

Beinum, Eduard van, eminent Dutch conductor; b. Arnhem, Sept. 3, 1900; d. Amsterdam, April 13, 1959. He studied violin with his brother, and piano with J.B. de Pauw; also took lessons in composition from Sem Dresden. He made his first appearance as a pianist with the Concertgebouw Orch. in Amsterdam in 1920; then devoted himself to choral conducting. In 1931 he was appointed associate conductor of the Concertgebouw; in 1945 he succeeded Mengelberg (who had been disfranchised for his collaboration with the Germans during their occupation of the Netherlands) as principal conductor of the orch. He was also a guest conductor of various European orchs.: the Leningrad Phil. (1937), the London Phil. (1946, 1949, 1950); he made his American debut with the Philadelphia Orch. on Jan. 8, 1954; in the autumn of 1954 toured the U.S. with the Concertgebouw. From 1957 until shortly before his death he was the principal guest conductor with the Los Angeles Phil. Beinum was regarded by most critics as an intellectual conductor whose chief concern was the projection of the music itself rather than the expression of his own musical personality. He was equally capable in the Classical, Romantic, and modern works.
BIBLIOGRAPHY: W. Paap, *Eduard van Beinum. 25 Years Conductor of the Concertgebouw Orchestra* (Amsterdam, 1956).

Beissel, Heribert, German conductor; b. Wesel-Niederrhein, March 27, 1933. He studied piano, composition, and conducting at the Hochschule für Musik in Cologne; then was a conductor at the City Theater in Bonn; also made appearances with the leading symph. orchs. in Germany. In 1972 he became chief conductor of the Hamburg Symph. Orch.; he also served as chief conductor of the Chur Kölnisches Orch. and Choir of Bonn; in addition, he taught at the Hochschule für Musik in Hamburg (from 1974). He has appeared as a guest conductor in Western Europe; also in Japan.

Beissel, Johann Conrad, German-American composer of religious music; founder of the sect of Solitary Brethren of the Community of Sabbatarians; b. Eberbach on the Neckar, Palatinate, March 1, 1690; d. Ephrata, Pa., July 6, 1768. He migrated to America in 1720 for religious reasons. His first attempt to build up a "solitary" residence failed, but in 1732 he started the community at Ephrata, which became a flourishing religious and artistic center. Beissel, who styled himself Bruder Friedsam (Brother Peaceful), was a prolific writer of hymns in fanciful German, publ. in various collections, some printed by Benjamin Franklin, some by the community at Ephrata. He composed tunes for his hymns and harmonized them according to his own rules. His compositions were collected in beautifully illuminated MSS, many of which are preserved at the Library of Congress and the Library of the Historical Society of Pa. Beissel was not a trained musician, but had original ideas; his religious fanaticism inspired him to write some startling music; in several of his hymns he made use of an antiphonal type of vocal composition with excellent effect. He left a tract explaining his harmonic theory and his method of singing. Beissel's hymns are collected chiefly in *Zionistischer Weyrauchs Hügel* (1739), *Das Gesang der einsamen und verlassenen Turtel Taube, das ist der christlichen Kirche* (1747), and *Paradisisches Wunder Spiel* (2 independent publications, 1754 and 1766). Only texts were printed in these volumes, but the 1754 issue was arranged so that the music could be inserted by hand. Beissel's life was first described in the *Chronicon Ephratense,* compiled by the brethren Lamech and Agrippa, publ. at Ephrata in a German edition in 1786, and in an Eng. trans. by J.M. Hark at Lancaster in 1889.

BIBLIOGRAPHY: J.F. Sachse, *The German Sectarians of Pennsylvania* (Philadelphia, 1899–1900); idem, *The Music of the Ephrata Cloister* (Lancaster, 1903); *Church Music and Musical Life in Pennsylvania in the 18th Century* (publ. by the Pennsylvania Society of the Colonial Dames of America, vol. II, pp. 26–84 and 242–53; Philadelphia, 1927); W.C. Klein, *J.C. Beissel: Mystic and Martinet* (Philadelphia, 1942); H.T. David, "Ephrata and Bethlehem in Pennsylvania: A Comparison," *Papers Read by Members of the American Musicological Society, 1941* (1946); T. Mann, *Doktor Faustus* (Stockholm, 1947, pp. 104–9; Eng. trans. by H.T. Lowe-Porter, N.Y., 1948, pp. 63–68); A. Briner, "Warheit und Dichtung um J.C. Beissel: Studie um eine Gestalt in Thomas Manns 'Dr. Faustus,'" *Schweizerische Musikzeitung* (Oct. 1958); L.G. Blakely, "Johann Conrad Beissel and Music of the Ephrata Cloister," *Journal of Research in Music Education* (Summer 1967).

Bekker, Paul, eminent writer on music; b. Berlin, Sept. 11, 1882; d. New York, March 7, 1937. He studied violin with Rehfeld, piano with Sormann, and theory with Horwitz; began his career as a violinist with the Berlin Phil. In 1909 he devoted himself mainly to writing. He was music critic of *Berliner Neueste Nachrichten* (1906–9) and of *Berliner Allgemeine Zeitung* (1909–11); also served as chief music critic at *Frankfurter Zeitung* from 1911. Later he was Intendant of the Kassel Stadttheater (1925); then in Wiesbaden (1927). In 1933 he left Germany,

being unable to cope with the inequities of the Nazi regime. He publ. biographies of Oskar Fried (1907) and Jacques Offenbach (1909); also *Das Musikdrama der Gegenwart* (1909); *Beethoven* (1911; in Eng., 1926); *Das deutsche Musikleben, Versuch einer soziologischen Musikbetrachtung* (1916); *Die Sinfonie von Beethoven bis Mahler* (1918; in Russian, 1926); *Franz Schreker* (1919); *Kunst und Revolution* (1919); *Die Weltgeltung der deutschen Musik* (1920); *Die Sinfonien G. Mahlers* (1921); *Richard Wagner* (1924; in Eng., 1931); *Von den Naturreichen des Klanges* (1924); *Musikgeschichte als Geschichte der musikalischen Formwandlungen* (1926; in French, 1929); *Das Opperntheater* (1930); *Briefe an zeitgenössische Musiker* (1932); *Wandlungen der Oper* (Zürich, 1934; Eng. trans. by Arthur Mendel as *The Changing Opera,* N.Y., 1935); *The Story of the Orchestra* (his last book; written in Eng.; N.Y., 1936).

Bekku, Sadao, Japanese composer; b. Tokyo, May 24, 1922. He studied theoretical physics at Tokyo Univ. (1943–50); then studied composition with Milhaud, Rivier, and Messiaen at the Paris Cons. (1951–54). Returning to Japan, he became engaged in pedagogy; was also a member of the Japanese section of the International Society for Contemporary Music from 1955 (president, 1968–73). His works are set in neo-Classical forms; some of them make use of authentic Japanese modalities.

WORKS: 3 operas: *Le Dit les trois femmes (The Story of 3 Women),* opera buffa (1964; Rome, 1964); *Prince Arima* (1963–67; Tokyo, March 13, 1967); *Aoi–no–ue* (1979); *Deux Prières (2 Prayers)* for Orch. (Tokyo, May 10, 1956); *Symphonietta* for String Orch. (Tokyo, Nov. 27, 1959); Symph. No. 1 (Tokyo, Jan. 18, 1962); Symph. No. 2 (1977); Violin Concerto (1969; Tokyo Radio, Nov. 13, 1969); Viola Concerto (Tokyo, March 3, 1972); Trio for Oboe, Clarinet, and Bassoon (1953); Flute Sonata (1954); 2 *Japanese Suites:* No. 1 for Wind Quintet (1955) and No. 2 for 12 Instruments and Percussion (1958); String Quartet No. 1 (1955); Piano Sonatina (1965); *Kaleidoscope,* suite for Piano (1966); Violin Sonata (1963–67); *3 Paraphrases* for Piano (1968); Viola Sonata (1969; rearrangement of the Violin Sonata); *Sonatina in Classical Style* for Piano (1969); choruses. He publ. a book, *The Occult in Music* (Tokyo, 1971).

Belafonte, Harry (Harold George, Jr.), American folksinger; b. New York, March 1, 1927, of a Jamaican mother and a Martiniquan father. As a youth he lived partly in N.Y., partly in Jamaica; worked as a janitor and a cart pusher in Manhattan. When his voice was discovered, he got singing jobs in Greenwich Village restaurants; acted the role of Joe in the film *Carmen Jones* (1954). From 1948–57 he was married to the black child psychologist Frances Marguerite Byrd; his second marriage was to Julie Robinson. His greatest success came as an interpreter of Calypso songs, which he performed with great dramatic power. He made numerous tours abroad.

Belaiev (Belaieff), Mitrofan, renowned Russian music publisher; b. St. Petersburg, Feb. 22, 1836; d. there, Jan. 10, 1904. His father, a rich lumber dealer, gave him an excellent education. After his father's death in 1885, Belaiev decided to use part of the income from the business for a music publishing enterprise devoted exclusively to the publication of works by Russian composers (the printing was done in Leipzig); he also established concerts of Russian music in St. Petersburg (10 symph. concerts and 4 concerts of chamber music each season) and provided funds for prizes awarded for the best compositions. He placed Rimsky-Korsakov, Glazunov, and Liadov on the jury for these multifarious activities. The "Belaiev Editions" became a vital factor in the development of Russian national music. Although a conservative, Belaiev was generous toward representatives of the modern school, such as Scriabin; early in Scriabin's career, Belaiev provided the financial means for him to travel in Europe. The catalogue of Belaiev's publications includes the greatest names in Russian music: Mussorgsky, Rimsky-Korsakov, Borodin, Balakirev, Cui, Scriabin, Glière, Glazunov, Gretchaninov, Liadov, Liapunov, Taneyev, and Nicolas Tcherepnin, as well as many lesser and even obscure composers, such as Akimenko, Alferaky, Amani, Antipov, Artzibushev, Blumenfeld, Kalafati, Kopylov, Sokolov, Steinberg, Wihtol, Zolotarev, and others. The complete list of Belaiev's editions is available in the *Verzeichnis der in Deutschland seit 1868 erschienenen Werke russischer Komponisten* (Leipzig, 1950).
BIBLIOGRAPHY: M. Montague-Nathan, "Belaiev, Maecenas of Russian Music," *Musical Quarterly* (July 1918).

Belaiev, Victor, Russian writer on music; b. Uralsk, Feb. 6, 1888; d. Moscow, Feb. 16, 1968. He studied at the St. Petersburg Cons. (1908–14) with Liadov, Wihtol, and Glazunov. In 1923 he was a founder of the Society of Contemporary Music in Leningrad, which presented numerous works by Western modern composers. He wrote about 20 biographical brochures on contemporary composers; also edited the correspondence between Scriabin and M.P. Belaiev (1922); contributed many valuable articles on folk music of Georgia, the Caucasus, and Central Asia.

Belcher, Supply, American hymn writer, dubbed "the Handel of Maine"; b. Stoughton, Mass., April 9, 1751; d. Farmington, Maine, June 9, 1836. He was a tavern keeper and original member (with Billings) of the Stoughton Musical Society, the earliest American performing group that held regular meetings. He served in the Revolutionary War under George Washington; subsequently lived in Farmington, Maine. He publ., in 1794, a collection of hymns, *Harmony of Maine.*

Belcke, Friedrich August, German trombone player; b. Lucka, Altenburg, May 27, 1795; d. there, Dec. 10, 1874. He was a member of the Gewandhaus Orch. in Leipzig (1815); a chamber musician in Berlin (1816–58); was the first concert virtuoso on the trombone, for which he wrote concertos and études.

Beliczay, Julius von, Hungarian composer; b. Komorn, Aug. 10, 1835; d. Budapest, April 30, 1893. He studied music in Pressburg with Joseph Kumlik; then moved to Vienna, where he had instruction in composition with Franz Krenn and Nottebohm; also took courses in engineering at the Vienna Technische Hochschule (1851–57). He remained in Vienna until 1871; in 1888 he was appointed prof. of music theory at the National Academy in Budapest. He wrote a Symphony; *Ave Maria* for Soprano, Chorus, and Orch.; a String Quartet; a *Serenade* for Strings; and a number of piano pieces and songs.
BIBLIOGRAPHY: A. Jenetschek, *Julius von Beliczay* (Carlsbad, 1889); I. Sonkoly, *Beliczay Gyula* (Budapest, 1943).

Belissen, Laurent, French composer; b. Aix-en-Provence, Aug. 8, 1693; d. Marseilles, Feb. 12, 1762. He studied in his native town; then went to Marseilles, where he served as maître de musique at the Abbey of St. Victor. He wrote mainly sacred music; composed a number of motets.

Belitz, Joachim, German composer; b. Brandenburg an der Havel, c.1550; d. Stargard, Pomerania, Dec. 26, 1592. He studied at the Univ. of Frankfurt an der Oder (1570); by 1584 he was cantor in Stargard, where he remained for the rest of his life. His works include 31 lieder (both secular and sacred) for 4 voices.

Belkin, Boris, violinist; b. Sverdlovsk, Russia, Jan. 26, 1948. He studied at the Moscow Cons. In 1972 he won first prize in the Soviet National Competition for violinists. In 1974 he left the Soviet Union and settled in Israel. He then played with several American orchs., including those of N.Y., Philadelphia, Boston, Cleveland, and Pittsburgh.

Bell, Donald, Canadian bass-baritone; b. South Burnaby, B.C., June 19, 1934. He studied at the Royal College of Music in London; made an impressive debut in a concert at Wigmore Hall in 1958; then sang at the Bayreuth Festivals (1958–60). In 1959 he made his American debut with the Philadelphia Orch. at Carnegie Hall in N.Y.; had guest engagements at the Glyndebourne Festival in 1963 and again in 1973–74. In 1963 he made a tour of Russia as a concert singer. He subsequently was a member of the Deutsche Oper am Rhein in Düsseldorf (1964–67).

Bell, Joshua, precocious American violinist; b. Bloomington, Ind., Dec. 9, 1967. He first studied violin with Mimi Zweig; made his debut as a soloist with the Bloomington Symph. Orch. in 1975 at the age of 7; subsequently studied with Josef Gingold at the Indiana Univ. School of Music; also took summer courses with Ivan Galamian and a master class with Henryk Szeryng. He won the grand prize in the first annual *Seventeen Magazine*/General Motors National Concerto Competition in Rochester, N.Y., which led to his appearance as a soloist with the Philadelphia Orch. under Riccardo Muti on Sept. 24, 1982; he was the youngest soloist ever to appear with it at a subscription concert.

Bell, William Henry, English composer; b. St. Albans, Aug. 20, 1873; d. Gordon's Bay, Cape Province, South Africa, April 13, 1946. He studied at his hometown; won the Goss Scholarship for the Royal College of Music in London (1889); studied organ with Stegall, violin with Burnett, piano with Izard, and composition with Corder and Stanford. He taught harmony at his alma mater (1903–12); in 1912 was appointed director of the South African College of Music in Cape Town; retired in 1935. He was extremely critical of himself as a composer, and destroyed many of his manuscripts. Among his surviving works are the operas *Hippolytus* (after Euripides; 1914) and *Isabeau* (1924). Other works include *Walt Whitman Symphony* (1899); Symph. No. 2 (1917–18); Symph. No. 3 (1918–19); *South African Symphony* (1927); Symph. in F minor (1932); *A Vision of Delight* (1906); *Arcadian Suite* (1908); the symph. poems *Love among the Ruins* (1908); *The Shepherd* (1908); *La Fée des sources* (1912); and *Veldt Loneliness* (1921); Viola Concerto; Violin Sonata.
BIBLIOGRAPHY: M. van Someren Godfrey, "The Symphonic Works of W.H. Bell," *Musical Times* (May/June 1920); H. du Plessis, ed., *Letters from William Henry Bell* (Cape Town and Johannesburg, 1973).

Bella, Ján Levoslav (Johann Leopold), Slovak composer; b. Lipto-Szentmiklós, Upper Hungary, Sept. 4, 1843; d. Bratislava, May 25, 1936. He studied theology in Banska Bystrica; then went to Vienna, where he studied composition with Sechter (1863–65). He was ordained a priest in 1866 and served as church music director at Kremnica (1869). In 1873 he received a scholarship to study in Germany and in Prague; in 1881 he relinquished his priesthood, and subsequently was organist at the Protestant church in Hermannstadt, Transylvania, and music director of the municipality there. He went to Vienna in 1921; in 1928 he returned to Bratislava. He wrote a great quantity of church music in the strict style; also composed an opera, *Wieland der Schmied* (Bratislava, April 28, 1926); a symph. poem, *Schicksal und Ideal* (Prague, March 19, 1876); some chamber music; songs; and piano pieces.
BIBLIOGRAPHY: Dobroslav Orel, *J.L. Bella* (Bratislava, 1924); J. Jindrá, "Ján Levoslav Bella," *Der Auftakt,* XIV (1934). K. Hudek, *J.L. Bella* (Prague, 1937); E. Zavárský, *Ján Levoslav Bella: Život a dielo* (Bratislava, 1955).

Bellaigue, Camille, French music critic; b. Paris, May 24, 1858; d. there, Oct. 4, 1930. Originally a law student, he took music courses at the Paris Cons. with Paladilhe and Marmontel; from 1885 was mu-sic critic for *La Revue des Deux Mondes;* also wrote for *Le Temps.* He bitterly opposed modern music and was particularly violent in his denunciation of Debussy, his classmate at the Paris Cons. His selected essays are publ. under the following titles: *L'Année musicale* (5 vols.; 1886–91); *L'Année musicale et dramatique* (1893); *Psychologie musicale* (1894); *Portraits et silhouettes de musiciens* (1896; in Eng., 1897; German, 1903); *Etudes musicales et nouvelles silhouettes de musiciens* (1898; Eng., 1899); *Impressions musicales et littéraires* (1900); *Etudes musicales* (2 vols.; 1903, 1907); *Mozart: biographie critique* (1906); *Mendelssohn* (1907); *Les Epoques de la musique* (2 vols.; 1909); *Gounod* (1910); *Paroles et musique* (1925); etc.
BIBLIOGRAPHY: L. Gillel, *Camille Bellaigue* (Paris, 1931).

Bellamann, Henry, American author and pianist; b. Fulton, Mo., April 28, 1882; d. New York, June 16, 1945. He studied at the Univ. of Denver (1898–1900), and in London and Paris. He was dean of the School of Fine Arts, Chicora College for Women, Columbia, S.C. (1907–24); served as chairman of the examining board of the Juilliard School (1924–26) and of the Rockefeller Foundation (1927–28); was dean of the Curtis Inst. (1931–32). Among his writings on music are: *A Music Teacher's Notebook* (1920); "Charles Ives, The Man and His Music," *Musical Quarterly* (Jan. 1933); etc. He was the author of a successful novel, *King's Row.*

Bellamy, Thomas (Ludford), English bass; b. London, 1770; d. there, Jan. 3, 1843. He was a chorister at Westminster Abbey; later studied with Tasca. He went to Dublin in 1797 as stage manager of the Theatre Royal; managed other theaters, but his ventures were not successful. He subsequently returned to London, where he sang at Covent Garden and the Drury Lane Theatre. He was choirmaster at the chapel of the Spanish Embassy from 1819–38; beginning in 1821, he appeared as principal bass at the Concerts of Antient Music series.

Bellasio, Paolo, Italian organist and composer; b. Verona, May 20, 1554; d. Rome, July 10, 1594. He was active as an organist in Rome beginning in 1584; he later traveled to Verona, returning to Rome in 1592. He publ. 5 books of madrigals (1578) and *Villanelle alla Romana* (1595).
BIBLIOGRAPHY: R. Casimiri, "Paolo Bellasio, musicista veronese 1554–1594: Nuovi documenti biografici," *Note d'Archivio per la Storia Musicale,* XIV (1937).

Bellazzi, Francesco, Venetian composer who flourished in the early 17th century. He was a pupil of Giovanni Gabrieli; later a follower of Monteverdi. From 1623–28 he was maestro di cappella at S. Francesco in Milano. He publ. a Mass, Psalms, motets, and other sacred music (1618).

Bellère (or **Bellerus,** properly **Beellaerts**), **Jean,** music publisher; b. Liège, 1526; d. Antwerp, Oct. 15, 1595. He was a partner of Pierre Phalèse, *fils*. His son **Balthasar Bellère** transferred the business to Douai, and printed much music up to 1625. His catalogue of compositions, publ. from 1603 to 1605, was found by Coussemaker in the Douai library.

BIBLIOGRAPHY: A. Goovaerts, *De muziekdrukkers Phalesius en Bellerus te Leuven* (Antwerp, 1882).

Bellermann, (Johann Gottfried) Heinrich, German music teacher and theorist, son of **Johann Friedrich Bellermann;** b. Berlin, March 10, 1832; d. Potsdam, April 10, 1903. He studied with Eduard Grell; from 1853 taught singing at Graues Kloster and in 1861 was appointed Royal Musikdirektor; in 1866 succeeded Marx as prof. of music at Berlin Univ. His book *Die Mensuralnoten und Taktzeichen des 15. und 16. Jahrhunderts* (Berlin, 1858; 4th enlarged ed., Berlin, 1963) gives an excellent exposition of the theory of mensural music; his treatise *Der Kontrapunkt* (1862; 4th ed., 1901) revives the theories of J.J. Fux's *Gradus ad Parnassum*. Bellermann attempted to justify his adherence to Fux in a pamphlet, *Die Grösse der musikalischen Intervalle als Grundlage der Harmonie* (Berlin, 1873). He also contributed valuable articles to the *Allgemeine Musikalische Zeitung* (1868–74) and publ. a biography of Eduard Grell (1899).

BIBLIOGRAPHY: O. Schneider, *H. Bellermann, Gedachtnisrede* (Berlin, 1903).

Bellermann, Johann Friedrich, German music scholar; b. Erfurt, March 8, 1795; d. Berlin, Feb. 5, 1874. He dedicated himself mainly to the study of ancient Greek music; his chief work was *Die Tonleitern und Musiknoten der Griechen*, explanatory of the Greek system of notation (Berlin, 1847). He further wrote *Die alten Liederbücher der Portugiesen* (Berlin, 1840) and *Die Hymnen des Dionysios und Mesomedes* (Berlin, 1840), and edited essays by authors of classical antiquity: *Anonymi scriptio de musica, Bacchii senioris introductio artis musicae* (Berlin, 1841).

BIBLIOGRAPHY: "Friedrich Bellermann; Seine Wirksamkeit auf dem Gebiet der Musik," reprint from the *Allgemeine Musikzeitung* (Leipzig, 1874, no. 9).

Belletti, Giovanni Battista, famous Italian baritone; b. Sarzana, Feb. 17, 1813; d. there, Dec. 27, 1890. He made his operatic debut in 1837 in Stockholm as Figaro in Rossini's *Il Barbiere di Siviglia;* made many appearances there with Jenny Lind; later toured with her in the U.S. He had his greatest successes in dramatic roles in Romantic operas.

Belleville-Oury, Caroline de. See **Oury, Anna Caroline.**

Bellezza, Vincenzo, Italian conductor; b. Bitonto, Bari, Feb. 17, 1888; d. Rome, Feb. 8, 1964. He studied piano with Alessandro Longo, composition with Nicola d'Arienzo, and conducting with Giuseppe Martucci at the Naples Cons. He made his conducting debut at the San Carlo Opera in Naples in 1908; then conducted throughout Italy; also had guest engagements at Covent Garden, London, from 1926–30 and again in 1935–36; served as guest conductor at the Metropolitan Opera in N.Y. (1926–35). After his return to Italy he was on the staff of the Rome Opera House.

Bell'Haver, Vincenzo, Italian organist; b. Venice, c.1530; d. there, Oct. 1587. He was a pupil of Andrea Gabrieli, and upon the latter's death, succeeded him as first organist of San Marco on Oct. 30, 1586; he himself died a year later, and his position was taken over by Gioseffo Guami. Bell'Haver publ. several books of madrigals (1567–75), of which only Book II, containing works for 5 Voices, is extant; single works survive in various collections.

BIBLIOGRAPHY: G. Benvenuti, *Andrea e Giovanni Gabrieli e la musica strumentale in San Marco*, vol. II of *Istituzioni e Monumenti dell'arte musicale italiano* (Milan, 1932).

Belli, Domenico, Italian composer; b. c.1590; d. (buried, May 5) 1627. He lived most of his life in Florence. On Sept. 19, 1619, he and his wife entered the service of the Medici court. As a composer, he was one of the earliest representatives of the new monodic style; Caccini praised his music. However, the claim that his short opera, *Il pianto d'Orfeo*, or *Orfeo Dolente* (Florence, 1616; reprinted Brussels, 1927, in Tirabassi's ed.), was the earliest opera ever written is questionable. Among his instrumental works is *Arie per sonarsi con il chitarrone* (Venice, 1616).

BIBLIOGRAPHY: E. Schmitz, *Geschichte der weltlichen Solokantate* (Leipzig, 1914; 2nd ed., revised, 1955); A. Tirabassi, "The Oldest Opera: Belli's 'Orfeo Dolente,'" *Musical Quarterly* (Jan. 1929); M. Bukofzer, *Music in the Baroque Era* (N.Y., 1947).

Belli, Girolamo, composer of the Venetian school; b. Argenta, near Ferrara, 1552; d. there, c.1618. He studied with L. Luzzaschi; was a singer at the Gonzaga court at Mantua. He publ. 3 books of madrigals *a* 6 (1583; 1584; 1593), 9 books of madrigals *a* 5 (1584; 1586; 9th ed., 1617); 2 books of canzonets *a* 4 (1584; 1593); Sacrae cantiones *a* 6 (1585), *a* 8 (1589), and *a* 10 (1594); 2 Magnificats (1610); and *Salmi a* 5; some 5-part madrigals in the collection *De'floridi virtuosi d'Italia* (1586).

Belli, Giulio, Italian composer; b. Longiano, c.1560; d. c.1621. He was a student of Cimello; joined the Franciscan order in 1789; held positions as maestro di cappella at Imola (1582), Carpi (1590), and Ferrara (1592–93). In 1594 he went to Venice, where he served at the church of the Cà Grande (1595), at Montagnana Cathedral (1596), and later at San Marco (1615). His interim posts included service at the court of Duke Alfonso II d'Este and at the Accademia della Morte in Ferrara (1597), at the Osimo Cathedral in Ferrara (1599), at the Ravenna Cathe-

dral (1600), and at Forlì (1603), San Antonio, Padua (1606–08), the Imola Cathedral (1611–13), the Cà Grande in Venice (1615–21), and again at Imola (1621). He was a prolific composer; publications of his works appeared between 1584 and 1615, some being reissued several times, among them madrigals and canzonets (1584; 1593); psalms and vespers (1596; 1604); masses (1586; 1595; 1599; 1608); *sacrae cantiones* (1600); motets (1605); *falsi bordoni* (1605, 1607); and *concerti ecclesiastici* (1613). Many of these works are provided with *basso continuo.*
BIBLIOGRAPHY: A. Brigidi, *Cenni sulla vita e sulle opera di Giulio Belli* (Modena, 1865).

Bellincioni, Gemma, Italian soprano who once enjoyed fame; b. Monza, Aug. 18, 1864; d. Naples, April 23, 1950. She studied singing with her father; made her operatic debut in Naples at the age of 15. In 1884 she made a concert tour of Spain; in 1885 she sang in Rome, and in 1886 made her debut at La Scala, Milan. She married the once-famous Italian tenor **Roberto Stagno,** and the marriage proved fortunate; they sang together in opera and in concert all over Europe and in Buenos Aires, but somehow she was never invited to the U.S. In 1906 she sang the title role in *Salome* in its Italian premiere; on May 17, 1890, she sang Santuzza in the first performance of *Cavalleria rusticana,* with her husband in the role of her operatic ex-lover. On Nov. 17, 1898, she sang at the Teatro Lirico in Milan the title role in *Fedora* by Giordano at its premiere, with Caruso in the role of her Russian paramour. Her husband died in 1897, but she continued to appear in opera and gave concert tours. From 1911 to 1915 she conducted an opera studio in Berlin; then lived in Rome and Naples; in 1933 she became a prof. of singing at the Cons. of Naples. She publ. an autobiography, *Io ed il palcoscenico* (Milan, 1920).
BIBLIOGRAPHY: Bianca Stagno Bellincioni, *Roberto Stagno e Gemma Bellincioni* (Florence, 1943).

Bellini, Renato, Italian conductor and composer; b. Naples, March 7, 1895. He studied piano and theory at the Naples Cons.; then was active as an opera coach. He was assistant conductor of the Chicago Opera Co. (1919–21). From 1921–34 he was in Europe; in 1934 he returned to the U.S. for a concert tour with Tito Schipa; settled in N.Y. in 1936 as a voice teacher. He has written numerous songs, including the popular *Ninna Nanna a Liana.*

Bellini, Vincenzo, famous Italian opera composer and a master of operatic bel canto; b. Catania, Sicily, Nov. 3, 1801; d. Puteaux, near Paris, Sept. 23, 1835. He was a scion of a musical family; his grandfather was maestro di cappella to the Benedictines in Catania, and organist of the Sacro Collegio di Maria in Misterbianco; his father also served as maestro di cappella. Bellini received his first musical instruction from his father and grandfather, and soon revealed a fine gift of melody. The Duke and Duchess of San Martino e Montalbo took interest in him and in 1819 arranged to have him enter the Real Col-

legio di Musica di San Sebastiano in Naples, where he studied harmony and accompaniment with Giovanni Furno and counterpoint with Giacomo Tritto; Carlo Conti supervised him as a *maestrino* and tutor. He further studied the vocal arts with Girolamo Crescentini and composition with Nicola Zingarelli. Under their guidance he made a detailed study of the works of Pergolesi, Jommelli, Paisiello, and Cimarosa, as well as those of the German classics. While still in school he wrote several sinfonias, two masses, and the cantata *Ismene* (1824). His first opera, *Adelson e Salvini,* was given at the Collegio in 1825; it was followed by an important production on the stage of the Teatro San Carlo in Naples of his 2nd opera, *Bianca e Gernando* (1826), a score later revised as *Bianca e Fernando* (1828). In 1827 Bellini went to Milan, where he was commissioned by the impresario Barbaja to write an "opera seria" for the famous Teatro alla Scala; it was *Il Pirata,* which obtained fine success at its production in 1827; it was also given in Vienna in 1828. It was followed by another opera, *La Straniera,* produced at La Scala in 1829; also in 1829 Bellini had the opera *Zaira* produced in Parma. He was then commissioned to write a new opera for the Teatro La Fenice in Venice, on a Shakespearean libretto; it was *I Capuleti ed i Montecchi;* produced in 1830, it had a decisive success. Even more successful was his next opera, *La Sonnambula,* produced in Milan in 1831 with the celebrated prima donna Giuditta Pasta as Amina. Pasta also appeared in the title role of Bellini's most famous opera, *Norma,* produced at La Scala in Milan in 1831, which at its repeated productions established Bellini's reputation as a young master of the Italian operatic bel canto. His following opera, *Beatrice di Tenda,* produced in Venice in 1833, failed to sustain his series of successes. He then had an opportunity to go to London and Paris, and it was in Paris that he produced in 1835 his last opera, *I Puritani,* which fully justified the expectations of his admirers. Next to *Norma,* it proved to be one of the greatest masterpieces of Italian operatic art; its Paris production featured a superb cast which included Grisi, Rubini, Tamburini, and Lablache. Bellini was on his way to fame and universal artistic recognition when he was stricken with a fatal affliction of amebiasis, and died 6 weeks before his 34th birthday. His remains were reverently removed to his native Catania in 1876.
Bellini's music represents the Italian operatic school at its most glorious melodiousness, truly reflected by the term "bel canto." In his writing, the words, the rhythm, the melody, the harmony, and the instrumental accompaniment unite in mutual perfection. The lyric flow and dramatic expressiveness of his music provide a natural medium for singers in the Italian language, with the result that his greatest masterpieces, *La Sonnambula* and *Norma,* remain in the active repertoire of opera houses of the entire world, repeatedly performed by touring Italian opera companies and by native forces everywhere.
For the libretti of his operas Bellini selected melodramatic subjects possessing a natural appeal to the public, with romantic female figures in the

center of the action. In *Il Pirata,* the heroine loses her reason when her lover is condemned to death for killing her unloved husband; in *La Sonnambula,* the sleepwalker innocently wanders into the bedroom of a lord and is suspected of infidelity by her lover but is exonerated when she is observed again walking in her sleep; in *Norma* a Druid priestess sacrifices herself when she ascends a funeral pyre with her Roman lover as a penalty for her betrayal of her sacred duty; in *I Puritani,* set in the period of the civil war in Britain, the heroine goes mad when she believes she has been betrayed by her beloved, but regains her reason when he accounts for his essentially noble actions.

WORKS: OPERAS: *Adelson e Salvini* (dramma semiserio, 1824–25; Real Collegio di Musica di San Sebastiano, Naples, between Feb. 10 and 15, 1825; 2nd version, 1826; not perf.); *Bianca e Gernando* (melodramma, 1825–26; Teatro San Carlo, Naples, May 30, 1826; revised version as *Bianca e Fernando,* 1828; Teatro Carlo Felice, Genoa, April 7, 1828); *Il Pirata* (opera seria, 1827; Teatro alla Scala, Milan, Oct. 27, 1827); *La Straniera* (opera seria, 1828–29; Teatro alla Scala, Milan, Feb. 14, 1829); *Zaira* (opera seria, 1829; Teatro Ducale, Parma, May 16, 1829); *I Capuleti ed i Montecchi* (tragedia lirica, 1830; Teatro La Fenice, Venice, March 11, 1830); *La Sonnambula* (melodramma, 1831; Teatro Carcano, Milan, March 6, 1831); *Norma* (opera seria, 1831; Teatro alla Scala, Milan, Dec. 26, 1831); *Beatrice di Tenda* (opera seria, 1833; Teatro La Fenice, Venice, March 16, 1833); *I Puritani* (melodramma serio, 1834–35; first perf. as *I Puritani e i cavalieri* at the Théâtre-Italien, Paris, Jan. 24, 1835).

BIBLIOGRAPHY: F. Gerardi, *Biografia di V. B.* (Rome, 1835); L. Scuderi, *Biografia di V. B.* (Catania, 1840); F. Cicconetti, *Vita di V. B.* (Prato, 1859); A. Pougin, *B.: Sa vie, ses œuvres* (Paris, 1868); A. Sciuto, *V. B.: Profilo biografico* (Catania, 1876); A. Tari, *V. B.: Reminiscenze* (Naples, 1876); F. Florimo, *B: Memorie e lettere* (Florence, 1882); M. Scherillo, *V. B.: Note aneddotiche e critiche* (Ancona, 1882); G. Salvioli, *Lettere inedite di B.* (Milan, 1884); M. Scherillo, *Belliniana: Nuove note* (Milan, 1885); F. Florimo and M. Scherillo, eds., *Album—B.* (Naples, 1886); F. Florimo, ed., *Album B.—Premio B.* (Naples, 1887); A. Amore, *V. B.: Arte—Studi e ricerche* (Catania, 1892); A. Amore, *V. B.: Vita—Studi e ricerche* (Catania, 1894); A. Cametti, *B. a Roma* (Rome, 1900); P. Voss, *V. B.* (Leipzig, 1901); A. Amore, *Belliniana (Errori e smentite)* (Catania, 1902); C. Reina, *V. B. (1801–35)* (Catania, 1902; 2nd ed. as *Il cigno catanese: B.—La vita e le opere,* Catania, 1935); W. Lloyd, *V. B.: A Memoir* (London, 1908); I. Pizzetti, *La musica di V. B.* (Milan, 1916); C. Gray, "V. B.," *Musical Times* (Jan. 1926); V. Ricca, *V. B.: Impressioni e ricordi, con documenti inediti* (Catania, 1932); L. Cambi, *B.* (Milan, 1934); N. Scaglione, *V. B. a Messina* (Messina, 1934); B. Condorelli, *Il Museo Belliniano: Catalogo storico-iconografico* (Catania, 1935); G. de Angelis, *V. B.: La vita, l'uomo, l'artista* (Brescia, 1935); A. Della Corte and G. Pannain, *V. B.: Il Carattere morale, i caratteri artistici* (Turin, 1935); G. Mezzatesta, *V. B. nella vita e nelle opere* (Palermo, 1935); F. Pastura, ed., *Le lettere di B.*

(1819–35) (Catania, 1935); G. Policastro, *V. B. (1801–19)* (Catania, 1935); O. Tiby, *V. B.* (Rome, 1935); I. Pizzetti, ed., *V. B.: L'uomo, le sue opere, la sua fama* (Milan, 1936); O. Tiby, *V. B.* (Turin, 1938); L. Cambi, ed., *V. B.: Epistolario* (Milan, 1943); P. Cavazzuti, *B. a Londra* (Florence, 1945); S. Pugliatti, *Chopin e B.* (Messina, 1952); F. Pastura, *B. secondo la storia* (the standard source on his life; Parma, 1959); F. Pastura, *V. B.* (Catania, 1959); F. Lippmann, "Quellenkundliche Ammerkungen zu einigen Opern V. B.s," *Analecta Musicologica,* 4 (Cologne and Graz, 1967); F. Lippmann, "V. B. und die italienische opera seria seiner Zeit," *Analecta Musicologica,* 6 (an exhaustive study of Bellini the composer; Cologne and Vienna, 1969); L. Orrey, *B.* (London and N.Y., 1969); H. Weinstock, *V. B.: His Life and His Operas* (the finest study in English; N.Y., 1971); F. Lippmann, "Belliniana: Nuovi documenti," *Il melodramma italiano dell'ottocento: Studi e ricerche per Massimo Mila* (Turin, 1977).

Bellinzani, Paolo Benedetto, Italian composer; b. probably in Mantua, c.1690; d. Recanati, Feb. 25, 1757. He became maestro di cappella at the Udine Cathedral in 1715; received the benefice of S. Ermacora; subsequently was made a censor in Ferrara. He went to Pergola in 1718; in 1721 he resigned from his position in Udine, and in 1724 became maestro di cappella at the Pesaro Cathedral. He was subsequently maestro di cappella at the Urbino Cathedral (1730–34) and the Ferrara Cathedral (1734–35). From 1737 until his death he was maestro di cappella at the Recanati Cathedral. He composed both sacred and secular vocal works of excellent quality, and also wrote instrumental sonatas.

Bellison, Simeon, Russian-American clarinetist; b. Moscow, Dec. 4, 1883; d. New York, May 4, 1953. He studied at the Moscow Cons.; was first clarinetist at the Moscow Opera (1904–14); toured the Far East and the U.S. with a chamber music group (1917–20); in 1920 became first clarinetist of the N.Y. Phil., retiring in 1948. He made transcriptions for clarinet of Hebrew melodies and of songs by Russian composers.

Bellman, Carl Michael, Swedish poet and composer; b. Stockholm, Feb. 4, 1740; d. there, Feb. 11, 1795. He publ. an important collection of songs to his own words; however, most of the music in it was taken from other sources, including publ. works by known composers. He also published lyric ballads expressive of folk life, *Fredmans epistlar* (1790) and *Fredmans sanger* (1791).

BIBLIOGRAPHY: Hendrik Van Loon, *The Last of the Troubadours, C.M. Bellman, His Life and His Music* (N.Y., 1939); P.B. Austin, *The Life and Songs of Carl Michael Bellman* (London, 1968); J. Massengale, "Did Bellman Write Music?" *Scandinavian Studies,* XLIV/3 (1972).

Bellmann, Karl Gottlieb, German organist; b. Muskau, Sept. 6, 1772; d. Schleswig, Dec. 26, 1861. He was an organist in Schleswig from 1813; composed the German national song *Schleswig-Holstein meerumschlungen;* a Christmas cantata; motets; etc.

Belloc-Giorgi, (Maria) Teresa, Italian contralto; b. San Benigno Cavanese, near Turin, July 2, 1784; d. San Giorgio Cavanese, May 13, 1855. She made her debut in Turin in 1801; sang in Paris in 1803, and at La Scala, Milan, from 1804 to 1824; then toured through Italy; also appeared in Paris and London; retired in 1828. Her repertoire comprised roles in 80 operas, Rossini's being her favorites.
BIBLIOGRAPHY: C. Boggio, *La cantante Teresa Belloc* (Milan, 1895).

Bellugi, Piero, Italian conductor; b. Florence, July 14, 1924. He attended the Cons. of Florence; studied composition with Luigi Dallapiccola. He then came to America and studied at the Berkshire Music Center. He was music director of the Oakland Symph. Orch. (1958–59) and the Portland (Oreg.) Symph. Orch. (1959–61). He then returned to Europe, conducting many of the major orchs. and also appearing as an opera conductor. In 1969 he was appointed chief conductor of the RAI (Radiotelevisione Italiana) Orch. of Turin.

Bělohlávek, Jiří, Czech conductor; b. Prague, Feb. 24, 1946. He studied piano with his father; also took cello lessons at the Prague Cons., and attended the master classes in conducting held by Sergiu Celibidache. In 1970 he won first prize in the Czech national competition for young conductors. From 1970 to 1972 he was assistant conductor of the Czech Phil. Orch. He then was conductor of the Brno State Phil. Orch. (1972–77); also toured the U.S. with this ensemble. In 1977 he was appointed chief conductor of the Prague Symph. Orch.

Bely, Victor, Soviet composer; b. Berdichev, Ukraine, Jan. 14, 1904. He studied violin at the Kharkov Cons. (1919–22) and the Moscow Cons., where he took courses in composition with Miaskovsky. In 1925, together with other Soviet composers, he organized the so-called Procoll (Production Collective) in order to promote collective composition by students. From 1929–32 he was a member of the Russian Assoc. of Proletarian Musicians. After its dissolution, he took part in various other organizations of Soviet composers; in 1957 he became editor in chief of the magazine *Musical Life* in Moscow. He also gave courses in composition at the Moscow Cons. (1935-48). In his works, mainly for chorus, he concentrates on the social themes of the revolution and class struggle. Many of his songs became popular. He wrote 4 piano sonatas (1923, 1926, 1942, 1946); also publ. collections of folk songs of the Ural nations.
BIBLIOGRAPHY: Yuri Korev, *Victor Bely* (Moscow, 1962).

Belza, Igor. See **Boelza, Igor.**

Bemberg, Herman, French dramatic composer; b. Paris, March 29, 1859; d. Bern, Switzerland, July 21, 1931. He studied at the Paris Cons. with Dubois, Franck, and Massenet; won the Rossini prize in 1885. Among his works are: cantata for Soprano and Orch., *La Mort de Jeanne d'Arc* (1886); short opera, *Le Baiser de Suzon* (Paris, 1888); grand opera, *Elaine* (Covent Garden, London, July 5, 1892; N.Y., Dec. 17, 1894). He also publ. numerous songs, of which *Chant hindou* became extremely popular.

Bembo, Antonia, composer; b. presumably in Venice, c. 1670; death date unknown. Between 1690 and 1695 she went to Paris; sang for Louis XIV, and received a pension from him enabling her to devote herself to composition. Extant works (in the Paris Bibliothèque Nationale): *Produzioni armoniche,* collection of 40 pieces (motets, duets, soli for soprano, etc., with figured bass or instrumental accompaniment, set to sacred Latin, French, and Italian texts); *Te Deum* for 3 Voices and String Orch.; *Divertimento* for 5-voiced Chorus with String Orch.; *Te Deum,* with Large Orch.; *Exaudiat* for 3 Voices, 2 "symphonie" parts, and Basso Continuo; an opera, *L'Ercole Amante* (1707); *Les Sept Psaumes de David* for various vocal combinations with instrumental accompaniment.
BIBLIOGRAPHY: Yvonne Rokseth, "A. Bembo, Composer to Louis XIV," *Musical Quarterly* (April 1937).

Bemetzrieder, Anton, music theorist; b. Dauendorf, Bas-Rhin, 1743; d. London, 1817. He was a Benedictine monk, but left the order when he became Diderot's pupil and follower in Paris, where he settled in 1770 as a music teacher. In 1781 he went to London. He wrote *Leçons de clavecin et principes d'harmonie* (Paris, 1771; London, 1778) and some other manuals of dubious value; he also publ. polemical pamphlets.
BIBLIOGRAPHY: R. Niklaus, "Diderot and the *Leçons de clavecin et principes d'harmonie* par Bemetzrieder (1771)," *Modern Miscellany Presented to Eugène Vinaver* (Manchester, 1969).

Ben-Haim, Paul, eminent Israeli composer; b. Munich, July 5, 1897; d. Tel Aviv, Jan. 14, 1984. His original name was **Frankenburger;** he changed it to the Hebrew name Ben-Haim after the capture of Germany by the anti-Semitic Hitlerites. He played the violin as a child; then entered the Munich Academy of Arts (1915–20); in 1920 he became an assistant conductor at the Munich Opera, and from 1924–31 conducted opera and a symph. orch. in Augsburg. He left Germany as soon as the country was taken over by the Nazis, and settled in Tel Aviv; there he engaged in a profound study of the folk music of the Middle East, and used it in many of his works, becoming a patriotic composer of his ancestral land. Still, he preserved his traditional learning of Baroque and Romantic European modalities, and contined to compose in the pragmatic forms of symphs. and concertos; several of his scores are fermented by Hebrew melos. He received the Israel

State Prize in 1957 for his work inspired by King David, *The Sweet Psalmist of Israel,* which was performed widely in Israel, and was conducted by Leonard Bernstein with the N.Y. Phil. in 1959. His *Kabbalai Shabbat (Friday Evening Service)* was performed in N.Y. in 1968 to mark the 20th anniversary of the founding of the State of Israel. Also popular was his Sonata in G for Violin Solo, which was frequently included in concert programs of Yehudi Menuhin.
WORKS: Symph. No. 1 (Tel Aviv, June 5, 1941, composer conducting); Symph. No. 2 (Tel Aviv, Feb. 2, 1948); Piano Concerto (Tel Aviv, Feb. 1, 1950); Sonata for Violin Solo (1953); *The Sweet Psalmist of Israel* for Harpsichord, Harp, and Orch. (Tel Aviv, Oct. 18, 1956); *To the Chief Musician* for Orch. (1958); *Vision of a Prophet* for Tenor, Chorus, and Orch. (1959); *Capriccio* for Piano and Orch. (Tel Aviv, Sept. 25, 1960); *Dance and Invocation* for Orch. (Tel Aviv, Feb. 2, 1961); Violin Concerto (Tel Aviv, March 20, 1962); *3 Psalms for San Francisco* for Voices and Orch. (1963); *Myrtle Blossoms from Eden* for Soprano, Contralto, and Piano (1965); *The Eternal Theme* for Orch. (Tel Aviv, Feb. 12, 1966); *Hodaya Min Hamidban (Thanksgiving from the Desert),* oratorio (first perf. at Kibbutz Yagour, Nov. 21, 1967); *Kabbalai Shabbat (Friday Evening Service;* 1968); Cello Concerto (Limburg, the Netherlands, Dec. 14, 1967); Sonata for String Instruments (1969).

Ben-Yohanan, Asher, Macedonian-born Israeli composer; b. Kavalla, May 22, 1929. He came to Palestine in 1935; studied composition privately with Ben-Haim in Tel Aviv; on a scholarship, studied with Copland in the U.S. at Tanglewood in Massachusetts (1966); worked with Nono in Venice (1966) and later at the Univ. of Cincinnati (1969–71); currently teaches at the Bar-Ilan Univ. in Ramat-Gan. His works use dodecaphony.
WORKS: *Festive Overture* (1957); *2 Movements* for Orch. (1959); *Prelude and Toccata* for Piano (1960); String Quartet (1962–64); *Music* for Orch. (1967); *Chamber Music for 6* (1968); *Quartetto concertato* for Piano, Clarinet, Trombone, and Cello (1969–70); *Mosaic,* after 5 poems by e.e. cummings, for Soprano and 10 Players (1970–71); *Meditations on a Folk Song* for Flute, Clarinet, and Piano (1972); Concerto for String Orch. (1973); *Songs of the Scorching Summer* for Baritone and Piano (1974); *Impressions* for Piano (1976); *Soliloquy* for Solo Violin (1977).

Benatzky, Ralph, Czech composer of light opera; b. Moravské-Budejovice, June 5, 1884; d. Zürich, Oct. 16, 1957. He studied in Prague with Veit and Klinger and in Munich with Mottl; then lived mostly in Vienna and Berlin. After the annexation of Austria by the Nazis in 1938, he went to America; after the war he settled in Switzerland. An exceptionally prolific composer, he wrote 92 stage works, about 250 motion picture scores, and perhaps 5,000 songs. His most successful operetta was *Im weissen Rössl,* first produced in Berlin, Nov. 8, 1930. His other operettas

are: *Der lachende Dreibund* (Berlin, Oct. 31, 1913); *Yuschi tanzt* (Vienna, April 3, 1920); *Adieu Mimi* (Vienna, June 9, 1926); *Casanova* (Berlin, Sept. 1, 1928); *Bezauberndes Fräulein* (1935); *Kleinstadtzauber* (1947); *Ein Liebestraum* (on Liszt's themes; 1951); *Don Juans Wiederkehr* (1953).

Benda, Franz (František), famous Bohemian violinist and important composer; brother of **George Anton (Jiří Antonín) Benda;** b. Alt-Benatek, Bohemia, Nov. (baptized, Nov. 22) 1709; d. Neuendorf, near Potsdam, March 7, 1786. In 1718 he became a chorister at the Church of St. Nicolas in Prague; in 1720 he was taken to Dresden, where he sang at the Hofkapelle. In 1723 he returned to Prague. It was not until much later that he began a serious study of music, with Löbel, Koniček, and J.S. Graun at Ruppin. In 1733 he joined the orch. of the Crown Prince (afterwards Friedrich II) as first violinist; in 1771 was named Konzertmeister. During his long years of service for Friedrich II he accompanied him at his flute concerts. Among his works are 17 violin concertos, 17 symphs., numerous solo sonatas, and various pieces of chamber music. His autobiography was publ. in the *Neue Berliner Musikzeitung* in 1856.
BIBLIOGRAPHY: F. Berten, *Franz Benda* (Cologne, 1928); F. Lorenz, *Die Musikerfamilie Benda. Franz Benda und seine Nachkommen* (Berlin, 1967).

Benda, Friedrich (Wilhelm Heinrich), German violinist, son of **Franz Benda;** b. Potsdam, July 15, 1745; d. there, June 19, 1814. He studied violin with his father, and music theory with J.P. Kirnberger. From 1765 to 1810 he served as a royal chamber musician at Potsdam.
WORKS: *Orpheus* (Berlin, Jan. 16, 1785; concert performance); *Alceste* (1786); *Das Blumenmädchen* (Berlin, July 16, 1806); 2 cantatas, *Pygmalion* and *Die Grazien;* 2 oratorios, *Die Junger am Grabe des Auferstandenen* and *Das Lob des Höchsten;* 2 violin concertos; 2 flute concertos; numerous piano pieces.

Benda, Friedrich Ludwig, German violinist and composer, son of **George Benda;** b. Gotha, Sept. 4, 1752; d. Königsberg, March 20, 1792. In 1775 he joined the orch. of the Seyler troupe in Gotha; after 1779 was employed as a violinist in theaters in Berlin and Hamburg. In 1782 he was engaged as violinist and Cammer-Compositeur to the Duke of Mecklenburg-Schwerin. In 1788 he settled in Königsberg. He composed the music for G.F. Grossmann's *Der Barbier von Sevilla* (Leipzig, May 7, 1776); also wrote cantatas and a number of instrumental works.
BIBLIOGRAPHY: H. Güttler, *Königsberger Musikkultur im 18. Jahrhundert* (Kassel, 1925).

Benda, George Anton (Jiří Antonín), important Bohemian composer, brother of **Franz Benda;** b. Alt-Benatek, June (baptized, June 30) 1722; d. Köstritz, Nov. 6, 1795. He was the third son of **Johann Georg Benda.** He studied at the Jesuit college in Jicin

(1739–42); then went to Prussia. In May 1750 he was appointed Kapellmeister to Duke Friedrich III of Saxe-Gotha. In 1765 he received a ducal stipend to go to Italy for half a year. In 1778 he went to Hamburg; also traveled to Vienna; finally settled in Köstritz. His works were distinguished for their dramatic use of rapidly alternating moods (*"Affekte"*), which became a characteristic trait of the North German School of composition and exercised considerable influence on the development of opera and ballad forms in Germany; his effective use of melodrama (spoken recitative accompanied by orch.) was an important innovation.

WORKS: Operas: *Ariadne auf Naxos* (Gotha, Jan. 27, 1775); *Medea* (Leipzig, May 1, 1775); *Philon und Theone,* also known as *Almansor und Nadine* (Gotha, Sept. 20, 1779); the singspiels *Der Dorfjahrmarkt* (1775), *Romeo und Julia* (1776), and *Der Holzhauer* (1778); cantatas, 3 piano concertos; 8 symphs.; 16 piano sonatas; flute sonata.

BIBLIOGRAPHY: R. Hodermann, *G.A. Benda* (Coburg, 1895); F. Brückner, *G.A. Benda* (Rostock, 1904); Vl. Helfert, *G. Benda und J.J. Rosseau* (Munich, 1908); Z. Pilková, *Dramatická tvorba Jiřiho Bendy* (Prague, 1960); F. Lorenz, *Die Musikerfamilie Benda. II. Georg Anton Benda* (Berlin, 1971).

Benda, Hans von, German conductor; b. Strasbourg, Nov. 22, 1888; d. Berlin, Aug. 13, 1972. He studied at the Stern Cons. in Berlin; also at the univs. of Berlin and Munich. He was director of music of the Berlin Radio (1926–33); then Intendant of the Berlin Phil. Orch. (1934–39); after 1939 he organized the Berlin Chamber Orch., with which he toured throughout Europe, South America, and the Far East. From 1954 to 1958 he served as director of music of Radio Free Berlin.

Benda, Karl Hermann Heinrich, German violinist, son of **Franz Benda**; b. Potsdam, May 2, 1748; d. Berlin, March 15, 1836. He studied with his father; entered the service of the Prussian Court about 1766; in 1802 he was appointed Konzertmeister. He was the teacher of King Friedrich Wilhelm III. Of his works, only a Violin Sonata is extant.

Bendel, Franz, German pianist; b. Schönlinde, Bohemia, March 23, 1833; d. Berlin, July 3, 1874. He was a pupil of Proksch (Prague) and Liszt (Weimar); from 1862 taught at Kullak's Academy in Berlin.

WORKS: Symphs.; 4 masses; Piano Concerto; Piano Trio; salon pieces for Piano; Violin Sonata; nocturnes, romances, several books of songs, etc.

Bendeler, Johann Philipp, German organ theorist; b. Riethnordhausen (near Erfurt), Nov. (baptized, Nov. 20) 1654; d. Quedlinburg, Dec. 26, 1709. He went to Quedlinburg in 1681 as an instructor at the Gymnasium there; in 1687 added the duties of cantor, which post he held for the rest of his life. As an organ theorist he belongs, with Werckmeister, to the middle German group whose ideas were realized in the organs of Arp Schnitger. His most impor-

tant work is *Organopoeia* (c.1690; reprinted in 1739 as *Orgelbaukunst;* facsimile ed., Amsterdam, 1972), a treatise on organ building. Other works are *Collegium Musicum de Compositione* (mentioned in Mattheson's *Ehrenpforte*); *Melopeia practica* (1686); and *Aerarium melopoeticum* (1688). In addition, he wrote 2 books on mathematics.

BIBLIOGRAPHY: Chr. Mahrenholz, *Die Berechnung der Orgelpfeifenmensuren* (Kassel, 1938).

Bender, Paul, German bass; b. Driedorf, July 28, 1875; d. Munich, Nov. 25, 1947. He studied with Luise Reuss-Belce and Baptist Hoffmann; made his operatic debut as Sarastro in *The Magic Flute* in Breslau (1900). He subsequently joined the Munich Opera Co. and was a member from 1903 to 1933. He made his American debut at the Metropolitan Opera in N.Y. on Nov. 17, 1922, and remained on its roster until 1927. He included both serious and comic roles in his repertoire; was particularly effective in the bass parts in Wagner's operas; in his concert recitals he performed a number of songs by Carl Loewe.

Bendinelli, Agostino, Italian composer and teacher; b. Lucca, April 26, 1635; d. there, c.1703. He was active as canon of St. John Lateran in Rome; also served as superintendent of the monastery of S. Frediano in Lucca and as prior of S. Agostino in Piacenza and S. Leonardo in Lucca. His most famous pupil was G.M. Bononcini. His only extant publ. in his *Psalmi vespertini ternis, quaternis, quinisque vocibus ad organum concinendi una cum litanis BVM,* op. 1 (Bologna, 1671).

Bendinelli, Cesare, Italian trumpeter; d. probably in Munich, 1617. He became a trumpeter in Vienna in 1567; was called to Munich in 1580 as chief trumpeter at the court, a post he held until his death. He prepared the earliest known trumpet method, *Tutta l'arte della trombetta* (publ. in Documenta Musicologica, 2nd series, V, 1975; Eng. trans., 1976).

BIBLIOGRAPHY: E.H. Tarr, "Cesare Bendinelli," *Brass Bulletin,* no. 17 (1977).

Bendinilli, Agostino, Italian composer and singer; b. Verona, c.1550; d. there, Nov. 23, 1598. He studied in Verona at the Scuola degli Accoliti; also took instruction from the maestro di cappella of the Cathedral, Gabriele Martinengo. He entered the priesthood and then was a singer in the Cathedral choir from 1580; also taught at the Scuola degli Accoliti. Between 1585 and 1594 he publ. 4 books of sacred vocal works.

Bendix, Max, American conductor and composer; b. Detroit, March 28, 1866; d. Chicago, Dec. 6, 1945. He studied in Germany; was concertmaster of the Metropolitan Opera House (1885), and the Thomas Orch. in N.Y. and Chicago (1886–96); later was an opera conductor in N.Y. He wrote a Violin Concerto; *Pavlova,* a valse-caprice for Orch.; also ballet scores for special productions.

Bendix – Benedito y Vives

Bendix, Otto, pianist; b. Copenhagen, July 26, 1845; d. San Francisco, March 1, 1904. He was a pupil of Niels Gade; then studied with Kullak in Berlin and Liszt at Weimar; taught piano at the Copenhagen Cons., and was oboist in a theater orch.; came to the U.S. in 1880; settled in Boston as a piano teacher at the New England Cons.; in 1895 moved to San Francisco, where he established his own music school; gave successful concerts in Europe and America; publ. some piano pieces.

Bendix, Victor Emanuel, Danish pianist and conductor, brother of **Otto Bendix;** b. Copenhagen, May 17, 1851; d. there, Jan. 5, 1926. He studied at the Copenhagen Cons. with Gade and J.P.E. Hartmann; also took piano lessons with Liszt in Weimar. Returning to Copenhagen, he was appointed to the piano faculty of the Royal Academy of Music; in 1897 he organized the Copenhagen Phil. Concerts and conducted them for many years. He wrote 4 symphs. in a Romantic vein, a Piano Concerto, and much choral music.

Bendl, Karl (Karel), Czech composer and conductor; b. Prague, April 16, 1838; d. there, Sept. 20, 1897. He studied at the Prague Organ School with Blažek, Pietsch, and Zvonar. In 1864–65 he was active as a conductor in Brussels, Amsterdam, and Paris. Returning to Prague in 1865, he conducted the male choral society Hlahol for 12 years; also was briefly deputy conductor at the Provisional Theater in Prague. He subsequently served as an organist at the church of St. Nicholas in Prague. He was an ardent supporter of Dvořák and Smetana in the cause of creating a national school of Czech music.
WORKS: Operas: *Lejla* (1867; Prague, Jan. 4, 1868); *Břetislav* (1869; Prague, Sept. 18, 1870); *Starý ženich* (1871–74); *Die Wunderblume* (1876; Czech Radio, Prague, Aug. 30, 1940, in Czech); *Indická princezna,* operetta (1876–77; Prague, Aug. 26, 1877); *Černohorci* (1881; Prague, Oct. 11, 1881); *Karel Š kréta* (1883; Prague, Dec. 11, 1883); *Gina* (1884; not performed); *Dítě Tabora* (1886–88; Prague, March 13, 1892); *Máti Míla* (1893–95; Prague, June 25, 1895); *Švanda dudák* (1895–96; Prague, April 29, 1907). Ballet: *Česká svatba* (1894; Prague, Feb. 13, 1895); 2 masses; 2 cantatas; about 450 songs and choruses.
BIBLIOGRAPHY: E. Krasnohorska, *Z mládí Karla Bendla* (Prague, 1897; 2nd ed. as *Z mého mládí,* 1920); J. Polák, *Karel Bendl* (Prague, 1938).

Bendler, Salomon, famous German bass, son of **Johann Philipp Bendeler;** b. Quedlinburg, 1683; d. Braunschweig, 1724. He studied with his father; then sang throughout Germany and Italy; later made appearances in London (1712–17). Upon return to Germany, he became a chamber singer at the court in Braunschweig, where he remained until his death.

Benedetti, Francesco Maria, Italian composer; b. Assisi, 1683; d. there, 1746. He was a Franciscan priest; served as maestro di cappella at S. Francesco in Turin (1710–13), at the Basilica in Assisi (1713–

16), at the Turin Cathedral and the Cathedral of Aosta (1716–28); in 1729 he resumed his post in Assisi, where he remained until 1744. He was a prolific composer of sacred music.

Benedetti Michelangeli, Arturo. See **Michelangeli, Arturo Benedetti.**

Benedict, Sir Julius, German-English conductor and composer; b. Stuttgart, Nov. 27, 1804; d. London, June 5, 1885. He was the son of a Jewish banker; from his earliest childhood he showed a decisive musical talent. He took lessons with J.C.L. Abeille in Stuttgart; then had further instruction with Hummel at Weimar. Hummel introduced him to Weber, and he became Weber's private pupil. In 1823, Benedict was appointed conductor of the Kärnthnerthor Theater in Vienna; in 1825 he obtained a similar post at the Teatro San Carlo in Naples and also at the Fondo Theater there. He produced his first opera, *Giacinta ed Ernesto,* in Naples in 1827. His second opera was *I Portoghesi in Goa,* produced in Naples on June 28, 1830. In 1834 Benedict went to Paris, and in 1835 he proceeded to London, where he remained for the rest of his life. In 1836 he became music director at the Opera Buffa at the Lyceum Theatre. He conducted opera at the Drury Lane Theatre from 1838 to 1848. His first opera in English, *The Gypsy's Warning,* was produced at Drury Lane under his direction on April 19, 1838. He also conducted at Covent Garden; led the Monday Popular Concerts; served as music director of the Norwich Festivals (1845–78); and conducted the Liverpool Phil. Society (1876–80). In recognition of his services, he was knighted in 1871. In 1850–52 he accompanied Jenny Lind on her American tours. His reputation as conductor and composer was considerable, both in Europe and America. Among his operas the most successful was *The Lily of Killarney,* which was produced at Covent Garden on Feb. 8, 1862; it was also staged in America and Australia. His other operas are *The Brides of Venice* (Drury Lane, April 22, 1844); *The Crusaders* (Drury Lane, Feb. 26, 1846); *The Lake of Glenaston* (1862); *The Bride of Song* (Covent Garden, Dec. 3, 1864). He also wrote the cantatas *Undine* (1860); *Richard Cœur-de-Lion* (1863); *The Legend of St. Cecilia* (1866); *Graziella* (1882); an oratorio, *St. Peter* (1870); a symph.; 2 piano concertos; and other instrumental works. He publ. biographies of Mendelssohn (London, 1850) and Weber (London, 1881; 2nd ed., 1913); both contained information from his personal acquaintance with Mendelssohn and Weber.

Benedictus Appenzeller. See **Appenzeller, Benedictus.**

Benedito y Vives, Rafael, Spanish conductor, pedagogue, and editor; b. Valencia, Sept. 3, 1885. He studied at the Madrid Cons.; in 1917 organized an orch. under his own name and a univ. chorus. In subsequent years he devoted himself to the organization of music festivals with folksinging. He publ.

several collections of songs of a popular nature; also pedagogical works: *El piano amigo del niño; Cómo se enseña el canto y la música;* etc.

Beneke, Tex (real name, **Gordon**), American jazz singer, tenor saxophonist, and bandleader; b. Fort Worth, Texas, Feb. 12, 1914. He worked with Ben Young (1935–37); then was a vocalist with the Glenn Miller orch. (1938–42); after serving in the U.S. Navy during World War II, he became leader of the Glenn Miller orch., which later toured as his own ensemble.

Beneken, Friedrich Burchard, German minister and composer; b. Kloster Wennigsen, near Hannover, Aug. 13, 1760; d. Wülfinghausen, near Hannover, Sept. 22, 1818. He studied theology in Göttingen; was a Protestant pastor in Ronneberg (1790–1802) and later in Wülfinghausen. He was a composer of numerous lieder; his *Wie sie so sanft ruhen* was highly popular in Germany.

Benelli, Antonio Peregrino (Pellegrino), Italian tenor and composer; b. Forlì, Romagna, Sept. 5, 1771; d. Börnichau, Saxony, Aug. 16, 1830. In 1790 he was first tenor at the Teatro San Carlo in Naples; held the same position in London in 1798, and in Dresden from 1801–22, when his voice failed; then taught singing at the Royal Theater School in Berlin; was dismissed in 1829 because of an unjust attack on his benefactor, Spontini. His most valuable work is a vocal method, *Gesangslehre* (Dresden, 1819; originally publ. in Italian as *Regole per il canto figurato,* 1814); also wrote *Bemerkungen über die Stimme* in the *Allgemeine Musikalische Zeitung* (Leipzig, 1824); composed many vocal pieces and some piano pieces.

Benet, John, English composer who flourished in the 15th century. He wrote mostly church music. The following works are extant: 2 motets, *Lux fulget ex Anglia* and *Tellus purpureum;* an isorhythmic motet, *Gaude pia Magdalena;* and several numbers from incomplete masses. Stylistically he belonged to the school of John Dunstable and Lionel Power. His *Sanctus* and *Agnus* are found in H. Wooldrige's *Early English Harmony* (2 vols., 1897 and 1913); *Gaude pia Magdalena* was edited in *Early English Church Music,* VIII (1968); *Lux fulget ex Anglia* and *Tellus purpureum* in B. Trowell's dissertation, *Music under the Plantagenets* (Univ. of Cambridge, 1960).

Benevoli, Orazio, Italian composer; b. Rome, April 19, 1605; d. there, June 17, 1672. He was the son of a French baker who Italianized his name when he settled in Rome. He studied with Vincenzo Ugolini and sang in the boys' choir in the school "dei francesi" in Rome (1617–23); also had some instruction from Lorenzo Ratti. After completion of his study period he had successive posts as maestro di cappella; served at Santa Maria in Trastevere (1624–30); at Santo Spirito, Sassia (1630–38); and at San Luigi dei Francesi (1638–44). In 1644 he went to Vienna, where he served at the Court until 1646; then returned to Rome as maestro di cappella at Santa Maria Maggiore; was also attached to the Vatican. His music shows influences of the Palestrina style combined with polychoral techniques of the Venetians; some of his sacred works call for 12 separate choirs. A considerable controversy arose when some music historians attributed to Benevoli the composition of the *Missa salisburgensis,* containing 53 separate parts, which was cited as an example of Benevoli's extraordinary contrapuntal skill. Such a Mass was indeed commissioned by Salzburg in 1628, but it was not composed by Benevoli; whoever wrote it, its performance did not take place until about 1682. This Mass and a hymn in 56 voices were reprinted in Denkmäler der Tonkunst in Österreich; another Mass, which was really composed by Benevoli and was performed at the Santa Maria sopra Minerva Church in Rome in 1650, is set for 12 choirs of 4 voices each.
BIBLIOGRAPHY: A. Cametti, "La Scuola dei pueri cantus di San Luigi dei francesi in Roma e suoi principali allievi," *Rivista Musicale Italiana* (Oct. 1915); M. Bukofzer, *Music in the Baroque Era* (N.Y., 1947); L. Feininger, ed., *O. Benevoli: Opera omnia* (Rome, 1966); L. Feininger, ed., "Orazio Benevoli (1605–672)," *I° congresso internazionale di musica sacra: Roma 1950;* E. Hintermaier, "The Missa Salisburgensis," *The Musical Times* (Nov. 1975); E. Hintermaier, "'Missa Salisburgensis': Neue Erkenntnisse über Entstehung, Actor und Zweckbestimmung," *Musicologica Austriaca,* I (1976).

Bengraf, Josef, German composer; b. Neustadt an der Saale, 1745 or 1746; d. Pest (buried, June 8), 1791. He studied music with his father; then went to Pest, where he was made regens chori at the principal Catholic church in 1784. He composed a great deal of music for the church, and some instrumental works.

Bengtsson, Gustaf Adolf Giburtius (Tiburt), Swedish conductor and composer; b. Vadstena, March 29, 1886; d. there, Oct. 5, 1965. He studied at the Stockholm Cons.; then in Berlin with Juon and in Leipzig with Riemann; returned to Sweden and settled in Karlstad as composer and teacher; from 1943 to 1949 was conductor of an orch. in Linköping.
WORKS: 3 symphs. (1908, 1910, 1921); Violin Concerto; Cello Concerto; *Sinfonia Concertante* for Violin, Viola, and Orch.; *Canone Concertante* for Violin, Viola, and Chamber Orch. (1950); *Vettern,* symph. poem (1950); String Quartet (1907); Piano Trio (1916); Violin Sonata; songs.

Bengtsson, (Lars) Ingmar (Olof), noted Swedish musicologist and editor; b. Stockholm, March 2, 1920. He studied piano at the Royal Cons. of Music in Stockholm and musicology at the univs. of Stockholm, Uppsala, and Basel; subsequently took his Ph.D. at the Univ. of Uppsala in 1955 with the dissertation *J.H. Roman och hans instrumental-*

Benguerel – Benjamin

musik: Käll och stilkritiska studier (publ. in Uppsala, 1955). Between 1942 and 1955 he made appearances as a pianist and harpsichordist; from 1943–59 wrote music criticism for *Svenska Dagbladet* in Stockholm. In 1947 he joined the faculty of the musicological inst. at the Univ. of Uppsala as a lecturer; in 1961 he was named a prof. there. In 1961 he was elected president of the Swedish Society for Musicology; also edited its journal. In 1962 he became editor of *Studia musicologica upsaliensia: Nova series*. He founded the Swedish Archive of the History of Music in 1965. He made a specialty of the musical developments in Sweden. He publ. the books *Bach och hans tid* (Stockholm, 1946); *Från visa till symfoni* (Uppsala, 1947; 5th ed., 1973); and *Handstilar och notpickturer i Kungl: Musikalska akademiens Roman-samling* (Uppsala, 1955; with R. Danielsson). He also edited *Modern nordisk musik* (Stockholm, 1957).

Benguerel, Xavier, Catalonian composer; b. Barcelona, Feb. 9, 1931. He was a pupil of Cristóbal Taltabull. His early works were influenced by French Impressionism; in 1958 he adopted the dodecaphonic techniques; then tilted toward extreme modernism, often in the manner of the New Polish School.

WORKS: Concerto for Piano and Strings (1955); *Contrasts* for Chamber Orch. (1959); *Cantata d'Amic i Amat* for Chamber Group, Contralto, and Chorus (1959); Concerto for 2 Flutes and Strings (1961); *Sinfonia Continua* (Bilbao, Oct. 21, 1962); *Nocturno de los avisos* for Soprano, Chorus, and Orch. (1963); Violin Concerto (Barcelona, Oct. 9, 1965); *Sinfonia per a un Festival* (Barcelona, Oct. 30, 1966); *Sinfonia per a Petita Orquestra* (Hagen, Germany, April 24, 1967); *Paraules de Cada Dia* for Voice and Chamber Orch. (1967); *Sinfonia per a Gran Orquestra* (Barcelona, Oct. 2, 1968); *Test Sonata* for 17 Instruments and Percussion (1968); *Musica per a Oboe* for Oboe and Chamber Group (1968); *Dialogue Orchestrale* (1969); *Musica Riservata* for Strings (1969); *Joc* for 7 Instruments and Percussion (1969); *Consort Music* for Strings (1970); Organ Concerto (Baden-Baden, Sept. 17, 1971); Guitar Concerto (Kassel, Germany, Feb. 17, 1972); *Quasi una fantasia* for Cello and Chamber Orch. (Barcelona, Oct. 22, 1972); *Arbor*, cantata to words of Goethe, Dante, Shakespeare, Hitler, Mussolini, Martin Luther King, and Ché Guevara, for Soli, 4 Speakers, Chorus, and Orch. (Barcelona, Oct. 22, 1972); *Destructio* for Orch. (Madrid, March 23, 1973); *Capriccio Stravagante* for Chamber Group (1974); *Thesis* for Chamber Group (1974); Concerto for Percussion and Orch. (1975); 2 violin sonatas (1953, 1959); String Quartet No. 1 (1954); *4 Estructuras: I* for Violin (1957); *II* for Flute (1959); *III* for Cello (1964); *IV* for Piano (1966); *Successions* for Wind Quintet (1960); *Duo* for Clarinet and Piano (1963); *Musica* for 3 Percussionists (1967); *Crescendo* for Organ (1970); *Intento a Dos* for Guitar and Percussion (1970); *Verses* for Guitar (1973); *El gran océano* for Soprano, Guitar, and Percussion (1975); *Vermelia* for 4 Guitars (1976).

Benincori, Angelo Maria, Italian composer; b. Brescia, March 28, 1779; d. Belleville, near Paris, Dec. 30, 1821. He studied in Parma with Rolla (violin) and counterpoint with Ghiretti; spent several years in Spain; in 1803 he settled in Paris, where he was active mostly as a violin teacher. He brought out 3 unsuccessful operas, but performed a meritorious service in completing Isouard's opera *Aladin.*

Benjamin, Arthur, Australian composer and pianist; b. Sydney, Sept. 18, 1893; d. London, April 9, 1960. He received his musical training in Brisbane; then went to London, where he studied piano with Frederick Cliffe and composition with Charles Stanford at the Royal College of Music. After serving in the British army during World War I, he was a piano instructor at the Sydney Cons. in Australia (1919–21). Later he taught at the Royal College of Music in London; was engaged as conductor of the Vancouver Symph. Orch. in Canada (1941–46); eventually returned to London.

WORKS: 5 operas: *The Devil Take Her* (London, Dec. 1, 1931); *Prima Donna* (1933; London, Feb. 23, 1949); *A Tale of Two Cities,* after Dickens (1949–50; BBC, London, April 17, 1953; prizewinner of Festival of Britain opera competition); *Mañana,* a television opera (1956); *Tartuffe,* after Molière (1960; completed by A. Boustead; performed posthumously, London, Nov. 30, 1964); *Orlando's Silver Wedding* (London, Festival of Britain, May 1951), ballet; Piano Concertino (1927); *Light Music,* suite (1928–33); Violin Concerto (1932); *Heritage,* ceremonial march (1935); *Romantic Fantasy* for Violin, Viola, and Orch. (London, March 24, 1938); *Overture to an Italian Comedy* (London, March 2, 1937); *Cotillon,* suite of 9 English dance tunes (1938); *2 Jamaican Pieces* (1938; includes the highly popular *Jamaican Rumba;* arranged also for One or 2 Pianos); *Prelude to Holiday* (Indianapolis, Jan. 17, 1941); Sonatina for Chamber Orch. (1940); Concerto for Oboe and Strings, transcribed from Cimarosa (1942); Symph. No. 1 (1944–45; Cheltenham Festival, June 30, 1948); Suite for Flute and Strings, transcribed from Scarlatti (1945); *Elegy, Waltz and Toccata,* concerto for Viola, and Orch. or Piano (1945); *From San Domingo* (1945); *Caribbean Dance* (1946); Ballade for Strings (1947); *Concerto quasi una fantasia* for Piano and Orch. (Sydney, Sept. 5, 1950, composer soloist); Harmonica Concerto (London, Aug. 15, 1953); *North American Square Dances* for 2 Pianos and Orch. (Pittsburgh, April 1, 1955); *3 Pieces* for Violin and Piano (1919); *3 Impressions* for Voice and String Quartet (1920); 2 string quartets: No. 1, *Pastorale Fantasia* (1924); No. 2 (1959); Violin Sonatina (1924); Suite for Piano (1927); Cello Sonatina (1938); *2 Jamaican Songs* for 2 Pianos (1949); *Le Tombeau de Ravel: Valse Caprice* for Clarinet or Viola, and Piano (1949); Divertimento for Wind Quintet (1960); songs and choral music.

Benjamin, William E., American composer; b. Montreal, Dec. 7, 1944. He attended McGill Univ. (1961–65), receiving his B.Mus.; studied composition with István Anhalt; also took piano lessons at the Conservatoire de Musique de la Province de Québec. In 1966 he enrolled at Princeton Univ., where his teachers were Milton Babbitt, Edward T. Cone, Peter Westergaard, and James K. Randall; received his M.F.A. in 1968. In 1970 he was appointed instructor of music at Wellesley College. In his music he strives to fashion a rational multidimensional musical space, in which dynamics, rhythm, and tonality are functional components in free serial arrangements. His works include *Mah Tovu* for Mixed Chorus a cappella (1965); *Variations* for 4 Players (1967); *At Sixes and Sevens,* a sextet (1968); Piano Concerto (1970).

Bennard, George, American hymn composer; b. Youngstown, Ohio, Feb. 4, 1873; d. Reed City, Mich., Oct. 10, 1958. He served as a Salvation Army officer from 1892–1907; subsequently traveled as an evangelist in the U.S. and Canada. He wrote a number of sacred songs, among them *God Bless Our Boys, The Old Rugged Cross, Sweet Songs of Salvation.*

Bennet John, English composer; b. c.1570, probably in Lancashire. In 1599 he publ. *Madrigalls to Foure Voyces,* containing 17 compositions. He contributed a well-known madrigal, *All creatures now are merry minded,* to *The Triumph of Oriana* (1601) and composed 6 songs for Ravenscroft's *Briefe Discourse* (1914). Bennet's works have been reprinted by Fellowes in *The English Madrigal School.*
BIBLIOGRAPHY: E.H. Fellowes, *The English Madrigal School* (1913–24; 2nd ed. revised by T. Dart as *The English Madrigalists,* 1956); E.H. Fellowes, *The English Madrigal Composers* (Oxford, 1921; 2nd ed., 1948).

Bennett, George John, English composer and organist; b. Andover, May 5, 1863; d. Lincoln, Aug. 20, 1930. He studied with G.A. Macfarren at the Royal Academy of Music in London (1878–84); then went to Germany for further studies (1874–87). Upon his return to London he was appointed to the faculty of his alma mater (1888). From 1895 till his death, he was organist of the Lincoln Cathedral. He was the author of the manuals *Florid Counterpoint* and *Elements of Music for Choir-boys.*
WORKS: *Festival Evening Service* (for dedication of St. Paul's Cathedral, 1890); 2 overtures; *Jugendträume* (1887) and *Cymbeline* (1895); Piano Trio (1893); piano pieces, songs, etc.

Bennett, Joseph, English critic and writer on music; b. Berkeley, Gloucestershire, Nov. 29, 1831; d. Purton, June 12, 1911. After serving in various musical positions in London, he wrote music criticism for *The Sunday Times, Pall Mall Gazette,* and *The Graphic;* was annotator of the programs of the Phil. Society (1885–1903) and of the Saturday Popular Concerts; also wrote libretti for several English composers.
WRITINGS: *Letters from Bayreuth* (1877); *The Musical Year* (1883); *History of the Leeds Musical Festivals, 1858–1889* (1892; with F.R. Spark); *Story*

of Ten Hundred Concerts (1887; an account of the origin and rise of the Saturday Popular Concerts, 1857–87); *Forty Years of Music* (1908).

Bennett, Richard Rodney, prolific and successful English composer; b. Broadstairs, Kent, March 29, 1936. He studied with Lennox Berkeley and Howard Ferguson at the Royal Academy of Music in London (1953–56); later took private lessons with Boulez in Paris (1957–58). Returning to London, he was engaged to teach at the Royal Academy of Music (1963–65); then went to the U.S. as a visiting prof. at the Peabody Cons. in Baltimore (1970–71). His music may be called "optimistic" in its facility of diatonic technique and felicity of songful expression; his instrumental works adhere to neo-Baroque forms. He is also adept in music for films, as illustrated in the atonal hippophilia of his background score for *Equus* (1977).
WORKS: FOR THE STAGE: *The Ledge,* chamber opera (Sadler's Wells Theatre, London, Sept. 11, 1961); 3-act opera, *The Mines of Sulphur* (London, Feb. 24, 1965); comic opera, *Penny for a Song* (London, Oct. 31, 1967); a children's opera, *All the King's Men* (Coventry, March 28, 1969); 3-act opera, *Victory,* after the novel by Conrad (Covent Garden, London, April 13, 1970); *Isadora,* ballet (Covent Garden, London, April 30, 1981).
FOR ORCH.: Horn Concerto (1956); *Journal* (1960); *Calendar* for Chamber Ensemble (London, Nov. 24, 1960); *Suite française* for Chamber Orch. (1961); *London Pastoral* for Chamber Ensemble (1961); *Nocturnes* for Chamber Orch. (1962); *A Jazz Calendar* for 12 Instruments (1963–64; produced as a ballet, Covent Garden, 1968); *Aubade* (London, Sept. 1, 1964); *Soliloquy* for Voice and Jazz Ensemble (1966); *Epithalamion* for Chorus and Orch. (1966); 2 symphs.: No. 1 (London, Feb. 10, 1966); No. 2 (N.Y., Jan. 18, 1968); Piano Concerto (Birmingham, Sept. 19, 1968); Concerto for Oboe and String Orch. (Aldeburgh Festival, June 6, 1971); Concerto for Guitar and Chamber Ensemble (London, Nov. 18, 1970); Viola Concerto (N.Y., July 3, 1973); Concerto for Orch. (Denver, Feb. 25, 1974); Violin Concerto (Birmingham, March 25, 1976); *Zodiac* (Washington, D.C., March 30, 1976); *Serenade* (London, April 24, 1977); *Acteon* for Horn and Orch. (London, Aug. 12, 1977); *Music for Strings* (Cheltenham, July 7, 1978); Double-bass Concerto (London, Oct. 15, 1978); *Sonnets to Orpheus* for Cello and Orch. (Edinburgh, Sept. 3, 1979); Harpsichord Concerto (St. Louis, Dec. 4, 1980); *Anniversaries* (London, Sept. 9, 1982); *Lamento* for Flute and Strings (1983).
CHAMBER MUSIC: 4 string quartets (1952, 1953, 1960, 1964); Sonatina for Solo Flute (1954); 4 improvisations for Solo Violin (1955); *Winter Music* for Flute and Piano (1960); Oboe Sonata (1961); Sonata for Solo Violin (1964); *Conversations* for 2 Flutes (1964); Trio for Flute, Oboe, and Clarinet (1965); Wind Quintet (1967–68); 5 impromptus for Solo Guitar (1968); *Commedia I* for 6 players (1972); *Commedia II* for Flute, Cello, and Piano (1972–73); *Commedia III* for 10 Instruments (1972–73); *Commedia IV* for Brass Quintet (1972–73); *Scena II* for Solo Cello

(1973); Oboe Quartet (1975); *Travel Notes,* No. 1 for String Quartet (1975); *Travel Notes,* No. 2 for Wind Quartet (1976); *Scena III* for Basset Horn (1977); Horn Sonata (1978); Violin Sonata (1978); *Metamorphoses* for String Octet (1980); *6 Tunes for the Instruction of Singing Birds* for Solo Flute (1981); Music for String Quartet (1981); Sonatina for Solo Clarinet (1981); *After Syrinx* for Oboe and Piano (1982).

VOCAL MUSIC: *The Aproaches of Sleep* for 4 Voices and 10 Instruments (1959); *The Music That Her Echo Is,* cycle for Tenor and Piano (1967); *Jazz Pastoral* for Voice and Jazz Ensemble (1969); *Crazy Jane* for Soprano, Piano, Clarinet, and Cello (1968–69); *Sonnet Sequence* for Tenor and Instrumental Ensemble (1971); *The House of Sleep* for 6 Male Voices (1971); *Tenebrae* for Baritone and Piano (1971); *Devotions* for Chorus a cappella (1971); *Nightpiece* for Soprano and Tape (1972); *Times Whiter Series* for Countertenor and Lute (1974); *Spells* for Soprano, Chorus, and Orch. (Worcester, Aug. 28, 1975); *Letters to Lindbergh* for Female Voices and Piano Duet (1982).

FOR PIANO: Sonata (1954); *5 Studies* (1962–64); *Capriccio* for Piano, 4-hands (1968); *Scena I* (1973); *4-Piece Suite* for 2 Pianos (1974); *Kandinsky Variations* for 2 Pianos (1977); *Noctuary,* ballet scene (1981).

FILM MUSIC: *The Nanny* (1965); *Billion Dollar Brain* (1967); *Nicholas and Alexandra* (about the last Imperial Romanovs; 1971); *Murder on the Orient Express* (1974); *Equus* (1977).

BIBLIOGRAPHY: C. Palmer and L. Foreman, "Richard Rodney Bennett," *British Music Now,* edited by L. Foreman (London, 1975); S. Bradshaw, "Richard Rodney Bennett: The Last Decade," *Musical Times* (Sept. 1982).

Bennett, Robert Russell, American composer and expert arranger and orchestrator; b. Kansas City, June 15, 1894; d. New York, Aug. 17, 1981. He was a member of a musical family; his father played in the Kansas City Phil. and his mother was a piano teacher. He studied music theory with Carl Busch, conductor of the Kansas City Symph. Orch.; in 1916 he moved to N.Y., where he earned a living copying music for G. Schirmer Co. He served in the U.S. Army in World War I; returning to civilian life, he began a career as orchestrator of musical comedy scores. Having earned enough money to travel, he went to Paris to study composition with Nadia Boulanger; in 1927 and 1928 he held a Guggenheim fellowship. He then undertook composition in earnest. Success haunted him. His music, which is distinguished by a facile flow of easily communicated melodies and rhythms in luscious harmonies and resplendent orchestration, found a receptive audience; he had no difficulties in having his works performed by top orchs. and celebrated conductors. However, his audience was limited to the U.S.; little of his music penetrated the cosmopolitan halls of Europe. He prospered mainly by his extraordinary expertise in arranging popular musical comedies in idiomatic instrumental colors. He provided arrangements for such successful shows as *Oklahoma!, Show Boat, South Pacific, The King and I, My Fair Lady,* and *The Sound of Music.* He received an Academy Award in 1955 for his scoring of the motion picture *Oklahoma!* He was also active as a conductor on the radio. His feats of organization and memory were extraordinary; he rarely had to revise his scoring, which he usually put down in calligraphic notation in the final copy.

WORKS: Operas, *Maria Malibran* (N.Y., April 8, 1935) and *The Enchanted Kiss* (N.Y., Dec. 30, 1945); operetta, *Endymion* (1927); for Orch.: *Charleston Rhapsody* (1926); *Paysage* (1928); *Sights and Sounds* (1929); March for 2 Pianos and Orch. (Los Angeles, July 18, 1930); *Abraham Lincoln Symphony* (Philadelphia, Oct. 24, 1931); *Adagio Eroico* (Philadelphia, April 25, 1935); Concerto Grosso for Band (Rochester, Dec. 9, 1932); *Hollywood Scherzo* (NBC, Nov. 15, 1936); 8 Etudes for Orch. (CBS, July 17, 1938); Symph. in D "for the Dodgers" (N.Y., Aug. 3, 1941); Violin Concerto (NBC, Dec. 26, 1941); *The Four Freedoms,* symph. sketch after 4 paintings by Norman Rockwell (Los Angeles, Dec. 16, 1943); Symph. (1946); *A Dry Weather Legend* (Knoxville, 1947); Piano Concerto (1948); Violin Sonata (1927); *Toy Symphony* for 5 Woodwinds (1928); Organ Sonata (1929); *Water Music* for String Quartet (1937); *Hexapoda* for Violin and Piano (1940); *Five Improvisations* for Trio (1946); *Sonatine* for Soprano and Harp (1947); *Six Souvenirs* for 2 Flutes and Piano (1948); Concerto for Violin, Piano, and Orch. (Portland, Oreg., March 18, 1963); Concerto for Guitar and Orch. (1970); *Suite on Old American Dances* for Band (1949); *Symphonic Songs* for Band (1958); Concerto for Wind Quintet and Wind Orch. (1958); Symph. (1963). He publ. a book on orchestration, *Instrumentally Speaking* (N.Y., 1975).

Bennett, Tony (real name, **Anthony Dominick Benedetto**), American singer of popular music; b. Queens, N.Y., Aug. 3, 1926. He studied commercial art at the Manhattan School of Industrial Art; after military service, he took vocal lessons with Miriam Spier; subsequently appeared in nightclubs and on television as a leading singer of popular music until the advent of rock 'n' roll. He resumed his career successfully in 1962 with his recording of the song *I Left My Heart in San Francisco.*

Bennett, Sir William Sterndale, distinguished English pianist, conductor, and composer; b. Sheffield, April 13, 1816; d. London, Feb. 1, 1875. His father, Robert Bennett, an organist, died when he was a child, and he was then placed in the care of his grandfather, John Bennett, who was also a musician. At the age of 8 he was admitted to the choir of King's College Chapel, Cambridge, and at 10 he became a pupil at the Royal Academy of Music in London, where he studied theory with Charles Lucas and piano with William Henry Holmes, and played violin in the academy orch. under Cipriani Potter; he later studied music theory there with William Crotch. Soon he began to compose; he was 16 years old when he was the soloist in the first performance of his Piano Concerto No. 1 in Cambridge on Nov. 28, 1832. In 1836 he made an extensive visit to Leipzig, where he became a close friend of Mendelssohn and Schumann; also appeared as a pianist and conductor of his own works with the Gewandhaus Orch. there. He continued to compose industriously, and played his Piano Concerto No. 4 with the Gewandhaus Orch. in Leipzig on Jan. 17, 1839. He visited Germany again in 1841–42. From 1843 to 1856 he gave a series of chamber music concerts in London; in 1849 he founded the Bach Society. From 1856 to 1866 he conducted the Phil. Society of London; concurrently he held the post of prof. of music at Cambridge Univ.; in 1866 he assumed the position of principal of the Royal Academy of Music. His reputation as a composer grew; Mendelssohn and Schumann were eloquent in praising his works. He amassed honors: in 1856 he received the honorary degree of D.Mus. from Cambridge Univ., which also conferred on him the degree of M.A. in 1867; he received the degree of D.C.L. from Oxford Univ. in 1870; in a culmination of these honors, he was knighted by Queen Victoria in 1871. The final honor was his burial in Westminster Abbey. His music seems to have been laid to posthumous immobility with his honored body; the great appreciation he enjoyed in Germany declined, and the desultory attempts to restore him to fame in England proved abortive; not a single work retained its erstwhile vitality. Yet at his best, Bennett could produce music not recognizably inferior to that of Schumann's lesser works. There is every reason and every chance for its natural resuscitation.

WORKS: Symph. No. 1, in E-flat major (London, June 16, 1832); Piano Concerto No. 1, in D minor, op. 1 (Cambridge, Nov. 28, 1832); Symph. No. 2, in D minor (1832–33); *The Tempest,* overture (1832); *Parisina,* overture, op. 3 (London, March 1835); Piano Concerto No. 2, in E-flat major, op. 4 (1833; London, May 24, 1834); Overture in D minor (1833); Symph. No. 4, in A major (1833–34; London, Jan. 5, 1835); *The Merry Wives of Windsor,* overture (1834); Piano Concerto No. 3, in C minor, op. 9 (1834; London, May 16, 1935; the original slow movement was rejected by the composer and replaced by a Romanza; the Adagio in G minor for Piano and Orch. was first perf. in Manchester on June 18, 1981); Symph. No. 5, in G minor (1835; London, Feb. 8, 1836); Piano Concerto in F minor (London, July 1, 1836); *The Naiads,* overture, op. 15 (1836; London, Jan. 25, 1837); Piano Concerto No. 4, in F minor, op. 19 (1838; Leipzig, Jan. 17, 1839); *The Wood Nymphs,* overture, op. 20 (1838; Leipzig, Jan. 24, 1839); *Caprice* in E major for Piano, op. 22 (London, May 25, 1838); Concert-Stück in A major for Piano and Orch. (1841–43; London, June 5, 1843); *Marie du Bois,* overture (1843; revised 1844; London, June 25, 1845); *Paradise and the Peri,* fantasia-overture, op. 42 (London, July 14, 1862); Symph. in G minor, op. 43 (London, June 27, 1864). Other works include *Zion,* an oratorio (1839); *The May Queen,* op. 39, a pastoral for Soprano, Alto, Tenor, Bass, Chorus, and Orch. (Leeds Festival, Sept. 8, 1858); *Ode for the Opening of the International Exhibition,* op. 40 (London, May 1, 1862); *Ode on the Installation of the Duke of Devonshire* (Cambridge, May 10, 1862); *The Woman of Samaria,* a cantata, op. 44 (Birmingham Festival, Aug. 28, 1867); also music to Sophocles' *Ajax* (1872?); String Quartet; Piano Sonata in A-flat major, op. 46, known as *The Maid of Orleans* (1873); numerous piano pieces; pedagogical works for piano; anthems; songs.

BIBLIOGRAPHY: The *Musical Times* publ. a series of articles on Sterndale Bennett in its issues of May–Aug. 1903; also an article by F. Corder in its issue of May 1916; see also J.R. Sterndale Bennett, *The Life of William Sterndale Bennett* (Cambridge, 1907); C. Stanford, "William Sterndale Bennett, 1816–1875," *Musical Quarterly* (Oct. 1916); G. Spink, "Schumann and Sterndale Bennett," *Musical Times* (June 1964); G. Bush, "Sterndale Bennett: The Solo Piano Works," *Proceedings of the Royal Musical Association,* XCI (1964–65); idem, "Sterndale Bennett: A Note on His Chamber and Piano Music," *Musical Times* (June 1972); N. Temperley, "Sterndale Bennett and the Lied," *Musical Times* (Nov.–Dec. 1975); A. Cope, "Sterndale Bennett's G minor Adagio," *Musical Times* (June 1981).

Bennewitz (Benevic), Antonín, Czech violinist and pedagogue; b. Prívaty, near Litomyše, March 1833; d. Doksy, near Litoměřice, May 29, 1926. He studied at the Prague Cons. (1846–52); in 1865 he was appointed a prof. of violin at the Prague Cons.; in 1882 he was named its director, a position he retained until 1901. Among his famous pupils were Ševčík, Suk, Halir, and Nedbal.

Benoist, André, French pianist; b. Paris, April 4, 1879; d. Monmouth Beach, N.J., June 19, 1953. He studied at the Paris Cons. with Pugno and Saint-Saëns; toured in Europe and America as accompanist to Casals, Heifetz, Albert Spalding, Tetrazzini, and other celebrated artists.

Benoist, François, French composer and organist; b. Nantes, Sept. 10, 1794; d. Paris, May 6, 1878. He studied at the Paris Cons. (1811–15) with Adam and Catel; won the Prix de Rome in 1815 with the cantata *Oenone;* returning from Italy in 1819, he was appointed to the staff of the Paris Cons., where he taught for 53 years; he was pensioned in 1872. He wrote mostly for the theater; among his operas are *Léonore et Félix,* produced at the Opéra-Comique in Paris on Nov. 27, 1821, and *L'Apparition* (Paris Opéra, June 16, 1848). He also wrote 4 ballets: *La Gipsy* (1839), *Le Diable amoureux* (1840), *Nisida, ou Les Amazones des Açores* (1848) and *Pâquerette* (1851). He publ. 12 books of organ pieces under the title *Bibliothèque de l'organiste.*

Benoit, Peter, foremost Flemish composer; b. Harlebeke, Belgium, Aug. 17, 1834; d. Antwerp, March 8, 1901. He studied at the Brussels Cons. with Fétis (1851–55); while there he earned his living by conducting theater orchs. He also wrote music for Flemish plays; at the age of 22 he produced his first opera in Flemish, *Het dorp in't gebergte (A Mountain Village),* staged in Brussels on Dec. 14, 1856.

With his cantata *Le Meurtre d'Abel* Benoit obtained the Belgian Prix de Rome (1857); however, he did not go to Italy, but traveled instead in Germany. As part of his duties he submitted a short *Cantate de Noël* to Fétis, who praised Benoit's music; he also wrote the essay *L'Ecole de musique flamande et son avenir,* proclaiming his fervent faith in the future of a national Flemish school of composition, of which he was the most ardent supporter. His one-act opera *Roi des Aulnes* was presented in Brussels (Dec. 2, 1859); the Théâtre-Lyrique of Paris tentatively accepted it; Benoit spent many months in Paris awaiting its production, which never took place; in the meantime he acted as 2nd conductor at the Bouffes-Parisiens. In 1863 he returned to Belgium, where he produced his 2nd Flemish opera, *Isa* (Brussels, Feb. 24, 1867). In 1867 he founded the Flemish Music School in Antwerp; he militated for many years to obtain official status for it. In 1898 it was finally granted, and the school became the Royal Flemish Cons.; Benoit remained its director to the end of his life. In Belgium Benoit is regarded as the originator of the Flemish musical tradition in both composition and education; but although he cultivated the Flemish idiom in most of his works, his musical style owes much to French and German influences. Apart from his successful early operas, he wrote the opera *Pompeja* (1895), which was not produced; Flemish oratorios: *Lucifer* (Brussels, Sept. 30, 1866; highly successful; considered his masterpiece); *De Schelde* (1868); *De Oorlog (War;* 1873); dramatic musical score, *Charlotte Corday* (1876); historic music drama, *De Pacificatie van Ghent* (1876); *Rubens Cantata* (1877; greatly acclaimed); children's oratorio, *De Waereld in (In the World;* 1878); cantatas: *Hucbald* (1880) and *De Genius van Vaderlands* (1880); oratorio, *De Rhijn* (1889); etc. Of his church music, the most important is his *Quadrilogie religieuse* (Antwerp, April 24, 1864), of which the component parts had been separately performed in 1860, 1862, and 1863; also *Drama Christi* (1871). Benoit wrote relatively little instrumental music; his symph. poems for piano with orch. and for flute with orch. have been performed. He also composed many songs in French and in Flemish. In his propaganda for national Flemish music, Benoit contributed numerous papers and articles, among them *Considérations à propos d'un projet pour l'institution de festivals en Belgique* (1874); *Verhandeling over de nationale Toonkunde* (2 vols.; Antwerp, 1877–79); *De Vlaamsche Muziekschool van Antwerpen* (1889; a history of the Antwerp School of Music); *De Oorsprong van het Cosmopolitisme in de Muziek* (1876). In 1880 he was elected a corresponding member of the Belgian Royal Academy; in 1882, a full member.

BIBLIOGRAPHY: M.E. Belpaire, *Een vlaamsche meester; Peter Benoit* (Belfort, 1901); C. Stoffels, *P. Benoit et le mouvement musical flamand* (Antwerp, 1901); Th. Radoux, "Paroles prononcées à l'annonce de la mort de P. Benoit," *Bulletins Lettres et Beaux-Arts* (Brussels, 1901); J. Sabbe, *P. Benoit; Zijn leven, zijne werken, zijne beteekenis* (Ghent, 1902); L. Mortelmans, *P. Benoit* (Antwerp, 1911); H. Baggaert, *P. Benoit, Een kampion der nacionale ge-dachte* (Antwerp, 1919); H.P. Morgan-Browne, "Peter Benoit, né Pierre Benoit," *Music and Letters* (1929); J. Horemans, *P. Benoit* (Antwerp, 1934); A.M. Pols, *Het leven van P. Benoit* (Antwerp, 1934); Ch. van den Borren, *Peter Benoit* (Brussels, 1942); R.R. Boschvogel, *P. Benoit* (Tiel, 1944); A. Corbet, *P. Benoit, Leven, werk en beteekenis* (Antwerp, 1944); G.-M. Matthijs, *P. Benoit* (Brussels, 1944); Floris van der Mueren, *Peter Benoit in het huidig perspectief* (Antwerp, 1968).

Bent, Ian D(avid), English musicologist; b. Birmingham, Jan. 1, 1938. He studied at St. John's College, Cambridge (B.A., 1961; B.Mus., 1962); subsequently taught at King's College, London. He received his Ph.D. in 1969 from the Univ. of Cambridge with the dissertation *The Early History of the English Chapel Royal, c.1066–1347.* In 1975 he became a prof. of music at the Univ. of Nottingham. With his wife, **Margaret Bent,** and B. Trowell, he edited the revised edition of Dunstable's works in the Musica Britannica series. He was a senior consulting editor of *The New Grove Dictionary of Music and Musicians* (London, 1980). He edited *Source Materials and the Interpretation of Music: A Memorial Volume to Thurston Dart* (London, 1981).

Bent, Margaret (Hilda), English musicologist; b. St. Albans, Dec. 23, 1940. She was an organ scholar at Girton College, Cambridge (B.A., 1962; B.Mus., 1963); also studied with Dart, receiving her Ph.D. in 1969 from the Univ. of Cambridge with the dissertation *The Old Hall Manuscript: A Palaeographical Study.* She taught at King's College (1965–75); also, concurrently, at Goldsmiths' College from 1972. In 1975 she joined the faculty of Brandeis Univ. at Waltham, Mass. With A. Hughes, she edited *The Old Hall Manuscript* in the Corpus Mensurabilis Musicae series, XLVI (1969–73); with her husband, **Ian Bent,** and B. Trowell, she edited the revised edition of Dunstable's works in the Musica Britannica series; also publ. a valuable study, *Dunstable* (London, 1981).

Bentoiu, Pascal, Rumanian composer; b. Bucharest, April 22, 1927. He studied composition with Mihail Jora in Bucharest (1943–48); was head of the Folklore Inst. there (1953–56). He composed a comic opera, *Amorul doctor (The Love Doctor;* 1964; Bucharest, Dec. 23, 1966); a radio opera, *Jertfirea Ifigeniei (The Immolation of Iphigenia;* 1968); an opera, *Hamlet* (1969; Bucharest, Nov. 19, 1971); Piano Sonata (1947); *Concert Overture* (1948; revised 1959); String Quartet (1953); 2 piano concertos (1954, 1960); *Suite Transylvania* for Orch. (1955); *Luceafărul (The Morning Star),* symph. poem (1957); Violin Concerto (1958); *Bucharest Images,* 3 symph. movements (1959); Violin Sonata (1962); Symph. (1965; Bucharest, Sept. 24, 1966). A detailed list of his works is found in Viorel Cosma's *Muzicieni români* (Bucharest, 1970).

Benton, Joseph. See **Bentonelli, Joseph.**

Benton, Rita, American musicologist and librarian; b. New York, June 28, 1918; d. Paris, March 23, 1980. She studied piano with James Friskin and music theory with Bernard Wagenaar at the Juilliard School of Music; then enrolled at the Univ. of Iowa; received her Ph.D. in musicology there in 1961. In 1967 she was appointed music librarian at the Univ. of Iowa and in 1975 became prof. of music there. In 1976 she became editor of *Fontes Artis Musicae,* and held this position until her death. Her specialty was French music history, a subject on which she contributed numerous articles to American and French magazines. She compiled a valuable catalogue of works by Ignace Pleyel (N.Y., 1977).

Bentonelli, Joseph, American tenor; b. Sayre, Okla., Sept. 10, 1900; d. Oklahoma City, April 4, 1975. His real name was **Benton,** but following the frequent practice among American singers, he adopted an Italian-sounding name when he embarked on a singing career. He studied voice with Jean de Reszke in Paris and made his public debut with the de Reszke Ensemble in Nice in 1925. He returned to the U.S. in 1934; sang with the Chicago Opera; then for 3 seasons sang with the Metropolitan Opera, where he made his debut as Des Brieux in *Manon* (Jan. 10, 1936). He had an extensive opera repertoire, and sang all leading Italian tenor parts.

Bentzon, Jørgen, Danish composer (cousin of **Niels Viggo Bentzon**); b. Copenhagen, Feb. 14, 1897; d. Hørsholm, July 9, 1951. He studied composition with Carl Nielsen (1915–18). At the same time he took courses in jurisprudence; subsequently he was attached to the Ministry of Justice in Denmark, and served as clerk of records of the Danish Supreme Court. He also taught piano and theory at a People's School of Music in Copenhagen. As a composer he followed the Romantic trends current in Scandinavia; an influence of his teacher Carl Nielsen pervades his music. WORKS: Opera, *Saturnalia* (Copenhagen, Dec. 15, 1944); *Dramatic Overture* (1923); *Variations on a Danish Folktune* for Piano, Strings, and Percussion (1928); 3 chamber concertos: No. 1, *Symphonic Trio,* for 3 instrumental groups of Violins, Horns, and Cellos (1928–29); No. 2, *Intermezzo Espressivo,* for Solo Oboe, Clarinet, Horn, Bassoon, Strings, and Percussion (1935); and No. 3, for Clarinet and Chamber Orch. (1941); *Fotomontage,* overture (1934); *Variations* for Chamber Orch. (1935); *Cyklevise-Rhapsody* for Orch. (1936); *Sinfonia seria* for School Orch. (1937); *Sinfonia buffa* for School Orch. (1939); 2 symphonies: No. 1, *Dickens-Symphonie* (1939–40) and No. 2 (1946–47); Sinfonietta for String Orch. (1943); *Racconti 1-6,* each piece for from 3 to 5 Instruments (1935–50); 5 string quartets (1921–28); String Trio (1921); Sonatina for Flute, Clarinet, and Bassoon (1924); *Variazioni interrotti* for Clarinet, Bassoon, and String Trio (1925); *Duo* for Violin and Cello (1927); *Mikrofoni No. 1* for Baritone, Flute, and Piano Trio (1937–39); *Variations* for Piano (1921); Piano Sonata (1946); *En romersk Fortaelling (A Roman Tale),* cantata for Soloists, Chorus, and

Piano (1937); songs; choruses.

Bentzon, Niels Viggo, eminent Danish composer; b. Copenhagen, Aug. 24, 1919. He is a descendant of **Johann Ernst Hartmann** (1726–93), an early German-born Danish composer. The musical tradition of the family continued through many generations (his cousin was **Jørgen Bentzon**). He studied piano with his mother; took classes in music theory with Knud Jeppesen. In 1950 he was appointed to the faculty of the Royal Danish Cons. in Copenhagen. In his early compositions he assimilated a neo-Classical idiom, distinguished by compact contrapuntal writing and harmonic clarity without avoidance of justifiable dissonance; later he adopted a metamorphic technique, characterized by an evolution of varied shapes emanating from the basic musical subject, exemplified in his Symph. No. 4, subtitled *Metamorphoses;* this metamorphism naturally led to the personal formulation of serial techniques. After 1960 his works vary in style, consisting of "happenings," audiovisual scores, 3rd-stream technique, graphic notation, and the like.
WORKS: FOR THE STAGE: 4 operas: *Faust III,* after Goethe, Joyce, and Kafka (1961–62; Kiel, Germany, June 21, 1964); *Jardin des Plantes* (1969); chamber opera, *Die Automaten,* based on motifs from *The Tales of Hoffmann* (1973; Kiel, May 1974); *The Bank Manager* (1974); 7 ballets: *Metaphor* (Copenhagen, March 31, 1950); *Kurtisanen* (*The Courtesan;* 1952; Copenhagen, Dec. 19, 1953); *Døren* (*The Door;* Copenhagen, Nov. 14, 1962); *Hommage à Jean Baptiste Lully* (1964); *Jenny von Westphalen* (1965; Aarhus, Sept. 9, 1965; new version, 1971); *Jubilaeumsballet 800* (1967; Copenhagen, 1967); *Duell* (1977; Stockholm, Nov. 12, 1977).
FOR ORCH.: 15 numbered symphs.: No. 1 (1942–43); No. 2, with Solo Piano (1944–45); No. 3 (1947); No. 4, *Metamorfosen* (1948–49; Copenhagen, June 18, 1949); No. 5, *Ellipser* (1950); No. 6, *Sinfonia piccola* (1950); No. 7, *De tre versioner* (1953; Copenhagen, April 21, 1953); No. 8 *Sinfonia discreta* (1957; Funen, Jan. 21, 1958); No. 9, *Aerosymfonien* (1960–61; Odense, May 29, 1961); No. 10, *Den hymniske* (1963; Aarhus, Oct. 26, 1964); No. 11, *Salzburg* (1965; Hamburg, Dec. 6, 1965); No. 12, *Tunis* (1965; Aarhus, Jan. 31, 1966); No. 13, *Militaer* (1965; Aalborg, Feb. 2, 1966); No. 14 (1971–72); and No. 15 (1980); *Mini-Symfoni* (1968); *Chamber Symphony* for 17 Instruments (1962); *Sinfonia* (1977); 26 concertos: 8 for Piano (1947–48; *Piccolo-concerto,* with Strings, 1950; 1952; 1954; 1963; 1966; 1967–69; 1982), 4 for Violin (1951, 1961, 1975, 1976), 3 for Cello (1956, 1973, 1982), 2 for Flute (1963, 1976), one each for Oboe (with Strings, 1952), Accordion (1962), Clarinet (1970–71), Viola (1973), Tuba (1975), 3 Clarinets (one soloist, 1975), (*Concerto barocco,* for Oboe and Strings 1978), and Horn (1982), and a Triple Concerto for Oboe, Clarinet, Bassoon, and Strings (1954); *Overture* for Chamber Orch. (1942); *Divertimento* for String Orch. (1942); *Orchestral Sonata* for Flute and Strings (1943); *Prelude and Rondo* (1949); Suite for String Orch. (1950); *Intrada* (1950); *Variazione breve* (1950); *Symphonic Variations* (1953); *Sym-*

phonic Suite (1955); Sinfonia concertante for Violin, Viola, Cello, Clarinet, Brass, and Timpani (1955–56); Pastorale (1956); Pezzi Sinfonici (1956; Louisville, Ky., March 13, 1957); Concerto for Strings (1957); Mutationer (1959); Fem Mobiler (5 Mobiles; 1959; Aarhus, Sept. 9, 1960); 2 Monkton Blues (1960); Ostinato (1961); Overture for Small Orch. (1961); Rhapsody for Piano and Orch. (1961); Gladsaxe, concerto for Orch. (1963); Symphonic Fantasy for 2 Pianos and Orch. (1958–63; Malmö, Sweden, March 10, 1964); Meet the Danes (1964); Suite for Foreigners (1964); Sinfonia concertante for 6 Accordions and Orch. (1965; Flensburg, Germany, Jan. 4, 1967); 6 Copenhagen Concertos for Various Solo Instruments, Strings, and Harpsichord (1965); Manfred Overture (1967); Eastern Gasworks No. 2 (1969); Chorus daniensis No. 2 (1969); Formula (in memory of Varèse, 1969; Graz, Austria, Oct. 20, 1970); Hucbald for Cello and Chamber Ensemble (1970); Extracts (1970); Ephitaph over Igor Stravinsky (1971); Busonism, audio-visual work for Piano and Orch. (1971); Saltholm, lyric intermezzo (1972); Reflection Suite for Strings (1972); Suite as Far as Jazz Music Is Concerned (1973); Trombones as trotyl (1973); Documenta 5, No. 1 (1973); Feature Article on René Descartes (1975); Leipziger Tage for Piano and Strings (1976); Still's for Piano, Orch., and Jazz Band (1975); Leipziger Tage for Piano and Strings (1976); Sinfonia concertante No. 2 (1976); Capriccio for Tuba and Small Orch. (1977); In an Atmosphere of Italian Futurism (1979); Fragment (1980); Variations without a Theme for Piano and Orch. (1980). FOR VOICE: Elementi aperti for Mezzosoprano and Orch. (1958); an oratorio, Torquilla, after Nevil Shute (1961; Aarhus, Oct. 23, 1961); a surrealistic cantata, Bonjour Max Ernst (1961; Aarhus, Oct. 22, 1962); Sagn (Myth) for Male Chorus, Brass, and Timpani (1964); An Arab in Cologne, 3 "Psalms of the common man" for Narrator, Flute, Violin, Viola, Xylophone, and Piano (1964); Mali for Soprano and Chamber Ensemble (1967); Det rustne menageri (The Rusty Menagerie), cantata for Narrator and Instruments (1972). CHAMBER MUSIC: Music for 7 Instruments (1943); Chamber Concerto for 3 Pianos, 2 Trumpets, Clarinet, Bassoon, Double Bass, and Percussion (1948); Elegi for 7 Instruments (1954); Concerto for 6 Percussionists (1957); Double Concerto for Solo Violin, Solo Piano, and Percussion (1965; Malmö, April 19, 1966); Sonata for 12 Instruments (1969); Sextet for Flute, Oboe, Clarinet, Horn, Bassoon, and Piano (1971); 5 wind quintets (with Piano, 1941; Variations, 1942; 1943; 1950; 1957); Quintet for Piano, Flute, Violin, Viola, and Cello (1960); Piano Quintet (1966); 11 string quartets (1940, 1944, 1951, 1954, 1956, 1959, 1964, 1967, 1968, 1974, 1976); Bagatelles for String Quartet (1944); Quartet for Flute, Oboe, Clarinet, and Bassoon (1943); Mosaïque musicale for Flute, Violin, Cello, and Piano (1950); Bop Serenade for Flute, Oboe, Clarinet, and Bassoon (1952); Quartet for Piano, Flute, Oboe, and Bassoon (1952–53); 4 quartets for 4 Flutes (1974, 1975, 1976, 1977); String Trio (1940); Trio for Flute, Oboe, and Clarinet (1942); 2 piano trios (1943, 1959); Trio for Horn, Trumpet, and Trombone (1952); Trio for Violin, Cel-

lo, and English Horn (1954); 2 trios for Clarinet, Cello, and Piano (1961, 1969); Trio for Cello, Flute, and Piano (1971); Observations, Psycho-biological Suite for Flute, Oboe, and Piano (1974); 7 violin sonatas (1940, 1943, 1943, 1959, 1965, 1971–72, 1973); Little Suite for Violin and Piano (1950); 4 cello sonatas (1946, 1967, 1971, 1972); sonatas for Horn (1947), Clarinet (1950), English Horn (1951), Trumpet (1951), Trombone (1971), Flute (1973), Bassoon (1973), and Saxophone (1973); 6 Variations for Flute and Piano (1942); Kvadratrod 3 (Square Root of 3) for Violin and Piano (1944); 2 Pieces for Oboe and Piano (1946); Duo for Violin and Cello (1954); 6 Pezzi for Violin and Viola (1956); Duet for Viola and Organ (1968); Suite for Violin and Piano (1973); Duo concertante for Violin and Piano (1973); Dialektism for Violin and Harmonica (1975); Dialog til en Horst for Flute and Organ (1975); Tuba Sonata (1976); Wiesbaden for Cello and Tuba (1977); Margarine for Double Bass and Piano (1977); 2 sonatas for Flute and Organ (1978; Die Schildkröte, 1978); Suite in the Form of Variations for Solo Violin (1942); Sonatina for Violin Solo (1950); Variations for Solo Flute (1953); Solo Cello Sonata (1956); In the Zoo for Solo Accordion (1964); Portrait of J.P. Sartre for Solo Accordion (1967); In the Forest, suite for Solo Horn (1968); Statics for Solo Cello (1972); 3 Sonatas and 3 Partitas for Solo Violin (1973) Variations on "The Volga Boatmen" for Solo Cello (1974); group of 3 solo cello sonatas (1974–75). FOR PIANO: 15 numbered sonatas (1940, 1946, 1946, 1949, 1951, 1952, 1959, 1966, 1966, 1967, 1973, 1974, 1974, 1981; Salzburg Sonata, 1981); Bonner Sonata (1967); Hoffmann Sonata (1969); Napolean Sonata (1970); Rossini Sonata (1970); Devrient Sonata (1970); Tekst Sonata (1972); Pièce héroïque for 3 Pianos (1967); 2 sonatas for 2 Pianos (1949, 1982); Prolog, Rondo, Epilog for 2 Pianos (1951); Sonata for Piano, 4-hands (1959); Propostae Novae for 2 Pianos (1960); Explosions for 2 Pianos (1968); Mozart Variations for 2 Pianos (1969); Bones and Flesh for 2 Pianos (1973); Dance and Contradance for Piano, 4-hands (1980); Theme and Variations for 2 Pianos (1982); Klaverfantasi (1939); 7 Small Pieces (1940); Toccata (1940); Rhapsody (1942); Bagatelles (1942); Passacaglia (1945); Prelude and Fugue (1945); Partita (1945); 3 Dance Compositions (1947); 3 Concert Etudes (1947); 5 Inventions (1947); Traesnit (Woodcuts; 1950); 2 Nocturnes (1950); Capriccio (1952); Kaleidoscope (1952); Pentachord (1954); Suite (1955); Variazione semplice (1955); 12 Preludes (1956–57); Epitaph (1962); Det temperered Klaver (The Tempered Clavier), 5 separate sets of 24 preludes and fugues (1964, 1976, 1977, 1978, 1979); 15 Two-part and 15 Three-part Inventions (1964); 2 Suites (1965); 10 Small Preludes (1965); Information and Scenery, cycle of 6 pieces in optical notation (1967); 6 Valses nobles et sentimentales (1967); 5 Mazurkas délicieuses (1967); 8 Nocturnes en couleurs (1967); 7 Etudes (1967); Scherzo (1967); Rondo amoroso (1967); Paganini Variations (1968); Vibrations for Prepared Piano (1969, in 2 versions); Hommage à Picasso (1971); Variazioni (1972); Utilized Termination of a Concert (1973); Documenta 5 No. 2 (1973); Micro-macro (1973); Pariser Suite (1982);

Piece for 12 Pianos (1954).

FOR ORGAN: *Prelude and Fugue* (1942); *Variations* (1955); *Mycelium* (1965); *Trivielle synonymer* (1965); *Toccata, Aria e Fuga* (1968); *Organsazione popolare I–IV* (1974); *Ariadne musica nova,* 17 preludes and fugues (1979); Sonata No. 1 (1980).

Benucci, Francesco, famous Italian bass; b. c.1745; d. Florence, April 5, 1824. He began his career in 1769; in 1783 he went to Vienna, where he created the roles of Figaro in *Le nozze di Figaro* (Vienna, May 1, 1786) and Guglielmo in *Così fan tutte* (Vienna, Jan. 26, 1790) by Mozart. He visited London in 1788–89; then lived again in Vienna. In 1795 he returned to Italy.

Benvenuti, Giacomo, Italian musicologist; b. Tremosina, Lake Garda, March 16, 1885; d. Barbarano di Saló, Jan. 20, 1943. He studied with his father, who was an organist; then had lessons in music theory with Vincenzo Sacchi and Paolo Chimeri in Brescia; received a diploma in composition at the Liceo Musicale in Bologna, where his teachers were Torchi and Bossi. He edited 2 vols. of selected works by Andrea and Giovanni Gabrieli for the *Istituzioni e monumenti dell'arte musicale italiana,* publ. in 1931–32 (with valuable documentary prefaces); 12 harpsichord sonatas by B. Galuppi; works by Cavazzoni (1919) and Paradies (with D. Cipollini; 1920); *35 Arie di vari autori del secolo XVII* (1922); etc. He also wrote an opera, *Juan José.*

Benvenuti, Nicola, Italian organist and composer; b. Pisa, May 10, 1783; d. there, Aug. 14, 1867. He studied music with his father, the organist at the Pisa Cathedral, and with Filippo Gherardeschi, the maestro di cappella at the church of the Cavalieri di S. Stefano; in 1804 he was appointed organist there. In 1810 he assumed the post of maestro di cappella at the Cathedral of Pisa, a post he held for 57 years. He also served as maestro di camera at the palaces of the Grand Duke of Tuscany in Florence and Pisa. In 1824 he founded in Pisa his own music school. He wrote mainly for the organ, and also left a number of ecclesiastical works.

Benvenuti, Tommaso, Italian opera composer; b. Cavarzere (Venice), Feb. 4, 1838; d. Rome, Feb. 26, 1906. When he was 18 years old, his opera *Valenzia Candiano* was announced for performance in Mantua, but was taken off after a rehearsal. The following year, he succeeded in having his 2nd opera, *Adriana Lecouvreur,* produced in Milan (Nov. 26, 1857). Other productions followed: *Guglielmo Shakespeare* (Parma, Feb. 14, 1861); *La Stella di Toledo* (Milan, April 23, 1864); *Il Falconiere* (Venice, Feb. 16, 1878); *Beatrice di Suevia* (Venice, Feb. 20, 1890); opera buffa, *Le baruffe Chiozzotte* (Florence, Jan. 30, 1895). Although Benvenuti's operas are workmanlike and effective, they failed to hold the stage after initial successes.

Benzell, Mimi, American soprano; b. Bridgeport,

Conn., April 6, 1922; d. Manhasset, Long Island, N.Y., Dec. 23, 1970. Her grandfather was a singer of Jewish folk songs in Russia before his emigration to America. She studied at the David Mannes Music School in N.Y.; appeared at the Metropolitan Opera on Jan. 5, 1945, in the role of the Queen of the Night in *The Magic Flute;* in the next 5 years she sang about 20 different roles with the Metropolitan, including Gilda in *Rigoletto* and Musetta in *La Bohème.* In 1949 she abandoned grand opera and became a popular singer in Broadway shows and in nightclubs.

Benzi, Roberto, French conductor; b. Marseilles, Dec. 12, 1937. He was educated at the Sorbonne in Paris; then appeared as a conductor with regional orchs. and opera houses of France. In 1973 he was named music director of the municipal orch. and opera at Bordeaux. He also was a guest conductor with the Philadelphia Orch. and with the Berlin Phil.

Berardi, Angelo, Italian organist and composer; b. S. Agata, Feltria, about 1630; d. Rome, April 9, 1694. He was a student of Mario Scacchi; served as maestro di cappella and organist at Tivoli (1673–79); was then at the Spoleto Cathedral (1681) and at the college of S. Angelo in Viterbo (1687). In 1693 he was a canon and maestro di cappella at S. Maria in Trastevere, Rome.

PUBLICATIONS: Several treatises on harmony and related theoretical subjects: *Ragionamenti musicali* (Bologna, 1681); *Documenti armonici* (Bologna, 1687); *Arcani musicale* (Bologna, 1690); *Il Perché musicale ovvero Staffetta armonica* (Bologna, 1936).

WORKS: *Missa pro defunctis* (1663); *Salmi concertati* (Bologna, 1668); *Concentus cum Missa* (Bologna, 1669); *Musiche diverse variemente concertate per camera* (Bologna, 1689); many canons.

Berat, Frédéric, French song composer; b. Rouen, 1800; d. Paris, Dec. 2, 1855. He was a friend of the poet Béranger, many of whose lyrics he set to music; wrote many popular romances and chansonettes: *A la frontière, Bibi, La Lisette de Béranger, Le Départ, Ma Normandie,* etc.

Berber, Felix, German violinist; b. Jena, March 11, 1871; d. Munich, Nov. 2, 1930. He studied with Adolf Brodsky at the Leipzig Cons.; served as concertmaster with the Gewandhaus Orch. there (1897–1903); then taught at the Royal Academy of Music in London (1904–7), at the Hoch Cons. in Frankfurt, and at the Geneva Cons. (1908). In 1910 he made a highly successful tour of the U.S. In 1912 he settled in Munich; in 1920 was appointed to the faculty of the Akademie der Tonkunst there.

Berberian, Cathy, versatile American mezzo-soprano; b. Attleboro, Mass., July 4, 1925; d. Rome, March 6, 1983. She was of Armenian parentage; she studied singing, dancing, and the art of pantomime;

took courses at Columbia Univ. and N.Y. Univ.; then went to Italy; attracted wide attention in 1958, when she performed the ultrasurrealist *Fontana Mix* by John Cage, which demanded a fantastic variety of sound effects. Her vocal range extended to 3 octaves, causing one bewildered music critic to remark that she could sing both Tristan and Isolde. Thanks to her uncanny ability to produce ultrahuman (and subhuman) tones, and her willingness to incorporate into her professional vocalization a variety of animal noises, guttural sounds, grunts and growls, squeals, squeaks and squawks, clicks and clucks, shrieks and screeches, hisses, hoots, and hollers, she instantly became the darling of inventive composers of the avant-garde, who eagerly dedicated to her their otherwise unperformable cantatas. She married one of them, **Luciano Berio,** in 1950, but they were separated in 1966. She could also intone classical music, and made a favorable impression with her recording of works by Monteverdi. Shortly before her death she sang her own version of the *Internationale* for an Italian television program commemorating the centennial of the death of Karl Marx (1983). She was an avant-garde composer in her own right; she wrote multimedia works, such as *Stripsody,* an arresting soliloquy of labial and laryngeal sounds, and an eponymously titled piano piece, *Morsicat(h)y.* She resented being regarded as a "circus freak," and insisted that her objective was merely to meet the challenge of the new art of her time.

Berbié, Jane, French mezzo-soprano; b. Villefranche-de-Lauragais, near Toulouse, May 6, 1934. She studied at the Toulouse Cons.; made her debut in 1958 at La Scala in Milan; in 1959 she became a member of the Paris Opéra. Her operatic roles include Despina, Marcellina, and Zerlina; she also gave solo recitals.

Berbiguier, Benoit-Tranquille, French flutist; b. Caderousse, Vaucluse, Dec. 21, 1782; d. Pont-Levoy, near Blois, Jan. 28, 1838. He was a pupil of Wunderlich at the Paris Cons.; wrote many important works for flute, among them 15 books of flute duos; 2 books of duos for flute and violin; 10 concertos; 7 books of sonatas, with cello or viola; 8 sets of variations, with piano or orch.; 6 books of flute trios.

Berchem (or **Berghem**), **Jachet (de)** (also **Jaquet, Jacquet**), Flemish composer; b. Berchem, near Antwerp, early in the 16th century; d. Ferrara, 1580. He was in the service of the Duke of Ferrara from 1555. He has been confused with his contemporary Jachet de Mantua; also with Jachet Buus and Giaches de Wert. Berchem's 27 madrigals for 5 Voices appeared in 1546, and 24 madrigals for 4 Voices in 1555; 3 books containing settings of stanzas from *Orlando furioso* and dedicated to Duke Alfonso II of Ferrara were publ. in 1561. Modern reprints of Berchem's works are included in the following editions: R. van Maldeghem, *Trésor musical* (1865–93), vols. XI and XX (chansons); vols. XXVII and XXVIII (madrigals); R. Eitner, *Publikationen älterer prak-* *tischer und theoretischer Musikwerke* (1873–1905), vols. IX and XI (chansons).
BIBLIOGRAPHY: R. Eitner, "Jachet da Mantua und Jachet Berchem," *Monatshefte für Musikgeschichte* (1889); A. Einstein, *The Italian Madrigal* (Princeton, 1949); G. Reese, *Music in the Renaissance* (N.Y., 1954).

Berens, Hermann, German pianist and pedagogue; b. Hamburg, April 7, 1826; d. Stockholm, May 9, 1880. He studied with his father, Karl Berens of Hamburg; then had instruction with Reissiger in Dresden, and later with Czerny. In 1847 he emigrated to Sweden; served as music director to the Hussar regiment in Örebro (1849–60); then was music director at Mindre Teatern, in Stockholm (1860). In 1861 he was appointed to the staff of the Stockholm Cons.; in 1868 was named prof. there. He wrote an operetta, *En sommarnattsdröm* (1856); the operas *Violetta* (1855); *Lully och Quinault* (1859); *En utflykt i det gröne* (1862); and *Riccardo* (1869), which sank without a trace. But his collection of piano studies. *Neueste Schule der Geläufigkeit,* modeled after Czerny's studies, remained popular with piano students and teachers for many years.

Beretta, Giovanni Battista, Italian music theorist; b. Verona, Feb. 24, 1819; d. Milan, April 28, 1876. He was director of the Bologna Cons.; then devoted himself to continuing the *Dizionario artistico-scientifico-storico-technologico-musicale* begun by A. Barbieri (publ. Milan, 1869–72), but did not complete it; also wrote a treatise on harmony, and another on instrumentation and orchestration; composed instrumental and sacred music.

Berezovsky, Maximus, Russian singer and composer; b. Glukhov, Oct. 27, 1740; d. St. Petersburg, April 2, 1777. He studied at the Kiev Ecclesiastic Academy; then was chorister at the Court Chapel in St. Petersburg. He attracted attention by his lyric voice, and in 1765 was sent by the Russian government to Bologna for further study. He became a pupil of Padre Martini, and wrote an opera, *Demofoonte* (1773), which was produced in Bologna. Upon his return to Russia, he was unable to compete with Italian musicians who had acquired all the lucrative positions in the field of vocal teaching and opera; he became despondent and cut his throat. In addition to his opera, he left a *Credo* and 17 other sacred works; in these he made an attempt to follow the natural accents of the Russian text, which was an innovation at the time.
BIBLIOGRAPHY: N. Lebedev, *Berezovsky and Bortniansky as Church Music Composers* (St. Petersburg, 1882).

Berezowsky, Nicolai, talented Russian composer; b. St. Petersburg, May 17, 1900; d. New York, Aug. 27, 1953. He studied piano, violin, and voice at the Imperial Chapel in St. Petersburg; graduated in 1916, and obtained work as a violinist in the orch. of the provincial opera theater in Saratov, on the Volga River; there he played until 1919, when he joined the orch. of the Bolshoi Theater in Moscow. He crossed the border to Poland in 1920, managed to obtain an American visa, and arrived in N.Y. in 1922. He was engaged as a violinist in the orch. of the Capital Theater; in 1923 he joined the N.Y. Phil., remaining there until 1929. At the same time he took violin lessons with Paul Kochanski and studied composition with Rubin Goldmark. In 1928 he became an American citizen. He began to compose in larger forms; his clarinet sextet was performed at a chamber music festival in Washington, D.C., on Oct. 7, 1926. In 1929 his orchestral *Hebrew Suite* was conducted by Mengelberg with the N.Y. Philharmonic. Soon Berezowsky obtained other opportunities; Koussevitzky let him conduct the Boston Symph. in performances of his First Symph. in 1931 and his Fourth Symph. in 1943; Koussevitzky himself conducted Berezowsky's Second and Third Symphs. The famous German violinist Carl Flesch played the solo part of Berezowsky's Violin Concerto with the Dresden Phil. in 1930; Primrose played his Viola Concerto in 1942; and Piatigorsky performed his *Concerto lirico* with Koussevitzky and the Boston Symph. Berezowsky continued to play violin and conduct. From 1932 to 1936 and from 1941 to 1946 he was violinist and assistant conductor with the Columbia Broadcasting System, and from 1935 to 1940 was a member of the Coolidge String Quartet. He held a Guggenheim fellowship in 1948. His cantata *Gilgamesh* (1947) was favorably received, and his children's opera *Babar the Elephant* (1953) had numerous performances. His music possesses a Romantic quality, ingratiatingly Russian in color; in his later works he introduced fine impressionistic harmonies. He died of intestinal congestion apparently caused by a suicidal dose of powerful sedative drugs. His first wife (he was married twice) wrote a sweet little memoir, *Duet with Nicky,* describing his happier days.

WORKS: Sinfonietta (NBC, N.Y., May 8, 1932; won a prize); Symph. No. 1 (Boston Symph., March 16, 1931, composer conducting); Symph. No. 2 (Boston Symph., Koussevitzky conducting, Feb. 16, 1934); Symph. No. 3 (Rochester, Jan. 21, 1937); Symph. No. 4 (Boston Symph., Oct. 22, 1943, composer conducting); *Hebrew Suite* for Orch. (1929); *Christmas Festival Overture* (N.Y., Dec. 23, 1943); *Soldiers on the Town* (N.Y., Nov. 25, 1943); Violin Concerto (Dresden, April 29, 1930, composer conducting; Carl Flesch, soloist); *Concerto lirico* for Cello and Orch. (Boston, Feb. 22, 1935, Koussevitzky conducting; Piatigorsky, soloist); Viola Concerto (CBS Orch., N.Y., Oct. 11, 1941); Harp Concerto (Philadelphia, Jan. 26, 1945); *Passacaglia* for Theremin and Orch. (N.Y., Feb. 29, 1948); *Fantaisie* for 2 Pianos and Orch. (N.Y., Feb. 12, 1932); *Introduction and Waltz* for Orch. (N.Y., Oct. 15, 1939); *Theme and Variations,* a sextet for Strings, Clarinet, and Piano (Washington, Oct. 7, 1926); Cantata, *Gilgamesh* (N.Y., May 16, 1947); *Babar the Elephant,* children's opera (N.Y., Feb. 21, 1953); Sextet Concerto for String Orch. (1953); Duo for Clarinet and Viola (1931); Woodwind Quintet (1941).

BIBLIOGRAPHY: Alice Berezowsky, *Duet with Nicky* (N.Y., 1943); David Ewen, *American Composers* (N.Y., 1982).

Berg, Adam, German music printer active at Munich between 1567 and 1599; d. Munich, 1610. He publ. the important collection *Patrocinium musices,* in 12 vols., printed between 1573 and 1598. Of these, 7 vols. are devoted to Orlandus Lassus.

Berg, Alban, greatly significant Austrian composer whose music combined classical clarity of design and highly original melodic and harmonic techniques that became historically associated with the New Viennese School; b. Vienna, Feb. 9, 1885; d. there, Dec. 24, 1935 (of an abscess that could have been cured by sulfa drugs overnight had such medication existed at his time). He played piano as a boy and composed songs without formal training. He worked as a clerk in a government office in Lower Austria; in 1904 he met Arnold Schoenberg, who became his teacher, mentor, and close friend; he remained Schoenberg's pupil for 6 years. A fellow classmate was Anton von Webern; together they initiated the radical movement known to history as the Second Vienna School of composition. In Nov. 1918 Schoenberg organized in Vienna the Society for Private Musical Performances (Verein für Musikalische Privataufführungen) with the purpose of performing works unacceptable to established musical society. So as to emphasize the independence of the new organization, music critics were excluded from attendance. The society was disbanded in 1923, having accomplished its purpose. In 1925 Alban Berg joined the membership of the newly created International Society for Contemporary Music, which continued in an open arena the promotion of fresh musical ideas.

Berg's early works reflected the Romantic style of Wagner, Hugo Wolf, and Mahler; typical of this period were his *3 Pieces for Orchestra* (1913–15). As early as 1917 Berg began work on his opera *Wozzeck* (after the romantic play by Büchner), which was to become his masterpiece. The score represents an ingenious synthesis of Classical forms and modern techniques; it is organized as a series of purely symph. sections in traditional Baroque forms, among them a passacaglia with 21 variations, a dance suite, and a rhapsody, in a setting marked by dissonant counterpoint. Its first production at the Berlin State Opera, on Dec. 14, 1925, precipitated a storm of protests and press reviews of extreme violence; a similarly critical reception was accorded to *Wozzeck* in Prague on Nov. 11, 1926. Undismayed, Berg and his friends responded by publishing a brochure incorporating the most vehement of these reviews so as to shame and denounce the critics. Leopold Stokowski, ever eager to defy convention, gave the first American performance of *Wozzeck* in Philadelphia on March 19, 1931; it aroused a great deal of interest and was received with cultured equanimity. Thereafter, performances of *Wozzeck* multiplied in Europe (including Russia), and in due time it became recognized as the modern masterpiece that it is. The original manuscript was acquired from the composer by the Library of Congress in Washington, D.C. Shortly after the completion of *Wozzeck,* Berg wrote a *Lyric Suite* for string quartet in 6 movements; it was first played in Vienna by the Kolisch Quartet on Jan. 8, 1927; in 1928 Berg arranged the 2nd, 3rd, and 4th movements for string orch., which were performed in Berlin on Jan. 21, 1929. Rumors of a suppressed vocal part for the 6th movement of the suite, bespeaking Berg's secret affection for a married woman, Hanna Fuchs-Robettin, impelled Douglas M. Greene to institute a search for the original score; he discovered it in 1976 and, with the help of the American scholar George Perle, decoded the vocal line in an annotated copy of the score that Berg's widow, understandably reluctant to perpetuate her husband's emotional aberrations, turned over to a Vienna library. The text proved to be Stefan Georg's rendition of Baudelaire's *De Profundis clamavi* from *Les Fleurs du mal.* Berg inserted in the score all kinds of semiotical and numerological clues to his affection in a sort of symbolical synthesis. The *Lyric Suite* with its vocal finale was played for the first time at Abraham Goodman House, N.Y., by the Columbia String Quartet and Katherine Ciesinski, mezzo-soprano, on Nov. 1, 1979.

Berg's second opera, *Lulu* (1929–35), to a libretto derived from 2 plays by Wedekind, was left unfinished at Berg's death; 2 acts and 2 fragments of the 3rd act were performed posthumously in Zürich on June 2, 1937. Again, Berg's widow intervened to forestall any attempt to have the work reconstituted by another musician. However, Berg's publishers, asserting their legal rights, commissioned the Viennese composer Friedrich Cerha to re-create the 3rd act from materials available in other authentic sources, or used by Berg elsewhere; the task required 12 years (1962–74) for its completion. After Berg's widow died, several opera houses openly competed for the Cerha version of the work; the premiere of the complete opera, incorporating this version, was first presented at the Paris Opéra on Feb. 24, 1979; the first American performance followed in Santa Fe, N.M., on July 28, 1979. As in *Wozzeck,* so in *Lulu,* Berg organized the score in a series of classical forms; but while *Wozzeck* was written before Schoenberg's formulation of the method of composition in 12 tones related solely to one another, *Lulu* was set in full-fledged dodecaphonic techniques; even so, Berg allowed himself frequent divagations, contrary to the dodecaphonic code, into triadic tonal harmonies.

Berg's last completed work was a violin concerto commissioned by the American violinist Louis Krasner, who gave its first performance at the Festival of the International Society for Contemporary Music in Barcelona, on April 19, 1936. The score bears the inscription "Dam Andenken eines Engels" ("To the memory of an angel"), the angel being the daughter of Alma Mahler and Walter Gropius who died of consumption at an early age. The work is couched in the 12-tone technique, with free and frequent interludes of passing tonality.

WORKS: OPERAS: *Wozzeck* after a play of Büchner (1917–21; Berlin, Dec. 14, 1925; Prague, Nov. 11, 1926; Philadelphia, March 19, 1931); *Lulu* (after Wedekind's plays, *Erdgeist* and *Die Büchse der Pandora;* incomplete; partial perf., Zürich, June 2, 1937; with a reconstructed and partially recomposed 3rd act by Friedrich Cerha, Paris, Feb. 24, 1979; Santa Fe, N.M., July 28, 1979). OTHER WORKS: Concerto for Violin and Orch. (Barcelona, April 19, 1936; Louis Krasner, soloist); *7 frühe Lieder* for Voice and Piano (1905–8; orchestrated in 1928); Piano Sonata, op. 1 (1908; revised 1920); *4 Lieder* for Medium Voice and Piano, op. 2 (1908–9; revised 1920); String Quartet, op. 3 (1910; revised 1924); *Altenberg Lieder,* "5 orch. songs" with Voice, op. 4 (1912); *3 Stücke* for Orch. (1913–15; revised 1929; first complete perf., Oldenburg, April 14, 1930); *4 Stücke* for Clarinet and Piano, op. 5 (1913); *Kammerkonzert* for Piano, Violin, and 13 Wind Instruments, (the thematic material based on letter-notes in the names of Arnold Schoenberg, Anton Webern, and Alban Berg; 1923–25; March 20, 1927; its *Adagio,* scored for Violin, Clarinet, and Piano, was arranged in 1934); *Lyrische Suite* for String Quartet (1925-26; first performed by the Kolisch Quartet in Vienna, Jan. 8, 1927); a version for String Orch. of 3 movements (Nos. 2, 3, and 4) was arranged in 1928 (first performed in Berlin, Jan. 21, 1929; the premiere of the *Lyrische Suite* with a newly discovered vocal finale took place at Abraham Goodman House, N.Y., with the Columbia String Quartet and Katherine Ciesinski, mezzo-soprano, on Nov.1, 1979); *Der Wein* for Soprano and Orch., after Baudelaire (Königsberg, June 4, 1930); piano arrangement of Schoenberg's *Gurre Lieder.*

WRITINGS: Musical analyses of Schoenberg's works; articles.

BIBLIOGRAPHY: Willi Reich, *Alban Berg* (Vienna, 1937; with contributions by Theodore Wiesengrund-Adorno and Ernst Krenek); Willi Reich, *Guide to Wozzeck* (in Eng., N.Y., 1931); Alban Berg issue of *Eine Wiener Musikzeitschrift* (Vienna, 1936); Hans Hollaender, "Alban Berg," *Musical Quarterly* (Oct. 1936); René Leibowitz, "Alban Berg's Five Orchestral Songs," *Musical Quarterly* (1948); René Leibowitz, *Schoenberg and His School* (N.Y., 1949); P.J. Jouvé and M. Fano, *Wozzeck, ou Le Nouvel Opéra* (Paris, 1953); H.F. Redlich, *Alban Berg* (Vienna, 1957; condensed Eng. version, N.Y., 1957); K. Vogelsang, *Alban Berg: Leben und Werk* (Berlin, 1959); Willi Reich, ed., *Alban Berg, Bildnis im Wort* (Zurich, 1959); G. Ploebsch, *Alban Bergs Wozzeck* (Vienna, 1968); Bernard Grund, ed., *Berg: Letters to His Wife* (N.Y., 1971); Mosco Carner, *Alban Berg: The Man and His Work* (London, 1975; 2nd revised ed., 1983); Erich Alban Berg, ed., *Alban Berg: Leben und Werk in Daten und Bildern* (Frankfurt, 1976); M. Tarakanov, *Muzykalnyi teatr Albana Berga* (in Russian, Moscow, 1976); Theodor W. Adorno, *Berg: Der Meister des kleinsten Übergangs* (Frankfurt, 1977); K. Monson, *Alban Berg* (Boston, 1979). The International Alban Berg Society, in the Graduate Center of the City Univ. of N.Y., issues a periodic newsletter.

Berg, Conrad Mathias, Alsatian pianist; b. Colmar, April 27, 1785; d. Strasbourg, Dec. 13, 1852. He studied at the Paris Cons. (1806–7); then settled in Strasbourg as a piano teacher (1808). He wrote 4 string quartets, 10 piano trios, 3 piano concertos, sonatas, and many other pieces for his instrument. His essay "Ideen zu einer rationellen Lehrmethode der Musik mit Anwendung auf das Klavierspiel" appeared in *Cäcilia* (vol. XVII, 1835); he also wrote *Aperçu historique sur l'état de la musique à Strasbourg pendant les 50 dernières années* (1840).

Berg, Gunnar, Danish composer; b. St. Gall, Switzerland, to Danish parents, Jan. 11, 1909. He studied composition with Jeppesen and piano with Hermann Koppel in Copenhagen (1935–48); went to Paris in 1948 to study with Honegger and stayed there until 1957; returning to Copenhagen, he joined the avant-garde groups with the aim of liberating music from unnecessary academism. In his works he employs a sui generis serial technique in which each theme is a "cell" consisting of 5 to 10 notes, a model suggested to him by the experiments in cellular biology conducted by the bacteriologist Gaffky.
    WORKS: *Hymnos* for String Orch. (1946); *Passacaglia* for Orch. (1948; Aarhus, Sept. 7, 1980); *Prosthesis* for Saxophone and Piano (1952); *Cosmogonie* for 2 Pianos (1952); ballet, *Mouture* (1953); *5 Etudes* for Double String Orch. (1955); *El triptico gallego* for Orch. (1957); *Pour piano et orchestre* (Danish Radio, Sept. 29, 1966); *Gaffky's,* piano cycle in 10 "assortments" (1959); *Pour violon et piano* (1960); 2 chamber cantatas: *Spring Thaw* (1961) and *Vision,* after Dylan Thomas (1962); *Frise* for Chamber Orch. and Piano (Copenhagen, May 17, 1961); *Pour clarinette et violon* (1962); *Pour quintette à vent* (1962); *Pour quatuor à cordes* (1966); *Uculang* for Piano and Orch. (1967; Danish Radio, April 15, 1969); *Random* for Cello and Percussion (1968); *Tronqué* for Xylophone, Cello, and Piano (1969); *Pour flûte, clarinet et violon* (1972); Flute Sonata (1972); *Pièce* for Trumpet, Violin, and Piano (1972); *Fresques I–III* for Solo Guitar (1976); *Mutationen* for Chamber Orch. (Danish Radio, Nov. 1, 1978); *Mouvement* for String Quartet (1978).

Berg, Johann von, Flemish music printer; b. Ghent; d. Nuremberg, Aug. 7, 1563. He lived in Ghent; in 1531, settled in Nuremberg, where he became Ulrich Neuber's partner.

Berg, Josef, Czech composer; b. Brno, March 8, 1927; d. there, Feb. 26, 1971. He studied with Petrželka at the Brno Cons. (1946–50); was music editor of Brno Radio (1950–53); wrote simple music for the Folk Art ensemble. Later he began using 12-tone techniques. His most original works are the satirical chamber operas, to his own texts: *The Return of Odysseus* (1962); *European Tourism* (1963); *Euphrides in Front of the Gates of Tymenas* (1964); *Breakfast at Slankenwald Castle* (1966). He also wrote 3 symphs. (1950, 1952, 1955); Viola Sonata (1958); Fantasia for 2 Pianos (1958); Sextet for Piano, Harp, and String Quartet (1959); *Songs of the New Werther* for Bass-baritone and Piano (1962); Nonet for 2 Harps, Piano, Harpsichord, and Percussion (1962); *Sonata*

in Modo Classico for Harpsichord and Piano (1963); *Organ Music on a Theme of Gilles Binchois* (1964); String Quartet (1966); 2 *Canti* for Baritone, Instrumental Ensemble, Organ, and Metronome (1966); *Ó Corino* for 4 Solo Voices and Classical Orch. (1967); *Oresteia* for Vocal Quartet, Narrator, and Instrumental Ensemble (1967).

Berg, (Carl) Natanaël, Swedish composer; b. Stockholm, Feb. 9, 1879; d. there, Oct. 14, 1957. He first studied surgery; then entered the Stockholm Cons., where he studied singing; later he went abroad and took courses in composition in Germany. His works are couched in a characteristically Scandinavian romantic manner.
    WORKS: 5 operas, all produced in Stockholm: *Leila* (Feb. 29, 1912); *Engelbrekt* (Sept. 21, 1929); *Judith* (Feb. 22, 1936); *Brigitta* (Jan. 10, 1942); *Genoveva* (Oct. 25, 1947); ballets: *Alvorna* (1914); *Sensitiva* (1919); *Hertiginnans friare* (*The Duchess's Suitors* 1920); 5 symphs. with subtitles: No. 1, *Alles endet was entstehet* (1913); No. 2, *Årstiderna* (*The Tides;* 1916); No. 3, *Makter* (*Power;* 1917); No. 4, *Pezzo sinfonico* (1918); No. 5, *Trilogia delle passioni* (1922); symph. poems: *Traumgewalten* (1911); *Varde ljus* (1914); *Reverenza; Suite* for Orch. (1930); oratorios: *Mannen och kvinnan* (*Man and Woman;* 1911); *Israels lovsång* (*Israel's Hymns;* 1915); *Das Hohelied* (1925); Violin Concerto (1918); Serenade for Violin and Orch. (1923); Piano Concerto (1931); Piano Quintet (1917); 2 string quartets (1917, 1919); songs.

Bergamo, Petar, Serbian composer; b. Split, Feb. 27, 1920. He studied composition at the Belgrade Academy of Music with Rajičič; in 1966 joined its faculty as assistant prof. His overture *Navigare necesse est* (Belgrade, Feb. 27, 1962) typifies his style and manner, with a reference to the necessity of navigating in finding one's way in the modern method of composition; his *Musica concertante* for Orch. (Belgrade, Feb. 18, 1963) points to a neo-Baroque formalism. He further wrote 2 symphs. (1957 and 1963); *Concerto abbreviato* for Clarinet Solo (1966); *Ritrovari per tre* for Piano Trio (1967); *I colori d'argento* for Flute, Harpsichord, and a Chamber Group (1968); a String Quartet (1958); and a ballet, *Steps* (1970).

Berganza, Teresa, Spanish mezzo-soprano; b. Madrid, March 16, 1935. She studied at the Madrid Cons.; in 1957 she sang at the Florence May Festival. She made her American debut in Dallas in 1958; also sang at the Glyndebourne Festival and at Covent Garden in London. On Oct. 11, 1967, she made her Metropolitan Opera debut as Cherubino in *The Marriage of Figaro;* also gave recitals.

Berge, Sigurd, Norwegian composer; b. Vinstra, July 1, 1929. He studied composition with Finn Mortensen (1956–59); later took courses in electronic music in the Netherlands and Poland.
    WORKS: *Dances from Gudbrandsdal* for Orch. (1955–56); Divertimento for Violin, Viola, and Cello

(1956); *Episode* for Violin and Piano (1958); *Pezzo orchestrale* (1958); *Raga,* a concerto-study in Indian music, for Oboe and Orch. (1959); *Sinus* for Strings and Percussion (1961); *Tamburo piccolo* for Strings and Percussion (1961); *Chroma* for Orch. (1963); *A* for Orch. (1964–65); *B* for Orch. (1965–66); *Flute Solo* (1966); *Oboe Solo* (1966); *Yang Guan* for Wind Quintet (1967); *Ballet* for 2 Dancers and Percussion (1967–68); *Gamma* for 7 Instruments (1970); *Epsilon* for Chamber Orch. (1970); *Delta* for Jazz Trio and Tape (1970); *Horn Call* for Solo Horn (1972); over 25 electronic pieces.

Bergel, Erich, conductor; b. Rosenau, Rumania, June 1, 1930. He studied in Bucharest; in 1959 he was appointed conductor of the Cluj Phil., but was shortly afterward (May 9, 1959) arrested on suspicion of subversive activities. He was released from prison on Oct. 4, 1962, and was engaged as a trumpet player by the Cluj Phil.; in 1965 became its conductor. In 1971 he left Rumania and settled in West Germany. In 1975 he made his American debut as guest conductor with the Houston Symph. Orch.; in 1979–81 he served as its principal guest conductor. He publ. a disquisition on Bach's *Art of the Fugue* (Bonn, 1979; first vol. only).

Berger, Andreas, German composer; b. Dolsenhaim, near Altenburg, Saxony, 1584; d. Ulm, Jan. 10, 1656. In 1606 he became a tenor at the court chapel in Stuttgart; from 1608–12 was court composer there. From 1624–34 he served as Kapellmeister to Count Ludwig Eberhard of Öttingen. He subsequently held posts as a public official in Augsburg, Leutkirch, and Ulm. He composed both sacred and secular vocal music.

Berger, Arthur, American composer and writer on music; b. New York, May 15, 1912. After a preliminary study with Vincent Jones at N.Y. Univ., he moved to Boston. From 1934 to 1937 he studied at the Longy School of Music in Cambridge, Mass., and later attended the Harvard Graduate School, where he took courses in composition with Walter Piston, and academic musical subjects with Archibald T. Davidson and Hugo Leichtentritt. Subsequently he went to Paris to study composition with Nadia Boulanger. Returning to the U.S. in 1939, he entered Mills College in Oakland, Calif., to study composition with Darius Milhaud. In 1942–43 he was on the staff of Brooklyn College; in 1953 he was appointed prof. of music at Brandeis Univ.; in 1973–74 he was visiting prof. of music at Harvard Univ.; in 1975–76 he was the recipient of a Guggenheim fellowship. His musical idiom reveals the influence of divergent schools of composition, including a sui generis serialism and the neo-Classical pragmatism of Stravinsky. His works, in whatever idiom, are characterized by a strong formal structure; the title of one of his most cogent scores, *Ideas of Order,* is a declaration of principles. Arthur Berger was also an able music critic; he covered concerts in N.Y. for the *New York Sun* (1943–46) and for the *New York Herald-Tribune* (1946–53). He also wrote a monograph on Aaron Copland (N.Y., 1953).

WORKS: *Two Episodes* for Piano (1933); *Three Songs of Yeats* for Voice, Flute, Clarinet, and Cello (1939); *Entertainment Piece* for 3 Dancers and "Modern-style Piano" (1940); Woodwind Quartet (1941); *Serenade Concertante* for Violin, Woodwind Quartet and Chamber Orch. (1944, Rochester, N.Y., Oct. 24, 1945); *Three Pieces* for Strings (N.Y., Jan. 26, 1946); *Duo* No. 1 for Violin and Piano (1948); *Duo* No. 2 for Violin and Piano (1950); *Duo* No. 3 for Oboe and Clarinet (1952); *Ideas of Order* for Orch. (N.Y. Phil., April 11, 1953, Mitropoulos conducting); *Polyphony* for Orch. (Louisville, Ky., Nov. 17, 1956); *Chamber Music for 13 Players* (Los Angeles, April 4, 1960); String Quartet (1958); *Chamber Concerto* for Orch. (1959; N.Y., May 13, 1962; revised 1978); *Septet* for Flute, Clarinet, Bassoon, Violin, Viola, Cello, and Piano (1966; Library of Congress, Washington, D.C., Nov. 25, 1966); *Trio* for Guitar, Violin, and Piano (1972); *Composition* for Piano, 4-hands (1976); *Five Songs* for Tenor and Piano (1979); Piano Trio (1980); *Improvisation for A.C.* for Piano (1981); numerous other piano pieces.

BIBLIOGRAPHY: J. Perkins, "Arthur Berger; The Composer as Mannerist," *Perspectives of New Music* (Fall/Winter 1966); David Ewen, *American Composers* (N.Y., 1982); B. Northcott, "Arthur Berger: An Introduction at 70" (*The Musical Times,* May 1982).

Berger, Erna, German soprano; b. Cossebaude, near Dresden, Oct. 19, 1900. She studied voice in Dresden with Melita Hirzel; made her operatic debut with the Dresden State Opera in 1925; sang there until 1930. On Nov. 21, 1949, she appeared at the Metropolitan Opera in N.Y. as Sophie in *Der Rosenkavalier;* remained on its roster until 1951; retired from the stage in 1955; returned to Germany and settled in Hamburg as a voice teacher. She gave her last solo recital in Munich on Feb. 15, 1968, at the age of 67. Her best operatic parts were Gilda in *Rigoletto* and Rosina in *Il Barbiere di Siviglia.*

BIBLIOGRAPHY: K. Höcker, *Erna Berger: Die singende Botschafterin* (Berlin, 1961).

Berger, Francesco, English pianist and composer; b. London, June 10, 1834; d. there (at the age of 98), April 25, 1933. He studied harmony with Luigi Ricci in Trieste, piano with Karl Lickl in Vienna; later studied with Hauptmann and Plaidy at Leipzig; returned to London, where he was a prof. of piano at the Royal Academy of Music and at the Guildhall School of Music; made frequent concert tours through Great Britain and Ireland; was for some years director and, from 1884–1911, honorary secretary of the Phil. Society. He composed an opera, *Il Lazzarone,* and a Mass; overtures and incidental music to Wilkie Collins's *The Frozen Deep* and *The Lighthouse;* many songs and piano pieces. He publ. *First Steps at the Pianoforte; Reminiscences, Impressions and Anecdotes; Musical Expressions, Phrases and Sentences;* and a *Musical Vocabulary in 4 Languages* (1922); in 1931 he publ. his memoirs, entitled (with reference to his age) *97.*

Berger, Jean, German-American choral conductor and composer; b. Hamm, Sept. 27, 1909. He studied music theory with Heinrich Besseler at the Univ. of Heidelberg (Ph.D., 1931), and also with Egon Wellesz at the Univ. of Vienna (1928–32). In 1931 he went to Paris, where he took lessons in composition with Louis Aubert; was also conductor of Les Compagnons de la Marjolaine, a mixed choral group specializing in his modern harmonizations of French folk tunes; in 1935 Berger acquired French citizenship. From 1939–41 he was in Rio de Janeiro, where he was employed as French opera coach at the Municipal Theater. In 1941 he went to N.Y. He taught at Middlebury College in Vermont (1948–59), at the Univ. of Illinois, Urbana (1959–61), at the Univ. of Colorado (1961–68), and at other colleges. As a composer, he writes mostly for voice, in a melodious pragmatic idiom. In 1937 his work *Le Sang des autres* won first prize at the International Competition in Zürich. His compositions of the American period include: *Brazilian Psalm* for Chorus (1941); *Caribbean Concerto* for Mouth Harmonica and Orch., possibly the first of its kind, commissioned by Larry Adler and performed by him with the St. Louis Symph. Orch. on March 10, 1942; *Vision of Peace* for Chorus (1948); *Creole Overture* (1949); *Short Symphony* (1952); *Magnificat* for Soprano, Flute, Percussion, and Chorus (1960); *The Fiery Furnace,* dramatic cantata (1962); *A Song of Seasons* (1967); *The Pied Piper* for Vocal Groups and Orch. (1968); liturgical drama, *The Cherry Tree Carol* (1975).

Berger, Ludwig, German composer and pianist; b. Berlin, April 18, 1777; d. there, Feb. 16, 1839. He studied flute and piano; went to Berlin in 1799; there he received instruction in harmony and counterpoint with Gürrlich. In 1804 he went to Russia, but fled in the face of Napoleon's invasion in 1812; in 1815 he returned to Berlin and was active mainly as a teacher; his students included Mendelssohn, Henselt, and Taubert. He wrote a Piano Concerto, 7 piano sonatas, songs, and numerous piano works.
BIBLIOGRAPHY: L. Rellstab, *Ludwig Berger* (Berlin, 1846); D. Siebenkäs, *Ludwig Berger: Sein Leben und seine Werke unter besonderer Berücksichtigung seines Liedschaffens* (Berlin, 1963).

Berger, Roman, Slovak composer; b. Těšín, Aug. 9, 1930. He studied piano at the municipal music school in Katowice, Poland (1949–52); then established himself in Bratislava, where he took lessons in composition with Kafenda (1952–56); taught piano at the Bratislava Cons. (1956–65) and theory and composition at the Bratislava Academy of Musical Arts (1969–73). His style of composition follows the tenets of the modern Vienna School, formally well disciplined, melodically atonal, and harmonically complex.
WORKS: 3 piano sonatas (1960, 1965, 1975); Trio for Flute, Clarinet, and Bassoon (1962); *Ukolébavka (Lullaby)* for Mezzo-soprano and Chamber Orch. (1962); Suite for Strings, Piano, and Percussion (1963); *Transformácie* for Orch. (1965); *Konvergen-*

zioni I for Violin and *II* for Viola; electronic pieces.

Berger, Rudolf, Czech opera singer; b. Brno, April 17, 1874; d. New York, Feb. 27, 1915. He began his career as a baritone with the Berlin Opera (1904–7); then went to N.Y. and studied with Oscar Saenger; changed his voice to tenor; and returned to Germany. He made his American debut at the Metropolitan Opera on Feb. 5, 1914, as Siegmund in *Die Walküre;* was on its roster until his death. His repertoire consisted of 96 baritone and 18 tenor roles; he sang Jokanaan in *Salome* 79 times. He was married to the soprano **Marie Rappold.**

Berger, Theodor, Austrian composer; b. Traismauer, May 18, 1905. He studied in Vienna with Franz Schmidt; evolved under Schmidt's influence a strong Romantic idiom within the framework of Classical forms. His music acquired many important supporters in Austria and Germany, but rarely penetrates beyond Central Europe.
WORKS: *Malinconia* for String Orch. in 25 parts (1938); Ballade for Orch. (1941); *Rondo ostinato* for Wind Instruments and Percussion (1947); *Homerische Symphonie* (1948); *La Parola* for Orch. (based on the sequitone scale of alternating whole tones and semitones; 1955); *Sinfonia Parabolica* (1956); *Sinfonia Macchinale* (1956); *Symphonischer Triglyph,* on themes from Schubert's chamber music (1957); *Jahreszeiten* for Orch. (1958); *Frauenstimmen im Orchester* for Women's Chorus, Harps, and Strings (1959); Violin Concerto (1963); Divertimento for Men's Chorus, 7 Wind Instruments, and Percussion (1968).

Berger, Wilhelm, German composer; b. Boston (of German parents); Aug. 9, 1861; d. Jena, Jan. 15, 1911. He was taken to Germany as a child; studied at the Hochschule für Musik in Berlin (1878–81). From 1888 to 1903 he taught at the Klindworth-Scharwenka Cons. in Berlin; in 1903 was named a member of the Akademie der Kunste in Berlin. He was a very prolific composer; wrote 105 opus numbers; his music, though lacking in originality, commanded respect for its technical skill.
WORKS: Symph. No. 1 (Boston, Nov. 4, 1899); Symph. No. 2; oratorio, *Euphorion;* Piano Quartet; numerous choral pieces; many songs.
BIBLIOGRAPHY: W. Altmann, *Wilhelm Berger;* catalogue (Leipzig, 1920); E. Krause, *Wilhelm Berger* (Leipzig, 1907); G. Ernest, *Wilhelm Berger: Ein deutscher Meister* (Berlin, 1931).

Berger, Wilhelm Georg, Rumanian composer and musicologist; b. Rupea, Dec. 4, 1929. He studied at the Bucharest Cons. (1948–52); was a viola player in the Bucharest Phil. (1948–57). In 1968 he was elected Secretary of the Rumanian Composers' Union.
WORKS: Oratorio, *Stefan Furtună* (1958); *Symphonic Variations* (1958); Concerto for String Orch. (1958); 13 symphs., all bearing descriptive subtitles: No. 1, *Lyric* (1960); No. 2, *Epic* (1962); No. 3, *Dramatic* (1964); No. 4, *Tragic* (1965); No. 5, *Solemn Music*

Berggreen – Bergman

(1968); No. 6, *Harmony* (1969); No. 7, *Energetic* (1970); No. 8, *The Morning Star,* with Chorus (1971); No. 9, *Melodie* (1974); No. 10, with Solo Organ (1975–76); No. 11, *Sarmizegetusa* (1975–77); No. 12, *To the Star,* for String Orch. (1977); No. 13, *Sinfonia solemnis* (1981); 2 viola concertos (1960, 1962); *Rhapsodic Images* for Orch. (1964); Violin Concerto (1965; Brussels, Jan. 11, 1966; winner of the 1966 Queen Elisabeth of Belgium Composition Contest in the concerto category); Cello Concerto (1967); *Meditations,* cycle of variations for Chamber Orch. (1968); Variations for Wind Orch. (1968); Concerto for 2 Violas and Orch. (1968); *Concert Music* for Flute, Strings, and Percussion (1972); Viola Sonata (1953); 12 string quartets (1954, 1956, 1957, 1959, 1961, 1965, 1966, 1966, 1967, 1967, 1967, 1967); Violin Sonata (1960); Sonata for Viola and Cello (1962); Piano Sonata (1962); Solo Violin Sonata (1964); Sonata for Flute, Viola, and Cello (1965); Solo Cello Sonata (1967); Sonata for Viola and Violin (1967); Solo Viola Sonata (1968). A detailed list of his works and writings on music is found in Viorel Cosma's *Muzicieni români* (Bucharest, 1970).

Berggreen, Andreas Peter, Danish composer; b. Copenhagen, March 2, 1801; d. there, Nov. 8, 1880. He studied law and turned to music late in life; occupied various teaching posts in Copenhagen. His opera *Billedet og Busten* (*The Portrait and The Bust*) was produced in Copenhagen on April 9, 1832; he also wrote incidental music to plays. His most important contribution to music literature is the compilation of 11 vols. of folk songs, *Folke-sang og melodier, faedre landske og fremmede* (Copenhagen, 1842–55; 2nd ed., enlarged, 1861–71); he further publ. 14 volumes of songs for use in schools (1834–76) and edited church anthems. Among his students was Niels Gade.
BIBLIOGRAPHY: C. Skou, *Andreas Peter Berggreen* (Copenhagen, 1895).

Bergh, Arthur, American composer and conductor; b. St. Paul, Minn., March 24, 1882; d. aboard the S.S. *President Cleveland* en route to Honolulu, Feb. 11, 1962. He studied violin; played in the orch. of the Metropolitan Opera (1903–8); then conducted a series of municipal concerts in N.Y. (1911–14); later became associated with various recording companies. Among his works are 2 melodramas with Orch., *The Raven* and *The Pied Piper of Hamelin;* romantic opera, *Niorada;* symph. chorale, *The Unnamed City;* 2 operettas: *In Arcady* and *The Goblin Fair;* about 100 songs; a number of violin pieces; etc. From 1941 Bergh lived in Hollywood as a librarian for motion picture companies.

Bergh, Rudolph, Danish composer and writer; b. Copenhagen, Sept. 22, 1859; d. Davos, Switzerland, Dec. 7, 1924. He studied biology and music in Copenhagen and Berlin; in 1922 was a member of the Board of the Copenhagen Cons. He composed the choral works *Requiem für Werther; Geister der Windstille;* and an oratorio, *The Mount of Holy Fire;* also about 150 songs; 50 piano pieces; chamber music; etc.

Berghem, Jachet de. See **Berchem, Jachet (de).**

Bergiron de Briou, Nicolas-Antoine, Seigneur du Fort Michon, French composer; b. Lyons, Dec. 12, 1690; d. there, before April 27, 1768. He studied classical literature and law at the Univ. of Paris; with J.P. Christin, he established in 1713 the Académie des Beaux-Arts in Lyons, and remained associated with it in various capacities until 1764. He composed a number of cantatas and motets; other works include divertissements and several operas.

Berglund, Joel, Swedish bass-baritone; b. Torsaker, June 4, 1903. He was educated at the Cons. in Stockholm; made his debut there in 1928. He then appeared in Zürich, Vienna, and Buenos Aires; also sang in Chicago. He sang at Bayreuth in 1942; after World War II, he returned to America, appearing at the Metropolitan Opera (1945–49). He then was director of the Royal Opera in Stockholm (1949–56); he retired from the stage in 1970. He was regarded as one of the leading Wagnerian singers of his generation.

Berglund, Paavo, Finnish conductor; b. Helsinki, April 14, 1929. He studied at the Sibelius Academy. In 1956 he became associate conductor of the Finnish Radio Symph. Orch. in Helsinki; in 1962 became its principal conductor. From 1972 to 1979 he served as music director of the Bournemouth Symph. Orch.; synchronously he conducted the Helsinki Phil. Orch. (1975–79). In 1981 he was appointed principal guest conductor of the Scottish National Orch. in Glasgow. He was named an Officer of the Order of the British Empire in 1977.

Bergman, Erik, Finnish composer; b. Uusikaarlepyy (Nykarleby), Nov. 24, 1911. He studied composition with Erik Furuhjelm at the Helsinki Cons. (1931–38); then with Heinz Tiessen at the Hochschule für Musik in Berlin, Joseph Marx in Vienna, and Wladimir Vogel in Switzerland. In 1963 he joined the staff of his Finnish alma mater, (renamed the Sibelius Academy); retired in 1976. Stylistically, Bergman cultivates varied techniques, ranging from medieval modality to dodecaphony. His predilection is for polyphonic vocal music. WORKS: FOR ORCH.: *Suite* for Strings (1938); *Burla* (1948); *Tre aspetti d'una serie dodecafonica* (1957); *Aubade* (1958); *Simbolo* (1960); *Circulus* (1965); *Colori ed improvvisazioni* (1973); *Dualis* for Cello and Orch. (1978); *Birds in the Morning* for Flute and Orch. (1979); *Arctica* (Utrecht, Nov. 2, 1979); Piano Concerto (1980–81; Helsinki, Sept. 16, 1981). CHORAL: *Rubaiyat,* to the text by Omar Khayyám, for Baritone, Male Chorus, and Orch. (1953); *Adagio* for Baritone, Male Chorus, Flute, and Vibraphone (1957); *Svanbild (Swan Picture)* for Baritone, Vocal Quartet, and Male Chorus (1958); *Aton,* on the text "Hymn to the Sun" by the Pharaoh Akhenaten, for Baritone, Reciter, Chorus, and Orch.

Bergmann – Bergsma

(1959); 4 *Galgenlieder* for 3 Reciters and Speaking Chorus (1960); *Sela* for Baritone, Chorus, and Chamber Orch. (1962); *Fåglarna (Birds)* for Baritone, Male Chorus, 5 Solo Voices, Percussion, and Celesta (1962); *Springtime* for Baritone and Chorus (1966); *Snö (Snow)* for Baritone, Male Chorus, and Flute (1966); *Jesurun* for Baritone, Male Chorus, 2 Trumpets, 2 Trombones, and Percussion (1967); *Canticum fennicum* for Baritone, Solo Voices, 2 Solo Quartets, Male Chorus, and Orch. (1968); *Annonssidan* for Baritone, 3 Tenors, Reciters, and Male Chorus (1969); *Nox* for Baritone, Chorus, Flute, English Horn, and Percussion (1970); *Requiem for a Dead Poet* for Baritone, Chorus, Brass, Percussion, and Organ (1970); *Missa in honorem Sancti Henrici* for Soloists, Chorus, and Organ (1971); *Samothrake*, dramatic scene for Reciter, Chorus, Instrumental Ensemble, and Choreography (1971); *Hathor Suite* for Soprano, Baritone, Chorus, and Small Ensemble (1971). VOCAL WORKS: *Majnätter (May Nights)* for Soprano and Orch. (1946); *Ensamhetens sånger (Songs of Solitude)* for Voice and Orch. (1947); *Livets träd (Tree of Life)*, chamber cantata for Soprano, Alto, Baritone, Horn, Clarinet, Percussion, Harp, and String Quartet (1947); *Bardo Thödol*, after the Tibetan Book of the Dead, for Narrator, Mezzo-soprano, Baritone, Mixed Chorus, and Orch. (1974); *Loleila* for Girls' and Boys' Choruses, Soprano, Tenor, and Orch. (1974); *Noa* for Baritone, Chorus, and Orch. (1976). CHAMBER MUSIC: Piano Trio (1937); Violin Sonata (1943); 3 Fantasies for Clarinet and Piano (1954); *Concerto da camera* for 8 Soloists (1961). Solo: Passacaglia and Fugue for Organ (1939); *Intervalles* for Piano (1949); Suite for Guitar (1949); *Espressivo* for Piano (1952); *Aspects* for Piano (1969); *Energien* for Harpsichord (1970).
BIBLIOGRAPHY: J. Parsons, *Erik Bergman: A Seventieth Birthday Tribute* (London, 1981).

Bergmann, Carl, German cellist and conductor; b. Ebersbach, Saxony, April 12, 1821; d. New York, Aug. 10, 1876. He was a pupil of Zimmermann in Zittau and of Hesse in Breslau; in consequence of his involvement in the revolutionary events of 1848–49, he left Germany and went to America. In 1850 he joined the traveling Germania Orch. as a cellist; later became its conductor; also led the Handel and Haydn Society of Boston (1852–54). In 1854 he went to N.Y. and became conductor of the German men's chorus "Arion." On April 21, 1855, he made an impressive debut as a guest conductor of the N.Y. Phil., and was named its sole conductor for the 1855–56 season; from 1856 to 1866 he shared the conductorship with Theodore Eisfeld. In 1866 he became permanent conductor of the N.Y. Phil., a position he held until his death. He continued to perform as a cellist, taking part in the Mason-Thomas chamber music concerts; furthermore, he led a series of Sacred Concerts, in programs of both choral and orch. music. He was a progressive musician, and presented works of Berlioz, Liszt, and Wagner at the time when their music did not suit the tastes of the American public.

Bergmans, Paul Jean Etienne Charles, Belgian musicologist; b. Ghent, Feb. 23, 1868; d. there, Nov. 14, 1935. He studied at the Univ. of Ghent (Dr.Phil., 1887); in 1892 became assistant librarian there; in 1919, chief librarian and prof. He was a member of the Royal Academy of Belgium; publ. a number of very valuable studies and books, the most important of which are: *P.J. Leblan, Carilloneur de la ville de Gand au XVIIIe siècle* (1884); *H. Waelput* (1886); *Variétés musicologiques* (3 vols.; 1891, 1901, 1920); *La Vie musicale gantoise au XVIIIe siècle* (1897); *Peter Philips* (1903); *Les Musiciens de Courtrai et du Courtraisis* (1912); *Notice sur Fl. van Duyse* (1919); *Corn. Verdonck* (1919); *Henri Vieuxtemps* (1920); *Le Baron Limnander de Nieuwenhove* (1920); *Quatorze lettres inédites du comp. Philippe de Monte* (1921); *Tielman Susato* (1923); *Notice sur le chevalier X. van Elewyck* (1925); *De l'histoire de la musique* (1927); *Les Origines belges de Beethoven* (1927); *Une Famille de musiciens belges du XVIIIe siècle: Les Loeillet* (Brussels, 1927; establishes for the first time accurate biographical data on members of the Loeillet family); *La Typographie musicale en Belgique au XVIe siècle* (1930). He also wrote an introduction to vol. I (1932; piano music, ed. by J. Watelet) of *Monumenta musicae Belgicae.*

Bergner, Wilhelm, Latvian organist; b. Riga, Nov. 4, 1837; d. there, June 9, 1907. He was organist of the English church at Riga (1861) and at the Riga Cathedral (1868–1906); exercised great influence on the development of musical culture in Latvia.

Bergonzi, Carlo, noted Italian tenor; b. Polisene, near Parma, July 13, 1924. He studied voice in Parma with Grandini; made his operatic debut as a baritone in Lecce in 1948, singing Figaro in *Il Barbiere di Siviglia;* then established himself as a tenor; in 1951 sang the role of Andrea Chénier in Bari; in 1953 he appeared at La Scala in Milan with much success; from 1953 sang in London. He made his U.S. debut with the Chicago Lyric Opera in 1955; on Nov. 13, 1956, he made his first appearance at the Metropolitan Opera in N.Y. as Radames in *Aida,* and continued to be on its roster in subsequent seasons. He was particularly distinguished in the lyrico-dramatic roles in Italian operas.

Bergonzi, Carlo, Italian violin maker; b. Cremona, c. 1683; d. there, 1747. He began manufacturing violins about 1720, working independently of Stradivarius and other violin makers of his time. His son, **Michael Angelo Bergonzi,** continued the trade, as did his grandsons, **Carlo, Nicola,** and **Zosimo Bergonzi.**

Bergsma, William Laurence, notable American composer; b. Oakland, Calif., April 1, 1921. His mother, a former opera singer, gave him piano lessons; he also practiced the violin. After the family moved to Redwood City, Bergsma entered Burlingame High School, where he had some music theory lessons. In 1937 he began to take lessons in composition with Howard Hanson, who was at that time

231

teaching a course at the Univ. of Southern Calif. in Los Angeles. He composed a ballet, *Paul Bunyan,* and Hanson conducted a suite from it with the Rochester Civic Orch. in Rochester, N.Y., on April 29, 1939. Bergsma also took courses at Stanford Univ.; from 1940 to 1944 he attended the Eastman School of Music in Rochester, studying general composition with Howard Hanson and orchestration with Bernard Rogers. He graduated in 1942, and received his M.M. degree in 1944. In 1944 Bergsma became an instructor in music at Drake Univ. in Des Moines. In 1946 and in 1951 he held Guggenheim fellowships. In 1946 he was appointed to the faculty of the Juilliard School of Music, N.Y., where he taught until 1963. From 1963 to 1971, Bergsma served as director of the School of Music of the Univ. of Washington in Seattle. During his teaching activities he continued to compose, receiving constant encouragement from an increasing number of performances of his works. His style of composition is that of classical Romanticism having a strong formal structure without lapsing into modernistic formalism. The Romantic side of his music is reflected in his melodious lyricism. He never subscribed to fashionable theories of doctrinaire modernity.

WORKS: OPERAS: *The Wife of Martin Guerre* (N.Y., Feb. 15, 1956); *The Murder of Comrade Sharik* (1973). Ballets: *Paul Bunyan* (San Francisco, June 22, 1939); *Senor Commandante* (Rochester, May 1, 1942). FOR ORCH.: Symphony for Chamber Orch. (Rochester, April 14, 1943); *Music on a Quiet Theme* (Rochester, April 22, 1943); Symphony No. 1 (1946–49; CBS Radio, May 20, 1950); *A Carol on Twelfth Night,* symph. poem (1953); *Chameleon Variations* (1960); *In Celebration: Toccata for the Sixth Day,* commissioned for the inaugural week concert of the Juilliard Orch. during the week of dedication of Phil. Hall at Lincoln Center for the Performing Arts (N.Y., Sept. 28, 1962); *Documentary One* (1963; suite from a film score); *Serenade, To Await the Moon* for Chamber Orch. (La Jolla, Calif., Aug. 22, 1965); Violin Concerto (Tacoma, Wash., May 18, 1966); *Documentary Two* (1967); Symphony No. 2, *Voyages* (Great Falls, Mont., May 11, 1976). CHAMBER MUSIC: *Concerto* for Wind Quintet (1958); *Fantastic Variations on a Theme from Tristan und Isolde* for Viola and Piano (Boston, March 2, 1961); Suite for Brass Quartet (1940); 4 string quartets (1942, 1944, 1953, 1970); *Showpiece* for Violin and Piano (1934); *Pieces for Renard* for Recorder and 2 Violas (1943); *Illegible Canons* for Clarinet and Piano (1969); *Changes for Seven* for Wind Quintet, Percussion, and Piano (1971); *Clandestine Dialogues* for Cello and Percussion (1972); *Blatant Hypotheses* for Trombone and Piano (1977); Quintet for Flute and Strings (1979). VOCAL MUSIC: *In a Glass of Water* (1945); *On the Beach at Night* (1946); *Confrontation* from the *Book of Job,* for Chorus and 22 Instruments (Des Moines, Iowa, Nov. 29, 1963); *Wishes, Wonders, Portents, Charms* for Chorus and Instruments (N.Y., Feb. 12, 1975); *In Space* for Soprano and Instruments (Seattle, May 21, 1975). For Piano: *3 Fanta-*

sies (1943); *Tangents* (1951).

BIBLIOGRAPHY: David Ewen, *American Composers* (N.Y., 1982).

Bergson, Michael, Polish-born composer; b. Warsaw, May 20, 1820; d. London, March 9, 1898. He studied music in Berlin; in 1840 he went to Paris, and in 1846 traveled to Italy, where he had his opera *Luisa di Montfort* produced in Florence in 1847. On his second visit to Paris he brought out an operetta, *Qui va à la chasse, perd sa place* (1859). In 1863 he taught piano at the Geneva Cons. He eventually settled in London. He wrote numerous pieces of piano music, clearly in imitation of Chopin (*Polonaise héroïque, 12 grandes études caractéristiques,* etc.); also brought out a manual, *Ecole du mécanisme.*

Berigan, Rowland Bernart ("Bunny"), American jazz trumpeter; b. Hilbert, Wis., Nov. 2, 1908; d. New York, June 2, 1942. He first took up violin, then turned to the trumpet; after playing in local bands, he went to N.Y., where he worked with Paul Whiteman, the Dorsey brothers, and Benny Goodman; from 1937 he led his own big band.

Berinbaum, Martin, American trumpet player; b. Philadelphia, June 14, 1942. He studied with James Stamp at the Univ. of Southern Calif. in Los Angeles; then toured Europe and the Near East with the Roger Wagner Chorale; played first trumpet in the West Point Military Academy Band (1966–69); subsequently enrolled as a student of William Vachiano at the Juilliard School of Music in N.Y., graduating in 1970, and developed a career as a trumpet soloist in concertos by Baroque composers.

Beringer, Oscar, pianist and pedagogue; b. Furtwangen, Baden, July 14, 1844; d. London, Feb. 21, 1922. His father, a political refugee, settled in London in 1849. Oscar Beringer received his rudimentary education at home; then enrolled in the Leipzig Cons., where he studied with Plaidy, Moscheles, and Reinecke (1864–66); he further studied in Berlin with Tausig; in 1869 became a prof. at Tausig's Schule des Höheren Klavierspiels; returned to London in 1871, and in 1873 established an Academy for the Higher Development of Pianoforte Playing, organized on the model of Tausig's Berlin school. From 1885 he was also a prof. at the Royal Academy of Music. He was a pianist of great perfection of method; his book of technical exercises is valuable for students. Among his publ. compositions are a piano concerto; 2 piano sonatinas; various minor piano pieces; songs. He also publ. *Fifty Years' Experience of Pianoforte Teaching and Playing* (1907).

Berio, Luciano, Italian composer of extreme musicoscientific tendencies; b. Oneglia, Oct. 24, 1925. He studied music with his father, an organist, then entered the Cons. of Milan, where he took courses in composition with Ghedini and in conducting with Giulini. In 1951 he went to the U.S. and attended a seminar given by Luigi Dallapiccola at Tangle-wood. In America he married an extraordinary singer named **Cathy Berberian,** who was willing and able to sing his most excruciating soprano parts; they were divorced in 1966, but magnanimously she continued to sing his music after their separation. Back in Italy, he joined the staff of the Italian Radio; founded the Studio di Fonologia Musicale for experimental work on acoustics; edited the progressive magazine *Incontri Musicali*; later on he joined the Institut de Recherche et de Coordination Acoustique/Musique (IRCAM) in Paris, working in close cooperation with its director, Pierre Boulez. From 1965 to 1972 he was on the faculty of the Juilliard School of Music in N.Y., and subsequently maintained a tenuous connection with America. Perhaps the most unusual characteristic of his creative philosophy is his impartial eclecticism, by which he permits himself to use the widest variety of resources, from Croatian folk songs to *objets trouvés*. He is equally liberal in his use of graphic notation; some of his scores look like expressionist drawings. He is one of the few contemporary composers who can touch the nerve endings of sensitive listeners and music critics, one of whom described his *Sinfonia* with ultimate brevity: "It stinks." (The last traceable use of the word was applied by Hanslick in 1875 to Tchaikovsky's Violin Concerto.) But if *Sinfonia* stank, then so did, by implication, the ample quotes from Mahler, Ravel, and Richard Strauss used as *objets trouvés* in this work. Apart from pure (or impure, depending on perception) music, Berio uses in his works all the artifacts and artifices of popular pageants, including mimodrama choreodrama, concrete noises, acrobats, clowns, jugglers, and organ grinders.

WORKS: *Concertino* for Clarinet, Violin, Harp, Celesta, and String Orch. (1949); *Opus No. Zoo* for Woodwind Quintet (1951); *2 Pezzi* for Violin and Piano (1951); *5 Variazioni* for Piano (1952); *Chamber Music,* to poems by James Joyce, for Voice, Clarinet, Cello, and Harp (1952); *Variazioni* for Chamber Orch. (1953); *Mimomusique,* ballet (1953); *Nones* for Orch. (1954); String Quartet (1955); *Allelujah I* for Orch. (1956); *Allelujah II* for 5 Instrumental Groups (1956–58); *Serenata* for Flute and 14 Instruments (1957); *Sequenze I* for Flute and 14 Instruments (1957); *Tempi concertati* for Chamber Orch. (1959); *Differences* for 5 Instruments and Stereophonic Tape (1959); *Circles,* to poems by e.e. cummings, for Voice, Harp, and Percussion (1960); *Quaderni* for Orch. (1960); *Sequenze II* for Harp (1963); *Traces,* for Voices and Orch. (1964); *Sincronie* for String Quartet (1964); *Epifanie* for Female Voices with Orch. (1959–63); *Chemins I* for Harp and Orch. (1965); *Chemins II* for Viola and 9 Instruments (1967); *Chemins II b* for Orch. (1969); *Chemins II c* for Orch. (1972); *Chemins III* for Viola, 9 Instruments, and Orch. (1968); *Chemins IV* for Oboe and Strings (1975); *Sequenza III* for Female Voice (1966); *Sequenze IV* for Piano (1966); *Sequenze V* for Trombone Solo (1966); *Sequenze VI* for Viola (1967); *Sequenze VII* for Oboe (1969); *Sequenze VIII* for Percussion (1975); *Sequenze IX* for Violin (1975); multifarious agglutinations and sonoristic amalga-

mations for electronic instruments (*Mutazioni, Perspectives, Omaggio a Joyce, Momento,* etc.); *Sinfonia,* containing a movement based on remembered fragments of works by Mahler, Ravel, Richard Strauss, etc. (N.Y., Oct. 10, 1968); *Air* for Soprano and Orch. (1969); *Bewegung* for Orch. (1970); *Opera,* spectacle for Mixed Media (Santa Fe, N.Mex., Aug. 12, 1970; completely revised 1976); *Memory* for Electronic Piano and Electronic Harpsichord (N.Y., March 12, 1971); *Prayer,* a speech sound event with Magnetic Tape Accompaniment (N.Y., April 5, 1971); *Recital* for Soprano and 17 Instruments (1971); *Amores* for 16 Vocal Soloists and 14 Instruments (1971–72); *Still* for Orch. (1973); Concerto for 2 pianos and Orch. (1973); *Eindrücke* for Orch. (1973–74); *Linea* for 2 Pianos, Marimba, and Vibraphone (1974); *Points on the Curve to Find ...* for Piano and 22 Instruments (1974); *Per la dolce memoria di quel giorno,* ballet (1974); *Après vidage* for Orch. (1974); *Coro* for 40 Voices and 40 Instruments (1974–76); *Il malato immaginario* for String Orch. (1975); Cello Concerto (1976); *Ritorno degli snovidenia (Return of Dreams;* "snovidenia" is a Russian word for "dream visions") for Cello and Orch. (Los Angeles, Jan. 25, 1979, composer conducting); *Mille Musiciens pour la paix* for 12 Wind Instruments (Lille, France, Nov. 22, 1981; composer conducting); *La vera storia,* opera to a highly diversified action, including Acrobats and featuring a Wordless Soprano (La Scala, Milan, March 9, 1982).

Bériot, Charles-Auguste de, celebrated Belgian violinist; b. Louvain, Feb. 20, 1802; d. Brussels, April 8, 1870. A precocious virtuoso, he played in Paris in 1821, and later toured in England. The famous singer **Maria Malibran** was often a joint artist at his recitals; they became intimate in 1830, and were married in 1836, but she died as a result of a riding mishap a few months after their marriage. Bériot himself developed various ailments and had to retire from a concert career because of a paralysis of his left arm. He taught violin at the Brussels Cons. from 1843 to 1852. He wrote 10 violin concertos and 11 sets of variations for Violin, as well as numerous minor pieces of chamber music. His violin methods, *Premier guide des violinistes* and *Méthode de violon* (Paris, 1858), were popular pedagogical works.

BIBLIOGRAPHY: E. Heron-Allen, "A Contribution towards an Accurate Biography of de Beriot and Malibran," *De Fidiculis Opuscula,* no. VI (1894); A. Bachmann, *Les Grands Violinistes du passé* (Paris, 1913); A. van der Linden, "L'Exotisme dans la musique de Charles de Bériot (1802–1870) et d'Henri Vieuxtemps (1820–1881)," *Bulletin de la Classe des Beaux-Arts de l'Académie Royale de Belgique,* LII/10–11 (1970).

Bériot, Charles-Wilfride de, French pianist; b. Paris, Feb. 21, 1833; d. Sceaux du Gâtinais, Oct. 22, 1914. He was a natural son of *Charles-Auguste de Bériot* and *Maria Malibran,* born before their marriage (which took place in 1836). He studied piano with Thalberg, and later became a prof. of piano, playing at the Paris Cons. He composed a symph. poem, *Fernand Cortez;* 3 piano concertos; and a collection of pieces for violin and piano entitled *Opéras sans paroles.* With his father he compiled a *Méthode d'accompagnement.*

Berkeley, Sir Lennox, significant English composer; b. Boar's Hill, near Oxford, May 12, 1903. He studied French and philosophy at Merton College, Oxford (1922–26); then took lessons in composition with Nadia Boulanger in Paris (1927–32). Returning to London in 1935, he was on the staff of the music dept. of the BBC (1942–45); then was a prof. of composition at the Royal Academy of Music in London (1946–68). He was attracted from the beginning by the spirit of neo-Classical music, and his early works bear the imprint of the Paris manner as exemplified by the neo-Baroque formulas of Ravel and Stravinsky; but soon he formed an individual idiom which may be termed "modern English," broadly melodious, richly harmonious, and translucidly polyphonic. He was knighted in 1974. WORKS: 4 operas: *Nelson,* in 3 acts (1951; preview with Piano accompaniment, London, Feb. 14, 1953; first complete perf., London Sept. 22, 1954; an orch. *Suite: Nelson* was drawn from it in 1955); *A Dinner Engagement,* in one act (1954; Aldeburgh Festival, June 17, 1954); *Ruth,* in one act (1956; London, Oct. 2, 1956); *Castaway* (Aldeburgh Festival, June 3, 1967); ballet, *The Judgement of Paris* (1938); oratorio, *Jonah* (1935); Overture (Barcelona, April 23, 1936); *Domini est Terra* for Chorus and Orch. (1937; International Society for Contemporary Music Festival, London, June 17, 1938); *Introduction and Allegro* for 2 Pianos and Orch. (1938); *Serenade* for String Orch. (1939); 4 symphs.: No. 1 (1940; London, July 8, 1943); No. 2 (1956–58; Birmingham, Feb. 24, 1959; revised 1976); No. 3, in one movement (1968–69; Cheltenham, July 9, 1969); No. 4 (1976–77); *Divertimento* for Orch. (1943); *Nocturne* for Orch. (1946); *4 Poems of St. Teresa* for Contralto and Strings (1947); *Stabat Mater* for 6 Solo Voices and 12 Instruments (1947); Concerto for Piano and Orch. (1947); 2-Piano Concerto (1948); *Colonus' Praise* for Chorus and Orch. (1949); Sinfonietta (1950); *Gibbons Variations* for Tenor, Chorus, Strings, and Organ (1951); Flute Concerto (1952; London, July 29, 1953); Suite for Orch. (1953); Concerto for Piano and Double String Orch. (1958; London, Feb. 11, 1959); *An Overture* for Light Orch. (1959); *Suite: A Winter's Tale* for Orch. (1960); *5 Pieces* for Violin and Orch. (1961; London, July 3, 1962); Concerto for Violin and Chamber Orch. (1961); *Batter My Heart* for Soprano, Chorus, Organ, and Chamber Orch. (1962); *4 Ronsard Sonnets* (Set 2) for Tenor and Orch. (1963; London, Aug. 9, 1963; version with Chamber Orch., Set 1, for 2 Tenors and Piano, 1952); *Partita* for Chamber Orch. (1965); *Signs in the Dark* for Chorus and Strings (1967); *Magnificat* for Chorus and Orch. (1968; London, July 8, 1968); *Windsor Variations* for Chamber Orch. (1969); *Dialogue* for Cello and Chamber Orch. (1970); *Sinfonia Concertante* for Oboe and Chamber Orch. (1973; London, Aug. 3, 1973); *Antiphon* for String Orch. (1973);

Voices of the Night for Orch. (1973; Birmingham, Aug. 22, 1973); Suite for Strings (1974); Guitar Concerto (1974; London, July 4, 1974); 3 string quartets (1935, 1942, 1970); Violin Sonatina (1942); String Trio (1943); Viola Sonata (1945); *Introduction and Allegro* for Solo Violin (1946); *Theme and Variations* and *Elegy* and *Toccata,* all for Violin and Piano (all 1950); Trio for Violin, Horn, and Piano (1954); Sextet for Clarinet, Horn, and String Quartet (1955); Concerto for Flute, Violin, Cello, and Harpsichord or Piano (1955); Sonatina for Solo Guitar (1957); Oboe Sonatina (1962); *Diversions* for 8 Instruments (1964); *Nocturne* for Harp (1967); Quartet for Oboe and String Trio (1967); *Theme and Variations* for Solo Guitar (1970); *Introduction and Allegro* for Double Bass and Piano (1971); Duo for Cello and Piano (1971); *In memoriam Igor Stravinsky* for String Quartet (1971); Quintet for Piano and Winds (1975); *Concert Studies* for Piano, sets 1 and 2 (1940, 1972); Sonata for Piano (1945); Sonatina for 2 Pianos (1959); Theme and Variations for 2 Pianos (1968); *3 Pieces* for Organ (1966–68); *Fantasia* for Organ (1976); numerous other pieces for piano; several songs, with piano, organ, harp, or guitar accompaniment; choruses.

Berkenhead, John L., blind organist who was active in the U.S. toward the end of the 18th century. He arrived in America in 1795; was organist at Trinity Church in Newport from 1796–1804. His piece for harpsichord, *Abolition of the Bastille,* was invariably featured at his concerts in Boston and other New England cities.

Berlijn, Anton (real name, **Aron Wolf**), Dutch composer; b. Amsterdam, May 2, 1817; d. there, Jan. 18, 1870. He studied with Friedrich Schneider in Berlin and with Spohr in Kassel; then went to Leipzig, where he took lessons with G.W. Fink; returning to Amsterdam in 1846, he became a conductor at the Royal Theater, but devoted himself mainly to composition. He wrote several operas, two of which were popular (*Die Bergknappen* and *Proserpina*); 7 ballets; an oratorio (*Moses auf Nebo*); and some instrumental music. He enjoyed a certain prestige in Holland; a memorial volume, *Nachruf an den verstorbenden Komponist A. W. Berlijn,* compiled by P. Böhm, was published in Amsterdam shortly after his death.

Berlin, Irving (real name, **Israel Balin**), famous American composer of popular music; b. Tyumen, Russia, May 11, 1888. He was brought to the U.S. in 1893. He never had any formal music training and never learned to read or write music, yet he succeeded in producing songs, most of them to his own lyrics, that are remarkable for their natural melodic patterns and rhythmic prosody, making a perfect blend of words and melodies. One of his songs, *God Bless America,* which he wrote in 1918 while serving in the American Expeditionary Force, acquired the informal status of a national anthem and is often performed at patriotic occasions; according to sales records compiled in 1978, it brought in

$673,939.46 in royalties, all of which Berlin donated to the Boy Scouts and Girl Scouts of America. Another great song, *White Christmas,* which Berlin wrote for the motion picture *Holiday Inn,* became a sentimental hit among American troops stationed in tropical bases in the Pacific during World War II; 113,067,354 records of this song and 5,566,845 copies of sheet music for it were sold in America between 1942 and 1978. In July 1954, Berlin received a Congressional Medal for his patriotic songs, particularly *God Bless America.* In 1973 he presented his upright piano to the Smithsonian Inst. in Washington, D.C.; this was an instrument fitted with a special mechanism which shifts the keyboard automatically to effect a modulation; according to his own statement, Berlin composed most of his songs in the key of F-sharp major, covering mainly the black keys, and then transposed the melody by ear. A man of exceptional modesty, Berlin rarely participated in public events in his honor. He celebrated his 90th birthday in 1978 at home with his wife of 52 years, 3 daughters, and 9 grandchildren. His financial interests were taken care of by his publishing enterprise, Irving Berlin Music, Inc., founded in 1919, and also by ASCAP, of which he was a member since its early years. His first copyrighted song was *Marie from Sunny Italy,* registered on May 8, 1907, for which he wrote only the lyrics.

WORKS: SONGS: *Marie from Sunny Italy* (1907; lyrics only); *Alexander's Ragtime Band* (1911; enormously popular); *Everybody's Doing It* (1911); *Ragtime Violin* (1911); *International Rag* (1913); *When that midnight choo-choo leaves for Alabam* (1912); *When I lost you* (1912); *I want to go back to Michigan* (1914); *When I leave the world behind* (1915); *What'll I Do?* (1924); *All Alone* (1924); *Remember* (1925); *Always* (1925); *The Song Is Ended but the Melody Lingers On* (1927); *Russian Lullaby* (1927); *Blue Skies* (1927; very popular); *White Christmas* (1942; enormously popular); *Mr. President* (1962). MUSICAL REVUES: *Watch Your Step* (1914); *Yip, Yip Yaphank,* containing the song *O how I hate to get up in the morning* (1918); 3 *Ziegfeld Follies* (1918, 1919, 1920; includes the celebrated songs *A pretty girl is like a melody* and *Mandy*); *Music Box Revues* (1921, 1922, 1923, 1925); *Face the Music* (1932); *As Thousands Cheer* (1933; includes the songs *Easter Parade* and *Heat Wave*); *Louisiana Purchase* (1940); *This Is the Army* (1942); *Annie Get Your Gun* (1946); *Miss Liberty* (1949); *Call Me Madam* (1950). FILM SCORES: *Top Hat* (1935); *Follow the Fleet* (1936); *On the Avenue* (1937); *Carefree* (1938); *Second Fiddle* (1939); *Holiday Inn* (1942); *Blue Skies* (1946); *Easter Parade* (1948).

BIBLIOGRAPHY: A. Woollcott, *The Story of Irving Berlin* (N.Y., 1925); D. Jay, *The Irving Berlin Songography* (New Rochelle, N.Y., 1969); M. Freedland, *Irving Berlin* (N.Y., 1974).

Berlin, Johan Daniel, German-born Norwegian organist and composer; b. Memel, May 12, 1714; d. Trondheim, Nov. 4, 1787. He studied organ with his father; in 1730 proceeded to Copenhagen, where he continued his studies with Andreas Berg. In 1737 he became a city musician in Trondheim, a position he held until 1767; he was also organist at the city Cathedral from 1740 until his death. In addition to his various musical duties for the city, he collected musical instruments and wrote several treatises on music. He was a founding member of the Royal Norwegian Scientific Assoc. (1760). He composed some organ music, but few of his works are extant.
BIBLIOGRAPHY: K. Michelesen, *Johan Daniel Berlin* (Diss., Univ. of Trondheim, 1971).

Berlinski, Jacques, Polish-American composer; b. Radon, Dec. 13, 1913. He went to France in 1931, and studied theory with Nadia Boulanger and Roger-Ducasse. He fought in the ranks of the French army, in the artillery unit, during World War II. In 1948 he received first prize in a N.Y. contest for composition, for his First Symph., dedicated to the memory of Churchill and subtitled *Symphony of Glory* (1965). In 1968 he settled in the U.S., becoming a naturalized citizen in 1973. For the American Bicentennial he wrote a choral symph. entitled *America, 1976,* which was performed for the first time in San Diego on May 6, 1976.

Berlioz, Gabriel Pierre, French composer (not related to Hector Berlioz); b. Paris, June 25, 1916. He studied in Paris with Roussel and d'Indy. He wrote Viola Concerto (1935); *Francezaic,* comic opera (1939); *Symphonie parisienne* (1942); *Jardin hanté,* ballet (1943); Piano Trio (1944); *Divertissement* for Violin, Cello, Piano, and String Orch. (1945); Concerto for Kettledrums and Orch. (1951; Paris, Jan. 25, 1953); Bassoon Concerto (1952); Symph. No. 2 (1953); pieces for tuba and piano, saxophone and piano, flute and piano, etc.

Berlioz, (Louis-) Hector, great French composer who exercised profound influence on the course of modern music in the direction of sonorous grandiosity, and propagated the Romantic ideal of program music, unifying it with literature; b. La Côte-Saint-André, Isère, Dec. 11, 1803; d. Paris, March 8, 1869. His father was a medical doctor who possessed musical inclinations; under his guidance Berlioz learned to play the flute, and later took up the guitar; however, he never became an experienced performer on any instrument. Following his father's desire that he study medicine, he went to Paris, where he entered the Ecole de Médecine; at the same time he began taking private lessons in composition from Jean François Lesueur. In 1824, he abandoned his medical studies to dedicate himself entirely to composition; his first important work was a *Messe solennelle,* which was performed at a Paris church on July 10, 1825; he then wrote an instrumental work entitled *La Révolution grecque,* inspired by the revolutionary uprising in Greece against the Ottoman domination. He was 22 years old when he entered the Paris Cons. as a pupil of his first music teacher, Lesueur, in composition, and of Anton Reicha in counterpoint and fugue. In 1826, Berlioz wrote an opera, *Les Francs-juges,* which never came to a complete performance. In 1827 he submitted his cantata *La Mort d'Orphée* for the Prix de Rome, but it was rejected. On May 26, 1828, he presented a concert of his works at the Paris Cons., including the *Resurrexit* from the *Messe solennelle*, *La Révolution grecque*, and the overtures *Les Francs-juges* and *Waverley*. Also in 1828 he obtained second prize for the Prix de Rome with his cantata *Herminie*. In 1828–29 he wrote *Huit scènes de Faust*, after Goethe; this was the score that was eventually revised and produced as *La Damnation de Faust*. In 1829, he applied for the Prix de Rome once more with the score of *La Mort de Cléopâtre*, but no awards were given that year. He finally succeeded in winning the first Prix de Rome with *La Mort de Sardanapale*; it was performed in Paris on Oct. 30, 1830. In the meantime, Berlioz allowed himself to be passionately infatuated with the Irish actress Harriet Smithson after he attended her performance as Ophelia in Shakespeare's *Hamlet*, given by a British drama troupe in Paris on Sept. 11, 1827. He knew no English and Miss Smithson spoke no French; he made no effort to engage her attention personally; conveniently, he found a surrogate for his passion in the person of Camille Moke, a young pianist. Romantically absorbed in the ideal of love through music, Berlioz began to write his most ambitious and, as time and history proved, his most enduring work, which he titled *Symphonie fantastique*; it was to be an offering of adoration and devotion to Miss Smithson. Rather than follow the formal subdivisions of a symphony, Berlioz decided to integrate the music through a recurring unifying theme, which he called *idée fixe*, appearing in various guises through the movements of the *Symphonie fantastique*. To point out the personal nature of the work he subtitled it "Épisode de la vie d'un artiste." The artist of the title was Berlioz himself, so that in a way the symphony became a musical autobiography. The five divisions of the score are: I. *Reveries, Passions;* II. *A Ball;* III. *Scene in the Fields;* IV. *March to the Scaffold;* V. *Dream of a Witches' Sabbath*. Berlioz supplied a literary program to the music: a "young musician of morbid sensibilities" takes opium to find surcease from amorous madness. Berlioz himself, be it noted, never smoked opium, but this hallucinogenic substance was in vogue at the time, and was the subject of several mystic novels and pseudo-scientific essays. In the *Symphonie fantastique* the object of the hero's passion haunts him through the device of the *idée fixe;* she appears first as an entrancing, but unattainable, vision; as an enticing dancer at a ball; then as a deceptive pastoral image. He penetrates her disguise and kills her, a crime for which he is led to the gallows. At the end she reveals herself as a wicked witch at a Sabbath orgy. The fantastic program design does not interfere, however, with an orderly organization of the score, and the wild fervor of the music is astutely subordinated to the symphonic form. The *idée fixe* itself serves merely as a recurring motif, not unlike similar musical reminiscences in Classical symphonies. Interestingly enough, in the *March to the Scaffold* Berlioz makes use of a section from his earlier score *Les Francs-juges*, and

merely inserts a few bars of the *idée fixe* in it to justify the incorporation of unrelated musical material. No matter; *Symphonie fantastique* with or without Miss Smithson, with or without *idée fixe*, emerges as a magnificent tapestry of sound; its unflagging popularity for a century and a half since its composition testifies to its evocative power. The *Symphonie fantastique* was first performed at the Paris Cons. on Dec. 5, 1830, with considerable success, although the conservatory director, the strict perfectionist Cherubini, who failed to attend the performance, spoke disdainfully of it from a cursory examination of the score. Nor did Miss Smithson herself grace the occasion by her physical presence. Incongruously, the published score of the *Symphonie fantastique* is dedicated to the stern Russian czar Nicholas I. That this apotheosis of passionate love should have been inscribed to one of Russia's most unpleasant czars is explained by the fact that Berlioz had been well received in Russia in 1847. Berlioz followed the *Symphonie fantastique* with a sequel entitled *Lélio, ou Le Retour à la vie*, purported to signalize the hero's renunciation of his morbid obsessions. Both works were performed at a single concert in Paris on Dec. 9, 1832, and this time La Smithson made her appearance. A most remarkable encounter followed between them; as if to prove the romantic notion of the potency of music as an aid to courtship, Berlioz and Smithson soon became emotionally involved and they were married on Oct. 3, 1833. Alas, their marriage proved less enduring than the music that fostered their romance. Smithson broke a leg (on March 16, 1833) even before the marriage ceremony; and throughout their life together she was beset by debilitating illnesses. They had a son, who died young. Berlioz found for himself a more convenient woman companion, one Maria Recio, whom he married shortly after Smithson's death in 1854. Berlioz survived his second wife, too; she died in 1862.

Whatever the peripeteia of his personal life, Berlioz never lost the lust for music. During his stay in Italy, following his reception of the Prix de Rome, he produced the overtures *Le Roi Lear* (1831) and *Rob Roy* (1832). His next important work was *Harold en Italie*, for the very unusual setting of a solo viola with orch.; it was commissioned by Paganini (although never performed by him), and was inspired by Lord Byron's poem *Childe Harold*. It was first performed in Paris on Nov. 23, 1834. Berlioz followed it with an opera, *Benvenuto Cellini* (1834–37), which had its first performance at the Paris Opéra on Sept. 10, 1838. It was not successful, and Berlioz revised the score; the new version had its first performance in Weimar in 1852, conducted by Liszt. About the same time, Berlioz became engaged in writing musical essays; from 1833 to 1863 he served as music critic for the *Journal des Débats;* in 1834 he began to write for the *Gazette Musicale*. In 1835 he entered a career as conductor. In 1837 he received a government commission to compose the *Grande messe des morts (Requiem)*, for which he demanded a huge chorus. It was first performed at a dress rehearsal in Paris on Dec. 4, 1837, with the public performance following the next day. On Dec. 16, 1838, Berlioz conducted a successful concert of his works in Paris; the legend has it that Paganini came forth after the concert and knelt in homage to Berlioz; if sources (including Berlioz himself) are to be trusted, Paganini subsequently gave Berlioz the sum of 20,000 francs. In 1839, Berlioz was named assistant librarian of the Paris Cons. and was awarded the Order of the Légion d'Honneur. On Nov. 24, 1839, Berlioz conducted, in Paris, the first performance of his dramatic symphony *Roméo et Juliette,* after Shakespeare; the work is regarded as one of the most moving lyrical invocations of Shakespeare's tragedy, rich in melodic invention and instrumental interplay. In 1849, Berlioz received another government commission to write a *Grande symphonie funèbre et triomphale.* This work gave Berlioz a clear imperative to build a sonorous edifice of what he imagined to be an architecture of sounds. The work was to commemorate the soldiers fallen in the fight for Algeria, and if contemporary reports can be taken literally, he conducted it with a drawn sword through the streets of Paris, accompanying the ashes of the military heroes to their interment in the Bastille column. The spirit of grandiosity took possession of Berlioz. At a concert after the Exhibition of Industrial Products in 1844 in Paris he conducted Beethoven's Fifth Symphony with 36 double basses, Weber's *Freischütz Overture* with 24 French horns, and the *Prayer of Moses* from Rossini's opera with 25 harps. He boasted that his 1,022 performers achieved an ensemble worthy of the finest string quartet. For his grandiose *L'Impériale,* written to celebrate the distribution of prizes by Napoleon III at the Paris Exhibition of Industrial Products in 1855, Berlioz had 1,200 performers, augmented by huge choruses and a military band. As if anticipating the modus operandi of a century thence, Berlioz installed 5 subconductors and, to keep them in line, activated an "electric metronome" with his left hand while holding the conducting baton in his right. And it was probably at Berlioz's suggestion that Vuillaume constructed a monstrous Octo-bass, a double bass 10 feet high, for use in a huge orch.; it was, however, never actually employed. Such indulgences generated a chorus of derision on the part of classical musicians and skeptical music critics; caricatures represented Berlioz as a madman commanding a heterogeneous mass of instrumentalists and singers driven to distraction by the music. Berlioz deeply resented these attacks and bitterly complained to friends about the lack of a congenial artistic environment in Paris.

But whatever obloquy he suffered, he also found satisfaction in the pervading influence he had on his contemporaries, among them Wagner, Liszt, and the Russian school of composers. Indeed, his grandiosity had gradually attained true grandeur; he no longer needed huge ensembles to exercise the magic of his music. In 1844 he wrote the overture *Le Carnaval romain,* partially based on music from his unsuccessful opera *Benvenuto Cellini.* There followed the overture *La Tour de Nice* (later revised under the title *Le Corsaire*). In 1845 he undertook the revision of his early score after Goethe,

which now assumed the form of a dramatic legend entitled *La Damnation de Faust.* The score included the *Marche hongroise,* in which Berlioz took the liberty of conveying Goethe's Faust to Hungary. The march became extremely popular as a separate concert number. In 1847, Berlioz undertook a highly successful tour to Russia, and in the following year he traveled to England. In 1849 he composed his grand *Te Deum;* he conducted its first performance in Paris on April 28, 1855, at a dress rehearsal; it was given a public performance two days later with excellent success. In 1852 he traveled to Weimar at the invitation of Liszt, who organized a festival of his music. Between 1850 and 1854 he wrote the oratorio *L'Enfance du Christ;* he conducted it in Paris on Dec. 10, 1854. Although Berlioz was never able to achieve popular success with his operatic productions, he turned to composing stage music once more between 1856 and 1860. For the subject he selected the great epic of Virgil relating to the Trojan War; the title was to be *Les Troyens.* He encountered difficulties in producing this opera in its entirety, and in 1863 divided the score into two sections: *La Prise de Troie* and *Les Troyens à Carthage.* Only the second part was produced in his lifetime; it received its premiere at the Théâtre-Lyrique in Paris on Nov. 4, 1863; the opera had 22 performances and the financial returns made it possible for Berlioz to abandon his occupation as a newspaper music critic. His next operatic project was *Béatrice et Bénédict,* after Shakespeare's play *Much Ado about Nothing.* He conducted its first performance in Baden-Baden on Aug. 9, 1862. Despite frail health and a state of depression generated by his imaginary failure as composer and conductor in France, he achieved a series of successes abroad. He conducted *La Damnation de Faust* in Vienna in 1866, and he went to Russia during the season 1867–68. There he had a most enthusiastic reception among Russian musicians, who welcomed him as a true prophet of the new era in music.

Posthumous recognition came slowly to Berlioz; long after his death some conservative critics still referred to his music as bizarre and willfully dissonant. No cult comparable to the one around the names of Wagner and Liszt was formed to glorify Berlioz's legacy. Of his works only the overtures and the *Symphonie fantastique* became regular items on symphony programs. Performances of his operas were still rare events. Since Berlioz never wrote solo works for piano or any other instrument, concert recitals had no opportunity to include his name in the program. However, a whole literature was published about Berlioz in all European languages, securing his rightful place in music history.

WRITINGS: *Grand Traité d'instrumentation et d'orchestration modernes* (Paris, 1843; numerous subsequent eds.; in Eng., 1858; eds. covering modern usages were published in German by Felix Weingartner, Leipzig, 1904, and Richard Strauss, Leipzig, 1905); *Le Chef d'orchestre, Théorie de son art* (Paris, 1855; in Eng. as *The Orchestral Conductor, Theory of His Art,* N.Y., 1902); *Voyage musical en Allemagne et en Italie, Etudes sur Beethoven, Gluck, et Weber. Mélanges et nouvelles* (2 vols., Paris,

1844); *Les Soirées de l'orchestre* (Paris, 1852; in Eng. as *Evenings in the Orchestra,* trans. by C. Roche, with introduction by Ernest Newman, N.Y., 1929; new Eng. trans. as *Evenings with the Orchestra* by J. Barzun, N.Y., 1956; 2nd ed., 1973); *Les Grotesques de la musique* (Paris, 1859); *A travers chants: Etudes musicales, adorations, boutades, et critiques* (Paris, 1862); *Les Musiciens et la musique* (a series of articles collected from the *Journal des Débats;* with introduction by A. Hallays, Paris, 1903); *Mémoires de Hector Berlioz* (Paris, 1870; 2nd ed. in 2 vols., Paris, 1878; in English, London, 1884; new trans. by R. and E. Holmes, with annotation by Ernest Newman, N.Y., 1932; another Eng. trans. by D. Cairns, N.Y., 1969; corrected ed., 1975). An incomplete edition of literary works of Berlioz was publ. in German by Breitkopf and Härtel: *Literarische Werke* (10 vols. in 5, Leipzig, 1903–4) and *Gesammelte Schriften* (4 vols., Leipzig, 1864).

WORKS: OPERAS: *Estelle et Némorin* (1823; not performed; score destroyed); *Les Francs-juges* (1826; not performed; revised, 1829 and 1833; overture and 5 movements extant); *Benvenuto Cellini* (1834–37; Paris Opéra, Sept. 10, 1838; revised, 1852; Weimar, Nov. 17, 1852); *La Nonne sanglante* (1841–47; score unfinished); *Les Troyens* (1856–58; revised, 1859–60; divided into 2 parts, 1863: I, *La Prise de Troie* [first performed in German under Mottl, Karlsruhe, Dec. 6, 1890]; II, *Les Troyens à Carthage* [first performed under Deloffre, Théâtre-Lyrique, Paris, Nov. 4, 1863]; first performance of both parts in French, with major cuts, Brussels, Dec. 26–27, 1906; first complete performance, *sans* cuts, alterations, etc., in Eng. under Alexander Gibson, Glasgow, May 3, 1969; in French, under Colin Davis, Royal Opera House, Covent Garden, London Sept. 17, 1969); *Béatrice et Bénédict* (1860–62; Baden-Baden, Aug. 9, 1862).

SYMPHONIES: *Symphonie fantastique: Episode de la vie d'un artiste,* op. 14a (1830; Paris, Dec. 5, 1830; revised, 1831); *Harold en Italie,* for Solo Viola and Orch., op. 16 (1834; Paris, Nov. 23, 1834); *Roméo et Juliette,* for Solo Voices, Chorus, and Orch., op. 17 (1839; Paris, Nov. 24, 1839); *Grande symphonie funèbre et triomphale,* op. 15 (1840; Paris, July 28, 1840).

OTHER WORKS FOR ORCH.: *Waverley,* overture, op.1 (1827–28; Paris, May 26, 1828); *Rob Roy,* full title *Intrata di Rob Roy Macgregor,* overture (1831: Paris, April 14, 1833); *Le Roi Lear,* overture, op. 4 (1831; Paris, Dec. 22, 1833); *Rêverie et caprice,* romance for Violin and Orch., op. 8 (1841); *Le Carnaval romain,* overture, op. 9 (1844; Paris, Feb. 3, 1844); *La Tour de Nice,* overture (1844; Paris, Jan. 19, 1845; revised 1851–52 as *Le Corsaire,* op. 21; Braunschweig, April 8, 1854); *Marche troyenne* (arranged from Act I of *Les Troyens;* 1864).

MAJOR CHORAL WORKS: *Mass* (1824; Saint-Roch, July 10, 1825; only Resurrexit extant); *La Révolution grecque,* scène héroïque (1825–26; Paris, May 26, 1828); *La Mort d'Orphée,* monologue et bacchanale (1827; first performed under Cortot, Paris, Oct. 16, 1932); *Huit scènes de Faust* (1828–29; one movement only performed, Paris, Nov. 29, 1829); *La Mort de Sardanapale* (1830; Paris, Oct. 30, 1830);

Fantaisie sur la Tempête de Shakespeare (1830; performed as *Ouverture pour la Tempête de Shakespeare,* Paris, Nov. 7, 1830); *Le Retour à la vie,* op. 14b, monodrame lyrique (1831–32; Paris, Dec. 9, 1832; revised, 1854, as *Lélio, ou Le retour à la vie*); *Grande messe des morts (Requiem),* op. 5 (1837; Paris, Dec. 4 [dress rehearsal], Dec. 5 [public performance], 1837; revised, 1852 and 1867); *La damnation de Faust,* légende dramatique, op. 24 (1845–46; Paris, Dec. 6, 1846); *Te Deum,* op. 22 (1849; Paris, April 28 [dress rehearsal], April 30 [public performance], 1855); *L'Enfance du Christ,* trilogie sacrée, op. 25 (1850–54; Paris, Dec. 10, 1854).

WORKS FOR SOLO VOICE AND ORCH.: *Herminie,* scène lyrique (1828); *La Mort de Cléopâtre,* scène lyrique (1829). Also more than 40 songs, including 9 songs after Thomas Moore (1829; 3 orchestrated); *La Captive,* op. 12 (1832; orchestrated, 1834 and 1848); *Les Nuits d'été,* 6 songs, op. 7 (1840–41; orchestrated, 1843–56); *La Mort d'Ophélie* (1842; orchestrated, 1848; published as *Tristia,* no. 2, 1849).

BIBLIOGRAPHY: COLLECTED EDITIONS, SOURCE MATERIAL: The first major edition of Berlioz's works (*Benvenuto Cellini, Les Troyens,* and several other scores excepted) was edited by C. Malherbe and F. Weingartner (20 vols., Leipzig, 1900–07); see Supplement 5 in J. Barzun's *Berlioz and the Romantic Century* (2 vols., Boston, 1950; 3rd ed., revised, 1969) for an extensive enumeration of its musical and other errors. A new critical edition of all of the extant works, the *New Berlioz Edition,* under the general editorship of Hugh Macdonald, began publication in Kassel in 1967.

The standard bibliography is C. Hopkinson, *A Bibliography of the Musical and Literary Works of Hector Berlioz 1803–1869 ...* (Edinburgh, 1951; 2nd ed. with additions and corrections by R. Macnutt, Tunbridge Wells, 1980). Another valuable source is M. Wright, *A Bibliography of Critical Writings on Hector Berlioz* (Library Association thesis, 1967).

CORRESPONDENCE: D. Bernard, ed., *Correspondance Inédite de B.* (Paris, 1879; Eng. trans. as *Life and Letters of B.,* I, 1882); *Lettres Intimes* (preface by Charles Gounod; Paris, 1882; Eng. trans. as *Life and Letters of B.,* II, 1882); La Mara, ed., *Briefe von H. B. an die Fürstin Carolyne Sayn-Wittgenstein* (Leipzig, 1903); J. Tiersot, ed., *H. B.: Les Années Romantiques (1819–1842)* (Paris, 1904), *H. B.: Le Musicien Errant (1842–1852)* (Paris, 1919), and *H. B.: Au Milieu du Chemin (1852–1855)* (Paris, 1930); G. Clarence, "Lettres inédites à B.," *La Revue Musicale,* 104 (1930); S. Ginsburg, "Correspondance russe inédite de B.," *La Revue Musicale,* 104 (1930); "Lettres inédites de B.," *La Revue Musicale,* 154 (1935); J. Barzun, ed. and trans., *Nouvelles lettres de B., 1830–1868; New Letters of B., 1830–1868* (N. Y., 1954); P. Citron, ed., *Correspondance générale de H. B.* (the definitive edition; 3 vols. to date: Paris, vol. I, 1803–1832 [1972]; vol. II, 1832–1842 [1975]; vol. III, 1842–1850 [1978]); R. Locke, "New Letters of B.," *19th Century Music,* 1 (1977).

BIOGRAPHICAL: W. Neumann, *B., Eine Biographie* (Kassel, 1855); E. de Mirecourt, *B.* (Paris, 1856); A. Jullien, *H. B.: La Vie et le Combat; Les Oeuvres* (Paris, 1882); J. Bennett, *B.* (London, 1883); E. Hippeau, *B.*

intime, d'après des documents nouveaux (Paris, 1883; 2nd ed., 1889); A. Jullien, *H. B.: Sa vie et ses œuvres* (Paris, 1888); M. Brenet, *Deux pages de la vie de B.* (Paris, 1889); E. Hippeau, *B. et son temps* (Paris, 1890); L. Pohl, *H. B.: Leben und Werke* (Leipzig, 1900); A. Hahn et al., *H. B.: Sein Leben und seine Werke* (Leipzig, 1901); G. Allix, *Sur les éléments dont s'est formée la personnalité artistique de B.* (Grenoble, 1903); R. Louis, *H. B.* (Leipzig, 1904); J.-G. Prod'homme, *H. B. (1803–1869): Sa vie et ses œuvres* (Paris, 1904; 3rd ed., 1927); A. Boschot wrote a major biography in 3 vols.; the work is flawed by many errors and marred by the author's lack of understanding of Berlioz's creative genius, although the revised volumes attempt to redress these shortcomings: *La Jeunesse d'un romantique; H. B., 1803–31* (Paris, 1906; revised ed., 1946), *Un Romantique sous Louis-Philippe; H. B., 1831–42* (Paris, 1908; revised ed., 1948), and *Le Crépuscule d'un romantique; H. B., 1842–69* (Paris, 1913; revised ed., 1950); B. Schrader, *B.* (Leipzig, 1907); A. Coquard, *B.* (Paris, n. d.); P.-L. Robert, *Etude sur H. B.* (Rouen, 1914); J. Kapp, *B.: Eine Biographie* (Berlin and Leipzig, 1917; 7th ed., 1922); A. Boschot, *Une Vie romantique: H. B.* (Paris, 1919; numerous subsequent printings); P.-M. Masson, *B.* (Paris, 1923); E. Rey, *La Vie amoureuse de B.* (Paris, 1929); L. Constantin, *B.* (Paris, 1934); W. Turner, *B.: The Man and His Work* (London, 1934); T. Wotton, *H. B.* (London, 1935); J. Elliot, *B.* (London, 1938; 4th ed., revised 1967); E. Lockspeiser, *B.* (London, 1939); G. de Pourtalès, *B. et l'Europe romantique* (Paris, 1939; revised ed., 1949); P. Mouthier, *H. B.* (Dilbeck, 1944); J. Daniskas, *H. B.* (Stockholm, 1947; in English, 1949); F. Knuttel, *H. B.* (The Hague, 1948); J. Barzun, *B. and the Romantic Century* (the standard modern study of the man and his music; invaluable for correcting many accepted but erroneous data; 2 vols., Boston, 1950; 3rd ed., revised, 1969); A. Ganz, *B. in London* (London, 1950); T. Tienot, *H. B.: Esquisse biographique* (Paris, 1951); H. Kühner, *H. B.: Charakter und Schöpfertum* (Olten, 1952); H. Barraud, *H. B.* (Paris, 1955; 2nd ed., 1966); H. Schonberg, *The Great Conductors* (N. Y., 1967; pp. 107–16); C. Ballif, *B.* (Paris, 1968); S. Demarquez, *H. B.: L'Homme et son œuvre* (Paris, 1969); J. Crabbe, *H. B.: Rational Romantic* (London, 1980); H. Macdonald, *B.* (London, 1982).

CRITICAL, ANALYTICAL: Important articles may be found in the *Berlioz Society Bulletin* and the *Bulletin de Liaison;* the latter is published by the Association Nationale Hector Berlioz in Paris (1964-). F. Liszt, "H. B. und seine Harold-Symphonie," *Sammlung Musikalische Vorträge,* 35–36 (1881; reprinted in vol. IV of Liszt's *Gesammelte Schriften,* L. Ramann, ed., Leipzig, 1882); A. Ernst, *L'Œuvre dramatique de H. B.* (Paris, 1884); R. Pohl, *H. B.: Studien und Erinnerungen* (Leipzig, 1884); J.-G. Prod'homme, *La Damnation de Faust* (Paris, 1896); E. Destranges, *Les Troyens de B.: Etude analytique* (Paris, 1897); J.-G. Prod'homme, *L'Enfance du Christ* (Paris, 1898); A. Hallays, "H. B., Critique musical," *Revue de Paris* (1903); J. Tiersot, *B. et la société de son temps* (Paris, 1904); J. Tiersot, "Berlioziana," *Le Ménestrel* (Jan. 3, 1904–Dec. 1, 1906); P. Magnette, *Les Grandes Etapes dans l'œuvre de B., I:*

Symphonie fantastique (1829–32) (Liège, 1908); E. Bernoulli, *H. B. als Ästhetiker der Klangfarben* (Zürich, 1909); A. Boschot, *Le Faust de B.* (Paris, 1910; revised ed., 1946); M. Emmanuel, "B.," *Le Correspondant* (1920); P.-L. Robert, *H. B.: Les Troyens* (Rouen, 1920); C. Koechlin, "Le Cas B.," *Revue Musicale* (Feb. 1922); T. Mantovani, *La damnazione di Faust di Ettore B.* (Milan, 1923); J. Tiersot, *La Damnation de Faust de B.* (Paris, 1924); H. Harty, "B.," *Music & Letters* (Jan., April, and Dec. 1926); F. Bonavia, "B.," *Monthly Musical Record* (Aug. 1929); J. Elliot, "B.," *Musical Times* (July 1929); C. Grey, "Letter on B. in Reply to Feste," *Musical Times* (July 1929); T. Wotton, "B. as Melodist," *Musical Times* (Sept. 1929); T. Wotton, *B.: Four Works* (London, 1929); J. Tiersot, "B. of the Fantastic Symphony," *Musical Quarterly* (July 1933); E. Lockspeiser, "B. and the French Romantics," *Music & Letters* (Jan. 1934); T. Wotton, "B. Funeral and Triumphal Symphony," *Musical Opinion* (July 1936); A. Boschot, *H. B., Critique musical* (Brussels, 1938); H. Bartenstein, *H. B.'Instrumentationskunst und ihre geschichtlichen Grundlagen* (Leipzig, 1939; revised ed., 1974); F. Schlitzer, *Il Grande Requiem di Ettore B.* (Naples, 1939); E. Harazsti, "B., Liszt and Rákóczy," *Musical Quarterly* (April 1940); E. Meyerstein, "An Approach to B.," *Music Review,* IX (1948); R. Collet, "B.: Various Angles of Approach to His Work," *The Score,* 10 (1954); R. Mendl, "B. and Shakespeare," *The Chesterian,* XXIX and XXX (1955); G. Court, "B. and Byron and Harold in Italy," *Music Review,* XVII (1956); A. Dickinson, "B. and the Trojans," *Durham University Journal,* XX (1958); P. Friedheim, "Radical Harmonic Procedures in B.," *Music Review,* XXI (1960); J. Klein, "B. as a Musical Dramatist," *The Chesterian,* XXXV (1960); C. Wallis, "B. and the Lyric Stage," *Musical Times* (June 1960); A. Court, *H. B.: The Role of Literature in His Life and Work* (Diss., Univ. of London, 1961); G. Fraenkel, "B., the Princess and 'Les Troyens,'" *Music & Letters* (July 1963); A. Dickinson, "B.'s Rome Prize Works," *Music Review,* XXV (1964); G. Sandford, *The Overtures of H. B.: A Study in Musical Style* (Diss., Univ. of Southern Calif., Los Angeles, 1964); J. Warrack, "B. and the 'Theatre of the Mind,'" *The Listener,* LXXII (1964); D. Cairns, "B.'s Epic Opera," *The Listener,* LXXVI (1966); K. Lucas, *H. B. and the Dramatic Symphony* (Diss., Univ. of Melbourne, 1966); E. Grabner, *B. and French Operatic Tradition* (Diss., Univ. of York, 1967); R. Weirauch, *The Orchestral Style of H. B.* (Diss., Univ. of Cincinnati, 1968); D. Cairns, "B.: A Centenary Retrospect," *Musical Times* (March 1969); A. Dickinson, "B.'s Songs," *Musical Quarterly* (July 1969); H. Macdonald, *B. Orchestral Music* (a valuable study; London, 1969); H. Macdonald, "H. B. 1969: A Centenary Assessment," *Adam,* XXXIV (1969); J. Barzun, "B. a Hundred Years After," *Musical Quarterly* (Jan. 1970); E. Cone, *B.: Fantastic Symphony* (N.Y., 1971); N. Temperley, "The Symphonie fantastique and Its Program," *Musical Quarterly* (Oct. 1971); A. Dickinson, *The Music of B.* (London, 1972); H. Cohen, *B. and the Opera (1829–1849)* (Diss., N.Y. Univ., 1973); B. Primmer, *The B. Style* (London, 1973); J. Rushton, "The

Berman – Bernacchi

Genesis of B's 'La Damnation de Faust,'" *Music & Letters* (April 1975); J. Barzun, "The Meaning of Meaning in Music: B. Once More," *Musical Quarterly* (Jan. 1980); D. Holoman, *The Creative Process in the Autograph Musical Documents of H. B., ca. 1818–1845* (Ann Arbor, 1980).

Berman, Lazar, brilliant Soviet pianist; b. Leningrad, Feb. 26, 1930. He studied with Goldenweiser at the Moscow Cons., graduating in 1953. In 1956 he obtained the fifth prize at the Brussels International Contest under the sponsorship of Queen Elisabeth of Belgium, and in the same year obtained the third prize at the Budapest Liszt contest. These were the modest beginnings of a brilliant career as a virtuoso pianist. In 1970 he made a highly successful tour of Italy; in 1976 he toured the U.S. with tremendous acclaim. In his repertoire he showed a distinct predilection for the Romantic period of piano music; among modern composers his favorites were Scriabin and Prokofiev. His titanic technique, astounding in the facility of bravura passages, did not preclude the excellence of his poetic evocation of lyric moods.

Bermudo, Juan, Spanish music theorist; b. Ecija, Seville, c.1510; d. Andalusia, after 1555. He first studied theology and devoted himself to preaching; later turned to music and studied at the Univ. of Alcalá de Henares. He spent 15 years as a Franciscan monk in Andalusia; in 1550 he entered the service of the Archbishop of Andalusia, where Cristóbal de Morales was choir director. The writings of Bermudo constitute an important source of information on Spanish instrumental music of the 16th century. His most comprehensive work is the *Declaración de instrumentos musicales* (Osuna, 1549 and 1555). It deals with theory, in which his authorities were Gafurius, Glareanus, and Ornithoparchus; instruments, including problems of tuning, technique of performance, and repertoire; and critical evaluation of contemporary composers, showing familiarity with the works of Josquin, Willaert, and Gombert. Bermudo also wrote *El Arte tripharia* (Osuna, 1550). Thirteen organ pieces by him are included in F. Pedrell, *Salterio Sacro-Hispano.*
BIBLIOGRAPHY: O. Kinkeldey, *Orgel und Clavier in der Musik des 16ten Jahrhundert* (1910); H. Collet, *Le Mysticisme musical espagnol au XVIᵉ siècle* (Paris, 1913); R. Mitjana, "La Musique en Espagne," in Lavignac's *Encyclopédie musicale;* H. Anglès and J. Subirá, *Catálogo Musical de la Biblioteca Nacional de Madrid* (vol. II); G. Reese, *Music in the Renaissance* (N.Y., 1954); R. Stevenson, *Juan Bermudo* (The Hague, 1960).

Bernabei, Ercole, Italian composer; b. Caprarola, Papal States, 1622; d. Munich, Dec. (buried, Dec. 6) 1687. He was a pupil of Orazio Benevoli, whom he succeeded in 1672 as chapel master at the Vatican; in 1674 he became court conductor in Munich. He wrote 5 operas, which were produced in Munich, and publ. a book of madrigals, *Concerto madrigalesco* (1669); also wrote masses, offertories, Psalms, and other sacred music.
BIBLIOGRAPHY: R. Casimiri, *Ercole Bernabei, Maestro di cappella musicale lateranse* (Rome, 1920); R. de Rensis, *Ercole Bernabei* (Rome, 1920).

Bernabei, Giuseppe Antonio, Italian composer; son of **Ercole Bernabei;** b. Rome, 1649; d. Munich, March 9, 1732. He studied with his father, and served with him as a vice-Kapellmeister in Munich beginning in 1677; after his father's death in 1687, assumed his post as principal Kapellmeister. He wrote 15 operas and much sacred music.
BIBLIOGRAPHY: Karl Forster, *G.A. Bernabei als Kirchenkomponist* (Munich, 1933).

Bernac, Pierre, French baritone; b. Paris, Jan. 12, 1899; d. Villeneuve-les-Avignon, Oct. 17, 1979. His real name was **Pierre Bertin,** which he changed in order to avoid confusion with another Pierre Bertin, an actor. He started on his career as a singer rather late in life, and was first engaged in finance as a member of his father's brokerage house in Paris. His musical tastes were decidedly in the domain of modern French songs; on May 2, 1926, he gave a recital in Paris with a program of songs by Francis Poulenc and Georges Auric; at other concerts he sang works by Debussy, Ravel, Honegger, and Milhaud. Eager to learn the art of German lieder, he went to Salzburg to study with Reinhold von Warlich. Returning to Paris, he devoted himself to concerts and teaching. He became a lifelong friend to Francis Poulenc, who wrote many songs for him and acted as his piano accompanist in many of their tours through Europe and America. He also conducted master classes in the U.S. and was on the faculty of the American Cons. at Fontainebleau. He publ. a valuable manual, *The Interpretation of French Songs* (N.Y., 1970; 2nd ed., 1976) and a monograph, *Francis Poulenc: The Man and His Songs* (N.Y., 1977).

Bernacchi, Antonio Maria, celebrated Italian singer; b. Bologna, June (baptized, June 23) 1685; d. there, March 13, 1756. He was a castrato; studied voice with Pistocchi and G.A. Ricieri. In 1700 he was sopranist at the church of S. Petronio in Bologna; made his operatic debut in Genoa in 1703; between 1709 and 1735 had a number of engagements in Venice, and between 1712 and 1731 made several appearances in Bologna. He also sang in Munich (1720–27). In 1716–17 he sang in London, and in 1729 he was engaged by Handel as a substitute for Senesino for the London seasons of the Italian Opera; however, he failed to please the British operagoers and returned to his native town of Bologna, where he opened a singing school. In his singing he cultivated the style of vocal embellishments in the manner of the French *roulades*. He composed some worthwhile pieces, among them *Grave et Fuga a 4; Kyrie a 5;* and *Justus ut palma a 5.*
BIBLIOGRAPHY: L. Frati, "Antonio Bernacchi e la sua scuola di canto," *Rivista Musicale Italiana* (Sept. 1922).

240

Bernard, Anthony, English conductor, pianist, and composer; b. London, Jan. 25, 1891; d. there, April 6, 1963. He studied piano with J. Holbrooke and L. Borwick, organ with T. Haigh, and composition with Bantock and Ireland; was active mainly as a church organist and choirmaster in London. In 1921 he founded the London Chamber Orch., which he led for many years. He was also music director of the Shakespeare Memorial Theatre in Stratford-upon-Avon (1932–42).

Bernard, Jean Emile Auguste, French composer and organist; b. Marseilles, Nov. 28, 1843; d. Paris, Sept. 11, 1902. He studied at the Paris Cons. with Benoist (organ) and with Marmontel (piano); was organist at Notre Dame des Champs (1887–95). He wrote 2 cantatas: *Guillaume le conquérant* and *La Captivité de Babylone;* an overture, *Béatrice;* Piano Quartet; Piano Trio; Cello Sonata; Violin Sonata; *Divertissement* for Wind Instruments; etc.

Bernard, Moritz (Matvey), Russian music publisher and pianist; b. Mitau, 1794; d. St. Petersburg, May 9, 1871. He studied piano with John Field in Moscow, and later was active as a piano teacher; in 1822 he moved to St. Petersburg, where he purchased a music store of Dalmas, and began publishing music. Bernard's printing press publ. songs by Glinka and Dargomyzhsky, and piano pieces by Anton Rubinstein and other important Russian composers. In 1840 he began publishing a musical monthly, *Nouvelliste,* which continued publication until 1914, many years after his death. Bernard's son took charge of the music store until 1885, when the stock was purchased by Jurgenson. Bernard composed an opera, *Olga,* which was performed in St. Petersburg in 1845; also publ. a valuable collection, *Songs of the Russian People* (St. Petersburg, 1847); a collection of children's pieces, *L'Enfant-pianiste;* and some original piano pieces and songs, some of which were printed in the Soviet Union.

Bernard, Paul, French pianist and teacher; b. Poitiers, Oct. 4, 1827; d. Paris, Feb. 24, 1879. He studied at the Paris Cons. with Halévy and Thalberg; wrote criticisms for *Le Ménestrel* and the *Revue et Gazette Musicale;* composed many piano pieces.

Bernard, Robert, Swiss-born composer, editor, and writer on music; b. Geneva, Oct. 10, 1900; d. Paris, May 2, 1971. He studied in Geneva with Templeton Strong, Barblan, and Lauber. In 1926 he settled in Paris; in 1937 he became a lecturer at the Schola Cantorum and a music critic; from 1939–51 he was editor of *La Revue Musicale.* He publ. monographs on Franck, Aubert, Roussel, and other French composers.
WORKS: Piano Concerto; Harp Concerto; Saxophone Quartet; Piano Trio; Trio for Oboe, Clarinet, and Trombone; a number of other piano pieces.

Bernardi, Bartolomeo, Italian violinist and composer; b. Bologna, c.1660; d. Copenhagen, May 23, 1732. He received an invitation from the Danish Court to serve as a violinist and composer, and began his work there on Jan. 1, 1703; after an absence of several years (1705–10), he returned to Copenhagen and was appointed director of court music. In Copenhagen he produced 2 operas, *Il Gige fortunato* and *Diana e la Fortuna;* he also wrote an opera, *La Libussa,* for a production in Prague in 1703; the music of these operas is lost. His trio sonatas were published in Bologna (1692, 1696).

Bernardi, Enrico, Italian conductor and composer; b. Milan, March 11, 1838; d. there, July 17, 1900. He toured in Italy as conductor of various opera companies; wrote several operas which he produced himself, and nearly 60 ballets, of which the first, *Illusioni d'un pittore* (Milan, 1854), was perhaps the most successful.

Bernardi, Francesco. See **Senesino, Francesco.**

Bernardi, Mario, Canadian conductor; b. Kirkland Lake, Ont., Aug. 20, 1930. He studied at the Royal Cons. of Music in Toronto; then went to London, becoming music director of the Sadler's Wells Opera (1966–69). In 1968 he returned to Canada as the first music director of the National Arts Centre Orch. in Ottawa.

Bernardi, Steffano, Italian composer; b. Verona, c.1575; d. 1636. He served as maestro di cappella at the church of the Santissima Madonna dei Monti in Rome; from 1611–22 was music director at the Cathedral of Verona; became Kapellmeister at the Salzburg Cathedral in 1628; left Salzburg in 1634.
WORKS: 2 books of masses for 8 Voices, and one for 4 and 5 Voices; a book of madrigals for 3 Voices (Rome, 1611), and 2 for 5 Voices (Venice, 1611; Rome, 1612); 2 books of *madrigaletti;* Psalms and motets; also instrumental works (trio sonatas, etc.). Reprints of some of his sacred works are to be found in Denkmäler der Tonkunst in Österreich (vol. 69; formerly 36.i). He also wrote the manual *Porta musicale per la quale il principiante con facile brevità all'acquisto delle perfette regole del contrapunto vien introdotto* (Verona, 1615; 7 subsequent eds.).
BIBLIOGRAPHY: F. Posch, *Steffano Bernardis weltliche Vokal- und Instrumental-Werke* (Munich, 1928).

Bernart de Ventadorn, Troubadour poet and composer; flourished in the 2nd half of the 12th century. His vita states that he was born in the castle of Ventadorn in the province of Limousin, and later was in the service of the Duchess of Normandy, Eleanor of Aquitaine, and of Raimon V, Count of Toulouse. He is believed to have entered a monastery in Dordogne, where he lived until his death. Some 45 poems are attributed to him, and 18 survive with complete melodies.
BIBLIOGRAPHY: S. Nichols and J. Galm, eds., *The Songs of Bernart de Ventadorn* (Chapel Hill,

N.C., 1962); M. Lazar, *Bernart de Ventadorn—Chansons d'amour* (Paris, 1966).

Bernasconi, Andrea, Italian composer and conductor; b. Milan, 1706; d. Munich, Jan. 29, 1784. It is known that he was maestro di cappella at the Ospedale della Rieta in Venice during the season 1746–47. In 1753 he was in Munich, where he taught music to Princess Maria Anna Josepha (1754–55) and Princess Josepha Maria (1754–65); he also gave musical instruction to the Elector, Maximilian III Joseph. He was appointed Kapellmeister at the Munich Court in 1755. He wrote 16 operas and 2 pasticcios, some of which were produced in Munich; he also composed sacred music.

BIBLIOGRAPHY: E.J. Weiss, *Andrea Bernasconi als Opernkomponist* (Munich, 1923).

Berneker, Constanz, German composer; b. Darkehmen, East Prussia, Oct. 30, 1844; d. Königsberg, June 9, 1906. He studied at the Institut für Kirchemusik and at the Akademie der Kunst in Berlin. In 1872 he was appointed director at the Königsberg Singakademie, and in 1873 was engaged as cathedral organist and teacher at the Königsberg Cons.; in 1885 he was named Royal Music Director; also was active as a music critic. He wrote a number of sacred and secular cantatas, and some instrumental music.

BIBLIOGRAPHY: O. Laudien, *Constanz Berneker* (Berlin, 1909).

Berner, Friedrich Wilhelm, German organist and composer; b. Breslau, May 16, 1780; d. there, May 9, 1827. He studied organ with his father and composition with Franz Gehirne. In 1815 he was appointed to the faculty of the Royal Academic Inst. for Church Music in Breslau; he wrote mostly sacred music. A biography of him by Hientsch was publ. in Breslau in 1829.

Berners, Lord (originally **Gerald Tyrwhitt**), eccentric British composer; b. Arley Park, Bridgnorth (Shropshire), Sept. 18, 1883; d. London, April 19, 1950. A scion of nobility and wealth, he was educated at Eton; lived many years in France, Italy, and Germany; studied music and art in Dresden and Vienna; then served as honorary attaché to the British diplomatic service in Constantinople (1909–11) and in Rome (1911–20). Returning to England, he joined the artistic smart set in London; was on intimate terms with George Bernard Shaw and H.G. Wells; took lessons in composition with Vaughan Williams; also had some friendly advice on orchestration from Casella and Stravinsky. As a composer, he was influenced by Satie's musical nihilism and affected bizarre social behavior; he was fond of practical jokes and elaborate spoofs; characteristic of his musical humor was a set of *3 Funeral Marches* for Piano (*For a Statesman, For a Canary, For a Rich Aunt,* the last in raucous dissonances). Possessing a facile literary gift, he publ. half a dozen novels and 2 autobiographical books written in an ironic and self-deprecatory vein, *First Childhood* (London, 1934) and *A Distant Prospect* (London, 1945). Overflowing with talents, he was also an amateur chef de cuisine and a passable painter; his oils were exhibited in London, in 1931 and 1936. He succeeded to the barony of Berners in 1918.

WORKS: Comic opera, *Le Carrosse du Saint-Sacrement,* after Mérimée (1923; Paris, April 24, 1924; revised 1926); 5 ballets: *The Triumph of Neptune* (1926; Diaghilev's Ballets Russes production, London, Dec. 3, 1926); *Luna Park* (1930; London Pavilion, 1930); *A Wedding Bouquet,* with Chorus, to a libretto by Gertrude Stein (1936; London, April 27, 1937); *Cupid and Psyche* (1938; London, April 27, 1939); *Les Sirènes* (1946; London, Nov. 12, 1946); *3 Pieces (Chinoiseries, Valse sentimentale,* and *Kasatchok*) for Orch. (1916; Manchester, March 8, 1919); *Fantaisie espagnole* for Orch. (1918–19); Fugue in C minor for Orch. (1924); *Adagio, Variations and Hornpipe* for String Orch. (arranged from *The Triumph of Neptune,* 1926); piano pieces: *3 Short Funeral Marches* (1914); *Le Poisson d'or* (1914); *3 fragments psychologiques* (1915); *Valses bourgeoises* for 2 Pianos (1919); scores for 3 films: *Halfway House* (1943), *Champagne Charlie* (1944), and *Nicholas Nickleby* (1946); songs.

BIBLIOGRAPHY: J. Holbrooke, *Berners,* in the Contemporary British Composers series (London, 1925); Harriett Bridgeman and Elizabeth Drury, *The British Eccentric* (N.Y., 1975).

Bernet, Dietfried, Austrian conductor; b. Vienna, May 14, 1940. He was educated at the Vienna Academy of Music; studied conducting with Hans Swarowsky and Dimitri Mitropoulos. In 1962 he won first prize in the Liverpool International Conductors' Competition. He then became a conductor at the Vienna Volksoper; also appeared with the Vienna State Opera and the Berlin Phil. In 1973 he made his American debut with the Chicago Symph. Orch. In 1974 he was named generalmusikdirektor of the City of Mainz.

Bernet Kempers, Karel Philippus, Dutch writer on music; b. Nijkerk, Sept. 20, 1897; d. Amsterdam, Sept. 30, 1974. He studied in Munich with Sandberger; received his Dr.Phil. in 1926; in 1929 was appointed teacher of music history at the Royal Cons. in The Hague and was secretary of the Federation of Dutch Composers. In 1946 he was appointed a prof. at the Amsterdam Univ. Among his writings are: *Jacobus Clemens non Papa und seine Motetten* (1928); *Italian Opera, Peri to Puccini* (1929; Eng. trans., 1947); *Muziekgeschiedenis* (Rotterdam, 1932; 4th ed., 1946); *Meesters der Muziek* (Rotterdam, 1939; 4th ed., 1948).

Bernhard, Christoph, German composer; b. Kolberg, Jan. 1, 1628; d. Dresden, Nov. 14, 1692. He studied with Paul Siefert in Danzig and with Schütz in Dresden. The Elector sent him to study singing in Italy (1649); in 1655 he became 2nd Kapellmeister in Dresden, but was forced to resign through the disaffection of his Italian associates. He then went to Hamburg, where he served as a cantor (1664–74);

was recalled by the Elector to Dresden and was appointed first Kapellmeister, as successor to Schütz. He enjoyed great respect as a composer, particularly for his mastery of counterpoint. He publ. *Geistliche Harmonien* (Dresden, 1665; new ed., Kassel, 1972) and *Prudentia prudentiana* (Hamburg, 1669); a treatise on composition and another on counterpoint are in MS. Three major treatises in translation with annotation by W. Hilse are publ. in "The Treatises of Christoph Bernhard," *Music Forum*, III (1973). Some of his cantatas were publ. by M. Seiffert in vol. VI of Denkmäler Deutscher Tonkunst.
BIBLIOGRAPHY: J.M. Müller-Blattau, *Die Kompositionslehre Heinrich Schützens in der Fassung seines Schülers Christoph Bernhard* (Leipzig, 1926); H. Rauschning, *Musikgeschichte der Stadt Danzing* (1926).

Bernhard der Deutsche (known also as **Bernardo di Steffanino Murer**), celebrated organist and the reputed inventor of organ pedals; b. Germany, early in the 15th century; d. 1459. He was an organist at San Marco in Venice.
BIBLIOGRAPHY: Michael Praetorius, *Syntagma musicum* (vol. I, part I, chapter 14, p. 145; vol. II, chapter 5, p. 96).

Bernheimer, Martin, American music critic; b. Munich, Sept. 28, 1936. He was taken to the U.S. as a child in 1940; studied music at Brown Univ. (B.A., 1958) and N.Y. Univ. (M.A., 1962); in the interim, took courses in music at the Munich Cons. (1958–59). Returning to the U.S., he was a member of the music faculty at N.Y. Univ. (1960–62); served as contributing critic for the *N.Y. Herald Tribune* (1959–62) and assistant music editor of *Saturday Review* (1962–65). In 1965 he was appointed music editor of the *Los Angeles Times;* in 1966 became instructor in the Rockefeller programs for training music critics at the Univ. of Southern Calif., Los Angeles; also was a member of the faculty of the Univ. of Calif., Los Angeles (since 1969). As a critic, he possesses a natural facility and not infrequently a beguiling felicity of literary style; he espouses noble musical causes with crusading fervor, but he can be aggressively opinionated and ruthlessly devastating to composers, performers, or administrators whom he dislikes; as a polemicist he is a *rara avis* among contemporary critics, who seldom rise to the pitch of moral or musical indignation; Bernheimer also possesses a surprising knowledge of music in all its ramifications, which usually protects him from perilous pratfalls. In 1981 he received the Pulitzer Prize for distinguished classical music criticism.

Bernier, Nicolas, French composer; b. Mantes, Seine-et-Oise, June 5, 1665; d. Paris, July 6, 1734. He held the post of organist at Chartres Cathedral (1694–98); in 1698 he was appointed maître de musique at St. Germain l'Aurerrois in Paris; then served at Sainte-Chapelle in Paris (1704–26). He publ. 8 books of "cantates profanes," of which *Les Nuits de Sceaux* is an important example of French secular cantatas. He also wrote a Te Deum. His *Principes de composition de M. Bernier* was trans. into Eng. by P. Nelson and publ. as *Nicolas Bernier: Principles of Composition* (Brooklyn, 1964).

Bernier, René, Belgian composer; b. Saint-Gilles, March 10, 1905. He studied at the Brussels Cons. and had private lessons from Paul Gilson. In 1925 he and 7 other pupils of Gilson formed the "Groupe des Synthetistes," whose aim was to combine modern technique with classical forms.
WORKS: 3 ballets: *Le Bal des ombres* (1954); *Symphonie en blanc* (1961; derived from the *Sinfonietta*); *Tanagras* (1969); *Mélopées et Rythmes* for Orch. (1932); *Ode à une Madone* for Orch. (1938; revised 1955); *Présages* for Voice and Orch. (1942–46); *Liturgies* for Voice and String Orch. (1946); *Sortileges ingénus (Ingenuous Charms),* 14 songs for Female or Children's Chorus, and Orch. or Piano (1947); *Eclaircies* for Voice and Orch. (1948); *Le Tombeau devant l'Escaut,* symph. poem (1952); *Notturno* for Orch. (1955); *Bassonniere* for Bassoon and Orch. (1956); *Sinfonietta* for String Orch. (1957); *Hommage à sax,* concertino for Saxophone and Orch. (1958); *Reverdies,* variations for Clarinet and Orch. (1960); *Epitaphe II* for Wind Orch. (1961); *Interludes* for Orch. (1966); *Ménestraudie* for Violin and Orch. (1970); *Sonata à deux* for Flute and Harp (1939); Trio for Flute, Cello, and Harp (1942); Sonatina for Flute and Harp (1943); *Liturgies* for a cappella Chorus (1940–41); *Chants Incantations* for a cappella Chorus (1968); songs.

Bernoulli, Eduard, Swiss music scholar; b. Basel, Nov. 6, 1867; d. Zürich, April 17, 1927. He studied at the Univ. of Leipzig, obtaining his doctorate in 1897 (Diss., *Die Choralnotenschrift bei Hymnen und Sequenzen im späteren Mittelalter*); subsequently edited several vols. of Denkmäler Deutscher Tonkunst. He publ. the valuable monographs *Berlioz als Ästhetiker der Klangfarben* (Zürich, 1909); *Aus Liederbüchern der Humanistenzeit* (1910); etc. From 1921 till his death, Bernoulli was a prof. at the Univ. of Zürich.

Berno von Reichenau, German theorist of the 11th century; b. c.970; d. in Cloister of Reichenau, June 7, 1048. In 1008 he was installed as Abbot of the Cloister of Reichenau; accompanied Emperor Henry II to Rome for coronation in 1014, and in 1027 attended the coronation in Rome of Emperor Conrad II. He wrote learned treatises on music, which can be found in J.P. Migne's *Patrologiae cursus completus* (vol. 142) and in Gerbert's *Scriptores* (vol. 2). A monograph on his system of music was publ. by W. Brambach (Leipzig, 1881).

Bernstein, Elmer, talented American composer of film music; b. New York, April 4, 1922. He studied with Roger Sessions and Stefan Wolpe at the Juilliard School of Music in N.Y.; served in the U.S. Air Force during World War II; after the end of the war he settled in Hollywood and became a highly successful composer of background scores, particularly in dramatic films; of these the most effective were *The Man with the Golden Arm; The Ten Commandments; Desire under the Elms; The Magnificent Seven; To Kill a Mockingbird; Walk on the Wild Side; The Great Escape; The Carpetbaggers; Hawaii.* He has also composed chamber music.

Bernstein, Leonard, greatly gifted American conductor and composer, equally successful in writing symph. music of profound content and strikingly effective Broadway shows, and, in the field of performance, a conductor of magnetic powers, exercising a charismatic spell on audiences in America and the world at large; b. Lawrence, Mass., Aug. 25, 1918, of a family of Russian-Jewish immigrants. His given first name was Louis, which at the age of 16 he had legally changed to Leonard to avoid confusion with other, pre-existent, Louis Bernsteins in the family. He studied piano with Helen Coates and Heinrich Gebhard in Boston. In 1935 he entered Harvard Univ. and took courses in music theory with Tillman Merritt, counterpoint and fugue with Walter Piston, and orchestration with Edward Burlingame Hill; he graduated in 1939. He then went to Philadelphia, where he studied piano with Isabelle Vengerova, conducting with Fritz Reiner, and orchestration with Randall Thompson at the Curtis Inst. of Music. During the summers of 1940 and 1941 he attended the Berkshire Music Center at Tanglewood, where he received instruction in conducting with Koussevitzky, who took great interest in his talent and made every effort to promote his career as a professional conductor. He also did some work for publishers, arranging music for band under the interlingual pseudonym **Lenny Amber** (Bernstein is the German word for "amber"). He conducted occasional concerts with local groups in Boston; in 1943 he obtained the job of assistant conductor to Arthur Rodzinski, then conductor of the N.Y. Phil.; his great chance to show his capacities came on Nov. 14, 1943, when he was called upon on short notice to conduct a difficult program in substitution for Bruno Walter, who was to lead that particular concert but happened to be indisposed, while Rodzinski was out of town. He acquitted himself brilliantly and was roundly praised for his courage in facing a trying situation with exemplary professional confidence. This was the beginning of one of the most brilliant conducting careers in American history. Bernstein became the first native-born American musician to become conductor of the N.Y. Phil., the post to which he acceded in 1958. He also filled other engagements, among them conducting the N.Y. City Center Orch. (1945–48), and was guest conductor of the International Music Festival in Prague in 1946. In 1958 he made a tour with the N.Y. Phil. in South America; in 1959 he took the orch. on a grand tour of Russia and 17 other countries in Europe and the Near East; in 1960 he toured Japan, Alaska, and Canada; on July 9, 1967, he led a memorable concert with the Israel Phil. in Jerusalem, at the conclusion of Israel's devastating Six Day War, in a program of works by Mendelssohn and Mahler. He was the first American conductor to lead a regular performance at La Scala in Milan, where he conducted Cherubi-

ni's opera *Medea* in 1953. In 1969 he resigned as permanent conductor of the N.Y. Phil. in order to have more time for composition and other projects; the orch. bestowed upon him the unprecedented honorific title of "laureate conductor," enabling him to give special performances with the orch. from time to time. In the summer of 1976 he took the orch. on a Bicentennial tour of 13 concerts in 11 European cities during a period of 17 days, in programs emphasizing American music. Ebullient with communicative talents, Bernstein initiated in 1958 a televised series of Young People's Concerts with the N.Y. Phil. in which he served as an astute commentator; these concerts were greatly popular with audiences extending beyond the eponymous youth. His eagerness to impart his wide knowledge in various fields to a willing audience found its expression in the classes he conducted at Brandeis Univ. (1951–55), and concurrently in the summer sessions at the Berkshire Music Center at Tanglewood. In 1972–73 he was a lecturer at the prestigious Norton series at Harvard Univ.; in 1974 he lectured at the Massachusetts Inst. of Technology. He was the recipient of many honors: the Order of Merit from Chile (1964); the Order of the Lion Commander from Finland (1965); that of Chevalier of the French Legion of Honor (1968); that of Cavaliere from Italy (1969); the Austrian Honorary Distinction in Science and Art (1976); the Albert Einstein Commemorative Award in the Arts from the Einstein College of Medicine; an International Education Award, presented to him by President Nixon, and the George Foster Peabody Award for his television programs. He also held an honorary doctorate of letters from the Univ. of Warwick in England (1974). An excellent pianist in his own right, Bernstein often appeared as a soloist in classical or modern concertos, playing and conducting the orch. from the keyboard. An intellectual by nature, and a litterateur by avocation, as well as an occasional poet, he took pride in publishing some excellent sonnets and other poems. An inevitable overflow of his spiritual and animal energy impelled him to display certain histrionic mannerisms on the podium, which elicited invidious comments on the part of some music critics who objected to his "choreography." But even the skeptics could not deny Bernstein's ardent devotion to music, both classical and modern. His interpretations of Mahler's symphs. seemed to respond to Mahler's innermost creative impulses. Whatever judgment may ultimately be rendered about Bernstein, he remains a phenomenal apparition. History knows of many significant composers who were also excellent conductors, but Bernstein seems to be unique in his protean power to be equally proficient as a symph. conductor, a composer of complex music, and last, not least, of highly original and enormously popular musical stage productions. In his *West Side Story* he created a significant social music drama, abounding in memorable tunes. In his score *The Age of Anxiety* he reflected the turbulence of modern life. A socially conscious individual, Bernstein espoused many libertarian causes, and was once derisively dubbed by a columnist as a devotee of "radical chic." Ever cognizant of his Jewish heritage, Bernstein wrote a devout choral symph., *Kaddish;* as a testimony to his ecumenical religious feelings, he produced a *Mass,* based on the Roman liturgy. On Sept. 9, 1951, he married the Chilean actress Felicia Montealegre (she died in 1978). (A debate rages as to the proper pronunciation of Bernstein's name; intimates used to refer to him as Bern*steen,* and he himself once said he preferred the "democratic Yiddish" Bern*steen* to the "aristocratic Germanic" Bern*styne,* but on his formal appearances on the radio or television, he reverted to the more universal "Bern*styne.*")

WORKS: FOR ORCH.: Symph. No. 1, subtitled *Jeremiah* (Pittsburgh, Jan. 28, 1944, composer conducting; received the N.Y. Music Critics' Circle Award); *The Age of Anxiety* (Symph. No. 2), after a poem by W.H. Auden, traversing many styles and moods, from the religious to the ultramodern, including a spectacular episode in the jazz idiom, scored for Piano and Orch. (Boston Symph. Orch., Koussevitzky conducting; Bernstein, piano soloist, April 8, 1949); *Fugue and Riffs* for Band (1949); *Serenade* for Violin Solo, Strings, and Percussion, after Plato's *Symposium* (Venice Festival, Sept. 12, 1954, Isaac Stern, soloist; Bernstein conducting); *Kaddish* (Symph. No. 3), for Narrator, Chorus, and Orch. (Tel Aviv, Dec. 9, 1963, Bernstein conducting); *Chichester Psalms* for Chorus and Orch. (commissioned by the Dean of Chichester, England; first performed by Bernstein and the N.Y. Phil., July 14, 1965); *Mass,* "a theater piece" for Orch., Chorus, a group of Boy Singers, Dancers, and Dancer-Singers, to a text partly consisting of the Roman liturgy in Latin, partly in vernacular (first produced at the opening of the John F. Kennedy Center for the Performing Arts, Washington, D.C., Sept. 7, 1971); *Songfest,* 12 pieces for 6 Singers and Orch. (Washington, D.C., Oct. 11, 1977); *Divertimento* (Boston, Sept. 25, 1980); *Halil* (Hebrew for "flute"), a Nocturne for Solo Flute, String Orch., and Percussion, dedicated to the memory of an Israeli soldier fallen in the 1973 war (1981; first performed, Tel Aviv, May 1981).

FOR THE STAGE: *Fancy Free,* ballet (N.Y., April 18, 1944); *On the Town,* musical comedy, derived from the scenario of the ballet *Fancy Free* (N.Y., Dec. 28, 1944); *Candide,* musical after Voltaire (N.Y., Dec. 1, 1956; new redaction, N.Y., Oct. 13, 1982, as an "opera-house version," produced by the N.Y. City Opera, with a revised orchestration by Bernstein, Hershy Kay, and John Mauceri, and a revised text, largely by Bernstein himself); *Facsimile,* "choreograhic observations in one scene" (N.Y., Oct. 24, 1946); *Trouble in Tahiti,* one-act opera to his own libretto (Brandeis Univ., June 12, 1952); *Wonderful Town,* musical comedy (N.Y., Feb. 25, 1953); *West Side Story,* social music drama, a perennial favorite (Washington, Aug. 19, 1957; N.Y., Sept. 26, 1957; also produced as a motion picture); *Dybbuk,* ballet (N.Y., May 16, 1974); the Bicentennial pageant *1600 Pennsylvania Avenue* (N.Y., May 4, 1976); film score, *On the Waterfront* (1954).

CHAMBER MUSIC: Clarinet Sonata (1942); *7 Anniversaries* for Piano (1942–43); *Elegy I* for Horn and Piano (1950); *Elegy II* for Solo Trombone (1950); *Elegy III* for Tuba and Piano (1950).

SONGS: *I Hate Music,* subtitled *5 Kid Songs* (1943); *La Bonne Cuisine,* 4 recipes for Voice and Piano (1945); *2 Love Songs* for Voice and Piano, to texts by Rilke (1949).

WRITINGS: *The Joy of Music,* a collection of television talks (N.Y., 1959; revised and amplified as *Young People's Concerts,* N.Y., 1970); *The Infinite Variety of Music* (N.Y., 1966); *Six Talks at Harvard* (Cambridge, Mass., 1976); *Findings* (N.Y., 1982).

BIBLIOGRAPHY: David Ewen, *Leonard Bernstein: A Biography for Young People* (N.Y., 1960); A. Holde, *Leonard Bernstein* (Berlin, 1961); J. Briggs, *Leonard Bernstein: The Man, His Work and His World* (Cleveland, 1961); Harold Schoenberg, *The Great Conductors* (N.Y., 1967); M. Cone, *Leonard Bernstein* (N.Y., 1970); Jack Gottlieb, *Leonard Bernstein: A Complete Catalogue of His Works, Celebrating His 60th Birthday* (N.Y., 1978); David Ewen, *Musicians since 1900* (N.Y., 1978); David Ewen, *American Composers* (N.Y., 1982).

Bernstein, Martin, American musicologist; b. New York, Dec. 14, 1904. He was educated at N.Y. Univ. (graduated in 1925; B.Mus., 1927); played the double bass in the N.Y. Symph. Orch. (1925), the N.Y. Phil. Orch. (1926–28), and the Chautauqua Symph. Orch. (1929–36). He was for 48 years a member of the faculty of N.Y. Univ. (1924–72); then a prof. of music at Lehman College, City Univ. of N.Y. (1972–73). He publ. *Score Reading* (1932; 2nd ed., 1949); the successful textbook *An Introduction to Music* (N.Y., 1937; 4th ed., 1972); contributed chapters on music to *An Intellectual and Cultural History of the Western World,* Harry Elmer Barnes, ed. (N.Y., 1937). A Festschrift, *A Musical Offering: Essays in Honor of Martin Bernstein,* edited by E.H. Clinkscale and C. Brook, was publ. in 1977. A brother, **Artie Bernstein** (b. Brooklyn, Feb. 3, 1909; d. Los Angeles, Jan. 4, 1964), a classically trained cellist, became a leading jazz bassist in the 1930s and '40s, playing with many big bands, including Jimmy Dorsey's; from 1939–41 he was part of the Benny Goodman Sextet; after World War II he became a studio musician.

Bernuth, Julius von, German conductor; b. Rees, Rhine Province, Aug. 8, 1830; d. Hamburg, Dec. 24, 1902. He was a practicing lawyer; studied music with Taubert and Dehn in Berlin, and at the Cons. of Leipzig, where he founded a chamber music society, "Aufschwung" (1857), and the "Dilettanten-Orchester-Verein" (1859); later became conductor of the Hamburg Phil. Orch.; in 1873 founded a cons. in Hamburg.

Béroff, Michel, French pianist; b. Epinal, Vosges, May 9, 1950. He studied piano with Yvonne Loriod at the Paris Cons., made his debut in Paris at 16; then toured as a concert pianist, often programming works of French avant-garde composers.

Berr, Friedrich, German clarinetist and bassoonist; b. Mannheim, April 17, 1794; d. Paris, Sept. 24, 1838. He studied with Fétis and Reicha in Paris, and settled there in 1823; served as the 2nd clarinetist at the Théâtre-Italien; in 1828 became first clarinetist. In 1931 he was appointed to the faculty of the Paris Cons.; in 1836 he became director of the new School of Military Music. He was the author of a *Traité complet de la clarinette à 14 clefs* (1836); also composed many works for clarinet and bassoon, and some 500 pieces of military music.

Berré, Ferdinand, Belgian composer; b. Ganshoren, near Brussels, Feb. 5, 1843; d. Brussels, July 29, 1880. He wrote the operas *L'Orage au moulin* and *Le Couteau de Castille;* publ. some 50 songs.

Berry, Chuck, black singer and guitarist; b. San Jose, Calif., Jan. 15, 1926. He was a carpenter's son; the family moved to Missouri when he was a child; he received his musical training as a chorister at the Antioch Baptist Church in St. Louis; learned to play a 6-stringed Spanish guitar, and improvised tunes in a then-current jazz manner. In 1955 he went to Chicago and sold his song *Maybelline* to a record company; it took off like a rocket, and reached No. 1 on the list in the 3 categories of rhythm-and-blues, country-and-western, and pop. This was followed by a brash bragging song with the lyrics "Roll over, Beethoven, tell Tchaikovsky the news; Roll over, Beethoven, dig these rhythm-and-blues." Moving into the big time, Berry opened in St. Louis the Chuck Berry Club Bandstand; it prospered, but he soon ran into trouble when a 14-year-old hatcheck girl employed in the club brought charges that he transported her across state lines for immoral purposes. He was found guilty and served 2 years in the federal penitentiary in Terre Haute, Ind. Jail failed to kill his spirit of happy-go-lucky insouciance, and he rebounded with the sexually oriented song *My Ding-a-Ling,* which made the coveted golden disk record. He became one of the most successful rock singers; when *Voyager 2* was launched into space on Aug. 20, 1977, it carried a sampler of terrestrial music on records, and next to Bach and Beethoven, the package included *Johnny B. Goode* by Chuck Berry.
BIBLIOGRAPHY: *Current Biography* (April 1977).

Berry, Jan, Californian rock artist; b. Los Angeles, April 3, 1941. With a high-school friend, Dean Torrance (b. Los Angeles, March 10, 1940), he formed a duo named Jan and Dean and began recording songs specializing in doomsday topics, in which surfing, cars, and girls were somehow mixed with murky speculations about death, with such titles as *Dead Man's Curve.* In April 1966, Jan Berry came very close to finality, when in a wild speed drive in his car he struck a parked truck in Los Angeles and went into a coma, suffering from paralysis of his right side and impediment of speech and vision. Miraculously, he emerged from this condition and returned to work. Of his doubles with Torrance, the most successful was *Ride the Wild Surf.* They also issued the mock-sentimental song *The Little Old Lady from Pasadena.*

Berry, Walter, Austrian bass-baritone; b. Vienna, April 8, 1929. He first studied engineering; later decided to engage in a musical career, and enrolled at the Vienna Academy of Music. In 1950 he sang at the Vienna State Opera. On Oct. 2, 1966, he made his American debut at the Metropolitan Opera in N.Y. as Barak in *Die Frau ohne Schatten* by Richard Strauss. He distinguished himself in Wagnerian operas. He was married to **Christa Ludwig** in 1957, and appeared with her numerous times in corresponding roles (Carmen and Escamillo, Ortrud and Telramund, etc.); they were divorced in 1970, but continued to sing in tandem in the same operas.

Bersa, Blagoje, Croatian composer; b. Ragusa, Dec. 21, 1873; d. Zagreb, Jan. 1, 1934. He studied music in Vienna, where he remained until 1919. He wrote 2 operas, *Fire* and *The Cobbler of Delft;* the symph. poems *Sunny Fields, Ghosts,* and *Hamlet;* a String Quartet, a Piano Trio, and songs. Bersa was for many years a prof. of composition at the Zagreb Cons., and influenced the development of the new generation of Croatian composers, several of whom were his pupils.

Bertali, Antonio, Italian violinist and composer; b. Verona, March 11, 1605; d. Vienna, April 1, 1669. He studied with Stefano Bernardi in Verona; in 1624 he went to Vienna, where he served as a court violinist; in 1649 he succeeded Giovanni Valentini as court conductor. He wrote about 11 operas and a number of secular cantatas and oratorios.

Bertalotti, Angelo Michele, Italian composer and teacher; b. Bologna, April 8, 1666; d. there, March 30, 1747. He studied in Bologna; then sang in the choirs of S. Luigi dei Francesi and S. Agostino in Rome (1687–90). In 1693 he became singing master at the Scuole Pie in Bologna; was a member of the choir of S. Petronio there from 1705 on. He publ. *Regole facilissime* (1706 and subsequent eds.); his *Solfeggi a canto e alto dati alle stampe per comodo delli putti delle Scuole pie* (1744; revised ed., 1764) retains its value as a choral method.

Bertani, Lelio, Italian composer; b. Brescia, c.1550; d. there, c.1620. He was appointed maestro di cappella at the Brescia Cathedral in 1584 and remained there until about 1590; from 1598–1604 he held a similar post at the Padua Cathedral. His madrigals were greatly appreciated.
WORKS: *Il primo libro de madrigali* for 5 Voices (Brescia, 1584); *Il primo libro de madrigali* for 6 Voices (Venice, 1585); *Madrigali spirituali* for 3 Voices (Brescia, 1585).

Berté, Heinrich, Hungarian composer; b. Galgócz, May 8, 1857; d. Vienna, Aug. 23, 1924. He studied with Hellmesberger, Fuchs, and Bruckner in Vienna. He produced ballets: *Das Märchenbuch* (Prague, 1890); *Amor auf Reisen* (Vienna, 1895); *Der Karneval in Venedig* (Vienna, 1900); and *Automatenzauber* (Vienna, 1901); operettas: *Die Schneeflocke*

(Prague, 1896); *Der neue Bürgermeister* (Vienna, 1904); *Die Millionenbraut* (Munich, 1905); *Der Kleine Chevalier* (Dresden, 1907); *Der schöne Gardist* (Breslau, 1907); *Der Glücksnarr* (Vienna, 1909); *Kreolenblut* (Hamburg, 1911); *Der Märchenprinz* (Hannover, 1914); *Das Dreimäderlhaus* (Vienna, Jan. 15, 1916). This last, based on Schubert melodies, was produced in English under the title *Blossom Time*, arranged by Romberg (N.Y., Sept. 21, 1921; very popular); also as *Lilac Time*, arranged by Clutsam (London, Dec. 22, 1922).

Berteau, Martin, famous French cellist; b. c.1700; d. Angers, Jan. 23, 1771. He studied the bass viol with Kozecz in Germany; then took up the cello, achieving mastery of its technique. He is regarded as the protagonist of the French school of cello playing. He also composed a number of effective pieces for cello.

Bertheaume, Isidore, French violinist; b. Paris, 1752; d. St. Petersburg, March 20, 1802. A precocious musician, he joined the orch. of the Paris Opéra in 1767 and served there until 1769 and again from 1775 to 1781. He conducted the Concert Spirituel during the Revolution (1789–91); then left France and went to Germany, and in 1801 emigrated to Russia, where he served as first violinist in the Imperial Orch. in St. Petersburg. He composed 2 symphs. concertantes for 2 violins; 3 sonatas for clavecin with violin; a Violin Concerto; and other works for violin.

Berthold, (Karl Friedrich) Theodor, German organist; b. Dresden, Dec. 18, 1815; d. there, April 28, 1882. He was a pupil of Julius Otto and Johann Schneider; in 1864 succeeded Schneider as court organist at Dresden. He wrote an oratorio, *Petrius;* a Symph.; much sacred music; was co-author with Fürstenau of the pamphlet *Die Fabrikation musikalischer Instrumente im Vogtlande* (1876).

Berti, Carlo, Italian composer and organist; b. probably in Florence, c.1555; d. Mantua, before Sept. 2, 1602. He became a novice in the Servite order at the Ss. Annunziata in Florence (1577); was ordained at the convent of the order in 1580. In 1592 he became maestro di cappella at Ss. Annunziata, remaining there until 1598. He went to Mantua in 1601. Only 3 books of his sacred music are extant, all publ. in Venice (1592, 1593, 1596).
BIBLIOGRAPHY: D. Nutter, *The Life and Works of Carlo Berti* (Diss., Rosary College, 1970).

Berti, Giovanni Pietro, Italian singer, organist, and composer; d. Venice, 1638. He was a tenor in the choir of San Marco in Venice; was named 2nd organist there in 1624, and remained at that post until his death. His songs, particularly his strophic arias, are of considerable historical importance; 56 songs for solo voice and continuo are extant.

Bertin, Louise-Angélique, French composer; b. Les Roches, near Paris, Feb. 15, 1805; d. Paris, April 26, 1877. She was a pupil of Fétis; composed the operas *Guy Mannering* (Les Roches, Aug. 25, 1825); *Le Loup-garou* (Paris, March 10, 1827); *Fausto* (Paris, March 7, 1831); *La Esmeralda* (to a libretto adapted by Victor Hugo from his novel *Notre-Dame de Paris;* Paris, Nov. 14, 1836). She also wrote a number of instrumental works, of which *Six Ballades* for Piano was publ.

Bertin de la Doué, Thomas, French composer; b. Paris, c.1680; d. there, 1745. He was maître de musique to the Princess of Orleans; then held the post of organist at the Théatins church in Paris; also served as violinist and keyboard musician with the Paris Opéra orch. (1714–34). As a composer, he was best known for his opera-ballet *Ajax* (Paris, April 30, 1716).

Bertini, Benoît-Auguste, French pianist; b. Lyons, June 5, 1780; d. London, 1830. He took lessons with Clementi in London from 1793 to 1799; in 1806 he returned to Paris, where he published a didactic tract, *Stigmatographie, ou L'Art d'écrire avec des points, suivie de la mélographie, nouvel art de noter la musique* (Paris, 1812), in which he claimed to simplify musical notation. In London he publ., in 1830, another didactic pamphlet, extravagantly titled *Phonological System for acquiring extraordinary facility on all musical instruments as well as in singing.*

Bertini, Domenico, Italian composer and music pedagogue; b. Lucca, June 26, 1829; d. Florence, Sept. 7, 1890. He studied at the Lucca Music School; later with Michele Puccini; in 1857 was director of the music institute and maestro di cappella at Massa Carrara; settled in Florence (1862) as a singing teacher and music critic; became director of the Cherubini Society. He contributed to musical periodicals, including *Boccherini* of Florence and *La Scena* of Venice; also wrote a *Compendio de' principi di musica, secondo un nuovo sistema* (1866); composed 2 operas; masses and other sacred music; chamber music.

Bertini, Gary, Russian-born Israeli conductor and composer; b. Briceni, May 1, 1927. He was taken to Palestine as a child and studied music in Tel Aviv; later went to Italy, where he studied at the Verdi Cons. in Milan; completed his musical education in Paris; graduated in conducting from the Paris Cons. in 1953. Returning to Israel, he was a frequent guest conductor with the Israel Phil. Orch.; also served as music director of the Jerusalem Symph. (1978–81); from 1981 to 1983 he was music adviser of the Detroit Symph. In 1983 he was appointed chief conductor of the Cologne Symph. Orch. He composed a Concerto for Horn, Strings, and Timpani (1952), a Solo Violin Sonata (1953), a ballet, *The Unfound Door* (1963), and incidental music to a number of plays.

Bertini, Giuseppe, Italian musicographer, son of

Salvatore Bertini; b. Palermo, Jan. 20, 1759; d. there, March 15, 1852. He studied at the Scuole Pie degli Scolopi; later entered the priesthood without abandoning his work in musical lexicography. He compiled the *Dizionario storico-critico degli scrittori di musica* (Palermo, 1814–15), which is still of some value for its entries on obscure Italian musicians.

Bertini, Henri (-Jérôme), known as "Bertini le jeune," pianist and composer; b. London, Oct. 28, 1798; d. Meylau, near Grenoble, Oct. 1, 1876. When 6 months old, he was taken to Paris, where he was taught music by his father and his elder brother, **Benoît-Auguste;** at the age of 12, made a concert tour through the Netherlands and Germany; then studied further in Paris and Great Britain; lived in Paris as a concert pianist from 1821–59, when he retired to his estate at Meylau. He wrote valuable technical studies, some of which have been publ. in editions by G. Buonamici and by Riemann; also arranged Bach's *48 Preludes and Fugues* for Piano, 4-hands; composed much chamber music, many piano pieces.

Bertini, Salvatore, Italian composer, father of **Giuseppe Bertini;** b. Palermo, 1721; d. there, Dec. 16, 1794. He studied in Palermo before entering the Jesuit College in Naples; subsequently took music courses with Fago and Leo at the Turchini Cons. In 1748 he was appointed substitute maestro di cappella at the Cappella Palatina in Palermo; was named maestro there in 1778. He composed mostly for the church.

Bertinotti (-Radicati), Teresa, Italian soprano; b. Savigliano, 1776; d. Bologna, Feb. 12, 1854. She studied with La Barbiera in Naples; married the singer **Felice Radicati** in 1801, and toured with him in a vocal duo, visiting Austria and Germany. She sang at the King's Theatre in London from 1810–12; then was in Lisbon from 1812–14. Upon her husband's death in 1820, she retired from the stage and devoted herself to teaching voice.

Bertoldo, Sperindio (Sper'in Dio), Italian organist and composer; b. Modena, c.1530; d. Padua, Aug. 13, 1570. He served as chief organist at the Cathedral of Padua. His surviving compositions include 2 books of madrigals in 5 Voices, publ. in Venice (book 1, 1561; book 2, 1562); the first book includes an *Echo a 6 voci* and a *Dialogo a 8 voci.* Several other madrigals are included in a collection by Cipriano and Annibale (Venice, 1561). Bertoldo's *Toccate, ricercari e canzoni francese . . . per sonar d'organo* (Venice, 1591) was publ. posthumously. Two ricercari for Organ are included in L. Torchi, *L'Arte musicale in Italia* (vol. III).

Bertolli, Francesca, Italian contralto; d. Bologna, Jan. 9, 1767. She sang in Bologna in 1728; then was engaged by Handel in 1729 for his Royal Academy of Music operatic performances in London at the King's Theatre; in 1733 she left Handel's company to join his rival's establishment, the Opera of the Nobility; in 1736–37 she was again a member of Handel's company; she then returned to Italy, where she retired shortly afterward. She was noted for her performances of male roles in lieu of castrati.

Berton, Henri-Montan, French conductor and composer, son of **Pierre-Montan Berton;** b. Paris, Sept. 17, 1767; d. there, April 22, 1844. He was a pupil of Rey and Sacchini; in 1782 he joined the orch. of the Paris Opéra as a violinist; in 1795 he was appointed to the staff of the Paris Cons., and in 1818 succeeded Méhul as prof. of composition. From 1807 to 1809 he conducted at the Opéra-Bouffe; in 1809 became chorusmaster at the Paris Opéra; in 1815 he was elected a member of the French Academy. He wrote 47 operas, of which the most successful were *Montano et Stéphanie* (1799), *Le Délire* (1799), and *Aline, reine de Colconde* (1803); other works included several oratorios, 8 cantatas, and 4 ballets. He also publ. some theoretical works expressing his own views on musical values; they are curious in content but otherwise devoid of significance.
    BIBLIOGRAPHY: D. Raoul-Rochette, *Notice historique sur la vie et les ouvrages de M. Berton* (Paris, 1846); H. Blanchard, *Henri-Montan Berton* (Paris, 1839); M.S. Selden, "Henri Berton as Critic," *Journal of the American Musicological Society* (Summer 1971).

Berton, Pierre-Montan, French composer; b. Maubert-Fontaines, Ardennes, Jan. 7, 1727; d. Paris, May 14, 1780. He studied organ and composition at the choir school of Senlis Cathedral; was a member of the chorus at the Paris Opéra; then became director of the Grand-Théâtre in Bordeaux. In 1755 he was appointed conductor of the Grand Opéra in Paris and was its general director from 1775 to 1778. In that capacity he supplemented the music of the operas of Lully, Rameau, and Gluck. He produced, in Paris, his operas *Erosine* (Aug. 29, 1766), *Théonis, ou Le Toucher* (Oct. 11, 1767), and *Adèle de Ponthieu* (Dec. 1, 1772).

Bertoni, Ferdinando Gioseffo, Italian organist and composer; b. island of Salò, near Venice, Aug. 15, 1725; d. Desenzano, Dec. 1, 1813. He studied with Padre Martini; in 1752 was appointed first organist of San Marco in Venice; made two trips to London, where several of his operas were produced; on Jan. 21, 1785, he succeeded Galuppi as maestro di cappella at San Marco; retired in 1808. From 1757 to 1797 he also served as choirmaster at the Cons. de' Mendicanti. He wrote about 50 operas; of these the following are important: *La Vedova accorta* (Venice, 1745); *Quinto Fabio* (Milan, Jan. 31, 1778); *Demofoonte* (London, Nov. 28, 1778); and *Nitteti* (Venice, Feb. 6, 1789). He also wrote a number of oratorios; harpsichord sonatas; and chamber music.
    BIBLIOGRAPHY: I. Haas, *Ferdinando Bertoni: Leben und Instrumentalwerk* (Vienna, 1958).

Bertouille, Gérard, Belgian composer; b. Tournai,

May 26, 1898. While studying philosophy and law, he took lessons in music with Absil, de Bourguignon, Marsick, and Souris. He began to compose rather late in life; in his music he pursues a median path in a restrained modern idiom.

WORKS: *Les Tentations de St. Antoine,* choreographic poem for Mezzo-soprano, Baritone, and Orch. (1958–59); *Requiem des hommes d'aujourd'hui (Requiem for Men of Today;* 1950); 2 symphs. (1947, 1955); *Sinfonia da Requiem* (1957); *Ouverture* (1937); *Prelude et Fugue* for Orch. (1939); *Passacaille* for Orch. (1940); *Sinfonietta* (1942); Concerto for Chamber Orch. (1942); 2 violin concertos (1942, 1970); *Fantaisie* for Orch. (1943); 2 piano concertos (1946, 1953); 2 trumpet concertos (with Strings, 1946; 1973); *Andante* for Strings (1955); *Ouverture* for Woodwind Trio, Strings, Timpani, and Piano (1956); *Aria et Divertimento* for Flute and Chamber Orch. (1956); *Prélude et Scherzo* for Flute and String Orch. (1958); Viola Concertino (1961); *Fantaisie-Passacaille* for Orch. (1963); *Fantaisie Lyrique* for Orch. (1969); Concertino for Clarinet and Strings (1970); *Musique* for Orch. (1972); Concerto for String Orch. (1974); 7 quartets: Nos. 1–3 and 5–7 are string quartets (1939; 1941; 1942; 1953; *Prélude,* 1953; 1957); No. 4 is for Flute and String Trio (1948); 5 violin sonatas (1936, 1942, 1946, 1953, 1971); Duo for Violin and Piano (1963–67); 2 string trios (1943, 1945); Trio for 2 Violins and Piano (1955); Prelude for 4 Harps (1956); Wind Quintet (1969); *6 Préludes et Fugues* for Piano (1940–42); Piano Sonata (1945); *Passacaille et Fugue* for 2 Pianos (1959); Concertino for 4 Clarinets (1977); songs.

Bertram, Theodor, German baritone; b. Stuttgart, Feb. 12, 1869; d. (suicide) Bayreuth, Nov. 24, 1907. He studied with his father, the baritone **Heinrich Bertram;** made his debut as the Hermit in *Der Freischütz* in Ulm in 1889; then sang at the Hamburg Opera (1891) and the Berlin Kroll Opera (1892); was a member of the Munich Court Opera (1893–99). He made his Metropolitan Opera debut in N.Y. on Jan. 6, 1900, as the Flying Dutchman, remaining on the roster for a year; he also sang at Covent Garden, London (1900, 1903, 1907), and at Bayreuth (1901–6). He was married to the soprano **Fanny Moran-Olden;** following her death, he became despondent and took his own life.

Bertrand, Aline, notable French harpist; b. Paris, 1798; d. there, March 13, 1835. She studied at the Paris Cons. with Naderman; then with Bochsa (1815); made her debut in 1820; then toured Europe, winning special acclaim upon her appearance in Vienna (1828). She publ. *Fantaisie sur la Romance de Joseph* (on themes of Méhul's opera) for harp, and various other arrangements.

Bertrand, Antoine de, French composer; b. Fontanges (Cantal), c.1540; d. c.1581. He composed 7 books of 4-part chansons: *Les Amours de P. de Ronsard* (2 vols., 1576); *Sonets chrestiens* (2 vols., 1580); *Chansons* (3 vols., 1578). His music shows harmonic daring in the use of chromatic progressions. Vols. 4–7 of H. Expert's *Monuments de la musique française au temps de la Renaissance* are devoted to Bertrand's works.

Bertrand, Jean-Gustave, French writer on music; b. Vaugirard, near Paris, Dec. 24, 1834; d. Paris, Feb. 9, 1880. He publ. the following books: *Histoire ecclésiastique de l'orgue* (1859); *Les Origines de l'harmonie* (1866); *De la réforme des études du chant au Conservatoire* (1871); *Les Nationalités musicales étudiées dans le drame lyrique* (1872).

Berutti, Arturo, Argentine opera composer; b. San Juan, March 27, 1862; d. Buenos Aires, Jan. 3, 1938. He was of Italian extraction, and naturalized the spelling of his last name as **Beruti.** He received his early training in music with his father; then went to Leipzig, where he became a student of Jadassohn. He subsequently lived in Italy, where he produced 3 of his operas: *La Vendetta* (Vercelli, May 21, 1892); *Evangelina* (Milan, Sept. 19, 1893); *Taras Bulba* (Turin, March 9, 1895). Returning to Argentina in 1896, he produced the following operas in various theaters in Buenos Aires: *Pampa* (July 27, 1897); *Yupanki* (July 25, 1899); *Khrise* (June 21, 1902); *Horrida Nox,* the first opera by a native Argentine composer, written to a Spanish libretto, which was produced in Argentina (Buenos Aires, July 7, 1908); *Los Heroes* (Aug. 23, 1919; his only opera produced at the Teatro Colón).

BIBLIOGRAPHY: E.M. Navarro, *San Juan en la historia de la música* (San Juan, Argentina, 1964).

Berwald, Franz Adolf, foremost Swedish composer of the 19th century; son of **Christian Friedrich Berwald;** brother of **Christian August Berwald;** cousin of **Johann Friedrich Berwald;** b. Stockholm, July 23, 1796; d. there, April 3, 1868. He was a member of a musical family of German extraction that settled in Sweden in the 18th century. He studied violin with his father and with his cousin Johann Friedrich Berwald; took lessons in composition with J.B.E. du Puy. He served as a violinist and violist in the orch. of the Royal Chapel in Stockholm (1812–28). In 1819 he played in Finland with his brother; also toured in Russia. In 1829 he went to Berlin and became engaged in business; in 1835 he opened an orthopedic establishment there. In 1841 he went to Vienna; then returned to Sweden, where he served as manager of a glassworks in Ångermanland (1850–58); in 1853 was a part owner of a sawmill. In 1864 he was made a member of the Swedish Royal Academy of Music in Stockholm; also gave courses at the Stockholm Cons. In his music Berwald followed the Romantic traditions of the German school of composition; his works reveal influences of Spohr, Weber, and Mendelssohn; there is in his music a certain nostalgia that exudes the sweet odor of slow decay. A renewed interest in Berwald led to a revival of his long-forgotten pieces. A complete edition of his works, *Franz Berwald: Sämtliche Werke,* began publ. in 1966.

WORKS: OPERAS: *Estrella di Soria* (1841; Stockholm, April 9, 1862; modern version by Moses Pergament, Göteborg, March 2, 1931); *Drottningen av Golconda* (1864; first perf. more than a century later, Stockholm, April 3, 1968); the early operas *Gustaf Wasa* (1827), *Leonida* (1829), and *Der Verräter* (1830) remain unperf. FOR ORCH.: *Sinfonie sérieuse,* No. 1 (Stockholm, Dec. 2, 1843); *Sinfonie capricieuse,* No. 2, (1842; perf. in a realization from short score in Stockholm, 72 years later, on Jan. 9, 1914); *Sinfonie singulière,* No. 3 (1845; first perf. 60 years later, Stockholm, Jan. 10, 1905); No. 4 (1845; Stockholm, April 9, 1878); Violin Concerto (Stockholm, March 3, 1821); *Concertstück* for Bassoon and Orch. (1827); Piano Concerto (1855; first perf. in Stockholm in 1904 with Berwald's granddaughter as soloist); 5 symph. poems: *Elfenspiel* and *Erinnerung an die norwegischen Alpen* (Vienna, March 6, 1842); *Ernste und heitere Grillen* (Stockholm, May 19, 1842); *Bayaderen-Fest* (Stockholm, Dec. 6, 1842); 5 piano trios and other chamber music; choral pieces.

BIBLIOGRAPHY: A. Hillman, *Franz Berwald* (Stockholm, 1920); R. Layton, *Berwald* (Stockholm, 1956; in Eng., London, 1959); I. Bengtsson, "Franz Berwald från vaggan till graven. En kronologisk tabell," *Musikrevy,* XXIII/6 (1968); S. Broman, "Franz Berwalds stanträd," *Svensk tidskrift för musikforskning* (1968); I. Andersson, *Franz Berwald. II: Källhänvisningar och personregister;* I. Bengtsson, N. Castegren, and E. Lömans, eds., *Franz Berwald: Die Dokumente seines Lebens* (London, 1980); A. Johnson, "Berwald and the *Queen of Golconda,*" *Musical Times* (Jan. 1982).

Berwald, Johan Fredrik (Johann Friedrich), Swedish violinist and composer; cousin of **Franz Berwald;** b. Stockholm, Dec. 4, 1787; d. there, Aug. 26, 1861. He was a member of a musical family of German nationality which settled in Sweden. A precocious musician, he played the violin in public at the age of 5; took lessons in composition with Abbé Vogler during the latter's stay in Sweden. At the age of 16 he went to St. Petersburg and served as concertmaster in the Russian Imperial Court orch. (1803–12). Returning to Sweden, he was appointed chamber musician to the King of Sweden, a post he held from 1815 until 1849; also conducted (from 1819) the Royal Orch. in Stockholm. He wrote his first symph. when he was 9 years old, but in his mature years he devoted himself mainly to theatrical productions. One of his light operas, *L'Héroïne de l'amour,* to a French libretto, was produced in St. Petersburg in 1811. In Stockholm he was also active as a teacher; among his pupils was his cousin Franz Berwald.

Berwald, William, German-American composer; b. Schwerin, Dec. 26, 1864; d. Loma Linda, Calif., May 8, 1948. He studied with Rheinberger at the Munich Cons. (1882–87), and with Faiszt in Stuttgart (1887–88). After a series of engagements as orch. conductor in Germany and Russia, he settled in the U.S. (1892); from 1921–24 he conducted the Syracuse Orch. Among his works are 3 cantatas: *Seven Last Words of Christ; Crucifixion and Resur-*

rection; From Old Japan; music drama, *Utopia* (1936); symph. poem, *Eros and Psyche* (1943); numerous choruses and instrumental pieces and about 250 anthems. He received many prizes for his works, and continued to compose to the end of his life.

Besanzoni, Gabriella, Italian contralto; b. Rome, Nov. 20, 1890; d. there, June 6, 1962. She made her debut as a soprano in *Norma* in 1913; after 1915 she sang mezzo-soprano and contralto; was particularly successful as Carmen. She appeared at the Metropolitan Opera in N.Y. as Amneris in *Aida* on Nov. 19, 1919, but sang there only one season. She made her home principally in Rio de Janeiro; in 1938 she returned to Italy.

Besard, Jean-Baptiste, French lutenist and composer; b. Besançon, 1567; d. probably in Augsburg, in 1625. He studied philosophy at the Univ. of Dôle; after his marriage in 1602, he went to Rome and studied with the lutenist Lorenzini. Later lived in Germany, publishing at Cologne his *Thesaurus harmonicus* (1603), and at Augsburg his *Novus partus, sive Concertationes musicae duodena trium . . .* (1617) and *Isagoge in artem testudinariam* (1617). Some of the compositions in these works have been trans. by O. Chilesotti in *Biblioteca di rarità musicali.*

BIBLIOGRAPHY: O. Chilesotti, *Di G.B. Besardo e del suo Thesaurus harmonicus* (Milan, 1886).

Besekirsky, Vasili. See **Bezekirsky, Vasili.**

Besler, Samuel, composer; b. Brieg, Silesia, Dec. 15, 1574; d. Breslau, July 19, 1625. He was rector (from 1605) of the Gymnasium zum Heiligen Geist in Breslau; wrote a large number of sacred pieces, most of which are preserved at the library of St. Bernardinus in Breslau.

Besly, Maurice, English composer and conductor; b. Normanby, Yorkshire, Jan. 28, 1888; d. Horsham, March 20, 1945. He studied at the Leipzig Cons.; took lessons in conducting with Ernest Ansermet in Switzerland; returning to England, he filled in engagements as church organist, and in 1924 was appointed conductor of the Scottish Orch. in Glasgow. He wrote a few orch. works with picturesque titles such as *Mist in the Valley* and *Chelsea China;* also many anthems, songs, and motets. He edited *Queen's College Hymn Book.*

Besozzi, Alessandro, celebrated Italian oboist; b. Parma, July 22, 1702; d. Turin, July 26, 1793. He was a musician at the ducal chapel in Parma (1728–31); made concert tours with his brother, Girolamo (see 3 below); appeared with him in Paris in 1735; then lived in Turin. He publ. numerous trio sonatas for Flute, Violin, and Cello; 6 violin sonatas (with Basso Continuo); etc. Other members of the family who specialized in wind instruments were: (1) **Antonio,** oboist, nephew of Alessandro (b. Parma, 1714; d. Turin, 1781); (2) **Carlo,** oboist, son of Antonio (b. Naples, c.1738; d. Dresden, March 22, 1791); played in the Dresden orch. (1754); wrote several oboe concertos; (3) **Girolamo,** bassoonist, brother of Alessandro (b. Parma, April 17, 1704; d. Turin, 1778); (4) **Gaetano,** oboist, nephew of Alessandro (b. Parma, 1727; d. London, 1794); (5) **Girolamo,** oboist, son of Gaetano (b. Naples, c.1750; d. Paris, 1785); (6) **Henri,** flutist, son of Girolamo; played at the Opéra-Comique; (7) **Louis-Désiré,** son of Henri (b. Versailles, April 3, 1814; d. Paris, Nov. 11, 1879), a student of Lesueur and Barbereau; he won the Prix de Rome in 1837, defeating Gounod.

Bessaraboff, Nicholas, Russian-American authority on musical instruments; b. Voronezh, Feb. 12, 1894; d. New York, Nov. 10, 1973. He trained as a mechanical engineer and a draftsman, but he also played the French horn and became interested in the mechanics and acoustics of musical instruments. After the completion of his studies at the polytechnical institute in St. Petersburg, he was sent in 1915 with a group of other Russian engineers to the U.S. in order to expedite the shipping of American military equipment for the Russian armed forces during World War I. He arrived in San Francisco in Dec. 1915, and remained in the U.S. after the Russian Revolution of 1917. He worked as a draftsman in Rochester, N.Y., at the same time doing extensive reading on the subject of musical instruments. In 1931 he moved to Boston, where he began working on cataloguing the collection of instruments in the Boston Museum of Fine Arts. In 1941 he publ. his magnum opus, *Ancient European Musical Instruments, An Organological Study of the Musical Instruments in the Leslie Lindsey Mason Collection at the Museum of Fine Arts, Boston.* In 1945 he officially changed his name to **Nicholas Bessaraboff Bodley,** adopting the maiden name of his American wife, Virginia Bodley.
BIBLIOGRAPHY: David Boyden, "Nicholas Bessaraboff's Ancient European Musical Instruments," *Notes* (Sept. 1971).

Bessel, Vasili, Russian music publisher; b. St. Petersburg, April 25, 1842; d. Zürich, March 1, 1907. He was the founder (1869) of the music publishing firm of Bessel & Co. at St. Petersburg, which has publ. works by many distinguished Russian composers (Anton Rubinstein, Rimsky-Korsakov, Tchaikovsky, Mussorgsky); also 2 short-lived periodicals, *Musical Leaflet* (1872–77) and the *Russian Musical Review* (1885–89). Bessel wrote *Reminiscences of Tchaikovsky,* who was his fellow student at the St. Petersburg Cons. In 1918 the firm was transferred to Paris, where it continued under the direction of Bessel's sons, Vasili and Alexander.

Besseler, Heinrich, eminent German musicologist; b. Hörde, Dortmund, April 2, 1900; d. Leipzig, July 25, 1969. He studied mathematics and natural sciences; then turned to musicology; attended the courses of Gurlitt in Freiburg, of Adler in Vienna, and of Ludwig in Göttingen. He received his doctorate in Frei-

burg in 1923; then taught classes at the univs. at Heidelberg (1928–48), Jena (1948–56), and Leipzig (1956–65). In 1967 he received the honorary degree of Doctor of Humane Letters of the Univ. of Chicago. A Festschrift in his honor was publ. on his 60th birthday. He contributed valuable articles to various music journals, mostly on the musical problems of the Middle Ages and the Renaissance, but also on general subjects of musical esthetics; wrote several basic articles for *Die Musik in Geschichte und Gegenwart.* He was also an editor of the collected works of Dufay, Okeghem, and other musicians of their period.
WRITINGS: *Die Musik des Mittelalters und der Renaissance* (Potsdam, 1931); *Fünf echte Bildnisse J.S. Bachs* (Kassel, 1956); *Das musikalische Hören der Neuzeit* (Berlin, 1959; in the report of the transactions of the Saxon Academy of Sciences, vol. 104); *Die Besetzung der Chansons im 15. Jahrhundert* (Utrecht, 1952); *Singstill und Instrumentenstil in der europäischen Musik* (Bamberg, 1953); "Zur Chronologie der Konzerte J.S. Bachs," in the Festschrift for Max Schneider (Leipzig, 1955); "Das Renaissanceproblem in der Musik," in the Festschrift for Br. Stäblein (Kassel, 1967). He brought out (with Max Schneider) the excellent edition *Musikgeschichte in Bildern* (begun serially in Leipzig, 1961; from 1968, his co-editor was W. Bachmann). A complete list of his writings (up to 1961) and editions is found in the Festschrift issued in his honor (Leipzig, 1961).

Bessems, Antoine, Belgian violinist; b. Antwerp, April 6, 1809; d. there, Oct. 19, 1868. He was a pupil of Baillot at the Paris Cons. (1826); in 1829 was first violinist at the Théâtre-Italien, Paris; then made long concert tours; taught for a time in Paris; returned to Antwerp and, from 1847–52, conducted the orch. of the Société Royale d'Harmonie. He composed a Violin Concerto; *12 Grandes Etudes* for Violin with Piano; *12 Grands Duos de concert* for Violin with Piano; many other violin pieces, masses, motets, Psalms, etc.

Best, William Thomas, eminent English organist; b. Carlisle, Aug. 13, 1826; d. Liverpool, May 10, 1897. He studied organ in Liverpool; held various posts as a church organist in Liverpool and London. At his numerous concerts he introduced arrangements of symph. works, thus enabling his audiences to hear classical works in musicianly manner at a time when orch. concerts were scarce. His own works, popular in type, though classical in form, included sonatas, preludes, fugues, concert studies, etc. for organ. He publ. *Handel Album* (20 vols.); *Arrangements from the Scores of the Great Masters* (5 vols.); *Modern School for the Organ* (1853); *The Art of Organ Playing* (1870); etc.
BIBLIOGRAPHY: O.A. Mansfield, "W.T. Best," *Musical Quarterly* (April 1918); J. Mewburn Levien, *Impressions of W.T. Best* (London, 1942).

Bethune, Thomas Greene (called **"Blind Tom"**), black American pianist and composer; b. Columbus,

Betti – Beurle

Ga., May 25, 1849; d. Hoboken, N.J., June 13, 1908. Born blind in slavery, he was purchased, along with his parents (Charity and Mingo Wiggins), by a Colonel Bethune in 1850. His master's wife was a music teacher who fostered his musical talent. At the age of 9 he was "leased" for 3 years to one Perry Oliver, who arranged concert appearances for him throughout the U.S., including a performance at the White House before President Buchanan. Col. Bethune then took full charge of Tom's career, obtaining legal custody and a major part of his earnings. Bethune played in Europe and in America; his programs usually included Bach, Liszt, Chopin, Gottschalk, and his own compositions, mostly improvised character pieces in salon manner, arranged and supplied with appropriate titles by his managers, e.g. *Rainstorm* (1865); *Wellenlänge* (1882; publ. under the pseudonym **François Sexalise**); *Imitation of the Sewing Machine* (1889); *Battle of Manassas* (1894); etc. He also improvised on themes given by members of the audience.

BIBLIOGRAPHY: J.M. Trotter, *Music and Some Highly Musical People* (Boston, 1885); G. Southall, "Blind Tom: A Misrepresented and Neglected Composer-Pianist," *Black Perspective in Music* (May 1975; the July 1976 issue of this journal reprints early testimonials by Charles Hallé, Ignaz Moscheles, and others, plus letters and articles, about Blind Tom).

Betti, Adolfo, Italian violinist; b. Bagni di Lucca, March 21, 1873; d. Lucca, Dec. 2, 1950. Of a musical family, he studied violin in Lucca; then with César Thomson in Liège (1892–96). In 1903 he became the first violinist of the famous Flonzaley Quartet and remained with it until it was disbanded in 1929; this group presented some 2,500 concerts in America and about 500 in Europe. In 1933 Betti was awarded the Coolidge Medal for eminent services to chamber music in America. He taught in N.Y. before returning to Italy. He publ. *La vita e l'arte di Francesco Geminiani* (Lucca, 1933); also edited Schubert's string quartets.

Bettinelli, Bruno, Italian composer; b. Milan, June 4, 1913. He studied with Paribeni at the Cons. of Milan; from 1941–61 he was an instructor at his alma mater; in 1961 he became a member of the Santa Cecilia Academy in Rome. In his works he follows the structural forms of classical Italian music while adorning the harmonies with permissible discords; he also explored the resources of Gregorian chant.

WORKS: *Sinfonia da camera* (1939); *Concerto per orchestra* (1940); *Fantasia e Fuga su temi gregoriani* for String Orch. (1942); *Sinfonia drammatica* (1943); *Messa da requiem* for Chorus a cappella (1945); *Fantasia concertante* for String Quartet and Orch. (1950); *Concerto da camera* (1952); *Sinfonia breve* (1954); 2 piano concertos (1953, 1968); opera, *La Smorfia* (Como, Sept. 30, 1959); Concerto for 2 Pianos and Orch. (1962); opera, *Il Pozzo e il Pendolo (The Pit and the Pendulum),* after Poe (1958; Bergamo, Oct. 24, 1967); *Improvvisazione* for

Violin and Piano (1968); opera, *Count Down* (Milan, March 26, 1970); *Variante per orchestra* (1970); 2 string quartets (1937, 1960); church music.

Betts, Lorne, Canadian composer; b. Winnipeg, Aug. 2, 1918. He studied music theory, piano, and organ in Winnipeg; then took courses in Toronto with John Weinzweig (1947–53); subsequently settled in Hamilton, Ontario, where he became a teacher and music critic.

WORKS: 2 operas: *Riders to the Sea* (1955) and *The Woodcarver's Wife* (1960); *Suite da chiesa* for Wind Ensemble and Percussion (1952); *Sinfonietta* (1952); 2 symphs. (1954, 1961); 2 piano concertos (1955, 1957); *2 Abstracts* for Orch. (1961); *A Cycle of the Earth,* 4 songs for Soprano and Orch. (1962–67); *Kanadario: Music for a Festival Occasion* for Orch. (1966); *Variants* for Orch. (1969); Concertino for Saxophone and Chamber Orch. (1972); *3 Saudades* for 11 Strings (1974); *Margarita Sorori* for Chorus and Orch. (1975); Suite in 3 Movements for Orch. (1975); Concerto for Cello, Piano, and Orch. (1976); Violin Sonata (1948); Clarinet Sonata (1949); 3 string quartets (1950, 1951, 1970); String Trio (1959); Quartet for Flute, Clarinet, Bass Clarinet, and Celesta (1960); Violin Sonatina (1970); Piano Sonata (1950); choruses and songs.

Betz, Franz, German baritone; b. Mainz, March 19, 1835; d. Berlin, Aug. 11, 1900. He made his debut in Hannover in 1856 as Heinrich in *Lohengrin;* then appeared at the Berlin Royal Opera on May 16, 1859, as Don Carlos in *Ernani;* was permanently engaged at the Berlin Royal Opera House until his retirement in 1897. He was best known for the roles of Han Sachs at Munich and Wotan at Bayreuth.

Beurhaus, Friedrich, German music theorist; b. Immecke, near Meinerzhagen, 1536; d. Dortmund, Aug. 6, 1609. He was educated in Münster and Dortmund; received his M.A. in 1560 from the Univ. of Cologne; subsequently was cantor in several towns before taking up the post of cantor of the Reinoldi school in Dortmund in 1567; was named its rector in 1582. He publ. the important treatise *Musicae erotematum libri duo, ex optimis huius artis scriptoribus vera perspicuaque methodo descripto* (Dortmund, 1573; 2nd ed. as *Erotematum musicae libri duo,* 1580; 4th ed., 1591; facsimile ed., prepared by W. Thoene, in *Beiträge zur rheinischen Musikgeschichte,* Cologne, 1959).

BIBLIOGRAPHY: W. Thoene, "Friedrich Beurhaus und seine Musiktraktate," *Beiträge zur rheinischen Musikgeschichte* (Cologne, 1959).

Beurle, Jürgen, German composer; b. Ludwigsburg, Feb. 27, 1943. He studied philology and music in Stuttgart, Tübingen, and Utrecht; in 1967 he attended Stockhausen's lectures at the Darmstadt Summer School for New Music. He is a confirmed constructionist in his musical design.

WORKS: *Sinus* for Soprano, Baritone, Violin, Viola, and Percussion (1966); *Variable Realizations* for Indeterminate Performers (1967); *Statisch-*

dynamisch for Orch. (1968); *Objets* for Chorus, Instruments, and Tape Recorder (1968); *Conditional* for Voice, Piano, and Tape Recorder (1969); *Madrigal* for Soprano, 2 Choruses, Percussion, and 5 Tape Recordings, with Audience participation (1969); *Differenz* for Indeterminate Performers grouped in 5 sections (1970).

Beversdorf, Thomas, American trombone player and composer; b. Yoakum, Texas, Aug. 8, 1924; d. Bloomington, Ind., Feb. 15, 1981. He studied trombone and baritone horn with his father, a band director; took courses in composition with Kent Kennan, Eric DeLamarter, and Anthony Donato at the Univ. of Texas (B.M., 1945) and with Bernard Rogers at the Eastman School of Music in Rochester, N.Y. (M.M., 1946); later attended a summer course in composition with Honegger and Copland at Tanglewood (1947); also had some lessons with Anis Fuleihan. He was trombone player with the Rochester Phil. (1945–46), the Houston Symph. (1946–48), and the Pittsburgh Symph. (1948–49); had special engagements as first trombonist with the Metropolitan Opera in N.Y., Ballets Russes de Monte Carlo, and Sadler's Wells Ballet in London. He was an instructor at the Univ. of Houston (1946–48); in 1951 joined the faculty of Indiana Univ. in Bloomington as prof. of composition; in 1977 lectured at the Univ. of Guadalajara in Mexico.
WORKS: 2 operas: *The Hooligan* (1964-69) and *Metamorphosis,* after Kafka (1968); mystery play, *Vision of Christ* (Bucknell Univ., Lewisburg, Pa., May 1, 1971); *Essay on Mass Production* for Orch. (1946); 4 symphs.: No. 1 (1946); No. 2 (1950); No. 3 for Winds and Percussion (1954; Bloomington, May 9, 1954; version for Full Orch., 1958; Bloomington, Oct. 10, 1958); No. 4 (1958); *Reflections* for Small Orch. (1947); *Mexican Portrait* for Orch. (1948; revised 1952); Concerto Grosso for Oboe and Chamber Orch. (Pittsburgh, April 28, 1950); 2-Piano Concerto (1951; Bloomington, March 17, 1967); *Ode* for Orch. (1952); *New Frontiers* for Orch. (Houston, March 31, 1953); Serenade for Small Orch. (1956); Serenade for Winds and Percussion (1957); oratorio, *The Rock,* after T.S. Eliot (Bloomington, March 16, 1958); *Danforth,* violin concerto (1959); ballet, *Threnody: The Funeral of Youth,* after Rupert Brooks (Bloomington, March 6, 1963; also known as Variations for Orch.); *Generation with the Torch* for Youth Orch. (Bayreuth, Germany, Aug. 5, 1965, by the touring Houston All-City Symph. Orch.); *Murals, Tapestries and Icons* for Symph. Band, with Electric Bass and Electric Piano (1975); Concerto for Tuba and Wind Orch. (Bloomington, Feb. 11, 1976); horn sonata, *Christmas* (1945); *Suite on Baroque Themes* for Clarinet, Cello, and Piano (1947); Prelude and Fugue for Wind Quintet (1950); 2 string quartets (1951, 1955); Sonata for Tuba and Piano (1956); Trumpet Sonata (1962); Violin Sonata (1964-65); Flute Sonata (1965–66); Cello Sonata (1967–69); *Walruses, Cheesecake and Morse Code* for Tuba and Piano (1973); *La Petite Exposition* for Solo Violin or Clarinet, and 11 Strings (Dallas, Feb. 28, 1976); Sonata for Violin and Harp (1976–77); *Corelliana*

Variations for 2 Flutes and Cello (1980).

Bevignani, Enrico, Italian conductor and composer; b. Naples, Sept. 29, 1841; d. there, Aug. 29, 1903. He produced an opera, *Caterina Bloom,* in Naples in 1863; then received an appointment as theater conductor in London; also conducted at the Metropolitan Opera in N.Y. (1894); eventually returned to Naples.

Bevilacqua, Alfredo Antonio, Argentinian composer of popular dances; b. Buenos Aires, Feb. 20, 1874; d. there, July 1, 1942. He earned a living by playing piano at María La Vasca's fashionable dancing bordello. His outstanding success was *Vénus* (1902).

Bevin, Elway, Welsh composer and organist; b. c.1554; d. Bristol, Oct. (buried, Oct. 19) 1638. He was a pupil of Tallis; served as organist of the Bristol Cathedral in 1589 and Gentleman Extraordinary of the Chapel Royal in 1605. He published *A Briefe and Short Instruction in the Art of Musicke* (London, 1631); wrote songs; among them, *Hark, Jolly Shepherds* was popular; also composed an anthem, arranged in a canon of 20 voices.

Bewerunge, Henry, German cleric and music editor; b. Letmathe, Westphalia, Dec. 7, 1862; d. Maynooth, Ireland, Dec. 2, 1923. He was ordained a priest in 1885; took courses in church music in Regensburg; then settled in Ireland and taught at St. Patrick's College in Maynooth (1888–1914) and at the Univ. of Dublin (1914–16). He published *Die Vatikanische Choralausgabe* (Düsseldorf, 1906; also in Eng. and French translations). In 1891–93 he edited *Lyra ecclesiastica.*

Bexfield, William Richard, English organist; b. Norwich, April 27, 1824; d. London, Oct. 29, 1853. He was organist in Lincolnshire and in London; took the degrees of B.Mus. at Oxford (1846) and D.Mus. at Cambridge (1849); wrote an oratorio, *Israel Restored* (1852); a cantata, *Hector's Death;* anthems; organ fugues; songs.

Beydts, Louis, French composer; b. Bordeaux, June 29, 1895; d. Caudéran, near Bordeaux, Sept. 15, 1953. After musical study in Bordeaux he became associated with the popular theater; wrote several operettas, 2 of them on a pseudo-Chinese subject: *Canards Mandarins* (Monte Carlo, 1931) and *Le Voyage de Tchong-Li,* based on a Chinese legend (1932); also wrote pieces for piano, violin, saxophone, and other instruments; choruses and songs.

Beyer, Frank Michael, German organist and composer; b. Berlin, March 8, 1928. He received his earliest musical training from his father, a writer and amateur pianist; spent his childhood in Greece, returning to Berlin in 1938. He studied sacred music and organ; took composition lessons with Ernst Pepping (1952–55). In 1960 he was appointed to the faculty of the Berlin Hochschule für Musik. He founded a concert series, "Musica Nova Sacra." As a composer, he applies the techniques of Bach's counterpoint to modern structures in the manner of Anton von Webern, with thematic materials based on secundal formations and the tritone; the rhythmic patterns of his music are greatly diversified; in dynamic coloration, he explores the finest gradations of sound, particularly in pianissimo.

WORKS: Concerto for Orch. (1957); 2 string quartets (1957, 1969); *Ode* for Orch. (1963); Flute Concerto (1964); Organ Concerto (1967); *Versi* for String Orch. (1968); *Maior Angelis,* cantata (1970); Wind Quintet (1972); *Rondo imaginaire* for Chamber Orch. (1973).

BIBLIOGRAPHY: W. Burde, "Der Komponist F.M. Beyer," *Musica* (May/June 1975).

Beyer, Johann Samuel, German choir director and composer; b. Gotha, 1669; d. Karlsbad, May 9, 1744. He served as a cantor in various churches in Saxony. Among his publications are *Primae lineae musicae vocalis* (1703) and *Geistlich-musikalische Seelenfreude* (1724).

Beyer, Johanna Magdalena, German-American composer and musicologist; b. Leipzig, July 11, 1888; d. New York, Jan. 9, 1944. She studied piano and music theory in Germany. In 1924 she went to America and studied at the David Mannes School in N.Y.; received a teacher's certificate in 1928. She also took private lessons with Dane Rudhyar, Ruth Crawford, Charles Seeger, and Henry Cowell. She wrote music and several plays for various projects in N.Y. During Cowell's term in San Quentin prison (1937–41), Johanna Beyer acted as his secretary and took care of his scores. Her own compositional style is dissonant counterpoint. She composed much chamber music; among her more interesting works are *4 Pieces for Oboe and Bassoon,* Clarinet Sonata, 4 string quartets, and *3 Songs for Soprano, Piano and Percussion.*

Beyschlag, Adolf, German conductor; b. Frankfurt, March 22, 1845; d. Mainz, Aug. 19, 1914. He studied in Mannheim; subsequently was active as a conductor; then went to England, where he conducted the Leeds Phil. Society; in 1902, returned to Germany. He publ. a valuable work, *Die Ornamentik der Musik* (Leipzig, 1908); also wrote dances for piano, 4-hands, in canon form; songs; etc.

Bezdek, Jan, American pianist and composer; b. St. Louis, Aug. 29, 1896. She studied piano with Rudolf Ganz and composition with Felix Borowski in Chicago; subsequently she obtained her Ph.D. at the Eastman School of Music in Rochester, N.Y., in 1946. She publ. a number of successful teaching pieces for Piano, among them *Bells, The Little Bird,* and *Marching.* Under the pseudonym **Julia Derleth,** she publ. easy pieces for piano.

Bezekirsky, Vasili, Russian violinist; b. Moscow,

Jan. 26, 1835; d. there, Nov. 8, 1919. He studied violin in Moscow; in 1858 he went to Brussels, where he took violin lessons with Leonard and lessons in composition with Damcke. Returning to Moscow in 1860, he was concertmaster at the Bolshoi Theater (1861–91); from 1882 to 1902 he was prof. at the Moscow Phil. Inst. As a violin virtuoso, he was greatly regarded in Russia. Tchaikovsky wrote about him: "Although not a Czar of the first magnitude, Bezekirsky is brilliant enough on the dim horizon of present violin playing." Bezekirsky was also a composer; he wrote a violin concerto (Moscow, Feb. 26, 1873); contributed cadenzas to the violin concertos of Beethoven and Brahms. He publ. a vol. of reminiscences, *From the Notebook of an Artist* (St. Petersburg, 1910).

Bezekirsky, Vasili, Russian violinist, son of the preceding; b. Moscow, Jan. 15, 1880; d. East Windham, N.Y., Nov. 8, 1960. He studied with his father; made several tours in Europe as a concert violinist; in 1914 he emigrated to the U.S.; played in various orchs. and taught in several music schools; from 1930–47 he was a violin teacher at the School of Music of the Univ. of Michigan at Ann Arbor.

Bhatkhande, Vishnu Narayan, eminent Indian musicologist; b. Bombay, Aug. 10, 1860; d. there, Sept. 19, 1936. He studied jurisprudence; concurrently investigated the systems of Indian ragas; while earning a living as a lawyer, he traveled throughout India to collect authentic ragas. In 1910 he abandoned his legal practice and dedicated himself exclusively to Indian folk music. His compilations of ragas are invaluable resources. He publ. *Hindusthāni sangit paddhati* (4 vols., Marathi, 1910–32), *Srimal-laksya sangitam* (Bombay, 1910), and *Kramik pustak mālikā* (6 vols., Marathi, 1919–37).

Biaggi, Girolamo Alessandro, Italian writer on music; b. Calcio, Bergamo, Feb. 2, 1819; d. Florence, March 21, 1897. He wrote an opera, *Martino della Scala.* He then went to Florence to teach at the newly established Reale Istituto Musicale; was active also as contributor to the *Gazetta d'Italia,* under the pen name **Ippolito d'Albano.** He publ. a valuable essay, *La riforma melodrammatica fiorentina.*

Bial, Rudolf, violinist, composer, and conductor; b. Habelschwerdt, Silesia, Aug. 26, 1834; d. New York, Nov. 13, 1881. He was a member of the Breslau Orch.; then toured Africa and Australia with his brother Karl; settled in Berlin as conductor of the Kroll Orch. and of the Wallner Theater, where his numerous farces, operettas, etc. were performed; later conducted at the Italian opera in Berlin. In 1878 he settled in N.Y.

Bialas, Günther, German composer; b. Bielschowitz, Silesia, July 19, 1907. His father was business manager of the local theater, and Bialas absorbed much music through personal connections with professional organizations. He pursued his formal studies at the Univ. of Breslau and at the Berlin Academy of Church and School Music. In 1940 he was appointed to teach music at the Univ. of Breslau; in 1950 he obtained a teaching post at the North-West German Academy of Music in Detmold, and in 1959 joined the faculty of the State Music School in Munich. In 1967 he received the music prize of the Bavarian Academy of Fine Arts, and in 1971 was awarded the Culture Prize of Upper Silesia. His idiom of composition is omnitonal; he uses dodecaphonic devices and folklike modalities with equal freedom; his music is pragmatic without being doctrinaire. He wrote 3 short operas: *Hero und Leander* (1966), *Die Geschichte von Aucassin und Nicolette* (1967–69), and *Der gestiefelte Kater* (1973–74); also several scores of incidental music for the theater. In his orch. works he adopts a Baroque manner à la moderne, exemplified by such works as *Kleine Konzertmusik* (1935), Viola Concerto (1940), Violin Concerto (1949), Cello Concerto (1962), and *Sinfonia piccola* (1960). His choral music comprises both sacred and secular works; he also wrote 3 string quartets (1936, 1949, 1969), a Viola Sonata (1946), Violin Sonata (1946), Flute Sonata (1946), and *Moments musicaux* for Cello and Harp (1970).

Bianchi, Antonio, Italian singer and composer; b. Milan, 1758; d. after 1817. He sang baritone roles in Milan, and later in Genoa; then went to Germany, where he became court singer to the Prince of Nassau Weilburg; sang at the Königliches Nationaltheater in Berlin from 1792–97; then made appearances in other German theaters; was also co-director of a touring opera company. He performed many roles in comic operas by Cimarosa, Sarti, and Paisiello, and himself composed the opera *Die Insel der Alcina* (Berlin, Feb. 16, 1794).

Bianchi, Bianca (real name, **Bertha Schwarz**), German soprano; b. Heidelberg, June 27, 1855; d. Salzburg, Feb. 1947. She studied in Heidelberg and Paris; made her debut as Barberina in *The Marriage of Figaro* at Karlsruhe (1873); sang in Vienna and London; in 1905 settled in Salzburg as a vocal teacher. She married her manager, Pollini, in 1897.

Bianchi, Francesco, Italian composer; b. Cremona, 1752; d. (suicide) London, Nov. 27, 1810. He studied in Naples with Jommelli and Cafaro. He wrote nearly 80 operas, some quite pleasing, but ephemeral. His first opera was *Giulio Sabino* (Cremona, 1772); it was followed by *Il Grand Cidde* (Florence, 1773). From 1775 to 1778 he was in Paris serving as maestro al cembalo at the Comédie Italienne; there he produced his opera *La Réduction de Paris* (Sept. 30, 1775). In 1778 he went to Florence; in 1783 he became 2nd maestro at the Cathedral of Milan, a post he held until 1793; concurrently he worked in Venice from 1785 to 1791, and again from 1793 to 1797, when he served as 2nd organist at San Marco. He subsequently was in Naples, where he produced

his most significant opera, *La Vendetta de Nino* (Nov. 12, 1790). In 1794 he went to London, where he officiated as conductor at the King's Theatre (1795–1801); several of his operas were produced there under his supervision. Apart from his operas, he wrote several pieces of instrumental music, and also publ. a theoretical treatise, *Dell' attrazione armonica*, which was publ. in excerpts, in Eng., in *The Quarterly Musical Magazine and Review* (1820–21). Bianchi was also a successful teacher; among his English pupils was Henry Bishop.

Bianchi, Valentina, Russian soprano; b. Vilna, 1839; d. Kurland, Feb. 28, 1884. She studied at the Paris Cons.; made her debut as a soprano in Frankfurt (1855); sang at Schwerin (1855–61), St. Petersburg (1862–65), and Moscow (until 1867); retired in 1870. She married chief forester von Fabian in 1865. Her range was extraordinary, extending from low alto through high soprano notes.

Bianchini, Domenico, Italian lutenist and composer; b. c.1510; d. Venice, c.1576. He worked as a mosaicist at San Marco in Venice (1540–76); as a composer, he publ. *Intavolatura de lauto ... di recercari, motetti, madrigali, napolitane et balli, libro primo* (Venice, 1546).
BIBLIOGRAPHY: R. de Morcourt, "Le Livre de tablature de luth de Domenico Bianchini (1546)," *La Musique instrumentale de la Renaissance: CNRS Paris 1954.*

Bianco, Pietro Antonio, Italian singer and composer; b. Venice, c.1540; d. Graz (buried, Feb. 2), 1611. He was a canon at S. Salvatore in Venice; became a tenor at the Hofkapelle in Graz in 1578; was named Hofkapellmeister there in 1595. He composed both secular and religious vocal music.
BIBLIOGRAPHY: H. Federhofer, "P.A. Bianco und seine Vorgänger A. Zweiller und P. Ragno an der Grazer Hofkapelle," *Kirchenmusikalisches Jahrbuch*, XXXVIII (1954).

Bibalo, Antonio, Italian-born Norwegian composer; b. Trieste, Jan. 18, 1922, of Slovak descent (his family name was **Bibalitsch**). He studied piano and composition at the Trieste Cons.; during the disruption caused by World War II, he earned his living as a nightclub pianist and a sanitation worker. He was in Australia briefly before going to England in 1953; studied advanced composition with Elisabeth Lutyens in London. In 1956 he went to Norway and became a naturalized citizen.
WORKS: He attracted the attention of the musical world with the production of his opera *The Smile at the Foot of the Ladder* (1958–62), after a short story by Henry Miller; the original libretto was in Italian as *Sorrisi ai piedi d'una scala*, but the production was in German under the name *Das Lächeln am Fusse der Leiter* at the Hamburg State Opera on April 6, 1965. His other works include a chamber opera, *Frøken Julie (Miss Julie),* after Strindberg (Århus, Denmark, Sept. 8, 1975); a ballet, *Pinocchio* (Hamburg, Jan. 17, 1969); a television bal-

let, *Nocturne for Apollo* (Norwegian Television, 1971); 2 piano concertos: No. 1 (1953; Oslo, Aug. 1, 1972) and No. 2 (1971; Bergen, Norway, April 27, 1972); *Piano Sonatina* (1953); 2 chamber concertos: No. 1 for Piano and Strings (1954) and No. 2 for Harpsichord, Violin, and Strings (1974); *Fantasy for Violin and Orch.* (1954; received 3rd prize at the Wieniawski Composer Competition, Warsaw, 1956); *4 Balkan Dances* for Piano or Orch. (1956); *12 Miniatures* for Piano (1956); *Concerto Allegorico* for Violin and Orch. (1957); *3 Hommages* for Piano (1957); Toccata for Piano (1957); *Pitture Astratte* for Orch. (1958); *Elegia per un'era spaziale (Elegy for a Space Age)* for Soprano, Baritone, Chorus, and Instrumental Ensemble (1963); *Sinfonia Notturna* (1968); *Overture,* after Goldoni's "Servant with Two Masters" (1968); *Autumnale,* suite de concert for Piano, Flute, Vibraphone, and Double Bass (1968); 2 sonatinas for Wind Quintet (1971, 1972); String Quartet No. 1 (1973); 2 piano sonatas (1974, 1975); Suite for Orch. (1974); *Games* for Trombone and Flute (1975).

BIBLIOGRAPHY: B. Kortsen, *Contemporary Norwegian Orchestral Music* (Bergen, 1969); B. Kortsen, *Contemporary Norwegian Chamber Music* (Bergen, 1971).

Biber, Heinrich Ignaz Franz von, famous Bohemian violinist and composer; b. Wartenberg, Bohemia, Aug. 12, 1644; d. Salzburg, May 3, 1704. He was in the service of the Emperor Leopold I, who ennobled him on Dec. 5, 1690; he also served at other courts. In 1670 he was a member of the Kapelle at Salzburg; in 1679 he was appointed Vice-Kapellmeister there, and in 1684 became Kapellmeister. He was one of the founders of the German school of violin playing and was among the first to employ the "scordatura," a system of artificial mistuning to facilitate performance. He publ. a number of violin sonatas, several of which were reprinted in David's *Hohe Schule* and in Denkmäler der Tonkunst in Österreich; composed 2 operas, *Chi la dura la vince* (Salzburg, 1687) and *L'ossequio de Salisburgo* (Salzburg, 1699); several scores of sacred music, including a requiem and numerous choruses.

BIBLIOGRAPHY: Thomas Russell, "The Violin 'Scordatura,'" *Musical Quarterly* (Jan. 1938); E. Schenk, "*Ein Singfundament* von Heinrich Ignaz Biber," in H. Becker and R. Gerlach, *Speculum musicae artis. Festgabe für Heinrich Husman* (Munich, 1970). S. Dahms, "Neues zur Chronologie der Opern von Biber und Moffat," *Österreichische Musikzeitschrift,* XXIX (1974).

Bibl, Andreas, Austrian organist; b. Vienna, April 8, 1807; d. there, April 30, 1878. He served for many years as organist at St. Stephen Cathedral in Vienna; was active as a teacher; among his pupils was his son, **Rudolf Bibl.**

Bibl, Rudolf, Austrian organist and composer; b. Vienna, Jan. 6, 1832; d. there, Aug. 2, 1902. He studied with his father, **Andreas Bibl;** occupied various posts as church organist in Vienna; he wrote 4 masses with orch. accompaniment, a Mass a cappella, 2 Requiems; much organ music; also a violin sonata and piano pieces. He publ. a valuable didactic volume, *Orgelschule.*

Bie, Oskar, German music critic; b. Breslau, Feb. 9, 1864; d. Berlin, April 21, 1938. He studied music with Philipp Scharwenka in Berlin; devoted himself principally to musical journalism, and publ. a number of informative monographs. In the spring of 1914 he accompanied Koussevitzky on his concert tour of the Volga and reported his impressions in a privately publ. illustrated edition in 1920. Among his publications are: *Das Klavier und seine Meister* (Munich, 1898; publ. in Eng. as *A History of the Pianoforte and Pianoforte Players,* London, 1899); *Intime Musik* (Berlin, 1904); *Tanzmusik* (Berlin, 1905); *Der Tanz* (Berlin, 1906; 1919; 1925); *Die moderne Musik und Richard Strauss* (Berlin, 1906; Leipzig, 1916, 1925); *Die Oper* (Berlin, 1913; many reprints); *Das Rätsel der Musik* (Leipzig, 1922); *Franz Schubert* (Berlin, 1925; publ. in Eng. under the title *Schubert the Man,* N.Y., 1929); *Das Deutsche Lied* (Berlin, 1926); *Richard Wagner und Bayreuth* (Zürich, 1931).

Biedermann, Edward Julius, American organist and composer; b. Milwaukee, Nov. 8, 1849; d. Freeport, N.Y., Nov. 26, 1933. He studied with his father, Julius Biedermann, and additionally in Germany (1858–64). Upon returning to N.Y., he occupied various posts as church organist and was also active as a teacher. He wrote much sacred music; also choruses for male voices, and several masses.

Biehle, Herbert, German voice teacher and theorist, son and pupil of **Johannes Biehle;** b. Dresden, Feb. 16, 1901. He studied composition with Georg Schumann, and musicology with Johannes Wolf. He became active mainly as a vocal pedagogue. He publ. several monographs dealing with vocal techniques, among them *Die Stimmkunst* (2 vols., Leipzig, 1931); also several informative essays on the role of the "Sprechstimme" in vocal literature, and a monograph dealing with contributions to the science of organ bells, invented by his father.

Biehle, Johannes, German organist; b. Bautzen, June 18, 1870; d. there, Jan. 4, 1941. He studied at the Dresden Cons.; served as music director and organist in Bautzen (1898–1914). He publ. 2 valuable vols. dealing with the acoustics of church and organ building: *Theorie der pneumatischen Orgeltraktur* (Leipzig, 1911) and *Theorie des Kirchenbaues* (Wittenberg, 1913). He was generally regarded as a founder of the modern organ carillon.

BIBLIOGRAPHY: Herbert Biehle, *Johannes Biehle als Begründer der Glockenwissenschaft* (1961).

Bielawa, Herbert, American composer; b. Chicago, Feb. 3, 1930, of Polish (paternal) and German (maternal) descent. He studied music at home; from

1954 to 1956 served in the U.S. Army in Germany, stationed in Frankfurt, where he also studied conducting with Bruno Vondenhoff. Returning to the U.S., he took courses in piano with Soulima Stravinsky at the Univ. of Illinois (B.M., 1954); enrolled at the Univ. of Southern Calif. in Los Angeles, and took courses in composition with Ingolf Dahl (1960–61), Halsey Stevens (1961–64), and Ellis Kohs (1961–63); also studied music for cinema with Miklós Rosza and David Raksin. In 1966 he was appointed to the faculty of San Francisco State Univ.; in 1967 established there the Electronic Music Studio. In his own music he makes use of the entire field of practical resources, without prejudice.

WORKS: *Concert Piece* for Orch. (1953); *Essay* for String Orch. (1958); *A Bird in the Bush,* chamber opera (1962); *Abstractions* for String Orch. (1965); *Four Legends* for Violins and Cellos (1967); *Divergents* for Orch. (1969); *A Dickinson Album* for Choir, Tape, Piano, and Guitar (1972); Quartet for Guitars (1978); electronic scores: *Additions* (1968); *Discoveries* (1972); *Laps, Caps* and *Overlaps* (1974); *Matrices* (1979); numerous organ pieces and choruses.

Bierdiajew, Walerian, Polish conductor; b. Grodno, March 7, 1885; d. Warsaw, Nov. 28, 1956. He studied composition with Max Reger and conducting with Arthur Nikisch at the Leipzig Cons.; began his conducting career in Dresden in 1906; in 1908 became regular conductor at the Maryinsky Opera Theater in St. Petersburg; then conducted in various Russian opera houses; from 1921–25 he lived in Poland; from 1925–30 was again engaged as a conductor in Russia and in the Ukraine. In 1930 he was appointed prof. of conducting at the Warsaw Cons.; in 1947–49 was conductor of the Cracow Phil.; then taught at the Cons. of Poznan (1949–54) and at the Warsaw Cons. (1954–56).

Bierey, Gottlob Benedikt, German conductor and composer; b. Dresden, July 25, 1772; d. Breslau, May 5, 1840. He was a pupil of Christian E. Weinlig at Dresden; then was director of a traveling opera troupe. He was appointed Kapellmeister at Breslau in 1808, succeeding Weber; retired in 1828. He composed 26 operas and operettas, 10 cantatas, masses, orch. and chamber music, etc.

Biernacki, Nikodem, Polish violinist; b. Tarnopol, 1826; d. Sanok, May 6, 1892. He studied piano and composition with Hauptmann and violin with David at the Leipzig Cons.; continued his studies with Spohr; then developed a career as a violinist in Europe; also played in the U.S. (1862) and Mexico (1864); later went to Stockholm, where he served as concertmaster of the Royal Orch. He finally settled in Poland as a teacher. He composed a number of works for the violin.

Bigard, "Barney" (Alban Leon Bigard), black American clarinetist; b. New Orleans, March 3, 1906; d. Los Angeles, June 27, 1980. He played in various local bands in New Orleans; in 1924 he went to Chicago, where he worked with King Oliver. In 1928 he joined Duke Ellington's band, with which he played until 1942. He later formed small bands of his own, working mostly in Los Angeles. He gradually acquired a reputation as one of the most ingenious jazz clarinet players; he also composed songs. As a sidekick for Duke Ellington, he co-authored *Mood Indigo,* which became one of the most famous meditation tunes in American popular music.

Biggs, E. Power (Edward George Power), eminent concert organist; b. Westcliff, England, March 29, 1906; d. Boston, March 10, 1977. He studied at Hurstpierpoint College (1917–24); then entered the Royal Academy of Music in London, graduating in 1929. In 1930 he came to the U.S. and became naturalized in 1937. He made his N.Y. debut as an organist at the Wanamaker Auditorium in 1932. He was an organist in Newport, R.I. (1929–31); then moved to Cambridge, Mass., where he served as organist at Christ Church, and later became music director of the Harvard Church in Brookline. In the interim he toured Europe, and made a wide survey of old church organs in England, Iceland, Sweden, Norway, Denmark, Germany, the Netherlands, Austria, Italy, and Spain in search of the type of organ that Bach and Handel played. His repertoire consisted mostly of the Baroque masters, but he also commissioned works from American composers, among them Walter Piston, Roy Harris, Howard Hanson, and Quincy Porter; Benjamin Britten also wrote a work for him. Biggs became well known to American music lovers through his weekly broadcasts of organ recitals over the CBS network, which he gave from 1942–58; he continued to give concerts until arthritis forced him to reduce his concert activities, but he was able to continue recording organ music, and he also edited organ works for publication. Biggs refused to perform on electronic organs, which in his opinion vulgarized and distorted the classical organ sound. His own style of performance had a classical austerity inspired by the Baroque school of organ playing.

Bignami, Carlo, renowned Italian violinist; b. Cremona, Dec. 6, 1808; d. Voghera, Oct. 2, 1848. He studied violin with his father and elder brother. He played in theater orchs. in Cremona and Milan; in 1829 he was appointed director of the Teatro Sociale in Mantua; then was in Milan and Verona. Returning to Cremona in 1837 as director and first violinist of the orch., he made it one of the best in Lombardy. Paganini called him *"il primo violinista d'Italia,"* but he may have meant this phrase to express his low opinion of other Italian violinists in comparison. Bignami wrote a number of violin pieces, including a concerto, a *Capriccio, Studi per violino, Grande Adagio, Polacca,* fantasias, variations, etc.

Bigot, Eugène, French conductor; b. Rennes, Feb. 28, 1888; d. Paris, July 17, 1965. He studied violin and piano at the Rennes Cons., and later at the Paris Cons. In 1913 he was named chorus master at the Théâtre des Champs-Elysées; subsequently toured

Europe with the Ballets Suédois; also conducted the Paris Cons. Orch. (1923–25); then served as music director at the Théâtre des Champs-Elysées (1925–27). In 1935 he became president and director of the Concerts Lamoureux, a post he held until 1950; also held the post of principal conductor of the Opéra-Comique (1936–47). In 1947 he became chief conductor of the Radio Orch. in Paris, a post he held until his death.

Bigot, Marie (née **Kiéné**), pianist; b. Colmar, Alsace, March 3, 1786; d. Paris, Sept. 16, 1820. After her marriage in 1804, she lived in Vienna, where she was known and esteemed by Haydn and Beethoven; went to Paris in 1808, where she gave piano lessons from 1812 on; Mendelssohn was briefly her pupil in Paris at the age of 7.

Bihari, János, Hungarian violinist; b. Nagyabony (baptized, Oct. 21), 1764; d. Pest, April 26, 1827. He led a Gypsy band in Pest, and improvised violin pieces in a Hungarian manner, which were later notated by an amanuensis (he himself could not read music); in this manner he became a mediator for Hungarian popular music, and his melodies were used as genuine source material by real composers in Hungary.
BIBLIOGRAPHY: E. Major, *Bihari János* (Budapest, 1928).

Bijvanck, Henk, Dutch composer; b. Kudus, Java, Nov. 6, 1909; d. Heemstede, near Haarlem, Sept. 5, 1969. He studied composition with Franz Schmidt and piano with Andrassy in Vienna; then was active as a pianist there; subsequently taught piano at the Amsterdam Music Lyceum (1945–47). His works include: Piano Concerto (1943); Liberation Symph. (1944); Lourdes Symph. (1952); Symph. No. 2; chamber music; vocal works.

Bikel, Theodore, Austrian-American singer and actor; b. Vienna, May 2, 1924. After the Anschluss in 1938, he fled with his family to Palestine; then made his way to London, where he studied at the Royal Academy of Dramatic Arts. He subsequently had a fine career as an actor on stage, screen, and television; concurrently established himself as a folksinger; in 1959 he scored a major Broadway success in the role of Georg von Trapp in the Rogers and Hammerstein musical *The Sound of Music.* He became an American citizen in 1961.

Bildstein, Hieronymus, important Austrian organist and composer; b. Bregenz, c.1580; d. c.1626. After studying music in Bregenz, he went to Konstanz, where he was active as court organist. He wrote 25 motets publ. as *Orpheus chritianus seu Symphoniarum sacrarum prodromus, 5–8 vocum cum basso generali* (Regensburg, 1624); publ. in a modern edition in the Denkmäler der Tonkunst in Österreich, CXXII (1971) and CXXVI (1976).
BIBLIOGRAPHY: W. Pass, "Hieronymus Bildstein und der Konstanzer Fürstbischof Jakob Fug-

ger," *Ausstellungskatalog "Musik im Bodenseeraum um 1600"* (Bregenz, 1974).

Bilhon (or **Billon**), **Jean de,** French composer who flourished c.1530. He was the author of several masses, Magnificats, and motets which are included in collections of church music publ. between 1534 and 1554.

Billeter, (Otto) Bernhard, Swiss organist, pianist, and musicologist; b. Zürich, July 26, 1936. He studied piano with Paul Baumgartner and organ with Anton Heiller; took courses in musicology with Kurt von Fischer at the Univ. of Zürich, where he received his Ph.D. in 1970. He publ. the valuable monograph *Frank Martin: Ein Aussenseiter der neuen Musik* (Frauenfeld, 1970).

Billings, William, pioneer American composer of hymns and anthems and popularizer of "fuging tunes"; b. Boston, Oct. 7, 1746; d. there, Sept. 26, 1800. A tanner's apprentice, he acquired the rudiments of music from treatises by Tans'ur; he compensated for his lack of education by a wealth of original ideas and a determination to put them into practice. His first musical collection, *The New England Psalm Singer* (Boston, 1770), contained what he described at a later date as "fuging pieces . . . more than twenty times as powerful as the old slow tunes." The technique of these pieces was canonic, with "each part striving for mastery and victory." His other publ. books were: *The Singing Master's Assistant* (1778); *Music in Miniature* (1779); *The Psalm Singer's Amusement* (1781); *The Suffolk Harmony* (1786); and *The Continental Harmony* (1794). In one instance, he harmonized a tune, *Jargon,* entirely in dissonances; this was prefaced by a "Manifesto" to the Goddess of Discord. There was further a choral work, *Modern Music,* in which the proclaimed aim was expressed in the opening lines: "We are met for a concert of modern invention—To tickle the ear is our present intention." Several of his hymns became popular, particularly *Chester* and *The Rose of Sharon;* an interesting historical work was his *Lamentation over Boston,* written in Watertown while Boston was occupied by the British. However, he could not earn a living by his music; appeals made to provide him and his large family with funds bore little fruit, and Billings died in abject poverty. The combination of reverence and solemnity with humor makes the songs of Billings unique in the annals of American music, and aroused the curiosity of many modern American musicians; Henry Cowell wrote a series of "fuging tunes" for Orch.
BIBLIOGRAPHY: O.G. Sonneck, *Early Concert Life in America* (Leipzig, 1907; reprinted 1949); E.H. Pierce, "The Rise and Fall of the Fugue Tune in America," *Musical Quarterly* (April 1930); I. Goldberg, "The First American Musician," *American Mercury,* 14; P. Scholes, *The Puritans and Music in England and New England* (Oxford, 1934); C.E. Lindstrom, "William Billings and His Times," *Musical Quarterly* (Oct. 1939); J. Barbour, *The Church*

Music of William Billings (East Lansing, 1960); D. McKay and R. Crawford, *William Billings of Boston* (Princeton, 1975); Hans Nathan, *William Billings, Data and Documents* (Detroit, 1976); H. Nathan, ed., *William Billings: Complete Works* (Charlottesville, 1977).

Billington, Elizabeth (née **Weichsel**), famous English soprano; b. London, Dec. 27, 1765; d. near Venice, Aug. 25, 1818. Her mother, a singer, was a pupil of Johann Christian Bach; Elizabeth, too, had some lessons with him. She received her early musical training from her father, a German oboist. She also studied with James Billington, a double-bass player by profession, whom she married on Oct. 13, 1783. Her operatic debut took place in Dublin (1784), as Eurydice in Gluck's opera; she went to London, where she appeared as Rosetta in *Love in a Village* at Covent Garden on Feb. 13, 1786. Her success was immediate; she was reengaged at Covent Garden and also sang at the Concerts of Antient Music in London. Her career was briefly disrupted by the publication, in 1792, of anonymous *Memoirs* attacking her private life. This was immediately followed by an equally anonymous rebuttal, "written by a gentleman," defending her reputation. In 1794 she went to Italy, where she sang for the King of Naples. He made arrangements for her appearances at the San Carlo, where she performed in operas by Bianchi, Paisiello, Paer, and Himmel, all written specially for her. Her husband died in 1794; she remained in Italy for 2 more years; then lived in France, where she married M. Felissent. Returning to London in 1801, she sang alternately at Drury Lane and Covent Garden, with great acclaim, at 4,000 guineas a season. This period was the peak of her success. She retired in 1809, except for occasional performances. After a temporary separation from Felissent, she returned to him in 1817; they settled at their estate at St. Artien, near Venice.

Billroth, Theodor, eminent surgeon and amateur musician; b. Bergen, on the island of Rügen, April 26, 1829; d. Abazzia, Feb. 6, 1894. He received a thorough musical education; was an intimate friend of Hanslick and Brahms; the musical soirees at his home in Vienna were famous. Almost all the chamber music of Brahms was played there (with Billroth as violist) before a public performance. He wrote the treatise *Wer ist musikalisch?* (1896, ed. by Hanslick). Billroth originated 2 crucial intestinal surgical operations, known in medical literature as Billroth I and Billroth II.
BIBLIOGRAPHY: J. Fischer, *Theodor Billroth und seine Zeitgenossen* (1929); A. Fränkel, *Th. Billroth* (1931); Otto Gottlieb, *Billroth und Brahms* (1934); *Briefe Billroths* (1895).

Bilse, Benjamin, German conductor; b. Liegnitz, Aug. 17, 1816; d. there, July 13, 1902. He was "Stadtmusikus" at Liegnitz (1843), and brought his orch. to a remarkable degree of perfection; then lived in Berlin (1868–84) and conducted at the Concerthaus; retired in 1894 with the title "Hofmusikus." He composed salon music.

Bilson, Malcolm, American pianist; b. Los Angeles, Oct. 24, 1935. He studied at the Vienna Academy of Music and at the Ecole Normale de Musique in Paris; subsequently received a Doctor of Musical Arts degree from the Univ. of Illinois at Urbana. In his concerts he revived the use of the fortepiano, performing on original instruments of the 18th century and modern replicas. In 1968 he became a prof. at Cornell Univ.

Bilstin (real name, **Bildstein**), **Yuri,** Russian cellist; b. Odessa, Feb. 10, 1887; d. New York, Dec. 15, 1947. He studied at the Tiflis Cons.; then at St. Petersburg. After the Russian Revolution he lived in Paris; in 1932 settled in the U.S. as a teacher. He wrote several works for cello; also *Invocation to the Light* for Viola da Gamba, Flute, and Piano (1932); *Variations diaboliques* for Cello and Piano; and *Méthode psycho-physiologique d'enseignement musical.*

Bilt, Peter van der, Dutch bass-baritone; b. Jakarta, Aug. 30, 1936. He studied voice in Amsterdam; made his debut there in 1960 as Dulcamara in *L'elisir d'amore;* in 1963 he sang Don Basilio in *Il Barbiere di Siviglia* at the San Francisco Opera; in 1964 he joined the Deutsche Oper am Rhein in Düsseldorf; also appeared as a guest artist throughout Europe, in both opera and concert.

Bimboni, Alberto, Italian-American pianist and composer; b. Florence, Aug. 24, 1882; d. New York, June 18, 1960. He studied in Florence; came to the U.S. in 1912 as an opera conductor. In 1930 he was appointed to the faculty of the Curtis Inst. in Philadelphia; taught opera classes at the Juilliard School of Music in N.Y. from 1933; appeared as a pianist in concerts with Ysaÿe, John McCormack, and other celebrated artists. He wrote the operas *Winona* (Portland, Oregon, Nov. 11, 1926); *Karina* (Minneapolis, 1928); *Il Cancelleto d'oro* (N.Y., March 11, 1936); *In the Name of Culture* (Rochester, N.Y., May 9, 1949); numerous songs (many of them publ.).
BIBLIOGRAPHY: E.E. Hipsher, *American Opera and Its Composers* (Philadelphia, 1927; pp. 72–76).

Binchois (de Binche), Gilles, Burgundian composer; b. Mons in Hainaut, c.1400; d. Soignies, near Mons, Sept. 20, 1460. His father was Jean de Binche, counselor to 2 rulers of Hainaut. Binchois was in the service of William de la Pole, Earl of Suffolk, in Paris (1424). From 1430 he was at the Burgundian court; advanced from 5th to 2nd chaplain; probably visited Italy at some time. Tinctoris considered him the equal of Dunstable and Dufay. He is best known for his secular works; his chansons rank with the finest. Modern reprints of his works are contained in: J. Marix, *Les Musiciens de la cour de Bourgogne au XVe siècle* (1937); L. Feininger, ed., *Documenta polyphoniae liturgicae Sanctae Ecclesiae Romanae,* Ser. I (1947); W. Gurlitt, ed., *Gilles Binchois, 16 weltliche Lieder zu 3 Stimmen,* in *Das Chorwerk,*

22; J. Stainer, ed., *Dufay and His Contemporaries* (1898); Denkmäler der Tonkunst in Österreich (vols. 14/15, 22, 61; formerly 7, 11.i, 31); A.W. Ambros, *Geschichte der Musik*, vol. II (1862–78, 1882); E. Droz and G. Thibault, eds., *Poètes et musiciens du XVe siècle* (1924); A. Schering, ed., *Geschichte der Musik in Beispielen* (Leipzig, 1931; reprinted N.Y., 1950); E. Droz, G. Thibault, and Y. Rokseth, eds., *Trois Chansonniers français du XVe siècle* (1927); H. Besseler, *Die Musik des Mittelalters und der Renaissance*, in Bücken's Handbuch series (1931); C. van den Borren, ed., *Polyphonia Sacra: A Continental Miscellany of the Fifteenth Century* (1932); O. Dischner, ed., *Kammermusik des Mittelalters. Chansons der 1. und 2. niederländischen Schule für drei bis vier Streichinstrumenten herausgegeben* (1927); A. Davison and W. Apel, eds., *Historical Anthology of Music*, vol. I (Cambridge, Mass., 1950); H.E. Wooldridge, *Oxford History of Music*, vol. II (1932); C. Parrish and J.F. Ohl, *Masterpieces of Music before 1750* (N.Y., 1951); G. de Van, "A Recently Discovered Source of Early Fifteenth Century Polyphonic Music, The Aosta Manuscript," *Musica Disciplina*, II (1948); J. Wolf, *Geschichte der Mensural-Notation von 1250–1460*, III (1904); J. Wolf, ed., *Music of Earlier Times* (1946); *Die Chansons von Gilles Binchois*, in *Musikalische Denkmäler*, 2.

BIBLIOGRAPHY: E. Closson, "L'Origine de Gilles Binchois," *Revue de Musicologie*, V (1924); A. Pirro, *Histoire de la musique de la fin du XIVe siècle à la fin du XVIe* (1940); Aurelio Gotti, *L'ars nova e il madrigale* in *Atti della Reale Accademia di Scienze, Lettere, e Arti di Palermo* (series IV, Vol. IV, Part II); W. Gurlitt in *Basler Kongressbericht* (1924); H. Funk, in *Acta musicologica*, IV; H. Riemann, *Handbuch der Musikgeschichte*, III; G. Reese, *Music in the Renaissance* (N.Y., 1954); M. Schuler, "Neues zur Biographie von Gilles Binchois," *Archiv für Musikwissenschaft*, XXIII (1976).

Binder, Abraham Wolfe, American composer and conductor; b. New York, Jan. 13, 1895; d. there, Oct. 10, 1966. He studied at Columbia Univ.; subsequently taught liturgical music at the Jewish Inst. of Religion, N.Y. He composed an opera, *A Goat in Chelm* (N.Y., March 20, 1960); a choral ballet, *Hora Vehodayah (Praise and Dance); The Legend of Ari* for Small Orch. (1963); and other symph. works on Jewish themes.

Binder, Christlieb Siegmund, German organist and composer; b. Dresden, July (baptized, July 29) 1723; d. there, Jan. 1, 1789. He was organist at the court church in Dresden from 1753; wrote prolifically, in an "elegant style" akin to that of C.P.E. Bach.

WORKS: Sonatas for harpsichord solo, and for harpsichord in various combinations with violin and cello; 76 organ preludes; harpsichord concertos; quartets with harpsichord; and trio sonatas for 2 violins with basso continuo. Some of his compositions have been reprinted by O. Schmid in *Musik am sächsischen Hofe.*

BIBLIOGRAPHY: H. Fleischer, *C.S. Binder* (Regensburg, 1941).

Binder, Karl, Austrian composer; b. Vienna, Nov. 29, 1816; d. there, Nov. 5, 1860. He was a theater conductor by profession; composed mostly for the stage: a melodrama, *Der Wiener Schusterhut* (1840); an opera, *Die Drei Wittfrauen* (1841); a vaudeville comedy, *Purzel* (1843); overture and choruses to the drama *Elmar;* a parody on *Tannhäuser* (1857).

Binenbaum, Janco, Bulgarian-French composer; b. Adrianopol, Dec. 28, 1880; d. Chevreuse (Seine-et-Oise), France, Feb. 4, 1956. He studied in Munich with Rheinberger and others; was active as a piano teacher in Germany and France, eventually settling in Chevreuse, where he remained until his death. He wrote a considerable amount of symph. and chamber music in an impressionistic vein, colored with Balkan rhythms, none of which was publ., and little ever performed. Nonetheless, Binenbaum found sincere admirers of his works, among whom M.D. Calvocoressi was the most vocal.

Binet, Jean, Swiss composer; b. Geneva, Oct. 17, 1893; d. Trélex, Feb. 24, 1960. He studied academic subjects at the Univ. of Geneva, and simultaneously obtained a diploma from the Institut Jaques-Dalcroze; then took lessons in musicology and composition with Otto Barblan, William Montillet, and Templeton Strong. In 1919 he went to America, where he organized the first school of Dalcroze eurhythmics, and also took lessons with Ernest Bloch. In 1921 he was instrumental in founding, with Bloch, the Cleveland Cons. In 1923 he returned to Europe, and lived in Brussels, where he taught the Dalcroze method. In 1929 he went back to Switzerland, and settled in Trélex. Many of his works are based on Swiss national folk songs. Binet's musical idiom is determined by pragmatic considerations of performance and does not transcend the natural borders of traditional harmonies.

WORKS: Primarily interested in the musical theater, he wrote 6 operettas and radiophonic cantatas; ballets; *L'Ile enchantée* (Zürich, 1947); *Le Printemps* (1950); *La Colline* for 5 Narrators and Orch. (1957); also several scores of incidental music for plays of Sophocles, Shakespeare, and contemporary writers. Other works include a number of sacred and secular choruses; songs with orch. accompaniment; String Quartet (1927); *Divertissement* for Violin and Orch. (1934); Sonatina for Flute and Piano (1942); *6 pièces* for Flute Solo (1947); *Petit concert* for Clarinet and String Orch. (1950); *Variations sur un chant de Noël* for Bassoon and Piano (1957); *3 Dialogues* for 2 Flutes (1957); educational pieces for piano; also harmonizations of popular melodies for chorus.

Bing, Sir Rudolf, international operatic impresario; b. Vienna, Jan. 9, 1902. He studied at the Univ. of Vienna; took singing lessons; then entered the managerial field in opera. After filling various positions with German agencies, he went to England in 1934; became a British subject in 1946. He was one of the most active organizers of the Edinburgh Festivals, and was their music director from 1947 to 1950. In 1950 he was appointed general manager of the Metropolitan Opera in N.Y., inaugurating one of the most eventful and, at times, turbulent periods in the history of the Metropolitan; his controversial dealings with prima donnas were legendary. He resigned in 1972; published an entertaining summary of his managerial experiences in a volume entitled *5,000 Nights at the Opera* (N.Y., 1972) and in his memoir, *A Knight at the Opera* (N.Y., 1981). In 1971 Queen Elizabeth II of England conferred on him the title of Knight Commander of the Order of the British Empire.

Binge, Ronald, English composer; b. Derby, July 15, 1910; d. Ringwood, Sept. 6, 1979. He earned a living by playing in cafés and theaters in London; then became an arranger for Mantovani; he also composed several works for brass instruments and *Saturday Symphony.*

Bingham, Seth, American organist and composer; b. Bloomfield, N.J., April 16, 1882; d. New York, June 21, 1972. He studied with Horatio Parker; later in Paris with d'Indy, Widor (composition), and Guilmant (organ). Returning to America, he graduated from Yale Univ. (B.A., 1904); took his M.B. at Yale in 1908, and taught there until 1919; was an instructor and associate prof. at Columbia Univ. until 1954.
WORKS: *Wall Street Fantasy* (1912; perf. as *Symphonic Fantasy* by the N.Y. Phil., Feb. 6, 1916); *La Charelzenn,* opera (1917); *Tame Animal Tunes* for 18 Instruments (1918); *Memories of France,* orch. suite (1920); *Wilderness Stone* for Narrator, Soli, Chorus, and Orch. (1933); Concerto for Organ and Orch. (Rochester, Oct. 24, 1946); *Connecticut Suite* for Organ and Strings (Hartford, March 26, 1954); Concerto for Brass, Snare Drum, and Organ (Minneapolis, July 12, 1954). Among his compositions for Organ, the following have been frequently performed: *Suite* (1926); *Pioneer America* (1928); *Harmonies of Florence* (1929); *Carillon de Château-Thierry* (1936); *Pastoral Psalms* (1938); *12 Hymn-Preludes* (1942); *Variation Studies* (1950); *36 Hymn and Carol Canons* (1952).

Bini, Pasquale, Italian violinist; b. Pesaro, June 21, 1716; d. there, April 1770. He studied with Tartini in Padua as a youth; then went to Rome, where he was, from 1738–47, in the service of Cardinal Acquaviva Troiano; then was active as a teacher and violinist in Pesaro. In 1754 he became director of concerts and chamber music at the court of the Duke of Württemberg. He returned to Pesaro about 1759. He left numerous compositions for the violin.

Binički, Stanislav, Yugoslav composer and conductor; b. Jasika, near Kruševca, July 27, 1872; d. Belgrade, Feb. 15, 1942. He studied at the Univ. of Belgrade; later took courses in composition with Rheinberger in Munich. Returning to Belgrade, he helped organize the Serbian School of Music; was also active as an opera conductor. He composed a number of incidental pieces for the theater; also the opera *Na uranku* (*Dawn;* Belgrade, Jan. 2, 1904), as well as choruses and songs.

Binkerd, Gordon, American composer and teacher; b. Lynch, Nebr., May 22, 1916. He studied piano in South Dakota; composition with Bernard Rogers at the Eastman School of Music in Rochester, N.Y., and with Walter Piston at Harvard Univ.; from 1949–71, was a member of the faculty of the Univ. of Illinois; received a Guggenheim fellowship in 1959.
WORKS: 4 symphs.: No. 1 (Univ. of Illinois, Urbana, March 20, 1955); No. 2 (Univ. of Illinois, Urbana, April 13, 1957); No. 3 (N.Y., Jan. 6, 1961); No. 4 (St. Louis, Oct. 12, 1963; dismembered and reduced to a *Movement for Orchestra*); *A Part of Heaven,* 2 romances for Violin and Orch. (1972); 2 string quartets (1956, 1961); Trio for Clarinet, Viola, and Cello (1955); Cello Sonata (1952); 3 songs for Mezzo-soprano and String Quartet; *Portrait Intérieur* for Mezzo-soprano, Violin, and Cello; Piano Sonata; *Entertainments* for Piano; numerous sacred choruses; songs.

Binns, Malcolm, English pianist; b. Gedling, Nottingham, Jan. 29, 1936. He studied at the Royal College of Music in London. He made his debut in London in 1957; subsequently appeared with the leading English orchs. and gave recitals. He taught piano at the Royal College of Music from 1962 to 1969.

Biordi, Giovanni, Italian composer; b. Rome, 1691; d. there, March 11, 1748. He was maestro di cappella at Tivoli Cathedral (1714–16); in 1717 he became a chapel singer to the Pope. He was named maestro di cappella at the church of S. Giacomo degli Spagnuoli in Rome in 1722, and remained in this post until his death. He also was a voice teacher at the Papal College from 1724; was named secretary (1730) and then chamberlain (1737) of the Sistine Chapel. He composed many sacred works.

Birchall, Robert, English music publisher; b. London, 1760; d. there, Dec. 19, 1819. He was the first to publ. Beethoven's works in England; letters from Beethoven to Birchall are found in Nohl's collection. The firm, which later became Birchall, Lonsdale & Mills, had one of the first circulating music libraries ever established.

Birchard, Clarence C., American music publisher; b. Cambridge Springs, Pa., July 13, 1866; d. Carlisle, Mass., Feb. 27, 1946. He established his firm in Boston in 1901 and specialized in educational books for public schools; of these, a 10-book series, *A Singing School,* introduced lavish profusion of color in design and illustration; the firm has also issued community songbooks, of which the most popular is *Twice 55 Community Songs* (several million copies sold). The catalogue includes orch. scores by many American composers (Berezowsky, Bloch, Converse, Hadley, Ives, Janssen, Josten, Kelley, Loeffler, Mason, Morris, Shepherd, and Sowerby); cantatas by Cadman, Converse, Hanson, Rogers, and Whithorne; and Copland's school opera, *Second Hurricane*. After Birchard's death, Thomas M. Moran succeeded to the presidency of the firm; after Moran's death in 1949, Donald F. Malin became president. The firm publishes a house organ, *The Birchard Broadsheet*.

Bird, Arthur, American composer; b. Belmont, Mass., July 23, 1856; d. Berlin, Dec. 22, 1923. He studied in Berlin with Loeschhorn; spent several months with Liszt at Weimar in 1885; returned to America briefly in 1886, and then lived in Berlin, identifying himself with conservative circles there. He was the Berlin correspondent for American music magazines; in his articles he violently attacked Richard Strauss and other modern composers. Among his own works is a Symph.; *2 Decimettes* for Wind Instruments (won a Paderewski prize in 1901); a comic opera, *Daphne* (N.Y., Dec. 13, 1897); and many piano pieces.
BIBLIOGRAPHY: W.L. Loring, "Arthur Bird, American Composer," *Musical Quarterly* (Jan. 1943).

Bird, Henry Richard, eminent English organist; b. Walthamstow, Nov. 14, 1842; d. London, Nov. 21, 1915. He was a pupil of his father; then studied with James Turle; came to London in 1859, where he held various positions as organist, and conducted the Chelsea Choral and Orch. Society; was appointed organist at St. Mary Abbott's in Kensington, and occupied this post until his death; was also a prof. of piano at the Royal College of Music and at Trinity College from 1896. He was famous throughout England as an unexcelled accompanist, and was in constant demand by the foremost artists.

Biriotti, León, Uruguayan conductor and composer; b. Montevideo, Dec. 1, 1929. He studied oboe, theory, and musicology; began to conduct experimentally without preliminary training; founded a string orch. in Montevideo; conducted the instrumental group Juventudes Musicales of Uruguay.
WORKS: 3 symphs. (1964, 1965, 1968); *Suite* for Violin and Cello (1952); String Sextet (1957); Trio for Oboe, Clarinet, and Bassoon (1963); String Quartet (1965); Violin Sonata (1967); songs and piano pieces.

Biriukov, Yuri, Russian composer; b. Moscow, April 1, 1908; d. there, Nov. 1, 1976. He studied piano with Feinberg and composition with Miaskovsky at the Moscow Cons., graduating in 1936. Among his works are two operas, *Peasant Gentlewoman* (after Pushkin, 1947) and *Knight of the Golden Star* (1956); a ballet, *The Cosmonauts* (1962); a musical, *The Blue Express* (1971); a symph. on Ingush themes (1968); 3 piano concertos (1941, 1945, 1970); 24 preludes and 4 toccatas for Piano; and much music for the theater and the cinema.

Birkenstock, Johann Adam, German violinist and composer; b. Alsfeld, Feb. 19, 1687; d. Eisenach, Feb.

26, 1733. He studied in Kassel with Ruggiero Fedeli; then in Berlin with Volumier and in Bayreuth with Fiorelli; was employed in the Kassel Court Orch. (1709–30); in 1730 went to Eisenach, where he served as Kapellmeister. His sonatas for violin with basso continuo (Amsterdam, 1722) are included in several anthologies.

Birnbach, Heinrich, German pianist and music pedagogue, son of **Karl Joseph Birnbach;** b. Breslau, Jan. 8, 1793; d. Berlin, Aug. 24, 1879. He studied piano with his father; taught in Breslau from 1814–21; settled in Berlin as a music teacher and founded a music institute. Among his pupils were Nicolai, Kücken, and Dehn. He composed 2 symphs.; 2 overtures; concertos for oboe, clarinet, and guitar; piano concertos; a Piano Quirtet; piano sonatas; piano duos; etc.; also publ. a treatise, *Der vollkommene Kapellmeister* (1845).

Birnbach, Karl Joseph, German composer; b. Köpernick, Silesia, 1751; d. Warsaw, May 29, 1805. During the last years of his life he was conductor at the German Theater in Warsaw. A prolific composer, he wrote 2 operas, 10 symphs., 16 piano concertos, 10 violin concertos, cantatas, masses, chamber music, piano pieces.

Birnie, Tessa, New Zealand pianist and conductor; b. Ashburton, July 19, 1934. She studied piano with Paul Schramm in Wellington; then went to Europe and took lessons with Lefebure in Paris and K.U. Schnabel in Como; subsequently toured as a pianist in Australia and Asia; also played in the U.S. She organized the Sydney Camerata Orch. in 1963, appearing with it as both pianist and conductor.

Birtner, Herbert, German musicologist; b. Hamburg, June 16, 1900; d. in battle at Voronezh, Russia, Sept. 27, 1942. He first studied medicine; then took courses in musicology with Gurlitt and Kroyer; was an assistant lecturer at the Univ. of Leipzig (1924–28); a prof. at the Univ. of Marburg (1938–40). In 1940 he was drafted into the German army and was killed on the Russian front. He contributed important studies on the music of the Reformation; his publ. works include *Joachim à Burck als Motettenkomponist* (Leipzig, 1924) and *Studien zur niederländisch-humanistischen Musikanschauung* (Marburg, 1929).

Birtwistle, Harrison, noted English composer; b. Accrington, Lancashire, July 15, 1934. He studied clarinet; won a scholarship in 1952 to the Royal Manchester College of Music, where he studied composition; also studied clarinet playing with Kell at the Royal Academy of Music in London. In 1966 he was visiting prof. at Princeton Univ.; in 1975 he became music director at the National Theatre, South Bank, London. In his compositions he departed completely from the folkloric trends popular in British modern music and adopted an abstract idiom, often with satirical overtones in his stage works.

WORKS: *Refrains and Choruses* for Wind Quintet (1957); *Monody for Corpus Christi* for Soprano Solo, Flute, Violin, and Horn (1959); *Précis* for Piano Solo (1959); *The World Is Discovered,* Instrumental motet (1960; Festival of the International Society for Contemporary Music, Copenhagen, June 2, 1964); *Chorales* for Orch. (1963); *Narration: The Description of the Passing of a Year* for a cappella Choir (1964); *3 Movements with Fanfares* for Chamber Orch. (1964); *Ring a Dumb Carillon* for Soprano, Clarinet, and Percussion (1965); *Verses* for Clarinet and Piano (1965); *Tragoedia* for Wind Quintet, Harp, and String Quartet (1965); *Carmen paschale* for Chorus and Organ (1965); *The Visions of Francesco Petrarca,* 7 sonnets for Baritone, Chamber Ensemble, and School Orch. (1966); *Punch and Judy,* chamber opera (1966–67; Aldeburgh Festival, June 8, 1968; revised version, London, March 3, 1970); *Monodrama* for Speaker and Instrumental Ensemble (London, May 30, 1967); *Nomos* for 4 Amplified Wind Instruments and Orch. (London, Aug. 23, 1968); *Linoi* for Clarinet and Piano (1968); *Down by the Greenwood Side,* dramatic pastorale (1968; Brighton, May 8, 1969); *Medusa* for Chamber Orch. and Percussion (London, Oct. 22, 1969; revised version, London, March 3, 1970); *4 Interludes* for Clarinet and Pre-recorded Tape (1970); *Verses and Ensembles* for 12 Players (London, Aug. 31, 1970); *Nenia on the Death of Orpheus* for Soprano and Instrumental Ensemble (1970); *The Triumph of Time* for Orch., after a painting of Breughel (1970; London, June 1, 1972); *Meridian* for Mezzo-soprano, Chorus, and an Instrumental Ensemble (1971); *Prologue to Agamemnon* by Aeschylus, for Tenor, Bassoon, Horn, 3 Trumpets, Trombone, Violin, and Double Bass (1971); *Chronometer* for 8-track Electronic Tapes (1971); *The Fields of Sorrow* for 2 Sopranos, Mixed Choir, and Instrumental Ensemble (1971); *An Imaginary Landscape* for Brass, Percussion, and 8 Double Basses (1971); *Epilogue: Full Fathom Five* for Tenor, Brass, and Percussion (1972); *La Plage,* 8 Arias of Remembrance for Soprano, 3 Clarinets, Piano, and Marimba (1972); *Tombeau,* in memory of Stravinsky (1972); *Grimethorpe Aria* for Brass Band (1973); *Orpheus,* opera (1974–77); *Melancholia I* for Clarinet, Harp, and 2 String Orchs. (1976); *Silbury Air* for Woodwind Quartet, Trumpet, Horn, Trombone, String Quintet, Piano, Harp, and Percussion (1977); *Frames, Pulses and Interruptions,* ballet (1977); *Bow Down,* musical theater (London, July 4, 1977); *For O, for O the Hobby Horse Is Forgot* for 6 Percussion Players (1977); *Carmen Arcadiae Mechanicae Perpetuum* for Instrumental Ensemble (1977); *Aventures des Mercures* for Instrumental Ensemble (1980); *On the Sheer Threshold of the Night,* madrigal (1980).

Bisaccia, Giovanni, Italian singer and composer; b. 1815; d. Naples, Dec. 20, 1897. He studied singing with Crescentini and composition with Raimondi and Donizetti; sang in the Nuovo and San Carlo theaters; later taught singing, and was maestro di cappella at the church of San Fernando, for which he wrote some music. In 1838 he brought out 2 musical farces, *I tre scioperati* and *Il figlio adottivo;* and in 1858, an opera buffa, *Don Taddeo.*

Bischoff, Georg Friedrich, German music director; b. Ellrich, Harz Mountains, Sept. 21, 1780; d. Hildesheim, Sept. 7, 1841. He was music director at Hildesheim from 1816; arranged the first Thuringian Festival at Frankenhausen (July 20 and 21, 1810), at which Spohr acted as both conductor and violin soloist.

Bischoff, Hans, German pianist and teacher; b. Berlin, Feb. 17, 1852; d. Niederschönhausen, near Berlin, June 12, 1889. He was a pupil of Theodor Kullak and Richard Wüerst; also studied at Berlin Univ. (Dr.Phil., 1873); taught piano at Kullak's Academy from 1873; conducted Monday Concerts of the Berlin Singakademie. He edited the 2nd and 3rd editions of Adolf Kullak's *Ästhetik des Klavierspiels* (Berlin, 1876 and 1889; Eng. trans., N.Y., 1895); also publ. *Auswahl Händel'scher Klavierwerke; Kritische Ausgabe von J.S. Bachs Klavierwerken;* etc.
BIBLIOGRAPHY: O. Stieglitz, *Dr. Hans Bischoff: Ein Lebensbild* (Berlin, 1889).

Bischoff, Hermann, German composer; b. Duisburg, Jan. 7, 1868; d. Berlin, Jan. 25, 1936. He was a pupil of Jadassohn at the Leipzig Cons.; lived for a time in Munich, where he was associated with Richard Strauss; then went to Berlin. He composed 2 symphs.; the First Symph. had its world premiere in Essen, May 24, 1906; was given by the Boston Symph. under Karl Muck twice in one season (Jan. 4, 1908, and Feb. 29, 1908); attracted a great deal of attention at the time, but sank into oblivion later on. He also composed the symph. poems *Pan* and *Gewittersegen;* publ. an essay, *Das deutsche Lied* (1905).

Bischoff, Kaspar Jakob, German composer and teacher; b. Ansbach, April 7, 1823; d. Munich, Oct. 26, 1893. He was a pupil of Franz Lachner in Munich (1842); studied in Leipzig (1848); settled in Frankfurt, where he taught singing, and founded an Evangelical Sacred Choral Society in 1850. He wrote an opera, *Maske und Mantilla* (Frankfurt, 1852); 3 symphs.; overture to *Hamlet;* chamber music; church music; also publ. a manual of harmony (1890).

Bischoff, Ludwig Friedrich Christian, German editor of music periodicals; b. Dessau, Nov. 27, 1794; d. Cologne, Feb. 24, 1867. He was a teacher at Wesel (1823–49); then settled in Cologne, where he founded and edited the *Rheinische Musikzeitung* (1850) and the *Niederrheinische Musikzeitung* (1853).

Bischoff, Marie. See **Brandt, Marianne.**

Bishop, Anna, English soprano; b. London, Jan. 9, 1810; d. New York, March 18, 1884. She was of

French descent (her maiden name was **Rivière**). She studied at the Royal Academy of Music in London; in 1831 she married **Henry Bishop.** She made her London debut on April 20, 1831. In 1839 she appeared in concerts with the French harpist Bochsa, with whom she apparently became intimate. In 1847 she went to America; she obtained a divorce in 1858 and married Martin Schultz. In 1866 she toured China and Australia; the ship she was on became grounded on a coral reef in the Marianas for 21 days, but despite this experience she completed her tour, eventually returning to N.Y.

Bishop, Sir Henry Rowley, noted English composer; b. London, Nov. 18, 1786; d. there, April 30, 1855. He was a pupil of Francesco Bianchi; attracted attention with his first opera, *The Circassian Bride* (Drury Lane, Feb. 23, 1809); from 1810–24, was conductor at Covent Garden; in 1813 was alternate conductor of the Phil.; in 1819 oratorio conductor at Covent Garden; in 1825 conductor at the Drury Lane Theatre; in 1830 music director at Vauxhall; took the degree of B.Mus. at Oxford (1839); from 1840 was music director at Covent Garden; then prof. of music at Edinburgh (1841–43); was knighted in 1842; conducted the Concerts of Antient Music in 1840–48; was then appointed (succeeding Dr. Crotch) prof. of music at Oxford, where he received the degree of D.Mus. in 1853. He was a remarkably prolific dramatic composer, having produced about 130 operas, farces, ballets, adaptations, etc. His operas are generally in the style of English ballad opera; some of the best are: *Cortez, or The Conquest of Mexico* (1823); *The Fall of Algiers* (1825); *The Knight of Snowdoun* (after Walter Scott, 1811); *Native Land* (1824). His *Clari, or The Maid of Milan* (Covent Garden, May 3, 1823) contains the famous song *Home Sweet Home,* with text by the American John Howard Payne; it appears repeatedly throughout the opera. The tune, previously publ. by Bishop to other words, was thought to have been of Sicilian origin, but after much litigation was accepted as Bishop's original composition (the MS is owned by the Univ. of Rochester in N.Y.). A version of the melody was used by Donizetti in his opera *Anne Boleyn,* giving rise to the erroneous belief that Donizetti was its composer. Bishop also wrote an oratorio, *The Fallen Angel;* a cantata, *The Seventh Day* (1834); many additions to revivals of older operas, etc.; his glees and other lyric vocal compositions are deservedly esteemed. Bishop also publ. vol. I of *Melodies of Various Nations;* and 3 vols. of *National Melodies,* to which Moore wrote the poems.
BIBLIOGRAPHY: F. Corder, "The Works of Sir Henry Bishop," *Musical Quarterly* (Jan. 1918); R. Northcott, *The Life of Sir Henry R. Bishop* (London, 1920).

Bishop-Kovacevich, Stephen, American pianist; b. Los Angeles, Oct. 17, 1940. He studied with Dame Myra Hess in London. His first public appearance came in 1951 in San Francisco. He made his London debut in 1961.

Bismillah Khan, Indian virtuoso on the shehnai; b. Dumraon, March 21, 1916. He studied instrumental and vocal music; earned great renown in India; appeared as soloist at the Commonwealth Arts Festival in London in 1965.

Bispham, David (Scull), American baritone; b. Philadelphia, Jan. 5, 1857; d. New York, Oct. 2, 1921. He first sang as an amateur in church choruses in Philadelphia; in 1886 went to Milan, where he studied with Vannuccini, and Francesco Lamperti; later studied in London with Shakespeare and Randegger; made his operatic debut as Longueville in Messager's *Basoche* (English Opera House, London, Nov. 3, 1891), in which his comic acting ability, as well as his singing, won praise; made his first appearance in serious opera as Kurwenal in *Tristan und Isolde* (Drury Lane, June 25, 1892). He was particularly effective in the Wagnerian baritone roles; made his American debut with the Metropolitan Opera as Beckmesser (Nov. 18, 1896); was on the Metropolitan roster 1896–97, 1898–99, and 1900–1903. He was a strong advocate of opera in English; a Society of American Singers was organized under his guidance, presenting light operas in the English language. He publ. an autobiography, *A Quaker Singer's Recollections* (N.Y., 1920). A Bispham Memorial Medal Award was established by the Opera Society of America in 1921 for an opera in English by an American composer; among its winners were Walter Damrosch, Victor Herbert, Henry Hadley, Deems Taylor, Charles Cadman, Louis Gruenberg, Howard Hanson, Otto Luening, Ernst Bacon, George Antheil, and George Gershwin. Bispham left all the biographical and bibliographical material connected with his career to the Music Division of the N.Y. Public Library.

Bissell, Keith, Canadian composer; b. Meaford, Ontario, Feb. 12, 1912. He studied composition with Leo Smith at the Univ. of Toronto, graduating in 1942; took some instruction in Munich with Carl Orff (1960) and was instrumental in introducing the Orff method of elementary music education to Scarborough (borough of Toronto), where he was chief coordinator of music for public schools (1955–76). A great believer in the propagation of music among semi-professionals, he composed works specifically designed for amateur performance.
WORKS: 2 operettas: *Rumpelstiltzkin* (1947) and *His Majesty's Pie* (1966); *3 Pieces* for String Orch. (1960); *Little Suite* for Trumpet and Strings (1962); Concertino for Piano and Strings (1963); *5 Dances* for Small Orch. (1963); Divertimento for String Orch. (1964); *Canada 1967* for Orch. (1967); *A Bluebird in March* for Chorus, and Orch. or Piano (1967); *Christmas in Canada* for Narrator, Soli, Chorus, and Orch. (1967); *Passion According to St. Luke* for Soli, Chorus, Children's Chorus, and Orch. (Toronto, April 9, 1971); *Andante e Scherzo* for Small Orch. (1971); *Variations on a Canadian Folksong* for String Orch. (1972); *Theme, Variation and Epilogue* for Chorus, Solo Viola, and String Orch. (1975); *God's Grandeur* for Chorus and Orch. (1975);

Andante and Allegro for Oboe and Strings (1976); *In Praise of Famous Men* for Soprano, Chorus, Organ, Brass Quintet, and String Orch. (Toronto, June 1, 1976); *Cantata Domino* for Female Chorus and Chamber Orch. (1977); Piano Sonata (1947); Violin Sonata (1948); Organ Sonata (1963); Serenade for Wind Quintet (1972); *Trio Suite* for Trumpet, Horn, and Trombone (1973); choruses; songs.

Bitetti (Ravina), Ernesto, Argentine guitarist; b. Rosario, July 20, 1943. He studied guitar in Santa Fe; made his debut in Rosario in 1958; then toured in the U.S., Europe, the Middle East, and the Orient. Several composers wrote guitar pieces especially for him.

Bitsch, Marcel, French composer; b. Paris, Dec. 29, 1921. He entered the Paris Cons. in 1939, studied composition with Busser, and won the second Prix de Rome, 1943; first Prix de Rome, 1945. He has written *6 Esquisses symphoniques* (1949); *Sinfonietta* (1950); cantata, *La Farce du Contrebandier* (1946); *Divertissement* for Flute, Clarinet, Oboe, and Bassoon (1947); *3 Sonatinas* for Flute and Piano (1952); Concertino for Piano and Orch. (Paris, Nov. 28, 1954); etc.

Bitter, Carl Hermann, German writer on music; b. Schwedt-an-der-Oder, Feb. 27, 1813; d. Berlin, Sept. 12, 1885. He studied at the Univ. of Berlin and at Bonn Univ.; pursued a career in government; served in the finance dept.; in 1879 he was appointed Prussian Minister of Finance by Bismarck. He retired in 1882. He publ. a book on Bach in 2 vols. (Berlin, 1865; revised ed., 1881; abridged Eng. ed., 1873). Other books: *Mozarts Don Juan und Glucks Iphigenie* (Berlin, 1866); *C.Ph.E. Bach und W.Fr. Bach und deren Brüder* (2 vols., Berlin, 1868); *Beiträge zur Geschichte der Oper* (1872); *Die Reform der Oper durch Gluck und Wagner* (1884).

Bittner, Albert, German conductor; b. Nuremberg, Sept. 27, 1900; d. Hamburg, Aug. 7, 1980. He studied at the Cons. of Nuremberg; was then active primarily as a theater conductor, at Gera, Berlin, Graz (1923–36), Oldenburg (1933–36), Essen (1936–43), Hamburg (1943–45), Braunschweig (1945–55), and then again in Hamburg as principal conductor of the Hamburg State Opera (1955–65). In 1965 he was appointed prof. at the Hamburg Musikhochschule.

Bittner, Julius, Austrian composer; b. Vienna, April 9, 1874; d. there, Jan. 9, 1939. He first studied law; then music with Bruno Walter and Josef Labor; was a magistrate in Vienna until 1920. At the same time he composed industriously. He devoted most of his energy to opera and also wrote his own librettos; composed 2 symphs., sacred choruses, and numerous songs for his wife, Emilie Bittner, a contralto. During his last years, he suffered from a crippling illness, necessitating the amputation of both legs. WORKS: Operas: *Die rote Gret* (Frankfurt, Oct. 26, 1907); *Der Musikant* (Vienna, April 12, 1910); *Der Bergsee* (Vienna, Nov. 9, 1911; revised 1938); *Der Abenteurer* (Cologne, Oct. 30, 1913); *Das höllisch Gold* (Darmstadt, Oct. 15, 1916); *Das Rosengärtlein* (Mannheim, March 18, 1923); *Mondnacht* (Berlin, Nov. 13, 1928); *Das Veilchen* (Vienna, Dec. 8, 1934); also operettas, ballets, and mimodramas.

BIBLIOGRAPHY: R. Specht, *Julius Bittner* (Munich, 1921); Ullrich Bittner, *Julius Bittner* (Vienna, 1969).

Bittoni, Bernardo, Italian organist, violinist, and composer; b. Fabriano, Aug. 20, 1756; d. there, May 18, 1829. He studied with his father, **Mario Gaetano Bittoni,** maestro di cappella of the Fabriano Cathedral. In 1779 he became maestro di cappella at the Rieti Cathedral; also served as organist at the Fabriano Cathedral. He wrote mostly church music.

Bizet, Georges (baptismal names, **Alexandre-César-Léopold**), great French opera composer; b. Paris, Oct. 25, 1838; d. Bougival, June 3, 1875. His parents were both professional musicians: his father, a singing teacher and composer; his mother, an excellent pianist. Bizet's talent developed early in childhood; at the age of 9 he entered the Paris Cons., his teachers being Marmontel (piano), Benoist (organ), Zimmermann (harmony), and (for composition), Halévy, whose daughter, Geneviève, married Bizet in 1869. In 1852 he won a first prize for piano, in 1855 for organ and for fugue, and in 1857 the Grand Prix de Rome. In the same year he shared (with Lecocq) a prize offered by Offenbach for a setting of a one-act opera, *Le Docteur miracle;* Bizet's setting was produced at the Bouffes-Parisiens on April 9, 1857. Instead of the prescribed Mass, he sent from Rome during his first year a 2-act Italian opera buffa, *Don Procopio* (not produced until March 10, 1906, when it was given in Monte Carlo in an incongruously edited version); later he sent 2 movements of a symph., an overture (*La Chasse d'Ossian*), and a one-act opera (*La Guzla de l'Emir;* accepted by the Paris Opéra-Comique, but withdrawn by Bizet prior to production). Returning to Paris, he produced a grand opera, *Les Pêcheurs de perles* (Théâtre-Lyrique, Sept. 30, 1863); but this work, like *La Jolie Fille de Perth* (Dec. 26, 1867), failed to win popular approval. A one-act opera, *Djamileh* (Opéra-Comique, May 22, 1872), fared no better. Bizet's incidental music for Daudet's play *L'Arlésienne* (Oct. 1, 1872) was ignored by the audiences and literary critics; it was not fully appreciated until its revival in 1885. But an orch. suite from *L'Arlésienne* brought out by Pasdeloup (Nov. 10, 1872) was acclaimed; a 2nd suite was made by Guiraud after Bizet's death. Bizet's next major work was his masterpiece, *Carmen* (based on a tale by Mérimée, text by Halévy and Meilhac), produced, after many difficulties with the management and the cast, at the Opéra-Comique (March 3, 1875). The reception of the public was not enthusiastic, and several critics attacked the opera for its lurid subject, and the music for its supposed adoption of Wagner's methods. Bizet received a generous sum (25,000 francs) for the score from the publisher Choudens and won other honors (he was named a Chevalier of the Légion d'Honneur on the eve of the premiere of *Carmen*); although the attendance was not high, the opera was maintained in the repertoire. There were 37 performances before the end of the season; the original cast included Galli-Marié as Carmen, Lhérie as Don José, and Bouhy as Escamillo. Bizet was chagrined by the controversial reception of the opera, but it is a melodramatic invention to state (as some biographers have done) that the alleged failure of *Carmen* precipitated the composer's death (he died on the night of the 31st perf. of the opera). Soon *Carmen* became a triumphant success all over the world; it was staged in London (in Italian at Her Majesty's Theatre, June 22, 1878), St. Petersburg, Vienna, Brussels, Naples, Florence, Mainz, N.Y. (Academy of Music, Oct. 23, 1878), etc. The Metropolitan Opera produced *Carmen* first in Italian (Jan. 9, 1884), then in French, with Calvé as Carmen (Dec. 20, 1893). It should be pointed out that the famous *Habanera* is not Bizet's own, but a melody by the Spanish composer Yradier; Bizet inserted it in *Carmen* (with slight alterations), mistaking it for a folk song. Bizet also wrote an operetta, *La Prêtresse* (1854); the operas *Numa* (1871) and *Ivan le Terrible*, in 4 acts (Bordeaux, Oct. 12, 1951; the score was believed to have been destroyed by Bizet, but was discovered among the manuscripts bequeathed to the Paris Cons. by the 2nd husband of Bizet's widow); the cantatas *David* (1856) and *Clovis et Clothilde* (1857); *Vasco da Gama,* symph. ode with Chorus (1859); *Souvenirs de Rome,* symph. suite in 3 movements (Paris, Feb. 28, 1869; publ. in 1880 as a 4-movement suite, *Roma*); orch. overture, *Patrie* (Paris, Feb. 15, 1874); *Jeux d'enfants* (suite for Piano, 4-hands); about 150 piano pieces of all kinds (Bizet was a brilliant pianist); etc. Bizet's First Symph., written at the age of 17, was discovered in the Bizet collection at the Paris Cons. in 1933, and was given its first performance anywhere by Felix Weingartner in Basel on Feb. 26, 1935; it rapidly became popular in the concert repertoire. Bizet also completed Halévy's biblical opera, *Noë* (1869).

BIBLIOGRAPHY: E. Galabert, *Georges Bizet* (Paris, 1877); Ch. Pigot, *Bizet et son œuvre* (1886; new ed., 1911); C. Bellaigue, *Bizet* (1891); P. Voss, *Bizet* (Leipzig, 1899); A. Weissmann, *Bizet* (Berlin, 1907); O. Séré, "Georges Bizet," in *Musiciens français d'aujourd'hui* (Paris, 1911); H. Gauthier-Villars, *Bizet; Biographie critique* (Paris, 1911); R. Brancour, *La Vie et l'œuvre de Bizet* (Paris, 1913); P. Landormy, "Bizet," in *Les Maîtres de la musique* (1924); Julius Rabe, *Bizet* (Stockholm, 1925); D.C. Parker, *Bizet, His Life and Works* (London, 1926); E. Istel, *Bizet und Carmen* (Stuttgart, 1927); J. Tiersot, "Bizet and Spanish Music," *Musical Quarterly* (Oct. 1925); J.W. Klein, "Nietzsche and Bizet," *Musical Quarterly* (Oct. 1925); M. Delmas, *Bizet* (1930); R. Laparra, *Bizet et l'Espagne* (Paris, 1934); Bizet issue of the *Revue de Musicologie* (Nov. 1938); M. Cooper, *Bizet* (London, 1938); W. Dean, *Georges Bizet: His Life and Work* (London, 1948; 3rd ed., 1975); Mina Curtiss, "Unpublished Letters by Georges Bizet," *Musical Quarterly* (July 1950); Mina Curtiss, *Bizet and His World* (N.Y., 1958).

Bjelinski, Bruno, Croatian composer; b. Trieste, Nov. 1, 1909. He studied law at the Univ. of Zagreb and music at the Cons. there; in 1945 he joined the faculty of the Cons. His music is marked by romantic coloring, often related to literary subjects.
WORKS: *Simfonija Ljeta (Summer Symphony;* Zagreb, Oct. 15, 1956); Symph. No. 2, *In Memoriam Poetae,* with Children's Chorus (1961); Symph. No. 3 (1964); Symph. No. 4 (1965); Symph. No. 5 (1969); Serenade for Trumpet, Piano, Strings, and Percussion (1957); *Mediterranean Sinfonietta* (Zagreb, Dec. 9, 1959); *Sinfonietta brasileira* (1961); operatic fairy tale, *Pčelica Maja (Maya the Bee;* 1952); *Sinfonietta concertante* (1967); Concertino for Horn and Orch. (1967); Clarinet Sonata (1966); several song cycles; piano pieces.
BIBLIOGRAPHY: K. Kovačević, *Hrvatski Kompozitori i Njihova Djela* (Zagreb, 1960).

Bjerre, Jens, Danish organist and composer; b. Aarhus, Oct. 13, 1903. He studied piano, organ, and theory at the Copenhagen Cons.; then went to Paris, where he took piano lessons with Lévy. Returning to Copenhagen in 1933, he became organist at the St. Stefanskirke; from 1955–72 he served as organist at the Garnisonskirke. He composed much music for the organ.

Bjoner, Ingrid, Norwegian soprano; b. Krakstad, Nov. 8, 1927. She studied at the Oslo Cons. and at the Hochschule für Musik in Frankfurt; made her opera debut as Donna Anna in Mozart's *Don Giovanni* at the Oslo Opera in 1957. She then sang at the Wuppertal Opera (1959–61). On Oct. 28, 1961, she made her American debut at the Metropolitan Opera in N.Y. as Elsa in *Lohengrin.* She distinguished herself as a Wagnerian singer at the Bayreuth Festivals.

Björkander, Nils (Frank Frederik), Swedish composer; b. Stockholm, June 28, 1893; d. Soedertälje, March 5, 1972. He studied at the Stockholm Cons.; in 1917 he established a music school of his own. Some of his piano pieces achieved considerable popularity, especially *Fyra Skärgårdsskisser (4 Sketches from the Skerries;* 1923); he also wrote *Concert-Fantasy* for Piano and Orch.; *Cavatina* for Violin and Orch.; Piano Quintet; Flute Sonata; Violin Sonata; etc.

Björlin, Ulf, Swedish conductor and composer; b. Stockholm, May 21, 1933. He studied conducting in Salzburg with Igor Markevitch and in Paris with Nadia Boulanger; from 1963–68 he was director of the Royal Dramatic Theater in Stockholm. He has written music mainly for the theater.
WORKS: *Pinocchio,* children's musical for Chamber Orch. (1966); *Ekon* for Orch. (1967); *Om fem år (In Five Years),* after García Lorca, opera for Actors and Chamber Ensemble (Stockholm, Oct. 27, 1967); *Epitaph for Lars Görling* for Orch. (1967); *Aft vaemod (Of Melancholy),* choreographic oratorio (1970); opera, *Den stora teatern (The Big Theater;* Göteborg, Feb. 25, 1972); short opera, *Balladen om*

Kasper Rosenröd, for Soli and Chamber Ensemble (Vålberg-Karlstad, Nov. 15, 1972); *Mandala* for Orch. (1974).

Björling, Jussi (baptismal names, **Johan Jonatan**), eminent Swedish tenor; b. Stora Tuna, Feb. 5, 1911; d. Siarö, near Stockholm, Sept. 9, 1960. He studied singing with his father, a professional singer; made his first public appearance in 1916 as a member of the vocal Björling Male Quartet, which included his father, David Björling (1873–26), and two other brothers, Johan Olof "Olle" (1909–65) and Karl Gustaf "Gösta" (1912–57), both of whom pursued careers as singers; another brother, Karl David "Kalle" (1917–75), was also a singer. The Björling Male Quartet gave concerts throughout Sweden (1916–19); made an extensive tour of the U.S. (1919–21); then continued to sing in Sweden until 1926. Jussi Björling had an excellent professional training with John Forsell at the Royal Academy of Music in Stockholm. He made his operatic debut as the Lamplighter in *Manon Lescaut* at the Royal Theater in Stockholm on July 21, 1930, and remained there until 1939; also sang as a guest artist with the Vienna State Opera, the Dresden State Opera, and at the Salzburg Festival. He made his professional U.S. debut in a concert broadcast from Carnegie Hall in N.Y. on Nov. 28, 1937, and his first appearance with the Metropolitan Opera as Rodolfo in *La Bohème* on Nov. 24, 1938; continued to sing there until 1941, when his career was interrupted by war. He resumed his appearances at the Metropolitan Opera in 1945 and sang there until 1954, and then again in 1956–57 and 1959. On March 15, 1960, he suffered a heart attack as he was preparing to sing the role of Rodolfo at the Royal Opera House, Covent Garden, London, but in spite of his great discomfort, went through with the performance. He appeared for the last time at a concert in Stockholm on Aug. 20, 1960. Björling was highly regarded for his fine vocal technique and his sense of style. He excelled in the Italian and French roles, and also essayed some Russian operas. He wrote an autobiography, *Med bagaget i strupen* (Stockholm, 1945). The Jussi Björling Memorial Archive was founded in 1968 to perpetuate his memory.

BIBLIOGRAPHY: J. Porter and H. Henrysson, *A Jussi Björling Discography* (a comprehensive discography with a biographical profile of his life; Indianapolis, 1982).

Björling, Sigurd, Swedish baritone; b. Stockholm, Nov. 2, 1907; d. Helsingborg, April 8, 1983. He studied at the Royal Cons. in Stockholm, made his debut in 1930 at the Royal Theater there; also had guest appearances at La Scala in Milan, Covent Garden in London, and in Paris. In 1951 he sang at the Bayreuth Festival; on Nov. 15, 1952, he made his Metropolitan Opera debut in N.Y. as Telramund in *Lohengrin;* then returned to Sweden. He was no relation to his famous namesake Jussi Björling.

Björnsson, Árni, Icelandic composer; b. Loni i Kelduhverfi, Dec. 23, 1905. He studied theory, composition, piano, and organ at the Reykjavik College of Music; later went to England, where he enrolled at the Royal Manchester College of Music; subsequently returned to Reykjavik, where he was appointed to the faculty of the College of Music. He composed orch. pieces and much choral music in a general Romantic vein.

Blacher, Boris, remarkable German composer; b. Newchwang, China (of half-German, quarter-Russian, and quarter-Jewish ancestry), Jan. 19 (Jan. 6 according to the Russian old-style calendar), 1903; d. Berlin, Jan. 30, 1975. His family moved to Irkutsk, Siberia, in 1914, remaining there until 1920. In 1922 Blacher went to Berlin; studied architecture, and then took a course in composition with F.E. Koch. From 1948 until 1970 he was prof. at the Hochschule für Musik in West Berlin, and from 1953 to 1970 served as its director. An exceptionally prolific composer, Blacher was equally adept in classical forms and in experimental procedures. He initiated a system of "variable meters," with time signatures following the arithmetical progression, alternatively increasing and decreasing, with permutations contributing to metrical variety. For the theater he developed a sui generis "abstract opera," incorporating an element of organized improvisation. In 1960 he was appointed director of the Seminar of Electronic Composition at the Technological Univ. in Berlin, and subsequently made ample use of electronic resources in his own compositions.

WORKS: OPERAS: *Habemeajaja* (1929; not extant); *Fürstin Tarakanowa* (1940; Wuppertal, Feb. 5, 1941); *Romeo und Julia,* after Shakespeare (1943; Berlin Radio, 1947); *Die Flut* (1946; Berlin Radio, Dec. 20, 1946; stage premiere, Dresden, March 4, 1947); *Die Nachtschwalbe (The Night Swallow),* "dramatic nocturne" (Leipzig, Feb. 22, 1948; aroused considerable commotion because of its subject, dealing with prostitutes and pimps); *Preussisches Märchen,* ballet-opera (1949; Berlin, Sept. 23, 1952); *Abstrakte Oper* No. 1 (text by Werner Egk, 1953; Frankfurt Radio, June 28, 1953; stage premiere, Mannheim, Oct. 17, 1953; revised version, Berlin, Sept. 30, 1957); *Rosamunde Floris* (1960; Berlin, Sept. 21, 1960); *Zwischenfälle bie einer Notlandung (Incidents at a Forced Landing),* "reportage in 2 phases and 14 situations" for Singers, Instruments, and Electronic Devices (1965; Hamburg, Feb. 4, 1966); *200,000 Taler,* after Sholom Aleichem (1969; Berlin, Sept. 25, 1969); *Yvonne, Prinzessin von Burgund* (1972; Wuppertal, Sept. 15, 1973); *Das Geheimnis des entwendeten Briefes,* after *The Purloined Letter* by Edgar Allan Poe (1974; Berlin, Feb. 14, 1975).

BALLETS: *Fest im Süden* (1935; Kassel, Feb. 4, 1935); *Harlekinade* (1939; Krefeld, Feb. 14, 1940); *Das Zauberbuch von Erzerum* (1941; Stuttgart, Oct. 17, 1942; revised, 1950, as *Der erste Ball;* Berlin, June 11, 1950); *Chiarina* (1946; Berlin, Jan. 22, 1950); *Hamlet* (1949; Munich, Nov. 19, 1950); *Lysistrata* (1950; Berlin, Jan. 22, 1951); *Der Mohr von Venedig,* after Shakespeare (1955; Vienna, Nov. 29, 1955); *Demeter* (1963; Schwetzingen, June 4, 1964); *Tristan*

(1965; Berlin, Oct. 10, 1965); incidental music for *Romeo and Juliet* (1951), *Lulu*, after Wedekind (1952), Molière's *Georges Dandin* (1955), *War and Peace*, after Tolstoy (1955), *Robespierre*, after Romain Rolland (1963), *Henry IV*, after Shakespeare (1970).

FOR ORCH.: Concerto for 2 Trumpets and 2 String Orchs. (1931); *Kleine Marchmusik* (1932; Berlin, Nov. 22, 1932); *Capriccio* (1933; Hamburg, May 14, 1935); Piano Concerto (1935; Stuttgart, Nov. 13, 1935); Divertimento for Wind Instruments (1936; Berlin, Feb. 24, 1937); *Geigenmusik* for Violin and Orch. (1936); *Concertante Musik* (1937; Berlin, Dec. 6, 1937); Symphony (1938; Berlin, Feb. 5, 1939); Concerto da camera for 2 Violins, Solo Cello, and String Orch. (1939); *Hamlet*, symph. poem (1940; Berlin, Oct. 28, 1940); Concerto for String Orch. (1940; Hamburg, Oct. 18, 1942); Partita for String Orch. and Percussion (1945); 16 Variations on a Theme of Paganini (1947; Leipzig, Nov. 27, 1947); Concerto for Jazz Orch. (1947); Piano Concerto No. 1 (1947; Göttingen, March 20, 1948); Violin Concerto (1948; Munich, Nov. 17, 1950); Concerto for Clarinet, Bassoon, Horn, Trumpet, Harp, and Strings (1950; Berlin, June 14, 1950); *Dialog* for Flute, Violin, Piano, and Strings (1950); Piano Concerto No. 2 (1952; Berlin, Sept. 15, 1952); *Orchester-Ornament*, based on "variable meters" (1953; Venice Festival, Sept. 15, 1953); *Studie im Pianissimo* (1953; Louisville, Kentucky, Sept. 4, 1954); *Zwei Inventionen* (1954; Edinburgh Festival, Aug. 28, 1954); Viola Concerto (1954; Cologne, March 14, 1955); *Orchester-Fantasie* (1955; London, Oct. 12, 1956); *Hommage à Mozart* (1956; Berlin, Dec. 10, 1956); *Music for Cleveland* (1957; Cleveland, Nov. 21, 1957); *Musica giocosa* (1959; Saarbrücken; April 30, 1959); Variations on a Theme of Muzio Clementi, for Piano and Orch. (1961; Berlin, Oct. 4, 1961); *Konzertstück* for Wind Quintet and Strings (1963; Donaueschingen, Oct. 19, 1963); Cello Concerto (1964; Cologne, March 19, 1965); *Virtuose Musik* for Solo Violin, 10 Wind Instruments, Percussion, and Harp (1966; Dartmouth College, Hanover, N.H., Aug. 19, 1967); arrangement of Bach's *Das musikalische Opfer* (1966); *Collage* (1968; Vienna, Oct. 5, 1969); Concerto for Trumpet and Strings (1970; Nuremberg, Feb. 11, 1971); Concerto for Clarinet and Chamber Orch. (1971; Schwetzingen, May 12, 1972); *Stars and Strings* for Jazz Ensemble and Strings (1972; Nuremberg, Jan. 12, 1973); *Poème* (1974; Vienna, Jan. 31, 1976); *Pentagram* for Strings (1974; Berlin, April 4, 1975).

CHAMBER MUSIC: 5 string quartets: No. 1 (1930; Frankfurt, Dec. 6, 1939); No. 2 (1940; Venice, 1941); No. 3 (1944); No. 4 (1951; Berlin, Jan. 25, 1953); No. 5, *Variationen über einen divergierenden c-moll-Dreiklang* (1967; Berlin, March 8, 1968); Cello Sonata (1940); *Divertimento* for Trumpet, Trombone, and Piano (1948; Berlin, Jan. 23, 1948); *Divertimento* for 4 Woodwinds (1951; Munich, Sept. 28, 1951); Violin Sonata (1951; Berlin, Jan. 27, 1952); *2 Poems* for Vibraphone, Double Bass, Percussion, and Piano (1957; N.Y., Nov. 14, 1958); *Perpetuum mobile* for Solo Violin (1963); Octet for Clarinet, Bassoon, Horn, and String Quintet (1965; Saarbrücken, Oct. 19, 1966); *4 Ornamente* for Violin and Piano (1969;

N.Y., Nov. 5, 1969); Piano Trio (1970); Sonata for 2 Cellos and 11 Instruments (1972; Berlin, Dec. 26, 1972); *Blues espagnola and Rumba philharmonica* for 12 Solo Cellos (1972; Tokyo, Oct. 28, 1973); Duo for Flute and Piano (1972); Quintet for Flute, Oboe, and String Trio (1973); *Tchaikovsky Variations* for Cello and Piano (1974).

FOR VOICE: *Jazz-Koloraturen* for Soprano, Saxophone, and Bassoon (1929); *5 Sinnsprüche Omars des Zeltmachers* for Voice and Piano (1931); *Der Grossinquisitor*, oratorio, after Dostoyevsky (1942; Berlin, Oct. 14, 1947); 4 choruses to texts by Villon (1944); *Es taget vor dem Walde*, cantata (1946; Berlin, June 29, 1946); *Francesca da Rimini* for Soprano and Violin (1954); *Träume vom Tod und vom Leben*, cantata (1955; Wuppertal, June 5, 1955); *13 Ways of Looking at a Blackbird*, to a text by Wallace Stevens, for Voice and Strings (1957; Vienna, Jan. 11, 1959); *Après-lude*, 4 lieder for Voice and Piano (1958); *Die Gesänge des Seeräubers O'Rourke und seiner Geliebten Sally Brown* for Soprano, Cabaret Singer, Baritone, Speaker, Chorus, and Orch. (1958; Vienna, Oct. 5, 1959); *Requiem* for Soprano, Baritone, Chorus, and Orch. (1958; Vienna, June 11, 1959); *Jüdische Chronik* for Soloists, Chorus, and Orch., a collective composition, with Dessau, K.A. Hartmann, Henze, and Wagner-Régeny (1961; Cologne, Jan. 14, 1966); 5 Negro Spirituals for Voice and Instruments (1962; Vienna, March 9, 1963); *Parergon* to *Eugene Onegin* for Mezzo-soprano and Chamber Ensemble (1966); Nursery Rhymes (1967); *For Seven* for Soprano, Percussion, and Double Bass (1973).

FOR PIANO: 2 sonatinas (1940 and 1941); *3 pièces* (1943); *Ornamente, 7 Studies* (1950); Sonata (1951); 24 Preludes (1974).

ELECTRONIC MUSIC: *Multiple Raumperspektiven* (1962); *Elektronische Studie über ein Posaunenglissando* (1962); *Persische elektronische Impulse* (1965); *Elektronisches Scherzo* (1965); *Musik für Osaka* (1969); *Ariadne*, duodrama for 2 Speakers and Electronics (1971).

BIBLIOGRAPHY: F. Burt, "The Teaching and Ideas of Boris Blacher," *The Score* (1954, No. 9); H.H. Stuckenschmidt, *Boris Blacher*, booklet of Blacher's publisher, Bote & Bock (Berlin, 1963); *Boris Blacher*, 56-page illustrated booklet issued by the Akademie der Künste in West Berlin to coincide with an exhibit of Blacher's archives (1973), with original essays by Chemin-Petit, Stuckenschmidt, Langner, and Jan Meyerowitz, with a complete list of his works through 1972.

Blachut, Beno, Czech tenor; b. Vítkovice, June 14, 1913. He studied at the Prague Cons.; made his debut in Olomouc in 1938; from 1941 was a leading member of the Prague National Theater; also appeared in concerts. He made it his specialty to perform the leading roles in Czech operas.

Black, Andrew, British baritone; b. Glasgow, Jan. 15, 1859; d. Sydney, Australia, Sept. 15, 1920. He studied singing in London with Randegger and Welch, then in Milan with Scafati; made his London debut at the Crystal Palace on July 30, 1887. In 1893 he was appointed prof. of singing at the Royal Manchester College of Music. In 1913 he settled in Australia.

Black, Frank, American conductor; b. Philadelphia, Nov. 28, 1894; d. Atlanta, Jan. 29, 1968. He studied piano with Raphael Joseffy in N.Y.; then devoted himself chiefly to conducting radio orchs.; in 1928 he organized the music dept. of the National Broadcasting Co.

Black, Stanley, English pianist and conductor; b. London, June 14, 1913. He studied at the Matthay School of Music in London, and began his career as a jazz pianist and arranger; then was a conductor of the BBC Dance Orch. (1944–52); subsequently worked as a music director for films. In 1968–69 he was principal conductor of the BBC Northern Ireland Orch.; also appeared as a guest conductor with various orch. groups in England.

Blackburn, Bonnie, American musicologist; b. Albany, N.Y., July 15, 1939. She studied at Wellesley College (B.A., 1961) and the Univ. of Chicago (M.A., 1963; Ph.D., 1970). From 1964 to 1976 she served as an assistant editor of its Monuments of Renaissance Music series. She was named a research associate of the Newberry Library in 1982. She contributed articles to *The New Grove Dictionary of Music and Musicians* (London, 6th ed., 1980); collaborated with Edward Lowinsky on the vol. *Josquin des Prez: Proceedings of the International Josquin Festival-Conference* (London, 1976); edited *Johannis Lupi Opera omnia* (3 vols., 1980). She is married to the musicologist **Edward Lowinsky.**

Blackmore, Richie, British "heavy metal" rock musician; b. Weston-super-Mare, April 14, 1945. He hit the guitar before puberty, and as a teenager played with Screaming Lord Sutch. In 1968 he moved to Hamburg, Germany, where he organized a band named Deep Purple, in a team with several other English boys. The group practiced high-decibel, wailing, screaming, screeching, deafening sound, which became the trademark of Blackmore. Typical of the din he created were his albums *Fireball, Machine Head,* and the big hit single *Smoke on the Water.*

Blackwood, Easley, American composer; b. Indianapolis, April 21, 1933. He studied piano in his hometown and appeared as a soloist with the Indianapolis Symph. at age 14; studied composition during summers at the Berkshire Music Center (1948–50), notably with Messiaen in 1949; then with Bernhard Heiden at Indiana Univ. and Hindemith at Yale (1949–51); received his M.A. from Yale in 1954; then went to Paris to study with Nadia Boulanger (1954–56). In 1958 he was appointed to the faculty of the Univ. of Chicago. His music is marked by impassioned Romantic éclat and is set in a highly evolved chromatic idiom. Blackwood is an accomplished pianist, particularly notable for his performances of modern works of transcendental difficulty, such as the Concord Sonata of Ives and the 2nd Piano Sonata of Boulez.

WORKS: 4 symphs.: No. 1 (1954–55; Boston, April 18, 1958; won the Koussevitzky Music Foundation prize); No. 2 (1960; Cleveland, Jan. 5, 1961; commissioned for the centenary of the music firm G. Schirmer); No. 3 for Small Orch. (1964; Chicago, March 7, 1965); No. 4 (Chicago, Nov. 22, 1978); Chamber Symph. for 14 Wind Instruments (1955); Clarinet Concerto (Cincinnati, Nov. 20, 1964); *Symphonic Fantasy* (Louisville, Sept. 4, 1965); Concerto for Oboe and String Orch. (1966); Violin Concerto (Bath, England, June 18, 1967); Concerto for Flute and String Orch. (Dartmouth College, Hanover, N.H., July 28, 1968); Piano Concerto (1969–70; Ravinia Festival, Highland Park, Ill., July 26, 1970); Viola Sonata (1953); 2 string quartets (1957, 1959); Concertino for 5 Instruments (1959); 2 violin sonatas (1960, 1975); Fantasy for Cello and Piano (1960); *Pastorale and Variations* for Wind Quintet (1961); Fantasy for Flute, Clarinet, Violin, and Piano (1965); *3 Short Fantasies* for Piano (1965); *Symphonic Movement* for Organ (1966); *Un Voyage à Cythère* for Soprano and 10 Players (1966); Piano Trio (1968).

Blaes, Arnold Joseph, noted Belgian clarinetist; b. Brussels, Dec. 1, 1814; d. there, Jan. 11, 1892. He studied with Bachmann at the Brussels Cons., winning first prize there in 1834; traveled on concert tour in Europe; while in Russia, he married the soprano **Elisa Blaes** in 1843. He taught at the Brussels Cons. from 1844–71; wrote an autobiography, *Souvenirs de ma vie artistique* (Brussels, 1888).

BIBLIOGRAPHY: P. Weston, *Clarinet Virtuosi of the Past* (London, 1971).

Blaes (née **Meerti**), **Elisa,** Belgian soprano; b. Antwerp, Nov. 2, 1817; d. Brussels, Nov. 6, 1878. She first gained distinction in Leipzig as a soloist with Mendelssohn and the Gewandhaus Orch. (1839, 1841–42); sang with the Phil. Society of London in 1839. In 1843 she appeared in Russia, where she married the Belgian clarinetist **Arnold Blaes;** she often appeared in concerts with him. In her later years she taught voice in Belgium.

Blagrove, Henry Gamble, English violinist; b. Nottingham, Oct. 20, 1811; d. London, Dec. 15, 1872. He was extremely precocious in his development; at the age of 12 he was admitted to the Royal Academy of Music in London at its opening in 1823. In 1832–34 he was in Germany and took lessons with Spohr in Kassel. He is credited with having established the first regular series of chamber music concerts in London in 1835.

Bláha, Ivo, Czech composer; b. Litomyšl, March 14, 1936. He studied with Řídký and Sommer at the Academy of Musical Arts in Prague, graduating in 1958; then joined the film-music dept. there.

WORKS: 2 string quartets (1957, 1966); Concerto for Orch. (1957); *3 Movements* for Violin and Piano

Bláha-Mikeš – Blake

(1961); Wind Quintet (1962); Concerto for Percussion and Orch. (1964); *Solitude,* sonata for Solo Violin (1965); *Music* for Wind Quintet (1965); *3 Toccata-Studies* for Piano (1967); Violin Concerto (1968); *Music to Pictures of a Friend* for Flute, Oboe, and Clarinet (1971); Cello Sonata (1972); *Oh, Love,* music to a poem of Jacques Prévert, for Narrator, Flute, Oboe, Clarinet, and Tape (1973); *2 Inventions* for Solo Flute (1974); *Variations on a Czech National Song* for 3 Flutes (1975); Duo for Bass Clarinet and Piano (1975).

Bláha-Mikeš, Záboj, Czech composer; b. Prague, Nov. 22, 1887; d. there, April 3, 1957. He was a pupil of Vítězslav Novák. As a composer, he wrote mostly vocal music; also composed a melodrama with Orch., *Tagore,* and sundry piano pieces.

Blahetka, Marie Léopoldine, Austrian pianist and composer; b. Guntramsdorf, near Vienna, Nov. 15, 1811; d. Boulogne, France, Jan. 12, 1887. She was a piano pupil of Kalkbrenner and Moscheles; also studied composition with Sechter. In 1840 she settled in Boulogne. She wrote a romantic opera, *Die Räuber und die Sänger,* which was produced in Vienna in 1830, and a considerable number of salon pieces for piano.

Blainville, Charles-Henri, French cellist and music theorist; b. probably in or near Rouen, 1710; d. Paris, c.1770. His claim to musicological attention resides in his "discovery" of a 3rd "mode hellénique" (actually the Phrygian mode); in 1751 he wrote a symph. in which he made use of this mode. Rousseau, always eager to welcome a "historical" discovery, expressed his admiration for Blainville. Among Blainville's theoretical writings are *L'Harmonie théorico-pratique* (1746); *Essai sur un troisième mode,* expounding the supposed "mode hellénique"(1751); *L'Esprit de l'art musical* (1754); and *Histoire générale, critique et philologique de la musique* (1767). He composed 5 symphs., publ. a book of sonatas "pour le dessus de viole avec la basse continue," and arranged Tartini's sonatas in the form of concerti grossi.

Blake, David (Leonard), British composer; b. London, Sept. 2, 1936. He studied music at Cambridge; then went to East Berlin, where he took lessons with Hanns Eisler. In 1964 he was appointed lecturer in music at York Univ. His early works were in a tonal idiom influenced by Bartók and Mahler, but later he began writing in the 12-tone system as promulgated by Schoenberg and Eisler. He then experimented in a wide variety of styles, including oriental scales and aleatory improvisation. While serving in the British army in the Far East, he learned Chinese.
WORKS: String Quartet No. 1 (1961–62); String Quartet No. 2 (1973); *It's a Small War,* musical for schools (1962); *3 Choruses* to poems by Robert Frost (1964); *Beata l'Alma* for Soprano and Piano (1966); Symph. for Chamber Orch. (1966); *Lumina,* cantata after Ezra Pound, for Soprano, Baritone, Chorus,

and Orch. (1968–69); *Metamorphoses* for Orch. (1971); *Scenes* for Solo Cello (1972); Nonet (1971; London, June 21, 1971); *The Bones of Chuang Tzu* for Baritone and Chamber Orch. (1972; Glasgow, March 25, 1975); *In Praise of Krishna* for Soprano and 9 Players (1973; Leeds, March 7, 1973); *Toussaint,* opera in 3 acts (1974–76; London, Sept. 28, 1977); Violin Concerto No. 1 (1976; London, Aug. 19, 1976); *Sonata alla Marcia* for Chamber Orch. (1978; London, May 17, 1978); *From the Mattress Grave* for High Voice and 11 Players (1978; Durham, Feb. 3, 1979); 9 Poems of Heine for High Voice and Piano (1978); *Cassation* for Wind Octet (1979; Sheffield, May 19, 1979); Clarinet Quintet (1980); *Capriccio* for 7 Players (1980); *The Spear* for Male Speaker, Mezzo-soprano, and 4 Players (1982); *Rise, Dove* for Baritone and Orch. (1982); String Quartet No. 3 (1982); Violin Concerto No. 2 (1983).

Blake, Eubie, black American centenarian jazz piano player, seeded buckdancer, vaudevillian, composer of musicals, rags, etudes, waltzes, and a plethora of miscellaneous popular numbers; b. Baltimore, Feb. 7, 1883; d. Brooklyn, Feb. 12, 1983, 5 days after reaching his 100th birthday. Both his parents were former slaves. He was baptized **James Hubert Blake;** relatives and friends called him Hubie, which was abbreviated to Eubie. He grew up in an atmosphere of syncopated music and sentimental ballads played on music boxes, and had some piano lessons from a friendly church organist in Baltimore. At the age of 15 he got a regular job as a standard pianist in a "hookshop" (a sporting house) run by Aggie Sheldon, a successful madam, which provided him with tips from both the inmates and their customers. He improvised rag music (his long fingers could stretch to 12 keys on the keyboard) and soon began to compose in earnest. In 1899 he wrote his *Charleston Rag,* which became a hit. In 1915 he joined a singer named Noble Sissle, and they appeared on the vaudeville circuit together, advertised as The Dixie Duo. They broke the tradition of blackface white comedians and devised an all-black musical, *Shuffle Along,* which opened in N.Y. on May 23, 1927, billed as "a musical mélange." The score included the song *I'm just wild about Harry,* which became a hit and was actually used as a campaign song for Harry Truman in 1948. Another hit song was *Memories of You,* which Eubie Blake wrote for the musical *Blackbirds of 1930.* Remarkably enough, he was moved by a purely scholarly interest in music and as late as 1949 took courses in the Schillinger System of Composition at N.Y. Univ. In 1969 he recorded the album *The Eighty-Six Years of Eubie Blake* and in 1972 he formed his own record company. As his centennial approached there was a growing appreciation of his natural talent, and a Broadway musical billed simply *Eubie!* was produced with resounding success. In 1981 he received the Medal of Freedom from President Reagan at the White House. He made his last public appearance at the age of 99, at Lincoln Center in N.Y., on June 19, 1982.
BIBLIOGRAPHY: Al Rose, *Eubie Blake* (N.Y.,

1979).

Blake, Ran, American composer; b. Springfield, Mass., April 20, 1935. He studied at Bard College (B.A., 1960) and at Columbia Univ. (1960–62), where he attended classes in improvisation with William Russo; later took lessons with Gunther Schuller, who inculcated him in "third stream" music (1960–67); also took straight jazz instruction at the Lenox School of Jazz. He composed mostly for piano, employing combined jazz-Baroque techniques and sonorities; his titles include *Aftermath, Chicken Monster, Crystal Trip, Glaciation, Interrogation at Logan Airport, Jim Crow, Klanwatch, Last Wave, Open City, Death Therapy, Deathwatch, East Wind, Field Cry, Police, Present Tense, Requiem for Mingus, Silver Fox, Sleep Secrets, Smoke after Smoke, Soul on Ice, Stoneciphering, Thursday, Touch of Evil, Turncoat, Vertigo,* and *Whirlpool;* also wrote many arrangements of original works for different ensembles, and improvisations on contemporary American songs. In 1967 he was appointed to the faculty of the New England Cons. in Boston.

Blakey, Art, black American jazz drummer; b. Pittsburgh, Oct. 11, 1919. He first studied piano, then turned to drums. In 1939 he joined Fletcher Henderson's orch.; later played in Mary Lou William's orch. (1941), with Billy Eckstine's orch. (1944–47), and with Buddy De Franco's Quartet (1952–53). In 1955 he formed a group, the Jazz Messengers. His hard-swing style was influential in the bop period of popular American music.

Blamont, François Colin de, French composer; b. Versailles, Nov. 22, 1690; d. there, Feb. 14, 1760. He was a pupil of Lalande; became superintendent of the King's music; wrote many court ballets, cantatas, and motets; publ. *Essai sur les goûts anciens et modernes de la musique française* (1754).

Blanc, Adolphe, French composer; b. Manosque, Basses-Alpes, June 24, 1828; d. Paris, May 1885. He studied at the Paris Cons. and privately with Halévy; for a short time he was conductor at the Théâtre-Lyrique. In 1862 he was awarded the Prix Chartier for chamber music. He wrote a one-act comic opera, *Une Aventure sous la Ligue* (1857); 2 operettas, *Les Deux Billets* (1868) and *Les Rêves de Marguerite;* a burlesque symph.; an overture; trios, quartets, quintets, and septets for strings, with and without piano; piano pieces.

Blanc, Giuseppe, Italian song composer; b. Bardonecchia, April 11, 1886; d. Santa Margherita Ligure, Dec. 7, 1969. He studied composition with Bolzoni; produced a number of comic operas, among them *La festa dei fiori* (Rome, Jan. 29, 1913). His only claim to fame is that he was the author of the song *Giovinezza,* which was adopted ex post facto by Mussolini as the national Fascist anthem.

Blancafort, Manuel, Spanish composer; b. Barcelona, Aug. 12, 1897. He studied in Barcelona with Lamote de Grignon. In his music he cultivates national Catalan subjects while adhering to the impressionistic idiom set in neo-Classical forms. He wrote *Sardana sinfónica* for Orch. (1951); *Rapsódia Catalana* for Cello and Orch. (1953); symph. suite, *Evocaciones* (1969); and a number of piano pieces of a descriptive character (*Le Parc d'attractions, Chants intimes, Pastorale, Chemins,* etc.).

Blanchard, Esprit Joseph Antoine, French composer; b. Pernes, Comtat-Venaissin, Feb. 29, 1696; d. Versailles, April 19, 1770. He studied with Poitevin at the choir school of the St. Sauveur Cathedral in Aix-en-Provence. In 1717 he became maître de musique to the chapter of St. Victor in Marseilles; was then maître de chapelle at the Toulon, Besançon, and Amiens cathedrals. He succeeded Bernier as sous-maître at the Chapelle du Roi in Versailles in 1738; was maître de chapelle there from 1761–65. He wrote mainly sacred choral music for performance at the churches where he was employed.

Blanchard, Henri-Louis, French musician; b. Bordeaux, Feb. 7, 1778; d. Paris, Dec. 18, 1858. He studied the violin; was conductor at the Théâtre des Variétés in Paris (1818–29); wrote music criticism; produced several operettas.

Blanchet, Emile R., Swiss pianist and composer; b. Lausanne, July 17, 1877; d. Pully, March 27, 1943. He studied with his father, Charles Blanchet (1833–1900); with Seiss, Franke, and Strässer at the Cologne Cons.; and with Busoni in Weimar and Berlin. From 1904–17 he was a teacher of piano at the Lausanne Cons. Among his works are *64 Preludes for Pianoforte in Contrapuntal Style,* a valuable pedagogical work; *Konzertstück* for Piano and Orch.; Violin Sonata; Ballade for 2 Pianos; many études and other piano works; songs; etc.

Blanck, Hubert de, conductor and educator; b. Utrecht, June 11, 1856; d. Havana, Nov. 28, 1932. He studied at the Liège Cons. with Ledent (piano) and Dupuy (composition); subsequently served as a theater conductor in Warsaw (1875); toured Europe as a pianist; visited South America with the violinist E. Dengremont (1880). After teaching at the N.Y. College of Music, he settled in Havana (1883) and founded the first cons. in Cuba, based upon European models (1885). He was exiled in 1896 for participation in the revolution; after the reestablishment of peace, he reopened his school in Havana and set up branches in other towns. He composed piano pieces and songs, but it is as an enlightened educator that he is honored in the annals of Cuban music.

Blanco, Juan, Cuban composer; b. Havana, June 29, 1920. He studied composition with José Ardévol; after a period of writing in traditional forms, he devoted himself to experimentation, making use of electronic devices with purposive spatial arrangement. In this manner he constructed *Texturas* for Orch. and Tape (1964); 4 sets of *Contrapunto espacial* for different groups distributed through the area of performance (1965–70); *Vietnam,* soundlike composition (1968).

Bland, James A., black American song composer; b. Flushing, N.Y., Oct. 22, 1854; d. Philadelphia, May 5, 1911. He learned to play the banjo and joined a minstrel troupe, improvising songs in the manner of Negro spirituals. His most famous ballad, *Carry Me Back to Old Virginny,* was publ. in 1878; in 1940 it was designated the official song of the state of Virginia. From 1881–1901 Bland lived in England, enjoying excellent success as an entertainer, including a command performance for Queen Victoria, but he dissipated his savings and died in abject poverty.
BIBLIOGRAPHY: E. Southern, *The Music of Black Americans* (N.Y., 1971).

Blandford, Walter, English horn player; b. London, Dec. 28, 1864; d. there, Jan. 23, 1952. He studied horn with T.E. Mann in London and with H.L. Merck in Brussels; played in several amateur orchs., and also publ. informative articles on brass instruments.

Blangini, Giuseppe Marco Maria Felice, Italian composer; b. Turin, Nov. 18, 1781; d. Paris, Dec. 18, 1841. He was a choirboy at Turin Cathedral; in 1799 his family moved to Paris, where he gave concerts, wrote fashionable *romances,* and came into vogue as an opera composer when he completed Della-Maria's opera *La Fausse Duègne* (1802); he was also popular as a singing teacher. After producing an opera in Munich, he was appointed court Kapellmeister (1806); later was Generalmusikdirektor at Kassel (1809); upon his return to Paris in 1814, was made superintendent of the King's music, court composer, and prof. of singing at the Cons., positions which he held until 1830.
WORKS: 30 operas; 4 masses with Orch.; 170 nocturnes for 2 Voices; 174 *romances* for One Voice; etc. See his autobiography, *Souvenirs de F. Blangini,* ed. by M. de Villemarest (Paris, 1834).

Blankenburg, Quirin van (full name, **Quirinus Gerbrandszoon van Blankenburg**), Dutch organist; b. Gouda, 1654; d. The Hague, May 12, 1739. He studied organ with his father and served as a church organist in Rotterdam (1671–76) and in Gorinchem (1676–81). Later on he went to Leiden for further study at the univ. there; his next engagement was as organist at the Hoofkerk in The Hague (1687–1702); he was then employed at the Nieuwe Kerk. He publ. *Elementa musica* (The Hague, 1729); compiled *Clavicembel en Orgelboek der gereformeerde Psalmen en Kerkgezangen* (1732; 3rd ed., 1772); also a method for flute.

Blanter, Matvei, Russian composer of popular songs; b. Potchep, Tchernigov district, Feb. 10, 1903. He studied in Moscow with G. Conus; then devoted himself exclusively to the composition of light music. He wrote an operetta, *On the Banks of the Amur* (1939), and some incidental music. Of his songs, the most popular is *Katyusha* (famous during World War II), which combines the melodic inflection of the typical urban ballad with the basic traits of a Russian folk song. Blanter is regarded in Russia as a creator of the new Soviet song style.
BIBLIOGRAPHY: V. Zak, *Matvei Blanter* (Moscow, 1971).

Blanton, James ("Jimmy"), black American jazz string bass player; b. Chattanooga, Tenn., Oct. 1918; d. Monrovia, Calif., July 30, 1942. He played the violin as a child; then began to play the string bass; in 1939 he joined Duke Ellington's orchestra, and continued as its member until his death.

Blaramberg, Pavel, Russian composer; b. Orenburg, Sept. 26, 1841; d. Nice, March 28, 1907. His father was a geographer of French origin; his mother was Greek. At the age of 14 he went to St. Petersburg; later became a functionary of the Central Statistical Committee there. He was largely self-taught in music, apart from occasional advice from Balakirev and Rimsky-Korsakov. In 1878 he settled in Moscow as an instructor at the newly founded Philharmonic Inst. In 1898 he went to the Crimea, then to France.
WORKS: Operas: *The Mummers* (1881); *Russalka* (Moscow, April 15, 1888); *Maria Tudor,* after Hugo (produced as *Mary of Burgundy* on account of the censor's objection to the original libretto; Moscow, Oct. 29, 1888); *Tushintsy* (Moscow, Feb. 5, 1895; his most successful opera; had several revivals); *The Waves* (1902). He also wrote a symph. poem, *The Dying Gladiator* (1882); a Symph. (1886); songs.

Blaserna, Pietro, Italian music theorist; b. Fiumicello, near Aquileja, Feb. 29, 1836; d. Rome, Feb. 26, 1918. He studied natural sciences in Vienna and Paris; later taught physics at the univs. of Palermo (1863) and Rome (1872). An exponent of the acoustic purity of intervals, he made important scientific contributions in the field of acoustics. His principal work is *La teoria del suono nei suoi rapporti colla musica* (1875).

Blasius, Mathieu-Frédéric, French composer; b. Lauterburg, Alsace, April 24, 1758; d. Versailles, 1829. He was also a violinist, clarinetist, flutist, and bassoonist; taught wind instruments at the Paris Cons. (1795–1802); conducted at the Opéra-Comique (1802–16). He wrote 3 operas, 3 violin concertos, many popular pieces for wind instruments in various combinations.

Blatný, Josef, Czech organist and composer, father of **Pavel Blatný;** b. Brno, March 19, 1891. He studied composition with Janáček at the Brno Organ School (1909–12); then served as his assistant;

subsequently became a prof. of organ at the Brno Cons., where he taught for 28 years (1928–56).

WORKS: *Sinfonia brevis* for String Orch. (1957); *2 Symphonic Dances* (1959); Chamber Symph. (1961); oratorio, *Lotr na pravici* (*The Thief on the Right;* 1953); 3 violin sonatas (1926, 1957, 1968); 3 string quartets (1929, 1954, 1962); Suite for 2 Flutes, Clarinet, and Bassoon (1947); Piano Trio (1950); Piano Quartet (1968); Piano Sonata (1960); many organ pieces; songs.

Blatný, Pavel, Czech composer and conductor, son of **Josef Blatný;** b. Brno, Sept. 14, 1931. He began his musical studies with his father; then studied piano and music theory at the Brno Cons. (1950–55) and musicology at the Univ. of Brno (1954–58); also took composition lessons with Bořkovec at the Prague Academy of Music (1955–59); attended summer courses of new music at Darmstadt (1965–69); in 1968 traveled to the U.S. and took lessons in jazz piano and composition at the Berklee College of Music. He became an exceedingly active musician in Czechoslovakia; wrote about 600 works, some of them paralleling the development of "third-stream music" initiated in the U.S. by Gunther Schuller, which constitutes a fusion of jazz and classical forms; played something like 2,000 piano recitals in programs of modern music; conducted a great many concerts and participated in programs of the Czech Radio; in 1971 he was appointed chief of the music division of the television station in Brno.

WORKS: *Per orchestra sintetica I* for Jazz Band and Wind Ensemble (1960); *Per orchestra sintetica II* for Jazz Band and Orch. (1971); *Study* for Quarter-tone Trumpet and Jazz Orch. (1964); *Tre per S + H* for Jazz Septet (1964); *Dialogue* for Soprano Saxophone and Jazz Band (1959–64); *Geschichte I* for Jazz Nonet (1968); *Geschichte II* for Jazz Septet (1969); *In modo classico* for String Quartet and Jazz Orch. (1973); *4 Movements* for Jazz Band (1973); *In modo archaico* for Piano and Jazz Orch. (1973); Concertino for Clarinet and Jazz Orch. (1974); *Picture* for Jazz Orch. (1976); *Chime* for Jazz Orch. (1978); *Zvony (The Bells),* symph. movement (1981); *Hommage à Gustave Mahler* for Symph. Orch. (1982); children's opera, *Domeček (Little House;* 1959); opera, *Fairy-tales of the Woods* (1976); several musicals; *Kaleidoscope* for Orch. (1970); *Continuum pro continuum* for Chamber Orch. (1973); cantata, *Allende,* dedicated to the memory of the democratic president of Chile (1974); a dozen suites for various instruments with piano; *2:3* for Wind Quintet (1973); *Discussion* for Violin, Accordion, and Guitar (1973); *Intermezzo* for Vocalist and Jazz Trio (1978); *Un Pezzo per due boemi* for Bass Clarinet and Piano (1981); pieces for Solo Piano, 2 Pianos, and 4 Pianos.

Blatt, František Tadeáš, Bohemian clarinetist and composer; b. Prague, 1793; d. there, March 9, 1856. He studied clarinet with Václav Farník and composition with Dionys Weber at the Prague Cons. He was a member of the orch. at the Prague Opera; also taught at the Prague Cons. He publ. a method for clarinet (1828) and also composed a number of works for the clarinet; other works include duets, trios, and piano music.

BIBLIOGRAPHY: P. Weston, *Clarinet Virtuosi of the Past* (London, 1971).

Blaukopf, Kurt, Austrian musicologist; b. Czernowitz, Feb. 15, 1914. He studied music theory with Wolpe and conducting with Scherchen in Vienna (1932–37); then went to Jerusalem, where he took courses in music history with Gerson-Kiwi (1940–42); later served as editor of the periodical *Phono* (1954–65). In 1962 he became a lecturer in music sociology at the Vienna Academy of Music; from 1965 was editor of the periodical *HiFi Stereophonie* in Vienna. His writings include *Muziksoziologie* (Cologne, 1952; 2nd ed., 1972); *Grosse Dirigenten* (Teufen, 1953; Eng. trans., 1955); *Grosse Virtuosen* (Teufen, 1954; French trans., 1955); *Gustav Mahler, oder Zeitgenosse der Zukunft* (Vienna, 1969; Eng. trans., 1973). He edited *Gustav Mahler: Sein Leben, sein Werk und seine Welt in zeitgenossischen Bildern und Texten* (Vienna, 1976; in Eng. as *Gustav Mahler: A Documentary Study,* N.Y., 1976).

BIBLIOGRAPHY: I. Bontinck and O. Brusatti, eds., *Festschrift Kurt Blaukopf* (Vienna, 1975).

Blauvelt, Lillian Evans, American soprano; b. Brooklyn, N.Y., March 16, 1874; d. Chicago, Aug. 29, 1947. After studying violin for several years, she took vocal lessons in N.Y. and Paris; gave concerts in France, Belgium, and Russia; made her operatic debut at Brussels (1893); sang before Queen Victoria (1899); sang the coronation ode and received the coronation medal from King Edward (1902); appeared for several seasons at Covent Garden. She married the composer **Alexander Savine** in 1914; created the title role in his opera *Xenia* (Zürich, 1919).

Blaze (called **Castil-Blaze**), **François-Henri-Joseph,** French writer on music; b. Cavaillon, Vaucluse, Dec. 1, 1784; d. Paris, Dec. 11, 1857. He studied with his father, a lawyer and amateur musician; went to Paris in 1799 as a law student; held various administrative posts in provincial towns in France. At the same time he studied music and compiled information on the opera in France. The fruit of this work was the publication in 2 vols. of his book *De l'opéra en France* (Paris, 1820; 1826). He became music critic of the influential Paris *Journal des Débats* in 1822, signing his articles "XXX." He resigned from this post in 1832 but continued to publ. books on music, including valuable compilations of musical lexicography: *Dictionnaire de musique moderne* (1821, 2 vols.; 2nd ed., 1825; 3rd ed., edited by J.H. Mees, with historical preface and a supplement on Netherlandish musicians, 1828, in one vol.); *Chapelle-musique des Rois de France* (1832); *La Danse et les ballets depuis Bacchus jusqu'à Mlle. Taglioni* (1832); *Mémorial du Grand Opéra* (from Cambert, 1669, down to the Restoration); "Le Piano; Histoire de son invention," *Revue de Paris* (1839–40); *Molière musicien* (1852); *Théâtres lyriques de Paris,* 2 vols., on the Grand Opéra (1855) and on the Italian opera (1856); *Sur l'opéra français; Vérités dures mais utiles* (1856); *L'Art des jeux lyriques* (1858); trans. into French many librettos of German and Italian operas. He himself wrote 3 operas; compiled a collection of *Chants de Provence;* some of his popular ballads attained considerable popularity.

Blaze, Henri, Baron de Bury, French music critic, son of **François Blaze;** b. Avignon, May 17, 1813; d. Paris, March 15, 1888. He wrote many essays for the *Revue des Deux Mondes* and other periodicals; these essays were subsequently collected as *Musiciens contemporains* (1856); *Meyerbeer et son temps* (1865); *Musiciens du passé, du présent, etc.* (1880); *Goethe et Beethoven* (1882); his most valuable book is *La Vie de Rossini* (1854).

Blažek, Zdeněk, Czech composer; b. Žarošice, May 24, 1905. He studied composition with Petrželka at the Brno Cons. (1924–29) and with Suk at the Prague Cons. (1933–35); became a prof. at the Brno Cons. in 1941 and was its director from 1947–57; in 1961 was appointed to the staff of the Univ. of Brno.
WORKS: Opera, *Verchovina (The Highlands;* 1950–51; Brno, 1956); Suite for String Orch. (1934); *Funereal Music* for Strings, 2 Harps, Gong, and Timpani (1968); Divertimento for String Orch. (1971); cantatas: *Song of My Native Land* (1938); *Ode to Poverty* (1958); *Home* (1962); Piano Trio (1929); 5 string quartets (1943, 1946–47, 1956, 1967, 1969); *Divertimento* for Woodwind Quartet (1946); String Quintet (1949); *Sonatina giocosa* for Clarinet and Piano (1949); *4 Romantic Compositions* for Horn and Piano (1952); *Music at Home* for String Trio (1953); *4 Romantic Compositions* for Violin and Piano (1953–54); Bassoon Sonatina (1958); *Sonatina balladica* for Cello and Piano (1962); Horn Sonata (1964); Wind Quintet (1971); choruses; songs.

Blazhkov, Igor, Ukrainian conductor and music scholar; b. Kiev, Sept. 23, 1936. He studied at the Kiev Cons., graduating in 1959; appeared as guest conductor in Moscow and Leningrad, specializing in modern music, including American works. From 1958–62 he was assistant conductor of the Ukrainian State Orch. in Kiev.

Blech, Harry, English violinist and conductor; b. London, March 2, 1910. He received his musical training at the Trinity College of Music in London and at the Royal Manchester College of Music; later was a violinist in the Hallé Orch. in Manchester (1929–30) and the BBC Symph. Orch., London (1930–36); organized the Blech String Quartet in 1933 (disbanded in 1950). In 1942 he founded the London Wind Players, in 1946 the London Symph. Players, and in 1949 the London Mozart Players; conducted numerous concerts with these ensembles, mostly in programs of Haydn and Mozart. In 1964 he was made an Officer of the Order of the British Empire.

Blech, Leo, eminent German opera conductor and composer; b. Aachen, April 21, 1871; d. Berlin, Aug. 25, 1958. As a young man he was engaged in a mercantile career; then studied briefly at the Hochschule für Musik in Berlin; returned to Aachen to conduct at the Municipal Theater there (1893–99); also took summer courses in composition with Humperdinck (1893–96). He was subsequently engaged as opera conductor in Prague (1899–1906); then became conductor at the Berlin Court Opera in 1906; was named Generalmusikdirektor in 1913. In 1923 he became conductor of the Deutsches Opernhaus in Berlin; in 1924 was with the Berlin Volksoper, and in 1925 with the Vienna Volksoper. In 1926 he returned to Berlin as a conductor with the Staatsoper, remaining there until 1937; then went to Riga as a conductor of the Riga Opera (1937–41). From 1941 to 1949 he conducted in Stockholm. In 1949 he returned to Berlin and served as Generalmusikdirektor of the Städtische Oper there, remaining at that post until 1953. He was considered a fine interpreter of the standard German and Italian repertoire, particularly in the works of Wagner and Verdi. His own music is in the Wagnerian tradition; his knowledge and understanding of instrumental and vocal resources enabled him to produce competent operas; however, after initial successes, they suffered total oblivion.
WORKS: Operas: *Aglaja* (1893), *Cherubina* (1894), *Das war ich,* an "opera-idl" (Dresden, Oct. 6, 1902), *Alpenkönig und Me chenfeind* (Dresden, Oct. 1, 1903, rewritten and p 'uced as *Rappelkopf* at the Berlin Opera, in 1917) *chenbrödel* (Prague, 1905), *Versiegelt* (Hamburg, 08; N.Y., 1912), *Die Strohwitwe,* operetta (Hamburg, 1920); 3 symph. poems, *Die Nonne, Waldwanderung, Trost in der Natur;* choruses, songs; piano pieces; *10 Kleinigkeiten* for Piano, 4-hands; music for children.
BIBLIOGRAPHY: E. Rychnowsky, *Leo Blech* (Prague, 1905); E. Rychnowsky, *Leo Blech,* in vol. III of Monographien moderner Musiker (Leipzig, 1909); W. Jacob, *Leo Blech* (Hamburg, 1931).

Bledsoe, Jules, black American   itone and composer; b. Waco, Texas, Dec. 29, 18 d. Hollywood, July 14, 1943. He studied at the Chicago Musical College (B.A., 1919); then went to Europe, taking singing lessons in Paris and Rome. Returning to America, he distinguished himself as a fine performer in musical comedies and opera. He sang the central role in the premiere of Jerome Kern's *Show Boat* (1927), appeared in grand opera as Rigoletto and Boris, and sang the title role in Gruenberg's opera *Emperor Jones.* As a composer, he wrote an *African Suite* for Orch. and several songs in the manner of Negro spirituals.

Blegen, Judith, American soprano; b. Missoula, Mont., April 23, 1941. She received her musical training, in violin as well as singing, at the Curtis Inst. in Philadelphia (1959–64). In 1962 she won the Philadelphia Award, entitling her to appear with the Philadelphia Orch.; she made her concert debut with it in 1963. In 1964 she won a Fulbright fellowship, and also sang at the Spoleto Festival; subsequently studied voice with Luigi Ricci in Italy. From 1963–66 she was a member of the Nuremberg Opera; in 1968 she made her debut at the Vienna State Opera, singing Rosina in *The Barber of Seville.* On Aug. 1, 1969, she sang at the Santa Fe Opera in the role of Emily in the American premiere of Menotti's satirical opera *Help! Help! the Globolinks!* (a role specially written for her). She made her Metropolitan Opera debut on Jan. 19, 1970, in N.Y. as Papagena in *The Magic Flute,* and has since been one of the principal sopranos of the Metropolitan Opera in a variety of roles, including Marzelline (*Fidelio*), Zerlina (*Don Giovanni*), Sophie (*Der Rosenkavalier*), and Mélisande. She sang Susanna in *The Marriage of Figaro* with the San Francisco Opera in 1972; made her appearance at the Salzburg Festival in 1974; sang at the Edinburgh Festival in 1976 and also at the Paris Opéra in 1977.

Bleichmann, Yuli, Russian composer; b. St. Petersburg, Dec. 6, 1868; d. there, Jan. 8, 1910. He studied with Rimsky-Korsakov at the St. Petersburg Cons.; later with Jadassohn and Reinecke in Leipzig. Returning to St. Petersburg, he founded the Popular Symph. Concerts in 1893; also conducted the Phil. Symph. Concerts. He composed 2 operas, greatly influenced by Wagner: *St. Sebastian* and *The Dream-Princess* (Moscow, Oct. 23, 1900); also songs.

Blessinger, Karl, German musicologist; b. Ulm, Sept. 21, 1888; d. Pullach, near Munich, March 13, 1962. He studied in Heidelberg and Munich; was theater conductor in Bremen and Bonn; was on the staff of the Akademie der Tonkunst in Munich (1920–45).
WRITINGS: *Ulmer Musikgeschichte im 17. Jahrhundert* (dissertation; Ulm, 1913); *Die musikalischen Probleme der Gegenwart* (1920); *Die Überwindung der musikalischen Impotenz* (1920); *Grundzüge der musikalischen Formenlehre* (1926); *Melodielehre als Einführung in die Musiktheorie* (1930); *Mendelssohn, Meyerbeer, Mahler* (1938); *Judentum und Musik; Ein Beitrag zur Kultur- und Rassenpolitik* (Berlin, 1944; a "scientific" apologia for the anti-Semitic policy of the Nazi regime).

Blewitt, Jonathan, English composer; b. London, July 19, 1782; d. there, Sept. 4, 1853. He studied with his father, and with Battishill; was an organist at several churches; served as conductor at the Theatre Royal in Dublin. Returning to London (1825), he was appointed music director at Sadler's Wells Theatre. He composed many popular ballads; was the author of a treatise on singing, *The Vocal Assistant.*

Bleyer, Georg, German composer, poet, and court functionary; b. Tiefurt, near Weimar, (baptized, Oct. 28) 1647; d. c.1694. He studied law and music in Jena (1664–66); was named chamber secretary at the court in Rudolstadt; was awarded the garland of poet laureate in 1672; then was active as a musician in Darmstadt at the court (1677–78). He composed sacred vocal music; also publ. a collection of dances for 4 and 5 instruments as *Lust-Music* (2 vols., Leipzig, 1670).
BIBLIOGRAPHY: C. Höfer, *Georg Bleyer: Ein thüringischer Tonsetzer und Dichter der Barockzeit* (*Zeitschrift des Vereins für thüringische Geschichte,* supplement XXIV, Jena, 1941).

Bleyer, Nicolaus, German violinist and composer; b. Stolzenau, Feb. 2, 1591; d. Lübeck, May 3, 1658. He studied with Brade (1614–17), and then joined the orch. of Count Ernst in Bückeburg; settled in Lübeck as town musician in 1621, remaining there until his death. About 1628 he publ. *Erster Theil neuer Paduanen, Galliarden, Balletten, Mascarden und Couranten.*

Bleyle, Karl, German composer; b. Feldkirch, Vorarlberg, May 7, 1880; d. Stuttgart, June 5, 1969. He studied with Wehrle (violin) and S. de Lange (composition) in Stuttgart and with Thuille (composition) in Munich. He was active as a teacher and a theater conductor in Graz, Weimar, and Munich; in 1923 he returned to Stuttgart.
WORKS: 2 operas: *Hannele und Sannele* (Stuttgart, 1923) and *Der Teufelssteg* (Rostock, 1924); many works for Soli, Chorus, and Orch: *An den Mistral, Lernt Lachen, Mignons Beisetzung, Heilige Sendung, Die Höllenfahrt Christi, Ein Harfenklang, Prometheus, Trilogie der Leidenschaft, Requiem,* etc.; orch. pieces: *Flagellantenzug, Gnomentanz, Siegesouverture, Reinecke Fuchs, Legende;* Symph.; Violin Concerto; String Quartet; Violin Sonata; songs; piano pieces; etc.

Blind Tom. See **Bethune, Thomas Greene.**

Bliss, Sir Arthur (Edward Drummond), significant English composer; b. London, Aug. 2, 1891; d. there, March 27, 1975. He studied at Pembroke College, Cambridge; then at the Royal College of Music in London, with Stanford, Vaughan Williams, and Holst. He served in the British Army during World War I; was wounded in 1916, and gassed in 1918. He resumed his musical studies after the Armistice; his earliest works, *Madam Noy,* for Soprano and 6 Instruments (1918), and *Rout,* for Soprano and Orch. (1919; Salzburg Festival, Aug. 7, 1922), were highly successful, and established Bliss as one of the most effective composers in the modern style. From 1923 to 1925 Bliss was in the U.S. as a teacher, living in California. Returning to London, he wrote the musical score for the film *Things to Come,* after H.G. Wells (1935). During World War II he was music director of the BBC (1942–44). He was knighted in 1950; in 1953 was named Master of the Queen's Musick as a successor to Sir Arnold Bax.
WORKS: OPERAS: *The Olympians* (London, Sept. 29, 1949) and *Tobias and the Angel* (London, BBC television, May 19, 1960).
BALLETS: *Checkmate* (Paris, June 15, 1937), *Miracle in the Gorbals* (London, Oct. 26, 1944), *Adam Zero* (London, April 8, 1946), and *The Lady of Shalott* (unofficially known also as *The Towers;* Berkeley, Calif., May 2, 1958).
FOR ORCH.: *Mêlée fantasque* (1921, revised 1965); *A*

Colour Symphony (the title refers to 4 heraldic colors, one for each movement: purple, red, blue, and green; premiere, Gloucester, Sept. 7, 1922, under the composer's direction; revised 1932); Concerto for 2 Pianos and Orch. (1924; originally for Piano, Tenor, Strings, and Percussion, 1921); *Introduction and Allegro* (1926, revised 1937); *Hymn to Apollo* (1926, revised 1966); *Things to Come,* concert suite from music to the film (1934–35); *Music for Strings* (1935); *Conquest of the Air,* concert suite from music to the film (1937); Piano Concerto (commissioned by the British Council for the British Week at the N.Y. World's Fair, dedicated "to the people of the United State of America"; N.Y., June 10, 1939); *Theme and Cadenza* for Violin and Orch. (1946); Violin Concerto (London, May 11, 1955); *Meditations on a Theme of John Blow* (Birmingham, England, Dec. 13, 1955); *Edinburgh,* overture (1956); *Discourse* (Louisville, Kentucky, Oct. 23, 1957; recomposed 1965); Cello Concerto (1969–70; Aldenburgh Festival, June 24, 1970; Rostropovich, soloist); *Metamorphic Variations* (London, April 21, 1973; Stokowski conducting; originally titled simply *Variations*); *2 Contrasts* for String Orch. (1972; from movements 2 and 3 of Quartet No. 2).

VOCAL MUSIC: *Madame Noy* for Soprano and 6 Instruments (1918); *Rhapsody* for Wordless Mezzo-soprano and Tenor, Flute, English Horn, String Quartet, and Double Bass (1919; London, Oct. 6, 1920); *Rout* for Soprano and Orch. (1920); *The Women of Yueh,* cycle for Voice and Chamber Ensemble (1923–24); *Pastorale* for Mezzo-soprano, Chorus, Strings, Flute, and Drums (1928); *Serenade* for Baritone and Orch. (1929); *Morning Heroes,* symphony for Orator, Chorus, and Orch., dedicated to his brother, killed in action (Norwich, Oct. 22, 1930); *The Enchantress* for Contralto and Orch. (1951); *A Song of Welcome,* for the return of Queen Elizabeth II from her Australian journey, for Soprano, Baritone, Chorus, and Orch. (BBC, May 15, 1954; Joan Sutherland, soprano soloist); *Elegiac Sonnet* for Tenor, String Quartet, and Piano (1955); *The Beatitudes,* cantata (Coventry Festival, May 25, 1962); *Mary of Magdala,* cantata (Birmingham, Sept. 1, 1963); *A Knot of Riddles* for Baritone and 11 Instruments (1963); *The Golden Cantata* (1964); *The World Is Charged with the Grandeur of God,* chamber cantata for Chorus, 2 Flutes, 3 Trumpets, and 4 Trombones (1969); *2 Ballads* for Female Chorus, and Orch. or Piano (1971); several song cycles with piano; motets; and anthems.

CHAMBER MUSIC: *Conversations* for Flute, Oboe, and String Trio (1920; a humorous work); Oboe Quintet (1927); Clarinet Quintet (1931); Viola Sonata (1933); 2 string quartets (1940, 1950; 2 earlier quartets are lost); *Flourish: Greeting to a City* for 2 Brass Choirs and Percussion (1961); *Belmont Variations* for Brass (1963).

PIANO MUSIC: Sonata (1952); *Triptych* (1971).

BIBLIOGRAPHY: L. Foreman, *Arthur Bliss: Catalogue of Complete Works* (Kent, England, 1980).

Bliss, Philip Paul, American hymn writer; b. in a log cabin in the woods of Clearfield County, Pa., July 9, 1838; d. in a train wreck near Ashtabula, Ohio, Dec. 29, 1876. He was an itinerant minstrel, traveling with a mechanical melodeon and an old horse. In 1864 he settled in Chicago, taught singing, and did some preaching. He publ. *Gospel Songs* (1874) and *Gospel Hymns* (1875), both highly successful.

BIBLIOGRAPHY: R.G. McCutchan, *Our Hymnody* (N.Y., 1937).

Bliss, P. Paul, American organist and music editor; b. Chicago, Nov. 25, 1872; d. Oswego, N.Y., Feb. 2, 1933. He studied in Philadelphia; then went to Paris, where he was a pupil of Guilmant (organ) and Massenet (composition). Returning to America, he was active as an organist in Oswego; served as music director with the John Church Co. (1904–10) and the Willis Music Co. (from 1911). He composed 3 operettas: *Feast of Little Lanterns; Feast of Red Corn; In India;* cantatas: *Pan on a Summer Day; Three Springs; The Mound-Builders;* piano suite, *In October;* many songs and choruses; also compiled *Graded Course for Piano* (4 vols.).

Blitheman, John, English organist and composer; b. c.1525; d. London, May 23, 1591. He was from 1558 a gentleman in the Chapel Royal; also held an annuity from Christ Church, Oxford. John Bull is said to have been one of his pupils. He composed liturgical organ music and several vocal pieces. See D. Stevens, ed., *The Mulliner Book,* in the Musica Britannica series, 1 (1951; 2nd ed., revised, 1962).

Blitzstein, Marc, significant American composer; b. Philadelphia, March 2, 1905; d. Fort-de-France, Martinique, Jan. 22, 1964, from a brain injury sustained after a political altercation with a group of men in a bar. He studied piano and organ in Pennsylvania; composition with Scalero at the Curtis Inst. in Philadelphia; also took piano lessons with Siloti in N.Y. In 1926 he went to Europe, and took courses with Nadia Boulanger in Paris and Schoenberg in Berlin. Returning to America, he devoted himself chiefly to the cultivation of theatrical works of "social consciousness" of the type created in Germany by Bertolt Brecht and Kurt Weill; accordingly he wrote his stage works for performances in small theaters of the cabaret type. In 1940 he received a Guggenheim fellowship; during World War II he was stationed in England with the U.S. Armed Forces. His theater works include *Triple Sec,* opera-farce (Philadelphia, May 6, 1929); *Parabola and Circula,* one-act opera-ballet (1929); *Cain,* ballet (1930); *The Harpies,* musical satire commissioned by the League of Composers (1931; first production, Manhattan School of Music, N.Y., May 25, 1953); *The Cradle Will Rock,* one-act opera of "social significance" (N.Y., June 16, 1937, with the composer at the piano); *No for an Answer,* short opera (N.Y., Jan. 5, 1941); musical play, *I've Got the Tune* (CBS Radio, Oct. 24, 1937); also musical revues, one of which, *Regina,* to Lillian Hellman's play *The Little Foxes,* was expanded into a full-fledged opera (Boston, Oct. 11, 1949). Shortly before his death the Ford Foundation commissioned Blitzstein to write an opera on the subject of Sacco and Vanzetti, for production by the Metropolitan Opera House, but the work was never finished. Blitzstein further composed *Gods* for Mezzo-soprano and String Orch. (1926); oratorio, *The Condemned* (1930); *Airborne Symphony* (N.Y., March 23, 1946); *Cantatina* for Women's Voices and Percussion; *Jig-Saw,* ballet-suite (1927); *Romantic Piece* for Orch. (1930); Piano Concerto (1931); *Freedom Morning,* symph. poem (London, Sept. 28, 1943); String Quartet; *Percussion Music* for Piano (1929); many other piano pieces. Blitzstein translated Kurt Weill's *Threepenny Opera* into English (1954), and his version scored great success.

BIBLIOGRAPHY: Henry Brant, "Marc Blitzstein," *Modern Music* (July 1946); *Composers of America,* vol. 5 (Washington, D.C., 1959); W. Mellers, *Music in a New Found Land* (N.Y., 1967; pp. 414–28).

Bloch, Alexander, American violinist and conductor; b. Selma, Ala., July 11, 1881; d. New York, March 16, 1983, at the age of 101. He studied violin with Edouard Herman in N.Y., with Otakar Sevčik in Vienna, with W. Hess and Henri Marteau in Berlin, and with Leopold Auer in St. Petersburg. He took conducting lessons with Chalmers Clifton in N.Y. From 1918 until 1930 he served as a teaching assistant to Auer in N.Y. He then devoted himself mainly to conducting; was conductor of the Central Florida Symph. Orch. at Winter Park (1936–43). In 1950 he took charge of the newly organized Florida West Coast Symph. Orch. in Saratoga; also had guest engagements with the National Symph. Orch. in Washington, D.C. He composed a Christmas opera, *The Lone Tree,* and a children's operetta, *Roeliffs Dream;* also publ. the violin studies *Principles and Practice of Bowing* and *How to Practice.*

Bloch, André, French composer; b. Wissembourg, Alsace, Jan. 18, 1873; d. Paris, Aug. 7, 1960. He studied at the Paris Cons. with Guiraud and Massenet; received the Premier Grand Prix de Rome in 1893. He was conductor of the orch. of the American Cons. at Fontainebleau. His works include operas: *Maida* (1909); *Une Nuit de Noël* (1922); *Broceliande* (1925); *Guignol* (1949); ballet, *Feminaland* (1904); symph. poems: *Kaa* (1933) and *L'Isba nostaligique* (1945); *Les Maisons de l'éternité* for Cello and Orch. (1930); *Suite palestinienne* for Cello and Orch. (Paris, Nov. 14, 1948; his most successful instrumental work).

Bloch, Augustyn, Polish composer and organist; b. Grudziadz, Aug. 13, 1929. He studied composition with Szeligowski, and organ at the Warsaw State College of Music (1950–58); then was employed at the Polish State Radio as music editor. In his compositions he follows the neo-Romantic trend of modern Polish music.

WORKS: One-act opera-mystery, *Ayelet, Jephta's Daughter* (Katowice, 1967); children's opera-pantomime, *The Sleeping Princess* (Warsaw, Sept. 29, 1974); 5 ballets: *Voci* (Warsaw Television, 1967); *Oczekiwanie (The Awaiting;* Warsaw, 1964); *Byk (The Bull;* 1965; Holland Festival, Amsterdam, June 24, 1965); *Gilgamesh* (1968); *The Looking Glass* for Tape (1975); Concertino for Violin, String Orch., Piano, and Percussion (1958); *Meditations* for Soprano, Organ, and Percussion (1961); *Télégramme* for Children's Chorus, 2 Pianos, and Percussion (1963); *Dialogues* for Violin and Orch. (1963); *Enfiando* for Orch. (1970); *Salmo gioioso* for Soprano and 5 Wind Instruments (1970); *Warsaw* for Narrator, Chorus, and Orch. (1974); *Wordsworth Songs* for Baritone and Chamber Ensemble (Warsaw, Sept. 23, 1976); *Clarinetto divertente* for Solo Clarinet (1976); piano pieces; songs.

Bloch, Ernest, remarkable Swiss-born American composer of Jewish ancestry; b. Geneva, July 24, 1880; d. Portland, Oreg., July 15, 1959. He studied solfeggio with Jaques-Dalcroze and violin with Louis Rey in Geneva (1894–97); then went to Brussels, where he took violin lessons with Ysaÿe and composition with Rasse (1897–99); while a student, he wrote a string quartet and a "symphonie orientale," indicative of his natural attraction to non-European cultures and coloristic melos. In 1900 he went to Germany, where he studied music theory with Iwan Knorr at the Hoch Cons. in Frankfurt and took private lessons with Ludwig Thuille in Munich; there he began the composition of his first full-fledged symphony, in C-sharp minor, with its 4 movements originally bearing titles expressive of changing moods. He then spent a year in Paris, where he met Debussy; Bloch's first published work, *Historiettes au crépuscule* (1903), shows Debussy's influence. In 1904 he returned to Geneva, where he began the composition of his only opera, *Macbeth,* after Shakespeare; the project of another opera, *Jézabel,* on a biblical subject, never materialized beyond a few initial sketches. As a tribute to his homeland, he outlined the orchestral work *Helvetia,* based on Swiss motifs, as early as 1900, but the full score was not completed until 1928. During the season 1909–10 Bloch conducted symphonic concerts in Lausanne and Neuchâtel. In 1916 he was offered an engagement as conductor on an American tour accompanying the dancer Maud Allan; he gladly accepted the opportunity to leave war-torn Europe, and expressed an almost childlike delight upon docking in the port of N.Y. at the sight of the Statue of Liberty. Maud Allan's tour was not successful, however, and Bloch returned to Geneva; in 1917 he received an offer to teach at the David Mannes School of Music in N.Y., and once more he sailed for America; he became an American citizen in 1924. This was also the period when Bloch began to express himself in music as an inheritor of Jewish culture; he explicitly articulated his racial consciousness in several verbal statements. His *Israel Symphony, Trois Poèmes juifs,* and *Schelomo,* a "Hebrew rhapsody" for Cello and Orch., mark the height of Bloch's greatness as a Jewish composer; long after his death, *Schelomo* still retains its popularity at symphony concerts. In America, he found sincere admirers and formed a group of greatly talented students, among them Roger Sessions, Ernst Bacon, George Antheil, Douglas Moore, Bernard Rogers, Randall Thompson, Quincy Porter, Halsey Stevens, Herbert Elwell, Isadore Freed, Frederick Jacobi, and Leon Kirchner. From 1920–25 he was director of the Inst. of Music in Cleveland, and from 1925–30, director of the San Francisco Cons. When the magazine *Musical America* announced in 1927 a contest for a symphonic work, Bloch won the first prize for his "epic rhapsody" entitled simply *America;* Bloch fondly hoped that the choral ending extolling America as the ideal of humanity would become a national hymn; the work was performed with a great outpouring of publicity in 5 cities, but as happens often with prizewinning works, it failed to strike the critics and the audiences as truly great, and in the end remained a mere by-product of Bloch's genius. From 1930–39 Bloch lived mostly in Switzerland; then returned to the U.S. and taught classes at the Univ. of Calif., Berkeley (1940–52); finally retired and lived at his newly purchased house at Agate Beach, Oreg. In his harmonic idiom Bloch favored sonorities formed by the bitonal relationship of 2 major triads with the tonics standing at the distance of a tritone, but even the dissonances he employed were euphonious. In his last works of chamber music he experimented for the first time with thematic statements of 12 different notes, but he never adopted the strict Schoenbergian technique of deriving the entire contents of a composition from the basic tone row. In his early Piano Quintet, Bloch made expressive use of quarter-tones in the string parts. In his Jewish works, he emphasized the interval of the augmented second, without a literal imitation of Hebrew chants.

WORKS: OPERA: *Macbeth* (1904–9; Opéra-Comique, Paris, Nov. 30, 1910). FOR ORCH.: *Poèmes d'automne,* songs for Mezzo-soprano and Orch. (1906); Prelude and 2 Psalms (Nos. 114 and 137) for Soprano and Orch. (1912–14); *Vivre-aimer,* symph. poem (1900; Geneva, June 23, 1901); Symph. in C-sharp minor (1901; first complete perf., Geneva, 1910; first American perf., N.Y. Phil., May 8, 1918, composer conducting); *Hiver-printemps,* symph. poem (1904–5; Geneva, Jan. 27, 1906); *Trois Poèmes juifs* (1913; Boston, March 23, 1917, composer conducting); *Israel,* symph. (1912–16; N.Y., May 3, 1917, composer conducting); *Schelomo,* Hebrew rhapsody for Cello and Orch. (1916; N.Y., May 3, 1917, composer conducting); Concerto Grosso No. 1 for Strings and Piano (1924–25; Cleveland, June 1, 1925, composer conducting); *America,* symph. poem (1926; N.Y., Dec. 20, 1928; next day simultaneously in Chicago, Philadelphia, Boston, and San Francisco); *Helvetia,* symph. poem (1928; Chicago, Feb. 18, 1932); *Voice in the Wilderness,* with Cello Obbligato (1936; Los Angeles, Jan. 21, 1937); *Evocations,* symph. suite (1937; San Francisco, Feb. 11, 1938); Violin Concerto (1938; first perf. by Szigeti, Cleveland, Dec. 15, 1938); *Suite symphonique* (Philadelphia, Oct. 26, 1945); *Concerto symphonique* for Piano and Orch. (Edinburgh, Sept. 3, 1949); *Scherzo*

fantasque for Piano and Orch. (Chicago, Dec. 2, 1950); *In Memoriam* (1952); *Suite hébraïque* for Viola and Orch. (Chicago, Jan. 1, 1953); *Sinfonia breve* (BBC, London, April 11, 1953); Concerto Grosso No. 2 for String Orch. (BBC, London, April 11, 1953); Symph. for Trombone Solo and Orch. (1953–54; Houston, April 4, 1956); Symph. in E-flat (1954–55; London, Feb. 15, 1956); *Proclamation* for Trumpet and Orch. (1955). CHAMBER MUSIC: *Episodes* for Chamber Orch. (1926); Quintet for Piano and Strings, with use of quarter-tones (1923; N.Y., Nov. 11, 1923); First String Quartet (N.Y., Dec. 29, 1916); 2 Suites for String Quartet (1925); 3 Nocturnes for Piano Trio (1924); Suite for Viola and Piano (won the Coolidge prize, 1919); First Violin Sonata (1920); 2nd Violin Sonata, *Poème mystique* (1924); *Baal Shem* for Violin and Piano (1923); *Méditation hébraïque* and *From Jewish Life,* both for Cello and Piano (1925); Piano Sonata (1935); 2nd String Quartet (London, Oct. 9, 1946; received the N.Y. Music Critics Circle Award for chamber music, 1947); 3rd String Quartet (1951); 4th String Quartet (Lenox, Mass., June 28, 1954); 5th String Quartet (1956); 3 Suites for Cello Unaccompanied (1956); Piano Quintet No. 2 (1956; Dec. 6, 1959); *Suite Modale* for Flute Solo and Strings (1957; Kentfield, Calif., April 11, 1965); 2 Suites for Unaccompanied Violin (1958); Suite for Unaccompanied Viola (1958; the last movement incomplete); *2 Last Poems* for Flute and Chamber Orch.: *Funeral Music* and *Life Again?* (1958; anticipatory of death from terminal cancer). PIANO MUSIC: *Poems of the Sea, In the Night, Nirvana, 5 Sketches in Sepia.* FOR VOICE: A modern Hebrew ritual, *Sacred Service* (1930–33; world premiere, Turin, Italy, Jan. 12, 1934); *Historiettes au crépuscule,* 4 songs for Mezzo-soprano and Piano (1903). Bloch contributed a number of informative annotations for the program books of the Boston Symph., N.Y. Phil., and other orchs.; also contributed articles to music journals, among them "Man and Music" in *Musical Quarterly* (Oct. 1933). An Ernest Bloch Society was formed in London in 1937 with the objective of promoting performances of Bloch's music, with Albert Einstein as honorary president and with vice-presidents including Sir Thomas Beecham, Havelock Ellis, and Romain Rolland.

BIBLIOGRAPHY: Paul Rosenfeld, in *Musical Portraits* (N.Y., 1920); G.M. Gatti, "Ernest Bloch," *Musical Quarterly* (1921); Roger Sessions, "Ernest Bloch," *Modern Music* (1927); R. Stackpole, "Ernest Bloch," *Modern Music* (1927); Mary Tibaldi Chiesa, *Bibliografia delle opere musicali di Ernest Bloch* (Turin, 1931); M.T. Chiesa, *Ernest Bloch* (Turin, 1933); Dika Newlin, "The Later Works of Ernest Bloch," *Musical Quarterly* (Oct. 1947); Henry Cowell, "Current Chronicle," *Musical Quarterly* (1954); D.Z. Kushner, "A Commentary on Ernest Bloch's Symphonic Works," *Radford Review* (Summer 1967); W.M. Jones, "Ernest Bloch's Five String Quartets," *Music Review* (May 1967); M. Griffel, "Bibliography of Writings on Ernest Bloch," *Current Musicology, 6* (1968); D.Z. Kushner, "Catalogue of the Works of Ernest Bloch," *American Music Teacher* (Feb./March 1969); A.V. Knapp, "The Jewishness of

Bloch: Subconscious or Conscious," *Proceedings of the Royal Music Association* (1970/71); D.Z. Kushner, *Ernest Bloch and His Music* (Glasgow, 1973); R. Strassburg, *Ernest Bloch, Voice in the Wilderness* (Los Angeles, 1977; contains a list of unpubl. works and of MSS in the Library of Congress in Washington, D.C., and in the Bloch Archive at the Univ. of Calif., Berkeley); Suzanne Bloch, *Ernest Bloch: Creative Spirit*, a program source book (by the composer's daughter, in collaboration with Irene Heskes; N.Y., 1976).

Bloch, Suzanne, lutenist and harpsichordist, daughter of **Ernest Bloch;** b. Geneva, Aug. 7, 1907. She came to the U.S. with her father; studied there with him and with Roger Sessions; then in Paris with Nadia Boulanger. She became interested in early polyphonic music and began to practice on old instruments to be able to perform music on the instruments for which it was written.

Blockx, Jan, significant Flemish composer; b. Antwerp, Jan. 25, 1851; d. Kapellenbos, near Antwerp, May 26, 1912. He studied organ with Callaerts and composition with Benoit. In 1885 he became a lecturer at the Flemish Music School; also was music director of the Cercle Artistique and other societies in Belgium. With Benoit, he is regarded as the strongest representative of the national Flemish school of composition; while the melodic and rhythmic materials in his music strongly reflect Flemish folk elements, the treatment, contrapuntal and harmonic, is opulent, approaching Wagnerian sonorities.
WORKS: Operas: *Jets vergeten* (Antwerp, Feb. 19, 1877); *Maître Martin* (Brussels, Nov. 30, 1892); *Herbergprinses* (Antwerp, Oct. 10, 1896; produced in French as *Princesse d'Auberge*, N.Y., March 10, 1909); *Thyl Uylenspiegel* (Brussels, Jan. 12, 1900); *De Bruid van Zee* (Antwerp, Nov. 30, 1901); *De Kapel* (Antwerp, Nov. 7, 1903); *Baldie* (Antwerp, Jan. 25, 1908; revised and performed under the title *Liefdelied;* Antwerp, Jan. 6, 1912); a ballet, *Milenka* (1887); *Rubens*, overture for Orch.; *Romance* for Violin and Orch.; several choral works with Orch., among them: *Vredezang; Het droom vant paradies; De klokke Roelandt; Op den stroom; Scheldezang.*
BIBLIOGRAPHY: L. Solvay, *Notice sur Jan Blockx* (1920); F. Blockx, *Jan Blockx* (1943).

Blodek, Wilhelm, Czech composer; b. Prague, Oct. 3, 1834; d. there, May 1, 1874. He studied with J.B. Kittl and A. Dreyschock; taught for 3 years in Poland; then returned to Prague, and became a prof. of flute at the Prague Cons. (1860–70). In 1870 he became insane and spent the rest of his life in an asylum. His opera in the Czech language, *V Studni (In the Well),* was produced with excellent success in Prague (Nov. 17, 1867); it was also given in German under the title *Im Brunnen* (Leipzig, 1893). His 2nd opera, *Zitek,* remained unfinished at his death; it was completed by F.X. Vana, and produced in Prague at the centennial of Blodek's birth (Oct. 3, 1934). Blodek also wrote Symph. in D minor (1859) and Flute Concerto (1862).
BIBLIOGRAPHY: R. Budiš, *Vilem Blodek* (Prague, 1964).

Blodgett, Benjamin Colman, American organist; b. Boston, March 12, 1838; d. Seattle, Sept. 22, 1925. He studied organ in Boston and was an organist at several churches there; then taught music at Smith College; from 1906–14 he was organist at Stanford Univ. in California. He finally settled in Seattle.

Blom, Eric, preeminent English writer on music; b. Bern, Switzerland, Aug. 20, 1888; d. London, April 11, 1959. He was of Danish and British extraction on his father's side; his mother was Swiss. He was educated in England. He was the London music correspondent for the *Manchester Guardian* (1923–31); then was the music critic of the *Birmingham Post* (1931–46) and of *The Observer* in 1949; edited *Music & Letters* from 1937–50 and from 1954 to the time of his death; he was also the editor of the Master Musicians series. In 1946 he was elected a member of the music committee of the British Council; in 1948, became member of the Royal Musical Assoc. In 1955 he was made a Commander of the Order of the British Empire in recognition of his services to music and received the honorary degree of D.Litt. from Birmingham Univ. In his writings Blom combined an enlightened penetration of musical esthetics with a literary capacity for presenting his subjects and stating his point of view in a brilliant journalistic manner. In his critical opinions he never concealed his disdain for some composers of great fame and renown, such as Rachmaninoff. In 1946 he was entrusted with the preparation of a newly organized and greatly expanded edition of *Grove's Dictionary of Music and Musicians,* which was brought out under his editorship in 1954, in 9 vols., and to which Blom himself contributed hundreds of articles and translated entries by foreign contributors. In his adamant determination to make this edition a truly comprehensive work, he insisted on the inclusion of complete lists of works of important composers and exact dates of performance of operas and other major works. In 1946 Blom publ. his first lexicographical work, *Everyman's Dictionary of Music,* which was reissued in an amplified edition by Jack Westrup in 1971. His other books include: *Stepchildren of Music* (1923); *The Romance of the Piano* (1927); *A General Index to Modern Musical Literature in the English Language* (1927; indexes periodicals for the years 1915–26); *The Limitations of Music* (1928); *Mozart* (1935); *Beethoven's Pianoforte Sonatas Discussed* (1938); *A Musical Postbag* (1941; collected essays); *Music in England* (1942; revised 1947); *Some Great Composers* (1944); *Classics, Major and Minor, with Some Other Musical Ruminations* (London, 1958).

Blomberg, Erik, Swedish composer; b. Järnskog, May 6, 1922. He studied with Erland von Koch and Gunnar Bucht; later went to Uppsala, where he became a music teacher.
WORKS: 5 symphs.: No. 1, *4 dramatiska skisser*

(1966); No. 2, *3 studier i melodik* (1968); No. 3, *Associationskedjor* (1971); No. 4 (1973); No. 5 (1974); *3 Orchestral Fragments* (1968); *Dialog* for Piano and Orch. (1969); *Debatt* for Wind Orch. (1970); *Vila i rörelse* for String Orch. (1970); *Vom Tod* for Soloists, Chorus, and Instruments (1970); *Die allerbeste Gabe* for Soloists, Chorus, and Orch. (1972); *Kompriment I–XIII* for various instrumental formations (1971–75); 3 string quartets; *4 Miniatures* for String Trio (1966); 3 piano sonatas (1965, 1968, 1971).

Blomdahl, Karl-Birger, significant Swedish composer; b. Växjö, Oct. 19, 1916; d. Kungsängen (near Stockholm), June 14, 1968. He studied composition with Hilding Rosenberg and conducting with Thor Mann in Stockholm; in 1946 he traveled in France and Italy on a state stipend; in 1954–55 he attended a seminar at Tanglewood on a grant of the American-Scandinavian Foundation. Returning to Sweden, he taught composition at the Royal College of Music in Stockholm (1960–64); in 1964 he was appointed music director at the Swedish Radio. He was an organizer (with Bäck, Carlid, Johanson, and Lidholm) of a "Monday Group" in Stockholm, dedicated to the propagation of an objective and abstract idiom as distinct from the prevalent type of Scandinavian romanticism. Blomdahl's early works are cast in a neo-Classical idiom, but he then turned to advanced techniques, including the application of electronic music. His 3rd symph., subtitled *Facetter (Facets),* utilizes dodecaphonic techniques. In 1959 he brought out his opera *Aniara,* which made him internationally famous; it pictures a pessimistic future when the remnants of the inhabitants of the planet Earth, devastated by atomic wars and polluted by radiation, are forced to emigrate to saner worlds in the galaxy; the score employs electronic sounds, and its thematic foundation is derived from a series of 12 different notes and 11 different intervals.
WORKS: Trio for Oboe, Clarinet, and Bassoon (1938); String Quartet No. 1 (1939); *Symphonic Dances* (Göteborg, Feb. 29, 1940); *Concert Overture* (Stockholm, Feb. 14, 1942); Suite for Cello and Piano (1944); Viola Concerto (Stockholm, Sept. 7, 1944); Symph. No. 1 (Stockholm, Jan. 26, 1945); Concerto Grosso (Stockholm, Oct. 2, 1945); *Vaknatten (The Wakeful Night),* theater music (1945); *3 Polyphonic Pieces* for Piano (1945); String Trio (1945); Suite for Cello and Piano (1945); *Little Suite* for Bassoon and Piano (1945); Concerto for Violin and String Orch. (Stockholm, Oct. 1, 1947); Symph. No. 2 (Stockholm, Dec. 12, 1952); *Dance Suite No. 1* for Flute, Violin, Viola, Cello, and Percussion (1948); String Quartet No. 2 (1948); *Pastoral Suite* for String Orch. (1948); *Prelude and Allegro* for Strings (1949); Symph. No. 3, *Facetter (Facets;* 1950; Frankfurt Festival, June 24, 1951); *Dance Suite No. 2* for Clarinet, Cello, and Percussion (1951); *I speglarnas sal (In the Hall of Mirrors),* oratorio of 9 sonnets from Erik Lindegren's "The Man without a Road," for Soli, Chorus, and Orch. (1951–52; Stockholm, May 29, 1953); Chamber Concerto for Piano, Woodwinds, and Percussion (Stockholm, Oct. 30, 1953);

Sisyfos, choreographic suite for Orch. (Stockholm, Oct. 20, 1954; produced as a ballet, Stockholm, April 18, 1957); Trio for Clarinet, Cello, and Piano (1955); *Anabase* for Baritone, Narrator, Chorus, and Orch. (Stockholm, Dec. 14, 1956); *Minotaurus,* ballet (Stockholm, April 5, 1958); *Aniara,* futuristic opera with electronic sound, after Harry Martinson's novel about an interplanetary voyage; libretto by Erik Lindegren (1957–59; Stockholm, May 31, 1959; numerous perfs. in Europe); *Fioriture* for Orch. (Cologne, June 17, 1960); *Forma ferritonans* for Orch. (Oxelösund, June 17, 1961); *Spel för åtta (Game for 8),* ballet (Stockholm, June 8, 1962; also a choreographic suite for Orch., 1964); *Herr von Hancken,* comic opera (Stockholm, Sept. 2, 1965); *Altisonans,* electronic piece from natural sound sources (1966); *. . . resan i denna natt (. . . the voyage in this night),* cantata, after Lindegren, for Soprano and Orch. (Stockholm, Oct. 19, 1966). At the time of his death, Blomdahl was working on an opera entitled *The Saga of the Great Computer,* incorporating electronic and concrete sounds, and synthetic speech.
BIBLIOGRAPHY: Gunnar Bucht, ed., *"Facetter" av och om Karl-Birger Blomdahl* (Stockholm, 1970; contains a complete catalogue of works and dates of first perfs.); R.K. Inglefield, "Karl-Birger Blomdahl: A Portrait," *Musical Quarterly* (Jan. 1972).

Blomstedt, Herbert, American-born Swedish conductor; b. Springfield, Mass., July 11, 1927. He was educated at the Royal Academy of Music in Stockholm and the Univ. of Uppsala, then studied conducting with Igor Markevitch in Paris, and with Jean Morel and Leonard Bernstein in N.Y. He was music director of the Norrköping Symph. Orch. (1954–61); then conductor of the Oslo Phil. Orch. (1962–68) and of the Danish State Radio Symph. Orch. of Copenhagen (1967–77). Subsequently he was appointed chief conductor of the Swedish Radio Symph. Orch. In 1975 he became principal conductor of the Dresden State Orch.; he toured the U.S. with this ensemble in the fall of 1979.

Blon, Franz von, German composer; b. Berlin, July 16, 1861; d. Seilershof, Oct. 21, 1945. He studied in Berlin; was active as a conductor. He wrote the operettas *Die Amazone* (1903) and *Die tolle Prinzess* (1913), and much instrumental music of a light variety, particularly waltzes and marches.

Blondeau, Pierre-Auguste-Louis, French violist and composer; b. Paris, Aug. 15, 1784; d. there, 1865. He studied at the Paris Cons. with Baillot, Gossec, and Méhul; won the Prix de Rome in 1808 with his cantata, *Maria Stuart;* was violist in the Grand Opéra until 1842. He wrote an opera, *Alla fontana;* a ballet; 3 overtures; church music; chamber music; piano pieces and songs; also a number of theoretical works.

Bloomfield, Fannie. See **Zeisler, Fannie Bloomfield.**

Bloomfield, Theodore, American conductor; b.

Cleveland, June 14, 1923. He studied piano at the Oberlin Cons. (Mus.B., 1944); then took courses in conducting at the Juilliard School in N.Y.; also studied piano with Claudio Arrau and conducting with Pierre Monteux. In 1946–47 he was apprentice conductor to George Szell at the Cleveland Orch.; then conducted the Cleveland Little Symph. and the Civic Opera Workshop (1947–52). He was subsequently music director of the Portland (Oreg.) Symph. (1955–59) and of the Rochester (N.Y.) Phil. (1959–63). He then settled in Germany; was first conductor of the Hamburg State Opera (1964–66) and generalmusik-direktor of Frankfurt (1966–68). In 1975 he became chief conductor of the West Berlin Symph. Orch. He has established a fine reputation for his programs of rarely performed works by old and contemporary composers.

Blow, John, great English composer and organist; b. Newark-on-Trent, Nottinghamshire, Feb. (baptized, Feb. 23) 1648 or 1649; d. Westminster (London), Oct. 1, 1708. In 1660–61 he was a chorister at the Chapel Royal, under Henry Cooke; he later studied organ with Christopher Gibbons. His progress was rapid, and on Dec. 3, 1668, he was appointed organist of Westminster Abbey. In 1679 he left this post and Purcell, who had been Blow's student, succeeded him. After Purcell's untimely death in 1695, Blow was reappointed, and remained at Westminster Abbey until his death; he was buried there, in the north aisle. He married Elizabeth Braddock in 1674; she died in 1683 in childbirth, leaving 5 children. Blow held the rank of Gentleman of the Chapel Royal from March 16, 1673 or 1674; on July 23, 1674, he succeeded Humfrey as Master of the Children of the Chapel Royal; was Master of the Choristers at St. Paul's (1687–1702 or 1703); in 1699 he was appointed Composer of the Chapel Royal. He held the honorary Lambeth degree of D.Mus., conferred on him in 1677 by the Dean of Canterbury. While still a young chorister of the Chapel Royal, Blow began to compose church music; in collaboration with Humfrey and William Turner, he wrote the *Club Anthem* ("I will always give thanks"); at the behest of Charles II, he made a 2-part setting of Herrick's poem "Goe, perjur'd man." He wrote many secular part-songs, among them an ode for New Year's Day 1681/82, "Great sir, the joy of all our hearts," an ode for St. Cecilia; 2 anthems for the coronation of James II; *Epicedium for Queen Mary* (1695); *Ode on the Death of Purcell* (1696). Blow's collection of 50 songs, *Amphion Anglicus,* was publ. in 1700. His best-known work is *Masque for the Entertainment of the King: Venus and Adonis,* written c.1685; this is his only complete score for the stage, but he contributed separate songs for numerous dramatic plays. Purcell regarded Blow as "one of the greatest masters in the world." Fourteen large works by Blow, anthems and harpsichord pieces, have been preserved; 11 anthems are printed in Boyce's *Cathedral Musick* (1760–78). Selected anthems are publ. in *Musica Britannica,* 7. The vocal score of his masque *Venus and Adonis* was publ. by G.E.P. Arkwright in the Old English Edition (No.

25; 1902); the complete score was publ. by the Editions de l'Oiseau Lyre, as ed. by Anthony Lewis (Paris, 1939).

BIBLIOGRAPHY: G.E.P. Arkwright's introduction to "Six Songs by Dr. John Blow" in the Old English Edition (No. 23; 1900); H.W. Shaw's "John Blow, Doctor of Music," in *Musical Times* (Oct.–Dec. 1937; also separately, London, 1943); id., "Blow's Use of the Ground Bass," in *Musical Quarterly* (Jan. 1938); id., "John Blow's Anthems," *Music & Letters* (Oct. 1938); H.L. Clarke, "John Blow: A Tercentenary Survey," *Musical Quarterly* (July 1949); W. Shaw, "The Autographs of John Blow," *Music Review,* XXV (1964); R. McGuinness, *English Court Odes 1660–1820* (Oxford, 1971); B. Wood, *John Blow's Anthems with Orchestra* (Diss., Cambridge Univ., 1977).

Blum, Robert, important Swiss composer; b. Zürich, Nov. 27, 1900. He studied at the Zürich Cons. with Andreae, Jarnach, and others; in 1924 he took some lessons with Busoni. Upon his return to Switzerland, he devoted himself to choral conducting and teaching. In 1943 he was appointed prof. at the Music Academy in Zürich. In his own compositions he cultivates polyphonic music in the traditional style, enhanced by modern harmonies and occasionally dissonant contrapuntal lines.
WORKS: Opera, *Amarapura* (1926); oratorio, *Kindheit Jesu* (1936); many sacred choral works and Psalms for Voice and Orch.; 6 symphs. (1924, 1926, 1935, 1959, 1961, 1969); *Passionskonzert* for Organ and String Orch. (1943); *Seldwyla-Symphonie* (1968); *4 Partite* for Orch. (1929, 1935, 1953, 1967); Concerto for Orch. (1955); *Overture on Swiss Themes* (1944); *Christ ist erstanden,* orch. variations (1962); *Lamentatio angelorum* for Chamber Orch. (1943); Viola Concerto (1951); Oboe Concerto (1960); Concerto for Wind Quintet (1962); Triple Concerto for Violin, Oboe, Trumpet, and Chamber Orch. (1963); Flute Quartet (1963); Sonata for Flute and Violin (1963); *Concertante Symphonie* for Wind Quintet and Chamber Orch. (1964); *Divertimento* on a 12-tone row for 10 Instruments (1966); *Le Tombe di Ravenna* for 11 Woodwind Instruments (1968); Quartet for Clarinet and String Trio (1970); String Quartet (1970); numerous songs, organ pieces, and arrangements of old vocal compositions.

Blume, Clemens, German music scholar; b. Billerbeck, Jan. 31, 1862; d. Königstein, April 8, 1932. He studied theology; then taught it at the Catholic Univ. in Frankfurt. He was regarded as an authority on texts of medieval Latin hymns. His books include *Cursus Sanctus Benedicti* (liturgical hymns of the 6th to 9th centuries; 1908); *Guide to Chevalier's "Repertorium Hymnologicum"* (1911); *Analecta hymnica medii aevi* (his standard work; 1896–1922; vols. 1–48, co-ed. with C.M. Dreves; some vols. with H.M. Bannister). A selection from this valuable source book of hymnological research was extracted as *Ein Jahrtausend lateinischer Hymnendichtung* (2 vols., 1909). Blume also publ. *Unsere* *liturgischen Lieder* (Pustet, 1932).

Blume, Friedrich, preeminent German musicologist and editor; b. Schlüchtern, Jan. 5, 1893; d. there, Nov. 22, 1975. He was the son of a Prussian government functionary; first studied medicine in Eisenach; in 1911 he went to the Univ. of Munich, where he began his musicological studies; then went to the univs. of Leipzig and Berlin. During World War I he was in the German army; was taken prisoner by the British and spent three years in a prison camp in England. In 1919 he resumed his studies at the Univ. of Leipzig, where he took his Ph.D. in 1921 with the dissertation *Studien zur Vorgeschichte der Orchestersuite im 15. und 16. Jahrhundert* (publ. in Leipzig, 1925); in 1923 he became a lecturer in music at the Univ. of Berlin; in 1925 he completed his Habilitation there with *Das monodische Prinzip in der protestantischen Kirchenmusik* (publ. in Leipzig, 1925); was made Privatdozent there that same year; also lectured in music history at the Berlin-Spandau School of Church Music from 1928 to 1934. In 1934 he joined the faculty of the Univ. of Kiel, where he was prof. from 1938 until his retirement in 1958; was then made prof. emeritus. He was an authority on Lutheran church music; his *Die evangelische Kirchenmusik* was published in Bücken's *Handbuch der Musikwissenschaft,* X (1931; 2nd ed., revised, as *Geschichte der evangelischen Kirchenmusik,* 1965; in Eng., as *Protestant Church Music: A History,* 1974). He prepared a collected edition of the works of M. Praetorius (21 vols., Berlin, 1928–41); was general editor of *Das Chorwerk,* a valuable collection of old polyphonic music (1929–38); also editor of *Das Erbe deutscher Musik* (1935–43). In 1943 he was entrusted with the preparation of the monumental encyclopedia *Die Musik in Geschichte und Gegenwart* (14 vols., Kassel, 1949–68); following its publication, he undertook the further task of preparing an extensive Supplement, which contained numerous additional articles and corrections of ascertainable errors; its publication was continued after his death by his daughter, Ruth Blume. He also wrote *Wesen und Werden deutscher Musik* (Kassel, 1944); *Johann Sebastian Bach im Wandel der Geschichte* (Kassel, 1947; Eng. trans. as *Two Centuries of Bach,* 1950); *Goethe und die Musik* (Kassel, 1948); *Was ist Musik?* (Kassel, 1959); *Umrisse eines neuen Bach-Bildes* (Kassel, 1962). His life's work was a study in the practical application of his vast erudition and catholic interests in musicological scholarship.
BIBLIOGRAPHY: A. Abert and W. Pfannkuch, eds., *Festschrift Friedrich Blume zum 70. Geburtstag* (Kassel, 1963); G. Feder, "Friedrich Blume zum 80. Geburtstag," and G. Henle, "Zum 80. Geburtstag von Friedrich Blume," in *Haydn Studien* (Jan. 1973).

Blumenfeld, Felix, Russian composer and conductor; b. Kovalevka, near Kherson, April 19, 1863; d. Moscow, Jan. 21, 1931. He studied piano in Elizavetgrad; then went to St. Petersburg, where he studied composition with Rimsky-Korsakov; upon gradua-tion in 1885, he joined the staff of the Cons. and taught there until 1905, and again from 1911–18; from 1895–1911 he was the conductor at the Imperial Opera in St. Petersburg; he was also a guest conductor in the Russian repertoire in Paris during the "Russian seasons" in 1908. He was a pianist of virtuoso caliber; was also active as an accompanist for Chaliapin and other famous singers. From 1918–22 he was a prof. of piano at the Cons. of Kiev, and from 1922 to his death he taught at the Moscow Cons. Among his piano students was Vladimir Horowitz. As a composer, Blumenfeld excelled mainly in his piano pieces and songs, many of them publ. by Belaiev. He also wrote a symph., entitled *To the Beloved Dead;* a String Quartet; some other pieces.

Blumenfeld, Harold, American composer; b. Seattle, Oct. 15, 1923. He studied composition with Bernard Rogers at the Eastman School of Music in Rochester, N.Y. (1941–43); after military service in World War II, he took courses in composition with Paul Hindemith at Yale Univ. (B.M., 1949; M.M., 1950); also studied conducting with Robert Shaw and Leonard Bernstein and operatic stage direction with Boris Goldovsky at the Berkshire Music Center at Tanglewood. In 1951 he became an assistant prof. at Washington Univ. in St. Louis; was director of the Opera Studio there (1963–71). From 1964 to 1968 he also was artistic director of the Opera Theatre of St. Louis.
WORKS: 3 operas: *Amphitryon 4,* after Molière (1962; the *Miniature Overture* has become successful as an orch. piece); *Fritzi* (1979); *Four-Score: An Opera of Opposites,* after Johann Nestroy's *Haus der Temperamente* (1984); *Transformations* for Piano (1963); *Expansions* for Woodwind Quintet (1964); *Movement* for Brass (1965); *War Lament* for a cappella Chorus, with Guitar obbligato, after Siegfried Sassoon (1970); *Eroscapes* for Coloratura Soprano, String Trio, and Woodwind Quintet, after poems of Isabella Gardner (1971); *Song of Innocence* for Soloists, Large Chorus, Chamber Chorus, and Orch., after Blake (1973); *Starfires,* cantata (1975); *Circle of the Eye,* song cycle after poems of Tom McKeown (1975); *Rilke* for Voice and Guitar (1975); *La Vie antérieure,* "spatial" cantata after Baudelaire (1976); *Voyages,* cantata after Hart Crane (1977); *Silentium,* song cycle after poems of Osip Mandelstam (1979); *La Voix reconnue,* cantata after Verlaine (1979); *La Face cendrée,* cantata after Rimbaud (1981).

Blumenschein, William Leonard, German-American composer and choral conductor; b. Brensbach, Germany, Dec. 16, 1849; d. Dayton, Ohio, March 27, 1916. He studied at the Leipzig Cons. with Reinecke (1869–72); then emigrated to the U.S. and settled in Dayton, Ohio, where he conducted several choral societies. He publ. some 50 piano pieces in an effective salon style; about 60 anthems; sacred choruses.

Blumental, Felicja, pianist; b. Warsaw, Dec. 28, 1918. She studied piano at the Warsaw Cons.; in 1945, she emigrated to Brazil and became a Brazilian citizen. Villa-Lobos dedicated his 5th Piano Concerto to her; she played this work many times under his direction. Penderecki wrote his *Partita for Harpsichord and Orchestra* for her.

Blumenthal, Jacob, German pianist; b. Hamburg, Oct. 4, 1829; d. London, May 17, 1908. He studied music in Hamburg and Vienna; in 1846 went to Paris, where he became a student of piano with Herz and of composition with Halévy. In 1848 he settled in London, where he became court pianist to Queen Victoria. He composed a number of melodious piano pieces in a fashionable salon style.

Blumer, Theodor, German conductor and composer; b. Dresden, March 24, 1881; d. Berlin, Sept. 21, 1964. He studied at the Dresden Cons. and was active as a pianist, and from 1925–31 as a conductor on Dresden Radio. From 1931–42 he conducted radio broadcasts in Leipzig and in 1952 moved to Berlin. He wrote several light operas, among them *Der Fünf-Uhr-Tee* (Dresden, 1911) and *Trau schau wem!;* 3 symphs.; several overtures; a considerable amount of chamber music, including duo sonatas, trios, quartets, quintets, and sextets; a goodly amount of songs.

Blumner, Martin, German choral conductor and composer; b. Fürstenberg, Mecklenburg, Nov. 21, 1827; d. Berlin, Nov. 16, 1901. He studied philosophy and mathematics at Berlin Univ.; then music with Siegfried Dehn. In 1847 he became a member of the Berlin Singakademie; was appointed associate conductor (1853), then chief conductor (1876). He composed oratorios: *Abraham* (1860) and *Der Fall Jerusalems* (1874); cantatas: *Columbus* (1852); *In Zeit und Ewigkeit* (1885); *Festival Cantata* (1891); a *Te Deum* in 8 parts; motets; Psalms; etc.
BIBLIOGRAPHY: E. Dryander, *Zum Gedächtnis Martin Blumner* (Berlin, 1901).

Blüthner, Julius (Ferdinand), celebrated German piano maker; b. Falkenhain, near Merseburg, March 11, 1824; d. Leipzig, April 13, 1910. In 1853 he founded his establishment at Leipzig with 3 workmen; by 1897 it had grown to a sizable company, producing some 3,000 pianos yearly. Blüthner's specialty was the "Aliquotflügel," a grand piano with a sympathetic octave-string stretched over and parallel with each unison struck by the hammers. He was awarded many medals for his contributions to the advancement of piano construction. He was co-author, with H. Gretschel, of *Der Pianofortebau* (1872; 3rd ed., revised by R. Hannemann, Leipzig, 1909).

Boatwright, Howard (Leake, Jr.), American violinist, conductor, and composer; b. Newport News, Va., March 16, 1918. His mother was a registered nurse, his father a dentist; both liked to paint and both were musical. Boatwright had some violin lessons as a child; then was sent to Norfolk, where he studied with a professional violinist, Israel Feldman; at the age of 17 he made a debut as soloist with

the Richmond (Va.) Symph. Orch. From 1943 to 1945 he taught violin at the Univ. of Texas in Austin; then decided to acquire a more solid training in composition and enrolled in the class of Paul Hindemith at Yale Univ. (1945–48). Subsequently he taught there (1948–64); concurrently served as music director at St. Thomas' Church in New Haven, Conn. (1949–64). From 1964 to 1972 he was dean of the music school at Syracuse Univ.; then taught music theory there. He continued to give violin recitals, usually with his wife, the soprano **Helen Boatwright,** as joint artist. From 1950 to 1962 he was concertmaster of the New Haven Orch., and from 1957 to 1960 conducted the Yale Univ. Symph. He became greatly interested in the musical folklore of Eastern nations. In 1959 he went to India on grants from Fulbright and from the Rockefeller Foundation, and wrote 2 valuable monographs, *A Handbook of Staff Notation for Indian Music* and *Indian Classical Music and the Western Listener,* both publ. in Bombay in 1960. In his own works he successfully attempted to revive the modalities of old church music, using modern harmonies and linear counterpoint. His best works are of this type, mostly written for chorus.
WORKS: *Variations* for Chamber Orch. (1949); Symph. (1976); 2 string quartets (1947, 1975); *Serenade* for 2 String Instruments and 2 Wind Instruments (1952); Clarinet Quartet (1958); 12 pieces for Solo Violin (1977); *Mass* in C (1958); *The Passion According to St. Matthew* for Chorus (1962); *Canticle of the Sun* for Chorus (1963); choral pieces and songs, including *6 Prayers of Kierkegaard* for Soprano and Piano (1978).
BIBLIOGRAPHY: David Ewen, *American Composers* (N.Y., 1982).

Boatwright, McHenry, black American baritone; b. Tenile, Ga., Feb. 29, 1928. He studied at the New England Cons. in Boston; made his concert debut in 1956; sang in London in 1962; was soloist with the N.Y. Phil., the Philadelphia Orch., and other orchs. in the U.S. He created the central role in Gunther Schuller's opera *The Visitation* (Hamburg, Oct. 12, 1968).

Boccherini, Luigi, famous Italian composer; b. Lucca, Feb. 19, 1743; d. Madrid, May 28, 1805. He grew up in a musical environment and became a cello player. In 1757 he was engaged as a member of the orch. of the Court Theater in Vienna. From 1761 to 1763 he was in Lucca; after a year in Vienna he returned to Lucca and played cello at the theater orch. there. He undertook a concert tour with the violinist Filippo Manfredi in 1766. Then he went to Paris, where he appeared at the Concert Spirituel in 1768. He became exceedingly popular as a performer, and his own compositions were publ. in Paris; his first publications were 6 string quartets and 2 books of string trios. In 1769 he received a flattering invitation to the Madrid Court, and became chamber composer to the Infante Luis; after the latter's death he served as court composer to Friedrich Wilhelm II of Prussia; was appointed to the German

Court on Jan. 21, 1786. After the death of the King in 1797 he returned to Madrid. In 1800 he enjoyed the patronage of Napoleon's brother, Lucien Bonaparte, who served as French ambassador to Madrid. Despite his successes at various European courts, Boccherini lost his appeal to his patrons and to the public. He died in Madrid; in a belated tribute to a native son, the authorities in Lucca had his remains transferred there and reinterred with great solemnity in 1927. Boccherini had profound admiration for Haydn; indeed, so close was Boccherini's style to Haydn's that this affinity gave rise to the saying, "Boccherini is the wife of Haydn." He was an exceptionally fecund composer, specializing almost exclusively in chamber music. The list of his works includes 20 chamber symphs.; 2 octets; 16 sextets; 125 string quintets; 12 piano quintets; 18 quintets for Strings and Flute (or Oboe); 102 string quartets; 60 string trios; 21 violin sonatas; 6 cello sonatas; also 4 cello concertos. He further wrote much guitar music, a Christmas cantata, and some sacred works.

BIBLIOGRAPHY: D.M. Cerù, *Cenni intorno alla vita e le opere di Luigi Boccherini* (Lucca, 1864); H.M. Schletterer, *Boccherini* (Leipzig, 1882); G. Malfatti, *Luigi Boccherini nell' arte, nella vita e nelle opere* (Lucca, 1905); L. Parodi, *Luigi Boccherini* (1930); A. Bonaventura, *Boccherini* (Milan, 1931); G. de Rothschild, *Luigi Boccherini* (Paris, 1962; London, 1965); Yves Gérard, *Thematic, Bibliographical and Critical Catalogue of the Works of Luigi Boccherini* (London, 1969); P. Carmirelli, ed., *Le opere complete di Luigi Boccherini* (Rome, 1970); M. Ophee, *Luigi Boccherini's Guitar Quintets: New Evidence* (Boston, 1981).

Bochsa, Robert-Nicolas-Charles, celebrated French harpist; b. Montmédy, Meuse, Aug. 9, 1789; d. Sydney, Australia, Jan. 6, 1856. He first studied music with his father; played in public at the age of 7; wrote a symph. when he was 9, and an opera, *Trajan,* at 15. He then studied with Franz Beck in Bordeaux, and later at the Paris Cons. with Méhul and Catel (1806). His harp teachers were Nadermann and Marin. Of an inventive nature, Bochsa developed novel technical devices for harp playing, transforming the harp into a virtuoso instrument. He was the court harpist to Napoleon, and to Louis XVIII. He wrote 8 operas for the Opéra-Comique (1813–16); several ballets, an oratorio, and a great number of works for the harp; also a method for harp. In 1817 he became involved in some forgeries, and fled to London to escape prison. He became very popular as a harp teacher in London society; organized a series of oratorio productions with Sir George Smart (1822). He was also the first prof. of harp at the Academy of Music in London, but in 1827 he lost his position when a story of his dishonest conduct became widely known. However, he obtained a position as conductor of the Italian Opera at the King's Theatre (1826–30). Another scandal marked Bochsa's crooked road to success and notoriety when he eloped with the soprano **Ann Bishop,** the wife of Sir Henry Bishop, in Aug. 1839. He gave concerts with her in Europe, America, and Australia, where he died.

BIBLIOGRAPHY: Arthur Pougin, "Un Musicien voleur, faussaire et bigame," *Le Ménestrel* (Jan. 19– March 9, 1907); J.B. Weidensaul, "Bochsa: A Biographical Sketch," *American Harp Journal* (Fall 1970).

Bock, Jerry (real given names, **Jerrold Lewis**), American songwriter of popular music; b. New Haven, Conn., Nov. 23, 1928. He studied at the Univ. of Wisconsin; subsequently settled in N.Y. He gained wide recognition with his Broadway musicals *Mr. Wonderful* (1956), *The Body Beautiful* (1958), and *Fiorello!* (1959), based on the life of Fiorello LaGuardia. His greatest success was *Fiddler on the Roof* (1964), which was also made into a movie.

Bockelmann, Rudolf, German bass-baritone; b. Bodenteich, April 2, 1892; d. Dresden, Oct. 9, 1958. He studied singing with Karl Scheidemantel and Oscar Lassner in Leipzig. He then sang at the Neues Theater (1921–26) and at the Stadttheater in Hamburg (1926–32); appeared at the Bayreuth Festival in 1928; in 1929 and in 1934–38 he sang at Covent Garden, London; from 1930 to 1932 he was on the roster of the Chicago Opera Co. In 1932 he returned to Germany and became a member of the Staatsoper in Berlin for the duration of the war. His crypto-Nazi inclinations precluded further engagements outside Germany. He was particularly noted for his congenial interpretations of villainous Wagnerian bass roles. His own notations on operatic techniques were publ. in the *Sammelbände der Robert-Schumann-Gesellschaft,* II/1966 (Leipzig, 1967).

Böckh, August, German authority on Greek literature and music; b. Karlsruhe, Nov. 24, 1785; d. Berlin, Aug. 3, 1867. He studied philology at the Univ. of Halle; received his doctorate with the treatise *De harmonice veterum* (1807). In 1811 he became a prof. at the Univ. of Berlin, a position which he retained until his death. He edited the works of Pindar with an introduction, *De metris Pindari,* from which modern research on old Greek music received a new impetus.

BIBLIOGRAPHY: M. Hoffmann, *A. Böckh* (Leipzig, 1901); G. Lehmann, *Theorie und Geschichte der griechischen Harmonik in der Darstellung durch August Böckh* (Würzburg, 1935).

Boda, John, American composer; b. Boyceswille, Wis., Aug. 2, 1922. He studied at the Eastman School of Music in Rochester, N.Y.; in 1946 joined the faculty of Florida State Univ. at Tallahassee. His *Sinfonia* was first performed in Knoxville, on Dec. 6, 1960.

Bodanzky, Artur, famous Austrian conductor; b. Vienna, Dec. 16, 1877; d. New York, Nov. 23, 1939. He studied at the Vienna Cons., and later with Zemlinsky. He began his career as a violinist at the

Vienna Opera. In 1900 he received his first appointment as a conductor, leading an operetta season in Budweis; in 1902 he became assistant to Mahler at the Vienna Opera; conducted in Berlin (1905) and in Prague (1906–9). In 1909 he was engaged as music director at Mannheim. In 1912 he arranged a memorial Mahler Festival, conducting a huge ensemble of 1,500 vocalists and instrumentalists. He conducted *Parsifal* at Covent Garden in London in 1914; his success there led to an invitation to conduct the German repertoire at the Metropolitan Opera House; he opened his series with *Götterdämmerung* (Nov. 18, 1915). From 1916–31 he was director of the Society of Friends of Music in N.Y.; in 1919 he also conducted the New Symph. Orch. He made several practical arrangements of celebrated operas (*Oberon, Don Giovanni, Fidelio,* etc.), which he used for his productions with the Metropolitan Opera. His style of conducting was in the Mahler tradition, with emphasis on climactic effects and contrasts of light and shade.

Böddecker, Philipp Friedrich, German organist, bassoonist, and composer; b. Hagenau, Alsace (baptized, Aug. 5), 1607; d. Stuttgart, Oct. 8, 1683. He first studied in Stuttgart with J.U. Steigleder; from 1626–29 served as organist and singing master in Buchsweiler, Alsace; was then organist and bassoonist at the courts in Darmstadt and Durlach. In 1638 he became organist at Frankfurt's Barfüsserkirche; in 1642 was appointed organist at the Strasbourg Cathedral; in 1648 received the post of organist and director of music at the Univ. of Strasbourg. In 1652 he settled in Stuttgart as organist at the collegiate church there. He publ. the treatise *Manuductio nova methodica-practica bassum generalem* (Stuttgart, 1701). He composed *Melos irenicum* for 6 Soloists, 4-part Chorus, and Instruments (Strasbourg, 1650); also 8 sacred concertos. His son, **Philipp Jakob Böddecker** (b. Frankfurt, 1642; d. Stuttgart, Feb. 1, 1707), was also an organist and composer; he succeeded his father as organist at the collegiate church in Stuttgart (from 1686).

Bode, Johann Joachim Christoph, German instrumentalist and composer; b. Barum, Jan. 12, 1730; d. Weimar, Dec. 13, 1793. He began his career as a bassoon player; also played cello in the collegium musicum in Helmstedt and oboe in Celle; in 1757 he went to Hamburg, where he was active as a teacher, writer, publisher, and translator; in 1778 he settled in Weimar as a diplomat. As a composer, he wrote several symphs., a Cello Concerto, a Violin Concerto, a Bassoon Concerto, and songs.
BIBLIOGRAPHY: E. Greeven, *Johann Joachim Christoph Bode, Ein Hamburger Uebersetzer, Verleger und Drucker* (Weimar, 1938).

Bode, Rudolf, German acoustician and theorist of rhythmic gymnastics; b. Kiel, Feb. 3, 1881; d. Munich, Oct. 7, 1970. He studied physiology and philosophy at the Univ. of Leipzig, and music theory at the Leipzig Cons. After attending the Dalcroze Inst. of Eurhythmics in Hellerau, he formulated a system of "rhythmic gymnastics." In 1911 he founded a school in Munich with courses embodying his body theories, intended to achieve perfect physical and mental health. He publ. a number of books and essays on the subject: *Der Rhythmus und seine Bedeutung für die Erziehung* (Jena, 1920); *Ausdruckgymnastik* (Munich, 1922; in English as *Expressions-Gymnastic,* N.Y., 1931); *Musik und Bewegung* (Kassel, 1930); *Energie und Rhythmus* (Berlin, 1939). He also wrote a manual of piano study as a rhythmic muscular action, *Rhythmus und Anschlag* (Munich, 1933).

Bodenschatz, Erhard, German theologian and music editor; b. Lichtenberg, 1576; d. Gross-Osterhausen, near Querfurt, 1636. He was a pupil of Calvisius in Pforta; then studied theology in Leipzig. In 1600 he became cantor in Schulpforta; in 1603 was pastor in Rehausen, and in 1608, in Gross-Osterhausen, where he remained until his death. He publ. several valuable collections of motets and hymns; particularly important is *Florilegium Portense* in 2 parts: the first part originally contained 89 motets (Leipzig, 1603; 2nd ed., with 120 motets, 1618) and the 2nd part (Leipzig, 1621) contained 150 motets, all by contemporary composers. There have been several reprints. He also publ. *Florilegium selectissimorum hymnorum* in 4 vols. (Leipzig, 1606). Bodenschatz's own compositions are not distinctive.
BIBLIOGRAPHY: Otto Riemer, *Erhard Bodenschatz und sein Florilegium Portense* (Leipzig, 1928).

Bodin, Lars-Gunnar, Swedish composer; b. Stockholm, July 15, 1935. He studied composition with Lennart Wenström (1955–59); attended the Darmstadt summer courses (1961); in 1972 became director of the electronic studio at the Stockholm Cons. In collaboration with the Swedish concrete poet and composer Bengt Emil Johnson, he produced a series of pieces described as "text-sound compositions."
WORKS: Brass Quartet (1960); *Arioso* for Piano, Percussion, Cello, Clarinet, and Trombone (1962); *Calendar Music* for Piano (1963); *Semicolon* for Piano and Semaphoring Chorus (1964); *My World Is Your World* for Organ and Tape (1966); *"... from any point to any other point"* for Electronic Sound (1968; also produced as a ballet, in Stockholm, Sept. 20, 1968); electronic pieces: *Place of Plays; Winter Events* (1967); *Toccata* (1969); *Traces I* and *II* (1970–71); *From the Beginning to the End* (1973); *Seeings (Earth, Sky, Winds)* (1973); television ballet, *Händelser och handlingar* (*Events and Happenings;* 1971); 3 compositions entitled *Dedicated to You* for Organ and Tape (1971).

Bodky, Erwin, German-American music scholar; b. Ragnit, March 7, 1896; d. Lucerne, Switzerland, Dec. 6, 1958. He studied piano and theory in Berlin with Dohnányi and Juon; later attended classes of Richard Strauss and Busoni at the Meisterschule für Komposition (1920–22). He subsequently taught at the Scharwenka School of Music. With the advent of the Nazi regime in 1933, Bodky went to Amsterdam, where he remained until 1938; then emigrated to the U.S., and taught at the Longy School of Music in Cambridge (1938–48); in 1949 was appointed a prof. at Brandeis Univ.

PUBLICATIONS: The valuable treatises *Der Vortag alter Klaviermusik* (Berlin, 1932), *Das Charakterstück* (Berlin, 1933), and *The Interpretation of J.S. Bach's Keyboard Works* (Cambridge, Mass., 1960; also in German, Tutzing, 1970).

BIBLIOGRAPHY: H. Slosbert et al., eds., *Erwin Bodky: A Memorial Tribute* (Waltham, Mass., 1965).

Bodley, Seóirse, Irish composer; b. Dublin, April 4, 1933. He studied at the Royal Irish Academy of Music and at Univ. College in Dublin (B.Mus., 1955). In 1957–59 he took courses in composition with Johann Nepomuk David in Stuttgart. Returning to Dublin, he was appointed lecturer at Univ. College (D.Mus., 1960). He devoted himself to a thorough study of Gaelic folksinging; his own music reflects this preoccupation; but he also experimented with serial techniques and novel instrumental combinations. His works include a Symph. (1958–59); Chamber Symph. (1964); Violin Sonata (1957); *Scintillae* for 2 Harps (1968); String Quartet (1969); choruses to English and Gaelic texts.

Boeck, August de, Belgian composer; b. Merchtem, May 9, 1865; d. there, Oct. 9, 1937. He studied organ at the Brussels Cons.; subsequently was church organist in Brussels; later taught harmony at the Royal Flemish Cons. at Antwerp and at the Brussels Cons. In 1930 he returned to his native town. He wrote operas and incidental music for stage plays; *Rapsodie Dahoméenne* for Orch., on exotic African themes (1893); an orch. fantasy on Flemish folk songs (1923); many songs to French and Flemish texts. Much of his orch. music is infused with impressionistic colors.

BIBLIOGRAPHY: F. Rasse, *A. De Boeck* (Brussels, 1943).

Boehe, Ernst, German composer and conductor; b. Munich, Dec. 27, 1880; d. Ludwigshafen, Nov. 16, 1938. He studied with Rudolf Louis and Thuille in Munich; in 1907 was associate conductor, with Courvoisier, of the Munich Volkssymphoniekonzerte; from 1913–20 was court conductor at Oldenburg; then conducted concerts in Ludwigshafen. His works are of a programmatic type, the orchestration emphasizing special sonorities of divided strings, massive wind instruments, and various percussive effects; his tone poems show a decisive Wagnerian influence, having a system of identification motifs. His most ambitious work was an orch. tetralogy on Homer's *Odyssey,* under the general title *Odysseus' Fahrten,* comprising: *Odysseus' Ausfahrt und Schiffbruch* (Munich, Feb. 20, 1903; Philadelphia, Dec. 3, 1904); *Die Insel der Kirke; Die Klage der Nausikaa;* and *Odysseus' Heimkehr;* also the symph. poem *Taormina* (Essen, 1906; Boston Symph., Nov. 29, 1907).

BIBLIOGRAPHY: Edgar Istel, "Ernst Boehe,"

Monographien moderner Musiker (Leipzig, 1909).

Boehmer, Konrad, German composer and writer on music; b. Berlin, May 24, 1941. He studied composition, musicology, sociology, and related sciences at Cologne Univ. (Ph.D., 1966); in 1967 he went to the Netherlands, where he lectured on music at the Royal Cons. in The Hague. He adopted a strong political stand of the extreme Marxist persuasion and delivered some sharp criticism against Stockhausen and other proponents of the avant-garde for their isolation from the musical masses, even classifying them as implicit adherents to imperialistic capitalism. In his own music he followed the ideas of Hanns Eisler; he also made use of electronic sound; typical of his belligerent sociomusical projections are *Potential* for Piano (1961); *Information* for Percussion and 2 Pianos (1964–65); and *Song without Words* for Voice and Chamber Orch., to a text by Ho Chi Minh.

Boekelman, Bernardus, Dutch pianist; b. Utrecht, the Netherlands, June 9, 1838; d. New York, Aug. 2, 1930. He studied with his father and at the Leipzig Cons. with Moscheles, Richter, and Hauptmann. In 1864 he emigrated to Mexico; in 1866 settled in N.Y. and then taught in various private schools. He publ. some piano pieces, edited the collection *Century of Music.* His analytical edition of Bach's *Well-Tempered Clavichord* and *2-Part Inventions* using colors to indicate part-writing is unique.

Boëllmann, Léon, French composer; b. Ensisheim, Alsace, Sept. 25, 1862; d. Paris, Oct. 11, 1897. He studied organ with Gigout; later was an organ teacher in Paris. He left 68 publ. works; his *Variations symphoniques* for Cello and Orch. became part of the repertoire of cello players. He wrote a symph., *Fantaisie dialoguée,* for Organ and Orch.; *Suite gothique* for Organ; Piano Quartet; Piano Trio; Cello Sonata; *Rapsodie carnavalesque* for Piano, 4-hands; publ. a collection of 100 pieces for organ under the title *Heures mystiques.*

BIBLIOGRAPHY: P. Locard, *L. Boëllmann* (Strasbourg, 1901).

Boëly, Alexandre Pierre François, French organist and composer; b. Versailles, April 19, 1785; d. Paris, Dec. 27, 1858. His father, a court musician, gave him his first instruction in music. Boëly studied piano and organ; occupied various positions as a church organist in Paris. As a teacher, he exercised a profound influence; Franck and Saint-Saëns owed much to him in the development of their style of composition for organ.

BIBLIOGRAPHY: A. Gastoué, "A Great French Organist: A. Boëly and His Works," *Musical Quarterly* (July 1944); this article gives a list of works and a bibliography of the principal studies on Boëly; N. Dufourcq, "Le 'cas' Boëly," *L'Orgue* (April/June 1971).

Boelza, Igor, Russian music scholar and composer;

b. Kielce, Poland, Feb. 8, 1904. He studied philology at the Univ. of Kiev; then taught at the Kiev Cons. (1929–41); then was on the staff of the Moscow Cons. (1942–49); was also a member of the board of the State Music Publishing House in Moscow (1941–48) and on the staff of the Inst. for the History of the Arts (1954–61); in 1961 he became a member of the Inst. for Slavonic Studies at the Academy of Sciences of the U.S.S.R. He contributed numerous informative articles dealing with the music of the Slavic countries to various publications; publ. *Handbook of Soviet Musicians* (London, 1943); *Czech Opera Classics* (Moscow, 1951); *History of Polish Musical Culture* (Moscow, 1954); and *History of Czech Musical Culture* (2 vols., Moscow, 1959–73).

Boepple, Paul, choral conductor and pedagogue; b. Basel, Switzerland, July 19, 1896; d. Brattleboro, Vt., Dec. 21, 1970. He took courses at the Dalcroze Inst. in Geneva, and adopted the Dalcroze system in his own method of teaching music; from 1918–26 he was a member of the faculty of the Inst. In 1926 he emigrated to the U.S.; directed the Dalcroze School of Music in N.Y. (1926–32); then taught at the Chicago Musical College (1932–34) and at Westminster Choir School in Princeton (1935–38); subsequently he taught at Bennington College in Vermont. As a choral conductor, he gave numerous performances of modern works.

Boero, Felipe, Argentine opera composer; b. Buenos Aires, May 1, 1884; d. there, Aug. 9, 1958. He studied with Pablo Berutti; received a government prize for further study in Europe and attended the classes of Vidal and Fauré at the Paris Cons. (1912–14). Returning to Buenos Aires, he became active as a teacher. Among his operas, the following were produced at the Teatro Colón: *Tucumán* (June 29, 1918); *Ariana y Dionisios* (Aug. 5, 1920); *Raquela* (June 25, 1923); *Las Bacantes* (Sept. 19, 1925); *El Matrero* (July 12, 1929); *Siripo* (June 8, 1937).

Boers, Joseph Karel, Dutch music scholar; b. Nimwegen, Aug. 4, 1812; d. Delft, Nov. 1, 1896. He was a pupil of Lübeck at The Hague Cons.; then was a theater conductor in the Netherlands and in France; in 1841 returned to Nimwegen as a teacher and choral conductor; in 1853 settled in Delft as a music director. He wrote an interesting treatise, *History of Musical Instruments in the Middle Ages;* also a complete bibliography of ancient and modern musical works produced in the Netherlands.

Boesch, Rainer, Swiss composer; b. Männedorf, Aug. 11, 1938. He studied in Zürich and Geneva; then took courses with Messiaen in Paris. After his return to Switzerland, he was active as a pianist. He composed a number of electronic and mixed-media works.

Boesmans, Philippe, Belgian composer; b. Tongeren, May 17, 1936. He studied composition with Froidebise and Pousseur, and piano at the Liège Cons. (1954–62). His music adheres to the abstract trends of cosmopolitan modernism, with structural formulas determining the contents. WORKS: *Etude I* for Piano (1963); *Sonance I* for 2 Pianos (1964); *Sonance II* for 3 Pianos (1967); *Impromptu* for 23 Instruments (1965); *Corrélations* for Clarinet and 2 Instrumental Ensembles (Brussels, Sept. 16, 1967); *Explosives* for Harp and 10 Instrumentalists (1968); *Verticles* for Orch. (1969); *Blocage* for Voice, Chorus, and Chamber Ensemble (1970); *Upon La, Mi* for Voice, Amplified Horn, and Instrumental Ensemble (1970); *Fanfare* for 2 Pianos (1971); *Intervalles I* for Orch. (1972); *Intervalles II* for Orch. (1973); *Intervalles III* for Voice and Orch. (1974); *Sur Mi* for 2 Pianos, Electric Organ, Crotale, and Tam-Tam (1974); *Multiples* for 2 Pianos and Orch. (1974); *Element—Extensions* for Piano and Chamber Orch. (1976).

Boësset, Antoine (Sieur de Villedieu), French composer of ballets; b. Blois, 1586; d. Paris, Dec. 8, 1643. He was court musician to Louis XIII, and wrote many *Airs du cour* for court performances; an Eng. edition of these works was publ. in 1629 under the title *French Court Aires;* a number of these were reprinted by H. Expert in *Chants de France et d'Italie.*

Boetius (or **Boethius**), **Anicius Manlius Torquatus Severinus,** Roman philosopher and mathematician; b. Rome, A.D. c.480; executed in 524 on suspicion of treason, by the Emperor Theodoric, whose counselor he had been for many years. Boetius wrote a treatise in 5 books, *De Institutione Musica,* which was the chief source book for the theorizing monks of the Middle Ages; this treatise was publ. in Venice (1491, 1499), in Basel (1570), in Leipzig (1867), and in a German trans. by Oscar Paul (Leipzig, 1872); a French trans. by Fétis remains in MS. Whether the notation commonly called "Boetian" (using Latin indices to denote traditional Greek notation) is properly attributable to him has been questioned for about 3 centuries (cf. Meibom, *Antiquae musicae auctores septem;* p. 7 of introduction on Alypius). For a defense of its authenticity, see F. Celentano, "La Musica presso i Romani," *Rivista musicale italiana* (1913). In this connection see also H. Potizon, *Boèce, théoricien de la musique grecque* (Paris, 1961). L. Schrade wrote several essays on Boetius: "Das propädeutische Ethos in der Musikanschauung des Boetius," *Zeitschrift für Geschichte der Erziehung und des Unterrichts* (1930); "Die Stellung der Musik in der Philosphie des Boetius," *Archiv für Geschichte der Philosophie* (1932); and "Music in the Philosophy of Boetius," *Musical Quarterly* (April 1947).

Boettcher, Wilfried, German cellist and conductor; b. Bremen, Aug. 11, 1929. He studied cello with Arthur Troester in Hamburg and with Pierre Fournier in Paris; also took some lessons with Pablo Casals; was subsequently principal cellist of the Hannover Opera (1956–58); in 1958 he became a prof. of cello at the Vienna Academy of Music; in 1959 he founded a chamber group, Die Wiener Solisten, and toured with it abroad. In 1965 he became a prof. at the Hochschule für Musik in Hamburg; was also chief conductor of the Hamburg Symph. Orch. (1967–71), and had engagements as a guest conductor in Germany, England, and France.

Boetticher, Wolfgang, noted German musicologist; b. Bad Ems, Aug. 19, 1914. He studied musicology at the Univ. of Berlin with Schering, Schünemann, Blume, and others; received his Ph.D. there in 1939 with the dissertation *Robert Schumann: Einführung in Persönlichkeit und Werk* (publ. in Berlin, 1941); completed his Habilitation in musicology there in 1943 with his *Studien zur solistischen Lautenpraxis des 16. und 17. Jahrhunderts* (publ. in Berlin, 1943). In 1948 he joined the faculty of the Univ. of Göttingen; was prof. of musicology (1956–59); from 1958 also taught at the Technical Univ. in Clausthal. He is an acknowledged authority on the music of the Renaissance and the 19th century; his writings on lute music, Orlando di Lasso, and Robert Schumann are valuable.
PUBLICATIONS: *Robert Schumann in seinen Schriften und Briefen* (Berlin, 1942); *Orlando di Lasso und seine Zeit* (2 vols., Kassel and Basel, 1958); *Von Palestrina zu Bach* (Stuttgart, 1959); *Dokumente und Briefe um Orlando di Lasso* (Kassel, 1960); *Aus Orlando di Lassos Wirkungskreis, Neue archivalische Studien zur Münchener Musikgeschichte* (Kassel and Basel, 1963); *Neue Forschungsergebnisse im Gebiet der musikali schen Renaissance* (Göttingen, 1964); *Die Familienkassette Schumanns in Dresden: Unbekannte Briefe an Robert und Clara Schumann* (Leipzig, 1974); *Robert Schumanns Klavierwerke: Entstehung, Urtext, Gestalt: Untersuchungen anhand unveröffentlichter Skizzen und biographischer Dokumente* (Wilhelmshaven, 1976—).
BIBLIOGRAPHY: H. Hüschen and D.-R. Moser, eds., *Convivium musicorum: Festschrift Wolfgang Boetticher zum sechzigsten Geburtstag* (Berlin, 1974).

Bogatyrev, Anatoly, Soviet composer; b. Vitebsk, Aug. 13, 1913. He studied composition with Zolotarev at the Belorussian Cons. in Minsk, graduating in 1937; was an instructor there from 1948. He wrote 2 patriotic operas: *In the Forests of Polesye* (Minsk, Aug. 28, 1939) and *Nadezhda Durova* (Minsk, Dec. 22, 1956); 2 symphs. (1946, 1947); cantatas: *The Leningraders* (1942); *Belorussia* (1949); *Glory Be to Lenin* (1952); Cello Concerto (1962); Concerto for Double Bass and Orch. (1964). In 1957 he reconstructed from Tchaikovsky's sketches the 7th Symph., in E-flat major.

Bogatyrev, Semyon, Russian musicologist and composer; b. Kharkov, Feb. 15, 1890; d. Moscow, Dec. 31, 1960. He studied law at the Univ. of Kharkov, graduating in 1912; then went to St. Petersburg, where he enrolled at the St. Petersburg Cons. in the

composition classes of Kalafati and Vitols and the orchestration class of Maximilian Steinberg. Upon graduating, he joined the faculty of the Kharkov Cons. (1917–19); subsequently was a lecturer at the Kharkov Inst. of Music and Drama (1922–41). In 1943 he was appointed to the faculty of the Moscow Cons., and remained there until his death. He publ. the valuable manuals *Double Canon* (Moscow, 1947) and *Retrograde Counterpoint* (Moscow, 1960). Bogatyrev undertook in 1957 the reconstruction and completion of Tchaikovsky's unfinished Symph. in E-flat major, which was publ. as the 7th Symph. His own compositions include works for orch., as well as 2 string quartets and 2 piano sonatas. A memorial vol. containing his writings was publ. in Moscow in 1972.

Bogdanov-Berezovsky, Valerian, Soviet composer and musicologist; b. Starozhilovka, near St. Petersburg, July 17, 1903; d. Moscow, May 13, 1971. He studied with Maximilian Steinberg and Liapunov at the Leningrad Cons., graduating in 1927; taught there from 1945–48, and was in charge of the artistic direction of the Leningrad Theater of Opera and Ballet from 1951–62. He wrote operas: *The Frontier* (1941); *The Leningraders* (1943); *Nastasia Filippovna,* after Dostoevsky's novel *The Idiot* (1964); several ballets, including *The Seagull,* after Chekhov (1959); 2 symphs. (1933, 1953); Piano Concerto; Violin Concerto; some chamber music; choruses. He was known chiefly as a critic and historian of Russian music, and wrote several monographs on Soviet composers and contributed numerous articles to Soviet journals.
BIBLIOGRAPHY: I. Gusin, *V. Bogdanov-Berezovsky* (Leningrad, 1966).

Boghen, Felice, Italian music editor and composer; b. Venice, Jan. 3, 1869; d. Florence, Jan. 25, 1945. He studied with Martucci, Sgambati, and Wolf-Ferrari; publ. the valuable collections *Fughe d'antichi Maestri italiani;* also edited works of Frescobaldi, Tartini, Alessandro Scarlatti, Bach, Clementi, and Liszt. As an occasional composer, he wrote an opera, *Alceste,* which, unlike Gluck's, was never produced, and also many passable piano pieces, which were seldom, if ever, played in public.

Bogianckino, Massimo, Italian pianist, musicologist, and administrator; b. Rome, Nov. 10, 1922. He studied piano with Casella at the Santa Cecilia Academy in Rome and with Cortot at the Ecole Normale de Musique in Paris; also took courses in musicology with Ronga at the Univ. of Rome and with P.M. Masson at the Sorbonne in Paris. He taught at the Carnegie Inst. in Pittsburgh (1948–51), at the Pesaro Cons. (1951–57), and at the Rome Cons. (1957–67). In 1967 he joined the faculty of the Univ. of Perugia. He served as artistic director of the Rome Opera (1963–68), the Spoleto Festival of Two Worlds (1968–71), La Scala in Milan (1972–74), and the Teatro Communale in Florence (from 1975). In 1983 he was appointed director of the Paris Opéra. He wrote the vols. *L'arte clavicembalistica di Domenico*

Scarlatti (Rome, 1956; in Eng. as *The Harpsichord Sonatas of Domenico Scarlatti,* Rome, 1968) and *Aspetti del teatro musicale in Italia e in Francia nell' età barocca* (Rome, 1968).

Boguslawski, Edward, Polish composer; b. Chorzów, Sept. 22, 1940. He studied composition with Szabelski in Katowice and with Haubenstock-Ramati in Vienna. In 1963 he joined the faculty of the State College of Music in Katowice. His music makes use of impressionistic techniques.

WORKS: *Intonazioni I* for 9 Instruments (1962); *Intonazioni II* for Orch. (1967); *Apocalypse* for Narrator, Chorus, and Instruments (1965); *Signals* for Orch. (1965–66); *Metamorphoses* for Oboe, Clarinet, 2 Violins, Viola, and Cello (1967); *Canti* for Soprano and Orch. (1967); Concerto for Oboe, Oboe d'Amore, English Horn, Musette, and Orch. (1967–68); *Versions* for 6 Instruments (1968); *Musica per Ensemble MW-2* for Flute, Cello, and 2 Pianos (1970); Trio for Flute, Oboe, and Guitar (1970); *Per Pianoforte* (1971); *Capriccioso-Notturno* for Orch. (1972); *Impromptu* for Flute, Viola, and Harp (1972); *L'Etre* for Soprano, Flute, Cello, and 2 Pianos (1973); *Pro Varsovia* for Orch. (1973–74); *Musica Notturna* for Musette and Piano (1974); *Evocations* for Baritone and Orch. (1974); *Divertimento* for Chamber Ensemble (1975); Concerto for Oboe, Soprano, and Orch. (1975–76).

Boháč, Josef, Czech composer; b. Vienna, March 25, 1929. After a preliminary course of music studies in Vienna, he went to Brno, where he studied with Petrželka at the Brno Academy of Musical Arts; upon graduation he became active in the musical programming on the radio. His music follows the median line of Central European modernism, with occasional resort to serial methods.

WORKS: Chamber opera, after Chekhov, *Námluvy (The Proposal;* 1967; Ustí nad Laben, Dec. 15, 1972); television opera, *Oči (The Eyes;* 1973; Prague Television, Oct. 5, 1974); opera, *Goya* (1972–77; Ostrava, 1977); Suite for String Quartet (1953); Cello Sonata (1954); *Rhapsody* for Orch. (1955); *Symphonic Prelude* (1964); *Sinfonietta Concertante* (1964–65; Prague, March 14, 1966); String Trio (1965); *Suita Drammatica* for Strings and Timpani (1969–70; Prague, March 23, 1974); *My Lute Sounds,* monodrama cycle of 12 songs on love, sickness, and death, for Tenor and Nonet (1971); *Southern Rainbow,* suite for Orch. (1971); *Sonetti per Sonatori* for Flute, Bass Clarinet, Percussion, and Piano (1974; for the chamber group Sonatori di Praga); Piano Concerto (1974; Prague, March 29, 1976).

Bohlmann, Theodor Heinrich Friedrich, pianist; b. Osterwieck, Germany, June 23, 1865; d. Memphis, Tenn., March 18, 1931. He was a pupil of Eugene d'Albert and Moszkowski; made his debut in Berlin in 1890; in the same year he emigrated to America and settled in Cincinnati as a teacher.

Böhm, Georg, German organist; b. Hohenkirchen, Thuringia, Sept. 2, 1661; d. Lüneburg, May 18, 1733.

He studied at the Univ. of Jena; was in Hamburg in 1693; in 1698 he became organist at the Johanneskirche in Lüneburg. His organ preludes and harpsichord pieces are exemplars of keyboard works of his time; Bach himself was influenced by Böhm's style of writing. A complete ed. of Böhm's work was begun by Johannes Wolgast in 1927 in 2 vols.; a revised ed. of both vols. was publ. in Wiesbaden in 1952 and 1963, respectively.

BIBLIOGRAPHY: J. Wolgast, *Georg Böhm* (Berlin, 1924).

Böhm, Joseph, violinist; b. Budapest, March 4, 1795; d. Vienna, March 28, 1876. He was a pupil of his father; at 8 years of age he made a concert tour to Poland and St. Petersburg, where he studied for some years under Pierre Rode. His first concert at Vienna (1815) was very successful; after a trip to Italy, he was appointed (1819) violin prof. at the Vienna Cons.; retired in 1848. He formed many distinguished pupils, including Joachim, Ernst, Auer, Rappoldi, and Hellmesberger (Sr.).

Bohm, Karl, German pianist; b. Berlin, Sept. 11, 1844; d. there, April 4, 1920. He studied with Löschhorn; lived most of his life in Berlin. He wrote a number of piano pieces in the salon genre; also songs, of which *Still wie die Nacht* became popular.

Böhm, Karl, Austrian conductor of great renown; b. Graz, Aug. 28, 1894; d. Salzburg, Aug. 14, 1981. He studied law before enrolling at the Cons. of Graz, where he took lessons in piano playing; subsequently he studied music theory with Mandyczewsky at the Cons. of Vienna. After service in the Austrian army during World War I he was appointed conductor at the Municipal Theater at Graz. He completed his studies of law, receiving a degree of Dr.Jur. in 1919. Although he never took formal lessons in conducting, he soon acquired sufficient technique to be engaged at the State Opera in Munich (1921). He made rapid progress in his career; in 1927 he was appointed Generalmusikdirektor in Darmstadt; having already mastered a number of works by Mozart, Wagner, and Richard Strauss, he included in his repertoire modern operas by Krenek and Hindemith. In 1931 he conducted *Wozzeck* by Alban Berg, a performance which Berg himself warmly praised. From 1931 to 1933 Böhm held the post of Generalmusikdirektor of the Hamburg Opera; from 1934 to 1943 he was music director of the Dresden State Opera, where he gave the first performances of two operas by Richard Strauss: *Die Schweigsame Frau* (June 24, 1935) and *Daphne* (Oct. 15, 1938), which Strauss dedicated to him. During the last two years of the raging war, he was conductor at the Vienna State Opera. The rumors were rife of his at least passive adherence to the Nazis, although he categorically denied that he was ever a member of the party. After the war he was not allowed by the Allied authorities to give performances pending an investigation of his political past; he was cleared and resumed his career in 1947. In 1950 he went to Argentina, where he organized and conducted a

German opera repertoire at the Teatro Colón in Buenos Aires; returning to Europe, he again served as principal conductor of the Vienna State Opera (1954–56). On Nov. 5, 1955, he conducted Beethoven's *Fidelio* at the opening in the reconstructed State Opera House. He made his first appearance in the U.S. with the Chicago Symph. Orch. on Feb. 9, 1956; on Oct. 28, 1957, he led the opening of the season at the Metropolitan Opera in N.Y. with Mozart's *Don Giovanni.* He continued to conduct occasional performances at the Metropolitan until 1974. He conducted a program of symphonic music with the N.Y. Phil. Orch. on Dec. 8, 1960; in 1961 he took the Berlin Phil. to the U.S., and in 1963–64 he made a tour in Japan with it. In 1975 he conducted an American tour with the Deutsche Oper of Berlin. In 1979 he brought the Vienna State Opera to America for its first U.S. tour. He also conducted radio and television performances. Böhm received numerous honors and tokens of distinction, among them the Golden Mozart Memorial Medal from the International Mozarteum Foundation in Salzburg, the Brahms Medal from Hamburg, and the Bruckner Ring from the Vienna Symph. On his 70th birthday in 1964 a Böhm Day was celebrated in Vienna; his 80th birthday was observed in 1974 in Salzburg and Vienna. In 1977 Böhm was elected president of the London Symph. Orch. In the annals of the art of conducting, Böhm may well be regarded as a worthy successor of the glorious pleiad of German and Austrian conductors such as Karl Muck, Bruno Walter, and Wilhelm Furtwängler. He was admired for his impeccable rendition of classical opera scores, particularly those of Mozart, in which he scrupulously avoided any suggestion of improper romanticization; he was equally extolled for his productions of the operas of Wagner and Richard Strauss, and he earned additional respect for his audacious espousal of modern music. He publ. *Begegnung mit Richard Strauss* (Munich, 1964) and a personal memoir, *Ich erinnere mich ganz genau (I Remember It Quite Clearly;* Zürich, 1968).
BIBLIOGRAPHY: F. Endler, *Karl Böhm: Ein Dirigentenleben* (Hamburg, 1981); H. Hoyer, *Karl Böhm an der Wiener Staatsoper: Eine Dokumentation* (Vienna, 1981).

Böhm, Theobald, German flutist and inventor of the "Böhm flute"; b. Munich, April 9, 1794; d. there, Nov. 25, 1881. He was the son of a goldsmith and learned mechanics in his father's workshop; studied the flute, achieving a degree of virtuosity that made him one of the greatest flute players of his time; he was appointed court musician in 1818; gave concerts in Paris and London. His system of construction marks a new departure in the making of woodwind instruments. To render the flute acoustically perfect, he fixed the position and size of the holes so as to obtain, not convenience in fingering, but purity and fullness of tone; all holes are covered by keys, whereby prompt and accurate "speaking" is assured; and the bore is modified, rendering the tone much fuller and mellower. He publ. *Über den Flötenbau und die neuesten Verbesserungen des-* *selben* (Mainz, 1847; Eng. trans. by W.S. Broadwood, London, 1882); *Die Flöte und das Flötenspiel* (Munich, 1871).
BIBLIOGRAPHY: Charles Welch, *History of the Boehm Flute* (London, 1883); V. Mahillon, *Etude sur le doigté de la flûte Boehm* (1885); R. Rockstro, *A Treatise on the Construction, the History and the Practice of the Flute* (London, 1890).

Böhme, Franz Magnus, German writer on music; b. Willerstedt, near Weimar, March 11, 1827; d. Dresden, Oct. 18, 1898. He was a pupil of Hauptmann and Rietz at Leipzig; taught at Dresden (1859–78) and at the Hoch Cons. in Frankfurt (1878–85); spent the remaining years of his life in Dresden.
WRITINGS: *Das Oratorium, Eine historische Studie* (Leipzig, 1861; revised ed., Gütersloh, 1887, under the title *Geschichte des Oratoriums*); *Altdeutsches Liederbuch,* a collection of German folk songs of the 12th to 17th centuries (Leipzig, 1877; later eds., 1913 and 1925); *Aufgaben zum Studium der Harmonie* (Mainz, 1880); *Kursus in Harmonie* (Mainz, 1882); *Geschichte des Tanzes in Deutschland* (2 vols., Leipzig, 1886); *Volkstümliche Lieder der Deutschen im 18. und 19. Jahrhundert* (Leipzig, 1895); *Deutsches Kinderlied und Kinderspiel* (1897). He edited Erk's *Deutscher Liederhort* (3 vols., 1893–94; new ed., 1925); also publ. several books of sacred songs and male choruses.

Böhme, Kurt, distinguished German bass; b. Dresden, May 5, 1908. He was educated at the Dresden Cons.; made his debut at the Dresden State Opera in 1930 as Kaspar in *Der Freischütz;* remained as a member there until 1950. On Nov. 11, 1954, he made his American debut at the Metropolitan Opera in N.Y. as Pogner in *Die Meistersinger von Nürnberg;* also sang there during the season of 1956–57.

Bohn, Emil, German music bibliographer; b. Bielau, near Neisse, Jan. 14, 1839; d. Breslau, July 5, 1909. He studied philology at Breslau, and then music; was organist of the Breslau Kreuzkirche and founder (1881) of the Bohn Choral Society.
WRITINGS: *Bibliographie der Musikdruckwerke bis 1700, welche auf der Stadtbibliothek ... zu Breslau aufbewahrt werden* (1883); *Die musikalischen Handschriften des 16. und 17. Jahrhunderts in der Stadtbibliothek zu Breslau* (1890); *Die Nationalhymnen der europäischen Völker* (1908). He also publ. the annotated chronicle of his choral society: *Bohn'scher Gesangverein; 100 historische Konzerte in Breslau* (1905).

Bohn, Peter, German organist and teacher; b. Bausendorf, Nov. 2, 1833; d. Trier, June 11, 1925. He was organist and teacher at Trier from 1852–1905; prepared German translations of Franco's *Ars cantus mensurabilis* (1880); *Dialogus de musica* of Odo de Clugny (1880); Glareanus's *Dodecachordon* (2 vols., 1888–89); and *Der Einfluss des tonischen Akzents auf die melodische und rhythmische Struktur der gregorianischen Psalmodie* (from *Paléographie musicale,* Solesmes, 1894); also publ. *Das liturgi-*

sche Rezitativ und dessen Bezeichnung in den liturgischen Büchern des Mittelalters (1887) and *Philipp von Vitry* (1890).

Bohnen, Michael, German bass-baritone; b. Cologne, May 2, 1887; d. Berlin, April 26, 1965. He studied at the Cologne Cons.; sang at several opera houses in Germany, Spain, and Sweden; made his American debut at the Metropolitan Opera, N.Y., on March 1, 1923, and created the leading role in the first American performance of Krenek's opera *Jonny spielt auf* (Jan. 19, 1929); remained at the Metropolitan until 1932; then was on the roster of the Deutsches Opernhaus (1933–45); subsequently assumed its administration when it was renamed the Städtische Oper, serving there until 1947.

Böhner, Ludwig, German composer; b. Töttelstedt, Gotha, Jan. 8, 1787; d. there, March 28, 1860. He studied with his father and with Johann Christian Kittel, a pupil of Bach. Having achieved considerable fame as a pianist and a composer, he failed to establish himself socially and economically, owing to his personal eccentricities. He wandered through Germany, often on foot, and worked irregularly as a theatrical conductor and a concert pianist. The claim he advanced, that other composers plagiarized him, is supported by the fact that Weber had unintentionally borrowed one of the themes in *Der Freischütz* from Böhner's piano concerto. Böhner's life and character are understood to have inspired the figure of the eccentric genius Kreisler in E.T.A. Hoffmann's *Capellmeister Kreisler* as well as Schumann's *Kreisleriana.*
BIBLIOGRAPHY: K.F. Bolt, *J.L. Böhner. Leben und Werk* (Hildburghausen, 1940).

Bohnke, Emil, viola player and composer; b. Zdunska Wola, Poland, Oct. 11, 1888; d. Pasewalk, Pomerania, May 11, 1928 (in an automobile accident, en route from Berlin to Swinemunde). He studied at the Leipzig Cons.; then was a violist in various chamber music groups. He wrote a Violin Concerto, a Piano Trio, a String Quartet, and several violin sonatas.

Boieldieu, François-Adrien, celebrated French opera composer; b. Rouen, Dec. 16, 1775; d. Jarcy, near Grosbois, Oct. 8, 1834. His father was a clerical functionary who at one time served as secretary to Archbishop Larochefoucauld; his mother owned a millinery shop; the parents were divorced in 1794, and Boieldieu received his musical instruction from Charles Broche; he then was apprenticed to Broche as an assistant organist at the church of St. André in Rouen. When he was 17 his first opera, *La Fille coupable* (to his father's libretto), achieved a production in Rouen (Nov. 2, 1793). He composed patriotic pieces which were in demand during the revolutionary period. His *Chant populaire pour la Fête de la Raison* for chorus and orch. was presented at the Temple of Reason (former cathedral) in Rouen on Nov. 30, 1793. His second opera, *Rosalie et Myrza,* was also staged in Rouen (Oct. 28, 1795). He

was befriended by the composer Louis Jadin and the piano manufacturer Erard; he met Cherubini and Méhul; made a tour in Normandy with the tenor Garat. His songs, of a popular nature, were printed in Paris; also publ. were his piano sonatas; a complete edition of these sonatas was reprinted by G. Favre in 2 albums (1944–45). A facile composer, Boieldieu produced one opera after another and had no difficulties in having them staged in Paris. Particularly successful was his opera *Le Calife de Bagdad* (Paris, Sept. 16, 1800), which appealed to the public because of its exotic subject and pseudo-oriental arias.
On March 19, 1802, Boieldieu married the dancer Clotilde Mafleurai, but separated from her the following year. Opportunely, he received an invitation to go to Russia. His contract called for an attractive salary of 4,000 rubles annually, in return for writing operas for the Imperial theaters in St. Petersburg. He attended to his duties conscientiously, and produced operas every year. His salary was raised, but Boieldieu decided to leave Russia in 1811 and return to Paris. His estranged wife died in 1826, and Boieldieu married the singer Jenny Phillis. True to his custom, he resumed composing operas for the Paris theaters. In 1817 he was appointed prof. of composition at the Paris Cons.; he resigned in 1826. In 1821 he was named a Chevalier of the Legion of Honor. After a number of insignificant productions, he achieved his greatest success with his Romantic opera *La Dame blanche,* fashioned after Walter Scott's novels *The Monastery* and *Guy Mannering;* the dramatic subject and the effective musical setting corresponded precisely to the tastes of the public of the time. It was produced at the Opéra-Comique in Paris on Dec. 10, 1825, and became a perennial success in Paris and elsewhere; it was produced in London on Oct. 9, 1826, and in N.Y. on Aug. 24, 1827. In 1833 he received a grant of 6,000 francs from the French government and retired to his country house at Jarcy, where he died. During the last years of his life he became interested in painting; his pictures show a modest talent in landscape. He was also successful as a teacher; among his pupils were Fétis, Adam, and P.J.G. Zimmerman.
Boieldieu composed about 40 operas, of which several were written in collaboration with Méhul, Berton, Hérold, Cherubini, Catel, Isouard, Kreutzer, and Auber; 9 of these operas are lost. Boieldieu's significance in the history of French opera is great, even though the nationalistic hopes of the French music critics and others that he would rival Rossini did not materialize; Boieldieu simply lacked the tremendous power of invention, both in dramatic and comic aspects, that made Rossini a magician of 19th-century opera. Boieldieu's natural son, **Adrien-Louis-Victor Boieldieu** (b. Paris, Nov. 3, 1815; d. Quincy, July 9, 1883), was also a composer; his mother was Thérèse Regnault, a singer. He wrote 2 operas, *Marguerite,* which was sketched by his father but left incomplete, and *L'Aïeule.*
WORKS: OPERAS: *La Fille coupable* (Rouen, Nov. 2, 1793); *Rosalie et Myrza* (Rouen, Oct. 28, 1795); *La Famille suisse* (Paris, Feb. 11, 1797); *Zoraine et Zul-*

nare (Paris, May 10, 1798); *La Dôt de Suzette* (Paris, Sept. 5, 1798); *Beniowski* (Paris, June 8, 1800); *Le Calife de Bagdad* (Paris, Sept. 16, 1800); *Ma tante Aurore* (Paris, Jan. 13, 1803); *Aline, reine de Golconda* (St. Petersburg, March 17, 1804); *Abderkhan* (St. Petersburg, Aug. 7, 1804); *Un Tour de soubrette* (St. Petersburg, April 28, 1806); *Télémaque dans l'isle de Calypso* (St. Petersburg, Dec. 28, 1806); *Les Voitures verseés* (St. Petersburg, April 16, 1808); *Rien de trop ou Les Deux Paravents* (St. Petersburg, Jan. 6, 1811); *Jean de Paris* (Paris, April 4, 1812); *Le Nouveau Seigneur de village* (Paris, June 29, 1813); *La Fête du village voisin* (Paris, March 5, 1816); *Le Petit Chaperon rouge* (Paris, June 30, 1818; highly successful); *La Dame blanche* (Paris, Dec. 10, 1825; his masterpiece; nearly 1,700 performances before 1914 in Paris alone). The following operas were products of collaboration: *La Prisonnière,* with Cherubini (1799); *Le Baiser et la quittance,* with Méhul, Kreutzer, and others (1803); *Bayard à Mézières,* with Cherubini, Catel, and Isouard (1803); *Les Béarnais, ou Henry IV en voyage,* with Kreutzer (1814); *Angéla, ou L'Atelier de Jean Cousin,* with Mme. Gail, a pupil of Fétis (1814); *Charles de France, ou Amour et gloire,* with Hérold (1816); *Blanche de Provence, ou La Cour des fées,* with Cherubini, Berton, and others (1821); *Les 3 Genres,* with Auber (1824); *La Marquise de Brinvilliers,* with Berton and others (1831).

INSTRUMENTAL WORKS: Piano Concerto (1797); Harp Concerto (1800); Duo for Violin and Piano; 4 Duos for Harp and Piano; 4 piano sonatas; numerous songs.

BIBLIOGRAPHY: G. Héquet, *A. Boieldieu, Sa vie et ses œuvres* (Paris, 1864); A. Pougin, *Boieldieu, Sa vie es ses œuvres* (Paris, 1875); E. Neukomm, *Trois jours à Rouen, Souvenirs du centenaire de Boieldieu* (Paris, 1875); H. de Thannberg, *Le Centenaire de Boieldieu, Anecdotes et souvenirs* (Paris, 1875); E. Duval, *Boieldieu, Notes et fragments inédits* (1883); P.L. Robert, "Correspondance de Boieldieu," *Rivista Musicale Italiana* XIX and XXII (also separately, Rouen, 1916); G. de Saint-Foix, "Les Premiers Pianistes parisiens: Boieldieu," *Revue Musicale* (Feb. 1926); G. Favre, "La Danseuse Clotilde Mafleurai, première femme d'Adrien Boieldieu," *Revue Musicale* (Jan. 1940); G. Favre, *Boieldieu, Sa vie, son œuvre* (part I, Paris, 1944; part II, Paris, 1945; an exhaustive work on the subject); also F. Clément and Larousse, *Dictionnaire des opéras* (Paris, 1906); L. Augé de Lassus, *Boieldieu,* in the series Les Musiciens Célèbres (Paris, 1908; contains catalogue of works); Alfred Loewenberg, *Annals of Opera* (lists the dates of first performances of Boieldieu's operas in all major opera houses).

Bois, Rob du, Dutch composer; b. Amsterdam, May 28, 1934. He had piano lessons as a child; then studied law; was mainly audodidact as a composer. His works are strongly contrapuntal in texture, following the classical Flemish tradition but applying ultramodern techniques, including serialism.

WORKS: Piano Concerto (1960; revised 1968); *Cercle* for Piano, 9 Winds, and Percussion (1963); Concertino for School Orch. (1963); *Simultaneous* for Orch. (1965; Utrecht, Sept. 29, 1966); *Breuker Concerto* for 2 Clarinets, 4 Saxophones, and 21 String Players (1968); *A Flower Given to My Daughter* for Orch. (1970); *Midas,* ballet (1970); *Le Concerto pour Hrisanide* for Piano and Orch. (1971; written for Rumanian virtuoso Alexandru Hrisanide); *Allegro* for Strings (1973); *3 Pezzi* for Orch. (1973); Suite No. 1 for Orch. (1973); Violin Concerto (1975); *Vandaag is het morgen van gisteren* for Narrator, Soprano, Youth Choir, Orch., and Brass Band (1975); *7 Pastorales:* No. 1 for Oboe, Clarinet, and Harp (1960; revised 1969); No. 2 for Recorder, Flute, and Guitar (1963; revised 1969); No. 3 for Clarinet, Bongos, and Double Bass (1963; revised 1969); No. 4 for Solo Guitar (1963); No. 5 for String Quartet (1964; revised 1966); No. 6 for Piano (1964); No. 7 for Recorder (1964); *Music* for Solo Flute (1961); *Bewegingen* for Piccolo and Piano (1961); Trio for Flute, Oboe, and Clarinet (1961); *Rondeaux per deux* for Piano and Percussion (1962; 2nd series, for Piano, 4-hands, and Percussion, 1964); *Spiel und Zwischenspiel* for Recorder and Piano (1962); *3 Pieces* for Flute, Oboe, and Cello (1962); *Chants et contrepoints* for Wind Quintet (1962); *Une Façon de dire que les hommes de cent vingt ans ne chantent plus* for Soprano, Piano, and 4 Percussion Instruments (1963); *Espaces à remplir* for 11 Musicians (1963); Oboe Quartet (1964); *7 Bagatelles* for Flute and Piano (1964); *Ad libitum* for Violin and Piano (1965); *Pour faire chanter la polonaise* for Flute, Soprano, and 3 Pianos (1965); *Pour 2 violons* (1966); *Words* for Mezzo-soprano, Flute, Cello, and Piano (1966); String Trio (1967); *Musica per quattro* for Horn, 2 Trumpets, and Trombone (1967); *Beat Music* for 2 Percussionists (1967); *Because Going Nowhere Takes a Long Time* for Medium Voice, Flute, and Piano (1967; version for Soprano, Clarinet, and Piano, 1969); *Rounds* for Clarinet and Piano (1967); *Ranta Music* for Percussionist (1968); *Music for a Sliding Trombone* (1968); *Musique d'atelier* for Clarinet, Trombone, Cello, and Piano (1968); *Enigma* for Flute, Bass Clarinet, Piano, and Percussion (1969); *Symposion* for Oboe, Violin, Viola, and Cello (1969); *Trio agitate* for Horn, Trombone, and Tuba (1969); *Réflexions sur le jour où Pérotin le Grand ressuscitera* for Wind Quintet (1969); *Polonaise* for a Pianist and a Percussionist (1971); *Fusion pour deux* for Bass Clarinet and Piano (1971); *The Dog Named Boo Has a Master Called Lobo* for Clarinet, Violin, and Piano (1972); *Because It Is* for 4 Clarinets (1973); *The Eighteenth of June, Springtime, and Yet Already Summer* for 4 Saxophones (1974); *Melody* for Bass Clarinet and String Quartet (1974); *Inferno,* after Dante, for Soprano, 2 Violins, Cello, and Harpsichord (1974); *Eine Rede* for Soprano, Clarinet, Basset Horn, and Bass Clarinet (1974); Piano Sonatina (1960); *Voices* for Piano (1964); *Just Like a Little Sonata* for Piano (1964); *A Combination of Voices* for 2 Pianos (1968); *New Pieces* for Piano (1972); *Cadences* for Piano (1975); songs.

Boise, Otis Bardwell, American organist; b. Oberlin, Ohio, Aug. 13, 1844; d. Baltimore, Dec. 2, 1912. He studied with Moscheles and Richter in Leipzig and with Kullak in Berlin. Returning to America in 1865, he occupied various posts as an organist and a teacher; eventually settled in Baltimore, where he taught at the Peabody Cons. Among his pupils were Ernest Hutcheson, Howard Brockway, and Arthur Nevin. He publ. the textbooks *Harmony Made Practical* (N.Y., 1900) and *Music and Its Masters* (N.Y., 1902).

Boismortier, Joseph Bodin de, French composer; b. Thionville (Moselle), Dec. 23, 1689; d. Roissy-en-Brie, Oct. 28, 1755. He lived in Metz and Perpignan before settling in Paris in 1724. A prolific composer of instrumental music, he wrote more than 100 opus numbers; of these there are several for block flutes (i.e., recorders) and transverse flutes; 2 suites for clavecin; trio sonatas, among them one with the viola da gamba (1732; modern ed., Mainz, 1967); collections of pieces designed for amateurs (in the positive sense of this abused word), scored with a drone instrument, either the musette (a wind instrument) or the vielle (a string instrument), and publ. under such coaxing titles as "Gentillesses," or "Divertissements de campagne." He also wrote 3 ballet-operas: *Les Voyages de L'Amour* (1736); *Don Quichotte* (1743); *Daphnis et Chloé* (1747), and a number of cantatas.
BIBLIOGRAPHY: H. Tribout de Morembert, "Bodin de Boismortier; Notes sur un musicien lorrain," *Revue de Musicologie* (1967); M. Pincherle, "A propos de Boismortier," *Journal Musical Français/Musica Disques* (Nov. 1968).

Boisselot, Xavier, French piano manufacturer; b. Montpellier, Dec. 3, 1811; d. Marseilles, March 28, 1893. He studied with Fétis and Lesueur in Paris; received the Grand Prix de Rome in 1836; then went to Marseilles, where he joined the piano manufacturing company founded by his father.

Boito, Arrigo, important Italian poet and opera composer; b. Padua, Feb. 24, 1842; d. Milan, June 10, 1918. He studied at the Milan Cons. with Alberto Mazzucato and Ronchetti-Monteviti; his 2 cantatas, *Il 4 Giugno* (1860) and *Le Sorelle d'Italia* (1861), written in collaboration with Faccio, were performed at the Cons., and attracted a great deal of favorable attention; as a result, the Italian government granted the composers a gold medal and a stipend for foreign travel for 2 years. Boito spent most of his time in Paris, and also went to Poland to meet the family of his mother (who was Polish); he also visited Germany, Belgium, and England. He was strongly influenced by new French and German music; upon his return to Milan, he undertook the composition of his first and most significant large opera, *Mefistofele,* which contains elements of conventional Italian opera but also dramatic ideas stemming from Beethoven and Wagner. It was performed for the first time at La Scala (March 5, 1868). A controversy followed when a part of the audience objected to the unusual treatment of the subject and the music, and there were actual disor-

ders at the conclusion of the performance. After the 2nd production, the opera was taken off the boards, and Boito undertook a revision to effect a compromise. In this new version, the opera had a successful run in Italian cities; it was also produced in Hamburg (1880), in London (in Italian, July 6, 1880), and in Boston (in Eng., Nov. 16, 1880). It was retained in the repertoire of the leading opera houses, but its success never matched that of Gounod's *Faust.* Boito never completed his 2nd opera, *Nerone,* on which he worked for more than half a century (from 1862–1916). The orch. score was revised by Toscanini and performed by him at La Scala on May 1, 1924. There are sketches for an earlier opera, *Ero e Leandro,* but not enough material to attempt a completion. Boito's gift as a poet is fully equal to that as a composer. He publ. a book of verses (Turin, 1877) under the anagrammatic pen name of **Tobia Gorrio;** he wrote his own librettos for his operas and made admirable translations of Wagner's operas (*Tristan und Isolde; Rienzi*); wrote the librettos of *Otello* and *Falstaff* for Verdi (these librettos are regarded as his masterpieces); also for *Gioconda* by Ponchielli, *Amleto* by Faccio, etc. Boito also publ. novels. He held various honorary titles from the King of Italy; in 1892 he was appointed inspector-general of Italian conservatories; was made honorary D.Mus. by Cambridge Univ. and Oxford Univ.; in 1912 he was made a senator by the King of Italy.
BIBLIOGRAPHY: P.G. Molmenti, *Impressioni letterarie* (Milan, 1875); A. Boccardi, *Arrigo Boito* (Trieste, 1877); D. Mantovani, *Letteratura contemporanea* (Turin, 1893); R. Giani, *Il Nerone di A. Boito* (Turin, 1901); R. Barbiera, *A. Boito, inverso l'ideale* (Milan, 1905); M. Risolo, *Il primo Mefistofele di A. Boito* (Naples, 1916); C. Trevor, "Boito's Nero," *Musical Times* (June 1916); A. Lualdi, "A. Boito, un' anima," *Rivista Musicale Italiana* (1919); A. Pompeati, *A. Boito* (Florence, 1919); C. Ricci, *A. Boito* (Milan, 1919); F. Torrefranca, "A. Boito," *La Critica Musicale* (Nov./Dec. 1919); F. Torrefranca, "A. Boito," *Musical Quarterly* (Oct. 1920); G.M. Gatti, "Boito's Nero," *Musical Quarterly* (Oct. 1924); V. Gui, *Il Nerone di Arrigo Boito* (Milan, 1924); A. Bonaventura, *A. Boito; Mefistofele* (Milan, 1924); G. Cesari, "Note per una bibliografia delle opere di A. Boito," *Rassegna di Coltura* (March 1924); R. de Rensis, *Franco Faccio e Boito, documento* (Milan, 1934); F. Ballo, *A. Boito* (Turin, 1938); R. de Rensis, *A. Boito; Aneddoti e bizzarrie poetiche e musicali* (Rome, 1942); P. Nardi, *Vita di A. Boito* (Verona, 1942; 2nd ed., Milan, 1944; complete documented biography); Massimiliano Vajro, *A. Boito* (Brescia, 1955); C. Orselli, "A. Boito: un riesame," *Chigiana* (1968); G. Mariani, *A. Boito* (Parma, 1973); G. Scarsi, *Rapporto poesia-musica in A. Boito* (Rome, 1973). Boito's letters were ed. by R. de Rensis (Rome, 1932), who also ed. Boito's articles on music (Milan, 1931).

Bok, Mary Louise Curtis, American patroness of music; b. Boston, Aug. 6, 1876; d. Philadelphia, Jan. 4, 1970. She inherited her fortune from Cyrus H.K. Curtis, founder of the Curtis Publishing Co. In 1924 she established in Philadelphia the Curtis Inst. of

Music and endowed it initially with a gift of $12.5 million in memory of her mother. The school had a faculty of the most distinguished American and European musicians, and it provided tuition exclusively on a scholarship basis; many talented composers and performers were its students; among them were Leonard Bernstein, Samuel Barber, and Lukas Foss. Josef Hofmann was engaged to head the piano dept.; from 1926 to 1938 he served as director of the Curtis Inst. Mrs. Bok was first married to Edward W. Bok, in 1896; he died in 1930; in 1943 she married **Efrem Zimbalist,** who was director of the Curtis Inst. from 1941 until 1968. She purchased in England the famous Burrell Collection of Wagneriana and brought it to the U.S. In 1932 she received an honorary doctorate from the Univ. of Pennsylvania, and in 1934, an honorary doctorate from Williams College.

Bokemeyer, Heinrich, German music theorist and composer; b. Immensen, near Lehrte, Lower Saxony, March 1679; d. Wolfenbüttel, Dec. 7, 1751. He attended the St. Martin's and St. Catherine's Church School in Braunschweig; in 1702 went to the Univ. of Helmstedt; he returned to Braunschweig in 1704 and served as cantor at St. Martin's; concurrently studied composition with Georg Oesterreich. In 1712 he became cantor in Husum; in 1717 he repaired to Wolfenbüttel; in 1720 he became cantor at the ducal palace there. He was a founding member of Mizler's Societät der Musikalischen Wissenschaften of Leipzig. Few of his compositions are extant, but several of his theoretical treatises survive. He collected a large music library. See H. Kümmerling, *Katalog der Sammlung Bokemeyer* (Kassel, 1970).

Bolck, Michel, Belgian pianist; b. Antwerp, June 12, 1937. He grew up in Mexico; made his debut as a soloist with the National Orch. in Mexico when he was 16; then went to N.Y., where he studied at the Juilliard School of Music. He made his N.Y. debut in 1959; then made a successful career as soloist with orchs. in the U.S. and Europe.

Bolck, Oskar, German composer; b. Hohenstein, March 4, 1837; d. Bremen, May 2, 1888. He studied at the Leipzig Cons. with Rietz and Moscheles; was active as a theater conductor in various German towns, and as a teacher at Riga, where his opera *Pierre und Robin* was produced (1876). He wrote 2 other operas, *Gudrun* and *Der Schmied von Gretna Green,* both of which remain unperformed.

Bolcom, William (Elden), American pianist and composer; b. Seattle, May 26, 1938. He studied at the Univ. of Washington in Seattle with John Verrall (B.A., 1958); took a course in composition with Darius Milhaud at Mills College in Oakland, Calif. (M.A., 1961); attended classes in advanced composition with Leland Smith at Stanford Univ. (D.M.A., 1964); also studied at the Paris Cons. (2nd prize in composition, 1965). He received Guggenheim fellowships in 1964–65 and 1968–69. He taught at the

Univ. of Washington in Seattle (1965–66), Queens College of the City Univ. of N.Y. (1966–68), and the N.Y. Univ. School of the Arts (1969–70). He joined the faculty of the school of music at the Univ. of Michigan in 1973; was made a full prof. in 1983. After absorbing a variety of techniques *sine ira et studio,* he began to experiment widely and wildly in serial thematics, musical collage, sophisticated intentional plagiarism, and microtonal electronics. He was also active as a pianist, recording and giving recitals of ragtime piano and, with his wife, the singer **Joan Morris,** in concerts of popular American songs from olden times. He publ., with Robert Kimbass, a book on the black American songwriting and musical comedy team of Noble Sissle and Eubie Blake, *Reminiscing with Sissle and Blake* (N.Y., 1973); also edited the collected essays of George Rochberg, under the title *The Aesthetics of Survival: A Composer's View of the 20th Century* (Ann Arbor, Mich., 1984).

WORKS: Stage works: *Dynamite Tonite,* an actors' opera (N.Y., Actors' Studio, Dec. 21, 1963); *Greatshot,* an actors' opera (1969); *Theatre of the Absurd* for Actor and Chamber Group (1970); *The Beggar's Opera,* an adaptation of John Gay's work, for Actors and Chamber Orch. (1978). For Orch.: Symph. (1957); Concertante for Violin, Flute, Oboe, and Orch. (1961); symph., *Oracles* (1964); *Concerto-Serenade* for Violin and String Orch. (1964); *Commedia* for "Almost" 18th-century Orch. (1971); *Summer Divertimento* for Chamber Orch. (1973); Piano Concerto (1976); *Humoresk* for Organ and Orchestra (1979); *Symphony for Chamber Orchestra* (1979); *Ragomania* for Orch. (1982); Concerto for Violin and Orch. (1983). Chamber music: *Décalage* for Cello and Piano (1961); Octet for Flute, Clarinet, Bassoon, Violin, Viola, Cello, Contrabass, and Piano (1962); several works, each entitled *Session,* for various instrumental ensembles and mandatory drum play (1965, 1966, 1967); *Dream Music No. 2* for Harpsichord and Percussion (1966); Duets for Quintet of Flute, Clarinet, Violin, Cello, and Piano (1971); *Whisper Moon* for Alto Flute, Clarinet, Violin, Cello, and Piano (1971); Duo Fantasy for Violin and Piano (1973); Piano Quartet (1976); *Afternoon,* rag suite for Clarinet, Violin, and Piano (1979); Brass Quintet (1980); *Aubade* for Oboe and Piano (1982); many works for keyboard, including *Frescoes* for 2 Pianists, each doubling on a Harmonium and Harpsichord (first perf. in Toronto, July 21, 1971, by Bruce Mather and Pierrette LePage); *3 Gospel Preludes* for Organ (3 books; 1979–81); also songs, including *Songs of Innocence and of Experience,* after Blake (1956–81; also for Soloists, Chorus, and Orch., 1982).

Boldemann, Laci, Finnish-born Swedish composer; b. Helsinki, April 24, 1921; d. Munich, Aug. 18, 1969. He grew up in Germany; went to Sweden in 1939, but was forced to return to Germany for military service. His music is of a lyrical nature, showing the influence of Sibelius.

WORKS: Fairy-tale opera, *Svart är vitt, sa kejsaren* (*Black Is White, Said the Emperor;* Stockholm, Jan. 1, 1965); opera-musical, *Dårskapens timme*

(*Hour of Madness;* Malmö, March 22, 1968); operatic scene, *Och så drömmer han om Per Jonathan* (*And He Dreams of Per Jonathan;* Stockholm, Nov. 29, 1969); *La Danza,* overture (1949–50); *Lieder der Vergänglichkeit,* cantata for Baritone and Strings (1951); *4 Epitaphs,* after Edgar Lee Masters, for Soprano and Strings (1952); Sinfonietta for Strings (1954); *Fantasia Concertante* for Cello and Orch. (1954); Piano Concerto (1956); *Notturno* for Soprano and Orch. (1958); Violin Concerto (1959); Symph. (Munich, Jan. 13, 1964); *John Bauer,* oratorio (1967); Trumpet Concerto (Malmö, Feb. 11, 1969); *Med bleck och med trä,* little overture for Winds (1969); Violin Sonata (1950); *6 Small Pieces without Pedal* for Piano (1950); String Quartet (1950–57); *Canto elegiaco* for Cello and Piano (1962); about 50 songs.

Bolden, Charles ("Buddy"), black American jazz cornetist; b. New Orleans, c.1868; d. Jackson, La., Nov. 4, 1931. He was a pioneering figure in early jazz; was active mainly in New Orleans. His career was broken by a cerebral dysfunction; he was confined to a state hospital in Jackson, in 1906, and lingered there for many years before succumbing.

Bolet, Jorge, brilliant Cuban-American pianist; b. Havana, Nov. 15, 1914. He went to the U.S. in 1926 and studied piano with David Saperton and conducting with Fritz Reiner at the Curtis Inst. in Philadelphia. In 1932 he took lessons with Leopold Godowsky and with Moriz Rosenthal; he also studied briefly with Rudolf Serkin. During World War II he was stationed in Japan; returning to the U.S., he took private lessons with Abram Chasins. Eventually he was appointed head of the piano dept. at the Curtis Inst. A virtuoso of maximal powers, he seems to be a natural heir of his teachers Godowsky and Rosenthal.

Bollius, Daniel, German organist and composer; b. Hechingen, c.1590; d. Mainz, c.1642. He studied at the Univ. of Dillingen; was court organist in Sigmaringen from 1613–19; in 1626 was appointed organist to the elector of Mainz. His oratorio, *Representatio harmonica conceptionis et nativitatis S. Joannis Baptistae,* is historically significant as an early example of the Italian oratorio form in Germany.

Bologna, Jacopo da. See **Jacopo da Bologna.**

Bölsche, Franz, German music editor; b. Wegenstedt, near Magdeburg, Aug. 20, 1869; d. Bad Oeynhausen, Oct. 23, 1935. He studied with Bargiel and Spitta in Berlin; became a teacher of theory at the Cologne Cons. (1896–1931). He was an editor for the Denkmäler Deutscher Tonkunst, and wrote the successful manual *Übungen und Aufgaben zum Studium der Harmonielehre* (Leipzig, 1911; 18th ed., 1938). Also composed a Symph., 4 overtures (*Tragödie der Menschen, Judith, Hero und Leander, Othello*), etc.

Bolshakov, Nicolai, Russian tenor; b. Kharkov, Nov. 23, 1874; d. Leningrad, Jan. 20, 1958. He studied in St. Petersburg; made his debut there with the Kharkov Opera Co. in 1899; in 1902 he went to Milan, where he studied voice with A. Brogi; then sang with the Maryinsky Theater in St. Petersburg (1906–29); participated in the spectacles of Diaghilev's "Russian Seasons" in Paris and London (1911–13). Returning to Russia, he gave solo recitals; from 1923 to 1953 taught voice at the Leningrad Cons. He was noted for his interpretations of Faust and Don José.

Bolzoni, Giovanni, Italian composer and conductor; b. Parma, May 14, 1841; d. Turin, Feb. 21, 1919. He studied at the Parma Cons.; was active as a conductor in Perugia; served as director and prof. of composition at the Liceo Musicale in Turin (1887–1916); also conducted at the Teatro Regio there (1884–89). He composed several operas; among them the most successful were *Il matrimonio civile* (Parma, 1870), *La stella delle Alpi* (Savona, 1876), and *Jella* (Piacenza, 1881). A melodious minuet from one of his string quartets became a perennial favorite in numerous arrangements.

Bombardelli, Silvije, Croatian conductor and composer; b. Split, March 3, 1916. He studied violin in Belgrade; returning to Split in 1945, he organized an orch., and also conducted opera. In his music he applies modernistic procedures, including modified serial techniques.
WORKS: Ballet, *Stranac* (*The Stranger;* Split, Jan. 25, 1956); *Plameni Vjetar* (*The Flaming Wind*) for Orch. and Speaking Chorus (Split, June 18, 1940); Symph. (Zagreb, Nov. 3, 1951); cantatas and choruses.
BIBLIOGRAPHY: K. Kovačević, *Hrvatski Kompozitori i Njihova Djela* (Zagreb, 1960).

Bomtempo, João Domingos, Portuguese pianist; b. Lisbon, Dec. 28, 1775; d. there, Aug. 18, 1842. He studied in Paris; then went to London, where he stayed until 1811. Returning to Lisbon, he was active on the concert stage; in 1816 he went to London again; finally went to Portugal in 1820. In 1822 he founded a phil. society in Lisbon; in 1833 became director of the Lisbon Cons. He wrote 6 symphonies, 4 piano concertos, 14 piano sextets, a piano quintet, and several piano sonatas; also an opera, *Alessandro in Efesso* (1816). He publ. a piano method (London, 1816).
BIBLIOGRAPHY: M.A. de Lima Cruz, *D. Bomtempo* (Lisbon, 1937).

Bon, Maarten, Dutch pianist and composer; b. Amsterdam, Aug. 20, 1933. He graduated from the Muzieklyceum in Amsterdam in 1954; studied piano with T. Bruins and Spaanderman, and composition with Baaren; then gave recitals with his wife, the violinist **Jeannelotte Hertzberger;** in 1971 was appointed pianist with the Dutch Radio Broadcasting Corp. His compositions are whimsical: *Caprichoso y Obstinato* for Solo Flute (1965); *Disturbing the Peace,* improvisation for 9 Players, more or less (1968–69); *Let's Go Out for a Drive (and Pollute the*

Air), improvisation for Trombone, 3 Pianists, and Conductor (1970–74); *Free or Not* for 21 Wind Players (1972); *Sieben, jedenfalls sieben* for Chamber Ensemble (1976).

Bon, Willem Frederik, Dutch composer and conductor; b. Amersfoort, June 15, 1940; d. Nijeholtpade, April 14, 1983. He studied clarinet, conducting, and composition at the Cons. of Amsterdam and The Hague, receiving a conducting diploma in 1971. In 1972 he became conductor of the Eindhoven Baroque Ensemble, and in 1973 he was named an assistant conductor of the Concertgebouw Orch. in Amsterdam. At the time of his death, he taught composition at the Groningen Cons.
WORKS: FOR THE STAGE: *Erik's wonderbaarlijke reis (Erik's Miraculous Journey),* instrumental opera for Children, Narrator, and Orch. (1979). FOR ORCH.: *Dialogues and Monologues* for Piano and Orch. (1968); *Nocturnes* for String Orch. (1968); *Variations on a Theme of Sweelinck* for Chamber Orch. (1969); 2 symphs.: No. 1, *Usher Symphony,* after Edgar Allan Poe's short story (1968–70; originally intended as material for an opera), and No. 2, *Les Prédictions* (1970); Concerto for String Orch. (1970); *Games* for 6 Wind Instruments, Piano, and String Orch. (1970); *To Catch a Heffalump* for Orch. and Tape (1971); *Circe,* prelude (1972); *Passacaglia in Blue* for 12 Wind Instruments and Double Bass (1972); *Aforismen* for 15 Strings (1972); Concerto for Oboes (Oboe, Oboe d'Amore, and Heckelphone) and Strings (1974); Symph. for Strings (1982). CHAMBER MUSIC: 2 wind quintets (1963–66, 1969); Cello Sonata (1966); *Sunphoneion I* for Flute, Vibraphone, and Piano (1968); *Sans paroles* for Clarinet, Bass Clarinet, and String Trio (1970); *Petite trilogie* for Solo Trumpet (1970); Sonata for Solo Bassoon (1970); *Riflessioni* for Flute and Harp (1971); *5 tours de passe-passe* for Flute and Piano (1971); *Allégorie* for Harp (1972); *3 Saturnien* for Piano Trio (1981). FOR PIANO SOLO: *Miniatures* (1966). FOR VOICE: *3 poèmes de Verlaine* for Mezzo-soprano, Flute, Cello, and Piano (1967); *Missa brevis* for Mixed Chorus and 9 Wind Instruments (1969); *Jadis et naguère* for Mezzo-soprano, Clarinet, Violin, and Piano (1970); *1999, 4 Prophesies of Nostradamus* for Soprano and Orch. (1973); *Le Grand Age Millième,* 4 quatrains after Nostradamus, for a cappella Male Chorus (1974); *Les Quatre Saisons de Verlaine,* each for a different Vocal Soloist and Orch.: *Le Printemps* for Soprano, *L'Eté* for Alto, *L'Automne* for Baritone, and *L'Hiver* for Tenor (1976–79); *Silence,* after Poe, for Mezzo-soprano, Wind Quintet, and Piano (1978); *Dag (Hello),* 4 songs for Mezzo-soprano and Percussion (1979).
BIBLIOGRAPHY: E. Vermeulen, "Bon: Usher Symphony," *Sonorum Speculum* No. 48 (Autumn 1971).

Bona, Giovanni, cardinal; b. Mondovi, Oct. 12, 1609; d. Rome, Oct. 28, 1674. His tract *De divina psalmodia . . . tractatus historicus, symbolicus, asceticus* (Rome, 1653) contains valuable information on church music. A complete ed. of his works was publ. in Rome in 1747.

Bona (or **Buona**), **Valerio,** Italian composer; b. Brescia, c.1560; date of death unknown, but he was still living in 1619. He was a Franciscan monk; maestro di cappella at the cathedrals of Vercelli (1591) and Mondovi, and at the Church of San Francesco in Milan (1596); musician at St. Francesco in Brescia (1611) and prefect at St. Fermo Maggiore in Verona (1614). He was a prolific composer, in polyphonic style, of sacred and secular vocal music (masses, litanies, Lamentations, motets, madrigals, etc.), many of which he wrote for 2 choirs. Also a theorist, he publ.: *Regole del contrapunto, et compositione brevemente raccolte da diuersi auttori* (Casale, 1595); *Esempii delli passagi delle consonanze, et dissonanze* (Milan, 1596); etc.

Bonanni, Filippo, Italian writer on music; b. Rome, Jan. 16, 1638; d. there, March 30, 1725. He was the author of the renowned manual *Gabinetto armonico pieno d'instromenti sonori, indicati, spiegati e di nuovo corretti ed accresciuti* (Rome, 1723, with 151 plates; 2nd ed., Rome, 1776).

Bonaventura, Anthony di, American pianist, brother of **Mario di Bonaventura;** b. Follansbee, W.Va., Nov. 12, 1930. A precocious talent, he played in public at the age of 13; then enrolled at the Curtis Inst. of Music in Philadelphia to study with Isabelle Vengerova. Upon graduation, he launched an ambitious career as a soloist with American and European orchs.; also played numerous recitals. He commissioned several composers of the avant-garde to write special works for him, among them Luciano Berio, Milko Kelemen, and György Ligeti. In 1974 he was appointed to the piano faculty of Boston Univ.

Bonaventura, Arnaldo, Italian musicologist; b. Livorno, July 28, 1862; d. Florence, Oct. 7, 1952. He studied law, violin, and music theory, but made musicology his career. He was a prof. of music history and librarian at the Royal Inst. of Music until 1932; then became director of the Cons. and prof. of music history and esthetics.
WRITINGS: *Manuale di storia della musica* (Livorno, 1898; 10th ed., 1920); *Elementi di Estetica musicale* (Livorno, 1905; 3rd ed., 1926, as *Manuale di Estetica musicale); Dante e la musica* (Livorno, 1904); *Storia degli stromenti musicali* (Livorno, 1908; many other eds.); "La vita musicale in Toscana" (Florence, 1910, in *La Toscana al fine del Granducato); Niccolò Paganini* (1911; 3rd ed., 1925); *Saggio storico sul teatro musicale italiano* (Livorno, 1913); *Storia e letteratura del pianoforte* (Livorno, 1918); *I violinisti italiani moderni; Verdi* (Paris, 1923); *Bernardo Pasquini* (Rome, 1923); *Giacomo Puccini* (Livorno, 1923); *Manuale di cultura musicale* (1924); "*Mefistofele" di Boito* (Milan, 1924); *Storia del violino, dei violinisti e della musica per violino* (Milan, 1925); *L'opera italiana* (1928); *Domenico del Mela* (1928); *Luigi Boccherini* (1931); *Musicisti livornesi* (1931); *Rossini* (1934); numerous essays in various journals. He was editor

of works of J. Peri, B. Strozzi, Frescobaldi, da Firenze, and others.

Bonaventura, Mario di, American conductor, educator, and music publisher; b. Follansbee, W.Va., Feb. 20, 1924. He studied violin; won an award at the N.Y. Phil. in the Young Composers' Composition Competition in 1941; in 1947 went to Paris to study composition with Nadia Boulanger; also took a course in piano accompaniment at the Paris Cons. He subsequently studied conducting with Igor Markevitch at the Mozarteum in Salzburg and later in Paris; received a prize at the 1952 International Conducting Competition at Besançon; in 1953 was awarded the Lili Boulanger Memorial Prize in Composition. In 1954–56 he served as staff pianist with the Pasdeloup Orch. in Paris; made jazz arrangements for the guitarist Django Reinhardt. Returning to the U.S., he conducted the Fort Lauderdale Symph. (1959–62); in 1962 was appointed to the faculty of Dartmouth College; in 1963 inaugurated there an auspicious series of summer festivals under the title "Congregation of the Arts" and commissioned a great number of special works from contemporary composers; all together, 389 modern works were performed during 7 summers, which included 38 world premieres. Among composers-in-residence during this period were Zoltán Kodály, Frank Martin, Boris Blacher, Hans Werner Henze, Ernst Krenek, Witold Lutoslawski, Luigi Dallapiccola, Roberto Gerhard, Walter Piston, Roger Sessions, Carlos Chávez, Easley Blackwood, Elliott Carter, Aaron Copland, Henry Cowell, Ross Lee Finney, Alberto Ginastera, Peter Mennin, and Vincent Persichetti. In 1968 Bonaventura produced and directed the 4th International Anton von Webern Festival; also initiated programs for the furtherance of new music, which awarded 55 commissions to composers in 19 countries. As a conductor, he led orchs. on several European tours. In 1974 he was appointed vice-president and director of publications of G. Schirmer/Associated Music Publishers, N.Y.; in that capacity, too, he promoted publications of modern music; he resigned in 1979 and dedicated himself mainly to univ. teaching.

Bonavia, Ferruccio, Italian-British writer on music; b. Trieste, Feb. 20, 1877; d. London, Feb. 5, 1950. He studied violin in Trieste and Milan; in 1898 went to England; earned his living as a violinist; mastered the English language and became music critic of the *Manchester Guardian* and of the London *Daily Telegraph.* He publ. a monograph on Verdi (London, 1930; 2nd ed., 1947); miniature biographies of Mozart (1938) and Rossini (1941); and a fanciful book of imaginary conversations, *Musicians in Elysium* (1949). He was also a composer; he wrote a violin concerto, a string octet, a string quartet, and some songs.

Bonawitz, Johann Heinrich, German conductor and composer; b. Dürkheim-on-Rhine, Dec. 4, 1839; d. London, Aug. 15, 1917. He studied at the Liège Cons. as a child; in 1852 his parents took him to America. He conducted an unsuccessful season of popular symph. concerts in N.Y. in 1872–73; then produced in Philadelphia 2 of his operas, *The Bride of Messina* (April 22, 1874) and *Ostrolenka* (May 3, 1874). He composed 2 other operas, *Irma* and *Napoleon;* also wrote some sacred choral music. He eventually returned to Europe.

Bonci, Alessandro, Italian lyric tenor; b. Cesena, Feb. 10, 1870; d. Viserba, Aug. 8, 1940. He studied with Carlo Pedrotti and Felice Coen in Pesaro; later took singing lessons with Della Sedie in Paris. He made his operatic debut in Parma on Jan. 20, 1896, as Fenton in *Falstaff;* then sang at La Scala, Milan, and later undertook a grand tour of Europe; also made appearances in South America and Australia. In 1906 he made his N.Y. debut at the new Manhattan Opera House, and remained on its roster for 3 seasons; on Nov. 22, 1907, he sang the role of the Duke in *Rigoletto* at his debut at the Metropolitan Opera, N.Y., and remained with it for 3 seasons. His voice was of great lyric charm; he was one of the few Italian artists to achieve distinction as a singer of German lieder.

Bond, Carrie Jacobs, American composer of sentimental songs; b. Janesville, Wis., Aug. 11, 1862; d. Glendale, Calif., Dec. 28, 1946. She was naturally gifted in music and painting, and improvised songs to her own words at the piano. She organized a music-selling agency and publ. her own songs under the imprint Carrie Jacobs Bond and Son. Although deficient in musical training, she succeeded in producing sweet melodies in lilting rhythms with simple accompaniment that became extremely popular in America. Her first song was *Is My Dolly Dead?* This was followed by her greatest hit, *A Perfect Day,* and a series of other successful songs: *I Love You Truly, God Remembers When the World Forgets, Life's Garden,* and many others. She publ. an autobiography, *The Roads of Melody* (1927), and an album of her poems with philosophical comments under the title *The End of the Road.*

Bond, Chapel, English organist and composer; b. Gloucester (baptized, Dec. 14), 1730; d. Coventry, Feb. 14, 1790. He studied with Martin Smith, the Cathedral organist; when he was 19 he became organist at St. Michael and All Angels in Coventry; from 1752 he also served as organist at Holy Trinity, retaining both posts until his death. He composed a number of effectively written instrumental pieces, including concerti grossi and concertos for trumpet and bassoon.

Bondeville, Emmanuel de, French composer; b. Rouen, Oct. 29, 1898. He studied organ in Rouen and composition with Jean Déré in Paris; subsequently held administrative positions as music director of the Eiffel Tower Radio Station (1935–49), artistic director of the Monte Carlo Opera (1945–49), and director of the Paris Opéra (1952–70). He wrote 2 operas, both produced at the Opéra-Comique in Paris: *L'École des maris* (June 19, 1935) and *Madame*

Bovary (June 1, 1951); also composed a symph. triptych after Rimbaud's poem *Illuminations: Le Bal des pendus* (Paris, Dec. 6, 1930), *Ophélie* (Paris, March 29, 1933), and *Marine* (Paris, March 11, 1934). Other works include *Symphonie lyrique* (1957); *Symphonie choréographique* (1966); choral pieces; a piano sonata; songs. In 1959 he was elected successor to Florent Schmitt as a member of the Académie des Beaux-Arts (Institut de France).

Bondon, Jacques, French composer; b. Boulbon (Bouches-du-Rhône), Dec. 6, 1927. He studied violin and painting in Marseilles. In 1945 he went to Paris, where he took courses in composition with Kœchlin, Milhaud, and Jean Rivier. After early experimentation with ultramodern techniques, he tergiversated to prudential modernism. He became associated with Martenot, and wrote a Concerto for Ondes Martenot and Orch. (1955); also composed music for films and for the radio.
WORKS: For Orch.: *La Coupole* (1954); *Le Taillis ensorcelé* (1954); *Suite indienne* (1958); *Musique pour un autre monde* (1962); *Concert de printemps* for Trumpet, Strings, and Percussion (1957); *Concerto de Mars* for Guitar and Orch. (Paris, Nov. 20, 1966); *Mélousine au rocher,* radio opera (Luxembourg, Oct. 30, 1969); *Le Soleil multicolore* for Flute, Harp, and Viola (1970); *Giocoso* for Violin Solo and String Orch. (1970); *Lumières et formes animées* for String Orch. (Paris, Oct. 6, 1970); opera, *Ana et l'albatros* (Metz, Nov. 21, 1970); a science-fiction opera-ballet, *i. 330* (Nantes, May 20, 1975).
BIBLIOGRAPHY: Jean Roy, *Musique française* (Paris, 1962; pp. 471–83); M.-J. Chauvin, "Entretien avec Jacques Bondon," *Courrier Musical de France* (Jan./April 1970).

Bonelli, Richard, American baritone; b. Port Byron, N.Y., Feb. 6, 1887; d. Los Angeles, June 7, 1980. His real name was **Bunn,** but he changed it to Bonelli when he began his career, since in his time it was difficult to succeed as a singer with an Anglo-Saxon name. He studied with Jean de Reszke in Europe; made his operatic debut as Valentine in *Faust* at the Brooklyn Academy of Music, N.Y., April 21, 1915; then sang at the Monte Carlo Opera, at La Scala in Milan, and in Paris. From 1925 to 1931 he was a member of the Chicago Opera Co.; he made his Metropolitan Opera debut as Germont in *La Traviata* on Dec. 1, 1932. He retired in 1945.

Bonfichi, Paolo, Italian organist and composer; b. Livraga, near Lodi, Oct. 6, 1769; d. Lodi, Dec. 29, 1840. He was self-taught as a keyboard performer; attended the Univ. of Parma, where he studied figured bass. He entered the order of Servi di Maria in 1787, but returned to music while in Rome as a student of counterpoint with Guglielmo. He then lived in a monastery in Poina (1796–1805); subsequently was in Milan; in 1829 became maestro di cappella at the Santa Casa di Loreto, where he remained until 1839. He composed mainly music for the church, including oratorios and cantatas.

Bongartz, Heinz, German conductor; b. Krefeld, July 31, 1894; d. Dresden, May 2, 1978. He studied piano with Elly Ney and conducting with Fritz Steinbach. He subsequently held numerous important positions as conductor in Berlin (1924–26), Meiningen (1926–30), Gotha (1930–33), Kassel (1933–37), and Saarbrücken (1937–44). In 1946–47 he taught at the Leipzig Hochschule für Musik; from 1947 to 1964 he served as chief conductor of the Dresden Phil.

Bonhomme, Pierre, South Netherlandish composer; b. c.1555; d. Liège, June 12, 1617. He was educated in Liège; received the tonsure in 1579; in 1594 was awarded a canonry at the collegiate church of Sainte-Croix in Liège, where he spent the rest of his life. He publ. the *Melodiae sacrae* for 5 to 9 Voices (Frankfurt, 1603) and the *Missae* for 6, 8, 10, and 12 Voices (Antwerp, 1616).

Boni, Guillaume, French composer; flourished in the 2nd half of the 16th century. He was maître de chapelle at the Cathedral in Toulouse. His sacred vocal works include motets and Psalms; he also composed secular sonnets after Ronsard.
BIBLIOGRAPHY: E. Droz, "Guillaume Boni de St. Flour en Auvergne, musicien de Ronsard," *Mélanges offerts à M. Abel Lefranc* (Paris, 1936).

Bonini, Severo, Italian composer, organist, and writer on music; b. Florence, Dec. 23, 1582; d. there, Dec. 5, 1663. He received the habit of the Vallombrosan Benedictines in 1595; professed in 1598; then studied theology and other subjects at the Univ. at Passignano; subsequently resided in an abbey in Florence. In 1611 he became organist at the abbey of Santa Trinità; in 1613 assumed a similar position at S. Mercuriale in Forlì. In 1615 he was made camarlingo at the abbey of S. Michele in Forcole, Pistoia, and in 1619 at S. Mercuriale in Forlì. In 1623 he became curate at S. Martino in Strada, where he remained until 1637. In 1640 he was named organist and maestro di cappella at Santa Trinità, posts he retained until his death. He wrote a valuable treatise on the beginnings of monody and opera, *Discorsi e regole sovra la musica et il contrappunto* (modern ed. and trans. by M. Bonino, Provo, Utah, 1978).
WORKS: *Madrigali e canzonette spirituali* for Voice and Instruments (Florence, 1607); *Il primo libro delle canzonette affettuose in stile moderno* for 4 Voices (Florence, 1608; not extant); *Il primo libro de' motetti* for 3 Voices, Organ, and Instruments (Venice, 1609); *Il secondo libro de' madrigali e motetti* for One and 2 Voices and Instruments (Florence, 1609); *Lamento d'Arianna in stile recitativo* for One and 2 Voices (Venice, 1613); *Affetti spirituali* for 2 Voices (Venice, 1615); *Serena aleste, Motetti* for One to 3 Voices (Venice, 1615).
BIBLIOGRAPHY: M. Bonino, *Don Severo Bonini (1582–1663): His "Discorsi e regole"* (Diss., Univ. of Southern Calif., 1971).

Boninsegna, Celestina, Italian soprano; b. Reggio Emilia, Feb. 26, 1877; d. Milan, Feb. 14, 1947. Without the benefit of vocal training, she made her debut at the age of 15 at Reggio Emilia as Norina; then enrolled at the Cons. in Pesaro; her official debut took place in Fano in 1896, when she appeared as Gilda; then sang in Milan, Rome, Genoa, and South America; also at Covent Garden, London (1904; 1905). On Dec. 21, 1906, she made her Metropolitan Opera debut as Aida, but remained on the roster for only that one season. Following her retirement, she taught voice; spent her last years in the Casa di Riposo in Milan.

Bónis, Ferenc, Hungarian musicologist; b. Miskolc, May 17, 1932. He was educated at the Budapest Academy of Music, studying composition with Szervánszky, Bartha, Kodály, and Szabolcsi (Ph.D., 1958, with the dissertation *Mosónyi Mihály*). He was an editor with Hungarian Radio (1950–52; 1957–70); became director of its programs in music for young audiences in 1970. From 1961 to 1973 he was engaged in musicological research at the Hungarian Academy of Sciences; was made a lecturer at the Budapest Academy of Music in 1972. He became editor a *Magyar Zenetudomány* in 1959, and also of *Magyar Zenetörteneti Tanulmányok* in 1968.
WRITINGS: *Erkel Ferenc* (Budapest, 1953; 2nd ed., 1954); *Bartók élete képekben* (Budapest, 1956; 4th ed., for the Bartók centenary, 1980; in German, 1964; in French, 1964; in Eng. as *Béla Bartók: His Life in Pictures*, 1964); *Kadósa Pál* (Budapest, 1965); ed. *Tóth Aladár válogatott zenekritikai* (Budapest, 1968); *Bartók Béla élete képekben és documentumokban* (Budapest, 1972; in German, 1972; in Eng. as *Béla Bartók: His Life in Pictures and Documents,* 1972).

Bonis, Mélanie (Mme. Albert Domange), French composer; b. Paris, Jan. 21, 1858; d. Sarcelles (Seine-et-Oise), March 18, 1937. She studied at the Paris Cons. with César Franck and Guiraud; wrote 22 chamber works (of which a Trio is still performed); 150 piano pieces; 27 choruses; Fantasy for Piano and String Orch. About 200 of her works are published.

Bonnet, Joseph, eminent French organist; b. Bordeaux, March 17, 1884; d. Ste. Luce-sur-Mer, Quebec, Aug. 2, 1944. He studied with his father, organist at Ste. Eulalie; at the age of 14 he was appointed regular organist at St. Nicholas, and soon after at St. Michel; entered the class of Guilmant at the Paris Cons. and graduated with the first prize. In 1906 he won the post of organist at St. Eustache over many competitors. After extensive tours on the Continent and in England, he became organist of the Concerts du Conservatoire as successor to Guilmant (1911). He made his American debut in N.Y. (Jan. 30, 1917), followed by successful tours of the U.S. He wrote many pieces for his instrument, and edited for publication all the works played in his series of N.Y. concerts as *Historical Organ Recitals* (6 vols.); also publ. an anthology of early French organ music (N.Y., 1942).
BIBLIOGRAPHY: H.B. Gaul, "Bonnet, Bossi,

Karg-Elert. Three Aperçus," *Musical Quarterly* (July 1918).

Bonno, Giuseppe, noted Austrian composer of Italian descent; b. Vienna, Jan. 29, 1711; d. there, April 15, 1788. His father, Lucrezio Bonno, was the imperial footman. He began his musical studies with Johann Georg Reinhardt, the court organist. Charles VI sent Bonno to Naples in 1726 for further musical education; there he studied composition with Durante and Leo. His first opera, *Nigella e Nise,* was performed in Naples in 1732. In 1736 he returned to Vienna, where he brought out his 2nd opera, *L'amore insuperabile.* In 1737 he was made a court scholar in composition, and in 1739 was named court composer. In 1739 he brought out his oratorio *Eleazaro,* which proved highly successful. He subsequently joined Gluck and Dittersdorf as a Kapellmeister to Field Marshall Joseph Friedrich, Prince of Sachsen-Hildburghausen, in Schlosshof and Mannersdorf. In 1774 he succeeded Gassmann as Imperial Court Kapellmeister. Bonno was greatly esteemed as a teacher; Dittersdorf and Marianne von Martinez were among his pupils. He was a friend of the Mozart family, and recognized the budding genius of Mozart at an early date.
WORKS: FOR THE STAGE (all perf. at the Burgtheater in Vienna, unless otherwise stated): *Nigella e Nise,* pastorale (Naples, 1732); *L'amore insuperabile,* festa di camera (July 26, 1736); *Trajano,* festa di camera (Oct. 1, 1736); *La gara del genio con Giunone,* serenata (Laxenburg, May 13, 1737); *Alessandro Severo,* festa di camera (Oct. 1, 1737); *La generosità di Artaserse,* serenata (Nov. 4, 1737); a pastorale (Nov. 19, 1737); *La pace richiamata,* festa di camera (July 26, 1738); *La pietà di Numa,* festa di camera (Oct. 1, 1738); *La vera nobilità,* festa di camera (July 26, 1739); *Il natale di Numa Pompilio,* festa di camera (Oct. 1, 1739); *Il nume d'Atene,* festa di camera (Nov. 19, 1739); *La generosa Spartana,* serenata (Laxenburg, May 13, 1740); *Il natale di Giove,* azione teatrale (Favorita, Vienna, Oct. 1, 1740); *Il vero omaggio,* componimento drammatico (Schloss Schönbrunn, Vienna, March 13, 1743); *La danza,* cantata (April 1744); *Danae,* opera (1744; not extant); *Ezio,* opera (1749; not extant); *Il Re pastore,* dramma per musica (Schloss Schönbrunn, Vienna, Oct. 27, 1751); *L'Ero cinese,* opera (Schloss Schönbrunn, Vienna, May 13, 1752); *L'isola disabitata,* azione teatrale (Sept. 23, 1754); *Didone abbandonata,* opera (1752; not extant); *Colloquio amoroso fra Piramo e Tisbe* (1757); *Complimento,* for the Prince of Sachsen-Hildburghausen (1761; not extant); *L'Atenaide ovvero Gli affetti più generosi,* azione teatrale (1762); *Il sogno di Scipione* (1763); also, in collaboration with others: *Catone in Utica* (1742) and *L'Armida placata* (Oct. 8, 1750). ORATORIOS (all perf. in Vienna): *Eleazaro* (1739); *San Paolo in Athene* (March 31, 1740); *Isacco figura del redentore* (March 18, 1759); *Il Giuseppe riconosciuto* (March 20, 1774). Also, masses and instrumental works.
BIBLIOGRAPHY: E. Wellesz, "Giuseppe Bonno: Sein Leben und seine dramatischen Werke," *Sam-*

melbände der Internationalen Musik-Gesell-schaft, XI (1909–10); A. Schienerl, *Die kirchlichen Kompositionen des Giuseppe Bonno* (Diss., Univ. of Vienna, 1925); K. Breitner, *Giuseppe Bonno und sein Oratorienwerk* (Diss., Univ. of Vienna, 1961).

Bononcini, Antonio Maria (not **Marco Antonio,** as he is often listed), Italian opera composer, son of **Giovannia Maria** and brother of **Giovanni;** b. Modena, June 18, 1677; d. there, July 8, 1726. He studied with his father; his first success came with the production of his opera *Il trionfo di Camilla, regina dei Volsci* (Naples, Dec. 26, 1696). This opera was produced in many other theaters in Italy, sometimes under different titles, as *Amore per amore, La fede in cimento,* etc. It was presented in London (March 31, 1706) with great acclaim. In 1702 Bononcini was in Berlin; from 1704–11 he was in Vienna, where he produced the operas *Teraspo* (Nov. 15, 1704); *Arminio* (July 26, 1706); *La conquista delle Spagne di Scipione Africano* (Oct. 1, 1707); *La presa di Tebe* (Oct. 1, 1708); *Tigrane, re d'Armenia* (July 26, 1710). Returning to Italy, he produced the following operas in Milan: *Il tiranno eroe* (Dec. 26, 1715); *Sesostri, re di Egitto* (Feb. 2, 1716); *Griselda* (Dec. 26, 1718). In his native town of Modena, he directed his operas *L'enigma disciolto* (Oct. 15, 1716) and *Lucio Vero* (Nov. 5, 1716). His last opera, *Rosiclea in Dania,* was staged in Naples (Oct. 1, 1721). He wrote 19 operas in all, and 3 oratorios. His most famous opera, *Il trionfo di Camilla,* has often been erroneously attributed to his brother; several songs from it were publ. in London by Walsh.

BIBLIOGRAPHY: L.F. Valdrighi, *I Bononcini da Modena* (Modena, 1882); for details of his operatic productions, see Loewenberg's *Annals of Opera* (1943; 2nd ed., 1955).

Bononcini, Giovanni (not **Giovanni Battista,** despite the fact that this name appears on some of his compositions), the best-known composer of the Bononcini family, son of **Giovanni Maria;** b. Modena, July 18, 1670; d. Vienna, July 9, 1747 (buried July 11). His first teacher was his father; he also studied with G.P. Colonna in Bologna, and took cello lessons from Giorgio. In 1687 he was a cellist in the chapel of San Petronio in Bologna; in the same year he became maestro di cappella at San Giovanni in Monte. He publ. his first work, *Trattenimenti da camera* for String Trio, in Bologna at the age of 15. This was followed in quick succession by a set of chamber concertos, "sinfonie" for small ensembles, masses, and instrumental duos (1685–91). In 1691 he went to Rome, where he produced his first opera, *Serse* (Jan. 25, 1694), and shortly afterward, another opera, *Tullo Ostilio* (Feb. 1694). In 1698 he went to Vienna as court composer; there he brought out his operas *La fede pubblica* (Jan. 6, 1699) and *Gli affetti più grandi vinti dal più giusto* (July 26, 1701). He spent 2 years (1702–4) at the court of Queen Sophie Charlotte in Berlin; at her palace in Charlottenburg he produced, in the summer of 1702, the opera *Polifemo;* here he also presented a new opera, *Gli amori di Cefalo e Procri* (Oct. 16, 1704). After the Queen's death (Feb. 1, 1705) the opera company was disbanded; Bononcini returned to Vienna and staged the following operas: *Endimione* (July 10, 1706); *Turno Aricino* (July 26, 1707); *Mario fuggitivo* (1708); *Abdolonimo* (Feb. 3, 1709); *Muzio Scevola* (July 10, 1710). In 1711 Bononcini returned to Italy with his brother (who had also been in Vienna). In 1719 he was in Rome, where he produced the opera *Erminia.* In 1720 he received an invitation to join the Royal Academy of Music in London, of which Handel was director, and the Italian Opera Co. connected with it. A famous rivalry developed between the supporters of Handel, which included the King, and the group of noblemen (Marlborough, Queensberry, Rutland, and Sunderland) who favored Bononcini and other Italian composers. Indicative of the spirit of the time was the production at the King's Theatre of the opera *Muzio Scevola,* with the first act written by Amadei, the 2nd by Bononcini (he may have used material from his earlier setting of the same subject), and the 3rd by Handel (April 15, 1721). By general agreement Handel won the verdict of popular approval; this episode may have inspired the well-known poem publ. at the time ("Some say, compar'd to Bononcini, That Mynheer Handel's but a ninny," etc.). Other operas brought out by Bononcini in London were: *Astarto* (Nov. 19, 1720); *Crispo* (Jan. 10, 1722); *Farnace* (Nov. 27, 1723); *Calpurnia* (April 18, 1724); *Astianatte* (May 6, 1727). He then suffered a series of setbacks, first the death of his chief supporter, Marlborough (1722), and then the revelation that a madrigal he had submitted to the Academy of Music was an arrangement of a work by Lotti, which put Bononcini's professional integrity in doubt. To this was added his strange association with one Count Ughi, a self-styled alchemist who claimed the invention of a philosopher's stone, and who induced Bononcini to invest his earnings in his scheme for making gold. After his London debacle, Bononcini went (in 1732) to Paris, where he was engaged as a cellist at the court of Louis XV. He was referred to in *Le Mercure de France* (Feb. 7, 1735) as the composer of 78 operas. In 1735 he was in Lisbon; in 1737, in Vienna, where he produced the oratorio *Ezechia* (April 4, 1737) and a *Te Deum* (1740). Reduced to poverty, he petitioned the young Empress Maria Theresa for a pension, which was granted in Oct. 1742, giving him a monthly stipend of 50 florins, received regularly until his death on July 9, 1747, at the age of 77. This date and the circumstances of his last years in Vienna were first made known in the valuable paper by Kurt Hueber, *Gli ultimi anni di Giovanni Bononcini, Notizie e documenti inediti,* publ. by the Academy of Sciences, Letters and Arts of Modena (Dec. 1954). Among Bononcini's works, other than operas, are 7 oratorios (including *Ezechia;* all on various biblical subjects), and instrumental works publ. in London by Walsh: several suites for harpsichord; *Cantate e Duetti,* dedicated to George I (1721); Divertimenti for Harpsichord (1722); *Funeral Anthem for John, Duke of Marlborough* (1722); *12 Sonatas or Chamber Airs for 2 Violins and a Bass* (1732); etc. For further details regarding Bononcini's operas, see Loewenberg's *Annals of Op-*

era (1943; 2nd ed., 1955).

Bononcini, Giovanni Maria, Italian composer; father of **Giovanni** and **Antonio Maria Bononcini;** b. Montecorone, Sept. 23, 1642; d. Modena, Nov. 18, 1678. In 1671 he was awarded a ducal appointment as violinist at the Cathedral of Modena; also served as chamber musician to the Dowager Duchess Laura d'Este. He had 8 children, of whom the only two who survived infancy were Giovanni and Antonio Maria Bononcini. He publ. 11 sets of instrumental works: *I primi frutti del giardino musicale* (Venice, 1666); *Varii fiori* (Bologna, 1669); *Arie, correnti, sarabande, gighe e allemande* (Bologna, 1671); *Sonate* (Venice, 1672); *Ariette, correnti, gighe, allemande e sarabande* (Bologna, 1673); *Trattenimenti musicali* (Bologna, 1675); *Arie e correnti* (Bologna, 1678); also vocal works: *Cantate da camara* for Solo Voice and 2 Violins (Bologna, 1677); *Madrigali* for 5 Voices (Bologna, 1678). He further publ. a didactic manual, *Musico prattico* (Bologna, 1673; a German trans. was publ. in Stuttgart, 1701).
BIBLIOGRAPHY: W. Klenz, *G. M. Bononcini of Modena: A Chapter in Baroque Instrumental Music* (Durham, N.C., 1962).

Bononcini, Marco Antonio. See **Bononcini, Antonio Maria.**

Bonporti, Francesco Antonio, Italian composer; b. Trento (baptized, June 11), 1672; d. Padua, Dec. 19, 1748. He studied theology in Innsbruck and Rome; in 1695 returned to Trento; was ordained a priest and served as a cleric at the Cathedral of Trento. He publ. 3 sets of 10 trio sonatas each (Venice, 1696, 1698, and 1703); 10 sonatas for Violin and Bass (Venice, 1707); 10 "concerti a 4" and 5 "concertini" for Violin and Bass; 6 motets for Soprano, Violin, and Bass. He also wrote 2 sets of minuets (50 in each set), which are lost. Four of his "invenzioni" were mistaken for Bach's works and were included in the Bachgesellschaft edition (XLV, part 1, p. 172). Henry Eccles publ. the 4th of these pieces as his own, incorporating it in his Violin Sonata No. 11.
BIBLIOGRAPHY: G. Barblan, *Un musicista trentino, F.A. Bonporti* (Florence, 1940); Ch. Bouvet, "Un Groupe de compositions musicales de Bonporti publiées sous le nom de Bach," *Union Musicologique* (The Hague, 1921); G. Barblan, ed., *Francesco A. Bonporti nel 3° centenario della nascita* (Trent, 1972); L. Feininger, *Francesco Antonio Bonporti: Catalogus thematicus operum omnium* (Trent, 1975).

Bonsel, Adriaan, Dutch flutist and composer; b. Hilversum, Aug. 4, 1918. He studied at the Amsterdam Cons.; appeared as a flute soloist in recitals and with various orchs.
WORKS: Suite for Flute and String Orch. (1946); *Folkloristic Suite* for Orch. (1948); Clarinet Concerto (1950); 2 symphs. (1956, 1957); Divertimento for Small Orch. (1957); *S.O.S.*, overture (1962); *Vrede-Oorlog-Vrede? (Peace-War-Peace?) Moto-perpetuo?* for Orch. (1975); *Minneliederen,* 6 love songs for Baritone, Chorus, and Small Orch. (1957); 2 wind quintets (1949, 1953); *Elegy* for Solo Viola (1961); *Concert Etudes* for Solo Flute (1963); *Musica* for Flute, Cello, and Piano (1971); *Anthriscus Sylvestris,* divertimento for 12 Flutes (1974); Octet for Winds (1975).

Bontempi (real name, **Angelini**), **Giovanni Andrea,** Italian singer and composer; b. Perugia, c.1624; d. Torgiano, July 1, 1705. He was a castrato, and sang in the choir of San Marco in Venice (1643–50). After studies with Mazzocchi, he was appointed joint Kapellmeister in Dresden, with Schütz and Vincenzo Albrici, in 1656. He assumed the name Bontempi after his patron, Cesare Bontempi. In 1680 he returned to Italy; sang at the Collegiata di S. Maria at Sapello, near Foligno, in 1682; was maestro di cappella there during the first half of 1686. He was one of the earliest composers of Italian operas and oratorios. His first opera, *Il Paride in musica,* to his own libretto, was produced in Dresden, on Nov. 3, 1662; it was the first Italian opera ever produced there. Two later operas, both produced in Dresden, were *Apollo e Dafne,* written in collaboration with Peranda and produced in Dresden on Sept. 3, 1671, and *Giove e Io* (also with Peranda), produced in Dresden on Jan. 16, 1673. He also composed an oratorio, *Martirio di San Emiliano;* published the treatises *Nova quatuor vocibus componendi methodus* (Dresden, 1660); *Tractus in quo demonstrantur occultae convenientiae sonorum systematis participati* (Bologna, 1690); *Historia musica, nella quale si ha piena cognitione della teorica e della pratica antica della musica harmonica secondo la dottrina de' Greci* (Perugia, 1695).
BIBLIOGRAPHY: G.B. Rossi Scotti, *Di Giovanni Andrea Bontempi di Perugia* (1878); F. Briganti, *Giovanni Andrea Angelini-Bontempi (1624–1705). Musicista, letterato, architto: Perugia-Dresda* (Florence, 1956).

Bonvin, Ludwig, choral conductor and scholar; b. Siders, Switzerland, Feb. 17, 1850; d. Buffalo, N.Y., Feb. 18, 1939. His musical training in early youth was irregular; as a musician he was chiefly self-taught; studied medicine in Vienna; in 1874 entered the Jesuit novitiate in the Netherlands, where he became organist and choirmaster; continued his musical studies, especially of early sacred works. He settled in Buffalo as a choral and orch. director at Canisius College (1887–1907); then devoted himself exclusively to music scholarship; promulgated a theory of mensural rhythm in Gregorian chant. He publ. much sacred music, including 8 masses; a Symph.; *Christmas Night's Dream* for String Orch.; many pieces for organ, piano, violin, and voice; his works exceed 125 opus numbers.
WRITINGS: "Gregorian Accompaniment," *Musica Sacra* (1931 and 1932); *Musical Accents in Gregorian Chant* (1932); "On Syrian Liturgical Chant," *Musical Quarterly* (Oct. 1918); "The 'Measure' in Gregorian Music," *Musical Quarterly* (Jan. 1929); etc.
BIBLIOGRAPHY: F.E. Bunse, "Ludwig Bonvin,"

Musica Sacra (Jan. 1933).

Bonynge, Richard, Australian conductor; b. Sydney, Sept. 29, 1930. He studied at the New South Wales Cons. of Music; began his career as a pianist. In 1954 he married **Joan Sutherland,** the famed Australian soprano. To assist her, Bonynge turned to conducting, making his debut in 1962. In 1976 he was named music director of the Australian Opera in Sydney. In 1977 he was made a Commander of the Order of the British Empire.

Bookspan, Martin, American music critic, administrator, and broadcaster; b. Boston, July 30, 1926. He was educated at the Boston Music School (violin and theory) and Harvard College (B.S. in German literature, 1947). He was executive director of the New England Opera Theater (1952–54); from 1956 to 1968 held various administrative positions with WQXR Radio in N.Y. In 1968 he was named coordinator for the symph. and concert activities of ASCAP. He was host and commentator for the Boston Symph. and Pops radio broadcasts (1957–68); since 1975 he has been host, commentator, and executive producer for the N.Y. Phil. radio broadcasts; from 1976 also commentator for the "Live from Lincoln Center" PBS telecasts. He has been a permanent member of the panel of critics for the "First Hearing" radio program; was a contributing editor to *Stereo Review Magazine* (1958–76); also wrote for the *New York Times* (1963–65). He publ. *101 Masterpieces of Music and Their Composers* (N.Y., 1968) and *Zubin: The Zubin Mehta Story* (N.Y., 1978).

Boom, Jan (Johannes) van, Dutch pianist and composer; b. Utrecht, Oct. 15, 1807; d. Stockholm, March 19, 1872. He studied piano with Hummel and Moscheles; undertook a concert tour in Scandinavia and settled in Stockholm; there he joined the staff of the Royal Academy of Music (1844–65). He composed some pleasing piano music in the salon manner.

Boone, Charles, American composer of the avantgarde; b. Cleveland, June 21, 1939. He studied with Karl Schiske at the Vienna Academy of Music (1960–61); after returning to the U.S., he took private lessons with Ernst Krenek and Adolph Weiss in Los Angeles (1961–62); attended the Univ. of Southern Calif. (B.M., 1963) and San Francisco State College (M.A., 1968); served as chairman of the San Francisco Composers' Forum and coordinator of the Mills College Performing Group and Tape Music Center. His music creates a sonic environment on purely structural principles, employing serial matrices, coloristic contrasts, and spatial parameters of performing instruments, with resulting styles ranging from lyrical pointillism to static sonorism. Electronic resources make up part of his musical equipment. WORKS: *Icarus* for Flute Solo (1964); *Song of Suchness* for Soprano, Flute, Piccolo, Viola, Piano, and Celesta (1964); *Parallels* for Violin and Piano (1964); *Oblique Formation* for Flute and Piano (1965); *Starfish* for Flute, E-flat Clarinet, Percussion, 2 Violins, and Piano (1966); *The Yellow Bird* for Orch. (1967); *Constant Comment* for Stereophonic Tape (1967); *Shadow* for Oboe Solo, Tape, and Orch. (1968); *The Edge of the Land* for Orch. (1968); *Not Now* for Clarinet Solo (1969); Quartet for Violin, Clarinet, Cello, and Piano (1970); *Zephyrus* for Oboe and Piano (1970); *Vermilion* for Oboe Solo (1970); *Chinese Texts* for Soprano and Orch. (1971); *Second Landscape* for Chamber Orch. (1973); *Raspberries* for 3 Drummers (1974); *Linea Meridiana* for Chamber Ensemble (1975); *San Zeno/Verona* for Chamber Ensemble (1976); *Fields/Singing* for Soprano and Chamber Ensemble (1976); *Shunt* for 3 Drummers (1978); *String Piece* for String Orch. (1978); *Streaming for Solo Flute* (1979); *Winter's End* for Soprano, Countertenor, Viola da Gamba, Harpsichord (1980); *The Watts Towers* for Solo Drummer (1981); *Trace* for Flute and 10 Players (1981).

Boone, Pat (Charles Eugene Boone), American singer of popular music; b. Jacksonville, Fla., June 1, 1934. He studied at North Texas State Teachers College in Denton; continued his studies at Columbia Univ. (B.S., 1958); He first came to prominence as a singer of popular music on television in 1955; later became active as an evangelist. His daughter **Debby (Deborah Anni;** b. Hackensack, N.J., Sept. 22, 1956) is also a singer.

Booren, Jo van den, Dutch composer; b. Maastricht, March 14, 1935. He studied trumpet with Marinus Komst and composition with Kees van Baaren and Klaus Huber; was active as an orch. trumpet player. In his music he pursues the goal of sonorous structuralism; some of his works bear ostentatiously abstract titles. WORKS: Trio for Oboe, Clarinet, and Bassoon (1960); Sonata for 3 Clarinets (1962); *Suite dionysienne* for English Horn and String Orch. (1963–64); *Estremi* for Oboe, Violin, Viola, and Cello (1967); *Spectra* for Wind Quintet (1967); *Capriccio* for Brass Orch. (1968); *Spiel I* for Oboe and Electronic Sound (1969); *Strofa I* for Solo Cello (1969); *Strofa II* for Solo Trumpet (1970); *Strofa III* for Solo Horn (1972); *Equilibrio* for Solo Flute (1970); *Ballade* for Solo Oboe (1971); *Intrada Festiva* for 4 Horns, 4 Trumpets, and 4 Trombones (1971); *Akirob* for Flute, Violin, and Viola (1972); *Potpourri 1973* for Brass Quintet (1973); *Sinfonia Jubilata* for Orch. (Tilburg, Oct. 3, 1975); *Birds,* a "story" for 5 Flutes (1975).

Boosey & Hawkes, British music publishers. **Thomas Boosey** was a London bookseller and a continental traveler since 1792. He was often asked to handle music, and in 1816 founded a music publishing house on Holles Street. On the Continent he met eminent musicians of the time; he visited Vienna and negotiated about publication with Beethoven (who mentions Boosey's name in one of his letters to the Royal Phil. Society in London). Boosey's main stock consisted of Italian and French operas; he owned copyrights of Bellini, Donizetti, and Verdi (until 1854); publ. inexpensive Eng. editions of standard European works. In the 1820s he put his son, **Thomas,** in charge of musical publications. In 1846 the firm of Boosey & Sons began publishing band music; in 1855 (in conjunction with the flutist R.S. Pratten) the manufacture of improved flutes was begun; in 1868 the firm acquired Henry Distin's factory for musical instruments, and supplied band instruments for the British and Colonial armies. It was this development that eventually brought about the merger of Boosey and Hawkes. **William Henry Hawkes** was a trumpeter-in-ordinary to Queen Victoria. He established in 1865 a workshop of band instruments and an edition of concert music for orch. and became a strong competitor of Boosey & Sons from 1885 on. Economic pressure forced the amalgamation of the two firms in 1930, combining valuable editions covering a whole century of music. A branch of Boosey & Sons had been established in N.Y. (1892), discontinued in 1900 and reestablished in 1906; after the merger, Boosey & Hawkes opened offices in N.Y., Chicago, and Los Angeles. In Canada, the business was inaugurated in 1913; the Editions Hawkes started a Paris branch in 1922; further affiliates were established in Australia (1933), India (1937), Argentina (1945), South Africa (1946), and Germany (1950). After World War II the factories for the manufacture of band instruments in London were greatly expanded; quantity production of wind instruments, harmonicas, and drums enabled the firm to extend the market to all parts of the world. For a few years after World War II Boosey & Hawkes leased Covent Garden. In 1927 the firm acquired the American rights of Enoch & Sons; in 1943 the catalogue of Adolph Fürstner, containing all the operas of Richard Strauss, was bought for certain territories. In 1947, the Koussevitzky catalogue (Edition Russe de Musique and Edition Gutheil) was purchased, including the major output of Stravinsky, Prokofiev, and Rachmaninoff. Other acquisitions include the copyrights of publications of Winthrop Rogers and Rudall Carte.

Boott, Francis, American composer; b. Boston, June 24, 1813; d. there, March 2, 1904. He was educated at Harvard (graduated in 1831); lived for a time in Florence, Italy, where he studied music; returned to the U.S. in 1874, settling in Cambridge, Mass. He bequeathed to Harvard Univ. $10,000 (which was increased through capital gains to $15,246 in 1960), the interest to form an annual prize for the best 4-part vocal composition written by a Harvard man. He was a prolific composer of secular and sacred songs, anthems, and chorales, many of which were included in the service book of King's Chapel in Boston. His songs *Here's a Health to King Charles, When Sylvia Sings,* and *Lethe* were once very popular.

Bopp, Wilhelm, German conductor and pedagogue; b. Mannheim, Nov. 4, 1863; d. Baden-Baden, June 11, 1931. He studied at the Leipzig Cons.; also took courses in conducting with Emil Paur at Mannheim; was a teacher at the Mannheim Cons.; in 1907 moved to Vienna, where he became director of the Conservatorium der Musikfreunde.

Borch, Gaston Louis Christopher, composer and conductor; b. Guines, France, March 8, 1871; d. Stockholm, Feb. 14, 1926. He studied in Paris with Massenet (composition) and Delsart (cello); then with Svendsen in Copenhagen; conducted various organizations in Norway (1896–99); came to the U.S. in 1899 as cellist with the Thomas Orch. in Chicago; then played in the Pittsburgh Orch. (1903–6); conducted various orchs. in Switzerland, France, Belgium, the Netherlands, and Germany. He composed 3 symph. poems: *Geneviève de Paris, Quo Vadis,* and *Frithjof;* made popular arrangements of standard classics for piano, violin, and cello. His one-act opera, *Silvio* (written as a sequel to *Cavalleria Rusticana*), was produced in Oslo in 1897. He publ. a *Practical Manual of Instrumentation* (Boston, 1918).

Borchard, Adolphe, French pianist and composer; b. Le Havre, June 30, 1882; d. Paris, Dec. 13, 1967. He studied at the Paris Cons. with Diémer and Lenepveu, where he won prizes for piano (1903) and composition (1905, 1907); toured extensively as a pianist, making his American debut in 1910; later settled in Paris as director of various musical activities sponsored by the French government. He composed *Es Kual Herria (The Basque Country)* for Piano and Orch. (Paris, 1922); *En Marge de Shakespeare* for Orch. (1923); *L'Elan* for Orch. (1923); *Sept estampes amoureuses* for Orch. (1927); numerous songs.

Borchers, Gustav, German vocal teacher; b. Woltwiesche (Braunschweig), Aug. 18, 1865; d. Leipzig, Jan. 19, 1913. He studied at the Leipzig Cons. (1887–89); then conducted various choral societies; in 1898 he founded a seminary for singing teachers, which later employed the methods of Jaques-Dalcroze ("rhythmical gymnastics") and Eitz ("Tonwort"). Borchers publ. a monograph on the "Tonwort" theory (1908).

Borchgrevinck, Melchior, Danish organist and composer; b. c.1570; d. Copenhagen, Dec. 20, 1632. He became a musician at the Danish court in 1587; found favor with King Christian IV, and in 1600 was named court organist; in 1603 he became chief instrumentalist; in 1618 was appointed director of court music. He composed madrigals, but most of his music is not extant.

Borck, Edmund von, talented German composer; b. Breslau, Feb. 22, 1906; killed in action near Nettuno, Italy, Feb. 16, 1944. He studied composition in Breslau (1920–26), and music history at the Univ. of Berlin; held several positions as opera conductor in Berlin and Frankfurt; then taught theory and composition in Berlin until drafted into the army in

1940. His progress as a composer was rapid; his early works indicated an original creative ability, and his death in combat was a great loss to German music. His style of composition is neo-Classical, with strong contrapuntal structure; the rather austere and reticent mode of expression assumes in Borck's music a colorful aspect through a variety of melodic and rhythmic devices, often in a rhapsodically romantic vein.

WORKS: Concerto for Alto Saxophone and Orch. (1932); Violin Sonata (1932); *Orchesterstücke* (1933); *Ländliche Kantate* (1934); Concerto for Orch. (1936); Sextet for Flute and Strings (1936); *Kleine Suite* for Unaccompanied Flute (1938); *2 Fantasiestücke* for Orch. (1940); Piano Concerto (1941); *Orphika,* "an Apollonian transformation" for Orch. (1941); an opera, *Napoleon* (Gera, 1942).

BIBLIOGRAPHY: K. Laux, "Edmund von Borck," in *Musik und Musiker der Gegenwart* (Essen, 1949); S. Borris, *Beiträge zu einer Musikkunde* (Berlin, 1948); K.H. Wörner, *Musik der Gegenwart* (Mainz, 1949).

Borde, Jean Benjamin de la. See **La Borde, Jean Benjamin de.**

Bordes, Charles, French choral conductor; b. Roche-Corbon, near Vouvray-sur-Loire, May 12, 1863; d. Toulon, Nov. 8, 1909. He studied piano with Marmontel and composition with César Franck. In 1894, in association with Guilmant and Vincent d'Indy, he organized the Schola Cantorum in Paris, and in subsequent years organized chapters of the Schola Cantorum in Avignon and Montpellier. He made numerous tours with his choral group. In 1889 he was commissioned by the French government to make a study of Basque folk songs; he publ. 100 of these in *Archives de la tradition basque.* He also wrote several pieces based on Basque motifs, among them *Suite basque* for Flute and String Quartet (1888) and *Rapsodie basque* for Piano and Orch. (1890); also edited several anthologies of old French music, publ. by the Schola Cantorum.

BIBLIOGRAPHY: *Charles Bordes, In memoriam* (Paris, Schola Cantorum, 1909); P. Alibert, *Charles Bordes à Maguelonne* (Paris, 1926); P. Dowd, *Charles Bordes and the Schola Cantorum of Paris* (Diss., Catholic Univ. of America, Washington, D.C., 1969).

Bordes-Pène, Léontine Marie, French pianist; b. Lorient, Nov. 25, 1858; d. Rouen, Jan. 24, 1924. She graduated with the first prize at the Paris Cons. in 1872; dedicated her concert career to propagandizing French music; she was the sister-in-law of Charles Bordes, and a friend of César Franck, Vincent d'Indy, etc. She suffered a paralytic stroke in 1890, and lived the rest of her life in Rouen.

BIBLIOGRAPHY: G. Samazeuilh, "Madame Bordes-Pène," *La Revue Musicale* (1924).

Bordier, Jules, French composer; b. Angers, Dec. 23, 1846; d. there, Jan. 29, 1896. He founded the concerts of the Association Artistique d'Angers in 1875; went to Paris (1894) as partner in the music publishing house of Baudoux & Cie. He composed a *Danse macabre* for Violin; the operas *Nadia* (Brussels, 1887) and *Le Fiancé de la Mer* (Rouen, 1895); choruses.

Bordogni, Giulio Marco, Italian tenor and singing teacher; b. Gazzaniga, near Bergamo, Jan. 23, 1789; d. Paris, July 31, 1856. He was a pupil of Simone Mayr; made his operatic debut in 1808, at La Scala, Milan. From 1819 to 1833 he was engaged at the Théâtre-Italien in Paris; later devoted himself primarily to teaching; he joined the staff of the Paris Cons. in 1820. He publ. a collection of 36 vocalises, in 2 vols., which became a standard book of vocal exercises throughout Europe.

Bordoni, Faustina. See **Hasse, Faustina.**

Borel-Clerc (real name, **Clerc**), **Charles,** French composer of popular music; b. Pau, Sept. 22, 1879; d. Cannes, April 9, 1959. He studied music at first in Toulouse; at the age of 17 he went to Paris, where he studied the oboe at the Paris Cons. with Gillet, and composition with Lenepveu; then played oboe in various Paris orchs. He wrote numerous operettas, music revues, and a great number of songs; his greatest success came with *La Matchiche* (1903), a song that became world-famous. His other celebrated songs were *C'est jeune et ça n'sait pas; Madelon de la Victoire* (1918; a sequel to the war song *Madelon* by Camille Robert); many chansonettes for Maurice Chevalier and other artists.

Boretz, Benjamin, American music critic, editor, and composer; b. New York, Oct. 3, 1934. He studied at Brooklyn College, Brandeis Univ., and Princeton Univ.; took courses in composition with Milton Babbitt, Irving Fine, Darius Milhaud, and Roger Sessions. From 1964 to 1969 he served on the faculty of N.Y. Univ.; then taught at Columbia Univ. (1969–72). In 1973 he became a prof. and chairman of the music dept. at Bard College in N.Y. In 1961 he co-founded, with Edward Cone, a non-periodical publication, *Perspectives of New Music,* radiating potent charges of musical profundity; he remained its editor until 1983; was engaged as music critic for the *Nation* from 1962 to 1969. Among his works is a Concerto Grosso (1965); Divertimento for Chamber Orch. (1955); Violin Concerto (1957); String Quartet (1958); Brass Quintet (1963); several "group variations" for the computer synthesizer.

Borg, Kim, noted Finnish bass; b. Helsinki, Aug. 7, 1919. He first studied chemistry; then enrolled in the Sibelius Academy of Music; also took singing lessons in Sweden, Denmark, Austria, Italy, and America. He began his operatic career at Aarhus in 1951; made his Metropolitan Opera debut in N.Y. on Oct. 30, 1959, as Count Almaviva in *Le nozze di Figaro,* remaining on its roster until 1962. He was one of the few non-Russian artists to sing the title role of *Boris Godunov* at the Bolshoi Opera in Moscow. In 1972 he became a member of the faculty of the Royal Cons. of Music in Copenhagen. He furthermore distinguished himself as a composer; wrote 3 trios, a String Quartet, a Trombone Concerto, and a Double-bass Concerto; published a didactic manual, *ABC for the Finnish Singer.*

Borgatti, Giuseppe, Italian tenor; b. Cento, March 17, 1871; d. Reno, Lago Maggiore, Oct. 18, 1950. He studied with Alessandro Busi in Bologna; made his operatic debut as Faust in Castelfranco Veneto in 1892; in 1896 he sang the title role in *Andrea Chenier* at La Scala, Milan; also sang tenor parts in Wagner's operas. He retired from the stage in 1914 owing to irreversible glaucoma; became totally blind in 1923. He publ. an autobiography, *La mia vita d'artista* (Bologna, 1927).

Borgatti, Renata, Italian pianist, daughter of the tenor **Giuseppe Borgatti;** b. Bologna, March 2, 1894. She studied in Bologna and Munich; has appeared as soloist with major orchs. in Europe; has given programs of complete works of Debussy; also played all of Bach's *Well-tempered Clavier* over the BBC network in London. After World War II she taught in Switzerland and Italy.

Borge, Victor (real name, **Borge Rosenbaum**), Danish pianist; b. Copenhagen, Jan. 3, 1909. He studied with his father, Bernhard Rosenbaum (1847–1932); then with V. Schioler. He developed a type of humorous piano concert *sui generis* and appeared in Danish musical revues. In 1940, he settled in the U.S. and became extremely successful in his specialty in radio and television; in autumn 1953 he opened a series of daily recitals on Broadway, billed as "comedy in music," which ran for two and a half seasons, unprecedented in N.Y. theatrical annals for a one-man show. In 1951 he was named "Funniest Man" in music.

Borghi, Adelaide, Italian mezzo-soprano; b. Bologna, Aug. 9, 1829; d. there, Sept. 28, 1901. Acting on the advice of Pasta, she trained herself for the stage; made her debut at Urbino (1846) in Mercadante's *Il Giuramento;* toured through Italy and in Vienna and Paris (1854–56); sang with the Grand Opéra in Paris (1856–59); appeared in London with great success (1860); then returned to Italy.

Borghi, Giovanni Battista, Italian composer; b. Camerino, Macerata, Aug. 25, 1738; d. Loreto, Feb. 25, 1796. He studied at the Cons. della Pietà dei Turchini in Naples (1757–59). From 1759–78 he was maestro di cappella at the Macerata Cathedral; from 1778, at Santa Casa of Loreto. He composed some 25 operas; *La morte di Semiramide* (Milan, Feb. 9, 1791) was moderately successful. He also wrote a number of oratorios and other sacred works.

Borghi, Luigi, Italian violinist and composer; b. c.1745; d. London, c.1806. He studied with Pugnani;

went to London about 1770; subsequently gained a fine reputation as a violinist. He composed a number of effective works for the violin, several of which were publ. in his lifetime.

Borgioli, Armando, Italian baritone; b. Florence, March 19, 1898; d. in an air raid on the Milan–Modena train near Codogno, Jan. 20, 1945. He made his debut as Amonasro at the Teatro Carcano in Milan in 1925; then sang at La Scala in Milan and Covent Garden in London. On Jan. 22, 1932, he made his Metropolitan Opera debut as Carlo in *La forza del destino;* continued on its roster until 1935. He was best known for his dramatic roles in Verdi's operas.

Borgioli, Dino, Italian tenor; b. Florence, Feb. 15, 1891; d. there, Sept. 12, 1960. He made his operatic debut at the Teatro Corso in Milan, in 1914; then sang leading parts in various Italian opera houses; also had guest engagements at Covent Garden, London. In 1924 he accompanied Nellie Melba on her farewell tour of Australia. On Dec. 31, 1934, he made his American debut at the Metropolitan Opera, N.Y., as Rodolfo in *La Bohème;* then returned to Italy, where he was active mainly as a voice teacher.

Borgström, Hjalmar, Norwegian critic and composer; b. Christiania, March 23, 1864; d. Oslo, July 5, 1925. He studied with Ursin, Svendsen, and Lindeman; also at Leipzig, Berlin, Paris, and London. In 1901 he returned to Oslo; was music critic of the *Aftenposten* from 1913.
 WORKS: 2 operas, *Thora fra Rimol* and *Fiskeren;* 2 symphs.; symphonic poems: *Hamlet; Jesus in Gethsemane; John Gabriel Borkman; Tanken; Reformation Cantata;* violin and piano concertos; chamber music, piano pieces, songs.

Bori, Lucrezia (real name, **Lucrecia Borja y Gonzalez de Riancho**), lyric soprano; b. Valencia, Dec. 24, 1887; d. New York, May 14, 1960. She studied with Melchior Vidal; made her debut in Rome on Oct. 31, 1908, as Micaëla; then sang in Milan, Naples, and, in 1910, in Paris as Manon Lescaut, with the Metropolitan Opera Co., then on a European tour. In 1911 she sang at La Scala; made her debut at the Metropolitan Opera House in N.Y. as Manon Lescaut on Nov. 11, 1912, and sang there until the end of the season 1914–15. After a period of retirement, occasioned by a vocal affliction, she reappeared in 1919 at Monte Carlo as Mimi, returning to the Metropolitan in 1921 in the same role. Thereafter she appeared in N.Y. with increasing success and popularity until the end of the 1935–36 season, when she retired permanently from opera.

Borisov, Lilcho, Bulgarian composer; b. Sofia, Nov. 1, 1925. He studied composition with Ghedini and clarinet at the Verdi Cons. in Milan, graduating in 1952.
 WORKS: *Cosmic Scenes* for Wind Quartet (1958); Trio for Clarinet, Bassoon, and Piano (1958); Violin

Sonata (1962); Clarinet Concerto (1966); *Scherzo* for Clarinet and Chamber Orch. (1966); *6 Etudes* for 2 Clarinets (1966); *Sonatina concertante* for Violin and Chamber Orch.; Concerto for Violin and Chamber Orch. (1971); *5 Pieces* for Violin and Piano (1973).

Borkh, Inge, famous German soprano; b. Mannheim, May 26, 1917. She first appeared as a stage actress, then decided upon a singing career. She studied at the Cons. in Milan and at the Mozarteum in Salzburg. She made her debut as Czipra in Johann Strauss's *Zigeunerbaron* at the Lucerne Opera in 1940; remained a member there until 1944; then sang at the Bern Opera until 1951. She made her American debut at the San Francisco Opera in 1953; on Jan. 24, 1958, she appeared at the Metropolitan Opera in N.Y. as Salome; she was on its roster also during the seasons of 1960–61 and 1970–71.

Bořkovec, Pavel, Czech composer; b. Prague, June 10, 1894; d. there, July 22, 1972. He originally studied philosophy and turned to composition rather late in life; took lessons with Jaroslav Křička and J.B. Foerster in 1919; in 1925–27 attended master classes of Josef Suk at the Prague Cons. From 1946–1964, he was on the faculty of the Academy of Musical Arts in Prague. His early works were in the manner of Dvořák and Suk; later he experienced the influence of neo-Classicism and adopted the technique of dissonant counterpoint in the Baroque framework; also cultivated topical subjects from the world of sports, exemplified by his symph. piece *The Start.* WORKS: 2 operas: *The Satyr,* after Goethe's poem (1937–38; Prague, Oct. 8, 1942), and *Paleček (Tom Thumb,* 1945–47; Czech Radio award, 1948; premiere, Prague, Dec. 17, 1958); a ballet, *Krysař (The Pied Piper,* 1939; concert perf., Prague, Jan. 15, 1941; first stage perf., Oct. 8, 1942, along with *The Satyr*); *Stmívání (Twilight),* symph. poem (1920); 3 symphs. (1926–27; 1955; 1959); *The Start,* symph. allegro (1929; Prague, March 26, 1930; also perf. at the Festival of the International Society for Contemporary Music in Liège, Sept. 6, 1930; 2 piano concertos (1931; 1949–50); Violin Concerto (1933); *Partita* for Orch. (1936); Concerto Grosso for 2 Violins, Cello, Orch., and Piano (1941–42); 2 *Symphoniettas* (for Chamber Orch., 1944; 1963–68); Cello Concerto (1950–51); *Silentium Turbatum,* symph. movement for Alto, Orch., and Electric Guitar (Prague, Feb. 28, 1965); *Te Deum* for Soli, Chorus, and Orch. (1968); Piano Quartet (1922); 5 string quartets (1924; 1928; 1940; 1947; 1961–62); Solo Viola Sonata (1931); Wind Quintet (1932); 2 violin sonatas (1934, 1956); Nonet (1941–42); Violin Sonatina (1942); *Intermezzo* for Horn and Piano (1965); Suite for Piano (1930); Partita for Piano (1935); *2 Pieces* for Piano (1941–42); a melodrama, *Jen jedenkrát (Only Once,* 1921); *Stadion (The Stadium)* for Voice, Wind Quintet, and Piano (1929); *Love Songs,* after Goethe and Villon, for Voice, and Piano or Small Orch. (1932); *5 Songs,* to poems of Pasternak (1935); *6 Madrigals about Time* for Chorus (1957).
BIBLIOGRAPHY: V. Holzknecht, *Hudební skupi-*

na Mánesa (Prague, 1968).

Borkowski, Bohdan, Polish composer; b. Teczynek, near Cracow, Nov. 7, 1852; d. Warsaw, Nov. 6, 1901. He studied piano with Nowakowski and harmony with Moniuszko at the Warsaw Inst. of Music; then continued his studies with Saar in Vienna. Upon his return to Warsaw, he was active as a teacher of piano and composition. He was known mainly for his sacred music; he composed 3 masses and a number of choral works.

Borland, John Ernest, English organist and writer on music; b. London, March 6, 1866; d. there, May 15, 1937. He was educated at Queen's College, Oxford, and at the Royal College of Music in London, and subsequently held positions as organist and music director at numerous churches. He was editor of *Musical News* (1895–1902); also prepared the music for the coronations of Edward VII, George V, and George VI. His writings include *The Instruments of the Orchestra* and *Musical Foundations.*

Bornefeld, Helmut, German organist and composer; b. Stuttgart-Untertürkheim, Dec. 14, 1906. He studied organ, piano, and composition at the Hochschule für Musik in Stuttgart; then was organist and choirmaster in Heidenheim. With Siegfried Reda, he organized the Heidenheim Arbeitstage für Neue Kirchenmusik in 1946, and remained actively engaged in its activities until 1960. His compositions include organ pieces and numerous choruses.
WRITINGS: *Das Positiv* (Kassel, 1941); *Orgelbau und neue Orgelmusik* (Kassel, 1952); *Orgelspiegel* (Kassel, 1966).

Bornschein, Franz Carl, American composer; b. Baltimore, Feb. 10, 1879; d. there, June 8, 1948. He studied at the Peabody Cons. in Baltimore (1895–1902), and became a teacher of violin and conductor of the student orch. there in 1906.
WORKS: *The Phantom Canoe,* Indian suite for Orch. (Baltimore, Nov. 24, 1916); *Onowa,* a cantata (1916); *The Sea God's Daughter,* symph. poem (Chicago, Feb. 10, 1924); *Old Louisiana,* symph. poem (1930); *The Willow Plate,* operetta (1932); *Leif Ericson,* symph. poem (Baltimore, Feb. 23, 1936); *Southern Nights,* symph. poem (Washington, D.C., March 1, 1936); *Moon over Taos* for Flute, Percussion, and String Orch. (1939); some chamber music and vocal compositions.

Borodin, Alexander, celebrated Russian composer; b. St. Petersburg, Nov. 12, 1833; d. there, Feb. 27, 1887. He was the illegitimate son of a Georgian prince, Ghedeanov; his mother was the wife of an army doctor. In accordance with customary procedure in such cases, the child was registered as the lawful son of one of Ghedeanov's serfs, Porfiry Borodin; hence, the patronymic, Alexander Porfirievich. He was given an excellent education; learned several foreign languages, and was taught to play the flute. He played 4-hand arrangements of

Haydn's and Beethoven's symphonies with his musical friend M. Shchiglev. At the age of 14 he tried his hand at composition; wrote a piece for flute and piano and a String Trio on themes from *Robert le Diable*. In 1850 he became a student of the Academy of Medicine in St. Petersburg, and developed a great interest in chemistry; he graduated in 1856 with honors, and joined the staff as assistant prof.; in 1858 received his doctorate in chemistry; contributed several important scientific papers to the bulletin of the Russian Academy of Sciences; traveled in Europe on a scientific mission (1859–62). Although mainly preoccupied with his scientific pursuits, Borodin continued to compose. In 1863 he married Catherine Protopopova, who was an accomplished pianist; she remained his faithful companion and musical partner; together they attended concerts and operas in Russia and abroad; his letters to her from Germany (1877), describing his visit to Liszt in Weimar, are of great interest. Of a decisive influence on Borodin's progress as a composer was his meeting with Balakirev in 1862; later he formed friendships with the critic Stasov, who named Borodin as one of the "mighty five" (actually, Stasov used the expression "mighty heap"), with Mussorgsky and other musicians of the Russian national school. He adopted a style of composition in conformity with their new ideas; he particularly excelled in a type of Russian orientalism which had a great attraction for Russian musicians at the time. He never became a consummate craftsman, like Rimsky-Korsakov; although quite proficient in counterpoint, he avoided purely contrapuntal writing; his feeling for rhythm and orchestral color was extraordinary, and his evocation of exotic scenes in his orch. works and in his opera *Prince Igor* is superb. Composition was a very slow process for Borodin; several of his works remained incomplete, and were edited after his death by Rimsky-Korsakov and Glazunov.

WORKS: OPERAS: *Prince Igor,* opera in 4 acts (begun in 1869, on the subject of the famous Russian medieval chronicle *Tale of Igor's Campaign;* completed posthumously by Rimsky-Korsakov and Glazunov; first perf., St. Petersburg, Nov. 4, 1890; London, June 8, 1914, in Russian; N.Y., Dec. 30, 1915, in Italian); an opera-farce, *Bogatyri* (*The Valiant Knights,* anonymously produced in Moscow on Oct. 29, 1867; rediscovered in 1932, and produced in Moscow, Nov. 12, 1936, with a new libretto by Demian Biedny, to serve propaganda purposes in an antireligious campaign, but 2 days later banned by the Soviet government for its mockery of Russian nationalism); sketches for the 4th act of an opera, *Mlada* (never produced), each act of which was to have been written by a different composer. FOR ORCH.: Symph. No. 1 in E-flat (1862–67; St. Petersburg, Jan. 16, 1869); Symph. No. 2 in B minor (1869–76; St. Petersburg, March 10, 1877); Symph. No. 3 in A minor (1886; unfinished; 2 movements orchestrated by Glazunov); symph. sketch, *In the Steppes of Central Asia* (1880); *Polovtzian Dances* from *Prince Igor* (perf. as an orch. piece, St. Petersburg, March 11, 1879). CHAMBER MUSIC: String Quartet No. 1 in A (1874–79); String Quartet No. 2 in D (1881); *Serenata*

alla Spagnola, 3rd movement of a quartet on the name B-la-f, for their publisher Be-la-ieff, by Borodin, Rimsky-Korsakov, Liadov, and Glazunov (1886); Scherzo for String Quartet in the collective set *Les Vendredis.* A String Trio (dated 1860) and a Piano Quintet were discovered in 1915. FOR PIANO: *Polka, Requiem, Marche funèbre,* and *Mazurka* in the series of paraphrases on the theme of the *Chopsticks Waltz* (includes variations by Borodin, other members of the Russian school, and Liszt; 1880); *Petite suite,* comprising 7 pieces (*Au couvent, Intermezzo, Deux mazurkas, Rêverie, Sérénade, Nocturne;* 1885). FOR VOICE: *Sérénade de 4 galants à une dame* for a cappella Male Quartet (comical; no date); songs: *Sleeping Princess* (1867); *The Princess of the Sea, The Song of the Dark Forest, The False Note, My Songs Are Full of Venom* (1867–68); *The Sea* (1870); *From My Tears* (1873); *For the Shores of Your Distant Country* (1881); *Conceit* (1884); *Arabian Melody* (1885); *The Wondrous Garden* (1885).

BIBLIOGRAPHY: V. Stasov, *A. Borodin* (St. Petersburg, 1882; French trans. by A. Habets, in 2 vols., Paris, 1893); Rosa Newmarch, *Borodin and Liszt* (London, 1895); E. Braudo, *Borodin* (Moscow, 1922); W. Kahl, "Die russischen Novatoren und Borodin," *Die Musik* (1923); G. Abraham, *Borodin, the Composer and His Music* (London, 1927); 2 vols. of Borodin's letters, ed. by S. Dianin (Moscow, 1928, 1936); G. Abraham, "Prince Igor: An Experiment in Lyrical Opera," *Musical Quarterly* (Jan. 1931); M. Rinaldi, "Borodin," *Musica d'oggi* (1933); G. Khubov, *Borodin* (Moscow, 1933); N. Rimsky-Korsakov, *Memoirs of My Musical Life* (3rd to 5th eds., with preface and notes by A. Rimsky-Korsakov; Moscow, 1932–35); Y. Kremlev, *Borodin* (Leningrad, 1934); G. Abraham, *Studies in Russian Music* (London, 1935); M.D. Calvocoressi and G. Abraham, *Masters of Russian Music* (London and N.Y., 1936); D. Brook, *Six Great Russian Composers* (London, 1946); M. Ilyin and E. Segal, *Borodin* (Moscow, 1953); S. Dianin, *Borodin* (Moscow, 1955; in English, 1963); W.B. Ober, "Alexander Borodin, M.D. (1833–1887): Physician, Chemist, Composer," *New York State Journal of Medicine* (March 1967); L. Velluz, *Du laboratoire au Prince Igor, pages sur Borodine* (Paris, 1971); M. Smirnov, *The Piano Works of Composers Comprising "The Five"* (Moscow, 1971); G. Golovinsky, *The Chamber Music of Borodin* (Moscow, 1972).

Borovsky, Alexander, Russian-American pianist; b. Mitau, March 18, 1889; d. Waban, Mass., April 27, 1968. He first studied with his mother (a pupil of Safonov), then with A. Essipova at the St. Petersburg Cons., winning the Rubinstein Prize in 1912. He taught master classes at the Moscow Cons. from 1915 to 1920; then went to Turkey, Germany, France, and England and gave a number of piano recitals; was a soloist with virtually all major European orchs.; he also made several successful tours in South America. In 1941 he settled in the U.S., and became a prof. at Boston Univ. (1956).

Borowski, Felix, English-American composer and critic; b. Burton, England, March 10, 1872; d. Chicago, Sept. 6, 1956. He studied violin with his father, a Polish émigré; took lessons with various teachers in London, and at the Cologne Cons.; then taught in Aberdeen, Scotland. His early *Russian Sonata* was praised by Grieg; this provided impetus to his progress as a composer. In 1897 he accepted a teaching engagement at the Chicago Musical College; was its president from 1916 to 1925. Subsequently he became active in musical journalism; in 1942 was appointed music editor of the *Chicago Sun;* also served as program annotator for the Chicago Symph. Orch., beginning in 1908. For 5 years he taught musicology at Northwestern Univ. (1937–42). Among his many musical works, the violin piece entitled *Adoration* became widely popular.

WORKS: *Boudour,* ballet-pantomime (Chicago, Nov. 25, 1919); *Fernando del Nonsensico,* satiric opera (1935); Piano Concerto (Chicago, 1914); *Allegro de Concert* for Organ and Orch. (Chicago, 1915); *Peintures* for Orch. (Chicago, Jan. 25, 1918); *Le Printemps passionné,* symph. poem (Chicago North Shore Festival, Evanston, Ill., 1920); *Youth,* fantasy-overture (Chicago North Shore Festival, Evanston, Ill., May 30, 1923); *Ecce Homo,* symph. poem (N.Y., Jan. 2, 1924); *Semiramis,* symph. poem (Chicago, Nov. 13, 1925); 3 symphs. (I, Chicago, 1933; II, Los Angeles, 1936; III, Chicago, 1939); *The Little Match Girl,* after Andersen, for Narrator and Orch. (1943); *Requiem for a Child* (1944); *The Mirror,* symph. poem (Louisville, Ky., Nov. 27, 1954); 3 string quartets; many pieces for violin, organ, and piano; songs. Borowski revised G.P. Upton's *The Standard Operas* in 1928, and *The Standard Concert Guide* in 1930.

Borras de Palau, Juan, Catalan writer on music; b. Barcelona, Sept. 24, 1868; d. there, Jan. 29, 1953. He was a lawyer by profession; publ. numerous songs, some of which became popular; was for more than 50 years music critic of the *Correo Catalan.*

Børresen, Hakon, Danish composer; b. Copenhagen, June 2, 1876; d. there, Oct. 6, 1954. He studied with Svendsen; was awarded the Ancker scholarship for composition in 1901. He was president of the Danish Composers Society from 1924 to 1949. His compositions include the operas *Den Kongelige Gaest* (Copenhagen, Nov. 15, 1919) and *Kaddara* (Copenhagen, March 16, 1921); a ballet, *Tycho Brahes Dröm* (*Tycho Brahe's Dream,* Copenhagen, March 1, 1924); 3 symphs.; a violin concerto; chamber music; piano works; songs.

Borris, Siegfried, German composer; b. Berlin, Nov. 4, 1906. He studied piano as a child, and began to compose tentatively while still a schoolboy. He entered the Univ. of Berlin as a student of economics; in 1927 became a pupil of Paul Hindemith at the Berlin Hochschule für Musik; in 1933 he obtained a B.Mus. at the Univ. of Berlin as a student of Arnold Schering, but with the advent of the Nazi regime he was compelled to abandon all his activities as a pianist and teacher. In 1945 he joined the staff of the Berlin Hochschule für Musik, and in 1967 became

director of the composition class at the Stern Cons. Borris is a prolific composer; he describes his idiom of composition as "vitalism," which connotes a pragmatic type of harmony and counterpoint enlivened by dance-like rhythms; functional tonality is preserved without excluding modernistic dissonant combinations.

WORKS: *Frühlingsgesellen,* "Liederspiel," to his own words (1951); *Die Rube,* fairy-tale opera (1953); *Ruf des Lebens,* scenic cantata (1954); radio operas: *Hans im Glück* (1947) and *Hirolas und Gerline* (1948); a ballet, *Das letzte Spiel* (1955); 5 symphs. (1940–53); Piano Concerto (1962); Organ Concerto (1965); Saxophone Concerto (1966); Horn Concerto (1967); Wind Quintet (1938); Wind Octet (1941); Octet for Clarinet, Bassoon, Horn, and String Quintet (1960); numerous lieder, mostly to his own texts; piano pieces; choruses. As a pedagogue he publ. *Praktische Harmonielehre* (10th ed., Berlin, 1948); *Einführung in die Moderne Musik* (Halle, 1951); *Modern Jazz* (Berlin, 1962); numerous articles in the musical press.

Bortkiewicz, Sergei, Russian pianist and composer; b. Kharkov, Feb. 28, 1877; d. Vienna, Oct. 25, 1952. He was a pupil of Liadov at the St. Petersburg Cons. (1896–99); later studied with Jadassohn in Leipzig. He made his debut as a pianist in Munich, in 1902, and subsequently made concert tours of Germany, Australia, Hungary, France, and Russia. From 1904 to 1914, he lived in Berlin, and taught at the Klindworth-Scharwenka Cons.; then went back to Russia; was in Vienna from 1920 to 1929; in Berlin from 1929 to 1934; and again in Vienna after 1934. His compositions include an opera, *Acrobats;* 2 symphs.; *Austrian Suite* and *Yugoslav Suite* for Orch.; 4 piano concertos; Violin Concerto; Cello Concerto; piano pieces; songs. He was the author of the book *Die seltsame Liebe Peter Tschaikowskys und der Nadezhda von Meck* (1938).

Bortniansky, Dimitri, Russian composer; b. Glukhov, Ukraine, 1751; d. St. Petersburg, Oct. 10, 1825. He was a choirboy in the court chapel, where he attracted the attention of Galuppi, who was at the time conductor there; was sent to Italy, where he studied with Galuppi and with other Italian masters in Venice, Bologna, Rome, and Naples (1769–79). In Italy he produced his operas *Creonte* (Venice, Nov. 26, 1776; lost) and *Quinto Fabio* (Modena, Dec. 26, 1778). In 1779 he returned to St. Petersburg and became director of vocal music at the court chapel (1796); as a conductor of the chapel choir he introduced radical reforms for improvement of singing standards; composed for his choir a number of sacred works of high quality, among them a Mass according to the Greek Orthodox ritual; 35 sacred concerti in 4 parts; 10 Psalms in 8 parts; 10 concerti for double choir; etc. He also continued to compose for the stage; produced the comic operas, in French, *Le Faucon* (Gatchina, Oct. 22, 1786) and *Le Fils rival* (Pavlovsk, Oct. 22, 1787). His sacred choral works are published in 10 vols., edited by Tchaikovsky.

BIBLIOGRAPHY: N. Findeisen, *History of Rus-*

sian Music (1929; vol. 2, pp. 260–76); B. Dobrohotov, *D. Bortniansky* (Moscow, 1950); A. Galkina, "About the Symphonism of Bortnjanskij," *Sovetskaja Muzyka* (Oct. 1973; in Russian).

Bortolotto, Mario, Italian physician and writer on music; b. Pordenone, Aug. 30, 1927. He publ. *Introduzione al lied romantico* (Milan, 1962) and *Fase seconda* (Milan, 1969), which aroused controversy; for the polemical exchange that followed its publication, see *Nuova Rivista Musicale Italiana* (Sept./Oct. 1969).

Börtz, Daniel, Swedish composer; b. Hässleholm, Aug. 8, 1943. He studied composition privately with Hilding Rosenberg; then with Blomdahl and Lidholm at the Royal Academy of Music in Stockholm; later attended seminars in electronic music at Utrecht.
WORKS: Chamber opera, *Landskab med flod,* after Hesse (1972); 2 liturgical operas: *Muren—Vägen —Ordet* (1971–72) and *Den heliga Birgittas död och Mottagande i himmelen* (Lund, Oct. 7, 1973); *Intrada* for Orch. (1964); *5 Preludes* for Flute (1964); *Il canto dei canti di Salomone* for Soprano and Instruments (1965); 4 *Monologhi: I* for Cello (1965–66), *II* for Bassoon (1966), *III* for Violin (1967), and *IV* for Piano and Tape (1970); 2 string quartets (1966, 1971); *In memoriam di . . .* for Orch. (Norrköping, May 29, 1969); *Voces* for 3 Voices, Tape, and Orch. (Stockholm, Sept. 19, 1968); *Josef K,* after Kafka, for Narrator, 8 Soli, Chorus, and Orch. (1969; Swedish Radio, Oct. 8, 1970); *Night Winds* for Vocal Quartet (1972); *Nightflies* for Mezzo-soprano and Chamber Ensemble (1973); *Sinfonia I* (Göteborg, March 7, 1974).

Borup-Jørgensen, Axel, Danish composer; b. Hjørring, Nov. 22, 1924. He grew up in Sweden; returned to Denmark after World War II and entered the Royal Cons. in Copenhagen, where he studied piano with Rachlew and orchestration with Schierbeck and Jersild (1946–51). His early compositions reflect the precise structural forms of Béla Bartók; later he experimented with the serial techniques of Anton von Webern.
WORKS: Concertino for Piano, Flute, Bassoon, and Strings (1948–49); *Fantasy* for Flute and String Orch. (1949); Clarinet Concerto (1949–50); 5 string quartets: No. 1 (1950), No. 2 (1951), No. 3 (1954–56), No. 4 (1960), and No. 5 (*Torso*), in the form of confrontations for two String Quartets, one of them pre-recorded (1965); *Chamber Concerto* for Violin and Small Orch. (1951); Viola Sonata (1952–53); *Partita* for Solo Viola (1953–54); *Improvisations* for String Quartet (1955); *Music* for Percussion and Viola (1955–56); *Microorganisms* for String Quartet (1956); *Sommasvit* for String Orch. (1957); Sonatina for 2 Violins (1958); *7 Preludes* for Piano (1958–59); *Winter Pieces* for Piano (1959); *Sonata breve* for Viola and Piano (1959–60); *Cretaufoni* for Orch. (1960–61); *Mobile* (after Calder) for Viola, Marimba, and Piano (1961); *Insulae* for String Orch. (1961–62); *Pocket Oratorium* for 16 Voices and Instruments

(1963–64); *Nordic Summer Pastoral* for Small Orch. (1964); *Stykker* for Orch. (1963–65); *Vinterstykke* for String Quartet (1967); *Marin* (after Langston Hughes) for 24 Male Voices (1969); *Marin* for Orch. (1963–70; Danish Radio, April 16, 1970); *Tagebuch im Winter* for Flute, String Quartet, and Piano (1970–72); *Distichon* for Violin and Piano (1972–73); *Malinconia* for String Quartet (1972–74); *Recostruzioni* for Wind Quintet (1973–74); *Vinter-epigrammer* for Piano (1975); *Epigrammer* for Piano (1976); *Carambolage* for Piano, Electric Guitar, and Percussion (1976–77); *Musica Autumnalis* for Wind Instruments, Percussion, and Electric Organ (1977).

Borwick, Leonard, English pianist; b. Walthamstow, Feb. 26, 1868; d. Le Mans, France, Sept. 15, 1925. He studied with Clara Schumann in Frankfurt; made his debut there (1889); then in London (May 8, 1889); made a concert tour in America and Australia (1911); also played in Europe. His programs included classics and moderns; in the last years of his career he played much music of Debussy and Ravel; made a transcription for piano of Debussy's *L'Après-midi d'un faune.*
BIBLIOGRAPHY: H. Plunket Greene, "L. Borwick," *Music & Letters* (1926).

Bory, Robert, Swiss writer on music; b. Geneva, April 1, 1891; d. Nyon, Oct. 9, 1960. He studied jurisprudence; at the same time took courses in composition with Jaques-Dalcroze and conducting with Gustave Doré; pursuing a legal career, he became a judge in Nyon in 1934. He publ. pictorial editions on Mozart, Beethoven, Wagner, Liszt, and Chopin.
WRITINGS: *Une Retraite romantique en Suisse: Liszt et la Contesse d'Agoult* (Geneva, 1923; 2nd ed., 1930); *La Vie de Franz Liszt par l'image* (Geneva, 1936); *Liszt et ses enfants, Blandine, Cosima et Daniel* (Paris, 1936); *Richard Wagner: Sein Leben und sein Werk in Bildern* (Frauenfeld, 1938); *La Vie et l'œuvre de Wolfgang-Amadeus Mozart par l'image* (Geneva, 1948; in Eng., 1948); *La Vie de Frédéric Chopin par l'image* (Geneva, 1951); *Le Séjour en Suisse de Wolfgang-Amadeus Mozart en 1766* (Lausanne, 1956); *La Vie et l'œuvre de Beethoven par l'image* (Zürich, 1960; in Eng., 1966).

Bos, Coenraad Valentyn, Dutch pianist and noted accompanist; b. Leiden, Dec. 7, 1875; d. Chappaqua, N.Y., Aug. 5, 1955. He was a pupil of Julius Röntgen at the Amsterdam Cons. (1892–95); later studied in Berlin. With 2 other countrymen, Jan van Veen (violin) and Jan van Lier (cello), he formed a trio in Berlin which enjoyed an enviable reputation during its active period (1896–1910). His masterly accompaniments on a tour with Ludwig Wüllner attracted more than ordinary attention, and made him one of the most celebrated accompanists both in Europe and the U.S., where he eventually settled. He was the accompanist of Julia Culp, Frieda Hempel, Helen Traubel, Fritz Kreisler, Ernestine Schumann-Heink, Pablo Casals, Elena Gerhard, Jacques Thibaud, Geraldine Farrar, and many others. He taught at the Juilliard School of Music from 1934 to

1952; publ. (in collaboration with Ashley Pettis) a book, *The Well-Tempered Accompanist* (1949).

Bosch, Pieter Joseph van den, Netherlandish organist; b. Hoboken, c.1736; d. Antwerp, Feb. 19, 1803. He became organist at the Antwerp Cathedral in 1765, remaining at this post until 1797. He composed a number of keyboard works.

Boschot, Adolphe, French music critic; b. Fontenay-sous-Bois, near Paris, May 4, 1871; d. Paris, June 1, 1955. He was music critic of *Echo de Paris* from 1910; of *Revue Bleue* from 1919; founded, with Théodore de Wyzewa, the Paris Mozart Society; was elected to the Institut de France in 1926, succeeding Widor as permanent secretary of the Académie des Beaux-Arts. His greatest work is an exhaustive biography of Berlioz in 3 vols.: *La Jeunesse d'un romantique, Hector Berlioz, 1803–31* (Paris, 1906); *Un Romantique sous Louis-Philippe, Hector Berlioz, 1831–42* (Paris, 1908); and *Crépuscule d'un romantique, Hector Berlioz, 1842–69* (Paris, 1913). For this work Boschot received a prize of the Académie. Other books are: *Le Faust de Berlioz* (1910; new ed., 1945); *Carnet d'art* (1911); *Une Vie romantique, Hector Berlioz* (an abridgement of his 3-vol. work, 1919; 27th ed., 1951; also in Eng.; a definitive ed. appeared in Quebec in 1965); *Chez les musiciens* (3 vols., 1922–26); *Entretiens sur la beauté* (1927); *La Lumière de Mozart* (1928); *Le Mystère musical* (1929); *La Musique et la vie* (2 vols., 1931–33); *Théophile Gautier* (1933); *Mozart* (1935); *La Vie et les œuvres d'Alfred Bruneau* (1937); *Musiciens-Poètes* (1937); *Maîtres d'hier et de jadis* (1944); *Portraits de musiciens* (3 vols., 1946–50); *Souvenirs d'un autre siècle* (1947). Boschot trans. into French the librettos of several of Mozart's operas. He was also prominent as a poet; publ. the collections *Poèmes dialogués* (1901) and *Chez nos poètes* (1925).

Boscovich, Alexander Uriah, significant Israeli composer; b. Klausenburg (Cluj), Transylvania, Aug. 16, 1907; d. Tel Aviv, Nov. 13, 1964. He studied in Budapest; later enrolled at the Vienna Academy, where he studied piano with Victor Ebenstein and composition with Richard Stöhr; then went to Paris, where he took courses with Paul Dukas and Nadia Boulanger; also had a few lessons in piano with Alfred Cortot. From 1930 to 1938 he was engaged as conductor at the State Opera in Cluj; in 1938 he emigrated to Palestine; taught at the Cons. of Tel Aviv (1945–64); wrote music criticism for the Israeli paper *Haaretz.*
WORKS: In his music he incorporates quasi-oriental motifs in the framework of Western music; in several works he makes use of authentic Jewish folk songs, adorning them with modernistic harmonies. In this manner he wrote his most popular piece, *Chansons populaires juives* for Orch. (Haifa, March 15, 1938; originally entitled *The Golden Chain*); Violin Concerto (1942); Oboe Concerto (1943); *Adonai Ro'i (The Lord Is My Shepherd)* for Alto Voice and Orch. (1946); *Semitic Suite* for Piano (1947; also for 2 Pianos, and for Orch.); *Piccola Suite*

for Flute, Snare Drum, and String Orch. (1956–57); *Psalm* for Violin and Piano (1957; contains thematic material from the Violin Concerto); *Cantico di ma'alot (Song of Ascent)* for Orch. (1960); *Bal Yisrael (Daughter of Israel),* cantata for Tenor, Chorus, and Orch. (1960–61); *With Joy and Gladness* for 2 Violins, with optional Drum and Triangle (1961); *Piece* for Oboe and Harpsichord (1961–62); *Lament* for Violin or Cello, and Piano (1962); *Concerto da Camera* for Violin and Chamber Ensemble (1962); *Ornaments* for Flute and 4 Orch. Groups (1964).
BIBLIOGRAPHY: M. Brod and Y. Cohen, *Die Musik Israels* (Kassel, 1976, pp. 64–66).

Bose, Fritz, German musicologist; b. Messenthin, July 26, 1906; d. Berlin, Aug. 16, 1975. He studied at the Humboldt Univ. in Berlin, where his teachers included Abert and Schering (musicology), Hornbostel (ethnomusicology), and Sachs (organology); received his Ph.D. there in 1934 with the dissertation *Die Musik der Uitoto* (publ. in Berlin, 1934). He was a lecturer of the Univ. of Berlin from 1934–45; in 1953 he was named director of the history dept. of the Institut für Musikforschung in Berlin, retiring in 1971; he also taught at the Technical Univ. of Berlin (1963–67). In 1966 he founded the Deutsche Gesellschaft für Musik des Orients, which he headed until 1972. He also served as editor of the *Jahrbuch für musikalische Volks- und Völkerkunde* from 1963 until his death. He wrote the study *Musikalische Völkerkunde* (Freiburg and Zürich, 1953).

Bose, Hans-Jürgen von, German composer; b. Munich, Dec. 24, 1953. He took courses at Hoch's Cons. (1969–72); then studied composition with Hans Ulrich Engelmann and piano with Klaus Billing at the Musikhochschule in Frankfurt.
WORKS: FOR THE STAGE: Chamber opera, *Blutbund* (1974; Hamburg, June 8, 1977); chamber opera, *Das Diplom,* after Pirandello (1975; Ulm, Nov. 26, 1976); "kinetic action" in 5 scenes, *Die Nacht aus Blei* (1980–81; Berlin, Nov. 1, 1981). FOR ORCH.: *Morphogenesis* (1975; Baden-Baden, Sept. 12, 1976); Symph. No. 1 (1976; Munich, March 10, 1978); *Music für ein Haus voll Zeit,* variations (1977); *3 Songs* for Tenor and Chamber Orch. (1977); *Travesties in a Sad Landscape,* variations for Chamber Orch. (1978); *Symphonic Fragment,* after Hölderlin, for Tenor, Baritone, Bass, Chorus, and Orch. (1980; Darmstadt, June 1, 1980); *Variations* for 15 Strings (1980; Frankfurt, March 29, 1981); *Idyllen* (1983; Berlin, April 23, 1983). CHAMBER MUSIC: 2 string quartets (1973, 1976–77); *5 Children's Rhymes* for Alto and 5 Instrumentalists (1974); *Threnos—Hommage à Bernd Alois Zimmermann,* a lament on his suicide, for Viola and Cello (1975); Solo Violin Sonata; *Variations* for Solo Cello (1978–79); *... vom Wege abkommen* for Solo Viola (1982); *Guarda el Canto,* 3 fragments after Bustos, for Soprano and String Quartet (1982).

Bose, Hans-Jürgen von, German composer; b. Munich, Dec. 24, 1953. He studied composition with

Hans Ulrich Engelmann and piano with Klaus Billing at the Hochschule für Musik in Frankfurt.

WORKS: 2 operas: *Blutbund (The Bond of Blood)* (1974; Hamburg, June 8, 1977) and *Das Diplom (The Diploma),* after Pirandello (1975; Ulm, Nov. 26, 1976); *Morphogenesis* for Orch. (1975; Baden-Baden, Sept. 12, 1976); Symph. No. 1 (1976; Munich, March 10, 1978); *Musik für ein Haus voll Zeit (Music for a House Full of Time),* variations for Chamber Orch. (1977); *3 Songs* for Tenor and Chamber Orch. (1977); *Travesties in a Sad Landscape,* variations for Chamber Orch. (1978); 2 string quartets (1973, 1976–77); *5 Children's Rhymes* for Alto and 5 Instrumentalists (1974); *Threnos—Hommage à Bernd Alois Zimmermann* for Viola and Piano (1975); Solo Violin Sonata (1978); *Variations* for Solo Cello (1978–79).

Bösendorfer, firm of piano makers at Vienna, specializing in concert grands. It was established by **Ignaz Bösendorfer** (b. Vienna, July 27, 1794; d. there, April 14, 1859) in 1828; later managed by his son **Ludwig** (b. Vienna, April 10, 1835; d. there, May 9, 1919). The firm, retaining its original name, was taken over by Carl Hutterstrasser (1863–1942). The Bösendorfer Saal (opened by Hans von Bülow in 1872, and used until 1913) was one of the finest chamber music concert halls in Europe.

Bosio, Angiolina, Italian soprano; b. Turin, Aug. 22, 1830; d. St. Petersburg, April 13, 1859. She studied in Milan with Cattaneo; made her stage debut there in 1846 as Lucrezia in Verdi's opera *I due foscari;* subsequently sang in Paris, N.Y., Philadelphia, Boston, and London; she later visited Russia, where she lived until her untimely death.

Boskoff, George, Rumanian pianist; b. Jassy, Sept. 2, 1882; d. Paris, Aug. 27, 1960. He studied piano with Anetta Boskoff in Jassy, and with Julius Wiest at the Bucharest Cons.; subsequently took lessons with Louis Diémer at the Paris Cons. He toured widely as a concert artist in Europe and South America.

Boskovsky, Willi, Austrian violinist and conductor; b. Vienna, June 16, 1909. He studied at the Vienna Academy of Music; in 1933 joined the Vienna Phil. and remained a member until 1970. In 1948 he organized the Wiener Oktet; in 1955 succeeded Clemens Krauss as conductor of the New Year's Day Concerts of the Vienna Phil. In 1969 he became principal conductor of the Johann Strauss Orch. of Vienna, originally founded by Eduard Strauss in 1890; the ensemble was reorganized by the nephew of the older Eduard Strauss, and namesake of the original founder, who died in 1966. Boskovsky assumed the direction of the ensemble as successor to Eduard Strauss, Jr. He resigned as conductor of the New Year's Day Concerts of the Vienna Phil. in 1979. Boskovsky conducted his orch. holding the violin relaxedly in his left hand à la Johann Strauss, and directing his group in an ingratiatingly, authentically Viennese manner in flowing waltz time or rapid polka rhythm, with expressive Luftpausen to emphasize the syncopation.

Bosmans, Henriette, Dutch pianist and composer; b. Amsterdam, Dec. 5, 1895; d. there, July 2, 1952. She studied piano with her mother at the Amsterdam Cons., and embarked on a career as a concert pianist. In 1927 she took lessons in composition with Willem Pijper. In her own music she cultivated an agreeable neo-Classical idiom, with coloristic éclat, suggesting the techniques and devices of French Impressionism; wrote many songs to texts by French poets. In her instrumental works she particularly favored the cello (her father was a well-known cellist, but he died when she was a year old).

WORKS: Cello Sonata (1919); 2 Cello Concertos (1922, 1924); *Poem* for Cello and Orch. (1926); Violin Sonata (1918); Piano Trio (1921); String Quartet (1928); Concertino for Piano and Orch. (1928; Geneva Festival of the International Society for Contemporary Music, April 6, 1929); *Konzertstück* for Flute and Orch. (1929); *Konzertstück* for Violin and Orch. (1934); *Doodenmarsch (March of the Dead)* for Narrator and Chamber Orch. (1946); piano pieces.

Bosquet, Emile, Belgian pianist; b. Brussels, Dec. 8, 1878; d. Uccle (Brussels), July 18, 1958. He studied with Tinel and Busoni; taught at the Cons. of Antwerp (1906–19) and in Brussels (from 1919); also made European tours. He publ. *La Musique de clavier* (Brussels, 1953).

Bosse, Gustave, music book publisher; b. Vienenburg (Harz), Feb. 6, 1884; d. Regensburg, Aug. 27, 1943. He founded his firm in 1912 at Regensburg; was publisher of *Zeitschrift für Musik* (since 1929) and *Deutsche Musikbücherei* (a collection of music books).

Bosseur, Jean-Yves, French composer; b. Paris, Feb. 5, 1947. He studied privately with Stockhausen and Pousseur. His music is marked by experimentation without specific serial procedures. Among his works is a symph. suite, *Un Arraché de partout* for Brass, Hammond Organ, 2 Electric Guitars, Vibraphone, Xylorimba, Marimbaphone, and Percussion (Paris, March 22, 1968). He is also a prolific writer of articles on current music and musical life.

Bossi, Costante Adolfo, Italian composer, brother of **Enrico Bossi;** b. Morbegno, Dec. 25, 1876; d. Milan, Jan. 4, 1953. He studied at the Milan Cons.; subsequently was a prof. there (1914–41). He wrote an opera, *La mammola e l'eroe* (Milan, 1916); a Requiem (1920); numerous choruses and songs.

Bossi, (Marco) Enrico, Italian composer; b. Salò, Brescia, April 25, 1861; d. at sea (en route from America to Europe), Feb. 20, 1925. Son and pupil of the organist **Pietro Bossi,** of Morbegno (1834–96), he studied at the Liceo Rossini in Bologna (1871–73), and at Milan (1873–81) under Sangali (piano), Fumagalli (organ), Campanari (violin), Boniforti (counterpoint), and Ponchielli (composition). He subsequently was maestro di cappella and organist at Como Cathedral (1881–89); then, until 1896, prof. of organ and harmony in the Royal Cons. San Pietro at Naples; prof. of advanced composition and organ at the Liceo Benedetto Marcello in Venice (1896–1902); and director of the Liceo Musicale at Bologna (1902–12). After a brief period of retirement from teaching, he was director of the Music School of the Santa Cecilia Academy in Rome (1916–23); toured Europe, England, and the U.S. as a pianist and organist.

WORKS: Operas: *Paquita* (Milan, 1881); *Il veggente* (Milan, 1890; rewritten and produced as *Il viandante*, Mannheim, 1896); *L'angelo della notte; Intermezzi Goldoniani* for String Orch.; *Concertstück* for Organ and Orch.; *Inno di Gloria* for Chorus and Organ; *Tota pulchra* for Chorus and Organ; *Missa pro Sponso et Sponsa* (Rome, 1896); *Il Cieco* for Solo, Chorus, and Orch. (1897); *Canticum Canticorum,* biblical cantata; *Il Paradiso Perduto* for Chorus and Orch. (Augsburg, 1903); *Surrexit pastor,* motet; *Giovanna d'Arco,* mystery play (Cologne, 1913); *Primavera classica* for 5-part Chorus a cappella; String Trio; Piano Trio; etc. He also wrote *Metodo di studio per l'organo moderno* (in collaboration with G. Tebaldini; Milan, 1893).

BIBLIOGRAPHY: H.B. Gaul, "Bonnet, Bossi, Karg-Elert, Three Aperçus," *Musical Quarterly* (July 1918); E. Dagnino, *M.E. Bossi, Cenni biografici* (Rome, 1925); L. Orsini, *Fascicolo commemorativo* (Milan, 1926); G.C. Paribeni, L. Orsini, and E. Bontempelli, *Marco Enrico Bossi: Il compositore, l'organista, l'uomo* (Milan, 1934); F. Mompellio, *M.E. Bossi* (Milan, 1952; contains a complete list of works).

Bossi, Renzo, Italian conductor and composer, son of **Enrico Bossi;** b. Como, April 9, 1883; d. Milan, April 2, 1965. He studied in Venice and in Leipzig; took a course in conducting with Nikisch; conducted at various cities in Italy; in 1916 was appointed instructor at the Verdi Cons. in Milan.

WORKS: Operas: *Passa la ronda* (Milan, March 3, 1919); *Volpino il calderaio* (Milan, Nov. 13, 1925); *La rosa rossa* (Parma, Jan. 9, 1940); ballet, *Il trillo del diavolo* (1948); Symph. in 5 movements; Violin Concerto; many minor pieces for various instruments.

BIBLIOGRAPHY: His biographical data and a complete list of works are appended to F. Mompellio's monograph on Enrico Bossi (Milan, 1952). See also S. Pintacuda, *Renzo Bossi* (Milan, 1955).

Bostelmann, Otto, German-American composer; b. Hamburg, Aug. 22, 1907. He settled in the U.S. in 1926; studied with Wesley La Violette in Los Angeles; there in 1957 he organized the Bohemian Composers Group. His works comprise 3 symphonies; 3 "crescendi" for orch.; much chamber music.

Bote & Bock, German music publishing firm established in Berlin in 1838 by **Eduard Bote** (retired 1847) and **Gustav Bock** (b. 1813; d. 1863); the directorship was assumed after Gustav Bock's death by his brother **Eduard Bock** (d. 1871), followed by his son **Hugo Bock** (b. Berlin, July 25, 1848; d. there, March 12, 1932), who handled the affairs of the firm for over 60 years. He acquired for the firm a great number of operas and operettas, and also a number of instrumental works by celebrated 19th-century composers. In 1904 Hugo Bock purchased the catalogue of Lauterbach & Kuhn of Leipzig, including the works of Max Reger (from op. 66 on). His successor was his son **Gustav Bock** (b. Berlin, July 17, 1882; d. July 6, 1953), who headed the firm until 1938, and again from 1947. The headquarters of the firm remained in Berlin; in 1948 a branch was formed in Wiesbaden. Apart from its musical publications, the firm publ. the *Neue Berliner Musikzeitung* (1847–96). A centennial vol. was issued in 1938 as *Musikverlag Bote & Bock, Berlin, 1838–1938.*

Botstiber, Hugo, Austrian music scholar and writer; b. Vienna, April 21, 1875; d. Shrewsbury, England, Jan. 15, 1941. He was a pupil of R. Fuchs, Zemlinsky, H. Rietsch, and Guido Adler; in 1896, assistant librarian of the Vienna Cons.; in 1900, secretary of the Konzertverein there; and in 1905, secretary of the Academy of Music; until 1938 was general secretary of the Vienna Konzerthaus-Gesellschaft; Knight of the Order of Franz Josef. He went to England in 1939. He edited the *Musikbuch aus Österreich* (1904–11); also organ compositions by Pachelbel, piano works of the Vienna masters, and waltzes of Johann Strauss for Denkmäler der Tonkunst in Österreich; was the author of *Joseph Haydn und das Verlagshaus Artaria* (with Franz Artaria; Vienna, 1911); *Geschichte der Ouvertüre* (Leipzig, 1913); *Beethoven im Alltag* (Vienna, 1927); completed Pohl's biography of Haydn (vol. III, 1927); publ. a new ed. of Kretzschmar's *Führer durch den Konzertsaal* (1932). Of special interest to American musicians is his article "Musicalia in der New York Public Library" in the bulletin of the Société Internationale de Musique (Oct. 1903), calling international attention for the first time to the important music collection of the N.Y. Public Library.

Bott, Jean Joseph, German violinist and conductor; b. Kassel, March 9, 1826; d. New York, April 28, 1895. He received primary education from his father, a court musician, and later with Hauptmann and Spohr; subsequently served as assistant conductor to Spohr (1852–56). He later served as court conductor at Meiningen (1857–65). He had trouble with excessive drinking, and in 1878 was forced to abandon his career after he appeared to be drunk while conducting Liszt's cantata *Die heilige Elisabeth.* In 1885 he went to N.Y. He wrote operas, overtures, and other music in a manner typical of Kapellmeister Musik, which had not even an infinitesimal value.

Botta, Luca, Italian tenor; b. Amalfi, April 16, 1882; d. New York, Sept. 29, 1917. He was a pupil of G. Vergine; made his operatic debut as Turiddu in *Cavalleria rusticana* (Naples, 1911); then sang in Malta, Turin, Mantua, Verona, Barcelona, Buenos Aires, and Milan; came to the U.S. in 1912 and sang with the Pacific Coast Opera Co. in San Francisco; made his Metropolitan Opera House debut as Rodolfo in *La Bohème* (N.Y., Nov. 21, 1914).

Bottée de Toulmon, Auguste, French writer on music; b. Paris, May 15, 1797; d. there, March 22, 1850. A lawyer by profession, he turned his attention to music, becoming a good amateur cellist; was the librarian of the Paris Cons. from 1831 to 1848.
WRITINGS: *L'Art musical depuis l'ère chrétienne jusqu'à nos jours* (Paris, 1836); "De la chanson en France au moyen-âge," *L'Annuaire historique* (1836); "Notice biographique sur les travaux de Guido d'Arezzo," *Mémoires de la Société des Antiquaires de France* (1837); "Des instruments de musique en usage au moyen-âge," *L'Annuaire historique* (1838); *Observations sur les moyens de restaurer la musique religieuse dans les églises de Paris* (Paris, 1841); *Notice des manuscrits autographes de Cherubini* (Paris, 1843).

Bottenberg, Wolfgang, German-born Canadian composer; b. Frankfurt, May 9, 1930. He emigrated to Canada in 1958; studied music theory with R.A. Stangeland at the Univ. of Alberta, graduating in 1961; then with Scott Huston, J. Takács, and P. Cooper at the Univ. of Cincinnati, obtaining his M.A. (1962) and D.Mus. (1970). Returning to Canada, he taught music at the Acadia Univ. in Wolfville, Nova Scotia (1965–73), and at Concordia Univ. in Montreal. In his compositions he makes eclectic use of tonal, atonal, and serial resources.
WORKS: Passacaglia for Orch. (1961; revised 1971); *Sinfonietta* (1961; revised 1969–70); Fantasia for Trumpet and Small Orch. (1966); *A Suite for Carols* for Orch. (1963–67); *Ritual,* a satire-collage on commercial slogans and sounds, for Chorus and Small Orch. (1970); *Fantasia Serena* for Orch. (1973); Concerto for Organ and Small Orch. (1975); Quartet for Flute, 2 Clarinets, and Bassoon (1960); Sonata for Flute and Clarinet (1960); Trio for Flute, Clarinet, and Bassoon (1963); Trio for Flute, Clarinet, and Piano (1964); Divertimento for 4 Flutes (1965); String Quartet (1968); *Variables* for Narrator, Wind Quartet, and String Quartet (1969); Octet (1972); *Fa So La Ti Do Re* for Soprano Saxophone and String Quartet (1972); songs; piano pieces.

Bottesini, Giovanni, Italian virtuoso on the double bass, conductor, and composer; b. Crema, Dec. 22, 1821; d. Parma, July 7, 1889. He took lessons in double-bass playing with Rossi at the Milan Cons. (1835–39); played in various orchs.; in 1847 he visited the U.S.; and in 1848 he went to England, where he appeared as a cello soloist; made his independent concert debut in London on June 26, 1849. In 1853 he was once more in America; also was active as a conductor in Paris, in Russia, and in Scandinavian countries. In 1871 he was invited by Verdi to conduct the world premiere of *Aida* in Cairo. He eventually retired to Parma as director of the cons. there. Bottesini was the first great virtuoso on the double bass, regarded as an unwieldy instrument, and thus became a legendary paragon for the few artists who essayed that instrument after him; thus Koussevitzky was often described as the Russian Bottesini during his early career as a double-bass player. Bottesini was the composer of a number of passable operas which had several performances in his lifetime.
WORKS: Operas: *Cristoforo Colombo* (Havana, 1847), *L'Assedio di Firenze* (Paris, Feb. 21, 1856), *Il Diavolo della notte* (Milan, Dec. 18, 1858), *Marion Delorme* (Palermo, Jan. 10, 1862), *Vinciguerra il bandito* (Monte Carlo, Feb. 22, 1870), *Alì Babà* (London, Jan. 18, 1871), *Ero e Leandro* (Turin, Jan. 11, 1879), and *La Regina di Nepal* (Turin, Dec. 26, 1880); oratorio, *The Garden of Olivet* (Norwich Festival, Oct. 12, 1887); overtures; and string quartets; as well as effective pieces for double bass, such as *Carnevale di Venezia* and *Tarantella*; also a valuable *Metodo complete per contrabasso,* in 2 parts, treating the double bass as an orchestral and as a solo instrument (in Eng., adapted by F. Clayton, London, 1870).
BIBLIOGRAPHY: L. Escudier, *Mes souvenirs: Les virtuoses* (Paris, 1868); C. Lesei, *G. Bottesini* (Milan, 1886); F. Warnecke, *Der Kontrabass* (Hamburg, 1909); A. Carniti, *In memoria di G. Bottesini* (Crema, 1922).

Bottje, Will Gay, American flutist and composer; b. Grand Rapids, Mich., June 30, 1925. He studied composition with Vittorio Giannini at the Juilliard School of Music, N.Y. (1943–47); then went to Europe and took courses with Henk Badings in the Netherlands and with Nadia Boulanger in Paris (1952–53); worked at the electronic studios at the Univ. of Utrecht (1962–63) and in Stockholm (1973). His music is of a highly experimental nature, awash with corrosive dissonances in a manner influenced primarily by the developments cultivated in the avant-garde music laboratories in Holland and in Sweden. His opera *Altgeld,* in mixed media, was produced at Southern Illinois Univ. in Carbondale, on March 6, 1968, while Bottje was the head of the electronic music laboratory there. Other works include 7 symphs. (1950–70); numerous pieces for quaquaversal instrumental combinations, with titles such as *Incognitos, Modules, Bandyings, Soundings, Mutations,* and *Fluctuations* (for 5 Clarinets).

Botto, Carlos, Chilean composer; b. Viña del Mar, Nov. 4, 1923. He studied in Valparaiso and later at the Santiago Cons. with Domingo Santa Cruz and Juan Orrego-Salas; in 1952 he was appointed to the faculty of the Chilean National Cons. of Music; in 1969 he became an instructor of composition at the Catholic Univ. of Chile. His works are unpretentious in style; among them are String Quartet (1954); Fantasia for Viola and Piano (1962); brief piano pieces; and songs.

Bottrigari, Ercole, Italian music theorist; b. Bologna (baptized, Aug. 24), 1531; d. San Alberto, near Bologna, Sept. 30, 1612. He was an illegitimate son of the nobleman Giovanni Battista Bottrigari; studied mathematics and music in the house of his father; learned to sing and play several instruments; his house teacher was Bartolomeo Spontone. In 1551 he married a rich lady. In his residence he met many celebrated poets of the day, including Tasso. Having acquired profound learning in several scientific and artistic disciplines, he devoted much of his energies to theoretical musical subjects; publ. numerous papers, many of a polemical nature.

WRITINGS: *Il Patricio ovvero de' tetracordi armonici di Aristosseno* (Bologna, 1593); *Il Desiderio ovvero de' concerti di vari stromenti musicali* (Venice, 1594, without Bottrigari's name, but under the pseudonym **Alemanno Benelli,** anagram of the name of his friend Annibale Melone; 2nd ed. with Bottrigari's name, Bologna, 1599; modern reprint of this ed., with introduction and annotations by Kathi Meyer, 1924; 3rd ed., Milan, 1601, under the name of Melone); *Il Melone, discorso armonico* (Ferrara, 1602). He left translations of Boetius and other writers in MS, preserved in the library of the Liceo Musicale in Bolonga.

BIBLIOGRAPHY: *Notizie biografiche intorno agli studi ed alla vita del Cavaliere Bottrigari* (Bologna, 1842); G. Gaspari, "Dei Musicisti Bolognesi al XVI secolo," in *Atti e Memorie* (Bologna, 1876).

Boucher, Alexandre-Jean, famous French violinist; b. Paris, April 11, 1778; d. there, Dec. 29, 1861. A brilliant violin virtuoso, he styled himself "l'Alexandre des violons." Boucher began his career at the age of 6, playing with the Concert Spirituel in Paris; was soloist in the court of Charles IV of Spain (1787–1805); traveled extensively on the Continent and in England. He wrote 2 violin concertos.

BIBLIOGRAPHY: G. Vallat, "Boucher, son temps," etc., in *Etudes d'histoire* (1890).

Boucourechliev, André, Bulgarian-French music critic; b. Sofia, July 28, 1925. He studied in Paris and settled there; in 1964 traveled in the U.S. He publ. a biography of Schumann (Paris, 1957; N.Y., 1959), a pictorial biography of Chopin (N.Y., 1962), and a biography of Beethoven (Paris, 1963); became a music critic; also composed music in an advanced idiom. For Beethoven's bicentennial he wrote *Ombres, Hommage à Beethoven* for String Orch. (Toulouse, June 8, 1970).

Boudreau, Robert Austin, American trumpeter and conductor; b. Bellingham, Mass., April 25, 1927. He studied trumpet with Georges Mager of the Boston Symph. and with William Vacchiano at the Juilliard School of Music in N.Y. He then taught music at Ithaca College (1951–52), Lehigh Univ. (1952–53), and Duquesne Univ. (1955–57). In 1957 he founded in Pittsburgh the American Wind Symph. Orch., specializing in contemporary music; it commissioned works from Henk Badings, Henry Brant, Paul Creston, Alan Hovhaness, Somers, Weinzweig, Penderecki, and Mayuzumi; the orch.'s performances take place aboard the *Point Counterpoint II,* a floating arts center that includes a theater and an art gallery.

Boughton, Rutland, English composer; b. Aylesbury, Jan. 23, 1878; d. London, Jan. 24, 1960. He studied at the Royal College of Music in London with Stanford and Walford Davies; without obtaining his diploma, he engaged in professional activity; was for a time a member of the orch. at Haymarket Theatre in London; taught at Midland Inst. in Birmingham (1905–11); also conducted a choral society there. He became a firm believer in the universality of arts on Wagnerian lines; formed a partnership with the poet Reginald Buckley; their book of essays, *The Music Drama of the Future,* expounding the neo-Wagnerian idea, was publ. in 1911. To carry out these plans, he organized stage festivals at Glastonbury, helped by his common-law wife, Christina Walshe. Boughton's opera, *The Immortal Hour,* was performed there on Aug. 26, 1914; his choral music drama *The Birth of Arthur* had a performance in 1920; these productions were staged with piano instead of an orch. After an interruption during World War I, Boughton continued the Glastonbury festivals until 1926. In 1927 he settled in the country, in Gloucestershire. He continued to compose, however, and produced a number of stage works, as well as instrumental pieces, few of which have been performed. His ideas of universal art had in the meantime been transformed into concepts of socialist realism, with an emphasis on the paramount importance of folk music as against formal constructions.

WORKS: FOR THE STAGE: *The Birth of Arthur* (1909; Glastonbury, Aug. 16, 1920); *The Immortal Hour* (1913; Glastonbury, Aug. 26, 1914); *The Round Table* (Glastonbury, Aug. 14, 1916); *The Moon Maiden,* choral ballet for girls (Glastonbury, April 23, 1919); *Alkestis,* music drama (1922; Glastonbury, Aug. 26, 1922; Covent Garden, London, Jan. 11, 1924); *The Queen of Cornwall,* music drama after Thomas Hardy (Glastonbury, Aug. 21, 1924); *May Day,* ballet (1926); *The Ever Young,* music drama (1928; Bath, Sept. 9, 1935); *The Lily Maid,* opera (1934; Gloucester, Sept. 10, 1934); *Galahad,* music drama (1944); *Avalon,* music drama (1946). FOR ORCH.: *The Skeleton in Armour,* symph. poem with Chorus (1898); *The Invincible Armada,* symph. poem (1901); *A Summer Night* (1902); *Oliver Cromwell,* symph. (1904); *Love and Spring* (1906); *Midnight* (1907); *Song of Liberty* for Chorus and Orch. (1911); *Bethlehem,* choral drama (1915; his most successful work); *Pioneers,* after Walt Whitman, for Tenor, Chorus, and Orch. (1925); *Deirdre,* symph. (1927); Symphony in B minor (1937); Trumpet Concerto (1943). CHAMBER MUSIC: Violin Sonata (1921); Quartet for Oboe and Strings (1930); String Trio (1944); Piano Trio (1948); Cello Sonata (1948); numerous choral works. He publ. several pamphlets and essays: *The Death and Resurrection of the Music Festival* (1913); *The Glastonbury Festival Movement* (1922); *Bach, the Master* (1930); *Parsifal: A Study* (1920); *The Nature of Music* (1930); *The Reality of Music* (1934).

BIBLIOGRAPHY: *The Self-Advertisement of Rutland Boughton* (anonymous pamphlet without date, c.1909); H. Antcliffe, "A British School of Music Drama: The Work of Rutland Boughton," *Musi-*

cal Quarterly (Jan. 1918); M. Hurd, *Immortal Hour: The Life and Period of Rutland Boughton* (London, 1962).

Bouhy, Jacques-Joseph André, Belgian-born French baritone; b. Pepinster, June 18, 1848; d. Paris, Jan. 29, 1929. He studied at the Liège Cons.; then went to Paris and entered the Paris Cons., where he studied piano, organ, and theory of composition, as well as singing. He made his debut as Méphistophélès in Gounod's *Faust* at the Paris Opéra on Aug. 2, 1871; on March 3, 1875, he sang Escamillo in the first performance of *Carmen* at the Opéra-Comique in Paris. He appeared at Covent Garden, London, on April 22, 1882; then sang at various opera houses in Europe, including that in St. Petersburg. In 1885 he went to N.Y. and served as director of the N.Y. Cons. (until 1889); was again in N.Y. from 1904 to 1907; then returned to Paris and settled there as a singing teacher.

Boulanger, Lili, talented French composer, sister of **Nadia Boulanger;** b. Paris, Aug. 21, 1893; d. Mézy (Seine-et-Oise), March 15, 1918. She studied composition with Paul Vidal at the Paris Cons. (1909–13), and attracted considerable attention when she won the Grand Prix de Rome at graduation with her cantata *Faust et Hélène,* as the first woman to receive this distinction. Her early death at the age of 24 was lamented by French musicians as a great loss. Her talent, delicate and poetic, continued the tradition of French Romanticism on the borderline of Impressionism. Besides her prize-winning cantata she wrote 2 symph. poems, *D'un soir triste* and *D'un matin de printemps;* her opera to Maeterlinck's play *La Princesse Maleine* remained incomplete. She also wrote several choral works with orch.: *Soir sur la plaine; Hymne au soleil; La Tempête; Les Sirènes; Sous bois; La Source; Pour les funerailles d'un soldat; 3 psaumes; Vieille prière bouddhique;* sacred chorus, *Pie Jesu,* for Voice, Strings, Harp, and Organ; cycle of 13 songs to texts of Francis Jammes, *Clairières dans le ciel;* some flute pieces.
BIBLIOGRAPHY: C. Mauclair, "La Vie et l'œuvre de Lili Boulanger," *Revue Musicale* (Aug. 1921); P. Landormy, "Lili Boulanger," *Musical Quarterly* (Oct. 1930); R. Dumesnil, *Portraits de musiciens français* (Paris, 1938); E. Lebeau, *Lili Boulanger* (Paris, 1968); Léonie Rosenstiel, *The Life and Works of Lili Boulanger* (1978).

Boulanger, Nadia, illustrious French composition teacher, sister of **Lili Boulanger;** b. Paris, Sept. 16, 1887; d. there, Oct. 22, 1979. Both her father and grandfather were teachers at the Paris Cons.; her mother, Countess Myshetskaya, was a Russian and a professional singer; it is from her that Nadia Boulanger received her Russian diminutive (for Nadezhda) name, and it was from her that she had her first music lessons. She entered the Paris Cons., where she studied organ with Guilmant and Vierne, and composition with Gabriel Fauré; she graduated with prizes in organ and theory; in 1908 she received the 2nd Prix de Rome for her cantata *La Sirène;* she

completed the composition of the opera by Raoul Pugno, *La Ville Morte,* left unfinished after his death; also composed cello music, piano pieces, and songs; realizing that she could not compare with her sister Lili in talent as a composer, she devoted herself to teaching, and it is in that profession, often regarded as ancillary and uncreative, that she found her finest vocation. She was assistant in a harmony class at the Paris Cons. (1909–24); was engaged as a teacher at the Ecole Normale de Musique in Paris (1920–39); when the American Cons. was founded in 1921 at Fontainebleau, she joined its faculty as a teacher of composition and orchestration; she became its director in 1950. She also had a large class of private pupils from all parts of the world; many of them achieved fame in their own right; among Americans who went to Paris to study with her were Aaron Copland, Roy Harris, Walter Piston, Virgil Thomson, Elliott Carter, David Diamond, Elie Siegmeister, Irving Fine, Easley Blackwood, Arthur Berger, John Vincent, and Harold Shapero; others were Igor Markevitch, Jean Françaix, Lennox Berkeley, and Dinu Lipatti. Not all of her students were enthusiastic about her methods; some of them complained about the strict, and even restrictive, discipline she imposed on them; but all admired her insistence on perfection of form and accuracy of technique. Her tastes were far from the catholicity expected of teachers; she was a great admirer of Stravinsky, Debussy, and Ravel, but had little appreciation of Schoenberg and the modern Vienna School. She visited the U.S. several times; played the organ part in Aaron Copland's Organ Symph. (which she advised him to compose) with the N.Y. Symph. Orch., under the direction of Walter Damrosch (Jan. 11, 1925), and was the first woman to conduct regular subscription concerts of the Boston Symph. Orch. (1938) and of the N.Y. Phil. (Feb. 11, 1939). During World War II she stayed in America; taught classes at Radcliffe College, Wellesley College, and the Juilliard School of Music; returning to Paris in 1946, she took over a class in piano accompaniment at the Paris Cons.; continued her private teaching as long as her frail health permitted; her 90th birthday was celebrated in September 1977, with sincere tributes from her many students in Europe and America.
BIBLIOGRAPHY: Alan Kendall, *The Tender Tyrant. Nadia Boulanger: A Life Devoted to Music* (London, 1977); Bruno Mosaingeon, *Mademoiselle: Entretiens avec Nadia Boulanger* (Luynes, 1980); Léonie Rosenstiel, *Nadia Boulanger: A Life in Music* (N.Y., 1982).

Boulez, Pierre, celebrated French composer and conductor; b. Montbrison, March 26, 1925. He studied composition with Olivier Messiaen at the Paris Cons., graduating in 1945; later took lessons with René Leibowitz, who initiated him into the procedures of serial music. In 1948 he became a theater conductor in Paris; made a tour of the U.S. with a French ballet troupe in 1952. In 1954 he organized in Paris a series of concerts called "Domaine Musical," devoted mainly to avant-garde music. In 1963

Boulnois

he delivered a course of lectures on music at Harvard Univ., and on May 1, 1964, made his American debut as conductor in N.Y. In 1958 he went to Germany, where he gave courses at the International Festivals for New Music in Darmstadt. It was in Germany that he gained experience as conductor of opera; he was one of the few Frenchmen to conduct Wagner's *Parsifal* in Germany; in 1976 he was engaged to conduct the *Ring* cycle in Bayreuth. The precision of his leadership and his knowledge of the score produced a profound impression on both the audience and the critics. He was engaged to conduct guest appearances with the Cleveland Orch., and in 1971 he was engaged as music director of the N.Y. Phil., a choice that surprised many and delighted many more. From the outset he asserted complete independence from public and managerial tastes, and proceeded to feature on his programs works by Schoenberg, Berg, Webern, Varèse, and other modernists who were reformers of music, giving a relatively small place to Romantic composers. This policy provoked the expected opposition on the part of many subscribers, but the management decided not to oppose Boulez in his position as music director of the orch. The musicians themselves voiced their full appreciation of his remarkable qualities as a professional of high caliber, but they described him derisively as a "French correction," with reference to his extraordinary sense of rhythm, perfect pitch, and memory, but a signal lack of emotional participation in the music. In America, Boulez showed little interest in social amenities and made no effort to ingratiate himself with men and women of power. His departure of the season 1977–78 and the accession of the worldly Zubin Mehta as his successor were greeted with a sigh of relief, as an antidote to the stern regimen imposed by Boulez. While attending to his duties at the helm of the N.Y. Phil., he accepted outside obligations; from 1971 to 1975 he served as chief conductor of the London BBC Symph. Orch.; as a perfect Wagnerite he gave exemplary performances of Wagner's operas both in Germany and elsewhere. He established his residence in Paris, where he had founded, in 1974, the Institut de Recherche & Coordination Acoustique/ Musique, a futuristic establishment generously subsidized by the French government; in this post he could freely carry out his experimental programs of electronic techniques with the aid of digital synthesizers and a complex set of computers capable of acoustical feedback. His own music is an embodiment of such futuristic techniques; it is fiendishly difficult to perform and even more difficult to describe in the familiar terms of dissonant counterpoint, free serialism, or indeterminism. He specifically disassociated himself from any particular modern school of music. He even publ. a pamphlet with the shocking title *Schoenberg est mort,* shortly after Schoenberg's actual physical death; he similarly distanced himself from other current trends.

WORKS: *Le Visage nuptial* for Soprano, Contralto Chorus, and Orch. (1946, revised 1951; Cologne, Dec. 4, 1957, composer conducting); *Le Soleil des eaux,* cantata for Soprano, Men's Chorus, and Orch. (original music for radio play, 1948, revised 1958 and 1965; Darmstadt, Sept. 9, 1958); *Livre pour quatuor* (1948–49; radically revised as *Livre pour cordes,* 1968; Brighton, Dec. 8, 1968, composer conducting); *Symphonie concertante* for Piano and Orch. (1950); *Polyphonie X* for 18 Solo Instruments (Donaueschingen Music Festival, Oct. 6, 1951); *Le Marteau sans maître,* cantata for Contralto, Flute, Viola, Guitar, Vibraphone, and Percussion (1953–55; International Festival of the Society for Contemporary Music, Baden-Baden, June 18, 1955); *Poésie pour pouvoir,* spatial work for 5-track Tape and 2 Orchs. (1958, revised 1982–83; Donaueschingen Festival, Oct. 19, 1958, under the direction of Boulez and Hans Rosbaud); *Pli selon Pli, Portrait de Mallarmé,* for Soprano and Orch. (Donaueschingen, Oct. 20, 1962); *Doubles* for Orch. (1958; Paris, March 16, 1958; expanded as *Figures-Doubles-Prismes* and performed at Strasbourg, Jan. 10, 1964); *Eclat* for Chamber Orch. (1965; Los Angeles, March 26, 1965; revised as *Eclats/Multiples;* London, Oct. 21, 1970); *Domaines,* for Solo Clarinet and 21 Instruments (1968; Brussels, Dec. 20, 1968, composer conducting); *cummings ist der dichter,* for 16 Voices and 24 Instruments (1970: Stuttgart, Sept. 25, 1970); . . . *explosante-fixe . . . .* for Vibraphone, Harp, Violin, Viola, Cello, Flute, Clarinet, Trumpet, and something called a Halaphone, run by a set of Computers (N.Y., Jan. 5, 1973; revised 1973–74; La Rochelle, July 6, 1974); *Rituel in memoriam Bruno Maderna* (1974–75; London, April 2, 1975, composer conducting); *Messagesquisse* for 7 Cellos (1977); *Pour le docteur Kalmus* for Clarinet, Flute, Violin, Cello, and Piano (1977); *Répons* for Chamber Orch. and 6 Solo Instruments with Computer (1981; Donaueschingen, Oct. 18, 1981; revised, London, Sept. 6, 1982); *Notations* for Orch. (1980; Paris, June 18, 1982); *Sonatine* for Flute and Piano (1946); Piano Sonata (1946); Sonata for 2 Pianos (Paris, April 29, 1950); *Structures I* for 2 Pianos (1951); *Structures II* for 2 Pianos (1956–61); Piano Sonata No. 2 (1948; Paris, April 29, 1950); Piano Sonata No. 3 (1957); music for the film *Symphonie mécanique* (1955); incidental music for Claudel's version of the *Oresteia* by Aeschylus (1955).

BIBLIOGRAPHY: A. Goléa, *Rencontres avec Pierre Boulez* (Paris, 1958); V.M. Ames, "What Is Music?," *Journal of Aesthetics and Art Criticism* (Winter 1967); S. Borris, "Pierre Boulez—Ein Komponistenporträt," *Musik im Unterricht,* B/LIV/5 (1968); J.P. Derrien, "Pierre Boulez," *Musique en Jeu* (1970); M. Fink, "Pierre Boulez: A Selective Bibliography," *Current Musicology,* 13 (1972); I. Stoianowa, "Pli selon pli, portrait de Mallarmé," *Musique en Jeu* (June 1973); Joan Peyser, *Boulez, Composer, Conductor, Enigma* (N.Y., 1976); P. Griffiths, *Boulez* (N.Y., 1979).

Boulnois, Joseph, French composer; b. Paris, Jan. 28, 1884; killed in battle at Chalaines, Oct. 20, 1918. He studied piano and composition at the Paris Cons.; later became church organist, and from 1909 was choir leader at the Opéra-Comique. He wrote an opera, *L'Anneau d'Isis,* a *Symphonie funèbre,* a Cello Sonata, and various pieces for organ, piano, and voice. His works remain mostly in MS. There has been a revival of interest in his music, which has resulted in some performances of his songs and choruses.

Boult, Sir Adrian (Cedric), eminent British conductor; b. Chester, April 8, 1889; d. Tunbridge Wells, Feb. 22, 1983. His mother, a professional writer on music, gave him piano lessons; at 12 he received some instruction in music from a science teacher, H.E. Piggott, at the Westminster School in London. At 19 he entered Christ Church in Oxford, where he sang in a school chorus under the direction of Sir Hugh Allen; earned a doctorate in music at Oxford Univ.; then went to Leipzig, where he was allowed to attend rehearsals of the Gewandhaus Orch., conducted by Nikisch, who offered him some advice on the technique of conducting; he also took courses in music theory at the Leipzig Cons. with Stephan Krehl and Hans Sitt, and had occasional lessons with Max Reger. He returned to England in 1913; held for a season a subsidiary position on the musical staff of Covent Garden; made his conducting debut with an amateur orch. at West Kirby in 1914. In 1915 he conducted a concert of the Liverpool Phil., and in 1918 led 4 concerts at Queen's Hall, London. During the season 1918–19 he was engaged by Diaghilev to conduct several productions of his Ballets Russes in London. On Jan. 30, 1919, he made his first appearance as guest conductor of the Royal Phil. Orch. in London; from 1919 to 1924 he led the British Symph., with the personnel of former soldiers of the British Army; concurrently, he taught a class in conducting at the Royal College of Music; in 1924–30 he also led a school orch. there. During the same period he conducted concerts of the Birmingham City Orch. (1924–28). In 1928 he was appointed music director of the British Broadcasting Co. and organized the BBC Symph., which eventually became one of the finest orch. groups in Europe. Boult led it on a European tour, visiting Brussels in 1933 and Vienna, Zürich, and Budapest in 1942. He remained its music director until 1950. From 1950 until 1957 he served as principal conductor of the London Phil. Orch. During the 1959–60 season he was music director of the Birmingham Symph. Orch. He also filled numerous guest engagements outside England; led a concert of British music at the Salzburg Festival in 1935, and also in 1935 conducted 4 concerts with the Boston Symph. Orch. In 1937 he was guest conductor with the NBC Symph. in N.Y.; on June 9 and 10, 1939, he presented at the N.Y. World's Fair the world premieres of the 7th Symph. of Arnold Bax and the Piano Concerto of Arthur Bliss. Throughout his career he consistently promoted the cause of British music, particularly that of Vaughan Williams; he gave first performances, in London, of his *Pastoral Symphony* (March 8, 1936), 4th Symph. (April 10, 1935), 6th Symph. (April 21, 1948), and 9th Symph. (April 2, 1958). In 1937 he was knighted. In 1952 he conducted at Westminster Abbey the music for the coronation of Queen Elizabeth II. His style of conducting was quite devoid of glamorous self-assertion; his ideal was to serve the music with a minimum display of histrionics; he was greatly respected by the musicians of the orchs. he conducted. He publ. *Thoughts on Conducting* (London, 1963) and an autobiography, *My Own Trumpet: Memoirs of Sir Adrian Boult* (London, 1973).

BIBLIOGRAPHY: Jerrold N. Moore, ed., *Music and Friends: Letters to Adrian Boult* (London, 1979); H. Simeone and S. Mundy, eds., *Sir Adrian Boult, Companion of Honor: A Tribute* (Tunbridge Wells, 1980).

Bour, Ernest, French conductor; b. Thionville, April 20, 1913. After musical studies at home, he entered the Univ. of Strasbourg, where he took courses in classical languages; later studied conducting with Fritz Munch and Hermann Scherchen. From 1935 to 1939 he was music director of Radio Strasbourg; from 1941–47 and from 1950–64 he was conductor of the Municipal Orch. there. From 1964–79 he served as principal conductor of the Southwest German Radio Symph. Orch. of Baden-Baden. In that capacity he continued the tradition of his predecessor Hans Rosbaud in presenting modern music in his programs. He further conducted guest appearances with the Hamburg State Opera, the German Opera in West Berlin, the Berlin Phil. Orch. and the Concertgebouw Orch. of Amsterdam. In 1976 he was appointed principal conductor of the Radio Kamerorkest in Hilversum.

Bourdin, Roger, French baritone; b. Lavallois, June 14, 1900; d. Paris, Sept. 14, 1974. He studied at the Paris Cons.; made his operatic debut as Lescaut in *Manon* in 1922 at the Opéra-Comique; also sang at the Paris Opéra; made his Covent Garden debut in London in 1930 as Pelléas in Debussy's opera. He was married to the soprano **Géori Boué.**

Bourgault-Ducoudray, Louis-Albert, French composer; b. Nantes, Feb. 2, 1840; d. Paris, July 4, 1910. At the age of 18 he composed his first opera, *L'Atelier de Prague* (Nantes, 1859); was a pupil of Ambroise Thomas at the Paris Cons., taking the Grand Prix de Rome in 1862 with a cantata, *Louise de Mézières.* He founded an amateur choral society in Paris (1868); spent some time in research in Greece, after which he publ. *Souvenirs d'une mission musicale en Grèce, 30 Mélodies populaires de Grèce et de l'Orient,* and *Etudes sur la musique ecclésiastique grecque* (1877). He was appointed prof. of music history at the Paris Cons. in 1878.
WORKS: 5 operas: *Thamara* (Paris Opéra, Dec. 28, 1891); *Michel Colomb* (Brussels, May 7, 1887); *Anne de Bretagne* (Nantes, Dec. 1892); *Myrdhin* (Nantes, March 28, 1912); *L'Atelier de Prague* (Nantes, 1958). For Orch.: *Le Carnaval d'Athènes* (from his *Danses grecques,* originally for Piano, 4-hands); *Rapsodie Cambodgienne.* For Voice: *François d'Amboise,* cantata (1866); *Stabat Mater* (1868); *La Conjuration des fleurs; Symphonie religieuse;* etc.; numerous songs, including *30 Mélodies populaires de la Basse-Bretagne,* with French translations (1885). He also wrote piano pieces.

BIBLIOGRAPHY: M. Emmanuel, *Eloge funère de Louis-Albert Bourgault-Ducoudray* (Paris, 1911; with complete catalogue of works); M. Poté, "Bourgault-Ducoudray," *Bulletin de la Société Archéologique et Historique de Nantes* (1965).

Bourgeois, Loys (Louis), French composer; b. Paris, c.1510; d. there, c.1561. He was a follower of Calvin, with whom he lived (1545–57) in Geneva; then returned to Paris; was still living in 1561. He is renowned for having composed, or adapted, almost all the melodies the Calvinists sang to Marot's and Bèze's French versions of the Psalms. Clément Marot, poet in the service of Francis I as "valet de chambre," trans. (1533–39) 30 Psalms in metrical form, which found great favor with the Court, who sang them to light melodies. However, the Sorbonne soon condemned them, and in 1542 Marot had to flee to Geneva. The first ed. of Calvin's Genevan Psalter, containing Marot's 30 Psalms, his versifications of the Paternoster and Credo, 5 Psalms of Calvin, and his versions of the Song of Simeon and the Decalogue, was publ. at Geneva in 1542; 17 of the melodies, all but 3 of which were more or less altered, were adapted by Bourgeois from the earlier Strasbourg Psalter of Calvin (1539), and 22 new ones were added. After arriving at Geneva, Marot added 19 other Psalms and the Song of Simeon; these, together with the 30 previously publ., compose the so-called "Cinquante Pseaumes," which, with Marot's Décalogue, Ave, and Graces (all with music), were added in the 1543 edition of the Psalter. By 1549, 17 of the melodies previously used were more or less altered by Bourgeois, and 8 others replaced; in 1551 he modified 4 and substituted 12 new tunes. Thus, several of the melodies are of later date than the Psalms. On Marot's death, in 1544, Théodore de Bèze undertook completing the Psalter. In 1551 he added 34 Psalms, in 1554 6 more, and in 1562 the remaining 60. Bourgeois composed, or adapted, the tunes to all except the last 40, these being set, supposedly, by Pierre Dubuisson, a singer. In 1557 Bourgeois left Geneva and severed his immediate contact with the work there, although he still continued his activity on the Psalter. Claude Goudimel publ. harmonized editions of the Genevan Psalter after 1562, thereby creating the erroneous belief that he was the author of the melodies themselves. Bourgeois himself harmonized, and publ. in 1547, 2 sets of Psalms in 4–6 parts, intended for private use only. His treatise *Le Droict Chemin de musique,* etc. (Geneva, 1550) proposed a reform in the nomenclature of the tones to fit the solmisation syllables, which was generally adopted in France (see Fétis, *Biographie des musiciens,* vol. II, p. 42).

BIBLIOGRAPHY: Douen, *Clément Marot et le Psaultier Huguenot* (2 vols.; Paris, 1878–79); G.A. Crawford, "Clément Marot and the Huguenot Psalter," *Musical Times* (June/Nov. 1881); G.R. Woodward, "The Genevan Psalter of 1562," *Proceedings of the Music Association, Session 44* (London, 1918); Sir Richard R. Terry, "Calvin's First Psalter," ibid., *Session 57* (Lecture; London, 1930); idem, *Calvin's First Psalter* (London, 1932; contains a facsimile and transcription into modern notation of the 1539 Strasbourg Psalter); W.S. Pratt, *The Music of the French Psalter of 1562* (N.Y., 1939); P.A. Gaillard, *L. Bourgeois: Sa vie, son œuvre comme pédagogue et compositeur* (Lausanne, 1948); P. Pidoux, "Loys Bourgeois Anteil am Huguenotten-Psalter," *Jahrbuch für Liturgik und Hymnologie* (1970).

Bourgeois, Thomas-Louis (-Joseph), French singer and composer; b. Fontaine-L'Evêque, Oct. 24, 1676; d. Paris, 1750. He was maître de musique at the Strasbourg Cathedral (1703–6); sang with the Paris Opéra (1708–11); then was in the service of the Duke of Bourbon (1715–21). As a composer, he produced a number of fine cantatas, of which 19 are extant; he also wrote divertissements and ballets.

BIBLIOGRAPHY: C. Lyon, "Thomas-Louis-Jos. Bourgeois," *L'Education populaire* (1882).

Bourguignon, Francis de, Belgian composer; b. Brussels, May 29, 1890; d. there, April 11, 1961. He studied at the Brussels Cons. with Léon Dubois and Edgar Tinel (composition) and Arthur de Greef (piano); entered the Belgian army and was wounded in 1915; was evacuated to England. After the war he made a tour as a pianist with Nellie Melba in Australia; went on concert tours in Canada, South America, Asia, and Africa; circled the globe 6 times. In 1925 he returned to Brussels, and took a course in composition with Paul Gilson; with 7 other pupils of Gilson he formed the "Groupe des Synthétistes" with the proclaimed objective of promoting modern music. He taught at the Brussels Cons. from 1939 to 1955.

WORKS: Chamber opera, *Le Mauvais Pari* (1937); ballet, *La Mort d'Orphée* (1928); radio play, *Congo* (1936); oratorio, *La Nuit* (1945); symph. poems: *Le Jazz vainqueur* (1929) and *Oiseaux de nuit* (Paris, June 28, 1937); symph. suites: *Puzzle* (1938) and *Juventus* (1941); Piano Concertino (1927); *2 esquisses sud-américaines* for Orch. (1928); *Fête populaire,* symph. movement (1929); *Prelude and Dance* (1929); *Eloge de la folie* for Orch. (1934); Symph. (1934); *Fantasy on 2 Themes of Eugène Ysaÿe* for Piano and Orch. (1938); Sinfonietta (1939); *Berceuse* (1940); Suite for Viola and Orch. (1940); *Recuerdos: 2 impressions sud-américaines* (1943); Concerto Grosso (1944); Violin Concerto (1947); Piano Concerto (1949); *Récitatif et Ronde* for Trumpet and Orch. (1951); Concertino for Piano and Chamber Orch. (1952); 2-piano Concerto (1953); *Ouverture martiale* (1960); String Trio; Piano Trio; 2 string quartets; Oboe Quintet; choral works; songs; several piano suites, including *Dans l'île de Pinang* (1925), *En Floride* (1927), and *2 danses* (1939).

BIBLIOGRAPHY: A. Vandernoot, *Francis de Bourguignon* (Brussels, 1949).

Bournonville, Jacques de, French harpsichordist and composer; b. probably in Amiens, c.1675; d. Paris, c.1754. He was either the grandson or the great-grandson of **Jean de Bournonville.** He studied with Bernier; subsequently established himself as a harpsichord player. His motets for one and 2 voices with continuo were publ. in 1711.

Bournonville, Jean de, French composer; b. Noyon, c.1585; d. Paris, May 27, 1632. In 1612 he was appointed director of music at the choir school of the collegiate church of St. Quentin; then was active in Amiens (1618–31). In 1631 he was named director of the choir school of the Sainte-Chapelle. He composed masses, Psalms, motets, and other church music.

Bournonville, Valentin de, French composer, son of **Jean de Bournonville;** b. probably in St. Quentin, c.1610; d. probably in Chartres, Dec. 1663. He studied with his father; became active as a musician in Amiens. In 1646 he became maître de musique at Notre Dame in Paris. In 1653 he was appointed choir director of the school in Chartres. In 1662 he returned to his former post at Notre Dame in Paris.

Bousquet, Georges, French conductor and music critic; b. Perpignan, March 12, 1818; d. St. Cloud, near Paris, June 15, 1854. He studied at the Paris Cons.; won the Prix de Rome (1838); conducted at the Opéra (1847) and at the Théâtre Italien (1849–51); wrote music criticism for *Le Commerce, l'Illustration,* and the *Gazette Musicale.* He composed 3 operas, which were performed in Paris: *l'Hôtesse de Lyon* (Paris Cons., 1844); *Le Mousquetaire* (Opéra-Comique, 1844); *Tabarin* (Théâtre-Lyrique, 1852); also a cantata; church music; chamber music.

Bousset, Jean-Baptiste, French composer and singer; b. Dijon, 1662; d. Paris, Oct. 3, 1725. He was active as maître de musique at the chapel of the Louvre, the Académie Française, and the Académies des Sciences et des Inscriptions. He composed many cantatas and motets. His son, **René Drouard de Bousset** (b. Paris, Dec. 11, 1703; d. there, May 19, 1760), was also a musician; he was active in Paris as an organist and composer.

Boutmy, Josse, Belgian organist and composer; b. Ghent, Feb. 1, 1697; d. Brussels, Nov. 27, 1779. He was a member of a musical family and received his training from his father, a church organist. In 1721 he went to Brussels, where he became a teacher of the clavecin; also was organist at the Royal Chapel (from 1744). He publ. 2 books of clavecin pieces (Brussels, 1738; 1750); partial reprints are in vol. V of *Monumenta Musicae Belgicae* (Antwerp, 1943), ed. by Suzanne Clercx, with a biographical essay in Flemish and French.

Boutry, Roger, French pianist, conductor, and composer; b. Paris, Feb. 27, 1932. He studied at the Paris Cons.; received first prize as a pianist at the age of 16; first prize as a conductor at 21; and the Premier Prix de Rome at 22. In 1963 he was awarded the Grand Prix Musical of the City of Paris. He embarked on a successful career as a pianist; toured in Europe, Russia, and Australia; as a conductor, he appeared with several orchs. in France; also conducted opera in Monte Carlo.

WORKS: Piano Concerto (1954); *Rapsodie* for Piano and Orch. (1956); *Ouverture-Tableau* for Orch. (1959); *Divertimento* for Saxophone and Orch. (1964); *Concerto-Fantaisie* for 2 Pianos and Orch. (Paris, Feb. 16, 1967); *Intermezzi* for Chamber Orch. (1970); Quartet for Trombones; Flute Concerto; 2 sextets; *Pastels et Contours* for 5 Harps; also didactic pieces for various instruments.

Bouvet, Charles, French musicologist; b. Paris, Jan. 3, 1858; d. there, May 24, 1935. He studied at the Paris Cons.; organized the Fondation J.S. Bach (1903–11); in 1924 he was appointed archivist of the Paris Opéra. He edited works of Bonporti and Couperin; also publ. *Les Couperin* (Paris, 1919); *L'Opéra* (1924); and *Massenet* (1929).

Bouzignac, Guillaume, French composer of the early 17th century. Biographical data are lacking, but several specimens of his music are extant. It is known that he was a choirboy at Narbonne; in 1609 was the "maître des enfants" at the Grenoble Cathedral. His creative period comprises the years 1610–40; he wrote a number of effective motets in the popular French style, distinguished by dramatic expression, as well as religious works. H. Quittard publ. several of these pieces in his paper "Un Musicien oublié du XVIᵉ siècle," *Bulletin de la Société Internationale de Musique* (Paris, 1905).

Bovery, Jules (real name, **Antoine-Nicolas-Joseph Bovy**), Belgian violinist and conductor; b. Liège, Oct. 21, 1808; d. Paris, July 17, 1868. He was employed in theater orchs. in France and the Netherlands; eventually settled in Paris. He was the author of several operettas and semi-popular instrumental pieces in the salon style.

Bovy, Vina, Belgian soprano; b. Ghent, May 22, 1900. She studied piano and voice at the Ghent Cons. (1915–17); made her operatic debut at the Théâtre Flamand in Ghent in 1918; then sang at the Théâtre de la Monnaie in Brussels (1922–25) and at the Opéra-Comique in Paris. After a series of performances in Italy, she was engaged by Toscanini to join La Scala in Milan. She made her American debut as Violetta in *La Traviata* at the Metropolitan Opera in N.Y. on Dec. 24, 1936, remaining there for a single season; she then returned to Europe. From 1947 to 1955 she served as managing director of the Ghent Opera. She retired from her active career in 1964.
BIBLIOGRAPHY: J. Deleersnyder, *Vina Bovy* (Ghent, 1965).

Bovy-Lysberg, Charles-Samuel, Swiss pianist and composer; b. Lysberg, near Geneva, Feb. 1, 1821; d. Geneva, Feb. 15, 1873. He went to Paris and was one of the few young pianists to study with Chopin (1835). Returning to Switzerland, he settled at Dardagny, near Geneva, in 1848; taught piano at the Geneva Cons., and gave recitals in the French cantons. His opera, *La Fille du Carillonneur,* was produced in Geneva in 1854; he also wrote a romantically inspired piano sonata, *L'Absence;* but he became known chiefly by his effective salon pieces for piano (numbering about 130), among them *La Napolitaine, Le Réveil des oiseaux, Le Chant du rouet, Idylle, Les Ondines, Sur l'onde,* etc. His real name was **Bovy,** but he hyphenated it with Lysberg, the name of his birthplace.

BIBLIOGRAPHY: Pauline Long, "Charles-Samuel Bovy-Lysberg," *Schweizerisches Jahrbuch für Musikwissenschaft,* III.

Bowen, Edwin York, English composer and pianist; b. London, Feb. 22, 1884; d. Hampstead, Nov. 23, 1961. He studied at the Royal Academy of Music, where he won the Erard and Sterndale Bennett scholarships; his teachers were Matthay (piano) and F. Corder (composition). Upon graduation, he was appointed instructor in piano there. A prolific composer, Bowen wrote 3 symphs.; 3 piano concertos; Violin Concerto; Viola Concerto; Rhapsody for Cello and Orch.; several symph. poems (*The Lament of Tasso, Eventide,* etc.); orch. suites; many practical piano pieces in miniature forms. Bowen was the author of a manual, *Pedalling the Modern Pianoforte* (London, 1936).

Bowers, Robert Hood, American composer; b. Chambersburg, Pa., May 24, 1877; d. New York, Dec. 29, 1941. He studied in Chicago, Baltimore, and Philadelphia; was active in radio and theatrical conducting; served for 16 years as a recording director of the Columbia Phonograph Co. His compositions include *The Anniversary,* one-act opera; operettas: *The Red Rose* (N.Y., 1911); *Old English* (1924); *Oh Ernest* (1927); *Listen In* (1929); etc.

Bowie, David, British rock musician, master of image manipulation; b. South London, Jan. 8, 1947. His real name was **David Jones,** which he changed to avoid confusion with a British singer, Davey Jones, of the American pop group The Monkeys. After some inconclusive attempts to fuse with the latest British fashion in punk rock, he switched to something called "flower power," associated with extra-terrestrial visions, which he embodied in his album *Space Oddity.* Dissatisfied with his directions, he opened the innovative Arts Lab, but was talked into returning to the punks. With the guitarist Mick Ronson and a drummer Woody Woodmansey, he put out a record, *The Man Who Sold the World,* with the cover showing him in drag; it gave the impetus to a subdivision of punk rock known as "glitter rock." The record was banned in the U.S. because the drag queen on the cover bore an uncanny resemblance to the movie star Lauren Bacall. Still carrying on his space obsession, Bowie released several "conceptual" albums, such as *Ziggy Stardust.* He also paid tribute to drug society in a number called *Rock-'n'-Roll Suicide.* His next avatar was in the "soul" sound of Philadelphia, exemplified by his hit song *Fame.* Then, all of a sudden, he decided to try his luck in the movies, and starred in the space fantasy *The Man Who Fell to Earth,* in which his somewhat introspective image and emaciated appearance fitted the hero's image. Always exploring new avenues, he took the role of the monstrously deformed *Elephant Man* on the legitimate stage (1980), depicting an actual case of a man afflicted by filariasis, a disease characterized by granulomatous lesions and resulting in gross expansion of the tissues of the face and scrotum. The play was a resounding success for Bowie, and gradually he moved away from rock to the stage.

Bowles, Paul Frederic, American composer and novelist; b. Jamaica, N.Y., Dec. 30, 1910. He studied at the Dunning School of Music in N.Y.; in 1928 enrolled in the School of Design and Liberal Arts in N.Y.; then went to Paris, where he earned his living as a telephone operator at the offices of the Paris *Herald Tribune.* He returned to N.Y. in 1930, and worked as a bookshop clerk. While thus occupied, he acquired some knowledge of composition, and was accepted as a private student of Aaron Copland in Saratoga, N.Y. In 1931 he studied counterpoint with Nadia Boulanger at the Ecole Normale de Musique in Paris; also took some lessons with Virgil Thomson. He became a habitué of the modernistic and surrealistic gatherings in Paris and wrote works in a post-impressionistic vein modeled after Erik Satie. To this period belong his Piano Sonatina No. 1 (1932), Flute Sonata (1932), Cantata, *Par le détroit* (1933), and *Scènes d'Anabase,* for Voice, Oboe, and Piano (1932). In 1936 he returned to the U.S., where he wrote his first stage work, the ballet *Yankee Clipper,* which was performed by the American Ballet Caravan in Philadelphia on July 19, 1937. He also wrote a number of scores of incidental music for various plays. Other works of the N.Y. period included the opera *Denmark Vesey* (1938), the ballet *Pastorela* (1941), and the opera *The Wind Remains,* to a text by García Lorca; it was produced in N.Y. in 1943, with Leonard Bernstein conducting. Always attracted by exotic lands and their art, Bowles went to Morocco, settling in Tangier. A total change in his artistic orientation occurred in 1949 when he publ. his first novel, *The Sheltering Sky,* with the action set in Morocco; it was acclaimed by sophisticated critics; in 1972 he publ. an autobiography entitled *Without Stopping.* From then on, literature became his vocation and music an avocation. In 1980 he opened in Tangier a writing workshop under the aegis of the School of Visual Arts, N.Y. He continued to compose. Among his later works are *A Picnic Cantata* for Women's Voices, 2 Pianos, and Percussion (N.Y., March 23, 1954); and *Yerma* (1959), to a libretto by García Lorca.

BIBLIOGRAPHY: David Ewen, *American Composers* (N.Y., 1982).

Bowman, Edward Morris, American organist; b. Barnard, Vt., July 18, 1848; d. New York, Aug. 27, 1913. He studied with William Mason in N.Y., and with Weitzmann in Berlin; was the first American to pass the examinations of the Royal College of Organists in London (1881). After his return to America he was active as an organist, a choir conductor, and a teacher in St. Louis and N.Y.; was director of the music dept. at Vassar College (1891–95). In 1884, with 15 others, he founded the American College of Musicians and was its first president. He publ. the Bowman-Weitzmann *Manual of Musical Theory* (1877; a compilation of notes, from oral communications, of Weitzmann's principles and rules of harmony; later trans. into German).

Bowman, James, English countertenor; b. Oxford, Nov. 6, 1941. He was educated at New College, Oxford; made his operatic debut as Oberon in Britten's *A Midsummer Night's Dream* in London in 1967; subsequently sang with the Glyndebourne Festival, the Royal Opera House, Covent Garden, the English National Opera, London, and the Scottish Opera, Glasgow; also appeared with the Early Music Consort of London. He gained distinction as an interpreter of the castrato roles in Handel's operas; also sang non-castrato songs in oratorios.

Boxberg, Christian Ludwig, German composer; b. Sondershausen, April 24, 1670; d. Görlitz, Dec. 1, 1729. He studied at the Thomasschule in Leipzig; from 1692–1702 was organist in Grossenhain; also was active as a librettist, composer, and singer at the Leipzig Opera. In 1702 he became organist at Ss. Peter and Paul in Görlitz. He wrote librettos for the operas of N.A. Strungk. His own operas include *Orion* (Ansbach, 1697); *Die verschwiegene Treue* (Ansbach, 1698); *Sardanapolus* (Ansbach, 1698); *Amyntas und Phyllis* (Leipzig, 1700). He also composed numerous cantatas.
BIBLIOGRAPHY: H. Mersmann, *Christian Ludwig Boxberg und seine Oper "Sardanapolus," Ansbach, 1698* (Diss., Univ. of Berlin, 1916).

Boyce, William, significant English musician, organist, and composer; b. London, Sept. (baptized, Sept. 11) 1711; d. Kensington, Feb. 7, 1779. As a youth he was a chorister in St. Paul's Cathedral under Charles King; then studied organ with Maurice Greene, the cathedral organist. In 1734–36 he was organist at the Earl of Oxford's Chapel; then was at St. Michael's, Cornhill, from 1736 to 1768. Concurrently he was named in 1736 composer to the Chapel Royal. In 1759 he was Master of the King's Musick. An increasing deafness forced him to abandon active musical duties after 1769. His main task consisted in providing sacred works for performance; he also contributed incidental music to theatrical productions. He conducted the Festivals of the Three Choirs (Gloucester, Worcester, Hereford) in 1737, and served as Master of the Royal Band in 1755. His magnum opus was the compilation of the collection *Cathedral Music,* in 3 vols. (1760, 1768, and 1773; 2nd ed., 1788; later eds., 1844 and 1849). This collection comprises morning and evening services, anthems, and other church music by a number of British composers, namely Aldrich, Batten, Bevin, Blow, Bull, Byrd, Child, Clarke, Creyghton, Croft, Farrant, Gibbons, Goldwin, Henry VIII, Humfrey, Lawes, Locke, Morley, Mundy, Purcell, Rogers, Tallis, Turner, Tye, Weldon, and Wise. Of his own

music, there are remarkable instrumental works: 12 overtures (London, 1720; reprinted in *Musica Britannica,* vol. XIII); 12 sonatas for 2 Violins and Bass (London, 1747); 8 symphs. (London, 1760; modern ed. by M. Goberman, Vienna, 1964); 10 voluntaries for Organ or Harpsichord (London, 1779). Two overtures erroneously attributed to Boyce, and publ. in Lambert's edition under the titles *The Power of Music* and *Pan and Syrinx,* were works by John Stanley, not by Boyce. His stage works include the following, all produced in London: *The Chaplet* (Dec. 2, 1749); *The Roman Father,* not extant (Feb. 24, 1750); *The Shepherd's Lottery* (Nov. 19, 1751); and *Harlequin's Invasion* (with M. Arne and T. Aylward, Dec. 31, 1759). Several of his vocal works were publ. in *Lyra Britannica* (1745–55); there were also 15 anthems (1780) and a collection of anthems (1750), which were republ. in Novello's edition in 4 vols.; also, various songs were originally publ. in the anthologies *The British Orpheus, The Vocal Musical Mask,* and others.
BIBLIOGRAPHY: D.A. Dawe, "New Light on William Boyce," *Musical Times* (Sept. 1968); John Hawkins, "Memoirs of Dr. William Boyce" (Introduction and notes by G. Beechey), *Musical Quarterly* (Jan. 1971); R. McGuinness, *English Court Odes 1660–1820* (Oxford, 1971).

Boyd, Anne, Australian composer; b. Sydney, April 10, 1946. She studied flute at the New South Wales Cons. (1960–63) and composition at the Univ. of Sydney (1963–66); concluded studies at York Univ. in England (1969–72; Ph.D., 1972); then became a lecturer at Sussex Univ.
WORKS: *Air and Variations* for Flute and Piano (1960); trio for Flute, Violin, and Piano (1962); *Infinity* for Piano (1964); *L'Altro* for Orch. (1964); *Exegesis No. 1* for 4 Flutes and 2 Piccolos (1964); *Synchrony No. 1,* trio for Oboe, Clarinet, and Bassoon (1964); *Chelidiones* for Solo Flute, Piccolo, and Tape (1965); *3 Piano Pieces* (1965); *The Fall of Icarus* for Flute, Clarinet, Cello, and Piano (1966); trio for Oboe, Violin, and Cello (1966); *The Stairway,* ballet for 4 Instruments and Percussion (1968); 2 string quartets (*The Fourth Generation,* 1968; 1973); *Games* for any number of Players (1969); *As Far as Crawls the Toad* for 5 Young Percussionists (1970); *Hidden in a White Cloud* for Wind Quintet, or for Flutes and Cellos (1970); *The Voice of the Phoenix* for Solo Piano, Guitar, and Harp (all amplified), 10 Percussionists, Orch. with Augmented Woodwinds, and an ad-lib VCS-3 Synthesizer (1971); *Greetings to Victor McMahon* for 12 Flutes (1971); *The Metamorphoses of the Solitary Female Phoenix* for Wind Quintet, Piano, and Percussion (1971); *The Rose Garden,* theater piece (1972); *Angklung* for Piano (1974).

Boyd, Charles N., American editor and writer on music; b. Pleasant Unity, Pa., Dec. 2, 1875; d. Pittsburgh, April 24, 1937. He was church organist and teacher of church music at the Western Theological Seminary (1903–37); director of the Pittsburgh Musical Inst. (1915–37). He publ. *Lectures on Church*

Boyden – Bozza

Music (1912).

Boyden, David D., American musicologist; b. Westport, Conn., Dec. 10, 1910. He studied at Harvard Univ. (A.B., 1932; M.A., 1938); was appointed to the staff at the Univ. of Calif., Berkeley, in 1938; was assistant prof. from 1943 to 1949, associate prof. from 1949 to 1955, and full prof. from 1955 to 1975. He publ. a number of valuable treatises on music history: *A Manual of Counterpoint Based on Sixteenth-century Practice* (N.Y., 1944; 2nd ed., 1953); *The History and Literature of Music, 1750 to the Present* (1948); *An Introduction to Music* (N.Y., 1956; 2nd ed., 1970); *The History of Violin Playing from Its Origins to 1761* (London, 1965); *Catalogue of the Hill Collection of Musical Instruments in the Ashmolean Museum, Oxford* (London, 1969).

Boykan, Martin, American pianist and composer; b. New York, April 12, 1931. He studied composition with Walter Piston at Harvard Univ., and also with Copland and Hindemith. As a pianist, he developed a remarkable technique entirely adequate for the most demanding contemporary compositions. As a composer, he writes mostly chamber music. His works include 2 string quartets (1949, 1967); Flute Sonata (1950); Duo for Violin and Piano (1951); Quintet for Flute, Piano, and Strings (1953); *Chamber Concerto* (1970). In 1957 he was appointed to the faculty of Brandeis Univ.

Boyle, George F., American pianist and composer; b. Sydney, Australia, June 29, 1886; d. Philadelphia, June 20, 1948. He received his early musical training from his parents; in 1905 went to Berlin, where he took piano lessons with Busoni. He began his career as an accompanist. In 1910 he settled in the U.S.; taught piano at the Peabody Cons. in Baltimore (1910–22), and at the Curtis Inst. in Philadelphia (1924–26); then taught privately. He was also a composer; wrote *Aubade* for Orch. (St. Louis, March 5, 1916); Piano Concerto (Worcester Festival, Sept. 28, 1911); Cello Concerto (Washington, D.C., Feb. 7, 1918); 3 piano trios; Violin Sonata; Viola Sonata; Cello Sonata; about 100 piano pieces and 50 songs.

Boyvin, Jacques, French organist and composer; b. Paris, c.1649; d. Rouen, June 30, 1706. He studied in Paris; then was organist at the Hôpital des Quinze-Vingts (1663–74); from 1674 until his death he was organist at Notre Dame Cathedral in Rouen; also served at St. Herbland (1697–1702). He composed mainly for organ; his organ works were publ. in Paris in 2 books (1689–90 and 1700). See A. Guilmant and A. Pirro, eds., *Jacques Boyvin: Œuvres complètes d'orgue* (Paris, 1905).
BIBLIOGRAPHY: N. Pierront, "Jacques Boyvin," *Etudes Normandes,* XXVI (1958).

Bozay, Attila, Hungarian composer; b. Balatonfüzfö, Aug. 11, 1939. He studied in Budapest first at the Bartók Cons. (1954–57) and then at the Academy of Music with Ferenc Farkas (1957–62). In his music he makes use of modified serial techniques.
WORKS: Opera, *Küngisz királynö (Queen Küngisz,* 1968–69); Duo for 2 Violins (1958); *Episodes* for Bassoon and Piano (1959); String Trio (1960; revised 1966); *Bagatelles* for Piano (1961); *Papírszeletek (Slips of Paper),* song cycle for Soprano, Clarinet, and Cello (1962); Wind Quintet (1962); *Ritornell* for Solo Violin (1963); *Kiáltasok (Outcries),* song cycle for Tenor and Chamber Ensemble (1963); 2 string quartets (1964, 1971); Variations for Piano (1964); *Pezzo concertato* for Orch. (1965); *Trapéz és korlát (Trapeze and Bars),* cantata (1966); *Pezzo sinfonico* for Orch. (1967); *Intervals* for Piano (1969); *Formations* for Solo Cello (1969); *Sorozat (Series)* for Chamber Ensemble (1970); *Improvisations* for Solo Zither (1972); *Malom (Mill)* for Wind Instruments, Portable Organ, and Percussion (1973); *Pezzo concertato* No. 2 for Zither and Orch. (1974–75).

Božič, Darijan, Slovenian composer; b. Slavonski Brod, April 29, 1933. He studied composition with Škerjanc and conducting with Švara at the Music Academy of Ljubljana; upon graduation, served as an opera conductor and artistic director of the Slovenian Phil. (1970–74). His music was at first influenced by jazz; later he adopted radical serial techniques.
WORKS: 3 operas: *Humoreske* (1958); *Spoštovanja vredna vlačuga* (1960); *Ares Eros;* a musical happening, *Jago;* a dramatic collage, *Polineikes* (1966); 2 ballets: *Baletska jednočinka* (1957) and *Gluha okna* (1967); Piano Concerto (1956); Saxophone Concerto (1958); Trombone Concerto (1960); Trumpet Concerto (1961); Symph. (1964–65); *Audiostructures* for Piano and Orch.; *Audiospectrum* for Orch. (1972); *Trije dnevni Ane Frank (Three Days of Anne Frank)* for 2 Narrators and Synthetic Sound (1963); *Gregora strniše* for Narrator and 7 Instruments (1965); *Kriki (Cries)* for Narrator, Brass Quintet, and Tape (1966); *Requiem (to the Memory of a Murdered Soldier—My Father),* sound collage for Narrator, Chorus, Instruments, and Concrete Sounds (1969); *Sonata in Cool I* for Flute and Piano (1961), *Sonata in Cool II* for Clarinet and Piano (1961); *Sonata in Cool III* for Flute, Bass Clarinet, and Harp (1965); *Pop-art-music* for String Quartet, Piccolo, and 2 Metronomes (1969); *Audiogemi I–IV* for String Quartet (1974).

Bozza, Eugène, French composer and conductor; b. Nice, April 4, 1905. He studied music at the Paris Cons.; received the Grand Prix de Rome in 1934. From 1939 to 1948 he was conductor of the Opéra-Comique in Paris; then moved to Valenciennes, where he was appointed director of the local cons.
WORKS: Opera, *Léonidas* (1947); lyric drama, *La Duchesse de Langeais* (Lille, 1967); ballets: *Fête romaine* (1942) and *Jeux de plage* (1946); Symph. (1948); Violin Concerto (1938); Cello Concerto (1947); *Luciolles* for 6 Clarinets; *Suite française* for 5 Woodwind Instruments; *3 Pieces* for 5 Trombones; and other compositions for unusual instrumental combinations.

Bradbury, William Batchelder, American music editor; b. York, Maine, Oct. 6, 1816; d. Montclair, N.J., Jan. 7, 1868. He studied with Lowell Mason; then went to Germany, where he took courses with Hauptmann and Moscheles in Leipzig. Returning to America, he became active in various musical enterprises; from 1854 to 1867 he was in business as a maker of pianos. He edited some 50 collections of songs and instrumental pieces; one of these collections, *Fresh Laurels for the Sabbath School* (1867), reached the circulation of 1,200,000 copies; other collections were *Bradbury's Golden Shower of Sunday School Melodies; Bright Jewels for the Sunday School; Musical Gems for School and Home.* He was the author of well-known hymn tunes: *He Leadeth Me; Saviour, Like a Shepherd Lead Me;* etc.
BIBLIOGRAPHY: A. Wingard, *The Life and Works of William Batchelder Bradbury (1816–1868)* (Diss., Southern Baptist Theological Seminary, Louisville, Ky., 1973).

Brade, William, English-born German violinist and composer; b. 1560; d. Hamburg, Feb. 26, 1630. He settled in Germany about 1590; thereafter was a court musician in various localities, including Brandenburg, Copenhagen, Bückeburg, Hamburg, Güstrow, and Berlin. He composed a number of popular collections of dances.
WORKS: *Newe ausserlesene Paduanen, Galliarden, Canzonen, Allmand und Coranten... auff allen musicalischen Instrumenten lieblich zu gebrauchen* (Hamburg, 1609); *Newe ausserlesene Paduanen und Galliarden... auff allen musicalischen Instrumenten und insonderheit auff Fiolen lieblich zu gebrauchen* (Hamburg, 1614); *Newe ausserlesene liebliche Branden, Intraden, Mascharaden, Balletten, All'manden, Couranten, Volten, Aufzüge und frembde Tänze... insonderheit auff Fiolen zu gebrauchen* (Hamburg and Lübeck, 1617); *Melodieuses paduanes, chansons, galliardes* (Antwerp, 1619); *Newe lustige Volten, Couranten, Balletten, Paduanen, Galliarden, Masqueraden, auch allerley arth newer frantzösischer Täntze* (Berlin, 1621).
BIBLIOGRAPHY: C. Huber, *The Life and Music of William Brade* (Diss., Univ. of North Carolina, 1965).

Bradshaw, Merrill, American composer and pedagogue; b. Lyman, Wyo., June 18, 1929. He received his academic education at Brigham Young Univ. in Salt Lake City and at the Univ. of Illinois; then began his musical studies; obtained an M.M. from Brigham Young Univ. in 1955 and a D.M.A. from the Univ. of Illinois in 1962. From 1957 he was engaged in teaching at Brigham Young Univ. As a member of the Mormon Church, he contributed a great deal to the formulation of classical Mormon music.
WORKS: FOR ORCH.: 5 symphs.: No. 1 (1957); No. 2 (1962); No. 3 (1967); No. 4 (1968; No. 5 (1978; Auckland, New Zealand, July 4, 1979); Piano Concerto (1955); Concerto for Viola and Orch., entitled *Homages* (Provo, Utah, July 14, 1979); Violin Concerto (Provo, March 5, 1981); *Facets* (1965); *Feathers*

(1968); *4 Mountain Sketches* (1974); *Nocturnes and Revels* (1974); *Lovers and Liars* (1976). CHAMBER MUSIC: *Dialogue* for Flute and Horn (1956); String Quartet No. 1 (1957); String Quartet No. 2 (1969); Violin Sonata (1957); Suite for Viola (1967); Suite for Oboe and Piano (1966); Brass Quintet (1969); Nocturne for 2 Horns and Strings (1977). FOR VOICE: *The Restoration,* oratorio (Provo, March 23, 1974); *Love and Death, 4 Elizabethan Lyrics* for Viola, Soprano, and Strings (Provo, Sept. 10, 1982); a musical, *The Title of Liberty* (1975); a cappella choruses; hymns; psalms; ballads. FOR PIANO: *6 Bagatelles* (1958); *Moments* (1968); *20 Mosaics* (1972); *6 plus 4* for 10 Pianos (1976).

Bradsky, Wenzel Theodor, Bohemian composer; b. Rakovník, Jan. 17, 1833; d. there, Aug. 10, 1881. He studied in Prague; then was a choir singer in Berlin; in 1874 he was given the title of court composer by Prince Georg of Prussia, whose drama *Iolanthe* he set to music. He wrote the operas *Roswitha* (Dessau, 1860); *Das Krokodil* (1862); *Jarmila* (Prague, 1879); *Der Rattenfänger von Hameln* (Berlin, 1881); also many choruses and solo songs.

Braein, Edvard Fliflet, Norwegian composer and conductor; b. Kristiansund, Aug. 23, 1924; d. Oslo, April 30, 1976. He was of a musical family; his grandfather was an organist and choirmaster; and his father, **Edvard Braein** (1887–1957), was a composer, organist, and conductor. E.F. Braein began his musical education at the Music Cons. in Oslo, graduating in 1943; then studied conducting with Odd Grüner-Hegge and composition with Bjarne Brustad; later took private lessons with Jean Rivier in Paris (1950–51). Upon returning to Oslo, he was active mainly as a choral conductor.
WORKS: FOR THE STAGE: Opera, *Anne Pedersdotter* (Oslo, 1971); opera buffa, *Den stundesløse (The Wastrel),* based on the play by L. Holberg (Oslo, 1975); ballet, *The Little Matchstick Girl,* after the tale by Hans Christian Andersen (1976; unfinished). FOR ORCH.: *Towards the Sea* for Chamber Orch. (1947); *Concert Overture* (1948); 3 symphs. (1949–50, 1951–54, 1967); *Serenade* (1951–52); *Adagio* for Strings (1953); *Capriccio* for Piano and Orch. (1956–57); Divertimento for Flute and Orch. (1958); *Symphonic Prelude* (1959); *Largo* for Strings (1960–61); *Intrata* (1961); *Overture in Miniature* (1962); *Little Serenade* (1963); *Ritmico e melodico* (1971); *Til Arendal,* festival overture for the city of Arendal (1972); *Havljom (Echo from the Sea;* 1973). CHAMBER MUSIC: Violin Sonata (1940); *The Merry Musicians* for Clarinet, Violin, Viola, and Cello (1947); Divertimento for Clarinet, Violin, Viola, and Cello (1962); String Trio (1964); *Humoresque* for Chamber Ensemble (1966).
BIBLIOGRAPHY: N. Grinde, *Contemporary Norwegian Music 1920–1980* (Oslo, 1981; pp. 93–96).

Braga, Francisco, Brazilian composer; b. Rio de Janeiro, April 15, 1868; d. there, March 14, 1945. He played clarinet in military bands in Rio de Janeiro; at the age of 18 he composed an overture, which was played at the inauguration of the Society of Popular Concerts in Rio de Janeiro. He then went to Paris, where he studied with Massenet; also traveled in Germany and Italy. Influenced mainly by Massenet and Mascagni, Braga wrote the opera *Jupira,* which was staged at Rio de Janeiro (March 20, 1899). From 1908 till 1933, he conducted symph. concerts in Rio. His symph. works include the programmatic pieces *Insomnia, Cauchemar, Paysage,* etc. Braga was the teacher of many Brazilian composers and contributed much to the musical culture of his country.

BIBLIOGRAPHY: Biography by T. Gomes (Rio de Janeiro, 1937); *Exposição Comemorativa do Centenario do Nascimento de Francisco Braga* (Rio de Janeiro, 1968).

Braga, Gaetano, Italian cellist and composer; b. Giulianova, Abruzzi, June 9, 1829; d. Milan, Nov. 21, 1907. He studied at the Naples Cons. with C. Gaetano (1841–52); made tours as a cellist in Europe and America; lived mostly in Paris and London. His *Leggenda valacca,* known in English as *Angel's Serenade,* originally written for voice with cello (or violin) obbligato, attained tremendous popularity and was arranged for various instrumental combinations. Braga wrote several operas: *Alina,* or *La spregiata* (1853); *Estella di San Germano* (Vienna, 1857); *Il ritratto* (Naples, 1858); *Margherita la mendicante* (Paris, 1859); *Mormile* (La Scala, Milan, 1862); *Ruy Blas* (1865); *Reginella* (Lecco, 1871); *Caligola* (Lisbon, 1873); sacred choruses; and a valuable *Metodo di violoncello.*

BIBLIOGRAPHY: V. Bindi, *Gaetano Braga: Da ricordi della sua vita* (Naples, 1927); A. de Angelis, "Gaetano Braga," *Rivista Musicale Italiana* (June 1929).

Braga-Santos, Joly. See **Santos-Braga, Joly.**

Bragard, Roger, Belgian musicologist; b. Huy, Nov. 21, 1903. He studied philology at the Univ. of Liège; received his Ph.D. with the dissertation *Les Sources du "De Institutione Musica" de Boèce* (1926); then studied in Paris with Pirro (musicology) and Vincent d'Indy (composition). In 1931 he worked in various European libraries on problems of medieval music. In 1935 he became prof. of music history at the Cons. of Brussels. He publ. a number of valuable papers, among them *Lambert de Sayve* (Liège, 1934); *Panorama de la musique belge du XIVᵉ au XVIIIᵉ siècle* (Brussels, 1938); *Boethiana* (Antwerp, 1945); *Histoire de la musique belge* (3 vols.; 1946, 1949, 1956); with F. De Hen, *Les Instruments de musique dans l'art et l'histoire* (Brussels, 1967; American ed., N.Y., 1968); etc.

Braham (real name, **Abraham**), **John,** renowned English tenor; b. London, March 20, 1774; d. there, Feb. 17, 1856. He studied with Leoni in London, with Rauzzini in Bath, and with Isola in Genoa. He made his debut at Covent Garden (April 21, 1787); then appeared at Drury Lane in 1796, in the opera *Mahmoud* by Storace. He was subsequently engaged to sing at the Italian Opera House in London. In 1798

he undertook an extensive tour in Italy; also appeared in Hamburg. Returning to England in 1801, he was increasingly successful. Endowed with a powerful voice of 3 octaves in compass, he knew no difficulties in operatic roles. He was the original Huon in Weber's *Oberon* (1826). As a ballad writer, he was very popular; he wrote much of the music for the operatic roles which he sang; often he added portions to operas by other composers, as in *The Americans* (1811), with its famous song *The Death of Nelson;* contributed incidental music to 12 productions. In 1831 he entered upon a theatrical business venture; he acquired the Colosseum in Regent's Park; in 1836 he had built the St. James's Theatre, but failed to recoup his investment and lost much of his considerable fortune. He made an American tour in 1840–42 despite the weakening of his voice with age; however, his dramatic appeal remained undiminished and he was able to impress the American public in concert appearances. He then returned to London; made his final appearance in 1852.

BIBLIOGRAPHY: J. Mewburn Levien, *The Singing of John Braham* (London, 1945).

Brahms, Johannes, great German composer; b. Hamburg, May 7, 1833; d. Vienna, April 3, 1897. His father, who played the double bass in the orchestra of the Phil. Society in Hamburg, taught Brahms the rudiments of music; later he began to study piano with Otto F.W. Cossel, and made his first public appearance as a pianist with a chamber music group at the age of 10. Impressed with his progress, Cossel sent him to his own former teacher, the noted pedagogue Eduard Marxsen, who accepted him as a scholarship student, without charging a fee. Soon Brahms was on his own, and had to eke out his meager subsistence by playing piano in taverns, restaurants, and other establishments (but not in brothels, as insinuated by some popular biographers). On Sept. 21, 1848, at the age of 15, Brahms played a solo concert in Hamburg under an assumed name. In 1853 he met the Hungarian violinist Eduard Reményi, with whom he embarked on a successful concert tour. While in Hannover, Brahms formed a friendship with the famous violin virtuoso Joseph Joachim, who gave him an introduction to Liszt in Weimar. Of great significance was his meeting with Schumann in Düsseldorf. In his diary of the time, Schumann noted: "Johannes Brahms, a genius." He reiterated his appraisal of Brahms in his famous article "Neue Bahnen" ("New Paths"), which appeared in the *Neue Zeitschrift für Musik* on Oct. 28, 1853; in a characteristic display of metaphor, he described young Brahms as having come into life as Minerva sprang in full armor from the brow of Jupiter. Late in 1853, Breitkopf und Härtel publ. his 2 piano sonatas and a set of 6 songs. Brahms also publ., under the pseudonym of G.W. Marks, a collection of 6 pieces for piano, 4-hands, under the title *Souvenir de la Russie* (Brahms never visited Russia). Schumann's death in 1856, after years of agonizing mental illness, deeply affected Brahms. He remained a devoted friend of Schumann's family; his correspondence with Schumann's widow Clara reveals a deep affection and spiritual intimacy, but the speculation about their friendship growing into a romance exists only in the fevered imaginations of psychologizing biographers. Objectively judged, the private life of Brahms was that of a middle-class bourgeois who worked systematically and diligently on his current tasks while maintaining a fairly active social life. He was always ready and willing to help young composers (his earnest efforts on behalf of Dvořák were notable). Brahms was entirely free of professional jealousy; his differences with Wagner were those of style. Wagner was an opera composer, while Brahms never wrote for the stage. True, some ardent admirers of Wagner (such as Hugo Wolf) found little of value in the music of Brahms, while admirers of Brahms (such as Hanslick) were sharp critics of Wagner, but Brahms held aloof from such partisan wranglings.

From 1857 to 1859 Brahms was employed in Detmold as court pianist, chamber musician, and choir director. In the meantime he began work on his first piano concerto. He played it on Jan. 22, 1859, in Hannover, with Joachim as conductor. Other important works of the period were the two serenades for orchestra and the first string sextet. He expected to be named conductor of the Hamburg Phil. Society, but the directoriat preferred to engage, in 1863, the singer Julius Stockhausen in that capacity. Instead, Brahms accepted the post of conductor of the Singakademie in Vienna, which he led from 1863 to 1864. In 1869 he decided to make Vienna his permanent home. As early as 1857 he began work on his choral masterpiece, *Ein deutsches Requiem;* he completed the score in 1868, and conducted its first performance in the Bremen Cathedral on April 10, 1868. In May 1868 he added another movement to the work (the 5th, "Ihr habt nun Traurigkeit") in memory of his mother, who died in 1865. The title of the German Requiem had no nationalistic connotations; it simply stated that the text was in German rather than Latin. His other important vocal scores include *Rinaldo,* a cantata; the *Liebeslieder* waltzes for vocal quartet and piano 4-hands; the *Alto Rhapsody;* the *Schicksalslied;* and many songs. In 1869 he publ. 2 vols. of *Hungarian Dances* for piano duet; these were extremely successful. Among his chamber music works, the Piano Quintet in F minor, the String Sextet No. 2 in G major, the Trio for French Horn, Violin, and Piano, the two string quartets, op. 51, and the String Quartet op. 67 are exemplary works of their kind. In 1872 Brahms was named artistic director of the concerts of Vienna's famed Gesellschaft der Musikfreunde; he held this post until 1875. During this time, he composed the *Variations on a Theme by Joseph Haydn,* op. 56a. The title was a misnomer; the theme occurs in a Feldpartita for military band by Haydn, but it was not Haydn's own; it was originally known as the St. Anthony Chorale, and in pedantic scholarly editions of Brahms it is called St. Anthony Variations. Otto Dessoff conducted the first performance of the work with the Vienna Phil. on Nov. 2, 1873.

For many years friends and admirers of Brahms urged him to write a symphony. He clearly had a symphonic mind; his piano concertos were symphonic in outline and thematic development. As early as 1855 he began work on a full-fledged symph.; in 1862 he nearly completed the first movement of what was to be his first symph. The famous horn solo in the finale of the first symph. was jotted down by Brahms on a picture postcard to Clara Schumann dated Sept. 12, 1868, from his summer place in the Tyrol; in it Brahms said that he heard the tune played by a shepherd on a Alpine horn; and he set it to a rhymed quatrain of salutation. Yet Brahms was still unsure about his symphonic capacity. (A frivolous suggestion was made by an irresponsible psychomusicologist that it was when Brahms grew his famous luxuriant beard that he finally determined to complete his symphonic essay; such pogonological speculations illustrate the degree to which musical criticism can contribute to its own ridiculosity.) The great C minor Symph., his first, was completed in 1876 and first performed at Karlsruhe on Nov. 4, 1876, conducted by Dessoff. Hans von Bülow, the German master of the telling phrase, called it "The Tenth," thus placing Brahms on a direct line from Beethoven. It was also Hans von Bülow who cracked a bon mot that became a part of music history, in referring to the three B's of music, Bach, Beethoven, and Brahms. The original saying was not merely a vacuous alphabetical generalization; Bülow's phrase was deeper; in answering a question as to what was his favorite key, he said it was E-flat major, the key of Beethoven's *Eroica,* because it had 3 B's in its key signature. (In German, B is specifically B flat, but by extension may signify any flat)—one for Bach, one for Beethoven, and one for Brahms. The witty phrase took wing, but its sophisticated connotation was lost at the hands of professional popularizers.

Brahms composed his 2nd symph. in 1877; it was performed for the first time by the Vienna Phil. on Dec. 30, 1877, under the direction of Hans Richter, receiving a fine acclaim. Brahms led a second performance of the work with the Gewandhaus Orch. in Leipzig on Jan. 10, 1878. In 1878 Brahms wrote his violin concerto; the score was dedicated to Joachim, who gave its premiere with the Gewandhaus Orch. on Jan. 1, 1879. Brahms then composed his 2nd piano concerto, in B-flat major, and was soloist in its first performance in Budapest, on Nov. 9, 1881. There followed the 3rd symph. in F major, first performed by the Vienna Phil., under the direction of Hans Richter, on Dec. 2, 1883. The 4th symph. in E minor followed in quick succession; it had its first performance in Meiningen on Oct. 25, 1885. The symph. cycle was completed in less than a decade; it has been conjectured, without foundation, that the tonalities of the four symphs. of Brahms—C, D, F, and E—correspond to the fugal subject of Mozart's Jupiter Symph., and that some symbolic meaning was attached to it. All speculations aside, there is an inner symmetry uniting these works. The four symphs. contain four movements each, with a slow movement and a scherzo-like Allegretto in the middle of the corpus. There are fewer departures from the formal scheme than in Beethoven, and there are

Brahms

no extraneous episodes interfering with the grand general line. Brahms wrote music pure in design and eloquent in sonorous projection; he was a true classicist, a quality that endeared him to the critics who were repelled by Wagnerian streams of sound, and by the same token alienated those who sought something more than mere geometry of thematic configurations from a musical composition.

The chamber music of Brahms possesses similar symphonic qualities; when Schoenberg undertook to make an orch. arrangement of the piano quartet of Brahms, all he had to do was to expand the sonorities and enhance instrumental tone colors already present in the original. The string quartets of Brahms are edifices of Gothic perfection; his 3 violin sonatas, his 2nd piano trio (the first was a student work and yet it had a fine quality of harmonious construction) all contribute to a permanent treasure of musical classicism. The piano writing of Brahms is severe in its contrapuntal texture, but pianists for a hundred years included his rhapsodies and intermezzos in their repertoire; and Brahms was able to impart sheer delight in his Hungarian rhapsodies and waltzes; they represented the Viennese side of his character, as contrasted with the profound Germanic quality of his symphs. The song cycles of Brahms continued the evolution of the art of the lieder, a natural continuation of the song cycles of Schubert and Schumann.

Brahms was sociable and made friends easily; he traveled to Italy, and liked to spend his summers in the solitude of the Austrian Alps. But he was reluctant to appear as a center of attention; he declined to receive the honorary degree of Mus.D. from the Univ. of Cambridge in 1876, giving as a reason his fear of seasickness in crossing the English Channel. He was pleased to receive the Gold Medal of the Phil. Society of London in 1877. In 1879 the Univ. of Breslau proffered him an honorary degree of Doctor of Philosophy, citing him as "Artis musicae severioris in Germania nunc princeps." As a gesture of appreciation and gratitude he wrote an *Akademische Festouvertüre* for Breslau, and since there was no Channel to cross on the way, he accepted the invitation to conduct its premiere in Breslau on Jan. 4, 1881; its rousing finale using the German student song "Gaudeamus igitur" pleased the academic assembly. In 1887 he was presented with the Prussian Order "Pour le Mérite." In 1889 he received the freedom of his native city of Hamburg; also in 1889, Franz Joseph, the Emperor of Austria, made him a Commander of the Order of Leopold. With success and fame came a sense of self-sufficiency, which found its external expression in the corpulence of his appearance, familiar to all from photographs and drawings of Brahms conducting or playing the piano. Even during his Viennese period Brahms remained a sturdy Prussian; his ideal was to see Germany a dominant force in Europe philosophically and militarily. In his workroom he kept a bronze relief of Bismarck, the "Iron Chancellor," crowned with laurel. He was extremely meticulous in his working habits (his manuscripts were clean and legible), but he avoided wearing formal dress, preferring a loosely fitting flannel shirt and a detachable white collar, but no cravat. He liked to dine in simple restaurants, and he drank a great deal of beer. He was indifferent to hostile criticism; still, it is amazing to read the outpouring of invective against Brahms by George Bernard Shaw and by American critics; the usual accusations were of dullness and turgidity. When Symph. Hall was opened in Boston in 1900 with the lighted signs Exit in Case of Fire, someone cracked that they should more appropriately announce Exit in Case of Brahms. Yet, at the hands of successive German conductors Brahms became a standard symphonist in N.Y., Boston, Philadelphia, and Baltimore. From the perspective of a century, Brahms appears as the greatest master of counterpoint after Bach; one can learn polyphony from a studious analysis of the chamber music and piano works of Brahms; he excelled in variation forms; his piano variations on a theme of Paganini are exemplars of contrapuntal learning, and they are also among the most difficult piano works of the 19th century. Posterity gave him a full measure of recognition; Hamburg celebrated his sesquicentennial in 1983 with great pomp. Brahms had lived a good life, but died a bad death, stricken with cancer of the liver.

WORKS: FOR ORCH.: 4 symphs.: No. 1 in C minor, op. 68 (1855–76; Karlsruhe, Nov. 4, 1876, Dessoff, conductor); No. 2 in D major, op. 73 (1877; Vienna, Dec. 30, 1877, Richter conductor); No. 3 in F major, op. 90 (1883; Vienna, Dec. 2, 1883, Richter, conductor); No. 4 in E minor, op. 98 (1884–85; Meiningen, Oct. 17, 1885, Brahms, conductor [private perf.]; public perf., Oct. 25, 1885, Bülow, conductor).

OTHER WORKS FOR ORCH.: Piano Concerto No. 1 in D minor, op. 15 (1854–58; Hannover, Jan. 22, 1859, Brahms, soloist; Joachim, conductor); Serenade No. 1 in D major, op. 11 (first version, for small orch., 1857–58; Hamburg, March 28, 1859, Joachim, conductor; 2nd version, for larger orch., 1859; Hannover, March 3, 1860, Joachim, conductor); Serenade No. 2 in A major, op. 16 (1858–59; Hamburg, Feb. 10, 1860, Brahms, conductor; revised, 1875); *Variations on a Theme by Joseph Haydn,* op. 56a (the theme, from the *St. Anthony Chorale,* may not be by Haydn; 1873; Vienna, Nov. 2, 1873, Dessoff, conductor); Violin Concerto in D major, op. 77 (1878; Leipzig, Jan. 1, 1879, Joachim, soloist; Brahms, conductor); Piano Concerto No. 2 in B-flat major, op. 83 (1878–81; Budapest, Nov. 9, 1881, Brahms, soloist; Erkel, conductor); *Akademische Festouvertüre,* op. 80 (1880; Breslau, Jan. 4, 1881, Brahms, conductor); *Tragische Ouvertüre,* op. 81 (1880; Vienna, Dec. 26, 1880, Richter, conductor; rev., 1881); Concerto in A minor for Violin and Cello, op. 102, the *Double* Concerto (1887; Cologne, Oct. 18, 1887, Joachim, violinist; Hausmann, cellist; and Wüllner, conductor); also 3 Hungarian Dances arranged for Orch. (1873): No. 1 in G minor, No. 3 in F major, and No. 10 in F major.

CHAMBER MUSIC: Piano Trio No. 1 in B major, op. 8 (1853–54; N.Y., Nov. 27, 1855; revised, 1889); Sextet No. 1 in B-flat major for 2 Violins, 2 Violas, and 2 Cellos, op. 18 (1858–60; Hannover, Oct. 20, 1860); Piano Quartet No. 1 in G minor, op. 25 (1861; Hamburg, Nov. 16, 1861); Piano Quartet No. 2 in A major, op. 26 (1861–62; Vienna, Nov. 29, 1862); Piano Quintet in F minor, op. 34 (1861–64; Paris, March 24, 1868); Sextet No. 2 in G major for 2 Violins, 2 Violas, and 2 Cellos, op. 36 (1864–65; Vienna, Feb. 3, 1867); Cello Sonata No. 1 in E minor, op. 38 (1862–65); Trio in E-flat major for Violin, Horn or Viola, and Piano, op. 40 (1865; Karlsruhe, Dec. 7, 1865); String Quartet No. 1 in C minor, op. 51 (1865?–73?; Vienna, Dec. 1, 1873); String Quartet No. 2 in A minor, op. 51 (1865?–73?; Vienna, Oct. 18, 1873); Piano Quartet No. 3 in C minor, op. 60 (1855–75; Ziegelhausen, Nov. 18, 1875); String Quartet No. 3 in B-flat major, op. 67 (1876; Berlin, Oct. 1876); Violin Sonata No. 1 in G major, op. 78 (1878–79; Vienna, Nov. 29, 1879); Piano Trio No. 2 in C major, op. 87 (1880–82; Frankfurt, Dec. 28, 1882); Quintet No. 1 in F major for 2 Violins, 2 Violas, and Cello, op. 88 (1882; Frankfurt, Dec. 28, 1882); Cello Sonata No. 2 in F major, op. 99 (1886; Vienna, Nov. 24, 1886); Violin Sonata No. 2 in A major, op. 100 (1886; Vienna, Dec. 2, 1886); Piano Trio No. 3 in C minor, op. 101 (1886; Budapest, Dec. 20, 1886); Violin Sonata No. 3 in D minor, op. 108 (1886–88; Budapest, Dec. 22, 1888); Quintet No. 2 in G major for 2 Violins, 2 Violas, and Cello, op. 111 (1890; Vienna, Nov. 11, 1890); Trio in A minor for Clarinet or Viola, Cello, and Piano, op. 114 (1891; Berlin, Dec. 1, 1891); Quintet in B minor for Clarinet and String Quartet, op. 115 (1891; Berlin, Dec. 1, 1891); Two sonatas: No. 1 in F minor and No. 2 in E-flat major for Clarinet or Viola and Piano, op. 120 (1894; Vienna, Jan. 7, 1895); also a Scherzo in C minor for Violin and Piano, a movement from the Sonata in A minor by Brahms, Schumann, and A. Dietrich. In 1924 a copy from the original score of a Trio in A major, presumably composed by Brahms when he was about 20 years old (see letter to R. Schumann, 1853), was discovered in Bonn; it was publ. in 1938.

FOR SOLO PIANO: Scherzo in E-flat minor, op. 4 (1851; Vienna, March 17, 1867); Sonata No. 1 in C major, op. 1 (1852–53; Leipzig, Dec. 17, 1853); Sonata No. 2 in F-sharp minor, op. 2 (1852; Vienna, Feb. 2, 1882); Sonata No. 3 in F minor, op. 5 (1853; Vienna, Jan. 6, 1863); *Variations on a Theme by Schumann* in F-sharp minor, op. 9 (1854; Berlin, Dec. 1879); 4 Ballades, op. 10: D minor, D major, B minor, and B major (1854); Gavotte in A minor (1854); Gavotte in A major (1855); 2 Gigues: A minor and B minor (1855); 2 Sarabandes: A minor and B minor (1855; Vienna, Jan. 20, 1856); *Variations [13] on a Hungarian Song* in D major, op. 21 (1853; London, March 25, 1874); *Variations [11] on an Original Theme* in D major, op. 21 (1857; Copenhagen, March 1868); *Variations [25] and Fugue on a Theme by Handel* in B-flat major, op. 24 (1861; Hamburg, Dec. 7, 1861); *Variations [28] on a Theme by Paganini* in A minor, op. 35 (1862–63; Zürich, Nov. 25, 1865); 16 Waltzes, op. 39 (1865); 8 Piano Pieces, op. 76 (1871–78; Leipzig, Jan. 4, 1880); 2 Rhapsodies: B minor and G minor, op. 79 (1879; Krefeld, Jan. 20, 1880); *Fantasien* [7], op. 116 (1892); 3 Intermezzos: E-flat major, B-flat minor, and C-sharp minor, op. 117 (1892); Piano Pieces [6], op. 118 (1892; London, Jan. 1894); Piano Pieces [4], op. 119 (1892; London, Jan. 1894); also 5 *Studien* for Piano (I, Study after Frédéric Chopin, in F minor, an arrangement of Chopin's

Etude No. 2, op. 25; II, Rondo after Carl Maria von Weber, in C major, an arrangement of the finale of Weber's *Moto perpetuo,* op. 24; III and IV, Presto after J.S. Bach, in G minor [2 arrangements of the finale of BWV 1001]; V, *Chaconne* by J.S. Bach, in D minor, (an arrangement of the finale of BWV 1016); Theme and Variations in D minor (an arrangement of the slow movement of the Sextet No. 1; 1860; Frankfurt, Oct. 31, 1865); Gavotte in A major (an arrangement from Gluck's *Paris ed Elena;* Vienna, Jan. 20, 1856; publ. 1871); 10 Hungarian Dances (an arrangement of nos. 1–10 from the original version for piano, 4-hands; publ. 1872); 51 Exercises (publ. 1893); cadenzas to concertos by Bach (Harpsichord Concerto No. 1 in D minor, BWV 1052), Mozart (Piano Concertos Nos. 17 in G major, K. 453, 20 in D minor, K. 466, and 24 in C minor, K. 491), and Beethoven (Piano Concerto No. 4 in G major, op. 58).

FOR PIANO, 4-HANDS: *Variations on a Theme by Schumann* in E-flat major, op. 23 (1861; Vienna, Jan. 12, 1864); 16 Waltzes, op. 39 (1865; Vienna, March 17, 1867); *Liebeslieder,* 18 waltzes, op. 52a (1874; an arrangement from the original version for 4 Voices and Piano, 4-hands); *Neue Liebeslieder,* 15 waltzes, op. 65a (1877; an arrangement from the original version for 4 Voices and Piano, 4-hands); Hungarian Dances (21 dances in 4 books; 1852–69).

FOR TWO PIANOS: Sonata in F minor, op. 34b (1864; Vienna, April 17, 1874); Variations on a Theme by Haydn, op. 56b (1873; Vienna, March 17, 1882); also arrangements of Joachim's *Demetrius* Overture and Overture to *Henry IV.*

FOR ORGAN: Fugue in A-flat minor (1856); *O Traurigkeit, O Herzeleid,* chorale prelude and fugue in A minor (1856; Vienna, Dec. 2, 1882); 2 preludes and fugues: A minor and G minor (1856–57); 11 *Choralvorspiele,* op. 122 (1896).

VOCAL MUSIC: Choral Works: *Geistliches Lied* for 4-part Chorus and Organ or Piano, op. 30 (1856); *Ein deutsches Requiem* for Soprano, Baritone, Chorus, and Orch., op. 45 (1857–68; first 3 movements, under Herbeck, Vienna, Dec. 1, 1867; movements 1–4 and 6, under Brahms, Bremen, April 10, 1868; first complete perf., under Reinecke, Leipzig, Feb. 18, 1869); *Ave Maria* for Women's Voices and Orch. or Organ, op. 12 (1858); *Begräbnisgesang* for Choir and Wind Instruments, op. 13 (1858; Hamburg, Dec. 2, 1859); *Marienlieder* for Mixed Chorus, op. 22 (7 songs; 1859); 4 Songs for Women's Voices, 2 Horns, and Harp, op. 17 (1859–60); *Der 13. Psalm* for Women's Voices and Organ or Piano, with Strings ad libitum, op. 27 (1859; Hamburg, Sept. 19, 1864); 2 Motets for 5-part Chorus a cappella, op. 29 (1860; Vienna, April 17, 1864); 3 Sacred Choruses for Women's Voices a cappella, op. 37 (1859–63); 5 *Soldatenlieder* for 4-part Male Chorus a cappella, op. 41 (1861–62); 3 Songs for 6-part Mixed Chorus with Piano ad libitum, op. 42 (1859–61); 12 Songs and Romances for Women's Voices with Piano ad libitum, op. 44 (1859–63); *Rinaldo,* cantata for Tenor, Male Chorus, and Orch., op. 50, after Goethe (1863–68; Vienna, Feb. 28, 1869); *Rhapsodie* for Contralto, Male Chorus, and Orch., op. 53, after Goethe's *Harzreise im Winter* (1869; Jena, March 3, 1870); *Schicksalslied* for Chorus and Orch., op. 54 (1868–71; Karlsruhe, Oct.

Brahms

18, 1871); Triumphlied for 8-part Chorus, Baritone, and Orch., op. 55 (1870–71; Karlsruhe, June 5, 1872); 7 Songs for 4- and 6-part a cappella Chorus, op. 62 (1874); *Nänie* for Chorus and Orch., op. 82, after Schiller (1880–81; Zürich, Dec. 6, 1881); Two Motets for 4- and 6-part a cappella Chorus, op. 74 (1877; 2nd motet probably composed between 1860 and 1865; Vienna, Dec. 8, 1878); *Gesang der Parzen* for 6-part Chorus and Orch., op. 89, after Goethe's *Iphigenie auf Tauris* (1882; Basel, Dec. 10, 1882); 6 Songs and Romances for 4-part a cappella Chorus, op. 93a (1883–84; Krefeld, Jan. 27, 1885); *Tafellied* for 6-part Chorus and Piano, op. 93b (1884; Krefeld, Jan. 28, 1885); Five Songs for 4- and 6-part a cappella Chorus, op. 104 (1888; Vienna, April 3, 1889); *Fest- und Gedenksprüche* for a Double a cappella Chorus, op. 109 (1886–88; Hamburg, Sept. 14, 1889); Three Motets for 4- and 8-part a cappella Chorus, op. 110 (1889; Cologne, March 13, 1890); also 13 Canons, for Women's Voices, op. 113 (1860–67); *Deutsche Volkslieder* (26 songs arranged for 4-part Chorus; 1854–73; publ. in 2 books, 1864 and 1926–27). Vocal quartets: For Soprano, Alto, Tenor, Bass, and Piano: 3 Quartets, op. 31 (1859–63); *Liebeslieder,* 18 waltzes, with Piano, 4-hands, op. 52 (1868-69; Vienna, Jan. 5, 1870); 3 Quartets, op. 64 (1862–74); *Neue Liebeslieder,* 15 waltzes, with Piano, 4-hands, op. 65 (1874; Mannheim, May 8, 1875); 4 Quartets, op. 92 (1877–84); *Zigeunerlieder,* op. 103 (1887); 6 Quartets, op. 112 (1888–91); also *Liebeslieder,* Nos. 1, 2, 4–6, 8, 9, and 11 from op. 52 and No. 5 from op. 65, with Orch. (1870); *Kleine Hochzeitskantate* (1874). Vocal duets: With Piano Accompaniment: 3 Duets for Soprano and Alto, op. 20 (1858–60; Vienna, Jan. 29, 1878); 4 Duets for Alto and Baritone, op. 28 (1860–62; Vienna, Dec. 18, 1862); 4 Duets for Soprano and Alto, op. 61 (1874); 5 Duets for Soprano and Alto, op. 66 (1875; Vienna, Jan. 29, 1878); 4 Ballads and Romances, op. 75 (1877–78). Songs: With Piano Accompaniment: 6 Songs, op. 7 (1851-52); 6 Songs, op. 3, for Tenor or Soprano (1852–53); 6 Songs, op. 6, for Soprano or Tenor (1852–53); 8 Songs and Romances, op. 14 (1858); 5 Poems, op. 19 (1858); Romances [15] from L. Tieck's "Magelone" (1861–68); Songs [9], op. 32 (1864); 7 Songs, op. 48 (1855–68); 4 Songs, op. 43 (1857–64); 5 Songs, op. 47 (1860–68); 4 Songs, op. 46 (1864–68); 5 Songs, op. 49 (1868); Songs [8], op. 57 (1871); Songs [8], op. 58 (1871); Songs [8], op. 59 (1871–73); Songs [9], op. 63 (1874); 4 Songs, op. 70 (1875–77); 9 Songs, op. 69 (1877); 5 Songs, op. 72 (1876–77); 5 Songs, op. 71 (1877); 6 Songs, op. 86 (1877–79); 6 Songs, op. 85 (1877–82); Romances and Songs [15] for one or 2 Female Voices, op. 84 (1881); 2 Songs for Alto, Viola, and Piano, op. 91 (first song may have been begun as early as 1864, the 2nd in 1878; publ. 1884); 5 Songs, op. 94 (1884); 7 Songs, op. 95 (1884); 4 Songs, op. 96 (1884); 6 Songs, op. 97 (1884–85); 5 Songs, op. 105 (1886); 5 Songs, op. 106 (1886); 5 Songs, op. 107 (1886); *Vier ernste Gesänge* for Baritone, op. 121 (1896); also *Mondnacht* (1854); *Regenlied* (1872); 5 *Songs of Ophelia* for Soprano, with Piano *ad libitum* (1873); 14 *Volkskinderlieder,* arrangements for Voice and Piano (1858); 28 *Deutsche Volkslieder,* arrangements for Voice and Piano (1858; publ. 1926); arrangement of Schubert's *Memnon* for Voice and Orch. (1862); arrangement of Schubert's *An Schwager Kronos* for Voice and Orch. (1862); arrangement of Schubert's *Geheimes* for Voice, Horn, and Strings; 8 *Gypsy Songs,* an arrangement of op. 103, nos. 1–7 and 11, for Voice and Piano (1887); 49 *Deutsche Volkslieder,* arrangements for Voice and Piano (1894).

BIBLIOGRAPHY: COLLECTED WORKS, SOURCE MATERIAL: H. Gál and E. Mandyczewski prepared the Gesellschaft der Musikfreunde edition; it was published as *Johannes Brahms: Sämtliche Werke* (26 vols., Leipzig, 1926–28).

A thematic catalogue was prepared by N. Simrock, *Thematisches Verzeichniss sämmtlicher im Druck erschienenen Werke von Johannes Brahms* (Berlin, 1897; 3rd ed., 1909; Eng. trans. and augmented ed. by J. Braunstein as *Thematic Catalogue of the Collected Works of Brahms,* N.Y., 1956; revised by D. McCorkle, N.Y., 1973). The standard thematic and bibliographic catalogue is found in D. McCorkle, *Johannes Brahms Thematisch-Bibliographisches Werkverzeichnis* (Munich, 1983).

Other sources include: O. Keller, "J. B.s-Literatur," *Die Musik,* XII/1 (1912–13); A. von Ehrmann, *J. B.: Thematisches Verzeichnis* (Leipzig, 1933); O. Deutsch, "The First Editions of B.," *Music Review,* XXI (1940); L. Koch, *B.-Bibliografia* (Budapest, 1943); "Filling the Gaps in B. Research," *Musical Times* (May 1983).

CORRESPONDENCE: A major edition of his correspondence was published by the Deutsche Brahmsgesellschaft as *J.B.: Briefwechsel* (16 vols., Berlin, 1906–22). See also B. Litzmann, ed., *Clara Schumann-J. B.: Briefe aus den Jahren 1853–1896* (2 vols., Leipzig, 1927; Eng. trans., n.d.); K. Geiringer, "J. B. im Briefwechsel mit Eusebius Mandyczewski," *Zeitschrift für Musikwissenschaft,* XV (1932–33); K. Stephenson, ed., *J.B.: Heimatbekenntnisse in Briefen an seine Hamburger Verwandten* (Hamburg, 1933); O.-G. Billroth, *Billroth und B. im Briefwechsel* (Vienna, 1935); K. Geiringer, "Wagner and B., with Unpublished Letters," *Musical Quarterly* (April 1936); F. Callomon, "Some Unpublished B. Correspondence," *Musical Quarterly* (Jan. 1943); R. Litterscheid, ed., *J. B. in seinen Schriften und Briefen* (Berlin, 1943); E. Müller von Asow, ed., *J. B. und Mathilde Wesendonck: Ein Briefwechsel* (Vienna, 1943); H. Barkan, ed., *J. B. and Theodore Billroth: Letters from a Musical Friendship* (Norman, Okla., 1957); A. Holde, "Suppressed Passages in the B.-Joachim Correspondence, Published for the First Time," *Musical Quarterly* (July 1959); K. Stephenson, *J. B. und Fritz Simrock, Weg einer Freundschaft: Briefe des Verlegers an den Komponisten* (Hamburg, 1961); K. Stephenson, *J. B. in seiner Familie: Der Briefwechsel* (Hamburg, 1973).

BIOGRAPHY: H. Deiters, "J. B. Eine Charakteristik," in *Sammlung musikalischer Vorträge* (Leipzig, 1880 and 1898); P. Spitta, "J. B.," *Zur Musik* (Berlin, 1892); H. Reimann, *J. B.* (Berlin, 1897; 6th ed., 1922); A. Dietrich, *Erinnerungen an J. B. in Briefen, besonders aus seiner Jugendzeit* (Liepzig, 1898: Eng. trans. by D. Hecht in *Recollections of J. B.,* London, 1899); J. Widmann, *J. B. in Erinnerungen* (Berlin 1898; 5th ed., 1947; Eng. trans. by D. Hecht in *Recol-*

lections of *J. B.*, London, 1899); J. Widmann, *Sizilien und andere Gegenden Italiens: Reisen mit J. B.* (Frauenfeld, 1898; 3rd ed., 1912); W. Hübbe, *B. in Hamburg* (Hamburg, 1902); M. Kalbeck, *J. B.* (the most detailed biography; 8 vols., Berlin, 1904–14); H. Antcliffe, *B.* (London, 1905); J. Erb, *B.* (London, 1905); R. von der Leyen, *J. B. als Mensch und Freund* (Düsseldorf and Leipzig, 1905); F. May, *The Life of J. B.* (2 vols., London, 1905; 2nd ed., 1948); G. Henschel, *Personal Recollections of J. B.* (Boston, 1907); W. Pauli, *Moderne Geister: B.* (Berlin, 1907); H. Colles, *J. B.* (London, 1908; 2nd ed., 1920); R. von Perger, *B.* (Leipzig, 1908); J. Fuller-Maitland, *B.* (London, 1911); W. Thomas-San-Galli, *J. B.* (Munich, 1912; 5th ed., 1922); L. Misch, *J. B.* (Bielefeld, 1913; 2nd ed., 1922); E. Lee, *B.: The Man and His Music* (London, 1915); W. Niemann, *J. B.* (Berlin, 1920; Eng. trans., N.Y., 1929); P. Landormy, *B.* (Paris, 1921; revised ed., 1948); G. Ophüls, *Erinnerungen an J. B.* (Berlin, 1921); W. Nagel, *J. B.* (Stuttgart, 1923); J. Pulver, *J. B.* (London 1926; new ed., 1933); J. Cooke, *J. B.* (Philadelphia, 1928); M. Komorn, *J. B. als Chordirigent in Wien und seine Nachfolger* (Vienna, 1928); R. Specht, *J. B.: Leben und Werk eines deutschen Meisters* (Hellerau, 1928; Eng. trans., 1930); W. Hutschenruyter, *B.* (The Hague, 1929); G. Ernest, *J. B.* (Berlin, 1930); P. Mies, *J. B.* (Leipzig, 1930); K. Geiringer, "B. als Musikhistoriker," *Die Musik*, XXV (1932–33); R. Schauffler, "B., Poet and Peasant," *Musical Quarterly* (Oct. 1932); G. Adler, "J. B.: Wirken, Wesen und Stellung," *Studien zur Musikwissenschaft*, XX (1933; Eng. trans. in *Musical Quarterly*, April 1933); A. von Ehrmann, *J. B.: Weg, Werk und Welt* (Leipzig, 1933); R. Fellinger, *Klänge um J. B.* (Berlin, 1933); K. Geiringer, "B. as a Reader and Collector," *Musical Quarterly* (April 1933); R. Hill, *B.* (London, 1933; 2nd ed., 1941); E. Hirschmann, *J. B. und die Frauen* (Vienna, 1933); L. Koch, *B. in Ungarn* (Budapest, 1933); M. Komorn, "B., Choral Conductor," *Musical Quarterly* (April 1933); J. Müller-Blattau, *J. B.* (Potsdam, 1933); W. Murdoch, *B.: With an Analytical Study of the Complete Pianoforte Works* (London, 1933); R. Schauffler, *The Unknown B.: His Life, Character and Works, Based on New Material* (N.Y., 1933); W. Schramm, *J. B. in Detmold* (Leipzig, 1933); K. Stephenson, *J. B.' Heimatbekenntnis* (Hamburg, 1933); S. Stojowski, "Recollections of B.," *Musical Quarterly* (April 1933); E. Blom, *J. B.* (N.Y., 1934); R. Hernried, *J. B.* (Leipzig, 1934); K. Geiringer, *J.B.: Leben und Schaffen eines deutschen Meisters* (a major study; Vienna, 1935; Eng. trans., London and N.Y., 1936; 3rd ed., rev. and enlarged, N.Y., 1981); K. Huschke, *J. B. als Pianist, Dirigent und Lehrer* (Karlsruhe, 1935); R. Lienau, *Erinnerungen an J. B.* (Berlin, 1935); K. Geiringer, "B.'s Family," *Musical Quarterly* (Jan. 1936); H.H. Stuckenschmidt, "J. B., 1833–1897," *Die grossen Deutschen* (Berlin, 1936); K. Geiringer, "B. and Chrysander," *Monthly Musical Record*, LXVII (1937); K. Huschke, *Frauen um B.* (Karlsruhe, 1937); A. Orel, *J. B.s Leben in Bildern* (Leipzig, 1937); R. Gerber, *J. B.* (Potsdam, 1938); M. Goss and R. Schauffler, *B., The Master* (N.Y., 1943); K. Laux, *Der Einsame: J. B., Leben und Werk* (Graz, 1944); W. and P. Rehberg, *J. B.: Sein Leben und Werk* (Zürich,

1947; 2nd ed., 1963); J. Culshaw, *B.: An Outline of His Life and Music* (London, 1948); H. Eppstein, *B.* (Stockholm, 1948); P. Latham, *B.* (London, 1948; revised ed. by J. Westrup, London, 1975); A. Orel, *J. B., Ein Meister und sein Weg* (Vienna, 1950); F. Grasberger, *J. B.: Variationen um sein Wesen* (contains a chronological and alphabetical list of his works; also new photographs; Vienna, 1952); L. Henning, *Die Freundschaft Clara Schumanns mit J. B.* (Zürich, 1952); A. Abell, *Talks with Great Composers* (N.Y., 1955); C. Rostand, *B.* (2 vols., Paris, 1954–55); L. Berger, *Vom Menschen J. B.* (Tübingen, 1959); F. Grasberger, "J. B. und Hugo Wolf," *Österreichische Muzikzeitschrift*, XV (1960); F. Müller-Blattau, *J. B.* (Königstein, 1960); H. Gál, *J. B.: Werk und Persönlichkeit* (particularly valuable for its critical survey of his music; Frankfurt, 1961; Eng. trans. as *J. B.: His Work and Personality*, N.Y., 1963); O. Goldhammer, "Liszt, B. und Reményi," *Studia musicologica Academiae scientiarum hungaricae*, V (1963); J. Laufer, *B.* (Paris, 1963); J. Bruyr, *B.* (Paris, 1965); W. Siegmund-Schultze, *J. B.* (Leipzig, 1966); F. Grasberger, "Das Jahr 1868," *Österreichische Musikzeitschrift*, XXIII (1968); Y. Tiénot, *B.: Son vrai visage* (Paris, 1968); K. Dale, *B.: A Biography with a Survey of Books, Editions & Recordings* (Hamden, Conn., and London, 1970); R. Heuberger, *Erinnerungen an J. B.: Tagebuchnotizen aus den Jahren 1875–97,* as ed. by K. Hofmann (Tutzing, 1971; 2nd ed., 1976); J. Clapham, "Dvorak's Relations with B. and Hanslick," *Musical Quarterly* (April 1971); J. Burnett, *B.: A Critical Study* (London, 1972); K. and I. Geiringer, "The B. Library in the Gesellschaft der Musikfreunde, Wein," *Notes* (Sept. 1973); J. Chissell, *B.* (London, 1977); K. Höcker, *J. B.: Begegnung mit dem Menschen* (Berlin, 1983); R. Pascall, ed., *B.: Biographical, Documentary and Analytical Studies* (Cambridge, 1983).

CRITICISM, ANALYSIS: L. Köhler, *J. B. und seine Stellung in der Musikgeschichte* (Hannover, 1880); E. Krause, *J. B. in seinem Werken* (Hamburg, 1892); W. Nagel, *B. als Nachfolger Beethovens* (Leipzig, 1892); G. Ophüls, *B.-Texte* (Berlin, 1898; 3rd ed., 1923); R. Barth, *J. B. und seine Musik* (Hamburg, 1904); G. Jenner, *J. B. als Mensch, Lehrer und Kunstler: Studien und Erlebnisse* (Marburg, 1905; 2nd ed., 1930); W. Thomas-San-Galli, *J. B. Eine musikpsychologische Studie* (Strasbourg, 1905); J. Knorr and H. Riemann, *J. B. Symphonien und andere Orchesterwerke erläutert* (Berlin, 1908); E. Howard-Jones, "B. in His Pianoforte Music," *Proceedings of the Musical Association*, XXXVII (1910–11); M. Burkhardt, *J. B.: Ein Führer durch seine Werke* (Berlin, 1912); E. Evans, *Historical, Descriptive and Analytical Account of the Entire Works of J. B.* (London; Vol. I, vocal works, 1912; Vols. II and III, chamber and orch. works, 1933 and 1935; Vol. IV, piano works, 1936); W. Hammermann, *J. B. als Liederkomponist* (Diss., Univ. of Leipzig, 1912); G. Jenner, "Zur Entstehung des d-moll Klavierkonzerts von J. B.," *Die Musik*, XII/1 (1912–13); R. Specht, "Zur Brahmsschen Symphonik," *Die Musik*, XII/1 (1912–13); H. Wetzel, "Zur Harmonik bei B.," *Die Musik*, XII/1 (1912–13); W. Vetter, "Der erste Satz von B.' e-moll-Symphonie: ein Beitrag zur Erkenntnis moderner Symphonik," *Die Musik,* XIII/3 (1913–14); W. Nagel, *Die Klaviersonaten von J. B.: technisch-ästhetische Analysen* (Stuttgart, 1915); M. Kalbeck, *B. als Lyriker* (Vienna, 1921); M. Friedländer, *B.' Lieder* (Berlin and Leipzig, 1922; Eng. trans., London, 1928); A. Orel, "Skizzen zu J. B.' Haydn-Variationen," *Zeitschrift für Musikwissenschaft,* V (1922–23); F. Wunsiedler, *Liederschlüsse bei J. B.* (Diss., Univ. of Erlangen, 1922); P. Mies, *Stilmomente und Ausdrucksstilformen im Brahmsschen Lied* (Leipzig, 1923); H. Schenker, "B.: Variationen und Fuge über ein Thema von Händel, op. 24," *Der Tonwille,* IV (1924); V. Urbantschitsch, *Die Sonatenform bei B.* (Diss., Univ. of Vienna, 1925); V. Urbantschitsch, "Die Entwicklung der Sonatenform bei B.," *Studien zur Musikwissenschaft,* XIV (1927); J. Wetzel, "Eine neue Volksliedersammlung aus B.' Jugendzeit," *Zeitschrift für Musikwissenschaft,* X (1927–28); E. Tetzel, "Die Schumann-Variationen von B.," *Zeitschrift für Musik,* XCVI (1929); G. Knepler, *Die Form in den Instrumentalwerken J. B.* (Diss., Univ. of Vienna, 1930); H. Meyer, *Linie und Form: Bach, Beethoven, B.* (Berlin, 1930); E. Markham Lee, *B.'s Orchestral Works* (London, 1931); D. Mason, "B.'s Third Symphony," *Musical Quarterly* (July 1931); H. Drinker, *The Chamber Music of B.* (Philadelphia, 1932); A. Schering, "B. und seine Stellung in der Musikgeschichte des 19. Jahrhunderts," *Jahrbuch Peters* (1932); A. Sturke, *Der Stil in J. B.' Werken* (Diss., Univ of Würzburg, 1932); W. Blume, *B. in der Meininger Tradition* (Stuttgart, 1933); P. Browne, *B.: The Symphonies* (London, 1933); H. Colles, *The Chamber Music of B.* (London, 1933); D. Mason, *The Chamber Music of B.* (N.Y. and London, 1933; 2nd ed., 1950); R. Specht, "B. der Sinfoniker," *Die Musik,* XXV/2 (1933); E. Kurzweil, *Der Klaviersatz bei B.* (Diss., Univ. of Vienna, 1934); G. Döhrn, *Die Volkslied-Bearbeitungen von J. B.* (Diss., Univ. of Vienna, 1936); H. Düsterbehn, "Ein Beitrag zur Entstehung der FAE-Freundschafts-Sonate," *Zeitschrift für Musikwissenschaft,* CIII (1936); F. Brand, *Das Wesen der Kammermusik von B.* (Diss., Univ. of Berlin, 1937); E. Bücken, "Ein neuaufgefundenes Jugendwerk von J. B.," *Die Musik,* XXX/1 (Berlin, 1937–38); F. Brand, "Das neue B.-Trio," *Die Musik,* XXXI/1 (1938–39); H. Feiertag, *Das orchestrale Klangbild in B.' Orchester-Werken* (Diss., Univ. of Vienna, 1938); F. Kurzweil, *Die Harmonik als formbildendes Element bei J. B.* (Diss., Univ. of Vienna, 1938); F. J. Harrison, *B. and His Four Symphonies* (London, 1939); R. Kratzer, *Die Kontrapunktik bei J. B. mit besonderer Berücksichtigung der grosskontrapunktischen Formen* (Diss., Univ. of Vienna, 1939); R. Fellinger, "Ist das Klaviertrio in A-dur ein Jugendwerk von J. B.?," *Die Musik,* XXXIV (1941–42); H. Hautz, *Die Harmonik der Brahms'schen Soloklavierwerke* (Diss., Univ. of Munich, 1942); J. Fry, "B.'s Conception of the Scherzo in Chamber Music," *Musical Times* (April 1943); E. Schenk, "Zur Inhaltsdeutung der Brahmsschen Worthersee-symphonie," *Festliche Jahresschrift des Musikvereins für Kärnten* (Klagenfurt, 1943); C. Mason, "B.'s Piano Sonatas," *Music Review,* V (1944); R. Gerber, "B. und das Volkslied," *Die Samm-*lung, III (1948); R. Gerber, "Das Deutsche Requiem als Dokument Brahmsscher Frommigkeit," *Das Musikleben,* II (1949); W. Gieseler, *Die Harmonik bei J. B.* (Diss., Univ. of Göttingen, 1949); B. Stäblein, "Die motivische Arbeit im Finale der ersten B.-Sinfonie," *Das Musikleben,* II (1949); W. Köser, *J. B. in seinen geistlichen Chorwerken a cappella* (Diss., Univ. of Hamburg, 1950); A. Schoenberg, "B. the Progressive," in *Style and Idea* (N.Y., 1950); R. Hasse, *Studien zum Kontrapunktischen Klaviersatz von J. B.* (Diss., Univ of Cologne, 1951); G. Jacob, "Schoenberg and B.'s Op. 25," *Music and Letters* (July 1951); W. Siegmund-Schultze, *Untersuchungen zum Brahmsstil und Brahmsbild* (Habilitationsschrift, Univ. of Halle, 1951); R. Tenschert, "Die Klangwelt von J. B.," *Österreichische Musikzeitschrift,* VI (1951); W. Hill, "B.' opus 51-a Diptych," *Music Review,* XXXIII (1952); S. Drinker, *B. and His Women's Choruses* (Merion, Pa., 1952); W. Morik, *J. B. und sein Verhältnis zum deutschen Volkslied* (Diss., Univ. of Göttingen, 1953); G. Gärtner, "Das Terzmotiv, Keimzelle der 1. Sinfonie von J. B.," *Die Musikforschung,* VIII (1955); S. Kross, "B. und der Kanon," in *Festschrift Joseph Schmidt-Görg zum 60. Geburtstag* (Bonn, 1957); S. Kross, *Die Chorwerke von J. B.* (Diss., Univ. of Bonn, 1957; published in an enlarged ed., Berlin, 1958; 2nd ed., 1963); O. Jonas, "Brahmsiana," *Die Musikforschung,* XI (1958); S. Kross, "Zur Frage der Brahmsschen Volksliedbearbeitung," *Die Musikforschung,* XI (1958); W. Siegmund-Schultze, "J. B.' Orchesterwerke," in K. Schönewolf, ed., *Konzertbuch Orchestermusik* (vol. I, Berlin, 1958); K. Giebeler, *Die Lieder von J. B.* (Diss., Univ. of Münster, 1959); I. Fellinger, *Über die Dynamik in der Musik von J. B.* (Berlin, 1961); H. Busch, "Die Orgelwerke von J. B.," *Ars organi,* XI (1963); A. Mitschka, *Der Sonatensatz in den Werken von J. B.* (Gütersloh, 1963); W. Newman, "A 'Basic Motive' in B.'s German Requiem," *Music Review,* XXIV (1963); H. Truscott, "B. and Sonata Style," *Music Review,* XXV (1964); C. Dahlhaus, *B., Klavierkonzert Nr. 1 d-moll op. 15, Meisterwerke der Musik,* III (Munich, 1965); H. Hollander, "Gedanken zum strukturellen Aufbau des Brahmsscher Requiems," *Schweizerische Musikzeitung/Revue musical suisse,* CV (1965); W. Moritz, *J. B. und sein Verhältnis zum deutschen Volkslied* (Tutzing, 1965); J. Fairleig, "Neo-Classicism in the Later Piano Works of B.," *Piano Quarterly* (Winter 1966–67); F. Kirby, "B. and the Piano Sonata," in *Paul A. Pisk: Essays in His Honor* (Austin, 1966); A. Brandes, *The Solo Piano Variations of J. B.* (Diss., Boston Univ., 1967); W. Czesla, "Motivischen Mutationen im Schaffen von J. B.," in S. Kross and H. Schmidt, eds., *Colloquium amicorum: Joseph Schmidt-Görg zum 70. Geburtstag* (Bonn, 1967); R. Rittenhouse, *Rhythmic Elements in the Symphonies of J. B.* (Diss., Univ. of Iowa, 1967); J. Wetschky, *Die Kanontechnik in der Instrumentalmusik von J. B.* (Regensburg, 1967); W. Czesla, *Studien zum Finale in der Kammermusik von J. B.* (Diss., Univ. of Bonn, 1968); S. Helms, *Die Melodienbildung in den Liedern von J. B. und ihr Verhältnis zu den Volksliedern und volkstümlichen Weisen* (Bamberg, 1968); J. Horton, *B. Orchestral Music* (London, 1968); R.

Klein, "Die konstruktiven Grundlagen der B.-Symphonien," *Österreichische Musikzeitschrift* XXIII (1968); K. Stahmer, *Musikalische Formung in soziologischem Bezug, dargestellt an der instrumentalen Kammermusik von J. B.* (Diss., Univ. of Kiel, 1968); H.-W. Kulenkampf, "Warum ist B. berühmt? Provokation eines unzeitgemassen Themas," *Neue Zeitschrift für Musik* (Sept. 1969); K. Reinhardt, "Motivisch-Thematisches im *Deutschen Requiem* von B.," *Musik and Kirche*, XXXIX (1969); V. Gotwals, "B. and the Organ," *Music/The A.G.O. Magazine*, IV/4 (1970); S. Helms, "J. B. und das deutsche Kirchenlied," *Der Kirchenmusiker*, XXI (1970); K. Blum, *Hundert Jahre "Ein deutsches Requiem" von J. B.* (Tutzing, 1971); M. Harrison, *The Lieder of B.* (N.Y., 1972); R. Pascall, *Formal Principles in the Music of B.* (Diss., Univ. of Oxford, 1972); E. Sams, *B. Songs* (London, 1972); K. Stahmer, "Korrekturen am B. Bild," *Die Musikforschung* (April–June 1972); C. Floros, ed., *B.-Studien*, 1 (Hamburg, 1974); R. Pascall, "Some Special Uses of Sonata Form by B.," *Soundings*, IV (1974); C. Jacobsen, *Das Verhältnis von Sprache und Musik in ausgewählten Liedern von J. B.* (Hamburg, 1975); R. Jacobson, *The Music of J. B.* (London, 1977); A. Craig Bell, *The Lieder of B.* (Darley, Harrogate, 1979); J. Webster, "The C-sharp minor Version of B.'s op. 60," *Musical Times* (Feb. 1980); J. Dunsby, *Structural Ambiguity in B.* (Ann Arbor, 1981); R. Pascall, "B.'s First Symphony Slow Movement: The Initial Performing Version," *Musical Times* (Oct. 1981); M. Musgrave, "B. the Progressive: Another view," *Musical Times* (May 1983); R. Pascall, "B. and Schubert," *Musical Times* (May 1983).

Brăiloiu, Constantin, Rumanian ethnomusicographer; b. Bucharest, Aug. 25, 1893; d. Geneva, Dec. 20, 1958. He studied in Austria and Switzerland; in 1928 founded the Archive of Folklore in Bucharest; also was a member of ethnomusicological organizations in Geneva and Paris.
WRITINGS: *Esquisse d'une méthode de folklore musical* (Paris, 1930); *La Musique populaire roumaine* (Paris, 1940); *Le Folklore musical* (Zürich, 1948); *Le Rythme aksak* (Paris, 1952); *La Rythmique enfantine* (Brussels, 1956); "Outline of a Method of Musical Folklore" (trans. by M. Mooney; ed. by A. Briegleb and M. Kahane), *Ethnomusicology* (Sept. 1970).
BIBLIOGRAPHY: T. Alexandra, "Constantin Brăiloiu," *Revista de etnografie și foleor* (1968); special Brăiloiu issue of *Cercetări de muzicologie*, II (1970); V. Cosma, *Muzicieni români* (Bucharest, 1970; pp. 75–79).

Brailowsky, Alexander, noted Russian pianist; b. Kiev, Feb. 16, 1896; d. New York, April 25, 1976. After study with his father, a professional pianist, he was taken to Vienna in 1911 and was accepted by Leschetizky as a pupil; made his debut in Paris after World War I; presented a complete cycle of Chopin's works in Paris (1924), and repeated it there several times. He made a highly successful tour all over the world; made his American debut at Aeolian Hall in N.Y., Nov. 19, 1924; made a coast-to-coast tour of the U.S. in 1936; first gave the Chopin cycle in America during the 1937–38 season, in 6 recitals in N.Y.

Brain, Aubrey, English French-horn player; b. London, July 12, 1893; d. there, Sept. 20, 1955. He studied at the Royal College of Music in London; joined the London Symph. Orch.; then played in the BBC Symph. Orch.; retired in 1945. He was appointed prof. at the Royal Academy of Music in 1923, and held this position for 30 years. His father was also a horn player, as was his brother **Alfred** and his son **Dennis.**

Brain, Dennis, English French-horn virtuoso; b. London, May 17, 1921; d. in a automobile accident in Hatfield, Hertfordshire, Sept. 1, 1957. He studied with his father, **Aubrey Brain;** served as first horn player in the Royal Phil., and later with the Philharmonia Orch. He rapidly acquired the reputation of a foremost performer on his instrument. Benjamin Britten's *Serenade* for Tenor, Horn, and Strings was written for Dennis Brain. He was killed when he drove at a high speed, at night, from Birmingham to London, and hit a tree. His death caused a profound shock among English musicians.
BIBLIOGRAPHY: S. Pettit, *Dennis Brain: A Biography* (London, 1976).

Braine, Robert, American composer; b. Springfield, Ohio, May 27, 1896; d. (suicide) New York, Aug. 22, 1940. He studied at the Cincinnati College of Music; acted as radio conductor in N.Y. He composed 3 operas: *The Eternal Light* (1924); *Virginia* (1926); *Diana* (1929); symph. pieces: *S.O.S. and The House of Usher, The Raven* for Baritone and Orch.; *Concerto in Jazz* for Violin and Orch.; *Barbaric Sonata* for Piano; many other piano pieces; also about 50 songs.

Braithwaite, Nicholas, English conductor; son of **Warwick Braithwaite;** b. London, Aug. 26, 1939. He was educated at the Royal Academy of Music in London; later went to Vienna, where he studied with Hans Swarowsky. He served as associate conductor of the Bournemouth Symph. Orch. (1967–70) and as associate principal conductor of the Sadler's Wells Opera (1970–74). From 1976 to 1980 he was music director of the Glyndebourne Touring Opera. In 1980 he was engaged as an assistant to Sir Georg Solti when the London Phil. Orch. made its tour of Japan and South Korea. In 1981 he became chief conductor of the Stora Theater Opera in Göteborg, Sweden.

Braithwaite, Sam Hartley, English composer; b. Egremont, Cumberland, July 20, 1883; d. Arnside, Westmoreland, Jan. 13, 1947. He studied at the Royal Academy of Music; upon graduation, joined its faculty as an instructor. His compositions include *Military Overture* and *A Night by Dalegarth Bridge,* a tone poem.

Braithwaite, Warwick, British conductor; b. Dunedin, New Zealand, Jan. 9, 1896; d. London, Jan. 18, 1971. He studied at the Royal Academy of Music in London; won the Challen Gold Medal and the Battison Hayes Prize. He began his career as a conductor with the O'Mara Opera Co.; then conducted with the British National Opera Co. He was assistant music director of the BBC; then went to its Cardiff studio in Wales as music director; also conducted the Cardiff Musical Society (1924–31). He was a founder of the Welsh National Orch. From 1932 to 1940 he was a conductor at the Sadler's Wells Opera; then he led the Scottish Orch. in Glasgow (1940–46). Later he was a ballet conductor at the Royal Opera, Covent Garden, in London (1950–53); then conducted the National Orch. of New Zealand and served as artistic director of the National Opera of Australia (1954–55). From 1956 to 1960 he was music director of the Welsh National Opera; then was again a conductor at Sadler's Wells until 1968. He publ. *The Conductor's Art* (London, 1952).

Brambach, Caspar Joseph, German composer; b. Oberdollendorf, near Königswinter, July 14, 1833; d. there, June 19, 1902. He studied composition at the Cologne Cons.; then taught there (1858–61); later was active as a teacher and composer in Bonn (1861–69). He wrote many secular cantatas, among them *Trost in Tönen, Das Eleusische Fest, Die Macht des Gesanges, Prometheus,* and *Columbus* (awarded the $1,000 prize at the Milwaukee Festival; performed there July 23, 1886); also an opera, *Ariadne;* concert overture, *Tasso;* Piano Concerto; Piano Sextet; String Sextet; 2 piano quartets; songs.

Brambach, Wilhelm, German musicologist, brother of **Caspar Joseph Brambach;** b. Bonn, Dec. 17, 1841; d. Karlsruhe, Feb. 26, 1932. He studied classical languages and musicology at the Univ. of Bonn; taught philology at the Univ. of Freiburg (1866–72); then was for 32 years librarian of the district library at Karlsruhe (1872–1904).
WRITINGS: *Das Tonsystem und die Tonarten des christlichen Abendlandes im Mittelalter* (Leipzig, 1881); *Die Musikliteratur des Mittelalters bis zur Blüte der Reichenauer Sängerschule* (Karlsruhe, 1883); *Hermanni Contracti musica* (Leipzig, 1884); *Die Verloren geglaubte "Historia de Sancta Afra Martyri" und das "Salve regina" des Hermannus Contractus* (Karlsruhe, 1892); *Gregorianische-bibliographische Lösung der Streitfrage über die Ursprung des Gregorianischen Gesangs* (Leipzig, 1895; 2nd ed., 1901).

Brambilla, Marietta, Italian contralto; b. Cassano d'Adda, June 6, 1807; d. Milan, Nov. 6, 1875. She was a member of a musical family; her 4 sisters were singers. She made her debut in London in 1827; then sang in Italy, Vienna, and Paris. She eventually settled in Milan as a teacher; publ. collections of vocalises.

Brambilla, Paolo, Italian composer; b. Milan, July 9, 1787; d. there, 1838. He wrote 4 operas, produced in Milan and Turin, and 6 ballets for La Scala. He was the father of **Marietta** and **Teresa Brambilla.**

Brambilla, Teresa, Italian opera singer, sister of **Marietta;** b. Cassano d'Adda, Oct. 23, 1813; d. Milan, July 15, 1895. She studied singing at the Milan Cons.; made her debut in 1831 in Milan and traveled through Europe, including Russia. Her appearances at La Scala were highly successful. After several seasons in Paris, she was engaged at the Teatro La Fenice in Venice, where she created the role of Gilda in *Rigoletto* (March 11, 1851).

Brancaccio, Antonio, Italian composer; b. Naples, 1813; d. there, Feb. 12, 1846. He studied at Naples, and produced his first opera, *I Panduri,* during the Carnival of 1843; his other operas included *L'Assedio di Constantina* (Venice, 1844); *Il Puntiglione* (Naples, 1845); *L'Incognita* (Venice, 1846); *Le sarte calabresi* (Naples, 1847; posthumous); *Lilla* (Venice, 1848; posthumous).

Brancour, René, French music critic; b. Paris, May 17, 1862; d. there, Nov. 16, 1948. Educated at the Paris Cons., he became curator of its collection of musical instruments; in 1906 began a course of lectures on esthetics at the Sorbonne; also wrote newspaper criticism. A brilliant writer, he poured invective on the works of composers of the advanced school; his tastes were conservative, but he accepted French music of the Impressionist period. He wrote biographies of Félicien David (1911) and Méhul (1912) in the series Musiciens Célèbres; of Massenet (1923) and Offenbach (1929) in Les Maîtres de la Musique. Other books are *La Vie et l'œuvre de Georges Bizet* (1913); *Histoire des instruments de musique* (1921); *La Marseillaise et le chant du départ;* etc.

Brand, Max, Austrian composer; b. Lemberg, April 26, 1896; d. Langenzersdorf, near Vienna, April 5, 1980. He studied with Franz Schreker at the Vienna Academy of Music. He made use of the 12-tone method of composition as early as 1927, but did not limit himself to it in his later works. His most spectacular work was the opera *Maschinist Hopkins,* to his own libretto, chosen as the best operatic work of the year by the Congress of German Composers, and first produced at Duisburg on April 13, 1929; it was later staged in 37 opera houses in Europe, including Russia; it marked the climactic point of the "machine era" in modern music between the two wars. Brand was also active in the field of experimental musical films in the triple capacity of author, composer, and director. From 1933–38 he remained in Vienna; then went to Brazil; in 1940 arrived in the U.S., becoming an American citizen in 1945. In 1975 he returned to Austria.
WORKS: *Nachtlied,* from Nietzsche's *Also sprach Zarathustra,* for Soprano and Orch. (1922); 3 songs to poems by Lao-Tse (Salzburg Festival, 1923); *Eine Nachtmusik* for Chamber Orch. (1923); String Trio (1923); *Die Wippe,* ballet (1925); *Tragœdietta,* ballet (1926); *5 Ballads,* a study in 12 tones (1927); *Maschinist Hopkins,* opera in 3 acts (1928);

The Chronicle, scenic cantata for Narrator, Soli, Chorus, and Orch. (1938); *Piece for Flute and Piano,* in 12 tones (1940); *Kyrie Eleison,* study in 12 tones for Chorus (1940; perf. by Villa-Lobos, Rio de Janeiro, 1940); *The Gate,* scenic oratorio, with Narrator (N.Y., May 23, 1944); *The Wonderful One-Hoss Shay,* symph. rondo for Orch., after Oliver Wendell Holmes (Philadelphia, Jan. 20, 1950); *Night on the Bayous of Louisiana,* tone poem (1953); *Stormy Interlude,* opera in one act, libretto by the composer (1955). About 1958 Brand became absorbed in electronic music; wrote *The Astronauts, An Epic in Electronics* (1962); *Ilian 1 & 2* (1966); numerous pieces of music for modern plays.

Brand, Oscar, Canadian folksinger and folklorist; b. Winnipeg, Feb. 7, 1920. He was brought to the U.S.; studied at Brooklyn College (B.A. in abnormal psychology, 1942); then served in the U.S. Army (1942–45). Following his discharge, he embarked upon a career as a folksinger; from 1945 was host of his own radio program in N.Y. He contributed informative articles on various aspects of folk music; his writings include *Bawdy Songs and Backroom Ballads* (1959), *Folk Songs for Fun* (1961), *The Ballad Mongers: Rise of the Modern Folksong* (1962), and *When I First Came to This Land* (1975).

Brandeis, Frederick, composer and pianist; b. Vienna, July 5, 1832; d. New York, May 14, 1899. He was a pupil of Carl Czerny; in 1849 settled in the U.S., where he was active as a solo pianist, conductor, and organist. He wrote numerous pieces for military band; a *Romanza* for Oboe and Orch.; a ballade, *The Sunken Cloister* (1882); some chamber music; and a variety of piano works and songs. His style of composition was entirely without distinction.

Brandl, Johann Evangelist, German composer; b. Kloster Rohr, near Regensburg, Nov. 14, 1760; d. Karlsruhe, May 25, 1837. He studied in various religious schools and monasteries as a youth; then decided to devote himself to music, and became proficient as an organist and violinist; was attached to the court of the Archduke of Baden as music director.
WORKS: Operas: *Germania* (1800); *Triumph des Vaterherzens* (Karlsruhe, Jan. 15, 1811); *Omar der Gute* (Karlsruhe, Aug. 24, 1811); *Nanthild, das Mädchen von Valbella* (Karlsruhe, May 19, 1813); a "Grande Symphonie"; Bassoon Concerto; a number of string quartets and string quintets; many songs; oratorios; masses.
BIBLIOGRAPHY: O. Danzer, *J.E. Brandls Leben und Werke* (Leipzig, 1936); F. Leinert, *J.E. Brandl als Lieder- und Kammermusik Komponist* (Wolfenbüttel, 1937).

Brandt, Jobst vom (or **Jodocus de Brant**), German musician; b. Waltersof, near Marktredwitz, Oct. 28, 1517; d. Brand, near Marktredwitz, Jan. 22, 1570. In 1530 he enrolled at Heidelberg Univ.; in 1548 had become Captain of Waldsassen and Administrator of Liebenstein. He was one of the most important composers of the Senfl school; his music is distinguished by deep feeling and a skillful use of counterpoint.
WORKS: 45 *Psalmen und Kirchengesänge* (Eger, 1572–73; preserved in the library of K. Proske); 55 vocal pieces in G. Forster's collection *Ein Auszug guter alter und neuer teutscher Liedlein* (III, Wittenberg, 1549; IV–V, 1556). Reprints are in R. von Liliencron's *Deutsches Leben im Volkslied 1530;* in Jöde's *Chorbuch,* III; in *Kaiserliederbuch für gemischten Chor;* in *Staatliches Jugendliederbuch;* in the *Chorsammlung für gemischten Chor des Arbeitsängerbundes;* in *Monatshefte für Musikgeschichte* (vol. 26); etc.

Brandt, Marianne (real name, **Marie Bischoff**), Austrian contralto; b. Vienna, Sept. 12, 1842; d. there, July 9, 1921. She studied voice in Vienna, and later with Pauline Viardot-Garcia in Baden-Baden (1869–70); she made her debut as Rachel in *La Juive* in Olmütz on Jan. 4, 1867; then sang in Hamburg and at the Berlin Opera (1868–82). In 1872 she appeared in London; made her American debut as Leonore at the Metropolitan Opera in N.Y. on Nov. 19, 1884, and remained on its staff until 1888; she also sang Italian roles in operas by Verdi and Meyerbeer. In 1890 she settled in Vienna as a singing teacher.
BIBLIOGRAPHY: La Mara, *Musikalische Studienköpfe* (Leipzig, 1902).

Brandt, Noah, American composer; b. New York, April 8, 1858; d. San Francisco, Nov. 11, 1925. He studied at the Leipzig Cons. with Ferdinand David (violin) and Jadassohn (theory); toured in Europe and the U.S. as a violinist; finally settled in San Francisco. He was the author of a light opera, *Captain Cook* (San Francisco, Sept. 2, 1895); his other operas, *Wing Wong* and *Daniel,* were not produced.

Brandts-Buys, Jan, composer; b. Zutphen, the Netherlands, Sept. 12, 1868; d. Salzburg, Dec. 7, 1933. He was a pupil of M. Schwarz and A. Urspruch at the Raff Cons. in Frankfurt; lived for a time in Vienna; later settled in Salzburg. His first opera, *Das Veilchenfest* (Berlin, 1909), met with opposition; a 2nd opera, *Das Glockenspiel* (Dresden, 1913), was received more kindly; while a 3rd, *Die drei Schneider von Schönau* (Dresden, April 1, 1916), was quite successful. Subsequent operas were: *Der Eroberer* (Dresden, 1918); *Micarême* (Vienna, 1919); *Der Mann im Mond* (Dresden, 1922); *Traumland* (Dresden, 1927). He also wrote a ballet, *Machinalität* (Amsterdam, 1928); 2 piano concertos; a *Konzertstück* for Cello and Orch.; chamber music; piano pieces; songs.

Brandukov, Anatol, eminent Russian cellist; b. Moscow, Dec. 22, 1856; d. there, Feb. 16, 1930. He studied cello at the Moscow Cons. with Fitzenhagen (1868–77), and also attended Tchaikovsky's classes in harmony. In 1878 he undertook a concert tour of Europe; lived mostly in Paris until 1906. His artistry was appreciated by Tchaikovsky, who dedicated his

Pezzo capriccioso for Cello and Orch. to him; he enjoyed the friendship of Saint-Saëns and Liszt. In 1906 he returned to Moscow, where he was prof. at the Phil. Inst.; from 1921 to 1930 he taught cello at the Moscow Cons. He composed a number of cello pieces and made transcriptions of works by Tchaikovsky, Rachmaninoff, and others.

BIBLIOGRAPHY: L. Ginsburg, *A.A. Brandukov* (Moscow, 1951).

Brannigan, Owen, English bass; b. Annitsford, March 10, 1908; d. there, May 10, 1973. He was educated at the Guildhall School of Music in London. He made his debut in 1943 at the Sadler's Wells Opera, becoming a member of the company (1944–49; 1952–58). He gained fame for creating several roles in the operas of Benjamin Britten. He also distinguished himself as a concert and oratorio singer.

Branscombe, Gena, Canadian-born American educator, chorus leader, and composer; b. Picton, Ontario, Nov. 4, 1881; d. New York, July 26, 1977. She attended the Chicago Musical College, where she studied piano with Rudolf Ganz and composition with Felix Borowski; then went to Berlin, where she took a course with Engelbert Humperdinck. Returning to America, she took conducting lessons with Frank Damrosch and Albert Stoessel; became a U.S. citizen in 1910. In 1935 she organized the Branscombe Chorale, a women's ensemble that she conducted until 1953. She composed mostly choral works, often to her own texts; of these the most notable are *Conventry's Choir, The Phantom Caravan, A Wind from the Sea, Youth of the World,* and *Pilgrims of Destiny,* a choral drama (1928–29). She also composed a symph. suite, *Quebec,* and some 150 songs. Amazingly energetic, she continued to be active until an improbable old age, and at the time of her death she was working on her autobiography.

Brant, Henry Dreyfus, American ultramodern composer and a pioneer of spatial music; b. Montreal, of American parents, Sept. 15, 1913. He learned the rudiments of music from his father, a violinist who taught at the McGill Univ. Conservatorium in Montreal. In 1929 his family moved to N.Y., where Brant studied piano with James Friskin and composition with Leonard Mannes at the Inst. of Musical Art; also took private lessons with Wallingford Riegger (1930–31) and George Antheil (1934–35) and attended classes of Rubin Goldmark at the Juilliard School of Music (1933); in 1938–39 he studied conducting with Fritz Mahler in N.Y. Having absorbed a totality of quaquaversal techniques of composition, he became a teacher; was on the faculty at Columbia Univ. (1945–52), at the Juilliard School of Music (1947–54), and at Bennington College in Vermont (1957–80). In 1982 he settled in Santa Barbara, Calif. He held Guggenheim fellowships in 1946 and 1955. An audacious explorer of sonic potentialities, he draws without prejudice on resources ranging from common objects of everyday American life, such as kitchen utensils and tin cans, to the outermost reaches of euphonious cacophony; he became a pioneer in the field of spatial music, in which the participating instruments are placed at specified points in space, on the stage, on the balcony, and on the aisles. In conducting his spatial music, he developed an appropriate technique, using body language, turnabouts of 90, 135, and 180 degrees to address his instrumentalists, and also resorting to verbal instructions. He is a minor virtuoso on blowing, squeaking, and squealing instruments, excelling on the flageolet, ocarina, and tin whistle. Brant expounded the rationale of spatial music in his article "Space as an Essential Aspect of Musical Composition" in *Contemporary Composers on Contemporary Music,* eds. E. Schwartz and B. Childs (N.Y., 1967). Among his future projects is the construction of a flexible concert hall of plywood parts changing configurations according to acoustical requirements.

WORKS: FOR ORCH.: *Variations* for Chamber Orch. (N.Y., Feb. 7, 1931); Double-bass Concerto (1932); *Angels and Devils* for a merry murmuration of Innumerable Flutes (N.Y., Feb. 6, 1933); *Lyric Piece* (N.Y., Oct. 16, 1933); *Coquette Overture* (1935); *Whoopee in D Major* (1938); *Fishermen's Overture* (1938); *Clarinet Concerto* (1938); *The Great American Goof,* ballet (N.Y., Jan. 11, 1940); Violin Concerto (1940); *Rhapsody* for Viola and Orch. (1940); Saxophone Concerto (1941; N.Y., May 12, 1945); *Downtown Suite* (1942); Symph. in F (1942); Symph. in B-flat (1945; Cincinnati, Nov. 19, 1948); *Dedication in Memory of Franklin D. Roosevelt* (1945); *Statements in Jazz* for Clarinet and Dance Orch. (1945); *Jazz Clarinet Concerto* for Clarinet and Dance Orch. (1946); *The Promised Land: A Symphony of Palestine* (1947); *Street Music* for Wind Instruments and Percussion (1949); *Millennium I* for 8 Trumpets, Chimes, and Glockenspiel (1950); *Sings and Alarms* for Wind Instruments and Percussion (1953); *Millennium II* for Multiple Brass and Percussion (1954); *Conclave* (1955); *Millennium III* for 6 Brass Instruments and Percussion (Bennington, Vt., June 20, 1957); *Millennium IV* for Brass (N.Y., March 2, 1964); *Chanticleer* for Clarinet, Piano, Percussion, and Strings (N.Y., March 9, 1968); *Nomads* for Wordless Text, Brass, and Percussion (Bennington, June 2, 1974).

CHAMBER MUSIC: *Variations* for 4 Instruments (1929); *Partita* for Flute and Piano (1932); *Requiem in Summer* for Woodwind Quintet (1934); *All Souls' Carnival* for Flute, Violin, Cello, Piano, and Accordion (1947); *Galaxy I* for Clarinet, Horn, Vibraphone, and Chimes (1954); *Conversations in an Unknown Tongue* for Strings (1958); *September Antiphonies* for 4 Clarinets and 4 Trumpets (1964); *Consort for True Violins* for Violins of 8 different sizes (1965); *Windjammer* for Woodwind Quintet (N.Y., May 3, 1969); *Crossroads* for 4 Violins (1971; East Hampton, N.Y., May 17, 1975); *Divinity* for Harpsichord and Brass Quintet (N.Y., March 15, 1973); *From Bach's Menagerie* for Saxophone Quartet (1974); *Prevailing Winds* for Woodwind Quintet (Brooklyn, Oct. 5, 1974); Piano Sextet (1976).

FOR VOICE: *Underground Cantata* (1946); *Behold the Earth,* a Requiem cantata (1951); *Ceremony* for

Voices to Wordless Texts and Instruments (N.Y., April 3, 1954); *December* for Speakers, Chorus, and Instruments (Dec. 15, 1964); *Dialogue in the Jungle* for Soprano, Woodwind Quintet, and Brass Quintet (1959; N.Y., May 25, 1964); *Feuerwerk* for Speaker, Fireworks, and Instruments (1961); *Voyage Four* for Wordless Text and Orch. (New Haven, Conn., Jan. 14, 1964); *Vita de Sancto Hieronymo* for Chorus and Instruments (1973); *Solomon's Gardens* for 7 Solo Voices, Chorus, 24 Handbells, and 3 Instruments (N.Y., March 23, 1974); *A Plan of the Air* for Voices, Percussion, and Brass (River Falls, Wis., April 24, 1975); *Long Life,* chorus a cappella "for 84 angels" composed for Nicolas Slonimsky's 83rd birthday (83 + 1, for luck; April 27, 1977).

WORKS FOR NONDESCRIPT ENSEMBLES: *5 & 10 Cent Store Music* for Violin, Piano, and Kitchen Hardware (1932); *Hommage aux frères Marx* for Solo Tin Whistle and other Plebeian Instruments (1938); *Kitchen Music* for Water Glasses, Bottles, and Tin Cans (1946); *Machinations* for an Imaginary Flute in E-flat, Double Flageolet, Double Ocarina, Ceramic Flute, Steel Harp, Organ, Glockenspiel, Xylophone, Chimes, and Timpani (1970); *Solar Moth* for Strings, a lot of Diversified Flutes, Harp, Piano, Marimba, Timpani, and Voice (1979).

SPATIAL WORKS: *Antiphony I* for 5 Synchronized Orch. Groups and 5 Synchronized Conductors (N.Y., Dec. 6, 1953); *Labyrinth* for 2 Synchronized Orchs. (1955); *Encephalograms* for Soprano and 7 Instruments (1955); *On the Nature of Things* for String Orch., Wind Instruments, and Glockenspiel (Bennington, Vt., Aug. 18, 1956); *Grand Universal Circus* for 8 Vocal Soloists, Chorus, and 16 Instruments (N.Y., May 19, 1956); *Hieroglyphics I* for Viola, Timpani, Chimes, Celesta, Harp, Organ, and Voice (1957); *Joquin* (the name of Brant's baby son) for Piccolo and 6 Instruments (1958); *In Praise of Learning* for 16 Sopranos and 16 Percussionists (1958); *Mythical Beasts* for Soprano and 16 Instruments (N.Y., Feb. 10, 1958); *The Children's Hour* for 6 Voices, Chorus, Brass, Organ, and Percussion (1958); *Atlantis* for Voices, Band, and Percussion (Poughkeepsie, N.Y., Jan. 31, 1960); *Quombex* for Viola d'Amore, Music Boxes, and Organ (1960); *The Fire Garden* for High Voice, Chorus, and Chamber Ensemble (1960); *Barricades* for Tenor and 9 Instruments (1961); *Fire in Cities* for Choruses, Orch., and 8 Timpani (1961); *Violin Concerto with Lights,* wherein kaleidoscopically activated beams of light are manipulated by 5 musicians manning (and/or womanning) 5 push buttons (N.Y., April 30, 1961); *Headhunt* for Trombone, Bass Clarinet, Bassoon, Cello, and Percussion (1962); *Odyssey—Why Not?* for Flutes and Orch. (Lausanne, Switzerland, Feb. 13, 1966); *Verticals Ascending* for 2 Separate Instrumental Groups (Pittsburgh, July 7, 1968); *Kingdom Come* for Wordless Text, Stage Orch., Balcony Orch., Sirens, Slide Whistles, Bells, and Buzzers (Oakland, Calif., April 14, 1970); *The Immortal Combat* for 2 Bands (N.Y., June 4, 1972); *Sixty* for 3 Wind Ensembles (New Haven, Conn., Feb. 22, 1974); *Nomads* for Wordless Text, Brass, and Percussion (Bennington, June 2, 1974); *An American Requiem* for 16 Woodwinds, 14 Brass, Percussion, and Church Bells (Mt. Lebanon, Pa., June 8, 1974); *Six Grand Pianos Bash Plus Friends* for 6 Grand Pianos, 3 Piccolos, Trumpet, Trombone, and Percussion (Riverdale, N.Y., Nov. 10, 1974); *Homage to Ives* for Baritone and 3 Orch. Groups (Denver, Feb. 21, 1975); *A Plan of the Air* for Voices, Percussion, and Brass (River Falls, Wis., April 24, 1975); *American Weather* for Voice and Instruments (1976); *American Debate* for Winds and Percussion (1976); *Antiphonal Responses* for 3 Bassoons, Piano, and Instruments (1978); *Cerberus* for Double Bass, Piccolo, Soprano, and Mouth Organ (1978); *Curriculum II* for Orch. Groups (1978); *Trinity of Spheres* for Orch. Groups (1978); *The $1,000,000 Confessions* for Brass Quintet (1978); *Spatial Concerto* for Piano Solo, 16 Women's Voices, and Orch. (Tucson, Ariz., Nov. 16, 1978; Hilde Somer, piano soloist); *Orbits* for 80 Trombones, Organ, and Soprano (1979); *The Glass Pyramid* for Voice, Strings, Winds, 2 Pianos, and Percussion (1980); *The Secret Calendar* for Voice and Instruments (1980); *Meteor Farm* for Orch., Jazz Band, Gamelans, West African Drums, South Indian Singers, and 2 Western Sopranos (Middletown, Conn., March 6, 1982); *Inside Track* for Piano, 2 Small Ensembles, Voice, and Projected Images (1982); *Stern Grove Grand Ceremonial Overtures* for 2 Chamber Orchs., Jazz Drummer, and 3 Karate Martial Artists, one of them being Brant's son Joquin Ives Brant (San Francisco, July 18, 1982); the title was subsequently changed to *Horizontals Extending.*

BIBLIOGRAPHY: David Ewen, *American Composers* (N.Y., 1982).

Brant, Jan, Polish composer and theologian; b. probably in Poznan, 1554; d. Lwow, May 27, 1602. He entered the Jesuit order in 1571; was ordained in 1578; then studied theology in Rome. He returned to Poland in 1584, and subsequently held positions in a number of Polish convents. Some of his MSS were discovered in 1972 in the archives of the Univ. of Uppsala.

BIBLIOGRAPHY: Z. Szweykowski, "Jan Brant (1554–1602) i jego nowo odkryta twórczość muzyczna," *Muzyka,* XVIII/2 (1973).

Branzell, Karin Maria, noted Swedish contralto; b. Stockholm, Sept. 24, 1891; d. Altadena, Calif., Dec. 14, 1974. She studied with Thekla Hofer in Stockholm, with Bachner in Berlin, and with Rosati in N.Y.; made her operatic debut in 1911. From 1912 to 1918 she was a member of the Stockholm Royal Opera; then sang with the Berlin State Opera (1919–23). She made her American debut as Fricka in *Die Walküre* with the Metropolitan Opera in N.Y. on Feb. 6, 1924, and remained on its roster for 20 seasons, retiring in 1944. Possessing a voice of exceptional range and power, she occasionally sang soprano roles. She was active as a voice teacher in N.Y.; in 1969 she moved to California.

Braslau, Sophie, American contralto; b. New York, Aug. 16, 1892; d. there, Dec. 22, 1935. She studied voice with Buzzi-Peccia; made her debut at the Met-

Brassens – Braunfels

ropolitan Opera in *Boris Godunov* (Nov. 26, 1914); was a member of the company until 1921; in 1931 toured Scandinavia and the Netherlands. A large collection of her programs, reviews, and biographical materials was given by the family to the Music Division of the N.Y. Public Library (1938).

Brassens, Georges, French chansonnier; b. Sète (Hérault), Oct. 22, 1921; d. there, Oct. 29, 1981. He began his career as a chansonnier, accompanying himself on the guitar in a repertoire of his own chansons which he called "lyrisme plébéien"; indeed, his texts voice proletarian discontent, as revealed by such titles as *La Mauvaise Réputation, Le Pornographe,* and *Je suis un voyau (I Am a Bum),* calculated to shock the self-contented bourgeoisie. But the Establishment apparently did not recoil from these verbal blows, and in 1967 the Académie Française honored him with a poetry prize. Brassens also wrote a novel, *La Tour des miracles* (Paris, 1953).
BIBLIOGRAPHY: J. Charpentreau, *Georges Brassens et la poésie quotidienne de la chanson* (Paris, 1960); A. Larue, *Brassens, ou La Mauvaise Herbe* (Paris, 1970).

Brassin, Leopold, pianist; b. Strasbourg, May 28, 1843; d. Constantinople, May 1890. He studied music with his brother **Louis Brassin;** was court pianist at Koburg; taught in the Bern Music School, and later in St. Petersburg and Constantinople; wrote concertos and many pieces for piano.

Brassin, Louis, French pianist; b. Aix-la-Chapelle, June 24, 1840; d. St. Petersburg, May 17, 1884. He was a pupil of Moscheles at the Leipzig Cons.; made concert tours with his brothers **Leopold** and **Gerhard;** taught at the Stern Cons. in Berlin (1866); at the Brussels Cons. (1869–79); then at the St. Petersburg Cons. He publ. the valuable *Ecole moderne du piano;* composed 2 piano concertos, salon pieces for piano, and songs. His effective piano transcription of the Magic Fire music from *Die Walküre* is well known.

Braudo, Eugen, Russian music scholar; b. Riga, Feb. 20, 1882; d. Moscow, Oct. 17, 1939. He studied natural science and musicology in Moscow, St. Petersburg, and Germany; in 1914 became a prof. at St. Petersburg Univ.; from 1924 taught at the Moscow Pedagogical Inst. and at the Inst. for Drama and Opera. He wrote a music history (1921–27; 3 vols.); publ. the monographs *E.T.A. Hoffmann* (1921); *A. Borodin* (1922); *Nietzsche, Philosopher and Musician* (1922); *Beethoven* (1927); trans. numerous books on music into Russian.

Brauel, Henning, German composer; b. Hannover, July 1, 1940. He studied piano and composition in Hannover, Salzburg, and Stuttgart; in 1968 he moved to Koblenz. His style is marked by structural cohesion within a framework of freely dissonant counterpoint. His works include *Symphonic Para-*

phrases on a Theme by Paganini (1968); *Notturno* for Bassoon and Chamber Orch. (1969); also 2 string quartets and other chamber music.

Brauer, Evald, Estonian flutist and composer; b. Väinjärve, July 26, 1904; d. Tallinn, Oct. 20, 1961. He studied flute at the Tallinn Cons., and then taught flute there (1935–40). He also publ. a textbook on flute playing in the Estonian language (1939). His compositions are set in an acceptable academic manner, with Estonian motifs lending an air of authenticity. In this ethnically colored idiom he wrote *Estonian Capriccio* for Orch. (1936); a symph. poem, *Mahtra* (1958); overtures and choruses.

Braun, Carl, German bass; b. Meisenheim, Prussia, June 2, 1885; d. Hamburg, April 19, 1960. He studied with Hermann Gausche in Kreuznach and later with Eugen Robert Weiss. He sang at the Wiesbaden Royal Opera (1906–11) and at the Vienna Opera (1911–12); then was engaged at the Berlin City Opera (1912–14). He also appeared at the Bayreuth Festivals (1906–11). In 1912 he made his American debut at the Metropolitan Opera, but was dismissed as an enemy alien in the spring of 1917 when the U.S. entered the war against Germany. In 1922–23 he made a South American tour; also sang in the U.S. in 1928 and 1931. In 1933 he was engaged as a stage director at the German Opera in Berlin, and in 1935–36 held similar posts at the Berlin Volksoper and at the Danzig Municipal Theater. In 1937 he retired from the stage and was thereafter active mainly as a concert agent in Hamburg.

Braun, Peter Michael, German composer; b. Wuppertal, Dec. 2, 1936. He studied in Dortmund; later took courses in Cologne with Frank Martin, Bernd Alois Zimmermann, and Herbert Eimert, and also in Detmold with Giselher Klebe. His musical style is governed by structural considerations; in his varied techniques he applies the resources of "organized sound" as formulated by Varèse, the theory of sets and devices of synthetic *musique concrète.* He wrote *Thesis-Medium* for Piano (1960); *Monophonie* for Electric Guitar (1961–67); *Wind Sextet* (1961); *Transfer* for Orch. (1968).

Braun, Wilhelm. See **Brown, William.**

Braunfels, Walter, German composer; b. Frankfurt, Dec. 19, 1882; d. Cologne, March 19, 1954. He studied piano in Vienna with Leschetizky and composition in Munich with L. Thuille. He became active both as an educator and a composer. From 1913 to 1925 he lived near Munich; in 1925 he became a co-director of the Hochschule für Musik in Cologne. With the advent of the Nazi regime, he was compelled to abandon teaching; from 1933 to 1937 he was in Godesberg; from 1937 to 1945 in Überlingen. He excelled mainly as an opera composer; the following operas are notable: *Prinzessin Brambilla* (Stuttgart, March 25, 1909; revised 1931); *Ulenspiegel* (Stuttgart, Nov. 9, 1913); *Die Vögel,* after Aristophanes (Munich, Dec. 4, 1920; his most successful opera; given also in Berlin and Vienna); *Don Gil* (Munich, Nov. 15, 1924); *Der gläserne Berg* (Cologne, Dec. 4, 1928); *Galathea* (Cologne, Jan. 26, 1930); *Der Traum, Ein Leben* (1937); *Die heilige Johanna* (1942); also a mystery play, *Verkündigung,* after Paul Claudel (1936). He further wrote 2 piano concertos; Organ Concerto; *Revelation of St. John* for Tenor, Double Chorus, and Orch.; piano music and songs. He believed in the artistic and practical value of Wagnerian leading motifs; in his harmonies he was close to Richard Strauss, but he also applied impressionistic devices related to Debussy.

Bravničar, Matija, Slovene composer; b. Tolmin, near Gorica, Feb. 24, 1897. He studied at Gorica; from 1915 to 1918 was in the Austrian army; from 1919 to 1945 was a violinist at the opera theater in Ljubljana; meanwhile he studied composition at the Cons. there, graduating in 1932; was director of the Ljubljana Academy of Music (1945–49) and later taught composition there (1952–68); was president of the Society of Slovene Composers (1949–52) and of the Union of Yugoslavian Composers (1953–57). In his works, Bravničar cultivates a neo-Classical style, with thematic material strongly influenced by the melorhythmic inflections of Slovenian folk music.

WORKS: Opera buffa, *Pohujšanje v dolini Sentflorijanski (Scandal in St. Florian's Valley;* Ljubljana, May 11, 1930); opera, *Hlapec Jernij in njegova pravica (Knight Jernej and His Justice;* Ljubljana, Jan. 25, 1941); a satirical revue, *Stoji, stoji Ljubljanca* (Ljubljana, Dec. 2, 1933); *Hymnus Slavicus* for Orch. (1931; Ljubljana, May 14, 1932); an overture, *Kralj Matjaž (King Mattias;* 1932; Ljubljana, Nov. 14, 1932); *Slavik Dance Burlesques* for Orch. (1932); *Divertissements* for Piano and Strings (1933); *Belokranjska rapsodija* for Orch. (1938); *Simfonič-na antiteza (Symphonic Antithesis;* 1940; Ljubljana, Feb. 9, 1948; also at the Salzburg Festival, June 29, 1952); 3 symphs.: No. 1 (1947; Ljubljana, Feb. 20, 1951); No. 2 (1951; Ljubljana, Oct. 27, 1952); No. 3 (1956); *Kurent,* symph. poem (1950); *Plesne metamorfoze* for Orch. (1955); *Marcia-Rondo* for Orch. (1960); Violin Concerto (1961); Horn Concerto (1963); *Fantasia rapsodica* for Violin and Orch. (1967); *Simfonični plesi (Symphonic Dances;* 1969); *Elegie* for Horn and Piano (1929); 2 wind quintets (1930, 1968); Trio for Flute, Clarinet, and Bassoon (1930); *Dialog* for Cello and Piano (1965); Sonata for Solo Violin (1966); piano pieces.

Bream, Julian, noted English guitarist and lutenist; b. London, July 15, 1933. He was educated at the Royal College of Music in London; made his debut at the age of 17. In 1960 he founded the Julian Bream Consort; also directed the Semley Festival of Music and Poetry from 1971. Through his numerous concerts and recordings he has helped to revive interest in Elizabethan lute music. He was named an Officer of the Order of the British Empire in 1964.

Breazul, George, Rumanian musicologist; b. Ol-

tenien, Sept. 26, 1887; d. Bucharest, Aug. 3, 1961. He studied at the Bucharest Cons. with Castaldi and Kiriac, and in Berlin with Hornbostel, Sachs, Stumpf, Schünemann, and Johannes Wolf. Upon returning to Bucharest, he organized a phonograph archive; publ. numerous articles dealing with Rumanian folklore. A Festschrift, in Rumanian, was publ. in his honor in 1966.

Brecher, Gustav, conductor and editor; b. Eichwald, near Teplitz, Bohemia, Feb. 5, 1879; d. Ostend, May 1940. His family moved to Leipzig in 1889, and he studied there with Jadassohn. His first major work, the symph. poem *Rosmersholm,* was introduced by Richard Strauss at a Liszt-Verein concert in Leipzig (1896); Brecher made his debut as a conductor there (1897); was vocal coach and occasional conductor of operas in Leipzig (1898); conducted in Vienna (1901); served as first Kapellmeister in Olmütz (1902), in Hamburg (1903), and Cologne (1911–16); then went to Frankfurt (1916–24) and Leipzig (1924–33). He committed suicide with his wife aboard a boat off the Belgian coast while attempting to flee from the advancing Nazi troops. His compositions include a symph. fantasia, *Aus unserer Zeit.* He was the author of several essays: *Über die veristische Oper; Analysen zu Werken von Berlioz und Strauss;* and *Über Operntexte und Opernübersetzungen* (1911).

Brecknock, John, English tenor; b. Long Eaton, Nov. 29, 1937. He received his vocal training in Birmingham; then joined the chorus of the Sadler's Wells Opera; in 1967 he appeared in a minor role there, soon rising to prominence as one of its principal members; also sang at Covent Garden, London, the Scottish National Opera, and the Glyndebourne Festival. He made his American debut with the Metropolitan Opera in N.Y. on March 23, 1977, as Tamino in *Die Zauberflöte.* He was especially praised for his performances of the early 19th-century Italian operatic repertoire.

Bredemeyer, Reiner, East German composer; b. Velez, Colombia, of German parents, Feb. 2, 1929. He studied composition with Karl Höller at the Akademie der Tonkunst in Munich (1949–53); then moved to East Germany, where he took courses with Wagner-Régeny at the Akademie der Künste in East Berlin (1955–57). In 1961 he was appointed conductor of the German Theater in East Berlin; in 1978 joined the faculty of the Akademie der Künste in East Berlin. In his own music he is an astute experimenter, but he adheres to the tenets of classical forms and avoids the extremes of modernism.

WORKS: FOR THE STAGE: *Leben der Andrea,* short opera after Brecht's *Galilei* (1971); *Die Galoschenoper,* after *The Beggar's Opera* (1978). FOR ORCH.: *Integration* (1961); *Variante* (1962); Violin Concerto (1963); *Komposition* for 56 Strings (1964); *Spiel* (1964); *Schlagstück 3* for Orch. and 3 Percussion Groups (1966); *Bagatellen für B.* for Piano and Orch. (1970); *Spiel zu 45* (1970); *Piano und . . .,* Piano Concerto (1972); *Oktoberstück* (1973); Symph. (1974);

Anfangen—aufhören (1974); Double Concerto for Harpsichord, Oboe, and Orch. (1974); *2 Tempi* for Flute, Recorder, and Strings (1976); *Auftakte* for 3 Orch. Groups (1976); Concerto for Oboe and Strings (1977); *4 Pieces* (1979). CHAMBER MUSIC: Quintet for Flute, Clarinet, Violin, Cello, and Double Bass (1956); Concertino for 12 (1957); Octet (1959); 2 quintets for Woodwinds (1959, 1969); *Schlagstück 1* for Solo Percussionist (1960); String Quartet (1961); String Quintet (1962); *5 Pieces* for Oboe and 3 Bassoons (1964); *Schlagstück 2* for Piano and Percussion (1965); *6 Serenades* for various instrumental combinations (1966–80); *Pointing* for 18 String Instruments (1966); Sonata for Violin, Viola, and Piano (1967); *Schlagquartett* for Piano, Double Bass, and 2 Percussionists (1967); *String Quartet 1968* (1968); *Schlagstück 5* for Piano and Percussion (1970); *Ab 14* for Piano and 13 String Instruments (1971); *(Cello)²* for Cello and Tape (1971); *8 Pieces* for String Trio (1971); 6 *Solos* for various Instruments (1973–80); *(Oboe)²* for Oboe and Tape (1975); *Grosses Duet* for 2 Instrumental Groups (1975); *Piano und ...⁵* for Piano, Flute, Horn, Trombone, Cello, and Double Bass (1976); *Interludium* for Soprano Saxophone, Flute, Cello, Double Bass, and Percussion (1977); *Piano und ...⁶* for Piano, 2 Cellos, Wind Instrument, and 3 Percussionists (1977); *5 Blechstücke* for 2 Trumpets and 2 Trombones (1979); *D für Paul Dessau* for 15 String Instruments (1980); Sextet (1980). FOR VOICE: *Cantata* for Alto and Female Choir (1961); *Wostock* for Choir and Orch. (1961); *Karthago* for Chorus and Chamber Ensemble (1961); *Sätze und Sentenzen* for Chorus and Orch. (1963); *Canto* for Alto, Male Chorus, and 10 Instruments (1965); *Synchronisiert-Asynchron* for Soprano, Oboe, Bassoon, Cello, Piano, Percussion, and Tape (1975); *Zum 13. 7. (Für Schönberg),* commemorative dedication on the 25th anniversary of Schoenberg's death, for Female Voice, Clarinet, Saxophone, and Percussion (1976); *Cantata 2* for 16 Voices and 16 Instruments (1977); *Madrigal, Rezitativ und Arie* for Tenor and 8 Instruments (1979); *Das Alltägliche* for Soprano, Tenor, and Orch. (1980); songs; piano pieces.
BIBLIOGRAPHY: Ursula Stürzbecher, *Komponisten in der DDR: 17 Gespräche* (Hildesheim, 1979).

Brediceanu, Tiberiu, Rumanian composer; b. Lugoj, Transylvania, April 2, 1877; d. Bucharest, Dec. 19, 1968. He studied music mainly in Rumania; was a founding member of the Rumanian Opera and National Theater in Cluj (1919) and the Society of Rumanian Composers in Bucharest (1920); later became director of the Astra Cons. in Brasov (1934–40) and director-general of the Rumanian Opera (1941–44). He publ. valuable collections of Rumanian songs and dances, including 170 Rumanian folk melodies, 810 tunes of the Banat regions, and 1,000 songs of Transylvania.
WORKS: Operas: *Poemul muzical etnografic* (1905; revised and retitled *Romania in port, joc si cintec,* 1929); *La şezătoare* (1908); *Seara mare,* lyric scene (1924); *Învierea,* a pantomime (1932); *La sece-*

riş (1936); *4 Symphonic Dances* (1951); 2 suites for Violin and Piano (1951); piano pieces; songs.

Bree, Jean Bernard van (Johannes Bernardus van), Dutch violinist and composer; b. Amsterdam, Jan. 29, 1801; d. there, Feb. 14, 1857. He was a pupil of Bertelman; in 1820–21 he played in the orch. of the Théâtre Français in Amsterdam; in 1830 he became conductor of the Felix Meritis Society; in 1841 he founded the Cecilia Society in Amsterdam; later became director of the Music School of the Society for the Promotion of Music.
WORKS: Operas: *Sappho* (in Dutch; Amsterdam, March 22, 1834); *Le Bandit* (in French; Amsterdam, Dec. 22, 1835); *Nimm dich in Acht* (in German; 1845); also 2 melodramas; several masses; cantatas; overtures; chamber music.
BIBLIOGRAPHY: H. Beijermann, *Jean Bernard van Bree* (1857).

Brehm, Alvin, American composer; b. New York, Feb. 8, 1925. He studied at the Juilliard School of Music and Columbia Univ.; also took lessons with Wallingford Riegger. A professional double-bass player, Brehm participates in chamber music concerts in N.Y. whenever a difficult part for the instrument is in the score. Among his compositions, a Divertimento for Brass Trio is often performed. His "extended overture," *Hephaestus* (N.Y., Nov. 22, 1966), was favorably received. He also wrote a set of variations for unaccompanied cello, a piece for bassoon and percussion, and a song cycle for voice and 10 instruments, to poems of García Lorca.

Brehme, Hans, German composer; b. Potsdam, March 10, 1904; d. Stuttgart, Nov. 10, 1957. He studied piano in Berlin with Wilhelm Kempff; taught at Stuttgart and elsewhere. A highly diligent composer, he wrote music in many genres; the idiom of his compositions is fundamentally Classical, with a generous admixture of moderately modern harmonies. He wrote an opera, *Der Uhrmacher von Strassburg* (1941); operetta, *Versiegelten Bürgermeister* (1944); 2 symphs.; 2 piano concertos; Flute Concerto; Sextet for Flute, Clarinet, Horn, Violin, Viola, and Cello; Clarinet Quintet; Saxophone Sonata; *Triptycon* for Orch., on a theme by Handel (highly successful); several works for Accordion.
BIBLIOGRAPHY: Karl Laux, *Musik und Musiker der Gegenwart* (Essen, 1949).

Bréhy, Hercule, Belgian organist and composer; b. Brussels (baptized, Sept. 13), 1673; d. there, (buried, Feb. 28) 1737. He was active as an organist in Brussels; from 1705 until his death he was singing master at Ste. Gudule. His works include masses, motets, and Lamentations.

Breil, Joseph Carl, American composer; b. Pittsburgh, June 29, 1870; d. Los Angeles, Jan. 23, 1926. He studied voice in Milan and Leipzig, and for a time sang in various opera companies. He was the composer of one of the earliest motion picture scores,

Queen Elizabeth (Chicago, 1912); wrote words and music for the comic operas *Love Laughs at Locksmiths* (Portland, Maine, Oct. 27, 1910); *Prof. Tattle* (1913); and *The Seventh Chord* (1913). His serious opera, *The Legend,* was produced by the Metropolitan Opera on March 12, 1919. His opera *Asra* (after Heine) had a single performance, in Los Angeles (Nov. 24, 1925).

BIBLIOGRAPHY: E.E. Hipsher, *American Opera and Its Composers* (Philadelphia, 1927; pp. 87–90).

Breitengraser, Wilhelm, German composer; b. Nuremberg, c.1495; d. there (buried, Dec. 23), 1542. He studied at the Univ. of Leipzig; then was active as a teacher and musician in Nuremberg. His works include masses, Psalms, and hymns.

BIBLIOGRAPHY: R. Wagner, "Wilhelm Breitengraser: Die Nürnberger Kirchen- und Schulmusik seiner Zeit," *Die Musikforschung,* II (1949).

Breithaupt, Rudolf Maria, German pianist, pedagogue, and music scholar; b. Braunschweig, Aug. 11, 1873; d. Ballenstedt, April 2, 1945. He studied jurisprudence, philosophy, and musicology before he began taking piano lessons with Teichmüller at the Leipzig Cons.; then went to Berlin and was appointed piano teacher at the Stern Cons. there. He publ. valuable studies on piano playing: *Die natürliche Klaviertechnik* (Leipzig, 1905; in French, Paris, 1923); *Die Grundlagen der Klaviertechnik* (Leipzig, 1906; in French, 1908; in Eng., 1909; in Russian, 1929); *Praktische Studien* (1916–21). He also publ. *Musikalische Zeit und Streitfragen* (Berlin, 1906).

Breitkopf & Härtel, important German firm of book and music publishers. As an established printing firm in Leipzig, it was bought in 1745 by **Bernhard Christoph Breitkopf** (b. Klausthal Harz, March 2, 1695; d. Leipzig, March 23, 1777). His son, **Johann Gottlob Immanuel** (b. Nov. 23, 1719; d. Jan. 28, 1794), entered the business in 1745; it was his invention which made the basis for the firm's position in the publication of music. In 1756 he devised a font with much smaller division of the musical elements, and this greatly reduced the cost of printing chords (and hence piano music). The firm soon began to issue numerous piano reductions of popular operas for amateur consumption. The earliest music publications, such as the *Berlinische Oden und Lieder* (3 vols., 1756, 1759, 1763), were made by Johann Gottlob Immanuel Breitkopf himself, and bore the imprint "Leipzig, Druckts und Verlegts Johann Gottlob Immanuel Breitkopf"; from 1765–77 the firm name appears as "Bernhard Christoph Breitkopf und Sohn"; from 1777–87 (after Christoph's death) Johann's name again appears alone; his second son, **Christoph Gottlob** (b. Leipzig, Sept. 22, 1750; d. there, April 4, 1800), joined the firm in 1787; from 1787–95 publications were issued as "im Breitkopfischen Verlage" (or Buchhandlung, or Musikhandlung); in 1795 (the year after Immanuel's death) Christoph Gottlob Breitkopf took as his partner his close friend **Gottfried Christoph Härtel** (b. Schneeburg, Jan. 27, 1763; d. near Leipzig, July 25, 1827); since

1795 the firm has been known as Breitkopf und Härtel, although no Breitkopf has been actively associated with the firm since Christoph Gottlob's death in 1800. Härtel's tremendous energy revitalized the firm. He added a piano factory; founded the important periodical *Allgemeine musikalische Zeitung* (1798; editor, J.F. Rochlitz); introduced pewter in place of the harder copper for engraving music; used Senefelder's new lithographic process for either title pages or music where suitable; issued so-called "complete" editions of the works of Mozart, Haydn, Clementi, and Dusek. The firm also began the practice of issuing catalogues with thematic indexes and keeping stocks of scores. From 1827–35 **Florenz Härtel** was head of the firm; **Hermann Härtel** (b. Leipzig, April 27, 1803; d. there, Aug. 4, 1875) and his brother, **Raimund Härtel** (b. Leipzig, June 9, 1810; d. there, Nov. 9, 1888), together dominated the book business of Leipzig (and thus all Germany) for many years; the sons of two sisters of Raimund and Hermann, **Wilhelm Volkmann** (b. Halle, June 12, 1837; d. Leipzig, Dec. 24, 1896) and **Dr. Oskar von Hase** (b. Jena, Sept. 15, 1846; d. Leipzig, Jan. 26, 1921), succeeded them. After Wilhelm Volkmann's death, his son, **Dr. Ludwig Volkmann** (1870–1947), headed the firm jointly with von Hase; von Hase's son, **Hermann** (1880–1945), entered the firm in 1904 and was a co-partner from 1910–14. Hermann von Hase publ. essays tracing the relation of J. Haydn, C.P.E. Bach, and J.A. Hiller to the firm; in 1915 he became a partner in the book business of K.F. Koehler. His brother **Dr. Hellmuth von Hase** (b. Jan. 30, 1891; d. Wiesbaden, Oct. 18, 1979) became director of the firm in 1919. The old house was destroyed during the air bombardment of Dec. 4, 1943; it was rebuilt after the war. In 1950 Dr.von Hase moved to Wiesbaden, where he established an independent business, reclaiming the rights for the firm in West Germany. Important enterprises of the firm throughout its existence are editions of Bach, Beethoven, Berlioz, Brahms, Chopin, Gluck, Grétry, Handel, Haydn, Lassus, Liszt, Mendelssohn, Mozart, Palestrina, Schein, Schubert, Schumann, Schütz, Victoria, and Wagner. The German government supported the publication by Breitkopf & Härtel of the two series of Denkmäler Deutscher Tonkunst (1892–1931 and 1900–1931). Other publications of the firm are: *Der Bär,* yearbook (since 1924); *Katalog des Archivs von Breitkopf und Härtel,* edited by Dr. F.W. Hitzig (2 vols., 1925–26); *Allgemeine musikalische Zeitung* (weekly; 1798–1848 and 1863–65); *Monatshefte für Musikgeschichte* (1869–1905); *Mitteilungen des Hauses Breitkopf und Härtel* (1876–1940; resumed in 1950); *Vierteljahrsschrift für Musikwissenschaft* (1869–1906); *Zeitschrift der Internationlen Musikgesellschaft* (monthly; Oct. 1899–Sept. 1914); *Sammelbände der Internationalen Musikgesellschaft* (quarterly; 1899–1914); *Korrespondenzblatt des Evangelischen Kirchengesangvereins für Deutschland* (monthly; 1886–1922); *Zeitschrift für Musikwissenschaft* (monthly; 1919–35); *Archiv für Musikforschung* (1936–43).

BIBLIOGRAPHY: B. Brook, ed., *The Breitkopf Thematic Catalogue . . . 1762–1787* (N.Y., 1966); R. Elvers, ed., *Breitkopf & Härtel 1719–1969. Ein his-*

torischer Überblick zum Jubiläum (Wiesbaden, 1968); I. Hempel, ed., *Pasticcio auf das 250 jahrige Bestehen des Verlages B. & H.* (Leipzig, 1968); Hase, O. von, *B. & H. Gedenkschrift und Arbeitsbericht* (3 vols.: I, 1542–1827; II, 1828–1918; III, 1918–68; Wiesbaden, 1968); R. Elvers, "B. & H.s Verlagsarchiv," *Fontes Artis Musicae* (Jan.–Aug. 1970).

Brel, Jacques, Belgian-born French singer and songwriter; b. Brussels, April 8, 1929; d. Paris, Oct. 9, 1978. He rose to fame in France in the 1950s as a singer and songwriter of popular music, which emphasized such themes as unrequited love, loneliness, death, and war. In 1967 he quit the concert stage and turned to the theater, as a producer, director, and actor. In 1968 the composer Mort Shuman brought Brel's songs to Broadway in his musical *Jacques Brel Is Alive and Well and Living in Paris.* The title proved ironic; stricken with cancer, Brel abandoned his career in 1974 and made his home in the Marquesas Islands; in 1977 he returned to Paris to record his final album, *Brel;* then died.

Brelet, Gisèle, French musicologist and pianist; b. Fontenay-le-Comte, Vendée, March 6, 1915; d. Sèvres, June 21, 1973. She studied piano at the Nantes Cons. and at the Paris Cons.; also took courses in biology and philosophy at the Sorbonne (Ph.D., 1949). In 1950 she became director of the Bibliothèque Internationale de Musicologie. She wrote the important studies *Esthétique et création musicale* (Paris, 1947); *Le Temps musical* (Paris, 1949); and *L'Interprétation créatrice* (Paris, 1951).

Brema, Marie (real name, **Minny Fehrman**), English mezzo-soprano of German-American parentage; b. Liverpool, Feb. 28, 1856; d. Manchester, March 22, 1925. She studied singing with Georg Henschel; made her concert debut in London performing Schubert's *Ganymed* on Feb. 21, 1891, under the name of **Bremer** (her father being a native of Bremen). In 1894 she sang at the Bayreuth Festival, the first English singer to be so honored. On Nov. 27, 1895, she appeared as Brangäne in *Tristan und Isolde* at the Metropolitan Opera in N.Y., and remained on its roster through the 1895–96 season. Returning to England, she taught singing at the Royal Manchester College of Music.

Brémond, François, French horn player and pedagogue; b. Nîmes, Nov. 1, 1844; d. Houilles, near Paris, July 15, 1925. He studied at the Paris Cons. with J.-B. Mohr, winning a premier prix in 1869. In 1878–88 he was principal horn of the Société des Concerts du Conservatoire in Paris; was also principal horn of the orch. at the Opéra-Comique. In 1891 he joined the faculty of the Paris Cons. He preferred to play the natural horn but in later years took up the valve horn as well.

Brendel, Alfred, eminent Austrian pianist; b. Wiesenberg, Moravia, Jan. 5, 1931. His principal teacher was Edwin Fischer; he also took some piano lessons with Paul Baumgartner, and later with Eduard Steuermann; he studied composition with Michl. He made his concert debut in Graz in 1948; then began a successful career in Europe. He played for the first time in America in 1963; also toured in South America, Japan, and Australia. He is particularly distinguished as an interpreter of the Vienna classics; but he also included in his active repertoire Schoenberg's difficult Piano Concerto. In May 1983 he presented in N.Y. a cycle of 7 concerts of the complete piano sonatas of Beethoven. He publ. *Musical Thoughts and Afterthoughts* (London, 1976; 2nd ed., 1982).

Brendel, Karl Franz, German writer on music; b. Stolberg, Nov. 26, 1811; d. Leipzig, Nov. 25, 1868. He was educated at the univs. of Leipzig and Berlin: studied piano with Wieck and through him entered the Schumann circle; edited Schumann's periodical *Neue Zeitschrift für Musik* from 1845 until his death in 1868; also was co-editor, with R. Pohl, of the monthly *Anregungen für Kunst.* In 1846 he joined the faculty of the Leipzig Cons.; was also one of the founders, in 1861, of the Allgemeiner Deutscher Musikverein. In his articles he boldly championed the cause of the new German music, as symbolized by the works of Wagner and Liszt. He publ. a successful general music history, *Geschichte der Musik in Italien, Deutschland und Frankreich von den ersten christlichen Zeiten bis auf die Gegenwart* (1852; 7th ed., ed. by Kienzl, 1888; new augmented ed., ed. by R. Hövker, 1902, and reissued in 1906); also publ. a treatise commenting on "the music of the future," *Die Musik der Gegenwart und die Gesamtkunst der Zukunft* (1854), and other similar publications dealing with new developments in German music.

Brendler, (Frans Fredric) Eduard, German-born Swedish flutist and composer; b. Dresden, Nov. 4, 1800; d. Stockholm, Aug. 16, 1831. He made his debut as a flutist in Stockholm when he was 10; later pursued a commercial career while continuing his interest in music. In 1823 he became a flutist in the Harmonisk Sällskap orch. His works include instrumental and choral pieces. His opera, *Ryno,* was completed by Prince Oscar in 1832 and was first performed at the Royal Opera in 1834. His early death was regretted by his admirers in Sweden.

Brenet, Michel (real name, **Marie Bobillier**), French musicologist; b. Lunéville, April 12, 1858; d. Paris, Nov. 4, 1918. After living in Strasbourg and Metz, she made her home in Paris from 1871.
WRITINGS: *Histoire de la symphonie à orchestre depuis ses origines jusqu'à Beethoven* (1882); *Grétry, Sa vie et ses œuvres* (1884); *Deux Pages de la vie Berlioz* (1889); *Jean d'Okeghem* (1893); *La Musique dans les processions* (1896); *Sébastien de Brossard* (1896); *La Musique dans les couvents de femmes* (1898); *Claude Goudimel* (1898); *Notes sur l'histoire du luth en France* (1899); *Les Concerts en France sous l'ancien régime* (1900); *Additions inédites de Dom Jumilhac à son traité* (1902); *La Jeu-*

nesse de Rameau (1903); *Palestrina* (1906, in Les Maîtres de la Musique; 3rd ed., 1910); *La Plus Ancienne Méthode française de musique* (1907); *Haydn* (1909, in Les Maîtres de la Musique; in English, 1926); *Les Musiciens de la Sainte-Chapelle: Documents inédits* (1910); *Musique et musiciens de la vieille France* (1911); *Handel* (1912, in Musiciens Célèbres); *La Musique militaire* (1917); *Dictionnaire pratique et historique de la musique* (posthumous; completed by A. Gastoué, Paris, 1926); valuable essays and articles in the *Grande Encyclopédie, Rivista Musicale Italiana,* and the *Musical Quarterly.*
BIBLIOGRAPHY: L. de La Laurencie, "Michel Brenet," *Bulletin de la Société française de Cologne* (1919, no. 4).

Brent, Charlotte, English soprano; b. c.1735; d. London, April 10, 1802. She studied with Arne; made her operatic debut in his *Eliza* at the Smock Alley Theatre in Dublin on Nov. 29, 1755; then sang at London's Drury Lane Theatre and at Covent Garden. She was noted for her performances of Polly in the *Beggar's Opera* and for corresponding roles in Handel's operas.

Brent-Smith, Alexander, English composer; b. Brookthorpe, Gloucestershire, Oct. 8, 1889; d. there, July 3, 1950. After the completion of his studies, he devoted himself to a pedagogical career. His works consist mainly of choral pieces and concertos for various instruments.

Brenta, Gaston, Belgian composer; b. Brussels, June 10, 1902; d. there, May 30, 1969. He studied music theory with Paul Gilson; in 1925, he and 7 other pupils of Gilson formed the Belgian "Groupe des Synthétistes," advocating a more modern approach to composition. From 1931 he was associated with the Belgian Radio, and from 1953 to 1967 he was music director of the French Services there. His music follows the traditions of cosmopolitan romanticism, with exotic undertones.
WORKS: Opera, *Le Khâdi dupé* (Brussels, 1929); 2 radio dramas: *Aucassin et Nicolette* (1934) and *Heracles* (1955); 3 full ballets: *Zo'har* (1928); *Florilège de Valses* (1940); *Candide* (1955); *Le Bal chez la Lorette* (1954), which forms a part of *Les Bals de Paris,* a large ballet consisting of passages contributed by several Belgian composers; oratorio, *La Passion de Notre-Seigneur* (1949). He also wrote *Variations sur un thème congolais* for Orch. (1926); Nocturne for Orch. (1934); *Arioso et Moto Perpetuo* for Orch. (1940); *War Music* for Orch. (1946); Symph. (1946); *In Memoriam Paul Gilson* for Orch. (1950); *Farandole Burlesque* for Orch. (1951); 2 piano concertos (1952, 1968); Concertino for Trumpet, Strings, and Timpani (1958); *Saxiana,* concertino for Saxophone, Strings, Timpani, and Piano (1962); *Airs variés pour de belles écouteuses (Various Tunes for Beautiful Listeners)* for Bassoon and String Orch. (1963); *Pointes sèches de la Belle Epoque* for Piano and String Orch. (1964); *Matinée d'été (Summer Morning)* for Orch. (1967); *Marche*

barbare for Piano (1926); *Impromptu* for Piano (1926); *Etude de Concert* for Piano (1931); String Quartet (1939); *Melopée* for Violin and Piano (1945); *Le Soldat fanfaron (The Boastful Soldier),* suite for Quintet (1952); Concertino for 5 Winds, Double Bass, Piano, and Percussion (1963); songs and choruses.

Brescianello, Giuseppe Antonio, Italian violinist and composer; b. probably in Florence, c.1690; d. Stuttgart, Oct. 4, 1758. He became a violinist at the Munich court in 1715; in 1716 he was made music director and master of the chamber music concerts at the Stuttgart court; was named chief Kapellmeister in 1717; in 1731 he was appointed Oberkapellmeister. He composed an opera, *La Tisbe* (1717–18); 2 cantatas; various instrumental pieces.
BIBLIOGRAPHY: J. Mitchell, *The Works of G.A. Brescianello* (Diss., Univ. of North Carolina, 1962).

Bresgen, Cesar, German composer; b. Florence (of German parents), Oct. 16, 1913. He studied composition with Haas in Munich; in 1939 he went to Salzburg, where he taught at the Mozarteum. After the war he devoted himself mainly to teaching. In his compositions he cultivates the spirit of pragmatic communication; his musical fairy tales and school operas have become widely known; among them the most successful are *Der Igel als Brautigam* (1950); *Brüderlein Hund* (1953); *Der Mann im Mond* (1958); short operas: *Die Freier* (1936); *Dornröschen* (1939); *Das Urteil des Paris* (1943); *Paracelsus* (1943); scenic cantatas: *Der ewige Arzt* (1955); *Salzburger Passion* (1966); Chamber Concerto for 8 Solo Instruments (1934); Concerto for 2 Pianos (1936); Chamber Concerto for Guitar and Small Orch. (1962); Wind Quintet (1964); numerous choral works for school performance. Bresgen has published articles and valuable collections of Austrian folk songs.
BIBLIOGRAPHY: D. Larese, *Cesar Bresgen* (Amriswil, 1968); R. Luck, *Gespräche mit Cesar Bresgen* (Vienna, 1975).

Breslaur, Emil, German music teacher and writer on music; b. Kottbus, May 29, 1836; d. Berlin, July 26, 1899. He studied at the Stern Cons. in Berlin (1863–67); taught at Kullak's Academy (1868–79); from 1863 was choirmaster at the Berlin Reformed Synagogue. A music teachers society founded by him in 1879 developed in 1886 into the Deutscher Musiklehrer-Verband. He was editor of the *Klavierlehrer,* and the author of several important works on piano playing: *Die technischen Grundlagen des Klavierspiels* (1874); *Führer durch die Klavierunterrichts-Literatur* (1887); *Zur methodischen Übung des Klavierspiels; Der entwickelnde Unterricht in der Harmonielehre; Über die schädlichen Folgen des unrichtigen Übens.* He also composed choral works, piano pieces, and songs.

Bresnick, Martin, American composer; b. New York, Nov. 13, 1946. He studied with Arnold Franchetti at the Hartt College of Music in Hartford, Conn., and with Leland Smith and John Chowning at Stanford Univ.; received a Fulbright fellowship for study in Vienna (1969–70); there he took courses in composition with Gottfried von Einem and Friedrich Cerha.

WORKS: Trio for 2 Trumpets and Percussion (1966); String Quartet (1968); *PCOMP*, a computer composition (Vienna, April 8, 1970); *Ocean of Storms* for Orch. (1970); also music for films, including a computer score for the film *Pour* (Prague, March 5, 1970).

Bressler-Gianoli, Clotilde, operatic contralto; b. Geneva (of Italian parents), June 3, 1875; d. there, May 12, 1912. She received her primary training at the Geneva Cons.; then enrolled at the Milan Cons., where she studied singing with Sangiovanni, Giocosa, and Ronconi. She made her operatic debut at the age of 19 in Geneva in *Samson et Dalila;* later sang at La Scala in Milan, at the Opéra-Comique in Paris, and with the San Carlo Co. at New Orleans. Her best roles were Carmen and Mignon.

Bret, Gustave, French organist and composer; b. Brignoles, Aug. 30, 1875; d. Fréjus, April 16, 1969. He studied with Widor and d'Indy in Paris; wrote music criticism. He composed mostly church music.

Bretan, Nicolae, remarkable Rumanian composer; b. Năsăud, April 6, 1887; d. Cluj, Dec. 1, 1968. He studied at the Cons. of Cluj, composition and singing with Farkas and violin with Gyémánt (1906–8); then at the Vienna Academy of Music (1908–9) and at the Magyar Királyi Zeneakademia in Budapest (1909–12) with Siklos (theory) and Szerémi (violin). His primary career was that of an opera singer, performing baritone parts at the opera houses in Bratislava, Oradea, and Cluj between 1913 and 1944, also acting as a stage director. At the same time he surprisingly asserted himself as a composer of operas and lieder in an effective veristic manner, marked by a high degree of professional expertise and considerable originality.

WORKS: One-act operas: *Luceafărul* (*The Evening Star;* in Rumanian; trans. by the composer into Hungarian and German; Cluj, Feb. 2, 1921); *Golem* (in Hungarian; trans. by the composer into Rumanian and German; Cluj, Dec. 23, 1924); *Eroii de la Rovine* (in Rumanian; Cluj, Jan. 24, 1935); *Horia* (in Rumanian; also trans. into German by the composer; Cluj, Jan. 24, 1937); *Arald* (in Rumanian; 1939); *Requiem;* mystery play, *An Extraordinary Seder Evening* (in Hungarian; also trans. into Eng.); *Mein Liederland,* about 230 songs to Rumanian, Hungarian, and German words.

Bretón y Hernández, Tomás, Spanish opera composer; b. Salamanca, Dec. 29, 1850; d. Madrid, Dec. 2, 1923. As a youth he played in restaurants and theaters; graduated from the Madrid Cons. (1872); conducted at the Madrid Opera; in 1901 joined the faculty of the Madrid Cons. A fertile composer, he contributed greatly to the revival of the zarzuela. He was at his best in the one-act comic type (*género chico*). Among his operas and zarzuelas (all produced in Madrid) are: *Los amantes de Teruel* (1889); *Juan Garín* (1892); *La Dolores* (1895); *El Domingo de Ramos* (1896); *La Verbena de la Paloma* (1894); *Raquel* (to his own libretto; Jan. 20, 1900); *El caballo del señorito* (1901); *Farinelli* (1903); *Tabaré* (1913). He also wrote an oratorio, *Apocalipsia* (Madrid, 1882), and works for Orch.: *Escenas Andaluzas; Funeral March for Alfonso XII;* Violin Concerto; etc.

BIBLIOGRAPHY: Angel S. Salcedo, *Tomás Bretón: Su vida y sus obras* (1924).

Breuer, Hans (real name, **Johann Peter Joseph**), German tenor; b. Cologne, April 27, 1868; d. Vienna, Oct. 11, 1929. He studied voice at the Cologne Cons. (1890–92); made his operatic debut in 1896 as Mime at Bayreuth, and appeared regularly there until 1914. He also sang at the Vienna Hofoper from 1900 until his death. He made his Metroplitan Opera debut in N.Y. in *The Flying Dutchman* on Jan. 6, 1900.

Breuning, Moritz Gerhard von, Austrian writer on music; b. Vienna, Aug. 28, 1813; d. there, May 6, 1892. He was a son of Beethoven's friend Stephan von Breuning; wrote *Aus dem Schwarzspanierhause* (Vienna, 1874; new ed., with additions by Kalischer, Berlin, 1907; 1970).

Breval, Jean-Baptiste Sébastien, outstanding French cellist and composer; b. Paris, Nov. 6, 1753; d. Colligis, Aisne, March 18, 1823. He studied cello with Jean-Baptiste Cupis; made his debut in 1778 at a Concert Spirituel performing one of his own sonatas; subsequently was a member of its orch. (1781–91); then played in the orch. of the Théâtre Feydeau (1791–1800). He composed a great quantity of instrumental music, including symphs., cello concertos, string quartets, trios, duos, and sonatas. He also wrote an opéra comique, *Ines et Leonore, ou La Soeur jalouse,* performed in Versailles on Nov. 14, 1788.

Bréval, Lucienne (stage name of **Bertha Schilling**), Swiss soprano; b. Männedorf, Switzerland, Nov. 4, 1869; d. Paris, Aug. 15, 1935. She studied piano in Lausanne and Geneva; later enrolled at the Paris Cons., where she studied voice. She made her operatic debut at the Paris Opéra as Selika in *L'Africaine* on Jan. 20, 1892; made her American debut at the Metropolitan Opera in N.Y. on Jan 16, 1901, as Chimène in *Le Cid,* and remained on its roster until 1902. She excelled in the French repertoire; eventually retired in Paris.

Brevig, Per, Norwegian trombonist; b. Berg by Halden, Sept. 7, 1936. He studied trombone in Copenhagen (1958); then went to the U.S. and enrolled at the Juilliard School of Music in N.Y., receiving a Mus.B. (1968), Mus.M. (1969), and D.M.A. (1971) there. Subsequently he took lessons in conducting with Stokowski in N.Y. (1966–67). From 1957 to 1965 he was first trombonist with the Bergen (Norway) Symph. Orch., and from 1965 to 1968, solo trombonist with the American Symph. Orch. under Stokowski; was then appointed first trombonist with the Metropolitan Opera Orch. In 1966 he became a member of the trombone faculty at the Juilliard School of Music. He specializes in performance of modern music; has publ. 2 books: *Avant-Garde Techniques in Solo Trombone Music* and *Problems of Notations and Execution.*

Brevik, Tor, Norwegian composer; b. Oslo, Jan. 22, 1932. He studied violin, viola, and music theory at the Cons. in Oslo, and in Sweden. He founded the Youth Chamber Orch. in Oslo (1958); was active as a music critic. He wrote an opera, *Da kongen kom til Spilliputt* (1973); *Adagio and Fugue* for String Orch. (1958); *Overture* (1958); Serenade for Strings (1959); Chaconne for Orch. (1960); Concertino for Clarinets and Strings (1961); *Music* for Solo Violin (1963); *Canto Elegiaco* for Orch. (1964); *Contrasts,* chamber ballet (1964); *Elegy* for Soprano, Viola, Double Bass, and Percussion (1964); Divertimento for Wind Quintet (1964); *Adagio Religioso* for Solo Horn (1967); String Quartet (1967); Chamber Concerto for Strings (1967); *Music* for 4 Strings (1968); *Intrada* for Orch. (1969); *Romance* for Violin, and Orch. or Piano (1972); *Andante Cantabile* for Violin and Strings (1975).

Bréville, Pierre-Onfroy de, French composer; b. Bar-le-Duc, Feb. 21, 1861; d. Paris, Sept. 24, 1949. He studied at the Paris Cons. with Théodore Dubois (1880–82) and later with César Franck. He was a prof. of counterpoint at the Schola Cantorum from 1898 to 1902; was active also as a music critic. He completed (with Vincent d'Indy and others) Franck's unfinished opera *Ghiselle;* in his own music he followed the traditions of French Romanticism. His opera, *Eros Vainqueur,* was produced in Brussels on March 7, 1910; he also wrote an overture to Maeterlinck's play *La Princesse Maleine,* and to his *Les Sept Princesses;* also composed the orch. suites *Nuit de décembre* and *Stamboul,* as well as numerous choral pieces.

Brewer, Sir (Alfred) Herbert, English organist and composer; b. Gloucester, June 21, 1865; d. there, March 1, 1928. He studied at the Royal College of Music with Parratt, Stanford, and Bridge; became organist of several churches, and director of musical societies. His compositions include many sacred cantatas (*Emmaus, The Holy Innocents, A Song of Eden,* etc.), which were performed at festivals in Gloucester, Worcester, Hereford, Cardiff, and Leeds; patriotic odes, such as *England, My England;* organ pieces; songs; etc. He was knighted in 1926.
BIBLIOGRAPHY: See A.H. Brewer, *Memories of Choirs and Cloisters* (London, 1931).

Brewer, John Hyatt, American organist and composer; b. Brooklyn, Jan. 18, 1856; d. there, Nov. 30, 1931. He studied organ and composition with Dudley Buck; was active as organist and music director of numerous local churches and musical societies. He was a prolific vocal composer; wrote the can-tatas (for women's voices) *Hesperus, The Sea and the Moon, Herald of Spring,* etc.; and (for men's voices) *Birth of Love, The Dunderberg,* etc.; also quartets, anthems, glees, and choruses.

Brewster, W. Herbert, black American gospel songwriter; b. Somerville, Tenn., July 2, 1899. He became minister at the East Trigg Baptist Church in Memphis, Tenn. He had a fine baritone voice and formed a Brewster Ensemble, but he acquired a solid reputation mainly as a writer of religious songs, to texts, somewhat altered, from the Bible; they bore an almost operatic character, allowing for metrical changes and use of extended melismatic cadenzas. His hymnal chant *Surely, God Is Able* was probably the first in gospel singing usage to employ triple meter within the time signatures of slow 12/8. Some of his moralistic songs, such as *How I Got Over,* sold more than a million copies, and he became an acknowledged monitor of gospel song practice.

Brian, Havergal, English composer of extraordinary fecundity and longevity; b. Dresden, Staffordshire, Jan. 29, 1876; d. Shoreham-by-the-Sea, Sussex, Nov. 28, 1972. He studied violin, cello, and organ with local teachers; left school at 12 to earn his living and help his father, who was a potter's turner. At the same time he taught himself elementary music theory and also learned French and German without an instructor. From 1904 to 1949 he engaged in musical journalism. He attained a reputation in England as a harmless eccentric possessed by inordinate ambitions to become a composer; he attracted supporters among English musicians, who in turn were derided as gullible admirers of a patent amateur. But Brian continued to write music in large symph. forms; some of his works were performed, mostly by non-professional organizations; amazingly enough, he increased his productivity with age; he wrote 22 symphs. after reaching the age of 80, and 7 more after the age of 90. The total number of symphs. at the time of his death was 32. Finally, English musicians, critics, conductors, and concert organizations became aware of the Brian phenomenon, and performances, mostly posthumous, followed. A Havergal Brian Society was formed in London, and there were a few timorous attempts to further the Brian cause outside of England. The slow acceptance of Brian's music was not due to his overindulgence in dissonance. Quite the contrary is true; Brian was not an innovator; he followed the Germanic traditions of Richard Strauss and Mahler in the spirit of unbridled grandiosity, architectural formidability, and rhapsodically quaquaversal thematicism. Brian's modernism tended to be programmatic, as in the ominous whole-tone progressions in his opera *The Tigers,* illustrating the aerial attacks on London by zeppelins during World War I. Brian's readiness to lend his MSS to anyone showing interest in his music resulted in the loss of several of his works; a few of them were retrieved after years of search.
WORKS: OPERAS: *The Tigers,* to his own libretto

(1916–19; orchestrated 1928–29; the score was regarded as lost, but was recovered in 1977, and a perf. was given by the BBC Radio, London, on May 3, 1983); *Deirdre of the Sorrows,* after Synge (1947; incomplete); *Turandot,* to a German libretto after Schiller (1950–51); *The Cenci,* after Shelley (1952); *Faust,* after Goethe (1955–56); *Agamemnon,* after Aeschylus, to an English libretto (1957).

32 SYMPHS: No. 1, *The Gothic,* for Vocal Soloists, Chorus, 4 Mixed Choirs, Children's Choir, 4 Brass Bands, and Very Large Orch. (1919–27; first perf., in London, June 24, 1961, by amateur forces; first professional perf., London, Oct. 30, 1966; broadcast to the U.S. by satellite, BBC-NPR, Washington, D.C., May 25, 1980); No. 2 (1930–31; Brighton, May 19, 1973); No. 3 (1931–32; private broadcast perf., BBC studios, London, Oct. 18, 1974); No. 4, *Das Siegeslied,* a setting of Psalm 68 in the Lutheran version, for Soprano, Double Mixed Chorus, and Orch., with a German text (1932–33; Manchester, July 3, 1967); No. 5, *Wine of Summer,* for Baritone and Orch., in one movement (1937; London, Dec. 11, 1969); No. 6, *Sinfonia tragica,* in one movement (1948; London, Sept. 21, 1966); No. 7 (1948; London, March 13, 1968); No. 8, in one movement (1949; London, Feb. 1, 1954); No. 9 (1951; London, March 22, 1958); No. 10, in one movement (1953–54; London, Nov. 3, 1958); No. 11 (1954; London, Nov. 5, 1959); No. 12, in one movement (1957; London, Nov. 5, 1959); No. 13, in one movement (1959; London, May 14, 1978); No. 14, in one movement (1959–60; London, May 10, 1970); No. 15, in one movement (1960; London, May 14, 1978); No. 16, in one movement (1960; private broadcast perf., BBC studios, London, June 18, 1975); No. 17, in one movement (1960–61; London, May 14, 1978); No. 18 (1961; London, Feb. 26, 1962); No. 19 (1961; Glasgow, Dec. 31, 1976); No. 20 (1962; London, Oct. 5, 1976); No. 21 (1963; London, May 10, 1970); No. 22, *Symphonia brevis* (1964–65; London, Aug. 15, 1971); No. 23 (1965; Univ. of Illinois, Urbana, Oct. 4, 1973); No. 24, in one movement (1965; private broadcast perf., BBC studios, London, June 18, 1975); No. 25 (1965–66; Glasgow, Dec. 31, 1976); No. 26 (1966; Stoke-on-Trent, May 13, 1976); No. 27 (1966; London, March 18, 1979); No. 28 (1967; London, Oct. 5, 1973); No. 29 (1967; Stoke-on-Trent, Nov. 17, 1976); No. 30 (1967; London, Sept. 24, 1976); No. 31, in one movement (1968; London, March 18, 1979); No. 32 (1968; London, Jan. 28, 1971).

OTHER WORKS FOR ORCH.: *Tragic Prelude* (1899–1900; lost); *Burlesque Variations on an Original Theme* (1903; lost; recovered in 1974; perf. by the City of Hull Youth Orch., March 13, 1980); *For Valour,* concert overture (1904; revised 1906); *Hero and Leander,* symph. poem (1904–5; London, Dec. 3, 1908); 5 *English Suites:* No. 1 (1904–6); No. 2, *Night Portraits* (1915; lost); No. 3 (1919–21; lost); No. 4, *Kindergarten* (1924); No. 5, *Rustic Scenes* (1953); *Fantastic Variations on an Old Rhyme* (1907; revised 1912; lost); *Festal Dance* (1908); *In Memoriam,* tone poem (1910); 3 *Comedy Overtures:* No. 1, *Doctor Merryheart* (1911–12); No. 2, *The Tinker's Wedding* (1948); No. 3, *The Jolly Miller* (1962); Violin Concerto in C (1934–35; London, June 20, 1969); *Elegy,* symph. poem (1954); Cello Concerto (1964; London,

Feb. 5, 1971); Concerto for Orch. (1964; Leeds College of Music, April 12, 1975); *Legend: Ave Atque Vale* (1968).

VOCAL WORKS: *Requiem* for Baritone, Chorus, and Orch. (1897; lost); *Psalm 23* for Tenor, Chorus, and Orch. (1904; reconstructed 1945; Hove, March 10, 1973); *By the Waters of Babylon* for Baritone, Chorus, and Orch. (1905; revised 1909; lost); *Carmilhan,* dramatic ballad for Soloists, Chorus, and Orch. (1906; lost); *Let God Arise (Psalm 68)* for Soloists, Chorus, and Orch. (1906–7; lost); *The Vision of Cleopatra,* tragic poem for Soloists, Chorus, Semichorus, and Orch. (1907; Stoke-on-Trent, July 7, 1907; lost); *Pilgrimage to Kevlaar,* ballad for Chorus and Orch. (1913–14; lost); *Prometheus Unbound,* lyric drama after Shelley, for Multiple Soloists, Double Chorus, Semi-chorus, and Orch. (1937–44; lost); choruses; songs.

CHAMBER MUSIC: String Quartet (1903; lost); *Legend* for Violin and Piano (1919); *Adagio e dolente* for Cello and Piano (1947; fragment only extant).

FOR PIANO: 3 *Illuminations* (1916); *Double Fugue* (1924); *Prelude and Fugue* in C minor (1924); *Prelude and Fugue* in D major and D minor (1924); *John Dowland's Fancy,* prelude (1934).

BIBLIOGRAPHY: R. Nettel, *Ordeal by Music: The Strange Experience of Havergal Brian* (London, 1945); R.L.E. Foreman, ed., *Havergal Brian: A Collection of Essays* (London, 1969); M. Macdonald, *Havergal Brian: Perspective on the Music* (London, 1972); idem, *The Symphonies of Havergal Brian,* vol. 1 (London, 1974), vol. 2 (London, 1978), and vol. 3 (London, 1983); R. Nettel, *Havergal Brian and His Music* (London, 1976); L. Foreman, *Havergal Brian and the Performance of His Orchestral Music: A History and a Sourcebook* (London, 1976); K. Eastaugh, *Havergal Brian: The Making of a Composer* (London, 1976); P. Rapoport, *Opus Est* (London, 1979).

Briard, Etienne, type-founder at Avignon, active in the early 16th century. In his engraving he employed round note heads instead of the ordinary angular ones, and separate notes instead of ligatures. Peignot holds that another printer, Granjon, used these methods prior to Briard (see his *Dictionnaire de la bibliologie,* supplement, p. 140). In any case, Briard's characters are much better formed and more easily read; Schmidt's *Ottaviano Petrucci* contains a facsimile of them. The *Liber primum missarum Carpentras* (works of Eleazar Genet, called "Il Carpentrasso"), printed with them at Avignon in 1532, is in the library of the Paris Cons.

BIBLIOGRAPHY: K. Meyer, "Music Printing, 1473–1934," *Dolphin* (N.Y., 1935).

Briccetti, Thomas, American conductor and composer; b. Mt. Kisco, N.Y., Jan. 14, 1936. He attended the Eastman School of Music and the Columbia Univ. School of Fine Arts; also studied privately with Samuel Barber and Peter Mennin. In 1958 he won the Prix de Rome, also held the Ford Foundation Composer's Fellowship (1960–61). In 1963 he helped to found the St. Petersburg (Fla.) Symph.;

then served as associate conductor of the Indianapolis Symph. (1968–72). In 1970 he became music director of the Fort Wayne Phil. In 1975 he was appointed music director of the Omaha Symph. and the Nebraska Sinfonia; in 1978 he initiated in Peru, Nebr., the Festival of a Thousand Oaks.

Briccialdi, Giulio, Italian flutist; b. Terni, Papal States, March 2, 1818; d. Florence, Dec. 17, 1881. A precocious musician, he held an appointment with the Santa Cecilia Academy at Rome at the age of 15; made concert tours in England and America; after 1842 lived chiefly in London. He wrote an opera, *Leonora de' Medici* (Milan, Aug. 11, 1855); many compositions for flute; also a method for flute.

Bricken, Carl Ernest, American pianist and composer; b. Shelbyville, Ky., Dec. 28, 1898; d. Sweet Briar, Va., Jan. 25, 1971. He studied piano with Alfred Cortot in Paris. Returning to America, he taught piano in N.Y., in Chicago, and at the Univ. of Wisconsin in Madison. From 1944 to 1948 he was conductor of the Seattle Symph. Orch. His compositions include a Symph. (1935) and several pieces of competent and agreeable chamber music, as well as piano pieces. In 1964 he relinquished his musical career and devoted himself to painting.

Bricktop, Ada Beatrice. See **Smith, Ada Beatrice Queen Victoria Louise Virginia.**

Brico, Antonia, American pianist and conductor; b. Rotterdam, June 26, 1902. She moved to California in 1906 and studied at the Univ. of Calif. at Berkeley, graduating in 1923; then went to Berlin, where she took lessons in conducting with Karl Muck at the State Academy of Berlin; also studied piano with Sigismund Stojowski. She gave piano recitals in Europe and America, but her prime interest was in conducting. Overcoming many difficulties, she organized a special concert with the Berlin Phil. on Jan. 10, 1930, which aroused considerable curiosity, women conductors being a rare species at the time. Returning to America, she obtained an engagement with the Los Angeles Phil. at the Hollywood Bowl (Aug. 1, 1930); also arranged a few concerts in N.Y., which she had to finance out of her own resources. After some disheartening experiences (a famous male singer on whom the management counted for public success refused to appear at the last moment), she sought opportunity in Europe; gave concerts in Finland and received a commendation from Sibelius for her conducting of his music. About 1949 she became associated with Albert Schweitzer, visiting his hospital in West Africa; he gave her some suggestions about performances of Bach. Eventually she settled in Denver as a piano teacher; to satisfy her unquenchable thirst for orch. conducting, she managed to lead concerts of the community orch. there. In 1974 she produced an autobiographical film called simply *Antonia,* in which she eloquently pleaded for equality of the sexes on the conducting podium; it was nominated for an Academy Award, and on the strength of it,

she was able to obtain several bona fide orch. engagements.

Bridge, Frank, distinguished English composer; b. Brighton, Feb. 26, 1879; d. Eastbourne, Jan. 10, 1941. He took violin lessons from his father; entered the Royal College of Music in 1899 and studied composition with Stanford, graduating in 1904; received an Arthur Sullivan Prize and the Gold Medal of the Rajah of Tagore for "the most generally deserving pupil." He specialized in viola playing; was a member of the Joachim String Quartet in 1906 and later of the English String Quartet. He also appeared as a conductor; was in charge of the New Symph. Orch. during Marie Brema's season (1910–11) at the Savoy Theatre in London; then conducted at Covent Garden during the seasons of Raymond Roze and Beecham; he also appeared as conductor at the Promenade Concerts. With a stipend from Elizabeth Sprague Coolidge, he toured the U.S. in 1923, conducting his own works with the orchs. of Rochester, Boston, Detroit, Cleveland, and N.Y.; he revisited the U.S. in 1934 and 1938. As a composer he received a belated recognition toward the end of his life, and posthumously; although he wrote a great deal of instrumental music, his name appeared but rarely in the programs of modern music festivals. Much of his music is generated by passionate emotionalism, soaring in the harmonic realms of euphonious dissonances, while most of his chamber music maintains a classical spirit of Baroque construction. Although he was greatly impressed by the works of the 2nd Vienna School, he never embraced serial methods of composition. Most remarkable of these advanced works was his 4th String Quartet, written in 1937. Benjamin Britten, who was an ardent student and admirer of Frank Bridge, wrote his *Variations on a Theme of Frank Bridge* based on the materials of this Quartet.
WORKS: FOR THE STAGE: *The Christmas Rose,* children's opera (1919–29; London, Dec. 8, 1932; composer conducting). FOR ORCH.: *Symphonic Poem* (1904); *The Hag* (1904); *Isabella,* symph. poem (London, Oct. 3, 1907); *Dance Rhapsody* (1908); incidental music for *The Two Hunchbacks* (London, Nov. 17, 1910; composer conducting); *The Sea,* orch. suite (London, Sept. 24, 1912); *Dance Poem* (1913; London, March 16, 1914; composer conducting); *Summer,* symph. poem (1914; London, March 13, 1916; composer conducting); *Two Poems* (London, Jan. 1, 1917); *Lament* for String Orch., in memory of the victims of the sinking of the *Lusitania* (London, Sept. 15, 1915); Suite for Strings (1908); incidental music for Frank Stayton's play *Threads* (1921; London, Aug. 23, 1921); *Sir Roger de Coverley* for String Orch. (London, Oct. 21, 1922); *Enter Spring* for Orch. (1926; Norwich, Oct. 27, 1927; composer conducting); *There Is a Willow Grows Aslant a Brook* (1927; London, Aug. 20, 1927); *Oration* for Cello and Orch. (1930; London, Jan. 17, 1936); *Phantasm* for Piano and Orch. (1931; London, Jan. 10, 1934); *Rebus* (1940; London, Feb. 23, 1941). CHAMBER MUSIC: Piano Trio No. 1 (London, Nov. 14, 1900); String Quartet No. 1 (London, March 14, 1901); String Quartet No.

2 (London, Dec. 4, 1901); Piano Quartet (London, Feb. 23, 1903); *Phantasie* for String Quartet (1905); *Three Idylls* for String Quartet (London, March 8, 1907); *Phantasie* for Piano Trio (1908); *Novellettes* for String Quartet (1910); *Phantasie* for Piano Quartet (1910); Viola Duos (1912); String Sextet (1912; London, June 18, 1913); Cello Sonata (1913–17; London, July 13, 1917); String Quartet No. 2 (1915); 2 old English songs, *Sally in Our Alley* and *Cherry Ripe*, for String Quartet (1916); *Sir Roger de Coverley* for String Quartet (1922; also arranged for Orch.); String Quartet No. 3 (1926–27; Vienna, Sept. 17, 1927); *Rhapsody* for String Trio (1928); Piano Trio No. 2 (1928–29; London, Nov. 4, 1929); Violin Sonata (1932); String Quartet No. 4 (1937; Pittsfield, Mass., Sept. 13, 1938); Piano Sonata (1922–25); *Four Characteristic Pieces* for Piano (1914). FOR VOICE: *Romeo and Juliet: A Prayer* for Chorus and Orch. (1916); *Blow Out, You Bugles* for Tenor and Orch. (1918); *Three Tagore Songs* (1922–25); about 100 other songs and choruses.

BIBLIOGRAPHY: P. Pirie, *Frank Bridge* (London, 1971); A. Payne and L. Foreman, *Frank Bridge* (London, 1976); Paul Hindmarsh, *Frank Bridge: A Thematic Catalogue* (London, 1983).

Bridge, Sir (John) Frederick, English organist, conductor, and composer; b. Oldbury, near Birmingham, Dec. 5, 1844; d. London, March 18, 1924. At the age of 14 he was apprenticed to John Hopkins, organist of Rochester Cathedral; later studied under John Goss; was principal organist at Westminster Abbey (1882–1918); took the degree of D.Mus. at Oxford in 1874 with his oratorio *Mount Moriah;* then taught harmony and organ at various music schools, including the Royal College of Music (from 1883); was conductor of the Highbury Phil. Society (1878–86), the Madrigal Society, and the Royal Choral Society (1896–1922); also served as chairman of Trinity College of Music. He was knighted in 1897.

WORKS: Cantatas: *Boadicea* (1880); *Rock of Ages* (1885); *Callirrhoë* (1888); *The Lobster's Garden Party, or The Selfish Shellfish* (1904); dramatic oratorio, *The Repentance of Nineveh* (Worcester, 1890); concert overture, *Morte d'Arthur* (1896); choral ballades. He publ. primers on counterpoint, canon, organ accompaniment, and other subjects; also *A Course of Harmony* (with Sawyer; 1899); *Samuel Pepys, Lover of Music* (1903); an autobiography, *A Westminster Pilgrim* (1918); *12 Good Musicians from John Bull to Henry Purcell* (1920); *The Old Cryes of London* (1921); *Shakespearean Music in the Plays and Early Operas* (1923); edited selected motets of Orlando Gibbons (1907).

Bridge, Joseph Cox, English organist and composer, brother of **John Frederick Bridge;** b. Rochester, Aug. 16, 1853; d. St. Albans, March 29, 1929. He studied with his brother and with John Hopkins; from 1877–1925 was organist of Chester Cathedral; in 1879 he revived the Chester Triennial Music Festival and became its conductor until 1900; also founded (1883) and conducted for 20 years the Chester Musical Society; from 1908 was a prof. of music at Durham Univ.

WORKS: Oratorio, *Daniel* (1885); cantatas: *Rudel* (1891) and *Resurgam* (1897); *Evening Service* with Orch. (1879); *Requiem Mass* (1900); operetta, *The Belle of the Area;* Symph. (1894); String Quartet; Cello Sonata; anthems, organ music, piano pieces, songs.

Bridgetower, George Auguste Polgreen, mulatto violinist; b. Biala, Poland, Oct. 11, 1778; d. Peckham, Surrey, Feb. 28, 1860. His father was an Abyssinian; his mother, of Polish extraction. He studied with Giornovichi; as a youth he went to England and entered the service of the Prince of Wales. In 1791, at the age of 13, he played in the violin section of the Haydn-Salomon Concerts in London. On Oct. 4, 1807, he was elected to the membership of the Royal Society of Musicians in London. In 1811 he received his Bachelor of Music degree from Cambridge Univ. From about 1829 to 1843 he resided mostly in Paris and Rome, eventually returning to England, where he married and settled in Surrey. His name is historically important because of his association with Beethoven; it was Bridgetower who gave the first performance, from MS, of the *Kreutzer Sonata,* with Beethoven himself at the piano, in Vienna on May 17, 1803. Beethoven spelled his name in a German orthography as Brischdower.

BIBLIOGRAPHY: *Musical Times* (Feb. 1981); relevant Beethoven literature.

Briegel, Wolfgang Carl, German organist and composer; b. Königsberg, May 1626; d. Darmstadt, Nov. 19, 1712. He received his musical training in Nuremberg; from 1645 to 1650 he was active in Schweinfurt; in 1650 was appointed cantor at the court of Gotha; in 1671 went to Darmstadt, where he served as court Kapellmeister until his death. He dedicated himself primarily to sacred choral composition, and publ. a number of collections for the Lutheran church service, among them *Evangelische Gespräch,* in 3 parts (1660, 1662, 1681); *Geistliche Arien,* in 2 parts (1660–61); *Evangelischer Blumengarten,* in 4 parts (1666–69); *Evangelischer Palmen-Zweig* (1685); *Evangelische Harpfen* (1685); *Apostolische Chormusik* (1697); *Letzter Schwanengesang* (1709). He also wrote instrumental works in dance forms, for instruments and voices, under such inviting Baroque titles as *Musicalisches Tafelkonfekt* (1672); a singspiel, *Das triumphierende Siegespiel der wahren Liebe;* and other theatrical music.

BIBLIOGRAPHY: K.F. Hirschmann, *W.D. Briegel* (Giessen, 1936); Elisabeth Noack, *W.C. Briegel: Ein Barock-Komponist in seiner Zeit* (Berlin, 1963).

Brilioth, Helge, Swedish tenor; b. Vaxjo, May 7, 1931. He was educated at the Royal Academy in Stockholm; then took courses at the Salzburg Mozarteum. Paradoxically, he began his career as a pianist and organist; then gave recitals as a baritone. After further vocal studies he made his debut as a tenor in 1965; then sang at Bayreuth and at

Herbert von Karajan's Easter Festival at Salzburg; since 1970 he has appeared regularly at Covent Garden, London. He made his American debut at the Metropolitan Opera in N.Y. as Parsifal, on Nov. 14, 1970.

Brindel, Bernard, American composer; b. Chicago, April 23, 1912. He studied violin and composition at the Chicago Musical College (B.M., 1945; M.M., 1946); played in the Illinois Symph. (1938–42) and was on the faculties of the Chicago Musical College (1946–54), Morton College (1954–79), and at Interlochen (1955–67); served as music director of Temple Sholom in Chicago.

WORKS: 2 concertinos for Cello and Orch.; Concertino for Horn and Orch.; Prelude for Orch.; 21 pieces for Strings and Orch.; 4 string quartets, *2 Songs* for Tenor and Orch.; Brass Quintet; chamber music; choral pieces.

Brînduş, Nicolae, Rumanian composer; b. Bucharest, April 16, 1935. He studied at the Bucharest Cons. with Zeno Vancea, Alfred Mendelsohn, Tudor Ciortea, and Anatol Vieru; in 1969 he became an instructor there. In his music, he experiments with novel sonorities.

WORKS: *Balada lui Pintea Viteazul (The Ballad of Pintea the Brave)* for Tenor, Chorus, and Orch. (1964); *3 Pieces for Orchestra* (1964); *Music* for Chamber Orch. (1964); Concerto for Piano, Percussion, and Orch. (1964); *Strigoii (The Ghosts),* lyric poem for Soloists, 3 Choral-Instrumental Ensembles, and Tape (1966); *Mărturie (The Witness),* cantata for Mezzo-soprano, Chorus, 2 Orch. Groups, Percussion, Organ, and Piano (1967); *Domnişoara Hus (Miss Hus),* cantata for 3 Basses and 3 Instrumental Groups (1968); *Phtora I,* symph. cycle for any group of Instruments over a given minimum scoring (1968); *Inscripţie (Inscription)* for Small Orch. and Tape (1969); *Match (Phtora II)* for 2 Percussionists, and 4 Instruments or Instrumental Groups (1969); *Cantus firmus (Phtora III)* for Electric Organ or Piano, and any number of different Instruments (1970); *Idéophonie, Psaume XIII (Phtora IV)* for 2–5 Antiphonal Groups of 5 combined Instrumentalists and Voices (1970); *Soliloque (Phtora V)* for Tape and Small Ensemble (1971); *Antiphonie* for a minimum of 18 String Instruments (1971); *Vos vassales les symétries* for 4 Trombones, 4 Double Basses, 4 String Quartets, 4 Wind Instruments, and 4 Choral Groups (1971); *Vagues* for Piano, Percussion, Clarinet, Violin, Viola, and Cello (1972).

Brinsmead, John, English piano maker; b. Weare Giffard, Devon, Oct. 13, 1814; d. London, Feb. 17, 1908. He founded his firm in London in 1835. In 1863 his sons, **Thomas** and **Edgar,** were admitted to partnership; in 1900 the firm was incorporated and assumed its permanent title, John Brinsmead & Sons, Ltd. In 1868 they patented an improvement in piano construction, "Perfect Check Repeater Action." In 1908, upon the death of John Brinsmead, the controlling interest was purchased by W. Savile, a director of J.B. Cramer & Co. The Brinsmead and Cramer pianos continued to be manufactured until 1967, when the firm was sold to Kemble & Co. **Edgar Brinsmead** (d. Nov. 28, 1907) wrote a *History of the Piano forte* (1868; revised and republ., 1879).

Bristow, George Frederick, patriotic American composer; b. Brooklyn, N.Y., Dec. 19, 1825; d. New York, Dec. 13, 1898. His father, **William Richard Bristow,** a professional English musician, came to America in 1824; he gave his son primary instruction in violin playing; Bristow's other teachers were Henry Christian Timm and Sir George Alexander Macfarren, who taught him orchestration. He also took violin lessons with Ole Bull. He began his career at the age of 13 by playing in the orch. of the Olympic Theater in N.Y.; in 1843 he joined the violin section of the newly formed N.Y. Phil., and remained with the orch. for 36 years; he also conducted the Harmonic Society, from 1851 to 1863 and the Mendelssohn Society from 1867 to 1871. He began to compose with a determination to prove the possibility and the necessity of forming a national American school of composition; he orated at various public occasions defending his cause. He even withdrew from the N.Y. Phil. for several months in 1854 in protest against the neglect of American music in favor of foreigners. Actually, the N.Y. Phil. frequently placed his works on its programs. He was the concertmaster of the circus orch. when P.T. Barnum brought Jenny Lind to America as a special attraction. He also played in the orch. at the N.Y. concerts led by the sensational French conductor Louis Antoine Jullien, and elicited from him a statement praising Bristow's String Quartet as a "truly classical work." Unfortunately, Bristow's own ostensibly American music sounded like a feeble imitation of German models. He merits his place in the annals of American music not for the originality of his own works but for his pioneering efforts to write music on American subjects.

WORKS: Opera, *Rip Van Winkle* (N.Y., Sept. 27, 1855); unfinished opera, *Columbus* (overture perf. by the N.Y. Phil., Nov. 17, 1866); oratorios: *Praise to God* (N.Y. Harmonic Society, March 2, 1861) and *Daniel* (N.Y., Dec. 30, 1867); cantatas: *The Great Republic* (Brooklyn Phil. Society, May 10, 1879) and *Niagara* for Soli, Chorus, and Orch. (Manuscript Society, Carnegie Hall, N.Y., April 11, 1898); Symph. in D minor (Jullien's concert, N.Y. Phil., March 1, 1856); Symph. in F-sharp minor (N.Y. Phil., March 26, 1859); *Arcadian Symphony* (N.Y. Phil., Feb. 14, 1874); overture, *Jibbenainosay* (Harlem Phil., N.Y., March 6, 1889); 2 string quartets; organ pieces; piano pieces; songs.

WRITINGS: *New and Improved Method for Reed or Cabinet Organ* (N.Y., 1888).

BIBLIOGRAPHY: J.T. Howard, *Our American Music* (4th ed., N.Y., 1965); G. Chase, *America's Music* (2nd ed., N.Y., 1966); David Ewen, *American Composers* (N.Y., 1982).

Britain, Radie, American composer; b. Amarillo, Texas, March 17, 1903. She studied piano at the

American Cons. in Chicago (B.M., 1924); then went to Germany, where she studied music theory in Munich. She excels in writing for chorus; several of her choral compositions were awarded prizes by the National Federation of Music Clubs, the National League of American Penwomen, and other organizations dedicated to the appreciation of artistic works by American women.

WORKS: *A Heroic Poem* for Orch., inspired by Lindbergh's flight to Paris in 1927 (won a prize at the Hollywood Bowl Contest; first perf. in Rochester, N.Y., March 3, 1932); *Light,* dedicated to Edison (received first prize in the National Contest for Women Composers in 1935; first perf. in Chicago, Nov. 29, 1938); *Ubiquity,* music drama (1937); *Southern Symphony* (Chicago, March 4, 1940); Fantasy for Oboe and Orch. (1941); *Cactus Rhapsody* for Orch. (1945); *Happyland,* operetta (1946); *Carillon,* short opera (1952); *The Spider and the Butterfly,* children's operetta (1953); *Radiation* for Orch. (1955); *Cowboy Rhapsody* for Orch. (1956); *Minha Terra* for Orch. (1958); *Kuthara,* chamber opera (1960); *Cosmic Mist Symphony* (1962); *Chipmunks* for Woodwinds, Harp, and Percussion (1964); 2 string quartets; several song cycles, including *Translunar Cycle,* celebrating the lunar landing of 1969, and dedicated to the National Aeronautics and Space Administration.

Britt, Horace, cellist; b. Antwerp, June 18, 1881; d. Austin, Texas, Feb. 3, 1971. He studied at the Paris Cons. with Jules Delsart (cello) and André Lavignac (harmony); was later a private pupil of André Caplet; made his American debut with the Chicago Symph. Orch. (1907); then toured extensively in the U.S. with Georges Barrère and Carlos Salzedo; was co-founder of the Barrère-Britt Concertino, a chamber music group organized in 1937.

Britten, Lord Benjamin, one of the most remarkable composers of England; b. Lowestoft, Suffolk, Nov. 22, 1913; d. Aldeburgh, Dec. 4, 1976. He grew up in moderately prosperous circumstances; his father was an orthodontist, his mother an amateur singer. He played the piano and improvised facile tunes; many years later he used these youthful inspirations in a symph. work which he named *Simple Symphony.* In addition to piano, he began taking viola lessons with Audrey Alston. At the age of 13 he was accepted as a pupil in composition by Frank Bridge, whose influence was decisive on Britten's development as a composer. In 1930 he entered the Royal College of Music in London, where he studied piano with Arthur Benjamin and Harold Samuel, and composition with John Ireland. He progressed rapidly; even his earliest works showed a mature mastery of technique and a fine lyrical talent of expression. His *Fantasy Quartet* for Oboe and Strings was performed at the Festival of the International Society for Contemporary Music in Florence on April 5, 1934. He became associated with the theater and the cinema and began composing background music for films. He was in the U.S. at the outbreak of World War II; returned to England in the spring of 1942; was exempted from military service as a conscientious objector. After the war he organized the English Opera Group (1947), and in 1948 founded the Aldeburgh Festival, in collaboration with Eric Crozier and the singer Peter Pears; this festival, devoted mainly to production of short operas by English composers, became an important cultural institution in England; many of Britten's own works were performed for the first time at the Aldeburgh Festivals, often under his own direction; he also had productions at the Glyndebourne Festival. In his operas he observed the economic necessity of reducing the orch. contingent to 12 performers, with the piano part serving as a modern version of the Baroque *ripieno.* This economy of means made it possible for small opera groups and univ. workshops to perform Britten's works; yet he succeeded in creating a rich spectrum of instrumental colors, in an idiom ranging from simple triadic progressions, often in parallel motions, to ultrachromatic dissonant harmonies; upon occasion he applied dodecaphonic procedures, with thematic materials based on 12 different notes; however, he never employed the formal design of the 12-tone method of composition. A sui generis dodecaphonic device is illustrated by the modulatory scheme in Britten's opera *The Turn of the Screw,* in which each successive scene begins in a different key, with the totality of tonics aggregating to a series of 12 different notes. A characteristic feature in Britten's operas is the inclusion of orchestral interludes, which become independent symph. poems in an impressionistic vein related to the dramatic action of the work. The cries of seagulls in Britten's most popular and musically most striking opera, *Peter Grimes,* create a fantastic quasi-surrealistic imagery. Britten was equally successful in treating tragic subjects, as in *Peter Grimes* and *Billy Budd;* comic subjects, exemplified by his *Albert Herring;* and mystical evocation, as in *The Turn of the Screw.* He was also successful in depicting patriotic subjects, as in *Gloriana,* composed for the coronation of Queen Elizabeth II. He possessed a flair for writing music for children, in which he managed to present a degree of sophistication and artistic simplicity without condescension. Britten was an adaptable composer who could perform a given task according to the specific requirements of the occasion. He composed a "realization" of Gay's *Beggar's Opera.* He also wrote modern "parables" for church performance, and produced a contemporary counterpart of the medieval English miracle play *Noye's Fludde.* Among his other works, perhaps the most remarkable is *War Requiem,* a profound tribute to the dead of many wars. In 1952 Britten was made a Companion of Honour; in 1965 he received the Order of Merit. In June 1976 he was elevated to the peerage of Great Britain by Queen Elizabeth II and became a Lord, the first composer to be so honored.

WORKS: OPERAS: *Paul Bunyan,* to a text by W.H. Auden (Columbia Univ., N.Y., May 5, 1941; revised 1974; BBC, Feb. 1, 1976; Aldeburgh, June 14, 1976); *Peter Grimes,* after a poem by Crabbe, Britten's most popular opera (London, June 7, 1945; originally commissioned by the Koussevitzky Foundation;

Tanglewood, Aug. 6, 1946, Leonard Bernstein conducting); *The Rape of Lucretia*, to a text by Ronald Duncan, after Shakespeare (Glyndebourne, July 12, 1946; Chicago, June 1, 1947); *Albert Herring*, after Maupassant (Glyndebourne, June 20, 1947, composer conducting; Tanglewood, Aug. 8, 1949); *The Beggar's Opera*, a new realization of the ballad opera by John Gay (Cambridge, May 24, 1948, composer conducting); *The Little Sweep*, or *Let's Make an Opera*, "an entertainment for young people" to a text by Eric Crozier, with optional audience participation (Aldeburgh, June 14, 1949; St. Louis, March 22, 1950); *Billy Budd*, after Melville (first version in 4 acts; Covent Garden, Dec. 1, 1951, composer conducting; NBC, N.Y., Oct. 19, 1952; revised version in 2 acts, 1960; BBC, Nov. 13, 1960; Covent Garden, Jan. 6, 1964, Solti conducting; Chicago, Nov. 6, 1970); *Gloriana*, on the subject of Elizabeth and Essex (first perf. during Coronation Week, June 8, 1953, at Covent Garden, conducted by Pritchard, in the disgruntled presence of Queen Elizabeth II, who was not amused by a stage presentation of her predecessor's amorous dallyings; Cincinnati, May 8, 1956); *The Turn of the Screw*, chamber opera after Henry James (Venice, Sept. 14, 1954, composer conducting; N.Y. College of Music, March 19, 1958); *Noye's Fludde*, one-act children's opera (Aldeburgh, June 18, 1958; N.Y., March 16, 1959); *A Midsummer Night's Dream*, after Shakespeare (Aldeburgh, June 11, 1960, composer conducting; San Francisco, Oct. 10, 1961); *Curlew River*, church parable (Aldeburgh, June 12, 1964, composer conducting; N.Y. Caramoor Festival, June 26, 1966); *The Burning Fiery Furnace*, church parable (Aldeburgh, June 9, 1966, composer conducting; N.Y. Caramoor Festival, June 25, 1967); *The Prodigal Son*, church parable (Aldeburgh, June 10, 1968, composer conducting; Katonah, June 29, 1969); *Owen Wingrave*, after Henry James (May 16, 1971, composer conducting; simultaneous production by the BBC and the NET Opera Theater in N.Y.; stage premiere, Covent Garden, London, May 10, 1973; Santa Fe, Aug. 9, 1973); *Death in Venice*, after Thomas Mann (Aldeburgh, June 16, 1973; N.Y., Metropolitan Opera, Oct. 18, 1974); 2 realizations of operas by Purcell: *Dido and Aeneas* (London, May 1, 1951, composer conducting) and *The Fairy Queen*, a shortened version for concert performance (Aldeburgh, June 25, 1967); a ballet, *The Prince of the Pagodas* (Covent Garden, Jan. 1, 1957, composer conducting).

VOCAL WORKS: *A Hymn to the Virgin*, anthem for Mixed Voices (1930; Lowestoft, Jan. 5, 1931); *A Boy Was Born*, choral variations (1933; BBC, Feb. 23, 1934; revised 1955); *Friday Afternoons* for Children's Voices (1935); *Te Deum in C* (1935; London, Jan. 27, 1936); *Our Hunting Fathers*, symph. cycle for High Voice and Orch. (1936; Norwich, Sept. 25, 1936, composer conducting; *On This Island*, 5 songs, to texts by W.H. Auden (1937; BBC, London, Nov. 19, 1937); *4 Cabaret Songs*, to texts by W.H. Auden (1937–39); *Ballad of Heroes* for High Voice, Chorus, and Orch. (London, April 5, 1939); *Les Illuminations* for High Voice and Strings, to poems by Rimbaud (1939; London, Jan. 30, 1940); *7 Sonnets of Michelangelo* for Tenor and Piano (1940; London,

Sept. 23, 1942); Hymn to St. Cecilia for 5-part Chorus (London, Nov. 22, 1942); *A Ceremony of Carols* for Treble Voices and Harp (Norwich, Dec. 5, 1942); *Rejoice in the Lamb* for Chorus, Soloists, and Organ (Northampton, Sept. 21, 1943); *Serenade* for Tenor, Horn, and Strings (London, Oct. 15, 1943); *Festival Te Deum* (1944; Swindon, April 24, 1945); *The Holy Sonnets of John Donne* for High Voice and Piano (London, Nov. 22, 1945); *Canticle I, "My Beloved Is Mine"* for High Voice and Piano (Aldeburgh, Nov. 1, 1947); *A Charm of Lullabies* for Mezzo-soprano and Piano (1947; The Hague, Jan. 3, 1948); *Saint Nicolas*, cantata (Aldeburgh, June 5, 1948); *Spring Symphony* for Soloists, Chorus, and Orch. (Amsterdam, July 9, 1949; Tanglewood, Aug. 13, 1949, Koussevitzky conducting); *5 Flower Songs* for Chorus (Dartington, South Devon, April 3, 1950); *Canticle II, Abraham and Isaac* (Nottingham, Jan. 21, 1952); *Choral Dances* from *Gloriana* (1953); *Winter Words* for High Voice and Piano, to poems by Thomas Hardy (Harewood House, Leeds, Oct. 8, 1953); *Canticle III, Still Falls the Rain*, for Tenor, Horn, and Piano, to a text by Edith Sitwell (London, Jan. 28, 1955); *Songs from the Chinese* for High Voice and Guitar (1957; Aldeburgh, June 17, 1958); *Nocturne* for Tenor, Obbligato Instruments, and Strings, to English poems (Leeds, Oct. 16, 1958); *Six Hölderlin Fragments* for Voice and Piano (Schloss Wolfsgarten, Nov. 20, 1958); *Cantata Accademica* for Soloists, Chorus, and Orch. (1959; Basel, July 1, 1960); *Missa Brevis in D* for Boys' Voices and Organ (London, July 22, 1959); *War Requiem*, to the texts of the Latin Requiem Mass and 9 poems of Wilfred Owen, for Soloists, Chorus, and Orch. (Coventry, May 30, 1962, composer conducting; Tanglewood, July 27, 1963); *Cantata Misericordium* for Soloists, Small Chorus, and Orch., for the centenary of the International Red Cross (Geneva, Sept. 1, 1963); *Songs and Proverbs of William Blake* for Baritone and Piano (Aldeburgh, June 24, 1965); *Voices for Today*, anthem for Chorus, for the 20th anniversary of the United Nations (triple premiere, N.Y., Paris, and London, Oct. 24, 1965); *The Poet's Echo* for High Voice and Piano, to texts by Pushkin (Moscow, Dec. 2, 1965); *The Golden Vanity*, vaudeville for Boys' Voices and Piano (1966; Aldeburgh, June 3, 1967, with the Vienna Boys' Choir); *Children's Crusade*, ballad for Children's Voices and Orch., to a text by Brecht (1968; London, May 19, 1969); *Who Are These Children?*, song cycle for Tenor and Piano (1969; Edinburgh, May 4, 1971); *Canticle IV, Journey of the Magi*, to a text by T.S. Eliot, for Tenor, Countertenor, Baritone, and Piano (Aldeburgh, June 26, 1971); *Canticle V, The Death of St. Narcissus* for Tenor and Harp, to a text by T.S. Eliot (1974; Schloss Elmau, Bavaria, Jan. 15, 1975); *Sacred and Profane*, 8 medieval lyrics for Chorus (Aldeburgh, Sept. 14, 1975); *A Birthday Hansel* for Voice and Harp, to poems by Robert Burns (1975; Cardiff, March 19, 1976); *Phaedra*, cantata for Mezzo-soprano and Chamber Orch. (1975; Aldeburgh, June 16, 1976); *Welcome Ode* for Children's Chorus and Orch. (1976; Ipswich, July 11, 1977); *8 British Folksongs*, arranged for Voice and Orch.; *6 French Folksongs*, arranged for Voice and Orch.; 6 vols. of British folk-song arrangements, with Piano Accompaniment (1943–61); realizations of Purcell's *Orpheus Britanicus,* with Peter Pears; *4 chansons françaises* for High Voice and Orch. (1928; first perf. in concert form at Aldeburgh, June 10, 1980).

FOR ORCH.: Sinfonietta (1932; London, Jan. 31, 1933); *Simple Symphony* (1934; Norwich, March 6, 1934, composer conducting); *Soirées musicales,* suite from Rossini (1936); *Variations on a Theme of Frank Bridge* for String Orch. (Salzburg, Aug. 27, 1937); *Mont Juic,* suite of Catalan dances, with Lennox Berkeley (1937; BBC, Jan. 8, 1938); Piano Concerto (London, Aug. 18, 1938; revised 1945; with an added 3rd movement, perf. in Cheltenham, July 2, 1946); Violin Concerto (1939; N.Y., March 28, 1940); *Young Apollo* for Piano, String Quartet, and Strings (1939; Toronto, Aug. 27, 1939); *Canadian Carnival* (1939; BBC, June 6, 1940); *Sinfonia da Requiem* (1940; N.Y., March 29, 1941); *An American Overture* (1942); *Diversions* for Piano, Left-hand, and Orch. (1940; revised 1954; Philadelphia, Jan. 16, 1942; Paul Wittgenstein, left-hand pianist, soloist); *Matinées musicales,* suite from Rossini (1941); *Scottish Ballad* for 2 Pianos and Orch. (Cincinnati, Nov. 28, 1941); *Prelude and Fugue* for 18 Strings (London, June 23, 1943); *4 Sea Interludes,* from *Peter Grimes* (Cheltenham, June 13, 1945); *The Young Person's Guide to the Orchestra,* variations and fugue on a theme of Purcell (Liverpool, Oct. 15, 1946); Symph. Suite from *Gloriana* (Birmingham, Sept. 23, 1954); *Pas de Six* from *The Prince of the Pagodas* (Birmingham, Sept. 26, 1957); *Cello Symphony* (1963; Moscow, March 12, 1964; composer conducting; Rostropovich, soloist); *The Building of the House,* overture for the opening of the Maltings concert hall (Aldeburgh, June 2, 1967; composer conducting); *Suite on English Folk Tunes* (1974; Aldeburgh, June 13, 1975); *Lachrymae, Reflections on a Song of John Dowland* for Viola and String Orch. (1976; Recklinghausen, May 3, 1977).

CHAMBER MUSIC: *Quartettino* for String Quartet (1930; London, May 23, 1983); *Phantasy in F minor* for String Quintet (1932; July 22, 1932); *Phantasy* for Oboe and String Trio (1932; Florence, April 5, 1934); Suite for Violin and Piano (1935; London, Jan. 27, 1936); *2 Insect Pieces* for Oboe and Piano (1935; Manchester, March 7, 1979); *3 Divertimenti* for String Quartet (1936; London, Feb. 25, 1936); *Temporal Variations* for Oboe and Piano (1936; London, Dec. 15, 1936); 3 string quartets: No. 1 (1941; London, April 28, 1943); No. 2 (1945; London, Nov. 21, 1945); No. 3 (1975; Aldeburgh, Dec. 19, 1976); *Lachrymae, Reflections on a Song of John Dowland* for Viola and Piano (1950; Aldeburgh; June 20, 1950); *6 Metamorphoses,* after Ovid, for Oboe Solo (1951; Thorpress, June 14, 1951); *Alpine Suite* for 3 Recorders (1955); Sonata in C for Cello and Piano (1961; Aldeburgh, July 7, 1961); *Nocturnal,* after John Dowland, for Guitar (1963; Aldeburgh, June 12, 1964); *3 Suites* for Solo Cello: No. 1 (1964; Aldeburgh, June 27, 1965); No. 2 (1967; Aldeburgh, June 17, 1968); No. 3 (1971; Aldeburgh, Dec. 21, 1974); String Quartet in D (1931; revised 1974; Aldeburgh, June 7, 1975); *Gemini Variations* for Flute, Violin, and Piano, 4-hands (1965; Aldeburgh, June 19, 1965); Suite for

Harp (1969; Aldeburgh, June 24, 1969).

FOR PIANO: 5 waltzes (1923–25; revised 1969); *Holiday Diary,* suite (1934); *Sonatina romantica* (1940; Aldeburgh, June 16, 1983).

BIBLIOGRAPHY: A whole literature has arisen about Benjamin Britten. A voluminous compendium, *Benjamin Britten: A Commentary on His Works from a Group of Specialists,* was publ. under the editorship of Donald Mitchell and Hans Keller (London, 1953); other biographical publications are E.W. White, *Benjamin Britten* (London, 1948; revised ed., 1970); *Tribute to Benjamin Britten on His 50th Birthday,* a collection of articles (London, 1963); Imogen Holst, *Britten* (London, 1966); Michael Hurd, *Benjamin Britten* (London, 1966); Percy M. Young, *Britten* (London, 1966); Patricia Howard, *The Operas of Benjamin Britten* (N.Y., 1969); A. Kendall, *Benjamin Britten* (1973); Donald Mitchell, *Benjamin Britten, 1913–1976; A Pictorial Biography* (N.Y., 1978); D. Herbert, ed., *The Operas of Benjamin Britten* (London, 1979); *The Music of Benjamin Britten* (London, 1979); Christopher Headington, *Britten* (London, 1981); Alan Blyth, *Remembering Britten* (London, 1981); R. Duncan, *Working with Britten: A Personal Memoir* (Welcombe, Devon, 1981); A. Whittall, *The Music of Britten and Tippet: Studies in Themes and Techniques* (Cambridge, 1982); P. Brett, *Peter Grimes* (Cambridge, 1983). In collaboration with Imogen Holst, Britten wrote *The Story of Music* (London, 1958) and *The Wonderful World of Music* (Garden City, N.Y., 1968; revised ed., 1970).

Brixi, Franz (František) Xaver, Bohemian composer of church music; b. Prague, Jan. 2, 1732; d. there, Oct. 14, 1771. He was a pupil of Segert in Prague; held several positions as a church organist; became Kapellmeister at St. Vitus's Cathedral in Prague on Jan. 1, 1759. He wrote a great number of sacred works: 105 masses; 263 offertories and anthems; 6 oratorios; 3 organ concertos; etc.

BIBLIOGRAPHY: O. Kamper, *Franz Xaver Brixi* (Prague, 1926); V. Novák, "Šimon a František Brixi . . . ," in *Zprávy Bertramky, jubilejní výtisk ke 40. výročí založení Mosartovy obce* (1967); idem, "Zur Katalogisierung von Werken der Familie Brixi," *Die Musikforschung* (July/Sept. 1969).

Brkanović, Ivan, Croatian composer; b. Skaljari, Bocca di Kotor, Dec. 27, 1906. He studied composition with Bersa at the Zagreb Music Academy, graduating in 1935; then went to Paris and studied with Léfebre at the Schola Cantorum. Returning to Zagreb, he taught at secondary schools (1935–51); was a music adviser at the Zagreb Opera (1951–54), director of the Zagreb Phil. (1954–57), and a visiting prof. at the Sarajevo Music Academy (1957–62). In his works, Brkanović derives thematic materials from national folk music, but his harmonic idiom follows modern usage.

WORKS: 2 operas: *Ekvinocij (Equinox;* 1945; Zagreb, Oct. 4, 1950) and *Zlato Zadra (The Gold of Zadar;* 1954; Zagreb, April 15, 1954); ballet, *Heloti* (1959; Zagreb, March 17, 1963); 5 symphs. (1935, 1946,

1947, 1948, 1949); Concertino for Strings (1955); *Sarajevska svita (Sarajevo Suite)* for Orch. (1957; Zagreb, Jan. 20, 1958); *Triptych* for Soloists, Chorus, and Orch. (1936); *Dalmatinski diptihon (Dalmatian Diptych)* for Soloists, Chorus, and Orch. (1953); 3 cantatas: *Bosnanska sjećanja* (1961); *Zelena zmija ljubavi* (1964); *Snatrenje* (1967); 2 string quartets (1933, 1938); *Theme and Variations* for Piano (1937).

BIBLIOGRAPHY: K. Kovačević, *Hravatski Kompozitori i Njihova Djela* (Zagreb, 1960).

Broadwood & Sons, oldest keyboard instrument manufacturer in existence; established in London in 1728 by the Swiss harpsichord maker **Burkhard Tschudi,** or **Shudi** (b. Schwanden, Switzerland, March 13, 1702; d. London, Aug. 19, 1773). **John Broadwood** (b. Cockburnspath, Scotland, 1732; d. London, 1812), a Scottish cabinetmaker, was Shudi's son-in-law and successor; in 1773 he began to build square pianos modeled after Zumpe's instruments; in 1780 he marketed his own square pianos, which he patented in 1783; in these, he dispensed with the old clavichord arrangement of the wrest-plank and tuning-pins and transformed the harpsichord pedals into damper and piano pedals; another important invention came in 1788, when he divided the long bridge, which until then had been continuous. Broadwood's improvements were soon adopted by other manufacturers. In 1794 the range of the keyboard was extended to 6 octaves. John Broadwood's sons, **James Shudi Broadwood** (b. London, Dec. 20, 1772; d. there, Aug. 8, 1851) and **Thomas Broadwood,** were admitted to the firm in 1795 and 1807, respectively, and the business was then carried on under the name of John Broadwood & Sons. Beethoven received a Broadwood piano in 1817. **Henry John Tschudi Broadwood** (d. Feb. 8, 1911), great-grandson of the founder, patented the so-called "barless" grand piano; he became a director of John Broadwood & Sons, Ltd., established in 1901, with W.H. Leslie as chairman. In 1925 the firm moved to new quarters in New Bond Street. Members of the Broadwood family are still active in its affairs.

BIBLIOGRAPHY: W. Dale, *Tschudi, the Harpsichord Maker* (London, 1913).

Broche, Charles, French organist and composer; b. Rouen, Feb. 20, 1752; d. there, Sept. 30, 1803. He studied with Desmazures at the Rouen Cathedral; then served as church organist in Lyons (1771–72); later went to Bologna, where he studied with Padre Martini. He returned to Rouen in 1777 and succeeded Desmazures as cathedral organist there. Among his pupils was Boieldieu. He publ. 3 piano sonatas (1782) and wrote some organ pieces.

BIBLIOGRAPHY: G. Favre, "Un Organiste de la Cathédrale de Rouen, Charles Broche," *Revue de Musicologie* (1937).

Brockway, Howard A., American composer and pianist; b. Brooklyn, Nov. 22, 1870; d. New York, Feb. 20, 1951. He studied in Berlin (1890–95); returning to the U.S., he settled in N.Y. as a teacher and concert

pianist; from 1903–10 taught at the Peabody Cons. in Baltimore.

WORKS: *Sylvan Suite* for Orch. (Boston, April 6, 1901); Symph. in D (Berlin, Feb. 23, 1895; Boston, April 6, 1907, Karl Muck conducting); *Moment musical* for Violin and Piano; many character pieces for piano (*Moods, Dance of the Sylphs,* etc.). He wrote piano accompaniments for 2 albums of Kentucky songs, which were publ. as *Lonesome Tunes* (N.Y., 1916) and *20 Kentucky Mountain Songs* (Boston, 1920).

Brod, Max, significant Czech-born writer and composer; b. Prague, May 27, 1884; d. Tel Aviv, Dec. 20, 1968. In Prague he associated himself with Kafka and other writers of the New School, and himself publ. several psychological novels. He studied music at the German Univ. in Prague and became a music critic in various Czech and German publications. In 1939 he emigrated to Tel Aviv, where he continued his literary and musical activities. Among his compositions are *Requiem Hebraicum* (1943); *2 Israeli Peasant Dances* for Piano and Small Orch. (Tel Aviv, April 24, 1947); several piano suites and 14 song cycles. He wrote an autobiography, *Streitbares Leben* (Munich, 1960), and a book on music in Israel (Tel Aviv, 1951).

Broder, Nathan, American musicologist and editor; b. New York, Dec. 1, 1905; d. there, Dec. 16, 1967. He studied at the College of the City of N.Y. In 1945 he became associate editor of the *Musical Quarterly*, a position he held until his death; from 1946–52 he was lecturer in music at Columbia Univ.; from 1959–62, adjunct prof. of music there. In 1956 he received a Guggenheim fellowship grant; received a Ford Foundation grant for research in 1961. From 1963 until his death he was music editor of W.W. Norton & Co.; also in 1963–64, president of the American Musicological Society. He publ. a monograph on Samuel Barber (N.Y., 1954); edited Mozart's piano sonatas and fantasies (Bryn Mawr, 1956); compiled *The Collector's Bach* (Philadelphia, 1958); was co-editor (with Paul Henry Lang) of *Contemporary Music in Europe* (N.Y., 1965).

Brodsky, Adolf, famous Russian violinist; b. Taganrog, April 2, 1851; d. Manchester, England, Jan. 22, 1929. A precocious violinist, he made his public debut at the age of 9 in Odessa; he was then sent to Vienna, where he studied with Joseph Hellmesberger, Sr., and played the 2nd violin in his string quartet. In 1866–68 he was appointed a violinist in the Vienna court orch.; in 1873 he returned to Moscow, where he studied with Ferdinand Laub, whom he succeeded in 1875 as prof. at the Moscow Cons. In 1881 he made a European tour, and on Dec. 4, 1881, in Vienna, gave the world premiere of Tchaikovsky's Violin Concerto, which Tchaikovsky in gratitude dedicated to him, after it had been rejected by Leopold Auer as unplayable. He was praised for his virtuosity, but Tchaikovsky's Violin Concerto was damned as badly written for the violin; the review by Eduard Hanslick, which described the music as emitting a stench, became notorious for its grossness, and caused Tchaikovsky great pain. From 1883 to 1891 Brodsky taught violin at the Leipzig Cons., and also organized a string quartet there (with Hugo Becker, Hans Sitt, and Julius Klengel), which enjoyed an international reputation. In 1891 he went to America and served as concertmaster of the N.Y. Symph. Orch. (until 1894); in 1895 he went to England, where he became concertmaster of the Halle Orch. in Manchester (1895–96); also taught violin at the Royal Manchester College of Music; in 1896 he became its principal. In England he changed the spelling of his first name to **Adolph.** His wife publ. *Recollections of a Russian Home* (London, 1904).

Brodsky, Vera. See **Lawrence, Vera Brodsky.**

Brody, Martin, American composer; b. Chicago, July 8, 1949. He studied at Amherst College (B.A., summa cum laude, 1972); then enrolled at the Yale School of Music, taking courses in composition with Yehudi Wyner and Robert Morris (M.M.A., 1976; D.M.A., 1981); also studied at Brandeis Univ. with Seymour Shifrin and Martin Boykan (1976–77); took a seminar in computer sound synthesis at the Mass. Inst. of Technology (1980). In 1980 he was appointed assistant prof. of music at Wellesley College. Apart from music in classical forms, he became active in electronic composition.
WORKS: *Saxifrage* for Piano (1976); *Duo* for Flute and Piano (1977); *Music for Cellos* (1977); Concertino for Orch. (1978); *3 Rituals* for Women's Chorus and Solo Violin (1978); *Nocturnes* for Solo Flute (1980); *Turkish Rondo* for Computer-synthesized Tape (1980); *Moments musicaux* for Piano and Computer-synthesized Tape (1981); *Apparitions* for Piano (1982); *Voices* for Solo Violin (1983).

Broekman, David, Dutch-born American conductor; b. Leiden, May 13, 1899; d. New York, April 1, 1958. He studied music with Van Anrooy in The Hague; came to the U.S. in 1924 as music editor for M. Witmark & Sons; then went to Hollywood, where he wrote film scores and conducted pageants and various other shows. He contributed the sound track for several motion pictures, including *All Quiet on the Western Front* and *The Phantom of the Opera;* he further wrote 2 symphs. (1934, 1947), and published an autobiography, *The Shoestring Symphony,* exhibiting a mandatory jaundiced view of Hollywood's life-style.

Brogi, Renato, Italian composer; b. Sesto Fiorentino, Feb. 25, 1873; d. San Domenico di Fiesole, Florence, Aug. 25, 1924. He studied music in Florence; then at the Milan Cons.; won the Steiner Prize in Vienna with his opera *La prima notte* (Florence, Nov. 25, 1898). He also composed the operas *L'Oblio* (Florence, Feb. 4, 1890) and *Isabella Orsini* (Florence, April 24, 1920); the operettas *Bacco in Toscana* and *Follie Veneziane* (both produced in Florence, 1923); Violin Concerto; String Quartet; Piano Trio; songs.

Brogue, Roslyn, American composer; b. Chicago, Feb. 16, 1919; d. Beverly, Mass., Aug. 1,1981. She studied languages at the Univ. of Chicago and music at Radcliffe College (Ph.D., 1947). In 1944 she married her private student Ervin Henning. Her music follows dodecaphonic precepts.
WORKS: Trio for Oboe, Clarinet, and Bassoon (1946); *Suite* for Small Orch. (1947); *Suite for Recorders* (1949); Piano Quartet (1949); String Quartet (1951); Trio for Violin, Clarinet, and Piano (1953); many songs with varied instrumental accompaniments.

Broman, Natanael, Swedish pianist and composer; b. Kolsva, Dec. 11, 1887; d. Stockholm, Aug. 27, 1966. He studied in Stockholm and later in Berlin. From 1925–51 he was in charge of the music division of Stockholm Radio. He was highly regarded as a pianist. In his compositions he follows the neo-Romantic trend with a strong undertow of Scandinavian melos. He composed a symph. poem, *Fritiof och Ingeborg* (1912); some violin pieces; and a number of songs.

Broman, Sten, eminent Swedish composer, conductor and music critic; b. Uppsala, March 25, 1902; d. Lund, Oct. 29, 1983. He studied at the German Music Academy in Prague, attending a master class in violin playing with Henri Marteau; subsequently studied musicology with Curt Sachs in Berlin. From 1929–51 he played the viola in various Swedish string quartets; from 1946 to 1966 was conductor of the Phil. Society in Malmö. He was an influential music critic; served as chairman of the Swedish section of the International Society for Contemporary Music from 1933 to 1962. A prolific composer, he wrote 8 symphs. and a number of chamber music pieces. In his idiom he followed a median line of Scandinavian Romanticism, but beginning about 1960 he adopted serial techniques and later experimented with electronic sound.
WORKS: *Choral Fantasia* for Orch. (1931); *Gothic Suite* for Strings (1932); a ballet, *Malmö Dances* (1952); 9 symphs.: No. 1, *Sinfonia ritmica* (Malmö, March 20, 1962); No. 2 (Stockholm, Nov. 16, 1963); No. 3 (Malmö, April 27, 1965); No. 4 (1965; Detroit, Nov. 17, 1966); No. 5, with Soprano Solo (Stockholm, April 19, 1968); No. 6, with Taped Organ Sounds (Lund, Sweden, Oct. 13, 1970); No. 7, with Electronic Sound (Stockholm, May 5, 1972); No. 8 (Stockholm, April 5, 1975); No. 9 (Swedish Radio, June 15, 1977); *Sententia crevit* for Orch. and Concrete Sound Tape (Lund, June 13, 1968); *Musica Cathedralis* for Soprano, Bass, 3 Choruses, Tape, Orch., and 2 Organs (Lund, April 4, 1973); *Overture* for Orch. (1979); *Canon* for Piano (1929); 3 string quartets (1929, 1933, 1970); Duo for Violin and Viola (1932); 3 suites for Viola and Piano (1935, 1937, 1942); Sextet for Strings, Percussion, and Piano (1963); Septet for Percussion, Celesta, and Piano (1968); Concerto for Brass (Malmö, Nov. 11, 1971); film music.

Bronner, Georg, German organist and composer; b. Hamburg (baptized, Feb. 17), 1667; d. there, (buried, March 8), 1720. In 1688 he became sacristan at the Heilig Geist hospital in Hamburg; in 1689 he also assumed the post of organist there, remaining in both positions until 1719. A number of his sacred works are extant.

Brons, Carel, Dutch composer; b. Groningen, Jan. 1, 1931; d. Hilversum, May 16, 1983. He studied piano with Luctor Ponse, organ with Cor Batenburg, and music theory with Johan Vetter (1949–55). He worked for Radio Holland (1954–72); after 1958 was music director of the Hilversum Radio. He adopted versatile idioms in his own compositions, making occasional use of serial methods.
WORKS: FOR ORCH.: *Varianten* (1966; orchestration of organ work); *Epitaphium* (1967); *Music for Strings* (1969); *They Are Telling Us* for 2 Harps and Chamber Orch. (1976–78); *Symphonic Fantasy* for Organ and Orch. (1980). CHAMBER MUSIC: *Balletto* for Wind Quintet (1961); *Dialogs I* for Oboe and Piano (1962); *Dialogs II* for Flute and Harp (1967); 3 string quartets (1962, 1969, 1977); *Serenata I* for Solo Flute (1963); *Serenata II* for Oboe, Clarinet, and Bassoon (1964); *Serenata III* for 4 Clarinets (1974); *Mutazione* for Wind Quintet (1964); *Monologue I* for Solo Oboe (1967); *Monologue II* for Solo Flute (1967); *Monologue III* for Solo Clarinet (1968); *Monologue IV* for Solo Bassoon (1968; revised 1974); *Monologue V* for Solo Trumpet (1970); Concertino for Clarinet, Violin, and Piano (1977); *Gentle Vision* for Flute and Piano (1978); *Threnody* for Solo Violin (1978); *Ballade '81* for Saxophone Quartet (1981); *Springtime Music* for 11 Instruments (1982–83). FOR VOICE: *Vox mea,* cantata for Soprano, Chorus, Instrumental Soloists, and Orch. (1974–76). FOR PIANO: *Imaginations I–III* (1966, 1966, 1974); *Telling a Story,* Nos. 1 and 2, for young Pianists (1970, 1978). FOR ORGAN: *Invenzione* (1963); *Reflecties* (1965); *Varianten* (1965; orchestrated 1966); *Prismen* (1967); *Astrabikon* (1968); *Cyclus* (1969); *Litany* (1971); *Reflections* for 2 Organs (1975); *Suite* (1979); *Structures in Music* (1980).

Bronsart von Schellendorf, Hans, German pianist and composer; b. Berlin, Feb. 11, 1830; d. Munich, Nov. 3, 1913. He studied piano with Kullak in Berlin and took lessons with Liszt in Weimar. In 1897 he undertook a concert tour through Germany, France, and Russia; from 1860–67 he was active as a conductor in Leipzig, Dresden, and Berlin. In his compositions he followed the Romantic trend in Schumann's tradition. His most successful was his youthful Piano Trio, his first opus number (1856); some of his piano pieces retained their popularity for a brief while. He also wrote a dramatic tone poem, *Manfred,* for Chorus and Orch., to his own text (Weimar, Dec. 1, 1901); 2 programmatic symphs. and choruses. In 1861 he married the pianist **Ingeborg Starck** (1840–1913).

Bronsart von Schellendorf, Ingeborg (née **Starck**), pianist and composer; b. (of Swedish parents) St. Petersburg, Aug. 24, 1840; d. Munich, June 17, 1913. She studied piano with Liszt at Weimar; in 1861 she married **Hans Bronsart von Schellendorf.** She composed 4 operas: *König Hjarne* (Berlin, 1891); *Jery und Bätely* (Weimar, 1873); *Die Sühne* (Dessau, 1909); *Die Gottin zu Sais;* also piano concertos, piano sonatas, salon pieces, violin pieces, cello pieces, and songs.

Bronskaya, Evgenya, Russian soprano; b. St. Petersburg, Feb. 1, 1882; d. Leningrad, Oct. 12, 1953. She first studied with her mother, E. de Hacke; then in Milan with Teresa Arkel; made her operatic debut in Tiflis in 1901; subsequently sang in Kiev (1902–3) and in Moscow (1904–5). From 1907 to 1910 she joined a traveling Italian opera troupe, and performed in Italy, France, and the U.S. (Boston, Chicago, and Philadelphia). Returning to Russia, she was a member of the Maryinsky Theater (1910–23); from 1923 to 1950 she taught voice at the Leningrad Cons. She was a brilliant coloratura soprano; was particularly impressive in the roles of Lucia, Gilda, and Violetta.

Brook, Barry Shelley, eminent American music scholar; b. New York, Nov. 1, 1918. He studied piano privately with Mabel Asnis; then entered the Manhattan School of Music, where he was a student of Louise Culver Strunsky in piano, of Hugh Ross in conducting, and of Roger Sessions in composition. He subsequently studied at the College of the City of N.Y., obtaining his B.S. in social sciences (1939); then took courses in musicology with Paul Henry Lang at Columbia Univ., receiving his M.A. with the dissertation *Clément Janequin* (1942). From 1942 to 1945 he was a member of the U.S. Air Corps. Selecting as his major subject French music history, he went to Paris, where he studied at the Sorbonne; in 1959 he received his doctorate with his dissertation *La Symphonie française dans la seconde moitié du XVIIIᵉ siècle.* In 1945 he was appointed to the faculty of Queens College; also taught at Brooklyn College. His other engagements were those of visiting prof. at N.Y. Univ. (1964–65), Université de Paris (1967–68), Eastman School of Music in Rochester, N.Y. (1973), Univ. of Adelaide in Australia (1974), and Aspen Music School (1975). From 1966 he served as editor in chief of RILM (Répertoire International de Littérature Musicale); from 1970 was also Chairman of RIdM (Répertoire International d'Iconographie Musicale); from 1977 he was acting president of the International Association of Music Libraries. The main subject of his studies was the music of the Renaissance; he was also an authority on French music of the 18th century. In appreciation of his work he received in 1965 the Dent Medal of the Royal Musical Association of Great Britain. An innovation in his bibliographical studies was the consistent use of modern computers.
WRITINGS: *La Symphonie française dans la seconde moitié du XVIIIe siècle* (3 vols., Paris, 1962); *The Breitkopf Thematic Catalogue, 1878–1962* (N.Y., 1966); *Musicology and the Computer* (N.Y., 1970); *Perspectives in Musicology* (with B. Downes and S. van Solkema; N.Y., 1972); *Thematic*

Catalogues in Music: An Annotated Bibliography (N.Y., 1972); numerous valuable articles in *Die Musik in Geschichte und Gegenwart, The New Grove,* and scholarly journals dealing with French symph. literature; also eds. of works of Gossec, Rigel, Bréval, and others (Paris, 1962–63).

Brook, Peter (Stephen Paul), noted English opera producer; b. London, March 21, 1925. He was educated at Oxford Univ.; then worked briefly at London's Covent Garden in producing opera; from 1962 he was a co-director of the Royal Shakespeare Co.; from 1970 he spent much time in Paris with his Centre International de Créations Théâtrales, where he attempted to synthesize theatrical elements in a total media art. In 1981 he produced in Paris a modernistically compressed version of *Carmen,* which he also staged in N.Y. in 1983.
BIBLIOGRAPHY: J. Trewin, *Peter Brook* (London, 1971).

Brooks, John Benson, American jazz pianist and composer; b. Houlton, Maine, Feb. 23, 1917. He attended John Cage's classes of modern music at the New School for Social Research in N.Y. and became immersed in dodecaphonic and aleatory lore. Moreover, he read books on astrology, numerology, and epistemology. Using the techniques of horoscopes, ink-blot tests, and extrasensory perception as catalytic agents to the imagination, he developed an individualized method of serial composition; by analogy with the principle of indeterminacy, he postulated that neither the velocity of musical particles nor their temporary positions at a given point can be precisely determined, and followed this idea in his improvisations, with *ostinatos* as departures from randomness. He composed the *Alabama Concerto* and a number of jazz songs.

Brooks, Patricia, American soprano; b. New York, Nov. 7, 1937. She studied at the Manhattan School of Music in N.Y.; also took dance lessons with Martha Graham. She made her operatic debut as Marianne in *Der Rosenkavalier* at the N.Y. City Opera on Oct. 12, 1960; also sang with opera companies in San Francisco, Chicago, New Orleans, Philadelphia, Houston, and Santa Fe. She made her Covent Garden debut in London in 1969. She gave an excellent account of the standard soprano roles; was especially praised as Gilda in *Rigoletto* and Lucia in *Lucia di Lammermoor.*

Broome, William Edward, Canadian organist and composer; b. Manchester, England, 1868; d. Toronto, Canada, May 10, 1932. He studied piano and organ with Dr. Roland Rogers at Bangor Cathedral in Wales (1876–90), was church organist in Bangor (1883–90); went to Canada and became an organist in Montreal (1894–1905) and Toronto. He won prizes at Welsh National Festivals for his dramatic cantata *The Siege of Cardiff Castle* (1908) and other works; publ. much church music, including *Hymn of Trust.*

Broonzy, "Big Bill" (real name, **William Lee Conley**), black American blues singer; b. Scott, Miss., June 26, 1893; d. Chicago, Aug. 14, 1958. He first took up the fiddle; after making his way to Chicago in 1920, he learned to play the guitar and subsequently began his career as a blues singer. He was as popular in Europe as in the U.S., making tours in 1951, 1955, and 1957.

Broqua, Alfonso, Uruguayan composer; b. Montevideo, Sept. 11, 1876; d. Paris, Nov. 24, 1946. He studied with Vincent d'Indy at the Schola Cantorum in Paris, where he settled. His works are characterized by a fine feeling for exotic material, which he presents in the brilliant manner of French modern music.
WORKS: Opera, *Cruz del Sur* (1918); *Thelen at Nagouëy,* Inca ballet (1934); *Isabelle,* romantic ballet (1936); *Tabaré,* poetic cycle for Soli, Women's Chorus, and Piano or Orch. (1908); *Poema de las Lomas,* triptych for Piano (1912); Piano Quintet; *3 Cantos del Uruguay* for Voice, Flute, and 2 Guitars (1925); *Cantos de Parana* for Voice and Guitar (1929); *Evocaciones Criollas,* 7 pieces for Guitar (1929); *3 Préludes Pampéens* for Piano (1938; also in orch. version).

Brosa, Antonio, Spanish violinist; b. Canonja, Tarragona, June 27, 1894; d. Barcelona, March 26, 1979. He studied in Barcelona and Brussels; then went to London, where he founded the Brosa String Quartet in 1925; made tours of Europe and the U.S. with it until 1938; then concentrated on a career as a soloist; lived in the U.S. during World War II; returned to Europe in 1946. He gave the world premiere of Benjamin Britten's Violin Concerto in N.Y. on March 28, 1940.

Broschi, Carlo. See **Farinelli.**

Broschi, Riccardo, Italian composer, brother of **Carlo Broschi;** b. Naples, c.1698; d. Madrid, 1756. He studied at the Cons. di Santa Maria di Loreto in Naples; brought out several operas in Naples, in which his brother sang. He later settled in Spain with his brother.

Brosig, Moritz, German church composer; b. Fuchswinkel, Upper Silesia, Oct. 15, 1815; d. Breslau, Jan. 24, 1887. He studied with Franz Wolf, organist at the Cathedral at Breslau, and succeeded him in 1842. He wrote 4 grand and 3 short instrumental masses; 7 books of graduals and offertories; 20 books of organ pieces; *Orgelbuch; Choralbuch; Modulationstheorie* (1865); *Harmonielehre* (1874; 4th ed., 1899, as *Handbuch der Harmonielehre und Modulation,* ed. by Thiel); also *Über die alten Kirchenkompositionen und ihre Wiedereinführung* (1880). Leuckart publ. a selection of his works in 5 vols.

Brosmann (à Sancto Hieronymo), Damasus, Moravian composer; b. Fulnek, Sept. 7, 1731; d. Příbor, Sept. 16, 1798. He studied violin and cello with Weissgräber in Fulnek; then devoted himself to the Piarist calling, serving in various capacities in Moravian towns. He wrote mostly sacred music.

BIBLIOGRAPHY: C. Gardavský, *Damasus Brosmann à Sancto Hieronymo* (Diss., Univ. of Brno, 1937).

Brossard, Noël-Matthieu, French writer on music; b. Chalons-sur-Saône, Dec. 25, 1789; date of death unknown. He was a judge; became interested in music; publ. *Théorie des sons musicaux* (Paris, 1847), a treatise on the variability of tones according to modulation (he reckoned 48 distinct tone-degrees within the octave).

Brossard, Sébastien de, French composer; b. Dompierre, Orne (baptized, Sept. 12), 1655; d. Meaux, Aug. 10, 1730. He studied theology at Caen (1670–76); was then in Paris (1678–87); in 1687 he went to Strasbourg; in 1689 became "maître de chapelle" at the Strasbourg Cathedral; in 1698 received a similar post at the Cathedral of Meaux; in 1709 he became canon there. His fame rests upon the authorship of what was erroneously regarded as the earliest dictionary of musical terms; it was in fact preceded by many publications: by the medieval compilation *De musica antica et moderna* (c.1100), the last section of which is a vocabulary of musical terms (to be found in Lafage's *Essais de dipthérographie musicale*, vol. I, pp. 404–7); by Joannes Tinctoris's *Terminorum musicae diffinitorium* (c.1475); and by Janowka's *Clavis ad thesaurum magnae artis musicae* (1701); Brossard had access to none of these, however. The title of Brossard's own volume is *Dictionnaire de musique, contenant une explication des termes grecs, latins, italiens et français les plus usités dans la musique,* etc. (Paris, 1703; 2nd ed., 1705; there is an Amsterdam reprint, marked 6th ed., but this designation is erroneous; Eng. trans. by Grassineau, 1740). Brossard also wrote *Lettre à M. Demotz sur sa nouvelle méthode d'écrire le plain-chant et la musique* (1729); a considerable variety of church music, including *Canticum Eucharisticum* on the Peace of Ryswick (1697; new ed. by F.X. Mathias); motets; etc. He brought out several vols. of *Airs sérieux et à boire.* His library of MSS was acquired by Louis XV in 1724, and formed the nucleus of the music collection of the Bibliothèque Nationale.

BIBLIOGRAPHY: M. Brenet, *Sébastien de Brossard* (Paris, 1896); also E. Lebeau, "L'Entrée de la collection musicale de Sébastien de Brossard à la Bibliothèque du Roi," *Revue de Musicologie* (Dec. 1950).

Brosses, Charles de, French magistrate and scholar; b. Dijon, Feb. 17, 1709; d. Paris, May 7, 1777. He first studied law, but later turned to science and literature, subjects on which he publ. several valuable dissertations; contributed the article "Musique" to the *Encyclopédie méthodique.* He was the first president of the parliament of Burgundy, and a member of the Académie des Belles-Lettres (1758).

BIBLIOGRAPHY: H. Mamet, *Le Président Charles de Brosses, Sa vie et ses ouvrages* (Lille, 1874); Cunisset-Carnot, "La Querelle de Voltaire et du président Charles de Brosses," *Revue des Deux Mondes* (Feb. 15, 1888).

Bros y Bertomeu, Juan (Joaquín Pedro Domingo), Spanish composer; b. Tortosa (baptized, May 12), 1776; d. Oviedo, March 12, 1852. He studied with Queralt in Barcelona; served as assistant maestro de capilla there at the church of S. Maria del Mar and as organist of the chapel of S. Severo. From 1806–23 he was maestro de capilla at the Cathedral of León; in 1824 was named maestro de capilla at the Cathedral of Oviedo. He wrote mostly church music.

BIBLIOGRAPHY: G. Bourligueux, "Juan Bros y Bertomeu (1776–1852), un maestro de capilla de la catedral de León: Semblanza biográfica," *Archivos Leoneses,* XXV/49 (1971).

Brott, Alexander, Canadian conductor, violinist, and composer; b. Montreal, March 14, 1915. He studied piano, violin, and composition at the McGill Cons. in Montreal (1928–35); then composition with Bernard Wagenaar, and conducting at Juilliard in N.Y. (1935–39). In 1939 he returned to Montreal, where he was engaged as concertmaster and assistant conductor of the Montreal Symph. Orch. (1945–58). In his music he follows the Romantic tradition, with impressionistic harmonies imparting an aura of modernity.

WORKS: Ballet, *Le Corriveau* (1966); for Orch.: *Oracle* (1938); *War and Peace* (1944); *Concordia* (1946); *From Sea to Sea,* suite (1947); Concerto for Violin and Chamber Orch. (Montreal, March 7, 1950); *Delightful Delusions* (1950); *Prelude to Oblivion* for Chamber Orch. (1951); *Fancy and Folly* (1953); *Scherzo* (1954); *Analogy in Anagram* (1955); *Israel* for Chorus and Orch. (1956); *Arabesque* for Cello and Chamber Orch. (1957); *The Vision of Dry Bones* for Baritone, Piano, and Strings (1958); *3 Astral Visions* for Strings (1959); *Spheres in Orbit* (1960); *Martlet's Muse* (1962); *Circle, Triangle, 4 Squares* for String Orch. (1963); *Profundium Praedictum* for Double Bass or Viola or Cello, and String Orch. (1964); *Centennial Celebration* for Narrator, Female Chorus, and Strings (1967); *Paraphrase in Polyphony* (Montreal, Nov. 3, 1967; variants based on a recently unearthed 10-bar canon written by Beethoven in 1825); *The Young Prometheus* (1969; 12 preludes and fugues based on Beethoven sketches); *The Emperor's New Clothes* for Narrator and Orch. (Kingston, Ontario, Feb. 21, 1971); Quintet for Recorder and String Quartet (1940); String Quartet (1941); *Critic's Corner* for String Quartet and Percussion (1950); *5 Miniatures* for 8 Players (1950); *Vignettes en Caricature* for Piano (1952); *Sept for Seven* for Narrator, String Trio, Clarinet, Saxophone, and Piano (1955); *3 Acts for 4 Sinners* for Saxophone Quartet (1961); *Mutual Salvation Orgy* for Brass Quintet (1962); *World Sophisticate* for Soprano, Brass Quintet, and Percussion (1962); *Berceuse* for Saxophone Quartet (1962); *3 on a Spree* for Flute, Oboe, and Harp (1963); *Mini-Minus* for Clarinet, Bassoon, Trumpet, Trombone, Violin, Double Bass, and Percussion (1968); *Spasms for Six* for 6 Percussionists (1971); *Saties-Faction* for String Quartet (1972); choral works with piano.

Brott, Boris, Canadian conductor, son of **Alexander Brott**; b. Montreal, March 14, 1944. He was educated at McGill Univ. and at the Cons. of Montreal. He also had instruction in conducting at various times in various places with Pierre Monteux, Igor Markevitch, and Leonard Bernstein. From 1963 to 1965 he was assistant conductor of the Toronto Symph. Orch.; then conducted the Northern Sinfonia of England (1964–68). In 1969 he became music director of the Hamilton (Ontario) Phil.

Brouillon-Lacombe, Louis. See **Lacombe, Louis.**

Brounoff, Platon, Russian conductor and composer; b. Elizavetgrad, May 10, 1863; d. New York, July 11, 1924. He studied at the St. Petersburg Cons. (1890) with Rimsky-Korsakov. In 1891 he went to the U.S., where he was conductor of the Modern Symph. Orch., the Russian Choral Society, and the People's Male Chorus in N.Y.
WORKS: Opera, *Ramona;* music dramas: *Xilona* and *Titanic; Angel,* cantata for 2 Solo Voices, Chorus, and Orch.; *The Glory of God,* oratorio; *Russia,* festival overture (N.Y., 1897); orch. suites: *Flower Garden* (1897); *Russian Village; Palestine* (1908); piano pieces; collections of Russian and Jewish folk songs. He was the author of *Ten Commandments of Piano Practice* (publ. privately, 1910).

Brouwenstijn, Gré, Dutch soprano; b. Den Helder, Aug. 26, 1915. She studied at the Cons. in Amsterdam. In 1940 she made her debut in *Tosca* at the Netherlands Opera. She first sang at Covent Garden in 1951; then appeared widely in Europe. She made her debut in America at the Chicago Lyric Opera in 1959.

Brower, Leo, Cuban guitarist and composer; b. Havana, March 1, 1939. He studied in the U.S. with Persichetti and Stefan Wolpe at the Juilliard School of Music in N.Y. and with Isadore Freed at Hartt College in Hartford. Returning to Cuba, he occupied various administrative posts on Havana Radio; also traveled abroad as a concert guitar player. In his own compositions he cultivated the most advanced contemporary techniques, including stylized pop art and multimedia productions.
WORKS: *Sonograma* for Prepared Piano (1963); *2 conceptos del tiempo* for 10 Players (1965); *Conmutaciones* for Prepared Piano and 2 Percussionists (1966); *Tropos* for Orch. (1967); *Hexahedron* for 6 Players (1969); Flute Concerto (1972); numerous guitar pieces in Cuban guitar rhythms.

Brown, Clifford ("Brownie"), black American jazz trumpeter; b. Wilmington, Del., Oct. 30, 1930; d.

in an automobile accident, June 26, 1956. He studied at Delaware State College and Maryland State College; gained experience playing in college jazz bands; later joined Tadd Dameron's group; toured Europe in 1953 with Lionel Hampton's orch.; returning to the U.S., he worked with Art Blakey; subsequently formed the Brown-Roach Quintet with Max Roach. Brown was particularly successful as a master of improvisation.

Brown, David, English musicologist; b. Gravesend, July 8, 1929. He studied at the Univ. of Sheffield (B.A., 1951; B.Mus., 1952); then was music librarian at the Univ. of London Library, Senate House (1959–62). In 1962 he was appointed a lecturer at the Univ. of Southampton. He was awarded a Ph.D. in 1971 by the Univ. of Southampton for his book *Thomas Weelkes: A Biographical and Critical Study* (London, 1969); also wrote *John Wilbye* (London, 1974); then specialized in Russian music; publ. *Mikhail Glinka* (London, 1974) and an extended 3-vol. biography of Tchaikovsky; its merits are marred by an easy acceptance of the untenable theory that Tchaikovsky committed suicide. He contributed articles on Russian music to the *New Grove Dictionary of Music and Musicians* (1980).

Brown, Earle, American composer of the avant-garde; b. Lunenburg, Mass., Dec. 26, 1926. He played trumpet in school bands; then enrolled in Northeastern Univ. in Boston to study engineering; played trumpet in the U.S. Army Air Force Band; also served as a substitute trumpet player with the San Antonio Symph. in Texas. Returning to Boston, he began to study the Schillinger system of composition; also took private lessons in music theory with Rosalyn Brogue Henning. He soon adopted the most advanced types of techniques in composition, experimenting in serial methods as well as in aleatory improvisation. He was fascinated by the parallelism existing in abstract expressionism in painting, mobile sculptures, and free musical forms; to draw these contiguities together he initiated the idea of open forms, using graphic notation with visual signs in musical terms. The titles of his works give clues to their contents: *Folio* (1952–53) was a group of 6 compositions in which the performer was free to vary the duration, pitch, and rhythm; *25 Pages* (1953) was to be played by any number of pianists up to 25, reading the actual pages in any desired order, and playing the notes upside down or right side up. Further development was represented by *Available Forms I* for 18 instruments, consisting of musical "events" happening in accordance with guiding marginal arrows. Brown made much use of magnetic tape in his works, both in open and closed forms. Apart from his creative endeavors, he had numerous lecturing engagements in Europe and the U.S. He was composer-in-residence with the Rotterdam Phil. in the Netherlands in 1947, and guest prof. at the Basel Cons. in Switzerland in 1975; also served as visiting prof. at the Univ. of Southern Calif. at Los Angeles (1978). He professes no *parti pris* in his approach to techniques and idioms of composition, whether dissonantly contrapuntal or serenely triadic; rather, his music represents a mobile assembly of plastic elements, in open-ended or closed forms. As a result, his usages range from astute asceticism and constrained constructivism to soaring sonorism and lush lyricism, *sine ira et studio.*

WORKS: *Perspectives* for Piano (1952); *Music* for Violin, Cello, and Piano (1952); *Folio,* a set of 3 pieces, each playable by any number of instruments and bearing titles indicating the chronology of composition: *November 1952* (subtitled *Synergy*), *December 1952,* and *1953; 25 Pages* for any number of Pianos not exceeding 25 (1953); *Octet I* for 8 Spatially Directed Magnetic Tapes (1953); *Indices* for Chamber Orch. (1954); *Pentathis* for Flute, Bass Clarinet, Trumpet, Trombone, Harp, Piano, Violin, Viola, and Celesta (1957); *Hodograph* for Flute, Piano, Celesta, Bells, Vibraphone, and Marimba (1959); *Available Forms I* for 18 Musicians (Darmstadt, Sept. 8, 1961); *Light Music* for Electric Lights and variable numbers of Instruments (1961); *Available Forms II* for 98 Musicians and 2 Conductors (1962); *Times 5* for 5 Instruments and Tapes (1963); *From Here* for 20 Musicians and 4 Optional Choruses (1963); *Corroboree* for 3 Pianos (1964); String Quartet (1965); *9 Rarebits* for Harpsichord (1965); *Chef d'orchestre/Calder Piece* for a Mobile Solo struck by Pursuing Percussionists and colliding with Other Musicians in the process (1967; first American perf. at the Contemporary Music Festival in Valencia, Calif., March 9, 1980); *Event: Synergy II* for Chamber Groups (1967–68); *Syntagm* for 8 Instruments (1970); *New Piece Loops* for 18 Instruments (1971); *Time Spans* for Orch. (1972); *Sign Sounds* for Chamber Ensemble (1972); *Centering* for Violin and 10 Instruments (1973); *Cross Sections and Color Fields* for Orch. (1973–75); *Patchen* for Chorus and Orch., in memory of the American surrealist poet Kenneth Patchen (1979); *Windsor Jambs* for Soprano and Chamber Orch. (1979).

Brown, Eddy, American violinist; b. Chicago, July 15, 1895; d. Abano Terme, Italy, June 14, 1974. He was given his first lessons in violin playing by his father; then was taken to Europe, and studied in Budapest with Jenö Hubay. He won a violin competition at the age of 11 playing the Mendelssohn Concerto in Budapest. He then proceeded to London, and eventually to Russia, where he became a pupil of Leopold Auer. Returning to the U.S. in 1915, he made several transcontinental tours; was a soloist with the N.Y. Phil., the Chicago Symph. Orch., the Philadelphia Orch., and the Boston Symph. Orch. In 1922 he founded the Eddy Brown String Quartet; in 1932 he became president of the Chamber Music Society of America, which he organized. He became active in educational programs over the radio; was music director of the Mutual Broadcasting System (1930–37) and of station WQXR in N.Y. (1936–55). From 1956–71 he was artistic coordinator of the Cincinnati College-Cons. of Music.

Brown, Howard Mayer, American musicologist; b. Los Angeles, April 13, 1930. He studied composition with Walter Piston and musicology with Otto Gombosi at Harvard Univ. (B.A., 1951; M.A., 1954; Ph.D., 1959). He held a Guggenheim fellowship in Florence (1963–64); returning to the U.S., he was a member of the faculty at Wellesley College (1958–60); in 1960 was appointed to the staff of the Univ. of Chicago; in 1967 was named prof. there; in 1970 became chairman of the music dept. In 1972–74 he taught at King's College, Univ. of London; then returned to the Univ. of Chicago. He publ. *Music in the French Secular Theater, 1400–1550* (Cambridge, Mass., 1963); *Instrumental Music Printed before 1600: A Bibliography* (Cambridge, Mass., 1965); *Music in the Renaissance* (Englewood Cliffs, N.J., 1976). In 1970 he was named editor of the compendium *Italian Opera, 1640–1770: Major Unpublished Works in a Central Baroque and Early Classical Tradition* (N.Y., 1977—; planned in 60 vols.).

Brown, Iona, English violinist and conductor; b. Salisbury, Siltshire, Jan. 7, 1941. She studied violin as a child; in 1955 joined the National Youth Orch. of Great Britain, remaining its member for 5 years; she also studied with Hugh Maguire in London, Remy Principe in Rome, and Henryk Szeryng in Paris and Nice. In 1963–66 she played in the Philharmonia Orch. of London; in 1964 she joined the Academy of St. Martin-in-the Fields, and served as its director in 1974. In 1980 she was named music director of the Norwegian Chamber Orch. in Oslo.

Brown, James, black American gospel-soul singer; b. Augusta, Ga., May 3, 1928. He banged on keyboards, beat drums, and plucked the string bass; then formed a group which he called The Famous Flames. In 1956 he produced a triply emphatic song, *Please, Please, Please,* which made the top of the charts. Other big-time hits were *Try Me, Prisoner of Love, It's a Man's World, Out of Sight,* and *Papa's Got a Brand New Bag.* He then formed the James Brown Revue and produced stage shows. His songs acquired a political flavor, such as his militant proclamation *Black Is Beautiful, Say It Loud, I'm Black and I'm Proud.* He cultivated vocal sex motifs in such songs as *I Got Ants in My Pants, Hot Pants, Body Heat,* and *Sex Machine.* He also made an admonitory gesture to junkies in his song *King Heroin.* At the height of his fame as a soul singer he was called "Soul Brother Number One," "Godfather of Soul," and "King of Soul."

Brown, James Duff, British music bibliographer; b. Edinburgh, Nov. 6, 1862; d. London, Feb. 14, 1914. He was librarian of the Clerkenwell Library of London from 1888; co-author (with Stephen S. Stratton) of the valuable reference work *British Musical Biography: A Dictionary of Musical Artists, Authors and Composers Born in Great Britain and Its Colonies* (1897). He also publ. *Biographical Dictionary of Musicians* (1886); *Guide to the Formation of a Music Library* (1893); *Characteristic Songs and Dances of All Nations,* with historical notes and a bibliography (in collaboration with Moffat, 1901);

and *Subject Classification* (1908). His *Manual of Library Economy* was publ. in several editions (3rd ed., London, 1920).

Brown, Dr. John, English writer; b. Rothbury, Northumberland, Nov. 5, 1715; d. (suicide) Newcastle upon Tyne, Sept. 23, 1766. He became vicar of Great Horkesley, Essex, in 1754, and of St. Nicholas's, Newcastle, in 1758. He is the author of *Dissertation on the Rise, Union, and Power, the Progressions, Separations and Corruptions of Poetry and Music, to which is prefixed The Cure of Saul, A Sacred Ode* (London, 1763). A revised edition was publ. in 1764 as *The History of the Rise and Progress of Poetry, through Its Several Species* (in French, Paris, 1768; in German, Leipzig, 1769; in Italian, 1772).

Brown, Les(ter Raymond), American bandleader; b. Reinerton, Pa., March 14, 1912. He studied at the Ithaca Cons. of Music; subsequently (1932–35) enrolled in Duke Univ., where he led the Duke Blue Devils band. In 1938 he organized his own band, which became quite successful in its renditions of popular music on radio, in films, and on television. His Band of Renown became closely associated with the comedian Bob Hope, and it accompanied him on many tours abroad to entertain American troops through the years of war and peace.

Brown, Maurice J(ohn) E(dwin), noted English writer on music; b. London, Aug. 3, 1906; d. Marlborough, Sept. 27, 1975. He received his education at the Univ. of London (B.Sc., 1929; B.Mus., 1939); then pursued a career as a high-school and grammar-school teacher; concurrently he devoted himself to musical research, studying various aspects of the life and works of Schubert; his *Schubert: A Critical Biography* (London, 1958; in German, 1969) is a standard source; he was also an authority on Chopin. In addition to many articles for music periodicals, he wrote *Schubert's Variations* (London, 1954); *Chopin: An Index of His Work in Chronological Order* (London, 1960); *Essays on Schubert* (London, 1966); with O.E. Deutsch, *Schubert: Die Erinnerungen seiner Freunde* (Leipzig, 1966); *Schubert Songs* (London, 1967); *Schubert Symphonies* (London, 1970).

Brown, Merton, American composer; b. Berlin, Vt., May 5, 1913. He studied both piano and violin; moved to N.Y. in 1935 and took piano lessons with Anne Hull, and studied composition privately with Wallingford Riegger (1939–42) and with Carl Ruggles (1943–45). From 1949–67 he lived in Rome; then returned to America, and settled in Boston. His music is set in dissonant counterpoint of great density without negating the lyrical flow of melody.
WORKS: *Consort for 4 Voices,* scored for 2 Pianos (N.Y., April 21, 1947); Piano Sonata (1948); *Chorale* for Strings (1948); *Duo in 3 Movements* for Violin and Piano (1956); *Concerto breve per archi* (Naples, Italy, Jan. 23, 1960); *Metamorfosi per piano* (1965); *Dialogo* for Cello and Piano (1970); *Concertino* for

String Orch. (1974); *Divertimento* for Piano, 4-hands (1975); *5 Pieces* for Clarinet and Piano (1976); *Psalm 13* (1976).

Brown, Nacio Herb, American composer of popular songs; b. Deming, N.Mex., Feb. 22, 1896; d. San Francisco, Sept. 28, 1964. He was a clothier and later a real-estate agent; learned a little about music at the Musical Arts High School in Los Angeles, where he began producing songs that seemed to be blessed with a dollar sign. Among his greatest hits were *Singin' in the Rain* (1929), made famous by Judy Garland in her movie *Little Nellie Kelly* (1940), and *Temptation,* glorified by Bing Crosby in the screen musical *Going Hollywood* (1933).

Brown, Newel Kay, American composer and pedagogue; b. Salt Lake City, Feb. 29, 1932. He studied composition with Leroy Robertson at the Univ. of Utah (B.F.A., 1953; M.F.A., 1954) and with Howard Hanson, Wayne Barlow, and Barnard Rogers at the Eastman School of Music in Rochester, N.Y. (Ph.D., 1967). From 1961 to 1967 he taught at Centenary College for Women at Hackettstown, N.J.; from 1967 to 1970 he was on the faculty of Henderson State College, Arkadelphia, Ark.; in 1970 became prof. of composition at North Texas State Univ. in Denton. As a member of the Mormon Church, he wrote a number of choral works which entered the permanent repertoire; of these, the Mormon children's choral work *I Hope They Call Me on a Mission* (1968) was translated into 17 languages.
WORKS: Saxophone Sonata (1968); *Four Pieces* for Flute and Clarinet (1968); Suite for 2 Trumpets (1968); Trombone Sonata (1969); Woodwind Quintet (1969); *Hopkins Set* for Baritone and Trombone (1971); *Postures* for Bass Trombone and Piano (1972); *Glaser Set* for Mezzo-soprano, Trumpet, Clarinet, and Piano (1974); *Anagrams* for Trumpet, Marimba, and Percussion (1977); *Windart I* for Tuba, Soprano, and Piano (1978); *Windart II* for Euphonium, 6 Clarinets, Vibraphone, and Percussion (1980); *Four Meditations* for Bass Voice, Alto Saxophone, and Percussion (1981); numerous sacred songs and choruses.

Brown, Rayner, American composer; b. Des Moines, Iowa, Feb. 23, 1912. He studied at the Univ. of Southern Calif., obtaining his M.Mus. in 1946; became active as a church organist in Los Angeles. In 1952 he became a prof. of music at Biola College in Los Angeles.
WORKS: 3 symphs. (1952, 1957, 1958); Concerto for Organ and Orch. (1959); Piano Quartet (1947); String Quartet (1953); 2 woodwind quintets (1955, 1957); Brass Quintet (1957); 2 flute sonatas (1944, 1959); 3 Fugues for 5 Flutes (1952); Trio for Flute, Clarinet, and Viola (1957); 12 sonatinas for Organ; Piano Sonata; etc.

Brown, Rosemary, British musical medium; b. London, July 27, 1917. She led a middle-class life as a housewife, and liked to improvise at the piano. Possessed of a certain type of musical mimicry, she began playing passages in the manner of her favorite compositions by Mozart, Beethoven, Schubert, Chopin, or Liszt; they usually consisted of short melodies invariably accompanied by broken triads and seventh-chords. Under the influence of popular literature dealing with communication with ghosts, she became convinced that the music she played was actually dictated to her by departed composers, and willingly recited stories about their human kindness to her (Chopin warned her to turn off the leaking faucet in the bathtub to prevent flooding). On an errand to a grocery store as a small child, she was approached by a tall, gray-haired gentleman who, observing that she carried a music book, introduced himself as Franz Liszt and volunteered to teach her piano without remuneration. She had similar happy encounters with other famous composers, and soon arranged to take dictation of posthumous works from them. She appeared on British television writing down notes under the dictation of Beethoven, but Beethoven's image failed to materialize on the screen, owing no doubt to some last-moment scruples on the part of the producers. She put out a couple of maudlin, maundering, meandering pamphlets dealing with her transcendental experiences, and a professional journalist publ. the story of her contacts with dead composers. Also transmitted were some postmortem essays by Tovey, well-known for his belief in spooks.

Brown, Wilfrid, English tenor; b. Horsham, April 5, 1921; d. Petersfield, March 5, 1971. He studied music with Charles Kennedy Scott at Trinity College of Music, and with Eric Greene; after 1951 he pursued a successful career in England as an oratorio singer; also sang with the Deller Consort, specializing in old English music.

Brown, William, flute player and composer who settled in America in the middle of the 18th century. He gave a concert on the flute in Baltimore on Jan. 30, 1784; then went to Philadelphia, where he participated in numerous benefit concerts; in 1785 he established a series of Subscription Concerts in N.Y. and Philadelphia (with Alexander Reinagle and Henri Capron). He composed *3 Rondos for the Pianoforte or Harpsichord* (dedicated to Francis Hopkinson). He was probably a German; may be identical with Wilhelm Braun of Kassel.
BIBLIOGRAPHY: J.D. Apell, *Galerie der vorzüglichsten Tonkünstler und merkwürdigen Musikdilettanten in Kassel* (1806); J.T. Howard, *Our American Music* (4th ed.; N.Y., 1965); Carl Engel, "Introducing Mr. Brown," *Musical Quarterly* (Jan. 1944).

Browne, Jackson, American folk-rock musician and songwriter; b. Heidelberg, Germany, Oct. 9, 1948; brought to California as a child. He sang in hootenannies before joining The Nitty Gritty Dirt Band. He reached the big time in 1969 when he opened a show with Linda Ronstadt at the Troubadour Club in Hollywood. In 1971 he got together with the versatile guitarist David Lindley, with whom he

produced *Doctor, My Eyes,* which became a smash hit. Another whammy was *Jamaica, Say You Will.* His record albums *Late for the Sky* and *The Pretender* made him a small fortune. Impassioned by the earnest desire to save the world from nuclear annihilation, he joined MUSE (Musicians United for Safe Energy) in 1979 and financed the movie *No Nukes.* He was briefly jailed in 1981 during a protest to obstruct the opening of the nuclear power plant at Diablo Canyon, Calif.

Browne, John Lewis, organist and composer; b. London, May 18, 1864; d. Chicago, Oct. 23, 1933. He was a pupil of his father, William Browne, a noted organist; later studied with S.P. Warren (1884) and F. Archer (1887); settling in America, he was active as an organist in San Francisco, Atlanta, Philadelphia, and Chicago; during his career he gave more than 500 organ recitals. He designed an organ for Medinah Temple in Chicago, and inaugurated it with the first performance of Felix Borowski's *Allegro de Concert,* commissioned for the occasion.
WORKS: Opera, *La Corsicana* (received an honorable mention in the Sonzogno Competition in 1902; first perf. in Chicago, Jan. 4, 1923); ode, *The Granite Walls Rise Fair* (1911); *Missa Solemnis* (1913); many songs.
BIBLIOGRAPHY: E.E. Hipsher, *American Opera and Its Composers* (Philadelphia, 1927; pp. 93–97).

Browning, John, brilliant American pianist; b. Denver, May 22, 1933. His father was a professional violinist, his mother an accomplished pianist. Browning studied with her from childhood; played a Mozart piano concerto at the age of 10, and was accepted as a student by Rosina Lhévinne, who was giving a master course in Denver at the time. The family later moved to Los Angeles, where Browning became a private student of Lee Pattison. He soon moved to N.Y., where he entered the class of Rosina Lhévinne at the Juilliard School of Music; in 1954 he received the $2,000 Steinway Centennial Award. In 1955 he won the Leventritt Award. He made his N.Y. debut in 1956; then went to Belgium to compete for the International Piano Competition sponsored by Queen Elisabeth; he won 2nd prize, after Vladimir Ashkenazy, who received first prize. Returning to the U.S., he developed a nonstop career of uninterrupted successes. On Sept. 24, 1962, he gave the world premiere of Samuel Barber's Piano Concerto with the Boston Symph., conducted by Erich Leinsdorf at Lincoln Center for the Performing Arts in N.Y. The work became his honorific cachet; it was modern, it was difficult to play, but he performed it, according to his own calculations, more than 400 times in the 20 years following its premiere. He has also performed virtually the entire standard repertoire of piano concertos from Beethoven to Prokofiev, 43 concertos in all. In 1965 Browning was soloist with the Cleveland Orch. on a European tour under the auspices of the State Dept.; the itinerary included the Soviet Union; so successful was he there that he was reengaged for appearances in the U.S.S.R. in 1967 and in 1970. In 1971 he played in Japan.

Brownlee, John (full name, **John Donald Mackensie Brownlee**), American baritone; b. Geelong, Australia, Jan. 7, 1900; d. New York, Jan. 10, 1969. He studied singing in Paris and made his operatic debut there in 1926; on June 8, 1926, he sang in Covent Garden in London, at the farewell appearance of Melba. He was subsequently a member of the Paris Opéra (1926–33); then joined the Metropolitan Opera in N.Y., making his debut there in *Rigoletto* on Feb. 17, 1937; he sang his last performance there on Dec. 20, 1956. He held the title of director at the Manhattan School of Music from 1956 to 1958; in 1958 was appointed its president, and held this post until his death.

Brubeck, Dave (David), American pianist and jazz improviser, brother of **Howard Brubeck;** b. Concord, Calif., Dec. 6, 1920. He played piano in jazz bands as a boy; then took lessons with Milhaud at Mills College, and with Schoenberg in Los Angeles. During World War II he was assigned to a band in Europe; after demobilization, he organized a highly successful band of his own. In his half-improvised compositions he employs a contrapuntal idiom combining elements of jazz with baroque textures. He wrote the oratorio *Truth Has Fallen* for the opening of the new Midland (Mich.) Center for the Arts, May 1, 1971. In the 1970s he drafted into his band his 3 rock-musician sons: **Darius** (named after Darius Milhaud), b. San Francisco, June 14, 1947 (plays acoustic and electric keyboards); **Chris,** b. Los Angeles, March 19, 1953 (trombone, bass, keyboards); and **Danny,** b. Oakland, Calif., May 5, 1955 (percussion).

Brubeck, Howard, American composer, brother of **Dave Brubeck;** b. Concord, Calif., July 11, 1916. After studying with Darius Milhaud and others, he devoted himself to teaching; was chairman of the music dept. at Palomar Junior College in San Marcos, Calif.
WORKS: *Elizabethan Suite* for Chamber Orch. and Women's Chorus (1944); *California Suite* for Orch. (1945); *Overture to the Devil's Disciple* (1954); *Four Dialogues* for Jazz Combo and Orch. (San Diego, Aug. 1, 1956); *The Gardens of Versailles,* suite for Orch. (1960); Woodwind Quintet (1950); choruses; piano pieces; arrangements for jazz combo and orch. on Dave Brubeck's themes.

Bruch, Max, celebrated German composer; b. Cologne, Jan. 6, 1838; d. Friedenau, near Berlin, Oct. 2, 1920. His mother, a professional singer, was his first teacher. He afterward studied theory with Breidenstein in Bonn; in 1852 he won a scholarship of the Mozart Foundation in Frankfurt for 4 years, and became a pupil of Ferdinand Hiller, Reinecke, and Breuning. At the age of 14, he brought out a symph. at Cologne, and at 20 produced his first stage work, *Scherz, List und Rache,* adapted from Goethe's Singspiel (Cologne, Jan. 14, 1858). Between 1858 and 1861 he taught music in Cologne; also made prolonged visits to Berlin, Leipzig, Dresden, and Munich; in 1863 he was in Mannheim, where he produced his first full-fledged opera, *Die Loreley* (April 14, 1863), to the libretto by Geibel, originally intended for Mendelssohn. About the same time he wrote an effective choral work, *Frithjof,* which was presented with great success in various German towns, and in Vienna. From 1865–67 Bruch was music director of a concert organization in Koblenz; there he wrote his First Violin Concerto (in G minor), which became a great favorite among violinists; then was court Kapellmeister in Sonderhausen. In 1870 he went to Berlin; his last opera, *Hermione,* based on Shakespeare's *The Winter's Tale,* was produced at the Berlin Opera on March 21, 1872. In 1880 he accepted the post of conductor of the Liverpool Phil., and remained in England for 3 years; in 1883 he visited the U.S. and conducted his choral work *Arminius* in Boston. From 1883–90 he was music director of an orch. society in Breslau; in 1891 he became a prof. of composition at the Hochschule für Musik in Berlin, retiring in 1910. Bruch was married to the singer **Clara Tuczek** (d. 1919). Cambridge Univ. conferred upon him the honorary degree of D.Mus. (1893); the French Academy elected him corresponding member; in 1918 the Univ. of Berlin gave him the honorary degree of Dr.Phil.
Bruch's music, although imitative in its essence and even in its melodic and harmonic procedures, has a great eclectic charm; he was a master of harmony, counterpoint, and instrumentation; he was equally adept at handling vocal masses. He contributed a great deal to the development of the secular oratorio, using soloists, chorus, and orch. In this genre he wrote *Odysseus, Arminius, Das Lied von der Glocke,* and *Achilleus;* also *Frithjof* for Baritone, Female Chorus, and Orch.; *Normannenzug* for Baritone, Male Chorus, and Orch.; and several other works for various vocal ensembles. Among his instrumental works, the so-called *Scottish Fantasy* for Violin and Orch. (1880) was extremely successful when Sarasate (to whom the work was dedicated) performed it all over Europe; but the most popular of all works by Bruch is his *Kol Nidrei,* a Hebrew melody for cello and orch., composed for the Jewish community of Liverpool in 1880; its success led to the erroneous assumption that Bruch himself was Jewish (he was, in fact, of a clerical Protestant family). His Concerto for 2 Pianos and Orch. was commissioned by the American duo-piano team Ottilie and Rose Sutro; when they performed it for the first time (Philadelphia Orch., Stokowski conducting, 1916), they drastically revised the original. In 1971 the authentic version was discovered in Berlin, and was given its first performance by Nathan Twining and Mer Berkofsky with the London Symph., Antal Dorati conducting, on May 6, 1974.
BIBLIOGRAPHY: Fritz Gysi, *Max Bruch* (Zürich, 1922); Hans Pfitzner, *Meine Beziehungen zu Max Bruch; persönliche Erinnerungen* (Munich, 1938); D. Kaemper, *Max Bruch-Studien. Zum 50. Todestag des Komponisten* (Cologne, 1970); Jacques Voois, "The Case of the Disappearing Double Piano Concerto," *Symphony News* (June 1974); K. Fellerer, *Max Bruch* (Cologne, 1974).

Bruchollerie, Monique de la, French pianist; b. Paris, April 20, 1915; d. there, Dec. 15, 1972. She studied with Isidor Philipp; graduated from the Paris Cons. at the age of 13; toured widely as a concert pianist; also was active as a teacher. In 1964 she made a bold proposal to modernize the piano as a performing instrument by constructing a crescent-shaped keyboard to facilitate simultaneous playing in high treble and low bass. She further proposed to install electronic controls enabling the pianist to activate a whole chord by striking a single key.
BIBLIOGRAPHY: *Time* (April 30, 1965).

Bruči, Rudolf, Serbian composer; b. Zagreb, March 30, 1917. He studied in Vienna with Uhl; returning to Serbia, he became a teacher and opera conductor in Novi Sad. In his works he employs polytonal and atonal devices, culminating in free dodecaphony.
WORKS: *Maskal,* symph. suite (1955); Concerto for Orch. (Belgrade, Nov. 25, 1959); *Čovek je vidik bez kraja,* cantata (Belgrade, Dec. 21, 1961); *Srbija,* cantata (Belgrade, May 24, 1962); *Sinfonia lesta* (received the Grand Prix at the Queen Elisabeth of Belgium Competition in Brussels, 1965); *Sinfonietta* for Strings (1965); *Salut au monde,* oratorio (1967).

Bruck (or **Brouck**), **Arnold von** (known also as **Arnold de Bruges** and **Arnoldo Flamengo**), Flemish composer; b. Bruges, c.1500; d. Linz, Feb. 6, 1554. He served as a choirboy in the chapel of Charles V; in 1527 he was named court Kapellmeister to Ferdinand I; retired on Dec. 31, 1545. Many of his motets, hymns, and German part-songs are preserved in MS collections of the 16th century; printed editions are found in Denkmäler der Tonkunst in Österreich, 72 (37.ii) and 99; R. Eitner in *Publikationen älterer Musik* (vol. 2); A. Schering in *Geschichte der Musik in Beispielen* (no. 110); J. Wolf in Denkmäler Deutscher Tonkunst (vol. 34); Otto Kade in A.W. Ambros's *Geschichte der Musik* (vol. 5); C.G. Winterfeld in *Der evangelische Kirchengesang;* A.T. Davison and W. Apel, *Historical Anthology of Music* (no. 111b); see also O. Wessely, ed., *A. von Bruck: Sämtliche lateinschule Motetten,* Denkmäler der Tonkunst in Österreich, XCIX (1961).

Bruck, Charles, Rumanian conductor; b. Timişoara, May 2, 1911. He studied composition with Nadia Boulanger in Paris, and conducting with Pierre Monteux. In 1949 he was appointed conductor of the Netherlands Opera in Amsterdam. He was subsequently conductor of the Strasbourg Radio Orch. (1956–65) and of the Orch. of the French Radio and Television (1965–70).

Brucken-Fock, Emil von, Dutch composer, brother of **Gerard von Brucken-Fock;** b. Koudekerke, Oct. 19, 1857; d. Aerdenhout, Jan. 6, 1944. He conducted a military band and wrote music criticism in Utrecht; influenced by Wagner, he composed the music drama *Seleneia.* He also wrote many songs.

Brucken-Fock, Gerard von, Dutch pianist and composer, brother of **Emil von Brucken-Fock;** b. Koudekerke, Dec. 28, 1859; d. Aerdenhout, Aug. 15, 1935. He studied with Friedrich Kiel and W. Bargiel. He wrote 2 symphs.; an oratorio, *De Wederkomst van Christus;* a Violin Sonata; etc. Some of his piano preludes and songs have acquired considerable popularity in the Netherlands.

Brückler, Hugo, German song composer; b. Dresden, Feb. 18, 1845; d. there, Oct. 4, 1871. He studied at the Dresden Cons.; publ. 2 groups of songs, both based on Scheffel's poem *Trompeter von Säckingen (Songs of Young Werner by the Rhine* and *Margaret's Songs;* also *Sieben Gesänge* (posthumous; selected and ed. by Adolf Jensen); a ballad, *Der Vogt von Tenneberg* (posthumous, ed. by Reinhold Becker); *Nordmännersang; Marsch der Bürgergarde.*
BIBLIOGRAPHY: R. Musiol, *Hugo Brückler* (Dresden, 1896).

Bruckner, (Josef) Anton, inspired Austrian composer; b. Ansfelden, Sept. 4, 1824; d. Vienna, Oct. 11, 1896. He studied music with his father, a village schoolmaster and church organist; also took music lessons at Hörsching with his cousin Johann Baptist Weiss. After his father's death in 1837, Bruckner enrolled as a chorister at St. Florian, where he attended classes in organ, piano, violin, and music theory. In 1840–41 he entered the special school for educational training in Linz, where he received instruction from J.N.A. Dürrnberger; he also studied music theory with Leopold Edler von Zenetti in Enns. While in his early youth, Bruckner held teaching positions in elementary public schools in Windhaag (1841–43) and Kronstorf (1843–45); later he occupied a responsible position as a schoolteacher at St. Florian (1845–55); also served as provisional organist there (1848–51). Despite his professional advance, he felt a lack of basic techniques in musical composition, and at the age of 31 went to Vienna to study harmony and counterpoint with the renowned pedagogue Simon Sechter. He continued his studies with him off and on until 1861. In 1856 he became cathedral organist in Linz, having successfully competed for this position against several applicants. Determined to acquire still more technical knowledge, he sought further instruction and began taking lessons in orchestration with Otto Kitzler, first cellist of the Linz municipal theater (1861–63). In the meantime he undertook an assiduous study of the Italian polyphonic school, and of masters of German polyphony, especially Bach. These tasks preoccupied him so completely that he did not engage in free composition until he was nearly 40 years old. Then he fell under the powerful influence of Wagner's music, an infatuation that diverted him from his study of classical polyphony. In 1865 he attended the premiere of *Tristan und Isolde* in Munich, and met Wagner. He also made the acquaintance of Liszt in Pest, and of Berlioz during his visit in Vienna. His adulation of Wagner was extreme; the dedication of his Third Symph. to Wagner reads: "To the eminent Excellency Richard Wagner the Unattainable, World-Famous, and Ex-

Bruckner

alted Master of Poetry and Music, in Deepest Reverence Dedicated by Anton Bruckner." Strangely enough, in his own music Bruckner never embraced the tenets and practices of Wagner, but followed the sanctified tradition of Germanic polyphony. Whereas Wagner strove toward the ideal union of drama, text, and music in a new type of operatic production, Bruckner kept away from the musical theater, confining himself to symphonic and choral music. Even in his harmonic techniques, Bruckner seldom followed Wagner's chromatic style of writing, and he never tried to emulate the passionate rise and fall of Wagnerian "endless" melodies depicting the characters of his operatic creations. To Bruckner, music was an apotheosis of symmetry; his symphs. were cathedrals of Gothic grandeur; he never hesitated to repeat a musical phrase several times in succession so as to establish the thematic foundation of a work. The personal differences between Wagner and Bruckner could not be more striking: Wagner was a man of the world who devoted his whole life to the promotion of his artistic and human affairs, while Bruckner was unsure of his abilities and desperately sought recognition. Devoid of social graces, being a person of humble peasant origin, Bruckner was unable to secure the position of respect and honor that he craved. A signal testimony to this lack of self-confidence was Bruckner's willingness to revise his works repeatedly, not always to their betterment, taking advice from conductors and ostensible well-wishers. He suffered from periodic attacks of depression; his entire life seems to have been a study of unhappiness, most particularly in his numerous attempts to find a woman who would become his life companion. In his desperation, he made half-hearted proposals in marriage to women of the people; the older he grew, the younger were the objects of his misguided affections; a notorious episode was his proposal in marriage to a chambermaid at a hotel in Berlin. Bruckner died a virgin.

A commanding trait of Bruckner's personality was his devout religiosity. To him the faith and the sacraments of the Roman Catholic Church were not mere rituals but profound psychological experiences. Following the practice of Haydn, he signed most of his works with the words *Omnia ad majorem Dei gloriam;* indeed, he must have felt that every piece of music he composed redounded to the greater glory of God. His original dedication of his *Te Deum* was actually inscribed *"an dem lieben Gott."* From reports of his friends and contemporaries, it appears that he regarded each happy event of his life as a gift of God, and each disaster as an act of divine wrath. His yearning for secular honors was none the less acute for that. He was tremendously gratified upon receiving an honorary doctorate from the Univ. of Vienna in 1891; he was the first musician to be so honored there. He successfully solicited similar degrees from the univs. of Cambridge, Philadelphia, and even Cincinnati. He eagerly sought approval in the public press. When Emperor Franz Josef presented him with a snuffbox as a sign of imperial favor, it is said that Bruckner pathetically begged the emperor to order Han-

slick to stop attacking him. Indeed, Hanslick was the nemesis of the so-called "New German School" of composition exemplified by Wagner and Liszt, and to a lesser extent, also by Bruckner. Wagner could respond to Hanslick's hostility by caricaturing him in the role of Beckmesser (whom he had originally intended to name Hanslich), and Liszt, immensely successful as a virtuoso pianist, was largely immune to critical attacks. But Bruckner was highly vulnerable. It was not until the end of his unhappy life that, thanks to a group of devoted friends among conductors, Bruckner finally achieved a full recognition of his greatness.

Bruckner himself was an inadequate conductor, but he was a master organist. In 1869 he appeared in organ recitals in France, and in 1871 he visited England, giving performances in the Royal Albert Hall and the Crystal Palace in London. He was also esteemed as a pedagogue. In 1868 he succeeded his own teacher Sechter as professor of harmony, counterpoint, and organ at the Vienna Cons.; also in 1868 he was named provisional court organist, an appointment formally confirmed in 1878. Concurrently he taught piano, organ, and music theory at St. Anna College in Vienna (1870–74). In 1875 he was appointed lecturer in harmony and counterpoint at the Univ. of Vienna. In failing health, Bruckner retired from the Vienna Cons. in 1891 and a year later relinquished his post as court organist; in 1894 he resigned his lecturer's position at the Univ. of Vienna. The remaining years of his life he devoted to the composition of his Ninth Symph., which, however, remained unfinished at his death.

Bruckner's symphs. constitute a monumental achievement; they are characterized by a striking display of originality and a profound spiritual quality. His sacred works are similarly expressive of his latent genius. Bruckner is usually paired with Mahler, who was a generation younger, but whose music embodied qualities of grandeur akin to those that permeated the symphonic and choral works of Bruckner. Accordingly, Bruckner and Mahler societies sprouted in several countries, with the express purpose of elucidating, analyzing, and promoting their music.

The textual problems concerning Bruckner's works are numerous and complex. He made many revisions of his scores, and dejectedly acquiesced in alterations suggested by conductors who expressed interest in his music. As a result, conflicting versions of his symphs. appeared in circulation. With the founding of the International Bruckner Society, a movement was begun to publ. the original versions of his manuscripts, the majority of which he bequeathed to the Hofbibliothek in Vienna. A complete edition of Bruckner's works, under the supervision of Robert Haas and Alfred Orel, began to appear in 1930; in 1945 Leopold Nowak was named its editor in chief. An excellent explication of the textual problems concerning Bruckner's works is found in Deryck Cook's article "The Bruckner Problem Simplified," in the *Musical Times* (Jan.–Feb., April–May, and Aug. 1969).

WORKS: Bruckner rejected his first symph. as a student work; it is in F minor and is known as his

Schul-Symphonie or *Studien-Symphonie (Study Symphony)* (1863; movements 1, 2, and 4 first perf. under Moissl, Klosterneuburg, March 18, 1924; movement 3 first perf. under Moissl, Klosterneuburg, Oct. 12, 1924). A second early symph., in D minor, apparently held some interest for him, as he marked it No. 0, "Die Nullte" (1863–64; revised, 1869; movements 3 and 4 first perf. under Moissl, Klosterneuburg, May 17, 1924; first complete perf. under Moissl, Klosterneuburg, Oct. 12, 1924). The following list of his nine symphs. is based upon the research of Leopold Nowak: No. 1 in C minor (Version I, "Linz," 1865–66; first perf. with minor additions and alterations, under Bruckner, Linz, May 9, 1868; Version II, "Vienna," 1890–91, a thorough revision; first perf. under Richter, Vienna, Dec. 13, 1891); No. 2 in C minor (Version I, 1871–72; first perf., with minor revisions, under Bruckner, Vienna, Oct. 26, 1873; Version II, 1876–77, with cuts and alterations); No. 3 in D minor, the "Wagner" Symph. (Version I, 1873; first perf. in the Nowak ed. under Schönzeler, Adelaide, March 19, 1978; Version II, 1876–77, a thorough revision; first perf. under Bruckner, Vienna, Dec. 16, 1877; Version III, 1888–89, a thorough revision; first perf. under Richter, Vienna, Dec. 21, 1890; a second Adagio [1876], unrelated to the other versions, was first perf. under C. Abbado, Vienna, May 24, 1980); No. 4 in E-flat major, the "Romantic" Symph. (Version I, 1874; first perf. in the Nowak ed. under K. Wöss, Linz, Sept. 20, 1975; Version II, 1877–78, with Finale of 1880, a thorough revision with a new Scherzo; first perf. under Richter, Vienna, Feb. 20, 1881; Version III, 1887–88, a major revision by Löwe, including a new Finale; first perf. under Richter, Vienna, Jan. 22, 1888); No. 5 in B-flat major (1875–76; minor revisions, 1876–78; first perf. in a recomposed version by F. Schalk, under his direction, Graz, April 8, 1894; first perf. in the Haas ed. under Hausegger, Munich, Oct. 20, 1935); No. 6 in A major (1879–81; Adagio and Scherzo under Jahn, Vienna, Feb. 11, 1883; with major cuts, under Mahler, Vienna, Feb. 26, 1899; first complete perf. under Pohlig, Stuttgart, March 14, 1901); No. 7 in E major (1881–83; first perf. under Nikisch, Leipzig, Dec. 30, 1884); No. 8 in C minor (Version I, 1884–87; first perf. in the Nowak ed. under Schönzeler, BBC, London, Sept. 2, 1973; Version II, 1889–90, a thorough revision; first perf. under Richter, Vienna, Dec. 18, 1892; first perf. in the Haas ed. [a composite version of I and II] under Furtwängler, Hamburg, July 5, 1939]; No. 9 in D minor (movements 1–3, 1887–94; Finale [unfinished], 1894–96; first perf. in a recomposed version by Löwe, under his direction, Vienna, Feb. 11, 1903, with Bruckner's *Te Deum* substituted for the Finale; first perf. in the Haas ed. under Hausegger, Munich, April 2, 1932). Other major works are 3 masses: D minor (1864; Linz, Nov. 20, 1864; revised, 1876 and 1881); E minor (1866; Linz, Sept. 29, 1869; revised, 1869, 1876, and 1882); F minor (1867–68; Vienna, June 16, 1872; many revisions); String Quintet in F major (1878–79); *Te Deum* (1881; revised, 1883–84; first perf. with orch. under Richter, Vienna, Jan. 10, 1886); Psalm 150 (1892; Vienna, Nov. 13, 1892). Selected minor works are a Mass in C major (1842?); *Requiem* in D minor (1848–49; St. Florian,

March 13, 1849); *Missa Solemnis* in B-flat minor (1854; St. Florian, Sept. 14, 1854); *Apollomarsch,* for Military Band (1862; authenticity not established); March in D minor, for Orch. (1862); 3 orch. pieces in E-flat major, E minor, and F major (1862); String Quartet in C minor (1862); Overture in G minor (1862–63; Klosterneuburg, Sept. 8, 1921); *Germanenzug,* for Male Choir and Brass Instruments (1863); March in E-flat major, for Military Band (1865); *Abendzauber,* for Male Choir and 4 Horns (1878); *Intermezzo,* for String Quintet (1879); *Helgoland,* for Male Choir and Orch. (1893); other choral settings; motets; etc.

BIBLIOGRAPHY: BIOGRAPHY: F. Brunner, *Dr. A. B.* (Linz, 1895); R. Louis, *A. B.* (Munich, 1905; 3rd ed., 1921); F. Gräflinger, *A. B.: Bausteine zu seiner Lebensgeschichte* (Munich, 1911; rev. ed., 1927); M. Morold, *A. B.* (Leipzig, 1912; 2nd ed., 1920); E. Decsey, *A. B., Versuch eines Lebens* (Berlin, 1920; 3rd ed., 1930); F. Gräflinger, *A. B.: Sein Leben und seine Werke* (Regensburg, 1921); A. Göllerich and M. Auer, *A. B.: Ein Lebens- und Schaffensbild* (an exhaustive study; 4 vols., Regensburg, 1922–37; 2nd ed., 1938); K. Grunsky, *A. B.* (Stuttgart, 1922); H. Tessmer, *A. B.* (Regensburg, 1922); R. Wetz, *A. B.: Sein Leben und Schaffen* (Leipzig, 1923); J. Daninger, *A. B.* (Vienna, 1924); G. Gräner, *A. B.* (Leipzig, 1924); E. Kurth, *A. B.* (2 vols., Berlin, 1925); A. Orel, *A. B.: Ein Österreichischer Meister der Tonkunst* (Altötting, 1926); F. Gräflinger, *A. B.: Leben und Schaffen* (Berlin, 1927); M. Auer, *A. B.: Sein Leben und Werk* (Vienna, 1931; 6th ed., 1966); G. Engel, *The Life of A. B.* (N.Y., 1931); R. Haas, *A. B.* (Potsdam, 1934); A. Orel, *A. B., 1824–1896: Sein Leben in Bildern* (Leipzig, 1936); W. Paap, *A. B.: Zijn land, zijn leven en zijn kunst* (Bilthoven, 1936); W. Wiora, "A. B.," *Die grossen Deutschen* (Berlin, 1936; revised ed., 1959); E. Schwanzara, *B.s Stamm- und Urheimat* (Berlin, 1937); K. Laux, *A. B.: Leben und Werk* (Leipzig, 1940; 2nd ed., 1947); L. van Vassenhove, *A. B.* (Neuchâtel, 1942); W. Wolff, *A. B.: Rustic Genius* (N.Y., 1942); A. Machabey, *La Vie et l'œuvre d'A. B.* (Paris, 1945); W. Reich, ed., *A. B.: Ein Bild seiner Persönlichkeit* (Basel, 1953); H. Redlich, *B. and Mahler* (London, 1955; revised ed., 1963); P. Benary, *A. B.* (Leipzig, 1956); W. Abendroth, *B.: Eine Bildbiographie* (Munich, 1958); E. Doernberg, *The Life and Symphonies of A. B.* (London, 1960); L. Nowak, *A. B.: Musik und Leben* (a brief study; Vienna, 1964); G. Wehle, *A. B. im Spiegel seiner Zeitgenossen* (Garmisch-Partenkirchen, 1964); J. Lassl, *Das kleine Brucknerbuch* (Salzburg, 1965; 2nd ed., 1972); H.-H. Schönzeler, *B.* (a perceptive study of the man and his music; N.Y., 1970; revised ed., 1978); J. Gallios, *B.* (Paris, 1971); L. Nowak, *A. B.: Musik und Leben* (a voluminous pictorial biography; Linz, 1973); H. Fischer, *A. B.: Sein Leben* (Salzburg, 1974); D. Watson, *B.* (a basic introduction to his life and works; London, 1975); Paul Langevin, *A. B., Apogée de la symphonie* (Lausanne, 1977); a complete catalogue of Bruckner's works, *Werkverzeichnis A. B.,* was compiled by Renate Grasberger (Tutzing, 1977).

CRITICAL, ANALYTICAL: A. Halm, *Die Symphonie A. B.s* (Munich, 1914; 2nd ed., 1923); A. Knapp, *A. B.: Zum Verständnis seiner Persönlichkeit und seiner*

Werke (Düsseldorf, 1921); A. Orel, *Unbekannte Frühwerke A. B.s* (Vienna, 1921); E. Schwebsch, *A. B.: Ein Beitrag zur Erkenntnis von Entwicklungen in der Musik* (Stuttgart, 1921; 2nd ed., 1923); K. Kobald, ed., *In memoriam A. B.* (Vienna, 1924); O. Lang, *A. B.: Wesen und Bedeutung* (Munich, 1924; 3rd ed., 1947); K. Singer, *B.s Chormusik* (Stuttgart, 1924); A. Orel, *A. B.: Das Werk, der Künstler, die Zeit* (Vienna, 1925); R. Wickenhausen, *A. B.s Symphonien: Ihr Werden und Wesen* (Leipzig, 1926–27); M. Auer, *A. B. als Kirchenmusiker* (Regensburg, 1927); F. Munch, "La Musique religieuse d'A. B.," *Le ménestrel* (Paris, 1928); H. Grunsky, *Das Formproblem in A. B.s Symphonien* (Augsburg, 1929); F. Grüninger, *A. B.: Der metaphysische Kern seiner Persönlichkeit und Werke* (Augsburg, 1930); H. Grunsky, *Formenwelt und Sinngefüge in den B.-Symphonien* (2 vols., Augsburg, 1931); K. Grunsky, *Fragen der B.-Auffassung* (Stuttgart, 1936); A. Köberle, *Bach, Beethoven, B. als Symbolgestalten des Glaubens* (Berlin, 1936; 4th ed., 1941); F. Grüninger, *Der Ehrfürchtige: A. B.s Leben dem Volke erzählt* (Freiburg, 1937); O. Loerke, *A. B.: Ein Charakterbild* (Berlin, 1938; 3rd ed., 1943); A. Mecklenburg, "Hugo Wolf and A. B.," *The Musical Quarterly* (July 1938); E. Wellesz, "A. B. and the Process of Musical Creation," *Musical Quarterly* (July 1938); W. Abendroth, *Die Symphonien A. B.s: Einführungen* (Berlin, 1940; 2nd ed., 1942); F. Wohlfahrt, *A. B.s symphonisches Werk* (Leipzig, 1943); P. Raabe, *Wege zu B.* (Regensburg, 1944); D. Newlin, *B., Mahler, Schoenberg* (N.Y., 1947; revised ed., 1978); L. Nowak, *Te Deum laudamus: Gedanken zur Musik A. B.s* (Vienna, 1947); E. Refardt, *Brahms, B., Wolf: Drei Wiener Meister des 19. Jahrhunderts* (Basel, 1949); F. Grüninger, *Der Meister von Sankt Florian-Wege zu A. B.* (Augsburg, 1950); E. Schenk, *Um B.s Persönlichkeit* (Vienna, 1951); G. Engel, *The Symphonies of A. B.* (N.Y., 1955); I. Krohn, *A. B.s Symphonien: Eine Untersuchung über Formenbau und Stimmungsgehalt* (3 vols., Helsinki, 1955–57); H. Raynor, "An Approach to A. B.," *The Musical Times* (Feb. 1955); N. Tschulik, ed., *A. B. im Spiegel seiner Zeit* (Vienna, 1955); M. Dehnert, *A. B.: Versuch einer Deutung* (Leipzig, 1958); L. Nowak, "Symphonischer und kirchlicher Stil bei A. B.," in the *Festschrift* for Karl Gustav Fellerer (Regensburg, 1962); A. Orel, "B. und Wien," *Hans Albrecht in Memoriam* (Kassel, 1962); R. Simpson, *B. and the Symphony* (London, 1963); F. Grasberger, ed., *B.-Studien: Leopold Nowak zum 60. Geburtstag* (Vienna, 1964); H. Winterberger, *A. B. in seiner Zeit* (Linz, 1964); R. Simpson, *The Essence of B.: An Essay towards the Understanding of His Music* (an excellent critical evaluation; London, 1967; Philadelphia, 1968); A. Howie, *The Sacred Music of A. B.* (Diss., Univ. of Manchester, 1969); O. Wessely, ed., *B.-Studien* (Vienna, 1975); C. Floros, *Brahms und B.* (Wiesbaden, 1980); A. Howie, "Traditional and Novel Elements in B.'s Sacred Music," *Musical Quarterly* (Oct. 1891).

CORRESPONDENCE: F. Gräflinger, ed., *A. B., Gesammelte Briefe* (Regensburg, 1924); M. Auer, ed., *A. B., Gesammelte Briefe*, new series (Regensburg, 1924); A. Orel, *B.-Brevier; Briefe, Dokumente, Berichte* (Vienna, 1953).

PERIODICALS: The International Bruckner Society of Vienna publ. *Bruckner-Blätter* from 1929 to 1937. The reconstituted Society has publ. *Mitteilungsblatt der Internationalen Bruckner-Gesellschaft* since 1971. The Bruckner Society of America publ. *Chord and Discord* from 1932 to 1941; it resumed publication in 1947.

Brückner-Rüggeberg, Wilhelm, German conductor; b. Stuttgart, April 15, 1906. He was educated in Munich, where he studied with August Schmid-Lindner and Siegmund von Hausegger; in 1936–37 he was a guest conductor with the Hamburg State Opera; in 1938 was appointed to its conducting staff, remaining on the roster until 1971; taught at the Hamburg Hochschule für Musik (prof. from 1955). In addition to his work as an opera conductor, he was esteemed for his performances of the classical choral masterworks.

Brudieu, Joan, French-Catalonian composer; b. in the diocese of Limoges, c.1520; d. Urgel, between April 22 and May 10, 1591. In 1539 he became choirmaster at the Urgel Cathedral, a post he held until 1577; then served as maestro de capilla and organist at Santa Maria del Mar in Barcelona (1578–79); subsequently resumed his Urgel post. His extant works include a 4-part Requiem Mass and Spanish madrigals.
BIBLIOGRAPHY: A. Mangeot, "The Madrigals of Joan Brudieu," *Score*, no. 7 (1952).

Brüggen, Frans, distinguished Dutch recorder player, flutist, and conductor; b. Amsterdam, Oct. 30, 1934. He studied the recorder with Kees Otten and flute at the Amsterdam Muzieklyceum; in addition, took courses in musicology at the Univ. of Amsterdam; then launched a major career as a virtuoso performer of music for the recorder; as a flute soloist, he was equally at home in performances of the Baroque masters and contemporary avant-garde composers; also gave informative lectures and illustrative performances of recorder music in Europe, and taught at the Royal Cons. in The Hague.

Brugnoli, Attilio, Italian composer; b. Rome, Sept. 7, 1880; d. Bolzano, July 10, 1937. He studied piano and composition at the Naples Cons. with Paolo Serrao (graduated in 1900); won the Rubinstein Prize in Paris (1905); taught at the conservatories of Parma (1907–21) and Florence (1921–37). His compositions include a Piano Concerto (1905); Violin Concerto (1908); piano suite, *Scene Napolitane* (1909); several songs; piano pieces; also a pedagogic work, *Dinamica pianistica* (Milan, 1926).

Bruhns, Nicolaus, German violinist, organist, and composer; b. Schwabstedt, 1665; d. Husum, March 29, 1697. He studied violin, organ, and composition with Buxtehude in Lübeck; then traveled to Copenhagen, where he served as a church organist; in 1689 he moved to Husum and was appointed organist at the Cathedral there. He was reputed to be an inventive virtuoso who could play the violin while providing the basso continuo on organ pedals. He was a reputable composer; his 12 church cantatas were notable; he also wrote fugues and chorales for organ.

BIBLIOGRAPHY: H. Kölsch, *Nicolaus Bruhns* (Kassel, 1958); M. Geck, *Nicolaus Bruhns: Leben und Werk* (Cologne, 1968).

Brüll, Ignaz, Austrian pianist and composer; b. Prossnitz, Moravia, Nov. 7, 1846; d. Vienna, Sept. 17, 1907. He studied in Vienna with Epstein (piano) and Dessoff (composition); subsequently made extended recital tours; eventually settled in Vienna, where he was a prof. of piano at the Horak Inst. (1872–78). He was an intimate friend of Brahms, who greatly valued his advice.

WORKS: Operas: *Die Bettler von Samarkand* (1864); *Das goldene Kreuz* (Berlin, Dec. 22, 1875; his most successful opera); *Der Landfriede* (Vienna, Oct. 4, 1877); *Bianca* (Dresden, Nov. 25, 1879); *Königin Marietta* (Munich, 1883); *Gloria* (Hamburg, 1886); *Das steinerne Herz* (Vienna, 1888); *Gringoire* (Munich, March 19, 1892); *Schach dem Könige* (Munich, 1893); *Der Husar* (Vienna, 1898; very successful); *Rübezahl* (unfinished); ballet, *Ein Märchen aus der Champagne* (1896); overture, *Im Walde;* 3 serenades and a Dance Suite for Orch.; 2 piano concertos; Violin Concerto; piano pieces; songs.

BIBLIOGRAPHY: H. Schwarz, *Ignaz Brüll und sein Freundeskreis* (1922); also many references in the biographies of Brahms.

Brumby, Colin, Australian composer; b. Melbourne, June 18, 1933. He graduated from the Melbourne Univ. Cons. of Music in 1957; studied in London with Alexander Goehr and John Carewe (1963). He lectured at the Brisbane Teacher's Training College (1959–64) and in 1964 became a senior lecturer at the Univ. of Queensland. His music is medium modern, with liberal application of avant-garde techniques.

WORKS: *Aegean Suite* for Flute and Strings (1957); *Mediterranean Suite* for Strings (1958); *4 Antiphons* for Organ (1961); *Partite* for Clarinet and Strings (1961); *Pantos* for Flute and Strings (1963); *Fibonacci Variations* for Orch. (1963); Wind Quintet (1964); *Antithesis* for Strings (1964); *Chance Piece* for Piano (1965); *Stabat Mater Speciosa,* a Christmas cantata (1965); Trio for Flute, Clarinet, and Horn (1965); *Doubles* for Wind Quartet (1965); *Diversion* for Horn and Orch. (1966); *Realisations* for Piano and Orch. (1966); *Antipodea* for Orch. (1966); *Bunyip,* ballet (1967); *French Suite* for 6 Horns (1967); *Gilgamesh,* cantata for Narrator, Chorus, Brass, and Percussion (1967); String Quartet (1968); *3 Italian Songs* for High Voice and String Quartet (1968); *Charlie Bubbles' Book of Hours* for Soli, Chorus, Tape, and Orch. (1969); *Five Days Lost* for Narrator and Orch. (1969); *Bring Out Your Christmas Masks* for Narrator, Soli, Chorus, Tape, and Orch. (1969); *The Seven Deadly Sins,* opera (1970); Violin Concerto (1970); Concerto for Horn and Strings (1971); *A Ballade for St. Cecilia,* cantata

(1971); *Celebrations and Lamentations* for Narrators, Soli, Chorus, and Orch. (1971); *Litanies of the Sun,* symph. suite (1971); *Doubles* for Piano (1972); Viola Concertino (1972); *Ishtar's Mirror,* opera (1972); *This Is the Vine* for Soli, Chorus, and Orch. (1972; Melbourne, Feb. 24, 1973); several children's operettas; songs and choral pieces; piano pieces.

Brumel, Antoine, celebrated Flemish (or French) musician, contemporary of Josquin des Prez; b. 1460; d. after 1520. He served as a chorister at the Cathedral of Notre Dame in Chartres in 1483; in 1486 became a Master of the Innocents at St. Peter's in Geneva, where he remained until 1492. In 1497 he was Canon at Laon Cathedral. He was a singer at the ducal court in Chambéry in 1501; took up his duties at the court of Alfonso I, Duke of Ferrara, in Aug. 1506; remained in his service there until the chapel was disbanded in 1510. A number of his sacred works were publ. during his lifetime; other pieces are scattered in various anthologies. A complete edition of his works was begun by A. Carapetyan in 1951 in Rome under the aegis of the American Inst. of Musicology. He composed masses, motets, Magnificats, and other sacred works. B. Hudson edited the collection *A. Brumel: Opera omnia,* Corpus Mensurabilis Musicae, V/1–6 (1969–72).

BIBLIOGRAPHY: A. Pirro, "Dokumente über Antoine Brumel, Louis van Pullaer und Crispin van Stappen," *Zeitschrift für Musikwissenschaft* (March 1929); Gustave Reese, *Music in the Renaissance* (N.Y., 1954).

Brun, Alphonse, German-Swiss violinist; b. Frankfurt, Oct. 25, 1888; d. Bern, March 27, 1963. He studied in Zürich and Berlin; in 1912 settled in Bern, where he organized a renowned string quartet; also was active as a teacher.

Brun, Fritz, Swiss composer and conductor; b. Lucerne, Aug. 18, 1878; d. Grosshöchstetten, Switzerland, Nov. 29, 1959. He studied in Lucerne (1892–95) and at Cologne (1896–1901); then lived in Berlin, London, and Dortmund; finally settled in Bern (1909), where he taught at the Cons. and conducted the Bern Symph. Orch. until 1943.

WORKS: 10 symphonies (1908–53); *Variations* for Piano and String Orch. (1944); Piano Concerto (1944); Cello Concerto; *Rhapsodie* for Orch. (1958); 4 string quartets (1898, 1921, 1943, 1949); Violin Sonata (1906); Cello Sonata (1953).

BIBLIOGRAPHY: *Kleine Festgabe für Fritz Brun* (Bern, 1941).

Brün, Herbert, Israeli composer; b. Berlin, July 9, 1918. In 1936 he emigrated to Palestine; studied composition in Jerusalem with Stefan Wolpe; later took courses at Columbia Univ. in N.Y. In 1950 he settled in Tel Aviv. In his music he explores the potentialities of computers as a catalytic factor for advanced techniques; the titles of his works often suggest paradoxical logic.

WORKS: 3 string quartets (1953, 1957, 1961); *Mo-*

bile for Orch. (1958); *Futility* for Electronic Sounds, and Voice on Tapes (1964); *Gestures for 11* for Chamber Ensemble (1964); *Sonoriferous Loops* for an Instrumental Ensemble and Tape (1964); a group of works for Varying Ensembles under the provocative title *Non sequitur* (1966); Trio for Trumpet, Trombone, and Percussion (1966); *Mutatis mutandis* for "Interpreters" (1968); Nonet (1969).

Bruna, Pablo, Spanish organist and composer; b. Daroca, near Saragossa (baptized, June 22), 1611; d. there, June 26 or 27, 1679. He was blinded by smallpox as a child and was later known as "El ciego de Daroca." He overcame his deficiency by successfully learning to play the organ, and was employed as a church organist in his native town. He also improvised a number of organ pieces which were notated by an amanuensis.

BIBLIOGRAPHY: P. Calahorra Martinez, "Pablo Bruna, 'El ciego de Daroca,' " *Analecta Musicologica,* XXII (1967).

Brune, Adolf Gerhard, composer; b. Bakkum, near Hannover, June 21, 1870; d. Chicago, April 21, 1935. He studied piano with his father; came to the U.S. in 1889 and was an organist in Peoria, Ill.; settled in Chicago in 1894; studied piano with Liebling and composition with Ziehn there, then taught piano and composition at Chicago Musical College (1898–1917). He wrote 3 symphs. and the symph. poems *Lied des Singschwans* and *Evangeline.*

Bruneau, (Louis-Charles-Bonaventure-) Alfred, French opera composer; b. Paris, March 3, 1857; d. there, June 15, 1934. In 1873 he entered the Paris Cons., where he was a pupil of Franchomme; won the first cello prize in 1876; later studied harmony with Savard and composition with Massenet; in 1881 he won the Prix de Rome with his cantata *Sainte-Geneviève.* He was a music critic for *Gil Blas* (1892–95); then for *Le Figaro* and *Le Matin;* from 1903–4 was first conductor at the Opéra-Comique; in 1900 he was made a member of the "Conseil Supérieur" at the Paris Cons. and in 1909 succeeded Reyer as inspector of music instruction. He made extensive tours of Russia, England, Spain, and the Netherlands, conducting his own works. He was made a Knight of the Légion d'Honneur in 1895; received the title "Commandeur de St.-Charles" in 1907; became a member of the Académie des Beaux Arts in 1925. His role in the evolution of French opera is of great importance; he introduced realistic drama on the French musical stage, working along lines parallel with Zola in literature. He used Zola's subjects for his most spectacular opera, *L'Ouragan,* and also for the operas *Messidor* and *L'Enfant-Roi.* In accordance with this naturalistic trend, Bruneau made free use of harsh dissonance when it was justified by the dramatic action of the plot.

WORKS: Operas (most of them produced in Paris at the Opéra-Comique): *Kérim* (June 9, 1887); *Le Rêve* (June 18, 1891); *L'Attaque du Moulin* (Nov. 23, 1893); *Messidor* (Feb. 19, 1897); *L'Ouragan* (April 29, 1901); *Lazare* (1902); *L'Enfant-Roi* (March 3, 1905);

Naïs Micoulin (Monte Carlo, Feb. 2, 1907); *La Faute de l'Abbé Mouret* (March 1, 1907); *Les Quatre Journées* (Dec. 25, 1916); *Le Roi Candaule* (Dec. 1, 1920); *Angelo, tyran de Padoue* (Jan. 16, 1928); *Virginie* (Jan. 7, 1931); ballets: *L'Amoureuse Leçon* (Feb. 6, 1913) and *Les Bacchantes* (after Euripides; Oct. 30, 1912); overtures: *Ode héroïque* and *Léda;* symph. poem, *La Belle au Bois dormant;* symph. poem, with Chorus, *Penthésilée;* a Requiem; *Lieds de France* and *Chansons à danser* (both to poems by C. Mendès); *Les Chants de la vie* (to poems by H. Bataille, F. Gregh, etc.); *Le Navire* for Voice and Orch.; pieces for various combinations of String and Wind Instruments. He publ. *Musiques d'hier et de demain* (1900); *La Musique française* (1901); *Musiques de Russie et musiciens de France* (1903; German trans. by M. Graf in *Die Musik,* Berlin, 1904); *La Vie et les œuvres de Gabriel Fauré* (1925); *Massenet* (1934).

BIBLIOGRAPHY: A. Hervey, "Alfred Bruneau," in *Living Masters of Music* (London, 1907); O. Séré in *Musiciens d'aujourd'hui* (Paris, 1911); J. Tiersot, *Un Demi-siècle de musique française* (1918); A. Boschot, *La Vie et les œuvres d'Alfred Bruneau* (Paris, 1937); for detailed lists of performances see A. Loewenberg, *Annals of Opera* (1943; new ed., 1955).

Brunelli, Antonio, Italian theorist and composer; b. Pisa, c.1575; d. there, c.1630. He was a pupil of G.M. Nanini; served as an organist at San Miniato in Tuscany from 1604 to 1607; then went to Prato, where he served as maestro di cappella at the Cathedral. On April 12, 1612, he was appointed maestro di cappella of the Grand Duke of Tuscany. Between 1605 and 1621 he publ. motets, canzonette, Psalms, madrigals, Requiems, and others sacred works; some of them were included in Donfried's *Promptuarium musicum* (1623). He publ. the theoretical treatises *Regole utilissime per li scolari che desiderano imparare a cantare* (Florence, 1606; one of the first publ. methods for voice); *Esercizi ad 1 e 2 voci* (Florence, 1607); and *Regole et dichiarazioni de alcuni contrappunti doppii* (Florence, 1610).

Brunetti, Domenico, Italian composer; b. Bologna, c.1580; d. there, April or May 1646. He was organist at the Church of S. Domenico (c.1609); then was maestro di cappella at the Bologna Cathedral (1618); with F. Bertacchi he founded the Accademia dei Filaschici (1633), which later was absorbed into the Accademia Filarmonica. His publications include *Euterpe* (Venice, 1606); *Varii Concentus unica, voce, duabus, tribus, quatuor vel pluribus cum gravi et acuto ad Organum* (Venice, 1609); *Canticum Deiparae Virginis Octies iuxta singulos Rhytmorum Sacrorum* (Venice, 1621). Several of his compositions (motets, madrigals, etc.) were publ. in contemporary collections (1611–26) of A. Schadeo, G. Donfried, A.N. di Treviso, F. Sammaruco, Z. Zanetti, and G.P. Biandrà.

Brunetti, Gaetano, Italian violinist and composer; b. probably in Fano, 1744; d. Culminal de Oreja, near Madrid, Dec. 16, 1798. He studied with Nardini, and

in about 1762 went to Madrid; in 1767 was appointed violinist in the Royal Chapel in Madrid; in 1788 became director of the Royal Chamber Orch., remaining in this post until his death. He composed many works for the Spanish Court, and also for the Duke of Alba; Boccherini, who was in Madrid during the same years as Brunetti, was also favored by the Court and the aristocracy, but there was apparently no rivalry between them, as commissions were plentiful. Brunetti's productivity was astounding; he wrote 32 symphs., 6 overtures, numerous dances for orch.; 12 sextets, 72 quintets, 50 quartets, 30 trios; 67 duos for violin and basso continuo; 23 divertimenti for violin, viola, and cello; also an opera, *Jason*, produced in Madrid on Oct. 4, 1768. The Library of Congress in Washington has a large collection of Brunetti's MSS.
BIBLIOGRAPHY: J. Subirá, *La música en la casa de Alba* (Madrid, 1927); Alice Belgray, *Gaetano Brunetti, An Exploratory Bio-bibliographical Study* (Diss., Univ. of Michigan, 1970).

Bruni, Antonio Bartolomeo, Italian violinist and composer; b. Cuneo, Jan. 28, 1757; d. there, Aug. 5, 1821. He studied with Pugnani in Turin. In 1780 he went to Paris, and on May 15, 1780, appeared as a violinist at the Concert Spirituel; then served as a member of the orch. of the Comédie-Italienne (1781–89). He was subsequently director of the orch. of the Opéra-Comique (1799–1801); then at the Opéra-Italienne (1801–6). He wrote 22 operas, of which the most successful were *Célestine* (Paris, Oct. 15, 1787), *Claudine* (Paris, March 6, 1794), and *La Rencontre en voyage* (Paris, April 28, 1798). He also wrote music for the violin; publ. a violin method and a viola method (the latter reprinted in 1928).
BIBLIOGRAPHY: G. Cesari, H. Closson, L. de La Laurencie, A. Della Corte, and C. Zino, *Antonio Bartolomeo Bruni, musicista cuneese* (Turin, 1931).

Brunold, Paul, French pianist, organist, and writer on music; b. Paris, Oct. 14, 1875; d. there, Sept. 14, 1948. He was a pupil of Marmontel (piano) and Lavignac (theory) at the Paris Cons.; later studied with Paderewski. In 1915 he became organist at St. Gervais, in Paris. With H. Expert, he edited the *Anthologie des maîtres français du clavecin des XVIIe et XVIIIe siècles;* with A. Tessier, he bought out a complete edition of Chambonnière's works; he also edited 2 vols. of works by Dieupart for the Lyre-Bird Press of Paris (*6 Suites pour clavecin* and *Airs et Chansons*). He publ. the book *Histoire du grand orgue de l'Eglise St. Gervais à Paris* (1934).

Brunswick, Mark, American composer; b. New York, Jan. 6, 1902; d. London, May 25, 1971. He studied theory of composition with Rubin Goldmark in N.Y. (1918–23); then took lessons with Ernest Bloch in Cleveland and with Nadia Boulanger in Paris (until 1929); later lived in Vienna. Returning to N.Y. in 1937, he taught at various schools; was a member of the music dept. of the College of the City of N.Y. from 1946–67.
WORKS: *2 Movements* for String Quartet (1925);

Lysistrata for Mezzo-soprano, Women's Chorus, and Orch. (1930); Fantasia for Viola (1932); Symphony in B-flat (Minneapolis, March 7, 1947); Quartet for Violin, Viola, Cello, and Double Bass (1957); Septet for Wind Quintet, Viola, and Cello (1958); 5 madrigals for Chorus, Viola, Cello, and Double Bass (1958–66); also *Eros and Death,* a choral symph. to texts from Greek and Roman poetry (1932–54). He left an unfinished opera, *The Master Builder,* after Ibsen.

Bruscantini, Sesto, Italian baritone; b. Porto Civitanova, Dec. 10, 1919. He studied law; then went to Rome to study music with Luigi Ricci. He made his debut at La Scala in Milan in 1949, singing the bass role as Don Geronimo in Cimarosa's *Il matrimonio segreto.* He then sang at several festivals in Glyndebourne (1951–54); in 1952 he appeared at the Salzburg Festival. In 1961 he made his U.S. debut with the Chicago Lyric Opera. He was particularly renowned for his buffo roles. In 1953 he married the singer **Sena Jurinac**.

Brusilovsky, Evgeni, Russian composer; b. Rostov-on-the-Don, Nov. 12, 1905; d. Moscow, May 9, 1981. He studied composition with Maximilian Steinberg at the Leningrad Cons., graduating in 1931. In 1933 he was commissioned by the Leningrad Union of Composers to go to Kazakhstan, promote musical education there, and help native composers to write music based on their own ethnic sources. Brusilovsky settled in Alma-Ata, capital of Kazakhstan, and taught at the Alma-Ata Cons. of Music. He wrote a number of works making use of native motifs; particularly notable are his operas on folk subjects.
WORKS: Operas (all produced in Alma-Ata): *Kyz-Zhybek* (1934); *Zhalbyr* (1935; 2nd version, 1938; 3rd version, 1946); *Er-Targyn* (1937; 2nd version, 1954); *Ayman-Sholpan* (1938); *Altyn Styk* (1940); *Guard, Alga!* (1942); *Amangeldy* (1945); *Dudaray* (1953); *The Inheritors* (1963); a ballet, *Bayan-Slu* (1971); 8 symphs. (1931, 1932, 1944, 1957, 1961, 1965, 1969, 1972); Piano Concerto (1948); Viola Concerto (1969); Trumpet Concerto (1967); 2 string quartets (1944, 1952); numerous choruses and songs; piano pieces; educational studies for various instruments.

Brusilow, Anshel (real name, **Brusilovsky**), American conductor; b. Philadelphia, Aug. 14, 1928, of Russian-Jewish parents. He studied violin at the Curtis Inst. of Music. Upon graduation, he served as concertmaster of the New Orleans Symph. (1954–55), associate concertmaster of the Cleveland Orch. (1955–59), and concertmaster of the Philadelphia Orch. (1959–66). He was also the founder of the Philadelphia Chamber Orch. (1961–65) and the Chamber Symph. of Philadelphia (1966–68). From 1970 to 1973 he was executive director and conductor of the Dallas Symph. In 1973 he joined the faculty of North Texas State Univ. in Denton.

Bruson, Renato, distinguished Italian baritone; b. Este, near Padua, Jan. 13, 1936. He studied at the

Padua Cons.; made his debut with the opera in Spoleto in 1961 as Count Di Luna in Verdi's *Il Trovatore;* then sang with other Italian opera houses; on Feb. 1, 1969, he made his Metropolitan Opera debut in N.Y. as Enrico in Donizetti's *Lucia di Lammermoor;* sang at La Scala in Milan and the Edinburgh Festival in 1972; in 1976 appeared at Covent Garden. He is primarily noted for his congenial interpretation of lyrico-dramatic parts in the operas of Verdi and Donizetti.

Brusselmans, Michel, Belgian composer; b. Paris (of Belgian parents) Feb. 12, 1886; d. Brussels, Sept. 20, 1960. He studied with Huberti, Tinel, and Gilson at the Brussels Cons.; won the Agniez Prix in 1914 for his symph. poem *Hélène de Sparte.* In 1922 he became editor for the Paris music publisher Jamin, and spent most of his life in France. His music is romantic in inspiration and programmatic in content.
WORKS: 3 ballets: *Les Néréides* (1911); *Kermesse flamande* (1912); *Les Sylphides* (on themes of Chopin); oratorio, *Jésus* (1936); *Psaume LVI* for Soprano, Chorus, and Orch. (1954); 3 symphs. (1924; 1934; *Levantine,* 1956–57); *Ouverture fériale* (1908); *Scènes Breugheliennes* for Orch. (1911); *Télémaque a gaulus* for Chamber Orch. (1923); *Esquisses flamandes* for Orch. (1927); *Légende du gapeau* for Horn, and Orch. or Piano (1930); *Rhapsodie flamande* for Orch. (1931); *Scènes provençales* for Orch. (1931); *Suite phrygienne* for Orch. (1932); *Suite d'après les Caprices de Paganini* for Orch. (1936); *Suite Divertissement* for Orch. (1937); *Rhapsodie* for Horn and Orch. (1938); Organ Concerto (1938); *Ouverture héroïque* (1942); Sinfonietta (1954); Violin Sonata (1915); Cello Sonata (1916); *Prelude and Fugue* for 8 Winds (1923); *Visages de Paris* for Piano (1946); songs.

Brustad, Bjarne, Norwegian composer; b. Oslo, March 4, 1895; d. there, May 22, 1978. He studied at the Oslo Cons.; then took violin lessons with Carl Flesch in Berlin (1915–16). From 1919 to 1922 he was violinist in the Oslo Phil., and from 1929 to 1943 played the first viola there. He also conducted orchs. in Oslo; in 1951 received a government life pension. His music is Romantic in its essence, and traditional in form.
WORKS: Opera, *Atlantis* (1945); 4 violin concertos (1922–61); Concertino for Viola and Chamber Orch. (1932); 9 symphs. (1948, 1951, 1953, 1957, 1967, 1970, 1971, 1972, 1973); Clarinet Concerto (1970); 3 string quartets (1919, 1929, 1959); 3 sonatas for Solo Violin (1935, 1956, 1957); Trio for Clarinet, Violin, and Viola (1938); Trio for Clarinet, Violin, and Bassoon (1947); Violin Sonata (1950); *Divertimento* for Solo Flute (1958).

Bruyck, Karl Debrois van, Austrian writer on music; b. Brünn, March 14, 1828; d. Waidhofen, Aug. 5, 1902. Originally a law student in Vienna, he turned to music in 1850. He publ. *Technische und ästhetische Analyse des Wohltemperierten Klaviers* (Leipzig, 1867; 3rd ed., 1925) and *Die Entwicklung der Klaviermusik von J.S. Bach bis R. Schumann* (1880).

Bruynèl, Ton, Dutch composer of electronic music; b. Utrecht, Jan. 26, 1934. He studied piano at the Utrecht Cons.; then worked in the studio for electronic music at the State Univ. of Utrecht; in 1957 organized a private electronic music studio. Most of his compositions involve instruments in combination with electronics, and some require theatrical visualizations.
WORKS: *Resonance I,* theater piece (ballet) in collaboration with Japanese-American sculptor Chinkichi Tajiri and American painter Sam Middleton (1960–62); *Reflexes* for Birma Drum (1961); *Resonance II,* theater piece in collaboration with the Dutch poet Gerrit Kouwenaar (1963); *Relief* for Organ and 4 Sound Tracks (1964); *Mobile* for 2 Sound Tracks (1965); *Milieu* for 2 Sound Tracks and Organ (1965–66); *Arc* for Organ and 4 Sound Tracks (1966–67); *Mekaniek* for Wind Quintet and 2 Sound Tracks (1967); *Decor,* a ballet score (1967); *Signs* for Wind Quintet, 2 Sound Tracks, and Video Projection (1969); *Ingredients* for Piano and Sound Tracks (1970); *Intra I* for Bass Clarinet and Sound Track (1971); *Elegy* for Female Voice and 2 Sound Tracks (1972); *Looking Ears* for Bass Clarinet, Grand Piano, and Sound Tracks (1972); *Phases* for 4 Sound Tracks and Orch. (Utrecht, Jan. 10, 1975); *Soft Song* for Oboe and 2 Sound Tracks (1975); *Dialogue* for Bass Clarinet and Sound Tracks (1976).

Bruzdowicz, Joanna, Polish composer; b. Warsaw, May 17, 1943. She studied music theory with Sikorski at the Warsaw State School of Music; then went to Paris, where she took lessons with Nadia Boulanger and Messiaen; worked there with the "Groupe de Recherches Musicales." Eventually she went to live in Belgium.
WORKS: 2 operas: *The Penal Colony,* after Kafka (Tours, 1972), and *Les Troyennes,* after Euripides (Saint-Denis, France, 1973); ballet, *Le Petit Prince,* after Saint-Exupéry (Brussels, Dec. 10, 1976); *Sketches from the Harbor,* cycle for Mezzo-soprano, Flute, and Percussion (1967); *Esquisses* for Flute, Piano, Viola, and Cello (1969); *Jour d'ici et d'ailleurs* for Narrator, Chorus, and Instruments (1971); *Episode* for Piano and 13 Instruments (1973); *Epitaph* for Harpsichord and Tape (1973); *Esitanza* for Piano, 4-hands (1973); *Le Beau Danube bleu* for 2 Pianos and Tape (1973–74); Piano Concerto (1974); Symph. (1975); Violin Concerto (1975–76).

Bryant, Allan, American composer; b. Detroit, July 12, 1931. He attended Princeton Univ.; then went to Germany, where he worked at the electronic studio in Cologne. Returning to the U.S., he wrote music with multimedia resources designed for theatrical representation. His works include *Quadruple Play* for Amplified Rubber Bands utilizing Contact Microphones and coordinated with an Audio-controlled Lighting System (1966); *Impulses* for a Variety of Percussion, Concussion, and Discussion Sounds (1967); *Bang-Bang* for Loud Instruments, including an Amplified Circular Violin (1967); *X-es Sex,* an intersexual happening, with Boots and Balloons (1967); also political works, e.g. *Liberate Isang Yun* (1967) for a Multimillion-decibel Electronic Sound calculated to reach the ears of the South Korean abductors of the dissident Korean composer Isang Yun from West Berlin (he was liberated in 1969 in response to the tremendous acoustical pressure of the Bryant piece).

Bryennius, Manuel, Byzantine writer on music, who flourished c.1320. His chief work, *Harmonicorum libri 3,* publ. in parallel Greek and Latin texts by Johannes Wallis in *Operum mathematicorum vol. 3* (Oxford, 1699), gives a comprehensive account of Greek music theories.
BIBLIOGRAPHY: R. Westphal, *Griechische Rhythmik und Harmonik* (Leipzig, 1867).

Brymer, Jack, distinguished English clarinetist; b. South Shields, Jan. 27, 1915. He studied at the Univ. of London; then served in the Royal Air Force in World War II. In 1947 he joined the Royal Phil. Orch. as principal clarinet; then held this position with the BBC Symph. Orch. (1963–71) and the London Symph. Orch. (from 1971). He was director of the London Wind Soloists; was prof. at the Royal Academy of Music, London (1950–59); also taught at Kneller Hall (1967–71). In 1960 he was made an Officer of the Order of the British Empire. He wrote an autobiography under the title *From Where I Sit,* publ. in 1979.

Bryn-Julson, Phyllis, American soprano; b. Bowdon, N.D., Feb. 5, 1945 (of Norwegian parentage). She studied piano, organ, violin, and voice at Concordia College, Moorhead, Minn.; then spent several summers at the Berkshire Music Center at Tanglewood and completed her studies at Syracuse Univ. In 1973 she made her first of many regular appearances with the N.Y. Phil.; also sang frequently with the Boston Symph. and other major American orchs. She is particularly renowned as a concert singer, at ease in all periods and styles of music.

Bryson, (Robert) Ernest, English composer; b. Liverpool, March 31, 1867; d. St. Briavels, Gloucestershire, April 20, 1942. He was engaged in trade, and music was his avocation. He wrote 2 symphs.; several orch. sketches; and an opera, *The Leper's Flute,* produced in Glasgow on Oct. 15, 1926.

Bubalo, Rudolph, American composer; b. Duluth, Minn., Oct. 21, 1927. He played jazz piano as a young man; then studied at the Chicago Musical College and Roosevelt Univ. with John Becker, Vittorio Rieti, Karel Jirak, Rudolph Ganz, and Ernst Krenek. Helped by numerous grants, he made rapid progress in writing works with unusual titles and of unusual content, among them *Valances, Soundposts,* and *Conicality;* most of his works employ electronic sound; perhaps the most striking is *Spacescape* for Orch. and Tape (Cleveland, Feb. 1, 1979), which con-

sists of a series of overlapping variations, with the main theme of 45-second duration.

Bucchi, Valentino, Italian composer; b. Florence, Nov. 29, 1916; d. Rome, May 9, 1976. He studied composition with Frazzi and Dallapiccola, and music history with Torrefranca at the Univ. of Florence, graduating in 1944; subsequently held teaching posts at the Florence Cons. (1945–52 and 1954–57), the Venice Cons. (1952–54), and the Cons. of Perugia (1957–58); was music director of the Accademia Filarmonica Romana (1958–60) and artistic director of the Teatro Communale in Bologna (1963–65). In his works he continued the national Italian tradition of the musical theater, while in his techniques he attempted to modernize the polyphony of the Renaissance along the lines established by Malipiero.
WORKS: Operas: *Il giuoco del barone* (Florence, Dec. 20, 1944); *Il Contrabasso,* after Chekhov (Florence, May 20, 1954); *Una notte in Paradiso* (Florence, May 11, 1960); *Il coccodrillo* (Florence, May 9, 1970); ballets: *Racconto siciliano* (Rome, Jan. 17, 1956) and *Mirandolina* (Rome, March 12, 1957); also *Ballata del silenzio* (1951); for Orch.: *Concerto lirico* for Violin and Strings (1958); *Concerto grottesco* for Double Bass and String Orch. (1967); String Quartet (1956); Concerto for Clarinet Solo (1969); *Ison* for Cello Solo (1971); *Colloquio corale* for Narrator, Vocal Solo, Chorus, and Orch. (1971).

Bucci, Mark, American composer; b. New York, Feb. 26, 1924. He studied with Jacobi and Giannini at the Juilliard School of Music and with Copland at the Berkshire Music Center in Tanglewood; adopted a pragmatic method of composition in a strong rhythmic style, in modern but tonal harmonies, particularly effective in his stage works.
WORKS: One-act operas: *The Boor* (after Chekhov, N.Y., Dec. 29, 1949); *The Dress* (N.Y., Dec. 8, 1953); *Sweet Betsy from Pike* (N.Y., Dec. 8, 1953); *The 13 Clocks* (N.Y., Dec. 29, 1953); *Tale for a Deaf Ear* (Tanglewood, Aug. 5, 1957); *The Hero* (Educational Television, N.Y., Sept. 24, 1965). His *Concerto for a Singing Instrument* was first performed as a *Concerto for Kazoo* by the N.Y. Phil., Leonard Bernstein conducting, on March 26, 1960, with Anita Darian as kazoo virtuoso.

Bucharoff (real name, **Buchhalter**), **Simon,** Russian-American pianist and composer; b. Berditchev, April 20, 1881; d. Chicago, Nov. 24, 1955. He settled in America as a youth; studied piano with Paolo Gallico in N.Y., and later with Julius Epstein and Emil Sauer in Vienna. He occupied various teaching posts; lived principally in Chicago and Hollywood.
WORKS: Operas: *A Lover's Knot* (Chicago Opera, Jan. 15, 1916); *Sakahra* (Frankfurt, Nov. 8, 1924; revised 1953); *Jewel; Wastrel;* several symph. poems (*Reflections in the Water; Drunk; Doubt; Joy Sardonic;* etc.); publ. *The Modern Pianist's Textbook* (N.Y., 1931).
BIBLIOGRAPHY: E.E. Hipsher, *American Opera and Its Composers* (Philadelphia, 1927; pp. 93–97).

Buchbinder, Rudolf, Austrian pianist; b. Leitmeritz, Dec. 1, 1946. He studied with Bruno Seidlhofer at the Vienna Academy of Music; in 1965 he made a tour of North and South America; in 1966 he won a special prize awarded at the Van Cliburn Competition; then made a tour with the Vienna Phil., and also appeared as a soloist in Paris, Milan, Madrid, and London. In 1975 he made a tour of Japan and the U.S. with the Vienna Symph. Orch.; in addition, he taught piano at the Basel Academy of Music.

Bücher, Karl, German economist and writer on music; b. Kirchberg, near Wiesbaden, Feb. 16, 1847; d. Leipzig, Nov. 12, 1930. As a prof. of economics at Leipzig Univ. (1892–1916), he became interested in the correlation between social conditions among primitive peoples and music; he publ. a book, *Arbeit und Rhythmus* (1896), in which the origin of music is traced to natural rhythmic exertions during manual labor, with group singing in unison as a natural expedient for teamwork. The book aroused a great deal of controversy, and went through several printings; the 6th edition was publ. in 1924.
BIBLIOGRAPHY: Lotte (Bucheim) Stratil-Sauer, *Volksliedhaftes unter Büchers deutschen Arbeitsliedern* (Leipzig, 1931); also Bücher's memoirs, *Lebenserinnerungen* (1919).

Buchmayer, Richard, German pianist and music editor; b. Zittau, April 19, 1856; d. Tams (Salzburg), May 24, 1934. He studied at the Dresden Cons.; later taught piano there. In his recitals he presented many unknown works by old masters. In 1903 he discovered, in the municipal library of Lüneburg, some valuable MSS of 17th-century organ and piano works, throwing new light on the subject of organ tablatures. The results of these studies were publ. in *Sammelbände der Internationalen Musik-Gesellschaft, Bach-Jahrbuch* (1908), *Signale,* etc. He edited Ch. Ritter's cantata *O sanctissime sponse, Jesu* and G. Böhm's cantata *Mein Freund ist mein;* also 5 vols. of piano and organ works of the 17th century (1927).

Buchner, Hans, German organist; b. Ravensburg, Württemberg, Oct. 26, 1483; d. probably in Constance, mid-Feb. 1538. His father, an organist, gave Buchner his first instruction. Hans Buchner became organist at the Cathedral of Constance on June 19, 1506, and was given permanent employment in 1512. His magnum opus was a *Fundamentum,* a manual for composition and improvisation on the organ (1551).

Buchner, Philipp Friedrich, German organist; b. Wertheim, Sept. 11, 1614; d. Würzburg, March 23, 1669. He was a chorister in Frankfurt; then served as organist in the Barfüsserkirche there (1634–36); subsequently was engaged as Kapellmeister in Cracow (c.1637–47). In 1648 he was in Mainz. His *Concerti ecclesiatici* was publ. in 2 books (Venice, 1642, 1644); he also wrote instrumental music for violins, violas, and cembalo.

Bucht, Gunnar, Swedish composer; b. Stocksund, Aug. 5, 1927. He studied musicology at Uppsala Univ. (1947–53); concurrently took lessons in theory with Blomdahl (1947–51); received his Ph.D. at Uppsala in 1953; later studied composition in Germany with Orff (1954), in Italy with Petrassi (1954–55), and in Paris with Max Deutsch (1961–62). He taught at Stockholm Univ. (1965–69); was also employed in diplomatic service as cultural attaché at the Swedish Embassy in Bonn (1970–73). In 1975 he was appointed prof. of composition at the Musikhögskolan in Stockholm. His music retains traditional forms while adopting diverse modern techniques.
WORKS: Opera, *Tronkrävarna,* after Ibsen (*The Pretenders,* 1961–64; Stockholm, Sept. 10, 1966); opera-oratorio, *Jerikos murar* (*The Walls of Jericho,* 1966–67; reworked as an electronic piece, 1970); 7 symphs.: No. 1 (1952; Swedish Radio, Dec. 6, 1953); No. 2 (1953; unperformed); No. 3 (1954; Swedish Radio, April 17, 1955); No. 4 (1957–58; Stockholm, April 3, 1959); No. 5 (1960; Stockholm, Jan. 14, 1962); No. 6 (1961–62; Stockholm, Nov. 20, 1963); No. 7 (1970–71; Norrköping, March 26, 1972); *Introduction and Allegro* for String Orch. (1950); *Meditation* for Piano and Orch. (1950); Cello Concerto (1954); *Symphonic Fantasy* for Orch. (1955); Divertimento for Orch. (1955–56); *Dagen svalnar (The Day Cools)* for Soprano, and Orch. or Piano (1956); *Envar sin egen professor* for Tenor, Chorus, and Orch. (1957); *La fine della diaspora,* after Quasimodo's "Auschwitz," for Chorus and Orch. (1958; Stockholm, Oct. 4, 1963); *Couplets et Refrains* for Orch. (1960); *Dramma per Musica* for Orch. (1963; symph. intermezzo from 2nd act of his opera *Tronkrävarna*); *Strangaspel* for Strings (1965); *Eine lutherische messe* for Soloists, Mixed and Children's Choruses, and Orch. (1972–73); *Winter Organ* for Orch. (1974); *Music for Lau* for Children's Chorus, Wind Orch., Percussion, Double Basses, and Tape (1974–75); *Theme and Variations* for Piano (1949); String Quintet (1949–50); 2 piano sonatas (1951, 1959); 2 string quartets (1951, 1959); *5 Bagatelles* for String Quartet (1953); Sonata for Piano and Percussion (1955); *Hommage à Edith Södergran* for Mixed Chorus (1956); *Kattens öron* for Narrator, Saxophone, Double Bass, and Percussion (1959); *Hund skenar glad (Dog Runs Happy),* chamber cantata for Voice, Female Chorus and 8 Instruments (1961); *Ein Wintermärchen* for Voice and Instrumental Ensemble (1962); *6 arstidssånger (Season Songs)* for Voice and Piano (1965); *Symphonie pour la musique libérée* for Tape (1969).

Büchtiger, Fritz, German composer; b. Munich, Feb. 14, 1903; d. Starnberg, Dec. 26, 1978. He studied organ, flute, voice, conducting, and music theory at the Music Academy of Munich; his instructors in composition were Beer-Walbrunn and Wolfgang von Waltershausen. He followed the contemporary trends of German music, but with the advent of the Nazis, when modernism became strictly *verboten,* he was compelled, as a certified Aryan, to write nationalistic and racially blatant stuff. In 1948 he swerved back to his original interests, formed a studio for new music in Munich, and began writing in a dodecaphonic idiom, adroitly applying it even to his religious compositions. He was also active internationally as chairman of the German section of "Jeunesses musicales."

WORKS: Oratorios: *Der weisse Reiter* (1948) and *Das gläserne Meer* (1953); *Himmelfahrt* (1957); *Die Verklärung* (1957); Christmas Oratorio (1959); *John the Baptist* (1962); Violin Concerto (1963); *Strukturen* for Nonet (1968); 4 string quartets (1948, 1957, 1958, 1969).

BIBLIOGRAPHY: L. Wismeyer, *Fritz Büchtiger* (Regensburg, 1963).

Buck, Dudley, noted American organist, composer, and pedagogue; b. Hartford, Conn., March 10, 1839; d. West Orange, N.J., Oct. 6, 1909. He studied piano with W.J. Babcock; then traveled to Germany, where he took courses at the Leipzig Cons. with Plaidy and Moscheles (piano), Hauptmann (composition), and J. Rietz (instrumentation); later was in Paris (1861–62). Returning to the U.S., he served as church organist in Hartford, Chicago, Boston, and Brooklyn. He was one of the first American composers to achieve recognition for his church music.

WORKS: Comic opera, *Deseret, or A Saint's Affliction* (N.Y., Oct. 11, 1880); grand opera, *Serapis;* symph. overture, *Marmion* (1880); cantata, *The Legend of Don Munio* (1874); *Canzonetta* and *Bolero* for Violin and Orch.; 2 grand sonatas for Organ; concert variations on *The Star Spangled Banner* for Organ; also several manuals for organ playing.

BIBLIOGRAPHY: *Dudley Buck: A Complete Bibliography* (N.Y., 1910).

Buck, Ole, Danish composer; b. Copenhagen, Feb. 1, 1945. Though largely self-taught, he began to compose energetically at an early age, adopting an elaborate serial idiom. Having reached an impasse on that primrose path, he experienced an epiphany upon contemplating Zen Buddhist paintings and reciting transcendental poetry, in which an act of sempiternal iteration becomes the guiding spirit of human art and music.

WORKS: *Kalligrafi* for Soprano and Orch. (1964); 2 sets of pieces, titled *White Flower Music:* No. 1 for 2 Flutes, 2 Clarinets, and Trumpet (1965) and No. 2 for Orch. (1973); *Envoi,* fragments for Orch. (1964–65); *Décor* for Chamber Orch. (1966; revised for Full Orch., 1969); *Prelude I–IV* for Chamber Orch. (1966–67); *Signes* for Wind Quintet (1967); *Punctuations* for Orch. (1968); *Masques* for 6 Percussion Groups (1969); *Fairies* for Soprano and Orch. (1972); *Felix Luna,* ballet, (1970–71; Copenhagen, Feb. 3, 1973); *Granulations* for Orch. (1971–72); *Kindergarten* for Flute, Oboe, Horn, and Violin (1972); *Christopher Columbus* for Chorus and Orch. (1973); *Pastorals* for Orch. (1975); choruses; songs; tape pieces.

Buck, Sir Percy Carter, English organist; b. London, March 25, 1871; d. there, Oct. 3, 1947. He studied at the Guildhall School and Royal College of Music; subsequently served as church organist. From 1901–27 he was music director at Harrow School; was prof. of music at Trinity College in Dublin (1910–20); at the Univ. of London (1925–37); also taught at the Royal College of Music in London. He was knighted in 1937. His works include an overture for Orch., *Cœur de Lion;* String Quartet; Piano Quintet; sonatas; piano pieces, etc. He was the author of *Ten Years of University Music in Oxford* (1894; with Mee and Woods); *Unfigured Harmony* (1911); *Organ Playing* (1912); *First Year at the Organ* (1912); *The Organ: A Complete Method for the Study of Technique and Style; Acoustics for Musicians* (1918); *The Scope of Music* (Oxford, 1924); *Psychology for Musicians* (London, 1944); also was editor of the introductory vol. and vols. I and II of the 2nd ed. of the *Oxford History of Music.*

Bücken, Ernst, eminent German musicologist; b. Aachen, May 2, 1884; d. Overath, near Cologne, July 28, 1949. He studied musicology at the Univ. of Munich with Sandberger and Kroyer; also took courses in composition with Courvoisier; received his Ph.D. there in 1912 with the dissertation *Anton Reicha; Sein Leben und seine Kompositionen* (publ. in Munich, 1912); completed his Habilitation at the Univ. of Cologne in 1920 with his *Der heroische Stil in der Oper* (publ. in Leipzig, 1924); was a prof. there from 1925 to 1945; then retired to Overath. His elucidation of musical styles remains an important achievement in his work as a musicologist; as such, he edited the monumental Handbuch der Musikwissenschaft in 10 vols., which began publication in 1927; for this series he contributed *Musik des Rokokos und der Klassik* (1927), *Die Musik des 19. Jahrhunderts bis zur Moderne* (1929–31), and *Geist und Form im musikalischen Kunstwerk* (1929–32); he was also editor of the series Die Grossen Meister der Musik from 1932. His further writings include *Tagebuch der Gattin Mozarts* (Munich, 1915); *München als Musikstadt* (Leipzig, 1923); *Führer und Probleme der neuen Musik* (Cologne, 1924); *Musikalische Charakterköpfe* (Leipzig, 1924); ed. of *Handbuch der Musikerziehung* (Wildpark-Potsdam, 1931); *Ludwig van Beethoven* (Wildpark-Potsdam, 1934); *Richard Wagner* (Wildpark-Potsdam, 1934; 2nd ed., 1943); *Deutsche Musikkunde* (Wildpark-Potsdam, 1935); *Musik aus deutscher Art* (Cologne, 1936); *Musik der Nationen* (Leipzig, 1937; 2nd ed., revised, as *Geschichte der Musik,* ed. by J. Völckers, 1951); ed. of *Richard Wagner: Die Hauptschriften* (Leipzig, 1937); *Das deutsche Lied: Probleme und Gestalten* (Hamburg, 1939); *Robert Schumann* (Cologne, 1940); *Wörterbuch der Musik* (Leipzig, 1940); *Musik der Deutschen: Eine Kulturgeschichte der deutschen Musik* (Cologne, 1941); *Wolfgang Amadeus Mozart: Schöpferische Wandlungen* (Hamburg, 1942); *Richard Strauss* (Kevelaar, 1949).

BIBLIOGRAPHY: W. Kahl, "Ernst Bücken," *Die Musikforschung,* III (1950).

Buckley, Emerson, American conductor; b. New York, April 14, 1916. He studied at Columbia Univ. (B.A., 1936) and the Univ. of Denver (L.H.D., 1959); made his debut as a conductor in N.Y. in 1936. After holding various posts with operatic and symph. groups, he became artistic director of the Miami Opera Guild in 1950; was also conductor of the Central City Opera (1956–69). He became music director of the Fort Lauderdale Symph. Orch. in 1963 while continuing to direct the Miami Opera.

Buckner, Milt (Milton), American jazz pianist; b. St. Louis, July 10, 1915. He played in Lionel Hampton's band; popularized the "locked-hands" technique of parallel block chords; perfected the rigid rhythmical patterns in the blues style; was the first to use the Hammond organ in jazz.

Buczynski, Walter, Canadian composer and pianist; b. Toronto, Dec. 17, 1933. He studied music theory at the Cons. of Toronto; took lessons in composition with Darius Milhaud in Paris in the summer of 1956, and also with Nadia Boulanger (1960 and 1962). He studied piano mainly in Warsaw, Poland, where he has ethnic roots. Returning to Canada in 1962, he was appointed teacher of piano and theory at the Cons. of Toronto. His music is influenced by the modern Polish school of composition; the titles of his works are in the spirit of aggressive modernism.
WORKS: Chamber opera, *From the Buczynski Book of the Living* for Soprano, Tenor, Clarinet, Piano, and Percussion (1972); Piano Trio (1954); Suite for Wind Quintet (1955); Divertimento for Violin, Cello, Clarinet, and Bassoon (1957); *Mr. Rhinoceros and His Musicians* for Narrator, Soprano, and Baritone (Canadian Radio, Dec. 25, 1965); *Do Re Mi* for Soprano, Tenor, 2 Actors, and Instrumental Ensemble (Canadian Radio, Dec. 13, 1967); *Two-and-a-Half Squares in a Circle* for Flute, Violin, Cello, and Strings (1967); *4 Movements* for Piano and Strings (1969); *Zeroing In No. 1* for Speaking Voice, Prepared Piano, and Tape (1971); *Zeroing In No. 2 (Distraction and Then)* for Orch. Groups in the audience and on-stage Strings (1971); *Zeroing In No. 3* for String Quartet and Orch. (1973); *Zeroing In No. 4 (Innards and Outards)* for Soprano, Flute, Piano, and Orch. (1972); *Zeroing In No. 5 (Dictionary of Mannerisms)* for Piano (1972); *Three Against Many* for Flute, Clarinet, Bassoon, and Orch. (1973); *27 Pieces for a 27-Minute Show* for Piano (1973); Concerto for Violin, Cello, and Orch. (1975); *Olympics '76* for Brass Quintet (1976); *The Tales of Nanabozho* for Narrator and Wind Quintet (1976); songs; piano pieces for young people; piano pieces for adults; piano pieces for diverse ages.

Budashkin, Nicolai, Russian composer; b. Lubakhovka, in Kaluga region, Aug. 6, 1910, of a peasant family. After working as a blacksmith, he went to Moscow and took a course with Miaskovsky at the Moscow Cons. He specializes in music for Russian popular instruments in symphonic combinations; he wrote 2 concertos for Domra and Orch. (1944, 1947); Concert Variations for Balalaika with Orch. on a Russian folk song (1946); and works for ensembles consisting entirely of such instruments. His early *Festive Overture* (1937) has achieved considerable success in Russia.

Budd, Harold, American composer of extreme avant-garde tendencies; b. Los Angeles, May 24, 1936. He studied composition and acoustics with Gerald Strang and Aurelio de la Vega at Calif. State Univ. at Northridge (B.A., 1963) and with Ingolf Dahl at the Univ. of Southern Calif. (M.Mus., 1966). From 1969 to 1976 he was on the faculty of the Calif. Inst. of the Arts. An exponent of optically impressive music, he judged the quality of a work by its appearance on paper, in the firm conviction that visual excellence is cosubstantial with audible merit. His compositions are mostly designed for mixed media; some of them are modular, capable of being choreographed one into another; some are mere verbalizations of the intended mode of performance, calculated to stultify, confuse, or exasperate the listening beholder. Perhaps the most arresting and bewildering of such misleading works in his catalogue is something called *Intermission Piece,* to be played at random with a "barely audible amplitude spectrum" during intermission, with the audience "physically or conceptually absent," so that the number of performances runs into thousands, including every time an intermission during a concert occurs any place in the world.
WORKS: *Analogies from Rothko* for Orch. (1964); *The Sixth This Year* for Orch. (1967); *September Music* (1967); *November* (1967; score displayed as a painting at the Museum of Contemporary Crafts in N.Y.); *Black Flowers,* a "quiet chamber ritual for 4 performers," to be staged in semidarkness on the threshold of visibility and audibility (1968); *Intermission Piece* (1968; first heard as musicians tuned their instruments and practiced various passages of the music scheduled to be played, during the intermission, at Hartford, Conn., Jan. 28, 1970); *One Sound* for String Quartet glissando (1968); *Mangus Colorado* for Amplified Gongs (1969; Buffalo, Feb. 4, 1970); *Lovely Thing* for Piano, telling the player: "Select a chord—if in doubt call me (in lieu of performance) at 213-662-7819 for spiritual advice" (first perf., Memphis, Tenn., Oct. 23, 1969); *Lovely Thing* for Strings (1969); *California 99* (1969); *The Candy-Apple Revision* (1970); *Wonder's Edge* for Piano, Electric Guitar, and Electronics (San Francisco, Feb. 26, 1982).

Budden, Julian, English musicologist; b. Holylake, Cheshire, April 9, 1924. He was educated at Queen's College, Oxford (B.A., 1948; M.A., 1951) and at the Royal College of Music, London (B.Mus., 1955); from 1951 he worked for the BBC, serving as a producer for music programs (1955–70), chief producer for opera (1970–76), and music organizer for external services (from 1976). His studies of 19th-century Italian opera are important; especially valuable is his publ. *The Operas of Verdi* (London, 1973).

Buelow, George, American musicologist; b. Chicago, March 31, 1929. He studied piano with Rudolph Ganz at the Chicago Musical College, where he received his M.B. (1950) and M.M. (1951) degrees; then studied musicology with Martin Bernstein, Sachs, and Reese at N.Y. Univ. (Ph.D., 1961, with the dissertation *Johann David Heinichen, "Der Generalbass in der Composition": A Critical Study with Annotated Translation of Selected Chapters*). In 1961 he joined the faculty of the Univ. of Calif. at Riverside; then was prof. of music at the Univ. of Kentucky at Louisville (1968–69) and Rutgers Univ. (1969–77). In 1977 he became prof. of musicology at Indiana Univ. in Bloomington. He is particularly noted for his studies of 17th- and 18th-century German music. He wrote *Thorough-bass Accompaniment according to Johann David Heinichen* (Berkeley, 1966).

Buffardin, Pierre-Gabriel, French flutist; b. Provence, c.1690; d. Paris, Jan. 13, 1768. He joined the Dresden court orch. in 1715; returned to France in 1750. He was highly regarded as a teacher; among his pupils were Johann Jacob Bach, the younger brother of J.S. Bach, and J.J. Quantz.

Bughici, Dumitru, Rumanian composer; b. Jassy, Nov. 14, 1921. After completing a course of elementary music at the Jassy Cons., he went to Leningrad, where he studied at the Cons. with Salmanov and Schnitke (1950–55). Returning to Rumania, he was appointed to the faculty of the Bucharest Cons.
WORKS: 2 ballets: *Lupta Luminii cu întunericul (Light and Darkness Wrestling;* 1965) and *Energie* (1965); Violin Concerto (1955); a symph. poem, *Evocare (Evocation;* 1956); *Poem concertant* for Cello and Orch. (1957); 3 sinfoniettas: No. 1, *Tinere ţii (Youth;* 1958); No. 2 (1962); No. 3, *Musică de concert* (1969); *4 Choreographic Pictures* for Orch. (1959); *Heroic Poem, Filimon Sîrbu* for Orch. (1959); *Poemul primăverii (Spring Poem)* for Violin and Orch. (1960); 3 symphs.: No. 1, *Simfonia-Poem* (1960–61); No. 2, *Simfonia-coregrafică* (1964; revised 1967); No. 3, *Ecouri de Jazz (Jazz Echoes;* 1966); *Poemul bucuriei (Poem of Joy)* for Orch. (1962); *Bolero* for Orch. (1963); *Monumentul (The Monument)* for Orch. (1964); *Partită* for Orch. (1965); *Dialoguri dramatica* for String Orch. and Flute (1967); *Omagiu* for Orch. (1967); *Baladă concertantă* for Violin and Orch. (1969); Sonata for String Orch. (1970); *Melodie, Ritm, Culoare (Melody, Rhythm, Color)*, a jazz concerto for Orch. (1970); *Sinfonietta da camera* for Strings, Flute, Oboe, and Percussion (1971); *Poem Iubirii (Poem to Love)* for Orch. (1971); *File de letopiset (Chronicle Pages)*, symph. in 6 pictures (1972); *Symphonic Fantasia*, in jazz rhythm, for Orch. (1973–74); Cello Concerto (1974); Concerto for Trumpet and Orch., in jazz rhythm (1975–76); *Symphonia 1907* (1975–76); Suite for Violin and Piano (1953); *Scherzo* for Cello and Piano (1954); 4 string quartets: No. 1 (1954); No. 2 (1968); No. 3, *Plaiurile copilăriei (Realm of Childhood;* 1971); No. 4 (1976–77); *Fantasia* for Trumpet and Piano (1960); *Divertimento* (Trio No. 1) for Violin, Cello, and Piano (1961); Violin Sonata (1963); *Mic (Small) Divertissement* for Violin, Viola, Cello, Piano, Clarinet, and Percussion (1967); Sonata for Solo Violin (1968); *Fantasia Quartet* (1969); *Minia-*

tures for Brass Quintet (1975); Trio No. 2 for Violin, Cello, and Piano (1977). He publ. (in Rumanian) the books *The Suite and the Sonata* (1965); *The Musical Forms: Lied, Rondo, Variations, and Fugue* (1969); *Dictionary of Musical Forms and Genera* (1976).

Bühler, Franz, German composer; b. Schneidheim, near Nördlingen, April 12, 1760; d. Augsburg, Feb. 4, 1823. He was a Benedictine monk at Donauwörth; a choral conductor at Botzen (1794) and at Augsburg Cathedral (1801); wrote an opera, *Die falschen Verdachte;* an oratorio, *Jesus, der göttliche Erlöser;* sonatas and preludes for organ; also several theoretical pamphlets.

Buhlig, Richard, American pianist; b. Chicago, Dec. 21, 1880; d. Los Angeles, Jan. 30, 1952. He studied in Chicago, and in Vienna with Leschetizky (1897–1900); made his debut in recital in Berlin (1901); then toured Europe and the U.S. (American debut with the Philadelphia Orch. in N.Y., Nov. 5, 1907). In 1918 he was appointed teacher of piano at the Inst. of Musical Arts in N.Y.; later returned to Europe; eventually settled in Los Angeles as a performer and teacher.

Bujarski, Zbigniew, Polish composer; b. Muszyna, 1933. He studied composition with Wiechowicz and conducting with Wodiczko at the State College of Music in Cracow. His music is dense in its contrapuntal entanglements, without becoming viscous.
WORKS: *Burning Bushes,* cycle for Soprano, and Chamber Ensemble or Piano (1958); *Triptych* for String Orch. and Percussion (1959); *Synchrony I* for Soprano and Chamber Ensemble (1959), and *II* for Soprano, Chorus, and Orch. (1960); *Zones* for Chamber Ensemble (1961); *Kinoth* for Orch. (1963); *Chamber Composition* for Voice, Flute, Harp, Piano, and Percussion (1963); *Contraria* for Orch. (1965); *El Hombre* for Soprano, Mezzo-soprano, Baritone, Chorus, and Orch. (1969–73; Warsaw, Sept. 21, 1974); *Musica domestica* for 18 String Instruments (1977).

Buketoff, Igor, American conductor; b. Hartford, Conn., May 29, 1915. He studied music at the Juilliard School in N.Y. (1939–42). In 1943 he began his conducting career; appeared as a guest conductor in America and in Europe; led the Young People's Concerts of the N.Y. Phil. (1948–53); then was director of the Fort Wayne (Ind.) Phil. (1948–66); also conducted the Iceland Symph. Orch. (1964–65); served as music director of the St. Paul Opera Assoc. (1968–74); was a visiting prof. at the Univ. of Houston (1977–79).

Bukofzer, Manfred F., eminent German-American musicologist; b. Oldenburg, March 27, 1910; d. Oakland, Calif., Dec. 7, 1955. He studied at the Hoch Cons. in Frankfurt, and at the univs. of Heidelberg, Berlin, and Basel (Dr.Phil., 1936); also took courses with Hindemith in Berlin. He lectured in Basel

(1933–39); also at the univs. of Oxford and Cambridge. In 1939 he settled in the U.S.; became a naturalized citizen in 1945. He taught at Case Western Reserve Univ. in Cleveland (1940–41). In 1941 he became a member of the faculty of the Univ. of Calif. at Berkeley; a year before his untimely death he was appointed chairman of the music dept. His numerous publications are distinguished by originality of historical and musical ideas coupled with precision of factual exposition; having mastered the English language, he was able to write brilliantly in British and American publications; he was also greatly esteemed as a teacher.

WRITINGS: *Geschichte des englischen Diskants und des Fauxbourdons* (Strasbourg, 1936; very valuable); "Über Leben und Werke von John Dunstable," *Acta musicologica* (1936); "Hegels Musikästhetik," in reports of *Deuxième Congrès d'Esthétique et de Science de l'Art* (Paris, 1937); "Kann die 'Blasquintentheorie' zur Erklärung primitiver Tonsysteme beitragen?" in *Anthropos* (1937); many other articles and important reviews in various magazines; also "Allegory in Baroque Music," *Journal of the Warburg Institute* (1939); *Sumer Is Icumen In: A Revision* (Berkeley, 1944), placing the date of this famous canon later than the generally accepted year 1240; *Music in the Baroque Era* (N.Y., 1947); *Studies in Medieval and Renaissance Music* (N.Y., 1950). He was also editor of the complete works of Dunstable (1954, vol. VIII of *Musica Britannica*).

BIBLIOGRAPHY: David D. Boyden, "In Memoriam: Manfred F. Bukofzer," *Musical Quarterly* (July 1956; contains a complete list of Bukofzer's writings).

Bull, John, famous English organist and composer; b. Old Radnor, Radnorshire, c.1562; d. Antwerp, March 12, 1628. He was a pupil of William Blitheman in the Chapel Royal; received his Mus.B. from Oxford in 1586. He was sworn in as a Gentleman of the Chapel Royal in Jan. 1586, becoming an organist in 1591. In 1596, on Queen Elizabeth's recommendation, he was appointed prof. of music at Gresham College, and on March 6, 1597, was elected first public lecturer there. He got into difficulties with Gresham College when he impregnated premaritally a maiden named Elizabeth Walter, and was forced to resign on Dec. 20, 1607; he hastened to take a marriage license 2 days later. In 1610 he entered the service of Prince Henry, but in 1613 was charged with adultery and had to flee England. In Sept. 1615 he became assistant organist at the Antwerp Cathedral in Belgium, and was named its principal organist on Dec. 29, 1617. In the Netherlands he became acquainted with the great Dutch organist and composer Sweelinck; both he and Bull exerted considerable influence on the development of contrapuntal keyboard music of the time. Altogether about 200 compositions are attributed to John Bull; they are listed in Ward's vol. *The Lives of the Professors of Gresham College* (1740). Exercises and variations for the virginal, as well as other works, were printed in the following collections: the *Fitzwilliam Virginal Book* (modern ed. by J.A. Fuller-Maitland and

W. Barclay Squire, London, 1899); *Benjamin Cosyn's Virginal Book* (23), *William Forster's Virginal Book* (3), Leighton's *The Tears or Lamentacions of a Sorrowfull Soule;* in *Parthenia* (pieces for virginal by Bull, Byrd, and Gibbons; new ed. by Margaret H. Glyn, London, 1927); and others. The complete keyboard works appear in *Musica Britannica*, XIV, ed. by J. Steele, F. Cameron, and T. Dart (1960; 2nd ed., revised, 1967), and XIX, ed. by T. Dart (1963; 2nd ed., revised, 1970). The conjecture put forward by some writers, notably Leigh Henry in his book *Dr. John Bull* (London, 1937), that Bull was the author of *God Save the King* does not have a scintilla of evidence in its support.

BIBLIOGRAPHY: Charles Van den Borren, *Les Origines de la musique de clavecin en Angleterre* (1913); Hugh Miller, "John Bull's Organ Works," *Music & Letters* (Jan. 1947); W. Mellers, "John Bull and English Keyboard Music," *Musical Quarterly* (July and Oct. 1954).

Bull, Ole (Bornemann), eccentric Norwegian violinist; b. Bergen, Feb. 5, 1810; d. Lyso, near Bergen, Aug. 17, 1880. He was extremely precocious, and played the violin experimentally even before acquiring the rudiments of music. At the age of 9 he played solos with the Bergen Harmonic Society. His teachers were then Niels Eriksen and J.H. Poulsen; later he had regular instruction with M. Ludholm. Ignoring academic rules, he whittled the bridge almost to the level of the fingerboard, so as to be able to play full chords on all 4 strings. He was sent by his father to Christiania (Oslo) to study theology, but failed the entrance examinations; instead, he organized a theater orch., which he led with his violin. In 1829 he played in Copenhagen and Kassel. In 1831 he went to Paris, where he heard Paganini and became obsessed with the idea of imitating his mannerisms and equaling his success, a fantasy devoid of all imagined reality because of Bull's amateurish technique. However, he developed a personal type of playing that pleased the public, particularly in localities rarely visited by real artists. During the season 1836–37 he played 274 concerts in England and Ireland; in 1839 he visited the great German violinist and composer Spohr in Kassel, in the hope of receiving useful advice from him. In 1840 he played Beethoven's *Kreutzer Sonata* in London, with Liszt at the piano. On July 23, 1849, he announced the formation of a Norwegian Theater in Bergen, which was opened on Jan. 2, 1850. While he failed to impress serious musicians and critics in Europe, he achieved his dream of artistic success in America; he made 5 concert tours across the U.S., playing popular selections and his own compositions on American themes with such fetching titles as *Niagara, Solitude of the Prairies,* and *To the Memory of Washington,* interspersing them with his arrangements of Norwegian folk songs. He entertained a strong conviction that Norway should generate its own national art, but the practical applications of his musical patriotism were failures because of his lack of formal study and a concentration on tawdry effects; still, it may be argued that he at least prepared the ground for the emergence of true Norwegian music; indeed, it is on his recommendation that Grieg was sent to study at the Leipzig Cons. Characteristically, Ole Bull became attracted by the then-current ideas of communal socialism. In 1852 he purchased 11,144 acres in Pennsylvania for a Norwegian settlement, but his lack of business sense led his undertaking to disaster. The settlement, planned on strict socialist lines, was given the name Oleana, thus establishing a personal connection with the name of its unlucky founder. Oleana soon collapsed, but Ole Bull earned admiration in Norway as a great national figure. Many of his violin pieces, mostly sentimental or strident in nature, with such titles as *La preghiera d'una madre, Variazioni di bravura, Polacca guerriera,* etc., were publ., but they sank into predictable desuetude.

BIBLIOGRAPHY: J. Lie, *Ole Bulls breve i utdreg* (Copenhagen, 1881); Sara C. Bull (his 2nd wife), *Ole Bull: A Memoir* (Boston, 1883; German ed., Stuttgart, 1886); O. Vik, *Ole Bull* (Bergen, 1890); C.A. Aarvig, *Den unge Ole Bull* (Copenhagen, 1935); A. Björndal, *Ole Bull og Norsk folkemusik* (Bergen, 1940); M.B. Smith, *The Life of Ole Bull* (Princeton, 1943); Z. Hopp, *Eventyret om Ole Bull* (Bergen, 1945); Ola Linge, *Ole Bull* (Oslo, 1953); I. Bull, *Ole Bull Returns to Pennsylvania* (N.Y., 1961).

Bullard, Frederick Field, American song composer; b. Boston, Sept. 21, 1864; d. there, June 24, 1904. He studied with Rheinberger at Munich; returned to Boston and became a music teacher; publ. about 40 songs, hymns, and anthems.

Bullock, Sir Ernest, English organist and educator; b. Wigan, Sept. 15, 1890; d. Aylesbury, May 24, 1979. He studied organ with Bairstow in Leeds; also took courses at the Univ. of Durham (B.Mus., 1908; D.Mus., 1914). After serving as suborganist at Manchester Cathedral (1912–15), he was organist and choirmaster at Exeter Cathedral (1919–27). In 1928 he was named organist and Master of the Choristers at Westminster Abbey, and as such participated in several coronations. He became Gardiner Prof. of Music at the Univ. of Glasgow in 1941. He was then director of the Royal College of Music in London from 1952 until his retirement in 1960. He was knighted by King George VI in 1951.

Bülow, Hans (Guido) von, celebrated German pianist and conductor of high attainment; b. Dresden, Jan. 8, 1830; d. Cairo, Egypt, Feb. 12, 1894. At the age of 9 he began to study piano with Friedrich Wieck and theory with Max Eberwein; then went to Leipzig, where he studied law at the univ. and took a music course with Moritz Hauptmann; he also studied piano with Plaidy. From 1846 to 1848 he lived in Stuttgart, where he made his debut as a pianist. In 1849 he attended the Univ. of Berlin; there he joined radical social groups; shortly afterward he went to Zürich and met Wagner, who was there in exile. After a year in Switzerland where he conducted theater music, Bülow proceeded to Weimar, where he began to study with Liszt. In 1853 he made a tour through Germany and Austria as a pianist. In 1855 he was appointed head of the piano dept. at the Stern Cons. in Berlin, retaining this post until 1864. He married Liszt's natural daughter, Cosima, in 1857. In 1864 he was called by Ludwig II to Munich as court pianist and conductor; the King, who was a great admirer of Wagner, summoned Wagner to Munich from exile. Hans von Bülow himself became Wagner's ardent champion; on June 10, 1865, he conducted at the court opera in Munich the first performance of *Tristan und Isolde,* and on June 21, 1868, he led the premiere of *Die Meistersinger von Nürnberg.* It was about this time that Wagner became intimate with Cosima; after her divorce she married Wagner, in 1870. Despite this betrayal, Bülow continued to conduct Wagner's music; his growing admiration for Brahms cannot be construed as his pique against Wagner. It was Bülow who dubbed Brahms "the third B of music," the first being Bach, and the second Beethoven. In fact, the context of this nomination was more complex than a mere alphabetical adumbration; according to reports, Bülow was asked to name his favorite key; he replied that it was E-flat major, the key signature of the *Eroica,* with the 3 B's (German colloquialism for flats) signifying Bach, Beethoven, and Brahms. Then he was asked why he did not rather nominate Bruckner for the 3rd B, and he is supposed to have replied that Bruckner was too much of a Wagnerian for him. Bülow was indeed renowned for his wit, and his aptitude for alliterative punning; his writings are of elevated literary quality. In 1872 Bülow lived in Florence; then resumed his career as a pianist, winning triumphant successes in England and Russia; during his American tour in 1875–76 he gave 139 concerts; he revisited America in 1889 and 1890. An important chapter in his career was his conductorship in Meiningen (1880–85). In 1882 he married a Meiningen actress, Marie Schanzer. He was conductor of the Berlin Phil. from 1887 to 1893, when a lung ailment forced him to seek a cure in Egypt. He died shortly after his arrival in Cairo.

As a conductor, Hans von Bülow was an uncompromising disciplinarian; he insisted on perfection of detail, and he was also able to project considerable emotional power on the music. He was one of the first conductors to dispense with the use of the score. His memory was fabulous; it was said that he could memorize a piano concerto by just reading the score, sometimes while riding in a train. The mainstay of his repertoire was Classical and Romantic music, but he was also receptive toward composers of the new school. When Tchaikovsky, unable to secure a performance of his First Piano Concerto in Russia, offered the score to Bülow, he accepted it, and gave its world premiere as soloist with a pickup orch. in Boston, on Oct. 25, 1875; however, the music was too new and too strange to American ears of the time, and the critical reactions were ambiguous. Hans von Bülow encouraged the young Richard Strauss, and gave him his first position as conductor. Bülow was a composer himself, but his works belong to the category of "Kapellmeister Musik," competent, well structured, but devoid of originality. Among his compositions were a symph. "mood picture," *Nirwana;* incidental music to Shakespeare's *Julius Caesar;* piano pieces and numerous songs. He made masterly transcriptions of the prelude to Wagner's *Meistersinger* and the entire opera *Tristan und Isolde;* also arranged for piano the overtures to *Le Corsaire* and *Benvenuto Cellini* by Berlioz. He annotated and edited Beethoven's piano sonatas, which were widely used by piano teachers, even though criticism was voiced against his cavalier treatment of some passages and his occasional alterations of Beethoven's original to enhance the resonance.

BIBLIOGRAPHY: E. Zabel, *Hans von Bülow* (Hamburg, 1894); R. Sternfeld, *Hans von Bülow* (Leipzig, 1894); Th. Pfeiffer, *Studien bei Hans von Bülow* (Berlin, 1894; 6th ed., 1909); Vianna da Motta, *Nachtrag zu den Pfeifferschen "Studien bei Hans von Bülow"* (Leipzig, 1895); W. Altmann, *Chronik des Berliner philharmonischen Orchesters, 1882–1901; zugleich ein Beitrag zur Beurteilung Hans von Bülows* (Berlin, 1902); G. Fischer, *Hans von Bülow in Hannover* (Hannover, 1902); H. Heimann, *Hans von Bülow: Sein Leben und sein Wirken* (Berlin, 1909); C. Krebs, *Meister des Takstocks* (1919); R. Du Moulin-Eckart, *Hans von Bülow* (1921); Marie von Bülow, *Hans von Bülow in Leben und Wort* (1925); Th.W. Werner, *Hans von Bülow in 75 Jahre Opernhaus Hannover* (1927); Walter Damrosch, "Hans von Bülow and the 9th Symphony," *Musical Quarterly* (April 1927); Ludwig Schemann, *Hans von Bülow im Lichte der Wahrheit* (Regensburg, 1935). Hans von Bülow's writings were publ. by his widow, Marie von Bülow, under the title *Briefe und Schriften Hans von Bülows* (8 vols., Leipzig, 1895–1908; vol. III, republ. separately in 1936, contains selected essays, while the other vols. contain letters); selected letters in Eng. trans. were publ. by C. Bache, *The Early Correspondence of Hans von Bülow* (London, 1896); F. Rösch, *Musikästhetische Streitfragen; Streitlichter zu den ausgewählten Schriften von Hans von Bülow* (Leipzig, 1897); La Mara, *Briefwechsel zwischen Franz Liszt und Hans von Bülow* (Leipzig, 1898); E. Förster-Nietzsche and P. Gast, *Friedrich Nietzsches gesammelte Briefe* (Berlin, 1905); vol. III contains the correspondence between Nietzsche and Hans von Bülow); Bülow's letters to Wagner, Cosima Wagner, Karl Klindworth, Karl Bechstein et al., ed. by R. Du Moulin-Eckart (Munich, 1927; in Eng., N.Y., 1931); H.C. Schonberg, *The Great Conductors* (N.Y., 1968); W.M. Freitag, "An Annotated Biography of Hans von Bülow in the Harvard College Library," *Harvard Library Bulletin* (July 1967); Harold Schonberg, *The Great Conductors* (N.Y., 1967; pp. 163–75); W. Stresemann, *The Berlin Philharmonic from Bülow to Karajan* (in German and Eng.; Berlin, 1979; pp. 43–57).

Bulthaupt, Heinrich, German dramatist and writer on music; b. Bremen, Oct. 26, 1849; d. there, Aug. 21, 1905. He studied jurisprudence at Göttingen, Leipzig, and Berlin; spent some time in Kiev with private teachers, and then made an extensive trip in the Orient. In 1879 he was appointed librarian of the Municipal Library at Bremen. Besides his purely literary work, he wrote librettos for Rubinstein, Eugene d'Albert, and others. His most important work dealing with music is *Dramaturgie der Oper* (2 vols.; Leipzig, 1887; 2nd ed., 1902). He also wrote a biography of Carl Loewe (1898) and *Richard Wagner als Klassiker* (1899).

Bumbry, Grace (Ann), greatly talented black American mezzo-soprano; b. St. Louis, Jan. 4, 1937. She sang in church choirs as a child; in 1955 went to Northwestern Univ. to study voice with Lotte Lehmann, and continued her lessons with her at the Music Academy of the West in Santa Barbara. She made her professional debut in a concert in London in 1959; then made a spectacular operatic appearance as Amneris at the Paris Opéra in 1960. In a lucky strike, Wieland Wagner engaged her to sing Venus in *Tannhäuser* at the Bayreuth Festival on July 23, 1961; she was the first Afro-American to be featured in the role of a goddess. This event created immediate repercussions in liberal circles, and Grace Bumbry was invited by Jacqueline Kennedy to sing at the White House on Feb. 20, 1962. She then undertook a grand tour of concerts in the U.S.; in 1963 she performed the role of Venus again at the Chicago Lyric Opera, and also sang it at Lyons, France. On Oct. 7, 1965, she made her Metropolitan Opera debut in N.Y. as Princess Eboli in Verdi's opera *Don Carlos.* In 1966 she sang Carmen at the Salzburg Festival under the direction of Herbert von Karajan; she repeated this role at the Metropolitan with extraordinary success. The sensational element of her race was no longer the exclusive attraction; the public and the press judged her impartially as a great artist. In 1970 she sang Salome in the Strauss opera at Covent Garden in London, and she sang it again, in German, at the Metropolitan Opera on Sept. 19, 1973. She proved her ability to perform mezzo-soprano and high soprano roles with equal brilliance by singing both Aida and Amneris in Verdi's opera, and both Venus and Elisabeth in *Tannhäuser.* In 1963 she married the Polish tenor **Erwin Jaeckel,** who also became her business manager.

Bümler, Georg Heinrich, German singer and chamber musician; b. Berneck, near Bayreuth, Oct. 10, 1669; d. Ansbach, Aug. 26, 1745. He studied at the Lateinschule in Münchberg; became a chamber descantist at the court in Bayreuth; there he studied voice and keyboard playing with Ruggiero Fedeli. He subsequently pursued a career as a singer in Wolfenbüttel, Hamburg, Berlin, and Bayreuth. In 1698 he became chamber musician at the Ansbach court; in 1717 he was made Kapellmeister there.

Bunger, Richard Joseph, American pianist and composer; b. Allentown, Pa., June 1, 1942. He studied at Oberlin College Cons. (B.Mus., 1964) and the Univ. of Illinois (M.Mus., 1965). In 1973 he was appointed to the faculty of Calif. State College, Dominguez Hills. He became absorbed in the modern techniques of composition, particularly in the new resources of prepared piano; publ. an illustrated vol., *The Well-Prepared Piano* (1973), with a foreword by John Cage; also evolved a comprehensive notational system called "Musiglyph" which incorporates standard musical notation and musical graphics indicating special instrumental techniques. He is the inventor of a "Bungerack," a music holder for the piano, particularly convenient for scores of large size.

Bungert, August, German composer; b. Mülheim, Ruhr, March 14, 1845; d. Leutesdorf, Oct. 26, 1915. He studied piano and composition at Cologne and Paris; lived mostly in Berlin. An ardent admirer of Wagner, Bungert devoted his life to the composition of a parallel work to Wagner's *Ring,* taking Homer's epics as the source of his librettos. The result of this effort was the creation of two operatic cycles: *The Iliad,* comprising *Achilleus* and *Klytemnestra;* and *The Odyssey,* a tetralogy. *The Iliad* was never completed for performance, but all four parts of *The Odyssey* were performed in Dresden: *Kirke* (Jan. 29, 1898); *Nausikaa* (March 20, 1901); *Odysseus' Heimkehr* (Dec. 12, 1896, prior to premieres of parts I and II); *Odysseus' Tod* (Oct. 30, 1903). There were also subsequent productions in other German cities, but everywhere Bungert's operas were received without enthusiasm, and the evident ambition to emulate Wagner without comparable talent proved his undoing. Among other works are the programmatic score *Zeppelins erste grosse Fahrt;* several symph. overtures; *Symphonia Victrix; German Requiem;* many songs. His most successful work was a comic opera, *Die Studenten von Salamanka* (Leipzig, 1884); he also wrote a mystery play, *Warum? woher? wohin?* (1908); incidental music to Goethe's *Faust,* etc.

BIBLIOGRAPHY: F.A. Geissler, "August Bungert," *Die Musik* (Dec. 1907); M. Chop, *August Bungert, Ein deutscher Dichterkomponist* (Leipzig, 1916).

Bunin, Revol, Soviet composer; b. Moscow, April 6, 1924. He studied music theory at the Moscow Cons. with Litinsky, Shebalin, and Shostakovich, graduating in 1945. In 1947 he became Shostakovich's assistant in composition at the Cons. of Leningrad. WORKS: Opera, *Masquerade* (1944); cantata, *Lead Us On* (1964); 8 symphs. (1943, 1945, 1959, 1961, 1966, 1968, 1970); Viola Concerto (1953); Concertante Symph. (1972); Concerto for Piano and Chamber Orch. (1963); Piano Quintet (1946); 2 string quartets (1943, 1956); Suite for Viola and Piano (1955); songs; film music.

Bunin, Vladimir, Russian composer; b. Skopin, Riazan district, July 24, 1908; d. Moscow, March 23, 1970. He studied at the Moscow Cons. with A. Alexandrov, graduating in 1938. In his music, Bunin follows the traditions of Russian classicism. He wrote 2 symphs. (1943, 1949); *Poem about Lenin* for Orch. (1969); Violin Concerto (1953); Piano Concerto

(1965); many piano pieces and songs.

Bunnett, Edward, English organist and composer; b. Shipdham, Norfolk, June 26, 1834; d. Norwich, Jan. 5, 1923. He was a chorister at Norwich Cathedral; then occupied various posts as organist; served as conductor of the Norwich Musical Union. He produced several cantatas at Norwich Festivals: *Rhineland* (1872); *Lora* (1876); and *De Profundis* (1880); also wrote numerous organ pieces. His *Nunc Dimittis* (1867) was for many years performed in English churches.

Bunning, Herbert, English conductor and composer; b. London, May 2, 1863; d. Thundersley, Essex, Nov. 26, 1937. He studied music with John Farmer at Harrow. After graduating from Oxford, he entered the army and served with the Queen's Own Hussars (1884); continued his musical studies in Milan with Vincenzo Ferroni and others (1886–91); upon his return to London, was appointed conductor of the Lyric Theatre (1892). WORKS: Opera, *Princess Osra* (Covent Garden, London, July 14, 1902); 2 overtures: *Mistral* (1897) and *Spring and Youth* (1897); Italian scena, *Ludovico il Moro* (1892); also *Shepherd's Call,* intermezzo for Horn and Strings (1893); *Village Suite* for Orch. (1896); *Sir Launcelot and Queen Guinevere* for Tenor and Orch. (1905); incidental music to *Robin Hood* (1906); songs.

Bunting, Edward, historiographer of Irish music; b. Armagh, Feb. 1773; d. Dublin, Dec. 21, 1843. He played organ at Belfast; then moved to Dublin. He publ. 3 collections of old Irish airs in 1796, 1809, and 1840; these were reprinted in 2 vols. in 1969 under the title *The Ancient Music of Ireland;* many of these were publ. for the first time; the first vol. contained songs by O'Conolan and O'Carolan; the 2nd included piano arrangements and a discussion of the Irish, British, and Egyptian harps; the 3rd contained a long dissertation on the history of Irish popular music. Bunting collected his material from old singers and harpers; his publications, therefore, have the value of authenticity.

Buonamente, Giovanni Battista, Italian composer; b. c.1600; d. Assisi, Aug. 29, 1642. He was maestro di cappella at the Austrian court in Vienna from 1626 to 1631; then served in a similar position at the Basilica of S. Francesco in Assisi, beginning in 1633. His importance rests on his sonatas for violin, some of which are the earliest examples of this form; he publ. 7 books of such works in Vienna during his stay there; also wrote trio sonatas for 2 violins and bass.

BIBLIOGRAPHY: Paul Nettl, "G.B. Buonamente," *Zeitschrift für Musikwissenschaft,* IX (1926–27).

Buonamici, Giuseppe, Italian pianist; b. Florence, Feb. 12, 1846; d. there, March 17, 1914. He first studied with his uncle, Giuseppe Ceccherini; then at the

Munich Cons. with Hans von Bülow and Rheinberger (1868–70); in 1873 returned to Florence, where he was active as a teacher and choral conductor. He publ. a compilation of the technical figures found in Beethoven's piano music, in the form of daily studies; edited the *Biblioteca del Pianista* and the complete Beethoven sonatas; also publ. piano pieces of his own.

Buongiorno, Crescenzo, Italian composer; b. Bonito, Province of Avellino, 1864; d. Dresden, Nov. 7, 1903. He studied with Serrao at the Naples Cons.; later settled in Dresden.
WORKS: 4 operas: *Etelka* (Naples, 1887); *Das Erntefest* (Leipzig, 1896); *Das Mädchenherz* (Kassel, 1901); *Michel Angelo und Rolla* (Kassel, 1903); also 12 operettas, including *Abukadabar* (Naples, 1889); *Circe e Calipso* (Turin, 1892); *La nuova Saltarella* (Trieste, 1894).

Buononcini. See **Bononcini.**

Burada, Theodor, Rumanian violinist and folklorist; b. Jassy, Oct. 3, 1839; d. there, Feb. 17, 1923. He studied in Rumania and at the Paris Cons. His significance lies in his pioneer work connected with Rumanian folklore and codifying folk melodies and popular ballads. He also wrote some violin music.

Burbure de Wesembeek, Léon-Philippe-Marie, Belgian music scholar; b. Dendermonde, Aug. 16, 1812; d. Antwerp, Dec. 8, 1889. A scion of an aristocratic family, he studied law at the Univ. of Ghent; he also received an excellent musical education at home with private teachers. In 1846 he settled in Antwerp, and became the keeper of Archives at the Cathedral. He made a profound study of materials on old music accessible to him, and publ. a number of valuable monographs dealing with the Renaissance music guilds of Antwerp, on lute makers, etc. He also composed some 200 works, including an opera, 25 orch. pieces, numerous choral works, etc.
WRITINGS: *Aperçu sur l'ancienne corporation des musiciens instrumentistes d'Anvers, dite de St. Job et de Ste. Marie-Madeleine* (Brussels, 1862); *Recherches sur les facteurs de clavecins et luthiers d'Anvers, depuis le XVIe jusqu'au XIXe siècle* (Brussels, 1869); *Notice sur Charles-Louis Hanssens* (Brussels, 1872); *Charles Luython (1550–1620), compositeur de musique de la Cour impériale* (Brussels, 1880); *Les Œuvres des anciens musiciens belges* (Brussels, 1882).
BIBLIOGRAPHY: F.A. Gevaert, *Notice sur le Chevalier Léon de Burbure* (Brussels, 1893).

Burck (real name, **Moller**), **Joachim à,** German church composer; b. Burg, near Magdeburg, 1546; d. Mühlhausen, Thuringia, May 24, 1610. In 1563 he settled in Mühlhausen; became organist at the Protestant Church of St. Blasius in 1566.
WORKS: *Harmoniae sacrae* (5 books of motets; Nuremberg, 1566); *Die deutsche Passion* (Wittenberg, 1568); *Crepundia sacra* (4 books; Mühlhausen, 1578); several books of motets, odes, and German songs, reprinted in various collections.
BIBLIOGRAPHY: A. Prüfer, *Untersuchungen über den aussernkirchlichen Kunstgesang in den evangelischen Schulen des 16. Jahrhundert* (Leipzig, 1890); R. Jordan, *Aus der Geschichte der Musik in Mühlhausen* (Mühlhausen, 1905).

Burco, Ferruccio, precocious Italian conductor; b. Milan, April 5, 1939; killed in an automobile accident near Ostuni, April 27, 1965. Phenomenally gifted, he was trained by his mother, a singer, and on May 30, 1943, at the age of 4, conducted an orch. in Milan by memorizing gestures to give cues. With his father acting as his manager, he was exhibited throughout Italy; in 1948 he was brought to the U.S. and conducted a concert at Carnegie Hall in N.Y.; also led sympathetic symph. groups in Philadelphia, Detroit, Boston, Chicago, Los Angeles, and San Francisco. At a special opera performance at the Triborough Stadium at Randalls Island in N.Y., he conducted *Cavalleria rusticana*, with his mother singing the role of Santuzza. During his American tour he weighed only 82 pounds. His subsequent development failed to do justice to his fantastic beginnings, and at the time of his death he was the leader of an itinerant provincial Italian band.

Burette, Pierre-Jean, French writer on music; b. Paris, Nov. 21, 1665; d. there, May 19, 1747. A physician by profession, he had an interest in musical subjects; was the author of the valuable treatise *La Musique et la danse des anciens,* dealing mainly with the problems of Greek music. It was publ. in the *Mémoires de l'Académie des Inscriptions* (nos. 1–17).

Burgess, Anthony, celebrated British novelist, author of *A Clockwork Orange* and other imaginative novels, who began his career as a professional musician; b. Manchester, England, Feb. 25, 1917. He played piano in jazz combos in England, at the same time studying classical compositions without a tutor. Despite his great success as a novelist, he continued to write music, and developed a style of composition that, were it not for his literary fame, would have earned him a respectable niche among composers. His music is refreshingly rhythmical and entirely tonal, but not without quirky quartal harmonies and crypto-atonal melodic flights. He publ. *This Man and Music* (London, 1982).
WORKS: 3 symphs. (1937; 1956, subtitled *Sinfoni Melayu,* and based on Malaysian themes; 1975); *Sinfonietta* for Jazz Combo (1941); symph. poem, *Gibraltar* (1944); *Song of a Northern City* for Piano and Orch. (1947); *Partita* for String Orch. (1951); *Ludus Multitonalis* for Recorder Consort (1951); Concertino for Piano and Percussion (1951); *Cantata for Malay College* (1954); Concerto for Flute and Strings (1960); Passacaglia for Orch. (1961); Piano Concerto (1976); Cello Sonata (1944); 2 piano sonatas (1946, 1951); incidental music for various plays; songs.

Burgess, Russell, English choral conductor; b. Leyton, Essex, July 3, 1931; d. there, Sept. 5, 1979. He studied at the Royal Academy of Music in London. In 1954 he became director of music at Wandsworth School in London, where he founded and conducted the Wandsworth School Boys' Choir; in 1964 he became an assistant to Wilhelm Pitz, the chorus master of the New Philharmonia Chorus; in 1971 he became its conductor.

Burghauser, Jarmil, Czech composer and conductor; b. Písek, Oct. 21, 1921. He studied composition with Křička and Jeremiáš (1933–49) and conducting with Talich and Dědeček at the Prague Cons. (1940–46); also took courses in musicology and psychology at the Charles Univ. in Prague (1945–48). In 1946–53 he was conductor at the National Theater in Prague. He began to compose in a customary Central European style, but later developed a system described by him as "harmonic serialism." Several of his works appeared under the nom de plume **Michal Hájků.**
WORKS: FOR THE STAGE: 4 operas: *Alladine and Palomide,* after Maeterlinck (1934; rewritten 1944); *Lakomec* (*The Miser;* 1949 Liberec, May 20, 1950); *Karolinka a lhář* (*Caroline and the Liar;* 1953; Olomouc, March 13, 1955); "anti-opera," *Most* (*The Bridge;* 1963–64; Prague, March 31, 1967); 3 ballets: *Honza a čert* (*Honza and the Devil;* 1954; Ostrava, Nov. 23, 1954; revised 1960); *Sluha dvou pánů* (*Servant of 2 Masters;* 1957; Prague, May 9, 1958); *Tristram a Izalda* (1968–69). FOR ORCH.: 3 symphs.: No. 1 (1933; revised 1974); No. 2 (1935; revised 1979); No. 3 (1938; revised 1950 and 1959); *Furiant* (1936; revised 1970); *Spring Rondo* (1937); *Suite* for Chamber Orch. (1939; revised 1977); Concerto for Wind Quintet and Strings (1942; Prague, Feb. 12, 1948); *Toccata* for Chamber Orch. (1947); *Symphonic Variations* (1952); *Sonata* (1954); *Symphonic Suite* (1957); *Sedm reliéfů* (*7 Reliefs;* 1962; Prague, Feb. 19, 1963); *Cesty* (*The Paths*), cycle of 8 movements for Strings, Percussion, Cimbalom, and Electric Guitar (1964; Prague, Feb. 21, 1965); *Barvy v čase* (*Colors in Time;* Wexford, Ireland, Oct. 25, 1967); *Strom života* (*The Tree of Life;* Graz, Austria, Oct. 22, 1969); *Ciaconna per il fine d'un tempo* for Piano and Orch (1981–82). CHAMBER MUSIC: 5 string quartets: No. 1 (1944; revised 1953); No. 2 (1938; revised 1953); No. 3 (1941); No. 4 (1944); No. 5 (1944–51); 4 wind quintets: No. 1 (1935; revised 1945); No. 2 (1935); No. 3 (1939); No. 4 (1940); 2 trios for Flute, Viola, and Guitar (1939, 1962); Solo Guitar Sonata (1943); *Partita* for 2 Flutes (1945; revised 1982); *Možnosti* (*Possibilities*) for Clarinet, Cimbalom, and Percussion (1965); *Deset Skic* (*10 Sketches*) for Solo Flute (1965); *Patero zamyšlení* (*5 Meditations*) for Viola and Guitar (1966); *Pět barevných střepin* (*5 Colored Splinters*) for Solo Harp (1966); *Sarabande and Toccata* for Solo Guitar (1968); *Druhá Suita* for 6 Clarinets (1970); *Neveselé vyprávění* (*Cheerless Tale*), sonata for Violin and Piano (1970); *Soumraky a svítání* (*Dusks and Dawns*) for Bass Clarinet and Piano (1971); *Stanze dell' ansieta e sperance,* 5 movements for Flute, Oboe, Harpsichord, Violin, Viola,

and Cello (1971); *Plochy a čáry* (*Surfaces and Lines*) for Violin, Cello, and Guitar (1972); *Partita* for 2 Flutes, Guitar, and Cello (1976). FOR VOICE: *Věčná oblaka* (*The Eternal Clouds*), small cantata for Soprano, Chorus, and Orch. (1942); *The Mystic Trumpeter,* after Whitman, cantata (1944); *Passion and Resurrection,* full-evening cantata (1937–46; Prague, May 26, 1946); *Zeme zamyslena* (*The Pensive Country*) for Narrator, Female Chorus, and Orch. (1966; Prague, March 24, 1968); *St. Luke Passion* for Soloists and Chorus a cappella (1977); choruses; songs. FOR PIANO: Sonata (1938); *Šest malých leptů* (*6 Little Etchings;* 1970). WORKS PUBL. UNDER THE NOM DE PLUME **Michal Hágků:** *Danse Burlesque* for Orch. (1971); *Impressions indiennes* for Orch. (New Delhi, Nov. 1972); *Indiánská symfonie* for Orch. (1974); *Proprium de Nativitate* for Soloists, Chorus, Organ, and Orch. (1978); Sinfonia in F (1980); *Missa brevis pastoralis* for Soloists, Chorus, Organ, and Orch. (1980). WRITINGS: *Orchestration of Antonín Dvořák's Symphonic Dances* (Prague, 1959); *Thematic Catalogue of Works by Antonín Dvořák* (Prague, 1960); *The Acoustical Fundamentals of Orchestration* (with A. Špelda, Prague, 1967; in German, 1971); *Modern Instrumentation* (begun by Jan Rychlík and completed by Burghauser, Prague, 1968).

Burgin, Richard, American violinist and conductor; b. Warsaw, Oct. 11, 1892; d. Gulfport, Fla., April 29, 1981. He studied violin with Auer at the St. Petersburg Cons.; played as a soloist with the Warsaw Phil. at the age of 11; in 1907 he made an American tour as a concert violinist. Abandoning a concert career, he served as concertmaster of the Helsingfors Symph. Orch. (1912–15) and of the Oslo Symph. Orch. (1916–19). In 1920 he went to the U.S.; was appointed concertmaster of the Boston Symph., and in 1927 became its assistant conductor; he also conducted orchs. in various cities in New England, and was for many years active as instructor in conducting at the Berkshire Music Center, Tanglewood. In 1967 he went to Tallahassee, Fla., where he continued his activities as a conductor and violin teacher. He was greatly esteemed by orch. members for his pragmatic and reliable technique; however, he never aspired to major orch. posts. He was married to the violinist **Ruth Posselt.**

Burgmüller, Johann August Franz, German organist and conductor; b. Magdeburg, April 28, 1766; d. Düsseldorf, Aug. 21, 1824. He was of a clerical family; having received a good education, he became a teacher and then a traveling theatrical conductor; he founded a musical society in Düsseldorf, and enjoyed a considerable reputation among musicians as a scholar. His two sons, **Johann Friedrich Franz** and **Norbert,** were both musicians.

Burgmüller, Johann Friedrich Franz, German composer of piano music; b. Regensburg, Dec. 4, 1806; d. Beaulieu, near Paris, Feb. 13, 1874. He was the son of **Johann August Franz Burgmüller,** and brother of **Norbert;** having settled in Paris, he adopted a light style to satisfy the demands of Parisian music lovers, and wrote numerous pieces of salon music for piano; he also publ. several albums of piano studies that have become standard works.

Burgmüller, Norbert, German composer, son of Johann August Franz and brother of Johann Friedrich Franz; b. Düsseldorf, Feb. 8, 1810; d. Aachen, May 7, 1836. He was extremely gifted, and composed music since his early childhood. After study at home, he took lessons with Spohr; wrote many songs and a symph. His 2nd Symph. remained incomplete at the time of his death at the age of 26; Schumann, who thought highly of him, orchestrated the 3rd movement, a scherzo; in this form, the symph. had many performances in Europe and America, and Norbert Burgmüller was mourned by musicians as another Schubert. The point of coincidence was that his unfinished symph. was in the same key as that of Schubert.

BIBLIOGRAPHY: H. Eckert, *Norbert Burgmüller* (Augsburg, 1932).

Burgon, Geoffrey, significant English composer; b. Hambledon, July 16, 1941. He studied with Peter Wishart and Lennox Berkeley at the Guildhall School of Music in London; earned his living as a jazz trumpeter. As a composer, he became particularly successful in providing background music for television shows; he wrote the score for Evelyn Waugh's *Brideshead Revisited* and for Le Carré's thriller *Tinker, Tailor, Soldier, Spy.* His wide range of musical expression includes the English ecclesiastical tradition as well as medieval French music.

WORKS: BALLETS: *The Golden Fish* (1964); *Ophelia* (1964); *The Calm* (1974); *Persephone* (1979); *Chamber Dances* (London, April 15, 1982). THEATER MUSIC: *Epitaph for Sir Walter Raleigh* (1968); *Joan of Arc* (1970). FOR ORCH.: Concerto for Strings (1963); 5 Pieces for Strings (1967); *Sanctus Variations* (London, Feb. 24, 1982); *Brideshead Variations* (London, March 21, 1982). VOCAL: Magnificat (1970); *The Golden Eternity* (1970); Requiem (1976); *The Fall of Lucifer* for Soloists, Chorus, and Orch. (1977); *Veni Spiritus* for Soprano, Baritone, Chorus, and Orch. (1979); *Orpheus,* dramatic oratorio (Wells Cathedral, July 17, 1982); *Hymn to St. Thomas of Hereford* (Hereford, Aug. 22, 1982); numerous settings for voice and piano, reflecting interest in mystical and devotional themes.

Burgstaller, Alois, German tenor; b. Holzkirchen, Sept. 21, 1871; d. Gmund, April 19, 1945. He was trained as a watchmaker, and also sang; encouraged by Cosima Wagner, he made a serious study of singing, and performed the role of Siegfried at the Bayreuth Festival in 1896. He made his American debut at the Metropolitan Opera in N.Y. as Siegmund in *Die Walküre* on Feb. 12, 1903; remained on it roster until his final appearance, again as Siegmund, on Jan. 14, 1909. He also sang the title role in the first staged American performance of *Parsifal,* in N.Y., on Dec. 24, 1903. In 1910 he re-turned to Germany.

Burian, Emil František, Czech composer; b. Pilsen, June 11, 1904; d. Prague, Aug. 9, 1959. He grew up in a musical family; his father, **Emil Burian** (1876–1926), was an operatic baritone; his uncle, **Karl Burian,** was a famous tenor. He studied with Foerster at the Prague Cons. From his first steps in composition, he adopted an extreme modernistic method—an eclectic fusion of jazz, Czech folk art, and French Impressionism; was also active as a film producer, dramatist, poet, jazz singer, actor, piano accompanist, and journalist. In 1927 he organized a "voice band" that sang according to prescribed rhythm but without a definite pitch; his presentation of the voice band at the Siena Festival of the International Society for Contemporary Music (Sept. 12, 1928) aroused considerable interest, and achieved further notoriety through his association with his Dada theater in Prague (1933–41, 1945–49). During World War II Burian was put in a concentration camp by the Nazis, but he survived and returned to active life.

WORKS: Fairy-tale opera, *Alladina and Palomid,* after Maeterlinck (1923); one-act musical drama, *Before Sunrise* (Prague, 1925); opera buffa, *Mister Ipokras* (1925; Prague, 1926; reworked into the opera farce *I Beg Your Pardon,* Prague, 1956); jazz opera, *Bubu from Montparnasse* (1927); opera, *Maryša* (Brno, April 16, 1940; his most important work); operatic parody, *The Emperor's New Clothes* (1947); musical comedy, *Lovers from the Kiosk* (1935); singspiel, *Opera from the Pilgrimage* (Prague, 1956); 4 ballets: *The Bassoon and the Flute* (1925; Prague, 1929); *Wooden Soldiers* (1926); *The Manège* (1927); *The Motorcoach* (1927; Prague, 1928); cantata, *May,* for Harp, 2 Pianos, Kettledrums, Solo Voice, and Chorus (1946); *Suita Poetica* for Orch., in 5 separate movements (1925, 1947, 1950, 1951, 1953); *Cocktails,* song cycle for Voice and Jazz Orch. (1926); Suite for Oboe and String Orch. (1928); *Reminiscence,* symph. suite (1929–36); symph., *Siréna* (1947; music used in film of the same title); Symph. No. 2, with Solo Piano (1948); Accordion Concerto (1949); *Overture to Socialism* (1950); Trio for Flute, Viola, and Cello (1924); *From Youth,* string sextet (1924); Duo for Violin and Cello (1925); *Requiem* for Voice Band and Jazz Band (1927); 8 string quartets (1927, 1929, 1940, 1947, 1948, 1949, 1951); Variations for Wind Quintet (1928); *Of Warm Nights,* suite for Violin and Piano (1928); *Passacaglia* for Violin and Viola (1929); *4 Pieces* for Wind Quintet (1929); Wind Quintet (1930); Suite for Cello and Piano (1935); *Children's Songs* for Voice and Nonet (1937); *Sonata Romantica* for Violin and Piano (1938); *Lost Serenade* for Flute and Piano (1940); Duo for Violin and Piano (1946); Fantasie for Violin and Piano (1954); *American Suite* for 2 Pianos (1926); Piano Sonata (1927); *Echoes of Czech Dances* for Piano (1953); Piano Sonatina (1954); songs; film music. He also wrote monographs: *Polydynamika* (1926); *Modern Russian Music* (1926); *Jazz* (1928); *Almanack of the Burian Brothers* (1929); *Emil Burian* (1947); *Karel Burian* (1948).

Burian, Karl, Czech tenor; b. Rusinov, near Rakovnik, Jan. 12, 1870; d. Senomaty, Sept. 25, 1924. He studied with F. Piwoda in Prague; made his operatic debut in Brno on March 28, 1891, as Jeník in Smetana's *The Bartered Bride;* then sang in Germany and Russia. In 1898 he was engaged to sing Parsifal at Bayreuth, and was extremely successful in this role. He sang the part of Herod in *Salome* at its world premiere in Dresden on Dec. 9, 1905. He made his American debut as Tannhäuser, on Nov. 30, 1906, at the Metropolitan Opera in N.Y.; remained on the Metropolitan's roster until 1913; then became a member of the Vienna Opera. In America he used the name **Carl Burrian.**

BIBLIOGRAPHY: E.F. Burian, *Karel Burian* (Prague, 1948).

Burk, John N., American writer on music; b. San José, Calif., Aug. 28, 1891; d. Boston, Sept. 6, 1967. He graduated from Harvard Univ. (A.B., 1916). In 1934 he succeeded Philip Hale as program annotator of the Boston Symph. Orch. He edited Philip Hale's Boston Symph. program notes (1935); annotated *Letters of Richard Wagner,* from the Burrell Collection (N.Y., 1950). He is the author of the books *Clara Schumann, A Romantic Biography* (N.Y., 1940); *The Life and Works of Beethoven* (N.Y., 1943); *Mozart and His Music* (N.Y., 1959).

Burkhard, Paul, Swiss conductor and composer; b. Zürich, Dec. 21, 1911; d. Tösstal, Sept. 6, 1977. He studied at the Cons. in Zürich. From 1932 to 1934 he conducted at the Bern Stadttheater; he was then engaged as a conductor at a Zürich theater (1939–45); then became conductor of the Beromünster Radio Orch. in Zürich (1945–57). As a composer he was successful mainly in light music; several of his operettas enjoyed considerable success in Switzerland; among them are *Hopsa* (1935; revised 1957), *Dreimal Georges* (1936), *Der schwarze Hecht* (1939; revived under a new title, *Feuerwerk,* 1950), *Tic-Tac* (1942), *Casanova in der Schweiz* (1944), *Die kleine Niederdorfoper* (1954), and *Die Pariserin* (1957). He also wrote the fairy-tale operas *Die Schneekönigin* (1964) and *Bunbury* (1966); and the Christmas opera *Ein Stern geht auf aus Jaakob* (1970).

Burkhard, Willy, significant Swiss composer; b. Evillard sur Bienne (Leubringen bei Biel), April 17, 1900; d. Zürich, June 18, 1955. He studied with Teichmüller and Karg-Elert in Leipzig (1921), Courvoisier in Munich (1922–23), and Max d'Ollone in Paris (1923–24). Returning to Switzerland, he taught at the Bern Cons. (1928–33) and at the Zürich Cons. (1942–55). His music is neo-Classical in form and strongly polyphonic in structure; his astringent linear idiom is tempered by a strong sense of modal counterpoint.

WORKS: Opera, *Die Schwarze Spinne (The Black Spider;* 1947–48; Zürich, May 28, 1949; revised 1954); oratorios: *Das Gesicht Jesajas (The Vision of Isaiah;* 1933–35; Basel, Feb. 18, 1936; his masterpiece); *Das Jahr (The Year;* 1940–41; Basel, Feb. 19, 1942); the cantatas, with Strings or Orch.: *Bibli-*

schen Kantate (1923); *Till Ulenspiegel* (1929); *Vorfrühling* (1930); *Spruchkantate* (1933); *Genug ist nicht genug* (1938–39; Basel, June 11, 1940); *Lob der Musik* (1939); *Cantate Domino* (1940); *Heimatliche Kantate* (1940); *Psalmen-Kantate* (1952); several chamber and a cappella cantatas. Other vocal works include *Te Deum* for Chorus, Trumpet, Trombone, Kettledrum, and Organ (1931); *Das ewige Brausen* for Bass and Chamber Orch. (1936); *Psalm 93* for Chorus and Organ (1937); *Kreuzvolk der Schweiz* for Chorus and Organ (1941); *Magnificat* for Soprano and Strings (1942); *Cantique de notre terre* for Soli, Chorus, and Orch. (1943); *Mass* for Soprano, Bass, Chorus and Orch. (1951; Zürich, June 28, 1951); *Psalm 148* for Chorus and Instruments (1954). For Orch.: *Ulenspiegel Variations* (1932); *Fantasy* for Strings (1934); *Small Serenade* for Strings (1935); Concerto for Strings (1937); Toccata for Strings (1939); *Laupen-Suite* for Orch. (1940); Concertino for Cello and Strings (1940); Violin Concerto (1943; Zürich, Jan. 26, 1946); Symph. in One Movement (1944); Organ Concerto (1945); *Hymne* for Organ and Orch. (1945); *Concertante Suite* (1946); *Piccola sinfonia giocosa* for Small Orch. (1949); *Fantasia mattutina* (1949); Toccata for 4 Winds, Percussion, and Strings (1951; Zürich, Dec. 7, 1951); *Sonata da camera* for Strings and Percussion (1952); Viola Concerto (1953); Concertino for 2 Flutes, Harpsichord, and Strings (1954); String Trio (1926); String Quartet (1929); Fantasie for Organ (1931); Piano Trio (1936); Violin Sonatina (1936); Suite for 2 Violins (1937); Solo Viola Sonata (1939); Piano Sonata (1942); String Quartet in One Movement (1943); Serenade for 8 Instruments (1945); *Romance* for Horn and Piano (1945); Violin Sonata (1946); Cello Sonata (1952); *Serenade* for Flute and Clarinet (1953); *Choral-Triptychon* for Organ (1953); Suite for Solo Flute (1954–55); *6 Preludes* for Piano (1954–55).

BIBLIOGRAPHY: Ernst Mohr, *Willy Burkhard: Leben und Werk* (Zürich, 1957); S. Burkhard and F. Indermühle, *Willy Burkhard (17. April 1900–18. Juni 1955) Werkverzeichnis* (issued by the Willy Burkhard Gesellschaft; Liebefeld, 1968); E. Schmidt, " 'Ahnung einer neuen Weltordnung'—Willy Burkhard," in U. von Brück, ed., *Credo musicale.... Festgabe zum 80. Geburtstag des ... Professor D. Dr. h.c. Rudolf Mauersberger* (Berlin, 1969).

Burkhardt, Max, German music analyst and composer; b. Löbau, Sept. 28, 1871; d. Berlin, Nov. 12, 1934. He studied at the Leipzig Cons.; received his degree of Dr.Phil. with the dissertation *Beiträge zum Studium des deutschen Liedes* (1897); then was a choral conductor in Cologne; in 1906 settled in Berlin as a teacher and writer. He publ. several useful music guides: *Führer durch Richard Wagners Musikdramen* (Berlin, 1909; 3rd ed., 1913); *Führer durch die Konzertmusik* (Berlin, 1911; analyzes 1,500 works); *Johannes Brahms: Ein Führer durch seine Werke* (Berlin, 1912). He also wrote the operas *König Drosselbart* (Cologne, 1904) and *Das Moselgretchen* (Schwerin, 1912); choral works and a series of *Lautenlieder* with lute accompaniment.

Burlas, Ladislav, Slovak composer; b. Trnava, April 3, 1927. He studied general musical subjects at Bratislava Univ. (1946–51) and composition with A. Moyzes at the Bratislava Cons. and at the Academy of Music there, graduating in 1955; then taught music theory at Comenius Univ. in Bratislava. He publ. monographs on J.L. Bella (Bratislava, 1953) and on A. Moyzes (Bratislava, 1956).

WORKS: *Symphonic Triptych* (1957); *Epitaph* for Orch. (1958); *Bagatelles* for String Orch. (1960); *Planctus* for String Orch. (1968); Concertino for Percussion and Winds (1971); *Wedding Songs* for Soloists, Chorus, and Orch. (1955); *The Miner's Cantata* (1955); *The Singing Heart,* string sextet (1960); Sonata for Solo Violin (1968); *Music* for String Quartet (1968–69); String Quartet No. 2, in memory of Prokofiev (1973); choruses; songs.

Burleigh, Cecil, American composer, violinist, and teacher; b. Wyoming, N.Y., April 17, 1885; d. Madison, Wis., July 28, 1980. In 1902 he went to Berlin, where he studied with Anton Witek (violin) and Hugo Leichtentritt (composition); returning to the U.S. in 1905, he studied with Felix Borowski and Emile Sauret at the Chicago Musical College. He subsequently taught at various colleges in Colorado, Iowa, and Montana (1909–19); was a concert violinist in N.Y. (1919–21); appeared in joint recitals with Rosa Ponselle, Louis Graveure, and Rudolf Ganz; in 1921, settled as a violin and composition teacher at the Univ. of Wisconsin. After retiring in 1955, he devoted himself mainly to painting.

WORKS: 3 violin concertos: No. 1 (1912), No. 2, *Indian* (1918), and No. 3 (1927); a trilogy of symphs., inspired by various books of the Bible (*Creation, Prophecy,* and *Revelation,* 1944; Univ. of Wisconsin, May 1, 1955); *Evangeline,* tone poem after Longfellow (1918); *Mountain Pictures* for Orch. (1918); *Two Sketches from the Orient* for Concert Band (1927); *From the Muses* for Small Orch. (1944); *2 Essays* for String Quartet (*Illusion* and *Transition,* 1945); 2 violin sonatas: *The Ascension* (1914) and *From the Life of St. Paul* (1926); descriptive violin and piano pieces (*4 Rocky Mountain Sketches, Up the Canyon, 4 Prairie Sketches, 5 Winter Evening Tales, 6 Nature Studies, The Avalanche, Elfin Lore,* etc.); songs.

Burleigh, Henry Thacker, black American baritone and songwriter; b. Erie, Pa., Dec. 2, 1866; d. Stamford, Conn., Sept. 12, 1949. He studied at the National Cons. in N.Y. In 1894 he became baritone soloist at St. George's Church in N.Y.; retired in 1946 after 52 years of service. He gained wide popularity as a songwriter. On May 16, 1917, the National Association for the Advancement of Colored People awarded him the Spingarn Medal for highest achievement by an American citizen of African descent during the year 1916.

BIBLIOGRAPHY: "In Retrospect ... Harry T. Burleigh (1866–1949)," *Black Perspective in Music* (Sept. 1974).

Burmeister, Joachim, German musician; b. Lüne-burg, March 5, 1564; d. Rostock, May 5, 1629. He received a master's degree from Rostock Univ.; publ. there the treatises *Hypomnematum Musicae Poeticae* (1599) and *Musicae Practicae sive artis canendi ratio* (1601); wrote several sacred songs, which were publ. in 1601.

BIBLIOGRAPHY: Martin Ruhnke, *Joachim Burmeister* (Kassel, 1955); C. Palisca, "Ut oratoria musica: The Theoretical Basis of Musical Mannerism," in *The Meaning of Mannerism* (Hanover, N.H., 1972).

Burmeister, Richard, German composer and pianist; b. Hamburg, Dec. 7, 1860; d. Berlin, Feb. 19, 1944. He studied with Liszt at Weimar, Rome, and Budapest, accompanying him on his travels; later taught at the Hamburg Cons., at the Peabody Inst. in Baltimore, Dresden Cons. (1903–6), and Klindworth-Scharwenka Cons. in Berlin (1907–25). Burmeister also made extensive concert tours of Europe and the U.S. His works include the symph. fantasy *Die Jagd nach dem Glück;* Piano Concerto; *The Sisters* (after Tennyson) for Alto with Orch.; Romanza for Violin and Orch.; songs; piano pieces. He also scored Chopin's F minor Concerto, Liszt's *Mephisto Waltz* and 5th Rhapsody (with new orch. accompaniment), and Weber's *Konzertstück* for Piano and Orch.

Burmester, Willy, German violinist; b. Hamburg, March 16, 1869; d. there, Jan. 16, 1933. He studied with his father, and with Joachim in Berlin; from 1886, made frequent concert tours throughout Europe and America. He composed a Serenade for String Quartet and Double Bass, and smaller virtuoso pieces; was the author of *Fünfzig Jahre Künstlerleben* (1926; in Danish, 1928).

Burney, Charles, celebrated English music historian; b. Shrewsbury, April 7, 1726; d. Chelsea, April 12, 1814. He was a pupil of Edmund Baker (organist of Chester Cathedral), of his eldest half brother, James Burney, and, from 1744–47, of Dr. Arne in London. In 1749 he became organist of St. Dionis-Backchurch, and harpsichord player at the subscription concerts in the King's Arms, Cornhill; resigned these posts in 1751, and until 1760 was organist at King's Lynn, Norfolk, where he planned and began work on his *General History of Music.* He returned to London in 1760; received the degrees of B.Mus. and D.Mus. from Oxford Univ. in 1769. Having exhausted such material as was available in London for his *History of Music,* he visited France, Switzerland, and Italy in 1770 and Germany, the Netherlands, and Austria in 1772, consulting the libraries, attending the best concerts of sacred and secular music, and forming contacts with the leading musicians and scholars of the period (Gluck, Hasse, Metastasio, Voltaire, etc.). The immediate result of these journeys was the publication of *The Present State of Music in France and Italy,* etc. (1771, in diary form) and *The Present State of Music in Germany, the Netherlands,* etc. (1773). His *General History of Music* appeared in 4 vols. (1776–89; new ed. by Frank Mercer in 2 vols. with "Critical and Historical Notes," London and N.Y., 1935), the first vol. concurrently with the complete work of his rival, Sir John Hawkins. From 1806 he received a government pension. Other publications: *La musica che si canta annualmente nelle funzioni della settimana santa nella Cappella Pontificia, composta de Palestrina, Allegri e Bai* (1771; a book of sacred works with Burney's preface); *An Account of the Musical Performances in Westminster Abbey . . . in Commemoration of Handel* (1785); *Memoirs of the Life and Writings of the Abate Metastasio* (3 vols., 1796); the articles on music for Rees's *Cyclopedia;* etc. He composed, for Drury Lane, music to the dramas *Alfred* (1745), *Robin Hood* and *Queen Mab* (1750), and *The Cunning Man* (1765; text and music adapted from *Le Devin du village* by Rousseau); also sonatas for piano and for violin; violin and harpsichord concertos, cantatas, flute duets, etc.

BIBLIOGRAPHY: Burney's daughter, Frances Burney (b. King's Lynn, Norfolk, June 13, 1752; d. London, Jan. 6, 1840), wrote the novel *Evelina* and *Memoirs of Dr. Burney* (publ. in 3 vols., 1832); cf. A.R. Ellis, *Early Diary of Frances Burney* (2 vols., 1889); C. Hill, *The House in St. Martin Street, Being Chronicles of the Burney Family* (London, 1906). On Charles Burney: L.M. Isaacs, "A Friend of Dr. Johnson," *Musical Quarterly* (Oct. 1915); C. Ricci, *Burney, Casanova e Farinelli in Bologna* (Milan, 1920); C.H. Glover, *Dr. Charles Burney's Continental Travels, 1770–72* (compiled from Burney's journals and other sources; London, 1927); P.A. Scholes, *The Great Dr. Burney* (a definitive biography; Oxford, 1948); Roger Lonsdale, *Dr. Charles Burney: A Literary Biography* (London, 1965); G. Stefani, "Musica, chiesa, società negli scritti dé Ch. Burney," *Nuova Rivista Musicale Italiana* (Jan.–Feb. 1971); J.C. Kassler, "Burney's *Sketch of a plan for a public music-school,*" *Musical Quarterly* (April 1972).

Burr, Willard, American composer; b. Ravenna, Ohio, Jan. 17, 1852; d. Boston, May 12, 1915. He studied with August Haupt in Berlin; then settled in Boston as a teacher. He wrote numerous works for piano, such as the suite *From Shore to Shore;* also anthems and art songs.

Burritt, Lloyd, Canadian composer; b. Vancouver, British Columbia, June 7, 1940. He studied with J. Coulthard and C. Hultberg at the Univ. of British Columbia, graduating in 1963 (M.M., 1968); then with G. Jacob and H. Howells in London at the Royal College of Music; later attended classes in conducting with Schuller, Leinsdorf, and Bernstein at the Berkshire Music Center at Tanglewood (summers of 1965 and 1966). Upon completing his studies, he was appointed music director of the Argyle School in North Vancouver. His music is modernistic in harmony, and he is apt to use some audacious effects in his audiovisual works, with correspondingly dramatic titles. WORKS: Symph. (1964); *3 Autumn Songs* for

Mezzo-soprano, Piano, and Orch. (1965); *Assassinations* for Orch. and Tape (Vancouver, Dec. 1, 1968); *Hollow Men,* after T.S. Eliot, for Chorus, Orch., and Tape (1968); *Landscapes,* after T.S. Eliot, for Soprano, Alto, and Tape (1968); *Acid Mass,* after T.S. Eliot, for Chorus, Dancers, and Film (1969); *Electric Tongue I* for Orch. and Tape (Vancouver, May 30, 1969; a version *II* included a direct telephone call by the conductor from London to Vancouver); *Cicada* for Orch. and Tape (1970); *New York* for Orch. and Tape (1970); *Overdose* for Orch. and Tape (1971); *Electric Chair* for Saxophone, Actress, and Tape (1971); *Rocky Mountain Grasshopper* for Chorus, Wind Orch., and 2 Tapes (1971); *Memo to RCCO* (Royal College of Canadian Organists) for Organ and Tape (1972); *Memo to NFBC* (National Film Board of Canada) for Keyboard and Tape (1972); *Spectrum* for Strings and Tape (1973); *David* for Soli, Chorus, Orch., and Tape (1977); several scores for theatrical plays.

Burrowes, John Freckleton, English composer; b. London, April 23, 1787; d. there, March 31, 1852. He was a pupil of William Horsley; was organist of St. James' Church in Piccadilly for many years. He wrote works for flute and other instruments, and made arrangements for operas. His 2 manuals, *Thorough-Bass Primer* and *The Pianoforte Primer,* were very successful and went through many editions before they became obsolete.

Burrowes, Norma, Welsh soprano; b. Bangor, April 24, 1944. She studied at the Queen's Univ. in Belfast and the Royal Academy, London; made her debut with the Glyndebourne Touring Opera in 1970; also in 1970 she sang at Covent Garden, London; in 1971 she joined the Sadler's Wells Opera; also appeared at the Bayreuth and Aix-en-Provence festivals; made her American debut at the Metropolitan Opera, N.Y., on Oct. 12, 1979.

Burrows, Stuart, Welsh tenor; b. Pontypridd, Feb. 7, 1933. He was educated at Trinity College, Carmarthen, Wales. He made his debut in 1963 at the Welsh National Opera. In 1967 he sang at the San Francisco Opera; in 1970 appeared at the Vienna State Opera. On April 13, 1971, he made his Metropolitan Opera debut in N.Y. as Ottavio in *Don Giovanni.* He is regarded as one of the finest interpreters of Mozart roles.

Burt, Francis, English composer; b. London, April 28, 1926. He studied at the Royal Academy of Music with Howard Ferguson (1948–51) and at the Hochschule für Musik in Berlin with Boris Blacher (1951–54); was awarded the German Mendelssohn Scholarship; went for further study to Rome; in 1956 he received a stipend from the Fondation Européenne de la Culture; from 1957 lived mostly in Vienna. WORKS: String Quartet (1953); *Iambics* for Orch. (1955); *Music* for 2 Pianos (1955); *The Skull,* cantata for Tenor and Orch. (1956); *Duo* for Clarinet and Piano (1956); *Bavarian Gentians* for Vocal Quartet and Piano (1957); *Espressione orchestrale* (1959);

Volpone, opera after Ben Jonson (Stuttgart, June 2, 1960); *The Golem,* ballet (1962); *Fantasmagoria* for Orch. (1963); one-act opera, *Barnstable, or Someone in the Attic* (Stuttgart, Nov. 30, 1969).

Burtius (also known as **Burci** or **Burzio**), **Nicolaus,** Italian theorist; b. Parma, c.1445; d. there, after 1518. He studied with J. Gallicus; received first clerical Orders in Parma in 1472; then studied ecclesiastical law in Bologna; in 1487 he publ. *Musices Opusculum,* which was one of the earliest printed books on music, containing mensural notes printed from woodblocks. In this work Burtius supports the Guidonian system opposing the innovations introduced by Ramos de Pareja.

Burton, Frederick Russell, American writer on music; b. Jonesville, Mich., Feb. 23, 1861; d. Lake Hopatcong, N.J., Sept. 30, 1909. He was a graduate of Harvard Univ. (1882); then went to N.Y., where he was active as a music teacher. He made a study of Indian music and publ. *Songs of the Ojibway Indians* (1903; later expanded into *American Primitive Music,* publ. posthumously, 1909).

Burton, Stephen Douglas, American composer; b. Whittier, Calif., Feb. 24, 1943. He studied piano and theory at Oberlin Cons.; then went to Vienna, where he studied with Morris Browda at the Vienna Cons. (1957–60); subsequently enrolled at the Mozarteum in Salzburg in classes of composition and conducting (1962–65); in 1963–64 he was music director of the Munich Kammerspiele; took private lessons with Hans Werner Henze (1966–67). In 1969 he held a Guggenheim fellowship. In 1974 he was appointed to the faculty of George Mason Univ. in Fairfax, Va. As a composer, Burton draws rapturously on the totality of modern resources, achieving impressive grandeur mitigated by beguiling dancing episodes, and producing audaciously euphonious sonorities unapologetically appealing to far-flung audiences. WORKS: FOR THE STAGE: *No Trifling with Love,* opera after Alfred de Musset (1970); *An American Triptych,* opera (1975); *The Duchess of Malfi,* opera (Wolf Trap, Va., Aug. 18, 1978); *Aimee,* opera (1983); *Finisterre,* ballet (Newport, R.I., Aug. 21, 1977). FOR ORCH.: Concerto da Camera (1963); *Ode to a Nightingale,* after Keats, for Soprano, Flute, Harp, and String Orch. (Berlin, Oct. 9, 1963); Symph. No. 1 (Berlin, Jan. 31, 1968); *Stravinskiana* for Flute and Orch. (Chicago, Feb. 14, 1972); *Dithyramb* (Washington, D.C., Oct. 10, 1972); Symph. No. 2, surnamed *Ariel,* to words of Sylvia Plath's poems, for Mezzosoprano, Baritone, and Orch. (Washington, D.C., Oct. 19, 1976); *Variations on a Theme of Mahler* for Chamber Orch. (Washington, D.C., Oct. 10, 1982); *The Pied Piper,* overture (Washington, D.C., Feb. 1, 1983); Violin Concerto (1983). CHAMBER MUSIC: *Burlesque* for Clarinet, Piano, and String Quartet (1972); *Notturno* for Cello Solo (1972); *Partita* for Violin Solo (1973); String Quartet (1974); *Divertimento* for Woodwind Quintet (1975); *Rhapsody* for Alto Saxophone and Piano (1975); Piano Trio (1975); *3 Poems* for Flute Solo (1976); *Fantocciata*

for Flute, Oboe, and Harpsichord (1976). VOCAL MUSIC: *6 Hebrew Melodies,* after Byron (Washington, D.C., Oct. 28, 1973); *Songs of the Tulpehocken* for Tenor and Orch., to anonymous Pennsylvania German texts (Reading, Pa., Feb. 22, 1976); *6 Songs* for Voice and 13 Instruments (Washington, D.C., May 7, 1977).

Bury, Edward, Polish composer and conductor; b. Gniezno, Sept. 18, 1919. He studied composition with Sikorski and conducting at the Warsaw Cons. (1937–44); from 1945–54 he taught at the Cracow Cons. He publ. 2 books on conducting, *Podstawy techniki dyrygowania* (*The Principles of Conducting Technique;* Cracow, 1961) and *The Technique of Reading Scores* (Cracow, 1971). WORKS: *Czech Fantasy* for Piano and Orch. (1948); *Little Suite* for Orch. (1950); *Triptych* for Orch. (1952); Violin Concerto (1954); *Concert Overture* (1954); *Suita giocosa* for Orch. (1956); *Maski (The Masks),* fantastic suite for Orch. (1957); 6 symphs.: No. 1, *Symfonia Wolności* (*Freedom Symphony,* 1960); No. 2 for 6 Concertante Instruments and Orch. (1962); No. 3, *Mówi Prezydent John F. Kennedy (President Kennedy Speaks)* for Male Speaker, Women's Speaking Chorus, Mixed Chorus, and Orch. (1964); No. 4, *De timpani a tutti,* for Solo Bass, Chorus, Tape, and Orch. (1966–67); No. 5, *Bohaterska* (*Heroic,* 1969); and No. 6, *Pacem in terris,* to a text from the encyclical of Pope John XXIII, for Narrator, Church Bells, and Orch. (1972); *The Millennium Hymn* for Chorus and Orch. (1965); chamber music; piano pieces; choruses.

Busby, Thomas, English writer on music; b. Westminster, Dec. 1755; d. London, May 28, 1838. He was a chorister in London; then studied with Battishill (1769–74); served as church organist at St. Mary's, Newington, Surrey, and St. Mary Woolnoth, Lombard Street. He obtained the degree of B.Mus. from Cambridge Univ. in 1801. In collaboration with Arnold, he publ. *A Complete Dictionary of Music* (1801); he then publ. *A Grammar of Music* (1818) and *A General History of Music* (2 vols., compiled from Burney and Hawkins; London, 1819; reprinted 1968). In 1825 he brought out a set of 3 little vols. entitled *Concert Room and Orchestra Anecdotes of Music and Musicians, Ancient and Modern,* a compilation of some topical value, even though many of the stories are apocryphal. He also publ. *A Musical Manual, or Technical Directory* (1828). His anthology of sacred music, *The Divine Harmonist* (1788), is valuable. His own compositions (oratorios and odes) are imitative of Handel. A melodrama, *Tale of Mystery,* with Busby's music, was produced at Covent Garden (Nov. 13, 1807). BIBLIOGRAPHY: K.G.F. Spence, "The Learned Doctor Busby," *Music & Letters* (April 1956).

Busch, Adolf, noted violinist, brother of **Hermann** and **Fritz Busch;** b. Siegen, Westphalia, Aug. 8, 1891; d. Guilford, Vt., June 9, 1952. He studied at Cologne and Bonn; then served as concertmaster of the Vienna Konzertverein (1912–18); subsequently taught at the Hochschule für Musik in Berlin. In 1919 he organized the Busch Quartet and the Busch Trio (with his younger brother Hermann Busch, and his son-in-law **Rudolf Serkin**). The Busch Quartet gained renown with the appointment of Gösta Andreasson and Karl Doktor as its members; Busch's brother Hermann became cellist in the Busch Trio in 1926 and in the Busch Quartet in 1930. Adolf Busch went to Basel in 1927; in 1939 he emigrated to America, and remained there until his death. In 1950 he organized the Marlboro School of Music in Vermont; Rudolf Serkin carried on his work after Busch's death.

Busch, Carl, Danish-American conductor and composer; b. Bjerre, March 29, 1862; d. Kansas City, Dec. 19, 1943. He studied at the Royal Cons. in Copenhagen with Hartmann and Gade; then went to Paris; in 1887 settled in Kansas City, where he was active as a conductor and teacher. From 1912–18 he was conductor of the Kansas City Symph.; also conducted his own works with various orchs. in the U.S., Denmark, and Germany.
WORKS: For Orch.: *The Passing of Arthur* (after Tennyson) and *Minnehaha's Vision; Elegy* for String Orch.; cantatas: *The Four Winds; King Olaf; The League of the Alps; America;* etc.; also many compositions for violin; songs.
BIBLIOGRAPHY: M.H. Barney, *Sir Carl Busch* (Kansas City, 1942).

Busch, Ernst, German actor and singer; b. Kiel, Jan. 22, 1900; d. East Berlin, June 8, 1980. He first worked for Krupp, but then turned to acting; went to Berlin in 1925, where he became associated with Bertolt Brecht and Kurt Weill in their collaboration. Long a member of the Communist Party, he left Germany in 1933; fought in the International Brigade during the Spanish Civil War; was imprisoned by the Gestapo during World War II but survived his ordeal; after the war, he settled in East Berlin.

Busch, Fritz, eminent German conductor (brother of **Adolf** and **Hermann Busch**); b. Siegen, Westphalia, March 13, 1890; d. London, Sept. 14, 1951. He studied at the Cologne Cons. with Steinbach, Boettcher, Uzielli, and Klauwell; was then conductor of the Deutsches Theater in Riga (1909–10); in 1912 he became music director of the city of Aachen, and then of the Stuttgart Opera in 1918. In 1922 he was named Generalmusikdirektor of the Dresden State Opera; during his tenure, he conducted many notable productions, including the world premieres of Strauss's *Intermezzo* and *Die Aegyptische Helena.* In 1933 he was dismissed from his Dresden post by the Nazi government; leaving Germany, he made many appearances as a conductor with the Danish Radio Symph. Orch. and the Stockholm Phil.; from 1934 to 1939 he served as music director of the Glyndebourne Festivals; from 1940 to 1945 he was active mainly in South America. On Nov. 26, 1945, he made his first appearance with the Metropolitan Opera in N.Y., conducting *Lohengrin;* he continued on its roster until 1949. He was equally distinguished as an operatic and symph. conductor; he was renowned for his performances of Mozart's works. He wrote an autobiography, *Aus dem Leben eines Musikers* (Zürich, 1949; in Eng. as *Pages from a Musician's Life,* London, 1953). Recordings and publications are issued by the Bruder-Busch Gesellschaft.
BIBLIOGRAPHY: G. Busch, *Fritz Busch, Dirigent* (Frankfurt, 1970); B. Dopheide, *Fritz Busch* (Tutzing, 1970).

Busch, Hermann, noted German cellist (brother of **Adolf** and **Fritz Busch**); b. Siegen, Westphalia, June 24, 1897; d. Bryn Mawr, Pa., June 3, 1975. He studied at the Cologne Cons. and the Vienna Academy of Music; played cello in the Vienna Symph. Orch. (1923–27); in 1926 became a member of the Busch Trio; was also a member of the renowned Busch Quartet from 1930 until the death of his brother Adolf in 1952; during his last years of life he taught at the Marlboro School of Music in Vermont.

Busch, William, English pianist and composer; b. London, June 25, 1901; d. Woolacombe, Devon, Jan. 30, 1945. Of German origin, he received his education in America and England; then studied in Germany with Leonid Kruetzer (piano) and Hugo Leichtentritt (theory). He made his debut in London (Oct. 20, 1927). His music shows competent craftsmanship; among his works are: Piano Concerto (1939); Cello Concerto (1941); Piano Quartet (1939); pieces for piano solo.

Buschkötter, Wilhelm, German conductor; b. Höxter, Westphalia, Sept. 27, 1887; d. Berlin, May 12, 1967. He studied medicine, and also played cello; then took lessons in general musicology with W. Klatte and A. Kieffel; in 1912 he received his Habilitation with a dissertation on Le Sueur. He then dedicated himself to theater conducting; was municipal conductor in Davos, Switzerland, in 1912; in Hamburg in 1913; in Altona in 1920; and in Åbo in 1923. From 1924 to 1926 he served as conductor with the Berlin Radio; from 1926 to 1936 was principal conductor with West German Radio in Cologne; then occupied the post of music director at Stuttgart Radio (1936–38) and at Dortmund (1937–39). From 1945 to 1949 he taught music privately in Berlin. In 1949 he was Kapellmeister in Sonderhausen; in 1950 he returned to his post at West German Radio in Cologne, which he retained until 1953; after 1954 he was active mainly as a guest conductor with various organizations. He publ. *Handbuch der internationalen Konzertliteratur* (Berlin, 1961).

Bush, Alan Dudley, notable English composer; b. Dulwich, Dec. 22, 1900. He studied piano with Matthay and composition with Corder at the Royal Academy of Music in London; also took private piano lessons with Artur Schnabel and composition with John Ireland. In 1929 he went to Berlin and took courses in musicology and philosophy. Returning to England, he was on the staff of the Royal Academy of Music, from 1925–55. In 1935 he joined the Communist Party; in 1936 he organized in London the Workers' Music Association, remaining its president for 40 years. His early works contain some radical modernistic usages, but in accordance with his political views on art, he adopted the precepts of socialist realism, demanding a tonal idiom more easily appreciated by audiences. He made numerous trips to Russia and other countries of the socialist bloc; several of his works had their first performance in East Germany.

WORKS: He wrote several operas on historical subjects dealing with social revolt: *Wat Tyler* (awarded a prize at the Festival of Britain in 1951, but not perf. in England; its first production took place in concert form on the Berlin Radio, to a German libretto, on April 3, 1952); *The Men of Blackmoor*, Nov. 18, 1956); *Guayana Johnny* (Leipzig, Dec. 11, 1966); *Joe Hill*, on the subject of the execution of the labor agitator Joe Hill in Salt Lake City on Nov. 19, 1915 (East Berlin, Sept. 29, 1970). Other works: Piano Concerto, with Baritone Solo and Male Chorus in the finale (1938); Symph. No. 1 (London, July 24, 1942, composer conducting); *Fantasia on Soviet Themes* for Orch. (London, July 27, 1945); *English Suite* for String Orch. (London, Feb. 9, 1946); *The Winter Journey*, cantata (Alnwick, Dec. 14, 1946); children's operetta, *The Press Gang* (Letchworth, March 7, 1947); *Piers Plowman's Day* for Orch. (Prague Radio, Oct. 16, 1947); Violin Concerto (London, July 16, 1948); Symph. No. 2, subtitled *Nottingham* (Nottingham, June 27, 1949); *Song of Friendship* for Bass Voice, Chorus, and Band (London, Nov. 6, 1949); *Defender of the Peace* for Orch. (Vienna Radio, May 24, 1952); cantata, *The Ballad of Freedom's Soldier* (1953); *Byron Symphony* for Chorus and Orch. (1960); *Time Remembered* for Chamber Orch. (1969); *Scherzo* for Wind Instruments and Percussion (1969); *Suite of 6* for String Quartet (1975). A *Tribute to Alan Bush* was publ. by the Workers' Music Association on the occasion of his 50th birthday (1950). He publ. an autobiography, *In My Seventh Decade* (London, 1971); also, *In My Eighth Decade and Other Essays* (London, 1980).

BIBLIOGRAPHY: R. Stevenson, ed., *Time Remembered—Alan Bush: An 80th Birthday Symposium* (Kidderminster, 1981).

Bush, Geoffrey, English organist, composer, and pedagogue; b. London, March 23, 1920. He studied at Oxford Univ.; received his B.M. degree in 1940 and D.M. in 1946; upon graduation, was active mainly as an organist, a teacher, and a music journalist. In 1952 he was appointed to the staff of the Univ. of London.

WORKS: Puppet opera, *The Spanish Rivals* (1948); *A Summer Serenade* for Chorus and Instruments (1949); Trio for Oboe, Bassoon, and Piano (1952); children's opera, *The Blind Beggar's Daughter* (1954); Symph. No. 1 (1954); one-act opera, *If the Cap Fits* (1957); Symph. No. 2 (1957); Concerto for Light Orch. (1958); *Dialogue* for Oboe and Piano (1960); Concerto for Piano, Trumpet, and Strings (1962); Wind Quintet (1963); opera, *The Equation* (1968). He publ. *Musical Creation and the Listener* (London, 1954; revised 1967) and *Left, Right and*

Centre (London, 1984).

Busi, Alessandro, Italian composer; b. Bologna, Sept. 28, 1833; d. there, July 8, 1895. He was a conductor of the Communal Theater in Bologna and taught at the Bologna Liceo. His works include a choral symph., *Excelsior; In alto mare* for Chorus and Orch.; many ballads for voice and piano; etc.

BIBLIOGRAPHY: L. Torchi, *Commemorazione di Alessandro Busi* (Bologna, 1896).

Busnois (properly, **De Busne**), **Antoine,** French musician, singer, and composer; b. Béthune, c.1430; d. Bruges, Nov. 6, 1492. In 1467 he entered the ducal chapel in Dijon as a singer; in 1477 he joined the court of Charles the Bold of Burgundy; was in the service of Mary of Burgundy, and remained in that post until her death in 1482. He professed to be a pupil of Okeghem, but there is no confirmation for that claim. Several of his works are found in various anthologies; 7 chansons were publ. by Petrucci (1501–3); a number of his masses, including one on *L'Homme armé,* are extant.

BIBLIOGRAPHY: Charles van den Borren, *Etudes sur le XVe siècle musical* (Antwerp, 1941).

Busoni, Ferruccio (Dante Michelangelo Benvenuto), greatly admired pianist and composer of Italian-German parentage; b. Empoli, near Florence, April 1, 1866; d. Berlin, July 27, 1924. His father played the clarinet; his mother, Anna Weiss, was an amateur pianist; Busoni grew up in an artistic atmosphere, and learned to play the piano as a child; at the age of 8 he played in public in Trieste. He gave a piano recital in Vienna when he was 10, and included in his program some of his own compositions. In 1877 the family moved to Graz, where Busoni took piano lessons with W. Mayer. He conducted his own choral work in Graz at the age of 12. At 15 he was accepted as a member of the Accademia Filarmonica in Bologna; he performed there his oratorio *Il sabato del villaggio* in 1883. In 1886 he went to Leipzig; there he undertook a profound study of Bach's music. In 1889 he was appointed a prof. of piano at the Helsingfors Cons., where among his students was Sibelius (who was actually a few months older than his teacher). At that time Busoni married Gerda Sjostrand, whose father was a celebrated Swedish sculptor; they had 2 sons, both of whom became well-known artists. In 1890 Busoni participated in the Rubinstein Competition in St. Petersburg, and won first prize with his *Konzertstück* for Piano and Orch. On the strength of this achievement he was engaged to teach piano at the Moscow Cons. (1890–91). He then accepted the post of prof. at the New England Cons. of Music (1891–94); however, he had enough leisure to make several tours, maintaining his principal residence in Berlin. During the season of 1912–13, he made a triumphant tour of Russia. In 1913 he was appointed director of the Liceo Musicale in Bologna. The outbreak of the war in 1914 forced him to move to neutral Switzerland; he stayed in Zürich until 1920; then returned to Berlin, remaining there until his death in 1924. In various cities, at various times, he taught piano in music schools; among his piano students were Brailovsky, Rudolf Ganz, Egon Petri, Mitropoulos, and Percy Grainger. Busoni also taught composition; Kurt Weill, Jarnach, and Wladimir Vogel were his pupils. He exercised great influence on Edgar Varèse, who was living in Berlin when Busoni was there; Varèse greatly prized Busoni's advanced theories of composition.

Busoni was a philospher of music who tried to formulate a universe of related arts; he issued grandiloquent manifestos urging a return to classical ideals in modern forms; he sought to establish a unifying link between architecture and composition; in his editions of Bach's works he included drawings illustrating the architectonic plan of Bach's fugues. He incorporated his innovations in his grandiose piano work *Fantasia contrappuntistica,* which opens with a prelude based on a Bach chorale, and closes with a set of variations on Bach's acronym, B-A-C-H (i.e., B-flat, A, C, B-natural). In his theoretical writings, Busoni proposed a system of 113 different heptatonic modes, and also suggested the possibility of writing music in exotic scales and subchromatic intervals; he expounded those ideas in his influential essay *Entwurf einer neuen Aesthetic der Tonkunst* (Trieste, 1907; Eng. trans. by T. Baker, N.Y., 1911). Busoni's other publications of significance were *Von der Einheit der Musik* (1923; in Italian, Florence, 1941; in Eng., London, 1957) and *Über die Möglichkeiten der Oper* (Leipzig, 1926). But despite Busoni's great innovations in his own compositions and his theoretical writing, the Busoni legend is kept alive, not through his music but mainly through his sovereign virtuosity as a pianist. In his performances he introduced a concept of piano sonority as an orchestral medium; indeed, some listeners reported having heard simulations of trumpets and French horns sounded at Busoni's hands. The few extant recordings of his playing transmit a measure of the grandeur of his style, but they also betray a tendency, common to Busoni's era, toward a free treatment of the musical text, surprisingly so, since Busoni preached an absolute fidelity to the written notes. On concert programs Busoni's name appears most often as the author of magisterial and eloquent transcriptions of Bach's works. His gothic transfiguration for piano of Bach's *Chaconne* for Unaccompanied Violin became a perennial favorite of pianists all over the world.

Busoni was honored by many nations. In 1913 he received the order of Chevalier de la Légion d'Honneur from the French government, a title bestowed on only 2 Italians before him: Rossini and Verdi. In 1949 an annual Concorso Busoni was established, with prizes given to contestants in piano playing. Another international award honoring the name of Busoni was announced by the Santa Cecilia Academy of Rome, with prizes given for the best contemporary compositions; at its opening session in 1950 the recipient was Stravinsky.

WORKS: OPERAS: *Sigune, oder Das vergessene Dorf* (1889; unperf.); *Die Brautwahl* (1908–11; Hamburg, April 13, 1912); *Arlecchino oder Die Fenster* (1916; Zürich, May 11, 1917, composer conducting; American concert perf., Carnegie Hall, N.Y., Oct. 11, 1951); *Turandot,* after Gozzi (1917; Zürich, May 11, 1917, composer conducting, on the same bill as *Arlecchino;* American premiere, N.Y., Oct. 10, 1967); *Doktor Faust* (1916–24; unfinished; completed by Philip Jarnach; perf. posthumously, Dresden, May 21, 1925; American concert perf., Carnegie Hall, N.Y., Dec. 1, 1964).

FOR ORCH.: *Symphonische Suite* (1883; Vienna, Nov. 25, 1883); *Konzertstück,* Introduction and Allegro for Piano and Orch. (1890; St. Petersburg, Aug. 27, 1890; won the Anton Rubinstein prize); *Konzert-Fantasie* for Piano and Orch. (1888–89; revised as *Symphonisches Tongedicht;* Boston, April 14, 1892); Suite No. 2 (1895; revised 1903; Berlin, Dec. 1, 1904); Violin Concerto (1896–97; Berlin, Oct. 8, 1897); *Lustspielouvertüre* (1897; Berlin, Oct. 8, 1897; revised 1904; Berlin, Jan. 11, 1907); Piano Concerto with Male Chorus in the finale (1903–4; Berlin, Nov. 10, 1904, composer soloist); *Turandot,* suite from incidental music (1904; Berlin, Oct. 21, 1905, composer conducting); *Berceuse élégiaque* (1909; adapted for Chamber Orch. from the original piano piece of 1907; conducted by Busoni at Mahler's last concert with the N.Y. Phil., Feb. 21, 1911); *Nocturne symphonique* (1912; Berlin, March 12, 1914); *Indianische Fantasie* for Piano and Orch. (1913; Berlin, March 12, 1914); *Die Brautwahl,* suite from the opera of the same title (1912; Berlin, Jan. 2, 1913); *Rondo arlecchinesco* (1915; Rome, March 5, 1916); *Indianisches Tagebuch,* book 1, subtitled *Gesang vom Reigen der Geister* (1915); *Concertino* for Clarinet and Orch. (1918; Zürich, Dec. 9, 1918); *Sarabande und Cortege,* 2 studies for *Doktor Faust* (1918–19; Zürich, March 31, 1919); Divertimento for Flute and Orch. (1920; Berlin, Jan. 13, 1921); *Tanzwalzer* (1920; Berlin, Jan. 13, 1921); *Romanza e scherzoso* for Piano and Orch. (1921; Basel, Dec. 10, 1921).

CHAMBER MUSIC: String Quartet No. 1 (1880–81); *Serenata* for Cello and Piano (1882); *Kleine Suite* for Cello and Piano (1886); *Bagatelles* for Violin and Piano (1888); String Quartet No. 2 for Violin and Piano (1888; Leipzig, Jan. 28, 1888); Violin Sonata No. 1 (1890); *Kultaselle,* 10 variations on a Finnish folk song for Cello and Piano (1890); Violin Sonata No. 2 (Helsingfors, Sept. 30, 1898); *Elegie* for Clarinet and Piano (1920).

FOR PIANO: *5 Pieces* (1877); *3 morceaux* (1877); *Suite campestra* (1878); *Una festa di villaggio,* 6 pieces (1882); *3 pezzi nello stile antico* (1882); *Danza antiche* (1882); *Danza notturna* (1882); 24 Preludes (1879–81); 6 Etudes (1883); *Macchiette medioevali,* 6 pieces (1883); *2 Klavierstücke* (1890); *Elegien,* 7 pieces, including the original version of *Berceuse élégiaque* (1907); *An die Jugend* (1908); *Fantasia nach J.S. Bach* (1909); *Fantasia contrappuntistica,* based on Bach's *The Art of the Fugue;* Busoni's Gothic masterpiece (1910; as *Grosse Fuge;* revised 1912); 6 sonatinas (1910, 1912, 1916, 1917, 1919, 1920); *Indianisches Tagebuch,* book I (1915); *2 Kontrapunktstudien nach J.S. Bach:* Fantasie and Fugue in A minor and *Canonic Variations* and Fugue (1917); Bach's *Klavierübung,* first ed. in 5 parts (1917); 2nd ed. in 10 parts (posthumous,

1925); *Toccata (Preludio, Fantasia, Ciacona)* (1921); *5 kurze Stücke zur Pflege des polyphonischen Spiels* (1923); arrangements of keyboard works of Bach; a concert version of Schoenberg's piano pieces, op. 11, No. 2. For 2 Pianos: *Improvisation* on Bach's chorale *Wie wohl ist mir* (1916); *Duettino concertante*, based on the finale of Mozart's 19th Piano Concerto (1919); a version of *Fantasia contrappuntistica* (1921; Berlin, Nov. 16, 1921).

VOCAL MUSIC: Mass (1879); *Le quattro stagioni* for Male Chorus and Orch. (1882); *Il sabato del villaggio*, to a poem by Leopardi, for Soloists, Chorus, and Orch. (1883); *2 Lieder*, to poems by Byron (1884); *Unter den Linden* for Soprano and Orch. (1893); *Zigeunerlied* and *Schlechter Trost* for Baritone and Orch., to Goethe's poems (1923); also cadenzas for Beethoven's 4th Piano Concerto and for 9 piano concertos of Mozart.

BIBLIOGRAPHY: Hugo Leichtentritt, *Ferruccio Busoni* (Leipzig, 1916); idem, "Ferruccio Busoni as a Composer," *Musical Quarterly* (Jan. 1917); H. Pfitzner, *Futuristengefahr* (Munich, 1917), polemical assault on Busoni's theories of new music); Giselda Selden-Goth, *Ferruccio Busoni* (Vienna, 1922); Augusta Cottlow, "My Years with Busoni," *Musical Observer* (June 1925); S. Nadel, *Ferruccio Busoni* (Leipzig, 1931); E.J. Dent, *Ferruccio Busoni, A Biography* (London, 1933); G.M. Gatti, "The Stage Works of Ferruccio Busoni," *Musical Quarterly* (July 1934); A. Santelli, *Busoni* (Rome, 1939); G. Guerrini, *Ferruccio Busoni, La vita, la figura, l'opera* (Florence, 1944); H.H. Stuckenschmidt, *Ferruccio Busoni, Zeittafel eines Europaers* (Zürich, 1967; in Eng. as *Ferruccio Busoni: Chronicle of a European*, London, 1970); Heinz Meyer, *Die Klaviermusik Ferruccio Busonis* (Zürich, 1969); H. Kosnick, *Busoni, Gestaltung durch Gestalt* (Regensburg, 1971); J. Kindermann, *Thematisch-chronologisches Verzeichnis der musikalischen Werke von Ferruccio Busoni* (Regensburg, 1980); S. Sablich, *Busoni* (Turin, 1982); A. Beaumont, *Busoni the Composer* (London, 1983).

Bussani, Dorothea, Austrian soprano; b. Vienna, 1763; d. after 1810. In 1786 she married the Italian bass **Francesco Bussani.** She created the roles of Cherubino in Mozart's *Le nozze di Figaro* (Vienna, May 1, 1786) and Despina in his *Così fan tutte* (Vienna, Jan. 26, 1790), opposite her husband's roles as Bartolo and Antonio. She made appearances in Italy with her husband between 1795 and 1805; subsequently appeared in Lisbon and London until she disappeared from the scene in 1810.

Bussani, Francesco, Italian bass; b. Rome, 1743; d. after 1807. He sang tenor roles; then turned to bass; was active from 1783–94 in Vienna, where he married the Austrian soprano **Dorothea Bussani** in 1786. He created the roles of Bartolo and Antonio in Mozart's *Le nozze di Figaro* (Vienna, May 1, 1786); also created Don Alfonso in *Così fan tutte* (Vienna, Jan. 26, 1790). His wife appeared in both, as Cherubino and Despina. He returned to Italy with his wife in 1795 and continued to make appearances there until they went to Lisbon in 1807.

Busschop, Jules-Auguste-Guillaume, French composer; b. Paris, Sept. 10, 1810; d. Bruges, Belgium, Feb. 10, 1896. He was entirely self-taught, and became successful as a composer of motets, cantatas, etc., including the prizewinning cantata *Le Drapeau belge* (1834) and a *Te Deum* (Brussels, 1860). He also wrote a Symph., several overtures, military music, etc.

Busser, Henri-Paul, French composer, organist, and conductor; b. Toulouse, Jan. 16, 1872; d. Paris, Dec. 30, 1973, at the age of 101. After primary musical studies in his native town, he went to Paris, where he studied with Guiraud at the Paris Cons.; also took private lessons with Gounod, Widor, and César Franck. He won 2nd Premier Prix de Rome in 1893 with his cantata *Antigone*. A year before, he was appointed organist at St. Cloud; later served as choirmaster of the Opéra-Comique; in 1902, appointed conductor of the Grand Opéra, a post which he held for 37 years until his resignation in 1939; was reappointed after the war in 1946, and served his term until 1951. He also was for several years president of the Académie des Beaux Arts. He taught composition at the Paris Cons. from 1930 until 1948. During his long career as a conductor, he led several important productions, including the 3rd performance of Debussy's opera *Pelléas et Mélisande*. His centennial was grandly celebrated in January 1972 with performances of his works by the leading Paris orchs. and by an exhibition of his MSS at the Opéra. In 1958 he married the French opera singer **Yvonne Gall** (1885–1972).

WORKS: *Daphnis et Chloë*, a scenic pastorale (Opéra-Comique, Paris, Dec. 14, 1897, composer conducting); operas: *Colomba* (Nice, Feb. 4, 1921); *Les Noces corinthiennes* (Paris, May 10, 1922); *La Carosse du Saint Sacrement* (1936); *Diafoirus 60* (Lille, 1963); *La Vénus d'Ille* (Lille, 1964); ballets: *La Ronde des saisons* (1905); *Le Vert Galant* (Paris, 1951); *Gayarni* (1963); *Le Sommeil de l'Enfant Jésus* for Violin and Orch.; *A la Villa Medicis*, symph. suite for Orch.; *Minerva*, concert overture for Orch.; *Hercule au jardin des Hespérides*, symph. poem; *Suite funambulesque* for Small Orch.; *A la lumière (Poème lyrique)*; *Suite brève* for Small Orch.; *Messe de Noël* for 4 Voices, and Organ or Orch.; *Pièce de Concert* for Harp and Orch.; *Appassionato* for Alto and Orch.; *Marche de Fête* for Orch.; *Hymne à la France* for Tenor and Orch.; *Impromptu* for Harp with Orch.; several preludes and fugues for Organ on themes by Gounod, Massenet, A. Thomas, etc. He completed and arranged for performance Bizet's unfinished opera *Ivan le Terrible;* publ. *Précis de composition* (Paris, 1943) and a vol. of memoirs, *De Pelléas aux Indes Galantes* (Paris, 1955).

Bussler, Ludwig, German music theorist and pedagogue; b. Berlin, Nov. 26, 1838; d. there, Jan. 18, 1900. His father was the painter, author, and privy councillor Robert Bussler; his maternal grandfather was the famous tenor singer **Karl Bader.** He studied with Dehn, Grell, and Wieprecht; then taught theory at the Ganz School of Music in Berlin (1865) and at the Stern Cons. (from 1879); was also active as a conductor at various Berlin theaters. In 1883 he became the music critic for the *National-Zeitung.* His eminently practical writings are: *Musikalische Elementarlehre* (1867; 3rd ed., 1882; Eng. trans., N.Y., 1895; also in Russian); *Der strenge Satz* (1877); *Harmonische Übungen am Klavier* (1877; in Eng., N.Y., 1890); *Kontrapunkt und Fuge im freien Tonsatz* (1878); *Musikalische Formenlehre* (1878; Eng. ed., N.Y., 1883); *Praktische musikalische Kompositionslehre:* Part I, *Lehre vom Tonsatz* (1878), and Part II, *Freie Komposition* (1879); *Instrumentation und Orchestersatz* (1879); *Elementar-Melodik* (1879); *Geschichte der Musik,* 6 lectures (1882); *Modulationslehre* (1882); *Lexikon der musikalischen Harmonien* (1889).

Bussotti, Sylvano, Italian composer of the avantgarde; b. Florence, Oct. 1, 1931. He studied violin; at the age of 9 was enrolled in the Cherubini Cons. in Florence, where he studied theory with Roberto Lupi, and also took piano lessons with Luigi Dallapiccola, while continuing his basic violin studies. In 1957 he went to Paris, where he studied privately with Max Deutsch. He became active as a theatrical director; also exhibited his paintings at European galleries. As a composer he adopted an extreme idiom, in which verbalization and pictorial illustrations are combined with aleatory discursions within the framework of multimedia productions. Many of his scores look like abstract expressionist paintings, with fragments of musical notation interspersed with occasional realistic representations of human or animal forms. WORKS: *Memoria* for Baritone, Chorus, and Orch. (1962); *Fragmentations* for Harp (1962); *La Passion selon Sade,* his crowning achievement, which makes use of theatrical effects, diagrams, drawings, surrealistic illustrations, etc., with thematic content evolving from a dodecaphonic nucleus, allowing great latitude for free interpolations, and set in an open-end form in which fragments of the music are recapitulated at will, until the players are mutually neutralized. The unifying element of the score is the recurrent motive D-Es-A-D-E, spelling the name De Sade, interwoven with that of B-A-C-H. The first production of *La Passion selon Sade* took place in Palermo on Sept. 5, 1965. His grand opera *Lorenzaccio,* in 23 scenes, employing a multitude of performers, which required 230 costumes, all designed by Bussotti himself, was produced at the opening of the Venice Festival of Contemporary Music on Sept. 7, 1972. Among Bussotti's other conceits is *5 Pieces for David Tudor* (1959), in which the dedicatee wears thick gloves to avoid hitting single and potentially melodious tones on the keyboard. Among his other works of various descriptions are 3 pieces for puppet theater: *Nottetempolunapark* (1954); *Arlechinbatocieria* (1955); *Tre mascare in gloria* (1956); *7 Fogli* for various instrumental combinations (1959); *Phrase à*

trois for String Trio (1960); *Torso* for Voices, Speaker, and Instrumentalists (1960–63); *La Partition ne peut se faire que dans la violence* for Orch. (1962); *I semi di Gramsci* for Quartet and Orch. (1967); *Tableaux vivants* for 2 Pianos (1965); *Rara requiem* to words in several languages (1969); *Opus Cygne* for Flute and Orch. (Baden-Baden, Oct. 20, 1979).

Bustabo, Guila, American violinist; b. Manitowoc, Wis., Feb. 25, 1919. She was a child prodigy; played at a benefit concert in Chicago at the age of 4; at age 10 was a soloist with the N.Y. Phil., performing a Wieniawski concerto (Nov. 2, 1929). She studied with Louis Persinger in N.Y. and with Enesco and Hubay in Europe. From 1964–70, she was on the faculty of the Cons. at Innsbruck in Austria.

Bustini, Alessandro, Italian composer; b. Rome, Dec. 24, 1876; d. there, June 23, 1970. He studied at the Santa Cecilia Academy with Sgambati (piano), Renzi (organ), and Falchi (composition), graduating in 1897. He was subsequently appointed to the faculty of Santa Cecilia, and was its president from 1952 to 1964. His works, all written in the traditional Italian manner, include the opera *Maria Dulcis* (Rome, April 15, 1902); 2 symphs. (1899, 1909); *Le Tentazioni,* a symph. poem (1914); *Le Stagioni* for Violin and Chamber Orch. (1934); 2 string quartets; songs; piano works.

Buswell, James Oliver IV, American violinist; b. Fort Wayne, Ind., Dec. 4, 1946. He was educated at Harvard College (B.A., 1970); studied violin with Ivan Galamian at the Juilliard School of Music; made his N.Y. recital debut in 1967. He was a visiting prof. at the Univ. of Arizona in Tucson (1972–73); in 1974 he joined the faculty of the Indiana Univ. School of Music in Bloomington.

Buths, Julius, German pianist; b. Wiesbaden, May 7, 1851; d. Düsseldorf, March 12, 1920. He was a pupil of his father; later of Hiller in Cologne and Kiel in Berlin; conducted the "Cecilia" at Wiesbaden (1871–72); traveled to Milan and Paris (1873–74); conducted in Breslau (1875–79) and in Elberfeld (1879–90); from 1890–1908 was music director at Düsseldorf, and conducted several Rhine music festivals; in 1902 was appointed director of the Düsseldorf Cons. He wrote a Piano Concerto; a Piano Quintet; a String Quartet; a Piano Suite; etc.

Butler (real name, **Whitwell**), **O'Brien,** Irish composer; b. Cahersiveen, c.1870; d. May 7, 1915 (lost on the *Lusitania*). He began his musical studies in Italy, then became a pupil of C.V. Stanford and W. Parratt at the Royal College of Music in London; later traveled extensively, and spent some time in India, where he wrote an opera, *Muirgheis,* the first opera to be written to a libretto in the Gaelic language; it was produced in Dublin, Dec. 7, 1903. Other compositions include a Sonata for Violin and Piano (on Irish themes) and songs.

Butt, Dame Clara, English contralto; b. Southwick, Sussex, Feb. 1, 1872; d. North Stoke, Oxfordshire, July 13, 1976. She studied with J.H. Blower at the Royal College of Music in London; later took lessons with Bouhy in Paris and Etelka Gerster in Berlin; made her operatic debut as Ursula in Sullivan's *Golden Legend* (London, Dec. 7, 1892); then sang at the music festivals at Hanley and Bristol. She visited the U.S. in 1899 and 1913; in 1913–14 made a world tour with her husband, **R. Kennerley Rumford,** a noted baritone. Several composers wrote special works for her, among them Elgar's *Sea-Pictures* and H. Bedford's *Romeo and Juliet.* In 1920 she was made a Dame of the British Empire.
BIBLIOGRAPHY: W. Ponder, *Clara Butt* (London, 1928).

Butterley, Nigel, Australian composer; b. Sydney, May 13, 1935. He began piano lessons at the age of 4; studied at the New South Wales State Cons. with Noel Nickson and Raymond Hanson (1952–55); then in London with Priaulx Rainier (1962). From 1955–72 he was music adviser to the Australian Broadcasting Commission.
WORKS: *Diversion* for Brass Quintet (1958); *Canticle of David* for Strings (1960); Oboe Sonatina (1960); *The Tell-Tale Heart,* after Poe, a ballet for 2 Pianos and Percussion (1961); *Laudes (Praises)* for Flute, Clarinet, Horn, Trumpet, Violin, Viola, Cello, and Piano (1963); String Quartet (1965); *Canticle of the Sun* for 3 amateur Instrumental Groups (1965); *The White-Throated Warbler* for Recorder and Harpsichord (1965); *In the Head the Fire,* a "radio tableau" for Narrator, Tenor, Baritone, Chorus, Winds, Piano, Organ, and Percussion (Italia Prize, 1966); *Interaction,* an "improvisation" for Painter and Orch. (1967; expanded into a television film); Variations for Wind Quintet, Piano, and Recorded Piano (Canberra, Sept. 30, 1967); *Meditations of Thomas Traherne* for Orch. and Recorder Ensemble (1968); *Carmina* for Voice and Wind Quintet (1968); Violin Concerto (1968–70); *Pentad* for 27 Wind Instruments (1969); *Refractions* for Wind Quintet and 28 String Instruments (1969); *Explorations* for Piano and Orch. (Sydney, May 2, 1970, in the presence of Queen Elizabeth II); *Voices* for Wind Quintet (1972); *First Day Covers,* a "philharmonic philatelia" for Narrator and Orch. (1972); *Fire in the Heavens* for Orch. (1973); *The 4 Elements* for Orch. (1973); *Watershore,* after Walt Whitman, for 4 Narrators, Improvising Group, 3 Cellos, and Piano Roll (1977).

Butterworth, George Sainton Kaye, talented English composer; b. London, July 12, 1885; killed in the battle of Pozières, Aug. 5, 1916. He inherited his love for music from his mother, a singer, Julia Wigan; learned to play organ at school in Yorkshire; then studied piano at Eton. He later entered Trinity College, Oxford; then engaged in music teaching and writing music criticism; also became an ardent collector of folk songs, and prepared material for Vaughan Williams's *London Symphony.* He made several arrangements of folk songs and wrote an orch. piece, *The Banks of Green Willows,* on folk themes (London, March 20, 1914). He enlisted in the British army at the outbreak of World War I. He wrote *Six Songs from "A Shropshire Lad"* (1911); 11 folk songs from Sussex (1912); *On Christmas Night* for Mixed Chorus (1912); *Cherry Tree,* a prelude for Orch. (1912); *Love Blows as the Wind Blows* for Baritone and String Quartet (1914).

Butting, Max, German composer; b. Berlin, Oct. 6, 1888; d. there, July 13, 1976. He studied organ in Berlin and composition in Munich. Returning to Berlin, he was a successful teacher, but in 1933 was deprived of his various positions for political reasons, being the former editor of a socialist publication. He was able to return to his professional activities after the end of the war. In 1948 he was appointed a lecturer in the music division of the East Berlin Radio; in 1968 he received an honorary doctor's degree from the Univ. of Berlin.
WORKS: Opera, *Plautus im Nonnenkloster* (Leipzig, Oct. 3, 1959); 10 symphs. (1923–63); *Sinfonietta with Banjo* (1929); Flute Concerto (1950); *Symphonic Variations* (1953); Sinfonietta op. 100 (1960); Piano Concerto (1965); *Legende* for Orch. (1966); *Triptychon* for Orch. (1967); *Concert Overture* (1973); 10 string quartets (1914–71); String Quintet (1916); Quintet for Violin, Viola, Cello, Oboe, and Clarinet (1921); Wind Quintet (1925); Piano Trio (1947); String Trio (1952); numerous minor pieces of chamber music; a considerable number of piano pieces, choruses, and songs. His music is animated by polyphonic purposefulness and is marked by rhythmic vitality and lyric meditation. Since many of his works were destined for amateur performances, Butting shunned modernistic involvements; however, in his 9th and 10th symphs. he applied dodecaphonic structures.
BIBLIOGRAPHY: Dietrich Brennecke, *Das Lebenswerk Max Buttings* (Leipzig, 1973).

Büttner, Erhard, German composer and writer on music; b. Römhild, Thuringia (baptized, July 19), 1592; d. (suicide) Coburg, Jan. 19, 1625. He studied at the Univ. of Jena; from 1616 until his death he was Kantor at the municipal school in Coburg. He took his own life, being stricken by the sin of having been unfaithful to his wife. He publ. *Rudimenta musica* (Coburg, 1623; 2nd ed., 1625).

Buttstett, Franz Vollrath, German composer; b. Erfurt, April 2, 1735; d. Rothenberg, May 7, 1814. He was a member of a musical family; may have been a grandson of the German organist **Johann Heinrich Buttstett.** He received his musical education at home. In 1766 he was appointed organist at Weikersheim; in 1767 went to Rothenberg. He wrote cantatas and instrumental sonatas.
BIBLIOGRAPHY: Hans Kern, *Franz Vollrath Buttstett; Eine Studie zur Musik des Spätbarock* (Würzburg, 1939).

Buttstett, Johann Heinrich, German organist and composer; b. Bindersleben, near Erfurt, April 25,

1666; d. Erfurt, Dec. 1, 1727. He studied with Johann Pachelbel; was appointed organist at the Reglerkirche in Erfurt in 1684; in 1691 became organist at the Predigerkirche there, a post he held for 36 years, until his death. In 1713 he publ. an album of keyboard pieces, *Musikalische Klavier-Kunst;* also wrote 5 masses and 36 chorale preludes. His *Harmonia aeterna* is a polemical pamphlet directed against Mattheson.

Buttykay, Akos, Hungarian pianist and composer; b. Halmi, July 22, 1871; d. Debrecen, Oct. 26, 1935. He studied at the Budapest Cons.; in 1894 went to Weimar for further courses in piano playing. He toured in Central Europe as a pianist; in 1907 settled in Budapest as a piano teacher at the Music Academy. He wrote several operettas which were modestly successful at their productions in Budapest: *The Flying Greek* (Budapest, Oct. 19, 1905); *Pompom* (1907); *Cinderella* (Budapest, Oct. 26, 1912); *A Love Storm* (Budapest, Feb. 6, 1920); 2 symphs. (1900, 1902); *Magyar Suite* for Orch. (1900); *Magyar Rhapsody* for Orch. (1931); Violin Sonata (1908); *Capriccio* for Violin and Piano (1928); many songs.

Buus, Jacques (**Jachet de** or **van Paus; Jacobus Bohusius**), Flemish contrapuntist; b. c.1500; d. Vienna, late August 1565. His first publications were 2 French songs, printed in Lyons in 1538. In 1541 he went to Italy and was engaged as assistant organist at San Marco in Venice; in 1550 he settled in Vienna. He publ., in Venice, 2 books of instrumental *Canzoni francese* (1543, 1550); 2 books of *Ricercari* (1547, 1549); and one book of *Motetti* (1549); several of his madrigals were publ. in various collections of the period, and also reprinted in a number of anthologies.
BIBLIOGRAPHY: G. Sutherland, "The Ricercari of Jacques Buus," *Musical Quarterly* (Oct. 1945); Walter Breitner, *Jacob Buus als Motettenkomponist* (Tutzing, 1977).

Buxtehude, Dietrich, great Danish organist and composer; b. Oldesloe (Holstein), c.1637; d. Lübeck, May 9, 1707. His father, **Johannes Buxtehude** (1602–74), an organist of German extraction, was active in Holstein, which was then under Danish rule. It is to be assumed that Dietrich Buxtehude received a thorough training from his father. He was about 20 years old when he was appointed organist at Helsingborg; in 1660 he became organist in Helsingor. On April 11, 1668, he was elected as successor to the famous organist Franz Tunder at the St. Mary Church in Lübeck; it was a custom in such successions that the newcomer was to marry the incumbent's daughter. Indeed, Dietrich Buxtehude did marry Tunder's daughter, on Aug. 3, 1668. In 1673 he revived the Abendmusik concerts in Lübeck which were originally organized by Tunder, and which were made up of organ music and concerted pieces for chorus and orch.; they were held annually on the 5 Sundays before Christmas, in the afternoon. Both Mattheson and Handel visited Buxtehude on Aug. 17, 1703, with the ostensible purpose of being con-

sidered as his successor, but it is a valid surmise that the notorious marriage clause which would have compelled Mattheson or Handel to marry one of Buxtehude's 5 daughters, allegedly lacking in feminine attraction, deterred them from further negotiations. In 1705 Bach, then 20 years old, was supposed to make a trip of some 200 miles from Arnstadt, where he was employed at the time, to Lübeck, to hear Buxtehude; however, the report of Bach's journey is open to serious doubts, for it would have been impossible for him to make such a trip in a short time during his leave of absence; and if he made it he was probably employed as a valet to a stagecoach traveler; any supposition that he walked to Lübeck and back, considering the usual inclement weather and the well-nigh impassable hilly terrain, is untenable. But there can be no doubt that Buxtehude exercised a profound influence on Bach, both as organist and composer. A complete edition of Buxtehude's organ works was publ. in 2 vols. by Spitta in 1875–76, and another edition was issued in 3 vols. by Josef Hedar in 1952. A complete edition of Buxtehude's vocal music under the editorship of W. Gurlitt, in 8 vols., was issued between 1927 and 1958. The complete vocal music began publication in 1925; the thematic catalogue was edited by G. Karstädt and publ. in Wiesbaden in 1974. The instrumental works are in vol. 11 of Denkmäler Deutscher Tonkunst; Abendmusiken and church cantatas are in vol. 14; 19 newly discovered keyboard suites by Buxtehude were brought out by E. Bangert (Copenhagen, 1942).
BIBLIOGRAPHY: H. Jimmerthal, *Buxtehude* (Lübeck, 1877); C. Stiehl, *Die Organisten an der Marienkirche und die Abendmusiken in Lübeck* (Leipzig, 1886); A. Pirro, *Buxtehude* (Paris, 1913); S.E.A. Hagen, *Diderik Buxtehude* (Copenhagen, 1920); W. Stahl, *Franz Tunder und Dietrich Buxtehude* (Leipzig, 1926); idem, *Buxtehude* (Kassel, 1937); J. Hedar, *Buxtehude's Orgelwerke* (Stockholm, 1951); F. Hutchins, *Dietrich Buxtehude: The Man, His Music, His Era* (Paterson, N.J., 1955); S. Sorensen, *Das Buxtehudebild im Wandel der Zeit* (Lübeck, 1972).

Buzzi-Peccia, Arturo, song composer and teacher; b. Milan, Oct. 13, 1854; d. New York, Aug. 29, 1943. He emigrated to America in 1898 and lived mostly in N.Y. as a vocal teacher. He publ. numerous songs and choral works; also a book, *How to Succeed in Singing* (1925).

Buzzolla, Antonio, Italian composer and conductor; b. Adria, March 2, 1815; d. Venice, March 20, 1871. He received his early education with his father, a professional theater conductor; then enrolled at the Naples Cons. as a student of Donizetti and Mercadante (1837–39). He was then active as a theater conductor in Italy, Germany, and France, returning to Venice in 1847. He wrote the operas *Ferramondo* (Venice, Dec. 3, 1836); *Mastino I della Scala* (Venice, May 31, 1841); *Gli Avventurieri* (Venice, May 14, 1842); *Amleto* (Venice, Feb. 24, 1848); *Elisabetta di Valois* (Venice, Feb. 16, 1850).

He also wrote an opera in Venetian dialect, *La Puta onorata,* which remained incomplete. In 1855 he was appointed maestro di cappella at San Marco, for which he subsequently wrote much sacred music.

BIBLIOGRAPHY: A. Casellati, "Antonio Buzzolla," *Musica d'Oggi* (July 1930).

Bychkov, Semyon, Russian-born American conductor; b. Leningrad, Nov. 30, 1952. He attended the Glinka Choir School in Leningrad as a youth; subsequently studied with Ilya Musin at the Leningrad Cons., graduating in 1974. In 1975 he emigrated to the U.S., where he received his Artist Diploma from the Mannes College of Music in 1976. In 1980 he became music director of the Grand Rapids Symph. Orch.; was concurrently associate conductor of the Buffalo Phil. Orch., and in 1981 became its principal guest conductor. He also appeared as a guest conductor with the Minnesota Orch., National Symph. of Washington, D.C., Detroit Symph., Indianapolis Symph., and Vancouver (B.C.) Symph.; also conducted in England, Israel, and Japan. On July 4, 1983, he gave a special concert of the Grand Rapids Symph. Orch. to mark his naturalization as a U.S. citizen.

Byrd, Henry Roeland, American blues pianist; b. Bogalusa, La., Dec. 19, 1918; d. New Orleans, Jan. 30, 1980. He received rudimentary instruction in music from his mother; subsequently developed an individual style of playing which utilized blues, New Orleans, and Caribbean elements; such musicians as Fats Domino, Huey Smith, and Allen Toussaint made his style popular outside New Orleans. His "erudite" synthetic techniques earned for him the nickname "Professor Longhair."

Byrd (or **Byrde, Bird**), **William,** great English composer; b. Lincoln, 1543; d. Stondon Massey, Essex, July 4, 1623. There are indications that Byrd studied music with Tallis. On March 25, 1563, Byrd was appointed organist of Lincoln Cathedral; in 1568 he married Juliana Birley; early in 1570 he was elected a member of the Chapel Royal, while retaining his post at Lincoln Cathedral until 1572; he then assumed his duties, together with Tallis, as organist of the Chapel Royal. In 1575, both Byrd and Tallis were granted a patent by Queen Elizabeth for the exclusive privilege of printing music and selling music paper for a term of 21 years; however, the license proved unprofitable and they petitioned the Queen in 1577 to give them an annuity in the form of a lease; this petition was granted. In 1585, after the death of Tallis, the license passed wholly into Byrd's hands. The earliest publication of the printing press of Byrd and Tallis was the first set of *Cantiones sacrae* for 5 to 8 Voices (1575), printed for them by Vautrollier and dedicated to the Queen; works issued by Byrd alone under his exclusive license were *Psalmes, Sonnets, and Songs of Sadness and Pietie* in 5 Voices (1588; publ. by Thomas East; reprinted as vol. XIV by Fellowes, *English Madrigal School*); *Songs of Sundrie Natures* for 3–6 Voices (1589; reprinted in vol. XV of the *English Madrigal School*); *Liber Primus Sacrarum Cantionum* for 5 Voices (1589); *Liber Secundus Sacrarum Cantionum* for 5–6 Voices (1591); also in 1591 appeared the famous collection of virginal music by Byrd, *My Ladye Nevells Booke* (42 pieces; modern ed. publ. by Hilda Andrews, London, 1926; reprinted, N.Y., 1969). In 1593 Byrd moved to Stondon Massey, Essex, between Chipping Ongar and Ingatestone; owing to various litigations and disputes concerning the ownership of the property, Byrd was limited to the publication of 3 masses, between c.1593 and 1595, separately, and lacking title pages. In 1605 he brought out the first book of *Gradualia;* 2 years later there followed the 2nd book (both books republ. in *Tudor Church Music,* Vol. 7). In 1611 the book of *Psalms, Songs and Sonnets* was publ. (reprinted in vol. XVI of the *English Madrigal School*); in the same year Byrd contributed several pieces to *Parthenia,* a collection of virginal compositions by Byrd, Bull, and Gibbons (newly ed. by Margaret H. Glyn, London, 1927); in 1614 he contributed 4 anthems to Leighton's *Teares or Lamentacions of a Sorrowful Soule;* separate numbers were publ. in various other collections (*Musica Transalpina,* 1588; Watson's *Italian Madrigales,* 1590; Barnard's *Selected Church Music,* 1641; Boyce's *Cathedral Music*); other music for virginal and organ in the *Virginal Book of Queen Elizabeth, Fitzwilliam Virginal Book* (70 pieces), *W. Forster's Virginal Book* (2 pieces). New editions (besides those previously mentioned): *Tudor Church Music* (vol. 2, English church music; vol. 9, masses, cantiones, and motets); Psalms, sonnets, and madrigals, by E.H. Fellowes (1920); *The Collected Works of William Byrd* by E.H. Fellowes (London, 1937–50; revised by T. Dart, P. Brett, and K. Elliott, London, 1962); the *Byrd Organ Book,* a collection of 21 pieces edited for piano from the virginal MSS by Margaret H. Glyn (London, 1923); 14 pieces for keyboard instruments, by J.A. Fuller-Maitland and W. Barclay Squire (London, 1923). A new publication of complete works, edited by P. Brett under the title *The Byrd Edition,* began publication in London in 1970.

BIBLIOGRAPHY: E.H. Fellowes, *The English Madrigal Composers* (Oxford, 1921; 2nd ed., 1948); idem, *William Byrd: A Short Account of His Life and Work* (Oxford, 1923; 2nd ed., 1928); F. Howes, *William Byrd* (London, 1928); E.H. Fellowes, *William Byrd* (Oxford, 1936; 2nd ed., 1948); I. Holst, *Byrd* (London, 1972); O. Neighbour, *The Consort and Keyboard Music of William Byrd* (Berkeley, 1978); J. Kerman, *The Masses and Motets of William Byrd,* vol. I of *The Music of William Byrd* (London, 1981). Individual articles dealing with specific aspects of Byrd's music: Margaret H. Glyn, *About Elizabethan Virginal Music and Its Composers* (London, 1924; revised ed., 1935); E.J. Dent, "William Byrd and the Madrigal," in the *Johannes Wolf Festschrift* (Berlin, 1929); J.A. Westrup, "William Byrd," *Music & Letters* (1943); W. Palmer, "Word-Painting and Suggestion in Byrd," *Music Review* (1952); idem, "Byrd and Amen," *Music & Letters* (1953); Fr.B. Zimmermann, "Advanced Tonal Design in the Part-Songs of William Byrd," in *Kon-*

gress Bericht (Cologne, 1958); T. Dart and P. Brett, "Songs by William Byrd in Manuscripts at Harvard," *Harvard University Bulletin* (1960); J. Kerman, "Byrd, Tallis and the Art of Imitation," in *Aspects of Medieval and Renaissance Music*, in the dedicatory vol. for Gustave Reese (N.Y., 1966); H. Andrews, *The Technique of Byrd's Vocal Polyphony* (London, 1966); W.B. Gray, "Some Aspects of Word Treatment in the Music of William Byrd," *Musical Quarterly* (1969).

Byrne, David, American rock musician and composer; b. Dumbarton, Scotland, May 14, 1952. He went to the U.S. as a youth, and studied art and music at The Rhode Island School of Design. He wrote a dance score, *The Catherine Wheel,* for Twyla Tharp (1980); but his main claim to fame is being the lead singer, guitarist, and composer for The Talking Heads, a foremost new-wave rock band. The sources of his creative imagination are manifold: primitive African rhythms, soul music, British art, rock, etc.

Byström, Oscar Fredrik Bernadotte, Swedish organist and composer; b. Stockholm, Oct. 13, 1821; d. there, July 22, 1909. After serving in the military, he became inspector of the conservatory of the Royal Academy of Music in 1866; was named prof. there in 1872. In addition to the music he wrote for the church, he also composed an opera, *Herman Vimpel;* a Symph. (1870–72; revised 1895); and chamber music.

C

Caamaño, Roberto, Argentinian pianist and composer; b. Buenos Aires, July 7, 1923. He studied at the Cons. Nacional in Buenos Aires; toured South America as a concert pianist; from 1961 to 1964 was artistic director of the Teatro Colón in Buenos Aires. In 1964 he was appointed a prof. of composition at the Pontífica Universita Católica Argentina. He was the editor of a valuable compendium in 3 vols., *La historia del Teatro Colón (1908–1968)*, publ. in Buenos Aires in 1969, illustrated with color plates, drawings, and photographs.

WORKS: *Magnificat* for Chorus and Orch. (1954); *Variaciones americanas* for Orch. (1954); *Bandoneon Concerto* (1954); 2 piano concertos (1957, 1971); Piano Quintet (1962); 2 string quartets (1946, 1947); *Cantata para la Paz* (1966); *Tripartita* for Wind Orch. (1967).

Caba, Eduardo, Bolivian composer; b. Potosí, Oct. 13, 1890; d. La Paz, March 3, 1953. He was educated in Buenos Aires; then went to study with Turina in Spain; in 1942 he settled in La Paz. His ballets and other music are inspired by the pentatonic structure of certain Bolivian folk songs.

Caballé, Montserrat, celebrated Spanish soprano; b. Barcelona, April 12, 1933. She learned to sing at a convent which she attended as a child; at the age of 9 she was accepted at the Conservatorio del Liceo in Barcelona; her teachers there were Eugenie Kemini, Conchita Badia, and Napoleone Annovazzi. She graduated in 1953; then went to Italy, where she sang some minor roles. After a successful appearance as Mimi in *La Bohème* at the Basel Opera, she advanced rapidly, singing Tosca, Aida, Violetta, and other standard opera parts; she also proved her ability to master such modern and difficult parts as Salome, Elektra, and Marie in *Wozzeck*. She filled guest engagements at the Vienna State Opera, then made a grand tour through Germany. In 1964 she sang Manon in Mexico City. She made a triumphant American debut on April 20, 1965, when she was summoned to substitute for another singer in the title role of Donizetti's *Lucrezia Borgia* in a concert performance at Carnegie Hall in N.Y.; the usually restrained N.Y. critics praised her without reservation for the beauty of her voice and expressiveness of her dramatic interpretation. There followed several other American appearances, all of which were highly successful. She made her debut at the Metropolitan Opera in N.Y. as Marguerite in *Faust* on Dec. 22, 1965; she continued her appearances with the Metropolitan Opera; among her most significant roles were Violetta, Mimi, Aida, Norma,

Donna Anna, and other roles of the standard operatic repertoire. In 1964 she married **Bernabé Marti**, a Spanish tenor. Subsequently they appeared together in joint recitals.

Cabanilles, Juan Bautista José, Spanish organist and composer; b. Algemesí, province of Valencia, Sept. 4, 1644; d. Valencia, April 29, 1712. He studied for the priesthood at Valencia and probably received his musical training at the Cathedral there; was appointed organist of the Valencia Cathedral, May 15, 1665 (succeeding J. de la Torre) and retained that post until his death; was ordained a priest on Sept. 22, 1668. He was the greatest of the early Spanish composers for organ, and the most prolific. He composed chiefly "tientos," remarkable for the ingenious use of the variation form (on liturgical or popular themes). A complete edition of his works, in 4 vols., has been edited by H. Anglès (Barcelona, 1927–52). The *Obras vocales* are edited by J. Climent (Valencia, 1971).
BIBLIOGRAPHY: H. Anglès, "Orgelmusik der Schola Hispanica vom XV.–XVI. Jahrhundert," in *P. Wagner-Festschrift* (Leipzig, 1926); M. Bradshaw, "Juan Cabanilles: The Toccatas and Tientos," *Musical Quarterly* (April 1973); A. Garcia Ferreras, *Juan Bautista Cabanilles: Sein Leben und sein Werk* (Regensburg, 1973).

Cabezón (Cabeçon), Antonio de, great Spanish organist and composer; b. Castrillo de Matajudíos, near Burgos, 1510 (the exact date is unknown; see S. Kastner's letter to the editor of *Music & Letters,* April 1955); d. Madrid, March 26, 1566. He became blind in infancy; went to Palencia about 1521 to study with the Cathedral organist García de Baeza and with Tomás Gómez. He was appointed organist to the court of the Emperor Charles V and Empress Isabel (1526); after her death, Cabezón entered the service of Prince Philip and accompanied him to Italy, Germany, the Netherlands (1548–51), and England (1554); he returned to Spain (1556) and remained court organist until his death. His keyboard style greatly influenced the development of organ composition on the Continent and the composers for the virginal in England; Pedrell called him "the Spanish Bach." The series Libro de Cifra Nueva (1557), which contains the earliest editions of Cabezón's works, was reprinted by H. Anglès in *La música en la corte de Carlos V* (1944). His son and successor at the court of Philip II, **Hernando** (b. Madrid; baptized, Sept. 7, 1541; d. Valladolid, Oct. 1, 1602), publ. his instrumental works as *Obras de música para tecla, arpa y vihuela* (Madrid, 1578). This vol. contains exercises in 2 and 3 parts, arrangements of hymn tunes, 4-part "tientos," arrangements of motets in up to 6 parts by Josquin and other Franco-Flemish composers, and variations on tunes of the day (*El caballero,* etc.). Copies are in the British Museum, in Sir Percy Wyndham's Collection, at Brussels, Berlin, Madrid, and Washington, D.C. A modern edition appears in *Hispaniae schola musica sacra* (F. Pedrell, 1898; 4 vols.). The Inst. of Medieval Music has issued several vols. of Cabezón's *Collected Works* (C. Jacobs, ed.; N.Y., 1967—). A short MS work for 5 voices is in the Medinaceli Library in Madrid.
BIBLIOGRAPHY: Otto Kinkeldey, *Orgel und Klavier in der Musik des 16. Jahrhunderts* (1910); Willi Apel, "Early Spanish Music for Lute and Keyboard Instruments," *Musical Quarterly* (July 1934); S. Kastner, *Antonio de Cabezón* (Barcelona, 1952); T. Dart, "Cavazzoni and Cabezón," *Music & Letters* (Jan. 1955; a rebuttal to Dart's conjecture concerning the relationship of Cavazzoni and Cabezón is found in Knud Jeppesen's article in the Summer 1955 issue of *Journal of the American Musicological Society*); special Cabezón issue of *Anuario Musical* (vol. XXI, 1966; publ. 1968); G. Bourligueux, "Antonio de Cabezón. Nota bibliográfia en su cuarto centenario," *Boletín de la Inst. Fernán González* (Jan.–June 1970); M. Kastner, *Antonio und Hernando de Cabezón: Ein Chronik* (Tutzing, 1977).

Caccini, Francesca (nicknamed **"La Cecchina"**), daughter of **Giulio Caccini**; b. Florence, Sept. 18, 1587; d. c.1640. She was probably the first woman composer of operas. Her opera-ballet *La liberazione di Ruggiero dall'isola d'Alcina* was produced at a palace near Florence on Feb. 2, 1625, and a book of songs from it was publ. in the same year. A modern reprint, edited by Doris Silbert, was publ. in Northampton, Mass. (1945). Francesca Caccini wrote further a *Ballo delle zingare* (Florence, Feb. 24, 1615) in which she acted as one of the gypsies. Her sacred opera *Il martirio di Sant' Agata* was produced in Florence, Feb. 10, 1622.
BIBLIOGRAPHY: A. Bonaventura, "Il ritratto della Cecchina," *La cultura musicale* (1922); D. Silbert, "F. Caccini called 'La Cecchina,'" *Musical Quarterly* (Jan. 1946); C. Raney, "Francesca Caccini's *Primo libro*," *Music & Letters* (Oct. 1967).

Caccini, Giulio, Italian composer (called **Romano,** because he lived mostly in Rome); b. Tivoli, c.1550; d. Florence, (buried, Dec. 10) 1618. He was a pupil of Scipione delle Palla in singing and lute playing. His first compositions were madrigals in the traditional polyphonic style, but the new ideas generated in the discussions of the artists and literati of the "Camerata," in the houses of Bardi and Corsi at Florence, inspired him to write vocal soli in recitative form (then termed "musica in stile rappresentativo"), which he sang with consummate skill to his own accompaniment on the theorbo. These first compositions in a dramatic idiom were followed by his settings of separate scenes written by Bardi, and finally by the opera *Il combattimento d'Apolline col serpente* (poem by Bardi); next was *Euridice* (1600; poem by Rinuccini) and *Il rapimento di Cefalo* (in collaboration with others; first perf., Oct. 9, 1600, at the Palazzo Vecchio in Florence). Then followed *Le nuove musiche,* a series of madrigals for solo voice, with bass (Florence, 1602; new eds., Venice, 1607 and 1615; a modern ed. of the 1602 publication, prepared by H. Wiley Hitchcock [Madison, Wis., 1970], includes an annotated Eng. trans. of Caccini's preface, realizations of the solo madrigals, airs, and the final section of *Il rapimento di Cefalo*, an introductory essay on Caccini, the music, the poetry, MSS, other editions, and a bibliography. A trans. of the preface is also available in O. Strunk, *Source Readings in Music History* [N.Y., 1950]). The song *Amarilli mia bella* from the first series became very popular. Caccini also publ. *Fuggilotio musicale* (Venice, 2nd ed., 1613; including madrigals, sonnets, arias, etc.). From 1565 Caccini lived in Florence as a singer at the Tuscan court. He was called, by abbate Angelo Grillo, "the father of a new style of music"; Bardi said of him that he had "attained the goal of perfect music." But his claim to priority in writing vocal music in the "stile rappresentativo" is not supported by known chronology. Caccini's opera *Il rapimento di Cefalo* was performed 3 days after Peri's path-breaking *Euridice;* the closeness in time of operatic productions by both Caccini and Peri is further emphasized by the fact that when Peri produced *Euridice* in Florence (1600), he used some of Caccini's songs in the score. Caccini later made his own setting of *Euridice* (1600), but it was not produced until Dec. 5, 1602. On the other hand, Caccini was undoubtedly the first to publish an operatic work, for his score of *Euridice* was printed early in 1601, before the publication of Peri's work of the same title.

BIBLIOGRAPHY: A. Ehrichs, *Giulio Caccini* (Leipzig, 1908); R. Marchal, "Giulio Caccini," *La Revue Musicale* (June 1925); F. Ghisi, *Alle fonti della monodia* (Milan, 1940); C. Morricone, "Considerazioni sul *Fuggilozio* de Giulio Caccini," *Rivista Italiana di Musicologia* (1968); L. Bianconi, "Giulio Caccini e il manierismo musicale," *Chigiana* XXV/5 (1968); H.W. Hitchcock, "Depriving Caccini of a Musical Pastime," *Journal of the American Musicological Society* (Spring 1972); idem, "A New Biographical Source for Caccini," ibid. (Spring 1973).

Cacioppo, George, American composer of the avant-garde; b. Monroe, Mich., Sept. 24, 1927. He studied with Ross Lee Finney at the Univ. of Michigan; received his M.A. in composition in 1952; then worked at Tanglewood, studying with Leon Kirchner. In 1960 he attended classes of Roberto Gerhard, then a visiting prof. at the Univ. of Michigan. Cacioppo was a co-founder of the ONCE Festival concerts in Ann Arbor in 1960. His technique partakes of the Schoenbergian credo while studiously avoiding the chronic chromaticism of atonal writing. Verbalization is an integral part of all of his music; aleatory principles are expressed in "open end" forms.

WORKS: *Pianopieces* for any number of Pianos, with their realizations on tape sounding synchronously or non-synchronously and lasting any practical, or impractical, length of time; *Holy Ghost Vacuum, or America Faints* for Electric`Qrgan (Ann Arbor, March 29, 1966, composer at the manuals); *Time on Time in Miracles* for Soprano, 2 Horns, 2 Trombones, Cello, Piano, and Percussion (1964); *Cassiopeia* for 2 Pianos (1964).

Cadman, Charles Wakefield, American composer; b. Johnstown, Pa., Dec. 24, 1881; d. Los Angeles, Dec. 30, 1946. His great-grandfather was Samuel Wakefield, the inventor of the so-called "Buckwheat Notation." Cadman studied organ with Leo Oehmler in Pittsburgh, and with Emil Paur. He was especially interested in American Indian music; gave lecture recitals with the Indian mezzo-soprano Tsianina Redfeather.

WORKS: For the stage: Opera, *Shanewis (The Robin Woman),* his most successful work (Metropolitan Opera, March 23, 1918); *The Sunset Trail,* operatic cantata (Denver, Dec. 5, 1922); *The Garden of Mystery* (N.Y., March 20, 1925); *A Witch of Salem* (Chicago, Dec. 8, 1926); radio play, *The Willow Tree* (NBC, October 3, 1933). For Orch.: *Thunderbird Suite* (Los Angeles, Jan. 9, 1917); *Oriental Rhapsody* (1917); *Dark Dancers of the Mardi Gras* (1933); *Suite on American Folktunes* (1937); symph. poem, *Pennsylvania* (Los Angeles, March 7, 1940). Cantatas: *Father of Waters* (1928); *House of Joy, Indian Love Charm* for Children's Choir; *The Vision of Sir Launfal* for Male Voices, written for the Pittsburgh Prize Competition (1909). Also, Piano Sonata; violin pieces; about 180 songs, of which *At Dawning* acquired enormous popularity.

BIBLIOGRAPHY: E.E. Hipsher, *American Opera and Its Composers* (Philadelphia, 1934; pp. 99–110).

Caduff, Sylvia, Swiss conductor; b. Chur, Jan. 7, 1937. She studied at the Lucerne Cons., receiving a piano diploma in 1961; then attended Karajan's conducting classes at the Berlin Cons.; continued conducting studies with Kubelik, Matacic, and Otterloo in Lucerne, Salzburg, and Hilversum (The Netherlands); made her debut with the Tonhalle-Orch. of Zürich. She won first prize in the 1966 Dimitri Mitropoulos conducting competition in N.Y.; as a result, she was an assistant conductor under Bernstein with the N.Y. Phil. (1966–67); taught orch. conducting at the Bern Cons. (1972–77). In 1977 she became the first woman in Europe to be appointed a Generalmusikdirektor, when she took that position with the orch. of the city of Solingen, Germany.

Cady, Calvin Brainerd, American music pedagogue; b. Barry, Ill., June 21, 1851; d. Portland, Oreg., May 29, 1928. He studied at Oberlin College and at the Leipzig Cons.; taught harmony and piano at Oberlin, the Univ. of Michigan, and the Chicago College of Music (1888–94); from 1907 he lectured on music at Columbia Univ. His teaching emphasized the understanding of music as a gateway to all liberal education. He publ. 3 vols. of a manual, *Musical Education* (1902–7).

Cafaro (Caffaro), Pasquale, Italian composer; b. San Pietro, in Galatina, Lecce, Feb. 8, 1716; d. Naples, Oct. 23, 1787. He studied at the Naples Cons.; became 2nd master at the Naples Cons. della Pietà in 1759, and first master in 1771.

WORKS: Operas: *Ipermestra* (Naples, Dec. 18, 1751); *La disfatta di Dario* (Naples, Jan. 20, 1756); *L'incendio di Troia* (Naples, Jan. 20, 1757); *L'Olim-*

piade (Naples, Jan. 12, 1769); *Antigono* (Naples, Aug. 13, 1770); 6 oratorios; 4 cantatas; a *Stabat Mater* in 2 parts, with Organ.

Caffarelli (real name, **Gaetano Majorano**), artificial soprano (*musico*); b. Bitonto, April 12, 1710; d. Naples, Jan. 31, 1783. A poor peasant boy, endowed with a beautiful voice, he was discovered by a musician, Domenico Caffarelli, who taught him, and later sent him to Porpora at Naples. In gratitude to his patron, he assumed the name of Caffarelli. He studied for 5 years with Porpora, who predicted a brilliant career for him. Caffarelli became a master of pathetic song, and excelled in coloratura as well; read the most difficult music at sight, and was an accomplished harpsichord player. His debut at the Teatro Valle (Rome, 1724) in a female role (as was the custom for artificial sopranos) was a triumph. From 1737 to 1745 he sang in London, then in Paris and Vienna. His last public appearance took place on May 30, 1754, in Naples. He was in Lisbon until the earthquake of 1755; he retired from the opera in 1756; upon his return to Naples, he bought the dukedom of Santo-Durato with the fortune he had amassed during his career, and assumed the title of duke.

Caffi, Francesco, Italian music scholar; b. Venice, June 14, 1778; d. Padua, Jan. 24, 1874. After a period of study in Venice, he produced an allegorical drama, *L'armonia richiamata,* which was performed at the opening of the Istituto Filarmonico there (Aug. 20, 1811). In 1827 he moved to Milan; in 1840 to Rovigo. His most important work was a *Storia della musica sacra nella gia Cappella Ducale di San Marco in Venezia dal 1318 al 1797* (2 vols., Venice, 1854–55; reprinted 1931). This was the first part of an ambitious project dealing with music in Venice; the 2nd part, *Storia della musica teatrale in Venezia durante la sua Repubblica,* was completed by Caffi shortly before his death, but remained in MS. He further publ. monographs on Bonaventura Furlanetto (1820); Zarlino (1836); Lotti; Benedetto Marcello (in Cicognia's *Venetiani iscritioni*); and Giammateo Asola (Padua, 1862). Caffi's grandson, F.A. Salvagnini, wrote his biography (Rome, 1905).

Cage, John, American composer of ultramodern tendencies; b. Los Angeles, Sept. 5, 1912. His father, John Milton Cage, Sr., was an inventor of devices for detection of submarines; his mother was active as a clubwoman in California. John Cage studied piano with Fannie Dillon and Richard Buhlig in Los Angeles and with Lazare Lévy in Paris; returning to America, he studied composition in California with Adolph Weiss and with Henry Cowell in N.Y.; also attended Schoenberg's classes at the Univ. of Calif., Los Angeles. He developed Cowell's piano technique, making use of tone clusters and playing directly on the piano strings, and initiated a type of procedure which he called "prepared piano." The "preparation" consists of placing on the piano strings a variety of objects, such as screws, copper coins, rubber bands, and the like, which alter the tone color of individual keys. As a performer on the "prepared piano," John Cage attracted considerable attention at his concerts in America and Europe. Eventually the term and the procedure gained acceptance among many avant-garde composers and was listed as a legitimate innovative method in many music dictionaries. On June 7, 1935, Cage married, in Los Angeles, Xenia Kashevaroff; they were divorced in 1945. In 1938–39 he was employed as an accompanist in a dance class at the Cornish School in Seattle, where he also organized a percussion group. He taught for a season at the School of Design in Chicago (1941–42); then moved to N.Y., where he began his fruitful association with the dancer Merce Cunningham, for whom he wrote many special works. An even more important association was his collaboration with the pianist David Tudor, who was able to reify Cage's exotic inspirations, works in which the performer shares the composer's creative role. In 1949 Cage received a Guggenheim fellowship. With the passing years he departed from the musical pragmatism of precise notation and definite ways of performance, electing instead to mark his creative intentions in graphic symbols and pictorial representations. He soon established the principle of indeterminacy in musical composition, borrowing the term from modern physics; in this sense no 2 performances of a composition can be identical. In the meantime he became immersed in the study of mycology, and acquired a formidable expertise in mushroom gathering; he even won a prize in Italy in competition with professional mycologists. He also became interested in chess and played demonstration games with Marcel Duchamps, the famous painter turned chessmaster, on chessboards designed by Lowell Cross to operate on aleatory principles with the aid of a computer and a system of laser rays. In his endeavor to achieve the ultimate in freedom of musical expression, he produced a piece entitled *4'33"*, "tacet, any instrument or combination of instruments," in 3 movements, during which no sounds are intentionally produced. It was "performed" in Woodstock, N.Y., on Aug. 29, 1952, by David Tudor, who sat at the piano playing nothing for the length of time stipulated in the title. This was followed by another "silent" piece, *0'00"*, an idempotent "to be performed in any way by anyone," presented for the first time in Tokyo, Oct. 24, 1962. Any sounds, noises, coughs, chuckles, groans, and growls produced by the captive listeners to silence are automatically regarded as an integral part of the piece itself, so that the wisecrack about the impossibility of arriving at a fair judgment of a silent piece, since one cannot tell whose music is not being played, is invalidated by the uniqueness of Cage's art. Cage is a consummate showman, and his exhibitions invariably attract music-lovers and music-haters alike, expecting to be exhilarated or outraged, as the case may be. In many such public happenings he departs from musical, unmusical, or even antimusical programs in favor of a free exercise of surrealist imagination, often instructing the audience to participate actively, as for instance going out in the street and bringing in garbage pails needed for percussion effects, with or without garbage. Cage is a brilliant writer, much influenced by the manner, grammar, syntax, and glorified illogic of Gertrude Stein. A detailed annotated catalogue of his works was publ. by Edition Peters (N.Y., 1962). In view of the indeterminacy of so many of Cage's works, such a catalogue can serve only as a list of titles and suggestions of contents. In order to eliminate the subjective element in composition, Cage resorts to a method of selecting the components of his pieces by dice throwing, suggested by the Confucian classic *I Ching*, an ancient Chinese oracle book; the result is a system of total serialism, in which all elements pertaining to acoustical pulses, pitch, noise, duration, relative loudness, tempi, combinatory superpositions, etc., are determined by previously drawn charts. In 1981 Cage was a recipient of the prestigious Mayor's Award of Honor in N.Y. City. On March 9, 1982, his 70th birthday was celebrated anticipatorily by a 13-hour-long exhibit, "Wall-to-Wall John Cage and Friends."

WORKS: Sonata for Solo Clarinet (1933); *Imaginary Landscape* No. 1 for 2 Variable-speed Phonograph Turntables, Muted Piano, and Cymbal (1939); *A Valentine Out of Season* for Prepared Piano (1944); ballet, *The Seasons,* for Chamber Orch. (N.Y., May 13, 1947); *Sonata and Interludes* for Prepared Piano (1948); String Quartet (1950); Concerto for Prepared Piano and Chamber Orch. (1951); *Imaginary Landscape* No. 4 for 12 Radios, 24 Players, and Conductor (1951); *Musical Changes* for Piano, according to the Chinese book of numbers *I Ching* (1951); *Water Music* for Pianist, Radio Receiver, and Drums (1952); *4'33",* tacet piece for Piano (unplayed by David Tudor in Woodstock, N.Y., Aug. 29, 1952); *Music for Piano 4–84* for 4, 5, 6 . . . , 84 Pianists (1953–56); *Winter Music* for 1, 2, 3, 4 . . . , 20 Pianists (1957); Concerto for Piano and Orch. (N.Y., May 15, 1958); *Fontana Mix* for 10 Transparencies permutated quaquaversally in 3 or more dimensions (N.Y., April 26, 1959); *Music for Amplified Toy Pianos* (Middletown, Conn., Feb. 25, 1960); *Cartridge Music* (Cologne, Oct. 6, 1960); *Atlas Eclipticalis* for Orch. (Montreal, Aug. 3, 1961); 0'00", silent piano piece (listened to but unheard, Tokyo, Oct. 24, 1962); *Cheap Imitation* for Piano, a memorized set of Erik Satie's pieces (1969; also for 24, 25, 26 . . . , 95 Pianists); *Reunion* for Electronic Chessboard (Toronto, March 5, 1968); *Renga* with *Apartment House 1776* for 2 Synchronized Orchs. and 4 Vocalists, a bicentennial work (Boston Symph., Sept. 29, 1976); *HPSCHD* ("harpsichord minus the vowels and the r's"), a multimedia event, with Lejaren Hiller, realized for 7 Amplified Harpsichords, Tapes, Slides, and Films programmed by a Computer with 52 Projectors and 52-channeled Tapes (Urbana, Ill., May 16, 1969); *32 études australes* for Piano (1970); *Lecture on the Weather* for 12 Vocalists reading excerpts from the writings of Thoreau, accompanied by electronically realized Wind, Rain, and Thunder (1975); *Roaratorio, An Irish Circus on Finnegans Wake* for 8 Irish Musicians spaced around the audience (1980); *Dance* for 4 Orchs. and 4 Conductors (Cabrillo Festival, Aptos, Calif., Aug.

22, 1982); a work played pizzicato on 8 Cactus Plants, as part of the television program "Good Morning, Mr. Orwell" (1984).

PUBLICATIONS: *Silence* (Middletown, Conn., 1961); *A Year from Monday* (Middletown, 1967); *Notations* (N.Y., 1969); *Writings '67–'72* (Middletown, 1973); *Empty Words: Writings '63–'78* (London, 1980); *For the Birds: John Cage in Conversation with Daniel Charles* (Boston and London, 1981).

BIBLIOGRAPHY: R. Kostelanetz, ed., *John Cage,* a collection of essays (N.Y., 1970); M. Nyman, *Experimental Music: Cage and Beyond* (London, 1974); P. Griffiths, *Cage* (London, 1981); Robert Stevenson, "John Cage on His 70th Birthday: West Coast Background," *Inter-American Music Review* (Fall 1982).

Cagnoni, Antonio, Italian composer; b. Godiasco, near Voghera, Feb. 8, 1828; d. Bergamo, April 30, 1896. He studied at the Milan Cons. (1842–47), where 3 of his operas were produced: *Rosalia di San Miniato* (1845), *I due Savoja* (1846), and his most successful work, *Don Bucefalo* (1847). From 1852–73 he was maestro di cappella in the Cathedral of Vigevano; from 1873, in the Cathedral of Novarra; from 1887, in Santa Maria Maggiore in Bergamo. From 1848–74 he brought out 15 operas in various Italian theaters.

Cahier, Mme. Charles (née Sarah Jane Layton-Walker), distinguished American contralto; b. Nashville, Jan. 8, 1870; d. Manhattan Beach, Calif., April 15, 1951. She studied in Paris with Jean de Reszke and in Vienna with Gustav Walter. She made her operatic debut in Nice (1904); married Charles Cahier on March 30, 1905. She was engaged at the Vienna Hofoper, and toured Europe and America for many years as a concert artist; later she taught at the Curtis Inst. of Music in Philadelphia. Her repertoire included Carmen, and Wagnerian contralto roles.

Cahn-Speyer Rudolf, Austrian conductor and musicologist; b. Vienna, Sept. 1, 1881; d. Florence, Dec. 25, 1940. He studied chemistry and music in Vienna; then in Leipzig and Munich; graduated from the Univ. of Munich in 1908 with the dissertation *Franz Seydelmann als dramatischer Komponist* (Leipzig, 1909). He began conducting in Kiel (1908); subsequently conducted in Hamburg (1909–11); taught in Berlin; became conductor of the Budapest Volksoper (1913). In 1933 he left Germany to live in Italy. He publ. *Zur Opernfrage; das Wesen der Oper und ihre Entwickelung in der Gegenwart* (Leipzig, 1913); and *Handbuch des Dirigierens* (1919).

Cahn, Sammy, American song composer; b. New York, June 18, 1913. He played violin in variety shows and organized a dance band; in 1940 he went to Hollywood and wrote film scores. In 1955 he started a music publishing company. His tune *High Hopes* became J.F. Kennedy's campaign song in 1960. Among his film title songs were *Three Coins in the Fountain, Pocketful of Miracles,* and *Come*

Blow Your Horn. He publ. *The Songwriter's Rhyming Dictionary* (N.Y.,1983).

Caillet, Lucien, brilliant orch. arranger; b. Dijon, France, May 22, 1891. He studied at the Dijon Cons. (graduated 1913); and with Paul Fauchet, Georges Caussade, and Gabriel Pares; settled in the U.S. in 1916, living first in Pennsylvania and later in California. He made a new orch. setting of Mussorgsky's *Pictures at an Exhibition* (1937), and of numerous other pieces. His own orch. compositions include *Memories of Stephen Foster* (1935); *Strains from Erin* (1936); variations on the theme *Pop! Goes the Weasel* (1938); many scores for Hollywood motion pictures.

Caix d'Hervelois, Louis de, French viola da gamba player; b. Amiens, c.1680; d. Paris, 1760. He probably studied with Sainte-Colombe and Marin Marais; was active as a musician in the court of the Duc d'Orléans. His works include 5 vols. of *Pièces de viole* (1725–52) and 2 vols. of *Pièces pour la flûte* (1726, 1731). Some of these compositions have been edited by Karl Schroeder; various arrangements of his viola da gamba pieces have been made for contemporary instruments.

Calabro, Louis, American composer and conductor; b. Brooklyn, Nov. 1, 1926. He studied with Persichetti at the Juilliard School of Music, graduating in 1952; in 1955 was appointed to the faculty at Bennington College, Vt. In 1971 he founded the Sage City Symph. in North Bennington. He received Guggenheim fellowships in 1954 and 1959 and National Endowment of the Arts fellowships in 1973 and 1976.
WORKS: Concerto for String Orch. (1950); *Statement* for Orch. (1951); Piano Concerto (1953); 3 symphs. (1956; for Strings, 1957; 1959–60); *10 Short Pieces* for Strings (1961); *Dadacantatadada* for Blues Singer and Orch. (1964); *Epitaphs* for Chorus and Orch. (1967); *Latitude 15.09° N (Longitude 108.5° E),* oratorio (1970); *Triple Concerto* for 3 Cellos and Orch. (1971); *The Young Pianist's Concertino* for Piano and Strings (1972); *Threnody* for String Orch. (1973); *Voyage,* Bicentennial work for Chorus and Orch. (1974–75); *Invention* for Symph. Band (1975); *Lunarlied* for Chorus and Strings (1976); *Eos* for English Horn and Strings (1977); trio for Clarinet, Cello, and Piano (1949); Piano Trio (1952); Violin Sonata (1953); 2 string quartets (1954, 1968); *Bodas de Sangre* for Piano, Violin, Clarinet, Cello, Timpani, and Guitar (1955); solo cello sonata (1956); *Dynamogeny* for Viola and Piano (1958); *Co-Instances—Music without Order* for Piano, Cello, Violin, and Clarinet (1958); *Environments* for 12 Brasses and Solo Clarinet (1969); *Memoirs: Part One* for Bassoon and Percussion (1973); *3 Pieces* for Solo Piccolo (1973); *Rare Birds* for Narrator and Flute (1976); *Kusehani* for 12 Players (1976); Piano Sonatina (1952); Piano Sonata (1954); *Diversities* for Piano (1966); *Piano Variations* (1968); songs.

Caland, Elisabeth, Dutch-German piano teacher and music editor; b. Rotterdam, Jan. 13, 1862; d. Berlin, Jan. 26, 1929. She studied piano with Deppe in Berlin. Her piano manuals, most of which have gone through several editions, include the authoritative exposition of Deppe's method, *Die Deppesche Lehre des Klavierspiels* (Stuttgart, 1897; in Eng. as *Artistic Piano-Playing,* 1903; also in French, Dutch, and Russian); *Technische Ratschläge für Klavierspieler* (Magdeburg, 1897; also in Eng. and Russian); *Die Ausnützung der Kraftquellen beim Klavierspiel* (Magdeburg, 1905); *Das künstlerische Klavierspiel in seinen physiologisch-physikalischen Vorgängen* (1910); *Praktische Lehrgänge für künstlerisches Klavierspiel* (Magdeburg, 1912); *Anhaltspunkte zur Kontrolle zweckmässiger Armbewegungen beim künstlerischen Klavierspiel* (1919).

Calcaño, José Antonio, Venezuelan composer and musicologist; b. Caracas, March 23, 1900; d. there, Sept. 11, 1980. After studies at the Escuela Superior de Música in Caracas, he went to Bern, Switzerland, for further training. Returning to Venezuela, he was appointed to the faculty of the Univ. of Caracas and organized an indigenous Coro Creole there; later taught at the Escuela de Música Padre Sojo. His works include a ballet, *Mirando en Rusia,* a Symph., 2 string quartets, choruses; he also arranged classical music for various ensembles, and publ. several informative books, among them a historical survey of music in Caracas, *400 años de música Caraqueña* (Caracas, 1967).

Caldara, Antonio, Italian cellist and composer; b. Venice, 1670; d. Vienna, Dec. 26, 1736. He was a pupil of Legrenzi; was maestro di cappella da chiesa e dal teatro to Ferdinando Carlo in Mantua (1699–1707); from 1709 served as maestro di cappella to Prince Ruspoli in Rome; on April 1, 1716, he was appointed assistant choirmaster to J.J. Fux in Vienna. He also lived in Milan, Bologna, and Madrid. Caldara composed 90 operas and sacred dramas, 43 oratorios, about 30 masses, other church music, chamber music, etc. A selection of his church music is reprinted in Denkmäler der Tonkunst in Österreich, 26 (formerly 13.i; ed. by Mandyczewski); other vocal works (cantatas, madrigals, and canons) are in vol. 75 (formerly 39; ed. by Mandyczewski, with introduction and explanatory notes by Geiringer); *Dafne,* ed. by C. Schneider and R. John, is in vol. 91; further vocal works are reprinted in *Musique d'église des XVIIe et XVIIIe siècles* (ed. by Charles Pineau); a madrigal and 18 canons were ed. by Geiringer in *Das Chorwerk* (1933); 28 3-part instrumental canons from Caldara's *Divertimenti musicali* are in *Spielkanons* (Wolfenbüttel, 1928).
BIBLIOGRAPHY: A. Schering on Caldara's 32 oratorios, in his *Geschichte des Oratoriums* (1911); A. Gmeyner, dissertation on Caldara's 87 operas (Vienna, 1927); C. Gray, "Antonio Caldara (1670–1736)," *Musical Times* (March 1929); U. Kirkendele, *Antonio Caldara: Sein Leben und seine venezianische-römischen Oratorien* (Graz, 1966); R. Freeman, "La verità nella ripetizione," *Musical Quar-*

terly (April 1968); Mario Rinaldi, "Contributo alla futura biografia di Antonio Caldara," *Rivista Musicale Italiana* (Sept.–Oct. 1970).

Caldicott, Alfred James, English conductor and composer; b. Worcester, Nov. 26, 1842; d. near Gloucester, Oct. 24, 1897. He received a B.M. degree at Cambridge (1878); was a prof. at the Royal College of Music in London (1883–1892). His works include the cantatas *The Widow of Nain* (1881) and *A Rhine Legend* for Women's Voices (1883); 13 operettas; numerous glees, especially the popular *Humpty Dumpty* (1878).

Caldwell, Sarah, remarkable American opera conductor; b. Maryville, Mo., March 6, 1924. She learned to play violin at home and appeared at local events as a child; then enrolled as a psychology student at the Univ. of Arkansas. She undertook serious violin study at the New England Cons. in Boston with Richard Burgin, concertmaster of the Boston Symph. Orch.; also studied viola with Georges Fourel. In 1947 she was engaged by Boris Goldovsky, head of the opera dept. at the New England Cons., as his assistant, which proved a valuable apprenticeship for her. In 1952 she was engaged as head of the Boston Univ. opera workshop. In 1957 she formed her own opera company in Boston, called Opera Group; this was the beginning of an extraordinary career, in which she displayed her peculiar acumen in building up an operatic enterprise with scant musical and financial resources. In 1965 she changed the name of her enterprise to Opera Co. of Boston, making use of a former vaudeville theater for her performances. In most of her productions she acts as producer, conductor, administrator, stage director, scenery designer, and publicity manager. Among her productions were *La Traviata* and *Falstaff* by Verdi, *Benvenuto Cellini* by Berlioz, *Don Quichotte* by Massenet, Bellini's *I Capuleti ed i Montecchi,* and several modern operas, among them Prokofiev's *War and Peace,* Schoenberg's *Moses and Aron,* Alban Berg's *Lulu,* Luigi Nono's *Intolleranza,* and *Montezuma* by Roger Sessions. She produced the American premieres in Boston of *The Ice Breaks* by Typpett and *The Soldiers* by Zimmermann. She was able to induce famous singers to lend their participation, among them Beverly Sills, Marilyn Horne, Tito Gobbi, Nicolai Gedda, and Placido Domingo. Because of her imposing corpulence (c.300 lbs.) she conducts performances sitting in a large armchair. Sober-minded critics heap praise on Sarah Caldwell for her musicianship, physical and mental energy, imagination, and a sort of genius for opera productions. On Jan. 13, 1976, she became the first woman to conduct at the Metropolitan Opera (in a perf. of *La Traviata*).

Calegari, Antonio, Italian composer and music theorist; b. Padua, Feb. 17, 1757; d. there, July 22, 1828. He studied with Scalabrin and Betoni in Venice; was active as a composer there and in Padua. He was a conductor at the Teatro Nuovo in Padua (c.1790–96); spent the last years of his life, from 1801, as organist at the Church of San Antonio in Padua. He brought out 3 operas in Venice: *Le Sorelle rivali* (1784), *L'amor soldato* (1786), and *Il matrimonio scoperto* (1789); the authorship of all 3 is dubious, the last perhaps attributable to Luigi Caligari. Antonio Calegari publ. a curious treatise on composition, *Gioco pittagorico musicale* (Venice, 1801), which was republ. in Paris, during his residence there, as *L'Art de composer la musique sans en connaître les éléments* (1802). A harmonic system, *Sistema armonico* (1829), and a vocal method, *Modi generali del canto* (1836), were publ. posthumously.

Calkin, John Baptiste, English pianist, organist, and composer; b. London, March 16, 1827; d. there, April 15, 1905. He studied music with his father; then was active as an organist in several churches in London; also taught at the Guildhall School of Music. He wrote many sacred choruses and organ pieces.

Callaerts, Joseph, Belgian organist and composer; b. Antwerp, Aug. 22, 1838; d. there, March 3, 1901. He studied with Lemmens at the Brussels Cons.; was organist of the Jesuit College and later of the Antwerp Cathedral; from 1876 taught organ at the Music School in Antwerp. He composed a comic opera, *Le Retour imprévu* (Antwerp, 1889); Symph. (1879); Piano Trio (1882); sacred music, organ pieces, piano pieces.

Callas, Maria, celebrated American soprano; b. New York, Dec. 3, 1923; d. Paris, Sept. 16, 1977. Her real name was **Maria Anna Sofia Cecilia Kalogeropoulos;** her father was a Greek immigrant. The family went back to Greece when she was 13; she studied voice at the Royal Academy of Music in Athens with the Spanish soprano Elvira de Hidalgo, and made her debut as Santuzza in the school production of *Cavalleria rusticana,* in Nov. 1938. Her first professional appearance was in a minor role in Suppé's *Boccaccio* at the Royal Opera in Athens when she was 16; her first major role, as Tosca, was there in July 1942. She went back to N.Y. in 1945; auditioned for the Metropolitan Opera Co. and was offered a contract, but decided to go to Italy, where she made her operatic debut in the title role of *La Gioconda* (Verona, Aug. 3, 1947). She was encouraged in her career by the famous conductor Tullio Serafin, who engaged her to sing Isolde and Aida at various Italian productions. In 1950 she was accepted as a member of the staff of La Scala in Milan. She was greatly handicapped by her absurdly excessive weight (210 lbs); by a supreme effort of will she slimmed down to 135 pounds; with her classical Greek profile and penetrating eyes, she made a striking impression on the stage; in the tragic role of Medea in Cherubini's opera she mesmerized the audience by her dramatic representation of pity and terror. Some critics opined that she lacked a true bel canto quality in her voice and that her technique was defective in coloratura, but her power of interpretation was such that she was soon acknowledged to be one of the greatest dramatic singers of the century. Her personal life was as tempestuous as that of any prima donna of the bygone era. In 1949 she married the Italian industrialist Meneghini (d. Jan. 20, 1981), who became her manager, but they separated 10 years later. Her romance with the Greek shipping magnate Aristotle Onassis was a recurrent topic of sensational gossip. Given to outbursts of temper, she made newspaper headlines when she walked off the stage following some altercation, or failed to appear altogether at scheduled performances, but her eventual return to the stage was all the more eagerly welcomed by her legion of admirers. Perhaps the peak of her success was her appearance as Norma at the Metropolitan on Oct. 29, 1956; then again she quit the company as a result of disagreement with the management; but once more an accommodation was reached, and she sang Violetta (N.Y., Feb. 6, 1958); she left the company later in 1956; eventually returned to sing Tosca in 1965, after which she abandoned the stage altogether. In 1971 she gave a seminar on opera at the Juilliard School of Music, and her magic worked even in the novel capacity as instructor; her classes were enthusiastically received by the students. In 1974 she went on a concert tour with the tenor Giuseppe di Stefano; then she returned to Europe. She died suddenly of a heart attack in her Paris apartment. Her body was cremated; her ashes were scattered on the Aegean Sea. A radio commentator's characterization of Callas was that "If an orgasm could sing, it would sound like Maria Callas." Pleonastically speaking, she was an incarnation of carnality.

BIBLIOGRAPHY: E. Gara and R. Hauert, *Maria Callas* (Geneva, 1957; in Eng., London, 1958); E. Callas, *My Daughter Maria Callas* (as told to L.G. Blochman; N.Y., 1960); G. Jellinek, *Callas* (N.Y., 1960); M.T. Picchetti and M. Teglia, *El arte de María Callas* (Buenos Aires, 1969); S. Galatopoulos, *Callas—La Divina: Art that Conceals Art* (Elmsford, N.Y., 1970); John Ardoin, *The Callas Legacy* (analysis of recordings; N.Y., 1977); P.-J. Remy, *Maria Callas: A Tribute* (N.Y., 1978); A. Stassinopoulos, *Maria Callas: The Woman behind the Legend* (London, 1980; N.Y., 1981); G.B. Meneghini (with Renzo Allegri), *My Wife Maria Callas* (N.Y., 1982).

Callaway, Paul (Smith), American organist, choirmaster, and conductor; b. Atlanta, Ill., Aug. 16, 1909. He attended Westminster College in Fulton, Mo. (1927–29); studied organ with Tertius Noble in N.Y. (1930–35), with Leo Sowerby in Chicago, and with Marcel Dupré in Paris. He served as organist and choirmaster at St. Thomas's Chapel in N.Y. (1930–35); then at St. Mark's Chapel in Grand Rapids, Mich.; in 1939 he began his 38-year regime as principal organist and music director of the Washington, D.C., National Cathedral, with an interruption during his service in the U.S. Army (1942–46). In 1941 he founded the Cathedral Choral Society; in 1962 was one of the founders of the College of Church Musicians at the Washington Cathedral, leading it until 1969. He was also music director of the Opera Society of Washington (1956–67) and directed the Lake George, N.Y., Opera Festival (1967–77); appeared as guest conductor of the National Symph. Orch. in Washington; conducted the notable first performances at the Library of Congress of Menotti's work *The Unicorn, the Gorgon, and the Manticore* (1956) and of Dallapiccola's *5 canti* (1956). Owing to his close affiliation with the Anglican Church, he was engaged to conduct the Cathedral Choir at Westminster Abbey in London during the celebration of the 900th anniversary of the Abbey (1966). On Nov. 30, 1977, he was made an honorary Member of the Order of the British Empire in ceremonies at the British Embassy in Washington. After becoming organist and choirmaster emeritus of the Washington Cathedral in 1977, he served on the faculty of the Univ. of Illinois at Carbondale, periodically returning to Washington to conduct the Cathedral Choral Society.

Callcott, John Wall, English organist and composer; b. London, Nov. 20, 1766; d. Bristol, May 15, 1821. Early in life he developed a particular talent for composing glees and catches; won 3 prize medals at a contest of the Catch Club of London (1785) for his catch *O Beauteous Fair;* a canon, *Blessed Is He;* and a glee, *Dull Repining Sons of Care.* He received his Mus.Bac. and Mus.Doc. from Oxford (1785, 1800); was a co-founder of the Glee Club (1787). During Haydn's visit to London in 1791, Callcott took a few lessons with him and wrote a symph. in imitation of his style. His mind gave way from overwork on a projected biographical dictionary of musicians, and he was institutionalized just before he reached the quirky letter Q. He recovered; but not sufficiently to continue his work, and was released in 1812. In addition to numerous glees, catches, and canons, he wrote *A Musical Grammar* (London, 1806), a standard elementary textbook that went through numerous editions in England and America. A 3-vol. collection of glees, catches, and canons, with a biographical memoir, was publ. posthumously by his son-in-law, William Horsley (London, 1824).

Calleja, Gómez Rafael, Spanish composer; b. Burgos, Dec. 23, 1874; d. Madrid, Feb. 7, 1938. He studied at the Madrid Cons.; subsequently conducted in Spain, Portugal, and South America. He composed about 300 revues and musical comedies, including *El Príncipe Carnaval* and *El mozo crúo;* publ. collections of folk songs from Santander, Galicia, and Asturias.

Calligaris, Sergio, Argentinian-Italian pianist; b. Rosario, Jan. 22, 1941. He studied with Jorge Fanelli in Buenos Aires; in 1964 he went to the U.S. and became a student of Arthur Loesser at the Cleveland Inst. of Music; then went to Italy, where he took lessons with Guido Agosti at the Santa Cecilia Academy in Rome; in 1970–72 he taught at the Calif. State Univ., Los Angeles; then returned to Italy, and in 1974 became an Italian citizen; also in 1974 he was appointed a prof. of piano at the Cons. of San Pietro a Majella in Naples. His playing is distinguished by a romantic élan and virtuoso technique.

Callinet, François, French organ manufacturer; b. Ladoix, Bourgogne, Oct. 1, 1754; d. Rouffach, Alsace, May 21, 1820. He was apprenticed to K. Riepp in Dijon, and later worked with Joseph Rabiny, with whom he became associated in organ building in 1786. His 2 sons, **Joseph** and **Claude-Ignace,** and the latter's son **Louis-François** carried on the family trade; **Louis Callinet,** a nephew of the founder of the firm, joined Daublaine & Co., and continued organ manufacture.

Callinet, Louis, French organ manufacturer; b. Weiler Ladoix, Bourgogne, April 19, 1786; d. Paris, Aug. 1, 1845. He was a nephew of **François Callinet.** He entered the partnership with Daublaine, who attended to the commercial interests of the firm known as Daublaine & Callinet, but broke with him and destroyed all the instruments that he had built.

Calloway, Cab, black American jazz singer; b. Rochester, N.Y., Dec. 25, 1907. He became a proponent of scat singing, characterized by nonsense syllabization and rapid glossolalia with the melodic line largely submerged under an asymmetric inundation of rhythmic heterophony. He led bands and appeared in the movies; also compiled *Hepster's Dictionary,* listing jazz terms (1938), and publ. an informal autobiography, *Of Minnie the Moocher and Me* (N.Y., 1976).

Calvé, Emma, famous French soprano; b. Décazeville (Aveyron), Aug. 15, 1858; d. Millau, Jan. 6, 1942. She studied voice with Puget in Paris and with Marchesi and Laborde; made her operatic debut as Marguerite in Gounod's *Faust* at the Théâtre de la Monnaie in Brussels, on Sept. 23, 1881; then sang at the Opéra-Comique in Paris 3 years later. She sang at La Scala in 1887. In 1892 she appeared at Covent Garden in London. She made her American debut at the Metropolitan Opera House on Nov. 29, 1893, and remained on its staff until 1904; her greatest role was that of Carmen. Subsequently she made sporadic, but successful, appearances in Europe and America; after 1910 she sang mainly in recitals. Calvé's biography was publ. in 1902 (A. Gallus, *Emma Calvé, Her Artistic Life*), and so great was the aura of her successes that her life was made the subject of a novel by Gustav Kobbé, *Signora, A Child of the Opera House* (N.Y., 1903). She publ. an autobiography, in Eng., *My Life* (N.Y., 1922); toward the end of her life she publ. an additional vol. of memoirs, *Sous tous les ciels j'ai chanté* (Paris, 1940). Forty of her letters, along with an extended biographical sketch, appear in A. Lebois, "Hommages à Emma Calvé (1858–1942)," *Annales, Faculté des Lettres de Toulouse* (Sept. 1967).

Calvisius, Sethus (real name, **Seth Kallwitz**), theorist; son of a poor peasant at Gorsleben, Thuringia; b. Feb. 21, 1556; d. Leipzig, Nov. 24, 1615. He supported himself while studying in the Gymnasia of Fran-

kenhausen and Magdeburg, and the univs. at Helmstadt and Leipzig. In Leipzig he became music director at the Paulinerkirche (1581); from 1582–92 he was cantor at Schulpforta, then cantor of the Thomasschule at Leipzig, and in 1594 became music director at the Thomaskirche and Nicolaikirche there. Calvisius was not only a musician, but a scholar of high attainments. His writings are valuable sources: *Melopoeia seu melodiae condendae ratio* (1582; 2nd ed., 1592); *Compendium musicae practicae pro incipientibus* (1594; 3rd ed. as *Musicae artis praecepta nova et facillima,* 1612); *Harmoniae cantionum ecclesiasticarum a M. Luthero et aliis viris piis Germaniae compositarum 4 voc.* (1596); *Exercitationes musicae duae* (1600); *Auserlesene teutsche Lieder* (1603); *Exercitatio musicae tertia* (1611); *Biciniorum libri duo* (1612).

BIBLIOGRAPHY: K. Benndorf, "Sethus Calvisius als Musiktheoretiker," *Vierteljahrsschrift für Musikwissenschaft* (1894); R. Wustmann, *Musikgeschichte von Leipzig,* vol. I (1909); G. Pietzch, "Sethus Calvisius und Joh. Kepler," *Die Musikpflege* I/8 (1930).

Calvocoressi, Michel Dimitri, eminent writer on music; b. (of Greek parents) Marseilles, Oct. 2, 1877; d. London, Feb. 1, 1944. He studied music in Paris, but was mostly autodidact; also pursued the social sciences. In 1914 he settled in London. He wrote music criticism and correspondences for French and other journals. He mastered the Russian language and became an ardent propagandist of Russian music; made excellent translations into English and French of Russian and German songs. Among his books are *La Musique russe* (Paris, 1907); *The Principles and Methods of Musical Criticism* (London, 1923; revised 1933); *Musical Taste and How to Form It* (London, 1925); *Musicians' Gallery: Music and Ballet in Paris and London* (London, 1933); also monographs on Liszt (Paris, 1906), Mussorgsky (Paris, 1908), Glinka (Paris, 1911), Schumann (Paris, 1912), Debussy (London, 1941); a new extensive biography of Mussorgsky was posthumously publ. (London, 1946). With Gerald Abraham he publ. the valuable *Masters of Russian Music* (London, 1936).

Calzabigi, Ranieri di, Italian poet and music theorist; b. Livorno, Dec. 23, 1714; d. Naples, July 1795. In 1750 he went to Paris, proceeded to Brussels in 1760; from 1761 until 1772 he remained in Vienna, and was in Pisa by 1775. He engaged in polemics regarding the relative merits of French and Italian operas; lent energetic support to Gluck in his ideas of operatic reform. He wrote for Gluck the libretti of *Orfeo, Alceste,* and *Paride ed Elena.* In 1780 he returned to Italy. He publ. *Dissertazione su le poesie drammatiche del Sig. Abate Pietro Metastasio* (1755), a controversial work concerning Metastasio and Hasse.

BIBLIOGRAPHY: Heinrich Welti, "Gluck und Calzabigi," *Vierteljahrsschrift für Musikwissenschaft* (1891); Ghino Lazzeri, *La vita e l'opera letteraria di Ranieri Calzabigi* (1907); J.-G. Prod'-

homme, "Deux Collaborateurs italiens de Gluck," *Rivista Musicale Italiana* (1916); R. Haas, *Gluck in Durazzo* (1924); H. Hammelmann and M. Rose, "New Light on Calzabigi and Gluck," *Musical Times* (June 1969).

Camarate, Salvador (a.k.a. **"Tutti"**), American composer and conductor of popular music; b. Glen Ridge, N.J., May 11, 1913. He studied composition at the Juilliard School of Music, N.Y., with Wagenaar and Jan Meyerowitz; earned his living by playing trumpet in dance bands around N.Y.; then was music director for Walt Disney Co., in Hollywood. He wrote a number of catchy tunes, among them *Hollywood Pastime* and *Moonlight Masquerade.*

Cambert, Robert, the first French opera composer, preceding Lully; b. Paris, c.1628; d. London, 1677. He was a pupil of Chambonnières. His first venture on the lyric stage was *La Pastorale,* written by Perrin and successfully produced at the Château d'Issy in 1659; it was followed by *Ariane, ou Le Mariage de Bacchus* (rehearsed in 1661) and *Adonis* (1662; not perf.; MS lost). In 1669 Perrin received letters patent for establishing the Académie Royale de Musique (the national operatic theater, now the Grand Opéra); he brought out, in collaboration with Cambert, the opera *Pomone* (1671); another opera, *Les Peines et les plaisirs de l'amour,* was written, and produced in Paris in March 1671, before Lully secured the patent. In 1673, Cambert's disappointment drove him to London, where he became a bandmaster.
BIBLIOGRAPHY: A. Pougin, *Les Vrais Créateurs de l'opéra français, Perrin et Cambert* (Paris, 1881).

Cambini, Giuseppe Maria (Gioacchino), Italian composer; b. Livorno, Feb. 13, 1746; d. Bicêtre, Dec. 29, 1825. He was a prolific composer of instrumental works, writing over 60 symphs. within a few years; also 149 string quartets; ballets, operas, and oratorios. He died in an almshouse.
BIBLIOGRAPHY: D.L. Trimpert, *Die "Quatuors concertants" von Giuseppi Cambini* (Tutzing, 1967); H. Bol, "Een rivaal van Mozart te Parijs, G.G. Cambini (1746–1825)," *Mens en Melodie* (March 1968).

Cambreling, Sylvain, French conductor; b. Amiens, July 2, 1948. He received his musical training at the Paris Cons.; in 1975 he became assistant conductor of the Orch. de Lyon; also conducted opera in Lyon; beginning with the 1979–80 season he appeared regularly as a conductor at the Paris Opéra. In 1981 he became joint music director (with John Pritchard) of the Théâtre Royal de la Monnaie in Brussels. He also conducted at the Glyndebourne Festival, the Frankfurt Opera, La Scala in Milan, in the U.S., and in Canada.

Camden, Archie, English bassoon virtuoso; b. Newark-upon-Trent, March 9, 1888; d. Wheathampstead, Feb. 16, 1979. He studied at the Royal Manchester College of Music. In 1906 he joined the Hallé Orch. of Manchester, where he played first bassoon from 1914 to 1933; during the same period he taught bassoon at the Royal Manchester College of Music. In 1933 he joined the BBC Symph. Orch.; then played with the Royal Phil. (1946–47); finally was a member of the London Mozart Players (1954–71). He did much to establish the bassoon as a solo instrument; his performances of works by Vivaldi, Mozart, and Weber were outstanding.

Cameron, Basil, English conductor; b. Reading, Aug. 18, 1884; d. Leominster, June 26, 1975. He studied music in York with Tertius Noble; then at the Berlin Hochschule für Musik, 1902–6; also took a course in composition with Max Bruch. Returning to England, he sought to obtain a conducting position by Germanizing his name as **Basil Hindenberg,** seeing that German conductors dominated the field in England, but changed it back to his real name when England went to war with Germany in 1914. He served in the British army and was wounded in action in 1918. He conducted the Hastings Municipal Orch. (1923–30); then was guest conductor of the San Francisco Symph. Orch.; from 1932 to 1938 he was conductor of the Seattle Symph. Orch.; during his tenure he played many new works by modern composers. He belonged to the category of "objective" conductors more interested in the music itself than in his individual communication, an attitude that in the end hampered his American success. He filled in a few engagements in Europe and eventually returned to London, where he was made a Commander of the Order of the British Empire in 1957.

Cametti, Alberto, Italian musicologist; b. Rome, May 5, 1871; d. there, June 1, 1935. He studied at the Cons. of the Santa Cecilia Academy; was a member of the commission appointed by Pope Pius X to investigate the condition of church music. In April 1914 he publ. a full description and complete thematic catalogue in the *Rivista Musicale Italiana* (XXI, 2) of 43 compositions for one to 3 voices with basso continuo (chiefly arias) by Orazio Michi, which he had discovered in various Italian libraries, and which prove Michi to have been one of the earliest and most important Roman masters of the monodic style.
WRITINGS: *Cenni biografici di G.P. da Palestrina* (Milan, 1894); *Il testamento di Jacobella Pierluigi* (1903); *Cristina di Suezia, l'arte musicale e gli spettacoli in Roma* (1911); *Documenti inediti su Luigi Rossi* (Leipzig, 1912); *Chi era l'Ippolita del cardinale di Montalto?* (1913); *L'accademia Filarmonica Romana, 1821–60* (1924); *I musici di Campidoglio dal 1524 al 1818* (1925); *La musica teatrale a Roma cento anni fa (1816–26)* (1928); *Dove fu sepolto il Palestrina?* (1929); *Bibliogr. delle opere di Costanzo Festa* (1931); biographical studies of Felice Anerio (1915), Giacomo Carissimi (1917), G.B. Costanzi (1924), Leonardo Vinci (1924), Ruggiero Giovanelli (1925), etc.; several valuable essays in *Rivista Musicale Italiana:* "Bellini a Roma" (1900); "Donizetti a Roma" (1904–7); "Mozart a

Camidge – Campanini

Roma" (1907); "Frescobaldi a Roma" (1908); etc.

Camidge, Matthew, English organist; b. York, May 25, 1764; d. there, Oct. 23, 1844. He was the son of **John Camidge, Sr.,** whom he succeeded at the Yorkminster on Nov. 11, 1799, and at St. Michaelle-' Belfry on July 2, 1801. He publ. *Cathedral Music; 24 Original Psalm- and Hymn-tunes;* piano sonatas and marches; a *Method of Instruction in Music by Questions and Answers;* etc.

Cammarano, Salvatore, Italian librettist; b. Naples, March 19, 1801; d. there, July 17, 1852. He wrote prose dramas, which were produced in Florence; after 1834 he devoted himself to writing opera libretti: Donizetti's *Lucia di Lammermoor;* Pacini's *Reggente, Buondelmonte, Saffo, Merope,* etc.; Verdi's *Alzira, Battaglia di Legnano, Luisa Miller,* and *Il Trovatore.*
BIBLIOGRAPHY: T. Mantovani, "Salvatore Cammarano," *Musica d'Oggi* (1926).

Camp, John Spencer, American organist and composer; b. Middletown, Conn., Jan. 30, 1858; d. Hartford, Conn., Feb. 1, 1946. After receiving an M.A. from Wesleyan Univ. (1881), he studied in N.Y. with Dudley Buck and with Dvořák; was organist and choirmaster at various churches in Connecticut; helped found the American Guild of Organists. He wrote numerous pieces for choir, organ, piano, and orch.; also anthems and songs.

Campagnoli, Bartolommeo, renowned Italian violinist; b. Cento di Ferrara, Sept. 10, 1751; d. Neustrelitz, Germany, Nov. 6, 1827. He studied in Bologna with Dall'Occa and in Florence with Nardini; for several years gave concerts in Italy; became music director to the Duke of Kurland in Dresden (1779–97); then was concertmaster at the Gewandhaus in Leipzig (1797–1818). He made several successful concert tours while in his service; from 1797–1818 was active as a violinist in Leipzig. He composed 41 *Capricci per l'alto viola* (revised by E. Kreuz and A. Consolini as *Caprices pour le viola,* 1922); a Violin Concerto; études for violin; chamber music. He was the author of several pedagogic manuals for the violin: *Nouvelle méthode de la mécanique progressive du jeu de violon* (1791; in Eng., 1856), and *Metodo per violino* (1797; his chief work; publ. and reprinted in all European languages).
BIBLIOGRAPHY: G. Atti, *Biografia di B. Campagnoli* (Bologna, 1892).

Campana, Fabio, Italian singing teacher and composer; b. Livorno, Jan. 14, 1819; d. London, Feb. 2, 1882. He studied in Bologna; produced the operas *Caterina di Guisa* (Livorno, 1838); *Giulio d'Este* (Livorno, 1841); *Vannina d'Ornano* (Florence, 1842); *Luisa di Francia* (Rome, 1844); then went to London, where he settled as a singing teacher. His opera *Almina* was staged in London at Her Majesty's Theatre (April 26, 1860); another opera, *Es-*

meralda, was produced in St. Petersburg (Dec. 20, 1869); Patti sang the title role in its productions in Western Europe. Campana also wrote hundreds of songs.

Campanari, Giuseppe, Italian dramatic baritone, brother of **Leandro Campanari;** b. Venice, Nov. 17, 1855; d. Milan, May 31, 1927. He began his career as a cellist; played in the orch. of La Scala, and started to study singing; went to the U.S. in 1884, and played cello in the Boston Symph. Orch. until 1893, when he joined Hinrich's Opera Co. in N.Y. as a baritone; made his debut (June 15, 1893) as Tonio in *Pagliacci;* after several years at the Metropolitan Opera he devoted himself to concert work and teaching.

Campanari, Leandro, Italian violinist and conductor, brother of **Giuseppe Campanari;** b. Rovigo, Oct. 20, 1857; d. San Francisco, April 22, 1939. He studied in Padua; attended the Milan Cons., graduating in 1877; after a tour of Europe, he came to the U.S. in 1881 and settled in Boston, where he organized the Campanari String Quartet. He became a proficient conductor and was in charge of the Grand Orch. Concerts at La Scala in Milan from 1897 till 1905. In Feb. 1907 he was engaged to complete the season of the Philadelphia Orch. after the sudden illness of the regular conductor, Fritz Scheel. Campanari failed to impress the orch. or the audience, and was not reengaged.

Campanella, Michele, Italian pianist; b. Naples, June 5, 1947. He was educated at the Cons. in Naples, winning the Casella Competition while still a student there in 1966; taught at the Milan Cons. (1969–73), and subsequently made tours as soloist with the leading orchs. of Europe and the U.S.

Campanini, Cleofonte, eminent Italian-American operatic conductor, brother of the famous tenor **Italo Campanini;** b. Parma, Sept. 1, 1860; d. Chicago, Dec. 19, 1919. He studied violin at the Parma Cons. and later at the Cons. of Milan; made his conducting debut with *Carmen* at Parma (1882); conducted the first American performance of *Otello* at the N.Y. Academy of Music (April 16, 1888) while his brother, Italo, was impresario. Between 1888 and 1906, he conducted in Italy, in England, and in South America. A larger field opened to him in 1906, when Hammerstein engaged him for the new Manhattan Opera House in N.Y. Differences with Hammerstein led him to resign in 1909. In the following year he was engaged as principal conductor of the newly formed Chicago Opera Co.; in 1913 he was appointed general director, which post he held until his death. Among opera conductors he occupied a place in the first rank; he seemed to be equally at home in all styles of music. He introduced many new operas in the U.S., among them Massenet's *Hérodiade,* Debussy's *Pelléas et Mélisande,* Charpentier's *Louise,* Wolf-Ferrari's *Il Segreto di Susanna,* etc. On May 15, 1887, he married, in Florence, **Eva Tetrazzini** (sister of **Luisa Tetrazzini**).

Campanini, Italo, famous Italian tenor, brother of **Cleofonte Campanini;** b. Parma, June 30, 1845; d. Corcagno, near Parma, Nov. 22, 1896. In his early years he was an apprentice in his father's blacksmith shop; joined Garibaldi's army and was wounded in the Italian struggle for unification. Subsequently, he studied with Griffini and Lamperti; appeared at Bologna in *Lohengrin* (Nov. 1, 1871), which started him on the road to fame. He made his London debut as Gennaro in *Lucrezia Borgia* (May 4, 1872), and his American debut, also as Gennaro, at the N.Y. Academy of Music (Oct. 1, 1873). He appeared in *Faust* at the opening of the Metropolitan Opera (Oct. 22, 1883); was on its roster until 1894; was briefly active as an impresario; brought over his brother Cleofonte Campanini to conduct the American premiere of Verdi's *Otello* at the N.Y. Academy of Music (April 16, 1888).

Campbell, Aline. Pen name of **Merle Montgomery.**

Campbell, Glen (Travis), American singer of country music and guitarist; b. Delight, Ark., April 22, 1938. He began his career as a singer and guitarist; worked as a studio musician on the West Coast; subsequently went to Nashville, Tenn., where he launched a solo career in country music. He gained much success in 1967 with his performances of *Gentle on My Mind* and *By the Time I Get to Phoenix.* His other hits included *Wichita Lineman, Houston,* and *Southern Nights.*

Campbell-Tipton, Louis, American composer; b. Chicago, Nov. 21, 1877; d. Paris, May 1, 1921. He studied at Leipzig (1896–99) with Carl Reinecke and Gustav Schreck; returned to Chicago and was an instructor of theory at the Chicago Musical College; then lived in Paris. He wrote chiefly for piano (*Sonata Heroic, Sea Lyrics, The 4 Seasons,* Suite, Serenade, etc.); *Suite pastorale* for Piano and Violin; also a number of very effective songs.

Campbell-Watson, Frank, American music editor; b. New York, Jan. 22, 1898. He studied at the Leipzig Cons. with Max Reger. Returning to the U.S., he held positions as editor with various publishing firms. He made transcriptions for string orch. of Bach, Reger, Mendelssohn, and Albéniz. He was also the author of *University Course of Music Study* (1923) and *Modern Elementary Harmony* (1930); edited *International Library of Music* (piano, 14 vols.; vocal, 12 vols.; violin, 14 vols.); *La mejor música del mundo* (in Spanish, also in Portuguese; for piano, 14 vols.).

Campenhout, François van, Belgian composer, author of the Belgian national anthem; b. Brussels, Feb. 5, 1779; d. there, April 24, 1848. Beginning as violinist in the Théâtre de la Monnaie, he studied singing under Plantade, and became a fine stage tenor, appearing in Belgium, Holland, and France. He wrote 6 operas, 9 cantatas, etc. He is, however, chiefly remembered as the composer of *La Braban-çonne,* which was written during the revolution of 1830, and eventually became the national anthem of Belgium.

Campion (Campian), Thomas, English physician, also poet, composer, and dramatist; b. London, Feb. 12, 1567; d. there, March 1, 1620. He studied at Cambridge from 1581–84, residing at Peterhouse; entered Gray's Inn on April 27, 1586. He received his M.D. degree from the Univ. of Caen in France on Feb. 10, 1605. He was first called a "Doctor of Physick" in an English publication in Barnabe Barnes's *Four Books of Offices* in 1606; earlier evidence of his having studied medical science is an oblique reference of Philip Rosseter in 1601, speaking of Campion's poetry and music as "the superfluous blossoms of his deeper studies." Campion was primarily a lyric poet; his music was to enhance the beauty of the poetry by supplying unobtrusive and simple harmonies; in this he differed from such contemporaries as John Dowland, who contrived elaborate lute accompaniments.

WORKS: 3 songs (1596); *A Booke of Ayres, Set Foorth to be sung to the Lute Orpherian, and Base Violl* (1601; consists of 2 separate books, one by Campion and one by Rosseter; Campion wrote both the words and the music for his half of the work); *First and Second Books of Airs* (1613?); *Third and Fourth Books of Airs* (1617?); songs for masques at the marriages of Sir James Hay (1607), Princess Elizabeth (1613), and Robert, Earl of Somerset (1613); songs for a masque at Caversham House (1613); *Songs of Mourning* (for Prince Henry; 1613; words by Campion, music by John Coperario); *A New Way for Making Foure Parts in Counterpoint* (1618; also in Playford's *Introduction to the Skill of Musick,* with additions by Christopher Simpson, 1655 and following years). Campion also publ. *Poemata,* a vol. of Latin epigrams and elegiacs (1595; reprinted 1619), *Observations on the Art of English Poesie* (1602; condemns "the vulgar and unartificial custom of riming"), etc. The 4 books of airs and the songs from Rosseter's *Booke of Ayres* are reprinted in E.H. Fellowes, *English School of Lutenist Song-Writers.*

BIBLIOGRAPHY: A.H. Bullen, *Thomas Campion, Songs and Masques* (1903; includes comments on Campion's music by Janet Dodge); Percival Vivian's ed. of the literary works of Thomas Campion (Oxford, 1909); Miles Kastendieck, *England's Musical Poet, Thomas Campion* (Oxford, 1938); W.R. Davis, ed., *The Works of Thomas Campion; Complete Songs, Masques, and Treatises* (Garden City, N.J., 1967); S.J. London, "Thomas Campion, M.D. (1567–1620)," *New York State Journal of Medicine* (Dec. 1967); J.T. Irwin, "Thomas Campion and the Musical Emblem," *Studies in English Literature, 1500–1900* (Winter 1970); E. Lowbury, T. Salter, and A. Young, *Thomas Campion: Poet, Composer, Physician* (N.Y., 1970).

Campioni, Carlo Antonio, French-born Italian composer; b. Lunéville, Nov. 16, 1720; d. Florence, April 12, 1788. He went to Florence in 1763, and was active there as a composer of church music and maestro di cappella to the ducal court at the Cathedral of S. Maria del Fiore, and in the oratory of S. Giovanni Battista. He also publ. instrumental works among them 6 sonatas for 2 violins, which were fraudulently issued in Amsterdam as the works of Haydn, and were reprinted still under Haydn's name in Mainz in 1953. The very fact that these pieces could pass as Haydn's for 2 centuries obliquely testifies to Campioni as a highly competent composer.

Campoamor, Manuel, Argentine composer of popular songs; b. Uruguay, Nov. 7, 1877; d. Buenos Aires, April 29, 1941. His best-known melody was *Sergento Cabral* (1899).

Campoli, Alfredo, Italian-born English violinist; b. Rome, Oct. 20, 1906. He studied with his father, a prof. at the Santa Cecilia Academy in Rome; made his debut in London at the age of 10; later made appearances as a conductor of his own ensemble. After World War II he resumed his career as a violinist, appearing as soloist with many of the major orchs. of England and the Continent; he made his U.S. debut in 1953 at Carnegie Hall in N.Y.

Campora, Guiseppe, Italian tenor; b. Tortona, Sept. 30, 1923. He studied voice in Genoa and Milan; made his debut in Bari in 1949; in 1951 he joined La Scala, Milan; also sang with other Italian opera houses. He made his Metropolitan Opera debut in N.Y. as Cavaradossi on Feb. 5, 1955.

Campos-Parsi, Hector, Puerto Rican composer; b. Ponce, Oct. 1, 1922. He studied at the New England Cons. in Boston, with Nadia Boulanger in Paris (1950–53), and with Copland at Tanglewood (summers of 1949 and 1956). Returning to Puerto Rico, he developed energetic activities as a composer, poet, journalist, music critic, educator, television commentator, and concert manager.
WORKS: *Incidente,* ballet (1948); *Music for 3 Violins* (1949); String Quartet (1950); *Versiculos* for Viola Unaccompanied (1950); *Melos,* ballet (1952); *Divertimento del Sur* for Flute, Clarinet, and Strings (1953); *Annunciation,* cantata (1954); *Juan Bobo,* ballet (1957); *Madrigales* for Contralto and Strings (1959); *Rapsodia elegiaca,* in memoriam Villa-Lobos (1960); *Duo tragico* for Piano and Orch. (1965); Piano Sonata; *Petroglifos* for Piano Trio (1966); Sonatina for Violin and Piano; choruses; songs.

Campo y Zabaleta, Conrado del, Spanish violinist and composer; b. Madrid, Oct. 28, 1879; d. there, March 17, 1953. He studied at the Madrid Cons.; in 1915 became a prof. of composition there. Most of his operas were produced at the Madrid Opera House.
WORKS: Operas: *El final de Don Alvaro* (1910); *Paolo e Francesca* (1911); *La tragedia del beso* (1911); *El Avapiés* (Madrid, March 8, 1919); *La Dama desconocida; La culpa; Leonor Teller; Romeo y Julieta; Dies irae; La Malquerida; Fantochines* (1922); *La flor del agua; El arbol de los ojos* (1930); *Lola, la piconera* (1949); *El pájaro de dos colores* (1951); symph. poems: *La divina comedia; Granada; Airinos;* oriental fantasy, *Kasida; Evocación medieval* for Chorus and Orch.; 12 string quartets, of which the *Caprichos románticos* (1908) became popular.
BIBLIOGRAPHY: T. Borrás, *Conrado del Campo* (Madrid, 1954).

Campra, André, historically important French opera composer; b. Aix (Provence), Dec. 4, 1660; d. Versailles, June 14, 1744. He studied with Guillaume Poitevin; then embraced an ecclesiastical vocation; was made chaplain at Aix on May 27, 1681; served as maître de musique at St. Etienne in Toulouse from 1683–94, and at Notre Dame from 1694–1700; then became conductor at the Paris Opéra. In 1723 he received a court appointment as sous-maître with Bernier and Gervais. His operas had numerous performances in Paris.
WORKS: (all produced in Paris): *L'Europe galante,* opéra-ballet (Oct. 24, 1697); *Le Carnaval de Venise,* ballet (Jan. 20, 1699; Act 3 includes the Italian opera *Orfeo nell' inferni*); *Hésione,* tragédie lyrique (Dec. 20, 1700); *Aréthuse, ou La Vengeance de l'Amour,* tragédie lyrique (July 14, 1701); *Tancrède,* tragédie lyrique (Nov. 7, 1702); *Les Muses,* opéra-ballet (Oct. 28, 1703); *Iphigénie en Tauride,* tragédie lyrique based on the unfinished work of Desmarets (May 6, 1704); *Télémaque,* extracts from operas by Campra et al. (Nov. 11, 1704); *Alcine,* tragédie lyrique (Jan 15, 1705); *Hippodamie,* tragédie lyrique (March 6, 1708); *Les Fêtes vénitiennes,* opéra-ballet (June 17, 1710); *Idoménée,* tragédie lyrique (Jan. 12, 1712); *Les Amours de Vénus et de Mars,* ballet (Sept. 6, 1712); *Téléphe,* tragédie lyrique (Nov. 28, 1713); *Camille, Reine des volsques,* tragédie lyrique (Nov. 9, 1717); *Ballet représenté à Lion devant M. le marquis d'Harlincourt,* ballet (Lyon, May 17, 1718; not exant); *Les Ages,* opéra-ballet (Oct. 9, 1718); *Achille et Deidamie,* tragédie lyrique (Feb. 24, 1735); several divertissements (most of them not exant); 3 books of *Cantates françoises* (1708, 1714, 1728); 5 books of motets (1695–1720); Mass (1700); 2 books of Psalms (1737–38).
BIBLIOGRAPHY: A. Pougin, *André Campra* (Paris, 1861); L. de la Laurencie, "Notes sur la jeunesse d'André Campra," *Sammelbände der Internationalen Musik-Gesellschaft,* X/2 (1909); idem, "André Campra, musicien profane," *L'Année Musicale* (1913); idem, *L'Ecole française de violon de Lulli à Viotti* (1922–24); M. Barthélemy, *André Campra* (Paris, 1957); C. Castle, *The Grand Motets of André Campra* (Diss., Univ. of Michigan, 1962); J. Anthony, *The Opera-Ballet of André Campra: A Study of the First Period French Opera-Ballet* (Diss., Univ. of Southern Calif., 1964); A. Baker, *The Church Music of André Campra* (Diss., Univ. of Toronto, 1978).

Camps, Pompeyo, Argentine composer; b. Paraná,

Oct. 27, 1924. After playing piano in bands in his native town, he settled in Buenos Aires in 1947; studied with Jaime Pahissa and adopted Pahissa's "intertonal system" of convertible counterpoint. In 1964 he modified this technique by incorporating serial procedures. He is also active as a music critic.

WORKS: Piano Sonata (1954); 2 string quartets (1957, 1974); *La pendiente,* opera in one act (1959); *Fantasia* for String Orch. (1961); *The Ballad of Reading Gaol* (1964) for Men's Choir, Narrator, and Orch.; *Sinfónia para un poeta* for Baritone and Orch. (obtained first municipal prize of Buenos Aires in 1967); *Tríptico arcáico* for Flute, Viola, Cello, and Guitar (1961); *Danzas* for Percussion (1966); *Reflejos* for 13 Brasses and Percussion (1968); *Ciudad sin tregua* for String Quartet (1974); songs; piano pieces.

Camussi, Ezio, Italian composer; b. Florence, Jan. 16, 1877; d. Milan, Aug. 11, 1956. He studied in Rome with Falchi and Sgambati; later with Massenet in Paris and at the Liceo Musicale in Bologna.

WORKS: Operas: *La Dubarry* (Milan, Nov. 7, 1912); *I fuochi di San Giovanni* (Milan, 1920); *Il donzello, Scampolo* (Trieste, Feb. 22, 1925); *La principessa lontana, I Romanzeschi, Intermezzi giocosi* for Puppet Theater; for Orch: *Baletto sinfonico, Pantomima romantica, Suita romanesca, Intermezzi Goldoniani; Fantasticherie* for Small Orch.; *Festival Miniature Overture; Scene medioevali* for Violin and Orch.; songs.

Canal, Marguerite, French composer; b. Toulouse, Jan. 29, 1890; d. there, Jan. 27, 1978. She studied at the Paris Cons. with Paul Vidal; in 1920 won the Grand Prix de Rome for her symph. scene *Don Juan.* In 1919 she was appointed to the faculty of the Paris Cons. Her works include a Violin Sonata (1922); *Spleen* for Cello and Chamber Ensemble (1926); several piano pieces; about 100 songs.

Caniglia, Maria, Italian soprano; b. Naples, May 5, 1905; d. Rome, April 16, 1979. She made her debut in Turin in 1930; from 1930 to 1943 she sang at La Scala, where she attained prominence. On Nov. 24, 1938, she made her Metropolitan Opera debut in N.Y. as Aida, but remained on its staff for only one season (1938–39). At the outbreak of World War II she returned to Italy. She was married to the Italian composer **Pino Donati.**

Cannabich, Christian, German composer, violinist, and conductor; b. Mannheim, Dec. 28, 1731; d. Frankfurt, Jan. 20, 1798. He studied with Johann Stamitz in Mannheim; became a violinist in the Mannheim Orch. (1746); was sent by the Elector to Rome, where he studied with Jommelli (1750–53); he returned to Mannheim and, after Stamitz's death (1757), became first violinist of the orch.; in 1774 was director of the instrumental music; in 1778 he moved to Munich. Cannabich is usually credited with bringing the Mannheim Orch. to a degree of perfection theretofore never attained, particularly in the carefully graduated crescendo and diminuendo. He was also a prolific composer.

WORKS: Some 90 symphs.; 3 violin concertos; 45 various pieces of chamber music; a singspiel, *Azakia* (Mannheim, 1778); melodrama, *Elektra* (Mannheim, 1781); 40 ballets. In Denkmäler der Tonkunst in Bayern appear a thematic index (vol. 4), a symph. and an overture (vol. 15), and a string quartet (vol. 27); H.T. David revised one of Cannabich's symphs. for an ed. publ. by the N.Y. Public Library (1937).

BIBLIOGRAPHY: H. Hofer, *C. Cannabich* (Munich, 1921); R. Kloiber, *Die dramatischen Ballette von C. Cannabich* (Munich, 1928).

Cannon, Beekman Cox, American musicologist; b. Teaneck, N.J., Dec. 25, 1911. He studied at Yale Univ. (B.A., 1934; Ph.D., 1939). He served in the U.S. Navy during World War II, returning to teaching at Yale in 1946; received a Guggenheim fellowship in 1950. He publ. a valuable monograph, *Johann Mattheson, Spectator in Music* (Yale Univ., 1947).

Cannon, Philip, English composer; b. Paris, Dec. 21, 1929, of English-French parentage. He was educated in England; studied composition with Imogen Holst; then at the Royal College of Music in London with Gordon Jacob. He subsequently took lessons with Hindemith. After graduation from the Royal College, he was appointed lecturer on music at the Univ. of Sydney in Australia; in 1952 he joined the staff of the Royal College of Music in London. His style of composition is neo-Romantic, but adheres to Classical forms, preserving a clear sense of tonality.

WORKS: *Morvoren,* opera on a Cornish legend (London, July 15, 1964); 2 Rhapsodies for Piano (1943); String Quartet No. 1 (1944); String Trio (1945); *In the Time of the Breaking of Nations,* after Thomas Hardy, for Voice and Piano Quintet (1945); Fantasia for String Quartet (1946); Sextet for Flute, Oboe, and String Quartet (1946); Sinfonietta for Chamber Orch. (1947); *Symphonic Study: Spring* for Orch. (1949); *Songs to Delight* for Women's Chorus and Strings (1950); *Galop Parisien* for 2 Pianos (1950); Sinfonietta for Strings (1952); *5 Chansons de Femme* for Soprano and Harp (1952); *L'Enfant s'amuse,* suite for Piano (1954); *Sonatine champêtre* for Piano (1959); Sonata for 2 Pianos (1960); *Son of Science,* cantata for the Machine Age, for Boys' Voices, Chorus, Tenor, Piano, Percussion, and Strings (Aylesbury, Dec. 2, 1961); *Fanfare to Youth* for 8 Trumpets (1963); String Quartet No. 2 (1964); *Kai-kaus* (*A Persian Suite*) for Chamber Group (1965); *Lacrimae mundi* for Piano Trio (1974); *Son of Man* for Chorus and Orch. (Liverpool, June 26, 1975).

Cantelli, Guido, brilliant Italian conductor; b. Novara, April 27, 1920; d. in an airplane crash at Orly, near Paris, Nov. 24, 1956. He played in his father's military band as a boy; studied piano at the Cons. of Milan. After Italy withdrew from the war in 1943 he, among others, was sent to a German concentration camp in Stettin. After the end of the war he conducted opera at La Scala in Milan. By invitation of Toscanini, he was engaged to conduct the NBC Symph. Orch. in N.Y., making his debut on January 15, 1949, and producing an immediate impression of great excellence. Possessing an extraordinary memory, he conducted both rehearsals and performances of operatic and symph. works without score. He lost his life flying to America to conduct a series of concerts with the N.Y. Phil.

BIBLIOGRAPHY: L. Lewis, *Guido Cantelli: Portait of a Maestro* (London, 1981).

Cantelo, April, English soprano; b. Purbrook, April 2, 1928. She studied piano and voice at the Royal College of Music in London; was subsequently a member of the New English Singers and the Deller Consort; also appeared in opera with the Glyndebourne Opera and the English Opera Group. Besides opera, she also gave solo recitals.

Canteloube (de Malaret), (Marie-) Joseph, French pianist, composer, and writer on music; b. Annonay, near Tournon, Oct. 21, 1879; d. Gridny (Seine-et-Oise), Nov. 4, 1957. His name was simply Canteloube, but he added "de Malaret" after the name of his ancestral estate. He studied piano in Paris with Amélie Doetzer, a pupil of Chopin, and composition with Vincent d'Indy at the Schola Cantorum. He became an ardent collector of French folk songs and arranged and publ. many of them for voice with instrumental accompaniment. His *Chants d'Auvergne* (4 sets for Voice, with Piano or Orch., 1923–30) are frequently heard. Among his other albums, *Anthologie des chants populaires français* (4 sets, 1939–44) is a comprehensive collection of regional folk songs.

WORKS: 2 operas: *Le Mas* (1910–13; Paris Opéra, April 3, 1929) and *Vercingetorix* (1930–32; Paris Opéra, June 26, 1933); symph. poem, *Vers la princesse lointaine* (1910–11); 3 symph. sketches: *Lauriers* (Paris, Feb. 22, 1931); *Pièces françaises* for Piano and Orch. (1935); *Poème* for Violin and Orch. (1937); *Rustiques* for Oboe, Clarinet, and Bassoon (1946). He also publ. a biography of Vincent d'Indy (Paris, 1949).

Capdevielle, Pierre, French composer and pianist; b. Paris, Feb. 1, 1906; d. Bordeaux, July 9, 1969. He studied at the Paris Cons. with Gédalge and Vidal, and privately with d'Indy; composed an opera, *Les Amants captifs* (1947–50); the orch. works *Incantation pour la mort d'un jeune spartiate* (1931), *Ouverture pour le pédant joué* (1943), and *Cantate de la France retrouvée* (1946); *Fille de l'homme,* lyric tragedy (Paris Radio, Nov. 9, 1967); 3 symphs. (1936; 1942; Chamber Symph., 1953); *Epaves retrouvées,* 4 symph. tableaux (1955); *Concerto del Dispetto* for Piano and Orch. (1959); Sonata concertante for Trombone and Piano (1963); *Sonatine pastorale* for Flute and Piano; String Quartet; etc.

Cape, Safford, American-Belgian choral conductor; b. Denver, June 28, 1906; d. Brussels, March 26, 1973. He studied in Europe, principally in Brussels,

with Charles van den Borren, whose daughter he married. In 1933 he established in Brussels a music society, Pro Musica Antiqua, with which he gave numerous performances of choral and instrumental works by medieval and Renaissance composers.

Capecchi, Renato, Italian baritone; b. Cairo, Egypt, Nov. 6, 1923. He studied violin; then went to Milan to study voice. In 1950 he joined La Scala, Milan; on Nov. 24, 1951, he made his Metropolitan Opera debut in N.Y. as Germont *père* in *La Traviata,* remaining on its roster for several subsequent seasons. He also sang at Covent Garden, London, and at many of the major European festivals.

Capell, Richard, English writer on music; b. Northampton, March 23, 1885; d. London, June 21, 1954. He studied cello in London and at the Lille Cons.; was music critic for the London *Daily Mail* (1911–33); then joined the *Daily Telegraph;* during World War II was its war correspondent in the French, Greek, and Italian campaigns. From 1928–33 he was an editor of the *Monthly Musical Record;* from 1950–54 edited *Music & Letters.* In 1946 he was made an Officer of the Order of the British Empire. He publ. *Schubert's Songs* (London, 1928), a biography of Gustav Holst (London, 1928), and *Opera* (London, 1930).

Capellen, George, German music critic; b. Salzuflen, Lippe, April 1, 1869; d. Hannover, Jan. 19, 1934. He studied philosophy and law at Tübingen, Göttingen, and Berlin. He publ. "Harmonik und Melodik bei Richard Wagner," *Bayreuther Blätter* (1901); *Die musikalische Akustik als Grundlage der Harmonik und Melodik* (Leipzig, 1903); *Die Freiheit oder Unfreiheit der Töne und Intervalle als Kriterium der Stimmführung* (Leipzig, 1904); *Die Abhängigkeitsverhältnisse in der Musik* (Leipzig, 1904); *Die Zukunft der Musiktheorie* (Leipzig, 1905); *Ein neuer exotischer Musikstil* (Stuttgart, 1906); *Fortschrittliche Harmonie und Melodielehre* (Leipzig, 1908).

Capet, Lucien, distinguished French violinist; b. Paris, Jan. 8, 1873; d. there, Dec. 18, 1928. He studied at the Paris Cons.; in 1896–99 was concertmaster of the Lamoureux Orch.; from 1899 to 1903 taught violin at the Cons. of Ste. Cécile in Bordeaux. In 1904 he founded the celebrated Capet Quartet, and played first violin in it until 1921, specializing particularly in the later Beethoven quartets. In 1924 he was appointed director of the Institut de Violon in Paris. He composed *Le Rouet,* symph. poem; *Prélude religieux* for Orch.; *Devant la mer* for Voice and Orch.; *Poème* for Violin and Orch.; 5 string quartets; 2 violin sonatas; 6 violin études. He publ. *La Technique supérieure de l'archet* (Paris, 1916); *Les 17 Quatuors de Beethoven;* also a philosophical work, *Espérances.*

Caplet, André, French composer; b. Le Havre, Nov. 23, 1878; d. Paris, April 22, 1925. He studied violin in Le Havre, and played in theater orchs. there and in Paris; entered the Paris Cons. (1896), where he studied with Leroux and Lenepveu; in 1901 received the Grand Prix de Rome for his cantata *Myrrha*. His *Marche solennelle* for the centennial of the Villa Medicis was performed in Rome (April 18, 1903). He was active in France as a choral and operatic conductor; conducted the first performance of Debussy's *Le Martyre de St. Sebastien* (Paris, May 22, 1911); also conducted opera in the U.S. with the Boston Opera Co. (1910–14) and in London at Covent Garden (1912). He served in the French army during World War I; later continued his musical activities. Caplet's music is unequivocally impressionistic, with a lavish use of whole-tone scales and parallel chord formations; he combined this impressionism with neo-archaic usages and mystic programmatic ideas.

WORKS: Oratorio, *Miroir de Jésus* (Paris, May 1, 1924); *Prières* for Voice and Chamber Orch.; *The Masque of the Red Death*, after Poe, for Harp and Orch. (Paris, March 7, 1909; later arranged for Harp and String Quartet and retitled *Conte fantastique;* perf. Paris, Dec. 18, 1923); *Epiphanie* for Cello and Orch. (Paris, Dec. 29, 1923); Double Wind Quintet (Paris, March 9, 1901); *Messe des petits de St. Eustache* (Paris, June 13, 1922); Sonata for Voice, Cello, and Piano; Septet for Strings and 3 Female Voices; *Suite persane* for Woodwind Instruments; piano duets; piano pieces; minor choral works and songs. He left unfinished a *Sonata da chiesa* for Violin and Organ (1924) and *Hommage à Ste. Cathérine de Sienna* for Organ and Orch. He was a close friend of Debussy; recent discoveries show that he collaborated with Debussy on several of his orch. works and even completed sections left unfinished by Debussy. His correspondence with Debussy was publ. in Monaco in 1957.

BIBLIOGRAPHY: M. Brillant, Roland-Manuel, and Arthur Hoerée, "André Caplet, musicien mystique," *La Revue Musicale* (July 1925); R. Dumesnil, *Portraits de musiciens français* (Paris, 1938); a memorial tribute, *André Caplet,* was publ. in Paris (1976).

Capobianco, Tito, Argentine opera director and administrator; b. La Plata, Aug. 28, 1931. He studied at the Univ. of Buenos Aires; then worked at the Teatro Colón (1958–62); was general director of the La Plata Opera (1959–61) and of the Chile Opera (1967–70). In 1975 he became general director of the San Diego Opera; in 1983 assumed a similar post with the Pittsburgh Opera. He also was a prof. at the Univ. of Chile (1954–56) and at the Academy of Vocal Arts in Philadelphia (1962–68); was director of the American Opera Center at the Juilliard School of Music in N.Y. (1967–69). In 1983 he became director of opera studies at the Music Academy of the West at Santa Barbara, Calif.

Capocci, Gaetano, Italian organist, composer, and teacher; b. Rome, Oct. 16, 1811; d. there, Jan. 11, 1898. He studied music with Valentino Fioravanti and organ with Sante Pascoli; at the same time he took courses in theology. In 1830 he was appointed organist and music director at the Church of S. Maria in Rome; was then organist at S. Maria Maggiore (from 1839) and at S. Giovanni in Laterano (from 1855). He had numerous students, among them Margherita of Savoy, the future Queen of Italy. His chief merit as a composer was a successful revival of the Classical oratorio. He wrote the oratorios *Il Battista* (Rome, March 31, 1833) and *Assalonne* (Rome, Dec. 8, 1842); numerous sacred choruses and organ pieces.

Capoianu, Dumitru, Rumanian composer; b. Bucharest, Oct. 19, 1929. He studied at the Bucharest Cons. (1941–47, 1947–53) with Jora, Mendelsohn, Vancea, Andricu, and Rogalski; from 1969 to 1973 he was music director of the Georges Enesco Phil. Orch.

WORKS: 2 suites for Orch. (1953, 1954); *Divertissement* for String Orch. and 2 Clarinets (1956); Violin Concerto (1957); *Cosmos 60,* ballet scene (1960); *5 Songs of Transylvania* for Female Chorus, Oboe, and Strings (1961); *Cinematographic Variations* for Orch. (1965); *Steel,* ballet (1965); *Curtea domnească (The Princely Courtyard),* a "spectacle" of sound and light (1969); *Moto perpetuo* for Solo Violin or Group of Violins, and Orch. (1972); Wind Quintet (1950); Viola Sonata (1952); 2 string quartets (1954, 1959); Trio for Violin, Viola, and Cello (1968); film music.

Capoul, Joseph-Amédée-Victor, brilliant French tenor; b. Toulouse, Feb. 27, 1839; d. Pujaudran-du-Gers, Feb. 18, 1924. He studied voice at the Paris Cons.; made his debut at the Opéra-Comique on Aug. 26, 1861; then sang opera in London and N.Y. In 1897 he was appointed manager of the Grand Opéra in Paris.

BIBLIOGRAPHY: A. de Lassus, *Victor Capoul,* in *La Revue Musicale* (May 1906).

Cappuccilli, Piero, Italian baritone; b. Trieste, Nov. 9, 1929. He studied voice privately; then made his debut at the Teatro Nuovo in Milan (1957). On March 26, 1960, he made his Metropolitan Opera debut in N.Y. as Germont *père* in *La Traviata.* In 1964 he joined La Scala Opera, Milan, achieving distinction in the roles in Verdi's operas.

Capron, Henri, prominent American cellist and composer of French origin. He was a pupil of Gaviniés in Paris (1768); first appeared in Philadelphia in 1785; became active as manager (with Reinagle, William Brown, and Juhan) of subscription concerts in Philadelphia and N.Y.; played in the Old American Co. orch. in N.Y., where he lived from 1788 to 1792; in 1794 he settled permanently in Philadelphia and later was principal of a French boarding school. He wrote *New Contredances;* some songs.

BIBLIOGRAPHY: O.G. Sonneck, *Early Concert Life in America* (N.Y., 1907).

Capuana, Franco, Italian conductor; b. Fano, Sept.

29, 1894; d. Naples, Dec. 10, 1969. He studied composition at the Naples Cons.; began his career as an opera conductor in 1915; from 1930–37 was music director of the Teatro San Carlo in Naples; from 1937–40 was conductor at La Scala in Milan, then its music director (1949–52). He specialized in Italian *verismo* operas, but also excelled in presenting the operas of Wagner, Strauss, and several modern composers.

Carabella, Ezio, Italian composer of light operas and orch. works; b. Rome, March 3, 1891; d. there, April 19, 1964. He studied at the Milan Cons. and at the Santa Cecilia Academy in Rome. He composed a number of singable operettas, among them *Bambù* (Florence, 1923), *La linea del cuore* (Rome, 1924), *Il Candeliere* (Genoa, 1939), and incidental music to various comedies.

Caracciolo, Franco, Italian conductor; b. Bari, March 29, 1920. He studied composition and piano at the Cons. in San Pietro. In 1949 he went to Naples as conductor of the Alessandro Scarlatti Orch. In 1964 he settled in Milan as principal conductor of RAI (Radiotelevisione Italiana). In his programs, Caracciolo revived many of the forgotten orch. works of Italian composers; also conducted contemporary works.

Caracciolo, Luigi, Italian composer and singing teacher; b. Andria (Bari), Aug. 10, 1847; d. London, July 22, 1887. He studied with Mercadante in Naples; went to Dublin in 1878; in 1881 settled in London. He wrote many popular songs, among them *Danza delle memorie, Un sogno fu!,* and *Rime popolari.*

Carafa de Colobrano, Michele Enrico, prolific composer of operas; b. Naples, Nov. 17, 1787; d. Paris, July 26, 1872. He was a son of Prince Colobrano, Duke of Alvito; began to study music at an early age. Though he became an officer in the army of Naples, and fought in Napoleon's Russian campaign, he devoted his leisure time to music, and after Waterloo adopted it as a profession. In 1827 he settled in Paris; succeeded Lesueur as a member of the Academy (1837); in 1840 was appointed a prof. of composition at the Paris Cons.
   WORKS: Operas: *Gabriella di Vergy* (Naples, July 3, 1816); *Ifigenia in Tauride* (Naples, June 19, 1817); *Berenice in Siria* (Naples, July 29, 1818); the following operas were produced at the Opéra-Comique in Paris: *Jeanne d'Arc* (March 10, 1821); *Le Solitaire* (Aug. 17, 1822); *Le Valet de chambre* (Sept. 16, 1823); *L'Auberge supposée* (April 26, 1824); *Sangarido* (May 19, 1827); *Masaniello* (Dec. 27, 1827; on the same subject as Auber's *La Muette de Portici,* staged at the Paris Opéra 2 months later; yet Carafa's *Masaniello* held the stage in competition with Auber's famous opera for 136 nights); *La Violette* (Oct. 7, 1828); *Jenny* (Sept. 26, 1829); *Le Livre de l'ermite* (Aug. 11, 1831); *La Prison d'Edimbourg* (July 20, 1833); *Une Journée de la Fronde* (Nov. 7, 1833); *La Grande Duchesse* (Nov. 16, 1835); *Thérèse* (Sept. 26, 1838). He also composed ballets, cantatas, and much church music.

Carapetyan, Armen, American musicologist of Armenian origin; b. Isfahan, Oct. 11, 1908. He studied philosophy in Paris and N.Y.; musicology at Harvard Univ. In 1945 he organized the American Inst. of Musicology, with headquarters in Rome and Cambridge, Mass.; he edited valuable collections, among them Corpus Mensurabilis Musicae, Corpus Scriptorum de Musica, Musicological Studies and Documents; contributed numerous articles, mainly on the music of the Renaissance, to American and European periodicals.

Cardew, Cornelius, English composer of extreme avante garde tendencies; b. Winchcombe, Gloucester, May 7, 1936; d. in a road accident, London, Dec. 13, 1981. He sang in the chorus at Canterbury Cathedral until puberty; then studied composition with Howard Ferguson at the Royal Academy of Music in London (1953–57); in 1957 he went to Cologne and worked at the electronic studio there as an assistant to Karlheinz Stockhausen (1958–60). Returning to England, he organized concerts of experimental music; in 1963–65 he was in Italy, where he had some private lessons with Goffredo Petrassi in Rome. In 1967 he was appointed to the faculty of the Royal Academy of Music in London. In 1969, together with Michael Parsons and Howard Skempton, he organized the Scratch Orchestra, a heterogeneous group for performances of new music, militantly latitudinarian and disestablishmentarian. Under the influence of the teachings of Mao Zedong, Cardew renounced his modernistic past as a bourgeois deviation detrimental to pure Marxism, and subsequently attacked his former associate, Stockhausen, in a book ominously entitled *Stockhausen Serves Imperialism* (London, 1974). He also repudiated his own magnum opus, *The Great Learning,* which was originally performed at the 1968 Cheltenham Festival, scored for a non-singing chorus to the words of Ezra Pound's translation of Confucius, a chorus which was admonished to bang on tapped stones, to whistle and shriek, but never to stoop to vocalizing. In the revised version of the work he appended to the title the slogan "Apply Marxism–Leninism–Mao Zedong Thought in a living way to the problems of the present." This version was first performed by the Scratch Orch. in the Promenade Concert in London on Aug. 24, 1972. His other works include *Volo Solo* for any handy musical instrument (1965); *3 Winter Potatoes* for piano and various assorted concrete sounds, as well as for newspapers, balloons, noise, and people working (Focus Opera Groups, London, March 11, 1968). He also publ. several pamphlets containing some confusing confutations of Confucius. In addition, he compiled a seminal manual, *Scratch Music* (London, 1970).

Cardus, Sir Neville, British writer on music and cricket; b. Manchester, April 2, 1889; d. London, Feb. 28, 1975. He studied singing, then turned to journalism; became an active contributor to the *Manchester Guardian;* wrote essays on numerous subjects, but primarily on cricket and music. He was cricket coach at Shrewsbury School (1912–16); in 1917 joined the staff of the *Manchester Guardian;* became its chief music critic (1927–39); from 1939–47 he was in Australia, writing on cricket and music for the *Syney Morning Herald.* Returning to London, he became music critic for the *Manchester Guardian* in 1951. He received the Wagner Medal of the City of Bayreuth in 1963; was knighted in 1967. His literary style is quasi-Shavian in its colloquial manner and stubborn persuasion.

WRITINGS: *A Cricketer's Book* (1921); *Autobiography* (1947); *Second Innings: More Autobiography* (1950); *Cricket All the Year* (1952); *A Composer's Eleven* (1958); *Sir Thomas Beecham: A Portrait* (1961); *The Playfair Cardus* (1963); *Gustav Mahler: His Mind and His Music,* Vol. I (1965); *The Delights of Music* (1966); *Full Score* (1970); R. Daniels, ed., *Conversations with Cardus* (London, 1976).

Carey, Bruce, Canadian choral conductor; b. Hamilton, Ontario, Nov. 16, 1876; d. there, May 8, 1960. He studied in London and Leipzig; returning to Canada, he devoted himself to teaching in his hometown. In 1927 he conducted the "sesquicentennial choir" of Philadelphia; also directed other choral groups in America and in Canada.

Carey, Francis Clive Savill, English baritone; b. Sible Hedingham, Essex, May 30, 1883; d. London, April 30, 1968. He studied voice at the Royal College of Music in London; after graduation he dedicated himself to teaching; was also for a few years (1931–39) an opera producer in London. He made a worldwide tour as a member of the group known as the English Singers.

Carey, Henry, English writer for the theater; b. probably in Yorkshire, c.1687; d. (suicide) London, Oct. 5, 1743. He was a natural son of Henry Savile, Lord Eland; studied music with Linnert, Roseingrave, and Geminiani; settled c.1710 in London, where he was active as a poet, librettist, playwright, and composer; wrote 6 ballad-operas, of which *The Contrivances* (Drury Lane, London, June 20, 1729) achieved the greatest success. He wrote the words of the popular song *Sally in Our Alley* and composed a musical setting for it, but his setting was replaced in 1790 by the tune *What though I am a Country Lass,* which has since been traditionally sung to Carey's original poem; also popular was his intermezzo with singing, *Nancy, or The Parting Lovers* (1739). He publ. a collection of 100 ballads, *The Musical Century* (2 vols., 1737 and 1740); also *6 Cantatas* (1732) and *3 Burlesque Cantatas* (1741). Carey's claim to the authorship of *God Save the King* was put forth by his son, George Savile Carey (1743–1807), more than 50 years after his father's death, without any supporting evidence; many anthologies still list Carey's name as the author of the British national anthem. For a complete account of this misattribution of the tune, see P.A. Scholes,

God Save the Queen! (London, 1954; Appendix I; pp. 284–88). Further discussion of the authorship of the anthem is to be found in W.H. Cummings, *"God Save the King," The Origin and History of the Music and Words* (London, 1902); O.G. Sonneck, *Report on the Star-Spangled Banner* (1909); F.S. Boas and J.E. Borland, *The National Anthem* (London, 1916); J.A. Fuller-Maitland, "Facts and Fictions about *God Save the King," Musical Quarterly* (Oct. 1916); E.A. Maginty, *"America:* The Origin of Its Melody," *Musical Quarterly* (July 1934).

Caridis Miltiades, conductor; b. Gdansk, Poland, May 9, 1923. He attended the Cons. in Athens and the Academy of Music in Vienna, where he studied conducting with Hans Swarowsky, Herbert von Karajan, and Hermann Scherchen. He conducted opera at Bregenz (1947–48), Graz (1945–59), and Cologne (1959–62). From 1960 to 1967 he was principal conductor of the Phil. Hungarica Orch. in Marl, West Germany; in 1964–67 toured the U.S. with his ensemble; in 1969 was appointed conductor of the Oslo Phil. Orch. From 1957 to 1981 he was Generalmusikdirektor of the Municipality of Duisburg. In 1979 he was appointed chief conductor of the Tonkünstler Orch. in Vienna.

Carissimi, Giacomo, Italian composer of sacred music; b. Marino, near Rome (baptized, April 18, 1605); d. Rome, Jan. 12, 1674. In 1625–27 he was organist at the Cathedral of Tivoli; from 1628 to his death, maestro di cappella in the Church of S. Apollinare in Rome; he also served as maestro di cappella of the Collegio Germanico in Rome. A prolific and original composer, he broke with the Palestrina tradition, devoting himself to perfecting the monodic style, as is evidenced by his highly developed recitative and more pleasing and varied instrumental accompaniments. His MSS were dispersed at the sale of the library of the Collegio Germanico, and many are lost, but a few printed works are still extant. There were publ. the 4 oratorios *Jephte* (his masterpiece), *Judicium Salomonis, Jonas, Balthazar;* 2 collections of motets *a* 2, 3, and 4 (Rome, 1664, 1667); masses *a* 5 and 9 (Cologne, 1663, 1667); *Arie de camera* (1667); and separate pieces in several collections. The finest collection of his works is that made by Dr. Aldrich at Christ-Church College, Oxford. Carissimi also wrote a treatise, publ. only in German: *Ars cantandi, etc.* (Augsburg; 2nd ed., 1692; 3rd ed., 1696; another ed., 1718). F. Chrysander publ. 4 oratorios (*Jephte, Judicium Salomonis, Balthazar, Jonas*) in Denkmäler der Tonkunst 2; *Jonas, Judicium Salomonis* and *Jephte* were also publ. in I Classici della Musica Italiana, No. 5 (Milan, 1919); vocal duets are reprinted in L. Landshoff's *Alte Meister des Bel canto* (1927); a motet was publ. in *Musique d'Eglise des XVIIᵉ et XVIIIᵉ siècles,* ed. by Ch. Pineau; *6 Solo Cantatas,* ed. with commentary by G. Rose (London, 1969). The complete works are being publ. by the Istituto Italiano per la Storia della Musica (1951—). Claudio Sartori has compiled *Carissimi, Catalogo delle opere attribuite* (1975).

BIBLIOGRAPHY: M. Brenet, "Les Oratorios de

Carissimi," *Rivista Musicale Italiana* (1897); A. Schering, *Geschichte des Oratoriums* (Leipzig, 1911); A. Cametti, "Primo contributo per una biografia di Giacomo Carissimi," *Rivista Musicale Italiana* XXIV/3 (1917); F.B. Pratella, "G. Carissimi ed i suoi oratori," *Rivista Musicale Italiana,* XXIX/1 (1920); J. Loschelder, "Nuovi contributi a una biografia di G. Carissimi," *Archiv für Musikwissenschaft* (1940); G. Massenkeil, "Die Wiederholungsfiguren in den Oratorien Giacomo Carissimis," ibid. (Jan. 1956); E. Rosend, "Four Oratorios by Giacomo Carissimi," *Amor Artis Bulletin* (Feb. 1967); L. Bianci, *Carissimi . . . e l'oratorio musicale* (Rome, 1969).

Carl, William Crane, American organist; b. Bloomfield, N.J., March 2, 1865; d. New York, Dec. 8, 1936. He first studied in N.Y.; in 1890 went to Paris, where he studied with Guilmant; returning to America, he was engaged as organist of the Old First Presbyterian Church in N.Y., a post which he held until his death. He made 7 tours to the Pacific coast and one to Alaska; was also active as a choral conductor in N.Y.; was a founder and served on the Council of the American Guild of Organists. He publ. *Masterpieces for the Organ; 30 Postludes for the Organ;* 2 vols. of *Novelties for the Organ; Master Studies for the Organ.*

Carlid, Göte, Swedish composer; b. Högbo, Dec. 26, 1920; d. Stockholm, June 30, 1953. He was a philosophy student at the Univ. of Uppsala; then served as a municipal librarian in Enköping (1946–48) and Sollentuna (1948–50). As a composer, he was largely autodidact, but from the outset he adopted a modern idiom, making use of impressionistic and expressionistic techniques. His last works before his early death show a learned approach to the problems of new music. WORKS: *Notturno* for String Orch. (1945); *Small Pieces* for Piano (1947); Piano Sonata (1948); *Quartetto elegiaco* for String Quartet (1948); *3 Songs* for Female Voice, Flute, Clarinet, and Cello (1946–49); *A Little Tea Music* for Flute, 2 Clarinets, and Cello (1949); *Mass* for Strings (1949); *Monologues* for Piano (1944–50); *Triad* for Saxophone and Piano (1950); *Hymnes à la Beauté* for Chorus and Orch., to poems by Baudelaire (the only Swedish entry in the 1952 Salzburg Festival of the International Society for Contemporary Music); *The Music Bus* for Soli, Children's Chorus, and Instruments (1952).

Carlos, Wendy (née **Walter**), transsexual American organist, composer, and electronics virtuoso; b. Pawtucket, R.I., Nov. 14, 1939. He played piano as a child; then studied music and physics at Brown Univ. and at Columbia Univ., where he took courses with Vladimir Ussachevsky. At the same time he began working with the electronic engineer Robert Moog in perfecting the Moog Synthesizer. The result of their experiments with versified tone-colors was a record album under the title "Switched-on-Bach," which became unexpectedly successful, especially among the wide-eyed, susceptible American youth, selling some million copies. This was followed in 1969 by "The Well-Tempered Synthesizer," engineered entirely by Carlos. In 1971 Carlos composed and synthesized the sound track for the film *A Clockwork Orange,* based on the futuristic novel by Anthony Burgess. Then, at the age of 32, he suddenly became aware of his sexual duality, a woman's psyche imprisoned in a man's body. To remedy this sundering nature, he underwent a transsexual operation with his penis being everted to create a fairly respectable and conceivably receptive vagina; on St. Valentine's Day, Feb. 14, 1979, he officially changed his first name Walter to Wendy. She/he described his sexual tergiversation in a candid interview in *Playboy* (May 1979), illustrated with photographs "before and after."

Carlson, Claudine, French mezzo-soprano; b. Mulhouse, Feb. 26, 1937. She studied in California and at the Manhattan School of Music in N.Y. with Jennie Tourel and Esther Andreas; then engaged on a successful career as a concert singer. In 1977 she made her debut at the Metropolitan Opera in N.Y. in Debussy's *Pelléas et Mélisande.* Gifted with a voice of fine quality, she gained renown in the French repertoire.

Carlstedt, Jan, Swedish composer; b. Orsa, June 15, 1926. He studied composition with Lars-Erik Larsson at the Royal Academy of Music in Stockholm (1948–52), and later in England (1952–53) and Italy (1954–55). Returning to Stockholm, he became active in furthering the cause of modern music; was a founder of the Society of Contemporary Music in Stockholm (1960). WORKS: 4 string quartets (1951–52, 1966, 1967, 1972); 2 symphs.: No. 1 (1952–54; revised 1960; Stockholm, Oct. 4, 1961); No. 2, in memory of Martin Luther King (1968; N.Y., Dec. 20, 1970); String Trio (1955–56); Sonata for String Orch. (1956); Sonata for 2 Violins (1956); *12 Miniatures* for Violin, Clarinet, and Cello (1958); 8 Duets for 2 Violins (1958); Sinfonietta for Wind Quintet (1959); Sonata for Solo Violin (1959); *Ballata* for Solo Cello (1960); Divertimento for Oboe and String Trio (1962); Wind Quintet (1962); *Pentastomos* for Wind Quintet (1972–73).

Carmichael, Hoagy, American jazz pianist and composer of popular music; b. Bloomington, Ind., Nov. 22, 1899; d. Rancho Mirage, near Palm Springs, Calif., Dec. 27, 1981. His ambition as a youth was to become a lawyer, and in fact, he graduated from the Indiana Univ. Law School, and played the piano only for relaxation. In 1929 he went to Hollywood but failed to obtain work as a musician. Working on his own, he organized a swing band and composed songs for it. Although unable to write music professionally, he revealed a natural gift for melody, and soon made a success with such songs as *Riverboat Shuffle* and *Washboard Blues.* He made a hit with his song *Stardust,* which became the foundation of his fame and fortune. Among his other popular tunes were *Ivy, I Get Along without You Very Well, Heart and Soul,* and *In the Cool, Cool, Cool of the*

Evening, which won the Academy Award as the best movie song for 1951.

BIBLIOGRAPHY: Hoagy Carmichael, *The Stardust Road* (N.Y., 1946); Hoagy Carmichael and Stephen Longstreet, *Sometimes I Wonder: The Story of Hoagy Carmichael* (N.Y., 1965); Alec Wilder, *American Popular Song* (N.Y., 1972).

Carmichael, Mary Grant, English pianist and composer; b. Birkenhead, 1851; d. London, March 17, 1935. She studied piano and composition in London; publ. a number of agreeable piano pieces and an operetta, *The Frozen Heart.*

Carmirelli, Pina, Italian violinist; b. Varzi, Jan. 23, 1914. She studied at the Cons. in Milan, graduating in 1930, and at the Santa Cecilia Academy in Rome. She began her concert career in 1937; in 1949 she founded the Boccherini Quintet, and in 1954 the Carmirelli Quartet, with which she toured throughout Europe. In 1941 she joined the faculty of the Rome Cons.; she also edited works by Boccherini and Vivaldi.

Carner, Mosco, Austrian-English musicologist and conductor; b. Vienna, Nov. 15, 1904. He studied at the New Vienna Cons.; then with Guido Adler at the Univ. of Vienna, where he received his Ph.D. in 1928 with the dissertation *Studien zur Sonatenform bei Robert Schumann;* was active conducting theater orchs. in Opava and Danzig until 1933, when the advent of the Nazi regime forced him to emigrate. He settled in London and devoted himself mainly to musical journalism; was critic for *Time and Tide* from 1949–62, and for the *Evening News* from 1957–61. He publ. a biography of Dvořák (London, 1941); contributed one vol. of the 2-vol. work *A Study of 20th-Century Harmony* (London, 1940–42); also wrote *Of Men and Music* (London, 1944); *The Waltz* (London, 1948); *Puccini: A Critical Biography* (London, 1958; revised 1974); *Alban Berg, The Man and His Work* (London, 1975; 2nd ed., revised, 1983); *Madama Butterfly* (London, 1979); *Major and Minor* (London, 1980); *Hugo Wolf's Songs* (London, 1982).

Carney, Harry, black American jazz baritone saxophonist; b. Boston, April 1, 1910; d. New York, Oct. 8, 1974. He learned to play the piano, clarinet, and saxophone; joined Duke Ellington's orch. in 1926; specialized on the baritone saxophone; he remained with Ellington throughout his long career, dying only a few months after the "Duke."

Carneyro, Claudio, Portuguese composer; b. Oporto, Jan. 27, 1895; d. there, Oct. 18, 1963. He studied composition with Lucien Lambert at the Oporto Cons. and later in Paris with Widor (1919–22) and Paul Dukas (1934); taught composition at the Oporto Cons. (1922–58); was its director in 1955–58. In his music, he made ample use of authentic Portuguese motives, adorning them by sonorous impressionistic harmonies.

WORKS: Piano Quartet (1914); *Pregões romarias e processões* for Orch. (1928); *Memento* for String Orch. (1933); *Cantarejo e dancara* for Orch. (1938); *Pavana e gelharda* for String Orch. (1939); *Catavento* for Piano and Chamber Orch. (1942); *Portugalesas* for Orch. (1949); *Khroma* for Viola and Orch. (1954); *Roda dos degredados* for Violin and Orch. (1960); *Bailadeiras* for Orch. (1962); *Gradualis* for Orch. (1962); Piano Quartet (1914); *Partita* for String Trio (1928–35); Violin Sonata (1929); String Quartet (1947); *Poemas em prosa* for Piano (1930–31); choruses; songs.

Carnicer, Ramón, Spanish composer; b. Tárrega, near Lérida, Oct. 24, 1789; d. Madrid, March 17, 1855. He studied in Barcelona with Francisco Queralt and Carlos Baguer; from 1818–20 conducted the Coliseo Theater orch. in Barcelona; in 1828–30 was conductor of the Royal Opera in Madrid; in 1830–54, was a prof. of composition at the Madrid Cons. One of the creators of Spanish national opera (the zarzuela), he composed 10 operas, wrote much church music, many symphs., Spanish songs, etc.; also *Dulce Patria,* the national hymn of Chile.

Carol-Bérard, French composer and theorist; b. Marseilles, April 5, 1881; d. Paris, Dec. 13, 1942. He studied with Albéniz in Barcelona; then settled in Paris. His music, impressionistic with an oriental flavor, remains largely unpubl. He evolved a theory of "chromophonie" (color in movement) and wrote several papers on the subject in *La Revue Musicale* and other publications. He also wrote poetry under the pseudonym **Olivier Realtor.**

WORKS: *Symphonie dansée; Symphonie des forces mécaniques* (in 3 movements: *Navire perdu; Gare nocturne; L'Aéroplane sur la ville,* utilizing phonograph records of noises); *L'Oiseau des îles,* lyric piece in 2 acts (to his own words); 3 piano suites: *Egypte, D'une existence antérieure,* and *Extrême-Asie;* humorous piano pieces: *Les Heures civiles et militaires* and *L'Elégie à jouer dans une cave;* a number of songs to poems of Verlaine and Mallarmé.

Carolan, Turlough, Irish song composer; b. near Nobber, County Meath, 1670; d. near Kilronan, March 25, 1738. He was an itinerant harper, and improvised Irish verses and tunes; these were publ. in various 18th-century collections of Irish music; the number of his original tunes is about 220. He is also known under the name **O'Carolan.**

BIBLIOGRAPHY: D. O'Sullivan, *Carolan: The Life, Times and Music of an Irish Harper* (London, 1958).

Caron, Philippe, famous Burgundian contrapuntist of the 15th century, a pupil of Binchois or Dufay. O.J. Gombosi, in his monograph *Jacob Obrecht, Eine stilkritische Studie* (Leipzig, 1925), groups Caron with composers of the Cambrai school interested in continuing Dufay's style; this work also contains a reprint of a 3-part chanson, *Vive Carloys,* MSS of which are in libraries at Rome and Florence. Other extant works include 4 masses *a* 4 in the Papal Chapel and a MS of 3- and 4-part chansons at Paris. Petrucci publ. a 5-part chanson, *Hélas que pourra deuenir,* in his *Odhecaton* (1501). The Inst. of Medieval Music (Brooklyn, N.Y.) began issuing the complete works in 1971.

Caron, Rose (née **Meuniez**), French dramatic soprano; b. Monerville, Nov. 17, 1857; d. Paris, April 9, 1930. She entered the Paris Cons. in 1880, leaving in 1882 to study with Marie Sasse in Brussels, where her debut was made as Alice in *Robert le Diable* (1884). She sang for 2 years at the Paris Opéra, and again in Brussels, creating Lorance (in *Jocelyn*), Richilde, and Salammbô (1890); in 1890 she returned to the Paris Opéra, where she sang Sieglinde (1893) and Desdemona (1894) in the first performances of *Die Walküre* and *Otello* in France; in 1898 she sang Fidelio at the Opéra-Comique. From 1900 she appeared almost exclusively on the concert stage; in 1902 she was appointed a prof. of singing at the Paris Cons.
BIBLIOGRAPHY: H. de Curzon, *Croquis d'artistes* (Paris, 1898).

Carpani, Giuseppe, Italian writer; b. Villalbese, Jan. 28, 1752; d. Vienna, Jan. 22, 1825. He studied and practiced law in Milan, later abandoning it for a literary career and writing on music. He was editor of the *Gazzetta di Milano* (1792–96); the French invasion forced him to go to Venice and then to Vienna. A great admirer of Haydn, he publ. a monograph, *Le Haydine ovvero Lettere su la vita e le opere del celebre Giuseppe Haydn* (Milan, 1812; enlarged ed., Padua, 1823). Stendhal printed a major part of this book as his own work, in French, under the pseudonym of Bombet (Paris, 1814); Carpani protested against this act of plagiarism in his pamphlet *Lettere dell'Autore delle Haydine* (Vienna, 1815), but Stendhal ignored the protest and republ. his book in 1817, this time under the signature Stendhal. Carpani also wrote a monograph on Rossini, *Le Rossiniane* (Padua, 1824).

Carpenter, John Alden, American composer; b. Park Ridge, Chicago, Feb. 28, 1876; d. Chicago, April 26, 1951. He received his B.A. degree from Harvard Univ. in 1897; also studied music there with John K. Paine; entered his father's shipping supply business, and from 1909–36 was vice-president of the firm. During his earlier years in business he continued his musical studies in Rome (1906) and with Bernard Ziehn in Chicago (1908–12); was made a Knight of the French Legion of Honor (1921); received an honorary M.A. from Harvard Univ. (1922) and an honorary Mus.Doc. from the Univ. of Wisconsin (1933). After his retirement from business in 1936, he devoted himself entirely to composing; in 1947 was awarded the Gold Medal of the National Inst. of Arts and Letters. From his musical contacts abroad he absorbed mildly modernistic and impressionistic techniques and applied them to his music based on American urban subjects, adding the resources of jazz rhythms. His first work in this

American idiom was a "jazz pantomime," *Krazy Kat,* after a well-known cartoon series (1921); he then wrote a large-scale musical panorama, *Skyscrapers* (1926), performed as a ballet and an orch. suite in America and abroad, attracting much critical comment as the first symph. work descriptive of modern American civilization; as such, the score has historical significance.
WORKS: Ballets: *Birthday of the Infanta* (Chicago Opera, Dec. 23, 1919); *Krazy Kat* (Chicago, Dec. 23, 1921); *Skyscrapers* (Metropolitan Opera, N.Y., Feb. 19, 1926; Munich, 1928); orch. suite, *Adventures in a Perambulator* (Chicago, March 19, 1915); Concertino for Piano and Orch. (Chicago, March 10, 1916; revised 1947); Symph. No. 1, in C (Litchfield County Choral Union Festival, Norfolk, Conn., 1917; revised for the 50th anniversary of the Chicago Symph. and perf. there, Oct. 24, 1940); *A Pilgrim Vision* for Orch. (Philadelphia, Nov. 23, 1920; for the tercentenary Mayflower Celebration); *Patterns* for Piano and Orch. (Boston, Oct. 21, 1932); *Sea-Drift,* symph. poem after Whitman (Chicago, Nov. 30, 1933; revised version, 1944); *Danza* for Orch. (Chicago, 1935); Violin Concerto (1936; Chicago, Nov. 18, 1937); Symph. No. 2 (N.Y., Oct. 22, 1942); symph. poem, *The Anxious Bugler* (N.Y., Nov. 17, 1943); *The 7 Ages,* symph. suite (N.Y., Nov. 29, 1945); *Carmel Concerto* for Orch. (1948); *Song of Faith* for Chorus and Orch. (Washington Bicentennial Commission, 1932); *Song of Freedom* for Chorus and Orch. (1941); Violin Sonata (1912); String Quartet (Elizabeth Coolidge Festival, Washington, D.C., 1928); Piano Quintet (1934); *Improving Songs for Anxious Children* (1904); *Gitanjali,* song cycle to poems by Tagore (1913; also arranged for Voice and Orch.); *Water Colors,* 4 Chinese songs with Chamber Orch. (1918); many other songs and piano pieces.
BIBLIOGRAPHY: Olin Downes, "J.A. Carpenter, American Craftsman," and Felix Borowski, "J.A. Carpenter," both in *Musical Quarterly* (Oct. 1930); W.T. Upton, *Art-Song in America* (N.Y., 1930; pp. 197–213); M. Goss, *Modern Music Makers* (N.Y., 1952; pp. 34–47). *Modern Music Index,* ed. by W. Shirley, W. and C. Lichtenwanger (N.Y. 1977; pp. 39–40).

Carpenter, Karen, American pop singer; b. New Haven, Conn., March 2, 1950; d. Downey, Calif., Feb. 4, 1983. She formed a pop-jazz group, playing drums, with her brother Richard on keyboards; they soon changed to vocals; she sang contralto. They became enormously popular with record albums selling into millions; she preferred soft, sentimental songs and rock singles, such as *We've Only Just Begun, Rainy Days and Mondays,* and *Close to You,* winning 2 Grammy awards in 1970. Their album *The Carpenters* won another Grammy award in 1971. Obsessed with thinning out her already fragile frame, she became a victim of anorexia nervosa and died of heart failure.

Carpentras (Il Carpentrasso in Italian; real name, **Elzéar Genet**), composer and priest; b. Carpentras (Vaucluse), c.1470; d. Avignon, June 14, 1548. In 1508 he was the leading singer in, and from 1513–21 maestro di cappella of, the Pontifical Chapel in Rome; in 1521 he was sent to Avignon on negotiations connected with the Holy See; in 1524 he made his last visit to Rome; in 1526 he went to France, where he became dean of St. Agricole. Four vols. of his works (masses, 1532; Lamentations, 1532; hymns, 1533; Magnificats, 1537), printed at Avignon by Jean de Channey, are of great interest for being the first works to introduce Briard's new types, with round instead of diamond-shaped and square notes, and without ligatures; a complete copy is in the Vienna Staatsbibliothek, an incomplete one in the Paris Cons. library. His works, though severe and dignified in style, were highly esteemed by his contemporaries. A few motets are printed in Petrucci's *Motetti della Corona* (vol. I, 1514; vol. III, 1519); other works in various contemporary collections, including the edition by A. Seay in Corpus Mensurabilis Musicae, LVIII (1972–73).

BIBLIOGRAPHY: Quittard, "E Genet de Carpentras," *Tribune de St. Gervais*, 7–9 (1899); Ch. Requin, "Elzéar Genet, dit il Carpentrasso," in *Mémoires de l'Académie de Vaucluse* (1918); J. Tiersot, "Elzéar Genet, dit Carpentras et la chanson 'a lombre d'ung buissonet,' " *Bulletin de la Société Française de Musicologie*, 3 (1918); C.A. Miller, "Jerome Cardan on Gombert, Phinot, and Carpentras," *Musical Quarterly* (July 1972).

Carr, Arthur, American pianist and composer; b. Pontiac, Mich., Feb. 29, 1908. He studied theory with David Stanley Smith and Richard Donovan at Yale Univ.; piano with Bruce Simonds; composition with Halsey Stevens at the Univ. of Southern Calif. (M.Mus., 1947). In 1942–46 he served as bandleader in the U.S. Army. His works include a symph. poem, *Desire* (1932); a comic opera, *Captain Jupiter* (1939); *Celtic Rondo* for Orch. (1941); *Thème varié* for String Quartet; piano pieces; songs. He made several tours in America and in Europe as a pianist and accompanist.

Carr, Benjamin, composer and publisher; b. London, Sept. 12, 1768; d. Philadelphia, May 24, 1831. He studied music with Samuel Arnold, Samuel Wesley, and Charles Wesley; established himself as a composer in London. He went to America with his father and brother in 1793; settled in Philadelphia and established Carr's Musical Repository, one of the most important early American music stores and music publishing houses; the following year (1794) they opened branches in N.Y. and Baltimore. He was co-founder in 1820 of the Musical Fund Society in Philadelphia. A versatile musician, he was proficient as a singer, pianist, and organist, and was an influential figure in early American musical life.

WORKS: *Philander and Silvia,* pastoral piece (London, Oct. 16, 1792); *The Archers, or Mountaineers of Switzerland,* ballad opera (N.Y., April 18, 1796); *Dead March for Washington* (1799); numerous songs and ballads. The N.Y. Public Library owns the only known copy of Carr's *Federal Overture*

(Philadelphia, 1794), a medley of popular airs, including the first printing of *Yankee Doodle.*

BIBLIOGRAPHY: O.G. Sonneck, "Early American Concert Life," *International Music Quarterly* 6; Wm. Henry Richards, *Carr Geneology* (1931); Virginia L. Redway, "The Carrs, American Music Publishers," *Musical Quarterly* (Jan. 1932); John T. Howard, *Our American Music* (N.Y., 4th ed., 1965); J. Mates, *The American Musical Stage before 1800* (1962).

Carr, Frank Osmond, English composer; b. Yorkshire, April 23, 1858; d. Uxbridge, Middlesex, Aug. 29, 1916. He received the Oxford degrees of Mus. Bac. (1882) and Mus.Doc. (1891).

WORKS: Comic operas: *The Rose of the Riviera* (1890); *Joan of Arc* (1891); *Blue-eyed Susan* (London, 1892); *In Town* (1892); *Morocco Bound* (1893); *Go Bang* (1894); *His Excellency* (1894; to a libretto by Gilbert); *Lord Tom Noddy* (1895); *The Clergyman's Daughter* (Birmingham, 1896; subsequently perf. in London under the title *My Girl*); etc.

Carr, Howard, English composer and conductor; b. Manchester, Dec. 26, 1880; d. London, Nov. 16, 1960. He was a conductor of light operas in London (1903–6) and in Australia (1906–8); after conducting in London, he again went to Australia in 1928; taught harmony and counterpoint at the Sydney Cons. until 1938, when he returned to London; then devoted himself to composing.

WORKS: Operettas: *Under The Greenwood Tree* and *Master Wayfarer;* 2 symphs.; orch. suite, *The Jolly Roger; The Bush* for Baritone Solo, Male Chorus, and Orch.

Carr, Vikki (Florencia Bisenta de Casillas Martinez Cardona), American singer of popular music; b. El Paso, Texas, July 19, 1942. She began her career as a vocalist with the Pepe Callahan Mexican-Irish Band in Los Angeles; then sang popular music in nightclubs; also appeared as an actress. Her hit songs included *It Must Be Him, With Pen in Hand,* and *Can't Take My Eyes Off You.*

Carranza, Gustavo Eduardo, Mexican-American pianist, teacher, and composer; b. Mexico City, June 14, 1897; d. Fullerton, Calif., Nov. 1, 1975. He was in the U.S. from 1911 to 1914; returned to Mexico for a year in 1914 and studied composition with Julian Carrillo in Mexico City; settled in the U.S. permanently in 1915; studied piano for a short time in N.Y. with Ethel Newcomb and Leopold Godowsky, while also pursuing intensive studies in philosophy. In 1930 he went to California; became a naturalized U.S. citizen in 1940.

WORKS: *Oriental Fantasy* for Orch.; 2 piano concertos, surnamed respectively *Medieval* and *American; Humoresque on Chopsticks* for 2 Pianos; and a large number of solo piano pieces, among them 5 sonatas, 24 concert études, 8 polonaises, 4 rhapsodies, and several suites, most of them surnamed for a specific nationality. His style of composition is Romantic, with a considerable infusion of exotic modalities.

Carraud, Michel-Gaston, French music critic and composer; b. Mée, near Paris, July 20, 1864; d. Paris, June 15, 1920. He studied with Massenet at the Paris Cons.; received the Premier Prix de Rome for his cantata *Cléopâtre.* He abandoned composition after 1905 and was mainly active as a music critic; publ. *La Vie, l'œuvre et la mort d'Albéric Magnard* (Paris, 1921).

Carré, Albert, French opera impresario, nephew of the librettist Michael Carré; b. Strasbourg, June 22, 1852; d. Paris, Dec. 12, 1938. He assumed the directorship of the theater at Nancy in 1884, and in 1885–90 headed the Cercle at Aix-les-Bains. From 1898–1912 he was director of the Opéra-Comique, succeeding Carvalho.

Carreño, Inocente, Venezuelan composer; b. Porlamar, Dec. 28, 1919. He studied French horn, clarinet, piano, and theory in Caracas; graduated in composition in 1946; subsequently became engaged in pedagogical work; also played the French horn in the Caracas Symph. Orch. and conducted choruses. His works include a symph. poem, *El Pozo* (1946); *Suite Breve* for String Orch. (1947); *Margariteña,* suite for Orch. (1954); Concerto for Horn and Strings (1958); *Sinfonieta satírica* for 11 Instruments (1965); *Dialogo* for Flute and Chamber Orch. (1965); chamber music and choruses.

Carreño, (Maria) Teresa, famous Venezuelan pianist; b. Caracas, Dec. 22, 1853; d. New York, June 12, 1917. As a child she studied with her father, an excellent pianist; driven from home by a revolution, the family in 1862 settled in N.Y., where she studied with Gottschalk. At the age of 8 she gave a public recital in N.Y. (Nov. 25, 1862). She began her career in 1866, after studying with Mathias in Paris and A. Rubinstein. She lived mainly in Paris from 1866 to 1870; then in England. She developed a singing voice and made an unexpected appearance in opera in Edinburgh as the Queen in *Les Huguenots* (May 24, 1872), in a cast that included Tietjens, Brignoli, and Mario; was again in the U.S. early in 1876, when she studied singing in Boston. For the Bolivar centenary celebration in Caracas (Oct. 29, 1885), she appeared as singer, pianist, and composer of the festival hymn, written at the request of the Venezuelan government; hence the frequent but erroneous attribution to Carreño of the national hymn of Venezuela, *Gloria al bravo pueblo* (the music of which was actually composed in 1811 by J. Landaeta, and officially adopted as the Venezuelan national anthem on May 25, 1881). In Caracas she once again demonstrated her versatility, when for the last 3 weeks of the season she conducted the opera company managed by her husband, the baritone **Giovanni Tagliapietra.** After these musical experiments she resumed her career as a pianist; made her German debut in Berlin, Nov. 18, 1889; in 1907 toured Australia. Her last appearance with an orch. was with the N.Y. Phil. Society (Dec. 8, 1916); her

last recital was in Havana (March 21, 1917). She impressed her audiences by the impetuous élan of her playing, and was described as "the Valkyrie of the piano." She was married 4 times: to the violinist **Emile Sauret** (June, 1873), to the baritone **Giovanni Tagliapietra** (1876), to **Eugène d'Albert** (1892–95), and to **Arturo Tagliapietra,** a younger brother of Giovanni (June 30, 1902). Early in her career, Teresa Carreño wrote a number of compositions, some of which were publ.: a String Quartet; *Petite danse tsigane* for Orch.; 39 concert pieces for piano; a waltz, *Mi Teresita,* which enjoyed considerable popularity; and other small pieces. She was one of the first pianists to play MacDowell's compositions in public; MacDowell took lessons from her in N.Y. She was greatly venerated in Venezuela; her mortal remains were solemnly transferred from N.Y., where she died, and reburied in Caracas, on Feb. 15, 1938.

BIBLIOGRAPHY: M. Milinowski, *Teresa Carreño* (New Haven, 1940); A. Marquez Rodriguez, *Esbozo biográfico de Teresa Carreño* (Caracas, 1953); W. Dinneen, in *Notable American Women* (Cambridge, Mass., 1971).

Carreras, José, Spanish tenor; b. Barcelona, Dec. 5, 1946. He was educated at the Barcelona Cons.; then sang at the Liceo there. In 1971 he appeared at the opera in Parma and scored a notable success; then sang at the N.Y. City Opera (1972) and Covent Garden, London (1974). He made his Metropolitan Opera debut in N.Y. as Cavaradossi on Nov. 18, 1974; then sang at La Scala, Milan (1975) and at the Salzburg Festival (1976). He possesses a fine lyrical voice and is regarded as one of the outstanding tenors of his generation.

Carrillo, Julián, Mexican composer; b. Ahualulco, San Luis Potosí, Jan. 28, 1875; d. Mexico City, Sept. 9, 1965. He was of Indian extraction; lived mostly in Mexico City, where he studied violin with Pedro Manzano and composition with Melesio Morales. He graduated from the National Cons. in 1899 and received a government stipend for study abroad as a winner of the President Diaz Prize. He took courses at the Leipzig Cons. with Hans Becker (violin), Jadassohn (theory), and Hans Sitt (orchestration); played violin in the Gewandhaus Orch. under Nikisch. In 1902–4 he studied at the Ghent Cons., winning first prize as violinist. He returned to Mexico in 1905 and made numerous appearances as a violinist; also conducted concerts; was appointed general inspector of music, and director of the National Cons. (1913–14 and again 1920–24). He visited the U.S. many times, and conducted his works in N.Y. and elsewhere. During his years in Leipzig he wrote a Symph., which he conducted there in 1902; at the same time he began experimenting with fractional tones; developed a theory which he named *Sonido 13,* symbolically indicating divisions beyond the 12 notes of the chromatic scale. He further devised a special number notation for quartertones, eighth-tones, and sixteenth-tones, and constructed special instruments for performance of his music in these intervals, such as a harpzither with 97 strings to the octave; his Concertino for Fractional Tones was performed by Leopold Stokowski with the Philadelphia Orch. on March 4, 1927. Carrillo also publ. several books dealing with music of fractional tones, and edited a monthly magazine, *El Sonido 13*, in 1924–25.

WORKS: Operas: *Ossian* (1903); *Matilda* (1909); *Zultil* (1922); Symph. No. 1 (1901); Symph. No. 2 (1905); Symph. No. 3 (1948); 3 symphs. for fractional tones (1926); Triple Concerto for Violin, Flute, Cello, and Orch. (1918); Concertino for Violin, Guitar, Cello, Piccolo, and Harp in fractional tones, with Orch. in normal tuning (1926); *Horizontes* for Violin, Cello, and Harp in fractional tones, and Orch. (1947; Pittsburgh, Nov. 30, 1951, Stokowski conducting); Concertino, subtitled *Metamorfoseador Carrillo*, for Piano in third-tones, and Orch. (1950; Brussels, Nov. 9, 1958); Concerto for Cello in quarter- and eighth-tones, and Orch. (1954; Brussels, Nov. 9, 1958); *Balbuceos* for Piano in sixteenth-tones, and Chamber Orch. (Houston, March 18, 1960); 2 concertos for Violin in quarter-tones, and Orch. (1963, 1964); chamber music: String Sextet (1902); Piano Quintet (1918); 4 atonal quartets (1928–48); *Preludio a Cristóbal Colón* for Soprano, with 5 Instruments in fractional tones (Mexico City, Feb. 15, 1925); Sonata in Quarter-Tones for Guitar (1925); also sonatas for string instruments in quarter-tones, with piano; *Mass for Pope John XXIII* for Chorus a cappella (1962).

WRITINGS: An autobiography, *Julián Carrillo, Su vida y su obra* (Mexico, 1945); *Leyes de metamórfosis musicales* (Mexico, 1949); several manuals of music theory.

BIBLIOGRAPHY: A. Pike, "The Discoveries and Theories of Julián Carrillo, 1875–1965," *Inter-American Music Bulletin*, IV (1966).

Carrodus (real name, **Carruthers**), **John Tiplady,** English violinist; b. Keighley, Yorkshire, Jan. 20, 1836; d. London, July 12, 1895. He studied with his father, a local musician of considerable attainments; played in public as a child; then commenced serious study with Molique in London and in Stuttgart, where he joined the court orch., of which Molique was first violinist. Upon his return to England, Carrodus occupied various positions in theatrical orchs.; was appointed violin instructor at the National Training School (1876); toured in South Africa in 1880. He publ. several pieces for the violin.

BIBLIOGRAPHY: A. Carrodus, *J.T. Carrodus, Violinist: A Life-Story* (London, 1897).

Carroll, Walter, English music pedagogue; b. Manchester, July 4, 1869; d. there, Oct. 9, 1955. He studied piano and theory privately; then at the Univ. of Manchester, obtaining his Mus.Doc. in 1900. He was on the faculty of the Manchester College of Music from 1893–1920 and musical adviser to the City of Manchester Education Committee from 1918–34. He specialized in methods of education for children; publ. a manual, *The Training of Children's Voices,* and various collections of children's songs.

Carron, Arthur, English tenor; b. Swindon, Dec. 12, 1900; d. there, May 10, 1967. He joined the Old Vic theater in 1929; also sang at the Sadler's Wells Opera and at Covent Garden; in 1936 he went to the U.S., where he won the Metropolitan Opera Auditions of the Air, and made his debut with the Metropolitan on May 29, 1936, as Canio in *Pagliacci;* he was chosen to sing the role of Nolan in the world premiere of Walter Damrosch's *The Man without a Country* on May 12, 1937; remained on the roster of the Metropolitan Opera until 1946; then returned to England, where he sang at Covent Garden until 1951.

Carruthers, John. See **Carrodus, John.**

Carse, Adam von Ahn, English composer and writer on music; b. Newcastle upon Tyne, May 19, 1878; d. Great Missenden, Buckinghamshire, Nov. 2, 1958. He studied with F. Corder and Burnett at the Royal Academy of Music in London; from 1909–22 taught music at Winchester College; taught harmony and composition at the Royal Academy of Music (1923–40). He assembled a collection of about 350 wind instruments, which he presented in 1947 to the Horniman Museum in London; publ. a catalogue of this collection in 1951.

WORKS: Symph. poems: *The Death of Tintagiles* (London, 1902) and *In a Balcony* (Promenade Concerts, Aug. 26, 1905); Symph. in C minor (London, July 3, 1906); Symph. in G minor (London, Nov. 19, 1908; revised for the Newcastle Festival, 1909); orch. suites: *The Merry Milkmaids* (1922) and *The Nursery* (1928); *Judas Iscariot's Paradise,* ballade for Baritone Solo, Chorus, and Orch. (1922); 2 sketches for String Orch. (1923); *Barbara Allen* for String Orch.; *Norwegian Fantasia* for Violin and Orch.; *The Lay of the Brown Rosary,* dramatic cantata; numerous choruses; chamber music; piano pieces; songs.

WRITINGS: *Summary of the Elements of Music; Practical Hints on Orchestration; Harmony Exercises* (2 vols., 1923); *The History of Orchestration* (1925); *Orchestral Conducting* (1929); *Musical Wind Instruments* (London, 1939); *The Orchestra in the 18th Century* (Cambridge, 1940; 2nd ed., 1950); *The Orchestra from Beethoven to Berlioz* (Cambridge, 1948); *The Orchestra* (London, 1948); *18th Century Symphonies* (London, 1951); *The Life of Jullien* (Cambridge, 1951).

Cartan, Jean, talented French composer; b. Nancy, Dec. 1, 1906; d. Bligny, March 26, 1932. His father was the famous mathematician Elie Cartan. Jean Cartan studied music with Marcel Samuel Rousseau; then with Paul Dukas at the Paris Cons. His works, composed within the brief period of 6 years, showed extraordinary promise, and his death at the age of 25 was mourned as a great loss to French music. He left a cantata, *Pater Noster;* 2 string quartets; a Sonatina for Flute and Clarinet (International Festival for Contemporary Music, Oxford, July 25, 1931); piano pieces and several cycles of songs.

BIBLIOGRAPHY: A. Roussel, "Jean Cartan," *La*

Revue Musicale (May 1932).

Carte, Richard D'Oyly, English impresario; b. London, May 3, 1844; d. there, April 3, 1901. He studied at Univ. College in London; wrote an opera, *Dr. Ambrosias,* and songs; later turned to music management; he represented, among others, Gounod, Adelina Patti, and the tenor Mario. He then became interested in light opera and introduced in England Lecocq's *Giroflé-Girofla,* Offenbach's *La Périchole,* and other popular French operettas. His greatest achievement was the launching of comic operas by Gilbert and Sullivan; he commissioned and produced at the Royalty Theatre their *Trial by Jury* (1875) and then formed a syndicate to stage other productions of works by Gilbert and Sullivan at the London Opéra-Comique Theatre. Dissension within the syndicate induced him to build the Savoy Theatre (1881), which subsequently became celebrated as the home of Gilbert and Sullivan productions, with Carte himself as the leading "Savoyard." He successfully operated the Savoy Theatre until his death; the enterprise was continued by his wife (Helen Lenoir) until her death in 1913; and thereafter by his sons. In 1887 Carte attempted to establish serious English opera through the building of a special theater (now known as Palace Theatre), and the production in 1891 of Sullivan's grand opera *Ivanhoe,* followed by commissions to other English composers (Hamish McGunn, F.H. Cowen, Goring Thomas) to write operas. D'Oyly Carte introduced many improvements in theatrical management, including the replacement of gaslight by electric illumination.

BIBLIOGRAPHY: F. Cellier and C. Bridgeman, *Gilbert, Sullivan and d'Oyly Carte* (London, 1914); Leslie Baily, the Gilbert and Sullivan Book (revised ed., London, 1966).

Carter, Bennett Lester ("Benny"), black American jazz alto saxophonist, trumpeter, and composer; b. New York, Aug. 8, 1907. He began to study piano as a child; later mastered the alto saxophone, and played in the bands of Horace Henderson, Duke Ellington, Fletcher Henderson, and Chick Webb; also played trumpet, and began to arrange music for bandleaders. In 1935 he went to Europe, where he played in Paris and Amsterdam. Returning to the U.S. in 1938, he led his own groups; then settled in Los Angeles as a film composer-arranger.

Carter, Betty, black American jazz singer; b. Flint, Mich., May 16, 1930. She studied piano at the Detroit Cons.; began singing in local jazz clubs, on the same bill with such celebrated jazz artists as Charlie Parker, Miles Davis, and Dizzy Gillespie; then joined Lionel Hampton's band (1948–51). She gained widespread acclaim at the Newport Jazz Festivals at Carnegie Hall in 1977 and 1978. She soon rose to the loftiest plateau on the jazz firmament; her voice was remarkable for its operatic qualities and resourceful adaptation to quaquaversal situations.

Carter, Elliott Cook, Jr., outstanding American composer; b. New York, Dec. 11, 1908. After graduating from the Horace Mann High School in 1926, Carter entered Harvard Univ., majoring in literature and languages; at the same time studied piano at the Longy School of Music in Cambridge, Mass. In 1930 he devoted himself exclusively to music, taking up harmony and counterpoint with Walter Piston, and orchestration with Edward Burlingame Hill; also attended in 1932 a course given at Harvard Univ. by Gustav Holst. He obtained his M.A. in 1932, and then went to Paris, where he studied with Nadia Boulanger at the Ecole Normale de Musique, receiving there a *licence de contrepoint;* in the interim he learned mathematics, Latin, and Greek. In 1935 he returned to America; was music director of the Ballet Caravan (1937–39); gave courses in music and also in mathematics, physics, and classical Greek at St. John's College in Annapolis, Md. (1939–41); then taught at the Peabody Cons. in Baltimore (1946–48). He was appointed to the faculty of Columbia Univ. (1948–50) and also taught at Yale Univ. from 1958 to 1962. In 1962 he was the American delegate at the East-West Encounter in Tokyo; in 1963 was composer-in-residence at the American Academy in Rome, and in 1964 held a similar post in West Berlin. In 1967–68 he was a professor-at-large at Cornell Univ. He held Guggenheim fellowships in 1945 and 1950, and the American Prix de Rome in 1953. In 1965 he received the Creative Arts Award from Brandeis Univ. In 1953 he received first prize in the *Concours International de Composition pour Quatuor à Cordes* in Liège for his First String Quartet; in 1960 he received the Pulitzer Prize for his 2nd String Quartet, which also received the N.Y. Music Critics Circle Award and was further elected as the most important work of the year by the International Rostrum of Composers. He again won the Pulitzer, for his 3rd String Quartet, in 1973. His reputation as one of the most important American composers grew with every new work he produced; Stravinsky was quoted as saying that Carter's Double Concerto was the first true American masterpiece. The evolution of Carter's style of composition is marked by his constant preoccupation with taxonomic considerations. His early works are set in a neo-Classical style. He later absorbed the Schoenbergian method of composition with 12 tones; finally he developed a system of serial organization in which all parameters, including intervals, metric divisions, rhythm, counterpoint, harmony, and instrumental timbres, become parts of the total conception of each individual work. In this connection he introduced the term "metric modulation," in which secondary rhythms in a polyrhythmic section assume dominance expressed in constantly changing meters, often in such unusual time signatures as 10/16, 21/8, etc. Furthermore, he assigns to each participating instrument in a polyphonic work a special interval, a distinctive rhythmic figure, and a selective register, so that the individuality of each part is clearly outlined, a distribution which is often reinforced by placing the players at a specified distance from one another.

WORKS: *Tom and Lily,* comic opera in one act (1934); Flute Sonata (1934); Tarantella for Male

Chorus and Orch. (1936); ballet, *The Ball Room Guide* (1937); *The Bridge,* oratorio (1937); *Madrigal Book* for Mixed Voices (1937); Concerto for English Horn (1937); ballet, *Pocahontas* (N.Y., May 24, 1939); *Heart Not So Heavy as Mine* for a cappella Chorus (1939); Suite for Quartet of Alto Saxophones (1939); *The Defense of Corinth,* after Rabelais, for Speaker, Men's Chorus, and Piano, 4-hands (Cambridge, Mass., March 12, 1942); Adagio for Viola and Piano (1943); Symph. No. 1 (Rochester, April 27, 1944); *The Harmony of Morning* for Female Chorus and Small Orch. (N.Y., Feb. 25, 1945); *Canonic Suite* for 4 Clarinets (1945); *Warble for Lilac Time,* after Walt Whitman, for Soprano and Instruments (Yaddo, Sept. 14, 1946); Piano Sonata (1946); *The Minotaur,* ballet (N.Y., March 26, 1947); *Holiday Overture* for Orch. (Baltimore, Jan. 7, 1948); Woodwind Quintet (N.Y., Feb 27, 1949); 8 pieces for 4 Timpani (1949; Nos. 3 and 6 composed and added in 1966); Cello Sonata (N.Y., Feb. 27, 1950); String Quartet (1951); 8 Etudes and a Fantasy, for Flute, Oboe, Clarinet, and Bassoon (N.Y., Oct. 28, 1952); Sonata for Flute, Oboe, Cello, and Harpsichord (N.Y., Nov. 19, 1953); Variations for Orch. (Louisville, Ky., April 21, 1956); 2nd String Quartet (1959); Double Concerto for Harpsichord and Piano with 2 Chamber Orchs. (N.Y., Sept. 6, 1961); Piano Concerto (Boston, Jan. 6, 1967); Concerto for Orch. (N.Y. Phil., Feb. 5, 1970); String Quartet No. 3 (1971); Brass Quintet (1974); Duo for Violin and Piano (1974); *A Mirror on Which to Dwell* for Soprano and 9 Players, to a cycle of 6 poems by Elizabeth Bishop (N.Y., Feb. 24, 1976); *A Symphony of 3 Orchestras* (N.Y., Feb. 17, 1977); *Syringa,* cantata for Soprano and Small Ensemble (N.Y., Dec. 10, 1978); *Night Fantasies* for Piano (1980); *In Sleep, in Thunder,* song cycle for Tenor and 14 Players, to poems by Robert Lowell (1981); *Triple Duo* for Paired Instruments: Flute/Clarinet; Violin/Cello; Piano/Percussion (1982; London, April 23, 1983); *Changes* for Guitar Solo (1983). BIBLIOGRAPHY: A. Skulsky, "Elliott Carter," *American Composers Alliance Bulletin* (Summer 1953); Richard F. Goldman, "The Music of Elliott Carter," *Musical Quarterly* (April 1957); *Modern Music: An Analytical Index,* compiled by Wayne Shirley, W. and C. Lichtenwanger (N.Y., 1976; pp. 40–41); Else Stone and Kurt Stone, eds., *The Writings of Elliott Carter. An American Composer Looks at Modern Music* (N.Y., 1977); David Schiff, *The Music of Elliott Carter* (N.Y., 1982); idem, "Elliott Carter," *Ovation* (Dec. 1983).

Carter, Ernest Trow, American organist and composer; b. Orange, N.J., Sept. 3, 1866; d. Stamford, Conn., June 21, 1953. He studied piano with Mary Bradshaw and William Mason (1874–84); then composition in Berlin with Wilhelm Freudenberg, Otis Boise, and others; returning to the U.S., he became organist and choirmaster at Princeton Univ. (1899–1901); he settled in N.Y. as an arranger, conductor, and composer. He received a B.A. from Princeton (1888) and an M.A. from Columbia Univ. (1899). WORKS: Operas: *The Blonde Donna, or The Fiesta of Santa Barbara* (N.Y., Dec. 9, 1931) and *The White Bird* (Chicago, March 6, 1924; Osnabrück, Germany, Nov. 15, 1927); ballet pantomime, *Namba, or The 3rd Statue* (N.Y., April 22, 1933); *Symphonic Suite* for Orch.; String Quartet; anthems, including *The Lord's Prayer* and *Out of the Depths;* male quartets; piano pieces; songs. BIBLIOGRAPHY: E.E. Hipsher, *American Opera and Its Composers* (Philadelphia, 1927; pp. 113–17).

Carter, Maybelle ("Mother"), American folk and country music singer; b. Nickelsville, Va., May 10, 1909; d. Nashville, Tenn., Oct. 23, 1978. With other members of her family, she formed the famous singing group known as the Carter Family in 1927; through recordings and radio broadcasts, they led the way to the widespread popularity of mountain folk and country music; among their greatest successes were their versions of *Wildwood Flower, It Takes a Worried Man to Sing a Worried Song, Will the Circle Be Unbroken, Wabash Cannonball,* and *Amazing Grace.* In later years she appeared as a soloist on the "Grand Ole Opry" radio program in Nashville, Tenn., where she displayed her talents as a guitarist, autoharpist, and songwriter. She also made appearances with her son-in-law, the singer Johnny Cash.

Cartier, Jean-Baptiste, French violinist and composer; b. Avignon, May 28, 1765; d. Paris, 1841. He was a pupil of Viotti; was a violinist at the Grand Opéra (1791–1821); in 1804, became a member of the Imperial Orch. under Paisiello; then of the Royal Orch. (1815–30). He composed 2 operas; 2 symphs.; sonatas, variations, duets, and études for violin; publ. a manual, *L'Art du violon* (Paris, 1798, 1801, 1803; reprinted, N.Y., 1973), containing selections from eminent French, Italian, and German masters of the 17th and 18th centuries.

Carulli, Ferdinando, Italian guitar player and composer; b. Naples, Feb. 20, 1770; d. Paris, Feb. 17, 1841. He went to Paris in 1808 and prospered there as a guitar teacher. He is generally regarded as the first guitarist to use his instrument for artistic performances; he publ. a method, *L'Harmonie appliquée à la guitarre* (Paris, 1825). His works number nearly 400 items, including concertos, quartets, trios, duos, fantasias, variations, and solos of all descriptions. In 1830 he composed a piece of program music for guitar entitled *Les Trois Jours,* descriptive of the days of the July 1830 revolution.

Caruso, Enrico, celebrated Italian tenor; b. Naples, Feb. 27, 1873; d. there, Aug. 2, 1921. He was the 18th child of a worker's family, his father being a machinist. All 17 children born before him died in infancy; 2 born after him survived. He sang Neapolitan ballads by ear; as a youth he applied for a part in *Mignon* at the Teatro Fondo in Naples, but was unable to follow the orch. at the rehearsal and had to be replaced by another singer. His first serious study was with Guglielmo Vergine (1891–94); he continued with Vincenzo Lombardi. His operatic debut took place at the Teatro Nuovo in Naples on

Nov. 16, 1894, in *L'Amico Francesco*, by an amateur composer, Mario Morelli. In 1895 he appeared at the Teatro Fondo in *La Traviata, La Favorita*, and *Rigoletto;* during the following few seasons he added *Aida, Faust, Carmen, La Bohème*, and *Tosca* to his repertoire. The decisive turn in his career came when he was chosen to appear as leading tenor in the first performance of Giordano's *Fedora* (Teatro Lirico, Milan, Nov. 17, 1898), in which he made a great impression. Several important engagements followed. In 1899 and 1900 he sang in St. Petersburg and Moscow; between 1899 and 1903 he appeared in 4 summer seasons in Buenos Aires. The culmination of these successes was the coveted opportunity to sing at La Scala; he sang there in *La Bohème* (Dec. 26, 1900), and in the first performance of Mascagni's *Le Maschere* (Jan. 17, 1901). At the Teatro Lirico in Milan he took part in the first performances of Franchetti's *Germania* (March 11, 1902) and Cilea's *Adriana Lecouvreur* (Nov. 6, 1902). In the spring season of 1902 he appeared (with Melba) in Monte Carlo, and was reengaged there for 3 more seasons. He made his London debut as the Duke in *Rigoletto* (Covent Garden, May 14, 1902) and was immediately successful with the British public and press. He gave 25 performances in London until July 28, 1902, appearing with Melba, Nordica, and Calvé. In the season of 1902–3, Caruso sang in Rome and Lisbon; during the summer of 1903 he was in South America. Finally, on Nov. 23, 1903, he made his American debut at the Metropolitan Opera, in *Rigoletto*. After that memorable occasion, Caruso was connected with the Metropolitan to the end of his life. He traveled with various American opera companies from coast to coast; he happened to be performing in San Francisco when the 1906 earthquake nearly destroyed the city. He achieved his most spectacular successes in America, attended by enormous publicity. In 1907 Caruso sang in Germany (Leipzig, Hamburg, Berlin) and in Vienna; he was acclaimed there as enthusiastically as in the Anglo-Saxon and Latin countries. A complete list of his appearances is given in the appendix of his biography by Pierre Key and Bruno Zirato (Boston, 1922). Caruso's fees soared from $2 as a boy in Italy in 1891 to the fabulous sums of $15,000 for a single performance in Mexico City in 1920. He made recordings in the U.S. as early as 1902; his annual income from this source alone netted him $115,000 at the peak of his career. He excelled in realistic Italian operas; his Cavaradossi in *Tosca* and Canio in *Pagliacci* became models which every singer emulated. He sang several French operas; the German repertoire remained completely alien to him; his only appearances in Wagnerian roles were 3 performances of *Lohengrin* in Buenos Aires (1901). His voice possessed such natural warmth and great strength in the middle register that as a youth he was believed to be a baritone. The sustained quality of his bel canto was exceptional and enabled him to give superb interpretations of lyrical parts. For dramatic effect, he often resorted to the "coup de glotte" (which became known as the "Caruso sob"); here the singing gave way to intermittent vocalization without tonal precision. While Caruso was criticized for such usages from the musical standpoint, his characterizations on the stage were overwhelmingly impressive. Although of robust health, he abused it by unceasing activity. He was stricken with a throat hemorrhage during a performance at the Brooklyn Academy of Music (Dec. 11, 1920), but was able to sing in N.Y. one last time, on Dec. 24, 1920. Several surgical operations were performed in an effort to arrest a pleurisy; Caruso was taken to Italy, but succumbed to the illness after several months of remission. He was known as a convivial person and a lover of fine food (a brand of macaroni was named after him). He possessed a gift for caricature; a collection of his drawings was publ. in N.Y. in 1922 (2nd ed., 1951). His private life was turbulent; his liaison (never legalized) with Ada Giachetti, by whom he had 2 sons, was painfully resolved by court proceedings in 1912, creating much disagreeable publicity; there were also suits brought against him by 2 American women. In 1906 the celebrated "monkey-house case" (in which Caruso was accused of improper behavior toward a lady while viewing the animals in Central Park) threatened for a while his continued success in America. On Aug. 20, 1918, he married Dorothy Park Benjamin of N.Y., over the strong opposition of her father, a rich industrialist. Caruso received numerous decorations from European governments, among them the Order of Commendatore of the Crown of Italy; the Légion d'Honneur; and the Order of the Crown Eagle of Prussia. A fictional film biography, *The Great Caruso*, was made of his life in 1950.

BIBLIOGRAPHY: E. Caruso, *How to Sing* (London, 1913; German trans. by A. Spanuth, *Wie man singen soll*, Berlin, 1914); J.H. Wagenmann, *E. C. und das Problem der Stimmbildung* (Altenburg, 1911); M.H. Flint, *C. and His Art* (N.Y., 1917); Pierre Key and Bruno Zirato, *E. C.* (Boston, 1922); Emil Ledtner, *Erinnerungen an C.* (1922); S. Fucito and B.J. Beyer, *C. and the Art of Singing* (N.Y., 1922); P.M. Marafioti, *C's Method of Voice Production* (N.Y., 1922; new ed., 1933); Dorothy B. Caruso and Mrs. T. Goddard, *Wings of Song: The Story of Caruso* (1928); C. Armin, *E. C.s Stimme und ihr Verhältnis zum Stauprinzip* (1929); Nicola Daspuro, *E. C.* (Milan, 1938); Eugenio Gara, *C., Storia di un Emigrante* (Milan, 1947); Dorothy Caruso, *E. C., His Life and Death* (N.Y., 1945); T.R. Ybarra, *C.: The Man of Naples and the Voice of Gold* (N.Y., 1953); F. Robinson, *Caruso: His Life in Pictures* (N.Y., 1957); J. Freestone and H. Drummond, *Enrico Caruso: His Recorded Legacy* (London, 1960); J. Bolig, *The Recordings of Enrico Caruso* (Dover, Del., 1973); P. Mario Marafioti, *Caruso's Method of Voice Production* (N.Y., 1981); H. Greensfeld, *Caruso* (N.Y., 1983).

Carvalho, Eleazar de, brilliant Brazilian conductor and composer; b. Iguatú (Ceará), July 28, 1912. His father was of Dutch extraction and his mother was part Indian. He studied in Fortaleza at the Apprentice Seaman's School; later joined the National Naval Corps in Rio de Janeiro and played tuba in the band. In 1941 he became assistant conductor of the Brazilian Symph. Orch. in Rio de Janeiro. In 1946 he went to the U.S. to study conducting with Koussevitzky at the Berkshire Music Center, and Koussevitzky invited him to conduct a pair of concerts with the Boston Symph. Orch. Carvalho demonstrated extraordinary ability and musicianship by leading all rehearsals and the concerts without score in a difficult program; his sense of perfect pitch is exceptional. He subsequently conducted a number of guest engagements with orchs. in America and in Europe. In 1963–68 he was conductor of the St. Louis Symph. Orch.; during his tenure he introduced many modern works into his programs, much to the discomfiture of the financial backers of the orch.; still, he lasted a few seasons in St. Louis. From 1969 to 1973 he was conductor of the Hofstra Univ. Orch. in Hempstead, N.Y., which offered him a more liberal esthetic climate; then returned to Brazil.

WORKS: 2 operas on Brazilian subjects: *Descuberta do Brasil* (Rio de Janeiro, June 19, 1939) and *Tiradentes* (Rio de Janeiro, Sept. 7, 1941, dealing with the exploits of a revolutionary dentist during the war of liberation); *Sinfonia branca* (1943); symph. poems: *A Traicao* (1941); *Batalha Naval de Riachuelo* (1943); *Guararapes* (1945); 3 overtures; 2 trios; 2 string quartets; Violin Sonata; songs. He is the husband of the avant-garde composer and pianist **Jocy de Oliveira.**

Carvalho (real name, **Carvaille**), **Léon,** distinguished French baritone and opera manager; b. Port-Louis, near Paris, Jan. 18, 1825; d. Paris, Dec. 29, 1897. He studied at the Paris Cons.; began his career as a singer; in 1853 married the French soprano **Marie Miolan.** From 1856–68 he was director of the Théâtre-Lyrique; from 1869–75 was chief producer at the Paris Opéra; concurrently was manager of the Théâtre du Vaudeville (1872–74); then acted as stage manager at the Opéra; in 1876–87 was director of the Opéra-Comique, succeeding du Locle. After the fire at the Opéra-Comique in 1887, in which 131 persons perished, he was arrested and sentenced to 6 months' imprisonment, but was acquitted on appeal, and reinstated in 1891. He had the reputation of an enlightened administrator, encouraging young artists and young composers.

Carvalho-Miolan, Caroline-Marie-Félix, French dramatic soprano; b. Marseilles, Dec. 31, 1827; d. near Dieppe, July 10, 1895. She entered the Paris Cons. at 12; studied under Duprez; made her operatic debut on Dec. 14, 1849, in *Lucia di Lammermoor* at the Opéra-Comique, where she was engaged from 1849–55; from 1856–67 she sang at the Théâtre Lyrique, where she created the soprano parts in Gounod's *Faust, Roméo et Juliette,* and *Mireille,* and in Clapisson's *La Fanchonette;* from 1868–85 she sang at the Paris Opéra and at the Opéra-Comique; also appeared in London, Berlin, Brussels, St. Petersburg, etc.; retired in 1885. In 1853 she married **Léon Carvalho.**

BIBLIOGRAPHY: E. Accoyer-Spoll, *Mme. Carvalho* (Paris, 1885); H. de Curzon, *Croquis d'artistes* (Paris, 1898).

Carver, Robert, Scottish composer; b. 1487; d. after 1546. He was a Monk of Scone Abbey; developed a melismatic style of composition; wrote masses on the medieval song *L'Homme armé* and many motets, one of them in 19 independent parts. He is regarded as an equal of Dunstable in melodic and rhythmic excellence. Vol. 1 of his collected works was publ. by the American Inst. of Musicology, edited by Denis Stevens, in 1959.

Cary, Annie Louise, celebrated American contralto; b. Wayne, Kennebec County, Maine, Oct. 22, 1841; d. Norwalk, Conn., April 3, 1921. She studied in Boston and Milan; made her operatic debut in Copenhagen as Azucena; studied under Mme. Viardot-García at Baden-Baden; was engaged at Hamburg, Stockholm, Brussels, London, and St. Petersburg. Returning to the U.S., she continued her operatic career in N.Y. theaters; was the first American woman to sing a Wagnerian role in the U.S. (Ortrud in *Lohengrin,* 1877). She married C.M. Raymond in 1882, and retired at the height of her powers. She appeared in concert or oratorio in all leading cities of America.

BIBLIOGRAPHY: G.T. Edwards, *Music and Musicians of Maine* (Portland, 1928; pp. 204-19); H. Earle Johnson, in *Notable American Women* (Cambridge, Mass., 1951, vol. 1; contains bibliography).

Casabona, Francisco, Brazilian composer and pedagogue; b. São Paulo, Oct. 16, 1894. He studied in Brazil and in Italy; attended classes of Alessandro Longo (piano), Camillo de Nardis (theory), and Giovanni Barbieri (composition) at the Cons. of Naples. Returning to Brazil, he became a prof. at the São Paulo Cons. In his music, Casabona follows an Italianate expressive style, excelling equally in vocal and instrumental works.

WORKS: Comic operas: *Godiamo la Vita* (Rome, 1917) and *Principessa dell'Atelier* (Naples, 1918); symph. poems: *Nero* (1915); *Crepúsculo Sertanejo* (1926); *Noite de São João* (1934); Sinfonia No. 1 (1937); Sinfonia No. 2 (1940); *La Fable d'Einstein* for Orch. (1946); *Maracatú,* Afro-Brazilian dance (1964); Violin Sonata; piano pieces in the Brazilian idiom; choruses and songs.

Casadesus, François Louis, French conductor and composer; b. Paris, Dec. 2, 1870; d. Suresnes, near Paris, June 27, 1954. He studied at the Paris Cons.; conducted the Opéra and the Opéra-Comique on tour in France (1890–92); in 1895 conducted the Opéra on a European tour; was the founder and director (1918–22) of the American Cons. at Fontainebleau; later was active as a radio conductor; wrote music criticism. A collection of valedictory articles was publ. in honor of his 80th birthday (Paris, 1950).

WORKS: Operas: *Cachaprès* (Brussels, 1914); *La Chanson de Paris* (1924); *Bertran de Born* (Monte Carlo, 1925); *Messie d'Amour* (Monte Carlo, 1928);

Symphonie scandinave; Au beau jardin de France for Orch.; Symph. in E major; smaller compositions for orch.; numerous songs.

Casadesus, Henri, French violinist, brother of the preceding; b. Paris, Sept. 30, 1879; d. there, May 31, 1947. He studied with Lavignac and Laforge in Paris; from 1910–17 was a member of the Capet Quartet; was a founder and director of the Société Nouvelle des Instruments Anciens, in which he played the viola d'amore; subsequently toured in the U.S., playing at the Elizabeth Sprague Coolidge Festivals, Library of Congress, Washington, D.C. Rare and ancient instruments collected by Casadesus are in the museum of the Boston Symph. Orch.

Casadesus, Jean, French pianist, son of **Robert** and **Gaby Casadesus;** b. Paris, July 7, 1927; d. in an automobile accident, near Renfrew, Ontario, Canada, Jan. 20, 1972. He studied piano with his parents; at the outbreak of World War II, he went to the U.S.; studied at Princeton Univ.; won the contest for young soloists held by the Philadelphia Orch. in 1946; appeared as soloist with the N.Y. Phil. and with major European orchs.; made tours of the U.S. and Canada.

Casadesus, Jean-Claude, French conductor, nephew of **Robert** and **Gaby Casadesus;** b. Paris, Dec. 7, 1935. He studied at the Paris Cons.; in 1959 he received first prize as a percussion player there; he was then engaged as timpanist of the Concerts Colonne and of the Domaine Musical; also studied conducting with Dervaux at the Ecole Normale de Musique and with Boulez in Basel. In 1969 he became resident conductor of the Paris Opéra and of the Opéra-Comique. In 1971 he became assistant conductor to Dervaux with the Orch. Phil. des Pays de la Loire in Angers. In 1976 he founded the Lille Phil. Orch.; also appeared as a guest conductor with the BBC Symph., Leningrad Phil., Scottish National Orch., Covent Garden, English National Opera, and other orchs. and opera houses in Europe. In 1983 he was named general secretary of the Major Council of Music in Paris. He was made an officer of the National Order of Merit for his services to French culture.

Casadesus, Marius, French violinist, brother of **François Casadesus;** b. Paris, Oct. 24, 1892; d. Suresnes (Paris), Oct. 13, 1981. He studied at the Paris Cons., graduating in 1914 with first prize in violin; subsequently toured in Europe and America; gave numerous sonata recitals with his nephew, the pianist **Robert Casadesus.** He was a founding member of the Société Nouvelle des Instruments Anciens (1920–40), organized with the purpose of reviving old string instruments, such as the Quinton and Diskantgambe. He wrote a number of pieces for the violin, some choral music, and songs, but his most notorious contribution to violin literature was the so-called Adelaide Concerto, supposedly composed by Mozart when he was 10 years old and dedicated to the oldest daughter of Louis XV, Adelaide (hence the nickname). It was performed in Paris on Dec. 24, 1931, with considerable publicity, but skepticism arose when Casadesus failed to produce either the manuscript or a contemporary copy of it. In 1977, in the course of a litigation for his copyright as the arranger of the "Adelaide Concerto," Casadesus admitted that the piece was entirely his own work. A detailed discussion of the whole hullabaloo is in the entry "Misattributed Compositions" in Percy A. Scholes, *The Oxford Companion to Music.*

Casadesus, Robert, eminent French pianist and composer; b. Paris, April 7, 1899; d. there, Sept. 19, 1972. A scion of a remarkable musical family, he absorbed music at home from his earliest childhood. His uncles were **Henri** and **François Casadesus;** another uncle, **Marcel Louis Lucien** (1882–1917), was a cellist, and his aunt **Rose** was a pianist. He received his formal musical education studying piano with Diémer and composition with Leroux at the Paris Cons. In 1922 he embarked on a wide-ranging tour as a concert pianist; after the outbreak of World War II he went to the U.S.; taught classes at various schools. After the war he taught at the American Cons. at Fountainebleau. He was a prolific composer; wrote 7 symphs., of which the last was performed posthumously in N.Y. on Nov. 8, 1972. He appeared with his wife, **Gaby Casadesus,** in his Concerto for 2 Pianos and Orch. with the N.Y. Phil. on Nov. 25, 1950. He also wrote a Concerto for 3 Pianos and String Orch., which he performed for the first time with his wife and his son **Jean** in N.Y., July 24, 1965. As a pianist, Casadesus was distinguished for his Gallic sense of balance and fine gradation of tonal dynamics.

BIBLIOGRAPHY: S. Stookes, *The Art of Robert Casadesus* (London, 1960).

Casals, Pablo (Pau Carlos Salvador Defilló), great Spanish cellist; b. Vendrell, Catalonia, Dec. 29, 1876; d. San Juan, Puerto Rico, Oct. 22, 1973. He was the second child of a progeny originally numbering 11, 7 of whom died at birth. Legend has it that Pablo Casals barely escaped the same fate when the umbilical cord became entangled around his neck and nearly choked him to death; another legend (supported by Casals himself) is that he was conceived when Brahms began his B-flat Major Quartet, of which Casals owned the original MS, and that he was born when Brahms completed its composition. This legend is rendered moot by the fact that the quartet in question was completed and performed before Casals was born. But even the ascertainable facts of the life of Casals make it a glorious legend. His father, the parish organist and choirmaster in Vendrell, gave Casals instruction in piano, violin, and organ. When Casals was 11 he first heard the cello performed by a group of traveling musicians, and decided to study the instrument. In 1888 his mother took him to Barcelona, where he enrolled in the Escuela Municipal de Música. There he studied cello with José García, and also took music theory with José Rodoreda, and studied piano with Joaquín Malats and Francisco Costa Llobera. His progress as a cellist was nothing short of prodigious, and he was able to give a solo recital in Barcelona at the age of 14, on Feb. 23, 1891; he graduated with honors in 1893. Albéniz, who heard him play in a café trio, gave him a letter of introduction to Count Morphy, the private secretary to María Cristina, the Queen Regent, in Madrid. Casals was asked to play at informal concerts in the palace, and was granted a royal stipend for study in composition with Tomás Bretón. In 1893 he entered the Cons. de Música y Declamación in Madrid, where he attended chamber music classes of Jesús de Monasterio. He also played in the newly organized Quartet Society there (1894–95). In 1895 he went to Paris and, deprived of his stipend from Spain, earned a living by playing the second cello in the theater orch. of the Folies Marigny. He decided to return to Spain, where he received, in 1896, an appointment to the faculty of the Escuela Municipal de Música in Barcelona; he was also principal cellist in the orch. of the Gran Teatro del Liceo. In 1897 he appeared as soloist with the Madrid Symph. Orch., and was awarded the Order of Carlos III from the Queen. His career as a cello virtuoso was now assured. In 1899 he played at the Crystal Palace in London, and was later given the honor of playing for Queen Victoria at her summer residence at Cowes, Isle of Wight. On Nov. 12, 1899, he appeared as a soloist at a prestigious Lamoureux Concert in Paris, and played with Lamoureux again on Dec. 17, 1899, obtaining exceptional success with both the public and the press. He toured Spain and the Netherlands with the pianist Harold Bauer (1900–1901); then made his first tour of the U.S. (1901–2). In 1903 he made a grand tour of South America. On Jan. 15, 1904, he was invited to play at the White House for President Theodore Roosevelt. In 1906 he became associated with the talented young Portuguese cellist Guilhermina Suggia, who studied with him and began to appear in concerts as Mme. P. Casals-Suggia, although they were not legally married. Their liaison was dissolved in 1912; in 1914 Casals married the American socialite and singer Susan Metcalfe; they became separated in 1928, but were not divorced until 1957. Continuing his brilliant career, Casals organized, in Paris, a concert trio with the pianist Cortot and the violinist Thibaud; they played concerts together until 1937. Casals also became interested in conducting, and in 1919 he organized, in Barcelona, the Orquesta Pau Casals and led its first concert on Oct. 13, 1920. With the outbreak of the Spanish Civil War in 1936, the Orquesta Pau Casals ceased its activities. Casals was an ardent supporter of the Spanish Republican Government, and after its defeat vowed never to return to Spain until democracy was restored there. He settled in the French village of Prades, on the Spanish frontier; between 1939 and 1942 he made sporadic appearances as a cellist in the unoccupied zone of southern France and in Switzerland. So fierce was his opposition to the Franco regime in Spain that he even declined to appear in countries that recognized the totalitarian Spanish government, making an exception when he took part in a concert of chamber music in the White House on Nov. 13, 1961, at the invitation of President Kennedy, whom he admired. In June 1950 he resumed his career as conductor and cellist at the Prades Festival, organized in commemoration of the bicentennial of the death of Bach; he continued leading the Prades Festivals until 1966. He made his permanent residence in 1956, when he settled in San Juan, Puerto Rico (his mother was born there when the island was still under Spanish rule). In 1957 an annual Festival Casals was inaugurated there. During all these years he developed energetic activities as a pedagogue, leading master classes in Switzerland; Italy; Berkeley, California; and Marlboro, Vermont; some of these sessions were televised. Casals was also a composer; perhaps his most effective work is *La sardana,* for an ensemble of cellos, which he composed in 1926. His oratorio *El pessebre* (*The Manger*) was performed for the first time in Acapulco, Mexico, on Dec. 17, 1960; in subsequent years he conducted numerous performances of the score. One of his last compositions was the *Himno a las Naciones Unidas* (*Hymm of the United Nations);* he conducted its first performance in a special concert at the United Nations on Oct. 24, 1971, 2 months before his 95th birthday. On Aug. 3, 1957, at the age of 80, Casals married his young pupil Marta Montañez; following his death, she married the pianist Eugene Istomin, on Feb. 15, 1975. Casals did not live to see the liberation of Spain from the Franco dictatorship, but he was posthumously honored by the Spanish government of King Juan Carlos I, which issued in 1976 a commemorative postage stamp in honor of his 100th birthday.

BIBLIOGRAPHY: L. Littlehales, *Pablo Casals* (N.Y., 1929; revised ed., 1948); A. Conte, *La Légende de Pablo Casals* (Perpignan, 1950); J. Corredor, *Conversations with Casals* (an Eng. trans. of the 1954 French ed. by A. Mangeot; London, 1956); A. Seiler, *Casals* (with many photographs by P. Moeschlin; Olten, 1956); P. and A. Kahn, *Joys and Sorrows: Reflections by Pablo Casals as Told to Albert E. Kahn* (N.Y., 1970; French trans., Paris, 1970; Japanese trans., Tokyo, 1973); H. Kirk, *Pablo Casals. A Biography* (N.Y., 1974); D. Blum, *Casals and the Art of Interpretation* (London, 1977).

Casamorata, Luigi Fernando, composer and music editor; b. Würzburg, of Italian parents, May 15, 1807; d. Florence, Sept. 24, 1881. He studied law and music in Florence; became co-editor of the Florentine *Gazzetta Musicale* from its start (1842) and was the founder of the Istituto Musicale in Florence (1860); publ. its history, *Origine, storia e ordinamento dell'Istituto musicale fiorentino;* also publ. *Manuale di armonia* (1876). His ballets and operas were unsuccessful, and he turned to instrumental and choral works, of which he wrote many.

Casanova, André, French composer; b. Paris, Oct. 12, 1919. He studied law as well as music; took lessons with René Leibowitz and others in Paris. His music is cast in a neo-Classical framework, with some atonal deviations.

WORKS: Symph. No. 1 (1949); Symph. No. 2 for

Chamber Orch. (1952; Nice, Feb. 20, 1971); *Ballade for Clarinet and Chamber Orch.* (1954–55); Capriccio for Oboe and Chamber Orch. (1960); *Anamorphoses* for Orch. (Strasbourg, June 21, 1963); Violin Concerto (1963); *La Clé d'argent,* lyric drama (1965); Trumpet Concerto (1966); *Le Bonheur dans le crime,* opera (1969); *Notturno,* ballet (Paris, June 20, 1972); Symph. No. 3, *Dithyrambe* (Paris, Feb. 13, 1973); *Récitatifs* for Orch. (Nice, Feb. 2, 1974).

Casanovas, Narciso, Spanish composer; b. Sabadell, near Barcelona, Feb. 17, 1747; d. Montserrat, April 1, 1799. He was a member of the famous Catalan school of Montserrat; was ordained a priest in 1763; served as organist at the Montserrat monastery. He wrote 5 motets, 13 Psalms, several litanies, and many works for organ. His Sonata in F (in Haydn's style) is reprinted in J. Nin's *17 sonates et pièces anciennes d'auteurs espagnols* (Paris, 1929).

Casavola, Franco, Italian composer; b. Modugno, July 13, 1891; d. Bari, July 7, 1955. He studied in Rome with Respighi; abandoned his academic pursuits, joined the futurist movement, and composed music glorifying the mechanical age; also wrote futurist poetry. Among his works in this genre are a ballet, *Fantasia meccanica,* and *La danza dell'elica* for Flute, Clarinet, Violin, Percussion, Wind Machine, and Blasting Machine. At a later period he changed his ideas and veered toward musical realism with Romantic overtones. His operas *Il gobbo del califfo* (1929), *Astuzie d'amore* (1936), and *Salammbô* (1948) have been produced with some success; he also wrote 2 ballets, *L'alba di Don Giovanni* (1932) and *Il castello nel bosco* (1931).

Casazza, Elvira, Italian mezzo-soprano; b. Ferrara, Nov. 15, 1887; d. Milan, Jan. 24, 1965. She studied in Ferrara and Milan; made her debut in Varese in 1909; then sang at La Scala in Milan (1915–42); also sang at Covent Garden, London (1926; 1931). After her retirement, she taught voice in Pesaro and Rome.

Case, Anna, American soprano; b. Clinton, N.J., Oct. 29, 1888; d. New York, Jan. 7, 1984. She studied voice in N.Y. with Mme. Ohrstrom-Renard; on Nov. 20, 1909, made her operatic debut at the Metropolitan Opera as a page in *Lohengrin;* remained on its roster until 1919; among the roles in which she excelled were Aida and Carmen. On July 18, 1931, she married Clarence H. Mackay, chairman of the board of the Postal Telegraph Corp., whose daughter, by his first marriage, was Ellin Mackay, who married Irving Berlin.

Casella, Alfredo, outstanding Italian composer; b. Turin, July 25, 1883; d. Rome, March 5, 1947. He began to play the piano at the age of 4 and received his early instruction from his mother; in 1896 he went to Paris, and studied with Diémer and Fauré at the Paris Cons.; won first prize in piano in 1899. He made concert tours as pianist in Europe, including

Russia; appeared as guest conductor with European orchs.; in 1912 conducted the Concerts Populaires at the Trocadéro; taught piano classes at the Paris Cons. from 1912–15; returned to Rome and was appointed a prof. of piano at the Santa Cecilia Academy, as successor to Sgambati. In 1917 he founded the Società Nazionale di Musica (later the Società Italiana di Musica Moderna; since 1923 as the Corporazione delle Musiche Nuove, Italian section of the International Society for Contemporary Music). On Oct. 28, 1921, Casella made his American debut with the Philadelphia Orch. in the triple capacity of composer, conductor, and piano soloist; he also appeared as a guest conductor in Chicago, Detroit, Cincinnati, Cleveland, and Los Angeles; was conductor of the Boston Pops in 1927–29, introducing a number of modern works, but failing to please the public. In 1928 he was awarded the first prize of $3,000 given by the Musical Fund Society in Philadelphia; in 1934 won the Coolidge Prize. In 1938 he returned to Italy, where he remained until his death. Apart from his activities as pianist, conductor, and composer, he was a prolific writer on music, and contributed numerous articles to various publications in Italy, France, Russia, Germany, and America; he possessed an enlightened cosmopolitan mind, which enabled him to penetrate the musical cultures of various nations; at the same time he steadfastly proclaimed his adherence to the ideals of Italian art. In his music he applied modernistic techniques to the old forms; his style may be termed neo-Classical, but in his early years he cultivated extreme modernism.

WORKS: OPERAS: *La donna serpente* (Rome, March 17, 1932); *La favola d'Orfeo* (Venice, Sept. 6, 1932); *Il deserto tentato,* mystery in one act (Florence, May 6, 1937). BALLETS: *Il convento veneziano* (1912; La Scala, Feb. 7, 1925); *La Giara,* "choreographic comedy" after Pirandello (Paris, Nov. 19, 1924; his most successful work); *La camera dei disegni,* for children (Rome, 1940); *La rosa del sogno* (Rome, 1943). ORCH. WORKS: Symph. No. I, in B minor (1905); Symph. No. II, in C minor (1908–9); Symph. No. III, op. 63 (Chicago, March 27, 1941); Suite in C (1909); *Italia,* rhapsody based on folk themes (Paris, April 23, 1910); *Le Couvent sur l'eau,* symph. suite based on the ballet *Il convento veneziano* (Paris, April 23, 1914); *Notte di Maggio* for Voice and Orch. (Paris, March 29, 1914); *Elegia eroica* (Rome, Jan. 21, 1917); *Pagine di guerra* (1916); *Pupazzetti,* 5 pieces for Puppets (1918); *Partita* for Piano and Orch. (N.Y., Oct. 29, 1925); *Scarlattiana,* on themes by Scarlatti, for Piano and Orch. (N.Y., Jan. 22, 1927); *Concerto romano* for Organ and Orch. (N.Y., March 11, 1927); Violin Concerto in A minor (Moscow, Oct. 8, 1928); *Introduzione, Aria e Toccata* (Rome, April 5, 1933); Concerto for Trio and Orch. (Berlin, Nov. 17, 1933); Concerto (Amsterdam, 1937); *Paganiniana,* on themes by Paganini (Vienna, 1942). VOCAL WORKS: *L'Adieu à la vie,* cycle of 4 Hindu lyrics after Tagore's *Gitanjali* (1915; also for Voice and Orch., 1926); *4 favole romanesche* (1923); *Ninna nanna popolare genovese* (1934); *3 canti sacri* for Baritone and Orch. (1943); *Missa solemnis pro pace* (1944). CHAMBER WORKS: *Barcarola e scher-*

zo for Flute and Piano (1904); 2 cello sonatas (1907, 1927); *Siciliana e burlesca* for Flute and Piano (1914; 2nd version for Piano Trio, 1917); *5 pezzi* for String Quartet (1920); Concerto for String Quartet (1923–24; also arranged for String Orch.); *Serenata* for Clarinet, Bassoon, Trumpet, Violin, and Cello (1927); *Sinfonia* for Clarinet, Trumpet, Cello, and Piano (1932); Piano Trio (1933). FOR PIANO: Many pieces, including 2 series of stylistic imitations, *A la manière de . . .*: Wagner, Fauré, Brahms, Debussy, Strauss, Franck (1911), and (in collaboration with Ravel) Borodin, d'Indy, Chabrier, Ravel (1913); Sonatina (1916); *A notte alta* (1917; also for Piano and Orch., 1921); *11 pezzi infantili* (1920); *2 ricercari sul nome Bach* (1932); 3 pieces for Pianola (1918). Casella orchestrated Balakirev's *Islamey;* edited Beethoven's sonatas and piano works of Albéniz; arranged Mahler's 7th Symph. for piano, 4-hands.
WRITINGS: *L'evoluzione della musica* (publ. in Italian, French, and Eng. in parallel columns; 1919); *Igor Stravinsky* (1926; new ed., Milan, 1951); *"21 + 26"* (about Rossini, Tolstoy, Busoni, etc.; 1931); *Il pianoforte* (1938); a manual of orchestration, *La tecnica dell'orchestra contemporanea* (completed by V. Mortari; Milan, 1950). In 1941 Casella publ. his memoirs, under the title *I segreti della Giara;* transl. into Eng. as *Music in My Time: The Memoirs of Alfredo Casella* (Oklahoma Univ. Press, 1955).
BIBLIOGRAPHY: L. Cortese, *Alfredo Casella* (Genoa, 1935); G.M. Gatti, *Musicisti moderni d'Italia e di fuori* (Bologna, 1925); a special number of *Rassegna Musicale* in honor of Casella's 60th birthday (May–June 1943); idem, "In Memory of A. Casella," *Musical Quarterly* (July 1947); F. d'Amico & G.M. Gatti, eds., *Alfredo Casella* (Milan, 1958).

Casella, Pietro, Italian composer who flourished in the 13th century. He was a personal friend of Dante; was long thought to be the earliest Italian madrigalist; however, this idea is now believed doubtful (see L. Ellinwood, "Origins of the Italian Ars Nova," *Papers of the American Musicological Society,* 1937; p. 30).

Cash, Johnny, American popular singer of partly Indian descent (one-quarter Cherokee); b. in a railroad shack near Kingsland, Ark., Feb. 26, 1932. He worked as a water boy in a farmer's family; sang Baptist hymns in church; at the age of 17 won $5 at a local amateur talent contest. In 1950 he enlisted in the U.S. Air Force; served in Germany, returning to the U.S. in 1954. He learned to play the guitar while in the service; in 1955 began a series of appearances on the radio and various country circuits specializing in country-western music, and soon began to compose his own songs, both lyrics and tunes. He could never learn to read the notes, a fact of no importance in his professional life. The subjects of his songs concern the miseries of common folks as well as prison life. His most popular songs are *Folsom Prison Blues* (inspired by his imprisonment overnight in El Paso on the charge of smuggling tranquilizer tablets from Mexico) and *I Walk the Line.* He publ. *Man in Black* (Grand Rapids, Mich., 1975).
BIBLIOGRAPHY: David Ewen, *All the Years of American Popular Music* (Englewood Cliffs, N.J., 1977; pp. 574–76).

Casimiri, Raffaele Casimiro, Italian musicologist; b. Gualdo Tadino, Nov. 3, 1880; d. Rome, April 15, 1943. He studied in Padua; dedicated himself to musical journalism; also conducted church choirs in the provinces. He founded the ecclesiastical magazines *Psalterium* (1907) and *Sacri concentus;* also *Note d'Archivio* (1924). His specialty was polyphonic music of the time of Palestrina, whose collected works he edited (1939–42). He contributed numerous articles to Italian publications; some of his findings on Palestrina have been disputed; his ingenious hoax, which he unveiled in *Note d'Archivio* of March 1924, claiming a discovery of a notebook of Palestrina establishing the date of Palestrina's birth, was deliberately contrived to confute his learned colleagues; he exposed it in a series of scurrilous letters. He also composed 2 oratorios, several masses, motets, and offertories.
BIBLIOGRAPHY: E. Dagnino, "R. Casimiri," *Rassegna Musicale* (April 1943).

Casini, Giovanni Maria, Italian organist and composer; b. Florence, Dec. 16, 1652; d. there, Feb. 25, 1719. He studied composition in Florence, and later in Rome with Matteo Simonelli and Bernardo Pasquini (organ). He became a priest and served as organist at the Cathedral of Florence from 1703; retired in 1711 owing to ill health. As a keyboard composer, Casini represents the late Baroque style. As a theorist, he was a follower of Nicolo Vicentino and Giovanni Battista Doni in their studies of the music of Greek antiquity.
WORKS: Existing publications of his works are: *Canzonette spirituali* (Florence, 1703); a collection of motets (in the style of Palestrina) in 4 Voices, op. 1 (Rome, 1706); *Responsori per la Settimana Santa,* op. 2 (Florence, 1706); *Pensieri per l'organo,* op. 3 (Florence, 1714); several oratorios. There is also an oratorio by Casini (in MS), *Il viaggio di Tobia.* Modern reprints of 2 numbers from his op. 3 are found in L. Torchi's *L'Arte Musicale in Italia* (vol. III).

Casken, John, British composer; b. Barnsley, July 15, 1949. He studied music theory with John Joubert and Peter Dickinson at the Univ. of Birmingham (1967–71). Upon graduation he received a Polish government scholarship, and in 1971 went to Warsaw, where he took courses with Andrzej Dobrowolski at the Warsaw Cons. Upon his return to England he joined the music dept. at Birmingham Univ.; in 1980 he became a lecturer of music at Durham Univ. As a composer, Casken was influenced by the developments of modern Polish music, and adopted a system of graphic music notation characteristic of modern techniques of composition in Poland and elsewhere. The influence of Lutoslawski is an important factor in Casken's music.
WORKS: *Kagura,* for 13 Wind Instruments, based

on a medieval Japanese court ritual (1972); *Music for the Crabbing Sun* for Flute, Oboe, Cello, and Harpsichord (1974); *Music for a Tawny-Gold Day* for Viola, Alto Saxophone, Bass Clarinet, and Piano (1976); *Arenaria* for Flute, Harp, Piano, Percussion, and 9 String Instruments (1976); *Tableaux des trois âges* for an Instrumental Ensemble (1977); *Ia Orana, Gaugin* for Soprano and Piano (1978); *Firewhirl* for Voice and Piano (1978); String Quartet (1981); Piano Concerto (1981; Manchester, Jan. 24, 1982).

Cassadó, Gaspar, distinguished Spanish cellist, son of **Joaquín Cassadó;** b. Barcelona, Sept. 30, 1897; d. Madrid, Dec. 24, 1966. He studied cello with Casals; toured Europe; made his debut in America, in N.Y., on Dec. 10, 1936; made another U.S. tour in 1949. He composed a Cello Sonata, a Cello Concerto, and other pieces for his instrument. His *Catalonian Rhapsody* for Orch. was performed by the N.Y. Phil. on Nov. 8, 1928. Cassadó also made arrangements for cello and orch. of a Mozart horn concerto and Weber's Clarinet Concerto.

Cassadó (Valls), Joaquín, Spanish organist and composer; b. Mataró, near Barcelona, Sept. 30, 1867; d. Barcelona, March 25, 1926. He served as a choir director and organist at several churches in Barcelona; wrote a comic opera, *El monjo negro* (Barcelona, Jan. 24, 1920); *Hispania* for Piano and Orch.; church music.

Cassily, Richard, American tenor; b. Washington, D.C., Dec. 14, 1927. He was educated at the Peabody Cons., Baltimore. After graduating, he went to N.Y. and appeared on the Broadway stage. He then sang at the N.Y. City Opera; made his European debut in Geneva in 1965. Also in 1965 he joined the Hamburg State Opera; from 1968 sang at Covent Garden, London. He made his debut at the Metropolitan Opera in N.Y., on Jan. 20, 1973, as Radames in *Aida.*

Cassiodorus, Magnus Aurelius, historian, statesman, and monk; b. Scyllacium (Squillace), Bruttii, c.485; d. Vivarese, Calabria, c.580. He was a contemporary of Boetius; held various civil offices under Theodoric and Athalaric until c.540, when he retired. He founded the monasteries of Castellum and Vivarium; at the latter he wrote his *De artibus ac disciplinis liberalium litterarum;* the section treating of music, *Institutiones musicae,* a valuable source, is printed in Gerbert's *Scriptores,* vol. I; a partial reproduction is to be found in Strunk's *Source Readings in Music History* (N.Y., 1950).

BIBLIOGRAPHY: A. Franz, *A. Cassiodorus* (1872); W. Brambach, *Die Musikliteratur des Mittelalters* (1883); H. Abert, "Zu Cassiodor," *Sammelbände der Internationalen Musik-Gesellschaft,* III/3; H. Abert, *Die Musikanschauung des Mittelalters* (pp. 132ff.; 1905); G. Pietzsch, *Die Klassifikation der Musik* (1929); idem, *Die Musik im Erziehungs- und Bildungsideal* (pp. 30ff.; 1932); G. Wille, *Musica Romana* (Amsterdam, 1967; pp. 700ff.).

Cassirer, Fritz, German conductor and writer on music; b. Breslau, March 29, 1871; d. Berlin, Nov. 26, 1926. He first studied philosophy (1889–92); then turned to music; was an orch. and operatic conductor in many German towns; also in London (1905–7).

WRITINGS: *Edgar,* a poem (1894); "Beethovens Briefe," *Die Musik* (1909); *Helldunkle Weltgeschichte* (1920; pseudonym: **Friedrich Leopold**); *Beethoven und die Gestalt* (1925).

Cassuto, Alvaro, Portuguese conductor and composer; b. Oporto, Nov. 17, 1938. He studied violin and piano as a small child; then took courses in composition with Artur Santos and Lopes Graça. During the season 1960–61 he attended classes in new music in Darmstadt, Germany, with Ligeti, Messiaen, and Stockhausen, and at the same time had instruction in conducting with Herbert von Karajan. He further studied conducting with Pedro de Freitas Branco in Lisbon and Franco Ferrara in Hilversum, the Netherlands. He served as an assistant conductor of the Gulbenkian Orch. in Lisbon (1965–68) and with the Little Orch. in N.Y. (1968–70). In 1970 he was appointed permanent conductor of the National Radio Orch. of Lisbon, and in 1975 was elected its music director. In 1974 he was appointed a lecturer in music and conductor of the Symph. Orch. of the Univ. of Calif. at Irvine, remaining there unitl 1979. He also was guest conductor of numerous orchs. in Europe, South America, and the U.S. In 1969 he received the Koussevitzky Prize in Tanglewood. A progressive-minded and scholarly musician, he amassed a large repertoire of both classical and modern works, displaying a confident expertise. He is also a composer of several orch. works in a modern idiom, as well as of chamber pieces.

WORKS: *Sinfonia breve No. 1* (Lisbon, Aug. 29, 1959); *Sinfonia breve No. 2* (1960); Variations for Orch. (1961); *Permutations* for 2 Orchs. (1962); String Sextet (1962); Concertino for Piano and Orch. (1965); *Cro (mo-no)fonia* for 20 String Instruments (1967); *Canticum in Tenebris* for Soloists, Chorus, and Orch. (1968); *Evocations* for Orch. (1969); *Circle* for Orch. (1971); *In the Name of Peace,* one-act opera (1971); *Song of Loneliness* for 12 Players (1972); *To Love and Peace,* symph. poem (1973).

Castagna, Bruna, Italian mezzo-soprano; b. Bari, Oct. 15, 1905; d. Pinamar, Argentina, July 10, 1983. She learned to play the piano; then went to Milan to study voice with Tina Scognamiglio; made her debut at Mantua in 1925; then traveled to South America, where she sang for 3 seasons at the Teatro Colón in Buenos Aires and in the provinces (1927–30). Returning to Italy, she sang at La Scala in Milan; then made guest appearances in the U.S. in Chicago, St. Louis, and San Francisco. On March 2, 1936, she successfully performed at the Metropolitan Opera House in N.Y. as Azucena in *Il Trovatore;* there followed a far-flung tour, in Australia, Brazil, Egypt, Rumania, and Spain. Eventually she made her home in Argentina. Her most applauded role was Carmen.

Castagnone, Riccardo, Italian pianist and composer; b. Brunate, Como, Sept. 10, 1906; d. Milan, Feb. 20, 1983. He was professionally active mainly as a piano accompanist; in 1956 joined the Virtuosi di Roma as a cembalo player. He composed *Sinfonia in tre tempi* (1940); 2 string quartets (1941, 1942); piano pieces; choruses; songs.

Castaldi, Alfonso, Italian-born Rumanian composer; b. Maddalone, April 23, 1874; d. Bucharest, Aug. 6, 1942. He studied at the Cons. in Naples with Francisco Cilea and Umberto Giordano; then went to Rumania; from 1904 to 1940 he taught at the Bucharest Cons., was greatly esteemed as a pedagogue. He wrote several operas in an Italianate style; the symph. poems *Thalassa* (1906) and *Marsyas* (1907); a Symph. (1920); 3 string quartets; other chamber music; numerous choruses.
BIBLIOGRAPHY: Z. Vancea, *Creatia muzicală romaneâscă sec. XIX–XX* (Bucharest, 1968); V. Cosma, *Muzicieni români* (Bucharest, 1970; pp. 102–3, containing a complete list of works).

Castaldo, Joseph, American composer; b. New York, Dec. 23, 1927. He studied in N.Y.; was a clarinetist; enrolled in the Santa Cecilia Academy in Rome. Returning to the U.S., he took composition lessons with Giannini and Persichetti. Among his works are a String Quartet; *Epigrams* for Piano and Orch.; *Flight,* cantata; *Dichotomy* for Woodwind Quintet; *Epiphonia* for Orch.; *Theoria* for 15 Winds, Piano, and Percussion (1971; revised 1972). In 1966 he was appointed president of the Philadelphia Music Academy.

Castan, Count Armand de. See **Castelmary.**

Castel, Louis-Bertrand, French acoustician; b. Montpellier, Nov. 11, 1688; d. Paris, Jan. 9, 1757. He became interested in Newton's observation on the correspondence, in proportionate breadth, of the 7 prismatic rays with the string-lengths required for the scale *re, mi, fa, sol, la, si, do;* acting upon this observation, he attempted the construction of a "clavecin oculaire," to produce color-harmonies for the eye as the ordinary harpsichord produces tone-harmonies for the ear. His theory is explained in an essay, *Nouvelles expériences d'optique et d'acoustique* (1735; Eng. trans., London, 1757).

Castelli, Ignaz Franz, Austrian opera librettist; b. Vienna, July 6, 1781; d. there, Feb. 5, 1862. He was employed as "court theater-poet" at the Kärnthner-tortheater in Vienna; was the founder and editor of the *Allgemeiner Musikalischer Anzeiger* (1829–40); he wrote numerous opera libretti; publ. a book of memoirs (4 vols., 1861).

Castelmary (stage name of Count **Armand de Castan**), French baritone; b. Toulouse, Aug. 16, 1834; d. New York, Feb. 10, 1897, on the stage of the Metropolitan Opera House, just after the first act of *Martha.* He made his operatic debut at the Paris Opéra (1863); remained there till 1870; then sang in London and N.Y.; made his debut at the Metropolitan on Nov. 29, 1893, as Vulcan in *Philemon;* was particularly successful as Méphistophélès in *Faust.*

Castelnuovo-Tedesco, Mario, greatly significant Italian-American composer; b. Florence, April 3, 1895; d. Los Angeles, March 16, 1968. He studied at the Cherubini Inst. with del Valle (piano) and Pizzetti (composition); he began to compose at an early age; his first organized composition, *Cielo di Settembre* for Piano, revealed impressionistic tendencies. He wrote a patriotic song, *Fuori i Barbari,* during World War I. He attained considerable eminence in Italy between the 2 wars, and his music was often heard at European festivals. Political events forced him to leave Italy; in 1939 he settled in the U.S. He became active as a composer for films in Hollywood, but continued to write large amounts of orch. and chamber music. His style is remarkably fluent and adaptable to the various moods evoked in his music, often reaching rhapsodic eloquence.
WORKS: OPERAS: *La mandragola* (libretto by the composer, after Machiavelli; Venice, May 4, 1926; won the National Prize); *The Princess and the Pea,* after Andersen, overture with Narrator (1943); *Bacco in Toscana,* dithyramb for Voices and Orch. (Milan, May 8, 1931); *Aucassin et Nicolette,* puppet show with Voices and Instruments (1938; first perf. in Florence, June 2, 1952); *All's Well That Ends Well,* after Shakespeare (1959); *Saul,* biblical opera (1960); *Il Mercante di Venezia,* after Shakespeare's play *The Merchant of Venice,* to the composer's libretto in Italian (won first prize at the International Competition at La Scala, Milan; first perf. at the Maggio Musicale, Florence, May 25, 1961); *The Importance of Being Earnest,* after Oscar Wilde, chamber opera (1962); *The Song of Songs,* scenic oratorio (Hollywood, Aug. 7, 1963); *Tobias and the Angel,* scenic oratorio (1965). BIBLICAL ORATORIOS: *Ruth* (1949) and *Jonah* (1951). FOR ORCH.: *Cipressi* (Boston Symph., Koussevitzky conducting, Oct. 25, 1940; originally for Piano, 1920); Piano Concerto No. 1 (Rome, Dec. 9, 1928); Piano Concerto No. 2 (N.Y. Phil., Nov. 2, 1939, composer soloist); 3 violin concertos: *Concerto italiano* (Rome, Jan. 31, 1926); *The Prophets* (Jascha Heifetz and the N.Y. Phil., Toscanini conducting, April 12, 1933); 3rd Violin Concerto (1939); Cello Concerto (N.Y. Phil., Jan. 31, 1935, Piatigorsky soloist; Toscanini conducting); *Variazioni sinfoniche* for Violin and Orch. (Rome, 1930); overtures to Shakespeare's plays: *The Taming of the Shrew* (1930); *Twelfth Night* (1933); *The Merchant of Venice* (1933); *Julius Caesar* (1934); *A Midsummer Night's Dream* (1940); *Coriolanus* (1947); etc.; *Poem* for Violin and Orch. (1942); *The Birthday of the Infanta* (1942; New Orleans, Jan. 28, 1947); *Indian Songs and Dances,* suite (Los Angeles, Jan. 7, 1943); *An American Rhapsody* (1943); Serenade for Guitar and Orch. (1943); *Octoroon Ball,* ballet suite (1947); *Noah's Ark,* movement for Narrator and Orch., from *Genesis,* a suite; other movements by Schoenberg, Stravinsky, Toch, Milhaud, Tansman, and N. Shilkret, who commissioned the work

(Portland, Oreg., Dec. 15, 1947). CHAMBER MUSIC: *Signorine: 2 profili* for Violin and Piano (1918); *Ritmi* for Violin and Piano (1920); *Capitan Fracassa* for Violin and Piano (1920); *Notturno adriatico* for Violin and Piano (1922); *I nottambuli* for Cello and Piano (1927); Cello Sonata (1928); First Piano Trio (1928); First String Quartet (1929); *Sonata quasi una fantasia* for Violin and Piano (1929); *The Lark* for Violin and Piano (1930); First Piano Quintet (1932); 2nd Piano Trio (1932); Toccata for Cello and Piano (1935); *Capriccio diabolico* for Guitar (1935; later arranged as a guitar concerto); Concertino for Harp and 7 Instruments (1937); *Ballade* for Violin and Piano (1940); Divertimento for 2 Flutes (1943); Sonata for Violin and Viola (1945); Clarinet Sonata (1945); Sonatina for Bassoon and Piano (1946); 2nd String Quartet (1948); Quintet for Guitar and Strings (1950); Sonata for Viola and Cello (1950); Fantasia for Guitar and Piano (1950); *Concerto da camera* for Oboe and Strings (1950); Sonata for Violin and Cello (1950); 2nd Piano Quintet (1951). FOR PIANO: *English Suite* (1909); *Questo fu il carro della morte* (1913); *Il raggio verde* (1916); *Alghe* (1919); *I naviganti* (1919); *La sirenetta e il pesce turchino* (1920); *Cantico* (1920); *Vitalba e Biancospino* (1921); *Epigrafe* (1922); *Alt-Wien*, Viennese rhapsody (1923); *Piedigrotta* (1924); *Le stagioni* (1924); *Le danze del Re David* (1925); *3 poemi campestri* (1926); *3 corali su melodie ebraiche* (1926); Sonata (1928); *Crinoline* (1929); *Candide*, 6 pieces (1944); *6 canoni* (1950). SONGS: *Le Roy Loys* (1914); *Ninna-Nanna* (1914; very popular); *Fuori i barbari*, a patriotic song (1915); *Stelle cadenti* (1915); *Coplas* (1915); *Briciole* (1916); *3 fioretti di Santo Francesco* (1919; also with Orch.); *Girotondo de golosi* (1920); *Etoile filante* (1920); *L'infinito* (1921); *Sera* (1921); *2 preghiere per i bimbi d'Italia* (1923); *1830*, after Alfred de Musset (1924); *Scherzi*, 2 series (1924–25); music to 33 Shakespeare songs (1921–25); *Indian Serenade* (1925); *Cadix* (1926); *3 Sonnets from the Portuguese*, after E.B. Browning (1926); *Laura di Nostra Donna* (1935); *Un sonetto di Dante* (1939); *Recuerdo* (1940); *Le Rossignol* (1942); *The Daffodils* (1944). FOR CHORUS: 2 madrigals a cappella (1915); *Lecho dodi*, synagogue chant for Tenor, Men's Voices, and Organ (1936); *Sacred Synagogue Service* (1943); *Liberty, Mother of Exiles* (1944). Numerous pieces for guitar, including: *Les Guitares bien temperées*, 24 preludes and fugues for 2 Guitars (1962); 2 guitar concertos (1939, 1953); Concerto for 2 Guitars and Orch. (1962); 3rd String Quartet (1964); Sonatina for Flute and Guitar (1965); Sonata for Cello and Harp (1966).

BIBLIOGRAPHY: Guido M. Gatti, *Musicisti moderni d'Italia e di fuori* (Bologna, 1925); G. Rossi-Daria, "Mario Castelnuovo-Tedesco," *Chesterian* (Jan.–Feb. 1926); Roland von Weber, "Mario Castelnuovo-Tedesco," in David Ewen, ed., *The Book of Modern Composers* (N.Y., 1942; 3rd ed., 1961); Nick Rossi, *Complete Catalogue of Works by Mario Castelnuovo-Tedesco* (N.Y., 1977).

Castéra, René d'Avezac, French composer; b. Dax (Landes), April 3, 1873; d. Angoume (Landes),

Oct. 8, 1955. He studied at the Schola Cantorum with Vincent d'Indy and Guilmant. In 1902 he founded the Edition Mutuelle for publication of works by French composers. He wrote an opera, some symph. pieces, a Piano Trio, Violin Sonata, songs, and character pieces for piano.

Castiglioni, Niccolò, Italian pianist and composer of avant-garde tendencies; b. Milan, July 17, 1932. He studied composition with Ghedini, Desderi, and Margola at the Verdi Cons. in Milan, and piano with Gulda at the Mozarteum in Salzburg; also took composition lessons with Blacher. He began his career as a pianist; in 1966 emigrated to the U.S.; was composer-in-residence at the Center of Creative and Performing Arts at the State Univ. of N.Y. in Buffalo (1966–67); then was on the faculty of the Univ. of Michigan (1967) and Univ. of Washington at Seattle (1968–69); in 1970 he was appointed instructor at the Univ. of Calif. in San Diego. In his music he follows a pragmatically modernistic line of composition, making use of any and all mannerisms of the neo-Classical, neo-Romantic, and experimental resources while preserving a necessary minimum of communicable sound production.

WORKS: Opera, *Uomini e no* (1955); radio opera, *Attraverso lo specchio* (*Through the Looking Glass*), after Lewis Carroll (1961; Italian Radio, Oct. 1, 1961); chamber opera, *Jabberwocky*, after Lewis Carroll (1962); one-act opera, *Sweet*, for Baritone, Piano, Bells, and Winds (Rome, 1968); opera-triptych, *3 Mystery Plays* (Rome, Oct. 2, 1968; material made up of *Silence, Chordination,* and *The Rise and Rebellion of Lucifer and Aria*); *Concertino per la notte di Natale* for Strings and Woodwinds (1952); Symph. No. 1 for Soprano and Orch., to a text by Nietzsche (Venice, Sept. 15, 1956); Symph. No. 2 (1956–57; Italian Radio, Nov. 23, 1957); *Canti* for Orch. (1956); *Ouverture in tre tempi* (1957); *Elegia* for 19 Instruments and Soprano (1957); *Impromptus* for Orch. (1957–58); *Inizio di movimento* for Piano (1958); *Movimento continuato* for Piano and 11 Instruments (1958–59); *Sequenze* for Orch. (1959); *Tropi* for 6 Players (1959); *Aprèslude* for Orch. (1959); *Cangianti* for Piano (1959); *Eine kleine Weihnachtsmusik (A Little Christmas Music)* for Chamber Orch. (1959–60); *Disegni* for Chamber Orch. (1960); *Gymel* for Flute and Piano (1960); *Rondels* for Orch. (1960–61); *Décors* for Orch. (1962); *Consonante* for Flute and Chamber Orch. (1962); *Synchromie* for Orch. (1963); Concerto for Orch. (1963); *A Solemn Music I*, after Milton, for Soprano and Chamber Orch. (1963); *Gyro* for Chorus and 9 Instruments (1963); *Caractères* for Orch. (1964); *A Solemn Music II*, a revised version of *I* (1964–65); *Figure*, a mobile for Voice and Orch. (1965); *Alef* for Solo Oboe (1965); *Anthem*, composition in 5 strophes for Chorus and Orch. (1966); *Ode* for 2 Pianos, Wind Instruments, and Percussion (1966); *Canzoni* for Soprano and Orch. (Naples, Oct. 18, 1966); *Carmina* for Chamber Ensemble (1967); *Sinfonia guerriere et amorose* for Organ (1967); *Granulation* for 2 Flutes and 2 Clarinets (1967); *Masques* for 12 Instruments, a bouillabaisse of poly-tonally arranged fragments of dimly remembered tunes by other composers (1967); *The New Melusine* for String Quartet (1969); *La Chant du signe*, concerto for Flute and Orch. (1969); *Sinfonia in Do*, after Ben Jonson, Dante, Shakespeare, and Keats, for Chorus and Orch. (1968–69; Rome, May 21, 1971).

Castil-Blaze. See **Blaze, François-Henri-Joseph.**

Castilla, Alberto, Colombian composer; b. Bogotá, April 9, 1883; d. Ibague, June 10, 1937. He studied engineering; was at one time connected with the government of Colombia. In 1898 he settled in Tolima, where he founded a music school. He wrote a number of songs, some of which achieved popularity. In 1954 the Colombian government issued a postage stamp in his honor.

Castillon, Alexis, French composer; b. Chartres, Dec. 13, 1838; d. Paris, March 5, 1873. He pursued a military career before turning to music. He studied with Victor Massé, and later took lessons with César Franck; was one of the founders of the Société Nationale de Musique. He composed mainly for chamber music groups; also wrote a Symph., 2 overtures, a Mass, and other religious music; his Piano Concerto was accepted for performance by Saint-Saëns, but was utterly unsuccessful.

Castleman, Charles, American violinist; b. Quincy, Mass., May 22, 1941. A *wunderkind* since his cradle, he appeared as a soloist with Arthur Fiedler and the Boston Pops Orch. at the age of 7; when he grew up he entered the Curtis Inst. of Music in Philadelphia as a student of Ivan Galamian; also received sporadic counsel from Josef Gingold, Henryk Szeryng, and David Oistrakh. In 1970 he founded the Quartet Program in Troy, N.Y., with the aim of promoting professional chamber groups. He played in the New String Trio of N.Y. (1972–75); then in the Raphael Trio, with which he made tours abroad. In 1975 he joined the violin faculty at the Eastman School of Music in Rochester, N.Y. He commissioned and gave the world premiere of David Amram's Violin Concerto in St. Louis in 1981.

Caston, Saul, American trumpet player and conductor; b. New York, Aug. 22, 1901. He studied at the Curtis Inst. in Philadelphia with Abram Chasins (piano), Scalero (composition), and Reiner (conducting); played trumpet in the Philadelphia Orch. (1918–45); taught trumpet at the Curtis Inst. (1924–42); was associate conductor of the Philadelphia Orch. (1936–45); conductor of the Reading Symph. Orch. (1941–44); in 1944 was appointed conductor of the Denver Symph. Orch., retiring in 1964.

Castriota, Samuel, Argentine composer of popular songs; b. Buenos Aires, Nov. 2, 1885; d. there, July 8, 1932. He made a good living as pianist in an elite bordello owned by La Gringa Adela. His most popular melodies were *La Yerra* (1903) and *Mi nocha triste* (1918).

Castro, Jean (Juan) de, composer who flourished in the 16th century; b. probably in Liège, c.1540; d. c.1611. From 1582–84 he was assistant choirmaster in Vienna; later (1593–96), in Cleve, near Cologne. WORKS: *Missae à 3* (Cologne, 1599); *Sacrae cantiones*, 5–8 parts (1571), 3 parts (1593, 1596), and 5–8 parts (1588); *Tricinia sacra* (1574); *Bicinia sacra* (1594); *Chansons, Odes et Sonnets par P. Ronsard à 4–8 voix* (1576); *Cantiones sacra* (1591; reprinted in Denkmäler rheinischer Musik, 16, 1972); *Chansons, Stances, Sonnets et Epigrammes à 2 voix* (Antwerp, 1592); *Quintines, Sextines, Sonnets à 5 voix* (1594). Many of these works are of interest because of the exact rhythmical arrangement of the verses.

Castro, José María, Argentine composer and conductor, brother of **Juan José Castro;** b. Avellaneda, near Buenos Aires, Dec. 15, 1892; d. Buenos Aires, Aug. 2, 1964. He studied in Buenos Aires; then went to Paris, and like his brother, took a course with Vincent d'Indy. Returning to Argentina in 1930, he became conductor of the Orquesta Filharmónica in Buenos Aires; from 1933 to 1953 also led the Banda Municipal de la Ciudad de Buenos Aires. WORKS: 3 ballets: *Georgia* (1937; Teatro Colón, Buenos Aires, June 2, 1939; composer conducting), *El sueño de la botella* (1948), and *Falarka* (1951); a monodrama, *La otra voz* for Voice and Orch. (1953); Concerto Grosso for Chamber Orch. (1932; Buenos Aires, June 11, 1933); *Obertura para una ópera cómica* (1934); Piano Concerto (Buenos Aires, Nov. 17, 1941; revised 1956); Concerto for Orch. (1944); Concerto for Cello and 17 Instruments (1945); *3 Pastorales* for Orch. (1945); *Preludio y Toccata* for String Quartet and String Orch. (1949); *Tema coral con variaciones* for Orch. (1952); Concerto for Violin and 18 Instruments (1953); *10 improvisaciones breves* for Chamber Orch. or Piano (1957); *Preludio, Tema con variaciones y Final* for Orch. (1959); *Sinfonía de Buenos Aires* (1963); *El libro de los sonetos* for Voice and Orch. (1947); *5 líricas* for Voice and Orch. (1958); 13 sonnets, *Con la patria adentro*, for Tenor and Orch. (1964); Violin Sonata (1918); Cello Sonata (1933); Sonata for 2 Cellos (1938); 3 string quartets (1944, 1947, 1956); *Sonata poética* for Violin and Piano (1957); 6 piano sonatas (1919; 1924; 1927; 1931; *Sonata de primavera*, 1939; *Sonata dramática*, 1944); piano pieces.

Castro, Juan José, eminent Argentine composer and conductor, brother of **José María Castro;** b. Avellaneda, near Buenos Aires, March 7, 1895; d. Buenos Aires, Sept. 3, 1968. After study in Buenos Aires he went to Paris, where he took a course in composition with Vincent d'Indy. Returning to Argentina in 1929, he organized in Buenos Aires the Orquesta de Nacimiento, which he conducted; in 1930 he conducted the ballet season at the Teatro Colón; conducted opera there from 1933; also became the music director of the Asociación del Profesorado Orquestal and Asociación Sinfónica, with which he gave first local performances of a number of modern works. In 1934 he received a Guggenheim Foundation grant. From 1947 to 1951 he conducted in Cuba and Uruguay; from 1952 to 1953 he was principal conductor of the Victorian Symph. Orch. in Melbourne, Australia; in 1955 he returned to Argentina; from 1956 to 1960 he was conductor of the Orquesta Sinfónica Nacional in Buenos Aires; from 1959 to 1964 was director of the Cons. of San Juan, Puerto Rico. He was proficient in all genres of composition, but his works were rarely performed outside of South America, and he himself conducted most of his symph. compositions.

WORKS: His most signal success on the international scene was the prize he received at the contest for the best opera at La Scala in Milan, for *Proserpina e lo straniero* (in the original Spanish, *Proserpina y el extranjero*), of which he conducted the first perf. at La Scala in Milan on March 17, 1952; his other operas were *La Zapatera prodigiosa,* after García Lorca (Montevideo, Dec. 23, 1949); *Bodas de sangre,* also after Lorca (Buenos Aires, Aug. 9, 1956); *Cosecha negra* (1961). Other works: Ballets: *Mekhano* (Buenos Aires, July 17, 1937) and *Offenbachiana* (Buenos Aires, May 25, 1940); 5 symphs.: No. 1 (1931); *Sinfonía bíblica* for Orch. and Chorus (1932); *Sinfonía Argentina* (Buenos Aires, Nov. 29, 1936); *Sinfonía de los campos* (Buenos Aires, Oct. 29, 1939); No. 5 (1956); *Dans le jardin des morts* (Buenos Aires, Oct. 5, 1924); *A una madre* (Buenos Aires, Oct. 27, 1925); *La Chellah,* symph. poem based on an Arabian theme (Buenos Aires, Sept. 10, 1927); *Allegro, Lento y Vivace* (1931); *Anunciación, Entrada a Jerusalem, Golgotha* (Buenos Aires, Nov. 15, 1932); *Corales criollos* No. 3, symph. poem (1953); won first prize at the Caracas Music Festival, 1954); *Epitafio en ritmos y sonidos* for Chorus and Orch. (1961); *Negro* for Soprano and Orch. (1961); *Suite introspectiva* (1961; Los Angeles, June 8, 1962); Violin Concerto (1962); Violin Sonata (1914); Cello Sonata (1916); String Quartet (1942); Piano Concerto (1941); 2 piano sonatas (1917, 1939); *Corales criollos* No. 1 and No. 2 for Piano (1947); songs.

BIBLIOGRAPHY: R. Arizaga, *Juan José Castro* (Buenos Aires, 1963).

Castro, Ricardo, Mexican composer and pianist; b. Durango, Feb. 7, 1864; d. Mexico City, Nov. 27, 1907. He studied with Melesio Morales in Mexico; in 1883 he appeared as pianist at the New Orleans Cotton Exposition. In 1902 he went to Europe and presented concerts of his works in Paris; he was soloist in his own piano concerto in Antwerp (Dec. 28, 1904). Returning to Mexico, he produced an opera, *La leyenda de Rudel* (Nov. 8, 1906). He composed 3 more operas (*Atzimba, Satán vencido,* and *La Rousalka*), 2 symphs. (1883, 1887), and a number of piano pieces.

Castro, Washington, Argentine composer, brother of **José María** and **Juan José Castro;** b. Buenos Aires, July 13, 1909. He studied cello; in 1947 devoted himself mainly to conducting and teaching.

WORKS: *Sinfonía primaveral* (1956); Piano Concerto (1960); *Sinfonía breve* for Strings (1960); Concerto for Orch. (1963); *Rhapsody* for Cello and Orch. (1963); *3 Pieces* for Orch. (1970); 3 string quartets (1945, 1950, 1965); piano pieces; songs.

Castrucci, Pietro, Italian violinist; b. Rome, 1679; d. Dublin, Feb. 29, 1752. He was a pupil of Corelli; came to London (1715) as leader of Handel's opera orch. He was a fine player on the "violetta marina," a stringed instrument invented by himself, and resembling the viola d'amore in tone. In *Orlando,* Handel wrote an air accompanied on 2 "violette marine" "per gli Signori Castrucci" (Pietro, and **Prospero,** his brother). Castrucci publ. violin concertos and 2 books of violin sonatas.

Catalani, Alfredo, greatly talented Italian composer; b. Lucca, June 19, 1854; d. Milan, Aug. 7, 1893. He studied music with his father, a church organist; in 1872 studied with Fortunato Magi and Bazzini at the Istituto Musicale Pacini in Lucca; then went to Paris, where he attended classes of Bazin (composition) and Marmontel (piano). He returned to Italy in 1873; in 1886 became the successor of Ponchielli as prof. of composition at the Milan Cons. It was in Milan that he became acquainted with Boito, who encouraged him in his composition; he also met young Toscanini, who became a champion of his music. Catalani was determined to create a Wagnerian counterpart in the field of Italian opera, and he selected for his libretti fantastic subjects suitable for dramatic action. After several unsuccessful productions he finally achieved his ideal in his last opera, *La Wally;* he died of tuberculosis the year after its production.

WORKS: His operas include *La Falce* (Milan, July 19, 1875); *Elda* (Turin, Jan. 31, 1880; revised and produced under the title *Loreley,* Turin, Feb. 16, 1890); *Dejanice* (Milan, March 17, 1883); *Edmea* (Milan, Feb. 27, 1886); *La Wally* (Milan, Jan. 20, 1892); he further composed *Sinfonia a piena orchestra* (1872); *Il Mattino,* romantic symph. (1874); *Ero e Leandro,* symph. poem (Milan, May 9, 1885); a number of piano pieces and songs.

BIBLIOGRAPHY: D.L. Pardini, *Alfredo Catalani* (Lucca, 1935); J.W. Klein, "Alfredo Catalani," *Musical Quarterly* (July 1937); A. Bonaccorsi, *Alfredo Catalani* (Turin, 1942); Carlo Gatti, *Alfredo Catalani* (Milan, 1953); J.W. Klein, "Toscanini and Catalani—A Unique Friendship," *Music & Letters* (July 1967).

Catalani, Angelica, Italian soprano; b. Sinigaglia, May 10, 1780; d. Paris, June 12, 1849. She was taught at the convent of Santa Lucia di Gubbio in Rome; made her operatic debut at the Teatro la Fenice in Venice (1795); then sang at La Pergola in Florence (1799), and at La Scala in Milan (1801). In 1801, while engaged at the Italian Opera in Lisbon, she married Paul Valabrègue, an attaché of the French embassy; subsequently gave highly successful concerts in Paris and London. In 1814–17 she undertook, without signal success, the management of the Théâtre des Italiens in Paris while continuing her singing career, appearing in major European cities and at provincial festivals until 1828, when she retired to her country home near Florence. She won great acclaim for her commanding stage presence, wide vocal range, and mastery of the bravura singing style.

Catel, Charles-Simon, French composer and music pedagogue; b. l'Aigle, Orne, June 10, 1773; d. Paris, Nov. 29, 1830. He studied in Paris with Gossec and Gobert at the Ecole Royale du Chant (later merged with the Cons.); served as accompanist and teacher there (1787); in 1790 was accompanist at the Opéra and assistant conductor (to Gossec) of the band of the Garde Nationale. In 1795, on the establishment of the Cons., he was appointed prof. of harmony, and was commissioned to write a *Traité d'harmonie* (publ. 1802; a standard work at the Cons. for 20 years thereafter). In 1810 with Gossec, Méhul, and Cherubini, he was made an inspector of the Cons., resigning in 1816; was named a member of the Académie des Beaux-Arts in 1817. As a composer, Catel was at his best in his operas, written in a conventional but attractive style of French stage music of the time.
WORKS: Operas, performed at the Paris Opéra and the Opéra-Comique: *Sémiramis* (May 4, 1802); *L'Auberge de bagnères* (April 23, 1807); *Les Artistes par occasion* (Jan. 22, 1807); *Les Bayadères* (Paris Opéra, Aug. 8, 1810; his most successful work); *Les Aubergistes de qualité* (June 11, 1812); *Bayard à Mézières* (Feb. 12, 1814); *Le Premier en date* (Nov. 3, 1814); *Wallace, ou Le Ménestrel écossais* (March 24, 1817); *Zirphile et Fleur de Myrte, ou Cent ans en jour* (June 29, 1818); *L'Officier enlevé* (May 4, 1819); also several symphs. and chamber works.
BIBLIOGRAPHY: J. Carlez, *Catel: Etude biographique et critique* (Caen, 1895); F. Hellouin and J. Picard, *Un Musicien oublié: Catel* (Paris, 1910); S. Suskin, *The Music of Charles-Simon Catel for the Paris Opéra* (Diss., Yale Univ., 1972).

Catelani, Angelo, Italian music historian; b. Guastalla, March 30, 1811; d. San Martino di Mugnano, Sept. 5, 1866. He studied piano with Asioli and harmony with M. Fusco; also at the Naples Cons. (1831) and privately with Donizetti and Crescentini; conducted at the Messina opera (1835–36) and at Correggio (1837); was appointed maestro di cappella at the Cathedral of Modena (1837–39); from 1860 served as assistant librarian of the Este Library; was appointed maestro di cappella at the court of Modena (1846). He composed 3 operas, of which one was successfully produced; then turned to writing on music.
WRITINGS: "Notizie su padre Aaron e su Nicola Vicentino," *Gazzetta Musicale di Milano* (1851); *Epistolario di autori celebri in musica* (1852–54); *Bibliografia di due stampe ignote di Ottaviano Petrucci da Fossombrone* (1858); *Della vita e delle opere di Orazio Vecchi* (1858); *Della vita e delle opere di Claudio Merulo da Correggio* (1860); *Delle opere di Alessandro Stradella* (1866).

Catlett, Sidney ("Big Sid"), black American jazz drummer; b. Evansville, Ind., Jan. 17, 1910; d. Chicago, March 25, 1951. After the family moved to Chica-

go, he took up drums; played with local musicians; then joined the bands of Fletcher Henderson (1936), Don Redman (1936–38), Louis Armstrong (1938–42), and others; led his own quartet from 1944 to 1947; then appeared with Armstrong's All Stars (1947–49); played at Carnegie Hall in N.Y. in 1950.

Catoire, Georgi Lvovitch, Russian composer of French descent; b. Moscow, April 27, 1861; d. there, May 21, 1926. While a student of mathematics at the Univ. of Berlin, he took lessons in piano with Klindworth and in composition with Rüfer; later studied with Liadov in St. Petersburg; lived in Moscow and devoted himself to composing; also taught composition at the Moscow Cons.
WORKS: Symph. in C minor; symph. poem, *Mtsyri;* Piano Concerto; cantata, *Rusalka;* 3 poems of Tiutchev for Female Voices, with Piano; String Trio; String Quartet; String Quintet; 4 preludes for Piano; violin sonata, *Poème;* Piano Quartet; Piano Quintet; many songs. He also publ. a manual on harmony (2 vols., 1924, 1925).
BIBLIOGRAPHY: V. Belayev, *G. Catoire* (in Russian and German; Moscow, 1926).

Catunda, Eunice, Brazilian pianist and composer; b. Rio de Janeiro, March 14, 1915. She studied piano and harmony; took special courses in modern music and orchestration with Camargo Guarnieri and H.J. Koellreuter; in 1948 she went to Europe and took a course in conducting with Scherchen. In 1946 she joined the modernistic group Musica Viva; in 1973 she was appointed a lecturer at the Univ. of Brasilia. Her compositions include a Piano Concerto (1955); *Hommage à Schönberg* for a Chamber Ensemble (1949); *Seresta* for 4 Saxophones (1958); several piano pieces; and songs.

Caturla, Alejandro García, Cuban composer; b. Remedios, March 7, 1906; assassinated at Remedios, Nov. 12, 1940. He studied with Pedro Sanjuán in Havana; then with Nadia Boulanger in Paris (1928); was founder (1932) and conductor of the Orquesta de Conciertos de Caibarién (chamber orch.) in Cuba; served as district judge in Remedios. His works have been performed in Cuba, Europe, and the U.S. In Caturla's music, primitive Afro-Cuban rhythms and themes are treated with modern techniques and a free utilization of dissonance.
WORKS: Suite of 3 Cuban dances: *Danza del tambor, Motivos de danzas, Danza Lucumí* (Havana, 1928; also perf. in Barcelona, Seville, and Bogotá); *Bembé* for 14 Instruments (Paris, 1929); *Dos poemas Afro-Cubanos* for Voice and Piano (Paris, 1929; also arranged for Voice and Orch.); *Yambo-O,* Afro-Cuban oratorio (Havana, Oct. 25, 1931); *Rumba* for Orch. (1931); *Primera suite cubana* for Piano and 8 Wind Instruments (1930); *Manita en el Suelo,* "mitologia bufa Afro-Cubana" for Narrator, Marionettes, and Chamber Orch., to the text of Alejo Carpentier (1934).
BIBLIOGRAPHY: Alejo Carpentier, *Música en Cuba* (Havana, 1946); Otto Mayer-Serra, *Música y músicos de Latino-América* (Mexico, 1947); Adolfo

Salazar, "La obra musical de Alejandro Caturla," *Revista Cubana* (Jan. 1938); Nicolas Slonimsky, "Caturla of Cuba," *Modern Music* (Jan. 1940); R. Nodal Consuegra, "La figure de Alejandro García Caturla en la musica cubana," *Exilo* (Summer 1971).

Cauchie, Maurice, French musicologist; b. Paris, Oct. 8, 1882; d. there, March 21, 1963. He was first a physicist and chemist; after 1917 devoted himself exclusively to music; specialized in the study of French music of the 16th and 17th centuries. He edited *Deux chansons à 5 voix de Clément Janequin* (1925); *Quinze chansons françaises du XVIe siècle à 4 et 5 voix* (1926); *Trente chansons de Clément Janequin* (1928); the collected works of Clément Janequin; wrote *La Pratique de la musique* (1948); numerous essays in French magazines on Ockeghem, Attaingnant, Janequin, Cléreau, Costeley, Boesset, Couperin, Gluck, Beethoven, etc.; compiled a thematic index of the works of François Couperin (1949).

Caudella, Edoardo, Rumanian violinist and composer of Italian origin; b. Jassy, June 3, 1841; d. there, April 15, 1924. He studied in Berlin and in Paris, where he took violin lessons with Vieuxtemps. Returning to Rumania, he taught at the Cons. of Jassy. He wrote 2 violin concertos; 4 operas: *Olteanca* (Jassy, March 8, 1880); *Hatmanul Baltag* (Bucharest, March 1, 1884); *Fata razesului* (Bucharest, March 2, 1893); *Petru Raresch* (Bucharest, Nov. 14, 1900).
BIBLIOGRAPHY: Z. Vancea, *Creaţia muzicală romaneâscă sec. XIX–XX* (Bucharest, 1968).

Caurroy, Eustache du. See **Du Caurroy, François-Eustache.**

Cavaccio, Giovanni, Italian composer; b. Bergamo, 1556; d. there, Aug. 11, 1626. He was maestro di cappella at the Cathedral of Bergamo (1581–98) and at Santa Maria Maggiore in Bergamo from 1604 until his death. Among his publ. works are collections of madrigals (1583, 1591, 1599); Psalms (1585); a Requiem (Milan, 1611); and a collection of keyboard pieces, *Sudori musicali* (Venice, 1626). Music by Cavaccio was included in a publication of Psalms dedicated to Palestrina (1592), and pieces by him were printed in Bonometti's *Parnassus Musicus. A Canzon francese per organo* and a toccata are reprinted in L. Torchi, *L'Arte Musicale in Italia* (vol. III.)

Cavaillé-Coll, Aristide, celebrated French organ builder; b. Montpellier, Feb. 4, 1811; d. Paris, Oct. 13, 1899. His father, Dominique Hyacinthe (1771–1862), was also an organ builder. Aristide went to Paris in 1833; built the organ at St.-Denis, and thereafter many famous organs in Paris (St.-Sulpice, Madeleine, etc.), the French provinces, Belgium, the Netherlands, and elsewhere. He invented the system of separate wind chests with different pres-

sures for the low, medium, and high tones; also the "flûtes octaviantes." He publ. *Etudes expérimentales sur les tuyaux d'orgues* (report for the Académie des Sciences, 1849) and *Projet d'orgue monumental pour la Basilique de Saint-Pierre de Rome* (1875).
BIBLIOGRAPHY: A. Peschard, *Notice biographique sur A. Cavaillé-Coll et les orgues électriques* (Paris, 1899); C. and E. Cavaillé-Coll, *A. Cavaillé-Coll: Ses origines, sa vie, ses œuvres* (Paris, 1928); M. Vanmackelberg, "L'Esthétique d'Aristide Cavaillé-Coll," *L'Orgue* (July–Sept. 1968).

Cavalieri, Emilio del, Italian composer; b. c.1550; d. Rome, March 11, 1602. He was a nobleman who served as Inspector-General of Art and Artists at the Tuscan court in Florence (1588). He was one of the "inventors" and most ardent champions of the monodic style, or "stile recitativo," which combines melody with accompanying harmonies. His chief work, *La rappresentazione di anima e di corpo* (publ. by A. Guidotti, Rome, 1600, with explanatory preface; reprints: L. Guidiccioni-Nicastro, Livorno, 1911; Munich, 1921), once regarded as the first oratorio, is really a morality play set to music; other dramatic works (*Il satiro,* 1590; *Disperazione di Filene,* 1590; *Giuoco della cieca,* 1595) exemplify in similar manner the beginnings of modern opera form. In all of Cavalieri's music there is a *basso continuato* with thoroughbass figuring; the melodies are also crudely figured. A facsimile ed. of the libretto for *La rappresentazione* was publ. by D. Alaleona (Rome, 1912); a facsimile ed. of the orch. score is to be found in Mantica's *Collezione di prime fioriture del melodramma italiano* (Rome, 1912).
BIBLIOGRAPHY: D. Alaleona, "Su E. Cavalieri," *Nuova Musica* (Florence, 1905); Henry Prunières, "Une lettre inédite d'Emilio de Cavalieri," *Revue Musicale* (1923); U. Rolandi, "Emilio de Cavalieri," *Rivista Musicale Italiana* (1929); B. Becherini, "La musica nelle Sacre Rappresentazioni fiorentini," *Rivista Musicale Italiana* (1951); T. Antonicek, "Emilio de'Cavalieri und seine *Rappresentazione di anima e di corpo,*" *Österreichische Musikzeitschrift* (Aug. 1969).

Cavalieri, Katharina, Austrian soprano of Italian descent; b. Währing, near Vienna, Feb. 19, 1760; d. Vienna, June 30, 1801. She studied with Salieri; sang with great success at the Italian Opera and then at the German Opera in Vienna. Although she never sang outside of Vienna, a passage in one of Mozart's letters, describing her as "a singer of whom Germany might well be proud," procured for her deserved recognition. She retired in 1793. Mozart wrote for her the role of Constanze in *Die Entführung,* and the aria "Mi tradi" in *Don Giovanni.*

Cavalieri, Lina, Italian dramatic soprano; b. Viterbo, Dec. 25, 1874; d. Florence, Feb. 8, 1944. As a young woman she was renowned for her beauty, and became the cynosure of the Paris boulevardiers when she appeared at the Folies-Bergère. During her Russian trip in 1900, she married Prince Baria-tinsky, who persuaded her to abandon vaudeville and engage in an operatic career. After a few singing lessons with Maddalena Mariani-Masi, she sang in opera in St. Petersburg and Warsaw. In 1906 she was engaged to sing at the Metropolitan Opera in N.Y. (debut Dec. 5, 1906, as Fedora), where she was praised for her dramatic performances as Tosca and Mimi. In 1907, after a Russian divorce from her aristocratic first husband, she contracted a lucrative marriage with the American millionaire Winthrop Chandler, but left him in a week, precipitating a sensational scandal that, given the mores of the time, caused the Metropolitan to break her contract; made her farewell appearance there in a concert on March 8, 1908. In 1909 she returned to N.Y. for guest appearances at the Manhattan Opera House. In 1913 she married the French tenor Lucien Muratore; in 1919 she abandoned him, and opened a beauty salon in Paris. She then married her 4th husband, Paolo D'Arvanni, and went to live at her Villa Cappucina near Florence. Her life ended tragically, when both she and her last husband were killed during an air raid in 1944. She was the subject of an Italian film under the telling title *La donna più bella dello mondo,* with Gina Lollabrigida in the role of Lina Cavalieri.

Cavalli (Caletti), Pier Francesco, historically significant Italian opera composer; b. Crema, Feb. 14, 1602; d. Venice, Jan. 14, 1676. His father, Giovanni Battista Caletti (known also as Bruni), was maestro di cappella at the Cathedral in Crema; he gave him his first instruction in music; as a youth he sang under his father's direction in the choir of the Cathedral. The Venetian nobleman Federico Cavalli, who was also mayor of Crema, took him to Venice for further musical training; and as it was a custom, he adopted his sponsor's surname. In December 1616 he entered the choir of San Marco in Venice, beginning an association there which continued for the rest of his life; he sang there under Monteverdi; also served as an organist at SS. Giovanni e Paolo (1620–30). In 1638, he turned his attention to the new art form of opera, and helped to organize an opera company at the Teatro San Cassiano. His first opera, *Le nozze di Teti e di Peleo,* was performed there on Jan. 24, 1639; 9 more were to follow within the next decade. In 1639 he successfully competed against 3 others for the post of second organist at San Marco. In 1660 Cardinal Mazarin invited him to Paris, where he presented a restructured version of his opera *Serse* for the marriage festivities of Louis XIV and Maria Theresa. He also composed the opera *Ercole Amante* while there, which was given at the Tuileries on Feb. 7, 1662. He returned to Venice in 1662; on Jan. 11, 1665, he was officially appointed first organist at San Marco; on Nov. 20, 1668, he became maestro di cappella there. After Monteverdi, Cavalli stands as one of the most important Venetian composers of opera in the mid-17th century. In recent years several of his operas have been revived; Raymond Leppard edited *L'Ormindo* (London, 1969) and *Calisto* (London, 1975); Jane Glover

edited *L'Eritrea* (London, 1977). Cavalli also composed much sacred music; several works are available in modern editions.

WORKS: Operas: *Le nozze di Teti e di Peleo* (Venice, Jan. 24, 1639); *Gli amori d'Apollo e di Dafne* (Venice, 1640); *Didone* (Venice 1641); *Amore innamorato* (Venice, Jan. 1, 1642; music not extant); *La virtù de' strali d'Amore* (Venice, 1642); *Egoisto* (Venice, 1643); *L'Ormindo* (Venice, 1644); *Doriclea* (Venice, 1645); *Titone* (Venice, 1645; music not extant); *Giasone* (Venice, Jan. 5, 1649); *Euripo* (Venice, 1649; music not extant); *Orimonte* (Venice, Feb. 20, 1650); *Oristeo* (Venice, 1651); *Rosinda* (Venice, 1651); *Calisto* (Venice, 1652); *L'Eritrea* (Venice, 1652); *Veremonda l'amazzone di Aragona* (Naples, Dec. 21, 1652); *L'Orione* (Milan, June 1653); *Ciro* (originally composed by Francesco Provenzale; prologue and arias added by Cavalli for Venice, Jan. 30, 1654); *Serse* (Venice, Jan. 12, 1655); *Statira principessa di Persia* (Venice, Jan. 18, 1656); *Erismena* (Venice, 1656); *Artemisia* (Venice, Jan. 10, 1657); *Hipermestra* (Florence, June 12, 1658); *Antioco* (Venice, Jan. 21, 1959; music not extant); *Elena* (Venice, Dec. 26, 1659); *Ercole Amante* (Paris, Feb. 7, 1662); *Scipione affricano* (Venice, Feb. 9, 1664); *Mutio Scevola* (Venice, Jan. 26, 1665); *Pompeo magno* (Venice, Feb. 20, 1666); *Eliogabalo* (composed in 1668; not perf.); *Coriolano* (Piacenza, May 27, 1669; music not extant); *Massenzio* (composed in 1673; not perf.; music not extant). The following operas have been ascribed to Cavalli but are now considered doubtful: *Narciso et Ecco immortalati; Deidamia; Il Romolo e 'l Remo; La prosperità infelice di Giulio Cesare dittatore; Torilda; Bradamante; Armidoro; Helena rapita da Theseo;* also *La pazzia in trono, overo Caligola delirante,* which is a spoken drama with some music. None of the music is extant for any of these works.

BIBLIOGRAPHY: H. Kretschmar, "Die Venetianische Oper und die Werke Cavallis und Cestis," *Vierteljahrsschrift für Musikwissenschaft,* VIII (1892); E. Wellesz, "Cavalli und der Stil der venezianischen Oper von 1640–1660," *Studien zur Musikwissenschaft,* I (1913); T. Wiel, "Francesco Cavalli e la sua musica scenica," *Nuovo archivio veneto,* XXVIII (1914); H. Prunières, *Cavalli et l'opéra venetien au dix-septième siècle* (Paris, 1931); U. Rolandi, "Le opere teatrali di Francesco Cavalli," *Accademia musicale chigiana; La scuola veneziana* (1941); B. Hjelmborg, "Une partition de Cavalli. Quelques remarques complémentaires aux recherches Cavalliennes," *Acta Musicologica,* XVI–XVII (1944–45); F. Bussi, *La Messa concertata et la musique sacrée de Pier Francesco Cavalli* (Paris, 1960); H. Powers, "Il Serse trasformato," *Musical Quarterly* (Oct. 1961 and Jan. 1962); B. Hjelmborg, "Aspects of the Aria in the Early Operas of Cavalli," in *Natalica musicologica: Knud Jeppesen, septuagenario collegis oblata* (Copenhagen, 1962); D. Arnold, "Francesco Cavalli: Some Recently Discovered Documents," *Music and Letters* (Jan. 1965); F. Bussi, "La produzione sacra di Cavalli e i suoi rapporti con quella di Monteverdi," *Rivista Italiana di Musicologica,* II/2 (1967); G. Crain, "Francesco Cavalli and the Venetian Opera," *Opera* (June

1967); R. Leppard, "Cavalli's Operas," *Proceedings of the Royal Musical Association,* XCIII (1967); H. Powers, *"L'Erismena travestita,"* in *Studies in Music History* (Princeton, N.J., 1968); D. Swale, "Cavalli: The *Erismena* of 1655," in *Miscellanea Musicologica, Adelaide Studies in Musicology,* III (1968); A. Hicks, "Cavalli and *La Calisto,*" *Musical Times* (May 1970); E. Rosand, *Aria in the Early Operas of Francesco Cavalli* (Diss., New York Univ., 1971); J. Glover, "Cavalli and Rosinda," *Musical Times* (Feb. 1973); L. Bianconi, *Francesco Cavalli und die Verbreitung der venezianischen Oper in Italien* (Diss., Univ. of Heidelberg, 1974); E. Rosand, "L'Ormindo travestito in Erismena," *Journal of the American Musicological Society,* XXVIII (1975); J. Glover, "Aria and Closed Form in the Operas of Francesco Cavalli," *Consort,* XXXII (1976); H. Powers, "*Il Mutio tramutato:* Sources and Libretto," in M. Muraro, ed., *Venezia e il melodramma nel seicento* (Florence, 1976); E. Rosand, "Aria as Drama in the Early Operas of Francesco Cavalli," ibid.; idem, "Comic Contrast and Dramatic Unity: Observations on the Form and Function of Aria in the Operas of Francesco Cavalli," *Music Review,* XXXVII (1976); J. Glover, *Cavalli* (N.Y., 1978); M. Turnbull, "Ercole and Hercule: Les goûts désunis?," *Musical Times* (May 1980); J. Glover, "Cavalli and L'Eritrea," ibid. (Feb. 1982).

Cavallo, Enrica, Italian pianist; b. Milan, May 19, 1921. She was educated at the Verdi Cons. in Milan. She married the Italian violinist **Franco Gulli;** in 1947 they formed the noted Gulli-Cavallo Duo; in subsequent years they toured all over the world; in addition, she taught at the Verdi Cons. In 1973 she was appointed to the faculty of the Indiana Univ. School of Music.

Cavazzoni, Girolamo, Italian organist and composer; b. Urbino, c.1520; d. Venice, c.1577. He was a son of **Marco Antonio Cavazzoni** and godson of Cardinal Pietro Bembo. He was organist at San Barbara in Mantua until 1577; supervised the building of the organ there in 1565–66. His *Intavolatura cioè Ricercari, Canzoni, Hinni, Magnificati* (Venice, 1542) contains the first examples of the polyphonic ricercare of the 16th century. His organ ricercari, though related to the motet, differ from it in their extension of the individual sections by means of more numerous entries of the subject and more definite cadences between sections. The 2 canzonas from the same work mark the beginnings of an independent canzona literature for the keyboard. Reprints of Cavazzoni's works are found in L. Torchi, *L'Arte Musicale in Italia* (vol. III); Tagliapietra, *Antologia di Musica* (vol. I); Davison and Apel, *Historical Anthology of Music;* and Schering, *Geschichte der Musik in Beispielen.* O. Mishiati edited his organ works (2 vols., Mainz, 1959 and 1961).
BIBLIOGRAPHY: C. Sartori, "Precisazioni bibliografiche sulle opere di Girolamo Cavazzoni," *Rivista Musicale Italiana* (1940).

Cavazzoni (also called **da Bologna** and **detta d'Ur-**

bino), **Marco Antonio,** Italian composer and singer, father of **Girolamo Cavazzoni;** b. Bologna, c.1490; d. c.1570 (the date appearing on his will is April 3, 1569). He went to Urbino about 1510 and became acquainted with Cardinal Pietro Bembo; then became a musician in the private chapel of Pope Leo X (1515). In Venice (1517) he was employed by Francesco Cornaro, nephew of the Queen of Cyprus. Back in Rome (1520) he was again in the employ of Pope Leo X. From 1522–24 and from 1528–31 he was in Venice, and in 1536–37 was organist at Chioggia. From 1545–59 he was a singer at San Marco (Venice), where Adriaen Willaert was maestro di cappella. As a youth Cavazzoni wrote a mass, *Domini Marci Antonii,* so named because he derived its theme from the solmization syllables of his Christian names. His most important work is a collection of keyboard pieces, *Recerchari, motetti, canzoni, Libro I* (Venice, 1523). The ricercari are toccata-like rather than contrapuntal, and the motets and canzonas are instrumental transcriptions of vocal pieces. Modern reprints (with biographical notes) are found in Benvenuti's *I classici musicali italiani* (Milan, 1941) and in K. Jeppesen, *Die italienische Orgelmusik am Anfang des Cinquecento* (Copenhagen, 1943).
BIBLIOGRAPHY: T. Dart, "Cavazzoni and Cabezón" (suggesting a conjecture that Marco Antonio may have been a brother of Cabezón, the latter being a possible Spanish form of Cavazzoni's name), *Music & Letters* (Feb. 1955); a rebuttal to this by Jeppesen appears in *Journal of the American Musicological Society* (Summer 1955), together with a final postscript by Dart.

Cavos, Catterino, Italian-Russian composer; b. Venice, Oct. 30, 1775; d. St. Petersburg, May 10, 1840. He studied with Francesco Bianchi; his first work was a patriotic hymn for the Republican Guard, performed at the Teatro Fenice (Sept. 13, 1797); he then produced a cantata, *L'eroe* (1798). That same year he received an invitation to go to Russia as conductor at the Imperial Opera in St. Petersburg. He was already on his way to Russia when his ballet *Il sotterraneo* was presented in Venice (Nov. 16, 1799). He remained in St. Petersburg for the rest of his life. His Russian debut as a composer was in a collaborative opera, *Rusalka* (adapted from *Das Donauweibchen* by F. Kauer; Nov. 7, 1803). This was followed by the operas *The Invisible Prince* (May 17, 1805), *The Post of Love* (1806), *Ilya the Bogatyr* (Jan. 12, 1807), *3 Hunchback Brothers* (1808), *The Cossack Poet* (May 27, 1812), and several ballets. His most significant work was *Ivan Susanin,* which he conducted at the Imperial Theater on Oct. 30, 1815. The subject of this opera was used 20 years later by Glinka in his opera *A Life for the Tsar;* the boldness of Cavos in selecting a libretto from Russian history provided the necessary stimulus for Glinka and other Russian composers. (Cavos conducted the premiere of Glinka's opera.) His subsequent operas were also based on Russian themes: *Dobrynia Nikitich* (1818) and *The Firebird* (1822). Cavos was a notable voice teacher; among his pupils were several Russian singers who later became famous.

BIBLIOGRAPHY: R. Aloys Mooser, "Un musicista veneziano in Russia: Catterino Cavos," *Nuova Rivista Musicale Italiana* (Jan.–Feb. 1969).

Cazden, Norman, American composer; b. New York, Sept. 23, 1914; d. Bangor, Maine, Aug. 18, 1980. He studied piano with Ernest Hutcheson; composition with Bernard Wagenaar at the Juilliard School of Music and with Walter Piston at Harvard Univ. (Ph.D., 1948). In 1968 he settled in Maine as a teacher. His works reflect some interesting technical ideas in a general format of acceptable modernity.

WORKS: Concerto for 10 Instruments (1937); Quartet for Clarinet and Strings (1939); Symph. (1948); *3 Ballads* for Orch. (1949); Woodwind Quintet (1966); other chamber music; piano pieces.

Cebotari, Maria, Moldavian soprano; b. Kishinev, Bessarabia, Feb. 23, 1910; d. Vienna, June 9, 1949. She sang in a church choir; in 1924–29 studied at the Kishinev Cons.; then went to Berlin, where she took voice lessons with Oskar Daniel at the Hochschule für Musik. In 1929 she sang with a Russian émigré opera troupe in Bucharest and in Paris. In 1931 she made an auspicious debut as Mimi in *La Bohème* at the Dresden Opera; also appeared at the Salzburg Festival. In 1935 she joined the Berlin State Opera; in 1943 became a member of the Vienna State Opera. She also filled guest engagements in other European opera houses. She had a large repertoire which included the standard soprano roles, among them Violetta, Madama Butterfly, Pamina, and Mañon; she also gave brilliant performances in modern operas; Richard Strauss greatly prized her abilities, and entrusted to her the role of Aminta in the premiere of his opera *Die schweigsame Frau*. Thanks to her cosmopolitan background, she sang the part of Tatiana in Russian in Tchaikovsky's opera *Eugene Onegin* and the part of Antonida in Glinka's *A Life for the Tsar*. She also appeared in sound films. She was married to the Russian nobleman Count Alexander Virubov; she divorced him in 1938 and married the film actor Gustav Diessl.

BIBLIOGRAPHY: A Mingotti, *Maria Cebotari, Das Leben einer Sängerin* (Salzburg, 1950).

Ceccato, Aldo, Italian conductor; b. Milan, Feb. 18, 1934. He studied at the Cons. of Milan, and at the Academy of Music in Berlin. In 1969 he won first prize in the International Competition of Italian Radio for young conductors. He made his American debut with the Chicago Lyric Opera in 1969; then conducted the N.Y. Phil. on Nov. 5, 1970, with excellent success. From 1973 to 1977 he was conductor of the Detroit Symph. Orch. In 1975 he was named Generalmusikdirektor of the Hamburg Phil.

Ceely, Robert, American composer; b. Torrington, Conn., Jan. 17, 1930. He studied composition at the New England Cons. in Boston (B.Mus., 1954) and at Mills College (M.A., 1961); in 1965 he was appointed to the faculty of the New England Cons.

WORKS: String Trio (1953); *Music for 10 Instruments* (1963); *Strati* for Magnetic Tape (1963); *Logs,* duet for Double Basses (1968); *Modules* for 7 Instruments (1968); *Spectrum* for Chamber Ensemble and Tape (1969); *Hymn* for Double Bass and Cello (1970); *Slide Music* for 4 Trombones (1975); *Rituals* for 40 Flutes (1976); *Roundels* for Wind Ensemble (1977).

Cehanovsky, George, Russian baritone; b. St. Petersburg, April 14, 1892. He entered the Russian navy during World War I and sustained a severe wound in a naval encounter. After the war he studied singing with his mother, who was a professional singer, and made his debut as Valentin in Gounod's *Faust* in Petrograd in 1921. In 1923 he emigrated to the U.S.; at first sang with various opera companies, and in 1926 was engaged by the Metropolitan Opera, with which he remained until 1966, the longest stretch of any member of the Metropolitan staff. He filled in 78 different roles during his career at the Metropolitan, all of them in *comprimario* parts, e.g. Wagner in *Faust,* Morales in *Carmen,* Sharpless in *Madama Butterfly,* and the 2nd policeman in *Jonny spielt auf.* In 1956 he married the German soprano **Elisabeth Rethberg.**

Čelanský, Ludvík Vítězslav, Czech conductor and composer; b. Vienna, July 17, 1870; d. Prague, Oct. 27, 1931. He studied at the Prague Cons.; then conducted theater orchs. in Pilsen and Zagreb. Returning to Prague, he made the Czech Phil. Orch. into an independent organization (1901), and conducted it for the first season and again in 1918–19; he also conducted opera and concerts abroad.

WORKS: Opera, *Camille* (Prague, Oct. 23, 1897); symph. trilogy, *Adam, Noë, Moïse* (1915–19); church music; songs.

BIBLIOGRAPHY: A valedictory brochure, ed. by V. Balthasar, was publ. in honor of his 50th birthday (Prague, 1920).

Celibidache, Sergiu, transcendently endowed Rumanian conductor; b. Roman, June 28, 1912. He studied at the Hochschule für Musik in Berlin with Kurt Thomas, Heinz Gmeindl, and Fritz Stein, and also attended the musicology classes of Schering and Schünemann at the Univ. of Berlin; apart from music, he studied advanced mathematics and formalistic philosophy. In 1945 he was suddenly thrust into the position of conductor pro tem of the Berlin Phil. until the regular conductor, Furtwängler, was cleared of any suspicion of Naziphilia. When Furtwängler took the Berlin Phil. on an American tour in 1948, Celibidache served as his assistant, and continued in this capacity in Berlin until 1952. From 1964 to 1971 he was engaged as music director of the Swedish Radio Symph. Orch.; in 1970 was named Knight of the Swedish Vasa Order; in 1971–77 he was conductor of the Stuttgart Radio Orch.; in 1980 was appointed Generalmusikdirektor of the Munich Phil. Orch. In 1983 he joined the faculty of the Curtis Inst. of Music in Philadelphia, where he also conducted the student orch. On Feb. 27, 1984, he conducted it at Carnegie Hall, N.Y., in his formal American debut as conductor, arousing hosannas and hurrahs from the delighted audience and astonishing critics, in a diversified program of works by Rossini, Wagner, Debussy, and Prokofiev. A cosmopolitan existentialist, he lectured on musical phenomenology at Mainz Univ., and composed music in his leisure time; he wrote 4 symphs., a Piano Concerto, and a variety of minor pieces. As an interpreter, he strives for humanly attainable perfection, and to achieve his goal demands an unconscionable number, sometimes as many as 18, of rehearsals; this precluded most American orch. managements from snaring him into permanent employment. His name is not unpronounceable, however (Cheh-lee-bee-dáh-key, with the stress on the 4th syllable).

Celis, Frits, Belgian conductor and composer, b. Antwerp, April 11, 1929. He studied composition at the Flemish Cons. in Antwerp, and harp at the Brussels Cons.; then attended the summer conducting course at the Mozarteum in Salzburg (1949–51) and similar courses at the Hochschule für Musik in Cologne (1953–54). He then became conductor of the Théâtre de la Monnaie in Brussels (1954–59) and also conducted in Czechoslovakia, the Netherlands, France, and Spain. In 1960 he was appointed to the faculty of the Flemish Cons. of Antwerp. His compositions are all written in a *laissez-faire* manner sparingly seasoned with atonality.
WORKS: *Music* for Strings (1951); Violin Sonata (1951); String Trio (1958); *De Geestelijke bruiloft* for Voice, and Piano or Chamber Orch. (1958); Cello Sonata (1963); *Elégie* for Orch. (Antwerp, Dec. 8, 1967); *3 Symphonic Movements* (1969); *Intrada and Toccata* for Oboe and Piano (1972); *Episodes* for Viola and Harpsichord (1973); *Variazioni* for Chamber Orch. (1974); choruses; songs.

Celletti, Rodolfo, Italian music critic; b. Rome, June 13, 1917. He obtained a law degree from the Univ. of Rome; then devoted himself to music criticism, writing for various newspapers in Milan. He also edited the valuable reference work *Le grandi voici: Dizionario critico-biografico dei cantanti* (Rome, 1964).

Cellier, Alfred, English conductor and composer; b. (of French parents) London, Dec. 1, 1844; d. there, Dec. 28, 1891. He was a chorister at St. James' Chapel Royal; studied music with Thomas Helmore; in 1866 was conductor, at Belfast, of the Ulster Hall concerts and the Phil.; in 1871–75 conducted at the Prince's Theatre in Manchester; in 1877–79 at the London Opéra-Comique, and (with Sullivan) the Promenade Concerts in Covent Garden. He then spent some years in America and Australia, returning to London in 1887.
WORKS: Light operas: *Charity Begins at Home* (London, 1870); *The Foster Brothers* (London, June 17, 1873); *The Sultan of Mocha* (Manchester, Nov. 16, 1874); *The Tower of London* (Manchester, Oct. 4, 1875); *Nell Gwynne* (Manchester, Oct. 16, 1876);

Dora's Dream (London, Nov. 17, 1877); *The Spectre Knight* (London, Feb. 9, 1878); *Bella Donna, or The Little Beauty and the Great Beast* (Manchester, April 27, 1878); *After All* (London, Dec. 16, 1878); *In the Sulks* (London, Feb. 21, 1880); *The Masque of Pandora,* after Longfellow (Boston, Jan. 10, 1881); *The Carp* (London, Feb. 11, 1886); *Dorothy* (London, Sept. 25, 1886); *Mrs. Jarramie's Genie* (London, Feb. 14, 1888); *Doris* (London, April 20, 1889); *The Mountebanks* (London, Jan. 4, 1892); also a setting of Gray's *Elegy,* written for the Leeds Festival (Oct. 10, 1883); a symph. suite; many popular songs.

Ceremuga, Josef, Czech composer; b. Ostrava-Kunčice, June 14, 1930. He studied composition with Řídký at the Music Academy in Prague and advance harmony with Alois Hába (1950–53); did postgraduate study with Dobiáš (1953–56). He then became a member of the staff of the Academy; later was a lecturer on the music for the cinema (1960–73). His own music reflects the modern Russian style, with broad neo-Romantic melos sharpened by euphonious dissonances.
WORKS: *Juraj Čup,* ballad-opera after Čapek (1958–60; Prague, April 27, 1963); 3 symphs. (1952, 1968, 1975); Violin Concerto (1955); *3 Symphonic Frescoes* (1958–59); Piano Concerto (Teplice, Jan. 21, 1963); *Hommage aux étudiants,* overture (1964); *Concerto da camera* for Wind Quintet and String Orch. (1970–71); 3 string quartets (1956, 1961, 1973); Piano Trio (1960); Cello Sonata (1957); Viola Sonata (1961); *4 Pictures* for Clarinet and Accordion (1961); 2 wind quintets (1964, 1967); songs.

Cererols, Joan, Catalan composer; b. Martorell, Sept. 9, 1618; d. Montserrat, Aug. 28, 1676. In 1636 he entered the Monastery of Montserrat; studied organ and violin there. He wrote a great number of sacred vocal works. The Monastery of Montserrat publ., in its series *Música Instrumental,* his Psalms and Vespers (vol. I, 1930), masses (vol. II, 1931), and villancicos (vol. III, 1932), ed. by Dom David Pujol.

Cerha, Friedrich, Austrian composer of the avant-garde; b. Vienna, Feb. 17, 1926. He studied violin with Vasa Prihoda and composition with Alfred Uhl at the Vienna Music Academy (1946–51); also attended courses in musicology and philosophy at the Univ. of Vienna (1946–50). Upon graduation, he became active in the modernistic movement as a violinist, conductor, and composer. In 1958 he organized (with Kurt Schwertsik) the Vienna concert ensemble Die Reihe, devoted to new music. In 1960 he became director of the electronic-music studio and a lecturer at the Vienna Academy, becoming a prof. in 1969. His music pursues the aim of "atomization of thematic materials" as a means toward total integration of infinitesimal compositional quantities, with minimal variations of successive temporal units.
WORKS: *2 éclats en reflexion* for Violin and Piano (1956); *Formation et solution* for Violin and Piano (1956–57); *Espressioni fondamentali* for Orch. (1956–57; Berlin, Nov. 17, 1960); *Relazioni*

fragili for Harpsichord and Chamber Orch. (1957; Vienna, May 16, 1960); *Enjambements* for 6 Players (1959; Paris, March 7, 1962); *Fasce* for Orch. (1959; fair-copied in 3 stages, 1967–68, 1972–73, and 1975; Graz, Oct. 8, 1975); *Intersecazioni I* (1959–61) and *II* (1959–73; Graz, Oct. 16, 1973) for Violin and Orch.; *Mouvements I–III* for Chamber Orch. (1960); *Spiegel I–VII* for Orch., some movements with Tape (1960–61; fair-copied 1961–71; first complete perf. of the entire 80-minute score, Graz, ISCM Festival, Oct. 9, 1972); *Exercises* for Baritone, Narrator, and Chamber Ensemble (1962–67); *Elegie* for Piano (1963); *Phantasme 63* for Organ (3 Players) and Chamber Orch. (1963); *Symphonien* for Winds and Timpani (1964); *Catalogue des objets trouvés* for Chamber Orch. (1968–69; West Berlin, Oct. 1, 1970); *Verzeichnis* for chorus a cappella (1969); *Langegger Nachtmusik I* and *II* for Orch. (1969, 1970); *Curriculum* for 12 Winds (1972); Symph. (1975); *Double Concerto* for Violin, Cello, and Orch. (1975); opera, *Baal,* after Brecht (1973–81); *Keintate* for Voice and 11 Instruments (1982–83); Double Concerto for Flute, Bassoon, and Orch. (1982; Graz, Oct. 7, 1983).

Černohorsky, Bohuslav. See **Czernohorsky, Bohuslav.**

Černušák, Gracian, Czech music lexicographer; b. Ptení, near Prostějov, Moravia, Dec. 19, 1882; d. Brno, Oct. 13, 1961. He studied music in Prague; then was active as a music teacher in Brno from 1919 to 1939 and again from 1945 to 1953; from 1945 to 1955 he also taught at the Univ. of Brno. He edited the *Hudební slovník nau-čný* (1937–40) and also prepared articles for the Czech music dictionary *Československý hudební slovník* (Prague, 1963–65). He contributed many entries on Czech composers to the 5th ed. of *Grove's Dictionary* (1954).

Černý, Ladislav, Czech viola player and composer; b. Pilsen, April 13, 1891; d. Dobříš, July 13, 1975. He studied violin at the Prague Cons.; then played viola at the opera in Ljubljana (1916–21); returning to Prague, he organized the Zik Quartet, known as the Prague Quartet from 1929; was a member until his death; taught at the Prague Cons. (1940–46); from 1946 to 1973 was a prof. at the Prague Music Academy. Hindemith dedicated his Sonata for Solo Viola to him.

Cerone, Domenico Pietro, Italian tenor and music theorist; b. Bergamo, 1566; d. Naples, 1625. In 1592 he went to Spain and became a singer in the court choir; later was appointed teacher of plainsong to the clergy of the church of the Annunciation at Naples; from 1610 until his death, sang in the Royal Chapel Choir there. He publ. the manual *Regole per il canto fermo* (Naples, 1609) and *El Melopeo y Maestro, tractado de música teórica y práctica* (Naples, 1613). This treatise, written in Spanish, numbers 1,160 pages, containing a compendium of early music theory; it is divided into 22 books and 849 chapters; its pedantic exposition and inordinate length were the main target of Eximeno's satirical

novel *Don Lazarillo Vizcardi;* Book XII is publ. in Eng. in O. Strunk's *Source Readings in Music History* (N.Y., 1950); in the U.S., copies of the entire work are to be found in the Library of Congress, the N.Y. Public Library, the Hispanic Society of N.Y., and the Sibley Music Library in Rochester, N.Y.
BIBLIOGRAPHY: F. Pedrell, *P. Antonio Eximeno* (1920); G. Pannain, *L'oratorio dei Filippini* (1934); Ruth Hannas, "Cerone, Philosopher and Teacher," *Musical Quarterly* (Oct. 1935), and "Cerone's Approach to the Teaching of Counterpoint," *Papers of the American Musicological Society* (1937); A. Howell, "Symposium on Seventeenth-century Music Theory," *Journal of Music Theory* (1972).

Cerquetti, Anita, Italian soprano; b. Montecòsaro, near Macerata, April 13, 1931. She studied in Perugia; made her debut as Aida in Spoleto in 1951; then sang throughout Italy; in 1955 she appeared with the Chicago Opera; in 1958 she sang in Rome and at La Scala in Milan. Her promising career came to an end because of a grave illness, and she had to retire.

Cerreto, Scipione, Italian composer, lutenist, and theorist; b. Naples, 1551; d. there, c.1632. He publ. 2 theoretical works containing valuable information on the music and musical instruments of his time: *Della prattica musica vocale e strumentale* (Naples, 1601) and *Arbore musicale* (Naples, 1608); a 3rd work, *Dialogo harmonico,* remained unpubl. (2 forms, 1628 and 1631).

Certon, Pierre, French contrapuntist; b. c.1510; d. Paris, Feb. 23, 1572. He was a pupil of Josquin des Prez; was choirmaster of the Sainte-Chapelle in Paris (from 1536); composed masses, motets, Psalms, Magnificats, and 4-part chansons, which were printed in the collections of Ballard, Attaignant, Susato, Phalèse, and others, between 1527 and 1560. Reprints of his masses (*Sur le pont d'Avignon; Adjuva me; Regnum mundi*) are to be found in H. Expert's *Monuments de la musique française au temps de la Renaissance,* vol. 2 (1925); 10 chansons in vol. 82 of *Das Chorwerk.*
BIBLIOGRAPHY: M. Brenet, *Les Musiciens de la Sainte-Chapelle* (Paris, 1910); a biographical account and bibliography, by A. Agnel, are included in the reprint *Pierre Certon: Chansons polyphoniques publiée par Pierre Attaingnant; Livre I (1533–39)* (Paris, 1967).

Cervantes (Kawanag), Ignacio, Cuban pianist and composer; b. Havana, July 31, 1847; d. there, April 29, 1905. He studied with Gottschalk (1859–61) and at the Paris Cons. (1866–68), with Alkan and Marmontel; in 1870 returned to Cuba; in 1898 went to Mexico; also visited the U.S. He was one of the pioneers of native Cuban music; in his *Danzas Cubanas* for Piano he employs Cuban rhythms in an effective salon manner; he also wrote 3 operas, *El submarino Peral, Los Saltimbanquis,* and *Maledetto* (1895; unfinished), and some orch. pieces.

BIBLIOGRAPHY: E. Sánchez de Fuentes, *Ignacio Cervantes Kawanag* (Havana, 1936); Alejo Carpentier, *La música en Cuba* (Mexico, 1946).

Červený, Wenzel Franz (Václav František), inventor of brass instruments; b. Dubeč, Bohemia, Sept. 27, 1819; d. Königgrätz, Jan. 19, 1896. He was a good performer on most brass instruments when he was only 12 years old; learned his trade with Bauer, a music instrument maker in Prague; worked at various times in Brünn, Bratislava, Vienna, and Budapest; in 1842 established his own shop at Königgrätz. He invented the following instruments: Cornon (1844), Contrabass (1845), Phonikon (1848), Baroxiton (1853), Contrafagotto in metal (1856), Althorn obbligato (1859), Turnerhorn, Jägerhorn, army trombones (1867), and Primhorn (1873). After the success of the Primhorn, he created the complete Waldhorn quartet, which he considered his greatest achievement. Then followed the Subcontrabass and the Subcontrafagotto, and finally an entire family of improved cornets ("Kaiserkornette") and the "Triumph" cornet. His "roller" cylinder-mechanism is an invention of the greatest importance. He also improved the Euphonion, the Russian Signal-horns, the Screw-drum, and the church kettledrum. His instruments took first prizes at exhibitions in Europe and America.

Cervetti, Sergio, Uruguayan composer; b. Dolores, Nov. 9, 1940. He studied in Uruguay; then went to the U.S. and attended classes of Ernst Krenek and Stefan Grove at the Peabody Cons. (1963–67). In 1970, he was appointed a teacher at the N.Y. Univ. School of the Arts.
WORKS: String Trio (1963); Piano Sonata (1964); *5 Sequences* for Flute, Horn, Cello, Electric Guitar, Piano, and Percussion (1966); *Orbitas* for Orch. (1967); *El Carro de Heno* for Small Chorus and Orch. (1967); *Zinctum* for String Quartet (Washington, D.C., June 24, 1968); *Dies tenebrarum* for Electric Organ, 3 Percussionists, Male Chorus, and Strings (1968); *Pulsar* for Brass Sextet (1969); *Prisons No. 1* for Singers, Dancers, Pantomime, 2 Trombones, Electric Organ, Electric Guitar, Double Bass, and Percussion (1969); *Prisons No. 2* for Speaking Chorus, Orch., and Tape (1970–71); *Peripetia* for 20–100 Singers and Instrumentalists (1970); *Cocktail Party* for Amplified Instruments and any number of Invitations (Malmö, Sweden, Nov. 9, 1970); *Plexus* for Small Orch. (Washington, May 18, 1971); *4 fragmentos de Pablo Neruda* for Soprano, Oboe, Guitar, Cello, and Percussion (1970); *Raga I* for Ensemble, *II* for Trombone and Tape (both 1971); *Graffiti* for Speaking Chorus, Orch., and Tape (1971); *. . . from the earth . . .* for Ensemble (1972).

Cervetto (real name, **Bassevi**), **Giacomo,** Italian cellist; b. c.1682; d. London, Jan. 14, 1783. In 1728 he settled in London, where he was a player and then manager of the Drury Lane Theatre; wrote some chamber music. He lived to be 100 years old. His son, **James Cervetto** (b. London, 1747; d. there, Feb. 5, 1837), was a cellist, too, and also lived to a very old age. He composed several cello pieces.

Cesana, Otto, American composer; b. Brescia, Italy, July 7, 1899; d. New York, Dec. 9, 1980. He came to the U.S. as a young man, and studied music with Julius Gold in California. He specialized in writing film music without, however, relinquishing his more ambitious pursuits. He wrote 6 symphs. and 6 concertos: one for Clarinet, one for Trumpet, one for Trombone, one for Piano, one for 2 Pianos, and one for 3 Pianos; also composed a ballet, *Ali Baba and the 40 Thieves,* and a jazzy piece entitled *Swing Septet,* which was performed in Indianapolis, on Jan. 23, 1942. He was the author of several manuals, among them *Course in Modern Harmony* (1939), *Course in Counterpoint* (1940), and *Voicing the Modern Dance Orchestra* (1946).

Cesari, Gaetano, Italian musicologist; b. Cremona, June 24, 1870; d. Sale Marasino, Oct. 21, 1934. He studied musicology in Germany; was a pupil of Mottl, Sandberger, and Kroyer at the Univ. of Munich. Returning to Italy, he was employed as a teacher, music critic, and librarian. He publ. several valuable essays on Italian music, among them "Musica e musicisti alla Corte Sforzesca," publ. in *Rivista Musicale Italiana* (1922); a monograph, *Amilcare Ponchielli nell' arte del suo tempo* (Cremona, 1934); and, in collaboration with A. Luzio, the important source book *I copialettere di Verdi* (1913).

Cesi, Beniamino, Italian pianist and pedagogue; b. Naples, Nov. 6, 1845; d. there, Jan. 19, 1907. He studied music with his father; then was a pupil of the celebrated pianist Thalberg; after a European tour he was a piano instructor at the Royal Collegio in Naples (1866–85) and at the St. Petersburg Cons. (1885–91). In 1895 he returned to the Cons. of Naples, where he taught until his death. His 2 sons, **Napoleone** and **Sigismondo,** were both pianists, whom he trained for a concert career; among other pupils were Martucci, Cilea, and A. Longo. He publ. a valuable *Metodo per pianoforte,* and also wrote an opera, *Vittor Pisani.*
BIBLIOGRAPHY: A. Longo, "Beniamino Cesi," *L'Arte Pianistica* (Jan. 1914).

Cesti, Antonio (baptismal name, **Pietro**), renowned dramatic composer; b. Arezzo, Aug. 5, 1623; d. Florence, Oct. 14, 1669. He was a choirboy in Arezzo; then joined the Franciscan order (1637) in Votterra; was probably a pupil of Carissimi at Rome in 1640–45; later was maestro di cappella to Ferdinand II de' Medici, at Florence; in 1660, became a tenor singer in the Papal choir; in 1666–68, was assistant Kapellmeister to Emperor Leopold I at Vienna; then he returned to Florence.
WORKS: His first opera, *Orontea* (Venice, Jan. 20, 1649), was much applauded; other dramatic ventures were also successful; *Cesare amante* (Venice, 1651); *Argia* (Innsbruck, 1655); *Dori* (Innsbruck, 1657; selections printed in vol. XII of *Publikationen der Gesellschaft für Musikforschung*); *Il Principe*

generoso (Vienna, 1665; authorship disputed); *Tito* (Venice, Feb. 13, 1666); *Nettuno e Flora festeggianti* (Vienna, July 12, 1666); *Il Pomo d'oro* (Vienna, 1667; publ. in its entirety in Denkmäler der Tonkunst in Österreich, 6, 9 [3.ii, 4.ii]); *Semiramide* (Vienna, June 9, 1667); *Le disgrazie d'Amore* (Vienna, 1667); *Argene* (Venice, 1668); *Genserico* (Venice, Jan. 31, 1669). Cesti wrote numerous cantatas which are preserved in various European libraries; his dramatic flair was reflected in the theatrical forms of his cantatas; he also wrote madrigals, songs, etc. A. Schering's *Geschichte der Musik in Beispielen* contains an aria from *Argia* (No. 203); H. Riemann's *Kantaten-Frühling* (Leipzig, 1912; no. 9), F. Vatielli's *Antiche cantate d'amore* (Bologna, 1920; no. 8), and G. Adler's *Handbuch* (2nd ed., 1930; pp. 439ff.).

BIBLIOGRAPHY: H. Kretzschmar, "Die venezianische Oper und die Werke Cavallis und Cestis," *Vierteljahrsschrift für Musikwissenschaft* (1892); E. Wellesz, "Ein Bühnenfestspiel aus dem 17. Jahrhundert," *Sämmelbande der Internationalen Musik-Gesellschaft* XV (1913; pp. 134ff.); F. Coradini, "Padre A. Cesti, Nuove notizie biografiche," *Rivista Musicale Italiana* (July 1923; very valuable for biographical documentation); A. Sandberger, in the bulletin of the Union Musicologique (1925; pp. 121–73); P. Nettl, "Ein verschollenes Tournierballett von M.A. Cesti," *Zeitschrift für Musikwissenschaft* (April 1926); A. Tessier, "L'Orontée de Lorenzani et l'Orontea du Padre Cesti," *La Revue Musicale* IX/8 (1928); W. Holmes, "Giacinto Andrea Cicognini's and Antonio Cesti's *Orontea* (1649)," in W. Austin, ed., *New Looks at Italian Opera* (Ithaca, N.Y., 1968); T. Antonicek, "Zum 300. Todestag Antonio Cestis," *Österreichische Musikzeitschrift* (Oct. 1969); D.H. Shock, "Costuming for *Il Pomo d'oro*," *Gazette des Beaux-Arts* (April 1967); T. Antonicek, "Antonio Cesti alla corte di Vienna," *Nuova Rivista Musicale Italiana* (March/April 1970); W.C. Holmes, "Cesti's *L'Argia:* An Entertainment for a Royal Convert," *Chigiana* (1969/70).

Cezar, Corneliu, Rumanian composer; b. Bucharest, Dec. 22, 1937. He studied composition at the Bucharest Cons., with Tudor Ciortea, Mihail Jora, Alfred Mendelsohn, and Anatol Vieru. After graduating, he was active mainly as a piano teacher. WORKS: Opera, after Brecht, *Galileo Galilei* (1962; Bucharest, Dec. 16, 1964); Piano Sonata (1959); Quartet for Flute, Violin, Viola, and Bassoon (1959); *Cronika* for Orch. and Tape (Bucharest, Feb. 1, 1968); a piece to a Polynesian text, *Taaroa,* for Narrator, 2 Prepared Pianos, Carillon on Tape, and Clarinet (1968); and numerous scores of incidental music for the theater.

Chabrier, (Alexis-) Emmanuel, famous French composer; b. Ambert, Puy de Dôme, Jan. 18, 1841; d. Paris, Sept. 13, 1894. He studied law in Paris (1858–61); also studied composition with Semet and Hignard, piano with Edouard Wolff, and violin with Hammer. He served in the government from 1861; at the same time cultivated his musical tastes; with Duparc, Vincent d'Indy, and others he formed a pri-

vate group of music lovers, and was an enthusiastic admirer of Wagner. He began to compose in earnest, and produced 2 light operas: *L'Étoile* (Paris, Nov. 28, 1877) and *Une Éducation manquée* (Paris, May 1, 1879). In 1879 he went to Germany with Duparc to hear Wagner's operas; returning to Paris, he publ. some piano pieces; then traveled to Spain; the fruit of this journey was his most famous work, the rhapsody *España* (Paris, Nov. 4, 1883), which produced a sensation when performed by Lamoureux in 1884. Another work of Spanish inspiration was the *Habanera* for piano (1885). In the meantime he served as chorus master for Lamoureux; this experience developed his knowledge of vocal writing; he wrote a brief cantata for mezzo-soprano and women's chorus, *La Sulamite* (March 15, 1885), and his 2 operas *Gwendoline* (Brussels, April 10, 1886) and *Le Roi malgré lui* (Opéra-Comique, Paris, May 18, 1887); another opera, *Briséis,* remained unfinished. In his operas Chabrier attempted a grand style; his idiom oscillated between passionate Wagnerianism and a more conventional type of French stage music; although these operas enjoyed a *succès d'estime,* they never became popular, and Chabrier's place in music history is secured exclusively by his *España,* and piano pieces such as *Bourrée fantasque* (1891; orchestrated by Felix Mottl); his *Joyeuse Marche* for Orch. (originally entitled *Marche française,* 1888) is also popular. Other works are *Ode à la musique* for Voices and Orch. (1890); *10 pièces pittoresques* for Piano (1880; 4 of them orchestrated and perf. as *Suite pastorale*); *3 valses romantiques* for 2 Pianos (1883); songs.

BIBLIOGRAPHY: O. Séré, *E. Chabrier,* in *Musiciens français d'aujourd'hui* (Paris, 1911); René Martineau, *E. Chabrier* (Paris, 1911); G. Servières, *E. Chabrier* (Paris, 1912); A. Cortot, "L'Œuvre pianistique de E. Chabrier," *La Revue Musicale* (Oct. 1926); Joseph Desaymard, *Chabrier d'après ses lettres* (Paris, 1934); J.–G. Prod'homme, "Chabrier in His Letters," *Musical Quarterly* (Oct. 1935); Francis Poulenc, *Emmanuel Chabrier* (Paris, 1961); Rollo Myers, *Emmanuel Chabrier and His Circle* (London, 1969); F. Robert, *Emmanuel Chabrier. L'Homme et son œuvre* (Paris, 1970); R. Delage and F. Durif, "Emmanuel Chabrier en Espagne," *Revue de Musicologie,* LVI/2 (1970); R. Delage, *Chabrier* (Geneva, 1982).

Chadwick, George Whitefield, eminent American composer; b. Lowell, Mass., Nov. 13, 1854; d. Boston, April 4, 1931. He first studied music with Eugene Thayer in Boston; then became head of the music dept. at Olivet College in Michigan (1876); from 1877–78 studied at the Leipzig Cons. with Reinecke and Jadassohn; his graduation piece was an overture to *Rip Van Winkle,* which he conducted with the Leipzig Cons. Orch. on June 20, 1879; then studied organ and composition at Munich under Rheinberger; in 1880 returned to Boston as organist of the South Congregational Church; in 1882 became a teacher of harmony and composition at the New England Cons.; in 1897 succeeded Faelten as director. He received the honorary degree of M.A.

from Yale, and an honorary LL.D. from Tufts College in 1905; received the Gold Medal of the Academy of Arts and Letters in 1928; for several seasons was conductor of the Worcester Music Festival; also head of music festivals in Springfield and Worcester, Mass.; was a member of the Boston Academy of Arts and Letters. Chadwick was one of the leading American composers; usually regarded as a pillar of the "Boston Classicists," he was actually an ardent romanticist; his musical style was formed under the influence of the German programmatic school; his harmonies are Wagnerian, his orchestration full and lush.

WORKS: FOR THE STAGE: Comic Operas: *The Quiet Lodging* (privately perf., Boston, 1892) and *Tabasco* (Boston, Jan. 29, 1894); *Judith,* lyric drama (Worcester Festival, Sept. 26, 1901); *The Padrone,* opera (1915); *Love's Sacrifice,* pastoral operetta (1916; Chicago, Feb. 1, 1923); incidental music to *Everywoman* (N.Y. and London, 1911). FOR ORCH.: 3 symphs.: No. 1, in C (1883–85); No. 2, in B-flat (Boston Symph., Dec. 11, 1886); No. 3, in F (Boston Symph., Oct. 20, 1894); overtures: *Rip Van Winkle, Thalia, The Miller's Daughter, Melpomene* (Boston, Dec. 24, 1887; also arranged for Piano, 4-hands), *Adonais* (Boston, Feb. 3, 1900), *Euterpe* (Boston Symph., April 23, 1904, composer conducting), and *Anniversary Overture* (Norfolk Festival, 1922); Serenade in F for String Orch.; *A Pastoral Prelude* (Boston, 1894); Sinfonietta in D (Boston, Nov. 21, 1904); symph. poems: *Cleopatra* (Worcester Festival, 1905) and *Angel of Death* (N.Y., 1919); *Symphonic Sketches,* suite (*Jubilee, Noël, Hobgoblin,* and *A Vagrom Ballad;* 1895–1904; Boston Symph., Feb. 7, 1908); Theme, Variations, and Fugue for Organ and Orch. (Boston, 1908; arranged by J. Wallace Goodrich for Organ Solo); *Suite symphonique* (Philadelphia, 1911; first prize of the National Federation of Music Clubs); *Aphrodite,* symph. fantasy (Norfolk Festival, 1912); *Tam O'Shanter,* symph. ballad (Norfolk Festival, 1915). CHORAL WORKS: *Dedication Ode* (1886) for Soli, Chorus, and Orch.; *Lovely Rosabelle,* ballad for Solo, Chorus, and Orch. (Boston, 1889); *The Pilgrims* for Chorus and Orch. (Boston, 1891); *Ode for the Opening of the Chicago World's Fair* for Chorus, with Piano or Orch. (1892); *Phoenix Expirans* for Soli, Chorus, and Orch. (Springfield Festival, 1892); *The Lily Nymph,* cantata (1893); *Lochinvar* for Baritone and Orch. (Springfield Festival, 1897); *Noël,* Christmas pastoral for Soli, Chorus, and Orch. (Norfolk Festival, 1908); *Aghadoe,* ballad for Alto and Orch.; numerous sacred works: *Ecce jam noctis* (Yale, 1897); *The Beatitudes; Jubilate;* etc.; many choruses for men's, women's, and mixed voices; also school choruses. CHAMBER MUSIC: 5 string quartets (I, in G minor; II, in C; III, in D; IV, in E minor; V, in D minor); Piano Quintet (1888); violin and cello pieces; etc. He composed about 100 songs with piano, organ, or orch. (*Allah, Ballad of the Trees and Masters, The Danza, Before the Dawn,* etc.). ORGAN WORKS: *10 Canonic Studies for Organ* (1885); *Progressive Pedal Studies for Organ* (1890); miscellaneous pieces (*Requiem, Suite in Variation Form,* etc.); also numerous piano pieces.

WRITINGS: He was the author of *Harmony, A Course of Study* (Boston, 1897; revised ed., 1922) and *Key to the Textbook on Harmony* (Boston, 1902); was co-editor of *A Book of Choruses for High Schools and Choral Societies* (N.Y., 1923).

BIBLIOGRAPHY: For a full list of works, with dates of composition, performance, and publication, see C. Engel, "G.W. Chadwick," *Musical Quarterly* (July 1924); also A.L. Langley, "Chadwick and the New England Conservatory," ibid., (Jan. 1935).

Chaffin, Lucien Gates, American organist and composer; b. Worcester, Mass., March 23, 1846; d. New York, May 26, 1927. He studied at Brown Univ. (graduated 1867); was active as a language teacher; studied music in Boston with Eugene Thayer; was organist in various churches in Boston, Buffalo, and N.Y.; was music editor of the Buffalo *Express* (1879–83) and the N.Y. *Commercial Advertiser* (1884–90); lectured on music and contributed articles to various music publications. He composed a cantata, *Holy Night;* many pieces for organ and piano; songs; made numerous arrangements for church of works by Grieg, Cornelius, Poldini, etc.; publ. a manual, *Song-writing and Song-making* (N.Y., 1923).

Chaikovsky. See **Tchaikovsky.**

Chailley, Jacques, eminent French musicologist; b. Paris, March 24, 1910. He studied composition with Nadia Boulanger, Delvincourt, and Busser; musicology with Pirro, Rokseth, and Smijers; conducting with Mengelberg and Monteux; also took courses in the history of medieval French literature at the Sorbonne (1932–36; received his Ph.D. there in 1952 with 2 dissertations: *L'Ecole musicale de Saint-Martial de Limoges jusqu'à la fin du XIe siècle* [publ. in Paris, 1960] and *Chansons de Gautier du Coinci* [publ. as *Les Chansons à la Vierge de Gautier de Coinci* in *Monuments de la musique ancienne,* XV, 1959]). He was general secretary (1937–47), vice-principal (1947–51), and prof. of the choral class (1951–53) at the Paris Cons.; in 1952 he became director of the Inst. of Musicology at the Univ. of Paris; also taught at the Lycée La Fontaine (1951–69); in 1962 he became director of the Schola Cantorum. He has written authoritatively on many subjects, including medieval music, the music of ancient Greece, musical history, and the music of Bach, Mozart, Wagner, and others. He also wrote 2 operas, a ballet, orch. works, etc.

WRITINGS: *Petite Histoire de la chanson populaire française* (Paris, 1942); *Théorie de la musique* (with H. Challan; Paris, 1949); *Histoire musicale du Moyen Age* (Paris, 1950; 2nd ed., 1969); *Les Notations musicales nouvelles* (Paris, 1950); *La Musique médiévale* (Paris, 1951); *Traité historique d'analyse musicale* (Paris, 1951); *Formation et transformations du langage musical* (Paris, 1954); *Chronologie musicale: I, années 300 à 1599* (Paris, 1955); ed. of *Précis de musicologie* (Paris, 1958); *40,-000 ans de musique: l'homme à la découverte de sa musique* (Paris, 1961, Eng. trans. as *40,000 Years of*

Music: Man in Search of Music, N.Y., 1964); *Les Passions de J.S. Bach* (Paris, 1963); *Tristan et Isolde de Wagner* (Paris, 1963; 2nd ed., 1972); ed. of *Alia musica* (Paris, 1965); *Cours d'histoire de la musique* (Paris, 1967—); *Expliquer l'harmonie?* (Lausanne, 1967); *La Musique et le signe* (Lausanne, 1967); *"La Flûte enchantée," opéra maçonnique: Essai d'explication du livret et de la musique* (Paris, 1968; Engl. trans. as *The Magic Flute, Masonic Opera*, N.Y., 1971; London, 1972); *"L'Art de la fugue" de J.S. Bach. Etude critique des sources* (Paris; I, 1971, II, 1972); *Le "Carnaval" de Schumann* (Paris, 1971); *Les Chorals d'orgue de Bach* (Paris, 1974); *La Musique* (Tours, 1975); *Le Voyage d'hiver de Schubert* (Paris, 1975); *Solfège-déchiffrage pour les jeunes pianistes* (Paris, 1975).

Chailly, Luciano, Italian composer; b. Ferrara, Jan. 19, 1920. He studied in Bologna and then with Renzo Bossi in Milan; in 1948 took courses with Hindemith in Salzburg. In 1962 he was appointed head of Rome Television. He was artistic director at La Scala in Milan in 1968–71 and in Turin from 1972; in 1969 joined the faculty at the Milan Cons. He composes in a communicative neo-Classical idiom, with some dodecaphonic incrustations and electronic effects.
WORKS: Operas: *Ferrovia sopraelevata* (Bergamo, Oct. 1, 1955); *Il canto del cigno* (Bologna, Nov. 16, 1957); *Una domanda di matrimonio*, after Chekhov (Milan, May 22, 1957); *La riva delle Sirti* (Monte Carlo, March 1, 1959); *Procedura penale* (Como, Sept. 30, 1959); *Il mantello*, surrealist opera (Florence, May 11, 1960); *Era probita* (Milan, March 5, 1963); *L'Idiota*, after Dostoyevsky (Rome, Feb. 14, 1970); also music for television.

Chailly, Riccardo, Italian conductor; b. Milan, Feb. 20, 1953. He studied music with his father, the renowned **Luciano Chailly.** As a young boy, he conducted a concert in Padua; then moved to Milan, which became his home town. He enrolled at the Giuseppe Verdi Cons. in the class of Bruno Bettinelli, and later went to Siena, where he took courses in conducting with the famous Franco Ferrara; his other teachers in conducting were Piero Guarino and Franco Caracciolo. He was only 19 when he was appointed assistant conductor at La Scala, in 1972. At 21 he was engaged to conduct *Madama Butterfly* with the Chicago Lyric Opera, marking the beginning of his international career. In 1976 he founded, with Hans Werner Henze, the Cantiere Internazionale d'Arte in Montepulciano. He made his debut as conductor of the Metropolitan Opera in N.Y. on March 8, 1982, in a new production of Offenbach's *Les Contes d'Hoffmann*. Apart from his operatic engagements, Chailly was appointed, in 1982, chief conductor of RIAS (West Berlin Radio Symph. Orch.); also in 1982, he became principal guest conductor of the London Phil.

Chaix, Charles, French-born composer and pedagogue; b. Paris, March 26, 1885; d. Thônex, near Geneva, Feb. 16, 1973. He studied music at the Ecole Niedermeyer in Paris; in 1904 he went to Geneva, where he studied with Otto Barblan at the Geneva Cons., graduating in 1908. He subsequently joined its staff (1910–14); served in the French army during World War I, returning to Geneva after the Armistice. He combined his pedagogical activities with service as a church organist; also conducted advanced classes in counterpoint at the Cons. of Lyons in France. He retired from teaching in 1961. His works include 2 symphs. (1914, 1928); a Piano Quintet (1941); String Quartet (1948); also choral works. He publ. a treatise on harmony, *Eléments d'écriture musicale* (Geneva, 1935).

Chajes, Julius, Polish pianist and composer; b. Lwow, Dec. 21, 1910. He studied piano with Richard Robert and Hedwig Rosenthal in Vienna; composition with Hugo Kauder; in 1933 won a prize at the International Contest for pianists in Vienna; in 1937 came to the U.S.; in 1940 became director of music at the Jewish Community Center in Detroit.
WORKS: *Fantasy* for Piano and Orch. (Vienna Radio, Oct. 9, 1928, composer soloist); Cello Concerto (Karlsbad, Aug 5, 1932); Piano Concerto (Vienna Radio, Nov. 25, 1953; Detroit Symph., Dec. 17, 1953, composer soloist); *Scherzo* (Detroit, Jan 11, 1970); several cantatas on biblical subjects; String Quartet; Piano Trio; Piano Sonata (1958).

Chalabala, Zdenek, noted Czech conductor; b. Uherske Hradiste, April 18, 1899; d. Prague, March 4, 1962. He was educated in Brno, his major teachers being František Neumann and Janáček. He conducted in Brno (1925–36); then settled in Prague. In 1953 he became chief conductor of the Prague National Theater. In addition to his notable opera performances, he was a distinguished symph. conductor.

Chaliapin, Feodor, celebrated Russian bass; b. Kazan, Feb. 13, 1873; d. Paris, April 12, 1938. He was of humble origin; at the age of 10 he was apprenticed to a cobbler; at 14 he got a job to sing in a chorus in a traveling opera company; his companion was the famous writer Maxim Gorky, who also sang in a chorus; together they made their way through the Russian provinces, often forced to walk the railroad tracks when they could not afford the fare. Chaliapin's wanderings brought him to Tiflis, in the Caucasus, where he was introduced to the singing teacher Dimitri Usatov (1847–1913), who immediately recognized Chaliapin's extraordinary gifts and taught him free of charge, helping him besides with board and lodgings. In 1894 Chaliapin received employment in a summer opera company in St. Petersburg, and shortly afterward he was accepted at the Imperial Opera during the regular season. In 1896 he sang in Moscow with a private opera company and produced a great impression by his dramatic interpretation of the bass parts in Russian operas. He also gave numerous solo concerts, which were sold out almost immediately; young music lovers were willing to stand in line all night long to obtain tickets. Chaliapin's first engagement outside Russia was in 1901, at La Scala in Milan, where he sang the role of Mefistofele in Boito's opera of that name; he returned to La Scala in 1904 and again in 1908. On Nov. 20, 1907, he made his American debut at the Metropolitan Opera as Mefistofele; then sang Mephistophélès in Gounod's *Faust* on Jan. 6, 1908; sang Leporello in Mozart's *Don Giovanni* on Jan. 23, 1908. He did not return to America until 1921, when he sang one of his greatest roles, that of the Czar Boris in *Boris Godunov* (Dec. 9, 1921); he continued to appear at the Metropolitan between 1921 and 1929. He sang in Russian opera roles at Covent Garden in London in 1913; returned to Russia in 1914, and remained there during World War I and the Revolution. He was given the rank of People's Artist by the Soviet government, but this title was withdrawn after Chaliapin emigrated in 1922 to Paris, where he remained until his death, except for appearances in England and America. The critical attitude toward Chaliapin in Russia on account of his emigration changed when he was recognized as a great Russian artist who elevated the art of Russian opera to the summit of expressive perfection; numerous articles dealing with Chaliapin's life and career were publ. in the Russian language. He was indeed one of the greatest singing actors of all time; he dominated every scene in which he appeared, and to the last he never failed in his ability to move audiences, even though his vocal powers declined considerably during his last years. He was especially famed for his interpretation of the role of Boris Godunov in Mussorgsky's opera; both dramatically and vocally he created an imperishable image. He was equally great as Mephistophélès in *Faust* and in the buffo roles of Don Basilio in *The Barber of Seville* and Leporello in *Don Giovanni*. He also played the title role in a film version of *Don Quixote*. His last American recital took place in N.Y. on March 3, 1935.

BIBLIOGRAPHY: F. Chaliapin, *Pages from My Life* (N.Y., 1926) and *Man and Mask* (N.Y., 1932); M. Yankovsky, *Chaliapin* (Leningrad, 1972); V. Drankov, *The Character of Chaliapin's Talent* (Leningrad, 1973).

Chamberlain, Houston Stewart, English writer on music; b. Portsmouth, Sept. 9, 1855; d. Bayreuth, Jan. 9, 1927. He received his earliest education at Versailles, and then studied at Cheltenham College in Gloucester. Because of ill health he was obliged to abandon his intention of following a military career (his father was a British admiral), and in 1870 he went to Stettin. His association with Prof. Kuntze there filled him with enthusiasm for Germanic culture and civilization, to the study of which he devoted many years. The results of these studies he publ. in a remarkable work, *Die Grundlagen des 19. Jahrhunderts* (Munich, 1899–1901; 10th ed., 1914; Eng. trans. by Lord Redesdale, London, 1910). The years 1879–81 he spent in Geneva, studying science at the Univ. (taking his degree with the dissertation *Recherches sur la sève ascendante*) and music with A. Ruthardt. During his residence at Dresden (1885–89) he began his activities as a contributor to various German, French, and

English journals, writing with equal facility in 3 languages. From 1889–1908 he lived in Vienna. In 1908 he married Wagner's daughter, Eva, then lived in Bayreuth. Chamberlain was one of the most ardent apostles of Wagner's art, and he was also the chief protagonist of Wagner's ideas of German supremacy, which Chamberlain presented in a simplified and vulgar manner, combined with pseudoscientific speculation and spiced with heavy doses of anti-Semitism. As early as 1923, Chamberlain was attracted to Hitler, but he did not live to see the full flowering of the Nazi millennium. Chamberlain's books on Wagner are of value as a reflection of the time, even though biographical sections are incomplete and out of focus.

WRITINGS: *Das Drama Richard Wagners* (Leipzig, 1892; 6th ed., 1921; French trans., 1894; Eng. trans., 1915); *Richard Wagner. Echte Briefe an F. Praeger* (Bayreuth, 1894; 2nd ed., 1908); *Richard Wagner* (Munich, 1896; 9th ed., 1936; Eng. trans., 1897; French trans., 1899); *Die ersten 20 Jahre der Bayreuther Bühnenfestspiele* (Bayreuth, 1896); *Parsifalmärchen* (Munich, 1900; 3rd ed., 1916); *Lebenswege meines Denkens*, autobiography (1919).

BIBLIOGRAPHY: L. von Schroeder, *Houston Stewart Chamberlain* (1918); Anna Chamberlain (his first wife, married 1878, divorced 1908), *Meine Erinnerungen an Houston Stewart Chamberlain* (1923).

Chambers, Stephen A. See **Hakim, Talib Rasul.**

Chambonnières, Jacques Champion (called **Champion de Chambonnières**), French clavecinist and composer; b. c.1601–2; d. Paris, April 1672. He was first chamber musician to Louis XIV until 1662, and the teacher of the elder Couperins, d'Anglebert, Le Bègue, Hardelle, and others. Considered the founder of the French clavecin school, he was famed throughout Europe and his style strongly influenced that of contemporary German composers, among them Froberger. Two books of his clavecin pieces were printed (Paris, 1670; reprint of *Les Pièces de clavessin* in the series Monuments of Music ... in Facsimile, Paris, 1967). Chambonnières's complete works were publ. by Brunold & Tessier (Paris, 1925; reprinted with Eng. trans. and new preface, 1961).

BIBLIOGRAPHY: H. Quittard, "Chambonnières," *Revue Internationale de Musique,* 12 (1898); idem., "Un Claveciniste français du XVIIᵉ siècle: Jacques Champion de Chambonnières," *Tribune de St. Gervais* (1901); B. Huys, "Jacques Champion de Chambonnières, humanist, klavicinist en komponist," *Vlaams Muziektijdschrift* (Oct. 1972); G.B. Sharp, "Gaultier and Chambonnières. Two French Tercentenaries," *Musical Times* (Dec. 1972).

Chaminade, Cécile, French composer and pianist; b. Paris, Aug. 8, 1857; d. Monte Carlo, April 13, 1944. She was a pupil of Lecouppey, Savard, and Marsick; later studied composition with Benjamin Godard. She became successful as a concert pianist; wrote a great number of agreeable piano pieces, in the salon style, which acquired enormous popularity in France, England, and America; her more serious works were much less successful. She made her American debut playing the piano part of her *Concertstück* with the Philadelphia Orch. (Nov. 7, 1908); also wrote a lyric symph., *Les Amazones* (Antwerp, 1888); 2 orch. suites; 2 piano trios; more than 200 piano pieces in a Romantic style, including *Etude symponique, Valse-Caprice, Les Sylvains, La Lisonjera, Arabesque, Impromptu, 6 Airs de ballet,* etc.; numerous songs.

Chamlee, Mario (real name, **Archer Cholmondeley**), American lyric tenor; b. Los Angeles, May 29, 1892; d. there, Nov. 13, 1966. He made his operatic debut as the Duke in *Rigoletto* (San Francisco Opera, 1917); from 1917–19 served with the U.S. Army in France; married the soprano **Ruth Miller** (d. Los Angeles, June 28, 1983, at the age of 90) on Oct. 2, 1919; first appeared with the Metropolitan Opera as Cavaradossi in *Tosca* (Nov. 22, 1920); made extensive concert tours of the U.S. In 1940 he settled in Hollywood as a voice teacher.

Champagne, Claude, Canadian composer; b. Montreal, May 27, 1891; d. there, Dec. 21, 1965. He studied violin, piano, and composition in Montreal; then went to Paris, where he took courses in composition with Gédalge, Koechlin, and Laparra (1921–29). Returning to Canada, he joined the staff of McGill Univ. in Montreal (1932–41). From 1942 to 1962 he served as associate coordinator at the Cons. of Quebec. In his music he follows the modern French tradition.
WORKS: *Hercule et Omphale,* symph. poem (1918; Paris, March 31, 1926); *Prelude et Filigrane* for Piano (1918); *Suite canadienne* for Chorus and Orch. (Paris, Oct. 20, 1928); *Habanera* for Violin and Piano (1929); *Danse villageoise* for Violin and Piano (1929; also orchestrated); *Quadrilha brasileira* for Piano (1942); *Images du Canada français* for Chorus and Orch. (1943; Montreal, March 9, 1947); *Evocation* for Small Orch. (1943); *Symphonie gaspésienne* (1945); Piano Concerto (1948; Montreal, May 30, 1950); String Quartet (1951); *Paysanna* for Small Orch. (1953); *Suite miniature* for Flute, Cello, and Harpsichord (1958); *Altitude* for Chorus and Orch., with Ondes Martenot (Toronto, April 22, 1960); *Concertino grosso* for String Orch. (1963); organ pieces; songs.

Champein, Stanislas, French composer; b. Marseilles, Nov. 19, 1753; d. Paris, Sept. 19, 1830. He studied under Peccico and Chavet in Paris; at 13 he became maître de musique at the Collegiate Church at Pignon, for which he wrote a Magnificat, a Mass, and Psalms; in 1776 he went to Paris, where some sacred works and 2 operettas made his name known. Up to 1792 he produced 30 works for the stage, the best of which were the operas *La Mélomanie* (1781), *Les Dettes* (1787), and *Le Nouveau Don Quichotte* (1789). From 1793–1804 he filled a government position; continued to compose for the stage, but without success; spent the last

years of his life in poverty; a pension, arranged for him through the efforts of Boieldieu and Scribe, came only 18 months before his death. Though Champein was one of the best-known stage composers of his time, his works are wholly forgotten.

Champion, Jacques. See **Chambonnières, Jacques Champion.**

Chanler, Theodore Ward, American composer; b. Newport, R.I., April 29, 1902; d. Boston, July 27, 1961. He studied in Boston with Hans Ebell (piano) and with Arthur Shepherd (composition); then at the Cleveland Inst. of Music with Ernest Bloch; later went to England, where he took courses at Oxford Univ. (1923–25); also studied with Nadia Boulanger in Paris. He returned to America in 1933. His music, mostly in smaller forms, is distinguished by a lyrical quality; his songs are particularly expressive; he employed the modern idiom of polytonal texture without overloading the harmonic possibilities; the melody is free, but usually within tonal bounds.
WORKS: 2 song cycles, *Epitaphs* (1937); *Pas de Trois,* ballet; *Ann Gregory* for Chorus; *Joyful Mystery,* fugue for 2 Pianos; *The Children,* song cycle; Violin Sonata (1927); *5 Short Colloquies,* piano suite (1936); *The Pot of Fat,* chamber opera (Cambridge, Mass., May 8, 1955).

Chanot, François, French violin maker; b. Mirecourt, March 25, 1788; d. Rochefort (Charente-Maritime), Nov. 12, 1825. He was the son of an instrument maker; became a naval engineer, was retired on half-pay, and during his forced inactivity constructed a violin on the principle that the vibratory power would be increased by preserving the longitudinal wood fibers intact as far as possible. Thus his violin had no bouts, but slight incurvations like a guitar; the sound holes were almost straight, and the belly nearly flat; the strings were attached to the edge of the belly, instead of to a tailpiece. The violin was submitted to the Academy, whose report after testing it rated it equally with those of Stradivari and Guarneri; despite this evaluation, Chanot's violin never became popular. His brother, a *luthier* at Paris, manufactured a number of them, but gave it up when a few years had demonstrated their unpractical character.

Chantavoine, Jean, French writer on music; b. Paris, May 17, 1877; d. Mussy-sur-Seine, July 16, 1952. He studied the history of music with Friedländer in Berlin (1898, 1901–2); in 1903–20 was music critic of *Revue Hebdomadaire* and *Excelsior* (1911–21); in 1921–23 lived in Wiesbaden as a member of the International Commission for the Rhine Province; in 1923 was appointed General Secretary of the Paris Cons., a post he held until 1937.
WRITINGS: He edited the biographical series Les Maîtres de la Musique, to which he contributed the monographs on Beethoven (1906) and Liszt (1910; 5th ed., 1950); publ. *Musiciens et poètes* (Paris, 1912; contains an account of Liszt's early opera *Don Sanche,* the score of which was found by Chantavoine);

De Couperin à Debussy (1921); *Les Symphonies de Beethoven* (1932); *Petit guide de l'auditeur de musique* (Paris, 1947); *Mozart dans Mozart* (1948).

Chapin, Harry, American singer and songwriter; b. New York, Dec. 7, 1942; d. in an automobile accident, Long Island, N.Y., July 16, 1981. With a blend of folk song and rock, he established himself as a popular balladeer of his own "story songs" which chronicled the misery of the poor. He was a dedicated social activist, and devoted much of his time and talents to radical causes. In 1979 he was appointed to the Presidential Council on World Hunger by President Carter. His most popular ballads included *Cat's in the Cradle, Sniper, I Still Remember You, You're the Only Song, All My Life's a Circle,* and particularly *Taxi.*

Chapí y Lorente, Ruperto, Spanish composer of light opera; b. Villena, near Alicante, March 27, 1851; d. Madrid, March 25, 1909. He studied at the Cons. of Madrid; received a stipend from the Spanish Academy for further study in Rome (1874); wrote some operas (*La hija de Jefte, La hija de Garcilaso,* etc.), but discovered that his talent found more suitable expression in the lighter zarzuela, in which form his first success was won with *La Tempestad* (1882); his work is noted for elegance, grace, and exquisite orchestration; of one of his last zarzuelas (*La revoltosa*), Saint-Saëns remarked that Bizet would have been proud to sign his name to the score. His last zarzuela, *Margarita la Tornera* (Madrid, Feb. 24, 1909), was produced shortly before his death. Chapí y Lorente wrote 155 zarzuelas and 6 operas. In 1893 he founded the Sociedad de Autores, Compositores y Editores de Música.
BIBLIOGRAPHY: A.S. Salcedo, *Ruperto Chapí, Su vida y sus obras* (Madrid, 1929); J. Aguilar Gómez, *Ruperto Chapi y su obra lirica* (Alicante, 1973).

Chapman, William Rogers, American choral conductor; b. Hanover, Mass., Aug. 4, 1855; d. Palm Beach, Fla., Mar. 27, 1935. He was a chorus leader and conductor in N.Y.; was founder and conductor of the Apollo (male voices) and Rubinstein (female voices) clubs, and from 1903 conductor of the annual Maine Festival at Bangor and Portland; wrote church music, choral works, piano pieces, songs, etc.

Chappell & Co., London music publishers, concert agents, and piano manufacturers. Founded in 1810 by Samuel Chappell, J.B. Cramer (the pianist), and F.T. Latour. Cramer retired in 1819, Latour in 1826, and S. Chappell died in 1834, when his son **William** (1809–88) became the head of the firm. In 1840 he established the Musical Antiquarian Society, for which he edited Dowland's songs; he also edited and publ. *A Collection of National English Airs* (2 vols., 1838–39), later enlarged as *Popular Music of the Olden Time* (2 vols., 1855–59; revised by H.E. Wooldridge and publ. in 2 vols., 1893); he left an unfinished *History of Music* (vol. I, London, 1874). His

brothers, **Thomas Patey** (1819–1902) and **S. Arthur** (1834–1904), were respectively the founder and manager of the Monday and Saturday Popular Concerts. In 1897 the partnership became a limited company, and Thomas was succeeded by his son, **T. Stanley** (d. 1933), as board chairman; later, William Boosey became managing director. In 1929 the firm was acquired by **Louis Dreyfus.** The American branch, under the direction of **Max Dreyfus,** brother of Louis, has publ. the songs and musical comedies of Richard Rodgers, Jerome Kern, Cole Porter, Harold Arlen, and other popular composers.

Chapple, Stanley, English conductor; b. London, Oct. 29, 1900. He studied at the London Academy of Music; became accompanist with the British National Opera Co. (1918–21); music director of the Vocalion Gramophone Co. (1924–29); and opera conductor at the Guildhall School of Music (1935–39). He had, meanwhile, been making annual summer appearances in the U.S. (1929–39) and was assistant conductor at the Berkshire Music Center (1939–47). In 1948 he became director of the School of Music at the Univ. of Washington in Seattle; resigned from there in 1971 and was then named a prof. emeritus.

Chapuis, Auguste, French composer; b. Dampierre-sur-Salon (Haute-Saône), April 20, 1858; d. Paris, Dec. 6, 1933. He studied at the Paris Cons. with Dubois, Massenet, and César Franck, winning first prize for organ playing. He was active as a church organist in Paris; in 1894 was appointed prof. of harmony at the Paris Cons.; retired from there in 1923. He wrote several operas which were produced without much success: *Enguerrande* (1892); *Tancrède* (1898); *Les Demoiselles de Saint-Cyr* (1921); also several oratorios and dramatic cantatas; numerous choruses; several pieces of chamber music. He publ. a harmony manual, *Traité d'harmonie théorique et pratique.*

Char, Friedrich Ernst (Fritz), German composer and conductor; b. Cleve, May 3, 1865; d. Velden, Sept. 21, 1932. He studied with Wüllner at Cologne (1883–86); then held various posts as an opera conductor. He wrote the text and music of a successful romantic opera, *Der Schelm von Bergen* (Zwickau, 1895); a cantata, *Spielmann;* Piano Concerto; numerous piano pieces; song cycles.

Charles, Ernest, American songwriter; b. Minneapolis, Nov. 21, 1895; d. Beverly Hills, Calif., April 16, 1984. He began his career as a singer in Broadway revues and in vaudeville; also wrote songs in an appetizing semi-classical genre, suitable for recitals. His first commercial success came in 1932 when the popular baritone John Charles Thomas sang his song *Clouds* in a N.Y. recital. Encouraged, Charles put out something like 50 solo songs, many of which made the top listing among recitalists: *Let My Song Fill Your Heart; My Lady Walks in Loneliness; When I Have Sung My Songs; If You Only Knew; Sweet Song of Long Ago; Oh, Lovely World.*
BIBLIOGRAPHY: Larry Wolz, "The Songs of Er-

nest Charles," *NATS Bulletin* (March/April 1983).

Charles, Ray, black American pianist and singer; b. Albany, Ga., Sept. 23, 1930. His full name was **Ray Charles Robinson,** but he shortened it to Ray Charles in order to avoid confusion with the boxer Sugar Ray Robinson. He began improvising on the piano as a small child; he was 6 years old when he began to lose his vision due to a form of glaucoma, and soon he became totally blind. He was then sent to the St. Augustine School for the Blind in Florida; soon his music became his full vocation; he joined a local band as a pianist and later formed his own group; also began to compose songs in the style of rhythm and blues; later expanded to "soul," jazz, and country and western. His first hit was *Hallelujah! I Love Her So,* which was recorded in 1956. In 1959 he composed his greatest hit, *Georgia on My Mind,* which in 1979 became the official song of the state of Georgia. Other hits were *I Can't Stop Loving You* and *Hit the Road, Jack.* There were setbacks due to his infatuation with narcotic drugs; he was twice arrested for possession of heroin (in 1955 and 1961), but was spared a long imprisonment. He soon became famous on the concert stage and radio, rating large fees for his appearances. A special resolution honoring Ray Charles was introduced in 1966 in the U.S. House of Representatives.

Charpentier, Gustave, famous French opera composer; b. Dieuze, Lorraine, June 25, 1860; d. Paris, Feb. 18, 1956. He studied at the Paris Cons. (1881–87), where he was a pupil of Massart (violin), Pessard (harmony), and Massenet (composition). He received the Grand Prix de Rome in 1887 with the cantata *Didon.* Charpentier evinced great interest in social problems of the working classes, and in 1900 formed the society L'Œuvre de Mimi Pinson, devoted to the welfare of the poor, which he reorganized during World War I as an auxiliary Red Cross society. He owes his fame to one amazingly successful opera, *Louise,* a "roman musical" to his own libretto (his mistress at the time was also named Louise, and like the heroine of his opera, was employed in a dressmaking shop), which was produced at the Opéra-Comique in Paris on Feb. 2, 1900. The score is written in the spirit of naturalism and includes such realistic touches as the street cries of Paris vendors. Its success was immediate, and it entered the repertoire of opera houses all over the world; its first American production, at the Metropolitan Opera in N.Y., took place on Jan. 15, 1921. Encouraged by this success, Charpentier wrote a sequel under the title *Julien* (June 4, 1913), but it failed to arouse interest comparable to that of *Louise.* Nor did Charpentier in his very long life (he lived to be 95) succeed in producing any other memorable scores. He wrote an orch. suite, *Impressions d'Italie* (1892); a cycle of songs, *Les Fleurs du mal,* to Baudelaire's words; etc.

BIBLIOGRAPHY: O. Séré, "Gustave Charpentier," *Musiciens français d'aujourd'hui* (Paris, 1911); André Homonet, *Louise* (Paris, 1922); Marc Delmas, *Gustave Charpentier et le lyrisme français* (Paris, 1931); K. O'D. Hoover, "Gustave Charpentier," Musical Quarterly (July 1939).

Charpentier, Jacques, French composer; b. Paris, Oct. 18, 1933. He studied piano with Maria Cerati-Boutillier; lived in Calcutta (1953–54), where he made a study of Indian music; prepared a valuable thesis, *Introduction à l'étude de la musique de l'Inde.* Upon his return to Paris he studied composition with Tony Aubin and musical analysis with Messiaen at the Paris Cons. In 1954 he was appointed organist at the church of St-Benoit-d'Issy; in 1966 was named chief inspector of music of the French Ministry of Cultural Affairs, and in 1975 was made Inspector General of the Secretariat of State for Culture; he traveled to Brazil and the U.S.S.R.; in 1974 was named official organist of the Church of St. Nicolas du Chardonnet in Paris. Several of his works are based on Hindu melorhythms. WORKS: Violin Concerto (1953); *4 psaumes de Toukaram* for Soprano and Orch. (1957); 4 symphs.: No. 1, *Symphonie brève,* for String Orch. (1958); No. 2, *Sinfonia sacra,* for String Orch. (1965); No. 3, *Shiva Nataraja (Shiva—the King of the Dance;* 1968; Paris, March 2, 1969); No. 4, *Brasil,* in homage to Villa-Lobos (1973); Concerto for Ondes Martenot and Orch. (1959); Concertino, *Alla francese,* for Ondes Martenot, Strings, and Percussion (1959–60); *Tantum ergo* for 4 Voices and Orch. (1962); Octuple Concerto for 8 Winds and Strings (1963); *La Croisade des pastoureaux,* oratorio (1964); *Prélude pour la Genèse* for String Orch. (1967); *Récitatif* for Violin and Orch. (1968); 7 concertos: No. 1 for Organ and Strings (1969); No. 2 for Guitar and Strings (1970); No. 3 for Harpsichord and Strings (1971); No. 4 for Piano and Strings (1971); No. 5 for Saxophone and Strings (1975); No. 6 for Oboe and Strings (1975); No. 7 for Trumpet and Strings (1975); *Musiques pour un Zodiaque,* oratorio (1971); 2 string quartets (1955, 1956); Piano Quintet (1955); Quartet for Ondes Martenot (1958); *Suite Karnatique* for Solo Ondes Martenot (1958); *Prelude and Allegro* for Bass Saxophone and Piano (1959); *Lalita* for Ondes Martenot and Percussion (1961); *Pour Diane* for Horn and Piano (1962); *Pour Syrinx* for Flute and Piano (1962); *Mouvement* for Flute, Cello, and Harp (1965); *Gavambodi 2* for Saxophone and Piano (1966); *Pour le Kama Soutra* for Percussion Ensemble (1969); *Pour une Apsara* for 2 Harps (1970); *Esquisses* for Flute and Piano (1972); *Tu dors mais mon cœur veille* for Solo Violin (1974); *Une Voix pour une autre* for 2 Female Voices, Flute, Clarinet, and Percussion (1974); *Prélude* for Harpsichord (1975); Toccata for Piano (1954); *Etudes Karnatiques* for Piano, in 4 cycles (1957–61); *Messe* for Organ (1964); *Repons* for Organ (1968).

Charpentier, Marc-Antoine, significant French composer; b. Paris, c.1645–50; d. there, Feb. 24, 1704. While he studied painting in Italy, his admiration for Carissimi's music led him to take up serious musical study with him. He then returned to Paris and was appointed maître de chapelle to the Dauphin, but lost the post through Lully's opposition.

This episode so embittered Charpentier against Lully that he totally eschewed Lully's style, often to the detriment of his own compositions. Louis XIV granted him a pension in 1683. He was appointed maître de musique and music teacher to Mlle. de Guise (until 1688); then intendant to the Duke of Orleans; maître de chapelle of the Jesuit collegial church and monastery; and maître de musique of Sainte-Chapelle, a post he held from 1698 until his death. He composed operas and lesser works for the stage; several "tragédies spirituelles" for the Jesuits; masses, motets, pastorales, drinking songs, etc. It has been claimed that Charpentier was Lully's superior in learning, if not in inventive power. Reprints: in *Musique d'Eglise des XVIIᵉ et XVIIIᵉ siècles* (ed. by Pineau); H.W. Hitchcock, ed., *Judicum Salomonis* (New Haven, Conn., 1964); *Médée* (facsimile of Paris ed., 1694; Ridgewood, N.J., 1968); D. Launay, ed., *Te Deum*, in *Le Pupitre* 13 (Paris, 1969); C. de Nys, ed., Mass for Soloists, Double Chorus, and Orch. (London, 1971). H. Wiley Hitchcock edited *The Works of Marc-Antoine Charpentier* (Paris, 1982).
BIBLIOGRAPHY: H. Quittard, "Notes sur un ouvrage inédit de Marc-Antoine Charpentier," *Zeitschrift der Internationalen Musikgesellschaft* (May 1905); M. Brenet, *Les Musiciens de la Sainte-Chapelle* (1910); L. de La Laurencie, "Un Opéra inédit de Marc-Antoine Charpentier, *La Descente d'Orfée*," *La Revue de Musicologie* 31; C. Crussard, *Un Musicien français oublié, Marc-Antoine Charpentier* (Paris, 1945); H. Wiley Hitchcock, "The Latin Oratorios of Marc-Antoine Charpentier," *Musical Quarterly* (Jan. 1955); R.W. Lowe, *Marc-Antoine Charpentier et l' Opéra de College* (Paris, 1966); T. Käser, *Die* Leçon de Ténèbres *im 17. und 18. Jahrhundert unter besonderer Berücksichtigung der einschlägigen Werk von M.-A. C.* (Bern, 1966); G. Massenkeil, "M.-A. C. als Messenkomponist," in S. Kross and H. Schmidt, eds. *Colloquium amicorum* (Bonn, 1967); L.M. Ruff, "M.-A. C.'s *Règles de composition*," *Consort*, 24 (1967); H.W. Hitchcock, "On M.-A. C.," *Amor Artis Bulletin* (Feb. 1968); idem, "M.-A. C. and the Comédie-Française," *Journal of the American Musicological Society* (Summer 1971); idem, "Problèmes d'edition de la musique de M.-A. C. pour *Le Malade imaginaire*," and "Deux 'nouveaux' manuscrits de M.-A. C.," *Revue de Musicologie* (1972); R.B. Petty, "C.'s Mass *Assumpta est Maria*," *Music Analysis* (Summer 1972); H.W. Hitchcock, "Some Aspects of Notation in an *Alma Redemptoris Mater* (c.1670) by M.-A. C. (d. 1704)," in E. Borroff, ed., *Notations and Editions* (Dubuque, Iowa, 1974).

Charpentier, Raymond, French composer and music critic; b. Chartres, Aug. 14, 1880; d. Paris, Dec. 27, 1960. He studied composition with André Gédalge; from 1921 to 1943 he was music director of the Comédie Française; then was active on the French radio (1944–50). Beginning in 1908, he wrote music criticism for various journals. As a composer, he wrote some 20 scores of incidental music for the plays produced at the Comédie Française and a comic opera, *Gérard et Isabelle* (Paris, 1912); also

several symph. overtures; 2 string quartets; Wind Quartet; Viola Sonata; piano pieces; songs to texts by Ronsard and Baudelaire.

Chase, Gilbert, eminent American musicologist; b. Havana, Cuba (of American parents), Sept. 4, 1906. He studied at Columbia Univ. and at the Univ. of North Carolina at Chapel Hill; also studied piano. From 1929 to 1935 he lived in Paris and was active as a music correspondent for British and American music periodicals. In 1935 he returned to the U.S.; during 1940–43 he was consultant on Spanish and Latin American music at the Library of Congress in Washington; simultaneously was active in an advisory capacity to musical radio programs. From 1951 to 1953 he was cultural attaché at the American Embassy in Lima, and from 1953 to 1955 served in the same capacity in Buenos Aires. He then became director of the School of Music at the Univ. of Oklahoma (1955–57); from 1958 to 1960 was cultural attaché in Belgium; from 1960 to 1966 he was a prof. of music and director of Latin American studies at Tulane Univ. in New Orleans; in 1965 he became editor of the *Yearbook of Inter-American Musical Research*. In 1963 he organized the First Inter-American Conference on Musicology in Washington. In 1955 the Univ. of Miami bestowed upon him the title of Honorary Doctor of Letters. He also taught at the State Univ. of N.Y. in Buffalo (1973–74) and at the Univ. of Texas in Austin from 1975.
WRITINGS: *The Music of Spain* (N.Y., 1941; new ed., 1959; in Spanish, Buenos Aires, 1943); *A Guide to the Music of Latin America* (Washington, 1962); *America's Music: From the Pilgrims to the Present* (N.Y., 1955; new revised ed., 1966; very valuable; also trans. into German, French, Portuguese, and Spanish); *Introducción a la música americana contemporánea* (Buenos Aires, 1958); *The American Composer Speaks: A Historical Anthology, 1770 to 1965* (Baton Rouge, 1966); *Two Lectures in the Form of a Pair: 1, Music, Culture and History; 2, Structuralism and Music* (Brooklyn, 1973).

Chasins, Abram, multitalented American pianist, composer, writer, educator, and adjudicator; b. New York, Aug. 17, 1903. He went to the Ethical Culture School in N.Y. as a child; then took courses at the Juilliard School of Music, where he studied piano with Ernest Hutcheson and composition with Rubin Goldmark; he was also a protégé of Josef Hofmann, the dean of the Curtis Inst. of Music in Philadelphia, who guided his progress as a concert pianist. At Hofmann's recommendation, Chasins was appointed, at the age of 23, a member of the faculty at the Curtis Inst. and also head of the supplementary piano dept. (1926–36). In the summer of 1931 he took a course in music analysis with Donald Tovey in London. In the meantime he developed a brilliant career as a pianist and composer. On Jan. 18, 1929, he appeared as soloist in his own Piano Concerto with the Philadelphia Orch., Ossip Gabrilowitsch conducting, and was again the soloist in his 2nd Piano Concerto on March 3, 1933, with the Philadelphia Orch. under the direction of Leopold Stokowski. He also wrote a set of 24 preludes for piano (1928), and made virtuoso arrangements for 2 pianos of excerpts from *Carmen* and an equally effective *Fantasy on Themes from Weinberger's Schwanda.* His *Narrative* is an evocative pianistic tone poem. But the most popular piano work of Chasins was his set of *3 Chinese Pieces* ("written with all the expertise of one who had never been near the Orient," as Chasins himself described it). Hofmann, Josef Lhévinne, and other famous pianists invariably included this number as an ultimate applause-maker in their programs. Toscanini became interested, and asked Chasins to orchestrate one of the numbers, *Flirtation in a Chinese Garden,* and also his piano piece *Parade;* Toscanini conducted both pieces at his concert with the N.Y. Phil. on April 8, 1931; this was the first time that Toscanini, so wary of American music, conducted the premiere of a work by a contemporary American composer (Chasins was only 27 years old at the time). In 1932 Chasins was invited by the Moore School of Engineering at the Univ. of Pa. to join Leopold Stokowski in conducting acoustical experiments; several of their findings were incorporated into the writings of the British physicist James Jeans. In 1939–40 Chasins was on the faculty of the Berkshire Center in Tanglewood, where he was engaged by Serge Koussevitzky to give a series of lectures on the niceties of ornamentation in Bach's B-minor Mass; among those who attended these lectures were Leonard Bernstein and Putnam Aldrich. Turning to the new potentialities of the radio, Chasins initiated a Master Class of the Air, broadcasting "Piano Pointers" over the national networks of CBS and NBC. In 1941 he began a series of classical music broadcasts over the radio station WQXR; it was continued under his direction until 1965. He taught and coached a number of brilliant pianists, among them William Kapell, Shura Cherkassky, Jorge Bolet, and **Constance Keene.** He married Constance Keen in 1949, and subsequently gave numerous duo-piano recitals with her. In 1972 he returned to school pedagogy as musician-in-residence at the Univ. of Southern Calif.; at the same time he was engaged as music director of the Univ. radio station, KUSC; he held this position until 1977. In 1976 Chasins received the Award of the National Federation of Music Clubs for "outstanding service to American music during the Bicentennial Year."

During his remarkable career, Chasins formed close relationships with the greatest artists of the century: Stokowski, Hofmann, Godowski. Rachmaninoff himself voiced appreciation of Chasins's piano music. His first publication, *Speaking of Pianists* (N.Y., 1957), records some of these associations. Then came *The Van Cliburn Legend,* telling the extraordinary story of an American winning the International Tchaikovsky Competition in Moscow (N.Y., 1959; also publ. in Russian trans. in Moscow); *The Appreciation of Music* (N.Y., 1966); *Music at the Crossroads* (N.Y., 1972); and *Leopold Stokowski: A Profile* (N.Y., 1979). He contributed articles and reviews to a number of national magazines, among them *Saturday Review* and the "Sunday Magazine" of the *New York Times.* As an

adjudicator, Chasins acted on the juries of several important competitions, including the Leventritt Foundation, Metropolitan Opera Auditions, N.Y. Phil. Youth Concerts, the Chopin Prize, the Rachmaninoff Award, and the prestigious Van Cliburn Competition. He also served as consultant on the Columbia Pictures film *The Competition.*

Chaumet, William, French composer; b. Bordeaux, April 26, 1842; d. Gajac, Gironde, Oct., 1903. He wrote several operas: *La Coche* (1865); *Le Péché de M. Géronte* (1873); *Hérode* (1885); an operetta, *La Petite Maison* (1903); also chamber music.

Chaun, František, Czech composer and painter; b. Kaplice, Jan. 26, 1921; d. Prague, Dec. 31, 1981. A pharmacist by profession and a painter by avocation, he studied music privately with Jindřich Feld and Klement Slavický in Prague (1954–61). Stylistically and ideologically he modeled his works after Stravinsky, with both the parody and classical formality in a curiously synthetic design.

WORKS: FOR ORCH.: *Fantasy* (1960); *Serenade for an Elderly Lady* (1962); Sinfonietta Concertante for Bassoon, Strings, and Piano (1963); Kafka Trilogy, comprised of 3 parts: *I, Proměna (The Metamorphosis,* 1968), *II, Zámek (The Castle,* 1964), and *III, Proces (The Trial,* 1967; Prague, Nov. 26, 1968); Divertimento for Violin and Chamber Orch. (1969); *Ghiribizzo* for Piano and Orch. (1969); *Sinfonietta buffa* (1970); *Hommage à Dubuffet,* double concerto for Violin, Cello, Strings, 2 Oboes, and 2 Horns (1970; Prague, March 4, 1971); *Pět obrázků (Five Pictures,* 1971; Prague, March 24, 1974); *Obrázek (Little Picture,* 1980; Prague, March 27, 1981). CHORAL: *Baptism of Hana Šindelářová,* cantata (1955); *150,000,000,* cantata to words of Mayakovsky (1963); *Co zpívávala babička (What Our Granny Used to Sing)* for Female Chorus (1975); *Hommage to E.F. Burian* for Female Chorus (1978); *Co jsem si zapamatoval z latiny (What I Remember from My Latin Lessons),* in "tender memory of Igor Stravinsky," for Madrigal Choir (1979). CHAMBER MUSIC: *Music* for Violin and Piano (1955); Trio for Flute, Violin, and Piano (1955); *Scherzino* for Violin and Piano (1960); *Divertimento* for 9 Winds (1961); *Andantino doloroso* for Violin and Piano (1962); *Pesante* for Violin and Bassoon (1962); Quartet for Flute, Oboe, Cello, and Bassoon (1963); Trio for Clarinet, Horn and Double Bass (1963); *Serenata rabbiosa* for Violin and 4 Double Basses (1964); *Adventures of a Violin and 9 Instruments* (1969); *Duo* for Viola and Double Bass (1969); *Ulysses* for String Quartet (1970); *Fuga solemnis,* collage for 6 Violins and 2 Violas (1970); *Decimetto* (1971); *Bruno* for String Quartet (1976). FOR PIANO: *Prelude, Improvisation and Scherzo* (1955); *Variations on Scales* (1960).

Chausson, (Amédée-) Ernest, distinguished French composer; b. Paris, Jan. 20, 1855; d. Limay, near Mantes, June 10, 1899 (in a bicycle accident). He studied with Massenet at the Paris Cons.; then took private lessons with César Franck, and began to compose. The influence of Wagner as well as that of Franck determined the harmonic and melodic elements in Chausson's music; but despite these derivations, he succeeded in establishing an individual style, tense in its chromaticism and somewhat flamboyant in its melodic expansion. The French character of his music is unmistakable in the elegance and clarity of its structural plan. He was active in musical society in Paris and was secretary of the Société Nationale de Musique. He composed relatively little music; possessing private means, he was not compelled to seek employment as a professional musician.

WORKS: Operas: *Les Caprices de Marianne* (1882–84); *Hélène* (1883–84); *Le Roi Arthus* (perf. posthumously, Brussels, Nov. 30, 1903); incidental music to *La Légende de Sainte Cécile* (Paris, Jan. 25, 1892); *Viviane,* symph. poem (1882; revised 1887); *Solitude dans les bois* (1886); Symph. in B-flat major (Paris, April 18, 1898; still in the repertoire); *Poème* for Violin and Orch. (Concerts Colonne, Paris, April 4, 1897; very popular among violinists); *Poème de l'amour et de la mer* for Voice and Orch. (1882–92; revised 1893); *Chanson perpetuelle* for Voice and Orch. (1898); *Hymne védique* for Chorus, with Orch. (1886); *Chant nuptial* for Women's Voices and Piano (1887); Piano Trio; Piano Quartet; String Quartet (unfinished); songs: *Chansons de Miarka,* to words by Jean Richepin; *Serres chaudes,* to words by Maeterlinck; *2 poèmes,* to words by Verlaine; etc.

BIBLIOGRAPHY: O. Séré, *Musiciens français d'aujourd'hui* (Paris, 1911); Special issue of *La Revue Musicale* (Dec. 1925; includes a catalogue of his works); H. Oulmont, *Musique de l'amour: Ernest Chausson et la "bande à Franck"...* (1935); J.P. Barricelli and Leo Weinstein, *Ernest Chausson* (Norman, Okla., 1955; a centennial biography); Jean Gallois, *Ernest Chausson: L'Homme et son œuvre* (Paris, 1967); L. Davies, *César Franck and His Circle* (Boston, 1970); R. Scott Grover, *Ernest Chausson: The Man and His Music* (London, 1980).

Chauvet, Charles-Alexis, French organist and composer; b. Marines (Seine-et-Oise), July 7, 1837; d. Argentan (Orne), Jan. 28, 1871. He studied organ and composition at the Paris Cons.; in 1869 he was appointed to the important post of chief organist at the Trinité in Paris. He publ. numerous organ works and piano pieces adaptable for teachers, students, and performers.

Chavanne, Irene von, Austrian contralto; b. Graz, April 18, 1868; d. Dresden, Dec. 26, 1938. She studied at the Vienna Cons.; in 1885 joined the Dresden Court Opera. She was praised for the volume and range of her voice.

Chavarri, Eduardo Lopez, Spanish composer; b. Valencia, Jan. 31, 1871; d. there, Oct. 28, 1970. He was a pupil of F. Pedrell; taught and conducted at the Valencia Cons.; founded a chamber orch. there. His compositions include *Acuarelas valencianas* for String Orch.; *Rapsodía valenciana* for Piano and Orch.; *Concerto español* for Piano and String Orch.; *Leyenda* for Chorus and Orch.; *Quarteto hispano;* quartets for 4 Violins; *Andaluza* for Cello and Piano; *Leyenda del Castillo Moro* for Piano; piano pieces; songs. He publ. a music history (2 vols.; 3rd ed., 1929); *Música popular española* (1927; 2nd ed., 1940); *Chopin* (Valencia, 1950); *Folklore musical español* (Madrid, 1955).

Chávez, Carlos, distinguished Mexican composer and conductor; b. Calzada de Tacube, near Mexico City, June 13, 1899; d. Mexico City, Aug. 2, 1978. He studied piano as a child with Pedro Luis Ogazón; studied harmony with Juan B. Fuentes and Manuel Ponce. He began to compose very early in life; wrote a symph. at the age of 16; made effective piano arrangements of popular Mexican songs and also wrote many piano pieces of his own. His first important work was a ballet on an Aztec subject, *El fuego nuevo,* which he wrote in 1921, commissioned by the Secretariat of Public Education of Mexico. Historical and national Mexican subject matter remained the primary source of inspiration in many works of Chávez, but he rarely resorted to literal quotations from authentic folk melodies in his works; rather, he sublimated and distilled the melorhythmic Mexican elements, resulting in a sui generis style of composition. In 1922–23 he traveled in France, Austria, and Germany, and became acquainted with the modern developments in composition. The influence of this period of his evolution as a composer is reflected in the abstract titles of his piano works, such as *Aspectos, Energía, Unidad.* Returning to Mexico, he organized and conducted a series of concerts of new music, giving the first Mexican performances of works by Stravinsky, Schoenberg, Satie, Milhaud, and Varèse. From 1926 to 1928 he lived in N.Y. In the summer of 1928 he organized the Orquesta Sinfónica de Mexico, of which he remained the principal conductor until 1949. Works of modern music occupied an important part in the program of this orch., including 82 first performances of works by Mexican composers, many of them commissioned by Chávez; Silvestre Revueltas was among those encouraged by Chávez to compose. During his tenure as conductor Chávez engaged a number of famous foreign musicians as guest conductors, as well as numerous soloists. In 1949 the orch. was renamed Orquesta Sinfónica Nacional; it remains a permanent institution. Chávez served as director of the Conservatorio Nacional de Música from 1928 to 1935 and was general director of the Instituto Nacional de Bellas Artes from 1946 to 1952. Beginning in 1936 Chávez conducted a great number of concerts with major American orchs., and also conducted concerts in Europe and South America. Culturally, Chávez maintained a close connection with progressive artists and authors of Mexico, particularly the painter Diego Rivera; his *Sinfonía proletaria* for Chorus and Orch. reflects his political commitment. In 1958–59 Chávez was Charles Eliot Norton Lecturer at Harvard Univ.; these lectures were publ. in book form under the title *Musical Thought* (Cambridge, 1960); Chávez also publ. a book of essays, *Toward a New Music*

(N.Y., 1937). A detailed catalogue of his works in 3 languages, Spanish, Eng., and French, was publ. in Mexico City in 1971.

WORKS: OPERA: *Panfilo and Lauretta,* first produced in Eng. (1953; N.Y., May 9, 1957; then revised and produced in a Spanish version as *El Amor propiciado,* Mexico City, Oct. 28, 1959; still later retitled *The Visitors*).

BALLETS: *El fuego nuevo* (1921; Mexico City, Nov. 4, 1928), *Los cuatro soles* (1925; Mexico City, July 22, 1930), *Caballos de Vapor* (1926; first produced in Eng. under the title *HP,* i.e., *Horsepower,* Philadelphia, March 31, 1932), *Antígona* (Mexico City, Sept. 20, 1940; originally conceived as incidental music for Sophocles' *Antigone,* 1932), *La hija de Cólquide* (*Daughter of Colchis,* 1943; presented by Martha Graham under the title *Dark Meadow,* N.Y., Jan. 23, 1946) and *Pirámide* (1968).

FOR ORCH.: *Sinfonía* (1915); *Cantos de Méjico* for Mexican Orch. (1933); *Sinfonía de Antígona,* Symph. No. 1, derived from his incidental music for *Antigone* (Mexico City, Dec. 15, 1933); *Obertura republicana* (Mexico City, Oct. 18, 1935); *Sinfonía India,* Symph. No. 2 (1935; broadcast, N.Y., Jan. 23, 1936; also Boston Symph. Orch., April 10, 1936; composer conducting); Concerto for 4 Horns (1937; Washington, D.C., April 11, 1937; composer conducting; revised 1964); Piano Concerto (1938–40; N.Y. Phil., Jan. 1, 1942); *Cuatro nocturnos* for Soprano, Contralto, and Orch. (1939); *Toccata* (1947); Violin Concerto (1948; Mexico City, Feb. 29, 1952); Symph. No. 3 (1951; Caracas, Dec. 11, 1954; composer conducting; N.Y. Phil., Jan. 26, 1956); *Sinfonía romántica,* Symph. No. 4 (1952; Louisville, Feb. 11, 1953; composer conducting); Symph. No. 5, for Strings (1953; Los Angeles, Dec. 1, 1953, composer conducting); Symph. No. 6 (1961; N.Y., May 7, 1964); *Soli No. 3* for Bassoon, Trumpet, Viola, Timpani, and Orch. (1965; Baden-Baden, West Germany, Nov. 24, 1965); Symph. No. 7 (1960—; unfinished); *Resonancias* (Mexico City, Sept. 18, 1964); *Elatio* (Mexico City, July 15, 1967); *Discovery* (Aptos, Calif., Aug. 24, 1969); *Clio,* symph. ode (Houston, Texas, March 23, 1970); *Initium* (1972); *Mañanas Mexicanas* (1974; originally for Piano, 1967); *Sonante* for String Orch. (1974); Trombone Concerto (1975–76; Washington, D.C., May 9, 1978; composer conducting).

CHORAL WORKS: *Tierra mojada* for Chorus, Oboe, and English Horn (Mexico City, Sept. 6, 1932); *El Sol* for Chorus and Orch. (Mexico City, July 17, 1934); *Sinfonía proletaria (Llamadas)* for Chorus and Orch. (Mexico City, Sept. 29, 1934); *La paloma azul* for Chorus and Chamber Orch. (1940); *Prometheus Bound,* cantata (1956; Aptos, Calif., Aug. 27, 1972).

CHAMBER MUSIC: Piano and String Sextet (1919); 3 string quartets (1921, 1932, 1944); *3 Pieces* for Guitar (1923); Violin Sonatina (1924); Cello Sonatina (1924); *Energía* for 9 Instruments (1925; Paris, June 11, 1931); Sonata for 4 Horns (1929); 3 of 4 pieces under the generic title *Soli* (No. 1 for Oboe, Clarinet, Trumpet, and Bassoon, 1933; No. 2 for Wind Quintet, 1961; No. 4 for Brass Trio, 1966); *3 Espirales* for Violin and Piano (1934); *Xochipilli Macuilxochitl* for 4 Wind Instruments and 6 Percussionists (N.Y., May 16, 1940; composer conducting); *Toccata* for 6 Percussionists (1942; Mexico City, Oct. 31, 1947); 2 of 3 instrumental pieces, under the generic title *Invention* (No. 2 for String Trio, 1965; No. 3 for Harp, 1967), introducing an inductive method of thematic illation in which each musical phrase is the logical consequent of the one immediately preceding it; *Upingos* for Solo Oboe (1957); *Fuga HAG,C* for Violin, Viola, Cello, and Double Bass (1964); *Tambuco* for 6 Percussionists (1964); Variations for Violin and Piano (1969).

FOR PIANO: 6 sonatas (*Sonata Fantasía,* 1917; 1919; 1928; 1941; 1960; 1961); *Berceuse* (1918); *7 Madrigals* (1921–22); *Polígonos* (1923); *Aspectos I* and *II* (1923); Sonatina (1924); *Blues* (1928); *Fox* (1928); *Paisaje* (1930); *Unidad* (1930); *10 Preludes* (1937); *Fugas* (1942); *4 Etudes* (1949); *Left Hand Inversions of 5 Chopin Etudes* (1950); *Invention* No. 1 (1958); *Estudio a Rubinstein,* in minor seconds (1974); *5 caprichos* (1975–76).

FOR VOICE AND PIANO: *3 exágonos* (1923); *Inutil epigrama* (1923); *Otros 3 exágonos* (1924); *3 poemas* (1938); *La casada infiel* (1941).

BIBLIOGRAPHY: H. Weinstock, "Carlos Chávez," *Musical Quarterly* (Oct. 1936); *Composers of the Americas,* vol. 3 (Washington, D.C., 1957); R.G. Morillo, *Carlos Chávez, vida y obra* (Buenos Aires, 1960); Rodolfo Halffter, compiler, *Carlos Chávez, Catalogo completo de sus obras* (Mexico City, 1971).

Chaynes, Charles, French composer; b. Toulouse, July 11, 1925. He studied violin at the Cons. of Toulouse; later took courses in harmony and counterpoint with Jean and Noël Gallon, and composition with Milhaud and Rivier at the Paris Cons. He received the Premier Grand Prix de Rome in 1951 and stayed at the Villa Medicis in Rome to compose; returned to France in 1955; in 1964 was appointed program director on the French Radio. In his music he makes use of "chromatic totality," which extends into free dodecaphony and aleatory usages.

WORKS: Concerto No. 1 for String Orch. (1953); dramatic overture, *Ode pour une mort tragique* (1954); Symph. (1955); Trumpet Concerto (1958); Violin Concerto (1958; Paris, March 14, 1961); *4 illustrations pour la flûte de jade* for Solo Flute, Strings, Harp, and Percussion (1960); Concerto for Piano and Chamber Orch. (1961); Concerto No. 2 for Orch. (1961); *3 études linéaires* for 13 Instruments and Percussion (1963); *Commentaires concertants* for Violin and Orch. (1964); *Expressions contrastées* for Orch., Piano, and Percussion (Strasbourg Festival, June 23, 1966); Concerto for Organ, Strings, and Percussion (1966); *Transmutations* for Orch. (1971); *Peintures noires* for Orch. (1975); Flute Sonatina (1951); Violin Sonata (1952); *Serenade* for Wind Quintet (1954); *Quadretti italiani* for Violin and Piano (1957); *Réflexes* for Violin and Piano (1963); *Concordances* for Piano and Percussion (1967); *Irradiations* for Violin, Cello, and Harpsichord (1968); *Interférences* for Cello and Piano (1972); *Tarquinia,* 3 fresques for Ondes Martenot, Piano, and Percussion (1973); *Joutes* for Organ and Harpsichord (1975); *Capriccio* for Piano (1954); *Substances convergentes* for Piano (1964); *M'zab,* suite for

Piano (1972); *Par ces chemins du cœur,* suite for Soprano and Orch. (1953); chamber cantata, *Joie aux âmes* (1962); *Alternances* for Alto and Piano (1965); *4 poèmes de Sappho* for Soprano and String Trio (1968).

Cheek, John, American bass-baritone; b. Greenville, S.C., Aug. 17, 1948. He received a B.Mus. degree from the North Carolina School of Arts; then studied in Italy with Gino Bechi at the Accademia Musicale Chigiana, where he received the Diploma of Merit; he subsequently served in the U.S. Army. He made his professional debut in 1975; in 1977 he sang with the N.Y. Phil. On Oct. 11, 1977, he made his Metropolitan Opera debut in N.Y. in the role of the physician in *Pelléas et Mélisande;* he later sang Pimen in *Boris Godunov,* Ferrando in *Il Trovatore,* Wurm in *Luisa Miller,* Klingsor in *Parsifal,* and also Panthée in *Les Troyens* at the opening-night celebration of the Metropolitan's centenary season in 1983-84.

Chélard, Hippolyte-André, French composer; b. Paris, Feb. 1, 1789; d. Weimar, Feb. 12, 1861. He studied with Fétis and Gossec at the Paris Cons.; won the Grand Prix de Rome in 1811; in Rome he studied with Baini, and then took lessons in Naples with Paisiello. Returning to Paris, he produced the opera *Macbeth* (to a libretto by Rouget de Lisle) on June 29, 1827, with meager success. He was much more fortunate in Germany as an opera composer; in Munich he produced a German version of *Macbeth;* a new opera, *Mitternacht* (June 19, 1831); and a German version of his French opera *La Table et le logement,* under the title *Der Student* (Feb. 19, 1832). These were followed by another German opera, *Die Hermannsschlacht.* From 1840 to 1852 he was court conductor at Weimar, where he brought out 2 comic operas, *Der Scheibentoni* (1842) and *Die Seekadetten* (1844). He also wrote a symph. poem in 8 movements entitled *La Symphonéide* (1848).

Chelius, Oskar von (pen name, **Siegfried Berger**), German composer; b. Mannheim, July 28, 1859; d. Munich, June 12, 1923. He was a pupil in Mannheim of E. Steinbach, in Kassel of Reiss, in Leipzig of Jadassohn; made his career in the army, rising to the rank of major general in 1911.
WORKS: Operas: *Haschisch* (Dresden, 1897) and *Die vernarte Prinzess* (Wiesbaden, 1905); symph. poem, *Und Pippa tanzt;* Requiem for Chorus and Orch.; Psalm 121; Violin Sonata; piano pieces; songs; etc.

Chelleri (real name, **Keller**), **Fortunato,** Italian composer and choral director; b. Parma, May 1690; d. Kassel, Dec. 11, 1757. He studied music with his uncle, F.M. Bassani, who was maestro di cappella at Piacenza Cathedral. His first opera, *Griselda* (Piacenza, 1707), was followed by 18 more, written for various Italian stages. He settled in Kassel in 1725 as court music director, and remained there until his death, except for brief journeys to London (1726) and Stockholm (1731). Besides his operas, he wrote 8 oratorios, including *Dio sul Sinai* (1731); overtures; church music; etc. He publ. a vol. of cantatas, and arias (London, 1726) and a collection of "Lessons" for harpsichord (London, 1750), containing 2 piano sonatas (really suites).

Chemin-Petit, Hans, German composer; b. Potsdam, June 24, 1902; d. Berlin, April 12, 1981. His family was of remote French origin; both his father and grandfather were professional musicians. He studied cello in Berlin with Hugo Becker and composition with Paul Juon; subsequently he was mostly active as a cello teacher; was on the staff of the Berlin Hochschule für Musik and later at the Akademie der Künste; in 1968 he was appointed director of its music dept. As a composer he followed the median line of neo-Classicism.
WORKS: Chamber operas: *Der gefangene Vogel* (1927), *Lady Monika* (1930), *König Nicolo* (1962), *Die Komödiantin* (1968), and *Die Rivalinnen* (1970); 2 symphs. (1932, 1949); Cello Concerto (1932); Concerto for Orch. (1944); Concerto for Organ, Strings, and Kettledrums (1963); *Music* for Orch. (1968); Symph. Cantata (1967); 2 sonatas for Recorder (1958, 1960); several cantatas; church music; piano pieces. He publ. a collection of choral arrangements of German folk songs (Berlin, 1949).

Chenoweth, Wilbur, American pianist, organist, and composer; b. Tecumseh, Nebr., June 4, 1899. He studied piano with Sigismund Stojowski and Alexander Lambert in N.Y., and organ and composition with Pietro Yon. In 1938 he moved to Los Angeles.
WORKS: Numerous effective piano pieces (*Concert Waltz; Cortege*); choruses (*Of the Father's Love Begotten; God of Comfort; Noel, Noel, Bells Are Ringing; Rise, Men Courageous*); songs (*Vocalise; The Arrow; The Song*). Among his works in larger forms is *Fiesta* for Piano and Orch. (also for 2 Pianos).

Cherbuliez, Antoine-Elisée, Swiss musicologist; b. Mulhouse, Alsace, Aug. 22, 1888; d. Zürich, Oct. 15, 1964. He studied science at the Univ. of Strasbourg and took private organ lessons with Albert Schweitzer. He studied music with his grandfather Adolphe Koekkert in Geneva, and took courses at the Zürich Cons. From 1913 until 1916 he studied privately with Max Reger in Jena. He served for a time as an organist; in 1923 was appointed instructor in musicology at the Univ. of Zürich. He wrote some chamber music and choruses, but devoted his energies mainly to writing. He publ. *Gedankliche Grundlagen der Musikbetrachtung* (Zürich, 1924); *Zum problem der religiösen Musik* (Basel, 1924); *Die Anwendung der Sievers'schen Theorien auf die musikalische Interpretation* (Zürich, 1925); *Peter Cornelius* (Zürich, 1925); *J.S. Bach* (Zürich, 1926); *Die Schweiz in der deutschen Musikgeschichte* (Zürich, 1926; a valuable and extensive account of Swiss music history); *Geschichte der Musikpedagogik in der Schweiz* (Bern, 1943); biographies of Handel, Haydn, Chopin, Grieg, Verdi, and Tchaikovsky; monographs on Mozart, Beethoven, and

Brahms; many articles for musical journals.

Cherepnin. See **Tcherepnin.**

Cherkassky, Shura, Russian pianist; b. Odessa, Oct. 7, 1911. He was a pupil of his mother; then studied with Josef Hofmann at the Curtis Inst. in Philadelphia. He played all over the world; was at his best in the Romantic repertoire; made his home in France.

Cherney, Brian, Canadian composer; b. Peterborough, Ontario, Sept. 4, 1942. He studied composition with Weinzweig and Dolin, and piano at the Univ. of Toronto, graduating in 1964 (M.M., 1967); had short periods of study at Columbia Univ. and at the international summer courses for new music in Darmstadt; taught at the Univ. of Victoria (1971–72) and since 1972 at McGill Univ. in Montreal. His music is determined by structural factors, and is largely atonal; visually it is drawn in graphic notation.
WORKS: 2 sets of *Variations* for Orch. (1962, 1967); *2 Songs* for Soprano and Chamber Orch. (1963); Violin Concerto (1964); *6 Miniatures* for Oboe and Strings (1968); *Mobile IV* for Soprano and Chamber Ensemble (1970); *7 Images* for 22 Players (1971); Violin Sonata (1961); *3 Pieces* for String Quartet (1961); *Suite* for Solo Oboe (1962); Quintet for Saxophone and String Quartet (1962); *Interlude and Variations* for Wind Quintet (1965); *Suite* for Viola and Piano (1965); Wind Quintet (1965); 2 string quartets (1966, 1970); *Mobile II* for Solo Cello (1968); *Kontakion (Quiet Music for 11 Players;* 1969*); Mobile IIIa* for Solo Oboe (1970); *Notturno* for Flute, Oboe, Clarinet, Bassoon, Horn, and Piano (1974); *Tangents* for Solo Cello, Tape, Piano, Double Bass and Piano (1975); *Chamber Concerto* for Viola and 10 Players (1975); *Fantasy* for Piano (1966); Piano Sonata (1966); *Interludes, Shapes and Patterns* for Piano (1968); *6 Miniatures* for Piano (1968); *Jest* for Piano (1968).

Cherry, Don(ald), black American jazz cornetist, trumpeter, and pianist; b. Oklahoma City, Nov. 18, 1936. He studied trumpet and harmony while attending high school in Los Angeles; began his career in 1951, appearing with Red Mitchell, Dexter Gordon, and other jazz musicians; he then went to N.Y., where he worked and recorded with Ornette Coleman; after 1963 he toured extensively in Europe, and also in Africa. A proponent of "free" jazz, he adopted instruments of other folk cultures in his performances.

Cherubini, Luigi (full baptismal name, **Maria Luigi Carlo Zenobio Salvatore**), famous Italian composer; b. Florence, Sept. 14, 1760; d. Paris, March 15, 1842. As a young child he studied music with his father, cembalist at the Pergola Theater; his subsequent teachers were Bartolomeo and Alessandro Felici; then Bizarri and Castrucci; in 1777 he was sent by Duke Leopold II of Tuscany (the future Emperor Leopold III) to Milan to perfect himself in counterpoint under Sarti. At 13 he had already written a Mass, and a stage-intermezzo for a society theater; at 15 he composed another intermezzo, *Il Giuocatore;* during his years of study with Sarti he confined himself to contrapuntal work and church music; in 1780, *Quinto Fabio* (perf. at Alessandria della Paglia) opened the series of his dramatic works; its cool reception spurred him to renewed study, and *Armida* (Florence, 1782), *Adriano in Siria* (Livorno, 1782), *Messenzio* (Florence, 1782), *Quinto Fabio* (revised; Rome, 1783), *Lo sposo di tre e marito di nessuna* (Venice, 1783), *Idalide* (Florence, 1784), and *Alessandro nelle Indie* (Mantua, 1784) received public approbation. Invited to London in the autumn of 1784, he brought out 2 operas: *La finta principessa* (1785), an opera buffa which had fair success; and *Giulio Sabino* (1786), which was less fortunate. Cherubini held the position of Composer to the King for one year, and in July 1786 went to Paris for a one-year visit; in 1788 he brought out *Ifigenia in Aulide* at Turin; then settled permanently in Paris. His first French opera, *Demofoonte* (Grand Opéra, 1788), was a failure owing to his attempt to adapt his style of flowing melody to the ill-turned style of Marmontel, the librettist. The next year Léonard, the Queen's hairdresser, obtained a license to establish Italian opera in a little playhouse called the Théâtre de la Foire de St.-Germain; and here Cherubini conducted, until 1792, the best works of Anfossi, Paisiello, and Cimarosa. During this period he developed, inspired by the text of his opera *Lodoiska* (Théâtre de Monsieur, 1791), a new dramatic style destined to work a revolution on the French stage; the increased breadth and force of the ensemble numbers, the novel and rich orch. combinations, and the generally heightened dramatic effect were imitated or expanded by a host of composers of the French school: Méhul, Berton, Lesueur, Grétry. Cherubini's next operas, *Eliza ou Le Voyage au mont St.-Bernard* (1794) and *Médée* (1797), were hampered by poor libretti. In 1795 Cherubini was appointed one of the Inspectors of the new Cons. Composing steadily, he brought out *L'Hôtellerie portugaise* (1798), *La Punition* (1799), *La Prisonnière* (1799; pasticcio, with Boieldieu), and in 1800, at the Théâtre Feydeau, *Les Deux Journées* (perf. in London, 1801, as *The Water-carrier;* in Germany as *Der Wasserträger*), his greatest operatic work. Cherubini had fallen into disfavor with Napoleon, whose opinion in musical matters he had slighted; but after the success of *Les Deux Journées,* he was able to produce at the Grand Opéra *Anacréon, ou L'Amour fugitif* (1803) and the ballet *Achille à Scyros* (1804), neither of which, however, had good fortune. At this juncture Cherubini was invited to write an opera for Vienna; *Faniska,* brought out in 1807 at the Kärnthnerthor Theater, was an overwhelming success; so much so that a Vienna critic who ventured the prophecy that Beethoven's *Fidelio* would one day be equally esteemed, was laughed at. Returning to Paris after the French occupation of Vienna, Cherubini wrote *Primmalione* for the Italian opera at the Tuileries (1808), but did not win the Emperor's favor, and retired for a time to the château of the Prince of Chimay, where he occupied his leisure with botanizing. The request to write a mass for the church of Chimay turned the current of his thoughts; he composed the celebrated 3-part Mass in F, the success of which was so marked that Cherubini thenceforward devoted more time to sacred than dramatic composition, though he did bring out *Le Crescendo* (1810), *Les Abencérages* (Opéra, April 6, 1813), *Bayard à Mézières* (1814), *Blanche de Provence* (1821), and *Ali Baba* (Opéra, July 22, 1833). On a visit to London, in 1815, he wrote for the Phil. Society a symph., an overture, and a Hymn to Spring. In this year he lost his place in the Cons. during the troublous times of the Restoration, but was recompensed by his appointment as superintendent of the Royal Chapel, succeeding Martini. In 1816 he was made prof. of composition at the Cons., and its director in 1821; he retired in 1841. Cherubini was one of the great modern masters of counterpoint, and his scores, particularly in his admirable sacred music, bear witness on every page to his skill and erudition. As an opera composer, his main failing was the undue musical prolongation of scenes in which swifter dramatic action would have been preferable.

WORKS: His own catalogue of his works, *Notice des manuscrits autographes de la musique composée par feu M.-L.-C.-Z.-S. Cherubini* (publ. 1843; reprinted, London, 1967), includes 15 Italian and 14 French operas (an uncatalogued, newly discovered opera, *Don Pistacchio,* was perf. at Dresden, Nov. 27, 1926); a ballet; 17 cantatas and "occasional" vocal works with orch.; many detached airs, romances, nocturnes, duets, etc.; 14 choruses; 4 sets of solfeggi (over 160 numbers); 11 Solemn Masses, 2 Requiems, many detached Kyries, Glorias, Credos, etc.; a Credo in 8 parts with Organ; an oratorio (Florence, 1777); motets, hymns, graduals, etc., with orch.; a Magnificat, a Miserere, a Te Deum (each with orch.); 4 litanies, 2 Lamentations, 20 antiphons, etc.; a Symph., an overture, 11 marches, 11 dances, etc.; 6 string quartets, a String Quintet; Sonata for 2 Organs; for piano: 6 sonatas, a grand fantasia, a minuet, a chaconne, etc.

WRITINGS: Cherubini's *Cours de Contrepoint et de Fugue* was prepared for publication by his pupil Halévy. It appeared in a German trans. by Stöpel (1835–36), in Eng. trans. by J. Hamilton (1837) and C. Clarke (1854). Two new German eds. were prepared by G. Jensen (1896) and R. Heuberger (1911).

BIBLIOGRAPHY: A. Bottée de Toulmon, *Notice des manuscrits autographes de Cherubini* (Paris, 1843); E. Bellasis, *Cherubini. Memorials Illustrative of His Life* (London, 1874; new augmented ed., Birmingham, 1912); F.J. Crowest, *Cherubini* (London and N.Y., 1890); M.E. Wittmann, *Cherubini* (Leipzig, 1895); M.Q. L'Epine, *Cherubini* (Lille, 1913); R. Hohenemser, *L. Cherubini, Sein Leben und seine Werke* (Leipzig, 1913); H. Kretzschmar, "Über die Bedeutung von Cherubini's Ouvertüren und Hauptopern für die Gegenwart," *Peters Jahrbuch* (1906); L. Schemann, *Cherubini* (Berlin, 1925); O.A. Mansfield, "Cherubini's String Quartets," *Musical Quarterly* (1929); H. Mersmann, *Kammermusikführer* (1932; analysis); P. Espil, *Les Voyages de Cherubini ou L'Enfance de Mozart* (Bayonne,

1946); G. Confalonieri, *Prigionia d'un artista: Il romanzo di Luigi Cherubini* (2 vols., Milan, 1948); A. Damerini, ed., *Luigi Cherubini nel II centenario della nascita* (Florence, 1962); Basil Deane, *Cherubini* (London, 1965); A.L. Ringer, "Cherubini's *Médée* and the Spirit of French Revolutionary Opera," in G. Reese and R.J. Snow, eds., *Essays in Music in Honor of Dragan Plamenac* (Pittsburgh, 1969).

Cheslock, Louis, American composer; b. London, Sept. 9, 1898; d. Baltimore, July 19, 1981. He was brought to the U.S. as a child; studied violin with Van Hulsteyn and Gittelson, and composition with Strube at the Peabody Cons., in Baltimore; in 1916 became violin instructor there; then taught theory of composition. He served as a violinist in the Baltimore Symph. Orch. (1916–37), and also appeared as guest conductor. His own music is of a neo-Romantic vein, with occasional incursions into modernity. He publ. *Introductory Study on Violin Vibrato* (Baltimore, 1931); edited *H.L. Mencken on Music* (N.Y., 1961).

WORKS: A one-act opera, *The Jewel Merchants* (Baltimore, Feb. 26, 1940); a Symph. (1932); tone poems for Orch.: *Cathedral at Sundown, 'Neath Washington Monument,* and *At the Railway Station* (Chicago, April 29, 1923); ballet, *Cinderella* (Baltimore, May 11, 1946; enlarged and revised 1958); oratorio, *The Congo* (Akron, Ohio, Oct. 30, 1942); Violin Concerto (Baltimore, Feb. 25, 1926); Horn Concerto (1936); *The Legend of Sleepy Hollow* for Orch. (1936); *Rhapsody in Red and White (An American Divertissement)* for Orch. (1941); *Set of Six* for Small Orch. (1946); piano pieces.

Chevalier, Maurice, popular French chansonnier; b. Paris, Sept. 12, 1888; d. there, Jan. 1, 1972. He began his career as a singer in Parisian cafés and music halls; then acted in films. In 1929 he went to Hollywood, and soon established himself as one of the foremost musical comedy stars, speaking and singing in English with an ingratiating French accent, affecting a debonair mien, carrying a cane, and wearing a straw hat. His early films included *The Innocents of Paris* (1929), *Love Me Tonight* (1932), and *The Merry Widow* (1934). He remained in France during the German occupation and gave shows for French prisoners of war in Germany. This activity led to accusations of collaboration with the enemy, but Chevalier was able to explain his conduct as a desire to maintain the public spirit among Frenchmen, and he was exonerated. His later films included *Gigi* (1958), *Can-Can* (1960), and *Fanny* (1961). A special Academy Award was presented to him in 1958 in appreciation of his contributions to popular entertainment.

Chevé, Emile-Joseph-Maurice, French music theorist; b. Douarnenez, Finistère, May 31, 1804; d. Fontenay-le-Comte, Aug. 26, 1864. A physician of great merit, he became a zealous advocate of Pierre Galin's method of musical instruction, explained in Galin's *Exposition d'une nouvelle méthode pour*

l'enseignement de la musique (1818; 3rd ed., 1831), which attained considerable popularity; married **Nanine Paris** (d. 1868) and collaborated with her in a *Méthode élémentaire de musique vocale* (Paris, 1844; later ed., 1863; German trans. by F.T. Stahl, 1878), in the preface to which he "exposes" and attacks the "defective" methods of the Cons. He and his wife also publ. *Méthode élémentaire d'harmonie* (with Galin; Paris, 1846); and Mme. Chevé wrote *Nouvelle théorie des accords, servant de base à l'harmonie* (Paris, 1844). He publ. a long series of essays and articles by which he vainly sought to draw out the profs. of the Cons. Acrimonious polemics raged for years, and numerous pamphlets were issued in Paris by adherents and foes of the Chevé method.
BIBLIOGRAPHY: A. Pagés, *La Méthode musicale Galin-Paris-Chevé* (Paris, 1860); A.L. Montandon, *Ecole Galin-Paris-Chevé; Problème musical, historique, pédagogique, prophétique* (Paris, 1861); O. Comettant, *Les Musiciens, les philosophes et les gaîtés de la musique en chiffres* (Paris, 1870).

Chevillard, Camille, French composer and conductor; b. Paris, Oct. 14, 1859; d. Chatou (Seine-et-Oise), May 30, 1923. He studied piano with Georges Mathias; was chiefly self-taught in composition. In 1897 he became assistant conductor of the Lamoureux Concerts; in 1899 succeeded Lamoureux as conductor after having married his daughter; from 1914 was conductor at the Grand Opéra.
WORKS: For Orch. (all perf. in Paris): *Ballade symphonique* (Feb. 23, 1890); *Le Chêne et le roseau* (March 8, 1891); *Fantaisie symphonique* (Oct. 21, 1894); also *Etude chromatique* for Piano; Piano Quintet, Piano Quartet, Piano Trio; String Quartet; Violin Sonata; Cello Sonata; songs with Orch., *L'Attente* and *Chemins d'amour.*
BIBLIOGRAPHY: R. Rolland, *Musiciens d'aujourd'hui* (1908); O. Séré, "Camille Chevillard," in *Musiciens français d'aujourd'hui* (Paris, 1911); R. Dumesnil, *Portraits des musiciens français* (Paris, 1938); H. Schonberg, *The Great Conductors* (N.Y., 1967).

Chevreuille, Raymond, Belgian composer; b. Brussels, Nov. 17, 1901; d. Montignies-le-Tilleul, May 9, 1976. He took a course in harmony at the Brussels Cons., but was largely self-taught in composition. From 1936 to 1959 he was employed as a sound engineer at the Belgian Radio. His style of composition embodies distinct elements of French impressionism, with its searing melodies and rich harmonies within a framework of emancipated tonality, often verging on polytonal syncretism.
WORKS: Chamber opera, *Atta Troll* (1952); 4 ballets: *Jean et les Argayons* (1934); *Cendrillon* (1946); *La Bal chez la portière* (1954); *Spéléomagie,* miniature ballet for TV (1959); 2 symph. radio plays: *D'un diable de briquet* (1950; Prix Italia, 1950) and *L'Elixir du révérend père Gaucher* (1951); 9 symphs.: No. 1 (1939); No. 2, *Symphonie des souvenirs,* with Soloists and Chorus optional (Brussels, Nov. 23, 1945); No. 3 (Brussels, June 25, 1952); No. 4, *Short Sympho-*ny (1952); No. 5, *Symphonie printanière* (1954); No. 6 (1957); Symph. for Chamber Orch. (1958); No. 7 (1964); No. 8 (1970); *Petite suite* for Orch. (1931); 3 piano concertos (1937, 1952, 1968); *Mouvements symphoniques* (1938); 2 cello concertos (1940, 1965); 3 violin concertos (1941, 1953, 1965); *Burlesque* for Cello and Orch. (1941); Concerto for Oboe, Clarinet, Bassoon, and Orch. (1943); Double Concerto for Piano, Saxophone or Viola, and Orch. (1946); *Divertissement* for Orch. (1946; extract from the ballet *Cendrillon*); Concerto for Orch. (1947); *Divertissement* for Chamber Orch. (1948); *Barbe-Bleu (Bluebeard)* for Orch. (1949); Horn Concerto (Brussels, July 12, 1950); Trumpet Concerto (1954); *Récréation de midi* for String Orch. (1955); *Mouvements,* suite for Brass (1956); *Carnaval à Ostende,* symph. suite (1959); *Presto Giocoso* for Orch. (1961); Concerto Grosso for 2 Trumpets and Orch. (1961); Concerto for Flute and Chamber Orch. (1961); *Bruegel, peintre des humbles,* symph. suite (1963); Concerto for Clarinet, String Orch., and Percussion (1968); *2 Airs* for Orch. (1971); 6 string quartets (1930, 1934, 1934, 1939, 1943, 1945); Piano Trio (1936); String Trio (1937); Piano Quartet (1938); Cello Sonata (1941); *Divertissement* for Wind Quintet (1942); *Musiques lilliputiennes* for 4 Flutes (1942); Quartet for 4 Cellos (1942); Piano Sonatina (1943); Suite for Piano (1943); Variations for Violin and Piano (1946); *Récit et Air gai* for Clarinet and Piano (1950); 5 Bagatelles for String Quartet (1952); Serenade for Wind Quintet (1958); Viola Sonatina (1959); *Récitatif et Marche* for Double Bass and Piano (1961); Wind Quartet (1964); Trio for Flute, Viola, and Double Bass or Piano (1961); Clarinet Quintet (1968); *Prelude, Scherzando et Marche* for Horn and Piano (1968); Clarinet Sonatina (1970); several cantatas: *Le Fléau* (1930); *Le Cantique de soleil* (1941); *L'Eléphant et le papillon* (1941); *La Dispute des orgues* (Brussels, Jan. 10, 1942); *Evasions* (1942); *Saisons* (1943); *Prière pour les condamnés à mort* for Narrator and Orch. (Brussels, Oct. 14, 1945); *Assonances* for Narrator and Chamber Orch. (1962); *Rhapsody* for Female Voice and Chamber Orch. (1969).

Chiari, Giuseppe, Italian composer of extreme avant-garde tendencies; b. Florence, Sept. 26, 1926. He studied piano; organized the group Musica e Segno in association with Sylvano Bussotti; participated in the Fluxus festival in Wiesbaden (1962), and in avant-garde manifestations in N.Y. (1964) and at the Centre de Musique in Paris (1965). Eventually he returned to Florence, where he owned a clothing store. In his productions he follows the most latitudinarian and disestablishmentarian trends of metadadaistic fragmentationarianism, both in tonal and verbal structures. He publ. *Musica senza contrappunto,* a varitype anthology of disjected observations (Rome, 1969). In it he launched the slogan "Musica gestuale," which deals with audiovisual and tactile events, volitional as well as aleatory. His works include: *Intervalli* for Piano (1956); *Per arco* for Cello (1962); *Teatrino* for Actor-Pianist, Rubber Dolls, Alarm Clocks, and Handsaw (1963); *Don't Trade Here* for Action Theater (1965).

Chiaromonte, Francesco, Italian musician of versatile attainments; b. Castrogiovanni, Sicily, July 26, 1809; d. Brussels, Oct. 15, 1886. He studied with Raimondi in Palermo and with Donizetti in Naples; began his musical career as a singing teacher, but was arrested for revolutionary activities in 1848 and, after serving 2 years in prison, was banished from Naples. He then proceeded to Paris, where he was employed as an opera chorus master; then went to Brussels in 1871 and was appointed prof. at the Brussels Cons. He produced several operas and oratorios; also publ. a valuable *Méthode de chant.*

Chickering, Jonas, American piano maker; b. New Ipswich, N.H., April 5, 1798; d. Boston, Dec. 8, 1853. In 1818 he was apprenticed to John Osborn, a Boston piano maker; in 1823, he founded (with James Stewart) the firm of Stewart & Chickering, from 1829 known as Chickering & Mackay (John Mackay, d. 1841), later as Chickering & Sons. Jonas Chickering pioneered in the development of the upright piano, and the full metal plate for square and grand pianos. His son and successor, **Col. Thomas E. Chickering** (b. Boston, Oct. 22, 1824; d. there, Feb. 14, 1871), was named a Chevalier of the Legion of Honor, in addition to taking the first prize for pianofortes at the Paris Exposition of 1867. His 3 sons and their successors carried on the factory, which was famous for quality and high rate of production, until 1908, when it became part of the American Piano Co., and the factory was moved from Boston to East Rochester, N.Y. Later the firm became a subsidiary of the Aeolian American Corp.
BIBLIOGRAPHY: R.G. Parker, *A Tribute to the Life and Character of Jonas Chickering* (Boston, 1854); *The Commemoration of the Founding of the House of Chickering* (Boston, 1904).

Chignell, Robert, English composer; b. Romsey, Hampshire, May 8, 1882; d. London, Feb. 27, 1939. He won a scholarship to the Royal College of Music, where his teachers were G. Garcia (voice) and Sir C.V. Stanford (composition); later continued vocal studies with C.W. Clark; was soloist with the Sheffield Choir on its world tour.
WORKS: Operas: *Romeo and Juliet; Herode; Aucassin and Nicolette;* 2 symph. poems; *Serenade humoresque* for Orch.; *The Jackdaw of Reims, Sunrise and Sunset,* and *The Monks of Bangor* for Chorus and Orch.; about 250 songs.

Chihara, Paul, American composer of Japanese descent; b. Seattle, July 9, 1938. After the outbreak of the war, his family was relocated, with many other Japanese-Americans, to Minadoka, Idaho. He studied piano as a child; took courses in English literature at the Univ. of Washington (B.A., 1960) and at Cornell Univ. (M.A., 1961); then went to Europe, where he studied composition with Nadia Boulanger in Paris (1962–63) and with Ernst Pepping in West Berlin (1965–66); in the interim he obtained his A.M.D. at Cornell Univ. (1965). From 1966 till 1974 he was on the music faculty of the Univ. of Calif., Los Angeles; traveled to Japan for research in 1967.

In his music he utilizes advanced forms of serial techniques, occasionally extending them to aleatory procedures. In his choral compositions he follows the time-honored polyphonic methods of the Renaissance.
WORKS: Viola Concerto (1963); String Quartet (1965); *Tree Music* for 3 Violas and 3 Trombones (1966); *Branches* for 2 Bassoons and Percussion (1966); *Magnificat* for Treble Voices (1966); *The 90th Psalm,* choral cantata (1966); Nocturne for 24 Solo Voices (1966); *Redwood* for Viola and Percussion (1967); *Willow, Willow* for Bass Flute, Tuba, and Percussion (1968); *Rain Music,* tape collage using brewery noises, commissioned by Rainier Breweries in Seattle (1968); *Forest Music* for Orch. (1968; Los Angeles, May 2, 1971); *Driftwood* for Violin, 2 Violas, and Cello (1969); *Logs XVI* for Amplified String Bass and Magnetic Tape (1970); *Ceremony I* for Oboe, 2 Cellos, Double Bass, and Percussion (1971); *Ceremony II* for Flute, 2 Cellos, and Percussion (1972); *Ceremony III* for Small Orch. (1973); *Ceremony IV* for Orch. (1974); *Ceremony V, Symphony in Celebration* (1973–75; Houston, Sept. 8, 1975); *Grass,* concerto for Double Bass and Orch. (1971; Oberlin (Ohio) Cons., April 14, 1972); *Wild Song* for Cello and Orch. (1972). *Missa Carminum* for Chorus a cappella (Los Angeles, Jan. 15, 1976); Saxophone Concerto (Boston, Jan. 30, 1981); Symph. No. 2 (Los Angeles, March 20, 1982); *Sequoia* for String Quartet and Tape (1984).

Child, William, English organist and composer of sacred music; b. Bristol, 1606; d. Windsor, March 23, 1697. He was a boy chorister at Bristol Cathedral under Elway Bevin; studied at Oxford (B.Mus., 1631); in 1632 was in Windsor as organist at St. George's Chapel (succeeding J. Mundy) and then in London at the Chapel Royal; in 1643–60 he apparently lived in retirement, devoting himself to composition; in 1660 he was appointed chanter at the Chapel Royal, and a member of the King's private band. He received his Mus.Bac. in 1631 or 1639; his Mus.Doc. from Oxford in 1663.
WORKS: He publ. Psalms (1639; later eds., 1650 and 1656), services, anthems, compositions in "Court Ayres," canons, catches, etc. (included in collections of Arnold Boyce, Hilton, Playford, and others); also instrumental works. Numerous services, anthems (including *O Lord, grant the King a long life*), a motet (*O bone Jesu*), and chants exist in MS.
BIBLIOGRAPHY: F. Hudson and W.R. Large, "William Child: A New Investigation of Sources," *Music Review* (Nov. 1970).

Childs, Barney, American composer; b. Spokane, Wash., Feb. 13, 1926. He studied sporadically and intermittently with Leonard Ratner, Carlos Chávez, Aaron Copland, and Elliott Carter; obtained a B.A. degree in English from the Univ. of Nevada (1949), an M.A. from Oxford Univ. as a Rhodes Scholar (1955), and a Ph.D. in literature from Stanford Univ. (1959). He taught English at the Univ. of Arizona (1956–65); then served as dean of Deep Springs College in California (1965–69). From 1969 to 1971 he taught music theory at Wisconsin College-Cons. in Milwaukee; in 1971 joined the faculty at Johnston College of the Univ. of Redlands in California; became a prof. there in 1973. Not overly concerned with public tastes and current fashions of cosmopolitan styles, he cultivates indeterminate structures. He edited, with Elliott Schwarz, *Contemporary Composers on Contemporary Music* (N.Y., 1967).

WORKS: 2 symphs. (1954, 1956); 8 string quartets (1951–74); 5 wind quintets (1951–69); Violin Sonata No. 1 (1950); Sonata for Solo Clarinet (1951); *Concerto da camera* for Trumpet and Woodwinds (1951); Trio for Flute, Oboe, and Clarinet (1952); Quartet for Clarinet and Strings (1953); Sonata for Bassoon and Piano (1953); *4 Involutions* for Solo English Horn (1955); *5 Considerations* for Solo French Horn (1955); *7 Epigrams* for Soprano and Clarinet (1955); Concerto for English Horn, Strings, Harp, and Percussion (1955); Violin Sonata No. 2 (1956); Quartet for Bassoons (1958); Sonata for Solo Oboe (1958); Brass Trio (1959); Flute Sonata (1960); Sonata for Solo Trombone (1961); 6 pieces under the generic title *Interbalances* for various groups (1941–64); *Take 5* for 5 Instruments (1962); *Stances* for Flute and Silence (1963); Quartet for Flute, Oboe, Double Bass, and Percussion (1964); *6 Events* for Band (1965); *Music* for Piano and Strings (1965); *Jack's New Bag* for 10 Players (1966); *The Golden Bubble* for Double Bass, Sarrusophone, and Percussion (1967); *Operation Flabby Sleep* for Any Instruments (1968); *Music* for 6 Tubas (1969); *Keet Seel* for Chorus a cappella (1970); Concerto for Clarinet and Orch. (1970); *Supposes: Imago Mundi* for Band (1970); *37 Songs* for Solo Piano (1971); *When Lilacs Last in the Dooryard Bloom'd ...* for Soloists, Chorus, and Band (1971); Trio for Clarinet, Cello, and Piano (1972); *Of Place, as Altered* for 5 Clarinets (1972); *Supposes: Cloud Busters* for Solo Tuba (1972); *Of Place, as Particular* for Soprano and Tape (1973); *A Music; That it Might be ...* for 2 Clarinets (1973); *Concert Piece for Tuba and Band* (1973); Quintet for Winds, Harp, and Percussion (1974); *The Golden Shore* for Band (1974); *Lanterns and Candlelight* for Marimba and Soprano (1975); *Bowling Again with the Champs* for 6 Improvisers and Tape (1976); *A Question of Summer* for Tuba and Harp (1976); *4 Pieces for 6 Winds* for Wind Quintet and Saxophone (1977); *Couriers of the Crimson Dawn* for Any Instruments (1977); *Quartet/Fantasy* for 4 Tubas (1977); *The Big New Improved Everybody Play Summer Music Clinic 12 Clarinet Fun Piece* (1977); *A Cello Piece* for Solo Cello (1978); *September with Band* for Band (1978); *Featuring: "Mighty" Joe Nowhere und die Greater Wairopi All*Stars* for 7 Equal Instruments (1978); *Overture to Measuring a Meridian* for Wind Sextet and Solo Percussion (1978); *As Endless Autumn* for High School Chorus, Horn, and Oboe (1978); *7 Quiet Studies for Solo Percussion* (1978); *6 Gamut Studies for Solo Marimba* (1978); *A Clarinet Piece* for Solo Clarinet (1978); *Since Then* for Solo Piano (1979); *The Word from Department R* for Clarinet and Alto Saxophone (1979); *Mosaic on a Theme of Balakirev* for Solo Alto Saxophone (1979); *A Continuance, in 7 Parts* for Band (1979); *Heaven to Clear When Day Did Close* for Solo Piano (1980); *Sky Visit* for Solo Cello (1980); *Clay Music* for 4 Players on special handmade clay instruments (1980); *!BANANA FLANNELBOARD!—the Historic First Album* for 3 Readers and Tape Delay (1980); *Orrery for Band* (1980); *Sleep, and Then Going On* for Clarinet and 2 Cymbals (1980); *13 Classic Studies for the Contrabass* (1981); *The Edge of the World* for Bass Clarinet and Organ (1981); *Real Music* for 2 Clarinets (1981); *81 Licks for Trombone* (1983); *Pastorale* for Bass Clarinet and Tape (1983); *Sunshine Lunchh, & Like Matters* for Bass Clarinet, Baritone, Percussion, and Electronic Music Machine (1984; "Lunchh" is the emphatically designated rendering by the composer); Horn Octet (1984).

Chilesotti, Oscar, Italian music historiographer; b. Basano, July 12, 1848; d. there, June 23, 1916. He was a graduate in law of Padua Univ.; was also a good flutist and cellist; self-taught in harmony. He lived in Milan, where he wrote regularly for the *Gazzetta Musicale.*

WRITINGS: *Biblioteca di rarità musicali* (9 vols., Milan, 1883), containing transcriptions from little-known works of the early 17th century, and (vol. IV) *Arianna* by Benedetto Marcello; *I nostri Maestri del passato* (Milan, 1882), biographical notes on the greatest Italian musicians, from Palestrina to Bellini; *Di G.B. Besardo e del suo "Thesaurus Harmonicus"* (Milan, 1886; French ed., 1901); *Sulla lettera critica di B. Marcello contra A. Lotti* (Bassano, 1885); *Sulla melodia popolare del cinquecento* (Milan, 1889); *Lautenspieler des 16. Jahrhunderts* (Leipzig, 1891); *L'evoluzione nella musica, appunti sulla teoria di H. Spencer* (Turin, 1911); etc. He publ. in modern notation Roncalli's *Capricci armonici* on the Spanish guitar (Milan, 1881) and trans. Schopenhauer's *Aphorismen* and *Die Welt als Wille und Vorstellung* into Italian.

BIBLIOGRAPHY: V. Fedeli, "Il Dr. O. Chilesotti," *Rivista Musicale Italiana,* XXIII/3–4 (1916).

Chiriac, Mircea, Rumanian composer; b. Bucharest, May 19, 1919. He studied harmony with Otescu and Jora at the Bucharest Cons. (1936–45); in 1966 was appointed to its faculty. He wrote a ballet, *Iancu Jianu* (1962); a symph. tableau, *Bucureştii de altădată (Bucharest of Old Times;* 1957); *Symphonic Triptych* (1971); *Divertissement* for String Orch. (1972); some chamber music.

Chisholm, Erik, Scottish composer; b. Glasgow, Jan. 4, 1904; d. Rondebosch, South Africa, June 7, 1965. He first studied music in Glasgow; then in London and in Edinburgh with Donald Tovey (composition) and Puishnov (piano); received his Mus.Bac. in 1931, and his Mus.Doc. from Edinburgh Univ. in 1934. He was conductor of the Glasgow Grand Opera Society in 1930–39; in 1940 joined the Carl Rosa Opera Co. as conductor; in 1943 toured with the Anglo-Polish Ballet; later went to the Far East; organized the Singapore Symph. Orch., and conducted 50 concerts in

Malaya; in 1946 was appointed prof. of music and director of the South African College of Music at Cape Town Univ.; also conducted operas in South Africa. His book, *The Operas of Leoš Janáček,* was publ. posthumously (N.Y., 1971). Chisholm's style of composition is marked by considerable complexity; elements of oriental scale formations are notable.

WORKS: Operas: *The Feast of Samhain* (1941); *The Inland Woman* (Cape Town, Oct. 21, 1953); *Dark Sonnet,* after O'Neill's drama *Before Breakfast* (Cape Town, Oct. 20, 1952); *Simoon,* after Strindberg (1953); *Dark Sonnet* and *Simoon* were later combined with a 3rd short opera, *Black Roses* (libretto by the composer), to form a trilogy entitled *Murder in 3 Keys* (perf. at the Cherry Lane Theater, Greenwich Village, N.Y., July 6, 1954). Ballets: *The Pied Piper of Hamelin* (1937); *The Forsaken Mermaid* (1940); *The Earth Shapers* (1941); *The Hoodie* (1947). For Orch.: *Straloch Suite* (1933); Symph. No. 1 (1938); Symph. No. 2 (1939); *The Adventures of Babar,* with Narrator (1940); *Piobaireachd Concerto* for Piano and Orch. (1940); *Pictures from Dante* (1948); *Hindustani Concerto* for Piano and Orch. (Cape Town, Nov. 22, 1949); Violin Concerto (Cape Town Festival, March 18, 1952); Concerto for Orch. (Cape Town, March 29, 1952). Chamber music: Double Trio for Clarinet, Bassoon, Trumpet, Violin, Cello, and Double Bass. Also choral works, songs, piano pieces.

Chladni, Ernest Florens Friedrich, eminent German acoustician; b. Wittenberg, Nov. 30, 1756; d. Breslau, April 3, 1827. At first a student and prof. of law at Wittenberg and Leipzig, he turned to physics, and made highly important researches in the domain of acoustics. He discovered the "Tonfiguren" (tone-figures; i.e., the regular patterns assumed by dry sand on a glass plate set in vibration by a bow); invented the Euphonium (glass-rod harmonica) and Clavicylinder (steel-rod keyboard harmonica). To introduce his ideas and inventions, he made long journeys and delivered many scientific lectures.

WRITINGS: His earlier publications, *Entdeckungen über die Theorie des Klanges* (1787), *Über die Longitudinal-schwingungen der Saiten und Stäbe,* and a series of minor articles in various periodicals, were followed by the important works *Die Akustik* (1802; 2nd ed., 1830; French trans., 1809); *Neue Beiträge zur Akustik* (1817); *Beiträge zur praktischen Akustik* (1821); *Kurze Übersicht der Schall- und Klanglehre* (1827).

BIBLIOGRAPHY: W. Bernhardt, *Dr. E. Chladni, der Akustiker* (Wittenberg, 1856).

Chlubna, Osvald, Czech composer; b. Brno, June 22, 1893; d. there, Oct. 30, 1971. He studied composition with Janáček in Brno (1914–15) and later at the Brno branch of the Master School of the Prague Cons. (1923–24); taught in Brno at the Cons. (1919–35) and at the Janáček Academy of Music (1953–59). His music is marked by rhapsodic élan; many of his works reflect national events. In 1948 he completed Janáček's unfinished symph. poem, *Dunaj* (*The Danube;* 1923–28).

WORKS: 8 operas: *Pomsta Catullova* (*Catullus's Revenge;* 1917; Brno, Nov. 30, 1921); *Aladina and Palomid,* after Maeterlinck (1921–22; Brno, May 31, 1925); *Nura* (1930; Brno, May 20, 1932); *Freje pana z Heslova* (*The Love Affairs of the Squire of Heslov;* 1939–40; Brno, Jan. 28, 1949); *Jiří of Kunštát and Poděbrady* (1941–42); *Kolébka* (*The Cradle;* 1952; Brno, 1953); *Eupyros* (1962); *Rytíř Jan z Linhartic* (*Knight Jan von Linhartic;* 1967); scenic mystery play, *V den počátku* (*The Day of Beginning;* 1935; Brno, Jan. 24, 1936); 7 cantatas: *České vzkříšení* (*The Czech Resurrection;* 1943); *My Land Is Beautiful* (1955); *In the Name of Life* (1959); *The Eternal Vigils of Life and Death* (1964); *Only Once,* chamber cantata (1967); *Leonydas,* chamber cantata (1968); *The Death of Caesar,* chamber cantata (1968); symph. poems: *Distance and Dreams* (1916); *Before I Grow Silent* (1918); *2 Fairy Tales* (1920); *A Song of Longing* (1922); *From Hills, Mountains and Forests* (1934); *Nature and Man* (a trilogy including the separate works *Spring, Summer Serenade,* and *Carnival of Autumn,* 1949–53); *This Is My Land* (a cycle including the separate works *The Fountains of Brno, The Abyss of Macocha, Pernštejn Castle, Moravian Slovakia,* and *Brno Portals and Frescoes,* 1956–62); Sinfonietta (1924); 3 symphs.: No. 1, *Symphony of Life and Love* (1927); No. 2, *Brno Symphony* (1946); No. 3 (1960); Fantasy for Viola and Orch. (1936); Piano Concerto (1937); Cello Concerto (1938); Violin Concerto (1950); *Andante* for Violin and Small Orch. (1951); 5 string quartets (1925, 1928, 1933, 1963, 1969); Sonata for Violin and Cello (1925); Wind Quintet (1936); Violin Sonata (1948); Cello Sonata (1948); Fantasy for String Trio (1953); Etudes for Oboe and Harp (1969); Etudes for Bass Clarinet (1969); Etude for Harpsichord and 12 Strings (1970); Viola Sonatina (1970); *Frescoes* for Solo Violin (1970); 5 Nocturnes for Piano (1933); Sonata-Fantasy for Piano (1959); *Elegies* for Piano (1968); choruses; songs.

BIBLIOGRAPHY: M. Černohorská, *Osvald Chlubna* (Brno, 1963).

Cholmondeley, Archer. See **Chamlee, Mario.**

Chop, Max (pen name, **Monsieur Charles**), German writer; b. Greuzen, Thuringia, May 17, 1862; d. Berlin, Dec. 20, 1929. A law student turned musician, he publ. several books of songs and ballades, 3 piano concertos, a Piano Trio, and 2 orch. suites; he lived from 1885–88 in Berlin as a writer of musical feuilletons; then, until 1902, in Neu-Ruppin as music critic and editor of the *Märkische Zeitung;* in 1902 he was again in Berlin; from 1920 until his death, was editor in chief of *Die Signale.* An ardent admirer of August Bungert, he publ. his detailed biography (Berlin, 1915) and analyses of his music dramas; was (from 1911) the editor of *Der Bund,* the official organ of the Bungert Association. He publ. *Zeitgenössische Tondichter* (2 vols., 1888–90, each containing 12 sketches); analyses of Liszt's symph. poems, Wagner's music dramas, etc.; a sketch of August Bungert in vol. III of *Monographien mo-*

derner Musiker (1903); *Vademecum für den Konzertsaal* (1904, et seq.); biographies of Delius (1907) and Rezniček (1920); *Führer durch die Musikgeschichte* (Berlin, 1912).

Chopin, (François-) Frédéric, incomparable genius of the piano who created a unique romantic style of keyboard music; b. Zelazowa Wola, near Warsaw, in all probability on March 1, 1810, the date given by Chopin himself in his letter of acceptance of membership in the Polish Literary Society in Paris in 1833 (but in his certificate of baptism the date of birth is given as Feb. 22, 1810); d. Paris, Oct. 17, 1849. His father, Nicolas Chopin, was a native of Marainville, France, who went to Warsaw as a teacher of French; his mother, Justyna Krzyzanowska, was Polish. He was brought up in his father's private school, among sons of the Polish nobility. Chopin's talent was manifested in early childhood; at the age of 8 he played in public a piano concerto by Gyrowetz, and he had already begun to compose polonaises, mazurkas, and waltzes. He received his primary musical instruction from the Bohemian pianist Adalbert Żywny, who resided in Warsaw at the time. A much more important teacher was Joseph Elsner, director of the Warsaw School of Music, who gave Chopin a thorough instruction in music theory and form. Chopin was 15 years old when his Rondeau for Piano was publ. in Warsaw as op. 1. In the summer of 1829 Chopin set out for Vienna, where he gave a highly successful concert on Aug. 11, 1829, and appeared there again on Aug. 18, 1829. While in Vienna he made arrangements to have his variations on Mozart's aria *Là ci darem la mano,* for Piano and Orch., publ. by Haslinger as op. 2. It was this work that attracted the attention of Schumann, who saluted Chopin in his famous article publ. in the *Allgemeine Musikalische Zeitung* of Dec. 7, 1831, in which Schumann's alter ego, Eusebius, is represented as exclaiming, "Hats off, gentlemen! A genius!" The common assumption in many biographies that Schumann "launched" Chopin on his career is deceptive; actually Schumann was some months younger than Chopin, and was referred to editorially merely as a student of Prof. Wieck. Returning to Warsaw, Chopin gave the first public performance of his Piano Concerto in F minor, op. 21, on March 17, 1830. On Oct. 11, 1830, he was soloist in his Piano Concerto in E minor, op. 11. A confusion resulted in the usual listing of the E minor Concerto as first, and the F minor Concerto as his 2nd; chronologically, the composition of the F minor Concerto preceded the E minor. He spent the winter of 1830–31 in Vienna. The Polish rebellion against Russian domination, which ended in defeat, determined Chopin's further course of action, and he proceeded to Paris, visiting Linz, Salzburg, Dresden, and Stuttgart on the way. He arrived in Paris in Sept. 1831, and was introduced to Rossini, Cherubini, and Paër. He also met Bellini, Meyerbeer, Berlioz, Victor Hugo, and Heinrich Heine; he became particularly friendly with Liszt. Paris was then the center of Polish emigration, and Chopin maintained his contacts with the Polish circle

there. He presented his first Paris concert on Feb. 26, 1832. He also taught the piano. The Paris critics found an apt Shakespearean epithet for him, calling him "the Ariel of the piano." In 1836 he met the famous novelist Aurore Dupin (Mme. Dudevant), who publ. her works under the affected masculine English name George Sand. They became intimate, even though quite incompatible in character and interests. George Sand was involved in social affairs and held radical views; Chopin was a poet confined within his inner world; it has been said that she was the masculine and he the feminine partner in their companionship. In the winter of 1838–39 Chopin accompanied George Sand to the island of Majorca, where she attended to him with total devotion; yet she portrayed Chopin in her novel *Lucrézia Floriani* as a weakling. Indeed, she was quite overt in her reference to Chopin as a lover; in a personal letter dated 1838 she said that she had difficulty in inducing Chopin to submit to a sensual embrace, and implied that she lived as an immaculate virgin most of the time they were together. They parted in 1847; by that time Chopin was quite ill with tuberculosis; a daguerreotype taken of him represents a prematurely aged man with facial features showing sickness and exhaustion, with locks of black hair partly covering his forehead. Yet he continued his concert career. He undertook a tour as pianist in England and Scotland in 1848; he gave his last concert in Paris on Feb. 16, 1848. *La Revue et Gazette Musicale* of Feb. 20, 1848, gives a precious account of the occasion: "The finest flower of feminine aristocracy in the most elegant attire filled the Salle Pleyel," the paper reported, "to catch this musical sylph on the wing." He died the following year; Mozart's Requiem was performed at Chopin's funeral at the Madeleine, with Habeneck conducting the orch. and chorus of the Paris Cons. and Pauline Viardot and Lablache singing the solo parts. Chopin was buried at Père Lachaise between the graves of Cherubini and Bellini; however, at his own request, his heart was sent to Warsaw for entombment in his homeland.

Chopin represents the full liberation of the piano from traditional orch. and choral influences, the authoritative assumption of its role as a solo instrument. Not seeking "orchestral" sonorities, Chopin may have paled as a virtuoso beside the titanic Liszt, but the poesy of his pianism, its fervor of expression, the pervading melancholy in his nocturnes and ballades, and the bounding exultation of his scherzos and études were never equaled. And, from a purely technical standpoint, Chopin's figurations and bold modulatory transitions seem to presage the elaborate transtonal developments of modern music.

WORKS: FOR SOLO PIANO: *Albumleaf (Moderato)* in E major (1843); *Allegro de concert,* op. 46 (1832–41); *Andante spianato* in G major, op. 22 (1834); *Andantino* in G minor (1838); ballades: G minor, op. 23 (1831–35); F major/A minor, op. 38 (1836–39); A-flat major, op. 47 (1840–41); F minor, op. 52 (1842); *Barcarolle* in F-sharp major, op. 60 (1845–46); *Berceuse* in D-flat major, op. 57 (1843–44); *Bolero* in C major/A major, op. 19 (1833); *2 Bourrées,* in G minor and A major (1846); *Canon* in F minor (1839?); *Cantabile* in B-flat major (1834); *Contredanse* in G-flat major (1827?); *3 Écossaises,* in D major, G major, and D-flat major, op. 72, no. 3 (1826); études: 4, in F major, F minor, A-flat major, and E-flat major, op. 10, nos. 8–11 (1829); 2, in G-flat major and E-flat minor, op. 10, nos. 5–6 (1830); 2, in C major and A minor, op. 10, nos. 1–2 (1830); C minor, op. 10, no. 12 (1830); C major, op. 10, no. 7 (1832); E major, op. 10, no. 3 (1832); C-sharp minor, op. 10, no. 4 (1832); 6, in A minor, E minor, G-sharp minor, D-flat major, G-flat major, and B minor, op. 25, nos. 4–6 and 8–10 (1832–34); A minor, op. 25, no. 11 (1834); F minor, op. 25, no. 2 (1836); C-sharp minor, op. 25, no. 7 (1836); 2, in F major and C minor, op. 25, nos. 3 and 12 (1836); A-flat major, op. 25, no. 1 (1836); *Fantaisie* in F minor/A-flat major, op. 49 (1841); *Fantaisie-impromptu* in C-sharp minor, op. 66 (1835); *Fugue* in A minor (1841–42); *Funeral March* in C minor, op. 72, no. 2 (1827); *Impromptu* in A-flat major, op. 29 (1837); *Impromptu* in F-sharp minor, op. 36 (1839); *Impromptu* in G-flat major, op. 51 (1842); *Introduction and Variations on the German air Der Schweizerbub* in E major (1826); *Introduction* in C major and *Rondo* in E-flat major, op. 16 (1832); *Introduction and Variations on Hérold's "Je vends des scapulaires" from Ludovic* in B-flat major, op. 12 (1833); *Largo* in E-flat major (1837?); mazurkas: D major (1820?); A-flat major (1825; earlier version of op. 7, no. 4); A minor (1825; earlier version of op. 17, no. 4); 2, in G major and B-flat major (1826); A minor, op. 68, no. 2 (1827); F major, op. 68, no. 3 (1829); C major, op. 68, no. 1 (1829); G major (1829); A minor (1829; earlier version of op. 7, no. 2); 4, in F-sharp minor, C-sharp minor, E major, and E-flat major, op. 6 (1830); 5, in B-flat major, A minor, F minor, A-flat major, and C major, op. 7 (1831); B-flat major (1832); 4, in B-flat major, E minor, A-flat major, and A minor, op. 17 (1832–33); C major (1833); A-flat major (1834); 4, in G minor, C major, A-flat major, and B-flat minor, op. 24 (1834–35); 2, in G major and C major, op. 67, nos. 1 and 3 (1835); 4, in C minor, B minor, D-flat major, and C-sharp minor, op. 30 (1836–37); 4, in G-sharp minor, D major, C major, and B minor, op. 33 (1837–38); E minor, op. 41, no. 2 (1838); 3, in E major, B major, and A-flat major, op. 41, nos. 1, 3, and 4 (1839–40); A minor (1840); A minor (1840); 3, in G major, A-flat major, and C-sharp minor, op. 50 (1842); 3, in B major, C major, and C minor, op. 56 (1843); 3, in A minor, A-flat major, and F-sharp minor, op. 59 (1845); 3, in B major, F minor, and C-sharp minor, op. 63 (1846); A minor, op. 67, no. 4 (1846); G minor, op. 67, no. 2 (1849); F minor, op. 68, no. 4 (1849); *Military March* (1817; not extant); nocturnes: E minor, op. 72, no. 1 (1827); C-sharp minor (1830); 3, in B-flat minor, E-flat major, and B major, op. 9 (1830–31); 2, in F major and F-sharp major, op. 15, nos. 1–2 (1830–31); G minor, op. 15, no. 3 (1833); C-sharp minor, op. 27, no. 1 (1835); D-flat major, op. 27, no. 2 (1835); 2, in B major and A-flat major, op. 32 (1836–37); C minor (1837); G minor, op. 37, no. 1 (1838); G major, op. 37, no. 2 (1839); 2, in C minor and F-sharp minor, op. 48 (1841); 2, in F minor and E-flat minor, op. 55 (1843); 2, in B major and E major, op. 62 (1846); polonaises: G minor (1817); B-flat major

(1817); A-flat major (1821); G-sharp minor (1822); D minor, op. 71, no. 1 (1825?); B-flat minor, *Adieu* (1826); B-flat major, op. 71, no. 2 (1828); F minor, op. 71, no. 3 (1828); G-flat major (1829); 2, in C-sharp minor and E-flat minor, op. 26 (1834–35); A major, op. 40, no. 1 (1838); C minor, op. 40, no. 2 (1839); F-sharp minor, op. 44 (1840–41); A-flat major, op. 53 (1842); *Polonaise-fantaisie* in A-flat major, op. 61 (1845–46); preludes: A-flat major (1834); 24, op. 28 (1836–39); C-sharp minor, op. 45 (1841); rondos: C minor, op. 1 (1825); F major, op. 5, "à la Mazur" (1826); C major (1828; earlier version of the Rondo in C major for 2 Pianos, op. 73); scherzos: B minor, op. 20 (1831–32); B-flat minor/D-flat major, op. 31 (1837); C-sharp minor, op. 39 (1839); E major, op. 54 (1842); sonatas: C minor, op. 4 (1828); B-flat minor, op. 35, *Funeral March* (1839; 3rd movement is a *Funeral March* in B-flat minor, composed in 1837); B minor, op. 58 (1844); *Tarantelle* in A-flat major, op. 43 (1841); *3 nouvelles études,* for Moscheles's *Methode* (1839); Variation No. 6, in E major, from the *Hexameron (Variations on the March from Bellini's I puritani)* (1837; other variations by Liszt, Thalberg, Pixis, Herz, and Czerny); Variations in A major, *Souvenir de Paganini* (1829); waltzes: A-flat major (1827); B minor, op. 69, no. 2 (1829); D-flat major, op. 70, no. 3 (1829); E major (1829); E-flat major (1829–30); E minor (1830); E-flat major, op. 18 (1831); A minor, op. 34, no. 2 (1831); G-flat major, op. 70, no. 1 (1833); A-flat major, op. 34, no. 1 (1835); A-flat major, op. 69, no. 1, *L'Adieu* (1835); F major, op. 34, no. 3 (1838); A-flat major, op. 42 (1840); E-flat major, *Sostenuto* (1840); F minor, op. 70, no. 2 (1841); A minor (1843?); 3, in D-flat major (*Minute*), C-sharp minor, and A-flat major, op. 64 (1846–47); B major (1848; not extant). — For Piano, 4-hands: *Introduction, Theme, and Variations* in D major (1826). — For 2 Pianos: Rondo in C major, op. 73 (1828; later version of Rondo in C major for Solo Piano).

FOR PIANO AND ORCH.: *Variations on Mozart's "Là ci darem la mano" from Don Giovanni* in B-flat major, op. 2 (1827); *Fantasia on Polish Airs* in A major, op. 13 (1828); *Krakowiak,* rondo in F major, op. 14 (1828); Piano Concerto No. 2, in F minor, op. 21 (1829–30; Warsaw, March 17, 1830, composer soloist; although listed as "No. 2," it was his first concerto in order of composition); Piano Concerto No. 1, in E minor, op. 11 (1830; Warsaw, Oct. 11, 1830, composer soloist; although listed as "No. 1," it was his 2nd concerto in order of composition); *Grand Polonaise* in E-flat major, op. 22 (1830–31).

CHAMBER MUSIC: *Variations on Rossini's "Non più mesta" from "La Cenerentola"* for Flute and Piano, in E major (1824); Piano Trio in G minor, op. 8 (1828–29); *Introduction and Polonaise* for Cello and Piano, in C major, op. 3 (1829–30); *Grand Duo on Themes from Meyerbeer's "Robert le diable"* for Cello and Piano, in E major (1832); Cello Sonata in G minor, op. 65 (1845–46).

SONGS: 17, op. 74 (to Polish texts; 1829–47).

BIBLIOGRAPHY: COLLECTED EDITIONS, SOURCE MATERIAL: A number of so-called complete editions of Chopin's works have been issued since the 19th century. The complete edition begun by Paderewski and publ. by the Chopin Inst. of Warsaw and Polskie Wydawnictwo Muzyczne of Cracow (26 vols., 1937–66) is extensively annotated but is unreliable in parts since the editors did not always have access to important sources. In 1967 a new "National Edition" was begun under the editorship of J. Ekier. Breitkopf & Härtel publ. a *Thematisches Verzeichniss der im Druck erschienenen Kompositionen von Friedrich Chopin* (Leipzig, 1852; 2nd ed., revised, 1888). Another thematic catalogue was prepared by F. Listy and H. Opieński (Warsaw, 1937). The most valuable is M.J.E. Brown, *Chopin: An Index of His Works in Chronological Order* (London, 1960; 2nd ed., revised, 1972). Other sources include the following: B. Sydow, *Bibliografia F.F. Chopina* (Warsaw, 1949; supplement, 1954); K. Michalowski, *Bibliografia chopinowska/A Chopin Bibliography 1849–1969* (Cracow, 1970); A. Hedley, *Catalogues des manuscrits de Frédéric Chopin* (Cracow, 1971); K. Kobylańska, *Frederic Chopin, Thematisch-bibliographisches Werkverzeichnis* (Munich, 1979).

CORRESPONDENCE: M. Karlowicz, ed., *Nie wydane dotychczas pamiatki po Chopinie* (*New Unpublished Souvenirs of Chopin;* Warsaw, 1904; French trans., 1904); B. Scharlitt, ed., *Friedrich Chopins gesammelte Briefe* (Leipzig, 1911); H. Opieński, ed., *Chopin; Collected Letters* (trans. from the original Polish and French, with a preface and editorial notes by E. Voynich; N.Y., 1931); B. Sydow, ed., *Korespondencja Fryderyka Chopina* (2 vols., Warsaw, 1955; French trans., 1953–60); A. Hedley, ed., *Selected Correspondence of Fryderyk Chopin* (London, 1962); Z. Lissa, "Chopins Briefe an Delfine Potocka," *Die Musikforschung,* XV (1962); J. Smoter, *Spór o "listy" Chopina do Delfiny Potockiej* (*The Controversy over Chopin's "Letters" to Delfina Potocka;* Cracow, 1967); M. Gliński, ed., *Chopin: Listy do Delfiny* (*Chopin: Letters to Delfina;* N.Y., 1972); K. Kobylańska, ed., *Korespondencja Fryderyka Chopina z rodziny* (*Chopin's Correspondence with His Family;* Warsaw, 1972).

In addition to the writings listed below, consult *Rocznik chopinowski/Annales Chopin* and *Chopin Jahrbuch* for important articles on his life and works.

BIOGRAPHICAL: G. Sand, *Un Hiver à Majorque* (Paris, 1842; 5th ed., 1929); idem, *Histoire de ma vie* (Paris, 1854; 7th ed., 1928); M. Karasowski, *Friedrich Chopin: Sein Leben, seine Werke und Briefe* (2 vols., Dresden, 1877; 4th ed., 1914; Eng. trans., London, 1879; 3rd ed., 1938); F. Niecks, *Frederick Chopin as a Man and Musician* (2 vols., London, 1888; German trans., Leipzig, 1890; 3rd Eng. ed., 1902); C. Willeby, *Frédéric François Chopin: A Biography* (London, 1892); J. Huneker, *Chopin: The Man and His Music* (N.Y., 1900; new ed., 1925); J. Hadden, *Chopin* (London, 1903; 2nd ed., revised, 1935); F. Hoesick, *Chopin* (Warsaw, 1904; revised, enlarged ed. as *Chopin: Życie i twórczość [Chopin: Life and Work],* 3 vols., 1910–11; further revised, 4 vols., Cracow, 1962–68); H. Leichtentritt, *Chopin* (Berlin, 1905); E. Ganche, *Frédéric Chopin: Sa vie et ses œuvres* (Paris, 1909; Eng. trans., 1922; 7th French ed., 1949); B. Scharlitt, *Chopin* (Leipzig, 1919); Z. Jachimecki, *Fryderyk Chopin* (Cracow, 1926;

French trans., 1930; 2nd Polish ed., 1949); G. de Pourtalès, *Chopin ou Le Poète* (Paris, 1927; Eng. trans. as *Frederick Chopin: A Man of Solitude,* 1927; 2nd ed. as *Polonaise: The Life of Chopin,* 1933; 10th French ed., 1963); E. Vuillermoz, *La Vie amoureuse de Chopin* (Paris, 1927; 2nd ed., revised, 1960); L. Binental, *Chopin* (Paris, 1934); W. Murdoch, *Chopin and His Life* (London, 1934); B. Ferra, *Chopin and George Sand in Majorca* (Palma de Mallorca, 1936); A. Hedley, *Chopin* (London, 1947; 3rd ed., revised, 1974); A.-E. Cherbuliez, *F. Chopin, Leben und Werk* (Zürich, 1948); M. Gliński, "Kiedy urodzil się Chopin?," *Ruch Muzyczny,* 19 (1948; an attempt to prove that Chopin was born on March 1, 1809); N. Slonimsky, "Chopiniana, Some Materials for a Biography," *Musical Quarterly* (Oct. 1948); B. Sydow, "O date urodzenia Fr. Chopina," *Ruch Muzyczny,* 10 (1948; the author argues in favor of acceptance of Chopin's birth date as March 1, 1810, and publishes, for the first time, a facsimile of Chopin's letter to the Polish Literary Society of Paris, giving this date); W. Rehberg, *Chopin, Sein Leben und seine Werke* (Zürich, 1949); H. Weinstock, *Chopin: The Man and His Music* (N.Y., 1949; 2nd ed., 1959); K. Wierzyński, *The Life and Death of Chopin* (N.Y., 1949; in Polish, 1953; 2nd Eng. ed., 1972); R. Bory, *La Vie de Frédéric Chopin par l'image* (Geneva, 1951); A. Cœuroy, *Chopin* (Paris, 1951); F. Zagiba, *Chopin und Wien* (Vienna, 1951); M. Idzikowski and B. Sydow, eds., *Portret Fryderyka Chopina* (45 plates and annotations to Chopin's portraits; Cracow, 1952; French trans., 1953; 2nd Polish ed., enlarged, 1963); J. Iwaszkiewicz, *Chopin* (Cracow, 1955; German trans., 1958; 2nd ed., 1964; French trans., 1966; 3rd Polish ed., 1965); K. Kobylańska, *Chopin w kraju: Dokumenty i pamiątki* (*Chopin in His Homeland: Documents and Souvenirs),* a lavish folio (Cracow, 1955; Eng. trans., 1955); E. Long, *A History of the Therapy of Tuberculosis and the Case of Frederic Chopin* (Lawrence, Kans., 1956); C. Bourniquel, *Chopin* (Paris, 1957; Eng. trans., 1960); J. Rousselot, *La Vie passionnée de Frédéric Chopin* (Paris, 1957); A. Czartkowski and Z. Jezewska, *Fryderyk Chopin* (Warsaw, 1958; 5th ed., 1975); M. Godeau, *Le Voyage à Majorque de George Sand et Frédéric Chopin* (Paris, 1959); I. Belza, *Fryderyk F. Chopin* (Moscow, 1960; Polish trans., 1969); A. Boucourechliev, *Chopin: A Pictorial Biography* (London, 1963); M. Gliński, *Chopin the Unknown* (Windsor, Ontario, 1963); J. Grenier, *Chopin* (Paris, 1964); V. Seroff, *Frederic Chopin* (N.Y., 1964); M. Mirska and W. Hordyński, *Chopin na obczyźnie: Dokumenty i pamiątki* (*Chopin Abroad: Documents and Souvenirs;* Cracow, 1965); A. Harasowski, *The Skein of Legends around Chopin* (Glasgow, 1967); A. Murgia, *The Life and Times of Chopin* (London, 1967); Smoter, *Spór o "listy" Chopina do Delfiny Potockiej* (Warsaw, 1967); L. Ripoll, *The Majorcan Episode of Chopin and George Sand 1838–1839* (Palma de Mallorca, 1969); W. Duleba (Cracow, 1975); A. Orga, *Chopin: His Life and Times* (Tunbridge Wells, 1976); A. Zamoyski, *Chopin: A New Biography* (Garden City, N.Y., 1979); J. Chomiński, *Fryderyk Chopin* (in German; London, 1980).

CRITICAL, ANALYTICAL: F. Liszt, *F. Chopin* (Paris,

1845; Eng. trans., London, 1877; German trans., Leipzig, 1880); J. Kleczyński, *Chopin w cenniejszych swoich utworach* (Warsaw, 1886; Eng. trans. as *Chopin's Greatest Works: How They Should Be Understood,* London, 1896; 2nd ed., 1898); G. Jonson, *A Handbook to Chopin's Works* (London, 1905; 2nd ed., revised, 1908); R. Koczalski, *Chopin-Zyklus: Vier Klavier-vorträge* (Leipzig, 1909); E. Kelley, *Chopin the Composer* (N.Y., 1913); J. Dunn, *Ornamentation in the Works of Frederick Chopin* (London, 1921; 2nd ed., 1930); H. Leichtentritt, *Analyse der Chopinschen Klavierwerke* (2 vols., Berlin, 1921 and 1922); E. Ganche, *Dans le souvenir de Frédéric Chopin* (Paris, 1925); H. Windakiewiczowa, *Die Urtypen Chopin'scher Melodik in der polnischen Volksmusik* (Cracow, 1926); S. Barbag, *Über die Lieder von Fr. Chopin* (Lwow, 1927); E. Ganche, *Voyages avec Frédéric Chopin* (Paris, 1934); J. Porte, *Chopin: The Composer and His Music: An Analytical Critique of Famous Traditions and Interpretations* (London, 1935); R. Koczalski, *Frédéric Chopin: Betrachtungen, Skizzen, Analysen* (Cologne, 1936); M. Ottich, *Die Bedeutung des Ornaments im Schaffen Friedrich Chopins* (Berlin, 1937); G. Abraham, *Chopin's Musical Style* (London, 1939; 4th ed., revised, 1960); L. Bronarski, *Etudes sur Chopin* (2 vols., Lausanne, 1944 and 1946); idem, *Chopin et l'Italie* (Lausanne, 1946); A. Gide, *Notes sur Chopin* (Paris, 1948; Eng. trans., 1949); A. Cortot, *Aspects de Chopin* (Paris, 1949; Eng. trans. as *In Search of Chopin,* London, 1951); B. von Pozniak, *Chopin: Praktische Anweisungen für das Studium der Chopin-Werke* (Halle, 1949); J. Holcman, *The Legacy of Chopin* (N.Y., 1954); J. Chomiński, *Sonaty Chopina* (*Chopin's Sonatas;* Cracow, 1960); Z. Lissa, ed., *The Book of the First International Musicological Congress Devoted to the Works of Frederick Chopin, Warsaw 16–22 February 1960* (Warsaw, 1963); A. Walker, ed., *Frédéric Chopin: Profiles of the Man and the Musician* (London, 1966; 2nd ed. as *The Chopin Companion,* 1973); F. McGinnis, *Chopin: Aspects of Melodic Style* (Diss., Indiana Univ., 1968); Z. Lissa, ed., *Studia nad twórczcia Fryderyka Chopina* (Cracow, 1970); D. Branson, *John Field and Chopin* (London, 1972); J. Holland, *Chopin's Teaching and His Students* (Diss., Univ. of North Carolina, 1973); D. Żebrowski, ed., *Studies in Chopin* (Warsaw, 1973).

Chorbajian, John, American composer; b. New York, June 2, 1936. He studied composition with Vittorio Giannini at the Manhattan School of Music, obtaining his M.M. in 1959. Subsequently he was a teacher of piano and music theory in N.Y.

WORKS: Violin Sonata (1956); *Antigone,* one-act opera (1959); *The Magic of Music,* scene for Mime with Orch. (1960); *The Crucifixion,* cantata for Mixed Chorus and Orch. (1962); *The Swing* for Children's Chorus, Flute, and Piano (1966); numerous choral pieces.

Chorley, Henry Fothergill, English writer on music; b. Blackley Hurst, Lancashire, Dec. 15, 1808; d. London, Feb. 16, 1872. He was at various times active as a dramatist, translator, art critic, poet, novelist, and journalist; from 1831–68 was music critic of the London *Athenaeum.* During his extensive travels he heard all the best music of the day and met many musical celebrities; a partisan of Mendelssohn and Spohr, he was intolerant toward new musical ideas and attacked Chopin, Schumann, and particularly Wagner, with extraordinary violence.

WRITINGS: *Music and Manners in France and Germany* (3 vols., London, 1841); *Modern German Music* (2 vols., 1854); *Thirty Years' Musical Recollections* (2 vols., 1862; abridged American ed., N.Y., 1926); an interesting *Autobiography, Memoirs and Letters* (2 vols., 1873; ed. by H.G. Hewlett); *National Music of the World* (1880; ed. by Hewlett; 3rd ed., 1911); *Handel Studies* (1859); a novel, *A Prodigy: A Tale of Music* (3 vols., 1866).

Choron, Alexandre Etienne, French music editor and theorist; b. Caen, Oct. 21, 1771; d. Paris, June 28, 1834. A student of languages, and passionately fond of music, he took interest in music theory and through it in mathematics, which he studied till the age of 25; then, by several years' serious application to the Italian and German theorists, he acquired a thorough knowledge of the theory and practice of music. Becoming (in 1805) a partner in a music publishing firm, he devoted his entire fortune to editing and publishing classic and theoretical works and compositions, meanwhile contributing new works of his own. In 1811 he became a corresponding member of the Académie Française; he was entrusted with the reorganization of the maîtrises (training schools for church choirs), and was appointed conductor of religious festivals. In 1816, as director of the Académie Royale de Musique, he reopened the Cons. (closed in 1815) as the Ecole Royale de Chant et de Déclamation. Losing his directorship (1817) because he favored new works by unknown composers, he established, with a very moderate subsidy, the Institution de Musique Classique et Religieuse, for which he labored indefatigably until the July Revolution (1830).

WRITINGS: *Principes d'accompagnement des écoles d'Italie* (1804); *Principes de composition des écoles d'Italie* (3 vols., 1808; 2nd ed., 6 vols., 1816); *Dictionnaire historique des musiciens* (2 vols., 1810–11; with Fayolle); *Méthode élémentaire de musique et de plainchant* (1811); Francœur's *Traité général des voix et des instruments d'orchestre* (1813); translations of Albrechtsberger's *Gründliche Anweisung zur Komposition* and *Generalbassschule* (1814, 1815; new ed., 1830; Eng. trans. by A. Merrick, 1835) and of Azopardi's *Musico prattico* (1816); *Méthode concertante de musique à plusieurs parties* (written for his Cons., 1818; new ed., 1833); *Méthode de plainchant* (1818); *Manuel complet de musique vocale et instrumentale, ou Encyclopédie musicale* (1836–39; 6 vols. letter press and 5 vols. plates; with Lafage).

BIBLIOGRAPHY: L.E. Gautier, *Eloge de Choron* (Caen, 1845); H. Réty, *Notice historique sur Choron et son école* (Paris, 1873); J. Carlez, *Choron, Sa vie et ses travaux* (Caen, 1880); G. Vauthier, *Choron sous l'Empire* (Poitiers, 1909).

Chorzempa, Daniel, American organist, harpsichordist, pianist, and composer; b. Minneapolis, Dec. 7, 1944. He was educated at the Univ. of Minnesota (Ph.D., 1971, with a dissertation on Reubke); then went to Germany and enrolled at the Hochschule für Musik in Cologne; became a member of the Studio für Elektronische Musik in Cologne in 1970, and composed works for the medium. He subsequently began a career as an organist, and made several wide-ranging tours giving solo recitals.

Chotzinoff, Samuel, American pianist and music critic; b. Vitebsk, Russia, July 4, 1889; d. New York, Feb. 9, 1964. He was brought to America as a child; studied piano with Oscar Shack and music theory with Daniel Gregory Mason at Columbia Univ., graduating in 1912. He subsequently became an expert accompanist; toured with Zimbalist and Heifetz. In 1925 he turned to music criticism; served as music critic of the *N.Y. World* (1925–30) and the *N.Y. Post* (1934–41). He then occupied various teaching and administrative positions; was for several years music director of the National Broadcasting Co. He wrote a novel on Beethoven's life, entitled *Eroica;* a book of reminiscences, *A Lost Paradise* (1955); and a monograph, *Toscanini, An Intimate Portrait* (N.Y., 1956). His autobiographical *Days at the Morn* and *A Little Night Music* were publ. posthumously in 1964.

Chouquet, (Adolphe-) Gustave, French writer on music; b. Le Havre, April 16, 1819; d. Paris, Jan. 30, 1886. He lived in America as a music teacher from 1840–56; in 1860 went to Paris. He twice won the Prix Bordin: in 1864 for a history of music from the 14th to the 18th century, and in 1868 for *Histoire de la musique dramatique en France depuis ses origines jusqu'à nos jours* (publ. 1873). From 1871, he was custodian of the collection of instruments in the Cons.; in 1875 he publ. a catalogue of them (2nd ed., 1884; supplemented by L. Pillaut, 1894, 1899, 1903).

Chou Wen-Chung, remarkable Chinese-American composer; b. Cheefoo, June 29, 1923 (corresponding to May 16, 1923, according to the lunar calendar in the Chinese Year of the Bear). He studied at the National Univ. of Chungking (1941–45); then went to the U.S.; took private lessons with Varèse in N.Y. and with N. Slonimsky in Boston; then entered Columbia Univ. where he was a student of Otto Luening (M.A., 1954). In 1957 he received a Guggenheim fellowship. In 1964 he joined the faculty of Columbia Univ. as a teacher of composition; became a prof. of music in 1972; was named vice-dean in 1976. His music combines Chinese elements of structure and scale formation with free dissonant counterpoint related to the theory of "organized sound" of Varèse. WORKS: *Landscapes* for Orch. (San Francisco, Nov. 19, 1953); *7 Poems of the T'ang Dynasty* for Tenor, 7 Wind Instruments, Piano, and Percussion (N.Y., March 16, 1952); *And the Fallen Petals,* triolet for Orch. (Louisville, Ky., Feb. 9, 1955); *In the Mode of Shang* for Chamber Orch. (N.Y., Feb. 2, 1957); *Metaphors* for Wind Instruments (1960–61); *Cursive* for Flute and Piano (1963); *Riding the Wind* for Wind Ensemble (1964); *Pien* for Piano, Wind Instruments, and Percussion (1966); *Yun* for Wind Instruments, 2 Pianos, and Percussion (1969). In 1968 Wen-Chung Chou completed Varèse's unfinished work *Nocturnal* for Voices and Instruments.

Christian, Charlie, black American guitarist and blues singer; b. Bonham, Texas, July 29, 1916; d. New York, March 2, 1942. His parents and his 4 brothers were musicians; as a child he played in the family band; at maturity he began playing electric guitar; from 1939 to 1941 he played in Benny Goodman's Sextet; later played with Dizzy Gillespie and Thelonious Monk. He was stricken with a paralyzing ailment and died at the age of 25.

Christiani, Adolf Friedrich, German pianist; b. Kassel, March 8, 1836; d. Elizabeth, N.J., Feb. 10, 1885. He went to London in 1855; then to America, teaching in Poughkeepsie, Pittsburgh, Cincinnati, and N.Y. He wrote a theoretical work, *The Principles of Musical Expression in Pianoforte-playing* (N.Y., 1886; German ed., Leipzig, as *Das Verständnis im Klavierspiel*).

Christiansen, Fredrik Melius, Norwegian-American choral conductor; b. Eidsvold, April 1, 1871; d. Northfield, Minn., June 1, 1955. He emigrated to the U.S. in 1888; studied at the Northwestern Cons. of Music; then went to Germany, where he took courses at the Leipzig Cons. (1897–99). Returning to America, he served as director of the School of Music at St. Olaf's College in Northfield, Minn.; he organized the important St. Olaf's Lutheran Choir there. He publ. several useful choral collections: *St. Olaf Choir Series* (6 vols., 1920); *Young Men's Choral Assembly for Schools* (1936); edited *50 Famous Hymns for Women's Voices* (1914); and publ. *Practical Modulation* (1916).
BIBLIOGRAPHY: L.N. Bergmann, *Music Master of the Middle West* (Minneapolis, 1944).

Christiansen, Olaf, American choral conductor of Norwegian descent, son of **Fredrik Melius Christiansen;** b. Minneapolis, Aug. 12, 1901; d. Northfield, Minn., April 12, 1984. He was trained by his father, and upon his death in 1955 succeeded him as director of the St. Olaf Lutheran Choir in Northfield, remaining at this post until his own retirement in 1968. He was also co-founder of the Christiansen Choral School, which had a very large attendance among choral conductors.

Christie, Winifred, English pianist; b. Stirling, Feb. 26, 1882; d. London, Feb. 8, 1965. She was the 2nd wife of the Hungarian pianist Emanuel Moór and made loyal propaganda for the Moór Duplex Piano, consisting of a double keyboard with a coupler between the 2 manuals. She was not successful in her task.

Christoff, Boris, eminent Bulgarian bass-baritone; b. Plovdiv, May 18, 1914. He studied law, and at the same time sang in a chorus in Sofia. A private stipend enabled him to go to Rome, where he studied voice with Stracciari. In 1946 he made a successful debut in a solo recital in Rome, and in 1947 sang at La Scala in Milan. He excelled particularly in the role of Boris Godunov, which he sang in Russia; his interpretation recalled that of Chaliapin; he made his American debut in that role at the San Francisco Opera House on Sept. 25, 1956 with great acclaim. His operatic repertoire includes about 40 parts in 6 languages.

BIBLIOGRAPHY: A monograph on Christoff by O. Deikowa was publ. in Bulgarian (Sofia, 1966); see also F. Barker, *Voice of the Opera: Boris Christoff* (London, 1951); G. Lauri-Volpi, *Voci parallele: Boris Christoff* (Milan, 1955).

Christoff, Dimiter, Bulgarian composer; b. Sofia, Oct. 2, 1933. He studied composition with Goleminov at the Bulgarian State Cons. (1951–56); later taught there. Like so many other Bulgarian composers, he utilized in his music the rich motivic resources and asymmetrical rhythmic figures of Balkan folk songs; however, these usages are not literal in his compositions, which are modernistic in their technique.

WORKS: Piano Concerto (1955); Sinfonietta for String Orch. (1956); *Poem* for Orch. (1957); 3 symphs. (1959, 1964, 1968); *Overture* (1961); *Symphonic Episodes* (1962); Violin Concerto (1966); *Chamber Suite* for Flute, Piccolo, and Chamber Orch. (1966); Cello Concerto (1969; Sofia, March 10, 1971); *Concert Miniatures* for Orch. or Piano (1970); *Overture with Fanfares* (1973); *Suite* for Wind Quintet (1953); *2 Dances* for Trumpet and Piano (1960); Solo Cello Sonata (1965); Concerto for 3 Small Drums and 5 Instruments (1967); String Quartet (1970); Quartet for Flute, Viola, Harp, and Harpsichord (1972); 4 piano sonatas (1962, 1974, 1974, 1974); choruses; songs. He publ. 6 theoretical works, including *Hypothesis about the Polyphonic Structure* (Sofia, 1970) and *The Composer and the Public Spirit* (Sofia, 1975).

Christopher, Cyril (Stanley), English organist and composer; b. Oldbury, Worcestershire, June 23, 1897. He studied organ with Alfred Hollins; held numerous posts as a church organist and a choral conductor; also taught music theory at the Birmingham School of Music. He wrote mainly for chorus; among his instrumental works are Fantasy-Trio for Clarinet, Violin, and Piano (1939); Trio for Oboe, Bassoon, and Piano (1954); Oboe Sonata (1956); Serenade for Wind Instruments, Cello, and Double Bass (1967); 2 short symph. poems, *Midsummer Night* and *The Lone Shore.*

Christoskov, Peter, Bulgarian composer and violinist; b. Sofia, March 8, 1917. He studied violin at the Bulgarian State Cons. in Sofia, graduating in 1936; then went to Berlin, where he continued his violin studies; returning to Bulgaria, he was appointed head of the instrumental dept. of the Bulgarian State Cons. In his own works he often applies the asymmetrical rhythms of Bulgarian folk songs, using dissonant harmonies for coloristic effects.

WORKS: *Moto Perpetuo* for String Orch. (1956); 2 violin concertos (1958, 1961); Concerto for Orch. (1964); *Children's Album* for Violin and Chamber Orch. (1966); Aria and Toccata for Violin and Orch. (1967); *Concerto-Improvisation* for Cello and Orch. (1970); Piano Concerto (1972); *Symphonic Sketches* (1973); *Concerto-Poem* for Cello and Orch. (1973).

Christou, Jani, remarkable Greek composer; b. Heliopolis, Egypt, Jan. 8, 1926, to Greek parents; d. in an automobile accident, with his wife, near Athens, on his 44th birthday, Jan. 8, 1970. He studied at Victoria College in Alexandria; then took courses in philosophy under Wittgenstein at King's College in Cambridge, England (M.A., 1948); concurrently studied composition with Hans Redlich in Letchworth (1945–48); then enrolled in the summer courses of the Accademia Musicale Chigiana in Siena (1949–50); during the same period he attended Karl Jung's lectures on psychology in Zürich. Christou returned to Alexandria in 1951; then lived on his family estate on the island of Chios. He evolved a system of composition embracing the totality of human and metaphysical expression, forming a "philosophical structure" for which he designed a surrealistic graphic notation involving a "psychoid factor," symbolized by the Greek letter psi; aleatory practices are indicated by the drawing of a pair of dice; a sudden stop, by a dagger, etc. His score *Enantiodromia (Opposed Pathways)* for Orch. (1965; revised 1968; first perf. in Oakland, Calif., Feb. 18, 1969), in such a graphic notation, is reproduced in the avant-garde publication *Source* 6 (1969). His notation also includes poetry, choreographic acting, special lighting, film, and projection meant to envelop the listener on all sides. At his death he left sketches for a set of 130 multimedia compositions of a category he called *Anaparastasis* ("proto-performances, meant to revive primeval rituals as adapted to modern culture").

WORKS: *Phoenix Music* for Orch. (1948–49); Symph. No. 1 (1950; London, April 29, 1951); *Latin Mass* for Chorus, Brass, and Percussion (1953; posthumous, Athens, Sept. 26, 1971); *David's Psalms* for Baritone, Chorus, and Orch. (1953); *6 Songs* for Voice and Piano, to poems by T.S. Eliot (1955; orchestrated 1957); Symph. No. 2 for Chorus and Orch. (1954–58; uses an adapted version of the *Latin Mass* as its finale); *Gilgamesh,* oratorio (1958); *Patterns and Permutations* for Orch. (1960; Athens, March 11, 1963); Symph. No. 3 (1959–62); Toccata for Piano and Orch. (1962); *The 12 Keys* for Mezzo-soprano and Chamber Ensemble (1962); *The Breakdown,* opera (1964); *Tongues of Fire,* Pentecost oratorio (1964; English Bach Festival, Oxford, June 27, 1964); *Mys-*

terion, oratorio for Soli, 3 Choirs, Actors, Orch., and Tape, to ancient Egyptian myths (1965–66); *Praxis for 12* for 11 Strings and Pianist-Percussionist-Conductor (1966; Athens, April 18, 1966; an alternate version exists, titled simply *Praxis,* for 44 Strings and Pianist-Percussionist-Conductor); *Oresteia,* unfinished "super-opera," after Aeschylus (1967–70). Performable works from the cycle *Anaparastasis* are: *The Strychnine Lady* for Female Viola Player, 2 groups of Massed Strings, Brass, Percussion, Tapes, Metal Sheet, Sound-producing Objects and Toys, Red Cloth, and 5 Actors (Athens, April 3, 1967); *Anaparastasis I (Astron)* for Baritone and Instrumental Ensemble (Munich, Nov. 12, 1968); *Anaparastasis III (The Pianist)* for Actor, Variable Instrumental Ensemble, and 3 Stereo Tapes (Munich, Nov. 13, 1969); *Epicycle* for Variable Instrumental Ensemble that may take a chiliad or a hebdomad, a nanosecond or a quindecillion of non-zero moments to perform (concise version, Athens, Dec. 15, 1968; extended version, Athens, Dec. 20, 1968); stage music for *The Persians* (1965), *The Frogs* (1966), and *Oedipus Rex* (1969).
BIBLIOGRAPHY: J. Papaioannou, *Jani Christou and the Metaphysics of Music* (London, 1970).

Christov, Dobri, noted Bulgarian composer; b. Varna, Bulgaria, Dec. 14, 1875; d. Sofia, Jan. 23, 1941. He was first a schoolteacher; then a pupil of Dvořák at Prague; spent the greater part of his career as director and teacher of composition of the Sofia Cons. He composed orch. suites based on folk tunes; an overture, *Jvailo;* the ballad *Zar Samuil;* 50 Bulgarian choral songs; he also edited Bulgarian folk songs.

Christy, Edwin P., American minstrel show promoter and performer; b. Philadelphia, Nov. 28, 1815; d. New York, May 21, 1862. In 1842 he founded the Christy Minstrels, which played a decisive role in the formation of a typical American variety show, consisting of songs, comic skits, and short plays and parodies. He opened his enterprise in Buffalo; in 1846 he introduced his troupe in N.Y. and played there for 8 years, then went to San Francisco; retired from performing in 1855. It was Christy who had Stephen Foster write his most famous "Ethiopian" songs for him; as was common in his time, Christy appropriated the authorship of these songs, but was decent enough to give Foster credit when the songs became greatly popular. Christy became mentally deranged and ended his life by jumping out of a window.

Chrysander, (Karl Franz) Friedrich, eminent German musicologist and editor; b. Lübtheen, Mecklenburg, July 8, 1826; d. Bergedorf, near Hamburg, Sept. 3, 1901. He began his career as a private tutor; in 1855 he received his Ph.D. from Rostock Univ. His major undertaking was a biography of Handel, but it remained incomplete, bringing the account only to 1740 (3 vols., 1858–67; reprint, 1966). With Gottfried Gervinus, the literary historian, he organized the Deutsche Händelgesellschaft in 1856 for the purpose of publishing a complete edition of

Handel's works. After the first vol. was issued in 1858, disagreements among the members caused Chrysander and Gervinus to carry the task alone. King George of Hannover granted them, in 1860, an annual subvention of 1,000 thaler, which they continued to receive until the annexation of Hannover by Prussia in 1866; in 1870, Prussia renewed the subvention from Hannover; after the death of Gervinus in 1871, Chrysander continued the task alone. The resulting publication, *Georg Friedrich Händels Werke: Ausgabe der Drutschen Handelgesellschaft* (100 vols., Leipzig and Bergedorf bei Hamburg, 1858–94; 6 supplementary vols., 1888–1902), was a monumental achievement, but it was superseded by the new critical edition edited by M. Schneider and R. Steglich (Kassel, 1955—). Chrysander also served as editor of the *Allgemeine Musikalische Zeitung* (1868–71 and 1875–82), to which he contributed many articles. He edited an important collection of essays in the *Jahrbuch für musikalische Wissenschaft* in 1863, and again in 1867. In 1885 he helped to found (with Philipp Spitta and Guido Adler) the *Vierteljahrsschrift für Musikwissenschaft,* and contributed to it until 1894. His other writings include *Über die Molltonart in den Volksgesängen* (Schwerin, 1853), *Über das Oratorium* (Schwerin, 1853), and *Händels biblische Oratorien in geschichtlicher Betrachtung* (Hamburg, 1897; 4th ed., 1922).
BIBLIOGRAPHY: A detailed biography and bibliography is found in R. Schaal, "Chrysander, Karl Franz Friedrich," in *Die Musik in Geschichte und Gegenwart;* see also B. Baselt, "Beiträge zur Chrysander-Forschung," *Händel-Jahrbuch* (1969/70).

Chrysanthos of Madytos, learned Greek cleric and music theorist; b. Madytos, Turkey (hence, known as "of Madytos"); c.1770; d. Bursa, Turkey, 1846. He was bishop of the Greek Orthodox Church in Istanbul, and taught at the music school of the Patriarchate there from 1815 to 1821. He subsequently served as bishop in Durazzo, in Smyrna, and finally in Bursa, where he died. He undertook the reform of the post-Byzantine music notation by reducing the number of neumes and interval indexes; also revived the division of scales into the ancient Greek modes—diatonic, chromatic, and enharmonic. He publ. 2 manuals in the Greek language: *Introduction into the Theory and Practice of Church Music* (Paris, 1821) and *Great Music Instruction* (Trieste, 1832).

Chueca, Federico, Spanish composer of zarzuelas; b. Madrid, May 5, 1846; d. there, June 20, 1908. He was a medical student; organized a band at the Univ. of Madrid; also conducted theater orchs. He began to compose for the stage in collaboration with Valverde, who helped him to harmonize and orchestrate his melodies. Thanks to his prodigious facility, he wrote a great number of zarzuelas, of which *La gran via,* produced in Madrid (July 2, 1886), became his greatest success, obtaining nearly 1,000 performances in Madrid alone; it has also been performed many times in Latin America and the U.S. The march from his zarzuela *Cadiz* served for a time as the Spanish national anthem; dances from his *El año pasado por agua* and *Locuras madrileñas* also enjoyed great popularity. Chueca is regarded as one of the creators of the "género chico" (light genre) of Spanish stage music.

BIBLIOGRAPHY: M. Zurita, *Historia del género chico* (Madrid, 1920); J. Delito y Piñuela, *Origen y apogeo del género chico* (Madrid, 1949).

Chung, Kyung-Wha, brilliant Korean violinist; sister of **Myung-Wha Chung** and **Myung-Whun Chung;** b. Seoul, March 26, 1948. She began to study the violin as a small child; made her orch. debut in Seoul at the age of 9, playing the Mendelssohn Concerto; in 1961 she went to the U.S., where she studied with Ivan Galamian at the Juilliard School of Music in N.Y. In 1967 she shared first prize with Pinchas Zukerman in the Leventritt Competition. In 1968 she appeared as soloist with the N.Y. Phil.; made her European debut in 1970 with the London Symph. Orch. She then embarked upon a wide-flung concert tour in Europe and Asia. She gave numerous trio concerts with her sister and brother, and also appeared as a soloist with her brother acting as conductor.

Chung, Myung-Wha, Korean cellist; sister of **Kyung-Wha Chung** and **Myung-Whun Chung;** b. Seoul, March 19, 1944. She studied cello in Seoul; made her orch. debut there in 1957; in 1961 she went to the U.S., where she studied at the Juilliard School of Music in N.Y.; then attended a master class given by Gregor Piatigorsky at the Univ. of Southern Calif. in Los Angeles. She appeared as soloist with orchs. in Europe and America; also played trio concerts with her sister and brother.

Chung, Myung-Whun, Korean pianist and conductor; brother of **Myung-Wha Chung,** and **Kyung-Wha Chung;** b. Seoul, Jan. 22, 1953. He began to play piano as a child in Seoul; then went to the U.S., where he studied at the Mannes College of Music; he received his diplomas in piano and conducting from the Juilliard School of Music in 1974. In 1971 he made his conducting debut in Seoul; in 1974 he won 2nd prize in the International Tchaikovsky Competition in Moscow as a pianist. He subsequently engaged in a double career as pianist and conductor; from 1978–81 he served as assistant conductor of the Los Angeles Phil. Orch.; also gave trio concerts with his sisters.

Chvála, Emanuel, Czech critic and composer; b. Prague, Jan. 1, 1851; d. there, Oct. 28, 1924. He was mainly active as a critic; he publ. articles in Czech and in German dealing with Czech music, of which *Ein Vierteljahrhundert böhmischer Musik* (Prague, 1887) was a pioneer work. He was also the composer of an opera, *Zaboj,* written in 1906–7, and produced in Prague on March 9, 1918.

Chwatal, Franz Xaver, Bohemian pianist and pedagogue; b. Rumburg, June 19, 1808; d. Elmen, June 24, 1879. He settled in Magdeburg as a piano teacher; publ. a great number of piano pieces; his 2 piano methods were much used.

Chybinski, Adolf, eminent Polish musicologist; b. Cracow, April 29, 1880; d. Poznan, Oct. 31, 1952. He studied at the Univ. of Cracow; later in Munich with Sandberger and Kroyer (1904–8); also with Thuille (1905–7); obtained his Dr.Phil. in Munich (1908). In 1917 he was an instructor at Lwow Univ.; in 1921, a prof. there; from 1916 to 1928 also a prof. of theory at the Cons.; in 1924, music counselor for the Polish State Art Dept. In 1945 he became head of the musicological inst. at Poznan Univ.

WRITINGS: (mostly in Polish): *Wagner's Meistersinger* (1908); *The Organ Tablatures of Joh. v. Lublin* (2 vols., 1911–14); *J.S. Bach* (2 vols., 1913); *Music Instruments of the Tatra* (1924–27); *Cracovian Music in the 17th Century* (Tarnov, 1928); *Musical Relations between Poland and France in the 16th Century* (Poznan, 1929); *Dictionary of Ancient Polish Musicians before 1800* (in Polish; Cracow, 1949). He also trans. German music books into Polish (Hausegger's *Musik als Ausdruck*); ed. Publications de Musique Ancienne Polonaise (17th vol. publ. in Warsaw, 1938; contains Bartolomei Perkiel's *Missa Pulcherrima ad instar Praenestini*).

Ciamaga, Gustav, Canadian electronic composer; b. London, Ontario, April 10, 1930. He studied music theory with Weinzweig and Beckwith at the Univ. of Toronto (1953–56); studied composition and musicology with Arthur Berger, Harold Shapero, and Irving Fine at Brandeis Univ.; in 1963 he was appointed to the music faculty at the Univ. of Toronto, where he is director of its electronic music studio. His electronic scores include: *Ottawa 1967* (1966); *Curtain Raiser* (1969); *One-Part Invention* (1965); 8 *2-Part Inventions* (1965–70); *Ragamuffin Nos. 1* and *2* (1967); he wrote several scores of computer music, among them *Canon for Stravinsky* (1972); for voice, instruments, and tape he composed *Solipsism while Dying* (1972).

Ciccolini, Aldo, Italian pianist; b. Naples, Aug. 15, 1925. He studied with Paolo Denza at the Naples Cons.; in 1949 he was the winner of the Long-Thibaud prize in Paris. He toured in France, Spain, and South America; on Nov. 2, 1950, he made his American debut with Tchaikovsky's Concerto No. 1 (N.Y. Phil.). He has since appeared with several major orchs. in the U.S., and has also continued his concerts in Europe. In 1971 he was appointed prof. at the Paris Cons. Ciccolini possesses a virtuoso technique combined with a lyrical sense of phrasing.

Ciconia, Jean (Johannes), Walloon theorist and composer; b. Liège, c.1335; d. Padua, between Dec. 11 and Dec. 24, 1411. Little is known about his life; he was in Italy from 1358 to 1367; was in Liège from 1372 until 1401. In 1402 he went to Padua, where he was a canon. A treatise by him entitled *De proportionibus musicae*, which he completed shortly before his death, is extant. Several of his musical compositions are preserved in Italian libraries; modern reprints are in Denkmäler der Tonkunst in Österreich (vols. VII and XXXI). Ciconia's significance lies in his early use of musical devices that did not become current until much later; he applied the technique of French isorhythmic style as well as canonic imitation.

BIBLIOGRAPHY: Suzanne Clercx, *Johannes Ciconia de Leodio* (Amsterdam, 1953); see also her addendum, "Question de Chronologie," *Revue Belge de Musicologie* (1955); S. Clercx, *Johannes Ciconia: Un Musicien liegeois et son temps* (includes valuable documentation, thematic catalogue, and works; Brussels, 1960.)

Ciesinski, Katherine, American mezzo-soprano; b. Wilmington, Del., Oct. 13, 1950. After vocal studies, she won first prizes at the Geneva International Competition and the Concours International de Chant in Paris; she then appeared in opera at the Spoleto Festival, the Santa Fe Opera, and the Chicago Lyric Opera; also sang duo recitals with her sister, the American soprano **Kristine Ciesinski** (b. Wilmington, Del., July 5, 1952), who also was a winner at the Geneva International Competition.

Cifra, Antonio, Italian composer; b. probably near Terracina, 1584; d. Loreto, Oct. 2, 1629. He was a choirboy in the church of San Luigi dei Francesi in Rome; in 1594–96, was a pupil of G.B. Nanino; also studied with Palestrina; in 1609, was maestro di cappella at the Collegio Germanico in Rome; in 1609–22 and from 1626, was maestro di cappella at Santa Casa di Loreto; in 1623–26, was maestro di cappella at San Giovanni in Laterano, Rome. A prolific composer, he is considered one of the best of the Roman school; he publ. (between 1600 and 1638) 5 books of motets; 3 of Psalms; 5 of masses; 10 sets of *concerti ecclesiastici* (over 200 numbers); many more motets and Psalms (in 2–12 parts); antiphons; litanies; madrigals; ricercari; *Scherzi ed arie a 1, 2, 3 e 4 voci, per cantar del clavicembalo;* etc.

BIBLIOGRAPHY: Article by A. Cametti, in *Rivista Musicale Italiana* XXI (1915).

Cigna, Gina, French soprano; b. Paris, March 6, 1900. She studied at the Paris Cons.; made her operatic debut at La Scala in Milan in 1927; returned every season from 1929 to 1943; sang at the Metropolitan Opera in N.Y. in 1937 (debut as Aida, Feb. 6, 1937). After a few more performances in N.Y., she returned to Europe, and settled in Milan as a voice teacher. She abandoned her singing career after World War II, following an auto accident. From 1953 to 1957 she taught at the Royal Cons. in Toronto.

Cikker, Ján, eminent Slovak composer; b. Banská Bystrica, July 29, 1911. He studied composition at the Prague Cons. with Jaroslav Křička and Vítězslav Novák; also took a course in conducting with Felix Weingartner in Vienna. In 1938–51 he was a prof. of theory at the Bratislava Cons.; then was a prof. of composition at the Bratislava Academy. An exceptionally prolific composer, Cikker is distinguished particularly in his works for the musical theater; his operas enjoyed greatly merited success in their productions in Czechoslovakia and Germany. In his music he has developed an idiom deeply rooted in the melorhythmic patterns of Slovak folk songs, while his harmonic and contrapuntal treatment is marked by effective modernistic devices, making use of unresolved dissonances and atonal melodic patterns.

WORKS: 6 operas: *Juro Jánošík* (1950–53; Bratislava, Nov. 10, 1954); *Beg Bajazid (Prince Bajazid;* Bratislava, Feb. 16, 1957); *Mr. Scrooge,* after Dickens's *A Christmas Carol* (1958–59; produced in a German version under the title *Abend, Nacht und Morgen,* Kassel, Oct. 5, 1963); *Vzkriesenie (Resurrection),* after Tolstoy's novel (1961; Prague, May 18, 1962; written in a highly tense, atonal, and Romantically expressive modern idiom); *Hra o láske a smrti (A Play about Love and Death),* after Romain Rolland (1967; Munich, Aug. 1, 1969); *Coriolanus,* after Shakespeare (1972; Prague, March 21, 1974); Symph. in C (1930); *Epitaph,* symph. poem (1931); *Symphonic Prologue* (1934); *Capriccio* for Orch. (1936); *Spring Symphony* (1937); Sinfonietta (1940; instrumentation of his Piano Sonatina); cantata, *Cantus Filiorum* (1940); symph. trilogy, *About Life: Léto (Summer;* 1941), *Vojak a matka (The Soldier and the Mother;* 1943), and *Ráno (Morning;* 1944–46); Piano Concertino (1942); *Slovak Suite* for Orch. (1942); *The Bucolic Poem,* ballet music (1944); *Spomienky (Recollections)* for 5 Wind Instruments and String Orch. (1947); *Dupák,* folk dance for Chamber Orch. (1950); *Dramatic Fantasia* for Orch. (1957); *Orchestrálne štúdie k činohre (Orchestral Studies on a Drama;* 1965); *Hommage à Beethoven* for Orch. (1970); *Variations on a Slovak Folk Song* for Orch. (1971; also for Piano); *Epitaph (Over an Old Trench),* symph. poem (1973); *Symphony 1945* (1974–75; Bratislava, May 22, 1975); 2 string quartets (1935); Piano Sonatina (1933); 3 Etudes *(Tatra Mountain Streams)* for Piano (1954); *What Children Told Me* for Piano (1957); film music.

BIBLIOGRAPHY: J. Šamko, *Jan Cikker* (Bratislava, 1955).

Cilèa, Francesco, Italian opera composer; b. Palmi, Calabria, July 23, 1866; d. Varazze, Nov. 20, 1950. He studied at the Naples Cons. (1881–89) with Cesi (piano) and Serrao (composition); taught piano there (1894–96); then harmony at the Istituto Musicale in Florence (1896–1904); was head of the Palermo Cons. (1913–16); director of the Majella Cons. in Naples (1916–35). He was a member of the Reale Accademia Musicale in Florence (1898) and a knight of the Order of the Crown of Italy (1893).

WORKS: Operas: *Gina* (Naples, Feb. 9, 1889); *La Tilda* (Florence, April 7, 1892); *L'Arlesiana,* after Daudet (Milan, Nov. 27, 1897; later revised from 4 to 3 acts and produced in Milan, Oct. 22, 1898); *Adriana Lecouvreur,* after Scribe (Milan, Nov. 6, 1902; Covent Garden, Nov. 8, 1904; Metropolitan Opera, Nov. 26, 1906; his most famous opera); *Gloria* (La Scala, Milan, April 15, 1907); *Il matrimonio Sel-*

vaggio (1909); *Poema sinfonico* for Solo, Chorus, and Orch. (Genoa, July 12, 1913); Piano Trio (1886); Cello Sonata (1888); Variations for Violin and Piano (1931); piano pieces; songs.

BIBLIOGRAPHY: Ettore Moschino, *Sulle opere di Francesco Cilèa* (Milan, 1932); C.P. Gaianus, *Francesco Cilèa e la sua nuova ora* (Bologna, 1939); T. d'Amico, *Francesco Cilèa* (Milan, 1960).

Cillario, Carlo Felice, Argentine-born Italian conductor; b. San Rafael, Argentina, Feb. 7, 1915. He studied violin and composition at the Cons. in Bologna; then went to Russia to continue his studies at the Odessa Cons. After World War II, he made concert apppearence in many countries. He is highly regarded as a competent opera conductor.

Cima, Giovanni Paolo, Italian organist and composer; b. Milan, c.1570; d. during the first half of the 17th century. In 1609 he was organist at the Cathedral of Milan. Publications of his works, including *Concerti ecclesiastici* and motets, appeared between 1598 and 1622. His *Partito de Ricercari e Canzoni alla francese* (Milan, 1606) is a keyboard collection with an appendix containing rules for tuning keyboard instruments. The *canzoni alla francese* of this collection are specially written for keyboard, and the ricercari are highly developed in their use of imitation. A modern reprint of *Ricercare per organo* is contained in L. Torchi's *L'Arte Musicale in Italia* (vol. III).

Cimadoro, Giovanni Battista, Italian composer; b. Venice, 1761; d. Bath, England, Feb. 27, 1805. After early successes in Italy, where he produced an opera, *Pimmaglione (Pygmalion;* Venice, Jan. 26, 1790), he settled in London; several arias from the opera were publ. in London, and acquired considerable popularity. While in England, he used a shortened form of his name, **Cimador.**

Cimara, Pietro, Italian conductor; b. Rome, Nov. 10, 1887; d. Milan, Oct. 1, 1967. He was educated at the Santa Cecilia Academy in Rome; made his debut as a conductor in 1916 in Rome. In 1933 he began conducting at the Metropolitan Opera; remained at this post for 26 years. He composed many songs, which were publ. in Italy and America.

Cimarosa, Domenico, eminent Italian composer; b. Aversa, near Naples, Dec. 17, 1749; d. Venice, Jan. 11, 1801. The son of a poor mason, and orphaned early, he attended the charity school of the Minorites; his first music teacher was Polcano, organist of the monastery. His talent was so marked that in 1761 he obtained a free scholarship to the Cons. di Santa Maria di Loreto, where he was taught singing by Manna and Sacchini, counterpoint by Fenaroli, and composition by Piccinni. In 1770 his oratorio *Giuditta* was performed in Rome; in 1772 he produced his first opera, *Le stravaganze del Conte,* at Naples, with moderate success. But with *La finta parigina,* given the next season at the Teatro Nuovo in Naples, he was fairly launched on a dramatic career singularly free from artistic reverses. His ease and rapidity of composition were phenomenal; in 29 years he wrote nearly 80 operas. His fame grew steadily, eventually rivaling that of Paisiello. In 1778 Cimarosa brought out *L'Italiana in Londra* in Rome, and lived, until 1781, alternately in Rome and Naples; following the custom of the period, he wrote one opera after another specially for the city in which it was to be performed. His speed of composition was such that during the year 1781 he brought out 2 operas in Naples, one in Rome, and 2 in Turin. His works became known far beyond the bounds of Italy; they were performed not only by Italian opera troupes in all European capitals, but also by foreign opera companies, in translation. After Paisiello's return from St. Petersburg, where he had served from 1776 to 1785 as court composer, his post was offered to Cimarosa. He accepted, and set out for St. Petersburg in the autumn of 1787. His journey there was like a triumphant procession; at the courts of Florence, Vienna, and Warsaw, he was overwhelmed with attentions; and he arrived in St. Petersburg on Dec. 2, 1787, wayworn and suffering from the wintry weather, but confident of success. Here he produced 3 operas, and during the 3 years of his stay wrote various other compositions for the court and nobility, including a ballet, *La felicità inaspettata* (Feb. 24, 1788), and a dramatic cantata, *Atene edificata* (June 29, 1788). But as Catherine the Great did not care for his choral works, he was replaced by Sarti, and in 1791 he left Russia; in the autumn of that year he arrived in Vienna, where Emperor Leopold engaged him at a salary of 12,000 florins as Kapellmeister. At Vienna, at the age of 42, he brought out his masterpiece, *Il matrimonio segreto* (Feb. 7, 1792), the success of which eclipsed not only that of his former works but that of the works of all rivals, not excepting Mozart. It is probably the sole survivor, on the present-day stage, of all Cimarosa's dramatic works. Cimarosa remained long enough in Vienna to write 2 more operas; 1793 found him once more at home in Naples, where his *Il matrimonio segreto* aroused unexampled enthusiasm, having 67 consecutive performances, the illustrious composer himself playing the cembalo for the first 7 representations. In 1794 he visited Venice to bring out *Gli Orazi e Curiazi;* in 1796 and 1798 he was in Rome, periodically returning to Naples, and all the time actively engaged in operatic composition. In 1798, he was seriously ill at Naples; the year after, having openly taken part in the Neapolitan revolutionary demonstration on the entrance of the French army into the city, he was imprisoned for a number of days. He then went to Venice, and was at work on a new opera, *Artemisia,* when death suddenly overtook him. It was rumored abroad that he had been poisoned by order of Queen Caroline of Naples, as a dangerous revolutionist; the rumor was so persistent, and popular embitterment so great, that the Pope's personal physician, Piccioli, was sent to make an examination; according to his sworn statement, Cimarosa died of a gangrenous abdominal tumor.

Comedy opera was Cimarosa's forte: in his happiest moments he rivals Mozart; even in "opera seria" many of his efforts are worthy of a place in the repertoire. The fluidity and fecundity of his melodic vein, his supreme command of form, and his masterly control of orch. resources still excite astonishment and admiration. He was the peer of his great Italian contemporary Paisiello.

WORKS: Of the 76 operas known to be his, some of the finest are: *La finta parigina* (Naples, 1773); *Il Fanatico per gli antichi Romani* (Naples, 1777); *L'italiana in Londra* (Rome, Dec. 28, 1778); *L'infedeltà fedele* (Naples, July 20, 1779); *Caio Mario* (Rome, Jan. 1780); *Il convito di pietra* (Venice, Dec. 27, 1781); *Giannina e Bernardone* (Venice, Nov., 1781); *La ballerina amante* (Naples, 1782); *Artaserse* (Turin, Dec. 26, 1784); *Le trame deluse* (Naples, Sept. 1786); *L'Impressario in angustie* (Naples, Oct. 1786); *Le vergine del sole* (St. Petersburg, Nov. 6, 1789); *Il matrimonio segreto* (Vienna, Feb. 7, 1792; given in Eng. with great success at the Metropolitan Opera in 1937); *Le astuzie femminili* (Naples, Aug. 16, 1794); *Orazi e Curiazi* (Venice, Dec. 26, 1796). He also produced at least 3 oratorios; several cantatas; masses in 4 parts, with instrumental accompaniment; Psalms, motets, Requiems, arias, cavatinas, solfeggi, and a great variety of other vocal works; 7 symphs.; cembalo sonatas (of which 32 were ed. and publ. by F. Boghen, Paris, 1926).

BIBLIOGRAPHY: P. Cambiasi, *Notizie sulla vita e sulle opere di D. Cimarosa* (Milan, 1901); F. Polidoro, "La vita e le opere di D. Cimarosa," in *Atti del' Accademia Pontiniana* (1902); A. della Corte, *L'opera comica italiana nel 1700* (1925); R. Vitale, *D. Cimarosa* (Aversa, 1929); G. Biamonti, *Il matrimonio segreto* (Rome, 1930); M. Tibaldi Chiesa, *Cimarosa e il suo tempo* (Milan, 1939); Carl Engel, "A Note on Cimarosa's *Il matrimonio segreto*," *Musical Quarterly* (April 1947); A. Mooser, *Annales de la musique et des musiciens en Russie au XVIIIe siècle* (Geneva, 1951; pp. 451-55); E. Ferrari Barassi, "Cimarosa clavicembalista," in *Scritti in onore di Luigi Ronga* (Milan, 1973); J. Johnson, *Domenico Chimarosa (1749-1801)* (Diss., Univ. College, Cardiff, 1976).

Ciortea, Tudor, Rumanian composer; b. Braşov, Dec. 11, 1903. He studied composition with Joseph Jongen in Brussels and with Nadia Boulanger and Paul Dukas in Paris; returning to Rumania, he took a course with Otescu at the Bucharest Cons.; in 1941-71 he was on its staff. In his music he adopts the models of French Impressionism; his songs to texts by Rumanian poets have a fine lyric quality.

WORKS: *Suită maramureşeană* for Orch. (1949); Passacaglia and Toccata for Orch. (1957); Concerto for String Orch. (1958); *Variaţiuni pe o temă de colind* for Piano and Orch. (1969); Clarinet Concerto (1973); Violin Sonata (1946); Cello Sonata (1946; revised 1958); 2 string quartets (1952, 1954); Piano Quintet (1957); Flute sonata (1959); octet, *The Adventures of Păcală* (1961; revised 1966); Clarinet Sonata (1962); *Canzona and Burlesque* for Horn and Piano (1962); Trumpet Sonata (1964); Brass Quintet (1970); *Danse tzigane* for Piano (1927); *Suite on*

Themes of Tirnave for Piano (1948); 3 piano sonatas (1950, 1953, 1959); *3 Pieces* for Piano (1955); Piano Sonatina (1960); *4 Songs from Maramures* for Piano (1969); many songs, with diverse instruments.

Cipollini, Gaetano, Italian composer; b. Tropea, Cantanzaro, Feb. 28, 1851; d. Milan, Oct. 1, 1935. He was a pupil of Francesco Coppa; composed an effective melodrama in 3 acts, *Gennariello* (Milan, June 1, 1891); *Il piccolo Haydn,* lyric comedy (Como, Jan. 24, 1893); *Ninon de Lenclos,* lyric comedy (Milan, Dec. 3, 1895); a large number of *romanze* for voice; piano pieces. A 5-act opera, *Simeta,* remained in MS.

Cipra, Milo, Croatian composer; b. Vares, Oct. 13, 1906. He studied composition with Bersa at the Zagreb Music Academy, graduating in 1933; taught there after 1941 and was its dean (1961-71). In his early composition he followed the national school, with thematic elements derived from folk-song patterns of Croatia; he then adopted a severe structural idiom, gradually increasing in modernity.

WORKS: 2 symphs. (1948, 1952); Sinfonietta (1934; revised 1946); *Dubrovački divertimento* for Chamber Orch. (1955-56); Concerto for Strings (1956); *Sunčev put (Sun's Way)* for Wind Orch., Piano, Harp, and Percussion (1958-59); *3 susreta (Encounters)* for Orch. (1961); *Epitaf* for Orch. (1961); *Leda,* symph. pantomime (1965); 5 string quartets (1930, 1932, 1935, 1938, 1972); Piano Trio (1937); Violin Sonata (1946); Cello Sonata (1946); *Musica sine nomine* for 5 Winds, Piano, and Voice (1963); *Svitanje (Aubade)* for Wind Quintet (1965); Piano Sonata (1954); songs.

Cirino, Giulio, Italian bass; b. Rome, Feb. 15, 1880; d. there, Feb. 26, 1970. He made his opera debut in Rome in 1903; subsequently sang at La Scala in Milan; was on the roster of the Teatro Colón in Buenos Aires from 1909 to 1923; retired from the stage in 1935. He was particularly successful in buffo roles, in the Italian repertoire; but he also sang in Wagner's operas.

Cisneros (née **Broadfoot**), **Eleanora de,** American contralto; b. New York, Nov. 1, 1878; d. there, Feb. 3, 1934. She studied singing in N.Y. with Mme. Murio-Celli and later in Paris with Jean de Reszke. In 1901 she married Count Francesco de Cisneros of Havana, Cuba, and appeared professionally under this name. She enjoyed a brilliant career; first appeared with the Metropolitan Opera Co. on tour in Chicago on Nov. 24, 1899, as Rossweisse in *Die Walküre;* then made her N.Y. Metropolitan Opera debut in the same role on Jan. 5, 1900; sang in Italy between 1902 and 1914, and annually in London from 1903 to 1908. Between 1906 and 1911 she was the principal contralto singer at the Manhattan Opera, and later was a member of the Chicago Opera. In 1915 she toured Australia; then lived in Paris until 1929, when she returned to N.Y.

BIBLIOGRAPHY: *Notable American Women* (Cambridge, Mass., 1971, vol. I; listing under De Cisneros).

Citkowitz, Israel, American composer; b. Skiernie-wice, Poland, Feb. 6, 1909; d. London, May 4, 1974. He was brought to the U.S. as a child; studied with Copland and Sessions in N.Y., and with Nadia Boulanger in Paris. He taught at the Dalcroze School of Music in N.Y. from 1939; in 1969 moved to London. He composed mainly for voice; his songs and choral works possess considerable expressive power.

Ciuciura, Leoncjusz, Polish composer; b. Grodzisk Mazowiecki, July 22, 1930. He studied with Szeligowski at the State College of Music in Warsaw. All of his works are essays in combinatorial permutation with optional instrumental or vocal additions, subtractions, multiplications, or divisions.
WORKS: *Canti al fresco* for 9 Female Voices and Instrumental Ensemble (1961); *Concertino de camera* for Chamber Orch. (1961); *Ornament* for Flute, Bassoon, Clarinet, and Strings (1962); *Penetrations* for 4 Orch. Groups, 4 Conductors, and Composer (1963); *Spirale I per uno* for Baritone and 36 Percussion Instruments (1964) and *Spirale II per uno e più* for Optional Instrumental Ensemble (1964); *Emergenza* for 3 Orch. Groups, 3 Conductors, and Composer (1964); *Incidenti* for Optional Voices and Instrumental Ensemble (1964); *Per 5* for a group which would include any combination of Flute, Oboe, Horn, Bassoon, and Trumpet (1972); *Creatoria I* and *II* for Optional Solo Voice or Instrument or Groups of Instruments or Voices (1975); *Music* for Solo Flute and 8 Instruments (1976).

Čiurlionis, Mikolajus, Lithuanian composer; b. Varena, Oct. 4, 1875; d. Pustelnik, near Warsaw, April 10, 1911. He studied composition with Noskowski, and at the Leipzig Cons. with Carl Reinecke and Jadassohn. From 1902 till 1909 he was active in Warsaw as a choral conductor. His music reflects the Germanic Romantic tendencies, but he also developed interesting theories of so-called "tonal ground formations," anticipating the serial methods of Schoenberg and Hauer. Čiurlionis was also a remarkable painter in an abstract expressionist manner; many of his paintings carry musical titles, such as "Prelude and Fugue," "Spring Sonata," etc. His musical works include the symph. poems *In the Forest* (1901) and *The Ocean* (1907); cantata, *De profundis* (1899); String Quartet; numerous piano pieces and songs.
BIBLIOGRAPHY: V. Čiurlionytė-Karužiene et al., *M.K. Čiurlionis. Bibliografia* (Vilnius, 1970); J. Čiurlionytė, *Atsiminimai apie M.K. Čiurlionis* (Vilnius, 1970); V. Landsbergis, *Spring Sonata. The Creative Activity of M.K. Čiurlionis* (Leningrad, 1971).

Civil, Alan, noted English horn–player; b. Northampton, June 13, 1929. He studied with Aubrey Brain in London and with Willy von Stemm in Hamburg. He was principal horn of the Royal Phil. Orch. (1952–55), and later co-principal horn, with Dennis Brain, of the Philharmonia Orch. (1955–57); after Brain's tragic death, was principal horn (1957–66); from 1966, principal horn of the BBC Symph. Orch. In 1966 he became a prof. of horn at the Royal College of Music in London.

Claassen, Arthur, American conductor and composer; b. Stargard, Prussia, Feb. 19, 1859; d. San Francisco, March 16, 1920. He studied in Weimar; his compositions aroused Liszt's interests, and he wrote a number of pieces in a Lisztian manner. In 1884 he was engaged as conductor of the choral group Arion in Brooklyn, and held this post for 25 years. In 1914 he took over the Beethoven Choral Society, a male chorus organization, in San Antonio, Texas; he also was engaged as conductor of the San Antonio Phil., which later became the San Antonio Symph. Simultaneously he organized the Mozart Society in San Antonio, a women's chorus, which enabled him to conduct choral works with the San Antonio Symph.; he left San Antonio in 1919. Among his works are the symph. poem *Hohenfriedberg; Waltz-Idyll* for String Orch.; and many choruses, of which *Der Kamerad* received a prize at the N.Y. Singing Festival.

Claflin, (Alan) Avery, American composer; b. Keene, N.H., June 21, 1898; d. Greenwich, Conn., Jan. 9, 1979. He studied law and banking, and pursued a business career; also took music courses at Harvard Univ. He attracted attention as a composer by his amusing choral work, a fiscal madrigal entitled *Lament for April 15* (1955), to the text of an Internal Revenue tax form. Among his other compositions are the operas *Hester Prynne* (after *The Scarlet Letter* of Hawthorne), of which Scene II of Act II was performed at Hartford on Dec. 15, 1934; *The Fall of Usher* (not performed); *La Grande Bretèche,* after Balzac's story (NBC Radio, Feb. 3, 1957); *Uncle Tom's Cabin* (1961–64); 2 symphs.; *Teen Scenes* for Strings (1955); *Pop Concert Concerto* for Piano and Orch. (1958); Piano Trio; other chamber music.

Clapham, John, English musicologist; b. Letchworth, July 31, 1908. He studied cello with Douglas Cameron, and took courses in harmony and counterpoint at the Royal Academy of Music in London; then studied at the Univ. of London (B.Mus., 1934; D.Mus., 1946). He was a lecturer at the Univ. College of Wales in Aberystwyth (1946–62); then was senior lecturer (1962–69) and lecturer (1969-73) at the Univ. of Edinburgh. He distinguished himself in studies of Czech music.
WRITINGS: *Antonín Dvořák: Musician and Craftsman* (London, 1966); *Smetana* (London, 1972); *Dvořák* (Newton Abbot, 1979).

Clapp, Philip Greeley, American composer and pedagogue; b. Boston, Aug. 4, 1888; d. Iowa City, April 9, 1954. He studied piano with his aunt Mary Greeley James (1895–99); and violin with Jacques Hoffman in Boston (1895–1905); also took lessons in music theory with John Marshall (1905). He then entered Harvard Univ., studying music theory and composition with Spalding, Converse, and Edward

Burlingame Hill; received his B.A. (1908), M.A. (1909), and Ph.D. (1911). He also studied composition and conducting in Stuttgart with Max von Schillings (1910). He became a teaching fellow at Harvard (1911–12); was music director at Dartmouth College (1915–18); in 1919 he was appointed director of the music dept. at the Univ. of Iowa, and remained at that post for the rest of his life. Clapp was a prolific composer and a competent teacher; he was also a brilliant pianist, but did not dedicate himself to a concert career; he also appeared as conductor of his own works and was in charge of the univ. orch. at Iowa City. His music is conceived in an expansive Romantic idiom much influenced by the modern German style of composition, and yet introducing some advanced melodic and harmonic patterns, such as building harmonies in fourths.

WORKS: For Orch.: 12 symphs.: No. 1, in E major (1910; first perf., Waterloo, Iowa, April 27, 1933, composer conducting); No. 2, in E minor (Boston Symph., April 10, 1914, composer conducting); No. 3, in E-flat major (Boston Symph., April 6, 1917, composer conducting); No. 4, in A major (1919; revised 1941; not perf.); No. 5, in D major (1926; revised 1941; Iowa City, July 26, 1944, composer conducting); No. 6, in B major, subtitled *Golden Gate* (1926; San Jose, Calif., June 5, 1951); No. 7, in A major (Boston, March 22, 1931, composer conducting); No. 8, in C major (1930; revised 1941; N.Y. Phil., Mitropoulos conducting, Feb. 7, 1952); No. 9, in E-flat minor, subtitled *The Pioneers* (1931; Iowa City, July 16, 1939); No. 10, in F major, subtitled *Heroic* (1935; Iowa City, May 23, 1951, composer conducting); No. 11, in C major (1942; revised 1950; not perf.); No. 12, in B-flat major (1944; not perf.); *Norge,* symph. poem, with Piano obbligato (Cambridge, Mass., Boston Symph., April 29, 1909; his most popular work); *Song of Youth,* symph. poem (1910); *Dramatic Poem with Solo Trombone* (Cambridge, Mass., April 24, 1912, composer conducting); *Summer,* orch. prelude (St. Louis, Jan. 16, 1914); *Overture to a Comedy* (1933); *A Highly Academic Diversion on 7 Notes* for Chamber Orch. (Iowa City, Feb. 17, 1933, composer conducting); *Fantasy on an Old Plain Chant* for Cello and Orch. (Iowa City, Jan. 17, 1940); Concerto for 2 Pianos (Iowa City, Dec. 20, 1945). Chamber music: Violin Sonata (1909); String Quartet (1909); Suite for Brass Sextet (1938); Concerto Suite for 4 Trombones (1939); *Prelude and Finale* for Woodwind Quintet (1939). Numerous choral works, among them *A Chant of Darkness* for Chorus and Orch., to the text by Helen Keller (1919; revised 1933; Iowa City, April 16, 1935, composer conducting); 2 operas, *The Taming of the Shrew,* after Shakespeare (1948), and *The Flaming Brand,* libretto by the composer on the exploit of John Brown (1949–53), neither of which was ever performed, nor are they likely to be performed in any foreseeable future century. All his MSS are in the Music Library of the Univ. of Iowa.

BIBLIOGRAPHY: Dorothy R. Holcomb, *P.G. Clapp* in *Books at Iowa* (Iowa City, 1972).

Clapton, Eric, British virtuoso on the electric guitar; b. Ripley, Surrey, March 30, 1945. He played guitar as a youth; at 18 he joined the Metropolis Blues Quartet, a group which later changed its name to The Yardbirds. Clapton played with it for a few months, but was turned off by its rank commercialism, and in 1965 joined John Mayall's Bluesbreakers; in another year he organized a group named simply Cream, which turned the rock world upside down by introducing prolonged improvisational jams. When in the course of human events Cream soured, Clapton organized a "supergroup," Blind Faith, with Ginger Baker, Stevie Winwood, and Rick Grech, but like so many men of little faith, Blind Faith soon gave up the ghost. Only Clapton's spiritual hymn *In the Presence of the Lord* maintained the flame. In 1970, Clapton formed Derek and the Dominoes, which received a certified Gold Award in 1971 with its album *Layla.* The group disbanded after a year or so of feverish activity. Depressed by these recurrent failures, Clapton went into crooning, fully aware that he was no Mick Jagger. His songs expressed his pessimism, as in *E.C. Was Here, There's One in Every Crowd,* and *No Reason to Cry.* In 1979, after a long period of doldrums, he hit the jackpot with *Lay Down Sally.* He also paid a debt to the middle-class fascination with coke with the promotional tunes *Tulsa Time* and *Cocaine.*

Clari, Giovanni Carlo Maria, Italian composer and choral director; b. Pisa, Sept. 27, 1677; d. there, May 16, 1754. He studied with his father and with Francesco Alessi in Pisa; then under Colonna at Bologna, where his opera *Il Savio delirante* was produced in 1695; from 1703 to 1724 he was in Pistoia as maestro di cappella of the Cathedral; then went to Pisa. His best-known work is a collection of madrigals for 2 and 3 voices (1720; reprinted by Carli, Paris, 1825); he also wrote masses, Psalms, a Requiem, and other sacred music.

BIBLIOGRAPHY: E.C. Saville, "Liturgical Music of Giovanni Clari: An Annotated Index," *Fontes Artis Musicae,* XV/1 (1968).

Claribel. See **Charlotte Barnard.**

Clark, Dick, American media entrepreneur; b. Mount Vernon, N.Y., Nov. 30, 1929. He was a school disc jockey at Syracuse Univ. while attending business classes. After graduation he had jobs as a radio announcer and, with the advent of television, organized a music-and-dance program, American Bandstand, which became a favorite TV waterhole for boppers. His subsequent program, Cavalcade of Stars, hit the top in the charts. Alas, Dick Clark himself became a falling star when he was summoned before the Senate Investigating Committee on charges of payola, a cynical slang term used to describe the eleemosynary donations from record companies and other interested parties in return for the promotion of their products on the air. He got away with only a nominal penalty, but the good name of the American Bandstand was badly besmirched. Clark retreated to Los Angeles, where he started a show called Where the Action Is. He also served as host of the quiz show $50,000 Pyramid, but it soon collapsed because of the bad odor lingering from the scandals of rigged quiz shows of the 1950s. Undaunted, he made one last attempt to get something out of his erstwhile popularity by publishing a book, *Looking Great, Staying Young.* It did not sell, but Clark recouped his losses by starting a successful television production company.

Clark, Edward, English conductor; b. Newcastle upon Tyne, May 10, 1888; d. London, April 29, 1962. He studied in Paris, in Vienna, and in Berlin with Schoenberg. He led the orch. for Diaghilev's London seasons (1924–26); was with the BBC (1927–36); in 1940 he founded the North Eastern Regional Orch. in Newcastle. In 1947 he was elected president of the International Society for Contemporary Music. He was married to the composer **Elizabeth Lutyens.**

Clark, Frederick Scotson, English clergyman, organist, and composer; b. London, Nov. 16, 1840; d. there, July 5, 1883. He studied with Sergent in Paris and with E.J. Hopkins; also studied at the Royal Academy of Music in London with Bennett, Goss, Engel, Pettit, and Pinsuti; received his religious education at Cambridge and Oxford; was organist of Exeter College, Oxford; took further music lessons in Leipzig and Stuttgart; returned in 1873 to London, where he founded the London Organ School; he was the representative English organist at the Paris Exposition of 1878.

WORKS: His organ compositions (15 marches, 48 voluntaries, 6 communions; offertories, improvisations, impromptus, etc.) are his best works; composed over 100 piano pieces; sacred vocal music, songs, etc.; he also played and composed for the harmonium.

Clark, Melville, one of the pioneers of the player-piano industry; b. Oneida County, N.Y., 1850; d. Chicago, Nov. 5, 1918. In 1875 he established himself as an organ builder in Oakland, Calif.; moved to Chicago in 1880; in 1894 he also opened a piano factory, after he had become interested in pneumatic actions; his experiments leading to practical results which convinced him of the possibilities of the player piano, he sold his organ factory, and, in 1900, organized the Melville Clark Piano Co., of which he was president. In 1901 he patented and placed on the market the 88-note roll, utilizing the full compass of the piano, and thus gave the impetus to the phenomenal player-piano industry which later developed. In 1911 he patented a recording mechanism which aimed to reproduce the actual performance of great pianists. He also held many other important patents.

Clark, Melville Antone, harpist and harp manufacturer, nephew of the preceding; b. Syracuse, N.Y., Sept. 12, 1883; d. there, Dec. 11, 1953. He received his first instruction on the harp from his father; was a pupil of Van Veachton Rogers (1896–99) and of John Aptommas in London (1908). While on a tour of Great Britain in 1908 he acquired a small Irish harp, formerly the property of the poet Thomas Moore; by the application of acoustic principles he improved the model and succeeded in producing a small, portable harp (39 inches high) of considerable tone volume; founded the Clark Harp Manufacturing Co. at Syracuse, which turned out the first small Irish harps in 1913; on a tour of the U.S. with John McCormack (1913–14) the inventor demonstrated the possibilities of the new instrument; took out 14 patents on improvements for the portable harp, and developed a new method of pedaling the concert harp; played about 4,000 recitals in the U.S., Canada, and England; was co-founder of the Syracuse Symph. Orch.; treasurer of the National Association of Harpists; president of the Clark Music Co. (1910).

WRITINGS: *How to Play the Harp, Romance of the Harp, Singing Strings.*

Clark, Roy (Linwood), American country-music singer and instrumentalist; b. Meherrin, Va., April 15, 1933. As a teenager he learned to play the banjo, guitar, and fiddle, later took up piano, trumpet, trombone, drums, and singing; at the age of 21 he formed his own band. In 1969 he became co-host (with Buck Owens) of the *Hee Haw* country-music television program; its jejune quality was relieved somewhat by Clark's natural gifts as a singer and instrumentalist. In addition to his many recordings, he toured the U.S. and Canada. In 1976 he made a successful tour of the Soviet Union.

Clarke, Henry Leland, American musicologist and composer; b. Dover, N.H., March 9, 1907. He studied piano and violin; then took courses at Harvard Univ. (M.A., 1929; Ph.D., 1947). In 1929 he went to Paris, where he took composition lessons with Nadia Boulanger at the Ecole Normale de Musique. Upon returning to the U.S., he occupied himself mainly with teaching; was on the faculty of Westminster Choir College (1938–42), the Univ. of Calif., Los Angeles (1947–58), and the Univ. of Washington, Seattle (1958–77). As a composer, Clarke applies a number of interesting innovations, e.g., "Intervalescent Counterpoint" (with interval values constantly changing from one voice to another), "Lipophony" (with certain notes systematically omitted), "Word Tones" (whenever a word recurs, it is assigned to the same pitch), and "Rotating Triskaidecaphony" (a 12-tone series returning to note one for the 13th note, with the next row starting and ending on note 2, etc.).

WORKS: *Danza de la muerte,* a choreography for Oboe and Piano (1937); *Monograph* for Orch. (1952); chamber opera, *The Loafer and the Loaf* (Stockbridge, Mass., July 1, 1954); *Nocturne* for Viola and Piano (1955); *Saraband for the Golden Goose* for Orch. (1957); *Points West* for Wind and Percussion (1960); *Encounter* for Viola and Orch. (1961); *Lysistrata,* opera (1969); *A Game That 2 Can Play* for Flute and Clarinet (1966); *Concatenata* for French Horn and Woodwind Quartet (1969); *Danza de la vida,* choreography for Oboe and Piano (1975);

These Are the Times That Try Men's Souls for Chorus, to the text of Thomas Paine (1976); *The Young Dead Soldiers* for Chorus, to words by Archibald MacLeish (1977); *Give and Take* for 2 Keyboards (1977); 3 string quartets.

Clarke, Hugh Archibald, organist; b. near Toronto, Canada, Aug. 15, 1839; d. Philadelphia, Dec. 16, 1927. He was a pupil of his father, **James Paton Clarke;** was organist in several churches in Philadelphia; in 1875 was elected prof. of the science of music at the Univ. of Pa.; retired in 1925.

WORKS: Music to Euripides' *Iphigenia in Tauris;* oratorio, *Jerusalem* (1891); piano music; songs.

WRITINGS: A treatise on harmony and one on counterpoint; textbooks for organ; a book of fiction, *The Scratch Club* (1888); *Music and the Comrade Arts* (1900); *Highways and Byways of Music* (1901).

Clarke, James Hamilton Smee, English organist; b. Birmingham, Jan. 25, 1840; d. Banstead, July 9, 1912. He was apprenticed to a land surveyor 1855–61; then turned to music, and in 1866 became organist to Queen's College, Oxford. In 1872 he succeeded Sullivan as organist of St. Peter's in South Kensington; was conductor of the D'Oyly Carte company on tour (1878); and also at the Lyceum Theatre, writing music for dramas given by Henry Irving. In 1893, he became first conductor of the Carl Rosa Co.

WORKS: He publ. about 400 works, including music to *Hamlet, The Merchant of Venice,* and *King Lear;* sacred cantata, *Praise;* 8-part anthem, *The Lord is my light;* 2 symphs.; 6 overtures; organ music.

Clarke, James Paton, Scottish organist; b. 1808; d. Toronto, Aug. 27, 1877. In 1829 he was the leader of psalmody in St. George's Church in Glasgow; in 1834 became organist of St. Mary's Episcopal Chapel, succeeding Thomas Macfarlane; he emigrated to Canada in 1835 and became a farmer; went to Toronto about 1845. In 1846 he took his Mus.Bac. degree at King's College with the 8-part anthem *Arise, O Lord God, forget not the poor.*

BIBLIOGRAPHY: H. Kallmann, "James Paton Clarke—Canada's Mus. Bac.," *Cahiers Canadiens de Musique* (Spring–Summer 1970).

Clarke, Jeremiah, English composer and organist; b. London, c.1673; d. there (suicide), Dec. 1, 1707. He was a chorister in the Chapel Royal; in 1700 was made Gentleman Extraordinary of the Chapel Royal; in 1704 was appointed joint organist (with Croft) there. A hopeless love affair caused Clarke to take his own life.

WORKS: He composed (with others) the stage works *The World in the Moon* (1697) and *The Island Princess* (1699); wrote incidental music to several plays; was the first composer to set Dryden's *Alexander's Feast* to music (for St. Cecilia's Day, Nov. 22, 1697); also wrote a cantata, an ode, anthems, songs, etc. He was the real author of the famous *Trumpet Voluntary,* erroneously ascribed to Purcell, and popularized by Sir Henry Wood's orch. arrangement.

BIBLIOGRAPHY: C.L. Cudworth, "Some New Facts about the Trumpet Voluntary," *Musical Times* (Sept. 1953); T.F. Taylor, "Jeremiah Clarke's Trumpet Tunes: Another View of Origins," *Musical Quarterly* (July 1970); R. McGuinness, *English Court Odes 1660–1820* (Oxford, 1971); T. Taylor, *Thematic Catalog of the Works of Jeremiah Clarke* (Detroit, 1977).

Clarke (Clarke-Whitfield), John, English organist and composer; b. Gloucester, Dec. 13, 1770; d. Holmer, near Hereford, Feb. 22, 1836. He studied organ at Oxford with Philip Hayes; received his B.Mus. degree in 1793; was church organist at Ludlow, Armagh, and Dublin; in 1799 he became organist at Trinity and St. John's College in Cambridge; from 1820 to 1833 he was organist at the Hereford Cathedral. He was stricken with paralysis; was forced to resign his post, and was an invalid for the rest of his life.

WORKS: 2 oratorios: *The Crucifixion* and *The Resurrection* (Hereford, 1822); 4 vols. of cathedral services and anthems (1805); 12 glees (1805); 12 songs; *Selection of Single and Double Chants;* etc. He also edited the *Vocal Works of Handel* (17 vols., 1809), with piano accompaniment.

Clarke, Kenny, black American jazz drummer; b. Pittsburgh, Jan. 9, 1914. While in school, he played piano, trombone, drums, and vibes. In 1935 he joined the band of Roy Eldridge, then played with Teddy Wilson's group; later appeared with Charlie Parker and Dizzy Gillespie. He was a founding member of the Modern Jazz Quartet in 1952, and played with it until 1955. Moving to Europe, he formed the Clarke-Boland Big Band with the Belgian pianist-arranger Francy Boland in Paris in 1960; it disbanded in 1973; he then worked with a small group in Europe, making occasional visits to the U.S.

Clarke, Rebecca, English composer and viola player; b. Harrow, Aug. 27, 1886; d. New York, Oct. 13, 1979. She studied composition at the Royal College of Music in London with Sir Charles Stanford. She was originally a violinist, but specialized later as a viola player. In 1916 she went to the U.S. Among her compositions are Piano Trio (1921), *Chinese Puzzle* for Violin and Piano (1922), Rhapsody for Cello and Piano (1923), and *3 Irish Country Songs* for Violin and Cello. Her music is quite advanced, on the fringe of atonality in melodic outline. She was actively at work in N.Y. until her death at the age of 93. An entry on her chamber music is found in Cobbett's *Cyclopedic Survey of Chamber Music* (London, 1929).

Clarke, Robert Coningsby, English song composer; b. Old Charlton, Kent, March 17, 1879; d. Walmer, Kent, Jan. 2, 1934. He studied with Sir John Frederick Bridge at Westminster Abbey; then served as church organist at Oxford. He wrote a number of popular ballads and piano pieces.

Clarke, William Horatio, American organist; b. Newton, Mass., March 8, 1840; d. Reading, Mass., Dec. 11, 1913. He was a church organist in Boston; retired in 1887 to his estate in Reading, where he built a chapel of music, Clarigold Hall, containing a large 4-manual organ with 100 stops.

Clarus, Max, German composer; b. Mühlberg, March 31, 1852; d. Braunschweig, Dec. 6, 1916. He studied with his father, who was a municipal music director, and with Löschhorn in Berlin. He became a theatrical conductor, traveling in Germany, Austria, and Hungary; composed mostly for the stage and for chorus.
WORKS: Operas (all produced in Braunschweig): *Des Königs-Rekrut* (1889); *Ilse* (1895; quite successful at the time); the fairy operas *Der Wunschpeter* (1910) and *Der Zwerg Nase* (1912); several ballets (*Opium-Träume,* etc.); *Die Wacht vor Samoa* for Baritone Solo, Male Chorus, and Orch.; numerous a cappella choruses.

Claudin le Jeune. See **Le Jeune, Claudin.**

Claussen, Julia (née **Ohlson**), dramatic mezzo-soprano; b. Stockholm, June 11, 1879; d. there, May 1, 1941. She studied at the Royal Academy of Music in Stockholm (1897–1902); then in Berlin with Prof. Friedrich. She made her debut as Leonora in *La Favorita* at the Stockholm Opera (Jan. 19, 1903); was engaged there from 1903 until 1912; made her debut at Covent Garden in London in 1914; was a member of the Chicago Opera Co. during World War I. She made her first appearance at the Metropolitan Opera House as Dalila on Nov. 23, 1917, and remained in the company until 1929; in 1934 she returned to Stockholm as a teacher at the Royal Academy of Music. After her death a memorial fund for vocal scholarships was established in Stockholm.

Clavé, José Anselmo, Spanish choral leader; b. Barcelona, April 21, 1824; d. there, Feb. 24, 1874. He was inspired by the success of the "orpheons" in France, and organized male singing societies in Spain on a similar scale. At the first singing festival in Barcelona in 1860 he conducted a chorus of 200 voices; in 1864 he augmented his ensemble to 2,000 singers, representing 57 organizations. Some of his songs and choruses, especially composed for his festivals, enjoyed great popularity.
BIBLIOGRAPHY: J. Subirá, *El Músico-poeta Clavé* (Madrid, 1924); T. Caballé y Clós, *J.A. Clavé y su tiempo* (Barcelona, 1949).

Clay, Frédéric, composer; b. (of English parents) Paris, Aug. 3, 1838; d. Great Marlow, near London, Nov. 24, 1889. He studied with Molique at Paris and with Hauptmann in Leipzig.
WORKS: His early operettas, *The Pirate's Isle* (1859) and *Out of Sight* (1860), were performed privately in London; his first operetta to be produced at Covent Garden was *Court and Cottage* (1862); other light dramatic works subsequently performed at Covent Garden included *Constance* (1865); *Ages Ago* (1869); *The Gentleman in Black* (1870); *Happy Arcadia* (1872); *Cattarina* (1874); *Princess Toto* (1876); *Don Quixote* (1876). He also composed 2 cantatas, *The Knights of the Cross* (1866) and *Lalla Rookh* (1877; including the well-known aria *I'll sing thee songs of Araby*).
BIBLIOGRAPHY: W.S. Gilbert, *Gilbert before Sullivan* (ed., with introduction, by J.W. Stedman; Chicago, 1967).

Clayton, Wilbur ("Buck"), black American jazz trumpeter; b. Parsons, Kans., Nov. 12, 1911. His father taught him to play the trumpet; he became a member of Count Basie's band (1936–43). After serving in the U.S. Army (1943–46), he resumed his career; also made arrangements for Basie, Benny Goodman, and other bandleaders; toured Europe (1949–50; 1953); later appeared at jazz festivals.

Clemencic, René, Austrian recorder player and conductor; b. Vienna, Feb. 27, 1928. He studied the recorder with Hans Staeps and Johannes Collette; also keyboard instruments with Eta Harich-Schneider. In 1958 he founded the Musica Antiqua in Vienna, which became the Ensemble Musica Antiqua in 1959; with this group he gave performances of music covering the period from the Middle Ages to the Baroque, utilizing authentic instruments. In 1969 he founded the Clemencic Consort, and led it in a vast repertoire, extending from the medieval period to the avant-garde.

Clemens, Charles Edwin, American organist; b. Plymouth, England, March 12, 1858; d. Cleveland, Dec. 26, 1923. He studied at the Royal College of Music in London; as a boy, played organ in churches; served as organist of the English Church in Berlin (1889–96); settled in Cleveland as organist at St. Paul's Church (1896–1911); also taught at Case Western Reserve Univ.
WRITINGS: He publ. 2 manuals: *Pedal Technique* (1894) and *Modern School for the Organ* (1903).

Clemens, Hans, German tenor; b. Bicken-Gelsenkirchen, July 27, 1890; d. Montrose, Colo., Aug. 25, 1958. After successful appearances in Germany and at Covent Garden in London, he came to the U.S.; made his N.Y. debut at the Metropolitan Opera House in *The Flying Dutchman* (Nov. 1, 1930); appeared also in other Wagnerian roles; was particularly effective as David in *Die Meistersinger,* a role which he sang more than 100 times. In 1938 he settled in Los Angeles as a vocal teacher.

Clemens (Clement), Jacobus (called **"Clemens non Papa"**), eminent Netherlandish contrapuntist; b. Ypres, c.1510; d. Dixmude, c.1556 (death date is surmised from the fact that vol. 1 of *Novum et insigne opus musicum,* publ. in 1558, contains the motet *Nanie,* composed by Jacob Vaet on Clemens's death). The exact meaning of "non Papa" is not clear; it was once thought to mean "not the Pope," to distinguish the composer from Clement VII; but a more recent interpretation suggests that "non Papa" was intended to differentiate Clemens from a poet also living in the town of Ypres, named Jacobus Papa. His teachers are not known; he was in France for a time; returned in 1540 to the Netherlands and settled in Bruges; in 1545 he went to Antwerp; later lived in Dixmude, where he was buried. WORKS: 15 masses, numerous motets, chansons, etc., publ. by Phalèse (Louvain, 1555–80); 4 books of *Souterliedekens a 3,* i.e., psalms set to popular Netherlandish tunes, publ. by T. Susato (Antwerp, 1556–57); and many miscellaneous pieces in collections of the period. Reprints are to be found in K. Proske's *Musica divina* (vol. II); R.J. van Maldeghem's *Trésor musical;* and F. Commer's *Collectio operum musicorum Batavorum.* El. Mincoff-Marriage republ. the text of the *Souterliedekens* (The Hague, 1922); a selection of 15 of these pieces, with music, was ed. by W. Blanke (Wolfenbüttel, 1929). BIBLIOGRAPHY: J. Schmidt, "Die Messen des Clemens non Papa," *Zeitschrift für Musikwissenschaft* (1926); K.P. Bernet Kempers, "Zur Biographie des Clemens non Papa," ibid. (1927); idem, *J. Clemens non Papa und seine Motetten* (Augsburg, 1928). A complete ed. of his works was publ. in Amsterdam (1951–76) under the editorship of K.P. Bernet Kempers.

Clément, Edmond, French tenor; b. Paris, March 28, 1867; d. Nice, Feb. 24, 1928. He was a pupil of Warot at the Paris Cons. in 1887; took first prize in 1889; his debut was at the Opéra-Comique, Nov. 29, 1889, as Vincent in Gounod's *Mireille.* His success was instantaneous, and he remained there until 1910 with frequent leave for extended tours; sang in the principal theaters of France, Belgium, Spain, Portugal, England, and Denmark; in 1909–10 sang at the Metropolitan Opera House; in 1911–13, with the Boston Opera Co. His voice was a light tenor of very agreeable quality, with a range of 2 octaves. He created the chief tenor parts in the following operas (all at the Opéra-Comique): Bruneau's *L'Attaque du Moulin* (1893); Saint-Saëns's *Phryné* (1893); Cui's *Le Flibustier* (1894); Godard's *La Vivandière* (1895); Dubois's *Xavière* (1895); Hahn's *L'Ile du rêve* (1898); Erlanger's *Le Juif polonais* (1900); Saint-Saëns's *Hélène* (1904); Dupont's *La Cabrera* (1905); Vidal's *La Reine Fiammette* (1908). He was particularly famous for his portrayal of Des Grieux in Massenet's opera *Manon.*

Clément, Félix, French writer on music; b. Paris, Jan. 13, 1822; d. there, Jan. 23, 1885. He devoted himself especially to historical studies; filled several positions as an organist and teacher, and finally became organist and choirmaster at the Church of the Sorbonne. In 1849 the government chose him to direct sacred music at the Ste.-Chapelle du Palais; during his tenure there he brought out a number of works of 13th-century music; they were publ. in full score as *Chants de la Sainte-Chapelle* (1849; 3rd ed.,

1855). He was active in establishing the Institution for Church Music. WRITINGS: *Méthode complète du plain-chant* (1854, 1872); *Histoire générale de la musique religieuse* (1860); *Les Musiciens célèbres depuis le XVIe siècle* (1868; 4th ed., 1887); *Dictionnaire lyrique, ou Histoire des opéras* (1869, 4 supplements up to 1881; new augmented ed. by A. Pougin, 1897 and 1904, under the title *Dictionnaire des opéras*); *Méthode d'orgue, d'harmonie et d'accompagnement* (1874; 2nd ed., 1894); *Histoire de la musique depuis les temps anciens jusqu'à nos jours* (1885); etc.

Clement, Franz, Austrian violinist and composer; b. Vienna, Nov. 17, 1780; d. there, Nov. 3, 1842. He learned to play the violin as a child, and at the age of 10 went to London, where he appeared as a soloist at concerts directed by Salomon and Haydn. Returning to Vienna, he continued his successful career; was conductor at the Theater an der Wien (1802–11); made a tour in Germany and Russia (1813–18); participated in the concerts of the famous singer Angelica Catalani. He was greatly esteemed as a violinist and musician by his contemporaries; Beethoven wrote his Violin Concerto for him, and Clement gave its first performance in Vienna (Dec. 23, 1806). He wrote 6 concertos and 25 concertinos for violin, as well as numerous technical studies. BIBLIOGRAPHY: Robert Haas, "The Viennese Violinist Franz Clement," *Musical Quarterly* (Jan. 1948).

Clement, Jacobus. See **Clemens, Jacobus.**

Clementi, Aldo, Italian composer of avant-garde tendencies; b. Catania, May 25, 1925. He took piano lessons as a child in Catania and later was a piano pupil of Pietro Scarpini in Siena; subsequently studied composition with Alfredo Sangiorgi, a pupil of Schoenberg, in Catania (1945–52) and with Petrassi in Rome (1952–54); then attended summer courses in new music at Darmstadt (1955–62). After an initial period of writing music in a neo-Baroque manner, he adopted serial techniques, employing rhythmic indeterminacy and dense, clustered sonics. WORKS: *3 piccoli pezzi* for Flute, Oboe, and Clarinet (1955); Sonata for Trumpet, Guitar, and Piano (1955); *2 studi* for Trumpet, Violin, and Piano (1956); *Concertino in forma di Variazioni* for 9 Instruments (1956); *3 studi* for Chamber Orch. (1956–57; Darmstadt, July 27, 1957); *Composizione No. 1* for Piano (1957); *Episodi* for Orch. (1958); *Ideogrammi No. 1* for 16 Instruments and *No. 2* for Flute and 17 Instruments (both 1959); *Triplum* for Flute, Oboe, and Clarinet (1960); *7 Scene* for Chamber Orch. (1961); *Informel 1* for 12 Percussion and Keyboard Instruments (1961), *2* for 15 Players (1962), and *3* for Orch. (1961–63; Palermo, Oct. 2, 1963); *Collage 1,* a one-act "musical action" for the stage, for Chamber Ensemble and Visuals (1961), *2* for Tape (1962), and *3, Dies irae,* for Tape (1966–67); *Intavolatura* for Harpsichord (1963); *Variante A*

Clementi

for Chorus and Orch. (1964; Rome, April 6, 1974) and *B* for Orch. (1964; Venice Festival, Sept. 12, 1964); *Reticolo: 11* for 11 Instruments (1966); *Silben* for Female Voice, Clarinet, Violin, and 2 Pianos (1966); Concerto for Wind Orch. and 2 Pianos (1967; Venice Festival, Sept. 12, 1970); *Reticolo: 4* for String Quartet (1968); *B.A.C.H.* for Piano (1970); Concerto for Piano and 7 Instruments (1970; Venice Festival, Sept. 10, 1972); *Reticolo: 12* for 12 Strings (1970); *Silbenmerz* (1971); *Replica* for Harpsichord (1972); *Manualiter* for Organ (1973); *Blitz,* "musical action" for Chamber Ensemble (1973); *Sinfonia da camera* (1974; Milan, April 22, 1974); Concerto for Piano, 24 Instruments, and Carillons (1975); *Reticolo: 3* for 3 Guitars (1975); *Clessidra* for 11 Instruments (1976).

Clementi, Muzio, celebrated Italian pianist and composer; b. Rome, Jan. 23, 1752; d. at his country seat at Evesham, England, March 10, 1832. His father, a goldsmith, was a devoted amateur of music, and had his son taught carefully, from early years, by Antonio Buroni, maestro di cappella in a Roman church. From 1759 the organist Condiceli gave him lessons in organ playing and harmony. So rapid was their pupil's progress that when but 9 he obtained a position as an organist, in competition with other, more mature, players. Until 14 years of age he pursued his studies in Italy, G. Carpani (composition) and Sartarelli (voice) being his next instructors. At a piano concert which Clementi gave in 1766, an English gentleman named Beckford was so delighted with his talent that he obtained the father's permission to educate the boy in England. Clementi lived and studied till 1770 in his patron's house in Dorsetshire; then, a thoroughly equipped pianist and musician, he took London by storm. In 1773 his op. 2 (3 piano sonatas dedicated to Haydn, and warmly praised by C.P.E. Bach) was publ.; it may be considered as finally establishing the form of the piano sonata. From 1777–80 he conducted, as cembalist, the Italian Opera. In 1781 he began a pianistic tour, giving concerts at Paris, Strasbourg, Munich and Vienna. Here, on Dec. 24, 1781, he met Mozart in "friendly" rivalry (Mozart's letters make no pretense of concealing his dislike of the "Italian" composer and player); though the palm of final victory was awarded to neither, yet Clementi tacitly admitted, by changing from a mechanically brilliant to a more suave and melodious piano style, the musical superiority of Mozart. In Vienna his opp. 7, 9, and 10 were publ. by Artaria. Excepting a concert season at Paris, in 1785, Clementi now remained in London for 20 years (1782–1802). He not only made his mark, and incidentally amassed quite a fortune, as a teacher, pianist, and composer, but also (after losses through the failure of Longman & Broderip, the instrument makers and music sellers) established, with John Longman, a highly successful piano factory and publishing house (now Collard & Collard). With his pupil Field, Clementi set out for St. Petersburg in 1802, passing through Paris and Vienna; their tour was attended by brilliant success, and Field was so well received in St. Petersburg that

he accompanied his master no further. Clementi resided for several years alternately in Berlin, Dresden, and St. Petersburg; then, after visiting Vienna, Milan, Rome, and Naples, he again settled in London. The businessman in Clementi now gained the upper hand; he no longer played in public, but devoted himself to composition and the management of his prosperous mercantile ventures. He never again went far from London, except during the winter of 1820–21, which he spent in Leipzig. As a teacher, Clementi trained many distinguished musicians: Field, Cramer, Moscheles, Kalkbrenner, Alexander Klengel, Ludwig Berger, Zeuner, even Meyerbeer, all owed much to his instruction.

WORKS: His compositions include symphs. (which failed in competition with Haydn's) and overtures for orch.; 106 piano sonatas (46 with violin, cello, or flute); 2 duos for 2 pianos; 6 4-hand duets; fugues, preludes, and exercises in canon form; toccatas, waltzes, variations, caprices; *Points d'orgue . . .* (op. 19); *Introduction à l'art de toucher le piano, avec 50 leçons,* etc. (Eng. trans., London, 1801; reprinted, N.Y., 1973); by far the greater part of these are wholly forgotten. But his great book of études, the *Gradus ad Parnassum* (publ. 1817), is a living reminder that he was one of the greatest of piano teachers. Bülow's excellent selection of 50 of these études has been outdone by several later complete eds. (German, Italian, Eng.), including that of Vogrich, arranged progressively (N.Y., 1898). The Library of Congress in Washington, D.C., acquired, largely through the efforts of Carl Engel, numerous MSS by Clementi, including 4 symphs. (almost complete); other fragments are in the British Museum. The first 2 of these symphs. were restored and ed. for publication by Alfredo Casella, who performed them (using Clementi's original instrumentation) for the first time (No. 1, Turin, Dec. 13, 1935; No. 2, Rome, Jan. 5, 1936). The *Collected Works* (5 vols., Leipzig, 1802–5) is now available in reprint (N.Y., 1973). Pietro Spada revised and edited Symphs. Nos. 1–4 and the 2 symphs. of op. 18.

BIBLIOGRAPHY: Giov. Froio, *Muzio Clementi, La sua vita, le sue opere e sua influenza sul progresso dell'arte* (Milan, 1876); O. Chilesotti, *I nostri maestri del passato* (Milan, 1882); F. Clément, *Les Musiciens célèbres depuis le XVIe siècle* (Paris, 1878); J.S. Shedlock, *The Pianoforte Sonata* (London, 1895); M. Unger, *Muzio Clementis Leben* (Leipzig, 1914); G.C. Paribeni, *Muzio Clementi nella vita e nell'arte* (1921); A. Longo, "Gradus ad Parnassum" (analysis), *Arte Pianistica* (1922); G. de Saint-Foix, "Muzio Clementi," *Musical Quarterly* (July 1923); idem, "Les Symphonies de Clementi," *Revue de Musicologie* (1924); idem, "Clementi: A Forerunner of Beethoven," *Musical Quarterly* (Jan. 1931); A. Stauch, *Muzio Clementis Klaviersonaten im Verhältnis zu den Sonaten von Haydn, Mozart, Beethoven* (Diss., Cologne, 1929); A. Casella, "Muzio Clementi et ses symphonies," *Revue Musicale* (March 1936); H. Simon, "The Clementi Manuscripts at the Library of Congress," *Musical Quarterly* (Jan. 1942); A.W. Tyson, *Thematic Catalogue of the Works of Muzio Clementi* (Tutzing, 1967); E.

Badura-Skoda, "Clementi's *Musical Characteristics* opus 19," in H.C.R. Landon and R. Chapman, eds., *Studies in Eighteenth-Century Music* (London, 1970); J. Bloch, "A Forgotten Clementi Sonata," *Piano Quarterly* (Fall 1972); L. Plantinga, "Clementi, virtuosity, and the 'German Manner,' " *Journal of the American Musicological Society* (Fall 1972). The Clementi-Archiv, in the Netherlands, issues the *Blätter aus dem Clementi-Archiv.*

Clemm, John (Johann Gottlob), German-American organ builder; b. Dresden, 1690; d. Bethlehem, Pa., May 5, 1762. Clemm reputedly learned organ making from A. Silbermann, probably while serving the Moravian Church settlement at Herrnhut, Saxony. He came to America with a group of Schwenkfelders in 1735, became a Separatist, and settled in Philadelphia in 1736. His first known organ was installed at Trinity Church in N.Y., in 1741. Subsequently, he assisted the Swedish-American organ builder Hesselius in Philadelphia. He reunited with the Moravians and moved to Bethlehem, Pa. (1756–58). There he continued his work with his assistant, David Tannenberg, until his death. His descendants were important music dealers and publishers in Philadelphia up to 1879. His son, **John Clemm, Jr.,** was the first organist at N.Y.'s Trinity Church.
BIBLIOGRAPHY: A. H. Messiter, *History of the Choir and Music of Trinity Church* (N.Y., 1907); Donald M. McCorkle, "The Moravian Contribution to American Music," *Music Library Association Notes* (Sept. 1956).

Cleonides, Greek writer on music; lived in the first half of the 2nd century A.D. His treatise *Eisagoge harmonike* (*Introductio harmonica*), based on the theories of Aristoxenus, was for a long time ascribed to the mathematician Euclid, because it had been publ. under Euclid's name by Pena (Paris, 1557) and Meibom (Amsterdam, 1652), although it had been printed with the real author's name by Valla (Venice, 1497). A new critical edition was publ. by K. von Jan in *Musici Scriptores Graeci.* There is a French trans. by Ruelle (1896); for an Eng. trans., see Strunk's *Source Readings in Music History* (N.Y., 1950).

Clérambault, Louis Nicolas, French composer and organist; b. Paris, Dec. 19, 1676; d. there, Oct. 26, 1749. He studied with André Raison; was organist at various Paris churches. He was a successful composer of theatrical pieces for the court: *Le Soleil vainqueur* (Paris, Oct. 21, 1721); *Le Départ du roi* (1745); etc. He also wrote a number of solo cantatas, in which genre he excelled; composed much organ music; some of his organ works are republ. in Guilmant's *Archives des maîtres de l'orgue.* His son, **César François Nicolas Clérambault** (1700–60), was also an organist and composer.

Clercx, Suzanne, Belgian musicologist; b. Houdeng-Aimeries, June 7, 1910. She studied at the Univ. of Liège; took courses in musicology with Charles van den Borren; obtained her Ph.D. in 1939 with the dissertation *Essai sur l'évolution de la musique instrumentale dans les Pays-Bas au XVIII siècle;* was then a librarian at the Royal Cons. in Brussels (1941–49); in 1945 was appointed lecturer at the Univ. of Liège; became a prof. in 1966.
WRITINGS: *Henri-Jacques de Croes* (Brussels, 1940); *Grétry, 1741–1813* (Brussels, 1944); *Le Baroque et la musique* (Brussels, 1948); *Pierre van Maldère* (Brussels, 1948); *Johannes Ciconia: Un musicien liégeois et son temps* (Brussels, 1960); contributed numerous factual essays to various musicological journals.

Cléreau, Pierre, 16th-century French composer. Virtually nothing is known about his life, except that he was a chorister in Toul as a youth. However, many of his sacred works and 3-part chansons have been preserved. The following are extant: 4 masses (Paris, 1554); *Missa pro mortuis* (Paris, 1554); *Missa* (Paris, 1557); 2 books of odes to Ronsard's words (Paris, 1566; several reprints); *Cantiques spirituels* (Paris, 1567).
BIBLIOGRAPHY: G. Thibault and L. Perceau, *Bibliographie des chansons de Ronsard mises en musique au XVIᵉ siècle* (Paris, 1941).

Clérice, Justin, opera composer; b. Buenos Aires, Oct. 16, 1863; d. Toulouse, Sept. 9, 1908. He left Argentina as a young boy and spent most of his life in Paris, studying at the Paris Cons. with Delibes and Pessard (1882). He wrote many comic operas, most of which were performed in Paris: *Figarella* (June 3, 1889); *Le 3ᵉ Hussards* (March 14, 1894); *Pavie* (Jan. 28, 1897); *L'Ordre de l'empereur* (March 3, 1902); etc. His most successful comic opera, *Le Meunier d'Alcala,* was first performed in Portuguese (Lisbon, April 11, 1887); he also wrote an operetta, *Phrynette* (1895); a pantomime, *Léda* (1896); a ballet-opera, *Au temps jadis* (Monte Carlo, 1905).

Cleva, Fausto, Italian conductor; b. Trieste, May 17, 1902; d. Athens (collapsed while conducting), Aug. 6, 1971. He studied in Milan; began his conducting career as a youth; in 1920 emigrated to the U.S.; became an American citizen in 1931. He was chorus master and later conductor of the Metropolitan Opera until 1942; then was conductor of the San Francisco Opera Co. (1942–44 and 1949–55); then again with the Metropolitan (1951 until his death). In 1971 he was presented with a gold cigarette case by the directors of the Metropolitan on the occasion of his 50th anniversary as a regular member, since the age of 18, of its conducting staff.

Cleve, Halfdan, Norwegian composer and pianist; b. Kongsberg, Oct. 5, 1879; d. Oslo, April 6, 1951. He studied with his father, an organist, and with Winter-Hjelms in Oslo; continued his studies in Berlin with O. Raif and with the Scharwenka brothers (1899–1903). He made his debut as a pianist in Berlin (1902); returned to Oslo in 1910, and settled as a pianist and teacher.
WORKS: 5 piano concertos (1902, 1904, 1906, 1910,

1916); Piano Quintet; Violin Sonata; Ballade for Cello and Piano; many piano pieces and songs.

Cliburn, Van (Harvey Lavan, Jr.), brilliant American pianist; b. Shreveport, La., July 12, 1934. He studied piano with his mother; then with Rosina Lhévinne at the Juilliard School of Music in N.Y., graduating in 1954. He made his debut with the Houston Symph. Orch. at the age of 13; appeared with the N.Y. Phil. in 1954; toured as a concert pianist in the U.S. He became suddenly famous when he won the Tchaikovsky Competition in Moscow in 1958, the first American to score such a triumph in Russia, where he became a prime favorite. Upon his return to N.Y. he received a hero's welcome in a street parade. In 1964 he made his debut as an orch. conductor. His playing combines a superlative technique with a genuine Romantic sentiment; this style is particularly effective in the music of Tchaikovsky and Rachmaninoff.
BIBLIOGRAPHY: A. Chasins, *The Van Cliburn Legend* (N.Y., 1959).

Clicquot, French family of organ builders, of whom the earliest was **Robert Clicquot,** builder of the organ in the Versailles Chapel for Louis XIV (1711), and organs in the cathedrals of Rouen (1689) and Saint-Quentin (1703). His sons **Jean-Baptiste** (b. Rheims, Nov. 3, 1678; d. Paris, March 16, 1746) and **Louis-Alexandre** (b. c.1680; d. Paris, Jan. 25, 1760) were his helpers. The most renowned of the family was **François-Henri Clicquot** (b. 1732; d. Paris, May 24, 1790), who constructed the great organ of Versailles Cathedral (installed Oct. 31, 1761) and the organ of St. Sulpice, with 5 manuals, 66 stops, and a 32-foot pedal (1781).
BIBLIOGRAPHY: F. Raugel, *Les Grandes Orgues des églises de Paris* (Paris, 1927); N. Dufourcq, *Les Clicquot* (Paris, 1942); J. Villard, *François-Henri Clicquot, Facteur d'orgues du roi* (Poitiers, 1975).

Cliffe, Frederick, English organist and composer; b. Bradford, Yorkshire, May 2, 1857; d. London, Nov. 19, 1931. He studied with his father, and showed such a precocious musical talent that at the age of 11 he performed his duties as organist at Wyke Parish Church; then was organist of the Bradford Festival Choral Society (1873–76); at the same time he continued his studies with Arthur Sullivan, Prout, Stainer, and Franklin Taylor as a scholarship student. In 1883 he joined the staff of the Royal College of Music, a post which he kept until his death.
WORKS: Symph. No. 1 (London, April 20, 1889); Symph. No. 2 (Leeds, 1892); tone poem, *Cloud and Sunshine* (1890); Violin Concerto (1896); *Ode to the North-East Wind* for Chorus and Orch. (1905); church music.

Clifton, Chalmers, American conductor; b. Jackson, Miss., April 30, 1889; d. New York, June 19, 1966. He studied at the Cincinnati College of Music; then at Harvard with E.B. Hill, Walter Spalding, and W.C. Heilman; further in Paris with Vincent d'Indy and Gédalge. Returning to America, he conducted the Cecilia Society of Boston (1915–17); enlisted in the U.S. Army, and served in the intelligence service. He was active in the Federal Music Project in N.Y. (1935–39); served in an advisory capacity with various musical organizations.

Cline, Patsy (née **Virginia Hensley**), American country-music singer; b. Winchester, Va., Sept. 8, 1932; d. in an airplane crash, Camden, Tenn., March 5, 1963. She became an accomplished singer of country music; in 1957 she won national recognition on Arthur Godfrey's "Talent Scouts" television program with her rendition of *Walkin' after Midnight;* among her hits were *Heartaches* and *Sweet Dreams of You.* In 1973 she was elected to the Country Music Hall of Fame. She was at the peak of her popularity when she met her untimely death.

Clippinger, David Alva, American choral conductor; b. Ohio, Sept. 2, 1860; d. Chicago, Feb. 20, 1938. He studied voice in London with William Shakespeare; then settled in Chicago, where he conducted the Madrigal Club; edited the *Musical Monitor* and *Western Musical Herald;* publ. numerous manuals on the voice: *Systematic Voice Training* (1910); *The Head Voice and Other Problems* (1917); *Collective Voice Training* (1924); *Fundamentals of Voice Training* (1929); *Sight-Singing Based on Rhythmic-Melodic-Harmonic Ear Training* (1931).

Clokey, Joseph Waddell, American organist; b. New Albany, Ind., Aug. 28, 1890; d. Covina, Calif., Sept. 14, 1960. He studied at Miami Univ. (B.A., 1912) and at the Cincinnati Cons. of Music (graduated 1915); in 1915–26 taught music theory at Miami Univ.; in 1926–39 taught organ at Pomona College in Claremont, Calif.; from 1939–46 was dean of the School of Fine Arts at Miami Univ.; retired and lived in Claremont. He wrote much music for schools.
WORKS: Short operas: *The Pied Piper of Hamelin* (Miami Univ., May 14, 1920); *The Nightingale,* after Andersen (Miami Univ., Dec. 12, 1925); *Our American Cousin* (Claremont, March 2, 1931); sacred cantatas: *The Vision; When the Christ Child Came; For He Is Risen; We Beheld His Glory; Adoramus Te; Christ Is Born;* organ pieces; songs. He publ. the manuals *Plainsong* (Boston, 1934) and *In Every Corner Sing: An Outline of Church Music for the Layman* (N.Y., 1945).
BIBLIOGRAPHY: E.E. Hipsher, *American Opera and Its Composers* (Philadelphia, 1927; pp. 122–25); *Compositions of Joseph W. Clokey, A.S.C.A.P.* (N.Y., 1945).

Closson, Ernest, Belgian writer on music; b. St. Josse ten Noode, near Brussels, Dec. 12, 1870; d. Brussels, Dec. 21, 1950. He was self-taught in music; occupied various posts as an archivist; was assistant curator for the collection of musical instruments at the Cons. of Brussels (1896–1924) and chief curator from 1924 to 1935; taught at the Brussels Cons. (1912–35) and the Cons. of Mons (1917); retired in 1935. From 1920–40 he was music critic of *L'In-*

dépendance Belge. In some of his writings he used the pen name **Paul Antoine.**

WRITINGS: *Siegfried de Wagner* (1891); *Edvard Grieg* (1892); *La Musique et les arts plastiques* (1897); *Chansons populaires des provinces belges* (1905; anthology with introduction and notes); *20 Noëls français anciens* (1911); *Le Manuscrit dit des basses-danses de la Bibliothèque de Bourgogne* (1912); *Notes sur la chanson populaire en Belgique* (1913); *Esthétique musicale* (1921); *L'Elément flamand dans Beethoven* (1928; 2nd ed., 1946; in Eng., London, 1936); "Grandfather Beethoven," *Musical Quarterly* (1933). Of his essays in various publications, "L'Instrument de musique comme document ethnographique," in *Guide musical* (1902), and "Le Dix-Neuvième Siècle et l'époque contemporaine," "Le Folklore," and "La Facture instrumentale," in *La Musique en Belgique du moyen-âge à nos jours* (1950), deserve mention. A collection, *Mélanges Closson,* dedicated to him (1948), contains a complete list of his writings.

Clough-Leighter, Henry, American music editor and composer; b. Washington, D.C., May 13, 1874; d. Wollaston, Mass., Sept. 15, 1956. He began to play piano as a child; then studied organ with G. Walter; held various positions as church organist. In 1901 he settled in Boston; was associate editor with Oliver Ditson & Co. (1901–8) and with the Boston Music Co. (1908–21); then in 1921–56, was editor in chief with E.C. Schirmer, Inc., of Boston. He composed several cantatas and a number of other choral works; edited numerous music collections.

Cluer, John, English publisher and engraver of music; d. London, 1728. He claimed to be the inventor of engraving on tin plates. He set up his shop in London about 1715. He engraved and publ. Handel's operas *Giulio Cesare* (1724), *Tamerlano, Scipione,* and others; also Handel's *Suites de pièces de clavecin* (1720) and an 8vo collection of operatic arias.

BIBLIOGRAPHY: F. Kidson, *British Music Publishers, Printers and Engravers* (London, 1900); C. Humphries and W. Smith, *Music Publishing in the British Isles* (London, 1954; 2nd ed., 1970).

Clutsam, George H., Australian pianist and composer; b. Sydney, Sept. 26, 1866; d. London, Nov. 17, 1951. As a young pianist, he made tours of Australia, India, China, and Japan; settled in London in 1889 and became a professional accompanist; gave concerts with Melba (1893). From 1908 until 1918 he was a music critic of the *Observer* in London; at the same time wrote music for the stage.

WORKS: Operas: *The Queen's Jester* (1905); *A Summer Night* (London, July 23, 1910); *After a Thousand Years* (1912); *König Harlekin* (Berlin, 1912); several musical comedies: *Gabrielle, Lavender, The Little Duchess* (Glasgow, Dec. 15, 1922). His greatest popular success was the production of *Lilac Time,* an arrangement of Heinrich Berté's operetta *Das Dreimäderlhaus,* based on Schubert's melodies; Clutsam's version in English was first staged in London on Dec. 22, 1922, and had many

revivals. Another theatrical medley, arranged from Chopin's melodies, was Clutsam's musical comedy *The Damask Rose* (London, June 17, 1929).

Cluytens, André, noted Belgian conductor; b. Antwerp, March 26, 1905; d. Neuilly, near Paris, June 3, 1967. He studied piano at the Antwerp Cons. His father, conductor at the Théâtre Royal in Antwerp, engaged him as a choral coach; later he conducted opera there (1927–32). He then settled in France, and became a French citizen in 1932. He served as music director at the Toulouse Opera (1932–35); in 1935 was appointed opera conductor in Lyons. In 1944 he conducted at the Paris Opéra; in 1947 he was appointed music director of the Opéra-Comique. In 1949 he was named conductor of the Société du Conservatoire de Paris, and in 1955 he became the first French conductor to appear at the Bayreuth Festival. On Nov. 4, 1956, he made his U.S. debut in Washington, D.C., as guest conductor of the Vienna Phil. during its first American tour. In 1960 he became chief conductor of the Orch. National de Belgique in Brussels, a post he held until his death. Cluytens was highly regarded as a fine interpreter of French music.

BIBLIOGRAPHY: B. Cavoty, *André Cluytens,* in the series Les Grands Interprètes (Geneva, 1955).

Cluzeau-Mortet, Luis, Uruguayan composer; b. Montevideo, Nov. 16, 1889; d. there, Sept. 28, 1957. He studied piano and theory with his maternal grandfather, who was the first Uruguayan to receive a prize at the Paris Cons. Cluzeau-Mortet played piano and the viola in radio bands in Montevideo and composed industriously. His music is marked by Romantic influences, with occasional excursions into cautious modernism. All of his orch. works were first performed by the radio orch. SODRE, in Montevideo, of which he was a member.

WORKS: *Llanuras* (Oct. 14, 1944); *Rancherío* (Aug. 2, 1947); *Artigas* (Aug. 13, 1955); *Sinfonía del Este* (unfinished; a movement, *La laguna negra,* was played on Aug. 16, 1958, as a posthumous act of homage); *Fantasía Concerto* for Piano and Chamber Orch.; *4 ritmos criollos* for String Quartet; *Bagatelas criollas* for 4 Flutes; songs and piano pieces. A complete catalogue of his works is found in Vol. 14 of the series Compositores de América (Washington, D.C., 1968).

Coates, Albert, eminent English conductor, b. St. Petersburg, Russia (of an English father and a mother of Russian descent), April 23, 1882; d. Milnerton, near Cape Town, South Africa, Dec. 11, 1953. He went to England for his general education; enrolled in the science classes of Liverpool Univ., and studied organ with an elder brother who was living there at the time. In 1902 he entered the Leipzig Cons., studying cello with Klengel, piano with Robert Teichmüller, and conducting with Artur Nikisch; served his apprenticeship there and made his debut as conductor in Offenbach's *Les Contes d'Hoffmann* at the Leipzig Opera. In 1906 he was appointed (on Nikisch's recommendation) as chief conductor of the opera house at Elberfeld; in 1910 he was a joint conductor at the Dresden Opera (with Schuch); then at Mannheim (with Bodanzky). In 1911 he received the appointment at the Imperial Opera of St. Petersburg, and conducted many Russian operas. From 1913 he conducted in England, specializing in Wagner and the Russian repertoire; was a proponent of Scriabin's music. In 1920 he made his American debut as guest conductor of the N.Y. Symph. Orch.; during 1923–25 he led conducting classes at the Eastman School of Music in Rochester, N.Y.; also conducted the Rochester Symph. Orch. and appeared as guest conductor with other American orchs. Subsequent engagements included a season at the Berlin State Opera (1931) and concerts with the Vienna Phil. (1935). In 1946 he settled in South Africa, where he conducted the Johannesburg Symph. Orch. and taught at the Univ. of South Africa at Cape Town. Coates was a prolific composer, but his operas and other works had few performances (usually conducted by himself).

WORKS: Symph. poem, *The Eagle* (Leeds, 1925; unsuccessful); operas: *Assurbanipal* (planned for perf. in Moscow in 1915, but abandoned in view of wartime conditions); *Samuel Pepys* (produced in German, Munich, Dec. 21, 1929); *Pickwick* (London, Nov. 20, 1936); *Tafelberg se Kleed* (Eng. title, *Van Hunks and the Devil;* produced at the South African Music Festival in Cape Town, March 7, 1952).

Coates, Edith (Mary), English mezzo-soprano; b. Lincoln, May 31, 1908; d. Worthing, Jan. 7, 1983. She studied at the Trinity College of Music in London; later took lessons with Clive Carey and Dino Borgioli; in 1924 she joined the Old Vic Theatre; sang major roles there from 1931; she appeared at Covent Garden in 1937; was on its roster from 1947 to 1967. She sang the leading roles in the world premieres of Britten's *Peter Grimes* (1945) and *Gloriana* (1953), and in *The Olympians* by Arthur Bliss (1949). In 1977 she was named an Officer of the Order of the British Empire.

Coates, Eric, English composer and viola player; b. Hucknall, Nottinghamshire, Aug. 27, 1886; d. Chichester, Dec. 21, 1957. He took instruction at the Royal Academy of Music with Tertis (viola) and Corder (composition). He was a member of the Hambourg String Quartet, with which he made a tour of South Africa (1908); was first violist in Queen's Hall Orch. (1912–19). In 1946 he visited the U.S., conducting radio performances of his works; in 1948 toured in South America. He gives a detailed account of his career in his autobiography *Suite in Four Movements* (London, 1953). As a composer, Coates specialized in semi-classical works for orch. His valse serenade *Sleepy Lagoon* (1930) attained enormous popularity all over the world, and was publ. in numerous arrangements. His *London Suite* (1933) was equally successful; its *Knightsbridge* movement became one of the most frequently played marches in England and elsewhere. He further wrote an orch. suite, *4 Centuries* (1941), tracing typical historical forms and styles in 4 sections

(*Fugue, Pavane, Valse, and Jazz*); *3 Elizabeths* for Orch.; a great number of songs and instrumental pieces.

Coates, Gloria, American composer; b. Wausau, Wis., Oct. 10, 1934. She studied with Helen Gunderson and Kenneth Klaus at Louisiana State Univ., with Alexander Tcherepnin at De Paul Univ. in Chicago, at Columbia Univ. with Otto Luening and Jack Beeson; also took courses in theater arts, developed a singing voice, and began a quaquaversal career as an actress, stage director, librettist, singer, impresario, and teacher. In 1971 she concentrated on composition; experimented with multiphonic techniques and gave demonstrations of her variegated prowesses at European festivals. In 1971 she organized in Munich a German-American Contemporary Music Series, which she supervised until 1984. In 1975 she inaugurated for the Univ. of Wisconsin a series of International Programs in Music; was also active as moderator and commentator for German radio programs in Cologne and Bremen. She traveled to Russia, India, China, and all over Europe, giving performances in her various capacities. He own music is compact and dense, replete with euphonious dissonances in the framework of involute counterpoint. When unable to earn an Existenz-Minimum to carry on, she cheerfully took on clerical jobs, as a cashier, shop supervisor, telephone operator, and domestic counselor. Her more or less permanent residence is in Munich.

WORKS: Sonatina for Violin and Piano (1961); *Fugue over Passacaglia* in 12 Tones for Piano (1962); *5 Abstractions* for Piano (1962); *Mathematical Equations* for Speaker, Soprano, and Piano (Baton Rouge, La., May 11, 1965); Trio for 3 Flutes (1965); 4 string quartets (1966, 1970, 1976, 1980); *Mobile* for String Quartet (1972); *5 Poems of Emily Dickinson* for Mezzo-soprano and Piano (1972); *Music on Open Strings* for Chamber Orch. (1974; Warsaw, Sept. 20, 1978); *Planets* for Orch. (1974; Hannover, Germany, Feb. 2, 1975); *Icarus,* ballet (1975); *Machine People,* ballet (1976); *6 Movements* for String Quartet (1976); *Sinfonietta della notte* (Lund, Sweden, July 4, 1982); several pieces for magnetic tape; electronic music.

Coates, John, English tenor; b. Girlington, Yorkshire, June 29, 1865; d. Northwood, Middlesex, Aug. 16, 1941. He studied with his uncle, J.G. Walton, at Bradford; sang as a small boy at a Bradford church; began serious study in 1893, and took lessons with William Shakespeare in London. He sang baritone parts in Gilbert & Sullivan operettas, making his debut at the Savoy Theatre in *Utopia Limited* (1894); toured in the U.S. with a Gilbert & Sullivan company. He made his debut in grand opera as Faust at Covent Garden (1901); also sang Lohengrin in Cologne and other German cities with considerable success; later sang nearly all the Wagner parts in English with the Moody-Manners Co., with the Carl Rosa Co., and with Beecham (1910); from 1911–13 he toured with Quinlan's opera company in Australia and South Africa. He served in the British army during World War I; in 1919, returned to London, devoting himself chiefly to teaching; also gave recitals of songs by English composers.

Cobbett, Walter Wilson, English patron of music; b. London, July 11, 1847; d. there, Jan. 22, 1937. He was a businessman and amateur violinist. An ardent enthusiast, he traveled widely in Europe and met contemporary composers. He was particularly active in promoting the cause of British chamber music, and arranged a series of Cobbett Competitions; also commissioned special works and established a Cobbett Medal for services to chamber music; the recipients included Thomas Dunhill (1924), Mrs. E.S. Coolidge (1925), and A.J. Clements (1926). Among composers who received the Cobbett commissions and awards were Frank Bridge, York Bowen, John Ireland, Vaughan Williams, James Friskin, Waldo Warner, and Herbert Howells. Cobbett edited the extremely valuable *Cobbett's Cyclopedic Survey of Chamber Music* (2 vols., London; vol. I, 1929; vol. II, 1930; a supplement to vol. I. was publ. in London in 1957; to vol. II, in 1963).

Cocchi, Gioacchino, Italian composer; b. Padua, c.1715; d. Venice, 1804. He was a teacher at the Cons. degli Incurabili in Venice by 1750; lived in London as an opera composer and music director of the Haymarket Theater, 1757–62; returned to Venice in 1773.
WORKS: His first opera was *Adelaide* (Rome, 1743); others were *Elisa* (1744); *Baiazette* (1746); *La Maestra* (Naples, 1747); *Arminio* (1749); *La Gismonda* (1750); *Semiramide riconosciuta* (1753); *Demofoonte* (1754); *Demetrio, re di Siria* (London, Nov. 8, 1757); *Zenobia* (London, 1758); *Ciro riconosciuto* (London, 1759); *La clemenza di Tito* (London, 1760); and *Tito Manlio* (London, 1761). He excelled in opera buffa and was also proficient in secular cantatas.

Coccia, Carlo, Italian opera composer; b. Naples, April 14, 1782; d. Novara, April 13, 1873. He studied music theory with Pietro Casella, singing with Saverio Valente, and composition with Paisiello; in 1820 went to Lisbon as maestro concertatore at the San Carlos Opera. In 1824–27 he was conductor at the King's Theatre in London, where he produced his own opera *Maria Stuarda* (1827). He returned to Italy in 1827. Coccia wrote 37 operas; 2 of them, *Clotilda* (Venice, June 8, 1815) and *Caterina di Guise* (Milan, Feb. 14, 1833), were fairly successful.

Cochereau, Pierre, French organist; b. St. Mandé, near Paris, July, 9, 1924; d. Lyons, March 6, 1984. He studied organ at the Paris Cons. with Marcel Dupré and composition with Maurice Duruflé; won prizes for organ, harmony, composition, and musicology. He served as organist at St. Roch in Paris (1942–54); in 1955 was engaged as organist at Notre Dame; was also director of the Le Mans Cons. (1950–56) and of the Cons. of Nice (from 1962). He made successful tours as an organist in Europe, the U.S., and the Far East. He composed 2 concertos for organ, and other pieces; like many other organists, he was proficient in effective improvisation.

Cochlaeus (real name, **Dobnek, Johannes**), German music theorist; b. Wendelstein, near Nuremberg, Jan. 10, 1479; d. Breslau, Jan. 10, 1552. He studied philosophy at the Univ. of Cologne (B.A., 1505; M.A., 1507); in 1509 became a prof. there. In 1510 he taught history and geography in Nuremberg. From 1515 he traveled in Italy; obtained the degree of doctor of theology in Ferrara (1517); then was ordained priest in Rome; subsequently held various ecclesiastical posts in Germany; during the last 7 years of his life he was at the Breslau Cathedral. Cochlaeus opposed Luther at the councils of Worms and Augsburg. He publ. numerous theological papers; was also the author of the treatise *Musica* (Cologne, 1507; enlarged ed., under the title *Tetrachordum musices,* Nuremberg, 1511, and 6 later eds.; Eng. trans. by C. Miller in *Musicological Studies and Documents,* XXIII, 1970).
BIBLIOGRAPHY: M. Spahn, *J. Cochlaeus* (Berlin, 1898).

Cocker, Joe, English vocalist in the American rhythm-and-blues style; b. Sheffield, May 20, 1944. He beat the drums, and began to croon as a boy. In 1963 he was lead vocalist of a group called The Avengers. His first success came with a blues version of the Beatles' song *With a Little Help from My Friends.* In 1969 he formed The Grease Band, with which he toured the U.S. The measure of his success can be gauged by the release of a record exclamatorily titled *Joe Cocker!* With his big vocal hit *She Came In through the Bathroom Window* he ascended to the top of the best-sellers. To emphasize his British allegiance in the world of psychedelic delirium tremens, he joined a group which annexed a line from Noël Coward, Mad Dogs and Englishmen. He excited the hordes of acid heads at the Woodstock Festival in 1969 with his epileptic twitches and facial contortions. Periodically, he freaked out and vanished into the starry vacuum, but invariably returned after a few months in outer mental space.

Cocks & Co., London firm of music publishers, founded 1823 by **Robert Cocks;** his sons, **Arthur Lincoln Cocks** and **Stroud Lincoln Cocks,** became partners in 1868. Upon the death of the original founder in 1887, **Robert Macfarlane Cocks** became the proprietor and carried on the business until 1898, when he retired and transferred the house to Augener and Co. The catalogue of publications comprised 16,000 numbers.

Cockshott, Gerald Wilfred, English composer; b. Bristol, Nov. 14, 1915; d. London, Feb. 3, 1979. He specialized in English literature; was head of the English dept. at Whittingehame College, Brighton (1948–64), and at Ifield Grammar School, Crawley, Sussex (1965–78). He studied composition privately with Vaughan Williams; became active primarily as a writer on musical subjects. His music is transparently tonal and is impressed with melorhythms of English folk songs, but its simplicity is of a sophisticated nature.

WORKS: 2 one-act operas: *Apollo and Persephone* (N.Y., Feb. 22, 1956) and *A Faun in the Forest* (Westport, Conn., Aug. 9, 1959); Symph. in B minor (1949); *Serenade* for Flute and Strings (1952); *3 Pieces on Appalachian Folk Tunes* for Cello and Piano (1962); songs; carols; choruses; numerous arrangements of American, English, French-Canadian, Danish, and Dutch songs.

Coclico, Adrianus Petit, Flemish musician and theorist; b. in Flanders, c.1500; d. Copenhagen, 1563 (of the plague). He was a disciple of Josquin; held a teaching post at the Univ. of Wittenberg (1545); then was in Frankfurt an der Oder (1546), in Königsberg (1547), and in Nuremberg (1550). In 1555 he was in Wismar; was compelled to leave Germany when a charge of bigamy was made against him; he settled in Copenhagen in 1556 as organist and singer at the court chapel. He was the author of the important tracts *Compendium musices* (1552; reproduced in facsimile [Kassel, 1955] in the series Documenta Musicologica, ed. by M. Bukofzer; Eng. trans. by A. Seay in Translations Series 5 [Colorado Springs, 1973]) and *Musica reservata* (1552).

BIBLIOGRAPHY: M. Van Crevel, *Adrianus Petit Coclico* (The Hague, 1940); G. Reese, *Music in the Renaissance* (N.Y., 1954; 2nd ed., revised, 1959).

Coelho, Ruy, eminent Portuguese composer; b. Alcaçer do Sal, March 3, 1891. He studied piano and composition in Lisbon; in 1910 he went to Germany, where he took lessons in composition with Engelbert Humperdinck, Max Bruch, and Schoenberg (1910–13); subsequently took a course at the Paris Cons. with Paul Vidal; returning to Portugal, he was active as a concert pianist; also wrote music criticism in the *Diario de Noticias.*

WORKS: As a composer, he devoted himself mainly to operas. Most of these were produced at the Lisbon Opera: *Inês de Castro* (Jan. 15, 1927); *Belkiss* (June 9, 1928); *Entre gestas* (1929); *Tá-Mar* (June 16, 1937); *Don João IV* (Dec. 1, 1940); *Rosas de todo o ano* (May 30, 1940); *A rosa de papel* (Dec. 18, 1947); *Auto da barca do Inferno* (Jan. 15, 1950); *Inês Pereira* (1952); *O vestido de novia* (Jan. 4, 1959); *Orfeu em Lisboa* (1963); *A bela dama sem pecado (Beautiful Lady without Sin;* 1968); *Auto da barca da Gloria* (1970); also *Serão da Infanta, Vagabundo, Soror Mariana,* and *Cavaleiro das mãos irresistiveis.* Ballets: *A Princesa dos sapatos de ferro* (1912); *A Feira* (1930); *Dom Sebastião* (1943); *Arraial na Ribeira* (1951); *Fatima,* oratorio (1960); *Oratorio da paz* (1967). Orch. works: *5 Sinfonias camoneanas* (1912, 1917, 1943, 1951, 1957); *Nun Alvares,* symph. poem (1922); *Rainha santa,* symph. legend (1926); *Suite Portuguesa No. 1* (1926) and *No. 2* (1928); *Petites symphonies* Nos. 1 and 2 (1928, 1932); *Sinfonia d'alem mar* (1969); Piano Concerto No. 1 (1909); Piano Concerto No. 2 (1948); Violin Sonata No. 1 (1910); Violin Sonata No. 2 (1924); Piano Trio (1916); *Cancões de Saudade e Amor* for

Voice and Piano (1917); songs.

Coenen, Franz, Dutch violinist; b. Rotterdam, Dec. 26, 1826; d. Leyden, Jan. 24, 1904. He was a pupil of his father, an organist; then of Vieuxtemps and Molique. After tours as a concert violinist with Henri Herz, and in South America with E. Lübeck, he settled in Amsterdam; until 1895 he was director at the Cons.

Coenen, Johannes Meinardus, Dutch bassoonist and conductor; b. The Hague, Jan. 28, 1824; d. Amsterdam, Jan. 9, 1899. He was a pupil of Lübeck at the Cons. there; from 1857 was conductor of the Felix Meritis orch.; in 1865, was conductor of the Grand Dutch Theater in Amsterdam; then at the Palais d'Industrie. The Palais Orch., which he founded, became world-famous. He retired in 1896.

Coenen, Willem, pianist, brother of **Franz Coenen;** b. Rotterdam, Nov. 17, 1837; d. Lugano, March 18, 1918. He traveled in South America and the West Indies; taught, gave concerts, and composed in London (1862–1909); then retired and lived near Lugano. He wrote an oratorio, *Lazarus* (1878); publ. piano music and songs; many cantatas, masses, etc., remain in MS.

Coerne, Louis Adolphe, American composer; b. Newark, N.J., Feb. 27, 1870; d. Boston, Sept. 11, 1922. He studied violin with Kneisel and composition at Harvard Univ. with J.K. Paine (1888–90); then went to Germany, where he took courses with Rheinberger in Munich. Returning to America, he became the first recipient of the degree of Ph.D. in music given by an American univ., with the thesis *The Evolution of Modern Orchestration* (1905; publ. in N.Y., 1908); he then occupied teaching positions at Harvard Univ., Smith College, the Univ. of Wisconsin, etc.

WORKS: Opera, *Zenobia* (1902; produced in Bremen, Germany, Dec. 1, 1905); *Hiawatha,* symph. poem (1893); *Romantic Concerto* for Violin and Orch.; *Beloved America,* patriotic hymn for Male Chorus and Orch.; many part-songs; *Swedish Sonata* for Violin and Piano; 3 piano trios in canon. Most of his MS works are in the Boston Public Library.

Coertse, Mimi, soprano; b. Durban, South Africa, June 12, 1932. She studied in Johannesburg and Vienna; made her debut with the Vienna State Opera on tour in Naples in 1955; then sang in Basel and at the Teatro San Carlo in Naples; in 1957 she became a member of the Vienna State Opera; also appeared in London, Cologne, Rome, Brussels, and other major European music centers.

Cœuroy André, (real name, **Jean Belime**), distinguished French music critic; b. Dijon, Feb. 24, 1891. He studied in Paris at the Ecole Normale Supérieure, and with Max Reger in Germany. He was in the French army in World War I, and was taken prisoner. He continued his musical activities in the

German prison camp, organizing instrumental bands and giving lectures on Wagner and other composers. After his release, he taught languages in Paris; lectured on French music in the U.S. (1930–31). He was a founder and associate editor of *La Revue Musicale* (1920) and wrote music criticism in various French newspapers. His musical works include several pieces for clarinet; also a Clarinet Quintet. His writings are valuable for originality of presentation as well as scholarship and accuracy.

WRITINGS: *La Musique française moderne* (Paris, 1921); *Essais de musique et littérature comparées* (1923); *Weber* (1924); *Le Jazz* (in collaboration with A. Schaeffner, 1926); *Le Phonographe* (1927); *Panorama de la musique contemporaine* (1928); *Panorama de la Radio* (in collaboration with J. Mercier, 1929); *Histoire de la musique avec l'aide du disque* (in collaboration with R. Jardillier, 1931); *La Musique et le peuple* (1942); *Histoire générale du jazz* (1943); *Les Lieder de Schubert* (1948); *R. Schumann* (1949); *La Musique et ses formes* (1950); *Chopin* (1951); *Dictionnaire critique de la musique ancienne et moderne* (Lausanne, 1956); *Wagner et l'esprit romantique* (Paris, 1965).

Cogan, Philip, Irish composer; b. Cork, 1748; d. Dublin, Feb. 3, 1833. He was a chorister at Cork; in 1772 went to Dublin, where he occupied various posts as a church organist. He acquired great renown as a teacher and performer; Michael Kelly and Thomas Moore were his pupils. Cogan wrote numerous pieces for the harpsichord and the piano, 2 piano concertos, and 2 comic operas: *The Ruling Passion* (Dublin, Feb. 24, 1778) and *The Contract* (Dublin, May 14, 1782; revived under the title *The Double Stratagem,* 1784). In some of his piano works he incorporated Irish rhythms, and is therefore regarded as a pioneer composer of instrumental music in Ireland.

Cohan, George M(ichael), celebrated American composer of popular songs; b. Providence, July 3, 1878 (Cohan, himself, believed that he was born on July 4, but the discovery of his birth certificate proves July 3 to be correct); d. New York, Nov. 5, 1942. He was a vaudeville performer and had a natural talent for writing verses and simple melodies in the ballad style. His greatest song, *Over There* (1917), became sweepingly popular during World War I. A congressional medal was given to him for this song. The film *Yankee Doodle Dandy* (1942) and the Broadway musical *George M!* (1968) were both based on his life.

BIBLIOGRAPHY: W. Morehouse, *George Michael Cohan, Prince of the American Theater* (N.Y., 1943).

Cohen, Harriet, distinguished English pianist; b. London, Dec. 2, 1895; d. there, Nov. 13, 1967. She studied piano with her parents; then took an advanced course in piano playing with Matthay; made her first public appearance as a solo pianist at the age of 13. She then engaged in a successful career in England, both as a soloist with major orchs. and in chamber music concerts. She made a specialty of old keyboard music, but also played many contemporary compositions; Vaughan Williams, Arnold Bax, and other English composers wrote special works for her. In 1938 she was made a Dame Commander of the Order of the British Empire in appreciation of her services. She publ. a book on piano playing, *Music's Handmaid* (London, 1936; 2nd ed., 1950). Her memoirs, *A Bundle of Time,* were publ. posthumously (London, 1969).

Cohen, Isidore, American violinist; b. New York, Dec. 16, 1922. He studied violin with Ivan Galamian at the Juilliard School of Music in N.Y.; from 1958–66 was a member of the Juilliard Quartet; in 1966 he joined the Beaux Arts Trio, and subsequently toured with it.

Cohen, Jules-Emile-David, French composer; b. Marseilles, Nov. 2, 1835; d. Paris, Jan. 13, 1901. He studied at the Paris Cons., piano with Marmontel, organ with Benoist, and composition with Halévy, and carried first prizes in each of these courses. He then served as an instructor of choral singing at the Paris Cons.; in 1877 was engaged as chorus master at the Grand Opéra. He produced several operas, none too successful, among them *Les Bleuets* (Paris, Oct. 23, 1867) and *Dea* (Paris, April 30, 1870); he also wrote 3 cantatas; several masses; symph. and chamber music; some 200 songs and 200 piano pieces.

Cohen, Leonard, Canadian balladeer; b. Montreal, Sept. 21, 1934. One of the few Jews who made it as a pop singer, he went into such highbrow stuff as writing poetry and publishing sentimental novels. At the same time, he strummed his guitar and sang such maudlin romances as *Suzanne* and such alienation tunes as *Stranger Song,* such heart-impinging implorations as *Hey, That's No Way to Say Goodbye,* and such beseeching tunes as *Sisters of Mercy.* He sang at the Newport Folk Festival in 1967 and teamed with Judy Collins in his American tour. Like Bob Dylan and other troubled songsters, Cohen periodically withdrew from public view to meditate about his alienation. His *Songs of Love and Hate* exemplified such psychological quaquaversality. He returned to the world at large and released an album symbolic of his healing graft, *New Skin for the Old Ceremony.*

Cohn, Al(vin Gilbert), American jazz tenor saxophonist and composer; b. New York, Nov. 24, 1925. He studied clarinet and piano; later took up the tenor saxophone; then played with several bands, including those of Buddy Rich (1947), Woody Herman (1948–49), and Artie Shaw (1949). He devoted much of his time to composing music for radio and television.

Cohn, Arthur, American composer, conductor, and publishing executive; b. Philadelphia, Nov. 6, 1910. He studied at the Combs Cons. of Music in Philadelphia (1920–28), and with William F. Happich;

also studied violin with Sascha Jacobinoff (1930–31); in 1933–34 he studied composition at the Juilliard School of Music with Rubin Goldmark. Returning to Philadelphia, he was appointed director of the Edwin A. Fleisher Collection at the Free Library of Philadelphia (1934–52); also served as executive director of the Settlement Music School in Philadelphia (1952–56). From 1942 to 1965 he conducted the Symph. Club of Philadelphia; also the Germantown Symph. Orch. (1949–55), the Philadelphia Little Symph. (1952–56), and in 1958 was appointed conductor of the Haddonfield, N.J., Symph. Orch.; made guest appearances at Children's Concerts with the Philadelphia Orch. From 1956 to 1966 he was head of symph. and foreign music at Mills Music Co., and from 1966 to 1972 held a similar position with MCA Music. In 1972 he was appointed Director of Serious Music at Carl Fischer.

WORKS: 6 string quartets (1928–45); *5 Nature Studies* (1932); *Retrospections* for String Orch. (Philadelphia, April 3, 1935); *Music for Brass Instruments* (1935); Suite for Viola and Orch. (1937); *Machine Music* for 2 Pianos (1937); 4 Preludes for String Orch. (N.Y., May 26, 1937); *4 Symphonic Documents* (1939); *Music for Ancient Instruments* (1939; awarded first prize in a contest of the American Society of Ancient Instruments); Quintuple Concerto for 5 Ancient Instruments, with Modern Orch. (1940); Concerto for Flute and Orch. (1941); Variations for Clarinet, Saxophone, and String Orch. (1945); *Music for Bassoon,* unaccompanied (1947); *Kaddish* for Orch. (1964). Perhaps the most remarkable of his works is *Quotations in Percussion* for 103 Instruments handled by 6 Players (1958). He publ. *The Collector's Twentieth-Century Music in the Western Hemisphere* (N.Y., 1961); *Twentieth-Century Music in Western Europe* (N.Y., 1965); *Musical Quizzical* (77 puzzles; N.Y., 1970; dedicated "to the most sagacious and needle-witted musician I know"); *Recorded Classical Music: A Critical Guide to Compositions and Performances* (N.Y., 1981).

Cohn, Heinrich. See **Conried, Heinrich.**

Cohn, James, American composer; b. Newark, N.J., Feb. 12, 1928. He studied with Wayne Barlow at the Eastman School of Music, with Roy Harris at Cornell Univ., and with Bernard Wagenaar at the Juilliard School of Music (B.S., 1949; M.S., 1950). Besides his compositions, he has several patents for devices that can be applied to keyboards or fingerboards to control pitch, intonation, loudness, vibrato, and tremolo.

WORKS: Opera, *The Fall of the City* (Columbus, Ohio, July 8, 1955). For Orch.: Symph No. 1 (1947); Symph. No. 2 (Brussels, Dec. 11, 1953), Symph. No. 3 (Detroit, Dec. 17, 1959); Symph. No. 4 (Florence, Italy, Oct. 1, 1960); Symph. No. 5 (1959); Symph. No. 6 (1965); Symph. No. 7 (1967); Symph. No. 8 (1978); Sinfonietta (1946); Variations on *The Wayfaring Stranger* (Detroit, Oct. 4, 1962); several overtures; Concerto for Concertina and Strings; Suite for String Orch. Chamber Music: 3 string quartets,

Wind Quintet; many piano and choral works.

Colasse, Pascal, French opera composer; b. Rheims, Jan. 22, 1649; d. Versailles, July 17, 1709. He was a pupil of Lully, who entrusted him with writing out the parts of his operas from the figured bass and melody. Later Colasse was accused of appropriating scores thrown aside by his master as incomplete. In 1683 he was appointed Master of the Music; in 1696, royal chamber musician. He was a favorite of Louis XIV, and obtained the privilege of producing operas at Lille, but the theater burned down; his opera *Polyxène et Pyrrhus* (1706) failed, and his mind became disordered. Of 10 operas, *Les Noces de Thétys et Pélée* (1689) was his best. He also composed songs, sacred and secular.

Colbran, Isabella (Isabel Angela Colbran), famous Spanish soprano; b. Madrid, Feb. 2, 1785; d. Bologna, Oct. 7, 1845. She studied with Pareja in Madrid, then with Marinelli and Crescentini in Naples; made her debut in a concert in Paris in 1801. After her successful appearances in Bologna (1807) and La Scala in Milan (1808), the impresario Barbaja engaged her for Naples in 1811; she became his mistress, only to desert him for Rossini, whom she married on March 16, 1822 (they were legally separated in 1837). She created the leading soprano roles in several of Rossini's operas, beginning with *Elisabetta, Regina d'Inghilterra* (1815) and concluding with *Semiramide* (1823); with her voice in decline, she retired from the stage in 1824. During the early years of the 19th century she was acclaimed as the leading dramatic coloratura soprano.

Colburn, George, American composer and conductor; b. Colton, N.Y., June 25, 1878; d. Chicago, April 18, 1921. He studied violin and singing at the American Cons. of Music in Chicago; then taught there (1903–15); conducted at Ravinia Park in 1913; from 1915 was director of municipal music at Winona, Minn. He wrote several symph. poems and scores for theatrical plays: *Masque of Montezuma* (1912); *Masque of Demeter and Persephone* (1913); *Anthony and Cleopatra* (1914); etc.; also some chamber music (Piano Quartet, etc.).

Colding-Jørgensen, Henrik, Danish composer; b. Riisskov, March 21, 1944. He studied composition with Holmboe at the Royal Cons. in Copenhagen, graduating in 1966; taught organ in Copenhagen (1967–70) and music theory at the Odense Cons. (1969–75). In 1975 he became active as a church organist and choirmaster in Copenhagen.

WORKS: FOR ORCH.: Symph. No. 1 (1965); *At elske musikken (To Love Music;* 1975; Copenhagen, May 6, 1976); *Ballade* for Tuba and Chamber Orch. (1979). CHAMBER MUSIC: Divertimento for 8 Instruments (1964); String Quartet No. 1 (1965); *Sinusrhapsodie* for 2 Cellos (1968); *Avnstrup Suite* for Recorder, Violin, and Guitar (1969); *Mourn* for Solo Guitar (1969); *Suite à deux* for Flute and Clarinet (1971); *Cello* for Solo Cello (1972); *Solo Grande* for Percussion (1972); *Balancer* for Violin and Percussion (1974); *Puer natus* for 5 Tubas (1976); *Boast* for Solo Tuba (1980). FOR VOICE: *Lapidary Landscapes* for Mezzo-soprano, Bass-baritone, Oboe, English Horn, Viola, Cello, and Percussion (1965); *Pä din taerskel (At Your Doorstep)* for Contralto and Orch. (1966); *Enfance III* for Contralto, Horn, and Harp (1967) and *IV* for Contralto and Piano (1968); *Barbare* for 6 Soloists, Choir, and Orch. (1967; Copenhagen Radio, Jan. 21, 1972); *Altid noget andet (Always Something Else)* for Tenor and Viola d'Amore (1973); *Ava Maria* for Contralto Solo (1974); *Fra först af (From the Beginning)* for Mixed Chorus, Trumpet, Trombone, and Organ (1975); *Victoria through the Wood* for Alto and Orch. (1975); *Det er mig der vaelter (It Is Me Who Is Overturned)* for Soprano, Mezzo-soprano, and Organ (1980). FOR ORGAN: *Logbogsblade (Logbook Sheets;* 1969); *Magnus* (1972).

Cole, Nat "King" (Nathaniel Adams Coles), black American pianist and singer; b. Montgomery, Ala., March 17, 1917; d. Santa Monica, Calif., Feb. 15, 1965. He worked as a jazz pianist in Los Angeles nightclubs; in 1939 formed the original King Cole Trio (piano, guitar, bass); then turned to singing. He was the first black artist to acquire a sponsor on a radio program; also had a brief series on television. He created a distinct style of velvet vocalization and satin softness in the rendition of intimate, brooding, sentimental songs. His appeal was universal; his tours in South America, Europe, the Middle East, and the Orient attracted great multitudes of admirers who knew him by his recordings. The sole exception was his native state; at his concert in Birmingham, Ala., on April 10, 1956, he was attacked by 6 white men and suffered a minor back injury.
BIBLIOGRAPHY: M. Cole and L. Robinson, *Nat King Cole: An Intimate Biography* (N.Y., 1971).

Cole, Rossetter Gleason, American composer; b. Clyde, Mich., Feb. 5, 1866; d. Lake Bluff, Ill., May 18, 1952. He studied music with C.B. Cady; in 1890 went to Germany, where he studied composition with Max Bruch in Berlin, and organ with Middleschulte. Returning to America in 1892, he occupied various posts as a teacher and organist in Wisconsin, Iowa, and Illinois; lived mostly in Chicago.
WORKS: *The Maypole Lovers,* opera (1931; a suite from it was perf. by the Chicago Symph. Orch., Jan. 9, 1936); *Hiawatha's Wooing* for Narrator and Orch. (1904); *King Robert of Sicily* for Narrator and Orch. (1906); *Ballade* for Cello and Orch. (Minneapolis, 1909); *Symphonic Prelude* (Chicago, March 11, 1915); *Pioneer Overture* (composed for the centenary of the state of Illinois; perf. by the Chicago Symph. Orch., composer conducting, March 14, 1919); *Heroic Piece* for Organ and Orch. (Chicago, Feb. 11, 1924); cantatas: *The Passing of Summer* (1902); *The Broken Troth* (1917); *The Rock of Liberty* (1920); Violin Sonata; several organ pieces; piano pieces (*From a Lover's Notebook, In Springtime, Sunset in the Hills,* etc.); songs (*Lilacs, Love's Invocation,* etc.). In 1896 he married the pianist **Fannie** Louise Gwinner.

Cole, Sidney Robert, English organist and music educator; b. London, Oct. 21, 1865; d. there, Nov. 28, 1937. He studied at the Royal College of Music; later was examiner there. In 1902 he went to Australia, settling as a teacher in Melbourne. He returned to England in 1932. His numerous compositions for organ, chorus, and piano, almost all in MS, are preserved in the library of the British Music Society in Melbourne.

Cole, Ulric, American composer and pianist; b. New York, Sept. 9, 1905. She studied with Goetschius and Rubin Goldmark (composition) and Josef Lhévinne (piano). She wrote 2 piano concertos; a Piano Quintet; 2 violin sonatas; and many piano pieces. She was the soloist in the premiere of her Divertimento for Piano and String Orch. with the Cincinnati Symph. (March 31, 1939).

Cole, William Randolph ("Cozy"), black American jazz drummer; b. East Orange, N.J., Oct. 17, 1909; d. Columbus, Ohio, Jan. 29, 1981. After taking up the drums while young, he began his career in 1928; he played with Jelly Roll Morton, Stuff Smith, and others before joining Cab Calloway's band in 1938; then appeared on radio; he played on Broadway in 1943 in the musical *Carmen Jones,* displaying his expertise in the number *Beat Out Dat Rhythm on a Drum;* also appeared in the 1945 production of *The Seven Lively Arts* with Benny Goodman's Quintet. He later played with Louis Armstrong; then formed his own band, which toured Africa in 1962; was also a member of the Jonah Jones Quintet (1969–76); then was artist-in-residence at Capital Univ. in Columbus, Ohio.

Coleman, Cy (real name, **Seymour Kaufman**), American composer of popular music; b. New York, June 14, 1929. He studied at the N.Y. College of Music, and began his career as a composer for radio and television. With the lyricist Joseph A. McCarthy, he composed the songs *I'm Gonna Laugh You Out of My Life* and *Why Try to Change Me Now?* To the words of Carolyn Leigh he wrote the song *Witchcraft;* as propelled through the pharynx and larynx of Frank Sinatra it became a hit. He also wrote the musical *Wildcat* (1960), best remembered for the song *Hey, Look Me Over; Little Me* followed in 1962. He achieved further success with *Sweet Charity,* composed in 1966, to the lyrics of Dorothy Fields.

Coleman, Ornette, black American jazz alto saxophonist and composer; b. Fort Worth, Texas, March 9, 1930. He was an autodidact; served his apprenticeship playing in carnival and "rhythm and blues" bands. His own studies of harmony and theory led him to develop a distinctive style in which the improvisational melodic line is independent of the pre-assigned harmonic scheme. He also writes concert music in a respectable modernistic idiom.

BIBLIOGRAPHY: A.B. Spellman, *Black Music: Four Lives in the Bebop Business* (N.Y., 1966; reprint, N.Y., 1970); E. Jost, "Zur Musik Ornette Colemans," *Jazzforschung* (1970).

Coleridge-Taylor, Samuel, British composer of African descent (his father was a native of Sierra Leone; his mother English); b. London, Aug. 15, 1875; d. Croydon, Sept. 1, 1912. He studied violin at the Royal Academy of Music (1890); won a composition scholarship (1893); studied under Stanford until 1896. In 1903 he founded at Croydon an amateur string orch. which was very successful; later he added professional woodwind and brass; was appointed a violin teacher at the Royal Academy of Music (1898); became a prof. of composition at Trinity College in London (1903) and at the Guildhall School (1910); was conductor of the London Handel Society (1904–12); lived as a composer and teacher in Croydon. He made 3 concert tours of the U.S., in 1904, 1906, and 1910, conducting his own works. From the very beginning his compositions showed an individuality that rapidly won them recognition, and his short career was watched with interest.

WORKS: 3-act opera, *Thelma;* operettas: *Dream Lovers* and *The Gitanos;* for Soli, Chorus, and Orch.: the successful trilogy *The Song of Hiawatha,* including *Hiawatha's Wedding Feast* (London, 1898), *The Death of Minnehaha* (North Staffordshire, 1899), and *Hiawatha's Departure* (Albert Hall, 1900); the entire trilogy was first performed in Washington, D.C. (Nov. 16, 1904, composer conducting); *The Blind Girl of Castel Cuille* (Leeds, 1901); *Meg Blane* (Sheffield, 1902); *The Atonement* (Hereford, 1903); *Kubla Khan* (Handel Society, London, 1906); *Endymion's Dream,* one-act opera (Brighton, England, Feb. 3, 1910); *A Tale of Old Japan* (London Choral Society, 1911); for orch.: Ballade for Violin and Orch.; Symph. in A minor (London, 1896); *Legend* for Violin and Orch.; Ballade in A minor (Gloucester Festival, 1898); *African Suite;* Romance for Violin and Orch.; *Solemn Prelude* (Worcester, 1899); *Scenes from an Everyday Romance,* suite (London Phil. Society, 1900); *Idyll* (Gloucester Festival, 1901); *Toussaint l'Ouverture,* concert overture (Queen's Hall Symph. Concerts, London, Oct. 26, 1901); *Hemo Dance; Ethiopa Saluting the Colours,* concert march; *4 Novelletten* for String Orch.; *Symphonic Variations on an African Air* (London, June 14, 1906, composer conducting); *Bamboula,* rhapsodic dance (Norfolk [Conn.] Festival, 1910); Violin Concerto in G minor (Norfolk Festival, 1911); *Petite suite de concert;* incidental music to Phillips's *Herod* (1900), *Ulysses* (1902), *Nero* (1906), *Faust* (1908), etc.; chamber music: Piano Quintet; Nonet for Piano, Strings and Woodwind (1894); *Fantasiestücke* for String Quartet (1895); Clarinet Quintet; String Quartet; Violin Sonata; vocal works: *Zara's Earrings,* rhapsody for Voice and Orch.; *Land of the Sun,* part-song; *In Memoriam,* 3 rhapsodies for Voice and Piano; *The Soul's Expression,* 4 songs for Contralto and Orch.; *Sea Drift,* rhapsody for Chorus; services, anthems, solo songs; for Piano: *Silhouettes; Cameos; Scènes de ballet;* etc. Also other compositions for violin and organ, and arrangements.

BIBLIOGRAPHY: M. Byron, *A Day with Samuel Coleridge-Taylor* (1912); *Golden Hours with Samuel Coleridge-Taylor* (1913); W.C.B. Sayers, *Samuel Coleridge-Taylor, His Life and Letters* (1915); Mrs. Samuel Coleridge-Taylor, *Samuel Coleridge-Taylor, A Memory Sketch* (1942); W. Tortolano, *Samuel Coleridge-Taylor: Anglo-Black Composer, 1875–1912* (Metuchen, N.J., 1977); A. Coleridge-Taylor, *The Heritage of Samuel Coleridge-Taylor* (London, 1979).

Coletti, Filippo, noted Italian baritone; b. Anagni, May 11, 1811; d. there, June 13, 1894. He studied with Alessandro Busti in Naples; made his debut there at the Teatro del Fondo in Rossini's *Il Turco in Italia* in 1834; subsequently established himself as a distinguished interpreter of roles in operas by Bellini, Donizetti, and Verdi.

Colgrass, Michael (Charles), American composer; b. Chicago, April 22, 1932. He studied at the Univ. of Illinois (Mus.B., 1956); attended classes at the Berkshire Music Center in Tanglewood (1952–54). His principal teachers were Darius Milhaud, Lukas Foss, Wallingford Riegger, and Ben Weber. A percussion player by profession, he was employed in various ensembles in N.Y. In his own music, percussion plays a significant melorhythmic role. He also studied theater arts, including special techniques of the Commedia dell' Arte of the Piccolo Teatro of Milan and physical training for actors at the Polish Theater Laboratory; wrote drama and poetry. He received Guggenheim fellowship awards in 1964 and 1968; won the Pulitzer Prize in 1978.

WORKS: *Chamber Music* for 4 Drums and String Quartet (1954); Percussion Quintet (1955); Divertimento for 8 Drums, Piano, and Strings (1960); Rhapsody for Clarinet, Violin, and Piano (1962); *Light Spirit* for Flute, Viola, Guitar, and Percussion (1963); *Sea Shadow* for Orch. (1966); *As Quiet As . . .* for Orch. (1966); *New People,* song cycle for Mezzo-soprano, Viola, and Piano (1969); *The Earth's a Baked Apple* for Chorus and Orch. (1969); *Letter from Mozart,* collage for Piano and Orch. (N.Y., Dec. 3, 1976); *Best Wishes, U.S.A.* for Black Chorus, White Chorus, Jazz Band, Folk Instruments, 4 Vocalists, and Orch. (1976); *Concertmasters,* concerto for 3 Violins and Orch. (1976). *Déjà vu,* concerto for 4 Percussionists and Orch. (1978; received the Pulitzer Prize); Piano Concerto (Miami, Fla., June 25, 1982), Viola Concerto (Toronto, Sept. 26, 1984).

Collaer, Paul, Belgian pianist and writer on music; b. Boom, June 8, 1891. He studied science at the Univ. of Brussels; then became interested in music; organized concerts; in 1937–53 was director of the Brussels Radio and promoted performances of modern music.

WRITINGS: *Stravinsky* (1930); *J.S. Bach* (1936); *Signification de la musique* (1943); *Darius Milhaud* (1947); *La Musique moderne* (1955); *A History of Modern Music* (amplified ed. of *La Musique mo-*

derne, N.Y., 1963); *Ozeanien* (Leipzig, 1965); *Amerika; Eskimo und indianische Bevölkerung* (Leipzig, 1967); with A. van der Linden, *Atlas historique de la musique* (Paris, 1960); *La Musique populaire traditionelle en Belgique* (Brussels, 1974).

Collard, a family of pianoforte makers in London. M. Clementi, in partnership with John Longman, bought out the music publishers Longman & Broderip in 1798. Longman left to establish his own enterprise, and Clementi entered into a new partnership including himself, Banger, F.A. Hyde, F.W. Collard, and Davis; after several changes, the firm was known as Clementi, Collard & Collard (1823); following Clementi's death in 1832, it has been known as Collard & Collard. While Clementi undoubtedly played an important part in the success of the business, it was Collard's patented inventions which gave the pianofortes their distinctive character, and established the firm's reputation in that field.

Collard, Jean-Philippe, French pianist; b. Mareuil, Jan. 27, 1948. He began piano studies as a child; then studied at the Paris Cons. with Pierre Sancan, graduating at age 16 with a first prize; subsequently won several honors, including the first prize in the Marguerite Long–Jacques Thibaud Competition; appeared as soloist with the leading European orchs. and in recitals. He made his American debut in 1973 with the San Francisco Symph. Orch.; then made a number of coast-to-coast tours of the U.S.; in 1983 appeared as soloist with the Indianapolis Symph. Orch. at Carnegie Hall in N.Y.

Colles, Henry Cope, eminent British music scholar; b. Bridgnorth, Shropshire, April 20, 1879; d. London, March 4, 1943. He studied at the Royal College of Music with Parry (music history), Walter Alcock (organ), and Walford Davies (theory). Subsequently he received a scholarship at Worcester College, Oxford, to study organ; then entered Oxford Univ., obtaining his B.A. (1902), Mus.Bac. (1903), and M.A. (1907); also received an honorary Mus.Doc. (1932). In 1905 he became music critic of the *Academy;* from 1906–19 was music critic of the *Times;* in 1919 was appointed teacher of music history and criticism at the Royal College of Music; was also music director of Cheltenham Ladies' College; in 1923, became member of the board of profs. at the Royal College of Music. He was the editor of the 3rd and 4th eds. of *Grove's Dictionary of Music and Musicians* (1927–29 and 1939–40). WRITINGS: *Brahms* (1908; in German, 1913); *The Growth of Music: A Study in Music History for Schools* (3 vols., 1912–16; 3rd ed., prepared by Eric Blom, 1956); *Voice and Verse, A Study in English Song* (1928); *The Chamber Music of Brahms* (1933); *English Church Music* (1933); *The Royal College of Music; A Jubilee Record, 1883–1933* (1933); *On Learning Music* (1940); *Walford Davies* (London, 1942). His *Essays and Lectures* were publ. posthumously in 1945. Articles: "Some Music Instruction Books of the 17th Century," in *Proceedings of the Music Academy* (1928–29); "Wagner," in D. Ewen's *From Bach to Stravinsky* (1933); "Sibelius," in *Great Contemporaries* (1933). Colles revised and added chapters to Sir Hubert Parry's *Evolution of the Art of Music* (new ed., 1930); edited vol. VII of *Oxford History of Music* (1934).

Collet, Henri, French music critic and composer; b. Paris, Nov. 5, 1885; d. there, Nov. 23, 1951. He was a pupil of J. Thibaut and Barès in Paris; then studied Spanish literature with Menéndez Pidal in Madrid, continuing his music studies under Olmeda. He coined the title Les Six Français for a group of young French composers comprising G. Auric, L. Durey, A. Honegger, D. Milhaud, F. Poulenc, and G. Tailleferre. WORKS: (compositions mostly in Spanish style): *El Escorial,* symph. poem; *Danses castillanes* for Orch.; *Gitanerías* for Orch.; *La cueva di Salamanca,* orch. intermezzo; *Impressions* (*Vers Burgos*) for String Quartet; *Rhapsodie castillane* for Viola and Orch.; *Romería castellana* for Woodwinds; Piano Quintet; String Quartet; *Trio castillan; Sonata castillane* for Violin and Piano; many songs (based on texts by F. James and on Spanish folk themes). WRITINGS: *Un tratado de Canto de órgano (siglo XVI) MS. en la Biblioteca Nacional de Paris* (Madrid, 1913); *Le Mysticisme musical espagnol au XVIᵉ siècle* (Paris, 1913); a biography of Victoria, in *Maîtres de la musique* (Paris, 1914); *Albéniz et Granados* (1926); *Samson et Dalila* (guide to Saint-Saëns's opera; 1926); "La Renaissance musicale en Espagne au XIXᵉ siècle," in *Encyclopédie du Conservatoire; L'Essor de la musique espagnole au XXᵉ siècle* (1929); also historical essays in *Bulletin Hispanique* and *L'Année Musicale.*

Collette, Buddy, black American jazz flutist and composer; b. Los Angeles, Calif., Aug. 6, 1921. He studied composition with Ernest Kanitz. He played flute with the Henry Mancini, Quincy Jones, and Benny Carter bands; appeared at the San Remo Festival in Italy in 1962. He favors the West Coast jazz style in an eloquently cool technique; his song *Blue Sands* has become a jazz standard.

Collier, Marie, Australian soprano; b. Ballarat, April 16, 1926; d. London, Dec. 7, 1971 (in an accidental fall from a window). She studied in Melbourne; then continued her musical training in Milan. In 1956 she sang in London. On March 17, 1967, she made her Metropolitan Opera debut in N.Y., creating the role of Christine Mannon in the opera *Mourning Becomes Electra* by Marvin David Levy. She was highly regarded for her performances of contemporary music.

Collier, Ronald, Canadian composer; b. Coleman, Alberta, July 3, 1930. He played trombone in a school band in Vancouver (1943–49); studied composition privately with Gordon Delamont in Toronto (1951); later studied with Hall Overton in N.Y. He was a trombonist in several orchs., including the Toronto Symph.; then formed his own jazz group, and was the first jazz composer to receive a Canada Council grant (1965); in 1971 became composer-in-residence at Humber College in Toronto.

WORKS: Pieces for jazz orch., including a ballet, *Aurora Borealis* (1967); music for a television drama, *Silent Night, Lonely Night* (1965); *Cambodian Suite* (1959); *The City,* with Narrator-Singer (1960); *Requiem for JFK* (1964); *Bonjour Canada Opening* (1967); *The Carnival,* with Narrator-Singer and Solo Flugelhorn (1969); *Celebration,* with Solo Piano (in collaboration with Duke Ellington, 1972); *Humber Suite* (1973); chamber pieces for jazz ensemble: *Invention Nos. 1* and *2* (1955); *Opus for Quintet* (1956); *Stratford Adventure* (1956); *Jazz Ballet* (1960); *2 Shades of Blue* (1962); *Impressions* (1963); *Hear Me Talkin' to Ya,* with Narrator and Singer (1964); *Walkin' Out* (1965); *Lyric for Trumpet* for Trumpet and Concert Band (1970) and *Waterfront, Night Thoughts* for Flute and Piano (1965).

Collingwood, Lawrance Arthur, English composer and conductor; b. London, March 14, 1887; d. Killin, near Perthshire, Dec. 19, 1982. He studied at the Guildhall School of Music and later at Exeter College. In 1912 he went to Russia and took courses at the St. Petersburg Cons. with Glazunov, Withol, Steinberg, and Tcherepnin; in 1918 he returned to England and became active as a conductor. On April 12, 1934, he conducted his opera *Macbeth* in London; his 2nd opera, *The Death of Tintagiles,* was produced in concert form in London on April 16, 1950. His 2 piano sonatas were published in Russia. He wrote a number of instrumental works and edited a collection of Breton folk songs.

BIBLIOGRAPHY: C.H. Glover, "Lawrance Collingwood," *Musical Quarterly* (April 1926).

Collins, Anthony, English conductor; b. Hastings, Sept. 3, 1893; d. Los Angeles, Dec. 11, 1963. He studied violin at the Royal College of Music in London, and composition there with Holst; was then a violist in the London Symph. Orch. and in the orch. of the Royal Opera House, Covent Garden; from 1936 he pursued a career as conductor, appearing with the Carl Rosa Opera Co., the Sadler's Wells Opera, and the London Symph. Orch. In 1939 he settled in the U.S., making his home in California as a conductor and composer for motion pictures. He wrote 2 symphs., 2 violin concertos, 4 operas, and other works.

Collins, Judy (Marjorie), American singer of folk and popular music; b. Seattle, Wash., May 1, 1939. She studied piano with Antonia Brico in hopes of a concert career, but deterred by the odds against success, she turned to folk music. After attending MacMurray College in Jacksonville, Ill., and the Univ. of Colorado in Denver, she began her career as a singer in 1959, accompanying herself on the guitar; she obtained a prestigious engagement at Carnegie Hall in N.Y. in 1965. She subsequently toured in Japan and other exotic lands. Her repertoire presents a wide spectrum from the traditional Anglo-American folk ballad to hard, loud rock.

Collum, Herbert, German organist and harpsichordist; b. Leipzig, July 18, 1914. He studied organ with Straube and Ramin at the Hochschule für Musik in Leipzig; also piano with Adolf Martienssen and composition with J.N. David. In 1934 he became organist of the Kreuzkirche in Dresden; founded the Collum Concerts (1935) and the Collum Choir (1946) of Dresden. He was a distinguished interpreter of the music of Bach, both as organist and as harpsichordist; also composed concertos for harpsichord and many vocal works.

Colobrano, Michele Enrico Carafa de. See Carafa de Colobrano, Michele Enrico.

Colombo, Pierre, Swiss conductor; b. La Tour-de-Peilz, May 22, 1914. He studied flute and theory at the Ribaupierre Inst.; conducting with Scherchen and H. Münch at the Basel Cons. and also with Clemens Krauss. He was conductor of the Lausanne Bach Choir (1947–63); from 1955 he served as program director of the radio service in Geneva. As a conductor, he was particularly known for his adequate performances of modern music.

Colonna, Giovanni Paolo, eminent Italian composer of church music; b. Bologna, June 16, 1637; d. there, Nov. 28, 1695. He studied organ with Filipucci in Bologna; composition in Rome with Carissimi, Benevoli, and Abbatini. In 1659 he became organist at San Petronio in Bologna; was appointed maestro di cappella in 1674. He was several times elected president of the Accademia Filarmonica.

WORKS: Mostly church music, but also several operas, including *Amilcare di Cipro* (1692), and 13 oratorios, *La profezia d'Eliseo* (1686) among them. Church music: *Motetti* for 2 and 3 Voices (1681); 3 books of *Salmi brevi* for 8 Voices and Organ (1681, 1686, 1694); *Motetti sacri a voce sola con due violini e bassetto di viola* (1681); *Litanie con le quattro antifone della B. Vergine* for 8 Voices (1682); *Messe piene* for 8 Voices, with Organ (1684); *Messa, salmi e responsori per li defonti* for 8 Voices (1685); *Compieta con le tre sequenze dell' anno* for 8 Voices (1687); *Sacre lamentazioni della settimana santa* for Solo Voice (1689); *Messa e salmi concertati* for 3 and 5 Voices with Instruments (1691); *Psalmi ad vesperas* for 3–5 Voices (1694); many other church works are also extant in MS.

BIBLIOGRAPHY: L. Frati, "Per la storia della musica in Bologna nel secolo XVII," *Rivista Musicale Italiana* (1925); A. Schnoebelen, "Performance Practices at San Petronio in the Baroque," *Acta Musicologica* (Jan./June 1969).

Colonne, Edouard (real name, **Judas**), French conductor and violinist; b. Bordeaux, July 23, 1838; d. Paris, March 28, 1910. He studied at the Paris Cons. under Girard and Sauzay (violin) and with Elwart and Ambroise Thomas (composition). In 1874 he founded the Concerts Nationaux (which later became famous as the Concerts du Châtelet; then Concerts Colonne), at which he brought out the larger works of Berlioz, and many new orch. scores by contemporary German and French composers. In 1878 he conducted the official Exposition concerts; was conductor at the Grand Opéra in 1892; appeared frequently as a visiting conductor in London; also in Russia and Portugal, and with the N.Y. Phil. (1905).

BIBLIOGRAPHY: H. Schonberg, *The Great Conductors* (N.Y., 1967).

Coltellini, Celeste, Italian mezzo-soprano; b. Livorno, Nov. 26, 1760; d. Capodimonte, near Naples, July 28, 1828. She studied with G.B. Mancini and G. Manzuoli; then sang at La Scala in Milan (1780); in 1781 she became a member of the Teatro dei Fiorentini in Naples. She was well known for her interpretations of roles in operas by Mozart, Paisiello, and Cimarosa.

Coltrane, John William, remarkable black American jazz musician, a virtuoso on the tenor saxophone, whose theory and practice stimulated the creation of sophisticated jazz performance which came to be known as "the new black music"; b. Hamlet, N.C., Sept. 23, 1926; d. Huntington, Long Island, N.Y., July 17, 1967. He studied at the Ornstein School of Music in Philadelphia; played in the bands of Dizzy Gillespie, Johnny Hodges, Miles Davis, and Thelonious Monk. He enhanced the resources of his style by studying ancestral African and kindred Asian music, absorbing the fascinating modalities of these ancient cultures.

BIBLIOGRAPHY: C.O. Simpkins, *Coltrane: A Biography* (N.Y., 1975); J.C. Thomas, *Chasin' the Trane: The Music and Mystique of John Coltrane* (N.Y., 1975); Bill Cole, *John Coltrane* (N.Y., 1976).

Combarieu, Jules (-Léon-Jean), eminent French music historian; b. Cahors, Lot, Feb. 4, 1859; d. Paris, July 7, 1916. He studied at the Sorbonne; later in Berlin with Spitta; received the degree of docteur ès lettres; was a prof. of music history at the Collège de France (1904–10).

WRITINGS: *Les Rapports de la poésie et de la musique considérées du point de vue de l'expression* (Diss., 1893); "L'Influence de la musique allemande sur la musique française," *Jahrbuch Peters* (1895); *Etudes de philologie musicale:* 1. *Théorie du rhythme dans la composition moderne d'après la doctrine antique* (1896; critique and simplification of Westphal); 2. *Essai sur l'archéologie musicale au XIXᵉ siècle et le problème de l'origine des neumes* (1896; these last 2 were awarded prizes by the Académie); 3. *Fragments de l'Enéide en musique d'après un manuscrit inédit* (1898); *Eléments de grammaire musicale historique* (1906); *La Musique: ses lois, son évolution* (1907; numerous eds.; in Eng., 1910); *Histoire de la musique des origines au début du XXᵉ siècle* (3 vols., Paris, 1913–19; an authoritative work; 8th ed. of vol. I, 1948; 6th ed. of vol. II, 1946; new ed. of vol. III, 1947).

Combe, Edouard, Swiss conductor and composer; b. Aigle, Sept. 23, 1866; d. Lausanne, Nov. 19, 1942. He studied in Paris; served as musical secretary to the conductor Lamoureux; was for a season a conductor in Cairo (1895–96). In 1896 was appointed to the staff of the Geneva Cons.; in 1902–14 he taught music history in Lausanne. He contributed numerous articles on music to the *Gazette Musicale de la Suisse Romande* and other music journals. He composed a symph. poem, *Les Alpes;* several overtures and marches.

Combs, Gilbert Raynolds, American organist; b. Philadelphia, Jan. 5, 1863; d. there, June 14, 1934. His father, a distinguished organist, was his first teacher. He originally studied medicine but made such progress in music that he decided to become a professional musician. He studied violin and cello as well as organ; in 1885 founded his own conservatory in Philadelphia. He publ. a number of piano pieces; also wrote a *Dramatic Symphony;* compiled the manuals *The Science of Piano Playing* and *Introductory Steps to the Science of Piano Playing.*

Comden, Betty, American musician, lyricist, and dramatist; b. Brooklyn, May 3, 1919. She received her B.S. degree from N.Y. Univ. in 1938; than sang, danced, and acted with "The Revuers"; worked in this group with the musician and playwright Adolph Green; their first venture as co-authors was *On the Town* (1944; music by Leonard Bernstein); subsequent successes included *Billion Dollar Baby, Two on the Aisle,* and *Bells Are Ringing.* She also authored successful screenplays; received Tony awards for her contributions to *Applause* (1970) and *On the 20th Century* (1978).

Comes, Juan Bautista, Spanish composer; b. Valencia, c.1582; d. there, Jan. 5, 1643. He studied with Juan Perez; was a choirboy at the Valencia Cathedral in 1594–96; in 1605 became choirmaster at the Cathedral of Lérida; then was at the Royal College in Valencia (1605–13); became maestro of the Cathedral there (1613); in 1618 was called by Philip III to Madrid, serving as vice-maestro of the Royal Chapel; from 1628 was again in Valencia; served as maestro of the Cathedral there in 1632–38. He left over 200 works, sacred (masses, Psalms, litanies, etc.) and secular (villancicos, tonadas), most of them in MS, preserved at the Escorial. Two vols. of selected numbers were publ. in Madrid in 1888.

BIBLIOGRAPHY: Manuel Palau, *La obra del músico Valenciano Juan Bautista Comes* (Valencia, 1943); J. Climent, *Juan Bautista Comes y su tiempo* (Madrid, 1977).

Comettant, Jean-Pierre-Oscar, French music critic and composer; b. Bordeaux, April 18, 1819; d. Montvilliers, near Le Havre, Jan. 24, 1898. He entered the Paris Cons. in 1839 and studied with Elwart and Carafa; developed considerable proficiency as a composer of semipopular songs and marches; also publ. piano transcriptions of famous operas, variations, and fantasias. From 1852–55 he lived in America, where he continued to write salon music. Returning to France, he became the music *feuilletoniste* for *Le Siècle,* and a contributor to various music journals; founded (with his wife, a singer) a musical inst. (1871).

WRITINGS: *Histoire d'un inventeur au 19e siècle: Adolphe Sax, ses ouvrages et ses luttes* (Paris, 1860); *Portefeuille d'un musicien; Musique et musiciens* (1862); *La Musique, les musiciens et les instruments de musique chez les différents peuples du monde* (1869); *Les Musiciens, les philosophes et les gaîtés de la musique en chiffres* (1870); *François Planté* (1874); *Les Compositeurs illustres de notre siècle* (1883); *La Norvège musicale à Paris* (1889); *Histoire de cent mille pianos et d'une salle de concert: Histoire de la Maison Pleyel, Wolff et Cie.* (1890); *La Musique de la Garde Républicaine en Amérique* (1894); etc.

Comissiona, Sergiu, Rumanian conductor; b. Bucharest, June 16, 1928. He studied violin and theory in Bucharest; conducting with Constantin Silvestri. He was one of the principal conductors of the Rumanian State Opera and the Bucharest Phil.; subsequently was music director of the Haifa Symph. Orch. (1959–64); was guest conductor with the London Phil. (1960–63), Stockholm Phil. (1964–66), Berlin Radio Symph. Orch. (1965–67); also was a guest conductor with major symph. orchs. in the U.S. In 1969 he was appointed music director and conductor of the Baltimore Symph. Orch. He was an Israeli citizen (1959–76); on July 4, 1976, he became a U.S. citizen. Symbolically, the ceremony was held at Fort McHenry in Baltimore Harbor, site of the battle which inspired the writing of *The Star-Spangled Banner.* From 1978 to 1982 Comissiona was principal conductor of the American Symph. Orch. in N.Y.; he led the Baltimore Symph. Orch. until 1984; in 1980 he became artistic director, and in 1983–84, music director, of the Houston Symph. Orch.; in 1982 he was also named principal guest conductor of the Radio Phil. Orch. in Hilversum, the Netherlands.

Commer, Franz, German music historian; b. Cologne, Jan. 23, 1813; d. Berlin, Aug. 17, 1887. He was a pupil of Leibl and Josef Klein at Cologne; in 1828, became organist of the Carmelite Church and chorister at the Cathedral. In 1832 he went to Berlin to study with A.W. Bach (organ) and A.B. Marx and Rungenhagen (composition). Commissioned to arrange the library of the Royal Inst. for Church Music, he pursued historical research, and edited the following important collections of old music: *Collectio operum musicorum Batavorum saeculi XVI.* (12 vols.); *Musica sacra XVI, XVII. saeculorum* (28 vols.); *Collection de compositions pour l'orgue des XVIe, XVIIe, XVIIIe siècles* (in 6 parts); and *Cantica sacra* of the 16th–18th centuries (2 vols.). He was the founder (1844), with Küster and Kullak, of the Berlin Tonkünstlerverein; wrote incidental music to Aristophanes' *The Frogs* and Sophocles' *Electra;* he also wrote masses, cantatas, and choruses.

Commette, Edouard, French organist; b. Lyons, April 12, 1883; d. there, April 21, 1967. He had his first appointment as church organist at the Church of Bon Pasteur in Lyons (1900–4); then for 59 years (1904–63) was organist at the Cathedral of Lyons; from 1928 he made recordings of the music of Bach. He wrote 34 organ works, and made many transcriptions for organ; also composed an opera and a symph.

Como, Perry (Pierino), American singer of popular music; b. Canonsburg, Pa., May 18, 1913. After a stint as a barber, he joined the Freddie Carlone Orch. as a singer; then sang with the Ted Weems Orch. (1937–43); subsequently he became one of the most successful popular vocalists through his numerous radio and television appearances. His recordings included such favorites as *I Think of You, It's Impossible,* and *Shadow of Your Smile.*

Compère, Loyset (real name, **Louis**), important composer of the Flemish School; b. Hainaut, c.1445; d. St. Quentin, Aug. 16, 1518. He was a chorister in St. Quentin; then a singer in the chapel of the Duke of Milan (1474–75); in 1486 was singer in the service of Charles VIII of France; was subsequently canon of St. Quentin. He was greatly esteemed by his contemporaries.

WORKS: Not many of his works are extant; they include pieces in collections publ. by Petrucci (21 vocal works in 3, 4, and 5 parts, in *Odhecaton, Canti B,* and *Canti C*), Petrejus, and Rhaw; masses, motets, a Magnificat, and chansons in MS. The motet *Omnium bonorum,* in which Compère mentions several Franco-Flemish composers beginning with Dufay and concluding with himself, was publ. from the Trent Codex 91 in vol. 14/15 (formerly 7) of Denkmäler der Tonkunst in Österreich. The *Opera Omnia,* in 6 vols., was edited by L. Finscher, and publ. as no. 15 of the Corpus Mensurabilis Musicae series of the American Inst. of Musicology in Dallas, Texas.

BIBLIOGRAPHY: O. Gombosi, "Ghizeghem und Compère; Zur Stilgeschichte der burgundischen Chanson," in *Adler-Festschrift* (Vienna, 1930); J. Delporte, "L'Ecole polyphonique franco-flamande; Louis Compère," *Revue Liturgique et Musicale* (July–Aug. 1932); L. Finscher, *Loyset Compère (c.1450–1518); Life and Works* (Rome, 1964).

Concone, Giuseppe, Italian singing teacher and composer; b. Turin, Sept. 12, 1801; d. there, June 1, 1861. From 1837 until 1848 he lived in Paris, where he became a popular singing teacher. His collection of solfeggi in 5 vols. (*50 Lezioni, 30 Esercizi, 25 Lezioni, 15 Vocalizzi,* and *40 Lezioni per Basso*) became a standard work for singing teachers, showing no signs of obsolescence and continuing much in use all over the world. He also wrote an opera, *Un episodio del San Michele,* which was produced in Turin in 1836.

Condon, Albert Edwin ("Eddie"), American jazz banjo player, guitarist, and bandleader; b. Good-land, Ind., Nov. 16, 1905; d. New York, Aug. 4, 1973. He first learned to play the ukelele; then took up the banjo and the guitar. He worked with Bix Beiderbecke, Louis Armstrong, Fats Waller, and Red Nichols. After settling permanently in N.Y., he led his own band and gave a series of jazz concerts at Town Hall. He operated his own club (1945–67); led his own band on tours to England (1957) and the Far East (1964); also appeared at the major jazz festivals in the U.S. His autobiography, *We Called It Music,* was publ. in 1948.

Cone, Edward T(oner), American composer, pianist, teacher, and writer on music; b. Greensboro, N.C., May 4, 1917. He studied composition with Roger Sessions at Princeton Univ. (B.A., 1939; M.F.A., 1942); also took piano lessons with Jeffrey Stoll, Karl Ulrich Schnabel, and Eduard Steuermann. After military service in World War II, he joined the faculty of Princeton Univ. in 1946; was made an associate prof. in 1952 and a full prof. in 1960. He received a Guggenheim fellowship in 1947. In addition to composing and teaching, he gave piano recitals. He was also active as a writer; was editor of the periodical *Perspectives of New Music* (1966–72).
WRITINGS: *Musical Form and Musical Performance* (N.Y., 1968); *The Composer's Voice* (Berkeley, 1974); co-ed. (with B. Boretz) of *Perspectives on Schoenberg and Stravinsky* (Princeton, 1968), *Perspectives on American Composers* (N.Y., 1971), and *Perspectives on Notation and Performance* (N.Y., 1975); ed. of *Roger Sessions on Music* (Princeton, 1979).
WORKS: For Orch.: Symph. (1953); *Elegy* (1953); *Nocturne and Rondo* for Piano and Orch. (1955–57); Violin Concerto (1959); *Music for Strings* (1964); *Variations for Orchestra* (1967–68); *Cadenzas* for Violin, Oboe, and String Orch. (1979). Chamber music: 2 string quartets (1939–49); 2 violin sonatas (1940, 1948); *Rhapsody* for Viola and Piano (1947); Piano Trio (1951); Piano Quintet (1960); *Funereal Stanzas* for Wind Quintet (1965); String Sextet (1966); Capriccio for String Quartet (1981); Piano Quartet (1983). For Voices: *Scarabs* for Soprano and String Quartet (1948); *Philomela* for Soprano and Chamber Ensemble (1954–70); *Around the Year* for Madrigal Group and String Quartet (1956); songs. For Piano: *Fantasy* (1950); *Prelude, Passacaglia and Fugue* (1957); *Fantasy* for 2 Pianos (1965).
BIBLIOGRAPHY: David Ewen, *American Composers* (N.Y., 1982).

Confalonieri, Giulio, Italian pianist and writer on music; b. Milan, May 23, 1896; d. there, June 29, 1972. He studied at the Univ. of Milan and the Cons. of Bologna; lived for some years in London; returned to Milan, where he settled as a teacher and music critic. He wrote an opera, *Rosaspina* (Bergamo, 1939); edited works by Cimarosa and Cherubini; publ. a comprehensive biography of Cherubini under the title *Prigionia di un artista: Il romanzo di Luigi Cherubini* (2 vols., Milan, 1948).

Conforti (Conforto), Giovanni Luca, Italian

theorist; b. Mileto (Calabria), c.1560; date and place of death unknown. He entered the Papal Choir in 1580 and remained there until Oct. 31, 1585, when he returned to Mileto; was chorister at the Papal Chapel again from Nov. 4, 1591. According to Baini, he was the first of his period to restore the "trillo."
WRITINGS: *Breve et facile maniera d'essercitarsi ad ogni scolaro . . . a far passaggi . . .* (Rome, 1593; facsimile ed., with trans., ed. by Johannes Wolf, Berlin, 1922) and *Passaggi sopra tutti li salmi . . .* (Venice, 1607; contains a set of vocal ornamentations to be used in the singing of the Psalms employed on Sundays and holidays throughout the year).

Confrey, Zez (Edward Elezear), American pianist and composer of light music, especially of a style known as "novelty piano"; b. Peru, Ill., April 3, 1895; d. Lakewood, N.J., Nov. 22, 1971. He studied at the Chicago Musical College and privately with Jessie Dunn and Frank Denhart. He appeared as piano soloist, along with George Gershwin, at Paul Whiteman's concert "Experiment in Modern Music" (1924), at which Gershwin's *Rhapsody in Blue* was premiered.
WORKS: *Kitten on the Keys* (1921; his most popular piece); *Stumbling* (1922); *Dizzy Fingers, Valse Mirage,* and *3 Little Oddities* (1923); *Concert Etude* (1922); *Buffoon* (1930); *Grandfather's Clock* (1933); *Oriental Fantasy* (1935); *Ultra Ultra* (1935); *Rhythm Venture* (1936); *Della Robbia* (1938); *Champagne;* etc.

Conley, Eugene, American tenor; b. Lynn, Mass., March 12, 1908; d. Denton, Texas, Dec. 18, 1981. He studied voice with Ettore Verna; began his career as a radio singer in 1939, when the National Broadcasting Co. put him on the air in a program entitled "NBC Presents Eugene Conley." He made his operatic debut at the Brooklyn Academy of Music as the Duke in *Rigoletto;* then sang with the San Carlo Opera Co. in N.Y., the Chicago Opera Co., and the Cincinnati Summer Opera. In 1942 he joined the Army Air Corps. In 1949 he became the first American opera singer to open the season at La Scala, Milan; he later appeared with the Opéra-Comique in Paris, the Covent Garden Opera in London, and the Royal Opera of Stockholm. On Jan. 25, 1950, he made his first appearance at the Metropolitan Opera in N.Y., in the title role of Gounod's *Faust.* He remained on its roster until 1956. In 1960 he was appointed artist-in-residence at North Texas State Univ. in Denton, retiring in 1978. He died of cancer.

Conlon, James, American conductor; b. New York, March 18, 1950. He was graduated from the Juilliard School of Music in N.Y., and conducted the Juilliard Orch. He was the youngest conductor ever invited to lead a subscription concert of the N.Y. Phil. He then appeared with virtually every major orch. in the U.S.; made his Metropolitan Opera debut in N.Y. in 1976. In 1979 he became music director of the Cincinnati May Festival.

Conniff, Ray, American conductor, arranger, and

composer of popular music; b. Attleboro, Mass., Nov. 6, 1916. He studied at the Juilliard School of Music in N.Y.; played trombone in various bands and arranged music for Artie Shaw and Harry James; also conducted his own groups.

Connolly, Justin Riveagh, English composer; b. London, Aug. 11, 1933. He studied composition with Peter Racine Fricker at the Royal College of Music in London; held a Harkness Fellowship at Yale Univ. (1963–65); was then instructor in music theory there (1965–66). Returning to London, he joined the faculty of his alma mater. As a composer he followed the structural techniques of the avant-garde; in this direction he was influenced by new American trends, such as the theory of combinatoriality of Milton Babbitt and the practice of metrical modulation of Elliott Carter; he also made use of electronic sound. His works are often arranged in sets unified by a generic title and a numerical rubric; in this he also paid tribute to the mathematical concepts of sets and matrixes).
WORKS: *Triads* (i.e., trios): No. 1 for Trumpet, Viola, and Piano; No. II for Double Bass, Piano, and Percussion; No. III for Oboe, Viola, and Cello; No. IV for Flute, 2 Percussion Instruments, and Recorded Sounds; No. V for Clarinet, Viola, and Cello. *Obbligati:* No. 1 for 13 Players; No. II for Flute, Clarinet, Violin, Cello, and Electronics; No. III for 20 Players; No. IV for Violin, Viola, Cello, and Strings; *Poems of Wallace Stevens:* No. I for Soprano and 7 Players; No. II for Soprano, Flute, and Piano; No. III for Soprano, Piano, and Electronics; *Tesserae:* No. I for Oboe and Harpsichord; No. II for Flute and Piano; *Phases-Phrases* for 48 Solo Players; *Antiphonies* for 36 Players; *Cinquepaces* for Brass Quintet; *M-piriform* (with reference to the piriform muscle of the thigh) for Soprano, Flute, Violin, and Electronics; *The Marriage of Heaven and Hell,* to a text by William Blake, for Soloists, Chorus, and Orch.; *Anima* for Viola and Orch.; *Diaphony* for Organ and Orch.; *Sestina* for Harpsichord and Instrumental Ensemble; *Poems of Henry Vaughan* for Mixed Chorus; *Waka* for Mezzo-soprano and Piano, to Japanese texts; *Sentences* for Chorus, Trumpets, Trombones, and Organ; *Chimera* for Dancer, Alto, Baritone, and Instrumental Ensemble. He also wrote an overture, *Rebus,* on the occasion of the 95th birthday of Havergal Brian, in 1971, constructed on rhythmic figures of 5 and 19 units as factors of 95.

Conradi, August, German opera composer; b. Berlin, June 27, 1821; d. there, May 26, 1873. He was a pupil of Rungenhagen (composition); organist of the "Invalidenhaus" in 1843; went in 1846 to Vienna, and brought out a symph. with marked success; was for years an intimate friend of Liszt at Weimar; then conducted in Stettin, Berlin, Düsseldorf, Cologne, and (from 1856) again in Berlin.
WORKS: Operas (all produced in Berlin): *Rübezahl* (1847); *Musa, der letzte Maurenfürst* (1855); *Die Braut des Flussgottes* (1850); *Die Sixtinische Madonna* (1864); *Knecht Ruprecht* (1865); *So sind*
die Frauen; Im Weinberge des Herrn (1867); *Das schönste Mädchen im Städtchen* (1868); also vaudevilles, farces, 5 symphs., overtures, string quartets, etc. He arranged many popular potpourris.

Conried (real name, **Cohn**), **Heinrich,** Austro-American operatic impresario; b. Bielitz, Austria, Sept. 13, 1848; d. Meran, Tyrol, April 27, 1909. He started as an actor in Vienna; in 1877 he managed the Bremen Municipal Theater; came to the U.S. in 1878 and took over the management of the Germania Theater in N.Y.; then was in charge of various theatrical enterprises; from 1892 was director of the Irving Place Theater in N.Y., which he brought to a high degree of efficiency. From 1903 till 1908 he was the manager of the Metropolitan Opera and was instrumental in engaging numerous celebrated artists, including Caruso. During his first season he gave the first American production of *Parsifal,* despite the heated controversy regarding the rights of Wagner's heirs; his decision to produce the opera *Salomé* by Richard Strauss in 1907 also aroused a storm of protests. Conried resigned in 1908 because of dissension within the management of the Metropolitan, and retired in Europe. He was decorated by several European governments; received an honorary M.A. from Harvard Univ.
BIBLIOGRAPHY: M.J. Moses, *Heinrich Conried* (N.Y., 1916).

Constant, Franz, Belgian composer and pianist; b. Montignies-le-Tilleul, Nov. 17, 1910. He studied music at the Charleroi Academy of Music and at the Brussels Cons., with M. Maas, L. Jongen, Bourguignon, and Absil; in Paris, studied with Tomasi. He became a concert pianist and formed a successful duo with his wife, **Jeanne Pellaerts.** In 1947 he was appointed to the faculty of the Brussels Cons. As a composer, he pursues the ideal of blending the modalities of the classical Belgian School with coloristic harmonies.
WORKS: Cantata, *Jeanne de Naples,* for Soprano, Narrator, Children's Voices, Speaking and Singing Choruses, and Orch. (1972); Rhapsodie for Violin and Orch. (1962); Saxophone Concerto (1963); Trumpet Concerto (1965); Sinfonietta for Flute, Oboe, and String Orch. (1968); Fantasia for Saxophone and Orch. (1969); Concertino for Flute and String Orch. (1970); Violin Concerto (1971); Rhapsodie for Orch. (1973); *Expressions* for Violin, Piano, and Strings (1973); Clarinet Concertino (1975); *Allegro* for Trumpet and Piano (1959); *4 séquences* for 4 Saxophones (1962); *Impressions* for 4 Clarinets (1964); Flute Sonata (1967); *Triade* for Voice, Saxophone, Piano, and Percussion (1967); *Evocation* for Flute and Piano (1969); *Suo tempore* for Violin and Piano (1969); *Dialogue* for Clarinet and Piano (1970); *Sonatine picturale* for Clarinet and Piano (1970); *Couleur provençale* for Horn and Piano (1970); *Pour la guitare I* and *II* (1971); *5 Miniatures* for Violin, Flute, and Piano (1971); Piano Quartet (1971); Divertissement for Bassoon and Piano (1972); *Rythme et expression* for Violin, Saxophone, Piano, and Percussion (1972); *Musique à deux* for Flute and Guitar

(1973); *Histoires du dimanche* for Children's Chorus, and Piano or Ensemble of 11 Instruments (1973); *Marée* for Oboe and Piano (1973); 2 piano sonatinas (1950, 1960); Toccata for Piano (1952); *Sonatine française* for 2 Pianos (1960); *Paysages* for Piano (1965); *Nuances* for Piano (1972); *Arcanes* for Piano (1974); songs.

Constant, Marius, Rumanian-born French composer and conductor; b. Bucharest, Feb. 7, 1925. He graduated from the Bucharest Cons. in 1944; then went to Paris, where he studied conducting with Fournet and composition with Messiaen, Nadia Boulanger, and Honegger (1945–49); he was director of the Ballets de Paris of Roland Petit (1956–66); was founder, president, and music director of Ars Nova (1963–71), a Parisian ensemble for new music; in 1967 he was a guest lecturer at Stanford Univ.; in 1970 gave lectures in Hilversum, the Netherlands. His early compositions are impressionistic; later he adopted serial and aleatory procedures, particularly in multimedia productions.

WORKS: Improvised opera, *La Serrure (The Lock;* 1969) other operas: *Le Souper* for Baritone and Vocal Orch. (1969) and *La Tragédie de Carmen* (Paris, Nov. 5, 1981); ballets: *Joueur de flûte (The Flute Player;* 1952); *Haut-Voltage* (1956); *Cyrano de Bergerac* (1960); *Éloge de la folie,* with Soprano (1966); *Paradise Lost* (1967); *Candide* (1970; Hamburg, Jan. 24, 1971; material reworked for a concert piece with Solo Harpsichord, 1971); *Le Jeu de Sainte Agnes,* "ecclesiastical action" on a 14th-century MS, for 6 Singers, 5 Actors, Dancer, Hammond Organ, Electric Guitar, Trombone, and Percussion (Besançon, Sept. 6, 1974); *Chants de Maldoror* for Narrator, Dancer-Conductor, 23 Improvising Instrumental Soloists, and 10 Cellos (1962); Piano Concerto (1954); *24 préludes* for Orch. (1957); Concerto for Tuba and String Orch. (1958); *Concert Music* for Saxophone and 11 Instruments (1960); *Turner,* 3 essays for Orch. (1961); *Chaconne et marche militaire* for Orch. (1967); *5 chants et une vocalise* for Dramatic Soprano and Orch. (1968); *Winds* for 13 Winds and Double Bass (1968); *Traits,* based on the 1930s game of surrealist poets, "exquisite corpse," for 6 to 25 Musicians (1969); *Equal* for 5 Percussionists (1969); *14 Stations* for 92 Percussion Instruments (one Player) and 6 Instrumentalists (1969–70); *Candide* for Amplified Harpsichord and Orch. (1971); *Strings* for Strings (1972); *Faciebat Anno 1973* for 24 Violins and Orch. (Paris, July 19, 1973); *Piano Personnage* for Piano and Chamber Ensemble (Paris, Jan. 15, 1974); *For Clarinet* for Solo Clarinet (1974); Symph. for Winds (Montreal, March 17, 1978); *Alleluias* for Trumpet and Organ (1980); *D'une élégie slave* for Solo Guitar (1981); *103 regards dans l'eau* for Violin and Orch. (1981); *Précis de décomposition* for Clarinet, Bassoon, Horn, String Quartet, and Tape (1982).

Constantinescu, Dan, Rumanian composer; b. Bucharest, June 10, 1931. He studied with Martian Negrea, Theodor Rogalski, and Mihail Jora at the Bucharest Cons.; later joined its staff as instructor in

music theory. He wrote *Divertissement in a Classical Style* for String Orch. (1954); *Toma Alimos,* ballad for Orch. (1955); *Partita* for Orch. (1957); Concerto for Piano and String Orch. (1963); Chamber Symph. (1968); *Sinfonia Concertante* for Orch. (1970); Concerto for 2 Pianos and Orch. (1972); Trio for Violin, Clarinet, and Piano (1964); Cello Sonata (1964); Clarinet Sonata (1965); Variations for Piano and String Trio (1966); String Quartet (1967); songs. His works are written in a compact neo-Classical idiom, with occasional melodic excursions into atonality.

Constantinescu, Paul, eminent Rumanian composer; b. Ploesti, July 13, 1909; d. Bucharest, Dec. 20, 1963. He studied composition at the Bucharest Cons. with Castaldi, Cuclin, and Jora; then went to Vienna, where he took courses with Schmidt and Joseph Marx. He was first engaged as a violinist in his native town of Ploesti (1927–34); then taught at the academy for religious music in Bucharest (1937–41). In 1941 he was appointed a prof. at the Bucharest Cons., and retained this post until his death.

WORKS: 2 operas: *O noapte furtunoasă* (Bucharest, Oct. 25, 1935; revised 1950; Bucharest, May 19, 1951) and *Pană Lesnea Rusalim* (Bucharest, June 27, 1956; enjoyed excellent success); 5 ballets: *Nunta în Carpați* (1938); *Spune, povesteste, spune* (1947); *Pe malul Dunării* (1947); *Tîrg pe muntele Găina* (1953); *Înfrățire* (1959); 2 Byzantine oratorios: *Patimile și Învierea Domnului* (1946; revised 1948) and *Nașterea Domnului* (1947); Violin Sonatina (1933); *Burlesque* for Piano and Orch. (1937); Sinfonietta (1937); Symph. (1944; revised 1955); Concerto for String Quartet (1947); Piano Concerto (1952); *Rapsodie oltenească* for Orch. (1956); Violin Concerto (1957); Harp Concerto (1960); *Sinfonia Ploieșteană* (1961); Concerto for Violin, Cello, Piano, and Orch. (1963; posthumous, Bucharest, Dec. 28, 1963); piano pieces; songs and choruses. His biography, by V. Tomescu, was publ. in Bucharest in 1967.

Conti, Carlo, Italian composer and pedagogue; b. Arpino, Oct. 14, 1796; d. Naples, July 10, 1868. He studied at the Naples Cons. with Zingarelli and J.S. Mayr; taught there in 1819–21; rejoined its faculty as a teacher of counterpoint in 1846–58; in 1862 became its assistant director. An industrious composer, he wrote 11 operas and much church music. Rossini called him "the best Italian contrapuntist of the day." His distinction lies principally in his excellence as a teacher; among his famous pupils was Bellini.

Conti, Francesco Bartolomeo, Italian composer; b. Florence, Jan. 20, 1681; d. Vienna, July 20, 1732. He was assistant court theorbist (1701–8), principal theorbist (1708–26), and court composer (from 1713); wrote about 30 stage works to Italian and German texts, of which the finest were *Clotilda* (Vienna, 1706) and *Don Chisciotte in Sierra Morena* (after Cervantes; Vienna, 1719); also 10 oratorios, many secular cantatas, and songs.

BIBLIOGRAPHY: C. Fruchtman and E. Fruchtman, "Instrumental Scoring in the Chamber Cantatas of Francesco Conti," in J.W. Pruett, *Studies in Musicology* (Chapel Hill, N.C., 1969); H. Williams, *Francesco Bartolomeo Conti: His Life and Operas* (Diss., Columbia Univ., 1964).

Conti-Guglia (originally **Contiguglia**), **Richard** and **John,** brilliant American duo-pianists; b. identical twins, New York, April 13, 1937. They began taking twin piano lessons in earliest childhood, and grew in parallel congruence; they played in a duo recital in public when they were 6 years of age; continued to develop in close consanguinity; they composed music for 2 pianos and transcribed solo works for their concerts. When they were 12, Percy Grainger invited them to play during one of his recitals; he subsequently befriended them and gave them valuable advice; later they took piano lessons with Jean Wilder and with Bruce Simonds at Yale Univ.; upon graduation, they received a Ditson Fellowship, which enabled them to study with Dame Myra Hess in London. They made their professional debut in London in 1962, playing piano 4-hands; in 1964 they made a major European tour. In addition to the standard literature for duo-pianos, they performed piano transcriptions for 2 pianos and for piano 4-hands of obscure works by forgotten composers. In 1971 they gave an all-Liszt concert in London, which included his piano transcriptions of his symph. poems *Mazeppa* and *Orpheus,* and of his arrangements of excerpts from Bellini's *Norma* and *La Sonnambula* and Mozart's *Don Giovanni.* In 1972 they played Liszt's transcriptions of Beethoven's 9th Symph. in London, arousing considerable curiosity, and repeated this exhibition in N.Y. in 1974. They further played duo-piano works by Bartók and Grainger. For better professional identification of their gemination, they split their original fetal name, Contiguglia, into two fungible parts, Conti-Guglia.

Contilli, Gino, Italian composer; b. Rome, April 19, 1907; d. Genoa, April 4, 1978. He studied at the Santa Cecilia Academy in Rome with Respighi. After 1942 he taught composition at the Liceo Musicale in Messina.
 WORKS: 2 concertos for Orch. (1936, 1942); *Sinfonia italiana* (1938); *Violin Sonata* (1947); *La notte,* lyric suite for Voice and Small Ensemble (1950); *In Lunam,* cantata (1957; Italian Radio, Nov. 20, 1964); *Espressioni sinfoniche* for Orch. (Venice, Sept. 21, 1960); *Offerta musicale* for Soprano and 5 Instruments (1959); *Immagini sonore* for Soprano and 11 Instruments (1964); *Preludi* for Orch. (1966).

Conus, Georgi, Russian composer and theorist; b. Moscow, Sept. 30, 1862; d. there, Aug. 29, 1933. He studied at the Moscow Cons. with Taneyev and Arensky; from 1891–99 he taught there; from 1902, was a prof. at the music school of the Phil. Society. He developed an original theory of metric analysis and publ. a brief outline of it; also wrote several symph. works, piano pieces, and songs.

Conus, Julius, Russian violinist and composer, brother of **Georgi Conus;** b. Moscow, Feb. 1, 1869; d. Malenki, Ivanov District, Jan. 3, 1942. He studied at the Moscow Cons.; later taught violin there. He was a friend of Tchaikovsky and was greatly esteemed in Moscow musical circles. His Violin Concerto, first performed by him in Moscow in 1898, has retained its popularity in Russia.

Conus, Sergei, Russian pianist and composer, son of **Julius Conus;** b. Moscow, Oct. 18, 1902. He studied music with his father, with his uncle, Leo Conus, and with Oskar Riesemann. In 1920 he went to Paris, where he studied piano with Cortot and Isidor Philipp; then lived in Serbia, Bulgaria, and Poland. He was again in France from 1937 to 1949, and in Morocco from 1949 to 1959; in 1959 settled in America; taught piano at the Boston Cons. His compositions are mostly for piano (24 preludes, many miniatures, a concerto); he also wrote a symph. His style is characteristically Russian, closely resembling that of Rachmaninoff.

Converse, Charles Crozat, American composer; b. Warren, Mass., Oct. 7, 1832; d. Englewood, N.J., Oct. 18, 1918. He studied at the Leipzig Cons. with Richter, Hauptmann, and Plaidy (1855–59). Upon his return to America he was a practicing lawyer in Erie, Pa.; then lived in Highwood, N.J.
 WORKS: A number of patriotic overtures and cantatas, among them *American Concert Overture* on "Hail, Columbia" (1869); *God for Us,* an American hymn (1887); etc.; also vocal quartets, music for strings, 2 symphs., 2 oratorios, etc. His hymn *What a Friend We Have in Jesus* is widely sung. In his writings he used the pen name **Karl Redan.** A man of many interests, he wrote articles on philosophical and philological subjects; proposed the use of the genderless pronoun of the 3rd person, "thon," which has been included in several dictionaries.

Converse, Frederick Shepherd, distinguished American composer; b. Newton, Mass., Jan. 5, 1871; d. Westwood, Mass., June 8, 1940. He graduated from Harvard Univ. (1893); studied music in Boston with Carl Baermann and Chadwick (1894–96); then in Munich at the Royal Academy of Music with Rheinberger, graduating in 1898. Returning to Boston, he taught harmony at the New England Cons. (1900–2) and 1920–36); was an instructor of composition at Harvard Univ. (1901–7). He was vice-president of the Boston Opera Co. (1911–14); served as a captain in the U.S. Army (1917–19); was dean of the New England Cons. (1931–37); received a Mus.Doc. from Boston Univ. (1933); became a member of the American Academy of Arts and Letters (1937). His early works reflect the influence of academic German training; later he began to apply more advanced harmonies; in his *Flivver Ten Million,* written to glorify the 10-millionth Ford car, he adopted a frankly modern idiom, modeled after Honegger's *Pacific 231.* He sketched some material for a 5th Symph. in 1937, but did not complete it. He had renumbered his symphs. in 1936, calling his previously unnumbered Symph. No. 1 and upping Nos. 1, 2, and 3 by one, giving the title of Symph. 5 to the undeveloped sketches for that work. But his Symphs. Nos. 2, 3, and 4 were premiered, respectively, as Nos. 1, 2, and 3.

WORKS: OPERAS: *The Pipe of Desire* (Boston Opera, Jan. 31, 1906; first American opera to be produced by the Metropolitan Opera Co., March 18, 1910; won the David Bispham medal); *The Sacrifice* (Boston, March 3, 1911); *Sinbad the Sailor* (1913; not perf.); *The Immigrants* (1914; not perf.). ORATORIOS: *Job,* dramatic poem for Soli, Chorus, and Orch. (Worcester Festival, Oct. 2, 1907; also in Hamburg, Nov. 23, 1908; the first American oratorio to be heard in Germany); *Hagar in the Desert,* dramatic narrative for Low Voice and Orch. (written for Mme. Schumann-Heink; sung by her in Hamburg, 1908). CANTATAS: *The Peace Pipe* (1914); *The Answer of the Stars* (1919); *The Flight of the Eagle* (1930). OTHER VOCAL WORKS: *La Belle Dame sans merci,* ballade for Baritone with Orch. (1902); psalm, *I Will Praise Thee, O Lord* (1924).

FOR ORCH.: Symphs.: in D minor, not numbered (Munich, July 14, 1898); No. 1 (Boston, Jan. 30, 1920); No. 2 (Boston, April 21, 1922); No. 3 (1936); No. 6 (posthumously perf. by the Indianapolis Symph. Orch., Nov. 29, 1940); concert overture, *Youth; Festival of Pan* (Boston, Dec. 21, 1900); *Endymion's Narrative* (1901; Boston, April 9, 1903); *Night* and *Day,* 2 poems for Piano and Orch. (Boston, Jan. 21, 1905); overture, *Euphrosyne* (Boston, 1903); orch. fantasy, *The Mystic Trumpeter* (Philadelphia, March 3, 1905; many subsequent perfs.); symph. poem, *Ormazd* (St. Louis, Jan. 26, 1912); symph. poem, *Ave atque Vale* (St. Louis, Jan. 26, 1917); Fantasia for Piano and Orch. (1922); *Song of the Sea* (Boston, April 18, 1924); *Elegiac Poem* (Cleveland, Dec. 2, 1926); fantasy, *Flivver Ten Million* (Boston, April 15, 1927); *California,* festival scenes (Boston, April 6, 1928); symph. suite, *American Sketches* (Boston, Feb. 8, 1935).

CHAMBER MUSIC: 3 string quartets; Violin Sonata; Cello Sonata; Piano Trio; also Violin Concerto, with Piano Accompaniment (1902); *Valzer poetici* for Piano, 4-hands; *Scarecrow Sketches* (excerpts from the photo-music-drama *Puritan Passions,* commissioned by the Film Guild of N.Y., 1923; originally for Piano; orchestrated and perf., Boston, Dec. 18, 1923); piano pieces and songs.

Conyngham, Barry, Australian composer; b. Sydney, Aug. 27, 1944. He studied jurisprudence; in 1966 entered the New South Wales Cons.; also took private lessons with Meale, and later with Sculthorpe at the Univ. of Sydney. In 1970 he traveled to Japan and had instruction in advanced techniques with Toru Takemitsu. Returning to Australia, he became a lecturer in Perth at the Univ. of Western Australia; then went to the U.S. to study electronic music at the Univ. of Calif. in San Diego and at Princeton Univ.; eventually received an appointment to teach at Melbourne Univ.

WORKS: Opera, *Ned Mark II* (1975–76); *Jazz Ballet* for Saxophone, Double Bass, Drums, Flute, and Piano (1964); Cello Sonata (1965); Piano Sonata (1966–67); *Dialogue* for String Trio (1967); *Lyric Dialogues* for 5 Flutes, Oboe, and Cello (1967); *Crises: Thoughts in a City* for 2 String Orchs. and Percussion (1968); *Prisms* for 6 Violins (1968); *Three* for 2 Percussion Groups and String Quartet (1969); *5 Windows* for Orch. (1969); *Ice Carving* for Amplified Violin and 4 String Orchs. (1970); *Water ... Footsteps ... Time* for Solo Piano, Harp, Electric Guitar, Tam-tam, and Orch. (1970–71); *Ends* for Piano (1970); theater piece, *Edward John Eyre,* for Female Voice, Actors, Wind Quintet, and String Orch. (1971); *Five* for Wind Quintet (1970–71); *Six* for 6 Percussionists and Orch. (1971); *Voss* for Female Voice, Chorus, Piano, and Orch. (1972); *Snowflake* for Electric Piano, interchangeable with Harpsichord and Celesta (1973); *Without Gesture* for Percussion and Orch. (1973); *Mirror Images* for 4 Actors, Saxophone, Cello, Double Bass, and Percussion (1975); Percussion Concerto (1977); *Sky* for Strings (1977); *The Apology of Bony Anderson,* musical theater for 4 Voices and Instrumental Ensemble (1978); *Shadows of Noh,* double-bass concerto (1978); *Mirages* for Orch. (1979); String Quartet (1979); *Horizons,* concerto for Orch. (1981); *Southern Cross,* double concerto for Violin, Piano, and Orch. (1981); *Basho* for Soprano and Instruments, after verses by Matsuo Basho (London, Oct. 13, 1981).

BIBLIOGRAPHY: James Murdoch, *Australia's Contemporary Composers* (Melbourne, 1972).

Cooke, Arnold, English composer; b. Gomersal, Yorkshire, Nov. 4, 1906. He studied at Cambridge (1925–29; B.A.; Mus.B.; Mus.D., 1948); also with Hindemith at the Berlin Hochschule für Musik to 1932; taught at the Royal Manchester College of Music (1933–38); was a prof. at the Trinity College of Music in London from 1947.

WORKS: Piano Concerto (1943); Concerto for String Orch. (1947); Symph. No. 1 (1949); Clarinet Concerto (1955); Oboe Sonata (1957); Violin Concerto (1958); Clarinet Sonata (1959); Suite for 3 Clarinets (1959); *Jabez and the Devil,* ballet (1961); Clarinet Quintet (1962); Symph. No. 2 (1963); *Variations on a Theme of Dufay* for Orch. (1966); Symph. No. 3 (1967); Piano Quintet (1970); Suite for Recorder, Strings, and Percussion (1972); 2 organ sonatas (1971, 1980); Cello Concerto (1972–73); Symph. No. 4 (1974); Symph. No. 5 (1978–79); Concerto No. 2 for Clarinet and Orch. (1981–82); other chamber works, including 2 cello sonatas (1941, 1979–80) and 5 string quartets (1933, 1945, 1967, 1976, 1978).

Cooke, Benjamin, English organist and composer; b. London, 1734; d. there, Sept. 14, 1793. He studied with Pepusch, whom he succeeded in 1752 as conductor at the Academy of Ancient Music; in 1757 he became choirmaster (after Gates), in 1758 lay vicar, and in 1762 organist, of Westminster Abbey; received a Mus.Doc. from Cambridge (1775) and from Oxford (1782); became organist of St. Martin-in-the-Fields, 1782; in 1789 he resigned the Academy conductorship in favor of Arnold. His best works are in the form of glees, canons, and catches, for which he took several Catch Club prizes (*Collection of 20 Glees, Catches, and Canons for 3-6 Voices in Score,* London, 1775; *9 Glees and 2 Duets,* 1795). He also wrote odes, instrumental concertos, church music, pieces for organ and harpsichord, etc., and added choruses and accompaniments to Pergolesi's *Stabat Mater* (1759) and Galliard's *Morning Hymn* (1772) for the Academy of Ancient Music. His son **Robert** (b. Westminster, 1768; d. Aug. 13, 1814) became organist of St. Martin-in-the-Fields after his father's death in 1793, and on the death of Dr. Arnold, in 1802, was appointed organist and choirmaster of Westminster Abbey; ended his life by drowning himself in the Thames. He publ. a collection of glees in 1805.

Cooke, Deryck, English musicologist; b. Leicester, Sept. 14, 1919; d. London, Oct. 26, 1976. He studied piano privately and composition at Cambridge Univ. with Patrick Hadley and Robin Orr, earning his B.A. in 1940, M.A. in 1943, and Mus.B. in 1947. From 1947 to 1959 he was a member of the music staff of the BBC (rejoined in 1965); after 1959, he devoted most of his time to writing on music and broadcasting. He attracted considerable attention by his scholarly and congenial arrangement of Mahler's unfinished 10th Symph., which he completed using authentic fragments from Mahler's sketch; this version was approved by Alma Mahler, the composer's widow. It was first performed at a BBC Henry Wood Promenade Concert at the Albert Hall in London, on Aug. 13, 1964. Cooke publ. *The Language of Music* (London, 1959) and *Mahler 1860–1911* (BBC centenary booklet, 1960); *I Saw the World End: A Study of Wagner's Ring* (London, 1979); *Gustav Mahler: An Introduction to His Music* (N.Y., 1980); *Variations: Essays on Romantic Music* (posthumous, London, 1982).

Cooke, James Francis, eminent American writer on music and composer; b. Bay City, Mich., Nov. 14, 1875; d. Philadelphia, March 3, 1960. He was educated in Brooklyn and studied music with R.H. Woodman and W.H. Hall; went to Germany in 1900, and continued his studies with Meyer-Obersleben and H. Ritter. As editor of the *Etude* for 40 years (1908–49), he brought it to a high degree of popularity by promoting special features (columns dealing with performance and technique; simple arrangements of classics; etc.). He composed a number of successful piano pieces (*White Orchids, Moon Mist, Ballet Mignon, Sea Gardens, Italian Lake Suite*), and songs.
WRITINGS: *A Standard History of Music* (Philadelphia, 1910); *Great Pianists on Piano Playing* (4th ed., 1914); *Mastering the Scales and Arpeggios* (1913); *Musical Playlets for Children* (1917); *Great Singers on the Art of Singing* (1921); *Great Men and Famous Musicians* (1925); *Young Folks' Picture-History of Music* (1925); *Light, More Light* (1925); *Johannes Brahms* (1928); *Claude Debussy* (1928); *Musical Travelogues* (1934); *How to Memorize Music* (1947); many non-musical works, including plays

and poems.

Cooke, Sam, black American balladeer; b. Chicago, Jan. 22, 1935; shot to death in Los Angeles, Dec. 11, 1964. He sang in a lyric tenor voice, avoiding the shouts and the screams that often covered up vocal incompetence among so many pop singers; rather, his songs recalled the Negro spirituals and the texts reflected religious sentiments, or else the throes of unrequited love. Among his big hits were *You Send Me, Chain Gang, Twistin' the Night Away,* and *Cupid.* He also sang gospel hymns such as *Nearer to Thee, Touch the Hem of His Garment, Wonderful, God Is So Wonderful,* and *Jesus, Wash Away My Troubles.* He was shot by a jealous girlfriend.

Cooke, Thomas Simpson, English composer and singing teacher; b. Dublin, 1782; d. London, Feb. 26, 1848. He studied with his father; while still a youth, served as concertmaster of the orch. at the Crow Street Theatre in Dublin. From 1806–12 he ran a music shop; also filled tenor parts at Drury Lane in London; in 1815 he became conductor and later music director there (1821–35). In 1846 he joined the ensemble of the Concerts of Antient Music as concertmaster. His versatility as an instrumentalist was displayed when, at one of his benefit concerts at Drury Lane, he performed alternately on the violin, flute, clarinet, bassoon, horn, cello, double bass, and piano. He also was esteemed as a singing teacher (Sims Reeves was his pupil); wrote 2 vocal treatises, *Singing exemplified in a series of Solfeggi* and *Singing in Parts* (London, 1942). He composed over 50 pieces of incidental music for Drury Lane.

Cooley, Spade (Donnell), American country fiddler, once renowned as the "King of Western Swing"; b. in a storm cellar under a shack near Saddle Paddle Creek, Okla., Dec. 17, 1910; d. Oakland, Calif., Nov. 23, 1969, while on a furlough from the Calif. State Medical Facility at Bakersfield, the minimum-security state prison where he was confined from 1961 for the murder of his wife, Ella Mae. Cooley was one-quarter Cherokee Indian; he joined the cowboy star Roy Rogers in Hollywood in his act, and acquired the nickname "Spade" after a spectacular poker game during which he filled several successive flushes in spades. He replenished his financial resources from these winnings and went into the real estate business. He was author of the song *Shame, Shame on You.*

Coolidge, Elizabeth Sprague (Mrs. Frederick Shurtleff Coolidge), American music patron and accomplished composer; b. Chicago, Oct. 30, 1864; d. Cambridge, Mass., Nov. 4, 1953. In 1918 she established at Pittsfield, Mass., the Berkshire Festivals of Chamber Music, which were held annually under her auspices and later transferred to Washington, D.C. She was the sponsor of the Elizabeth Sprague Coolidge Foundation in the Library of Congress, created in 1925 for the purpose of producing concerts, music festivals, awarding prizes, etc., under the administration of the Music Division of the Library. Numerous modern composers, including Loeffler, Schoenberg, Malipiero, Bartók, Casella, Stravinsky, Prokofiev, Piston, and Hanson, have written works commissioned for it. The auditorium of the Library, of Congress was likewise a gift of Mrs. Coolidge. In 1932 she founded the Elizabeth Sprague Coolidge Medal "for eminent services to chamber music," awarded annually (until 1949) to one or more persons; its recipients included Adolfo Betti, Walter W. Cobbett, Carl Engel, and E.T. Rice. She also initiated performances of modern and classical chamber music throughout the U.S. and Europe. Her sponsorship of the appearances of artists in the U.S. and abroad (the Pro Arte, Coolidge, Roth quartets, etc.) was an important factor in the musical life of the U.S. In recognition of her many cultural contributions she was made honorary M.A. (Yale Univ., Smith College, Mills College), L.D. (Mt. Holyoke College), Mus.Doc. (Pomona College), LL.D. (Univ. of Calif.). She received the Cobbett Medal and various foreign decorations.

Cools, Eugène, French composer; b. Paris, March 27, 1877; d. there, Aug. 5, 1936. He studied at the Paris Cons. with Gédalge, Fauré, and Widor; won the Prix Crescent for his Symph. (1906); was assistant of Gédalge at the Cons. (1907–23); taught at the Ecole Normale de Musique (1919); was music critic for *Le Monde Musical;* in 1928 he was appointed editor in chief for Max Eschig, a Paris music publisher.
  WORKS: 2 operas: *Le Jugement de Midas* (1922) and *Kymris;* opera buffa, *Beaumarchais,* on themes by Rossini; operettas: *Magda, Les Violettes de la Malmaison,* and *Ravioli;* symph. poem, *La Mort de Chénier; Hamlet,* symph. suite; *2 pièces russes* for Orch. (most of these pieces are also available in piano arrangements); Piano Quintet; String Quartet; Violin Sonata; Flute Sonata; about 80 songs; many piano pieces.

Coombs, Charles Whitney, American organist and composer; b. Bucksport, Maine, Dec. 25, 1859; d. Orange, N.J., Jan 24, 1940. He studied piano and composition in Germany; was organist of American Church in Dresden (1887–91); returned to America, and took charge of the music in the Church of the Holy Communion in N.Y., holding the position till 1908; was at St. Luke's, 1908–28; retired in 1928. He was made an honorary Mus.Doc. by Syracuse Univ. (1922).
  WORKS: Cantatas: *The Vision of St. John, Hymn of Peace, The First Christmas, The Ancient of Days, The Sorrows of Death; Song of Judith,* motet for Soprano and Baritone Soli and Chorus; a number of sacred songs, anthems, etc.; about 75 secular songs.

Cooper, Alice, American rocker and female impersonator; b. Detroit, Feb. 4, 1948. His real name was **Vincent Furnier.** The family moved to Phoenix, Ariz., where he went to school and formed a band. In 1967 he moved to Los Angeles and decided to dress like a female. His notoriety as a transvestite skyrocketed on a wave of revulsion mixed with sexual titillation.

Cooper, Emil, Russian conductor; b. Kherson, Dec. 20, 1877; d. New York, Nov. 16, 1960. He studied at the Odessa Cons., then went to Vienna, where he took lessons in violin with Joseph Hellmesberger; later studied in Moscow with Taneyev. At the age of 22 he began to conduct at the Kiev Opera. In 1909 he conducted the Russian Ballet and Opera with the Diaghilev troupe in Paris. He then conducted in Moscow; in 1923 he went abroad; in 1929 he conducted the Chicago Civic Opera; in 1944–50 was on the staff of the Metropolitan Opera Co.; then became music director of the Montreal Opera Guild; subsequently lived in N.Y.

Cooper, George, English organist; b. London, July 7, 1820; d. there, Oct. 2, 1876. His father was an organist, and he served his apprenticeship at an early age; when he was 13 played organ at St. Benet Church; 5 years later became assistant organist at St. Paul's; in 1856, appointed organist of the Chapel Royal. An able performer, he did much to elevate the public taste, especially by his playing of Bach's organ works. He publ. *The Organist's Assistant,* selections from classical authors; *The Organist's Manual; Organ Arrangements* (3 vols.); *Classical Extracts for the Organ; Introduction to the Organ;* songs.

Cooper, Kenneth, highly talented American harpsichordist; b. New York, May 31, 1941. He studied harpsichord playing with Sylvia Marlowe at the Mannes College of Music in N.Y.; also took harpsichord lessons with Fernando Valenti; then entered Columbia Univ. (B.A., 1962; M.A., 1964; Ph.D. in musicology, 1971). He subsequently developed an energetic schedule of teaching; was an instructor of music at Barnard College (1967–71), lecturing on all academic music subjects; an adjunct assistant prof. at Brooklyn College (1971–73); in 1975 was appointed prof. of harpsichord at the Mannes College of Music. A man of latitudinarian and panoramic faculties, Kenneth Cooper encompasses a 360° range of activities, specializing in playing piano and harpsichord, improvisation, authentication of performing usages of the Baroque, translation from musically important languages (Italian, German), and last but not least, revivification of ragtime. He has publ. a number of scholarly articles dealing with the Baroque period; directed stage performances of neglected operas by Handel; and gave concerts of Bach's music at midnight. He has further commissioned works for harpsichord to composers of the avant-garde; played recitals in England, at the Salzburg Festival; traveled as a concert artist in Russia, Rumania, and Greece under the auspices of the U.S. Dept. of State; made frequent appearances with his wife, the soprano **Josephine Mongiardo,** whom he married in 1969.

Cooper, Martin, English music critic; b. Winchester, Jan. 17, 1910. He was educated at Hertford College, Oxford (B.A., 1931); then studied with Egon

Wellesz in Vienna (1932–34); was music critic for the *London Mercury* (1935–38) and the *Daily Herald* (1946–50); in 1950 he joined the staff of the *Daily Telegraph,* where he was chief music critic from 1954 until 1976. He also was editor of the *Musical Times* from 1953 to 1956.

WRITINGS: *Gluck* (London, 1935); *Bizet* (London, 1938); *Opéra comique* (London, 1949); *Profils de musiciens anglais* (Paris, 1950); *French Music from the Death of Berlioz to the Death of Fauré* (London, 1951); *Russian Opera* (London, 1951); *Ideas and Music* (London, 1966); *Beethoven: the Last Decade* (London, 1970); he also edited *The Concise Encyclopedia of Music and Musicians* (London, 1958; 3rd ed., revised, 1975) and Vol. X, *The Modern Age 1890–1960,* of *The New Oxford History of Music* (London, 1974), for which he wrote section III, "Stage Works: 1890–1918."

Cooper, Paul, American composer; b. Victoria, Ill., May 19, 1926. He studied at the Univ. of Southern Calif. under Ernest Kanitz and Roger Sessions (M.A., 1953; D.M.A., 1956); was a private student of Nadia Boulanger in Paris (1953–54). Upon return to the U.S., he held the posts of prof. of music at the Univ. of Michigan (1955–67) and composer-in-residence at the Univ. of Cincinnati (1968–74) and at Rice Univ. in Houston (1974). He held two Guggenheim fellowships (1965, 1972).

WORKS: FOR ORCH.: Sinfonia for Strings (1952); 4 symphs. (1954; 1956; *Lamentations* for Strings, 1971; *Landscape,* 1973); Overture (1953); Concerto for Orch. (1966); Violin Concerto (1967); *A Shenandoah* (for the centennial of Charles Ives, 1974); Symph. in 2 Movements (Houston, Sept. 10, 1983). For Wind Ensemble: Sinfonia (1958); Concerto for Winds, Percussion, and Piano (1968); *Liturgies* (1969); *Antiphons* for Oboe and Winds (1973). CHAMBER MUSIC: 5 string quartets (1953; 1954; 1959; 1964; *Umbrae,* 1973); *Canonic Variations* for Wind Quintet (1960); Viola Sonata (1961); Concerto for Harpsichord and Organ (1962); Violin Sonata (1962); Cello Sonata (1962); Sonata for Flutes and Piano (1963); Double bass Sonata (1964); *Concert for 2* for Cello and Piano (1965); *Concert for 4* for Flute, Oboe, Harpsichord, and Double Bass (1965); *Concert for 5* for Wind Quintet (1965); *Epitaphs* for Alto Flute, Harp, and Double Bass (1969); *Soliloquies* for Violin and Piano (1970); *Chimera,* piano quartet (1972); *Variants II* for Viola and Piano (1972); *Aegina Music* for Violin, Cello, and Piano (1973). FOR PIANO: 2 sonatas (1949, 1963); *3 Small Sonatas* (1953); *Momentos* (1957); *Partimento* (1967); *Cycles* (1969). FOR ORGAN: Concerto for Antiphonal Organs (1954); Toccata (1959); *Variants I* (1971). CHORAL MUSIC: *Missa Brevis* (1954); *Chorales of Nativity* (1954); *4 Madrigals* (1956); *Genesis II* (1969); *Credo* for Double Chorus and Orch. (1970); *?for Boys' Chorus* (1972); *Cantigas* for Double Chorus and Orch. (1972). He publ. a textbook, *Perspectives in Music Theory* (1973).

Coopersmith, Jacob Maurice, American musicologist; b. New York, Nov. 20, 1903; d. Washington, D.C., May 12, 1968. He attended N.Y. Univ. (B.S., 1929), Columbia Univ. (M.A., 1930), Harvard Univ. (Ph.D., 1932); also studied organ with Samuel A. Baldwin and Dr. A.M. Richardson; won the Schepp Foundation Scholarship (Harvard, 1930–31), John K. Paine Traveling Fellowship (1932), Charles E. Ditson Traveling Fellowship (1933), Juilliard Foundation Grant (1934); was connected, as a librarian, with various radio stations. In 1949 he was appointed senior music cataloguer at the Library of Congress; has publ. many articles relating to Handel, and an edition of *Messiah* based on the original sources.

BIBLIOGRAPHY: M. Picker, "Jacob Maurice Coopersmith," *Journal of the American Musicological Society* (Fall 1969); G. Reese, "Jacob Maurice Coopersmith," *Notes* (Dec. 1969).

Coperario (**John Cooper,** an Englishman who Italianized his patronymic after study in Italy), famous lutenist and viola da gamba player; b. c.1575; d. London, 1626. He went to Italy about 1600, and upon his return to England became an acknowledged authority in the field of instrumental and vocal music, patterned closely on the Italian model. He became music teacher to the children of James I, and of Henry and William Lawes. His improvisations on the organ were greatly admired. He wrote a set of "Fancies" for organ, and a set for viols; music for 2 masques; songs (*Funeral Teares,* 1606; *Songs of Mourning,* 1613, etc.). Two of his anthems are included in Leighton's *Teares of Lamentations;* numerous works for string instruments, with organ, are in the Christ Church library at Oxford; compositions for viols are preserved at the Royal College of Music in London, and other works at the British Museum. His treatise *Rules How to Compose* (c.1610) was publ. in facsimile in Los Angeles in 1951, with an introduction by the editor, Manfred Bukofzer.

BIBLIOGRAPHY: J. Pulver, in *Monthly Musical Record* (April 1927); idem, in his *Biographical Dictionary of Old English Music and Instruments* (2nd ed., 1927); Ernst Hermann Meyer, *Die mehrstimmige Spielmusik des 17. Jahrhunderts in Nord- und Mitteleuropa* (Kassel, 1934); G. Dodd, "Coperario or Bull?" and "The Coperario-Lupo Five-part Books at Washington," *Chelys* (1969).

Copland, Aaron, a greatly distinguished and exceptionally gifted American composer; b. Brooklyn, Nov. 14, 1900. He was educated at the Boys' High School in Brooklyn; began to study piano with Victor Wittgenstein and Clarence Adler as a young child. In 1917 he took lessons in harmony and counterpoint with Rubin Goldmark in N.Y., and soon began to compose. His first publ. piece, *The Cat and the Mouse* for piano (1920), subtitled *Scherzo humoristique,* shows the influence of Debussy. In 1921 he went to Paris, where he studied composition and orchestration with Nadia Boulanger. Returning to America in 1924, he lived mostly in N.Y.; became active in many musical activities, not only as a composer but also as a lecturer, pianist, and organizer in various musical societies. He attracted the attention of Serge Koussevitzky, who gave the first performance of his early score *Music for the Theater* with the Boston Symph. Orch. in 1925; then engaged Copland as soloist in his Concerto for Piano and Orch. in 1927; the work produced a considerable sensation because of the jazz elements incorporated in the score, and there was some subterranean grumbling among the staid subscribers to the Boston Symph. concerts. Koussevitzky remained Copland's steadfast supporter throughout his tenure as conductor of the Boston Symph. Orch., and later as the founder of the Koussevitzky Music Foundation. In the meantime, Walter Damrosch conducted in N.Y. Copland's Symph. for Organ and Orch., with Nadia Boulanger as soloist. Other orchs. and their conductors also performed his music, which gained increasing recognition. Particularly popular were Copland's works based on folk motifs; of these the most remarkable are *El Salón México* (1933–36) and the American ballets *Billy the Kid* (1938), *Rodeo* (1942), and *Appalachian Spring* (1944). A place apart is occupied by Copland's *Lincoln Portrait* for narrator and orch. (1942), with the texts arranged by the composer from speeches and letters of Abraham Lincoln; this work has had a great many performances, with the role of the narrator performed by such notables as Adlai Stevenson and Eleanor Roosevelt. His patriotic *Fanfare for the Common Man* (1942) achieved tremendous popularity and continued to be played on various occasions for decades; Copland incorporated it *in toto* into the score of his 3rd Symph. He was for many years a member of the board of directors of League of Composers in N.Y.; with Roger Sessions he organized the Copland-Sessions Concerts (1928–31), and was also a founder of the Yaddo Festivals (1932) and of the American Composers' Alliance (1937); was also a participant in such organizations as the Koussevitzky Music Foundation, the Composers Forum, the Cos Cob Press, etc. He was head of the composition dept. at the Berkshire Music Center at Tanglewood from 1940 to 1965, and from 1957 to 1965 was chairman of the faculty. He has lectured extensively and has given courses at The New School for Social Research in N.Y. and at Harvard Univ. (1935 and 1944); was the Charles Eliot Norton Lecturer at Harvard in 1951–52. He is the recipient of many awards: Guggenheim fellowship (1925–27); RCA Victor award of $5,000 for his *Dance Symphony;* Pulitzer Prize and N.Y. Music Critics' Circle Award for *Appalachian Spring* (1945); N.Y. Music Critics' Circle Award for the 3rd Symph. (1947); Oscar award for the film score *The Heiress* from the Academy of Motion Picture Arts and Sciences (1950); Gold Medal for Music from the American Academy of Arts and Letters (1956); Presidential Medal of Freedom (1964); Howland Memorial Prize of Yale Univ. (1970); was also decorated with a Commander's Cross of the Order of Merit in West Germany; was elected to honorary membership of the Santa Cecilia Academy in Rome. He holds numerous honorary doctor's degrees: Princeton Univ. (1956); Brandeis Univ. (1957); Wesleyan Univ. (1958); Temple Univ. (1959); Harvard Univ. (1961); Rutgers Univ. (1967); Ohio State

Univ. (1970); N.Y. Univ. (1970); Columbia Univ. (1971); also York Univ. in England (1971). About 1955 Copland developed a successful career as a conductor, and has led major symph. orchs. in Europe, the U.S., South America, and Mexico; he also traveled to Russia under the auspices of the State Dept. As a composer, Copland makes use of a broad variety of idioms and techniques, tempering dissonant textures by a strong sense of tonality. He enlivens his musical textures by ingenious applications of syncopation and polyrhythmic combinations; but in such works as Piano Variations he adopts an austere method of musical constructivism. He uses a modified 12-tone technique in his Piano Quartet (1950) and an integral dodecaphonic idiom in the score of *Connotations* (1962). A chronological list of his works was publ. by Boosey & Hawkes in 1960.

WORKS: FOR THE STAGE: *Grohg,* ballet in one act (1922–25; not perf.; material incorporated into *A Dance Symphony*); *Hear Ye! Hear Ye!,* ballet (1934); *The 2nd Hurricane,* play-opera for high school (1936; N.Y., April 21, 1937); *Billy the Kid,* ballet (Ballet Caravan Co., Chicago, Oct. 16, 1938; N.Y., May 24, 1939); *From Sorcery to Science,* music for a puppet show (1939); *Rodeo,* ballet in one act (Ballets Russes de Monte Carlo, N.Y., Oct 16, 1942); *Appalachian Spring,* ballet (Martha Graham Ballet, Washington, D.C., Oct. 30, 1944); *The Tender Land,* opera (N.Y., April 1, 1954); *Dance Panels,* ballet in 7 movements (1959; revised 1962; Munich, Dec. 3, 1963, composer conducting; arranged for Piano, 1965).

FILM MUSIC: *The City* (1939); *Of Mice and Men* (1939); *Our Town* (1940); *North Star* (1943); *The Cummington Story* (1945); *The Red Pony* (1948); *The Heiress* (1948; received an Academy Award, 1949); *Something Wild* (1961).

INCIDENTAL MUSIC TO PLAYS: *Miracle at Verdun* (1931); *The 5 Kings* (1939); *Quiet City* (1939).

FOR ORCH.: *Music for the Theater* (N.Y., League of Composers, Nov. 28, 1925, Koussevitzky conducting); Symph. for Organ and Orch. (N.Y., Jan. 11, 1925, Nadia Boulanger, organist; Walter Damrosch conducting; revised version without organ, designated as Symph. No. 1, 1928; also as *Prelude* for Chamber Orch., 1934); Concerto for Piano and Orch. (1926; Boston, Jan. 28, 1927, composer soloist, Koussevitzky conducting); *Symphonic Ode* (1927–29; composed for the 50th anniversary of the Boston Symph. Orch.; Boston Feb. 19, 1932, Koussevitzky conducting; revised 1955 for the 75th anniversary of the Boston Symph. Orch. and rededicated to the memory of Koussevitzky; Boston, Feb. 3, 1956, Munch conducting; *A Dance Symphony* (1930; based on the ballet *Grohg;* received the RCA Victor Competition prize; Philadelphia, April 15, 1931, Stokowski conducting; *Short Symphony* (Symph. No. 2) (1932–33; Mexico City, Nov. 23, 1934, Chávez conducting); *Statements* (1932–35; first complete perf., N.Y., Jan. 7, 1942); *El Salón Mexico* (1933–36; Mexico City, Aug. 27, 1937, Chávez conducting); *Music for Radio (Prairie Journal),* subtitled *Saga of the Prairie* (CBS, N.Y., July 25, 1937); *An Outdoor Overture* (N.Y., Dec. 16, 1938; arranged for Band, 1941); *John Henry* for Chamber Orch. (CBS, N.Y., March 5, 1940;

revised 1952); *Our Town,* suite from the film (CBS, N.Y., June 9, 1940); *Quiet City,* suite from the film, for English Horn, Trumpet, and Strings (1939; N.Y., Jan. 28, 1941); *Billy the Kid,* suite from the ballet (Boston, Jan. 30, 1942); *Lincoln Portrait* for Speaker and Orch. (commissioned by Kostelanetz; Cincinnati, May 14, 1942, Carl Sandburg, speaker; Kostelanetz conducting; highly successful; numerous perfs. by orchs. in America and abroad); *Rodeo,* 4 dance episodes from the ballet (1942); *Music for Movies* for Chamber Orch. (from the films *The City, Of Mice and Men,* and *Our Town;* 1942; N.Y., Feb. 17, 1943); *Fanfare for the Common Man* for Brass and Percussion (1942; Cincinnati, March 12, 1943, Goossens conducting; highly successful on television and radio); *Letter from Home* (N.Y. broadcast, Oct. 17, 1944; revised 1962); *Variation of a Theme by Eugene Goossens* (with 9 other composers; 1944; Cincinnati, March 23, 1945, Goossens conducting); *Appalachian Spring,* suite from the ballet (N.Y., Oct. 4, 1945, Rodzinski conducting; Copland's most popular orch. work; received the Pulitzer Prize for 1945); *Danzón Cubano* (originally for 2 Pianos, 1942; orch. version, 1944; Baltimore, Feb. 17, 1946); Symph. No. 3 (in memory of Mme. Natalie Koussevitzky; 1944–46; Boston, Oct. 18, 1946, Koussevitzky conducting); Concerto for Clarinet, Strings, Harp, and Piano (1947–48; N.Y., Nov. 6, 1950, Benny Goodman, soloist; Reiner conducting); *The Red Pony,* suite from the film (Houston, Nov. 1, 1948); *Preamble for a Solemn Occasion* for Speaker and Orch. (N.Y., 1949, Laurence Olivier, speaker, Bernstein conducting; arranged for Organ, 1953; arranged for Band, 1973); Orch. Variations (orch. version of the Piano Variations; 1930; 1957); *Connotations* (composed entirely in the 12-tone technique; commissioned for the opening of Phil. Hall, Lincoln Center, N.Y., Sept. 23, 1962, Bernstein conducting); *Music for a Great City* (symph. suite descriptive of life in N.Y. City; London, May 26, 1964, composer conducting); *Emblems* for Band (1964); *Down a Country Lane* for School Orch. (1965); *Inscape* (commissioned by the N.Y. Phil. and first perf. by that orch. at the Univ. of Michigan, Ann Arbor, Sept. 13, 1967, Bernstein conducting); *Inaugural Fanfare* (1969; revised 1975); *3 Latin American Sketches: Estribillo, Paisaje mexicano, Danza de Jalisco* (N.Y., June 7, 1972, Kostelanetz conducting).

VOCAL MUSIC: Choral: 4 Motets (1921); *The House on the Hill* for Women's Voices (1925); *An Immorality* for Soprano, Women's Voices, and Piano (1925); *What Do We Plant?* for Women's Voices and Piano (1935); *Lark* for Bass and Mixed Chorus (1938); *Las agachadas* for Mixed Chorus (1942); *Song of the Guerrillas* for Baritone, Men's Voices, and Piano (1943); *The Younger Generation* for Mixed Chorus and Piano (1943); *In the Beginning* for Mezzo-soprano and Mixed Chorus (commissioned for the Harvard Symposium; Cambridge, Mass., May 2, 1947, Robert Shaw conducting); *Canticle of Freedom* (1955; revised 1965). Songs: *Melancholy* (1917); *Spurned Love* (1917); *After Antwerp* (1917); *Night* (1918); *A Summer Vacation* (1918); *My Heart Is in the East* (1918); *Simone* (1919); *Music I Heard* (1920); *Old Poem* (1920); *Pastorale* (1921); *As It Fell Upon a Day* (1923); *Poet's Song* (1927); *Vocalise* (1928); *12 Poems of Emily Dickinson* (1949–50); *Old American Songs* for Voice and Orch. (arrangements in 2 sets, 1950 and 1959); *Dirge in Woods* (1954).

CHAMBER MUSIC: *Capriccio* for Violin and Piano; *Poem* for Cello and Piano; *Lament* for Cello and Piano; *Preludes* for Violin and Piano; String Quartet (unfinished); Piano Trio (unfinished); *Rondino* for String Quartet (1923); *Nocturne* for Violin and Piano (1926); *Ukelele Serenade* for Violin and Piano (1926); *Lento molto* for String Quartet (1928); *Vitebsk, Study on a Jewish Theme* for Piano Trio (1928; League of Composers, N.Y., Feb. 16, 1929); *Elegies* for Violin and Viola (1932); Sextet for Clarinet, Piano, and String Quartet (arranged from *Short Symphony;* 1932–33; 1937; N.Y., Feb. 26, 1939); Sonata for Violin and Piano (1942–43); Quartet for Piano and Strings (Washington, D.C., Oct. 29, 1950); *Nonet* for 3 Violins, 3 Violas, and 3 Cellos (1960; Washington, March 2, 1961, composer conducting); Duo for Flute and Piano (1971); *Threnody I: Igor Stravinsky, In Memoriam* for Flute and String Trio (1971); *Vocalise* for Flute and Piano (arrangement of *Vocalise;* 1928; 1972); *Threnody II: Beatrice Cunningham, In Memoriam* for G-Flute and String Trio (1973).

FOR PIANO: *Moment musical* (1917); *Danse caractéristique* for Piano Duet or Orch. (1918); *Waltz Caprice* (1918); Sonnets, 1–3 (1918–20); *Moods* (3 esquisses): *Amertume, pensif, jazzy* and *Petit portrait,* a supplement (1920–21); Piano Sonata in G major (1920–21); *Scherzo humoristique: Le Chat et la souris* (1920); Passacaglia (1921–22); *Sentimental Melody* (1926); Piano Variations (1930; orch. version, 1957); *Sunday Afternoon Music (The Young Pioneers)* (1935); Piano Sonata (1939–41; Buenos Aires, Oct. 21, 1941, composer pianist); 4 Piano Blues (1926–48); Piano Fantasy (1952–57); *Down a Country Lane* (1962); *Rodeo* (arrangement from the ballet; 1962); *Danza de Jalisco* for 2 Pianos (1963; orch. version, 1972); *Dance Panels* (arrangement from the ballet; 1965); *In Evening Air* (excerpt arranged from the film score *The Cummington Story;* 1969); *Night Thoughts (Homage to Ives)* (1972).

WRITINGS: He has publ. the following books: *What to Listen for in Music* (N.Y., 1939; 2nd ed., 1957; trans. into German, Italian, Spanish, Dutch, Arabic and Chinese); *Our New Music* (N.Y., 1941; 2nd ed., revised and enlarged as *The New Music, 1900–1960,* N.Y., 1968); *Music and Imagination,* a collection of lectures delivered at Harvard in 1951–52 (Cambridge, Mass., 1952); *Copland on Music* (N.Y., 1960).

BIBLIOGRAPHY: P. Rosenfeld, *An Hour with American Music* (Philadelphia, 1929; pp. 126–43); T. Chanler, "Aaron Copland," in H. Cowell, ed., *American Composers on American Music* (Stanford, 1933); A. Berger, "The Music of Aaron Copland," *Musical Quarterly* (Oct. 1945); idem, *Aaron Copland* (N.Y., 1953); J. Smith, *Aaron Copland: His Work and Contribution to American Music* (N.Y., 1955); R. Goldman, "Aaron Copland," *Musical Quarterly* (Jan. 1961); E. Cone, "Conversation with Aaron Copland," *Perspectives of New Music* (Spring/Summer 1968); C. Peare, *Aaron Copland. His Life* (N.Y.,

1969); D. Hamilton, "Aaron Copland: A Discography of the Composer's Performances," *Perspectives of New Music* (Fall/Winter 1970); special issue of *Tempo*, devoted to Copland on the occasion of his 70th birthday (Winter 1970/71); B. Northcott, "Notes on Copland," *Musical Times* (Nov. 1980).

Coppet, Edward J. de, American patron of art and founder of the Flonzaley Quartet; b. New York, May 28, 1855; d. there, April 30, 1916. A man of wealth and refined artistic tastes, he engaged various artists for private quartet performances at his residence. When he realized that constant practice was indispensable for the attainment of a perfect ensemble, he commissioned A. Pochon, in 1902, to find 4 men of the highest artistic standing who were willing to devote all their time to quartet playing. In the summer of the following year Adolfo Betti, Alfred Pochon, Ugo Ara, and Ivan d'Archambeau (first violin, 2nd violin, viola, and cello, respectively) began to practice at Flonzaley, de Coppet's summer residence near Lausanne, Switzerland; in the spring of 1904 they made their first European tour, arousing admiration by the perfection of their ensemble; on Dec. 5, 1905, they gave their first public concert in America (Carnegie Chamber Music Hall, N.Y.), with overwhelming success. They then appeared regularly in America and Europe. After de Coppet's death, his son, **André,** continued the original policy until 1929, when the quartet disbanded.
BIBLIOGRAPHY: D.G. Mason, "Edward J. de Coppet," *Musical Quarterly* (Oct. 1916); E.T. Rice, "The de Coppet Music Room in New York and Switzerland," *Musical Quarterly* (Oct. 1937).

Coppola, Piero, Italian conductor and composer; b. Milan, Oct. 11, 1888; d. Lausanne, March 13, 1971. He studied at the Milan Cons., graduating in 1909; in 1913 he filled engagements as a conductor at La Scala; in 1914 was in London; in 1921 settled in Paris, where he was active as music director of the recording company "His Master's Voice" (1923–34); eventually settled in Switzerland. He wrote 2 operas, *Sirmione* and *Nikita* (1914); a Symph. (Paris, Nov. 13, 1924, composer conducting); a symph. sketch, *La Ronde sous la cloche* (1924); and various other pieces.
BIBLIOGRAPHY: W.A. Holmes, "Episodes in the Life and Times of an Artist: The Story of Piero Coppola," in *Le Grand Baton* (Sept.–Dec. 1973).

Coppola, Pietro Antonio (Pierantonio), Italian composer; b. Castrogiovanni, Sicily, Dec. 11, 1793; d. Catania, Nov. 13, 1877. For a short time he studied at the Naples Cons.; then began to compose operas, which obtained sufficient success to enable his friends and admirers to present him as a rival to Rossini.
WORKS: From the time he was 19, he produced one opera after another, but without much success until he composed *La Pazza per amore* (Rome, Feb. 14, 1835). This was his 5th opera and it became popular all over Europe (presented in Paris under the title *Eva*). In 1839–43, and again from 1850 till 1871,

he was conductor of the Lisbon Royal Opera. His other operas were: *Gli Illinesi* (Turin, Dec. 26, 1835); *Enrichietta di Baienfeld* (Vienna, June 29, 1836); *La bella Celeste degli Spadari* (Milan, June 14, 1837); *Giovanna prima di Napoli* (Lisbon, Oct. 11, 1840); *Il folletto* (Rome, June 18, 1843). He also wrote church music, notably a *Salve Regina* which was highly regarded. His son publ. his biography (1899).

Coquard, Arthur, French composer and music critic; b. Paris, May 26, 1846; d. Noirmoutier, Vendée, Aug. 20, 1910. He took private lessons with César Franck (1862–66); was music critic for *Le Monde* and *Echo de Paris.* He publ. *De la musique en France depuis Rameau* (Paris, 1892), which received a prize from the Académie des Beaux-Arts.
WORKS: Operas: *L'Epée du roi* (Angers, 1884); *Le Mari d'un jour* (Paris, 1886); *L'Oiseau bleu* (Paris, 1894); *La Jacquerie* (Paris, 1895); *Jahel* (Lyons, 1900); *La Troupe Jolicœur* (Paris, May 30, 1902); oratorio, *Jeanne d'Arc.*
BIBLIOGRAPHY: N. Dufourcq, *Autour de Coquard, Franck et d'Indy* (Paris, 1952).

Corboz, Michel (-Jules), Swiss conductor; b. Marsens, Feb. 14, 1934. He was educated at the Ecole Normale in Fribourg; then became a director of church music in Lausanne, where he organized the Ensemble Vocal et Instrumental de Lausanne, with which he has given numerous performances of Baroque vocal and orch. music.

Corder, Frederick, English composer and eminent teacher of composition; b. London, Jan. 26, 1852; d. there, Aug. 21, 1932. He was a pupil at the Royal Academy of Music (1873–75); in 1875 won the Mendelssohn Scholarship; studied with Ferdinand Hiller at Cologne (1875–78); was conductor of the Brighton Aquarium Concerts from 1880 to 1882, and greatly improved their quality; from 1886, was a prof. of composition at the Royal Academy of Music and, from 1889, also curator. In 1905 he founded the Society of British Composers. He was remarkably successful as a teacher, many prominent British composers having been his pupils; a zealous apostle of Wagner, he and his wife made the first English translation of *The Ring of the Nibelung, Die Meistersinger,* and *Parsifal* for the original scores publ. by Schott; was also a contributor to *Grove's Dictionary.*
WORKS: Operas: *Morte d'Arthur* (1877); *Nordisa* (Liverpool, Jan. 26, 1887; Drury Lane, London, May 4, 1887); *Ossian* (1905); operettas: *Philomel* (an operatic satire, 1880); *A Storm in a Teacup* (1880); *The Nabob's Pickle* (1883); *The Noble Savage* (1885); cantatas: *The Cyclops* (1881); *The Bridal of Triermain* (Wolverhampton Festival, 1886); *The Blind Girl of Castel-Cuillé* (1888); *The Sword of Argantyr* (Leeds Festival, 1889). For Orch.: *Evening on the Sea Shore,* idyll (1876); *Im Schwarzwald,* suite (1876); *Ossian,* overture (1882); *Nocturne* (1882); *Prospero,* overture (1885); *Roumanian Suite* (1887); *Pippa Passes,* orch. poem (1897); *A Fairy Tale* (1913);

incidental music to *The Tempest* (1886), *The Termagant* (1898), *The Black Tulip* (1899); *Dreamland,* ode for Chorus and Orch. (1883); *Roumanian Dances* for Violin and Piano (1883); *The Minstrel's Curse,* ballad for declamation, with Orch. (1888); *True Thomas,* musical recitation (1895); *The Witch's Song* (1904); *Elegy* for 24 Violins (1908); *Empire Pageant Masque* (1910); *The Angels,* biblical scene for 6 Choirs (1911); *Sing unto God,* 50-part motet (1912).

WRITINGS: *Exercises in Harmony and Musical Composition* (1891); *The Orchestra and How to Write for It* (1895; 2nd ed., 1902); *Modern Composition* (1909); *Musical Encyclopaedia* (1915); *History of the Royal Academy of Music* (1922).

BIBLIOGRAPHY: *Musical Times* (Nov. 1913).

Corder, Paul, English composer, son of **Frederick Corder;** b. London, Dec. 14, 1879; d. there, Aug. 6, 1942. He entered the Royal Academy of Music in 1895, studied piano with Oscar Beringer and Tobias Matthay, composition with his father; studied violin, viola, horn, clarinet, etc. He was appointed a prof. of harmony and composition at the Royal Academy of Music in 1907; was elected an associate of the Academy in 1905.

WORKS: 2 operas: *Grettir the Strong* and *Rapunzel* (finished 1917); *The Moon Slave,* terpsichorean fantasy; *Cyrano de Bergerac,* overture; *Dross,* music drama without words; op. 8, *Morar,* a "Gaelic fantasy"; *The Dryad,* ballet; *Prelude and Fugue; Sea-Songs; 2 Choral Songs; Heroic Elegy;* many piano works (*Transmutations, 9 Preludes, Passacaglia,* etc.); songs.

Cordero, Roque, Panamanian composer; b. Panama, Aug. 16, 1917. He first studied in Panama; then came to the U.S. (1943); studied with Krenek in Minneapolis and with Stanley Chapple (conducting) at the Berkshire Music Center at Tanglewood. He was a prof. at the National Inst. of Music in Panama in 1950–66, and its director in 1953–64; taught at Indiana Univ. in Bloomington (1966–69) and at Illinois State Univ. from 1972; was also active as a conductor.

WORKS: *Capriccio interiorano* for Band (1939); Piano Concerto (1944); Symph. No. 1 (1947); *8 Miniatures* for Orch. (1948); *Rapsodia campesina* for Orch. (1949); Quintet for Flute, Clarinet, Violin, Cello, and Piano (1949); Symph. No. 2 (1956); *5 mensajes breves* for Orch. (1959); 2 string quartets (1969, 1968); Cello Sonata (1962); Violin Concerto (1962); Symph. No. 3 (1965); *Sonata breve* for Piano (1966); *Circunvoluciones y moviles* for 57 Players (1967); *Permutaciones 7* for 7 Instrumentalists (1967); *Paz, Paix, Peace* for 4 Trios and Harp (1969); *Variations and Theme for 5* for Woodwind Quartet and Horn (1975).

Cordon, Norman, American baritone; b. Washington, N.C., Jan. 20, 1904; d. Chapel Hill, N.C., March 1, 1964. He attended the Fishburne Military School; later studied at the Univ. of N.C. and at the Nashville Cons. of Music; was a voice student of Gaetano de Lucas and Hadley Outland; in 1933 made his debut at the Civic Opera in Chicago, of which he was a member until 1936; from 1936 to 1946 he was a member of the Metropolitan Opera; he also appeared with the San Francisco Opera, the Cincinnati Summer Opera, and on Broadway.

Corea, "Chick" (Armando Anthony Corea), American jazz pianist; b. Chelsea, Mass., June 12, 1941. He began his career as a sideman with Mongo Santamaria, Willie Bobo, Blue Mitchell, and Herbie Mann; also worked with Miles Davis. After leading a group known as The Circle (1970–71), he worked with Stan Getz. His popularity grew as he turned to rock music, playing with a group known as Return to Forever.

Corelli, Arcangelo, famous Italian violinist and composer; b. Fusignano, near Imola, Feb. 17, 1653; d. Rome, Jan. 8, 1713. His violin teacher was G. Benvenuti in Bologna; he learned counterpoint with Matteo Simonelli. Little is known of his early life; about 1671 he went to Rome, where he was a violinist at the French Church (1675); in the beginning of 1679, he played in the orch. of the Teatro Capranica; Rome remained his chief residence to the end of his life, except for visits to Modena (1689–90) and Naples (1702). There is no substance to the story that in 1672 he went to Paris and was driven out by the intrigues of Lully; biographers mention also his stay at the court of the Elector of Bavaria in Munich about 1680, but there is no documentary evidence of this stay. Equally unfounded is the story that while he was in Naples, a mediocre violinist, Giuseppe Valentini, won the favor of the Roman public so that Corelli returned to Rome a broken man and died shortly afterward. Quite contrary to these fanciful legends, Corelli enjoyed respect, security, and fame. In Rome he had a powerful protector in Cardinal Benedetto Panfili; later he lived in the palace of Cardinal Pietro Ottoboni, conducting weekly concerts which were attended by the elite of Roman society. One of Corelli's admirers was Queen Christina of Sweden, who lived in Rome at the time. Among his pupils were Baptiste Anet, Geminiani, Locatelli, and Giovanni Somis. Corelli was famous as a virtuoso on the violin and may be regarded as the founder of modern violin technique; he systematized the art of proper bowing, and was one of the first to use double stops and chords on the violin. His role in music history is very great despite the fact that he wrote but few works; only 6 opus numbers can be definitely attributed to him. His greatest achievement was the creation of the concerto grosso. Handel, who as a young man met Corelli in Rome, was undoubtedly influenced by Corelli's instrumental writing. Corelli was buried in the Pantheon in Rome.

WORKS: 12 *sonate a 3, 2 violini e violone o arcileuto col basso per l'organo,* op. 1 (Rome, 1681; dedicated to Queen Christina of Sweden); 12 *sonate da camera a 3, 2 violini e violone o cembalo,* op. 2 (Rome, 1685); 12 *sonate a 3, 2 violini e violone o arcileuto, col basso per l'organo,* op. 3 (Rome, 1689);

12 *sonate a 3*, op. 4 (Rome, 1694; in Amsterdam as *Balleti da camera*); 12 *sonate a violino e violone o cembalo*, op. 5 (Rome, 1700; later arranged by Geminiani as *Concerti grossi;* the 12th sonata of op. 5 is *La Follia*, the celebrated set of variations for Violin); *Concerti grossi con 2 violini e violoncello di concertino obbligati, e 2 altri violini, viola, e basso di concerto grosso ad arbitrio che si potranno raddoppiare*, op. 6 (Amsterdam, 1714). All these were variously reprinted at the time; an important ed. is by Pepusch (London, opp. 1–4 and 6); Joachim and Chrysander issued the "complete works" in 1888–91 (London; opp. 1–6); a new critical ed. has been started at the Musikwissenschaftliches Institut der Universität Basel (1976—).
BIBLIOGRAPHY: C. Piancastelli, *In onore di Corelli* (Bologna, 1914); A. Einstein in *Sammelbände der Internationalen Musik-Gesellschaft*, IX (pp. 414ff.); F.T. Arnold, "A Corelli Forgery" (about a forged Antwerp ed. of 1693), in *Proceedings of the Musical Association* (London, 1921); A. Moser, in *Archiv für Musikwissenschaft*, I (pp. 358ff.); idem, in *Zeitschrift für Musikwissenschaft*, I (pp. 287ff.) and III (pp. 415ff.); A. Cametti, "Corelli à Saint-Louis des Français à Rome," *Revue Musicale* (Jan. 1922); F. Vatielli, "Il Corelli e i maestri bolognesi del suo tempo," *Arte e Vita Musicale a Bologna* (1927); A. Toni, "Arcangelo Corelli, cenni biografici," *Bolletino Bibliografico Musicale* (1927); H. Engel, *Das Instr.-Konzert* (Leipzig, 1932); M. Pincherle, *Corelli* (Paris, 1933; completely revised ed., 1954; Eng. trans., N.Y., 1956); C. Sartori, "Le 44 edizioni italiane delle sei opere di Corelli" (listing full titles of original eds. and reprints), *Rivista Musicale Italiana* (Jan.–March 1953); M. Rinaldi, *Arcangelo Corelli* (Milan, 1953; a comprehensive biography, bibliography, and catalogue of works); Bernhard Paumgartner, detailed article in *Die Musik in Geschichte und Gegenwart;* D.D. Boyden, "The Corelli 'Solo' Sonatas and Their Ornamental Additions ... ," *Musiqua Antiqua*, III (Bydgoszcz, 1972); D. Libby, "Interrelationships in Corelli," *Journal of the American Musicological Society* (Summer 1973).

Corelli, Franco, outstanding Italian tenor; b. Ancona, April 8, 1921. He studied naval engineering at the Univ. of Bologna; in 1947 entered the Pesaro Cons. to study voice; dissatisfied with the academic training, he left the Cons. and proceeded to learn the repertoire by listening to recordings of great singers. He made his operatic debut at the Spoleto Festival in 1952 as Don José in *Carmen;* then sang at the Rome Opera in 1953 and at La Scala, Milan, in 1954; he appeared at London's Covent Garden in 1957. On Jan. 27, 1961, he made his Metropolitan Opera debut in N.Y. as Manrico in *Il Trovatore;* from that time he appeared with most of the major opera houses of the world. Among his finest roles are Radames, Ernani, and Don Alvaro.

Corena, Fernando, Swiss bass; b. Geneva, Dec. 22, 1916. He was educated in Geneva and Milan. He made his debut in Trieste as Varlaam in *Boris Godunov* in 1947. On Feb. 6, 1954, he appeared for the first time at the Metropolitan Opera in N.Y. as Leporello in *Don Giovanni;* remained with the company for several seasons. He made his debut at Covent Garden, London, on May 16, 1960, as Dr. Bartolo in *Il Barbiere di Siviglia*. He is particularly known for his buffo roles.

Coria, Miguel Angel, Spanish composer; b. Madrid, Oct. 24, 1937. He studied at the Cons. of Madrid, and later took a course in electronic music in Utrecht, the Netherlands. Returning to Spain, he organized the ultramodern studio Alea, promoting aleatory and electronic music.
WORKS: *Imágenes* for Flute, Oboe, Vibraphone, Violin, and Viola (1963); *Vértices* for Small Ensemble (1964); *Volúmenes* for Small Ensemble (1967); *Joyce's Portrait* for Chamber Orch. (1968); several pieces for Small Ensemble under the generic name *Lúdica.*

Corigliano, John, American violinist; b. New York, Aug. 28, 1901; d. Norfolk, Conn., Sept. 1, 1975. He studied with Leopold Auer in N.Y.; gave violin recitals; in 1935 he was appointed assistant concertmaster of the N.Y. Phil., and in 1943 concertmaster; he resigned his position in 1966; subsequently served as concertmaster of the San Antonio Symph.

Corigliano, John, American composer, son of the violinist **John Corigliano;** b. New York, Feb. 16, 1938. He studied at Columbia Univ. with Otto Luening (B.A., 1959), with Vittorio Giannini at the Manhattan School of Music, and privately with Paul Creston. He was subsequently employed as a scriptwriter for radio station WQXR in N.Y. and as assistant director for musical television shows there; later he was in charge of the music section at WBAI. He held a Guggenheim fellowship in 1968–69. In 1971 he joined the faculty of the Manhattan School of Music, and from 1973 taught at Lehman College. His style of composition shows a fine capacity for lyrical expression, and an incisive sense of rhythm, in the generic tradition of Béla Bartók and Prokofiev. Despite the dissonant freedom of his polyphonic writing, his music retains a firm tonal anchorage.
WORKS: *Kaleidoscope* for 2 Pianos (1959); *Pastorale* for Cello and Piano (1958); *Fern Hill* for Chorus and Orch., to words by Dylan Thomas (N.Y., Dec. 19, 1961); Violin Sonata (1963; received first prize in the Spoleto Festival Competition of 1964); *The Cloisters,* cycle of songs (1965); *Elegy* for Orch. (San Francisco, June 1, 1966); *Tournaments Overture* (1967); Piano Concerto (San Antonio, Texas, April 7, 1968, Hilde Somer, soloist); *Poem in October* for Tenor and 8 Instruments (1969); Oboe Concerto (N.Y., Nov. 9, 1975); *Poem on His Birthday* for Baritone, Chorus, and Orch. (Washington, D.C., April 24, 1976); Clarinet Concerto (N.Y., Dec. 6, 1977); *3 Hallucinations for Orchestra,* derived from his score for the film *Altered States* (1981). Also incidental music for Molière's *Le Malade imaginaire,* Sheridan's *The Rivals,* Sophocles' *Oedipus Rex,* Brecht's *Galileo;* special scores for the N.Y. Shakespeare Festival of 1970. He arranged Bizet's *Carmen* for

singers, rock and pop groups, Moog synthesizer, and instruments, issued on a record under the title *The Naked Carmen*.

Cornelis, Evert, Dutch conductor and pianist; b. Amsterdam, Dec. 5, 1884; d. Bilthoven, Nov. 23, 1931. He was a pupil of de Pauw at the Amsterdam Cons.; in 1904, won the organ prize; was conductor at the Amsterdam Opera (1908); assistant conductor of the Concertgebouw Orch. (1910–19); from 1922 conductor of the orch. at Utrecht, later choral director at Rotterdam; conductor of the Netherlands Bach Society (1927); toured Europe, the Dutch East Indies, Australia, etc., as a guest conductor. He pioneered extensively for modern music.

Cornelius, Peter, Danish tenor; b. Labjerggaard, Jan. 4, 1865; d. Copenhagen, Dec. 25, 1934. He studied in Copenhagen; made his debut as a baritone there in 1892; then studied in Berlin with Hermann Spiro and Julius Lieban; made his debut as a tenor in Copenhagen in 1899, where he sang at the Royal Danish Theater until 1922; also sang at Bayreuth (1906) and Covent Garden in London (1907–14); made guest appearances in Paris, Stockholm, Oslo, Karlsruhe, and other cities; after his retirement, he taught voice in Copenhagen. He was particularly renowned for his Wagnerian roles. A biography of him by C. Cornelius was publ. in 1925.

Cornell, John Henry, American organist and writer on music; b. New York, May 8, 1828; d. there, March 1, 1894. He studied in N.Y., Germany, and England; was organist in several N.Y. churches (1848, St. John's Chapel; 1868–77, St. Paul's Church; 1877–82, Old Brick Church). His sacred compositions were highly esteemed.
WRITINGS: *Primer of Modern Musical Tonality; Practice of Sight-Singing; Theory and Practice of Musical Form* (after L. Bussler); *Easy Method of Modulation; Manual of Roman Chant; Congregational Tune Book; The Introit Psalms as prescribed by the First Prayer book of Edward VI, set to Original Chants* (N.Y., 1871).

Corner, Philip, American composer; b. New York, April 10, 1933. He studied piano; began composing autogenetically at 13, gestated a 3-minute piano piece in 9 months, learned to play the trombone. In 1955 he went to Paris, where he took a course in musical philosophy with Olivier Messiaen; spent a year in Korea studying oriental calligraphy in order to apply it to the needs of graphic music notation. In 1958 he turned to serial music, but mitigated its stern doctrines by aleatory indeterminacy; he often composes works after their first performance to avoid the stigma of premeditation. The titles of his compositions show a surrealistic flavor: *Passionate Expanse of the Law, Certain Distilling Processes, Expressions in Parallel, Air Effect,* and *Music Reserved until Now.* In his *Punishment Piece,* using the naked strings of a grand piano, musical material is determined by tossing spotted transparent paper on the manuscript. In 1965 he composed a time-less piece for indefinitely prolonged chanting on a single note. In 1968 he verbalized a work with the injunction: "One anti-personnel type CBU bomb will be thrown into the audience" (publ. in *Source 6,* 1969, but never perf).

Coronaro, Gaetano, Italian violinist and composer; b. Vicenza, Dec. 18, 1852; d. Milan, April 5, 1908. He studied with Faccio at the Milan Cons. and briefly in Germany; upon returning, to Italy, produced a choral work, *Un Tramonto* (Milan, 1873); was for several years a prof. of harmony at the Milan Cons. He wrote the operas *La Creola* (Bologna, 1878), *Malacarne* (Brescia, 1894), and *Un curioso accidente* (Turin, 1903); also some instrumental music.
BIBLIOGRAPHY: E. Oddone, *Gaetano Coronaro* (Rome, 1922).

Coronaro, Gellio Benvenuto, Italian pianist and composer; b. Vicenza, Nov. 30, 1863; d. Milan, July 26, 1916. He was 8 years old when he made his debut as a pianist; at 13, was theater conductor at Marosteca, and chorus master at 15; in 1882 he entered the Liceo Rossini at Bologna, where his teachers were Busi, Parisini, and Mancinelli; he graduated in 1883, winning the first prize with a one-act opera, *Jolanda,* which was produced at the Milan Cons. (1883). Other works: one-act dramatic sketch, *Festa a Marina* (took first Sonzogno Prize in 1892); operetta, *Minestrone napoletano* (Messina, 1893); 2-act opera, *Claudia* (Milan, 1895); *Bertoldo* (Milan, 1910); he also wrote 2 masses, a String Quartet, songs, piano pieces, etc.

Correa de Arauxo, Francisco, one of the most important Spanish organists of the Renaissance; b. Seville, c.1576; d. Segovia, Oct. 31, 1654. He held the post of organist at the Church of San Salvador in Seville (1599–1636), at the Cathedral of Jaen (1636–40), and at Segovia (from 1640 until his death). His *Facultad orgánica* (originally publ. in Alcaláde Henares, 1626) contains 70 pieces for organ in tablature (most of them his own compositions), reproduced in the series Monumentos de la Música Española, ed. by Santiago Kastner (Madrid, 1950).
BIBLIOGRAPHY: The biography by Charles Jacobs, *Francisco Correa de Arauxo* (The Hague, 1973), contains errors, pointed out by Robert Stevenson in the *Journal of the American Musicological Society* (Spring 1975). See also idem, "Francisco Correa de Arauxo," *Revista Musical Chilena* (Jan.–March 1968).

Correa de Azevedo, Luis Heitor, Brazilian musicologist; b. Rio de Janeiro, Dec. 13, 1905. He studied at the Instituto Nacional de Música in Rio de Janeiro; in 1932 was appointed librarian there; in 1939 became prof. of national folklore; in 1943 organized the Centro de Pesquisas Folklóricas at the Escuela Nacional de Música. He publ. numerous valuable studies on Brazilian music: *Escala, ritmo e melodia na música dos Indios brasileiros* (Rio de Janeiro,

1938); *Relação das operas de autores brasileiros* (Rio de Janeiro, 1938); *A música brasileira e seus fundamentos* (Washington, D.C., 1948); *Música e músicos do Brasil* (Rio de Janeiro, 1950); *150 años de música no Brasil* (Rio de Janeiro, 1956); *La Musique en Amérique latine* (Paris, 1957); several informative articles in Brazilian, French, and American magazines. From 1947 to 1965 he was in charge of the music division of UNESCO in Paris; in 1967–68 he gave lectures at the Newcomb College of Tulane Univ. in Louisiana.

Corri, Domenico, Italian composer; b. Rome, Oct. 4, 1744; d. London, May 22, 1825. He was a pupil of Porpora in Naples; in 1781 went to Edinburgh as an opera conductor. His attempt to organize his own opera company and a publishing firm there was a failure, and he sought better fortune in London (1790). There he engaged in various enterprises as a publisher, composer, and impresario. His opera, *The Travelers, or Music's Fascination,* was given at Drury Lane on Jan. 22, 1806, with little success. He publ. 4 music manuals in English: *A Complete Musical Grammar* (1787); *A Musical Dictionary* (1798); *The Art of Fingering* (1799); and *The Singer's Preceptor* (1810). His daughter, **Sophia Giustina,** a talented pianist and singer, married Dussek; his sons, **Montague Corri** (1784–1849) and **Haydn Corri** (1785–1860), were also musicians.

BIBLIOGRAPHY: P.J. Revitt, "Domenico Corri's 'New System' for Reading Thorough-Bass," *Journal of the American Musicological Society* (Spring 1968).

Corsi (Corso), Giuseppe (called **Celano** after his birthplace), Italian composer; b. Celano, May 1630; d. May 1690. He studied with Carissimi; served as maestro di cappella at Santa Maria Maggiore in Rome (1659–61); at the Lateran Palace chapel (1661–65); at Santa Casa di Loreto (1668–75); then returned to Rome, but because of his dissemination of books placed on the Church Index, was persecuted and forced to leave (1678); from 1681 to 1688 he was at the court of the Duke of Parma. Among his pupils were Jacopo Perti (at Parma) and Petronio Franceschini. He publ. *Motetti a 2, 3 e 4 voci* (Rome, 1667), *Miserere a 5,* and *Motetti a 9;* various other vocal works, in MS, are preserved in the library of the Liceo Musicale and the Archivio Musicale di S. Petronio at Bologna. Several of his works appeared in collections of the time. He is mentioned in Giuseppe Pitoni's *Guida armonica.*

Corsi, Jacopo, Florentine nobleman and patron of art; b. Florence, July 17, 1560; d. there, Dec. 29, 1602. In his palace, as in that of his friend Bardi, were held the memorable meetings of the "Camerata" in which Peri, Caccini, Emilio del Cavaliere, Galilei, the poet Rinuccini, and others took part, leading to the creation of the earliest operas. Corsi was a good musician, a skillful player on the harpsichord, and a composer; he wrote the concluding 2 numbers of the first opera by Peri, *Dafne,* which was performed at his home in 1598; these settings are preserved in the library of the Brussels Cons.; they were publ. in Solerti's *Albori del Melodramma* (Milan, 1905).

BIBLIOGRAPHY: W. Porter, "Peri and Corsi's *Dafne:* Some New Discoveries and Observations," *Journal of the American Musicological Society,* XVIII (1965).

Corso, Giuseppe. See **Corsi, Giuseppe.**

Corte, Andrea della. See **Della Corte, Andrea.**

Corteccia, Francesco Bernardo (baptismal names, **Pier Francesco**), Italian composer and organist; b. Florence, July 27, 1502; d. there, June 27, 1571. He studied music with Bernardo Pisano; was a choirboy at S. Giovanni Battista in Florence; later prepared for the priesthood, and was chaplain at S. Giovanni in 1527–31; in 1531 was organist at S. Lorenzo, then at S. Giovanni (1535–39); was maestro di cappella there and at the Florence Cathedral from 1540 until his death. He wrote musical intermezzi for the opera *Il furto* by Francesco d'Ambra (1544); wedding music (for Duke Cosimo the Great); 9 pieces a 4, 6, and 8 (Venice, 1539); 3 books of madrigals (1544, 1547, 1547); *Responsoria et lectiones* (1570); 32 hymns a 4; *Canticorum liber primus* (1571); many others. Modern editions of his works include *Francesco Corteccia: Hinnario secondo l'uso della chiesa romana e fiorentina,* ed. by G. Haydon (Cincinnati, 1958 and 1960); A.C. Minor and B. Mitchell, eds., *A Renaissance Entertainment: Festivities for the Marriage of Cosimo I, Duke of Florence, in 1539* (Columbia, Mo., 1968); *Francesco Corteccia: Eleven Works to Latin Texts,* ed. by A. McKinley in *Recent Researches in the Music of the Renaissance,* XXVI (1969).

BIBLIOGRAPHY: O.G. Sonneck, *Miscellaneous Studies in the History of Music* (N.Y., 1921).

Cortés, Ramiro, American composer of Mexican extraction; b. Dallas, Nov. 25, 1933; d. Salt Lake City, July 2, 1984. He studied with Henry Cowell in N.Y. and at the Univ. of Southern Calif. with Halsey Stevens and Ingolf Dahl. From 1956 to 1958 he was in Rome on a Fulbright fellowship; there he studied with Petrassi. Returning to America in 1959, he had sessions with Roger Sessions at Princeton Univ.

WORKS: *Elegy* for Flute and Piano (1952); Divertimento for Flute, Clarinet, and Bassoon (1953); Piano Quintet (1953); Piano Sonata (1954; awarded Steinway Centennial prize); *Sinfonia sacra* for Orch. (1954; received George Gershwin Memorial Award; N.Y. Phil., April 9, 1955; revised 1959); *Night Music* for Chamber Orch. (1954; received first prize of Broadcast Music Incorporated Awards); *Yerma,* symph. portrait after a play by García Lorca (1955); *Xochitl* for Orch. (1955; Hollywood, April 22, 1956); Chamber Concerto for Cello Solo and 12 Wind Instruments (1958; first prize of Broadcast Music Incorporated Awards); Symph. (1953–58); *Sinfonia breve* (1955–58); String Quartet (1958); Piano Trio (1959); *Prometheus,* opera in one act (1960); *The Eternal Return* for Orch. (1963; revised 1965); Violin Concerto (1965); Wind Quintet (1967–68); *Hom-*

age to Jackson Pollock for Solo Viola (1968); *Charenton,* suite for Chamber Orch. (1968–71); *Movements in Variation* for Orch. (1972).

Cortese, Luigi, Italian pianist and composer; b. Genoa, Nov. 19, 1899; d. there, June 10, 1976. He studied music with Mario Ferrari in Genoa, with Casella in Rome, and with Gédalge in Paris. From 1951 to 1964 he served as director of the Istituto Musicale in Genoa. He was a prolific composer, and was also active as a music critic.

WORKS: 3 operas: *Prometeo* (1941–47; Bergamo, Sept. 22, 1951), *La notte veneziana* (1953–55; Turin Radio, 1955) and *Le notte bianche* (1970); an oratorio, *David* (1938; Genoa, Feb. 20, 1941); *Prelude and Fugue* for Orch. (1936); *Serenata* for Orch. (1936); *Canto notturno* for Orch. (1940); *4 odes de Ronsard* for Voice and Orch. (1948–57; Naples, Aug. 4, 1961); Symphony (1953–56); Violin Concerto (1961); *Fantasia* for Orch. (1964); *Sinfonia Sacra,* subtitled *Inclina, Domine, aurem tuam,* for Chorus and Orch. (1967; Turin, April 24, 1969); *3 Salmi* for Soprano and Orch. (1975); Violin Sonatina (1935); *Salmo VIII* for Female Voice, Flute, and Piano (1943); Horn Sonata (1955); Cello Sonata (1960); *Improvviso* for Viola and Piano (1966); *Invenzione* for 2 Flutes (1973); numerous piano pieces and songs. He publ. the monographs *Alfredo Casella* (Genoa, 1935), *Il Bolero di Ravel* (1944), and *Chopin* (1949).

Cortesi, Francesco, Italian composer; b. Florence, Sept. 11, 1826; d. there, Jan. 3, 1904. He studied at Bologna under Rossini and others; became a conductor and a composer of many light stage works; settled in Florence about 1880 as a singing master and was appointed head of the vocal dept. in the government music school. Many celebrated singers were his pupils.

WORKS: Operas: *Il Trovatore* (Trieste, 1852; then at Florence, as *La Schiava*); *Almina* (Rome, 1859); *La dama a servire* (Ancona, 1859); *La colpa del cuore* (Florence, 1870); *Mariulizza* (Florence, 1874); *L'Amico di casa* (Florence, 1881); all fairly successful.

Cortolezis, Fritz, German composer and conductor; b. Passau, Feb. 21, 1878; d. Bad Aibling, Bavaria, March 13, 1934. He studied in Munich with H. Bussmeyer (piano) and with L. Thuille (composition) from 1899–1902; was répétiteur at the opera in Schwerin (1903); chorus master at the National Theater in Berlin (1904); first conductor in Regensburg (1905) and in Nuremberg (1906); upon Mottl's recommendation he was appointed conductor of the court opera in Munich; was engaged by Beecham in 1911 for the Wagner and Strauss performances in London; in 1912 was first conductor at the Kurfürstenoper in Berlin; then in Karlsruhe (1913–24) and at the Breslau Opera (1925–28).

WORKS: Operas: *Rosemarie* (Bremen, 1919); *Das verfemte Lachen* (Rostock, 1924); *Der verlorene Gulden* (Breslau, 1928).

Cortot, Alfred (Denis), famous French pianist; b. (of a French father and a Swiss mother) Nyon, Switzerland, Sept. 26, 1877; d. Lausanne, June 15, 1962. He was a pupil at the Paris Cons., and studied with Decombes, Rouquou, and Diémer; he won the first prize for piano in 1896; the same year he made his debut in Paris, playing Beethoven's C minor Concerto at one of the Colonne concerts, and won signal success; he went to Bayreuth (1898) and studied Wagner's works with J. Kniese, and acted as répétiteur at the festivals from 1898–1901. Returning to Paris, he began a most active propaganda for the works of Wagner; on May 17, 1902, he conducted the French premiere of *Götterdämmerung* at the Théâtre du Château d'Eau, and in the same year established the Association des Concerts A. Cortot, which he directed for 2 years, educating the public to an appreciation of Wagner; in 1904 he became conductor of the orch. concerts of the Société Nationale and of the Concerts Populaires at Lille (till 1908). In 1905, together with Jacques Thibaud (violin) and Pablo Casals (cello), he formed a trio, which soon gained a great European reputation. He founded, with A. Mangeot, the Ecole Normale de Musique (1919), and became its director, also giving a summer course in piano interpretation there annually; gave many lecture recitals and appeared as a guest conductor with various orchs.

WRITINGS: Articles on the piano works of Debussy, Fauré, Franck, and Chabrier in *Revue Musicale* (1920–26); he publ. a new working ed. of Chopin's Preludes and Etudes; also publ. *Principes rationnels de la technique pianistique* (French and Eng., Paris, 1928; American ed., Boston, 1930); *La Musique française de piano* (vol. I, 1930; Eng. trans., London, 1932; vol. II, 1932); *Cours d'interprétation* (vol. I, Paris, 1934; in Eng., London, 1937); *Aspects de Chopin* (Paris, 1949; in Eng., as *In Search of Chopin,* London, 1951). The publication of a classified catalogue of Cortot's library, entitled *Bibliothèque Alfred Cortot,* ed. by F. Goldbeck and A. Fehr with preface by H. Prunières, was begun in 1936.

BIBLIOGRAPHY: Bernard Gavoty, *Alfred Cortot* (Paris, 1977).

Cosma, Viorel, Rumanian musicologist; b. Timişoara, March 30, 1923. He studied composition with Mihail Jora, Ion Dumitrescu, Paul Constantinescu, Theodor Rogalski; musicology with Zeno Vancea. He was active as a choral conductor; joined the faculty at the Bucharest Cons. in 1951; then devoted himself mainly to music criticism; publ. several valuable monographs on Rumanian musicians (Ciprian Porumbescu, Ion Ivanovici, and others). He compiled a uniquely useful biographical dictionary of Rumanian composers and musicologists, *Muzicieni Români* (Bucharest, 1965; revised and augmented ed., 1970); he also edited *Interpreti romani lexicon,* a dictionary of performing Rumanian musicians (Bucharest, 1977).

Cossa, Dominic, American baritone; b. Jessup, Pa., May 13, 1935. He studied with Anthony Marlow and Robert Weede; made his debut at the N.Y. City Opera in 1961; then made appearances in Europe; in

1967 he sang at the San Francisco Opera; made his Metropolitan Opera debut in N.Y. on Jan. 30, 1970, as Silvio in *Pagliacci.*

Cossetto, Emil, Croatian composer; b. Trieste, Oct. 12, 1918. He studied in Zagreb. His compositions, based mostly on patriotic themes, include *Borbena kantata (Cantata of the Struggle;* 1947), inspired by the wartime resistance in Yugoslavia; *Zagreb kantata* (Zagreb, May 7, 1950); *Konjanik,* a "cavalcade" for Men's Voices and Orch. (Zagreb, Dec. 9, 1957); numerous choruses.

Cossmann, Bernhard, German cellist; b. Dessau, May 17, 1822; d. Frankfurt, May 7, 1910. He was a pupil of Espenhahn and Drechsler; also of Theodor Müller and Kummer (in Dresden); was a member of the Italian Opera Orch. in Paris (1840); London (1841); Opéra-Comique, Paris (till 1846); was a member of the Gewandhaus Orch. in Leipzig (1847–48), as solo cellist, also studying composition under Hauptmann; at Weimar with Liszt (in 1850); was a prof. at the Moscow Cons. (1866–70); lived at Baden-Baden (1870–78); thereafter, was a prof. of cello at the Frankfurt Cons.

Cossotto, Fiorenza, Italian contralto; b. Crescentino, Vercelli, near Turin, April 22, 1935. She studied at the Turin Cons.; sang at La Scala in Milan as a student; made her formal debut there as Sister Mathilde in *Les Dialogues de Carmélites* (Jan. 26, 1957); also sang at the Vienna State Opera, at Covent Garden in London, in Paris, in South America, and in Russia. She made her American debut in 1964 at the Lyric Opera in Chicago; was soloist in Verdi's *Requiem* in N.Y. with the orch. of the Teatro alla Scala during its American visit in 1967. On Feb. 6, 1968, she sang Amneris at her Metropolitan Opera debut. Among her most successful roles was that of Santuzza in *Cavalleria rusticana.* She is married to the Italian bass **Ivo Vinco.**

Cossutta, Carlo, Italian tenor; b. Trieste, May 8, 1932. He was taken to Argentina while young; received his musical training there. He sang at the Teatro Colón in Buenos Aires in 1958; in 1964 appeared at Covent Garden, London. On Feb. 17, 1973, he made his Metropolitan Opera debut in N.Y. as Pollione in *Norma.* He also sang with the Chicago Lyric Opera, the Paris Opéra, and the Vienna State Opera. He distinguished himself in dramatic roles.

Costa, Don, American conductor and film composer; b. Boston, June 10, 1925; d. New York, Jan. 19, 1983. He moved to Calif. early in his career and became active as a composer for films and television, as well as a conductor of theater music. His movie scores included *Rough Night in Jerico, Madigan,* and *The Impossible Years.* He also put out, with his 10-year-old daughter, Nikka, an album, *Out Here On My Own,* which sold into the millions of copies.

Costa, Mary, American soprano; b. Knoxville, Tenn., April 5, 1932. She received her primary musical training in Los Angeles; sang at the Hollywood Bowl and with the San Francisco Opera. On Jan. 6, 1964, she made her debut at the Metropolitan Opera in N.Y. as Violetta in *La Traviata;* in 1970 she sang opera at the Bolshoi Theater in Moscow. She also made many concert appearances.

Costa, Sir Michael (properly, **Michele**), eminent conductor and opera composer; b. Naples, Feb. 4, 1806; d. Hove, England, April 29, 1884. He studied with his maternal grandfather, **Giacomo Tritto;** with his father, **Pasquale Costa** (a composer of church music); and with Giovanni Furno. He then studied at the Naples Cons. with Crescentini (singing) and Zingarelli (composition). His operas *Il sospetto funesto* (Naples, 1826), *Il delitto punito* (1827), *Il carcere d'Ildegonda* (Naples, 1828), and *Malvina* (Naples, 1829) were well received; when Zingarelli was commissioned to write a Psalm (*Super Flumina Babilonis*) for the Music Festival at Birmingham, England, he sent Costa to conduct it. When Costa arrived in Birmingham, the directors of the Festival refused to accept him as a conductor owing to his extreme youth, but offered to pay him a similar fee for performance as tenor in Zingarelli's Psalm and in other works. He was compelled to accept, but his debut as a singer was disastrous. Despite this setback, he decided to remain in England, a decision in which he was encouraged by Clementi, who was impressed by Costa's scoring of a Bellini aria. In 1830 Costa was engaged as maestro al cembalo at the King's Theatre in London; in 1832 he became music director; and in 1833, director and conductor. During this time he produced 3 of his ballets, *Kenilworth* (1831), *Une Heure à Naples* (1832), and *Sir Huon* (1833, for Taglioni). In 1846 he became conductor of the Phil. and of the Royal Italian Opera; in 1848–82, he conducted the Sacred Harmonic Society. From 1849 he was the regular conductor of the Birmingham Festivals; from 1847 to 1880, of the Handel Festivals. He was knighted in 1869; was appointed "director of the music, composer, and conductor" at Her Majesty's Opera, Haymarket, in 1871, serving till 1881. He produced 2 operas in London: *Malek Adel* (May 18, 1837; a revision of *Malvina*) and *Don Carlos* (June 20, 1844).

BIBLIOGRAPHY: H. Schonberg, *The Great Conductors* (N.Y., 1967).

Costeley, Guillaume, French organist; b. probably at Pont-Audemer (Normandy), 1531; d. Evreux, Jan. 28, 1606. The theory that he was an Irishman named Costello who settled in France, as well as the theory that he was of Scottish extraction, has been discarded. He was court organist to Charles IX of France. In 1571 he became the first annually elected "prince" or "maître" of a society organized in honor of St. Cecilia, which, beginning in 1575, awarded a prize each year for a polyphonic composition. Costeley excelled as a composer of polyphonic chansons; his *Musique,* a book of such works for 4–6 voices, appeared in 1570. Modern editions of some

of those for 4 voices are in H. Expert, Maîtres Musiciens de la Renaissance Française (vols. III, XVIII, XIX); an example for 5 voices in Cauchie's *Quinze chansons.*
BIBLIOGRAPHY: M. Cauchie, "Documents pour servir à une biographie de Guillaume Costeley," *Revue de Musicologie* (May 1926); I. Godt, *Guillaume Costeley, Life and Works* (Diss., N.Y. Univ., 1969).

Costello, Elvis, new-wave British rocker and songwriter; born nobody knows where and when, but apparently his real name was **Declan McManus,** and he spent his childhood in Liverpool, the city of the Beatles. When he was quite young he managed to get a contract with a company called Stiff Records. His songs were permeated with the feeling of doom, personal as well as universal. A typical title was *Waiting for the End of the World.* Among his first hits were *Less than Zero, Watching the Detectives,* and a love ballad, *Alison,* all on his album *My Aim Is True.* His next album, *This Year's Model,* increased his popularity.

Cotapos, Acario, Chilean composer; b. Valdivia, April 30, 1889; d. Santiago, Nov. 22, 1969. He studied music in Santiago; in 1916 went to N.Y., where he took lessons with 10 teachers, among them Ernest Bloch. He lived in France until 1934; then went to Spain to work in defense of the Loyalists during the Spanish Civil War; in 1939 he returned to Chile. An experimenter by nature, he adopted an advanced quasi-serial technique of monothematic mottoes of 8 or more notes. He wrote a music drama, *Voces de gesta* (1933); several symph. preludes; String Quartet; *Sonata fantasia* for Piano (1924); songs; piano pieces.

Čotek, Pavel, Czech composer; b. Fryšava, March 12, 1922. He studied at the Prague Cons. and the Janáček Academy in Brno; then was active as a choirmaster and music critic.
WORKS: *Concertino Grosso* for Oboe, Clarinet, Horn, and Strings (1964); *Symphonic Etudes* (1965); Concerto for 2 Solo Percussionists and Orch. (Olomouc, Oct. 22, 1968); *Responsoria* for Organ and Orch. (1969); *3 Romantic Compositions* for Horn and Piano (1954); *Dance Suite* for Wind Quintet (1955); Suite for Violin and Piano (1958); *3 Compositions* for Flute and Piano (1962); Violin Sonata (1962); *Portrait of a Bird,* melodrama for 2 Narrators, Flute, Viola, Bass Clarinet, Celesta, and Harp (1963); *Chamber Music* for String Quartet and Percussion (1963); *5 Short Movements* for Clarinet and Piano (1964–69); *Wind Music* for Piccolo, Trumpet, Bass Trumpet, Bass Trombone, and Piano (1970); *Agoge* for Viola and Piano (1973); choruses; songs.

Cotogni, Antonio, Italian baritone; b. Rome, Aug. 1, 1831; d. there, Oct. 15, 1918. He studied voice with Achille Faldi; made his operatic debut in Rome in 1852 in the role of Belcore in *L'elisir d'amore;* subsequently sang at La Scala in Milan (1860), at Covent Garden in London (1867), and at other European opera houses. He had an enormous repertoire of Italian and French operas. He retired in 1894 and devoted the rest of his life to teaching. Among celebrated singers who were his pupils were Jean de Reszke, Battistini, Lauri-Volpi, Gigli, and Stabile.

Cotrubas, Ileana, Rumanian soprano; b. Galatz, June 9, 1939. She studied at the Bucharest Cons.; made her debut at the Bucharest Opera in Debussy's *Pelléas et Mélisande* in 1964; then appeared with increasing acclaim at the Salzburg Festival, the Frankfurt Opera, the Royal Opera House in London, and the Paris Opéra. She made her American debut with the Chicago Lyric Opera in 1973; appeared for the first time at the Metropolitan Opera in N.Y. in 1977. She is especially distinguished in lyrico-dramatic roles.

Cottlow, Augusta, American pianist; b. Shelbyville, Ill., April 2, 1878; d. White Plains, N.Y., April 11, 1954. She received her first instruction from her mother; performed in public as a child; went to Berlin in 1896 to study with Busoni; played concerts in Germany, England, and Russia. In 1912 she married Edgar E. Gerst of Berlin; returned to America in 1917. She publ. a memoir, "My Years with Busoni," *Musical Observer* (June 1925).

Cotton, John (or **Johannis Cottonis;** also **Joannes Musica, Johannes filius Dei,** and **Johannes of Afflighem**), early music theorist (11th to 12th century), probable author of the treatise *Epistola ad Fulgentium* (printed by Gerbert in *Scriptores,* vol. II), a valuable work on music describing the modal system of the time and a phase of the development of organum. Six MS copies are preserved: one each in Leipzig, Paris, Antwerp, and the Vatican Library, and 2 in Vienna. Various theories have been advanced concerning its authorship. In the copies at Antwerp and Paris the author is referred to as Cotton or Cottonius, while 2 others give the author's name as Joannes Musica. In an anonymous work, *De script. eccles.,* quoted by Gerbert, there is a reference to a certain Joannes, an erudite English musician; the dedication of this volume, "Domino et patri sua venerabili Anglorum antistiti Fulgentio," adds further strength to the contention that the author of the *Epistola* was English. However, J. Smits van Waesberghe identifies him with the Flemish theorist Johannes of Afflighem, author of the treatise *De Musica cum tonario* (reprinted Rome, 1950). Other sources suggest that Cotton is also one Johannes filius Dei.
BIBLIOGRAPHY: L. Ellinwood, "John Cotton or John of Afflighem?" *Notes* (Sept. 1951); J. Smits van Waesberghe's reply in *Musica Disciplina* (1952; pp. 139–53); J. Pulver, "John Cotton," *Musical Times* (Oct. 1933); E.F. Flindell, "Johannis Cottonis, Corrigenda et Addenda," *Musica Disciplina* XXIII (1969).

Cottrau, Teodoro, Italian composer of Neapolitan ballads; b. Naples, Nov. 27, 1827; d. there, March 30, 1879. His father, **Guglielmo Louis Cottrau** (b. Paris, Aug. 9, 1797; d. Naples, Oct. 31, 1847), was also a composer of Neapolitan canzonettas (some of them used by Liszt in his piano work *Venezia e Napoli*), as was his brother **Giulio Cottrau** (b. Naples, Oct. 29, 1831; d. Rome, Oct. 25, 1916). Teodoro Cottrau was the composer of the perennial favorite *Santa Lucia* (1850).

Coulthard, Jean, Canadian pianist and composer; b. Vancouver, Feb. 10, 1908. She studied piano with her mother; went to London to study composition with Vaughan Williams (1929–30); had lessons at various times and at various places with Arthur Benjamin (1939), Milhaud (1942), Bartók (1944), Wagenaar (1945, 1949), Nadia Boulanger (1955), and Gordon Jacob (1965–66). In 1947 she joined the staff of the newly created dept. of music at the Univ. of British Columbia; retired in 1973. In her music she rarely strays from conventional usages, but it is not devoid of occasional modernistic whimsicalities.
WORKS: *Canadian Fantasy* for Orch. (1939); *Excursion,* ballet (1940); *Ballade (A Winter's Tale)* for String Orch. (1940); *Song to the Sea,* overture (1942); *Music on a Quiet Song* for Flute and Strings (1946); Symph. No. 1 (1950–51); *Nightwind,* song cycle for Mezzo-soprano, and Orch. or Piano (1951); *Rider on the Sands* for Orch. (1953); *A Prayer for Elizabeth* for Strings (1953); *Music for St. Cecilia* for Strings, Organ, and Tape (1954; revised 1969); Violin Concerto (1955–59); *The Devil's Fanfare: 4 Bizarre Dances,* ballet for Violin, Piano, and 3 Dancers (1958–60); Fantasie for Piano, Violin, and Chamber Orch. (1960–61); *Musenade* for String Orch. (1961); *The Bird of Dawning Singeth All Night Long* for Violin, 9 Strings, and Harp (1962); Piano Concerto (1963; revised 1967); *Endymion* for Orch. (1964); *Symphonic Ode* for Cello and Orch. (1965); *This Land,* choral symph., with Tape (1966–67); *Pastorale Cantata* for Narrator, Chorus, Brass Quintet, and Organ (1967); *2 Visionary Songs* for Soprano, Flute, and Strings (1970); *Kalamalka (Lake of Many Colors)* for Orch. (1974); *Canadian Mosaic* for Orch. (1974); Piano Quintet (1932); 2 violin sonatinas (1945); Cello Sonata (1947); Oboe Sonata (1947); Piano Sonata (1947–48); *3 Shakespearean Sonnets* for Soprano and String Quintet (1948); 2 string quartets (1948; 1953, revised 1969); 2 violin sonatas: *Duo Sonata* (1952) and *Correspondence* (1964); Piano Quartet (1957); *Sonata Rhapsody* for Viola and Piano (1962); Divertimento for Wind Quintet and Piano (1968); *The Pines of Emily Carr* for Narrator, Contralto, String Quintet, Piano, and Timpani (1969); *12 Essays on a Cantabile Theme,* string octet (1972); *The Birds of Lansdowne* for Violin, Cello, Piano, and Bird Songs on Tape (1972); *4 Prophetic Songs* for Contralto, Flute, Cello, and Piano (1975); *Symphonic Ode* for Viola and Chamber Orch. (1977); piano pieces; songs.

Couperin, a renowned family of French musicians. Its musical prominence dates from the 3 sons of **Charles Couperin,** merchant and organist of Chaume, in the dept. of Brie (now part of the dept. of Seine et Marne), and his wife, Marie Andry. The eldest of these, **Louis,** established the family in Par-

is, where it remained until the extinction of the male line in 1826. He was also the first of his name to hold the post of organist at St.-Gervais in Paris. He was followed in this position by his youngest brother, **Charles; François le Grand,** son of Charles, and the family's most illustrious representative; **Nicolas,** son of **François** (called **Sieur de Crouilly**); **Armand-Louis,** son of Nicolas; and by the 2 sons of Armand-Louis, **Pierre-Louis** and **Gervais-François.** The following articles, arranged alphabetically, give the individual histories of the members of the Couperin family.

Couperin, Armand-Louis (son of **Nicolas**), b. Paris, Feb. 25, 1727; d. there, Feb. 2, 1789. His virtuosity on the organ was extraordinary; in 1748, succeeded his father as organist at St.-Gervais; was also organist to the King (1770–89), and held appointments at St.-Barthélemy, Ste.-Marguerite, Ste.-Chapelle, St.-Jean-en-Grève, etc. He was one of the 4 organists of Notre-Dame. He died a violent death, having been knocked down by a runaway horse. His compositions include sonatas, a trio, motets, and other church music. His wife, **Elisabeth-Antoinette** (née **Blanchet;** b. Paris, Jan. 14, 1729), was also a remarkable organist and clavecinist, still playing in public at the age of 81 (in 1810). She was the daughter of **Blanchet,** the famous clavecin maker, and sister-in-law to **Pascal Joseph Taskin,** the court instrument keeper under Louis XV. D. Fuller edited *A.-L. Couperin: Selected Works for Keyboard* (Madison, Wis., 1975).

Couperin, Charles, b. Chaumes (baptized, April 9), 1638; d. Paris, 1679. He succeeded his brother **Louis** as organist at St.-Gervais in 1661. He married Marie Guérin (Feb. 20, 1662), and is principally remembered as being the father of the celebrated **François le Grand.**
BIBLIOGRAPHY: C. Bouvet, "Quelques précisions biographiques sur Charles Louis Couperin," *Revue de Musicologie* (Paris, 1930).

Couperin, François, b. Chaumes, c.1631; d. Paris, after 1708. He was a pupil of Chambonnières in harmony and clavecin playing; was active as a music teacher and organist. His daughter, **Marguerite Louise** (b. Paris, 1676; d. Versailles, May 30, 1728), was a well-known singer and harpsichordist. She was a fellow member of the Chambre du Roi with her cousin **François le Grand,** who wrote for her the verset *Qui dat nivem* and other pieces.

Couperin, François (surnamed **le Grand** on account of his superiority in organ playing), the most illustrious member of a distinguished family, and one of the greatest of early French composers; b. Paris, Nov. 10, 1668; d. there, Sept. 11, 1733. He was the son of **Charles Couperin,** who was his first teacher; later was a pupil of Jacques-Denis Thomelin, organist of the King's chapel; in 1685 he became organist of St.-Gervais, which post he held until his death; on Dec. 26, 1693, after a successful competition, he succeeded Thomelin as organist of the Chapelle Royale, receiving the title of "organiste du roi"; in 1701 he was appointed "claveciniste de la chambre du roi, et organiste de sa chapelle," and in 1717 he received the title "Ordinaire de la musique de la chambre du roi"; also was made a chevalier of the Order of Latran; he was music master to the Dauphin and other members of the royal family, and ranked high in the favor of Louis XIV, for whom he composed the *Concerts royaux,* which, during 1714–15, were played in Sunday concerts in the royal apartments. He married Marie-Anne Ansault (April 26, 1689), by whom he had 2 daughters: **Marie-Madeleine** (b. Paris, March 9, 1690; d. Montbuisson, April 16, 1742), who became organist of the Abbey of Montbuisson, and **Marguerite-Antoinette** (b. Paris, Sept. 19, 1705; d. there, 1778), who was a talented clavecin player; from 1731–33, she substituted for her father as clavecinist to the King, being the first woman to hold this position (cf. C. Bouvet, "Les Deux d'Anglebert et Marguerite-Antoinette Couperin," *Revue de Musicologie,* 1928); there were also 2 sons, **Nicolas-Louis** (b. July 24, 1707), who died young, and **François-Laurent,** b. c.1708. Famed as an organist, Couperin also acquired a high reputation for his remarkable ability as a performer on the clavecin.

WORKS: His compositions may be conveniently divided into 3 categories: those written for the church, those for the King, and those for the general public. More than half of his creative life was taken up with the religious compositions of the first 2 periods. These include *Pièces d'orgue consistantes en deux Messes* (1690, a total of 42 pieces), formerly attributed to his uncle **François,** and, indeed, publ. under the latter's name in vol. 5 of *Archives des maîtres de l'orgue,* ed. by Guilmant, but now established, through the researches of A. Tessier and P. Brunold, as the early work of **Couperin le Grand;** motets; *Elévations; Leçons de ténèbres;* etc. Couperin's last and most prolific period was concerned exclusively with instrumental works, and in this field he achieved his greatest and most enduring distinction. In 1713, 1716, 1722, and 1730, he publ. the 4 vols. of his *Pièces de clavecin,* consisting of about 230 pieces or 27 "Ordres" or Suites, each suite being a series of dance forms, programmatic in title and content (*La Majestueuse, La Nanette, Les Petits Moulins à vent, Le Carillon de Cythère, Les Barricades mystérieuses, Les Tic-Toc-Choc ou Les Maillotins,* etc.). In 1716 he publ. an expository work pertaining to the execution of his clavecin pieces, *L'Art de toucher le clavecin,* which attained wide celebrity, and which influenced the keyboard style of Couperin's great contemporary, J.S. Bach. Couperin also introduced the trio sonata to France, his first works in this form being an imitation of Corelli. Later, in 1726, he publ. 4 sonatas, *Les Nations,* described as "Sonades" or "Suites de symphonies en trio," 3 of which are partial reworkings of earlier pieces. They are composed alternately in the strict primitive form, *sonata de chiesa,* and the more flexible composite of dance forms, *sonata de camera.* The 3rd of the series, *L'Impériale,* perhaps represents his most mature and inspired style. Living at a time during which the rivalry between French and Italian music reached its climax, Couperin sought to adapt the new Italian forms to his own personal, and essentially French, style. In his *Les Goûts réunis* (1724), a series of concerted pieces with strings very similar in form and spirit to the *Pièces de clavecin,* one finds titles such as *Sicilienne* and *Ritratto dell' amore.* In the following year he publ. an *Apothéose de Lully,* in which the rivals, Lully and Corelli, are made to unite for the furtherance of art. Couperin's style of composition was based on the basso continuo, the most important voices usually being the uppermost, carrying the melody, and the bass. Nevertheless, his music sometimes attains considerable complexity (on occasion requiring as many as 3 harpsichordists for its proper execution). His melodic invention, particularly in his use of the rondeau, was virtually inexhaustible, his themes swift and expressive. An outstanding feature was his inventive mode of ornamentation, in the "gallant style" of the period. In 1933 the Lyrebird Press in Paris publ. a "complete" ed. of Couperin's works, in 12 vols., under the chief editorship of Maurice Cauchie, assisted by P. Brunold, A. Gastoué, A. Tessier, and A. Schaeffner. The contents are as follows: Vol. I, Didactic works: *Règle pour l'accompagnement* and *L'Art de toucher le clavecin;* Vols. II–V, the 4 books of *Pièces de clavecin;* Vol. VI, *Pièces d'orgue consistantes en deux Messes;* Vols. VII–X, chamber music, including *Concerts royaux, Les Goûts réunis ou Nouveaux concerts à l'usage de toutes les sortes d'instruments de musique, Les Nations, Le Parnasse ou l'Apothéose de Corelli, Apothéose de Lully, Pièces de violes avec la basse chiffrée,* and *Sonades inédites;* Vols. XI and XII, secular vocal music and religious music I and II. More recent eds. are in the LePupitre series, vols. 8 (*Leçons de ténèbres;* 1968), 21–24 (*Pièces de clavecin,* books 1-4; 1969–72), 45 (*9 motets;* 1972), and 51 (*Pièces de violes;* 1974), also separate eds. of *Pièces de clavecin,* ed. by M. Cauchie (1968–72) and by K. Gilbert (1969–72).

BIBLIOGRAPHY: H. Quittard, *Les Couperins* (Paris, 1913); C. Bouvet, *Une Dynastie de musiciens français: Les Couperins . . .* (Paris, 1919); L. de La Laurencie, *L'Ecole française de violon de Lully à Viotti* (1922–24); Joan Llongueras, *Couperin o la Gracia* (1925); A. Tessier, *Couperin* (Paris, 1926); J. Tiersot, *Les Couperins* (Paris, 1926); J. Tiersot, "Two Centuries of a French Musical Family—The Couperins," *Musical Quarterly* (July 1926); P. Brunold, *Le Grand Orgue de St.-Gervais à Paris* (Paris, 1934); M. Riemann, *Untersuchungen zur Formgeschichte der französischen Klavier-Suite . . .* (1940; reprinted Regensburg, 1968); P. Brunold, *François Couperin* (Eng. trans., Monaco, 1949); M. Cauchie, *Thematic Index of the Works of Couperin* (Monaco, 1949); W. Mellers, *François Couperin and the French Classical Tradition* (London, 1950); M. Antoine, "Autour de François Couperin," *Revue de Musicologie* (Dec. 1952); P. Citron, *Couperin* (Paris, 1956); *Mélanges François Couperin. Publiés à l'occasion du tricentenaire de sa naissance* (Paris, 1968); V. Schwarz, "F. C. und seine Zeit. Zum 300. Geburtstag des Meisters," *Österreichische Musikzeitschrift* (Nov. 1968); T. Dart, "On Couperin's Harpsichord Music,"

Musical Times (June 1969); N. Dufourcq, "F. C., Musicien de la terre, de la ville, de l'église, de la cour," *XVIIᵉ siècle,* 82 (1969); F. Neumann, "Couperin and the Downbeat Doctrine for Appoggiaturas," *Acta Musicologica* (Jan.–June 1969); M. Pincherle, "F. C. et la conciliation des 'goûts' français et italien," *Chigiana,* XXV/5 (1968); N. Dufourcq, "*Les Baricades mistérieuses* de F. C.," *Recherches sur la Musique Française,* XIII (1973); D. Tunley, *Couperin* (London, 1982).

Couperin, Gervais-François, 2nd son of **Armand-Louis;** b. Paris, May 22, 1759; d. there, March 11, 1826. He succeeded his brother, **Pierre-Louis,** as organist at St.-Gervais in 1789, also taking over his other appointments. He composed sonatas, variations, etc. He was the last of the Couperins to serve as organist at St.-Gervais, although his daughter, **Céleste** (b. 1793; d. Belleville, Feb. 14, 1860), played there at the time of her father's death. She was a teacher of singing and piano at Beauvais for about 10 years.
BIBLIOGRAPHY: C. Bouvet, "La Fin d'une dynastie d'artistes: Gervais-François Couperin et sa fille," *Revue de Musicologie* (1926).

Couperin, Louis, b. Chaumes, c.1626; d. Paris, Aug. 29, 1661. He went to Paris with Chambonnières, whose pupil he was; in 1653 became organist of St.-Gervais, a post in which he was succeeded, without interruption, by other members and descendants of the Couperin family until 1826; from 1656, he was a violinist and violist in the orchs. of the court ballets, and musician of the Chambre du Roi. He composed *Pièces de clavecin, Carillons* for Organ, violin pieces, etc. He was one of the earliest of French composers for the harpsichord in the new harmonic style employing the basso continuo, possibly being preceded only by his teacher, Chambonnières. The Lyrebird Press in Paris publ. a "complete" edition of his works, ed. by P. Brunold. His *Pièces de clavecin* is publ. as vol. 18 of Le Pupitre (1970).
BIBLIOGRAPHY: A. Pirro, "Louis Couperin," *Revue de Musicologie* (1930).

Couperin, Nicolas, son of **François de Crouilly;** b. Paris, Dec. 20, 1680; d. there, July 25, 1748. In 1733 he succeeded his cousin **François le Grand** as organist at St.-Gervais.

Couperin, Pierre-Louis (called **"M. Couperin l'aîné"** or **"Couperin fils"**), son of **Armand-Louis;** b. Paris, March 14, 1755; d. there, Oct. 10, 1789. He was organist to the King, later at Notre-Dame, St.-Jean, St.-Merry, and at St.-Gervais (succeeded his father early in 1789; died 8 months later). Some of his compositions were publ. in contemporary collections; others are in MS.

Cour, Niels la, Danish composer; b. Copenhagen, Nov. 14, 1944. He studied music theory and history at the Royal Cons. of Copenhagen, graduating in 1969; subsequently taught at the Funen Academy of

Music in Odense (1969–77).
WORKS: *Imago* for Flute, Clarinet, Violin, Viola, Cello, and Piano (1967); 6 string quartets: No. 1, *Das innere Licht (The Inner Light,* 1968), No. 2, *Mild und leise (Mild and Gentle,* 1969), No. 3, *Communio* (1971), No. 4, *Quatuor classique* (1972), No. 5 (1977), and No. 6 (1977); *5 Stilleben (Still Lives)* for Viola and Piano (1969); *Mythos* for String Orch. (1969; Copenhagen, Oct. 29, 1971); *Archetypon* for Organ (1970); *Imago* for Orch. (1971); *Vinger (Wings)* for Female Chorus a cappella (1973); 2 wind quintets (1972–73, 1975); *Symphonic Fragments* (1974); *De profundis* for Organ (1974); *3 Intermezzi* for Organ (1974); *Divertimento* for Orch. (1976); *5 Motets* for Chorus a cappella (1977).

Couraud, Marcel, French conductor; b. Limoges, Oct. 20, 1912. He studied organ with André Marchal; then enrolled in music theory courses at the Ecole Normale in Paris; also took lessons in composition with Nadia Boulanger and in conducting with Charles Munch. In 1945 he formed the Marcel Couraud Vocal Ensemble, which he conducted until 1954; in 1967 he was appointed artistic director of the ORTF choirs in Paris.

Courboin, Charles Marie, American organist; b. Antwerp, April 2, 1884; d. New York, April 13, 1973. He studied at the Cons. of Brussels with J. Blockx and A. Mailly; in 1904 emigrated to the U.S.; made several transcontinental tours of the U.S. and Canada, and 2 European tours; in 1919 he played the organ in the first performance of Widor's *6th Symphony* (dedicated to Courboin) with the Philadelphia Orch. under Stokowski. He designed 144 important organs in the U.S., among them Wanamaker's in N.Y.

Courtois, Jean, Franco-Flemish contrapuntist of the first half of the 16th century. He was maître de chapelle at Cambrai Cathedral in 1539, when a 4-part motet of his, *Venite populi terrae,* was performed before Charles V of Spain. Many of his motets, Psalms, and songs appeared in publications of the period (printed at Paris, Lyons, Antwerp, Nuremberg, etc.); H. Expert reprinted some of his songs in Les Maîtres Musiciens de la Renaissance Française. Masses, motets, and songs in MS are in the Munich State Library and the library at Cambrai.

Courvoisier, Karl, violinist; b. Basel, Nov. 12, 1846; d. Liverpool, Jan. 31, 1908. He studied with David and Röntgen at Leipzig Cons. (1867–69), and Joachim in Berlin (1869–70). In 1885 he settled in Liverpool as a teacher. He publ. *Die Violintechnik* (1878; Eng. trans. by H.E. Krehbiel, *The Techniques of Violin Playing;* 2nd ed., N.Y., 1896); *Ecole de la vélocité* for violin; and *Méthode de violon* (text in German, Eng., and French; London, 1892).

Courvoisier, Walter, Swiss composer and conductor; b. Riehen, near Basel, Feb. 7, 1875; d. Locarno,

Dec. 27, 1931. He first studied medicine (M.D., 1900), later music with Thuille in Munich (whose son-in-law he became); taught composition at the Academy of Music in Munich (1910–30).

WORKS: Operas: *Lanzelot und Elaine* (Munich, 1917) and *Die Krähen* (Munich, 1921); oratorio, *Totenfeier;* chamber music; piano pieces; about 150 songs.

Coussemaker, Charles-Edmond-Henri de, French music scholar; b. Bailleul, Nord, April 19, 1805; d. Bourbourg, Jan. 10, 1876. He studied music as a child. His main profession was the law; while studying law at the Univ. of Paris, he took private lessons with Pellegrini in singing and Anton Reicha in harmony. He continued his studies with Lefebvre in Douai, after becoming a practicing lawyer. At this time (1831–35) he found leisure to compose music of the most varied description, all of which, with the exception of a few *romances* and 2 sets of songs, is unpubl., and apparently lost. His interest in history and archaeology led him to the study of the authentic documents of music; he was also influenced by the scholarly articles in *La Gazette et Revue Musicale* (then edited by Fétis). During successive terms as judge in Hazebrouck, Dunkirk, and Lille, he continued to accumulate knowledge of musical documentation; he assembled a vast library; 1,075 items in his library are listed in the *Catalogue de's livres, manuscrits et instruments de musique du feu M. Charles Coussemaker* (Brussels, 1877; issued for an auction).

WRITINGS: A great number of valuable treatises and collections: *Mémoire sur Hucbald* (Paris, 1841); *Notice sur les collections musicales de la bibliothèque de Cambrai . . .* (1843); "Essai sur les instruments de musique au moyen-âge," in Dindron, *Annales archéologiques,* illustrated; *Histoire de l'harmonie au moyen-âge* (1852); *Trois chants historiques* (1854); *Chants populaires des Flamands de France* (1856); *Drames liturgiques du moyen-âge* (1860); *Les Harmonistes des XIIᵉ et XIIIᵉ siècles* (1865); a great work, intended for a supplement to Gerbert, entitled *Scriptorum de musica medii ævi nova series* (4 vols., 1864–76; new ed., Graz, 1908; anastatic reprint, 1931, by *Bolletino Bibliografico Musicale*); *L'Art harmonique aux XIIᵉ et XIIIᵉ siècles* (1865); *Œuvres complètes d'Adam de la Halle* (1872); etc.

BIBLIOGRAPHY: A. Desplanque, *Etude sur les travaux d'historie et d'archéologie de M. Edmond de Coussemaker* (Paris, 1870); R. Debevere, "Edmond de Coussemaker (1805–1876), Een belangrijk frans-vlaming," *Ons Erfdeel* XII/2 (1968).

Coverly, Robert, Portuguese composer of light music; b. Oporto, Sept. 6, 1864; d. there, Sept. 19, 1944. He studied in London and N.Y.; composed a great number of effective marches and songs, of which *The Passing Regiment,* a military march for band, achieved great popularity.

Coward, Sir Noel, British playwright and author of musical comedies; b. Teddington, Middlesex, Dec. 16, 1899; d. Port Maria, Jamaica, March 25, 1973. At the age of 11, he appeared on the stage, and was associated with the theater ever since, in the triple capacity of actor, playwright, and producer. Having had no formal education in music, he dictated his songs to a musical amanuensis. Among the musical comedies for which he wrote both words and music are *This Year of Grace* (N.Y., Nov. 7, 1928); *Bitter Sweet* (London, July 18, 1929); *Conversation Piece* (London, Feb. 16, 1934); *Pacific 1860* (London, Dec. 19, 1946); *Ace of Clubs* (London, July 7, 1950); *After the Ball,* to Wilde's *Lady Windermere's Fan* (London, June 10, 1954); 51 songs from his musical plays are publ. in the *Noel Coward Song Book* (N.Y., 1953) with the author's introduction. He also publ. an autobiography, *Present Indicative* (London, 1937); 2nd vol., *Future Indefinite* (London, 1954). He was knighted in 1970.

BIBLIOGRAPHY: Cole Lesley (Noel Coward's valet-companion), *Remembered Laughter* (N.Y., 1976); G. Payn and S. Morley, eds., *The Noël Coward Diaries* (London, 1982).

Coward, Sir Henry, English choral conductor; b. Liverpool, Nov. 26, 1849; d. Sheffield, June 10, 1944. He was apprenticed to be a cutler but attended classes of solfeggio. He organized a choral group at Sheffield and became its conductor. After a period of hard study, he obtained the B.Mus. degree at Oxford (1889), and later D.Mus. (1894). He organized spectacular choral festivals in Sheffield, in which thousands of choristers participated; gave concerts with his chorus in Germany (1906); in 1908 he presented 16 concerts in Canada with members of the Sheffield Choral Union, headed by him. There followed in 1911 a world tour, which included the U.S., Canada, Australia, and South Africa. Coward was the leader of choral groups at Leeds and Glasgow; acted as a judge at competition festivals. He was knighted in 1926. He composed several cantatas and other choral works; ed. a collection of Methodist hymns (1901); publ. *Choral Technique and Interpretation* (1914) and *Reminiscences* (1919).

BIBLIOGRAPHY: J.A. Rodgers, *Dr. Henry Coward, The Pioneer Chorus-master* (London, 1911).

Cowell, Henry Dixon, remarkable, innovative American composer; b. Menlo Park, Calif., March 11, 1897; d. Shady, N.Y., Dec. 10, 1965. His father, of Irish birth, was a member of a clergyman's family in Kildare; his mother was an American of progressive persuasion. Cowell studied violin with Henry Holmes in San Francisco; after the earthquake of 1906, his mother took him to N.Y., where they were compelled to seek support from the Society for the Improvement of the Condition of the Poor; they returned to Menlo Park, where Cowell was able to save enough money, earned from menial jobs, to buy a piano. He began to experiment with the keyboard by striking the keys with fists and forearms; he named such chords "tone clusters" and at the age of 13 composed a piece called *Adventures in Harmony,* containing such chords. Later he began experimenting in altering the sound of the piano by placing various objects on the strings, and also by playing directly under the lid of the piano *pizzicato* and *glissando*. He first exhibited these startling innovations on March 5, 1914, at the San Francisco Musical Society at the St. Francis Hotel, much to the consternation of its members, no doubt. The tone clusters per se were not new; they were used for special sound effects by composers in the 18th century to imitate thunder or cannon fire. The Russian composer Vladimir Rebikov applied them in his piano piece *Hymn to Inca,* and Charles Ives used them in his *Concord Sonata* to be sounded by covering a set of white or black keys with a wooden board. However, Cowell had a priority by systematizing tone clusters as harmonic amplifications of tonal chords, and he devised logical notation for them. The tone clusters eventually acquired legitimacy in the works of many European and American composers. Cowell also extended the sonorities of tone clusters to instrumental combinations and applied them in several of his symph. works. In the meantime Cowell did not neglect formal studies; he began taking lessons in composition with E.C. Strickland and Wallace Sabin at the Univ. of Calif. in Berkeley, and later with Frank Damrosch at the Inst. of Musical Art in N.Y., and privately, with Charles Seeger (1914–16). After brief service in the U.S. Army in 1918, where he was employed first as a cook and later as arranger for the U.S. Army Band, he became engaged professionally to give a series of lectures on new music, illustrated by his playing his own works on the piano. In 1928 he went to Russia, where he attracted considerable attention as the first American composer to visit there; some of his pieces were publ. in a Russian edition, the first such publications by an American. Upon return to the U.S., he was appointed lecturer on music at The New School in N.Y.

In 1931 he received a Guggenheim fellowship grant, and went to Berlin to study ethnomusicology with Erich von Hornbostel. This was the beginning of his serious study of ethnic musical materials. He had already experimented with some Indian and Chinese devices in some of his works; in his *Ensemble* for Strings (1924) he included Indian thundersticks; the piece naturally aroused considerable curiosity. In 1931 he formed a collaboration with the Russian electric engineer Leon Theremin, then visiting the U.S.; with his aid he constructed an ingenious instrument which he called the Rhythmicon; it made possible the simultaneous production of 16 different rhythms on 16 different pitch levels of the harmonic series. He demonstrated the Rhythmicon at a lecture-concert in San Francisco on May 15, 1932. He also wrote an extensive work entitled *Rhythmicana,* but it did not receive a performance until Dec. 3, 1971, at Stanford Univ., using advanced electronic techniques. In 1927 Cowell founded the *New Music Quarterly* for publication of ultramodern music, mainly by American composers.

Cowell's career was brutally interrupted in 1936, when he was arrested in California on largely contrived and falsified evidence, on charges of homosexuality (then a heinous offense in California) involving the impairment of the morals of a minor.

Lulled by the deceptive promises of a wily district attorney of a brief confinement in a sanatorium, Cowell pleaded guilty to a limited offense, but he was vengefully given a maximum sentence of imprisonment, up to 15 years. Incarcerated at San Quentin, he was assigned to work in a jute mill, but indomitably continued to write music in prison. Thanks to interventions in his behalf by a number of eminent musicians, he was paroled in 1940 to Percy Grainger as a guarantor of his good conduct; he was pardoned in the spring of 1941. On Sept. 27, 1941, he married Sidney Robertson, a noted ethnomusicologist. He was now able to resume his full activities as editor and instructor; he held teaching positions at The New School for Social Research in N.Y. (1940–62), the Univ. of Southern Calif., Mills College, and the Peabody Cons. of Music in Baltimore (1951–56); was also appointed adjunct prof. at summer classes at Columbia Univ. (1951–65). In 1951 Cowell was elected a member of the National Academy of Arts and Letters; received an honorary Mus.D. from Wilmington College (1953) and from Monmouth (Ill.) College (1963). In 1956–57 he undertook a world tour with his wife through the Near East, India, and Japan, collecting rich prime materials for his compositions, which by now had acquired a decisive turn toward the use of ethnomusicological melodic and rhythmic materials, without abandoning, however, the experimental devices which were the signposts of most of his works. In addition to his symph. and chamber music, Cowell publ. in 1930 an important book, *New Musical Resources.* He also edited a symposium, *American Composers on American Music;* in collaboration with his wife he wrote the basic biography of Charles Ives (1955).

WORKS: FOR THE STAGE: Unfinished opera, *O'Higgins of Chile* (1949); a pageant, *The Building of Bamba* (Halcyon, near Pismo Beach, Calif., Aug. 18, 1917).

16 HYMN AND FUGUING TUNES (based on fuguing tunes of William Billings): No. 1 for Band (1943); No. 2 for String Orch. (1944); No. 3 for Orch. (1944); No. 4 for 3 Instruments (1944); No. 5 for String Orch. (1945; version for Orch. incorporated into Symph. No. 10); No. 6 for Piano (1946); No. 7 for Viola and Piano (1946); No. 8 for String Quartet or String Orch. (1947–48); No. 9 for Cello and Piano (1950); No. 10 for Oboe and Strings (1955); No. 11, became *A Thanksgiving Psalm from the Dead Sea Scrolls* for Male Chorus and Orch. (1956); No. 12 for 3 Horns (1957); No. 13 for Trombone and Piano (1960); No. 14 for Organ (1961); No. 15 for 2 Violins or any combination (1961); No. 16 for Orch. (1965; posthumous, N.Y., Oct. 6, 1966).

20 SYMPHS.: No. 1 (1916–17); No. 2, *Anthropos* (*Mankind,* 1938); No. 3, *Gaelic Symphony* (1942); No. 4, *Short Symphony* (1946; Boston, Oct. 24, 1947); No. 5 (1948; Washington, D.C., Jan. 5, 1949); No. 6 (1950–55; Houston, Nov. 14, 1955); No. 7 (1952; Baltimore, Nov. 25, 1952); No. 8, *Choral,* for Chorus and Orch. (1952; Wilmington, Ohio, March 1, 1953); No. 9 (1953; Green Bay, Wis., March 14, 1954); No. 10 for Chamber Orch. (1953; U.S. premiere, N.Y., Feb. 24, 1957); No. 11, *Lines from the Dead Sea Scrolls* (1953;

Louisville, May 29, 1954); No. 12 (1955–56; Houston, March 28, 1960); No. 13, *Madras Symphony,* for Small Orch. and 3 Indian Instruments (1957–58; Madras, India, March 3, 1959); No. 14 (1960–61; Washington, D.C., April 27, 1961); No. 15, *Thesis* (1961; Louisville Orch., Murray, Ky., Oct. 7, 1961); No. 16, *Icelandic Symphony* (1962; Reykjavik, March 21, 1963); No. 17, *Lancaster* (1962); No. 18 (1964); No. 19 (1965; Nashville, Oct. 18, 1965); No. 20 (1965).

OTHER WORKS FOR ORCH.: *Vestiges* (1914–20); *Some Music* (1915); *Some More Music* (1915–16); *Communication* (1920); Sinfonietta for Small Orch. (1924–28; Boston, Nov. 23, 1931, Slonimsky conducting); Suite for Solo String and Percussion Piano, and Chamber Orch. (1928; Boston, March 11, 1929, Slonimsky conducting; a scoring of the piano pieces *The Banshee, Leprechaun,* and *Fairy Bells* with Chamber Orch. accompaniment); Piano Concerto (1929; first complete perf., Havana, Cuba, Dec. 28, 1930; first complete U.S. perf., Omaha, Oct. 12, 1978); *Irish Suite* for Chamber Orch. (1929); *Polyphonica* for 12 Instruments (1930); *Synchrony* (1930; Paris, June 6, 1931, Slonimsky conducting); *Reel No. 1* and *No. 2* (1930, 1932); *2 Appositions* for String Orch. (1931); *Rhythmicana,* Concerto for Rhythmicon and Orch. (1931; Stanford Univ. Orch., Dec. 3, 1971); 3 pieces for Chamber Orch.: *Competitive Sport, Steel and Stone,* and *Heroic Dance* (all 1931); *4 Continuations* for String Orch. (1933); *Old American Country Set* (1937; Indianapolis, Feb. 28, 1940); *American Melting Pot* (1939); *Symphonic Set* (1939; orchestration of *Toccanta*); *Celtic Set* (1939; also for band); *Shoonthree* (*Sleep Music,* 1939; also for band); *Pastoral & Fiddler's Delight* (1940; N.Y., July 26, 1949, Stokowski conducting); *Ancient Desert Drone* (1940); *Tales of Our Countryside* for Piano and Orch. (1940; Atlantic City, May 11, 1941, Cowell, soloist; Stokowski conducting; based on piano pieces written 1922–30); *Vox Humana* (1940); *Little Concerto* for Piano, and Orch. or Band (1942; also known as *Concerto Piccolo;* Suite for Piano and String Orch. (1943); *American Pipers* (1943); *United Music* (1944); *Big Sing* (1945); *Festival Overture* for 2 Orchs. (1946); *Saturday Night at the Firehouse* (1948); *Aria* for Violin and String Orch. (1952); *Rondo* (1953); *Ballad* for Strings (1955); *Variations* (1956); *Persian Set* for 12 Instruments (1956–57); *Music 1957* (1957); *Ongaku* (1957; Louisville, March 26, 1958); *Antiphony* for 2 Orchs. (1958); Percussion Concerto (1958; Kansas City, Jan. 7, 1961); *Mela and Fair* (New Delhi, India, Dec. 11, 1959); *Characters* (1959); *Chiaroscuro* (1960); *Variations on Thirds* for 2 Solo Violas and Strings (1960); *Concerto Brevis* for Accordion and Orch. (1960); Harmonica Concerto (1960); *Air and Scherzo* for Saxophone and Small Orch. (1961); *Duo Concertante* for Flute, Harp, and Orch. (1961; Springfield, Ohio, Oct. 21, 1961); 2 koto concertos: No. 1 (1963; Philadelphia, Dec. 18, 1964) and No. 2 (1965); *Concerto Grosso* for 5 Instruments and Orch. (1963; Univ. of Miami, Fla., Jan. 12, 1964); Harp Concerto (1965); *Carol* (1965; new orchestration of slow movement of Koto Concerto No. 1).

OTHER WORKS FOR BAND: *A Curse and a Blessing* (1938); *Shoonthree* (1940; also for Orch.); *Celtic Set* (1943; originally for Orch., 1939); *Animal Magic*

(1944); *Grandma's Rumba* (1945); *Fantaisie* (U.S. Military Academy Band, West Point, N.Y., May 30, 1952); *Singing Band* (1953).

OTHER WORKS FOR VOICE: *The Thistle Flower* for Women's Voices a cappella (1928); *Vocalise* for Voice, Flute, and Piano (1937); *Chrysanthemums* for Soprano, 2 Saxophones, and 4 Strings (1937); *Toccanta* for Soprano, Flute, Cello, and Piano (1938); *The Coming of Light* for Chorus a cappella (1939); *Fire and Ice,* after Frost's poem, for 4 Male Soloists, and Orch. or Band (1942); Sonatina for Baritone, Violin, and Piano (1942); *American Muse* for Soprano, Alto, and Piano (1943); *To America* for Chorus a cappella (1947); *The Commission,* cantata for 4 Soloists and Orch. (1954); *... if He Please* for Mixed and either Boys' or Women's Choruses, and Orch. (1954); Septet for 5 Voices without words, Clarinet, and Piano (1955–56); *A Thanksgiving Psalm from the Dead Sea Scrolls* for Male Chorus and Orch. (1956; originally *Hymn and Fuguing Tune* No. 11); *Edson Hymns and Fuguing Tunes* for Chorus and Orch. (1960); *The Creator* for Chorus and Orch. (1963); *Ultima Actio* for Chorus a cappella (1965).

OTHER CHAMBER WORKS: *Quartet Romantic* for 2 Flutes, Violin, and Viola (1915–17); 5 string quartets: No. 1, *Pedantic* (1915–16); *Quartet Euphometric* (1916–19); No. 3, *Movement* (1934); No. 4, *Mosaic* (1935); No. 5, *United* Quartet (1936), based on folk melodies of the world; No. 6 (1956; revised 1962); also unnumbered *Ensemble* for 2 Violins, Viola, 2 Cellos, and 3 Thundersticks (1924; version for String Orch. without Thundersticks, 1959); 7 *Paragraphs* for String Trio (1925); Suite for Violin and Piano (1927); *Exultation* for 10 Strings (1928); Suite for Wind Quintet (1930); 3 works for Percussion: *Pulse, Return,* and *Ostinato Pianissimo* (1930–34); *6 Casual Developments* for Clarinet and Piano (1935); *Sound-form for Dance* for Flute, Clarinet, Bassoon, and Percussion (1936); *Sarabande* for Oboe, Clarinet, and Percussion (1937); *Trickster Coyote* for Flute and Percussion (1941); *Action in Brass* for 5 Brasses (1943); Violin Sonata (1945, revised 1947); Saxophone Quartet (1946); *Tall Tale* for Brass Sextet (1947); *Set for Two* for Violin and Piano (1948); *4 Declamations and Return* for Cello and Piano (1949); *Set of 5* for Violin, Piano, and Percussion (1951); *Set* for Harpsichord, Flute, Oboe, and Cello (1953); *Set of 2* for Harp and Violin (1955); *Homage to Iran* for Violin and Piano (1957); *Iridescent Rondo* for Solo Accordion (1959); *Air and Scherzo* for Saxophone and Piano (1961); Quartet for Flute, Oboe, Cello, and Harp (1962); *Gravely and Vigorously,* in memory of John F. Kennedy, for Solo Cello (1963); *26 Simultaneous Mosaics* for Violin, Cello, Clarinet, Piano, and Percussion (N.Y., Dec. 1, 1964); Piano Trio (1965); *Cleistogamy* (self-pollinating flowerlets), a collection of pieces written between 1941 and 1963.

FOR PIANO: *The Tides of Manaunaun* (1912); *Advertisements* (1914, revised 1959); *Dynamic Motion* (1914); *6 Ings: Floating-Fleeting-Wafting-Seething-Frisking-Scooting* (1916); *It Isn't It* (1922); *The Snows of Fujiyama* (1922); *Aeolian Harp* (1923); *Piece for Piano with Strings* (Paris, 1924); *The Ban-*

shee (1925); *Lilt of the Reel* (1925); *Sinister Resonance* (1925); *Tiger* (1927); *2 Woofs* (1930); *Hilarious Curtain Opener and Ritournelle* (1937); hundreds of other pieces with similar fanciful titles; also some organ pieces.

WRITINGS: *New Musical Resources* (N.Y., 1930); ed., *American Composers on American Music: A Symposium* (Stanford, Calif., 1933; reprinted, N.Y., 1962); *Charles Ives and His Music* (N.Y., 1955; in collaboration with his wife, Sidney Cowell).

BIBLIOGRAPHY: N. Slonimsky, "Henry Cowell," in *American Composers on American Music: A Symposium* (Stanford, Calif., 1933; reprinted, N.Y., 1962); Madeleine Goss, *Modern Music-Makers* (N.Y., 1952; pp. 266–81); Hugo Weisgall, "The Music of Henry Cowell," *Musical Quarterly* (Oct. 1959); Oliver Daniel, "Henry Cowell," *Stereo Review* (Dec. 1974; pp. 72–82). Rita H. Mead, *Henry Cowell's New Music, 1925–1936* (N.Y., 1981); Martha L. Manion, *Writings about Henry Cowell: An Annotated Bibliography* (N.Y., 1982). A somewhat incomplete listing of his works to 1955 is found in *Composers of the Americas,* vol. 2 (Washington, D.C., 1956).

Cowen, Sir Frederic Hymen, English composer; b. Kingston, Jamaica, Jan. 29, 1852; d. London, Oct. 6, 1935. His evident talent for music caused his parents to take him to England to study at the age of 4. He was a pupil of Benedict and Goss in London; studied at Leipzig under Hauptmann, Moscheles, Reinecke, Richter, and Plaidy (1865–66); in Berlin under Kiel (1867–68); was conductor of the Phil. Society of London (1888–92), succeeding Sullivan, and again from 1900–7; was music director of the Melbourne Centennial Exhibition (1888–89); conductor of the Liverpool Phil. from 1896–1913; Sir Charles Hallé's successor as conductor of the Manchester Concerts (1896–99); conducted the Handel Triennial Festival (Crystal Palace, 1903–12); the Cardiff Festival (1902–10). He received the degree of Mus.Doc. from Edinburgh Univ. (1910); was knighted in 1911.

WORKS: 4 operas; *Pauline* (London, Nov. 22, 1876); *Thorgrim* (London, April 22, 1890); *Signa* (London, June 30, 1894); *Harold, or The Norman Conquest* (London, June 8, 1895); oratorios: *The Deluge* (1878); *St. Ursula* (1881); *Ruth* (1887); *The Veil* (Cardiff Festival, Sept. 20, 1910; his most successful work); cantatas. For Orch.: 6 symphs.: No.1, in C minor (1869); No.2, in F minor (1872); No. 3, in C minor, *Scandinavian* (1880); No. 4, in B-flat minor, *Welsh* (1884); No. 5, in F (1887); No. 6, in E, *Idyllic* (1897); 3 suites: *The Language of Flowers, In the Olden Time, In Fairyland;* Sinfonietta; Piano Concerto; 4 overtures; *Of Life and Love,* fantasy. Chamber music: 2 piano trios; 2 string quartets; piano pieces; over 250 songs; etc. He publ. his memoirs as *My Art and My Friends* (London, 1913), and an amusing glossary of musical terms, *Music as she is wrote* (London, 1915); also, for the Masterpieces of Music series, books (with biography and music) on Haydn, Mozart, Mendelssohn, and Rossini.

BIBLIOGRAPHY: *Musical Times* (Nov. 1898).

Cowie, Edward, English composer; b. Birmingham, Aug. 17, 1943. He studied at Trinity College, and later took courses at the univs. of Southampton and Leeds with Fricker, Goehr, and Lutoslawski. An artist of wide-ranging attainments, he studied not only music but also painting and ornithology; often his compositions portrayed his pictorial visions of birds, not by literal imitation or suggestion but rather through inner kinship; his intellectual inspirations were Leonardo da Vinci and Goethe in their universal thinking and practice. Eschewing musicological pedantry, he used techniques ranging from static triadic tonality to serialistic atonality, from abstract tonal formations to concrete references to external objects.

WORKS: *Dungeness Choruses* (1970); *Endymion Nocturnes* for Tenor and Instruments (1973); *Somnus ei inductus* for 4 Trombones (1973); *Shinkokinshu* for Voice and Instruments (1968); *Leviathan,* symph. poem (1975); Clarinet Concerto No. 2 for Orch. minus Woodwinds (1975); *Gesangbuch* for 24 Voices and 12 Instruments (1976); *Piano Variations* (1976; revised, 1981); Piano Concerto (1976–77); *L'Or de la trompette d'été* for 18 String Instruments (1977); *Cathedral Music* for Brass (1977); String Quartet No. 2 (1977); *Commedia,* opera in 4 acts to a scenario by the composer (1976–78); *Columbine* for 14 Instruments (1979); *Brighella's World* for Baritone and Piano (1979); *Harlequin* for Harp (1980); *The Falls of Clyde* for 2 Pianos (1980); *Commedia Lazzi* for Guitar (1980); *Madrigals,* 2 vols. for 12 Voices (1980–81); Concerto for Orch. (1979–80; Liverpool, Feb. 2, 1982).

Cowles, Walter Ruel, American composer; b. New Haven, Conn., Sept. 4, 1881; d. Tallahassee, Fla., Dec. 8, 1959. He graduated from Yale Univ. (B.A. 1906; Mus.Bac. 1907); studied with Horatio Parker; then at the Schola Cantorum in Paris; was an instructor of piano at the Yale Music School (1911–19); a prof. of music theory at Florida State College for Women (1930–51); won the Steinert prize for composition at Yale. He composed a Piano Concerto; a Piano Trio; songs; piano pieces.

Cox, Jean, American tenor; b. Gadsen, Ala., Jan. 16, 1922. He studied at the Univ. of Alabama, and at the New England Cons. in Boston. He sang with the New England Opera Theater; then went to Europe; made his debut with the Kiel Stadttheater in 1954; in succeeding years he appeared with many of the major European and American opera houses; also sang at Bayreuth. He made his Metropolitan Opera debut in N.Y. on April 2, 1976, as Walther in *Die Meistersinger.*

Crabbé, Armand, Belgian baritone; b. Brussels, April 23, 1883; d. there, July 24, 1947. He studied with Désiré Demest at the Brussels Cons. (1902–4); made his debut at the Théâtre de la Monnaie in Brussels as the Night Watchman in *Die Meistersinger* in 1904; there he also created the role of the Friar in Massenet's *Jongleur de Nôtre-Dame* (also sung by him for the first time at Covent Garden, N.Y., Boston, etc.). In 1907 he joined Hammerstein's Manhattan Opera in N.Y.; then was with the Chicago Grand Opera (1910–14); returning to Europe, he settled in Brussels as a voice teacher. He wrote an opera, *Les Noces d'or* (in collaboration with Auguste Maurage).

Craft, Marcella, American lyric soprano; b. Indianapolis, Aug. 11, 1880; d. Riverside, Calif., Dec. 12, 1959. She studied with Charles Adams in Boston (1897–1900) and with F. Mottino in Milan (1901–5); made her debut in Italy; sang in Germany until the outbreak of World War I, when she returned to the U.S.; subsequently appeared with the San Carlo Opera Co.; settled in Riverside as a singing teacher.

Craft, Robert, American conductor and brilliant writer on music; b. Kingston, N.Y., Oct. 20, 1923. He studied at the Juilliard School of Music and the Berkshire Music Center; took courses in conducting with Monteux. During World War II he was in the U.S. Army Medical Corps. In 1947 he conducted the N.Y. Brass and Woodwind Ensemble. A decisive turn in his career was his encounter with Stravinsky, whom he greatly impressed by his precise knowledge of Stravinsky's music; gradually he became Stravinsky's closest associate. He was also instrumental in persuading Stravinsky to adopt the 12-tone method of composition, a momentous turn in Stravinsky's creative path. He collaborated with Stravinsky on 6 vols. of a catechumenical and discursive nature: *Conversations with Igor Stravinsky* (N.Y., 1959); *Memories and Commentaries* (N.Y., 1960); *Expositions and Developments* (N.Y., 1962); *Dialogues and a Diary* (N.Y., 1963); *Themes and Episodes* (N.Y., 1967); *Retrospections and Conclusions* (N.Y., 1969). Resentful of frequent referral to him as a musical Boswell, Craft insists that his collaboration with Stravinsky was more akin to that between the Goncourt brothers, both acting and reacting to an emerging topic of discussion, with Stravinsky evoking his ancient memories in his careful English, or fluent French, spiced with unrestrained discourtesies toward professional colleagues on the American scene, and Craft reifying the material with an analeptic bulimia of quaquaversal literary, psychological, physiological, and culinary references in a flow of finely ordered dialogue. His other publications include *Prejudices in Disguise* (N.Y., 1974); *Stravinsky in Photographs and Documents* (London, 1976; N.Y., 1978); *Current Convictions: Views and Reviews* (N.Y.,1977).

Cramer, Johann Baptist, famous German pianist and pedagogue, eldest son of **Wilhelm Cramer;** b. Mannheim, Feb. 24, 1771; d. London, April 16, 1858. He was brought to London as an infant, and throughout his life regarded it as his home. He received a fine musical education, first from his father, then from Clementi (1783–84) and C.F. Abel (1785). He began to travel as a concert pianist in 1788; visited Vienna, where he met Haydn and Beethoven (1799–1800); in later years (1832–45) spent considerable time as a teacher in Munich and Paris, finally returning to London. His greatest work is his piano method, *Grosse Praktische Pianoforte Schule* (1815) in 5 parts, the last of which, *84 Studies* (op. 50; later revised and publ. as op. 81, including *16 nouvelles études*) is famous in piano pedagogy. Hans von Bülow made a selection of 50 studies from this collection, later revised and annotated in collections of 52 and 60; Henselt issued a different selection, with accompaniment of a 2nd piano; other eds. of Cramer's studies are by Coccius, Riemann, Pauer, Lack, and Lickl; *100 Progressive Etudes* is also well known. Apart from his pedagogic collections, Cramer wrote 9 piano concertos; over 50 piano sonatas; 2 piano quartets; 2 piano quintets; and numerous piano pieces of the salon type; but all these are quite forgotten, while his piano studies, with those of Czerny, maintained their value for more than a century. He first entered the music publishing business in 1805, as head of the firm Cramer & Keys; was in partnership with Samuel Chappell (1810–19). In 1824, together with R. Addison and T.F. Beale, Cramer established a music publishing house (now J.B. Cramer & Co., Ltd.), of which he was director until 1842; in 1844 Addison retired and was succeeded by W. Chappell, the firm then becoming Cramer, Beale & Chappell; after Cramer's death in 1858, and Chappell's retirement in 1861, G. Wood became Beale's partner; about 1862 the firm began to devote much attention to the manufacture of pianos; on Beale's death in 1863, Wood became sole director, continuing it successfully until his death in 1893, although devoting more consideration to piano manufacture than to music publishing. His 2 nephews succeeded him. In 1897 the firm became a limited company.

BIBLIOGRAPHY: J. Pembaur, *Die 84 Etüden von J.B. Cramer; Anleitung zu gründlichem Studieren und Analysieren derselben* (Leipzig, 1901); Th. Schlesinger, *J.B. Cramer und seine Klavier-Sonaten* (Munich, 1928); A. Hyatt King, "Mozart and Cramer," in *Mozart in Retrospect: Studies in Criticism and Bibliography* (London, 1955; 3rd ed., 1970); P.F. Ganz, "Johann Baptist Cramer and His Celebrated Etudes," *Clavier* (Feb. 1967); H. Goldschmidt, "Beethovens Anweisungen zum Spiel der Cramer-Etüden," in H.A. Brockhaus and K. Niemann, *Bericht über den Int. Beethoven-Kongress 10.–12. Dezember 1970* (Berlin, 1971).

Cramer, Wilhelm, German violinist, father of **Johann Baptist Cramer;** b. Mannheim, June (baptized, June 2) 1746; d. London, Oct. 5, 1799. He received his musical training from his father, Jacob Cramer (1705–70), who was a violinist in the Mannheim Orch., and also studied with Johann Stamitz and Cannabich; in 1752–69 he was a member of the Mannheim Orch.; then went to Paris. In 1772 he went to London, where he became a successful violinist and conductor. He was concertmaster of the orch. of the Anacreontic Society during its most prestigious years (1773–91); was chamber musician to the King. He wrote 11 violin concertos, 6 string quartets, 6 violin sonatas, and other string music.

Cranz, August, music publishing firm in Hamburg, founded 1813 by August Heinrich Cranz (1789–1870). His son **Alwin** (b. 1834; d. Vevey, April 10, 1923), who succeeded him in 1857, bought the firm of C.A. Spina of Vienna in 1876, and in 1886 the firm of C.A. Böhme of Hamburg. Alwin's son, **Oskar** (pen name, **Anton Toska;** d. Boston, Aug. 24, 1929), entered as a partner in 1896. In 1897 the firm removed to Leipzig. Branches were established in Vienna (1876), Brussels (1883), and London (1896). After World War II its permanent headquarters were in Wiesbaden.

Cras, Jean Emile Paul, French composer; b. Brest, May 22, 1879; d. there, Sept. 14, 1932. He was an officer in the French navy, reaching the rank of vice-admiral; he grew up in a musical atmosphere and when still a child began to compose; took lessons with Henri Duparc. Under the influence of Duparc's style, Cras composed a number of miniatures in an impressionistic vein; he was at his best in lyrical songs and instrumental pieces.
WORKS: Opera, *Polyphème* (Paris, Opéra-Comique, Dec. 28, 1922; won the Prize of the City of Paris); *Journal de Bord,* symph. suite (1927); *Légende* for Cello and Orch. (1929); Piano Concerto (1931); for Voice and Orch.: *L'Offrande lyrique* (1920); *Fontaines* (1923); *3 Noëls* (1929); many pieces of chamber music; a number of songs.
BIBLIOGRAPHY: René Dumesnil, "Jean Cras," in *Portraits de musiciens français* (Paris, 1938; pp. 153–60).

Crass, Franz, German bass-baritone; b. Wipperfurth, Feb. 9, 1928. He made his debut at Krefeld in 1954; gained prominence as a member of the Vienna State Opera; also appeared at the German Opera in West Berlin, La Scala in Milan, and at the Bayreuth Festival. He is generally recognized as one of the foremost interpreters of bass roles in the operas of Mozart and Wagner.

Crawford, Robert M., baritone and conductor; b. Dawson, Yukon Territory, Canada, July 27, 1899; d. New York, March 12, 1961. He studied at Princeton Univ., and also took courses at the Juilliard Graduate School and at the American Cons. at Fontainebleau, France. Returning to the U.S., he held various posts as a choral teacher and conductor; was in charge of the Newark Symph. Orch. and the Chautauqua Orch. (1933); composed several orch. suites and songs, of which the most popular is *The U.S. Air Force.* ("Off we go . . .").

Crawford, Ruth Porter, remarkable American composer; b. East Liverpool, Ohio, July 3, 1901; d. Chevy Chase, Md., Nov. 18, 1953. She studied composition with **Charles Seeger,** whom she later married; her principal piano teacher was Heniot Lévy. She dedicated herself to teaching and to collecting American folk songs; when still very young, she taught at the School of Musical Arts in Jacksonville, Fla. (1918–21); then gave courses at the American Cons. in Chicago (1925–29) and at the Elmhurst College of Music in Illinois (1926–29). In 1930 she re-

ceived a Guggenheim fellowship. She became known mainly as a compiler of American folk songs; publ. *American Folk Songs for Children* (1948), *Animal Folk Songs for Children* (1950), and *American Folk Songs for Christmas* (1953). Her own compositions, astonishingly bold in their experimental aperçus and insights, often anticipated many techniques of the future avant-garde; while rarely performed during her lifetime, they had a remarkable revival in the subsequent decades.
WORKS: Violin Sonata (1926); Suite for Piano and Woodwind Quintet (1927; perf. for the first time in Cambridge, Mass., Dec. 14, 1975); *4 Diaphonic Suites* for Various Instruments (1930); *3 Songs* for Contralto, Oboe, Percussion, and Piano, to words by Carl Sandburg (*Rat Riddles; Prayers of Steel; In Tall Grass;* perf. at the Amsterdam Festival of the International Society for Contemporary Music, June 15, 1933); String Quartet (1931; contains a slow movement anticipating the "static" harmonies and "phase shifts"); *Sacco and Vanzetti* for Chorus (Workers' Olympiad, 1933); *Risselty Rosselty* for Small Orch. (1941); Suite for Wind Quintet (1952); several sets of piano pieces; *2 Ricercari* for Voice and Piano (*Sacco, Vanzetti; Chinaman, Laundryman;* 1932).
BIBLIOGRAPHY: Charles Seeger, "Ruth Crawford," in Henry Cowell's symposium, *American Composers on American Music* (Stanford, 1933); M. Gaume, *Ruth Crawford Seeger: Her Life and Works* (Diss., Indiana Univ., 1973); D. Nichols, "Ruth Crawford Seeger: An Introduction," *Musical Times* (July 1983).

Creatore, Giuseppe, band conductor; b. Naples, June 21, 1871; d. New York, Aug. 15, 1952. He studied at the Naples Cons. with Nicola d'Arienzo and Camillo de Nardis. In 1900 he came to the U.S., organized his own band, and toured from coast to coast and in Canada. In 1906 he returned to Italy, where he established a band which he brought to America for a tour. He then settled in N.Y. and was active as impresario of various opera companies which, however, were not successful; conducted band concerts during summer seasons in various U.S. cities.

Crécquillon (Créquillon), Thomas, Franco-Flemish contrapuntist; b. probably in Ghent; d. Béthune, 1557. It is known that he was maître de chapelle at Béthune in 1540; was court musician to Charles V of Spain; later was canon at Namur, Termonde, and Béthune. His works, which rank with the best of that period, consist of 16 masses in 4 and 5 parts, 116 motets, *cantiones,* and 192 French chansons in 4, 5, and 6 parts. Reprints appear in Commer's *Collectio operum musicorum Batavorum saeculi XVI* and Maldeghem's *Trésor musical.* An edition of his works was publ. by N. Bridgman and B. Hudson, *Thomas Crécquillon: Opera omnia,* in Corpus Mensurabilis Musicae, LXIII/1 (1974—). For a complete list of his works (publ. mostly between 1545 and 1636) and a detailed bibliography, see the article on him in *Die Musik in Geschichte und Gegenwart.*

515

Crescentini, Girolamo, one of the last and finest of the Italian artificial mezzo-sopranos; b. Urbania, near Urbino, Feb. 2, 1762; d. Naples, April 24, 1846. He studied singing with Gibelli at Bologna, and made a highly successful debut at Rome in 1783; subsequent successes in other European capitals earned him the surname of "Orfeo Italiano." He sang at Livorno, Padua, Venice, Turin, London (1786), Milan, and Naples (1788–89). Napoleon, having heard him in 1805, decorated him with the Iron Crown, and engaged him to teach singing to his family in 1806–12; Crescentini then retired from the stage and left Paris, on account of vocal disorders induced by the climate; in 1816 he became a prof. of singing in the Royal Cons. in Naples. Cimarosa wrote his *Orazi e Curiazi* for him. Crescentini publ. several collections of *Ariette* (Vienna, 1797) and a *Treatise on Vocalization in France and Italy,* with vocal exercises (Paris, 1811).

Creser, William, English organist and composer; b. York, Sept. 9, 1844; d. London, March 13, 1933. He was taught by his father, in whose choir (at St. John's Church) he sang; studied later with G.A. Macfarren (organ and composition); as early as 1856 he occasionally acted as Sir J. Barnby's substitute at Holgate Road Church; was appointed organist at Holy Trinity in Micklegate in 1859, and later succeeded Barnby; then filled various other positions; was organist at the Chapel Royal, St. James' (1891–1902); from 1902 examiner of Trinity College of Music, in which capacity he made frequent visits to musical institutions throughout the British colonies; received a Mus.Bac. (1869) and a Mus.Doc. (1880) from Oxford. His wife (née **Amelia Clarke**) was a well-known mezzo-soprano.
WORKS: Oratorio, *Micaiah;* cantatas: *Eudora* (Leeds, 1882); *The Sacrifice of Freia* (Leeds, 1889); *The Golden Legend; Tegner's Drapa;* Mass; 2 Psalms; *Old English Suite* for Orch.; String Quartet; Piano Trio; Violin Sonata; organ music.

Crespin, Régine, French soprano; b. Marseilles, Feb. 23, 1927. She studied pharmacology; then began taking voice lessons with Suzanne Cesbron-Viseur and Georges Jouatte in Paris. She made her debut in Mulhouse as Elsa in 1950 and then sang at the Paris Opéra. She later acquired a European reputation as one of the best Wagnerian singers; she sang Kundry in *Parsifal* at the Bayreuth Festivals (1958–60); appeared also at La Scala in Milan, at Covent Garden in London, and on Nov. 19, 1962, made her debut with the Metropolitan Opera in N.Y. in the role of the Marschallin in *Der Rosenkavalier;* she remained on the staff of the Metropolitan since 1971; sang the parts of Elsa in *Lohengrin,* Sieglinde in *Die Walküre,* and Amelia in *Un ballo in maschera.;* also appeared as a concert singer. Her sonorous, somewhat somber voice suits dramatic parts excellently.

Creston, Paul (real name, **Giuseppe Guttoveggio**), distinguished American composer; b. New York, Oct. 10, 1906. He studied piano with Randegger and Déthier and organ playing with Yon; he was essentially autodidact in composition. He adopted the name Creston, an anglicized version of his high-school nickname, Crespino, a role he acted in a play. He began to compose tentatively at the age of 8, but he did not compose his full-fledged first opus, *5 Dances* for piano, until he was 26. In 1938 he obtained a Guggenheim fellowship, and in a few years advanced to the front ranks of American composers, with an impressive catalogue of major works. He filled various jobs as a theater organist for silent movies; then obtained the post of organist at St. Malachy's Church in N.Y. (1934–67); concurrently he taught at the N.Y. College of Music (1963–67). From 1968–75 he was a prof. of music at Central Washington State College. In 1976 he moved to San Diego. He has written more than 100 major compositions, including 6 symphs. and 15 concertos for various instruments, as well as 35 other symph. works, chamber music for various instrumental combinations, choral works, piano pieces, and songs. His music is characterized by engaging spontaneity, with strong melodic lines and full-bodied harmonies; his instrumental writing is highly advantageous for virtuoso performance. He publ. 2 books: *Principles of Rhythm* (N.Y., 1964) and *Creative Harmony* (N.Y., 1970). In his theoretical writings, he militates against the illogic of binary meters and proposes to introduce such time signatures as 6/12 or 3/9; some of these metrical designations he uses in his own works.
WORKS: FOR ORCH.: 6 symphs.: No. 1 (N.Y., Feb. 22, 1941; received N.Y. Music Critics' Circle Award); No. 2 (N.Y., Feb. 15, 1945; highly successful); No. 3 (Worcester Festival, Oct. 27, 1950); No. 4 (Washington, D.C., Jan. 30, 1952); No. 5 (Washington, April 4, 1956); No. 6 for Organ and Orch. (Washington, June 28, 1982); Partita for Flute, Violin, and Strings (1937); *Threnody* for Orch. (1938); *2 Choric Dances* for Woodwinds, Piano, Percussion, and Strings (1938); Concertino for Marimba and Orch. (1940); *Prelude and Dance* for Piano, Strings, and Orch. (1941); *Pastorale and Tarantella* for Piano, Strings, and Orch. (1941); Saxophone Concerto (1941; N.Y., Jan. 27, 1944); *A Rumor,* symph. sketch (N.Y., Dec. 13, 1941); *Dance Variations* for Soprano and Orch. (1942); *Frontiers* for Orch. (Toronto, Oct. 14, 1943); *Poem* for Harp and Orch. (1945); Fantasy for Trombone and Orch. (Los Angeles, Feb. 12, 1948); Piano Concerto (1949); Concerto for 2 Pianos and Orch. (1951; Montevallo, Ala., Nov. 18, 1968); *Walt Whitman,* symph. poem (1952); *Invocation and Dance* for Orch. (Louisville, Ky., May 15, 1954); *Dance Overture* (1954); *Lydian Ode* (1956); Violin Concerto No. 1 (1956; Detroit, Jan. 14, 1960); Toccata (1957); *Pre-Classic Suite* for Orch. (New Orleans, April 3, 1958); Accordion Concerto (1958); *Janus* for Orch. (Denver, July 17, 1959); Violin Concerto No. 2 (Los Angeles, Nov. 17, 1960); *Corinthians XIII,* symph. poem (Phoenix, March 30, 1964); *Choreografic Suite* for Orch. (1966); *Pavane Variations* for Orch. (La Jolla, Calif., Aug. 21, 1966); *Chthonic Ode,* an "homage to Henry Moore" (Detroit, April 6, 1967); *The Psalmist* for Contralto and Orch. (1967); *Anatolia (Turkish Rhapsody)* for Symph. Band (1967);

Thanatopsis for Orch. (1971); *Square Dance 76* for Wind Symph. Orch. (1975); *Suite for Strings* (1978); *Sadhana,* op. 117, for Cello and Chamber Orch., inspired by the philosophy of the Indian poet Rabindranath Tagore, cast in the form of a theme and variations (Los Angeles, Oct. 3, 1981).

CHAMBER MUSIC: Suite for Saxophone and Piano (1935); String Quartet (1936); Suite for Viola and Piano (1937); Suite for Violin and Piano (1939); Sonata for Saxophone and Piano (1939); Suite for Flute, Viola, and Piano (1952); Suite for Cello and Piano (1956); Concertino for Piano and Woodwind Quintet (1969); *Ceremonial* for Percussion Ensemble (1972); *Rapsodie* for Saxophone and Organ (1976); Trio for Piano, Violin, and Cello (1979). CHORAL WORKS: *3 Chorales from Tagore* (1936); *Requiem Mass* for Tenor, Bass, and Organ (1938); *Missa Solemnis* (1949); *Isaiah's Prophecy,* Christmas oratorio (1961); *The Northwest* for Chorus and Orch. (1969); *Hyas Illahee* for Chorus and Orch. (Shreveport, La., March 14, 1976); *Thanksgiving Anthem* for Chorus and Orch. (1982); also liturgical vocal works, with piano or organ accompaniment; piano pieces (*5 Little Dances, 5 Inventions,* etc.).

BIBLIOGRAPHY: Henry Cowell, "Paul Creston," *Musical Quarterly* (Oct. 1948).

Crews, Lucile, American composer; b. Pueblo, Colo., Aug. 23, 1888; d. San Diego, Calif., Nov. 3, 1972. She studied at the New England Cons.; later went to Europe, where she took private lessons with Nadia Boulanger in Paris and Hugo Kaun in Berlin. She wrote a symph. poem, *To an Unknown Soldier* (1926); a miniature opera, *Ariadne and Dionysus* (1935); a "grand opera" in one act entitled *Eight Hundred Rubles* (1926); *Suite* for Strings and Woodwinds; Viola Sonata; piano pieces; songs.

Crimi, Giulio, Italian tenor; b. Paterno, May 10, 1885; d. Rome, Oct. 29, 1939. He made his debut in Palermo in 1910; then sang at Covent Garden in London (1914). On Dec. 14, 1918, he sang at the Metropolitan Opera in N.Y. in the world premieres of Puccini's *Gianni Schicchi* (as Rinuccio) and *Il Tabarro* (as Luigi); continued to sing there until 1921; also made appearances in Chicago (1916–18; 1922–24); then sang in Milan and Rome. After his retirement, he taught voice; one of his most famous pupils was Tito Gobbi.

Crist, Bainbridge, American composer; b. Lawrenceburg, Ind., Feb. 13, 1883; d. Barnstable, Mass., Feb. 7, 1969. He studied piano and flute; later law at the George Washington Univ. (LL.B.); was a lawyer in Boston for 6 years (until 1912), continuing his music as an avocation. He went to Europe to complete his musical training (theory with P. Juon in Berlin and C. Landi in London, and singing with William Shakespeare); he taught singing in Boston (1915–21) and Washington, D.C. (1922–23); returned to Europe (1923) and spent 4 years in Florence, Paris, Lucerne, and Berlin; then came back to the U.S. and settled in Washington. WORKS: FOR THE STAGE: *Le Pied de la momie,*

choreographic drama in 2 scenes (1915; Bournemouth Festival, England, 1925); *Pregiwa's Marriage,* Javanese ballet in one scene (1920); *The Sorceress,* choreographic drama (1926). FOR ORCH.: *Egyptian Impressions,* suite (Boston Pops, June 22, 1915); *Abhisarika* for Violin and Orch. (1921); *Intermezzo* (1921); *Chinese Dance* (1922); *Arabian Dance* (1922); *Nautch Dance* (1922); *Dreams* (1924); *Yearning* (1924); *Nocturne* (1924); *An Old Portrait* (1924); *La Nuit revécue* (1933; Radio City, N.Y., March 8, 1936); *Vienna 1913* (1933); *Frivolité* (1934); *Hymn to Nefertiti* (1936); *Fête espagnole* (1937); *American Epic 1620,* tone poem (Washington, Feb. 28, 1943). FOR VOICE AND ORCH.: *A Bag of Whistles* (1915); *The Parting,* poem (1916); *Rhymes* (1917); *O Come Hither!* (1918); *Drolleries* (1920); *Colored Stars,* suite of 4 songs (1921); *Remember* (1930); *The Way That Lovers Use* (1931); *Noontime* (1931); *Evening* (1931); *By a Silent Shore* (1932). Choral works for mixed, male, and female voices; piano pieces; songs. He is author of *The Art of Setting Words to Music* (N.Y., 1944).

BIBLIOGRAPHY: J.T. Howard, *Bainbridge Crist* (N.Y., 1929); W.T. Upton, *Art-Song in America* (N.Y., 1930; pp. 236–49).

Cristoforeanu, Florica, Rumanian soprano; b. Rimnicu-Sarat, Aug. 16, 1887; d. Rio de Janeiro, March 1, 1960. She studied at the Milan Cons. with Filippi and Bodrilla; made her debut in Capodristia in 1908 as Lucia; then sang operetta in Bucharest; from 1927 to 1932 she appeared at La Scala, Milan. She also sang in Rome and South America; retired in 1940. In addition to her classical roles, she was known for her performances of works by contemporary Italian composers.

Cristofori, Bartolommeo, celebrated Italian instrument maker; b. Padua, May 4, 1655; d. Florence, Jan. 27, 1731. He was the inventor of the first practical piano as opposed to the clavichord (which also employs a type of hammer action), although 2-keyed instruments called "Piano e Forte" are known to have existed in Modena in 1598, and a 4-octave keyboard instrument shaped like a dulcimer, with small hammers and no dampers, dating from 1610, is yet in existence. He was a leading maker of clavicembali in Padua; about 1690 went to Florence, where he was instrument maker to Ferdinando de' Medici; on the latter's death in 1713, he was made custodian of the court collection of instruments by Cosimo III. According to an article by Maffei (publ. 1711, *Giornale dei Letterati d'Italia*), Cristofori had up to that year made 3 "gravecembali col piano e forte," these having, instead of the usual jacks plucking the strings with quills, a row of little hammers striking the strings from below. The principle of this hammer action was adopted, in the main, by Gottfried Silbermann, the Streichers, and Broadwood (hence called the "English action"). Following the designation by its inventor, the new instrument was named piano-forte. A piano of Cristofori's make is in the possession of the Metropolitan Museum of Art in N.Y.

BIBLIOGRAPHY: F. Casaglia, *Per le onoranze a Bartolommeo Cristofori* (1876).

Crivelli, Giovanni Battista, Italian composer of the Lombardy school; b. Scandiano, Modena; d. Modena, 1652. He was organist at the Reggio Emilia Cathedral (1614–19); then served as director at the Accademia dello Spirito Santo in Ferrara (1626); subsequently was organist at the electoral court in Munich. He became maestro di cappella at the Milan Cathedral (1638–42) and at S. Maria Maggiore in Bergamo (1642–48). He publ. *Motetti concertati* (1626; 3rd ed., 1635) and *Madrigali concertati* (1626; 2nd ed., 1633).

Croce, Giovanni, eminent Venetian composer; b. Chioggia (hence surnamed "**il Chiozzotto**"), c.1560; d. Venice, May 15, 1609. He was a pupil of Zarlino; was chorister at San Marco; succeeded Donato as maestro di cappella there in 1603.
WORKS: Sonatas *a* 5 (1580); 2 vols. of motets *a* 8 (1589, 1590; vol. II reprinted 1605 with organ bass; both vols. with organ bass in 1607); 2 vols. of madrigals *a* 5 (1585, 1588); *Triacca musicale* (caprices, or humorous songs in Venetian dialect, *a* 4–7; went through 4 eds. (1596, 1601, 1607, 1609), and was his most popular and famous work; it includes the contest between the cuckoo and the nightingale, judged by the parrot); madrigals *a* 5–6 (1590–1607); *Cantiones sacrae a* 8, with Basso Continuo, for Organ (1622; a 2nd vol. was publ. in 1623); canzonette *a* 4 (1588; new eds., 1595, 1598); masses *a* 8 (1596); Lamentations *a* 4 (1603, 1605) and *a* 6 (1610); Magnificats *a* 6 (1605); vesper psalms *a* 8 (1589); etc. Younge printed some of Croce's madrigals in his *Musica Transalpina* (1588), and a selection of his church music was publ. with Eng. words as *Musica sacra, Penetentials for 6 voyces,* in London in 1608. Modern reprints include 3 masses publ. at Regensburg in 1888, 1891, and 1899, and other works in Proske's *Musica Divina,* Haberl's *Repertorium,* Torchi's *L'Arte musicale in Italia,* Bäuerle's *12 Hymnen und Motetten alter Meister,* and the publications of the Motet Society (London).
BIBLIOGRAPHY: F.X. Haberl, "Giovanni Croce," in *Kirchenmusikalisches Jahrbuch* (1888); L. Torri, in *Rivista Musicale Italiana* (1900); Denis Arnold, "Giovanni Croce and the Concertato Style," *Musical Quarterly* (Jan. 1953).

Croes, Henri-Jacques de, Belgian composer; b. Antwerp, Sept. 19, 1705; d. Brussels, Aug. 16, 1786. He was violinist and assistant conductor at St.-Jacques in Antwerp (1723); in 1729, became music director to the Prince of Thurn and Taxis, at Brussels, Frankfurt, and Regensburg. He went to Brussels in 1744 as first violinist in the chapel of Charles of Lorraine; in 1746–55 was maître de chapelle to Charles of Lorraine.
WORKS: Masses, motets, anthems, and other church music; also symphs., sonatas, etc.
BIBLIOGRAPHY: S. Clercx, *Henri-Jacques de Croes, Compositeur et Maître de Musique du Prince Charles de Lorraine* (Brussels, 1940).

Croft (or **Crofts**), **William,** English organist and composer; b. Nether Ettington, Warwickshire (baptized, Dec. 30), 1678; d. Bath, Aug. 14, 1727 (buried in Westminster Abbey). He was a chorister in the Chapel Royal, under Dr. Blow; became a Gentleman of the Chapel Royal in 1700, and (with J. Clarke) joint organist in 1707; he succeeded Blow as organist of Westminster Abbey, Master of the Children, and Composer of the Chapel Royal (1708).
WORKS: *Musica sacra,* numerous anthems *a* 2–8, and a burial service in score (1724; in 2 vols.; the first English work of church music engraved in score on plates); *Musicus apparatus academicus* (2 odes written for his degree of Mus.Doc., received from Oxford, 1713); overtures and act tunes for several plays; violin sonatas; flute sonatas; etc. Modern editions include H. Ferguson and C. Hogwood, eds., *William Croft: Complete Harpsichord Works* (London, 1974); R. Platt, ed., *William Croft: Complete Organ Works* (London, 1976–77).
BIBLIOGRAPHY: F.G.E., "Dr. William Crofts," *Musical Times* (Sept. 1900); A. R. Carpenter, "William Croft's Church Music," *Musical Times* (March 1971).

Crooks, Richard Alexander, American tenor; b. Trenton, N.J., June 26, 1900; d. Portola Valley, Calif., Sept. 29, 1972. He studied voice for 5 years with Sydney H. Bourne and also took lessons with Frank La Forge; was a boy soprano soloist in N.Y. churches, later tenor soloist; after his war service, made his debut with the N.Y. Symph. Orch. under Damrosch in 1922; gave concerts in London, Vienna, Munich, Berlin, and in the U.S. (1925–27); made his American debut as Cavaradossi with the Philadelphia Grand Opera Co. (Nov. 27, 1930); debut as Des Grieux at the Metropolitan Opera (Feb. 25, 1933); toured Australia (1936–39); gave concerts from coast to coast in the U.S. and Canada; appeared in recitals, as an orch. soloist, and in festivals.

Crosby, Bing (real name, **Harry Lillis**), popular American singer; b. Tacoma, Wash., May 2, 1901; d. while playing golf at La Moraleja golf course outside Madrid, Oct. 14, 1977. He was a drummer in school bands; intermittently attended classes in law at Gonzaga Univ. in Spokane, Wash.; when he became famous, the school gave him an honorary degree of doctor of music. In 1926 he went to Los Angeles, where he filled engagements as a singer. He made his mark on the radio, and his success grew apace; he used his limited vocal resources to advantage by a cunning projection of deep thoracic undertones. He never deviated from his style of singing—unpretentious, sometimes mock-sentimental, and invariably communicative; he became a glorified crooner. Apart from his appearances in concert and with bands, he also made movies; his series with Bob Hope, beginning with *Road to Morocco,* made in 1942, with their invariable girl companion Dorothy Lamour, became classics of the American cinema. He continued his appearances until the last months of his life. The origin of his nickname is in dispute; it was derived either from the popular comic strip "The Bingville Bugle," or from his habit of popping a wooden gun in school, shouting, "Bing! Bing!" In 1953 he publ. his autobiography under the title *Call Me Lucky.* His brother **Bob Crosby** is a bandleader; Bing Crosby's 4 sons from his first marriage are also crooners.

BIBLIOGRAPHY: Ted Crosby, *The Story of Bing Crosby* (N.Y., 1937; 2nd ed., 1946); Barry Ulanov, *The Incredible Crosby* (N.Y., 1947); Charles Thompson, *Bing* (N.Y., 1976); Gary Crosby, *Going My Own Way,* an anti-paternal account of life with a famous father by a disrespectful son (N.Y., 1983).

Crosby, John, American opera impresario; b. New York, July 12, 1926. He studied violin and piano with his mother. Upon graduating from high school in 1944, he was drafted into the U.S. Army, serving in the infantry as a corporal; he played various instruments in the dance band of his regiment; after the end of the war he played trombone and double bass in dance orchs. He then entered Yale Univ., where he studied composition with Hindemith, receiving his B.A. in music in 1950. In 1951 he took courses in conducting at Columbia Univ. with Rudolph Thomas; later he attended conducting seminars in Maine under Pierre Monteux. In 1956 Crosby persuaded his father, an affluent lawyer, to give him enough money to build an outdoor opera house in Santa Fe, New Mexico. He inaugurated the Santa Fe Festival in the summer of 1957, producing a season of classical and modern operas. The theater burned down in 1967, but Crosby collected enough money to build a new fireproof building for his enterprise, which eventually became known as the Santa Fe Opera. Crosby was able to persuade Stravinsky to conduct a performance of his opera *The Rake's Progress;* Hindemith was engaged to conduct his own opera *Neues vom Tage.* Weather has been an uncertain factor through the Santa Fe seasons, and once or twice a cloudburst forced the postponement of a performance. In 1975 he took over the presidency of Opera America, a cartel coordinating 43 opera companies; in 1976 he became president of the Manhattan School of Music.

BIBLIOGRAPHY: Winthrop Sargeant, "A Miracle in the Desert," *New Yorker* (Aug. 1, 1975).

Cross, Joan, English soprano; b. London, Sept. 7, 1900. She was educated at Trinity College, London. In 1931 she joined Sadler's Wells Opera; also appeared at Covent Garden. Subsequently she helped to found the English Opera Group in London, devoted to performances of new works; sang in several first performances of Benjamin Britten's operas. In 1948 she founded the Opera School (now the National School of Opera), serving as one of its teachers for many years. In 1955 she began to produce opera at Sadler's Wells and Covent Garden.

Cross, Lowell Merlin, American composer and electro-musicologist; b. Kingsville, Texas, June 24, 1938. He studied mathematics and music at Texas Technological College, graduating in 1963; then entered the Univ. of Toronto in Canada, obtaining his M.A. in musicology in 1968; attended classes of Marshall McLuhan in environmental technology there; took a course in electronic music with Myron Schaeffer and Gustav Ciamaga. In 1970 he served as resident programmer for Experiments in Art and Technology at Expo '70 in Osaka, Japan, and guest consultant in electronic music at the National Inst. of Design in Ahmedabad, India; in 1971 he was engaged as artist-in-residence at the Univ. of Iowa's Center for New Performing Arts. Eschewing any preliminary serial experimentation, Cross espoused a cybernetic totality of audiovisual, electronic, and theatrical arts.

WORKS: *4 Random Studies* for Tape (1961); *0.8 Century* for Tape (1962); *Eclectic Music* for Flute and Piano (1964); *Antiphonies* for Tape (1964); *After Long Silence* for Soprano and Quadraphonic Tape (1964); *3 Etudes* for Tape (1965); *Video I* and *Video II* for Variable Media, including Tape, Audio System, Oscilloscope, and Television (1965–68); *Musica Instrumentalis* for Acoustical Stereophonic Instruments, Monochrome and Polychrome Television (1965–68); *Video III* for Television and Phase-derived Audio System (1968); *Reunion* for Electronic Chessboard (constructed by Cross and first demonstrated in Toronto, March 5, 1968, the main opponents in the chess game being John Cage and the painter Marcel Duchamp, who won readily); *Electro-Acustica* for Instruments, Laser Deflection System, Television, and Phase-Derived Audio System (1970–71). The notation of Cross's audiovisual compositions consists of color photographs of television images resulting from the programmed manipulation of sound-producing mechanisms in the acoustical space (see his technical paper *Audio/Video/Laser,* publ. in *Source,* Sacramento, Calif., No. 8, 1970). He compiled a valuable manual, *A Bibliography of Electronic Music* (Toronto, 1967). As a pioneer in astromusicology, he created the selenogeodesic score *Lunar Laser Beam* (broadcast as a salutatory message on Nicolas Slonimsky's 77th birthday, April 27, 1971, purportedly via Leningrad, the subject's birthplace; the Sea of Tranquillity on the moon; and the Ciudad de Nuestra Señora Reina de Los Angeles in California). As director of the Video/Laser Laboratory at the Univ. of Iowa, Cross was responsible for the production of Scriabin's *Prometheus* by the Iowa Univ. Orch., conducted by James Dixon, with color projections coordinated with the "color organ" *(luce)* as prescribed in the score (Iowa City, Sept. 24, 1975).

Cross, Ronald, American musicologist; b. Fort Worth, Texas, Feb. 18, 1929. He studied at Guilmant Organ School in N.Y., at Centenary College of Louisiana, and at N.Y. Univ. (Ph.D., 1961). In 1955 he received a Fulbright fellowship to travel in Italy. In 1959 he was appointed to the faculty of Notre Dame College of Staten Island. In 1968 he joined the faculty of Wagner College in N.Y.; became chairman of the music dept. and director of the Collegium Musicum. He wrote a number of choral pieces; also chamber music; edited the collected works of Matthaeus Pipelare; contributed articles and reviews to musicological journals.

Crosse, Gordon, English composer; b. Bury, Lancashire, Dec. 1, 1937. He studied at Oxford Univ., where he took courses in music history with Egon Wellesz; did postgraduate work in medieval music. In 1962 he went to Rome, where he attended the classes of Goffredo Petrassi at the Santa Cecilia Academy. Returning to England, he taught at Birmingham Univ. (extramurally); in 1969 was appointed to the music dept. of Essex Univ. His absorption in the studies of old music, in combination with an engrossment in modern techniques, determines the character of his own compositions.
WORKS: *Concerto da camera* for Violin and Orch. (Violin Concerto No. 1, 1962; London, Feb. 18, 1968); *Carol* for Flute and Piano (1962); *For the Unfallen* for Tenor, Horn, and Strings (1963; Liverpool, Sept. 17, 1968); *Meet My Folks,* a multi-child presentation for Voices, Instruments, and Adults (1964); Symphs. for Chamber Orch. (Birmingham, Feb. 13, 1965); *Sinfonia Concertante* for Orch. (Cheltenham, July 15, 1965); *Changes,* nocturnal cycle for Soprano, Baritone, Chorus, and Orch. (1965); *Purgatory,* opera after Yeats (Cheltenham, July 7, 1966); *Ceremony* for Cello and Orch. (London, Aug. 4, 1966); *The Grace of Todd,* one-act opera (Aldeburgh, June 7, 1967); *The Demon of Adachigahara* for Speaker, Adolescent Chorus, Mime, and Instruments (1968); Concerto for Chamber Orch. (Budapest, July 3, 1968); Violin Concerto No. 2 (Oxford, Jan. 29, 1970); *The History of the Flood* for Children's Voices and Harp (London, Dec. 6, 1970); *Some Marches on a Ground* for Orch. (1970); *Memories of Morning: Night,* monodrama for Soprano and Orch. (London, Dec. 8, 1971); *Wheel of the World,* "entertainment" based on Chaucer's *Canterbury Tales,* for Actors, Children's Chorus, Mixed Chorus, and Orch. (Aldeburgh Festival, June 5, 1972); *Ariadne* for Solo Oboe and 12 Players (Cheltenham Festival, July 11, 1972); *The Story of Vasco,* opera (London, March 13, 1974); *Celebration* for Chorus (London, Sept. 16, 1974); *Holly from the Bongs,* opera (Manchester, Dec. 9, 1974); *Potter Thompson,* children's opera (London, Jan. 9, 1975); Symph. No. 2 (London, May 27, 1975); *Epiphany Variations: Double Variations for Orchestra* (N.Y., March 18, 1976); *Playground* for Orch. (1977; Manchester, March 2, 1978); *Wildboy* for Clarinet and Ensemble (1977; version for Full Orch., 1980); *Dreamsongs* for Chamber Orch. (1978); Cello Concerto (1979); String Quartet (1980); sacred and secular choruses.

Crossley, Ada (Jessica), Australian mezzo-soprano; b. Tarraville, Gippsland, March 3, 1874; d. London, Oct. 17, 1929. She was a pupil of Fanny Simonson (voice) in Melbourne; having sung in several churches, she made her concert debut with the Melbourne Phil. Society in 1892; came to London in 1894, studied with Santley, and later with Mme. Marchesi in Paris; made her London debut at Queen's Hall on May 18, 1895; her success was so emphatic that she sang by command 5 times before Queen Victoria within the next 2 years; appeared as a soloist at all important English festivals; her tour of Australia in 1904 was a succession of triumphs; also made successful tours of the U.S. and South Africa.

Crossley, Paul, English pianist; b. Dewsbury, Yorkshire, May 17, 1944. He attended Oxford Univ. as an organ scholar at Mansfield College there; also studied piano with Fanny Waterman in Leeds. In 1967 he received a scholarship from the French government to continue his studies with Messiaen and Yvonne Loriod. In 1968 he made his first major tour, garnering praise in England and on the Continent as an interpreter of the Romantic repertoire.

Crossley-Holland, Peter, English ethnomusicologist and composer; b. London, Jan. 28, 1916. He studied physiology at St. John's College, Oxford (B.A., 1936; M.A., 1941); then took courses in composition with Ireland, Seiber, and Julius Harrison at the Royal College of Music in London (B.Mus., 1943); subsequently pursued postgraduate work in Indian music at the London School of Oriental and African Studies. From 1943 to 1945 he was regional director of the British Arts Council; in 1948–63 was engaged in the music division of the BBC; then became assistant director of the Inst. of Comparative Music Studies and Documentation in Berlin. In 1969 he joined the faculty at the Univ. of Calif. in Los Angeles; became a prof. there in 1972; retired in 1984. In 1965 he became editor of the *Journal of the International Folk Music Council.* As an ethnomusicologist, he has concentrated mostly on Celtic, Tibetan, and native American music. He edited *Music in Wales* (London, 1948) and *Artistic Values in Traditional Music* (Berlin, 1966); also publ. *Music: A Report on Musical Life in England* (London, 1949). He composed songs; also pieces for chorus and for recorders.

Crotch, William, eminent English composer; b. Norwich, July 5, 1775; d. Taunton, Dec. 29, 1847. His extraordinary precocity may be measured by the well-authenticated statement (Burney's paper, "Account of an Infant Musician," in the *Philosophical Transactions* of 1779) that when 2 and a half years old he played on a small organ built by his father, a master carpenter. In 1779, he was brought to London, and played in public. At the age of 11 he became assistant to Dr. Randall, organist of Trinity and King's colleges at Cambridge; at 14, he composed an oratorio, *The Captivity of Judah* (Cambridge, June 4, 1789); he then studied for the ministry (1788–90); returning to music, he was organist of Christ Church, Oxford; graduated from Oxford with a Mus.Bac. in 1794; received a Mus.Doc. in 1799. In 1797 he succeeded Hayes as prof. of music at the Univ. and as organist of St. John's College. Crotch lectured in the Music School (1800–4), and in the Royal Institution in London (1804, 1805, 1807, and again from 1820); was principal of the new Royal Academy of Music from 1822 to 1832.
WORKS: 2 oratorios: *Palestine* (London, April 21, 1812) and *The Captivity of Judah* (Oxford, June 10,

1834; a different work from his juvenile oratorio of the same name); 10 anthems (1798); 3 organ concertos; piano sonatas; an ode, *Mona on Snowdown calls;* a glee, *Nymph, with thee;* a motet, *Methinks I hear the full celestial choir* (these last 3 were very popular); other odes; other glees, fugues; he also wrote *Elements of Musical Composition* (London, 1812; reprint, 1833; 2nd ed., 1856); *Practical Thorough-bass;* etc. A complete list of his compositions appeared in *Musical News* (April 17 and 24, 1897). The Crotch Society of London promotes research and performances.

BIBLIOGRAPHY: J. Rennert, *William Crotch* (London, 1975).

Crouch, Frederick Nicholls, English conductor and composer; b. London, July 31, 1808; d. Portland, Maine, Aug. 18, 1896. He studied with Bochsa (cello), and entered the Royal Academy of Music in 1822 (teachers: Crotch, Attwood, Howes, Lindley, and Crivelli). At the age of 9 he was a cellist in the Royal Coburg Theater; played in Queen Adelaide's private band till 1832; was a teacher and singer in Plymouth, and cellist in various theaters. He went to N.Y. in 1849; was in Philadelphia in 1856 as conductor of Mrs. Rush's Saturday Concerts; served in the Confederate Army, and settled in Baltimore as a singing teacher. Cora Pearl, the famous Parisian courtesan of the Second Empire, was his daughter. He composed 2 operas; many collections of songs, some original (including the well-known *Kathleen Mavourneen*).

Crowest, Frederick J., English writer on music; b. London, Nov. 30, 1850; d. Edgbaston, June 14, 1927. He joined the editorial staff of Cassell, Petter & Galpin in 1886; held various editorial positions; in 1901 was appointed general manager and editor of Walter Scott Publishing Co., Ltd.; retired in 1917.

WRITINGS: *The Great Tone Poets* (1874); *Book of Musical Anecdote* (1878; 2 vols.; revised ed., 1902, as *Musicians' Wit, Humour and Anecdote*); *Phases of Musical England* (1881); *Musical History and Biography in the Form of Question and Answer* (1883); *Advice to Singers* (many eds.); *Musical Groundwork;* "Cherubini" (in Great Musicians Series); *Dictionary of British Musicians* (1895); *The Story of British Music* (vol. I, 1895); *Catechism of Musical History* (many eds.); *Story of Music* (1902; in America as *Story of the Art of Music*); *Verdi: Man and Musician* (1897); *Beethoven* (1899).

Crozier, Catharine, American organist; b. Hobart, Okla., Jan. 18, 1914. She studied organ at the Eastman School of Music, where she received a master's degree in music; then taught organ there (1938–53); became head of the organ dept. in 1953. She subsequently was prof. of organ at Rollins College, Winter Park, Fla. (1955–69). She was married to the organist and musicologist **Harold Gleason.**

Crüger, Johann, noted German composer of church music; b. Grossbreesen, near Guben, April 9, 1598; d. Berlin, Feb. 23, 1662. A student of divinity at Wittenberg in 1620, he had received thorough musical training at Regensburg under Paulus Homberger. He then traveled in Austria and Hungary; spent some time in Bohemia and Saxony before settling in Berlin, where he was cantor at the Nicolaikirche from 1622 until his death. His fame rests on the composition of many fine chorales (*Jesu, meine Freude; Jesu, meine Zuversicht; Nun danket alle Gott;* etc.), which were originally publ. in the collection *Praxis pietatis melica* (Berlin, 1644; reprinted in 45 eds. before 1736). In addition, he publ. the following collections: *Neues vollkömmliches Gesangbuch Augsburgischer Konfession . . .* (1640); *Geistliche Kirchenmelodeyen . . .* (1649); *Dr. M. Luthers wie auch andrer gottseliger christlicher Leute Geistliche Lieder und Psalmen* (1657); *Psalmodia sacra . . .* (1658); the valuable theoretical works *Synopsis musica* (1630; enlarged 1634), *Praecepta musicae figuralis* (1625), and *Quaestiones musicae practicae* (1650).

BIBLIOGRAPHY: E.C.G. Langbecker, *J. Crügers Choral-Melodien* (Berlin, 1835); E. Fischer-Krückeberg's articles: "Johann Crüger als Musiktheoretiker," *Zeitschrift für Musikwissenschaft,* XII; "Johann Crügers Choralbearbeitungen," ibid., XIV; "Johann Crüger und das Kirchenlied des 17. Jahrhundert," *Monatsschrift für Gottesdienst und kirchliche Kunst,* XXXIV, 2; Otto Brodde, *Johann Crüger, Sein Weg und sein Werk* (Leipzig, 1936); J. Hoffmeister, *Der Kantor zu St. Nicolai: Beschreibung des Lebens von Johann Crüger* (Berlin, 1964).

Crumb, George (Henry Jr.), distinguished and innovative American composer; b. Charleston, W.Va., Oct. 24, 1929. He was brought up in a musical environment; his father played the clarinet and his mother was a cellist; he studied music at home; began composing while in school, and had some of his pieces performed by the Charleston Symph. Orch. He then took courses in composition at Mason College in Charleston (B.M., 1950); later enrolled at the Univ. of Illinois (M.M., 1952) and continued his studies in composition with Ross Lee Finney at the Univ. of Michigan (D.M.A., 1959); in 1955 he received a Fulbright fellowship for travel to Germany, where he studied with Boris Blacher at the Berlin Hochschule für Musik. He further received grants from the Rockefeller (1964), Koussevitzky (1965), and Coolidge (1970) foundations; in 1967 held a Guggenheim fellowship, and also was given the National Inst. of Arts and Letters Award. In 1968 he was awarded the Pulitzer Prize in music for his *Echoes of Time and the River.* Parallel to working on his compositions, he was active as a music teacher. From 1959 to 1964 he taught piano and occasional classes in composition at the Univ. of Colorado at Boulder; in 1965 he joined the music dept. of the Univ. of Pa.; in 1983 he was named Annenberg Prof. of the Humanities there. In his music, Crumb is a universalist. Nothing in the realm of sound is alien to him; no method of composition is unsuited to his artistic purposes; accordingly, his music can sing as sweetly as the proverbial nightingale, and it can be as rough, rude, and crude as a primitive man of the mountains. The vocal parts especially demand extraordinary skills of lungs, lips, tongue, and larynx to produce such sound effects as percussive tongue clicks, explosive shrieks, hissing, whistling, whispering, and sudden shouting of verbal irrelevancies, interspersed with portentous syllabification, disparate phonemes, and rhetorical logorrhea. In startling contrast, Crumb injects into his sonorous kaleidoscope citations from popular works, such as the middle section of Chopin's *Fantaisie-Impromptu,* Ravel's *Bolero,* or some other "objet trouvé," a procedure first introduced facetiously by Erik Satie. In his instrumentation, Crumb is no less unconventional. Among the unusual effects in his scores is instructing the percussion player to immerse the loudly sounding gong into a tub of water, having an electric guitar played with glass rods over the frets, or telling wind instrumentalists to blow soundlessly through their tubes. Spatial distribution also plays a role: instrumentalists and singers are assigned their reciprocal locations on the podium or in the hall. All this is, of course, but an illustrative décor; the music is of the essence. Like most composers who began their work around the middle of the 20th century, Crumb adopted the Schoenbergian idiom, seasoned with pointillistic devices. After these preliminaries, he wrote his unmistakably individual *Madrigals,* to words by the martyred poet Federico García Lorca, scored for voice and instrumental groups. There followed the most extraordinary work, *Ancient Voices of Children,* performed for the first time at a chamber music festival in Washington, D.C., on Oct. 31, 1970; the text is again by Lorca; a female singer intones into the space under the lid of an amplified grand piano; a boy's voice responds in anguish; the accompaniment is supplied by an orch. group and an assortment of exotic percussion instruments, such as Tibetan prayer stones, Japanese temple bells, a musical saw, and a toy piano. A remarkable group of 4 pieces, entitled *Makrokosmos,* calls for unusual effects; in one of these, the pianist is ordered to shout at specified points of time. Crumb's most grandiose creation is *Star-Child,* representing, in his imaginative scheme, a progression from tenebrous despair to the exaltation of luminous joy. The score calls for a huge orch., which includes 2 children's choruses and 8 percussion players performing on all kinds of utensils, such as pot lids, and also iron chains and metal sheets, as well as ordinary drums; it had its first performance under the direction of Pierre Boulez with the N.Y. Phil. on May 5, 1977.

WORKS: Sonata for Solo Cello (1955); *Variazioni* for Orch. (1959; Cincinnati, May 8, 1965); *5 Pieces for Piano* (1962); *Night Music I* for Soprano, Piano or Celesta, and Percussion, to verses by Federico García Lorca (1963; Paris, Jan. 30, 1964); *4 Nocturnes (Night Music II)* for Violin and Piano (1963; Buffalo, N.Y., Feb. 3, 1965); *Madrigals, Book I* for Soprano, Contrabass, and Vibraphone, to a text by García Lorca (1965; Philadelphia, Feb. 18, 1966); *Madrigals, Book II* for Soprano, Flute, and Percussion, to a text by García Lorca (1965; Washington, D.C., March 11, 1966); *11 Echoes of Autumn, 1965*

(Echoes I) for Violin, Alto Flute, Clarinet, and Piano (Brunswick, Maine, Aug. 10, 1966); *Echoes of Time and the River (Echoes II: 4 Processionals for Orchestra)* (Chicago, May 26, 1967); *Songs, Drones, and Refrains of Death* for Baritone, Electric Guitar, Electric Contrabass, Amplified Piano (and Amplified Harpsichord), and 2 Percussionists, to a text by García Lorca (1968; Iowa City, Iowa, March 29, 1969); *Madrigals, Book III* for Soprano, Harp, and One Percussion Player, to a text by García Lorca (1969; Seattle, March 6, 1970); *Madrigals, Book IV* for Soprano, Flute, Harp, Contrabass, and One Percussion Player, to a text by García Lorca (1969; Seattle, March 6, 1970); *Night of the 4 Moons* for Alto, Alto Flute, Banjo, Electric Cello, and One Percussion Player, to a text by García Lorca (Washington, Pa., Nov. 6, 1969); *Black Angels (13 Images from the Dark Land: Images I)* for Electric String Quartet (Ann Arbor, Mich., Oct. 23, 1970); *Ancient Voices of Children* for Soprano, Boy Soprano, Oboe, Mandolin, Harp, Electric Piano (and Toy Piano), and 3 Percussion Players, to a text by García Lorca (Washington, D.C., Oct. 31, 1970); *Lux aeterna for 5 Masked Players* for Soprano, Bass Flute (and Soprano Recorder), Sitar, and 2 Percussion Players (1971; Richmond, Va., Jan. 16, 1972); *Vox balaene (Voice of the Whale) for 3 Masked Players* for Electric Flute, Electric Cello, and Amplified Piano (1971; Washington, D.C., March 17, 1972); *Makrokosmos, Volume I (12 Fantasy-Pieces after the Zodiac for Amplified Piano)* (1972; Colorado Springs, Feb. 8, 1973); *Makrokosmos, Volume II (12 Fantasy-Pieces after the Zodiac for Amplified Piano)* (1973; N.Y., Nov. 12, 1974); *Music for a Summer Evening (Makrokosmos III)* for 2 Amplified Pianos and 2 Percussion Players (Swarthmore, Pa., March 30, 1974); *Dream Sequence (Images II)* for Violin, Cello, Piano, One Percussion Player, and 2 Offstage Musicians playing Glass Harmonica (1976); *Star-Child,* a parable for Soprano, Antiphonal Children's Voices, Male Speaking Choir, Bell Ringers, and Large Orch., demanding the coordinating abilities of 4 conductors (N.Y. Phil. May 5, 1977, under the general direction of Pierre Boulez); *Celestial Mechanics (Makrokosmos IV),* cosmic dances for Amplified Piano, 4-hands (N.Y., Nov. 18, 1979); *Apparitions,* elegiac songs and vocalises for Soprano and Amplified Piano, to a text by Walt Whitman (1979; N.Y., Jan. 13, 1981); *A Little Suite for Christmas, A.D. 1979* for Piano (Washington, D.C., Dec. 14, 1980); *Gnomic Variations* for Piano (1981); *Pastoral Drone* for Organ (1982); *Processional* for Piano (1983); *A Haunted Landscape* for Orch. (N.Y. Phil., June 7, 1984).

BIBLIOGRAPHY: David Ewen, *American Composers* (N.Y., 1982); D. Cope, *George Crumb: A Biography* (N.Y., 1984; with annotated list of works compiled by D. Gillespie).

Crusell, Bernhard Henrik, noted Finnish clarinetist and composer; b. Uusikaupunki, near Turku, Oct, 15, 1775; d. Stockholm, July 28, 1838. He took clarinet lessons from a member of the military band at Svaeborg Castle; then moved to Stockholm in 1791; there he had a chance to study with the renowned

German music scholar and composer Abbé Vogler, who was a frequent visitor to Sweden. While improving his general knowledge of music, Crusell continued to play the clarinet; in 1798 he went to Berlin to study with Franz Tausch. In 1803 he went to Paris, where he studied composition with Berton and Gossec. In his instrumental music Crusell followed the tradition of Gluck; his vocal works reveal Nordic traits. In Sweden he acted as translator of opera librettos for Stockholm productions; among these were Beethoven's *Fidelio,* Rossini's *The Barber of Seville,* Meyerbeer's *Robert le Diable,* and Auber's *La Muette de Portici.* The Swedish Academy awarded him its gold medal shortly before his death.

WORKS: 3 clarinet concertos (1811, 1818, 1828); *Concertante* for Horn, Bassoon, Clarinet, and Orch. (1816); *Introduction et air suédois* for Clarinet and Orch. (1830); *Concertino* for Bassoon and Orch. Chamber Music: 3 quartets for Clarinet and Strings (1811, 1817, 1823); 3 clarinet duos (1821); *Divertimento* for Oboe and Strings (1823); Vocal Music: 37 songs for 4-part Chorus; *Den lilla slavinnan* (*The Little Slave Girl;* Stockholm, Feb. 18, 1824).

Cruz, Ivo, Portuguese conductor and composer; b. Corumbá, Brazil, May 19, 1901. He was taken to Portugal as a child; studied law at Lisbon Univ. (1919–24); then went to Munich, where he studied composition and conducting with Richard Mors and August Reuss (1925–30); took courses in musicology at Munich Univ.; returned to Portugal in 1931; organized a choral society in Lisbon; founded the Lisbon Phil. Orch. in 1937 and was its conductor until 1971; from 1938 to 1971 served as director of the National Cons. of Music in Lisbon. His music cultivates Portuguese themes.

WORKS: Ballet, *Pastoral (Poemas de amor e saudade),* with optional Female Chorus (1942); orch. suite, *Nocturnos da Lusitania* (1928); 2 "Portuguese" piano concertos, subtitled "Symbolic Poems": No. 1, *Coimbra* (1945), and No. 2, *Lisboa* (1946); *Sinfonia de Amadis* (1952); *Idilio de Miraflores* for Orch. (1952); *Sinfonia de Quelez* (1964); song cycles with Orch.: *Triptico* (1941) and *Os amores do poeta* (1942); Violin Sonata (1922). For Piano: *Aguarelas* (1921); *Homenagens (Homages,* 1955); *Caleidoscopio* (1957). Songs: *Cancões perdidas* (1923); *Baladas lunaticas* (1944); *Cancões profanes* (1968); *Cancões sentimentais* (1972).

Cruz-Romo, Gilda, Mexican soprano; b. Guadalajara, Feb. 12, 1940. She studied at the Cons. of Mexico; made her debut there in 1962. On May 8, 1970, she appeared at the Metropolitan Opera in N.Y. as Maddalena in *Andrea Chénier;* continued to sing there in subsequent seasons; also sang in Chicago, Houston, Dallas, etc. In Europe, she appeared in London, Milan, Moscow, Paris, and Vienna.

Crzellitzer, Franz, German-born Israeli composer; b. Berlin-Charlottenburg, Nov. 1, 1905. In 1934 he settled in Tel Aviv.

WORKS: *Charaktermarsch* for Orch. (1939); 2 unnumbered symph. (1940–41, 1968–70); a ballet pantomime, *Pied Piper of Hamelin* (1944–46); *Improvisation* for Orch. (1951); 3 *Suites* for String Orch. (1952, 1968–74, 1974); 2 *Symphonic Fantasies* for Orch. (1958, 1959); *Fantasy* for Violin and Orch. (1960); *Fantasy* for Cello and Orch. (1962); 2-piano Concerto (1966); Trumpet Concerto (1967); Viola Concerto (1967); *Capriccio* for Piano and Chamber Orch. (1970); Concertino for Clarinet and String Orch. (1971); *Concert Piece* for Trombone and Orch. (1971); Sinfonietta (1972); *Concert Piece* for Horn, Clarinet, and Strings (1972); *Die Wüste (The Desert),* passacaglia for Orch. (1974); Concertino for Bassoon and Strings (1975); Concertino for Flute and Strings (1975); Concertino for Violin and Strings (1976); *Concert Piece* for Organ and Orch. (1976); *Concert Piece* for Orch. (1977); 2 violin sonatas (1948); Piano Quintet (1949); 2 string quartets (1954, 1963); Oboe Quartet (1955); Wind Quintet (1966); 2 piano trios (1968, 1971); Cello Sonata (1971); Flute Sonata (1972); Trio for Horn, Violin, and Piano (1973); Viola Sonata (1974); Brass Quintet (1975); *5 Preludes* for Piano (1947); *7 Preludes* for Piano (1968–69); *Theme and Variations* for Piano (1973); *Toccata and 2 Etudes* for Piano (1976); *Passacaglia* for Organ (1972).

Csiky, Boldizsár, Rumanian composer; b. Tîrgu-Mureş, Oct. 3, 1937. He studied at the Tîrgu-Mureş Music College (1953–55) and with Demian, Toduţa, and Jodál at the Cons. in Cluj (1956–61); taught at Tîrgu-Mureş in 1961–68. In his music he applies dissonant sonorism, striving for coloristic effects.

WORKS: Chamber opera, *Görog Ilona* (1966); *Octombrie,* cantata (1960); *Purtătorii de Făclii,* cantata (1961); Overture (1960); Sinfonia (1960); *Cîntec de Vitejie* for Chamber Orch. (1971); *Recitativo, Adagio and Fugue* for Flute and Piano (1958); 2 piano sonatas (1960, 1964); choruses; songs.

Ctesibius, inventor of the hydraulis. He flourished between 246 and 221 B.C., and is known in literature as Ctesibius of Alexandria. The weight of evidence collected by H.G. Farmer tends to demonstrate that the first hydraulis was indeed constructed by Ctesibius.

BIBLIOGRAPHY: P. Tannery, "Athénée sur Ctesibius et l'hydraulis," *Revue des Etudes Grecques* (1896); H.G. Farmer, *The Organ of the Ancients* (London, 1931).

Cubiles, José, Spanish pianist and conductor; b. Cadiz, May 15, 1894; d. Madrid, April, 1971. He studied in Paris with Diémer; gave concerts in Europe; returning to Spain, he devoted himself mainly to teaching.

Cuclin, Dimitri, prolific Rumanian composer; b. Galatz, April 5, 1885; d. Bucharest, Feb. 7, 1978. He studied with Castaldi in Bucharest; in 1907 went to Paris, where he took courses with Vincent d'Indy at the Schola Cantorum. Returning to Rumania, he taught violin at the Bucharest Cons. (1918–22). From 1924 to 1930 he was in America as violin teacher at the Brooklyn College of Music; in 1930 he returned to Rumania, devoting himself mainly to teaching and composition; he continued to write symph. and other music well into his 90s.

WORKS: 20 symphs.: No. 1 (1910); No. 2, subtitled *Triumph of the People's Union* (1938); No. 3 (1942); No. 4 (1944); No. 5, with Soloists and Chorus (1947); No. 6 (1948); No. 7 (1948); No. 8 (1948); No. 9 (1949); No. 10, with Chorus (1949); No. 11 (1950); No. 12, with Soloists and Chorus (1951); No. 13 (1951); No. 14 (1952); No. 15 (1954); No. 16, subtitled *Triumph of Peace* (1959); No. 17 (1965); No. 18 (1967); No. 19 (1971); No. 20 (1972); 5 operas: *Soria* (1911), *Trian si dochia* (1921), *Agamemnon* (1922), *Bellérophon* (1924), and *Meleagridele;* Violin Concerto (1920); Piano Concerto (1939); *Rumanian Dances* for Orch. (1961); Clarinet Concerto (1968); 3 string quartets (1914, 1948, 1949) and numerous other chamber works; piano pieces; sacred choruses; songs. A detailed list of Cuclin's works and his theoretical publications, as well as an extensive bibliography, is contained in Viorel Cosma's *Muzicieni romani* (Bucharest, 1970).

Cudworth, Charles, British librarian and musicologist; b. Cambridge, Oct. 30, 1908; d. there, Dec. 26, 1977. He served at the Music Division of the Library of Cambridge Univ. from 1943 on; in 1946–73 was curator of the Pendlebury Library of Music there; in 1965 was elected a Fellow of the Univ. College at Cambridge; in 1968 was a visiting prof. at the Univ. of Southern Calif., Los Angeles. His specialty was the music of the 18th century. He publ. *Thematic Index of English Eighteenth Century Overtures and Symphonies* (London, 1953) and *Handel* (London, 1972); contributed numerous valuable articles to British and American music journals.

BIBLIOGRAPHY: C. Hogwood and R. Luckett, eds., *Music in Eighteenth-century England: Essays in Memory of Charles Cudworth* (Cambridge, 1983).

Cuénod, Hugues (-Adhémar), Swiss tenor; b. Corseaux-sur-Vevey, June 26, 1902. He studied voice in Lausanne, Basel, Geneva, and Vienna. After a long sojourn in Paris, he toured the U.S. (1937–39); during the war he taught at the Geneva Cons. (1940–46); then resumed his career as an opera singer; he appeared at La Scala in Milan in 1951, and at Covent Garden in London in 1954. Then he turned almost exclusively to Baroque music; founded the Ensemble Baroque in Lausanne; eventually settled in Vevey.

Cugat, Xavier, Spanish-American bandleader; b. Barcelona, Jan. 1, 1900. As a youth he came to the U.S.; studied violin with Franz Kneisel; played at concerts with Caruso; became a cartoonist for the *Los Angeles Times.* In 1928 he organized a dance orch.; led a combo, with his niece, the actress Margo, as a dancer. In 1933 he was engaged as bandleader of the Hotel Astoria in N.Y.; played numerous engagements at hotels and nightclubs, achieving popularity by his astute arrangements of Latin American dances; invented a congat (a cross breed

of bongos and a conga). He was married to the singers **Carmen Castillo** (1929–45), **Lorraine Allen** (1946–50), and **Abbe Lane** (1952–63). He publ. an autobiography, *The Rumba Is My Life* (N.Y., 1949).

Cugley, Ian, Australian composer; b. Melbourne, June 22, 1945. He studied with Peter Sculthorpe and Peter Maxwell Davies at the Univ. of Sydney (1963–66); in 1967 was appointed to the faculty of the Univ. of Tasmania; also was percussionist in the Tasmanian Symph. Orch.; organized a contemporary music ensemble, Spectrum. His music represents a curious polarization of techniques, in which starkly primitive melorhythms enter a tangential relationship with total serialism.

WORKS: Variations for Flute, Oboe, and Horn (1963); *Adagio* for 4 Horns or String Quartet (1964); *Pan, the Lake* for Flute, Horn, Cello, Strings, and Percussion, including 8 Indonesian Kulintang Gongs (1965); Prelude for Orch. (1965); Sonata for Flute, Viola, and Guitar or Harp (1966); *Canticle of All Created Things* for Chorus, Harp, and Percussion (1966); *Canticle II (In Cenerem Reverteris)* for Soli, Chorus, and Orch. (1967); *5 Variants* for String Orch. (1968); *3 Pieces* for Chamber Orch. (1968); *The 6 Days of Creation,* cantata (1969); *Chamber Symphony* for 11 Wind Instruments (1971); *Aquarelles* for Piano (1972); *Sonata Movement* for Violin and Piano (1972); Violin Concerto (1973); numerous works for school orchs.; 3 electronic studies (1967–72); sacred music.

Cui, César, Russian composer, one of "The Five"; b. Vilna, Jan. 18, 1835; d. Petrograd, March 26, 1918. He was the son of a soldier in Napoleon's army who remained in Russia, married a Lithuanian noblewoman, and settled as a teacher of French in Vilna. Cui learned musical notation by copying Chopin's mazurkas and various Italian operas; then tried his hand at composition on his own. In 1849 he took lessons with Moniuszko, who was in Vilna at the time. In 1850 he went to St. Petersburg, where he entered the Engineering School in 1851 and later the Academy of Military Engineering (1855). After graduation in 1857 he became a topographer and later an expert in fortification. He participated in the Russo-Turkish War of 1877; in 1878 he became a prof. at the Engineering School and was tutor in military fortification to Czar Nicholas II. In 1856 Cui met Balakirev, who helped him master the technique of composition. In 1858 he married Malvina Bamberg; for her he wrote a scherzo on the theme *BABEG* (for the letters in her name) and *CC* (his own initials). In 1864 he began writing music criticism in the St. Petersburg *Vedomosti* and later in other newspapers, continuing as music critic until 1900. Cui's musical tastes were conditioned by his early admiration for Schumann; he opposed Wagner, against whom he wrote vitriolic articles; he attacked Strauss and Reger with even greater violence. He was an ardent propagandist of Glinka and the Russian national school, but was somewhat critical toward Tchaikovsky. He publ. the first comprehensive book on Russian music, *Musique en*

Russie (Paris, 1880). Cui was grouped with Rimsky-Korsakov, Mussorgsky, Borodin, and Balakirev as one of the "Mighty Five"; the adjective in his case, however, is not very appropriate, for his music lacks grandeur; he was at his best in delicate miniatures, e.g., *Orientale*, from the suite *Kaleidoscope*, op. 50.

WORKS: 6 operas produced in St. Petersburg: *The Mandarin's Son* (1859; Dec. 19, 1878); *The Prisoner of the Caucasus* (1857–58; 1859; rewritten 1881; produced Feb. 16, 1883); *William Ratcliff* (Feb. 26, 1869); *Angelo* (Feb. 13, 1876); *The Saracen* (Nov. 14, 1899); *The Captain's Daughter* (1907–9; Feb. 27, 1911). Other operas: *Le Flibustier* (Opéra-Comique, Paris, Jan. 22, 1894); *Mam'zelle Fifi* (Moscow, Nov. 16, 1903); *Matteo Falcone* (Moscow, Dec. 27, 1907). *A Feast in Time of Plague*, written originally as a dramatic cantata, was produced as a one-act opera (Moscow, Nov. 23, 1901). Children's operas: *The Snow Giant; Little Red Ridinghood; Puss in Boots; Little Ivan the Fool.* Orch. works: *Tarantella* (1859); *Marche solennelle* (1881); *Suite miniature* (1882); *Suite concertante* for Violin, and Orch. or Piano (1884); *2 morceaux* for Cello, and Orch. or Piano (1886); Suite No. 2 (1887); Suite No. 4, *A Argenteau* (1887); Suite No. 3, *In modo populari;* (1890); 3 Scherzos (op. 82; 1910). Chamber music: 3 string quartets (c. 1890, 1907, 1913); *5 Little Duets* for Flute and Violin; violin pieces: *2 Miniatures;* Violin Sonata; *Petite Suite; 12 Miniatures* (op. 20); *Kaleidoscope*, 24 numbers; *6 Bagatelles* (op. 51); many songs; piano pieces; choruses. Cui contributed a number to a set of variations on "Chopsticks" (with Borodin, Liadov, and Rimsky-Korsakov). In 1914–16 Cui completed Mussorgsky's opera *The Fair at Sorotchinsk.* A vol. of his *Selected Articles* (1864–1917) was publ. in Leningrad in 1953.

BIBLIOGRAPHY: Louise Mercy-Argenteau, *César Cui, Esquisse critique* (Paris, 1888); N. Findeisen, "C.A. Cui," *Russian Musical Gazette* (1894); A. Koptyayev, "César Cui as a Composer for the Pianoforte," ibid., (1895); P. Weimarn, *César Cui as a Songwriter* (St. Petersburg, 1896); *Musical Festival in Honor of C.A. Cui*, a symposium (St. Petersburg, 1910); G. Abraham, *Studies in Russian Music* (N.Y. and London, 1935); M.D. Calvocoressi and G. Abraham, *Masters of Russian Music* (N.Y., 1936); M. Smirnov, *The Piano Works of Composers Comprising "The Five"* (Moscow, 1971); E. Guglielmi, "César Cui e l'Ottocento musicale russo," *Chigiane* XXV/5 (1968). See also the biographical note in the Appendix to Cui's *Musique en Russie* (1880).

Culbertson, Alexander (Sascha), violinist; b. Bessarabia, Aug. 10, 1894; d. New York, April 16, 1944. He received his first instruction on the violin from Zuckovsky, and at the age of 9 entered the Rostov Cons.; was a pupil of Sevčik in Prague (1905–8); made his debut at Vienna (1908); toured Europe with extraordinary success (1908–14); joined the U.S. Army (1918); had his debut in the U.S. in 1919; gave concerts throughout the U.S. (1919–27); returned to Europe, residing in Paris as a performer and teacher (1927–37); finally settled in N.Y. as a teacher.

Culp, Julia, Dutch contralto; b. Groningen, Oct. 6, 1880; d. Amsterdam, Oct. 13, 1970. She first studied violin as a child; then became a voice pupil of Cornelia van Zanten at the Amsterdam Cons. (1897), and later of Etelka Gerster in Berlin; made her formal debut in Magdeburg in 1901; her tours of Germany, Austria, the Netherlands, France, Spain and Russia were highly successful from an artistic standpoint, establishing her as one of the finest singers of German lieder. Her American debut took place in N.Y. on Jan. 10, 1913; for many years, she visited the U.S. every season. In private life Mme. Culp was the wife of Erich Merten; after his death in 1919 she married an Austrian industrialist, Willy Ginzkey; lived in Czechoslovakia; after his death (1934) she returned to Amsterdam.

Culshaw, John, English recording producer; b. London, May 28, 1924; d. there, April 27, 1980. He studied music while serving in the British army. From 1954 to 1967 he was manager and chief producer with the Decca Recording Co.; from 1967 to 1975 he held the same post with the BBC. He was awarded the rank of Officer of the Order of the British Empire in 1966. He made a mark in the recording industry by introducing the stereo-reproduction process, which created a three-dimensional effect. His principal achievement was the stereophonic recording of the entire *Ring of the Nibelung*, issued by the Decca Record Co. under the direction of Sir Georg Solti. Culshaw related the background of this undertaking in his books *Ring Resounding* (London, 1967) and *Reflections on Wagner's Ring* (London, 1976). His other publications are *Sergei Rachmaninoff* (London, 1949) and *A Century of Music* (London, 1952). He also publ. an autobiography, *Odyssey of a Recording Pioneer: Putting the Record Straight* (N.Y., 1981; posthumous).

Culwick, James C., English organist and composer; b. W. Bromwich, Staffordshire, April 28, 1845; d. Dublin, Oct. 5, 1907. He was a pupil of T. Bedsmore; assistant organist at Lichfield Cathedral and organist at various churches until 1881, when he was appointed to the Chapel Royal at Dublin, where he remained till his death; also was a prof. of piano and theory at Alexandra College, and conductor of the Harmonic Society and Orpheus; received a Mus.Doc. *(honoris causa)* from Dublin Univ. in 1893. He wrote a dramatic cantata, *The Legend of Stauffenberg* (1890); piano pieces (suite, ballade, sonatina, etc.); several anthems and church services.

WRITINGS: *Rudiments of Music* (1880; 2nd ed., 1882); *The Study of Music and Its Place in General Education* (1882); *The Works of Sir R. Stewart* (1902).

Cumberland, Gerald (real name, **C.F. Kenyon**), English critic and writer; b. Eccles, May 7, 1881; d. Southsea, June 14, 1926. He was music critic of the

Manchester Courier (1909–12), the *Daily Citizen* (1921–25), and of various American papers; publ. books and pamphlets: *How to Memorize Music; Set Down in Malice* (1918); *Written in Friendship* (1923); *Imaginary Conversations with Great Composers* (1924).

Cumberworth, Starling, American composer; b. Remson Corners, Ohio, July 25, 1915. He studied at the Cleveland Inst. of Music with Herbert Elwell and Arthur Shepherd; then at Yale Univ. with Quincy Porter and Paul Hindemith (M.M., 1948) and at the Eastman School of Music in Rochester, N.Y., with Bernard Rogers and Howard Hanson (Ph.D., 1956). In 1956 he joined the staff of the Cleveland Music School Settlement, remaining there until 1971. Among his works are an opera, *Home Burial* (1955); 2 string quartets; Suite for Oboe and Piano; Suite for Flute and Piano; Violin Sonata; Trio for Violin, Clarinet, and Piano.

Cummings, William Hayman, English singer and music antiquarian; b. Sidbury, Devonshire, Aug. 22, 1831; d. London, June 6, 1915. He was a chorister in London at St. Paul's and at the Temple Church; was organist of Waltham Abbey (1847); tenor singer in the Temple, Westminster Abbey, and Chapel Royal; was a prof. of singing at the Royal Academy of Music (1879–96); from 1882–88 was conductor of the Sacred Harmonic Society; was precentor of St. Anne's, Soho (1886–98); principal of the Guildhall School of Music (1896–1910); received an honorary degree of Mus.Doc. from Trinity College in Dublin (1900). He was a cultivated singer and a learned antiquarian; was instrumental in founding the Purcell Society, and edited its first publications; was the author of a biography of Purcell (in the Great Musicians Series; London, 1882; 2nd ed., 1911); also publ. *Primer of the Rudiments of Music* (1877), and *Biographical Dictionary of Musicians* (1892); contributed to *Grove's Dictionary.* His library of 4,500 vols. contained many rare autographs. He composed a cantata, *The Fairy Ring* (1873); sacred music; glees; part-songs; etc.

Cundell, Edric, English composer and conductor; b. London, Jan. 29, 1893; d. Ashwell, Hertfordshire, March 19, 1961. He was first a horn player, then a pianist; taught at Trinity College (1914); was conductor of the Westminster Orch. Society (1920) and of the Stock Exchange Orch. (London, 1924). In 1935, he founded the Edric Cundell Chamber Orch.; in 1938, succeeded Sir Landon Ronald as director of the Guildhall School of Music; retired in 1959; in 1949 was made a Commander of the Order of the British Empire. WORKS: A Symph.; symph. poems: *Serbia* (1919) and *The Tragedy of Deirdre* (1922); sonnet, *Our Dead,* for Tenor and Orch. (1922); Piano Concerto; Piano Quartet, String Sextet, String Quartet, Rhapsody for Viola and Piano; miscellaneous piano pieces (*Valse Fantastique; The Water Babies;* etc.); songs.

Curci, Giuseppe, Italian composer; b. Barletta, June 15, 1808; d. there, Aug. 5, 1877. He studied in Naples with Zingarelli and Crescentini; became a singing teacher; composed several operas, including *Il Proscritto* (Turin, 1837) and *Don Desiderio* (Venice, 1837); traveled in Germany and Austria; taught voice in Paris (1848–56), where his opera *Il Baccelliere* was produced; then returned to his native town. He publ. a manual, *Il bel canto.*

Curran, Pearl Gildersleeve, American composer; b. Denver, June 25, 1875; d. New Rochelle, N.Y., April 16, 1941. She studied music privately; publ. about 40 songs, many of them to her own texts. The most successful include *Dawn; Life; Rain; Nursery Rhymes; Nocturne.*

Curry, Arthur Mansfield, American composer and pedagogue; b. Chelsea, Mass., Jan. 27, 1866; d. Atlanta, Ga., Dec. 30, 1953. He studied with Franz Kneisel (violin) and Edward MacDowell (composition); taught at the New England Cons. (1915–39). WORKS: Orch. overture, *Blomidon* (Worcester, Mass., 1902); symph. poem, *Atala,* after Chateaubriand (Boston Symph., April 21, 1911, composer conducting); *The Winning of Amarac,* Celtic legend for Narrator, Women's Chorus, and Orch. (Boston, 1934); choruses for Men's, Women's, and Mixed Voices; piano pieces and many songs (*Before Night; The Fiddler of Dooney;* etc.).

Curschmann, Karl Friedrich, German composer; b. Berlin, June 21, 1805; d. Langfuhr, near Danzig, Aug. 24, 1841. Originally a law student, he devoted himself to music, studying with Hauptmann and Spohr at Kassel, where his one-act opera *Abdul und Erinnieh* was produced (Oct. 29, 1828). His songs possess a fine poetic quality; a collection of 83 lieder and 9 duets and trios was publ. posthumously in 2 vols. (Berlin, 1871). He was also a noted singer and gave concerts in Germany and Italy. BIBLIOGRAPHY: G. Meissner, *Karl Friedrich Curschmann* (Bautzen, 1899); D. Curschman-Undenheim, *Das Geschlecht Curschmann* (Oppenheim am Rhein, 1937).

Curti, Franz (Francesco), German composer; b. Kassel, Nov. 16, 1854; d. Dresden, Feb. 6, 1898. He studied medicine; became a dentist by profession; at the same time took music courses in Dresden with Kretschmer and Schulz-Beuthen. He wrote several operas: *Hertha* (Altenburg, 1887); *Reinhardt von Ufenau* (Altenburg, 1889); *Erlöst* (Mannheim, 1894); melodrama, *Schneefried* (Mannheim, 1895); one-act Japanese fairy opera, *Lili-Tsee* (Mannheim, 1896; N.Y., 1898); *Das Rösli vom Säntis* (Zürich, 1898); also a cantata, *Die Gletscherjungfrau;* music to *Die letzten Menschen,* by W.E. Kirchbach; songs. A catalogue of his works appeared in 1898.

Curtin, Phyllis, American soprano; b. Clarksburg, W.Va., Dec. 3, 1922. She studied with Olga Avierino in Boston; sang with the New England Opera Co.;

was a member of the N.Y. City Opera; made successful appearances at the Teatro Colón in Buenos Aires (1959) and at the Vienna State Opera (1960–61). She made her debut with the Metropolitan Opera Co. on Nov. 4, 1961. Among her most successful roles is Salome; she also sang leading parts in first performances of several American operas. She was married to Phillip Curtin in 1946; divorced and married Eugene Cook in 1956. She taught master classes at the Berkshire Music Center in Tanglewood; then was head of the voice dept. at Yale Univ., and later dean of the School of Fine Arts at Boston Univ.

BIBLIOGRAPHY: David Ewen, *Musicians since 1900* (N.Y., 1978).

Curtis, Alan (Stanley), American musicologist, harpsichordist, and conductor; b. Mason, Mich., Nov. 17, 1934. He studied at Michigan State Univ. (B.Mus., 1955) and the Univ. of Illinois (M.Mus., 1956; Ph.D., 1963); also studied the harpsichord with Gustav Leonhardt in Amsterdam (1957–59). He joined the faculty of the Univ. of Calif. at Berkeley in 1960; became a full prof. there in 1970. He wrote *Sweelinck's Keyboard Music: A Study of English Elements in 17th-century Dutch Composition* (London and Leiden, 1969).

Curtis, Natalie, American writer on folk music; b. New York, April 26, 1875; d. Paris, Oct. 23, 1921. She studied with Arthur Friedheim, with Busoni in Berlin, Alfred Giraudet in Paris, and Julius Kniese at the "Wagner-Schule" in Bayreuth; returning to the U.S., she became an ardent investigator of songs, legends, and customs of the North American Indians. She was married to Paul Burlin of N.Y. (July 25, 1917).

WRITINGS: *Songs of Ancient America* (1905); *The Indian's Book* (1907; contains over 200 songs of 18 different tribes); songs from *A Child's Garden of Verse: Negro Folk Songs* (4 vols., 1918–19; collected in the South and recorded for the Hampton Inst. in Virginia); *Songs and Tales from the Dark Continent* (1920).

Curtiss (née **Kirstein**), **Mina,** American writer; b. Boston, Oct. 13, 1896. She was educated at Smith College (M.A., 1918); was an associate prof. of English literature there (1920–34). Apart from her literary publications, she has contributed articles to the *Musical Quarterly;* wrote *Bizet and His World* (N.Y., 1958). In 1977 she publ. a memoir, *Other People's Letters.*

Curwen, Rev. John, English music theorist; b. Heckmondwike, Yorkshire, Nov. 14, 1816; d. Manchester, May 26, 1880. He was a Congregational minister; studied at Wymondley College and Univ. College in London; in 1844 was pastor at Plaistow, Essex. Becoming interested in Miss S.A. Glover's "Tonic Sol-Fa" system of teaching, he labored to improve it; established the Tonic Sol-Fa Assoc. and the *Tonic Sol-Fa Reporter* in 1853, and the Tonic Sol-Fa College in 1869, having resigned his pastorate in 1867 to devote himself entirely to propagating

the system. His numerous publications relate chiefly to Tonic Sol-Fa (issued by Novello). In 1863 Curwen founded the firm of John Curwen & Sons, publishers of works for school use, choral music. etc., also of the periodicals *Musical News and Herald* (weekly) and *Sackbut* (monthly; discontinued in 1934). In 1923 the business merged with F. & B. Goodwin.

BIBLIOGRAPHY: J.S. Curwen (John Curwen's son), *Memorials of John Curwen* (London, 1882).

Curwen, John Spencer, English music theorist, son of the **Rev. John Curwen;** b. Plaistow, Sept. 30, 1847; d. London, Aug. 6, 1916. He was a pupil of his father and G. Oakey, and later of G.A. Macfarren, Sullivan, and Prout at the Royal Academy of Music. Like his father, he was an active promoter of the Tonic Sol-Fa system; became president of the Tonic Sol-Fa College in 1880; was a frequent contributor to the *Tonic Sol-Fa Reporter* and its continuation, the *Musical Herald.* He publ. *Studies in Worship Music* (1880) and a 2nd series in 1885; *Memorials of John Curwen* (London, 1882); *Musical Notes in Paris* (1882); etc.

Curzon, Sir Clifford, eminent English pianist; b. London, May 18, 1907; d. there, Sept. 1, 1982. His father was an antique dealer; both he and his wife were music lovers and they encouraged their son's studies, first in violin playing and then as a pianist. In 1919 he enrolled at the Royal Academy of Music, where he studied piano with Charles Reddie and Katharine Goodson; he won two scholarships and the Macfarren Gold Medal. At the age of 16, he made a prestigious appearance as soloist at the Queen's Hall in London. He was only 19 years old when he was given a post as a teacher at the Royal Academy of Music, but he decided to continue his studies and went to Berlin, where he was tutored by Artur Schnabel, and then to Paris, where he took courses with Wanda Landowska in harpsichord and with Nadia Boulanger in general music culture. On Feb. 26, 1939, he made an auspicious American debut in N.Y., and in subsequent years made regular concert tours in the U.S. One of his last American appearances took place on May 2, 1978, when he played the Mozart C-minor Concerto with the Philadelphia Orch. Curzon was a scholarly virtuoso who applied his formidable technique with a careful regard for the music. He was particularly praised for his congenial interpretations of works by Romantic composers, especially Schubert, Schumann, and Brahms. He was a recipient of many official honors in England. In 1958 he was made a Commander of the Order of the British Empire. He received the degree of D.Mus. *honoris causa* from Leeds Univ. in 1970. He was knighted by Queen Elizabeth II in 1977. In 1980 he received the Gold Medal of the Royal Phil. Society in London.

Curzon, (Emanuel-) Henri (-Parent) de, French music critic and writer; b. Le Havre, July 6, 1861; d. Paris, Feb. 25, 1942. He was keeper of the government archives at Paris from 1882 until 1926; then became librarian of the Opéra-Comique; was music critic of the *Gazette de France* (1889–1918); contributed to the *Guide Musical, Bulletin de la Société de l'Histoire du Théâtre*, etc. WRITINGS: *Les Dernières Années de Piccini à Paris* (1890); *La Légende de Sigurd dans l'Edda; L'Opéra d'E. Reyer* (1890); *Musiciens du temps passé* (1893); *Croquis d'artistes* (1898); *Les Lieder de Schubert* (1899); "Biographie critique de Franz Schubert," *Revue des Etudes Historiques* (1899); *Etat sommaire des pièces et documents concernant la musique* (1899); *Guide de l'amateur d'ouvrages sur la musique* (1901); *Felipe Pedrell et "Les Pyrénées"* (1902); *Les Lieder de Beethoven* (1905); *Essai de bibliographie mozartienne* (1906); *Grétry, biographie critique* (1907); *L'Evolution lyrique au théâtre* (1908); *Meyerbeer, biographie critique* (1910); *Documents inédits sur le "Faust" de Gounod* (with A. Soubies; 1912); *La Vie artistique aux XVIIᵉ et XVIIIᵉ siècles;* "La Musique," *Bibliothèque française* (1914); *Mozart, biographie critique* (1914); "Rossini, biographie," *Les Maîtres de la Musique* (1920); *L'Œuvre de R. Wagner à Paris et ses interprètes* (1920); *A. Thomas* (1921); *G. Fauré* (1923); *E. Reyer* (1924); *Jean Elleviou* (1930); *Cosima Wagner et Bayreuth* (1930); *Berlioz, L'Homme et le musicien* (1932); "Les Opéras-comiques de Boieldieu," *Revue Musicale* (Nov. 1933); "Les Archives anciennes de l'Opéra-Comique, Paris," *Le Ménestrel* (1934). Translations: *Lettres complètes de Mozart* (1888, 1898); *Ecrites de Schumann sur la musique et les musiciens* (1894, 1898); *Hoffmann: Fantaisies dans la manière de Callot* (1891); also several German, Italian, and Spanish opera libretti.

Cusins, Sir William George, English organist; b. London, Oct. 14, 1833; d. Remouchamps (Ardennes), Aug. 31, 1893. He was a choirboy of the Chapel Royal (1843); was a pupil of Fétis at the Brussels Cons. (1844), and of Bennett, Potter Lucas, and Sainton at the Royal Academy of Music (1847). He took the King's Scholarship in 1847 and 1849; in the latter year he was appointed organist of the Queen's private chapel, and became a violinist in the Italian Opera orch. In 1851 he was a prof. at the Royal Academy of Music; succeeded Bennett (1867–83) as conductor of the Phil., and also became conductor of the Royal Band in 1870; served as Master of Music to the Queen from 1870 until his death; also succeeded Bennett as examining prof. at Queen's College (1875); was a prof. at Trinity College and a prof. of piano at the Guildhall School of Music (1885). He was knighted in 1892. WORKS: *Royal Wedding Serenata* (1863); 2 concert overtures: *Les Travailleurs de la mer* (1869) and *Love's Labour's Lost* (1875); oratorio, *Gideon* (Gloucester Festival, 1871); Piano Concerto; Septet for Winds and Double-bass; piano pieces; songs.

Custer, Arthur, American composer; b. Manchester, Conn., April 21, 1923. He studied composition with Paul Pisk at the Univ. of Redlands, Calif., and with Philip Bezanson at the Univ. of Iowa; after graduation, he took a course of studies in composi-

tion with Nadia Boulanger. Subsequently he held numerous teaching jobs; also served as music consultant to the U.S. Information Agency in Madrid (1960–62). In 1970 he was appointed director of the Arts in the Education Project of the Rhode Island Council on the Arts; resigned from this post in 1973, but continued as composer-in-residence there until 1975. WORKS: Sextet for Woodwinds and Piano (1959); *Colloquy* for String Quartet (1961); Sinfonia de Madrid (Madrid, April 28, 1962); *Cycle* for a Heterogeneous Ensemble (1963); Concertino for 2nd Violin and Strings, in reality his String Quartet No. 2 (1964); *2 Movements* for Wind Quintet (1964); *Permutations* for Violin, Clarinet, and Cello (1967); Concerto for Brass Quintet (1968); *Rhapsodality Brass!* for Orch. (1969); *Interface I* for String Quartet and 2 Recording Engineers, being (minus affectation) his String Quartet No. 3 (1969) and a thing entitled *Rhapsodality Brown!* for Piano (1969); *Parabolas* for Trombone and Percussion (1969); *Parabolas* for Viola and Piano (1969); *Doubles* for Violin and Chamber Orch. (1972; revised 1975); *Eyepiece* for Oboe and Tape (1974); *Sweet Sixteen* for Clarinet and Piano (1976); *Interface II* for Ensemble, Slide Projectors, and Audience (1976). He also contributed informative articles on American and Spanish music to various music journals.

Cutler, Henry Stephen, American organist and hymn writer; b. Boston, Oct. 13, 1824; d. there, Dec. 5, 1902. He studied in Germany; returning to the U.S., he held posts as a church organist in Boston, N.Y., and Philadelphia. His anthem *The Son of God Goes Forth to War* is well known.

Cuvillier, Charles, French composer of light opera; b. Paris, April 24, 1877; d. there, Feb. 14, 1955. He studied privately with Fauré and Messager, and with Massenet at the Paris Cons.; then became interested in the theater; his first operetta, *Avanthier matin*, was produced at the Théâtre des Capucines in Paris (Oct. 20, 1905); at the same theater, Cuvillier produced *Son petit frère* (April 10, 1907); *Algar* (1909); *Les Muscadines* (1910); and *Sapho* (1912). His most successful operetta, *La Reine s'amuse*, was first staged in Marseilles (Dec. 31, 1912); was revised and produced in Paris as *La Reine joyeuse* (Nov. 8, 1918) and in London as *The Naughty Princess* (1920). His other operettas were *La Fausse Ingénue* (Paris, 1918); *Bob et moi* (1924); *Boufard et ses filles* (Paris, 1929); etc. Cuvillier was also active in musical administration as music director at the Odéon in Paris. The waltz from *La Reine joyeuse* has retained its popularity in numerous arrangements.

Cuyler, Louise, American musicologist; b. Omaha, March 14, 1908. She studied at the Eastman School of Music in Rochester, N.Y. (B.M., 1929; Ph.D., 1948) and at the Univ. of Michigan (M.M., 1933), where she was a member of the staff from 1929 to 1975, with wartime leave (1942–45) for service with the American Red Cross in the Pacific. In 1975 she went to Smith College as Neilson Distinguished Professor. She contributed a number of informative papers to various scholarly publications, among them "Mozart's Quartets Dedicated to Haydn" in the memorial vol. for Curt Sachs (N.Y., 1965); "Music in Biographies of Emperor Maximilian" in the Festschrift for Gustave Reese (N.Y., 1966); also edited music: Isaac's *Choralis Constantinus*, Part III (Ann Arbor, Mich., 1950); *Five Polyphonic Masses of Heinrich Isaac* (Ann Arbor, 1956). She also publ. *The Emperor Maximilian I and Music* (London, 1973) and *The Symphony* (N.Y., 1973).

Cuzzoni, Francesca, celebrated Italian soprano; b. Parma, c.1700; d. Bologna, 1770. She studied with Lanzi; sang in Parma, Bologna, Genoa, and Venice (1716–18); was engaged at the Italian opera in London, making her debut as Teofane in Handel's opera *Ottone* (Jan. 12, 1723). She made a profound impression on London opera lovers, and was particularly distinguished in lyric roles; but later her notorious rivalry with Faustina Bordoni nearly ruined her career. Following some appearances in Venice, she returned to London (1734); after several seasons she went to the Netherlands, where she became impoverished and was imprisoned for debt. Eventually, she returned to Bologna, where she subsisted by making buttons.

Czernohorsky (Černohorsky), Bohuslav, Bohemian composer; b. Nimburg, Feb. 16, 1684; d. Graz, July 1, 1742. He studied at Prague Univ. A Minorite monk, he was organist at Assisi in 1710–15 (Tartini was one of his pupils) and choirmaster at San Antonio in Padua, in 1715–20. Returning to Bohemia, he was Kapellmeister at the Teinkirche in Prague, and (1735) at St. Jacob's (Gluck was among his pupils); he was again organist in Padua in 1731–41. Many of his MSS were lost at the burning of the Minorite monastery (1754). An offertory *a* 4 and several organ fugues and preludes were publ. by O. Schmid in *Orgelwerke altböhmischer Meister;* 5 organ fugues have been ed. by K. Pietsch; a *Regina Coeli* for Soprano, Organ, and Cello obbligato, and a motet, *Quem lapidaverunt,* are also extant; *Composizioni per organo* constitute vol. 3 of *Musica antiqua Bohemica* (Prague, 1968). The contrapuntal skill of Czernohorsky's fugal writing is remarkable; Kretzschmar described him as "the Bach of Bohemia"; Czech writers refer to him as "the father of Bohemian music" despite the fact that Czernohorsky never made thematic use of native rhythms or melodies.

BIBLIOGRAPHY: O. Schmid, *Die böhmische Altmeisterschule Czernohorskys* (1900); A. Hnilička, *Porträte* (1922); Z. Culka, "Varhanní skladby Bohuslava Matěje Černohorského?" *Hudební Věda,* V/4 (1968).

Czerny, Carl, celebrated Austrian pianist, composer, and pedagogue; b. Vienna, Feb. 20, 1791; d. there, July 15, 1857. He was of Czech extraction (*czerny* means "black" in Czech), and his first language was Czech. He received his early training from his fa-

ther, Wenzel Czerny, a stern disciplinarian who never let his son play with other children and insisted on concentrated work. Czerny had the privilege of studying for 3 years with Beethoven, and their association in subsequent years became a close one. Czerny also received advice as a pianist from Hummel and Clementi. He made trips to Leipzig (1836); visited Paris and London (1837) and Italy (1846); with these exceptions, he remained all his life in Vienna. His self-imposed daily schedule for work was a model of diligence; he denied himself any participation in the social life of Vienna and seldom attended opera or concerts. Very early in life he demonstrated great ability as a patient piano teacher; Beethoven entrusted to him the musical education of his favorite nephew. When Czerny himself became a renowned pedagogue, many future piano virtuosos flocked to him for lessons, among them Liszt (whom he taught without a fee), Thalberg, Theodore Kullak, Döhler, Jaëll, and Ninette Belleville-Oury. Despite the heavy teaching schedule, Czerny found time to compose a fantastic amount of piano music, 861 opus numbers in all, each containing many individual items; these included not only piano studies and exercises, for which he became celebrated, but also sonatas, concertos, string quartets, masses, and hymns. In addition, he made numerous piano arrangements of classical symphs., including all of Beethoven's, and wrote fantasies for piano on the themes from famous operas of the time. So dedicated was he to his chosen work that he renounced all thoughts of marriage (but a secret confession of his Platonic adoration of an unnamed female person was found among his MSS); in this wistful deprivation, Czerny's fate paralleled Beethoven's. For a century there has been a fashion among musical sophisticates to deprecate Czerny as a pathetic purveyor of manufactured musical goods; his contemporary John Field, the originator of the genre of piano nocturnes, described Czerny as a "Tintenfass"—an inkpot. A quip was circulated that Czerny hated children, and that he publ. his voluminous books of piano exercises to inflict pain on young pianists. Of late, however, there has been a change of heart toward Czerny as a worthy composer in his own right. Stravinsky expressed his admiration for Czerny, and modern composers have written, with a half-concealed smile, pieces "à la manière de Czerny." Czerny was unexpectedly revealed to be a musician of imaginative fancy and engaging pedantic humor, as for instance in his Brobdingnagian arrangement of Rossini's Overture to *William Tell* for 16 pianists playing 4-hands on 8 pianos; pieces for 3 pianists playing 6-hands on a single keyboard; etc. Obsessed by an idea of compassing all musical knowledge at once, he publ. an *Umriss der ganzen Musikgeschichte* (Mainz, 1851), and also a vol. in English entitled *Letters to a Young Lady on the Art of Playing the Pianoforte from the Earliest Rudiments to the Highest State of Cultivation* (the young lady in the title was never identified). Of his studies the most famous are *Schule der Geläufigkeit,* op. 299, and *Schule der Fingerfertigkeit,* op. 740; others are *Die Schule des Legato und Staccato,* op. 335; *40 Täg-*

liche Studien, op. 337; *Schule der Verzierungen*, op. 355; *Schule des Virtuosen*, op. 365; *Schule der linken Hand*, op. 399; etc. His Sonata, op. 7, was popular; among his piano transcriptions to be mentioned is *Fantaisie et Variations brilliantes* on an aria from Persiani's opera *Ines de Castro*. Czerny's autobiography, *Erinnerungen aus meinem Leben*, was ed. by W. Kolneder (Baden-Baden, 1968; publ. in part in Eng. in the *Musical Quarterly*, July 1956).

Czerwenka, Oskar, Austrian bass; b. Linz, July 5, 1924. He made his debut in Graz in 1947; in 1951 he joined the Vienna State Opera; from 1953 he sang at Salzburg. He made his American debut at the Metropolitan Opera in N.Y., on Feb. 13, 1960, as Rocco in *Fidelio,* but he did not remain with the company, and continued to pursue his career in Europe, principally in Vienna. He was best known for his buffo roles.

Czibulka, Alphons, Hungarian bandmaster and composer; b. Szepes-Várallya, May 14, 1842; d. Vienna, Oct. 27, 1894. Originally a pianist, he became Kapellmeister at the Karltheater in Vienna in 1865; was bandmaster of the 17th Regiment, and later of the 25th Regiment at Prague; finally settled in Vienna, where he brought out the operetta *Pfingsten in Florenz* (Dec. 20, 1884). Other stage works are *Der Glücksritter* (1887); *Gil Blas* (Hamburg, 1889); *Der Bajazzo* (Vienna, 1892); *Signor Annibale* (1893).

Cziffra, György, noted Hungarian pianist; b. Budapest, Sept. 5, 1921. He studied with Dohnányi at the Budapest Academy of Music; his education was interrupted by World War II, when he served in the Hungarian army; after the war he continued his studies at the Budapest Academy of Music with Ferenczi, but was once more distracted from music when he was arrested in 1950 for his rebellious political views. He was released from jail in 1953, but was again endangered by the abortive Hungarian revolt in 1956. Convinced that he could have no peace under Communist rule, he went to Paris, where he made successful appearances as a concert pianist; eventually he became a French citizen. He was best known for his interpretations of the works of the Romantic repertoire; especially brilliant are his renditions of the music of Liszt.

Czyż, Henryk, Polish conductor and composer; b. Grudziadz, June 16, 1923. He studied law at Torun Univ.; then went to the Poznan Academy of Music, where he studied conducting with Bierdiajew and composition with Szeligowski. In 1952 he was appointed conductor at the Poznan Opera; from 1953–56 he conducted the Polish Radio Symph. Orch. in Warsaw. He was subsequently chief conductor of the Lodz Phil. (1957–60); from 1964–68 he conducted the Cracow Phil.; in 1971–74 served as Generalmusikdirektor of the Düsseldorf Symph.; in 1972–80 again assumed the post of chief conductor of the Lodz Phil. He made his American debut with the Minnesota Orch. in 1973. In 1980 he became a prof. at the Warsaw Academy. His works include *Etude for Orch.* (1949); *Symphonic Variations* (1952); the musical *Bialowlosa* (1960); and the comic opera *Kynolog w rosterce* (1964).

D

Da-Oz, Ram, German-born Israeli composer; b. Berlin, Oct. 17, 1929. He came to Palestine as a child in 1934; studied oboe and piano at the Cons. in Tel Aviv, and composition with André Hajos at the Music Academy there; he lost his eyesight during the Israeli war for independence.

WORKS: *Von Trauer und Trost* for Orch. (1960); Concerto for Violin and String Orch. (1961); *Dmuyoth umassechot (Changing Phantoms),* movements for Chamber Ensemble (1967); *Improvisation on a Song* for 10 Instruments (1968); *Quartet* for Narrator and Small Orch. (1970); *Rhapsody on a Jewish Yemenite Song* for Piano and Strings (1971); *3 Romances* for Violin and Small Orch. (1975); 4 string quartets (1955–70); Violin Sonata (1960); String Trio (1961); *Suite* for Harpsichord, Flute, Oboe, and Cello (1963); Piano Trio (1963); *Dialogue* for 2 Clarinets (1965); *Illumination* for Solo Violin (1966); *4 Miniatures* for Recorders and Piano (1975); *3 Snacks* for Brass Quartet (1977); songs. For Piano Solo: 2 sonatas (1955; *Movimenti quasi una sonata,* 1963); *5 Contrasts* (1958); *Capriccio* (1960); *8 Little Pictures* (1962); *Aspects* (1969); *Bells* (1973); *Mood Ring* (1976).

Dachs, Joseph, pianist and pedagogue; b. Regensburg, Sept. 30, 1825; d. Vienna, June 6, 1896. He studied in Vienna with Czerny and Sechter; in 1861 was appointed prof. of piano at the Vienna Cons.; he had numerous distinguished pupils, among them Vladimir de Pachmann, Laura Rappoldi, and Isabelle Vengerova. He also gave concerts which were well received in Vienna.

Dadelsen, Georg von, distinguished German musicologist; b. Dresden, Nov. 7, 1918. He studied musicology at the Univ. of Kiel, at Humboldt Univ. in Berlin, and at the Free Univ. of Berlin (Ph.D., 1951, with the dissertation *Alter Stil und alte Techniken in der Musik des 19. Jahrhunderts*); completed his Habilitation at the Univ. of Tübingen in 1958 with his *Beiträge zur Chronologie der Werke J.S. Bachs* (publ. in Trossingen, 1958). He was an assistant lecturer at the Univ. of Tübingen (1952–58); was then prof. of musicology at the Univ. of Hamburg (1960–71); after 1971 held the same title at the Univ. of Tübingen. He is particularly noted for his valuable contribution to the study of Bach's music.

WRITINGS: *Bemerkungen zur Handschrift J.S. Bachs, seiner Familie und seines Kreises* (Trossingen, 1957); *Editionsrichtlinien musikalischer Denkmäler und Gesamtausgaben* (Kassel, 1967).

Daffner, Hugo, German composer and musicologist; b. Munich, June 2, 1882; perished in the concentration camp in Dachau, Oct. 9, 1936. He studied composition with Thuille and musicology with Sandberger and Kroyer at the Royal Academy in Munich; received his degree of Dr.Phil. in 1904; subsequently took private lessons with Max Reger. He conducted at the Munich opera house in 1904–6; was active as a music critic in Königsberg and Dresden. After World War I he decided to study medicine, and obtained the degree of M.D. in 1920; in 1924 he went to live in Berlin as a practicing physician. He became a victim of the Nazi program of extermination of Jews.

WORKS: 3 operas: *Macbeth, Truffaldino, Der eingebildeste Kranke* (after Molière); 2 symphs.; 2 string quartets; 2 piano trios; 2 piano quintets; various other pieces. He publ. several monographs, including his dissertation *Die Entwicklung des Klavierkonzerts bis Mozart* (Leipzig, 1908); edited writings by Nietzsche and C.P.E. Bach.

Dahl, Ingolf, distinguished composer; b. Hamburg, Germany (of Swedish parents), June 9, 1912; d. Frutigen, near Bern, Switzerland, Aug. 6, 1970. He studied composition at the Cons. of Cologne and musicology at the Univ. of Zürich. He came to the U.S. in 1935; settled in California (1938), where he became active as a conductor and composer; was appointed an assistant prof. at the Univ. of Southern Calif. (1945); received 2 Guggenheim fellowships (1952 and 1960). He taught at the Berkshire Music Center, Tanglewood, in the summers of 1952–55. As a composer, he adhered to an advanced polyphonic style in free dissonant counterpoint.

WORKS: *Andante and Arioso* for Flute, Clarinet, Oboe, Horn, and Bassoon (1942); *Music for Brass Instruments* (1944); *Concerto a tre* for Clarinet, Violin, and Cello (1946); Duo for Cello and Piano (1946); Divertimento for Viola and Piano (1948); Concerto for Saxophone and Wind Orch. (1949); *Symphony concertante* for 2 Clarinets and Orch. (1953); *Sonata seria* for Piano (1953); *The Tower of Saint Barbara,* symph. legend (Louisville, Jan. 29, 1955); Piano Quartet (1957); *Sonata Pastorale* for Piano (1960); *Serenade* for 4 Flutes (1960); *Sinfonietta* for Concert Band (1961); Piano Trio (1962); *Aria sinfonica* (Los Angeles, April 15, 1965); *Elegy Concerto* for Violin and Small Orch. (1963; completed by Donal Michalsky, 1971); *Duo concertante* for Flute and Percussion (1966); *Sonata da camera* for Clarinet and Piano (1970); *Intervals* for String Orch. (1970).

BIBLIOGRAPHY: J. Berdahl, *Ingolf Dahl: His Life and Works* (Diss., Univ. of Miami, 1975).

Dahl, Viking, Swedish composer; b. Osby, Oct. 8, 1895; d. Stockholm, Jan. 1, 1945. He studied at the Malmö and Stockholm conservatories; later in Paris and London with Vidal, Viñes, and Ravel; studied dancing with Isadora Duncan.

WORKS: Ballets: *Oriental Suite* (Stockholm, 1919) and *Maison des fous* (Paris, 1920); *Pastorale* for Oboe and Orch.; chamber music; many songs.

Dahlhaus, Carl, eminent German musicologist and editor; b. Hannover, June 10, 1928. He studied musicology at the Univ. of Göttingen with Gerber; also at the Univ. of Freiburg with Gurlitt; received his Ph.D. from the Univ. of Göttingen in 1953 with the dissertation *Studien zu den Messen Josquins des Prés.* He was a dramatic adviser for the Deutsches Theater in Göttingen from 1950 to 1958; from 1960 to 1962 was an editor of the *Stuttgarter Zeitung;* then joined the Inst. für Musikalische Landesforschung of the Univ. of Kiel; completed his Habilitation there in 1966 with his *Untersuchungen über die Entstehung der harmonischen Tonalität* (publ. in Kassel, 1968). In 1966–67 he was a research fellow at the Univ. of Saarbrücken; in 1967 he became prof. of music history at the Technical Univ. of Berlin. He is the editor in chief of the complete edition of Wagner's works, which began publication in 1970; was also an editor of the Supplement to the 12th edition of the *Riemann Musik-Lexikon* (2 vols., Mainz, 1972, 1975) and (with Hans Eggebrecht) of the *Brockhaus-Riemann Musik-Lexikon* (2 vols., Wiesbaden and Mainz, 1978); in addition, was co-editor of the *Neue Zeitschrift für Musik* (from 1972) and of the *Archiv für Musikwissenschaft* (from 1973).

WRITINGS: *Musikästhetik* (Cologne, 1967; Eng. trans. by William Austin as *Esthetics of Music,* Cambridge, 1982); as editor, *Studien zur Trivialmusik des 19. Jahrhunderts* (Regensburg, 1967); *Analyse und Werturteil* (Mainz, 1970); *Die Bedeutung des Gestischen in Wagners Musikdramen* (Munich, 1970); as ed., *Das Drama Richard Wagners als musikalisches Kunstwerk* (Regensburg, 1970); as ed., *Einführung in die systematische Musikwissenschaft* (Cologne, 1971); *Richard Wagners Musikdramen* (Velber, 1971; Eng. trans. as *Richard Wagner's Music Dramas,* Cambridge, 1979); as ed., *Richard Wagner: Werk und Wirkung* (Regensburg, 1971); *Wagners Konzeption des musikalischen Dramas* (Regensburg, 1971).

Dahms, Walter, German music critic; b. Berlin, June 9, 1887; d. Lisbon, Oct. 5, 1973. He studied with Adolf Schultze in Berlin (1907–10), then engaged in music criticism; also composed some minor piano pieces and songs. About 1935 he went to Lisbon, Portugal, where he changed his name to **Gualtério Armando,** and continued to publ. books on music in the German language, but for some unfathomable reason he persistently denied his identity. The reasons for his leaving Germany are obscure; he was not a Jew (in fact, he wrote some anti-Semitic articles, directed against Schoenberg and others as early as 1910), and presumably had nothing to fear from the Nazi government, unless he regarded it as unduly liberal. A clue to his true identity was the synonymity of his first names in German (Walter) and in Portuguese (Gualtério).

WRITINGS: *Schubert* (Berlin, 1912); *Schumann* (1916); *Mendelssohn* (1919); *Die Offenbarung der Music: Eine Apotheose Friedrich Nietzsches* (Munich, 1921); *Music des Südens* (1923), *Paganini* (Berlin, 1960); *Liszt* (Berlin, 1961); and *Wagner* (Berlin, 1962).

Dalayrac, Nicolas (-Marie), French composer; b. Muret (Haute-Garonne), June 8 (baptized, June 13), 1753; d. Paris, Nov. 26, 1809. (He signed his name **d'Alayrac,** but dropped the nobiliary particle after the Revolution.) His early schooling was in Toulouse; returning to Muret in 1767, he studied law and played violin in a local band. He then entered the service of the Count d'Artois in his Guard of Honor, and at the same time took lessons in harmony with François Langlé at Versailles; he also received some help from Grétry. In 1781 he wrote 6 string quartets; his first theater work was a one-act comedy, *L'Eclipse totale* (Paris, March 7, 1782). From then on, he devoted most of his energies to the theater. He wrote over 56 operas; during the Revolution he composed patriotic songs for special occasions. He also enjoyed Napoleon's favors later on. During his lifetime, and for some 3 decades after his death, many of his operas were popular not only in France but also in Germany, Italy, and Russia; then they gradually disappeared from the active repertoire, but there were several revivals even in the 20th century. Dalayrac's natural facility enabled him to write successfully in all operatic genres. The list of his operas produced in Paris (mostly at the Opéra-Comique) includes the following: *Le Petit Souper, ou L'Abbé qui veut parvenir* (1781); *Le Chevalier à la mode* (1781); *Nina* (May 15, 1786; one of his most successful operas); *Sargines* (May 14, 1788); *Les Deux Petits Savoyards* (Jan. 14, 1789); *Raoul, Sire de Créqui* (Oct. 31, 1789); *La Soirée orageuse* (May 29, 1790); *Camille* (March 19, 1791); *Philippe et Georgette* (Dec. 28, 1791); *Ambroise* (Jan. 12, 1793); *Adèle et Dorsan* (April 27, 1795); *Marianne* (July 7, 1796); *La Maison isolée* (May 11, 1797); *Gulnare* (Dec. 30, 1797); *Alexis* (Jan. 24, 1798); *Adolphe et Clara* (Feb. 10, 1799); *Maison à vendre* (Oct. 23, 1800; many revivals); *Léhéman* (Dec. 12, 1801); *L'Antichambre* (Feb. 26, 1802); *La Jeune Prude* (Jan. 14, 1804); *Une Heure de mariage* (March 20, 1804); *Gulistan* (Sept. 30, 1805); *Deux mots* (June 9, 1806); *Koulouf* (Dec. 18, 1806); *Le Poète et le musicien* (posthumous, Paris, May 30, 1811).
BIBLIOGRAPHY: R.C.G. de Pixérécourt, *Vie de Dalayrac* (includes a complete list of his operas; Paris, 1810); A. Fourgeaud, *Les Violons de Dalayrac* (Paris, 1856); G. Cucuel, *Les Créateurs de l'opéra-comique français* (Paris, 1914); W. Kloppenburg, "Nicolas Dalayrac," *Mens en melodie,* IX (1954).

Dalberg, Johann Friedrich Hugo, German pianist, composer, and writer on music; b. Aschaffenburg, May 17, 1760; d. there, July 26, 1812. He studied theology; became a canon in Trier; was also counsellor to the Elector of Trier at Coblenz. He traveled in Italy (1775) and England (1798); gave private concerts as a pianist. Although he was not a professional musician, his compositions and particularly his writings reveal considerable musical culture. He publ. many vocal works; set to music Schiller's *Ode an die Freude* (1799); also wrote songs to Eng. and French texts.
WRITINGS: *Blicke eines Tonkünstlers in die Musik der Geister* (Mannheim, 1787); *Vom Erfinden und Bilden* (Frankfurt, 1791); *Untersuchungen über den Ursprung der Harmonie* (Erfurt, 1800); *Die Äolsharfe, Ein allegorischer Traum* (Erfurt, 1801); etc.; trans. Jones's *The Musical Modes of the Hindus* (1802).

D'Albert, Eugène. See **Albert, Eugène d'.**

Dalcroze, Emile Jaques. See **Jaques-Dalcroze, Emile.**

Dale, Benjamin James, English composer; b. Crouch Hill, July 17, 1885; d. London, July 30, 1943. He studied at the Royal Academy of Music with F. Corder; was organist at St. Stephen's Ealing; then taught composition at the Royal Academy of Music.
WORKS: Overture, *The Tempest* (1902); Piano Sonata in D minor (1905; was frequently performed); suites for Piano and Viola (1907); *Before the Paling of the Stars* for Chorus and Orch. (1912); *Songs of Praise* for Chorus and Orch. (1923); *Rosa mystica* and *Cradle Song* for Mixed Chorus; 2 songs (after Shakespeare) for Voice, with Viola obbligato; Sextet for Violas; Violin Sonata; piano pieces; songs; etc. His last work was *The Flowing Tide* for Large Orch., completed in 1943 from sketches made in 1924. For analysis of his chamber music, see Cobbett's *Cyclopedic Survey of Chamber Music* (London, 1929, I, 310–13).

Dale, Clamma, black American soprano; b. Chester, Pa., July 4, 1948. She began to study piano as a child; later studied clarinet and singing; at 14 she began to study voice at Philadelphia's Settlement Music School; subsequently enrolled at the Juilliard School of Music in N.Y. (B.Mus., 1970; M.S., 1975); her teachers were Hans Heinz, Alice Howland, and Cornelius Reed. She made her debut with the N.Y. City Opera as Antonia in *Les Contes d'Hoffmann* in 1975; her other roles were Nedda in *Pagliacci,* Musetta in *La Bohème,* Countess Almaviva in *Le nozze di Figaro,* Pamina in *The Magic Flute,* and Bess in *Porgy and Bess.*
BIBLIOGRAPHY: *Current Biography* (April 1979).

D'Alembert, Jean le Rond. See **Alembert, Jean le Rond d'.**

Dalhart, Vernon (real name, **Marion Try Slaughter**), American country music singer; b. on a ranch near Jefferson, Texas, April 6, 1883; d. Bridgeport, Conn., Sept. 14, 1948. He studied at the Dallas Cons. of Music; then went to N.Y., where he sang in opera and operetta; he also became a successful recording artist, mostly of popular music. In 1924 he recorded *The Wreck of the Old '97* and *The Prisoner's Song;* with these recordings the commercial country music industry was vigorously launched; he remained a leading figure in country music until the Great Depression, when the success of Jimmie Rodgers, the Carter Family, and others obscured his pioneering efforts.

D'Alheim, Marie. See **Olénine d'Alheim, Marie.**

D'Alheim, Pierre, French journalist; b. Laroche (Yonne), Dec. 8, 1862; d. Paris, April 11, 1922. In 1893 he married the singer **Marie Olénine,** and organized her concerts in Moscow and in Paris. He became a propagandist of Russian music; publ. a book on Mussorgsky (Paris, 1896), and trans. into French the librettos of *Boris Godunov* and *Khovanshchina* and Mussorgsky's songs.

Dalis, Irene, American mezzo-soprano; b. San Jose, Calif., Oct. 8, 1925. She studied voice with Edyth Walker and Paul Althouse in N.Y., with Otto Müller in Milan, and with Margarete Klose in Berlin; made her debut in Oldenburg in 1953; then sang with the Städtische Oper in Berlin. She made her Metropolitan Opera debut in N.Y. as Eboli in *Don Carlos,* on March 16, 1957; also sang at Covent Garden, London, the Chicago Lyric Opera, and at the Bayreuth Festival.

Dall'Abaco, Evaristo Felice. See **Abaco, Evaristo Felice dall'.**

Dall'Abaco, Joseph. See **Abaco, Joseph Marie Clément dall'.**

Dallapiccola, Luigi, distinguished Italian composer; b. Pisino (Pazin), Istria (now a part of Yugoslavia), Feb. 3, 1904; d. Florence, Feb. 19, 1975. He took piano lessons at an early age; went to school at the Pisino Gymnasium (1914–21), except for a period of over a year (1917–18) in which his family was politically exiled in Graz; studied piano and harmony in nearby Trieste (1919–21); in 1922 moved to Florence, where he took courses at the Cherubini Cons., studying piano with Ernesto Consolo (graduated 1924) and composition with Vito Frazzi (graduated 1931); was active in the Italian section of the International Society for Contemporary Music (ISCM) from the early 1930s. In 1934 Dallapiccola was appointed to the faculty of the Cherubini Cons., where he stayed until 1967. As a composer Dallapiccola became interested from the very first in the melodic application of atonal writing; in 1939 he adopted the dodecaphonic method of Schoenberg with considerable innovations of his own (for example, the use of mutually exclusive triads in thematic structure and harmonic progressions). He particularly excelled in his handling of vocal lines in a difficult modern idiom. He visited London in 1946 and traveled on the Continent; taught several courses in American colleges: Berkshire Music Center, Tanglewood, Mass. (1951); Queens College, N.Y. (1956, 1959); the Univ. of Calif., Berkeley (1962); Dartmouth College (summer, 1969); Aspen Music School (1969); and Marlboro (1969).
WORKS: FOR THE STAGE: *Volo di notte (Night Flight),* one-act opera after the St. Exupéry novel *Vol de nuit* (1937–39; Florence, May 18, 1940); *Il Pri-*

gioniero (The Prisoner), one-act opera with a prologue, after Villiers de l'Isle and Charles de Coster (1944–48; revised in 1950 for Reduced Orch.; Turin Radio, Dec. 4, 1949; stage premiere, Florence, May 20, 1950); *Ulisse,* 2-act opera with prologue, after Homer's *Odyssey* (1959–68; premiere, as *Odysseus,* Berlin, Sept. 29, 1968, to a German libretto; in Italian, Milan, 1969); *Marsia,* ballet in one act (1942–43; Venice Music Festival, Sept. 9, 1948). INSTRUMENTAL WORKS: *Partita* for Orch., with Soprano in the last movement (1930–32; Florence, Jan. 22, 1933); *Musica* for 3 Pianos (1935); *Piccolo Concerto per Muriel Couvreaux* for Piano and Chamber Orch. (1939–41; Rome, May 1, 1941); *Sonatina canonica,* after Paganini's *Caprices,* for Piano (1942–43); *Ciaccona, Intermezzo e Adagio* for Solo Cello (1945); *Due studi* for Violin and Piano (1946–47); *Due pezzi* for Orch. (1947; arrangement and elaboration of the *Due studi*); *Tartiniana,* divertimento on themes from Tartini sonatas, for Violin and Chamber Orch. (1951; Bern, March 4, 1952); *Quaderno musicale di Annalibera* for Piano (1952, revised 1953; transcribed for organ by Rudy Shackelford, 1970); *Variazioni per orchestra* (1953–54; Louisville, Ky., Oct. 2, 1954; orch. version of the *Quaderno musicale di Annalibera); Piccola musica notturna* for Orch. (1954; Hannover, June 7, 1954; arranged for 8 Instruments, 1961); *Tartiniana seconda* for Violin and Piano (1955–56; chamber orch. version made with an added movement, 1956; chamber orch. version, Turin Radio, March 15, 1957); *Dialoghi* for Cello and Orch. (1959–60; Venice, Sept. 17, 1960); *Three Questions with Two Answers* for Orch. (1962; based on material from *Ulisse;* New Haven, Conn., Feb. 5, 1963). VOCAL WORKS: *Due Canzoni di Grado* for Mezzo-soprano, Small Female Chorus, and Small Orch. (1927); *Dalla mia terra,* song cycle for Mezzo-soprano, Chorus, and Orch. (1928); *Due laudi di Fra Jacopone da Todi* for Soprano, Baritone, Chorus, and Orch. (1929); *La Canzone del Quarnaro* for Tenor, Male Chorus, and Orch. (1930); *Due liriche del Kalewala* for Tenor, Baritone, Chamber Chorus, and 4 Percussion Instruments (1930); *3 Studi* for Soprano and Chamber Orch. (1932; also based on the Kalevala epos); *Estate* for Male Chorus a cappella (1932); *Rhapsody* for Voice and Chamber Orch. (1934); *Divertimento in quattro esercizi* for Soprano, Flute, Oboe, Clarinet, Viola, and Cello (1934); *Cori de Michelangelo* in 3 sets: I for Chorus a cappella (1933), II for Female Chorus and 17 Instruments (1935), and III for Chorus and Orch. (1936); *3 Laudi* for Soprano and Chamber Orch. (1936–37); *Canti de prigionia (Songs of Captivity)* for Chorus, 2 Pianos, 2 Harps, and Percussion (1938–41; first complete perf., Rome, Dec. 11, 1941); *Liriche greche* in 3 sets: I, *Cinque frammenti di Saffo* for Voice and 15 Instruments (1942); II, *Due liriche de Anacreonte* for Soprano, 2 Clarinets, Viola, and Piano (1945); III, *Sex carmina Alcaei,* for Soprano and 11 Instruments (1943); *Roncesvals* for Voice and Piano (1946); *Quattro liriche di Antonio Machado* for Soprano and Piano (1948; version with Chamber Orch., 1964); *3 Poemi* for Soprano and Chamber Ensemble (1949); *Job,* biblical drama for 5 Singers, Narrator, Chorus, Speaking Chorus, and Orch.

(1949–50; Rome, Oct. 30, 1950); *Goethe-Lieder* for Female Voice and 3 Clarinets (1953); *Canti di liberazione (Songs of Liberation)* for Chorus and Orch. (1951–55; Cologne, Oct. 28, 1955); *An Mathilde,* cantata for Female Voice and Orch. (1955); *Cinque canti* for Baritone and 8 Instruments (1956); *Concerto per la notte di Natale dell'anno 1956 (Christmas Concerto for the Year 1956)* for Soprano and Chamber Orch. (1957; Tokyo, Oct. 11, 1957); *Requiescant* for Mixed Chorus, Children's Chorus, and Orch. (1957–58; Hamburg Radio, Nov. 17, 1959); *Preghiere (Prayers)* for Baritone and Chamber Orch. (1962; Berkeley, Calif., Nov. 10, 1962); *Parole di San Paolo* for Medium Voice and Chamber Ensemble (1969; Washington, D.C., Oct. 10, 1969); *Sicut umbra...* for Mezzo-soprano and 4 Instrumental Groups (1969–70; Washington, Oct. 30, 1970); *Tempus destruendi/Tempus aedificandi* for Chorus a cappella (1970–71); *Commaito* for Soprano and Chamber Ensemble (1972; Styrian Autumn Festival, Murau, Austria, Oct. 15, 1972; his last completed work). The *Revue Musical Suisse* dedicated a special issue to Dallapiccola (July/Aug. 1975). A complete catalogue of his works is publ. in the March 1976 issue of *Tempo* (No. 115). A collection of Dallapiccola's own essays was publ. under the title *Appunti incontri meditazioni* (Milan, 1970).

BIBLIOGRAPHY: G.M. Gatti, "Luigi Dallapiccola," *Monthly Musical Record* (Feb. 1937); Domenico de Paoli, "An Italian Musician: Luigi Dallapiccola," *Chesterian* (July 1938); "Nota bio-bibliografica," *Rassegna Musicale* (1950); Hans Nathan, "The Twelve-Tone Compositions of Luigi Dallapiccola," *Musical Quarterly* (April 1958); Bruno Zanolini, *Luigi Dallapiccola; La conquista di un linguaggio* (Padua, 1974); "The Genesis of the *Canti di Prigionia* and *Il Prigioniero,"* autobiographical fragment in *Musical Quarterly* (July 1953).

Dallapozza, Adolf, Italian-born Austrian tenor; b. Bolzano, March 14, 1940. His parents settled in Austria when he was 5 months old. He received his musical education at the Vienna Cons.; then joined the Chorus of the Volksoper; in 1962 made his debut as soloist in the role of Ernesto in Donizetti's *Don Pasquale.* In 1967 he became a member of the Vienna State Opera; also sang with the Bavarian State Opera in Munich and made appearances in Milan, Basel, Hamburg, Zürich, and Buenos Aires. In 1976 the President of Austria made him a Kammersänger. He is highly regarded for his versatility, being equally competent in opera, oratorio, and operetta.

Dalla Rizza, Gilda, Italian soprano; b. Verona, Oct. 2, 1892; d. Milan, July 4, 1975. She received her musical training in Bologna; made her debut there in 1912; in 1915 she sang at La Scala; Puccini so admired her singing that he created the role of Magda in *La Rondine* for her (Monte Carlo, March 27, 1917). Toscanini engaged her at La Scala in Milan, and she remained on its roster until 1939. She subsequently taught voice at the Cons. of Venice.

Dal Monte, Toti, Italian coloratura soprano; b. Mo-

gliano, near Treviso, June 27, 1893; d. Pieve di Soligo, Treviso, Jan. 26, 1975. Her original name was **Antonietta Meneghelli.** She studied piano and singing; made her operatic debut at La Scala in Milan in 1916; made her first American appearance at the Metropolitan Opera House in N.Y. in *Lucìa di Lammermoor* on Dec. 5, 1924, remaining at the Metropolitan for the 1924–25 season; also sang in Chicago in 1924–28; at Covent Garden in London in 1926; toured Australia in 1929. After the end of her operatic career, about 1949, she devoted herself to teaching. She publ. her autobiography, *Una voce nel mondo* (Milan, 1962).

Dalmorès, Charles, French dramatic tenor; b. Nancy, Jan. 1, 1871; d. Hollywood, Dec. 6, 1939. After taking first prizes at the local Cons. for solfeggio and French horn at 17, he received from the city of Nancy a stipend for study at the Paris Cons., where he took first prize for horn at 19; played in the Colonne Orch. (2 years) and the Lamoureux Orch. (2 years); at 23, became a prof. of horn playing at the Lyons Cons. His vocal teacher was Dauphin, the bass singer; his debut as a tenor took place on Oct. 6, 1899, at Rouen; later he sang at the Théâtre de la Monnaie in Brussels; 7 seasons at Covent Garden; at the Manhattan Opera House in N.Y. (1906–10; debut as Faust, Dec. 7, 1906); then was with the Chicago Opera Co. (1910–18). His repertoire was large, and included Wagnerian as well as French operas; in Chicago he sang Tristan and the title role in the first performance of *Parsifal* to be presented there.

d'Alvimare, Martin-Pierre. See **Dalvimare, Martin-Pierre.**

Dalvimare (real name, **d'Alvimare**), **Martin-Pierre,** French harpist and composer for harp; b. Dreux (Eure-et-Loire), Sept. 18, 1772; d. Paris, June 13, 1839. In 1800 he was harpist at the Paris Opéra; became harpist to Napoleon in 1806; harp teacher to the Empress Josephine (1807); retired to his estate at Dreux in 1812. He wrote several sonatas for harp and violin; duets for 2 harps, for harp and piano, for harp and horn; fantasies, variations, etc.

Damase, Jean-Michel, French composer and pianist; b. Bordeaux, Jan. 27, 1928. He studied with Delvincourt at the Paris Cons.; received the Grand Prix de Rome in 1947; made his U.S. debut April 20, 1954, in N.Y. as a pianist-composer.

WORKS: Ballets: *Le Saut du Tremplin* (Paris, 1944); *La Croqueuse de diamants* (Paris, 1950); *Interludes* for Orch. (Nice, 1948); Rhapsody for Oboe and String Orch. (Paris Radio, 1948); Piano Concerto (Cannes, 1950); Violin Concerto (Paris, Dec. 22, 1956); 2nd Piano Concerto (Paris, Feb. 6, 1963); chamber music: Quintet for Violin, Viola, Cello, Flute, and Harp (1947); Trio for Flute, Harp, and Cello (1949); piano pieces and songs; operas: *Colombe* (Bordeaux, May 5, 1961) and *Eurydice* (Bordeaux Festival, May 26, 1972). A list of works and bibliography is publ. in C. Chamfray, "Jean-Michel Damase," *Courrier Musical de France,* 18 (1967).

Dambois, Maurice, Belgian cellist; b. Liège, March 30, 1889; d. there, Nov. 12, 1969. He studied at the Cons. there (1899–1905) and won many prizes (piano, harmony, chamber music, fugue, cello); made his debut at 12 with Saint-Saëns's A-minor Concerto; toured Germany (1905), England (1906–8), France, Portugal, and the Netherlands; was appointed director of the Académie de Musique at Liège (1910), and prof. of cello at the Brussels Cons. (1912). After the outbreak of the war he went to England (until 1916); went to the U.S. in 1917 with Ysaÿe; made his American debut in N.Y., April 21, 1917, followed by successful tours. In 1926 he settled in Brussels, and resumed his post as prof. of cello at the Cons., retaining it for 30 years.

Damcke, Berthold, German conductor; b. Hannover, Feb. 6, 1812; d. Paris, Feb. 15, 1875. He was a pupil of Alexander Schmitt and F. Ries at Frankfurt; in 1837, became conductor of the Potsdam Phil. Society, and of the Choral Union for operatic music (grand concerts, 1839–40); was active in St. Petersburg (1845), Brussels (1855), and Paris (1859). He was a friend and devoted admirer of Berlioz. He revised and edited, with F. Pelletan, Gluck's 2 *Iphigénies;* composed oratorios, part-songs, and piano pieces.
BIBLIOGRAPHY: *Berthold Damcke, Etude biographique et musicale* (Paris, 1895).

Damerini, Adelmo, Italian musicologist; b. Carmignano, near Florence, Dec. 11, 1880; d. there, Oct. 12, 1976. He studied with Edgardo Binelli and Giannotto Bastianelli. He held teaching positions at the American Methodist Inst. in Rome, at the Palermo Cons. (1922), and at the Cons. Boito in Parma; from 1933 till 1962 was a prof. at the Cons. of Florence. He publ. *Origine e svolgimento della sinfonia* (Pistoia, 1919); *Le sinfonie di Beethoven* (Rome, 1921); *Lorenzo Perosi* (Rome, 1924; 2nd ed., revised, 1953); *Classicismo e romanticismo nella musica* (Florence, 1942); *Il R. Conservatorio di musica "Luigi Cherubini" di Firenze* (Florence, 1942); *L'Istituto Giovanni Pacini di Lucca* (Florence, 1942); *Boezio: Pensieri sulla musica* (Florence, 1955); *Profilo delle grandi epoche musicale* (Milan, 1955); *Guglielmo de Machaut e l' "Ars nova" italiana* (Florence, 1960); with G. Roncaglia, *Volti musicale di Falstaff* (Siena, 1961); *Luigi Cherubini nel II centenario della nascita* (Florence, 1962).

Dameron, "Tadd" (Tadley Ewing), black American jazz pianist; b. Cleveland, Feb. 21, 1917; d. New York, March 8, 1965. He was inspired to follow a career as a jazz musician by his brother Caesar, a saxophone player; he subsequently played piano with Freddie Webster, Zack White, and Blanche Calloway; also became an accomplished arranger, working in Chicago and N.Y. His career was plagued by his addiction to narcotics, as a result of which he served time in jail.

Damone, Vic, American singer of popular music; b. Brooklyn, June 12, 1928. He first came to promi-
nence on the radio; subsequently became a successful nightclub singer; also appeared on television. He made several film appearances as an actor, but concentrated mainly on his vocal career.

Damoreau, Laure-Cinthie (née **Montalant;** first known as **"Mlle. Cinti"**), noted French operatic soprano; b. Paris, Feb. 6, 1801; d. Chantilly, Feb. 25, 1863. She studied at the Paris Cons.; made her debut in 1819 at the Théâtre Italien; later was engaged at the Opéra (1826–35). Rossini wrote leading roles for her in *Le Siège de Corinthe* and *Mosè*, as did Auber, during her engagement (1835–43) at the Opéra-Comique (*Domino noir, L'Ambassadrice,* etc.). Retiring from the stage, she made concert tours to England, the Netherlands, and Russia, and (with Artôt, the violinist) to the U.S. and Havana (1843). She was a prof. of singing at the Paris Cons. in 1834–56; then retired to Chantilly. Her husband was an actor at Brussels. She publ. *Album de romances* and *Méthode de chant.*

Da Motta, José Vianna, noted Portuguese pianist; b. on Isle St. Thomas, Portuguese Africa, April 22, 1868; d. Lisbon, May 31, 1948. His family returned to Lisbon when he was a year old; he studied with local teachers; gave his first concert at the age of 13; then studied piano in Berlin with Xaver Scharwenka and composition with Philipp Scharwenka. In 1885 he went to Weimar, where he became a pupil of Liszt; also took lessons with Hans von Bülow in Frankfurt (1887). He then undertook a series of concert tours throughout Europe (1887–88), the U.S. (1892–93; 1899), and South America (1902). He was in Berlin until 1915; then became director of the Geneva Cons. In 1919 he returned to Lisbon and was appointed director of the Lisbon Cons., retiring in 1938. At the height of his career he was greatly esteemed as a fine interpreter of Bach and Beethoven. He was also the author of many articles in German, French, and Portuguese; wrote *Studien bei Bülow* (1896); *Betrachtungen über Franz Liszt* (1898); *Die Entwicklung des Klavierkonzerts* (as a program book to Busoni's concerts); essays on Alkan; critical articles in the *Kunstwart, Klavierlehrer, Bayreuther Blätter,* etc. He was a prolific composer; among his works are *Die Lusiaden* for Orch. and Chorus; Symph.; String Quartet; many piano pieces, in some of which (e.g., the *5 Portuguese Rhapsodies* and the Portuguese dance *Vito*) he employs folk themes with striking effect.
BIBLIOGRAPHY: F. Lopes Graça, *Vianna da Motta; Subsidios para una biographia* (Lisbon, 1949).

Damrosch, Frank, German-American choral conductor, son of **Leopold Damrosch;** b. Breslau, June 22, 1859; d. New York, Oct. 22, 1937. He studied with Bruckner, Jean Vogt, and von Inten, and composition with his father and Moszkowski. In 1882–85 he was conductor of the Denver (Colo.) Chorus Club, and in 1884–85, supervisor of music in public schools, and organist at different churches. In 1885–91, he was chorus master and assistant conductor at the Metropolitan Opera House in N.Y.; till 1887 was conductor of the Newark Harmonic Society; in 1892, organized the People's Choral Union, an enterprise for the popularization of choral singing, for which he publ. in 1894 *Popular Method of Sight Singing*; in 1897–1905, he was supervisor of music in N.Y. City public schools; conducted the Oratorio Society (1898–1912). In 1893 he founded the Musical Art Society, a chorus of 60 trained voices for the performance of a cappella music, which he conducted till 1920. In 1905 he established an exemplary organization, the splendidly equipped Inst. of Musical Art, which, in 1926, became affiliated with the Juilliard School of Music; he retained his position as dean until his retirement in 1933. He received the degree of D.Mus. (*honoris causa*) from Yale Univ. in 1904; publ. vocal numbers (songs, choruses); also wrote *Some Essentials in the Teaching of Music* (N.Y., 1916) and *Institute of Musical Art, 1905–26* (N.Y., 1936).

BIBLIOGRAPHY: E.T. Rice, "A Tribute to Frank Damrosch," *Musical Quarterly* (April 1939); L.P. and R.P. Stebbins, *Frank Damrosch* (1945).

Damrosch, Leopold, eminent German-American conductor and violinist; b. Posen, Oct. 22, 1832; d. New York, Feb. 15, 1885. He studied with Ries, Dehn, and Böhmer; took the degree of M.D. at Berlin Univ. in 1854, but then, against his parents' wishes, embraced the career of a musician; he appeared at first as a solo violinist in several German cities, later as a conductor at minor theaters, and in 1885 procured, through Liszt, the position of solo violinist in the Grand Ducal Orch. at Weimar. While here he was intimate with Liszt and many of his most distinguished pupils, and won Wagner's lifelong friendship; in Weimar, too, he married the singer **Helene von Heimburg** (b. Oldenburg, 1835; d. New York, Nov. 21, 1904). In 1858–60, Damrosch was conductor of the Breslau Phil. Concerts; gave up the post to make tours with von Bülow and Tausig; organized the Breslau Orch. Society in 1862. Besides this, he founded quartet *soirées,* and a choral society; conducted the Society for Classical Music, and a theater orch. (for 2 years); frequently appeared as a solo violinist. In 1871 he was called to N.Y. to conduct the Arion Society, and made his debut, on May 6, 1871, as conductor, composer, and violinist. In N.Y. his remarkable capacity as an organizer found free scope; besides bringing the Arion to the highest pitch of efficiency and prosperity, he founded the Symphony Society in 1878, the latter's concerts succeeding those of the Thomas Orch. at Steinway Hall. In 1880 Columbia College conferred on him the degree of D.Mus.; in 1881 he conducted the first major music festival held in N.Y., with an orch. of 250 and a chorus of 1,200; in 1883 he made a highly successful Western tour with his orch.; in 1884–85 he organized the German Opera Co., and, together with Anton Seidl, conducted a season of German opera at the Metropolitan Opera House, presenting Wagner's *Ring des Nibelungen, Tristan und Isolde,* and *Die Meistersinger* for the first time in the U.S. He composed 7 cantatas; Symph. in A; music to

Schiller's *Joan of Arc*; marches for orch.; 3 violin concertos; several pieces for violin and orch., and for solo voice and orch.; choruses for mixed voices and male voices; duets; many songs.

BIBLIOGRAPHY: E.T. Rice, "Personal Recollections of Leopold Damrosch," *Musical Quarterly* (July 1942); George Martin, *The Damrosch Dynasty: America's First Family of Music* (N.Y., 1983).

Damrosch, Walter Johannes, famous German-American conductor, composer, and educator, son of **Leopold Damrosch;** b. Breslau, Jan. 30, 1862; d. New York, Dec. 22, 1950. He studied harmony with his father, also with Rischbieter and Draeseke in Dresden; piano with von Inten, Boekelmann, and Max Pinner in the U.S.; and conducting with his father and with Hans von Bülow. He was conductor of the N.Y. Oratorio Society (1885–98) and of the N.Y. Symph. Society (1885–1903); assistant conductor of German opera at the Metropolitan Opera House (1885–91); organized the Damrosch Opera Co. (1894), which he directed for 5 seasons, giving German opera (chiefly Wagner) in the principal cities of the U.S.; among the artists whom he first brought to the U.S. were Mmes. Klafsky, Gadski, and Ternina. On March 3, 1886, he presented *Parsifal* in N.Y., in concert form for the first time in America; in 1900–1902 he conducted Wagner's operas at the Metropolitan; then was conductor of the N.Y. Phil. Society (1902–3); in 1903 the N.Y. Symph. Society was reorganized with Damrosch as its regular conductor, a post he held until 1927; he again conducted the Oratorio Society (1917); organized at the request of General Pershing the American Expeditionary Force bands and founded schools for bandmasters in Chaumont, France (1918); conducted a concert by the N.Y. Symph. Society Orch. in the first chain broadcast over the network of the newly organized NBC (Nov. 15, 1926); was appointed musical adviser to NBC (1927, retired 1947); was conductor of the NBC Symph. Orch. in a weekly series of music appreciation hours for the schools and colleges of the U.S. and Canada (1928–42). He conducted many famous works for the first time in the U.S. (Brahms' 3rd and 4th symphs.; Tchaikovsky's 4th and 6th symphs.; etc.); was U.S. delegate at the Paris International Music Congress (1937). He received degrees of D.Mus. (*honoris causa*) from Columbia Univ. (1914), Princeton Univ. (1929), Brown Univ. (1932), Dartmouth College (1933), and N.Y. Univ. (1935); was awarded the David Bispham medal (1929) and the gold medal of the National Inst. of Arts and Letters (1938).

WORKS: Operas: *The Scarlet Letter* (Damrosch Opera Co., Boston, Feb. 10, 1896); *Cyrano de Bergerac* (Metropolitan Opera House, Feb. 27, 1913; revised 1939); *The Man without a Country* (Metropolitan, May 12, 1937); *The Opera Cloak*, one-act opera (N.Y. Opera Co., Nov. 3, 1942); comic opera, *The Dove of Peace* (Philadelphia, Oct. 15, 1912). Other works: *Manila Te Deum* (N.Y., 1898); *An Abraham Lincoln Song* (N.Y., 1936); incidental music to Euripides' *Iphigenia in Aulis* and *Medea* (Berkeley, Calif., 1915), and to Sophocles' *Electra*

(N.Y., 1917); Violin Sonata; *At Fox Meadow* (1899); *Dunkirk,* a setting of R. Nathan's poem, for Baritone, Solo, Male Chorus, and Chamber Orch. (NBC broadcast, May 2, 1943); many songs, including *Death and General Putnam* (1936), *Danny Deever,* etc. He publ. an autobiography, *My Musical Life* (N.Y., 1923; 2nd ed., 1930); was co-editor, with Gartlan and Gehrkens, of the Universal School Music Series.

BIBLIOGRAPHY: W.J. Henderson, "Walter Damrosch," *Musical Quarterly* (Jan. 1932); Gretchen Damrosch Finletter, *From the Top of the Stairs* (reminiscences of Walter Damrosch's daughter; Boston, 1946).

Dan, Ikuma, Japanese composer; b. Tokyo, April 7, 1924. He studied at the Tokyo Music Academy with K. Shimofusa and S. Moroi; taught at the Tokyo Music School (1947–50); has been active as a film music director and composer and, since 1967, has presented pop music concerts on television.

WORKS: 5 operas: *Yûzuru* (*The Twilight Crane;* 1950–51; Tokyo, Jan. 30, 1952; revised 1956); *Kikimi-mi-zukin* (*The Listening Cap;* 1954–55; Tokyo, March 18, 1955); *Yang Kwei-fei* (1957–58; Tokyo, Dec. 11, 1958); *Chanchiki* (*Cling-Clang;* 1961–63); *Hikarigoke* (1972; Osaka, April 27, 1972); *Symphonic Poem* (1948); 5 symphs. (1949–50, 1955–56, 1959–60, 1964–65, 1965); *Sinfonia Burlesca* (1953; Tokyo, Jan. 26, 1959); dance suite for Orch., *The Silken Road* (1953–54; Tokyo, June 23, 1955); *Journey through Arabia,* symph. suite (1958); *Olympic Games Overture* (1964); *Festival Overture* (1965); *Japanese Poem* No. 1 for Orch. (1967; Tokyo, Sept. 25, 1967, Arthur Fiedler conducting); *Hymn to the Sai-kai* for Chorus and Orch. (1969); *A Letter from Japan* No. 2 for Orch. (1969); *Rainbow Tower* for Orch. (1970); String Trio (1947); Piano Sonata (1947); String Quartet (1948); Divertimento for 2 Pianos (1949); *Futari Shizuka,* dance drama for Flute, Percussion, and String Ensemble (1961); Concerto Grosso for Harpsichord and String Ensemble (1965); choruses.

Dana, William Henry, American music pedagogue; b. Warren, Ohio, June 10, 1846; d. there, Feb. 18, 1916. He studied at Kullak's Academy of Music in Berlin and at the Royal Academy of Music in London (1881). He was a founder of the American Music Teachers' National Assoc. He publ. several manuals: *Practical Thorough-bass* (1873), *Orchestration* (1875), *Instrumentation for Military Bands* (1876), *Practical Harmony* (1884). He also composed a *De profundis* for Soli, Chorus, and Orch.; motets, songs, piano pieces.

Danbé, Jules, French violinist and composer; b. Caen, Nov. 16, 1840; d. Vichy, Nov. 10, 1905. He was a pupil at the Paris Cons.; 2nd director of the Cons. concerts till 1892; conductor at the Opéra-Comique (1877–98); from 1899 until his death, was conductor at the Théâtre Lyrique, where he successfully revived Gluck's *Iphigénie en Tauride* after a long period of neglect.

Danckert, Werner, German musicologist; b. Erfurt, June 22, 1900; d. Krefeld, March 5, 1970. He studied natural science and mathematics at the Univ. of Jena, then musicology at the Univ. of Leipzig with Riemann and Abert, at the Univ. of Erlangen with Becking, and at the Leipzig Cons. with Schering. He received his Ph.D. in 1924 at the Univ. of Erlangen with the dissertation *Geschichte der Gigue* (publ. in Leipzig, 1924); he completed his Habilitation at the Univ. of Jena in 1926 with his *Personale Typen des Melodiestils* (publ. in an enlarged ed. as *Ursymbole melodischer Gestaltung* in Kassel, 1932). He was Becking's assistant at the Univ. of Erlangen (1924–25); then taught piano at the Weimar Academy of Music (1929–32) and was a music critic in Erfurt (1932–37). He became a lecturer at the Univ. of Berlin in 1937, prof. in 1939, and head of the musicology dept. in 1943; then was in Graz (1943–45). He was briefly a prof. at the Univ. of Rostock in 1950, but returned to West Germany that same year; then lived in Krefeld.

WRITINGS: *Beiträge zur Bachkritik* (Kassel, 1934); *Das europäische Volkslied* (Berlin, 1939; 2nd ed., 1970); *Grundriss der Volksliedkunde* (Berlin, 1939); *Claude Debussy* (Berlin, 1950); *Goethe: Der mythische Urgrund seiner Weltenschau* (Berlin, 1951); *Offenes und geschlossenes Leben: Zwei Daseinsaspekte in Goethes Weltenschau* (Bonn, 1963); *Unehrliche Leute: Die verfemten Berufe* (Bern and Munich, 1964); *Das Volkslied im Abendland* (Bern and Munich, 1966); *Tonreich and Symbolzahl in Hochkulturen und in der Primitivenwelt* (Bonn, 1966); *Symbol, Metaphor, Allegorie im Lied der Völker* (Bonn, 1977).

Danckerts, Ghiselin, Flemish contrapuntist and theorist; b. Tholen, Zeeland, c.1510; d. c.1565. He entered the Papal Chapel in Rome as a chorister in 1538; was pensioned in 1565. He publ. (1559) 2 books of motets for 4–6 voices; single motets are included in Augsburg collections of 1540 and 1545. His ingenuity in counterpoint is demonstrated in the so-called Chessboard Canon for 4 voices with alternating black and white notes. His autograph MS, pronouncing judgment on the theoretical dispute between Vincentino and Lusitano on the nature of ancient modes, is in the Vatican Library in Rome.

Dancla, Arnaud, French cellist, brother of **Jean-Baptiste-Charles Dancla;** b. Bagnères-de-Bigorre, Jan. 1, 1819; d. there, Feb. 1, 1862. He was the author of a method for cello; composed études, duos, and melodies for his instrument.

Dancla, (Jean-Baptiste-) Charles, French violinist and composer; b. Bagnères-de-Bigorre, Dec. 19, 1817; d. Tunis, Nov. 9, 1907. He entered the Paris Cons. in 1828, his teachers being Baillot (violin), Halévy, and Berton. In 1834, he was a violinist in the Opéra-Comique orch.; became renowned by his playing in the Société des Concerts, and was appointed prof. of violin at the Paris Cons. in 1857. His quartet *soirées* were famous. Besides 4 symphs., he composed some 130 works for violin; 14 string quartets; 4 piano trios.

WRITINGS: *Méthode élémentaire et progressive pour le violon; Ecole du mécanisme; L'Ecole de la mélodie; Ecole de l'expression;* and (with Panseron) *L'Art de moduler sur le violon;* also books of essays, *Les Compositeurs chefs d'orchestre* (1873), and *Miscellanées musicales* (1876).

BIBLIOGRAPHY: *Charles Dancla, Notes et souvenirs* (Paris, 1893; 2nd ed., 1898; contains catalogue of works).

Dancla, Léopold, French violinist, brother of the preceding; b. Bagnères-de-Bigorre, June 1, 1823; d. Paris, April 29, 1895. He was a pupil of Baillot at the Paris Cons., taking first prize in violin in 1842. He wrote 3 string quartets; *airs variés;* fantasies and studies for the violin.

Danco, Suzanne, Belgian soprano; b. Brussels, Jan. 22, 1911. She studied at the Brussels Cons.; in 1936 won the International Bel Canto Prize at Venice; in 1948 was engaged as soloist at the Edinburgh Festival; also sang in Milan; in 1950 made her American debut. She has gained a fine reputation in Europe and America for her musicianly performances in opera (ranging from Mozart to Alban Berg) and in concert recitals (notably in Debussy's songs).

Dandara, Liviu, Rumanian composer; b. Miorcani, near Botoşani, Dec. 3, 1933. He studied with Paul Constantinescu, Ion Dumitrescu, and Tudor Ciortea at the Bucharest Cons. (1953–59).

WORKS: 2 cantatas: *1907* (1957) and *Construcţii* (1969); *Sinfonietta lirica* (1958); *Ouverture solennelle* (1959); Suite for Orch. (1962); *Divertissement* for Orch. (1964); *Expresii umane* for Orch. (1968); *Spaţii,* stereophonic music for 32 Instruments and Amplifiers (1971); Piano Concerto (1972); *3 Slow Movements* for Clarinet and Piano (1963); *Ipostaze* for Wind Quartet (1966); Sonata for Solo Clarinet (1966); *Dialoguri cu axa timpului* for Flute, Violin, Piano, and Percussion (1968); *Pentaedre per la "Musica Nova,"* quintet for Clarinet, Violin, Viola, Cello, and Piano (1969; "Musica Nova" is a Rumanian ensemble); *Bamba!* for Wind Instruments, or Voices and Percussion (1971); *Miniatures* for Piano (1959); Piano Sonatina (1961); Toccata for Piano (1965); *Sonata brevis* for Piano (1966); *Quadriforium* for Piano and Tape (1970; variable timing); *Timpul suspendat* for Tape (1971); *Imnurile verii,* 3 madrigals for Double Chorus, Xylophone, and Vibraphone (1967); songs; film music.

Dandelot, Georges, French composer, son of the impresario **Arthur Dandelot** (1864–1943); b. Paris, Dec. 2, 1895; d. St.-Georges de Didonne (Charente-Maritime), Aug. 17, 1975. He studied with Widor at the Paris Cons.; later took lessons with Dukas and Roussel. He was in the French army during World War I, and received the Croix de Guerre for valor. In 1919 he became an instructor at the Ecole Normale de Musique in Paris; in 1942, was appointed a prof. at the Paris Cons. Dandelot composed an oratorio, *Pax* (first prize at the International Exposi-

tion in Paris, 1937); 2 operas: *Midas* (1947) and *L'Ennemi* (1948); ballets: *Le Souper de famine* (1943); *Le Jardin merveilleux* (1944); *Pierrot et la rose* (1948); Symph. (1941); Piano Concerto (Paris, Jan. 7, 1934); *Concerto romantique* for Violin and Orch. (1944); chamber music; songs.

Dandrieu, Jean François, French composer; b. Paris, 1682; d. there, Jan. 17, 1738. He was organist at Saint-Merry, Paris, in 1704; in 1721 became organist at the Royal Chapel. He publ. *Livre de sonates en trio* (1705); *Livre de sonates* for Solo Violin (1710); *Principes de l'accompagnement du clavecin* (1718); *Pièces de clavecin* (3 albums, 1724); organ pieces, airs. His importance lies in his works for clavecin, written in a style closely resembling Couperin's.

BIBLIOGRAPHY: P. Brunold, *Dandrieu* (Paris, 1954).

Daneau, Nicolas, Belgian composer; b. Binche, June 17, 1866; d. Brussels, July 12, 1944. He studied at the Ghent Cons. with Adolphe Samuel, graduating in 1892; won the 2nd Prix de Rome in 1895. He was director of the Cons. of Tournai (1896–1919), and of the Cons. of Mons (1919–31).

WORKS: *Linario,* lyric drama (Tournai, 1906); *Myrtis,* opera-idyll (Tournai, 1910); *Le Sphynx,* opera; *La Brute,* lyric drama. For Orch.: *Villes d'Italie; Adima et Hevah; Arles; Mardi-Gras; Petite suite.* Chamber music: Suite for Violin and Piano; String Quartet; Piano Quintet. His daughter, **Suzanne Daneau** (b. Tournai, Aug. 17, 1901), was his pupil. She has written orch. works, chamber music, and piano pieces, mostly based on native folk songs.

BIBLIOGRAPHY: L.J. Beatrice, *Daneau; Histoire d'une famille d'artistes* (Brussels, 1944).

Danhauser, Adolphe-Léopold, French composer and teacher; b. Paris, Feb. 26, 1835; d. there, June 9, 1896. He studied at the Paris Cons. with Halévy and Reber; won first prize in harmony (1857); first prize in fugue (1859); 2nd Prix de Rome (1862); was chief inspector of instruction in singing in the communal schools in Paris and prof. of solfeggio at the Cons. He wrote *Théorie de la musique;* publ. *Soirées orphéoniques,* a collection of 3-part choruses for equal voices. He composed *Le Proscrit,* a musical drama with choruses, which was produced (1866) in a religious institution at Auteuil; a 3-act opera, *Maures et Castillans* (not perf.). His *Solfège des solfèges* (3 vols.; trans. into Eng. and Spanish) is still in use throughout the U.S. and South America.

Daniel, Oliver, American music critic and editor; b. De Pere, Wis., Nov. 24, 1911. He was editor of the American Composers' Alliance (1951–54); in 1954 became director of the Concert Music Administration of Broadcast Music, Inc. He was co-founder, with Leopold Stokowski, of the Contemporary Music Society in 1952; represented the U.S. at the International Music Council of UNESCO. He edited the collections *The Harmony of Maine, Down East Spirituals,* and *The Music of William Billings.*

Daniel – Dankevich

Daniel, Salvador (real name, **Francisco Daniel;** also known as **Salvador-Daniel**), French composer and political revolutionary; b. Bourges, Feb. 17, 1831; killed during the Paris Commune, May 23, 1871. For a brief time he was director of the Paris Cons. under the Commune. He taught music in an Arab school in Algiers; studied native folk songs of North Africa; wrote a valuable book, *La Musique arabe* (Algiers, 1863, publ. in Eng. as *The Music and Musical Instruments of the Arabs,* London, 1915).

Daniel-Lesur. See **Lesur, Daniel.**

Daniélou, Alain, French musicologist, authority on music of Asia; b. Paris, Oct. 4, 1907. He devoted himself mainly to the study of Asian music; lived mostly in India; lectured at the Univ. of Benares (1949–54); was director of research in Madras (1954–56) and at the Inst. of Indology in Pondicherry (1956–59). In 1959 he was appointed instructor at the Ecole Français d'Extrême Orient in Paris. In 1963 he assumed the post of director of the International Inst. for Comparative Studies.
WRITINGS: *Introduction to the Study of Musical Scales* (London, 1943); *Northern Indian Music* (2 vols., Calcutta, 1949, 1953; 2nd ed., revised, as *The Ragas of Northern Indian Music,* 1968); *La Musique du Cambodge et du Laos* (Pondicherry, 1957); *Traité de musicologie comparée* (Paris, 1959); *Purānas: Texts des Purānas sur la théorie musicale* (Pondicherry, 1959); *Bharata, Muni, Le Gitālamkāra* (Pondicherry, 1960); *Inde* (Paris, 1966); *Sémantique musicale* (Paris, 1967); *La Situation de la musique et des musiciens dans les pays d'orient* (Florence, 1971; Eng. trans., 1971).

Daniels, Charlie, American country-music violinist; b. Wilmington, N.C., Oct. 28, 1936. He played in a group known as the Jaguar band; then joined the country-music ensembles of Earl Scruggs and Marty Robbins; in 1971 he founded his own Charlie Daniels Band, which won a Grammy award in 1980 and became one of the most popular country-and-western groups before the public.

Daniels, Mabel Wheeler, American composer; b. Swampscott, Mass., Nov. 27, 1878; d. Boston, March 10, 1971. She studied at Radcliffe College (B.A., magna cum laude, 1900) and with Chadwick in Boston; then with Thuille in Munich; was director of the Radcliffe Glee Club (1911–13); head of music at Simmons College in Boston in 1913–18; received an honorary M.A. from Tufts College in 1933; an honorary D.Mus. from Boston Univ. in 1939. As a composer, she excelled in vocal writing; her instrumental pieces are cautiously modernistic.
WORKS: Operetta, *The Court of Hearts* (Cambridge, Mass., Jan. 2, 1901; she sang the part of Jack of Hearts); operatic sketch, *Alice in Wonderland Continued* (Brookline, Mass., May 20, 1904). Vocal works with Orch.: *The Desolate City* (1913); *Peace with a Sword* (Handel and Haydn Society, Boston, 1917); *Songs of Elfland* (St. Louis Symph. Orch., Feb. 2, 1924); *The Holy Star* (1928); *Exultate Deo* (for the 50th anniversary of Radcliffe College; Boston, May 31, 1929); *Song of Jael,* cantata for Dramatic Soprano, Mixed Voices, and Orch. (Worcester Festival, Oct. 5, 1940); *A Psalm of Praise* (composed for the 75th anniversary of the founding of Radcliffe College; Cambridge, Dec. 3, 1954; Boston Symph. Orch., April 27, 1956); choral cycle for Women's Voices, *In Springtime* (1910); 3-part women's choruses, with Piano and 2 Violins: *Eastern Song* and *The Voice of My Beloved* (prize of the National Federation of Music Clubs, 1911); sacred choruses a cappella (*The Christ Child, Salve festa dies,* etc.); duets; part-songs. For Orch.: *Deep Forest,* prelude for Small Orch. (Barrère Little Symph., N.Y., June 3, 1931; re-scored for Full Orch., 1934; Boston Symph., April 16, 1937, Koussevitzky conducting); *Pirates' Island* (Harrisburg Symph., Feb. 19, 1935). Chamber music: *Pastoral Ode* for Flute and Strings (1940); *3 Observations* for Oboe, Clarinet, and Bassoon (1943); *Digressions,* a ballet for Strings (Boston, 1947). She wrote a lively book, *An American Girl in Munich* (Boston, 1905).

Danjou, Jean-Louis-Félix, French music teacher; b. Paris, June 21, 1812; d. Montpellier, March 4, 1866. He studied organ with François Benoist at the Paris Cons.; then played organ at various churches from 1830; was organist at Notre Dame from 1840 till 1847. With his essay *De l'état de l'avenir du chant ecclésiastique* (1844), he became the pioneer in the movement for reforming plainchant; and his journal *Revue de la Musique Religieuse, Populaire et Classique* (1845–49) showed profound erudition gained by assiduous historical research. He was the discoverer (1847) of the celebrated "Antiphonary of Montpellier." He labored to promote organ building in France; made a special study of organ manufacture in Germany and the Netherlands; entered into partnership with the organ builders Daublaine & Callinet of Paris, but lost his entire capital, gave up music, and in 1849 became a political journalist in Marseilles and Montpellier.

Dankevich, Konstantin, eminent Ukrainian composer; b. Odessa, Dec. 24, 1905. He studied with Zolotarev at the Odessa Cons., graduating in 1929. In 1942 he was artistic director of the Red Army Ensemble of Songs and Dance in Tiflis. From 1944 to 1953 he was a prof. of composition at the Odessa Cons.; in 1953 he was appointed to the faculty of the Kiev Cons. In his works he successfully presents the motifs of Ukrainian and Russian folk songs. He first attracted attention with his opera *Bogdan Khmelnitzky* (Moscow, June 15, 1951), on a subject from Ukrainian history; the opera was attacked for its libretto and its unsuitable music, and Dankevich revised the score, after which it gained favorable notices in Russia. He also wrote the opera *Nazar Stodolya* (Kharkov, May 28, 1960). His most popular score is *Lileya,* a ballet, produced in 1939 and retained in the repertoire of the Russian theater. Other works include 2 symphs. (1937, 1945), several overtures, and patriotic choruses, including *Poem of the Ukraine* (1960) and the ideological cantata to his own words, *The Dawn of Communism Has Risen over Us* (1961). A monograph on Dankevich was publ. in Ukrainian in Kiev (1959).

Danks, Hart Pease, American song composer; b. New Haven, Conn., April 6, 1834; d. Philadelphia, Nov. 20, 1903. He studied at Saratoga Springs with Dr. L.E. Whiting; in 1851 moved to Chicago, where he became a photographer, and also sang bass in church. In 1864 he settled in N.Y. and developed energetic activity as a prolific composer of sacred hymns and popular songs; publ. a total of about 1,300 separate numbers; also compiled books of church anthems; wrote 2 operettas: *Pauline, or the Belle of Saratoga* (1872) and *Conquered by Kindness* (1881). Of his sacred songs, the most popular was *Not Ashamed of Christ* (1873); in the light genre, his greatest successes were the songs *Don't be angry with me, darling* and *Silver threads among the gold.*

BIBLIOGRAPHY: G.L. Howe, *A Hundred Years of Music in America* (Chicago, 1889, pp. 98–99).

Dankworth, John, English alto saxophonist, clarinetist, bandleader, and composer-arranger; b. London, Sept. 20, 1927. He studied at the Royal Academy of Music (1944–46); then played alto saxophone and clarinet in jazz groups; formed his own septet in 1950, then his own jazz orch. in 1953. After his marriage to the singer **Cleo Laine** in 1958, he toured with her, appearing as a guest conductor in England and the U.S. His compositions include *Improvisations* (1959; composed with Mátyás Seiber); *Escapade* (1967); *Tom Sawyer's Saturday* for Narrator and Orch. (1967); String Quintet (1971); Piano Concerto (1972). In 1974 he was made a Commander of the Order of the British Empire.

Dannreuther, Edward George, pianist and music scholar, brother of **Gustav;** b. Strasbourg, Nov. 4, 1844; d. London, Feb. 12, 1905. He went with his parents in 1849 to Cincinnati, where he was taught by F.L. Ritter; then studied at the Leipzig Cons. with Richter, Moscheles, and Hauptmann (1859–63). On April 11, 1863, he made his debut in London, playing Chopin's Concerto in F minor. He introduced into England the piano concertos of Liszt, Grieg, and Tchaikovsky. In 1872 he founded the London Wagner Society, and conducted its concerts in 1873–74; was an active promoter of the Wagner Festival (1877); was appointed a prof. at the Royal Academy of Music in 1895. An indefatigable champion of the new composers, he was equally active on behalf of the older masters; the chamber music concerts that he gave at his home (1874–93) were famous. Dannreuther visited the U.S. several times.

WRITINGS: "Richard Wagner and the Reform of the Opera," *Monthly Musical Record* (separately, London, 1873; 2nd ed., revised, 1904); *Richard Wagner, His Tendencies and Theories* (London, 1873); *Musical Ornamentation* (2 vols., London, 1893–95; a valuable work, despite some misapprehensions exposed by later investigations); *The Romantic Period,* vol. VI of the *Oxford History of Music* (London,

1905; 3rd ed., 1931). He trans. into Eng. several of Wagner's literary works: *Wagners Briefe an einen französischen Freund* (1873); *Das Kunstwerk der Zukunft* (1873); *Beethoven* (1880); *Über das Dirigieren* (1885; 4th ed., 1940).

Dannreuther, Gustav, American violinist, brother of **Edward;** b. Cincinnati, July 21, 1853; d. New York, Dec. 19, 1923. He studied at the Hochschule für Musik, Berlin, under de Ahna and Joachim (violin) and Heitel (theory); then lived in London; in 1877 he joined the Mendelssohn Quintette Club of Boston, traveling through the U.S., Canada, and Newfoundland. In 1882–84 he was director of the Buffalo Phil. Society (a chamber music organization), and during this period gave 60 concerts. In 1884 he founded the Beethoven String Quartet of N.Y. (renamed the Dannreuther Quartet in 1894). From 1907 he taught violin at Vassar College.

Danon, Oskar, Yugoslav conductor; b. Sarajevo, Feb. 7, 1913. He was educated at the Prague Cons. and the Univ. of Prague (Ph.D., 1938). In 1940 he became a conductor at the Belgrade Opera; eventually became chief conductor there. He also conducted throughout Europe, both opera and symph. concerts.

Danzi, Franz, German composer and teacher; b. Schwetzingen, June 15, 1763; d. Karlsruhe, April 13, 1826. He received primary instruction in music from his father, **Innocenz Danzi,** a cellist; later took theory lessons with Abbé Vogler. In 1783 he joined the court orch. in Munich; then (1807–12) served as assistant Kapellmeister at Stuttgart, where he was the teacher of Carl Maria von Weber.

WORKS: *Cleopatra,* duodrama (Mannheim, Jan. 30, 1780); *Azakia,* comedy (Mannheim, June 6, 1780); *Die Mitternachtsstunde,* singspiel (Munich, April 1788); *Der Sylphe,* singspiel (Munich, 1788); *Der Triumph der Treue,* melodrama (Munich, Feb. 1789; not extant); *Der Quasi-Mann,* comedy (Munich, Aug. 1789; not extant); *Deucalion et Pirrha,* opera (c.1795); *Der Kuss,* comedy (Munich, June 27, 1799); *El Bondocani,* singspiel (Munich, 1802; not extant); *Iphigenie in Aulis,* grand opera (Munich, Jan. 27, 1807); *Dido,* melodrama (Stuttgart, 1811; not extant); *Camilla und Eugen oder Der Gartenschlüssel,* comedy (Stuttgart, March 15, 1812); *Rubezahl,* singspiel (Karlsruhe, April 19, 1813); *Malvina,* singspiel (Karlsruhe, Dec. 20, 1814); *Turandot,* singspiel (Karlsruhe, Feb. 9, 1817); *Die Probe,* opera (Karlsruhe, Oct. 1817); *L'Abbe de Attaignant oder Die Theaterprobe,* opera (Karlsruhe, Sept. 14, 1820); oratorios, cantatas; masses; the 128th Psalm for Chorus and Orch.; symphs., quintets, quartets, concertos, sonatas. He was an excellent singing teacher, and wrote vocal exercises of practical value.

BIBLIOGRAPHY: E. Reipschläger, *Schubaur, Danzi und Poissl als Opernkomponisten* (Diss., Univ. of Rostock, 1911); M. Herre, *Franz Danzi* (Diss., Univ. of Munich, 1924).

Da Ponte, Lorenzo, famous librettist; b. Ceneda,

near Venice, March 10, 1749; d. New York, Aug. 17, 1838. His real name was **Emanuele Conegliano;** he was of a Jewish family; was converted to Christianity at the age of 14, and assumed the name of his patron, Bishop of Ceneda Lorenzo da Ponte. He then studied at the Ceneda Seminary and at the Portogruaro Seminary, where he taught in 1770–73; in 1774 obtained a post as prof. of rhetoric at Treviso, but was dismissed in 1776 for his beliefs concerning natural laws. He then went to Venice, where he led an adventurous life, and was banished in 1779 for adultery; subsequently lived in Austria and in Dresden; in 1782 he settled in Vienna and became official poet to the Imperial Theater; met Mozart and became his friend and librettist of his most famous operas, *Le nozze di Figaro, Don Giovanni,* and *Così fan tutte.* In 1792–98 he was in London; traveled in Europe; then went to N.Y. in 1805. After disastrous business ventures, with intervals of teaching, he became interested in various operatic enterprises. In his last years he was a teacher of Italian at Columbia College. He publ. *Memorie* (4 vols., N.Y., 1823–27; Eng. trans., London, 1929, and Philadelphia, 1929).

BIBLIOGRAPHY: A. Marchesan, *Della vita e delle opere di Lorenzo da Ponte* (Treviso, 1900); J.L. Russo, *Lorenzo da Ponte, Poet and Adventurer* (N.Y., 1922); A. Fitzlyon, *The Libertine Librettist* (London, 1955).

Daquin, Louis-Claude, French organist and composer; b. Paris, July 4, 1694; d. there, June 15, 1772. He was a pupil of Marchand; at 6 played on the clavecin before Louis XIV; at 12 became organist at St.-Antoine, where his playing attracted crowds of curious listeners. From 1727 until his death he was organist at St.-Paul, having won the position in competition with Rameau. He publ. a book of *Pièces de clavecin* (1735; contains the celebrated piece *Le Coucou;* selections reprinted in Expert's *Les Maîtres du clavecin;* also revised by Brunold in 1926); a collection of *Noëls pour l'orgue ou le clavecin* (reprinted by Guilmant in *Archives des Maîtres de l'Orgue*), and a cantata, *La Rose.* The first complete modern edition of his *Pièces de clavecin* was edited by Christopher Hogwood (London, 1983).

D'Aranyi, Jelly. See **Aranyi, Jelly.**

D'Archambeau, Iwan. See **Archambeau, Iwan.**

Darclée, Hariclea (real name, **Haricly Hartulary**), Rumanian soprano; b. Brǎila, June 10, 1860; d. Bucharest, Jan. 10, 1939. She studied in Bucharest and Paris; made her debut as Marguerite at the Paris Opéra in 1888; then sang at La Scala in Milan, creating La Wally in 1892; also sang in Rome, N.Y., St. Petersburg, Moscow, and in South America. She retired in 1918. She was particularly distinguished for her Italian repertoire; she created the role of Tosca; also was known for her performances of soprano roles in Wagner's operas.

Darcy, Robert, French-born Belgian cellist and composer; b. Paris, Nov. 10, 1910; d. Schaerbeek, near Brussels, June 6, 1967. He obtained the Premier Prix in cello at the Lyons Cons. (1928); studied composition with Francis Bousquet and Paul Vidal; played the cello in orchs. in Paris and Brussels. Mobilized in 1939, he was taken prisoner of war in June 1940; while in captivity, he organized a prisoners' orch.; returned to Belgium, becoming a citizen in 1949. His style is rooted in neo-Classicism, with an admixture of atonal elements.

WORKS: *Scherzo* for Orch. (1923); *Rêverie* for Orch. (1931); *7 Sketches* for Small Orch. (1933); Suite for Wind Orch. (1935); Suite for String Orch. (1936); Concerto for 4 Cellos and Wind Orch. (1936); *Piece* for 2 Cellos and Orch. (1937); Fantasie for Cello and Orch. (1937); *3 Marines* for Orch. (1939); Concerto for 4 Saxophones and Orch. (1939); *Danses Mosanes* for Orch. (1943); Trumpet Concerto (1948); Piano Concerto (1951); Symph. (1953); Concerto for Orch. (1965); 3 quartets for 4 Cellos (1935–37); 3 string quartets (1936–1950); *Caprice* for Wind Quintet (1936); Sextet for Winds (1937); *6 Pieces* for 4 Cellos (1937); Trio for Oboe, Clarinet, and Bassoon (1938); Quartet for 4 Saxophones (1938); Bassoon Sonata (1948); *Piece* for Wind Quintet (1962); songs.

Dargomyzhsky, Alexander, outstanding Russian composer; b. in Tula province, Feb. 14, 1813; d. St. Petersburg, Jan. 17, 1869. From 1817 he lived in St. Petersburg; studied piano with Schoberlechner and Danilevsky, and violin with Vorontsov. At 20 he was a brilliant pianist; in 1827–43 he held a government position, but then devoted himself exclusively to music, studying assiduously for 8 years; visited Germany, Brussels, and Paris in 1845; at Moscow (Dec. 17, 1847) produced an opera, *Esmeralda* (after Victor Hugo's *Notre-Dame de Paris*), with great success (excerpts publ. in piano score, Moscow, 1948). In 1845–55 he publ. over 100 minor works (vocal romances, ballads, airs, and duos; waltzes, fantasies, etc.); on May 16, 1856, he brought out his best opera, *Rusalka,* at St. Petersburg (vocal score, with indications of instruments, publ. at Moscow, 1937); in 1867, an opera-ballet, *The Triumph of Bacchus* (written in 1845; perf. in Moscow, Jan. 23, 1867); a posthumous opera, *Kamennyi gost* (*The Stone Guest,* after Pushsky's poem of the same title), was scored by Rimsky-Korsakov and produced at St. Petersburg on Feb. 28, 1872; of *Rogdana,* a fantasy-opera, only a few scenes were sketched. At first a follower of Rossini and Auber, Dargomyzhsky gradually became convinced that dramatic realism with nationalistic connotations was the destiny of Russian music; he applied this realistic method in treating the recitative in his opera *The Stone Guest* and in his songs (several of these to satirical words). His orch. works (*Finnish Fantasia, Cossack Dance, Baba-Yaga,* etc.) enjoyed wide popularity. In 1867 he was elected president of the Russian Music Society.

BIBLIOGRAPHY: N. Findeisen, *A.S. Dargomyzhsky: His Life and Work* (Moscow, 1902); S.B. Fried, *A.S. Dargomyzhsky* (St. Petersburg, 1913); A.N. Drozdov, *A.S. Dargomyzhsky* (Moscow, 1929); M. Pekelis, *Alexander Dargomyzhsky and His Circle*

(2 vols., Moscow, 1966, 1973).

Darin, Bobby, American pop crooner; b. New York, May 14, 1936; d. there, Dec. 20, 1973. His real name was **Robert Walden Cassoto.** He slogged drums, banged on the piano keys, and ripped the guitar strings as a child. He changed his name to avoid the ethnic curse and began to compose music in the rhythm-and-blues manner. His songs were marked by kinetic vitality, exemplified in such tunes as *Splish Splash* and *Queen of the Hop.* In a more romantic mood he wrote *Dream Lover.*

Darke, Harold Edwin, English organist and composer; b. London, Oct. 29, 1888; d. Cambridge, Nov. 28, 1976. He studied organ with Parratt and composition with Stanford at the Royal College of Music in London; from 1916 to 1966 he served as organist at St. Michael's Church, Cornhill, London. He wrote several cantatas and other sacred music, as well as organ pieces and songs.

Darnton, Charles, English composer and organist; b. Islington, Oct. 10, 1836; d. London, April 21, 1933. He was almost entirely self-taught; was organist of St. Jude's Church in Canonbury (1860–67), Park Chapel in Camden Town (1867–91), and Gospel Oak in Hampstead (1892–1901); composed 90 anthems (prize anthem: *I will sing of the mercies of the Lord,* London, 1897); many other sacred works; operettas; piano pieces; etc.

Darnton, Christian, English composer and writer; b. near Leeds, Oct. 30, 1905; d. Hove, April 14, 1981. He took piano lessons at the age of 4 and began to compose at 9; then studied piano with Craxton and composition with Benjamin Dale, Charles Wood, and Rootham at Cambridge; went to Berlin in 1928 and took some lessons in composition with Butting. In 1952 he decided to abandon composition and to devote himself to the writing of philosophical essays and poetry. His works include 3 symphs., 2 piano concertos, a Viola Concerto, choral works, and chamber music. He publ. a book, *You and Music* (London, 1940).

Darré, Jeanne-Marie, French pianist; b. Givet, July 30, 1905. She studied with Marguerite Long and Isidor Philipp in Paris; after numerous concerts in France and elsewhere in Europe, she made a successful series of tours in the U.S., appearing with major American orchs. A virtuoso in a grand manner, she produced a sensation by playing several piano concertos on a single night.

Darrell, Robert Donaldson, American writer on music; b. Newton, Mass., Dec. 13, 1903. He studied at the New England Cons. of Music; contributed to the *Phonograph Monthly Review* and became its editor and publisher in 1930; received a Guggenheim fellowship in 1939; was, from 1956, a contributing editor of *High Fidelity,* and continued in that capacity until 1984. He publ. the valuable compilations

Gramophone Shop Encyclopedia of Recorded Music (1936) and *Schirmer's Guide to Books on Music and Musicians* (annotated bibliography of books in Eng. available in print; N.Y., 1951); also *Good Listening* (N.Y., 1953).

Dart, (Robert) Thurston, eminent English musicologist; b. London, Sept. 3, 1921; d. there, March 6, 1971. He studied keyboard instruments at the Royal College of Music in London (1938–39); also took courses in mathematics at Univ. College, Exeter (B.Sc., 1942). In 1947 he became an assistant lecturer in music at the Univ. of Cambridge, then a full lecturer in 1952, and finally a prof. of music in 1962. In 1964 he was named King Edward Prof. of Music at King's College of the Univ. of London. As a performing musician, he made numerous appearances on the harpsichord; also appeared as organist and performer on Baroque keyboard instruments. He served as editor of the *Galpin Society Journal* (1947–54) and secretary of the documentary edition *Musica Britannica* (1950–65). His magnum opus was *The Interpretation of Music* (London, 1954; 4th ed., 1967; also in German, under the title *Practica musica,* Bern, 1959, and in Swedish, Stockholm, 1964). He also edited works by Morley, Purcell, John Bull, and others.
BIBLIOGRAPHY: I. Bent, ed., *Source Materials and the Interpretation of Music: A Memorial Volume to Thurston Dart* (London, 1981).

Darvas, Gábor, Hungarian composer; b. Szatmárnémeti, Jan. 18, 1911. He studied at the Liszt Academy in Budapest with Kodály; in 1939–48 lived in Chile, where he was an assistant conductor to Erich Kleiber. He returned to Hungary in 1948; worked mainly on orch. arrangements of classical compositions.
WORKS: *Harvest Festival* for Orch. (1935); *Autumn Pastorale* for Orch. (1936); *Symphonic Movement* (1937); *Improvisations symphoniques* for Piano and Orch. (1963); *Sectio Aurea* for 3 Percussion Groups and Orch. (1964); *Medaille* for Soprano, Percussion, Keyboard Instruments, and 2 Loudspeakers (1965); *Der Turm* for Soloists, Chorus, Percussion, 2 Pianos, and String Orch. (1967); *Rotation for 5* for 5 Instrumental Groups (1968); *Gyermekzene (Children's Music)* for Soprano and 12 Performers, 11 of whom play on child-sized instruments (1969); *Antiphon* for Tape (1970).

Dārziņš, Emils, Latvian composer and writer on music; b. Lunpiebama, Nov. 3, 1875; d. (run over by a train) Riga, Aug. 31, 1910. From 1898 to 1901 he was a pupil in composition of Rimsky-Korsakov at the St. Petersburg Cons. Returning to Latvia, he became active as a choral conductor and music critic while continuing to compose. He excelled particularly in vocal music; among his choral works, *Broken Pines* and *In the Faraway Land of Dreams* are best known. His style is marked by a fine mastery of old-fashioned Germanic Romanticism, reflected through Slavic harmonic and melodic folkways. Among his symph. pieces, only his

543

Melancholy Waltz survives. A program of his songs was presented in N.Y. by the Latvian singer Janis Klavins on Jan. 25, 1976.

Dasch, George, American violinist and conductor; b. Cincinnati, May 14, 1877; d. Chicago, April 12, 1955. He studied with Brockhoeven (theory) and L. Campanari (violin) at the Cincinnati College of Music; was a member of the Cincinnati Symph. Orch. (1895–98) and the Chicago Symph. Orch. (1898–1923); then organized his own string quartet. He was the conductor of the Chicago Civic Orch., the Joliet (Illinois) Symph. Orch., and the Evansville Phil.

Daser (Dasser, Dasserus), Ludwig, German composer; b. Munich, c.1525; d. Stuttgart, March 27, 1589. He preceded Orlando di Lasso as Kapellmeister at Munich to Duke Albert V of Bavaria; held that post until 1559.
WORKS: He publ. a Passion *a* 4 (1578), plus motets in the *Orgeltabulaturbuch* of J. Paix.
BIBLIOGRAPHY: A. Sandberger, *Beiträge zur Geschichte der Beyerischen Hofkopelle I.* (1894); B.A. Wallner, *Musikalische Denkmäler der Steinätzkunst* (1912).

Dasser, Ludwig. See **Daser, Ludwig.**

Daublaine et Callinet, firm of Paris organ builders; founded in 1838 as Daublaine et Cie. Daublaine was the business partner, Callinet the practical mechanician, and Danjou, (the initiator of the business), an intelligent and progressive theorist. After a quarrel in 1843, Callinet demolished the new work partly finished for the organ of St.-Sulpice, dissolved the partnership, and entered Cavaillé's workshops. The firm name became Ducroquet et Cie. in 1845; in 1855 it was succeeded by a limited company, later by Merklin, Schütze et Cie. from Brussels; subsequently Merklin continued the business alone until his death in 1905. As a manufacturer of instruments, the firm no longer exists.

Dauney, William, British music historian; b. Aberdeen, Scotland, Oct. 27, 1800; d. Georgetown, British Guiana, July 28, 1843. In the Advocates' Library at Edinburgh he discovered what is now known as the "Skene MS," a collection of 114 English and Scottish dances, ballads, and songs (written in tablature between 1614 and 1620), containing the oldest known (and probably original) versions of *John Anderson My Jo, The Flowers of the Forest,* etc. Dauney transcribed these into modern notation, and publ. them in 1838 as *Ancient Scottish Melodies from a MS. of the Reign of King James VI,* together with *An Introductory Enquiry Illustrative of the History of Music of Scotland.*

Dauprat, Louis-François, celebrated French horn player and composer for horn; b. Paris, May 24, 1781; d. there, July 16, 1868. He studied with Kenn at the Paris Cons.; joined the band of the Garde Nationale, and in 1799 the band of the Garde des Consuls, with which he passed through the Egyptian campaign. In 1801–5 he studied theory at the Cons. under Catel and Gossec, and studied again with Reicha in 1811–14; in 1806–8 was first horn at the Bordeaux Theater; succeeded Kenn in the Opéra orch., and Duvernoy (as *cor solo*), retiring in 1831. He was chamber musician to Napoleon (1811) and Louis XVIII (1816); in 1816 he was appointed prof. of horn in the Cons., resigning in 1842.

Dauriac, Lionel Alexandre, French psychologist and writer on music; b. Brest, Finisterre, Nov. 19, 1847; d. Paris, May 26, 1923. He graduated from the Ecole Normale Supérieure of Brest in 1867; received the degree of *docteur ès lettres* from the Univ. of Paris in 1878 (with the dissertations *Des Notions de matière et de force dans les sciences de la nature* and *De Heraclito Ephesio*); held teaching positions in philosophy at Brest, Toulouse, and Montpellier; was a lecturer at the Sorbonne on musical psychology (1896–1903); a laureate of the Academy of Moral and Political Sciences (awarded the Prix Gegner, 1916); first president of the Paris section of the International Music Society; from 1907, its honorary president. Besides many works dealing with philosophy, he publ. the following concerning music: *Introduction à la psychologie du musicien* (Paris, 1891); *La Psychologie dans l'opéra français* (Paris, 1897); *Essai sur l'esprit musical* (Paris, 1904); *Rossini, biographie critique* (Paris, 1905); *Le Musicien-poète Richard Wagner* (Paris, 1908); *Meyerbeer* (Paris, 1913).

Daussoigne-Méhul, Louis-Joseph, French composer; b. Givet, Ardennes, June 10, 1790; d. Liège, March 10, 1875. He was the nephew and foster son of **Etienne-Nicolas Méhul;** studied under him and Catel at the Cons.; took the Grand Prix de Rome in 1809; after writing 4 operas, which were rejected, he at length produced his one-act *Aspasie* at the Grand Opéra (1820) with moderate success. He did still better with *Valentine de Milan,* a 3-act opera left unfinished by his foster father which he completed. In 1827 he accepted the directorship of the Liège Cons., which he retained, with great benefit to the school, until 1862. Daussoigne-Méhul was an associate of the Royal Academy, Brussels. He brought out a cantata with full orch. in 1828, and a choral symph., *Une Journée de la Révolution,* in 1834.

Dauvergne, Antoine, French composer and conductor; b. Clermont-Ferrand, Oct. 3, 1713; d. Lyons, Feb. 11, 1797. He received his first instruction from his father, went for further study to Paris in 1739, and was appointed a violinist in the Royal Orch. (1741); in 1755 was appointed composer to the Royal Orch.; in 1762, conductor of the Concert Spirituel; after 1769 was active as a conductor and manager of various enterprises until his retirement to Lyons in 1790. He introduced into France the forms of the Italian intermezzo, substituting spoken dialogue for the recitative, and thus was the originator of a style that soon became typical of French dramatic composition. He wrote 15 operas, the first of which, *Les*

Troqueurs, was produced at Paris in 1753, and is regarded as the first opéra-comique; wrote 2 books of symphs., 12 sonatas for Violin and Basso Continuo, etc.

Davenport, Francis William, English composer; b. Wilderslowe, near Derby, April 9, 1847; d. Scarborough, April 1, 1925. He studied law at Oxford, but preferred music, and became the pupil (later son-in-law) of Sir G.A. Macfarren. In 1879, he became a prof. at the Royal Academy of Music, and in 1882 at the Guildhall School of Music.
WORKS: 2 symphs.; overture, *Twelfth Night;* 6 pieces for Piano and Cello; *Pictures on a Journey,* a series of piano pieces; part-songs and songs.

Davenport, Marcia (née **Abigail Gluck**), American writer on music; b. New York, June 9, 1903. She studied at Wellesley College and at the Univ. of Grenoble, France (graduated 1925). She has written successful novels, including one on a musical subject (*Of Lena Geyer,* based to some extent on the life of her mother, **Alma Gluck,** 1936); a biography of Mozart (1932); and memoirs, *Too Strong for Fantasy* (N.Y., 1967).

Davey, Henry, English musicologist; b. Brighton, Nov. 29, 1853; d. Hove, Sussex, Aug. 28, 1929. He entered the Leipzig Cons. in 1874, devoting himself chiefly to theoretical studies; lived for several years in Brighton as a teacher. He publ. *The Student's Musical History* (London, 1895; 2nd ed., 1921), a valuable work, the result of original research; *History of English Music* (1921; reprint, N.Y., 1969).

Davico, Vincenzo, Italian composer; b. Monaco, Jan. 14, 1889; d. Rome, Dec. 8, 1969. He studied in Turin, and later in Leipzig with Max Reger; graduated from the Leipzig Cons. in 1911; then he settled in Rome.
WORKS: Operas: *La dogaressa* (Monte Carlo, Feb. 26, 1920) and *La Principessa prigioniera* (Bergamo, Sept. 29, 1940); ballets: *L'agonia della rosa* (Paris, May 2, 1927) and *Narciso* (San Remo, Feb. 19, 1935); oratorio, *La Tentation de Saint Antoine* (Monte Carlo, Dec. 15, 1921); *Requiem per la morte d'un povero* (1950); for Orch.: *La Principessa lontana* (after Rostand's *Princesse lointaine;* won the Augusteo prize, 1911); *Poema erotico* (also won the Augusteo prize, 1913); *Polifemo,* symph. poem (Turin, 1920); *Impressioni dal mio diario di viaggio* (1949); piano pieces and numerous songs.
BIBLIOGRAPHY: G. Franchi, *Vincenzo Davico* (1924); Raymond Petit, *Les Mélodies de Vincenzo Davico* (Nice, 1925); Massimo Gaglione, "Vincenzo Davico," in his book *I Giovani.*

David, Félicien (-César), French composer; b. Cadenet, Vaucluse, Apr. 13, 1810; d. St.-Germain-en-Laye, Aug. 29, 1876. Of precocious talent, he was taught in the maîtrise of St.-Sauveur at Aix in 1818–25. He had a fine voice, and composed hymns, motets, and other music. He then studied in the Jesuit college for 3 years; became assistant conductor in the theater at Aix, and in 1829 maître de chapelle at St.-Sauveur; but in 1830 a longing to widen his musical horizons drew him to Paris, where he submitted specimens of his compositions to Cherubini, and was admitted to the Cons., studying harmony with Reber and Millault, counterpoint and fugue with Fétis, and organ with Benoist. In 1831, when the meager allowance given him by a rich and avaricious uncle had been withdrawn, he joined the socialistic movement of the St.-Simonists at Ménilmontant; here he composed a series of 4-part *hymnes* for men's voices (later publ. with the words, as the *Ruche harmonieuse*). On the dispersion of the society in 1833, David went to Marseilles with a group of the brotherhood, giving concerts on the way; they proceeded to Constantinople, Smyrna, and Egypt, where they finally dispersed; with an imagination stimulated by his long sojourn in the East, David returned alone to Paris in 1835. He now publ. a collection of *Mélodies orientales;* they met with small success, and he retired to the country, giving himself up to study and composition (2 symphs., 24 small string quintets, 2 nonets for wind instruments, romances, etc.). In 1838 his First Symph. was produced. On Dec. 8, 1844, he at last reaped the fruit of many years' study: his symph. ode *Le Désert* was received at its first performance in the hall of the Cons. with "delirious" applause, and a series of repeat performances were given to crowded houses at the Salle Ventadour for a month. The oratorio *Moïse au Sinaï* followed in 1846, but, like a 2nd symph. ode, *Christophe Colomb* (Paris, March 7, 1847), and *L'Eden* (a "mystery" in 2 parts, Grand Opéra, Aug. 25, 1848), it met with a cool reception. However, his opera *La Perle du Brésil* (Théâtre-Lyrique, Nov. 22, 1851) was quite successful; a 2nd, *Le Dernier Amour,* was rejected by the Grand Opéra and by the Théâtre-Lyrique; but the Grand Opéra accepted it in 1859 as *Herculanum,* and for this opera the great state prize of 20,000 francs was awarded to David in 1867. *Lalla Roukh* (May 12, 1862) and *Le Saphir* (March 8, 1865) were given at the Opéra-Comique (the former with great success, the latter with scarcely a *succès d'estime*). David now abandoned dramatic composition, withdrawing his last opera, *La Captive.* In 1869 he was elected to the Académie, taking Berlioz's chair, and succeeding him also as librarian of the Cons. Besides the above works, he wrote 12 melodies for cello; *Les Brises d'Orient,* piano pieces; *Les Minarets,* 3 piano pieces; *Les Perles d'Orient,* 6 melodies for Voice and Piano; etc.
BIBLIOGRAPHY: A. Azevedo, *Félicien David, Sa vie et son œuvre* (Paris, 1863); C. Bellaigue, "Félicien David," in *Etudes musicales et nouvelles silhouettes* (Paris, 1898); J.-G. Prod'homme, "Félicien David d'après sa correspondance inédite," in *Mercure Musical,* II, III (1907); R. Brancour, *Félicien David* (Paris, 1911); R. Locke, "Notice biographique sur Félicien David," in *Célébration du centenaire de la mort: Félicien David* (Cadenet, 1976).

David, Ferdinand, German violinist and pedagogue; b. Hamburg, Jan. 19, 1810; d. near Klosters, Switzerland, July 18, 1873. In 1823–24 he studied with Spohr and Hauptmann at Kassel; played in the Gewandhaus Orch. in Leipzig, 1825; in 1826–29 was a member of the Königstadt Theater in Berlin. In 1829 he became the first violinist in the private string quartet of the wealthy amateur Baron von Liphardt of Dorpat, Russia, whose daughter he married. He remained in Russia until 1835, giving concerts in Riga, Moscow, and St. Petersburg with great acclaim. In 1836, at Mendelssohn's suggestion, he was appointed first violinist of the Gewandhaus Orch., of which Mendelssohn was the conductor. They became warm friends; Mendelssohn had a great regard for him, and consulted him constantly while writing his Violin Concerto; it was David who gave its first performance (Leipzig, March 13, 1845). When the Leipzig Cons. was established in 1843, David became one of its most important teachers; his class was regarded as the finishing school of the most talented violinists in Europe; among his pupils were Joachim and Wilhelmj. He publ. many valuable editions of violin works by classical composers, notably *Die hohe Schule des Violinspiels*, containing French and Italian masterpieces of the 17th and 18th centuries. His pedagogical activities did not interfere with his concert career; he played in England in 1839 and 1841 with excellent success and was compared with Spohr as a virtuoso; also made occasional appearances on the Continent.

WORKS: 5 violin concertos; many other pieces for violin; an opera, *Hans Wacht* (Leipzig, 1852); 2 symphs.; string quartets and other chamber music. His violin pieces, *Bunte Reihe*, were transcribed for piano by Liszt.

BIBLIOGRAPHY: J. Eckardt, *Ferdinand David und die Familie Mendelssohn-Bartholdy* (Leipzig, 1888); A. Bachmann, "Ferdinand David," in *Les Grands Violinistes du passé* (Paris, 1913).

David, Giacomo, Italian tenor, father of **Giovanni David;** b. Presezzo, near Bergamo, 1750; d. Bergamo, Dec. 31, 1830. He studied in Naples; made his debut in 1773 in Milan; then made many appearances at La Scala in Milan (1782–83; 1799–1800; 1802–3; 1806–8); also sang in concert in London (1791); was a featured singer at the first performances given at the Teatro Nuovo in Trieste (1801) and at the Teatro Carcano in Milan (1803).

David, Giovanni, Italian tenor, son of **Giacomo David;** b. Naples, Sept. 15, 1790; d. St. Petersburg, 1864. He studied with his father; made his debut in 1808 in Siena; created the role of Narciso in Rossini's *Il Turco in Italia* at La Scala in Milan on Aug. 14, 1814; also created other roles in Rossini operas; sang in London in 1818 and 1831; quit the stage in 1839 and later became manager of the St. Petersburg Opera.

Dávid, Gyula, Hungarian composer; b. Budapest, May 6, 1913; d. there, March 14, 1977. He studied with Kodály at the Academy of Music in Budapest; won the Erkel Prize in 1952 and 1955 and the Kos-

suth Prize in 1957. His music is marked by a fashionable modernism, while retaining the traditional virtues of euphonious tonality.

WORKS: 4 symphs. (1947, 1957, 1960, 1970); Viola Concerto (1950); Sinfonietta (1960); *Felhőtlenég (Cloudless Skies),* cantata (1964); Violin Concerto (1966); *Égő szavakkal (With Flaming Words),* cantata (1969); Horn Concerto (1971); 5 wind quintets (1949, 1955, 1964, 1967, 1968); Flute Sonata (1955); Piano Sonata (1955); 2 string quartets (1962, 1974); *Miniatures* for Brass Sextet (1968); Violin Sonata (1968); Viola Sonatina (1969); Sonata for Violin Solo (1971); Piano Trio (1972); incidental music; songs and motets.

BIBLIOGRAPHY: J. Breuer, *Dávid Gyula* (Budapest, 1966).

David, Hal, American lyrics writer, brother of **Mack David;** b. New York, May 25, 1921. He studied journalism at N.Y. Univ.; then became collaborator with Bacharach and other composers of popular songs. His lyrics for *Raindrops Keep Falling on My Head* (1969) won an Academy Award. The titles he wrote for Bacharach include *Here Am I, Magic Moments, My Little Red Book, Love Can Break a Heart, Send Me No Flowers, The Story of My Life, What's New, Pussycat?* and *Wives and Lovers.* He also contributed lyrics to several films, among them *Lost Horizon, Butch Cassidy and the Sundance Kid,* and *Moonraker.*

David, Hans Theodor, American musicologist; b. Speyer, Palatinate, July 8, 1902; d. Ann Arbor, Mich., Oct. 30, 1967. He studied at the univs. of Tübingen and Göttingen; received the degree of Dr.Phil. at Berlin (1928). In 1936 he emigrated to the U.S.; occupied various positions as a researcher and librarian; headed the dept. of musicology at Southern Methodist Univ. in Dallas, Texas (1945–50); in 1950 was appointed to the faculty of the Univ. of Michigan. He publ. *J.S. Bach's Musical Offering, History, Interpretation and Analysis* (N.Y., 1945); edited, with A. Mendel, *The Bach Reader* (N.Y., 1945; 2nd ed., revised, 1966); was co-author, with A.G. Rau, of *A Catalogue of Music of American Moravians, 1742–1842, from the Archives of the Moravian Church at Bethlehem, Pa.* (Bethlehem, Pa., 1938); edited Bach's *Art of the Fugue, Musical Offering,* and *Overture in the French Manner* (first version); *English Instrumental Music of the 16th and 17th Centuries;* etc.

BIBLIOGRAPHY: *Quarterly Journal of the Riemenschneider Bach Inst.* (July 1970; biographical sketch).

David, Johann Nepomuk, outstanding Austrian composer; b. Eferding, Nov. 30, 1895; d. Stuttgart, Dec. 22, 1977. He studied with Joseph Marx at the Vienna Academy (1920–33); in 1934 was engaged as a prof. of composition at the Leipzig Cons., becoming its director in 1939. He was subsequently director at the Salzburg Mozarteum (1945–47). In 1947 he was appointed a prof. of composition at the Musikhochschule in Stuttgart, serving until 1963. David's music is severely polyphonic in its structure; almost all of his instrumental works are cast in forms of late Baroque; his mastery of counterpoint is revealed in his many choral pieces.

WORKS: FOR ORCH.: Concerto Grosso for Chamber Orch. (1923); Flute Concerto (1934); 2 partitas (1935, 1940); 8 numbered symphs. (1936; 1938; 1940; 1948; 1951, revised 1953; 1954; 1956; 1964–65); *Kume, kum, geselle min,* divertimento on old folk songs (1939; also a sextet for Winds and Piano); *Variations on a Theme of J.S. Bach* for Chamber Orch. (1942); *Symph. Variations on a Theme of H. Schütz* for Chamber Orch. (1942); 3 concertos for String Orch. (1949, 1949, 1975); 2 violin concertos: No. 1 (1952; Stuttgart, April 25, 1954) and No. 2 (1957; Munich, April 22, 1958); *Sinfonia preclassica super nomen H-A-S-E* for 2 Flutes, 2 Horns, and Strings (1953); *Deutsche Tänze* for Strings (1953); *Sinfonia breve* (1955); *Melancholia* for Solo Viola and Chamber Orch. (1958); *Magische Quadrate,* fantasy on serial principles (1959; Recklinghausen, March 23, 1960); *Sinfonia per archi* (1959); *Spiegelkabinett,* waltzes (1960); Organ Concerto (1964–65; Cologne, Nov. 28, 1966); *Variations on a Theme of Josquin des Pres* for Flute, Horn, and Strings (1966); Concerto for Violin, Cello, and Small Orch. (1969); Chaconne (1972).

FOR VOICE: *Requiem chorale* for Soloists, Chorus, and Orch. (1956; Vienna, June 11, 1957); *Ezzolied,* oratorio (1957; West Berlin, May 17, 1960); *Komm, Heiliger Geist,* cantata for 2 Choruses and Orch. (1972; Linz, March 26, 1974); *Stabat Mater,* in 6 parts, for a cappella Chorus (1927); *Deutsche Messe* for a cappella Chorus (1952); *O, wir armen Sünder,* cantata for Alto, Chorus, and Organ (1966); several motets.

CHAMBER MUSIC: Clarinet Quintet (1924); 3 string quartets; String Trio (1931, revised 1935); *Duo concertante* for Violin and Cello (1937); Sonata for Flute, Viola, and Guitar (1939); *Introitus, Choral, and Fugue* for Organ and 9 Winds (1939); Trio for Flute, Violin, and Viola (1942); Solo Sonatas for Flute, for Viola, for Cello, and for Lute (1942–44); 2 Solo Sonatas for Violin (1943 and 1963); Sonata for 2 Violins (1945); 4 string trios (1945–48); Partita for Solo Violin (1949); Sonata for 3 Cellos (1962); Trio for Flute, Violin, and Cello (1973); Partita for Violin and Organ (1975). Also numerous organ works (*Ricercare, Chaconne, Fantasia super L'Homme armé, Toccata and Fugue, Partita,* etc.). He wrote a study of Mozart's Jupiter Symph. (2nd ed., 1956).

David, José, French composer, son of the singer **Léon David;** b. Sables-d'Olonne, Jan. 6, 1913. He entered the Paris Cons. in 1933; studied with Fauchet, Jacques de la Presle, and Henri Busser; also took organ lessons with Marcel Dupré and music history with Maurice Emmanuel. He was mobilized in 1939 and served in the artillery regiment of the French army during World War II. After the Armistice he returned to Paris.

WORKS: *Impressions de Vendée* for Piano (1944; also for Orch.); *La Ballade de Florentin Prunier* for Voice, Violin, Cello, and Piano (1947); *Symphonie*

for Ondes Martenot and Orch. (1948); ballet, *Jacquet le Prioux* (1950); Violin Sonata (1955); *Laudate Dominum* for 3 Male Voices and Organ (1960); *2 Poems* for Voice and Piano (1973). He collaborated with Nicolas Obouhov in *Traité d'harmonie tonale et atonale* (Paris, 1947).

David, Karl Heinrich, Swiss composer; b. St. Gall, Dec. 30, 1884; d. Nervi, Italy, May 17, 1951. He studied in Cologne and Munich; taught at the Basel Cons. (1910–14); then at Cologne and Berlin (1914–17); in 1918 returned to Switzerland. He was the editor of the *Schweizer Musikzeitung* in Zürich (1928–41).

WORKS: Operas: *Aschenputtel* (Basel, Oct. 21, 1921); *Der Sizilianer* (Zürich, Oct. 22, 1924); *Jugendfestspiel* (Zürich, June 8, 1924); *Traumwandel* (Zürich, Jan. 29, 1928); *Weekend,* comic opera (1933). Other works: Piano Concerto (1929); *Ballet* for Orch. (1931); *Pezzo sinfonico* (1945); Concerto for Saxophone and String Orch. (1947); *Symphonie de la côte d'argent* 1948); *Mascarade,* overture (1950); *Andante and Rondo* for Violin and Chamber Orch.; 2 Pieces for Piano and 9 Woodwinds; Viola Suite; Piano Trio; Quartet for Saxophone, Violin, Cello, and Piano (1946); Duet for Horn and Piano (1951); *Das hohe Lied Salomonis* for Soprano, Tenor, Female Chorus, and Orch.; songs.

David, Léon, French tenor; b. Sables-d'Olonne, Dec. 18, 1867; d. there, Oct. 27, 1962. He studied singing at the Cons. of Nantes and later at the Paris Cons.; made his debut at the Opéra-Comique in Paris in 1892; appeared subsequently in Brussels, Monte Carlo, Marseille, Bordeaux, Cairo, Lisbon, Bucharest, etc. He was a prof. of singing at the Paris Cons. from 1924 to 1938.

David, Mack, American lyricist and composer, brother of **Hal David;** b. New York, July 5, 1912. He studied at Cornell Univ. and at St. John's Univ. Law School. Turning to writing for Broadway and for films, he collaborated with Count Basie, Burt Bacharach, Ernest Gold, Elmer Bernstein, David Raksin, Henry Mancini, and other composers. Among his best-known songs are *Bibbidi, Bobbidi, Boo* (1948); *Cat Ballou* (1965); *The Hanging Tree* (1959); *It's a Mad, Mad, Mad, Mad World* (1963); *My Own True Love* (1954). Mack David won a spectacular lawsuit for copyright infringement of his song *Sunflower* (1948) which he claimed was plagiarized by Jerry Herman for the latter's sensationally popular song *Hello, Dolly* (1964). The sum paid in an out-of-court settlement to Mack David was in excess of half a million dollars.

David, Samuel, French composer; b. Paris, Nov. 12, 1836; d. there, Oct. 3, 1895. He studied at the Cons. with Halévy; won the Grand Prix de Rome (1858) for his cantata *Jephté,* and another prize for a work for male chorus and orch., *Le Génie de la terre,* performed by a chorus of 6,000 singers (1859); was a prof. at the Collège de Sainte-Barbe (1861) and a music director in Paris synagogues (1872). He wrote several operas, 4 symphs., choruses, and songs.

Davidenko, Alexander, Russian composer; b. Odessa, April 13, 1899; d. Moscow, May 1, 1934. He organized, with Belyi, the Procoll (Production Collective of Composers) in Russia in 1925; wrote workers' songs. His most important work is the opera *1905* (written in 1929–33, with Boris Schechter); another opera, *Down the Cliff,* was left incomplete.
BIBLIOGRAPHY: M. Koval, "At the Side of Alexander Davidenko," *Sovietskaya Muzyka* (Feb. 1967); N. Martynov, ed., *Alexander Davidenko* (Leningrad, 1968).

Davidov, Carl, outstanding Russian violoncellist; b. Goldingen, Latvia, March 15, 1838; d. Moscow, Feb. 26, 1889. He studied cello in Moscow with Heinrich Schmidt and in St. Petersburg with K. Schuberth; in 1859 went to Leipzig, where he studied composition with Hauptmann. In 1860, at the age of 22, he was appointed an instructor at the Leipzig Cons. In 1862 he returned to Russia; from 1862 till 1887 was a prof. at the St. Petersburg Cons., and acting director from 1876 to 1887. He made several European tours, during which he played recitals with Anton Rubinstein, Saint-Saëns, and Liszt. Davidov was also a reputable composer; he wrote 4 cello concertos; a fantasy on Russian songs for Cello and Orch.; a symph. poem, *The Gifts of the Terek River;* String Quartet; String Sextet; Piano Quintet; songs. He also publ. a cello method (Leipzig, 1888; Russian ed., supervised by L. Ginsburg, Moscow, 1947).
BIBLIOGRAPHY: V. Hutor, *Carl Davidov und seine Art das Violoncell zu behandeln* (Moscow, 1899); S. Ginsburg, *Carl Davidov* (Moscow, 1950).

Davidovich, Bella, Russian pianist; b. Baku, July 16, 1928. She studied at the Moscow Cons. with Igumnov and Flier, graduating in 1951; in 1962 she joined the faculty of the Moscow Cons. In 1949 she won the first prize at the International Chopin Contest. In 1977 she emigrated to the U.S. She achieved success as soloist with American and European orchs. and in recital, being praised particularly for her peculiarly "Russian" interpretation of 19th-century music, marked by a pervasive Romantic quality.

Davidovsky, Mario, Argentinian composer; b. Buenos Aires, March 4, 1934. He studied there with Ernesto Epstein and others; went to the U.S. in 1958; held 2 consecutive Guggenheim fellowships (1960–62); worked in the electronic music centers of Columbia Univ. and Princeton Univ. In 1971 he was appointed a prof. at the City College of N.Y.; in 1981 he joined the faculty at Columbia Univ. His method of composition tends toward mathematical parameters; his series of *Synchronisms* derives from the numerical coordinates of acoustical elements; electronic sound is integral to most of his work.
WORKS: String Quartet No. 1 (1954); Clarinet Quintet (1956); Nonet (1957); Concerto for Strings and Percussion (1957); String Quartet No. 2 (1958);

Suite sinfónica para el Payaso (1958); *Serie sinfónica* (1959); *Planos* for Orch. (1961); *2 Studies* for Electronic Sound (1961, 1962); *Contrasts* for Strings and Electronic Sound (1962); *Inflexions* for 14 Instruments (1965); 7 pieces under the generic title *Synchronisms:* Nos. 1–6 for different Instrumental Groups (1963–70) and No. 7 for Orch. and Tape (1974; N.Y. Phil., Dec. 4, 1975); *Chacona* for Piano Trio (1972); cantata-opera, *Scenes from Shir Hashirim,* for 4 Voices and Chamber Ensemble (1975–76). His *Synchronisms No. 6* for Piano and Electronic Sound was awarded the 1971 Pulitzer Prize.

Davidson, Harold Gibson, American pianist and composer; b. Low Moor, Va., Feb. 20, 1893; d. Glendale, Calif., Dec. 14, 1959. He studied at the Cincinnati Cons.; taught at several schools; settled in California. His music is of an experimental nature, exemplified by such titles as *Auto Accident* and *Hell's Bells* (for Percussion); *2 Minor Disturbances and One Major Calamity,* piano suite; *Legend of the Flying Saucers;* etc.

Davidson, Lyle, American composer; b. Randolph, Vt., Feb. 25, 1938. He studied at the Univ. of Vermont (1956–58); then entered the New England Cons. (B.M., 1962; M.M., 1964); subsequently attended Brandeis Univ. and Boston Univ. In 1971–73 he was a lecturer in music at the Mass. Inst. of Technology; in 1977–78 was a visiting lecturer in music at Harvard Univ. He became active promoting the cause of avant-garde music in Boston; composed for the theater, dance, and films. His own works are marked by concision, brevity, and immediacy of aural receptivity; in other words, he composes for the people, albeit in highly modernized techniques. The titles of his pieces, most of them brief, are indicative of their intent: *Crystals* for Piano; *Blocks* for Flute, Clarinet, Violin, and Piano; *Phrase* for 2 Trumpets; *Detours* for any 3 String Instruments; *March Detours* for Viola, Cello, and Electronic Tape; *And a Certain Gurgling Melodiousness* for Double Bass; and *Furies of Complexity* for Various Small Groups. For electronic works he is apt to dip into high math, e.g., *Fibonacci Rehearsed.* He was a consultant of Project Zero and Aphasia Research. He also wrote a paper on the etiology of brain damage among composers. For a complete list of works and dates of performance, see *The Boston Composers Project* (Cambridge, Mass., 1983).

Davies, Ben (Benjamin) Grey, Welsh tenor; b. Pontardawe, near Swansea, South Wales, Jan. 6, 1858; d. Bath, England, March 28, 1943. He studied at the Royal Academy of Music under Randegger, winning the bronze, silver, and gold medals for best declamatory English singing. His debut was in Birmingham, Oct. 11, 1881, in *The Bohemian Girl.* He made several American tours, beginning in 1893.

Davies, Dennis Russell, American conductor; b. Toledo, Ohio, April 16, 1944. He studied at the Juilliard School of Music in N.Y.; became a member of its faculty (1968–71) and co-founder, with Luciano

Berio, of the Juilliard Ensemble. He was subsequently music director of the Norwalk (Conn.) Symph. Orch. (1968–73); then was music director of the St. Paul Chamber Orch. (1972–80). In 1980 he became Generalmusikdirektor of the Württemberg State Theater in Stuttgart.

Davies, Fanny, English pianist; b. Guernsey, June 27, 1861; d. London, Sept. 1, 1934. She studied at the Leipzig Cons. with Reinecke and Paul (piano) and Jadassohn (theory) in 1882–83, and at the Hoch Cons. in Frankfurt with Clara Schumann (1883–85); also was a pupil of Scholz in fugue and composition. Her London debut took place at the Crystal Palace, Oct. 17, 1885; then she made successful tours in England, Germany, France, and Italy.

Davies, Meredith, English organist, conductor, and educator; b. Birkenhead, July 30, 1922. He studied at the Royal College of Music, London, Keble College, Oxford, and the Santa Cecilia Academy, Rome; served in the armed forces in World War II; then resumed his activities as organist and choral conductor at several cathedrals. He also appeared as symph. conductor; was associate conductor of the City of Birmingham Symph. (1957–59); also director of the City of Birmingham Choir (1957–64). He then served as music director of the English Opera Group, London (1963–65), and of the Vancouver Symph. (1964–71). He was chief conductor of the BBC Touring Orch. (1969–72); made numerous appearances as guest conductor at home and abroad. In 1979 he was named principal of the Trinity College of Music in London.

Davies, Peter Maxwell, remarkable British composer of variegated avant-garde pursuits; b. Manchester, Sept. 8, 1934. He went to Leigh Grammar School and then to the Royal Manchester College of Music and Manchester Univ. In 1957 he won a scholarship from the Italian government and proceeded to Rome, where he studied with Goffredo Petrassi; his orch. work *Prolation* (named after the medieval metrical division) received the Olivetti Prize in 1958 and was performed at the Festival of the International Society for Contemporary Music in Rome on June 10, 1959. Returning to England, he served as director of music at Cirencester Grammar School (1959–62); it was there that he introduced for the first time his neo-Socratic method of schooling, encouraging his students to exercise their curiosity. In 1962 he went to the U.S. on a Harkness fellowship and took a fruitful succession of sessions with Sessions at Princeton Univ. In 1965 he joined the UNESCO Conference on Music in Education and traveled around the world on a lecture tour. In 1966–67 he served as composer-in-residence at the Univ. of Adelaide in Australia. In 1967 he organized with Harrison Birtwistle in London an ensemble called the Pierrot Players; in 1970 they decided to rename it The Fires of London, with programs of provocative modernistic works. In 1970 Davies made his home in the Orkney Islands; in 1977 he organized there the annual St. Magnus Festival, which gave its presentations at the Norse Cathedral of St. Magnus; there he also staged many of his own compositions, inspired by medieval chants. Despite the remoteness of the Orkney Islands from musical centers, the festival attracted attention. In 1979 Maxwell Davies was awarded an honorary doctorate of music at Edinburgh Univ.; he was also appointed successor to Sir William Glock as director of music at Dartington Summer School and was named Composer of the Year by the Composers' Guild of Great Britain. He was commissioned to write a symph. for the Boston Symph. Orch. on the occasion of its centennial in 1981. In his own works Maxwell Davies combines seemingly incongruous elements, which include reverential evocations of medieval hymnody, surrealistic depictions of historical personages, and hedonistic musical theatrics. His most arresting work in this synthetic manner is a set of *8 Songs for a Mad King,* a fantastic suite of heterogeneously arranged pieces representing the etiology of the madness of King George III; at the other end of the spectrum is *Vesalii Icones,* inspired by the anatomical drawings of Christ's Passion and Resurrection by the Renaissance artist Vesalius. Davies is a fervent political activist, a participant in the movement combating the spread of nuclear weapons, and a staunch defender of the planetary environment against industrial pollution.

WORKS: FOR THE STAGE: *Nocturnal Dances,* ballet (London, May 31, 1970); *Blind Man's Buff,* masque for High Voice, Mime, and Chamber Orch. (London, May 29, 1972); *Taverner,* opera to a libretto by Davies, descriptive of the life of the English composer Taverner (1962–70; London, July 12, 1972); *The Martyrdom of Saint Magnus,* chamber opera in 9 scenes (Kirkwall, Orkney, June 18, 1977); *The 2 Fiddlers,* opera for young people (Kirkwall, Orkney, June 16, 1978); *Le Jongleur de Notre Dame,* masque (Kirkwall, Orkney, June 18, 1978); *Salome,* ballet (Copenhagen, Nov. 10, 1978; concert suite drawn from the score, London, March 6, 1979); *The Lighthouse,* chamber opera (1979; Edinburgh, Sept. 2, 1980); *Cinderella,* pantomime for Child Actors (Kirkwall, Orkney, June 21, 1980; first American perf., Washington, D.C., April 16, 1982); *The Rainbow,* theatrical work for children (Kirkwall, Orkney, June 20, 1981).

FOR ORCH.: *Antechrist* for Chamber Ensemble (London, May 30, 1967); *Stedman Caters* for Chamber Ensemble (London, May 30, 1968); *Worldes Blis* (London, Aug. 28, 1968); *Vesalii Icones* for Dancer, Solo Cello, and Instruments, in 14 movements, after 14 anatomical drawings by Andreas Vesalius depicting Christ's Passion and Resurrection (London, Dec. 9, 1969); *Ave Maris Stella* for Chamber Ensemble (Bath, May 27, 1975); Symph. No. 1 (1976; London, Feb. 2, 1978); Symph. No. 2, commissioned by the Boston Symph. Orch. for its centennial (1980; Boston, Feb. 26, 1981); *Image, Reflection, Shadow* (Lucerne Festival, Switzerland, Aug. 22, 1981); *Sinfonia Concertante* for Chamber Orch. (1982; Aug. 12, 1983); *Sinfonietta Accademica* (Edinburgh, Oct. 6, 1983).

CHAMBER MUSIC: Sonata for Trumpet and Piano

(1955); *Alma Redemptoris Mater* for Flute, Oboe, 2 Clarinets, Horn, and Bassoon (1957); *St. Michael* for 17 Wind Instruments (London, July 13, 1959); *Hymnos* for Clarinet and Piano (1967); *Canon in Memoriam Igor Stravinsky* for Flute, Clarinet, Harp, and String Quartet (London, June 17, 1972); *All Sons of Adam* for Flute, Clarinet, Marimba, Celesta, Guitar, Viola, and Cello (London, Feb. 20, 1974); *Little Quartet* for String Quartet (1980); *A Welcome to Orkney* for Flute, Oboe, Clarinet, Bassoon, Horn, 2 String Quartets, and Double Bass (Kirkwall, Orkney, June 20, 1980); Brass Quintet (1981; N.Y., March 19, 1982); *Birthday Music for John* for Viola, Flute, and Cello (London, Jan. 25, 1983).

VOCAL WORKS: *O Magnum Mysterium,* 4 carols for Chorus a cappella (Cirencester, Dec. 8, 1960); *Leopardi Fragments* for Soprano, Contralto, and Instruments (1962); *Veni Sancte Spiritus* for Solo Soprano, Contralto, and Bass, plus Chorus and Chamber Ensemble (Cheltenham Festival, July 10, 1964); *The Shepherds' Calendar* for Chorus and Instruments (Sydney, Australia, May 20, 1965); *Revelation and Fall* for Soprano and 16 Instruments (London, Feb. 26, 1968, composer conducting); *8 Songs for a Mad King* for Male Voice and Instruments, his most important and popular work (London, April 22, 1969, composer conducting); *From Stone to Thorn* for Mezzo-soprano and Instrumental Ensemble (Oxford, June 30, 1971, composer conducting); *Hymn to Saint Magnus* for Mezzo-soprano obbligato and Instrumental Ensemble (London, Oct. 13, 1972, composer conducting); *Notre Dame des Fleurs* for Soprano, Mezzo-soprano, Countertenor, and Instruments, to an obscene French text by the composer (London, March 17, 1973); *Dark Angels* for Mezzo-soprano and Guitar (1974); *Miss Donnithorne's Maggot* for Mezzo-soprano and Instruments (Adelaide Festival, March 9, 1974, composer conducting); *Fiddlers at the Wedding* for Mezzo-soprano and Instruments (Paris, May 3, 1974); *The Blind Fiddler,* song cycle for Soprano and Instrumental Ensemble (Edinburgh, Feb. 16, 1976, composer conducting); *Anakreontika* for Mezzo-soprano and Instrumental Ensemble (London, Sept. 17, 1976) composer conducting); *Westerlings* for Chorus a cappella (London, Oct. 15, 1977); *Solstice of Light* for Tenor Solo, Chorus, and Organ (St. Magnus Festival, Kirkwall, Orkney, June 18, 1979); *Black Pentecost,* cantata for Mezzo-soprano, Baritone, and Orch., decrying industrial air pollution (1979; London, May 11, 1982); *The Yellow Cake Revue* for Singers and Piano, to texts by the composer inveighing against the ominous threat of uranium mining in the Orkney Islands (Kirkwall, Orkney, June 21, 1980, composer conducting); *Into the Labyrinth,* cantata (Kirkwall, Orkney, June 22, 1983).

FOR SOLO INSTRUMENTS: Organ Fantasia from *O Magnum Mysterium* (Cirencester, Dec. 8, 1960); *The Door of the Sun* for Viola (1975); *Farewell to Stromness* (a town in the Orkney Islands), piano interlude from *The Yellow Cake Revue* (St. Magnus Festival, Kirkwall, Orkney, June 21, 1980, composer conducting); Piano Sonata (1981); Organ Sonata (1982); *Sea Eagle* for Solo Horn (1982).

WORKS FOR YOUNG PERFORMERS: *5 Klee Pictures* for School Orch. (1959; revised 1976); *3 Studies for Percussion* for 11 Percussionists (1975); *Kirkwall Shopping Songs* for Children's Voices, Recorders, Percussion, and Piano, to words by the composer (1979); *Songs of Hoy* for Children's Voices and Instruments, to a text by the composer (1981); *7 Songs Home* for Unaccompanied Children's Voices, to texts by Davies (1981).

BIBLIOGRAPHY: J. Arnold, compiler, *Peter Maxwell Davies: The Complete Catalogue of Printed Works* (London, 1981); P. Griffiths, *Peter Maxwell Davies* (London, 1982).

Davies, Ryland, Welsh tenor; b. Cwm, Ebbw Vale, Feb. 9, 1943. He studied at the Royal Manchester College of Music; made his debut as Almaviva in 1964 with the Welsh National Opera; then sang in Glasgow, Glyndebourne, and in London (1969). He sang in San Francisco in 1970; made his Metropolitan Opera debut in N.Y. on Oct. 15, 1975, as Fernando in *Così fan tutte.*

Davies, Tudor, Welsh tenor; b. Cymmer, Nov. 12, 1892; d. London, April 2, 1958. He studied in Cardiff and at the Royal Academy of Music in London; then appeared at the Old Vic; joined the British National Opera Co. in 1922; created the title role in *Hugh the Drover* by Vaughan Williams (London, July 14, 1924); in 1928 he sang in the U.S. with the Civic Opera in Philadelphia; then was a principal singer with the Old Vic and the Sadler's Wells Opera (1931–41); was a member of the Carl Rosa Opera Co. (1941–46); also appeared in concerts.

Davies, Sir (Henry) Walford, eminent English organist, educator, and composer; b. Oswestry, Sept. 6, 1869; d. Wrington, Somerset, March 11, 1941. He was a pupil of Sir Walter Parratt at St. George's Chapel in Windsor, where he also served as organist (1885–90); then held positions as organist at Christ Church, Hampstead (1891–98), at the Temple Church (1898–1918), and at St. George's Chapel (1927–32); was a prof. of music at the Univ. of Wales (1919–26). Between 1924 and 1934 he led the novel broadcasting series "Music Lessons in Schools." He was knighted in 1922; was appointed Master of the King's Musick in 1934. He composed mostly sacred choruses.

WORKS: Choruses: *The Temple* (1902); *Lift Up Your Hearts* (1906); *5 Sayings of Jesus* (1911); *Heaven's Gate* (1916); *Men and Angels* (1925); *Christ in the Universe* (1929); several orch. overtures: *Dedication Overture* (1893); *Festal Overture* (1910); many works for school performance, including *A Children's Symphony* (1927) and *London Calling the Schools* for Piano, Orch., and Radio Announcer (1932); *Conversations* for Piano and Orch. (London, Oct. 14, 1914); 2 violin sonatas (1894, 1896); *Peter Pan* for String Quartet (1909); numerous part-songs. He publ. *The Musical Outlook in Wales* (London, 1926); *The Pursuit of Music* (London, 1935); *Music and Worship* (with Harvey Grace, London, 1935).

BIBLIOGRAPHY: H.C. Colles, *Walford Davies, A Biography* (London, 1942).

Davis, Andrew, English conductor; b. Ashbridge, Feb. 2, 1944. He studied at King's College, Cambridge, and at the Royal Academy of Music in London; then went to Rome, where he studied conducting with Franco Ferrara at the Santa Cecilia Academy. Returning to England, he served as assistant conductor of the BBC Scottish Symph. Orch. in Glasgow (1970–73); later was assistant conductor of the New Philharmonia Orch. in London. In 1975 he was named music director of the Toronto Symph. Orch. He also made an American tour as guest conductor.

Davis, Sir Colin (Rex), eminent English conductor; b. Weybridge, Sept. 25, 1927. He studied the clarinet at the Royal College of Music in London, and played in the band of the Household Cavalry while serving in the army. He began his conducting career with the semi-professional Chelsea Opera Group; in 1958 he conducted a performance of *Die Entführung aus dem Serail* at London; from 1961–65 served as music director of Sadler's Wells. He made his U.S. debut as a guest conductor with the Minneapolis Symph. Orch. on Dec. 30, 1960; subsequently had engagements with the N.Y. Phil., the Philadelphia Orch., and the Los Angeles Phil. From 1972–83 he served as principal guest conductor of the Boston Symph. Orch. On Jan. 20, 1967, he made his Metropolitan Opera debut in N.Y., conducting *Peter Grimes*. From 1967–71 he was chief conductor of the BBC Symph. Orch. in London. In 1965 he conducted at the Royal Opera at Covent Garden; he succeeded Solti as its music director in 1971. Among his notable achievements was the production at Covent Garden of the entire cycle of *Der Ring des Nibelungen* in 1974–76; in 1977 he became the first British conductor to appear at the Bayreuth Festival, conducting *Tannhäuser*. He conducted the Royal Opera during its tours in South Korea and Japan in 1979. In 1983 he was appointed chief conductor of the Bavarian Radio Symph. Orch. in Munich, while continuing his regular engagements in London. He was made a Commander of the Order of the British Empire in 1965, and was knighted in 1980.

BIBLIOGRAPHY: A. Blyth, *Colin Davis* (London, 1972).

Davis, Eddie ("Lockjaw"), black American jazz tenor saxophonist; b. New York, March 2, 1921. He taught himself to play the tenor saxophone; began his career as a musician in Harlem; later worked with Cootie Williams, Andy Kirk, Louis Armstrong, and Count Basie; subsequently led his own combos.

Davis, Ivan, American pianist; b. Electra, Texas, Feb. 4, 1932. He studied piano with Silvio Scionti at North Texas State Univ. in Denton and later at the Santa Cecilia Academy in Rome with Carlo Zecchi. He also took private lessons with Vladimir Horowitz, beginning in 1961. He obtained first prizes at the Busoni Competition in Bolzano (1958), the Casella Competition at Naples (1958), and the Franz Liszt Competition in N.Y. (1960). He appeared as a soloist with the N.Y. Phil., Boston Symph. Orch.,

Philadelphia Orch., Chicago Symph., London Symph., Concertgebouw Orch. in Amsterdam, etc. In 1970 he was artist-in-residence at the Univ. of Miami at Coral Gables, Fla.

Davis, John David, English composer and music teacher; b. Birmingham, Oct. 22, 1867; d. Estoril, Portugal, Nov. 20, 1942. He studied music at Frankfurt and Brussels; returned to England in 1889; taught in various schools in Birmingham; in 1905, was appointed prof. of composition at the Guildhall School of Music in London. He wrote an opera on a Russian subject, *The Zaporogue Cossacks,* which was produced in Birmingham on May 7, 1895; also a concert overture, *Germania;* 2 string quartets; 2 violin sonatas; piano pieces and songs.

Davis, (Morris) Mac, American singer and songwriter of country and rock music; b. Lubbock, Texas, Jan. 21, 1942. He took up the guitar as a teenager; then attended Emory Univ. in Atlanta and organized his own rock group; also took a few courses at Georgia State College. He gained commercial success when a number of his songs were sung by Bobby Goldsboro, Kenny Rogers, and Glen Campbell; he also wrote songs for Elvis Presley. At the perihelion of his luminary career, he made lucrative tours and television appearances. Among his most popular songs are *In the Ghetto, Don't Cry Daddy, I Believe in Music,* and *Stop and Smell the Roses.*

Davis, Miles (Dewey), Jr., black American jazz trumpeter; b. Alton, Ill., May 25, 1926. He organized a band with Sonny Stitt and Clark Terry; as a youngster: contributed to the flowering of bebop in the company of "bird" Charlie Parker, Coleman Hawkins, Benny Carter, and Billy Eckstine. His bebop syle was modified in 1948 when a band which he led included such an untypical jazz instrument as the French horn (played by Gunther Schuller), and which was exemplified by such numbers as *Boplicity.* He introduced a "cool" manner of playing as contrasted with the frantic "hot" bebop. His arranger was Gil Evans; he had John Coltrane on the saxophone and Philly Joe Jones on the drums. In his own songs he introduced the lyrical and quiet "modal" type of setting, favoring the Lydian scale with its enervating tritone base, and he found suitable harmonies for it. By 1958 he abandoned standard pop practices and plunged into the mystical depths of exotic jazz in such far-out numbers as *Nefertiti* and *Sorcerer.* Then he annexed electronics, forming a "fusion style" with hard rock. To emphasize his departure from his native territory, he affected pseudo-African vestments at his public appearances. Inevitably, or so it seemed, he began to use hallucinogenic drugs, and had some close encounters with unfeeling law enforcers. As he prospered from megamillion sales of record discs, he became the target of extortionists eager to muscle in on the action; some inartistic malefactors peppered his snazzy Ferrari car with machine-gun bullets; he suffered a hip injury which required the implantation of an artificial bone. Davis summarized his creative evolution in his 1981 album egotistically named *We Want Miles.*

BIBLIOGRAPHY: Ian Carr, *Miles Davis* (N.Y., 1982).

Davis, Sammy, Jr., popular black American singer; b. New York, Dec. 8, 1925. His father, Sammy Senior, was a vaudeville dancer; his mother, a chorus girl. He was taken on tour with them as a child; at the age of 8 he obtained a role in a film musical; very soon he became enormously successful as an all-around entertainer; sang in the Broadway musicals *Mr. Wonderful* (1956) and *Golden Boy* (1964); also made numerous appearances on television and in nightclubs. His autobiography, *Yes, I Can,* was publ. in 1965.

Davison, Archibald Thompson, eminent American music educator; b. Boston, Oct. 11, 1883; d. Brant Rock, Cape Cod, Mass., Feb. 6, 1961. He studied at Harvard Univ. (B.A., 1906; M.A., 1907; Ph.D., 1908); took lessons in organ with Widor in Paris. Returning to America, he was organist and choirmaster at Harvard Univ. (1910–40); conducted the Harvard Glee Club (1912–33) and the Radcliffe Choral Society (1913–28); he was a prof. of music at Harvard until his retirement in 1954. He held numerous honorary degrees, including those of D.Mus. at Williams College and Oxford Univ.; Fellow of the Royal College of Music, London; Litt.D. from Washington Univ. (1953); and L.H.D. from Temple Univ. (1955). He wrote a musical comedy, *The Girl and the Chauffeur,* upon his graduation from Harvard (perf. in Boston, April 16, 1906) and the overtures *Hero and Leander* (1908) and *Tragic Overture* (1918). His greatest achievement was as an educator and popularizer of musical subjects: his lectures on music appreciation were broadcast and enjoyed considerable success among radio listeners. He was associate editor, with Thomas W. Surette, of a multivolume collection of vocal and instrumental pieces, the Concord Series, for which he made numerous arrangements.

WRITINGS: *Music Education in America* (1926); *Protestant Church Music in America* (1920; enlarged ed., 1933); *Harvard University Hymn Book* (with E.C. Moore, 1926); *Choral Conducting* (1945); *The Technique of Choral Composition* (Cambridge, Mass., 1946); ed., with W. Apel, *Historical Anthology of Music* (Cambridge, 2 vols., 1946; revised ed., 1949); *Bach and Handel: The Consummation of the Baroque in Music* (Cambridge, 1951); *Church Music: Illusion and Reality* (Cambridge, 1952). A dedicatory vol., *Essays on Music in Honor of A.T. Davison by His Associates,* was publ. at Cambridge in 1957.

Davison, James William, renowned English music critic; b. London, Oct. 5, 1813; d. Margate, March 24, 1885. He was editor of the *Musical Examiner* (1842–44) and the *Musical World* (1844–85); a contributor to the *Saturday Review, Pall Mall Gazette,* and *Graphic;* and was the influential critic of the *Times* (1846–79). In 1860 he married his pupil **Ara-**

bella Goddard. He wrote the analytical program books for the Popular Concerts and the Hallé recitals; composed a few songs, several piano pieces, and a dramatic overture (for Piano Duet) to *Fortunatus,* a fairy tale. His memoirs were publ. by H. Davison as *From Mendelssohn to Wagner* (1912).

Davison, William Edward ("Wild Bill"), American jazz cornetist and bandleader; b. Defiance, Ohio, Jan. 5, 1906. He first took up the mandolin, banjo, and guitar; then turned to the mellophone and cornet; after working with local bands, he played in Chicago (1927–32) and Milwaukee (1933–41); was also active as a bandleader. He served in the U.S. Army during World War II; then resumed his career, playing with Eddie Condon. He was a major figure in Chicago jazz circles.

Davy, Gloria, black American soprano; b. New York, March 29, 1931. She attended the Juilliard School of Music; then toured widely in the production of *Porgy and Bess* in 1953. In 1957 she made her European operatic debut in Nice. She sang at the Metropolitan Opera in N.Y. for the first time on Feb. 12, 1958, as Aida; then appeared at the Vienna State Opera (1959) and Covent Garden (1960). She was particularly noted for her fine performances of contemporary music.

Davy, John, English song composer and violinist; b. Upton-Helions, near Exeter, Dec. 23, 1763; d. London, Feb. 22, 1824. He studied at Exeter, and then settled in London, where he played the violin at Covent Garden. He wrote the music to a number of plays: *A Pennyworth of Wit* (London, April 18, 1796); *Alfred, the Great,* a "grand historical ballet" (London, June 4, 1798); etc. *The Bay of Biscay, O!,* one of the songs from his incidental music to a play, *Spanish Dollars,* was extremely popular.

Dawson, Ted, Canadian composer; b. Victoria, British Columbia, April 28, 1951. He studied violin, viola, and piano at the Victoria Cons. (1964–68); took courses in music theory with Cherney and Komorous at the Univ. of Victoria (1968–72), then in composition with Hambraeus and electronic music with Alcides Lanza at McGill Univ. in Montreal (1973–74); he subsequently engaged in teaching.

WORKS: *Pentad* for String Quartet (1971); *Concerto Grosso I* for Quadraphonic Tape, or Amplified Viola, Amplified Bassoon, Trombone, Percussion, and Stereo Tape (1973–74); *Concerto Grosso II* for 5 Instrumental Soloists and Orch. (1973); *Chameleon* for Solo Amplified Viola (1974); *Chameleon* for Solo Amplified Flute (1974–75); *The Clouds of Magellan* for 3 Slide Projectors, Computerized Dissolver, Synchronization Tape, and Quadraphonic Audiotape (1976–77); *Binaries in Lyrae* for 4 Dancers, 2 Amplified Percussion Ensembles, Amplified Piano, and Lights (1977–78); *Megatherium* for 2 Amplified Pianos, Synthesizer, and Audiotape (1977–78).

Dawson, William Levi, American composer; b.

Anniston, Ala., Sept. 26, 1898. At the age of 13, he ran away from home to enter the Tuskegee Inst.; later played trombone on the Redpath Chautauqua Circuit; graduated from the Tuskegee Inst. in 1921; later studied with Carl Busch in Kansas City and at the American Cons. in Chicago. He received his M.A. in 1927. He played first trombone in the Chicago Civic Orch. (1926–30); then conducted the Tuskegee Choir. Among his works is a Negro folk symph. in 3 movements (Philadelphia Orch., Stokowski conducting, Nov. 16, 1934).

Day, Major Charles Russell, English writer on music; b. Horstead, Norwich, in 1860; d. Paardeberg, South Africa, Feb. 18, 1900. He was a soldier in the British army from 1880; served in India and later in South Africa, where he was killed in battle. His chief work was *Music and Musical Instruments of Southern India and the Deccan* (London, 1891); he also publ. *A Descriptive Catalogue of the Musical Instruments Recently Exhibited at the Royal Military Exhibition, London, 1890* (London, 1891) and papers and pamphlets on national and military music.
BIBLIOGRAPHY: A.J. Hipkins, *Musical Times* (April 1900; obituary).

Dayas, William Humphreys, American organist and teacher; b. New York, Sept. 12, 1863; d. Manchester, England, May 3, 1903. He studied piano with Joseffy; then went to Germany, and was one of Liszt's last pupils at Weimar; also studied there with Kullak, Haupt, Ehrlich, and Urban. He was a piano teacher at the Helsingfors Cons. (1890); taught in Düsseldorf (1894), Wiesbaden, and Cologne; returned for a while to N.Y., and then settled in Manchester (1896), where he taught at the Music College.

De Ahna, Heinrich Karl Hermann, Austrian violinist; b. Vienna, June 22, 1835; d. Berlin, Nov. 1, 1892. He studied in Vienna with Mayseder and at the Prague Cons. with Mildner; made his debut as a violinist at the age of 12, playing in Vienna, London, etc. He settled in 1862 in Berlin as a member of the Royal Orch., becoming its concertmaster in 1868.

Deák, Csaba, Hungarian-born Swedish composer; b. Budapest, April 16, 1932. He studied clarinet and composition in Budapest (1949–56); came to Sweden in 1957 and took lessons in composition with Hilding Rosenberg. In 1971 he was appointed to the staff of the Univ. of Göteborg. In his music he applies a modified type of dodecaphonic techniques.
WORKS: Chamber opera, *Fäderna (The Ancestors),* for 3 Singers, Percussion, and Tape (Stockholm, Oct. 16, 1968); *Rondo* for Piano (1957); *Jubilemus Salvatori,* chamber cantata (1958); Sonatina for Solo Clarinet (1958); 2 string quartets (1959, 1967); *Duo Suite* for Flute and Clarinet (1960); *Danaiderna* for Narrator and Chorus (1964); Wind Quintet (1965); *Klarinettofoni* for Electronically Altered Clarinets (1968); *I 21* for Winds, Percussion, and Double Bass (1969); electronic ballet, *Etyd om*

våren (Spring Etude, 1970); Trio for Flute, Cello, and Piano (1971); *Ska vi göra musik?* for Children's Voices, Cello, Percussion, and Tape (1972); *Andante and Rondo* for Wind Quintet (1973); *Piri* for Chorus and Percussion (1973); music for theater productions.

Deakin, Andrew, English publisher and bibliographer; b. Birmingham, April 13, 1822; d. there, Dec. 21, 1903. While serving his apprenticeship as a printer, he taught himself music; established a publishing house in Birmingham, and held several positions as an organist. His chief work is *Outlines of Musical Bibliography* (Birmingham, 1899), a catalogue of works on music printed in England from the 15th to the 18th century.

Dean, Stafford, English bass; b. Kingswood, Surrey, June 20, 1937. He studied at the Royal College of Music; later took lessons with Howell Glynne and Otakar Kraus; then sang with Opera for All in London; subsequently made appearances at Glyndebourne (1964), Sadler's Wells (1964), and Covent Garden (1969). He made his Metropolitan Opera debut in N.Y. on Feb. 6, 1976, as Figaro.

Dean, Winton, English writer on music; b. Birkenhead, March 18, 1916. He pursued studies in the liberal arts at Kings College, Cambridge (B.A., 1938; M.A., 1941); took private music lessons with Philip Radcliffe; then devoted himself to musicological research; publ. several valuable biographical essays on Handel, Bizet, and others.
WRITINGS: *Bizet* (London, 1948; 2nd ed., revised 1965, as *Georges Bizet: His Life and Work;* 3rd ed., 1976); *Carmen* (London, 1949); *Franck* (London, 1950); *Introduction to the Music of Bizet* (London, 1950); *Handel's Dramatic Oratorios and Masques* (London, 1959); *Handel and the Opera Seria* (Berkeley, 1969).

De Angelis, Nazzareno, noted Italian bass; b. Aquila, Nov. 17, 1881; d. Rome, Dec. 14, 1962. As a boy he sang in the Sistine and Justine chapel choirs in Rome; made his operatic debut in Aquila in 1903; then appeared with major Italian opera houses; in America, he was on the roster of the Manhattan Opera House in N.Y. (1909–10); then of the Chicago Opera (1910–11; 1915–20); later made appearances with the Rome Opera (until 1938); also gave song recitals. He was regarded as one of the most cultured bass singers of the Italian school of opera; and he was equally appreciated in Wagnerian roles.

Debain, Alexandre-François, the inventor of the harmonium; b. Paris, 1809; d. there, Dec. 3, 1877. He established a factory of pianos and organs in Paris (1834), and after long experimentation with free reeds patented his harmonium in 1840. He also invented the antiphonel and the harmonichorde, and improved the accordion.

De Boeck, Auguste, Belgian composer; b. Merch-

Debussy

tem, near Brussels, May 9, 1865; d. there, Oct. 9, 1937. He studied composition with Paul Gilson; taught organ (1893–1902) and harmony (1920–30) at the Brussels Cons. and was director of the Cons. at Mechelen (1920–30); also taught organ at the Antwerp Cons. (1909–21).

WORKS: 5 operas: *Théroigne de Méricourt* (1901); *Winternachtsdroom* (*Le Songe d'une nuit d'hiver;* 1903); *De Rijndevergen* (*Les Gnomes du Rhin;* 1906); *Reinaert le Renard* (1909); *Francesca* (*La Route d'Emeraude;* 1921); 3 ballets: *Assepoes* (*Cendrillon;* 1895); *De Nachtvlinder* (*La Phalène;* 1896); *La Tentation du Poète* (1929); *Rhapsodie Dahoméenne* for Orch. (1893); Symph. (1896); *Fantaisie sur deux airs flamande* for Orch. (1923); Violin Concerto (1925); various pieces for piano; songs; etc.

Debussy, Claude (Achille-Claude), great French composer; b. St.-Germain-en-Laye, Aug. 22, 1862; d. Paris, March 25, 1918. Mme. de Fleurville, a pupil of Chopin, prepared him for the Paris Cons., where he was admitted at the age of 10. Here he continued his study of piano with Marmontel, and won 2nd prize in 1877; in the solfeggio class of Lavignac he won the medal 3 years in succession (1874, 1875, 1876). Emile Durand was his teacher in harmony (1876–80); he received no awards there. After his graduation in 1880, Debussy was recommended to Mme. Nadezhda von Meck, Tchaikovsky's patroness, as a household pianist to teach piano to her children and play 4-hands with them. She summoned him to Switzerland, where she was traveling (he was not quite 18 at the time), and took him to Italy and Russia; he stayed with her family in Moscow and at her country estate in the summers of 1881 and 1882. There he had an opportunity to acquaint himself with the music of Borodin and Mussorgsky, which was to influence him greatly in the subsequent period of his creative activity. Although he played Tchaikovsky's scores for Mme. von Meck (including the MS of the 4th Symph., dedicated to her), Debussy did not evince great interest in Tchaikovsky's works. Another influence in his youth was Mme. Vasnier, an excellent singer, whom he met during the years he was preparing for the Grand Prix (1881–84); he spent much of his time at the Vasnier residence at Ville-d'Avray; the first of his *Fêtes galantes,* on poems of Verlaine (as well as some other works), is dedicated to her. In the composition class of Guiraud he won a prize for counterpoint and fugue in 1882; the next year he was the winner of the 2nd Prix de Rome, and finally, in 1884, he won the much coveted Grand Prix, with his cantata *L'Enfant prodigue.* From the Villa Medici in Rome he sent as the fruit of the first year a fragment of a choral work, *Zuleïma* (after Heine's *Almanzor*), which he later destroyed; he also worked on a composition for the stage, *Diane au bois,* which he had begun in Paris, but this was never finished. The 2nd year he wrote *Printemps,* a symph. suite, which found no favor with the jury at the Academy. This did not prevent Debussy from following the path on which he had commenced, and, returning to Paris,

he composed another cantata, *La Damoiselle élue,* even more advanced; at this time (1887) he also visited London. The work of the last year in Rome (1888) was a *Fantaisie* for Piano and Orch. The customary performance of the "envois de Rome" never took place; the committee refused to put *Printemps* on the program, and Debussy insisted that either all or none be produced. At about that time Debussy became an intimate of a group of French poets of the symbolist school, and was particularly fascinated by Mallarmé; he also made a visit to Bayreuth (1888), where he heard *Parsifal;* he repeated this visit in 1889; in that year he also became greatly interested in the oriental music which was presented at the Paris Exposition, and acquired a taste for exotic musical colors. His early enthusiasm for Wagner soon petered out, and he became actually antagonistic to Wagner's ideas. Contacts with the impressionist movement, added to the influence of modern French poetry, contributed to Debussy's mature style, in which formal structure becomes less important, while mood, atmosphere, and color assume special significance. His *Ariettes oubliées* (1888), to Verlaine's words, and *Cinq poèmes* (1890), to Baudelaire's verses, are the first revelations of this new style. He wrote *Petite suite* for Piano, 4-hands (1889; arranged for orch. by H. Busser); in 1890 he began *Suite bergamasque* for Piano, which includes the most celebrated single piece by Debussy, *Clair de lune* (the title is from Verlaine's poem, which also contains the word "bergamasque," adopted by Debussy); it is interesting to observe that in the framework of a classical suite, Debussy applies his novel methods of musical coloring. The year 1892 marked the beginning of the composition of his orchestral *Prélude à l'Après-midi d'un faune* (after Mallarmé; Paris, Dec. 23, 1894) and his only opera, *Pelléas et Mélisande.* Debussy continued his productive work; he wrote a String Quartet (1893; designated as *Premier Quatuor,* although it was the only quartet he wrote); the song vols. *Proses lyriques* (1894) and *Chansons de Bilitis* to poems of Pierre Louÿs (1898), the latter being one of his most poetic invocations; another work, also entitled *Chansons de Bilitis,* for 2 Flutes, 2 Harps, and Celesta was performed semi-privately (Paris, Feb. 7, 1901), in the form of a mimo-melodrama. Debussy's major composition at the turn of the century was *3 Nocturnes* for Orch. (the first 2, *Nuages* and *Fêtes,* were perf. in Paris, Dec. 9, 1900; the 3rd, *Sirènes,* for Orch. and Wordless Choir of Women's Voices, was perf. with the others on Oct. 27, 1901).

On Oct. 19, 1899, Debussy married Rosalie Texier. (The *Nocturnes* are dedicated to her under the affectionate name "Lily-Lilo.") However, in 1904 he eloped with Mme. Emma Bardac, the wife of a banker; Rosalie shot herself in despair, but recovered; the divorce followed on Aug. 2, 1904, and Debussy finally married Mme. Bardac on Oct. 15, 1905. A daughter born to this marriage ("Chouchou," to whom Debussy dedicated his *Children's Corner*) died at the age of 14 on July 14, 1919.

Pelléas et Mélisande was produced at the Opéra-Comique on April 30, 1902, after many difficulties, among them the open opposition of Maeterlinck, on whose play the opera was based. Mary Garden sang Mélisande, arousing admiration as well as wonderment as to the reason why an American singer with imperfect French pronunciation should have been selected; Maeterlinck's own choice for the part was his mistress, Georgette Leblanc. The opera was attacked violently by some critics for its decadent character, and for many years was a center of musical controversy. Performances followed, but slowly; it was produced at the Manhattan Opera House in N.Y. on Feb. 19, 1908; at Covent Garden in London on May 21, 1909; at the Metropolitan Opera House in N.Y. on March 21, 1925. At various times it was reported that Debussy had completed other dramatic works; in fact, the Metropolitan even announced its acquisition of the rights to the production of *Le Diable dans le beffroi, La Chute de la maison Usher,* and *La Légende de Tristan;* 2 versions of Debussy's libretto for *La Chute de la maison Usher* are in existence, but nothing is known of any music for these works beyond mention of it in correspondence or conversations. *La Mer,* his next important composition, was completed at Eastbourne, England, in March 1905; it was first performed by Chevillard in Paris, Oct. 15, 1905. Then followed the orch. suite *Images,* of which *Ibéria* (1908), descriptive of a Spanish fiesta, with guitarlike strumming on the violins, was the most successful. On Dec. 18, 1908, Harold Bauer played the first performance, at the Cercle Musical in Paris, of Debussy's *Children's Corner;* an orchestration by Caplet was performed in Paris on March 25, 1911. In 1908 Debussy conducted *La Mer* and *Prélude à l'Après-midi d'un faune* in London; in 1909 he appeared there again to conduct the *Nocturnes;* following this he filled various engagements as a conductor in Paris, Vienna, and Budapest (1910), Turin (1911), Moscow and St. Petersburg (1913), and The Hague, Amsterdam, and Rome (1914). Diaghilev produced his ballet *Jeux* in Paris on May 15, 1913. Debussy contemplated an American tour with the violinist Arthur Hartmann in 1914, but abandoned the idea because of illness; thereafter his health failed rapidly owing to cancer, and, after 2 operations, he finally succumbed. Debussy's last appearance in public was on May 5, 1917, when he played (with Gaston Poulet) the piano part in his Violin Sonata.

Debussy is regarded as the creator and chief protagonist of musical Impressionism, despite the fact that he deprecated the term and denied his role in the movement. This, however, cannot alter the essential truth that, like Monet in painting and Mallarmé in poetry, Debussy created a style peculiarly sensitive to musical mezzotint from a palette of half-lit, delicate colors. To accomplish the desired effect, Debussy introduced many novel technical devices. He made use of the óriental pentatonic scale for exotic evocations, and of the whole-tone scale (which he did not invent, however; samples of its use are found in Glinka and Liszt); he emancipated dissonance, so that unresolved discords freely followed one another; he also revived the archaic practice of consecutive perfect intervals (particularly fifths and fourths). In Debussy's formal constructions, traditional development is abandoned and the themes themselves are shortened and rhythmically sharpened; in instrumentation, the role of individual instruments is greatly enhanced and the dynamic range subtilized. These applications aroused intense criticism on the part of traditionalists; a book, *Le Cas Debussy* (1910), gave expression to this opposition; see also N. Slonimsky, *Lexicon of Musical Invective* (N.Y., 1953).

WORKS: PUBLISHED: FOR THE STAGE: *Pelléas et Mélisande,* opera (1892–1902); *Le Martyre de Saint Sébastien,* music to the mystery play by d'Annunzio, for Soli, Chorus, and Orch. (1911); ballets: *Jeux* (1912) and *Khamma* (1912).

CHORAL WORKS: *Printemps* for Women's Voices (1882); *Invocation* for Men's Voices (1883); *L'Enfant prodigue,* cantata (1884); *La Damoiselle élue* for Soli, Chorus, and Orch. (1887–88); *3 Chansons de Charles d'Orléans* for Unaccompanied Chorus (1908); *Ode à la France* for Solo, Chorus, and Orch. (1916–17).

FOR ORCH.: *Printemps,* symph. suite (1886–87); *Fantaisie* for Piano and Orch. (1888–89); *Prélude à l'Après-midi d'un faune* (1892–94); *Nocturnes* (1893–99); *La Mer,* 3 symph. sketches: *De l'aube à midi sur la mer, Jeux de vagues, Dialogue du vent et de la mer* (1903–5); incidental music to Shakespeare's *King Lear* (1904); *Danse sacrée* and *Danse profane* for Harp and Strings (1904); *Images: Gigues, Ibéria, Rondes de Printemps* (1906–12).

CHAMBER MUSIC: String Quartet (1893); *Rapsodie* for Saxophone and Piano (1903–5; also with Orch.); *Première rapsodie* for Clarinet and Piano (1909–10); *Petite pièce* for Clarinet and Piano (1910); *Syrinx* for Flute alone (1912); Cello Sonata (1915); Sonata for Flute, Viola, and Harp (1915); Violin Sonata (1916–17).

FOR PIANO SOLO: *Danse bohémienne* (1880); *2 arabesques* (1888); *Rêverie, Ballade, Danse, Valse romantique, Nocturne* (1890); *Suite bergamasque* (1890–1905); *Mazurka* (1891); *Pour le piano* (1896–1901); *Estampes* (1903); *D'un cahier d'esquisses* (1903); *Masques* (1904); *L'Isle joyeuse* (1904); *Images,* first series (1905); *Images,* 2nd series (1907); *Children's Corner* (1906–8); *Hommage à Haydn* (1909); *La Plus que lente* (1910); *12 préludes* (first book, 1910; 2nd book, 1910–13); *La Boîte à joujoux,* children's ballet (1913); *Berceuse héroïque pour rendre hommage à S.M. le Roi Albert Ier de Belgique et à ses soldats* (1914); 2 books of *12 études* (1915).

FOR PIANO DUET: One movement of a *Symphonie en si* (1880; intended for Orch.); *Triomphe de Bacchus* (1881); *Petite suite* (1889); *Marche écossaise sur un thème populaire* (1891; also for Orch.); *6 épigraphes antiques* (1914).

FOR 2 PIANOS: *Lindaraja* (1901); *En blanc et noir* (1915). 60 songs to texts by Verlaine, Bourget, Villon, Baudelaire, Louÿs, Girod, Mallarmé, and others; various arrangements and orchestrations; also *Masques et Bergamasques,* scenario for a ballet written in 1910.

WORKS: UNPUBLISHED: FOR THE STAGE: *Rodrigue et Chimène,* opera (1891–92; unfinished); *F.E.A. (Frères en art),* 3 scenes of a play (1900; with René Peter); *Le Diable dans le beffroi,* opera after Poe's *The Dev-*

il in the Belfry (1902–3; unfinished; only notes for the libretto and a sketch for Scene I are extant); 2 versions of a libretto for *La Chute de la maison Usher* (after Poe; 1908–18).

CHORAL WORKS: *Daniel,* cantata (1880–84); *Le Gladiateur* (1883).

FOR ORCH.: *Intermezzo* (after a passage from Heine's *Intermezzo;* 1882; also arranged for Piano Duet).

CHAMBER MUSIC: Trio in G for Piano, Violin, and Cello (1880); *Chansons de Bilitis,* incidental music for Louÿs's poems, for 2 Flutes, 2 Harps, and Celesta (1900).

SONGS: *Caprice* (1880); *Chanson espagnole* for 2 Voices, *Rondel chinois, Romance, Aimons-nous, La Fille aux cheveux de lin, Eclogue* (1880–84); *Berceuse* for the play *La Tragédie de la mort* (1908). An Intermezzo for Cello and Piano was found by Gregor Piatigorsky in Paris in 1938.

WRITINGS: Debussy contributed numerous criticisms and essays to the *Revue Blanche, Gil Blas, Musica, Mercure de France, La Revue S.I.M.,* etc. Collected essays and criticisms publ. in various journals were issued as *Monsieur Croche, Antidilettante* (Paris, 1923; Eng. trans. 1928, 1948; new ed. with commentary by F. Lesure, Paris, 1971).

BIBLIOGRAPHY: L. Gilman, *D.'s "Pelléas et Mélisande"* (N.Y., 1907); Mrs. F. Liebich, *C.-A. D.* (London, 1908); L. Laloy, *C. D.* (Paris, 1909); F. Santoliquido, *Il Dopo-Wagner, C. D. e R. Strauss* (Rome, 1909); C. Caillard and J. de Berys, *Le Cas D.* (Paris, 1910); G. Setaccioli, *D. è un innovatore?* (Rome, 1910); M. Rivière, *Etudes* (Paris, 1911); O. Séré, *Musiciens français d'aujourd'hui* (Paris, 1911); R. Rolland, *Musiciens d'aujourd'hui* (Paris, 1912); D. Chennevière, *D. et son œuvre* (Paris, 1913); C. Paglia, *Strauss, Debussy, e compagnia bella* (Bologna, 1913); G. Jean-Aubry, *La Musique française d'aujourd'hui* (Paris, 1916); E. Newman, "The Development of D.," *Musical Times* (May, Aug. 1918); G. Jean-Aubry, "Some Recollections of D.," ibid., (May 1918; full list of compositions and writings); L.S. Liebich. "An Englishwoman's Memories of D.," ibid., (June 1918); G. Jean-Aubry, "C. D.," *Musical Quarterly* (Oct. 1918); J.-G. Prod'homme, "C.-A. D.," ibid., (Oct. 1918); A. Lualdi, "C. D. La sua arte e la sua parabola," in *Rivista Musicale Italiana,* XXV/2 (1918); Guido M. Gatti, "The Piano Works of C. D.," *Musical Quarterly* (July 1921); A. Cortot, *The Piano Music of C. D.* (1922); L. Fabian, *D.* (Munich, 1923); André Suarès, *D.* (Paris, 1923; new ed., 1936); E. Gianturco, *C. D.* (Naples, 1923); J.G. Palache, "D. as Critic," *Musical Quarterly* (July 1924); L. Perrachio, *L'opera pianistica di Cl. D.* (Milan, 1924); F.H. Shera, *D. and Ravel* (London, 1925); M. Emmanuel, *Pelléas et Mélisande* (Paris, 1926); Rient van Sant, *D.* (Hague, 1926); F. Gysi, *D.* (Zürich, 1926); M. Arconada, *En torno a D.* (Madrid, 1926); J. Durand, *Lettres de C. D. à son editeur* (Paris, 1927); Léon Vallas, *Les Idées de D., musicien français* (Paris, 1927; in Eng., 1929); Ch. Koechlin, *D.* (Paris, 1927); J. F. Cooke, *D.* (Philadelphia, 1928); A. Coeuroy, *D.* (1930); M. Boucher, *D.* (1930); J. Lépine, *La Vie de C. D.* (1930); R. Peter, *D.* (1931; augmented ed., 1944); M. Dumesnil, *How to Play and Teach D.* (N.Y., 1932);

Ernst Decsey, *D.* (1933; new ed., 1936); Léon Vallas, *C. D. et son temps* (Paris, 1932; in Eng., London, 1933); Andreas Liess, *C. D. Das Werk in Zeitbild* (2 vols., Strasbourg, 1936); E. Lockspeiser, *D.* (London, 1936; revised 1951); idem, "Mussorgsky and D.," *Musical Quarterly* (Oct. 1937); Oscar Thompson, *D., Man and Artist* (N.Y., 1937); H.F. Kölsch, *Der Impressionismus bei D.* (Düsseldorf, 1937); M. Dumesnil, *C. D., Master of Dreams* (N.Y., 1940); H. Strobel, *C. D.* (Zürich, 1940); R. Paoli, *D.* (Florence, 1941); D.: *Lettres à deux amis* (Paris, 1942); G. Schaeffner, *C. D. und das Poetische* (Bern, 1943); L. Laloy, *C. D.* (Paris, 1944); Léon Vallas, *C. D.* (Paris, 1944); D.: *Correspondance avec Pierre Louÿs* (Paris, 1945); D.: *Correspondance avec d'Annunzio* (Paris, 1948); Guy Ferchault, *C.D., musicien français* (Paris, 1948); Rollo H. Myers, *D.* (London, 1948); H.B. Harvey, *Claude of France: The Story of Debussy* (N.Y., 1948); W. Danckert, *C. D.* (Berlin, 1948); E. Robert Schmitz, *The Piano Works of C. D.* (N.Y., 1950); A. Gauthier, *D., Documents iconographiques* (Geneva, 1952); A. Colea, *Pelléas et Mélisande, Analyse poétique et musicale* (Paris, 1952); J. van Ackere, *Pelléas et Mélisande* (Brussels, 1952); Germaine and D.E. Inghelbrecht, *D.* (Paris, 1953); J. d'Almendre, *Les Modes grégoriens dans l'œuvre de C. D.* (Paris, 1953); Victor Seroff, *D., Musician of France* (N.Y., 1956); E. Vuillermoz, *C. D.* (Geneva, 1957); E. Lockspeiser, ed., *Lettres inédites à André Caplet, 1908–1914* (Monaco, 1957); J.L. Pasteur Vallery-Radot, *Tel était C. D.* (with letters to the author; Paris, 1958); Y. Tiénot and O. d'Estrade-Guerra, *D.: L'Homme, son œuvre, son milieu* (Paris, 1961); M. Dietschy, *La Passion de C. D.* (Neuchâtel, 1962); *C. D., Revue Musicale,* special issue, 258 (1964); E. Lockspeiser, *D.: His Life and Mind* (2 vols., London, 1962, 1965); F. Lesure, ed., *C. D., Textes et documents inédits,* special issue of *Revue de musicologie* (1962); A. Goléa, *C. D.* (Paris, 1965); E. Weber, ed., *D. et l'évolution de la musique au XXᵉ siècle* (Paris, 1965); P. Young, *D.* (London, 1966); E. Hardeck, *Untersuchungen zu den Klavierliedern C. D.* (Regensburg, 1967); V. Jankélévitch, *La Vie et la mort dans la musique de D.* (Neuchatel, 1968); F. Dawes, *D.'s Piano Music* (London, 1969); W.W. Austin, ed., Norton Critical Score edition of *Prelude to "The Afternoon of a Faune"* (contains background, criticism, analysis; N.Y., 1970); S. Jarocinski, *D., Impressionisme et symbolisme* (Paris, 1970; trans. from Polish); H. Barraud, *Les Cinq Grands Opéras* (includes analysis of *Pelléas;* Paris, 1972); S. Jarocinski, *D. Kronika zycia, dziela, epoki* (Cracow, 1973); A.B. Wenk, *C. D. and the Poets* (1976); M. Cobb, ed., *The Poetic D.: A Collection of His Song Texts and Selected Letters* (annotated; Boston, 1982); R. Orledge, *D. and the Théâtre* (Cambridge, 1982); R. Howat, *D. in Proportion: A Musical Analysis* (Cambridge, 1983). The periodical *Cahiers Debussy* began publication in 1974, issued by the Centre de Documentation Claude Debussy, Saint Germain-en-Laye, France.

Decadt, Jan, Belgian composer; b. Ypres, June 21, 1914. He studied with Joseph Ryelandt at the Cons.

of Ghent, and later with Jean Absil in Brussels. He was director of the music school in Harelbeke in 1945, and in 1957 was appointed prof. of fugue at the Antwerp Cons.; from 1971 taught composition at the Ghent Cons. His musical style is marked by strong polyphonic structures with impressionistic coloration.

WORKS: *Variations on "Sir Halewijn"* for Orch. (1943); *Ballada op een boom (Ballade on a Tree)* for Soprano, Flute, Oboe, and String Trio (1945); Piano Concerto (1953); Symph. No. 1 (1958); *Constant Permeke*, cantata (1963); *Monographie musicale d'un grand peintre* for Orch. (Johannesburg, Nov. 17, 1964); *Concerto Overture* for Flute, Oboe, and String Orch. (1964); Suite for Trumpet and Chamber Orch. (1967); *Petite planète* for Narrator, Soprano, Flute, Viola, and Cello (1967); *Concertante Fantasia* for Oboe and Piano (1970); *Introduction and Capriccio* for Clarinet and Piano (1972); Saxophone Concerto (1973); Quartet for Saxophones (1974).

Decaux, Abel, French organist and composer; b. Auffay, 1869; d. Paris, March 19, 1943. He studied organ with Widor and Guilmant and composition with Massenet at the Paris Cons. He served as organist at the church of Sacré-Cœur in Montmartre; then was prof. of organ playing at the Schola Cantorum; from 1923 to 1937 he taught organ at the Eastman School of Music in Rochester, N.Y. Decaux composed very little; but he attracted posthumous attention by the discovery, and performance, of his group of piano pieces under the title *Clairs de Lune* (the plural being of the essence): *Minuit passe, La Ruelle, Le Cimétière,* and *La Mer,* written between 1900 and 1907 and publ. in 1913, seem to represent early examples of piano writing usually associated with Debussy and Ravel; the similarity of styles is indeed striking, which indicates that Impressionism was "in the air," and in the ears, of impressionable French musicians early in the new century.

Dechevrens, Antoine, Swiss musicologist; b. Chêne, near Geneva, Nov. 3, 1840; d. Geneva, Jan. 17, 1912. He entered the Jesuit order in 1861; was a prof. of theology and philosophy at Univ. of Angers; devoted himself to the study of Gregorian chant and of neume notation. He publ. *Du rythme dans l'hymnographie latine* (1895); *Etudes de science musicale* (3 vols., Paris, 1898); *Composition musicale et composition littéraire* (Paris, 1910); also publ. a study on Chinese music in *Sammelbände der Internationalen Musik-Gesellschaft,* vol II.

Decker, Franz-Paul, German conductor; b. Cologne, June 23, 1923. He was educated at the Univ. of Cologne. In 1945 he became a conductor at the Opera there. He then conducted at the opera houses in Wiesbaden, Bochum, and Aachen, and served as chief conductor of the Rotterdam Phil. Orch. (1962–68). In 1967 he became music director of the Montreal Symph. Orch., a post he held until 1975. He then was principal guest conductor and music adviser of the Calgary (Alberta) Phil. Orch. (1975–77). In 1981 he was appointed artistic adviser of the Winnipeg Symph. Orch..

Decoust, Michel, French composer; b. Paris, Nov. 19, 1936. He studied at the Paris Cons. with Olivier Messiaen and others; received the Premier 2nd Grand Prix de Rome (1963). His works include *Mouvement* for Strings and Percussion (1964); Etudes for Flutes and Cellos (1966); *Polymorphée* for Orch. (Royan, April 1, 1967); *Instants-Stabiles* for Chamber Ensemble (1967); *Actions* for Voice and Piano, with Audience Participation (Angers, April 18, 1972); *T'Ai* for Double Bass, Electric Guitar, Percussion, Harpsichord, and Voice (Paris, Jan. 25, 1972); *Et, ée* for Chorus and Orch. (Paris, July 23, 1973).

Decreus, Camille, French pianist; b. Paris, Sept. 23, 1876; d. Fontainebleau, Sept. 26, 1939. He studied piano with Pugno at the Paris Cons.; had a successful career as a pianist; made tours in England and Germany; after several concerts as assisting artist and accompanist in the U.S., he settled in Washington, D.C., as a private teacher in the family of Senator W. Clark; then returned to France. In 1924 he was appointed director of the American Cons. at Fontainebleau, a post which he held until his death.

Decsey, Ernst, German-Austrian writer on music; b. Hamburg, April 13, 1870; d. Vienna, March 12, 1941. He studied law in Vienna (receiving a doctorate in law in 1894); then studied composition with Bruckner and Robert Fuchs at the Vienna Cons.; was active as a music critic in Graz and in Vienna. He was the author of the standard biography of Hugo Wolf (in 4 vols., Berlin, 1903–6; several subsequent printings; an abridged one-vol. ed. appeared in 1921). He also wrote the monographs *Anton Bruckner* (Berlin, 1920); *Johann Strauss* (Stuttgart, 1922; 2nd ed., 1947); *Franz Lehár* (Vienna, 1924); *Franz Schubert* (Vienna, 1924); *Maria Jeritza* (Vienna, 1931); *Claude Debussy* (Graz, 1936); and *Debussys Werke* (Graz and Vienna, 1948).

Dedler, Rochus, Austrian composer; b. Oberammergau, Jan. 15, 1779; d. Vienna, Oct. 15, 1822. He wrote the music of the Passion play still in use at Oberammergau.

Deering (or **Dering**), **Richard,** English composer; b. Kent, c.1580; d. London (buried, March 22), 1630. He was educated in Italy; returned to England as a well-known musician and practiced in London; in 1610, took the degree of B.Mus. at Oxford; in 1617, became organist at the convent of English nuns at Brussels; in 1625, was appointed organist to Queen Henrietta Maria.

WORKS: *Cantiones sacrae sex vocum cum basso continuo ad organum* (Antwerp, 1597); *Cantiones sacrae quinque vocum* (1617); *Cantica sacra ad melodium madrigalium elaborato senis vocibus* (Antwerp, 1618); *Cantiones sacrae quinque vocum* (1619); 2 books of *Canzonette,* one for 3 Voices and one for 4 (1620; author's name given as Richardo

Diringo Inglese); *Cantica sacra ad duos et tres voces, composita cum basso continuo ad organum* (posthumous; London, 1662). Sir Frederick Bridge ed. and publ. an elaborate work of Deering's entitled *The Cryes of London.* Various other compositions (anthems, motets, viol music) are preserved in MS in the libraries of the British Museum, Christ Church, Oxford, the Royal College of Music, Peterhouse, Cambridge, Durham Cathedral, etc.

BIBLIOGRAPHY: Jeffrey Pulver, *Biographical Dictionary of Old English Music* (1923; 2nd ed., 1927); E.H. Meyer, *Die mehrstimmige Spielmusik des 17. Jahrhunderts in Nord- und Mitteleuropa* (Kassel, 1934); P. Platt, "Deering's Life and Training," *Music & Letters* (Jan. 1952); E. Brennecke, "The Country Cryes of Richard Deering," *Musical Quarterly* (July 1956).

DeFabritiis, Oliviero, Italian conductor; b. Rome, June 13, 1902; d. there, Aug. 12, 1982. He studied with Setaccioli and Refice; made his conducting debut at the Teatro Adriano in Rome in 1920; subsequently was a conductor at the Rome Opera (1934–61). He made numerous guest appearances with the major European opera houses; also conducted in the U.S.

Defauw, Désiré, Belgian conductor and violinist; b. Ghent, Sept. 5, 1885; d. Gary, Ind., July 25, 1960. He was a pupil of Johan Smit (violin); in 1914–18, led his own quartet (with L. Tertis, C. Woodhouse, and E. Doehard); was a prof. at the Antwerp Cons.; later conductor of the Defauw Concerts in Brussels; was also conductor of the Royal Cons. Orch. there and director of the National Inst. of Radio. In 1938 he was a guest conductor with the NBC Symph. Orch. in N.Y.; in Sept. 1940 he returned to the U.S.; was conductor of the Chicago Symph. Orch. (1943–47) and the Gary Symph. Orch. (1950–58).

Deffés, Pierre-Louis, French composer; b. Toulouse, July 25, 1819; d. there, June 10, 1900. He was a pupil of Halévy at the Paris Cons., taking the Grand Prix de Rome in 1847 for the cantata *L'Ange et Tobie.*

Defossez, René, Belgian composer and conductor; b. Spa, Oct. 4, 1905. He studied with his father, then at the Liège Cons. with Rasse; received the Belgian Prix de Rome in 1935 for his opera-cantata *Le Vieux Soudard.* He was then active as a conductor; from 1936 to 1959 was conductor of the Théâtre Royal de la Monnaie in Brussels; in 1946 succeeded Defauw as prof. of conducting at the Brussels Cons.; retired from there in 1971. He was an inspector of state-subsidized music schools (1961–71). In 1969 he was elected a member of the Royal Belgian Academy.

WORKS: Operas: *Le Subterfuge improvisé* (1938); *A chacun son mensonge; Les Surprises de l'amour; A chacun sa vérité; L'Amour est Roi* (1946); opera-cantatas: *La Conversion de St. Hubert* (1933) and *Le Vieux Soudard* (1935); oratorios: *Bê Pretimps d'amour* for Soprano and Orch. (1939) and *La Frise empourprée* for Soprano and Orch. (1939); ballets: *Floriante* (1942); *Le Sens du Divin* (1947); *Le Rêve de l'astronome* (1950); *Les Jeux de France* (1959); *Le Regard* (1970; Charleroi, March 27, 1971); ballet cantata, *Le Pêcheur et son âme (The Fisherman and His Soul,* after Wilde; 1965); *Lieges libertés,* historic fresco in 10 scenes (1981); *Aquarium,* 3 symph. impressions (1927); *Images sous-marines* for Orch. (1930); *Symphonie wallonne* (1935); *Poème romantique* for String Orch. (1935); *Amaterasu,* symph. legend, with Solo Soprano (1935); Variations for Piano and Orch. (1938); *Adagio et Scherzo* for Flute and Orch. (1941); *Recitativo et Allegro* for Trumpet and Orch. (1945); *Marche funebre* for Orch. (1946); *Minutes heureuses,* small suite for Orch. (1947); Trombone Concerto (1948); *Marche triomphale* for Wind Orch. (1950); Violin Concerto (1951); Piano Concerto (1956); 2-piano Concerto (1963; revision of the Piano Concerto); *La Chasseur d'images* for Orch. (1966); *Aria et Moto Perpetuoso* for Orch. (1968); *Duo concertante* for Trumpet, Percussion, and Strings; *Concerto romantique* for Piano and Orch.; *Mini-symphonie; Le Culte sans paroles* for Orch.; *Fantaisie* for Orch.; *Sinfonietta de printemps* (1975); 2 string quartets (1934, 1950); Ballad for Clarinet and Piano (1942); Wind Trio (1946); *4 églogues* for 4 Flutes and 2 Percussionists; *Petit quartet* for Violin, Piano, Saxophone, and Percussion (1973); *3 farces* for Piano (1937; orchestrated 1942); Variations for Piano (1941); *Les Caprices de ma poupée* for 2 Pianos (1950; revised for Wind Quartet, 1965); Piano Sonatina (1958); choruses; songs.

De Franco, "Buddy" (Boniface Ferdinand Leonardo), American jazz clarinetist; b. Camden, N.J., Feb. 17, 1923. He took up the clarinet at the age of 12; worked with many leading jazz musicians, including Gene Krupa (1941–42), Charlie Barnet (1943–44), Tommy Dorsey (1944–46), and Count Basie (1950); then organized his own big band (1951) and quartet (1952), appearing with the latter for many years with much success. He led the Glenn Miller Orch. from 1966 to 1974; then resumed touring on his own.

DeGaetani, Jan, remarkable American mezzo-soprano; b. Massillon, Ohio, July 10, 1933. She studied with Sergius Kagen at the Juilliard School of Music in N.Y.; in 1973 was appointed prof. of voice training at the Eastman School of Music in Rochester, N.Y. She achieved distinction as a virtuoso vocalist in her performances of ultramodern works requiring accurate rendition of unusual intervallic skips, and often quarter-tones and other fractional intervals, in addition to special effects such as percussive tongue-clicking and a variety of finely calibrated dynamic nuances. In this field she has become a unique phenomenon; several vocal works have been written specially for her by grateful modern composers. As a lieder singer, DeGaetani excels in an analytical capacity to express the most minute vocal modulations of the melodic line while parsing the words with exquisite intellectual penetration of their meaning, so that even experienced music critics are rendered helpless in search of congenial superlatives to describe her artistry.

Degen, Helmut, German composer; b. Aglaster-hausen, near Heidelberg, Jan. 14, 1911. He studied piano, composition, and conducting at the Hochschule für Musik in Cologne; then took courses at the Univ. of Bonn with Schiedermair and Schrade; taught at the Cons. of Duisburg; after the war he taught music at Trossingen.

WORKS: A prolific composer, he wrote 3 symphs. (1945, 1947, 1948); *Symphonisches Spiel I* (1956), *II* for Violin, Cello, Piano, and Orch. (1957), and *III* (1960); Piano Concerto (1940); Organ Concerto (1943); Concertino for 2 Clarinets and Orch. (1944); Cello Concerto (1945); Concerto for Harpsichord and 6 Instruments (1945); *Triptychon* (1952); 2 string quartets (1941, 1950); Piano Trio (1943); Trio for Flute, Viola, and Clarinet (1950); Saxophone Sonata (1950); Nonet for Wind Instruments and Strings (1951); 4 piano sonatas; numerous concert studies; choruses. His music is couched in a well-defined, neo-Classical idiom, with strong points of reference to Baroque forms. He also publ. a *Handbuch der Formenlehre* (Regensburg, 1957).

BIBLIOGRAPHY: K. Laux, *Musik und Musiker der Gegenwart* (Essen, 1949; pp. 57–64).

Degeyter, Pierre, wood-carver and author of the famous workers' song *Internationale* (1888); b. Oct. 8, 1848; d. St. Denis, near Paris, Sept. 27, 1932. The authorship of the song was contested by Pierre's brother, Adolphe, a blacksmith (b. 1858; d. Lille, Feb. 15, 1917), but after 18 years of litigation, the Paris Appellate Court decided in favor of Pierre.

Degner, Erich Wolf, German composer; b. Hohenstein-Ernstthal, April 8, 1858; d. Berka, near Weimar, Nov. 18, 1908. He studied at the grand-ducal school of music at Weimar, and later at Würzburg; taught at Regensburg and Gotha; in 1885 became director of the music school at Pettau, Styria; in 1888, instructor at the grand-ducal music school at Weimar; in 1891, director of the music school of the Styrian Music Society at Graz; in 1902 was again in Weimar as director of the music school.

WORKS: Symph. for Organ and Orch.; *Maria und die Mutter* for Soli, Chorus, and Orch.; pieces for piano; songs. He publ. *Anleitung und Beispiele zum Bilden von Kadenzen* (1902).

BIBLIOGRAPHY: R. Mojsisowicz, *Erich Wolf Degner* (1909).

De Guide, Richard, Belgian composer; b. Basècles, March 1, 1909; d. Brussels, Jan. 12, 1962. He studied with Paul Gilson and Jean Absil; worked for the Inst. National de Radiodiffusion (1938–45); was director of the music academy of Woluwé-St.-Pierre in Brussels (1946–61); also taught at the Liège Cons. (1950–53) and at the Mons Cons. (1961).

WORKS: *Mouvements symphoniques* (1938); *Illustration pour un Jeu de l'Oie* for Voice, and Piano or Orch. (1939–41); *Concerto for 11* for Winds and Percussion (1940); 3 symphs.: No. 1 (1943); No. 2, with Organ (1951); No. 3 for Strings, Harp, and Timpani (1957); *Vincti non devicti,* symph. poem (1948); piano concerto, *Le Téméraire* (1952); *Le Tombeau de Montaigne,* symph. suite (1955); ballet, *Les Danaïdes* (1956); *Hommage à Hindemith* for Chamber Orch. (1958); *Humoresque* for Piano (1927); *Préludes* for Organ (1942); Duo for 2 Trumpets (1944); Duo for 2 Violins (1945); *Speciosa miracula,* sextet for Wind Quintet and Piano (1948); *Préludes and Toccata* for Piano (1949); *2 nômes* for Flute (1951); *Suite "Les caractères du trombone"* for Trombone and Piano (1958); *4 symptômes* for Piano, left-hand (1960). He wrote a monograph, *Jean Absil, vie et œuvre,* publ. posthumously (Tournai, 1965).

Dehn, Siegfried Wilhelm, famous German music theorist; b. Altona, Feb. 24, 1799; d. Berlin, April 12, 1858. He was a law student at Leipzig in 1819–25; also studied harmony and cello playing. He studied theory assiduously with Bernhard Klein in Berlin; at Meyerbeer's insistence he was appointed librarian of the music dept. of the Royal Library in 1842. In 1842–48 he was also editor of the *Caecilia;* then was a prof. at the Royal Academy of Arts (1849–58). Dehn was a profound theorist, and very successful as a teacher of theory, numbering among his pupils Anton Rubinstein and Glinka.

WRITINGS: *Theoretisch-praktische Harmonielehre* (Berlin, 1840; 2nd ed., Leipzig, 1860; his most important work); *Analyse dreier Fugen aus J.S. Bachs Wohltemperiertem Clavier und einer Vokaldoppelfuge G.M. Buononcinis* (Leipzig, 1858); *Eine Sammlung älterer Musik aus dem 16. und 17. Jahrhundert* (Berlin; 12 books of vocal compositions a 4–10); trans. Delmotte's work on Orlandus Lassus, *Biogr. Notiz über Roland de Lattre* (Vienna, 1837). A posthumous *Lehre vom Kontrapunkt, dem Kanon und der Fuge* (Berlin, 1859; 2nd ed., 1883) was ed. by B. Scholz.

Deis, Carl, American pianist, music editor, and composer; b. New York, March 7, 1883; d. there, July 24, 1960. He studied piano at home from early childhood under the guidance of his father, who was a trombone player; then was a pupil at the National Cons. of Music and the N.Y. College of Music. In 1906 he became a choral conductor and voice teacher at various private schools in N.Y.; was engaged as organist at the Society for Ethical Culture (1919–33). In 1917 he was appointed music editor of G. Schirmer, Inc.; retired in 1953. He wrote several attractive songs, among them *New Year's Day, The Flight of the Moon, Come down to Kew, The Drums, Were I a Star.*

Deiters, Hermann, German writer on music; b. Bonn, June 27, 1833; d. Koblenz, May 11, 1907. He studied jurisprudence in Bonn, where he took the degrees of Dr.Jur. (1854) and Dr.Phil. (1858). He taught in the gymnasia at Bonn (1858) and Düren (1869); was director of gymnasia at Konitz (1874), Posen (1878), and Bonn (1883); "Provincial-Schulrath" at Koblenz (1885–93); assistant in the Ministry of Public Worship at Berlin (1890); he retired in

1903, living thereafter in Koblenz. Deiters wrote many articles on music for the *Deutsche Musik-zeitung,* the *Allgemeine Musikalische Zeitung,* and other journals. He contributed several music biographies to Meyer's *Konversations-Lexikon* (3rd ed.); wrote a biography of Brahms in Waldersee's *Sammlung musikalischer Vorträge* (1882, 1898). His greatest achievement was his masterly trans. into German of Thayer's *Life of Beethoven,* with critical comments by Deiters (3 vols., Berlin, 1866–79; 2nd ed., with 2 additional vols. ed. by Riemann, Berlin, 1910–11).

Dejoncker, Theodore, Belgian composer; b. Brussels, April 11, 1894; d. Asse, July 10, 1964. He studied with Gilson; in 1925, founded, with 7 other composers, the progressive Groupe des Synthétistes.
WORKS: *Sinfonia la classica* (1939); *Symphonie burlesque; Symphonie romantique;* overture, *Brutus; Prologue symphonique; Portrait de Bernard Shaw* for Orch.; String Quartet; Saxophone Quartet; String Trio (1960).

De Jong, Conrad, American composer; b. Hull, Iowa, Jan. 13, 1934. He studied trumpet at North Texas State Univ. in Denton, majoring in music education; received his B.M.Ed. in 1954; later studied composition with Bernhard Heiden at Indiana Univ. in Bloomington, obtaining his M.M. in 1959. He was appointed to the music faculty of Wisconsin State Univ. at River Falls in 1959.
WORKS: *Unicycle* for Harpsichord (1960); *3 Studies* for Brass Septet (1960); *Music for 2 Tubas* (1961); *Essay* for Brass Quintet (1963); String Trio (1964); *Fun and Games* for Any Instrument with Piano (1966); *Aanraking (Contact)* for Solo Trombone (1969); *Hist Whist* for Soprano, Flute, Viola, and Percussion (1969); *Grab Gab* for Tuba Ensemble (1970); *Peace on Earth* for Unison Chorus and Organ (1970).

De Jong, Marinus. See **Jong, Marinus de.**

De Koven, (Henry Louis) Reginald, American composer; b. Middletown, Conn., April 3, 1859; d. Chicago, Jan. 16, 1920. He was educated in Europe from 1870, taking his degree at St. John's College, Oxford, in 1879. Before this he studied piano under W. Speidel at Stuttgart, and after graduation studied there another year under Lebert (piano) and Pruckner (harmony). After a 6-month course in Frankfurt under Dr. Hauff (composition), he studied singing with Vannucini at Florence, and operatic composition under Genée in Vienna and Delibes in Paris. In 1902 he organized the Phil. Orch. at Washington, D.C., which he conducted for 3 seasons. He was music critic for the *Chicago Evening Post* (1889–90), *Harper's Weekly* (1895–97), *N.Y. World* (1898–1900 and 1907–12), and later for the *N.Y. Herald.*
WORKS: He wrote several successful operettas: *The Begum* (Philadelphia, Nov. 7, 1887); *Don Quixote* (Boston, Nov. 18, 1889); *Robin Hood* (his best-known work; Chicago, June 9, 1890; London, Jan. 5,

1891; the celebrated song *O Promise Me* was introduced into the score shortly after its first perf.; it was originally publ. as a separate song in 1889); *The Fencing Master* (Boston, 1892); *The Knickerbockers* (Boston, 1893); *The Algerian* (Philadelphia, 1893); *Rob Roy* (Detroit, 1894); *The Tzigane* (N.Y., 1895); *The Mandarin* (Cleveland, 1896); *The Paris Doll* (Hartford, Conn., 1897); *The Highwayman* (New Haven, 1897); and the following, all of which had their premieres in N.Y.: *The Tree Dragoons* (1899); *Red Feather* (1903); *Happyland* (1905); *Student King* (1906); *The Golden Butterfly* (1907); *The Beauty Spot* (1909); *The Wedding Trip* (1911); *Her Little Highness* (1913). A grand opera, *The Canterbury Pilgrims,* was produced at the Metropolitan Opera House on March 8, 1917; another opera, *Rip van Winkle,* was performed by the Chicago Opera Co. (Jan. 2, 1920). In addition, he wrote some 400 songs and a Piano Sonata.
BIBLIOGRAPHY: Anna de Koven, *A Musician and His Wife* (N.Y., 1926).

Dela, Maurice, French-Canadian composer and organist; b. Montreal, Sept. 9, 1919; d. Montreal, April 28, 1978. He studied composition with Champagne at the Montreal Cons. and orchestration with Leo Sowerby in Chicago. He subsequently became a church organist in the province of Quebec. His music is pragmatic in style and idiom, tending toward Baroque consistency but energized by an injection of euphonious dissonance.
WORKS: Ballade for Piano and Orch. (1945); Piano Concerto (1946); *Ronde* for Soprano, and Small Orch. or Piano (1949); *Le Chat, la belette et le petit lapin* for Narrator and Orch. (1950; revised 1965); *Les Fleurs de Glais* for Narrator and Orch. (1951); *Scherzo* for Orch. (1953); *Adagio* for String Orch. (1956); Piano Concertino (1962); *2 esquisses* for Orch. (1962); *Projection* for Orch. (1966); 2 symphs. (1968, 1972); *3 Dances* for Orch. (1971); *Triptyque* for Orch. (1974); *Suite 437* for Band (1977); *Petite suite maritime* for Wind Instruments (1946); Suite for Flute, Cello, and Piano (1953–54); 2 string quartets (1960, 1963); *Divertissement* for Brass Quintet (1962); *Miniatures* for 3 Recorders (1968); *Hommage* for Piano (1950); *2 Impromptus* for Piano (1964); songs; arrangements of folk songs of Quebec province.

Delacôte, Jacques, French conductor; b. Remiremont, Vosges, Aug. 16, 1942. He studied conducting with Hans Swarowsky at the Vienna Academy of Music; in 1971 he won the Mitropoulos Competition in N.Y.; in 1972 he appeared as a conductor with the N.Y. Phil.; subsequently conducted at the Hamburg State Opera, the Düsseldorf Opera, the Paris Opéra, and Covent Garden in London. As a symph. conductor, he had engagements with the London Symph., the Cleveland Orch., and the San Francisco Symph. Naturally, he is especially praised for his congenial performances of French operas.

Delage, Maurice, French composer; b. Paris, Nov. 13, 1879; d. there, Sept. 19, 1961. He was engaged as a clerk in a maritime agency in Paris and in a fishery in Boulogne; in 1900 was in the army; then became interested in music and took lessons with Ravel. Subsequently he made voyages to the Orient, and was greatly impressed with Japanese art. His music reveals oriental traits in subject matter as well as in melodic progressions. An ardent follower of Debussy's principles, Delage wrote music in a highly subtilized manner with distinctive instrumental colors. After 1920 he lived mostly in Paris.

WORKS: Symph. poem, *Conte par la mer;* several songs, with Small Orch.; *4 poèmes hindous* (1921); *Roses d'Octobre* (1922); *7 Haï-Kaï* (1923); *3 chants de la jungle* (1935); *2 fables de La Fontaine* (1949); *In Morte* (1951); String Quartet (1948).

Delalande, Michel-Richard, French organist and composer; b. Paris, Dec. 15, 1657; d. Versailles, June 18, 1726. He was the 15th child of a Paris tailor; was apprenticed as a boy chorister at the Saint-Germain Auxerrois; when his voice broke, he began to study organ playing, in which he succeeded so well that Louis XIV entrusted him with giving keyboard lessons to the royal princesses. In 1683 he received the position of "surintendant" of the Royal Chapel. In 1704 he became master of the Royal Chapel; in 1722, he was joined in this directorship by Campra, Bernier, and Gervais.

WORKS: Delalande was the composer of excellent ballets, even though they yielded in quality to those of Lully; of these, *Ballet de la jeunesse* (1686), *Le Palais de Flore* (1689), *Adonis* (1698), *Le Ballet des fées* (1699), *L'Hymen champestre* (1700), *Le Ballet de la paix* (1713), and *Les Folies de Gardenio* (1720) were produced at the court in Versailles. With Destouches, he wrote the ballet *Les Elements,* which was produced at the Tuileries Palace in Paris on Dec. 31, 1721. (Vincent d'Indy edited the score and publ. it in 1883.) Delalande also wrote 42 motets, which were publ. in 1729, and a number of "symphonies pour les soupers du roi" (intermezzos to be played at court dinners) and "symphonies de Noël" (instrumental interludes for performances at Christmas time at the court); 22 "Noëls" (arranged in a series of 4 "symphonies") by Delalande were ed. by A. Cellier (Paris, 1937).

BIBLIOGRAPHY: N. Dufourcq, ed., *Notes et références pour servir à une histoire de Michel-Richard Delalande* (Paris, 1957; contains a thematic catalogue).

De Lamarter, Eric, American organist, music critic, and composer; b. Lansing, Mich., Feb. 18, 1880; d. Orlando, Fla., May 17, 1953. He studied organ with Fairclough in St. Paul, Middleschulte in Chicago, and Guilmant and Widor in Paris (1901–2); then was organist of various churches in Chicago till 1936; assistant conductor of the Chicago Symph. Orch. in 1918–36; also conducted the Chicago Civic Orch. He was music critic of the *Chicago Record-Herald* (1908–9), *Chicago Tribune* (1909–10), and *Inter-Ocean* (from 1910); held teaching positions at the Chicago Musical College and Olivet College.

WORKS: Ballet, *The Betrothal* (N.Y., Nov. 19, 1918); ballet suite, *The Black Orchid* (Chicago Symph. Orch., Feb. 27, 1931, composer conducting); 4 symphs. (1914, 1926, 1931, 1932); overture, *The Faun* (1914); *Serenade* for Orch. (1915); overture, *Masquerade* (1916); *Fable of the Hapless Folktune* for Orch. (1917); 2 organ concertos (1920, 1922); *Weaver of Tales* for Organ and Chamber Orch. (1926); ballet suite, *The Dance of Life* (1931); *The Giddy Puritan,* overture on 2 early New England tunes (1921; NBC, June 6, 1938; Chicago Symph., March 9, 1942); organ works; songs.

Delamont, Gordon, Canadian composer; b. Moose Jaw, Saskatchewan, Oct. 27, 1918; d. Toronto, Jan. 16, 1981. He played trumpet in his father's band in Vancouver; in 1945 organized his own dance band. From the very first he embraced jazz as a medium of composition, but treated the popular idiom in a modernistic manner. Among his works are *Allegro and Blues* for Jazz Orch. (1964); *3 Entertainments* for Saxophone Quartet (1970); and *Moderato and Blues* for Brass Quintet (1972). He also publ. texts on practical arranging techniques and *Modern 12-tone Technique* (N.Y., 1973).

De Lancie, John Sherwood, American oboe virtuoso; b. Berkeley, Calif., July 26, 1921. His father was an electrical engineer and an amateur clarinet player; his brother played the violin. In 1935 he won an audition for the Philadelphia Orch., and was also accepted to study oboe in the class of Marcel Tabuteau at the Curtis Inst. of Music. He was engaged as principal oboist with the Pittsburgh Symph. under Fritz Reiner, who was also conductor of the Curtis Student Orch. He was then engaged as oboist with the Denver Orch.; in 1942 he was drafted into the U.S. Army as a member of the U.S. Army Band; in 1943 the band was sent to Algiers, to Eisenhower's headquarters; he was subsequently employed by the Office of Strategic Services (now the CIA). After the war De Lancie succeeded Tabuteau as first oboist of the Philadelphia Orch. In 1977 he was appointed Director of the Curtis Inst., succeeding Rudolf Serkin. De Lancie rapidly advanced to the position of one of the greatest virtuosos on his instrument. An interesting episode in his career concerns his meeting with Richard Strauss, during which he asked Strauss why he would not compose a concerto for oboe, in view of the fact that there are so many beautiful oboe solos in many of his works. This suggestion bore fruit, but De Lancie was not the first to play it; the first performance was given by Marcel Saillet on Feb. 26, 1946, in Zürich.

Delaney, Robert Mills, American composer; b. Baltimore, July 24, 1903; d. Santa Barbara, Calif., Sept. 21, 1956. He studied music in the U.S., later in Italy, then in Paris (1922–27) with Capet (violin) and Nadia Boulanger and Arthur Honegger (composition). He won the Guggenheim fellowship in 1929; in 1933 he received a Pulitzer Traveling Fellowship for his music to Stephen Vincent Benét's *John Brown's Song*. He then occupied various teaching posts; settled in Santa Barbara.

WORKS: *Don Quixote Symphony* (1927); *John Brown's Song,* choral symph. (1931); *Night* for Chorus, String Orch., and Piano, after William Blake (1934); *Work 22,* overture (1939); Symph. No. 1 (1942); *Western Star* for Chorus and Orch. (1944); 3 string quartets.

Delannoy, Marcel, French composer; b. La Ferté-Alais, July 9, 1898; d. Nantes, Sept. 14, 1962. He served in the French army in World War I; then took lessons with Gédalge and Honegger. After a few years of instruction, he produced an effective stage work, *Poirier de Misère* (Paris, Feb. 21, 1927), which obtained excellent success. Other works are the ballet-cantata *Le Fou de la dame* (in concert form, Paris, Nov. 9, 1928; stage production, Geneva, April 6, 1929); *Cinderella,* ballet (Chicago, Aug. 30, 1931; revised and perf. as *La Pantoufle de vair* at the Opéra-Comique, Paris, May 14, 1935); a Symph. (Paris, March 15, 1934); *Ginevra,* comic opera in 3 acts (Paris, Opéra-Comique, July 25, 1942); *Arlequin radiophile,* chamber opera (Paris, April 1, 1946); *Puck,* fairy opera after Shakespeare (Strasbourg, Jan. 29, 1949); *Concerto de mai* for Piano and Orch. (Paris, May 4, 1950); *Travesti,* ballet (Enghien-les-Bains, June 4, 1952); ballet, *Les Noces fantastiques* (Paris, Feb. 9, 1955); Symph. for Strings and Celesta (1952–54); *Le Moulin de la galette,* symph. poem (1958).

De Lara (real name, **Cohen**), **Isidore,** English composer of operas; b. London, Aug. 9, 1858; d. Paris, Sept. 2, 1935. He began to study the piano at the age of 10 with H. Aguilar; also studied singing with Lamperti and composition with Mazzucato at the Milan Cons. He then went to Paris to study with Lalo; returning to London, he wrote one opera after another, and easily secured performances.
WORKS: *The Light of Asia* (1892); *Amy Robsart* (London, July 20, 1893); *Moina* (Monte Carlo, March 14, 1897); *Messalina* (Monte Carlo, March 21, 1899; his most successful work); *Sanga* (Nice, Feb. 21, 1906); *Solea* (Cologne, Dec. 12, 1907); *Les Trois Masques* (Marseilles, Feb. 24, 1912); *Naïl* (Paris, April 22, 1912); *Les Trois Mousquetaires* (Cannes, March 3, 1921).

Delcroix, Léon Charles, Belgian composer; b. Brussels, Sept. 15, 1880; d. there, Nov. 14, 1938. He studied piano with J. Wieniawski, organ with A. Mailly, and composition with Théophile Ysaÿe in Brussels and Vincent d'Indy in Paris. He conducted theater orchs. in Belgium (1909–27); then devoted his entire time to composition.
WORKS: For the stage: *Ce n'était qu'un rêve* (one act); *La Bacchante,* ballet (Ghent, 1912); *Le Petit Poucet,* opera (Brussels, Oct. 9, 1913). For Orch.: Symph. (won the award of the Belgian Academy); *Le Roi Harald, Çunacépa, Soir d'été à Lerici, Le Val harmonieux; Rapsodie languedocienne; Marche cortège; Sérénade* for Clarinet, Piano, and Orch.; *Elégie et Poème* for Violin and Orch.; many chamber music works (quartets, quintets, sonatas, etc.); piano works; church music (*Pie Jesu, Resurrexi,*

Ecce panis); songs. He wrote a biography of his teacher J. Wieniawski (Brussels, 1908).

Delden, Lex van, Dutch composer; b. Amsterdam, Sept. 10, 1919. He studied medicine at the Univ. of Amsterdam; then turned to music; wrote criticism in Dutch newspapers. In composition, he was entirely autodidact; yet he wrote a number of works, including 8 symphs.
WORKS: 3 oratorios: *De Vogelvrijheid (The Phoenix;* 1956); *Anthropolis* (1962); *Icarus,* radiophonic oratorio, with Tape (1963); 8 symphs.: No. 1, *De stroom, Mei 1940 (The Torrent, May 1940)* for Soprano, Chorus, 8 Instruments, and Percussion (1952; alternate version with orch. scoring, 1954; describes the destruction of Rotterdam at the beginning of World War II); No. 2, *Sinfonia giocosa* (1953); No. 3, *Facetten (Facets;* 1955); No. 4 (1957); No. 5 (1959); No. 6 (1963); No. 7, *Sinfonia concertante,* for 11 Winds (1964); No. 8 for String Orch. (1964); *Allegretto* for Orch. (1949); *Introduction and Allegro,* small concerto for Violin, Piano, and Orch. (1951); Harp Concerto (1951); *In memoriam* for Orch. (1953); Trio for String Orch. (1954); *Tij en Ontij,* ballet music (1956); Trumpet Concerto (1956); 2-oboe Concerto (1959); Piano Concerto (1960); *Piccolo Concerto* for 12 Winds and Percussion (1960); Concerto for 2 String Orchs. (1961); *Piccolo musica concertata* for 3 Trombones and String Orch. (1963); Flute Concerto (1965); Concerto for Violin, Viola, Double Bass, and Orch. (1965); Concerto for 2 Soprano Saxophones and Orch. (1967); *Musica sinfonica* (1967); Concerto for Percussion, Celesta, and String Orch. (1968); Organ Concerto (1973); *Rubáiyát* for Soprano, Tenor, Chorus, 2 Pianos, and Percussion (1947); *Het spoorboekje (The Railway Timetable)* for a cappella Chorus (1952; a setting of a number of sections from the regulations of Dutch railways); *Canto della guerra* for Chorus and Orch. (1967); Suite for Violin and Piano (1939); *Ballet* for Flute, Viola, Bassoon, and Guitar (1946); Piano Sonata (1949); *Introduction and Dance (Judith)* for Flute, Clarinet, Violin, Viola, Cello, and Piano (1950); Duo for Flute and Harp (1950); *Small Suite* for 12 Harps (1951; in collaboration with Marius Flothuis); Saxophone Sonatina (1952); 2 string quartets (1954, 1965); 4 Pieces for Piano (1954); *Impromptu* for Harp (1955); *Sonatina eroica* for Piano (1956); Quartet for Flute, Violin, Viola, and Cello (1957); Solo Cello Sonata (1958); *Intrada and Dance* for 6 Harps (1961); Concertino for 2 Harps (1962); Violin Sonata (1964); Fantasia for Harp and 8 Winds (1965); *Musica notturna a 5* for 4 Cellos and Harp (1967); Piano Trio (1969); Quartet for Flute, Oboe, Violin, and Cello (1970); *Sestetto* for 6 Strings (1971); songs.

Deldevez, Edouard-Marie-Ernest, French conductor and composer; b. Paris, May 31, 1817; d. there, Nov. 6, 1897. He studied violin with Habeneck and music theory with Halévy and Berton at the Paris Cons. In 1859 he was appointed assistant conductor at the Grand Opéra and of the Conservatoire Concerts; in 1872–75 was principal conductor; concurrently was principal conductor of the Paris Opéra

(1873–77); taught orchestral playing at the Paris Cons. (1874–85).

WORKS: Ballets: *Eucharis* (1844); *Paquita* (1846); *Vert-Vert* (1851, with Tolbecque); operas: *Samson* and *Le Violon enchanté;* 3 symphs.; chamber music; sacred choruses and songs.

WRITINGS: Monograph, *Curiosités musicales* (1873); *La Notation de la musique classique comparée à la notation de la musique moderne, et de l'exécution des petites notes en général; L'Art du chef d'orchestre* (1878); *La Société des Concerts de 1860 à 1885* (1887); *De l'exécution d'ensemble* (1888); *Le Passé à propos du présent* (1892), a continuation of his personal recollections publ. in 1890 as *Mes mémoires.*

BIBLIOGRAPHY: Ch. Malherbe, "Notice sur Deldevez," *Revue Internationale de Musique* (1899).

De Leone, Francesco B., American composer; b. (of Italian parents) in Ravenna, Ohio, July 28, 1887; d. Akron, Ohio, Dec. 10, 1948. He studied at Dana's Musical Inst., Warren, Ohio (1901–3), and at the Royal Cons. of Naples (1903–10); returned to the U.S. and established his home in Akron, where he founded the De Leone School of Music, and organized and directed the music dept. of the Univ. of Akron; also conducted the Akron Symph. Orch. He wrote the operas *Alglala* (Akron, May 23, 1924); *A Millionaire Caprice* (in Italian; Naples, July 26, 1910); *Cave Man Stuff,* operetta; *Princess Ting-Ah-Ling,* operetta; the sacred musical dramas *Ruth, The Prodigal Son, The Golden Calf,* and *David; The Triumph of Joseph,* oratorio; pieces for Symph. Orch.: 6 *Italian Dances, Italian Rhapsody, Gibraltar Suite;* over 400 songs; piano pieces.

Delgadillo, Luis Abraham, Nicaraguan composer; b. Managua, Aug. 26, 1887; d. there, Dec. 20, 1961. He studied at the Milan Cons.; returning to Nicaragua, he became a band conductor and opened a music school, which later became a cons. His music is permeated with native rhythm and melos; virtually all of his output is descriptive of some aspect of Latin American culture and history.

WORKS: For Orch.: *Sinfonia indigena* (1921); *Sinfonia mexicana* (1924); *Teotihuacan* (1925); *Sinfonia incaica* (1926; Caracas, May 20, 1927, composer conducting); *Sinfonia serrana* (1928); 12 short symphs., all composed in one year (1953) and couched in different styles, from classical to modernistic; overtures in the styles of Debussy and Schoenberg (*Obertura Debussyana* and *Obertura Schoenbergiana,* 1955); 7 string quartets; church music; piano pieces in various forms.

Delibes, (Clément-Philibert-) Léo, famous French composer; b. St.-Germain-du-Val, Sarthe, Feb. 21, 1836; d. Paris, Jan. 16, 1891. He received his early musical training with his mother and an uncle; then enrolled in the Paris Cons. in 1847 as a student of Tariot; won a premier prix in solfège in 1850; also studied organ with Benoist and composition with Adam. In 1853 he became organist of St. Pierre de Chaillot and accompanist at the Théâtre-Lyrique. In 1856 his first work for the stage, *Deux sous de charbon,* a one-act operetta, humorously subtitled "asphyxie lyrique," was produced at the Folies-Nouvelles. His 2nd work, the opérette bouffe *Deux vielles gardes,* won considerable acclaim at its premiere at the Bouffes-Parisiens on Aug. 8, 1856. Several more operettas were to follow, as well as his first substantial work for the stage, *Le Jardinier et son seigneur,* given at the Théâtre-Lyrique on May 1, 1863. In 1864 he became chorus master of the Paris Opéra. With Louis Minkus he collaborated on the ballet score *La Source,* which was heard for the first time at the Paris Opéra on Nov. 12, 1866. It was with his next ballet, *Coppelia, ou La Fille aux yeux d'émail,* that Delibes achieved lasting fame after its premiere at the Paris Opéra, on May 25, 1870. Another ballet, *Sylvia, ou La Nymphe de Diane* (Paris Opéra, June 14, 1876), was equally successful. He then wrote a grand opera, *Jean de Nivelle* (Opéra-Comique, March 8, 1880), was moderately successful; it was followed by his triumphant masterpiece, the opera *Lakmé* (Opéra-Comique, April 14, 1883), in which he created a most effective lyric evocation of India; the "Bell Song" from *Lakmé* became a perennial favorite in recitals. In 1881 he was appointed prof. of composition at the Paris Cons.; in 1884 was elected a member of the Institut. His last opera, *Kassya,* was completed but not orchestrated at the time of his death; Massenet orchestrated the score, and it was premiered at the Opéra-Comique on March 24, 1893. Delibes was a master of melodious elegance and harmonious charm; his music possessed an autonomous flow in colorful timbres, and a finality of excellence that seemed effortless while subtly revealing a mastery of the Romantic technique of composition.

BIBLIOGRAPHY: E. Guiraud, *Notice sur la vie et les œuvres de Léo Delibes* (Paris, 1896); O. Séré, *Musiciens français d'aujourd'hui* (2nd ed., Paris, 1911); H. de Curzon, *Léo Delibes* (Paris, 1927).

Delius, Frederick (baptismal names, **Fritz Theodor Albert**), significant English composer of German parentage; b. Bradford, Jan. 29, 1862; d. Grez-sur-Loing, France, June 10, 1934. His father was a successful merchant, owner of a wool company; he naturally hoped to have his son follow a career in industry, but did not object to his study of art and music. Delius learned to play the piano and violin. At the age of 22 he went to Solano, Florida, to work on an orange plantation owned by his father; a musical souvenir of his sojourn there was his symph. suite, *Florida.* There he met an American organist, Thomas F. Ward, who gave him a thorough instruction in music theory; this study, which lasted 6 months, gave Delius a foundation for his further progress in music. In 1885 he went to Danville, Virginia, as a teacher. In 1886 he enrolled at the Leipzig Cons., where he took courses in harmony and counterpoint with Reinecke, Sitt, and Jadassohn. It was there that he met Grieg, becoming his friend and admirer. Indeed Grieg's music found a deep resonance in his own compositions. An even more powerful influence was Wagner, whose principles of continuous melodic line and thematic development Delius adopted in his own works. Euphonious serenity reigns on the symph. surface of his music, diversified by occasional resolvable dissonances. In some works he made congenial use of English folk motifs, often in elaborate variation forms. Particularly successful are his evocative symphonic sketches *On Hearing the First Cuckoo in Spring, North Country Sketches, Brigg Fair, A Song of the High Hills,* etc. His orch. nocturne *Paris: The Song of a Great City* is a tribute to a city in which he spent many years of his life. Much more ambitious in scope is his choral work *A Mass of Life,* in which he draws on passages from Nietzsche's *Also sprach Zarathustra.*

Delius settled in Paris in 1888; in 1897 he moved to Grez-sur-Loing, near Paris, where he remained for the rest of his life, except for a few short trips abroad. In 1903 he married the painter Jelka Rosen. His music began to win recognition in England and Germany; he became a favorite composer of Sir Thomas Beecham, who gave numerous performances of his music in London. But these successes came too late for Delius; a syphilitic infection which he had contracted early in life eventually grew into an incurable illness accompanied by paralysis and blindness; as Beecham phrased it, "Delius had suffered a heavy blow in the defection of his favorite goddess Aphrodite Pandemos who had returned his devotions with an affliction which was to break out many years later." Still eager to compose, Delius engaged as his amanuensis the English musician Eric Fenby, who wrote down music at the dictation of Delius, including complete orch. scores. In 1929, Beecham organized a Delius Festival in London (6 concerts; Oct. 12 to Nov. 1, 1929), and the composer was brought from France to hear it. In the same year Delius was made Companion of Honour by King George V and an Hon.Mus.D. by Oxford. A motion picture was made by the British filmmaker Ken Russell on the life and works of Delius. However, Delius remains a solitary figure in modern music. Affectionately appreciated in England, in America, and to some extent in Germany, his works are rarely performed elsewhere.

WORKS: FOR THE STAGE: *Zanoni,* incidental music (1888); *Irmelin,* opera (1890–92; first perf., Oxford, May 4, 1953, Beecham conducting); *The Magic Fountain,* opera (1893–95; first perf., BBC, London, Nov. 20, 1977); *Koanga,* opera (1895–97; Elberfeld, March 30, 1904; first English perf., London, Sept. 23, 1935); *Folkeraadet,* incidental music for G. Heiberg's drama (1897; Christiania, Oct. 1897, Delius conducting); *A Village Romeo and Juliet,* opera (1900–1; Berlin, Feb. 21, 1907; first English perf., London, Feb. 22, 1910); *Margot la Rouge,* opera (1902; first perf., BBC, London, Feb. 21, 1982); *Fennimore and Gerda,* opera after J.P. Jacobsen's novel *Niels Lhyne* (1909–10; Frankfurt, Oct. 21, 1919); *Hassan, or The Golden Journey to Samarkand,* incidental music for J.E. Flecker's drama (1920–23; Darmstadt, June 1, 1923; first English perf., a full version of the score, London, Sept. 23, 1923).

FOR ORCH.: *Florida Suite* (1887; first perf. privately, Leipzig, 1888; first public perf., London, April 1,

1937); *Hiawatha,* tone poem (1888); *Marche Caprice* and *Schlittenfahrt* (1887–88); *Rhapsodic Variations* (unfinished; 1888); *Pastorale* for Violin and Orch. (1888); *Petite Suite* (1889); *Idylle de Printemps* (1889); *Summer Evening* (1890; first perf., London, Jan. 2, 1949); *Legends* for Piano and Orch. (unfinished; 1890); *Paa Vidderne (Sur les Cimes),* concert overture after Ibsen (1890–91; Christiania, Oct. 10, 1891); *Legend* for Violin and Orch. (1893; London, May 30, 1899); *Over the Hills and Far Away,* tone poem (1895; London, May 30, 1899); Piano Concerto in C minor (first version in 3 movements, 1897; 2nd version in one movement, 1906; London, Oct. 22, 1907); *La Ronde se déroule,* tone poem (1899; London, May 30, 1899; revised 1901, as *Life's Dance;* 2nd revision, 1912; Berlin, Nov. 12, 1912); *Paris: The Song of a Great City* (1898; Elberfeld, 1901); *Appalachia,* orch. variations with final chorus (1898–1902; Elberfeld, 1904); *Brigg Fair, An English Rhapsody* (1907; Basel, 1907; first English perf., Liverpool, Jan. 18, 1908); *In a Summer Garden,* rhapsody (1908; London, Dec. 11, 1908, Delius conducting); *Dance Rhapsody* No. 1 (1908; Hereford, Sept. 8, 1909, Delius conducting); *Summer Night on the River* (1911) and *On Hearing the First Cuckoo in Spring* (1912; Leipzig, Oct. 2, 1913; first English perfs. of both pieces, London, Jan. 20, 1914); *North Country Sketches* (1913–14; London, May 10, 1915); *Air and Dance* for Strings (1915; London, Oct. 16, 1929); Double Concerto for Violin, Cello, and Orch. (1915–16; London, Feb. 21, 1920); Violin Concerto (1916; London, Jan. 30, 1919); *Dance Rhapsody* No. 2 (1916); *Eventyr (Once Upon a Time),* ballad for Orch. (1917; London, Jan. 11, 1919); *A Song before Sunrise* for Small Orch. (1918); Cello Concerto (1921; Frankfurt, Jan. 30, 1921); *Caprice and Elegy* for Cello and Chamber Orch. (1930); *A Song of Summer* (dictated by Delius to Eric Fenby in France, 1930; London, Sept. 17, 1932); *Fantastic Dance* (1931; London, Jan. 12, 1934).

VOCAL WORKS: *Paa Vidderne,* after Ibsen, for Reciter with Orch. (1888); *Sakuntala* for Tenor and Orch. (1889); *Maud,* after Tennyson, song cycle for Tenor and Orch. (1891); *Seven Danish Songs* for Voice and Orch. (1897; Paris, 1901, d'Indy conducting); *Mitternachtslied (Zarathustra's Night Song),* after Nietzsche (1898); *Sea Drift,* setting of extract of Walt Whitman's *Out of the Cradle Endlessly Rocking,* for Baritone, Chorus, and Orch. (1903–4; Essen, May, 24, 1906; first English perf., Sheffield, Oct. 7, 1908); *A Mass of Life,* after Nietzsche's *Also sprach Zarathustra,* for Soprano, Alto, Tenor, Baritone, Chorus, and Orch. (1904–5; London, June 7, 1909); *Cynara,* to words by Ernest Dowson, for Baritone and Orch. (1907; London, Oct. 18, 1929); *Songs of Sunset,* after poems of Ernest Dowson, for Mezzo-soprano, Baritone, Chorus, and Orch. (1908; London, June 16, 1911); *On Craig Dhu* (1907) and *Midsummer Song* (1908), both for Unaccompanied Chorus; *Wanderer's Song* for Unaccompanied Men's Chorus (1908); *A Song of the High Hills* for Wordless Chorus and Orch. (1911; London, Feb. 20, 1920); *Arabesk* for Baritone, Chorus, and Orch. (1911; Newport, 1920; first London perf., Oct. 18, 1929); *Requiem,* after Nietzsche, for Soprano, Baritone, Chorus, and Orch., dedicated "to the memory of all young artists fallen in the war" (1914–16; London, March 23, 1922); *Songs of Farewell,* after Walt Whitman, for Double Chorus and Orch. (1930; London, March 21, 1932); *Idyll: Once I Passed through a Populous City,* after Walt Whitman, for Soprano, Baritone, and Orch. (1930–32; London, Oct. 3, 1933; reworking of portions of *Margot la Rouge*) also numerous songs, including several of the above to original piano accompaniments.

CHAMBER MUSIC: 2 string quartets (1888 and 1893; unpubl.); Violin Sonata No. 1 (1905–14); String Quartet (1916; London, Feb. 1, 1919); Cello Sonata (1916; London, Jan. 11, 1919); Violin Sonata No. 2 (1923; London, Oct. 7, 1924); Violin Sonata No. 3 (1930; London, Nov. 6, 1930); also pieces for piano, and a Dance for Harpsichord (1919).

BIBLIOGRAPHY: P. Heseltine, *Frederick Delius* (London, 1923; 2nd ed., revised, 1952); R. Hull, *Frederick Delius* (London, 1928); E. Blom, "Delius and America," *Musical Quarterly* (July 1929); C. Delius, *Frederick Delius, Memories of My Brother* (London, 1935); E. Fenby, *Delius as I Knew Him* (London, 1936; 3rd ed., 1966); A. Hutchings, *Delius, A Critical Biography* (London, 1948); T. Beecham, *Frederick Delius* (London, 1959; 2nd ed., revised, 1975); G. Jahoda, *The Road to Samarkand: Frederick Delius and His Music* (N.Y., 1969); E. Fenby, *Delius* (London, 1971); W. Randel, "Frederick Delius in America," *Virginia Magazine of History & Biography* (July 1971); L. Carley and R. Threlfall, *Delius and America* (London, 1972); A. Jefferson, *Delius* (London, 1972); R. Lowe, *Frederick Delius, 1862–1934; A Catalogue of the Music Archives of the Delius Trust, London* (London, 1974); L. Carley, *Delius: The Paris Years* (London, 1975); C. Palmer, *Delius: Portrait of a Cosmopolitan* (London, 1976); C. Redwood, ed., *A Delius Companion* (London, 1976); L. Carley and R. Threlfall, *Delius: A Life in Pictures* (London, 1977); R. Threlfall, *A Catalogue of the Compositions of Frederick Delius* (London, 1977).

Della Casa, Lisa, noted Swiss Soprano; b. Burgdorf, Feb. 2, 1919. She was educated at the Cons. in Bern, and later at the Zürich Cons. She made her debut in Biel in 1941; from 1943 to 1950 she sang at the Stadttheater in Zürich; also appeared at Salzburg, Glyndebourne, and Munich. From 1952 she was a leading member of the Vienna State Opera. On Nov. 20, 1953, she made her debut at the Metropolitan Opera in N.Y. as the Countess in *The Marriage of Figaro;* continued to make appearances there until 1968; retired in 1974.

Della Ciaia, Azzolino Bernardino, Italian organist and composer; b. Siena, March 21, 1671; d. Pisa, Jan. 15, 1755. He was an organist and also an experienced organ builder; constructed a large organ with 4 manuals and 100 stops for the St. Stephen Church in Pisa. He publ. *Salmi concertati* for 4 Voices, with Instruments (Bologna, 1700); *Cantate de camera* (Lucca, 1701); *Sonate per cembalo* (Rome, 1727). Much of his church music is extant in MS. He is regarded by some as an Italian originator

of the sonata form; his instrumental music, however, is more interesting for its florid ornamentation than for strict formal development.

BIBLIOGRAPHY: Fausto Torrefranca, "L'impressionismo ritmico e le sonate del Della Ciaia," *Rivista dei Amici della Musica in Milano* (1913); F. Vatielli, "Una lettera biografica di A. Della Ciaia," *Critica Musicale,* IV/8–9. Béla Bartók made a piano transcription of a keyboard sonata by Della Ciaia, in *XVIIth and XVIIIth Century Italian Cembalo and Organ Music Transcribed for Piano* (N.Y., 1930). Luigi Silva arranged *Toccata e Canzona* for cello and piano (1952). Alessandro Esposito ed. and arranged Della Ciaia's *12 soggetti, 6 ricercari, messa,* and 12 cembalo pieces (Padua, 1956).

Della Corte, Andrea, eminent Italian musicologist; b. Naples, April 5, 1883; d. Turin, March 12, 1968. He was self-taught in music; devoted himself mainly to musical biography and analysis. He taught music history at the Turin Cons. (1926–53) and at the Univ. of Turin (from 1939). From 1919 till 1967 he was music critic of *La Stampa.*

WRITINGS: A prolific writer, he publ. *Paisiello* (Turin, 1922); *Saggi di critica musicale* (Turin, 1922); *L'opera comica italiana del 1700* (2 vols., Bari, 1923); *Piccola antologia settecentesca, XXIV pezzi inediti o rari* (Milan, 1925); *Disegno storico dell'arte musicale* (Turin, 5th ed., 1950); *Antologia della storia della musica* (2 vols., Turin, 1927–29; 4th ed., 1945); *Niccolò Piccinni* (Bari, 1928); *Scelta di musiche per lo studio della storia* (Milan, 3rd ed., 1949); *La vita musicale di Goethe* (Turin, 1932); *Vincenzo Bellini* (in collaboration with Guido Pannain, Turin, 1936); *Ritratto di Franco Alfano* (Turin, 1936); *Pergolesi* (Turin, 1936); *Un Italiano all'estero: Antonio Salieri* (Turin, 1937); *Tre secoli di opera italiana* (Turin, 1938); *Verdi* (Turin, 1939); *Toscanini* (Vicenza, 1946; in French, Lausanne, 1949); *Satire e grotteschi di musiche e di musicisti d'ogni tempo* (Turin, 1947); *Le sei più belle opere di Verdi: Rigoletto, Il Trovatore, La Traviata, Aida, Otello, Falstaff* (Milan, 1947); *Gluck* (Florence, 1948); *Baldassare Galuppi* (Siena, 1949); *Arrigo Serato* (Siena, 1949); *Storia della musica* (3 vols., in collaboration with Guido Pannain, Turin, 3rd ed., 1952; 2nd ed., trans. into Spanish, 1950); *L'interpretazione musicale e gli interpreti* (Turin, 1951). He ed. song textbooks for the Italian schools. With Guido M. Gatti, he compiled a valuable *Dizionario di musica* (1926; 6th ed., 1959).

Della Maria, Pierre-Antoine-Dominique, French opera composer; b. Marseilles, June 14, 1769; d. Paris, March 9, 1800. Son of an Italian mandolinist, he was remarkably precocious; played the mandolin and cello at an early age, and at 18 produced a grand opera at Marseilles. He then studied composition in Italy (for a time with Paisiello) and produced in Naples a successful opera, *Il maestro di cappella* (1792). He went to Paris in 1796; obtaining a libretto *(Le Prisonnier)* from Duval, he set it to music in 8 days, brought it out at the Opéra-Comique (Jan. 29, 1798), and was at once famous. Before his death he finished 6 more operas, 4 of which were produced during his lifetime; a posthumous opera, *La Fausse Duègne* (completed by Blangini), was produced at Paris in 1802; several church compositions are in MS.

Deller, Alfred, English countertenor; b. Margate, May 31, 1912; d. while visiting Bologna, Italy, July 16, 1979. He studied voice with his father; began singing as a boy soprano, later developing the alto range. He sang in the choirs of the Canterbury Cathedral (1940–47) and at St. Paul's in London. In 1950 he formed his own vocal and instrumental ensemble, the Deller Consort, acting as conductor and soloist in a repertoire of old English music. This unique enterprise led to a modest revival of English madrigals of the Renaissance. In 1963 he founded the Stour Music Festival in Kent. Britten wrote the part of Oberon in his *A Midsummer Night's Dream* for Deller. In 1970 Deller was named a Commander of the Order of the British Empire.
BIBLIOGRAPHY: Michael and Mollie Hardwick, *Alfred Deller: A Singularity of Voice* (London, 1968; 2nd ed., revised, 1982).

Delle Sedie, Enrico, Italian baritone and singing teacher; b. Livorno, June 17, 1822; d. Garennes-Colombes, near Paris, Nov. 28, 1907. His teachers were Galeffi, Persanola, and Domeniconi. After imprisonment as a revolutionist (1848), he resumed the study of singing and made his debut in San Casciano (1851) in Verdi's *Nabucco.* Until 1861 he sang in the principal Italian cities; appeared in London in 1861; was then engaged at the Théâtre des Italiens, Paris, and appointed prof. of singing in the Cons. (1867–71); was regarded as one of the best singing teachers in Paris. His basic manuals, *Arte e fisiologia del canto* (Milan, 1876; in French as *L'Art lyrique,* Paris, 1876) and *L'estetica del canto e dell'arte melodrammatica* (Milan, 1886), were publ. in N.Y. in Eng. as *Vocal Art* (3 parts) and *Esthetics of the Art of Singing, and of the Melodrama* (4 vols.). A condensation (by the author) of both manuals was publ. in one vol. as *A Complete Method of Singing* (N.Y., 1894).

Dellinger, Rudolf, German composer and conductor; b. Graslitz, Bohemia, July 8, 1857; d. Dresden, Sept. 24, 1910. He was a pupil at the Prague Cons.; played clarinet in the city orch. at Brünn; became 2nd conductor there in 1880; in 1883, occupied the same post at the Carl Schulze Theater in Hamburg; from 1893 till his death, was conductor at the Residenz-Theater in Dresden. He produced the operettas *Don Caesar* (Hamburg, March 28, 1885; highly popular), *Lorraine* (Hamburg, 1886), *Capitän Fracassa* (Hamburg, 1889), *Saint-Cyr* (Hamburg, 1891), *Die Chansonnette* (Dresden, 1894; Prague, 1895, as *Die Sängerin*), *Jadwiga* (Dresden, 1901), and *Der letzte Jonas* (1910).

Dello Joio, Norman, able American composer of pleasurable music; b. New York, Jan. 24, 1913, of an Italian-American family whose original surname was Ioio. His father, his grandfather, and his great-grandfather were church organists. Dello Joio acquired skill as an organist and pianist at home; at the age of 12 he occasionally substituted for his father on his job at the Church of Our Lady of Mount Carmel in Manhattan. He took additional organ lessons from his well-known godfather, **Pietro Yon,** and studied piano with Gaston Déthier at the Inst. of Musical Art (1933–38); in the meantime he played jazz piano in various groups in N.Y. From 1939 to 1941 he studied composition with Bernard Wagenaar at the Juilliard School of Music; in 1941 he enrolled in the summer class of composition led by Hindemith at the Berkshire Music Center in Tanglewood; he continued to attend Hindemith's courses at Yale Univ. in 1941–43. During this period he wrote several works of considerable validity, among them a piano trio, a ballet entitled *The Duke of Sacramento,* a Magnificat, a piano sonata, and other pieces. He taught composition at Sarah Lawrence College (1945–50); held two consecutive Guggenheim fellowships (1944, 1945); and composed music with utmost facility and ingratiating felicity. His *Concert Music* was played by the Pittsburgh Symph., conducted by Fritz Reiner, on Jan. 4, 1946, and his *Ricercari* for Piano and Orch. was introduced by the N.Y. Phil. on Dec. 19, 1946, with George Szell conducting, and the piano part played by Dello Joio himself. There followed a number of major works in a distinctive Joioan manner, some of them deeply rooted in medieval ecclesiasticism, profoundly liturgical, and yet overtly modern in their neo-modal moderately dissonant counterpoint. He also exhibited a flair for writing on topical American themes, ranging from impressions of the Cloisters in N.Y. to rhythmic modalities of Little Italy. On May 9, 1950, at Sarah Lawrence College, where he taught, he produced his first opera, *The Triumph of St. Joan;* he later used its thematic material in a symph. in 3 movements, *The Triumph of St. Joan,* originally titled *Seraphic Dialogue.* He then wrote another opera on the subject of St. Joan, to his own libretto, *The Trial of Rouen,* first performed on television by the NBC Opera Theater, April 8, 1956; still another version of the St. Joan theme was an opera in which Dello Joio returned to the original title, *The Triumph of St. Joan,* but composed the music anew; it had its production at the N.Y. City Opera on April 16, 1959. In 1957 Dello Joio received the Pulitzer Prize for his *Meditations on Ecclesiastes,* scored for string orch.; it was first performed in Washington on Dec. 17, 1957, but the material was used previously for a ballet, *There Is a Time.* In 1961 Dello Joio produced an opera, *Blood Moon,* brought out by the San Francisco Opera, to a scenario dealing with the life and times of an adventurous actress, Adah Menken, who exercised her charms in New Orleans at the time of the Civil War. Returning to liturgical themes, Dello Joio composed three masses, in 1968, 1975, and 1976. He continued his activities as a teacher; from 1956 to 1972 he was on the faculty of the Mannes College of Music in N.Y.; from 1972 to 1979 he taught at Boston Univ. In 1964 he traveled to Rumania, Bulgaria, and the Soviet Union under the auspices of the Cultural

Program of the State Dept. He held honorary doctorates in music from Lawrence College in Wisconsin (1959), Colby College in Maine (1963), and the Univ. of Cincinnati (1969). On Feb. 16, 1958, he was the subject of a CBS television documentary titled "Profile of a Composer." He received the N.Y. Music Critics' Award twice, in 1947 and 1959.

WORKS: FOR THE STAGE: Operas on the subject of St. Joan: *The Triumph of St. Joan* (Sarah Lawrence College, May 9, 1950); *The Trial at Rouen,* to the composer's libretto (NBC-TV Opera Theater; April 8, 1956); *The Triumph of St. Joan,* a new version of the St. Joan theme, bearing the identical title of the original work (N.Y. City Opera, April 16, 1959; received a N.Y. Music Critics' Circle Award). Other operas: *The Ruby* (Bloomington, Ind., May 13, 1955); *Blood Moon* (San Francisco, Sept. 18, 1961).

FOR DANCE: *The Duke of Sacramento* (1942); *Diversion of Angels,* dance by Martha Graham (New London, Conn., Aug. 13, 1948); *Seraphic Dialogue,* choreographed by Martha Graham (Louisville, Ky., Dec. 5, 1951; material taken from *The Triumph of St. Joan Symphony*).

FOR ORCH.: Sinfonietta (1940); Concerto for 2 Pianos and Orch. (1941); *Magnificat* (1942); *To a Lone Sentry* for Chamber Orch. (1943); *On Stage* (Cleveland, Nov. 23, 1945); *Concert Music* (Pittsburgh, Jan. 4, 1946); *Ricercari* for Piano and Orch. (N.Y., Dec. 19, 1946, composer soloist with the N.Y. Phil., George Szell conducting); Harp Concerto (N.Y., Oct. 20, 1947); *Variations, Chaconne and Finale* (originally titled *3 Symphonic Dances;* Pittsburgh, Jan. 30, 1948); *Concertato* for Clarinet and Orch. (Chautauqua, May 22, 1949); *Serenade* (Cleveland, Oct. 20, 1949); *New York Profiles* (La Jolla, Calif., Aug. 21, 1949); *The Triumph of St. Joan Symphony* (Louisville, Dec. 5, 1951); *Epigraph* (Denver, Jan. 29, 1952); *Meditations on Ecclesiates* for String Orch. (Washington, D.C., Dec. 17, 1957; received the Pulitzer Prize); *Air Power,* suite (1957); *Anthony and Cleopatra* for Chamber Group (1960); *Fantasy and Variations* for Piano and Orch. (Cincinnati, March 9, 1962); *Variants on a Medieval Tune* for Band (Duke Univ., May 8, 1963); *From Every Horizon* for Band (1964); *Antiphonal Fantasy on a Theme of Vincenzo Albrici,* dedicated to the memory of Hindemith (1966); *5 Images* (1967); *Homage to Haydn* (Little Rock, Ark., June 3, 1969); *Songs of Abélard* for Band (1969; earlier version titled *A Time of Snow*); *Satiric Dances for a Comedy by Aristophanes* for Band (Concord, Mass., July 17, 1975); *Colonial Variants* (Philadelphia, May 27, 1976); *Ballabili* (1981).

CHAMBER MUSIC: Quartet for Bassoons (1937); Sextet for 3 Recorders, Violin, Viola, and Cello (1941); *Fantasia on a Gregorian Theme* for Violin and Piano (1943); Trio for Flute, Cello, and Piano (N.Y., March 1, 1944); *Due Concertato* for Cello and Piano (1945); *Variations and Capriccio* for Violin and Piano (1948); *Colloquies* for Violin and Piano (1964); *Developing Flutist* for Flute and Piano (1972); 3 Essays for Clarinet and Piano (1974); *Lyric Fantasies* for Viola, String Quartet, and Double Bass (1973); String Quartet (1974); Trumpet Sonata (1981).

FOR PIANO: 3 sonatas (1933, 1943, 1948); *Aria and Toccata* for 2 Pianos (1952); *Family Album* for Piano, 4-hands (1962); *Capriccio on the Interval of a Second* (1969); *Lyric Pieces for the Young* (1971); *Diversions* (1975).

VOCAL MUSIC: 3 masses: Mass for Chorus, Brass, and Organ (1968); Mass in Honor of the Blessed Virgin Mary (Washington, Dec. 8, 1975); Mass in Honor of the Eucharist for Chorus, Brass, Strings, and Organ (1976); *The Mystic Trumpeter,* cantata after Walt Whitman (1943); *The Assassination* for Low Voice and Piano (1947); *Song of Affirmation,* symph. cantata (1952); *Song of the Open Road* for Chorus, Trumpet, and Piano, after Walt Whitman (1952); *The Lamentation of Saul* for Baritone and Orch. (1954); *As of a Dream* for Narrator, Chorus, and Orch., after Walt Whitman (Midland, Mich., May 18, 1979); *Love Songs of Parting* (Indianapolis, Nov. 7, 1982).

BIBLIOGRAPHY: David Ewen, *American Composers* (N.Y., 1982).

Dell'Orefice, Giuseppe, Italian composer; b. Fara, Abruzzio Chietino, Aug. 22, 1848; d. Naples, Jan. 3, 1889. He was a pupil of Fenaroli and Miceli at the Naples Cons.; from 1878, was conductor at the San Carlo Theater in Naples; wrote the ballet *I fantasmi notturni* (Naples, 1872) and the operas *Romilda de' Bardi* (Naples, 1874), *Egmont* (Naples, 1878), *Il segreto della Duchesa* (Naples, 1879), and *L'oasi* (Vicenza, 1886); also songs and piano pieces.

Delmar, Dezso, Hungarian-American composer; b. Timişoara, July 14, 1891. He studied piano with Béla Bartók and theory with Kodály at the Royal Academy of Music in Budapest, graduating in 1913; concurrently took courses in jurisprudence, obtaining a law degree. He served in the Austro-Hungarian army in World War I; after demobilization, devoted himself entirely to music. He came to the U.S. in 1922; lived in N.Y. until 1929, then moved to Los Angeles; in 1946 settled in Sacramento as a teacher of piano and theory. His works include a Symph. (1949); *Hungarian Sketches* for Orch. (1947); 3 string quartets, String Trio, Violin Sonata, etc.; choral music; many piano pieces and songs. His works reflect the melorhythmic modalities of Hungarian folk music.

Del Mar, Norman, English conductor; b. London, July 31, 1919. He studied composition with R.O. Morris and Vaughan Williams at the Royal College of Music in London; also played the violin and the French horn in the student orch. He then took lessons in conducting with Constant Lambert. During World War II he played in the Royal Air Force bands and visited the U.S. with the Royal Air Force Symph. in 1944. After the war he organized the Chelsea Symph. Orch. in London; in 1948 he conducted the Sadler's Wells Ballet during its tour in Germany. He was principal conductor of the English Opera Group from 1949–55; was conductor and prof. at the Guildhall School of Music (1953–60); then conducted the BBC Scottish Symph. (1960–65), the Göteborg (Sweden) Symph. (1969–73), and the

Chamber Orch. of the Royal Academy of Music (1973–77). In 1972 he was appointed instructor in conducting at the Royal College of Music. In 1975 he was made a Commander of the Order of the British Empire. In 1982 he was named principal guest conductor of the Bournemouth Sinfonietta. He publ. several valuable monographs: *Paul Hindemith* (London, 1957); *Richard Strauss, A Critical Commentary of His Life and Works* (3 vols., London, 1962, 1968); *Modern Music and the Conductor* (London, 1960; paperback ed., 1970); *Anatomy of the Orchestra* (London and Berkeley, 1981).

Delmas, Jean-François, famous French dramatic bass; b. Lyons, April 14, 1861; d. St. Alban de Monthel, France, Sept. 29, 1933. He was a pupil of the Paris Cons., where he won first prize for singing in 1886; made his debut at the Grand Opéra in 1886, as St.-Bris in *Les Huguenots;* then was a regular member of the Opéra, idolized by the public, and unexcelled as an interpreter of Wagner, in whose works he created the principal bass parts at all the French premieres; he created also the chief roles in Massenet's *Le Mage* (1891) and *Thaïs* (1894), Leroux's *Astarté* (1901), Saint-Saëns's *Les Barbares* (1901), Erlanger's *Le Fils de l'étoile* (1904), etc.; besides an enormous French repertoire, he also sang in the operas of Gluck, Mozart, and Weber.
BIBLIOGRAPHY: H. Curzon, *Croquis d'artistes* (Paris, 1898).

Delmas, Marc-Jean-Baptiste, talented French composer; b. St. Quentin, March 28, 1885; d. Paris, Nov. 30, 1931. He was a pupil of Vidal and Leroux; won the Prix de Rossini (1911), t¹ ᵌ Grand Prix de Rome (1919), the Chartier Prix for chamber music, the Prix Cressent, and other awards for various compositions. He also wrote the books *G. Bizet* (Paris, 1930) and *G. Charpentier et le lyrisme française* (1931).
WORKS: OPERAS: *Jean de Calais* (1907); *Laïs* (1909); *Stéfano* (1910); *Cyrce* (1920; perf. 1927); *Iriam* (1921); *Anne-Marie* (1922); *Le Giaour* (1925). ORCH. MUSIC: *Les Deux Routes* (1913); *Au pays wallon* (1914); *Le Poète et la fée* (1920); *Le Bateau ivre* (1923); *Penthésilée* (1922); *Rapsodie ariégeoise* for Cello and Orch.; chamber music; piano pieces.

Del Monaco, Mario, powerful Italian tenor; b. Florence, July 27, 1915; d. Mestre, near Venice, Oct. 16, 1982. His father was a government functionary, but his mother loved music and actually sang. Del Monaco haunted provincial opera theaters, determined to be a singer; indeed, he was allowed to sing a minor part in a theater at Mondolfo, near Pesaro, when he was only 13. Rather than take regular voice lessons, he listened to operatic recordings; at 19 he entered the Rossini Cons. in Pesaro, but left it after an unhappy semester of academic vocal training with unimaginative teachers. In 1935 he won a prize in a singing contest in Rome. On Jan. 1, 1941, he made his professional debut in Milan as Pinkerton in *Madama Butterfly,* but had to serve time out in the Italian army during the war. After the war's end he developed a busy career singing opera in a number of Italian theaters, including La Scala of Milan. In 1946 he sang at the Teatro Colón in Buenos Aires, and also in Rio de Janeiro and Mexico City. On Sept. 26, 1950, he sang the role of Radames in *Aida* at the San Francisco Opera; on Nov. 27, 1950, he made his Metropolitan Opera debut in N.Y. as Des Grieux in *Manon Lescaut;* he continued to sing at the Metropolitan until 1959 in virtually every famous tenor part, as Don José in *Carmen,* Manrico in *Il Trovatore,* Cavaradossi in *Tosca,* Canio in *Pagliacci,* etc. On Nov. 16, 1954, he scored considerable success in the role of Andrea Chénier. He sang 102 times at the Metropolitan and appeared in its tours 38 times. Numerically, the maximum of his appearances in the same role was as Otello, which he sang at various opera theaters 427 times. In 1973 he deemed it prudent to retire, and he spent the rest of his life in a villa near Venice, devoting his leisure to his favorite avocations, sculpture and painting. Unlike most Italian tenors who tend to grow corpulent with success, Del Monaco managed to preserve his lean, slender figure, which ensured his mobility on the stage and enabled him to honor the Italian operatic tradition of scurrying to the footlights at the approach of the high C. So energetic was he at climactic scenes that he nearly broke the wrist of Risé Stevens when he threw her down in the last act of *Carmen.* Del Monaco was buried in his Otello costume, while the funeral hymns were intoned in his own voice on a phonograph record.

Delna (real name, **Ledan**), **Marie,** French contralto; b. Meudon, near Paris, April 3, 1875; d. Paris, July 23, 1932. She made her debut at the Opéra-Comique, June 9, 1892, as Dido in Berlioz's *Les Troyens;* sang there for 6 years with great success; in 1898–1901 was at the Opéra; then again at the Opéra-Comique in 1903 she married a Belgian, A.H. de Saone, and retired temporarily from the stage; her reappearance at the Opéra-Comique in 1908 was acclaimed with great applause; after that she was a prime favorite. In 1910 she sang Orfeo (in Gluck's opera) and Marcelline in Bruneau's *L'Attaque du moulin* at the New Theater, making a deep impression; then returned to Paris, where she continued to sing at the Opéra-Comique for many years.

Delogu, Gaetano, Italian conductor; b. Messina, April 14, 1934. He studied violin as a child, but began his university education as a law student. He then decided upon a musical career; studied conducting with Franco Ferrara. In 1964 he won first prize at the Florence Young Conductors' Competition. In 1968 he won first prize in the Mitropoulos Competition in N.Y. He then embarked upon an international career, conducting many of the major orchs. of Europe and the U.S. In 1979 he became music director of the Denver Symph. Orch.

Del Tredici, David (Walter), remarkable American composer; b. Cloverdale, Calif., March 16, 1937. He studied piano, and made his debut as a soloist with the San Francisco Symph. at the age of 16; then enrolled at the Univ. of Calif. in Berkeley, studying composition with Seymour Shifrin, Andrew Imbrie, and Arnold Elston (B.A., 1959). He undertook additional studies at Princeton Univ., where his teachers were Earl Kim and Roger Sessions (M.F.A., 1964). He also continued his pianistic practice, taking private lessons with Robert Helps in N.Y. During the summers of 1964 and 1965 he served as pianist at the Berkshire Music Center in Tanglewood. In 1966 he received a Guggenheim fellowship award; in 1966–67 he was resident composer at the Marlboro Festival in Vermont. From 1966 to 1972 he was assistant prof. of music at Harvard Univ.; in 1973 he joined the music faculty at Boston Univ. While thus retained by pedagogy, he composed avidly. Fascinated by the creation of new literary forms and the novel language of James Joyce, he wrote the work *I Hear an Army,* based on a Joyce poem, scored for soprano and string quartet, which was performed at Tanglewood on Aug. 12, 1964, and immediately caught the fancy of the cloistered but influential cognoscenti, literati, and illuminati; another significant Joyce poem set by Del Tredici was *Night Conjure-Verse* for soprano, mezzo-soprano, woodwind septet, and string quartet, which he conducted in San Francisco on March 4, 1966. Yet another work inspired by the verbal music of James Joyce was *Syzygy* for soprano, horn, bells, drums, and chamber orch., performed in N.Y. on July 6, 1968. For these works Del Tredici plied a modified dodecaphonic course in a polyrhythmic context, gravid with meaningful pauses without fear of triadic encounters. But Del Tredici achieved rare fame with a series of brilliant tone pictures after *Alice in Wonderland* by Lewis Carroll, in which he projected, in utter defiance of all modernistic conventions, overt tonal proclamations, fanfares, and pretty tunes that were almost embarrassingly attractive, becoming melodiouser and harmoniouser with each consequent tone portrait of Alice. And in a couple of the *Alice* pieces he disarmingly attached a personal signature, the vocal countdown of 13, his last name Tredici, in Italian. In 1980 he received the Pulitzer Prize for his score *In Memory of a Summer Day.*

WORKS: : *Soliloquy* for Piano (1958); 4 songs to poems of James Joyce for Voice and Piano (1959); String Trio (1959); *Fantasy Pieces* for Piano (1960); *Scherzo* for Piano, 4-hands (1960); *I Hear an Army* for Soprano and String Quartet, to words of James Joyce (Berkshire Music Center, Tanglewood, Aug. 12, 1964); *Night Conjure-Verse* for Voices and Instruments, to words by James Joyce (1965); *The Last Gospel* for Soprano (amplified), Rock Group, and Orch. (San Francisco, June 15, 1968, composer conducting); *Syzygy* for Soprano, Horn, Bells, and Chamber Orch., to words by James Joyce (N.Y., July 6, 1968); *Pop-Pourri* for Voices, Rock Group, and Orch., to text from Lewis Carroll (La Jolla, Calif., July 28, 1968); *The Lobster Quadrille* for Soprano, Folk Group, Mandolin, Banjo, Accordion, and Orch. (London, Nov. 14, 1969, Aaron Copland conducting; revised 1974; first perf., Aspen Festival, Colo., July 29, 1975); *Vintage Alice* for Soprano, Folk Group, and Chamber Orch. (1971; Saratoga, Calif., Aug. 5,

1972, composer conducting); *Adventures Underground* (1971; Buffalo, April 13, 1975); *An Alice Symphony (Illustrated Alice;* San Francisco, Aug. 8, 1976, composer conducting); *Final Alice* (1975–76; Chicago, Oct. 7, 1976, Solti conducting); *Child Alice,* Part I, *In Memory of a Summer Day* for Soprano (amplified) and Orch. (St. Louis, Feb. 23, 1980; received the Pulitzer Prize); *Child Alice,* Part II, *Happy Voices* for Soprano and Orch. (San Francisco, Sept. 16, 1980); *Child Alice,* Part III, for Soprano (amplified) and Orch. (Philadelphia, May 8, 1981); *All in the Golden Afternoon* for Orch. (Rotterdam, the Netherlands, March 11, 1983).

BIBLIOGRAPHY: : David Ewen, *American Composers* (N.Y., 1982); John Rockwell, *All American Music* (N.Y., 1983).

De Luca, Giuseppe, Italian baritone; b. Rome, Dec. 25, 1876; d. New York, Aug. 26, 1950. He studied music with Vinceslao Persichini at the Santa Cecilia Academy in Rome; made his first professional appearance in Piacenza (Nov. 6, 1897) as Valentine in *Faust;* then sang in various cities of Italy; from 1902, was chiefly in Milan at the Teatro Lirico, and from 1903 at La Scala; he created the principal baritone role in the world premiere of Cilea's *Adriana Lecouvreur* and in *Madama Butterfly.* He made his American debut at the Metropolitan Opera as Figaro in *Il Barbiere di Siviglia* on Nov. 25, 1915, with excellent success, immediately establishing himself as a favorite; on Jan. 28, 1916, he sang the part of Paquiro in the world premiere of *Goyescas* by Granados, at the Metropolitan Opera, of which he became a member until 1935; after a sojourn in Italy, he returned to the U.S. in 1940, and made a few more appearances at the Metropolitan, his vocal powers undiminished by age; he made his farewell appearance in N.Y. in 1947. He sang almost exclusively the Italian repertoire; his interpretations were distinguished by fidelity to the dramatic import of his roles; he was praised by the critics for his finely graduated dynamic range and his mastery of bel canto.

De Lucia, Fernando, famous Italian tenor; b. Naples, Oct. 11, 1860; d. there, Feb. 21, 1925. He made his debut in Naples on March 9, 1885, as Faust; then appeared in London at Drury Lane (1887); on Oct. 31, 1891, he created in Rome the role of Fritz in Mascagni's *L'Amico Fritz;* on Jan. 10, 1894, he made his American debut at the Metropolitan Opera, again as Fritz in Mascagni's opera; then returned to Europe. He retired from the stage in 1917, and taught voice in Naples; sang for the last time in public at Caruso's funeral (1921). De Lucia was one of the finest representatives of the *bel canto* era; he was especially praised for his authentic interpretations of Italian operatic roles.

Delune, Louis, Belgian composer and conductor; b. Charleroi, March 15, 1876; d. Paris, Jan. 5, 1940. He studied with Tinel at the Brussels Cons.; won the Belgian Prix de Rome with his cantata *La Mort du roi Reynaud* (1905); then traveled as accompanist for César Thomson. He lived many years in Paris, and wrote most of his works there; composed *Symphonie chevaleresque;* the opera *Tania;* a ballet, *Le Fruit défendu;* Piano Concerto; violin pieces; etc.

Del Valle de Paz, Edgardo, Italian writer on music; b. Alexandria, Egypt, Oct. 18, 1861; d. Florence, April 5, 1920. He studied at the Naples Cons. under B. Cesi (piano) and P. Serrao (composition); made pianistic tours in Italy and Egypt; in 1893 he established the Circolo Del Valle at Florence, and in 1896–1914 was director of the journal *La Nuova Musica* and a prof. in the Florence Cons. (from 1890). He publ. *Scuola pratica del pianoforte,* adopted by several Italian music schools. His opera, *Oriana,* was produced at Florence (1907).

Delvaux, Albert, Belgian composer; b. Louvain, May 31, 1913. He studied first at the Cons. in Louvain and completed his studies with Joseph Leroy at the Liège Cons. He won a 3rd prize (1957, for *Esquisses*) and a first prize (1961, for *Sinfonia burlesca*) in the Queen Elisabeth International Composition Competition in Brussels.
WORKS: *Héro et Léandre* for Soloists, Chorus, and Orch. (1941); *5 Pieces* for String Orch. (1942); *Scherzo* for Orch. (1942); *Symphonic Poem* (1943); *Symphonic Suite* (1948); Symph. Variations (1948); *Sinfonietta* (1952); Concerto for Cello and Chamber Orch. (1957); *Esquisses (Schetsen)* for Chamber Orch. (1956); *Concerto da camera* for Chamber Orch. (1957); *Sinfonia burlesca* (1960); *5 Bagatelles* for Chamber Orch. (1960); *Miniatures* for Orch. (1960); 2 violin concertos (1961, 1974); *Sinfonia concertante* for Violin, Viola, and Strings (1963); *Mouvement symphonique* (1966); Concerto for Flute, Oboe, Clarinet, Bassoon, and Chamber Orch. (1967); *Sinfonia* (1969); Concerto for Violin, Cello, and Strings (1970); *Introduction e Allegro* for Strings (1971); 2 string trios (1939, 1961); Sonata for Flute, Oboe, Clarinet, and Bassoon, (1940); 4 string quartets (1943, 1945, 1955, 1961); Trio for Oboe, Clarinet, and Bassoon (1948); Oboe Sonatina (1956); *5 Impromptus* for Flute, Oboe, Clarinet, and Piano (1959); Violin Sonata (1962); *Sonata a 4* for 4 Clarinets, or Flute, Oboe, Clarinet, and Bassoon (1964); *Walliser Suite* for Wind Quintet (1966); *Cassazione* for Violin, Oboe, Clarinet, and Cello (1966); *Andante e Scherzando* for Violin and Piano (1972); choruses.

Delvincourt, Claude, outstanding French composer; b. Paris, Jan. 12, 1888; d. in an automobile accident in Orbetello, province of Grosseto, Italy, April 5, 1954. He studied with Boellmann, Busser, Caussade, and Widor at the Paris Cons.; in 1913 received the Prix de Rome for his cantata *Faust et Hélène* (sharing the prize with Lili Boulanger). He was in the French army in World War I, and on Dec. 31, 1915, suffered a crippling wound. He recovered in a few years, and devoted himself energetically to musical education and composition. In 1931 he became director of the Cons. of Versailles; in 1941 he was appointed director of the Paris Cons. His

music is distinguished by strong dramatic and lyric quality; he was most successful in his stage works.
WORKS: *Offrande à Siva,* choreographic poem (Frankfurt, July 3, 1927); *La Femme à barbe,* musical farce (Versailles, June 2, 1938); *Lucifer,* mystery play (Paris Opéra, Dec. 8, 1948); 2 orch. suites from the film score *La Croisière jaune: Pamir* (Paris, Dec. 8, 1935) and *Films d'Asie* (Paris, Jan. 16, 1937). He also wrote *Ce monde de rosée* for Voice and Orch. (Paris, March 25, 1935); some chamber music (Trio for Oboe, Clarinet, and Bassoon; Violin Sonata; etc.); piano pieces.
BIBLIOGRAPHY: W.L. Landowski, *L'Œuvre de Claude Delvincourt* (Paris, 1947).

De Main, John, American conductor; b. Youngstown, Ohio, Jan. 11, 1944. He studied piano with Adele Marcus at the Juilliard School of Music in N.Y. (B.M., 1966) and conducting there with Jorge Mester (M.S., 1968). He served as associate conductor of the St. Paul Chamber Orch. (1972–74); in 1974–76 was music director of the Texas Opera Theater; in 1979 he assumed the post of music director of the Houston Grand Opera, and from 1983 concurrently conducted the opera company in Omaha.

Demantius, (Johannes) Christoph, German composer; b. Reichenberg, Dec. 15, 1567; d. Freiberg, Saxony, April 20, 1643. He became cantor at Zittau in 1597; was at Freiberg in 1604–43; as a prolific composer of sacred and secular music, he ranks with Hassler, M. and H. Prätorius, and Eccard. He wrote *Deutsche Passion nach Johannes* (1631; ed. and publ. by F. Blume, 1934); *Triades precum vespertinarum* (1602); etc. He was the author of an instruction book, *Isagoge artis musicae* (Nuremberg, 1605; 10th ed., 1671).

Demarest, Clifford, American organist and composer; b. Tenafly, N.J., Aug. 12, 1874; d. there, May 13, 1946. He was organist at the Church of the Messiah in N.Y.; wrote 2 cantatas, *The Shepherds of Bethlehem* and *The Cross Victorious; Pastoral Suite* for Organ; *Rip van Winkle* for Organ (1925); about 30 anthems; songs; etc.; also publ. *Hints on Organ Accompaniment.*

Demarquez, Suzanne, French composer; b. Paris, July 5, 1899; d. there, Oct. 23; 1965. She studied at the Paris Cons.; composed chamber music, including a sprightly *Sonatine* for Flute and Piano (1953). She publ. valuable monographs: *André Jolivet* (Paris, 1958); *Manuel de Falla* (Paris, 1963; in Eng., Philadelphia, 1968); *Hector Berlioz* (Paris, 1969).

Demény, Desiderius, Hungarian composer; b. Budapest, Jan. 29, 1871; d. there, Nov. 9, 1937. He was a pupil of V. Herzfeld and S. von Bacho; was ordained as a priest at Gran in 1893; became court chaplain (1897); on 3 different occasions he won the Géza Zichy Prize (with *Ungarische Tanzsuite, Festouvertüre,* and *Rhapsodie*); in 1902 he founded *Zeneközlöny,* an important Hungarian music journal.

WORKS: 8 masses; *Hungarian Suite* for Mixed Chorus; *Scherzo* for Male Chorus; 2 *Bilder aus Algier; Serenata sinfonica;* operetta, *Der sieghafte Tod;* several melodramas; many other choral and vocal works, including about 100 songs (most to German texts).

Demessieux, Jeanne, French organist; b. Montpellier, Feb. 14, 1921; d. Paris, Nov. 11, 1968. At the age of 12 she played organ at the church of Saint-Esprit; she studied at the Paris Cons. with Tagliafero, Jean and Noël Gallon, and Dupré; won premiers prix in harmony (1937), piano (1938), and fugue and counterpoint (1940). She gave her first public recital in Paris in 1946; then toured widely in Europe; made her first highly successful visit to the U.S. in 1953. In 1952 she became a prof. at the Liège Cons.; also served as organist at the Madeleine in 1962. She possessed a phenomenal technique and was regarded as one of the most brilliant improvisers on the organ.

Demian, Wilhelm, Rumanian composer and conductor; b. Brasov, June 22, 1910. He studied music in his hometown (1925–28); then in Vienna (1929–33); from 1935 to 1940 conducted the Phil. in Cluj; after 1949 was also conductor of the Hungarian State Opera there. His music is marked by a distinct neoclassical idiom in the manner of the modern German school. Among his works are an opera, *Capcana* (1964); Symph. (1947); Piano Concertino (1953); Violin Concerto (1956); *Liberté,* cantata (1957); Oboe Concerto (1963); musical, *Attention! On tourne!* (1972).

De Mol, Pierre, Belgian composer; b. Brussels, Nov. 7, 1825; d. Alost, July 2, 1899. He was a pupil at the Brussels Cons.; took the Grand Prix de Rome (1855); was first cellist at the Besançon Theater and a teacher at the Cons.; later was director of the Cons. at Alost.

WORKS: 3 cantatas: *Les Chrétiens Martyrs; Le Dernier Jour d'Herculaneum; La Fête de Belsazar;* oratorio, *St. Cecilia;* Mass; 12 string quartets; opera, *Quentin Metsys.*

Demougeot, Marcelle, French soprano; b. Dijon, June 18, 1871; d. Paris, Nov. 24, 1931. She studied in Dijon and Paris; made her operatic debut at the Paris Opéra in 1902 as Donna Elvira in *Don Giovanni;* continued to sing there until 1925. She was one of the foremost French Wagnerian sopranos of her time, noted for her fine renditions as Brünnhilde, Elisabeth, Kundry, and Venus.

Demus, Jörg, noted Austrian pianist; b. St. Polten, Dec. 2, 1928. At the age of 11 he entered the Vienna Academy; also took lessons in conducting with Swarowsky and Krips and in composition with Joseph Marx; continued his piano studies with Gieseking at the Saarbrücken Cons.; then worked with Kempff, Benedetti Michelangeli, and Edwin Fischer. He made his debut as a concert pianist at the age of 14 in Vienna; made his London debut in 1950; then toured South America (1951). In 1956 he won the Busoni prize of the International Competition for Pianists. Apart from his solo recitals, he distinguished himself as a lieder accompanist to Dietrich Fischer-Dieskau and other prominent singers. Demus assembled a large collection of historic keyboard instruments; publ. a book of essays, *Abenteuer der Interpretation,* and, with Paul Badura-Skoda, an analysis of Beethoven's piano sonatas.

Demuth, Leopold, Austrian baritone; b. Brno, Nov. 2, 1861; d. (during a concert) Czernowitz, March 4, 1910. His real Czech name was **Leopold Pokorný,** but he changed it for professional use. He studied with Joseph Gänsbacher in Vienna; made his debut in 1889 in Halle as Hans Heiling; sang in Leipzig (1891–95) and Hamburg (1895–97); then joined the Vienna Court Opera, remaining on its roster until his death; he also sang at Bayreuth (1899), where he gained recognition as a fine Wagnerian singer.

Demuth, Norman, English composer and writer on music; b. London, July 15, 1898; d. Chichester, April 21, 1968. He studied with Parratt and Dunhill at the Royal College of Music in London. As a youth he joined the British army, in 1915. After the war he played organ in London churches. Later he became a choral conductor; in 1930 became a prof. of composition at the Royal Academy of Music. His works are influenced mainly by French music; in later years he became better known as the author of many books and unorthodox essays on music.

WORKS: 5 symphs. (2 of which are entitled *Symphonic Study*); *Threnody* for Strings (1942); *Overture for a Joyful Occasion* (1946); Violin Concerto (1937); Saxophone Concerto (1938); Piano Concerto (1943); Piano Concerto for the Left Hand (1947); 3 violin sonatas; Cello Sonata; Flute Sonata; many piano pieces.

WRITINGS: (all publ. in London except the last): *The Gramophone and How to Use It* (1945); *Albert Roussel* (1947); *Ravel,* in the Master Musicians Series (1947); *An Anthology of Musical Criticism* (1948); *César Franck* (1949); *Paul Dukas* (1949); *The Symphony: Its History and Development* (1950); *Gounod* (1950); *Vincent d'Indy* (1951); *A Course in Musical Composition* (1951); *Musical Trends in the 20th Century* (1952); *Musical Forms and Textures* (1953); *French Piano Music: A Survey with Notes on Its Performance* (1959); *French Opera: Its Development to the Revolution* (Sussex, 1963).

Dencke, Jeremiah, American Moravian minister, organist, and composer; b. Langenbilau, Silesia, Oct. 2, 1725; d. Bethlehem, Pa., May 28, 1795. In 1748 he became organist at Herrnhut, the center of the European Moravians; came to America (1761) and served the Moravian settlements in Pennsylvania in various capacities. During the Revolutionary War he was warden of the Bethlehem congregation. Dencke was apparently the first individual to compose vocal concerted church music in the Moravian settlements in Pennsylvania, and possibly the first to write such music in colonial America. He was an able composer. The earliest work he is known to have composed in America is a simple anthem for chorus, strings, and figured bass, written for a *Liebesmahl* ("love feast," a service of spiritual devotion and earthly fraternalism, composed of hymn singing and a light meal of a roll and beverage) on Aug. 29, 1765. His finest works are 3 sets of sacred songs for soprano, strings, and organ, composed in 1767–68. The first, written for the annual festival of the "choir" of small girls, is included in the first vol. of the series Music of the Moravians in America, issued by the N.Y. Public Library in 1938. The other sets of solos were written for Christmas services. Dencke's compositions are listed in A.G. Rau and H.T. David, *A Catalogue of Music by American Moravians, 1742–1842* (Bethlehem, Pa., 1938).

BIBLIOGRAPHY: H.T. David, "Musical Life in the Pennsylvania Settlements of the *Unitas Fratrum*," *Transactions of the Moravian Historical Society* (1942; reprinted as Moravian Music Foundation Publication No. 6, Winston-Salem, N.C., 1959); "Recent Discoveries in the Foundation Archives," *Moravian Music Foundation Bulletin* (Spring–Summer 1974).

Dendrino, Gherase, Rumanian composer and conductor; b. Turnu-Măgurele, Sept. 16, 1901; d. Bucharest, Jan. 4, 1973. He studied with Kiriac and Castaldi at the Bucharest Cons. (1920–27); after holding various theater conducting posts, he was conductor of the State Operetta Theater in Bucharest. He wrote 4 light operettas: *Lăsaţi-mă să cînt* (1953); *Poveste pe strune şi pe clape* (1955); *De luni pînă luni* (1958); and his particularly successful *Lysistrata* (Bucharest, Dec. 15, 1960); also, film music and popular music.

Denéréaz, Alexandre, Swiss composer and musicologist; b. Lausanne, July 31, 1875; d. there, July 25, 1947. He studied at the Lausanne Cons. with Blanchet and at the Dresden Cons. with Draeseke and Döring; in 1896 was appointed a prof. at the Lausanne Cons.; also taught musicology at Lausanne Univ.; publ. an original theory of harmony.

WORKS: 3 symphs.; many symph. poems; cantatas; Concerto Grosso for Orch. and Organ; string quartets; organ works; a male chorus; music to René Morax's *La Dime.* He was also the author, in collaboration with C. Bourguès, of *La Musique et la vie intérieure: Histoire psychologique de l'art musical* (appendix entitled *L'Arbre généalogique de l'art musical;* 1919).

Dengremont, Maurice, Brazilian violinist; b. Rio de Janeiro, March 19, 1866, of French parents; d. Buenos Aires, Sept. 1893. As a child prodigy, he attracted general notice in Europe in 1877, but his early death did not allow him to develop his gifts.

Denis, Didier, French composer; b. Paris, Nov. 5, 1947. He studied at the Paris Cons. with Henri Challan, Marcel Bitsch, Olivier Messiaen, and Jean Rivi-er, graduating in 1968.

WORKS: Trio for Flute, Clarinet, and Bassoon (1966); *Sagesse, Force, Beauté, l'Amour* for Coloratura Soprano, 12 Instruments, and 6 Percussion Instruments (1967); *Cinq fois je t'aime* for Speaker, Soprano, and Orch. (1968); *Fugue indoue* for 2 groups of Percussion Instruments (1968); *Chants de Tse Yeh* for Piano and 12 Instruments (1969); *Puzzle* for Voice, Spanish Guitar, and Percussion (1970).

Denisov, Edison, remarkable, innovative Soviet composer; b. Tomsk, April 6, 1929. He was named after Thomas Alva Edison by his father, an electrical engineer; another aspect in so naming him was that the surname Denisov is anagrammatic with Edison, leaving out the last letter. He studied mathematics at the Univ. of Moscow, graduating in 1951, and composition at the Moscow Cons. with Shebalin (1951–56). In 1959 he was appointed to the faculty of the Cons. An astute explorer of tonal possibilities, Denisov writes instrumental works of an empirical genre; typical of these is *Crescendo e diminuendo* for Harpsichord and 12 String Instruments, composed in 1965, with the score written partly in graphic notation. The titles of his pieces reveal a lyric character of subtle nuances, often marked by impressionistic colors: *Aquarelle, Silhouettes, Peinture, Le Vie en rouge, Signes en blanc, Nuages noires.*

WORKS: FOR THE STAGE: Opera, *Soldier Ivan* (1959); *L'Ecume des jours,* lyric drama (1981); *Confession,* ballet after Alfred de Musset (1984). FOR ORCH.: Symph. in C (1955); *Sinfonietta on Tadzhik Themes* (1957); *Peinture* (Graz, Oct. 30, 1970); Cello Concerto (Leipzig, Sept. 25, 1973); Flute Concerto (Dresden, May 22, 1976); Violin Concerto (Milan, July 18, 1978); Piano Concerto (Leipzig, Sept. 5, 1978); *Partita* for Violin and Orch. (Moscow, March 23, 1981); Concerto for Bassoon, Cello, and Orch. (1982); *Tod ist ein langer Schlaf,* variations on a theme by Haydn, for Cello and Orch. (Moscow, May 30, 1982); Chamber Symph. (Paris, March 7, 1983); *Epitaphe* for Chamber Orch. (Reggio Emilia, Italy, Sept. 11, 1983). CHAMBER MUSIC: Sonata for 2 Violins (1958); *Musique* for 11 Wind Instruments and Timpani (Leningrad, Nov. 15, 1965); String Quartet No. 2 (1961); Violin Sonata (1963); *Crescendo e diminuendo* for Harpsichord and 12 String Instruments (Zagreb, May 14, 1967); *Ode in Memory of Ché Guevara* for Clarinet, Piano, and Percussion (Moscow, Jan. 22, 1968); *Musique romantique* for Oboe, Harp, and String Trio (Zagreb, May 16, 1969); *3 Pieces* for Cello and Piano (1969); String Trio (1969); *D-S-C-H,* a monogram for Shostakovich (1969); Wind Quintet (1969); *Silhouettes* for Flute, 2 Pianos, and Percussion (1969); *Chant des oiseaux* for Prepared Piano and Tape (1969); Sonata for Alto Saxophone and Piano (1970); Piano Trio (1971); Cello Sonata (1971); *Solo per flauto* (1971); *Solo per oboe* (1971); *Canon in Memory of Igor Stravinsky* for Flute, Clarinet, and Harp (1971); Sonata for Clarinet Solo (1972); *3 Pieces* for Harpsichord and Percussion (1972); *2 Pieces* for Alto Saxophone and Piano (1974); *Choral varié* for Trombone and Piano

(1975); *Aquarelle* for 24 String Instruments (1975); *4 Pieces* for Flute and Piano (1977); *Concerto piccolo* for 4 Saxophones and 6 Percussionists (Bordeaux, April 28, 1979); Sonata for Flute and Guitar (1977); Sonata for Solo Violin (1978); Concerto for Guitar Solo (1981); Trio for Oboe, Cello, and Harpsichord (1981); Sonata for Bassoon Solo (1982); Sonata for Violin and Organ (1982); *Musique de chambre* for Viola, Harpsichord, and Strings (1982); 5 études for Bassoon Solo (1983); Sonata for Flute and Harp (1983); *Es ist genug,* variations for Viola and Piano on a theme of Bach (1984); *Diane dans le vent d'automne* for Viola, Vibraphone, Piano, and Double Bass (1984). FOR VOICES: *Canti di Catulli* for Bass and 3 Trombones (1962); *Soleil des Incas* for Soprano and Instrumental Ensemble, to poems by Gabriela Mistral (Leningrad, Nov. 30, 1964); *Chansons italiennes* for Soprano, Flute, Horn, Violin, and Harpsichord (1966); *Pleurs* for Soprano, Piano, and Percussion, on texts from Russian folk songs (1966); *5 Geschichten vom Herrn Keuner* for Tenor and 7 Instruments, to Brecht's poems (1968); *Automne,* 13 poems to surrealist vocables by Khlebnikov (1969); 2 songs for Soprano and Piano, to poems by Bunin (1970); *Chant d'automne* for Soprano and Orch., to poems by Baudelaire (1971); *La Vie en rouge* for Voice, Flute, Clarinet, Violin, Cello, and Piano (1973); *Requiem* for Soprano, Tenor, Chorus, and Orch. (1980); *Colin et Chloé,* suite from the opera *L'Ecume des jours,* for Soloists, Chorus, and Orch. (1981); *Lumière et ombres* for Bass and Piano, to poems by Vladimir Soloviev (1982); *Ton image charmante* for Voice and Orch., to words by Pushkin (1982); *Venue du printemps* for Chorus a cappella (1984). FOR PIANO: *Variations* (1961); *3 Pieces* for Piano, 4-hands (1967); *Signes en blanc* (1974); also *Feuilles mortes* for Harpsichord. ORCHESTRATIONS: Mussorgsky: *Nursery Songs, Sunless,* and *Songs and Dances of Death;* Mossolov: *Advertisements,* arranged for Voice and Orch.; also several Schubert dances.

Dennée, Charles (Frederick), American pianist and pedagogue; b. Oswego, N.Y., Sept. 1, 1863; d. Boston, April 29, 1946. At the New England Cons. in Boston he studied piano with A.D. Turner and composition with S.A. Emery; also studied piano with Hans von Bülow during von Bülow's last visit to the U.S. (1889–90); in 1883 he was appointed a teacher of piano at the New England Cons.; an accident to his right wrist caused his retirement in 1897, after he had played almost 1,100 recitals; subsequent devotion to teaching was fruitful, for many of his pupils held prominent positions on the faculties of various conservatories and music colleges. He was among the first to give illustrated lecture-recitals in the U.S. A selection of his essays was publ. as *Musical Journeys* (Brookline, Mass., 1938). Some of his teaching pieces achieved steady popularity with piano students; he also publ. a manual, *Progressive Technique.*

Denny, William D., American composer and pedagogue; b. Seattle, July 2, 1910; d. Berkeley, Calif., Sept. 2, 1980. He studied at the Univ. of Calif., Berkeley (A.B., 1931; M.A., 1933); after graduation he went to Paris, where he took lessons with Paul Dukas at the Ecole Normale de Musique. He returned to the U.S. in 1935, and taught at Vassar and Harvard. In 1945 he was appointed to the faculty of his alma mater in Berkeley, where he remained until his retirement in 1978. His compositions are marked by a strong contrapuntal texture, with the fugal element much in evidence. WORKS: For Orch.: Concertino (1937; San Francisco, April 25, 1939, composer conducting); Symph. No. 1 (1939; first perf., CBS Radio, May 1939); Sinfonietta for Strings (1940; NBC Radio, 1940); Suite for Chamber Orch. (1940); Overture for Strings (1945; San Francisco, May 2, 1946); *Praeludium* (1946; San Francisco, Feb. 5, 1947, composer conducting); Symph. No. 2 (1949; San Francisco, March 22, 1951, composer conducting); Symph. No. 3 (1955–57; San Francisco, Jan. 16, 1963, composer conducting). Chamber music: 3 string quartets (1938, 1952, 1955); Viola Sonata (1943–44); Trio for Strings (1965); Partita for Organ (1958); Toccata, Aria, and Fugue for Organ (1966). Choral music: Cantata, *Most Glorious Lord of Life* (1943); 3 motets (1946–47).

Densmore, Frances, specialist in American Indian music; b. Red Wing, Minn., May 21, 1867; d. there, June 5, 1957. She studied at the Oberlin (Ohio) Cons. (hon. M.A., 1924); then took courses with Leopold Godowsky (piano) and J.K. Paine (counterpoint); began study of Indian music in 1893 at the World's Fair in Chicago, continuing privately until 1907, when she began systematic research for the Bureau of American Ethnology (Smithsonian Inst.), including an exhaustive study of the Cheyenne, Arapaho, Maidu, Santo Domingo Pueblo, and New Mexican Indian tribes. She lectured extensively on Indian music, and publ. a number of books and articles on the subject. WRITINGS: *Chippewa Music,* a collection of Indian songs in 2 vols. (1910–13); *Poems from Sioux and Chippewa Songs* (words only; 1917); *Tetom Sioux Music* (1918); *Indian Action Songs* (1921); *Northern Ute Music* (1922); *Mandan and Hidatfa Music* (1923); *The American Indians and Their Music* (1926; 2nd ed., 1936); *The Music of the Tule Indians of Panama* (1926); *Some Results of the Study of American Indian Music* (reprinted from the *Journal of the Washington Academy of Sciences,* XVIII/14; 1928); *Pawnee Music* (1929); *Papago Music* (1929); *What Intervals Do Indians Sing?* (reprinted from the *American Anthropologist,* April/June, 1929); *Yaman and Yaqui Music* (U.S. Bureau of American Ethnology, Bulletin 110; 1932); *Menominee Music* (ibid., Bulletin 102; 1932); *Cheyenne and Arapaho Music* (Southwest Museum, 1936); *Alabama Music* (Texas Folk-Lore Society, 1937); *Music of Santo Domingo Pueblo, New Mexico* (Southwest Museum, 1938); *Nootka and Quileute Music* (Washington, D.C., 1939); *Music of the Indians of British Columbia* (Washington, 1943); *Choctaw Music* (1943); *Seminole Music*

(1956). The April 1956 issue of *Ethnomusicology* contains a complete bibliography of her writings up to 1955 (pp. 13–29). A Frances Densmore ethnological library has been established at Macalester College in St. Paul, Minn.

Densmore, John H., American composer; b. Somerville, Mass., Aug. 7, 1880; d. Boston, Sept. 21, 1943. He was educated at Harvard Univ. (B.A., 1904); wrote operettas for the Hasty Pudding Club. His mature works (mostly for chorus) are distinguished by practical adaptability.

Dent, Edward Joseph, eminent English musicologist, teacher, and critic; b. Ribston, Yorkshire, July 16, 1876; d. London, Aug. 22, 1957. He studied music with C.H. Lloyd at Eton College; then went to Cambridge to continue his studies with Charles Wood and Stanford (Mus.B., 1899; M.A., 1905); he was elected a Fellow of King's College there in 1902, and subsequently taught music history, harmony, counterpoint, and composition until 1918. He was also active in promoting operatic productions in England by preparing translations of libretti for performances at Cambridge, particularly of the operas of Mozart. From 1918 he wrote music criticism in London; in 1919 he became one of the founders of the British Music Society, which remained active until 1933. The International Society for Contemporary Music came into being in 1922 largely through his efforts, and he served as its president until 1938 and again in 1945; he also was president of the Société Internationale de Musicologie from 1931 until 1949. In 1926 he was appointed prof. of music at Cambridge, a position he held until 1941. He was made an honorary Mus.D. at Oxford (1932), Harvard (1936), and Cambridge (1947) univs. After his death, the Royal Musical Association created, in 1961, the Dent Medal, which is given annually to those selected for their important contributions to musicology. A scholar of the widest interests, he contributed numerous articles to music journals, encyclopedias, dictionaries, and symposia.

WRITINGS: *Alessandro Scarlatti* (London, 1905; 2nd ed., revised by F. Walker, 1960); *Mozart's Operas: A Critical Study* (London, 1913; 3rd ed., revised, 1955); *Terpander, or Music and the Future* (London, 1926); *Foundations of English Opera: A Study of Musical Drama in England during the Seventeenth Century* (Cambridge, 1928); *Ferruccio Busoni* (London, 1933; 2nd ed., 1966); *Handel* (London, 1934); *Opera* (Harmondsworth, 1940; 5th ed., revised, 1949); *Notes on Fugue for Beginners* (Cambridge, 1941); *A Theatre for Everybody: The Story of the Old Vic and Sadler's Wells* (London, 1945; 2nd ed., revised, 1946); *The Rise of Romantic Opera* (ed. by W. Dean; Cambridge, 1976); *Selected Essays* (ed. by H. Taylor; Cambridge, 1979).

BIBLIOGRAPHY: L. Haward, "Edward J. Dent: Bibliography," *Music Review*, VII (1946; publ. separately, Cambridge, 1956); W. Dean, "Edward J. Dent: A Centenary Tribute," *Music & Letters* (Oct. 1976); P. Radcliffe, *E.J. Dent: A Centenary Memoir* (Rickmansworth, 1976).

Denver, John (real name, **Henry John Deutschendorf, Jr.**), popular American singer and songwriter; b. Roswell, N.M., Dec. 31, 1943. He played guitar as a youngster; for a time attended Texas Tech. Univ. in Lubbock; then made his way to N.Y., where he played in the Mitchell Trio and wrote the popular song *Leaving on a Jet Plane*. In 1968 he launched a solo career, appearing in concerts all over the U.S.; also made television appearances and recordings. His successful songs included *Rocky Mountain High, Take Me Home,* and *Country Roads*. He appeared in the movie *Oh, God!*

Denza, Luigi, Italian song composer; b. Castellammare di Stabia, Feb. 24, 1846; d. London, Jan. 26, 1922. He studied with Serrao and Mercadante at the Naples Cons. Besides the opera *Wallenstein* (Naples, May 13, 1876), which was not especially successful, he wrote about 600 songs (some in Neapolitan dialect), many of which won great popularity. In 1879 he settled in London; was appointed prof. of singing at the Royal Academy of Music (1898); was made a Chevalier of the order of the Crown of Italy. His most famous song is *Funiculi-Funicula,* which was used (under the mistaken impression that it was a folk song) by Richard Strauss in *Aus Italien.*

Denzler, Robert, Swiss conductor and composer; b. Zürich, March 19, 1892; d. there, Aug. 25, 1972. He studied with Volkmar Andreae in Zürich; held posts as conductor at the Municipal Theater in Zürich (1915–27), at the Berlin Opera (1927–32), and again in Zürich (1934–47). He wrote a piano concerto, several instrumental suites, and songs.

De Peyer, Gervase, English clarinetist; b. London, April 11, 1926. He studied at the Royal College of Music with Frederick Thurston; also in Paris with Louis Cahuzac. In 1955 he became first clarinetist of the London Symph. Orch.; in 1959 was appointed to the faculty of the Royal Academy of Music. He made appearances also as a soloist, and encouraged composers to write works for the clarinet, of which he gave first performances.

Deppe, Ludwig, famous German piano pedagogue; b. Alverdissen, Lippe, Nov. 7, 1828; d. Bad Pyramont, Sept. 5, 1890. He was a pupil of Marxsen at Hamburg in 1849; later of Lobe at Leipzig. He settled in Hamburg in 1857 as a music teacher, and founded a singing society, which he conducted till 1868. He went to Berlin in 1874, and from 1886 to 1888 was court conductor; also conducted the Silesian Musical Festivals established by Count Hochberg in 1876. He wrote a symph. and 2 overtures, *Zriny* and *Don Carlos.*

BIBLIOGRAPHY: Amy Fay, "Deppe as Teacher," in her book *Music Study in Germany* (1897); H. Klose, *Deppesche Lehre des Klavierspiels* (Hamburg, 1886); Elisabeth Caland, *Die Deppesche Lehre des Klavierspiels* (Stuttgart, 1897; 5th ed., 1921; in Eng. as *Artistic Piano Playing,* 1903).

De Preist, James, greatly talented black American

conductor; b. Philadelphia, Nov. 21, 1936. He was educated in his native city. He conducted the Contemporary Music Guild there (1959–62); then was a music specialist for the U.S. State Dept. in Bangkok, Thailand. In 1964 he won first prize in the Mitropoulos Competition in N.Y.; served for a season as assistant conductor of the N.Y. Phil. (1965–66). He then was associate conductor of the National Symph. Orch. in Washington, D.C. (1972–75). In 1976 he was appointed music director of the Quebec Symph. Orch.; in 1980 became music director of the Oregon Symph. at Portland, but continued at his Quebec post until 1982. He is a nephew of the renowned singer **Marian Anderson.**

Déré, Jean, French composer; b. Niort, June 23, 1886; d. Sainte Suzanne (Mayenne), Dec. 6, 1970. He studied at the Paris Cons. with Caussade, Diémer, and Widor; won the 2nd Prix de Rome (1919). Among his works are the symph. poem *Krischna;* incidental music for Marlowe's *Faustus; 3 esquisses* for Piano and Orch.; chamber music; piano pieces; songs.

De Rensis, Raffaello, Italian music critic; b. Casacalenda, Campobasso, Feb. 17, 1879; d. Rome, Nov. 3, 1970. He founded the weekly magazine *Musica* in 1908; wrote music criticism in daily newspapers. He publ. a number of monographs: *Il Cantore del popolo, B. Gigli* (Rome, 1934); *F. Faccio e Verdi* (Milan, 1934); *Ottorino Respighi* (Turin, 1935); *E. Wolf-Ferrari* (Milan, 1937); *A. Boito* (Florence, 1942); *U. Giordano e R. Leoncavallo* (Siena, 1949); *F. Cilèa* (Palmi, 1950); also a collection of essays, *Musica vista* (Milan, 1960).

De Reszke, Edouard, famous Polish bass, brother of the tenor **Jean de Reszke** and of the soprano **Josephine de Reszke;** b. Warsaw, Dec. 22, 1853; d. Garnek, May 25, 1917. He studied with an Italian teacher, Ciaffei, in Warsaw; also was trained by his older brother, Jean, and by Steller and Coletti. He then went to Italy, where he continued his study with various teachers. His professional debut was at the Théâtre des Italiens in Paris, when he sang Amonasro in *Aida* under Verdi's direction (April 22, 1876). He continued to make appearances in Paris for 2 seasons, and later sang at La Scala in Milan. In 1880–84 he sang in London with extraordinary success. He made his American debut in Chicago as the King in *Lohengrin* (Nov. 9, 1891); then as Frère Laurent in *Roméo et Juliette* at the Metropolitan Opera House in N.Y. (Dec. 14, 1891); his brother Jean made his N.Y. debut as Roméo at the same performance. Edouard de Reszke's greatest role was that of Méphistophélès in *Faust;* he sang this part at its 500th performance at the Paris Opéra (his brother Jean sang the title role), on Nov. 4, 1887; he made a special final appearance at a Metropolitan gala on April 27, 1903, in the last act of *Faust.* He then retired, and died in extreme poverty as a result of the depredations brought on by World War I.
BIBLIOGRAPHY: H. Klein, "E. de Reszke: The Career of a Famous Basso," *Musical Times* (July 1917).

De Reszke, Jean (Jan Mieczislaw), celebrated Polish tenor, brother of **Edouard** and **Josephine de Reszke;** b. Warsaw, Jan. 14, 1850; d. Nice, April 3, 1925. His mother gave him his first singing lessons; he then studied with Ciaffei and Cotogni. He sang at the Warsaw Cathedral as a boy; then went to Paris, where he studied with Sbriglia. He was first trained as a baritone, and made his debut in Venice (1874) as Alfonso in *La Favorita* under the name of **Giovanni di Reschi.** He continued singing in Italy and France in baritone parts; his first appearance as a tenor took place in Madrid on Nov. 9, 1879, in *Robert le Diable.* He created the title role of Massenet's *Le Cid* at the Paris Opéra (Nov. 30, 1885) and became a favorite tenor there. He appeared at Drury Lane in London as Radames on June 13, 1887 (having previously sung there as a baritone in 1874). He then sang at Covent Garden (until 1900). On Nov. 9, 1891, he made his American debut with the Italian Opera Co.; he made his Metropolitan Opera debut in N.Y. on Dec. 14, 1891, as Roméo; he remained with the Metropolitan for 11 seasons. In order to sing Wagnerian roles, he learned German, and made a sensationally successful appearance as Tristan (N.Y., Nov. 27, 1895). His last appearance at the Metropolitan was as Tristan on April 29, 1901, in Act 2 during a postseason gala performance. The secret of his success rested not so much on the power of his voice (some baritone quality remained in his singing to the end) as on his controlled interpretation, musical culture, and fine dynamic balance. When he retired from the stage in 1902, settling in Paris as a voice teacher, he was able to transmit his method to many of his students, several of whom later became famous on the opera stage.
BIBLIOGRAPHY: Clara Leiser, *Jean de Reszke and the Great Days of Opera* (London, 1933); P.G. Hurst, *Jean de Reszke: 40 Years of Opera, 1874–1914* (London, 1958).

De Reszke, Josephine, Polish soprano, sister of **Jean** and **Edouard de Reszke;** b. Warsaw, June 4, 1855; d. there, Feb. 22, 1891. She studied at the St. Petersburg Cons.; first appeared in public under the name of **Giuseppina di Reschi** at Venice in 1875; sang Marguerite in Gounod's *Faust* (Aug. 1, 1874), with her brother Jean as Valentin; then was engaged at the Paris Opéra, where she made her debut as Ophelia in *Hamlet* by Ambroise Thomas (Paris, June 21, 1875); later sang in Madrid and Lisbon; appeared as Aida at Covent Garden in London on April 18, 1881. She retired from the stage upon her marriage in 1885 and settled in Poland.

Dering, Richard. See **Deering, Richard.**

Dérivis, Henri Etienne, French bass, father of **Prosper Dérivis;** b. Albi, Aug. 2, 1780; d. Livry, Feb. 1, 1856. He made his debut at the Paris Opéra as Sarastro in the French version of *Die Zauberflöte* under the title of *Les Mystères d'Isis* in 1803; during the next 25 years he was a principal singer there, creating roles in works by Spontini (*La Vestale, Fernand Cortez,* and *Olympie*), Cherubini (*Les Abencérages*), Rossini (*Le Siège de Corinthe*), and others.

Dérivis, Prosper, distinguished French bass, son of **Henri Etienne Dérivis;** b. Paris, Oct. 28, 1808; d. there, Feb. 11, 1880. He studied with Pellegrini and Nourrit in Paris; made his debut at the Paris Opéra in 1831; subsequently created roles there in operas by Berlioz (*Benvenuto Cellini*), Meyerbeer (*Les Huguenots*), Donizetti (*Les Martyrs*), etc.; appeared at La Scala in Milan (1842–43), singing in the premieres of Verdi's *Nabucco* and *I Lombardi;* also sang in the first performance of Donizetti's *Linda di Chamounix* in Vienna in 1842; retired from the stage in 1857; then taught voice in Paris.

Dermota, Anton, tenor; b. Kropa (now in Yugoslavia), June 4, 1910. He studied at the State Academy in Ljubljana and at the Vienna Academy of Music. In 1936 he became a member of the Vienna State Opera; also sang at the Salzburg Festival. After retirement he joined the faculty of the Vienna Academy of Music.

Dernesch, Helga, Austrian soprano; b. Vienna, Feb. 3, 1939. She was educated at the Vienna Cons.; made her operatic debut at the Bern Stadttheater in 1961; then sang in Wiesbaden and Cologne; subsequently appeared at the Bayreuth Festivals; in 1969 Herbert von Karajan chose her for his Salzburg Easter Festival; in 1970 she made her debut at Covent Garden, London; also sang with the Hamburg State Opera, the Berlin Städtische Oper, and the Vienna State Opera. She sang many Wagnerian dramatic roles and those of Richard Strauss; from 1979 she turned her attention to mezzo-soprano parts.

De Rogatis, Pascual, Argentine composer; b. Teora, Italy, May 17, 1880; d. Buenos Aires, April 2, 1980, a few weeks before his 100th birthday. He was taken to Buenos Aires as a child; studied piano and composition with Alberto Williams and violin with Pietro Melani and Rafael Albertini. He subsequently established himself in Buenos Aires as a violin teacher and composer. His music followed the Italian tradition, but he often selected local subjects from history and folklore for his operas and choral works. The following operas by him were produced in Buenos Aires: *Anfión y Zeto,* Greek tragedy (Aug. 18, 1915); *Huémac,* to a story of ancient Mexico (July 22, 1916); *La novia del hereje* (*The Heretic's Bride;* June 13, 1935). He further composed a symph. poem, *Atipac* (Buenos Aires, April 7, 1928), and numerous vocal pieces on Argentine themes.

De Rose, Peter, American composer of popular music; b. New York, March 10, 1900; d. there, April 24, 1953. After a desultory musical education, he formed a radio team, The Sweethearts of the Air, with May Singhi Breen, whom he married. He gained fame with a piano piece entitled *Deep Purple;* it was introduced in an orch. version by Paul Whiteman (N.Y., May 10, 1934) and subsequently converted into a saccharine ballad with lachrymose lyrics which became a commercial hit. Other lucrative songs by De Rose are *The Lamp Is Low* (derived from a malformed fragmentation of Ravel's *Pavane*) and *As Years Go By*, a sentimentalized misinterpretation of Brahms's *Hungarian Dance No. 4.*

Dervaux, Pierre, noted French conductor; b. Juvisy-sur-Orge, Jan. 3, 1917. He entered the Paris Cons. at the age of 9, studying piano and composition. In 1934 he became timpanist of the Pasdeloup Orch. in Paris; made his debut as conductor with that orch. in 1945. In 1948 he became chief conductor of the Opéra-Comique. In 1956 he was appointed chief conductor of the Paris Opéra. He later served as chief conductor of the Co'ogne Orch.; also conducted the regional orch. in Angers and the Quebec Symph. Orch. His performances of the French repertoire are noted for their authentic color and technical brilliance.

De Sabata, Victor, outstanding Italian conductor and composer; b. Trieste, April 10, 1892; d. Santa Margherita Ligure, Dec. 11, 1967. He studied with Michele Saladino and Giacomo Orefice at the Milan Cons. (1901–11). An extremely versatile musician, he could play piano with considerable élan, and also took lessons on cello, clarinet, oboe, and bassoon. He was encouraged in his career as conductor by Toscanini; at the same time he began to compose operas; his first production was *Il Macigno,* first performed at the La Scala Opera in Milan on March 30, 1917. His symph. poem *Juventus* (1919) was conducted at La Scala by Toscanini. De Sabata's style of composition involved Romantic Italian formulas, with lyric and dramatic episodes receiving an equal share of his attention. In the meantime he filled engagements as an opera and symph. conductor in Italy. In 1927 he conducted concerts in N.Y. and Cincinnati, in 1936 he conducted opera at the Vienna State Opera, in 1939 he was a guest conductor with the Berlin Phil. Orch., and in 1946 he conducted in Switzerland. On April 21, 1946 he was invited to conduct a symph. concert in London, the first conductor from an "enemy country" to conduct in England after the war. He conducted the Chicago Symph. Orch. in Oct. 1949; in March 1950 he conducted 14 concerts at Carnegie Hall with the N.Y. Phil.; the following August he was guest conductor with the Boston Symph. Orch. In April 1951 he conducted 6 concerts with the N.Y. Phil. in Carnegie Hall. He became popular with American audiences, and in 1952 was engaged to conduct in N.Y., Philadelphia, Washington, Baltimore, St. Louis, and Detroit. In 1953 he conducted in Philadelphia, Los Angeles, San Francisco, and Santa Barbara, Calif. He returned to Italy in 1955; on Feb. 18, 1957, he conducted at the funeral of Toscanini; this was his last appearance on the podium. He died of a heart attack at Santa Margherita Ligure during the night of Dec. 10–11, 1967.

WORKS: Operas; *Il Macigno* (*The Rock;* La Scala, Milan, March 30, 1917; 2nd version, *Driada,* Turin,

Nov. 12, 1935); *Lisistrata* (1920); theater music for Max Reinhardt's production of *The Merchant of Venice* (*Il Mercanto di Venezia;* Venice, July 18, 1934); ballet, *Le mille e una notte* (La Scala, Milan, Jan. 20, 1931); symph. poems, *Juventus* (1919); *La notte di Platon* (1924); *Gethsemani* (1925).

BIBLIOGRAPHY: R. Mucci, *Victor de Sabata* (Lanciano, 1937); Teodoro Celli, *L'arte di Victor de Sabata* (Turin, 1978).

Desarzens, Victor, Swiss conductor; b. Château d'Oex, Oct. 27, 1908. He received his musical education at the Lausanne Cons.; studied conducting with Franz von Hoesslin. He played violin in the Orchestre de la Suisse Romande in Geneva; also led a series of chamber music concerts there and later served as conductor of the Lausanne Chamber Orch. In 1945 he was appointed music director of the Musikkollegium of Winterthur, a post he held until his retirement in 1976.

Deschamps-Jehin, (Marie-) Blanche, outstanding French contralto; b. Lyons, Sept. 18, 1857; d. Paris, June 1923. She studied at the Cons. in Lyons; later at the Paris Cons.; made her debut in Brussels in 1874; then sang at the Théâtre Royal de la Monnaie in Brussels (1879–85); during her tenure there, she created the role of Hérodiade in Massenet's opera; then sang at the Opéra-Comique in Paris (1885–91) and the Paris Opéra (1891–1902), and at Covent Garden in London (1891); in later years she appeared mainly in concerts. She was married to the conductor **Léon Jehin.**

Desderi, Ettore, Italian composer; b. Asti, Dec. 10, 1892; d. Florence, Nov. 23, 1974. He studied with Luigi Perrachio at the Turin Cons. and then with Franco Alfano in Bologna. In 1933–41 he was a director of the Liceo Musicale in Alessandria; in 1941–51, a teacher of composition at the Milan Cons. From 1951 to 1963 he was director of the Cons. of Bologna.

WORKS: *Intermezzi all' Antigone* for Orch. (1924); *Job,* biblical cantata (1927); *Sinfonia Davidica* for Soli, Chorus, and Orch. (1929); Violin Sonata; Cello Sonata; many choral works. He publ. *La musica contemporanea* (Turin, 1930) and numerous articles in Italian and German journals.

BIBLIOGRAPHY: A. Bonacorsi, "Ettore Desderi," *Il Pianoforte* (July 1926); Mario Rinaldi, *Ettore Desderi* (Tivoli, 1943); a festive vol., *A Ettore Desderi nel suo 70 compleanno* (Bologna, 1963).

De Segurola, Andrés, Spanish bass; b. Valencia, March 27, 1874; d. Barcelona, Jan. 22, 1953. He studied with Pietro Farvaro; sang at the Teatro Liceo in Barcelona; made his American debut at the Metropolitan Opera as Alvise in *La Gioconda* (Nov. 15, 1909). For 20 years (1931–51) he lived in Hollywood as a teacher; then returned to Spain.

Deshevov, Vladimir, Russian composer; b. St. Petersburg, Feb. 11, 1889; d. there (Leningrad), Oct. 27,

1955. He studied with Steinberg and Liadov at the Cons. there. Many of his themes are drawn from folk sources. Among his works are the revolutionary operas *The Red Hurricane* (Leningrad, Oct. 29, 1924), *Ice and Steel,* based on the Kronstadt rebellion of 1921 (Leningrad, May 17, 1930), and *The Hungry Steppe,* about socialist distribution of land in Uzbekistan.

Deslandres, Adolphe-Edouard-Marie, French composer; b. Batignolles, Monceaux, Jan. 22, 1840; d. Paris, July 30, 1911. He was a pupil of Leborne and Benoist at the Paris Cons.; in 1862 was appointed organist at Ste.-Marie. He wrote the operas *Dimanche et lundi* (1872), *Le Chevalier Bijou* (1875), and *Fridolin* (1876); *Ode à l'harmonie; La Banque brisée;* a patriotic dirge, *Les Sept Paroles;* many sacred choruses.

Des Marais, Paul, American composer; b. Menominee, Mich., June 23, 1920. He was taken to Chicago as an infant; studied there with Leo Sowerby; then with Nadia Boulanger in Cambridge, Mass., and with Walter Piston at Harvard Univ. (B.A., 1949; M.A., 1953). He received the Lili Boulanger prize (1947–48); the Boott prize in composition from Harvard (1949); a John Knowles Paine Traveling Fellowship (1949–51); joined the staff of the Univ. of Calif., Los Angeles, in 1960; received the Inst. of Creative Arts Award there in 1964–65. His early music was oriented toward neo-classicism, with pandiatonic excrescences in harmonic structures; in 1959 he evolved a decaphonic idiom using series of no more than 10 notes, while preserving a free, not necessarily nontonal, style of writing.

WORKS: Mass a cappella (1949); 2 piano sonatas (1947, 1952); *Theme and Changes* for Harpsichord (1953); Motet for Mixed Voices, Cellos, and Double Basses (1959); *Psalm 121* for Chorus a cappella (1959); *Capriccio* for 2 Pianos, Percussion, and Celesta (1962; Los Angeles, March 18, 1963); *Epiphanies,* chamber opera with intervening film sequences (1964–68). In 1970–73 he held the Thorne Music Fund award, enabling him to work on his project on the sounds produced by underwater mammals as a foundation of musico-marine electronic and acoustical works.

Desmarets, Henri, important French composer; b. Paris, Feb. 1661; d. Lunéville, Sept. 7, 1741. He was a boy soprano in the Paris Royal Chapel until 1678; was maître de chapelle at Louise-le-Grand, a Jesuit college. He was regarded as one of the most skillful musicians during the reign of Louis XIV. His first stage work produced was the opera *Endymion* (Versailles, March 16, 1682; not extant); there followed (all at Paris) *Didon* (Sept. 11, 1693); *Circé* (Oct. 1, 1694); *Théagène et Cariclée* (Feb. 3, 1695); *Les Amours de Momus,* ballet (May 25, 1695); *Vénus et Adonis,* serious opera (March 17, 1697); *Les Fêtes galantes,* ballet (May 10, 1698); *Iphigénie en Tauride,* opera (May 6, 1704); *Renaud, ou La Suite d'Armide* (March 5, 1722); etc. His personal life was stormy and included an abduction, for which he was sentenced to death in absentia, prompting him to flee France for Brussels (1699). He was then musician to Philip V of Spain, and intendant of music to the Duke of Lorraine at Lunéville (from 1707). He was able to return to France in 1722 after his marriage to the abducted woman was recognized as valid by the French courts.

BIBLIOGRAPHY: M. Brenet, "Desmarets, un compositeur oublié du 17e siècle," *Le Ménestrel,* 39–40 (1883); M. Antoine, *Henri Desmarets* (Paris, 1965).

Desmond, Paul, American jazz alto saxophonist; b. San Francisco, Nov. 25, 1924; d. New York, May 30, 1977. His real name was **Paul Emil Breitenfeld;** he picked up his professional name from a telephone book at random. He gained the rudiments of music from his father, who played the organ for silent movies; Desmond played the clarinet in the school orch.; then switched to the alto saxophone. He made rapid strides toward recognition and modest fame when he joined the Dave Brubeck Quartet, and continued with it until it was disbanded in 1967. He wrote some pieces for the Brubeck Quartet, of which *Take Five,* a jazz composition in 5/4 meter, was adopted as their signature song and became popular.

Desormière, Roger, brilliant French conductor; b. Vichy, Sept. 13, 1898; d. Paris, Oct. 25, 1963. He studied at the Paris Cons.; conducted the Swedish Ballet in Paris (1924–25) and the Ballets Russes (1925–29), and later at La Scala, at Covent Garden, and in Monte Carlo; was at the Opéra-Comique (1937–46); at the Grand Opéra (1945); conducted the BBC in London (1946–47). In 1950 he was stricken with aphasia and other disorders, and was compelled to give up his career.

BIBLIOGRAPHY: D. Mayer and P. Souvchinsky, *Roger Desormière et son temps* (Monaco, 1966).

Despalj, Pavle, Yugoslav conductor; b. Blato na Korčuli, March 18, 1934. He studied at the Zagreb Academy of Music with Stjepan Šulek; played violin in the Zagreb Phil.; then emigrated to the U.S.; in 1968 he was named associate conductor of the Florida Symph. Orch. in Orlando; from 1970 to 1984 was its music director. Returning to Yugoslavia, he was appointed chief conductor of the Zagreb Phil. in 1980, and in 1981 led it on an American tour. He composed a Violin Concerto (1960), Concerto for Alto Saxophone and String Orch. (1963), and some minor pieces for various groups.

Despalj, Valter, cellist; b. Zadar, Yugoslavia, Nov. 5, 1947. He was taken to the U.S. as a child; studied cello with Leonard Rose at the Juilliard School of Music in N.Y., graduating in 1969; from 1970 to 1972 he was a graduate student at the Moscow Cons., where he studied with Galina Kozolupova; also took master classes with Pablo Casals, André Navarra, and Pierre Fournier. He toured widely as a soloist, appearing in the major music centers of Europe, the U.S., Asia, and Australia; in 1981 he toured the U.S. as a soloist with the Zagreb Phil. He is the brother of the conductor **Pavle Despalj.**

Des Prez, Josquin, the greatest of the Franco-Flemish contrapuntists; b. c.1440 in Hainault or Henegouwen (Burgundy); d. Condé-sur-Escaut, as provost of the Cathedral Chapter, Aug. 27, 1521. His surname was variously spelled: *Després, Desprez, Deprés, Depret, Deprez, Desprets, Dupré,* and by the Italians *Del Prato* (Latinized as *a Prato, a Pratis, Pratensis*), etc.; while Josquin (contracted from the Flemish Jossekin, "little Joseph") appears as *Jossé, Jossien, Jusquin, Giosquin, Josquinus, Jacobo, Jodocus, Jodoculus,* etc. His epitaph reads *Jossé de Prés.* However, in the motet *Illibata Dei Virgo* (contained in vol. 9 of the Josquin ed.), of which the text is quite likely of Josquin's authorship, his name appears as an acrostic, thus: *I, O, S, Q, V, I, N, D[es], P, R, E, Z;* this seems to leave little doubt as to its correct spelling. Few details of Josquin's early life are known. He was a boy chorister of the Collegiate Church at St.-Quentin, later becoming canon and choirmaster there; possibly was a pupil of Okeghem, whom he greatly admired (after Okeghem's death, in 1495, he wrote *La Déploration de Johan Okeghem*); from 1459–72 he sang at the Milan Cathedral; by July 1474, was at the Court of Duke Galeazzo Maria Sforza, Milan, as chorister; in 1486–94, was a singer in the Papal choir under the Popes Innocent VIII and Alexander VI; he was also active, for various periods, in Florence, where he met the famous theorist Pietro Aron; in Modena; and in Ferrara (where Isaac was also) as maestro di cappella in 1503–4. Later Josquin returned to Burgundy, settling in Condé-sur-Escaut (1504), where he became provost of Notre Dame. As a composer, he was considered by contemporary musicians and theorists to be the greatest of his period, and he had a strong influence on all those who came into contact with his music or with him personally, as a teacher; Adriaan Petit Coclicus, one of Josquin's distinguished pupils (publ. a method in 1552, entitled *Compendium musices,* based on Josquin's teaching), termed him "princeps musicorum." His works were sung everywhere, and universally admired; in them he achieves a complete union between word and tone, thereby fusing the intricate Netherlandish contrapuntal devices into expressive and beautiful art forms. Two contrasting styles are present in his compositions: some are intricately contrapuntal, displaying the technical ingenuity characteristic of the Netherlands style; others, probably as a result of Italian influence, are homophonic.

WORKS: Masses: (In Petrucci's Lib. I, Venice, 1502): *L'Omme armé; La sol fa re mi; Gaudeamus; Fortunata desperata; L'Omme armé, sexti toni.* (Ibid., II, 1505): *Ave Maris stella; Hercules, dux Ferrarae; Malheur me bat; Lami Baudichon; Una musque de Buscaya; Dung aultre amor.* (Ibid., III, 1514): *Mater patris; Faysans regrets; Ad fugam; Di dadi; De Beata Virgine; Sine nomine.* (These 3 books republ. by Junta, Rome, 1526.)—(In Graphäus's *Missae III*): *Pange lingua; Da pacem; Sub tuum praesidium.* Some of these are scattered in other collections, and fragments are found in still others; several more masses are in MS at Rome, Munich, and Cambrai. Motets were publ. by Petrucci (8 in the *Odhecaton*, 1501; others in his books of motets); by Peutinger (*Liber selectarum cantionum*, 1520); and by others of the period. French chansons were publ. by T. Susato (1545), P. Attaignant (1549), and Du Chemin (1553). A complete ed. of Josquin's works was issued (1921–69; 55 vols.) by the Vereeniging voor Nederlandsche Muziekgeschiedenis under the general editorship of A. Smijers, M. Amlonowycz, and W. Elders.

BIBLIOGRAPHY: E. Van der Straeten, *La Musique aux Pays-Bas avant le XIXe siècle,* VI (Brussels, 1882); F. de Ménil, *Les Grands Musiciens du Nord: Josquin de Prés* (Paris, 1897); A. Schering, *Die niederländische Orgelmesse im Zeitalter des Josquin* (Leipzig, 1912); A. Gastoué, "J. des Prés, ses précurseurs et ses émules," *La Tribune de St. Gervais* (1921; pp. 201–23); T.W. Werner, "Anmerkungen zur Kunst Josquins und zur Gesamt-Ausgabe seiner Werke," *Zeitschrift für Musikwissenschaft,* VII (1924); O. Ursprung, "Josquin Des Prez; Eine Charakterzeichnung," *Bulletin of the Union Musicologique,* VI/1 (1926); A. Smijers, in *Proceedings of the Musical Association, Session 53* (London, 1926–27; pp. 95–116); E.E. Lowinsky, *Secret Chromatic Art in the Netherlands Motet* (N.Y., 1946); C. van den Borren, *Geschiedenis van de muziek in de Nederlanden* (Antwerp, 1948); M. Antonowitsch, *Die Motette "Benedicta Es" von Josquin Des Prez* (Utrecht, 1951); G. Reese, *Music in the Renaissance* (N.Y., 1954; 2nd ed., revised, 1959); C. Sartori, article in *Annales Musicologiques* (1956; discusses birth date); H. Osthoff, *Josquin Desprez* (2 vols., Tutzing, 1962, 1965); W. Elders, *Studien zur Symbolik in der Musik der alten Niederländer* (Bilthoven, 1968); idem.; "Das Symbol in der Musik von Josquin des Prez," *Acta Musicologica* (July–Dec. 1969); A. Ghislanzoni, *Josquin Des Prez (Joducus Pratensis)* Florence, 1976); S. Charles, *Josquin des Pres: A Guide to Research* (N.Y. and London, 1983). The International Josquin Festival Conference was held in N.Y. on June 21–25, 1971; reports appeared in *Journal of the American Musicological Society* (Fall 1971), *Die Musikforschung* (Oct.–Dec. 1971), and *Current Musicology,* 14 (1972); papers presented at the Conference were publ. under the editorship of Edward Lowinsky (London, 1976).

Dessau, Bernhard, German violinist; b. Hamburg, March 1, 1861; d. Berlin, April 28, 1923. He studied violin with Joachim and Wieniawski; held various posts as concertmaster in Germany and the Netherlands; in 1906 was appointed a prof. at the Berlin Cons. He was a prolific composer; his Violin Concerto "im alten Stil" was widely known.

Dessau, Paul, German composer of socialist convictions; b. Hamburg, Dec. 19, 1894; d. East Berlin, June 27, 1979. He learned to play the violin at an early age and gave a concert when he was 11 years old. In 1910 he enrolled at the Klindworth-Scharwenka Cons. in Berlin, where he studied violin with Florian Zajic and composition with Eduard Behm and Max Loewengard. In 1913 he worked as répétiteur at the Hamburg City Theater; in 1914 he was drafted into the German army. After the Armistice in 1918 he became engaged as a composer and conductor in various chamber groups in Hamburg; then served as coach and conductor at the Cologne Opera (1919–23) and in Mainz (1924). In 1925 he was appointed conductor at the Städtische Oper in Berlin, holding this position until 1933; with the usurpation of power by the Nazis, he left Germany, lived in various European cities, and also visited Palestine. In 1939 he emigrated to America; lived for some time in N.Y., and in 1944 went to Hollywood, where he worked on the background scores for 14 films as a composer or orchestrator. He returned to Berlin in 1948 and took an active part in German musical life, aligning himself with the political, social, and artistic developments in the German Democratic Republic; he became closely associated with Bertolt Brecht and composed music for several of his plays. Dessau's operas, choral works, songs, and instrumental music are imbued with the progressive ideals of socialist realism; while he believed in the imperative of music for the masses, he made use of modern techniques, including occasional applications of Schoenberg's method of composition with 12 tones.

WORKS: FOR THE STAGE: Opera, *Lanzelot und Sanderein* (Hamburg, 1918); 2 children's operas: *Das Eisenbahnspiel* (1931) and *Tadel der Unzuverlässigkeit* (1931); opera, *Die Verurteilung des Lukullus,* after Brecht (Berlin, March 17, 1951; original title, *Das Verhör des Lukullus;* new version, 1968); *Geschäftsbericht,* "minimal" opera of 600 seconds' duration (Leipzig, April 29, 1967); stage music for Brecht's plays: *Furcht und Elend des Dritten Reiches* (1938; originally entitled *99%*); *Mutter Courage und ihre Kinder* (1946); *Der gute Mensch von Sezuan* (1947); *Herr Puntila und sein Knecht Matti* (1949); *Mann ist Mann* (1951); *Der kaukasische Kreidekreis* (1954); also music to Brecht's productions of classical drama: *Faust,* after Goethe (1949); *Don Juan,* after Molière (1953); *Coriolan,* after Shakespeare (1964).

FOR ORCH.: Symph. No. 1 (1926); Symph. No. 2 (derived from *Hommage à Bartók;* 1962); *Sozialistische Festouvertüre* (originally, *Symphonischer Marsch,* 1953; revised 1963); *In memoriam Bertolt Brecht* (1957); *Bach-Variationen* (on themes of J.S. Bach and C.P.E. Bach, 1963); *Divertimento* for Chamber Orch. (1964); *Meer der Stürme,* symph. poem (East Berlin, Oct. 14, 1967); *Lenin,* with a choral finale (1970).

CHAMBER MUSIC: 5 string quartets (1932, 1943, 1946, 1948, 1955); Suite for Saxophone and Piano (1935); *5 Tanzstücke* for Mandolin; Guitar, and Accordion (1951); *Jewish Dance* for Violin and Piano (1940); *Quattuordrama* 1965 for 4 Cellos, 2 Pianos, and 2 Percussionists (1965).

FOR PIANO: Sonata (1914); 12 etudes (1932); *10 Kinderstücke* (1934); *Zwölfton Versuche* (1937); *Guernica* (1938); *11 Jüdische Volktänze* (1946); Sonatine (1955); *4 kleine Klavierstücke* (1955); *3 Intermezzi* (1955).

VOCAL MUSIC: Symphonische Kantate (1917); scenic oratorio, *Haggada* (1936); *Deutsches Miserere* (1944–47); *5. März 1953, 21 Uhr 50* (day and hour of Stalin's death; composed in 1954); *Hymne auf den Beginn einer neuen Geschichte der Menschheit* (1959; commemorating the 10th anniversary of the German Democratic Republic); *Appell der Arbeiterklasse* (1961); *Requiem für Lumumba* (1963); *Armeebefehl No. 13* for Speaker, Chorus, and 9 Instruments (1967); several funerary odes: *Grabschrift für Gorki* (1947); *Grabschrift für Rosa Luxemburg* (1948); *Grabschrift für Karl Liebknecht* (1948); *Grabschrift für Lenin* (1951); numerous a cappella choruses to biblical texts; also a setting of the Communist manifesto, *Proletarier aller Länder, vereinigt euch* (1948); a number of mass songs to politically inspired texts.

WRITINGS: Manual, *Musikarbeit in der Schule* (Berlin, 1968); book of reminiscences, *Aus Gesprächen* (Leipzig, 1975). Dessau's other writings are edited by F. Hennenberg, as *Notizen und Noten* (Leipzig, 1974).

BIBLIOGRAPHY: F. Hennenberg, *Dessau-Brecht, Musikalische Arbeiten* (Berlin, 1963); J. Hennenberg, *Paul Dessau* (Leipzig, 1965; contains list of works); F.K. Prieberg, *Musik im anderen Deutschland* (Cologne, 1968).

Dessauer, Joseph, composer; b. Prague, May 28, 1798; d. Mödling, near Vienna, July 8, 1876. He studied piano with Tomaschek and composition with Dionys Weber in Prague. He wrote several operas: *Lidwina* (Prague, 1836); *Ein Besuch in Saint-Cyr* (Dresden, May 6, 1838; his best work); *Paquite* (Vienna, 1851); *Domingo* (1860); and *Oberon* (not perf.); also overtures, string quartets, piano pieces, etc.

Dessoff, (Felix) Otto, eminent German conductor; b. Leipzig, Jan. 14, 1835; d. Frankfurt, Oct. 28, 1892. He studied at the Leipzig Cons. with Moscheles, Hauptmann, and Rietz; then was a theater conductor in various German cities (1854–60). In 1860–75 he was a conductor of the Vienna Opera; also conducted the Vienna Phil. Orch., and taught at the Vienna Cons. In 1875–81 he occupied similar posts at Karlsruhe; in 1881 he became an opera conductor in Frankfurt. He was greatly esteemed by his many celebrated friends for his musicianship; his correspondence with Brahms was publ. by the Brahms Society. He also wrote chamber music (Piano Quintet; Piano Quartet; etc.).

Dessoff, Margarethe, Austrian choral conductor; b. Vienna, June 11, 1874; d. Locarno, Switzerland, Nov. 19, 1944. She was educated at the Frankfurt Cons.; taught there in 1912–17. She organized a madrigal singing group, and traveled with it in Germany (1916–21). In 1922 she settled in America, where she presented interesting programs of choral music (gave the first complete perf. in N.Y. of Vecchi's *L'Amfiparnaso,* 1933). In 1936 she went to Switzerland, where she remained until her death. The leadership of the Dessoff Choir, which she established

in N.Y., was taken over in 1936 by Paul Boepple.

Destinn (real name, **Kittl**), **Emmy,** famous dramatic soprano; b. Prague, Feb. 26, 1878; d. Budějovice (Bohemia), Jan. 28, 1930. She first studied the violin; her vocal abilities were revealed later by Mme. Loewe-Destinn, whose second name she adopted as a token of appreciation. She made her debut as Santuzza at the Kroll Opera in Berlin (July 19, 1898) and was engaged at the Berlin Opera as a regular member until 1908. She then specialized in Wagnerian operas, and became a protégée of Cosima Wagner in Bayreuth; because of her ability to cope with difficult singing parts, Richard Strauss selected her for the title role in the Berlin and Paris premieres of his *Salome.* She made her London debut at Covent Garden on May 2, 1904, as Donna Anna; her success in England was spontaneous and unmistakable, and she continued to sing opera in England until the outbreak of World War I. She made her American debut in *Aida* with the Metropolitan Opera Co., Toscanini conducting, on Nov. 16, 1908, and remained with the company until 1914. She returned to America after World War I to sing *Aida* at the Metropolitan (Dec. 8, 1919); retired from the opera stage in 1920 but continued to make concert appearances until shortly before her death. For a few years following World War I she used her Czech name, **Ema Destinnová,** but dropped it later on. Her voice was a pure soprano of great power; she was a versatile singer; her repertoire included some 80 parts. A film biography of her life, *The Divine Emma,* was produced in Czechoslovakia in 1982.

BIBLIOGRAPHY: L. Brieger-Wasservogel, *Emmy Destinn und Maria Laiba* (1908); A. Rektorys, *Ema Destinnová* (Prague, 1936); M. Martínková, *Život Emy Destinnová* (Pilzen, 1946); V. Holzknecht and B. Trita, *E. Destinnová ve slovech a obrazech* (*Destinn in Words and Pictures;* Prague, 1972); M. Pospíšil, *Veliké srdce. Život a umění Emy Destinové* (*A Great Heart: The Life and Art of Destinn;* Prague, 1974; with discography).

Destouches, André-Cardinal, French operatic composer; b. Paris, April (baptized, April 6) 1672; d. there, Feb. 7, 1749. After attending a Jesuit school in Paris, he went as a boy to Siam with his teacher, the missionary Gui Tachard (1686). He returned to France in 1688; served in the Royal Musketeers (1692–94), and later took lessons from André Campra, contributing 3 airs to Campra's opera-ballet *L'Europe galante* (1697). After this initiation, Destouches produced his first independent work, *Issé,* a "heroic pastorale" in 3 acts (Fontainebleau, Oct. 7, 1697); its popularity was parodied in several productions of a similar pastoral nature (*Les Amours de Vincennes* by P.F. Dominique, 1719; *Les Oracles* by J.A. Romagnesi, 1741). Among his other operas, the following were produced in Paris: *Amadis de Grèce* (March 22, 1699), *Omphale* (Nov. 10, 1701), and *Callirhoé* (Dec. 27, 1712). With Delalande, he wrote the ballet *Les Eléments,* which was produced at the Tuileries Palace in Paris on Dec. 22, 1721. In 1713 Louis XIV appointed him inspector general of the

Académie Royale de Musique; in 1728 he became its director, retiring in 1730. A revival of *Omphale* in 1752 evoked Baron Grimm's famous *Lettre sur Omphale*, inaugurating the so-called "Guerre des Bouffons" between the proponents of the French school, as exemplified by Destouches, and Italian opera buffa.

BIBLIOGRAPHY: K. Dulle, *A.C. Destouches* (Leipzig, 1908); A. Tessier, "Correspondance d'A.C. Destouches et du Prince Antoine 1er de Monaco," *Revue Musicale* (Dec. 1926–May 1927); D.R.B. Kimbell, "The Amadis Operas of Destouches and Handel," *Music & Letters* (Oct. 1968).

Destouches, Franz (Seraph) von, German composer; b. Munich, Jan. 21, 1772; d. there, Dec. 10, 1844. He was a pupil of Haydn in Vienna in 1787; was appointed music director at Erlangen (1797); then was 2nd concertmaster at the Weimar theater (1799), later becoming first concertmaster and director of music (1804–8); in 1810 was a prof. of theory at Landshut Univ.; then a conductor at Hamburg (1826–42); retired to Munich in 1842.

WORKS: *Die Thomasnacht,* opera (Munich, Aug. 31, 1792); *Das Missverständniss,* operetta (Weimar, April 27, 1805); comic opera, *Der Teufel und der Schneider* (1843; not perf.); incidental music: to Schiller's version of Gozzi's *Turandot* (1802); to Schiller's *Die Braut von Messina* (1803), *Die Jungfrau von Orleans* (1803), and *Wilhelm Tell* (1804); to Kotzebue's *Die Hussiten vor Naumburg* (1804); and to Zacharias Werner's play *Wanda, Königin der Sarmaten* (1808); also a Piano Concerto; piano sonatas; fantasias; variations for piano; Piano Trio; Clarinet Concerto; Mass; oratorio, *Die Anbetung am Grabe Christi.*

BIBLIOGRAPHY: Ernst von Destouches, *Franz von Destouches* (Munich, 1904).

Destranges, Louis Augustin Etienne Rouillé, French music critic; b. Nantes, March 29, 1863; d. there, May 31, 1915. He publ.: *L'Œuvre théâtrale de Meyerbeer* (1893); *L'Evolution musicale chez Verdi* (1895); *Les Femmes dans l'œuvre de Richard Wagner* (1899); *Consonances et dissonances* (1906).

Deswert, Jules, Belgian cellist and composer; b. Louvain, Aug. 15, 1843; d. Ostend, Feb. 24, 1891. He studied with Servais at the Brussels Cons.; became a prof. at the Hochschule für Musik in Berlin (1869–73). He was in Leipzig in 1881, and in 1888 was appointed director of the Ostend Music School and a prof. at the Ghent and Bruges conservatories. He wrote 2 operas, *Die Albigenser* (Wiesbaden, Oct. 1, 1878) and *Graf Hammerstein* (Mainz, 1884); a symph., *Nordseefahrt;* 3 cello concertos; romances, fantasias, duos, and solo pieces for cello.

Déthier, Edouard, Belgian violinist, brother of **Gaston-Marie Déthier;** b. Liège, April 25, 1886; d. New York, Feb. 19, 1962. He studied at the Liège Cons. (1895–1901); then at the Brussels Cons. (1901–2); subsequently taught there (1902–4). He settled in the U.S. in 1906, appearing in recitals with the principal orchs.; taught at the Inst. of Musical Art and at the Juilliard Graduate School.

Déthier, Gaston-Marie, Belgian organist, brother of **Edouard Déthier;** b. Liège, April 18, 1875; d. New York, May 26, 1958. He studied at the Liège Cons. and later with Guilmant in Paris; came to the U.S. in 1894; was organist at St. Francis Xavier's, N.Y.; taught at the Inst. of Musical Art; in 1915, gave a series of successful sonata recitals as a pianist, with his brother playing violin.

Detoni, Dubravko, Croatian pianist and composer; b. Križevci, Feb. 22, 1937. He graduated in piano from the Zagreb Academy of Music in 1960; studied with Alfred Cortot in Siena (1960–61); then took lessons in composition with Šulek at the Zagreb Academy, graduating in 1965; had advanced studies with Bacewicz and Lutoslawski at the experimental studio of the Polish Radio in Warsaw (1966–67) and with Stockhausen and Ligeti in Darmstadt. He was the founder and artistic leader of ACEZANTEZ, the Ensemble of the Center for New Tendencies in Zagreb. His music rejects all established formulas and seeks new conceptions in sound through serial, aleatory, and musical-theater resources.

WORKS: *Passacaglia* for 2 Pianos and Strings (1962); *Musica a cinque* for Orch. (1962); *Tri koralne predigre* for Piano (1963); *Preobrazbe (Transfigurations)* for Orch. (1963; Zagreb, June 7, 1965); *Dramatski prolog* for Orch. (1965); *Quatorze moments dodécaphoniques* for Piano (1966); *Stravaganze* for Wind Quintet (1966); *Likovi i plohe (Forms and Surfaces)* for Chamber Orch. (1967; Graz, Austria, Sept. 26, 1968); *Phonomorphia 1* for Electronic and Concrete Sounds (1967), *2* for Piano and Tape (1968), and *3* for Voices, Instrumental Ensemble, and Tape (1969); *Šifre* for Piano and 4 Loudspeakers (1967); *Grafika I* for Organ (1968), *II* for Chamber Ensemble (1968), *III* for Vocal Ensemble, 6 Flutes, Ondes Martenot, Organ, and Piano (1969), *IV* for ad libitum Chamber Ensemble (1971), and *V,* instrumental "theater" for Chamber Ensemble (1972; Graz, Oct. 14, 1973); *Assonanze No. 1* for Cello and Piano (1968); *Assonanze No. 2* for Cello and Orch. (1971); *Elucubrations* for Piano and Orch. (1969; Zagreb, Jan. 7, 1970); *Forte-Piano, Arpa, Crescendo* for 2 Pianos and Percussion (1969); *Notturni* for 4 Vocal Groups, 4 Instrumental Ensembles, Organ, and Tape (1970); *d,* scene for Harpsichord and Electronic Instruments (1971); *Einflüsse* for 2 Cellos and Orch. (1971); *Monos 1–3,* cycle for variable orchestration (1970–72); *Music, or Tract about the Superfluous* for Narrating Actor, Organ, Piano, Percussion, Clarinet, and Orch. (1973); *Fable,* synthetic music (1973); *10 Beginnings* for String Quartet (1973); *Dokument 75* for Chamber Ensemble (1975); *Fragment 75* for Chamber Ensemble (Graz, Oct. 11, 1975).

Dett, R(obert) Nathaniel, distinguished black composer, conductor, and anthologist; b. Drummondville, Quebec, Canada, Oct. 11, 1882; d. Battle Creek, Mich., Oct. 2, 1943. He came from a musical family; both his parents were amateur pianists and singers. In 1893 the family moved to Niagara Falls, N.Y.; Dett studied piano with local teachers. He earned his living by playing at various clubs and hotels; then enrolled at the Oberlin (Ohio) Cons., where he studied piano with Howard Handel Carter and theory of composition with Arthur E. Heacox and George Carl Hastings, obtaining his B.Mus. in 1908. He also conducted a school choir; eventually, choral conducting became his principal profession. Upon graduation he occupied various teaching jobs, at Lane College in Jackson, Tenn. (1908–11), the Lincoln Inst. in Jefferson, Mo. (1911–13), the Hampton Inst. in Virginia (1913–32), and Bennett College in Greensboro, N.C. (1937–42). Concerned about his lack of technical knowledge in music, he continued taking courses, mostly during summers, when he was not engaged in teaching and choral conducting; he took lessons with Karl Gehrkens at Oberlin in 1913; attended classes at Columbia Univ., the American Cons. of Music in Chicago, Northwestern Univ., the Univ. of Pa., and, during the academic year 1919–20, Harvard Univ., where he studied composition with Arthur Foote. In the summer of 1929, at the age of 47, he went to France to study with Nadia Boulanger at the American Cons. in Fontainebleau; during the year 1931–32 he attended the Eastman School of Music in Rochester, N.Y., obtaining his M.Mus. in 1932. In the meantime he developed the artistic skills of the Hampton Choir, which toured in Europe in 1930 with excellent success, receiving encomiums in England, France, Belgium, the Netherlands, Germany, and Switzerland. He also periodically led his choir on the radio; in 1943 he became a musical adviser for the USO, and worked with the WAC (Women's Army Corps) on service duty at Battle Creek, where he died. His dominating interest was in cultivating Negro music, arranging Negro spirituals, and publishing collections of Negro folk songs. All of his works were inspired by black melos and rhythms; some of his piano pieces in Negro idiom became quite popular, among them, the suite *Magnolia* (1912); *In the Bottoms* (1913), which contained the rousing *Juba Dance;* and *Enchantment* (1922). He also wrote a number of choral pieces, mostly on biblical themes, such as his oratorios *The Chariot Jubilee* (1921) and *The Ordering of Moses* (Cincinnati, May 7, 1937). His choruses *Listen to the lambs, I'll never turn back no more,* and *Don't be weary, traveler,* became standard pieces of the choral repertoire. He publ. the anthologies *Religious Folk Songs of the Negro* (1926) and *The Dett Collection of Negro Spirituals* (4 vols., 1936). His piano compositions were reprinted in 1973 in Evanston, Ill., with introductory articles by Dominique-René de Lerma and Vivian McBrier.

BIBLIOGRAPHY: W.F. McBrier, *R. Nathaniel Dett, His Life and Works* (Washington, D.C., 1977); *Biographical Dictionary of Afro-American and African Musicians,* ed. by Eileen Southern (Westport, Conn., 1982); M. Stanley, "R.N. Dett of Hampton Institute" (*Musical America,* July 1918); R. Nathaniel Dett, "From Bell Stand to Throne Room" (*Etude,* Feb. 1934).

Dettmer, Roger (Christian), American music critic; b. Cincinnati, Aug. 2, 1927. He practiced piano, clarinet, and drums before puberty; precociously produced, directed, and starred in a school pageant-drama at 10; then took up music seriously at the Univ. of Cincinnati (1945–47), Columbia Univ. (1948), and the Univ. of Michigan (B.A., 1950); also studied composition privately with Vittorio Giannini. He composed sundry pieces for piano and other instruments, mostly in B-flat major, but destroyed the MSS. Relieved of the composing itch, he engaged in musical journalism. He was music editor of *Chicago Today* (1969–74); also contributed articles to various European publications.

Deutekom, Cristina, Dutch soprano; b. Amsterdam, Aug. 28, 1932. She was educated in Amsterdam; sang with the Netherlands Opera; also appeared in Munich, Hamburg, Vienna, London, and Milan. She made her American debut at the Metropolitan Opera in N.Y., as the Queen of the Night in *Die Zauberflöte,* on Sept. 28, 1967; also appeared in concerts. She was acknowledged as one of the finest coloratura sopranos of her generation.

Deutsch, Max, Austrian-born French composer, conductor, and pedagogue; b. Vienna, Nov. 17, 1892; d. Paris, Nov. 22, 1982. He studied composition privately with Schoenberg; also took courses at the Univ. of Vienna. He began his career by conducting operetta in Vienna; in 1923 he went to Berlin, where he organized his own orch. group concentrating mainly on modern music, emulating Schoenberg's Society for Private Performances of Vienna. In 1925 he settled in Paris, where he founded a Jewish theatrical ensemble, Der Jiddische Spiegel; also conducted concerts of modern music. From 1933–35 he was in Madrid, where he was in charge of a film enterprise; in 1939 he went to France; served in the Foreign Legion until 1945; then returned to Paris, where he devoted himself to teaching, using Schoenberg's method. In 1960 he founded the Grands Concerts de la Sorbonne. In his own compositions, he pursued novel ideas; he was the first to write a complete film symph., in 5 movements, for the production of the German motion picture *Der Schutz* (1923); he furthermore composed 2 symphs. and a choral symph., *Prière pour nos autres mortels,* after the text of Charles Peguy.

Deutsch, Otto Erich, eminent Austrian musicologist; b. Vienna, Sept. 5, 1883; d. there, Nov. 23, 1967. He studied literature and the history of art at the univs. of Vienna and Graz; was the art critic of Vienna's *Die Zeit* (1908–9); then served as an assistant at the Kunsthistorisches Institut of the Univ. of Vienna (1909–12); later was a bookseller, and then music librarian of the important collection of Anthony van Hoboken in Vienna (1926–35); In 1939 he emigrated to England and settled in Cambridge; in 1947 he became a British subject, but returned to Vienna in 1951. A scholar of impeccable credentials, he was considered one of the foremost authorities on Handel, Mozart, and Schubert; his documentary biographies of these composers constitute primary sources; he was also responsible for initiating the critical edition of Mozart's letters, which he edited with W. Bauer and J. Eibl as *Mozart: Briefe und Aufzeichnungen* (7 vols., Kassel, 1962–75).

WRITINGS: *Schubert-Brevier* (Berlin, 1905); *Beethovens Beziehungen zu Graz* (Graz, 1907); *Franz Schubert: Die Dokumente seines Lebens und Schaffens* (in collaboration, first with L. Scheibler, then with W. Kahl and G. Kinsky), which was planned as a comprehensive work in 3 vols. containing all known documents, pictures, and other materials pertaining to Schubert, arranged in chronological order, with a thematic catalogue, but of which only 2 vols. were publ.: vol. III, *Sein Leben in Bildern* (Munich, 1913), and vol. II, part 1, *Die Dokumente Seines Lebens* (Munich, 1914; Eng. trans. by Eric Blom, titled *Schubert: A Documentary Biography*, London, 1946; American ed., titled *The Schubert Reader: A Life of Franz Schubert in Letters and Documents*, N.Y., 1947; a 2nd German ed., enlarged, publ. in the *Neue Ausgabe sämtlicher Werke* of Schubert, in 1964); *Franz Schuberts Briefe und Schriften* (Munich, 1919; in Eng., London, 1928; 4th German ed., Vienna, 1954); *Die historischen Bildnisse Franz Schuberts in getreuen Nachbildungen* (Vienna, 1922); *Die Originalausgaben von Schuberts Goethe-Liedern* (Vienna, 1926); *Franz Schubert: Tagebuch: Faksimile der Originalhandschrift* (Vienna, 1928); *Mozart und die Wiener Logen* (Vienna, 1932); *Leopold Mozarts Briefe an seine Tochter* (with B. Paumgartner; Salzburg, 1936); *Das Freihaustheater auf der Wieden 1787–1801* (Vienna, 1937); *Wolfgang Amadé Mozart: Verzeichnis aller meiner Werke. Faksimile der Handschrift mit dem Beiheft "Mozarts, Werkverzeichnis 1784–1791"* (Vienna, 1938; in Eng., 1956); *Schubert: Thematic Catalogue of All His Works in Chronological Order* (with D. Wakeling; London, 1951; in German as *Franz Schubert: Thematisches Verzeichnis seiner Werke*, publ. in the *Neue Ausgabe sämtlicher Werke* of Schubert in a revised ed., 1978); *Handel: A Documentary Biography* (N.Y., 1954; London, 1955); *Franz Schubert: Die Erinnerungen seiner Freunde* (Leipzig, 1957; in Eng., 1958); *Mozart: Die Dokumente seines Lebens* (Kassel, 1961; in Eng. as *Mozart: A Documentary Biography*, Palo Alto, Calif., 1965; 2nd ed., 1966; supplement, 1978); *Mozart und seine Welt in zeitgenössischen Bildern* (completed by M. Zenger, Kassel, 1961); also numerous articles on Mozart, Haydn, Beethoven, and others contributed to German, English, and American music publications. BIBLIOGRAPHY: *Otto Erich Deutsch zum 75. Geburtstag* (Vienna, 1958); W. Gerstenberg, J. LaRue, and W. Rehm, eds., *Festschrift Otto Erich Deutsch* (Kassel, 1963).

Devčić, Natko, Croatian composer; b. Glina, June 30, 1914. He studied piano and composition at the Zagreb Academy of Music, graduating in 1939; after the war he studied with Joseph Marx in Vienna (1949–50) and Jean Rivier in Paris (1953); attended courses led by Boulez at Darmstadt (summer 1965)

and researched the potentialities of electronic sound with Davidowsky at the Columbia-Princeton Electronic Studio in N.Y. (1966–67). His early works are based on folklore resources; later on, he experimented with advanced techniques.

WORKS: Opera, *Labinska vještica (The Witch of Labin;* Zagreb, Dec. 25, 1957); ballet, *Dia...* (Zagreb, May 20, 1971); *Scherzo* for Orch. (1936); *Nocturne* for Orch. (1941; revised 1956); *Istarska suite (Istrian Suite)* for Orch. (Zagreb, Dec. 8, 1948); Symph. (1953); *Balada* for Piano and Orch. (1953); Concertino for Violin and Chamber Orch. (1958); *Prolog* for Winds and Percussion (1965); *Fibula* for 2 Orchs. (Zagreb, May 12, 1967); Concerto for Voice, Ondes Martenot, and Chamber Ensemble (Graz, Austria, Oct. 23, 1969); *Panta rei (All Things Change,* a motto of Heraclitus) for Piano and Orch. (1973); *Entre nous* for Orch. (Zagreb, March 26, 1975); *Kantata o bezimenima (Cantata about a Nameless One)* for Chamber Chorus and 12 Instruments (1959); *Ševa (The Lark),* cantata (Zagreb, March 30, 1960); *Igra riječi (Play of Words)* for 2 Narrators, Chorus, Instrumental Ensemble, and Tape (1969; Zagreb, May 9, 1969); *8 Minutes* for Piano and Chamber Ensemble (1965); *Odrazi (Reflections)* for Chamber Ensemble (1965); *Micro-tune* for Viola and Piano (1971); *Sonata-Fantasy* for Piano (1940); *Koraci (Steps),* 5 movements for Piano (1962); *Micro-suite* for Piano (1965); *Structures transparentes* and *Structures volantes* for Solo Harp (1966, 1971); *Columbia 68* for Tape (1968). BIBLIOGRAPHY: K. Kovačević, *Hrvatski Kompozitori i Njihova Djela* (Zagreb, 1960).

Devienne, François, versatile French musician; b. Joinville, Haute-Marne, Jan. 31, 1759; d. in the insane asylum at Charenton, Sept. 5, 1803. A flutist and bassoonist, member of the band of the Gardes Suisses, bassoonist at the Théâtre de Monsieur (1789–1801), and a prof. at the Paris Cons. (from 1795), he was an extraordinarily prolific composer of peculiar importance from the impulse which he gave to perfecting the technique of wind instruments.

WORKS: 12 operas; many concerted pieces for various wind instruments, with orch.; overtures; concertos, quartets, trios, sonatas, etc., for flute, piano, and other instruments; *12 suites d'harmonies à 8 et 12 parties;* numerous romances, chansons, etc.; also a valuable *Méthode de flûte* (Paris, 1795), which went through several editions. BIBLIOGRAPHY: W. Montgomery, *The Life and Works of François Devienne, 1759–1803* (Diss., Catholic Univ. of America, 1975).

De Vito, Gioconda, Italian violinist; b. Martina Franca (Lecce), July 26, 1907. She studied at the Liceo Musicale in Pesaro, graduating in 1921; then taught at the Bari Cons.; made her debut with the London Phil. in 1948. In 1946–53 she gave concerts in England. She married David Bicknell, an English record company executive, in 1949.

Devlin, Michael, American baritone; b. Chicago,

Nov. 27, 1942. He studied at Louisiana State Univ. (B.Mus., 1965); also took vocal lessons with Norman Treigle and Daniel Ferro in Santa Fe; made his operatic debut as Spalanzani in *Les Contes d'Hoffmann* in 1963 with the New Orleans Opera; in 1979 sang the role of Don Giovanni at Covent Garden in London. He made his Metropolitan Opera debut in N.Y. in 1980 as Eugene Onegin, and was a visiting artist at the San Francisco Opera in 1983.

De Vocht, Lodewijk, Belgian conductor and composer; b. Antwerp, Sept. 21, 1887; d. 's Gravenzel, near Antwerp, March 27, 1977. He studied with Gilson and Mortelmans at the Royal Flemish Cons. in Antwerp; played the violin in the newly formed orch. of the Société des Concerts Nouveaux (1903) and became its conductor in 1921; conducted the choir of the Antwerp Cathedral (1912–50); for more than half a century led the Chorale Caecilia that he had founded (1915–68); also the Assoc. des Concerts of the Antwerp Cons. (1935–53); taught music at the Flemish Cons. (1921–53). His own compositions are in a Romantic style.
WORKS: 3 symphs. (No. 1, with Chorus, 1932); Violin Concerto (Antwerp, May 20, 1944); Cello Concerto (1955); Concerto for Recorder and Orch. (1957); *Primavera,* pastoral poem for Soprano, Tenor, Chorus, and Orch. (1963–65); *Scaldis aeterna,* cantata (1966); several symph. poems, among them *Sortilèges des bois;* Wind Trio (1955); *Tylliederen,* 7 ballads for Baritone, and Guitar or Piano (1968); *Suite champêtre* for Guitar (1971–73); many choruses; 2 piano sonatas; preludes and fugues for organ.

Devreese, Frédéric, Belgian conductor and composer, son of **Godefroid Devreese;** b. Amsterdam, June 2, 1929. He studied first at the Cons. in Malines, then took courses in composition from Poot and conducting from Defossez at the Brussels Cons.; subsequently studied with Pizzetti at the Santa Cecilia Academy in Rome (1952–55). Returning to Belgium, he became associated with Flemish Television, as program director.
WORKS: An opera that won the 1964 Prix Italia, *Willem van Saeftinghe* (Brussels TV, Sept. 28, 1964; first stage perf., Antwerp, Nov. 21, 1964); TV opera, *De vreemde ruiter* (1966); 2 ballets: *Mascarade* (1955; Aix-les-Bains, France, 1956) and *L'Amour de Don Juan* (1973); 3 piano concertos (1949, 1952, 1955–56); Violin Concerto (1951); Symph. (1953); *Mouvement lent* for String Orch. (1953); *Recitativo et Allegro* for Trumpet and Orch. (1959); *Mouvement vif* for String Orch. (1963); *Evocation,* suite for Orch. (1967); Divertimento for String Orch. (1970); *Complainte* for Cello or Oboe, and Piano (1951); Quintet for Flute, Clarinet, Bassoon, Piano, and Percussion (1957); *Ensorbeelden,* suite for Brass Quintet (1972).

Devreese, Godefroid, Belgian conductor and composer; b. Kortrijk, Jan. 22, 1893; d. Brussels, June 4, 1972. He studied at the Brussels Cons. with Ysaÿe and César Thompson (violin) and Rasse and Gilson (composition); was a conductor of the Antwerp Opera (1919–20); a violinist with the Concertgebouw Orch. in Amsterdam (1925–30); director of the Cons. of Malines (1930–58), concurrently giving courses at the Brussels Cons. (1944–59).
WORKS: Ballet, *Tombelène* (1927); *Poème héroïque* for Orch. (1923); *Symphonic Variations on a Popular Scottish Theme* (1923); Concertino for Cello and Chamber Orch. (1926); *In memoriam* for Orch. (1928); 2 violin concertos (1936, 1970); Piano Concerto (1938); 4 symphs.: No. 1, *Gothique* (1944); No. 2, *Goethe,* with Chorus (1952); No. 3, *Sinfonietta* (1962); No. 4 (1965–66); Rhapsodie for Clarinet and Orch. (1948); *Allegro* for Trumpet and Orch. (1950); Suite for Orch. (1953); Sinfonietta for String Orch. (1962); *6 Variations on a Popular Theme* for String Orch. (1963); *Capriccio* for Violin and String Orch. (1963); *Stabat Mater* for Soprano, Chorus, and Orch. (1965); *Te Deum* for Chorus and Orch. (1967; posthumous, Brussels, March 30, 1973); Violin Sonata (1924); Cello Sonata (1926); String Quartet (1937); Piano Trio (1950); *Scherzo de concert* for Piano (1921); *Danse lente* for Piano (1924); 7 piano sonatinas (1944–45); Piano Sonata (1945); songs.

Devrient, Eduard, German writer on musical subjects; b. Berlin, Aug. 11, 1801; d. Karlsruhe, Oct. 4, 1877. He studied singing and thorough-bass with Zelter; gave his first public performance as a baritone in 1819; then joined the Royal Opera, but after the loss of his voice (1834) went over to the spoken drama, without losing his interest in music. He sang the role of Christ in the famous performance of Bach's *St. Matthew Passion* under Mendelssohn on March 11, 1829; was chief producer and actor at the Dresden Court Theater (1844–46) and director at the Karlsruhe Court Theater (1852–70); he was the author of the text to Marschner's *Hans Heiling,* and also created the title role (1833). His chief work is *Geschichte der deutschen Schauspielkunst* (5 vols., 1848–74); his works concerning music are *Briefe aus Paris* (1840, about Cherubini) and *Meine Erinnerungen an Felix Mendelssohn-Bartholdy und seine Briefe an mich* (Leipzig, 1869). Within weeks after publication of the latter, Wagner issued a polemical pamphlet entitled *Herr Eduard Devrient und sein Styl* (Munich, 1869) under the pseudonym Wilhelm Drach, violently attacking Devrient for his literary style. Devrient's book was publ. in Eng. in the same year (London, 1869; 3rd ed., 1891).
BIBLIOGRAPHY: J. Bab, *Die Devrients* (Berlin, 1932).

Devries, Herman, American bass; b. New York, Dec. 25, 1858; d. Chicago, Aug. 24, 1949. He studied in Paris; in 1879, made his debut at the Paris Opéra as the Grand Inquisitor in *L'Africaine;* in 1880–88, was at the Opéra-Comique; then appeared in Brussels, Marseilles, Aix-les-Bains, and Vichy; made his debut at the Metropolitan Opera on Dec. 17, 1898, appearing through that season; established his own studio in Chicago in 1900. He was music critic of the *Chicago American;* composed various songs and several pieces for piano and orch.

Deyo, Felix, American composer and pianist; b. Poughkeepsie, N.Y., April 21, 1888; d. Baldwin, N.Y., June 21, 1959. He studied piano with his mother, **Mary Forster Deyo** (1857–1947); then at the Brooklyn Cons. of Music; after graduation, he taught there (1911–39). In 1939 he became director of the Baldwin (Long Island) Cons. of Music; wrote 3 symphs.: *A Lyric Symphony* (Babylon, Long Island, Dec. 8, 1949); *An Ancient Symphony; A Primeval Symphony;* also 2 piano sonatas, a Violin Sonata, and numerous piano pieces of a programmatic nature (*Flight of the Dodo Bird,* etc.). His wife, **Asta Nygren Deyo** (1898–1953), was a piano teacher.

Deyo, Ruth Lynda, American pianist (second cousin of **Felix Deyo**); b. Poughkeepsie, N.Y., April 20, 1884; d. Cairo, March 4, 1960. She studied piano with William Mason and Teresa Carreño; composition with MacDowell; made her debut at the age of 9 at the World's Columbian Exposition in Chicago (1893); made her concert debut in Berlin (March 23, 1904); subsequently played with major orchs. in the U.S. and in Europe; appeared in recitals with Kreisler and Casals. In 1925 she settled in Egypt and devoted herself mainly to composition. In 1930 she completed the full score of a large opera on Egyptian themes, *The Diadem of Stars* (libretto by her husband, Charles Dalton; unperf.). The Prelude to this opera was performed by Stokowski with the Philadelphia Orch. (April 4, 1931).

Dezède (Deziades, De Zaides), Nicolas, opera composer; b. in Slovenia, c.1740; d. Paris, Sept. 11, 1792. He was active in Paris, where over 15 of his stage works were produced, including *Julie* (1772), *Le Stratagème découvert* (1773), *Cécile* (1781), *Blaise et Babet* (1783), *Alexis et Justine* (1785), and *Alcindor* (1787). The overture of his opera *Blaise et Babet* and a Finale for Piano figured frequently on early American concert programs.
BIBLIOGRAPHY: O.G. Sonneck, *Early Concert-Life in America,* Leipzig, 1907; A. Pougin, *Dezède* (Paris, 1862).

D'Hoedt, Henri-Georges, Belgian composer; b. Ghent, June 28, 1885; d. Brussels, May 14, 1936. He was a student of Emile Mathieu and Leo Moeremans; became director of the Cons. at Louvain in 1924, serving until his death. He was one of the first Belgian composers to depart from late-19th-century Romanticism and come under the influence of French Impressionism.
WORKS: Opera, *Klaas au Pays de Cocagne* (*Klaas in t'Luilekkerland;* Antwerp, 1926); satirical symph. study, *Les Brèves Chroniques de la vie bourgeoise* (1934); *Narcisse* for Orch.; *L'Ile de Cythère* for Chorus and Orch.; *La Vocation de Siddartha,* symph. trilogy; *Dionysos,* symph. poem; *Poème pantagruélique* for Orch.; chamber music.

Diabelli, Anton, Austrian composer and publisher; b. Mattsee, near Salzburg, Sept. 5, 1781; d. Vienna, April 8, 1858. He was a choirboy in the monastery at Michaelbeurn, and at Salzburg Cathedral; studied for the priesthood at the Munich Latin School, but continued his musical work, submitting his compositions to Michael Haydn, who encouraged him. On the secularization of the Bavarian monasteries, Diabelli, who had already entered that at Raichenhaslach, embraced the career of a musician, went to Vienna (where Joseph Haydn received him kindly), taught piano and guitar for a living, and in 1818 became a partner of Cappi, the music publisher, assuming control of the firm (Diabelli & Co.) in 1824. He publ. much of Schubert's music, but underpaid the composer, and complained that he wrote too much. In 1852 he sold his firm to C.A. Spina. A facile composer, Diabelli produced an opera, *Adam in der Klemme* (Vienna, 1809; one perf.), masses, cantatas, chamber music, etc., which were consigned to oblivion; his sonatinas are still used for beginners. His name was immortalized through Beethoven's set of 33 variations (op. 120) on a waltz theme by Diabelli.

Diack, John Michael, British vocal pedagogue; b. Glasgow, June 26, 1869; d. London, Feb. 2, 1946. He lived in London as head of the publishing house of Paterson Sons & Co.; publ. valuable pedagogic works: *Vocal Exercises on Tone-Placing and Enunciation* (1920); *Song Studies* (1920); *Five Minutes Daily Exercises on Vocal Technique* (Glasgow, 1920); *Tone Color and Interpretation* (1926); edited *New Scottish Orpheus* (2 vols.; 200 songs); *The Burns Song Book* (50 songs); and choral works of Bach and Handel.

Diaghilev, Sergei, creator and director of the famous Russian Ballet; b. Gruzino, Novgorod district, March 31, 1872; d. Venice, Aug. 19, 1929. He was associated with progressive artistic organizations in St. Petersburg, but his main field of activity was in western Europe. He established the Ballets Russes in Paris; he commissioned Stravinsky to write the ballets *The Firebird, Petrouchka,* and *Le Sacre du Printemps;* also commissioned Prokofiev, Milhaud, Poulenc, Auric, and other composers of the younger generation. Ravel and Manuel de Falla also wrote works for Diaghilev. The great importance of Diaghilev's choreographic ideas lies in the complete abandonment of the classical tradition; in this respect Diaghilev was the true originator of the modern dance.
BIBLIOGRAPHY: Diaghilev issue of *La Revue Musicale* (Dec. 1930); *The Russian Ballet* (London, 1931); C.W. Beaumont, *Sergei Diaghilev* (London, 1933); A.L. Haskell, *Diaghilev, His Artistic and Private Life* (London, 1935); V. Kamenev, *Russian Ballet through Russian Eyes* (London, 1936); Serge Lifar, *Serge Diaghilev: His Life, His Work, His Legend* (London, 1940); C.W. Beaumont, *The Diaghilev Ballet in London, A Personal Record* (London, 1940); S.L. Grigoriev, *The Diaghilev Ballet* (London, 1953); Richard Buehle, *In Search of Diaghilev* (N.Y., 1956); Boris Kochno, *Diaghilev and the Ballets Russes* (N.Y., 1970); R. Buckle, *Diaghilev* (N.Y., 1979).

Diamond, David, outstanding American composer; b. Rochester, N.Y., July 9, 1915. He studied composition with Bernard Rogers at the Eastman School of Music in his hometown (1930–34); then took courses with Roger Sessions in N.Y. In 1936 he went to Paris, where he studied with Nadia Boulanger and became associated with the most important musicians and writers of the time. Returning to N.Y., he devoted his time exclusively to composition; various grants and awards enabled him to continue his work in relative financial prosperity. He received the Juilliard Publication Award for his *Psalm* (1937), 3 Guggenheim fellowships (1938, 1941, 1958), an American Academy in Rome award (1942), the Paderewski Prize (1943), and a grant of $1,000 from the National Academy of Arts and Letters (1944). In 1965–67 he taught at the Manhattan School of Music, and in 1973 joined the faculty at the Juilliard School of Music. His early music is marked by a great complexity of harmonic writing, with the sense of tonality clearly present; the element of rhythm, often inspired by natural folklike patterns, is very strong in all of his works. In his later symphs. he adopted a modified dodecaphonic method of composition, while keeping free of doctrinaire serialism. His instrumental and vocal writing is invariably idiomatic, which makes his music welcome to performers and audiences alike.

WORKS: FOR ORCH.: 8 symphs.: No. 1 (N.Y., Dec. 21, 1941); No. 2 (Boston, Oct. 13, 1944); No. 3 (1945; Boston, Nov. 3, 1950); No. 4 (Boston, Jan. 23, 1948); No. 5 (1947–64; N.Y., April 28, 1966); No. 6 (Boston, March 8, 1957); No. 7 (N.Y., Jan. 26, 1962); No. 8 (N.Y., Oct. 26, 1961, prior to Symph. No. 7); *To Music,* choral symph. for Soloists, Chorus, and Orch. (1967); 3 violin concertos: No. 1 (N.Y., March 24, 1937); No. 2 (Vancouver, Feb. 29, 1948); No. 3 (N.Y., April 1, 1976); *Hommage à Satie* (1934); *Threnody* (1935); *Psalm* for Orch. (Rochester, Dec. 10, 1936); first suite from the ballet *Tom* (1936); *Variations on an Original Theme* (1937; Rochester, April 23, 1940); *Elegy in Memory of Maurice Ravel* for Brass, Harp, and Percussion (Rochester, April 28, 1938); *Heroic Piece* (Zürich, July 29, 1938); Cello Concerto (1938; Rochester, April 30, 1942); *Concert Piece* (N.Y., May 16, 1940); Concerto for Chamber Orch. (Yaddo, N.Y., Sept. 7, 1940, composer conducting); *Rounds* for String Orch. (Minneapolis, Nov. 24, 1944; his most successful work); *Romeo and Juliet* (N.Y., Oct. 20, 1947); *The Enormous Room,* after e.e. cummings (Cincinnati, Nov. 19, 1949); *Timon of Athens,* symph. portrait after Shakespeare (Louisville, 1949); Piano Concerto (1949; N.Y., April 28, 1966); *Ahavah* for Narrator and Orch. (Washington, D.C., Nov. 17, 1954); *Diaphony* for Brass, 2 Pianos, Timpani, and Organ (N.Y., Feb. 22, 1956); *Sinfonia concertante* (Rochester, March 7, 1957); *World of Paul Klee,* orch. suite (Portland, Oreg., Feb. 15, 1958); *Music for Chamber Orch.* (1969); *A Buoyant Music,* overture No. 2 (1970). CHAMBER MUSIC: Partita for Oboe, Bassoon, and Piano (1935); Concerto for String Quartet (1937); String Trio (1937); Quintet for Flute, String Trio, and Piano (1937); Piano Quartet (1938); Cello Sonata (1938); 10 string quartets (1940, 1943, 1946, 1951, 1960, 1962, 1963, 1964, 1966–68, 1966); Violin Sonata (1945); *Canticle for Perpetual Motion* for Violin and Piano (1947); Chaconne for Violin and Piano (1947); Quintet for Clarinet, 2 Violas, and 2 Cellos (1951); Piano Trio (1951); Nonet for 3 Violins, 3 Violas, and 3 Cellos (1962). VOCAL MUSIC: *This is the Garden,* Chorus a cappella (1935); *3 Madrigals,* after James Joyce, for Chorus a cappella (1937); *Young Joseph,* after Thomas Mann, for Women's Chorus and String Orch. (1944); *L'Ame de Claude Debussy,* extracts from Debussy's letters to Jacques Durand (1949); *The Midnight Meditation,* cycle of 4 songs (1950); *This Sacred Ground* for Chorus, Male Voice, and Orch. (Buffalo, Nov. 17, 1963); *A Secular Cantata,* to texts from James Agee's *Permit Me Voyage* (N.Y., Feb. 5, 1977). FOR PIANO: Sonatina (1935); Concerto for 2 Pianos (1941); *Album for the Young* (1946); Sonata (1947).

Diamond, Neil (Leslie), enormously popular American singer and songwriter; b. New York, Jan. 24, 1941. After a brief interlude as a medical student in N.Y., he plunged into the nightclubs of N.Y., singing his own songs with subtly sexual undertones and overtones, *Solitary Man, I Got the Feelin', Kentucky Woman, I'm a Believer,* and *I Am, I Said.* His recording albums, such as *Hot August Night, Jonathan Livingston Seagull, Beautiful Noise,* etc. hit the populace with inexplicable impact; soon he rose to a high plateau in the world of commercial music; his concerts began to attract mobs of plebs in quest of easy thrills, and the wave of success never abated as he, still unmellowed, reached his middle age.

Dianda, Hilda, Argentinian composer; b. Córdoba, April 13, 1925. She studied in Europe with Scherchen and Malipiero; in 1958–62 worked at Radiodiffusion Française in Paris. Upon returning to Argentina, she devoted herself to composition and organization of concerts of ultramodern music.

WORKS: 3 string quartets (1947, 1960, 1962); Concertante for Cello and Chamber Orch. (1952); Trio for Flute, Oboe, and Bassoon (1953); Wind Quintet (1957); *Díptico* for 16 Instruments (1962); *Núcleos* for String Orch., 2 Pianos, and Percussion (1964); works for various ensembles under the generic titles *Resonancias* and *Ludus* (1964–69).

Dianin, Sergei, Russian writer on music; b. St. Petersburg, Dec. 26, 1888; d. in the village of Davidovo, Vladimir district, Oct. 26, 1968. A son of Borodin's assistant in chemistry, he became a mathematician by profession; having access to Borodin's archives, he publ. 4 vols. of Borodin's letters (Moscow, 1928, 1936, 1949, 1950) and a biography, *Borodin, Life, Materials, Documents* (Moscow, 1955; 2nd ed., 1960; in Eng., London, 1963).

Dianov, Anton, Russian composer; b. Moscow, Feb. 19, 1882; d. there, March 25, 1939. He was a pupil of the Moscow Cons., graduating in 1912; in 1920 became director of the Music School in Moscow. He wrote effective piano pieces, music for violin and piano (*Lyrische Fragmente*), and many songs.

Diaz (de la Peña), Eugène (-Emile), French composer, son of the celebrated painter; b. Paris, Feb. 27, 1837; d. Coleville, Sept. 12, 1901. He was a pupil at the Paris Cons., studying with Halévy and Reber; produced the comic opera *Le Roi Candaule* (Paris, 1865) and won the government prize for the opera *La Coupe du roi de Thulé* (Paris, Jan. 10, 1873), which, however, proved a complete failure.
BIBLIOGRAPHY: A. Jullien, *Airs variés* (Paris, 1877; pp. 202–10).

Diaz, Justino, Puerto Rican bass; b. San Juan, Jan. 29, 1940. He received his primary training in Puerto Rico; then enrolled at the New England Cons. of Music in Boston, and sang with the New England Opera Theater. On Oct. 23, 1963, he made his Metropolitan Opera debut in N.Y. as Monterone in *Rigoletto;* in 1966 he created there the role of Antony in Samuel Barber's *Antony and Cleopatra.*

Diaz, Rafaelo, American tenor; b. (of Spanish-American parents) San Antonio, Texas, 1884; d. New York, Dec. 12, 1943. He studied music in Berlin, voice in Italy; made his opera debut with the Boston Opera Co., Dec. 6, 1911; was a member of the Metropolitan Opera Co. in 1918–36; then sang mostly in concerts.

Dibdin, Charles, English composer; b. Dibdin, near Southampton (baptized, March 4), 1745; d. London, July 25, 1814. In 1756–59 he was a chorister at Winchester Cathedral; took lessons there from Kent and Fussell, but was chiefly self-taught in composition; at 15 went to London; was engaged at Covent Garden as a singing actor, and soon began to write for the stage. His first piece, *The Shepherd's Artifice,* was produced at his benefit performance, at Covent Garden, on May 21, 1764. He was engaged at Birmingham in 1763–65, and at Covent Garden again till 1768, when he went over to Drury Lane. Falling out with Garrick, he went to France in 1776 to avoid imprisonment for debt, remaining there until 1778, when he was appointed composer to Covent Garden, having up to that time brought out 8 operas. In 1782–84, he was manager of the newly erected Royal Circus (later the Surrey Theatre). After the failure of certain theatrical enterprises, and a projected journey to India, he commenced a series of monodramatic "table-entertainments," of which song was a principal feature, and which were extremely popular from 1789 to 1805; in these Dibdin appeared as author, composer, narrator, singer, and accompanist. He then built and managed a small theater of his own, which opened in 1796; he retired in 1805 on a pension, which was withdrawn for a time, but subsequently restored. Dibdin also composed numerous sea songs which were very popular at the time. He publ. *The Musical Tour of Mr. Dibdin* (1788), *History of the Stage* (5 vols., 1795), *The Professional Life of Mr. Dibdin* (4 vols., 1803), and various novels. His grandson, **Henry Edward Dibdin** (b. London, Sept. 8, 1813; d. Edinburgh, May 6, 1866), was an organist, harpist, and teacher who compiled the collection *The Standard Psalm Tune Book* (1851).
BIBLIOGRAPHY: E.R. Dibdin, *A Charles Dibdin Bibliography* (Liverpool, 1937); E. Holmes, *Charles Dibdin* (Diss., Univ. of Southampton, 1974).

di Bonaventura, Anthony and **Mario.** See **Bonaventura.**

Di Capua, Eduardo, Italian composer of Neapolitan ballads; b. Naples, 1864; d. there, 1917. He earned his living by playing in small theaters and cafés in and around Naples, and later in the cinemas; also gave piano lessons. His most famous song was *O sole mio* (1898); its popularity was immense, and never abated. Other celebrated songs were *Maria Marì* (1899); *Torna maggio* (1900); *Canzona bella;* etc. Di Capua sold these songs to publishers outright, and so did not benefit by their popularity. He died in extreme poverty.

Dichter, Misha, talented American pianist; b. Shanghai, of Polish-Jewish refugees, Sept. 27, 1945. He was reared in Los Angeles; at the age of 15 he won a contest of the Music Educators National Conference, Western Division. While attending the Univ. of Calif. at Los Angeles, he enrolled in a master class conducted by Rosina Lhévinne; later joined her class at the Juilliard School of Music in N.Y. In 1966 he entered the International Tchaikovsky Competition in Moscow and won 2nd prize, scoring popular acclaim among Russian audiences. Returning to the U.S., he made his Boston Symph. Orch. debut as soloist at the Tanglewood Festival in 1966; numerous appearances with major American and European orchs. followed; he also gave recitals. His wife, **Cipa** (b. Rio de Janeiro, May 20, 1944), is a fine pianist in her own right; they frequently appear together in duo recitals. Dichter's natural predilections lie in the Romantic repertoire; his playing possesses a high emotional appeal; but he also can render full justice to Classical masterpieces, as demonstrated by his appropriate rendition of Mozart's concertos.

Dick, Marcel, Hungarian-American violinist and composer; b. Miskolcz, Hungary, Aug. 28, 1898. He came from a musical family; the famous Hungarian violinist **Eduard Reményi** was his great-uncle. Dick studied violin with Joseph Bloch and composition with Kodály. He was first violist in the Vienna Symph. Orch. (1924–27), and was also a member of the Kolisch Quartet and of the Rosé Quartet. In 1934 he went to the U.S.; was first violist of the Cleveland Orch. (1943–49); in 1948 was appointed head of the dept. of theory of the Cleveland Inst. of Music; he retired in 1973. He wrote a Symph. (Cleveland, Dec. 14, 1950) and a Symph. for 2 String Orchs. (1964); also some chamber music and songs.

Dickenson, Victor ("Vic"), black American jazz trombonist; b. Xenia, Ohio, Aug. 6, 1906. He learned to handle the trombone; played with Blanche Calloway (1933–36), Benny Carter (1939), Count Basie

(1940–41), and Sidney Bechet (1941). In 1949 he formed his own band, and appeared at the major U.S. jazz festivals.

Dickie, Murray, Scottish tenor; b. Bishopton, April 3, 1924. He received his musical training in Glasgow and London. He sang in London at Covent Garden and in Milan at La Scala; eventually became a member of the Vienna State Opera. On Oct. 18, 1962, he made his debut at the Metropolitan Opera in N.Y. as David in *Die Meistersinger von Nürnberg.*

Dickinson, Clarence, American composer; b. Lafayette, Ind., May 7, 1873; d. New York, Aug. 2, 1969. He studied music with Weidig in Chicago; then went to Germany, where he took courses with Riemann; further had piano lessons with Moszkowski; he moved to Paris, where he became a pupil of Guilmant in organ playing and with Pierné in composition. Returning to America in 1909, he settled in N.Y. as a church organist; in 1912–45 he served as director of sacred music at the Union Theological Seminary; also made lecture tours in the U.S., Canada, France, England, and Spain. He composed the operas *The Medicine Man* and *Priscilla;* numerous organ pieces and songs; edited the collections *Historical Recitals for Organ* (50 numbers), *Book of 80 Amens,* and *Book of 40 Antiphons.* He also publ. *Excursions in Musical History* (1917); *Troubadour Songs* (1920); *Technique and Art of Organ Playing* (1921).

Dickinson, Edward, American music historian; b. West Springfield, Mass., Oct. 10, 1853; d. Oberlin, Ohio, Jan. 25, 1946. He studied organ with Eugene Thayer at the New England Cons.; also traveled to Germany and attended classes with Spitta in Berlin. In 1883–92 he was director of music at Elmira College; and in 1893 was appointed a prof. of music history at Oberlin College. He publ. *Music in the History of the Western Church* (1902); *The Study of the History of Music* (1905); *The Education of a Music Lover* (1911); *Music and the Higher Education* (1915); *The Spirit of Music* (1925).

Dickinson, George Sherman, American music educator; b. St. Paul, Minn., Feb. 9, 1888; d. Chapel Hill, N.C., Nov. 6, 1964. He studied at Oberlin College (B.A., 1909); at the Oberlin Cons. of Music (Mus.Bac., 1910); and at Harvard Univ. (M.A., 1912); also studied with Kaun and Juon in Berlin (1913–14). He taught at the Oberlin Cons. in 1914–16, and was a member of the faculty of Vassar College in 1922–53. He wrote *The Growth and Use of Harmony* (vol. 4 of *Fundamentals of Musical Art;* N.Y., 1927); *Classification of Musical Compositions* (Poughkeepsie, 1938); *The Pattern of Music* (Poughkeepsie, 1939); *Music as a Literature: An Outline* (Poughkeepsie, 1953); *The Study of Music as a Liberal Art* (Poughkeepsie, 1953); *The Study of the History of Music in the Liberal Arts College* (N.Y., 1953); *A Handbook of Style in Music* (N.Y., 1965).

Dickinson, Helen Adell, Canadian-American author; b. Port Elmsley, Ontario, Canada, Dec. 5, 1875; d. Tucson, Ariz., Aug. 25, 1957. She studied at Queen's Univ. in Kingston, Canada (M.A., 1895), and at Heidelberg Univ. (Ph.D., 1901); in 1904 she married Clarence Dickinson. She publ. *Metrical Translation of 150 Ancient Carols* (1930); *A Book of Antiphons* (1919); *The Coming of the Prince of Peace: A Nativity Play of Ancient Christmas Carols* (1919); *A Treasury of Worship* (1926).

Dickinson, Peter, English composer; b. Lytham St. Annes, Lancashire, Nov. 15, 1934. Of a musical family, he studied piano and began to compose early in life. He entered Cambridge Univ.; after obtaining his M.A. degree in music there, he went to the U.S. on a Rotary Foundation fellowship, and studied with Bernard Wagenaar at the Juilliard School of Music in N.Y. (1958–60). Returning to England, he became a lecturer at the College of St. Mark and St. John in London (1962–66); then at the Univ. of Birmingham (1966–70). In 1973 he became a prof. at Keele Univ. In his music he combines the esoteric techniques of serialism with pragmatic considerations for performance.

WORKS: *Postlude on Adeste Fideles* for Organ (1954); *Jesus Christ Is Risen Today* for Chorus a cappella (1955); Sonatina for Flute and Piano (1955); *4 W.H. Auden Songs* for Voice and Piano (1956); Variations for Piano (1957); *5 Blake Songs* for Tenor, Horn, Clarinet, and Bassoon (1957); String Quartet (1958); *Air* for Solo Flute (1958); *Monologue* for String Orch. (1959); *A Dylan Thomas Song Cycle* for Baritone and Piano (1959); *Study in Pianissimo* for Organ (1959); Fantasia for Solo Violin (1959); *Vitalitas,* ballet (1960); Violin Sonata (1961); 4 Duos for Flute and Cello (1962); Trio for Flute, Oboe, and Harpsichord (1962); *5 Forgeries* for Piano Duet (1963); *5 Diversions* for Keyboard Instruments (1963); *Carillon* for Organ (1964); *The Judas Tree,* musical drama for Speakers, Singers, Chorus, and Chamber Orch. (London, May 27, 1965); *Outcry* for Chorus and Orch. (Leamington, May 10, 1969); *Diversions* for Small Orch. (Leamington, Nov. 23, 1969); *Transformations: Homage to Satie* for Orch. (Cheltenham, July 3, 1970); Organ Concerto (Gloucester Cathedral, Aug. 22, 1971); Concerto for Strings, Percussion, and Electronic Organ (Birmingham, Jan. 22, 1971).

BIBLIOGRAPHY: R. Norrington, "Peter Dickinson," *Musical Times* (Feb. 1965).

Diderot, Denis, illustrious projector and editor of the celebrated "Encyclopédie"; b. Langres, Oct. 5, 1713; d. Paris, July 30, 1784. In his work *Mémoirs sur différents sujets de mathématiques* (The Hague, 1748) are the essays "Des principes d'acoustique" and "Projet d'un nouvel orgue," the latter being an impracticable idea for a new kind of barrel organ.

Di Domenica, Robert, American composer and flutist; b. New York, March 4, 1927. He graduated in music education from N.Y. Univ. in 1951; then studied composition privately with Wallingford Riegger; also took flute lessons with Harold Bennett

(1949–55). He performed as a flutist with the Metropolitan Opera and various orch. groups, and also with the Modern Jazz Quintet. He taught flute privately in N.Y.; in 1969 he was appointed to the faculty of the New England Cons. in Boston; in 1976 became dean there.

WORKS: Opera, *The Balcony* (1972); Flute Sonata (1957); Sextet for Piano, Flute, Oboe, Clarinet, Horn, and Bassoon (1957); Piano Sonatina (1958); Quartet for Violin, Flute, Horn, and Piano (1959); *4 Movements* for Piano (1959); Quartet for Flute, Violin, Viola, and Cello (1960); *The First Kiss of Love* for Soprano and Piano (1960); String Quartet (1960); Symph. (1961; first complete perf., Boston, Nov. 15, 1972); *Variations on a Tonal Theme* for Solo Flute (1961); Concerto for Violin and Chamber Orch. (1962; N.Y., April 15, 1965); Wind Quintet (1969); Piano Concerto (1963); Concerto for Wind Quintet, Strings, and Timpani (1964); Quintet for Clarinet and String Quartet (1965); Trio for Flute, Bassoon, and Piano (1960); Violin Sonata (1966); *Saeculum Aureum* for Flute, Piano, and Tape (1967); *Music for Flute and String Orch.* (1967); Saxophone Sonata (1968); *11 Short Pieces* for Piano (1973); *Improvisations* for Piano (1974); *4 Short Songs* for Soprano, Flute, Clarinet, Violin, Viola, Cello, and Piano (1975); *Songs from 12th Night* for Tenor, Flute, Viola da Gamba, and Harpsichord (1976); *Black Poems* for Baritone, Piano, and Tape (1976).

Didur, Adamo, famous Polish bass; b. Wola Sekowa, near Sanok, Galicia, Dec. 24, 1874; d. Katowice, Jan. 7, 1946. He studied with Wysocki and Emerich; in 1894 made his operatic debut in Rio de Janeiro, thereafter appearing at the La Scala Opera in Milan, at the Warsaw Opera, in Moscow, St. Petersburg, Barcelona, Madrid, London, and Buenos Aires; in 1907–8 he appeared with the Manhattan Opera Co.; in 1908, made his debut as Méphistophélès at the Metropolitan Opera House, of which he was a leading member until 1932. After his retirement from the Metropolitan, he returned to Poland; eventually settled in Katowice, where he taught voice and founded an opera company; also served as director of the Katowice Academy of Music.

Didymus, grammarian of Alexandria; b. 63 b.c. The number of his works was estimated by Seneca at 4,000; he wrote a tract on music, now known only by an epitome of Porphyry's, and some quotations by Ptolemy. In his system the octave of the diatonic genus is formed by 2 precisely similar tetrachords, and in all 3 species of tetrachord (diatonic, chromatic, enharmonic) the ratio for the interval of the major third is 4:5. He also recognized the difference between the major and minor whole tone; this difference $(9/8 : 10/9 = 81:80)$ is, therefore, rightly termed the "comma of Didymus." Salinas and Doni have written on his musical system.

Diémer, Louis, distinguished French pianist; b. Paris, Feb. 14, 1843; d. there, Dec. 21, 1919. He was a pupil of Marmontel at the Paris Cons., where he took first piano prize in 1856; also of Ambroise Thomas and Bazin for composition, taking first harmony prize, 2d organ prize, and first prize for fugue. He played with great success at the Alard, Pasdeloup, and Paris Cons. concerts; succeeded Marmontel (1887) as prof. of piano at the Cons. The immense success of his series of historical recitals, in 1889, made him resolve to specialize in early music, and led to his establishing the Société des Anciens Instruments. Widor, Saint-Saëns, Lalo, and others wrote pieces for him which he played at the Colonne and Lamoureux concerts. He edited a number of old French keyboard pieces; his collection *Clavecinistes français* was publ. posthumously in 1928.

Dienel, Otto, German organist; b. Tiefenfurth, Silesia, Jan. 11, 1839; d. Berlin, March 7, 1905. He studied music in Berlin at the Royal Inst. for Church Music, and at the Royal Academy. He taught music, and was organist at the Marienkirche in Berlin. He wrote compositions for organ, and choruses; was the author of *Die moderne Orgel* (1889, 2nd ed., 1891).

Diepenbrock, Alphons, eminent Dutch composer; b. Amsterdam, Sept. 2, 1862; d. there, April 5, 1921. He learned to play violin and piano in his childhood. In 1880 he entered the Univ. of Amsterdam, where he studied classical philology; received his Ph.D. in 1888; taught academic subjects at the grammar school at 's-Hertogenbosch (1888–94); then abandoned his pedagogical activities and devoted himself primarily to music; studied works of the Flemish School of the Renaissance, and later perused the scores of Berlioz, Wagner, and Debussy. Despite this belated study, he succeeded in developing a rather striking individual style of composition, in which Wagnerian elements curiously intertwine with impressionistic modalities. However, he had difficulty in putting the results into definite shape, and he left more than 100 incomplete MSS at his death. His Catholic upbringing led him to concentrate mainly on the composition of sacred choral music; he wrote no symphs., concertos, or instrumental sonatas.

WORKS: *Stabat Mater* for Men's Chorus; *Missa in Die festo* for Tenor, Male Chorus, and Organ (1890–91); *Les Elfes* for Soprano, Baritone, Women's Chorus, and Orch. (1896); *Te Deum* for Soloists, Double Chorus, and Orch. (1897); 2 *Hymnen an die Nacht,* after Novalis, one each for Soprano and Contralto, with Orch. (1899); *Vondel's vaart naar Agrippine (Vondel's Journey to Agrippina)* for Baritone and Orch. (1902–3); *Im grossen Schweigen,* after Nietzsche, for Baritone and Orch. (Amsterdam, May 20, 1906); *Hymne aan Rembrandt* for Soprano, Women's Chorus, and Orch. (1906); incidental music to Verhagen's mythical comedy *Marsyas of De betooverde bron (Marsyas or The Enchanted Well;* 1909–10); *Die Nacht,* after Hölderlin, for Mezzo-Soprano and Orch. (1910–11); *Lydische Nacht* for Baritone and Orch. (1913); incidental music to Aristophanes' *The Birds* (1917; a concert overture from this music is fairly popular); incidental music to Goethe's *Faust* (1918); incidental music to Sophocles' *Electra* (1920); numerous choruses and songs. A collection of Diepenbrock's writings, *Verzamelde geschriften*, ed. by Eduard Reeser, was publ. in Utrecht (1950); a catalogue of his works was issued in Amsterdam in 1962. Eduard Reeser brought out *Brieven en documenten* (letters and documents of Diepenbrock; 2 vols., Amsterdam, 1962–67); he also wrote "Some Melodic Patterns in the Music of Alphons Diepenbrock," *Composers' Voice, 3* (1976/1; pp. 16–25).

Dieren, Bernard van, important composer and writer; b. Rotterdam, Dec. 27, 1884; d. London, April 24, 1936. After studying in Germany and the Netherlands, he settled in 1909 in London as music correspondent of the *Nieuwe Rotterdamsche Courant;* later devoted his time exclusively to composing. His works show radical tendencies.
WORKS: *6 Sketches* for Piano (1911); 4 string quartets (1912; 1917, perf. at the Donaueschingen Music Festival in 1920; 1919; 1923, perf. at the Frankfurt International Music Festival in 1925); Symph. for Soli, Chorus, and Orch. on Chinese texts (1914); *Diaphony* for Baritone and Chamber Orch., on 3 Shakespearean sonnets; *Overture to an Ideal Comedy* (1916); *Les Propous des Beuveurs*, introit for Orch. (after Rabelais; London, 1921); *Sonata Tyroica* for Violin and Piano (1927); many songs (also with string quartet and chamber orch.). He wrote a book on the modern sculptor Jacob Epstein (1920); and a collection of essays, *Down among the Dead Men* (London, 1935).
BIBLIOGRAPHY: E. Davis, "B. van Dieren," *Musical Quarterly* (April 1938); G. Grouse, "Bernard van Dieren—Three Early Songs in Relation to His Subsequent Development," *Music Review* (May 1968).

Diet, Edmond-Marie, French dramatic composer; b. Paris, Sept. 25, 1854; d. there, Oct. 30, 1924. He was a pupil of César Franck and Guiraud; produced the operas *Stratonice* (1887), *Le Cousin Placide* (1887), *Fleur de Vertu* (1894), *La Revanche d'Iris* (1905); also ballets and pantomimes: *Scientia* (1889); *La Grève; Masque rose; M. Ruy-Blas* (1894); *La Belle et la bête* (1895); *L'Araignée d'or* (1896); *Rêve de Noël* (1896); *Watteau* (1900; with Pujet); 3-act operetta, *Gentil Crampon* (Paris, 1897); songs; church music.

Diether, Jack, Canadian-American musicologist; b. Vancouver, British Columbia, Feb. 26, 1919. He was educated at the Univ. of British Columbia; served in the Canadian army and air force during World War II. In 1955 he settled in the U.S.; was employed at the Pickwick Bookshop in Hollywood and at G. Schirmer's music store in N.Y. In the meantime he wrote for music journals, concentrating on the clarification of obscure periods in the lives and works of Bruckner and Mahler; contributed valuable articles to the journal of the Bruckner Society of America, *Chord and Discord,* of which he became the editor in 1969; wrote annotations for orch. programs and for phonograph records. His valuable article "Notes on Some Mahler Juvenilia,"

Chord and Discord, 3/1 (1969), settles some moot questions regarding Mahler's early development.

Dietrich, Albert Hermann, German conductor; b. Forsthaus Golk, near Meissen, Aug. 28, 1829; d. Berlin, Nov. 19, 1908. He was a pupil of J. Otto in Dresden and of Moscheles and Rietz at Leipzig (1847–51); studied with Schumann (was one of Schumann's best pupils) at Düsseldorf (1851–54). In 1855–61 he was a concert conductor, and from 1859 municipal music director, at Bonn; from 1861, at Oldenburg; he retired in 1890 and lived in Berlin; was made Royal Prof. in 1899. He wrote *Erinnerungen an Johannes Brahms in Briefen, besonders aus seiner Jugendzeit* (Leipzig, 1898; in Eng., 1899).

Dietrich (or Dieterich), Sixtus, composer; b. Augsburg, c.1492–94; d. St. Gall, Switzerland, Oct. 21, 1548. He was a boy chorister at Constance in 1504–6; in 1508–9, studied in Freiburg; in 1517 was a choirmaster in Constance, becoming a priest in 1522; in 1540 and 1544 he was in Wittenberg. He was one of the most important early Protestant composers of sacred music. A book of Magnificats (1535) and 2 collections of antiphons *a* 4 (1541, 1545) were publ.; motets, songs, etc., are scattered through various German collections printed in 1536–68; 5 pieces are in Glareanus' *Dodecachordon* (1547). Reprints have been publ. in Denkmäler Deutscher Tonkunst, 34, and by H. Zenck (13 hymns).
BIBLIOGRAPHY: H. Zenck, *S. Dietrich, Ein Beitrag zur Musik und Musikanschauung im Zeitalter der Reformation* (Leipzig, 1928).

Dietsch, Pierre-Louis-Philippe, French conductor; b. Dijon, March 17, 1808; d. Paris, Feb. 20, 1865. He was a pupil of Choron at the Paris Cons.; in 1830 became maître de chapelle at St.-Eustache, and later at Ste.-Madeleine; in 1860–63 was conductor at the Paris Opéra; composed 25 masses and other sacred music. He would have been forgotten long ago were his name not connected with that of Wagner. In 1842 he brought out at the Opéra *Le Vaisseau fantôme*, written on Wagner's original sketch of *Der fliegende Holländer*, and in 1861 he conducted (most incompetently) the notorious 3 Paris performances of *Tannhäuser*. See references to Dietsch in Wagner's *Mein Leben* (vols. I and III).

Dietz, Howard, American lyricist; b. New York, Sept. 9, 1896; d. (of Parkinson's disease) July 30, 1983. He began writing lyrics for popular songs in 1918; wrote texts for Jerome Kern, Gershwin, and Vernon Duke; also collaborated in writing lyrics with Arthur Schwartz. In 1919 he joined the Goldwyn Pictures Corp. as publicity director; when the firm merged into Metro-Goldwyn-Mayer in 1924 he remained with it, becoming its vice-president in 1940. He devised its pseudo-Latin logo, Ars Gratia Artis (the correct word sequence would be Ars Artis Gratia). In 1974 he publ. an autobiography, *Dancing in the Dark*. Of his hobbies, to be noted is the invention of the 2-handed bridge game which was named after him. He also painted and translated librettos.

As a publicity man for Metro-Goldwyn-Mayer, he popularized, and possibly made up, Greta Garbo's line "I want to be alone," which became famous.

Dietz, Max, Austrian musicologist; b. Vienna, April 9, 1857; d. there, Aug. 5, 1928. Having obtained his degree (Dr.Phil.) from the Univ. of Vienna, he spent some time in France in research work, the results of which he publ. in his *Geschichte des musikalischen Dramas in Frankreich während der Revolution bis zum Direktorium* (1885), a most valuable contribution to the history of opera; in 1886 he established himself as docent of musicology at the Univ. of Vienna; edited several masses, a *Stabat Mater* and Requiem by Emperor Leopold I (1891), and *Recitativo e Duetto fra l'anima e Gesù Cristo* by A. de Liguori (1895).

Dieupart, Charles François, French violinist and harpsichordist; b. c.1670; d. London, c.1740. He went to London in 1700; was maestro al cembalo, for several years, of Handel's operas; and died almost destitute. He publ. *6 Suites de clavecin ... composées et mises en concert pour un violon et une flûte, avec basse de viole et un archiluth.* Bach copied 2 of Dieupart's clavecin suites, and used various themes in his own *English Suites.* The Lyrebird Press of Paris publ. 2 vols. of Dieupart's works, edited by P. Brunold (vol. I, *6 suites pour clavecin;* vol. II, *Airs et Chansons*).

Dijk, Jan van, Dutch pianist and composer; b. Oostzaan, June 4, 1918. He studied composition with Willem Pijper in Rotterdam (1936–46); gave piano recitals; taught at the Brabant Cons. in Tilburg from its founding in 1955, and at the Royal Cons. in The Hague from 1961. A prolific composer, he wrote hundreds of works, not counting orchestrations of piano pieces by classical composers. He also produced music in the 31-tone system devised by the Dutch physicist Adriaan Fokker.
WORKS: OPERAS: *Flying Dutchman* (1953) and *Protesilaus and Laodamia* (1968). FOR ORCH.: Dance Suite for Orch. and Jazz Combo (1961); Concertino for Flute, Piano, Percussion, and Strings (1938); 3 sinfoniettas (1940, 1952, 1956); *Cassatio* for Strings and Piano obbligato (1943); 4 symphs. (1944, 1947, 1948, 1951); *Capriccio* for Viola and Orch. (1946); 4 piano concertinos (1948–49, 1953, 1966, 1966); Concertino for 2 Pianos and String or Wind Orch. (1949); *Suite pastorale* for Oboe, English Horn, and Small Orch. (1953); 3 *Suites da Sonar* (1954, 1955, 1958); *Cortège en Rondeau* for Orch. (1955); Saxophone Concertino (1956); Toccata for String Orch. (1957); Concertino for Recorder and Chamber Orch. (1958); Serenade for Winds, Percussion, and Piano (1959); *4 Bagatelles* for Orch. (1960); Concertino for Accordion and String Orch. (1960); *17 Projections* for Orch. (1962); Double-bass Concerto (1962); *Salon symphonique* (1963); Concerto for Piano, 4-hands, and Small Orch. (1963); *Contrasts* for Orch. and Jazz Combo (1964); *Décorations et décompositions* for Orch. (1964); *Duetto accompagnato* for Saxophone, Trombone, and String Orch. (1964); 2 serenades for

Small Orch. (1966, 1970); *Jardin public,* divertimento for Flute and Orch. (1967); Triple Concerto for Flute, Recorder, Harpsichord, and Orch. (1968); *Makedonski,* suite for Chamber Orch. (1969); *2 Résumés* for Piano and Small Orch. (1970); *Touch after Finish* for Trumpet, Organ, Piano, and Strings (1971); *Fantaisie* for Double Bass and Orch. (1972); *About* for Orch. (1973); *Kleine Concertante* for 2 Flutes and Chamber Orch. (1974); *Affiche pour le réouverture du magasin* for Orch. (1974); *Accomplishement* for Small Orch. (1975); *Sinfonia e Fughetta* for Orch. (1976); *Parties sur l'amitié* for Orch. (1977). VOCAL WORKS: *Jaergetijde* for Chorus and Orch. (1944); *Het masker van den Rooden Dood (The Mask of the Red Death),* after Edgar Allan Poe, for Narrator and Chamber Orch. (1952); *Zwartbaard* for Male Chorus and Orch. (1953); *De Kommandeur* for Soloists, Narrator, Boys' Chorus, and String Quartet or String Orch. (1958); *Heer en Knecht,* cantata (1963); *Coornhert,* cantata (1964); *Quodlibet* for Chorus and Orch. (1967); *Pros romaious,* cantata (1968); *Ars vivendi* for Chorus and Orch. (1977). CHAMBER MUSIC: 5 string quartets (1940, 1941, 1942, 1965, 1974); Divertimento for Clarinet, Viola, and Cello (1941); Septet (1949–50); Piano Trio (1950); Divertimento for 2 Violins and Cello (1951); Duo for Cello and Piano (1953); Cello Sonatina (1953); Violin Sonatina (1953); Saxophone Sonata (1953); Sonatina for Violin and Piano (1954); Serenade for Trumpet and Horn (1955); Suite for 2 Flutes and Piano (1957); 2 sonatas for Solo Flute (1961, 1966); *Musica sacra I* for 2 Violins, Viola, and Organ (1966), *II* for Flute, Cello, and Piano (1968), and *III* for Clarinet, Violin, and Piano (1975); *Musique à trois* for Flute, Recorder, and Harpsichord (1967); Solo Violin Sonata (1968); *Quintetto* for Mandolin, Bass Clarinet, Percussion, Organ, and Piano (1969); *4 Caprices* for Accordion (1969); *Pet* for Flute, Saxophone, Trumpet, Violin, and Double Bass (1973); *Concertino à 3* for Flute, Violin and Viola, (1975). FOR PIANO: Sonata (1942); 18 sonatinas (1944–74); *Rondino* (1955); Sonatina for 4-hands (1956); 2 *Kantieks* (1964, 1976); *Couple* (1969); *Something for 2 Piano Players* (1969); *Partita piccola* (1970); *Alba Communis* (1973); *3 Inventions* (1976). 31-TONE PIECES: *7 Pieces* for Organ (1948); *Musica per organo trentunisono I* for 31-tone Organ (1950–51) and *II,* 7 pieces for 31-tone Organ (1957); Concertino for Trombone, Violin, and Cello (1961).

Diller, Angela, American pianist and pedagogue; b. Brooklyn, Aug. 1, 1877; d. Stamford, Conn., April 30, 1968. She studied music at Columbia Univ. with Edward MacDowell and Percy Goetschius; also with Johannes Schreyer in Dresden; in 1899–1916 was head of the theory dept. of the Music School Settlement in N.Y.; in 1916–21, was an administrator at the David Mannes School; then director of the Diller-Quaile School of Music in N.Y.; was on the faculty of the Univ. of Southern Calif. (1932), Mills College (1935), and the New England Cons. (1936 and 1937); was co-founder, with Margarethe Dessoff, of the Adesdi Chorus and A Cappella Singers of N.Y.; edited, with E. Quaile, K. Stearns Page, and

Harold Bauer, many educational music works. In 1953 she received a Guggenheim fellowship award. She publ. *First Theory Book* (1921); *Keyboard Harmony Course* (4 books, 1936, 1937, 1943, 1949), and *The Splendor of Music* (1957).

Dilling, Mildred, noted American harpist; b. Marion, Indiana, Feb. 23, 1894; d. New York, Dec. 30, 1982. She studied with Louise Schellschmidt-Koehne and later, in Paris, with Henriette Renié. After her concert debut in Paris, she played in N.Y. (1913) with the Madrigal Singers of the MacDowell Chorus; appeared in joint recitals in Europe with the de Reszkes and Yvette Guilbert, and in the U.S. with Alma Gluck and Frances Alda; toured the U.S. and Great Britain many times; also made concert tours in South America, in the Middle East, and in the Orient. She had 7 engagements to play at the White House. She had numerous private pupils who became well-known harp players; her most famous student was the comedian Harpo Marx. She cultivated calluses on her fingers to achieve sonority. She was the owner of a large collection of harps which she acquired in different parts of the world. She publ. *Old Tunes for New Harpists* (1934) and *30 Little Classics for the Harp* (1938).

Dillon, Fannie Charles, American pianist; b. Denver, March 16, 1881; d. Altadena, Calif., Feb. 21, 1947. She studied at Claremont College in Pomona, Calif., and in Berlin (1900–8) with Godowsky and Hugo Kaun; later in N.Y. with Rubin Goldmark; she made her debut as a pianist in 1908; taught at Pomona College (1910–13), and from 1918 in Los Angeles high schools.
WORKS: *Celebration of Victory* (1918); *The Cloud* (1918); *A Letter from the Southland; Mission Garden; The Alps* (1920); *Chinese Symph. Suite;* etc.; many piano pieces (*Birds at Dawn*, etc.); songs; anthems.

Dillon, Henri, French composer; b. Angers, Oct. 9, 1912; d. in Indo-China, in combat, July 9, 1954. He studied at the Military School in St.-Cyr; was in the army during World War II. He was largely self-taught in music, and adopted a classical style of composition, derived mainly from the melodic patterns of French folk songs.
WORKS: Cello Concerto (1949); Violin Concerto (1949); Viola Concerto (1952); Concerto for 2 Trumpets and Orch. (1953); *Arlequin*, divertimento for String Orch. (1949); *Cassation* for 12 Wind Instruments (1953); Sonata for Saxophone and Piano (1949); Violin Sonata (1952); Concerto for 2 Pianos (Paris, Dec. 15, 1952); Piano Sonata (1953); various works for piano.

Dima, Gheorghe, Rumanian composer; b. Brasov, Oct. 10, 1847; d. Cluj, June 4, 1925. He was a pupil of Giehne in Karlsruhe, of Uffmann in Vienna, of Thieriot in Graz, and of Richter, Jadassohn, and Reinecke at the Leipzig Cons.; directed musical societies and church choirs in Sibiu and Brasov; also taught music in those cities.

WORKS: *La Mère d'Etienne le Grand*, oratorio; *Voilà la hora qui tourne* for Mixed Chorus and Orch.; *Salvum fac regem* for Voices and Orch.; etc.

Dimov, Bojidar, Bulgarian composer; b. Lom, Jan. 31, 1935. He studied composition with Veselin Stoyanov in Sofia and with Karl Schiske in Vienna. In 1968 he settled in Cologne, where he founded a group for promotion of new music, called Trial and Error. His own compositions follow the experimental method symbolized by the name of this group, striving to obtain a pragmatic modern style and technique.
WORKS: *Incantations I–III* for Soprano and Chamber Orch. (1963–69); *Komposition I* for Piano (1963), *II* for String Quartet (1964), and *III* for Orch. (1967–68); *Continuum,* subtitled *Trauerminuten für Dana Kosanova,* for Chamber Orch., commemorating a 15-year-old Czech girl student killed in the course of the Soviet invasion of Czechoslovakia in 1968 (Graz, Oct. 25, 1969); *Raumspiel* for Piano and Chamber Orch., a work of spatial music (1969); *Symphonies* for Voice and Chamber Orch. (1970); *Dual* for 7 Instruments (1971).

Dimov, Ivan, Bulgarian composer; b. Kazanlak, Dec. 13, 1927. He studied composition with Goleminov at the Bulgarian State Cons., graduating in 1953; then went to Moscow, where he took courses in advanced composition at the Moscow Cons.
WORKS: 2 operas: *They Have Stolen the Council* (1966) and *The Emigrant* (1973); ballet, *Laughter of Africa* (1966); *Pieces* for Oboe and Piano (1955); *Kardjalii,* dance drama for Orch. (1959); Violin Concertino (1961); *Dramatic* Poem for Orch. (1964); String Quartet in 2 parts (1971); *Miniatures* for Piano (1973); choruses; songs.

D'Indy, Vincent. See **Indy, Vincent d'**.

Dinicu, Grigoraş, Rumanian composer of light music; b. Bucharest, April 3, 1889; d. there, March 28, 1949. He was of a family of musicians; in 1902 studied violin with Carl Flesch, who taught at the Bucharest Cons. At his graduation in 1906, Dinicu played a violin piece of his own based on popular Rumanian rhythms, *Hora staccato;* Jascha Heifetz made a virtuoso arrangement of it in 1932. Subsequently Dinicu played in hotels, restaurants, nightclubs, and cafés in Bucharest and in Western Europe. Apart from *Hora staccato,* he composed numerous other pieces of light music in the gypsy and Rumanian manner.
BIBLIOGRAPHY: Viorel Cosma, *Figuri de Lautari* (Bucharest, 1960; pp. 189–229).

Dippel, Andreas, dramatic tenor and impresario; b. Kassel, Germany, Nov. 30, 1866; d. Hollywood, May 12, 1932. In 1882–87 he was employed in a banking house at Kassel, meanwhile beginning vocal study with Frau Zottmayr, a well-known singer at the court theater; he was engaged at the Bremen Stadttheater (1887–92); made his American debut at the Metropolitan Opera in N.Y. (Nov. 26, 1890); then sang at Covent Garden in London, in Munich, and at Bayreuth. His repertoire included nearly 150 roles; he was particularly successful in Wagner's operas. In 1908 he became administrative manager of the Metropolitan; in 1910 he assumed control of the Chicago Opera Co.; was its manager till 1913; then organized his own company, specializing in light opera.

Diruta, Girolamo, celebrated Italian organist; b. Deruta, province of Perugia, c.1554; d. after 1610. He was a pupil, in Venice, of Zarlino, Costanzo Porta, and Claudio Merulo, the last of whom mentions the fact with pride in the preface of Diruta's *Il Transilvano.* In 1574, Diruta was in the Minorite monastery at Correggio; then was church organist in Venice (1582–93); was at the Cathedral of Chioggia (1593–1603); and at Agobbio (Gubbio) Cathedral (1609–12). His *Il Transilvano* is a valuable treatise on organ playing, the first work to treat the organ and its playing technique as distinct and separate from the clavier. It is in 2 parts, in dialogue form: *Dialogo sopra il vero modo di sonar organi e istromenti da penna* (Venice, 1593; further eds., 1597, 1609, 1612, 1625) and *Dialogo diviso in quattro libri ... il vero modo e la vera regola d'intavolare ciascun canto* (Venice, 1609; 2nd ed., 1622). Dannreuther, in his *Musical Ornamentation,* gives a thorough analysis of Diruta's system of ornamentation. Vol. III of L. Torchi's *L'arte musicale in Italia* contains a Ricercare and 2 toccatas for organ by Diruta.
BIBLIOGRAPHY: F. Briganti, "Il primo libro dei Contrapunti di Girolamo Diruta," *Perugia,* VI (Sept. 23, 1950).

Di Stefano, Giuseppe, noted Italian tenor; b. Motta Santa Anastasia, near Catania, July 24, 1921. He studied with Luigi Montesanto in Milan; then was conscripted into the Italian army in the infantry, and was taken prisoner; he escaped and went to Switzerland. Returning to Italy after the war, he made his operatic debut in Reggio Emilia in 1946; then sang in Rome and at La Scala in Milan. On Feb. 25, 1948, he made his debut as the Duke of Mantua in *Rigoletto* at the Metropolitan Opera in N.Y.; he was on its roster until 1952, and again in 1955–56 and 1964–65. On Oct. 8, 1950, he sang the role of Rodolfo in *La Bohème* at the San Francisco Opera. He also appeared as a guest artist with the Chicago Lyric Opera during the season 1965–66; his other engagements were at La Scala, the Vienna State Opera, the Berlin State Opera, Covent Garden in London, the Paris Opéra, and Teatro Colón in Buenos Aires. In 1973–74 he made a much-publicized concert tour with Maria Callas. His opera roles were limited almost exclusively to the Italian repertoire, but he also sang Faust in Gounod's opera, Don José in *Carmen,* and Des Grieux in *Manon.*

Distler, Hugo, important German composer; b. Nuremberg, June 24, 1908; d. (suicide) Berlin, Nov. 1, 1942. He studied at the Leipzig Cons. with Grabner and Martienssen. In 1931 he became a church

organist at Lübeck; joined the faculty of the Lübeck Cons. (1933–37); also was a teacher at an ecclesiastical school in Spandau (1933–37); taught at the Hochschule für Musik in Wurttemberg (1937–40); from 1940 he was in Berlin. His early training and his connection with church music determined his style as a composer; his music is marked by a strong sense of polyphony. He wrote few works, mostly chamber music and choral pieces: Concerto for Cembalo and String Orch. (1935–36); cantatas: *An die Natur* (1933); *Das Lied von der Glocke* (1933–34); *Lied am Herde* (1940). His oratorio *Die Weltalter* (1942) remained unfinished. Distler's works have been heard in frequent performances since his death. He also publ. *Funktionelle Harmonielehre* (Kassel and Basel, 1941).
BIBLIOGRAPHY: Karl Laux, *Musik und Musiker der Gegenwart* (Essen, 1949); L.G. Palmer, *Hugo Distler and His Church Music* (St. Louis, 1967); U. Herrmann, *Hugo Distler—Rufer und Mahner* (Berlin, 1972).

Ditson, Oliver, American music publisher, founder of the firm of **Oliver Ditson & Co.;** b. Boston, Oct. 20, 1811; d. there, Dec. 21, 1888. He established himself as a music seller and publisher in Boston in 1835; became a partner of G.H. Parker, his employer, under the firm name of Parker & Ditson; carried on the business in his own name (1842–57); when J.C. Haynes joined the firm, Ditson changed its name to O. Ditson & Co. His eldest son, **Charles,** took charge of the N.Y. branch (**Ch. H. Ditson & Co.**) in 1867, the business being continued until his death. A Philadelphia branch, opened in 1875 by **J. Edward Ditson** as **J. E. D. & Co.,** was in existence until 1910. A branch for the importation and sale of instruments, etc., was established at Boston in 1860 as John C. Haynes & Co. On Oliver Ditson's death, the firm of Oliver Ditson & Co. was reorganized as a corporation, with J.C. Haynes as president (d. May 3, 1907); from 1907 until his death, on May 14, 1929, Charles H. Ditson managed the business; he was succeeded by H.H. Porter. In 1931 Theo. Presser Co., of Philadelphia, took over the management of the firm; its catalogue embraced about 52,000 titles; it publ. the *Musical Record* (a monthly periodical) from 1878 to 1903, the *Musician* from 1896 to 1918, and several library series. The music house Lyon & Healy was founded by Oliver Ditson in Chicago in 1864 as a western branch.
BIBLIOGRAPHY: W.A. Fisher, *Notes on Music in Old Boston* (Boston, 1918); idem, *One Hundred and Fifty Years of Music Publishing in the U.S.* (Boston, 1933).

Dittersdorf, Karl Ditters von (original name, **Karl Ditters**), eminent Austrian composer and violinist; b. Vienna, Nov. 2, 1739; d. Schloss Rothlhotta, Neuhof, Bohemia, Oct. 24, 1799. He played violin as a child; then studied with König and Ziegler; the Prince of Sachsen-Hildurghausen made it possible for him to take private violin lessons with Trani and to study composition with Bono; he played in the Prince's orch. from 1751 to 1761. In 1761 he went to Vienna, where he was engaged as a member of the court theater orch. (until 1764). He was befriended by Gluck, who took him along on his Italian journey, where he had an occasion to appear in public as a violinist. In 1765 he assumed the post of Kapellmeister to the Bishop of Grosswardein in Hungary, where he remained until 1769. His career as a composer began in earnest at this time; he wrote an oratorio, *Isacco, figura del redentore;* several cantatas; and many pieces of orch. and chamber music. In 1770 he became Kapellmeister to the Prince-Bishop of Breslau, Count von Schaffgotsch, at Johannisberg in Silesia. There he wrote mostly for the stage, bringing out 12 works between 1771 and 1776. However, he wrote his most important dramatic works in Vienna and for the ducal theater in Oels. He gained fame with his first singspiel, *Doctor und Apotheker,* produced in Vienna on July 11, 1786; it was followed by other successful stage works, *Betrug durch Aberglauben, Die Liebe im Narrenhause, Das rote Käppchen,* and *Hieronymus Knicker.* He received several honors during his lifetime; in 1770 the Pope bestowed upon him the Order of the Golden Spur; in 1773 he was ennobled by the Emperor as von Dittersdorf. Upon his death of the Prince-Bishop in 1795, he was granted a small pension, and found himself in straitened circumstances until a friend, Baron von Stillfried, took him into his castle, Rothlhotta, where he remained until his death. Dittersdorf was an important figure in the Viennese Classical school of composition, although he lacked the genius of Haydn and Mozart. He was able to fuse the common folksong elements of the period with brilliant ensembles characteristic of opera buffa. His singspiels reveal a jovial humor, melodic charm, and rhythmic vitality. His symphs. and concertos are also of interest as characteristic specimens of the period.

WORKS: FOR THE STAGE: *Il viaggiatore americano in Joannesberg,* farce (Johannisberg, May 1, 1771; not extant); *L'amore disprezzato (Pancratio; Amore in musica),* operetta buffa (Johannisberg, 1771); *Il finto pazzo per amore,* operetta giocosa (Johannisberg, June 3, 1772); *Il tutore e la pupilla,* dramma giocoso (Johannisberg, May 1, 1773); *Lo sposo burlato,* operetta giocosa (Johannisberg, 1773 or 1775; another version as *Der gefoppte Bräutigam*); *Il tribunale di Giove,* serenade with prologue (Johannisberg, 1774); *Il maniscalco,* operetta giocosa (Johannisberg, May 1, 1775); *La contadina fedele,* opera giocoso (Johannisberg, 1776); *La moda ossia Gli scompigli domestici,* dramma giocoso (Johannisberg, June 3, 1776); *L'Arcifanfano, re de' matti,* opera giocosa (Johannisberg, 1776); *Il barone di rocca antica,* operetta giocosa (Johannisberg, 1776); *I visionari* (Johannisberg, 1776; not extant); *Doctor und Apotheker (Der Apotheker und der Doctor),* singspiel (Vienna, July 11, 1786); *Betrug durch Aberglauben oder Die Schatzgräber (Der glückliche Betrug; Die dienstbaren Geister),* singspiel (Vienna, Oct. 3, 1786); *Democrito corretto,* opera giocosa (Vienna, Jan. 24, 1787; performed under various titles); *Die Liebe im Narrenhause,* singspiel (Vienna, April 12, 1787); *Das rote Käppchen oder Hilft's nicht so schadt's nicht (Die rote Kappe;*

Das Rotkäppchen), comic operetta (Vienna, 1788); *Im Dunkeln ist nicht gut munkeln oder Irrung über Irrung (25,000 Gulden),* comic opera (Vienna, Feb. 1789); *Hieronymus Knicker (Lucius Knicker; Chrisostomus Knicker; Hokus Pokus oder Die Lebensessenz),* singspiel (Vienna, July 7, 1789); *Die Hochzeit des Figaro,* singspiel (Brno, 1789?; music not extant); *Der Schiffspatron oder Der neue Gutsherr,* singspiel (Vienna, 1789); *Hokus-Pokus oder Der Gaukelspiel,* comic opera (Vienna, 1790); *Der Teufel ein Hydraulikus,* comedy (Gratz, 1790); *Der Fürst und sein Volk,* pasticcio (Leipzig, March 5?, 1791; music not extant; in collaboration with F. Piterlin and F. Bertoni); *Das Gespenst mit der Trommel (Geisterbanner),* singspiel (Oels, Aug. 16, 1794); *Don Quixote der Zweyte (Don Chisciotto),* singspiel (Oels, Feb. 4, 1795); *Gott Mars und der Hauptmann von Bärenzahn (Gott Mars oder Der eiserne Mann),* singspiel (Oels, May 30, 1795); *Der Durchmarsch,* an arrangement of J. Paneck's *Die christliche Judenbraut* (Oels, Aug. 29, 1795); *Der Schach von Schiras,* singspiel (Oels, Sept. 15, 1795); *Die befreyten Gwelfen (Die Guelfen),* prologue (Oels, Oct. 29, 1795); *Ugolino,* serious singspiel (Oels, June 11, 1796); *Die lustigen Weiber von Windsor,* singspiel (Oels, June 25, 1796); *Der schöne Herbsttag,* dialogue (Oels, Oct. 29, 1796); *Der Ternengewinnst oder Der gedemütigte Stolz (Terno secco),* singspiel (Oels, Feb. 11, 1797); *Der Mädchenmark,* singspiel (Oels, April 18, 1797); *Die Opera buffa,* comic opera (Vienna, 1798); *Don Coribaldi ossia L'usurpata prepotenza,* drama (Dresden, 1798?); *Ein Stück mit kleinen Liedern,* opera based on *Frau Sybilla trinkt keinen Wein* and *Das Reich der Toten*; comic opera version based on *Amore in musica* (Grosswardein, 1767?; not extant); etc.

OTHER VOCAL WORKS: *Isacco, figura del redentore,* oratorio (Grosswardein, 1766); *Il Davide nella Valle di Terebintho (Davidde penitente),* oratorio (Johannisberg, 1771); *L'Esther ossia La Liberatrice del popolo giudaico nella Persia,* oratorio (Vienna, Dec. 19, 1773); *Giobbe (Hiob),* oratorio (Vienna, April 8–9, 1786); also several cantatas, both sacred and secular; masses; offertories; graduals; motets; etc.

FOR ORCH: A great number of symphs. have been attributed to Dittersdorf, with over 100 being most likely by him. Most famous are the 12 symphs. on Ovid's *Metamorphoses*; only Nos. 1–6 are extant, although Nos. 7–12 have survived in arrangements for Piano, 4–hands, by Dittersdorf. He also composed many concertos, including 18 for violin, 3 for 2 violins, one for cello, 5 for viola, 4 for oboe, 5 for harpsichord, and one for flute.

CHAMBER MUSIC: 15 divertimentos, including *Il combattimento dell'umane passioni;* 4 string serenades (with 2 horns); numerous string quartets; many sonatas for 4-hands; preludes; etc.

WRITINGS: "Briefe über Behandlung italienischer Texte bei der Composition," *Allgemeine musikalische Zeitung* (Leipzig, 1799); an autobiography publ. as *Karl von Dittersdorfs Lebensbeschreibung, Seinem Sohne in die Feder diktiert* (Leipzig, 1801; Eng. trans., London, 1896; new ed. by N. Miller, Munich, 1967).

BIBLIOGRAPHY: C. Krebs, *Dittersdorfiana* (Berlin, 1900); K. Holl, *Carl Ditters von Dittersdorfs Opern für das wiederhergestellte Johannisberger Theater* (Diss., Univ. of Bonn, 1913); H. Kralik, *Carl Ditters von Dittersdorfs Symphonien und Konzerte* (Diss., Univ. of Vienna, 1913); L. Riedinger, "Karl von Dittersdorf als Opernkomponist," *Studien zur Musikwissenschaft,* II (1914); G. Rigler, "Die Kammermusik Dittersdorf," *Studien zur Musikwissenschaft,* XIV (1927); F. Souper, "The Music of Dittersdorf," *Music and Letters,* XI (1930); M. Grave, *Dittersdorf's First-movement Form as a Measure of His Symphonic Development* (Diss., N.Y. Univ., 1977).

Dittrich, Paul-Heinz, German composer; b. Gornsdorf, Erzgebirge, Dec. 4, 1930. He studied composition with Fidelio Finke and choral conducting with Günther Ramin at the Leipzig Hochschule für Musik (1951–56). Later he took a seminar in advanced composition with Rudolf Wagner-Régeny at the Academy of Arts in East Berlin (1958–60). He was a choral director in Weimar (1956–58) and taught counterpoint and harmony at the Hanns Eisler Hochschule für Musik in East Berlin (1963–76). In 1980 he visited America. In his music, Dittrich reveals himself as an astute creator of modern forms and technical idioms, while carefully observing and preserving the pragmatic elements of instrumental and vocal components. He obtained numerous awards for his compositions, among them a prize of the International Society for Contemporary Music (1975) and a UNESCO prize (1976). WORKS: Violin Sonata (1956); String Quartet (1959); *Pentaculum* for Wind Quintet (1960); Sextet for Wind Instruments, Percussion, and Guitar (1960); *Orchestermusik* (1960); *Irische Harfe,* 3 songs for Voice and Orch., to words by W.B. Yeats (1965); *Golgotha,* oratorio for Soloists, Chorus, and Orch. (1967); *3 Lieder* for Soprano and 13 Instruments (1967); *Fables and Parables* for Mixed Chorus (1968); *Musik* for Piano and 4 Speakers (1969); *Stabiles and Mobiles* for Orch. and Vocal Ensemble (1969); *Les Fleurs de Baudelaire* for 3 Sopranos and Instruments (1969); *Kammermusik I* for 4 Woodwinds, Piano, and Tape (1970); *Begegnung* for 9 Instruments (1970); *Schlagzeilen* for 2 Pianos, 2 Percussionists, and Tape (1971); String Quartet with Electronic Instruments (1971); *Memento Vitae* for Baritone Solo, 12 Voices, 4 Choral Groups, and 9 Percussions, to words by Brecht (1971); *Die anonyme Stimme* for Oboe, Trombone, and Tape (1972); *Vokalblätter* for Soprano Solo and 12 Voices, to words by James Joyce, Brecht, and Goethe (1972–73); *Areae sonantes* for Instrumental and Vocal Groups (1972–73); Concerto for Oboe and Chamber Orch. (1973–74); *Collage* for Oboe, Cello, Piano, and Electronic Sounds (1973); *Rondo à la Rossini* for Cello and Double Bass (1974); *Kammermusik II* for Oboe, Cello, Piano, and Tape (1974); *Kammermusik III* for Wind Quintet and Baritone (1974); Concerto for Cello and Orch. (1974–75); *Cello-Einsatz* for Solo Cello (1975); *Aktion-Reaktion* for Oboe, Tape, and Synthesizer (1975); *Cantus I* for Orch. (1975); *Illuminations* for Orch. (1976); *Concerts avec plusieurs instruments No. 1* for Harpsichord and 7 Instruments (1976–77); *Kammermusik IV* for Soprano, Piano, Flute, Clarinet, Violin, Cello, Guitar, Percussion, and Synthesizer (1977); *Kammermusik V* for Wind Quintet and Electronic Sounds (1977); *Rondeau* for Flute Solo (1977); *Cantus II* for Soprano, Cello, Orch., and Tape, to words by Eluard (1977); *Concerts avec plusieurs instruments No. 2* for Viola, Cello, and 2 Orch. Groups (1978); *Concerts avec plusieurs instruments No. 3* for Flute, Oboe, Orch., and Synthesizer (1978); Double Concerto for Flute, Oboe, and Orch. (1979).

Divitis (de Ryche, le Riche), Antonius (Antoine), celebrated French (or Flemish) contrapuntist of the late 15th and early 16th centuries; b. Louvain, c.1475; d. probably after 1526, in which year he is mentioned as very likely being at St. Peter's in Rome as **Antonius Richardus.** He was a singer and choirmaster at St. Donatien in Bruges (Brugge) in 1501–4; in 1504–5, was choirmaster at St. Rombaut in Malines; then was in the service of Philippe le Beau in Brussels; was a chapel singer to Louis XII from 1506 to 1515. WORKS: Motets and chansons are scattered in collections, e.g., *Motetti de la corona* (1514), and others printed by Rhaw, Attaignant, etc. At Cambrai is a mass in MS; at Munich, 2 credos and a Salve Regina *a* 5; at Rome, *Quem dicunt homines* for 4 Voices. BIBLIOGRAPHY: G. van Doorslaer, "Antonius Divitis," *Tijdschrift der Vereeniging voor Nederlandsche Muziekgeschiedenis,* XIII, 1 (1929); W. Nugent, *The Life and Works of Antonius Divitis* (Diss., North Texas State Univ., 1970).

Dixon, Dean, black American conductor; b. New York, Jan. 10, 1915; d. Zug, near Zürich, Nov. 3, 1976. He showed a musical talent as a child and began to take violin lessons. At the age of 17 he organized at his high school in the Bronx a group that he was pleased to call the Dean Dixon Symphony Society. He studied violin at the Juilliard School of Music (1932–36); on a conducting fellowship he took lessons with Albert Stoessel at the Juilliard Graduate School (1936–39); also enrolled in academic classes at Columbia Univ. Teachers College, receiving an M.A. in 1939. Eleanor Roosevelt became interested in his career, and helped him to obtain some conducting engagements, including an appearance with the N.Y. Phil. at the Lewisohn Stadium on Aug. 10, 1941, making him the first of his race to conduct this orch. In 1944 Dixon organized the American Youth Orch., which had a limited success. In 1949 he went to Europe in the hopes of securing wider opportunities. These hopes were fully realized; he was engaged as music director of the Hessian Radio Orch. in Frankfurt (1961–75); concurrently he served as music director of the Sydney (Australia) Symph. (1964–67); also filled special engagements in France, Italy, Spain, and Austria. Returning briefly to the U.S. in 1970, he was guest conductor for a series of N.Y. Phil. summer concerts in Central

Park, then went back to Europe and settled in Switzerland in 1974. His career was cut short when he underwent open-heart surgery in 1975; yet he managed to conduct several engagements in Europe before suffering a final collapse.

BIBLIOGRAPHY: Raoul Abdul, *Blacks in Classical Music* (N.Y., 1977; pp. 191–93).

Dixon, James, American conductor; b. Estherville, Iowa, April 26, 1928. He studied at the Univ. of Iowa (B.M., 1952; M.M., 1956); was conductor of the U.S. 7th Army Symph. Orch. in Germany (1951–54); the Univ. of Iowa Symph. Orch. in Iowa City (1954–59); the New England Cons. Symph. Orch. in Boston (1959–61). In 1962 he returned to the Univ. of Iowa Symph. Orch. as its permanent conductor; from 1965, served as conductor of the Tri-City Symph. Orch. in Davenport, Iowa, and Rock Island, Ill. In addition, he was associate conductor of the Minneapolis Symph. Orch. (1961–62); guest conductor with the following orchs.: National Orch. of Greece in Athens (1955, 1959, 1961), Norddeutscher Rundfunk (1963), Westdeutscher Rundfunk (1964), Tanglewood (1965), Chicago Civic Symph. (1967), and Chicago Symph. Orch. (1972). He was the recipient of the Gustav Mahler Medal in 1963. As an interpreter, he follows the style of Mitropoulos, under whose influence he began his career, combining precision of rhythmic flow with expressive shaping of melodic phrases.

Dizi, François-Joseph, famous French harpist; b. Namur, Jan. 14, 1780; d. Paris, Nov., 1847. He set out for London when only 16; lost his harp on the way but went on without it, and introduced himself to Erard, who gave him a harp and obtained pupils for him. Besides winning fame as a concert player and as a harpist at the principal theaters, he invented the "perpendicular harp" (which was unsuccessful), and composed sonatas, romances, variations, studies, etc., for harp; also publ. *Ecole de Harpe, Being a Complete Treatise on the Harp* (London, 1827). In 1830 he went to Paris, and established a harp factory with Pleyel, which did not do well. There he was appointed harp teacher to the royal princesses.

Dlabacz, Gottfried Johann, Bohemian music scholar; b. Brod, July 17, 1758; d. Prague, Feb. 4, 1820. He was librarian and choirmaster of the Premonstratensian monastery in Prague; publ. a valuable reference work, *Allgemeines historisches Künstlerlexikon für Böhmen* (3 vols., 1815–18), and contributed articles to Riegger's *Statistik von Böhmen.*

Dlugoszewski, Lucia, American composer; b. Detroit, June 16, 1931. She studied piano, and concurrently attended classes in physics at Wayne State Univ. (1946–49). Fascinated with the mathematical aspects of music, she began to study with Edgar Varèse, whose works illuminated this scientific relationship for her. Accordingly, in her own works she emphasizes the sonorific element of music; inspired by the example of Varèse's *Ionisation,* she invented or perfected a number of percussion instruments; one of her inventions is the timbre piano, in which she makes use of bows and plectra on the piano strings. In 1960 she joined the Foundation for Modern Dance as a teacher and composer.

WORKS: Her dance scores include *Openings of the Eye* for Flute, Percussion, and Timbre Piano (1958); *8 Clear Places* for Percussion Ensemble (1958–61); *Geography of Noon* for New Percussion Instruments (1964); *Dazzle on a Knife's Edge* for Timbre Piano and Orch. (1966); *Agathlon Algebra* for Timbre Piano and Orch. (1968); and a series of works for various instrumental combinations under the title *Lords of Persia.* Other works are: *50 Transparencies* "for everyday sounds" (1951); *Arithmetic Points* for Orch. (1955); *Instants in Form and Movements* for Timbre Piano and Chamber Orch. (1957); *Delicate Accidents in Space* for Rattle Quintet (1959); *Archaic Aggregates* for Timbre Piano, Ladder Harps, Tangent Rattles, Unsheltered Rattles, and Gongs (1961); *4 Attention Spans* for Orch. (1964); *Strange Tenderness of Naked Leaping* for Orch. (Santa Fe, N.Mex., Nov. 13, 1977); several pieces entitled *Beauty Music,* and *Music for the Left Ear in a Small Room* and other bafflingly and provocatively yclept productions.

Doane, William Howard, American hymn writer; b. Preston, Conn., Feb. 3, 1832; d. South Orange, N.J., Dec. 24, 1915. He served as a clerk and later entered the manufacturing business. He composed more than 2,000 gospel songs and a Christmas cantata, *Santa Claus.* His hymn *Pass Me Not* was popular.

BIBLIOGRAPHY: R.G. McCutchan, *Our Hymnody* (N.Y., 1937).

Döbber, Johannes, German composer; b. Berlin, March 28, 1866; d. there, Jan. 26, 1921. He was a pupil, in the Stern Cons., of R. Radecke, L. Bussler (composition), and C. Agghazy (piano). He taught the first piano class in the Kullak Cons.; became Kapellmeister at Darmstadt; then was at Coburg-Gotha as tutor in music to Princess Beatrice; was a teacher and music critic of the *Volkszeitung* in Berlin (1908).

WORKS: Operas: *Die Strassensängerin* (Gotha, 1890); *Der Schmied von Gretna-Green* (Berlin, 1893); *Dolcetta* (Brandenburg, 1894); *Die Rose von Genzano* (Gotha, 1895); *Die Grille* (Leipzig, 1897); *Die drei Rosen* (Coburg, 1902); *Der Zauberlehrling* (Braunschweig, 1907); *Die Franzosenzeit* (Berlin, 1913); song-play, *Fahrende Musikanten* (Magdeburg, 1917); operettas: *Die Millionenbraut* (Magdeburg, 1913) and *Des Kaisers Rock* (Berlin, 1915); Symph.; piano pieces; over 60 songs; quartets, duets, etc.

Dobbs, Mattiwilda, American soprano; b. Atlanta, July 11, 1925. She studied with Lotte Lehmann; also in Paris with Pierre Bernac. She began her concert career in Europe in 1948; won first prize in the International Competition for Singers in Geneva in 1951; then sang at La Scala, Glyndebourne, and other leading European opera houses. She made her Metropolitan Opera debut in N.Y. on Nov. 9, 1956, as Gilda in Verdi's *Rigoletto.*

Dobiáš, Václav, Czech composer; b. Radčice, near Semily, Sept. 22, 1909; d. Prague, May 18, 1978. He studied violin and composition at the Prague Cons., where he also took courses in microtonal music with Alois Hába, and wrote a *Lento* for 3 Harps (1940) and a Violin Concerto (1941) making use of quarter-tones. After 1945 he became involved in the political problems of musical education; in conformity with the ideology of the Communist Party, he began to write music for the masses in the manner of socialist realism; in 1958 he was elected to the Central Committee of the Communist Party of Czechoslovakia, and was a member of the National Assembly from 1960 to 1969.

WORKS: Chamber Symph. (1939); 2 numbered symphs. (1943, 1956–57); Sinfonietta (1946–47; revised 1962); Sonata for Piano, Wind Quintet, Strings, and Timpani (1947); *The Grand Procession,* symph. poem (1948); cantatas: *Stalingrad* (1945); *The Order No. 368* (1946); and *Build Up Your Country and Strengthen Peace,* also known as *Czech Polka* (1947–50); *Praho Jediná (Only Prague),* a song cycle with Orch. (1960–61); a plethora of mass choruses; 4 string quartets (1931, 1936, 1938, 1942); Violin Sonata (1936); Cello Sonata (1939); *Říkadla (Rhymes)* for 9 Instruments (1938); *Pastoral Wind Quintet* (1943); *4 Nocturnes* for Cello and Piano (1944); *Quartettino* for String Quartet (1944); *Dance Fantasy* for 9 Instruments (1948); 2 piano sonatas (1931, 1940); a fistful of playable piano pieces and a scattering of songs.

Dobos, Kálmán, Hungarian composer; b. Szolnok, July 22, 1931. He became nearly blind at the age of 14, but pursued studies of music at the Academy of Music in Budapest, graduating in 1957; later he worked on the Hungarian State Radio. He composed a Cello Sonata (1956); Symph. (1957); Piano Sonata (1957); a cappella *Missa brevis* (1957); *Adagio and Fugue* for String Quartet (1959); *2 Movements* for Piano Trio (1960); *Musica da camera* for Violin and Piano (1962); String Trio (1963); *Villanások (Flashes)* for Soprano and Piano Trio (1963); *3 Hungarian Dances* for Orch. (1964); *Meditation* for Piano (1964); *Sound Phenomena* for Orch. (1968); *Manifestations* for String Quartet, Piano, and Percussion (1969); *Belsö mozdulatok (Inner Movements)* for Clarinet, Piano, and Percussion (1970); *Ringató (Rocking)* for Piano (1972); *Vetületek (Projections)* for Orch. (1973).

Dobronić, Antun, Croatian composer; b. Jelsa, island of Hvar, April 2, 1878; d. Zagreb, Dec. 12, 1955. He studied music with Novák in Prague; then returned to Yugoslavia; in 1921 was appointed a prof. at the Cons. of Zagreb. He wrote many stage works, among them the operas *Ragusean Diptych; The Man of God; Mara; Dubrovnički triptihon* (1925); *Udovica Rozlinka* (1934); *Rkac* (1938); *Goran* (1944); ballet, *The Giant Horse;* 8 symphs.; symph. poems: *Au long de l'Adriatique* (1948) and *Les*

Noces (1949); chamber music in the national style, including a Piano Quintet, subtitled *Bosnian Rhapsody;* 5 string quartets; choruses and songs. Dobronić is the author of "A Study of Yugoslav Music," *Musical Quarterly* (Jan. 1926).

Dobrowen, Issay, Russian conductor; b. Nizhny-Novgorod, Feb. 27, 1891; d. Oslo, Dec. 9, 1953. His real name was **Barabeichik;** his orphaned mother was adopted by Israil Dobrovel; Issay Dobrowen changed his legal name, Dobrovel, to Dobrowein, and later to Dobrowen. He studied at the Nizhny-Novgorod Cons. as a small child (1896–1900); then entered the Moscow Cons. and studied with Igumnov (piano) and Taneyev (composition); went to Vienna for additional study with Leopold Godowsky (piano). Returning to Moscow, he became conductor of the Moscow Opera; in 1922 he led the Dresden State Opera in the German premiere of Mussorgsky's opera *Boris Godunov;* in 1924 he conducted opera in Berlin; during the season 1927–28 he conducted opera in Sofia, Bulgaria. In 1931 he made his American debut; conducted the San Francisco Symph. Orch.; was guest conductor with the Minneapolis Symph. Orch., Philadelphia Orch., and the N.Y. Phil. However, he was received indifferently by American audiences, and returned to Europe. He was a regular conductor of the Budapest Opera in 1936–39; at the outbreak of World War II he went to Sweden, where he won his greatest successes, as conductor of both opera and symph., at the Stockholm Opera and the Phil. of Göteborg. In 1948 he conducted at La Scala in Milan. On frequent occasions Dobrowen acted as stage director as well as conductor in German, Italian, and Swedish opera houses. He was a prolific composer; wrote several piano concertos and pieces for piano solo, in a Romantic vein; also an orch. fairy tale, *1,001 Nights* (Moscow, May 27, 1922).

Dobrowolski, Andrzej, Polish composer; b. Lwow, Sept. 9, 1921. He studied organ, singing, clarinet, theory, and composition at the State College of Music in Cracow (1947–51); in 1954 joined the faculty of the Warsaw State College of Music; in 1976 was appointed to the faculty of the Graz Hochschule für Musik. His music is a paradigm of modern structuralism and textural abstraction.

WORKS: *Symphonic Variations* (1949); *Overture* (1950); Oboe Concerto (1953); *Popular Overture* (1954); Trio for Oboe, Clarinet, and Bassoon (1954); Symph. No. 1 (1955); *8 Studies* for Oboe, Trumpet, Bassoon, and Double Bass (1959); *Music No. 1* for Tape (1962); *Music* for Strings and 4 Groups of Wind Instruments (1964); *Music* for Tape and Solo Oboe (1965); *Music* for Strings, 2 Groups of Wind Instruments, and 2 Loudspeakers (1966); *Music* for Orch. (1968–69); *Krabogapa* for Clarinet, Trombone, Cello, and Piano (1969); *Music No. 2* for Orch. (1970); *Music* for Tape and Solo Piano (1972); *Music* for Solo Tuba (1972); *Music No. 3* for Orch. (1972–73); *Music No. 4* for Orch. (1974); *Music* for Chorus, 2 Groups of Winds, Double Bass, and Percussion (1975).

Dobrzynski, Ignacy Feliks, Polish pianist; b. Romanov, Volhynia, Feb. 15, 1807; d. Warsaw, Oct. 10, 1867. The son of a violinist, **J. Dobrzynski** (1777–1841), he was taught by his father; then, being a fellow pupil and close friend of Chopin, by Chopin's teacher Elsner; on subsequent pianistic tours to Leipzig, Dresden, and Berlin (1845–46), he had great success. For a time he conducted the opera in Warsaw, where he finally settled. He wrote an opera, *Monbar or The Filibuster* (Warsaw, 1861); *Symphonie caractéristique;* String Sextet; 2 string quintets; 2 string quartets; Piano Trio; Violin Sonata; a nocturne for Violin and Piano, *Les Larmes;* mazurkas for piano; songs. His son **Bronislaw Dobrzynski** publ. a monograph on him (Warsaw, 1893).

Doche, Joseph-Denis, French composer; b. Paris, Aug. 22, 1766; d. Soissons, July 20, 1825. He was a chorister at the Cathedral of Meaux; then was organist at Coutances in Normandy. He played string instruments in a theater orch. in Paris from 1794 till 1810; then became a conductor, retiring in 1823. He wrote numerous successful vaudevilles; also operas: *Point du bruit* (Oct. 25, 1802); *Les Deux Sentinelles* (Sept. 27, 1803); others.

Dodds, Baby (real first name, **Warren**), black American drummer, brother of **Johnny Dodds;** b. New Orleans, Dec. 24, 1898; d. Chicago, Feb. 14, 1959. He played on showboats; joined the King Oliver Creole Band. He was praised by the cognoscenti as a rhythmician of versatile gifts. His autobiography "as told to Larry Gara" was publ. posthumously in Los Angeles in 1959.

Dodds, Johnny, black American jazz clarinetist; b. New Orleans, April 12, 1892; d. Chicago, Aug. 8, 1940. He studied with Lorenzo Tio, Jr., and Charlie McCurdy; worked with Kid Ory; then played with King Oliver and Freddie Keppard; he also made recordings with Louis Armstrong and Jelly Roll Morton; later formed his own group. His brother, **Warren ("Baby") Dodds,** was a drummer.

Dodds, Warren ("Baby"), black American jazz drummer; b. New Orleans, Dec. 24, 1898; d. Chicago, Feb. 14, 1959. He was the youngest of 6 children, hence his nickname; he studied drums with Dave Perkins, Walter Brundy, and Louis Cottrell, Sr.; then began his career with local groups in New Orleans; made appearances with King Oliver in San Francisco and Chicago; made recordings with Louis Armstrong, Jelly Roll Morton, and others. Though plagued by ill health from 1949, he continued to play until 1957. He was one of the pioneer jazz drummers. His brother, **Johnny Dodds,** was a clarinetist.

Dodge, Charles, American composer; b. Ames, Iowa, June 5, 1942. He studied composition with Philip Benzanson at the Univ. of Iowa (B.A., 1964); Darius Milhaud at the Aspen Summer School (1961); Gunther Schuller and Arthur Berger at the Berkshire Music Center in Tanglewood (1964); and

Jack Beeson, Chou Wen-Chung, Otto Luening, and Vladimir Ussachevsky at Columbia Univ. (M.A., 1966). He subsequently was on the faculty of Columbia (1967–77) and Princeton (1969–70) univs., teaching electronic music; in 1977 joined the faculty at Brooklyn College; received numerous commissions, grants, and awards, including one from the Koussevitzky Foundation in 1969. He composes in an empirical manner, following serial ideas; in most of his works he makes use of electronic media. WORKS: *Folia* for 7 Instruments and Percussion (1963); *Rota* for Orch. (1966); *Changes* for Electronic Tape with the aid of a digital computer storing a succession of numbers made audible by an analog converter (first perf. at the Coolidge Festival, Washington, D.C., Oct. 31, 1970); *Palinode* for Computerized Tape and Orch. (N.Y., Feb. 7, 1977).

Doebler, Curt, German composer of sacred music; b. Kottbus, Jan. 15, 1896; d. Berlin, June 19, 1970. He studied organ with A. Dreyer. In 1919–32 he was organist and choral leader at the Catholic church in Charlottenburg; after occupying various positions as an organist and a teacher elsewhere, he returned to Charlottenburg (1950). In his music Doebler attempts to establish a modern style based on Palestrina's polyphony. His numerous choruses a cappella enjoy considerable renown in Germany.

Doenhoff, Albert von, American pianist; b. Louisville, Ky., March 16, 1880; d. New York, Oct. 3, 1940. He studied at the Cincinnati College of Music and then in N.Y. with Rafael Joseffy; made his professional debut in N.Y. on March 8, 1905; subsequently developed a successful career as a concert pianist. He publ. many pieces for piano (*Arabesque, Revery,* etc.); also pedagogical material (*Three Modern Etudes for the Virtuoso; Six Special Studies Adapted to Small Hands;* etc.); edited and revised numerous editions of classics for G. Schirmer, Inc.

Doflein, Erich, German musicologist; b. Munich, Aug. 7, 1900; d. Kirchzarten, Oct. 29, 1977. He studied with Weismann, Auerbach, and Praetorius, and later with Kaminski; was a music instructor in Freiburg im Breisgau (1924–41); taught in Breslau (1941–44); was a prisoner of war in Russia (1944–46). After his return to Germany, he taught at the Musikhochschule in Freiburg im Breisgau, retiring in 1965; he prepared modern editions of 6 sonatas by Boismortier (in 2 books, 1960); concertos by Fr. Durante (1967); etc. A Festschrift was publ. in Mainz in 1972 in his honor.

Döhler, Theodor, Italian pianist and composer; b. Naples, April 20, 1814; d. Florence, Feb. 21, 1856. He was a pupil of Julius Benedict at Naples and of Czerny (piano) and Sechter (composition) at Vienna. In 1831 he became pianist to the Duke of Lucca; lived for a time in Naples; made brilliant pianistic tours in 1836–46 in Germany, Italy, France, the Netherlands, and England; in 1843 went to Copenhagen, thence to Russia, and in 1846 to Paris; settled in Florence in 1848. In 1846 the Duke, his patron, ennobled him, and he married a Russian countess. He wrote an opera, *Tancreda,* which was performed posthumously in Florence in 1880; many piano pieces; nocturnes; tarantellas; *12 études de concert; 50 études de salon;* variations, fantasias, and transcriptions.

Dohnányi, Christoph von, eminent German-born conductor; grandson of **Ernö (Ernst von) Dohnányi;** b. Berlin, Sept. 8, 1929. He began to study the piano as a child; his musical training was interrupted by World War II. His father, Hans von Dohnányi, a jurist, and his uncle, Dietrich Bonhoeffer, the Protestant theologian and author, were executed by the Nazis for their involvement in the July 20, 1944, attempt on Hitler's life. After the war, he studied jurisprudence at the Univ. of Munich; in 1948 he enrolled at the Hochschule für Musik in Munich, and won the Richard Strauss Prize for composition and conducting. Making his way to the U.S., he continued his studies with his grandfather at Florida State Univ. at Tallahassee; also attended sessions at the Berkshire Music Center at Tanglewood. Returning to Germany, he received a job as a coach and conductor at the Frankfurt Opera (1952–57). Progressing rapidly, he served as Generalmusikdirektor in Lübeck (1957–63) and Kassel (1963–66), chief conductor of the Cologne Radio Symph. Orch. (1964–70) and director of the Frankfurt Opera (1968 –77). From 1977 to 1984 he was Staatsopernintendant of the Hamburg State Opera. In 1984 he assumed the position of music director of the Cleveland Orch., having been appointed music director-designate in 1982, succeeding Lorin Maazel. In the meantime he had engagements as guest conductor of the Vienna State Opera, Covent Garden in London, La Scala in Milan, the Metropolitan Opera in N.Y., the Berlin Phil., the Vienna Phil., and the Concertgebouw Orch. in Amsterdam. Both as symph. and opera conductor, Dohnányi proved himself a master technician and a versatile musician capable of congenial interpretation of all types of music, from Baroque to the avant-garde. He is regarded as a leading exponent of the works of the Modern Vienna School, excelling in fine performances of the works of Schoenberg, Berg, and Webern. He is married to the noted German soprano **Anja Silja.**

Dohnányi, Ernö (Ernst von), eminent Hungarian pianist, composer, conductor, and pedagogue; b. Pressburg (Bratislava), July 27, 1877; d. New York, Feb. 9, 1960. He began his musical studies with his father, an amateur cellist; then studied piano and music theory with Károly Forstner. In 1894 he entered the Royal Academy of Music in Budapest, where he took courses in piano with István Thomán and in composition with Hans Koessler. In 1896 he received the Hungarian Millennium Prize, established to commemorate the thousand years of existence of Hungary, for his symph. He graduated from the Academy of Music in 1896, and then went to Berlin for additional piano studies with Eugen d'Albert. He made his debut in a recital in Berlin on Oct.

1, 1897; on Oct. 24, 1898, he played Beethoven's 4th Piano Concerto in London; then followed a series of successful concerts in the U.S. Returning to Europe, he served as prof. of piano at the Hochschule für Musik in Berlin (1908–15). He then returned to Budapest, where he taught piano at the Royal Academy of Music; served briefly as its director in 1919, when he was appointed chief conductor of the Budapest Phil. Orch. In 1928 he became head of the piano composition classes at the Academy of Music; in 1934 he became its director. In 1931 he assumed the post of music director of the Hungarian Radio. As Hungary became embroiled in war and partisan politics which invaded even the arts, Dohnányi resigned his directorship in 1941, and in 1944 he also resigned his post as conductor of the Budapest Phil. Personal tragedy also made it impossible for him to continue his work as a musician and teacher: both of his sons lost their lives; one of them, the German jurist Hans von Dohnányi, was executed for his role in the abortive attempt on Hitler's life; the other son was killed in combat. Late in 1944, Dohnányi moved to Austria. At the war's end rumors were rife that Dohnányi used his influence with the Nazi overlords in Budapest to undermine the position of Bartók and other liberals, and that he acquiesced in anti-Semitic measures. But in 1945 the American occupation authorities exonorated him of all blame; even some prominent Jewish-Hungarian musicians testified in his favor. In 1947–48 he made a tour of England as a pianist; determined to emigrate to America, he accepted the position of piano teacher at Tucumán, Argentina; in Sept. 1949 he reached the U.S., where he became composer-in-residence at Florida State Univ. in Tallahassee.

Dohnányi was a true virtuoso of the keyboard, and was greatly esteemed as a teacher; among his pupils were Georg Solti, Geza Anda, and Bálint Vázsonyi. His own music represented the terminal flowering of European Romanticism, marked by passionate eloquence of expression while keeping within the framework of Classical forms. Brahms praised his early efforts. In retrospect, Dohnányi appears as a noble epigone of the past era, but pianists, particularly Hungarian pianists, often put his brilliant compositions on their programs. Dohnányi's most popular work with an orch. is *Variations on a Nursery Song;* also frequently played is his Orch. Suite in F-sharp minor. Dohnányi himself presented his philosophy of life in a poignant pamphlet under the title *Message to Posterity* (Jacksonville, Fla., 1960). His grandson **Christoph von Dohnányi** is a talented conductor.
WORKS: FOR THE STAGE: *Der Schleier der Pierrette (Pierrette's Veil),* op. 18, pantomime (1908–9; Dresden, Jan. 22, 1910); *Tante Simona,* op. 20, comic opera (1911–12; Dresden, Jan. 20, 1913); *A vajda tornya (The Tower of the Voivod),* op. 30, opera (1915–22; Budapest, March 19, 1922); *Der Tenor,* op. 34, comic opera (1920–27; Budapest, Feb. 9, 1929).
FOR ORCH.: Symph. in F major (not numbered) and *Zrinyi,* overture (both were awarded the Hungarian Millennium Prize in 1896; first perf., Budapest, June 3, 1897); Piano Concerto No. 1 in E minor, op. 5 (1897–98; Budapest, Jan. 11, 1899; won the Bösen-

dorfer Prize in Vienna, 1899); Symph. No. 1 in D minor, op. 9 (1900–1; Manchester, Jan. 30, 1902); *Konzertstück* for Cello and Orch., op. 12 (1903–4; Budapest, March 7, 1906); Suite in F-sharp minor for Orch., op. 19 (1908–9; Budapest, Feb. 21, 1910); *Variationen über ein Kinderlied (Variations on a Nursery Song),* for Piano and Orch., op. 25 (1913; Berlin, Feb. 17, 1914, Dohnányi, soloist); Violin Concerto No. 1 in D minor, op. 27 (1914–15, Copenhagen, March 5, 1919); *Ünnepi nyitány (Festival Overture),* op. 31 (1923); *Ruralia hungarica,* 5 pieces for Orch., op. 32b (1924; Budapest, Nov. 17, 1924, Dohnányi, conductor); *Szimfonikus percek (Symphonic Minutes),* op. 36 (1933); *Suite en valse,* op. 39 (1942–43); Symph. No. 2 in E major, op. 40 (1943–44; London, Nov. 23, 1948; revised 1953–56; Minneapolis, March 15, 1957; Piano Concerto No. 2 in B minor, op. 42 (1946–47; Sheffield, England, Dec. 3, 1947); Violin Concerto No. 2, op. 43 (scored for Orch. without Violins; 1949–50; San Antonio, Jan. 26, 1952); Concertino for Harp and Chamber Orch., op. 45 (1952); *American Rhapsody,* op. 47 (1953; Athens, Ohio, Feb. 21, 1954, Dohnányi, conductor).

VOCAL WORKS: *Magyar hiszekegy (Hungarian Credo)* for Tenor, Choir, and Orch. (1920); *Missa in Dedicatione Ecclesiae (Mass of Szeged)* for Soloist, Chorus, Organ, and Orch., op. 35 (1930; consecration of the Cathedral of Szeged, Oct. 25, 1930); *Cantus vitae,* symph. cantata, op. 38 (1939–41); *Stabat Mater* for 3 Soloists, Children's Chorus, and Orch., op. 46 (1952–53; Wichita Falls, Kans., Jan. 16, 1956); also songs, including 6 Poems, op. 14 (1905–6); *Im Lebenslenz,* op. 16 (1906–7); 3 Songs, with Orch., op. 22 (1912); Hungarian Folk Songs (1922).

CHAMBER MUSIC: Piano Quintet No. 1, op. 1 (1895); String Quartet No. 1, op. 7 (1899); Sonata for Cello and Piano, op. 8 (1899); *Serenade* for String Trio, op. 10 (1902); String Quartet No. 2, op. 15 (1904); Sonata for Violin and Piano, op. 21 (1912); Piano Quintet No. 2, op. 26 (1914); *Ruralia hungarica,* 3 pieces for Violin and Piano, op. 32c (1924); *Ruralia hungarica,* 1 piece for Cello or Violin and Piano, op. 32d (1924); String Quartet No. 3, op. 33 (1926); Sextet for Piano, Clarinet, Horn, and String Trio, op. 37 (1935); *Aria,* for Flute and Piano (1958); *Passacaglia* for Flute, op. 48 (1959).

FOR PIANO: 4 Pieces, op. 2: *Scherzo* in C-sharp minor, *Intermezzo* in A minor, *Intermezzo* in F minor, *Capriccio* in B minor (1896–97); *Waltz* in F-sharp minor, for 4 hands, op. 3 (1897); Variations and Fugue on a Theme of E(mma) G(ruber), op. 4 (1897); Gavotte and Musette in B-flat major (1898); Passacaglia in E-flat minor, op. 6 (1899); 4 Rhapsodies, in G minor, F-sharp minor, C major, E-flat minor, op. 11 (1902–3); *Winterreigen,* 10 bagatelles: *Widmung, Marsch der lustigen Bruder, An Ada, Freund Viktor's Mazurka, Sphärenmusik, Valse aimable, Um Mitternacht, Tolle Gesellschaft, Morgengrauen, Postludium,* op. 13 (1905); *Humoresken in Form einer Suite:* March, Toccata, Pavane with Variations, Pastorale, Introduction, and Fugue, op. 17 (1907); 3 Pieces: *Aria, Valse impromptu, Capriccio,* op. 23 (1912); Fugue, for left hand or 2 hands (1913); *Suite im alten Stil:* Prelude, Allemande, Courante, Sarabande, Menuet, Gigue, op. 24 (1913); 6 Concert

Etudes, op. 28 (1916); Variations on a Hungarian Folk Song, op. 29 (1917); Pastorale, Hungarian Christmas Song (1920); *Ruralia hungarica,* 7 pieces, op. 32a (1923); Essential Finger Exercises (1929); *Suite en valse* for 2 pianos, op. 39a (1945); 6 Pieces: Impromptu, Scherzino, Canzonetta, Cascade, Ländler, Cloches, op. 41 (1945); 12 Short Studies for the Advanced Pianist (1950); 3 Singular Pieces: *Burletta, Nocturne (Cats on the Roof), Perpetuum mobile,* op. 44 (1951); Daily Finger Exercises (3 vols., 1960).

BIBLIOGRAPHY: V. Papp, *Dohnányi Ernö* (Budapest, 1927); M. Reuth, *The Tallahassee Years of Ernst von Dohnányi* (Diss., Florida State Univ., 1962); L. Podhradszky, "The Works of Ernö Dohnányi," *Studia musicologica Academiae scientiarum hungaricae,* VI (1964); B. Vázsonyi, *Dohnányi Ernö* (Budapest, 1971).

Doire, René, French composer and conductor; b. Evreux, June 13, 1879; d. Paris, July 9, 1959. He studied in Rouen and later in Paris, with Widor and Vincent d'Indy; then was engaged as a bandleader in the casinos of various French spas. He composed a one-act opera, *Morituri* (1903); a cycle of songs, *Reflets de Jeunesse,* for Voice and Piano, or Orch. (1902); *Vision d'Espagne* for Violin and Orch. (1916); Violin Sonata (1918); *Dramatico* for Piano and Orch. (1923); songs.

Dokshitcher, Timofei, Soviet trumpet virtuoso; b. Nezhin, Dec. 13, 1921. He studied trumpet with Tabakov in Moscow, and conducting at the Moscow Cons., graduating in 1957. In 1945 he became a member of the Bolshoi Theater orch. He enjoys a reputation as one of the finest artists on his instrument.

Doktor, Paul, Austrian-American violist; b. Vienna, March 28, 1919. He studied with his father, **Karl Doktor,** violinist of the renowned Busch String Quartet; graduated as a violinist at the State Academy of Music in Vienna in 1938, but subsequently changed to viola, and in 1942 received the first prize for viola at the International Music Competition in Geneva. He left Vienna in 1938; in 1939–47 was solo violist of the Lucerne Orch.; emigrated to the U.S. in 1947. He edited several collections of viola music for G. Schirmer, Inc. (*Solos for the Viola Player,* Schubert's Arpeggione Sonata, 2 sonatas by Brahms, Mozart's duets for violin and viola, etc.). In 1953 he was appointed to the faculty of the Mannes College of Music in N.Y.; taught at the Philadelphia Academy from 1970 and at the Juilliard School of Music from 1971.

Dolega-Kamiénski. See **Kamiénski, Lucian.**

Doles, Johann Friedrich, German composer; b. Steinbach, April 23, 1715; d. Leipzig, Feb. 8, 1797. He was a student of theology in Leipzig; then became a pupil of Bach (1740–44), who recommended him for the post of cantor at Salzburg. In 1743–44 he conducted a series of concerts in Leipzig which

proved to be the precursor to the famous concerts of the Gewandhaus Orch. In 1756 he became cantor at the St. Thomas School in Leipzig; was also director of the St. Thomas Church until 1789, when he resigned owing to old age. He wrote a great number of sacred works, a full list of which is given in *Die Musik in Geschichte und Gegenwart.*
BIBLIOGRAPHY: H. Banning, *J.F. Doles: Leben und Werke* (Leipzig, 1939).

Doležálek, Jan Emanuel, Czech musician; b. Chotěboř, May 22, 1780; d. Vienna, July 6, 1858. He studied music in Vienna with Beethoven's teacher, Albrechtsberger, and through him came to know Beethoven himself. It is owing chiefly to this association that Doležálek's name is known in music history. He arranged a number of Czech songs, and publ. a collection of them.

Dolin, Samuel, Canadian composer; b. Montreal, Aug. 22, 1917. He studied piano in Montreal and Toronto; later took lessons in composition with Weinzweig and Krenek. In 1945 he was appointed to the faculty of the Toronto Cons.; was active in various musical organizations; served as president of the Canadian League of Composers (1969–73).
WORKS: Opera, *Casino (Greed;* 1966–67); *Drakkar,* "an entertainment" for Narrator, Mezzo-soprano, 2 Baritones, 2 Dancers, Chamber Ensemble, 2 Synthesizers, and Amplifiers (1972; Toronto, Feb. 17, 1973); Sinfonietta (1950; the *Scherzo* movement is often played as a separate piece); Serenade for Strings (1951); 3 symphs. (1956, 1957, 1976); *Isometric Variables* (*Bassooneries in Free Variations*) for Bassoon and Strings (1957); Sonata for String Orch. (1962); Fantasy for Piano and Chamber Orch. (1967); Piano Concerto (1974); Violin Sonatina (1954); Violin Sonata (1960); *Portrait* for String Quartet (1961); *Barcarolle* for Violin and Piano (1962); Concerto Grosso (*Georgian Bay*) for Percussion, Accordion, and Tape (1970); Sonata for Solo Accordion (1970); *Marchbankantata* for Baritone, Chorus, Piano, and Synthesizer (1971); Mass for 6 Voices, Congregation, and Organ (1972); 3 sonatas: for Solo Violin, Solo Flute, and Solo Cello, each with Tape (all 1973); *Ricercar* for Solo Guitar (1974); *Adikia* for one to 5 Accordions in any combination, and Tape (1975); *4 Miniatures* for Piano (1943); 3 Preludes for Piano (1949); Piano Sonata (1950); *Little Toccata* for Piano (1959); Piano Sonatina (1959); Variation for 2 Pianos (1967); *If* for Piano (1972); choruses; songs.

Dolmetsch, Arnold, English music antiquarian; b. Le Mans, France, Feb. 24, 1858; d. Haslemere, Surrey, Feb. 28, 1940. While apprenticed in his father's piano factory he learned to play both piano and violin, making such marked progress on the latter instrument that his father sent him to Brussels, where he became a pupil of Vieuxtemps (1881–83); then went to the Royal College of Music in London, where he studied violin with Henry Holmes and harmony with Bridge; after completing his studies he went to Dulwich, was appointed instructor of violin at the College, and soon won a reputation as a teacher (1885–89). From his earliest years he had shown a decided predilection for the music of Bach and the old masters; when by chance he became the possessor of a well-preserved viola d'amore, he did not rest until he had mastered the instrument; gradually he acquired the same skill on all the members of the viol family. He then gave up his large class of violin pupils and devoted his entire time to lecturing and giving recitals on the old instruments. In his quest for old music he found in the British Museum MSS of almost-forgotten English composers (Simon Ives, Matthew Locke, Thomas Tomkins, John Jenkins, etc.). To become an authoritative interpreter of all this music, he found it necessary to extend his investigations to the virginal, spinet, harpsichord, and clavichord. He began by collecting old books in which those instruments were described by contemporary authorities; the mechanical skill he had acquired in his father's shop he turned to account in repairing the instruments he collected, and before long he was acknowledged as an authority on old music and instruments; he was not only a connoisseur and skilled workman, but also a masterly performer on every instrument in his large collection; with his wife and a pupil, **Kathleen Salmon,** he established the Dolmetsch Trio, devoted exclusively to the performance of old music on the original instruments. A tour of the U.S. attracted so much attention that Chickering & Sons, of Boston, placed their factory and a force of their best workmen at Dolmetsch's disposal. The beginning was made with the restoration of a virginal by Hans Ruckers (1620); then a number of stringed and keyed instruments were built after the best models extant. The interest excited by the revival of these instruments induced several other artists (Wanda Landowska, Fuller-Maitland, the brothers Casadesus, etc.) to give recitals on them. In 1902–9 Dolmetsch lived in Boston, supervising the construction of his instruments and concertizing; he went to Paris to work for Gaveau in 1911–14; after that, he resided in England. In 1925 he founded at Haslemere, Surrey, annual historical chamber music festivals, where the works were played (many by himself) on modern reconstructions of the original historic instruments (clavichord, harpsichord, viols, recorders, etc.). The Dolmetsch Foundation, a society for the purpose of cultivating old music and making his ideas more widely known, was founded by his friends in 1929.
WRITINGS: *Select English Songs and Dialogues of the 16th and 17th Centuries* (2 vols., London, 1898, 1912) and *The Interpretation of the Music of the 17th and 18th Centuries* (London, 1915; new ed., 1944).
BIBLIOGRAPHY: R. Donington, *The Work and Ideas of Arnold Dolmetsch* (Haslemere, 1932); Percy Grainger, "Arnold Dolmetsch, Musical Confucius," *Musical Quarterly* (April 1933); M. Dolmetsch, *Personal Recollections of Arnold Dolmetsch* (London, 1958); M. Campbell, *Dolmetsch: The Man and His Work* (London, 1975).

Dolmetsch, Carl Frederick, French specialist in

recorder music, son of **Arnold Dolmetsch;** b. Fontenay-sous-Bois, near Paris, Aug. 23, 1911. He received thorough training in instrumentation from his father; eventually succeeded him as a leader of the Haslemere Festival. He devoted himself mainly to the publication of music for the recorder; publ. a survey, *Recorder and German Flute during the 17th and 18th Centuries* (London, 1957), and *An Introduction to the Recorder in Modern British Music* (London, 1960). He also publishes the annual bulletin *The Consort.*

Dolukhanova, Zara, Russian mezzo-soprano of Armenian extraction; b. Moscow, March 5, 1918. She studied with private teachers; joined the Moscow Radio staff in 1944; was awarded the Lenin Prize in 1966. A lyric singer, she excels in the Romantic Russian repertoire. In 1959 she made her first American tour, enjoying great acclaim; she toured America again in 1970.

Domaniewski, Boleslaus, Polish pianist; b. Gronówek, Russian Poland, July 16, 1857; d. Warsaw, Sept. 11, 1925. He studied at the St. Petersburg Cons.; in 1890–1900 taught at the Cons. of Cracow; in 1900 he became director of the Warsaw Cons. His piano method, *Vademecum pour le pianiste,* enjoyed considerable popularity.

Domarkas, Ionas, Lithuanian composer; b. Lengiru, May 23, 1934. He studied at the Lithuanian Cons. in Vilna, and was subsequently active in radio broadcasting and teaching. Among his works are *Symphonic Dances* for Orch. (1969); a Violin Sonata (1972); and several pieces for clarinet, oboe, and bassoon, as well as for piano.

Domgraf-Fässbander, Willi, German baritone; b. Aachen, Feb. 19, 1987; d. Nuremberg, Feb. 13, 1978. He made his debut in Aachen in 1922; then sang in Berlin, Düsseldorf, and Stuttgart. From 1928–48 he was a principal member of the Berlin State Opera; he then made appearances in Hannover, Vienna, Munich, and Nuremberg. In 1954 he became a member of the faculty at the Nuremberg Cons. of Music. His daughter, **Brigitte Fässbander,** is a well-known mezzo-soprano.

Domingo, Placido, Spanish operatic tenor; b. Madrid, Jan. 21, 1941. He went to Mexico at the age of 9 with his parents, who were performers of Spanish zarzuelas; took part in these performances as a child; learned to play the piano and soon developed a pleasing baritone voice, from which he changed to a fine tenorino. He studied operatic parts, accompanying himself at the piano. His first important engagement was in Tel Aviv, where he was engaged as an opera singer for 2 years. He then went to America, where his first engagement was at the N.Y. City Opera as Pinkerton in *Madama Butterfly,* on Oct. 17, 1965; he made his debut with the Metropolitan Opera in N.Y. at the Lewisohn Stadium as Turiddu in a concert performance of *Cavalleria*

rusticana, on Aug. 9, 1966. In quick succession he sang Canio in *Pagliacci,* Cavaradossi in *Tosca,* Pinkerton in *Madama Butterfly,* Manrico in *Il Trovatore,* Alfredo in *La Traviata,* Rhadames in *Aida,* and Don José in *Carmen.* He also sang in Hamburg, Milan, and other European cities. Addicted to precise statistics, he calculated the number of his appearances from 1966 to April 1977 at the Metropolitan as 108, and the total of his appearances since his very first engagement up to the same terminal date as 1,209 in 74 roles. His voice possesses a liquidity that is the essence of bel canto; he excels particularly in lyric parts in Italian operas, but he has also essayed Wagnerian roles. He publ. his autobiography, *My First Forty Years* (N.Y., 1983).

Dominiceti, Cesare, Italian composer; b. Desenzano, July 12, 1821; d. Sesto di Monza, June 20, 1888. He studied in Milan, where all his operas were brought out; lived for a long time in Bolivia; made a fortune there. Some years after his return to Italy, he was appointed prof. of composition at the Milan Cons. He wrote the operas *Due mogli in una* (Milan, June 30, 1853), *La maschera* (Milan, March 2, 1854), *Morovico* (Milan, Dec. 4, 1873), *Il lago delle fate* (Milan, May 18, 1878), and *L'Ereditiera* (Milan, Feb. 14, 1881).

Domino, "Fats" (Antoine, Jr.), black American pianist and bandleader; b. New Orleans, Feb. 26, 1928. Although he sustained a severe hand injury as a youth, he pursued his career as a pianist; gained fame during the early years of the rock-'n'-roll era by mixing blues elements with straight rock; he was successful in nightclubs and movies as a purveyor of popular, jazz, and blues genres.

Dommer, Arrey von, German musicographer; b. Danzig, Feb. 9, 1828; d. Treysa, Feb. 18, 1905. A theological student, he turned to music, and in 1851 became the pupil of Richter and Lobe (composition) and Schallenberg (organ) at Leipzig. He taught music at Leipzig, and went to Hamburg in 1863. He publ. *Elemente der Musik* (1862); *Musikalisches Lexikon* (1865; a revised ed. of Koch's); *Handbuch der Musikgeschichte* (1867; 2nd ed., 1878; 3rd ed., entirely rewritten and brought up to date by A. Schering, 1914).

Donalda, Pauline (real name, **Lightstone,** translated by her father from **Lichtenstein** when he became a British subject), dramatic soprano; b. Montreal, March 5, 1882; d. there, Oct. 22, 1970. She received her first musical training at Royal Victoria College in Montreal, and then was a private pupil of Duvernoy in Paris; made her debut as Manon (Massenet) at Nice, Dec. 30, 1904; the next year she appeared at La Monnaie in Brussels and at Covent Garden; in 1906–7, at the Manhattan Opera House in N.Y.; then chiefly at the Opéra-Comique. From the time of her retirement, in 1922, to 1937, she had a singing school in Paris; in 1937, returned to Montreal. In 1938 she presented her valuable music library (MSS, autographs, and music) to McGill Univ. In

1940 she founded the Opera Guild in Montreal, serving as its president until it ceased operations in 1969. In 1967 she was made an Officer of the Order of Canada. Her stage name was taken in honor of Sir Donald Smith (later Lord Strathcona), who endowed the Royal Victoria College and was her patron (1975).

BIBLIOGRAPHY: C. Brotman, *Pauline Donalda* (1975).

Donaldson, Walter, American pianist and composer; b. Brooklyn, Feb. 15, 1893; d. Santa Monica, Calif., July 15, 1947. He worked for Wall Street brokerage firms before engaging in music; went to Hollywood in 1929 and wrote film scores and also single songs, among them *Yes, Sir, That's My Baby* (1925), which became a perennial hit. Another song that became exceptionally popular, for which Donaldson wrote both lyrics and music, was *You're Driving Me Crazy.*

Donath, Helen, American soprano; b. Corpus Christi, Texas, July 10, 1940. She was educated at Del Mar College. She then settled in West Germany; made her debut at the Cologne Opera in 1962; sang with fine success in Hannover, Frankfurt, and Munich; also appeared at Bayreuth, being one of the few American singers to gain such distinction. In America, she sang at the San Francisco Opera. She was a favorite singer at Herbert von Karajan's annual Easter Festival in Salzburg.

Donati (Donato), Baldassare, famous Italian composer of motets and madrigals; b. Venice, c.1530; d. there, 1603. He was choirmaster of the so-called "small choir" at San Marco in Venice in 1562–65; this was disbanded by Zarlino when he was appointed maestro di cappella in 1565, and Donati became a simple chorister; he was appointed maestro di canto to the Seminario Gregoriano di San Marco (1580); in 1590, he succeeded Zarlino as maestro di cappella. His compositions are distinguished by their well-defined rhythm and originality. Extant works include *Canzoni Villanesche alla Napoletana* (1550–58); several books of madrigals for 4 parts (1550–68); a vol. of madrigals for 5–6 parts (1553; new eds., 1557, 1560); a vol. of motets for 5–8 parts (1597); etc.

Donati, Ignazio, Italian composer; b. Casalmaggiore, c.1570; d. Milan, Jan. 21, 1638. He was maestro di cappella at the Urbino Cathedral (1612–16); then at Ferrara (1616–18); Casalmaggiore (1618–23); Novara and Lodi (1626–30). In 1631 he became maestro di cappella at the Cathedral of Milan. He publ. 8 books of *concerti ecclesiastici,* 7 books of motets, masses, and Psalms.

Donati, Pino, Italian composer and conductor; b. Verona, May 9, 1907; d. Rome, Feb. 24, 1975. He studied violin; then took composition lessons with G.C. Paribeni. He served as artistic coordinator of the Chicago Lyric Opera from 1958. He wrote 2 operas: *Corradino lo Svevo* (Verona, April 4, 1931) and *Lancillotto del lago* (Bergamo, Oct. 2, 1938); also chamber music.

Donato, Anthony, American violinist and composer; b. Prague, Nebr., March 8, 1909. He studied at the Eastman School of Music in Rochester, N.Y., with Hanson, Rogers, and Royce; obtained the degrees of M.Mus. (1937) and Ph.D. (1947). He was a violin teacher at Drake Univ. (1931–37); Iowa State Teachers College (1937–39); the Univ. of Texas (1939–46); Northwestern Univ. (1947–77).

WORKS: 2 symphs. (1944, 1945); opera, *The Walker through Walls* (Evanston, Ill., Feb. 26, 1965, composer conducting); *March of the Hungry Mountains* for Chorus and Orch. (1949); *Solitude in the City* for Narrator and Instruments (1954); *Centennial Ode* for Orch., commissioned by the Nebraska State Centennial (Omaha, Dec. 11, 1967); *Improvisation* for Orch. (Kansas City, May 3, 1969); 4 string quartets (1941, 1947, 1951, 1975; the *Andante* from String Quartet No. 1 is also arranged for String Orch.); 2 violin sonatas (1938, 1949); *Pastorale and Dance* for 4 Clarinets (1947); Sonatina for 3 Trumpets (1949); Sonata for Horn and Piano (1950); Piano Trio (1959); Sonata for Clarinet and Piano (1966); *Discourse* for Flute and Piano (1969); many choral works and piano teaching pieces. He publ. *Preparing Music Manuscript* (Englewood Cliffs, N.J., 1963).

BIBLIOGRAPHY: *Composers of the Americas,* vol. 15 (Washington, D.C., 1969).

Donatoni, Franco, Italian composer; b. Verona, June 9, 1927. He studied with Desderi in Milan, Liviabella in Bologna, and Pizzetti at the Santa Cecilia Academy in Rome, graduating in 1953. He was then an instructor at the Cons. of Bologna, the Verdi Cons. in Milan, the Verdi Cons. in Turin, and, since 1970, at the Accademia Musicale Chigiana in Siena. In his music he adopts a system of serial techniques while retaining a fairly strict Baroque structure.

WORKS: String Quartet (1950); Viola Sonata (1952); Concerto for Bassoon and Strings (1952); Concertino for Strings, Brass, and Percussion (1952); *Sinfonia* for Strings (1953); Overture (1953); *Divertimento I* for Violin and Orch. (1954); *5 Pieces* for 2 Pianos (1954); *La Lampara,* ballet (1954); *Quartetto II* for String Quartet (1958); *Serenata* for Soprano and 16 Instruments, to words by Dylan Thomas (1959); *Strophes* for Orch. (Radio Rome, Jan. 30, 1960); *Movimento* for Harpsichord, Piano, and 9 Instruments (1959); *Sezioni (Sections)* for Orch. (1960; Hamburg Radio, May 14, 1962); *Quartetto III* for 4-track Tape (1961); *Puppenspiel I,* study for stage music, for Orch. (Palermo, Oct. 8, 1962); *Per orchestra* (1962; Warsaw Autumn Festival, Sept. 24, 1963); *Quartetto IV* for String Quartet (1963; an aleatory work); *Asar* for 10 String Instruments (1964); *Black and White* for 37 String Instruments (1964); *Divertimento II* for String Orch. (1965); *Puppenspiel II* for Flute and Orch. (Valdagno, Sept. 17, 1966); *Souvenir,* subtitled *Kammer-*

Donaudy – Donizetti

symphonie, for 15 Instruments (Venice Festival, Sept. 12, 1967); *Etwas ruhiger im Ausdruck* for Flute, Clarinet, Violin, Cello, and Piano (1968; the title is taken from an expression mark in bar 8 of the 2nd of Schoenberg's *5 Piano Pieces*, op. 23); *Black and White No. 2*, exercises for 10 fingers for Keyboard Instrument (1968); *Orts (Souvenir No. 2)* for 14 Instruments with Optional Lecturer (1969); *Solo II* for 10 String Instruments (1969); *Doubles II* for Orch. (Rome, June 13, 1970; as a ballet, Venice, Jan. 15, 1971); Lied for 13 Instruments (1972); *Voci* for Orch. (1972–73; Rome, Feb. 3, 1974); *Lumen* for 6 Instruments (1975); *Diario 1976* for 4 Trombones and 4 Trumpets (1976); *Ash* for 8 Instruments; 4 works under the generic title *Estratto (Extract)*: No. 1 for Piano (1969); No. 2 for Harp, Harpsichord, and Piano (1970); No. 3 for Piano and 8 Wind Instruments (1975); No. 4 for 8 Instruments (1975).

Donaudy, Stefano, composer; b. (of a French father and an Italian mother) Palermo, Feb. 21, 1879; d. Naples, May 30, 1925. He was a pupil at the Palermo Cons. of G. Zuelli in 1896–1900; wrote the operas *Folchetto* (Palermo, 1892); *Scampagnata* (Palermo, 1898); *Theodor Körner* (Hamburg, Nov. 27, 1902); *Sperduti nel buio* (Palermo, April 27, 1907); *Ramuntcho* (Milan, March 19, 1921); *La Fiamminga* (Naples, April 25, 1922); symph. poem, *Le Rêve de Polysende; 12 airs de style ancien* for Voice and Piano; and numerous piano pieces.

Donfrid, Johannes, German editor of church music; b. Veringenstadt, 1585; d. Rottenburg, Aug. 4, 1650. He was rector of a school, and cantor at St. Martin's Church in Rottenburg. His most important publication is the *Promptuarium musicum* (3 vols., Strasbourg, 1622–27), containing sacred works by various composers; he also publ. a collection of songs, *Viridarium Musico-Marianum* (Strasbourg, 1627); and *Corolla musica,* including 37 masses (Strasbourg, 1628).

Doni, Antonio Francesco, Italian writer; b. Florence, May 16, 1513; d. Monselice, near Padua, in Sept., 1574. For several years he was a member of the Servite fraternity in Florence; after leaving it in 1539, he led a wandering life as a lay priest. He publ., besides various non-musical treatises, a *Dialogo sulla musica* (1544; includes a list of 17 composers living in Venice at the time, with works of each) and a *Libraria* (2 vols., Venice, 1550–51), containing a description of all publ. and unpubl. musical books in Italian known at the time, as well as a list of the music academies then in existence and details of their foundation.

Doni, Giovanni Battista, Italian music theorist, b. 1594; d. Florence, Dec. 1, 1647. He studied literature and philosophy at Bologna and Rome; in 1613–18 he was a law student at Bourges, France, and took his degree at Pisa. In 1621 he accompanied Cardinal Corsini to Paris, where he zealously pursued his literary and antiquarian studies; went to Rome in 1622, at the invitation of Cardinal Barberini, who

was passionately fond of music, and with whom he traveled. In the intervals of his profound study of ancient music, he found time to construct the "Lira Barberina," or "Amphichord," a species of double lyre which he dedicated to Pope Urban VIII. Recalled to Florence in 1640 by deaths in his family, he settled there, married the next year, and accepted a professorship of elocution offered him by the Grand Duke. His criticism and discussions of the earliest operas are very valuable, and were publ. for the first time by A. Solerti in *Origini del melodramma. Testimonianze dei contemporanei* (Turin, 1903).

WRITINGS: *Compendio del trattato de' generi e de' modi della musica* (Rome, 1635); *Annotazioni* on the above (Rome, 1640); *De praestantia musicae veteris libri tres* (Florence, 1647); and several essays in MS (some still extant in the library of the Santa Cecilia Academy in Rome).

BIBLIOGRAPHY: A.M. Blandini, *Commentarium de vita et scripts G.B. Doni* (Florence, 1755); F. Vatielli, *La lira barberina di G.B. Doni* (Pesaro, 1909).

Donington, Robert, distinguished English musicologist; b. Leeds, May 4, 1907. He studied at Queen's College, Oxford (B.A., 1930; B. Litt., 1946); also took a course in composition with Egon Wellesz at Oxford; became associated with Arnold Dolmetsch in his workshop in Haslemere and studied the technique of old instruments; in the capacity of an expert, he contributed to the revival of Elizabethan instruments and music. He was a member of the English Consort of Viols (1935–39); then played with the London Consort (1950–60); in 1956 he founded the Donington Consort, and led it until 1961. He lectured extensively in the U.S.; in 1974 was appointed a prof. at the Univ. of Iowa. He was made a Commander of the Order of the British Empire in 1979.

WRITINGS: *The Work and Ideas of Arnold Dolmetsch* (Haslemere, 1932); *A Practical Method for the Recorder* (with Edgar Hunt; 2 vols., London, 1935); *The Instruments of Music* (London, 1949; 3rd ed., revised, 1970); *Music for Fun* (London, 1960); *Tempo and Rhythm in Bach's Organ Music* (London, 1960); *The Interpretation of Early Music* (N.Y., 1963; 3rd ed., revised, 1974); *Wagner's "Ring" and Its Symbols* (London, 1963; 3rd ed., revised and enlarged, 1974); *A Performer's Guide to Baroque Music* (London, 1973); *String-playing in Baroque Music* (London, 1977); *The Opera* (London, 1978); *The Rise of Opera* (London, 1981).

Donizetti (real name, **Ciummei**), **Alfredo,** composer; b. Smyrna, Sept. 2, 1867; d. Rosario, Argentina, Feb. 4, 1921. He studied (1883–89) at the Milan Cons. under Ponchielli and Dominiceti; then settled in Argentina. He wrote the operas *Nama* (Milan, 1890) and *Dopo l'Ave Maria* (Milan, 1896); also piano pieces and songs.

Donizetti, Gaetano, one of the brilliant triumvirate (Donizetti, Rossini, and Bellini) of Italian opera composers in the first half of the 19th century; b. Bergamo, Nov. 29, 1797; d. there, April 8, 1848. His father, a weaver by trade, later obtained a position in the local pawnshop and desired that his son should become a lawyer. But Donizetti's inclinations were toward art; besides being strongly attracted to music, he studied drawing. His father finally allowed him to enter the Bergamo school of music; his teachers were Salari (voice), Gonzales (piano), and J.S. Mayr (harmony). In 1815 he enrolled in the Bologna Liceo Filarmonico, here completing his contrapuntal studies under Pilotti and Padre Mattei. From his earliest attempts at composition Donizetti was determined to write operas. His first opera was *Il Pigmalione,* which was not produced; but he gained production with his next opera, *Enrico di Borgogna* (Venice, 1818). Two operas —*Una follia* (1818) and *I piccoli, virtuosi ambulanti* (1819)—intervened before the success of *Il Falegname di Livonia* (Venice, 1819; given at first as *Pietro il Grande, Czar delle Russie*). However, *Le nozze in villa* (Mantua, 1820) was a failure. At least a year before his next successful opera, *Zoraide di Granata* (Rome, Jan. 28, 1822), he was exempted from military service thanks to the intercession of an influential noblewoman. In 7 years, between 1822 and 1829, he produced no fewer than 23 operas, none of which left a lasting impression. But with the next production, *Anna Bolena* (Milan, 1830), Donizetti established himself as a master of the musical theater. Written for Pasta and Rubini, after the Italian fashion of adapting roles for singers, its vogue was more than local; in 1831 it was produced in London, with the bass Lablache as Henry VIII. There followed *L'elisir d'amore* (Milan, 1832), the tragic *Lucrezia Borgia* (La Scala, Milan, 1833), and the immensely popular *Lucia di Lammermoor* (Naples, 1835). Donizetti's life was now spent in traveling from place to place, bringing out opera after opera. He visited Paris in 1835, and produced *Marino Faliero* at the Théâtre des Italiens. In May 1837, he succeeded Zingarelli as director of the Naples Cons. On July 30, 1837, he suffered a grievous loss when his wife died after 9 years of happy marital life. The censor's veto prevented the production of *Poliuto* (written for Nourrit after Corneille's *Polyeucte*) in Naples, and Donizetti decided to go to France. He produced at the Opéra-Comique in Paris the highly successful *La Fille du régiment* (1840), and, at the Grand Opéra, *Les Martyrs,* a revision of the forbidden *Poliuto* (1840). His next opera, *La Favorite* (1840), made a veritable sensation at its production at the Grand Opéra. After this series of Paris successes, Donizetti went back to Italy, where he produced *Adelia* (Rome, 1841) and *Maria Padilla* (Milan, 1841). His next travels took him to Vienna, where his new opera *Linda di Chamounix* evoked such enthusiasm that the Emperor conferred on him the titles of court composer and Master of the Imperial Chapel. In the interim, Donizetti composed a *Miserere* and an *Ave Maria* for the Austrian Court Chapel, in a severe purity of style. After the production of *Don Pasquale* (Paris, 1843), Donizetti had reached the height of his fame and prosperity; but he began to suffer from nervous fatigue and circulatory disturbance. The last opera produced in his lifetime was *Caterina Cornaro* (Naples, 1844); in 1845 he had a paralytic stroke from which he never recovered; he died a madman 3 years later. Posthumous works were *Rita,* produced in 1860; *Gabriella di Vergy* (1869); and *Le Duc d'Albe* (1882). Besides operas, Donizetti wrote many songs, ariettas, duets, and canzonets; 7 masses, one being a Requiem; cantatas; vespers, Psalms, motets; 12 string quartets; piano music.

WORKS: OPERAS: *Il Pigmalione* (1817; not produced in Donizetti's lifetime, but had a modern revival in Bergamo, Oct. 13, 1960); *Enrico di Borgogna* (Venice, Nov. 14, 1818); *Una follia* (Venice, Dec. 15, 1818); *Pietro il Grande, Czar delle Russie,* better known under the title *Il Falegname di Livonia* (Venice, Dec. 26, 1819); *Le nozze in villa* (Mantua, Jan. 23, 1821); *Zoraide di Granata* (Rome, Jan. 28, 1822); *La Zingara* (Naples, May 12, 1822); *La lettera anonima* (Naples, June 29, 1822); *Chiara e Serafina* (Milan, Oct. 26, 1822); *Alfredo il Grande* (Naples, July 2, 1823); *Il fortunato inganno* (Naples, Sept. 3, 1823); *L'Aio nell' imbarazzo* (Rome, Feb. 4, 1824); *Emilia di Liverpool* (Naples, July 28, 1824); *I voti dei sudditi,* cantata (Naples, March 6, 1825); *Alahor di Granata* (Palermo, Jan. 7, 1826); *Elvida* (Naples, July 6, 1826); *Olivo e Pasquale* (Rome, Jan. 7, 1827); *Gli Esiliati in Siberia,* commonly known as *Otto Mesi in due ore* (Naples, May 13, 1827); *Il Borgomastro di Saardam* (Naples, Aug. 19, 1827); *Le convenienze ed inconvenienze teatrali* (Naples, Nov. 21, 1827); *L'Esule di Roma* (Naples, Jan. 1, 1828); *Alina, regina di Golconda* (Genoa, May 12, 1828); *Gianni di Calais* (Naples, Aug. 2, 1828); *Il Paria* (Naples, Jan. 12, 1829); *Elisabetta al Castello di Kenilworth* (Naples, July 6, 1829); *I Pazzi per progetto* (Naples, Feb. 7, 1830); *Il diluvio universale* (Naples, Feb. 28, 1830); *Il ritorno desiderato,* cantata, which may be identical with *Il fausto ritorno* (Naples, may have been perf. in Aug. 1830 as a ceremonial piece to celebrate the return of Francesco I and Isabella Maria from Spain); *Imelda de' Lambertazzi* (Naples, Aug. 23, 1830); *Anna Bolena* (Milan, Dec. 26, 1830); *Francesca di Foix* (Naples, May 30, 1831); *La Romanziera e l'uomo nero* (Naples, date cannot be established); *Fausta* (Naples, Jan. 12, 1832); *Ugo, conte di Parigi* (Milan, March 13, 1832); *L'elisir d'amore* (Milan, May 12, 1832); *Sancia di Castiglia* (Naples, Nov. 4, 1832); *Il Furioso all'isola di San Domingo* (Rome, Jan. 2, 1833); *Parisina* (Florence, March 17, 1833); *Torquato Tasso* (Rome, Sept. 9, 1833); *Lucrezia Borgia* (Milan, Dec. 26, 1833); *Rosmonda d'Inghilterra* (Florence, Feb. 26, 1834); *Maria Stuarda* (Naples, Oct. 18, 1834); *Gemma di Vergy* (Milan, Dec. 26, 1834); *Marino Faliero* (Paris, March 12, 1835); *Lucia di Lammermoor* (Naples, Sept. 26, 1835); *Belisario* (Venice, Feb. 4, 1836); *Il campanello di notte* (Naples, June 1, 1836); *Betly* (Naples, Aug. 24, 1836); *L'assedio di Calais* (Naples, Nov. 19, 1836); *Pia de' Tolomei* (Venice, Feb. 18, 1837); *Roberto Devereux,* known also as *Il Conte d'Essex* (Naples, Oct. 29, 1837); *Maria di Rudenz* (Venice, Jan. 30, 1838); *Gianni di Parigi* (Milan, Sept. 10, 1839); *La Fille du régiment* (Paris, Feb. 11, 1840); *Les Martyrs* (Paris, April 10, 1840; French version of his Neapolitan opera *Poliuto*); *La Favorite* (Paris, Dec. 2, 1840; derived from his unfinished opera *L'Ange de Nisida*); *Adelia* (Rome, Feb. 11, 1841); *Maria Padilla* (Milan, Dec. 26, 1841); *Linda di Chamounix* (Vienna, May 19, 1842); *Don Pasquale* (Paris, Jan. 3, 1843); *Maria di Rohan* (Vienna, June 5, 1843); *Dom Sébastien, roi de Portugal* (Paris, Nov. 13, 1843; revised several times by Donizetti and Giacomo Panizza); *Caterina Cornaro* (Naples, Jan. 12, 1844); *Rita, ou Le Mari battu* (1840; Paris, May 7, 1860; posthumously produced); *Il Duca d'Alba* (written for the Paris Opéra in 1839, but the score was incomplete; it was largely supplemented by Matteo Salvi, with new material added, for the Rome premiere on March 22, 1882; Thomas Schippers ed. the original Donizetti score and orchestrated parts of it for his perf., in Italian, in Spoleto in 1959; the libretto was by Scribe, who also wrote the book on the same subject for Verdi's opera, *Les Vêpres siciliennes,* 1855).

BIBLIOGRAPHY: F. Cicconetti, *Vita di Donizetti* (Rome, 1864); F. Alborghetti and Galli, *Donizetti e S. Mayr* (Bergamo, 1875); Ch. Malherbe, *Catalogue biographique di la Section française à l'exposition de Bergame* (Paris, 1897); E.C. Verzino, *Le opere de G. Donizetti, contributo alla loro storia* (Milan, 1897); Ippolito Valetti, *Donizetti* (Rome, 1897); Adolfo Calzado, *Donizetti e l'opera italiana in Spagna* (Paris, 1897); A. Gabrielli, *Gaetano Donizetti* (Turin, 1904); A. Cametti, *Donizetti a Roma, con lettere e documenti inediti* (Milan, 1907); C. Caversazzi, *Donizetti* (Bergamo, 1924); G. Donati-Petteni, *Donizetti* (Milan, 1930); G. Gavazzeni, *G. Donizetti* (Milan, 1935); Gino Monaldi, *G. Donizetti* (Turin, 1938); G. Zavadini, *G. Donizetti: Vicende della sua vita e catalogo* (Bergamo, 1941); A. Fraccaroli, *Donizetti* (Milan, 1944); G. Barblan, *L'opera di Donizetti nell' eta romantica* (Bergamo, 1948); G. Zavadini, *Donizetti: Vita, musiche, epistolario* (Bergamo, 1948; consists largely of Donizetti's correspondence, 1,019 pp.); Lea Bossi, *Donizetti* (Brescia, 1956); H. Weinstock, *Donizetti and the World of Opera in Italy, Paris and Vienna in the First Half of the 19th Century* (N.Y., 1964); G. Barblan, "Lettura di un'opera dimenticata: *Pia de' Tolomei* di Donizetti," *Chigiana,* XXIV/4 (1967); P. Rattalino, "Il processo compositivo nel *Don Pasquale*," *Nuova Rivista Musicale Italiana* (Jan.–April 1970); J.D. Freeman, "Donizetti in Palermo and *Alahor in Granata,*" *Journal of the American Musicological Society* (Summer 1972); John Allitt, *Donizetti and the Tradition of Romantic Love* (1975); W. Ashbrook, *Donizetti and His Operas* (a major study; Cambridge, 1982). The Donizetti Society in London issues an annual journal and a quarterly newsletter.

Donizetti, Giuseppe, Italian bandmaster and composer, brother of **Gaetano Donizetti;** b. Bergamo, Nov. 9, 1788; d. Constantinople, Feb. 10, 1856. In 1832 he was summoned by the sultan of Turkey to take charge of Turkish military bands. He accepted, and successfully accomplished the task of introducing Western instruments and modernizing the repertoire. The sultan richly rewarded him with honors and money, and Donizetti remained in Constantinople to the end of his life.

Donner, Henrik Otto, Finnish composer; b. Tampere, Nov. 16, 1939. He studied composition at the Sibelius Academy in Helsinki with Nils-Eric Fougstedt and Joonas Kokkonen; then attended seminars in electronic music in Bilthoven, the Netherlands; also took private lessons with Ligeti. For some years he earned his living as a jazz trumpeter in Helsinki; staged "happenings," with free improvisation on pre-programmed themes.

WORKS: *3 Pieces* for Flute and Piano (1962); *Cantata profana* (1962); *Ideogramme I* for Flute, Clarinet, Trombone, Percussion, and 12 Radios (1962); *Ideogramme II,* employing 20 Musicians, a Tape Recording, and renting a Promenade Room (1963); *For Emmy 2* for 3 Female Voices and an Amplified Chamber Ensemble (1963); *Kinetique* for Jazz Band and Chamber Ensemble (1964); *Moonspring, or Afforderung zum ... or Symphony 1,* subtitled "Hommage à Ives," for Strings, Guitar, Harp, and Hammond Organ (1964); 6 *Bagatelles* for String Quartet (1965); *Gilbert,* a musical (1965); *To Whom It May Concern* for Orch., with Jazz Drums (1966); *XC* for Soprano, Chorus, and Chamber Orch., on a text by Ezra Pound (1969); String Quartet No. 1, with Baritone Solo, on a text of Lenin (1970); *In the Afternoon* for Viola (1971); *Notte* for Guitar (1971); *Etyd för sommarvind* (*Etude for Summer Wind*) for Male Chorus (1971); music for films.

Donohoe, Peter, talented English pianist; b. Manchester, June 18, 1953. He studied at Chetham's School of Music in Manchester; made his debut at the age of 12 playing Beethoven's 3rd Piano Concerto at Manchester's Free Trade Hall; then enrolled in the Royal Manchester College of Music; took lessons in Paris with Yvonne Loriod. International recognition followed in 1982, when he became joint first-prize winner in the International Tchaikovsky Competition in Moscow. He subsequently made several world tours, performing in Japan, Canada, the U.S., Australia, and throughout Europe; he was particularly popular in Russia. His repertoire includes the entire range of Classical and Romantic works, but he also cultivates modern piano music, delivering such transcendentally difficult pieces as Liszt's opera transcriptions and Stravinsky's *Petrouchka.*

Donostia, José Antonio de, Basque composer and student of folklore; b. San Sebastián, Jan. 10, 1886; d. Lecároz, Navarra, Aug. 30, 1956. Donostia is his Basque name, corresponding to Dominus Sebastianus, or San Sebastián, his religious name; his full family name was José Antonio Zulacia y Arregui. He attended the Capuchin College in Lecaroz (Navarra); at the age of 16 entered the Franciscan order; was ordained a priest. He studied organ and violin with various teachers; composition with Eugène Cools in Paris. He lived many years in France; also traveled in South America; was compelled to leave Spain during the civil war of 1936–39. He was one of the founders of the Instituto Español de Musicología, and corresponding member of the

Academia de Bellas Artes in Madrid. His chief accomplishment is the collection of more than 1,000 Basque folk songs, which he wrote down and transcribed during his methodical journeys through the Basque countryside; 493 of these were publ. in his Basque cancionero, *Euskel Eres-Sorta* (1912); he also publ. *De la música popular vasca; Como canta el vasco;* etc. He wrote several cantatas (*La Vie profonde de Saint François d'Assise; Les Trois Miracles de Sainte Cécile; La Quête héroïque de Graal*); *Préludes basques* for Piano; many motets and other sacred choruses; *Itinerarium mysticum* for Organ (3 vols., based on Gregorian themes); compiled a bibliography of Basque folk music.

Donovan, Richard Frank, American organist and composer; b. New Haven, Conn., Nov. 29, 1891; d. Middletown, Conn., Aug. 22, 1970. He studied music at Yale Univ. and at the Inst. of Musical Art in N.Y. (M.B., 1922); also took lessons in organ playing with Widor in Paris. Returning to America, he served as organist in several N.Y. churches; in 1923–28 he was on the faculty of Smith College; in 1928 he was appointed to the School of Music at Yale Univ.; was a prof. of theory there from 1947 to 1960. He conducted the New Haven Symph. Orch. from 1936 till 1951; was also organist and choirmaster of Christ Church in New Haven. As a composer, he adopted a modern polyphonic style in his choral works, while his instrumental scores often reveal impressionistic traits.
WORKS: For Orch.: *Smoke and Steel*, symph. poem (1932); Symph. for Chamber Orch. (1936); *New England Chronicle*, overture (1947); *Passacaglia on Vermont Folk Tunes* (1949); Symph. in D (1956); *Epos* (1963). Chamber music: *Wood-Notes* for Flute, Harp, and Strings (1925); Sextet for Wind Instruments and Piano (1932); Piano Trio No. 1 (1937); Serenade for Oboe, Violin, Viola, and Cello (1939); *Terzetto* for 2 Violins and Viola (1950); Woodwind Quartet (1953); *Soundings* for Trumpet, Bassoon, and Percussion (1953); *Music for 6* (1961); Piano Trio No. 2 (1963). Choral works: *Fantasy on American Folk Ballads* for Men's Voices and Piano (1940); *Mass for Unison Voices* with Organ, 3 Trumpets, and Timpani (1955); *Forever, O Lord* for Chorus a cappella (1965). For Keyboard: 2 suites for piano; numerous organ works.
BIBLIOGRAPHY: Alfred Frankenstein, "Richard Donovan," *American Composers Alliance Bulletin* (1956); *Composers of the Americas,* vol. 15 (1969).

Dont, Jakob, Austrian violinist, teacher, and composer; b. Vienna, March 2, 1815; d. there, Nov. 17, 1888. He was the son of the cellist **Joseph Valentin Dont** (b. Georgenthal, Bohemia, April 15, 1776; d. Vienna, Dec. 14, 1833); was a pupil of Böhm and Hellmesberger (Sr.) at the Vienna Cons.; joined the orch. of the Hofburgtheater in 1831, and the court orch. in 1834. He taught in the Akademie der Tonkunst and the Seminary at St. Anna; Leopold Auer was his pupil. From 1873 he was a prof. at the Vienna Cons. His book of violin studies, *Gradus ad Parnassum,* is widely known; he publ. altogether some

50 works.

Dooley, William, American baritone; b. Modesto, Calif., Sept. 9, 1932. He studied at the Eastman School of Music in Rochester, N.Y.; then went to Germany; made his operatic debut as Rodrigo in *Don Carlos* in Heidelberg in 1957. On Feb. 15, 1964, he made his debut at the Metropolitan Opera in N.Y. in the title role of Tchaikovsky's *Eugene Onegin.* He also made successful appearances as a concert singer, both in the U.S. and in Europe.

Door, Anton, Austrian pianist; b. Vienna, June 20, 1833; d. there, Nov. 7, 1919. He was a pupil of Czerny (piano) and Sechter (composition). He gave successful concerts in Germany; after a tour in Sweden (1856–57) he went to Russia; taught at the Moscow Cons. (1864). In 1869 he returned to Vienna and became prof. of the advanced piano class at the Vienna Cons., a post he held for 32 years (1869–1901).

Doorslaer, George van, Belgian music scholar; b. Malines, Sept. 27, 1864; d. there, Jan. 16, 1940. He studied medicine; music was his avocation. In association with Charles van den Borren, he began a detailed study of old Belgian music; became particularly interested in the history of the carillon.
WRITINGS: *Le Carillon et les carilloneurs de la Tour Saint-Rombaut, à Malines* (1893); *Les Waghevens, fondeurs de cloches* (1908); *Le Carillon, son origine et son développement* (1911); numerous papers on Philippe de Monte, whose works he edited. For a complete list of publications see Albert van der Linden's article in *Die Musik in Geschichte und Gegenwart.*

Dopper, Cornelis, eminent Dutch composer and conductor; b. Stadskanaal, near Groningen, Feb. 7, 1870; d. Amsterdam, Sept. 18, 1939. He studied at the Leipzig Cons.; returning to the Netherlands, he became assistant conductor of the Concertgebouw Orch. in Amsterdam (1908), and was associated with that orch. until 1931. He also traveled as an opera conductor in America (1906–8).
WORKS: 4 operas: *Het blinde meisje von Castel Cuille* (1892); *Het Eerekruis* (Amsterdam, 1894); *Fritjof* (1895); *Willem Ratcliff* (1901); ballet, *Meidevorn,* with Soli and Chorus; 8 symphs.: No. 1, *Diana,* ballet symph. (1896); No. 2 (1903; finished after the 3rd); No. 3, *Rembrandt* (1892; later rewritten); No. 4, *Symphonietta* (1906); No. 5, *Symphonia epica,* with Chorus and Soli (1914); No. 6, *Amsterdam* (1912); No. 7, *Zuiderzee;* No. 8; symph. rhapsody, *Paris;* 5 suites; Divertimento; *Ciaconna gotica,* symph. variations (his best-known work; Concertgebouw, Amsterdam, Oct. 24, 1920, composer conducting); Concertino for Trumpet and 3 Kettledrums; Cello Concerto; 2 overtures; String Quartet; violin sonatas; Cello Sonata; Scherzo for Woodwinds and Piano; many choral works; songs; piano pieces.
BIBLIOGRAPHY: Sem Dresden, *Het Muziekleven in Nederland sinds 1880* (Amsterdam, 1923).

Doppler, Albert Franz, Austrian composer and conductor; b. Lwow, Oct. 16, 1821; d. Baden, near Vienna, July 27, 1883. He studied music with his father; played first flute in the Pest Opera Orch.; in 1858 settled in Vienna as ballet conductor at the court opera; taught flute at the Vienna Cons. from 1865. His first opera, *Benjowsky,* was well received in Budapest (Sept. 29, 1847) and had several revivals under the title *Afanasia;* the following operas were also produced in Budapest: *Ilka* (Dec. 29, 1849); *Wanda* (Dec. 16, 1856); *2 Hussars* (March 12, 1853); his last opera, *Judith,* was produced in Vienna (Dec. 30, 1870). He also wrote 15 ballets.

Doppler, Árpád, Hungarian pianist, son of **Karl Doppler;** b. Pest, June 5, 1857; d. Stuttgart, Aug. 13, 1927. He went to Stuttgart as a young man and studied there; was engaged to teach in N.Y. and spent 3 years there (1880–83); later returned to Stuttgart and taught at the Cons. He publ. a number of salon pieces for piano; also wrote a comic opera, *Caligula* (Stuttgart, 1891).

Doppler, Karl, Austrian composer and conductor, brother of **Albert Franz Doppler;** b. Lwow, Sept. 12, 1825; d. Stuttgart, March 10, 1900. Like his father and his brother, he became an excellent flute player; gave concerts in all the major cities of Europe. He was then appointed as court Kapellmeister in Stuttgart, and held this position for 33 years (1865–98). He wrote an opera and pieces for the flute.

Doran, Matt, American composer; b. Covington, Ky., Sept. 1, 1921. He studied at the Univ. of Southern Calif. with Ernst Toch; also took courses in composition with Hanns Eisler and Gail Kubik in Los Angeles, and orchestration with Caillet. His works include 2 one-act operas, *The Committee* (produced in Corpus Christi, Texas, May 25, 1955) and *Marriage Counselor* (Los Angeles, March 12, 1977); 3 symphs.; Double Concerto for Flute, Guitar, and Strings (Los Angeles, May 21, 1976); Flute Concerto (1953); Horn Concerto (1954); String Quartet; Woodwind Quintet; Clarinet Sonata; Flute Sonata; Suite for Flute and Percussion; Quartet for Cellos; Sonatine for 2 Violins; Suite for Flute and Percussion; Trio for Oboe, Violin, and Viola; many songs and piano pieces.

Dorati, Antal, distinguished Hungarian-American conductor and composer; b. Budapest, April 9, 1906. He studied harmony with Leo Weiner and composition with Kodály at the Liszt Academy in Budapest (1920–24). He made his debut as an opera conductor in Budapest at the age of 18; was on the staff of the Budapest Opera (1924–28); then conducted at the Dresden Opera (1928–29); was named Generalmusikdirektor at the Münster State Opera (1929–32). As the political situation, both racially and artistically, darkened in Central Europe in 1933, Dorati went to France, where he conducted the Ballets Russes de Monte Carlo, which he took over to Australia. He made his American debut with the National Symph. Orch. in Washington (1937); settled in the U.S. in 1940, and became a naturalized American citizen in 1947. In America he held with great distinction the posts of symph. conductor and music director of the Dallas Symph. Orch. (1945–49) and Minneapolis Symph. Orch. (1949–60); then was engaged as chief conductor of the BBC Symph. Orch. in London (1963–66), and of the Stockholm Phil. (1966–70); subsequently was conductor of the National Symph. Orch. in Washington, D.C. (1970–77). In 1977–81 he was conductor and music director of the Detroit Symph. Orch. Simultaneously, he held the position of principal conductor of the Royal Phil. Orch. of London (1975–79); was then named conductor laureate. Through the years he has acquired the reputation of an orch. builder able to handle not only the music but also the musicians; not only the public, but also the business management. He recorded all of the Haydn symphs. Dorati was married to the pianist **Ilse von Alpenheim;** in 1984 was made an Honorary Knight Commander of the Most Excellent Order of the British Empire. He is an active composer; among his works are a String Quartet; String Octet; Oboe Quintet; *Divertimento* for Orch.; ballet, *Graduation Ball,* arranged from the waltzes of Johann Strauss; dramatic cantata, *The Way of the Cross* (Minneapolis, April 19, 1957); Symph. (Minneapolis, March 18, 1960); *7 Pieces* for Orch. (1961; perf. as a ballet, *Maddalena*); Piano Concerto (1974; Washington, Oct. 28, 1975); Cello Concerto (Louisville, Ky., Oct. 1, 1976).

Doret, Gustave, Swiss composer; b. Aigle, Sept. 20, 1866; d. Lausanne, April 19, 1943. He received his first instruction at Lausanne; studied violin with Joachim in Berlin; then entered the Paris Cons. as a pupil of Marsick (violin) and Dubois and Massenet (composition); was conductor of the Concerts d'Harcourt and of the Société Nationale de Musique in Paris (1893–95); of the concerts at the National Exposition at Geneva (1896); of the Saint-Saëns Festival at Vevey (1913); at the Opéra-Comique (1907–9); also appeared as a visiting conductor in Rome, London, and Amsterdam. Doret was a member of the commission for editing Rameau's collected works. In his music Doret cultivated the spirit of Swiss folk songs; his vocal writing is distinguished by its natural flow of melody.

WORKS: Operas: *Les Armaillis* (Paris, Oct. 23, 1906; enlarged version, Paris, May 5, 1930); *Le Nain du Hasli* (Geneva, Feb. 6, 1908); dramatic legend, *Loÿs* (Vevey, 1912); *La Tisseuse d'Orties* (Paris, 1926); *Voix de la Patrie,* cantata (1891); oratorio, *Les Sept Paroles du Christ* (1895); *La Fête des vignerons* (1905); incidental music to Shakespeare's *Julius Caesar* and to plays by René Morax: *Henriette, Aliénor, La Nuit des quatre-temps, Wilhelm Tell, Davel* (all produced at Mézières); String Quartet; Piano Quintet; about 150 songs. He publ. *Musique et musiciens* (1915); *Lettres à ma nièce sur la musique en Suisse* (1919); *Pour notre indépendance musicale* (1920); *Temps et contretemps* (1942).

BIBLIOGRAPHY: J. Dupérier, *Gustave Doret* (Paris, 1932).

Dörffel, Alfred, German music editor; b. Waldenburg, Jan. 24, 1821; d. Leipzig, Jan. 22, 1905. He went to Leipzig at the age of 14, and studied with G.W. Fink and K.G. Müller. Mendelssohn and Schumann became interested in his musical education; in 1845 Schumann recommended him as an arranger to Breitkopf & Härtel. In 1861 he opened a circulating library in Leipzig; it was later purchased by C.F. Peters and became the nucleus of the *Musikbibliothek Peters* at Leipzig. The fame of the *Edition Peters* is in large measure due to Dörffel's careful editorship. He publ. a catalogue of his library (1861; with supplement, 1890); a German trans. of Berlioz's *Traité d'instrumentation* (1863, authorized by Berlioz himself; 4th ed., 1888); *Führer durch die musikalische Welt* (1868); *Geschichte der Gewandhauskonzerte 1781–1881* (Leipzig, 1884; a very valuable compilation, with commentary, of programs given by the Gewandhaus Orch. for 100 seasons); a thematic catalogue of Bach's instrumental works and of Schumann's complete works (1871).

Dorfmann, Ania, Russian-American pianist; b. Odessa, July 9, 1899; d. New York, April 21, 1984. As a very young child in Russia she teamed up with Jascha Heifetz in duo recitals; then went to Paris and was accepted at the age of 12 at the Paris Cons., where her teacher was Isidor Philipp. She returned to Russia just before the Revolution, but was able to leave again in 1920; she toured in Europe as a concert pianist; in 1936 she emigrated to America; gave her first American recital in N.Y. on Nov. 27, 1936; on Dec. 2, 1939, she appeared as a soloist with Toscanini and the NBC Symph. Orch. She then devoted herself mainly to teaching; for several years was on the faculty of the Juilliard School of Music in N.Y.

Dorian, Frederick (real name, **Friedrich Deutsch**), eminent Austrian-born American music scholar and commentator; b. Vienna, July 1, 1902. He studied musicology with Guido Adler at the Univ. of Vienna (Dr.Phil., 1925); also took piano lessons with Eduard Steuermann and studied composition privately with Anton von Webern. He was also closely associated with Schoenberg; Dorian's family apartment housed the headquarters of the famous Society for Private Musical Performances, organized by Schoenberg, Alban Berg, and Webern. He also took courses in conducting, achieving a high degree of professionalism. He served as music critic of the *Berliner Morgenpost* (1930–33); with the advent of the Nazi regime to power in Germany, he emigrated to the U.S., becoming an American citizen in 1941. From 1936–54 he was a member of the Carnegie-Mellon Univ. in Pittsburgh (formerly named Carnegie Inst. of Technology); there he organized an opera dept., and conducted its inaugural performance; from 1971–75 he served as Andrew Mellon Lecturer there. From 1975–77 he was visiting lectures on music history at the Curtis Inst. in Philadelphia. In 1978 he gave lectures on musicology at the Hebrew Univ. in Jerusalem. He also served, beginning in 1945, as program annotator for the Pittsburgh Symph. program magazine.

PUBLICATIONS: "Die Fugenarbeit in den Werken Beethovens," in *Studien zur Musikwissenschaft* (1927; publ. under his original name, Friedrich Deutsch); *Hausmusik alter Meister* (3 vols., Berlin, 1933); *The History of Music in Performance* (N.Y., 1942; 2nd ed., 1966; also publ. in Spanish, Hebrew, and Japanese, and in the Braille Edition for the Blind at the Library of Congress, Washington, D.C., 1965); *The Musical Workshop* (N.Y., 1947; in Spanish, Buenos Aires, 1961; in French, Paris, 1962); *Commitment to Culture* (Pittsburgh, 1964).

Doring, Ernest Nicholas, American specialist in violins; b. New York, May 29, 1877; d. Fort Worth, Texas, July 9, 1955. He studied violin in Chicago; in 1894 he joined the violin maker John Friedrich of N.Y. and remained with the firm for 33 years (until 1927). In 1933 he moved back to Chicago; was manager of the rare violin dept. of the Wurlitzer Co. In 1938 he began publishing the magazine *Violins and Violinists.* He wrote *How Many Strads?* (Chicago, 1945) and *The Guadagnini Family of Violin Makers* (Chicago, 1949).

Döring, (Carl) Heinrich, German piano pedagogue; b. Dresden, July 4, 1834; d. there, March 26, 1916. He was a pupil at the Leipzig Cons. (1852–55) and studied with Hauptmann, Lobe, Plaidy, and Richter; in 1858 joined the staff of the Dresden Cons. He publ. the piano collection *Die Grundpfeiler des Klavierspiels* in 3 parts: *Praktische Studien und Übungsstücke für das polyphone Klavierspiel; Technische Hülfs- und Bildungsmittel; Rückblicke auf die Geschichte der Erfindung des Hammerklaviers im 18. Jahrhundert* (Dresden, 1898).

Dorn, Alexander (Julius Paul), prolific composer, son of **Heinrich Dorn;** b. Riga, June 8, 1833; d. Berlin, Nov. 27, 1901. He studied with his father; traveled as a pianist and choral conductor; spent 10 years in Egypt (1855–65); then settled in Berlin, where he taught piano at the Hochschule für Musik. He wrote more than 400 compositions, including masses and operettas; also a number of salon pieces for piano.

Dorn, Heinrich (Ludwig Egmont), German composer, conductor, and pedagogue; b. Konigsberg, Nov. 14, 1800; d. Berlin, Jan. 10, 1892. He was a law student at Königsberg in 1823, but studied music diligently, continuing in Berlin under L. Berger (piano), Zelter, and B. Klein. After teaching in Frankfurt, he became Kapellmeister of the Königsberg Theater in 1828; in 1829, became music director (and Schumann's teacher) at Leipzig, where he met young Wagner; was music director at the Cathedral of St. Peter's in Riga (1831–42); Kapellmeister and city music director at Cologne (1843), where he founded (1845) the Rheinische Musikschule (which became the Cologne Cons. in 1850); in 1844–47, he conducted the Lower Rhenish Music Festivals. In 1849–69 he was court Kapellmeister at the Royal Opera, Berlin; was pensioned, with the title of Royal Professor, and busied himself with teaching and musical criticism.

WORKS: Operas: *Die Rolandsknappen* (Berlin, 1826); *Der Zauberer* (Berlin, 1827); *Die Bettlerin* (Königsberg, 1827); *Abu Kara* (Leipzig, 1831); *Das Schwärmermädchen* (Leipzig, 1832); *Der Schöffe von Paris* (Riga, 1838); *Die Musiker von Aix-la-Chapelle* (1848); *Artaxerxes* (Berlin, 1850); *Die Nibelungen* (Berlin, March 27, 1854; anticipating Wagner in the operatic treatment of the subject, but, despite initial successes, failing completely in the end); *Ein Tag in Russland,* comic opera (Berlin, 1856); *Der Botenläufer von Pirna* (Mannheim, March 15, 1865); operetta, *Gewitter bei Sonnenschein* (Dresden, 1865); ballet, *Amors Macht* (Leipzig, 1830); *Missa pro defunctis* (Berlin, 1851); cantatas; symphs.; orch. pieces (*Siegesfestklänge,* 1866); piano music; songs. He publ. an autobiography, *Aus meinem Leben,* with a collection of various essays (7 vols., 1870–86).

BIBLIOGRAPHY: W. Neumann, *Die Componisten der neueren Zeit,* IV (Kassel, 1854); Adam Rauh, *Heinrich Dorn als Opernkomponist* (Munich, 1939).

Dorsey, Jimmy (James), American clarinet and saxophone player, brother of **Tommy Dorsey;** b. Shenandoah, Pa., Feb. 29, 1904; d. New York, June 12, 1957. He played clarinet in school bands, and at one time led a band of his own; later joined his brother's group, rapidly climbing the ladder of commercial success, epitomized in the film *The Fabulous Dorseys* (1947).

Dorsey, Tommy (Thomas), American trombonist and bandleader, brother of **Jimmy Dorsey;** b. Mahoney Plains, Pa., Nov. 19, 1905; d. Greenwich, Conn., Nov. 26, 1956. He played trumpet and other instruments in school bands; then took up the trombone and developed a virtuoso technique using a unique method of convex breathing that enabled him to maintain miraculously long passages legato. His brother regularly played the clarinet and alto saxophone in his band from 1953 on. The film *The Fabulous Dorseys* (1947) bears eloquent testimony to the brothers' fame.

Dostal, Nico, Austrian composer of light music; b. Korneuburg, Nov. 25, 1895. He was brought up in a musical family; his uncle, **Hermann Dostal** (1874–1930), was a composer of celebrated military marches. Dostal studied in Linz and Vienna; specialized in arrangements of popular music, and began to compose on his own much later in life. Eventually he went to Salzburg to live.

WORKS: Numerous successful operettas: *Clivia* (Berlin, 1933); *Die Vielgeliebte* (Berlin, 1934); *Prinzessin Nofretete* (Cologne, 1935); *Extrablätter* (Bremen, 1937); *Monika* (Stuttgart, 1937); *Die Flucht ins Glück* (Stuttgart, 1940); *Manina* (Berlin, 1942); *Zirkusblut* (Bielefeld, 1951); *Dr. Eisenbart* (Nuremberg, 1952); *Rhapsodie der Liebe* (Nuremberg, 1963).

Dotzauer, (Justus Johann) Friedrich, famous German cellist; b. Hässelrieth, near Hildburghau-

sen, June 20, 1783; d. Dresden, March 6, 1860. He was a pupil of Heuschkel (piano), Gleichmann (violin), and Rüttinger (composition) at Hildburghausen, and of Hessner for cello; he took further lessons with Kriegck at Meiningen, where he played in the court orch. (1801–5); then was a member of the Leipzig Orch. (1806–11). He joined the Dresden Orch. in 1811; became first cellist in 1821 and was pensioned in 1852. Among his pupils were Karl Schuberth, Drechsler, Kummer, and his own son, **K.L. Dotzauer.**

WORKS: Opera, *Graziosa* (Dresden, 1841); symphs., overtures, masses, and, more especially, cello concertos; sonatas, variations, exercises for cello.

Dotzauer, Karl Ludwig (Louis), German cellist; b. Dresden, Dec. 7, 1811; d. Kassel, July 1, 1897. He studied with his father, **Friedrich Dotzauer;** from his youth to his death, for 67 years, he was cellist of the court orch. in Kassel (1830–1897).

Doubrava, Jaroslav, Czech composer; b. Chrudim, April 25, 1909; d. Prague, Oct. 2, 1960. He studied privately with Otakar Jeremiáš (1931–37); was active mainly in the musical theater. He wrote the operas *A Midsummer Night's Dream,* after Shakespeare (1942–49; completed by Jiří Jaroch, 1966; posthumous premiere, Opava, Dec. 21, 1969), and *Lazy John* (1952); *Balada o lásce* (*Ballad of Love;* 1959–60; completed by Jan Hanuš; posthumous premiere, Prague, June 21, 1962); 3 ballets: *The Tale of the Pea* (1935); *King Lavra* (1951); *Don Quixote* (1954–55); 3 symphs.: No. 1, with Chorus (1938–40); No. 2, *Stalingrad* (1943–44); No. 3 (1956–58); oratorio, *The Message* (1939–40); *Ballad about a Beautiful Death* for Women's Chorus and Orch. (1941); symph. marches: *Partisan March* and *Festive March* (1945); *Autumn Pastorale* (1960; fragment of his unfinished 4th Symph., arranged by Otmar Mácha); Piano Sonatina (1937); 2 violin sonatas (1942, 1958); Sonata for Solo Violin (1942); Piano Sonata (1948–49); piano pieces for children; song cycles.

Dougherty, Celius, American pianist and composer; b. Glenwood, Minn., May 27, 1902. He studied piano and composition at the Univ. of Minnesota with Donald Ferguson, and later at the Juilliard School with Rubin Goldmark (composition) and Josef Lhévinne (piano). He became a highly successful accompanist and toured with many celebrated singers. He publ. a number of songs, some of which became popular in recitals (*Weathers, Song for Autumn, Five American Sea-Chanties*). He also wrote an opera, *Many Moons,* based on a story of James Thurber, which was first performed at Vassar College on Dec. 6, 1962.

Douglas, Clive, Australian composer; b. Rushworth, Victoria, July 27, 1903; d. Brighton, Victoria, April 30, 1977. He studied at the Melbourne Cons. (1929–34; D.Mus., 1958); was attached to the Australian Broadcasting Commission as a resident staff conductor in various cities (1936–66); taught at the Melbourne Cons. (1953–66). His music draws on indigenous Australian subjects and melorhythmic patterns; some abstractions suggesting serial techniques are found in his chamber music.

WORKS: 4 operas: *The Scarlet Letter*, after Hawthorne (1927–28); *Ashmadai* (1935); *Kaditcha* (1937–38); opera-trilogy, *Eleanor* (1940–43); 3 symphs. (*Jubilee*, 1951; *Namatjira*, 1956; 1963); symph. poems: *Carwoola* (1939) and *Sturt 1829* (1952); *Symphonic Fantasy* (1938); *Festival of Perth*, sinfonietta (1961); *Symphonic Variations* (1961); *Divertimento No. 2* for 2 Pianos and Chamber Orch. (1962); *3 Frescoes* for Orch. (1969); *Pastoral* for Orch. (1970); *Discourse* for Strings (1971); *The Hound of Heaven* for Baritone, Chorus, and Orch. (1932–33); *Terra Australis* for Narrator, Soprano, Chorus, and Orch. (1959); 2 string quartets (1933, 1935); *Divertimento No. 1* for Wind Quintet (1962–63).

Dounias, Minos, musicologist; b. Cetate, Rumania, Sept. 26, 1900, of Greek parents; d. Athens, Oct. 20, 1962. He studied violin; musicology at the Univ. of Berlin with Abert and Schering; publ. a dissertation, *Die Violinkonzerte Giuseppe Tartinis* (Berlin, 1935). In 1936 he settled in Athens as a music critic.

Dounis, Demetrius Constantine, Greek-American violinist and teacher; b. Athens, Dec. 7, 1886; d. Los Angeles, Aug. 13, 1954. He studied violin with Ondříček in Vienna and simultaneously enrolled as a medical student at the Univ. of Vienna; made several tours as a violinist in Europe, including Russia; after World War I he was appointed prof. at the Salonika Cons. He then lived in England and eventually settled in America; established his N.Y. studio in 1939; went to Los Angeles in 1954. He originated the technique of the "brush stroke," in which the bow is handled naturally and effortlessly.

WRITINGS: Numerous manuals, including: *The Artist's Technique of Violin Playing; The Absolute Independence of the Fingers; Advanced Studies for the Development of the Independence of the Fingers in Violin Playing on a Scientific Basis; The Development of Flexibility;* etc.

BIBLIOGRAPHY: V. Leland, *Dounis Principles of Violin Playing* (London, 1949).

Dowland, John, great English composer of songs and famous lutenist; b. probably in London, 1563; d. there (buried, Feb. 20) 1626. In 1580 he went to Paris in the service of Sir Henry Cobham; by 1584 he was back in England, where he eventually married; on July 8, 1588, he was admitted to his Mus.B. from Christ Church, Oxford; in 1592 he played before the Queen. Unsuccessful in his effort to secure a position as one of the Queen's musicians, he set out in 1594 for Germany, where he received the patronage of the Duke of Braunschweig in Wolfenbüttel and the Landgrave of Hesse in Kassel; he then went to Italy and visited Venice, Padua, Genoa, Ferrara, and Florence; in Florence he played before Ferdinando I, the Grand Duke of Tuscany; he then made his way home, returning to England in 1595. In 1598 he was appointed lutenist to King Christian IV of Denmark, remaining in his service until 1606;

he then returned to England, where he became lutenist to Lord Howard de Walden. In 1612 he became one of the lutenists to King Charles I. Dowland was a foremost representative of the English school of lutenist-composers. He was also noted for his songs, in which he made use of novel chromatic developments; he treated the accompanying parts as separate entities, thereby obtaining harmonic effects quite advanced for his time.

WORKS: *The First Booke of Songes or Ayres of fowre partes with Tableture for the Lute . . .* (London, 1597); *The Second Booke of Songs or Aires, of 2. 4. and 5. parts; With Tableture for the Lute or Orpherian . . .* (London, 1600); *The Third and Last Booke of Songs or Aires . . .* (London, 1603); *Lachrimae, or Seven Teares Figvred in Seaven Passionate Pauans, . . . set forth for the Lute, Viols, or Violons, in fiue parts* (London, 1604); songs in *A Mvsicall Banquet* (London, 1612) and *A Pilgrimes Solace. Wherein is contained Musicall Harmonie of 3. 4. and 5. parts, to be sung and plaid with the Lute and Viols* (London, 1612).

WRITINGS: He trans. into Eng. *The Micrologus* of Ornithoparcus [Andreas Vogelsang] (London, 1609; modern ed. in Eng. and Latin, ed. by G. Reese and S. Ledbetter, by the American Musicological Association and the Music Library Association, N.Y., 1973); also with his son Robert, the *Necessarie Observations Belonging to the Lute, and Lvte playing, by John Baptisto Besardo* [Jean-Baptiste Besard] *of Visconti: with choise varietie of Lvte-lessons . . .* (includes compositions by John Dowland; London, 1610).

EDITIONS: These include E. Fellowes's eds. of *The First Book of Songs* (London, 1920; revised ed., 1965, by T. Dart), *The Second Book of Songs* (London, 1922; revised ed., 1969, by T. Dart), *The Third and Last Book of Songs* (London, 1923; revised ed., 1970, by T. Dart), *A Pilgrimes Solace* (London, 1924; revised ed., 1969, by T. Dart), and *Seven Hymn Tunes . . . Lamentatio Henrici Noel* (London, 1934); P. Warlock, *Lachrimae or Seven Tears . . . Transcribed from the original edition of 1605* (without tablature; London, 1927); T. Dart and N. Fortune, eds., *Ayres for Four Voices*, in *Musica Britannica* (vol. 6, London, 1953; 2nd ed., revised, 1963); D. Poulton and B. Lam, eds., *The Collected Lute Music of John Dowland* (London, 1974).

BIBLIOGRAPHY: E. Fellowes, *The English Madrigal Composers* (London, 1921; 2nd ed., 1948); P. Warlock, *The English Ayre* (London, 1926); D. Poulton, "Dowland's Songs and Their Instrumental Settings," *The Monthly Musical Record*, LXXXI (1951); C. Hill, "John Dowland: Some New Facts and a Quatercentenary Tribute," *Musical Times* (Nov. 1963); P. Brown, "Influences on the Early Lute Songs of John Dowland," *Musicology*, 3 (1968–69); V. Reed, "Doleful Dowland," *English Language Notes* (Sept. 1968); D. Poulton, *John Dowland: His Life and Works* (Berkeley and Los Angeles, 1972; 2nd ed., revised, 1982).

Dowland, Robert, English composer and lute player, son of **John Dowland;** b. London, 1591; d. there,

Nov. 28, 1641. He remained in London after his father went to Denmark; in 1626, succeeded his father as lutenist to Charles I. He publ. *Varietie of Lute Lessons* (1610); edited *A Musicall Banquett,* a collection of English, French, Spanish, and Italian airs (reprinted in *The English Lute Songs,* vol. 20).

Downes, Edward (Thomas), English conductor; b. Aston (Birmingham), June 17, 1924. He studied at the Univ. of Birmingham (1941–44), taking a B.A. in music; and at the Royal College of Music in London (1944–46), studying horn, theory, and composition. In 1948 he was awarded the Carnegie Scholarship, which he used for taking a course in conducting with Hermann Scherchen. His first professional post as conductor was with the Carl Rosa Opera (1950); in 1952 he became a staff conductor at the Covent Garden Opera in London, with which he conducted every work in the repertoire, including the complete *Ring of the Nibelung* cycle; in 1969 he left the Covent Garden staff as a regular member in order to devote himself to symph. conducting, but continued to fill in occasional opera engagements. In 1972–76 he was music director of the Australian Opera; in 1980 became chief conductor of the Omroeporkest in Hilversum. He conducted the world premiere of Richard Rodney Bennett's opera *Victory* (April 13, 1970). He also conducted the world premieres of Havergal Brian's 14th and 21st symphs. with the London Symph. Orch. on May 10, 1970.

Downes, Edward O(lin) D(avenport), American music critic and lecturer, son of **Olin Downes;** b. Boston, Aug. 12, 1911. He studied at Columbia Univ. (1929–30), the Univ. of Paris (1932–33), the Univ. of Munich (1934–36, 1938), and Harvard Univ. (Ph.D., 1958). Under the tutelage of his father, he entered the career of a music critic; wrote for the *N.Y. Post* (1935–38), the *Boston Transcript* (1939–41), and the *N.Y. Times* (1955–58); was program annotator for the N.Y. Phil. (1960–74); from 1958 acted as quizmaster for the Metropolitan Opera broadcasts. He was a lecturer in music at Wellesley College (1948–49), Harvard Univ. (1949–50), the Univ. of Minnesota (1950–55), and (from 1966) Queens College. WRITINGS: *Verdi, The Man and His Letters* (trans. of correspondence, N.Y., 1942); *Adventures in Symphonic Music* (N.Y., 1943); *The New York Philharmonic Guide to the Symphony* (N.Y.,1976); co-edited J.C. Bach's opera *Temistocle* (Vienna, 1965); also *Perspectives of Musicology* (N.Y., 1972); contributed a great number of articles on a variety of subjects to music periodicals.

Downes, Olin, eminent American music critic; b. Evanston, Ill., Jan. 27, 1886; d. New York, Aug. 22, 1955. He studied piano with L. Kelterborn and Carl Baermann; harmony with Homer Norris, Clifford Heilman and J.P. Marshall; then devoted himself mainly to musical journalism. From 1906 to 1924 he was music critic of the *Boston Post;* in 1924 was appointed music critic of the *N.Y. Times;* held this post until his death. He was awarded the Order of Commander of the White Rose, Finland (1937); an

hon. Mus.Doc., Cincinnati Cons. of Music (1939). WRITINGS: *The Lure of Music* (1918); *Symphonic Broadcasts* (1931); *Symphonic Masterpieces* (1935). He edited *Select Songs of Russian Composers* (1922); compiled and annotated *Ten Operatic Masterpieces, from Mozart to Prokofiev* (1952). A selection from his writings was publ. in 1957 under the title *Olin Downes on Music,* edited by his widow, Irene Downes.

Downes, Ralph, English organist; b. Derby, Aug. 16, 1904. He studied at the Royal College of Music (1922–25); then was an organ scholar at Keble College, Oxford. Making his way to the U.S., he was music director and organist at Princeton Univ. (1928–36); he then returned to London, where he became organist of Brompton Oratory; in 1948 he became resident organist of the London Phil. Orch. He was appointed a prof. at the Royal College of Music in 1954. In 1969 he was made a Commander of the Order of the British Empire.

Downey, John, American composer; b. Chicago, Oct. 5, 1927. He studied music theory with Leon Stein at De Paul Univ. in Chicago (1945–49) and advanced composition with Alexander Tcherepnin, Krenek, and Rieti at the Chicago Musical College of Roosevelt Univ. (M.M., 1951); went to Paris and took private lessons with Nadia Boulanger, Milhaud, and Honegger (1952–58); returning to the U.S., he was appointed in 1964 to the music faculty of the Univ. of Wisconsin in Milwaukee. WORKS: *La Joie de la paix* for Orch. (1956); *Chant to Michelangelo* for Orch. (1958); Concerto for Harp and Chamber Orch. (1964); ballet, *Ageistics* (1967); *Jingalodeon* for Orch. (1968); *Prospectations III–II–I* for 3 Simultaneous Youth Orchs. (1970); *Almost 12* for Wind Quintet, Strings, and Percussion (1970); *Symphonic Modules 5* for Orch. (1972); *Fantasy* for Bassoon and Orch. (1978); String Trio (1953); Violin Sonata (1954); Wind Octet (1954); 2 string quartets (1964, 1975); *Eartheatrics* for 8 Percussionists (1967); *Tabu* for Solo Tuba (1967); *Ambivalences I* for any chamber combination (1972); *What If?,* after e.e. cummings, for Chorus, Brass Octet, Timpani, and 3 Gongs (1973); *A Dolphin* for High Voice, Flute, Viola, Piano, and Percussion (1974); *Crescendo* for 13 Percussionists (1976); *High Clouds and Soft Rain* for 24 Flutes (1977); *Earthplace,* ballet for Tape (1973); 2 piano sonatas (1949, 1951); *Adagio Lyrico* for 2 Pianos (1953); *Eastlake Terrace* for Piano (1959); *Edges* for Piano (1960); *Pyramids* for Piano (1961); *Ambivalences II* for Piano (1973); choruses; songs.

Doyen, Albert, French composer; b. Vendresse (Ardennes), April 3, 1882; d. Paris, Oct. 22, 1935. He studied composition with Widor at the Paris Cons. In 1917 he established the choral society Fêtes du Peuple, and subsequently conducted more than 200 concerts. Among his works are a Symph., an ode in memory of Zola, String Quartet, Piano Trio, Violin Sonata, and numerous choral compositions.

Dozier, Lamont, black American songwriter; b. Detroit, June 16, 1941. He sang in a church choir directed by his grandmother and as a youth joined the Motown organization dedicated to the promotion of "soul" music as urbanized in the Motown sound, the name being a reference to Motor Town, that is, Detroit. He teamed with Brian Holland (b. Detroit, Feb. 15, 1941) and Eddie Holland (b. Detroit, Oct. 30, 1939), and together they created the great Motown hits *Heat Wave, Nowhere to Run, Mickey's Monkey, How Sweet It Is (to Be Loved by You), Reach Out, I'll Be There, Where Did Our Love Go, Baby Love, Stop! In the Name of Love, I Hear a Symphony, My World Is Empty without You, Heaven Must Have Sent You,* etcetera, ad infinitum.

Draeseke, Felix (August Bernhard), significant German composer; b. Coburg, Oct. 7, 1835; d. Dresden, Feb. 26, 1913. He studied privately with Julius Rietz in Leipzig; became a friend of Liszt and Wagner, and an ardent champion of the New German School. In 1862 he went to Switzerland; taught at the Cons. of Lausanne (1864–74) and later in Geneva. In 1876 he returned to Germany and became a prof. at the Dresden Cons. A Wagnerian in his youth, he was regarded as a radical, but he never accepted the modern tendencies of the 20th century, which he attacked in his pamphlet *Die Konfusion in der Musik* (1906), directed chiefly against Richard Strauss. He was a prolific composer, but his works are virtually unknown outside Germany. A Draeseke Society was formed in Germany in 1931, and issued sporadic bulletins.
WORKS: 6 operas: *König Sigurd* (1853–57; only a fragment perf., in Meiningen, 1867); *Herrat* (1879; Dresden, March 10, 1892); *Gudrun* (Hannover, Jan. 11, 1884); *Bertrand de Born* (1894); *Fischer und Kalif* (Prague, April 15, 1905); *Merlin* (perf. posthumously, Gotha, May 10, 1913); choral trilogy, *Christus* (his major work), consisting of a prelude, *Die Geburt des Herrn;* I. *Christi Weihe,* II. *Christus der Prophet,* III. *Tod und Sieg des Herrn* (produced in its entirety in Dresden and Berlin, 1912); Symph. in G (1872); Symph. in F (1876); *Symphonia tragica* (1886); *Symphonia comica* (1912); sacred and secular choruses; many songs; Piano Concerto; Violin Concerto; 3 string quartets; Quintet for Piano, Violin, Viola, Cello, and Horn; Clarinet Sonata, etc. A complete list of works is found in H. Stephani's article on Draeseke in *Die Musik in Geschichte und Gegenwart.* Draeseke's theoretical publications include: *Anweisung zum kunstgerechten Modulieren* (1875); *Zur Beseitigung des Tritonus* (1876); a versified *Lehre von der Harmonia* (1885); *Der gebundene Stil: Lehrbuch für Kontrapunkt und Fugue* (Hannover, 1902).
BIBLIOGRAPHY: H. Platzbecker, *Felix Draeseke,* in vol. III of *Monographien moderner Musiker* (Leipzig, 1909); E. Röder, *Felix Draeseke* (2 vols., Dresden and Berlin, 1932, 1937); A. Kruecke, *The Symphonies of Felix Draeseke* (Diss., Univ. of Zürich, 1967).

Draga, George, Rumanian composer; b. Bîrsa-Aldeşti, April 26, 1935. He studied with Vancea, Vieru, and Ion Dumitrescu at the Bucharest Cons. (1957–63); in 1963 became editor of the periodical *Muzica.*
WORKS: Piano Sonata (1962); Clarinet Sonata (1963); *Se construieşte lumea noastră,* cantata (1963); Symphony (1965); *Cantata festiva* (1967); Concert Music for Orch. (1968); String Quartet (1968); *Eterofonii* for Strings, Brass, and Percussion (1969); *Concert Overture* (1969); Prelude for Orch. (1971).

Draghi, Antonio, Italian composer of operas and oratorios; b. Rimini, 1635; d. Vienna, Jan. 16, 1700. He was a singer in Venice; in 1658 he settled in Vienna; became Kapellmeister to the Empress Eleanora in 1669; was appointed Hoftheater-Intendant to Leopold I in 1673; named Imperial Court Kapellmeister in 1682. In 1661–99 he produced 67 operas, 116 festival plays ("feste teatrali") and serenades, 32 oratorios, 11 cantatas, 2 masses, etc. Reprints are in Denkmäler der Tonkunst in Österreich, 46 (23.i; 2 masses, a Stabat Mater, and 2 hymns) and in A. Schering's *Geschichte der Musik in Beispielen,* no. 226 (an opera scene).
BIBLIOGRAPHY: M. Neuhaus, "A. Draghi," *Studien zur Muzikwissenschaft,* I (1913); H. Seifert, *Neues zu Antonio Draghis Weltlichen Werken* (Vienna, 1978).

Draghi, Giovanni Battista, Italian harpsichordist; lived in London from 1667 to 1706. He was organist to the Queen from 1677; also music teacher to Queen Mary and Queen Anne. He wrote the music to Dryden's ode *From Harmony* and (with Locke) to Shadwell's *Psyche* and d'Urfey's *The Wonders in the Sun, or The Kingdom of Birds* (London, 1706); also many songs, and instructive harpsichord lessons.

Drăgoi, Sabin, eminent Rumanian composer and folklorist; b. Selişte, June 18, 1894; d. Bucharest, Dec. 31, 1968. He studied with Novák and Ostrčil in Prague (1920–22); from 1924 to 1942 taught at the Timişoara Cons.; then was a prof. at the Cluj Cons. (1942–46); was director of the Folklore Inst. of Bucharest (1950–64) and a prof. of folklore at the Bucharest Cons. (1950–52).
WORKS: Operas: *Năpasta (Disaster;* 1927; Bucharest, May 30, 1928; revised 1958; Bucharest, Dec. 23, 1961); *Kir Ianulea* (1937; Cluj, Dec. 22, 1939); *Horia* (1945); *Păcală* (1956; Brasov, May 6, 1962); oratorio, *Povestea bradului* (1952); 3 cantatas: *Slăvită lumină* (1937); *Mai multă lumină* (1951); *Cununa* (1959); *3 Symphonic Tableaus* (1922); *Divertissement Rustic* for Orch. (1928); *Divertissement sacru* for Chamber Orch. (1933); Piano Concerto (1941); Concertino for Tarogato and Orch. (1953); *7 Popular Dances* for Orch. (1960); *Suită tătară* for Small Orch. (1961); *Suită lipovană* for Small Orch. (1962); Violin Sonata (1949); String Quartet (1952); *Dixtour* for Winds, Strings, and Piano (1955); *50 Colinde* for Piano (1957); *10 Miniatures* for Piano (1960); *12 Miniatures* for Piano (1968); songs; film music.

BIBLIOGRAPHY: N. Rădulescu, *Sabin V. Drăgoi* (Bucharest, 1971).

Dragon, Carmen, American conductor of popular music; b. Antioch, Calif., July 28, 1914; d. Santa Monica, Calif., March 28, 1984. He learned to play piano, double bass, accordion, trumpet, and trombone. He studied music at San Jose State College; then went to San Francisco, where he played the piano in a nightclub. His next move was to Hollywood, where he effloresced as an arranger for movie stars who could not read music. He conducted background music for radio shows. In a higher elevation, he composed a patriotic band piece, *I'm an American.* His concerts supplied pleasurable fare for contented music-lovers. His son **Daryl Dragon** became one-half of the popular music team Captain and Tennille.

Dragonetti, Domenico, noted Italian double-bassist; b. Venice, April 7, 1763; d. London, April 16, 1846. The "Paganini of the contra-basso" was self-taught, excepting a few lessons from Berini, bassist at San Marco, whom he succeeded in 1782; he had already played in the orchs. of the Opera Buffa and Opera Seria for 5 years, and composed concertos with double-bass parts impracticable for anyone but himself. He appeared at London in 1794; with the cellist Lindley, his close friend for 52 years, he played at the Antient Concerts and the Phil. As late as 1845, his virtuosity still unimpaired, he led the double basses, at the unveiling of the Beethoven monument in Bonn, in the C minor Symph. To the British Museum he left a remarkable collection of scores, engravings, and old instruments; to San Marco, his favorite cello (a Gasparo da Salò).
BIBLIOGRAPHY: F. Caffi: *Vita di D. Dragonetti* (Venice, 1846).

Drake, Earl R., American violinist and composer; b. Aurora, Ill., Nov. 26, 1865; d. Chicago, May 6, 1916. He studied violin in Chicago, and later with Joachim in Berlin. He was head of the violin dept. at the Gottschalk Lyric School in Chicago (1893–97); organized his own school of music in Chicago in 1900.
WORKS: *The Blind Girl of Castel-Cuille,* opera and ballet (Chicago, Feb. 19, 1914); *The Mite and the Mighty,* light opera (Chicago, 1915); *Dramatic Prologue* for Orch.; *Ballet* for Orch.; *Gypsy Scenes* for Violin and Orch.; pieces for violin and piano (*Polish Dance, Mazurka, An Alpine Farewell,* etc.).
BIBLIOGRAPHY: E.E. Hipsher, *American Opera and Its Composers* (Philadelphia, 1934, pp. 162–64).

Drangosch, Ernesto, Argentine pianist and composer; b. Buenos Aires, Jan. 22, 1882; d. there, June 26, 1925. He studied in Buenos Aires with Alberto Williams and Aguìrre, and in Berlin with Max Bruch, Humperdinck, and Ansorge; later toured Europe and America as a pianist; returned to Buenos Aires (1905), and founded his own cons. His piano pieces have been publ.

Dranishnikov, Vladimir, Russian conductor; b. St. Petersburg, June 10, 1893; d. Kiev, Feb. 6, 1939. He studied at the St. Petersburg Cons. with Mme. Essipoff (piano); Steinberg, Liadov, and Wihtol (composition); and Nicolas Tcherepnin (conducting). He was employed as a rehearsal pianist at the St. Petersburg Imperial Opera (1914–18); in 1918 became conductor there, earning great esteem for his professional skill in both the classical and modern repertoire; he conducted the first Soviet performance of Alban Berg's *Wozzeck,* and of numerous Soviet operas; in 1930 he was appointed conductor of the Kiev Opera. He also wrote symph. works and choruses.

Drdla, Franz, Bohemian composer and violinist; b. Saar, Moravia, Nov. 28, 1868; d. Gastein, Sept. 3, 1944. After 2 years at the Prague Cons. he studied at the Vienna Cons. under Hellmesberger (violin) and Krenn (composition), winning first prize for violin and the medal of the Gesellschaft der Musikfreunde; for several years was a violinist in the orch. of the Hofoper; then made successful tours of Europe; in 1923–25, lived in the U.S.; then in Vienna and Prague. His pieces for violin and piano have won enormous popularity, especially *Souvenir, Vision,* and the first Serenade in A (dedicated to, and played by, Jan Kubelik); he also composed 2 operettas, *Das goldene Netz* (Leipzig, 1916) and *Die Ladenkomtesse* (Prague, 1917).

Drechsler, Joseph, Austrian composer; b. Wällisch-Birken, Bohemia, May 26, 1782; d. Vienna, Feb. 27, 1852. He was a pupil of the organist Grotius at Florenbach; chorus master and Kapellmeister (1812) at the Vienna Court Opera, then conductor in the theaters at Baden (near Vienna) and Pressburg; returning to Vienna, he became organist of the Servite church; in 1816 precentor at St. Ann's; in 1823 Kapellmeister at the University church and the Hofpfarrkirche; in 1822–30 he was also Kapellmeister at the Leopoldstadt Theater, and from 1844, Kapellmeister at St. Stephen's.
WORKS: 6 operas, and about 30 operettas, vaudevilles, and pantomimes; a Requiem, 10 other masses, 3 cantatas, offertories, etc.; string quartets, organ fugues, piano sonatas, other piano music, songs, etc.; a method for organ, and a treatise on harmony. He reedited Pleyel's *Piano School,* and publ. a theoretico-practical guide to preluding.
BIBLIOGRAPHY: C. Preiss, *Joseph Drechsler* (Graz, 1910).

Dregert, Alfred, German conductor; b. Frankfurt an der Oder, Sept. 26, 1836; d. Elberfeld, March 14, 1893. He studied piano with Hans von Bülow in Berlin; after a brief concert career, devoted himself to opera conducting; also led choral societies.

Dreier, Per, Norwegian conductor; b. Trondheim, Dec. 25, 1929. He studied conducting with Paul van Kempen and Willem van Otterloo at the Royal Cons. of Music in The Hague. He made his debut in his home town with the Trondheim Symph. Orch. in

1953. He then was a conductor at the Württemberg State Theater at Stuttgart (1953–57) and chief conductor and artistic director of the Aarhus Symph. Orch. (1957–73); also served as chief conductor of the Jutland Opera (1957–71). He has done much to promote contemporary Norwegian music.

Drejsl, Radim, Czech composer; b. Dobruska, April 29, 1923; d. (suicide) Prague, April 20, 1953. He studied piano at the Prague Cons. and then took composition with Bořkovec at the Academy of Musical Arts in Prague (1946–50); was music director of the Vít Nejedlý Army Artistic Ensemble from 1949 until his death. WORKS: 2 suites for Piano (1945, 1946); 2 piano sonatas (1946, 1947); Flute Sonatina (1947); Bassoon Sonatina (1948); *Spring* for Wind Quintet (1948); Symph. for Strings (1948); Piano Concerto (1948–49); *Dožinková Suite (Harvest Home Suite)* for Oboe or English Horn, and Piano (1949–50); military marches; choruses; songs.

Dresden, Sem, notable Dutch composer; b. Amsterdam, April 20, 1881; d. The Hague, July 30, 1957. He studied first in Amsterdam with Zweers; then went to Berlin, where he took a course in composition with Hans Pfitzner (1903–5). Returning to the Netherlands, he was active as a choral conductor; from 1919 to 1924 taught composition at the Amsterdam Cons.; then became its director (1924–37); subsequently was director of The Hague Cons. (1937–49, with a break during World War II). From 1914 till 1926 he led the Motet and Madrigal Society in Amsterdam. As a composer, Sem Dresden was influenced primarily by German neo-Romanticism, but his harmonic idiom reveals some impressionistic usages; in many of his works there is a distinctive strain of Dutch melodic rhythms. WORKS: Opera, *François Villon* (1956–57, piano score only; orchestrated by Jan Mul and presented posthumously at the Holland Festival in Amsterdam, June 15, 1958); operetta, *Toto* (1945); oratorios: *Saint Antoine* (1953) and *St. Joris* (1955); *Carnival Cantata* for Soprano, Male Chorus, and Orch. (1954); *Chorus tragicus* for Chorus, 5 Trumpets, 2 Bugles, and Percussion (1927); *4 Vocalises* for Mezzo-soprano and 7 Instruments (1935); *O Kerstnacht* for Chorus and Strings (1939); *Chorus symphonicus* for Soprano, Tenor, Chorus, and Orch. (1943–44; revised 1955); *Psalm 99* for Chorus, Organ, and 4 Trombones (1950); *Psalm 84* for Soprano, Tenor, Chorus, and Orch. (1954); *De wijnen van Bourgondië (The Wines of Burgundy)* for Chorus and Orch. (1954); *Catena musicale* for Soprano, Solo Woodwind Quartet, Solo String Trio, and Orch. (1956); *Rembrandt's "Saul and David"* for Soprano and Orch. (1956). For Orch.: Theme and Variations (Amsterdam, March 29, 1914); 2 violin concertos (1936, 1942); *Symphonietta* for Clarinet and Orch. (1938); Oboe Concerto (1939); Piano Concerto (1942–46); Flute Concerto (1949); *Dansflitsen (Dance Flashes)* for Orch. (The Hague, Oct. 20, 1951); Organ Concerto (1952–53). Chamber music: 3 sextets (1910, 1913, 1920); 2 piano trios (1902, 1942); Violin Sonata (1905);

Trio for 2 Oboes and English Horn (1912); 2 cello sonatas (1916, 1942); Sonata for Flute and Harp (1918); String Quartet (1924); Solo Violin Sonata (1943); Suite for Solo Cello (1943–47); piano pieces; organ pieces; choruses; songs. WRITINGS: *Het muziekleven in Nederland sinds 1880* (Amsterdam, 1923); *Stromingen en Tegenstromingen in de muziek* (Haarlem, 1953); co-editor of the new ed. of van Milligen's *Music History* and (with Worp and Milligen) of *Algemeene muziekleer* (1931). BIBLIOGRAPHY: P.F. Sanders, *Moderne nederlandsche componisten* (The Hague, 1930); C. Backers, *Nederlandse componisten van 1400 tot op onze tijd* (The Hague, 1949); J. Wouters, "Sem Dresden," *Sonorum Speculum,* 25 (Winter 1965).

Dresel, Otto, German pianist and composer; b. Geisenheim, Dec. 20, 1826; d. Beverly, Mass., July 26, 1890. He was a pupil of Hiller at Cologne, and of Mendelssohn at Leipzig. He went to N.Y. as a concert pianist and teacher in 1848; revisited Germany, but in 1852 settled in Boston, where for some 15 years he was very influential in introducing German music to the American public. He publ. only a few songs and piano pieces.

Dressel, Erwin, German composer; b. Berlin, June 10, 1909; d. there, Dec. 17, 1972. He studied with Wilhelm Klatte and Paul Juon in Berlin; then was active as a conductor and arranger. Among his works are the comic operas *Armer Columbus* (1928); *Der Kuchentanz* (1929); *Die Zwillingsesel* (1932); *Die Laune der Verliebten* (1949); *Der Bär* (1963); 4 symphs.; Oboe Concerto (1951); Clarinet Concerto (1961); Saxophone Concerto (1965); Viola Concerto (1969); 2 string quartets; String Trio; songs; piano pieces.

Dreves, Guido Maria, German music historian; b. Hamburg, Oct. 27, 1854; d. Mitwitz, near Kronach, June 1, 1909. He entered the Jesuit order; lived in Vienna and Würzburg. For distinguished service to the cause of hymnology and medieval music, the Univ. of Munich made him a Dr.Phil. (*honoris causa*). WRITINGS: Co-editor, with C. Blume and H.M. Bannister, of the great *Analecta hymnica medii aevi* (53 vols., 1886–1911); *Cantiones Bohemicae* (1886); *Die Hymnen des Johannes von Jenstein* (1886); *Aurelius Ambrosius, der Vater des Kirchengesanges* (1893); *Psalteria rhythmica* (1901); *Die Kirche der Lateiner in ihren Liedern* (1908).

Drew, James, American composer, pianist, and conductor; b. St. Paul, Minn., Feb. 9, 1929. He studied at the N.Y. School of Music (1954–56); also had private sessions with Edgar Varèse (1956) and Wallingford Riegger (1956–59); continued his studies at Tulane Univ. (M.A., 1964). He occupied several teaching posts, at Northwestern Univ. (1965–67), Yale Univ. (1967–73), Louisiana State Univ. (1973–76), Calif. State Univ. in Fullerton (1976–77), and the Univ. of Calif. in Los Angeles (1977–78). In 1972–73 he held a Guggenheim fellowship. He developed a sui generis program of performance arts in which he acted interchangeably as composer, conductor, pianist, conferencier, and entertainer. In 1980 he was appointed director of music and experimental theater at the Contemporary Arts Center in New Orleans. Drew's style of composition is built on flexible techniques, both polythematic and monothematic, often deriving from varying elements of instrumental Klangfarbe; sometimes literal repetition of whole sections is used for emphasis. The stylistic sources of his music can be found in the works of Scriabin and Varèse. A professional pianist, he often appears as a soloist in programs of contemporary music, including jazz. A polymath in his vocations and avocations, Drew drew the Downbeat International Jazz Critics Award in the New Star category in 1961.

WORKS: *Passacaglia* for Orch. (1957); *Indigo Suite* for Piano, Double Bass, and Percussion (1959); *Divisiones* for 6 Percussionists (1962); Piano Trio (1962); *Polifonica I* for Flute, Clarinet, Oboe, String Quartet, and Piano (1963); *The Lute in the Attic* for Voice, Flute, Clarinet, Cello, and 3 Gongs (1963); *4 Pieces* for String Quartet (1964); *Contrappunto* for Orch. (1965); *Polifonica II* for Flute and Percussion (1966); Symph. No. 1 for Chamber Orch. (1968); *Symphonies* for Orch., Chorus, and 3 Conductors (1969); *October Lights* for Orch. (New Haven, Oct. 18, 1969); Concerto for Violino Grande and Orch. (1970); *Metal Concerto* for Percussion (N.Y., Feb. 2, 1971); Symph. No. 2 for Chorus and Orch. (Norfolk, Va., Aug. 20, 1971); *Almost Stationary* for Piano Trio (1971); *Gothic Lights* for Brass Ensemble (1972); Concerto for Percussion (N.Y., March 21, 1973); *Tango* for Cello Solo (1973); *West Indian Lights* for Orch. (Tanglewood, Aug. 9, 1973); *Epitaphium pour Stravinsky* for 3 Trombones, Horn, Tuba, and Piano (Atlanta, Feb. 14, 1974); *Crucifixus Domini Christi*, dramatic stage work (Baton Rouge, Jan. 30, 1975); *The Fading of the Visible World,* oratorio (1975); *Suspense Opera* for Voices and Chamber Ensemble (1975); *Metal Assemblage* for Wind Orch. (1976); Symph. No. 3 (1977); Violin Concerto (1977); String Quartet No. 2 (1977); *Dr. Cincinnati,* dramatic entertainment for Actors, Dancers, Singers, Instrumentalists, and Magnetic Tape Segments (1977); *The Orangethorpe Aria* for Soprano, Piano Trio, and Clarinet (1978); *All Saints' Chorales* (1978); *St. Dennis Variations* for Clarinet (1978); *Trio for the Fiery Messengers* for Piano Trio (1979); Sonata for Violin and Piano (1979); Sonata for Cello and Piano (1980); *St. Mark Triple Concerto* for Violin, Cello, Piano, and Brass/Winds (1981); *5 O'Clock Ladies,* dramatic stage work (1981); *Himself, the Devil,* dramatic stage work (1982); *Whisper,* dramatic video work (1982); Sonata for Solo Viola (1983); *Open/Closed Forms* for Chamber Ensemble (1983); *Trinity* for Soprano and Chamber Ensemble (1983); *American Elegy* for Brass Quintet (1983); *Courtyard Music* for Chamber Orch. and specially designed instruments called Kinisones (1983); *Faustus, An Epilogue* for 2 Pianos, Viola, and Chamber Ensemble (1984); *Becket: The Final Moments,* automated drama (1984); *One Last Dance,* theater and/

or video piece (1984).

Drewanz, Hans, German conductor; b. Dresden, Dec. 2, 1929. He studied conducting with Kurt Thomas and Sir Georg Solti; then was conductor of the Wuppertal Opera (1959–63). In 1963 he became Generalmusikdirektor at Darmstadt.

Dreyer, Johann Melchior, German organist and composer; b. Röttingen, Württemberg, June 24, 1747; d. Ellwangen, March 22, 1824. He studied in Ellwangen, where he became a church organist; wrote chiefly church music, adopting a modern homophonic style. Among his publ. works are *6 Missae breves et rurales ad modernum genium* (1790); *24 Hymni brevissimi ad vesperas* (1791); *Sehr kurze und leichte Landmessen* (1793); *Deutsche Messe* (1800); etc.; also organ music.

Dreyfus, George, German-born Australian composer, bassoonist, and conductor; b. Wuppertal, July 22, 1928. His family left Germany in 1939, settling in Australia. He studied clarinet and then bassoon at the Melbourne Univ. Cons.; played the bassoon in various Australian orchs.; founded the Dreyfus Chamber Orch. in Melbourne. His music is pragmatically constructed and designed for performance by any competent instrumentalists or vocalists.

WORKS: Opera for 8 Characters and Chamber Orch., *Garni Sands* (1965–66; Sydney, July 12, 1972); opera, *The Gilt-Edged Kid* (1970; Melbourne, April 11, 1976); 12-minute opera for Children's Choruses, *Song of the Maypole* (1968); school opera, *The Takeover* (1969); ballet, *The Illusionist* (1965); Trio for Flute, Clarinet, and Bassoon (1956); *Galgenlieder* for Baritone, Flute, Clarinet, Bassoon, and Violin (1957); *Songs Comic and Curious* for Baritone, Flute, Oboe, Clarinet, Horn, and Bassoon (1959); *Wilhelm Busch Lieder* for High Voice and Wind Trio, to words from a famous German children's book (1959); *Music in the Air* for Baritone, Flute, Viola, and Percussion (1961); *From Within Looking Out* for Soprano, Flute, Viola, Vibraphone, and Celesta (1962); *The Seasons* for Flute, Viola, Vibraphone, and Percussion (1963); *Ned Kelly Ballads*, 3 folk songs for Folksinger, 4 Horns, and Rhythm Section (1963); Wind Quintet (1965); *Music for Music Camp* for Orch. (1967); 2 symphs. (1967, 1976); *Jingles*, 5 pieces for Orch. (1968; a potpourri of styles from Mahler, Stravinsky, rock and roll, ballads, and the Tijuana Brass); Wind Quintet (No. 2), after the notebook of J.G. Noverre (1968); *Reflections in a Glass-House*, an image of Captain James Cook, for Narrator, Children's Chorus, and Orch. (1969); Sextet for Didjeridu and Wind Quintet (1971); *MO* for Baritone and String Orch. (1971); *. . . and more Jingles*, 5 further pieces for Orch. (1972); *The Grand Aurora Australis Now Show* for Orch. (1973); *Old Melbourne* for Bassoon and Guitar (1973); *Hallelujah for Handel* for Orch. (1976); *Kaffeekonzert* for Soprano and Piano Trio (1977); *Terrigal* for Chorus and Orch. (1977); Concerto for Bassoon and Strings (1978); film and television scores.

Dreyschock, Alexander, brilliant Bohemian pianist; b. Zack, Oct. 15, 1818; d. Venice, April 1, 1869. A student of Tomaschek, he acquired a virtuoso technique and was regarded as a worthy rival of Liszt in technical dexterity. At 8 he was able to play in public; toured North Germany (1838); spent 2 years in Russia (1840–42); visited Brussels, Paris, and London, then the Netherlands and Austria. In 1862 he was called to St. Petersburg as a prof. at the newly founded Cons. In 1868, he went to Italy, where he died. His astounding facility in playing octaves, double sixths, and thirds, and performing solos with the left hand alone cast a glamour about his performance; he reached the zenith of his fame about 1850.
WORKS: Opera, *Florette, oder Die erste Liebe Heinrichs des IV.*; Overture for Orch.; Rondo for Orch.; String Quartet; 140 piano pieces of the salon type.

Dreyschock, Felix, German pianist, son of **Raimund Dreyschock**; b. Leipzig, Dec. 27, 1860; d. Berlin, Aug. 1, 1906. He studied under Grabau, Ehrlich, Taubert, and Kiel; gave successful concerts, and was a prof. at the Stern Cons. in Berlin. His piano pieces are well-written and effective; he also publ. a Violin Sonata and songs.

Dreyschock, Raimund, Bohemian violinist, brother of **Alexander Dreyschock**; b. Zack, Bohemia, Aug. 20, 1824; d. Leipzig, Feb. 6, 1869. He was a pupil of Pixis in Prague; was concertmaster at the Gewandhaus concerts (1850–69) and a violin teacher in the Cons. at Leipzig. His wife, **Elizabeth** (b. Cologne, 1832; d. there, July, 1911), was a contralto singer who founded and managed a vocal academy in Berlin.

Drieberg, Friedrich von, German music historian and composer; b. Charlottenburg, Dec. 10, 1780; d. there, May 21, 1856. He served in the Prussian army until 1804, when he went to Paris to study composition with Spontini; also traveled to Vienna. He produced 2 operas, *Don Cocagno* (Berlin, 1812) and *Der Sänger und der Schneider* (Berlin, Nov. 23, 1814), but became known mainly through his speculative publications concerning Greek music, promulgating theories and conclusions that were utterly unfounded. However, they were publ. and seriously discussed, if only in refutation. These are *Die mathematische Intervallenlehre der Griechen* (1818); *Aufschlüsse über die Musik der Griechen* (1819); *Die praktische Musik der Griechen* (1821); *Die pneumatischen Erfindungen der Griechen* (1822); *Wörterbuch der griech. Musik* (1835); *Die griechische Musik, auf ihre Grundgesetze zurückgeführt* (1841); *Die Kunst der musikalishen Composition ... nach griechischen Grundsätzen bearbeitet* (1858).

Driessler, Johannes, German composer; b. Friedrichsthal, near Saarbrücken, Jan. 26, 1921. He studied organ and theory with Karl Rahner at the Cons. of Saarbrücken. By the age of 13 he was filling a regular position as church organist. In 1946 he was engaged as an instructor at the Music Academy in Detmold; in 1960 became its director. He devoted himself mainly to choral composition, in which he attained such an outstanding practical craft that his works entered the active repertoire of both sacred and secular institutions in Germany.
WORKS: Choral: *Sinfonia sacra* (1948); *Dein Reich komme* (1949); *Cantica nova* (1950); *Triptychon* (1950); secular oratorio, *Gaudia mundana* (1951); *De profundis* (1952); oratorio, *Der Lebendige* (1956); oratorio, *Der grosse Lobgesang* (1959); 2 *Concerti sacri* (1961); lyric opera, *Claudia amata* (1952); 3 symphs. with subtitles of spiritual connotations: No. 1, *Dum spiro spero* (1964); No. 2, *Dum ludo laudo* (1966); No. 3, *Amo dum vivo* (1969); works for chamber ensembles and numerous teaching pieces.

Drigo, Riccardo, Italian composer and conductor; b. Padua, June 30, 1846; d. there, Oct. 1, 1930. He studied music in Venice; conducted opera in Venice and Milan. In 1879 he was engaged to conduct the Italian opera in St. Petersburg; in 1886 became permanent ballet conductor of the Imperial Theater there; conducted first performances of Tchaikovsky's ballets *The Sleeping Beauty* and *The Nutcracker*. After Tchaikovsky's death, Drigo edited the score of the ballet *Swan Lake* and orchestrated a number of Tchaikovsky's piano pieces. Drigo's own ballets, melodious and easy to listen to, also enjoyed excellent success in Russia. Particularly popular was his ballet *Les Millions d'Arlequin (Harlequin's Millions)*, which includes the famous *Serenade* for a soulful cello solo and the ingratiating *Valse Bluette*. Drigo conducted the first performance of this ballet in St. Petersburg on Feb. 10, 1900. In 1914–16 he was in Italy; in 1916–20 he was again in St. Petersburg, finally returning to Italy and remaining there until his death.
BIBLIOGRAPHY: S. Travaglia, *Riccardo Drigo, L'uomo e l'artista* (Padua, 1929).

Dring, Madeleine, English violinist, pianist, singer, and composer; b. Hornsey, Sept. 7, 1923; d. London, March 26, 1977. She studied violin at the Junior Dept. of the Royal College of Music in London, and also acquired professional skill as a pianist, singer, and actress. She took courses in composition at the Royal College of Music with Hubert Howells and Vaughan Williams; developed a knack for writing attractively brief pieces. She also wrote a short opera called *Cupboard Love*, several trios, a suite for Harmonica and Piano, and incidental-music scores for radio and television.

Drinker, Henry S., Jr., American music scholar and translator; b. Philadelphia, Sept. 15, 1880; d. Merion, Pa., March 9, 1965. He was by profession a lawyer. He trans. the texts of all the Bach cantatas and of the complete vocal works of Brahms and Schumann; was the author of *The Chamber Music of Johannes Brahms* (Philadelphia, 1932). He founded the Drinker Library of Choral Music, which he eventually donated to the Free Library of

Philadelphia.

Drobisch, Moritz Wilhelm, German scholar; b. Leipzig, Aug. 16, 1802; d. there, Sept. 30, 1896. In 1826 he became a prof. extraordinary of mathematics, and in 1842 a prof. ordinary of philosophy, at Leipzig Univ. Besides various works on mathematics and philosophy, he wrote several valuable essays on musical subjects.
WRITINGS: *Über die mathematische Bestimmung der mus. Intervalle* (1846); *Über mus. Tonbestimmung und Temperatur* (1852); *Nachträge zur Theorie der mus. Tonverhältnisse* (1855); "Über ein zwischen Altem und Neuem vermittelndes Tonsystem," *Allegemeine Musikalische Zeitung* (1871); *Über reine Stimmung und Temperatur der Töne* (1877).

Drouet, Louis François-Philippe, famous French flute player and composer; b. Amsterdam, April 14, 1792; d. Bern, Sept. 30, 1873. He studied composition at the Paris Cons.; at the age of 16, was appointed solo flutist to King Louis of the Netherlands, and at 19 became solo flutist to Napoleon; after Napoleon's defeat, he played the flute with fine impartiality for King Louis XVIII. In 1817 he went to London, and subsequently made concert tours across Europe. In 1840 he was appointed Kapellmeister at Coburg; in 1854 he visited America for a few months; then lived in Gotha and Frankfurt before going to Switzerland, where he died. He composed mainly for the flute; among his works are 10 flute concertos; 2 fantasias for flute and piano; 3 trios for 3 flutes; numerous sonatas and variations for flute and assorted instruments. Drouet is credited with the arrangement of the French popular air *Partant pour la Syrie,* supposedly sung for him by Queen Hortense of the Netherlands.

Drozdov, Anatol, Russian pianist, pedagogue, and writer on music; b. Saratov, Nov. 4, 1883; d. Moscow, Sept. 10, 1950. He studied piano at the St. Petersburg Cons., graduating in 1909; then engaged in teaching; was a prof. of piano at the conservatories of Ekaterinoder (1911–16), Saratov (1918–20), and Moscow (1920–24). He publ. a number of articles in Russian music journals; also composed 2 piano sonatas, other piano pieces, and chamber music.

Drozdowski, Jan, Polish pianist; b. Cracow, Feb. 2, 1857; d. there, Jan. 21, 1918. He studied at the Vienna Cons. with Dachs and Epstein; also took lessons with Bruckner. In 1889 he was appointed prof. of piano at the Cracow Cons. and retained that post till his death. He publ. a piano method, *Systematic School of Pianoforte Technique* (1887; German ed., Munich, 1889, under the pseudonym **Jan Jordan**).

Druckman, Jacob, outstanding American composer; b. Philadelphia, June 26, 1928. He took private lessons in composition as a youth with Louis Gesensway in Philadelphia; played jazz trumpet as a teenager. Then he entered the Juilliard School of Music in N.Y. and studied with Bernard Wagenaar, Vincent Persichetti, and Peter Mennin (B.S., 1954; M.S., 1956); also in Tanglewood with Aaron Copland (1949, 1950). In 1954–55 he was at the Ecole Normale de Musique in Paris, where he studied with Tony Aubin. In 1957 he was appointed instructor in the dept. of literature and materials of music at Juilliard; from 1967 he was also an associate at the Columbia-Princeton Electronic Music Center; taught at Brooklyn College from 1972 to 1974; in 1975 was appointed a prof. at Yale Univ. He held Guggenheim grants in 1957 and 1968. In 1972 he received the Pulitzer Prize for music for his orch. work *Windows.* In his music he happily combines the strict elements of polyphonic structure, harking back to Palestrina, with modern techniques of dissonant counterpoint, while refusing to adhere to any doctrinaire system of composition. In his orchestration he makes use of a plethora of percussion instruments, including primitive drums; electronic sonorities also have an increasing importance in his works.
WORKS: Violin Concerto (1956); *4 Madrigals* for Chorus (1959); *Dark upon the Harp* for Mezzo-soprano, Brass Quintet, and Percussion (1962); *Antiphonies* for 2 Choruses (1963); *The Sound of Time* for Soprano and Orch. (1965); *Animus I* for Trombone and Tape (1966); *Incenters* for 13 Players (1968); *Animus II* for Mezzo-soprano, Percussion, and Tape (1969); *Animus III* for Clarinet and Tape (1969); *Windows* for Orch. (Chicago Symph. Orch., May 16, 1972); *Lamia* for Soprano and Orch. (1974); *Valentine* for Double-bass Solo (1975); *Chiaroscuro* for Orch. (1976); Viola Concerto (N.Y., Nov. 2, 1978); *Bo* for Marimba, Harp, and Bass Clarinet (N.Y., Juilliard, March 3, 1979); *Aureole* (N.Y., June 6, 1979); 2 string quartets; other chamber music; songs.

Drury, Stephen, American pianist; b. Spokane, Wash., April 13, 1955. His mother taught him piano; he then went to Harvard Univ., where he worked at the Electronic Music Studio. In 1977 he continued his piano studies in N.Y., with William Masselos; then returned to Harvard and organized an Experimental Music Festival, during which he gave a complete performance of Satie's piano piece *Vexations,* repeated 840 times. He also played the piano sonatas of Ives and piano pieces by John Cage. While preoccupied with avant-garde music, he took occasional lessons in classical piano playing with Claudio Arrau in N.Y. On the musical far-out frontier, he became a member of a conceptual team called Beaux Eaux Duo.

Drysdale, Learmont, Scottish composer; b. Edinburgh, Oct. 3, 1866; d. there, June 18, 1909. He was a pupil at the Royal Academy of Music, and winner of the Lucas prize for composition (1890). He composed the orch. overtures *Tam O'Shanter* (1891; awarded a prize by the Glasgow Society of Musicians) and *Herondean* (1894); also an opera, *The Red Spider* (1898); some choral works.

Dubensky, Arcady, Russian-American violinist

and composer; b. Viatka, Oct. 15, 1890; d. Tenafly, N.J., Oct. 14, 1966. He studied violin at the Moscow Cons. with Jan Hřimaly and composition with Ilyinsky, graduating in 1909; was a violinist at the Moscow Opera (1910–19); then left Russia; played in hotels and restaurants in Constantinople (1920); settled in the U.S. in 1921; was a member of the N.Y. Symph. Orch., and then of the N.Y. Phil. Orch., retiring in 1953. His music is conservative in its idiom; however, an impression of originality is created by his adroit use of unusual combinations (such as a quartet for double basses, a fugue for 18 violins, a suite for 9 flutes).

WORKS: *Romance with Double Bass,* comic opera after Chekhov (N.Y., Oct. 31, 1936); *Russian Bells,* symph. poem (N.Y., Dec. 29, 1927, composer conducting); Prelude and Fugue (1932; Boston Symph. Orch., Koussevitzky conducting, April 12, 1943); *Tom Sawyer,* overture (for Mark Twain's centennial, Philadelphia, Nov. 29, 1935); *Political Suite* for Orch. (*Russian Monarchy, Nazi and Fascist, Communist;* N.Y. radio broadcast, Sept. 17, 1936); *Fantasy on a Negro Theme* for Tuba and Orch. (Indianapolis, 1938); *Stephen Foster,* symph. suite (Indianapolis, Jan. 31, 1941); *Trumpet Overture* for 18 Toy Trumpets and 2 Bass Drums (N.Y., Dec. 10, 1949); *Trombone Concerto* (1953); *Gossips* for Strings (Philadelphia, Nov. 24, 1928); Fugue for 18 Violins (his most successful work; Philadelphia, April 1, 1932, Stokowski conducting); Prelude and Fugue for 4 Bassoons (Brooklyn, Feb. 16, 1947); Suite for 9 Flutes, including a Piccolo and Basset Horn (N.Y., Jan. 26, 1936, composer conducting); other chamber works for various combinations of instruments.

Dubinsky, Vladimir, Russian cellist; b. Russia, Sept. 10, 1876; d. Syracuse, N.Y., Jan. 10, 1938. He studied cello at the Cons. of Moscow; emigrated to the U.S. in 1905, and became cellist with the Tollefsen Trio in N.Y., where he lived for many years as a teacher.

Dubois, Léon, Belgian conductor and composer; b. Brussels, Jan. 9, 1859; d. Boitsfort, Nov. 19, 1935. He won the Prix de Rome at the Brussels Cons. in 1885; conducted opera at the Théâtre de la Monnaie (1892–97); was director of the Louvain Music School (1899–1912); then director of the Brussels Cons. (1912–26). He wrote the operas *Son Excellence ma femme* (1884), *La Revanche de Sganarelle* (1886), and *Edénie* (Antwerp, 1912); a ballet, *Smylis* (Brussels, 1891); the mimodrama *La Mort* (Brussels, 1894); chamber music.

Dubois, Pierre-Max, French composer; b. Graulhet (Tarn), March 1, 1930. He studied at the Cons. in Tours, obtaining a prize in piano at the age of 15; later studied composition with Darius Milhaud at the Paris Cons. His works include *Impressions foraines* for Orch. (1951); *Divertissement* for Saxophone and Orch. (1952); *Sérénades* for Bassoon and Orch. (1953); *Capriccio* for Violin and Orch. (1954); *Concertstück* for Saxophone and Piano (1955); Vio-

lin Concerto (Strasbourg, June 20, 1957); Cello Concerto (1958); Concerto for Saxophone and String Orch. (1959); Symph. No. 1, subtitled *Drame pour Epidaure* (1960); *Le Docteur OX,* ballet-bouffe, after Jules Verne (Lyons, Feb. 23, 1964); Quartet for 4 French Horns (1961); Quartet for 4 Flutes (1961); Quartet for 4 Trombones (1961); *Concerto italien* for 2 Pianos and Orch. (1962); Concerto for Violin, Piano, and Orch. (Besançon, Sept. 15, 1963); Quartet for 4 Clarinets (1962); Symph. No. 2 (*Symphonie-Sérénade*) for Strings (1964); *Musique pour un Western* for Orch. (1964); *Cover Girls,* a choreographic spectacle (1965); *Concerto ironico* for Bassoon and Orch. (1968); Concertino for 4 Saxophones and Orch. (1969); *Beaujency concerto* for Clarinet and Orch. (1969); *Sinfonia militaire* (1969).

Dubois, (Clément-François) Théodore, eminent French organist and composer; b. Rosnay, Marne, Aug. 24, 1837; d. Paris, June 11, 1924. He entered the Paris Cons. in 1853, working under Marmontel (piano), Benoist (organ), and Bazin and Ambroise Thomas (composition); he graduated in 1861; was the recipient of the Grand Prix de Rome with the cantata *Atala,* after having taken first prizes in all depts. Returning to Paris, he was maître de chapelle at Sainte-Clothilde until 1869 and at the Madeleine until 1877, and then succeeded Saint-Saëns there as organist. In 1871 he was made prof. of harmony at the Paris Cons., succeeding Elwart; in 1891 became prof. of composition; in 1894 was elected to the chair in the Academy left vacant by Gounod's death; in 1896 he succeeded Ambroise Thomas as director of the Paris Cons.; retired in 1905.

WORKS: Comic operas: *La Guzla de l'émir* (Paris, April 30, 1873) and *Le Pain bis, ou La Lilloise* (Opéra-Comique, Feb. 26, 1879); *Aben Hamet* (produced in Italian, Théâtre du Châtelet, Dec. 16, 1884); "idylle dramatique," *Xavière* (Opéra-Comique, Nov. 26, 1895); ballet, *La Farandole* (Paris Opéra, Dec. 14, 1883); 2 oratorios: *Les Sept Paroles du Christ* (1867) and *Le Paradis perdu* (1878; won the City of Paris prize); several cantatas (*L'Enlèvement de Proserpine, Hylas, Bergerette, Les Vivants et les morts, Délivrance*); masses and other church music; many orch. works: *Marche heroïque de Jeanne d'Arc; Fantaisie triomphale* for Organ and Orch.; *Hymne nuptiale; Méditation-Prière* for Strings, Oboe, Harp, and Organ; *Concerto-Capriccio* for Piano; 2nd Piano Concerto; Violin Concerto; 2 symph. poems: *Notre Dame de la Mer* and *Adonis; Symphonie française* (1908); *Fantasietta* (1917); piano pieces (*Chœur et danse des lutins; 6 poèmes sylvestres*); pieces for organ and for harmonium; a cappella choruses; etc. Dubois publ. a practical manual, *Traité de contrepoint et de fugue* (1901), which was a standard work at the Paris Cons.

BIBLIOGRAPHY: M. Widor, *Notice sur la vie et les travaux de Théodore Dubois* (Paris, 1924).

Dubrovay, László, Hungarian composer; b. Budapest, March 23, 1943. He studied in Budapest at the Academy of Music, graduating in 1966; then attended classes of Stockhausen in Germany; was a répétiteur with the Hamburg State Opera (1971–72). In his music he experiments with mathematically conceived forms.

WORKS: *5 Pieces* for Bassoon and Piano (1967); *6 Duos* for Violin and Percussion (1968); *Verificazione* for Orch. (1969); String Quartet (1969); Brass Quintet (1969); *Succession* for Orch. (1973); *E-Trio* for Violin, Percussion, and Synthesizer (1974); *Sequence* for Flute and Synthesizer (1974); *Magic Square* for Violin and Cimbalom (1975); *A²* for Violin, Cello, Piano, Percussion, and Synthesizer (1975); *Geometrum 1* for Tape (1975); *Geometrum 2* for String Quartet or 4 String Instruments (1976); *Interferences* for 2 Cimbaloms (1976); *Numberplay No. 1* for 20 Instruments (1976); *Numberplay No. 2* for Chorus (1977); *Oscillations No. 1* for Electric Organ and Synthesizer; *Oscillations No. 2* for Cello, Cimbalom, Electric Organ, and Synthesizer; *Oscillations No. 3* for Piano and Synthesizer (1976–77); *Matuziáda Nos. 1–4* for 4 Flutes (1976–77); *Caput* for Chorus, Electric Organ, and Phase Shifter (1977).

Dubuc, Alexander, Russian pianist, composer, and teacher; b. Moscow, March 3, 1812; d. there, Jan. 8, 1898. He was a pupil of John Field, about whom he publ. a vol. of memoirs; was a prof. at the Moscow Cons. (1866–72). He wrote piano pieces, songs, and a work on piano technique (1866).

Du Cange, Charles Du Fresne, Sieur, French scholar; b. Amiens, Dec. 18, 1610; d. Paris, Oct. 23, 1688. He belonged to the famed group of 17th-century French writers who established the precepts of modern historical criticism; he is important to musicology because he included definitions of Latin musical terms in his lexicographies. The most valuable of his many works are the *Glossarium ad scriptores mediae et infimae latinitatis* (Paris, 3 vols., 1678; 6 vols., 1733–36; 7 vols., 1840–50; 10 vols., 1883–87) and the *Glossarium ad scriptores mediae et infimae graecitatis* (Lyons, 1688; Breslau, 1889). Almost all his works are preserved in the Bibliothèque Nationale in Paris.

BIBLIOGRAPHY: H. Hardouin, *Essai sur la vie et sur les ouvrages de Du Cange* (Amiens, 1849); L.J. Feugère, in the *Journal de l'Instruction Publique* (Paris, 1852).

Du Caurroy, François-Eustache, Sieur de St.-Frémin; French composer; b. Beauvais (baptized, Feb. 4), 1549; d. Paris, Aug. 7, 1609. He was a member of the French nobility; his father was "procureur du roi." He entered the Royal Chapel as a singer in 1569; in 1575 received a prize for a chanson, *Beaux yeux;* in 1578 he was "sous-maître"; in 1599 became superintendent of "la musique du roi." Influenced by Le Jeune, he began to compose "musique mesurée"; advanced in the favor of the court, receiving honors and awards; held the ecclesiastical titles of canon at the Ste. Chapelle of Dijon, Ste. Croix of Orleans, and other provincial posts. His greatest work was the collection *Meslanges de la musique,* containing Psalms, "chansons mesurées," noëls, in

4, 5, and 6 voices (posthumously publ., Paris, 1610; some specimens reprinted in Expert's *Maîtres musiciens,* vol. XIII). Other works: *Missa pro defunctis;* 2 vols. of *Preces ecclesiasticae;* instrumental *Fantaisies* for 3, 4, 5, and 6 parts (Paris, 1610; several nos. publ. separately by Expert); 5 vols. of his works in score are in the Bibliothèque Sainte-Geneviève in Paris.

BIBLIOGRAPHY: M.Th. Luillier, *Note sur quelques artistes-musiciens dans la Brie* (1870); N. Dufourcq, "A propos d'Eustache Du Caurroy," *Revue de Musicologie* (Dec. 1950); F. Lesure, "La Carrière et les fonctions de Du Caurroy," ibid. (1952).

Ducis (Duch), Benedictus, distinguished composer of the 16th century; b. probably near Constance, c.1490; d. Schalckstetten, near Ulm, 1544. He may or may not be identical with **Benedictus de Opitiis,** who was organist at the Antwerp Cathedral (1514–16) and at the Chapel Royal in London (1516–22). It is known for a certainty that Benedictus Ducis was in Vienna c.1515; he probably studied there; in 1532 he applied for a pastorate at Ulm (under the name **Benedict Duch**), but failed to obtain it. In 1533 he succeeded in receiving a pastorate at Stubersheim, near Geislingen; in 1535 he became pastor at Schalckstetten and remained there till his death. Benedictus Ducis has been confused by many writers with Benedictus Appenzeller; the long list of Ducis's works given by Fétis is spurious; Barclay Squire, in *Sammelbände der Internationalen Musik-Gesellschaft* (Jan. 1912), brought conclusive evidence that a considerable number of these works must be attributed to Benedictus Appenzeller. Two works by Ducis were publ. in facsimile by M. Nijhoff (The Hague, 1925); 10 sacred motets are reprinted in Denkmäler Deutscher Tonkunst, vol. XXXIV (ed. by Johannes Wolf).

BIBLIOGRAPHY: F. Spitta, "Benedictus Ducis," *Monatsschrift für Gottesdienst und kirchliche Kunst* (Jan.–March 1913); Charles Van den Borren, "Benedictus de Opitiis," *Musica sacra* (Sept. 1927); D. Bartha, *Benedictus Ducis und Appenzeller* (Wolfenbüttel, 1930).

Duckles, Vincent Harris, American musicologist and librarian; b. Boston, Sept. 21, 1913. He studied at Columbia Univ. and at the Univ. of Calif., Berkeley (Ph.D., 1953); in 1947, was appointed head of the music library at Berkeley; was a prof. of music there from 1962. He specializes in 17th-century English song literature, music bibliography, and history of musical scholarship. He has held 2 Fulbright fellowships (1950, Cambridge; 1957, Univ. of Göttingen); a grant-in-aid from the American Council of Learned Societies (1964, Florence). He publ. a valuable manual, *Music Reference and Research Materials: An Annotated Bibliography* (N.Y., 1964; 3rd ed., 1974).

Ducloux, Walter, Swiss-American conductor; b. Kriens, April 17, 1913. He studied at the Univ. of Munich (1932–35) and at the Academy of Music in Vienna (1935–37); was assistant to Toscanini at the

Lucerne Festivals (1938–39); came to America and conducted opera in N.Y. (1940–42); became a bandleader in the U.S. Army (1943–46); then was active in California and in Texas as an opera conductor.

Dudarova, Veronica, Russian conductor; b. Baku, Dec. 5, 1916. She studied piano in Leningrad and took a course in conducting at the Moscow Cons. with Leo Ginsburg, graduating in 1947; in the same year became associate conductor of the Moscow State Orch. She is one of the foremost women conductors of the Soviet Union.

Dufallo, Richard, American clarinetist and conductor; b. East Chicago, Ind., Jan. 30, 1933. He played clarinet as a youngster; then enrolled at the American Cons. of Music in Chicago. He subsequently studied composition with Lukas Foss at the Univ. of Calif., Los Angeles; in 1957 he joined the Improvisation Chamber Ensemble organized by Foss, and showed an exceptional talent for controlled improvisation in the ultramodern manner. He then joined Lukas Foss as his associate conductor with the Buffalo Phil. (1962–67); also served on the faculty of the State Univ. of N.Y. at Buffalo (1963–67), where he directed its Center of Creative and Performing Arts. He attended a conducting seminar with William Steinberg in N.Y. (1965); Pierre Boulez gave him additional instruction in Basel (1969). In 1967 he went to Japan and other Asian countries as assistant tour conductor with the N.Y. Phil. In 1971 he made his European conducting debut in Paris. He served as conductor of the "Mini-Met," an adjunct to the Metropolitan Opera in N.Y. (1972–74), and was director of the series of new music sponsored by the Juilliard School of Music in N.Y. (1972–79). In 1970 he became artistic director of the Aspen Music Festival's Conference on Contemporary Music. From 1980 he has also served as artistic adviser of Het Gelders Orkest in Arnhem, the Netherlands. He made guest appearances with the Concertgebouw Orch. of Amsterdam, London Symph., Chicago Symph., Berlin Phil., Pittsburgh Symph., and Philadelphia Orch.

Dufau, Jenny, French soprano; b. Rathau, Alsace, July 18, 1878; d. Pau, France, Aug. 29, 1924. She was a pupil of Etelka Gerster in Berlin (1901–5); studied subsequently with Mme. Marchesi, P. Vidal, A. Selva, and G. Benvenuti; sang at the Berlin Opera (1910–11); from 1911, was with Chicago Opera Co.; later, appeared in vaudeville.

Dufay, Guillaume, chief representative of the Burgundian school, and famed particularly for his 3-part chansons, masses, and motets; b. probably at Hainault, c.1400; d. Cambrai, Nov. 27, 1474. The last name is pronounced "du-fah-ee," in 3 syllables, as indicated by the way he set his name to music in *Ave regina caelorum,* asking for the Lord's mercy: "Miserere tui labentis *Du-fa-y.*" He was a choirboy at the Cathedral of Cambrai, where he received an excellent training; his teachers were Loqueville and Grenon. He was in Rimini and Pesaro (1419–26);

then returned to Cambrai, where he was chapel master (1426–28); then member of the Papal Chapel in Rome (1428–33); in the service of the Duke of Savoy (1433); again in Cambrai (1434); entered again the Papal Chapel (1435–37; not in Rome, however, but in Florence and Bologna); was again in Savoy (1438–44); studied jurisprudence at the Univ. of Turin, obtaining the degree "Baccalarius in decretis" (c.1445). In 1445 he settled at Cambrai, holding the important position of canon at the cathedrals of Cambrai and Mons. Under these fortunate circumstances, which enabled him to live in comfort, he spent the rest of his life, greatly esteemed by both the Church authorities and musicians; he was described by Compère as "the moon of all music, and the light of all singers." Dufay wrote music in almost every form practiced in his time, and was successful in each. A complete list of works, including MS sources and approximate dates of composition, is found in Charles E. Hamm's *A Chronology of the Works of Guillaume Dufay* (1964). The *Opera omnia* (issued by the American Inst. of Musicology, Rome, 1947–50; first ed. by Guillaume de Van, continued by Heinrich Bessler) also contains a valuable commentary.

BIBLIOGRAPHY: F.X. Haberl, "Wilhelm du Fay," *Bausteine für Musikgeschichte,* vol. I (Leipzig, 1885); H. Besseler, "Studien zur Musik des Mittelalters," *Archiv für Musikwissenschaft* (June 1925); Charles Van den Borren, *Guillaume Dufay: Son importance dans l'évolution de la musique au XVe siècle* (Brussels, 1926); K. Geiringer, "Dufay's 'Gloria ad modum tubae,' " *Zeitschrift für Musikwissenschaft* (Jan. 1927); K. Dèzes, "Das Dufay zugeschriebene 'Salve Regina,' eine deutsche Komposition," ibid. (Feb. 1928); H. Besseler, *Die Musik des Mittelalters und der Renaissance,* in Bücken's Handbuch der Musikwissenschaft series (1931–34); Charles Van den Borren, "Guillaume Dufay, Light of the 15th Century," *Musical Quarterly* (July 1935); H. Besseler, "Neue Dokumente zum Leben und Schaffen Dufays," *Archiv für Musikwissenschaft* (Sept. 1952); D. Plamenac, "An Unknown Composition by Dufay?," *Musical Quarterly* (April 1954); chap. 2 in Gustave Reese, *Music in the Renaissance* (N.Y., 1954); H. Besseler's article in *Die Musik in Geschichte und Gegenwart* incorporates new documentary discoveries on Dufay's life (many of them made by Besseler himself); C. Van den Borren, "Dufay and His School," in D.A. Hughes and G. Abraham, *Ars Nova and the Renaissance* (London, 1960); Charles E. Hamm, *A Chronology of the Works of Guillaume Dufay Based on a Study of Mensural Practice* (Princeton, N.J., 1964); L. Treitler, "Tone System in the Secular Works of Guillaume Dufay," *Journal of the American Musicological Society* (1965); A.E. Planchart, "Guillaume Dufay's Masses: Notes and Revisions," *Musical Quarterly* (Jan. 1972); F. Otterbach, *Kadenzierung und Tonalität im Kantilenensatz Dufays* (1974); D. Fallows, *Dufay* (London, 1982); idem, "Dufay's Mass for St. Anthony of Padua: Reflections on the Career of His Most Important Work," *Musical Times* (July 1982). A Dufay Quincentennial Conference was held at Brooklyn College on Dec. 6–7, 1974;

a compilation of the papers read at the Conference was publ. in 1976 (ed. by Allan Atlas).

Dufourcq, Norbert, distinguished French music historian and organist; b. St. Jean-de-Braye (Loiret), Sept. 21, 1904. He was educated at the Sorbonne (1921–23), where he studied history and geography; then at the Ecole Nationale des Chartes (1924–28), graduating as an archivist-palaeographer; also studied piano and music history with Gastoué (1913–20), organ with André Marchal (1920–40), and harmony, counterpoint, and fugue with Marie-Rose Hublé. He took his Ph.D. at the Univ. of Paris in 1935 with the dissertation *Esquisse d'une histoire de l'orgue en France: XIIIe–XVIIIe siècles* (publ. in Paris, 1935). He was a teacher of history at the Collège Stanislas in Paris (1935–46); also prof. of Music History and Musicology at the Paris Cons. (1941–76). In addition to other teaching positions, he also appeared as an organist. He edited performing and scholarly editions of works for the organ and harpsichord of 17th- and 18th-century French composers.
WRITINGS: *Documents inédits pour servir à l'histoire de l'orgue* (Paris, 1935); *Les Clicquot, Facteurs d'orgues du Roy* (Paris, 1942); *Jean-Sébastien Bach: génie allemand, génie latin?* (Paris, 1947; 2nd ed., 1949); *Jean-Sébastien Bach, le maître de l'orgue* (Paris, 1948; 2nd ed., 1973); *L'Orgue* (Paris, 1948; 5th ed., 1976); *César Franck* (Paris, 1949); *La Musique française* (Paris, 1949; 2nd ed., augmented, 1970); *Le Clavecin* (Paris, 1949; 2nd ed., 1967); *Autour de Coquard, César Franck et Vincent d'Indy* (Paris, 1952); *Nicolas Lebègue* (Paris, 1954); *Jean-Baptiste Boesset, surintendant de la Musique du Roi* (Paris, 1963); *Le livre de l'orgue français, 1589–1789* (Paris, 1969—); *Les Grandes Dates de l'histoire de la musique* (with M. Benoit and B. Gagnepain; Paris, 1969; 2nd ed., 1975).

Dufranne, Hector, French baritone; b. Mons, Belgium, Oct. 25, 1870; d. Paris, May 3, 1951. He made his debut as Valentine in *Faust* at the Théâtre de la Monnaie in Brussels on Sept. 9, 1896; at the Opéra-Comique in Paris on June 18, 1900. He sang with the Manhattan Opera House in N.Y. (1908–10), and with the Chicago Opera Co. (1910–22).

Dugan, Franjo, Croatian composer and organist; b. Krapinica, Sept. 11, 1874; d. Zagreb, Dec. 12, 1948. He studied music with Max Bruch in Berlin, and also attended classes in mathematics. He settled in Zagreb as a church organist; taught at the Zagreb Cons.; publ. manuals on orchestration and musical form; composed many organ pieces.

Dugazon, Louise Rosalie, famous opera singer; b. Berlin, June 18, 1755; d. Paris, Sept. 22, 1821. She was brought up in the atmosphere of the theater; her father, F.J. Lefebvre, was a French dancer at the Berlin Opera; she herself began her career as a ballet dancer; then she became a singer, encouraged mainly by Grétry, who thought highly of her talent. She made her debut in Paris in Grétry's opera *Syl-*

vain (June 19, 1774); in 1775 she married an actor who used the professional name Dugazon; although they were soon separated, she adopted this name for her professional appearances. She sang mostly at the Opéra-Comique; created some 60 new roles; her last public appearance was at the Paris Opéra on Feb. 29, 1804. She was greatly admired by her contemporaries, and her name became a designation of certain types of operatic parts ("jeune Dugazon"; i.e., an ingenue).
BIBLIOGRAPHY: H. and A. Leroux, *La Dugazon* (Paris, 1926).

Duggan, Joseph Francis, Irish pianist and composer; b. Dublin, July 10, 1817; d. London, 1900. He was engaged at the Italian Opera in N.Y.; taught in Philadelphia, Baltimore, and Washington; then lived in London; became a prof. of singing in the Guildhall School of Music. He wrote 2 successful operas, *Pierre* (London, 1853) and *Leonie* (London, 1854); 2 symphs.; 6 string quartets; numerous piano pieces; also publ. *The Singing Master's Assistant* and translations of Albrechtsberger's *Science of Music* (Philadelphia, 1842) and Fétis's *Counterpoint and Fugue.*

Duhamel, Antoine, French composer, son of the famous writer Georges Duhamel; b. Paris, July 30, 1925. He studied with René Leibowitz and from the very first began to compose in the dodecaphonic technique; has written a quintet for piano and wind instruments; also publ. a book, *L'Opéra depuis Wagner* (Liège, 1950).

Duiffoprugcar (properly, **Tieffenbrucker**), **Gaspar,** Bavarian viol maker; b. Tieffenbrugg, Bavaria, 1514 (date established by Dr. Coutagne of Lyons, in his work *Gaspar Duiffoproucart et les luthiers lyonnais du XVIe siècle*, Paris, 1893); d. Lyons, Dec. 16, 1571. He was long reputed to be the first maker of violins; but Vidal, in his *Les Instruments à archet*, states that all the so-called Duiffoprugcar violins are spurious, having been made by Vuillaume, who in 1827 conceived the idea of making violins after the pattern of a viola da gamba by Duiffoprugcar. Apparently, the latter learned his trade in Italy, the usual spellings of his name showing it to be Italianized rather than gallicized; he settled in Lyons in 1553, and was naturalized in 1559.

Dukas, Paul, famous French composer; b. Paris, Oct. 1, 1865; d. there, May 17, 1935. In 1882–88 he was a student at the Paris Cons., studying under G. Mathias (piano), Théodore Dubois (harmony), and E. Guiraud (composition); won first prize for counterpoint and fugue in 1886, and the 2nd Prix de Rome with a cantata, *Velléda* (1888); began writing music reviews in 1892; was music critic of the *Revue Hebdomadaire* and *Gazette des Beaux-Arts*; also a contributor to the *Chronique des Arts, Revue Musicale*, etc.; in 1906, was made a Chevalier of the Légion d'Honneur; in 1910–13, and again in 1928, was prof. of the orch. class at the Cons.; in 1918, was elected Debussy's successor as a member of the

Conseil de l'enseignement supérieur there; in 1927, was appointed prof. of composition at the Paris Cons.; also taught at the Ecole Normale de Musique; assisted in the revising and editing of Rameau's complete works for Durand of Paris. Although he was not a prolific composer, he wrote a masterpiece of modern music in his orch. scherzo *L'Apprenti Sorcier;* his opera *Ariane et Barbe-Bleue* is one of the finest French operas in the impressionist style. Shortly before his death he destroyed several MSS of his unfinished compositions.

WORKS: 3 overtures: *King Lear* (1883); *Götz von Berlichingen* (1884); *Polyeucte* (1891); Symph. in C (Paris, Jan. 3, 1897); *L'Apprenti Sorcier* (May 18, 1897; his most famous work); opera, *Ariane et Barbe-Bleue* (Opéra-Comique, May 10, 1907); ballet, *La Péri* (Paris, April 22, 1912); *Villanelle* for Horn and Piano (1906); for Piano: Sonata in E-flat minor; *Variations, Interlude et Finale,* on a theme by Rameau; *Prélude élégiaque.* Together with Saint-Saëns, he completed Guiraud's opera *Frédégonde.*

BIBLIOGRAPHY: O. Séré, *Musiciens français d'aujourd'hui* (1911; revised ed., Paris, 1921); G. Samazeuilh, *Paul Dukas* (Paris, 1913; 2nd ed., 1936); G. Jean-Aubry, *La Musique française d'aujourd'hui* (1916); V. d'Indy, *E. Chabrier et Paul Dukas* (1920); A. Cœuroy, *La Musique française moderne* (1922); A. Cortot, *La Musique française de piano;* I. Schwerke, "Paul Dukas," *Musical Quarterly* (1928); G. Samazeuilh, *Paul Dukas, musicien français* (Paris, 1936); Dukas issue of the *Revue Musicale* (May–June 1936); G. Favre, *Paul Dukas: Sa vie, son œuvre* (Paris, 1948); F. Lesure, *Catalogue de l'exposition* (Paris, 1965); G. Favre, *L'Œuvre de Paul Dukas* (Paris, 1969); idem, ed., *Correspondence de Paul Dukas* (Paris, 1971). See also *Les Écrits de Paul Dukas sur la musique* (Paris, 1948).

Duke, John, American pianist and composer; b. Cumberland, Md., July 30, 1899. He studied at the Peabody Cons. in Baltimore with G. Strube (composition) and H. Randolph (piano); later studied in Europe with Schnabel and Nadia Boulanger. From 1923 to 1967 he taught piano at Smith College.

WORKS: String Trio (1937); Concerto for Piano and Strings (1938); *Carnival Overture* (1941); Piano Trio (1943); one-act opera, *Captain Lovelock* (N.Y., Feb. 20, 1956); String Quartet (1969); *6 Song Settings of Emily Brontë's Poems* (1970); many songs.

Duke, Vernon. See Dukelsky, Vladimir.

Dukelsky, Vladimir (pen name as composer of light music: **Vernon Duke**), versatile composer of both "serious" and popular music; b. Oct. 10, 1903, in the railroad station of the Russian village of Parfianovka (during his mother's trip to Pskov); d. Santa Monica, Calif., Jan. 16, 1969. He was a pupil at the Kiev Cons. of Glière and Dombrovsky; left Russia in 1920 and went to Turkey, coming to the U.S. shortly afterward; later lived in Paris and London; settled in N.Y. in 1929 (naturalized, 1936); was a lieutenant in the Coast Guard (1939–44); went back to France (1947–48), but then returned to the U.S. to live in N.Y. and Hollywood. He began to compose at a very early age; was introduced to Diaghilev, who commissioned him to write a ballet, *Zéphyr et Flore,* the production of which put Dukelsky among the successful group of ballet composers. Another important meeting was with Koussevitzky, who championed Dukelsky's music in Paris and in Boston. In the U.S. Dukelsky began writing popular music; many of his songs, such as *April in Paris,* have enjoyed great popularity. At George Gershwin's suggestion, he adopted the name Vernon Duke for popular music works; in 1955 he dropped his full name altogether, and signed both his serious and light compositions Vernon Duke.

WORKS: FOR THE STAGE: *Zéphyr et Flore* (Paris, Jan. 31, 1925); *Demoiselle Paysanne,* opera in 2 acts (1928); *Le Bal des blanchisseuses,* ballet (Paris, Dec. 19, 1946); *Souvenir de Monte Carlo,* ballet (1949–56). FOR ORCH.: Piano Concerto (1924; not orchestrated); 3 symphs.: No. 1 (Paris, June 14, 1928); No. 2 (Boston, April 25, 1930); No. 3 (Brussels Radio Orch., Oct. 10, 1947); *Ballade* for Piano and Small Orch. (1931); *Dédicaces* for Soprano, Piano, and Orch. (Boston Symph., Dec. 16, 1938); Violin Concerto (Boston, March 19, 1943); Cello Concerto (Boston, Jan. 4, 1946); *Ode to the Milky Way* (N.Y., Nov. 18, 1946). CHORAL MUSIC: *Dushenka,* duet for Women's Voices and Chamber Orch. (1927); *Epitaph* (on the death of Diaghilev) for Soprano Solo, Chorus, and Orch. (Boston Symph., April 15, 1932); *The End of St. Petersburg,* oratorio (Schola Cantorum, N.Y., Jan. 12, 1938); *Moulin-Rouge* for Mixed Chorus (1941). CHAMBER MUSIC: Trio (Variations) for Flute, Bassoon, and Piano (1930); Etude for Bassoon and Piano (1932); *Capriccio mexicano* for Violin and Piano (1933); *3 Pieces* for Woodwind (1939); Violin Sonata (1949); String Quartet (1956). SONGS: *The Musical Zoo,* 20 songs to Ogden Nash's lyrics (1946); *A Shropshire Lad,* song cycle (1949). FOR PIANO: Sonata (1927); *Surrealist Suite* (1944); *Souvenir de Venise* (1948); *Serenade to San Francisco* (1956). He wrote songs for the musical comedies *The Show Is On, Garrick Gaieties, Walk a Little Faster, Three's a Crowd, Americana, Ziegfeld Follies, Cabin in the Sky,* etc.; added 2 ballets and several songs to *Goldwyn Follies,* an unfinished film score by George Gershwin (1937). He publ. an amusing autobiography, *Passport to Paris* (Boston, 1955), and the polemical book *Listen Here! A Critical Essay on Music Depreciation* (N.Y., 1963). See Igor Stravinsky, "A Cure for V.D.," in the unperiodical magazine *Listen* (Sept. 1964), a curiously undignified polemical incursion.

Dulcken, Ferdinand Quentin, pianist and composer; b. London, June 1, 1837; d. Astoria, N.Y., Dec. 10, 1901. He was the son of **Luise Dulcken** and nephew of **Ferdinand David;** was a pupil of Moscheles and Gade at the Leipzig Cons.; also received encouragement from Mendelssohn. He subsequently taught at the Warsaw Cons., and also at Moscow and St. Petersburg; made many concert tours in Europe as a pianist with Wieniawski, Vieuxtemps, and others. In 1876 he emigrated to America and gave concerts with Reményi; settled in N.Y. as a teacher and composer. He publ. nearly 400 piano pieces of the salon type and also some vocal works.

Dulcken (née **David**), **Luise,** pianist, sister of **Ferdinand David;** b. Hamburg, March 29, 1811; d. London, April 12, 1850. She was taught by C.F.G. Schwencke and Wilhelm Grund; played in public (in Germany) when 11 years of age. She married in 1828, and went to London, where she met with brilliant success as a pianist and teacher. Queen Victoria was one of her many pupils.

Dulichius (Dulich, Deilich, Deulich), Philippus, German composer and music theorist; b. Chemnitz, Dec. 18 (baptized, Dec. 19), 1562; d. Stettin, March 24 (buried, March 25), 1631. He studied at the Univ. of Leipzig; there is no evidence that he went to Italy and studied with Gabrieli, although this assertion appears in his biographies. He was a cantor in Stettin from 1587 until his retirement in 1630; was also in Danzig in 1604–5 to deputize for the cantor of the Marienkirche.
WORKS: (EXCLUSIVELY VOCAL): *Novum opus musicum duarum partium continens dicta insigniora ex evangeliis* (Stettin, 1599); *Centuriae octonum et septenum vocum harmonias sacras laudibus sanctisimae Triados consecratas continentes* (4 parts, Stettin 1607). R. Schwartz publ. 7 choruses from the *Centuriae* (1896); the complete *Centuriae* are publ. in Denkmäler Deutscher Tonkunst (XXXI, XLI).
BIBLIOGRAPHY: R. Schwartz, "Philippus Dulichius," *Monatsschrifte für Gottesdienst und kirchliche Kunst* (1896).

Du Locle, Camille Théophile Germain du Commun, French librettist; b. Orange, Vacluse, July 16, 1832; d. Capri, Oct. 9, 1903. He was secretary of the Opéra under Perrin's direction; later, director of the Opéra-Comique. He commissioned Bizet to compose *Carmen;* was also instrumental in the preparation of the libretto for Verdi's opera *Aida.*

Dülon, Friedrich Ludwig, blind German flutist; b. Oranienburg, near Potsdam, Aug. 14, 1769; d. Würzburg, July 7, 1826. He was taught by his father (flute) and Angerstein (theory); in 1783 his concert travels began, and extended all over Europe. In 1793–94 he was chamber musician at the St. Petersburg court (gave his first concert in St. Petersburg on March 30, 1793); then settled (1823) in Würzburg. He wrote an autobiography: *Dülons des blinden Flötenspielers Leben und Meinungen, von ihm selbst bearbeitet* (Zürich, 2 vols., 1807–8, ed. by Wieland).

Dumbraveanu, Corneliu, Rumanian conductor; b. Cerneuti, Sept. 26, 1933. He studied the double bass; after playing in orchs. in Ploesti and Galatz, he became conductor of the State Phil. Orch. in Satu-Mare in 1967; then led the State Phil. Orch. in Ploesti (1969–75); in addition, he toured Hungary and the Soviet Union. In 1977 he settled in the Netherlands;

made his debut there with the Utrecht Symph. Orch. in 1978; in 1979 he became its chief conductor.

Dumesnil, Maurice, French-American pianist; b. Angoulême, Charente, April 20, 1886; d. Highland Park, Mich., Aug. 26, 1974. He studied at the Paris Cons. with Isidor Philipp, graduating in 1905. He received personal coaching from Debussy in playing Debussy's piano works, and was subsequently considered as an authority on the subject. He publ. *How to Play and Teach Debussy* (1933) and *Claude Debussy, Master of Dreams* (1940). Apart from his principal occupation as a piano teacher, he was also active as a conductor in Mexico (1916–20); eventually settled in N.Y.

Dumesnil, René, French writer; b. Rouen, June 19, 1879; d. Paris, Dec. 24, 1967. He studied literature at the Sorbonne; was active as a literary critic. Besides his publications dealing with literature, he wrote a number of books on music.
WRITINGS: *Le Rythme musical* (1921; 2nd augmented ed., 1949); *Le Monde des musiciens* (1924); *Le Don Juan de Mozart* (1927; 2nd ed., 1955); *Musiciens romantiques* (1928); *Richard Wagner* (1929); *La Musique contemporaine en France* (1930; 2nd ed., 1949); *Le Livre du disque* (with P. Hemardinquer; 1931); *Histoire illustrée de la musique* (1934); *Portraits de musiciens français* (1938); *La Musique romantique française* (1944); *La Musique en France entre les deux guerres* (Geneva, 1946); *L'Envers de la musique* (Paris, 1949); *Histoire illustrée du théâtre lyrique* (Paris, 1953; received the Grand Prix for musical literature); *Richard Wagner* (Paris, 1954; a much larger work than his first Wagner book of 1929); *L'Opéra* (Paris, 1964); *Mozart présent dans ses œuvres lyriques* (Brussels, 1965).

Dumitrescu, Gheorghe, Rumanian composer, brother of **Ion Dumitrescu;** b. Oteşani, Dec. 28, 1914. He studied with Cuclin, Perlea, and Jora at the Bucharest Cons. (1934–41); was active as a violinist; served as director at the National Theater in Bucharest (1935–46); was composer-counselor for the Armatei artistic ensemble (1947–57); in 1951 was appointed a prof. at the Bucharest Cons. His music is marked by a vivacious quality typical of the operetta style.
WORKS: Operetta, *Tarsiţa şi Roşiorul* (1949); 5 operas: *Ion Vodă cel Cumplit (Ion Voda the Terrible;* 1955); *Decebal* (1957); *Răscoala* (1959); *Fata cu garoafe* (1961); *Meşterul Manole* (1969); oratorios: *Tudor Vladimirescu* (1950); *Griviţa noastră* (1963); *Zorile de aur* (1964); *Din lumea cu dor în cea fără dor* (1966); *Pămînt dezrobit* (1968); numerous cantatas and other vocal-symphonic works; 4 symphs.: No. 1 (1945); No. 2, *A Republicii,* with Chorus (1962); No. 3 (1965); No. 4 (1970); *Poem rustic* for Orch. (1939); *Poemul amurgului* for Orch. (1941); *Suită pitorească* for Orch. (1942); *4 Symphonic Frescoes* (1943); *Suită primaverii* for Orch. (1944); Cello Concerto (1947); *Suită cîmpenească* for Orch. (1963); 2 piano sonatas (1938, 1939); Viola Sonata (1939); Violin Sonata (1939); Piano Quintet (1940); songs; cho-

ruses.

Dumitrescu, Ion, Rumanian composer, brother of **Gheorghe Dumitrescu;** b. Oteşani, June 2, 1913. He studied conducting with Perlea and composition with Cuclin at the Bucharest Cons. (1934–41); was a composer and conductor at the National Theater in Bucharest (1940–47); has taught at the Bucharest Cons. since 1944. He writes in classical forms with undertones of Rumanian folk music.

WORKS: 3 suites for Orch. (1938, 1940, 1944); *2 Pieces* for Orch. (1940); *Poeme* for Cello and Orch. (1940); Symph. No. 1 (1948); *Symphonic Prelude* (1952); Concerto for String Orch. (1956); Suite from the film *Muntele Retezat* (1956); *Sinfonietta* (1955–57); Piano Sonata (1938); *Suite in stil vechi* for Viola and Piano (1939); Piano Sonatina (1940); *2 Pieces* for Piano (1942); String Quartet No. 1 (1949; transcribed for String Orch., 1961); film music; songs.

Dumler, Martin G., American composer; b. Cincinnati, Dec. 22, 1868; d. there, Oct. 19, 1958. He studied at the Cincinnati College of Music (graduated 1901); was subsequently vice-president of the board of trustees; also president of the Bruckner Society. His compositions are chiefly settings of sacred texts.

Dumont (Du Mont), Henri (Henry), significant Belgian-French composer of motets; b. Villers l'Evèque, near Liège, 1610; d. Paris, May 8, 1684. He served as a chorister at Maastricht, and was ordained a priest at Liège; then was organist at St. Paul's Church in Paris (1640–63); maître de chapelle at the French court (1663–83); concurrently was maître de la musique for the Queen of France (1673–81).

WORKS: *5 Messes Royales en plain-chant* (Paris, 1699; 4th ed., 1701); 5 books of *Meslanges,* containing polyphonic choral works (only books 2 and 3 are extant, publ. in 1657 and 1661); 5 books of motets in 2, 3, and 4 voices (1652–86). Two of his organ pieces are found in *Les Maîtres français de l'orgue,* ed. by F. Raugel (Paris, 1939); 4 motets are reproduced in *Anthologie du motet latin polyphonique en France,* ed. by D. Launay (Paris, 1963).

BIBLIOGRAPHY: H. Quittard, *Un musicien en France au XVIIe siècle, Henri Dumont* (Paris, 1906); A. Gastoué, *Les Messes Royales de Henri Dumont* (Paris, 1912); L.-H. Collard, "Quelques documents sur Henry Du Mont," *Recherches sur la musique française classique,* XV (1975).

Dunayevsky, Isaak, Soviet composer of popular songs; b. Lokhvitza, near Poltava, Jan. 30, 1900; d. Moscow, July 25, 1955. He studied piano as a child; then entered the Kharkov Cons. and studied violin with Joseph Achron. He devoted himself mainly to popular music; some songs from his operettas and film scores have become famous. At one time he experimented with jazz rhythms. He received many honors from the Soviet government; in 1941 he won the first Stalin Prize for his music to the film *The Circus.*

BIBLIOGRAPHY: L. Danilevitch, *Isaak Duna-*

yevsky (Moscow, 1947); A. Tchernov, *Isaak Dunayevsky* (Moscow, 1961).

Dunbar, Rudolph, black conductor and composer; b. British Guiana, April 5, 1907. He played in a local military band as a child; in 1919 came to the U.S. and entered the Juilliard School of Music, graduating in 1928. He made his London debut as a conductor on April 26, 1942, and in Paris on Nov. 18, 1944.

Duncan, William Edmondstoune, English composer and writer on music; b. Sale, Cheshire, April 22, 1866; d. there, June 26, 1920. He studied at the Royal College of Music with Parry and Stanford; then acted as music critic and correspondent for British and American music magazines. He wrote an opera, *Perseus* (1892); a setting of Milton's sonnet *To a Nightingale* for Soprano and Orch. (1895); etc. He also publ. several books on music: *Schubert* (1905; 2nd ed., 1934; in Spanish, Buenos Aires, 1942); *The Story of Minstrelsy* (1907); *A History of Music* (1908); *The Story of the Carol* (1911); *Encyclopedia of Musical Terms* (1914); *Ultra-Modernism in Music* (1917).

Dunham, Henry Morton, American organist; b. Brockton, Mass., July 29, 1853; d. Brookline, Mass., May 4, 1929. He studied at the New England Cons.; was an organist at various churches in and around Boston; taught at the New England Cons. for 52 years (1876–1929). His works include 3 organ sonatas, marches, preludes, fugues, passacaglias, and other organ music; also numerous arrangements. He publ.: *Organ School* (in 4 books); *A System of Technique for Piano; The Choir Manual; Hymn Music.* His autobiography, *The Life of a Musician, Woven into a Strand of History of the New England Conservatory of Music,* was publ. posthumously (N.Y., 1931).

Dunhill, Thomas Frederick, English composer; b. London, Feb. 1, 1877; d. Scunthorpe, Lincolnshire, March 13, 1946. He entered the Royal Academy of Music in 1893, and studied with Franklin Taylor (piano) and Stanford (theory); in 1905 was appointed a prof. at the Royal Academy of Music; in 1907 he founded the Concerts of British Chamber-Music, which he conducted until 1916.

WORKS: Operas: *The Enchanted Garden* (London, 1927); *Tantivy Towers* (London, Jan. 16, 1931); *Happy Families* (Guildford, Nov. 1, 1933); ballet, *Gallimaufry* (Hamburg, Dec. 11, 1937); *Phantasy* for String Quartet; Piano Quintet; Quintet for Violin, Cello, Clarinet, Horn, and Piano; Quintet for Horn and String Quartet; Piano Quartet; Viola Sonata; 2 violin sonatas; *The Wind among the Reeds,* song cycle for Tenor and Orch.; violin pieces; compositions for cello. He publ.: *Chamber Music* (a treatise for students, 1912); *Mozart's String Quartets* (2 vols., 1927); *Sullivan's Comic Operas* (1928); *Sir Edward Elgar* (1938).

Duni, Egidio Romoaldo, Italian composer of opera; b. Matera, Feb. 9, 1708; d. Paris, June 11, 1775. He first studied in the Cons. "della Madonna di Loreto," then in the Cons. "della Pietà de' Turchini." His first opera, *Nerone* (Rome, May 21, 1735), was a popular success. He went to London (1737) and the Netherlands (1738); in 1739 he returned to Italy; in 1743 he was maestro di cappella at S. Nicolo di Bari, in Naples; became tutor at the Court of Parma, where, encouraged by the Duke, he began composing French operettas, one of which, *Le caprice amoureux ou Ninette à la cour* (Parma, 1756), was so well received that Duni decided to try his fortune in Paris, where he brought out light and frivolous stage pieces which suited the prevailing taste; he is regarded by some music historians as a founder of French opéra-bouffe. He wrote about 13 Italian operas, and 22 in French.

Dunkley, Ferdinand (Luis), organist and composer; b. London, July 16, 1869; d. Waldwick, N.J., Jan. 5, 1956. At the Royal Academy of Music he was a pupil of Parry, Bridge, Martin, Gladstone, Sharpe, and Barnet; then was organist of St. Jude's, London (1885–87) and of St. Aubyn's, London (1888–93). In 1893 he was engaged as music director at St. Agnes' School in Albany, N.Y.; was organist at Temple Sinai, New Orleans (1924–34); in 1934 was appointed a prof. at Loyola Univ., New Orleans. He made his last public appearance on his 82nd birthday, when he gave an organ recital.
WORKS: *The Wreck of the Hesperus,* ballade for Soli, Chorus, and Orch.; choral works: *Praise the Lord* (1919); *Green Branches* (1919); *God is my strong salvation* (1921); *Street Cries* (1924); *Blessed is the man* (1937); etc.

Dunlop, Isobel, Scottish violinist and composer; b. Edinburgh, March 4, 1901; d. there, May 12, 1975. She studied with Tovey and Dyson; gave concerts presenting her own works.

Dunn, James Philip, American composer; b. New York, Jan. 10, 1884; d. Jersey City, N.J., July 24, 1936. He studied at the College of the City of N.Y. (B.A., 1903); then at Columbia Univ. with MacDowell, and subsequently with Cornelius Rybner. He was then active as a teacher and church organist in N.Y. and elsewhere. As a composer, he attracted attention by his symph. poem descriptive of Lindbergh's transatlantic flight, *We* (N.Y., Aug. 27, 1927). He also wrote an *Overture on Negro Themes* (N.Y., July 22, 1922), some chamber music, and organ pieces.
BIBLIOGRAPHY: John Tasker Howard, *James Philip Dunn* (N.Y., 1925).

Dunn, John, English concert violinist; b. Hull, Feb. 16, 1866; d. Harrogate, Dec. 18, 1940. He received his first instruction from his brother, who was conductor of the Hull Theatre Orch.; then was a pupil at the Leipzig Cons. of Schradieck (violin) and Jadassohn (theory); toured England and Germany. He wrote a violin concerto and a spate of short violin pieces; publ. *Manual of Violin Playing* (London, 1898).

Dunn, John Petri, Scottish pianist and writer on music; b. Edinburgh, Oct. 26, 1878; d. there, Feb. 4, 1931. He studied in London with Matthay; toured Europe as accompanist of Jan Kubelik in 1904; later was a prof. at the Stuttgart and Kiel conservatories; in 1914, returned to Great Britain; was a prof. of music at the Univ. of Edinburgh from 1920 until his death.
WRITINGS: *Ornamentation in the Works of Chopin* (London, 1921); *A Student's Guide for Orchestration* (London, 1928); *The Basis of Pianoforte Playing* (London, 1933).

Dunn, Mignon, American mezzo-soprano; b. Memphis, Tenn., June 17, 1932. At the age of 17 the Metropolitan Opera awarded her a scholarship for vocal studies; she made her operatic debut with the N.Y. City Opera in 1956 as Carmen; on Oct. 29, 1958, she made her first appearance at the Metropolitan Opera, and within a few years became a member of the company; also sang with the Vienna State Opera, the Paris Opéra, at Covent Garden, London, the San Francisco Opera, and the Chicago Lyric Opera. A versatile artist, her repertoire includes roles in Italian and French operas, as well as those of Wagner.

Dunn, Thomas, American conductor; b. Aberdeen, S.D., Dec. 21, 1925. He studied at the Peabody Cons. of Music, Johns Hopkins and Harvard univs., and the Amsterdam Cons.; his teachers included Virgil Fox and E. Power Biggs (organ) and Robert Shaw (choral conducting) in the U.S., and Gustav Leonhardt (harpsichord) and Anton van der Horst (conducting) in the Netherlands. He began his career as a church music director in Baltimore and Philadelphia; in 1959 he was appointed director of the Cantata Singers in N.Y.; also organized the Festival Orch. there, and led it from 1959 until 1969. In 1967 he became music director of the Handel and Haydn Society of Boston.

Dunstable (Dunstaple), John, English composer; b. probably at Dunstable, Bedfordshire, between 1380 and 1390; d. Dec. 24, 1453; buried in St. Stephen's Walbrook, London. He was the most important English composer of the early 15th century, rivalling his contemporaries Binchois and Dufay; was also an astrologer and mathematician. From April 28, 1419, to May 1440 he was canon of Hereford Cathedral and prebendary of Putson Minor; for some time he was in the service of John, Duke of Bedford; the Duke, as Regent of France, represented King Henry V in Paris for a number of years, and probably took his musicians with him. Practically nothing further is known of Dunstable's life. Much of his music is contained in the 6 MSS discovered by F.X. Haberl in the library of the Cathedral of Trent in 1884 ("Trent Codices"). The *Complete Works* are publ. as vol. VIII of *Musica Britannica*, ed. by M.F. Bukofzer (London, 1953; 2d ed., revised, 1970). An examination of these compositions reveals not only the existence of a highly developed art in England early in the 15th century, antedating the full flowering of the Burgundian school (Binchois, Dufay), but also Dunstable's most important contributions to the music of the period in making use of the declamatory motet (in which the rhythm of the spoken word largely governs the musical rhythm) and, apparently, introducing the motet with double structure (which provided the predominant technique of composition of masses in the 15th century).

BIBLIOGRAPHY: C. Stainer, "Dunstable and the Various Settings of *O Rosa Bella*," *Sammelbände der Internationalen Musik-Gesellschaft,* II/1 (1900–1901); H. Riemann, *Handbuch der Musikgeschichte* (Leipzig, 1907, II, 1, p. 106 ff.); R. von Ficker, in Adler's *Studien zur Musikwissenschaft* (VII and XI; on the "Trent Codices"); C. Van den Borren, "The Genius of Dunstable," *Proceedings of the Musical Association* (London, 1921); Dom Anselm Hughes, in *Laudate* (1936); M. Bukofzer, *John Dunstable and the Music of His Time,* in the *Proceedings of the Musical Association* (London, 1938); idem, "Über Leben und Werke von Dunstable," *Acta Musicologica,* 8; idem, "John Dunstable: A Quincentenary Report," *Musical Quarterly* (Jan. 1954); R.L. Greene, "John Dunstable: A Quincentenary Supplement," ibid. (July 1954); E. Kovarik, "A Newly Discovered Dunstable Fragment," *Journal of the American Musicological Society* (Spring 1968); M. Bent, *Dunstable* (London, 1981).

Dunstan, Ralph, English composer and writer on music; b. Carnon Downs, Truro, Nov. 17, 1857; d. London, April 2, 1933. He obtained his Mus.Doc. from Cambridge in 1892. He edited *A Manual of Music* (1918); *A Cyclopedic Dictionary of Music* (1925); *Composer's Hand Book;* composed church music (21 masses, anthems), cantatas, and songs for school use.

Duparc, Henri, one of the chief innovators in the domain of French song; b. Paris, Jan. 21, 1848; d. Mont-de-Marsan, Feb. 12, 1933. He studied with César Franck, who regarded him as his most talented pupil. Duparc suffered from a nervous affliction, which forced him to abandon his composition and seek rest in Switzerland. He destroyed the MS of his Cello Sonata, and several symph. suites; of his instrumental works only a few MSS have survived, including the symph. poems *Aux étoiles* (perf. in Paris, April 11, 1874) and *Lénore* (1875) and a suite of 6 piano pieces, *Feuilles volantes.* His songs, to words by Baudelaire and other French poets, are distinguished by exquisitely phrased melodies arranged in fluid modal harmonies; among the best are: *Invitation au voyage, Extase, Soupir, Sérénade, Chanson triste, La Vague et la cloche, Phidilé, Elégie, Testament, Lamento,* and *La Vie antérieure.*

BIBLIOGRAPHY: Guy Ferchault, *Henri Duparc* (Paris, 1944); S. Northcote, *The Songs of Henri Duparc* (London, 1949); N. Van Der Elst, *Henri Duparc: L'Homme et son œuvre* (Diss., Univ. of Paris; Lille, 1972; contains a complete catalogue of works, correspondence, and bibliography).

Dupin, Paul, prolific French composer; b. Roubaix, Aug. 14, 1865; d. Paris, March 6, 1949. He worked in a factory; then was a menial clerk, but turned to music against all odds; took some lessons with Emile Durand, and then proceeded to compose with fanatic compulsion; somehow he managed to have more than 200 works actually publ. Of these, the most original were about 500 canons for 3–12 voices, and 40 string quartets titled *Poèmes;* he wrote much other chamber music; some pretty piano pieces with fanciful titles such as *Esquisse fuguées, Dentelles,* etc.; he even wrote a grand opera, *Marcelle,* which he later hopefully renamed *Lyszelle* for exotic effect. He was much admired in Paris for his determination to succeed, but his works were rarely performed.

BIBLIOGRAPHY: R. Rolland, "Paul Dupin," *Bulletin Français de la S.I.M.* (Dec. 15, 1908); C. Koechlin, "Dupin," *Revue Musicale* (Jan. 1923); P. Ladmirault, *Les Chœurs en canon de Paul Dupin: Notice biographique et analytique* (Paris, 1925).

Dupont, Gabriel, French composer; b. Caen, March 1, 1878; d. Vésinet, Aug. 2, 1914. He was a pupil of his father, the organist at the Cathedral; later, of Gédalge; then of Massenet and Widor at the Paris Cons.; won the 2nd Prix de Rome in 1901. In a contest conducted in 1903 by Sonzogno, the publishing house in Milan, his opera *La Cabrera* was selected, along with 2 others, to be performed and judged by the public (237 works were submitted); it was produced at Milan on May 17, 1904, with great success, thereby winning for Dupont the prize of 50,000 lire. He wrote other operas: *La Glu,* libretto by Jean Richepin (Nice, Jan. 24, 1910); *La Farce du cuvier* (Brussels, March 21, 1912); *Antar* (1913; the outbreak of war in 1914 prevented its planned production, and the opera was staged posthumously at the Paris Opéra on March 14, 1921); also *Les Heures dolentes* for Orch., 4 pieces from a suite of 14 compositions for Piano (1903–5); *Poèmes d'automne* for Piano; symph. poems: *Hymne à Aphrodite* and *Le Chant de la destinée; Poème* for Piano Quintet; many other piano pieces; etc.

BIBLIOGRAPHY: M. Léna, "Gabriel Dupont, Souvenirs," and H. Collet, "Antar," in *Le Ménestrel* (March 18, 1921); E. Vuillermoz, "Antar de Gabriel Dupont à l'Opéra," *Revue Musicale* (April 1921); M. Dumesnil, "Gabriel Dupont, Musician of Normandy," *Musical Quarterly* (Oct. 1944).

Dupont, Pierre, French songwriter; b. Rochetaillée, near Lyons, April 23, 1821; d. St. Etienne, July 25, 1870. The son of a laborer, and himself uneducated, he attracted attention by his political and rustic ditties. He wrote the words, and then sang the airs to Reyer, who put them into shape. His political songs (*Le Pain, Le Chant des ouvriers,* etc.) created such disturbances that he was banished in 1851, but in 1852 he was pardoned. His song *Les Bœufs* enjoyed some popularity.

Duport, Jean-Louis, famous French cellist; b. Paris, Oct. 4, 1749; d. there, Sept 7, 1819. He made his public debut at the Concerts Spirituels (1768); joined his brother, Jean Pierre, in Berlin at the outbreak of the Revolution; returning in 1806, he became musician to Charles IV, the ex-king of Spain, at Marseilles; in 1812 returned to Paris, where he was soon regarded as the foremost French cellist; taught at the Paris Cons. (1813–15). He wrote 6 cello concertos, sonatas, duos, airs variées, 9 nocturnes (for harp and cello), etc. His *Essai sur le doigté du violoncelle et la conduite de l'archet, avec une suite d'exercises* is still a standard textbook, and practically laid the foundations of modern cello virtuosity.

Duprato, Jules-Laurent, French composer; b. Nîmes, Aug. 20, 1827; d. Paris, May 20, 1892. He studied with Leborne at the Paris Cons.; in 1848, won the Prix de Rome. He composed operettas, cantatas, songs, etc.; also recitatives for Hérold's *L'Illusion* and Balfe's *The Bohemian Girl.*
BIBLIOGRAPHY: F. Clauzel, *Jules Duprato* (1896).

DuPré, Jacqueline, English cello player; b. Oxford, Jan. 26, 1945. The Gallic name of her family dates back to Norman times. Both her parents were musicians; her mother even wrote a ballet score. Jacqueline DuPré studied cello at the Guildhall School of Music in London and later with Paul Tortelier in Paris, in Switzerland with Casals, and with Rostropovich in Moscow. She owns the famous "Davidov cello" made by Stradivarius in 1712. She made her American debut in N.Y. on May 14, 1965, with electrifying success, playing Elgar's Cello Concerto and eliciting rapturous reviews from the critics. On June 15, 1967, she married the Israeli pianist and conductor **Daniel Barenboim.** In 1972 she was stricken with multiple sclerosis and was obliged to give up her public appearances. In 1976 she was made an Officer of the Order of the British Empire.
BIBLIOGRAPHY: W. Woodsworth, ed., *Jacqueline DuPré: Impressions* (London, 1983).

Dupré, Marcel, celebrated French organist and composer; b. Rouen, May 3, 1886; d. Meudon, near Paris, May 30, 1971. He was a pupil of his father, **Albert Dupré;** also an organist; studied organ with Guilmant in 1898; he then entered the Paris Cons. (1902–14) and studied with Vierne, Diémer, and Widor, winning first prizes for organ (1907) and for fugue (1909); in 1914 he won the Grand Prix de Rome for the cantata *Psyché.* He was interim organist at Notre-Dame in 1916; in 1920 he gave at the Paris Cons. a cycle of 10 recitals of Bach's complete organ works, playing from memory. On Nov. 18, 1921, he made his N.Y. debut, followed by a transcontinental tour, performing 94 recitals in 85 American cities; a 2nd U.S. tour in 1923 included 110 concerts; he made his 10th tour of the U.S. in 1948. In 1939 he gave 40 concerts in Australia on his world tour. He had, meanwhile, been appointed prof. of organ at the Paris Cons. in 1926; in 1934 he succeeded Widor as organist at St. Sulpice; continued there until his death at the age of 85; became general

director of the American Cons. in Fontainebleau in 1947 and was appointed director of the Paris Cons., in succession to Delvincourt, in 1954 (until 1956). Dupré wrote his first work, the oratorio *La Vision de Jacob,* at the age of 14; it was performed on his 15th birthday at his father's house in Rouen, in a domestic production assisted by a local choral society. Most of his organ works are products of original improvisations. Thus *Symphonie-Passion,* first improvised at the Wanamaker organ in Philadelphia (Dec. 8, 1921), was written down much later and performed in its final version at Westminster Cathedral in London (Oct. 9, 1924). Similarly, *Le Chemin de la Croix* was improvised in Brussels (Feb. 13, 1931) and performed in a definitive version in Paris the following year (March 18, 1932). Among precomposed works there are symphs. for Organ: No. 1 (Glasgow, Jan. 3, 1929) and No. 2 (1946); Concerto for Organ and Orch. (Groningen, Netherlands, April 27, 1938, composer soloist); *Psalm XVIII* (1949); 76 chorales and several a cappella choruses; also numerous "verset-préludes." He is the author of *Traité d'improvisation à l'orgue* (1925) and *Méthode d'orgue.*
BIBLIOGRAPHY: R. Delestre, *L'Œuvre de Marcel Dupré* (Paris, 1952); B. Gavoty, *Marcel Dupré* (Monaco, 1955).

Duprez, Louis-Gilbert, French tenor; b. Paris, Dec. 6, 1806; d. there, Sept. 23, 1896. His fine boy-voice gained him admission to Choron's Inst.; after diligent vocal and theoretical study, he made his debut as Count Almaviva at the Odéon, in 1825. Dissatisfied with the results, he subjected himself to a long course of training in Italy, and in 1836 succeeded Nourrit at the Opéra. He was appointed prof. of lyrical declamation at the Cons. in 1842, but resigned in 1850 to establish a vocal school of his own, which flourished. He publ. the vocal methods *L'Art du chant* (1845) and *La Mélodie, Etudes complémentaires vocales et dramatiques de l'Art du chant* (1846); also wrote *Souvenirs d'un chanteur* (1880); composed several operas.
BIBLIOGRAPHY: A.A. Elwart, *Duprez, sa vie artistique* (Paris, 1838).

Dupuis, Albert, outstanding Belgian composer; b. Verviers, March 1, 1877; d. Brussels, Sept. 19, 1967. He studied piano, violin, and flute at the Music Academy in Verviers; later entered the classes of Vincent d'Indy at the newly created Schola Cantorum in Paris (1897); returned to Belgium in 1899 and later won the Belgian Prix de Rome with his cantata *La Chanson d'Halewyn* (Brussels, Nov. 25, 1903; arranged and perf. as a 3-act opera, Antwerp, Feb. 14, 1914). He became director of the Verviers Cons. in 1907, retiring in 1947.
WORKS: His other operas, the largest body of lyrical works by a Belgian composer, include *Bilitis* (Verviers, 1899); *Jean Michel* (1901–2; Brussels, March 5, 1903); *Martille* (1904; Brussels, March 3, 1905); *Fidélaine* (Liège, 1910); *Le Château de la Grande Bretèche* (Nice, 1913); *La Passion* (Monte Carlo, April 2, 1916; over 150 perfs. in Europe); *La*

Captivité de Babylone (biblical drama); *La Barrière* (Verviers, 1920); *La Délivrance* (Lille, 1921); *Le Sacrifice* (Antwerp, 1921); *La Victoire* (Brussels, 1923); *Ce n'était qu'un rêve* (Antwerp, 1935); *Hassan,* oriental fairy tale (Brussels, 1938); *Un Drame sous Philippe II* (Brussels, Jan. 18, 1938); oratorios: *Les Cloches nuptiales* (1899); *Œdipe à Colone; Psalm 118;* ballets: *Rêve d'enfant,* after Schumann (1951); *Au temps jadis* (1952); *Evocations d'Espagne* (1954); cantatas: *Vers le progrès, Pour la Paix, La Gileppe,* and a *Cantata jubilaire* for Belgian independence; 2 symphs. (1904, 1922–23); *Fantaisie rhapsodique* for Violin and Orch. (1906); *Poème oriental* for Cello and Orch. (1924); *Hermann et Dorothée,* overture; Cello Concerto (1926); *Epitaphe* for Orch. (1929); *Aria* for Viola and Orch. (1933); Piano Concerto (1940); *Caprice rhapsodique* for Orch. (1941); Violin Concerto (1944); *Caprice* for Flute and Orch.; *Solo de concours* for Horn and Orch. and for Trombone and Orch.; *Valse Joyeuse* for Orch.; *La Navarraise* for Orch.; 2 concertinos for Timpani and Orch.; Violin Sonata (1904); String Quartet; 2 piano trios; Piano Quartet; *Scherzo* for Solo Horn; Variations for Solo Horn; *5 pièces paradoxales* for Piano; many other works for piano; choruses; songs; etc. In 1955 he was awarded a prize by the Société des Auteurs Lyriques de Paris for his creative output.
BIBLIOGRAPHY: J. Dor, *Albert Dupuis* (Liège, 1935); R. Michel, *Un grand musicien belge méconnu: Albert Dupuis* (Verviers, 1967).

Dupuis, Sylvain, Belgian conductor; b. Liège, Oct. 9, 1856; d. Bruges, Sept. 28, 1931. He was a pupil at the Liège Cons., winning the Prix de Rome in 1881; became a teacher of counterpoint there; was conductor of the singing society *La Légia;* established in 1888 the *Nouveaux Concerts Symphoniques;* was appointed first conductor at Théâtre de la Monnaie in Brussels in 1900, and conductor of the *Concerts Populaires;* from 1911 until 1926 was director of the Cons. at Liège.
WORKS: 2 operas: *Cour d'Ognon* and *Moïna;* 3 cantatas: *La Cloche de Roland, Camoëns,* and *Chant de la Création;* a symph. poem, *Macbeth;* Concertino for Oboe and Orch.; 2 suites for Orch.; pieces for violin; choruses.

Durand, Emile, French composer; b. St.-Brieuc, Feb. 16, 1830; d. Neuilly, May 6, 1903. In 1850, while still a student at the Paris Cons., he was appointed teacher of an elementary singing class; in 1871 he became prof. of harmony there. He publ. *Traité d'harmonie* and *Traité de composition musicale;* also wrote several light operas.

Durand, Marie-Auguste, French organist and publisher; b. Paris, July 18, 1830; d. there, May 31, 1909. He studied organ with Benoist; in 1849, was organist at St. Ambroise; then at Ste.-Geneviève, St.-Roch, and (1862–74) St. Vincent de Paul. He also occupied himself with music criticism and composition (his Chaconne and *Valse* for piano are especially popular). In 1870 he entered into partnership with Schönewerk (acquiring Flaxland's music publishing business), the firm then being known as Durand & Schönewerk; when his son, **Jacques** (b. Paris, Feb. 22, 1865; d. Bel-Ebat, Aug. 22, 1928), replaced Schönewerk in 1891, the title became Durand & Fils. The house is now known as Durand & Cie.; it has made a specialty of publishing works of the outstanding French composers (Joncières, Lalo, Massenet, Debussy, Saint-Saëns, Chausson, Ravel, and many others), and has also brought out French editions of Wagner's *Tannhäuser, The Flying Dutchman,* and *Lohengrin,* as well as several editions of old masters, including a complete critical edition of Rameau, edited by Saint-Saëns. Jacques Durand publ. the following works: *Cours professionel à l'usage des employés du commerce de musique* (2 vols., 1923); *Quelques souvenirs d'un éditeur de musique* (2 vols., 1924–25); *Lettres de Cl. Debussy à son éditeur* (Paris, 1927).

Durante, Francesco, celebrated Italian church composer and noted teacher; b. Frattamaggiore, near Naples, March 31, 1684; d. Naples, Sept. 30, 1755. He studied in Rome and, under the guidance of his uncle, D. Angelo, at the Cons. di Sant' Onofrio, where he taught in 1710–11; then became maestro at the Cons. di Santa Maria di Loreto, and at the Cons. dei Poveri di Gesù Cristo from 1742; again at Sant' Onofrio from 1745 until his death. After Alessandro Scarlatti, and with Leo, Durante ranks as one of the founders and a chief representative of the "Neapolitan school" of composition. He devoted himself almost exclusively to sacred music, in which the breadth, vigor, and resourcefulness of his style are more in evidence than marked originality. He was a very great teacher; his pupils, Duni, Traetta, Vinci, Jommelli, Piccinni, Guglielmi, Pergolesi, Paisiello, and others, took almost complete possession of the European lyric stage during the latter half of the 18th century. The library of the Paris Cons. contains a rich collection of his works.
WORKS: 13 masses, and fragments of masses; 16 Psalms; 19 motets; several antiphons and hymns; 12 madrigals; 6 harpsichord sonatas; etc. His *Lamentations of Jeremiah* and *Pastoral Mass* are in the Vienna Library (in MS). The libraries of the Naples and Bologna Cons. also possess MSS of Durante. Karmrodt of Halle printed a grand Magnificat (with additional accompaniments by Robert Franz); Breitkopf & Härtel publ. 12 *duetti da camera;* H. Schletterer ed. a selection of his keyboard pieces; other reprints of keyboard pieces were publ. by A. Diversi in *Arte antica e moderna* (vol. I; 3 studies), F. Boghen in *Antichi maestri italiani* (4 fugues, 3 toccatas), A. Longo in *Biblioteca d'oro* (vol. II; *Aria danzante*), G. Tagliapietra in *Antologia di musica antica e moderna* (vol. XI), M. Vitali in *Composizioni scelte* (vol. II). A. Diversi publ. a 4-voiced *Christe eleison* in his *Biblioteca mus. sacra.* Concertos for orch. are printed in Le Pupitre, 26.
BIBLIOGRAPHY: R. Fimmanó, "F. Durante," *Musica d'Oggi* (Aug.–Sept. 1936); V. de Rubertis, *Dos Bajetes de Francesco Durante, erroneamente interpretados por Fétis y de Nardis* (Buenos Aires, 1947;

reproduces in facsimile Durante's birth registry).

Durey, Louis, French composer; b. Paris, May 27, 1888; d. St. Tropez, July 3, 1979. He studied music with Léon Saint-Requier (1910–14); became known as a member of Les Six, a group of young French composers dedicated to modern music, the other 5 being Darius Milhaud, Arthur Honegger, Georges Auric, Francis Poulenc, and Germaine Tailleferre. Durey wrote music fashionable during a wave of anti-Romanticism, proclaiming the need of constructive simplicity in modern dress, with abundant use of titillating discords. Although he was the oldest of Les Six, he wrote the least music; most of his works are in miniature forms. Durey's esthetic code was radically altered in 1936 when he joined the French Communist Party. During the German occupation of France he was active in the Resistance, for which he wrote anti-Fascist songs. In 1948 he was elected vice-president of the Association Française des Musiciens Progressives; in 1950 he became the music critic of the Paris Communist newspaper *L'Humanité*. He subscribed to the tenets of the Prague Manifesto of 1948, which called upon progressive musicians to initiate a "democratization of musical forms," to abandon artistic individualism, and to write music derived from national folk songs. In 1961 he received the Grand Prix de la Musique Française.

WORKS: *Le Navire* for Voice and Orch., to words by André Gide (1916); *Le Bestiaire* for Voice and 12 Instruments, after Apollinaire (1919); *Le Printemps au fond de la mer* for Voice and Wind Instruments, to a text by Jean Cocteau (1920); *L'Occasion*, lyric drama after Mérimée (1928); *Fantaisie concertante* for Cello and Orch. (1947); *3 poèmes de Paul Eluard* for Voice and Orch. (1952); *Trio-Serenade* for Violin, Viola, and Cello, in memory of Béla Bartók (1955); overture, *Ile-de-France* (1955); Concertino for Piano, 16 Wind Instruments, Double Bass, and Timpani (1956); *10 chœurs de métiers* for Chorus, 2 Flutes, Clarinet, Violin, Celesta, and Piano (1957); *3 Polyphonies vocales et intrumentales* for Vocal Quartet and 8 Instruments (1963); *Mouvement symphonique* (1964); *Les Soirées de Valfère* for Wind Instruments (1964); *Cantate de la rose et de l'amour* for Soprano and Strings (1965); Sinfonietta (1966); *4 octophonies* for 8 String Instruments (1966); *Dilection* for Strings (1969); *Obsession* for Wind Instruments, Harp, Double Bass, and Percussion (1970); political cantatas, *Paix aux hommes par millions*, to words by Mayakovsky (1949); *La Longue Marche*, after Mao Tse-tung (1949); 3 string quartets; numerous solo songs; piano pieces.

BIBLIOGRAPHY: F. Robert, *Louis Durey, L'Aîné des Six* (Paris, 1968).

Durkó, Zsolt, Hungarian composer; b. Szeged, April 10, 1934. He studied composition at the Academy of Music at Budapest with Ferenc Farkas (1955–60) and at the Santa Cecilia Academy in Rome with Petrassi (1961–63). Many of his works have scientific connotations, at least in their titles; but some are rooted in Hungarian melorhythmic patterns.

WORKS: *11 Pieces* for String Quartet (1962); *Episodi sul tema B-A-C-H* for Orch. (1962–63); *Organismi* for Violin and Orch. (1963–64); *Psicogramma* for Piano (1964); *Una rapsodia ungherese (A Hungarian Rhapsody)* for 2 Clarinets and Orch. (1964–65); *Improvisations* for Wind Quintet (1965); *Dartmouth Concerto* for Soprano and Chamber Orch. (1966); 2 string quartets (1966, 1969); *Fioriture* for Orch. (1966); *Altimara* for Chorus and Orch. (1967–68); *Cantilene* for Piano and Orch. (1968); *Symbols* for Horn and Piano (1968–69); *Colloïdes* for Flute, Piccolo, Bassoon, String Quartet, and 5 Alto Voices (1969); *Quartetto d'Ottoni* for 2 Trumpets, Trombone, and Tuba or 2nd Trombone (1970); Concerto for 12 Flutes and Orch. (1970); *2 Iconographies:* No. 1 for 2 Cellos and Harpsichord (1970) and No. 2 for Horn and Chamber Ensemble (1971); *Fire Music* for Flute, Clarinet, Piano, and String Trio (1970–71); Cantata No. 1 (1971); Cantata No. 2 (1972); *Assonance* for Organ (1972); *Halotti beszéd (Funeral Oration)*, oratorio (1972); *Colloïdes* for Flute, Chamber Ensemble, and 3 Contraltos (1975); *Turner Illustrations* for Solo Violin and 14 Instruments (1976); opera, *Moses* (Budapest, May 15, 1977).

Durlet, Emmanuel, Belgian pianist and composer; b. Antwerp, Oct. 11, 1893; d. there, Feb. 7, 1977. He studied piano with Frans Lenaerts; took a 2-year course in Vienna with Leopold Godowsky (1912–14). Returning to Belgium, he developed a brilliant career as a pianist; gave a cycle of all 32 sonatas by Beethoven. He held the post of prof. of advanced piano playing at the Cons. of Antwerp for 39 years (1920–59). Among his works are a Piano Concerto, a Violin Concerto, a Violin Sonata, and numerous teaching pieces for piano in a Romantic vein, as well as songs.

Durme, Jef van. See **Van Durme, Jef.**

Dürr, Alfred, distinguished German musicologist and editor; b. Charlottenburg, March 3, 1918. He studied musicology at the Univ. of Göttingen, receiving his Ph.D. there in 1950 with the dissertation *Studien über die frühen Kantaten Johann Sebastian Bachs* (publ. in Leipzig, 1951). In 1951 he joined the Johann-Sebastian-Bach-Inst. in Göttingen as a research assistant; in 1962 he became its director. From 1953 he edited (with W. Neumann) the *Bach-Jahrbuch;* also edited works for the Bach *Neue Ausgabe sämtlicher Werke*. His books include *Johann Sebastian Bach, Weihnachts oratorium* (Munich, 1967) and *Die Kantaten von Johann Sebastian Bach* (Kassel and Munich, 1971).

Dürrner, Ruprecht Johannes Julius, German conductor and composer; b. Ansbach, Bavaria, July 15, 1810; d. Edinburgh, June 10, 1859. He was a pupil of Friedrich Schneider at Dessau; in 1831–42, was a cantor at Ansbach, then studied under Mendelssohn and Hauptmann at Leipzig, and settled in Edinburgh as a conductor and vocal teacher. His choruses and quartets for male voices won great favor.

Duruflé, Maurice, noted French organist, teacher, and composer; b. Louviers, Eure, Jan. 11, 1902. He studied piano and organ with local teachers; in 1919 went to Paris, where he studied organ with Tournemire, Guilmant, and Louis Vierne. In 1920 he enrolled at the Paris Cons., where he took courses in organ playing with Gigout (first prize, 1922), harmony with Jean Gallon (first prize, 1924), fugue with Caussade (first prize, 1924), and composition with Paul Dukas (1928). In 1930 he was appointed organist of the church of St. Etienne-du-Mont in Paris. In 1943 he became a prof. at the Paris Cons., remaining on its staff until 1969. He composed a number of sacred works and organ pieces. His best known compositions are a Requiem (1947) and a Mass (1967).

Dushkin, Samuel, American violinist; b. Suwalki, Poland, Dec. 13, 1891; d. New York, June 24, 1976. He was brought to America as a child and was adopted by the composer Blair Fairchild, who gave him primary musical education. He studied violin with Leopold Auer in N.Y. and later took several lessons with Fritz Kreisler. He made his European debut as a violinist in 1918, and subsequently toured widely in Europe and America. In 1928 he became associated with Stravinsky and helped him in solving the technical problems in the violin part of his Violin Concerto, and was the soloist in the first performance of this work in Berlin on Oct. 23, 1931, with Stravinsky conducting. He also gave the first performance of Stravinsky's *Duo Concertant* for Violin and Piano, with Stravinsky playing the piano part (Berlin, Oct. 28, 1932). He recounted the details of his collaboration with Stravinsky in his article "Working with Stravinsky," publ. in the Merle Armitage collection *Stravinsky* (N.Y., 1936).

Dussek or **Dušek (Dusík), Franz (František Xaver),** Bohemian pianist and composer; b. Chotěborky, Bohemia, Dec. 8, 1731; d. Prague, Feb. 12, 1799. He studied in Prague with F. Habermann and in Vienna with Wagenseil. He settled in Prague by 1770, as a teacher and performer; was a close friend of Mozart. He wrote several keyboard sonatas and concertos, symphs., quartets, and trios.
BIBLIOGRAPHY: V. Sýkora, *František Xaver Dušek: Život a dílo* (*Life and Works;* Prague, 1958; contains a thematic catalogue of his works).

Dussek (Dusík), Jan Ladislav, outstanding composer; b. Čáslav (Tschaslau), Bohemia, Feb. 12, 1760; d. St.-Germain-en-Laye, March 20, 1812. At first a boy soprano at the Minorite church in Iglau, he was taught music by Father Špinar while attending the Jesuit college; was organist at the Jesuit church in Kuttenberg for 2 years, and while studying theology at Prague Univ. found time to get a thorough musical training so that after graduation he obtained, through Count Männer, his patron, the post of organist at the church of St.-Rimbaut in Malines (now Mechelen). Thence he went to Bergen-op-Zoom, and in 1782 to Amsterdam; then spent a year at The Hague, and in 1783 studied under C.P.E.

Bach at Hamburg; won renown as a pianist and as a performer on Hessel's "harmonica" in Berlin and St. Petersburg, then accepted an appointment from Prince Radziwill, with whom he lived in Lithuania for over a year. He played before Marie Antoinette in 1786, in Paris; soon went to Italy, and returned to Paris in 1788, whence the Revolution drove him to London. Here he married **Sofia Corri,** a singer, in 1792, and undertook a music business with his father-in-law; but his careless habits, and love of luxury and ease, ill fitted him for commercial pursuits; the enterprise failed, and he fled to Hamburg in 1800 to escape his creditors. Here he appears to have stayed about 2 years, giving concerts and teaching. In 1802 he gave a concert at Prague, and paid a visit to his father at Čáslav; he then entered the service of Louis Ferdinand of Prussia (1804–6), whose heroic death in battle (1806) inspired one of Dussek's finest pieces, *Elégie harmonique* for Piano. Afterward, he was briefly attached to the Prince of Isenburg (1806–7); then went to Paris as maître de chapelle to Prince Talleyrand. Dussek's significance in music history is unjustly obscured; he was a master craftsman; some canonic devices in his piano sonatas are remarkable for their skill; his piano writing had both brilliance and science; there are some idiomatic harmonies that presage Schumann and Brahms. He was a virtuoso at the keyboard; with Clementi he shares the honor of having introduced the "singing touch." A composer of amazing industry, Dussek wrote 16 piano concertos (one for 2 pianos), numerous accompanied sonatas, string quartets, a Piano Quartet, Piano Quintet, 53 violin sonatas (some interchangeable with flute), about 40 piano sonatas, 9 sonatas for piano, 4-hands, a number of sets of variations, dances, etc., for piano, as well as topical pieces on world events (*The Sufferings of the Queen of France; The Naval Battle and Total Defeat of the Dutch Fleet by Admiral Duncan;* etc.). He also wrote an opera, *The Captive of Spilberg* (London, Nov. 14, 1798) and incidental music to Sheridan's play *Pizarro* (London, May 24, 1799); publ. a piano method. His *Collected Works* were publ. in Leipzig in 1813–17 (12 vols.; reprinted in 6 vols., N.Y., 1973).
BIBLIOGRAPHY: F.L. Schiffer, *Johann Ladislaus Dussek: Seine Sonaten und seine Konzerte* (Leipzig, 1914; reprinted, N.Y., 1973); H. Truscott, "Dussek and the Concerto," *Music Review* (Feb. 1955); H. Craw, *A Biography and Thematic Catalog of the Works of Jan Ladislav Dussek* (Diss.,Univ. of Southern Calif., 1964).

Dustmann (née **Meyer**), **Marie Luise,** dramatic soprano; b. Aix-la-Chapelle, Aug. 22, 1831; d. Charlottenburg (Berlin), March 2, 1899. She made her debut in Breslau (1849); after this she was engaged at Kassel (under Spohr), Dresden (1853), Prague (1854), and Vienna (1857). In 1858 she married a book dealer, Dustmann, and adopted her married name professionally.

Dutilleux, Henri, talented French composer; b. Angers, Jan. 22, 1916. He studied at the Paris Cons. with

H. Busser and with Jean and Noël Gallon; won the first Grand Prix de Rome in 1938; was director of singing at the Paris Opéra in 1942; subsequently was active on the Paris radio (1943–63). In 1961 he was a prof. at the Ecole Normale de Musique and in 1970 at the Paris Cons. He has developed a modernistic style which incorporates many procedures of Impressionism. His instrumental works have had numerous performances in France, England, and America; his most impressive work is his Symph. No. 1 (Paris, June 7, 1951; also perf. in Germany, England, and America). Other works: *Les Hauts de Hurle-Vent,* symph. suite; *Symphonie de danses; Salmacis,* ballet; *Sarabande* for Orch. (1941); Sonatine for Flute and Piano (1943); *La Gioie* for Voice and Orch. (1944); *La Princesse d'Elide,* incidental music to Molière's play (1946); Piano Sonata (1946–48); *Monsieur de Pourceaugnac,* incidental music to Molière's play (1948); *Le Loup* (Paris, March 18, 1953); Symph. No. 2 (Boston, Dec. 11, 1959); *5 métaboles* for Orch. (Cleveland, Jan. 14, 1965); *Tout un monde lointain* for Cello and Orch. (Aix-en-Provence, July 25, 1970); *Timbres, espace, mouvement* for Orch. (Washington, D.C., Jan. 10, 1978); chamber music; piano pieces; film music and songs.

BIBLIOGRAPHY: R. Jacobs, *Henri Dutilleux* (Paris, 1974); P. Mari, *Henri Dutilleux* (Paris, 1974).

Dutoit, Charles, Swiss conductor; b. Lausanne, Oct. 7, 1936. He was of multinational heritage: his father was Swiss French; his mother was part German, part English, and, in her remote ancestry, part Brazilian. He learned to play the violin, viola, piano, and drums; studied conducting by watching Ansermet's rehearsals with the Suisse Romande. He studied music theory at the Lausanne Cons. and at the Academy of Music in Geneva; acquired fluency in the major European languages. He then took courses at the Accademia Musicale in Siena and at the Cons. Benedetto Marcello in Venice; also attended a summer seminar at the Berkshire Center in Tanglewood. Returning to Switzerland, he joined the Lausanne Chamber Orch. as a viola player. He made his conducting debut with the Bern Symph. Orch. in 1963; in 1964 he conducted *Le Sacre du printemps,* and was engaged as music director of the Bern Orch. Later he served in a similar capacity with the Tonhalle Orch. in Zürich. In 1967 he became conductor and artistic director of the Zürich Radio Orch.; then undertook a tour of South America, Australia, Japan, Israel, and Egypt. For several years he was artistic director of the National Orch. in Mexico City. In 1975 he was appointed conductor of the Göteborg Symph. Orch. in Sweden. In 1977 he was engaged as permanent conductor and music director of the Montreal Symph. Orch.; he found the work congenial, since it was centered on French culture; he greatly expanded the orch.'s repertoire; conducted 25 Haydn symphs., much music of Mozart and Beethoven and especially French music, beginning with Berlioz and including Debussy and Ravel. He also promoted new Canadian music. Articulate in several languages, he speaks volubly of his future plans, which include new op-

era productions, and guest appearances in the U.S. In 1983 he was appointed principal guest conductor of the Minnesota Orch. in Minneapolis. Dutoit was married 3 times; his 2nd wife was the pianist **Martha Argerich.**

BIBLIOGRAPHY: Herbert Kupferberg, "Charles Dutoit," *Ovation* (Jan. 1984).

Duval, Denise, French soprano; b. Paris, Oct. 23, 1921. She studied at the Paris Cons.; sang with the Bordeaux Opera and the Folies-Bergère in Paris. In 1947 she joined the Paris Opéra; also sang at the Opéra-Comique; then toured in the U.S., Italy, and England; upon her retirement in 1965, she became a voice teacher. She was best known for her roles in French operas.

Duvernoy, Charles, French clarinetist; b. Montbéliard, 1776; d. Paris, Feb. 28, 1845. He came to Paris in 1810, and was first clarinet at the Théâtre de Monsieur and the Feydeau, retiring in 1824. Till 1802 he was also a prof. at the Cons. He wrote several clarinet sonatas and clarinet duets.

Duvernoy, Henri-Louis-Charles, French composer, son of **Charles;** b. Paris, Nov. 16, 1820; d. there, Jan. 1906. He was a pupil of Halévy and Zimmermann at the Paris Cons.; in 1848 was appointed a prof. there. He publ. (with Kuhn) *Nouveaux choix de psaumes et de cantiques* (1848); *Solfège des chanteurs* (1855); *Solfège à changements de clefs* (1857); and *Solfège artistique* (1860); also some 100 light piano pieces.

Duvernoy, Victor-Alphonse, French pianist and composer; b. Paris, Aug. 30, 1842; d. there, March 7, 1907. He was a pupil of Bazin and Marmontel at the Paris Cons., taking the first prize for piano (1855). In 1869 he founded, together with Léonard, Stiehle, Trombetta, and Jacquard, a series of chamber music concerts; he devoted his time otherwise to composing and teaching, and held a professorship at the Cons. For some 11 years, he was music critic of the *République française;* he was made a Chevalier of the Legion of Honor, and was an officer of public instruction.

WORKS: As a dramatic composer, he produced the 3-act opera *Sardanapale* (Liège, 1892), the "scène lyrique" *Cléopâtre* (at the Concerts Colonne), and the 4-act opera *Hellé* (Grand Opéra, 1896). His symph. poem *La Tempête,* produced at the Concerts Colonne, won the City of Paris prize in 1880; he also wrote a ballet, *Bacchus* (1902); an overture, *Hernani;* much piano music.

Duvosel, Lieven, Belgian composer; b. Ghent, Dec. 14, 1877; d. Sint-Martens-Latem, Belgium, April 20, 1956. He studied in Antwerp and Paris; lived for a time in Berlin (where Nikisch and R. Strauss performed his works), later in The Hague and Haarlem.

WORKS: His most representative work is the symph. cycle in 5 parts *Leie:* 1. *De Morgen;* 2. *De*

Leie; 3. *De Liefde aan der Leie;* 4. *Kerstnacht (Christmas);* 5. *Het Leieland.* Other compositions: 3 symphs.; the symph. poem *Den Avond (Evening); Wereldwee (World's Grief);* many cantatas; male and mixed choruses; songs; and the earlier works *Vers la Lumière, La Charité,* and *La Tristesse et la consolation.*

BIBLIOGRAPHY: F. van Durme, *Lieven Duvosel* (Antwerp, 1943); E. Collumbien, *Lijst der werken van Duvosel* (Ghent, 1950).

Dux, Claire, soprano; b. Bydgoszcz, Poland, Aug. 2, 1885; d. Chicago, Oct. 8, 1967. She studied voice with Teresa Arkel in Berlin; made her operatic debut in Cologne in 1906; in 1911–18, was a member of the Berlin State Opera (made her debut in *La Bohème* with Caruso); in 1912–14, sang at Covent Garden in London; in 1918–21, was a member of the Royal Opera in Stockholm; came to the U.S. in 1921 and joined the Chicago Civic Opera Co.; toured the U.S.; then retired. She was married to Charles Swift of Chicago, where she settled.

Dvarionas, Balis, Lithuanian composer; b. Leipaia, June 19, 1904; d. Vilnius, Aug. 23, 1972. He studied at the Leipzig Cons. with Teichmüller (piano) and Karg-Elert (composition). In 1926 he went to Kaunas and taught piano there, until 1940; in 1947 he became a prof. at the Lithuanian Cons. in Vilna; also conducted the Lithuanian Phil. Orch. there (1940–41 and 1958–61). Among his works are: Symph. (1947); Violin Concerto (1948; received a State Prize); 2 piano concertos (1958, 1962); opera, *Dalia* (1959); many choral works. He wrote the music for the national anthem of the Lithuanian Soviet Socialist Republic (1950).

Dvořáček, Jiří, Czech composer; b. Vamberk, June 8, 1928. He studied organ at the Prague Cons. (1943–47); entered the Prague Academy and studied composition with Řídký and Dobiáš (1949–53); in 1953 he joined its faculty, becoming a senior lecturer in 1967. He represents a median course of Central European modernism.
WORKS: Opera, *The Island of Aphrodite* (1967; Dresden, Feb. 13, 1971); Symph. (1953); *Symphonic Suite* for Orch. (1958); *Overture* (1958); *Inventions* for Trombone, and String Orch. or Piano (1961); *Concertante Suite* for Orch. (1962); *Ex post,* symph. movement for Piano and Orch. (1963); *Quattro Episodi,* sinfonietta for Orch. (1970); *Sonata capricciosa* for Violin and Piano (1956); *Meditations for Clarinet* for Clarinet and Percussion (1964); *3 Miniatures* for 2 Trumpets and Trombone (1966); *Due per Duo,* 2 rondos for Horn and Piano (1969); *Dialogues* for Flute and Piano (1973); Brass Quintet (1973); *April Sketches,* variations for Piano (1955); *Etudes,* 3 compositions for Piano (1959); *Sonatina di bravura* for Piano (1960); choruses; songs.

Dvořák, Antonín, famous Bohemian composer; b. Mühlhausen, Sept. 8, 1841; d. Prague, May 1, 1904. His father, an innkeeper, wished him to enter the butcher's trade; but he, having learned to play the violin from the village schoolmaster, left home at the age of 16 and entered the Prague Organ School, studying under Pitzsch and earning a precarious livelihood as a violinist in a small orch. For about a decade (1861–71), he played the viola in the orch. of the National Theater in Prague. It was not until 1873 that he brought out an important work, *Hymnus* for Mixed Chorus and Orch., which was performed on March 9 of that year and attracted wide notice; in 1875 he was awarded the Austrian State Prize for his Symph. in E-flat (perf. in Prague by Smetana in 1874), and he received that stipend repeatedly thereafter. He then devoted himself to composition with increasing success, becoming the most celebrated of Czech national composers. Liszt, Brahms, and Hans von Bülow, by securing performances and publication of his work, did much to obtain for his compositions the vogue they deservedly enjoy. In 1873 Dvořák gave up playing in orchs. when he was appointed organist at St. Adalbert's Church in Prague. His fame as a composer spread, and numerous pupils flocked to him; finally, a professorship in composition at the Prague Cons. was offered him. In 1884 he was invited to conduct his *Stabat Mater* in London. It was received with such enthusiasm that in the fall of the same year he conducted it at the Worcester Festival, and was commissioned to write a new work for the Birmingham Festival of 1885 (*The Spectre's Bride*). The following year (1886) he visited England again to direct his oratorio *St. Ludmila* at the Leeds Festival; in 1891 he was made an honorary Mus.Doc. by Cambridge Univ. and an honorary Dr.Phil. by the Czech Univ. in Prague. In 1892 he accepted an invitation to head the National Cons. in N.Y. It was in America that he wrote his most celebrated work, the symph. *From the New World* (first perf. by the N.Y. Phil., Dec. 15, 1893); the themes seemed to reflect Negro spirituals, but Dvořák denied any conscious design in this approximation. The work, though, by proposing the use of Negro themes—or Negro-like themes—in symphonic music, had an enormous impact on American musical nationalism. He discussed the idea further in an article, "Music in America," *Harper's New Monthly Magazine* (Feb. 1895), stating that although Americans had accomplished marvels in most fields of endeavor, in music they were decidedly backward and were content to produce poor imitations of European music; the way to salvation, he suggested, was in the development of a national style, a style based on the melodies of Negroes and Indians. This proposal was greeted with enthusiasm by one segment of America's musical world, but by another, fearing a musical miscegenation, it was rejected with disdain. The controversy that ensued raged for more than 2 decades. Upon returning to Prague in 1895, Dvořák resumed his professorship at the Cons.; was appointed its artistic director in 1901. He was the first musician to be made a life member of the Austrian House of Lords. He was a composer of singular versatility and fecundity; the most prominent characteristics of his music are an inexhaustible, spontaneous melodic invention, rhythmic variety, free employment of national folk tunes, and an intensity of harmony which, in his finest works, has an electrifying effect, though sometimes bordering on the crude. His musical style was eclectic; the conflicting influences of Brahms and Wagner occasionally effected an inner incompatibility; however, his very lack of startling originality, combined with an uninhibited emotionalism, contributed to the lasting success of his music.

WORKS: 10 OPERAS (All except the first produced in Prague): *Alfred*, without op. (1870; posthumous, Olomouc, Dec.10, 1938); *Král a uhlíř (The King and the Coal Burner)*, op. 14 (1871; Nov. 24, 1874); *Tvrdé palice (The Blockheads* or *The Pig-Headed Peasants)*, op. 17 (1874; Oct. 2, 1881); *Vanda*, op. 25 (April 17, 1876); *Selma sedlák (The Peasant a Rogue)*, op. 37 (1877; Jan. 27, 1878); *Dimitrij*, op. 64 (Oct. 8, 1882; revised 1883, 1894); *Jakobin*, op. 84 (*The Jacobin*, 1887–88; Feb. 12, 1889; revised 1897); *Čert a Káča (The Devil and Kate)*, op. 112 (Nov. 23, 1899); *Rusalka*, op. 114 (1900; March 31, 1901; Dvořák's most popular opera); *Armida*, op. 115 (1902–3; March 25, 1904).

FOR ORCH.: 9 symphs., in a chronological renumbering: No. 1, *The Bells of Zlonice*, in C minor, op. 3 (1865; recovered in Prague in 1936 and first perf. there, Oct. 4, 1936); No. 2, in B-flat, op. 4 (1865); No. 3, in E-flat, op. 10 (1873); No. 4, in D minor, op. 13 (1874); No. 5, in F, op. 76 (originally op. 24; 1875); No. 6, in D, op. 60 (1880); No. 7, in D minor, op. 70 (1884–85); No. 8, in G, op. 88 (1888); No. 9, *From the New World*, in E minor, op. 95 (1892–93; N.Y. Phil., Dec. 15, 1893); Piano Concerto in G minor, op. 33 (1875); Violin Concerto in A minor, op. 53 (1879–80); Cello Concerto in B minor, op. 104 (1894–95); *Romance* for Violin and Orch., op. 11 (1873); *Mazurek* for Violin and Orch., op. 49 (1879); *Silent Woods* for Cello and Orch., op. 68 (1893); *Rondo* for Cello and Orch., op. 94 (1892); *Nocturne* in B for Strings, op. 40 (1870); *Serenade* in E for Strings, op. 22 (1875); *Symphonic Variations on an Original Theme*, op. 78 (1877); *Serenade* in D minor, op. 44, for Winds, Cellos, and Double Basses (1878); *Czech Suite* in D, op. 39 (1879); *10 Legends*, op. 59 (1881; originally for Piano, 4-hands); *American Suite* in A, op. 98b (1895; originally for Piano); 5 symph. poems: *The Watersprite*, op. 107 (1896); *The Midday Witch*, op. 108 (1896); *The Golden Spinningwheel*, op. 109 (1896); *The Wood Dove*, op. 110 (1896); *Heroic Song*, op. 111 (1897); overtures: *Dramatic (Tragic) Overture* (1870; from the opera *Alfred*); *My Home*, op. 62 (1881); *Husitská*, op. 67 (1883); *Amid Nature*, op. 91 (1891); *Carnival*, op. 92 (1891); *Othello*, op. 93 (1892); 3 *Slavonic Rhapsodies*, op. 45 (1878); *Slavonic Dances*, in 2 sets, opp. 46, 72 (1878, 1886).

VOCAL WORKS: *Hymnus*, from Hálek's "The Heirs of the White Mountain," op. 30, for Chorus and Orch. (1872; revised 1880); *Stabat Mater*, op. 58, oratorio (1876–77); *Psalm 149*, op. 79, for Chorus and Orch. (1879); *The Spectre's Bride*, op. 69, cantata (1884); *St. Ludmila*, op. 71, oratorio (1885–86; amplified and perf. as an opera, *Svatá Ludmila*, Prague, Nov. 30, 1901); Mass in D, op. 86, for Solo Voices and Chorus (1887); *Requiem*, op. 89, for Soloists, Chorus, and Orch. (1890); *Te Deum*, op. 103, for Soprano, Baritone, Chorus, and Orch. (1892); *The*

American Flag, op. 102, cantata (1893); choruses.

CHAMBER MUSIC: 3 string quintets (1861, 1875, 1893); 14 string quartets (1862–95); 2 piano quintets (1872, 1887); 2 piano quartets (1875, 1889); 4 piano trios (1875, 1876, 1883, 1891); String Sextet in A, op. 48 (1878); Bagatelles for 2 Violins, Cello, and Harmonium or Piano, op. 47 (1878); Violin Sonata in F, op. 57 (1880); *Terzetto* for String Trio, op. 74 (1887); *4 Romantic Pieces*, op. 75, for Violin and Piano (1887); Violin Sonatina in G, op. 100 (1893); piano pieces. A complete ed. of Dvořák's works, under the general editorship of O. Šourek, was begun in Prague in 1955 and continued after Šourek's death in 1956 by a committee of Czech scholars.

BIBLIOGRAPHY: J. Zubatsky, *Antonin Dvořák, Biographische Skizze* (Leipzig, 1886; in Eng. by W.H. Hadow in *Studies in Modern Music*, 2nd series, London, 1895; 2nd ed., 1904); D.G. Mason, *From Grieg to Brahms* (N.Y., 1902); V. Joss, *Antonin Dvořák* (1903); K. Hoffmeister, *Antonin Dvořák* (in Eng. by R. Newmarch, London, 1928); O. Šourek, *Antonin Dvořák* (in Czech, 4 vols., Prague 1916–33; in German as *Dvořák, Leben und Werk*, one vol., abridged by Paul Stefan from the original materials, Vienna, 1935; in Eng., N.Y., 1954); O. Šourek, *Dvořáks Werke: Ein vollständiges Verzeichnis in chronologischer, thematischer und systematischer Anordnung* (Berlin, 1917); H. Sirp, *Antonin Dvořák* (Potsdam, 1939); P. Stefan, *Antonin Dvořák* (N.Y., 1941); A. Robertson, *Dvořák* (London, 1945); J. Van Straaten, *Slavonic Rhapsody, The Story of Antonin Dvořák* (N.Y., 1948); H. Boese, *Zwei Urmusikanten: Smetana, Dvořák* (Zürich, 1955; contains bibliography); J. Burghauser, *Antonin Dvořák: Thematic Catalogue, Bibliography, and Survey of Life and Work* (in Czech, German, and Eng., Prague, 1960); A. Hetschko, *Antonín Dvořák* (Leipzig, 1965); J. Clapham, *Antonin Dvořák: Musician and Craftsman* (N.Y., 1966); Gervase Hughes, *Dvořák: His Life and Music* (N.Y., 1967); I. Spector, "Dvořák's American Period," *Illinois Quarterly* (Feb. 1971); L. Davis, "Dvořák and American Music," in J. Riedel, *A Tribute to Donald N. Ferguson* (Minneapolis, 1972); W. Beyer and E. Kapst, *Antonin Dvořák: Zur Ästhetik seines sinfonischen Schaffens* (Leipzig, 1973); M. Kantor and H. Pinsker, "Musical Expression and Psychopathology," *Perspectives in Biology and Medicine* (Winter 1973). The Dvořák Society of Epsom, England, issues a journal.

Dvořáková, Ludmila, Czech soprano; b. Kolin, July 11, 1923. She made her professional debut at Ostrava in 1949; also sang in Bratislava, Prague, and Vienna (1956). She then appeared in Berlin (1960) and Bayreuth (1965). On Jan. 12, 1966, she made her Metropolitan Opera debut in N.Y. as Leonore in *Fidelio*. In addition to the German repertoire, she sang many roles in Verdi's operas.

Dwight, John Sullivan, American music critic, and editor of *Dwight's Journal of Music;* b. Boston, May 13, 1813; d. there, Sept. 5, 1893. He graduated from Harvard in 1832, and was one of the founders and most active members of the Harvard Musical

Assoc. After studying for the ministry, in 1840 he took charge of the Unitarian Church at Northampton, Mass. His literary and socialistic proclivities, however, gained the mastery; he gave up his pastorate, and entered the ill-starred Brook Farm Community as a teacher of German music and the classics. Returning to Boston in 1848, after the failure of the socialistic experiment, he devoted himself to literature, founded the journal in 1852, and remained its editor in chief until its discontinuance in 1881. A prominent feature in this periodical was the valuable historical essays of A.W. Thayer. The entire journal is available in reprint (N.Y., 1968). Dwight also publ. the excellent *Translations of Select Minor Poems from the German of Goethe and Schiller, with Notes.*
BIBLIOGRAPHY: George Willis Cooke, *J.S. Dwight, Brook-Farmer, Editor, and Critic of Music* (Boston, 1898); Cooke's ed. of Dwight's correspondence with George William Curtis (Boston, 1898); Edward N. Waters, "J.S. Dwight, First American Critic of Music," *Musical Quarterly* (Jan. 1935).

Dyer, Louise (Mrs. Louise B.M. Hanson), patroness of music and publisher; b. Melbourne, Australia, July 16, 1890; d. Monaco, Nov. 9, 1962. She established in Monaco an important publishing enterprise, L'Oiseau-Lyre (The Lyre-Bird Press), financing it entirely out of her own resources. The Lyre-Bird Press has issued a great number of unpubl. or obscure works of medieval and Renaissance French music.

Dyer-Bennet, Richard, American ballad singer; b. Leicester, England, Oct. 6, 1913. He emigrated to the U.S. in 1925; became a naturalized citizen in 1935. He studied voice with Cornelius Reid, and guitar playing with José Rey De La Torre. He made his concert debut in N.Y. in 1944; also sang in nightclubs. In 1970 he joined the State Univ. of N.Y. at Stony Brook as an instructor in the theater arts dept. He acquired popularity mainly as a singer of English and American ballads, but he was also praised for his performance of Schubert song cycles, especially *Die schöne Müllerin* in his own trans., under the title "The Lovely Milleress."

Dykema, Peter, American music pedagogue; b. Grand Rapids, Mich., Nov. 25, 1873; d. Hastings-on-Hudson, N.Y., May 13, 1951. He studied law at the Univ. of Michigan (M.L., 1896); then took lessons in singing and in music theory at the Inst. of Musical Art in N.Y. (1911–12); later supplemented his musical education in Germany; returning to America, he held numerous teaching positions in high schools in Illinois and Indiana; in 1913–24 was on the faculty of the Univ. of Wisconsin; in 1924–39 was a prof. of music education at Teacher's College, Columbia Univ. He publ. a number of music handbooks for schools, among them: *Twice 55 Community Songs* (6 vols., 1919–27); *School Music Handbook* (1931; revised ed., by Hannah M. Cundiff, Boston, 1955); *Singing Youth* (1935); *Golden Key Orchestral Series* (1937); *Modern Band Training Series* (with N.

Church, 1938); *The Teaching and Administration of High School Music* (with K.W. Gehrkens, Boston, 1941).

Dykes, Rev. John Bacchus, English composer of hymn tunes; b. Kingston-upon-Hull, March 10, 1823; d. in an asylum at Ticehurst, Sussex, Jan. 22, 1876. He was educated at Cambridge, was ordained a minor canon and precentor at Durham Cathedral in 1849; took the degree of Mus.Doc. in 1861; in 1862 became vicar of St. Oswald, Durham. He composed numerous anthems and part-songs.
BIBLIOGRAPHY: J.T. Fowler, *Life and Letters of John Bacchus Dykes* (London, 1897).

Dylan, Bob (real name, **Robert Zimmerman**), American folksinger and songwriter; b. Duluth, Minn., May 24, 1941. He adopted the name Dylan out of admiration for the poet Dylan Thomas. Possessed by wanderlust, he rode freight trains across the country; played guitar and crooned in the coffeehouses of N.Y. He also improvised songs to his own lyrics. His nasalized country-type semi-Western style, and his self-haunted soft guitar-strumming captured the imagination not only of untutored adolescents but also of certified cognoscenti in search of convincing authenticity. In 1966 he broke his neck in a motorcycle accident, which forced him to interrupt his charismatic career for 2 years. In 1970 he was awarded an honorary doctorate from Princeton Univ., the first such honor given to a popular singer innocent of all academic training. A group of militants in the Students for a Democratic Society adopted the name "Weathermen" after a line from Dylan's song *Subterranean Homesick Blues,* "You don't need a weatherman to know which way the wind blows." The Weathermen claimed credit for several bombings in N.Y. City during 1969 and 1970.
BIBLIOGRAPHY: Daniel Kramer, *Bob Dylan* (N.Y., 1967); Bob Dylan, *Tarantula* (N.Y., 1971).

Dyson, Sir George, English composer; b. Halifax (Yorkshire), May 28, 1883; d. Winchester, Sept. 28, 1964. He studied at the Royal College of Music in London; was its music director in 1937–52. He was knighted in 1941. His works include a Symph. (1937); Violin Concerto (1943); an oratorio, *Quo Vadis* (1949); Suite for Small Orch.; *3 Rhapsodies* for String Quartet; piano pieces; numerous pedagogic pieces and songs. His cantata *The Canterbury Pilgrims,* to words modernized from Chaucer's *Canterbury Tales,* is his best-known work; the overture to it was extracted in 1946, and performed separately under the title *At the Tabard Inn.* He further composed numerous sacred choruses; publ. the books *The New Music* (1924), *The Progress of Music* (1932), and a candid autobiography, *Fiddling While Rome Burns: A Musician's Apology* (London, 1954).

Dzegelenok, Alexander, Russian composer; b. Moscow, Aug. 24, 1891; d. there, Jan. 31, 1969. He studied at the Phil. Inst. in Moscow with Koreshchenko. He composed an orch. suite, *Egypt;* also

Hiawatha for Voice and Instruments; piano pieces and songs.

Dzerzhinsky, Ivan, Russian composer; b. Tambov, April 9, 1909; d. Moscow, Jan. 18, 1978. He studied with Asafiev at the Leningrad Cons. (1932–34). As a composer he espoused the doctrine of socialist realism. Possessing a facile gift of flowing melodiousness, he made a mark in Soviet music by his first opera, *Quiet Flows the Don,* to a libretto from the novel by the Soviet writer Sholokhov; in it he made use of peasant folk-song elements, emphasizing mass choruses. It was produced in Leningrad on Oct. 22, 1935, and became immediately successful when Stalin attended a performance in Moscow and personally congratulated the composer on his ability to create music in a characteristically Soviet style. He followed it with a sequel, *Virgin Soil Upturned,* which was produced in Moscow on October 23, 1937. His subsequent operas were *The Storm* (after Ostrovsky, 1940); *The Blood of the People* (Leningrad, Jan. 21, 1942); *The Blizzard* (after Pushkin, 1946); *Nadezhda Svetlova* (Orenburg, Sept. 8, 1943); and *A Man's Destiny* (Moscow, Sept. 30, 1961). He further wrote 3 piano concertos (1932, 1934, 1945); numerous piano pieces; songs.

BIBLIOGRAPHY: O.M. Tompakova, *Essays on the Life and Work of Ivan Dzerzhinsky* (Leningrad, 1964).

E

Eames, Emma, famous soprano; b. of American parentage in Shanghai, China, Aug. 13, 1865; d. New York, June 13, 1952. Her mother, who was her first teacher, took her to America as a child; she then studied with Clara Munger in Boston and with Mme. Marchesi in Paris. She made her operatic debut at the Grand Opéra, March 13, 1889, as Juliette in Gounod's *Roméo et Juliette.* She subsequently sang at Covent Garden in London, and on Dec. 14, 1891, made her debut at the Metropolitan Opera House in N.Y., again in the role of Juliette. She remained with the Metropolitan until 1909, appearing as Marguerite in *Faust,* Desdemona in *Otello,* Elisabeth in *Tannhäuser,* Aida, Tosca, and Donna Anna in *Don Giovanni.* From 1923 to 1936 she made her home intermittently in Paris and Bath, Maine; in 1936 she settled in N.Y., where she remained until her death. She received the Jubilee Medal from Queen Victoria, and was decorated by the French Academy with the order of Les Palmes Académiques. Her emotional life was turbulent; she married the painter Julian Story in 1891, but they were separated in the midst of a widely publicized scandal; in 1911 she married the baritone **Emilio de Gogorza,** but left him too. She publ. an autobiography, *Some Memories and Reflections* (N.Y., 1927).

Eames, Henry Purmort, American pianist and music educator; b. Chicago, Sept. 12, 1872; d. Claremont, Calif., Nov. 25, 1950. After completing preliminary music education in the U.S., he went to Europe, where he took piano lessons with Clara Schumann and Paderewski; after a career as a concert pianist, he devoted himself to teaching; was on the faculty at the Univ. of Nebraska (1898–1908), and eventually at the American Cons. in Chicago (1923–28). He then settled in California, where he taught at Scripps College, Claremont. He was also a composer; wrote for chorus, voice, and piano.

Earhart Will, American music educator; b. Franklin, Ohio, April 1, 1871; d. Los Angeles, April 23, 1960. From 1900 to 1912 he was a school supervisor in various localities in Ohio and Indiana; in 1912 he went to Pittsburgh, where he lectured on music education at the Univ. of Pittsburgh and at the Carnegie Inst. of Technology. He publ. a number of books on musical education, among them *Music in the Public Schools* (1914); *Music in Secondary Schools* (with O. McConathy; 1917); *Music to the Listening Ear* (1932); *The Meaning and Teaching of Music* (1935); and *Elements of Music Theory* (with C.N. Boyd; 2 vols., 1938); ed. *Art Songs for High Schools* (1910); *The School Credit Piano Course* (with others; 1918).

BIBLIOGRAPHY: C.V. Buttelman, ed., *Will Earhart: Teacher, Philosopher, Humanitarian* (Washington, D.C., 1962).

Easdale, Brian, English composer; b. Manchester, Aug. 10, 1909; studied at the Royal College of Music in London (1925–33). He became interested in theatrical music; wrote 3 operas, *Rapunzel* (1927), *The Corn King* (1935), and *The Sleeping Children* (1951); incidental music to Shakespeare's plays; also several film scores, of which the most successful was *The Red Shoes*. Other works include a Piano Concerto and several orch. pieces of a descriptive nature (*Dead March; The Phoenix; Bengal River;* etc.); also a *Cavatina* for Brass Ensemble (1961).

East (Easte, Este), Thomas, English music printer and publisher of Elizabethan madrigals; b. London, c.1535; d. there, Jan. 1608. He received his license as a printer in 1565; his first musical publication was Byrd's collection *Psalmes, Sonets and Songs of Sadnes and Pietie* (1588); he was also the assignee of Byrd's patent for printing music paper and musical compositions. In 1592 he brought out *The Whole Booke of Psalmes, with their wonted tunes as they are sung in Churches, composed in four parts*, containing harmonizations by Allison, Blancks, Cavendish, Cobbold, Dowland, Farmer, Farnaby, Hooper, Johnson, and Kirbye (republ. 1594 and 1604; reprinted in score by the Musical Antiquarian Society, 1844). This collection is of historical significance, for it was the first to be printed in score rather than in separate part-books; also for the first time, the tunes were design ated by specific names, such as "Kentish" and "Cheshire." Other works printed by East are Yonge's *Musica Transalpina* (1588); Byrd's *Songs of Sundrie Natures* (1589); Watson's *Madrigals* (1590); Byrd's *Cantiones Sacrae* (2 books, 1589, 1591); Morley's *Canzonets* (1593); Mundy's *Songs and Psalmes* (1594); Kirbye's *Madrigals* (1596); Wilbye's *Madrigals* (1598); Dowland's *Ayres* (1600); Bateson's *Madrigals* (1603); Michael East's *Madrigals* (1604); Pilkington's *Songs or Ayres* (1604); Byrd's *Gradualia* (1605); Youll's *Canzonets* (1607). East's presumed son **Michael East** (c.1580–1648) was a composer; his set of madrigals was publ. by Thomas East in 1604. He served as organist at Lichfield Cathedral; received the degree of B.Mus. at Cambridge (1606); he publ. 6 sets of vocal pieces (madrigals, anthems, etc.) and a set of instrumental works (1638).

BIBLIOGRAPHY: F. Kidson, *British Music Publishers* (London, 1900); E.H. Fellowes, *The English Madrigal Composers* (London, 1921; 2nd ed., 1948).

Eastman, George, American industrialist; b. Waterville, N.Y., July 12, 1854; d. (suicide, when he learned he had cancer) Rochester, March 14, 1932. Eastman made important and far-reaching contributions to the cause of education; invested immense sums in scientific institutions, particularly the Univ. of Rochester, which includes the Eastman Theater and School of Music (one of the leading music schools of the U.S.). This alone he endowed with $3.5 million.

BIBLIOGRAPHY: Carl W. Ackerman, *George Eastman* (1930).

Easton, Florence, operatic soprano; b. South Bank, Yorkshire, Oct. 25, 1882; d. New York, Aug. 13, 1955. She studied singing with Agnes Larkcom and piano with Charles Reddie at the Royal Academy of Music in London, and singing with Elliott Haslam in Paris. Made her debut at Covent Garden in 1903; in 1906 she married the tenor **Francis Maclennan** (divorced in 1929); her 2nd husband was Stanley Rogers. She toured the U.S. with the Savage Grand Opera; then was engaged at the Berlin Opera (1907–13) and at Hamburg (1912–15). She was with the Chicago Opera from 1915 to 1917; from 1917 to 1929 she was a member of the Metropolitan Opera Co.; after a sojourn in Europe, she reappeared meteorically on leap-year day in 1936 at the Metropolitan as Brünnhilde in *Die Walküre*.

Eaton, John, American composer; b. Bryn Mawr, Pa., March 30, 1935. He received his A.B. and M.F.A. degrees from Princeton Univ., where he studied composition with Milton Babbitt, Edward Cone, and Roger Sessions; subsequently won 3 American Prix de Rome awards and two Guggenheim grants. In 1970 he became prof. of music at the Indiana Univ. School of Music in Bloomington. He lectured at the Salzburg Center in American Studies (1976) and was composer-in-residence at the American Academy in Rome (1976–77). In his works he avails himself of all resources of modern music, including serial techniques, microtones, and electronic media. In several of his scores he makes use of the Syn-Ket (a portable electronic synthesizer built by the Roman sound engineer Ketoff).

WORKS: Operas: *Ma Barker* (1957); *Heracles* (1964; Turin, Italy, Oct. 10, 1968); *Myshkin,* after Dostoevsky's novel *The Idiot* (1971; Bloomington, Ind., April 23, 1973); *The Lion and Androcles,* for children (1973; Indianapolis, May 1, 1974); *Danton and Robespierre* (1978; Bloomington, April 21, 1978); *The Cry of Clytaemnestra* (1979; Bloomington, March 1, 1980). Other Works: *Song Cycle on Holy Sonnets of John Donne,* for Voice and Piano (1956); Piano Variations (1957); String Quartet (1958); *Tertullian Overture* (1958); *Adagio and Allegro* for Flute, Oboe, and Strings (1960); *Concert Piece* for Clarinet and Piano (1960); *Concert Music* for Solo Clarinet (1961); *Songs for R.P.B.* for Voice, Piano, and Synthesizer (1964); *Microtonal Fantasy* for 2 Pianos (1965); *Concert Piece* for Syn-Ket (1966); *Thoughts on Rilke* for Soprano, 2 Syn-Kets, and Syn-Mill (1966); *Concert Piece* for Syn-Ket and Symph. Orch. (1966; Berkshire Music Festival, Tanglewood, Mass., Aug. 9, 1967); *Soliloquy* for Electronic Sound Synthesizer (1967); *Vibrations* for 2 Oboes, 2 Clarinets, and Flute (1967); Duet for Syn-Ket and Moog Synthesizer (1968); *Blind Man's Cry* for Soprano and Orch. of Electronic Synthesizers (1968); Mass for Soprano, Clarinet, 3 Syn-Kets, Moog Synthesizer, and Syn-Mill (1970); *Sonority Move-*

ment for Flute and 9 Harps (1971); *In Memoriam Mario Cristini,* piano trio (1971); *Ajax* for Baritone and Orch., after Sophocles (1972); *Guillen Songs* for Voice and Piano (1974); *Duo* for Mixed Chorus (1977); *A Greek Vision* for Soprano, Flute, and Electronics (1981; Chicago, Dec. 7, 1981); Symph. No. 2 (1980–81).

Eaton, Louis, American violinist; b. Waltham, Mass., Feb. 24, 1872; d. Hartford, Conn., May 4, 1927. He studied violin with Loeffler and Bernard Listemann, and piano with **Jessie Downer** (b. Middlebury, Vt., Nov. 17, 1872; d. Hartford, Nov. 22, 1936), whom he married in 1899. In 1915 they settled in Hartford as teachers. With the cellist Arthur Hadley, they formed the Downer-Eaton Trio, which presented first American performances of a number of chamber works.

Ebel, Arnold, German composer and choral conductor; b. Heide, Holstein, Aug. 15, 1883; d. Berlin, March 4, 1963. He studied at Berlin Univ.; also took private lessons with Max Bruch; from 1909 was active in Berlin as an organist, choral conductor, and teacher; served as president of the German Composers' Association (1920–33, and again from 1949). He wrote numerous piano pieces and songs; also a *Sinfonietta giocosa* for Orch.

Eben, Petr, Czech composer; b. Žamberk, Jan. 22, 1929. He studied composition with Bořkovec at the Prague Academy (1948–54); upon graduation he taught musicology at the Charles Univ. in Prague. In his own compositions he follows the traditions of Central European classicism, with modern techniques adding zest to old forms. WORKS: Organ Concerto, subtitled *Symphonia Gregoriana* (1954); Piano Concerto (1961); *Vox clamantis,* symph. movement for 3 Trumpets and Orch. (1969); *Apologio Sokratus,* oratorio based on the Greek text of Plato's defense of Socrates, for Alto, Baritone, Children's Chorus, Mixed Chorus, and Orch. (1961–67); 2 cantatas: *The Lover's Magic Spell,* small cantata for Solo Female Voice and Chorus (1957), and *Bitter Earth* for Baritone, Chorus, and Organ (1959); *Ballads* for Soloists, Chorus, and Orch. (1956); Oboe Sonata (1950); *Suite Baladica* for Cello and Piano (1955); *Duetti* for 2 Trumpets (1956); *Sonatina semplice* for Violin or Flute, and Piano (1957); *Ordo Modalis* for Oboe and Harp (1964); Wind Quintet (1965); *Fantasia Verpertina* for Trumpet and Piano (1967); *Variations on a Chorale* for Brass Quintet (1969); Trio for Oboe, Bassoon, and Piano (1970); *Okna (Windows)* for Trumpet and Organ (1976); Piano Sonata (1950); *Love and Death* for Chorus, to folk texts (1958); *Ubi Caritas et Amor,* antiphon (1964); songs, among them *Písně nelaskavé (Loveless Songs)* for Contralto and 6 Violas (1963).

Eberhardt, Siegfried, German violin pedagogue, son of the violinist and pedagogue **Goby Eberhardt** (1851–1926); b. Frankfurt, March 19, 1883; d. Zwickau, June 29, 1960. He studied violin with Dessau at the Stern Cons. in Berlin, and then with Serato; was a teacher of violin at the Stern Cons. (1908–35); then lived in Halle and Lübeck; in 1945 founded the Hochschule für Theater und Musik in Halle and the Zwickau Academy. WRITINGS: *Der beseelte Violinton* (with Carl Flesch; Dresden, 1910; 4 eds.; also in Eng.); *Treffsicherheit auf der Violine* (1911; 22 eds.; also in Eng., French, and Swedish); *Virtuose Violintechnik* (1920); *Paganinis Geigenhaltung* (1921); *Die Lehre der organischen Geigenhaltung* (1922); *Der Körper in Form und Hemmung* (Munich, 1926); *Wiederaufstieg oder Untergang der Kunst der Geigen* (1956). BIBLIOGRAPHY: K. Schröter, *Flesch-Eberhardt, Naturwidrige oder natürliche Violintechnik?* (1924).

Eberl, Anton Franz Josef, Austrian pianist and composer; b. Vienna, June 13, 1765; d. there, March 11, 1807. On Feb. 27, 1787, he produced the singspiel *La Marchande des modes;* there followed several other stage works, including *Die Zigeuner* (1793). His symphs. and piano music were praised by Mozart and Gluck. He made a concert tour with Mozart's widow in 1795; lived in St. Petersburg from 1796 to 1799; revisited Russia in 1801; gave concerts there on Dec. 8, 15, and 28, 1801, presenting the first performances in Russia of Haydn's *The Creation;* returned to Vienna early in 1802; traveled through Germany in 1806. Besides 4 more stage works, he wrote 2 cantatas, symphs., piano concertos, much chamber music, many piano works (especially sonatas), songs, etc. BIBLIOGRAPHY: Fr.J. Ewens, *Anton Eberl* (Dresden, 1927; with thematic catalogue); R. Haas, "Anton Eberl," *Mozart-Jahrbuch 1951* (Salzburg, 1953); A. White, *The Piano Works of Anton Eberl (1765–1807)* (Diss., Univ. of Wisconsin, 1971).

Eberlin (Eberle), Johann Ernst, German composer; b. Jettingen, Bavaria, March 27, 1702; d. Salzburg, June 19, 1762. He studied at Benedictine Univ. in Salzburg in 1721–23; was 4th organist at the Salzburg Cathedral (1726), and from 1729, organist and choirmaster there; from 1749, was court Kapellmeister to the Prince-Archbishop in Salzburg. WORKS: *Der Blutschwitzende Jesus* (in Denkmäler der Tonkunst in Österreich, 55 [28.i]; *XI Toccate e Fughe per l'organo* (Augsburg, 1747; several reprints); fugues and toccatas (in Commer's *Musica sacra*); 2 motes (publ. by Schott); 2 sonatas (publ. by Haffner); 5 pieces in L. Mozart's *Der Morgen und der Abend* (Augsburg, 1759). In MS: 13 oratorios in Regensburg (Proske's Library); an offertory and Miserere (Berlin Library); a volume of organ pieces (Royal Inst. for Church Music, Berlin); other works in the Vienna Library (a 4-voiced Mass with organ motets, cantatas, etc.), the Munich Library (18 masses and other pieces), and in the libraries of Kremsmünster and Salzburg (37 masses with Orch., 75 oratorios, 43 Psalms with Orch., 3 Te Deums, etc.). BIBLIOGRAPHY: Robert Haas, "Eberlins Schuldramen und Oratorien," in *Studien zur Musikwissenschaft* (1921); C. Schneider, *Geschichte der Musik in Salzburg* (Salzburg, 1935); K.A. Rosenthal, "Mozart's Sacramental Litanies and Their Forerunners," *Musical Quarterly* (Oct. 1941); H. Herbort, *Die Messen des Johann Ernst Eberlin* (Diss., Univ. of Münster, 1961); M. Cucay-Schneider, *Die Instrumentalwerke Johann Ernst Eberlins* (Diss., Univ. of Salzburg, 1975).

Ebert, Carl, noted German opera producer and administrator; b. Berlin, Feb. 20, 1887; d. Santa Monica, Calif., May 14, 1980. He studied acting with Max Reinhardt; then appeared in theaters in Berlin and Frankfurt. In 1927 he became general administrator of the State Theater in Darmstadt and began to produce operas there. He then held a similar post at the Berlin City Opera (1931–33); he left Germany when the Nazis came to power. Ebert was one of the founders of the famous Glyndebourne Festival (1934); in 1936 he organized the Turkish National Theater and Opera in Ankara, serving as its administrator. In 1948 he came to the U.S. and served as head of the opera dept. of the Univ. of Southern Calif., Los Angeles. He was again general administrator of the Berlin City Opera (1956–61). In addition to his work as producer at Glyndebourne (1947–59), he also worked at the Metropolitan Opera in N.Y., La Scala in Milan, and Vienna. As a producer, he gave much importance to the fusion of the music with the dramatic action on stage.

Eberwein, Carl, German composer; b. Weimar, Nov. 10, 1786; d. there, March 2, 1868. He was a member of a musical family; after a study of general subjects at the Weimar Hochschule für Musik he received an appointment as a court musician at the age of 16. He then studied with Zelter in Berlin; returning to Weimar, he held the posts of chamber musician (1810–18), music director of the Weimar town church (1818–26), and conductor of the Weimar Opera (1826–49). He was a friend of Goethe, who often mentions him, and for whom he composed some songs.
WORKS: 3 operas: *Die Heerschau; Der Graf zu Gleichen; Der Teppichhändler;* several cantatas written for various state occasions; some chamber music; a great number of songs with piano accompaniment.
BIBLIOGRAPHY: W. Bode, *Goethes Schauspieler und Musiker* (1912, with autobiographical sketch of Eberwein); H.J. Moser, *Goethe und die Musik* (Leipzig, 1949).

Eberwein, Traugott Maximilian, German composer, brother of **Carl Eberwein;** b. Weimar, Oct. 27, 1775; d. Rudolstadt, Dec. 2, 1831. He played the violin in the Weimar court orch. as a very young man; like his brother, he was a protégé of Goethe; wrote 2 operas, *Claudine von Villa Bella* (1815) and *Der Jahrmarkt von Plundersweilen* (1818), to texts by Goethe; he further composed church music and instrumental concertos.

Eccard, Johannes, eminent German composer; b. Mühlhausen, 1553; d. Berlin, 1611. He was a chorister in the Kapelle at the Weimar court from 1567–71; then in the Bavarian Hofkapelle in Munich, where he was a pupil (1571–74) of Orlandus Lassus; was director of J. Fugger's private orch. at Augsburg (1577); in 1578 he moved to Königsberg, as a member of the Prussian chapel; in 1580 became its assistant conductor, and in 1604, chief conductor. In 1608 he was called to Berlin to serve as court musician to the Elector. He was an important composer of sacred music.
WORKS: He publ. (with Burgk): *Odae sacrae* (1574) and *Crepundia sacra* (in 2 parts, 1578); his own works include *Neue deutsche Lieder mit 4 und 5 Stimmen,* dedicated to J. Fugger (1578); *Neue geistliche und weltliche Lieder mit 4 und 5 Stimmen* (1589; ed. in score by R. Eitner, in *Publikationen älterer Musik,* vol. 25); *Geistliche Lieder auf den Choral mit 5 Stimmen,* 51 songs (2 parts, 1597; ed. by Teschner and Fr. von Baussnern, 1928); *Preussische Festlieder auf das ganze Jahr für 5–8 Stimmen* (posthumous in 2 parts, 1642–44; ed. by Teschner, 1858); also occasional songs (many in the Königsberg Library).
BIBLIOGRAPHY: C. von Winterfeld, *Der evangelische Kirchengesang . . . ,* I and II; A. Mayer-Reinach, "Zur Geschichte der Königsberger Hofkapelle," *Sammelbände der internationalen Musik-Gesellschaft;* H.E. Brinckmann, "Neue Forschungen zum Leben der grossen Mühlhauser Musiker," in the *Armin Tille Festschrift* (Weimar, 1930); H. Heckmann, "Johannes Eccards Gelegenheitskompositionen," in M. Ruhnke, ed., *Festschrift Bruno Stäblein* (Cassel, 1967).

Eccles, Henry, English violinist, brother of **John Eccles;** b. London, c.1670; d. Paris, c.1742. He was a member of the King's Band (1689–1710), and then of the French court orch. In 1720 he publ. under his own name 12 violin solos, adaptations of works by Giuseppe Valentini and others.

Eccles, John, English violinist and composer; b. London, c.1668; d. Kingston, Surrey, Jan. 12, 1735. He was the son and pupil of the violist **Solomon Eccles** (1618–83). He became a member of the Queen's Band in 1694, and Master of it in 1700. He was active as a composer for the theater; in 1694 wrote music for *Don Quixote* (with Purcell) and *Don Carlos, Prince of Spain* (after T. Otway); in 1700, for Congreve's *The Judgment of Paris* (March 1701) and *The Way of the World* (March 1700); in 1710, he publ. a collection of his own songs (about 100), which enjoyed wide popularity. He also publ. 3 vols. of "Theatre Music" (c.1700). In all, he wrote music for 12 masques and 62 pieces of incidental music for the stage.
BIBLIOGRAPHY: John Jeffreys, *The Eccles Family* (Enfield, 1951); S. Lincoln, *John Eccles: The Last of a Tradition* (Diss., Oxford Univ., 1963).

Echaniz, José, Cuban pianist; b. Havana, June 4, 1905; d. Pittsford, N.Y., Dec. 30, 1969. He studied piano in Havana; appeared as a soloist with major American orchs., receiving praise for his brilliant interpretations. In 1944 he joined the staff of the Eastman School of Music in Rochester, N.Y. He also served as conductor of the Grand Rapids Symph. Orch.

Eckard (Eckardt, Eckart), Johann Gottfried, German composer of keyboard music; b. Augsburg, Jan. 21, 1735; d. Paris, July 24, 1809. He was a copper engraver by profession and learned music in his spare time. In 1758 he was taken to Paris by the piano manufacturer J.A. Stein, and remained there. He acquired a great facility as a pianist, and gave successful concerts in Paris. In the preface to his album of 6 sonatas he states that his task was to compose music suitable for any keyboard instrument, but the indications of dynamics in the MS show that he had mainly the then-novel piano in view. Mozart admired Eckard's works, and there are traits in Mozart's keyboard music of the Paris period that may be traced to Eckard's usages. A complete edition of Eckard's works for piano, ed. by Eduard Reeser and annotated by J. Ligtelijn, has been publ. (Amsterdam, 1956).

Eckardt, Hans, German musicologist, authority on Japanese music; b. Magdeburg, Oct. 9, 1905; d. Berlin, Feb. 26, 1969. He studied philology in Leipzig, Berlin, Paris, and Heidelberg (1925–29); musicology with Sachs, Hornbostel, and Schünemann (1925–32). From 1932 to 1935 he taught at Imperial Univ. in Fukuoka, Japan; in 1938–47 he was in Kyoto, as director of the Japanese-German Research Inst. of Cultural History. In 1948 he settled in Heidelberg; in 1958 he joined the faculty at the Free Univ. in Berlin. He contributed articles on the music of Asia to *Die Musik in Geschichte und Gegenwart;* wrote several papers in Japanese for *Monumenta Nipponica.*

Eckelt, Johann Valentin, German organist; b. Werningshausen, near Erfurt, May (baptized, May 8) 1673; d. Sondershausen, Dec. 18, 1732. From 1696 he was organist at Wernigerode; from 1703, at Sondershausen.
WORKS: *Experimenta musicae geometrica* (1715); *Unterricht, eine Fuge zu formieren* (1722); *Unterricht, was ein Organist wissen soll.* His MS Passion, cantatas, and organ works are of interest. His valuable library was acquired by E.L. Gerber, who utilized it in the compilation of his dictionary.
BIBLIOGRAPHY: E. Jacobs, "Der Orgelspieler und Musikgelehrte J.V. Eckelt," *Vierteljahrsschrift für Musik-Wissenschaft* (1893).

Eckerberg, Sixten, Swedish conductor, pianist, and composer; b. Hjältevad, Ingatorp, Sept. 5, 1909. He studied at the Stockholm Cons. (1927–32); received a Jenny Lind stipend to study conducting with Weingartner in Basel (1932–34); also was a piano pupil of Emil Sauer in Vienna and of Isidor Philipp in Paris. In 1937 he was appointed conductor of the Göteborg Symph. Orch.

WORKS: 3 symphs. (1941, 1944, 1965); *Sommarmusik* for Orch. (1941); *Sub luna,* symph. poem (1942); 3 piano concertos (1943, 1949, 1971); *Visione* for Orch. (1961); Piano Concertino (1962); *Triologi* for Voice, Flute, and Percussion (1969); *La danza della vita* for Orch. (1970); Nocturne for Alto and Orch. (1970–71); *Promenade Suite* for Winds and Percussion (1971); *Sagan om asarna* for Orch. (1971); Serenade for Orch. (1972); *Skogssuset* for Orch. (1973); *Anger,* musical after Maupassant (1972; Radio Sweden, July 22, 1975); Cello Concerto (1974); chamber music; piano pieces. He publ. an autobiography, *Musiken och mitt lif* (Stockholm, 1970).

Eckert, Karl Anton Florian, German composer and conductor; b. Potsdam, Dec. 7, 1820; d. Berlin, Oct. 14, 1879. At the age of 6 he was considered a prodigy; the poet F. Förster became interested in him and sent him to the best teachers; he studied piano with Rechenberg and Greulich, violin with Botticher and Ries, and composition with Rungenhagen. At 10 he wrote an opera, *Das Fischermädchen;* at 13, an oratorio, *Ruth.* After study (for a time at Leipzig under Mendelssohn) he went to the U.S. with Henriette Sontag; was then conductor of the Italian opera in Paris (1852); in 1854–60 he was conductor and music director of the Vienna Opera; from 1860 to 1867 he held a similar post in Stuttgart; he was in Baden-Baden from 1867–69; then was called to Berlin to succeed Heinrich Dorn as director of the Berlin Opera. He wrote 4 operas, several oratorios, and a Cello Concerto which had little success; his songs, however, proved more popular; of these the *Swiss Echo Song* is the best known.

Eckhard, Jacob, one of the early German organists in America; b. Eschwege (Hesse), Nov. 24, 1757; d. Charleston, S.C., Nov. 10, 1833. He came to the U.S. in 1776 and settled in Richmond, Va. In 1786 he was organist of St. John's Lutheran Church in Charleston; in 1809 received the post of organist at St. Michael's Episcopal Church. He publ. a hymn book (printed in Boston, 1816); wrote 2 patriotic naval songs, *The Pillar of Glory* and *Rise, Columbia, Brave and Free.*
BIBLIOGRAPHY: G.W. Williams, "Jacob Eckhard and His Choirmaster's Book," *Journal of the American Musicological Society* (Spring 1954).

Eckhardt-Gramatté, Sonia (Sophie-Carmen), violinist, pianist, and composer; b. Moscow, Jan. 6, 1899; d. Stuttgart, Dec. 2, 1974, in a traffic accident while visiting Europe. She received early piano training from her mother, a former student of Anton Rubinstein; was taken to Paris, where she studied violin and piano at the Cons. there. She made her concert debut in Berlin at the age of 11 on the piano and violin, playing Beethoven sonatas for each instrument; later took violin lessons with Bronislaw Huberman; after World War I, she toured Europe as a duo-pianist with Edwin Fischer. In 1920 she married the painter Walter Gramatté; they lived in Barcelona from 1924 until his death in 1929.

In 1934 she returned to Germany and married the art critic Ferdinand Eckhardt, adding his name to that of her first husband in her patronymic. She took additional courses in composition with Max Trapp (1936–42). In 1953 she moved to Winnipeg, Canada. Her own compositions are marked by impressive craftsmanship.

WORKS: 2 piano concertos (1925, 1946); 2 symphs. (1939; *Manitoba*, 1969–70); *Capriccio Concertante* for Orch. (1940); Concertino for String Orch. (1947); *Markantes Stück* for 2 Pianos and Orch. (1946–50); Triple Concerto for Trumpet, Clarinet, Bassoon, Strings, and Timpani (1949); Bassoon Concerto (1950); 2 violin concertos (1951, 1952); Concerto for Orch. (1953–54); *Symphony-Concerto* for Piano and Orch. (1966–67); 4 suites for Solo Violin (1922–68); 6 piano suites (1923–52); Concerto for Solo Violin (1925); *10 Caprices* for Solo Violin (1924–34); *6 Caprices* for Piano (1934–36); 3 string quartets (1938, 1943, 1962–64); 2 duos for 2 Violins (1944); Duo for Viola and Cello (1944); Duo for 2 Cellos (1944); Wind Quartet (1946); 2 string trios (1947); *Ruck-Ruck Sonata* for Clarinet and Piano (1947); Wind Trio (1947); *Duo Concertante* for Flute and Violin (1956); *Duo Concertante* for Cello and Piano (1959); Wind Quintet (1962–63); Nonet (1966); Piano Trio (1967); Woodwind Trio (1967); Concerto for Viola da Gamba and Harpsichord (1971); *Fanfare* for 8 Brasses (1971).

Eckstein, Pavel, Czech musicologist; b. Opava, April 27, 1911. He studied jurisprudence at Charles Univ. in Prague, graduating in 1935; received his musical education there. During the German occupation (1941–45) he was in a concentration camp in Lodz, Poland, but survived and returned to Prague, where he became active as an organizer of music festivals, an editor, and a writer on music.

Eckstine, Billy (William Clarence), black American jazz singer and bandleader; b. Pittsburgh, July 8, 1914. He worked in nightclubs as a crooner; formed a band of his own in 1944, proselytizing for bebop, in association with such bop figures as Dizzy Gillespie and Miles Davis; later became successful as a balladeer of "cool" jazz.

Ecorcheville, Jules, French writer on music; b. Paris, July 17, 1872; d. Feb. 19, 1915 (fell in battle at Perthesles-Hurlus). He was a pupil of César Franck, 1887–90; a student of literature and art history in Paris and (1904–5) Leipzig; received a doctorat ès lettres (Paris, 1906); was editor of *La Revue Musicale S.I.M.* and a writer on the history and esthetics of music.

WRITINGS: *De Lully à Rameau: 1690–1730, L'Esthétique musicale* (1906); *Corneille et la musique* (1906); *Actes d'état civil des musiciens insinués au Châtelet de Paris de 1539 à 1650* (1907); *Catalogue du fonds de musique ancienne de la Bibliothèque Nationale* (thematic list of 10,000 items, to be completed in 10 vols.; only 8 vols. were publ.); "Un Livre inconnu sur la danse" (F. de Lauze's *Apologie de la danse,* 1623), in *Riemann-Fest-schrift,* 1909; also edited *Vingt suites d'orchestre du XVIIᵉ siècle français* (1906; facsimile and transcription).

BIBLIOGRAPHY: *Le Tombeau de Jules Ecorche-ville: suivi de lettres inédites* (Paris, 1916).

Eda-Pierre, Christiane, French soprano; b. Fort-de-France, Martinique, March 24, 1932. She studied at the Paris Cons.; made her operatic debut in 1962 at the Paris Opéra in the title role of Donizetti's *Lucia di Lammermoor;* subsequently appeared as a guest artist with the Deutsche Oper in Berlin, the Hamburg State Opera, and the Chicago Lyric Opera. On April 3, 1980, she made her Metropolitan Opera debut in N.Y. as Constanze in Mozart's *Die Entführung aus dem Serail.* An outstanding coloratura soprano, she possesses a large operatic repertoire.

Eddy, Clarence, distinguished American organist; b. Greenfield, Mass., June 23, 1851; d. Chicago, Jan. 10, 1937. He studied with Dudley Buck in N.Y.; in 1871 he went to Berlin to study piano with Loeschhorn. He made frequent tours in America and Europe; appeared at the Vienna Exposition of 1873; at the Philadelphia Centennial in 1876; gave a series of 100 organ recitals in Chicago (1879) with completely different programs; appeared at the Chicago Columbian Exposition in 1893, etc. He wrote many pieces for organ; publ. *The Church and Concert Organist* (2 vols., 1882–85); *The Organ in Church* (1887); *A Method for Pipe Organ* (1917); and trans. K.A. Haupt's *Theory of Counterpoint and Fugue* (1876).

Eddy, Nelson, popular American baritone; b. Providence, R.I., June 29, 1901; d. Miami Beach, March 6, 1967. He studied voice with W. Vilonat in N.Y.; then in Dresden and Paris; was for 4 years a member of the Philadelphia Opera Co.; then sang on the radio with sensational success; also acted in musical films.

Edelmann, Jean-Frédéric, Alsatian musician of considerable accomplishments and a tempestuous and tragic life; b. Strasbourg, May 5, 1749; executed by guillotine in Paris, July 17, 1794. He studied law, matriculating from the Univ. of Strasbourg in 1770. In 1774 he went to Paris, where he became a successful music teacher; among his students was the opera composer Méhul. It was Edelmann who in his teaching and in his compositions made the piano a fashionable instrument in Paris. He joined the Jacobins during the Revolution, and this proved his undoing when the Revolution took a more violent turn.

WORKS: His keyboard pieces are in the manner of Couperin; he affected suggestive subtitles, such as *La Coquette* and *La Caressante.* He also wrote an oratorio, *Esther,* which was performed at the Concert Spirituel in Paris on April 8, 1781; on Sept. 24, 1782, the Paris Opéra presented 2 of Edelmann's lyric dramas, *Feu* and *Ariane dans l'isle de Naxos.* Many of his keyboard works were publ. in his lifetime; of these there are 2 albums of *6 sonates pour le clavecin* (Paris, 1775, 1777); *Divertissements pour le clavecin* (1776); *Sinfonie pour le clavecin,* accompanied by 2 Violins, 2 Horns, and Cello ad libitum (1776); *4 quatuors* for Clavecin, 2 Violins, and Viola (1781); *4 sonates* for Clavecin and Violin (1782); Concerto for Clavecin, 2 Violins, 2 Oboes, 2 Horns, and Bass ad libitum (1782); *4 sonates en quatuor* for Clavecin, 2 Violins, and Bass (1784); *3 concerts* for Clavecin, 2 Violins, and Viola (1785); *4 divertissements* for Clavecin, 2 Violins, and Viola (1786); *Airs pour clavecin ou le forte piano* (1788). A thematic catalogue of Edelmann's works was publ. by Rita Benton in *Fontes Artis Musicae,* XI/2 (1964).

BIBLIOGRAPHY: Vogeleis, *Bausteine und Quellen zu einer Geschichte der Musik im Elsass* (Strasbourg, 1911); G. de Saint-Foix, "Les Premiers Pianistes parisiens: J.F. Edelmann," *La Revue Musicale* (June 1924); Rita Benton, "Jean-Frédéric Edelmann, A Musical Victim of the French Revolution," *Musical Quarterly* (April 1964).

Edelmann, Otto, noted Austrian bass; b. Vienna, Feb. 5, 1917. He studied at the Vienna Academy of Music; in 1949 he became a member of the Vienna State Opera. He later appeared at the Bayreuth Festival, at the Salzburg Festival, at La Scala, Milan, and other prestigious European music centers. On Nov. 11, 1954, he made his debut at the Metropolitan Opera in N.Y. as Hans Sachs in *Die Meistersinger von Nürnberg,* a role in which he particularly excelled.

Eder, Helmut, Austrian composer; b. Linz, Dec. 26, 1916. He studied at the Bruckner Cons. in his hometown; was drafted into the army during World War II; after the end of the war, he resumed his musical studies, taking composition lessons with Carl Orff and Johann Nepomuk David. In 1950, he joined the staff of his alma mater in Linz, and proceeded to modernize its curriculum, establishing an electronic studio and organizing a series of disturbing avant-garde concerts. In 1967 he was appointed to the faculty of the Music Academy at the Mozarteum in Salzburg, and quieted down.

WORKS: Operas: *Oedipus* (1960); *Der Kardinal* (1965); *Die weisse Frau* (1968); television opera, *Konjugation 3* (1969); ballets: *Moderner Traum* (1957); *Anamorphase* (1963); *Infahrten des Odysseus* (1969); 3 symphs. (1952, 1960, 1962); String Quartet (1948); Trio for Flute, Clarinet, and Bassoon (1952); Concerto for Piano, 15 Wind Instruments, Double Basses, and Percussion (1952); Partita for 2 Guitars (1954); Piano Concerto (1958); *Concerto semiserio* for 2 Pianos and Orch. (1962); *Concerto a dodici* for Strings (1963); Violin Concerto (1964); Oboe Concerto (1966); *Syntagma* for Orch. (1967); *Nil admirari* for Chamber Orch. (1967); *L'Homme armé* for Organ and Orch. (1969); *Septuagesima instrumentalis* for Wind Quintet (1969); *Metamorphosen* for Orch. (1970); Septet for Winds (1970); Piano Trio (1970); *Memento* for Organ Positive and 2 String Groups (1971); *Melodia-ritmica* for 12 Cellos (1973); *Melodia* for String Orch. (1973); *Divertimento* for Soprano and Orch. (1975); choruses; songs.

Edmunds, Christopher, English organist and composer; b. Birmingham, Nov. 26, 1899. He studied with Bantock; was organist at Aston; from 1945 to 1957 was a prof. at the Birmingham School of Music. He wrote an opera, *The Blue Harlequin;* 2 symphs.; chamber music.

Edmunds, John (baptismal names, **Charles Sterling**), American composer and music scholar; b. San Francisco, June 10, 1913. He studied with Rosario Scalero at the Curtis Inst. in Philadelphia, with Walter Piston at Harvard Univ. (M.A., 1941), with Roy Harris at Cornell Univ., and with Otto Luening at Columbia Univ.; subsequently traveled to England, where he took private lessons with Arnold Goldsbrough and Thurston Dart. He was the recipient of the Bearns Prize at Columbia Univ. for a group of 40 songs (1937), a Fulbright fellowship for a treatise on the songs of Purcell (1951), an Italian government grant for work on the solo cantatas of Alessandro Scarlatti and Benedetto Marcello (1954–56), a Folger Shakespeare Library grant for work on the vocal works of Campion and Dowland (1967), a fellowship from the American Council of Learned Societies for work on Purcell songs (1968), and a Guggenheim fellowship for an edition of his own songs and folk song settings (1969). He held lectureships at Syracuse Univ. (1946–47) and at the Univ. of Calif. at Berkeley (1965–66). From 1946 to 1953 he led festivals of the Campion Society in San Francisco, of which he was the founder and which presented much unfamiliar music, including modern American works. From 1957 to 1961 Edmunds was head of the Americana Collection in the Music Division of the N.Y. Public Library; in collaboration with Gordon Boelzner, he publ. a valuable edition, in 2 vols., of *Some 20th-Century American Composers: A Bibliography.* From 1968 to 1976 he worked in England, returning to San Francisco in 1977. His output of original works is impressive; most of them are choral works, masques, and ballets, in the manner of the late Renaissance and early Baroque; among his stage works are *The Pastoral Kingdom,* a masque (1963); *The Voyage to Ararat,* a ballet (1973); *The Parliament of Fowls,* a ballet (1974); *The Book Called the Governor,* a ballet (1974); *Choric Requiem,* a ballet (1968–75); *The Lord of Misrule,* a masque (1978). He further wrote numerous songs, carols, hymns, and solo piano pieces, under such engaging titles as *Various Animals* and *Flowers and Vegetables.* Of great importance are his astute editions of Elizabethan songs and realizations of the basso continuo of classical Italian songs; he also compiled a 12-volume anthology of songs and solo cantatas by 17-century English composers.

Edson, Lewis, American musician; b. Bridgewater, Mass., Jan. 22, 1748; d. Woodstock, N.Y., 1820. Originally a blacksmith by trade, he became very active as a music teacher. He went to N.Y. in 1776; moved to Woodstock in 1817. He compiled (with Thomas Seymour) *The New York Collection of Sacred Music;* composed the hymn tunes *Bridgewater, Lenox, Greenfield,* and others.

Edwards, Clara, American musician of varied accomplishments as singer, pianist, and song composer; b. Mankato, Minn., April 18, 1887; d. New York, Jan. 17, 1974. She studied voice in Vienna; returned to America in 1914 and became active as a singer and pianist. She wrote a number of songs to her own words, among them *By the Bend of the River* and *Into the Night;* also composed music for children's plays and animated cartoons.

Edwards, Henry John, English composer; b. Barnstaple, Devon, Feb. 24, 1854; d. there, April 8, 1933. He received his first instruction from his father, organist of the Barnstaple Parish Church; from 1874–76 studied with H.C. Banister (harmony), G. Macfarren (composition), and S. Bennett (piano and orchestration); at Oxford he took the degrees of Mus.Bac. (1876) and Mus.Doc. (1885); succeeded his father in 1886; also conducted for the Barnstaple Music Festival Society and the Exeter Oratorio Society (1896–1921); retired in 1926. He wrote 2 oratorios, *The Ascension* (Exeter Festival, 1888) and *The Risen Lord* (Exeter Festival, 1906); a cantata, *The Epiphany* (1891); motets; etc.

Edwards, Henry Sutherland, English writer on music; b. Hendon (London), Sept. 5, 1829; d. London, Jan. 21, 1906. For many years he was critic of the *St. James Gazette;* among his numerous books the following are the most important: *The Russians at Home* (1861); *History of the Opera from Its Origin in Italy to the Present Time* (1862; 2nd ed., publ. in same year as *History of the Opera, from Monteverdi to Donizetti*); *Life of Rossini* (1869; in condensed form in Great Musicians Series, 1881); *The Lyric Drama* (2 vols., 1881); *Famous First Representations* (1886); *The Prima Donna* (2 vols., 1888).

Edwards, Julian, operetta composer; b. Manchester, England, Dec. 11, 1855; d. Yonkers, N.Y., Sept. 5, 1910. He was a pupil in Edinburgh of Sir H. Oakeley, and in London of Sir George Macfarren; conducted the Royal English Opera Co. (1877) and the English Opera at Covent Garden (1883); came to the U.S. in 1888, settling in Yonkers and devoting himself entirely to composition. Some of his comic operas achieved more than average success, among them *Victoria* (Sheffield, March 6, 1883); *Jupiter* (N.Y., April 14, 1892); *Friend Fritz* (N.Y., Jan. 26, 1893); *King Rene's Daughter,* lyric drama (N.Y., Nov. 22, 1893); *Madeleine* (N.Y., July 31, 1894); *The Goddess of Truth* (N.Y., Feb. 26, 1896); *Brian Boru,* romantic Irish opera (N.Y., Oct. 19, 1896); *The Wedding Day* (N.Y., April 8, 1897); *The Patriot* (1907; N.Y., Nov. 23, 1908; revived, July 24, 1975, at the Newport, R.I., Music Festival; the libretto deals with an attempted assassination of George Washington).

Edwards, Richard, English composer; b. Somerset-

shire, near Yeovil, c.1522; d. London, Oct. 31, 1566. He studied at Oxford (M.A. in 1547); was (from 1561) master of the children of the Chapel Royal. With these choirboys he presented in 1565 his musical play *Damon and Pithias* (publ. in 1571). Edwards is best known for his madrigal "In going to my naked bed," written about 20 years before the madrigal became popular in England (this piece is reprinted by Fellowes in *The English Madrigal School,* 36).

Edwards, Ross, Australian composer; b. Sydney, Dec. 23, 1943. He studied at the New South Wales State Cons. (1959–62); privately with Richard Meale (1963) and Peter Sculthorpe (1965); at the Univ. of Adelaide with visiting composers Peter Maxwell Davies and Sándor Veress (1966–69).
WORKS: *Chamber Symphony* (1962); Piano Sonata (1962); *2 Pieces* for Piano (1962); Wind Quintet No. 1 (1963); Trio for Flute, Harp, and Viola (1965); *Music* for Flute and Tape (1965); Wind Quintet No. 2 (1965); Sextet for Flute, Clarinet, Horn, Harp, Viola, and Cello (1966); Sonata for Wind Quintet, Violin, Viola, Cello, and Harp (1967); 3 string quartets (1968, 1969, 1972); Etude for Orch. (1969; Sydney, April 3, 1971); *Monos I* for Cello (1970), *II* for Piano (1970), *III* for Violin (1971); *Choros* for Piano and Orch. (1971); *Kan-Touk* for Female Voice, Harp, 2 Pianos, 2 Percussion Instruments, and Tape (1973); *Antiphon* for Chorus, 3 Trumpets, 3 Trombones, Organ, and Tam-Tams (1973).

Eeden, Jean-Baptiste van den, Belgian composer; b. Ghent, Dec. 26, 1842; d. Mons, April 4, 1917. He was a pupil in the conservatories at Ghent and Brussels, winning at the latter the first prize for composition (1869) with the cantata *Faust's laatste nacht.* In 1878, he was appointed director of the Mons Cons., succeeding Huberti.
WORKS: Operas: *Numance* (Antwerp, Feb. 2, 1897) and *Rhena* (Brussels, Feb. 15, 1912); oratorios: *Brutus; Jacqueline de Bavière; Jacob van Artevelde; Le Jugement dernier;* dramatic scene for 3 Voices, *Judith;* 2 cantatas: *Het Woud* and *De Wind;* symph. poem, *La Lutte au XVIᵉ siècle; Marche des esclaves;* etc.; also choruses and songs.
BIBLIOGRAPHY: Paul Bergmans, "Notice sur Jean van den Eeden," in the annual publication of the Académie Royale (Brussels, 1924; pp. 375–436; contains a complete catalogue of works); M. Delsaux, *Jean van den Eeden et son œuvre* (Mons, 1925).

Effinger, Cecil, American composer; b. Colorado Springs, July 22, 1914. He studied violin and oboe; then went to Paris, where he attended classes in composition with Nadia Boulanger. Returning to America, he was first oboist in the Denver Symph. Orch.; then served as bandmaster in the U.S. Army in France (1942–45). Beginning with 1936, he taught music at the Univ. of Colorado, in Boulder, retaining this post until 1981; then continued as composer-in-residence there. In his own music, he maintains a median modern style, making use of polytonal and atonal procedures, without abandoning the ba-

sic sense of tonality. Effinger is the inventor of a practical music typewriter patented in 1955 under the name "Musicwriter."
WORKS: Opera, *Cyrano de Bergerac* (Univ. of Colorado, Boulder, July 21, 1965); children's opera, *Pandora's Box* (1962); 5 symphs. (1946–58); 2 sinfoniettas (1945, 1958); Piano Concerto (1946); Choral Symph. (Denver, Dec. 2, 1952); cantata, *The St. Luke Christmas Story* (1953); *Symphonie concertante* for Harp, Piano, and Orch. (1954); *Tone Poem on the Square Dance* for Orch. (1955); oratorio, *The Invisible Fire* (1957); *Trio concertante* for Trumpet, Horn, Trombone, and Chamber Orch. (1964); 4 string quartets (1943, 1944, 1948, 1963); Viola Sonata (1944); Suite for Cello and Piano (1945); *Pastoral* for Oboe and Strings (1948); *Landscape* for Brass and Strings (1966); Violin Concerto (1974); *The Long Dimension* for Baritone, Chorus, and Orch., (1970); *A Cantata for Easter* (1971); *Quiet Evening* for Flute, Marimba, and Strings (1972); *This We Believe,* oratorio (1975); *Capriccio* for Orch. (1975); music drama, *The Gentleman Desperado and Miss Bird* (1976).

Egenolff, Christian, early German music printer; b. Hadamar, July 26, 1502; d. Frankfurt, Feb. 9, 1555. He publ. 2 collections of 4-part songs, *Gassenhawerlin* and *Reutterliedlin* (1535; facsimile ed. publ. by Moser, Augsburg, 1927), which are of decided value.
BIBLIOGRAPHY: H. Grotefend, *Christian Egenolff* (Frankfurt, 1881).

Egge, Klaus, prominent Norwegian composer; b. Gransherad, Telemark, July 19, 1906; d. Oslo, March 7, 1979. He studied piano with Nils Larsen and composition with Fartein Valen; after a brief period of further instruction at the Hochschule für Musik in Berlin, he became engaged in organizational work in Norway; was president of the Society of Norwegian composers from 1945. In 1949 he received the State Salary of Art (a government life pension for outstanding artistic achievement). His style of composition is conditioned by Scandinavian modalities, within a framework of euphonious and resonantly modernistic harmonies. He likes to sign his scores with the notes E-g-g-e of his name, a motto which also serves him occasionally as a basic theme.
WORKS: 3 piano concertos: No. 1 (Oslo, Nov. 14, 1938); No. 2 (Oslo, Dec. 9, 1946); No. 3 (Bergen, April 25, 1974); *Sveinung Vreim* for Soli, Chorus, and Orch. (Oslo, Dec. 1, 1941); *Fjell-Norig (Mountainous Norway)* for Voice and Orch. (Oslo, Oct. 1, 1945); *Noreg-songer (The Norway Song)* for Chorus and Orch. (Oslo, May 2, 1952); 5 symphs.: No. 1, *Lagnadstonar (Sounds of Destiny;* Oslo, Oct. 4, 1945); No. 2, *Sinfonia giocosa* (Oslo, Dec. 9, 1949); No. 3, commissioned by the Louisville Orch. (Louisville, Ky., March 4, 1959); No. 4, *Sinfonia seriale sopra B.A.C.H—E.G.G.E* (Detroit, March 28, 1968); No. 5, *Sinfonia dolce quasi passacaglia* (Oslo, Sept. 27, 1969); *Elskhugskvaede (Love Song)* for Voice and Strings (1942); *Draumar i stjernesno (Starsnow Dreams),* 3 songs for Soprano and Orch. (1943); *Fanitullen (Devil's Dance),* ballet (Oslo, 1950); *Tårn over Oslo,* overture (1950); Violin Concerto (Oslo,

Nov. 5, 1953); Cello Concerto (Oslo, Sept. 9, 1966); Violin Sonata (1932); 2 piano sonatas: No. 1, *Draumkvede (Dream Vision;* 1933), and No. 2, *Patética* (1955); String Quartet (1933; revised 1963); 3 Fantasies for Piano in the rhythms of the Norwegian dances Halling, Springar, and Gangar, (1939); 2 wind quintets (1939, 1976); Piano Trio (1941); *Duo concertante* for Violin and Viola (1950); Sonatina for Harp (1974); choruses and songs.

Eggebrecht, Hans Heinrich, eminent German musicologist and editor; b. Dresden, Jan. 5, 1919. He attended the Gymnasium in Schleusingen, of which his father was superintendent; was drafted into the army during World War II, through which he went unscathed, and then studied music education in Berlin and Weimar; he received his teacher's certificate in 1948. He subsequently studied musicology with H.J. Moser, R. Münnich, and M. Schneider; received his Ph.D. in 1949 from the Univ. of Jena with the dissertation *Melchior Vulpius.* He was assistant lecturer under W. Vetter in music history at the Univ. of Berlin from 1949 to 1951; then did lexicographical work in Freiburg and taught musicology at the univ. there (1953–55); he completed his Habilitation there in 1955 with his *Studien zur musikalischen Terminologie* (publ. in Mainz, 1955; 2nd ed., 1968). He was Privatdozent at Erlangen Univ. (1955–56) and taught musicology at the Univ. of Heidelberg (1956–57). In 1961 he succeeded W. Gurlitt as prof. of musicology at the Univ. of Freiburg. In 1964 he became editor of the *Archiv für Musikwissenschaft.* One of his major musicological contributions was his publ. of the vol. on musical terms and historical subjects (*Sachteil*) for the 12th edition of the *Riemann Musik-Lexikon* (Mainz, 1967), in which he settles many debatable points of musical terminology. Equally important has been his editorship of the *Handwörterbuch der musikalischen Terminologie* since 1972. He also was an editor of the *Brockhaus-Riemann Musik-Lexikon* with Carl Dahlhaus (2 vols., Wiesbaden and Mainz, 1978).
WRITINGS: *Heinrich Schütz: Musicus poeticus* (Göttingen, 1959); *Ordnung und Ausdruck im Werk von Heinrich Schütz* (Kassel, 1961); *Die Orgelbewegung* (Stuttgart, 1967); *Schütz und Gottesdienst* (Stuttgart, 1969); *Versuch über die Wiener Klassik: die Tanzszene in Mozarts Don Giovanni* (Wiesbaden, 1972); *Zur Geschichte der Beethoven-Rezeption: Beethoven 1970* (Wiesbaden, 1972).

Eggen Arne, Norwegian composer; b. Trondheim, Aug. 28, 1881; d. Baerum, near Oslo, Oct. 26, 1955. He studied in Oslo and in Leipzig; toured Norway and Sweden giving organ recitals from 1927 to 1945 was president of the Society of Norwegian Composers. In 1934 he received the Norwegian State Salary of Art (a government life pension).
WORKS: 2 operas: *Olav Liljekrans,* after Ibsen (1931–40; Oslo, 1940), and *Cymbeline,* after Shakespeare (1943–48; Oslo, 1951); Symph. (Oslo, 1920); *King Olav,* oratorio (1930); Chaconne for Organ (1918); 2 violin sonatas; Piano Trio; many songs and

choral works.

Eggen, Erik, Norwegian composer and musicologist, brother of **Arne Eggen;** b. Trondheim, Nov. 17, 1877; d. Ringsaker, June 7, 1957. He was a schoolteacher in southern Norway (1898–1939); was editor of *Norsk Toneblad* (1910–17); concurrently devoted himself to the study of folk music; composed *Norsk rapsodi* for Orch., a cantata, and choral works, mostly in a folk-song vein; publ. a monograph on Grieg (1911).

Egghard, Julius (pen name of **Count Hardegen**), Austrian pianist; b. Vienna, April 24, 1834; d. there, March 23, 1867. He was a pupil of Czerny and became a concert pianist; wrote a number of piano pieces in salon style, which were extremely popular.

Egidi, Arthur, German organist and composer; b. Berlin, Aug. 9, 1859; d. there, June 3, 1943. He studied in Berlin; taught at Hoch's Cons. in Frankfurt (1885–92); then was organist and choral conductor in Berlin. He composed mostly for the organ; publ. a collection of reprints of works by old German masters under the title *Musikschätze der Vergangenheit.*

Egk, Werner, significant German composer; b. Auchsesheim, near Donauwörth, May 17, 1901; d. Inning, near Munich, July 10, 1983. His original name was **Mayer,** and rumor had it that he took the name Egk as a self-complimentary acronym for "ein grosser (or even ein genialer) Komponist." Egk himself rejected this frivolous suspicion, offering instead an even more fantastic explanation that Egk was a partial acronym of the name of his wife Elisabeth Karl, with the middle guttural added "for euphony." He studied piano with Anna Hirzel-Langenhan and composition with Carl Orff in Munich, where he made his permanent home. Primarily interested in theater music, he wrote several scores for a Munich puppet theater; was also active on the radio; then wrote ballet music to his own scenarios and a number of successful operas. He was also active as opera conductor and music pedagogue. He conducted at the Berlin State Opera from 1938 to 1941, and was head of the German Union of Composers from 1941 to 1945. He was commissioned to write music for the Berlin Olympiad in 1936, for which he received a Gold Medal. He also received a special commission of 10,000 marks from the Nazi Ministry of Propaganda. The apparent favor that Egk enjoyed during the Nazi reign made it necessary for him to stand trial before the Allied Committee for the de-Nazification proceedings in 1947; it absolved him of political taint. In 1950–53 he was director of the Berlin Hochschule für Musik. As a composer, Egk continued the tradition of Wagner and Richard Strauss, without excluding, however, the use of acidulous harmonies, based on the atonal extension of tonality. The rhythmic investiture of his works is often inventive and bold.
WORKS: Piano Trio (1922); Passacaglia for Strings (1923); String Quartet (1924); String Quintet (1924); radio opera, *Columbus* (Munich, July 13, 1933; first stage perf., Frankfurt, Jan. 13, 1942); *Die Zaubergeige,* opera in 3 acts (Frankfurt, May 19, 1935); *Fürchtlosigkeit und Wohlwollen* (Baden-Baden, April 3, 1936); *Olympische Festmusik* for Orch. (Berlin Olympiad, Aug. 1, 1936); cantatas: *Natur-Liebe-Tod* and *Mein Vaterland* (both perf. at Göttingen, June 26, 1937); *Peer Gynt,* opera (Berlin, Nov. 24, 1938, composer conducting; highly successful despite the inevitable comparisons with Grieg); *Joan von Zarissa,* ballet (Berlin, Jan. 20, 1940); *La Tentation de Saint Antoine* for Contralto and String Quartet (Baden-Baden, May 18, 1947); Piano Sonata (1947); *Abraxas,* ballet (Baden-Baden Radio, Dec. 7, 1947; stage perf., June 6, 1948, in Munich); *Circe,* opera after Calderón (Berlin, Dec. 18, 1948, composer conducting); 2 sonatas for Orch. (1948, 1969); *Französische Suite,* after Rameau, for Orch. (Munich, Jan. 28, 1950); *Ein Sommertag,* ballet (Berlin, June 11, 1950); *Allegria,* suite for Orch. (Baden-Baden radio, April 25, 1952); *Die chinesische Nachtigall,* ballet after Andersen (Munich, May 6, 1953); *Chanson et Romance* for Coloratura Soprano and Chamber Orch. (Aix-en-Provence, July 19, 1953); *Irische Legende,* opera after Yeats (Salzburg, Aug. 17, 1955); *Der Revisor,* opera after Gogol (Schwetzingen, May 9, 1957); *Variations on a Caribbean Theme* for Orch. (Baden-Baden, Jan. 18, 1960); *Die Verlobung in San Domingo,* opera (Munich, Nov. 27, 1963); *17 Days & 4 Minutes,* burlesque opera (Stuttgart, June 2, 1966); *Casanova in London,* ballet (Munich, Nov. 23, 1969); *Moria* for Orch. (Nuremberg, Jan. 12, 1973).
BIBLIOGRAPHY: B. Kohl and E. Nölle, eds., *Werner Egk: Das Bühnenwerk* (Munich, 1971); E. Krause, *Werner Egk: Oper und Ballet* (Wilhelmshaven, 1971).

Egli, Johann Heinrich, Swiss composer; b. Seegraben, near Zürich, March 4, 1742; d. Zürich, Dec. 19, 1810. He studied voice, violin, piano, and composition; diligently perused theoretical works by Kirnberger and Carl Philip Emanuel Bach. He composed mainly sacred choruses; publ. several song collections, among them *Lieder der Weisheit und Tugend* (Zürich, 1790); also publ. arrangements of Swiss folk songs, *Schweizerlieder* (Zürich, 1787).
BIBLIOGRAPHY: A. Nef, *Das Lied in der deutschen Schweiz* (Zürich, 1909).

Egmond, Max von, Dutch bass-baritone; b. Semarang (Java), Feb. 1, 1936. He received his musical training in the Netherlands; gained experience by entering voice competitions in Brussels and Munich. His career was enhanced by appearances in concerts and oratorios. He sang widely in Europe, and also had engagements in America.

Egorov, Yuri, talented Russian pianist; b. Kazan, May 28, 1954. He learned to play piano as a child in Kazan; in 1971 he won a prize at the Marguerite Long–Jacques Thibaud competition in Paris, then studied with Yakov Zak at the Moscow Cons. In 1974 he received 3rd place at the Tchaikovsky Competition in Moscow; subsequently launched a successful concert career; made his N.Y. debut in 1978; then gave numerous recitals and appeared as soloist with American orchs. He made his first tour of England in 1980; then settled in the Netherlands, but continued to tour widely in Europe and America, with notable acclaim. His playing is marked by an accomplished virtuoso technique and spontaneity of interpretation, particularly of the Romantic literature.

Ehlers, Alice, Austrian-American harpsichordist; b. Vienna, April 16, 1887; d. Los Angeles, March 1, 1981. She studied piano with Leschetizky in Vienna; during World War I she took lessons in harpsichord playing with Wanda Landowska in Berlin. In 1936 she emigrated to the U.S. From 1941 to 1967 she taught harpsichord at the Univ. of Southern Calif. in Los Angeles; she also gave courses at the Juilliard School of Music in N.Y. and at the Univ. of Calif. in Berkeley. She continued to appear in concert as a harpsichordist and gave occasional performances even as a nonagenarian.

Ehlert, Louis, German composer, conductor, and writer on music; b. Königsberg, Jan. 13, 1825; d. Wiesbaden, Jan. 4, 1884. In 1845 he entered the Leipzig Cons., where he studied with Mendelssohn and Schumann; then took music courses in Vienna and Berlin, where he lived from 1850 to 1863. He visited Italy; conducted the Società Cherubini in 1869; from 1869 to 1871 taught piano at Tausig's school for advanced pianists; then was active in Meiningen and Wiesbaden mainly as a piano teacher. He wrote a great many piano pieces; also *Frühlingssinfonie* and *Requiem für ein Kind.* His collection of essays, *Aus der Tonwelt* (Berlin, 1877), was publ. also in Eng. under the title *From the Tone World* (N.Y., 1885); he also wrote an entertaining vol., *Briefe über Musik an eine Freundin* (Berlin, 1859), which was issued in an Eng. trans. as *Letters on Music, to a Lady* (Boston, 1870).

Ehmann, Wilhelm, German musicologist; b. Freistatt, Dec. 5, 1904. He studied musicology at the univs. of Freiburg and Leipzig; received his Ph.D. in 1934 with the dissertation *Adam von Fulda als Vertreter der ersten deutschen Komponisten-Generation* (Berlin, 1936) from the Univ. of Freiburg; completed his Habilitation there with his *Der Thibaut-Behaghel-Kreis* in 1937. From 1934 to 1940 he was on the faculty of the Univ. of Freiburg; from 1940 to 1945 he taught at the Univ. of Innsbruck. In 1948 he founded and became director of the church-music school in Westphalia (later named the Hochschule für Kirchenmusik); he retired in 1972. He also taught at the Univ. of Münster (1948–54).
WRITINGS: *Die Chorführung* (2 vols., Kassel, 1949; 3rd ed., 1956; vol. II, in English, Minneapolis, 1938); *Tibilustrium: Das geistliche Blasen, Formen und Reformen* (Kassel, 1950); *Erziehung zur Kirchenmusik* (Gütersloh, 1951); *Erbe und Auftrag musikalischer Erneuerung: Entromantisierung der Singbewegung* (Kassel, 1951); *J.S. Bach in un-*
serem Leben (Wolfenbüttel, 1952); *Das Chorwesen in der Kulturkrise* (Regensburg, 1953); *Kirchenmusik, Vermächtnis und Aufgabe* (Darmstadt, 1958); *Alte Musik in der neuen Welt* (Darmstadt, 1961); *Der Bläserchor: Besinnung und Aufgabe* (Kassel, 1969).

Ehrenberg, Carl Emil Theodor, German conductor and composer; b. Dresden, April 6, 1878; d. Munich, Feb. 26, 1962. He studied with Draeseke at the Dresden Cons. (1894–98); from 1898 on was engaged as a conductor in Germany; in 1909–14 conducted concerts in Lausanne, Switzerland; in 1915–18 was an opera conductor in Augsburg; conducted concerts in Bad Homburg (1918–22); then became conductor at the Berlin State Opera (1922–24). Subsequently he devoted himself mainly to teaching; was a prof. at the Cologne Hochschule für Musik (1924–35) and at the Akademie der Tonkunst in Munich (1935–45).
WORKS: 2 operas: *Und selig sind* (1904) and *Anneliese* (after a tale by Hans Christian Andersen, 1922); several overtures; 2 symphs.; Sinfonietta; Cello Concerto; 4 string quartets; Piano Trio; Wind Quartet; String Trio; Violin Sonata; many choruses; songs; piano pieces.

Ehrlich, Abel, German-born Israeli composer; b. Cranz, Sept. 3, 1915. He studied music in Germany; then studied at the Music Academy of Zagreb (1934–38). He went to Palestine in 1939 and studied composition with Solomon Rosowsky at the Jerusalem Academy of Music (1939–44); attended the summer courses in new music led by Stockhausen, Nono, and others at Darmstadt (1959, 1961, 1963, 1967). In Israel he has taught in various schools, since 1964 at the Tel Aviv Academy. Until 1955 he based his music on Middle Eastern themes and folklore; since then he has developed a personal amalgam of traditional Jewish cantillation and modern serialism.
WORKS: *Immanuel Haromi,* musical spectacle in 3 scenes (1971); *Carolus-Music* for Instrumental Ensemble (1975); *arpmusic* for Baritone, Mime, 8 Instruments, and Electro-Acoustics, a tribute to the surrealist sculptor Hans Arp (1971); 6 string quartets (1947, 1947, 1952, 1962, 1967, 1969); *Bashrav* for Solo Violin (1953); *A Game of Chess* for Winds, Percussion, Piano, and Double Bass (1957); *The Towers and the Shadows* for Narrator, Singers, and Instruments (1960); *Testimony* for 2 Flutes (1961); *The Writing of Hezekiah* for Soprano, Violin, Oboe, and Bassoon (1962); 4 wind quintets (1966–70); *Radiations* for Piano (1967); *And Though Thou Set Thy Nest among the Stars* for Orch. (1969); *Music for Solo Cello* (1970); *Evolution* for Orch. (1970); *The Answer* for Tenor, Flute, and Saxophone (1970); *Deliver Them That Are Drawn unto Death* for String Orch. (1970); *Trio for Violins* (1970); *Improvisations with a Game in Hell* for String Trio (1970); Trio for Horn, Cello, and Percussion (1970); *The Unicorn* for 12 Singers, 3 Percussionists, and 3 Oboes (1971); *7 Minutes* for Strings (1971); *Seeing . . .* for Singer, Violin, and Cello (1971); Divertimento for Oboe, Clarinet, 2 Horns, and Strings (1971); *Job 7,*

11–16 for Baritone, Chorus, and Orch. (1971); *Ne subito . . .* for Chorus and Orch. (1971); *Comedy* for Orch. (1971); Trio for Violin, Flute, and Bassoon (1971); Trio for Horn, Violin, and Piano (1972); Piano Sonata (1973); Music for Violin, Cello, Piano, and 2 Tape Recorders (1974); *Diario* for Solo Flute (1975); *A Vision of God* for 8 Groups, each consisting of Soprano, Alto, Violin, and Viola (1975); *Personal Boxes* for Soprano and Instruments (1976); *Many Wonders* for Soprano and Wind Quintet (1977); *Sonnets,* after Shakespeare, for Soprano, Baritone, Chorus, Oboe, Violin, and Viola (1977).

Ehrlich, (Karl) Heinrich (Alfred), Austrian pianist and writer on music; b. Vienna, Oct. 5, 1822; d. Berlin, Dec. 30, 1899. He was a pupil of Henselt and Thalberg (piano), and of Sechter (composition). For several years he lived at Hannover as court pianist; then at Wiesbaden (1855–57), London, Frankfurt, and Berlin. He was a piano teacher at the Stern Cons. from 1864 to 1872; and again from 1886 to 1898. He was also music critic of the *Berliner Tageblatt.*
WRITINGS: *Schlaglichter und Schlagschatten aus der Musikwelt* (1872); *Für den Ring des Nibelungen gegen Bayreuth* (1876); *Wie übt man am Klavier?* (1879; 2nd ed., 1884; Eng. trans. as *How to Practice on the Piano,* 2nd ed., 1901); *Die Musikästhetik in ihrer Entwickelung von Kant bis auf die Gegenwart* (1881); *Lebenskunst und Kunstleben* (1884); *Wagnersche Kunst und wahres Christentum* (1888); *Aus allen Tonarten* (1888); *Musikstudium und Klavierspiel* (1891); *Dreissig Jahre Künstlerleben* (1893); *Berühmte Klavierspieler der Vergangenheit und Gegenwart* (1893; in Eng. as *Celebrated Pianists of the Past and Present Time,* 1894); *Berühmte Geiger der Vergangenheit und Gegenwart* (1893; in Eng. as *Celebrated Violinists, Past and Present,* 1897); *Die Ornamentik in Beethovens Sonaten* (1896); *Die Ornamentik in Beethovens Klavierwerken* (1896; in French and Eng., 1898); also the novels *Abenteuer eines Emporkömmlings* (1858); *Kunst und Handwerk* (1862); *Vier Noveletten aus dem Musikantenleben* (1881).

Ehrling, Sixten, noted Swedish pianist and conductor; b. Malmö, April 3, 1918. He studied piano, organ, composition, and conducting at the Royal Academy of Music's Cons. in Stockholm. After a brief career as a concert pianist he joined the staff of the Royal Opera in Stockholm as a rehearsal pianist, and made his conducting debut there in 1940. He then took conducting lessons with Karl Böhm in Dresden (1941) and, after the end of the war, with Albert Wolff in Paris. In 1942 he was appointed conductor in Göteborg; in 1944 he became a conductor at the Royal Opera in Stockholm, where he served as chief conductor from 1953 to 1960. From 1963 to 1973 he was music director of the Detroit Symph. Orch.; then headed the orch. conducting class at the Juilliard School of Music, N.Y. In 1978 he became music adviser and principal guest conductor of the Denver Symph. Orch., and from 1979, principal guest conductor. He excels in the repertoire of Romantic music, and particularly in his authentic interpretation of works by Scandinavian composers.

Eibenschütz, José, German conductor; b. Frankfurt, Jan. 8, 1872; d. Sülzhayn, Harz, Nov. 27, 1952. He studied at the Hoch Cons. in Frankfurt; in 1894 was appointed orch. conductor in Åbo, Finland; there he remained until 1905; subsequent positions as conductor were at Görlitz (1905–8) and with the Verein Hamburgischer Musikfreunde (1908–20), the Oslo Phil. (1921–27), and North German Radio (1928–33). From 1938–46 he conducted in Scandinavia and in Russia; he returned to Germany in 1946.

Eichberg, Julius, German violinist and composer; b. Düsseldorf, June 13, 1824; d. Boston, Jan. 19, 1893. His first teachers were J. Fröhlich (at Würzburg) and J. Rietz (at Düsseldorf); he then (1843–45) attended the Brussels Cons., studying under Fétis, Meerts, and Bériot; in 1846 was appointed prof. of violin and composition at the Geneva Cons.; in 1856 came to N.Y.; settled in Boston in 1859 as director of the Museum Concerts (till 1866). He also became director of the Boston Cons. and superintendent of music in the public schools; he founded the Eichberg School for Violin.
WORKS: Light operas: *The Doctor of Alcantara* (Boston, April 7, 1862); *The Rose of Tyrol* (1865); *The 2 Cadis* (Boston, March 5, 1868); studies, duets, and characteristic pieces for violin; trios and quartets for strings; songs.

Eichborn, Hermann, German composer, writer, and inventor; b. Breslau, Oct. 30, 1847; d. Gries, near Bozen, April 15, 1918. He studied jurisprudence; then became interested in music and took organ lessons with the organist of the Breslau Cathedral. His income from a wine-brewing business in Gries enabled him to devote himself to writing and the invention of instruments. He also supported a local orch. which performed several of his works. In 1882 he patented his invention of the soprano French horn in F, which he called Oktav Waldhorn, and which was adopted in many Silesian bands.
WORKS: Sonata for Waldhorn and Piano; *Rondo brillant* for Waldhorn and Orch.; *Trompeters Berglied,* "echo piece" for 2 Trumpets; *Trompeter blas! Nur ein Spass!* for 2 Trumpets and Orch.; several operettas.
WRITINGS: Numerous pamphlets on instruments: *Die Trompete in alter und neuer Zeit* (Leipzig, 1881; new ed., Wiesbaden, 1968); *Das alte Clarinblasen auf Trompeten* (Leipzig, 1894); *Die Dämpfung beim Horn* (Leipzig, 1897); *Militarismus und Musik* (Leipzig, 1909).

Eichheim, Henry, American composer and violinist; b. Chicago, Jan. 3, 1870; d. Montecito, near Santa Barbara, Calif., Aug. 22, 1942. He received his elementary musical training from his father, **Meinhard Eichheim,** a cellist in the Theodore Thomas Orch.; then studied with C. Becker and L. Lichtenberg at the Chicago Musical College. After a season as a violinist in the Thomas Orch. in Chicago, he was a member of the Boston Symph. Orch. (1890–

1912); then devoted himself to concert work and composition. He made 4 trips to the Orient (1915, 1919, 1922, 1928) and collected indigenous instruments, which he subsequently used in his orch. music. All of his works are on oriental subjects.

WORKS: *Oriental Impressions,* or *The Story of the Bell* (Boston Symph., March 24, 1922, composer conducting); *The Rivals,* ballet based on an ancient Chinese legend (Chicago, Jan. 1, 1925; as an orch. piece, under the title *Chinese Legend* Boston Symph., April 3, 1925, composer conducting); *Malay Mosaic* (International Composers' Guild, N.Y., March 1, 1925); *Impressions of Peking* and *Korean Sketch* for Chamber Orch. and a group of Oriental Instruments (Venice Festival of the International Society for Contemporary Music, Sept. 3, 1925); *Burma,* symph. poem (Neighborhood Playhouse Co., N.Y., March 16, 1926, as incidental music for a play; Chicago Symph. Orch., Feb. 18, 1927, composer conducting; *Java* (Philadelphia Orch., Nov. 8, 1929, composer conducting; contains a "gamelan" section, with 45 instruments); *Bali* (Philadelphia Orch., Stokowski conducting, April 20, 1933, at a Youth Concert); Violin Sonata (1934); other chamber music. The harmonic idiom of these works is derived from Debussy and Scriabin.

Eichhorn, Kurt, German conductor; b. Munich, Aug. 4, 1908. He studied with Hermann Zilcher; made his professional debut at the Bielefeld Opera in 1932. In 1941 he conducted at the Dresden State Opera. After World War II, he returned to Munich as a conductor at the Gärtnerplatz Theater; also conducted at the Bavarian State Opera. From 1967 to 1975 he served as chief conductor of the Munich Radio Orch.

Eichner, Ernst, German composer and bassoon virtuoso; b. Arolsen, Hesse, Feb. (baptized, Feb. 15) 1740; d. Potsdam, 1777. He was concertmaster at the court of Duke Christian IV of Zweibrücken in 1769–72; visited Paris with the orch. in 1770, and after a very successful season in London (1773) was appointed a member of the orch. of Prince Frederick William of Prussia.

WORKS: 31 symphs. (thematic catalogue in Denkmäler der Tonkunst in Bayern, 13, formerly 7.ii); piano concertos; piano trios; piano sonatas; duets for violin and viola; quartets for flute, violin, viola, and cello; quintets for flute and string quartet. His Symph. in D was publ. by Riemann in Denkmäler der Tonkunst in Bayern, 15 (formerly 8.ii); some chamber music, in vols. 27 and 28 (15, 16); his Symph. in F (1772) was revised for violin and piano by R. Sondheimer in 1923.

BIBLIOGRAPHY: A. Volk, *Ernst Eichner* (Cologne, 1943); Marianne Reissinger, *Die Sinfonien Ernst Eichners* (Wiesbaden, 1970).

Eijken, Jan Albert van. See **Eyken, Jan Albert van.**

Eilers, Albert, German bass; b. Cöthen, Dec. 21, 1830; d. Darmstadt, Sept. 4, 1896. He studied at the Cons. of Milan; made his opera debut in Dresden

(1854); sang at the German Theater in Prague (1858–65). In 1876 Wagner selected him to sing the part of the giant Fasolt at Bayreuth. In 1882 he became a member of the Darmstadt Opera. He wrote a fairly successful comic opera, *Die Johannisnacht* (Koblenz, 1889).

Eimert Herbert, German music theorist; b. Bad Kreuznach, April 8, 1897; d. Düsseldorf, Dec. 15, 1972. He studied at the Cons. and the Univ. of Cologne (musicology and philosophy); became interested in new musical techniques and publ. several essays on the subject, among them *Atonale Musiklehre* (Leipzig, 1924) and *Lehrbuch der Zwölftontechnik* (Wiesbaden, 1950). He composed several pioneering electronic works including *Chimes* (1953–54); *Etude on Sound Mixtures* (1954); and *5 Compositions* (1955–56).

Einem, Gottfried von, outstanding Austrian composer; b. Bern, Switzerland (where his father was attached to the Austrian embassy), Jan. 24, 1918. He went to Germany as a child; studied at Plön, Holstein; then was opera coach at the Berlin Staatsoper. In 1938 he was arrested by the Gestapo, and spent 4 months in prison. After his release he studied composition with Boris Blacher in Berlin (1941–43); was later (1944) in Dresden, where he became resident composer and music adviser at the Dresden State Opera; was then active in Salzburg. In 1953 he visited the U.S.; then settled in Vienna; in 1965 was appointed prof. at the Hochschule für Musik there. Having absorbed the variegated idioms of advanced techniques, Einem produced a number of successful short operas and ballets; in his music he emphasized the dramatic element by dynamic and rhythmic effects; his harmonic idiom is terse and strident; his vocal line often borders on atonality, but remains singable.

WORKS: OPERAS: *Dantons Tod* (Salzburg, Aug. 6, 1947); *Der Prozess (The Trial),* after Kafka (Salzburg Festival, Aug. 17, 1953); *Der Zerrissene* (Hamburg, Sept. 17, 1964); *Der Besuch der alten Dame,* after Dürrenmatt's play (Vienna, May 23, 1971); *Kabale und Liebe,* after Schiller's play (Vienna, Dec. 17, 1976); *Jesu Hochzeit* (Vienna, May 18, 1980; caused a scandal for depicting Christ as having taken a wife). BALLETS: *Prinzessin Turandot* (Dresden, Feb. 5, 1944); *Rondo vom goldenen Kalb* (Hamburg, Feb. 1, 1952); *Pas de cœur* (Munich, July 22, 1952); *Glück, Tod und Traum* (Alpbach, Aug. 23, 1954); *Medusa* (Vienna, Jan. 16, 1957; revised 1971). FOR ORCH.: *Capriccio* (Berlin, March 3, 1943); Concerto for Orch. (1943; Berlin, April 3, 1944, Karajan conducting); *Orchestra Music* (1947; Vienna, June 21, 1948, Böhm conducting); *Serenade* for Double String Orch. (1949; Berlin, Jan. 31, 1950); *Hymnus* for Alto, Chorus, and Orch. (1949; Vienna, March 31, 1951); *Meditations* (Louisville, Nov. 6, 1954); Piano Concerto (1955; Berlin, Oct. 6, 1956); *Symphonic Scenes* (1956; Boston, Oct. 11, 1957); *Ballade* (1957; Cleveland, March 20, 1958, Szell conducting); *Das Stundenlied* for Chorus and Orch., after Brecht (Hamburg, March 1, 1959); *Dance Rondo* (Munich, Nov.

13, 1959); *Nachtstück* (1960; Kassel, Nov. 16, 1962); *Von der Liebe*, lyrical fantasies for High Voice and Orch. (Vienna, June 18, 1961); *Philadelphia Symphony* (Vienna, Nov. 11, 1961, Solti conducting; Philadelphia, Nov. 9, 1962); *Chamber Songs* for Voice and Orch. (1964); Violin Concerto (1966; Vienna, May 31, 1970); *Hexameron* (1969; Los Angeles, Feb. 19, 1970); *Bruckner Dialog* (1971; Linz, March 23, 1974); *Rosa Mystica* for Voice and Orch. (1972; Vienna, June 4, 1973; Fischer-Dieskau, soloist); *An die Nachgeborenen* for Soloists, Chorus, and Orch. (N.Y., Oct. 4, 1976); *Wiener Symphonie* (1976; Minneapolis, Nov. 16, 1977); *Arietten* for Piano and Orch. (1977; Berlin, Feb. 20, 1978); *Ludi Leopoldini*, variations on a theme of Emperor Leopold I (Berlin, Oct. 12, 1980). CHAMBER WORKS: Sonata for Violin and Piano (1949); *Sacred Sonata* for Soprano, Trumpet, and Organ (1971); *Die traumenden Knaben* for Chorus, Bassoon, and Clarinet (1972); 3 string quartets (1975, 1977, 1980); Wind Quintet (1975); Sonata for Solo Violin (1976); Sonata for Solo Viola (1980); *Steinbeis Serenade* for 8 Instruments (1981); 8 sets of lieder (1944–80).

Einstein, Alfred, preeminent German musicologist; b. Munich, Dec. 30, 1880; d. El Cerrito, Calif., Feb. 13, 1952. Although he was friendly with Albert Einstein, the two were not related; a search through the genealogies of both revealed no common ancestor. Alfred Einstein first studied law, then turned to music and took courses with Sandberger and Beer-Walbrunn at the Univ. of Munich, receiving a Dr.Phil. in 1903 with the thesis *Zur deutschen Literatur für Viola da Gamba im 16. und 17. Jahrhundert* (Leipzig, 1905); in 1918–33 he was editor of the *Zeitschrift für Musikwissenschaft;* lived in Munich until 1927 as music critic of the *Münchner Post;* in 1927–33 he was an influential critic of the *Berliner Tageblatt;* in 1933 he left Germany; lived in London and Italy (near Florence); in 1938 settled in the U.S.; taught at Smith College (retired, 1950); was naturalized as an American citizen on March 2, 1945.

WRITINGS: Revised eds. of Riemann's *Musiklexikon* (9th ed., 1919; 10th eds., 1922; 11th enlarged ed., 1929); *Neues Musiklexikon* (German ed. of A. Eaglefield-Hull's *Dictionary of Modern Music and Musicians,* 1926); *Geschichte der Musik,* with *Beispielsammlung zur älteren Musikgeschichte* (1917–18; 6th ed., revised, 1953); new ed. (3rd) of Köchel's *Mozart Verzeichnis* (Leipzig, 1937; very valuable; reprint ed. with numerous corrections, Ann Arbor, 1947); *A Short History of Music* (London, 1936; N.Y., 1937; 4th ed., 1954; trans. of *Geschichte der Musik*); *Gluck* (London, 1936). He contributed a great many valuable papers to the publications of the International Music Society and to other learned editions, to Festschriften, Jahrbücher, etc.; his articles for the *Musical Quarterly* are especially notable: "The Madrigal" (Oct. 1924); "Dante, on the Way to the Madrigal" (Jan. 1939; also "A Supplement," Oct. 1939); etc. He also prepared a modern ed. of Andrea Antico's publication of 1517, *Canzoni, Sonetti, Strambotti, et Frottole*

(Northampton, Mass., 1941); ed. a collection, *The Golden Age of the Madrigal* (N.Y., 1942). His writings in America (publ. in Eng. trans. from his original German) include: *Greatness in Music* (N.Y., 1941; German ed., *Grösse in der Musik,* Zürich, 1951); *Mozart: His Character, His Work* (N.Y., 1945; 4th ed., 1949; German original, 1947); *Music in the Romantic Era* (N.Y., 1947; German ed., *Die Romantik in der Musik,* Vienna, 1950); *The Italian Madrigal* (3 vols., Princeton, 1949; of fundamental importance); *Schubert: A Musical Portrait* (N.Y., 1950; German trans., 1952); *Essays on Music,* ed. by P. Lang (N.Y., 1956; posthumous; 2nd ed., revised, 1958). A profound scholar, Einstein was also a brilliant journalist, with a vivid, richly metaphorical style, capable of conveying to the reader an intimate understanding of music of different eras.

Eisenberg, Maurice, outstanding cellist; b. Königsberg, Feb. 24, 1900; d. (while teaching a cello class at the Juilliard School of Music) New York, Dec. 13, 1972. He was brought to the U.S. as a child; studied violin; then, at the age of 12, took up the cello. He played as a youth in café orchs., and studied at the Peabody Cons. in Baltimore; was a cellist of the Philadelphia Orch. (1917–19); then joined the N.Y. Symph. (under Walter Damrosch). He went to Europe in 1927 and studied in Berlin with Hugo Becker; in Leipzig with Julius Klengel; in Paris with Alexanian; and in Spain with Casals; then taught at the Ecole Normale in Paris (1930–37); returning to the U.S., he gave a concert in N.Y. (Dec. 27, 1937) with excellent success; then appeared with major symph. orchs.; taught at various colleges; publ. a book, *Cello Playing of Today* (1957).

Eisenberger, Severin, Polish pianist; b. Cracow, July 25, 1879; d. New York, Dec. 11, 1945. He studied with Leschetizky in Vienna; was a prof. at the Cracow Cons. from 1914–21; lived several years in Vienna, and later came to the U.S. He played as a soloist with the Cincinnati Symph. Orch. in 1935, and gave recitals in Cleveland and elsewhere in the U.S.

Eisfeld, Theodor, German conductor; b. Wolfenbüttel, April 11, 1816; d. Wiesbaden, Sept. 2, 1882. He conducted at the Wiesbaden court theater (1839–43); then in Paris. He occasionally visited Italy; took lessons with Rossini at Bologna; became an honorary member of the Santa Cecilia Academy. From 1848–66, he lived in N.Y.; conducted the N.Y. Phil. for several years, and the Harmonic Society from its foundation; established quartet soirées in 1851 with Noll, Reyer, and Eichhorn, joined also by Otto Dresel as pianist. Till 1865 he alternated with Bergmann in conducting the Phil. Concerts in N.Y.; retired to Wiesbaden in 1866.

Eisler, Hanns, remarkable German composer; b. Leipzig, July 6, 1898; d. Berlin, Sept. 6, 1962. He studied at the New Vienna Cons.; was a pupil of Arnold Schoenberg in composition; won the Music Prize of the City of Vienna (1924); taught in Berlin from 1925 to 1933; came to the U.S. in 1933; lectured on music at The New School for Social Research in N.Y. (1935–36); was musical assistant to Charlie Chaplin in Hollywood (1942–47); left the U.S. under the terms of "voluntary deportation" in 1948, on account of his radical political past; then lived in Vienna and in Berlin. Under Schoenberg's influence, he adopted the 12-tone method of composition; most of his symph. works are in this advanced style. However, he demonstrated his capacity for writing simple songs for use of choral ensembles; several of his choruses for workers and for the Red Army have become popular in Russia. Eisler was the author of the music of the national anthem of the German Democratic Republic, *Auferstanden aus Ruinen,* adopted in 1949. An edition of his collected works was initiated by the German Academy of the Arts in East Berlin in connection with the Hanns Eisler Archive in 1968, in 3 vols.: I, vocal music; II, instrumental music; III, writings and documents.

WORKS: Opera, *Johannes Faustus* (East Berlin, March 11, 1953); over 40 scores of incidental music, to plays by Brecht (*Rote Revue; Die Rundköpfe und die Spitzköpfe; Galileo Galilei; Die Tage der Kommune;* etc.), Ernst Toller (*Feuer aus dem Kesseln*), Feuchtwanger (*Kalkutta, 4. Mai*), Shakespeare, Schiller, Aristophanes; about 40 film scores (*Der Rat der Götter; Die Hexen von Salem; Trübe Wasser;* etc.); cantatas (*Tempo der Zeit; Die Massnahme; Kalifornische Ballade;* etc.); several cantatas to texts by Brecht (*Die Weissbrotkantate; Kantate im Exil; Kriegskantate; Kantate auf den Tod eines Genossen;* etc.); *Deutsche Symphonie* for Soli, 2 Speakers, Chorus, and Orch. (Paris, June 25, 1937); 6 orch. suites (Nos. 2–6 from film scores; 1930–34); *Kleine Symphonie* (1931–32); *5 Orchestral Pieces* (1938); *Kammersinfonie* (1940); *Rhapsody* for Orch. and Soprano (1949); *Ernste Gesänge* for Baritone and String Orch. (1962); chamber music: 2 nonets (1939); 2 septets (1941–47); *Divertimento* for Wind Quintet (1923); *14 Arten, den Regen zu beschreiben* for Flute, Clarinet, Violin, Cello, and Piano (1947); String Quartet (1941); Quintet for Flute, Clarinet, Violin, Cello, and Piano (1941–44); Sonata for Flute, Oboe, and Harp (1935); Duo for Violin and Cello (1925); Violin Sonata (1937); 3 piano sonatas (1922, 1923, 1943); piano albums for children; numerous choruses; mass songs, among them several to Brecht's words (*Das Einheitsfrontlied,* etc.). He publ. a book, *Composing for the Films* (N.Y., 1947).

BIBLIOGRAPHY: Hanns Eisler, *Reden und Aufsätze* (Leipzig, 1961); I. Nestyev, *Hanns Eisler and His Songs* (Moscow, 1962); N. Notowicz, *Hanns Eisler Quellennachweise* (Leipzig, 1966); E. Klemm, *Hanns Eisler: Für Sie porträtiert* (Leipzig, 1973); A. Betz, *Hanns Eisler: Musik seiner Zeit* (Munich, 1976; in Eng. as *Hanns Eisler: Political Musician;* Cambridge, 1982); G. Mayer, ed., *Hans Eisler: Musik und Politik. Schriften, 1948–1962* (Leipzig, 1982).

Eisler, Paul, Austrian pianist and conductor; b. Vienna, Sept. 9, 1875; d. New York, Oct. 16, 1951. He was a pupil of Bruckner at the Vienna Cons.; conducted in Riga, Vienna, and at the Metropolitan Opera in N.Y.; made numerous tours as accompanist for Caruso, Ysaÿe, and other celebrated artists; composed several operettas (*Spring Brides; The Sentinel; The Little Missus; In the Year 1814*).

Eisma, Will, Dutch violinist and composer; b. Sungailiat, island of Bangka, Indonesia, May 13, 1929. He learned violin from his father; then studied theory with Kees van Baaren at the Rotterdam Cons. (1948–53); in 1959–61 he took a course with Petrassi at the Santa Cecilia Academy in Rome; also studied electronic music in Bilthoven. He was employed as an orch. violinist with the Rotterdam Phil. (1953–59) and since 1961 with the Hilversum Radio Chamber Orch., where he joined a group of avant-garde musicians, Instrumental Circuitry Ensemble. In his works he cultivates a strong polyphonic idiom in an uncompromisingly dissonant counterpoint, while the titles reflect preoccupations with structural abstractions.

WORKS: 3 orch. concertos (1958, 1959, 1960); Concerto for 2 Violins and Orch. (1961); *Taurus* for Orch. (1963); *Volumina* for Orch. (1964); *Diaphora* for 15 Strings, Harpsichord, Marimbaphone, and Percussion (1964); *Pages from Albion Moonlight* for 2 Mezzo-sopranos, Baritone, Chorus, and Orch. (1968); *5 Roses for Diana* for 16 Amplified Winds (1969); *Orchestral Music with Voice* for Soloists, Chorus, and Orch. (1969); *Vanbridge Concerto* for Horn Player (on 2 different Horns, and Tuba) and Orch. (Einhoven, Nov. 18, 1970); *Little Lane,* Concerto for Oboe and Orch. (Hilversum, Feb. 15, 1974); *Le Choix du costume est libre,* concerto for Solo String Trio and Chamber Orch. (1974); Duo for Violin and Viola (1956); *Concert Piece* for Violin and Piano (1956); Septet (1959); Sonata for Clarinet, Horn, Violin, Viola, and Cello (1959); Solo Flute Sonatina (1959); Violin Sonatina (1960); 4 Duos for Violins (1961); String Quintet (1961); 2 Madrigals for Violin and Piano (1962); *Diaphonia* for Oboe, Violin, Viola, and Cello (1962); *Archipel* for String Quartet (1964); *Affairs II* for Recorder and Harpsichord (1964), and *III* for Oboe, Clarinet, and Bassoon (1965); *Fontemara* for Wind Quintet (1965); *World within World* for Oboe, Violin, Viola, and Cello (1966); *Klein protokol* for Violin and Cello (1966); *Non-lecture IV* for Solo Violin (1967); *Hot Powdery Stones* for Solo Alto Recorder (1968); *Because It Is* for Oboe, Harpsichord, and Percussion (1968); *Non-lecture III* for Solo Viola (1970); *Gezang XXIII* for Violin and Percussion (1970); *La Sonorité suspendue* for String Trio (1970); *If . . .* for Wind and String Quartets (1970); *Non-lecture II* for Solo Saxophone (1971); *Le Gibet* for Baritone, 7 Instruments, and Live Electronics (1971); *The Light of the Cold Still Moon* for Cello and Piano (1972); *10 Flutes and Tape* (1973); *Collected Papers II* for Solo Instrument, Percussion, and Synthesizer (1973–74); *Concert à vapeur* for Violin, Tape, and Synthesizer (1974); *Helena Is Coming Later* for 2 Violins, Viola, Cello, and Synthesizer (1975); *Le Cheval mort* for Mezzo-soprano, Bass Clarinet, Piano, Percussion, 2 Synthesizers, and Tape (1976); tape pieces; songs.

Eitler, Esteban, Austrian-Chilean composer; b. Bolzano, Tyrol, June 25, 1913; d. São Paulo, Brazil, June 25, 1960. He studied at the Univ. of Budapest; left Europe in 1936; went to Buenos Aires, where he was associated with modernist music groups; in 1945 he settled in Santiago, Chile.

WORKS: *Microsinfonia politonal* (1943) for Full Orch. and *Policromía* (1950) for String Orch.; *Serie Boliviana* for Flute and String Orch. (1941); Concertino for Piano and 11 Instruments (1947); Concertino for Horn and 11 Instruments (1949); Wind Quintet (1945); Quartet for Piccolo, Flute, Trumpet, and Saxophone (1945); Quartet for Flute, Violin, Viola, and Cello (1950); *Microsinfonia atonal* for Orch. (1956).

Eitner, Robert, eminent German musicologist; b. Breslau, Oct. 22, 1832; d. Templin, Feb. 2, 1905. He was a pupil of M. Brosig; settled (1853) in Berlin as a teacher, and gave concerts (1857–59) of his own compositions. He established a piano school in 1863, and publ. *Hilfsbuch beim Klavierunterricht* (1871). He devoted himself chiefly to musical literature, and especially to research on works of the 16th and 17th centuries. One of the founders of the Berlin *Gesellschaft für Musikforschung,* he edited its *Monatshefte für Musikgeschichte* from 1869 till his death; also the *Publikationen älterer praktischer und theoretischer Musikwerke.*

WRITINGS: "Verzeichnis neuer Ausgaben alter Musikwerke aus der frühesten Zeit bis zum Jahr 1800," *Monatshefte* (1871); *Bibliographie der Musiksammelwerke des 16. und 17. Jahrhunderts* (with Haberl, Lagerberg, and Pohl); "Verzeichnis der gedruckten Werke von Hans Leo Hassler und Orlandus de Lassus," *Monatshefte* (1873–74); "S.G. Staden's 'Seelewig,' " *Monatshefte* (1881); *Die Oper von ihren ersten Anfängen bis 1750* (3 vols., 1881–85); *Quellen und Hilfswerke beim Studium der Musikgeschichte* (1891); *Buch- und Musikaliendrucker nebst Notenstecher* (1904; as supplement to *Monatshefte*). His principal work is the great *Biographisch-bibliographisches Quellenlexikon der Musiker und Musikgelehrten der Christlichen Zeitrechnung bis zur Mitte des 19. Jahrhunderts* (10 vols., Leipzig, 1899–1904; additions and corrections publ. from 1913–16 in a quarterly, *Miscellanea Musicae Bio-bibliographica,* ed. by H. Springer, M. Schneider, and W. Wolffheim; reprinted N.Y., 1947). Among Eitner's compositions (several of which were publ.) are a biblical opera, *Judith;* an overture; a piano fantasia on themes from *Tristan und Isolde;* songs.

Eitz, Karl Andreas, German singing teacher; b. Wehrstedt, near Halberstadt, June 25, 1848; d. Eisleben, April 18, 1924. He originated a new system of solmisation ("Tonwortmethode"), somewhat similar to the English tonic sol-fa system; it is widely used in German music schools.

WRITINGS: *Das mathematisch-reine Tonsystem* (1891); *100 geistliche Liedweisen in Tonsilben gesetzt* (1893); *Deutsche Singfibel* (1899); *Tonwort-Wandtafel* (1907); *Bausteine zum Schulgesangunterricht im Sinne der Tonwortmethode* (Leipzig, 1911; 2nd ed., edited by F. Bennedik, 1928).

BIBLIOGRAPHY: G. Borchers, *Karl Eitz* (1908); O. Messmer, *Die Tonwortmethode von Karl Eitz* (Würzburg, 1911); F. Bennedik, *Historische und psychologisch-musikalische Untersuchungen über die Tonwortmethode von Eitz* (Langensalza, 1914); M. Koch, *Kurzgefasste Einführung in das Eitzsche Tonwort* (1925); F. Bennedik and A. Strube, *Handbuch für den Tonwortunterricht* (1926); R. Junker and R.M. Breithaupt, *Tonwort-Klavierschule* (1933); W. Stolte, *Carl Eitz in seiner Bedeutung für Wissenschaft und Schule* (Detmold, 1951).

Ek, Gunnar, Swedish organist, cellist and composer; b. Asarum, Blekinge, June 21, 1900; d. Lund, June 21, 1981. He studied organ, cello, and composition at the Stockholm Cons.; played cello in the Swedish film industry orch. (1928–37). In 1942 he went to Lund, where he was employed as an organist.

WORKS: 3 symphs. (1928, revised 1942; 1932; 1936); *Swedish Fantasy* for Orch. (1935); Fantasy for Violin and Orch. (1939); Piano Concerto (1944); *Doomsday Cantata* (1946); *Dig vare lov och pris, o Krist,* choral fantasy for Chorus, Organ, and Strings (1950; Malmö, Dec. 13, 1964); *Fantasy, Fugue and Coda* for Strings (1963); Suite for Organ (1966); *Dorisk Suite* for Strings and 5 Winds (1966; revised 1968–69); *Variations on a Chorale Theme* for Strings (1969); Wind Octet (1970); Concertino for Strings (1971); songs.

Ekier, Jan, Polish pianist and composer; b. Cracow, Aug. 29, 1913. He studied composition with K. Sikorski and piano with Z. Drzewiecki; became a concert pianist; taught piano at the State College of Music in Warsaw. Among his works are *Highland Suite* for Chamber Orch. (1936); *Variations and Fugue* for String Quartet (1937); Piano Concerto (1949); *Melodies in Color* for Mixed Chorus and Orch., to words from folk songs in Polish, Russian, German, French, and English (1951).

Eklund, Hans, Swedish composer; b. Sandviken, July 1, 1927. He studied at the Royal Academy of Music in Stockholm with Lars-Erik Larsson (1949–52); then went to Berlin, where he took lessons with Ernst Pepping (1954). His music follows a tradition of neo-Classicism; most of his instrumental works are set in Baroque forms.

WORKS: Radio opera, *Moder Svea (Mother Svea)* for Soloists, Chorus, Trumpet, and Strings (Swedish Radio, Oct. 7, 1972); Variations for Strings (1952); *Symphonic Dances* (1954); 6 numbers of *Musica da camera:* No. 1, for Cello and Chamber Orch. (1955); No. 2, *Art Tatum in Memoriam,* for Trumpet, Piano, Percussion, and Strings (1956); No. 3, for Violin and Chamber Orch. (1957); No. 4, for Piano and Orch. (1959); No. 5, Fantasia, for Cello and String Orch. (1970); No. 6, for Oboe and Chamber Orch. (1970); 4 symphs.: No. 1, *Sinfonia seria* (1958); No. 2, *Sinfonia breve* (1964); No. 3, *Sinfonia rustica* (1967–68); No. 4, *Hjalmar Branting in memoriam,* for Narrator, Orch., and Tape (1973–74); *Music for*

Orchestra (1960); *Bocetos españoles* for Chamber Orch. (1961); *Songs from Stahl,* cantata (1961); *Variazioni brevi* for Orch. (1962); *Introduzione-Versioni e Finale* for Strings (1962–63); *Facce* for Orch. (1964); *Toccata* for Orch. (1966); *Interludio* for Orch. (1967); *Primavera* for Strings (1967); *Pezzo elegiaco* for Cello, Percussion, and Strings (1969); *Introduction and Allegro* for Harpsichord and String Orch. (1972); Concerto for Trombone, Winds, and Percussion (1972); 4 string quartets (withdrawn, 1954, 1960, 1964); *Little Serenade* for Violin, Clarinet, and Double Bass (1954); Solo Violin Sonata (1956); *Improvisata* for Wind Quintet (1958); *Canzona and Dance* for Solo Violin (1962); Piano Trio (1963); *4 Pieces* for Solo Clarinet (1963); *Invocazione* for Chorus, Piano, and Percussion (1963); *4 Temperamenti* for 4 Clarinets (1963); *Zodinai* for Flute, 2 Clarinets, Bassoon, and Piano (1966); *Per Violoncello* (1967); *Sommarparafras* for Wind Quintet (1968); Toccata and Fugue for Piano (1971); *Notturno,* 3 pieces for Piano (1972); *5 Bagatelles* for Solo Oboe (1973); *4 Pieces* for Solo Bassoon (1973).

Ekman, Karl, Finnish pianist and conductor; b. Kaarina, near Åbo, Dec. 18, 1869; d. Helsinki, Feb. 4, 1947. He studied in Helsinki (1889–92); in 1892–95, was a pupil of H. Barth in Berlin and A. Grünfeld in Vienna; in 1895, a piano teacher at the Helsinki Cons., and in 1907–11, director there; in 1912–20, he was conductor of the orch. at Åbo. He arranged Swedish and Finnish folk songs, and edited a piano method; publ. a biography of Sibelius (Stockholm, 1935; Eng. trans., 1936). His wife, **Ida** (b. Helsinki, April 22, 1875; d. there, April 14, 1942), a concert singer, studied in Helsinki, Paris, and Vienna; she distinguished herself by her performances of Sibelius's songs.

El-Dabh, Halim, Egyptian composer; b. Cairo, March 4, 1921. He studied agriculture, and graduated from Cairo Univ. as an agrarian engineer (1945); then became interested in Egyptian musical instruments and composition; in 1950 received a Fulbright fellowship for music study in America; took courses at the New England Cons. in Boston and at the Berkshire Music Center in Tanglewood, Mass. (with Irving Fine and Copland). From 1966 to 1968 he taught at Howard Univ., and from 1969 at Kent State Univ. in Ohio, specializing in African ethnomusicology. Most of his music is derived from authentic Egyptian melodies and rhythms, but the contrapuntal and harmonic accoutrements are of a Western modern type.
WORKS: 3 symphs. (1952–56); Concerto for an Egyptian Drum with String Orch. (1955); *Tahmela,* symph. poem (Cairo, Jan. 22, 1960); *Ballet of Lights* (*Cairo, Before the Sphinx,* July 23, 1960); *Opera Flies,* on the story of the Kent State Univ. killings of 1969, the "flies" in the title being an ironically bitter reference to the student victims (Washington, D.C., May 5, 1971); String Quartet (1951); Sextet for Wind Instruments and Percussion (1952); songs; and music for drums (for which he devised his own system of notation).

El-tour, Anna, Russian soprano; b. Odessa, June 4, 1886; d. Amsterdam, May 30, 1954. She studied at the St. Petersburg Cons. (voice with Mme. von Hecke; piano with Essipova). From 1913–20, she taught in Moscow; then left Russia; from 1922–25 was in Berlin; from 1925–48, she taught at the Cons. Internationale de Paris. After 1948, she was a prof. of singing at the Amsterdam Cons. She traveled widely in the Far East; gave recitals in Israel in 1953.

Elder, Mark, English conductor; b. Corbridge, June 2, 1947. He was educated at Cambridge Univ. Upon graduation he served as apprentice conductor of several British orchs. In 1970 he was appointed to the music staff of the Royal Opera House, Covent Garden, and the Glyndebourne Festival. In 1974 he became associate conductor of the English National Opera in London, and in 1979 its music director; in 1980 he was engaged as principal guest conductor of the London Mozart Players. In 1981 he made a satisfactory appearance conducting Wagner at the Bayreuth Festival.

Eldridge, "Roy" (David), black American jazz trumpeter, drummer, and singer; b. Pittsburgh, Jan. 30, 1911. He learned to play the trumpet from Joe and P.M. Williams, then hit the road with his own group. After working with various bands, he played with Fletcher Henderson (1935–36), Gene Krupa (1941–43), and Artie Shaw (1944–45); also played in a quintet with Coleman Hawkins. He made many appearances at jazz festivals in the U.S. and Europe.

Elewijck, Xavier Victor van, Belgian music scholar; b. Brussels, April 24, 1825; d. in the insane asylum at Zickemont, April 28, 1888. He was the author of several monographs: *Discours sur la musique religieuse en Belgique* (1861); *Mathias van den Gheyn* (1862); and *De l'état actuel de la musique en Italie* (1875).

Elgar, Sir Edward (William), eminent English composer; b. Broadheath, near Worcester, June 2, 1857; d. Worcester, Feb. 23, 1934. He received his musical education from his father, who was organist at St. George's Roman Catholic Church in Worcester for 37 years. At an early age he assisted his father at the organ, and took part in the rehearsals and concerts at the Worcester Glee Club; in 1879 he took a few violin lessons in London from Adolf Pollitzer; in the same year, he accepted an appointment as bandmaster at the County Lunatic Asylum in Worcester; he also played in Stockley's orch. in Birmingham; in 1882, was appointed conductor of the Worcester Amateur Instrumental Society; in 1885 succeeded his father as organist at St. George's. After his marriage (1889) to a daughter of Sir Henry Roberts, he tried his fortune in London but found conditions unfavorable, and in 1891 settled in Malvern, where he remained for 13 years. He went to Hereford in 1904, and later to London, until 1920, when he returned to Worcester following the death of his wife. The first composition of Elgar that had a public performance was an orchestral intermezzo (Birmingham, Dec. 13, 1883); his first signal success was with the concert overture *Froissart* (Worcester Festival, Sept. 9, 1890). His cantata *The Black Knight* was produced by the Festival Choral Society in Worcester (April 18, 1893) and was also heard in London, at the Crystal Palace (Oct. 23, 1897); the production of his cantata *Scenes from the Saga of King Olaf* at the North Staffordshire Festival (Oct. 30, 1896) attracted considerable attention; from then on, Elgar's name became familiar to the musical public. There followed the cantata *Caractacus* (Leeds Festival, Oct. 5, 1898), and Elgar's masterpiece, the oratorio *The Dream of Gerontius* (Birmingham Festival, Oct. 3, 1900). In the meantime, Elgar gave more and more attention to orchestral music. On June 19, 1899, Hans Richter presented the first performance in London of Elgar's *Variations on an Original Theme* (generally known as *Enigma Variations*). This work consists of 14 sections, each marked by initials of fancied names of Elgar's friends; in later years, Elgar issued cryptic hints as to the identities of these persons, which were finally revealed. Elgar also stated that the theme itself was a counterpoint to a familiar tune, but the concealed subject was never discovered; various guesses were advanced in the musical press from time to time; a contest for the most plausible answer to the riddle was launched in America by the *Saturday Review* (1953) with dubious results. It is most probable that no such hidden theme existed, and that Elgar, who had a stately sense of humor, indulged in harmless mystification. The success of the *Enigma Variations* was followed (1901–30) by the production of Elgar's *Pomp and Circumstance* marches, the first of which became Elgar's most famous piece through a setting to words by Arthur Christopher Benson, used by Elgar in the *Coronation Ode* (1902), and then publ. separately as *Land of Hope and Glory;* another successful orch. work was the *Cockaigne Overture* (London, June 20, 1901). Elgar's 2 symphs., written in close succession in 1908 and 1910, received respectful attention in England, but never became popular elsewhere. His Violin Concerto, first performed by Fritz Kreisler (London, Nov. 10, 1910), was more successful; there was also a Cello Concerto (London, Oct. 26, 1919). The emergence of Elgar as a major composer about 1900 was all the more remarkable since he had no formal academic training. Yet he developed a masterly technique of instrumental and vocal writing. His style of composition may be described as functional Romanticism; his harmonic procedures remain firmly within the 19th-century tradition; the formal element is always strong, and the thematic development logical and precise. Elgar had a melodic gift, which asserted itself in the earliest works such as the popular *Salut d'amour;* his oratorios, particularly *The Apostles,* were the product of Elgar's fervent religious faith (he was a Roman Catholic); however he avoided archaic usages of Gregorian chant; rather, he presented the sacred subjects in a communicative style of secular drama. Elgar's stature in England is very great. During his lifetime he was a recipient of many honors. He was knighted in 1904. He received honorary degrees of Mus.Doc. from Cambridge (1900), Oxford (1905), Aberdeen (1906); also an LL.D., from Leeds (1904). During his first visit to the U.S. in 1905 he received a D.Mus. degree from Yale Univ.; in 1907 he received the same degree from the Univ. of Western Pa. (now the Univ. of Pittsburgh). He received the Order of Merit in 1911; was made K.C.V.O. in 1928 and a baronet in 1931; was appointed Master of the King's Musick in 1924, succeeding Sir Walter Parratt. Although he was not a proficient conductor, he appeared on various occasions with orchs. in his own works; during the 3rd of his 4 visits to the U.S. (1905, 1906, 1907, 1911) he conducted his oratorio *The Apostles* (N.Y., 1907); also led the mass chorus at the opening of the British Empire Exhibition in 1924.

WORKS: OPERA: *The Spanish Lady,* in 2 acts, to a libretto based on Ben Jonson, op. 89 (unfinished; sketches date from 1878; 15 excerpts orchestrated by Percy M. Young; BBC, London, Dec 4, 1969). ORATORIOS: *The Light of Life,* op. 29 (Worcester, 1896); *The Dream of Gerontius,* op. 38 (Birmingham, 1900); *The Apostles,* op. 49 (Birmingham, 1903); *The Kingdom,* op. 51 (Birmingham, 1906).

CANTATAS: *The Black Knight,* op. 25 (1893); *Scenes from the Saga of King Olaf,* op. 30 (1896); *The Banner of St. George,* op. 33 (1897); *Caractacus,* op. 35 (1898); *Coronation Ode,* op. 44 (Sheffield, 1902); *The Music Makers* op. 69 (Birmingham, 1912).

CHORAL WORKS WITH ORCH.: *Star of the Summer Night,* op. 23 (1892); *Scenes from the Bavarian Highlands,* op. 27 (1896); *The Spirit of England,* op. 80 (1916).

FOR ORCH.: *The Wand of Youth,* suite in 7 movements, op. 1a (subtitled *Music to a Child's Play,* written at the age of 12 and orchestrated 37 years later; London, Queen's Hall Orch., Dec. 14, 1907); 2nd suite, *The Wand of Youth,* op. 1b (1908); *Sevillana,* op. 7; *3 Pieces* op. 10 (Mazurka, Sérénade mauresque, Contrasts); *Salut d'amour* op. 12 (Crystal Palace, London, Nov. 11, 1889); *2 Pieces,* op. 15 (*Chanson du Matin, Chanson du soir;*) *Froissart,* op. 19, overture (1890); *Serenade* for String Orch. op. 20 (1892); *Imperial March,* op. 32, for Queen Victoria's Diamond Jubilee (1897); *Enigma Variations,* op. 36 (1899); *Pomp and Circumstance,* op. 39, 4 military marches (1901–7; a 5th composed in 1930); *Cockaigne,* op. 40, overture (1901); *Dream Children,* op. 43, 2 pieces for Small Orch. (London Symph. Orch., March 8, 1905, composer conducting); *Introduction and Allegro* for Strings, op. 47 (London, March 8, 1905); *In the South,* op. 50, overture (1904); Symph. No. 1, op. 55 (Manchester, Dec. 3, 1908); *Elegy* for Strings, op. 58 (1909); Violin Concerto, op. 61 (London, Nov. 10, 1910); *Romance,* op. 62, for Bassoon and Orch. (1910); Symph. No. 2, op. 63 (London, May 24, 1911); *Coronation March* op. 65 (1911); *Falstaff,* op. 68, symph. study (Leeds Festival, Oct. 2, 1913, composer conducting); *Sospiri,* op. 70, for String Orch., Harp, and Organ (1914); *Carillon,* op. 75, for Recitation, with Orch. (1914); *Polonia,* op. 76, symph. prelude (1915); *Une voix dans le désert,* op. 77, for Recitation, with Orch. (1915); *Le Drapeau belge,* op. 79, for Recitation with Orch. (1917); Cello

Concerto, op. 85 (1919); *Severn Suite,* op. 87, for Brass Band (1930); *Nursery Suite* for Orch. (1931); incidental music for *Grania and Diarmid,* op. 42; *The Crown of India,* op. 66, masque (1912); *The Starlight Express,* op. 78 (1915); music for Laurence Binyon and J.M. Harvey's play *King Arthur* (London, 1923).

CHAMBER MUSIC: Quintet for Wind Instruments, op. 6; String Quartet, op. 8 (MS destroyed); Violin Sonata, op. 9; Violin Sonata in E minor, op. 82 (MS destroyed); String Quartet in C minor, op. 83 (1918); Piano Quintet, op. 84 (1919). Organ works: Voluntaries, op. 14; Sonata in G, op. 28; also choruses and solo songs.

BIBLIOGRAPHY: R.J. Buckley, *Sir Edward Elgar* (London, 1904; new ed., 1925); E. Newman, *Elgar* (London, 1906); D.G. Mason, "A Study of Elgar," *Musical Quarterly* (April 1917); J.F. Porte, *Sir Edward Elgar* (London, 1921); J.H. Shera, *Elgar's Instrumental Works* (London, 1931); J.F. Porte, *Elgar and His Music* (London, 1933); B.S. Maine, *Elgar, His Life and Works* (2 vols., London, 1933); A.J. Sheldon, *Edward Elgar* (London, 1933); A.H. Fox-Strangways, "Elgar," *Music & Letters* (Jan. 1934); R.C. Powell, "Elgar's Enigma," ibid. (July 1934); special Elgar issue, ibid. (Jan. 1935); C. Barber, "Enigma Variations," ibid. (April 1935); William H. Reed, *Elgar as I Knew Him* (London, 1936; new ed., 1973); Mrs. Richard Powell, *Edward Elgar: Memories of a Variation* (London, 1937; 2nd ed., 1947); William H. Reed, *Elgar* (London, 1939; contains a complete list of works); W.R. Anderson, *Introduction to the Music of Elgar* (London, 1949); Diana McVeagh, *Edward Elgar, His Life and Music* (London, 1955); Percy Young, *Elgar, O.M.* (London, 1955; new ed., 1973); idem, ed., *Letters of Edward Elgar and Other Writings* (London, 1956); idem, ed., *Letters to Nimrod from Edward Elgar* (London, 1965); M. Kennedy, *Portrait of Elgar* (London, 1968); M. Hurd, *Elgar* (London, 1969); R. Fiske, "The Enigma: A Solution," *Musical Times* (Nov. 1969); E. Sams, "Elgar's Cipher Letter to Dorabella," ibid. (Feb. 1970); idem, "Variations on an Original Theme (Enigma)," ibid. (March 1970); I. Parrott, *Elgar* (London, 1971); M. De-la-Noy, *Elgar, the Man* (London, 1983); C. Redwood, ed., *An Elgar Companion* (Ashbourne, 1983); R. Anderson, "Elgar and Some Apostolic Problems," *Musical Times* (Jan. 1984); J. Moore, *Spirit of England: Edward Elgar, A Creative Life* (London, 1984). The Elgar Society in Northwood, Middlesex, England, publishes the *Elgar Society Newsletter* triennially.

Elías, Alfonso de, Mexican composer, father of **Manuel Jorge de Elías;** b. Mexico City, Aug. 30, 1902. He studied piano with José Velasquez, orchestration with Gustavo Campa, and composition with Rafael Tello at the National Cons. of Mexico (1915–27); was subsequently active as a pianist and conductor; taught at the Universidad Autónoma of Mexico from 1958 and at the National Cons. from 1963. His music is cast in a Romantic idiom, much in the manner of Tchaikovsky, and contains few concessions to modern usages.

WORKS: Ballet, *Las Biniguendas de plata* (1933; concert version, Mexico City, Nov. 21, 1940); *El jardín encantado,* symph. triptych (1924); 3 symphs. (1926, 1934, 1968); *Variaciones sobre un tema mexicano (Las mañanitas)* for Orch. (1927); symph. poems: *Leyenda mística del Callejón del Ave María* (1930) and *Cacahuamilpa* (1940); *Tlalmanalco,* suite for Clarinet, Bassoon, Trumpet, Piano, and Strings (1936); 2 string quartets (1930, 1961); Violin Sonata (1932); *6 Pieces* for String Quartet; *Suite antiqua* for 4 Recorders (or 2 Flutes and 2 Clarinets); *5 Pieces* for Violin and Piano, and *4 Pieces* for Cello and Piano (all 1937–66); Organ Sonata (1963); piano pieces; commemorative masses for soloists, organ, and strings; motets. A complete list of his works through 1972 is in *Composers of the Americas,* vol. 18 (Washington, D.C., 1972).

Elías, Manuel Jorge de, Mexican composer, son of **Alfonso de Elías;** b. Mexico City, June 5, 1939. He received his early musical training from his father; he then entered the Autonomous National Univ. of Mexico and the National Cons., where he studied piano, organ, flute, violin, and cello (1959–62); in Mexico City he also attended courses by visiting lecturers: on *musique concrète,* given by Jean-Etienne Marie (1967), and on new music, by Stockhausen (1968); had lessons in conducting with Herrera de la Fuente (1968–72); attended a class in electronic music at Columbia Univ. in N.Y. (1974); then traveled to Belgium and enrolled in a workshop in opera and ballet conducting with Edgar Doneux in Brussels (1974–75); returning to Mexico, he founded in 1976 the Inst. of Music of the Univ. of Veracruz. His music is hedonistically pragmatic and structurally precise, but allows interpolation of aleatory passages.

WORKS: *Pequeños corales* for Chorus a cappella (1954–57); *Suite romántica,* 10 pieces for Piano (1954–56); *Suite de miniaturas* for Wind Quartet (1957); *Sonata breve* for Piano (1958); *Estampas Infantiles,* suite for Strings (1959); Sinfonietta (1958–61); *Vitral No. 1* for Chamber Orch. (1962), *No. 2* for Chamber Orch. and Tape (1967), and *No. 3* for Orch. (Mexico City, Nov. 7, 1969); *Fantasía* for Solo Cello (1962); *Elegía* for Solo Clarinet (1962); *Divertimento* for Percussion (1963); ballet, *Jahel,* for 2 Pianos (1964); *Aforismo No. 1, Pájaros perdidos* for Chorus a cappella (1963); *Aforismo No. 2* for Flute and Tape (1968); *Guanajuato,* overture-divertimento for Orch. (1964); *Impresiones sobre una Estampa Colonial,* divertimento for Orch. (1965); *Microestructuras* for Piano (1965); *Ciclos elementarios* for Wind Quartet (1965); *Speculamen* for 2 Violins, 2 Violas, 3 Cellos, and Double Bass (1967); *Elegía heroica,* symph. poem (1967); *Memento* for Recorder, Chorus, Strings, and Narrator (1967); String Quartet No. 1 (1967); *Música nupcial* for Contralto, and Brass or Strings (1967); *Aforismo* for Solo Flute (1968); 2 solo violin sonatas (1968, 1969); *Pro Pax* for Tape (1968); *Nimyé* for Solo Flute (1969); 3 *Quimeras* for 2 Pianos (1969, 1973, 1974); 3 *Kaleidoscopios* for Organ (1969, 1973, 1974); *Sonante (Sonority) No. 1* for Piano (1971), *No. 2* for Solo

Clarinet (1970), *No. 3* for Trumpet, Trombone, and Horn (1970; version for Orch., 1974), *No. 4* for Orch. (Mexico City, March 26, 1971), *No. 5* for Orch. (Mexico City, Nov. 24, 1972), *No. 6, Homenaje a Neruda,* for String Orch. (1973), and *No. 7* for Orch. (Brussels, Dec. 1974); *Parametros I* for Synthesizer (1971); *Ludus* for 3 Choruses (1972–73); *Concertante No. 1* for Violin and Orch. (1973); *Música domestica* for Recorder and Percussion (1973); *Sine nomine* for String Quartet and Piano (1975); *Jeux* for Horn, Trumpet, and Bassoon (1975); *Obertura-Poema* for Soloists, Chorus, Organ, and Wind Orch. (1975); *Preludio* for Solo Violin (1975); *To Play Playing* for Solo Flute (1976); *Preludio* for Solo Guitar (1976); *Preludio* for Solo Viola (1976); further choruses; songs. For a list of his works through 1969, see *Composers of the Americas,* vol. 15 (Washington, D.C., 1969).

Elias, Rosalind, American mezzo-soprano; b. Lowell, Mass., March 13, 1929. She studied at the New England Cons. of Music in Boston and at the Santa Cecilia Academy in Rome. In 1954 she joined the Metropolitan Opera; on Jan. 15, 1958, she sang the role of Erika in the first performance of Samuel Barber's *Vanessa;* also appeared as a concert singer.

Elias, Salomon (Salomonis), French monk at Sainte-Astère, Périgord. He wrote in 1274 a treatise, *Scientia artis musicae* (printed by Gerbert, *Scriptores,* vol. III), of value as the first practical work giving rules for improvised counterpoint.

BIBLIOGRAPHY: E.T. Ferand, *Die Improvisation in der Musik* (Zürich, 1938); idem, "The 'Howling in Seconds' of the Lombards," *Musical Quarterly* (July 1939).

Eliasson, Anders, Swedish composer; b. Borlänge, April 3, 1947. He studied in Stockholm with Ingvar Lidholm and Soderholm. His music emphasizes the structural elements in freely dissonant texture.

WORKS: *In Medias* for Solo Violin (1970); *Kantillation* for Mezzo-soprano and Organ (1970); a String quartet, *Melos* (1970); *Picnic* for Wind Quintet (1972); *Tider* for Mezzo-soprano, Trombone, Cello, Electric Organ, Marimba, Vibraphone, and Percussion (1972); *Glasdans* for Orch. (1973; Swedish Television, Jan. 9, 1974); *Inför logos (In the Presence of Logos),* after Kafka, for Chorus and Tape (1973); *Quo Vadis* for Mezzo-soprano, Electric Organ, and Tape (1973); church opera, *En av oss (One of Us;* 1974); *Disegno della pioggia* for Piano, 4-hands, Cello, and Xylophone (1974); *Disegno* for String Quartet (1975); *Disegno* for 6 Brasses (2 Trumpets, Horn, 2 Trombones, and Tuba; 1975); several electronic pieces.

Elizalde, Federico, Spanish composer; b. Manila, Philippines (of Spanish parents), Dec. 12, 1908; d. there, Jan. 16, 1979. He entered the Madrid Cons. as a child and received the first prize as pianist at the age of 14. Later he went to California, and studied law at Stanford Univ. At the same time he took composition lessons with Ernest Bloch. He was subsequently active as a conductor of hotel orchs. in England; also visited Germany. Returning to his native islands, he became conductor of the Manila Symph. Orch. (1930). On April 23, 1936, he conducted his *Sinfonia Concertante* at the Festival of the International Society for Contemporary Music in Barcelona. He was in France during World War II; in 1948 he assumed the post of president of the Manila Broadcast Co., but continued his travels in both hemispheres. His music is influenced mainly by Mañuel de Falla; beginning with dancelike works in the Spanish vein, Elizalde has gradually changed his style toward neo-Classicism. He wrote the opera *Paul Gauguin* for the centennial of Gauguin's birth (1948); a Violin Concerto (1943); a Piano Concerto (1947); much chamber music.

Elizza, Elise, Austrian soprano; b. Vienna, Jan. 6, 1870; d. there, June 3, 1926. She studied in her native city; then appeared as an operetta singer. In 1895 she joined the Vienna Opera, rapidly becoming one of its principal singers. She retired in 1919; then taught voice. She possessed a fine coloratura voice.

Elkan, Henri, American conductor and music publisher; b. Antwerp, Nov. 23, 1897. He studied viola and piano at the conservatories of Antwerp (1914) and Amsterdam (graduated 1917); in 1920 came to the U.S.; played the viola in the Philadelphia Orch. (1920–28); was conductor of the Philadelphia Grand Opera Co. (1928–36) and of the Philadelphia Ballet Co. (1926–39). In 1926 he founded the Henri Elkan Music Publishing Co. in Philadelphia; it became the Elkan-Vogel Music Publishing Co. in 1928, when Adolphe Vogel, a cellist in the Philadelphia Orch., joined Elkan; the partnership was dissolved in 1952; in 1956 Elkan formed a publishing firm under his own name, specializing in works by American and Latin American composers.

Elkus, Albert (Israel), American composer and teacher; b. Sacramento, April 30, 1884; d. Oakland, Feb. 19, 1962. He studied piano with Hugo Mansfeldt in San Francisco, and later with Harold Bauer and Josef Lhévinne; went to Vienna, where he took lessons in conducting with Franz Schalk and counterpoint with Karl Prohaska; then took courses with Robert Fuchs and Georg Schumann in Berlin. Returning to the U.S., he taught at the Dominican College in San Rafael, Calif. (1924–31); was on the faculty of the San Francisco Cons. (1923–25 and 1933–37); was its director from 1951 to 1957; he also taught at Mills College in Oakland (1929–44). Among his compositions are *Concertino on Lezione III of Ariosto* for Cello and String Orch. (1917); *Impressions from a Greek Tragedy* (San Francisco, Feb. 27, 1921); a chorus for Men's Voices, *I Am the Reaper* (1921).

Elkus, Jonathan, American conductor, pedagogue, and composer, son of **Albert Elkus;** b. San Francisco, Aug. 8, 1931. He started his musical career as a bassoon player; was bassoonist in the California National Guard (1949–57); enrolled at Stanford Univ., studying composition with Ernst Bacon and Leonard Ratner (M.A., 1954); then took a course with Darius Milhaud at Mills College in Oakland in 1957. He served as conductor of the Univ. Bands at Lehigh Univ. in Bethlehem, Pa. (1957–73); concurrently taught music courses there (1965–73); after 1973 he was engaged mainly as a music editor and band arranger. His compositions are directed mainly at high school and college workshops.

WORKS: OPERAS: *Tom Sawyer* (San Francisco, May 22, 1953); *The Outcasts of Poker Flat* (Lehigh Univ., April 16, 1960); *Treasure Island,* after R.L. Stevenson (1961); *The Mandarin* (N.Y., Oct. 26, 1967); *Helen in Egypt* and *Medea* (Milwaukee, Nov. 13, 1970). FOR BAND: *Camino Real* (1955); *The Apocalypse* (1974); *Chiaroscuro* (1977). CHAMBER MUSIC: *5 Sketches* for 2 Clarinets and Bassoon (1954); *Triptych* for 4 Bassoons and Mezzo-soprano (1962); *The Charmer* for Clarinet, Trombone, and Piano (1972); choruses and songs. He arranged for band *Decoration Day* by Charles Ives, Wagner's *Siegfried's Funeral March,* and numerous college songs and popular tunes. He publ. a monograph, *Charles Ives and the American Band Tradition: A Centennial Tribute* (Exeter, England, 1974).

Ella, John, English writer on music; b. Leicester, Dec. 19, 1802; d. London, Oct. 2, 1888. He studied violin in London; then enrolled as a harmony student at the Royal Academy of Music; in 1827 went to Paris to study with Fétis. Returning to London, he played in theater orchs.; was director of Lord Saltoun's musical society until 1846; in 1845 he established The Musical Union, presenting morning concerts of chamber music, and was its director until 1880; in 1850 opened a series of "Music Winter Evenings" which continued until 1859. For these organizations he wrote analytical program notes, of excellent quality for the time. He was a contributor of reviews and music articles to the *Morning Post,* the *Musical World,* and the *Athenaeum.*

WRITINGS: *Lectures on Dramatic Music Abroad and at Home* (1872); *Musical Sketches Abroad and at Home,* (3 eds., 1861, 1869, 1878); *Record of the Musical Union* (1845–80); *Personal Memoir of Meyerbeer* (1868); other publications. BIBLIOGRAPHY: John Ravell, "John Ella," *Music & Letters* (Jan. 1953).

Ellberg, Ernst Henrik, Swedish composer and pedagogue; b. Söderhamn, Dec. 11, 1868; d. Stockholm, June 14, 1948. He studied violin and composition at the Stockholm Cons., and was a teacher there from 1904 to 1933; among his pupils were Hilding Rosenberg, Dag Wirén, and Gunnar de Frumerie. He wrote an opera, *Rassa,* which received a prize; several ballets and concert overtures; some chamber music.

Ellegaard, France, Danish pianist; b. Paris (of Danish parents), Oct. 10, 1912. She studied at the Paris Cons. (1922–33), then toured in Germany, France, and England. In 1949 she married the Finnish painter Birger Carlstedt. In 1969 she was ap-

pointed prof. at the Sibelius Academy in Helsinki.

Eller, Heino, noted Estonian composer and pedagogue; b. Dorpat (Tartu), March 7, 1887; d. Tallinn, June 16, 1970. He studied law at St. Petersburg Univ. (1908–11), and later took music courses at the Cons. there, graduating in composition in 1920 in the class of Kalafati. From 1920 to 1940 he taught at the music high school in Tartu; in 1940 he joined the faculty of the Cons. in Tallinn. Together with Artur Kapp, Eller established the modern national school of Estonian music, derived from folk materials but framed in modern harmonic structures. He was also renowned as a pedagogue.

WORKS: 3 symphs. (1936, 1947, 1962); several symph. poems, including *Öö hüded* (*Nocturnal Sounds;* 1920; revised 1960); *Symphonic Scherzo* (1921); Violin Concerto (1933; revised 1965); *Fantasy for Violin and Orch.* (1916; revised 1963); 5 string quartets (1925, 1930, 1945, 1954, 1959); 2 violin sonatas (1922, 1946); 4 piano sonatas (1920, 1937, 1944, 1958).

Eller, Louis, Austrian violinist; b. Graz, June 9, 1820; d. Pau, July 12, 1862. He studied with Hysel; from 1836 made tours in central Europe; traveled to Spain and Portugal with Gottschalk. He wrote several effective pieces for the violin: *Valse diabolique, Menuet sentimental,* etc.

Ellert, Laurence B., American music editor; b. Louisville, Jan. 3, 1878; d. Washington, D.C., Oct. 25, 1940. He attended Georgetown Univ.; from 1900–2, was director of the Mandolin Club there; studied piano and harmony privately; in 1902 entered the music business; in 1919, became associated with the sales dept. of G. Schirmer, Inc.; in 1920 became general manager of the Willis Music Co. in Cincinnati; in 1923, he was again in N.Y., as director of publications for the Boston Music Co. and the Willis Music Co., specializing in educational music.

Ellerton, John Lodge (real name, **John Lodge**), English poet and prolific composer; b. Cheshire, Jan. 11, 1801; d. London, Jan. 3, 1873. An Oxford graduate, he studied counterpoint under Pietro Terriani in Rome, where he composed 9 Italian operas. Besides, he lived for some time in Germany, where he wrote 2 German operas. Besides his operas, he wrote an oratorio, *Paradise Lost;* 6 symphs., 4 concert overtures; 3 quintets; 50 string quartets; 3 string trios; 8 trios for various instruments; 13 sonatas; 61 glees; 83 vocal duets; songs.

Elleviou, Jean, French operatic tenor; b. Rennes, June 14, 1769; d. Paris, May 5, 1842. He made his debut in Monsigny's *Déserteur* at the Comédie Italienne in Paris in 1790, and sang there until 1813. The revival of interest in the works of Grétry in 1801 was largely due to his influence and excellent interpretations; Méhul wrote his *Joseph* (1807) and Boieldieu his *Jean de Paris* (1812) for him. BIBLIOGRAPHY: E.H.P. de Curzon, *Jean Elle-*

viou (Paris, 1930).

Ellicott, Rosalind Frances, English composer; b. Cambridge, Nov. 14, 1857; d. London, April 5, 1924. She studied at the Royal Academy of Music (1875–76), and later with Thomas Wingham (1885–92); she received several commissions to write works for the Gloucester and Cheltenham Festivals; among them were the cantatas *Radiant Sister of the Dawn* (Cheltenham, 1887) and *Elysium* (Gloucester, 1889). She retired from active musical work in 1900.

Elling, Catharinus, Norwegian composer and folklorist; b. Christiania, Sept. 13, 1858; d. Oslo, Jan. 8, 1942. He studied music with native teachers; then in Leipzig (1877–78) and Berlin (1886–96). In 1908 a subvention was granted him by the state for the pursuit of his studies of Norwegian folk songs, on which he publ. various essays; he also wrote biographies of Ole Bull, Grieg, Svendsen, and Kjerulf, and publ. a book. *Norsk Folkemusik* (Oslo, 1922). He composed an opera, *Kosakkerne* (1897); an oratorio, *The Prodigal Son;* a Symph.; incidental music to *A Midsummer Night's Dream;* chamber music; many songs.

Ellington, Edward Kennedy (known as **Duke Ellington**), black American pianist, bandleader, and composer; one of the most remarkable musicians of jazz; b. Washington, D.C., April 29, 1899; d. New York, May 24, 1974. He played ragtime as a boy; worked with various jazz bands in Washington during the 1910s and early 1920s, and in 1923 went to N.Y., where he organized a "big band" (originally 10 pieces) that he was to lead for the next half-century, a band that revolutionized the concept of jazz: no longer was jazz restricted to small combos of 4–6 "unlettered" improvisers; with the Ellington band complex arrangements were introduced, requiring both improvising skill and the ability to read scores; eventually these scores were to take on the dimensions and scope of classical compositions while retaining an underlying jazz feeling. In the early days his chief collaborator in composition and arrangements was trumpeter James "Bubber" Miley; baritone saxophonist Harry Carney, another arranger, was with the band from its inception until Ellington's death; from 1939 the main collaborator was pianist-composer Billy Strayhorn. Ellington possessed a social elegance and the gift of articulate verbal expression that inspired respect, and he became known as "Duke" Ellington. He was the only jazz musician to receive an honorary degree from Columbia Univ. (1973). He was also the recipient of the Presidential Medal of Freedom on his 70th birthday at the White House in 1969. He made several European trips under the auspices of the State Dept.; toured Russia in 1970 and also went to Latin America, Japan, and Australia. So highly was he esteemed in Africa that the Republic of Togo issued in 1967 a postage stamp bearing his portrait. Since Duke's death, his band has been led by his son **Mercer Ellington** (b. Washington, D.C., March 11, 1919).
WORKS: More than 1,000 compositions, including *East St. Louis Toodle-Oo* (pronounced "toad-lo"; 1926); *Black and Tan Fantasy* and *Creole Love Song* (1927); *Mood Indigo* (1930); *Sophisticated Lady* (uses a whole-tone scale; 1932); *Diminuendo and Crescendo in Blue* (1937); *Black, Brown and Beige,* (a tonal panorama of black history in America (1943); *Liberian Suite* (1948); *My People,* commissioned for the 100th anniversary of the Emancipation Proclamation (1963); *First Sacred Concert* (first perf., Grace Cathedral, San Francisco, 1965); *Second Sacred Concert* (first perf., Cathedral of St. John the Divine, N.Y., 1968); *The River,* ballet (1970). He publ. a book, *Music Is My Mistress* (Garden City, N.Y., 1973).
BIBLIOGRAPHY: B. Ulanov, *Duke Ellington* (N.Y., 1946); P. Gammond, *Duke Ellington, His Life and Music* (London, 1958); S. Dance, *The World of Duke Ellington* (N.Y., 1970); Derek Jewell, *Duke, A Portrait of Duke Ellington* (N.Y., 1977); D. George, *The Real Duke Ellington* (London, 1982). The Duke Ellington Society, in N.Y., promotes lectures, performances, and scholarships.

Ellinwood, Leonard Webster, American musicologist; b. Thomaston, Conn., Feb. 13, 1905. He studied at Aurora College in Illinois and at the Eastman School of Music in Rochester, N.Y., where he received the degrees of M.M. and Ph.D. He subsequently held a number of teaching positions until 1939, when he became cataloguer at the Library of Congress in Washington; he retired from there in 1975. He compiled *Musica Hermanni Contracti* (Rochester, 1936); edited works of Francesco Landini (1939), *The History of American Church Music* (N.Y., 1953), and a *Bio-bibliographical Index of Musicians in the U.S.A. since Colonial Times* (Washington, D.C., 1941; 2nd ed., 1956); also contributed to the Episcopal songbook *The Hymnal Companion* (1951).

Ellis (real name, **Sharpe**), **Alexander John,** English writer on musical science; b. Hoxton (London), June 14, 1814; d. Kensington, Oct. 28, 1890. He studied at Trinity College, Cambridge, graduating in 1837; his subjects were mathematics and philology; he also studied music; was elected Fellow of the Royal Society (1864) and was president of the Philological Society; publ. valuable papers in the *Proceedings of the Royal Society:* "On the Conditions . . . of a Perfect Musical Scale on Instruments with Fixed Tones" (1864); "On the Physical Constitutions and Relations of Musical Chords" (1864); "On the Temperament of Instruments with Fixed Tones" (1864); and "On Musical Duodenes; or, The Theory of Constructing Instruments with Fixed Tones in Just or Practically Just Intonation" (1874). Papers containing new theories, etc., for the Musical Association are as follows: "The Basis of Music" (1877); "Pronunciation for Singers" (1877); and "Speech in Song" (1878). He was awarded a silver medal for his writings on musical pitch for the *Proceedings of the Society of Arts* (1877, 1880, and 1881; publ. separately, 1880–81; and in summary form in the Appendix to the 2nd ed. of his trans. of Helmholtz's *Lehre von* *den Tonempfindungen* under the title *On the Sensations of Tone, as a Physiological Basis for the Theory of Music;* first ed., 1875; 6th ed., 1948); he also wrote "Tonometrical Observations, or Some Existing Non-harmonic Scales" (Royal Society, 1884) and "On the Musical Scales of Various Nations" (Society of Arts, 1885).

Ellis, Don, American trumpet player and jazz music arranger; b. Los Angeles, July 25, 1934; d. Hollywood, Dec. 17, 1978. He studied composition at Boston Univ. with Gardner Read, and later at the Univ. of Calif., Los Angeles, with John Vincent; in the interim he took trumpet lessons with 7 teachers in Boston, N.Y., and Los Angeles. He played with numerous bands; eventually formed his own group. In his arrangements he boldly introduced asymmetrical meters. His major work is *Contrasts* for 2 Orchs. and Trumpet (1965).

Elman, Mischa, remarkable Russian violinist; b. Talnoy, Jan. 20, 1891; d. New York, April 5, 1967. At the age of 6 he was taken by his father to Odessa, where he became a violin student of Fidelmann and a pupil of Brodsky. His progress was extraordinary, and when Leopold Auer heard him play in 1902, he immediately accepted him in his class at the St. Petersburg Cons. In 1904 he made his debut in St. Petersburg with sensational acclaim; his tour of Germany was equally successful; in 1905 he appeared in England, where he played the Glazunov Violin Concerto. On Dec. 10, 1908, he made his American debut in N.Y. and was hailed as one of the greatest virtuosos of the time; he played with every important symph. orch. in the U.S.; with the Boston Symph. alone he was a soloist at 31 concerts. In the following years he played all over the world, and, with Jascha Heifetz, became a synonym for violinistic prowess. His playing was the quintessence of Romantic interpretation; his tone was mellifluous but resonant; he excelled particularly in the concertos of Mendelssohn, Tchaikovsky, and Wieniawski; but he could also give impressive performances of Beethoven and Mozart. He publ. several violin arrangements of Classical and Romantic pieces, and he also composed some playable short compositions for his instrument. His father publ. a sentimental book, *Memoirs of Mischa Elman's Father* (N.Y., 1933).

Elmendorff, Karl, eminent German conductor; b. Düsseldorf, Oct. 25, 1891; d. Hofheim am Taunus, Oct. 21, 1962. He studied at the Hochschule für Musik in Cologne; conducted opera there, then in Munich, Wiesbaden, and Mannheim. From 1927 to 1942 he conducted at the Bayreuth Festival. He appeared infrequently outside Germany, and his reputation rests entirely on his interpretations of German operas.

Elmo, Cloe, Italian mezzo-soprano; b. Lecce, April 9, 1910; d. Ankara, May 24, 1962. She studied voice in Rome; made her debut in Cagliari in 1934; from 1936 she was a prominent member of La Scala; on Nov.

19, 1947, she made an impressive debut at the Metropolitan Opera in N.Y. as Azucena in *Il Trovatore;* in 1948 she returned to Italy. Eventually she made her home in Ankara, where she taught at the Cons. from 1954 until her death.

Elmore, Robert Hall, American organist and composer; b. Ramapatnam, India, Jan. 2, 1913 (of American parentage). He studied organ with Pietro Yon, composition with Harl McDonald, and at the Univ. of Pa. (B.Mus., 1937); from 1936 to 1953 he was an organ teacher at the Clarke Cons. of Music in Philadelphia; in 1940 he joined the faculty at the Univ. of Pa. He wrote a tone poem, *Valley Forge* (Philadelphia Orch., April 9, 1937, Stokowski conducting); Organ Concerto; String Quartet; many sacred songs and cantatas; secular songs; etc.

Eloy, Jean-Claude, French composer; b. Mont-Saint-Aignan (Seine-Maritime), June 15, 1938. He studied in Paris with Darius Milhaud and in Basel with Pierre Boulez. From his earliest works he adopted the advanced techniques of serialism; his main influences are Boulez, Varèse, and Webern; there is an extreme miniaturization in his instrumental music. He composed *Etude III* for Orch. (1962); *Equivalences* (1963); *Polychronies* (1964), *Macles* (1967), and *Faisceaux-Diffractions* (1970), all for Chamber Orch.; also *Kamakala* for Chorus and 3 Orch. Ensembles (1971); *Kshara-Akshara* for Soprano Chorus and 3-sectioned Orch. with 3 Conductors (1974); *Shanti* (Tibetan for "good fortune"), an electronic work lasting 2½ hours without interruption, probably the longest uninterrupted piece ever composed (London, April 6, 1975).

Elsenheimer, Nicholas J., German music educator; b. Wiesbaden, June 17, 1866; d. Limburg, July 12, 1935. He was a pupil of his father; took the degree of LL.D. at Heidelberg; studied under G. Jacobsthal in Strasbourg. In 1890 he went to America; taught at the Cincinnati College of Music (1890–1906); after 1907 taught in N.Y.; then went back to Germany.

Elsner, Joseph, noted Polish composer, teacher of Chopin; b. Grottkau, June 1, 1769 (of German descent); d. Elsnerowo, near Warsaw, April 18, 1854. He studied violin, voice, and organ at Grottkau, Breslau, and Vienna. In 1791 he became concertmaster of the Brünn Opera Theater; then was Kapellmeister at Lemberg (from 1792 to 1799). He was Chopin's teacher at Warsaw, and founded a school there for organists which later became the Warsaw Cons. He also headed the Opera there for 25 years. His autobiography (1840–49), written in German, was publ. posthumously in a Polish trans. (1855; new ed., Cracow, 1957).
WORKS: 32 operas, including *King Wladislaw* (Warsaw, April 3, 1818), duo-dramas, and musical plays, of which 2 were produced in German at Lemberg (*Die seltenen Brüder*, 1794; *Der verkleidete Sultan*, 1796) and the rest in Warsaw; 17 masses; several ballets; sacred and secular choral works; 8 symphs.; 11 string quartets; 2 piano quartets; 3 vio-

lin sonatas (a number of these works were publ. by Breitkopf & Härtel and by French and Polish publishers). He also publ. 2 treatises on the vocal treatment of Polish texts (Warsaw, 1818). A medal was struck in his honor in 1849, on the occasion of his 80th birthday.

BIBLIOGRAPHY: F. Hoesick, *From Elsner's Memoirs* (Warsaw, 1901, in Polish); J. Reiss, *Joseph Elsner* (Katowice, 1936).

Elson, Arthur, American writer on music, son of **Louis C. Elson;** b. Boston, Nov. 18, 1873; d. New York, Feb. 24, 1940. He studied with J.K. Paine at Harvard Univ. and at the New England Cons. of Music; received fundamental training from his father. He was a graduate of Harvard and of the Mass. Inst. of Technology.

WRITINGS: *A Critical History of the Opera* (1901; new ed., 1926, as *A History of Opera*); *Orchestral Instruments and Their Use* (1902; new ed., Boston, 1930); *Woman's Work in Music* (1903; new ed., 1931); *Modern Composers of Europe* (1905; new ed., 1922); *Music Club Programs from All Nations* (1906; new ed., 1928); *The Musician's Guide* (1913); *The Book of Musical Knowledge* (1915; new ed., N.Y., 1934); *Pioneer School Music Course* (1917).

Elson, Louis Charles, American music historian; b. Boston, April 17, 1848; d. there, Feb. 14, 1920. He studied voice with Kreissmann at Boston and music theory with Karl Gloggner Castelli in Leipzig. Returning to Boston, he was for many years music editor of the *Boston Advertiser;* in 1880 became lecturer on music history at the New England Cons.; was also editor in chief of the *University Encyclopedia of Music* (10 vols., 1912). In his music criticism he attacked the modernists with vicious eloquence, reserving the choicest invective for Debussy; he called *La Mer* "Le Mal de Mer," and said that the faun of *L'Après-midi d'un faune* needed a veterinary surgeon.

WRITINGS: *Curiosities of Music* (1880); *History of German Song* (1888); *The Theory of Music* (1890; revised by F. Converse, 1935); *European Reminiscences* (Chicago, 1891; new ed., Philadelphia, 1914); *The Realm of Music* (1892); *Great Composers and Their Work* (1898); *The National Music of America and Its Sources* (1899; new ed., revised by Arthur Elson, 1924); *Famous Composers and Their Works* (with Philip Hale; new series, Boston, 1900); *Shakespeare in Music* (1901); *History of American Music* (N.Y., 1904; 2nd ed., 1915; revised ed. by A. Elson, 1925); *Music Dictionary* (1905); *Pocket Music Dictionary* (1909; many reprints); *Folk Songs of Many Nations* (1905); *Mistakes and Disputed Points in Music* (1910); *Woman in Music* (1918); *Children in Music* (1918).

Elvey, Sir George (Job), English organist and composer; b. Canterbury, March 27, 1816; d. Windlesham, Surrey, Dec. 9, 1893. He was a chorister at Canterbury Cathedral; studied with Skeats, Potter, and Dr. Crotch at the Royal Academy of Music. From 1835 until 1882 he served as organist and master of the boys at St. George's Chapel, Windsor; received a Mus.Bac. (1838) and a Mus.Doc. (1840) from Oxford; was knighted in 1871.

WORKS: 2 oratorios, which were moderately successful: *The Resurrection and Ascension* (London, Dec. 2, 1840) and *Mount Carmel* (London, June 30, 1886); also many pieces of church music; glees, part-songs; organ pieces. His widow publ. a memoir, *Life and Reminiscences of George J. Elvey* (London, 1894).

Elvey, Stephen, English organist and composer, brother of **Sir George Elvey;** b. Canterbury, June 27, 1805; d. Oxford, Oct. 6, 1860. He was a chorister at Canterbury Cathedral, and a pupil of Skeats there; in 1830 he became organist of New College, Oxford; received a Mus.Bac. (1831) and a Mus.Doc. (1838) from Oxford; was Choragus there from 1840 until his death. He wrote mostly church music, and publ. a successful handbook, *The Psalter, or Canticles and Psalms, Pointed for Chanting, upon a New Principle* (London; 6 eds. to 1866).

Elvira, Pablo, Puerto Rican baritone; b. Santurce, Sept. 24, 1938. He was born into a musical family; entered the Casals Cons., where he studied voice. In 1966 he became a finalist in the Metropolitan Opera auditions, and subsequently sang with the N.Y. City Opera, the Chicago Lyric Opera, and the San Francisco Opera. In 1977 he made his Metropolitan Opera debut in N.Y. as Tonio in *Pagliacci*. His finest roles include Figaro in *Il Barbiere di Siviglia,* Lescaut in *Manon Lescaut,* Renato in *Un ballo in maschera,* Germont in *La Traviata,* and Rigoletto.

Elwart, Antoine-Aimable-Elie, French writer on music and composer; b. Paris, Nov. 18, 1808; d. there, Oct. 14, 1877. A chorister at St.-Eustache when 10 years old, he was apprenticed at 13 to a mechanic, but ran away, and joined a small theater orch. as a violinist. From 1825–34 he studied at the Paris Cons., taking the Grand Prix de Rome in 1834; taught at the Paris Cons. from 1836 to 1871. Among his pupils were Gouvy, Grisar, and Weckerlin.

WORKS: Opera, *Les Catalans* (Rouen, 1840); "oratorio-symphonie," *Noé, ou Le Déluge universel* (Paris, 1845); oratorio, *La Naissance d'Eve* (Paris, 1846); *Les Noces de Cana,* mystery; *Ruth et Booz,* vocal symph.; masses, cantatas, a Te Deum, a Miserere, and other church music; symphs., overtures, chamber music, etc. He is better known by his musico-literary works: *Duprez, sa vie artistique, avec une biographie authentique de son maître A. Choron* (1838); *Théorie musicale (Solfège progressif,* etc., 1840); *Feuille harmonique* (1841); *Le Chanteur accompagnateur* (1844); *Traité de contrepoint et de la fugue; Essai sur la Transposition; Etudes élémentaires de musique* (1845); *L'Art de chanter en chœur; L'Art de jouer impromptu de l'alto-viola; Solfège de jeune âge; Le Contrepoint et la fugue appliqués au style idéal; Lutrin et Orphéon* (theoretical and practical vocal studies); *Histoire de la Société des Concerts du Conservatoire* (1860; 2nd ed., 1863); *Manuel des aspirants aux grades de chef et de souschef de musique dans l'armée fran-çaise* (1862); *Petit manuel d' instrumentation* (1864); *Histoire de concerts populaires* (1864). His projected complete ed. of his own compositions (1867–70) reached only vol. III.

Elwell, Herbert, American composer and music critic; b. Minneapolis, May 10, 1898; d. Cleveland, April 17, 1974. He studied at the Univ. of Minnesota; then took courses with Ernest Bloch in N.Y. (1919–21) and Nadia Boulanger in Paris (1921–24); received a Prix de Rome in 1923; from 1924 to 1927 held a fellowship at the American Academy in Rome. Returning to the U.S., he held a post as teacher of composition at the Cleveland Music Inst. (1928–45); from 1932 to 1964 served as music critic for the Cleveland *Plain Dealer*.
WORKS: His most successful work was the ballet *The Happy Hypocrite*, after Max Beerbohm (an orch. suite drawn from the score was perf. in Rome on May 21, 1927, with Elwell himself conducting); *Introduction and Allegro* for Orch. (N.Y., July 12, 1942); *I Was with Him*, cantata for Male Chorus, Tenor Solo, and 2 Pianos (Cleveland, Nov. 30, 1942); *Blue Symphony* for Voice and String Quartet (Cleveland, Feb. 2, 1945); *Lincoln: Requiem Aeternam* for Chorus and Orch. (Oberlin, Feb. 16, 1947); *Pastorale* for Voice and Orch. (Cleveland, March 25, 1948); *Ode* for Orch. (1950); *The Forever Young* for Voice and Orch. (Cleveland, Oct. 29, 1953); *Concert Suite* for Violin and Orch. (Louisville, Feb. 5, 1958); 2 string quartets; Piano Sonata; Violin Sonata; etc.

Elwes, Gervase, English tenor; b. Billing Hall, near Northampton, Nov. 15, 1866; d. Boston, Jan. 12, 1921. He began his career as a diplomat; while stationed in Vienna (1891–95), he studied singing; during his sojourn in Paris he took voice lessons with Bouhy, and soon achieved competence as a concert singer. He made a tour of Germany in 1907 and 2 tours in the U.S. (1909 and 1921; died on his 2nd tour, killed by a train in the railroad station in Boston). He excelled in oratorio; sang Elgar's *Dream of Gerontius* about 150 times. Winifred and Richard Elwes publ. an impassioned family monograph, *Gervase Elwes: The Story of His Life* (London, 1935).

Emerson, Luther Orlando, American composer and conductor; b. Parsonsfield, Maine, Aug. 3, 1820; d. Hyde Park, Mass., Sept. 29, 1915. He was a competent composer of church music, a popular conductor of the early musical conventions, and a compiler of numerous successful collections of songs and hymn tunes: *The Romberg Collection* (1853); *The Golden Wreath* (1857, Sunday-school music); *The Golden Harp* (1860); *The Sabbath Harmony* (1860); *The Harp of Judah* (1863); *Merry Chimes* (1865); *Jubilate* (1866); *The Chorus Wreath*.

Emery, Stephen Albert, American music teacher, writer, and composer; b. Paris, Maine, Oct. 4, 1841; d. Boston, April 15, 1891. His first teacher was H.S. Edwards, of Portland, Maine; in 1862 he went to Leipzig, where he studied with Plaidy, Papperitz,

Richter, and Hauptmann. He returned to Portland in 1864; went to Boston in 1866; taught at the New England Cons. there from 1867. He publ. 2 textbooks, *Foundation Studies in Piano Playing* and *Elements of Harmony* (1879; several later eds.).

Emery, Walter, English organist and writer; b. Tilshead, Wiltshire, June 14, 1909; d. Salisbury, June 24, 1974. He studied organ at the Royal Academy of Music in London; then was engaged as a church organist; from 1937 to 1969 he was an associate at Novello & Co. in the editorial dept.; publ. several valuable books and pamphlets: *The St. Matthew Passion: Its Preparation and Performance* (with Sir Adrian Boult; London, 1949); *Bach's Ornaments* (London, 1953); commentaries on Bach's organ works; etc.

Emmanuel, Maurice, eminent French music scholar; b. Bar-sur-Aube, May 2, 1862; d. Paris, Dec. 14, 1938. He received his primary education in Dijon; sang in the church choir in Beaune; then studied at the Paris Cons. (1880–87) with Savard, Dubois, Delibes, and Bourgault-Ducoudray; then specialized in the musical history of antiquity under Gevaert in Brussels; also studied ancient languages at the Sorbonne, receiving a licencié ès lettres (1887) and a docteur ès lettres (1895) with the theses *De saltationis disciplina apud Graecos* (publ. in Latin, Paris, 1895) and *La Danse grecque antique d'après les monuments figurés* (Paris, 1896; in Eng. as *The Antique Greek Dance after Sculptured and Painted Figures*, N.Y., 1916). He was a prof. of art history at the Lycée Racine and Lycée Lamartine (1898–1905); maître de chapelle at Ste.-Clotilde (1904–7); in 1909 he succeeded Bourgault-Ducoudray as prof. of music history at the Paris Cons., and held this post until 1936; he edited vols. 17 and 18 of the complete works of Rameau; also Bach's works in Durand's ed. of the classical masters.
WRITINGS: *Histoire de la langue musicale* (2 vols., Paris, 1911; new ed., 1928); *Traité de l'accompagnement modal des psaumes* (Lyons, 1912); *La Polyphonie sacrée* (with R. Moissenet; Dijon, 1923); *Pelléas et Mélisande de Claude Debussy* (Paris, 1926); *César Franck* (Paris, 1930); *Antonin Reicha* (Paris, 1937); also articles in the *Revue Musicale, Musical Quarterly*, etc.
WORKS: Opera, *Salamine* (Paris, June 28, 1929); opéra-bouffe, *Amphitryon* (Paris, Feb. 20, 1937); 2 symphs. (1919, 1931); 2 string quartets and other chamber music; 6 piano sonatinas; vocal music (much of it publ.).
BIBLIOGRAPHY: Special issue of the *Revue Musicale* devoted to Maurice Emmanuel (1947).

Emmett, Daniel Decatur, American composer of *Dixie* and other popular songs; b. Mt. Vernon, Ohio, Oct. 29, 1815; d. there, June 28, 1904. He began his career as a drummer in military bands; then joined the Virginia Minstrels, singing and playing the banjo; later was a member of Bryant's Minstrels. He wrote the lyrics and the music of *Dixie* in 1859, and it was performed for the first time in N.Y., on April

4, 1859; upon publication, the popularity of the song spread, and it was adopted as a Southern fighting song during the Civil War (even though Emmett was a Northerner). His other songs, *Old Dan Tucker, The Road to Richmond, Walk Along,* etc., enjoyed great favor for some years, but were eclipsed by *Dixie.*

BIBLIOGRAPHY: Ch. B. Galbreath, *Daniel Decatur Emmett* (Columbus, Ohio, 1904); R.B. Harwell, *Confederate Music* (Chapel Hill, N.C., 1950); Hans Nathan, "Dixie," *Musical Quarterly* (Jan. 1949); H.O. Wintermute, *Daniel Decatur Emmett* (Mt. Vernon, 1955); Hans Nathan, *Dan Emmett and the Rise of Early Negro Minstrelsy* (Norman, Okla., 1962).

Enacovici, George, Rumanian composer; b. Focşani, May 4, 1891; d. Bucharest, Jan. 26, 1965. He studied at the Bucharest Cons. with Kiriac and Castaldi (1905–12); studied composition, with d'Indy, and violin at the Schola Cantorum in Paris (1914–18); taught violin at the Bucharest Cons. (1919–54) and was concertmaster of the Bucharest Phil. (1920–21) and the Bucharest Radio Orch. (1928–33). He was a founder-member of the Society of Rumanian Composers (1920).

WORKS: *Intermezzo* for String Orch. and Harp (1912); *Poem* for Violin and Orch. (1920); *Suite in a Rumanian Style* for Orch. (1928); *Symphonic Episode* (1933); *Rapsodie română* for Orch. (1934); *Amfitrita,* symph. poem with Violin obbligato (1940); *Arlequinada,* capriccio for 2 Violins and Chamber Orch. (1941); Symph. (1954); Violin Concerto (1956); 3 string quartets; Violin Sonata; Piano Sonata; minor pieces in various genres.

Encina, Juan del, Spanish poet and composer; b. Salamanca, July 12. 1468; d. León, Aug. 29 or 30, 1529. He was the son of a shoemaker of Salamanca named Juan de Fermoselle; became chorister at Salamanca Cathedral; studied music under his elder brother, Diego de Fermoselle, and under Fernando de Torrijos; took his degree in law at Salamanca Univ., where he enjoyed the favor of the chancellor, Don Gutiérrez de Toledo. In 1492 he entered the household of the 2nd Duke of Alba, for whom he wrote a series of pastoral eclogues that form the foundation of the Spanish secular drama. These eclogues included "villancicos," or rustic songs, for which Encina composed the music. He went to Rome in 1500; on May 12, 1500, was appointed canon at the Cathedral of Salamanca; from Feb. 2, 1510, until 1512, he was archdeacon and canon of Málaga; on May 2, 1512, he again went to Rome; his *Farsa de Plácida e Vittoriano* was performed there in the presence of Julius II on Jan. 11, 1513. In 1517, he was "subcollector of revenues to the Apostolic Chamber." In 1519 he was appointed prior of León, and that same year made a pilgrimage to Jerusalem, where he was ordained a priest. He described his sacred pilgrimage in *Tribagia o Via Sacra de Hierusalem* (Rome, 1521). After the death of Leo X in 1521, Encina returned to Spain and spent his last years as prior at León. Besides being the creator of the Spanish drama, Encina was the most important Spanish composer of the reign of Ferdinand and Isabella; he cultivated with notable artistry a type of part-song akin to the Italian "frottola," setting his own poems to music; 68 of these songs are preserved in the valuable *Cancionero musical de los siglos XV y XVI,* ed. by F. A. Barbieri (Madrid, 1890; new ed., in 3 vols., by H. Anglès, 1947, 1951, 1953). Another modern ed. was publ. by C. Terni, *Juan del Encina: L'opera musicale* (Florence, 1974—). No religious music by Encina is known to exist.

BIBLIOGRAPHY: E. Diaz-Jiménez, *Juan del Encina en León* (Madrid, 1909); R. Mitjana, *Estudios sobre algunos músicos españoles del siglo XVI* (Madrid, 1918); R. Espinosa Maeso, "Nuevos datos biográphicos de Juan del Encina," *Boletín de la Royal Academia Española* (1921); J. Subirá, *La música en la Casa de Alba* (1927); F. Pedrell, *Cancionero musical popular español* (new ed., 2 vols., Barcelona, 1936); J.P. Wichersham Crawford, *Spanish Drama Before Lope de Vega* (revised ed., Philadelphia, 1937); G. Chase, "Origins of the Lyric Theater in Spain," *Musical Quarterly* (July 1939); G. Chase, "Juan del Encina, Poet and Musician," *Music & Letters* (Oct. 1939); C. Terni, "Juan del Encina," *Chigiana* (1968).

Enckhausen, Heinrich Friedrich, German organist and composer; b. Celle, Aug. 28, 1799; d. Hannover, Jan. 15, 1885. He studied with Aloys Schmitt in Berlin, succeeding him as court organist. He wrote an opera, *Der Savoyard* (Hannover, 1832), and sacred music; publ. a book of chorales.

Ende, Heinrich vom, German music publisher; b. Essen, Aug. 12, 1858; d. Cologne, Jan. 20, 1904. He publ. popular manuals on music, such as *Schatzkästlein;* also composed a considerable number of male choruses (*Das Kätzchen; Es ist ein Brünnlein geflossen;* etc.) songs, and piano pieces.

Endo, Akira, Japanese-American conductor; b. Shido, Nov. 16, 1940. He studied violin with Vera Barstow and Eudice Shapiro; received B.M. and M.M. degrees from the Univ. of Southern Calif. at Los Angeles; was a member of the Trojan and Pacific string quartets. He conducted the Long Beach, Calif., Symph. Orch. (1966–69) and the West Side Symph. Orch. in Los Angeles (1968–69) was then music director of the American Ballet Theater (1969–79) and of the Austin (Texas) Symph. Orch. (1975–83). In 1981 he was appointed music director of the Louisville Orch.

Enesco (Enescu), Georges, foremost Rumanian composer and violinist; b. Liveni-Virnaz, Aug. 19, 1881; d. Paris, May 4, 1955. He began to play violin when only 4 years old, taking lessons with a Rumanian gypsy violinist, Nicolas Chioru; then studied with the violinist and composer Caudella; from 1888–93 he was a pupil at the Vienna Cons. under Hellmesberger (violin) and R. Fuchs (theory), winning first prize in violin and harmony (1892); in 1894–99 he studied at the Paris Cons. with Marsick (violin), Fauré and Massenet (composition); won 2nd *accessit* for counterpoint and fugue (1897) and first prize for violin (1899); at the same time he studied cello, organ, and piano, attaining more than ordinary proficiency on all these instruments. His talent for composition manifested itself very early, his first efforts dating from his student days in Vienna; on June 11, 1897, when he was not quite 16, he presented in Paris a concert of his own works (String Quintet, Piano Suite, Violin Sonata, and songs), which attracted the attention of Colonne, who produced the following year the youthful composer's op. 1, *Poème roumain.* On March 8, 1903, he conducted in Bucharest the first performances of his 2 *Rumanian Rhapsodies,* the first of which was to become his most enduring work. He was appointed court violinist to the Queen of Rumania; gave master classes in violin interpretation at the Ecole Normale de Musique; among his pupils was Yehudi Menuhin. In 1912 he offered an annual prize for Rumanian composers (won by Jora, Enacovici, Stan Golestan, Otescu, and others); then toured Europe; first visited the U.S. in 1923, making his debut as conductor, composer, and violinist in a N.Y. concert of the Philadelphia Orch. (Jan. 2, 1923); returned to the U.S. in 1937, and conducted the N.Y. Phil. on Jan. 28, 1937, and several subsequent concerts with remarkable success; reengaged in 1938 and conducted the N.Y. Phil. in 14 concerts; appeared twice as a violinist; also conducted 2 concerts of Rumanian music at the N.Y. World's Fair (May 1939). The outbreak of World War II found Enesco in Rumania, where he lived on his farm in Sinaia, near Bucharest. He remained there through the war years; in 1946 he came again to the U.S. to teach in N.Y. On Jan. 21, 1950, on the 60th anniversary of his first public appearance at the age of 8, he played a farewell concert in N.Y. in the multiple capacity of violinist, pianist, conductor, and composer, in a program comprising Bach's Double Concerto (with Enesco's pupil Yehudi Menuhin), his own Violin Sonata (playing the piano part with Menuhin), and his *First Rumanian Rhapsody* (conducting the orch.). He then returned to Paris; in July 1954 he suffered a stroke, and became an invalid for his remaining days. In homage to his accomplishment in Rumanian music, his native village was renamed Enescu and a street in Bucharest was also named after him. Periodical Enescu Festivals and international performing contests were established in Bucharest in 1958. Enesco had an extraordinary range of musical interests. His compositions include artistic stylizations of Rumanian folk strains; his style was neo-Romantic, but he made occasional use of experimental devices, such as quarter-tones in his opera *Œdipe.* He possessed a fabulous memory and was able to play complete symph. works without the scores.

WORKS: LYRIC TRAGEDY: *Œdipe* (1931; Grand Opéra, Paris, March 10, 1936; Bucharest, posthumous production, Sept. 22, 1958). FOR ORCH.: 3 early symphs., unnumbered (1895, 1896, 1898); 5 numbered symphs.: No. 1 (Paris, Jan. 21, 1906); No. 2 (Bucharest, March 28, 1915); No. 3 (1918; Bucharest, May 25, 1919); No. 4 (1934; unfinished); No. 5, with

Tenor and Women's Chorus (1941; unfinished); *Ballad* for Violin and Orch. (1895); *Tragic Overture* (1895); Violin Concerto (1896; Paris, March 26, 1896, at a Paris Cons. concert); Fantasy for Piano and Orch. (1896; Bucharest, March 26, 1900); *Rumanian Poem* (1897; Paris, Feb. 9, 1898); *Pastorale* (1899; Paris, Feb. 19, 1899); *Rumanian Rhapsody No. 1* (1901) and *No. 2* (1902; both perf. for the first time in Bucharest, March 8, 1903, composer conducting); *Symphonie concertante* for Cello and Orch. (1901; Paris, March 14, 1909); Suite No. 1 (1903; Paris, Dec. 11, 1904); Suite No. 2 (1915; Bucharest, March 27, 1916, composer conducting); Suite No. 3, *Villageoise* (1938; N.Y. Phil., Feb. 2, 1939, composer conducting); *Concert Overture on Popular Rumanian Themes* (1948; Washington, D.C., Jan. 23, 1949, composer conducting); *Symphonie de chambre* (1954; Paris, Jan. 23, 1955); *Vox maris,* symph. poem (1955; posthumous, Bucharest, Sept. 10, 1964). CHAMBER MUSIC: *Ballad* for Violin and Piano (1895); Piano Quintet (1895); Violin Sonata No. 1 (1897); *Nocturne et Saltarelle* for Cello and Piano (1897); Cello Sonata No. 1 (1898); Violin Sonata No. 2 (1899); *Aubade* for String Trio (1899); Octet for 4 Violins, 2 Violas, and 2 Cellos (1900); *Intermezzo* for Strings (1903); *Allegro de concert* for Harp and Piano (1904); *Dixtuor* for Wind Instruments (1906); *Au soir,* nocturne for 4 Trumpets (1906); *Legenda* for Trumpet and Piano (1906); *Konzertstück* for Viola and Piano (1906); Piano Quartet No. 1 (1909); String Quartet No. 1 (1920); Violin Sonata No. 3, "in popular Rumanian character" (1926); Cello Sonata No. 2 (1935); Piano Quintet No. 2 (1940); *Impressions d'enfance* for Violin and Piano (1940); Piano Quartet No. 2 (1944); String Quartet No. 2 (1951). FOR PIANO: *Variations on an Original Theme* for 2 Pianos (1899); 2 suites for Piano Solo: No. 1, *Dans le style ancien* (1897), and No. 2 (1903); *Pièces impromptues* (1915–16); 3 sonatas (1924, 1927, 1934). VOCAL WORKS: *La Vision de Saul,* cantata (1895); *L'Aurore,* cantata (1898); *Waldgesang* for Chorus (1898); many songs to words by the Queen of Rumania, who wrote poetry in German under the pen name Carmen Sylva, among them *Armes Mägdlein* (1898); *Der Schmetterlingskuss* (1898); *Schlaflos* (1898); *Frauenberuf* (1898); *Sphynx* (1898); *Königshusarenlied* (1899); *Ein Sonnenblick* (1901); *Regen* (1903); *Entsagen* (1907); *Morgengebet* (1908); also several cycles of songs to French texts.

BIBLIOGRAPHY: B. Gavoty, *Les Souvenirs de Georges Enesco* (Paris, 1955); G. Balan, *George Enescu* (Bucharest, 1962); B. Kotlyarov, *George Enescu* (Moscow, 1965); M. Voicana et al., eds., *George Enescu,* a symposium (2 vols., Bucharest, 1971). A complete list of works and an extensive bibliography is found in Viorel Cosma, *Muzicieni Români* (Bucharest, 1970).

Engel, Carl, German musical historiographer; b. Thiedeweise, near Hannover, July 6, 1818; d. by suicide, London, Nov. 17, 1882. He studied organ with Enckhausen at Hannover and piano with Hummel at Weimar. After residing in Hamburg, Warsaw, and Berlin, he went to Manchester, England, in

1846, and in 1850 to London. There he became an influential writer, and an authority on musical history and musical instruments.

WRITINGS: *The Pianist's Handbook* (1853); *Piano School for Young Beginners* (1855); *Reflections on Church Music* (1856); his lifework began with *The Music of the Most Ancient Nations, Particularly of the Assyrians, Egyptians, and Hebrews* (1864), followed by *An Introduction to the Study of National Music* (1866); *Musical Instruments of All Countries* (1869); *Catalogue of the Special Exhibition of Ancient Musical Instruments* (2nd ed., 1873); *Descriptive Catalogue of the Musical Instruments in the South Kensington Museum* (1874); *Musical Myths and Facts* (1876); *The Literature of National Music* (1879); *Researches into the Early History of the Violin Family* (1883). Among his unpublished MSS is a large history of the musical instruments of the world (4 quarto vols. with over 800 illustrations).

BIBLIOGRAPHY: Carl Engel, "Some Letters to a Namesake," *Musical Quarterly* (July 1942); Gustave Reese, "More about the Namesake," in *A Birthday Offering to Carl Engel* (N.Y., 1943).

Engel, Carl, distinguished American musicologist and writer on music; b. Paris, July 21, 1883; d. New York, May 6, 1944. He was a great-grandson of **Josef Kroll,** founder of Kroll's Etablissement in Berlin, and grandson of **J.C. Engel,** who made the Kroll Opera famous. Carl Engel was educated at the univs. of Strasbourg and Munich; studied composition in Munich with Thuille. He came to the U.S. in 1905 and established himself as an editor, musicologist, librarian, and publisher. He was editor and musical adviser of the Boston Music Co. (1909–21); chief of the Music Division of the Library of Congress (1922–34); president of G. Schirmer, Inc. (1929–32); in 1929 became editor of the *Musical Quarterly;* remained with it until 1942; from 1934 was again president of G. Schirmer, Inc., and honorary consultant in musicology for the Library of Congress; was U.S. delegate to the Beethoven Centenary, Vienna, 1927; U.S. representative of the International Society of Musicology; first chairman of the Committee on Musicology, American Council of Learned Societies; president of the American Musicological Society (1937–38); was an honorary member of the Harvard Musical Association; also a Fellow of the American Academy of Arts and Letters; received an honorary Mus.Doc. from Oberlin College (1934); was made a Chevalier of the Légion d'Honneur (1937); was a recipient of the Elizabeth Sprague Coolidge medal "for eminent services rendered to chamber music" (1935). A writer with a brilliant style and of wide learning, Carl Engel contributed valuable essays to the *Musical Quarterly* (*Views and Reviews;* articles on Chadwick, Loeffler, etc.); publ. 2 collections of essays: *Alla Breve, from Bach to Debussy* (N.Y., 1921) and *Discords Mingled* (N.Y., 1931). Carl Engel was also a composer; his music was in the French tradition, in an impressionistic vein; his songs, particularly his settings of poems by Amy Lowell, were often sung (the best known among them is *Sea-*

Shell); other works include *Triptych* for Violin and Piano; *Perfumes* for Piano (an album of 5 pieces); *Presque valse* for Piano was publ. posthumously.

BIBLIOGRAPHY: G. Reese, ed., *A Birthday Offering to Carl Engel* (N.Y., 1943); Harold Bauer, "Carl Engel," *Musical Quarterly* (July 1944); G. Reese, "A Postscript" (ibid.); H. Putnam and E.S. Coolidge, "Tributes to Carl Engel," *Musical Quarterly* (April 1945).

Engel, David Hermann, German organist and composer; b. Neuruppin, Jan. 22, 1816; d. Merseburg, May 3, 1877. He studied in Breslau; in 1848 became organist at Merseburg; wrote a comic opera, *Prinz Carneval* (Berlin, 1862); publ. *Beitrag zur Geschichte des Orgelbauwesens* (1855).

Engel, Gabriel, American writer, violinist, and composer; b. Beregszasz, Hungary, May 4, 1892; d. Vergennes, Vt., Aug. 1, 1952. He was the author of *The Life of Anton Bruckner* (N.Y., 1931) and *Gustav Mahler—Song-Symphonist* (N.Y., 1932); also editor of *Chord and Discord,* the magazine of the Bruckner Society of America. During the last 15 years of his life he was engaged in the rare-books business.

Engel, Gustav Eduard, German music critic and singing teacher; b. Königsberg, Oct. 29, 1823; d. Berlin, July 19, 1895. He was music critic of the *Vossische Zeitung* from 1861; taught singing at Kullak's Academy from 1862; among his pupils was Lola Beeth. He publ. *Sängerbrevier* (daily vocal exercises, 1860), *Ästhetik der Tonkunst* (1884), and other books and articles.

Engel, Hans, eminent German musicologist; b. Cairo, Egypt, Dec. 20, 1894; d. Marburg, May 15, 1970. He studied at the Akademie der Tonkunst in Munich with Klose and at the Univ. of Munich with Sandberger; received his Ph.D. from the Univ. of Munich in 1925 with the dissertation *Die Entwicklung des deutschen Klavierkonzertes von Mozart bis Liszt* (publ. in Leipzig, 1927); completed his Habilitation at the Univ. of Greifswald in 1926; then taught there (1926–35). He was on the faculty of the Univ. of Königsberg (1935–46) and Marburg Univ. (1946–63).

WRITINGS: *Carl Loewe* (Greifswald, 1934); *Franz Liszt* (Potsdam, 1936); *Deutschland und Italien in ihren musikgeschichtlichen Beziehungen* (Regensburg, 1944); *Johann Sebastian Bach* (Berlin, 1950); *Musik der Völker und Zeiten* (Hannover, 1952; revised ed., 1968); *Luca Marenzio* (Florence, 1956); *Musik in Thüringen* (Cologne and Graz, 1966).

Engel, Joel, Russian writer on music; b. Berdiansk, April 16, 1868; d. Tel Aviv, Feb. 2, 1927. He studied at Kharkov; later with Taneyev and Ippolitov-Ivanov in Moscow. In 1922 he went to Berlin, where he organized a publishing house for propaganda of Jewish music; issued a collection of Jewish folk songs in 3 vols. His publications in Russian are: *Pocket Music*

Dictionary (Moscow, 1913); *Essays on Music History* (Moscow, 1911); *In the Opera* (1911).

Engel, Johann Jakob, German musician and writer; b. Parchim, Mecklenburg, Sept. 11, 1741; d. there, June 28, 1802. He was tutor to the Crown Prince (later Friedrich Wilhelm III); publ. an interesting essay, *Über die musikalische Malerei* (1780).

Engel, Karl, Swiss pianist; b. Birsfeld, June 1, 1923. He studied in Bern and Paris; his principal teachers were Paul Baumgartner and Alfred Cortot. In 1952 he won second prize at the Queen Elisabeth Competition in Brussels; gave many recitals and played at the leading festivals in Europe. In addition, he became one of the most distinguished accompanists of singers, among them Dietrich Fischer-Dieskau. In 1959 he was appointed prof. at the Hannover Hochschule für Musik.

Engel, Lehman, American composer, conductor, and writer on music; b. Jackson, Miss., Sept. 14, 1910; d. New York, Aug. 29, 1982. He began to take piano lessons with local teachers as a child; then went to Cincinnati, where he studied with Sidney Durst at the Cincinnati College of Music (1927–29) and later with Eduardo Trucco in N.Y.; in 1930–34 he took courses in composition with Rubin Goldmark at the Juilliard School of Music and also took private composition lessons with Roger Sessions (1931–37). While still a student, he began to write music for ballet and theatrical plays; in 1934 he wrote incidental music for Sean O'Casey's play *Within the Gates,* which he conducted. From 1935 to 1939 he led the Madrigal Singers for the Works Progress Administration; later worked with the Mercury Theater as composer and conductor. During World War II Engel enlisted in the U.S. Navy and conducted a military orch. at the Great Lakes Naval Training Stations; later was appointed chief composer of the Navy's film division in Washington, D.C. He wrote a great many scores of incidental music for Broadway productions, which he also conducted, among them for T.S. Eliot's *Murder in the Cathedral* and Tennessee Williams's *A Streetcar Named Desire.* As a composer, Engel was happiest in writing for the theater; he had a special knack for vivid musical illustration of the action on the stage. Of importance are his numerous books on the American music theater. He was also active as a teacher of composition and led in N.Y. a seminar on musical lyrics. He conducted the first American performance of Kurt Weill's *The Threepenny Opera;* also conducted the productions of *Showboat, Brigadoon, Annie Get Your Gun, Fanny, Guys and Dolls,* and *Carousel.* Engel received 2 Antoinette Perry (Tony) Awards, in 1950 for conducting Menotti's opera *The Consul,* and in 1953 for conducting the operettas of Gilbert and Sullivan. In 1971 he received the honorary degree of D.M. from the Univ. of Cincinnati. WORKS: OPERAS: *Pierrot of the Minuet* (Cincinnati, April 3, 1928); *Malady of Love* (N.Y., May 27, 1954); *The Soldier* (N.Y., Nov. 25, 1956, a concert version); *Golden Ladder,* a musical (Cleveland,

May 28, 1953). BALLETS: *Phobias* (N.Y., Nov. 18, 1932); *Ceremonials* (N.Y., May 13, 1933); *Transitions* (N.Y., Feb. 19, 1934); *The Shoebird* (Jackson, Miss., April 20, 1968). INCIDENTAL MUSIC TO SHAKESPEARE'S PLAYS: *Hamlet* (1938); *Macbeth* (1941); *Julius Caesar* (1955); *The Tempest* (1960); also music to plays by contemporary authors. FOR ORCH.: 2 symphs. (1939, 1945); Viola Concerto (1945); *The Creation* for Narrator and Orch. (1947); overture, *Jackson* (Jackson, Miss., Feb. 13, 1961). CHAMBER MUSIC: Cello Sonata (1945); Violin Sonata (1953). FOR CHORUS: *Rain* (1929); *Rest* (1936); *Chansons innocentes* (1938); *Let Us Now Praise Famous Men* (1955). WRITINGS: *The Bright Day,* an autobiography (N.Y., 1956; revised 1974); an instruction book, *Planning and Producing the Musical Show* (N.Y., 1957; revised 1966); *The American Musical Theater: A Consideration* (N.Y., 1967); ed. the collection *Three Centuries of Choral Music: Renaissance to Baroque* (N.Y., 1939–56); *The Musical Book* (N.Y., 1971); *Words and Music* (N.Y., 1972); *Their Words Are Music* (N.Y., 1975); *Getting the Show On: The Complete Guidebook for Producing a Musical in Your Theater* (N.Y., 1983). A detailed list of Lehman Engel's works for the theater is found in Walter Rigdon, ed., *Who's Who of the American Theater* (N.Y., 1966).

Engelke, Bernhard, German musicologist; b. Brunswick, Sept. 2, 1884; d. Kirchbarkau, near Kiel, May 16, 1950. He studied at Halle with H. Abert and at Leipzig Univ. with Riemann (Dr.Phil., 1908, for his dissertation on J.F. Fasch). In 1912 he went to Magdeburg as teacher and choirmaster at the Cathedral; in 1925 he settled in Kiel. He publ. numerous articles in music journals dealing mainly with German church music and musicians.

Engelmann, Hans Ulrich, German composer; b. Darmstadt, Sept. 8, 1921. He had piano lessons while in high school; after the end of the disrupting war, he took courses in composition with Wolfgang Fortner in Heidelberg (1945–49); in 1948–50 he attended the classes of René Leibowitz and Ernst Krenek in Darmstadt; enrolled at the Univ. of Frankfurt (1946–52), taking classes in musicology (with Gennrich and Osthoff) and philosophy (with Adorno); in 1952, received his Dr.Phil. with a thesis on Béla Bartók's *Mikrokosmos* (publ. in Würzburg, 1953). Parallel to these pursuits, he took courses in architecture. In 1949 he held a Harvard Univ. stipend at the Salzburg Seminar in American Studies; was active in radio programming and in composition for films and for the theater; spent a season in Iceland (1953–54); then was theater composer in Darmstadt (1954–61). In 1969 he was appointed an instructor at the Frankfurt Hochschule für Musik. His early works are impregnated by chromaticism with an impressionistic tinge. He adopted the 12-tone method of composition, expanding it into a sui generis "field technique" of total serialism, in which rhythms and instrumental timbres are organized systematically. In his theater music he utilizes aleatory devices, *musique concrète,* and electronic sonorities. WORKS: *Klangstück* for Violin and Piano (1947);

Concerto for Cello and String Orch. (1948); *Doktor Fausts Höllenfahrt,* chamber opera (Hamburg, Jan. 11, 1951); *Orchester-Fantasie* (1951); String Quartet (1953); *Komposition in 4 Teilen* (1953; his first work in the 12-tone technique); Partita for 3 Trumpets, Percussion, and Strings (1953); *Integrale* for Saxophone and Piano (1954); *Strukturen* for Chamber Orch. (1954); *Atlantische Ballade* for Voices, Strings, and Percussion (1955); *Die Mauer,* dramatic cantata after Langston Hughes (radio production, Hamburg, Oct. 4, 1955; stage premiere, Darmstadt, March 21, 1960); *Metall,* "chronicle" for Soloists, Chorus, and Orch. (1958); *Der verlorene Schatten,* opera (1960); *Trias* for Piano, Orch., and Magnetic Tape (1962); *Serpentina* (1963); *Noche de Luna,* ballet (Lübeck, June 1, 1965); *Duplum* for 2 Pianos (1965); *Manifest vom Menschen,* oratorio (1966); *Capricciosi* for Orch. (1967); *Der Fall Van Damm,* radio opera (Cologne, June 7, 1968); *Sinfonies* for Orch. (1968); *Ophelia,* music for action theater (Hannover, Feb. 1, 1969); *Drei Kreise* for Orch. Groups (1970); *Commedia humana* for 2 Mixed Choruses, Amplified Cello, and Tape (1972).

Englert, Giuseppe Giorgio, Italian organist and composer; b. Fiesole, near Florence, July 22, 1927. He studied composition with Willy Burkhard at the Zürich Cons. (1945–48); in 1949 went to Paris, where he took organ lessons with André Marchal (1949–56), became his assistant as organist of the St. Eustache Church (1957–62); in 1970 he was appointed a lecturer at the Univ. of Paris at Vincennes. WORKS: *Rime serie* for Wind Quintet (1958–61); *Au jour ultime liesse,* cantata for Voice and 6 Instruments (1961–63); *Les Avoines folles* for String Quartet (1962–63); *Aria* for Timpani and 13 Instruments (1965); *La Joute des lierres* for String Quartet (1965–66); *Tarok,* musical game for 3–6 String Instruments (1967); *Vagans animula* for Organ and Tape (1969); *Maquillage,* theatrical composition for Voice, Scenic Apparatus, and Tape (1967–71); *Cantus plumbeus* for Organ (1972); *Non pulsando* for Organ (1972); *Caracol* for 15 Instruments (1974).

English, Granville, American composer; b. Louisville, Ky., Jan. 27, 1895; d. New York, Sept. 1, 1968. He was educated at the Chicago Musical College (Mus.Bac., 1915). WORKS: *Ugly Duckling,* cantata (1924); *Among the Hills,* orchestral scherzo (Oklahoma City, March 9, 1952); *Mood Tropicale* for Orch. (Baltimore, Feb. 5, 1955); *Evenings by the Sea,* symph. poem (Port Washington, Long Island, N.Y., Jan. 20, 1956); *Song of the Caravan* for Male Chorus (1937); piano pieces; violin pieces; songs.

Englund, Einar, Finnish composer; b. Ljugarn, Gotland, Sweden, June 17, 1916. He studied at the Sibelius Academy in Helsinki (1933–45); in 1949 he took a course in composition with Aaron Copland at Tanglewood. Returning to Finland, he became a teacher at the Sibelius Academy (1958). WORKS: Piano Quintet (1941); Symph. No. 1 (1946); *Epinikia,* symph. poem (1947); Symph. No. 2 (1948); *The Great Wall of China,* symph. suite from incidental music to Max Frisch's play (1949); Cello Concerto (1954); Piano Concerto No. 1 (1955); *Odysseus,* symph. suite (1959); *Sinuhe,* symph. suite from the ballet (1965); Chaconne for Chorus, Trombone, and Double Bass (1969); *Introduzione e Capriccio* for Violin and Piano (1970); Symph. No. 3, *Cholecystitis* (Helsinki, May 12, 1972); Piano Concerto No. 2 (1974); Symph. No. 4 for Strings and Percussion (1976); Symph. No. 5, *Fennica* (1977); Piano Sonata (1978); Violin Sonata (1979); Concerto for 12 Solo Cellos (1980); *De profundis* for 14 Brasses (1980); Violin Concerto (1981); also music for numerous radio plays and films.

Enna, August, eminent Danish composer; b. Nakskov, May 13, 1859; d. Copenhagen, Aug. 3, 1939. He was partly of German and Italian blood; his grandfather, an Italian soldier in Napoleon's army, married a German girl, and settled in Denmark. Enna was brought to Copenhagen as a child, and went to school there. He learned to play piano and violin; had sporadic instruction in theory; later became a member of a traveling orch. and played with it in Finland (1880). Upon his return to Copenhagen, he taught piano and played for dancers; in 1883 he conducted a theater orch. and wrote his first stage work, *A Village Tale,* which he produced the same year. After these practical experiences, he began to study seriously; took lessons with Schjorring (violin), Matthesson (organ), and Rasmussen (composition) and soon publ. a number of piano pieces, which attracted the attention of Niels Gade, who used his influence to obtain a traveling fellowship for Enna; this made it possible for Enna to study in Germany (1888–89) and acquire a complete mastery of instrumental and vocal writing. WORKS: He followed the German Romantic school, being influenced mainly by Weber's type of opera, and by Grieg and Gade in the use of local color; the first product of this period was his most successful work, in the opera *Heksen* (*The Witch*), produced in Copenhagen (Jan. 24, 1892), then in Germany. Enna's other operas also enjoyed a modicum of success; these are *Cleopatra* (Copenhagen, Feb. 7, 1894); *Aucassin and Nicolette* (Copenhagen, Feb. 2, 1896); *The Match Girl,* after Andersen (Copenhagen, Nov. 13, 1897); *Lamia* (Antwerp, Oct. 3, 1899); *Ung Elskov* (first produced in Weimar, under the title *Heisse Liebe,* Dec. 6, 1904); *Princess on the Pea,* after Andersen (Aarhus, Sept. 15, 1900); *The Nightingale,* also after Andersen (Aarhus, Sept. 15, 1900); *The Nightingale,* also after Andersen (Copenhagen, Nov. 10, 1912); *Gloria Arsena* (Copenhagen, April 15, 1917); *Comedians,* after Victor Hugo's *L'Homme qui rit* (Copenhagen, April 8, 1920); *Don Juan Mañara* (Copenhagen, April 17, 1925). He further wrote the ballets *The Shepherdess and the Chimney Sweep* (Copenhagen, Oct. 6, 1901); *St. Cecilia's Golden Shoe* (Copenhagen, Dec. 26, 1904); *The Kiss* (Copenhagen, Oct. 19, 1927); also a Violin Concerto, 2 symphs.; an overture, *Hans Christian Andersen;* choral pieces.

Enríquez, Manuel, Mexican composer and violinist; b. Ocotlán, June 17, 1926. He studied violin with Camarena and composition with Bernal Jiménez at the Guadalajara Cons. (1942–50); then went to N.Y. and took lessons in composition with Peter Mennin and violin with Ivan Galamian at the Juilliard School of Music (1955–57); also had private theory lessons with Stefan Wolpe and attended the Columbia-Princeton Electronic Music Center (1971). Returning to Mexico, he was concertmaster of the Guadalajara Symph. Orch.; later supervised music courses at the Inst. of Fine Arts in Mexico City. In 1975 he went to France under a special commission from the Mexican government. As a composer, he follows the median line of cosmopolitan modernism, making use of a severe constructivist idiom, employing graphic optical notation.
WORKS: *Suite* for Violin and Piano (1949); 2 violin concertos (1955, 1966); Symph. No. 1 (1957); 3 string quartets (1959, 1967, 1974); *Preámbulo* for Orch. (1961); Sonatina for Solo Cello (1962); *Divertimento* for Flute, Clarinet, and Bassoon (1962); *4 Pieces* for Viola and Piano (1962); *Obertura lírica* for Orch. (1963); *Pentamúsica* for Wind Quintet (1963); *3 formas concertantes* for Violin, Cello, Clarinet, Bassoon, Horn, Piano, and Percussion (1964); Violin Sonata (1964); *3 invenciones* for Flute and Viola (1964); *Módulos* for 2 Pianos (1965); *Transición* for Orch. (1965); *Poema* for Cello and Small String Orch. (1966); *Ego* for Female Voice, Flute, Cello, Piano, and Percussion (1966); *Trayectorias* for Orch. (1967); *Ambivalencia* for Violin and Cello (1967); *Si Libet* for Orch. (1968); *5 Plus 2* for Flute, Viola, Trombone, Piano, and Percussion, with Actress and Director (1969); *Concierto para 8* (1969); *Ixamatl* for Orch. (1969); *Díptico I* for Flute and Piano (1969); *Díptico II* for Violin and Piano (1971); *Presagios* for Piano (1970); *Móvil I* for Piano (1969); Piano Concerto (1971); *El y Ellos* for Solo Violin and Orch. Ensemble (1973).

Enriquez de Valderrabano, Enrique, 16th-century Spanish lutenist; native of Peñaranda de Duero. He wrote the tablature book *Libro de música de vihuela, intitulado Silva de Sirenas* (Valladolid, 1547), containing transcriptions for vihuela (large 6-stringed guitar) of sacred and secular vocal works (some arranged for 2 vihuelas), also some original pieces.
BIBLIOGRAPHY: G. Morphy, *Les Luthistes espagnols du XVIᵉ siècle* (1902); J.B. Trend, *Luis Milán and the Vihuelistas* (1925); W. Apel, "Early Spanish Music for Lute and Keyboard Instruments," *Musical Quarterly* (July 1934).

Enthoven, Emile, Dutch composer; b. Amsterdam, Oct. 18, 1903; d. New York, Dec. 26, 1950. He studied composition with Johan Wagenaar in Utrecht, and at the age of 15 wrote an adolescent but well-crafted symphony, which Mengelberg performed with the Concertgebouw Orch. in Amsterdam (1918). But this precocious success was not a manifestation of enduring talent; his later works lacked originality. Soon he abandoned composition altogether and took up jurisprudence; for a time he lectured on political science at the Univ. of Leiden; in 1939 emigrated to America and settled in N.Y.

Entremont, Philippe, eminent French pianist and conductor; b. Rheims, June 6, 1934. Both his parents were professional musicians and teachers, and he received his first training from them. He subsequently studied piano with Marguerite Long; then entered the Paris Cons.; won first prize in solfège at 12, in chamber music at 14, and in piano at 15. In 1951 he was the winner of the Belgian State Competition in Brussels. He then toured in Europe; on Jan. 5, 1953, he made his American debut with the National Orch. Association in N.Y.; appeared also as soloist with other American orchs. In 1976 he became music director of the Vienna Chamber Orch.; in 1980 was appointed music adviser and principal conductor of the New Orleans Phil., and in 1981–84 was its music director; in 1982 he took that orch. on a European tour.

Eppert, Carl, American composer; b. Carbon, Ind., Nov. 5, 1882; d. Milwaukee, Oct. 1, 1961. He studied in Chicago and in Germany; founder and conductor of the Civic Symph. Orch. in Milwaukee (1923–26).
WORKS: 7 symphs.; *Escapade* for Orch. (Indianapolis, Jan. 3, 1941); symph. fantasy, *Traffic* (NBC Orch., May 8, 1932); 2 symph. poems: *City Shadows* and *Speed* (both perf. at Rochester, N.Y., Oct. 30, 1935); *2 Symphonic Impressions* (Chicago, Feb. 13, 1941; received first prize in the Chicago Symph. Orch. Golden Jubilee in 1940–41).

Epstein, David M(ayer), American composer, conductor, and writer on music; b. New York, Oct. 3, 1930. He learned to play the piano and clarinet and took part in jazz bands. He studied at Antioch College (A.B., 1952); then took courses with Carl McKinley at the New England Cons. of Music (M.M., 1953), with Irving Fine, Harold Shapero, and Arthur Berger at Brandeis Univ. (M.F.A., 1954), and with Milton Babbitt and Roger Sessions at Princeton Univ. (M.F.A., 1956; Ph.D., 1968, with the dissertation *Schoenberg's Grundgestalt and Total Serialism: Their Relevance to Homophonic Analysis*). In 1955–56 he took lessons in composition with Darius Milhaud at Aspen. In conducting, his mentors were, at various times, at various places, Max Rudolf, Izler Solomon, and George Szell. He taught at Antioch College (1957–62); became an associate prof. of music at the Mass. Inst. of Technology in 1965; was named a prof. there in 1971. He also served as music director of the M.I.T. Symph. Orch. from 1965. In addition, he was music director of the Harrisburg (Pa.) Symph. Orch. (1974–78). In 1983 he was appointed conductor of the New Orch. of Boston. He publ. *Beyond Orpheus: Studies in Musical Structure* (Cambridge, Mass., 1979). In his music he follows a serial method, cleansed of impurities and reduced to a euphonious, albeit contrapuntally dissonant, idiom.
WORKS: For Orch.: *Movement* (1953); Symph. (1958); *Sonority-Variations* (1968); *Ventures, 3*

Pieces for Symphonic Wind Ensemble (Rochester, N.Y., Dec. 11, 1970); Cello Concerto (1979). Chamber music: Piano Trio (1953); String Trio (1964); String Quartet (1971). For Voices: *Excerpts from a Diary,* song cycle (1953); *The Seasons,* song cycle to poems by Emily Dickinson (1956); *Night Voices* for Narrator, Children's Choir, and Orch. (1974); *The Concord Psalter* for Choir (1979); *The Lament of Job* for Choir (1982); also Piano Variations (1961); film music.

BIBLIOGRAPHY: David Ewen, *American Composers* (N.Y., 1982)

Epstein, Julius, Austrian pianist; b. Agram, Croatia, Aug. 7, 1832; d. Vienna, March 1, 1926. He was a pupil at Agram of Ignaz Lichtenegger, and at Vienna of Anton Halm (piano) and Johann Rufinatscha (composition). From 1867 to 1901 he was a prof. of piano at the Vienna Cons.; one of the editors of Breitkopf & Härtel's monumental edition of Schubert's works. Among his pupils were Gustav Mahler and Ignaz Brüll.

BIBLIOGRAPHY: H. Schuster, *J. Epstein: Ein tonkünstlerisches Charakterbild zu seinem 70. Geburts-Feste* (Vienna, 1902).

Epstein, Peter, German musicologist; b. Strasbourg, Nov. 12, 1901; d. Breslau, June 9, 1932. He studied in Frankfurt, in Berlin, and at the Univ. of Breslau. He publ. catalogues of church music MSS of the Library of the City of Frankfurt (1926; in collaboration with C. Süss), and of musical instruments in the Breslau Museum (1932); ed. Schutze's *St. Luke Passion* (1930).

Epstein, Richard, Austrian pianist, son of **Julius Epstein;** b. Vienna, Jan. 26, 1869; d. New York, Aug. 1, 1919. He was a pupil at the Vienna Cons. of his father and R. Fuchs (composition); was a prof. of piano at the Vienna Cons.; lived in London (1904–14); then in N.Y. He excelled as an accompanist, in which capacity he was frequently heard with such artists as Sembrich, Fremstad, Culp, Gerhardt, Destinn, Elman, and Kreisler; and as assisting artist with famous chamber music organizations, including the Joachim, Rosé, and Bohemian Quartets.

Equiluz, Kurt, Austrian tenor; b. Vienna, June 13, 1929. He sang in the Vienna Boys Choir; then studied at the Vienna Academy of Music; sang in the Vienna Akademie-Kammerchor. After winning the Vienna Mozart Competition in 1949, he joined the chorus of the Vienna State Opera; made his solo debut there in 1957. He gained wide recognition as an outstanding concert and oratorio singer; was also a member of the faculty of the Hochschule für Musik in Graz.

Erard, Sébastien, famous maker of pianos and harps; b. Strasbourg, April 5, 1752; d. in his château, La Muette, near Paris, Aug. 5, 1831. His family name was originally **Erhard;** his father was a cabinetmaker by trade, and in his shop Sébastien worked until he was 16, when his father died. He was then engaged by a Paris harpsichord maker, who dismissed him "for wanting to know everything"; under a 2nd employer his ingenuity made a stir in the musical world, and the invention of a "clavecin mécanique" (described by Abbé Roussier, 1776) made him famous. The Duchess of Villeroy became his patroness, and fitted up in her home a workshop for Erard in which (1777) he finished the first pianoforte made in France. In the meantime, his brother, **Jean-Baptiste,** joined him, and they founded an instrument factory in the Rue Bourbon. Their growing success led to a conflict with the fan-makers' guild (to which the brothers did not belong), which tried to prevent them from working. But the Erards obtained a special "brevet" from Louis XVI for the manufacture of "forté-pianos" and this enabled them to continue their trade unmolested. In the following years, Erard invented the "piano organisé" with 2 keyboards, one for piano and the other for a small organ; he also became interested in the harp, and invented the ingenious double-action mechanism, perfected in 1811. From 1786–96 he was in London; returning to Paris, he made his first grand piano, and employed the English action until his invention, in 1809, of the repetition action, which is regarded as his supreme achievement. An "orgue expressif," built for the Tuileries, was his last important work. His nephew, **Pierre Erard** (1796–1855), succeeded him; he publ. *The Harp in its present improved state compared with the original Pedal Harp* (1821), and *Perfectionnements apportés dans le mécanisme du piano par les Erards depuis l'origine de cet instrument jusqu'à l'exposition de 1834* (1834). Pierre's successor was his wife's nephew, **Pierre Schäffer** (d. 1878); the firm is still the leading French manufacturer of pianos and harps.

BIBLIOGRAPHY: F. Fétis, *Notice biographique sur Sébastien Erard* (Paris, 1831).

Eratosthenes, Greek philosopher; b. Cyprene, c.276 B.C.; d. Alexandria, Egypt, c.194 B.C. He wrote on numerous subjects, chiefly mathematics, and was custodian of the Alexandria library. The *Catasterismi,* attributed to Eratosthenes, contain scattered notes on Greek music and instruments, especially the "lyra" (German trans. by Schaubach, 1795; Bernhardy publ. in 1822 an ed. of the original text). His work on music is lost; Ptolemy quotes his division of the tetrachord.

Erb, Donald, significant American composer; b. Youngstown, Ohio, Jan. 17, 1927. His family moved to Cleveland when he was a child; he studied cornet with a local musician. After a period of service in the U.S. Navy, he enrolled at Kent State Univ. in Ohio, where he continued to study trumpet and also took courses in composition with Harold Miles and Kenneth Gaburo (B.S., 1950), earning his living by playing trumpet in dance bands. In 1950 he entered the Cleveland Inst. of Music, in the class of Marcel Dick (M.M., 1953). On June 10, 1952, he married Lucille Hyman, and went with her to Paris to study with Nadia Boulanger. Returning to Cleveland, he was engaged as a member of the faculty of the Cleveland Inst. (1953). In 1961 he moved to Bloomington, Ind., where he studied composition with Bernard Heiden at Indiana Univ., receiving his doctorate in music in 1964. In 1964–65 he was an assistant prof. of composition at Bowling Green State Univ. In 1965 he received a Guggenheim fellowship grant. In 1965–67 he was a visiting assistant prof. for research in electronic music at Case Inst. of Technology in Cleveland; in 1966–81 was composer-in-residence at the Cleveland Inst. of Music; in 1975–76, visiting prof. of composition at Indiana Univ. in Bloomington. In the summer of 1968 he headed the composition workshop at the centennial Alaska Festival. From 1969–74 he served as staff composer at the Bennington Composers Conference in Vermont. In 1981 he was appointed prof. of composition at the Southern Methodist Univ. in Dallas. As a composer, he is exceptionally liberal in experimenting in all useful types of composition, from simple folklike monody to the strict dodecaphonic structures; as a former trumpeter in jazz bands, he also makes use of the jazz idiom as freely as of neo-Classical pandiatonic techniques. His most popular composition, *The 7th Trumpet* for Orch., is an epitome of his varied styles. He furthermore applied electronic sound in several of his works. In his band compositions he achieves an extraordinary degree of pure sonorism, in which melody, harmony, and counterpoint are subordinated to the purely aural effect. He also cleverly introduces strange-looking and unusual-sounding musical and unmusical and antimusical instruments, such as euphonious goblets, to be rubbed on the rim, and telephone bells. Thanks to the engaging manner of Erb's music, even when ultradissonant, his works safely traverse their premieres and endure through repeated performances.

WORKS: FOR ORCH.: Chamber Concerto for Piano and Chamber Orch. (Chicago, Feb. 12, 1961); *Spacemusic* for Symph. Band (1963); *Symphony of Overtures* (1964; Bloomington, Feb. 11, 1965); Concerto for Solo Percussion and Orch. (Detroit, Dec. 29, 1966); *Christmasmusic* (Cleveland, Dec. 21, 1967); *The 7th Trumpet* (Dallas, April 5, 1969; his most successful work; received the UNESCO Award in 1971); *Treasures of the Snow* for Youth Orch. (1973; Bergen, N.J., June 8, 1974); Cello Concerto (1975; Rochester, N.Y., Nov. 4, 1976); Trombone Concerto (St. Louis, March 11, 1976); Concerto for Keyboards and Orch. (1978; Akron, Ohio, March 23, 1981); Trumpet Concerto (1980; Baltimore, April 29, 1981); *Sonneries* for Orch. (1981; Rochester, N.Y., March 18, 1982); *Prismatic Variations* for Orch. and Children (St. Louis, Jan. 28, 1984).

CHAMBER MUSIC: *Dialog* for Violin and Piano (1958); String Quartet No. 1 (1960); *Music for Brass Choir* (1960); Quartet for Flute, Oboe, Alto Saxophone, and Double Bass (1961); Sonata for Harpsichord and String Quartet (1962); *Four* for Percussion (1962); *Dance Pieces* for Violin, Piano, Trumpet, and Percussion (1963); *Hexagon* for Flute, Alto Saxophone, Trumpet, Trombone, Cello, and Piano (1963); *Concertante* for Harpsichord and Strings (1963); *Antipodes* for String Quartet and

Percussion Quartet (1963); *Phantasma* for Flute, Oboe, Double Bass, and Harpsichord (1965); *Diversion for 2 (other than sex)* for Trumpet and Percussion (1966); *Andante* for Piccolo Flute and Alto Flute (1966); String Trio for Violin, Electric Guitar, and Cello (1966); *Reconnaissance* for Violin, Double Bass, Piano, Percussion, and 2 Electronic Setups (1967); *3 Pieces* for Brass Quintet and Piano (1968); *Trio for 2* for Alto Flute, Percussion, and Double Bass (1968); *Fanfare* for Brass and Percussion (1971); *Harold's Trip to the Sky* for Viola, Piano, and Percussion (1972); Quintet for Violin, Cello, Flute, Clarinet, and Piano (1976); Trio for Piano, Electric Piano, and Celesta (1977); Sonata for Clarinet and Percussion (1980); *3 Pieces* for Harp and Percussion (1981); *Déjà Vu*, 6 études for Double-bass Solo (1981); *The St. Valentine's Day* for Brass Quintet (1981); *Aura* for String Quartet (1981); *The Last Quintet* for Woodwinds (1982); *Devil's Quickstep* for Flute, Clarinet, Violin, Cello, Electric Piano, Harp, Percussion, Harmonicas, Tuned Goblets, Telephone Bells, and Audience (1982); *Fantasy for Cellist and Friends* for 8 to 12 Participants (1983).

VOCAL MUSIC: *Cummings Cycle* for Mixed Chorus and Orch. (1963); *Fallout* for Narrator, Chorus, String Quartet, and Piano (1964); *God Love You Now* for Chorus, Hand Percussion, and Harmonicas (1971); *New England's Prospect* for Choruses, Narrator, and Orch., commissioned for the 100th anniversary of the Cincinnati May Festival (Cincinnati, May 17, 1974).

FOR ELECTRONIC SOUND: *Reticulation* for Symph. Band and Electronic Tape (1965); *Reconnaissance* for Moog Synthesizer (1965); *Stargazing* for Dance and Electronic Tape (1966); *Fission* for Electronic Tape, Soprano Saxophone, Piano, Dancers, and Lights (1968); *In No Strange Land* for Tape, Trombone, and Double Bass (1968); *Basspiece* for Double Bass and 4 tracks of prerecorded Double Bass (1969); *Souvenir* for Tape, Instruments, Lights, etc. (1970); *Klangfarbenfunk I* for Orch., Rock Band, and Electronic Sound (Detroit, Oct., 1, 1970); *Z milosci do Warszawy* for Piano, Clarinet, Cello, Trombone, and Electronic Sound (1971); *The Purple-roofed Ethical Suicide Parlor* for Wind Ensemble and Electronic Sound (1972); *Autumnmusic* for Orch. and Electronic Sound (New Haven, Oct. 20, 1973); *The Towers of Silence* for Electronic Quartet (1974); *Music for a Festive Occasion* for Orch. and Electronic Sound (1975; Cleveland, Jan. 11, 1976).

BIBLIOGRAPHY: David Ewen, *American Composers* (N.Y., 1982).

Erb, John Lawrence, American music pedagogue and author; b. Reading, Pa., Feb. 5, 1877; d. Eugene, Oreg., March 17, 1950. He studied at the Metropolitan College of Music in N.Y.; then was director of the Wooster, Ohio, Cons. (1905–13) and cf the School of Music, Univ. of Illinois (1914–21); was lecturer at the American Inst. of Applied Music in N.Y. (1921–24); from 1923 was at the Connecticut College for Women. He publ. *Brahms,* a biography (1895; 1905; revised ed., London, 1934); *Hymns and Church Music* (1911); *Elements of Harmony* (1911); *Elemen-*

tary Theory (1911); *Music Appreciation for the Student* (1926); *Select Songs for the Assembly* (1931). He also composed songs, piano pieces, organ music, anthems, and music for pageants.

Erb, John Warren, American music educator and composer; b. Massillon, Ohio, April 17, 1887; d. Pittsburgh, July 2, 1948. He studied in Berlin with Xaver Scharwenka, Siegfried Ochs, and Felix Weingartner, and in the U.S. with Stillman Kelley. After completing his musical education, he occupied various teaching positions in small colleges and music clubs; wrote some pieces for chorus, etc.

Erb, Karl, noted German tenor; b. Ravensburg, July 13, 1877; d. there, July 13, 1958. He was self-taught; made his debut in Stuttgart in 1907; then sang in Lübeck (1908–10), Stuttgart (1910–13), and Munich (1913–25). In 1925 he joined the Berlin City Opera; later embarked on a series of appearances as a concert and oratorio singer.

Erb, Marie Joseph, Alsatian composer and organist; b. Strasbourg, Oct. 23, 1858; d. Andlau, July 9, 1944. He studied at first in Strasbourg; then (1875–80) in Paris, under Saint-Saëns, Gigout, and Loret, at the Ecole de Musique Classique; returned to Strasbourg as teacher of piano and organ, and organist in the Johanniskirche (Roman Catholic) and at the Synagogue.
WORKS: Operas (all first perf. in Strasbourg, unless otherwise noted): *Der Letzte Ruf* (1895); *Der glückliche Taugenichts* (1897); *Abendglocken* (1900); *Eifersüchtig* (Leipzig, 1901); *Der Riese Schletto* (1901); *Der Zaubermantel* (1901); *Die Vogesentanne* (1904); *Der Heimweg* (ballet-opera, 1907); *Prinzessin Flunkerli* (1912); Symph. in G; 3 violin sonatas; Cello Sonata; 2 string quartets; String Trio; Octet for Wind and Strings; *Sonata liturgica* (1919); *Suite liturgique; Danses et pièces alsaciennes* (1924 and 1925); 8 masses; organ pieces; pieces for piano (2- and 4-hands); songs; also 2 vols. of Alsatian folk songs.
BIBLIOGRAPHY: *Marie Joseph Erb, sa vie et son œuvre,* ed. by P. de Bréville (Strasbourg, 1948).

Erbach, Christian, German organist and composer; b. Hesse, 1570; d. Augsburg (buried, June 14), 1635. He was the successor of Hassler as town organist in Augsburg (1602); in 1625 became organist of the Cathedral there. He publ. 3 books of *Modi sacri* (1600, 1604, 1611; under varying titles) for 4–10 voices; several works by him are included in contemporary collections; 12 motets are in A.B. Gottron, *Christian Erbach* (Mainz, 1943). His collected keyboard works were ed. by C. Raynor in *Corpus of Early Keyboard Music,* XXXVI (1971—).

Erbse, Heimo, German composer; b. Rudolstadt (Thuringia), Feb. 27, 1924. He studied in Weimar, and in Berlin with Boris Blacher; in 1957 he moved to Salzburg.
WORKS: Sonata for 2 Pianos (1951); *Capriccio* for

Piano, Strings, and Percussion (1952); Piano Trio (1953); 12 *Aphorismen* for Flute, Violin, and Piano (1954); *Sinfonietta giocosa* (1955); *Dialog* for Piano and Orch. (1955); *Tango-Variationen* for Orch. (1958); *Julietta,* opera semi-seria (Salzburg, Aug. 17, 1959); Wind Quartet (1961); Piano Concerto (1962); 2 symphs. (1963–64, 1969–70); comic opera, *Der Herr in Grau* (1966); *5 Songs* for Baritone and Orch. (1969).

Erdélyi, Miklós, Hungarian conductor; b. Budapest, Feb. 9, 1928. He studied at the Franz Liszt Academy of Music in Budapest; served as music director of the Hungarian Radio Choir (1950–52); from 1951 was a principal conductor of the Hungarian State Opera. He made a successful debut with the Berlin Phil. in 1974; led the Hungarian State Orch. on a tour of England. In 1976 he took the Bamberg Symph. of West Germany on an extensive tour of the major European festivals. He made his American debut with the San Antonio Symph. in 1972. He wrote *Schubert* (1961; 2nd ed., 1979), a biographical study.

Erdmann, Eduard, Latvian pianist and composer; b. Tsezis (Wenden), March 5, 1896; d. Hamburg, June 21, 1958. He studied in Riga; then went to Berlin, where he studied piano with Konrad Ansorge (1914–17) and composition with Heinz Tiessen (1915–18). From 1925–35 he was a prof. at the Cologne Cons.; then was active as a concert pianist (1935–50); in 1950, was appointed prof. of piano at the Hochschule für Musik in Hamburg. He wrote 4 symphs.; piano pieces; songs.

Erdmannsdörfer, Max von, German conductor; b. Nuremberg, June 14, 1848; d. Munich, Feb. 14, 1905. He studied at the Leipzig Cons. (1863–67), and in Dresden (1868–69). From 1871 to 1880 he was court conductor at Sondershausen; then was active in Vienna, Leipzig, and Nuremberg. In 1882 he was engaged as conductor of the Imperial Musical Society in Moscow; in 1885 became prof. at the Moscow Cons. His symph. concerts in Moscow were of great importance to Russian music; he introduced many new works by Russian composers, and his influence was considerable in Moscow musical circles, despite the mediocrity of his conducting. Returning to Germany, he became conductor of the Bremen Phil. Concerts (until 1895); in 1897 he settled in Munich.

Erede, Alberto, Italian conductor; b. Genoa, Nov. 8, 1908. He studied at the Milan Cons. (piano, cello, theory); then in Basel with Weingartner (conducting). He conducted opera in England (1934–39); from 1951 to 1955 was a guest conductor at the Metropolitan Opera in N.Y.; from 1958 to 1962 was Generalmusikdirektor of the German Opera Theater in Düsseldorf; in 1961 became conductor of the Göteborg (Sweden) Orch.; first conducted in Bayreuth in 1968, leading a performance of *Lohengrin.*
BIBLIOGRAPHY: L. Rognoni, *Alberto Erede* (Arzignano, 1954).

Erhardt, Otto, German opera director; b. Breslau, Nov. 18, 1888; d. near Buenos Aires, Jan. 18, 1971. He studied violin; took courses in music and art at Breslau, Munich, Oxford, and London. He played violin in various orchs. (1908–11); then became a stage director; acted in this capacity with the Stuttgart Opera (1920–27) and the Dresden Opera (1927–32); directed the festivals at Salzburg (1933–36). In 1938 he went to Buenos Aires, where he was stage director at the Teatro Colón; subsequently divided his time between South America, Europe, and the U.S. He publ. a book, *Die Operndichtung der deutschen Romantik* (Breslau, 1911); also a biography of Richard Strauss (Buenos Aires, 1950, in Spanish; German ed., 1953).

Erickson, Robert, American composer; b. Marquette, Mich., March 7, 1917. He studied music with Wesley La Violette at the Chicago Cons.; with Ernst Krenek at Hamline Univ. in St. Paul (B.A., 1943); in 1950, attended a seminar in composition under Roger Sessions at the Univ. of Calif., Berkeley; in 1966 held a Guggenheim fellowship. In 1967 he was appointed prof. of composition at the Univ. of Calif., San Diego. In his music he explores electronic and serial techniques.
WORKS: *Introduction and Allegro* for Orch. (Minneapolis, March 11, 1949); Piano Sonata (1948); String Quartet No. 1 (1950); Piano Trio (1953); Divertimento for Flute, Clarinet, and Strings (1953); Fantasy for Cello and Orch. (1953); String Quartet No. 2 (1956); Variations for Orch. (1957); Duo for Violin and Piano (1959); *Chamber Concerto* (1960); Toccata for Piano (1962); Concerto for Piano and 7 Instruments (1963); *Sirens and Other Flyers* for Orch. (1965); *Piece for Bells and Toy Pianos* (1965); *Ricercar a 5* for Trombone and Tape (1966); *Scapes,* a "contest for 2 groups" (1966); *Birdland* for Electronic Tape (1967); *Ricercar a 3* for Solo Double Bass and Electronic Tape (1967); *Cardenitas,* dramatic aria for Singer, Mime, Conductor, 7 Musicians, and Stereophonic Prerecorded Tape (1968); *Pacific Sirens* for Instruments and Tape (1969); *General Speech* for Trombone (1969); *The Idea of Order at Key West* for Voice and Instruments (1979).

Ericson, Eric, Swedish conductor; b. Boras, Oct. 26, 1918. He was educated at the Stockholm Music Academy; then served as organist and choir director in several churches in Stockholm. In 1945 he joined the faculty of the Stockholm Music Academy; was made a prof. in 1968. He made his American debut with the National Symph. Orch. of Washington, D.C., in 1974.

Erk, Ludwig (Christian), German music scholar and educator; b. Wetzlar, Jan. 6, 1807; d. Berlin, Nov. 25, 1883. He received good training in music from his father, **Adam Wilhelm Erk** (1779–1820), who was organist at Wetzlar. His further studies were under André in Offenbach and Spiess in Frankfurt. In 1826 he became a prof. at the seminary in Mörs, where he taught until 1835; from 1836 to 1840 he was an instructor in liturgical singing at Berlin, and conducted a choir. In 1852, he founded the Erk Gesangverein for mixed voices. During his years as a conductor of choral societies, he became interested in folk songs, and accumulated a great collection of authentic materials on the subject; also publ. songbooks for schools, which attained considerable popularity; some of these were written jointly with his brother **Friedrich Erk,** and his brother-in-law, **Greef.** He also publ. *Die deutschen Volkslieder mit ihren Singweisen* (1838–45); *Volkslieder, alte und neue* (1845–46); *Deutscher Liederhort* (folk songs; vol. 1 publ. 1856; MS of the remainder was bought—with the rest of his valuable library—for the Royal Hochschule für Musik in Berlin; continued and ed. by Magnus Böhme, and publ. in 4 vols., 1894); *Mehrstimmige Gesänge* (1833–35); *Volksklänge* (1851–60); *Deutscher Liederschatz* (1859–72); *Vierstimmige Choralgesänge der vornehmsten Meister des 16. and 17. Jahrhunderts* (1845); *J.S. Bachs mehrstimmige Choralgesänge und geistliche Arien* (1850–65); *Vierstimmiges Choralbuch für evangelische Kirchen* (1863); *Choräle für Männerstimmen* (1866); *Methodischer Leitfaden für den Gesangunterricht in Volksschulen* (1834, Part I).
BIBLIOGRAPHY: *Chronologisches Verzeichnis der musikalischen Werke und literarischen Arbeiten von Ludwig Erk* (compiled by a group of friends; Berlin, 1867); K. Schultze, *Ludwig Erk* (Berlin, 1876); H. Schmeel, *Ludwig Erk, Ein Lebensbild* (Giessen, 1908).

Erkel, Franz (Ferenc), the creator of Hungarian national opera; b. Gyula, Hungary, Nov. 7, 1810; d. Budapest, June 15, 1893. He was taught by his father; at 24 became director of the Kaschau opera troupe, and went with it to Pest, where he was appointed conductor at the National Theater on its opening in 1837. He was the founder and director of the Budapest Phil. Concerts (1853), and first prof. of piano and instrumentation at the National Musical Academy. His numerous songs, in the national vein, became very popular. He composed the Hungarian National Hymn (1845).
WORKS: Operas (all first presented in Budapest): *Báthory Mária* (Aug. 8, 1840); *Hunyady László* (Jan. 27, 1844; the first truly national Hungarian opera; given almost 300 perfs. in the first 50 years); *Erzsébet* (May 6, 1857); *Kúnok* (1858); *Bánk-Bán* (March 9, 1861; highly successful in Hungary); *Sarolta,* comic opera (June 26, 1862); *Dózsa György* (April 6, 1867); *Brankovics György* (May 20, 1874); *Névtelen hosök* (Nov. 30, 1880); *István király* (March 14, 1885); music for plays; *Festival Overture* for Orch. (1887); many songs and anthems. A symposium of essays on Erkel was publ. in *Zenetudományi Tanulmányok* (Budapest, 1954, II) under the editorship of B. Szabolcsi.
BIBLIOGRAPHY: K. Abrányi, *Franz Erkel* (Budapest, 1895); F. Scherer, *Franz Erkel* (Gyula, 1944).

Erkin, Ulvi Cemal, Turkish composer; b. Istanbul, March 14, 1906; d. Ankara, Sept. 15, 1972. He studied piano with Isidor Philipp in Paris and composition with Nadia Boulanger in Fontainebleau. Returning to Turkey, he became a piano instructor at the Ankara Cons.

WORKS: *Bayram*, tone poem (Ankara, May 11, 1934); Symph. No. 1 (Ankara, April 20, 1946); Symph. No. 2 (1948–51); Violin Concerto (Ankara, April 2, 1948); chamber music; piano pieces.

Erlanger, Camille, French composer; b. Paris, May 25, 1863; d. there, April 24, 1919. He was a pupil of the Paris Cons. under Delibes, Durand, and Matthias; in 1888, took the Grand Prix de Rome for his cantata *Velléda*. He earned fame with his opera *Le Juif polonais* (Paris, April 11, 1900), which has remained in active repertoire; other operas are: *Kermaria* (Paris, Feb. 8, 1897); *Le Fils de l'étoile* (Paris, April 20, 1904); *Aphrodite* (Paris, March 27, 1906); *Bacchus triomphant* (Bordeaux, Sept. 11, 1909); *L'Aube rouge* (Rouen, Dec. 29, 1911); *La Sorcière* (Paris, Dec. 18, 1912); *Le Barbier de Deauville* (1917); *Forfaiture* (perf. posthumously at the Opéra-Comique in 1921). He also wrote several symph. poems (*Maître et serviteur*, after Tolstoy, etc.) and a French Requiem.

d'Erlanger, Baron Frédéric, member of the family of bankers; composer and opera director; b. Paris, May 29, 1868; d. London, April 23, 1943. In 1897 he assumed the pseudonym **Regnal**, formed by reading backward the last 6 letters of his name. He lived in London, where for many years he was one of the directors of the Covent Garden Opera.

WORKS: Operas: *Jehan de Saintre* (Aix-les-Bains, Aug. 1, 1893); *Inez Mendo* (London, July 10, 1897, under the pseudonym Regnal); *Tess*, after Thomas Hardy (Naples, April 10, 1906); *Noël* (Paris, Dec. 28, 1910; Chicago, 1913); Piano Quintet; String Quartet; Violin Concerto (London, March 12, 1903, Kreisler soloist); Violin Sonata; *Andante* for Cello and Orch.

d'Erlanger, Rodolphe, French musicologist, specialist in Arab studies; b. Boulogne-sur-Seine, June 7, 1872; d. Sidi-bou-Sadi, Tunisia, Oct. 29, 1932. He went to Tunis in 1910, and began a thorough study of the theory and history of Arabian music. The result was a series of publications of primary importance, most of them issued posthumously, including a monumental work in 6 volumes under the general title *La Musique arabe* (Paris, 1930–59).

Erlebach, Philipp Heinrich, important German composer; b. Esens, East Frisia, July 25, 1657; d. Rudolstadt, April 17, 1714. He was Hofkapellmeister at Rudolstadt from at least 1681; remained there until 1714. His style was strongly influenced by that of Lully. He wrote orch. suites (6 overtures, publ. 1693); suites for violin, viola da gamba, and continuo (1694), one of which was reprinted by Einstein in *Zur deutschen Literatur für Viola da Gamba* (1905); cantatas; sacred and secular songs, including *Harmonische Freude* (2 parts: 1697, 1710; reprinted by Kinkeldey in vol. 46/47 of Denkmäler deutscher Tonkunst); organ works; etc. Examples

from his *Gottgeheiligte Singstunde* (1704) are printed in M. Friedlaender's *Das deutsche Lied im 18. Jahrhundert* (1902).

Erlebach, Rupert, English composer; b. London, Nov. 16, 1894. He studied at the Royal Academy of Music with Stanford and Vaughan Williams. As a composer, he makes considerable use of English folk material.

WORKS: *Before Dawn, Aubade, A Memory, High Noon, Lark's Song at Evening;* for Orch.: Rhapsody for Cello and Orch.; *Folksong Poems* for String Orch.; Rhapsody for Flute, Oboe, Violin, Viola, and Cello; *Moods* for String Quartet; *Legends* for Violin and Piano; Sonata for Violin and Piano; 2 sonatas for Cello and Piano (one, *Folksong Sonata*); piano pieces; organ pieces; songs; choral works.

Ermatinger, Erhart, Swiss composer; b. Winterthur, Feb. 16, 1900; d. Arnhem, July 14, 1966. He studied at the Zürich Cons. with Jarnach, then at the Berlin Hochschule für Musik; in 1922–23 was chorus master at the Zürich Opera; later a private teacher there; in 1925–26, was a teacher of theory at the Freiburg Univ.; lived in Berlin, then in the Netherlands. He wrote an opera, *Gijsbrecht van Amstel* (1947); 3 symphs.; 2 string quartets; songs; publ. a book, *Bildhafte Musik: Entwurf einer Lehre von der musikalischen Darstellungskunst* (Tübingen, 1928).

Ernesaks, Gustav, Estonian composer; b. Chariu, Dec. 12, 1908. He studied composition at the Tallinn Cons. with Arthur Kapp; then was active as a choral conductor. He wrote the music drama *Tormide Rand (Stormy Coast;* Tallinn, Sept. 29, 1949), and a comic opera, *Bridegrooms* (1960); also many choruses in Estonian.

Ernst, Alfred, French writer and critic; b. Périgueux, April 9, 1860; d. Paris, May 15, 1898. A pupil of the Ecole Polytechnique, he abandoned science for art; was a passionate admirer and defender of Wagner. Besides many contributions to musical journals, he publ. *L'Œuvre dramatique de Berlioz* (1884); *Richard Wagner et le drame contemporain* (1887); *L'Art de Richard Wagner, L'Œuvre poétique* (1893; a projected 2nd vol. on *L'Œuvre musicale* remained unfinished); *Etude sur "Tannhäuser,"* analysis and thematic guide (1895; with E. Poirée). He trans. *Die Meistersinger* and *Der Ring des Nibelungen* into French.

Ernst, Heinrich Wilhelm, violinist and composer; b. Brünn, May 6, 1814; d. Nice, Oct. 8, 1865. He was a pupil of Böhm (violin) and Seyfried (composition) in Vienna, with further study under Mayseder; from 1832–38, lived in Paris. From 1838 to 1850 he was almost continually on concert tours; then settled in London (1855). His works for violin are brilliant and effective; the *Elégie,* the Concerto in F-sharp minor (new ed. by Marteau, 1913), and *Carnaval de Venise* are a few of the most celebrated.

BIBLIOGRAPHY: A. Heller, *Heinrich Wilhelm Ernst im Urteile seiner Zeitgenossen* (Brünn, 1904).

Ernster, Deszö, Hungarian bass; b. Pécs, Nov. 23, 1898; d. Zürich, Feb. 15, 1981. He studied in Budapest and Vienna; then sang in Plauen, Gera, and Düsseldorf; in 1929 he appeared at the Berlin State Opera, and 1931 at the Bayreuth Festival, and in 1933 at the Vienna State Opera; then joined the Graz Opera. He made his first visit to the U.S. during the 1938–39 season, when he sang in N.Y. with the Salzburg Opera Guild. On Nov. 20, 1946, he made his Metropolitan Opera debut in N.Y. as Marke in *Tristan und Isolde;* remained on its roster until 1963; in 1964 he settled in Zürich.

BIBLIOGRAPHY: J. Fábián, *Ernster* (Budapest, 1969).

Erös, Peter, Hungarian conductor; b. Budapest, Sept. 22, 1932. He studied piano with Lajos Hernadi, composition with Zoltán Kodály, conducting with Lászlo Somogyi, and chamber music with Leo Weiner. After the abortive revolution in Hungary in 1956, he emigrated to the Netherlands. There he served as assistant to Otto Klemperer at the Holland Festival of 1958; from 1958–61 was assistant to Ferenc Fricsay, working with the Deutsche Grammophon Gesellschaft; in 1960 he attended the master classes at Bayreuth. His subsequent professional engagements were: assistant conductor of the Concertgebouw Orch. in Amsterdam (1960–65); chief conductor of the Malmö Symph. Orch. (1966–68); permanent guest conductor of the Melbourne Symph. (1969–70). In 1972 he was appointed music director and conductor of the San Diego Symph. Orch.; was active as conductor of the West Australian Symph. Orch. of the Australian Broadcasting Commission. He was also a guest conductor of orchs. all over the world. He resigned from the San Diego Symph. post in 1980, and in 1982 was appointed conductor of the Peabody Symph. Orch. in Baltimore.

Erpf, Hermann, German musicologist; b. Pforzheim, April 23, 1891; d. Stuttgart, Oct. 17, 1969. He studied at Heidelberg and with Riemann at Leipzig; received his Ph.D. from the Univ. of Leipzig in 1913 with the dissertation *Der Begriff der musikalischen Form* (publ. in Stuttgart, 1914); was in the army (1914–18); taught at Pforzheim (1919–23) and at the Univ. of Freiburg (1923–25); was assistant director at the Academy of Speech and Music in Münster (1925–27); was in charge of the Folkwangschule in Essen (1927–43). In 1943–45, and again in 1952–56, was director of the Hochschule für Musik in Stuttgart.

WRITINGS: *Entwicklungszüge in der zeitgenössischen Musik* (Karlsruhe, 1922); *Studien zur Harmonie- und Klangtechnik der neueren Musik* (Leipzig, 1927; 2nd ed., 1969); *Harmonielehre in der Schule* (Leipzig, 1930); *Vom Wesen der neuen Musik* (Stuttgart, 1949); *Neue Wege der Musikerziehung* (Stuttgart, 1953); *Gegenwartskunde der Musik* (Stuttgart, 1954); *Form und Struktur in der Musik* (Mainz, 1967). He composed a Mass, numerous cantatas, 3 string quartets, and piano music.

Ershov, Ivan, celebrated Russian tenor; b. in the village of Maly Nesvetai, near Novocherkassk, Nov. 20, 1867; d. Tashkent, Nov. 21, 1943. He studied voice in Moscow with Alexandrova-Kochetova and in St. Petersburg with Gabel and Palečck. In 1893 he made his operatic debut at the Maryinsky Theater in St. Petersburg as Faust, which became one of his most popular roles; then went to Italy for a year and took voice lessons with Rossi in Milan; appeared in Turin as Don José in *Carmen.* He returned to Russia in 1894 and joined the Kharkov Opera; in 1895 he became a member of the Maryinsky Opera Theater, and served with it until 1929. He achieved fabulous success as the greatest performer of the tenor roles in the Russian repertoire, and he also was regarded by music critics and audiences as the finest interpreter of the Wagnerian operas; he sang Siegfried, Tannhäuser, Lohengrin, and Tristan with extraordinary lyric and dramatic penetration; as an opera tenor in his time he had no rivals on the Russian stage. In 1929, at the age of 62, he sang Verdi's Otello; he also appeared in oratorio and solo recitals. From 1916 to 1941 he taught voice at the Petrograd (Leningrad) Cons. At the beginning of the siege of Leningrad in 1941, Ershov was evacuated with the entire personnel of the Cons. to Tashkent in Central Asia, where he died shortly afterward.

BIBLIOGRAPHY: V. Bogdanov-Berezovsky, *Ivan Ershov* (Leningrad, 1951).

Erskine, John, American educator and writer on music; b. New York, Oct. 5, 1879; d. there, June 1, 1951. He studied piano with Carl Walter; composition with MacDowell; then took up an academic and literary career, becoming highly successful as a novelist and essayist. He was educated at Columbia Univ. (B.A., 1900; M.A., 1901; Ph.D., 1903; LL.D., 1929); was a prof. of English there (1909–37), then prof. emeritus. In 1923 he resumed piano study under Ernest Hutcheson; played as soloist with the N.Y. Symph. Orch. and the Baltimore Civic Orch.; was president of the Juilliard School of Music in N.Y. (1928–37); president of the Juilliard Music Foundation from 1948 until his death. He was editor of *A Musical Companion* (1935). He received the degree of Mus.Doc. from Rollins College in Florida (1931), Cornell College, Iowa (1935); also the degree of Litt.D. from Amherst College (1923) and the Univ. of Bordeaux, France (1929). Erskine was an Officer of the French Legion of Honor. He publ. books on music, including *Is There a Career in Music?* (N.Y., 1929); *Song without Words: The Story of Felix Mendelssohn* (1941); *The Philharmonic-Symphony Society of N.Y., Its First Hundred Years* (N.Y., 1943); *What Is Music?* (Philadelphia, 1944); *The Memory of Certain Persons* (Philadelphia, 1947); *My Life as a Teacher* (N.Y., 1948); *My Life in Music* (N.Y., 1950).

Ertel, (Jean) Paul, German pianist and composer; b. Posen, Jan. 22, 1865; d. Berlin, Feb. 11, 1933. He studied with L. Brassin (piano) and later took lessons with Liszt; also studied law; was music critic of the *Berliner Lokal Anzeiger* and editor of *Deutscher Musikerzeitung* (1897–1905). He wrote several symph. poems in a general Lisztian vein (*Der Mensch, Die nächtliche Heerschau,* etc.); many ballads for voice and instruments; a violin sonata and other chamber music.

Eschenbach, Christoph, remarkably talented German pianist and conductor; b. Breslau, Feb. 20, 1940. His real name was Christoph Ringman; his mother died in childbirth, and his father died shortly afterward. He was adopted by his mother's relatives, whose name was Eschenbach; this became his legal name. His foster mother, a professional musician, gave him his first music lessons. He later studied piano with Eliza Hansen in Hamburg and Hans-Otto Schmidt in Cologne. His career proceeded most auspiciously; he won several school prizes; in 1962 he received the important prize of the International Competition in Munich; in 1965 he won the first prize of the Haskil Competition in Lucerne; in the same year he was soloist in a recording of Beethoven's First Piano Concerto with the Berlin Phil. under the direction of Herbert von Karajan. He was selected to represent West Germany at Expo 1967 in Montreal, Canada; on Jan. 16, 1969, he made his first appearance in the U.S., playing Mozart's Piano Concerto in F major with the Cleveland Orch. under the direction of George Szell. Eschenbach became interested in modern music; he gave the premiere of Hans Werner Henze's Second Piano Concerto in 1969. From then on, Eschenbach made several world tours which took him to Russia, South America, South Africa, Israel, and Japan. In 1976 he turned to conducting; on Aug. 10, 1976, he conducted in N.Y. a Mozart program, leading the orch. from the keyboard in two Mozart concertos. He made his home in the Canary Islands, while continuing his tours. He is regarded as one of the finest interpreters of the piano concertos of Mozart and Beethoven; he has also distinguished himself in conducting the Classical repertoire.

Escher, Rudolf, noted Dutch composer; b. Amsterdam, Jan. 8, 1912; d. De Koog (Texel), March 17, 1980. He studied harmony, violin, and piano at the Toonkunst Cons. in Rotterdam (1931–37); was a student in composition of Pijper (1934); worked in the electronic music studios in Delft (1959–60) and in Utrecht (1961). He taught at the Amsterdam Cons. (1960–61) and at the Inst. for Musical Science at the Utrecht Univ. (1964–75). In 1977 he was awarded the Johan Wagenaar Prize for his compositions. Escher's music was very much influenced by the modern French school.
WORKS: FOR ORCH.: *Sinfonia in memoriam Maurice Ravel* (1940); *Musique pour l'esprit en deuil* (*Music for the Soul in Mourning;* 1941–43; Amsterdam, Jan. 19, 1947); Passacaglia (1945; withdrawn); Concerto for Strings (1947–48; withdrawn); *Hymne de Grand Meaulnes* (1950–51); 2 symphs.: No. 1 (1953–54) and No. 2 (1958; revised 1964 and 1971); *Summer Rites at Noon* for 2 facing Orchs. (1962–68); orchestration of Debussy's *6 épigraphes antiques* for Piano Duet (1976–77; Hilversum Radio, July 6, 1978).
FOR VOICE: *3 poèmes de Tristan Corbière* for Soprano and Piano (1936); *Horcajo* for Mezzo-soprano and Piano (1941); *Lettre du Mexique* for Baritone and Piano (1942); *Protesilaos en Laodamia,* musical comedy for Mezzo-soprano, Tenor, Baritone, and Orch. (1946–48; withdrawn); *De poort van Ishtar,* incidental music for Chorus and Orch. (1947; withdrawn); *Poèmes de Vion Dalibray* for Tenor and Piano (1947–49); *Chants du désir* for Mezzo-soprano and Piano (1951); *Nostalgies* for Tenor and Orch. (1951; revised 1961); *Strange Meeting,* after Owen, for Baritone and Piano (1952); *Le Vrai Visage de la paix,* after Eluard, for Chorus a cappella (1953; revised 1957); *Song of Love and Eternity,* after Dickinson, for Chorus a cappella (1955); *Ciel, air et vents,* after Ronsard, for Chorus a cappella (1957); *De Perzen (The Persians),* after Aeschylus, incidental music for Narrator, Men's Choir, and Orch. (1963); *Univers de Rimbaud,* 5 songs after Rimbaud for Tenor and Orch. (1970); *3 Poems by W.H. Auden* for Chorus a cappella (1975).
CHAMBER MUSIC: *Sonata concertante* for Cello and Piano (1943); Sonata for 2 Flutes (1944); Solo Cello Sonata (1945); Trio for Oboe, Clarinet, and Bassoon (1946); Solo Flute Sonata (1949); Sonata for Violin and Piano (1950); *Le Tombeau de Ravel* for Flute, Oboe, Violin, Viola, Cello, and Harpsichord (1952); *Air pour charmer un lézard* for Solo Flute (1953); Trio for Violin, Viola, and Cello (1959); Wind Quintet (1966–67); *Monologue* for Solo Flute (1969); Solo Clarinet Sonata (1973); *Sinfonia* for 10 Instruments (1976); Sonata for Flute and Piano (1975–77); Trio for Clarinet, Viola, and Piano (1978).
FOR PIANO: Sonata No. 1 (1935); *Arcana Musae Dona,* suite (1944); *Habanera* (1945); *Due voci* (1949); *Non troppo,* 10 easy pieces (1949); Sonatina (1951).
He also wrote a Passacaglia for Organ (1937) and electronic music for *The Long Christmas Dinner,* after Thornton Wilder (1960).
WRITINGS: The monographs *Toscanini en Debussy* (Rotterdam, 1938) and "Maurice Ravel," *Groot Nederland* (July 1939); "Debussy and the Musical Epigram," *Key Notes, 10* (1979/2).
BIBLIOGRAPHY: Elmer Schönberger, "Rudolf Escher: Thinking in and about Music," *Key Notes, 5* (1977/1).

Eschig, Max, French music publisher; b. Opava, now Czechoslovakia, May 27, 1872; d. Paris, Sept. 3, 1927. He settled in Paris and founded a publishing firm under his name in 1907, prospering continually and forming an impressive catalogue of modern works by Ravel, Manuel de Falla, and many other French, Spanish, and English composers.

Eschmann, Johann Karl, Swiss pianist and pedagogue; b. Winterthur, April 12, 1826; d. Zürich, Oct. 27, 1882. He studied in Leipzig with Moscheles, and also had some lessons with Mendelssohn. He then settled in Zürich as a piano teacher; publ. a valuable manual, *Wegweiser durch die Klavierliteratur* (Zürich, 1879; 8th ed., 1914), and *100 Aphorismen aus dem Klavierunterricht* (2nd ed., 1899).

Escobar, Luis Antonio, Colombian composer; b. Villapinzón, near Bogotá, July 14, 1925. He studied music at the Bogotá Cons.; then took courses with Nicolas Nabokov at the Peabody Cons. in Baltimore and with Boris Blacher in Berlin. He returned to Bogotá in 1953, and received the post of prof. at the Cons., which he held until 1962.
WORKS: Flute Concertino (1951); ballet, *Avirama* (1955); *Sinfonía Cero* (1955); *Sinfonía X* (1955); Harpsichord Concertino (1958); Piano Concerto (1959); *Los Hampones,* opera for Soloists, Chorus, and Percussion (1961); *Juramento a Bolívar* for Male Chorus and Orch. (1964); *Little Symphony* (Washington, D.C., May 7, 1965); 2 string quartets; 2 violin sonatas; 5 piano sonatinas (1950–59); etc. His style is brisk and terse in the modern manner; but there is in his music also a melorhythmic pattern of Spanish-American dances.

Escobar-Budge, Roberto, Chilean composer; b. Santiago, May 11, 1926. He studied composition with René Amengual and Alfonso Letelier; was active as a music critic; taught at the Catholic Univ. of Chile in Santiago. He publ. *Músicas sin pasado* (Santiago, 1971).
WORKS: Wind Quintet (1957); *Diferencias sinfónicas* for Orch. (1962); *Los Bisontes,* symph. suite (1964); Nonet (1965); *Cuarteto estructural* for Strings (1965); *Sinfonía Valparaíso* (1967); *Incógnita* for Harpsichord, Trumpet, Bassoon, Cello, and Percussion (1967); choruses; piano pieces.

Escobedo, Bartolomé, Spanish composer; b. Zamora, c.1515; d. Nov. 1563 as canon at Segovia. From 1536–41, and again from 1545–54, he was a singer in the Papal Choir at Rome. He was a judge in the famous dispute between Nicola Vicentino and Vincento Lusitano (1551) over the qualities of Greek modes. He composed 2 masses and a number of motets.

Escot, Pozzi, Peruvian-born American composer of French parentage; b. Lima, Oct. 1, 1931. She studied with the Belgian-born Peruvian composer Andrés Sás; in 1953 emigrated to the U.S.; took courses in composition with William Bergsma at the Juilliard School of Music in N.Y. and with Philipp Jarnach at the Hochschule für Musik in Hamburg (1957–61); subsequently was appointed to the faculty of Wheaton College in Massachusetts. Her musical idiom follows the tenets of modern structural formalism with modified serial procedures.
WORKS: 3 piano sonatinas (1950, 1951, 1952); 4 string quartets (1951; 1954; 1956; *Credo,* with Soprano, 1958); 3 symphs. (*Little Symphony,* 1952–1953; Symph. for Strings, 1955; 1957); *And Here I Rest,* cantata (1958); *3 Poems of Rilke* for Narrator and String Quartet (1959); *3 Movements* for Violin and Piano (1960); *Differences, Group I* and *II* for

Piano (1961, 1963); *Lamentus* for Soprano, 2 Violins, 2 Cellos, Piano, and 3 Percussionists (Madrid, Oct. 22, 1964); *Cristos* for 3 Violins, Alto Flute, Double Bassoon, and Percussion (1963); *Visione* for Solo Double Bass, Flute, Saxophone, Soprano, "Ghost" Speaker, and Percussion (N.Y., Nov. 20, 1964); *Sands . . .* for 9 Double Basses, 17 Violins, 5 different Saxophones, Electric Guitar, and 4 Bass Drums of varying sizes (Caracas, May 6, 1966); *Interra* for Piano, Tape, Spotlights, and simultaneous Slide Projections (1968–69); *Ainu* for 20 Vocal Soloists (1970–71); *Fergus Are* for Organ (1974–75). She is the co-author of a book, *Sonic Design: The Nature of Sound and Music* (N.Y., 1976).

Escudier, Léon, French music journalist; b. Castelnaudary, Aude, Sept. 17, 1816; d. Paris, June 22, 1881. He was a brother and partner of **Marie Escudier** (b. Castelnaudary, June 29, 1809; d. Paris, April 18, 1880). In 1838, the brothers began publishing the periodical *La France Musicale* and soon afterward established a music shop. Industrious writers, they issued jointly the following works: *Etudes biographiques sur les chanteurs contemporains* (1840); *Dictionnaire de musique d'après les théoriciens, historiens et critiques les plus célèbres* (2 vols., 1844; reprinted in 1854 as *Dictionnaire de musique, théorique et historique*); *Rossini, sa vie et ses œuvres* (1854); *Vie et aventures des cantatrices célèbres, précédées des musiciens de l'Empire, et suivies de la vie anecdotique de Paganini* (1856). Léon broke up partnership with his brother in 1862, retaining the music business; he established a new paper, *L'Art Musical,* which continued to appear until Sept. 27, 1894. Marie retained the publishing and editorial rights to *La France Musicale,* which ceased publication in 1870.

Eshpai, Andrei, Soviet composer, son of **Yakov Eshpai;** b. Kozmodemiansk, May 15, 1925. He studied with Aram Khatchaturian in Moscow; during the war he acted as a translator from German. In his music he makes use of folk motifs of the Mari nation from which he descended.
WORKS: 4 symphs. (1959, 1962, 1964, 1982); *Symphonic Dances* (1951); *Hungarian Melodies* for Violin and Orch. (1952); 2 piano concertos (1954, 1972); 2 violin sonatas (1966, 1970); Concerto for Orch., with Solo Trumpet, Vibraphone, Piano, and Double Bass (1967); *Festival Overture* for Chorus, 12 Violins, 8 Cellos, 6 Harps, 4 Pianos, and Orch. (1970); ballet, *The Circle* (Kuibishev, Feb. 23, 1981); Oboe Concerto (1982).
BIBLIOGRAPHY: L. Novosiolova, *The Creative Work of A. Eshpai* (Moscow, 1981).

Eshpai, Yakov, Russian composer of Mari extraction; b. near Zvenigorodsk, Oct. 30, 1890; d. Moscow, Feb. 20, 1963. He studied violin and singing in Kazan, and later at the Moscow Cons. He publ. important collections of national songs of the Ural region, particularly of the Mari ethnic group; also wrote vocal and instrumental music on native themes.

Eslava y Elizondo, Miguel Hilarión, Spanish composer and scholar; b. Burlada, Navarra, Oct. 21, 1807; d. Madrid, July 23, 1878. He was a choirboy at the Cathedral of Pamplona; studied organ and violin; in 1827 he went to Calahorra, where he studied with Francisco Secanilla; at the age of 21 he was appointed music director at the Cathedral of Burgo de Osma, where he was ordained a priest. In 1832 he became music director at Seville; in 1847 he obtained the appointment as chapel master to Queen Isabella in Madrid; in 1854 he became a prof. at the Madrid Cons. He also edited a periodical, *Gaceta Musical de Madrid* (1855–56). He wrote 3 operas with Italian texts: *Il Solitario del Monte Selvaggio* (Cádiz, 1841), *La tregua di Ptolemaide* (1842), and *Pietro il crudele* (1843); his fame rests, however, not on his musical compositions, but on his great collection in 10 vols., *Lira sacro-hispana* (Madrid, 1869), an anthology of Spanish sacred music from the 16th to the 19th century, including some of Eslava's own works (Requiem, Te Deum, etc.). He also publ. *Método de solfeo* (1846) and *Escuela de Armonía y Composición* (1861).
BIBLIOGRAPHY: G. Chase, "Miguel Hilarión Eslava," *Musical Quarterly* (Jan. 1938).

Espagne, Franz, German music editor; b. Münster, April 21, 1828; d. Berlin, May 24, 1878. He studied with Dehn; after Dehn's death, he became head of the music dept. of the Royal Library in Berlin; edited new classical editions (works by Palestrina, Beethoven, and others).

Espinosa, Guillermo, Colombian conductor; b. Cartagena, Jan. 9, 1905. He studied music in Milan and in Berlin. After appearing as a guest conductor in Italy, Switzerland, Denmark, and France, he returned to Colombia, and in 1936 founded the National Symph. Orch. at Bogotá, which he led for 10 years. In 1947, he settled in Washington, D.C., as an official of the Division of Music in the Pan American Union; in 1953, succeeded Charles Seeger as chief; retired in 1975.
BIBLIOGRAPHY: F.C. Lange, "Guillermo Espinosa y la Sinfónica Nacional," *Bolletín Latino-Americano de Música* (1938).

Esplá, Oscar, Spanish composer; b. Alicante, Aug. 5, 1886; d. Madrid, Jan. 6, 1976. He at first studied engineering and philosophy; then turned to music, traveling and studying for some years in Germany. He was the first president of the Junta Nacional de Música under the Spanish Republic (1934) and in 1936 was director of the Madrid Cons.; then lived in Brussels and Paris; eventually returned to Spain.
WORKS: *La bella durmiente,* opera (Vienna, 1909); *La Balteira,* opera (1939); ballets: *Ciclopes de Ifach* and *El contrabandista* (1930); orch. works: *Suite levantina; El sueño de Eros; Don Quixote; Ambito de la danza; Las cumbres;* scenic cantata, *Nochebuena del diablo* (1924); *Sonata del sur* for Piano and Orch. (1936–43); *Sinfonía Aitana* (Madrid, Oct. 31, 1964); String Quartet (1947); *De profundis* for 4 Soloists, Chorus, and Orch. (1967);

piano pieces; songs. He publ. the books *El arte y la musicalidad* and *Las actividades del espíritu y su fundamento estético.*
BIBLIOGRAPHY: A. Iglesias, *Oscar Esplá* (Madrid, 1960).

Esposito, Michele, Italian composer and conductor; b. Castellammare, near Naples, Sept. 29, 1855; d. Florence, Nov. 23, 1929. He studied at the Cons. San Pietro at Naples with Cesi (piano) and Serrao (theory); for a time he gave piano concerts in Italy; from 1878–82 was in Paris; in 1882 he was engaged as a piano teacher at the Irish Academy of Music in Dublin; he organized the Dublin Orch. Society in 1899 and conducted it until 1914, and again in 1927. He held the honorary degree of Mus.Doc. of Trinity College, Dublin.
WORKS: He composed several works on Irish subjects: Irish operetta, *The Post Bag* (London, Jan. 27, 1902); incidental music for *The Tinker and the Fairy* (Dublin, 1910); *Suite of Irish Dances* for Orch.; 2 Irish rhapsodies; several arrangements of Irish melodies. He received first prizes for his cantata *Deirdre* (Irish Festival, Dublin, 1897); *Irish Symphony* (Irish Festival, Dublin, 1902); also wrote 2 string quartets, 2 violin sonatas, cello sonatas, etc.

Esser, Heinrich, German composer; b. Mannheim, July 15, 1818; d. Salzburg, June 3, 1872. He studied in Vienna with Lachner and Sechter. In 1847 he became conductor of the Vienna Opera, succeeding Otto Nicolai; in 1869 retired and lived in Salzburg. He was a competent opera conductor; also had a modicum of success as an opera composer; 3 of his operas were performed: *Sitas* (Mannheim, 1839); *Thomas Riquiqui* (Frankfurt, 1843); and *Die zwei Prinzen* (Munich, 1844); also numerous vocal works; 5 symphs.; arrangements of Bach's organ works; a string quartet.
BIBLIOGRAPHY: Karl-Josef Müller, *Heinrich Esser als Komponist* (Mainz, 1969).

Esser, Heribert, German conductor; b. Rheinhausen, Jan. 12, 1929. He studied at the Cologne Cons. and at the Univ. of Cologne. In 1958 he became first conductor of the Wiesbaden Opera. He also conducted at the Cologne Opera. In 1961 he became Generalmusikdirektor at Braunschweig.

Essipoff (Essipova), Anna, famous Russian pianist and pedagogue; b. St. Petersburg, Feb. 13, 1851; d. there, Aug. 18, 1914. She was a pupil of **Leschetizky,** and married him in 1880 (divorced 1892). She made her debut in St. Petersburg; subsequently made long concert tours throughout Europe and in America; her distinguishing artistic quality was a singing piano tone and "pearly" passage work. From 1870 to 1885 she gave 669 concerts. In 1893 she was engaged as a prof. of piano at the St. Petersburg Cons., and continued to teach there until the last years of her life. Many famous pianists and composers, Prokofiev among them, were her students.

Esswood, Paul, English countertenor; b. West

Bridgford, June 2, 1942. He studied with Gordon Clinton at the Royal College of Music, London; then was lay vicar at Westminster Abbey (1964–71). He made his formal debut as countertenor in 1965 in a performance of the *Messiah;* his operatic debut took place in Berkeley, Calif., when he sang in Cavalli's *Erismena.* He was a founder of the Pro Cantione Antiqua, an a cappella male vocal group.

Esteban, Julio, noted pianist and pedagogue; b. Shanghai (of Spanish parentage), March 18, 1906. In 1907 he was taken to Spain; gave concerts in Spain from 1919 to 1924; in 1925 went to Manila, where he taught at the Cons. of Music of the Univ. of the Philippines until 1947, when he was appointed director of the Cons. of Music at the Univ. of Santo Tomás there. He traveled through the Orient; gave concerts in Hong Kong and in Japan in 1952; also played for the U.N. troops in Korea. In 1955 he left Manila and joined the faculty of the Peabody Cons. in Baltimore.

Estes, Charles E., American organist; b. Somersworth, N.H., Aug. 28, 1882; d. Dover, N.H., Sept. 16, 1968. He studied at Dartmouth College with Charles S. Morse and at Teachers College, Columbia Univ.; also with Widor in Paris (1917–18) and Seth Bingham in N.Y. (1924–25); was head of the music dept. of the Robert College in Constantinople from 1910 to 1917, and again from 1926 to 1947. In 1948 he returned to America and served as organist at the First Parish Church in Dover.

Estes, Simon, black American bass-baritone; b. Centerville, Iowa, March 2, 1938. He studied voice at the Juilliard School of Music in N.Y.; then began his career as a singer of oratorio and lieder. On June 10, 1976, he made his Metropolitan Opera debut in N.Y. as Oroveso in *Norma;* he also appeared at La Scala in Milan, the Bolshoi Theater in Moscow, and the Hamburg State Opera. In 1978 he sang at the Bayreuth Festival in the title role of *Der Fliegende Holländer.* His major operatic roles include Wotan, Boris Godunov, and King Philip in Verdi's *Don Carlos.*

Esteve, Pablo, Catalonian composer; b. c.1730, probably in Barcelona; d. Madrid, June 4, 1794. He went to Madrid about 1760; was maestro di cappella to the Duke of Osuna; in 1778 was appointed official composer for the municipal theaters of Madrid. He composed over 300 tonadillas, and some zarzuelas. His song *El jilguerito con pico de oro* has been arranged for soprano and orch. by Joaquín Nin.
BIBLIOGRAPHY: F. Pedrell, *Teatro lírico español anterior al siglo XIX* (5 vols. in one, 1879–98); J. Nin, *Les Classiques espagnols du chant* (2 vols., Paris, 1926); J. Subirá, *Tonadillas teatrales inéditas* (Barcelona, 1932; contains score of Esteve's *Los signos del año*).

Estévez, Antonio, Venezuelan composer; b. Calabozo, Jan. 3, 1916. He studied composition in Caracas with Vicente Emilio Sojo; played the oboe in the Caracas Symph. Orch. At the age of 50 he became interested in electronic music and obtained a scholarship from the Venezuelan National Inst. of Culture and Fine Arts to study electronic techniques in Paris.
WORKS: *Suite Llanera* for Orch. (1942); Concerto for Orch. (1949–50); *Cantata criolla* for Voices and Orch. (1954); choruses; piano pieces; a group of electronic works under the title *Cosmovibrafonía* (1968).

Estrada, Carlos, Uruguayan composer and conductor; b. Montevideo, Sept. 15, 1909; d. there, May 7, 1970. He studied in Paris with Roger-Ducasse and Henri Busser (composition) and with Philippe Gaubert (conducting). Returning to Montevideo, he was associated with the State Radio (1940–54) and later became director of the National Cons. in Montevideo (1954–68). He wrote 2 symphs. (1951, 1967); chamber music; effective piano pieces. A complete list of his works is found in vol. 16 of *Composers of the Americas* (Washington, D.C., 1970).

Estrada, Garcia Juan Agustín, Argentine composer; b. Buenos Aires, Nov. 8, 1895. He studied law; then went to Paris, where he took lessons in composition with Jacques Ibert. Returning to Argentina, he became a municipal judge.
WORKS: *Tres aires argentinos* for Orch. (Paris, Feb. 28, 1929); opera, *La Cuarterona* (Buenos Aires, Aug. 10, 1951); a number of songs.

Etcheverry, Henri-Bertrand, French bass-baritone; b. Bordeaux, March 29, 1900; d. Paris, Nov. 14, 1960. He studied in Paris; made his debut at the Paris Opéra in 1932; also sang at the Opéra-Comique; made several appearances at Covent Garden in London. In addition to the French operatic roles, he was one of the best performers of Russian roles, such as Boris Godunov.

Etler, Alvin Derald, American oboist and composer; b. Battle Creek, Mich., Feb. 19, 1913; d. Northampton, Mass., June 13, 1973. He studied at the Univ. of Illinois, Case Western Reserve Univ., and Yale Univ. He subsequently was on the faculty of Yale Univ. (1942–46), at Cornell Univ. (1946–47), at the Univ. of Illinois (1947–49), and from 1949 at Smith College. He held 2 Guggenheim fellowships (1941, 1963). His music is marked by stately formality of design.
WORKS: FOR ORCH.: *Music* for Chamber Orch. (1938); 2 sinfoniettas (1940, 1941); *Passacaglia and Fugue* for Orch. (1947); Concerto for String Quartet and String Orch. (1948); Symph. (1951); *Dramatic Overture* (1956); Concerto for Orch. (1957); *Elegy* for Small Orch. (1959); Concerto for Wind Quintet and Orch. (1960; Tokyo, Oct. 18, 1962); *Triptych* for Orch. (1961); Concerto for Clarinet and Chamber Ensemble of 3 Trumpets, 3 Trombones, 2 Double Basses, and 3 Percussionists (1962; N.Y., Dec. 20, 1965); Concerto for Brass Quintet, String Orch., and Percussion (1967); Concerto for String Quartet and Orch. (1968; Milwaukee, June 13, 1968); *Conviviali-*

ties for Orch. (1968); Concerto for Cello, with Chamber Group (N.Y., March 2, 1971). CHAMBER MUSIC: Suite for Oboe, Violin, Viola, and Cello (1936); Sonata for Oboe, Clarinet, and Viola (1944); Bassoon Sonata (1951); 2 clarinet sonatas (1952, 1969); Oboe Sonata (1952); 2 wind quintets (1955, 1957); Cello Sonata (1956); Concerto for Violin and Wind Quintet (1958); Sonata for Viola and Harpsichord (1959); 2 string quartets (1963, 1965); Brass Quintet (1963); *Sonic Sequence* for Brass Quintet (1967); also *Onomatopoësis* for Men's Chorus, Winds, Brass, and Percussion (1965).

Eto, Toshiya, Japanese violinist; b. Tokyo, Nov. 9, 1927. After preliminary study in Japan he went to the U.S. and enrolled as a student of Efrem Zimbalist at the Curtis Inst. of Music in Philadelphia; then was on its faculty (1953–61). In 1961 he returned to Japan as a prof. at the Toho School of Music. He continued to appear widely as a soloist, and received praise for his technical ability in performances of contemporary music. He made his American debut as a soloist at Carnegie Hall in N.Y., in 1951.

Ett, Kaspar, German organist and composer; b. Eresing, Jan. 5, 1788; d. Munich, May 16, 1847. From 1816, he was court organist at St. Michael's Church in Munich. He was active in reviving the church music of the 16th and 17th centuries; his own sacred compositions (of which but a few graduals and *cantica sacra* were printed) follow these early works in style. He composed 273 separate works; a complete enumeration is given by F. Bierling, *Kaspar Ett* (1906).
BIBLIOGRAPHY: K.F.E. von Schafhäutl, "Erinnerungen an Kaspar Ett," *Kirchenmusikalisches Jahrbuch* (1891).

Ettinger, Max, German composer and conductor; b. Lemberg (Lwow), Dec. 27, 1874; d. Basel, July 19, 1951. He studied in Berlin and Munich; was active as a conductor in Munich (1900–20), Leipzig (1920–29), and Berlin (1929–33). In 1938 he went to Switzerland, where he remained until his death.
WORKS: Operas: *Judith* (Nuremberg, 1921); *Der eifersüchtige Trinker,* after Boccaccio (Nuremberg, 1925); *Juana* (Nuremberg, 1925); *Clavigo,* after Goethe (Leipzig, 1926); *Frühlings Erwachen* (Leipzig, 1928); oratorio, *Weisheit des Orients,* after Omar Khayyám (Nuremberg, 1924); *Jewish Requiem* (1947); also chamber music and songs.

Euclid, famous Greek geometer; lived at Alexandria about 300 B.C. He is the reputed author of a treatise on music, *Katatomè kanonos (Sectio canonis),* following the theories of Pythagoras (new critical ed. by K. von Jan in *Musici scriptores graeci).* For another treatise long ascribed to Euclid, see the entry on Cleonides.

Eulenburg, Ernst, German music publisher, b. Berlin, Nov. 30, 1847; d. Leipzig, Sept. 11, 1926. He stud-

ied at the Leipzig Cons.; in 1874 established in Leipzig the publ. house bearing his name; after his acquisition of Payne's *Kleine Partitur-Ausgabe* (1892) he enormously increased the scope of that publication so that large orch. scores could be included. Upon his death the firm was taken over by his son **Kurt Eulenburg.**

Eulenburg, Kurt, German music publisher, son of **Ernst Eulenburg;** b. Berlin, Feb. 22, 1879; d. London, April 10, 1982 (at the age of 103!). Apprenticed by his father, he joined the Eulenburg firm in 1911, and upon his father's death in 1926 became its sole owner. He extended the dept. of miniature scores and also publ. the original text ("Urtext") of many of Mozart's works, edited by Alfred Einstein, Blume, Kroyer, and others. During the war, he lived in Switzerland. He settled in London in 1945 and took over the management of the London branch of his publishing business. He retired in 1968.

Euler, Leonhard, great mathematician; b. Basel, April 15, 1707; d. St. Petersburg, Sept. 18, 1783. He was a prof. of mathematics at St. Petersburg (1730) and Berlin (1741); publ. several important works on music theory and acoustics, chief among them being the *Tentamen novae theoriae musicae* (1739). Euler was the first to employ logarithms to explain differences in pitch.
BIBLIOGRAPHY: Schulz-Euler, *Leonhardt Euler* (Frankfurt, 1907); also Treubner's ed. of Euler's *Opera omnia,* series 3, vol. I (1926).

Euting, Ernst, English musicologist; b. London, Feb. 7, 1874; d. Berlin, April 21, 1925. From 1892–96 he attended the Hochschule für Musik in Berlin, then devoted himself to musicology at the Univ. there, and became a Dr.Phil. with the thesis *Zur Geschichte der Blasinstrumente im 16. und 17. Jahrhundert* (1899); in the same year he founded the *Deutsche Instrumentenbau-Zeitung,* of which he was the editor; also edited the *Zeitschrift der Internationalen Musikgesellschaft* (1902–3).

Evangelisti, Franco, Italian composer; b. Rome, Jan. 21, 1926; d. there, Jan. 29, 1980. He first studied engineering at the Univ. of Rome; then went to Germany, where he took courses in composition at the Univ. of Freiburg; also attended summer courses with Ernst Krenek and René Leibowitz at Darmstadt. In his own music he explored the musical resources of electronics; the titles of his works betray his preoccupation with mathematical terminology, as exemplified by *4!* (factorization of the numbers from 1 to 4) for Violin and Piano (1955); *Ordini* for Orch. (1955); *Random or Not Random* for Orch. (1956–62); *Proporzioni* for Flute (1958); *Campi integrati* (1959); *Aleatorio* for String Quartet (1959); *Condensazioni* for Orch. (1962). He also lectured on electronic music.

Evans, Bill (William John Evans), American jazz pianist and composer; b. Plainfield, N.J., Aug. 16,

1929; d. New York, Sept. 15, 1980. After taking up the piano, he joined the band of Miles Davis and soon became a leading jazz pianist; after making the classic jazz recording of *Kind of Blue* with the Davis group, he formed his own jazz trio. He received Grammy awards for his recordings *Conversations with Myself* (1963), *Alone* (1970), and *The Bill Evans Album* (1971).

Evans, David Emlyn, Welsh music editor and composer; b. near Newscastle Emlyn, Wales, Sept. 21, 1843; d. London, April 19, 1913. He was established in business at Cheltenham, but devoted his leisure hours to music; took part in many Welsh music festivals (Eisteddfodau), his works invariably winning prizes; after the Eisteddfod at Wexham in 1876, when he carried off all 4 prizes, he voluntarily withdrew from further competitions, but frequently acted as judge; at the National Eisteddfod in London in 1887, he was awarded a prize for his *Biography of Welsh Musicians;* for many years he was editor of *Y Cerddor (The Musician).* His chief work is *Alawon Fy Ngwlad* (2 vols., 1896), a collection of 500 Welsh airs in piano arrangements; his publ. compositions include 2 cantatas, *The Christian's Prayer* and *The Fairy-tribe;* many glees, anthems, and part-songs.

Evans, Edwin, Jr., English writer on music, son of **Edwin Evans, Sr.;** b. London, Sept. 1, 1874; d. there, March 3, 1945. He studied for a business career; was engaged in telegraphy, railroads, and finance from 1889 to 1913; then devoted himself exclusively to musical pursuits. He was music critic of the *Pall Mall Gazette* (1914–23) and other London papers; was one of the founders of the International Society for Contemporary Music (1922); in 1938 was elected its president, retaining this post until his death. He wrote *Tchaikovsky* (London, 1906; revised ed., 1935); *The Margin of Music* (London, 1924); *Music and the Dance* (posthumous; London, 1948).

Evans, Edwin, Sr., English organist and writer; b. London, 1844; d. there, Dec. 21, 1923. An assiduous and thorough scholar, he publ. basic analytic vols. on Beethoven and Brahms: *Beethoven's 9 Symphonies, fully described and analyzed* (London, 1923–24) and the remarkable 4-vol. edition (1,581 pages; over 1,000 musical examples) *Historical, Descriptive and Analytical Account of the Entire Works of Johannes Brahms:* vol. I, vocal works (1912); vol. II, chamber and orch. music up to op. 67 (1933; reprinted 1950); vol. III, chamber and orch. music from op. 68 to the end (1935; reprinted 1949); vol. IV, piano works (1936; reprinted 1950). Vols. II, III, and IV were publ. posthumously. He also wrote *Accompaniment of Plainchant* (1911); *Wagner's Teachings by Analogy* (1915); *How to Compose; How to Accompany at the Piano* (London, 1917); *Method of Instrumentation* (vol. I, *How to Write for Strings*); *Technics of the Organ* (London, 1938); trans. Wagner's *Oper und Drama;* made organ arrangements of operatic overtures.

Evans, Sir Geraint, Welsh baritone; b. Pontypridd, South Wales, Feb. 16, 1922. He studied in Hamburg and Geneva; was associated with the Glyndebourne Festivals from 1949 to 1961; appeared in San Francisco in 1959, and also sang at La Scala in Milan in 1960 and at the Vienna Opera in 1961. He made his Metropolitan Opera debut in N.Y. on March 25, 1964, as Falstaff. He distinguished himself particularly in the roles of Figaro, Leporello, and Papageno. He was knighted in 1969 after having been made a Commander of the Order of the British Empire in 1959. He publ. *A Knight at the Opera* (London, 1984).

Evans, Gil, Canadian jazz pianist and composer of Australian parentage; b. Toronto, May 13, 1912. He taught himself to play the piano; then led his own band in Stockton, Calif. (1933–38); in 1941 he became an arranger for Claude Thornhill; later he toured as a pianist and bandleader.

Everding, August, German opera producer and administrator; b. Bottrop, Oct. 31, 1928. He was educated in Bonn and Munich. He began his career as a theater producer for stage plays. In 1973 he was named Intendant of the Hamburg State Opera; in 1976, of the Bavarian State Opera in Munich; in 1982 he assumed the post of General Intendant for all of the Munich theaters.

Everly, Don, American country and western singer; b. Brownie, Ky., Feb. 1, 1937. With his brother, **Phil Everly** (b. Brownie, Ky., Jan. 19, 1939), he appeared at the age of 8 on a radio show managed by their parents at Shenandoah, Iowa. Both brothers then toured with their parents around the country. When they grew up they moved to Nashville and began playing rock'n'roll in a synthetic style of rhythm-and-blues, pop, and country-and-western. Their hits were *Bye, Bye Love, Wake Up, Little Susie, All I Have to Do Is Dream,* and *Cathy's Clown.* Alas, brotherly love did not last forever; they split apart in 1973; their divergent ways led to a sad impasse, but happily their fraternal records survived, and continued to provide joy to a new generation of bobby-soxers and their hippie mates.

Evett, Robert, American composer; b. Loveland, Colo., Nov. 30, 1922; d. Takoma Park, Md., Feb. 3, 1975. He studied with Roy Harris in Colorado Springs (1941–46) and with Persichetti at the Juilliard School of Music in N.Y. (1951–52); settled in Washington, D.C., as a music critic.

WORKS: 4 piano sonatas (1945, 1952, 1953, 1954); Cello Concerto (1954); Piano Quintet (1954); Sonata for Cello and Harpsichord (1955); *Variations* for Clarinet and Orch. (1955); Piano Concerto (1957); Viola Sonata (1958); Symph. No. 1 (1960); Violin Sonata (1960); Concerto for Harpsichord and Orch. (Washington, D.C., April 25, 1961); Piano Quartet (1961); Sonata for Harpsichord (1962); *Anniversary Concerto* for Orch. (Washington, Oct. 19, 1963); Sonata for Oboe and Harpsichord (1964); Symph. No. 2, subtitled *Billy Ascends,* for Voices and Orch., to a text by Melville (Washington, May 7, 1965); Symph. No. 3 (Washington, June 6, 1965); *The Windhover,* concerto for Bassoon and Orch. (5th Inter-American Music Festival, Washington, May 20, 1971); songs; piano pieces.

Evseyev, Sergei, Russian composer and pedagogue; b. Moscow, Jan. 24, 1893; d. there, March 16, 1956. He studied piano with Medtner as a youth; then entered the Moscow Cons., where he continued to study piano with Goldenweiser and also attended classes in composition with Taneyev; upon graduation, he devoted himself to teaching music theory at the Moscow Cons., where he introduced a special seminar in modern harmony; he also taught a course of specific Russian folk-song polyphony; furthermore, he conducted classes in musical education by correspondence on an experimental basis (1936–41).

WORKS: 3 symphs. (1925, 1933, 1943); 2 piano concertos (1932); Clarinet Concerto (1943); 2 string quartets (1935, 1945); *Dramatic Sonata* for Cello and Piano (1941); many piano pieces (most of them influenced by Medtner).

Ewald, Victor, Russian composer; b. St. Petersburg, Nov. 27, 1860; d. Leningrad, April 26, 1935. He studied engineering; from 1895 to 1915 was a prof. at the Inst. of Civil Engineering. Music was his avocation; he played the cello and the French horn; took part in Belaieff's quartet evenings and wrote a number of chamber music works; of these, his brass quintet is still popular. After the Revolution he continued to work in his primary profession as a civil engineer and instructor; also was active as an ethnomusicologist and participated in the expeditions in the north of European Russia collecting folk songs. His daughter **Zinaida** (1894–1942) continued his work in folklore and publ. several collections of Russian songs, in collaboration with her husband, **Evgeny Gippius** (b. 1903).

Ewen, David, prolific American writer on music; b. Lwow, Poland, Nov. 26, 1907. He came to the U.S. in 1912. He attended the College of the City of N.Y.; studied music theory with Max Persin; was enrolled as a student at the Music School Settlement and at Columbia Univ. He was music editor of *Reflex Magazine* (1928–29) and *The American Hebrew* (1935); was active briefly as a publisher (1946–49); in 1965 joined the music faculty of the Univ. of Miami, which awarded him in 1974 the honorary degree of D.Mus.. In all probability, Ewen has publ. more books on music and edited more reference publications than anyone else in the 20th century (82 at the last count in 1984). Some of his publications have been trans. into 17 languages.

WRITINGS: (not including revisions publ. with the amplificatory modifier "New"): *The Unfinished Symphony* (1931); *Hebrew Music* (1931); *Wine, Women, and Waltz* (1933); *Composers of Today* (1934); *The Man with the Baton* (1936); *Composers of Yesterday* (1937); *Men and Women Who Make Music* (1939); *Musical Vienna* (with Frederic Ewen, 1939); *Living Musicians* (1940); *Pioneers in Music* (1941); *Music Comes to America* (1942; revised 1947); *Dictators of the Baton* (1943; revised 1948); *Men of Popular Music* (1944; revised 1952); *Music for the Millions* (1944; revised 1946, 1949; publ. under title *Encyclopedia of Musical Masterpieces,* 1950); *American Composers Today* (revised ed., 1949); *The Story of Irving Berlin* (1950); *The Story of Arturo Toscanini* (1951; in Italian, Milan, 1952); *Fun with Musical Games and Quizzes* (with N. Slonimsky, 1952); *The Complete Book of 20th Century Music* (1952); *European Composers Today* (1953); *The Story of Jerome Kern* (1953); *The Milton Cross Encyclopedia of Great Composers and Their Music* (with Milton Cross, 1953); *Encyclopedia of the Opera* (1955); *A Journey to Greatness, George Gershwin* (1956; rewritten in 1970 under the title *George Gershwin: His Journey to Greatness*); *Panorama of American Popular Music* (1957); *Complete Book of the American Musical Theater* (N.Y., 1958; extremely valuable; brought up to date as *The New Complete Book of the American Musical Theater,* 1970); *Encyclopedia of Concert Music* (N.Y., 1959); *The World of Jerome Kern* (N.Y., 1960); *Leonard Bernstein* (N.Y., 1960; revised 1967); *History of Popular Music* (N.Y., 1961); *The Story of America's Musical Theater* (N.Y., 1961; revised 1969); *Ewen's Lighter Classics in Music* (N.Y., 1961); *David Ewen Introduces Modern Music* (N.Y., 1962; revised 1969); *The Book of European Light Opera* (N.Y., 1962); *Popular American Composers* (N.Y., 1962); *The Complete Book of Classical Music* (N.Y., 1963); *The Life and Death of Tin Pan Alley* (N.Y., 1964); *American Popular Songs: From the Revolutionary War to the Present* (N.Y., 1966); *Great Composers: 1300–1900* (N.Y., 1966); *The World of 20th-Century Music* (N.Y., 1968); *Composers since 1900* (N.Y., 1969); *Great Men of American Popular Songs* (N.Y., 1970); *Composers of Tomorrow's Music* (N.Y., 1971); *New Encyclopedia of the Opera,* a radical revision of *Encyclopedia of the Opera* (1971); *Popular American Composers: First Supplement* (N.Y., 1972); *Mainstreams of Music* (in 4 vols., N.Y., 1972, 1973, 1974, 1975); *All the Years of American Popular Music* (Englewood Cliffs, N.J., 1977); *Musicians since 1900* (N.Y., 1978); *American Composers: A Biographical Dictionary* (N.Y., 1982). He also publ. a number of books for young people (on Gershwin, Bernstein, Haydn, Irving Berlin, Toscanini, Johann Strauss, Jerome Kern, Richard Rodgers, and Cole Porter). He rewrote, revised, and expanded the *Milton Cross Encyclopedia of Great Composers* (N.Y., 1960). Revised eds. of *The Book of Modern Composers,* originally publ. in 1943, appeared as *The New Book of Modern Composers* in 1960 and 1967. He further edited *From Bach to Stravinsky* (1933) and *The World of Great Composers* (Englewood Cliffs, N.J., 1962).

Ewing, Maria (Louise), American soprano; b. Detroit, March 27, 1950. She studied at the Cleveland Inst. of Music with Eleanor Steber and Jennie Tourel; made her professional debut in 1973 at the Ravinia Festival with the Chicago Symph. Orch.;

subsequently appeared with opera companies in Chicago, Washington, D.C., Santa Fe, and Houston. She made her Metropolitan Opera debut in N.Y. in 1976 as Cherubino in *Le nozze di Figaro;* in 1976 she sang at La Scala in Milan. She returned to the Metropolitan Opera to sing the part of Dorabella in a new production of *Così fan tutte.* She was a periodic soloist at the Glyndebourne Festival, where her husband, **Sir Peter Hall,** was artistic director.

Excestre, William, English singer and composer who flourished c.1390–1410. He was clerk of the Chapel Royal in 1393, and received a prebend in St. Stephen's, Westminster, in 1394. He was one of the composers whose music is contained in the *Old Hall Manuscript;* a Gloria, a Credo, and a Sanctus (all for 3 voices) are extant.

Eximeno (y Pujades), Antonio, one of the most important Spanish writers on music; b. Valencia, Sept. 26, 1729; d. Rome, June 9, 1808. He entered the Company of Jesus at the age of 16; became a prof. of rhetoric at the Univ. of Valencia; in 1764 was appointed prof. of mathematics at the military academy in Segovia. When the Jesuits were expelled from Spain in 1767, he went to Rome, and in 1768 began to study music. In 1774 he publ. *Dell' origine e delle regole della musica colla storia del suo progresso, decadenza e rinnovazione* (Rome; Spanish trans. by Gutierrez, 1776, 3 vols.), in which he protested against pedantic rules and argued that music should be based on the natural rules of prosody. His theories were strongly controverted, especially by Padre Martini; in answer to the latter, Eximeno publ. *Dubbio di Antonio Eximeno sopra il Saggio fondamentale, pratico di contrappunto del Maestro Giambattista Martini* (Rome, 1775). His dictum that the national song should serve as a basis for the art-music of each country was taken up by Pedrell and led to the nationalist movement in modern Spanish music. Eximeno also wrote a satirical musical novel, *Don Lazarillo Vizcardi,* directed against the theories of Pietro Cerone (publ. by Barbieri, 1872–73, 2 vols.).

BIBLIOGRAPHY: F. Pedrell, *Padre Antonio Eximeno* (Barcelona, 1921).

Expert, Henry, eminent French music editor; b. Bordeaux, May 12, 1863; d. Tourettes-sur-Loup (Alpes-Maritimes), Aug. 18, 1952. He attended a Jesuit school in Bordeaux; went to Paris in 1881 and studied with César Franck and Eugène Gigout; taught at the Ecole Nationale de Musique Classique, and lectured at the Ecole des Hautes Etudes Sociales; from 1909, he was deputy-librarian of the Paris Cons.; became chief of the library in 1921; was the founder (in 1903, with Maury) of the Société d'Etudes Musicales et Concerts Historiques, also of the choral society Chanterie de la Renaissance (1924). In 1933 he retired. His life work was the editing and publication of Franco-Flemish music of the 15th and 16th centuries, in 6 parts: I. *Les Maîtres-Musiciens de la Renaissance française* (works by Orlando di Lasso, Goudimel, Costeley, Janequin,

Brumel, La Rue, Mouton, Fevin, Mauduit, Claude Le Jeune, Regnart, Du Caurroy, Gervaise, and Attaingnant's collection of chansons, all in modern notation, with facsimiles, etc.; 23 vols., publ. 1894–1908); II. *Bibliographie thématique* (2 vols., catalogue of publications of Attaingnant); III. *Les Théoriciens de la musique au temps de la Renaissance* (works of Michel de Menhou); IV. 2 vols. of music by Antoine de Bertrand; V. *Commentaires;* VI. *Extraits des Maîtres Musiciens* (selected single compositions, arranged for modern use; a large number have been publ., including works by some composers not found in Part I, viz.: Bertrand, Bonnet, Certon, De La Grotte, Gardanne, Josquin des Prez, Le Heurteur, Le Pelletier, Passereau, Thoinot-Arbeau). In 1924 Expert began the publication of a new series of French music of the 16th century entitled *Monuments de la musique française au temps de la Renaissance* (with scores in modern notation), of which 10 vols. were publ.; these contain works by Le Jeune, in 2 vols. (*Octonaires de la vanité et inconstance du monde);* Certon (3 masses); Le Blanc (*Airs de plusieurs musiciens);* Bertrand, in 4 vols. (*Amours de P. de Ronsard);* Goudimel (*Messes à 4 voix);* L'Estocart (*Octonaires de la vanité du monde).* Expert also edited *Chansons mondaines des XVIIe et XVIIIe siècles français* (80 songs); *Airs français des XVIe et XVIIe siècles* (Boesset, Guedron, Tessier, Lambert) *Florilège du concert vocal de la Renaissance* (1928–29), in 8 parts (Janequin, Lassus, Costeley, Bonnet, Le Jeune, Mauduit); *Les Maîtres du clavecin des XVIIe et XVIIIe siècles* (Dandrieu, Daquin, Corrette); *Amusements des maîtres français du XVIIIe siècle* (Chédeville, J. Aubert, Baton); *Répertoire de musique religieuse et spirituelle* (Campra, Charpentier, Dumont, Lully, Bernier, Couperin le Grand, Clérambault, Lalande, Rameau, etc.); *La Fleur des musiciens de P. de Ronsard* (1923); instrumental *Fantaisies* by Le Jeune and Du Caurroy; and *Le Pseautier huguenot du XVIe siècle* (the Huguenot Psalter; 1902). He contributed the chapter on the music of France during the 16th century to Lavignac's *Encyclopédie de la Musique.*

Eybler, Joseph, Austrian composer; b. Schwechat, near Vienna, Feb. 8, 1765; d. Schönbrunn, July 24, 1846. He studied with Albrechtsberger in Vienna; was a friend of Haydn and Mozart; in 1792, became choirmaster at the Carmelite Church; was tutor to the princes in 1810, and first court Kapellmeister in 1824, on Salieri's retirement. He composed symphs., concertos, quartets, sonatas, etc.; also 2 oratorios, 32 masses, a Requiem, 7 Te Deums, and 30 offertories.

BIBLIOGRAPHY: Hildegard Herrmann, *Thematische Verzeichnis der Werke von Joseph Eybler* (thematic catalogue, Munich, 1976).

Eyken (Eijken), Jan Albert van, Dutch organist; b. Amersfoort, April 26, 1823; d. Elberfeld, Sept. 24, 1868. He studied at the Leipzig Cons., and afterward at Dresden with Schneider. In 1848, he became organist of the Remonstrantenkerk in Amsterdam; in 1853, of the Zuyderkerk, and teacher at the music school in Rotterdam; in 1854, he became organist at

Elberfeld. His organ pieces (150 chorales with introductions, 25 preludes, a toccata and fugue on B–A–C–H, 3 sonatas, variations, transcriptions, etc.) are well and favorably known.

Eymieu, Henry, French composer and writer on music; b. Saillans, Drôme, May 7, 1860; d. Paris, March 21, 1931. He studied law; then turned to music, taking lessons with Widor; settling in Paris, he wrote for *Le Ménestrel* and other musical publications; publ. *Etudes et biographies musicales* (Paris, 1892); composed a great variety of piano pieces, songs, and duets for piano and violin (58 publ. opus numbers in all); also produced a stage piece, *Un Mariage sous Né ron* (Paris, 1898), and an oratorio, *Marthe et Marie* (Asnières, 1898).

Eyser, Eberhard, Polish-born Swedish violinist, violist, and composer; b. Kwidzyn (Marienwerder), East Prussia, Aug. 1, 1932. He studied at the Music Academy in Hannover (1952–57); also attended seminars of Alois Hába in Prague, Hauer in Vienna, and Xenakis. In 1961 he became a violist in the Royal Opera House Orch. in Stockholm.
WORKS: FOR THE STAGE: 2 one-act operas: *Carmen 36*, after Strindberg, for 2 Singing Voices, Speaking Voice, Chamber Orch., and Tape (1972; Umeå, Nov. 5, 1975) and *Kalifens son* (1970–73); 2 chamber operas, after Strindberg: *Molonne* (Stockholm, Oct. 27, 1970) and *Sista resan (Last Voyage)* for 2 Voices, Clarinet, and Tape (1972–73; Vadstena, July 24, 1974); miniature opera, *Hjärter Kung eller Trägen vinner,* for 9 Voices and Instrumental Ensemble (1973; Vadstena, June 6, 1973); 3 "operettinas": *I, Drömmen om mannen (Dream of Man)* for 7 Voices, Small Girls' Chorus, and Chamber Orch. (1972), *II* for 2 Voices a cappella (1971), and *III* for 4 Voices and 2 Pianists on one Piano (1971). His other works include a Toccata for Orch. (1957); *Iberian Suite* for Chamber Orch. (1957); *Serenata spagnola* for English Horn and String Quartet (1959); *Capriccio svedese* for 12 Solo Strings (1964); *Metastrophý* for Orch. (1965); *Podema* for String Quartet (1969); *Capriccio 68* for Orch. (1968); *Colludo* for 3 to 8 String and Wind Instruments (1971); Concertino for Horn and Chamber Orch. (1971); *Constructo* for Optional Instrumental Ensemble (1971); *Solo* for Double Bass (1971); Sonata for Bass Clarinet, Cymbal, and Piano (1972); *Petite nocturne*

for Double Bass, Harpsichord, and String Orch. (1972); Sonata for Solo Bassoon (1973); Serenade for Flute, Viola, and Cello (1973); *Stochasta 57–74* for Winds and Percussion (1974); *Symphonie orientale* for Chamber Orch. (1974); Passacaglia for Solo Cello (1974); *Ottoletto* for 8 Clarinets (1975); *Circus Overture* for 12 Winds, Percussion, and Double Bass (1976).

Eysler, Edmund S., Austrian operetta composer; b. Vienna, March 12, 1874; d. there, Oct. 4, 1949. He produced a great number of stage works; in 1915 he wrote no fewer than 4 operettas (*Leutnant Gustl, Der grosse Gabriel, Ein Tag im Paradies, Die oder Keine*). His most successful operetta was *Bruder Straubinger* (Vienna, Feb. 20, 1903; over 100 perfs. in that year). Other successful operettas: *Pufferl* (Vienna, April 13, 1905); *Künstlerblut* (1906); *Das Glückschweinchen* (1908); *Der unsterbliche Lump* (1910); *Das Zirkuskind* (1911); *Die goldene Meisterin* (Vienna, Sept. 13, 1927).
BIBLIOGRAPHY: R. Prosl, *Edmund Eysler* (Vienna, 1947).

Ezaki, Kenjiro, Formosan-born Japanese composer; b. Tainan, Oct. 27, 1926. He studied at the Nihon Univ. in Tokyo (1953–57); also in the U.S. at the Univ. of Illinois Experimental Music Studio, and with Ussachevsky at the Columbia-Princeton Electronic Music Center. Returning to Japan, he operated his own electronic music studio in Tokyo; in 1971 was appointed to the faculty of the Univ. of Tokyo. He uses electronic sound in many of his works.
WORKS: *Discretion* for a Female Voice (1961); *Concretion* for String Trio (1962); *Dim Light* for Chorus and 6 Instruments (1962); *Contention* for Soprano and Guitar (1963); *Presage* for Orch., in mobile configuration (1964); *Omen* for Modified Orch. (1964); Piano Trio (1964); *Pharos No. 1* and *No. 2* for Chorus, Flute, Clarinet, Oboe, and Piano (1965); *Music I* and *II* for Guitar and Tape (1967, 1971); *Ensemble* for a Piano and 2 Playback Devices (1967); *Composition 5* for Flute, 2 Guitars, Cello, Percussion, and Soprano (1968); *Musicronics No. 1* for Piano, Percussion, and Tape (1968); *Zamuzara*, ballet music for Tape (1968); *Requiem 1970* for Soprano and Tape (1969); *Computer Music No. 1* (1969; composed on the FACOM 270–30 computer); *Liaison* for 12-channel Tape (1971).

F

Faber, Heinrich (known as **Magister Henricus Faber**), German theorist; b. Lichtenfels, c.1500; d. Ölsnitz, Saxony, Feb. 26, 1552. He entered the Univ. of Wittenberg in 1542; received the degree of Master of Liberal Arts in 1545; was then rector of the school of St. George's Monastery near Naumburg; in 1551 was appointed lecturer at Wittenberg Univ.; then was rector at Ölsnitz. He publ. *Compendiolum musicae pro incipientibus* (1548; reprinted many times and also issued in German trans. as *Musica, Kurtzer Inhalt der Singkunst*, 1572; ed. by Adam Gumpelzhaimer and publ. as *Compendium musicae pro illius artis tironibus*, 1591). Faber further publ. *Ad Musicam practicam introductio* (1550); a *Musica poetica* remains in MS.

Fabini, Eduardo, Uruguayan composer; b. Solís del Mataojo, May 18, 1882; d. Montevideo, May 17, 1950. He studied violin in Montevideo, and later in Europe with César Thomson at the Brussels Cons., winning first prize; then gave concerts as a violinist in South America and in the U.S. (1926); eventually returned to Montevideo, and was active there as a composer and educator. His music is inspired entirely by South American folklore; the idiom is mildly modernistic, with lavish use of whole-tone scales and other external devices of Impressionism.

WORKS (all first perf. in Montevideo): Ballets: *Mburucuyá* (April 15, 1933) and *Mañana de Reyes* (July 31, 1937); symph. poem, *Campo* (April 29, 1922); overture, *La isla de los Ceibos* (Sept. 14, 1926); *Melga sinfónica* (Oct. 11, 1931); Fantasia for Violin and Orch. (Aug. 22, 1929); choral works; piano pieces; songs.

Fabricius, Johann Albert, eminent bibliographer, son of **Werner Fabricius;** b. Leipzig, Nov. 11, 1668; d. Hamburg, April 30, 1736. A learned man, he was a prof. of elocution; publ. important books of reference, valuable to musicology for the information they contain on musical topics: *Thesaurus antiquitatum hebraicarum* (7 vols., 1713); *Bibliotheca latina mediae et infimae aetatis* (6 vols., 1712–22; 2nd ed., 1734); *Bibliotheca graeca sive notitia scriptorum veterum graecorum* (14 vols., 1705–28).

Fabricius, Werner, German composer; b. Itzehoe, April 10, 1633; d. Leipzig, Jan. 9, 1679. He studied with Thomas Selle and Heinrich Scheidemann in Hamburg; then took courses in law in Leipzig, where he also served as organist of the Nicolaikirche and Paulinerkirche.

WORKS: He publ. a collection of pavanes, allemandes, etc., for viols and other instruments, under the title *Deliciae harmonicae* (Leipzig, 1656); also *Geistliche Lieder* (Jena, 1659); *Geistliche Arien, Dialogen, Concerten, etc.* (Leipzig, 1662); motets; etc.

Faccio, Franco, Italian composer and conductor; b. Verona, March 8, 1840; d. near Monza, July 21, 1891. His first teacher was G. Bernasconi; in 1855–64 he studied at the Milan Cons.; Arrigo Boito was his fellow pupil and friend; they wrote together a patriotic music drama, *Le Sorelle d'Italia,* which was produced by the students; the 2 served together under Garibaldi in 1866. His first opera was *I profughi fiamminghi* (La Scala, Nov. 11, 1863); this was followed by the Shakespearian opera *Amleto,* for which Boito wrote the libretto (Genoa, May 30, 1865). In 1866–68 Faccio made a tour in Scandinavia as a symph. conductor; in 1868 he became a prof. at the Milan Cons., and in 1871 succeeded Terziani as conductor at La Scala; on April 25, 1886, he conducted for the 1,000th time there. His performances of Verdi's operas were regarded as most authentic; he gave the world premiere of *Otello* at La Scala (1887).
BIBLIOGRAPHY: R. de Rensis, *Franco Faccio e Verdi* (Milan, 1934).

Fachiri, Adila, Hungarian violinist, grandniece of **Joachim,** sister of **Jelly d'Aranyi;** b. Budapest, Feb. 26, 1886; d. Florence, Dec. 15, 1962. She studied with Joachim, and received from him a Stradivarius violin. In 1909 she settled in London, where she married Alexander Fachiri, a lawyer. She appeared many times with her sister in duets; on April 3, 1930, the sisters gave in London the first performance of Holst's Concerto for 2 Violins, written especially for them.
BIBLIOGRAPHY: J. Macleod, *The Sisters d'Aranyi* (London, 1969).

Faelten, Carl, pianist and teacher, brother of **Reinhold Faelten;** b. Ilmenau, Thuringia, Dec. 21, 1846; d. Readfield, Maine, July 20, 1925. He studied in Frankfurt, and profited by advice from Raff. In 1878–82 he taught at the Hoch Cons. in Frankfurt; then was engaged at the Peabody Inst. in Baltimore (1882–85) and at the New England Cons. in Boston (1885–97); was director of the Cons. from 1890 until 1897, when with his brother he founded the Faelten Pianoforte School in Boston.
WORKS: *The Conservatory Course for Pianoforte* (1888); *Fundamental Training Course for Pianoforte* (in collaboration with his brother; 1895); also *Technische Übungen* for piano; *30 Characteristic Studies* (transcribed for piano from the violin sonatas of Bach); *30 Instructive Pieces* by G.F. Handel; transcriptions of 6 songs by Schubert; etc.

Faelten, Reinhold, pianist and teacher, brother of **Carl Faelten;** b. Ilmenau, Thuringia, Jan. 17, 1856; d. Worcester, Mass., July 17, 1949. He was a pupil of Klughard and Gottschalk at Weimar; taught in Frankfurt, Baltimore, and Boston; in 1897 he founded, with his brother, the Faelten Pianoforte School

in Boston. Jointly with his brother, he wrote several books on the Faelten method: *100 Ear-training Exercises; Keyboard Harmony;* also a *Transposition System.*

Faerber, Jörg, German conductor; b. Stuttgart, June 18, 1929. He studied at the Stuttgart Hochschule für Musik; then began his career in Stuttgart as a theater conductor. In 1960 he founded the Württemberg Chamber Orch. in Heilbronn, and subsequently established it as one of the finest ensembles of its kind in Europe. He was especially distinguished as an interpreter of the Baroque repertoire.

Fagan, Gideon, South African conductor and composer; b. Somerset West, Cape Province, Nov. 3, 1904; d. Cape Town, March 21, 1980. He studied at the South African College of Music in Cape Town with W.H. Bell (1916–22) and later in London at the Royal College of Music (1922–26), where his teachers were Boult and Sargent (conducting) and Vaughan Williams (composition). With the exception of a brief return to South Africa (1926–27), Fagan established residence in London, where he led theatrical companies, arranged light music for broadcasts and films, and acted as guest conductor with the BBC and other orchs. In 1949 he went back to South Africa, where he became active as arranger and conductor at the Johannesburg Radio (SABC); later was appointed its head of music (1963–66). He also taught composition and conducting at the Univ. of Cape Town (1967–73). In 1979 he received the Medal of Honor of the South African Academy for Science and Art.
WORKS: *Nocturne* for Woodwinds and Strings (1926); *Ilala,* tone poem for Orch. (1941); *South African Folk-tune Suite* for Orch. (1942); symph. poem, *Ilala* (1942); *5 Orchestral Pieces* (1948–49); Concert Overture in D (1954); *Heuwelkruin (Hill Crest),* suite for Piano and Orch. (1954); *Concert Overture* (1954); *Tears,* symph. poem, after Whitman, for Soloist, Chorus, and Orch. (1954); *Heuwelkruin,* suite for Piano and Orch. (1954); Nonet (1958); *My Lewe,* 6 poems for Baritone, Flute, Clarinet, Piano, and String Quartet (1969); *Albany,* overture (1970); *Ex Unitate Vires,* symph. sketch (1970); Suite for Strings (1974); *Quintics* for 5 Brasses (1975); *Karoosimfonie* (1976–77); *Een Vaderland,* oratorio (1977–78); piano pieces; songs; film music.

Fago, Nicola, Italian composer, called "Il Tarantino" after his place of birth; b. Taranto, Feb. 26, 1677; d. Naples, Feb. 18, 1745. He was a pupil of Provenzale at the Cons. della Pietà in Naples (from 1693); he became his assistant in 1697 and his successor in 1705. From 1704 to 1708 he was maestro di cappella at the Cons. di Sant' Onofrio; from 1709 to 1731, maestro di cappella at the Tesoro di San Gennaro; retired on a modest pension in 1740. He was the teacher of Leonardo Leo, Francesco Feo, Jommelli, and Sala. His son **Lorenzo Fago** (b. Naples, Aug. 13, 1704; d. there, April 30, 1793), an organist and composer, was his successor at the Tesoro di San Gennaro (1731–66 and 1771–80), and taught at the Cons. della Pietà dei Turchini for 56 years (1737–93) until his death.

WORKS: 4 operas: *Radamisto* (1707); *Astarto* (1709); *La Cassandra indovina* (1711); *Lo Masillo* (1712); 3 oratorios, including *Faraone sommerso* and *Il monte fiorito;* a Te Deum and other sacred music, much of it still preserved in the archives of Naples, Paris, and London.

BIBLIOGRAPHY: E. Faustini-Fasini, *Nicola Fago, Il Tarantino e la sua famiglia* (Taranto, 1931).

Fahrbach, Philipp, Austrian conductor and composer; b. Vienna, Oct. 26, 1815; d. there, March 31, 1885. He was a pupil of Lanner; conducted his own orch. for years, and then a military band. His dances and marches (over 400 works) were very popular. His 3 brothers, his son, and his nephews were all active as band musicians.

BIBLIOGRAPHY: P. Fahrbach, *Alt-Wiener Erinnerungen* (the composer's memoirs, publ. on the 50th anniversary of his death, 1935); O. Schneider, "Die Fahrbachs: Eine Wiener Musikerfamilie der Strauss-Zeit," *Österreichische Musikzeitschrift* (Jan. 1967).

Faignient, Noë, Flemish 16th-century contrapuntist; b. c.1540; d. Antwerp, c.1595. His compositions, written in the style of Orlando di Lasso, consist of 2 sets of chansons, madrigals, and motets for 4, 5, and 6 voices (1568, 1569). Two of his madrigals are included in Maldeghem's *Trésor musical.*

Failoni, Sergio, Italian conductor; b. Verona, Dec. 18, 1890; d. Sopron, July 25, 1948. He received his musical education in Verona and Milan; conducted opera throughout Italy; from 1932 he made appearances with the La Scala Opera in Milan. From 1928 to 1947 he was chief conductor of the State Opera in Budapest. In 1947 he was invited to make his debut at the Metropolitan Opera in N.Y.; however, he suffered a stroke and died the following year. He was regarded as one of the leading interpreters of the Italian repertoire.

Fain, Sammy, American composer of popular music; b. New York, June 17, 1902. He moved to California as a youth and wrote music for films. Gifted with a simple talent for facile tunes, he wrote several hit songs, among them *When I Take My Sugar to Tea, Dear Hearts and Gentle People,* and *Love Is a Many-Splendored Thing.*

Fairchild, Blair, American composer; b. Belmont, Mass., June 23, 1877; d. Paris, April 23, 1933. He studied composition with J.K. Paine and Walter Spalding at Harvard Univ. (B.A., 1899); then took courses with Giuseppe Buonamici in Florence. From 1901 till 1903 he was an attaché in the American embassies in Turkey and Persia. From 1905 he lived mostly in Paris, where he continued his musical studies with Charles Widor. Influenced by his travels in the Orient, and fascinated by the resources of exotic melos and rhythm, he wrote a number of pieces for orch. and for piano, and many songs in a pseudo-oriental manner; despite the imitative qualities of his music, Fairchild must be regarded as one of the few Americans who tried to transplant exotic folkways, both in subject matter and in melodic turns.

WORKS: Symph. poems: *East and West* (1908); *Légende* for Violin and Orch. (1911); *Taminch,* symph. sketch after a Persian legend (1913); *6 chants nègres* for Piano (also orchestrated and perf. by the Boston Symph. Orch., Dec. 6, 1929); *12 Indian Songs and Dances* for Piano; Violin Sonata; 5 sets of *Stornelli Toscani* for Piano; song cycles, among them *Persian Folk Songs and 5 Sea Prayers.*

BIBLIOGRAPHY: W.T. Upton, *Art-Song in America* (N.Y., 1930; pp. 169–76); idem, "Our Musical Expatriates," *Musical Quarterly* (Jan. 1928); John Tasker Howard, *Dictionary of American Biography,* Supplement I.

Fairclough, George Herbert, American organist and composer; b. Hamilton, Canada, Jan. 30, 1869; d. Saratoga, Calif., March 27, 1954. He studied at the Toronto Cons. (1887–90); then went to Berlin, where he took organ lessons at the Hochschule für Musik with Karl Heinrich Barth and with Bargiel. Returning to America, he served from 1900 until 1937 as organist at St. John's Episcopal Church in St. Paul; concurrently taught organ at the Univ. of Minnesota (1917–37); then retired. He composed a number of organ works and some sacred music.

Fairlamb, James Remington, American composer; b. Philadelphia, Jan. 23, 1838; d. Ingleside, N.Y., April 16, 1908. As a youth he played the organ in several Philadelphia churches; in 1858 went to Paris; studied piano there with Marmontel. While in Europe, he was appointed by Abraham Lincoln as American Consul at Zürich (1861) and stayed in Zürich until 1865, when he returned to the U.S. He organized an amateur opera company with which he brought out his 4-act grand opera *Valérie, or Treasured Tokens* (Philadelphia, Dec. 15, 1869). In 1872–98 he was church organist in Philadelphia, Jersey City, and N.Y. Besides *Valérie,* he wrote another grand opera, *Lionello* (which was never perf.), and 2 light operas: *Love's Stratagem* and *The Interrupted Marriage;* some 50 of his choral works and nearly 150 songs and organ pieces are publ. He was one of the founders of the American Guild of Organists.

Faisst, Immanuel Gottlob Friedrich, German composer; b. Esslingen, Württemberg, Oct. 13, 1823; d. Stuttgart, June 5, 1894. He studied theology at Tübingen, and also learned to play the organ; subsequently took lessons with Dehn in Berlin. He became active as a choral conductor and organist; in 1847 organized a society for classical church music in Stuttgart, where he settled. He was the founder of the *Schwäbischer Sängerbund* (1849); with Lebert, Stark, Brachmann, and others he established the Stuttgart Cons. (1857); became its director in 1859. He received a Dr.Phil. at Tübingen Univ. for his essay *Beiträge zur Geschichte der Klavier-*

sonate (*Cäcilia,* 1846; reprinted in the *Neues Bee-thovenjahrbuch,* 1, 1924). He was the editor (with Lebert) of the famous edition of classical piano works *Instruktive ausgewählte classische Werke,* publ. by Cotta; also (with Stark) of *Elementar- und Chorgesangschule* (2 vols., Stuttgart, 1880–82). Faisst was a prolific composer; a number of his songs, ballads, choral works, etc., were publ. during his lifetime, but then were completely forgotten. He also publ. several school manuals on harmony.

Faith, Percy, American conductor and arranger of popular music; b. Toronto, April 7, 1908; d. Los Angeles, Feb. 9, 1976. He studied with Louis Waizman and Frank Wellman at the Toronto Cons.; played piano in movie theaters and in dance bands. In 1931 he joined the Canadian Broadcasting Corp. and conducted the radio orch. in popular programs of Canadian music; in 1940 moved to the U.S. to fill a conducting post for the NBC Carnation Contented Hour; in 1950 he became music director of Columbia Records and made more than 45 albums of his own. He composed numerous film scores for Hollywood movies and in 1955 won an Academy Award nomination for *Love Me or Leave Me.* An amiably disposed composer of music "for listening pleasure," he described his goal as "satisfying the millions of devotees of that pleasant American institution known as the quiet evening at home, whose idea of perfect relaxation is the easy chair, slippers and good music."

Falabella Correa, Roberto, Chilean composer; b. Santiago, Feb. 13, 1926; d. there, Dec. 15, 1958. Paralyzed by polio since childhood, Falabella was educated at home; studied privately with Lucila Césped (1945–46), Alfonso Letelier (1949–50), Gustavo Becerra (1952), Miguel Aguilar and Esteban Eitler (1956–57). His music is Classical in form, Romantic in content, and modernistic in technique. WORKS: Chamber opera, *Epitafios fúnebres* (1952); miniature opera, *Del diario morir* (1954); 2 piano sonatas (1951, 1954); *Dueto* for Flute and Violin (1952); *Preludios episódicos* for Piano (1953); ballet, *El peine de oro* (1954); *Palimpsestos* for Contralto, Bassoon, Horn, and Percussion (1954); Violin Sonata (1954); Cello Sonata (1954); *Impresiones* for Piano (1955); Symph. No. 1 (1955); 2 divertimenti for Strings (1955); *Emotional Studies* for Piano (1957; also for Orch., 1957); ballet, *Andacollo,* for Voices, Piano, and Percussion (1957); String Quartet (1957); *Retratos* for Piano (1957); *La Lámpara en la tierra,* cantata for Baritone and Orch. (1958; Santiago, Oct. 21, 1960).

Falchi, Stanislao, Italian composer; b. Terni, Jan. 29, 1851; d. Rome, Nov. 14, 1922. He studied in Rome with C. Maggi and S. Meluzzi; in 1877 he became a teacher at the Santa Cecilia Academy; from 1902 till 1915 was its director. Among his pupils were A. Bonaventura, A. Bustini, V. Gui, B. Molinari, L. Refice, and F. Santoliquido. He wrote the operas *Lorhelia* (Rome, Dec. 4, 1877), *Giuditta* (Rome, March 12, 1887), and *Il Trillo del diavolo* (Rome,

Jan. 29, 1899); also a Requiem for the funeral of Victor Emmanuel II (Jan. 17, 1883).

Falcinelli, Rolande, French organist and composer; b. Paris, Feb. 18, 1920. She studied at the Paris Cons. with Samuel-Rousseau, and Simone Pié-Caussade; also took courses with Henri Büsser. She received first prize in organ playing in the class of Marcel Dupré (1942); also in 1942 she received the Grand Prix de Rome. She subsequently taught at the American Cons. in Fontainebleau; in 1955 she became organ teacher at the Paris Cons. She composed a number of sacred works for chorus and organ pieces, written in an amiable French manner.

Falcon, Marie-Cornélie, French soprano; b. Paris, Jan. 28, 1814; d. there, Feb. 25, 1897. She studied with Bordogni and A. Nourrit; made her debut at the Paris Opéra on July 20, 1832, as Alice in *Robert le Diable.* She sang at the Paris Opéra with excellent success; appeared as Valentine in *Les Huguenots* on Jan. 15, 1838, when, though still a very young woman, she unaccountably lost her voice. She made an unsuccessful attempt to return to the stage in a special benefit performance at the Paris Opéra on March 14, 1840; in desperation she resorted to consuming all sorts of quack medicines provided by bogus doctors, but in the end had to give up her career. She retired to her villa near Paris; she lived another 60 years. Still, her singing in the roles of Valentine in *Les Huguenots* and Rachel in *La Juive* became a legendary memory, so that the description "Falcon type" was applied to singers who excelled in her roles.
BIBLIOGRAPHY: C. Bouvet, *Cornélie Falcon* (Paris, 1927).

Falconieri, Andrea, Italian composer and lutenist; b. Naples, 1586; d. there, July 29, 1656. He was in the service of the house of Farnese at Parma; studied with Santino Garsi there until 1614; in 1615 was in Florence; in 1616, in Rome; in 1619, again in Florence; in 1620–21, at the court of Modena; then traveled in Spain and France; in 1629–35, was again at Parma; from 1639, was maestro di cappella at the royal court in Naples; in 1642, was in Genoa; in 1650, was in Naples. His *Libro Primo di Villanelle a 1, 2 e 3 voci* (with alphabetical tablature for Spanish guitar) was publ. in Rome, 1616 (reprinted by Gardano at Venice); various other books followed, the *Libro V delle musiche* appearing in 1619; probably one of his last works was the valuable instrumental collection *Primo Libro di Canzone, Sinfonie, Fantasie, Capricci per Violini e Viole, overo altri Strumenti a 1, 2 e 3 voci con il basso continuo* (Naples, 1650). Reprints: arias (2 books) in the *Raccolta nazionale delle musiche italiane;* in A. Parisotti's *Arie antiche* and *Piccolo album di musica antica;* in L. Torchi's *Eleganti canzoni ed arie italiane del secolo XVII* and *L'arte musicale in Italia* (vol. VII); *17 Arie a una voce,* publ. by G. Benvenuti; *2 Villanelle a 3,* ed. by C. Sabatini; 4 songs in *La Flora,* ed. by Knud Jeppesen (Copenhagen, 1949).
BIBLIOGRAPHY: L. Valdrighi, *Atti* (1883; p. 488);

L. Torchi, in *Rivista Musicale Italiana* (1898; p. 65).

Falik, Yuri, greatly talented Soviet cellist and composer; b. Odessa, July 30, 1936. He studied cello with A. Strimer at the Leningrad Cons.; in 1962 won first cello prize at the International Competition in Helsinki. He composed music from adolescence; in 1955 enrolled in the composition class of Boris Arapov at the Leningrad Cons., graduating in 1964. He subsequently joined the staff of the Leningrad Cons., teaching both cello and composition. In his own music Falik reveals a quasi-Romantic quality, making use of tantalizingly ambiguous melodic passages approaching the last ramparts of euphonious dissonance. His angular rhythms, with their frequently startling pauses, suggest a theatrical concept.
WORKS: For the stage: *Till Eulenspiegel,* "mystery ballet" (1967); *Oresteia,* choreographic tragedy (1968). For Orch.: Concertino for Oboe and Chamber Orch. (1961); Symph. for String Orch. and Percussion (1963); Concerto for Orch. on the themes of *Till Eulenspiegel* (1967); *Music for Strings* (1968); *Easy Symphony* (1971); Violin Concerto (1971); *Elegiac Music in Memoriam Igor Stravinsky* for Chamber Orch. (1975); Concerto for Orch. No. 2, *Symphonic Etudes* (1977). Chamber music: 5 string quartets (1955, 1965, 1974, 1976, 1978); Trio for Oboe, Clarinet, and Piano (1959); Wind Quintet (1964); *The Tumblers* for 4 Woodwinds, 2 Brasses, and 19 Percussion Instruments (1966); *Inventions* for Vibraphone, Marimba, and 5 Tam-tams (1972); *English Divertimento* for Flute, Clarinet, and Bassoon (1978). Vocal music: *Solemn Song,* cantata (1968); *Winter Songs* for Chorus a cappella (1975); solo songs.

Falk, Richard, German-American opera conductor; b. Moringen, April 29, 1878; d. New York, March 3, 1949. He studied at the Leipzig Cons. with Jadassohn and Riemann; conducting with Nikisch. After graduation in 1908 he began to conduct theater orchs. in Berlin and other German cities; in 1939 he settled in the U.S. He adapted and produced a number of 18th-century Italian operas.

Falkner, Sir (Donald) Keith, English bass-baritone; b. Sawston, Cambridgeshire, March 1, 1900. He was a chorister at New College School, Oxford, and Perse School, Cambridge; then served in the Royal Naval Air Service during World War I. It was only after the Armistice that he began to study singing in earnest, taking lessons first with Plunkett Greene in London, then far afield, with Lierhammer in Vienna, with Grenzebach in Berlin, and with Dossert in Paris. Returing to England, he made it a specialty to sing Elizabethan songs in recital. He also appeared with the British National Opera Co. During World War II he served in the Royal Air Force. In 1950 he went to the U.S., and taught voice at Cornell Univ. In 1960 he returned to England, and was appointed director of the Royal College of Music in London, retiring in 1974. He was knighted in 1967.

Fall, Fritz (Frederick), opera conductor, nephew of

Leo Fall; b. Vienna, July 25, 1899; d. Washington, D.C., Nov. 24, 1974. He studied at the Vienna Academy; was an opera conductor in Austria, Germany, and Czechoslovakia (1925–37); in 1937 he went to America; in 1938–42, conducted and taught in Tyler, Texas; during World War II was with the Office of Strategic Services of the U.S.; in 1945–48, was with the Allied Military Government in Europe; from 1948, taught and conducted the Dept. of Agriculture Symph. Orch. in Washington, D.C. He changed his first name from Fritz to Frederick after becoming an American citizen.

Fall, Leo(pold), Austrian composer of light opera; b. Olmütz, Feb. 2, 1873; d. Vienna, Sept. 16, 1925. His father was a military bandmaster, and it was from him that Leo Fall received his training in practical music making; then he took up academic courses at the Vienna Cons. with Johann Fuchs and others. For some years he was a theater conductor in Berlin, Hamburg, and Cologne, but lived for most of his life in Vienna. His operettas are typical Viennese products, light-hearted, romantic, and melodious. Although they never reached the height of international success obtained by such masters of the genre as Lehár, at least one of them, *Die Dollarprinzessin* (Vienna, Nov. 2, 1907), was famous for many years. The list of his operettas includes also *Der fidele Bauer* (Mannheim, July 27, 1907), *Eternal Waltz* (London, Dec. 22, 1911), *Die Rose von Constantinople* (Vienna, Dec. 2, 1916), and *Mme. Pompadour* (Vienna, March 2, 1923). His operetta *Der Rebell,* a failure at its first production (Vienna, Nov. 29, 1905), was revised and staged under the new title *Der liebe Augustin* (Berlin, Feb. 3, 1912), scoring excellent success.
BIBLIOGRAPHY: W. Zimmerli, *Leo Fall* (Zürich, 1957).

Falla (y Matheu), Manuel de, one of the greatest Spanish composers; b. Cádiz, Nov. 23, 1876; d. Alta Gracia, in the province of Córdoba, Argentina, Nov. 14, 1946. He studied with J. Tragó (piano) and F. Pedrell (composition) in Madrid; composed some zarzuelas, which he later discarded. His opera, *La vida breve,* won the prize awarded by the Academia de Bellas Artes, Madrid, in 1905; in that year he also won the Ortiz y Cussó Prize for pianists. In 1907 he went to Paris, where he became friendly with Debussy, Dukas, and Ravel, who aided and encouraged him. Under their influence he adopted the principles of Impressionism without, however, giving up his personal and national style; in 1914 he returned to Spain and in 1921 made his home in Granada, frequently touring Europe as conductor of his own works. In May 1938 he was made president of the Instituto de España. In 1939, at the end of the Spanish Civil War, he went to Argentina; after conducting a few concerts of his music in Buenos Aires, he withdrew to the small locality of Alta Gracia, where he lived the last years of his life in seclusion. His art is rooted both in the folk music of Spain and in the purest historical traditions of Spanish music. Up to 1919 his works were cast chiefly in the Andalusian idiom, and his instrumental technique was often conditioned by effects peculiar to Spain's national instrument, the guitar. In *El retablo de Maese Pedro* he turns to the classical tradition of Spanish (especially Castilian) music; the keyboard style of his Harpsichord Concerto shows, in the classical lucidity of its writing, a certain kinship with Domenico Scarlatti (who lived in Spain for many years). Falla taught composition privately, his most gifted pupils being Ernesto Halffter and Joaquín Nin-Culmell.

WORKS: Opera, *La vida breve* (Nice, 1905; revised 1913; April 1, 1913; Metropolitan Opera, N.Y., March 7, 1926); *El retablo de Maese Pedro* for Marionettes and Singers (1919–22; perf. in Madrid, in concert form, March 23, 1923; a private stage perf. was given in the salon of the Princesse de Polignac, in Paris, on June 25, 1923; first public stage perf., Paris, Nov. 13, 1923, under the composer's direction); ballets: *El amor brujo* (Madrid, April 15, 1915; a tremendously effective work; numerous perfs. as an orch. suite) and *El sombrero de tres picos* (London, July 22, 1919; very successful); *Noches en los jardines de España* for Piano and Orch. (1909–15; Madrid, April 9, 1916); Concerto for Harpsichord (or Piano), Flute, Oboe, Clarinet, Violin, and Cello, written at the suggestion of Wanda Landowska (Barcelona, Nov. 5, 1926, composer conducting; Wanda Landowska, soloist); *Homenajes*, in 4 parts: 1. *Pour le tombeau de Debussy* (originally for Guitar, 1920); 2. *Fanfare pour Arbós* (1933); 3. *Pour le tombeau de Paul Dukas* (originally for Piano, 1935); 4. *Pedrelliana* (1938; first perf. of the entire suite, Buenos Aires, Nov. 18, 1939, composer conducting); for Piano: *4 pièces espagnoles: Aragonesa, Cubana, Montañesa, Andaluza; Fantasia Bética*; songs: *3 mélodies* (1909); *7 canciones populares españolas* (1914; very popular); *Psyché* for Voice, Flute, Harp, Violin, Viola, and Cello (1924); *Soneto a Córdoba* for Voice and Harp (1927). A posthumous opera, *La Atlántida*, begun in 1928 and based on M.J. Verdaguer's Catalan poem, was completed by Ernesto Halffter and produced at La Scala in Milan on June 18, 1962. Falla's writings on music were collected and ed. by F. Sopeña and publ. as *Escritos sobre música y músicos* (Buenos Aires, 1950); another collection, in German trans. and ed. by J. Grünfeld, is *Spanien und die neue Musik. Ein Lebensbild in Schriften, Bildern Erinnerungen* (Zürich, 1968); in Eng., trans. by D. Urman and J. Thomson, as *On Music and Musicians* (London, 1979).

BIBLIOGRAPHY: G. Jean-Aubry, "Manuel de Falla," *Musical Times* (April 1917); M. Castelnuovo-Tedesco, in "Il pianoforte" (Jan. 1923); E. Istel, "Manuel de Falla," *Musical Quarterly* (Oct. 1926); Roland-Manuel, *Manuel de Falla* (Paris, 1930); J.B. Trend, *Manuel de Falla and Spanish Music* (N.Y., 1929; new ed., 1934); G. Chase, "Falla's Music for Piano Solo," *Chesterian* (1940); Jaime Pahissa, *Vida y obra de Manuel de Falla* (Buenos Aires, 1947; also publ. in Eng., London, 1954); J.M. Thomas, *Manuel de Falla en la Isla* (Palma, 1947); J. Jaenisch, *Manuel de Falla und die spanische Musik* (Freiburg, 1952); Kurt Pahlen, *Manuel de Falla und die Musik in Spanien* (Olten, 1953); Suzanne Demarquez,

Manuel de Falla (Paris, 1963; also in Eng., Philadelphia, 1968); J.J. Vinegra and Lasso de la Vega, *Vida intima de Manuel de Falla* (Cadiz, 1966); A. Saeardia, *Vida y obra de Manuel de Falla* (Madrid, 1967); A. Campoamor Gonzales, *Manuel de Falla, 1876–1946* (Madrid, 1976); *Modern Music in an Analytic Index* (N.Y., 1976, p. 69); E. Franco, *Manuel de Falla* (Madrid, 1977); B. James, *Manuel de Falla and the Spanish Musical Renaissance* (London, 1979); R. Crichton, *Falla* (London, 1982).

Faller, Nikola, Croatian conductor and composer; b. Varaždin, April 22, 1862; d. Zagreb, Feb. 28, 1938. He studied with Bruckner in Vienna and with Massenet in Paris. He was active as an opera conductor in Split and Zagreb; composed choral works and dances.

Famintsyn, Alexander, Russian critic and composer; b. Kaluga, Nov. 5, 1841; d. Ligovo, near St. Petersburg, July 6, 1896. He studied with Jean Vogt in St. Petersburg, and then with Hauptmann and Richter in Leipzig. He taught music history at the St. Petersburg Cons. (1865–72); translated into Russian the textbooks *Allgemeine Musiklehre* by Marx and *Harmonielehre* by Richter. However he soon abandoned his teaching activities and devoted himself chiefly to music criticism, taking a very conservative attitude; he indulged in frequent polemics against the Russian composers of the National School; Mussorgsky caricatured Famintsyn in his satirical song *The Classicist* and in a section of his burlesque *Rayok*. Famintsyn's publications on Russian instruments are valuable; he publ. essays on the gusli (1890) and the domra (1891). He was also a composer; his opera *Sardanapal* was produced in St. Petersburg on Dec. 5, 1875, but without any success; his other opera, *Uriel Acosta* (1883), was not performed. He further wrote a Piano Quintet, String Quartet, and some songs.

Fanciulli, Francesco, Italian conductor and composer; b. Porto San Stefano, July 17, 1850; d. New York, July 17, 1915. He studied in Florence; after some years as an opera conductor in Italy, he came to America (1876) and earned his living as an organist and theatrical conductor; in 1893 he succeeded Sousa as conductor of the Marine Band in Washington, D.C.; was then bandmaster of the 71st Regiment in N.Y. (1898–1904); after that, conducted his own band. He wrote an opera, *Priscilla*, which was produced in Norfolk, Va., on Nov. 1, 1901.

Fanelli, Ernest, French composer; b. Paris, June 29, 1860; d. there, Nov. 24, 1917. He played drums in orchs. as a small boy; entered the Paris Cons. in 1876, in the class of Delibes. He worked as a copyist and music engraver for many years; in 1912 he applied to Gabriel Pierné for work, submitting the score of his own symph. poem *Thèbes* as a specimen of his handwriting. This score, composed by Fanelli as early as 1883, seemed to anticipate the instrumental and harmonic usages of Debussy and other composers of impressionist music, and Pierné decided to perform it as a curiosity; he conducted it at the Colonne concert in Paris (March 17, 1912), and the novelty created a mild sensation in French musical circles; other works by Fanelli (*Impressions pastorales; L'Effroi du Soleil; Suite rabelaisienne;* etc.), all written before 1893, were also found interesting. However, the sensation proved of brief duration, and the extravagant claims for Fanelli's talent collapsed.

BIBLIOGRAPHY: M.-D. Calvocoressi, "An Unknown Composer of Today," *Musical Times* (April 1912).

Faning, Eaton, English conductor and composer; b. Helston, Cornwall, May 20, 1850; d. Brighton, Oct. 28, 1927. He studied at the Royal Academy of Music in London with Sterndale Bennett and Arthur Sullivan, winning the Mendelssohn Scholarship (1873) and the Lucas medal (1876); received the degrees of Mus.Bac. (1894) and Mus.Doc. (1899) from Cambridge Univ. From 1878 he taught piano at the Royal Academy of Music; in 1885 became music director at Harrow School (until 1901); thereafter occupied various educational posts, and was a member of examination boards. He wrote a Symph., some chamber music, and several operettas. An account of his career is found in the *Musical Times* of Aug. 1901.

Fano, Guido Alberto, Italian composer and writer on music; b. Padua, May 18, 1875; d. Tauriano di Spilimbergo (Udine), Aug. 14, 1961. He studied with Pollini in Padua and Martucci in Bologna; at the same time he took courses in law; received the degree of Dr.Juris from Bologna Univ. in 1898. In 1900 he was appointed a teacher of piano at the Liceo Musicale in Bologna; was director of the Cons. of Parma (1905–11); then taught piano at Naples (1912–17), Palermo (1917–21), and Milan (1921–38). He wrote an opera, *Iuturna,* and a symph. poem, *La tentazione di Gesù;* also publ. several books: *Pensieri sulla musica* (Bologna, 1903); *Nella vita del ritmo* (Naples, 1916); *Lo studio del pianoforte* (3 vols., Milan, 1923–34).

Fara, Giulio, Italian writer on music and composer; b. Cagliari, Sardinia, Dec. 3, 1880; d. Pesaro, Oct. 9, 1949. He studied singing and composition; became an instructor in public schools of Sardinia; collected Sardinian folk songs and used some of them in his own compositions, notably in the opera *Elia.* He publ. a biography of Rossini (1915) and a collection of essays, *L'anima musicale d'Italia* (1921); contributed to the *Rivista Musicale Italiana* and other Italian publications. His collection of Sardinian songs was publ. by Ricordi (1924).

Farberman, Harold, American conductor and composer; b. New York, Nov. 2, 1929. He studied at the Juilliard School of Music in N.Y. and the New England Cons. in Boston; served as percussion player with the Boston Symph. Orch. (1952–63); then engaged on an independent career as a symph. conductor; from 1971 to 1979 he conducted the Oakland (Calif.) Symph. Orch. In his own music he often cultivates the idiom of jazz and rock.

WORKS: Rock Opera, *Medea* (Boston, March 26, 1961); *The Losers,* opera (N.Y., March 26, 1971); *Evolution* for Soprano, Horn, and Percussion (1954); Timpani Concerto (1962); Trio for Violin, Piano, and Percussion (1963); Concerto for Bassoon and String Orch.; *5 Images* for Brass Quintet (1964); *Elegy, Fanfare and March* for Orch. (1964–65); Concerto for Saxophone and String Orch. (1965); Symph. No. 1 for Strings and Percussion; *Greek Scene* for Soprano and Orch.; *Progressions* for Flute, Percussion, and Orch.; *Variations* for Piano, Percussion, and Orch.; *Paramount Concerto* for Piano and Orch.; *If Music Be* for Rock Group, Jazz Organ, and Orch. (1969); *Pilgrim's Progress* for Jazz Organ and Orch. (1969); *There's Us, There's Them ... Together?* for Voice, Jazz Combo, and Orch.; *Initiation Ballet* for Jazz Quartet and Orch. (from the opera *The Losers*); Violin Concerto (1972); *Impressions* for Oboe, Strings, and Percussion; *War Cry on a Prayer Feather* for Soprano, Baritone, and Orch. (Colorado Springs, Nov. 11, 1976).

Fariñas, Carlos, Cuban composer; b. Cienfuegos, Nov. 28, 1934. He studied with José Ardévol and Harold Gramatges at the Havana Cons.; in 1956 went to the U.S. to take courses at the Berskire Music Center in Tanglewood, where he studied composition with Aaron Copland and conducting with Eleazar de Carvalho. Returning to Cuba, he was active as composer for television; in 1961–63 he was in Moscow for further study at the Moscow Cons. He also traveled in Europe as a lecturer, conductor, and composer. His music partakes of a wide variety of methods, techniques, and applications, ranging from triadic structures to serial procedures, making use also of electronic sound.

WORKS: *Despertar,* ballet (1960); *Relieves* for 5 Instrumental Groups with Audience Participation (1969); *Muros, Rejas y Vitrales* for Orch. and Various Objects (1972); Concerto for Violin and Percussion (1975); *El Bosque ha echado a andar* for Orch., dedicated to the memory of Ché Guevara (Metamusik Festival, Berlin, Oct. 9, 1976); Sonata for Violin and Cello (1961); String Quartet (1963); *Tiento I* for Clarinet, Guitar, Piano, and Percussion (1966); *Tiento II* for 2 Pianos and Percussion (1969).

Farinelli (real name, **Carlo Broschi**), celebrated Italian artificial soprano; b. Andria, Jan. 24, 1705; d. Bologna, Sept. 16, 1782. His father was a merchant of flour (*farina* in Italian), and called him Farinelli ("little flour"); at puberty, he had him castrated to promote his singing career. Porpora took the boy as a pupil, and he became famous in Naples as "il ragazzo" (the boy) singing in the streets. At the age of 16 he sang in Rome in Porpora's opera *Eomene;* his fame spread in Italy and abroad. In 1727 he met the famous castrato singer Bernacchi in Bologna; in a singing contest with him, Farinelli acknowledged defeat, and persuaded Bernacchi to give him lessons to achieve virtuosity in coloratura. He visited Vienna in 1724, 1728, and 1731. In 1734 he was sent by Porpora to London to join the Italian opera there. He made his London debut on Oct. 27, 1734, in *Artaserse* by Hasse, appearing with Senesino and Cuzzoni; he remained in London for 2 years, amassing a fortune; he then went to Paris, and in 1737 to Madrid, where he attained unparalleled success as court singer to King Philip V; his duty was to sing several arias every night to cure the king's melancholy. His influence on the ailing monarch, and on the Queen, was such that he was able to command considerable funds to engage famous performers at the Madrid court. He also persuaded Philip V to cut his beard. When Farinelli's voice began to fail, he undertook to serve as impresario, decorator, and stage director. He continued to enjoy the court's favor under Philip's successor, Ferdinand VI, but at the accession to the Spanish throne of Carlos III in 1759, Farinelli was dismissed. He went back to Italy in possession of great wealth; he assembled his family in a palatial villa which he built near Bologna, and spent his last 20 years of life in contentment.

BIBLIOGRAPHY: G. Sacchi, *Vita del Cavaliere Don Carlo Broschi, detto Farinelli* (Venice, 1784); J. Desastre, *G. Broschi* (Zürich, 1903); G. Monaldi, *Cantanti evirati celebri* (Rome, 1919); F. Haböck, *Die Gesangskunst der Kastraten* (Vienna, 1923); R. Bouvier, *Farinelli, le chanteur des rois* (Paris, 1943).

Farinelli, Giuseppe, prolific Italian composer; b. Este, May 7, 1769; d. Trieste, Dec. 12, 1836. In 1785 he entered the Cons. della Pietà dei Turchini at Naples, his teachers being Barbiello, Fago, Sala, and Tritto; his first opera, *Il Dottorato di Pulcinella*, produced in 1792, was followed by 50 or 60 others, not original, but in very happy imitation of Cimarosa's style and chiefly comic. During 1810–17 he lived at Turin; then went to Trieste as organist at the Cathedral of San Giusto. He also wrote several oratorios, cantatas, 5 masses, 2 Te Deums, and other church music.

Farjeon, Harry, English composer; b. Hohokus, N.J. (of English parents), May 6, 1878; d. London, Dec. 29, 1948. He was a son of the English novelist B.L. Farjeon, and grandson of the famous actor Joseph Jefferson. He was educated in England, taking music lessons with Landon Ronald and John Storer; then studied composition with Corder at the Royal Academy of Music; won the Lucas Medal and other prizes. In 1903 he became an instructor at the Academy. WORKS: Opera, *Floretta* (1899), and 2 operettas, *The Registry Office* (1900) and *A Gentleman of the Road* (1902), all performed in London; Piano Concerto (1903); *Hans Andersen Suite* for Small Orch. (London, 1905); 2 song cycles: *Vagrant Songs* and *The Lute of Jade.* The score of a symph. poem, *Summer Vision* (regarded by the composer as his best work), was sent to Germany shortly before World War I and was lost.

Farkas, Edmund, Hungarian composer; b. Puszta-

Monostor, 1851; d. Klausenburg, Sept. 1, 1912. He studied engineering at the Univ. of Budapest; then took courses at the Budapest Academy of Music with Erkel, Volkmann, and others. Upon graduation he was appointed director at the Klausenburg Cons. There he organized an orch., established a musical journal, and promoted national Hungarian music. WORKS: Operas (all first perf. in Budapest): *Bayadere* (Aug. 23, 1876); *Valentin Balassa* (Jan. 16, 1896); *The Inquest* (Oct. 5, 1900); *The World of Kurucz* (Oct. 26, 1906); several symph. poems in a Romantic vein (*Dusk, Storm,* etc.); church music; 5 string quartets; several piano pieces in the Hungarian style. He also publ. (in Hungarian) several papers on school music.

Farkas, Ferenc, Hungarian composer; b. Nagykanizsa, Dec. 15, 1905. He began to study piano as a child; took courses with Leo Weiner and Albert Siklós at the Academy of Music in Budapest (1923–28); a state scholarship enabled him to study with Respighi at the Santa Cecilia Academy in Rome (1929–31); later he was engaged as conductor of incidental music to films in Vienna and Copenhagen (1933–35). Returning to Hungary, he was a music teacher at the municipal school in Budapest (1935–41); from 1941 to 1944 he taught at the Cons. of Kolozsvár (Cluj); was director of the music school in Székesfehérvár (1946–48); in 1949–75 was a prof. of composition at the Academy of Music in Budapest. In 1950 he was awarded the Kossuth Prize and in 1960 the Erkel Prize.

WORKS: FOR THE STAGE: *The Magic Cupboard,* comic opera (1938–42; Budapest, April 22, 1942; also a separate overture, 1952); *The Sly Students,* ballet (1949); *Csinom Palkó,* musical play (1950; revised 1960); *Vidróczki,* opera (1964); *Piroschka,* musical comedy (1967); *Story of Noszty Junior with Mari Tóth,* musical comedy (1971); *Panegyricus,* ballet with Narrator and Chorus (1972). FOR ORCH.: Fantasy for Piano and Orch. (1929); Divertimento (1930); Harp Concertino (1937; revised 1956); *Dinner Music* for Chamber Orch. (1938); *Rhapsodia Carpathiana* (1940); *Marionette's Dance Suite* (1941); *Musica Pentatonica* for String Orch. (1945); Prelude and Fugue (1947; originally titled *Musica Dodecatonica*); Piano Concertino (1948); *Lavotta,* suite (1951); Symph. (1951–52); *Scherzo Sinfonico* (1952); *Symphonic Overture* (1952); *Sketches from the Bükk* (1955); *Piccola musica di concerto* for String Orch. (1961); *Trittico concertato* for Cello and String Orch. (1964); *Gyász és vígasz* (*Planctus et Consolationes;* 1965); *Concerto all'Antica* for Baryton (Viola da Gamba) and String Orch. (1965); *Serenata concertante* for Flute and String Orch. (1967). CHORAL AND OTHER VOCAL: *Cantata Lirica* (1945); *Cantus Pannonicus,* cantata to the Latin verses of the 15th-century Hungarian archbishop Janus Pannonius (1959; Budapest, April 3, 1959); *Laudatio Szigethiana,* oratorio (1967); other works for voice and/or chorus and orch. CHAMBER WORKS: 3 violin sonatinas (1930, 1931, 1959); String Quartet (1970–72); other chamber pieces. FOR PIANO: Sonata (1930); Toccata (1945); *Correspondences* (1957); *Hybrids* (1957);

3 Monograms (1962); *Naptár (Calendar)* for Soprano, Tenor, and Piano or Chamber Ensemble (1956) and other songs; incidental music.

Farley, Carole Ann, American soprano; b. LeMars, Iowa, Nov. 29, 1946. She studied at Indiana Univ.; then with Marianne Schech at the Hochschule für Musik in Munich, and with Cornelius Reid in N.Y. She made her debut in Linz, Austria, in 1969; married José Serebrier. Her singing of the title role in Alban Berg's *Lulu* at the Metropolitan Opera in N.Y. in 1977 placed her at the foremost rank of musicianly artists and singing intellectuals. She also appeared as Lulu in Cologne. Other roles are: Manon, Donna Anna, Mimi, Violetta.

Farmer, Henry George, eminent musicologist; authority on oriental music; b. Birr, Ireland, Jan. 17, 1882; d. Law, Lanarkshire, Dec. 30, 1965. He studied piano and violin, and as a boy joined the Royal Artillery Orch. in London, playing the French horn at its concerts. He then studied philosophy and languages at Glasgow Univ. An extremely prolific writer, he publ. a number of original works, dealing with such varied subjects as military music and Arabic musical theories. He was the founder and conductor of the Glasgow Symph. Orch. (1919–43); wrote several overtures and some chamber music.
WRITINGS: *Memoirs of the Royal Artillery Band* (1904); *The Rise and Development of Military Music* (1912); *The Arabian Influence on Musical Theory* (1925); *Byzantine Musical Instruments in the 9th Century* (1925); *The Arabic Musical MSS. in the Bodleian Library* (1926); *A History of Arabian Music to the 13th Century* (1929); *Music in Medieval Scotland* (1930); *Historical Facts for the Arabian Musical Influence* (1930); *The Organ of the Ancients* (1931); *Studies in Oriental Musical Instruments* (1931); *An Old Moorish Lute Tutor* (1931); *Al-Farabi's Arabic-Latin Writings* (Glasgow, 1934); *Turkish Instruments of Music in the 17th Century* (1937); *New Mozartiana* (1938); *Sa'adyah Gaon on the Influence of Music* (1943); *A History of Music in Scotland* (London, 1947); *Music Making in the Olden Days* (1950); *Military Music* (1950); *Oriental Studies, Mainly Musical* (London, 1953); *The History of the Royal Artillery Band* (1954); *British Bands in Battle* (London, 1965). For a comprehensive bibliography of his writings on oriental music see *Notes* (March and June, 1949).

Farmer, John, Elizabethan madrigal composer, active from 1591 to 1601. In 1595 he was organist at the Christ Church Cathedral in Dublin; in 1599 he left Dublin and went to London. Among his madrigals the best known are *Fair Phyllis I saw sitting all alone, You pretty flowers,* and *A little pretty bonny lass,* included in his *First Set of English Madrigals to Foure Voices* (London, 1599; reprinted in vol. 8 of E.H. Fellowes's *English Madrigal School*). He contributed a 6-part madrigal, *Fair Nymphs, I heard one telling,* to *The Triumphes of Oriana,* and several canticles and hymns to Thomas East's *Whole Booke of Psalmes* (1592). Extant MSS are in the Christ Church Library and Music School at Oxford, and in the British Museum. Farmer was also the author of *Divers and sundry waies of two parts in one* (London, 1591).
BIBLIOGRAPHY: E.H. Fellowes, *English Madrigal Verse, 1588–1632* (London, 1920; 3rd ed., revised, 1967); idem, *The English Madrigal Composers* (Oxford, 1921; 2nd ed., 1948).

Farmer, John, English composer; b. Nottingham, Aug. 16, 1836; d. Oxford, July 17, 1901. He studied at the Leipzig Cons. and later at Coburg; then lived in Switzerland, returning to England in 1862; taught at Harrow School (1862–85). He composed an oratorio, *Christ and His Soldiers* (1878); fairy opera, *Cinderella* (1882); comic cantata, *Froggy Would A-wooing Go* (1887); settings of nursery rhymes for chorus and orch.; church music; chamber music; Piano Quintet, other chamber music.

Farnaby, Giles, English composer; b. probably in Cornwall, c.1565; d. London, Nov. (buried, Nov. 25) 1640. He graduated from Oxford in 1592, receiving the degree of B.Mus.; later moved to London, where he remained until his death.
WORKS: *Canzonets to Fowre Voyces* (1598; includes an added madrigal for 8 Voices, one of the few such works in the English school; reprint by E.H. Fellowes, in vol. 20 of the *English Madrigal School*); vocal religious works in various collections, and motets, psalms, etc.; more than 50 virginal pieces in the *Fitzwilliam Virginal Book* (ed. by J.A. Fuller-Maitland and W. Barclay Squire, London, 1899); a madrigal, *Come, Charon,* is in MS at the Royal College of Music; part of another is in the British Library. Farnaby's son, **Richard Farnaby,** was also a gifted composer.
BIBLIOGRAPHY: E.H. Fellowes, *The English Madrigal Composers* (Oxford, 1921; 2nd ed., 1948); R. Marlow, *The Life and Music of Giles Farnaby* (Diss., Cambridge Univ., 1966).

Farnadi, Edith, Hungarian-born Austrian pianist; b. Budapest, Sept. 25, 1921. She entered the Budapest Academy of Music at the age of 9; studied with Bartók and Weiner; made her debut at 12; was granted her diploma at 16. She made appearances with the violinists Hubay and Hubermann; taught at the Budapest Academy; then moved to Austria and became a teacher in Graz. She is noted for her performances of Hungarian music.

Farnam, W. Lynnwood, Canadian-American organist; b. Sutton, Quebec, Jan. 13, 1885; d. New York, Nov. 23, 1930. He studied with his mother and local teachers; came to America in 1904; was organist at several churches in N.Y. and Boston.

Farncombe, Charles, English conductor; b. London, July 29, 1919. He first studied engineering at the Univ. of London; after military service in World War II he enrolled at the Royal School of Church Music, Canterbury, and the Royal Academy of Music, London. In 1955 he organized the Handel Opera Society, serving as its music director and conductor. In 1970 he assumed the post of chief conductor of the Royal Court Theater in Drottningholm, Sweden. In 1977 he was made a Commander of the Order of the British Empire.

Farnsworth, Charles Hubert, music educator; b. Cesarea, Turkey, Nov. 29, 1859; d. Thetford, Vt., May 22, 1947. He studied organ in Worcester, Mass.; held various positions as organist; was head of the music dept. at Colorado Univ. (1888–1900); then was on the faculty at Teachers College, Columbia Univ. (1900–25); retired and lived in Vermont. He publ. several pamphlets on music education, among them *The Why and How of Music Study* (1927) and *Short Studies in Musical Psychology* (N.Y., 1930). An appreciation of his work was publ. in the *Musician* (1933).

Farquhar, David, New Zealand composer; b. Cambridge, England, April, 5, 1928. He studied first at Victoria Univ. in Wellington; went to England and studied at Cambridge Univ. and took composition from Benjamin Frankel at the Guildhall School of Music in London. His music is contrapuntal in structure and neo-Romantic in mood.
WORKS: *Ring around the Moon,* dance suite for Orch. (1954); *Harlequin Overture* (1958); Symph. (1959; Wellington, Aug. 13, 1960; the first symph. by a New Zealand composer to be given a premiere at a public concert); Concertino for Piano and Strings (1960); 2 *Anniversary Suites* for Orch. (1961, 1965); *Elegy for Strings* (1961); an opera, *A Unicorn for Christmas* (1962); *3 Pieces* for Violin and Piano (1967).

Farrant, John, English organist and composer, active in the 16th century. He served as lay clerk at Salisbury, and subsequently organist at the Salisbury Cathedral (1587–92); he was briefly organist at Hereford (1593). Contemporary records testify to his intractable temper, which resulted in physical clashes with the dean of the Salisbury Cathedral, and led to his expulsion from there. As a composer, Farrant is chiefly distinguished for his Service in D minor (misattributed in a 19th-century ed. to Richard Farrant). His son, also named **John Farrant** (baptized in Salisbury, Sept. 28, 1575; d. there, 1618), was a chorister at the Salisbury Cathedral in 1585, and organist there from 1598 till 1616. Another John Farrant, possibly related to the preceding, was organist at Christ Church, Newgate, London; he was the author of a Magnificat; this work, sometimes referred to as "Farrant in G minor," is often confused with Richard Farrant's Cathedral Service in A minor.

Farrant, Richard, English composer; b. c.1530; d. Windsor, probably Nov. 30, 1580. He was a Gentleman of the Chapel Royal during the reign of Edward VI; then became master of the choristers (1564) at St. George's Chapel, Windsor; also served as a lay clerk and organist there. Beginning with 1567 Farrant presented a play annually before the Queen. In 1569 he returned to the Chapel Royal. Farrant wrote mainly church music; his Cathedral Service in A minor and 2 anthems, *Hide Not Thou Thy Face* and *Call to Remembrance,* are regarded as the most beautiful examples of English sacred music of the 16th century. A Service in D minor was publ. as by Richard Farrant, but this was a misattribution, the real author being John Farrant of Salisbury. Several of Richard Farrant's works are in the British Library and at Durham Cathedral.

Farrar, Ernest Bristow, English organist and composer; b. London, July 7, 1885; d. in the battle of the Somme, France, Sept. 18, 1918. He studied at the Royal College of Music with Stanford and Parratt; served as organist of the English Church in Dresden (1909); then at various churches in England (1910–14). His orch. suite *English Pastoral Impression* won the Carnegie Award; he further wrote the orch. pieces *The Open Road, Lavengro, The Forsaken Merman,* and *Heroic Elegy;* also *3 Spiritual Studies* for Strings; variations on an old English sea song, for Piano and Orch.; the cantatas *The Blessed Damozel* and *Out of Doors;* chamber music (*Celtic Suite* for Violin and Piano, etc.); songs; preludes for organ; etc.

Farrar, Geraldine, celebrated American soprano; b. Melrose, Mass., Feb. 28, 1882; d. Ridgefield, Conn., March 11, 1967. She studied music with Mrs. J.H. Long of Boston; at 17, she went to Europe; took lessons with Emma Thursby in N.Y., Trabadello in Paris, and Graziani in Berlin; made a successful debut at the Berlin Opera on Oct. 15, 1901, as Marguerite, under the direction of Karl Muck; then studied with Lilli Lehmann. She sang at the Monte Carlo Opera for 3 seasons (1903–6). Her career in Europe was well established before her American debut as Juliette at the Metropolitan Opera (Nov. 26, 1906); she remained on the staff for 16 years; made her farewell appearance in *Zaza* on April 22, 1922, but continued to sing in concert; gave her last public performance at Carnegie Hall in 1931; then retired to Ridgefield, Conn. Her greatest success was *Madama Butterfly,* which she sang with Caruso in its American premiere at the Metropolitan on Feb. 11, 1907; subsequently sang this part in America more than 100 times. Her interpretation of Carmen was no less remarkable. She also appeared in silent motion pictures between 1915 and 1919; her film version of Carmen aroused considerable interest. On Feb. 8, 1916, she married the actor Lou Tellegen, from whom she was subsequently divorced. She made adaptations of pieces by Kreisler, Rachmaninoff, and others, for which she publ. the lyrics. She wrote an autobiography, *Such Sweet Compulsion* (N.Y., 1938; reprinted in 1970), which had been preceded in 1916 by *Geraldine Farrar: The Story of an American Singer.* Her scrapbooks, many letters, the fan she used in *Madama Butterfly,* etc., are in the Music Division of the Library of Congress in Washington, D.C.
BIBLIOGRAPHY: H.T. Finck, *Success in Music*

(N.Y., 1909); E. Wagenknecht, *Geraldine Farrar: An Authorized Record of Her Career* (Seattle, 1929); Oscar Thompson, *The American Singer* (N.Y., 1937); E. Nash, *Always First Class: The Career of Geraldine Farrar* (Washington, D.C., 1982).

Farrell, Fileen, brilliant American soprano; b. Willimantic, Conn., Feb. 13, 1920. Her parents were vaudeville singers; she received her early vocal training with Merle Alcock in N.Y., and later studied with Eleanor McLellan. In 1940 she sang on the radio; in 1947–48 made a U.S. tour as a concert singer; toured South America in 1949. Her song recital in N.Y. on Oct. 24, 1950, was enthusiastically acclaimed and secured for her immediate recognition. She was soloist in Beethoven's 9th Symph. with Toscanini and the NBC Symph. Orch.; also appeared many times with the N.Y. Phil. She made her operatic debut as Santuzza with the San Carlo Opera in Tampa, Fla., in 1956. In 1958 she joined the San Francisco Opera Co. and in 1957 became a member of the Lyric Opera of Chicago. On Dec. 6, 1960, she made a successful debut with the Metropolitan Opera Co. in N.Y., in Gluck's *Alcestis;* she remained on its roster until 1964; then returned in 1965–66; was a Distinguished Professor of Music at the Indiana Univ. School of Music in Bloomington from 1971 to 1980.

Farrenc, Aristide, French flutist and music editor; b. Marseilles, April 9, 1794; d. Paris, Jan. 31, 1865. He studied flute; went to Paris in 1815, and studied at the Cons.; at the same time was engaged as 2nd flutist at the Théâtre Italien. In 1821 he established a music shop and printing press; publ. French editions of Beethoven; also composed music for the flute. He married **Louise Dumont,** a talented musician in her own right. He diligently collected material for the rectification of existing biographies, but generously turned it over to Fétis for use in the 2nd edition of his great work, of which Farrenc also read proofs. Jointly with Fétis's son, Edouard, he began the publication of *Le Trésor des pianistes* (23 vols., 1861–72; reprinted N.Y., 1977, foreword by Bea Friedland), a collection of piano music from the 16th century to Mendelssohn, with historical notes; it was continued after his death by his wife. From 1854 he contributed papers to *La France Musicale* and other journals.

Farrenc (neé **Dumont**), **Louise,** French pianist and composer; b. Paris, May 31, 1804; d. there, Sept. 15, 1875. She studied music with Reicha; in 1821 married **Aristide Farrenc,** but was not entirely eclipsed by his acknowledged eminence. While most female composers of her time hardly ever rose above the level of barely tolerable salon music, she actually labored and produced works of such competence that they might well have been written by Onslow or some other male contemporary. Her 3 symphs. had respectable performances: No. 1 in Brussels, Feb. 23, 1843; No. 2 in Paris, May 3, 1846; No. 3 in Paris, April 22, 1849; the latter received an accolade in the prestigious, and definitely male-oriented, *Ga-zette Musicale,* which conceded that "she revealed, alone among her sex in musical Europe, genuine learning, united with grace and taste." She also wrote a Piano Concerto; 30 études in all major and minor keys for Piano; 4 piano trios; Cello Sonata; 2 violin sonatas; 2 piano quintets; a Sextet and a Nonet for Winds and Strings; one of her overtures (1840) was reviewed by Berlioz, who remarked that it was orchestrated "with a talent rare among women." Louise Farrenc was a brilliant pianist; she taught piano at the Paris Cons. from 1842 till 1872, the only woman ever to hold a permanent position as an instrumentalist there in the 19th century. Her daughter **Victorine** (1827–59) was also a talented pianist whose promising career was cut short by an early death. After the death of her husband in 1865, Louise Farrenc assumed the editorship of the monumental collection *Le Trésor des pianistes* begun by him.

BIBLIOGRAPHY: Bea Friedland, "Louise Farrenc, Composer, Performer, Scholar," *Musical Quarterly* (April 1974).

Farrow, Norman D., Canadian baritone; b. Regina, May 6, 1916. He studied at the Juilliard School of Music and at N.Y. Univ.; took voice lessons with Mack Harrell and others; was one of the organizers of the Bach Aria Group. He toured as soloist with choral ensembles; in 1960 he was engaged as artist-in-residence at Southern Methodist Univ. in Dallas.

Farwell, Arthur, American composer and music educator; b. St. Paul, Minn., April 23, 1872; d. New York, Jan. 20, 1952. He studied at the Mass. Inst. of Technology, graduating in 1893; then studied music with Homer Norris in Boston, Humperdinck in Berlin, and Guilmant in Paris. He was a lecturer on music at Cornell Univ. (1899–1901); in 1909–14 was on the editorial staff of *Musical America;* then directed municipal concerts in N.Y. City (1910–13); was director of the Settlement Music School in N.Y. (1915–18); in 1918 he went to California; lectured on music there; was acting head of the music dept. at the Univ. of Calif., Berkeley (1918–19); in 1919 he founded the Santa Barbara Community Chorus, which he conducted until 1921; was the first holder of the composers' fellowship of the Music and Art Association of Pasadena (1921–25); taught music theory at Michigan State College in East Lansing (1927–39); eventually settled in N.Y. Farwell was a pioneer in new American music, and tirelessly promoted national ideas in art. He contributed to various ethnological publications. In 1901–11 he operated the Wa-Wan Press (Newton, Mass.), a periodical (quarterly, 1901–7; monthly, 1907–11) that printed piano and vocal music of "progressive" American composers of the period, the emphasis being on works that utilized indigenous (black, Indian, and cowboy) musical materials (reprinted N.Y., 1970, under the direction of Vera Lawrence Brodsky). Disillusioned about commercial opportunities for American music, including his own, he established at East Lansing, in April 1936, his own lithographic handpress, with which he printed his music, handling the entire process of reproduction, including the cover designs, by himself.

WORKS: For Orch.: *Symbolistic Study No. 3*, after Walt Whitman (1905; revised 1922; Philadelphia Orch., March 30, 1928); *Pageant Scene* (1913); *The Gods of the Mountain* (Minneapolis Symph. Orch., Dec. 13, 1929); music for pageants, including Percy MacKaye's *Caliban by the Yellow Sands* (N.Y., May 1916; written for the Shakespeare tercentenary); *Pilgrimage Play* (Hollywood, 1921); *Symphonic Song on "Old Black Joe"* (Hollywood, 1923); *Symphonic Hymn on "March! March!"*; also *The Hako* for String Quartet (1922); Violin Sonata (1928); Concerto for 2 Pianos and String Orch., a version of *Symbolistic Study No. 6* (1931; won first prize of the National Federation of Music Clubs Competition; broadcast by CBS, May 28, 1939); numerous school choruses, and vocal compositions; piano pieces (many of them arranged for various instrumental ensembles); several collections of American Indian melodies and folk songs of the South and West; arrangements of Indian melodies (*Dawn*, a fantasy on Indian themes, in various versions, dated between 1901 and 1926, is characteristic of these works).

BIBLIOGRAPHY: E. Kirk, *Toward American Music: A Study of the Life and Music of Arthur George Farwell* (Diss., Univ. of Rochester, 1958); G. Chase, *Dictionary of American Biography,* Supplement V; Brice Farwell et al., *Guide to the Music of Arthur Farwell and to the Microfilm Collection of His Work* (Briarcliff Manor, N.Y., 1971).

Fasano, Renato, Italian conductor; b. Naples, Aug. 21, 1902; d. Rome, Aug. 3, 1979. He studied piano and composition at Naples, specializing in Renaissance music; in 1941 he founded the Collegium Musicum Italicum of Rome; in 1947 he organized the distinguished chamber group I Virtuosi di Roma, and led its performances on European tours. In 1957 he also founded the Piccolo Teatro Musicale Italiano; in 1960 he was named director of the Santa Cecilia Academy in Rome. Fasano was greatly esteemed for his effort to revive a proper appreciation of Italian music of the Renaissance period.

Fasch, Johann Friedrich, German composer; b. Buttelstadt, near Weimar, April 15, 1688; d. Zerbst, Dec. 5, 1758. He studied with Kuhnau at Leipzig, and later (1713) with Graupner and Grunewald at Darmstadt; in 1721 he went to Lukaveč, Bohemia, as Kapellmeister to Count Morzin; after 1722, was Kapellmeister at Zerbst. A catalogue of his works, compiled in 1743, enumerates 12 complete series of church cantatas, 16 masses and Mass sections, 4 operas, over 90 overtures, 61 concertos (for violin, flute, oboe, etc.), some of which have been printed in modern editions; most of his vocal works are not extant. Many scores are preserved in MS in the libraries of Darmstadt, Dresden, Leipzig, and Brussels; in the archives of the Thomasschule at Leipzig are the parts of 5 orch. suites of Fasch in the handwriting of J.S. Bach, who entertained a very high opinion of the works of his contemporary. Hugo Riemann publ. 5 trio sonatas and a String Quartet

in *Collegium Musicum* and 2 orch. suites in Breitkopf & Härtel's *Orchesterbibliothek;* a Violin Concerto in D was ed. by A. Hoffmann (Wolfenbüttel, 1961). Fasch's autobiography appeared in vol. III of F.W. Marpurg's *Historisch-kritische Beyträge zur Aufnahme der Musik* (Berlin, 1754–78).

BIBLIOGRAPHY: J.A. Hiller, *Lebensbeschreibungen berühmter Musikgelehrten und Tonkünstler neuerer Zeit* (Leipzig, 1784); B. Engelke, *Johann Friedrich Fasch, Sein Leben und seine Tätigkeit als Vokalkomponist* (Leipzig, 1908); B. Engelke, "Johann Friedrich Fasch, Versuch einer Biographie," *Sammelbände der Internationalen Musik-Gesellschaft* (1909); C.A. Schneider, *J. Fr. Fasch als Sonatenkomponist* (Münster, 1936); G. Küntzel, "Die Instrumentalkonzerte von Johann Friedrich Fasch," *Die Musikforschung* (Oct.–Dec. 1969); D.A. Sheldon, "Johann Friedrich Fasch: Problems in Style Classification," *Musical Quarterly* (Jan. 1972).

Fasch, Karl Friedrich Christian, German composer, son of **Johann Friedrich Fasch;** b. Zerbst, Nov. 18, 1736; d. Berlin, Aug. 3, 1800. He learned to play the violin and harpsichord as a child; studied all musical subjects with Hertel at Strelitz. At the age of 15, he joined the violinist Franz Benda as his accompanist, and at the age of 20 he was recommended by Benda as harpsichordist to Frederick the Great, jointly with C.P.E. Bach. He also taught music and composed contrapuntal pieces of considerable ingenuity and complexity. He was conductor at the Berlin Opera (1774–76). In 1790 he organized a choral society, which led to the foundation of the famous Singakademie. Fasch was greatly admired by musicians for his contrapuntal skill; the renown of his name was still strong in the first part of the 19th century; in 1839, 6 vols. of his sacred works were publ. by the Singakademie.

BIBLIOGRAPHY: K.F. Zelter, *Biographie von Karl Friedrich Christian Fasch* (Berlin, 1801); M. Blummer, *Geschichte der Berliner Singakademie* (Berlin, 1891); G. Schünemann, *Die Singakademie zu Berlin* (Regensburg, 1941).

Fassbänder, Brigitte, German mezzo-soprano; b. Berlin, July 3, 1939. She studied with her father, the noted baritone **Willi Domgraf-Fassbänder.** She made her debut at the Bavarian State Opera, Munich, in 1961; soon established herself as one of its leading singers. She also made appearances at La Scala, Milan, the Vienna State Opera, Covent Garden, London, etc. Her repertoire ranges from Gluck to Richard Strauss in opera; she is also adept in lieder.

Fassbender, Zdenka, soprano; b. Děčín, Bohemia, Dec. 12, 1879; d. Munich, March 14, 1954. She studied voice in Prague; made her operatic debut in Karlsruhe in 1899; from 1906 to 1919 she was one of the principal singers at the Munich Opera; she also sang at Covent Garden in London (1910, 1913). The famous conductor **Felix Mottl** married her on his deathbed to sanction a lifelong alliance.

Fattorini, Gabriele, Italian composer; b. Faenza in the latter part of the 16th century; date of death unknown. He was maestro di cappella at Faenza, and possibly in Venice. His compositions include *Sacri Concerti a due voci* (Venice, 1600; further eds., 1602, 1608); *Completorium Romanum* (Venice, 1602); motets, madrigals, etc. Several of his works appeared in contemporaneous collections between 1605 and 1622 (Bodenschatz, Donfried, Diruta, etc.). Two of his ricercari for organ are in vol. III of Torchi's *L'arte musicale in Italia.* Banchieri mentions Fattorini in his *Conclusioni del suono dell'Organo* (Lucca, 1591; Bologna, 1609). For bibliographical details, see F. Ghisi's article on Fattorini in *Die Musik in Geschichte und Gegenwart.*

Fauchet, Paul Robert, French composer; b. Paris, June 27, 1881; d. there, Nov. 12, 1937. He studied at the Paris Cons., and later taught harmony there; also was maître de chapelle of Saint-Pierre de Chaillot in Paris. He wrote a number of sacred works, but is remembered mainly for his *Symphonie* for Band, the earliest example of a classical symph. written for the medium (1936); its *Scherzo* is profusely enmeshed with whole-tone scales.

Fauchey, Paul, French composer; b. Paris, March 18, 1858; d. there, Nov. 15, 1936. He was active in the theater as a chorus master and then began to compose light operas, of which *La Carmagnole* (Paris, 1897) was quite popular for a time.

Faulkes, William, English organist and composer; b. Liverpool, Nov. 4, 1863; d. there, Jan. 25, 1933. He studied with W. Dawson and H. Dillon-Newman; from 1886 he was active in Liverpool as an organist and teacher; composed mostly for organ; publ. several albums of organ pieces.

Fauré, Gabriel-Urbain, great French composer; b. Pamiers (Ariège), May 12, 1845; d. Paris, Nov. 4, 1924. His father was a provincial inspector of primary schools; noticing the musical instinct of his son, he took him to Paris to study with Louis Niedermeyer; after Niedermeyer's death in 1861, Fauré studied with Saint-Saëns, from whom he received a thorough training in composition. In 1866 he went to Rennes as organist at the church of Saint-Sauveur; returned to Paris on the eve of the Franco-Prussian War in 1870, and volunteered in the light infantry. He was organist at Notre-Dame de Clignancourt, Saint-Honoré d'Eylau, and Saint-Sulpice (1871–74); subsequently became 2nd organist, and in 1877 choirmaster, at the Madeleine; in 1896 he was appointed chief organist there, and prof. of composition at the Paris Cons. He was an illustrious teacher; among his students were Ravel, Enesco, Koechlin, Roger-Ducasse, Laparra, Florent Schmitt, Louis Aubert, and Nadia Boulanger. In 1905 he succeeded Théodore Dubois as director; resigned in 1920, when growing deafness and ill health made it impossible for him to continue to direct the Cons. From 1903 till 1921 he wrote occasional music reviews in *Le Figaro* (publ. as *Opinions Musicales;* posthumous, Paris,

1930); he was elected a member of the Académie des Beaux Arts in 1909; became a Commander of the Légion d'Honneur in 1910. Fauré's stature as composer is undiminished by the passage of time. He developed a musical idiom all his own; by subtle application of old modes he evoked the aura of eternally fresh art; by using unresolved mild discords and special coloristic effects in his instrumental music, he anticipated the procedures of Impressionism; in his piano works he shunned virtuosity in favor of the classical lucidity of the French masters of the clavecin; the precisely articulated melodic line of his songs is in the finest tradition of French vocal music. Several of his works (significantly, those of his early period) have entered the general repertoire: the great Requiem, First Violin Sonata, *Elégie* for Cello and Piano; also songs (*Ici-bas, Les Roses d'Ispahan, Clair de lune, Au cimetière,* etc.).

WORKS: FOR THE STAGE: *Caligula,* incidental music to a play by A. Dumas, Jr. (Paris, Nov. 8, 1888); *Shylock,* after Shakespeare (Paris, Dec. 17, 1889); *Pelléas et Mélisande,* after Maeterlinck (London, June 21, 1898; often perf. as an orch. suite); *Prométhée,* lyric tragedy (Béziers, Aug. 27, 1900); *Le Voile du bonheur,* incidental music for Clémenceau's play (Paris, Nov. 4, 1901); *Pénélope* (Monte Carlo, March 4, 1913); *Masques et bergamasques,* stage music (Monte Carlo, April 10, 1919). FOR ORCH.: Symph. in D minor (Paris, March 15, 1885); Suite (1875; only one movement, *Allegro symphonique,* was publ.); *Pavane* (1887); Ballade for Piano and Orch. (Paris, April 23, 1881); Romance for Violin and Orch. (1882); *Fantaisie* for Piano and Orch. (1919). CHORAL WORKS: *Cantique de Jean Racine* for Mixed Chorus, Harmonium, and String Quartet (1873); *Les Djinns* for Chorus and Orch. (1875); *La Naissance de Vénus* for Soli, Chorus, and Orch. (1882; Paris, April 3, 1886); *Messe de Requiem* for Soli, Chorus, Organ, and Orch. (1887); *Ave Verum* and *Tantum Ergo* for Female Voices and Organ (1894); offertories and other church music. CHAMBER MUSIC: 2 violin sonatas (1876, 1916); 2 piano quartets (1879, 1886); 2 piano quintets (1906, 1921); 2 cello sonatas (1918, 1922); Piano Trio (1923); String Quartet (1924); *Berceuse* for Piano and Violin (1879); *Elégie* for Piano and Cello (1894); Andante for Violin and Piano (1894); *Papillon* for Cello and Piano (1897); *Sicilienne* for Cello and Piano (1893); *Sérénade* for Cello and Piano (1908); *Fantaisie* for Flute and Piano (1898). PIANO WORKS: 13 nocturnes; 13 barcarolles; 5 impromptus; 4 waltzes; *Dolly,* 6 pieces for 4-hands (1889; orchestrated by Rabaud); 96 songs: 4 to words by Victor Hugo, 4 after Théophile Gautier, 3 after Baudelaire, 16 after Paul Verlaine (including the cycle *La Bonne Chanson*), etc.

BIBLIOGRAPHY: O. Séré, *Musiciens français d'aujourd'hui* (Paris, 1911); L. Vuillemin, *Gabriel Fauré et son œuvre* (Paris, 1914); the special Fauré issue of *La Revue Musicale* (Oct. 1922); Aaron Copland, "Gabriel Fauré: A Neglected Master," *Musical Quarterly* (Oct. 1924); Alfred Bruneau, *La Vie et les œuvres de Gabriel Fauré* (Paris, 1925); C. Koechlin, *Gabriel Fauré* (Paris, 1927; Eng. trans., London, 1945); Ph. Fauré-Fremiet, *Gabriel Fauré* (Paris, 1929); G. Servières, *Gabriel Fauré* (Paris, 1930); Paul

Landormy, "Gabriel Fauré," *Musical Quarterly* (July 1931); V. Jankélévitch, *Gabriel Fauré et ses mélodies* (Paris, 1938; enlarged ed., 1951); G. Faure, *Gabriel Fauré* (Paris, 1945); Claude Rostand, *L'Œuvre de Gabriel Fauré* (Paris, 1945); Norman Suckling, *Fauré* (in the Master Musicians Series; London, 1946); G. Samazeuilh, *Musiciens de mon temps* (Paris, 1947); Max Favre, *Gabriel Faurés Kammermusik* (Zürich, 1948); Ph. Fauré-Fremiet, ed., *Fauré, Lettres intimes* (Paris, 1951); E. Vuillermoz, *Gabriel Fauré* (Paris, 1960; in Eng., Philadelphia, 1969); R. Orledge, *Gabriel Fauré* (London, 1979); J.-M. Nectoux, ed., *Gabriel Fauré: Correspondence* (Paris, 1980); Florent Schmitt's article on Fauré's chamber music in *Cobbett's Cyclopedia of Chamber Music;* the article by Fauré's son, Philippe Fauré-Fremiet, in *Die Musik in Geschichte und Gegenwart,* contains a very extensive bibliography on Fauré.

Faure, Jean-Baptiste, famous French baritone; b. Moulins, Allier, Jan. 15, 1830; d. Paris, Nov. 9, 1914. He was a choirboy at the Madeleine and other Paris churches; entered the Paris Cons. at the age of 21; after a short period of study he made his debut at the Opéra-Comique, in Massé's opera *Galathée* (Oct. 20, 1852); from 1861–76 he was on the staff of the Paris Opéra; his farewell appearance was in the title role of *Hamlet* by Ambroise Thomas (May 13, 1876), the role that he created in 1868. Subsequently he sang in concerts, appearing with enormous success in Vienna and in London. He was particularly impressive in dramatic roles in Meyerbeer's operas and also in Gounod's *Faust,* as Méphistophélès. He wrote a number of songs, of which several became fairly successful (*Crucifix, Les Rameaux,* etc.).
BIBLIOGRAPHY: H. de Curzon, "Jean-Baptiste Faure," *Musical Quarterly* (April 1918); H. de Curzon, *Jean-Baptiste Faure* (Paris, 1923).

Favarger, René, French pianist; b. Dun-sur-Auron, Cher, Feb. 25, 1815; d. Etretat, Aug. 3, 1868. He was successful as a teacher in Paris and in London; composed a number of salon pieces for piano.

Favart, Charles-Simon, French librettist; b. Paris, Nov. 13, 1710; d. Belleville, near Paris, March 12, 1792. He publ. satirical plays as a youth; after a successful performance of one of his vaudevilles at the Opéra-Comique, he was appointed stage manager there; in 1758 he became its director. He wrote about 150 plays used for operas by Duni, Philidor, and Gluck; he was also the author of *Les Amours de Bastien et Bastienne* (1753), used by Mozart in a German version for his early opera (1768).

Favart, Marie, French soprano; b. Avignon, June 15, 1727; d. Paris, April 21, 1772. Her maiden name was **Marie-Justine-Benoît Buronceray;** she married the impresario **Charles-Simon Favart** in 1745; went with him to Paris, where she sang soubrette roles at the Théâtre-Italien with notable success, often appearing in works for which her husband had prepared the librettos. She became involved in various theatrical intrigues in Paris; an account of these was publ. by Pougin in his book *Madame Favart* (1912).

Favero, Mafalda, Italian soprano; b. Ferrara, Jan. 6, 1905; d. Milan, Sept. 3, 1981. She studied in Bologna; then sang in Cremona and Parma. In 1929 Toscanini invited her to sing at La Scala in Milan. She was engaged by Covent Garden in London in 1937; on Nov. 24, 1938, she sang Mimi at her Metropolitan Opera debut in N.Y. From 1945 to 1950 she once again sang at La Scala. She was at her best in Italian and French roles.
BIBLIOGRAPHY: I. Buscaglia, *Mafalda Favero nella vita e nell'arte* (1946).

Fay, Amy, American pianist; b. Bayou Goula, La., May 21, 1844; d. Watertown, Mass., Feb. 28, 1928. She studied in Berlin with Tausig and Kullak; then became a pupil of Liszt in Weimar. She publ. a vivid book of impressions, *Music-Study in Germany* (Chicago, 1881), which went through more than 20 printings and was trans. into French and German. See H.L. Kaufman in *Notable American Women* (Cambridge, Mass., 1971), vol. 1.

Fay, Maud, American soprano; b. San Francisco, April 18, 1879; d. there, Oct. 7, 1964. She studied in Dresden; became a member of the Munich Opera (1906–16); appeared at Covent Garden in London in 1910, and with the Thomas Beecham Opera Co. in 1914. After the outbreak of World War I she returned to America; sang with the Metropolitan Opera in 1916; also appeared with the Chicago Opera Co. She was particularly distinguished in Wagnerian roles.

Fayer, Yuri, Soviet conductor; b. Kiev, Jan. 17, 1890; d. Moscow, Aug. 3, 1971. He studied violin at the Moscow Cons.; played in various orchs.; in 1909–10 conducted opera in Riga; in 1916 joined the orch. of the Bolshoi Theater in Moscow; from 1923 to 1963 conducted ballet there; toured Europe, America, and China with the ballet troupe. He publ. an autobiography, *Of Me, of Music, of Ballet* (1970).

Fayolle, François-Joseph-Marie, French writer on music and literature; b. Paris, Aug. 15, 1774; d. there, Dec. 2, 1852. A man of brilliant faculties, he was equally proficient in mathematics and poetry; also studied harmony and cello; after 1814 he lived in London; returned to Paris in 1830; he died in an almshouse. He contributed a number of articles to Fétis's *Biographie Universelle;* together with Choron, he publ. *Dictionnaire historique des musiciens* (Paris, 1810–11); his other writings on music include *Notices sur Corelli, Tartini, Gaviniès, Pugnani et Viotti* (Paris, 1810); *Sur les drames lyriques et leur exécution* (Paris, 1813); *Paganini et Bériot* (Paris, 1830).

Fayrfax, Robert, English composer; b. Deeping Gate, Lincolnshire (baptized, April 23), 1464; d. St. Alban, Hertfordshire, Oct. 24, 1521. He was a Gentleman of the Chapel Royal in 1496, and organist at St. Alban's Abbey and at King's Chapel (1497–98); received a B.Mus. (1501) and a D.Mus. (1504) from Cambridge Univ. and a D.Mus. from Oxford Univ. (1511; with his mass *O quam glorifica*). In 1520 he led the Royal Singers accompanying King Henry VIII to the Field of the Cloth of Gold in France. Of his works, 29 are extant: 6 masses (4 are in the Oxford Museum School Collection), 2 Magnificats, 10 motets, 8 part-songs, 3 instrumental pieces. His sacred and secular vocal works are in the *Fayrfax Book* (British Library MS Add. 5465); lute arrangements of several sacred compositions and an instrumental piece for 3 parts are in the British Library. Reprints of some of his compositions are in J. Stafford Smith's *Musica Antiqua* (1812). E. Warren edited *Robert Fayrfax: Collected Works,* in Corpus Mensurabilis Musicae, XVII/1–3 (1959–66).

BIBLIOGRAPHY: J. Pulver, "Robert Fayrfax," *Musical News* (Feb. 10, 1917; Dom Anselm Hughes, "An Introduction to Fayrfax," *Musica Disciplina* (1952); E. Warren, *Life and Works of Robert Fayrfax, 1464–1521,* in Musicological Studies and Documents, XXII (1969).

Feather, Leonard, British-American writer on music, expert on jazz; b. London, Sept. 13, 1914. He studied at St. Paul School in London; in 1935 he came to the U.S.; was naturalized in 1948. He held various jobs as an arranger, lyricist, adviser for jazz festivals, radio commentator, and lecturer; specialized in the field of jazz and folk music; publ. *Inside Bebop* (N.Y., 1949); a compendious *Encyclopedia of Jazz* (N.Y., 1955), which he supplemented by the *New Encyclopedia of Jazz* (1960) and the *Encyclopedia of Jazz in the 60's* (1966). He makes his home in Hollywood.

Fechner, Gustave Theodor, German music theorist; b. Gross-Särchen, Niederlausitz, April 19, 1801; d. Leipzig, Nov. 18, 1887. He was a prof. of physics at the Univ. of Leipzig from 1834. He publ. *Repertorium der Experimentalphysik,* in which musical phenomena are treated; also *Elemente der Psychophysik* (2 vols., 1860) and *Vorschule der Aesthetik* (2 vols., 1870), valuable as establishing a basis of musical esthetics.

Fedeli, Vito, Italian composer; b. Foligno, June 19, 1866; d. Novara, June 23, 1933. He was a pupil of Terziani in Rome; was director of the Cons. at Novara from 1904.

WORKS: Operas: *La Vergine della Montagna* (Reggio-Calabria, Sept. 6, 1897) and *Varsovia* (Rome, Dec. 15, 1900); several masses a cappella; also pieces for orch. He contributed valuable historical articles to the *Rivista Musicale Italiana* and the *Zeitschrift der Internationalen Musik-Gesellschaft;* also wrote a book, *Giacomo e Gaudenzio Battistini* (1932).

BIBLIOGRAPHY: G. Bustico, *Bibliografia di un musico novarese, Vito Fedeli* (1925).

Feder, (Franz) Georg, German musicologist; b. Bochum, Nov. 30, 1927. He studied composition in Bochum; then served as director of stage music at the local Schauspielhaus; subsequently studied musicology at the univs. of Tübingen, Göttingen, and Kiel; received his Ph.D. from the Univ. of Kiel in 1955 with the dissertation *Bachs Werke in ihren Bearbeitungen 1750–1950, I: Die Vokalwerke.* In 1957 he became assistant to Jens Peter Larsen at the Joseph-Haydn-Inst. in Cologne; he succeeded Larsen as its director in 1960; as such, he became chief editor of the complete edition of Haydn's works; he also served as editor of the publ. *Haydn-Studien* from 1965.

Federhofer, Helmut, Austrian musicologist; b. Graz, Aug. 6, 1911. He studied piano and theory in Graz; then continued his studies at the Vienna Academy of Music with Stöhr and Kabasta, graduating in 1936 with a diploma in conducting. He also took private lessons in composition with Alban Berg, Ernst von Sauer, and Oswald Jonas. He took courses in musicology with Alfred Orel and Robert Lach at the Univ. of Vienna; received his Ph.D. there in 1936 with the dissertation *Akkordik und Harmonik in frühen Motetten der Trienter Codices.* From 1937 to 1944 he was State Librarian. He completed his Habilitation in 1944 at the Univ. of Graz with his *Musikalische Form als Ganzheit* (publ. as *Beiträge zur musikalischen Gestaltanalyse,* Graz, 1950). He became Privatdozent at the Univ. of Graz in 1945; in 1951 prof. of musicology. In 1962 he became the director of the Musicological Inst. at the Johannes Gutenberg Univ. in Mainz. That same year he became editor of *Acta Musicologica.* His publications range widely, covering the history of Austrian court music, biographical data of little-known composers of the Renaissance, and abstruse points of old and new music theory. He has also edited works by Fux and Mozart. His books include *Musikpflege und Musiker am Grazer Habsburgerhof der Erzherzöge Karl und Ferdinand von Innerösterreich (1564–1619)* (Mainz, 1967) and *Neue Musik: Ein Literaturbericht* (Tutzing, 1977). He also contributed a great number of articles to various publications dealing with the musical history of Graz.

Federici, Vincenzo, Italian dramatic composer; b. Pesaro, 1764; d. Milan, Sept. 26, 1826. He became an orphan at 16; lived in Turin, where he produced his first opera, *L'Olimpiade* (Dec. 26, 1789). He then made his way to London, where he became cembalist at the Italian Opera; returned to Italy in 1802; in 1814 he became a teacher of harmony at the Milan Cons.

Federlein, Gottfried H., American organist, son of **Gottlieb Federlein;** b. New York, Dec. 31, 1883; d. there, Feb. 26, 1952. He studied with his father; then with Goetschius; in 1915 became organist at Temple Emanu-El in N.Y. He publ. a number of anthems and organ pieces.

Federlein, Gottlieb (Heinrich), organist and vocal

pedagogue; b. Neustadt-an-der-Aisch, near Nuremberg, Nov. 5, 1835; d. Philadelphia, April 29, 1922. He studied with Rheinberger in Munich; was active as an organist and singing teacher in N.Y.; publ. numerous songs and a manual, *Practical School of Voice Culture* (N.Y., 1880).

Fedorov, Vladimir, music librarian and historian; b. near Chernigov, Aug. 18, 1901; d. Paris, April 9, 1979. He studied at the Univ. of Rostov; emigrated to Turkey in 1920; then settled in Paris, where he studied art, archeology, and music; took lessons with Gédalge and Vidal; later took additional courses in Germany. In 1933 he became librarian at the Sorbonne; later took a post in the music division of the Bibliothèque Nationale in Paris (1946–66). He publ. *Moussorgsky, Biographie critique* (Paris, 1935); contributed numerous articles on musical subjects to French publications; was editor of *Fontes Artis Musicae* from 1954 to 1976.

Fehr, Max, Swiss musicologist; b. Bülach, near Zürich, June 17, 1887; d. Winterthur, April 27, 1963. He studied at the Univ. of Zürich with Eduard Bernoulli (Ph.D., 1912). In 1917 he became librarian, and in 1923, president, of the Allgemeine Musikgesellschaft of Zürich; retired as librarian in 1957.
WRITINGS: *Spielleute im alten Zürich* (Zürich, 1916); *Die Meistersinger von Zürich,* satirical novelette (Zürich, 1916); *Unter Wagners Taktstock* (Winterthur, 1922); *Geschichte des Musikkollegiums Winterthur, I. Teil: 1629–1830* (1929); *Richard Wagners Schweizer Zeit,* in 2 vols. (Aarau, 1934, 1953); *Die Familie Mozart in Zürich* (Zürich, 1942); *Die wandernden Theatertruppen in der Schweiz: Verzeichnis der Truppen, Aufführungen und Spieldaten für das 17. und 18. Jahrhundert* (Einsiedeln, 1949); *Der junge Mozart in Zürich* (with L. Caflisch; Zürich, 1952); *Musikalische Jagd* (Zürich, 1954).
BIBLIOGRAPHY: E. Nievergelt, *Max Fehr* (Zürich, 1968).

Feicht, Hieronim, Polish musicologist; b. Mogilno, near Poznan, Sept. 22, 1894; d. Warsaw, March 31, 1967. He studied theology; then turned to music and took courses in composition with Wallek-Walewski in Cracow, and with Soltys and Chybinski in Lwow (Ph.D., Univ. of Lwow, 1925). He taught at the Cracow Cons. in 1927–30 and again in 1935–39; in the interim was a prof. at the State College of Music in Warsaw (1930–32). From 1946–52 he was chairman of the musicology dept. at the Univ. of Wroclaw; subsequently was rector of the State College of Music in Wroclaw (1948–52), and a prof. of music history at the Univ. of Warsaw (1952–64). He publ. important essays on Polish music: *Musik-historische Bemerkungen über die Lemberger Handschriften des Bogarodzica-Liedes* (Poznan, 1925); *Wojciech Debolecki, Ein polnischer Kirchenkomponist aus der 1. Hälfte des 17. Jahrhunderts* (Lwow, 1926); *Polifonia renesansu* (Cracow, 1957); also edited works by Polish composers. A Festschrift was publ. in honor of his 70th birthday in 1964.

Feinberg, Samuel, eminent Russian pianist and composer; b. Odessa, May 26, 1890; d. Moscow, Oct. 22, 1962. He moved to Moscow in 1894; studied piano with Goldenweisser at the Moscow Cons.; also took theory lessons with Zhilayev; graduated in 1911. In 1922 he was appointed prof. of piano at the Cons., holding this post until his death; also gave regular piano recitals in Russia in programs emphasizing new Russian music; he performed all of Beethoven's sonatas and the complete set of Bach's *Wohltemperiertes Clavier,* as well as Chopin and Schumann. As a composer he limited himself almost exclusively to piano music, which was influenced mainly by Chopin and Scriabin in its fluidity and enhanced tonality. His 6th Piano Sonata was played at the Venice Festival in 1925.
WORKS: 3 piano concertos (1931; 1944; 1947, revised 1951); 12 piano sonatas (1915, 1916, 1917, 1918, 1921, 1923, 1924, 1933, 1939, 1940, 1954, 1960); 2 fantasias for Piano (1916–17, 1924); 4 preludes for Piano (1922); 3 preludes for Piano (1923); 2 suites for Piano (1926, 1936); 10 songs to words by Pushkin (1922, 1937); 7 songs to Lermontov's words; and 13 songs to words by Alexander Blok.
BIBLIOGRAPHY: V. Belayev, *Samuel Feinberg* (Moscow, 1927; in Russian and German); D. Gojowy, *Neue sowjetische Musik der 20er Jahre* (Regensburg, 1980).

Feinhals, Fritz, distinguished German baritone; b. Cologne, Dec. 4, 1869; d. Munich, Aug. 30, 1940. He studied in Milan and Padua; made his operatic debut in Essen in 1895; in 1898 he joined the Munich Opera, where he remained until his retirement in 1927. On Nov. 18, 1908, he made his debut at the Metropolitan Opera in N.Y. as Wotan in *Die Walküre,* but was on its roster for only the 1908–9 season. He also made appearances in London, Paris, and Vienna. He was a Wagnerian singer par excellence; his portrayal of Wotan was imperious in its power; he was also successful in the role of Hans Sachs.

Felciano, Richard, American composer; b. Santa Rosa, Calif., Dec. 7, 1930. He studied with Darius Milhaud at Mills College; subsequently took courses at the Paris Cons. In 1958–59 he took private lessons with Luigi Dallapiccola in Florence. He holds a Ph.D. from the Univ. of Iowa (1959). He was the recipient of the Guggenheim fellowship in 1969 and 2 fellowships from the Ford Foundation (1964, 1971–73). He is also the holder of the American Academy of Arts and Letters Award (1974). In 1967 he was appointed resident composer at the National Center for Experiments in Television in San Francisco. At the same time he was also on the music faculty of the Univ. of Calif. at Berkeley.
WORKS: Opera, *Sir Gawain and the Green Knight* (San Francisco, April 4, 1964); *4 Poems from the Japanese* for 5 Harps, Women's Voices, and Percussion (1964); *The Captives* for Chorus and Orch. (1965); *Contractions,* theatrical mobile for Woodwind Quintet (1965); *Mutations* for Orch. (1966); *Aubade* for String Trio, Harp, and Piano (1966);

Glossolalia for Organ, Baritone, Percussion, and Tape (1967); *Spectra* for Piccolo, Flute, Alto Flute, and Double Bass (1967); *Noosphere I* for Alto Flute and Tape (1967); *Noosphere II* for Electronic Tape (1967); *Trio* for Speaker, Screen, and Viewer, a videotape (1968); Quintet for Piano, Strings, and Electronic Tape (1970); *Lamentations for Jani Christou* for 12 Instruments and Electronic Tape (1970); *Soundspace for Mozart* for Flute, Electronics, and Tape (1970); *Galactic Rounds* for Orch. (1972); *Chod* for Violin, Violoncello, Double Bass, Piano, Percussion, and Electronics (1975); *The Passing of Enkidu* for Chorus, Piano, Percussion, and Tape (1976); *In Celebration of Golden Rain*, utilizing Indonesian Gamelan and Occidental Pipe Organ (1977); *Lumen*, duo for Soprano and Organ (1980); *Orchestra* for Orch. (San Francisco, Sept. 24, 1980).

Feld, Jindřich, Czech composer; b. Prague, Feb. 19, 1925. He studied violin with his father; took composition with Hlobil at the Prague Cons. (1945–48) and with Řídký at the Prague Academy of Music (1948–52); also studied musicology at Charles Univ. (1945–52). During the academic year 1968–69 he was a visiting prof. at the Univ. of Adelaide in Australia; returning to Prague, he was appointed to the staff of the Prague Cons. His early music is in a neo-Baroque manner, but he soon adopted a variety of modern means.
WORKS: Children's opera, *Postácká opera (The Postman's Tale)*, after Čapek (1956); *Divertimento* for String Orch. (1950); *Furiant* for Orch. (1950); Concerto for Orch. (1951; revised 1957); *Comedy Overture* (1953); Flute Concerto (1954; Czech Radio, Oct. 26, 1956); *Rhapsody* for Violin and Orch. (1956); Concerto in C for Chamber Orch. (1956–57); Cello Concerto (1958); Bassoon Concerto (1958–59); *May 1945*, dramatic overture (1959–60); Suite for Chamber String Orch. (1960–61); *Thuringian Ouverture* (1961); *3 Frescoes* for Orch. (Prague, Feb. 21, 1964); *Concert Music* for Oboe, Bassoon, and Orch. (1964); *Serenata giocosa* for Chamber Orch. (1966); *Concert Piece* for Horn and Orch. (1966); Symph. No. 1 (Prague, Jan. 23, 1969); *Dramatic Fantasy* for Orch. (1968–69); Oboe Concerto (1970); Piano Concerto (1973); Saxophone Concerto (1980); Suite for Clarinet and Piano (1948–49); 4 string quartets (1949, 1952, 1962, 1965); 2 wind quintets (1949, 1968); Sonatina for 2 Violins (1952–53); *2 Compositions* for Cello and Piano (1954–55); Viola Sonata (1955); *Rhapsody* for Violin and Piano (1956); Flute Sonata (1957); *Chamber Suite* for Nonet (1960); String Trio (1961); Trio for Flute, Violin, and Cello (1963); *Capriccio* for Wind Quartet and Guitar (1964); Suite for Solo Accordion (1965); *4 Intermezzos* for Accordion (1967); *Miniatures* for Violin, Guitar, and Accordion (1967–68); Brass Quintet (1969–70); *Concertante Suite* for Bass Clarinet and Piano (1971); Cello Sonata (1972); Prelude and Toccata for 2 Pianos (1960); Piano Sonata (1971–72); *Rhapsody* for Organ (1963); *3 Inventions* for Chamber Chorus (1966); *Mockery of Names* for Women's Chorus, Oboe, Clarinet, Bass Clarinet, Ocarina, Double Bass, Piano, and Percussion (1974); *Elegy* for Saxophone and Piano (1981); Oboe Sonata (1981–82); many educational pieces for various instruments.

Feldbrill, Victor, Canadian conductor; b. Toronto, April 4, 1924. He studied violin with Kathleen Parlow in Toronto and conducting with Monteux in Maine; later took lessons in conducting with Otterloo in Hilversum and Zallinger in Salzburg. He was assistant conductor of the Toronto Symph. (1956–57); then was music director of the Winnipeg Symph. (1958–68); in 1968 he joined the staff of the Univ. of Toronto, where he became conductor of its symph. orch. He also served as acting music director of the London, Ontario, Symph. in 1979–80. In most of his programs he has included works by contemporary Canadian composers.

Feldbusch, Eric, Belgian cellist and composer; b. Grivegnée, March 2, 1922. He studied cello at the Liège Cons. (1934–39); later took courses in composition with Quinet and Legley (1947–48). He divided his time between concert activity as a cellist and teaching; was director of the Cons. of Mons (1963–72); in 1973 was appointed director of the Brussels Cons.
WORKS: Opera, *Orestes* (1969); ballet, *El Diablo Cojuelo* (1972); *Variations sur un air connu* for Orch. (1955); *Contrastes* for Orch. (1956); *5 Brief Pieces* for String Orch. and Piano (1957); *Les Moineaux de Baltimore*, suite for Orch. (1958; also as a radio play); *Adagio* for String Orch. (1958); *Adagio* for 3 Cellos and String Orch. (1960); *Mosaïque* for String Orch. (1961); *Overture* for String Orch. (1961); *Shema Israël* for String Orch. (1962); *Choral* for a group of Wind Instruments (1963); *3 poèmes de Federico García Lorca* for Voice and Orch. (1964); *Ode à des enfants morts* for Orch. (1965–66); Violin Concerto (1967); *Fantaisie-Divertissement* for Orch. (1967); *Cantique des cantiques* for Soprano and Orch. (1970); *Piccola musica* for String Orch. (1971); *Kadisch* for Baritone, Solo Violin, and Strings (1974); *Aquarelles* for Wind Quintet (1947); Sonata for Violin and Cello (1955); *Cadence and Allegro* for Cello and Piano (1956); Violin Sonata (1957); *3 pièces* for Viola, Cello, and Oboe (1957); Duo for Violin and Piano (1958); 4 string quartets (1955, 1958, 1963, 1971); *Mosaïque* for Solo Cello (1958); Piano trio (1958); Duo for Flute and Piano (1959); *Variations extra-formelles* for Cello and Piano (1959); Trio for Flute, Violin, and Cello (1961); Duo for Flute and Viola (1963); Septet for Soprano, 2 Violins, Double Bass, Flute, Trumpet, and Percussion (1969); *Arabesques* for Piano; *3 Movements* for Piano; *Dicht am Flüsschen*, variations for Piano (1960); incidental music for theater plays.

Felderhof, Jan, Dutch composer; b. Bussum, near Amsterdam, Sept. 25, 1907. He studied theory of composition with Sem Dresden at the Amsterdam Cons. In 1934 he was appointed to its faculty; remained there until 1954; during intervening years taught at the music school in Bussum (1944–54), and later at the Utrecht Cons. (1956–67); in 1958 he was named chief theory teacher at the Amsterdam Cons., and assistant director in 1971. He composed a radio opera, *Vliegvuur* (*Wildfire;* 1959–64; Dutch Radio, Nov. 10, 1965); a cantata, *Tot wien zullen wij henengaan* (*To Whom Shall We Make Our Way;* 1935–41); *Music* for 15 Winds and Percussion (1930); *5 Dance Sketches* for Orch. (1930); 2 sinfoniettas (1932, 1962); Suite for Flute and Small Orch. (1933); *Rhapsodie* for Oboe and Small Orch. (1937); Symph. (1949); *Ouverture* (1955); Concerto for Flute, String Orch., and Percussion (1955); *Omaggio* for Orch. (1974); *Complimento* for String Orch. (1975); 3 violin sonatas (1932, 1939, 1965); 4 string quartets (1932, 1936, 1938, 1957); Suite for Flute and Piano (1933); String Trio (1934); Cello Sonata (1935); Piano Trio (1936); Divertimento for Brass Quartet (1950); Violin Sonatina (1953); *Rondo* for Oboe, Clarinet, and Bassoon (1960); Trio for 3 Different Clarinets (1968); Suite for Flute, Oboe, and Piano (1974); 5 piano sonatinas (1933–62); piano and organ pieces; songs. All of these works have an agreeable veneer of simple musicality, and all are excellently written for the instruments.

Feldhoff, Gerd, German baritone; b. Radervormwald, near Cologne, Oct. 29, 1931. He studied at the Northwest German Music Academy in Detmold; made his operatic debut in Essen in 1959 as Figaro in *Le nozze di Figaro;* then sang at the Städtische Oper in Berlin, the Hamburg State Opera, and the Frankfurt Opera. He made his Metropolitan Opera debut in N.Y. as Kaspar in *Der Freischütz* on Sept. 28, 1971. He is especially noted as a dramatic baritone; apart from opera he also made tours as a concert artist.

Feldman, Ludovic, Rumanian composer; b. Galati, June 6, 1893. He studied violin in his hometown; then at the Bucharest Cons. and with František Ondriček at the Vienna Cons. (1911–13). He was a violinist with the Bucharest Philharmonia and at the State Opera (1926–40). Then, after a long career as a violinist, he began to study composition with Mihail Jora; wrote numerous works for orch. and chamber groups, adopting a fairly modern idiom within a classical framework. WORKS: Symph. (1947); 5 suites for Orch. (1948, 1949, 1951–52, 1960, 1960); *Fantaisie concertante* for Cello and Orch. (1949); *Poème concertant* for Violin and Orch. (1951); *8 scènes de ballet* (1952); Ballade for Violin and Orch. (1952); Concerto for Flute and Chamber Orch. (1952); *Ode solennelle* for Orch. (1954); *6 Symphonic Pieces* (1956); Concerto for 2 String Orchs., Celesta, Piano, and Percussion (1958); *Rapsodie dobrogeană* for Orch. (1960); *5 Symphonic Pieces* (1961); Sinfonietta (1962); *Sonata concertante* for Cello and Chamber Orch. (1964); *3 Symphonic Images* (1965); *Symphonic Variations* (1966); *De profundis* for Orch. (1967); Chamber Symph. (1969); *Suite de concert* for Bassoon and Orch. (1969); *Ombres et lumières* for Orch. (1969); *Alternances,* symph. triptyque (1970); Symph. for 15 Instruments (1970); *Sinfonia concertante* for String Orch. (1971); 2 suites for Violin and Piano

(1947, 1948); 2 viola sonatas (1953, 1965); String Trio (1955); String Quartet (1957); Wind Quintet (1957); Violin Sonata (1963); Cello Sonata (1963–66); *3 Concert Pieces* for String Quartet and Percussion (1968); piano pieces; songs.

Feldman, Morton, American composer of the avant-garde; b. New York, Jan. 12, 1926. He studied piano with Vera Maurina-Press and had composition lessons with Wallingford Riegger in 1941 and with Stefan Wolpe in 1944. Profoundly impressed by the abstract expressionism of modern painting in the late 1940s and by his first meeting with John Cage in 1950, Feldman evolved a congenial set of musical concepts and introduced an element of predetermined indeterminacy into the performance of his music, as exemplified in his *Projections I–IV* for different instrumental combinations (1950–51). In such works he indicates only an approximation of the notes to be played in a musical "action," specifying the instrumental range (high, medium, low) and the number of notes per time unit in any voluntary or involuntary rhythmic distribution. He uses graphic optical notation optionally, transcribing it into traditional scores for practical performance; he abandoned graphic notation altogether during two periods (1953–58 and in the early 1960s), employing precise notation. WORKS: *Projections I–IV* (1950–51); *Intersections I* for Orch. (1951), *II* and *III* for Piano (1952, 1953), and *IV* for Cello (1953); *Marginal Intersection* for Orch. (1951); *4 Songs to E.E. Cummings* for Soprano, Cello, and Piano (1951); *Extensions I* for Violin and Piano (1951), *III* for Piano (1952), *IV* for 3 Pianos (1952–53), and *V* for 2 Cellos; *Intermissions I–VI* (1951–53); *Intersection* for Tape (1951); *Structures* for String Quartet (1951); *2 Pieces* for 2 Pianos (1954); *3 Pieces* for String Quartet (1954–56); *Piece* for 4 Pianos (1957); *2 Pianos* for 2 Pianos (1957); *2 Instruments* for Cello and Horn (1958); *Atlantis* for Orch. (1958); *Last Pieces* for Piano (1959); Trio for 3 Pianos (1959); Trio for 2 Pianos and Cello (1959); a ballet, *Ixion (Summerspace)* for 10 Instruments or 2 Pianos (1960; as a classical ballet, N.Y., April 14, 1966; choreographed by Merce Cunningham); a cantata, *The Swallows of Salangan,* for Chorus and 23 Instruments (1960); *Out of "Last Pieces"* for Orch. (1960–61); *Journey to the End of the Night* for Soprano and 4 Wind Instruments (1960); *Structures* for Orch. (1960–62); *Intervals* for Baritone and Instruments (1961); *2 Pieces* for Clarinet and String Quartet (1961); *Philip Guston* for Small Orch. (1962); *For Franz Kline* for Soprano, Violin, Cello, Horn, Chimes, and Piano (1962); *The Straits of Magellan* for 7 Instruments (1963); *De Kooning* for Piano, Violin, Cello, Horn, and Percussion (1963); *4 Instruments* for Violin, Cello, Glockenspiel, and Piano (1963); *Chorus and Instruments I–II* (1963, 1967); *Vertical Thoughts I–V* for different instrumental combinations (1963); *Numbers* for 9 Instruments (1964); *Rabbi Akiba* for Soprano and 10 Instruments (1964); *The King of Denmark* for Percussion (1965); *Christian Wolff at Cambridge* for Chorus a cappella (1965); *2 Pieces* for 3 Pianos

(1966); *First Principles* for Large Instrumental Ensemble (1966–67); *In Search of an Orchestration* for Orch. (1967); *False Relationships and the Extended Ending* for Violin, Cello, Trombone, 3 Pianos, and Chimes (1968); *On Time and the Instrumental Factor* for Orch. (1969); *Between Categories* for 2 Pianos, 2 Chimes, 2 Violins, and 2 Cellos (1969); *Madame Press Died Last Week at Ninety* for Chamber Ensemble (St. Paul de Vence, July 20, 1970; Foss conducting); *The Viola in My Life I* for Solo Viola and 6 Instrumentalists, *II* for Solo Viola and 7 Instrumentalists, *III* for Viola and Piano, and *IV* for Viola and Orch. (1970–71); *3 Clarinets, Cello and Piano* (1971); *Chorus and Orchestra I–II* (1971–72); *I Met Heine on the Rue Fürstenberg* for Voice and 6 Instrumentalists (1971); *The Rothko Chapel* for Solo Viola, Chorus, and Percussion (1971; Houston, April 9, 1972); *Cello and Orchestra* (1971–72); *Voice and Instruments I* for Soprano and Chamber Orch. (1972), and *II* for Voice, Clarinet, Cello, and Double Bass (1974); *Voices and Instruments I* for Chorus and 9 Instrumentalists, and *II* for 3 Voices, Flute, 2 Cellos, and Double Bass (both 1972); *Pianos and Voices I* for 5 Pianists that hum, and *II* for 5 Pianos and 5 Voices (both 1972); *For Frank O'Hara* for 7 Instrumentalists (1973); *String Quartet and Orchestra* (1973); *Voices and Cello* for 2 Voices and Cello (1973); *Instruments I* for 5 Instruments, and *II* for 9 Instrumentalists (1974–75); *Piano and Orchestra* (1975); *4 Instruments* for piano quartet (1975); *Oboe and Orchestra* (1976); *Orchestra* (1976); *Voice, Violin and Piano* (1976); *Routine Investigations* for Oboe, Trumpet, Piano, Viola, Cello, and Double Bass (1976); *Elemental Procedures* for Chorus and Orch. (1976); *The Spring of Chosroes* for Violin and Piano (1977); *Neither,* monodrama after an original text by Beckett, for Soprano and Orch. (1977; Rome, May 13, 1977; N.Y., Nov. 21, 1978).

Feliciano, José, blind singer, guitarist, and songwriter; b. Larex, Puerto Rico, Sept. 10, 1945. His family moved to N.Y. when he was 5; he taught himself to play the guitar, and then appeared in Greenwich Village clubs; his self-exclamatory record album *Feliciano!* brought him fame (it included his soulful version of the song *Light My Fire,* notable for its sexual and narcotic overtones). His blues rendition of *The Star-Spangled Banner* at the 1968 World Series in Detroit caused a furor, leading many radio stations to boycott him. After a hiatus of several years, he was able to renew his career. He toured in the U.S. and in Europe.

Felix, Hugo, Austrian composer of operettas; b. Vienna, Nov. 19, 1866; d. Hollywood, Aug. 24, 1934. He produced several operettas in Vienna: *Husarenblut* (1894); *Das Kätzchen* (1892); etc.; and several in Berlin (*Madame Sherry,* 1902; etc.). After World War I he settled in America; wrote an operetta with an English text, *The Sweetheart Shop* (Chicago, 1920); also incidental music to Otis Skinner's *Sancho Panza,* and other plays.

Felix, Václav, Czech composer; b. Prague, March 29, 1928. He studied composition with Bořkovec and Dobiáš at the Prague Academy of Arts and Music (1949–53); then theory with K. Janeček (1953–56), obtaining a Ph.D. in philosophy. From 1961 to 1976 he was on the staff of the Prague Academy, as a prof. of composition. His own music follows the golden mean of agreeable Central European modernism.

WORKS: 2 comic operas: *What Matures Men* (1966) and *The Timid Casanova* (1975); *Concerto romantico* for Violin, Clarinet or Viola, Harp, and String Orch. (1953); *Fantasy* for Clarinet and Orch. (1959); *Concertant Variations* for Orch. (1962); Suite for String Orch. (1969); *Joyful Prelude* for Orch. (1971); Symph. for Mezzo-soprano and Orch. (1974); oratorio, *Legend about Lenin* (1956); 2 cantatas: *Scientific Songs* (1963) and *Where Do the Months Come From* (1965); 2 double-bass sonatinas (1951, 1970); Duo for Violin and Cello (1962); 3 piano trios (1955, 1956, 1962); Cello Sonata (1960); String Trio (1961); *The Story of Snow White,* quintet for Harp and String Quartet (1963); 2 violin sonatinas (1963, 1968); *Sonata a tre* for Violin, Viola, and Harp (1967); *Sonata da Requiem* for Horn or Bass Clarinet, and Piano (1969); *Terzetto* for Oboe, Clarinet, and Bassoon (1971); Wind Quintet (1972); Brass Quintet (1972); Trio for Violin, Horn, and Piano (1973); *Open House,* chamber cantata for Contralto, Tenor, and Piano (1961); Piano Sonata (1950); 3 piano sonatinas (1969); choruses; songs. He also publ. monographs on Vít Nejedlý (Prague, 1968) and Václav Kálik (Opava, 1973).

Fellagara, Vittorio, Italian composer; b. Milan, Nov. 4, 1927. He studied physics and mathematics at the Univ. of Milan (1945–50); concurrently took lessons in music theory with Luciano Chailly at the Verdi Cons. in Milan, graduating in 1951. He subsequently taught at the Donizetti Cons. in Bergamo. His own music follows neo-Baroque models.

WORKS: A ballet, *Mutazioni* (1962; La Scala, Milan, Jan. 27, 1965); 4 symphonic fragments (Copenhagen ISCM Festival, May 28, 1964); *Invenzioni* for Piano (1949); *Ricercare Fantasia* for Piano (1951); Concerto for Orch (1952; Turin, Feb. 28, 1957); *Preludio, Fuga e Postludio* for Piano (1952–53); *Ottetto* for Winds (1953); *Concert breve* for Chamber Orch. (1956); *Sinfonia 1957* (Rome, June 28, 1958); *Requiem di Madrid* for Chorus and Orch. (1958; Turin, Oct. 17, 1959); *Dies Irae* for Chorus, 6 Trumpets, Cymbals, and 7 Percussionists (1959); *Frammenti I* for Chamber Orch. (1960); *Serenata* for Chamber Orch. or 9 Instruments (1960); *Variazioni (Frammenti II)* for Chamber Orch. (1961); *Epitaphe* for 2 Sopranos and 5 Instrumentalists (1964); *Cantata* for 2 Female Voices and Orch. (1966; Donaueschingen, Oct. 23, 1966); *Madrigale* for Vocal Quintet and 14 Instruments (1969); *Chanson* for Soprano and Chamber Orch. (1974; Milan, Nov. 29, 1975); *Omaggio a Bach* for Piano (1975).

Fellerer, Karl Gustav, eminent German musicologist and editor; b. Freising, July 7, 1902; d. Munich, Jan. 7, 1984. He studied at the Regensburg School of

Church Music and took courses in composition with Heinrich Schmid and Joseph Haas in Munich; then studied musicology at the Univ. of Munich with Sandberger and at the Univ. of Berlin with Hornbostel, Abert, Wolf, and Sachs; received his Ph.D. in 1925 from the Univ. of Munich with the dissertation *Beiträge zur Musikgeschichte Freisings von den ältesten christlichen Zeiten bis zur Auflösung des Hofes 1803* (Freising, 1926); completed his Habilitation in 1927 at the Univ. of Münster with his *Der Palestrina stil und seine Bedeutung in der vokalen Kirchenmusik des 18. Jahrhunderts* (Augsburg, 1929). In 1927 he became a lecturer at the Univ. of Münster; in 1931 prof. in Freiburg, Switzerland; in 1934 he became head of the dept. of musicology at the Univ. of Münster; in 1939 he succeeded Theodor Kroyer as prof. of music history at the Univ. of Cologne; he retired in 1970. Fellerer distinguished himself as an outstanding authority on the history of music of the Roman Catholic church; he contributed valuable studies on the music of the Middle Ages, the Renaissance, and the 19th century; he also served as editor of several important music journals and other publications. His 60th birthday was honored by the publication of three *Festschriften*.

WORKS: *Die Deklamationsrhythmik in der vokalen Polyphonie des 16. Jahrhunderts* (Düsseldorf, 1928); *Orgel und Orgelmusik; Ihre Geschichte* (Augsburg, 1929); *Palestrina* (Regensburg, 1930; 2nd ed., revised, 1960); *Studien zur Orgelmusik des ausgehenden 18. und frühen 19. Jahrhunderts* (Kassel, 1932); *Beiträge zur Choralbegleitung und Choralverarbeitung in der Orgelmusik des ausgehenden 18. und beginnenden 19. Jahrhunderts* (Leipzig, 1932); *Die Aufführung der katholischen Kirchenmusik in Vergangenheit und Gegenwart* (Einsiedeln, 1933); *Mittelalterliches Musikleben der Stadt Freiburg im Uechtland* (Regensburg, 1935); *Der gregorianische Choral im Wandel der Jahrhunderte* (Regensburg, 1936); *Giacomo Puccini* (Potsdam, 1937); *Geschichte der katholischen Kirchenmusik* (Düsseldorf, 1939); *Deutsche Gregorianik im Frankenreich* (Regensburg, 1941); *Edvard Grieg* (Potsdam, 1942); *Einführung in die Musikwissenschaft* (Berlin, 1942); 2nd ed., revised 1953); *Georg Friedrich Händel: Leben und Werk* (Hamburg, 1953); *Mozarts Kirchenmusik* (Salzburg, 1955); *Soziologie der Kirchenmusik* (Cologne, 1963); *Bearbeitung und Elektronik als musikalisches Problem in Urheberrecht* (Berlin and Frankfurt, 1965); *Klang und Struktur in der abendländischen Musik* (Cologne, 1967); *Das Problem Neue Musik* (Krefeld, 1967); *Monodie und Polyphonie in der Musik des 16. Jahrhunderts* (Brussels, 1972); *Der Stilwandel in der abendländischen Musik um 1600* (Cologne, 1972); *Geschichte der katholischen Kirchenmusik* (Kassel, 1972–76); *Max Bruch* (Cologne, 1974); *Der Akademismus in der deutschen Musik des 19. Jahrhunderts* (Opladen, 1976).

Fellowes, Rev. Edmund Horace, eminent English musicologist and editor; b. London, Nov. 11, 1870; d. Windsor, Dec. 20, 1951. He attended Winchester and Oriel Colleges, Oxford; studied music with P.C. Buck, Fletcher, and L. Straus; received a Mus.Bac. degree from Oxford (1896); honorary Mus.Doc. degrees from Dublin Univ. (1917), Oxford (1938), and Cambridge (1950). In 1897–1900, he was precentor at Bristol Cathedral; in 1900, canon; in 1923–27, conductor at St. George's Chapel, Windsor Castle; in 1918, librarian at St. Michael's College, Tenbury; in 1927–29, he toured the U.S. and Canada with the Choir of St. George's Chapel and Choristers of Westminster Abbey; also lectured on old English music at various univs.; in 1932–33, was a lecturer on music at Liverpool Univ. He ed. the valuable collections *The English Madrigal School,* including the works of Thomas Morley, Orlando Gibbons, John Wilbye, John Farmer, Thomas Weelkes, William Byrd, Henry Lichfild, John Ward, Thomas Tomkins, Giles Farnaby, Thomas Bateson, John Bennet, George Kirbye, etc. (36 vols., 1913–36), and *The English School of Lutenist Songwriters,* containing the collected works of John Dowland, Thomas Campion, Thomas Ford, Francis Pilkington, Robert Jones, etc. (32 vols., 1920–32); was co-editor of the Carnegie edition *Tudor Church Music,* including works of White, Tallis, Taverner, Byrd, and Gibbons (10 vols., 1919–47); was also ed. of collected works of William Byrd (20 vols., 1937–50); 11 fantasies for Strings by Orlando Gibbons (1925); songs of Fletcher and Beaumont; etc. Fellowes was also a composer of church music; in his early years he wrote many anthems, *Morning and Evening Service,* songs, and a String Quartet.

WRITINGS: *English Madrigal Verse* (1920; 2nd ed., 1931); *The English Madrigal Composers* (1921; 2nd ed., 1948); *William Byrd, A Short Account of His Life and Work* (1923; 2nd ed., 1928); *Orlando Gibbons* (1925; 2nd ed., 1951); *The English Madrigal* (London, 1925); *Windsor Castle, St. George's Chapel and Choir* (1927); *Repertory of English Cathedral Music* (in collaboration with C.H. Stewart, 1930); *The Catalogue of the Manuscripts at St. Michael's College, Tenbury* (1934); *William Byrd* (1936; an entirely different book from the monograph of 1923, and much larger in scope; 2nd ed., 1948); *Westminster Abbey and Its Music; Organists and Masters of the Choristers of St. George's Chapel in Windsor Castle* (1939); *English Cathedral Music from Edward VI to Edward VII* (1941; revised 1945). He wrote an autobiography, *Memoirs of an Amateur Musician* (London, 1946).

Felsenstein, Walter, influential Austrian opera producer; b. Vienna, May 30, 1901; d. East Berlin, Oct. 8, 1975. He studied at a Graz technical college; then went to Vienna, where he enrolled in drama courses at the Burgtheater. In 1923 he appeared as an actor in Lübeck; in 1924 went to Mannheim. In 1925 he became dramatic adviser and producer in Beuthen, Silesia; in 1927 he was called to Basel to become chief opera and drama producer at the Stadttheater; in 1929 he went to Freiburg im Breisgau as both actor and dramatic adviser and producer. He served as chief producer at the Cologne Opera in 1932 and at the Frankfurt Opera in 1934. Despite his differences with the policies of the Nazi authorities, he as able to continue producing operas and dramas. From 1938–40 he produced plays in Zürich; he then served as producer in Berlin (1940–44); he was drafted by the military despite his age, and served for a year. After the war he was director of the Komische Oper in East Berlin, a position he held until his death. During his tenure, the Komische Oper established itself as one of the best opera houses of Europe; his productions of *Die Fledermaus, Carmen, Le nozze di Figaro, Otello, Les Contes d'Hoffmann,* and *Die Zauberflöte* were artistically of the first rank. He also made operatic films and gave courses on theater arts. Among his students were the opera producers Götz Friedrich and Joachim Herz. With S. Melchinger, he compiled *Musiktheater* (Bremen, 1961); with G. Friedrich and J. Herz, he publ. *Musiktheater: Beiträge zur Methodik und zu Inszenierungs-Konzeptionen* (ed., S. Stomper; Leipzig, 1970).

BIBLIOGRAPHY: R. Münz, *Untersuchungen zum realistischen Musiktheater Walter Felsensteins* (Diss., Humboldt Univ., Berlin, 1964); G. Friedrich, *Walter Felsenstein: Weg und Werk* (Berlin, 1967); P. Fuchs, ed. and translator, *The Music Theater of Walter Felsenstein: Collected Articles, Speeches and Interviews by Felsenstein and Others* (N.Y., 1975).

Felsztyn (Felstin, Felstinensis, Felsztynski), Sebastian von, notable Polish theorist and composer; b. Felsztyn, Galicia, c.1490; d. c.1543. He studied (1507–9) at the Univ. of Cracow (bachelor's degree); was chaplain at Felsztyn, later at Przemysl; then was provost in Sanok. He wrote a compendium on Gregorian chant and mensural music, publ. in several eds. (1515, 1519, 1522, 1534, 1539) as *Opusculum utriusque musicae tam choralis quam etiam mensuralis.* He further publ. a practical manual for church singing, *Directiones musicae ad cathedralis ecclesiae Premisliensis usum* (Cracow, 1543); edited St. Augustin's *Dialogus de musica* (with comments); and composed a vol. of hymns, *Aliquot hymni ecclesiastici vario melodiarum genere editi* (Cracow, 1522; partly lost). His significance as a composer lies in the fact that he was the first Polish musician to employ consistent 4-part writing; one selection for 4 voices is reprinted in Surzynski's *Monumenta musices sacrae in Polonia* (vol. II).

BIBLIOGRAPHY: A. Chybinski, *The Relationship of Polish and West-European Music of the 15th and 16th Centuries* (1909; in Polish); A. Chybinski, *The Mensural Theory in Polish Musical Literature of the 1st Half of the 16th Century* (1911); S. Lobaczewska, *Sebastian Felsztyn as Composer* (1928). See also Zofia Lissa's article in *Die Musik in Geschichte und Gegenwart.*

Felumb, Svend Christian, Danish composer; b. Copenhagen, Dec. 25, 1898; d. there, Dec. 16, 1972. He studied in Copenhagen with L. Nielsen and Bruce, and in Paris with Blenzel and Vidal; from 1924 till 1947 he was an oboist in the Danish Royal Orch.; in 1947–1962 he conducted the Tivoli Orch. He was the founder of the Ny Musik society in Copenhagen and a leader of the movement for modern national Danish music.

Fenaroli, Fedele, Italian music theorist; b. Lanciano, April 25, 1730; d. Naples, Jan. 1, 1818. He studied with his father, who was a church organist; then went to Naples, where he became a pupil of Francesco Durante and Leonardo Leo at the Cons. of Santa Maria di Loreto; in 1762 became 2nd master there, and in 1777 the first; also taught at the Cons. della Pietà. He trained many famous musicians (Cimarosa, Conti, Mercadante, Zingarelli, etc.); his theoretical manuals were highly regarded, not only in Italy, but in France; he publ. *Partimento ossia Basso numerato* (Rome, 1800); *Studio del contrappunto* (Rome, 1800); *Regale musicali per i principianti di cembalo* (Naples, 1775). He was a prolific composer of church music, which, however, did not sustain its initial renown; composed 2 oratorios, *Abigaille* (1760) and *L'arca nel Giordano.*

BIBLIOGRAPHY: T. Consalvo, *La teoria musicale del Fenaroli* (1826); G. de Napoli, "F. Fenaroli nel secondo centenario della nascita," *Musica d'Oggi* (March 1930).

Fenby, Eric, English composer; b. Scarborough, April 22, 1906. He studied piano and organ; after a few years as an organist in London, he went (1928) to Grez-sur-Loing, France, as amanuensis for Frederick Delius, taking down his dictation note by note, until Delius's death in 1934. Two years later he publ. his experiences in a book entitled *Delius as I Knew Him* (London; 4th ed., N.Y., 1981). He was director of music of the North Training School (1948–62); from 1964 was a prof. of composition at the Royal Academy of Music. Because of the beneficent work he undertook, he neglected his own compositions; however he also wrote some pleasant music for strings.

BIBLIOGRAPHY: C. Redwood, ed., *A Delius Companion: A 70th Birthday Tribute to Eric Fenby* (London, 1976).

Fendler, Edvard, German-American conductor; b. Leipzig, Jan. 22, 1902. He studied conducting with G. Brecher and composition with Leichtentritt; conducted in Germany, France, and the Netherlands (1927–41); was conductor of the National Symph. Orch., Ciudad Trujillo, the Dominican Republic (1942–44); then was in the U.S. (1945–47); was conductor of the National Symph. Orch. in San José, Costa Rica (1948–49); returned to the U.S. in 1949; from 1952 till 1970 he was conductor of the Mobile (Ala.) Symph. Orch.

Fennell, Frederick, American band conductor; b. Cleveland, July 2, 1914. He began conducting during the summers of 1931–33 at the National Music Camp at Interlochen, Mich.; went on to study at the Eastman School of Music in Rochester, N.Y. (B.M., 1937; M.M., 1939); then served on its faculty as conductor of the Little Symph. and Symph. Band (1939–65). In 1952 he founded the Eastman Wind Ensemble, with which he made numerous record albums; he was also a guest conductor at the Boston Pops. In 1965 he was appointed conductor-in-residence of the Univ. of Miami School of Music at Coral Gables, Fla.; he also made European tours with the School Orch. of America (1965, 1966) and produced a series of specially recorded concerts at the Library of Congress, using 19th-century band instruments and music (1972, 1973, 1977). He is the recipient of an honorary Mus.D. degree from the Univ. of Oklahoma City; in 1958 was made an Honorary Chief by the Kiowa Indian tribe. He publ. *Time and the Winds* (Kenosha, Wis., 1954) and *The Drummer's Heritage* (Rochester, 1957).

Fennelly, Brian, American composer; b. Kingston, N.Y., Aug. 14, 1937. He attended Union College in Schenectady (1954–58), earning a bachelor's degree in mechanical engineering; served in the Air Force (1958–61); upon discharge, returned to Union College, obtaining the degree of B.A. in 1963. He then took postgraduate courses at Yale Univ. School of Music, where he studied with Mel Powell, Gunther Schuller, and Allen Forte (M.M., 1965; Ph.D., 1968); also took cello lessons. As a doctoral student, he wrote the dissertation *A Descriptive Notation for Electronic Music.* In 1968 he was appointed to the faculty of the School of Arts and Sciences at N.Y. Univ. In 1980 he received the Guggenheim fellowship grant. He traveled widely as a pianist, conductor, and lecturer; was delegate to World Music Days, under the auspices of the International Society for Contemporary Music, in Iceland, the Netherlands, France, Austria, Czechoslovakia, Finland, Greece, and Israel. He is extremely liberal in his choice of idiom for his own music, free of fashionable elitism, willing and eager to use all effective means of composition, ranging from stark homophony to dodecaphonic structuralism, traversing on the way through the unblushing expression of soulful Romanticism. For purely practical purposes he produced 9 pieces, each for a solo instrument, under the general title *Tesserae* (that is, regularly shaped pieces of stone or glass used for mosaic material; the word itself, meaning "four" in Greek, refers to a 4-cornered plate). He also made use of electronic sound. WORKS: FOR ORCH.: *In Wildness Is the Preservation of the World,* orch. fantasy after Thoreau (1975; Davenport, Iowa, Nov. 5, 1976); *Concert Piece* for Trumpet and Orch. (1976); *Quintuplo* ("fivefold five") for Brass Quintet and Orch. (1977–78); *Scintilla prisca* for Cello and Orch. (1980); *Tropes and Echos* for Clarinet and Orch. (1981). CHAMBER MUSIC: Duo for Violin and Piano (1964); *2 Movements* for Oboe, Clarinet, Trumpet, and Trombone (1965); Wind Quintet (1967); *Evanescences* for Alto Flute, Clarinet, Violin, Cello, and Electronic Tape (1969); String Quartet (1971); *Prelude and Elegy* for Brass Quintet (1973); *Consort I* for Trombone Quintet (1976); *Empirical Rag* for Brass Quintet (1977); *Scintilla prisca* for Cello and Piano (1979); *Canzona* for Clarinet, Violin, Viola, Cello, and Piano (1981–82); *3 Intermezzi* for Bass Clarinet and

Marimba (1983). FOR SOLO INSTRUMENTS: Suite for Double Bass (1963; revised 1981); *For Solo Flute* (1964; revised 1976); *Divisions* for Solo Violin (1968; revised 1981); *Sonata seria* for Piano (1976); *Empirical Rag* for Piano (1978; also for other instruments); 9 pieces entitled *Tesserae* (i.e., mosaics), numbered in Roman numerals: I for Harpsichord (1971), II for Cello (1972), III for Viola (1976), IV for Double-bass Trombone (1976), V for Tuba (1980), VI for Trumpet (1976), VII for Clarinet (1979), VIII for Alto Saxophone (1980), IX for Percussion (1981). VOCAL MUSIC: *Songs with Improvisation* for Mezzo-soprano, Clarinet, and Piano, to texts by e.e. cummings (1964; revised 1969); Psalm XIII for Chorus and Brass (1965); *Sunyata* for 4-channel Magnetic Tape (1970); *Festive Psalm* for Chorus, Narrator, Organ, and Electronic Tape (1972); *Praise Yah* for Chorus and Organ (1974); *Winterkill* for Chorus and Piano (1981).

Feo, Francesco, celebrated Italian composer; b. Naples, 1691; d. there, Jan. 18, 1761. He was a pupil of Andrea Basso and Nicola Fago at the Cons. della Pietà from 1704; his first opera was *Amor tirannico* (Naples, Jan. 18, 1713); then followed *La forza della virtù* (Naples, Jan. 22, 1719), *Teuzzone* (Naples, Jan. 20, 1720), *Siface, re di Numidia* (Naples, Nov. 4, 1720), *Andromaca* (Rome, Feb. 5, 1730), *Arsace* (Turin, Dec. 26, 1740), etc. He also wrote pieces for special occasions, including a serenade for the marriage of Charles of Bourbon, King of the 2 Sicilys, to Princess Maria Amalia of Poland (1737) and a piece for the Spanish King's birthday (1738). Feo spent most of his life in Naples; he was first maestro di cappella at the Cons. of Sant' Onofrio (1723–39); then at the Cons. dei Poveri di Gesù Cristo (1739–43). Most of his works (over 150 in all) are extant in MS at Naples.

Ferand, Ernst Thomas, Hungarian music scholar; b. Budapest, March 5, 1887; d. Basel, May 29, 1972. He studied at the Budapest Academy of Music, graduating in 1911; then collaborated with Jaques-Dalcroze in Dresden-Hellerau and Geneva; taught at the Fodor Cons. of Music in Budapest (1912–19) and at the Dalcroze School in Hellerau (1920–25); directed the Hellerau-Laxenburg College in Vienna (1925–38). In 1938 he emigrated to the U.S. and taught at The New School for Social Research in N.Y. (1939–65); then went to Basel. He publ. a textbook on harmony in Hungarian (Budapest, 1914); *Die Improvisation in der Musik* (Zürich, 1938); an anthology of improvised music, *Die Improvisation in Beispielen aus neun Jahrhunderten abendländischer Musik* (Cologne, 1956; 2nd ed., revised, 1961; Eng. trans., 1961); contributed valuable articles to music magazines.

Ferchault, Guy, French musicologist; b. Mer (Loire-et-Cher), Aug. 16, 1904. He studied philosophy and music at the Sorbonne; held teaching positions in music education in Paris, Orléans (1941), Poitiers (1942–49), Tours (1948–51), and Roubaix (from 1952); from 1943–67 he was also a prof. of music history at the Cons. Régional de Musique in Versailles.

WRITINGS: *Henri Duparc, Une Amitié mystique, d'après ses lettres à Francis Jammes* (Paris, 1944); *Les Créatures du drame musical: De Monteverdi à Wagner* (Paris, 1944); *Introduction à l'esthétique de la mélodie* (Gap, 1946); *Claude Debussy, musicien français* (Paris, 1948); *Faust, J.-S. Bach et l'esthétique de son temps* (Zürich, 1950).

Fere, Vladimir, Russian composer and ethnomusicologist; b. Kamyshin, in the Saratov district, May 20, 1902; d. Moscow, Sept. 2, 1971. He studied piano with Goldenweiser and composition with Glière and Miaskovsky at the Moscow Cons. (1921–29). In 1936 he went to Frunze, Kirghizia; composed (in collaboration with Vlasov) a number of operas based on native folk motifs; all these operas were first produced in Frunze: *Golden Girl* (May 1, 1937); *Not Death but Life* (March 26, 1938); *Moon Beauty* (April 15, 1939); *For People's Happiness* (May 1, 1941); *Patriots* (Nov. 6, 1941); *Son of the People* (Nov. 8, 1947); *On the Shores of Issyk-Kul* (Feb. 1, 1951); *Toktogul* (July 6, 1958); *The Witch* (1965); *One Hour before Dawn* (1969). He wrote several symph. pieces on Kirghiz themes; numerous choruses; also chamber music.

Ferencsik, János, eminent Hungarian conductor; b. Budapest, Jan. 18, 1907; d. there, June 12, 1984. He studied organ and music theory at the Budapest Cons.; then served as choral conductor at the Hungarian State Opera. In 1930–31 he was an assistant at the Bayreuth Festival. In 1948–50 he conducted the Vienna State Opera. From 1957 to 1974 he was chief conductor of the Hungarian State Opera, and concurrently led concerts of the Hungarian National Phil. Orch. In 1951 and again in 1961 he was awarded and prestigious Kossuth Prize. In 1958 he undertook a series of tours as a guest conductor in Europe and America. On his 70th birthday, in 1977, the Hungarian government bestowed upon him the Order of the Banner.

Ferenczy, Oto, Slovak composer; b. Brezovice, March 30, 1921. He studied philosophy, esthetics, and musicology at the Comenius Univ. in Bratislava; is mainly self-taught in composition. In 1954 he joined the staff of the Bratislava Academy of Music and Dramatic Arts; in 1962 was appointed its rector. His music is entrenched well within the inoffensive idiom of Central European neo-Classicism; it is expertly crafted.

WORKS: Comic opera, *Nevšedna humoreska (An Uncommon Humoresque;* 1966–67); *Merry-Making,* dance suite for Orch. (1951); *Hurbanovská,* overture (1952); *Serenade* for Harp, Flute, Clarinet, Bassoon, and String Orch. (1955); *Capriccio* for Piano and Orch. (1957); *Elegy* for Orch. (1957); *Finale* for Orch. (1958); *Partita* for Chamber Orch. (1963–65); *Symphonic Prologue* (1975); *The Star of the North,* cantata (1960); *Music* for 4 String Instruments (1947; revised 1973); Concerto for 9 Instruments (1949); String Quartet (1962); Violin Sonata

(1964); Concertino for 12 Instruments (1965); piano pieces; choruses; solo songs.

Ferguson, Donald Nivison, American music educator; b. Waupun, Wisc., June 30, 1882. He studied at the Univ. of Wisconsin (B.A., 1904); then went to London, where he studied composition with Josef Holbrooke and piano with Michael Hambourg. In 1913 he joined the faculty of the Univ. of Minnesota; was named full prof. in 1927; retired in 1950, but returned to teach as prof. emeritus there from 1953 to 1956. Concurrently he was head of the music dept. at Macalester College in Minneapolis (1950–59). From 1930 to 1960 he served as program annotator for the Minneapolis Symph. Orch. He celebrated his centennial in 1982 but, ignoring the connotations of melancholy longevity, persevered in bringing to completion his final book, *The Forgotten Purpose of Music Making.*

WRITINGS: *A History of Musical Thought* (N.Y., 1935; 3rd ed., revised, 1959); *A Short History of Music* (N.Y., 1943); *Piano Music of 6 Great Composers* (N.Y., 1947); *Masterworks of the Orchestral Repertoire* (Minneapolis, 1954); *Music as Metaphor; The Elements of Expression* (Minneapolis, 1960); *Image and Structure in Chamber Music* (Minneapolis, 1964); *The Why of Music* (Minneapolis, 1969).

BIBLIOGRAPHY: J. Slettom, "Donald Ferguson at 100: A Life in Music," *Minnesota Monthly* (Sept. 1982).

Ferguson, Howard, British composer and music editor; b. Belfast, Oct. 21, 1908. He studied composition with R.O. Morris at the Royal College of Music in London; piano with Harold Samuel; conducting with Sargent. From 1948 to 1963 he was a prof. at the Royal Academy of Music in London. His music is neo-Classical in its idiom; in some of his compositions he makes use of English, Scottish, and Irish folk songs.

WORKS: 5 *Irish Folktunes* for Cello or Viola, and Piano (1927); 2 *Ballads* for Baritone, Chorus, and Orch. (1928–32); Violin Sonata No. 1 (1931); 3 *Medieval Carols* for Voice and Piano (1932–33); Octet for Clarinet, Bassoon, Horn, String Quartet, and Double Bass (1933); 5 *Pipe Pieces* for 3 Bamboo Pipes (1934–35); *Partita* for Orch. (1935–36; also for 2 Pianos); 4 *Short Pieces* for Clarinet or Viola and Piano (1932–36); 4 *Diversions on Ulster Airs* for Orch. (1939–42); Flute Sonata (1938–40); 5 *Bagatelles* for Piano (1944); Violin Sonata No. 2 (1946); *Chauntecleer,* ballet (1948); Concerto for Piano and Strings (1950–51; London, May 29, 1952, Myra Hess, soloist); *Discovery* for Voice and Piano (1951); 3 *Sketches* for Flute and Piano (1932–52); 2 *Fanfares* for 4 Trumpets and 3 Trombones (1952); *Overture for an Occasion* for Orch. (1952–53); 5 *Irish Folksongs* for Voice and Piano (1954); *Amore langueo* for Tenor, Chorus, and Orch. (1955–56); *The Dream of the Rood* for Soprano or Tenor, Chorus, and Orch. (1958–59); piano pieces. He edited many old keyboard works, among them those by Purcell (1964) and Blow (1965); also the anthologies *Style and Interpretation* (4 vols., 1963–64), *Early French Keyboard Mu-*

sic (2 vols., 1966); *Early Italian Keyboard Music* (2 vols., 1968); *Early German Keyboard Music* (2 vols., 1970); *Early English Keyboard Music* (1971); also edited *W. Tisdall: Complete Keyboard Works* (London, 1958); with C. Hogwood, *W. Croft: Complete Harpsichord Works* (2 vols., London, 1974); *Anne Cromwell's Virginal Book, 1638* (London, 1974); *F. Schubert, Piano Sonatas* (London, 1979); *Keyboard Works of C.P.E. Bach* (4 vols., London, 1983). BIBLIOGRAPHY: A. Burn, "The Music of Howard Ferguson," *Musical Times* (Aug. 1983).

Ferguson, Maynard, Canadian jazz trumpeter and bandleader; b. Montreal, May 4, 1928. He played violin and piano as a child; then learned to play wind instruments; subsequently studied at the Montreal Cons. He began his career by playing in the bands of Boyd Ferguson, Jimmy Dorsey, Charlie Barnet, and Stan Kenton; in 1956 he formed his own band, and led it until 1967; then spent some time in India and England. He was adept in the pop and the rock genres as well as in traditional jazz.

Fernándes, Armando José, Portuguese composer; b. Lisbon, July 26, 1906. He studied piano with Rey Colaço and Varela Cid, musicology with Freitas Branco, and composition with A.E. da Costa Ferreira at the National Cons. in Lisbon; then went to Paris, where he took piano lessons with Cortot and composition with Nadia Boulanger (1933–36). Returning to Lisbon, he taught composition at the National Cons. WORKS: A ballet, *O homem do cravo* (1941); *Fantasia sobre temas populares portugueses* for Piano and Orch. (1945); Violin Sonata (1946); Violin Concerto (1948); Concerto for Piano and String Orch. (1951); *O terramoto de Lisboa,* symph. poem descriptive of the devastating earthquake of 1765 in Lisbon (1962); *Suite Concertante* for Harpsichord and Chamber Orch. (1967); piano pieces.

Fernandez, Oscar Lorenzo, Brazilian composer; b. Rio de Janeiro, Nov. 4, 1897; d. there, Aug. 26, 1948. He studied music at the Instituto Nacionale de Musica, and appeared as composer, conductor, and pianist in his own works in Brazil and other Latin American countries. He won several prizes. In 1925 he became a prof. at the Instituto Nacionale, and organized a choral society there. In his music he adopted a strongly national style, derived from Brazilian folk songs but without actual quotation. WORKS: Opera, *Malazarte* (Rio de Janeiro, Sept. 30, 1941, composer conducting; ballet on Inca themes, *Amayá* (Rio de Janeiro, July 9, 1939); suite for Orch., *Imbapará* (Rio de Janeiro, Sept. 2, 1929); suite for Orch., *Reisado do pastoreio* (Rio de Janeiro, Aug. 22, 1930; the last movement of this suite, *Batuque,* a Brazilian dance, became popular); Violin Concerto (1942); Symph. (perf. posthumously by the Boston Symph. Orch., Eleazar de Carvalho conducting, Feb. 25, 1949); also a number of chamber music compositions: *Trio Brasileiro* (1924); Suite for Flute, Oboe, Clarinet, Bassoon, and Horn (Rio de Janeiro, Sept. 20, 1927); several piano works; songs.

A complete bibliography of magazine articles on Fernandez is found in Vasco Mariz, *Dicionario Bio-Bibliografico Musical* (Rio de Janeiro, 1948).

Fernández Arbós, Enrique. See **Arbós, Enrique Fernández.**

Fernández Bordas, Antonio, eminent Spanish violinist; b. Orense, Jan. 12, 1870; d. Madrid, Feb. 18, 1950. He studied at the Madrid Cons. with Jesús de Monasterio, and at the age of 11, won first prize for violin students; gave concerts in England, France, and other European countries; returning to Spain, he became a prof. of violin at the Madrid Cons.; in 1921 he was elected director.

Fernández Caballero, Manuel, Spanish composer; b. Murcia, March 14, 1835; d. Madrid, Feb. 20, 1906. He was a precocious musician; learned to play the violin, piano, and piccolo as a child, and at the age of 7, played in a school band. He then studied violin with Soriano Fuertes in Murcia; in 1850 he entered the Madrid Cons., where his teachers were Eslava and Pedro Albéniz; in 1856 he received first prize in composition; then conducted various orchs. and became interested in theatrical composition. During his career as a conductor and composer, he wrote more than 200 zarzuelas, several of which attained great popularity: *Los dineros del Sacristan* and *Los Africanistas* (Barcelona, 1894); *El cabo primero* (Barcelona, 1895); *La rueda de la fortuna* (Madrid, 1896); *Los estudiantes* (Madrid, 1900). He also wrote sacred music.

Ferneyhough, Brian, English composer; b. Coventry, Jan. 16, 1943. He studied at the Birmingham School of Music (1961–63); then took courses with Lennox Berkeley and Maurice Miles at the Royal Academy of Music in London (1966–67); furthermore, received instruction in advanced composition with Ton de Leeuw in Amsterdam and Klaus Huber in Basel (1969–73). In 1971 he was appointed to the faculty at the Hochschule für Musik in Freiburg, Germany; in 1976, 1978, and 1980, lectured at the Darmstadt summer courses. WORKS: *4 Miniatures* for Flute and Piano (1965); *Coloratura* for Oboe and Piano (1966); Sonata for 2 Pianos (1966); *Prometheus* for Wind Sextet (1967); *Sonatas* for String Quartet (1967); *Epicycle* for 20 Strings (Hilversum, Sept. 7, 1969); *Missa Brevis* for 12 Solo Voices (1971); *Firecycle Beta* for Orch., with 5 Conductors (1969–71); *7 Sterne* for Organ (1971); *Time and Motion Study I* for Solo Bass Clarinet (1971–77), *II* for Cello and Electronics (1973–75), and *III* for 16 Solo Voices and Percussion (1974); *Transit* for 6 Amplified Voices and Chamber Orch. (1972–76; London Sinfonietta in Royan, France, March 25, 1975; first British perf., London, Nov. 16, 1977); *Perspectivae Corporum Irregularum* for Oboe, Viola, and Piano (1975); *Unity Capsule* for Solo Flute (1975–76); *Funérailles,* version I, for String Sextet, Double Bass, and Harp (1969–77); *La Terre est un homme* for Orch. (1976–79); *Funérailles,* version II, for 7 Strings and Harp (1980); String Quartet No. 2

(1980); *Lemmacon-Epigram* for Piano (1981); *Superscriptio* for Solo Piccolo (1981); *Carceri d'Invenzione* for Chamber Ensemble (London, Nov. 16, 1982).

Ferni-Giraldoni, Carolina, Italian soprano; b. Como, Aug. 20, 1839; d. Milan, June 4, 1926. She studied violin in Paris and Brussels; later took voice lessons with Pasta; made her debut as Leonora in *La Favorita* in Turin in 1862; sang at La Scala in Milan (1866–68); retired in 1883 and taught voice. She was married to the baritone **Leone Giraldoni;** their son **Eugenio Giraldoni** was the famous baritone; Caruso was one of her pupils.

Fernström, John (Axel), Swedish conductor and composer; b. I-Chang, Hupei, China (the son of a Swedish missionary), Dec. 6, 1897; d. Hälsingborg, Oct. 19, 1961. He studied first at the Cons. in Malmö, then took violin lessons in Copenhagen, where he also studied with P. Gram (1923–30). He took courses in conducting at Sonderhausen, Germany, and later settled in Hälsingborg.
WORKS: An exceptionally prolific composer, he wrote 3 operas: *Achnaton* (1931); *Isissystrarnas bröllop* (1942); *Livet en dröm* (1946); 12 symphs.: No. 1 (1920); No. 2 (1924); No. 3, *Exotica* (1928); No. 4 (1930); No. 5 (1932); No. 6 (1938); No. 7, *Sinfonietta in forma di sonata de chiesa* (1941); No. 8, *Amore studiorum* (1942); No. 9, *Sinfonia breve* (1943); No. 10, *Sinfonia discrète* (1944); No. 11, *Utan mask* (1945); No. 12 (1951); *Symphonic Variations* (1930); 2 violin concertos (No. 2, 1952); Chaconne for Cello and Orch. (1936); Clarinet Concerto (1936); Viola Concerto (1937); Concertino for Flute, Female Chorus, and Small Orch. (1941); Bassoon Concerto (1946); Cello Concertino (1949); *Ostinato* for Strings (1952); Mass for Soli, Chorus, and Orch. (1931); *Stabat Mater* for Soli, Chorus, and Strings (1936); *Songs of the Sea,* suite for Soprano and Strings (1943); *Den mödosamma vä gen,* profane oratorio (1947); 8 string quartets (1920, 1925, 1931, 1942, 1945, 1947, 1950, 1952); many other chamber works; songs and choral works. He publ. an autobiographical book, *Confessions* (1946).

Ferrabosco, Alfonso, Italian composer, son of **Domenico Ferrabosco;** b. Bologna, Jan. (baptized, Jan. 18) 1543; d. there, Aug. 12, 1588. He went to England as a youth; in 1562 he was in the service of Queen Elizabeth; went back to Italy in 1564; was again in England from 1564 to 1569. He lived in France for some time, and married a woman from Antwerp; after another sojourn in England (1572–78) he was in Turin in the service of the Duke of Savoy, whom he accompanied to Spain (1585); eventually he returned to Bologna. The historical position of Alfonso Ferrabosco is important for the influence of Italian music that he brought to the court of Queen Elizabeth. Some of his madrigals are found in Young's *Musica transalpina* (London, 1588, 1597), Morley's *Madrigals to Five Voyces* (London, 1598), Pevernage's *Harmonia celesta* (1593), and other collections up to 1664; further composi-

tions appear in collections of P. Phalèse (1583, 1591, 1593), A. Morsolina (1588), G.B. Besardo (1603), etc. MSS are in the Bodleian Library and Music School at Oxford, British Library, St. Michael's College, Tenbury, and Royal College of Music Library.
BIBLIOGRAPHY: G.E.P. Arkwright, "Un compositore italiano alla corte di Elisabetta, Alfonso Ferrabosco di Bologna," *Rivista Musicale Italiana* (1897); S. Cordero di Pamparato, *Musici alla Corte di Carlo Emanuele I di Savoia* (Turin, 1930); A. Einstein, *The Italian Madrigal* (Princeton, 1949); see also J. Kerman, "Master Alfonso and the English Madrigal," *Musical Quarterly* (April 1952).

Ferrabosco, Alfonso, Italian-English composer, natural son of the preceding; b. Greenwich, England, c.1575; d. there, March (buried, March 11) 1628. He was educated in England, and remained there after his father returned to Italy in 1578. He was supported from the funds of the English court; was one of the King's Musicians for the Violins from about 1602 until his death; was named teacher to the Prince of Wales in 1604. In 1626 he was made Composer of the King's Music; also Composer of Music in Ordinary to the King. He was highly regarded as composer of the music for masques of Ben Jonson, of whom he was a close friend: *The Masque of Blackness* (1604–5); *The Masque of Hymen* (1605–6); *The Masque of Beauty* (1607–8); *The Masque for Lord Haddington's Marriage* (1607–8); and *The Masque of Queens* (1608–9). In 1609 he publ. a vol. of *Ayres* (dedicated to Prince Henry) and a book of *Lessons for 1, 2 and 3 Viols;* also contributed 3 compositions to Leighton's *Teares or Lamentacions* (1614). MSS are in libraries of the British Museum, the Music School and Church, Oxford, and the Royal College of Music. His works for viol demonstrate extraordinary ability in contrapuntal writing, while preserving the rhythmic quality of the dance forms (pavans, etc.) and the free ornamental style of the fantasies.
BIBLIOGRAPHY: G.E.P. Arkwright, "Notes on the Ferrabosco Family," *Musical Antiquary* (July 1912); G. Livi, "The Ferrabosco Family," ibid. (April 1913); J. Duffy, *The Songs and Motets of Alfonso Ferrabosco, the Younger* (Ann Arbor, 1980).

Ferrabosco, Domenico Maria, Italian composer; b. Bologna, Feb. 14, 1513; d. there, Feb. 1574. He was maestro di cappella at San Petronio in Bologna; in 1546 he was at the Vatican, returning to Bologna in 1548; was again at the Vatican from 1550 until 1555; eventually returned to Bologna. He is chiefly known as a composer of madrigals; his book of 45 madrigals, *Il primo libro de' madrigali a 4 voci,* was publ. by Gardano in 1542; Gardano also publ. motets (1554) and other madrigals (1557) by Ferrabosco; some madrigals and a 4-voiced canzona, the latter in lute tablature, appeared in 1584 (publ. by Scotto).

Ferrani, Cesira, Italian soprano; b. Turin, May 8, 1863; d. Pollone, near Biella, May 4, 1943. Her original name was **Cesira Zanaggio.** She studied with Antonietta Fricci in Turin; was chosen to create the roles of Manon Lescaut (1893) and Mimi in *La Bohème* (1896); from 1894 she sang at La Scala in Milan; retired in 1909. In addition to her Italian repertoire, she was also renowned for her Wagnerian roles.

Ferrara, Franco, Italian conductor; b. Palermo, July 4, 1911. He studied piano, violin, organ, and composition at the Cons. of Palermo and Bologna; made his debut as a conductor in Florence in 1938; in 1959 went to the Netherlands, where he gave courses in conducting with the Holland Radio Phil. Among his students was Edo de Waart.

Ferrari, Benedetto, Italian opera librettist and composer, called "Della Tiorba" from his proficiency on the theorbo; b. Reggio, c.1603; d. Modena, Oct. 22, 1681. He studied music in Rome; served as a choirboy at the Collegio Germanico in Rome (1617–18); subsequently was a musician at the Farnese court in Parma (1619–23). In 1637 he proceeded to Venice; there he wrote the libretto for Manelli's opera *L'Andromeda,* produced at the Teatro di San Cassiano in 1637; it was the first opera performed in a theater open to the public. He then wrote libretti for *La Maga fulminata* by Manelli (1638); *L'inganno d'Amore* by Bertoli (Regensburg, 1653); *La Licasta* by Manelli (Parma, 1664); and 4 of his own operas, all produced in Venice: *Armida* (Feb. 1639); *Il Pastor regio* (Jan. 23, 1640), *La Ninfa avara* (1641), and *Il Principe giardiniero* (Dec. 30, 1643). In 1651–53 he was in Vienna. From 1653–62 he served as court choirmaster in Modena; after a hiatus of employment, he was reinstated in 1674, remaining in this post until his death. In Modena he produced the opera *Erosilda* (1658) and 2 cantatas; *Premo il giogo delle Alpi* and *Voglio di vita uscir* (reprinted in Riemann's *Kantaten Frühling,* vol. 1, Leipzig, 1909). Six of Ferrari's libretti were publ. in Milan in 1644 under the title *Poesie drammatiche.*

Ferrari, Carlotta, Italian composer of operas; b. Lodi, Jan. 27, 1837; d. Bologna, Nov. 23, 1907. She studied with Strepponi and Mazzucato at the Milan Cons.; then devoted herself to the composition of operas to her own librettos. The following operas were produced: *Ego* (Milan, 1857), *Sofia* (Lodi, 1866), and *Eleanora d'Armorea* (Cagliari, 1871).

Ferrari, Domenico, Italian composer and violinist; b. Piacenza, c.1722; d. Paris, 1780. He studied with Tartini; traveled as a concert violinist, obtaining great success; in 1753 he joined the orch. of the Duke of Württemberg in Stuttgart; in 1754 he went to Paris, where he became extremely successful; he excelled as a virtuoso; his employment of passages in octaves, and particularly of harmonics, was an innovation at the time. He wrote several sets of violin sonatas and also trio sonatas, which were published.

Ferrari, Gabrielle, French pianist and composer; b. Paris, Sept. 14, 1851; d. there, July 4, 1921. She stud-

ied at the Milan Cons. and later in Paris, where she had lessons with Gounod. She wrote a number of effective piano pieces (*Rapsodie espagnole, Le Ruisseau, Hirondelle,* etc.) and songs (*Larmes en songe, Chant d'exil, Chant d'amour,* etc.); finally ventured to compose operas, producing *Le Dernier Amour* (Paris, June 11, 1895), *Sous le masque* (Vichy, 1898), *Le Tartare* (Paris, 1906), and *Le Cobzar,* which proved to be her most successful opera (Monte Carlo, Feb. 16, 1909; several subsequent revivals).

Ferrari, Giacomo Gotifredo, Italian composer; b. Rovereto, Tyrol (baptized, April 2), 1763; d. London, Dec. 1842. He studied piano at Verona with Marcola and theory with Marianus Stecher at the Monastery of Mariaberg in Switzerland. He then went to Naples, where he studied with Latilla. There he met Chevalier Campan, household master for Marie Antoinette; he was then appointed as court musician at the Tuileries. He arrived in Paris in 1787; after the Revolution he went to London, where he settled as a singing teacher. He produced in London the operas *I due Svizzeri* (May 14, 1799), *Il Rinaldo d'Asti* (March 16, 1802), *L'eroina di Raab* (April 8, 1813), and *Lo sbaglio fortunato* (May 8, 1817); he also wrote 2 ballets and several instrumental works (4 septets, 2 piano concertos, etc.). WRITINGS: *Concise Treatise on Italian Singing* (1818); *Studio di musica pratica, teorica* (1830); and a book of reminiscences, *Anedotti piacevoli ed interressanti* (London, 1830, in Italian; contains some vivid recollections of Haydn and other celebrities; new ed., Palermo, 1920). BIBLIOGRAPHY: D.G. Fino, *Giacomo Gotifredo Ferrari, musicista roveretano* (Trent, 1928); G. de Saint-Foix, "A Musical Traveler," *Musical Quarterly* (Oct. 1939).

Ferrari, Gustave, Swiss pianist and composer; b. Geneva, Sept. 28, 1872; d. there, July 29, 1948. He studied at the Geneva Cons., and later in Paris. In 1900 he went to London, where he remained for many years. From 1917 till 1925 he conducted operetta in America; then returned to Europe and toured with Yvette Guilbert, as her accompanist in a repertoire of French folk songs; later on he gave song recitals himself, singing with his own accompaniment folk songs of France and French Canada; also lectured on the subject, and edited collections of French folk music. As a composer, he wrote mostly incidental music for the stage; composed a cantata for the Rousseau Festival (Geneva, 1912); *The Wilderness,* a Greek dance ballad (London, 1915); other choral works; a song cycle, *Le Livre pour toi.*

Ferrari-Fontana, Edoardo, Italian operatic tenor; b. Rome, July 8, 1878; d. Toronto, Canada, July 4, 1936. As a young man he served in the Italian consulate in South America; also studied singing. Returning to Italy in 1908, he sang in operetta; given a chance to appear as Tristan in Turin (Dec. 23, 1909), he scored a signal success, and in a few years became well known as a principal Italian tenor in Wagner's repertoire. He sang in the U.S. during the 1913–14 season of the Boston Opera Co. and with the Metropolitan Opera in N.Y., and later at the Chicago Opera. In 1926 he settled in Toronto as a singing teacher. He was married (June 26, 1912) to **Margarete Matzenauer,** but they separated after a few years.

Ferrari-Trecate, Luigi, Italian composer; b. Alessandria, Piedmont, Aug. 25, 1884; d. Rome, April 17, 1964. He studied with Antonio Cicognani at the Cons. of Pesaro, and also with Mascagni. Subsequently he was engaged as a church organist; was prof. of organ at the Liceo Musicale in Bologna (1928–31); in 1929–55 was director of the Parma Cons. He wrote several operas which had considerable success: *Pierozzo* (Alessandria, Sept. 15, 1922); *La Bella e il mostro* (Milan, March 20, 1926); *Le astuzie di Bertoldo* (Genoa, Jan. 10, 1934); *Ghirlino* (Milan, Feb. 4, 1940); *Buricchio* (Bologna, Nov. 5, 1948); *L'Orso Re* (Milan, Feb. 8, 1950); *La capanna dello Zio Tom* (*Uncle Tom's Cabin;* Parma, Jan. 17, 1953); *La fantasia tragica; Lo spaventapasseri* (1963); he also wrote music for a marionette play, *Ciottolino* (Rome, Feb. 8, 1922); a sacred cantata, *In hora calvarii* (1956); and *Contemplazioni* for Orch. (1950).

Ferras, Christian, French violinist; b. Le Touquet-Paris-Plage, June 17, 1933; d. Paris, Sept. 15, 1982. He received his musical education in Nice and Paris. He then began his career as a soloist with many European orchs. His performances were marked by stylistic fidelity to the music and a fine virtuosity.

Ferrata, Giuseppe, Italian-American composer; b. Gradoli, Romagna, Jan. 1, 1865; d. New Orleans, March 28, 1928. At the age of 14 he won a scholarship to study at the Santa Cecilia Academy in Rome, where he took courses with Sgambati and Terziani, graduating in 1885; then had the good fortune of benefiting from the last lessons that Liszt gave; in 1892 came to the U.S.; taught at Tulane Univ. in New Orleans. He wrote a Symph., a Piano Concerto, a String Quartet, numerous songs, to Italian and English texts (*Night and the Curtains Drawn, A Song of Thanksgiving, On Music, Alla musa,* etc.); piano pieces (*Humoresque, A Wave, An Eagle, Leonard Serpent, Serenade triste*); compiled a book of scales and *Esthetic Exercises of Technique.*

Ferrer, Mateo, Catalan composer; b. Barcelona, Feb. 25, 1788; d. there, Jan. 4, 1864. A highly gifted musician, he was famous for his improvisations on the organ. He was organist at the Barcelona Cathedral for 52 years, from 1812 until his death. His Sonata (1814), printed by Joaquín Nín in his collection *16 sonates anciennes d'auteurs espagnols* (Paris, 1925), shows a certain affinity with early Beethoven.

Ferrer, Rafael, Spanish conductor; b. St.-Celoni, near Barcelona, May 22, 1911. He studied with Luis

Millet and Enrique Morera (composition) and Eduardo Toldrá (violin). He played the violin in various orchs. in Spain; then devoted himself mainly to conducting. He specializes in Spanish music, and has revived many little-known works of Granados, Turina, and other Spanish composers.

Ferrero, Willy, precocious Italian conductor; b. Portland, Maine, May 21, 1906; d. Rome, March 24, 1954. He was taken to Italy in his infancy; as a child of 6 he conducted a performance at the Teatro Costanzi in Rome; at age 8 he conducted symph. concerts in European capitals with sensational success, and was the object of extravagant praise as a phenomenal musician. World War I interrupted his career; he continued to conduct operas and concerts in Italy, but failed to fulfill the extraordinary promise of his early youth. He received an excellent academic education; studied at the Vienna Academy (graduated in 1924); composed a symph. poem, *Il mistero dell' aurora,* and some chamber music.

BIBLIOGRAPHY: Alberto de Angelis, "Willy Ferrero," *Noi e il Mondo* (Rome, 1919).

Ferretti, Dom Paolo, eminent Italian musicologist; b. Subiaco, Dec. 3, 1866; d. Bologna, May 23, 1938. He studied theology at the Benedictine College of San Anselmo in Rome; then taught in Malta, Genoa, and Parma; was abbot of the Benedictine Monastery of San Giovanni in Parma; in 1922 was appointed by Pope Pius XI director of the Scuola Pontificia (until 1931, when it became the Pontifical Inst. of Sacred Music). During the summers of 1925, 1927, and 1928 he taught courses in Gregorian chant at the Pius X School of Liturgical Music in N.Y. The importance of his investigations lies in a scholarly analysis of the rhythmic treatment and especially the forms of Gregorian chant. He publ. *Principii teorici e practici del Canto Gregoriano* (Rome, 1905); *Il Cursus Metrico e il ritmo delle melodie del Canto Gregoriano* (Rome, 1913); *Estetica gregoriana* (Rome, 1934; also in French, Tournai, 1938).

Ferri, Baldassare, celebrated Italian artificial soprano; b. Perugia, Dec. 9, 1610; d. there, Nov. 18, 1680. At the age of 11 he was choirboy in Orvieto to Cardinal Crescenzio, in whose service he remained until 1625, when he entered the service of Prince Ladislaus of Poland in Warsaw, remaining with him until 1655, with some interruptions for trips to Italy. From 1655 he was in Vienna at the court of Ferdinand III; appeared briefly in London (about 1671); then returned to Italy. His success at the various courts, and with the public in several countries, must have been great, for he accumulated a fortune. According to contemporary accounts (e.g., A. Bontempi, *Historia Musica,* 1695), he possessed a phenomenal voice.

BIBLIOGRAPHY: G. Conestabile, *Notizie biografiche di Baldassare Ferri* (Perugia, 1846); G. Monaldi, *Cantanti evirati celebri* (Rome, 1919).

Ferrier, Kathleen, remarkable English contralto; b. Higher Walton, Lancashire, April 22, 1912; d. London, Oct. 8, 1953. She grew up in Blackburn, where she studied piano; also began voice lessons there with Thomas Duerden; for a time she was employed as a telephone operator. In 1937 she won first prizes for piano and singing at the Carlisle Competition; she then decided on a career as a singer, and subsequently studied voice with J.E. Hutchinson in Newcastle upon Tyne and with Roy Henderson in London. After an engagement as a soloist in the *Messiah* at Westminster Abbey in 1943, she began her professional career in full earnest. Britten chose her to create the title role in his *Rape of Lucretia* (Glyndebourne, July 12, 1946); she also sang Orfeo in Gluck's *Orfeo ed Euridice* there in 1947 and at Covent Garden in 1953. She made her American debut with the N.Y. Phil. on Jan. 15, 1948, singing *Das Lied von der Erde,* with Bruno Walter conducting. She made her American recital debut in N.Y. on March 29, 1949. Toward the end of her brief career, she acquired in England an almost legendary reputation for vocal excellence and impeccable taste, so that her untimely death (from cancer) was greatly mourned. In 1953 she was made a Commander of the Order of the British Empire; she also received the Gold Medal of the Royal Phil. Society.

BIBLIOGRAPHY: N. Cardus, ed., *Kathleen Ferrier, a Memoir* (London, 1955; 2nd ed., revised, 1969); W. Ferrier, *The Life of Kathleen Ferrier* (London, 1955); C. Rigby, *Kathleen Ferrier* (London, 1955); W. Ferrier, *Kathleen Ferrier, Her Life* (London, 1959); P. Lethbridge, *Kathleen Ferrier* (London, 1959).

Ferris, William, American organist, choral conductor, and composer; b. Chicago, Feb. 26, 1937. He studied composition with Alexander Tcherepnin at the De Paul Univ. School of Music (1955–60) and took private lessons with Leo Sowerby in Chicago (1957–62). In 1960 he founded the William Ferris Chorale, specializing in the music of the Renaissance and that of 20th-century composers. He served as organist of Holy Name Cathedral in Chicago (1954–58, 1962–64) and as director of music at Sacred Heart Cathedral in Rochester, N.Y. (1966–71); in 1973 he joined the faculty of the American Cons. of Music in Chicago. His compositions are mostly liturgical.

WORKS: *Concert Piece* for Trumpet, Horn, and String Orch. (1960); *October–November,* symph. movement (1962; Rochester, Nov. 6, 1968); *Concert Piece* for Organ and String Orch. (1963; Boston Symph., Worcester, Mass., Nov. 19, 1967); *Celebrations,* overture (1966); Trio for Flute, Bassoon, and Piano (1957); String Trio (1958); Piano Sonata (1976). Vocal works: *De Profundis* (Fordham Univ., Nov. 22, 1964); *Ed e subito sera,* solo cantata for Tenor and String Quartet (1965); *The Angelic Salutation: Glory to God in the Highest* for Chorus, Organ, and Orch. (Rochester, Nov. 6, 1968); *Durobrivae,* music for Tenors, Basses, 5 Brasses, and Kettledrums (1970); *A Canticle of Celebration* for Chorus, Brasses, and Kettledrums (1971); *Make We Joy,* cantata (Chicago, Dec. 12, 1976); *A Song of Light,* cantata (Chicago, Oct. 11, 1977); *Acclamations* for Organ and Orch. (1981–82; Chicago, Jan. 27, 1983); numerous works for chorus and organ; a cappella

choruses; songs.

Ferroni, Vincenzo Emidio Carmine, Italian composer and educator; b. Tramutola, Feb. 17, 1858; d. Milan, Jan. 10, 1934. He studied at the Paris Cons. (1876–83) with Savard and Massenet; in 1888 returned to Italy, where he became a prof. of composition at the Milan Cons., succeeding Ponchielli; resigned in 1929. He wrote 3 operas: *Rudello* (Milan, 1892); *Ettore Fieramosca* (Como, 1896); *Il Carbonaro* (Milan, 1900); 2 symphs.; a symph. poem, *Risorgimento;* many works in smaller forms.

Ferroud, Pierre-Octave, French composer; b. Chasselay, near Lyons, Jan. 6, 1900; d. near Debrecen, Hungary (killed in an automobile accident), Aug. 17, 1936. He attended the Univ. of Lyons, and studied there and in Strasbourg with Erb, Ropartz, Witkowski, and Florent Schmitt; in 1923 settled in Paris, where he developed varied activities as a composer, music critic, and adviser for radio broadcasting. He first attracted attention with the performance of his ballet *Le Porcher* (Ballets Suédois, Paris, Nov. 15, 1924); there followed the symph. poem *Foules* (Paris, March 21, 1926); an operatic sketch, *Chirurgie,* after Chekhov (Monte Carlo, March 20, 1928); and Symph. in A (Paris, March 8, 1931, Monteux conducting; also at the Prague Festival of the International Society for Contemporary Music, Sept. 6, 1935); other works are the ballets *Jeunesse* (Paris, April 29, 1933) and *Vénus ou L'Equipée planétaire* (1935); Cello Sonata (1933); *Andante cordial* for Violin, Cello, and Piano; Trio for Oboe, Clarinet, and Bassoon (1934); also several song cycles and piano pieces. Ferroud's music is distinguished by an adroit application of contrapuntal methods to compositions of an essentially popular style; his chief influence was Florent Schmitt, about whom he wrote a book, *Autour de Florent Schmitt* (Paris, 1927).

BIBLIOGRAPHY: René Dumesnil, "Pierre-Octave Ferroud," *Revue Musicale* (Oct.–Nov. 1931).

Fesca, Alexander Ernst, German pianist and composer, son of **Friedrich Ernst Fesca;** b. Karlsruhe, May 22, 1820; d. Braunschweig, Feb. 22, 1849. He studied with his father, and later with Taubert. He was extremely successful as a concert pianist in 1839; in 1841 he became chamber musician to Prince Fürstenberg; settled in Braunschweig in 1842, where he brought out his operas *Der Troubadour* (July 25, 1847) and *Ulrich von Hutten* (1849); he also wrote a piano sextet, 2 piano trios, a violin sonata, and many songs, some of which became popular. His early death at the age of 28 was regretted by many admirers who believed that he was a composer of uncommon talent.

Fesca, Friedrich Ernst, German composer; b. Magdeburg, Feb. 15, 1789; d. Karlsruhe, May 24, 1826. He studied violin; made a debut in his own Violin Concerto; in 1806 he joined the orch. of the Duke of Oldenburg; in 1808 he obtained a similar position at the Westphalian court at Kassel; in 1813 he was in

Vienna; in 1814 became a member of the Karlsruhe Orch. He was a prolific composer of chamber music (20 quartets and 5 quintets); also wrote 2 operas, *Cantemire* (Karlsruhe, April 27, 1820) and *Omar und Leila* (Karlsruhe, Feb. 26, 1824); 3 symphs.; 4 overtures; etc.

Fesch, Willem de, Flemish organist; b. Alkmaar, Aug. 25, 1687; d. London, Jan. 3, 1761. He was organist at Antwerp; in 1731 went to London, where he produced his oratorios *Judith* (1733) and *Joseph* (1745).
   BIBLIOGRAPHY: F. van den Bremt, *Willem de Fesch, Nederlands Componist en Virtuoos* (Louvain, 1949).

Festa, Costanzo, Italian composer; b. Rome, c.1480; d. there, April 10, 1545. He was a singer in the Pontifical Chapel from about 1517. He was a composer of much importance, being regarded as a forerunner of Palestrina, whose works were strongly influenced by those of Festa; was the first important Italian musician who successfully fused the Flemish and Italian styles, melodically and harmonically. He may well be considered one of the first, if not the first, of the native Italian madrigalists. The earliest known publ. work of his appeared in 1519. Of his numerous compositions, many sacred works were publ. in various collections from 1513 till 1549; a *Te Deum a 4* (publ. in Rome, 1596) is still sung in the Vatican on solemn festivals. A complete list of Festa's works, together with reprints, is found in A. Cametti's "Per un precursore del Palestrina: Il compositore piemontese Costanzo Festa," *Bollettino Bibliografico Musicale* (April 1931); also, A. Main edited *Costanzo Festa, Opera omnia,* in Corpus Mensurabilis Musicae, XXV (1962–68).

Festing, Michael Christian, English violinist; b. London, c.1680; d. there, July 24, 1752. He was a pupil of Richard Jones and Geminiani. In 1735 he joined the king's private band and became first violin in an amateur group called the Phil. Society; in 1737, was appointed director of the Italian Opera; in 1742, conductor at Ranelagh Gardens. In 1738 he established, with Dr. Greene and others, the Society of Musicians, for the maintenance of impoverished musicians and their families. He wrote numerous solos and concertos for violin; 18 sonatas for violins and bass; cantatas; songs.

Fétis, Edouard-Louis François, Belgian music editor, son of **François-Joseph Fétis;** b. Bouvignes, near Dinant, May 16, 1812; d. Brussels, Jan. 31, 1909. He edited his father's *La Revue Musicale* (1833–35); was for years librarian of the Brussels Library. He publ. *Les Musiciens belges* (1848) and *Les Artistes belges à l'étranger* (1857–65), and compiled a catalogue of his father's library. His brother, **Adolphe-Louis-Eugène Fétis** (b. Paris, Aug. 20, 1820; d. there, March 20, 1873), was a pupil of his father, and of Herz (piano); lived in Brussels and Antwerp, and from 1856 in Paris as a music teacher. He composed music for piano and harmonium.

Fétis, François-Joseph, erudite Belgian musical theorist, historian, and critic; b. Mons, March 25, 1784; d. Brussels, March 26, 1871. He received primary instruction from his father, an organist at the Mons Cathedral; learned to play the violin, piano, and organ when very young, and in his 9th year wrote a Concerto for Violin, with Orch.; as a youth, was organist to the Noble Chapter of Sainte-Waudru. In 1800 he entered the Paris Cons., where he studied harmony with Rey and piano with Boieldieu and Pradher; in 1803 he visited Vienna, there studying counterpoint, fugue, and masterworks of German music. Several of his compositions (a symph., an overture, sonatas and caprices for piano) were publ. at that time. In 1806 Fétis began the revision of the plainsong and entire ritual of the Roman Church, a vast undertaking, completed, with many interruptions, after 30 years of patient research. A wealthy marriage in the same year, 1806, enabled him to pursue his studies at ease for a time; but the fortune was lost in 1811, and he retired to the Ardennes, where he occupied himself with composition and philosophical researches into the theory of harmony; in 1813 he was appointed organist for the collegiate church of St.-Pierre at Douai. In 1818 he settled in Paris; in 1821 became a prof. of composition at the Paris Cons.; in 1824 his *Traité du contrepoint et de la fugue* was publ. and accepted as a regular manual at the Cons. In 1827 he became librarian of the Cons., and in the same year founded his unique journal *La Revue Musicale,* which he edited alone until 1832; his son edited it from 1833 until 1835, when its publication ceased. Fétis also wrote articles on music for *Le National* and *Le Temps.* In 1828 he competed for the prize of the Netherlands Royal Inst. with the treatise *Quels ont été les mérites des Néerlandais dans la musique, principalement aux XIVᵉ–XVIᵉ siècles . . . ;* Kiesewetter's essay on the same subject won, but Fétis's paper was also printed by the Inst. In 1832 he inaugurated his famous series of historical lectures and concerts. In 1833 he was called to Brussels as maître de chapelle to King Leopold I, and director of the Cons.; during his long tenure in the latter position, nearly 40 years, the Cons. flourished as never before. He also conducted the concerts of the Academy, which elected him a member in 1845. Fétis was a confirmed believer in the possibility of explaining music history and music theory scientifically; in his scholarly writings he attempted a thorough systematization of all fields of the art; he was opinionated and dogmatic, but it cannot be denied that he was a pioneer in musicology. He publ. the first book on music appreciation, *La Musique mise à la portée de tout le monde* (Paris, 1830; numerous reprints and translations into Eng., German, Italian, Spanish, Russian); further pedagogical writings are: *Solfèges progressifs* (Paris, 1837); *Traité complet de la théorie et de la pratique de l'harmonie* (Brussels, 1844). As early as 1806 Fétis began collecting materials for his great *Biographie universelle des musiciens et bibliographie générale de la musique* in 8 vols. (Paris, 1833–44; 2nd ed., 1860–65; supplement of 2 vols., 1878–80; edited by A. Pougin). This work of musical biography was unprecedented in its scope; entries on composers and performers whom Fétis knew personally still remain prime sources of information. On the negative side are the many fanciful accounts of composers' lives taken from unreliable sources; in this respect Fétis exercised a harmful influence on subsequent lexicographers for a whole century. His *Histoire générale de la musique,* in 5 vols., goes only as far as the 15th century (Paris, 1869–76); this work exhibits Fétis as a profound scholar, but also as a dogmatic philosopher of music propounding opinions without convincing evidence to support them. Of interest are his *Esquisse de l'histoire de l'harmonie considerée comme art et comme science systématique* (Paris, 1840); *Notice biographique de Nicolo Paganini* (Paris, 1851; with a short history of the violin); *Antoine Stradivari* (Paris, 1856; with a commentary on bowed instruments); reports on musical instruments at the Paris Expositions of 1855 and 1867; etc. Fétis was also a composer; between 1820 and 1832 he wrote 7 operas, serious and light, for the Opéra-Comique; composed church music, 3 string quartets, 3 string quintets, 2 symphs., and a Flute Concerto. His valuable library of 7,325 vols. was acquired after his death by the Bibliothèque Royale of Brussels; a catalogue was publ. in 1877.

BIBLIOGRAPHY: K. Gollmick, *Herr Fétis, Vorstand des Brüsseler Conservatoriums als Mensch, Kritiker, Theoretiker und Komponist* (Leipzig and Brussels, 1852); L. Alvin, *Notice sur François-Joseph Fétis* (Brussels, 1874); R. Wangermée, *F.-J. Fétis, musicologue et compositeur* (Brussels, 1951); B. Huys et al., *F.-J. Fétis et la vie musicale de son temps: 1784–1871* (Brussels, 1972).

Fetler, Paul, American composer; b. Philadelphia, Feb. 17, 1920. His family moved to Europe when Fetler was a child, and he had early musical studies in Latvia, Holland, Sweden, and Switzerland. He returned to the U.S. in 1939 and studied composition with Van Vactor at Northwestern Univ., graduating in 1943. He studied briefly with Celibidache in Berlin (1945–46) and, returning to the U.S., with Quincy Porter and Hindemith and Yale Univ. (1946–48). In 1948 he was appointed a teacher at the Univ. of Minnesota and in 1960 became a prof. there. His numerous awards include two Guggenheim grants (1953, 1960) and National Endowment grants (1975, 1977).

WORKS: An opera for youth, *Sturge Maclean* (St. Paul, Oct. 11, 1965); *Passacaglia* for Orch. (1942); 4 Symphs. (1948, 1951, 1954, 1968); Suite for Orch. (1950); *A Comedy Overture* (1952); *Gothic Variations,* after a Machaut theme, for Orch. (1953); *Of Earth's Image* for Chorus, Orch., and Solo Soprano (Minneapolis, May 2, 1958); *Contrasts* for Orch. (Minneapolis, Nov. 7, 1958); *Nothing but Nature,* comedy cantata after Ogden Nash, for Chorus and Small Orch. (St. Paul, Feb. 12, 1961); *Soundings* for Orch. (1962); *Cantus Tristis,* in memory of J.F.K., for Orch. (1964); *This Was the Way,* a sacred cantata (Minneapolis, May 7, 1969); Violin Concerto (St. Paul, March 27, 1971); *3 Poems by Walt Whitman* for Narrator and Orch. (1975); *Celebration* for

Orch. (1976); *3 Impressions* for Guitar and Orch. (1977; Minneapolis, May 31, 1978); *Song of the Forest Bird* for Chorus and Orch. (1978; Rochester, N.Y., Feb. 11, 1979); Sextet for Clarinet, Horn, and Strings (1942); String Quartet (1947); Violin Sonata (1950); *3 Pieces* for Violin and Piano (1952); *Belloc's Beasts* for Soprano, Baritone, and Piano (1959); *A Contemporary Psalm,* dedicated to Martin Luther King, Jr., for Chorus, Soprano, Baritone, Organ, and Percussion (1968); *Cycles* for Percussion and Piano (1970); *Lamentations* for Chorus, Narrator, Flute, Piccolo, Organ, and Percussion (1973); *Dialogue* for Flute and Guitar (1973); *Pastoral Suite* for Piano Trio (1976); *5 Piano Games* for Piano (1979); *6 Songs of Autumn* for Guitar (1979).

Feuermann, Emanuel, greatly gifted Austrian-born American cellist; b. Kolomea, Galicia, Nov. 22, 1902; d. New York, May 25, 1942. As a child he was taken to Vienna where he first studied cello with his father; subsequently studied cello with Friedrich Buxbaum and Anton Walter; made his debut in Vienna in 1913 in a recital. He went to Leipzig in 1917 to continue his studies with Julius Klengel; his progress was so great that he was appointed to the faculty of the Gürzenich Cons. in Cologne by Abendroth at the age of 16; he also was first cellist in the Gürzenich Orch. and was a member of the Bram Eldering Quartet. In 1929 he was appointed prof. at the Hochschule für Musik in Berlin; as a Jew he was forced to leave Germany after the advent of the Nazis to power; he then embarked on a world tour (1934–35). He made his American debut on Dec. 6, 1934, with the Chicago Symph. Orch.; then appeared as soloist with many of the leading American orchs.; also played chamber music with Schnabel and Huberman, and later with Rubinstein and Heifetz.

BIBLIOGRAPHY: David Ewen, *Musicians since 1900* (N.Y., 1978); S. Itzkoff, *Emanuel Feuermann, Virtuoso: A Biography* (University of Ala., 1979).

Fevin, Antoine de, French composer; b. probably in Arras, 1474; d. Blois, Jan. 1512. He was a younger contemporary of Josquin des Prez, whose style he emulated. He composed 12 masses, 6 of which were printed in collections by Petrucci (1515) and Antico (1516); also 29 motets, 3 Magnificats, and Lamentations (publ. by Montanus in 1549); 3 works by Fevin are in the archives of Toledo Cathedral (cf. F. Rubio Piqueras, *Música y músicos toledanos,* 1923); 6 motets were printed in Petrucci's *Motetti della corona* (1514), and some French chansons in various collections. Fevin's mass *Mente tota* is reprinted in Expert's *Maîtres musiciens* (vol. 5); a 6-voice motet and parts of masses are in Eslava's *Lira sacro-hispana;* a 4-voice *Kyrie* in Burney's *General History of Music* (vol. 2); the mass *Ave Maria* and *Benedictus et Hosanna* is in Delporte's *Collection de polyphonie classique;* several motets were reprinted by B. Kahmann (Amsterdam, 1951).

BIBLIOGRAPHY: P. Wagner, in *Geschichte der Messe* (vol. I); J. Delporte, *Revue Liturgique et Musicale* (Jan.–Feb. 1935); E. Clinkscale, *The Com-*

plete Works of Antoine de Fevin (Diss., N.Y. Univ., 1965).

Fevin, Robert, French composer; a native of Cambrai, probably a relative of **Antoine de Fevin.** He was maestro di cappella to the Duke of Savoy at the beginning of the 16th century. One mass, *Le Vilain jaloux,* probably by Robert Fevin, was printed by Petrucci as by Antoine Fevin; another, on *La sol fa re mi,* is in the Munich Library.

Février, Henri, French opera composer; b. Paris, Oct. 2, 1875; d. there, July 6, 1957. He studied at the Paris Cons. with Fauré, Leroux, Messager, Pugno, and Massenet; composed the operas *Le Roi aveugle* (Paris, May 8, 1906); *Monna Vanna* (Paris, Jan. 13, 1909); *Gismonda* (Chicago, Jan. 14, 1919; Paris, Oct. 15, 1919); *La Damnation de Blanche-Fleur* (Monte Carlo, March 13, 1920); *La Femme nue* (Monte Carlo, March 23, 1929); operettas: *Agnès, dame galante* (1912); *Carmosine* (1913); *Ile désenchantée* (Paris, Nov. 21, 1925); etc. Février wrote the monograph *André Messager; Mon maître, mon ami* (Paris, 1948).

Ffrangcon-Davies, David Thomas (real name, **David Thomas Davis;** the surname Ffrangcon was taken from the Nant-Ffrangcon mountain range near his birthplace), prominent British baritone; b. Bethesda, Caernarvon, Wales, Dec. 11, 1855; d. London, April 13, 1918. He was ordained a priest in 1884, but later left the church to take up a musical career; studied singing with Richard Latter, Shakespeare, and Randegger in London; made his concert debut in Manchester (Jan. 6, 1890), his stage debut at Drury Lane Theatre (April 26, 1890). In 1896–98, he sang in festivals throughout the U.S. and Canada; then lived in Berlin (1898–1901); from 1903, he was a prof. of singing at the Royal College of Music in London. After a nervous breakdown in 1907 he gave up public singing. His book, *The Singing of the Future* (London, 1905; preface by Elgar), was republ. by his daughter, Marjorie Ffrangcon-Davies, as Part II of *David Ffrangcon-Davies, His Life and Book* (London, 1938; introduction by Ernest Newman).

Fiala, George, Russian-born Canadian composer; b. Kiev, March 31, 1922. He took piano lessons at the music school for gifted children in Kiev; then studied composition at the Kiev Cons. with Revutsky, Liatoshinsky, and others (1939–41). When the Germans occupied Kiev in 1942, he went to Berlin, where he continued his studies despite wartime difficulties; also took courses in conducting with Furtwängler. In 1945 he moved to Belgium, where he became a student of Léon Jongen at the Brussels Cons. In 1949 he emigrated to Canada; settled in Montreal; became a Canadian citizen in 1955. Besides his activities as a composer, pianist, and teacher, he also became a music producer with the Russian section of Radio-Canada International. His compositions still retain traces of Russian and Ukrainian modalities; the settings are formally in a Classical vein.

WORKS: Piano Concerto (1946); *Autumn Music* for Orch. (1949); Symph. in E minor (1950); Concertino for Solo Piano, Trumpet, Timpani, and Strings (1950); *Suite concertante* for Oboe and Strings (1956); *Introduction and Fugato* for English Horn and Strings (1961); *Capriccio* for Piano and Orch. (1962); *Shadows of Our Forgotten Ancestors,* symph. poem (1962); *Divertimento concertante* for Violin and Orch. (1965); *Eulogy,* in memory of President Kennedy, for Orch. (1965); *Canadian Credo* for Chorus and Orch. (1966); *Montréal,* symph. suite (1968); *Musique concertante* for Piano and Orch. (1968); *Serenada concertante* for Cello and Strings (1968); *Sinfonietta concertata* for Solo Free-bass Accordion, Harpsichord, and Strings (1971); *Overture Burlesque* (1972); *5 Ukrainian Songs* for Voice and Orch. (1973); Violin Concerto (1973); Symph. No. 4, *Ukrainian* (1973; Toronto, Nov. 21, 1982); *Ukrainian Suite* for Cello and Piano (1948); Wind Quintet (1948); Trio for Oboe, Cello, and Piano (1948); Woodwind Octet (1948); 2 saxophone quartets (1955, 1961); String Quartet (1956); Quartet for 4 Cellos (1957); Piano Quartet (1957); Violin Sonatina (1959); Cello Sonata (1969); Violin Sonata (1969); *Musique à trois* for String Trio (1970); Saxophone Sonata (1970); *Duo Sonata* for Violin and Harp (1971); *Sonata Fantasia* for Cello and Piano (1971); *Sonata da camera* for Soprano Saxophone and Free Bass Accordion (1971); *Musique à quatre* for String Quartet (1972); *Concertino canadese* for 4 Harps (1972); *Sonata breve* for Clarinet and Harp (1972); Piano Quintet (1982); 8 piano sonatas (No. 7, 1947; No. 8, 1970); *10 Postludes* for Piano (1947; revised 1968); *Australian Suite* for Piano (1963); *3 Bagatelles* for Piano (1968); 2-piano Sonata (1970).

Fibich, Zdenko (Zdeněk), significant Czech composer; b. Seboriče, Dec. 21, 1850; d. Prague, Oct. 15, 1900. He studied first in Prague, then at the Leipzig Cons. with Moscheles (piano) and Richter (theory). Upon his return to Prague, he occupied the posts of deputy conductor and choirmaster at the Provisional Theater (1875–78) and director of the Russian Church choir (1878–81). From then on, he continued to live in Prague, devoting himself mainly to composition. In his music, he was greatly influenced by Wagner, and applied quasi-Wagnerian methods even when treating national Bohemian subjects. His main distinction was a gift for facile melody, and he was at his best in his short pieces, such as *Poème,* op. 41, no. 6, for piano, which has become extremely popular through many arrangements for various instrumental combinations.

WORKS: Operas (produced at Prague): *Bukovín* (April 16, 1874); *Blaník* (Nov. 25, 1881); *Nevěsta Messinská* (*The Bride of Messina;* March 28, 1884; very popular); *Bouře* (*The Tempest;* March 1, 1895); *Hědy,* after Byron's *Don Juan* (Feb. 12, 1896); *Šárka* (Dec. 28, 1897); *Pad Arkuna* (*The Fall of Arkun;* produced posthumously, Nov. 9, 1900; his most important work); music to the dramatic trilogy *Hippodamia* by Vrchlický, a sequence of 3 scenic melodramas with actors reciting to orch. accompaniment: *Námluvy, Pelopovy* (*The Wooing of Pelops;* Feb. 21, 1890); *Smír Tantalúv* (*The Atonement of Tantalus;* June 2, 1891); *Smrt Hippodamie* (*Hippodamia's Death;* Nov. 8, 1891). For Orch.: 3 symphs.: No. 1 (1883); No. 2 (1893); No. 3, in E minor (1898); symph. poems: *Othello* (1873); *Zaboj, Slavoj a Luděk* (1873); *Toman a lesni panna* (*Toman and the Wood Nymph;* 1875); *Bouře* (*The Tempest;* 1880); *Vesna* (*Spring;* 1881); *Vigiliae* for Small Orch. (1883); *V podvečeř* (*At Twilight;* 1893); choral ballad, *Die Windsbraut;* melodramas: *Stědrý den* (*Christmas Day;* 1875); *Vodník* (*The Water Sprite;* 1883); *Hákon* (1888); *Věčnost* (*Eternity;* 1878); *Spring Romanza* for Chorus and Orch. (1880); 2 string quartets; Piano Quartet; *Romance* for Violin and Piano; piano pieces; songs; choruses. He also publ. a method for piano.

BIBLIOGRAPHY: C.L. Richter, *Zdenko Fibich* (Prague, 1899); Z. Nejedlý, *Fibich* (Prague, 1900); O. Hostinský, *Erinnerungen an Fibich* (1909); J. Bartoš, *Zdenko Fibich* (1913); A. Rektorys, *Zdenko Fibich* (2 vols., Prague, 1952).

Ficher, Jacobo, Russian-Argentine composer; b. Odessa, Jan. 14, 1896; d. Buenos Aires, Sept. 9, 1978. He studied violin with Stolarsky and Korguev in Odessa and composition with Kalafati and Steinberg at the St. Petersburg Cons., graduating in 1917. In 1923 he left Russia and emigrated to Argentina. In 1956 he was appointed prof. of composition at the National Cons. of Music in Buenos Aires. His music is characterized by a rhapsodic fluency of development and a rich harmonic consistency. A prolific composer, he wrote for the stage, for orch., and for voice; he particularly excelled in chamber music. WORKS: FOR THE STAGE: Chamber operas: *The Bear* (1952) and *Proposal in Marriage* (1955), both after Chekhov; ballets: *Colombina de Hoy* (1933); *Los Invitados* (1933); *Golondrina* (1942). FOR ORCH.: 8 symphs. (1932, 1933, 1940, 1946, 1947, 1956, 1959, 1964); *Sulamita,* symph. poem (Buenos Aires, July 20, 1929); *Obertura patética* (Buenos Aires, May 17, 1930); Violin Concerto (1942); 3 piano concertos (1945, 1954, 1960); Harp Concerto (1956); Flute Concerto (1965). CHAMBER MUSIC: 4 string quartets (1927, 1936, 1943, 1952); Piano Quintet (1961); Wind Quintet (1967); 3 violin sonatas (1929, 1945, 1959); *Suite en estilo antiguo* for Woodwind Quintet (1930); Sonata for Viola, Flute, and Piano (1931); Sonatina for Saxophone, Trumpet, and Piano (1932); Piano Trio (1935); Flute Sonata (1935); Clarinet Sonata (1937); Oboe Sonata (1940); Cello Sonata (1943); Sonata for Flute and Clarinet (1949); Sonata for Flute, Oboe, and Bassoon (1950); Viola Sonata (1953); 8 piano sonatas; several sets of piano pieces (including 2 groups of effective "fables," descriptive of animals). CANTATAS: *Salmo de alegría* (1949); *Mi aldea* (1958); *Kadisch* (1969).

BIBLIOGRAPHY: B. Zipman, *Jacobo Ficher* (Buenos Aires, 1966).

Fickenscher, Arthur, American composer and pianist; b. Aurora, Ill., March 9, 1871; d. San Francisco, April 15, 1954. He studied at the Munich Cons.; toured the U.S. as accompanist to famous singers, among them Bispham and Schumann-Heink. From 1920 till 1941 he was head of the music dept. of the Univ. of Virginia, Charlottesville. In 1947 he settled in San Francisco. A musician of an inquisitive mind, he elaborated a system of pure intonation; contrived the "Polytone," an instrument designed to play music in which the octave is subdivided into 60 tones; publ. an article, "The Polytone and the Potentialities of a Purer Intonation," *Musical Quarterly* (July 1941).

WORKS: His major work was the *Evolutionary Quintet,* evolved from a violin sonata and an orch. scherzo written in the 1890s; the MSS were burned in the San Francisco earthquake and fire of 1906; the musical material was then used from memory for a quintet for piano and strings, in 2 movements; the 2nd movement, entitled *The 7th Realm,* became a separate work. He also wrote *Willowwave and Welloway* for Orch. (1925); *The Day of Judgment* for Orch. (1927; Grand Rapids, Feb. 10, 1934); *Out of the Gay Nineties* for Orch. (Richmond, Va., Dec. 4, 1934, composer conducting); *Variations on a Theme in Medieval Style* for String Orch. (1937); *Dies Irae* for Chamber Orch. (1927); *The Chamber Blue,* mimodrama for Orch., Soli, Women's Chorus, and Dancers (Univ. of Virginia, April 5, 1938); large choral work, with Orch., *The Land East of the Sun and West of the Moon* (after William Morris).

Ficker, Rudolf von, distinguished German musicologist; b. Munich, June 11, 1886; d. Igls, near Innsbruck, Aug. 2, 1954. In 1905–12 he studied at the Univ. of Vienna with Adler (musicology), and in Munich with Thuille and Courvoisier (composition); received his Ph.D. from the Univ. of Vienna with the dissertation *Die Chromatik im italienischen Madrigal des 16. Jahrhunderts.* He taught at the Univ. of Innsbruck from 1920; became a prof. there in 1923; at the Univ. of Vienna in 1927; and in 1931 at the Univ. of Munich. He was a specialist in early Gothic music.

WRITINGS: "Die Musik des Mittelalters und ihre Beziehungen zum Geistesleben," *Vierteljahrsschrift für Literaturwissenschaft und Geistesgeschichte* (1925); "Polyphonic Music of the Gothic Period," *Musical Quarterly* (Oct. 1929); "Agwillare, A Piece of Late Gothic Minstrelsy," *Musical Quarterly* (April 1936); "Probleme der modalen Notation," *Acta Musicologica* (1946). He edited vol. XXVII, 1 (4th selection from the Trent Codices; in collaboration with A. Orel) and vol. XXXI (5th selection) Denkmäler der Tonkunst in Österreich; likewise the *Sederunt principes* of Pérotin (1930).

Fiedler, Arthur, highly popular American conductor; b. Boston, Dec. 17, 1894; d. Brookline, Mass., July 10, 1979. Of a musical family, he studied violin with his father, **Emanuel Fiedler,** a member of the Boston Symph. Orch.; his uncle, **Benny Fiedler,** also played violin in the Boston Symph. In 1909 Fiedler was taken by his father to Berlin, where he studied violin with Willy Hess, and attended a class of chamber music with Ernst von Dohnányi; he also had some instruction in conducting with Arno Kleffel and Rudolf Krasselt. In 1913 he formed in Berlin the Fiedler Trio with 2 other Fiedlers. In 1915, with the war raging in Europe, Fiedler returned to America, and joined the 2nd-violin section of the Boston Symph. Orch. under Karl Muck; later he moved to the viola section; he also doubled on the celesta, when required. In 1924 he organized the Arthur Fiedler Sinfonietta, a professional ensemble of members of the Boston Symph. In 1929 he started a series of free open-air summer concerts at the Esplanade on the banks of the Charles River in Boston, presenting programs of popular American music intermingled with classical numbers. The series became a feature in Boston's musical life, attracting audiences of many thousands each summer. In 1930 Fiedler was engaged as conductor of the Boston Pops, which he led for nearly half a century. Adroitly combining pieces of popular appeal with classical works and occasional modern selections, Fiedler built an eager following, eventually elevating the Boston Pops to the status of a national institution. He was seemingly undisturbed by the clinking of beer steins, the pushing of chairs, the shuffling of feet, and other incidental sound effects not provided for in the score but which were an integral part of audience participation at Pops concerts. For Fiedler was a social man, gregarious, fond of extracurricular activities; one of his favorite pastimes was riding on fire engines; this addiction was rewarded by a number of nominations as honorary chief of the fire depts. of several American cities. He became commercially successful and willingly accepted offers to advertise for whisky or for orange juice ("that is not only for breakfast anymore"); this popularity, however, cost him a degradation to a lower rank of music-makers, so that his cherished ambition to conduct guest engagements in the regular subscription series of the Boston Symph. Orch. never materialized. On Jan. 4, 1977, President Gerald Ford bestowed upon him the Medal of Freedom. As a mark of appreciation from the city of Boston, a footbridge near the Esplanade was named after him, with the first 2 notes of the Prelude to *Tristan and Isolde,* A and F, marking the initials of Arthur Fiedler's name, engraved on the plaque. His death was mourned by Boston music-lovers in a genuine outpouring of public grief.

BIBLIOGRAPHY: R. Moore, *Fiedler, The Colorful Mr. Pops* (Boston, 1968); C.G. Wilson, *Arthur Fiedler, Music for the Millions* (N.Y., 1968); J.R. Holland, *Mr. Pops* (N.Y., 1972); H.E. Dickson, *Arthur Fiedler and the Boston Pops* (Boston, 1981).

Fiedler, Max, German conductor; b. Zittau, Dec. 31, 1859; d. Stockholm, Dec. 1, 1939. He was a piano pupil of his father, and studied the organ and theory with G. Albrecht; attended the Leipzig Cons. (1877–80). In 1882 he was appointed a teacher at the Hamburg Cons.; in 1903, became its director. In 1904 he succeeded Barth as conductor of the Hamburg Phil. Society; remained there until 1908. Although he had won an enviable reputation as a concert pianist, he soon abandoned that career and rapidly won distinction as a conductor. He was guest conductor of the N.Y. Phil. Orch. during the season of 1905–6; in 1907, conducted the London Symph. Orch. The climax of his career was the prestigious appointment as conductor of the Boston Symph. Orch., the position he held from 1908 to 1912. In 1916 he was named music director in Essen, Germany; after 1933 appeared as conductor with the Berlin Phil. and the Berlin Radio. In 1934 he conducted in Sweden. He composed a Symph., a Piano Quintet, a String Quartet, a *Lustspiel* overture, piano pieces, and songs.

BIBLIOGRAPHY: G. Dejmek, *Max Fiedler; Werden und Werken* (Essen, 1940).

Field, John, remarkable Irish pianist and composer; b. Dublin, July 26, 1782; d. Moscow, Jan. 23, 1837. His father was a violinist; his grandfather, an organist; it was from his grandfather that he received his first instruction in music. He then had lessons with Clementi, and was also employed in the salesrooms of Clementi's music establishment in London. In 1802 he accompanied Clementi to Paris, and in 1803 to St. Petersburg, where Field settled as a teacher and performer. After many concert tours in Russia, he returned to England temporarily, and performed his Concerto in E-flat with the Phil. Society of London (Feb. 27, 1832); he continued a European tour in 1833, playing in Paris, in Switzerland, and in Italy. He was stricken with an ailment at Naples, and remained in a hospital for 9 months; at the end of his resources, he was persuaded by a friendly Russian family to return to Moscow. On the way, he was able to give a concert in Vienna, with extraordinary success; but the combination of alcoholism and general ill health led to his death 2 years after arriving in Moscow. Field's historical position is of importance, even though his music in itself does not reveal a great original talent. He was undoubtedly a precursor of Chopin in his treatment of piano technique; he was also the originator of keyboard nocturnes. He greatly developed the free fantasias and piano recitative, while following the basic precepts of Classical music. Like Chopin after him, Field wrote mainly for the piano; he composed 7 piano concertos, 4 sonatas, 18 nocturnes, polonaises, and other pieces; also Quintet for Piano and Strings and 2 divertimenti for Piano, Strings, and Flute.

BIBLIOGRAPHY: F. Liszt, *Über John Fields Nocturnes* (Hamburg, 1859; also in vol. IV of Liszt's *Gesammelte Schriften,* Leipzig, 1882); H. Dessauer, *John Field, Sein Leben und seine Werke* (Langensalza, 1912); W.H. Grattan Flood, *John Field of Dublin* (Dublin, 1920); E. von Tidebőhl, "Reminiscences of John Field," *Monthly Musical Record* (1923); E. Blom, "John Field," *Chesterian* (1930); A. Nikolaev, *John Field* (Moscow, 1960; Eng. trans., 1973); C. Hopkinson, *A Bibliographical Thematic Catalogue of the Works of John Field* (London, 1961); G. Southall, *John Field's Piano Concertos: An Analytical and Historical Study* (Diss., Univ. of Iowa, 1966); D. Branson, *John Field and Chopin* (London, 1972); Patrick Piggott, *The Life and Music of John Field* (London, 1973); R. Langley, "John Field and the

Genesis of a Style," *Musical Times* (Feb. 1982).

Fields, James, American pianist; b. Los Angeles, Nov. 1, 1948. He studied piano with Ethel Leginska and Victor Aller; appeared in public as a child. In 1965 he won a debut grant of the Young Musicians Foundation in California, which catapulted him into a promising concert career.

Fielitz, Alexander von, German conductor and composer; b. Leipzig, Dec. 28, 1860; d. Bad Salzungen, July 29, 1930. He was of partly Slavic origin; his mother was Russian. He studied piano with Julius Schulhoff and composition with Kretschmer in Dresden; in conducting he profited by the advice of Nikisch. He conducted opera in various German towns; a nervous disorder caused him to take a prolonged rest in Italy (1887–97); then he settled in Berlin as a teacher. In 1905–8 he was in Chicago, where he organized an orch. and conducted it for a season; in 1908 he returned to Berlin as a teacher at, and later (1916) director of, the Stern Cons. He wrote a number of songs and piano pieces; his song cycle *Eliland* and his songs based on Tuscan folk music were quite popular; he also wrote 2 operas, *Vendetta* (Lübeck, 1891) and *Das stille Dorf* (Hamburg, March 13, 1900).

Fiévet, Paul, French composer; b. Valenciennes, Dec. 11, 1892; d. Paris, March 15, 1980. His father, **Claude Fiévet** (1865–1938), was a composer in his own right. Paul Fiévet studied piano and music theory at the Paris Cons., where he was a student of Xavier Leroux, Caussade, and Widor, obtaining first prize in harmony in 1913, and first prize in composition in 1917, 1918, and 1919. He received the Grand Prix International in Ostende in 1931 and the Grand Prix of Paris in 1932. Among his works are an operetta, *Le Joli Jeu* (Lyons, 1933), and several symph. suites of the type of "landscape music," e.g., *Les Horizons dorés* (Paris, 1932), *Puerta del Sol* (Paris, 1933), *Images de France* (Paris, 1964), *Orient* (Paris, 1929), *En hiver,* etc. He also wrote several string quartets (one of which he whimsically entitled *Sputnik*), a Brass Sextet, and numerous choruses and piano pieces.

Figner, Medea, famous Italian-Russian soprano; b. Florence, April 3, 1858; d. Paris, July 8, 1952. Her complete name was **Zoraide Amedea Mei.** She studied voice with Bianchi, Carlotta Carozzi-Zucchi, and Panofka in Florence; made her debut as Azucena in Sinalunga, near Florence, in 1875; then sang in the opera theaters of Florence. From 1877 to 1887 she toured in Italy, Spain, and South America; she met the celebrated Russian tenor **Nicolai Figner** during her travels, and followed him to Russia; they were married in 1889, divorced in 1903. She became extremely successful on the Russian operatic stage; was a member of the Maryinsky Imperial Opera Theater in St. Petersburg until 1912. She then devoted herself mainly to voice teaching. In 1930 she emigrated to Paris. Her voice was described by contemporary critics as engagingly soft, rich, "velvety," and "succulent." She could sing mezzo-soprano roles as impressively as those in the soprano range. She was fortunate in having been coached by Tchaikovsky in the role of Liza in his opera *The Queen of Spades,* which she sang in its first production; her husband sang the role of her lover in the same opera. Her other successful roles were Tosca, Mimi, Donna Anna, Elsa, Brünnhilde, Marguerite, Desdemona, Aida, Amneris, and Carmen. In 1912 she publ., in St. Petersburg, her memoirs.

Figner, Nicolai, celebrated Russian tenor; b. Nikiforovka, in the Kazan government, Feb. 21, 1857; d. Kiev, Dec. 13, 1918. He was a lieutenant in the Russian navy before his voice was discovered; made his debut in Naples in 1882; then he studied diligently in Milan; in 1887 he returned to Russia and was engaged as a tenor at the Imperial Theater in St. Petersburg. He was the favorite tenor of Tchaikovsky and was selected to sing the leading role in the premiere of *The Queen of Spades;* his interpretation of Lensky in *Eugene Onegin* was also famous. In 1889 he married the Italian soprano **Medea Mei,** who wrote a book of memoirs (St. Petersburg, 1912) in which she described their careers.
BIBLIOGRAPHY: L.M. Kutateladse, *Nicolai Figner: Recollections, Letters, Materials* (Leningrad, 1968).

Figueredo, Carlos, Venezuelan composer; b. Valencia, Aug. 15, 1910. He studied with Vicente Emilio Sojo at the Caracas School of Music, graduating in 1947. In 1948 he entered the diplomatic service as a cultural attaché at the Venezuelan Embassy in Paris, consul in Copenhagen, and then in Madrid. However, he did not abandon music; he wrote 4 competent symphs. (1947, 1948, 1951, 1953), some acceptable chamber music, and tolerable choruses.

Figulus (real name, **Töpfer**), **Wolfgang,** German writer on music; b. Naumburg, c.1525; d. Meissen, Sept. 1589. He studied in Leipzig; in 1549–51 was cantor at the Thomaskirche in Leipzig; in 1551–88, at the Fürstenschule in Meissen. He wrote *Elementa musicae* (1555; many other eds.); revised Martin Agricola's *Deutsche Musica* (1560); publ. a book of motets, *Precationes* (Leipzig, 1553); *Cantiones sacrae* (1575); and *Hymni sacri et scholastici* (revised by his son-in-law, Friedrich Birck, 1604); a collection of Christmas songs, containing works of his own, of Martin Agricola, and others, was publ. posthumously in 2 books (1594 and 1605).

Figuš-Bystrý, Viliam, Slovak composer; b. Banská Bystrica, Feb. 28, 1875; d. there, May 11, 1937. He spent many years collecting Slovak folk melodies, which he publ. in 5 vols. (1906–15) for voice and piano; also publ. a collection of 1,000 arranged for piano only (1928). He further wrote an opera, *Detvan* (Bratislava, Aug. 1, 1928); a cantata, *Slovenská Piesen* (1913); an orch. suite, *From My Youth;* Piano Quartet; Piano Trio; 3 sonatines for Violin and Piano; violin pieces; piano works; choruses and songs.

Filev, Ivan, Bulgarian composer and conductor; b. Kazanluk, June 22, 1941. He studied conducting with Iliev and composition with Goleminov and Raichev at the Bulgarian State Cons. in Sofia, graduating in 1968. He is currently conductor of the National Opera in Ruse.

WORKS: 2 piano concertinos (1963, 1967); String Quartet (1964); *Music* for Strings, Winds, and Piano (1966); Symph. for String Orch. (1967); *5 Pieces* for Orch. (1967); Rondo for String Orch. (1968); Prelude and Fugue for Orch. (1968); *Symphonic Forms* (1970); Concerto for Orch. (1973).

Filiasi, Lorenzo, Italian composer; b. Naples, March 25, 1878; d. Rome, July 30, 1963. He studied at the Cons. di S. Pietro a Majella with Nicola d'Arienzo. His first success came with the opera *Manuel Menendez,* which won the Sonzogno Competition Prize in 1902 and was produced in Milan (May 15, 1904); his other operas included *Fior di Neve* (La Scala, April 1, 1911) and *Messidoro* (1912). He also wrote a pantomime, *Pierrot e Bluette* (1895); a choral work, with Orch., *La preghiera del marinaio italiano; Visioni romantiche* for Orch.; violin pieces; many songs.

Filippi, Filippo, Italian composer and critic; b. Vicenza, Jan. 13, 1830; d. Milan, June 24, 1887. He studied law at Padua, taking his degree in 1853. In 1852 he began his career as a music critic with a warm defense of Verdi's *Rigoletto;* from 1858 till 1862 was editor of the *Gazzetta Musicale,* and in 1859 music critic of the newly founded *Perseveranza.* He publ. a collection of essays on great musicians, *Musica e musicisti* (Milan, 1876); as a zealous Wagnerite he wrote a pamphlet, *Riccardo Wagner* (in German, as *Richard Wagner: Eine musikalische Reise in das Reich der Zukunft,* 1876); also publ. a monograph, *Della vita e delle opere di Adolfo Fumagalli* (Milan, 1857); composed a String Quintet; 9 string quartets; Piano Trio; piano pieces; songs.

Filke, Max, German composer; b. Steubendorf-Leobschütz, Silesia, Oct. 5, 1855; d. Breslau, Oct. 8, 1911. He studied with Brosig in Breslau and with Haberl at the Kirchenmusikschule in Regensburg (1877); then with Piutti at the Leipzig Cons. (1880); was engaged as choirmaster at Straubing (1881) and conductor of the Sängerkreis at Cologne (1890); then became director at the Cathedral in Breslau and prof. at the inst. for church music there. His numerous compositions for the church assign him a distinguished position among composers of sacred music.

Filleul, Henry, French composer; b. Laval, May 11, 1877; d. Saint-Omer, May 1, 1959. He studied at the Paris Cons. with Lavignac and Casadesus; in 1908 became director of the Ecole Nationale de Musique at St. Omer, France.

WORKS: *Le Jugement de Triboulet,* comic opera (1923); oratorios: *Le Christ vainqueur* (1925); *Le Miracle de Lourdes* (1927); *Les Doulces Joyes de Nostre Dame* (1928); *Jeanne d'Arc* (1929); *Eva* (1931); *Variations symphoniques sur un thème languedocien* (1939); *Fantaisie concertante* for Piano and Orch. (1950); Cello Concerto; violin pieces, with organ; motets; male choruses; etc.

BIBLIOGRAPHY: *Hommage à Henri Filleul* (St. Omer, 1952).

Fillmore, Henry (full name, **James Henry Fillmore, Jr.**), American bandleader and composer; b. Cincinnati, Feb. 3, 1881; d. Miami, Fla., Dec. 7, 1956. His paternal grandfather was August Damerin Fillmore (2nd cousin of President Millard Fillmore); his father, James Henry Fillmore, and his uncles Fred A. and Charles M. Fillmore were the founders of the Cincinnati music publishing firm of Fillmore Bros. Co. Henry Fillmore was educated at the Miami (Ohio) Military Inst., and later at the Cincinnati College of Music. As a bandmaster, he led the Syrian Shrine Band of Cincinnati to national prominence in the period 1920–26, making several transcontinental tours; in 1915 he founded the Fillmore Band, which was one of the earliest bands to make regular radio broadcasts (1927–34). In 1938 he moved to Miami, Fla., where he conducted bands at the Orange Bowl. He is best known, however, as the composer of numerous popular marches (*Americans We, Men of Ohio, His Honor* et al.), 2nd only to Sousa's in their tuneful liveliness. He was also the leading proponent of the "trombone smear," a humorous effect of the trombone glissando. He used numerous pseudonyms in his publ. pieces (**Al Hayes, Harry Hartley, Ray Hall, Gus Beans, Henrietta Moore,** and **Harold Bennett,** under which name he publ. the popular *Military Escort March*). He was also a compiler of sacred songs and tune books. In 1956 he received an honorary D.Mus. degree from the Univ. of Miami, Fla.

BIBLIOGRAPHY: Paul E. Bierley, *Hallelujah Trombone: The Story of Henry Fillmore* (Columbus, Ohio, 1983); idem, *The Music of Henry Fillmore and Will Huff* (Columbus, 1983).

Fillmore, John Comfort, American music educator; b. New London, Conn., Feb. 4, 1843; d. there, Aug. 15, 1898. He was a pupil of G.W. Steele at Oberlin College in Ohio; then at the Leipzig Cons. (1865–67). He was director of the music dept. at Oberlin College (1867); at Ripon College in Wisconsin (1868–78); at Milwaukee College for Women (1878–84). He founded (1884) the Milwaukee School of Music, of which he was director until 1895, when he took charge of the School of Music of Pomona College in Claremont, Calif.

WRITINGS: *Pianoforte Music: Its History, with Biographical Sketches and Critical Estimates of Its Greatest Masters* (Chicago, 1883); *New Lessons in Harmony* (1887); *Lessons in Music History* (1888); *A Study of Omaha Indian Music* (with Alice C. Fletcher and F. La Flesche, 1893).

Filtz, Anton, talented German composer; b. Eichstätt, Sept. (baptized, Sept. 22) 1733; d. Mannheim, March (buried, March 14) 1760. He was a pupil of J. Stamitz; from 1754, first cellist in the Mannheim Orch. He belongs to the school of Mannheim Symphonists, early practitioners of classic instrumental style. That his works must have enjoyed great popularity seems to be proved by the numerous reprints issued at London and Amsterdam, pirated from the original Paris editions. He was exceptionally prolific; in the span of his brief life he completed 41 symphs., many trio sonatas, string trios, sonatas for violin, cello, flute, etc., and concertos for various instruments. Riemann publ. 4 symphs. by Filtz in Denkmäler der Tonkunst in Bayern (4 and 13; formerly 3.i and 7.ii); 2 trios (ibid., 27; formerly 15); and one in *Collegium Musicum.*

Finagin, Alexei, Russian musicologist; b. St. Petersburg, March 16, 1890; d. Leningrad, Feb. 4, 1942. He publ. *Russian Folksongs* (Petrograd, 1923); *Fomin: His Life and Works* (in vol. 1 of *Music and Musical Life of Old Russia;* Leningrad, 1927); contributed to various periodicals.

Finck, Heinrich, German composer; b. Bamberg, 1445; d. in the Schottenkloster, Vienna, June 9, 1527. He was in the service of 3 Polish kings: Johann Albert (1492), Alexander (1498), and Sigismund (1506); was in Cracow from at least 1491; in 1492 visited Budapest, Vienna, and Torgau, but returned to Poland; in 1510–13 was Kapellmeister to Duke Ulrich at Stuttgart; then at the court of Maximilian I, in Augsburg; in 1520 was appointed composer of the Cathedral chapter at Salzburg; in 1525–26, Hofkapellmeister to Ferdinand I at Vienna, where he was succeeded by his pupil Arnold von Bruck. WORKS: *Schöne auserlesene Lieder des hochberühmten Heinrich Finckens* (Nuremberg, 1536; reprinted in R. Eitner's *Publikationen,* vol. VIII); other songs publ. by Salblinger (1545) and by Rhaw (1542). Reprints are to be found in Blume's *Das Chorwerk* (hymns ed. by R. Gerber; the *Missa in summis*); in A.W. Ambros's *Geschichte der Musik* (vol. 5); in the Denkmäler der Tonkunst in Österreich (72; formerly 37.ii); in H.J. Moser's *Kantorei der Spätgotik* and in L. Hoffmann-Erbrecht's *Heinrich Finck: Ausgewählte Werke,* I, in *Das Erbe deutscher Musik* (1962). BIBLIOGRAPHY: H. Riemann, in *Kirchenmusikalisches Jahrbuch* (1897); P. Wagner, in *Geschichte der Messe* (I, 275).

Finck, Henry Theophilus, American music critic and editor; b. Bethel, Mo., Sept. 22, 1854; d. Rumford Falls, Maine, Oct. 1, 1926. He was brought up in Oregon; then entered Harvard Univ., where he studied with J.K. Paine. After graduation in 1876 he went to Germany; studied comparative psychology in Berlin and Vienna, and publ. a book, *Romantic Love and Personal Beauty* (1887), propounding a theory that romantic love was unknown to the ancient nations. He was music editor of the *N.Y. Evening Post* from 1881 to 1924, and occasionally wrote for other journals. Finck was a brilliant journalist; in his books on music he stressed the personal and psychological elements. WRITINGS: *Chopin, and Other Musical Essays* (1889); *Wagner and His Works* (2 vols., N.Y., 1893; reprinted 1968); *Pictorial Wagner* (1899); with others, *Anton Seidl: A Memorial by His Friends* (1899); *Songs and Song Writers* (1900); *Edward Grieg* (1906); *Grieg and His Music* (1909); *Success in Music and How It Is Won* (1909); *Massenet and His Operas* (1910); *Richard Strauss* (1917); *Musical Progress* (1923); *My Adventures in the Golden Age of Music* (1926). He edited *50 Master Songs* (1902); *50 Schubert Songs* (1903); *50 Grieg Songs* (1909).

Finck, Hermann, German composer, great-nephew of **Heinrich Finck;** b. Pirna, Saxony, March 21, 1527; d. Wittenberg, Dec. 28, 1558. He was educated at the court chapel of King Ferdinand of Bohemia; studied at Wittenberg Univ. (1545); then taught music there (1554); was appointed organist in 1557. His major work is the treatise *Practica musica,* publ. by Rhaw (1556), and subdivided into 5 parts. Some of Hermann Finck's works are reprinted by Eitner in his *Publikationen* (vol. VIII, 1879). BIBLIOGRAPHY: P. Matzdorf, *Die Practica musica Hermann Fincks* (Frankfurt, 1957); F. Kirby, *Hermann Finck's Practica musica: A Comparative Study in 16th Century German Musical Theory* (Diss., Yale Univ., 1957).

Findeisen, Nicolai, Russian music historian and editor; b. St. Petersburg, July 23, 1868; d. Leningrad, Sept. 20, 1928. He studied with Nicolai Sokolov; in 1893 he founded the *Russian Musical Gazette* and remained its editor until it ceased publication in 1917. His writings include monographs on Verstovsky (1890), Serov (1900), Dargomyzhsky (1902), Anton Rubinstein (1905), and Rimsky-Korsakov (1908); he publ. a series of brochures and books on Glinka; the first vol. of a projected large biography, *Glinka in Spain,* appeared in 1896; a catalogue of Glinka's MSS, letters, and portraits was publ. in 1898; he also edited Glinka's correspondence (1908). Findeisen's major achievement was the extensive history of Russian music up to the year 1800, publ. in 2 vols. (partly posthumously) in Leningrad (1928–29) under the title *Sketches of Music in Russia from the Most Ancient Times until the End of the 18th Century.*

Findeisen, Otto, German composer of operettas and theater conductor; b. Brünn, Dec. 23, 1862; d. Leipzig, Jan. 23, 1947. He conducted in Magdeburg from 1890, and produced 2 of his operettas there: *Der alte Dessauer* (1890) and *Hennigs von Treffenfeld* (1891). Other light operas were: *Frau Holle* (Berlin, 1904); *Kleopatra* (Hamburg, 1897); *Der Spottvogel* (Bremen, 1898); *Der Sühneprinz* (Leipzig, 1904); *Sonnenguckerl* (Vienna, 1908); *Meister Pinkebank* (Vienna, 1909); etc.

Fine, Irving, remarkable American composer; b. Boston, Dec. 3, 1914; d. there, Aug. 23, 1962. He studied with Walter Piston at Harvard Univ. (B.A., 1937; M.A., 1938) and with Nadia Boulanger in Cambridge, Mass. (1938), and in France (1939); also took a course in choral conducting with A.T. Davison. He was an assistant prof. of music at Harvard (1947–50); in 1950 was appointed prof. at Brandeis Univ.; also was a member of the faculty at the Berkshire Music Center in Tanglewood, Mass. (1946–57). He was at first influenced by Stravinsky and Hindemith, and adopted a cosmopolitan style of composition in which contrapuntal elaboration and energetic rhythm were his main concerns; later on, however, he developed a distinctive style of his own, with a lyrical flow of cohesive melody supported by lucid polyphony.

WORKS: Violin Sonata (1946); *Toccata concertante* for Orch. (Boston, Oct. 22, 1948); Partita for Wind Quintet (1948); *Alice in Wonderland,* suite for Chorus and Orch. (1949); Nocturne for Strings and Harp (1951); String Quartet (1952); *Serious Song,* lament for String Orch. (1955); Fantasy for String Trio (1956–57); *Diversions* for Orch. (1958–68); several ingenious piano pieces for children; and his capital work, *Symphony 1962* (Boston Symph. Orch., March 23, 1962).

Fine, Vivian, American composer; b. Chicago, Sept. 28, 1913. She was accepted as a piano student at the Chicago Musical College at an incredible one-digit age; as she grew she took piano lessons with Djane Lavoie-Herz, who claimed to be a pupil of Scriabin, and who instilled the love of Scriabin's polychromatic, anxious melorhythms in Vivian Fine herself. She then had harmony lessons with Ruth Crawford; later received instruction in modern composition from Henry Cowell; also had some help from Adolph Weidig. Progressing precociously, she wrote a piece for oboe solo, which rated a performance in N.Y.; in 1931 her *4 Pieces* for 2 flutes was performed at the Bauhaus in Dessau, Germany. She settled in N.Y. in 1931 and for fully 10 years had sessions with Sessions; she also took piano lessons with Abby Whiteside (1937–45) and had a brief series of lessons in orchestration with George Szell. In 1935 she married the sculptor Benjamin Karp, but continued her career under her maiden name. Although her musical environment in N.Y. was suffused with atonality and dodecaphony, she wrote basically tonal music; she was particularly adept in intimate theatrical productions for a chamber ensemble with voices, and for ballet. In 1974 she received a grant from the National Endowment for the Arts to write an opera; the result was a rather pleasing opus, to her own libretto, *The Women in the Garden,* produced in San Francisco on Feb. 12, 1978. The women in the plot were Emily Dickinson, Isadora Duncan, Gertrude Stein, and Virginia Woolf, disporting themselves in their characteristically erratic fashion. Vivian Fine held several teaching jobs: at N.Y. Univ. (1945–48); at the Juilliard School of Music in N.Y., for a brief semester in 1948; at the College School of Dance in Connecticut (1963–64), and at Bennington College in Vermont (from 1964). She further gave lectures at various small artistic schools in places like Oshkosh (1968). In 1980 she received a Guggenheim fellowship and also became a member of the National Academy and Inst. of Arts and Letters.

WORKS: FOR THE STAGE: *A Guide to the Life Expectancy of a Rose* for Soprano, Tenor, and Chamber Ensemble (N.Y., May 16, 1956); *The Women in the Garden,* chamber opera for 5 Singers and 9 Instruments (1977; San Francisco, Feb. 12, 1978); the ballets *The Race of Life* (1937; N.Y., Jan. 23, 1938), *Opus 51* (Bennington Dance Festival, Aug. 6, 1938), *Tragic Exodus* (N.Y., Feb. 19, 1939), *They Too Are Exiles* (N.Y., Jan. 7, 1940), *Alcestis* (N.Y., April 29, 1960), and *My Son, My Enemy* (Connecticut College, Aug. 14, 1965). FOR ORCH.: Concertante for Piano and Orch. (1944); *Drama* for Orch. (San Francisco, Jan. 5, 1983). CHAMBER MUSIC: *Solo* for Oboe (1929); *4 Pieces* for 2 Flutes (1930); Sonatina for Oboe and Piano (1939); *Capriccio* for Oboe and String Trio (1946); *Divertimento* for Cello and Percussion (1951); Violin Sonata (1952); String Quartet (1957); *Duo* for Flute and Viola (1961); *Fantasy* for Cello and Piano (1962); *Melos* for Solo Double Bass (1964); *The Song of Persephone* for Solo Viola (1964); Concertino for Piano and Percussion Ensemble (1965); Chamber Concerto for Cello and 6 Instruments (1966); Quintet for Violin, Viola, Cello, Trumpet, and Harp (1967); Concerto for Piano Strings and Percussion for One Performer (1972); *The Flicker* for Solo Flute (1973); *3 Buddhist Evocations* for Violin and Piano (1977); Brass Quartet (1978); *Nightingales,* motet for 6 Instruments (1979); *Music* for Flute, Oboe, and Cello (1980); Piano Trio (1980). VOCAL MUSIC: *The Passionate Shepherd to His Love and Her Reply* for 3-part Women's Chorus (1938; Madison, Wis., April 23, 1975); *4 Elizabethan Songs* (1938–41); *The Great Wall of China* for Voice, Flute, Cello, and Piano, to the text of Kafka (1947); *Valedictions* for Mixed Chorus, Soprano, Tenor, and 10 Instruments (1959); *Morning* for Mixed Chorus, Narrator, and Organ (1962); *Paean* for Women's Chorus, Brass Ensemble, and Narrator (1969); *Sounds of the Nightingale* for Soprano, Chorus, and Chamber Orch. (1971); *Missa brevis* for 4 Cellos and Taped Voice (1972); *Teisho* for 8 Singers and String Quartet (1975); *Meeting for Equal Rights: 1866,* cantata (N.Y., April 23, 1976); *Oda a las Ranas* for Women's Chorus, Flute, Oboe, Cello, and Percussion (1980); piano pieces; songs.

BIBLIOGRAPHY: David Ewen, *American Composers* (N.Y., 1982).

Fink, Christian, German organist and composer; b. Dettingen, Aug. 9, 1822; d. Esslingen, near Stuttgart, Sept. 5, 1911. He studied at the Leipzig Cons.; became organist there (1856–60); in 1863 was appointed church organist at Esslingen; publ. numerous organ works. He was greatly esteemed in Germany; his choral works and organ pieces were often performed.

Fink, Gottfried Wilhelm, German writer on music and editor; b. Sulza, Thuringia, March 8, 1783; d. Leipzig, Aug. 27, 1846. He studied music and theology in Leipzig; wrote criticism in the *Allgemeine Musikalische Zeitung* from 1808; in 1827 he became editor of this influential publication (until 1841); also contributed articles on music and musicians to various German encyclopedias. His extensive music history remains in MS. Among his publications are the collections of German songs *Musikalischer Hausschatz* (Leipzig, 1843) and *Die deutsche Liedertafel* (Leipzig, 1846). For a complete list of his writings, see the article by W. Boetticher in *Die Musik in Geschichte und Gegenwart*.

Finke, Fidelio Fritz, significant German composer and pedagogue; b. Josefsthal, Northern Bohemia, Oct. 22, 1891; d. Dresden, June 12, 1968. He studied with Vítězslav Novák at the Prague Cons.; from 1915–20 was on its faculty. In 1920 he was named supervisor of German music schools in Czechoslovakia; in 1926 was appointed prof. at the Prague Cons. From 1927–58 he was a prof. of composition at the Hochschule für Musik in Leipzig, and in 1959 held a similar post at the Hochschule für Musik in Dresden. As a composer, he followed the evolutionary path of German music, from the classicism of Brahms through the deeply contrapuntal constructions of Max Reger, finally adopting the liberating precepts of the New Vienna School, with its integration of thematic elements and concomitant emancipation of dissonance. As a pedagogue, he was highly regarded in the academic community.

WORKS: Operas: *Die versunkene Glocke* (1915–18); *Die Jakobsfahrt* (Prague, 1936); *Der schlagfertige Liebhaber* (1950–54); *Der Zauberfisch* (Dresden, June 3, 1960). For Orch.: *Pan*, a symph. (1919); Piano Concerto (1930); Concerto for Orch. (1931); *Das Lied der Zeit*, choreographic tone poem (1946); 2 *Symphonische Märsche* (1960); *Festliche Musik* (1964); 8 suites for various Instrumental Groupings (1947–61). Chamber music: 5 string quartets (1914–64); Sonata for Harp Solo (1945); Horn Sonata (1946); Clarinet Sonata (1949); Viola Sonata (1954); Wind Quintet (1955); *Primula veris* for Violin and Piano (1957); *Divertimento* for Chamber Orch. (1964); numerous choruses; Toccata for Piano, Left-hand; organ works; songs.

BIBLIOGRAPHY: G. Hofmeyer, *Vorläufiges Verzeichnis der Kompositionen von Fidelio F. Finke* (1966); D. Hartwig, *Fidelio F. Finke, Leben und Werk* (Leipzig, 1970).

Finko, David, Russian pianist, composer, and conductor; b. Leningrad, May 15, 1936. He studied at the Leningrad School of Performing Arts (1950–58), and subsequently at the Leningrad Cons. (1960–65). In 1979 he emigrated to the U.S.; was then a visiting lecturer in the history and theory of Russian music at the Univ. of Pa. (1979–81). In 1981 he became a lecturer and composer-in-residence at the Univ. of Texas at El Paso. He was awarded a number of grants and fellowships, including ones from ASCAP, the Fromm Foundation, and the Memorial Foundation for Jewish Culture. Some of his works reflect the tragic aspects of Jewish history.

WORKS: OPERAS: *Polinka*, after Anton Chekhov (1965; first perf. El Paso, Feb. 26, 1983); *In a Torture Chamber of the Gestapo* (1970); *The Lodger from the Garret* (1976–78; score lost); *The Enchanted Tailor*, after Sholem Aleichem (1983). FOR ORCH.: 6 tone poems (1965, 1967, 1968, 1970, 1975, 1978); *Holocaust*, overture (1965; revised 1983); Symph. No. 1 (1969); Concerto for Piano and Orch. (1971); Concerto for Viola and Orch. (1971); Symph. No. 2 (1972); Double Concerto for Violin, Viola, and Orch. (1973); Double Concerto for Viola, Double Bass, and Orch. (1975); Concerto for Harp and Orch. (1976); Concerto for Viola d'Amore, Lute, and Orch. (1978); Concerto for 3 Violins and Orch. (1981); *Pilgrimage to Jerusalem* (Detroit, April 20, 1983); *The Wailing Wall* (1983); CHAMBER MUSIC: *Mourning Music* for Violin, Viola, and Cello (1968); *Mass without Words* for Violin and Organ (1968); *Lamentations of Jeremiah* for Solo Violin (1969); *Fromm Septet* for Oboe, Clarinet, Bass Clarinet, Violin, Cello, Double Bass, and Percussion (Philadelphia, April 24, 1983); FOR PIANO: *Russia in Darkness*, poem for Piano (1961); Piano Sonata (1962).

Finley, Lorraine Noel, American pianist and composer; b. Montreal, December 24, 1899; d. Greenwich, Conn., Feb. 13, 1972. She studied in Europe; then enrolled at Wellesley College; later took courses at the Juilliard School of Music and Columbia Univ., where she studied with Percy Goetschius and Rubin Goldmark. She was married to **Theodore F. Fitch,** with whom she gave recitals announced as "Mr. and Mrs. Composer." She wrote some instrumental pieces and several songs.

Finney, Ross Lee, distinguished American composer and teacher; b. Wells, Minn., Dec. 23, 1906. He studied at the Univ. of Minn. with Donald Ferguson; received a B.A. in 1927 from Carleton College. In 1928 he went to Paris, where he took lessons with Nadia Boulanger; returning to America, he enrolled at Harvard Univ., where he studied with Edward Burlingame Hill; in 1935 had instructive sessions with Sessions. From 1929–49 he was on the faculty of Smith College; concurrently taught at Mt. Holyoke College (1938–40). In 1931–32 he was in Vienna, where he took private lessons with Alban Berg; in 1937 he studied with Gian Francesco Malipiero in Asolo. He then taught composition at the Hartt School of Music in Hartford, Conn. (1941–42), and at Amherst College (1946–47). In the interim he served with the Office of Strategic Services in Paris; was slightly injured when he stepped on a land mine while working in the war zone; this earned him the Purple Heart and Certificate of Merit. His professional career was facilitated by 2 Guggenheim fellowships (1937, 1947) and a Pulitzer traveling fellowship (1937). In 1948–49 he was a visiting lecturer at the Univ. of Michigan in Ann Arbor; from 1949–73 he was a prof. there, and also served as chairman of the dept. of composition; furthermore, he established there an electronic laboratory. Because of the wide diversification of his stylistic propensities, Finney's works represent a veritable encyclopedic inventory of styles and idioms, from innocently pure modalities to highly sophisticated serialistic formations. About 1950 Finney devised a sui generis dodecaphonic method of composition which he called "complementarity." In it a 12-tone row is formed by 2 mutually exclusive hexachords, often mirror images of each other; tonal oases make their welcome appearances; a curious air of euphony of theoretically dissonant combinations is created by the contrapuntal superposition of such heterophonic ingredients, and Finney's harmonies begin to sound seductively acceptable despite their modernity.

WORKS: FOR ORCH.: 4 symphs.: No. 1, subtitled *Communiqué* (1942); No. 2 (1958; Philadelphia, Nov. 13, 1959); No. 3 (1960; Philadelphia, March 6, 1964); No. 4 (1972; Baltimore, March 31, 1973); Violin Concerto No. 1 (1935; revised 1952); *Barbershop Ballad* (CBS Radio, Feb. 6, 1940); *Overture for a Drama* (Rochester, N.Y., Oct. 28, 1941); *Slow Piece* for String Orch. (1940); *Variations, Fuguing, and Holiday* for Orch., based on a hymn tune of William Billings (1943; Los Angeles, May 17, 1947); Piano Concerto No. 1 (1948); *Variations* for Orch. (1957; Minneapolis, Dec. 30, 1965); *Three Pieces* for Chamber Orch. and Tape Recorder (1962); Concerto for Percussion and Orch. (1965); Symph. Concertante (1967); Piano Concerto No. 2 (1968); *Landscapes Remembered* (1971); *Summer in Valley City* for Concert Band (Ann Arbor, April 1, 1971); *Spaces* (Fargo, N. Dak., March 26, 1972); Violin Concerto No. 2 (1973; Dallas, March 31, 1976; revised 1977); Concerto for Alto Saxophone, with Wind Orch. (1974); *Variations on a Memory* for 10 Players (1975); *Narrative* for Cello and 14 Instruments (1976); Concerto for Strings (1977; N.Y., Dec. 5, 1977); Chamber Concerto for 7 Players (1981). CHAMBER MUSIC: 8 string quartets (1935–60); 2 piano trios (1938, 1954); Piano Quartet (1948); 2 piano quintets (1953, 1961); *Chromatic Fantasy* for Solo Cello (1957); String Quintet (1958); *Fantasy in 2 Movements* for Solo Violin (1958; commissioned by Yehudi Menuhin and first perf. by him at the World's Fair in Brussels, June 1, 1958); *Divertissement* for Piano, Clarinet, Violin, and Cello (1964); *Three Studies in Four* for Solo Percussionists (1965); *Two Acts for Three Players* for Clarinet, Percussion, and Piano (1970); *Two Ballades* for Flutes and Piano (1973); *Tubes I* for one to 5 Trombones (1974); *Quartet* for Oboe, Cello, Percussion, and Piano (1979); *Two Studies* for Saxophones and Piano (1981); also 2 viola sonatas; 2 cello sonatas; 3 violin sonatas. FOR SOLO PIANO: 5 piano sonatas (1933–61); *Fantasy* (1939); *Nostalgic Waltzes* (1947); *Variations on a Theme by Alban Berg* (1952); *Sonata quasi una fantasia* (1961). CHORAL WORKS: *Pilgrim Psalms* (1945); *Spherical Madrigals* (1947); *Edge of Shadow* for Chorus and Orch. (1959); *Still Are New Worlds* for Narrator, Tape, Choir, and Orch. (1962; Ann Arbor, May 10, 1963); *Nun's Priest's Tale,* after Chaucer, for Folksinger, Electric Guitar, and Small Orch. (Hanover, N.H., Aug. 21, 1965); *The Martyr's Elegy* for High Voice, Chorus, and Orch. (Ann Arbor, April 23, 1967); *The Remorseless Rush of Time* for Choir and Orch. (1969); *Earthrise* for Soloist, Choir, and Orch. (1978; Ann Arbor, Dec. 11, 1979).

PUBLICATIONS: Editions of Geminiani's 12 sonatas for Violin and Piano (Northampton, Mass., 1935); a book, *The Game of Harmony* (N.Y., 1947). BIBLIOGRAPHY: P. Cooper, "The Music of Ross Lee Finney," *Musical Quarterly* (Jan. 1967); David Ewen, *American Composers* (N.Y., 1982).

Finney, Theodore Mitchell, American music educator and historian, brother of **Ross Lee Finney;** b. Fayette, Iowa, March 14, 1902. He studied at the Univ. of Minnesota (B.A., 1924); then at the American Cons. at Fontainebleau (1926) and in Berlin (1927–28). He was a member of the viola section in the Minneapolis Symph. Orch. (1923–25); then an assistant prof. of music at Carleton College (1925–32) and a lecturer at the Smith College Summer School (1930–38). In 1936–68 he was head of the music dept. at the Univ. of Pittsburgh. He publ. a practical college textbook, *A History of Music* (N.Y., 1935; revised ed., 1946); also *Hearing Music, A Guide to Music* (N.Y., 1941); *We Have Made Music* (essays; Pittsburgh, 1955); *A Union Catalogue of Music and Books on Music Printed before 1801 in Pittsburgh Libraries* (2nd ed., 1963); some scholarly articles in music journals.

Finnila, Birgit, Swedish contralto; b. Falkenberg, Jan. 20, 1931. She studied in Göteborg; later took courses at the Royal Academy of Music in London with Roy Henderson; made her concert debut in Göteborg in 1963; then made numerous appearances with the major orchestras of Europe; later sang in America, Australia, and Israel.

Finnissy, Michael, English composer; b. London, March 17, 1946. He studied composition with Searle and Bernard Stevens at the Royal College of Music (1964–66); taught in the music dept. of the London School of Contemporary Dance (1969–74). WORKS: FOR THE STAGE: *Mysteries,* musical theater in 8 parts to Latin texts from the Bible, for varying vocal and instrumental combinations (1972–79; the separately performable parts are titled *The Parting of Darkness, The Earthly Paradise, Noah and the Great Flood, The Prophesy of Daniel, The Parliament of Heaven, The Annunciation, The Betrayal and Crucifixion of Jesus of Nazareth,* and *The Deliverance of Souls); Circle, Chorus and Formal Act* for Soloists, Choruses, Percussionists, Instrumentalists, Dancers, and Mimes (1973); *Orfeo* for Soloists and Instrumentalists (1974–75); *Medea* for Soloists, Actors, and Instrumentalists (1973–76); *Tom Fool's Wooing* for 14 a cappella Voices (1975–78); *Mr. Punch* for Voice and Instrumentalists (1976–77). FOR ORCH.: 5 concertos for Piano and Ensemble: No. 1 (1975); No. 2 (1975–76); No. 3 (1978); No. 4 for Piano Alone (1978–80); No. 5, with Mezzo-soprano (1980); *Offshore* (1975–76); *Long Distance* for Concertante Piano and Chamber Orch. (1977–78); *Alongside* for Chamber Orch. (1979); *Sea and Sky* (1979–80). CHAMBER MUSIC: *Song 2, 4, 6,* and *10* for Chamber Ensemble (1967–68); *Transformation of the Vampire* for Clarinet, 3 Percussionists, Violin, and Viola (1968–71); *Alice III* for

Cello and Percussionist (1970–75); *Kagami-Jashi* for Flute and Harp (1979). FOR PIANO: *Song 5, 7, 8,* and *9* (1963–68); *Jazz* (1976); *All Fall Down* (1977); Piano Concerto No. 4 (1978–80); *Grainger* (1979); *Boogie-Woogie* (1980); *Nancarrow* (1980). VOCAL WORKS: *World* for 6 Voices and 27 Instruments (1968 –74); *Jeanne d'Arc* for Soprano, Tenor, Solo Cello, and Chamber Orch. (1967–71); *Babylon* for Mezzo-soprano and Ensemble (1971); *Goro* for Tenor and Ensemble (1978); *Sir Tristan* for Mezzo-soprano and Instruments (1978); *Talawva* for Mezzo-soprano and Instruments (1979).

Fino, Giocondo, Italian composer; b. Turin, May 2, 1867; d. there, April 19, 1950. He studied oriental languages and theology; concurrently took music lessons with Giovanni Bolzoni; he remained in Turin practically all his life. He wrote the operas *La festa del grano* (Turin, 1910) and *Campana a gloria* (Turin, 1916); several stage works in the Piedmont dialect; biblical cantata, *Noemi e Ruth* (Bergamo, 1908); ballets, pantomimes, choral works; chamber music and piano pieces.

Finzi, Gerald, English composer; b. London, July 14, 1901; d. Oxford, Sept. 27, 1956. He began his study of music with Ernest Farrar (1914–16) and Edward Bairstow (1917–22); studied counterpoint with R.O. Morris in 1925. He was a teacher of composition at the Royal Academy of Music in London (1930–33); in 1939 he organized the Newbury String Players, which did much to develop interest in 18th-century English music. He edited overtures by Boyce for the Musica Britannica. As a composer, Finzi's music reflects the influence of Elgar and Vaughan Williams, while the basic materials are rooted in English folk songs.
WORKS: *A Severn Rhapsody* (1923; Bournemouth, June 4, 1924); *By Footpath and Stile,* song cycle for Baritone and String Quartet to poems by Thomas Hardy (1921–22; London, Oct. 23, 1923); *Introit,* for Violin and Small Orch. (1925; London, May 4, 1927; revised, 1935 and 1942); *Interludium* for Oboe and String Quartet (1936); *Dies Natalis,* cantata for Soprano or Tenor Solo and Strings (1938–39; London, Jan. 26. 1940); *Prelude and Fugue* for String Trio (1942); *Farewell to Arms* for Tenor and Chamber Orch. (1944; Manchester, April 1, 1945); *Let Us Garlands Bring,* 5 Shakespeare songs for Baritone and Strings (1929–42); BBC, London, Oct. 18, 1942); 5 cycles for Voice and Piano of settings of poems by Thomas Hardy: *Before and after Summer* (1932), *Earth and Air and Rain* (1928–32), *I said to Love* (1928), *Till Earth Outwears* (1927), and *A Young Man's Exhortation* (1926–29); *Intimations of Immortality,* ode after Wordsworth for Tenor, Chorus, and Orch. (1949–50; Gloucester, Sept. 5, 1950); *Nocturne: New Year Music* for Orch. (1949); *For St. Cecilia,* ceremonial ode for Tenor, Chorus, and Orch. (1947; London, Nov. 22, 1947); Concerto for Clarinet and Strings (1948–49; Hereford, Sept. 9, 1949); *Grand Fantasia and Toccata* for Piano and Orch. (1953); Cello Concerto (1951–55; Cheltenham, July 19, 1955); *In Terra Pax,* Christmas scene for

Soprano, Baritone, Chorus, Strings, and Antique Cymbals (1954; revised 1956).

Finzi, Graciane, French composer; b. Casablanca, Morocco, July 10, 1945. She enrolled in the Paris Cons. and studied theory with Elsa Barriane and Tony Aubin. Returning to Casablanca, she became active as an organizer of music festivals. Among her works are a Cello Concerto, a Wind Quintet, a Piano Trio, and Oboe Sonata, piano pieces, and songs.

Fiocco, Jean-Joseph, Belgian composer, 2nd son of **Pietro Antonio Fiocco** (of the first marriage); b. Brussels, Dec. (baptized, Dec. 15) 1686; d. there, March 30, 1746. He succeeded his father as music master at the ducal chapel, and held this post for 30 years (1714–44); wrote 5 oratorios, 8 Psalms, 9 Requiems, motets, etc. Two copies of his *Sacri concentus* for 4 Voices and 3 Instruments are known to exist; most of his other works are lost.
BIBLIOGRAPHY: Christiane Stellfeld, *Les Fiocco* (Brussels, 1941).

Fiocco, Joseph-Hector, Belgian composer, 8th child of **Pietro Antonio Fiocco** (of his 2nd marriage); b. Brussels, Jan. 20, 1703; d. there, June 22, 1741. He was sous-maître at the royal chapel c.1729–31; from 1731 to 1737 was maître de chapelle at the Antwerp Cathedral; was master of the collegiate church of SS. Michel and Gudule in Brussels until his death. He wrote numerous sacred works, publ. in *Monumenta Musicae Belgicae* (vol. III); also wrote *Pièces de clavecin* (2 suites of 12 pieces each).
BIBLIOGRAPHY: Christiane Stellfeld, *Les Fiocco* (Brussels, 1941).

Fiocco, Pietro Antonio, Italian composer; b. Venice, c.1650; d. Brussels, Sept. 3, 1714. He traveled to Germany, then settled in Brussels, marrying a Belgian lady in 1682; she died in 1691, and Fiocco remarried in 1692. He was music master of the ducal chapel in Brussels; in 1694 he established an opera enterprise; until 1698 was director, with Giovanni Paolo Bombarda, of the Opéra du Quai du Forn; wrote special prologues for the operas of Lully; also wrote music for the court; his pastoral play *Le Retour du printemps* was produced in 1699. A collection of his sacred concertos was publ. in Antwerp (1691). Among his instrumental works only a few, including *Sonate à 4,* are extant. Two of his sons, **Jean-Joseph** and **Joseph-Hector,** became professional musicians.
BIBLIOGRAPHY: Christiane Stellfeld, *Les Fiocco* (Brussels, 1941).

Fioravanti, Valentino, Italian composer; b. Rome, Sept. 11, 1764; d. Capua, June 16, 1837. He studied in Rome with Jannacconi and with Sala and Fenaroli in Naples. Returning to Rome in 1782, he began his career as a prolific composer of operas. He visited Naples quite often; was in Paris in 1807; succeeded Zingarelli as maestro di cappella at St. Peter's in

Rome in 1816; during his last period he wrote much church music.

WORKS: His earliest work, an intermezzo, was *Le avventure di Bertoldino* (Rome, 1784); he produced a comic opera, *Gl' inganni fortunati*, in Naples (1786); there followed *Il furbo contro al furbo* (Venice, Dec. 29, 1796). His greatest success was achieved by his comic opera *Le Cantatrici villane*, first produced in Naples (1799) and then in Venice in a new version under the title *Le Virtuose ridicole* (Dec. 28, 1801); there were performances all over Europe, including Russia; the opera was particularly in favor with German audiences (under the title *Die Dorfsängerinnen*); other operas were *La capricciosa pentita* (Milan, Oct. 2, 1802) and *I Virtuosi ambulanti* (Paris, Sept. 26, 1807); Fioravanti produced 77 operas in all between 1784 and 1824. His autobiographical sketch was reprinted by G. Roberti in *La Gazzetta Musicale* (1895).

Fioravanti, Vincenzo, Italian composer, son of **Valentino Fioravanti;** b. Rome, April 5, 1799; d. Naples, March 28, 1877. He studied with his father, and also with his father's teacher, Jannacconi; he also took lessons with Donizetti. He wrote a number of operas in the Neapolitan dialect; only a few of them (trans. into conventional Italian) were produced outside Italy. He composed about 40 operas in all.

Fiorillo, Dante, American composer; b. New York, July 4, 1905. He studied the cello, and later began to compose without formal instruction. He held Guggenheim fellowships in composition for 4 successive years (1935–39). Extraordinarily prolific, he wrote 12 symphs.; 11 string quartets; piano quintets and trios; piano sonatas; choral music.

Fiorillo, Federigo, violinist and composer; b. Braunschweig, Germany (baptized, June 1), 1755; d. after 1823. He was taught by his father, **Ignazio Fiorillo;** he traveled as a violinist and conductor; appeared as a violinist in St. Petersburg in 1777, then in Poland (1780–81); conducted in Riga (1782–84); in 1785 he went to Paris, where he participated in the Concert Spirituel; in 1788 he was in London, where he played the viola in Salomon's quartet. He probably remained in London until c.1815; then he was in Amsterdam and again in Paris. He was a prolific composer for violin and various combinations of string instruments; but he is known chiefly through his useful collection *Etudes de violon*, comprising 36 caprices, which was frequently reprinted.

Fiorillo, Ignazio, Italian composer, father of **Federigo Fiorillo;** b. Naples, May 11, 1715; d. Fritzlar, near Kassel, Germany, June 1787. He studied with Durante and Leo in Naples; composed his first opera, *Mandane*, at the age of 20 (Venice, 1736). Other operas were *Artimene* (Milan, 1738), *Partenope nell' Adria* (Venice, 1738), and *Il Vincitor di se stesso* (Venice, 1741). He traveled as a theater conductor; was appointed court conductor at Braunschweig (1754); in 1762 he received a similar post at Kassel, retiring in 1780. He wrote a number of Ger-

man operas in Braunschweig and 3 Italian operas in Kassel. An oratorio, *Isacco;* a Requiem; and other church works are also noteworthy.

Fiqué, Karl, German organist; b. St. Magnus, near Bremen, April 17, 1867; d. Brooklyn, N.Y., Dec. 7, 1930. After studying at the Leipzig Cons. with Carl Reinecke, he emigrated to the U.S. (1887) and settled in Brooklyn, where he served as church organist and lectured at the Brooklyn Inst. of Arts and Sciences (1897–1915). He married the soprano **Katherine Noack** (d. 1940). He wrote 2 comic operas in German: *Priesewitz* (Brooklyn, 1893) and *Der falsche Mufti* (N.Y., 1901); a String Quartet, several choral works, and numerous piano pieces. Shortly before his death, he finished an operetta, *Merry Madrid.*

Firkušný, Rudolf, eminent Czech pianist; b. Napajedla, Feb. 11, 1912. Janáček, impressed by his musical talent, accepted him as a private pupil in composition in 1919; he also studied piano with Růžena Kurzová at the Brno Cons. He made his concert debut in Prague on June 14, 1920, at the age of 8, as soloist in a Mozart piano concerto. He also studied music theory with Vilém Kurz and Rudolf Karel at the Prague Cons. He began his professional career in Czechoslovakia. On Jan. 13, 1938, he made his American debut in N.Y.; also took private piano lessons with Artur Schnabel, who lived in N.Y. at the time. In 1943 he toured South America; in 1944 he made a tour of Mexico, Cuba, and Central America. In 1946 he participated in the Prague Festival; but this was his last professional appearance in Czechoslovakia. Eventually, he became an American citizen; he was soloist with the Boston Symph. Orch. on Nov. 2, 1945, in the world premiere of Menotti's Piano Concerto, and again on Dec. 31, 1948, in the premiere of Howard Hanson's Piano Concerto. Bohuslav Martinu wrote for Firkušný his 3rd Piano Concerto, which he performed for the first time with the Dallas Symph. on Nov. 20, 1949; he also gave the first performance of Martinu's 4th Piano Concerto with the Symph. of the Air in N.Y., under Leopold Stokowski, on Oct. 4, 1956. In 1958–59 he toured Australia and the politically available countries in Asia. By 1973, the count of his tours aggregated to 25 in Europe, 10 in South America, 12 in Mexico, 3 in Israel, and 2 in Australia; to these must be added a greater number of American concerts. In all of his programs he included works by Czech composers, particularly those by his teacher Janáček. In 1982, on his 70th birthday, he celebrated his 60th anniversary as a concert pianist. In his career he shunned the appurtenances and perquisites of a typical virtuoso; even his physical appearance did not suit the consecrated image of a flamboyant matinée idol; he was too deeply concentrated on the proper interpretation of the music he played to flaunt the externals; he earned the admiration of critics for his musical integrity. His technical equipment was always of the highest caliber; his lyrical talent enhanced the physical aspects of his virtuosity. Firkušný was also a composer; he wrote a Piano Concerto and a number of attractive piano études and miniatures. In 1979 he began the publication, with the violinist Rafael Druian, of a complete edition of the Mozart violin sonatas. An excellent teacher, he gave master classes in piano at the Juilliard School of Music in N.Y. and at the Aspen Music School in Colorado.

BIBLIOGRAPHY: David Ewen, *Musicians since 1900* (N.Y., 1978).

Fischer, Annie, distinguished Hungarian pianist; b. Budapest, July 5, 1914. She studied at the Academy of Music in Budapest with Ernst von Dohnányi; in 1933 she won first prize in the International Liszt Competition in Budapest. Her career was interrupted by World War II, but she eventually resumed her concert activities. She became well known for her authentic performances of the piano music of Mozart and Beethoven.

Fischer, Carl, music publisher; b. Buttstädt, Thuringia, Dec. 7, 1849; d. New York, Feb. 14, 1923. He studied music in Gotha; entered a partnership in an instrument manufacturing business with his brother **August Emil Fischer** in Bremen. In 1872 he went to N.Y. and opened a music store at 79 East 4th Street; in 1923 the store was moved to 62 Cooper Square. He secured the rights for republishing orch. scores and parts by German composers, eventually becoming one of the most important of American music publishing firms. From 1907 to 1931 the firm publ. a monthly periodical, the *Musical Observer,* edited by Gustav Sänger; in 1923 the business was incorporated and Carl Fischer's son **Walter S. Fischer** (b. New York, April 18, 1882; d. there, April 26, 1946) became president; after his death, Frank H. Connor (1903–77) was elected president; upon his death he was succeeded by his son. In 1909 the firm established a branch in Boston, which was expanded in 1960 through the purchase of the Charles Homeyer Music Co. of Boston; in 1935 a branch was also opened in Los Angeles, and in 1969 one in San Francisco. In 1947 the firm occupied a new building in N.Y. at 165 West 57th Street, which also housed a concert hall. The catalogue of the firm is representative of all genres of musical composition; early acquisitions were works by composers living in America, including Rachmaninoff and Ernest Bloch; in the last quarter of the century, the firm publ. a number of instrumental and vocal works by composers of the avant-garde, including some in graphic notation.

Fischer, Edwin, eminent Swiss pianist; b. Basel, Oct. 6, 1886; d. Zürich, Jan. 24, 1960. He studied with Hans Huber in Basel and Martin Krause in Berlin; then taught at the Stern Cons. in Berlin (1905–14); taught at the Berlin Hochschule für Musik from 1931; between 1926 and 1932 he was also engaged as a conductor in Lübeck, Munich, and Berlin. In 1942 he returned to Switzerland. He was renowned as one of the most intellectual pianists of his time and a distinguished pedagogue. He founded the Edwin-Fischer-Stiftung to assist needy and young musicians. He also publ. several valuable books on mu-

sic: *J.S. Bach* (Potsdam, 1945); *Musikalische Betrachtungen* (Wiesbaden, 1949; in Eng. as *Reflections on Music,* London, 1951); *Beethovens Klaviersonaten* (Wiesbaden, 1956; Eng. trans., 1959); and *Von den Aufgaben des Musikers* (Wiesbaden, 1960).

BIBLIOGRAPHY: B. Gavoty, *Edwin Fischer* (Geneva, 1954); H. Haid, ed., *Dank an Edwin Fischer* (Wiesbaden, 1962).

Fischer, Emil, German operatic bass; b. Braunschweig, June 13, 1838; d. Hamburg, Aug. 11, 1914. He received his vocal training entirely from his parents, who were opera singers; made his debut in Graz in 1857; then was with the Danzig Opera (1863–70); in Rotterdam (1875–80); and with the Dresden Opera (1880–85); then went to America; made his debut with the Metropolitan Opera Co. on Nov. 23, 1885, and remained on the staff for 5 years; lived mostly in N.Y. as a vocal teacher; returned to Germany shortly before his death. On March 15, 1907, a testimonial performance was held in his honor at the Metropolitan Opera, at which he sang one of his greatest roles: that of Hans Sachs in *Die Meistersinger* (Act 3, Scene 1). He was particularly famous for his Wagnerian roles.

Fischer, Erich, German music editor and composer; b. Kreuzlingen, April 8, 1887. He studied musicology in Berlin at the Univ. under Kretzschmar, Stumpf, and Friedländer; received his Dr.Phil. in 1909 with the dissertation *Über die Musik der Chinesen;* in 1914 he founded in Berlin the Musikalische Hauskomödien, a society for the performance of little-known music by German composers, arranged as singspiels with new words; for this venture he organized his own company of singers.

Fischer, Frederick, German conductor; b. Munich, May 25, 1868; d. St. Louis, April 17, 1931. He studied at the Royal Academy of Music in Munich; then came to the U.S., where he conducted the Calif. Opera Co.; in 1904 he settled in St. Louis and was assistant conductor of the St. Louis Symph.; was also guest conductor of the Boston People's Orch., choral societies, etc.; wrote music to the pageant *Missouri 100 Years Ago,* choral works, and songs.

Fischer, Irwin, American composer, organist, and conductor; b. Iowa City, July 5, 1903; d. Wilmette, Ill., May 7, 1977. He graduated in 1924 from the Univ. of Chicago; studied organ with Middelschulte, piano with Robyn, and composition with Weidig at the American Cons. in Chicago (M.M., 1930); later studied composition briefly with Nadia Boulanger in Paris (1931) and Kodály in Budapest (1936); took lessons in conducting with Palmgartner at the Salzburg Mozarteum (1937). In 1928 he joined the faculty of the American Cons. in Chicago; conducted several community orchs., including the West Suburban Symph. in Hinsdale (1955–77). As a composer, he held fast to the historically justified tonal techniques; but upon occasion he ventured into the alluring field of serialism.

WORKS: FOR ORCH.: *Rhapsody of French Folk*

Tunes (1933); Piano Concerto (1935; Chicago, Feb. 23, 1936); *Marco Polo,* fantasy overture (1937); *Hungarian Set* (1938); *Lament* for Cello and Orch. (1938); *Chorale Fantasy* for Organ and Orch. (1940); Symph. No. 1 (1943); *Variations on an Original Theme* (1950); *Legend* (1956); *Poem* for Violin and Orch. (1959); *Passacaglia and Fugue* (1961); *Overture on an Exuberant Tone Row* (1964–65); *Short Symphony* (1970–71; Hinsdale, April 16, 1972; orchestration of Piano Sonata); *Concerto Giocoso* for Clarinet and Orch. (1971; Hinsdale, Jan. 21, 1973); *Orchestral Adventures of a Little Tune* for Narrator and Orch. (1974; Chicago, Nov. 16, 1974). VOCAL MUSIC: *5 Symphonic Psalms* for Soprano, Chorus, and Orch. (1967); *Statement 1976* for Soprano, Chorus, Brass, Strings, and Percussion (1976; New Haven, April 25, 1976); choruses; songs. CHAMBER MUSIC: *Divertimento* for Flute, Clarinet, Bassoon, Horn, Trumpet, Violin, Cello, and Double Bass (1963); *Fanfare* for Brass and Percussion (1976). FOR PIANO: *Introduction and Triple Fugue* (1929); *Rhapsody* (1940); Piano Sonata (1960).

Fischer, Ivan, Hungarian conductor; b. Budapest, Jan. 20, 1951. He studied cello and composition at the Bartók Cons. in Budapest (1965–70); then took lessons in conducting with Hans Swarowsky at the Vienna Academy of Music; during the 1975–76 season he conducted concerts in Milan, Florence, Vienna, and Budapest; beginning in 1976, he filled engagements with the BBC Symph. Orch. in London and the BBC regional orchs. From 1979–82 he was music director of the Northern Sinfonia Orch. at Newcastle upon Tyne. In 1983 he took the London Symph. Orch. on a tour of the Far East. Also in 1983 he made his first appearance in the U.S., as a guest conductor with the Los Angeles Phil., and was appointed music director of the Kent Opera.

Fischer, Jan, Czech composer; b. Louny, Sept. 15, 1921. He studied at the Prague Cons. (1940–45) and took lessons in composition from Řídký at the master class there (1945–48). His music occupies the safe ground of Central European Romanticism, not without some audacious exploits in euphonious dissonance.
WORKS: 5 operas: *Ženichové* (*Bridegrooms;* 1956; Brno, Oct. 13, 1957); *Romeo, Julie a tma* (*Romeo, Juliet and Darkness;* 1959–61; Brno, Sept. 14, 1962); *Oh, Mr. Fogg,* comic chamber opera after Jules Verne's *Around the World in 80 Days* (1967–70; Saarbrücken, June 27, 1971); *Miracle Theater,* radio opera (1970); *Decamerone,* chamber opera (1975–76); ballet, *Eufrosyne* (1951; Pilsen, 1956); *Pastoral Sinfonietta* (1944); Violin Concerto (1946); *Essay* for Jazz Orch. and Solo Piano (1947); *Popular Suite* for Wind Orch. and Piano (1950); *Dance Suite* for Orch. (1957); *Fantasia* for Piano and Orch. (1953); Symph. No. 1, *Monothematic* (1959); Clarinet Concerto (1965); *Obrazy* (*Pictures*) *I* and *II* for Orch. (1970, 1973); Harp Concerto (1972); Flute Sonata (1944); Suite for Wind Sextet (1944); Suite for English Horn and Piano (1945); *Ballada* for String Quartet and Clarinet (1949); Piano Quintet (1949); *Ut stellae* for

Soprano, 2 Pianos, Flute, Bass Clarinet, Percussion, and Tape (1966); *Amoroso* for Clarinet and Piano (1970); Wind Quintet (1971); *4 Studies* for Solo Harp (1971).

Fischer, Johann Caspar Ferdinand, German composer of keyboard music; b. c.1665; d. Rastatt, Aug. 27, 1746. He served as house musician to the Margrave of Baden (1696–1716); continued to serve the court after it moved to Rastatt in 1716.
WORKS: During his lifetime he publ. the following: *Le Journal du printemps,* op. 1 (airs and ballet numbers in the style of Lully; 1696; reprinted in the Denkmäler Deutscher Tonkunst, X/1); *Les Pièces de clavecin,* op. 2 (1696; reprinted 1698, under the title *Musikalisches Blumen-Büschlein*); *Vesper Psalms,* op. 3 (1701); *Ariadne musica neo-organoedum,* op. 4 (Schlackenworth, 1702; contains 20 preludes and fugues for Organ in 20 different keys, thus foreshadowing Bach's *Well-Tempered Clavier*); *Litaniae Lauretanae,* op. 5 (1711); also *Musikalischer Parnassus* (9 keyboard suites named after the 9 Muses; Augsburg, 1738) and *Blumenstrauss* (Augsburg, 1732; a series of 8 preludes and fugues in 8 church modes). His *Sämtliche Werke für Klavier und Orgel,* ed. by E.V. Werra, was publ. in Leipzig, 1901.
BIBLIOGRAPHY: For discussion of Fischer's influence on Bach, see Max Seiffert, *Geschichte der Klavier-Musik,* vol. 1 (Berlin, 1899); also R. Oppel, "Über J.K.K. Fischers Einfluss auf Bach," *Bach-Jahrbuch* (1910); W. Lebermann, "Johann Caspar Fischer der Jüngere," *Die Musikforschung,* XXIII (1970).

Fischer, Joseph, music publisher; b. Silberhausen, Germany, April 9, 1841; d. Springfield, Ohio, Nov. 24, 1901. He emigrated to the U.S. as a youth, and in 1864 established the firm of J. Fischer & Bro. in Dayton, Ohio, with his brother **Ignaz Fischer;** in 1875 the firm moved to N.Y. Joseph Fischer was succeeded, at his death, by his sons **George** and **Carl;** the sons of George Fischer, **Joseph** and **Eugene,** became proprietors of the firm in 1920. During its early years, J. Fischer & Bro. specialized in music for the Roman Catholic Church, but later expanded its activities to include instrumental music by contemporary composers, organ works, and also light opera.

Fischer, Kurt von, distinguished Swiss musicologist; b. Bern, April 25, 1913. He studied piano at the Bern Cons. with F.J. Hirt and with Czeslaw Marek; later took the courses in musicology with Kurth and Gurlitt at the Univ. of Bern, where he received his Ph.D. in 1938 with the dissertation *Griegs Harmonik und die nordländische Folklore* (publ. in Bern, 1938); subsequently completed his Habilitation in 1948 there with his *Die Beziehungen von Form und Motiv in Beethovens Instrumentalwerken* (publ. in Strasbourg, 1948; 2nd ed., 1972). He taught piano at the Bern Cons. from 1939–57, and concurrently was lecturer in musicology at the Univ. of Bern (1948–57). In 1957 he became prof. of musicology and chairman of the dept. at the Univ.

of Zürich. In 1965 he assumed the post of co-editor of the *Archiv für Musikwissenschaft.* In 1967–72 he served as president of the International Musicological Society.

WRITINGS: *Studien zur italienischen Musik des Trecento und frühen Quattrocento* (Bern, 1956); *Arthur Honegger* (Zürich, 1977).

BIBLIOGRAPHY: H.H. Eggebrecht and M. Lütolf, eds., *Studien zur Tradition in der Musik: Kurt von Fischer zum 60. Geburtstag* (Munich, 1973).

Fischer, Ludwig, German bass; b. Mainz, Aug. 18, 1745; d. Berlin, July 10, 1825. He first studied violin and cello; then took vocal lessons with Anton Raaff in Mannheim; in 1772 he was named virtuoso da camera at the Mannheim court; followed the court when it moved to Munich in 1778; proceeded to Vienna, where he sang opera in 1780–83; then obtained excellent success in Paris (1783) and Italy; also sang in Prague and Dresden (1785) and in Regensburg (1785–88). In 1788 he was granted a lifetime appointment in Berlin; retired in 1815. Mozart wrote the part of Osmin in *Die Entführung aus dem Serail* for Fischer.

Fischer, Michael Gotthard, German organist and composer; b. Alach, near Erfurt, June 3, 1773; d. Erfurt, Jan. 12, 1829. He was a pupil of Kittel; also concert conductor and teacher in the seminary at Erfurt. He wrote about 50 organ pieces; symphs., concertos, chamber music, piano pieces, motets, chorales, etc.; publ. *Evangelisches Choral-Melodienbuch.*

Fischer, Res, German contralto; b. Berlin, Nov. 8, 1896; d. Stuttgart, Oct. 4, 1974. She studied in Stuttgart and Prague; then took lessons in Berlin with Lilli Lehmann; made her debut in 1927 in Basel, where she sang until 1935; then appeared with the Frankfurt Opera (1935–41); in 1941 she joined the Stuttgart Opera, remaining on its roster until 1961; was made its honorary member in 1965. She also sang at the festivals of Salzburg and Bayreuth, and with the state operas in Vienna, Hamburg, and Munich. She created the title role in Orff's *Antigonae* (Salzburg, 1949) and sang in the first performance of Wagner-Régeny's *Bergwerk von Falun* (Salzburg, 1961).

Fischer, Wilhelm, eminent Austrian musicologist; b. Vienna, April 19, 1886; d. Innsbruck, Feb. 26, 1962. He studied with Guido Adler at the Univ. of Vienna, where he received his Ph.D. with the dissertation *Matthias Georg Monn als Instrumentalkomponist* in 1912; he obtained his Habilitation there with his *Zur Entwicklungsgeschichte des Wiener klassischen Stils* in 1915; then joined the faculty of the Univ. of Vienna in 1919; subsequently was lecturer in musicology at the Univ. of Innsbruck from 1928 until the Anschluss of 1938, when he was removed from this position and was conscripted as a forced laborer; after World War II, he was restored to the faculty of the Univ. of Innsbruck as a prof., serving there from 1948 until his retirement in 1961. In 1951

he was elected president of the Central Inst. of Mozart Research at the Mozarteum in Salzburg; he publ. numerous essays on Mozart and other Classical composers; among his most important writings, apart from his *Habilitationsschrift,* are *Zur Geschichte des Fugenthemas* (Leipzig, 1925) and *Beethoven als Mensch* (Regensburg, 1928). In 1956 he was presented with a Festschrift on the occasion of his 70th birthday.

Fischer, William Gustavus, American hymn-tune writer; b. Baltimore, Oct. 14, 1835; d. Philadelphia, Aug. 13, 1912. He sang in a Baltimore German church; was a bookbinder by trade and a choral conductor by avocation; then entered the retail piano business and, under its imprint, Gould & Fischer, printed a number of Sunday-school leaflets. Of his songs, *Coming to the Cross,* first sung at a National Camp meeting at Hamilton, Mass., June 22, 1870, is the best known.

BIBLIOGRAPHY: R.G. McCutchan, *Our Hymnody* (N.Y., 1937).

Fischer-Dieskau, Dietrich, celebrated German baritone; b. Zehlendorf, a suburb of Berlin, May 28, 1925. His original family name was Fischer, but his grandfather made it Fischer-Dieskau, after the name of a small castle near Leipzig that the family owned in years past. Both his parents were musical, and he studied piano and took voice lessons with Georg Walter; in 1942 he entered the Berlin Hochschule für Musik as a student of Hermann Weissenborn, but was soon conscripted into the German army, to tend horses. In 1945 he was taken prisoner of war in Italy, during which time he was allowed to make appearances as a singer; finally released in 1947, he returned to Berlin and resumed his vocal studies with Weissenborn. He made his operatic debut as Posa in *Don Carlos* at the Berlin Städtische Oper in 1948; he then sang opera in Munich, Vienna, Milan, and Bayreuth; he also made numerous appearances in song recitals and concerts. In a few years he established himself as a master of the art of German song; and he sang with equal penetration the Italian and French repertoire. His specialty became complete cycles of Schubert's great lieder; he elicited great encomiums for such performances from the British critics after his London recitals in 1950 and 1951. He made his American debut as soloist with the Cincinnati Symph. on April 5, 1955, singing the baritone part in the *German Requiem* of Brahms. On May 2, 1955, he gave a recital in N.Y., in a program of Schubert's lieder, with excellent acclaim. Remarkably, he achieved equal successes in opera and in concert; critics and commentators freely referred to him as one of the greatest singers of the century; remarkable also was his ability to embrace the largest repertoire in opera and concerts; as a matter of course, he sang the major baritone parts in standard operas, among them Don Giovanni, Count Almaviva in *Le nozze di Figaro,* Hans Sachs, Wolfram, Valentin, Rigoletto, Renato, and Falstaff; he demonstrated his extraordinary musicianship by singing the title role in Alban

Berg's opera *Wozzeck;* the baritone solo part in Stravinsky's sacred ballad *Abraham and Isaac;* the title role in Busoni's opera *Doktor Faust;* Mandryka in Richard Strauss's *Arabella;* roles in operas of Hindemith; and Mittenhofer in the world premiere of Hans Werner Henze's *Elegy for Young Lovers* (Schwetzingen, May 20, 1961). In his recital programs he audaciously tackled the songs of Charles Ives. He proved his ability in oratorio, both traditional and modern, no less than in opera and concert. Bravely, he ventured into the circumscribed field of conducting; he made his American debut with the Los Angeles Phil. on March 24, 1974. Then, in an apparent effort to round off the entire domain of music, he publ. books of surprising excellence: *Auf den Spuren der Schubert-Lieder* (Wiesbaden, 1971; Eng. trans. as *Schubert: A Biographical Study of His Songs,* London, 1976), *Wagner und Nietzsche* (Stuttgart, 1974; Eng. trans., N.Y., 1976), and *The Fischer-Dieskau Book of Lieder* (N.Y., 1976). He married often. His 4th wife, **Julia Varadi**, is a soprano.

BIBLIOGRAPHY: K. Whitton, *Dietrich Fischer-Dieskau—Mastersinger: A Documented Study* (London, 1981).

Fischhof, Joseph, Austrian pianist; b. Butschowitz, Moravia, April 4, 1804; d. Vienna, June 28, 1857. He studied piano with Anton Halm in Vienna; then became a private teacher there, with growing success, and in 1833 was appointed a prof. in the Vienna Cons. He publ. many piano pieces (rondos, variations, fantasias, dances, marches, etc.) and *Versuch einer Geschichte des Klavier-Baus* (Vienna, 1853). He gathered a remarkable collection of musical MSS, including one of Bach's *Wohltemperierte Clavier,* and authentic materials for a Beethoven biography collected by Hotschewar (the guardian of Beethoven's nephew); these MSS were given, after Fischhof's death, to the Berlin State Library.

Fišer, Luboš, outstanding Czech composer; b. Prague, Sept. 30, 1935. He studied composition with Hlobil at the Prague Cons. (1952–56) and with Bořkovec at the Prague Academy of Music, graduating in 1960. In 1971 he emigrated to the U.S.; was a composer-in-residence with the American Wind Symph. Orch. in Pittsburgh. His music is often associated with paintings, archeology, and human history; his style of composition employs effective technical devices without adhering to any particular doctrine. WORKS: FOR THE STAGE: Chamber opera, *Lancelot* (1959–60; Prague, May 19, 1961); musical, *Dobrý voják Švejk (The Good Soldier Schweik;* Prague, 1962); ballet, *Changing Game* (1971). FOR ORCH.: *Suite* (1954); 2 symphs. (1956, 1958–60); *Symphonic Fresco* (1962–63); *Chamber Concerto* for Piano and Orch. (1964; revised 1970); *15 Prints after Dürer's Apocalypse* (1964–65; Prague, May 15, 1966; his most successful work; winner of a UNESCO prize in Paris, 1967); *Pietà* for Chamber Ensemble (1967); *Riff* (1968); *Double* (1969); *Report* for Wind Instruments (1971; commissioned by the American Wind Symph. Orch.); *Kreutzer Etude* for Chamber Orch. (1974);

Labyrinth (1977); *Serenade for Salzburg* for Chamber Orch. (1978); *Albert Einstein,* portrait for Organ and Orch. (1979); Piano Concerto (1980); *Meridian* (1980); *Romance* for Violin and Orch. (1980); *Centaures* (1983). CHAMBER MUSIC: *4 Compositions* for Violin and Piano (1955); String Quartet (1955); Sextet for Wind Quintet and Piano (1956); *Ruce (Hands),* sonata for Violin and Piano (1961); *Crux* for Violin, Kettledrums, and Bells (1970); Cello Sonata (1975); *Variations on an Unknown Theme* for String Quartet (1976); Piano Trio (1978); Sonata for 2 Cellos and Piano (1979); *Testis* for String Quartet (1980); Sonata for Solo Violin (1981). FOR VOICE: *Caprichos* for Vocalists and Chorus, after a text drawn from Goya's paintings (1966); Requiem for Soprano, Baritone, 2 Choruses, and Orch. (Prague, Nov. 19, 1968); *Lament over the Destruction of the City of Ur,* after Ur-Sumerian tablets, for Soprano, Baritone, 3 Narrators, Chorus, Children's and Adult's Speaking Choruses, 7 Timpani, and 7 Bells (1969; as a ballet, 1978); *Ave Imperator* for Solo Cello, Male Chorus, 4 Trombones, and Percussion (1977); *The Rose* for Chorus a cappella (1977); *Per Vittoria Colona* for Solo Cello and Female Chorus (1979); *Istanu,* melodrama for Narrator, Alto Flute, and 4 Percussionists (1980); *Znameni (The Sign)* for Soloists, Chorus, and Orch. (1981); *Address to Music,* melodrama for Narrator and String Quartet (1982). FOR PIANO: 6 sonatas: No. 1 (1955); No. 2 (1957); No. 3, *Fantasia* (1960); No. 4 (1962–64); No. 5 (1974); No. 6, *Fras* (1978).

Fisher, Avery, American pioneer in audio equipment and munificent patron of music; b. New York, March 4, 1906. He was educated at N.Y. Univ. (B.S., 1929); then worked for the publishing house of Dodd, Mead as a graphics designer (1933–43). In 1937 he founded the Phil. Radio firm, later known as Fisher Radio; it became one of the foremost manufacturers of audio equipment in the world, producing high-fidelity and stereophonic components. Having amassed a substantial fortune, he sold the firm in 1969. In 1973 he gave the N.Y. Phil. $10 million to renovate the interior of Phil. Hall; in 1976 it was inaugurated at a gala concert in which it was officially renamed Avery Fisher Hall in his honor. He also created the Avery Fisher Prize, which is awarded to outstanding musicians of the day.

Fisher, Eddie (Edwin Jack Fisher), American singer of popular music; b. Philadelphia, Aug. 10, 1928. He won an Arthur Godfrey Talent Scouts contest in 1948; then sang successfully on radio and television. His career was highlighted by his romantic marriages and sensational divorces successively to the movie stars Debbie Reynolds, Elizabeth Taylor, and Connie Stevens.

Fisher, Sylvia, Australian soprano; b. Melbourne, April 18, 1910. She studied at the Melbourne Cons.; then sang in local productions. In 1948 she became a member of the Covent Garden Opera in London, remaining on its roster until 1958. In 1959 she sang in Chicago; then was a member of the English Opera Group (1963–71). She created the role of Miss Wingrave in Britten's *Owen Wingrave* (London, BBC, May 16, 1971); also sang in other contemporary operas.

Fisher, William Arms, American music editor and publisher; b. San Francisco, April 27, 1861; d. Boston, Dec. 18, 1948. He studied theory with Horatio Parker; singing with William Shakespeare in London. When Dvořák came to N.Y. in 1892, Fisher became his pupil. In 1897 he settled in Boston as editor and director of music publication for O. Ditson & Co.; was its vice-president in 1926–37; then retired. He edited several vocal albums, among them *60 Irish Folksongs* (Boston, 1915) and *Ye Olde New England Psalm Tunes* (Boston, 1930). He wrote the words of the song *Goin' Home,* to the melody of the slow movement of Dvořák's *New World Symphony,* a setting that became enormously popular. See H. Earle Johnson in *Dictionary of American Biography,* Supplement IV.

WRITINGS: *Notes on Music in Old Boston* (1918); *The Music That Washington Knew* (1931); *One Hundred and Fifty Years of Music Publishing in the U.S.* (1933); *Music Festivals in the U.S.* (1934).

Fisk, Eliot, American guitarist; b. Philadelphia, Aug. 10, 1954. He studied with Oscar Ghiglia at the Aspen School of Music (1970–76); also studied with Ralph Kirkpatrick and Albert Fuller at Yale Univ. (B.A., 1972; M.M., 1977). He was on the faculty at the Aspen School of Music (1973–82), at Yale (1977–82), and at the Mannes College of Music in N.Y. (1978–82); in 1982 he became a prof. at the Cologne Hochschule für Musik.

Fissot, Alexis-Henri, French pianist and composer; b. Airaines (Somme), Oct. 24, 1843; d. Paris, Jan. 28, 1896. He entered the Paris Cons. as a child of 9, and studied piano with Marmontel, organ with Benoist, and composition with Ambroise Thomas till 1860, taking successively all first prizes. He then taught piano at the Paris Cons. (from 1887). He wrote many effective piano pieces: *12 préludes; 2 ballades; 3 feuillets d'album; 12 pièces de genre;* etc.

Fistoulari, Anatole, Russian conductor; b. Kiev, Aug. 20, 1907. He studied with his father, the opera conductor **Gregory Fistoulari;** a child prodigy, he conducted Tchaikovsky's 6th Symph. at the age of 8; in 1920 went to Rumania and Germany; was in Paris as a ballet conductor in 1933; later toured with the Ballet Russe de Monte Carlo in the U.S. (1937). He was in the French army in 1939; in 1940 made his way to London, where he settled as an orch. and theatrical conductor.

Fitelberg, Gregor, eminent Polish conductor and composer; b. Dvinsk, Latvia, Oct. 18, 1879; d. Katowice, June 10, 1953. He studied at the Warsaw Cons. with Barcewicz and Noskowski; then played the violin in the Warsaw Phil.; became its concertmaster,

and eventually (1908) conductor. After the outbreak of World War I he went to Russia as a conductor of symph. concerts; in 1921 he went to Paris; conducted performances of Diaghilev's Ballets Russes; in 1923 he returned to Poland and conducted the Warsaw Phil. (1923–34); then founded and led the Polish Radio Symph. Orch. in Warsaw from 1934 to 1939; in 1940 he was in Buenos Aires, after fleeing Warsaw via Vienna, Italy, and Paris; from 1942–45 he was in the U.S.; in 1947 he went back to Poland, and became conductor at the Polish Radio Symph. Orch. in Katowice. At his symph. concerts he gave many performances of works by Polish composers; was one of the best interpreters of Szymanowski. In 1951 the Polish government awarded him a state prize. Fitelberg was also a composer; he wrote 2 symphs. (1903, 1906); 2 Polish rhapsodies for Orch. (1913, 1914); symph. poem, *In der Meerestiefe* (1913); Violin Concerto (1901); and some chamber music; his Violin Sonata received the Paderewski prize in 1896.

Fitelberg, Jerzy, talented Polish composer, son of **Gregor Fitelberg;** b. Warsaw, May 20, 1903; d. New York, April 25, 1951. He received his musical education mainly from his father; then took courses in the Hochschule für Musik in Berlin. In 1933 he went to Paris; in May 1940 he came to the U.S., where he remained until his death. In 1936 he received an Elizabeth Sprague Coolidge award for his String Quartet No. 4, which was performed at the Coolidge Festival of Chamber Music in Washington, D.C. (1937); his orch. and chamber music was often performed in Europe; much of it was publ. His works are couched in the neo-Classical style, and are cosmopolitan in thematic substance; they are distinguished by energetic rhythm and strong contrapuntal texture; only a few of his compositions reflect Polish melos.

WORKS: 3 suites for Orch. (1926–30); Concerto for String Orch. (1928; arrangement of the 2nd String Quartet); Violin Concerto No. 1 (Vienna Festival of the International Society for Contemporary Music, June 20, 1932); Violin Concerto No. 2 (Paris Festival, June 22, 1937); *The Golden Horn* for String Orch. (1942); Nocturne for Orch. (N.Y. Phil., March 28, 1946, Rodzinski conducting); Octet for Wind Instruments; 5 string quartets; Sonata for 2 Violins and 2 Pianos; Sonatina for 2 Violins; *3 Polish Folksongs* for Women's Voices (1942).

BIBLIOGRAPHY: Emilia Elsner, "Jerzy Fitelberg," *Chesterian* (Sept.–Oct. 1939); *Modern Music . . . An Analytic Index* (N.Y., 1976; p. 73).

Fitzgerald, Ella, black American jazz singer; b. Newport News, Va., April 25, 1918. She began singing in small clubs in Harlem in the early 1930s; discovered by Chick Webb (one of Harlem's most popular musicians) in 1935, she joined his band; upon his death in 1939, she became its leader; in 1942 she became a free-lance singer and has since worked with most major jazz musicians and groups. She is particularly adept at scat singing and improvising, frequently creating new melodies over given harmonies much in the manner of a jazz instrumentalist. Stylistically, she is equally at ease in swing and bebop; developing, over the years, a superlative blend of musicianship, vocal ability, and interpretive insight, she has achieved a popularity and respect rarely acquired by jazz singers.

Fitzwilliam, Viscount Richard, wealthy British collector of paintings, engravings, books, and musical MSS; b. Richmond, Surrey, Aug. 1745; d. London, Feb. 4, 1816. He bequeathed his library to Cambridge Univ. The musical MSS include especially valuable works: the immensely important *Fitzwilliam Virginal Book* (often wrongly termed *Virginal Booke of Queen Elizabeth*), anthems in Purcell's hand, sketches by Handel, and many early Italian compositions. Vincent Novello edited and publ. 5 vols. of the Italian sacred music as *The Fitzwilliam Music* (London, 1825); J.A. Fuller-Maitland and A.H. Mann made a complete catalogue of it (1893). The entire contents of the *Fitzwilliam Virginal Book* were edited and publ. by J.A. Fuller-Maitland and William Barclay Squire (2 vols., Leipzig and London, 1894–99; facsimile reprint, N.Y., 1954).
BIBLIOGRAPHY: E.W. Naylor, *An Elizabethan Virginal Book* (London, 1905).

Fiume, Orazio, Italian composer; b. Monopoli, Jan. 16, 1908. He studied piano and theory in Palermo and Naples; was later a student of Pizzetti (composition) and Molinari (conducting) in Rome. He taught harmony at the Cons. of Parma (1941–51), in Milan (1951–59), and in Pesaro (1959–60); in 1961 became director of the Cons. of Trieste. His music follows the tradition of expansive Italian Romanticism. He wrote *3 Pieces* for Chamber Orch. (1937); Symph. (1956); opera, *Il tamburo di panno* (Rome, April 12, 1962); 2 concertos for Orch. (1945, 1956); cantata, *Ajace* (1940); songs.

Fizdale, Robert, American pianist; b. Chicago, April 12, 1920. He studied with Ernest Hutcheson at the Juilliard School of Music; formed a piano duo with Arthur Gold; they made a professional debut at N.Y.'s New School for Social Research in 1944, in a program devoted entirely to John Cage's music for prepared pianos. They toured widely in the U.S., Europe, and South America; works were written specially for them by Samuel Barber, Milhaud, Poulenc, Auric, Virgil Thomson, Norman Dello Joio, and Ned Rorem. With Arthur Gold he publ. a successful book, *Misia* (N.Y., 1979), on the life of Maria Godebsky, a literary and musical figure in Paris early in the century.

Fjeldstad, Oivin, Norwegian conductor; b. Oslo, May 2, 1903. He studied at the Cons. in Oslo; then went to Leipzig and Berlin for further studies. He began his career as a violinist. In 1931 he made his debut as conductor with the Oslo Phil. Orch. In 1946 he became chief conductor of the Norwegian State Broadcasting Co.; also conducted at the Oslo Opera. In 1962 he was named chief conductor of the Oslo Phil. Orch., a post he held until 1969.

Flack, Roberta, black American pop singer; b. Black Mountain, N.C., Feb. 10, 1939. Her mother was a church organist who taught her the rudiments of piano playing. The family moved to Arlington, Va., and she began taking music lessons with Alma Blackmon of Washington, D.C. She then enrolled in Howard Univ. (B.A., 1958), and upon graduation started a teaching career in public schools. Concurrently, she served as voice coach and accompanist. A complete change in her musical direction came in 1968, when she received an opportunity to perform in nightclubs; she suddenly revealed herself as a stunningly successful interpreter of popular songs; in this field she frequently teamed with the brilliant black singer Donny Hathaway. Among her most popular renditions were *The First Time Ever I Saw Your Face* and *Killing Me Softly with His Song.*

Flackton, William, English organist and composer; b. Canterbury, March 1709; d. there, Jan. 5, 1798. He was organist at Faversham in 1735–52; wrote church music; also 6 "overtures" for Harpsichord; 6 sonatas for 2 Violins and Cello; 3 cello sonatas and 3 viola sonatas; song, *The Chase* (with Horn obbligato).

Flagello, Ezio, American bass; b. New York, Jan. 28, 1933. He studied with Friedrich Schorr; made his debut at the Rome Opera in 1956; in 1957 he won the Metropolitan Opera Auditions of the Air and sang there in the same year; also appeared at La Scala in Milan, the Vienna State Opera, the San Francisco Opera, and the Deutsche Oper in Berlin.

Flagello, Nicolas (Oreste), prolific and brilliant American composer and conductor; b. New York, March 15, 1928. He was of Italian antecedents; his father, a professional dress designer, loved music and played the oboe; his mother assisted him tastefully in his successful shop, and also sang. His maternal grandfather, Domenico Casiello, was a musician in Naples. With such genetic endowment, it was inevitable that Flagello should become a musician. He began his piano lessons at the incredible age of 3, or so they say, and played in public at 5, according to undocumented reports. At 6 he began taking violin lessons with Francesco di Giacomo. He also learned to play the oboe, and was a member of the school band, performing on these instruments according to demand. In 1945–46 he played the violin in Stokowski's All-American Youth Orch. in N.Y. In 1946 he entered the Manhattan School of Music (B.M., 1949; M.M., 1950), studying with a variety of teachers in multifarious subjects (Harold Bauer, Hugo Kortschak, Hugh Ross, Vittorio Giannini). He also took conducting lessons with Mitropoulos. It was with Giannini that he had his most important training in composition, for 15 years, from 1935 to 1950, and it was Giannini who influenced him most in his style of composition—melodious, harmonious, euphonious, singingly Italianate, but also dramatically modern. After obtaining his master's degree, Flagello went to Italy, where he took lessons with Ildebrando Pizzetti at the Santa Cecilia Academy in Rome (Mus.D., 1956). Returning to the U.S., he taught composition and conducting at the Manhattan School of Music until 1977; appeared as a guest conductor with the Chicago Lyric Opera and the N.Y. City Opera; also toured as accompanist to Tito Schipa, Richard Tucker, and other singers.

WORKS: *Lyra* for 6 Brass Instruments (1945); *Beowulf*, symph. poem (1949); Piano Concerto No. 1 (1950); *Mirra*, opera in 3 acts (1953); *The Wig*, one-act opera (1953); Piano Concerto No. 2 (1955); Violin Concerto (1956); *Rip Van Winkle*, children's operetta (1957); *Missa sinfonica* for Orch. without Voices (1957); *The Sisters*, one-act opera (1958; N.Y., Feb. 23, 1961); Concerto for String Orch. (1959); *The Judgment of St. Francis*, one-act opera (1959; N.Y., March 18, 1966); Divertimento for Piano and Percussion (1960); *Capriccio* for Cello and Orch. (1961); *Burlesca* for Flute and Guitar (1961); Piano Concerto No. 3 (1962); Concertino for Piano, Brass, and Timpani (1963); Concerto for Harp (1963); Violin Sonata (1963); *Lautrec*, ballet suite (1965); Symph. No. 1 (1967; N.Y., April 23, 1971); *Passion of Martin Luther King* for Soloists, Orch., and Chorus (1968); *Te Deum for All Mankind* for Chorus and Orch. (1968); *The Piper of Hamelin*, children's opera to Flagello's own libretto (1970); Symph. No. 2, *Symphony of the Winds*, for Wind Instruments and Percussion (1970); *Philos* for Brass Quintet (1970); *Ricercare* for Brass and Percussion (1971); *Remembrance* for Soprano, Flute, and String Quartet (1971); *Credendum* for Violin and Orch. (1973); *Benedictus* for a cappella Chorus (1974); *Prisma* for Horn Septet (1974); Piano Concerto No. 4 (1975); *Canto* for Soprano and Orch. (1978); *Furanna* for Flute (1978); *Diptych* for Brass Trio (1979); *Odyssey* for Symphonic Band (1981); *Quattro amori*, song cycle for Mezzo-soprano and Piano (1983); *Beyond the Horizon*, 3-act opera (1983).

Flagg, Josiah, American bandmaster; b. Woburn, Mass., May 28, 1737; d. c.1795. He organized and drilled the first regular militia band of Boston (most probably the first group of that nature in America); on June 29, 1769, presented its first concert, and on Oct. 28, 1773, gave a "final Grand Concert" at Faneuil Hall with about 50 players. Subsequently he settled in Providence and served there as lieutenant colonel during the Revolution; little is known of his other activities. He publ. *A Collection of the best Psalm Tunes in 2, 3 and 4 parts ... To which is added some Hymns and Anthems, the Greater part of them never before printed in America* (1764; introduced the anthem to the English colonies; engraved by Paul Revere) and *Sixteen Anthems ... To which is added a few Psalm Tunes* (1766). Flagg was the first in America to establish a connection between sacred and secular music. That he was an educated practical musician and was acquainted with European music is evidenced by the type of programs he conducted.

BIBLIOGRAPHY: O.G. Sonneck, *Early Concert Life in America* (Leipzig, 1907); *Dictionary of American Biography,* vol. VI (N.Y., 1931); R.F. Camus, *Military Music of the American Revolution* (Chapel Hill, N.C., 1976).

Flagler, Isaac Van Vleck, American organist; b. Albany, May 15, 1844; d. Auburn, N.Y., March 16, 1909. He studied with H.W.A. Beale at Albany, Edouard Batiste in Paris, and others. He was an organist at and music director of various churches; co-founder of the American Guild of Organists. He publ. *The Organist's Treasury, Flagler's New Collection of Organ Music,* and *Flagler's New Collection for Choirs and Soloists.*

Flagstad, Kirsten, famous Norwegian soprano; b. Hamar, July 12, 1895; d. Oslo, Dec. 7, 1962. She studied with her mother (coach at the Oslo Opera) and with Ellen Schytte-Jacobsen in Oslo; in 1912 she made her debut there at the National Theater as Nuri in d'Albert's opera *Tiefland;* then sang in oratorio, operettas, and musical comedies in Oslo; in 1928–30 was engaged at the Storm Theater at Göteborg; in 1931-32, again at the National Theater; in 1933 and 1934, appeared at the Bayreuth Festival. On Feb. 2, 1935, she made a very successful debut at the Metropolitan Opera in N.Y. as Sieglinde in *Die Walküre,* and sang Isolde (her most celebrated role), Brünnhilde, Elisabeth, Elsa, and Kundry in her first season there; appeared at Covent Garden in London, as Isolde, on May 18, 1936. She also sang with the San Francisco Opera (1935–38) and the Chicago City Opera (1937), and made numerous guest appearances through the U.S. and Australia. In 1941 she returned to Norway; in 1951 she reappeared at the Metropolitan Opera, singing Isolde and Leonore; made her farewell appearance there on March 19, 1952. She was director of the Norwegian Opera from 1958 to 1960.

BIBLIOGRAPHY: *The Flagstad Manuscript* (an autobiography narrated to Louis Biancolli, N.Y., 1952); E. McArthur, *Flagstad: A Personal Memoir* (N.Y., 1965).

Flament, Edouard, French composer, conductor, and bassoon virtuoso; b. Douai, Aug. 27, 1880; d. Bois-Colombes (Seine), Dec. 27, 1958. He studied at the Paris Cons. with Bourdeau (bassoon), Lavignac, Caussade, and Lenepveu (composition). After graduation (1898), he played the bassoon in the Lamoureux Orch. (1898–1907) and in the Société des Instruments à Vent (1898–1923); conducted opera and concerts in Paris (1907–12), Algiers (1912–14), and Marseilles (1919–20); summer concerts at Fontainebleau (1920–22); then with the Diaghilev ballet in Monte Carlo, Berlin, London, and Spain (1923–29). In 1930 he became conductor at the Paris Radio.

WORKS: An exceptionally prolific composer, he wrote between 1894 and 1957 some 175 opus numbers, including the operas *La Fontaine de Castalie, Le Cœur de la rose,* and *Lydéric et Rosèle;* 8 symphs.; *Oceano Nox,* symph. poem; *Variations radio-phoniques;* 5 piano concertos; *Concertstück* for Bassoon and Orch.; Divertimento for 6 Bassoons; Quintet for 5 Bassoons; Quartet for 4 Bassoons; 3 string quartets; Violin Sonata, Viola Sonata, 2 cello sonatas, etc.; about 180 film scores. Few of his works are publ.; most of the larger ones remain unperformed.

Flammer, Harold, American music publisher; b. New York, Sept. 19, 1889; d. Bronxville, N.Y., Oct. 23, 1939. He studied at Princeton Univ. (Litt.B., 1911). In 1913 he entered G. Schirmer, Inc.; in 1917, established Harold Flammer, Inc.; in 1929–34 was vice-president and business manager of G. Schirmer; in 1934, re-established his own firm. During the years 1932–36 he was at various times treasurer, president, and vice-president of the Publishers Music Assoc. of the U.S. He publ. piano compositions, songs, and many song texts and translations.

Flanagan, William, American composer; b. Detroit, Aug. 14, 1923; d. New York, Aug. 31, 1969 (found dead in his apartment, a victim of an overdose of barbiturates). He studied composition at the Eastman School of Music in Rochester, N.Y., with Burrill Phillips and Bernard Rogers; then at the Berkshire Music Center in Tanglewood with Arthur Honegger, Arthur Berger, and Aaron Copland; also, in N.Y., with David Diamond. Concurrently, he became engaged in musical journalism; was a reviewer for the *N.Y. Herald Tribune* (1957–60). His style of composition is characterized by an intense pursuit of an expressive melodic line, projected on polycentric but firmly tonal harmonies.
WORKS: One-act opera, *Bartleby*, after Melville's short story (1952–57; N.Y., Jan. 24, 1961); *A Concert Ode* for Orch. (1951; Detroit, Jan. 14, 1960); *A Concert Overture* (1948; N.Y., Dec. 4, 1959); *Divertimento for Classical Orchestra* (1948; Toledo, Ohio, Jan. 9, 1960); *Notations* for Large Orch. (1960); *Chapter from Ecclesiastes* for Mixed Chorus and String Quintet (N.Y., March 21, 1963); *Narrative* for Orch. (Detroit, March 25, 1965); Divertimento for String Quartet (1947); Chaconne for Violin and Piano (1948); Passacaglia for Piano (1947); Piano Sonata (1950); song cycles. He wrote background music for Edward Albee's plays *The Sandbox* (1961) and *The Ballad of the Sad Café* (1963).
BIBLIOGRAPHY: A catalogue of his works appears in *Composers of the Americas,* vol. 12 (Washington, D.C., 1966).

Flatt, Lester (Raymond), American country-music singer and guitarist; b. Overton County, Tenn., June 19, 1914; d. Nashville, May 11, 1979. He joined Bill Monroe's Blue Grass Boys as a singer in 1944; then formed a duo with Earl Scruggs, the banjo player; they organized their own band, the Foggy Mountain Boys, and soon established themselves as leading figures in country music. Flatt became famous for his "Lester Flatt G Run" on the guitar, accompanied by Scruggs's 3-finger banjo style. After their partnership came apart in 1969, Flatt played with the remaining members of the band, which later adopted the name The Nashville Brass. Among the best-known songs of Flatt and Scruggs were *Roll in My Sweet Baby's Arms, Old Salty Dog Blues, The Ballad of Jed Clampett* (from the inane

television comedy series "The Beverly Hillbillies"), and *Foggy Mountain Breakdown* (the theme song of the film *Bonnie and Clyde*).

Flaxland, Gustave-Alexandre, French music publisher; b. Strasbourg, Jan. 26, 1821; d. Paris, Nov. 11, 1895. He studied at the Paris Cons.; founded a music publishing business in 1847, and, by acquiring copyrights of compositions of Schumann and Wagner, made it prominent. He sold his firm to Durand et Schönewerk in 1869, and commenced making pianos.

Flecha, Mateo, Spanish composer; b. Prades, Tarragona, 1530; d. Solsona, Lérida, Feb. 20, 1604. He received his musical education from his uncle, also named **Mateo Flecha** (1481–1553); was boy chorister in the court chapel at Arevalo. In 1564 he entered the imperial chapel in Vienna; by 1579 was in Prague with the Emperor; Philip III made it possible for him to return to Spain as abbot of Portella in 1599. He publ. a book of madrigals in Venice (1568), and the collection *Las ensaladas* (Prague, 1581), containing "ensaladas" (quodlibets, comic songs) by his uncle, and some by himself. This collection was brought out in a modern edition by Higinio Anglés, with an introductory essay on the Flechas (Barcelona, 1954).

Fleck, Henry T., American music educator; b. Buffalo, April 28, 1863; d. Rockaway Beach, Long Island, N.Y., Sept. 6, 1937. He studied music with Wüllner at Cologne; upon returning to the U.S., he organized in N.Y. the Euterpe Choral Society (1889) and the Harlem Phil. Society (1890), which he conducted till 1901; also established free concerts of chamber music in N.Y. From 1901 until his death he was a prof. of music at Hunter College in N.Y.

Fleetwood, Mick, English pop musician; b. Redruth, July 24, 1947. He began his career as a drummer in a local band; then played with John Mayall's Bluesbreakers. In 1967 he teamed up with the string bass player John McVie (b. London, Nov. 26, 1945) and, annexing his Scottish prefix "Mc," formed a band named Fleetwood Mack. The personnel of Fleetwood Mack was anything but stable. A procession of British rockers, most notably Peter Green, came and went as though through a revolving door into the body of Fleetwood Mack; McVie married a woman providentially named Christine Perfect (b. Greenodd, Lancashire, July 12, 1943), who became an integral part of the group. The group flew to California and took shape with the addition of Stephanie "Stevie" Nicks (b. Phoenix, Ariz., May 26, 1948) and Lindsey Buckingham (b. Palo Alto, Calif., Oct. 3, 1949). Following the Zeitgeist of the United Kingdom and the disunited state of California, the band drifted away from blues into cosmopolitan pop. In this Anglo-Californian incarnation Fleetwood Mack reached the empyrean heights of the pop charts in the ultra-platinum category. Songs: *Future Games, Over My Head, Say You Love Me, Rhianon, Go Your Own Way, You Make*

Loving Fun. Their album *Fleetwood Mac, Rumours* sold over 14 million copies.

Flégier, Ange, French composer; b. Marseilles, Feb. 25, 1846; d. there, Oct. 8, 1927. He studied first at the Cons. of Marseilles and then at the Paris Cons. (1866–69), returning to Marseilles in 1870. He wrote *Fatima,* comic opera; *Ossian,* lyric poem for Soli, Chorus, and Orch.; *Françoise de Rimini,* cantata; miscellaneous orch. pieces (*Valse du rêve, Badinage, Habanera, Minuet, Berceuse, Mignardise,* etc.); many songs, of which *Le Cor* is the best known.

Fleischer, Anton, Hungarian conductor and composer; b. Makó, May 30, 1891; d. Budapest, Oct. 30, 1945. He studied in Budapest with Kodály; in 1913–15, conducted at the Budapest Municipal Theater; conducted at the Budapest Opera (1915) and taught at the National Cons. from 1918; won the Hungarian State Prize with his symph. on Oscar Wilde's *The Nightingale and the Rose* (1915).

Fleischer, Oskar, eminent German musicologist; b. Zörbig, Nov. 2, 1856; d. Berlin, Feb. 8, 1933. He studied philology at Halle (1878–83); then musicology in Berlin under Spitta. In 1892 he became Privatdozent at the Univ. of Berlin; promoted to professorship in 1895. He was a founder and first president of the Internationale Musik-Gesellschaft (1899); together with Johannes Wolf edited its publications, *Zeitschrift* and *Sammelbände,* until 1904. In 1892 he represented the Prussian government at the Vienna Exhibition, on which he publ. an exhaustive report, *Die Bedeutung der internationalen Musik-und Theaterausstellung in Wien für Kunst und Wissenschaft der Musik* (Leipzig, 1894).

WRITINGS: *Führer durch die königliche Sammlung alter Musikinstrumente* (Berlin, 1892); *Musikinstrumente aus deutscher Urzeit* (1893); *W.A. Mozart* (1899); *Führer durch die Bachausstellung* (Berlin, 1901); *Neumen-Studien* (4 vols.: 1895; 1897; 1904, with facsimiles of late Byzantine notation; 1923, *Die germanischen Neumen als Schlüssel zum altchristlichen und gregorianischen Gesang).* He also wrote short biographies of the masters of music in *Grosse Männer* (1922–23); contributed valuable articles to various German music journals.

Fleisher, Edwin A., American patron of music; b. Philadelphia, July 11, 1877; d. there, Jan. 9, 1959. He studied at Harvard Univ. (B.A., 1899). He founded a Symph. Club in Philadelphia (1909) and engaged conductors to rehearse an amateur orch. there; at the same time he began collecting orch. scores and complete sets of parts, which became the nucleus of the great Edwin A. Fleisher Collection, presented by him to the Free Library of Philadelphia. A cumulative catalogue covering the period from 1929 to 1977 was publ. in Boston in 1979.

Fleisher, Leon, distinguished American pianist; b. San Francisco, July 23, 1928, of Jewish-Russian immigrant parents. His father was a tailor; his mother a singing teacher. He received the rudiments of music from his mother; then studied piano with Lev Shorr. He played in public at the age of 6; then was sent to Europe for studies with Artur Schnabel at Lake Como, Italy; continued his studies with him in N.Y. At the age of 14 he appeared as soloist with the San Francisco Symph. Orch.; at 16 he was soloist with the N.Y. Phil. (Nov. 4, 1944); in 1952 he became the first American to win first prize at the Queen Elisabeth of Belgium International Competition in Brussels; this catapulted him into a brilliant career. He made several European tours; in 1958 played at the Bayreuth and Salzburg festivals; also gave highly successful recitals in South America. In 1961–62 he was a soloist with the San Francisco Symph. Orch. to observe its 75th anniversary. At the peak of his career, a pianistic tragedy befell him; he was stricken with a mysterious and mystifying neurological ailment that made the fingers of his right hand curl up on itself, completely incapacitating him as a pianist; this thing was diagnosed as carpaltunnel syndrome. A possible treatment was surgical, by cutting the ligament and removing the tenosynovium around the tendons to relieve the pressure on the nerve. Disabled as he was, Fleisher turned to piano works written for left hand alone commissioned by Paul Wittgenstein, the Austrian pianist who lost his right arm during World War I, to Ravel, Prokofiev, and others. Fleisher learned these concertos and performed them successfully. He also began to conduct. He studied conducting with Pierre Monteux in San Francisco and at the conducting school established by Monteux in Hancock, Maine; he also profited from advice from George Szell. In 1968 he became artistic director of the Theater Chamber Players in Washington, D.C.; in 1970 he became music director of the Annapolis Symph. Orch. as well. From 1973 to 1977 he was associate conductor of the Baltimore Symph. Orch.; then was its resident conductor in 1977–78. He appeared as a guest conductor at the Mostly Mozart Festival in N.Y., and also with the Boston Symph., San Francisco Symph., Cincinnati Symph., and the Los Angeles Chamber Orch. A treatment with cortisone injections and even acupuncture and the fashionable biofeedback to control the electrophysiological motor system did not help. In 1981 he decided to undergo surgery; it was miraculously successful, and on Sept. 16, 1982, he made a spectacular comeback as a bimanual pianist, playing the *Symphonic Variations* by César Franck with Sergiu Comissiona and the Baltimore Symph. He then resumed his active career.

Fleisher devoted much time to teaching; he joined the faculty of the Peabody Cons. of Music in Baltimore in 1959, and subsequently was named to the Andrew W. Mellon Chair in Piano; was also a visiting prof. at the Rubin Academy of Music in Jerusalem. Among his brilliant pupils were André Watts and Lorin Hollander.

BIBLIOGRAPHY: David Ewen, *Musicians since 1900* (N.Y., 1978).

Fleming, Robert, Canadian pianist and composer;

b. Prince Albert, Saskatchewan, Nov. 12, 1921; d. Ottawa, Nov. 28, 1976. He studied piano with Arthur Benjamin and composition with Herbert Howells at the Royal College of Music in London (1937–39); served in the Canadian Air Force during World War II; after the war he continued his musical education at the Toronto Cons. with Healey Willan and others. He subsequently joined the National Film Board of Canada in 1946 and was its music director from 1958 to 1970; taught at Carleton Univ. in Ottawa from 1970 until his death. He wrote music for some 250 films.

WORKS: Ballets: *Chapter 13* (1950); *Shadow on the Prairie* (1951); *Ballet Introduction* (1960); 3 puppet plays; *Around the House,* suite for Orch. (1942); *Rondo* for Orch. (1942); *6 Variations on a Liturgical Theme* for String Orch. (1946); *Kaleidoscope* for Small Orch. (1949); *Red River Country* for Small Orch. (1953); *Hymn to War* for Baritone and Strings (1954); *Recollections* for Violin and Strings (1954); *Summer Suite* for Orch. (1957); *Suite Short and Simple* for Piano and Strings (1959); Piano Concerto (1963); *3 Contrasts* for School Orch. (1964); *Concerto '64* for Piano and Orch. (1964); Tuba Concerto (1966); *4 Fantasias on Canadian Folk Themes* for Orch. or Symph. Band (1966); Divertimento for Organ, 2 Oboes, and Strings (1970); *Hexad* for Small Orch. (1972); *Our Mind Was the Singer,* cycle for Baritone and Orch. (1972); *3 Scenarios* for Symph. Band (1974); *Of a Timeless Land* for Contralto and Orch. (1974); *Bella Bella Sonatina* for Violin and Piano (1943); Violin Sonata (1944); *Colors of the Rainbow* for Wind Quartet, String Quartet, and Harp (1962); *Maritime Suite* for Wind Quartet, String Quartet, and Harp (1962); *3 Miniatures* for Brass Quintet (1962); *Go for Baroque* for Flute, Oboe, and Harpsichord (1963); *3 Dialogues* for Flute or Oboe, and Piano or Harpsichord (1964); *A Quartet for Strings* (1969); *Threo* for Soprano Saxophone and Piano (1972); piano pieces; choruses.

Flesch, Carl, celebrated violinist and pedagogue; b. Moson, Hungary, Oct. 9, 1873; d. Lucerne, Switzerland, Nov. 14, 1944. He was a violin pupil of Grün at the Vienna Cons. (1886–89), then of Sauzay and Marsick at the Paris Cons. (1890–94). From 1897 to 1902 he was a prof. at the Cons. in Bucharest; in 1903–8, a prof. at the Cons. in Amsterdam. From 1924 till 1928 Flesch was head of the violin dept. of the Curtis Inst. in Philadelphia; then divided his time between the U.S. and Germany; in 1933 he went to England; eventually went to Hungary and then to Switzerland, where he taught at the Lucerne Cons. He issued the standard pedagogic work for violin, *Die Kunst des Violinspiels* in 2 vols. (Berlin, 1923, 1928; new ed., 1954), which was translated into English (Boston, 1924–30), Italian (Milan, 1953), Polish (Cracow, 1964), and Russian (vol. 1, Moscow, 1964); also wrote *Das Klangproblem im Geigenspiel* (Berlin, 1931; in Eng., N.Y., 1934). His MS work *Die Hohe Schule des Violin-Fingersatzes* was publ. first in Italian (Milan, 1960), then in Eng., as *Violin Fingering, Its Theory and Practice* (N.Y., 1966). His *Erinnerungen eines Geigers* was publ. posthumously

(Freiburg im Breisgau, 1960), and appeared previously in English translation, edited by Hans Keller and C.F. Flesch, under the title *The Memoirs of Carl Flesch* (London, 1957; 3rd ed., 1974). Carl Flesch publ. new editions of Kreutzer's études, Mozart's violin sonatas (with Schnabel), 20 études of Paganini, and the violin concertos of Beethoven, Mendelssohn, and Brahms.

Fleta, Miguel, Spanish tenor; b. Albalate, Dec. 28, 1893; d. La Coruña, May 30, 1938. He studied at the Barcelona Cons.; also took vocal lessons in Italy with **Louisa Pierrich,** who became his wife. He made his debut in Trieste on Nov. 14, 1919. After several busy tours in Europe, Mexico, and South America, he came to the U.S. in 1923; made his debut at the Metropolitan Opera in N.Y. on Nov. 8, 1923, as Cavaradossi in *Tosca;* remained on its roster until 1925; in 1924 and 1926 sang as La Scala in Milan, where he appeared in the premiere of *Turandot.* In 1926 he returned to Spain.

Fleta, Pierre, French tenor, son of **Miguel Fleta;** b. Villefranche-sur-Mer, July 4, 1925. He studied with his mother, **Louise Pierrick-Fleta,** a member of La Scala; then sang as a boy soprano at Cannes; went to London, where he was engaged as a professional singer before making his opera debut in Barcelona in 1949. He made a concert tour in the Middle East in 1951; then was engaged as first tenor at the Théâtre de la Monnaie in Brussels (1952). He has also developed a repertoire of French, Italian, Spanish, and English folk songs.

Fletcher, Alice C., American ethnologist; b. Cuba (of American parents), March 16, 1838; d. Washington, D.C., April 6, 1923. She devoted her life to the study of North American Indians, among whom she lived for a number of years; in 1896, became vice-president of the American Assoc. for the Advancement of Science; then president of the American Anthropological Society (1903) and the American Folk Lore Society (1905). She is the author of *Indian Story and Song from North America* (1900); *A Study of Omaha Indian Music* (1903); *Indian Games and Dances* (1915); numerous articles in the *Journal of American Folk Lore;* etc.

BIBLIOGRAPHY: *Dictionary of American Biography,* vol. VI (N.Y., 1931).

Fletcher, Grant, American composer; b. Hartsburg, Ill., Oct. 25, 1913. He studied music theory with Bessie Louise Smith at Illinois Wesleyen Univ. (1932–35); took a course in conducting with Thor Johnson; for 3 summers (1937–39) attended composition classes with Ernst Krenek at the Univ. of Michigan; then took classes with Healy Willan in Toronto; later studied at the Eastman School of Music in Rochester, N.Y., where his teachers were Bernard Rogers and Howard Hanson (1947–49); also had private lessons with Herbert Elwell in Cleveland. In 1945–48 he was conductor of the Akron (Ohio) Symph. Orch.; from 1949–51 he was on the faculty of the Chicago Musical College; later was on the staff of the Arizona State Univ. at Tempe (1956–78). In his music he follows the median line of modern techniques; he adopts the Baroque forms in most of his compostions while diversifying the contrapuntal and harmonic ingredients, achieving considerable originality. He is ingenious in combining instrumental ensembles.

WORKS: FOR THE STAGE: Buffa-fantasy opera, *The Carrion Crow,* after J.J. Niles (1948); ballet-pantomime, *Lomotawi* (N.Y., 1957); opera, *The Sack of Calabasas,* after J.M. Myers (1964–66). FOR ORCH.: *Rhapsody* for Flute and Strings (1935; withdrawn); *A Rhapsody of Dances* for Chamber Orch. (1935; for Wind Instruments, 1970; for Full Orch., 1972); *Nocturne* (1938); *Song of Honor,* on Yugoslav themes (1944; first perf. as *A Song for Warriors,* Rochester, Oct. 25, 1945); *An American Overture* (1945; Duluth, April 23, 1948); *Panels from a Theater Wall* (1949; Rochester, April 27, 1949); Symph. No. 1 (1950; Rochester, April 24, 1951); Symph. No. 2 (1982–83); *The Pocket Encyclopedia of Orchestral Instruments,* with optional Narrator (1953; also perf. as *Dictionary of Musical Instruments*); 4 concertos: No. 1 for Piano and Orch. (1953); No. 2, *Regency Concerto,* for Piano and Strings (1966); No. 3, *Concerto for Winds* (1969); No. 4, *Multiple Concerto for 5 Solo Winds,* for one Soloist playing on 5 different Wind Instruments, with Wind Ensemble (1970); *Sumare* and *Wintare* (1956); *7 Cities of Cibola* (1961); *Retrospection (Rhapsody III)* for Flute, 9 Strings, and Tape (1965; revision of *Rhapsody* of 1935); *Dances from the Southwest* for Strings and Piano (1966); *Glyphs* for Band (1970); *Diversion III* for Strings (1971; *I* and *II* are for Piano); ballet suite, *The 5th of May* (1972); *Aubade* for Wind Instruments (1974); *Celebration of Times Past* (1976); *A More Proper Burial Music for Wolfgang* for Wind Instruments (1977); *Saxsōn II* for Saxophone and Strings (1977; *I* is for Solo Saxophone); *Serenade* (1979); *Symphonic Suite* (1980). FOR VOICE: *The Crisis,* after Thomas Paine, for Chorus and Orch. (1945; Walla Walla, Wash., Feb. 22, 1977); *House Made of Dawn* for Alto, Piano, Flute, Indian Drum, and Rattle (1957); 4 sacred cantatas: No. 1, *O Childe Swete* (1965); No. 2 (1967); No. 3, *The Branch* (1970); No. 4, *Judas* (1978); *Who Is Sylvia?* for Baritone, Flute, Oboe, Bassoon, and Guitar (1969); *Psalm I* for Chorus and Organ (1979); choruses; songs. CHAMBER MUSIC: *Musicke for Christening:* No. 1 for Cello and Piano (1945); No. 2 for Saxophone and Piano (1979); No. 3 for Clarinet and Piano (1979); *Heralds* for Brass and Timpani (1949); *Tower Music* for Brass (1957); 5 sonatas: No. 1 for Clarinet and Piano (1958); No. 2, *Sōn,* for Cello and Piano (1972); No. 3 for Saxophone and Piano (1974); No. 4 for Solo Viola (1977); No. 5 for Solo Violin (1983); *Prognos* for Brass Quintet (1965–67); *Uroboros* for Percussion (1967); *Octocelli* for 8 Solo Cellos or their multiples (1971); Trio for Flute, Guitar, and Piano (1973); *Toccata II* for Marimba (1979; *I* is for Piano); *Quadra* for Percussion (1975); String Quartet (1975; 4 earlier quartets were withdrawn); *Zortzicos* No. 2 for Double Bass and Piano (1977); *Zortzicos* No. 3 for Bassoon and Piano (1979); *Zortzicos* No. 4 for Cello and Piano (1979); *Zortzicos* No. 5 for Clarinet and Piano

(1980); *Zortzicos* No. 6 for Viola and Piano (1980; *Zortzicos* No. 1 is the last movement of the piano piece *Izquierdas*); *Saxsōn I* for Saxophone Solo (1977); *Trio Bulgarico* for Flute, Oboe, and Bassoon (1980); *Palimpsest* for Flute Choir (1980); *Madrigals* for Clarinet Choir (1981). FOR PIANO: *2 Books of Nocturnes* (1935); *4 American Dance Pieces* (1944); *Openend Triptych* (1957); *Izquierdas* for Left Hand (1967); *Toccata I* (1974); also *Dodecachordon* for Organ (1967).

WRITINGS: *Fundamental Principles of Counterpoint* (Rock Hill, S.C., 1942); *Syullabus for Advanced Integrated Theory* (Tempe, Ariz., 1962; revised 4th ed., 1976); *Rhythm: Notation and Production* (Tempe, 1967).

Fletcher, Percy E., English composer; b. Derby, Dec. 12, 1879; d. London, Sept. 10, 1932. He went to London in 1899 as a conductor at various theaters there; he composed many works in a light, melodious style, including the orch. pieces *Woodland Pictures, Sylvan Scenes, Parisian Sketches, 3 Frivolities,* and the overture *Vanity Fair;* also a short sacred cantata, *Passion of Christ.*

Fleury, André, French organist and composer; b. Neuilly-sur-Seine, July 25, 1903. He studied with his father; later with Gigout, Marcel Dupré, and Louis Vierne. In 1930 he became organist at St. Augustin, Paris; in 1943 he was appointed prof. of organ playing at the Ecole Normale de Musique; after World War II he taught at the Cons. of Dijon. Fleury wrote 2 symphs. for Organ (1947, 1949) and numerous other works for his instrument.

Fleury, Louis, eminent French flutist; b. Lyons, May 24, 1878; d. Paris, June 11, 1926. He studied at the Paris Cons.; from 1905 until his death was head of the famous Société Moderne d'Instruments à Vent, also (from 1906) of the Société des Concerts d'Autrefois, with which he gave concerts in England; made appearances with Melba and Calvé. Debussy composed *Syrinx* for Unaccompanied Flute for him. He edited much old flute music, including sonatas and other pieces by Blavet, Naudet, Purcell, J. Stanley, etc., and contributed to French and English periodicals ("Souvenirs d'un flûtiste," *Le Monde Musical;* etc.).

Flipse, Eduard, Dutch conductor; b. Wissekerke, Feb. 26, 1896; d. Etten-Leur, Sept. 11, 1973. He studied piano and composition in Rotterdam and conducting in Utrecht. In 1930 he became chief conductor of the Rotterdam Phil. Orch., a post he retained until 1965. In 1952 he became the chief conductor of the Holland Festival, and was later chief conductor of the Antwerp Phil. Orch. (1961–70). During his long tenure in Rotterdam, he introduced works of numerous contemporary composers. He was also a passionate propagandist of the music of Gustav Mahler.

Flodin, Karl, Finnish composer; b. Wasa (Vaasa),

July 10, 1858; d. Helsinki, Nov. 30, 1925. He studied music with Faltin in Helsinki (1877–83), and with Jadassohn at the Leipzig Cons. (1890–92). In 1908 he went to Buenos Aires as music critic for a German paper there; returned to Finland in 1921. He publ. numerous essays on Finnish music (in Finnish and German); wrote a biography of Martin Wegelius (1922); composed a *Cortège* for Horn and Orch., as well as incidental music to various plays; publ. some 80 piano pieces. He was married to the singer **Adée Leander** (1873–1935).

Floersheim, Otto, editor and composer; b. Aix-la-Chapelle, March 2, 1853; d. Geneva, Nov. 30, 1917. He was a pupil of Ferdinand Hiller at Cologne; went to N.Y. in 1875; became editor of the *Musical Courier* in 1880, and from 1894 to 1904 was manager of its Berlin branch. As a music journalist and a man of musical affairs, he was very influential in America; he was also a composer of competently put together piano pieces and songs in a German Romantic vein.

Flood, (William Henry) Grattan, Irish organist and music historian; b. Lismore, Nov. 1, 1859; d. Enniscorthy, Aug. 6, 1928. He served as a church organist in Dublin; achieved recognition as a writer on Irish music and musicians. He publ. *History of Irish Music* (1895; 4th ed., 1927); *Story of the Harp* (1905); *Story of the Bagpipe* (1911); *W. Vincent Wallace, A Memoir* (1912); *John Field of Dublin* (Dublin, 1920); *Introductory Sketch of Irish Musical History* (1921); *Early Tudor Composers* (1925); *Late Tudor Composers* (1929); was the editor of *Songs and Airs of O'Carolan, Moore's Irish Melodies, Armagh Hymnal,* and *The Spirit of the Nation.*

Floquet, Etienne Joseph, French composer; b. Aix-en-Provence, Nov. 23, 1748; d. Paris, May 10, 1785. After studying in his native town, he went to Paris; there he wrote the opera-ballet *L'Union de l'amour et des arts,* produced with great success at the Académie Royale de Musique (Sept. 7, 1773); his 2nd opera, *Azolan, ou Le Serment indiscret* (Nov. 22, 1774, also at the Académie), was a fiasco. Floquet then went to Italy, where he perfected his knowledge by studying with Sala in Naples and with Martini in Bologna. Returning to Paris, he had 2 operas performed at the Académie: *Hellé* (Jan. 5, 1779) and *Le Seigneur bien-faisant* (Dec. 14, 1780). He also wrote a comic opera, *La Nouvelle Omphale* (Comédie-Italienne, Nov. 22, 1782). In an attempt to challenge Gluck's superiority, Floquet wrote the opera *Alceste* on the same subject as Gluck's famous work, but it was never produced.
BIBLIOGRAPHY: A. Pougin, *Etienne-Joseph Floquet* (Paris, 1863); F. Huot, *Etude biographique sur Etienne-Joseph Floquet* (Aix, 1903).

Florence (real name, **Houghton**), **Evangeline,** American soprano; b. Cambridge, Mass., Dec. 12, 1873; d. London, Nov. 1, 1928. She studied with Henschel and Lilli Lehmann; made her debut in London, in 1892, and carried on her entire concert career in England.

Flores, Bernal, Costa Rican composer; b. San José, July 28, 1937. After acquiring the rudiments of music in Costa Rica, he came to the U.S. and enrolled at the Eastman School of Music in Rochester, N.Y. (M.M., 1962; Ph.D., 1964). Returning to Costa Rica, he became a prof. at the Cons. of San José.
WORKS: Symph. No. 1 for Strings (1965); Symph. No. 2 (1966); Concerto for Piano, Percussion, and Orch. (1963); Clarinet Concerto (1968); piano pieces; songs.

Floridia, Pietro, Italian composer; b. Modica, Sicily, May 5, 1860; d. New York, Aug. 16, 1932. He studied in Naples with Cesi (piano) and Lauro Rossi (composition); while at the Naples Cons. he publ. several piano pieces which became quite popular. On May 7, 1882, he brought out in Naples a comic opera, *Carlotta Clepier.* From 1888 to 1892 he taught at the Cons. of Palermo; then lived in Milan. In 1904 he emigrated to the U.S.; taught at the Cincinnati College of Music (1906–8); in 1908 settled in N.Y.; in 1913 organized and conducted an Italian Symph. Orch. there. His music (mostly for the stage) is written in a competent manner, in the style of the Italian *verismo.*
WORKS: Operas: *Maruzza* (Venice, Aug. 23, 1894); *La colonia libera* (Rome, May 7, 1899); *Paoletta* (Cincinnati, Aug. 29, 1910); also *The Scarlet Letter* (1902; not produced) and *Malia* (completed in 1932; not produced). Floridia edited a valuable collection in 2 vols., *Early Italian Songs and Airs* (Philadelphia, 1923).

Florimo, Francesco, Italian musician and historian; b. S. Giorgio Morgeto, Calabria, Oct. 12, 1800; d. Naples, Dec. 18, 1888. In 1817 he entered the Collegio di Musica at Naples; Furno, Elia, Zingarelli, and Tritto were his teachers; in 1826–51 he was librarian there. He was Bellini's closest friend; in 1876 he escorted the latter's remains from Paris to Catania, and publ. the pamphlet "Trasporto delle ceneri di Bellini a Catania"; composed *Sinfonia funebre per la morte di Bellini;* founded the Bellini Prize, a competition open to Italian composers not over 30.
WRITINGS: His chief work is *Cenno storico sulla scuola musicale di Napoli* (2 vols., Naples, 1869–71; republ. 1880–84, in 4 vols., as *La scuola musicale di Napoli e i suoi Conservatori*), a complete musical history of Naples and its conservatories, their teachers and pupils, etc.; despite numerous errors, it remains an invaluable guide; also, *Riccardo Wagner ed i Wagneristi* (Naples, 1876); *Bellini, Memorie e lettere* (Florence, 1882); *Album Bellini* (Naples, 1886), containing opinions by many eminent musicians on Bellini's works; and *Metodo di canto,* adopted by the Paris Cons. and described as "magistrale" by Rossini. Florimo was also an excellent singing teacher.
BIBLIOGRAPHY: G. Megali del Giudice, *Francesco Florimo* (Naples, 1901).

Florio, Caryl (real name, **William James Robjohn**), organist and composer; b. Tavistock, Devon, Nov. 3,

1843; d. Morganton, N.C., Nov. 21, 1920. He left England at the age of 14 and settled in N.Y.; was engaged as a singer and organist at various churches in N.Y., Baltimore, Indianapolis, etc.; conducted choral societies in N.Y.; eventually settled in Asheville, N.C. He wrote 2 operas (the first work written for such an ensemble); Piano Concerto; 4 violin sonatas; 2 piano sonatas.

Flosman, Oldřich, Czech composer; b. Plzen, April 5, 1925. He studied composition with K. Janeček at the Prague Cons. and with Bořkovec at the Prague Academy, graduating in 1950. In his music he follows the neo-Romantic tradition of the Czech school of composition, with strong formal design and an animating rhythmic pulse; the influence of Prokofiev's lyrical dynamism is much in evidence.
WORKS: Pantomime, *Pierrot and Columbine* (1957); ballets: *The Woman Partisan* (1959); *The Taming of the Shrew* (1960); *Maska* (*The Mask;* 1968); cantatas: *Tři zastavení* (*3 Stoppings;* 1960); *Count Sámo* (1970); *Moments of Victory* for Male Chorus and Chamber Ensemble (1972); Double Concerto for Harp, Clarinet, and Orch. (1950); Clarinet Concerto (1954); Bassoon Concertino (1956); 2 violin concertos (1958, 1972); *Dances* for Harp, and String Quartet or String Orch. (1961); *Cuban Overture* (1962); 2 symphs. (1964, 1974); *3 Studies* for Strings and Piano (1965); *Concertante Music* for Wind Quintet and Chamber Orch. (1965); Sonata for Soprano and Strings (1967); Flute Concerto (1969); Horn Concerto (1970); Fugues for Strings (1970); *Fires on the Hills,* symph. prelude (1973); 2 wind quintets (1948, 1962); *Bagatelles* for Winds and Piano (1950); Sonatina for Clarinet and Piano (1952); *Jeseník Suite* for Viola and Piano (1956); 3 string quartets (1956, 1963, 1966); *Dreaming about a Violin* for Violin and Piano (1962); *Romance and Scherzo* for Flute and Harp (1962); Nonet No. 2 (1967); Sonata for Wind Quintet and Piano (1970); *Chamber Music* for Flute, Oboe, Violin, Viola, and Cello (1971); Sonata for Violin, Cello, and Piano (1971); *Letters to You,* 4 songs for Soprano, Flute, and Piano (1973); *Motýli zde nežijí (Butterflies Don't Live Here Any Longer),* piano sonata inspired by the film about children's drawings from a Nazi concentration camp (1961); *4 Fugues* for Piano (1967); *5 Madrigals* for Chorus a cappella (1965).

Flothuis, Marius, eminent Dutch composer; b. Amsterdam, Oct. 30, 1914. He received his rudimentary musical education at home from his uncle, who taught him piano; then had piano lessons with Arend Koole and studied music theory with Brandts-Buys. He took academic courses at the Univ. of Amsterdam, and musicology at the Univ. of Utrecht (1932–37); served as assistant manager of the Concertgebouw Orch. After the occupation of the Netherlands by the Germans in 1940 he was dismissed from his job (his wife was half Jewish).

On Sept. 18, 1943, he was arrested by the Nazis on the charge of hiding Jews, and transported to the concentration camp in Vught, the Netherlands, and a year later to a German labor camp. His liberation came on May 4, 1945, in a forest near Schwerin; he returned to Amsterdam and was reinstated at his managerial job at the Concertgebouw. From 1955 till 1974 he was artistic director of the Concertgebouw. In 1974 he was appointed prof. of musicology at the Univ. of Utrecht. He publ. several books, including a monograph on W.A. Mozart (The Hague, 1940) and the essay *Mozarts Bearbeitungen eigener und fremder Werke* (Kassel, 1969). In his compositions he adopts the motivic method of melodic writing and its concomitant form of variations in freely dissonant counterpoint and largely neo-Classical format. Dissatisfied with his youthful works, he destroyed his MSS dating before 1934, including some perfectly acceptable symph. pieces.
WORKS: *4 Songs* for Soprano, and Small Orch. or Piano (1937–38); Concertino for Small Orch. (1940); *Sonnet* for Mezzo-soprano and Small Orch. (1939–40); *Small Overture* for Soprano and Orch. (1942); *Dramatic Overture* (1943–46); Flute Concerto (Utrecht, Dec. 19, 1945); *2 Sonnets* for Mezzo-soprano and Orch. (1945); Concerto for Horn and Small Orch. (1945); *Valses sentimentales* for Small Orch. (1946; also for Piano, 4-hands); Concerto for Piano and Small Orch. (1946–48); *To an Old Love* for Mezzo-soprano and Orch. (1948); *4 Trifles* for High Voice and Small Orch. (1948–50); *Capriccio* for Wind Orch. or String Orch. (1949); Concerto for Violin and Small Orch. (1950; Utrecht, Jan. 14, 1952); Fantasia for Harp and Small Orch. (1953; Amsterdam, May 26, 1955); *Sinfonietta concertante* for Clarinet, Saxophone, and Small Orch. (1954–55; Amsterdam, June 2, 1955); *Concert Overture* (1955); *Rondo festoso* for Orch. (Amsterdam, July 7, 1956); Clarinet Concerto (1957); *Symphonic Music* for Orch. (1957); *Spes Patriae,* sinfonietta for Small Orch. (1962); *Espressioni cordiali,* 7 bagatelles for String Orch. (1963); *Canti e Giouchi (Songs and Games)* for Wind Quintet and String Orch. (1964); *Celdroom,* radiophonic scene for Speakers, Chorus, and Orch. (1964); *Hymnus* for Soprano and Orch. (1965); Concertino for Oboe and Small Orch. (1968); *Fantasia quasi una cantate* for 12 Strings, Harpsichord, and Soprano (1968); *Per Sonare ed Ascoltare,* 5 canzonas for Flute and Orch. (1971); *Cantata silesiana* for Chorus, Flute, String Quartet, and Harpsichord (1946); *Love and Strife,* cantata for Contralto, Flute, Oboe d'Amore, Viola, and Cello (1948–49); *Een Amsterdams lied,* cantata for Solo Soprano and Baritone, Flute, Clarinet, 2 Violins, Viola, Cello, Double Bass, and Piano (1951); *Negro Lament,* after Langston Hughes, for Contralto, Saxophone, and Piano (1953); *Odysseus and Nausikaa,* madrigal for Soprano, Contralto, Tenor, Baritone, and Harp (1958–60); Solo Cello Sonata (1937–38); Nocturne for Flute, Oboe, and Clarinet (1941); Quintet for Flute, Oboe, Clarinet, Bass Clarinet, and Bassoon (1941–42); *Sonata da camera* for Flute and Piano (1943); *2 Pieces* for Guitar (1944); *Aria* for Trumpet and Piano (1944); *Aubade* for Solo Flute (1944); *3 Pieces* for 2 Horns (1945); *Ronde cham-*

pêtre for Flute and Harpsichord (1945); Solo Violin Sonata (1945); Sonatina for Horn, Trumpet, and Trombone (1945); Partita for Violin and Piano (1950); *Pour le tombeau d'Orphée* for Solo Harp (1950); *Trio serio* for Piano Trio (1950–51); *Sonata da camera* for Flute and Harp (1951); *Small Suite* for 12 Harps (1951; in collaboration with Lex Van Delden); String Quartet (1951–52); *Small Suite* for Oboe, Trumpet, Clarinet or Saxophone, and Piano (1952); Divertimento for Clarinet, Bassoon, Horn, Violin, Viola, and Double Bass (1952); *4 invenzioni* for 4 Horns (1963); Partita for 2 Violins (1966); Concertino for Oboe, Violin, Viola, and Cello (1967); *Allegro vivace* for 2 Harps (1969); *Caprices roumains* for Oboe and Piano (1975); *Adagio* for Piano, 4-hands, and Percussion (1975); *Romeo's Lament* for Solo Horn (1975); Sonata for Flute and Alto Flute (1975); Suite for Piano (1937–38); *Divertimento on a Theme of Kees Stokvis* for 2 Pianos (1946); *6 moments musicaux* for Piano (1946–47); *5 Epigrams and a Capriccio* for Piano (1970); songs.

BIBLIOGRAPHY: "Marius Flothuis on Himself," *Key Notes*, 4 (Amsterdam, 1976).

Flotow, Friedrich (Adolf Ferdinand) von, famous German opera composer; b. Teutendorf, April 27, 1813; d. Darmstadt, Jan. 24, 1883. He was a scion of an old family of nobility; he received his first music lessons from his mother; then was a chorister in Güstrow. At the age of 16 he went to Paris, where he entered the Cons. to study piano with J.P. Pixis and composition with Reicha. After the revolution of 1830, he returned home, where he completed his first opera, *Pierre et Cathérine,* set to a French libretto; it was premiered in a German translation in Ludwigslust in 1835. Returning to Paris, he collaborated with the Belgian composer Albert Grisar on the operas *Lady Melvil* (1838) and *L'Eau merveilleuse* (1839). With the composer Auguste Pilati, he composed the opera *Le Naufrage de la Méduse* (Paris, May 31, 1839; performed in a German trans. as *Die Matrosen,* Hamburg, Dec. 23, 1845). He scored a decisive acclaim with his romantic opera, *Alessandro Stradella,* based on the legendary accounts of the life of the Italian composer; it was first performed in Hamburg on Dec. 30, 1844, and had numerous subsequent productions in Germany. He achieved an even greater success with his romantic opera *Martha, oder Der Markt zu Richmond* (Vienna, Nov. 25, 1847); in it he demonstrated his ability to combine the German sentimental spirit with Italian lyricism and Parisian elegance. The libretto was based on a ballet, *Lady Henriette, ou La Servante de Greenwich* (1844), for which Flotow had composed the music for Act I; the ballet in turn was based on a vaudeville, *La Comtesse d'Egmont;* the authentic Irish melody *The Last Rose of Summer* was incorporated into the opera by Flotow, lending a certain nostalgic charm to the whole work. Flotow's aristocratic predilections made it difficult for him to remain in Paris after the revolution of 1848; he accepted the post of Intendant at the grand ducal court theater in Schwerin (1855–63); then moved to Austria; he returned to Germany in 1873, settling in Darmstadt in 1880.

WORKS: OPERAS: *Pierre et Cathérine* (first perf. in a German version, Ludwigslust, 1835); *Die Bergknappen; Alfred der Grosse; Rob-Roy* (Royaumont, Sept. 1836); *Sérafine* (Royaumont, Oct. 30, 1836); *Alice* (Paris, April 8, 1837); *La Lettre du préfet* (Paris, 1837; revised 1868); *Le comte de Saint-Mégrin* (Royaumont, June 10, 1838; revised as *Le Duc de Guise,* Paris, April 3, 1840; in German, Schwerin, Feb. 24, 1841); *Lady Melvil* (with Albert Grisar; Paris, Nov. 15, 1838); *L'eau merveilleuse* (with Grisar; Paris, Jan. 30, 1839); *Le Naufrage de la Méduse* (with Auguste Pilati; Paris, May 31, 1839; in German as *Die Matrosen,* Hamburg, Dec. 23, 1845); *L'Esclave de Camoëns* (Paris, Dec. 1, 1843; subsequent revisions under different titles); *Alessandro Stradella* (Hamburg, Dec. 30, 1844); *L'Ame en peine (Der Förster;* Paris, June 29, 1846); *Martha, oder Der Markt zu Richmond* (Vienna, Nov. 25, 1847); *Sophie Katharina, oder Die Grossfürstin* (Berlin, Nov. 19, 1850); *Rübezahl* (Retzien, Aug. 13, 1852, private perf.; Frankfurt, Nov. 26, 1853, public perf.); *Albin, oder Der Pflegesohn* (Vienna, Feb. 12, 1856; revised as *Der Müller von Meran,* Königsberg, 1859); *Herzog Johann Albrecht von Mecklenburg, oder Andreas Mylius* (Schwerin, May 27, 1857); *Pianella* (Schwerin, Dec. 27, 1857); *La Veuve Grapin* (Paris, Sept. 21, 1859; in German, Vienna, June 1, 1861); *La châtelaine (Der Märchensucher,* 1865); *Naida* (St. Petersburg, Dec. 11, 1865); *Zilda, ou La Nuit des dupes* (Paris, May 28, 1866); *Am Runenstein* (Prague, April 13, 1868); *L'Ombre* (Paris, July 7, 1870; in German as *Sein Schatten,* Vienna, Nov. 10, 1871); *Die Musikanten,* or *La Jeunesse de Mozart* (Mannheim, June 19, 1887).

BALLETS: *Lady Henriette, ou La Servante de Greenwich* (Act II by R. Burgmüller and Act III by E. Deldevez; Paris, Feb. 21, 1844); *Die Libelle,* or *La Demoiselle, ou Le Papillon ou Dolores* (Schwerin, Aug. 8, 1856); *Die Gruppe der Thetis* (Schwerin, Aug. 18, 1858); *Der Tannkönig* (Schwerin, Dec. 22, 1861); *Der Königsschuss* (Schwerin, May 22, 1864).

INSTRUMENTAL MUSIC: Symph. (1833; not extant); 2 piano concertos (1830 and 1831); *Jubel-Ouverture* (1857); also *Trio de salon* for Violin, Piano, and Cello (1845); Violin Sonata (1861); songs.

BIBLIOGRAPHY: G. von Flotow, *Beiträge zur Geschichte der Familie von Flotow* (Dresden, 1844); A. Bussensius, *Friedrich von Flotow: Eine Biographie* (Kassel, 1855); F. von Flotow, "Erinnerungen aus meinem Leben," in J. Lewinsky, ed., *Vor den Coulissen* (Berlin, 1882); B. Bardi-Poswiansky, *Flotow als Opernkomponist* (Diss., Univ. of Königsberg, 1924); J. Weissmann, *Flotow* (London, 1950); R. Stockhammer, "Friedrich von Flotows Beziehungen zu Wien," *Österreichische Musikzeitschrift,* XVII (1962).

Flower, Sir Newman, English publisher and writer on music; b. Fontmell Magna, Dorset, July 8, 1879; d. Dorset, March 12, 1964. He joined the firm of Cassel & Co. in 1906; purchased it in 1927. He became deeply interested in music; publ. an extensive biography, *George Frederick Handel: His Personality* and His Times (London, 1923; 2nd ed., revised, 1947); Sir Arthur Sullivan: His Life, Letters and Diaries (London, 1927; 2nd ed., revised, 1950); Franz Schubert: The Man and His Circle (London, 1928; 2nd ed., revised, 1949); also prepared a Catalogue of a Handel Collection Formed by Newman Flower (Sevenoaks, 1921); publ. a vol. of memoirs, Just As It Happened (London, 1950). He was knighted in 1938.

BIBLIOGRAPHY: A. Walker, George Frederick Handel: The Newman Flower Collection (Manchester, 1972).

Floyd, Carlisle, American opera composer; b. Latta, S.C., June 11, 1926. He studied at Syracuse Univ. with Ernst Bacon (A.B., 1946; M.A., 1949); also took private lessons with Rudolf Firkušný. and Sidney Foster. In 1947 he joined the staff of the School of Music of Florida State Univ., Tallahassee; in 1976 became a prof. of music at the Univ. of Houston. His musical drama in 2 acts and 10 scenes, Susannah, was produced there (Feb. 24, 1955); it was later staged at the City Center in N.Y. (Sept. 27, 1956); received the N.Y. Music Critics Circle Award as the best opera of the year. Floyd's other works include Slow Dusk, a musical play in one act (1949); Fugitives, a musical drama in 3 acts (1951); operas: Wuthering Heights (Santa Fe, July 16, 1958); The Passion of Jonathan Wade (N.Y., Oct. 11, 1962); The Sojourner and Mollie Sinclair (Raleigh, N.C., Dec. 2, 1963); Markheim (New Orleans, March 31, 1966); Of Mice and Men, after John Steinbeck's novel (Seattle, Jan. 22, 1970); Bilby's Doll, for the Bicentennial (Houston, Feb. 29, 1976); Willie Stark (Houston, April 24, 1981); All the King's Men (1981). He further wrote the ballet Lost Eden for 2 Pianos (1952); Pilgrimage, a cycle of 5 songs (1955); The Mystery (5 Songs of Motherhood) for Soprano and Orch. (1962); In Celebration: An Overture (1970); other vocal and instrumental pieces.

Flummerfelt, Joseph, American conductor; b. Vincennes, Ind., Feb. 24, 1937. He studied at DePauw Univ. (B.Mus., 1958), the Philadelphia Cons. of Music (M.Mus., 1962), and the Univ. of Illinois (D.M.A., 1971); also had private lessons with Julius Herford in San Diego (1958) and Nadia Boulanger in Fontainebleau (1964). He was director of choral activities at DePauw Univ. (1964–68) and Florida State Univ. (1968–71); in 1971 was appointed choral director at Westminster Choir College; in 1982 he became artistic director and principal conductor there. He served as choral director of the Spoleto Festival in Italy (from 1971) and in the U.S. (from 1976); also held the posts of director of the N.Y. Choral Artists and of chorus master of the N.Y. Phil.

Flury, Richard, Swiss composer; b. Biberist, March 26, 1896; d. there, Dec. 23, 1967. He studied musicology in Basel, Bern, and Geneva, then theory and composition with Kurth, Hubert, Lauber, and Marx; conducted orchs. and choral societies in Switzerland (Zürich, Bern, and Solothurn); taught at the Solothurn Canton School.

WORKS: Operas: Eine florentinische Tragödie

(1926); Die helle Nacht (1932); Casanova e l'Albertolli (1937); ballet, Die alte Truhe (1945); several festival music scores; 7 symphs.: No. 1 (1923); Fastnachts-Symphonie (1928); Tessiner Symphonie (No. 2, 1936); Waldsymphonie (1942); Bucheggbergische Symphonie (No. 3, 1946); Liechtensteinische Symphonie (No. 4, 1951); No. 5 (1955–56); 6 symph. overtures; 4 violin concertos (1933, 1940, 1944, 1965); 2 piano concertos (1927, 1943); Caprice for Violin and Orch. (1967); chamber music: Oboe Sonata (1926); 3 cello sonatas (1937, 1941, 1966); 7 string quartets (1926, 1929, 1938, 1940, 1955, 1958, 1964); Piano Quintet (1948); 11 violin sonatas (Nos. 5–11, 1940–61); Piano Sonata (1920); 50 romantische Stücke for Piano; 24 preludes for Piano; 15 military marches and other music for Band; choruses; about 150 songs. He wrote an autobiography, Lebenserinnerungen (1950; with a list of works).

Flynn, George, American composer; b. Miles City, Mont., Jan. 21, 1937. He studied composition with Ussachevsky (1960–64), Beeson (1964–66), and Luening at Columbia Univ. (D.M.A., 1972). He subsequently joined the faculty at his alma mater (1966–73) and also taught at City College of the City Univ. of N.Y. (1973–76). In 1977 he was appointed chairman of the composition dept. at DePauw Univ. in Chicago; he was a co-founder of Chicago Soundings, a performing group for contemporary music. His own music is of a quaquaversal nature, disdaining nothing, absorbing anything of modernistic applicability.

WORKS: FOR THE STAGE: Ballet, Mrs. Brown, for Chamber Orch. and Tape (1965). FOR ORCH.: 2 symphs.: No. 1, Music for Orchestra (1966); No. 2 (Chicago, May 19, 1980); Lammy for Strings (1973); Javeh (1973); Meditations, Praises (Chicago, June 20, 1981); Focus for Chamber Orch. (1983); Coloration for Chamber Orch. (1983); Quietude for Chamber Orch. (1983); Lost and Found for Youth Orch. (1984). FOR VOICE: Tirades and Dreams for Actress, Soprano, and Chamber Orch. (1972); Songs of Destruction, 5 duos for Soprano and Piano (1973–74); American Songs, 6 settings for Chorus, Horn, and Piano (1983–84); choruses. CHAMBER MUSIC: Piano Quartet (1963); Solo and Duos for Violin and Piano (1964); Wind Quintet (1965, revised 1983); 4 Pieces for Violin and Piano (1965); Duo for Clarinet and Piano (1966); Duo for Trumpet and Piano (1974); Duo for Viola and Piano (1974); American Rest for Clarinet, Viola, Cello, and Piano (1975, revised 1982); American Festivals and Dreams for String Quartet (1976); Duo for Cello and Piano (1977); Celebration for Violin and Piano (1980); Saxophone Quartet (1980); 4 Fantasy-Etudes for Solo Violin (1981); Diversion for Flute, Clarinet, Violin, Cello, and Piano (1984). FOR PIANO: Fuguing (1962); 4 Preludes (1965); Fantasy No. 1 (1966); Music for Piano, 4-hands (1966); Wound (1968); Canal (1976); Fantasy No. 2 (1980–82); also Drive for Harpsichord (1973).

Foch (real name, **Fock**), **Dirk,** composer and conductor; b. Batavia, Java (where his father was governor general of the Dutch East Indies), June 18, 1886; d.

Locarno, Switzerland, May 24, 1973. He studied in the Netherlands and Germany; began his career in Sweden; conducted the Göteborg Symph. Orch. (1913–15); was guest conductor of the Concertgebouw Orch. in Amsterdam and of the orch. at The Hague (1917–19). He made his American debut as conductor with a specially assembled orch. at Carnegie Hall in N.Y., April 12, 1920; also conducted orch. groups elsewhere in the U.S., and in Vienna.

WORKS: *Ein hohes Lied,* 5 fragments from the Bible for Recitation and Orch. (Amsterdam, 1931); a musical pageant in the style of the medieval mystery plays, *From Aeon to Aeon;* 3 ballades for Piano (1913); a cycle of songs from the Chinese (1921); *Java Sketches* for Piano (1948).

Fodi, John, Hungarian-born Canadian composer; b. Nagyteval, March 22, 1944. He came to Canada as a child; studied music theory with Lorne Betts in Hamilton; then went to Toronto, where he took courses in composition with Weinzweig and Beckwith at the Toronto Cons. (1966–70); also studied composition with Anhalt and Pedersen at McGill Univ. in Montreal (1970–71). Fodi's own compositions partake of multifarious techniques of ultramodern music; the titles alone point to a preoccupation with abstract textures and mathematical processes, e.g., *Contrasts 4, Pi, Divisions, Signals, Segments,* and even *Erro.*

WORKS: 6 string quartets (1963; 1963; 1965; *Fantasia,* 1967; *Ch'ien,* 1969; *Concerto a 4,* 1973); *Movement* for Wind Quintet and String Quartet (1964); *Prelude* for Small Orch. (1964); Piano Sonata (1964–66); Symph. (1964–66); *Contrasts 4* for Piano (1964–66); *Chamber Symphony* for Flute, Horn, Piano, and String Quartet (1967); *Polyphony* for 2 Woodwinds and 2 Strings (1967); *7 Fantasias* for Solo Flute (1968); *Tettares* for Percussion Quartet (1968); *Pi* for Trombone and Piano (1968); Harpsichord Sonata (1968); *Signals* for Soprano Saxophone, Tenor Saxophone, Trombone, Percussion, and Piano (1969); *Divisions I* for Piano (1970), *II* for Piano and Harpsichord (1972), *III* for Solo Viola (1971), and *IV* for Solo Guitar (1974–77); *Symparanekromenoi* (Greek polynome; translatable as *Those Who, for Some Cause or Another, Are Living Lives That Are Spiritually or Mentally Entombed and Isolated*) for Orch. (1969–71; first complete perf., Toronto, July 25, 1974); *Segments* for Piano (1971); *Variations I* for Flute, Clarinet, Percussion, and 3 Strings (1972) and *II* for Wind Quintet (1975); Concerto for Viola and 2 Wind Ensembles (1972); *Erro* for Organ (1974); *An Investigation,* graphic score for Oboe, Organ, Viola, and Percussion, in any combination (1974); *Iz Ist in der Werlt Wol Schin* for High Voice and Viola (1975); *Dragon Days* for Orch. (1974–76); *Partimento: Here the Forsaken Virgin Rests . . .* for Flute, Oboe, Cello, Piano, Electric Organ, Spinet, and Percussion (1976); Trio for Flute, Viola, and Harpsichord (1976–77); *Capriccio* for Solo Double Bass (1977); *Patrem Omnipotentem* for Flute, Trombone, Viola, Cello, Piano, and Percussion (1977); 5 pieces for tape.

Fodor, Eugene, American violinist of Hungarian-Italian extraction; b. Turkey Creek, Colo., March 5, 1950. His great-great-grandfather founded the Fodor Cons. in Hungary. Eugene Fodor studied violin with Harold Wippler in Denver; in 1967 he went to N.Y. and studied with Galamian; later took lessons in the master class of Jascha Heifetz at the Univ. of Southern Calif. In 1972 he won the Paganini Competition in Genoa, Italy. In 1974 he shared 2nd prize with 2 Soviet violinists (no first prize was awarded) at the Tchaikovsky Violin Contest in Moscow. Returning to America, he was given the honors of the state of Colorado, and on Sept. 12, 1974, played at a state dinner at the White House for the premier of Israel, Rabin.

BIBLIOGRAPHY: *Current Biography* (April 1976).

Fodor-Mainvielle, Joséphine, famous French soprano; b. Paris, Oct. 13, 1789; d. Saint-Génis, near Lyons, Aug. 14, 1870. She made her debut in 1808 in St. Petersburg in Fioravanti's *Le Cantatrici villane;* gained renown for her performances in the operas of Mozart and Rossini at the King's Theatre in London (1816–18); was likewise successful in her many engagements in Paris, Naples, and Vienna. During a performance of the title role of *Sémiramide* in Paris on Dec. 9, 1825, she suddenly lost her voice and was eventually compelled to quit the stage. She went to Naples in the hopes of recovery under the warm sun, but her attempts to renew her career in 1828 and 1831 failed, and she spent the rest of her long life in retirement.

Foerster, Adolph Martin, American composer; b. Pittsburgh, Feb. 2, 1854; d. there, Aug. 10, 1927. He owed his first musical training to his mother; studied at the Leipzig Cons. with Richter; then returned to Pittsburgh, where he was active as a teacher of singing and piano. He composed *Dedication March* for the opening of the Carnegie Music Hall in Pittsburgh (Nov. 7, 1895); symph. poem, *Thusnelda;* Violin Concerto; 2 piano trios; 2 piano quartets; 2 string quartets; numerous piano works; songs.

Foerster, Joseph Bohuslav, significant Czech composer; b. Prague, Dec. 30, 1859; d. Nový Vestec, near Stará Boleslav, May 29, 1951. He was the son of the Czech organist **Joseph Förster** (1833–1907). He studied at the Prague Organ School; in 1882–88 was organist at St. Vojtěch; subsequently was choirmaster of Panna Marie Sněžná (1889–94); also wrote music criticism. He married the opera singer **Berta Lauterer** in 1888; when she was engaged to sing at the Municipal Theater of Hamburg in 1893, Foerster followed her, and became a prof. at the Hamburg Cons. in 1901 and also music critic of the *Hamburger Nachrichten,* the *Neue Hamburger Zeitung,* and the *Hamburger Freie Presse.* Subsequently his wife was engaged by Mahler for the Vienna Court Opera (1903), and Foerster obtained a position at the New Cons. in Vienna. In 1918 he returned to Prague, where he held teaching positions: taught composition at the Prague Cons. (1919–22); then taught at its master school (1922–31) and at the Univ. of Prague (1920–36). He was president of the Czech Academy (1931–39); in 1945 received the honorary title of National Artist of the Republic of Czechoslovakia. He continued to teach privately and to compose almost to the end of his very long life; many Czech composers of the 20th century were his students. Foerster wrote in every genre; his music is suffused with lyric melos, and reveals characteristic national traits in his treatment of melodic and rhythmic material. His harmonic idiom represents the general style of Central European Romanticism, stemming from Dvořák, and ultimately from Wagner and Brahms.

WORKS: Operas (all first perf. in Prague): *Deborah* (Jan. 27, 1893); *Eva* (Jan. 1, 1899); *Jessika* (April 16, 1905); *Nepřemožení* (*The Conquerers;* Dec. 19, 1918); *Srdce* (*The Heart;* Nov. 15, 1923); *Bloud* (*The Simpleton;* Feb. 28, 1936); incidental music for Shakespeare's plays *Love's Labour's Lost, Twelfth Night,* and *Julius Caesar,* and for Strindberg's *Journey of Fortunate Peter;* 4 masses; oratorio, *St. Venceslas* (1928); cantata, *May* (1936); cantata on the subject of the Thirty Years' War (1940); *1945,* cantata written to celebrate the liberation of Czechoslovakia; 5 symphs. (1888, 1893, 1895, 1905, 1929); symph. poems: *My Youth* (1900) and *Enigma* (1909); symph. suite, *Cyrano de Bergerac* (1903); *Solemn Overture* (1907); 2 violin concertos (1911, 1926); Cello Concerto (1931); *Capriccio* for Flute and Small Orch. (1940); 4 string quartets (1882, 1893, 1907, 1944); 3 piano trios (1883, 1894, 1921); String Quintet (1886); Wind Quintet (1909); Nonet for String and Wind Instruments (1931); 2 violin sonatas (1889, 1892); *Sonata quasi una fantasia* for Violin and Piano (1943); Suite for Viola and Piano (1940). He publ. a book of memoirs, *Poutník v Cizině* (Prague, 1947; in German as *Der Pilger,* 1955).

BIBLIOGRAPHY: Z. Nejedlý, *J.B. Foerster* (Prague, 1910); J. Bartoš, *J.B. Foerster* (Prague, 1923); a symposium, *J.B. Foerster,* by various Czech writers, was publ. for his 90th birthday (Prague, 1949); F. Pala, *Josef Bohuslav Foerster* (Prague, 1962).

Foerstrová-Lautererová, Berta, Czech soprano; b. Prague, Jan. 11, 1869; d. there, April 9, 1936. She studied in Prague; made debut as Agathe in *Der Freischütz* at the Prague National Theater in 1887; during her tenure there, she created roles in Dvořák's operas *Jakobín* and *Dimitrij;* was a member of the Hamburg Opera (1893–1901); then sang with the Vienna Court Opera (1901–13), appearing under the name of **Foerster-Lauterer;** she retired in 1914. He husband was the composer **Josef Bohuslav Foerster.**

Fogg, Eric, English organist and composer; b. Manchester, Feb. 21, 1903; d. London, Dec. 19, 1939. He studied organ with his father; composition with Granville Bantock. He was active as an organist in Manchester; then was music director with the British Broadcasting Corp. He wrote an overture to the *Comedy of Errors* (1922); *Poem* for Cello and Piano;

Suite for Violin, Cello, and Harp; songs (*Love and Life, The Little Folk,* etc.); piano pieces; choral works; etc.

Foggia, Francesco, Italian composer; b. Rome, 1604; d. there, Jan. 8, 1688. He was a pupil of A. Cifra and of P. Agostini; served at several German courts; returning to Rome, he was maestro di cappella at the Lateran (1636–61); at San Lorenzo in Damaso (1661); and, from 1677, at Santa Maria Maggiore. A prolific and masterly composer, he continued the traditions of the Roman School. He wrote the oratorios *David fugiens a facie Saul* and *San Giovanni Battista* (1670); numerous masses a cappella (also a few with organ); litanies, motets, etc.

Fogliani (Fogliano), Ludovico, Italian theorist; b. Modena, 2nd half of the 15th century; d. there, 1538. He was famous for his book *Musica theorica ...* (Venice, 1529; modern facsimile ed., Bologna, 1970), in which he preceded Zarlino in declaring the correct proportion of the major third to be 4:5, and in distinguishing between the major and minor (greater and lesser) semitones. In Petrucci's *Frottole* (1504–8) are some specimens of his compositions.

BIBLIOGRAPHY: J. Barbour, *Tuning and Temperament* (East Lansing, Mich., 1951; 2nd ed., 1953).

Fogliano, Giacomo, Italian theorist and composer, brother of **Ludovico Fogliani;** b. Modena, 1468; d. there, April 10, 1548. He was chorister in the Papal Chapel in Rome (1513–14); later was choirmaster of the Modena Cathedral.

Foldes, Andor, Hungarian pianist; b. Budapest, Dec. 21, 1913. He was given piano lessons by his mother as a child, and at the age of 8 already played a Mozart concerto with the Budapest Phil. From 1922 to 1932 he studied composition with Leo Weiner, conducting with Ernst Unger, and piano with Dohnányi at the Liszt Academy of Music in Budapest; in 1933 he received the Liszt Prize, and in 1934 began his first European tour as a concert pianist. In 1939 he went to N.Y., and became a naturalized American citizen in 1948; then he returned to Europe; lived in Germany and in Switzerland. In 1969 he toured India and South Japan; also gave concerts in Argentina and South Africa. Apart from the regular piano repertoire, Foldes played almost all piano works by Bartók. With his wife, **Lili Foldes,** he publ. an entertaining booklet, *Two on a Continent* (N.Y., 1947); he further publ. a lively piano manual, *Keys to the Keyboard* (N.Y., 1948), which was translated into German, Hungarian, Italian, Spanish, Norwegian, Polish, Dutch, Japanese, and Korean, and *Gibt es einen Zeitgenössischen Beethoven-Stil und andere Aufsätze* (Wiesbaden, 1963).

Foley, "Red" (Clyde Julian), American country-music singer; b. Blue Lick, Ky., June 17, 1910; d. Fort Wayne, Ind., Sept. 19, 1968. He studied briefly at Georgetown (Ky.) College; in 1937 he formed his own Renfro Valley Barn Dance program, and appeared regularly at the Grand Ole Opry in Nashville. He made popular such country-music classics as *Chattanooga Shoeshine Boy, Peace in the Valley,* and *Beyond the Sunset.* In 1967 he was elected to the Country Music Hall of Fame in recognition of his prominent place among modern country-music performers. He died while on tour with the Grand Ole Opry.

Foli (real name, **Foley**), **A(llan) J(ames),** Irish bass; b. Cahir, Tipperary, Aug. 7, 1835; d. Southport, Oct. 20, 1899. He was a pupil of Bisaccia in Naples. Following a widespread fashion among aspiring English opera singers, he changed his name to an Italian-sounding homonym, Foli, and made a career as "Signor Foli." He made his professional debut as Elmiro in Rossini's *Otello* in Catania in 1862; then sang throughout Italy; appeared in London at Her Majesty's Theatre in 1865; and later at Covent Garden and Drury Lane; toured the U.S. with Mapleson's opera company (1878–79); also traveled in South Africa, Australia, and Russia.

Folville, Eugénie-Emilie Juliette, Belgian pianist and composer; b. Liège, Jan. 5, 1870; d. Dourgne, France, Oct. 28, 1946. She studied piano with her father and violin with César Thomson; took lessons in composition with Radoux at the Liège Cons. She was only 17 when her *Chant de Noël* was performed at the Liège Cathedral. In 1898 she was appointed prof. at the Liège Cons. After the outbreak of World War I in 1914 she lived in Bournemouth, England; later returned to the Continent. She wrote an opera, *Atala* (Lille, 1892), a Violin Concerto, a Piano Concerto, and assorted piano solo pieces and songs.

Fomin, Evstignei, one of the earliest Russian national composers; b. St. Petersburg, Aug. 16, 1761; d. there, April 27, 1800. He was sent to Bologna to study with Padre Martini; returned to St. Petersburg in 1785; then became a singing teacher and operatic coach at the theatrical school there. He composed about 10 operas, including *Novgorod Hero Vassily Boyeslavich* (St. Petersburg, Dec. 8, 1786); *Yamshchiki (Coachmen;* St. Petersburg, Jan. 13, 1787); *Orpheus and Eurydice* (St. Petersburg, Jan. 13, 1792); and *The Americans* (St. Petersburg, Feb. 19, 1800; the title refers to the Russians in Alaska; vocal score publ. in 1893; the opera was revived in a perf. at Moscow, Jan. 17, 1947). A number of other operas were erroneously attributed to Fomin, among them the popular *Miller, Wizard, Cheat, and Marriage-Broker,* produced in Moscow on Jan. 31, 1779, the music of which was actually written by an obscure violinist named Sokolovsky.

BIBLIOGRAPHY: A. Finagin, "E. Fomin," in the collection *Music in Old Russia* (Leningrad, 1927); N. Findeisen, "The Earliest Russian Operas," *Musical Quarterly* (July 1933); A. Rabinovich, *Russian Opera before Glinka* (Moscow, 1948; pp. 50–57 and 85–105); B. Dobrokhotov, *Evstigney Fomin* (Moscow, 1968).

Fongaard, Björn, prolific Norwegian composer

and guitarist; b. Oslo, March 2, 1919; d. there, Oct. 26, 1980. He played guitar at an early age; began his formal music education in 1942 at the Oslo Cons. with Per Steenberg and Bjarne Brustad; later took a course in advanced techniques with Karl Andersen. He then taught guitar at the Oslo Cons., and also gave guitar recitals. As a composer, he became interested in the potentialities of fractional intervals, and devised special guitars for playing microtonal music with the aid of electronic techniques; he dubbed the resulting sound "orchestra microtonalis." His fascination with science is reflected in titles such as *Uran 235, Galaxy, Kosmos, The Solar System,* and *M.1 Crab Nebula in Taurus.* Possessed with indefatigable energy and astounding diligence, he continued to work to the end of his life, producing an enormous number of works in every conceivable genre.

WORKS: FOR THE STAGE: *Skapelse II (Creation II),* church opera, with Lights, Dancers, and Tape (1972); *Andromeda,* ballet music for Tape (orch. microtonalis; San Diego, Calif., 1972); *Dimensions,* ballet music for Tape (orch. microtonalis; 1974).

FOR ORCH.: 2 sinfoniettas (1951, 1968); *3 Pieces* for Strings, op. 10 (1953); Concertino for Piano and Strings (1953); *3 Pieces* for Strings, op. 22 (1954); *3 Novelettes* (1954); Sonata Concertante for Guitar and Orch. (1963); *Uran 235,* symph. poem glorifying the energy of the fissionable isotope (1963); *Visions* for Strings (1964); *Kosmos* for Strings and Percussion (1964); *3 Novasjoner* for Chamber Orch. (1966); Serenade for Strings (1967); *Ochestra Antiphonalis* for Orch. divided into 2 groups (1968); *Legende* (1968); *Fantasia* for Strings (1968); *Klangbilder* for Strings (1968); *Symphony of Space I–III* (all 1969); cycle of 5 symph. poems: *Mare Tranquillitatis, Callisto, Titan, Triton,* and *Sinus Iridum* (1969); *Sinfonia Geo-Paleontologica I–V* (1970); *Universum,* symph. poem (1970); *Relativity: Symphony I–III* (1970); *Angelicum,* symph. poem (1970); *Sanheten (The Verity),* symph. poem (1971); *Die Pflanzenwelt,* symph. (1971); *Naturen,* symph. poem (1971); *Livet (Life),* symph. poem (1971); 23 piano concertos (1973–76); 7 violin concertos (1973–77); Viola Concerto (1977); 3 cello concertos (1977); Double-bass Concerto (1977); Concerto for Piccolo and Orch. (1973); 3 flute concertos (1973–76); 2 oboe concertos (1976); English Horn Concerto (1976); 2 clarinet concertos (1976); Bass-clarinet Concerto (1976); Saxophone Concerto (1976); Bassoon Concerto (1976); 3 horn concertos (1973–77); 2 trumpet concertos (1977); Trombone Concerto (1977); 5 organ concertos (1977–78); Harp Concerto (1977); Guitar Concerto (1977); Accordion Concerto (1977); Percussion Concerto (1977); 3 serenades for Orch. (1978); *Svalbard. Nasjonal-epos* (1979); *Frans av Assisi* (1979); *Hjemmefronten* (1979); 7 symphs. for Strings (1980).

CHAMBER MUSIC: 2 *Lyrical Suites* for Guitar (1945, 1955); 2 sonatas for Guitar (1947, 1963); Suite for Solo Horn (1953); Suite for Violin and Cello (1953); Serenade for String Trio (1953); *Vision* for Cello and Piano (1959); *3 Aleatory Pieces* for Chamber Ensemble (1964); 3 concertinos for Quarter-tone Guitar and Percussion (1964); 2 sonatas for Microtonal Guitar (1965, 1975); *Galaxy* for 3 Quarter-tone Guitars,

Electronically Altered (1965); Sonata for Solo Oboe, op. 52, No. 1 (1967); Sonata for Oboe and Organ, op. 52, No. 2 (1967); Sonata for a Single Tam-tam, Electronically Metamorphosed (1968); Sonata for Solo Oboe, op. 70, No. 1 (1968); Sonata for Saxophone and Microtonal Guitar (1970); *Microtonal Structures for Organ, Microtonal Guitar, Percussion, Violin, Viola, and Cello* (1971); Sonata for Solo Bassoon (1972); Sonata for Oboe and Organ, op. 109, No. 3 (1970); Harp Sonata (1971); Trio for Flute, Viola, and Harp (1971); 120 preludes for Harp (1972); Solo Saxophone Sonata (1973); 21 string quartets (1973; some with Tape); 57 solo sonatas, for virtually every instrument (1973); *Microtonal Syntèse* for String Quartet and Tape (1974); 9 wind quintets (1974); 31 sonatinas for Solo Instrument and Piano (1974); 17 duos for Various Instruments (1974); Suite for Vibraphone (1975); 9 wind trios (1975); 6 wind quartets (1975); 12 string trios (1975); Sonata for Violin and Piano, op. 134 (1975); 41 concertos for Solo Instrument and Tape (orch. microtonalis; 1976–77); *Capriccio* for Accordion (1977); Sonata for Renaissance Instruments, Percussion, and Tape (1977); Sonata for Accordion Duo (1978).

FOR PIANO: *Tonal Studies,* 341 instructive pieces (1953); 2 sonatas and a suite, op. 9, Nos. 1–3 (1953); 12 sonatinas (1954); *24 Novelettes* (1954); *12 Lyrical Pieces* (1954); 6 sonatinas (1954); *12 Inventions* (1954); Concerto No. 1 (*Space Concerto*) for Piano and Tape (orch. microtonalis; 1971), No. 2 (1973), and No. 3 (1975); *6 peintures* (1970) Sonata, op. 110, No. 1 (1972); *Ex Flora et Fauna,* 37 sonatas (1969–72); *Fantasia* for Piano and Tape (1975); 28 suites (1975).

FOR ORGAN: 16 sinfonias, with subtitles such as *Messier 31 i Andromeda, M.42 i Oreon, Cluster of Nebulae in Corona Borealis, M.1 Crab Nebula in Taurus,* etc. (1969–72); *Sinfonia per Organum* (1972); *Caritas* (1973); *En kirkes historie* (1974); *Fantasia* (1974); *Peintures sur verre,* 34 liturgical character studies (1974); 12 suites (1976); *Aeternitas,* symph. (1976); *Symphonic Variations* (1976).

FOR VOICE: 24 songs, with Piano, each for various soloists, after Norwegian writers (1953); organi and motets to scientific texts, for a cappella Chorus (1953); *2 Reflections* for Narrator and Quarter-tone Guitar (1964); *Orafoni I* for Male Speaking Chorus, Percussion, and Strings (1964) and *II* for Male Speaking Chorus and Electronics (1965); *The Solar System,* after Willy Ley, for Solo Baritone (1964); *Reflections* for Narrator, Percussion, and Tape (orch. microtonalis; 1967); *Skapelsen (Creation)* for Narrator and Tape (orch. microtonalis; 1970); *Mora parva infinitatis* for Soprano, String Quartet, and Tape (1970); *Die Erkentnis* for Soprano, Violin, and Percussion (1976).

FOR TAPE ALONE: *Homo Sapiens* for Orch. Microtonalis (1966); *Epos* for Orch. Microtonalis (1967) *Elektrofonia I–VII* for Orch. Microtonalis (1970); *Sinfonia Microtonalis I–V* (1970); *Legend* for Orch. Microtonalis (1978).

BIBLIOGRAPHY: Nils Grinde, *Contemporary Norwegian Music 1920–1980* (Oslo, 1981).

Fonseca, Julio, Costa Rican composer; b. San José,

May 22, 1885; d. there, June 22, 1950. He received elementary musical training at home from his father, a military band musician. A government grant enabled him to pursue serious study in Europe, at the Cons. of Milan and in Brussels. Returning to Costa Rica, he became active as a teacher at music schools in San José and a church organist. His works consist mostly of pleasant salon music for piano and effective band pieces, much of it based on native folk rhythms, such as his band pieces *Suite tropical* (1934) and *Gran fantasia sinfónica sobre motivos folklóricos* (1937).

Fontanelli, Alfonso, Italian madrigal composer; b. Reggio Emilia, Feb. 15, 1557; d. Rome, Feb. 11, 1622. He was in the service of Duke Alfonso II of Este in Ferrara (1588–97) and of his successor, Cesare II, until 1601, when Fontanelli left the court to save himself from prosecution for suspected complicity in the assassination of his 2nd wife's lover. However, he was again in the service of the Estes in 1605, when he was in Rome as emissary of the Duke of Modena; in 1608 he was in Modena; in 1612–13, at the Spanish court. He took Holy Orders in 1621. He was a friend of Gesualdo, Prince of Venosa, and may have been influenced by him in his madrigals. He publ. anonymously 2 books of madrigals in 5 voices: *Primo libro* (Ferrara, 1595; reprint, Venice, 1603); *Secondo libro* (Venice, 1604; reprints 1609 and 1619). He was greatly esteemed by his contemporaries; Orazio Vecchi contributed an introduction to the 1603 edition of his *Primo libro,* praising him for the inventiveness and dignity of his music.

BIBLIOGRAPHY: F. Vatielli, *Il Principe di Venosa e Leonora d'Este* (Milan, 1941); A. Einstein, *The Italian Madrigal* (Princeton, 1949; vol. 2, p. 703).

Fontyn, Jacqueline, Belgian composer; b. Antwerp, Dec. 27, 1930. She studied piano with Marcel Maas in Brussels (1935–48); then took lessons in composition with Marcel Quinet and with Max Deutsch in Paris; also attended courses at the Akademie für Musik und Darstellende Kunst in Vienna and at the Chapelle Musicale Reine Elisabeth in Brussels (1956–59). She taught at the Royal Flemish Cons. in Antwerp (1963–70) and at the Brussels Cons. Her music has won numerous international prizes. She was married to the Belgian composer **Camille Schmit.**

WORKS: Ballet, *Piedigrotta* (1958); 2 cantatas: *La Trapéziste qui a perdu son cœur* for Mezzo-soprano and Chamber Orch. (1953) and *Psalmus Tertius* for Baritone, Chorus, and Orch. (1959); *Petite suite* for Orch. (1951); Divertimento for Strings (1953); *Danceries* for Orch. (1956); *Prelude and Allegro* for Orch. (1957); *Mouvements concertants* for 2 Pianos and Strings (1957); *2 estampies* for Orch. (1961); *Digressions* for Chamber Orch. (1962); *6 ébauches (6 Sketches)* for Orch. (1964); *Digressions* for Cello, and Chamber Orch. or Piano (1964); *Galaxie* for 17 Instruments (1965); Piano Concerto (1969); *Colloque* for Chamber Orch. (1970); *Pour 11 cordes (For 11 Strings;* 1971); *Evoluon* for Orch. (1973); *Per Archi* for 11 Strings (1973); Flute Sonata (1952); *Danceries* for Violin and Piano (1953); Wind Quintet (1954); Piano Trio (1956); String Quartet (1958); *Mosaïci* for 4 Clarinets (1965); *Musica a 4* for Violin, Viola or Clarinet, Cello, and Piano (1966); *Mosaïques* for Clarinet and Piano (1967); *Dialogues* for Saxophone and Piano (1969; an adaptation of *Digressions* for Cello and Chamber Orch.); Nonet (1969); *Filigrane* for Flute and Harp (1970); *6 climats* for Cello and Piano (1972); *Strophes* for Violin and Piano (1972); *2 Impromptus* for Piano (1950); *Capriccio* for Piano (1954); Ballade for Piano (1963); *Mosaïci* for Piano (1964); *Spirales* for 2 Pianos (1972); *Digitale* for Harpsichord (1973); Violin Concerto (1975); choruses; songs.

Foote, Arthur (William), eminent American composer; b. Salem, Mass., March 5, 1853; d. Boston, April 8, 1937. He studied piano with a local teacher in Salem; in 1870 he entered Harvard Univ., studying composition with J.K. Paine; he received the A.M. degree in 1875 (the first such degree in music given in America). He also studied organ with B.J. Lang. In 1876 he attended the Wagner Festival in Bayreuth. In 1878 he became organist in the Boston First Unitarian Church, a post that he held until 1910. In 1881 he organized in Boston a series of chamber music concerts which continued until the end of the century; he was frequently pianist with the Kneisel Quartet (1890–1910), performing several of his own works. For 50 years, from 1883, he was a successful teacher in Boston. He was a member of the Music Teachers National Assoc.; a founding member of the American Guild of Organists, and its president from 1909–12; was also a member of the National Inst. of Arts and Letters and a Fellow of the American Academy of Arts and Sciences. His music is distinguished by a fine lyrical feeling, in a Romantic tradition. WORKS: Many of his orch. works were presented for the first time by the Boston Symph. Orch.: overture, *In the Mountains* (Feb. 5, 1887; also perf. at the Paris Exposition, July 12, 1889); Suite for Strings in D, op. 21 (Nov. 23, 1889); symph. prologue, *Francesca da Rimini* (Jan. 24, 1891); Suite in D minor, op. 36 (March 7, 1896); Suite for Strings in E, op. 63 (April 16, 1909; particularly popular). Other works include: Serenade in E for Strings, op. 25; *4 Character Pieces,* after Omar Khayyám, op. 48, for Orch.; Cello Concerto; *A Night Piece* for Flute and Strings; cantatas (for Chorus, and Piano or Orch.): *The Farewell of Hiawatha* for Men's Voices, op. 11; *The Wreck of the Hesperus,* op. 17; *The Skeleton in Armor,* op. 28. Chamber music: 3 string quartets; 2 piano trios; Violin Sonata; Piano Quartet; Piano Quintet; Cello Sonata; various pieces for instruments with piano accompaniment; more than 100 songs, of which the following are the best known: *The Night Has a Thousand Eyes; I Know a Little Garden Path; Constancy; In Picardie; Ashes of Roses;* also vocal quartets; church music. WRITINGS: He was the author of several manuals: *Modern Harmony in Its Theory and Practice* (jointly with W.R. Spalding, 1905; reprinted 1936; revised 1959; republ. as *Harmony,* 1969); *Some Prac-*

tical Things in Piano-Playing (1909); *Modulation and Related Harmonic Questions* (1919); also trans. Richter's *Treatise on Fugue;* ed. vol. 9 of *The American History and Encyclopedia of Music* (1908–10). His autobiography was privately printed by his daughter, Katharine Foote Raffy (Norwood, Mass., 1946). See also his article "A Bostonian Remembers," *Musical Quarterly* (Jan. 1937). BIBLIOGRAPHY: N. Slonimsky, in *Dictionary of American Biography,* Supplement II; W. Cipolla, *A Catalog of the Works of Arthur Foote* (Detroit, 1980).

Foote, George, American composer; b. Cannes, France, of American parents, Feb. 19, 1886; d. Boston, March 25, 1956. He studied with E.B. Hill at Harvard Univ.; then in Berlin with Koch and Klatte. Upon his return to the U.S., he was a member of the staff in the music dept. of Harvard Univ. (1921–23) and president of the South End Music School in Boston (until 1943). WORKS: *Variations on a Pious Theme* for Orch. (Boston Symph., Feb. 11, 1935); *In Praise of Winter,* symph. suite (Boston Symph., Jan. 5, 1940); *98th Psalm* for Chorus and Organ (1934); religious pantomime, *We Go Forward* (1943); Trio for Flute, Harp, and Violin; other chamber music.

Forbes, Elliot, American choral conductor and music educator; b. Cambridge, Mass., Aug. 30, 1917. He studied at Harvard Univ. (B.A., 1941; M.A., 1947); also took courses at the Mozarteum in Salzburg (1937). He subsequently joined the staff of the music dept. of Princeton Univ. (1947–57). In 1958 he was appointed prof. at Harvard Univ. and conductor of the Harvard Glee Club and Radcliffe Choral Society, a post he retained until 1970; conducted the Harvard Glee Club in a tour around the world in 1961 and the Harvard-Radcliffe Chorus in a North American tour in 1964. In 1965 he taught at the Berkshire Music Center in Tanglewood. He is the editor of the revision of Thayer's *Life of Beethoven* (Princeton, 1964; 2nd ed., revised, 1967), of *Harvard-Radcliffe Choral Music,* and of the *Harvard Song Book* (Boston, 1965).

Forbes, Henry, English composer; b. London, 1804; d. there, Nov. 24, 1859. He studied with Sir George Smart in London, and with Moscheles and Hummel in Germany; was engaged as a church organist, and publ. a collection of psalm tunes, *National Psalmody* (1843). His opera *The Fairy Oak* was produced in London (Oct. 18, 1845) with considerable success.

Forbes, Sebastian, Scottish composer, organist, and choral conductor; b. Amersham, Buckingham, May 22, 1941. He is the son of the Scottish violist **Watson Forbes** (b. St. Andrews, Nov. 16, 1909), a performer in several English chamber groups, prof. of viola at the Royal Academy of Music in London, and head of the music dept. of the BBC for Scotland. Sebastian Forbes studied with Howard Ferguson at the Royal Academy (1958–60) and with Philip Radcliffe and Thurston Dart at King's College of Cambridge Univ. (1960–64). He subsequently held positions as conductor of the Aeolian Singers (1965–69) and Seiriol Singers (1969–72), and was a univ. lecturer at Bangor (1968–72) and Surrey (since 1972).

WORKS: *Pageant of St. Paul,* suite for orch. (1964); Piano Trio (1964); *Antiphony* for Violin and Piano (1965); Partita for Clarinet, Cello, and Piano (1966); Chaconne for Orch. (1967); *Sequence of Carols* for Chorus a cappella (1967); *Second Sequence of Carols* for Male Chorus, String Orch., and Organ (London, May 1, 1968); String Quartet (1969); *Essay* for Clarinet and Orch. (London, July 28, 1970); *Third Sequence of Carols* for Chorus a cappella (1971); Symph. in 2 movements (Edinburgh Festival, Sept. 2, 1972); *Fantasy* for Solo Cello (1974).

Ford, Ernest, English conductor and composer; b. London, Feb. 17, 1858; d. there, June 2, 1919. He was a pupil of Arthur Sullivan at the Royal Academy of Music and of Lalo in Paris; for some years was conductor at the Royal English Opera House (where he conducted the premiere of Sullivan's *Ivanhoe* in 1891), then at the Empire Theatre, and in 1897–1908 at the Royal Amateur Orch. Society; from 1916, was a prof. of singing at the Guildhall School of Music; was a Fellow of the Royal Academy of Music from 1899. He wrote operas and operettas; a motet, *Domine Deus* (for the 250th anniversary of Harvard Univ.); songs, duets, etc.; publ. *Short History of Music in England* (1912).

Ford, "Tennessee" Ernie, American country-music singer; b. Bristol, Tenn., Feb. 13, 1919. He studied at the Cincinnati Cons. of Music; then was a bombardier during World War II; after his discharge, he spent a period of time as a disc jockey in California; finally launched a career as a country-music singer. He gained enormous success in 1955 with his recording of *Sixteen Tons.*

Ford, Thomas, English composer and lutenist; b. c.1580; d. Nov. (buried, London, Nov. 17) 1648. He was appointed musician to Prince Henry in 1611, and to Charles I in 1626. He was especially successful in the "ayre," a type of composition developed by Dowland, in which melodic prominence is given to the upper voice. These "ayres" appear in alternative settings, either as solo songs with lute accompaniment or as 4-part a cappella songs. He wrote *Musicke of Sundrie Kindes* (1607; the first part contains 11 ayres); 2 anthems in Leighton's *Teares;* canons in Hilton's *Catch that catch can;* and the famous madrigal *Since first I saw your face.* MSS are at Christ Church, Oxford, and at the British Library.

Fordell, Erik, Finnish composer; b. Kokkola, July 2, 1917; d. Kaarlela, Dec. 21, 1981. He studied at the Sibelius Academy and the Helsinki Inst. of Church Music. He was unquestionably the most prolific symph. composer in Finland. He wrote 45 symphs. in 32 years: No. 1 (1949); No. 2 (1949); No. 3 (1952); Nos. 4–9 (1956); No. 10 (1956); Nos. 11–13 (1957); No. 14 (1958); No. 15 (1961); No. 16 (1955; revised 1966); No. 17 (1966); No. 18 (1955; revised 1966); No. 19 (1967); Nos. 20–21 (1968); Nos. 22–25 (1969); No. 26, *Kaustby* (1970); No. 27 (1973–74); No. 28, *Chou-En-lai* (1974); No. 29 (1974); No. 30, *China's Folk* (1974); Nos. 31–34 (1976); No. 35 (1977); Nos. 36–39 (1978); No. 40 (1978–79); Nos. 41–42 (1979); No. 43 (1980); and 2 unnumbered symphs.: *Nature Symphony* (1970–71) and Symph. in One Movement (1981). He also wrote 2 violin concertos (1955, 1959); 4 piano concertos (1961, 1962, 1962); Horn Concerto (1956); *Oratorium profanum* (1968); *Trilogy* for Orch. (1969); *Symphonic Trilogy* (1970); 8 suites for Strings; 5 cantatas; 4 wind quintets; 7 string quartets; Violin Sonata; Flute Sonata; songs; choral music; piano pieces.

Forkel, Johann Nikolaus, erudite German music historian; b. Meeder, near Coburg, Feb. 22, 1749; d. Göttingen, March 20, 1818. He was a chorister at Lüneburg (1762–66) and at Schwerin (1766). In 1769 he began the study of law in Göttingen, supporting himself by teaching music. He served as a church organist; in 1778 was appointed music director at the Univ. of Göttingen.

WRITINGS: *Über die Theorie der Musik, sofern sie Liebhabern und Kennern derselben nothwendig und nützlich ist* (1774); *Musikalischkritische Bibliothek* (3 vols., Gotha, 1778–79); *Über die beste Einrichtung öffentlicher Concerte* (1779); *Genauere Bestimmung einiger musikalischer Begriffe* (1780); *Musikalischer Almanach für Deutschland* (1782, 1783, 1784, and 1789); *Allgemeine Geschichte der Musik* (Leipzig, 1788 and 1801, 2 vols., covering the period up to 1550; his materials for later times went to the publisher Schwickert); *Allgemeine Literatur der Musik, oder Anleitung zur Kenntniss musikalischer Bücher* (1792; important as the pioneer work of its class); *Über Johann Sebastian Bachs Leben, Kunst und Kunstwerke* (Leipzig, 1802; the first full biography of Bach, based on information supplied by Bach's sons; in Eng., London, 1820; new trans., London, 1920, by Terry). Forkel's unique transcriptions, in modern notation, of Graphäus's *Missae XIII* (1539) and of the *Liber XV. missarum* of Petrejus (1538; masses by Ockeghem, Obrecht, Josquin, and others) were engraved, and a proof pulled, but the invading French army melted down the plates for cannonballs. The proof sheets, corrected by Forkel, are in the Berlin Library. His publ. compositions include piano sonatas and songs; in MS are the oratorio *Hiskias;* 2 cantatas: *Die Macht des Gesangs* and *Die Hirten an der Krippe zu Bethlehem;* symphs., trios, choruses, etc.

BIBLIOGRAPHY: Heinrich Edelhoff, *J.N. Forkel* (Göttingen, 1935); W. Franck, "Musicology and Its Founder, J.N. Forkel," *Musical Quarterly* (Oct. 1949).

Formes, Karl Johann, German bass; b. Mülheim, Aug. 7, 1815; d. San Francisco, Dec. 15, 1889. He made his opera debut as Sarastro in Cologne on Jan. 26, 1842; then sang at the Kärntnertor in Vienna; in 1843–48 he was engaged at Mannheim; appeared at Drury Lane in London in 1849; made his Covent

Garden debut as Caspar in *Der Freischütz* on March 16, 1850; sang there until 1868; in 1852–57 also sang at the Royal Italian Opera in London; in 1857 he made his first American tour; then divided his time between Europe and America. He wrote an autobiography, *Aus meinem Kunst- und Bühnenleben* (1888; in Eng., San Francisco, 1891).

Formes, Theodor, German tenor, brother of **Karl Formes;** b. Mülheim, June 24, 1826; d. Endenich, near Bonn, Oct. 15, 1874. He made his debut at Ofen (1846); then sang opera in Vienna (1848) and Berlin (1851–66); made a tour in America with his brother. He lost his voice temporarily; returned to the stage for a few years; then suffered a setback, became insane, and died in an asylum.

Formichi, Cesare, Italian baritone; b. Rome, April 15, 1883; d. there, July 21, 1949. He studied in Rome; made his debut at the Teatro Lirico in Milan in 1911; then sang at the Teatro Colón in Buenos Aires, in Madrid, in Barcelona, and at the Paris Opéra; appeared with the Chicago Opera Co. (1922–32); also sang at Covent Garden in London. He was particularly effective in dramatic roles, such as Rigoletto, Iago, and Scarpia.

Fornerod, Aloys, Swiss violinist and composer; b. Montet-Cudrefin (Vaud), Nov. 16, 1890; d. Fribourg, Jan. 8, 1965. He studied violin and theory at the Cons. of Lausanne and at the Schola Cantorum in Paris. Returning to Switzerland, he was a member of the Lausanne Symph. Orch.; in 1954 he was appointed director of the Fribourg Cons. As a composer, he followed the French modern style, in the spirit of fin-de-siècle Impressionism. He publ. *Les Tendances de la musique moderne* (Lausanne, 1924); was for 40 years a critic for *La Tribune de Lausanne.*
WORKS: *Geneviève,* one-act comic opera (Lausanne, May 20, 1954); *Te Deum* for Soloists, Chorus, and Orch. (1955); *Hymne à la Très Sainte Trinité* for Chorus and Brass (1961); *Le Voyage de printemps,* symph. suite (1943); Piano Concerto (1944); Violin Sonata (1925); Concerto for 2 Violins and Piano (1927); Cello Sonata (1934); choruses and songs.

Fornia-Labey, Rita (née **Newman**), American soprano; b. San Francisco, July 17, 1878; d. Paris, Oct. 27, 1922. She adopted the name Fornia from her native state of California; married J.P. Labey in 1910. She studied in Paris with Jean de Reszke; began her career as a coloratura soprano; then changed to mezzo-soprano. She made her debut in Germany; came to the U.S. in 1906 as a member of H.W. Savage's Opera Co.; in 1907–22 she was on the staff of the Metropolitan Opera; also made appearances at Covent Garden in London. She was particularly effective in Wagnerian roles.

Foroni, Jacopo, Italian conductor and composer; b. Verona, July 25, 1825; d. Stockholm, Sept. 8, 1858 (of cholera). He settled in Stockholm in 1849, and became court conductor there; was very successful at his public concerts, and also as a composer. He wrote several operas, among them *I Gladiatori* (Milan, Oct. 7, 1851). His opera *Advokaten Patelin,* performed posthumously in Stockholm (Dec. 4, 1858), was revived several times until 1926.

Forqueray, Antoine, French player on the viola da gamba; b. Paris, 1672; d. Mantes, June 28, 1745. He held an appointment as royal chamber musician to Louis XIV from 1690; publ. pieces for his instrument and also *Pièces de clavecin* (ed. by C. Tilney, 1970). His brother, **Michel Forqueray** (b. Chaumes-en-Brie, Feb. 15, 1681; d. Montfort l'Amaury, May 30, 1757), was a Paris organist. **Jean Baptiste Forqueray** (b. Paris, April 3, 1699; d. there, Aug. 15, 1782), a son of **Antoine Forqueray**'s, was also a player on the viola da gamba; transcribed for the harpsichord some of his father's pieces. **Nicolas Gilles Forqueray** (b. Chaumes-en-Brie, Feb. 15, 1703; d. there, Oct. 22, 1761), another son of **Antoine**'s, was a church organist.

Forrest, Hamilton, American composer; b. Chicago, Jan. 8, 1901. He sang as a chorister in Chicago churches; studied with Adolf Weidig; has written mainly for the stage, including the operas *Yzdra* (1925; received the Bispham Memorial Medal of the American Opera Society of Chicago) and *Camille* (Chicago, Dec. 10, 1930, with Mary Garden in the title role); ballet music; and *Watercolors* for 14 Wind Instruments and Harp.

Forrester, Maureen, outstanding Canadian contralto; b. Montreal, July 25, 1930. She studied piano as a child; had vocal training in Montreal with Sally Martin, and later with Frank Rowe and Bernard Diamant. She made her professional debut in a recital in Montreal on March 29, 1953; then traveled to Paris, and gave a recital there on Feb. 14, 1955. She made her American debut at N.Y.'s Town Hall on Nov. 12, 1956; on Feb. 17, 1957, she was soloist in Mahler's *Resurrection Symphony* with the N.Y. Phil. under Bruno Walter, scoring a remarkable success. From 1965–74 she was a member of the Bach Aria Group. She made her first appearance with the Metropolitan Opera in N.Y. on Feb. 10, 1975, as Erda in *Das Rheingold.* She also taught voice; served as head of the voice dept. of the Philadelphia Academy of Music (1966–71).

Forsell, (Carl) Johan (John), famous Swedish baritone; b. Stockholm, Nov. 6, 1868; d. there, May 30, 1941. He was in the Swedish army before embarking on his vocal studies. He made his debut in 1896 at the Stockholm Opera; sang there from 1896 to 1901, and again in 1903–9. He was on the roster of the Metropolitan Opera during the season of 1909–10. In 1924 he was appointed director of the Stockholm Opera, a post he held until 1939; also taught singing at the Stockholm Cons. from 1924 until 1931. A jubilee collection of essays, *Boken om J. Forsell,* was publ. on his 70th birthday (Stockholm, 1938).

BIBLIOGRAPHY: E. Ljungberger, *John Forsell* (Stockholm, 1916); K. Liliedahl, *John Forsell: A Discography* (Trelleborg, 1972).

Förster, Alban, German violinist; b. Reichenbach, Oct. 23, 1849; d. Neustrelitz, Jan. 18, 1916. He was a pupil, in Reichenbach, of R. Blume; later studied at the Dresden Cons.; in 1871 was court musician at Neustrelitz, also conducting the Singakademie; in 1881 was a teacher at the Dresden Cons., and conductor of the Liedertafel; in 1882–1908 was court Kapellmeister at Neustrelitz. He wrote a ballet, *Träumerei in der Waldmühle* (Zwickau, 1896); orch. and chamber music (string trios and quartets); violin music; instructive piano pieces; songs.

Förster, August, German piano manufacturer; b. Löbau, July 30, 1829; d. there, Feb. 18, 1897. He founded a piano factory in Bohemia; also owned the Förster Saal in Berlin. His firm constructed the first quarter-tone piano with 2 manuals (1924).

Förster, Emanuel Aloys, German composer and theorist; b. Niederstein, Silesia, Jan. 26, 1748; d. Vienna, Nov. 12, 1823. After service in the Prussian army, during which he played the oboe in a band, he went to Vienna for a thorough course in music, eventually becoming a teacher himself, although without a school position. He became friendly with Beethoven, who expressed esteem for him. Förster was a prolific composer; he wrote 48 string quartets, 5 oboe concertos, 10 violin sonatas, 21 piano sonatas, etc. His variations on arias from operas by Mozart, Sarti, and others enjoyed great popularity. He also publ. a manual, *Anleitung zum Generalbass* (1805; several later eds.).

BIBLIOGRAPHY: N. Saltscheff, *Emanuel Alois Förster* (Diss., Univ. of Munich, 1911).

Forster, Georg, German composer and compiler of music; b. Amberg, c.1510; d. Nuremberg, Nov. 12, 1568. He sang at the Heidelberg chapel in 1521, matriculating in classical studies in 1528. In 1531 he undertook medical studies at Ingolstadt; in 1534–39, studied humanities in Wittenberg with Melanchthon. In 1544 he received his degree of doctor of medicine at Tübingen Univ.; then was a medical practitioner in Amberg, Würzburg, Heidelberg, and Nuremberg (1544–47). He edited the valuable collection *Ein Auszug guter alter und neuer teutscher Liedlein* (in 5 parts; Nuremberg, 1539–56). Reprints are found in Jöde's *Das Chorbuch* and Schering's *Geschichte der Musik in Beispielen* (no. 88). Part II of the collection is publ. in R. Eitner's *Publikationen,* vol. 29. The first 3 parts were publ. in *Das Erbe deutscher Musik:* XX (1942), LX (1969), and LXI (1976); the other 2 parts are in preparation.

BIBLIOGRAPHY: H.J. Moser in *Jahrbuch Peters* (1928; pp. 45ff.); H. Kallenbach, *Georg Forsters Frische teutsche Liedlein* (Diss., Univ. of Fiessen, 1931).

Förster, Joseph, Czech organist and composer; b. Osojnitz, Bohemia, Feb. 22, 1833; d. Prague, Jan. 3, 1907. He was organist in several churches in Prague, and a prof. of theory at the Prague Cons. He wrote organ pieces, church music, and a treatise on harmony. He was the father of the celebrated Czech composer **Joseph Bohuslav Foerster.**

Forsyth, Cecil, English composer and writer on music; b. Greenwich, Nov. 30, 1870; d. New York, Dec. 7, 1941. He received his general education at Edinburgh Univ.; then studied at the Royal College of Music with Stanford and Parry. He joined the viola section in the Queen's Hall Orch.; also was connected with the Savoy Theatre, where he produced 2 of his comic operas, *Westward Ho!* and *Cinderella.* After the outbreak of World War I he went to N.Y., where he remained for the rest of his life. He composed a Viola Concerto and *Chant celtique* for Viola and Orch.; also songs, sacred music, and instrumental pieces. He was the author of a comprehensive manual, *Orchestration* (N.Y., 1914; 2nd ed., 1935; reprinted 1948); *Choral Orchestration* (London, 1920); also a treatise on English opera, *Music and Nationalism* (London, 1911). He publ. (in collaboration with Stanford) *A History of Music* (London, 1916) and a collection of essays, *Clashpans* (N.Y., 1933).

Forsyth, Josephine, American song composer; b. Cleveland, July 5, 1889; d. there, May 24, 1940. She was married to P.A. Meyers on April 29, 1928, and wrote a setting of the Lord's Prayer for her wedding. This setting later attained considerable popularity, and was sung for many years at Easter sunrise ceremonies at the Hollywood Bowl.

Forsyth, Malcolm, South African–born Canadian composer and trombonist; b. Pietermaritzburg, Dec. 8, 1936. He studied composition with Mátyás Seiber, Erik Chisholm, and Stefans Grové; trombone and conducting at the Univ. of Cape Town (1959–63; M.M., 1966; D.Mus., 1972); further composition studies with Ronald Stevenson. He was a trombonist in the Cape Town Symph. Orch. (1960–67); in 1968 went to Canada and became trombonist with the Edmonton (Alberta) Symph. Orch.; also taught trombone and theory at the Univ. of Alberta; became a Canadian citizen in 1974. His music is highly colorful and rhythmic, making use of African folk tunes in a modern Western dressing.

WORKS: *Erewhon,* overture (1962); *Jubilee Overture* (1964); *Essay for Orchestra: 67,* variations on a ground bass for Orch. (Cape Town, Dec. 15, 1967); 2 symphs.: No. 1 (1968–72; Cape Town, Sept. 4, 1972) and No. 2, *... a host of nomads ...* (1976); *Sketches from Natal* for 2 Oboes, 2 Horns, and Strings (Edmonton, March 23, 1970); Piano Concerto (1973–75); 2 concerti grossi for Brass Quintet and Orch.: No. 1, *Sagittarius* (1975; Banff, Alberta, Aug. 16, 1975), and No. 2, *Quinquefid* (1976–77); *Quartet 61* for 4 Trombones (1961); *Poem* for Brass (1964–66); *Pastorale and Rondo* for 4 Wind Instruments and Piano (1968–69); *Aphorisms* for Brass (1969–71); *Music for*

Mouths, Marimba, Mbira, and Roto-Toms for Chorus and Percussion (1973); *Quartet 74* for 4 Trombones (1974); *Salterello,* ballet score for Brass Quintet and Tape (1976–77).

Forti, Anton, famous Austrian tenor and baritone; b. Vienna, June 8, 1790; d. there, June 16, 1859. He first sang in Esterháza (1807–11); then went to Vienna, where he appeared at the Theater an der Wien (1811–13); in 1813 he joined the Court Theater, singing both tenor and baritone roles; also sang in Prague, Hamburg, and Berlin; continued to sing until late in his life. He was particularly esteemed for his performances in the roles of Figaro and Don Giovanni.

Fortlage, Karl, German theorist; b. Osnabrück, June 12, 1806; d. Jena, Nov. 8, 1881. He studied theology and philosophy; was a prof. at Jena Univ. from 1846. In connection with his study of Greek philosophy, he became interested in the Greek musical system; publ. one of the earliest comprehensive works on the subject, *Das musikalische System der Griechen in seiner Urgestalt* (Leipzig, 1847).

Fortner, Wolfgang, important German composer; b. Leipzig, Oct. 12, 1907. He studied composition with Hermann Grabner at the Leipzig Cons., and musicology with Theodore Kroyer at the Univ. there (1927–31). Upon graduation he was engaged for 22 years as instructor in music theory at the Inst. of Sacred Music in Heidelberg; then was a prof. of composition at the Music Academy in Detmold (1954–57) and held a similar position at the Hochschule für Musik in Freiburg im Breisgau (1957–73). Concurrently he led the concerts of Music Viva in Heidelberg, Freiburg, and Munich; and after 1954 was also a lecturer at the Academy of the Arts in West Berlin. In 1961 he was engaged to conduct a seminar at the Berkshire Music Center at Tanglewood; he visited the U.S. again in 1968. His music is marked by exceptional contrapuntal skills, with the basic tonality clearly present even when harmonic density reaches its utmost; in some of his works since 1947, Fortner gives a dodecaphonic treatment to melodic procedures; in his textures he often employs a "rhythmic cell" device. He is equally adept in his works for the musical theater and purely instrumental compositions; the German tradition is maintained throughout, both in the mechanics of strong polyphony and in rational innovations. WORKS: FOR THE STAGE: 5 operas: *Bluthochzeit* (after García Lorca's *Bodas de Sangre,* 1956; Cologne, June 8, 1957; revised 1963), which is a reworking of a dramatic scene, *Der Wald,* for Voices, Speaker, and Orch. (Frankfurt, June 25, 1953); *Corinna,* opera buffa (1958; Berlin, Oct. 3, 1958); *In seinem Garten liebt Don Perlimlín Belisa* (also after García Lorca's *Bodas de Sangre,* 1961–62; Schwetzingen, May 10, 1962); *Elisabeth Tudor* (1968–71; Berlin, Oct. 23, 1972); *That Time (Damals),* after Beckett, for Mime, Narrator, Mezzo-soprano, Baritone, Harpsichord, Guitar, Piano, and Live

Electronics (1977; Baden-Baden, April 24, 1977). 3 ballets: *Die weisse Rose* (after Wilde's *The Birthday of the Infants,* 1949; concert perf., Baden-Baden, March 5, 1950; stage premiere, Berlin, April 28, 1951); a pantomime, *Die Witwe von Ephesus* (1952; Berlin, Sept. 17, 1952); *Carmen,* a Bizet-collage (1970; Stuttgart, Feb. 29, 1971). FOR ORCH.: *Suite,* on music of Sweelinck (1930); Concerto for Organ and String Orch. (1932; reused as a Harpsichord Concerto, 1935); Concerto for String Orch. (1933); Concertino for Viola and Small Orch. (1934); *Capriccio und Finale* (1939); *Ernste Musik* (1940); Piano Concerto (1942); *Streichermusik II* for String Orch. (1944); Violin Concerto (1946; Baden-Baden, Feb. 16, 1947); Symph. (1947; Baden-Baden, May 2, 1948; his first use of dodecaphony); *Phantasie über die Tonfolge B-A-C-H* for 2 Pianos, 9 Solo Instruments, and Orch. (1950); Cello Concerto (1951; Cologne, Dec. 17, 1951); *Mouvements* for Piano and Orch. (1953; Baden-Baden, Feb. 6, 1954; as a ballet, Essen, Feb. 26, 1960); *La Cecchina,* Italian overture after Piccini (1954); *Impromptus* (1957; Donaueschingen, Oct. 20, 1957); *Ballet blanc* for 2 Solo Violins and String Orch. (1958; as a ballet, Wuppertal, Dec. 30, 1959); *Aulodie* for Oboe and Orch. (1960, revised 1966); *Triplum* for Orch. and 3 Obbligato Pianos (1965–66; Basel, Dec. 15, 1966; as a ballet, Munich, 1969); *Immagini* for Small or Large String Orch. (1966–67; also version for Large String Orch. and Soprano); *Marginalien* (1969; Kiel, Jan. 12, 1970); *Zyklus* for Cello, Winds, Harp, and Percussion (1969; originally for Cello and Piano, 1964); *Prolegomena* (concert suite from the opera *Elisabeth Tudor,* 1973; Nuremberg, April 19, 1974); *Prismen* for Flute, Oboe, Clarinet, Harp, Percussion, and Orch. (1974; Basel, Feb. 13, 1975); *Triptychon* (1976–77; consists of 3 parts: *Hymnus I* for 6 Brasses; *Improvisation* for Large Orch., and *Hymnus II* for 18-Voice String Orch.; first complete performance, Düsseldorf, April 6, 1978). FOR VOICE: *Fragment Maria,* chamber cantata (1969); *Grenzen der Menschheit,* cantata (1930); *Nuptiae Catulli* for Tenor, Chamber Chorus, and Chamber Orch. (1937; Basel, April 5, 1939); *An die Nachgeborenen,* cantata (1947; Baden-Baden, April 4, 1948); *2 Exerzitien* for 3 Female Voices and 15 Instruments (1948); *Mitte des Lebens,* cantata for Soprano and 5 Instruments (1951); *Isaaks Opferung,* oratorio-scene for 3 Soloists and 40 Instruments (1952; Donaueschingen, Oct. 12, 1952); *The Creation,* after James Weldon Johnson's poem, for Voice and Orch. (1954; Basel, Feb. 18, 1955; Fischer-Dieskau, soloist); *Chant de naissance,* cantata for Soprano, Chorus, Solo Violin, Strings, Winds, Percussion, and Harp (1958; Hamburg, April 12, 1959); *Berceuse royale* for Soprano, Solo Violin, and String Orch. (a section from *Chant de naissance,* 1958; revised in 1975 for Soprano and 7 Instruments); *Prélude und Elegie,* parergon to the Orch.; *Impromptus* for Soprano and Orch., after Hölderlin (1959); *Die Pfingstgeschichte nach Lukas,* for Tenor, Chorus, 11 Instruments or Chamber Orch., and Organ (1962–63; Düsseldorf, May 7, 1964); *Der 100. Psalm* for Chorus, 3 Horns, 2 Trumpets, and 2 Trombones (1962); *"Versuch eines Agon um...?"* for 7

Singers and Orch. (1973; Hannover, Nov. 8, 1973); *Gladbacher Te Deum* for Baritone, Chorus, Tape, and Orch. (1973; Mönchengladbach, June 6, 1974); *Machaut-Balladen* for Voice and Orch. (1973; Saarbrücken, Jan. 19, 1975); choruses; songs.

CHAMBER MUSIC: 4 string quartet (1929, 1938, 1948, 1975); *Suite* for Solo Cello (1932); Violin Sonata (1945); *Serenade* for Flute, Oboe, and Bassoon (1945); Flute Sonata (1947); Cello Sonata (1948); String Trio (1952); *6 Madrigals* for Violins and Cellos (1954); *New-Delhi-Musik* for Flute, Violin, Cello, and Harpsichord (1959); *5 Bagatelles* for Wind Quintet (1960); *Zyklus* for Cello and Piano (1964); *Theme and Variations* for Solo Cello (1975); *9 Inventionen und ein Anhang* for 2 Flutes (1976).

FOR PIANO: Sonatina (1935); *Kammermusik* (1944); *7 Elegies* (1950); *Epigramme* (1964).

FOR ORGAN: *Toccata and Fugue* (1930); *Preamble and Fugue* (1935); *Intermezzi* (1962).

Fortune, Nigel (Cameron), English musicologist; b. Birmingham, Dec. 5, 1924. He studied at the Univ. of Birmingham (B.A., 1950); received his Ph.D. in 1954 from Gonville and Caius College, Cambridge with the dissertation *Italian Secular Song from 1600 to 1635: The Origins and Development of Accompanied Monody.* He was music librarian at the Univ. of London (1956–59); in 1959 he became a lecturer at the Univ. of Birmingham; in 1969 was appointed a reader in music there. He was a senior consulting editor of the *New Grove Dictionary of Music and Musicians* (London, 1980). With D. Arnold, he edited *The Monteverdi Companion* (London, 1968) and *The Beethoven Companion* (London, 1971). He also edited works by Dowland and Purcell.

Foss, Hubert James, English writer on music; b. Croydon, May 2, 1899; d. London, May 27, 1953. He attended Bradfield College; in 1921 became a member of the educational dept. of the Oxford Univ. Press, and in 1924 founded the music dept., which he headed till 1941. He composed *7 Poems by Thomas Hardy* for Baritone, Male Chorus, and Piano; instrumental pieces; songs. He was the author of *Music in My Time* (1933); *The Concertgoer's Handbook* (London, 1946); *Ralph Vaughan Williams* (London, 1950); collected and edited *The Heritage of Music, Essays . . .* (2 vols., London, 1927–34). His book *London Symphony: Portrait of an Orchestra* remained unfinished at his death, and was completed by Noël Goodwin (London, 1954).

Foss, Lukas (real surname, **Fuchs**), brilliant American pianist, conductor, and composer; b. Berlin, Aug. 15, 1922. He was a scion of a cultural family; his father was a prof. of philosophy; his mother, a talented modern painter. He studied piano and music theory with Julius Goldstein-Herford. When the dark shadow of the Nazi dominion descended upon Germany, the family prudently moved to Paris; there Foss studied piano with Lazare Lévy, composition with Noël Gallon, and orchestration with Felix Wolfes. He also took flute lessons with Marcel Moÿse. In 1937 he went to the U.S. and enrolled at

the Curtis Inst. in Philadelphia, where he studied piano with Isabelle Vengerova, composition with Rosario Scalero, and conducting with Fritz Reiner; spent several summers at Tanglewood, Mass., where he studied conducting with Koussevitzky at the Berkshire Music Center; in 1940–41 he took a course in advanced composition with Hindemith at Yale Univ. He became a naturalized American citizen in 1942. Foss began to compose at a very early age; was the youngest composer to be awarded a Guggenheim fellowship (1945); in 1960 he received his 2nd Guggenheim fellowship. His first public career was that of a concert pianist, and he elicited high praise for his appearances as a piano soloist with the N.Y. Phil. and other orchs. He made his conducting debut with the Pittsburgh Symph. Orch. in 1939. From 1944 to 1950 he was pianist of the Boston Symph. Orch.; then traveled to Rome on a Fulbright fellowship (1950–52). From 1953 to 1962 he taught composition at the Univ. of Calif. in Los Angeles, where he also established the Improvisation Chamber Ensemble to perform music of "controlled improvisation." In 1960 he traveled to Russia under the auspices of the U.S. State Dept. In 1963 he was appointed music director and conductor of the Buffalo Phil. Orch.; during his tenure there he introduced ultramodern works, much to the annoyance of some regular subscribers; he resigned his position there in 1970. In 1964–65 he led in N.Y. a series of "Evenings for New Music." In 1965 he served as music director of the American-French Festival at Lincoln Center, N.Y. In 1971 he became principal conductor of the Brooklyn Philharmonia; also established the series "Meet the Moderns" there. From 1972–75 he conducted the Jerusalem Symph. Orch. In 1980 he was appointed music director of the Milwaukee Symph. Orch.; also conducted several guest engagements with the N.Y. Phil. Throughout the years he evolved an astounding activity as conductor, composer, and lately college instructor, offering novel ideas in education and performance. As a composer he traversed a protean succession of changing styles, idioms, and techniques. His early compositions were marked by the spirit of Romantic lyricism, adumbrating the musical language of Mahler; some other works reflected the neo-Classical formulas of Hindemith; still others suggested the hedonistic vivacity and sophisticated stylization typical of Stravinsky's productions. But the intrinsic impetus of his music was its "pulse," which evolves the essential thematic content into the substance of original projection. His earliest piano pieces were publ. when he was 15 years old; there followed an uninterrupted flow of compositions in various genres. Foss was fortunate in being a particular protégé of Koussevitzky, who conducted many of his works with the Boston Symph.; and he had no difficulty in finding other performers. As a virtuoso pianist he often played the piano part in his chamber music, and he conducted a number of his symph. and choral works.

WORKS: Incidental music to Shakespeare's play *The Tempest* (N.Y., March 31, 1940); *The Prairie,* cantata after Carl Sandburg's poem (N.Y., May 15, 1944; an orch. suite from it was performed earlier by the Boston Symph. Orch., Oct. 15, 1943); Piano Concerto No. 1 (1944); *Symphony in G* (Pittsburgh, Feb. 4, 1945, composer conducting); *Ode* for Orch. (N.Y., March 15, 1945); *Gift of the Magi*, ballet after O. Henry (Boston, Oct. 5, 1945); *Song of Anguish*, biblical solo cantata (1945; Boston, March 10, 1950); *Song of Songs*, biblical solo cantata (Boston, March 7, 1947); String Quartet (1947); *Recordare* for Orch. (Boston, Dec. 31, 1948); Oboe Concerto (N.Y., radio premiere, Feb. 6, 1950); opera, *The Jumping Frog of Calaveras County*, after Mark Twain (Bloomington, Ind., May 18, 1950); Piano Concerto No. 2 (Venice, Oct. 7, 1951, composer soloist; revised 1953; N.Y. Music Critics' Award, 1954); *A Parable of Death*, cantata after Rilke (Louisville, Ky., March 11, 1953); opera, *Griffelkin* (NBC Television, Nov. 6, 1955); *Psalms* for Voices and Orch. (N.Y., May 9, 1957); *Symphony of Chorales*, based on Bach's chorales (Pittsburgh, Oct. 24, 1958); *Introductions and Goodbyes*, miniature opera (N.Y., May 6, 1960); *Time Cycle*, suite for Soprano and Orch. in 4 movements to texts by Auden, Housman, Kafka, and Nietzsche with intercalative improvisations by a combo of Clarinet, Cello, Percussion, and Piano (N.Y., Oct. 21, 1960; won the N.Y. Music Critics' Award); *Echoi* for Piano, Percussion, Clarinet, and Cello (N.Y., Nov. 11, 1963); *Elytres* for 21 Instruments (Los Angeles, Dec. 8, 1964); *Fragments of Archilochos* for Contratenor, Narrator, 4 Small Choruses, Large Chorus ad lib., Mandolin, Guitar, and Percussion (1965); *For 24 Winds* (1966); *Phorion* for Electric Guitar, Electric Piano, and Electric Organ, with thematic material derived from Bach's E-major Partita for Solo Violin (hence the title, *Phorion*, meaning "borrowed" in Greek; first perf., N.Y., April 27, 1967; later incorporated into *Baroque Variations*, consisting of the *Largo* from Handel's Suite in E, Scarlatti's Sonata in E, and *Phorion*); *Concert* for Cello and Orch. (N.Y., March 5, 1967; Rostropovich, soloist); *Geod* (abbreviation of Geodesics), musical action for Orch. (Hamburg, Dec. 6, 1969, composer conducting); *MAP* (acronym for "Men at Play"), musical play for 5 Instrumentalists (1970); *Paradigm* for Percussionist, Electric Guitar, and 3 Instruments (Buffalo, N.Y., 1969); *The Cave of the Winds*, wind quintet (1972); *Orpheus* for Cello or Viola or Guitar, with Orch. (1972); *Divertissement* for String Quartet (1972; Ojai, Calif., 1973); *Ni bruit ni vitesse* for 2 Pianists playing on the Keyboard and 2 Percussionists playing on Piano Strings (1973); *Fanfare* for Chamber Orch. with 3 Folk Instruments (Istanbul, June 28, 1973); *The Percussion Concerto* for Chamber Orch. with a "percussionist/magician" perambulating about the stage telling the players what to do, and a "mechanical metronomic conductor" (1975); *Folksong* for Orch. (Baltimore, Jan. 21, 1976); *Quartet Plus* for Narrator and Double String Quartet (N.Y., April 29, 1977); *American Cantata* for Tenor, Soprano, 2 Speakers, Chorus, and Orch. (N.Y., Dec. 1, 1977); *Quintets for Orchestra* (Cleveland, May 2, 1979); *Round a Common Center* for Piano Quartet or Piano Quintet, with or without Voice, with or without Narration (Lake Placid, N.Y., Jan. 30, 1980); *Curriculum vitae* with a "Time-Bomb" for a Miscellaneous Ensemble, ending with a Cap-gun Explosion; *Exeunt,* dissertation for Orch. (1982); *Solo Observed* for Chamber Orch. (1983).

BIBLIOGRAPHY: David Ewen, *American Composers* (N.Y., 1982); H. Kupferberg, "Lucas Foss," *Ovation* (April 1984).

Foster, Fay, American composer; b. Leavenworth, Kans., Nov. 8, 1886; d. Bayport, N.Y., April 17, 1960. She studied at the Munich Cons. with Schwartz (piano) and Jadassohn (composition); studied piano further with M. Rosenthal and Sophie Menter; won a prize at the International Waltz Competition (Berlin, 1910); first prize in the American Composers' Contest (N.Y., 1913); made several tours as a pianist; eventually settled in N.Y. She wrote 3 operettas; over 100 songs (*The Americans Come!, My Journey's End*, etc.); piano studies; etc.

Foster, Lawrence, American conductor; b. Los Angeles, Oct. 23, 1941. He made his first conducting appearance with the Young Musicians Foundation Debut Orch. in 1960. At the age of 24 he was appointed assistant conductor of the Los Angeles Phil. Orch.; in 1966 received the Koussevitzky Memorial Conducting Prize at the Berkshire Music Festival in Tanglewood, Mass. In 1969–74 he was chief guest conductor of the Royal Phil. Orch. of London. In 1971–78 he was conductor-in-chief of the Houston Symph. Orch. He became Generalmusikdirektor in the city of Duisburg, West Germany, in 1981. He is particularly notable for his dynamic interpretations of modern works, but has also been acclaimed for his precise and intelligent presentations of the Classical and Romantic repertoire.

Foster, Muriel, English contralto; b. Sunderland, Nov. 22, 1877; d. London, Dec. 23, 1937. In 1896 she entered the Royal College of Music. She sang before Queen Victoria in 1900; in 1901 toured Canada with Mme. Albani. After her marriage to Ludwig Goetz, in 1906, she appeared infrequently in public.

Foster, Myles Birket, English organist; b. London, Nov. 29, 1851; d. there, Dec. 18, 1922. He was a pupil of Hamilton Clarke; later of Arthur Sullivan, Prout, and Westlake at the Royal Academy of Music; served as organist at the Foundling Hospital (1880–92); from 1888 was Examiner of Trinity College, London, in which capacity he spent many years in Australia and South Africa. He publ. *Anthems and Anthem-Composers* (1901), *History of the London Philharmonic Society, 1813–1912* (1913), and pedagogic works.

Foster, Sidney, American pianist; b. Florence, S.C., May 23, 1917; d. Boston, Feb. 7, 1977. He began playing piano when he was 4 years old, and at the age of 10 was admitted to the Curtis Inst. in Philadelphia, where he studied with Isabelle Vengerova and David Saperton. In 1940 he won the first Leventritt Foundation Award, which entitled him to an appearance as soloist with the N.Y. Phil. This was the beginning of a brilliant international career. In

1964 he played 16 concerts in Russia. He taught piano at Florida State Univ. (1949–51); in 1952 he joined the piano faculty of Indiana Univ. at Bloomington.

Foster, Stephen Collins, American composer of famous songs; b. Lawrenceville, Pa., July 4, 1826; d. New York, Jan. 13, 1864. He learned to play the flute as a child; publ. a song, *Open Thy Lattice, Love,* at the age of 18. His father was a government worker and businessman, active in politics; his brothers were engaged in commerce. About 1846 he went to Cincinnati as accountant for his brother Dunning. Foster wrote a total of 189 songs, for most of which he wrote both words and music. Of these, *Old Folks at Home,* sometimes referred to as *Swanee Ribber* (from its initial line, "Way down upon de Swanee ribber"), was publ. on Oct. 21, 1851, with the subtitle "Ethiopian Melody as sung by Christy's Minstrels." E.P. Christy (1815–62) was the organizer of one of the first traveling minstrel companies; his name was given as author, in consideration of a small sum of money received by Foster, whose name was not attached to the song until 1879, upon the expiration of the original copyright. About 40,000 copies of this song were sold during the year after publication. Foster was greatly encouraged and, as he wrote to Christy, hoped to establish himself as "the best Ethiopian song writer." Of other songs, the most notable are *Oh! Susanna* (1848; became popular in the gold rush of 1849), *My Old Kentucky Home, Massa's in de Cold Ground, Jeanie with the Light Brown Hair, Old Black Joe, Nelly Was a Lady, Laura Lee,* etc. The title page of *Beautiful Dreamer* (publ. 1864) bears the legend "the last song ever written by Stephen C. Foster. Composed but a few days previous to his death," but this maudlin claim (an appeal for sales) is false, as the work was prepared for publication in 1862. It is not known which song was Foster's last. On July 22, 1850, Foster married Jane McDowell in Pittsburgh; they had a daughter, but the marriage was not happy. In 1853 Foster went to N.Y. and stayed there alone for a year; in 1854 he was living in Hoboken, N.J.; went to N.Y. again in 1860, while his wife remained with relatives. Foster died penniless at Bellevue Hospital, yet his earnings were not small; in 1849–60 he received about $15,000 in royalties. Apart from the songs, Foster wrote 12 instrumental pieces in salon music style, and made numerous arrangements for flute, guitar, violin, etc., for the collection *Foster's Social Orchestra* (N.Y., 1854). He had some knowledge of instrumental writing; his harmonies, though simple, are adequate. The extant MSS are mostly in the Foster Hall Collection at the Univ. of Pittsburgh (dedicated on June 2, 1937); bibliographical bulletins are issued periodically by this organization. A one-cent stamp bearing Foster's picture was brought out by the U.S. post office in 1940. In 1915 W.R. Whittlesey and O.G. Sonneck publ. a *Catalogue of First Editions of S. Foster.* There are hundreds of reprints of Foster's songs, but almost all are in "improved" arrangements. A facsimile reprint of the original sheet music of 40 songs was publ., with valuable commentary by Richard Jackson, in N.Y. in 1974.

BIBLIOGRAPHY: M. Foster (brother), *Biography, Songs and Musical Compositions of Stephen Foster* (1896; not always accurate); H.V. Milligan, *S.C. Foster* (N.Y., 1920); J.T. Howard, *Stephen Foster, America's Troubadour* (N.Y., 1934; new ed., 1953); idem, ed., "Stephen Foster and His Publishers," *Musical Quarterly* (Jan. 1934); idem, *Newly Discovered Fosteriana* (N.Y., 1935); G.P. Jackson, *Stephen Foster's Debt to American Folk-Songs* (N.Y., 1936); R. Walters, *Stephen Foster: Youth's Golden Gleam* (Princeton, N.J., 1936); J.T. Howard, *The Literature on Stephen Foster* (Washington, D.C., 1944); Evelyn Foster Morneweck, *Chronicles of Stephen Foster's Family* (2 vols., Pittsburgh, 1944); Otto Gombosi, "Stephen Foster and 'Gregory Walker,' " *Musical Quarterly* (April 1944); F. Hodges, Jr., "Stephen Foster, Democrat," *Lincoln Herald* (June 1945; publ. separately, Pittsburgh, 1946); G. Chase, *America's Music* (2nd ed., N.Y., 1966); H. Wiley Hitchcock, "Stephen Foster," *HiFi/Stereo Review* (Jan. 1967); idem, *Music in the United States* (Englewood Cliffs, N.J., 1969; 2nd ed., 1974); W.W. Austin, *Susanna, Jeanie, and The Old Folks at Home: The Songs of Stephen Foster from His Time to Ours* (N.Y., 1975).

Fotek, Jan, Polish composer; b. Czerwinsk on the Vistula, Nov. 28, 1928. He studied composition with Wiechowicz at the State College of Music in Cracow and with Szeligowski at the State College of Music in Warsaw.

WORKS: *Opus concertante* for Organ, Piano, and Percussion (1959); *Gregorian Hymn* for Chorus and Orch. (1963); *A Cycle of Verses* for Children's Chorus and Orch. (1963); *Trimorphie* for 3 Flutes, Harpsichord, and Piano (1966); *Epitasis* for Orch. (1967); *Galileo,* musical drama (1969); *The Last War,* rhapsody for Narrator, Chorus, and Orch. (1971); *Cantata Copernicana* (1973); *Partita* for 12 Bassoons and 3 Double Bassoons (1973).

Fou Ts'ong, Chinese pianist; b. Shanghai, March 10, 1934. He studied piano in his native city; then won third prizes in the Bucharest Piano Competition (1953) and the Warsaw International Chopin Competition (1955); continued his studies at the Warsaw Cons. In 1958 he decided to make his home in London; appeared with many of the major orchs. of Europe and the U.S.; also gave many recitals. He was particularly noted for his expressive playing of works by Chopin and Debussy.

Fougstedt, Nils-Eric, Finnish conductor and composer; b. Raisio (near Turku), May 24, 1910; d. Helsinki, April 12, 1961. He studied composition in Helsinki with Furuhjelm, in Italy with Carlo Felice Boghen, and in Berlin with Max Trapp. Upon returning to Finland in 1932, he lectured in music theory at the Music Inst. in Helsinki; was also active as a conductor; led the Finnish Radio Orch. from 1951 until his death.

WORKS: Piano Trio (1933); Divertimento for

Wind Quintet (1936); Suite for Orch. (1936); Violin Sonata (1937); Violin Concertino (1937); 2 symphs. (1938, 1949); String Quartet (1940); Cello Concerto (1942); Piano Concerto (1944); *Tulukset (The Tinder Box)*, cantata after Hans Christian Andersen (1950); *Trittico sinfonico* (1958); many choruses and songs.

Foulds, John Herbert, significant English composer and musical theorist; b. Manchester, Nov. 2, 1880; d. Calcutta, April 24, 1939. He was precocious and began to compose at a single-digit age; learned to play cello; earned a living by playing in theater orchs. In 1900 he joined the prestigious Hallé Orch. in Manchester, until 1910; then moved to London, where he served as music director for the London Central YMCA (1918–23); also conducted at the Univ. of London Music Society (1921–26). In 1935 he left England and went to India; there he undertook a thorough study of Indian folk music; served as director of European music for the All-India Radio at Delhi Station and at Calcutta Station (1937–39); he also formed an experimental "Indo-European" orch., which included both European and Asian instruments. He was the first English composer to experiment with quarter-tones, and as early as 1898 wrote a string quartet with fractional intervals; he also composed semi-classical pieces using traditional Indian instruments. Unfortunately, most of his MSS are lost, but enough remain to confute the Kipling dictum that East and West shall never meet.
WORKS: For the stage: Concert opera, *The Vision of Dante* (1905–8); miniature opera, *Cleopatra* (1909; lost); *The Tell-Tale Heart,* melodrama after Edgar Allan Poe, for Actor and Chamber Orch. (1910); 3-act opera, *Avatara* (1919–30; lost); music for the ritual play *Veils* (1926; unfinished). For orch.: *Undine Suite* (c.1899); *Epithalamium* (London, Oct. 9, 1906); *Lento e scherzetto* for Cello and Orch. (c.1906); 2 Cello Concertos (1908–9; Manchester, March 16, 1911); *Apotheosis* for Violin and Orch. (1908–9); *Mirage,* symph. poem (1910); *Suite française* (1910); *Keltic Suite* (1911); *Music Pictures (Group III),* suite (London, Sept. 4, 1912); *Hellas* for Double String Orch., Harp, and Percussion (1915–32); *Miniature Suite* (1915); *Peace and War,* meditation (1919); *3 Mantras* (1919–30); *Le Cabaret,* overture to a French comedy (1921); *Suite fantastique* (1922); *Music Pictures (Group IV)* for Strings (c.1922); *Saint Joan Suite* (1924–25); *Henry VIII Suite* (1925–26); *April-England,* tone poem (1926–32); *Dynamic Triptych* for Piano and Orch. (1929; Edinburgh, Oct. 15, 1931); *Keltic Overture* (1930); *Indian Suite* (1932–35); *Pasquinades symphoniques,* symph. in 3 movements (1935; finale left unfinished); *Deva-Music* (1935–36; only fragments remain); *Chinese Suite* (1935); *3 Pasquinades* (c.1936); *Symphony of East and West* for European and Indian Instruments (1937–38; lost); *Symphonic Studies* (1938; lost). For voice: *The Song of Honor* for Speaker, Chamber Orch., and ad lib. Female Chorus (1918); *A World Requiem* for 4 Soloists, Small Boys' Chorus, Mixed Chorus, and Orch. (1919–21; London, Nov. 11, 1923; perf. each Armistice

Night in London from 1923 to 1926); choruses; songs. Chamber music: 10 string quartets: Nos. 1–3 (before 1899; lost), No. 4 (1899), No. 5 (lost), No. 6, *Quartetto romantico* (1903), No. 7 (lost), No. 8 (1907–10), No. 9, *Quartetto intimo* (1931–32), and No. 10, *Quartetto geniale* (1935; only the 3rd movement, *Lento quieto,* is extant); Cello Sonata (1905; revised 1927); *Impromptu on a Theme of Beethoven* for 4 Cellos (1905); *Music Pictures (Group I)* for Piano Trio (1910; lost); *Ritornello con variazioni* for String Trio (1911); *Aquarelles (Music Pictures—Group II)* for String Quartet (c.1914); *Sonia* for Violin and Piano (1925). For piano: *Dichterliebe,* suite (1897–98); *Essays in the Modes,* 6 studies (1920–27); *Egotistic,* modal essay (1927); *2 Landscapes* (c.1928); *Scherzo chromatico* (1927; lost).
WRITINGS: *Music To-Day: Its Heritage from the Past, and Legacy to the Future* (London, 1934).
BIBLIOGRAPHY: M. MacDonald, *John Foulds: His Life in Music* (London, 1975); M. MacDonald, *John Foulds, A centenary brochure from Musica Viva* (1979); M. MacDonald, "John Foulds and the String Quartet," *Tempo* (Feb. and March 1980).

Fountain, "Pete" (Peter Dewey Fountain, Jr.), American jazz clarinetist; b. New Orleans, July 3, 1930. Growing up in the jazz milieu of New Orleans, he mastered the clarinet in his youth; in 1949 he joined the Dukes of Dixieland, remaining with them until 1954; was then a member of Lawrence Welk's Orch. (1957–60); then founded his own group, with which he toured widely in the U.S. With the aid of an experienced ghostwriter he publ. the book *A Closer Walk: The Pete Fountain Story* (Chicago, 1972).

Fountain, Primous, III, American composer; b. St. Petersburg, Fla., Aug. 1, 1949. He studied at De Paul Univ. and at the Berkshire Music Center. In 1974 he became the youngest person to win a Guggenheim Foundation fellowship. His music shows quaquaversal influences, in a spectrum ranging from Stravinskian neo-Classicism to hot jazz.
WORKS: *Evolutio Quaestionis* for Soprano and Ensemble (1967); *3 Pieces* for Flute, Violin, and Piano (1967); *Will* for Flute, Clarinet, Horn, and Piano (1967); *Meditation on a Theme* for Piano (1967); a ballet, *Manifestation* (1968; Chicago, March 13, 1970); *Ritual Dances of the Amaks* for Orch. (1972); *Exiled* for Orch. (1974); *Osiris* for Orch. (1975); *Ricia* for Piano Trio (1977); Cello Concerto (1976; Minneapolis, Dec. 28, 1977); *Poème* for 17 Wind Instruments (1978); *Caprice* for Orch. (1978; N.Y., May 12, 1980); Concerto for Harp and Chamber Orch. (1981).

Fourdrain, Félix, French composer; b. Nice, Feb. 3, 1880; d. Paris, Oct. 22, 1923. He studied with Widor; wrote operas: *Echo* (Paris, 1906); *La Légende du point d'Argentan* (Paris, April 17, 1907); *La Glaneuse* (Lyons, 1909); *Vercingétorix* (Nice, 1912); *Madame Roland* (Rouen, 1913); *Les Contes de Perrault* (Paris, 1913); *Les Maris de Ginette; La Mare au diable; La Griffe;* operettas: *Dolly* (Paris, 1922);

L'Amour en cage; Le Million de Colette; La Hussarde (Paris, 1925); incidental music to Cain's *Le Secret de Polichinelle* (Cannes, 1922); *Anniversaire* for Orch.; many songs (*Le Papillon, Sérénades, Revanche d'amour, Pays des cours,* etc.).

Fourestier, Louis, French composer and conductor; b. Montpellier, May 31, 1892; d. Boulogne-Billancourt, Sept. 30, 1976. He studied at the Paris Cons. under Gédalge and Leroux; won the Rossini Prize in 1924 (for his cantata *Patria*), the Grand Prix de Rome in 1925 (for the cantata *La Mort d'Adonis*), and the Heugel Prize in 1927 (for the symph. poem *Polynice*); served as a conductor in Marseilles and Bordeaux; in 1938 was appointed conductor at the Paris Opéra; in 1945–63 was a prof. at the Paris Cons.; on Nov. 11, 1946, he made his conducting debut at the Metropolitan Opera in N.Y.; conducted also in 1947–48; then returned to Paris.

Fouret, Maurice, French composer; b. St.-Quentin, Nov. 28, 1888; d. Paris, Jan. 22, 1962. He studied with Ravel, Charpentier, and Busser. He composed several symph. poems on exotic subjects, among them *Aladdin* (Paris, Nov. 28, 1920) and *Danse de Sita* (1922); the ballets *Le Rustre imprudent* (1931) and *La Jeune Fille aux joues roses* (1934); a group of symph. suites inspired by Alsatian folklore; songs.

Fournet, Jean, distinguished French conductor; b. Rouen, April 14, 1913. He studied at the Paris Cons., graduating with the highest honors. He then became conductor of the French Radio Orch.; also conducted at the Paris Opéra and the Opéra-Comique. Concurrently he taught conducting at the Ecole Normale de Musique. In 1961 he was appointed a permanent conductor of the Radio Phil. Orch. at Hilversum, the Netherlands. He also was chief conductor of the Rotterdam Phil. Orch. (1968–73). He is especially renowned for his interpretations of new French music, tempering its orchestral brilliance with Classical restraint.

Fournier, Emile-Eugène-Alix, French composer; b. Paris, Oct. 11, 1864; d. Joinville-le-Pont, Sept. 12, 1897. He was a pupil of Delibes and Dubois at the Paris Cons.; took 2nd Grand Prix de Rome in 1891 and the Prix Cressent in 1892 for the one-act opera *Stratonice* (Paris, 1892); publ. a number of songs.

Fournier, Pierre, famous French cellist; b. Paris, June 24, 1906. He studied cello with Paul Bazelaire and G. Hekking at the Paris Cons. He taught at the Ecole Normale de Musique (1937–39) and at the Paris Cons. (1941–49); then he decided to devote himself entirely to his concert career, which took him all over the world, including South America, Japan, Australia, New Zealand, and South Africa; he also made regular appearances in the U.S.; was praised for his natural *bel canto* quality on his instrument, as well as for his impeccable musical taste. Several composers wrote special works for him; he gave first performances of the cello concertos of Albert

Roussel, Frank Martin, Bohuslav Martinů, and Jean Martinon. He also possessed the entire repertoire of cello works of Bach, Beethoven, and Brahms. In 1970 he settled in Switzerland, where he holds summer courses in interpretation in Zürich. In 1953 he was made a Chevalier of the Legion of Honor.
BIBLIOGRAPHY: B. Gavoty, *Pierre Fournier* (Geneva, 1957).

Fournier, Pierre-Simon, French cutter and founder of music type; b. Paris, Sept. 15, 1712; d. there, Oct. 8, 1768. Instead of the lozenge-shaped types in the style of Hautin's (1525), Fournier introduced round-headed notes, described in his *Essai d'un nouveau caractère de fonte . . .* (1756); he also publ. a *Traité historique sur l'origine et le progrès des caractères de fonte pour l'impression de la musique* (Paris, 1765).

Fowler, Jennifer, Australian composer; b. Bunbury, Western Australia, April 14, 1939. She attended the Univ. of Western Australia, graduating in the arts (1961) and later in music (1968); studied electronic music at the Univ. of Utrecht (1968–69); then went to live in England.
WORKS: *Variations* for Voice, Violin, Clarinet, and Percussion (1966); String Quartet (1967); *Fanfare* for Brass and Strings (1968); *Sculpture in 4 Dimensions* for Orch. (1969); *Chimes, Fractured* for Antiphonally Placed Chamber Ensemble (1970); *Hours of the Day* for 4 Mezzo-sopranos, 2 Oboes, and 2 Clarinets (1970); *Revelation* for String Quintet (1970–71); *Look on This Oedipus* for Orch. (1973); *Piece for an Opera House* for 2 Pianos, or for Piano and Tape (1973); *Chant with Garlands* for Orch. (1974).

Fox, Carol, American opera singer and administrator; b. Chicago, June 15, 1926; d. there, July 21, 1981. She studied singing in Chicago, N.Y., and Italy; in 1952 she helped to found the Lyric Theater of Chicago, which later became known as the Lyric Opera; in 1956 she was appointed its general manager, holding this post until her last year of life.

Fox, Charles Warren, American musicologist; b. Gloversville, N.Y., July 24, 1904; d. there oct. 15, 1983. He took courses in psychology at Cornell Univ. (B.A., 1926; Ph.D., 1933); also studied musicology there with Otto Kinkeldey. In 1932 he became a part-time instructor in psychology at the Eastman School of Music in Rochester, N.Y.; in 1933 began giving courses in music history and musicology; he retired in 1970. From 1952–59 he was editor of the *Journal of the American Musicological Society.* From 1954–56 he served as president of the Music Library Association.

Fox, Charlotte (née **Milligan**); b. Omagh, Ireland, 1860; d. London, March 26, 1916. She was an enthusiastic musical amateur, especially interested in Irish music; in 1904 she founded the Irish Folk Song Society; in her will she left the Bunting MSS to Belfast Univ. She publ. *Annals of the Irish Harpers* (London, 1911); composed the well-known song *The Foggy Dew.*

Fox, Felix, pianist and teacher; b. Breslau, May 25, 1876; d. Boston, March 24, 1947. He studied at the Leipzig Cons. with Reinecke (piano) and Jadassohn (theory); then with Isidor Philipp in Paris, where he gave several recitals introducing works by MacDowell. In 1897 he returned to the U.S. and settled in Boston as a pianist and teacher; in 1898 he established, with C. Buonamici, a piano school which enjoyed an excellent reputation; after Buonamici's death in 1920 it became the Felix Fox School of Pianoforte Playing; it was discontinued in 1935. Fox wrote many piano pieces and songs; made transcriptions of MacDowell's works; also edited numerous piano works.

Fox Strangways, A(rthur) H(enry), noted English writer on music and ed.; b. Norwich, Sept. 14, 1859; d. Dinton, near Salisbury, May 2, 1948. He studied at Wellington College, London; received his M.A. in 1882 from Balliol College, Oxford; then was a schoolmaster at Dulwich College (1884–86) and Wellington College (1887–1910). From 1911–25 he wrote music criticism for the *Times* of London; in 1925 he became music critic of the *Observer.* In 1920 he founded the quarterly journal *Music & Letters,* which he edited until 1937 (he was succeeded by Eric Blom). He was a specialist on Indian music and wrote several books on the subject, including *The Music of Hindostan* (Oxford, 1914); also publ. a collection of essays, *Music Observed* (London, 1936), and a biography of Cecil Sharp (with M. Karpeles; London, 1933; 2nd ed., 1955). He contributed the article "Folk-Song" to the introductory vol. of *The Oxford History of Music* (London, 1929).

BIBLIOGRAPHY: *Music & Letters,* Oct. 1939 (articles by Blom, Colles, Dent, Vaughan Williams et al.) and July 1948; also F. Howes, "A.H. Fox Strangways," in the same journal (1969).

Fox, Virgil, American concert organist; b. Princeton, Ill., May 3, 1912; d. Palm Beach, Fla., Oct. 25, 1980. He studied piano as a child, but soon turned to the organ as his favorite instrument. He played the organ at the First Presbyterian Church in his hometown at the age of 10, and gave his first public recital in Cincinnati at 14. He then enrolled in the Peabody Cons. in Baltimore, graduating in 1932. To perfect his playing he went to Paris, where he took lessons with Marcel Dupré at St. Sulpice and Louis Vierne at Notre Dame. He returned to the U.S. in 1938 and became head of the organ dept. at the Peabody Cons. In 1946 he was appointed organist at the Riverside Church in N.Y., where he played on a 5-manual 10,561-pipe organ specially designed for him. He then launched a remarkable career as an organ soloist. He was the first American to play at the Thomaskirche in Leipzig, where Bach had served as organist, and also played at Westminster Abbey in London. As a solo artist, he evolved an idiosyncratic type of performance in which he em-

bellished the stodgy Baroque music with romantic extravaganza; he also took to apostrophizing his audiences in a whimsical mixture of lofty sentiment and disarming self-deprecation. This type of personalized art endeared him to the impatient emancipated musical youth of America, and he became one of the few organists who could fill a concert hall. He also displayed a robust taste for modern music; he often played the ear-stopping discordant arrangement of *America* by Charles Ives. Wracked by cancer, he gave his last concert in Dallas on Sept. 26, 1980.

Fracassi, Américo, composer, brother of **Elmérico Fracassi;** b. Lucito, Campobasso, Italy, Feb. 29, 1880; d. Goya, Argentina, Aug. 15, 1936. With his brother, he left his native Italy as a very young man and settled in Buenos Aires, where he taught various musical subjects at a music school. He composed some songs and piano pieces.

Fracassi, Elmérico, composer, brother of **Américo Fracassi;** b. Lucito, Campobasso, Italy, Dec. 19, 1874; d. Buenos Aires, Oct. 12, 1930. He was taken to Buenos Aires as a boy, but returned to Italy in 1890 for his musical training (Cons. of Naples, with Rossomandi and D'Arienzo); toured Europe twice as a concert pianist; in 1904 was appointed director (together with G. d'Andrea) of the Almagro Cons. in Buenos Aires. He composed 2 operas, *Finlandia* (Turin, 1914) and *Merletti di Burano;* Piano Concerto; Violin Sonata; piano studies; songs; and 4 Argentine anthems, one of which, *Himno al Centenario,* won a prize from the Argentine government.

Frackenpohl, Arthur (Roland), American composer; b. Irvington, N.J., April 23, 1924. He studied at the Eastman School of Music in Rochester, N.Y., with Bernard Rogers; also with Milhaud at the Berkshire Music Center in Tanglewood, Mass., and with Nadia Boulanger at Fontainebleau. In 1949 he was appointed a member of the faculty at the State Univ. Teachers' College in Potsdam, N.Y.

WORKS: Sonatina for Clarinet and Piano (1948); Brass Quartet (1949); Trio for Oboe, Horn, and Bassoon (1949); cantata, *A Child This Day Is Born* (1951); Suite for Strings (1953); *An Elegy on the Death of a Mad Dog* (1955); *Allegro Giocoso* (1955); *A Jubilant Overture* for Orch. (1956); cantata, *The Natural Superiority of Men* (1959); Symph. No. 2 for Strings (1960); chamber opera, *Domestic Relations ("To Beat or Not to Beat"),* after O. Henry (1964); Suite for Trumpet and Strings (1964); String Quartet (1971); *French Suite* for Woodwind Quintet (1972); *American Folk Song Suite* for Band (1973); Variations for Tuba and Winds (1974); Duo for Clarinet and Percussion (1974).

Fradkin, Fredric, American violinist; b. Troy, N.Y., April 2, 1892; d. New York, Oct. 3, 1963. At the age of 5 he became a pupil of Schradieck; later studied with Max Bendix and Sam Franko in N.Y.; then went to Paris; studied at the Cons. there with Lefort, graduating in 1909 with first prize. He was concertmaster of the Bordeaux Opera Co.; then took instruction with Ysaÿe in Brussels. Returning to America, he made his debut as a concert violinist in N.Y. on Jan. 10, 1911; then gave concerts in Europe; in 1918–19 he was concertmaster of the Boston Symph. Orch.; later settled in N.Y. as a private teacher.

Fraemcke, August, German pianist and pedagogue; b. Hamburg, March 23, 1870; d. New York, Jan. 18, 1933. He studied at the Hamburg Cons.; then at the Vienna Cons., where he won the Beethoven Prize. In 1891 he emigrated to the U.S., and joined the staff of the N.Y. College of Music, in 1906 becoming its co-director. He was active in the Bohemian Club in N.Y.

Fraenkel, Wolfgang, German composer; b. Berlin, Oct. 10, 1897; d. Los Angeles, March 8, 1983. He studied violin, piano, and music theory at the Klindworth-Scharwenka Cons. in Berlin; at the same time took courses in jurisprudence and was a judge in Berlin until the advent of the Nazi regime in 1933; he was interned in the Sachsenhausen concentration camp, but as a 50 percent Jew (his mother was an Aryan, as was his wife), he was released in 1939, and went to China, where he enjoyed the protection of Chiang Kai-shek, who asked him to organize music education in Nanking and Shanghai. In 1947, when China exploded into a civil war, he emigrated to the U.S. and settled in Los Angeles. He earned a living by composing background music for documentary films in Hollywood, supplementing his income by copying music (he had a calligraphic handwriting). Fraenkel's own music was evolved from the standard German traditions, but at a later period he began to experiment with serial methods of composition.

WORKS: Opera, *Der brennende Dornbusch* (1924 –27); 3 string quartets (1924, 1949, 1960; the 3rd Quartet received the Queen Elisabeth Prize and was performed at the Liège Festival of the International Society for Contemporary Music in 1962); Flute Concerto (1930); *Der Wegweiser*, cantata (1931); Cello Sonata (1934); Violin Sonata (1935); *Filippo* for Speaker and Orch. (1948); Sonata for Solo Violin (1954); *Variations and a Fantasy on a Theme by Schoenberg* for Piano (1954); *Frescobaldi*, transcription for Orch. of 5 organ pieces by Frescobaldi (1957); Viola Sonata (1963); *Klavierstück* for Tape and Piano (1964); *Symphonische Aphorismen* for Orch. (1965; awarded first prize at the International Competition of the City of Milan); *Joseph* for Baritone and Orch., to a text by Thomas Mann (1968); *Missa aphoristica* for Chorus and Orch. (1973); String Quintet (1976). All his works, both publ. and in MS, are deposited in the Moldenhauer Archive in Spokane, Wash.

Frager, Malcolm, American pianist; b. St. Louis, Jan. 15, 1935. He studied languages at Columbia Univ.; majored in Russian, graduating in 1957. He studied piano with Carl Friedberg in N.Y. (1949–55); received various prizes in the U.S. In 1960 he won

the Queen Elisabeth of Belgium International Competition, which marked the beginning of his worldwide career; he was particularly successful in Russia.

Framery, Nicolas Etienne, French composer, writer on music, and poet; b. Rouen, March 25, 1745; d. Paris, Nov. 26, 1810. He composed the text and music for the comic opera *La Sorcière par hasard* (1768); its performance at Villeroy earned him the position of superintendent of music with the Count of Artois. The opera was played at the Comédie-Italienne (Paris, Sept. 3, 1783), but suffered a fiasco because of the antagonism against Italian opera generated by the adherents of Gluck. He also wrote librettos for Sacchini, Salieri, Paisiello, Anfossi, and other Italian composers; edited the *Journal de Musique* in Paris from 1770 till 1778, and *Calendrier Musical Universal* (1788–89); compiled, together with Ginguéne and Feytou, the musical part of vol. I of *Encyclopédie méthodique* (1791; vol. II by Momigny, 1818); besides smaller studies, he wrote *De la nécessité du rythme et de la césure dans les hymnes ou odes destinées à la musique* (1796); translated into French Azopardi's *Musico prattico* (*Le Musicien pratique;* 2 vols., 1786).

BIBLIOGRAPHY: J. Carlez, *Framery, Littérateur-musicien* (Caen, 1893).

Frampton, Peter (Kenneth), English rock singer and guitarist; b. Beckenham, Kent, April 20, 1950. He learned to play the guitar and began working with several rock groups, becoming a sort of rock celebrity himself by the age of 16. He formed the band Humble Pie with Steve Marriott, and toured with it throughout England and the U.S. In 1976 he issued a sensational album titled, with egotistical narcissism, *Frampton Comes Alive!* which sold something like 12 million copies. His music has been characterized by some deep-browed analysts as romantic pop rather than hard rock.

Françaix, Jean, talented French composer; b. Le Mans, May 23, 1912. He first studied at the Le Mans Cons., of which his father was director; then at the Paris Cons. with Isidor Philipp (piano) and Nadia Boulanger (composition). In his music, Françaix associates himself with the new French school of composers, pursuing the twofold aim of practical application and national tradition; his instrumental works represent a stylization of Classical French music; in this respect, he comes close to Ravel.

WORKS: FOR THE STAGE: Comic chamber opera, *Le Diable boiteux* (1937; Paris, June 30, 1938, Nadia Boulanger conducting); opera, *La Main de gloire* (1945; Bordeaux, May 7, 1950; comic operas: *Paris à nous deux* (Fontainebleau, Aug. 7, 1954) and *La Princesse de Clèves* (1961–65); ballets: *Scuola di Ballo* (1933); *Les Malheurs de Sophie* (1935); *Le Roi nu,* after Andersen's tale (Paris, June 15, 1936); *Le Jeu sentimental* (1936); *La Luthérie enchantée* (1936); *Verreries de Venise* (1938); *Le Jugement du fou* (1938); *Les Demoiselles de la nuit* (1948); *La Dame*

dans la lune (Paris, Feb. 11, 1958); *L'Apostrophe,* musical comedy, after Balzac (1940; Amsterdam, July 1, 1951); oratorio, *L'Apocalypse selon St. Jean* (Paris, June 11, 1942); *Cantate de Méphisto* for Bass Solo and Strings (Paris, Oct. 8, 1955). FOR ORCH.: Symph. (Paris, Nov. 6, 1932); Concertino for Piano and Orch. (1932); Suite for Violin and Orch. (1934); *Sérénade* for Chamber Orch. (1934); *Fantaisie* for Cello and Orch. (1934; revised 1955); *Quadruple Concerto* for Flute, Oboe, Clarinet, Bassoon, and Orch. (1935); *Au Musée Grévin,* suite for Orch. (1936); Piano Concerto (Berlin, Nov. 8, 1936); *Musique de cour,* suite for Flute, Violin, and Orch. (1937); *Invocation à la volupté* for Baritone and Orch. (1946); *Les Bosquets de Cythère,* 7 waltzes for Orch. (1946); *La Douce France,* suite for Orch. (1946); *Rhapsodie* for Viola and Small Orch. (1946); Symph. for Strings (1948); *Les Ziques de Mars,* "petit ballet militaire" for Orch. (1950); Symph. (1953; La Jolla, Calif., Aug. 9, 1953); *Si Versailles m'était conté,* suite for Orch. from the film (1954); *Sérénade B E A,* "game" for String Orch. on 3 notes (1955); *Divertimento* for Horn and Small Orch. (1958); Concerto for Harpsichord and Instrumental Ensemble (1959); *Le Dialogue des Carmelites,* suite for Orch. (1960); *L'Horloge de Flore,* suite for Oboe and Orch. (Philadelphia, March 31, 1961); *6 préludes* for Chamber String Orch. (1963); 2-Piano Concerto (1965); Flute Concerto (Schwetzingen, May 13, 1967); *Jeu poétique en 6 mouvements* for Harp and Orch. (1969); *Les Inestimables Chroniques du grand Gargantua* for Narrator and String Orch. (1970); Violin Concerto (1970); *Theme and Variations* for Orch. (Bochum, Germany, Dec. 12, 1973); *Fantaisie-Burlesque* for Orch. (Nuremberg, March 15, 1974); Concerto for Double Bass and Orch. (Frankfurt, Nov. 1, 1974); *Cassazione per 3 orchestre* (1975). CHAMBER MUSIC: *Divertissement* for Violin, Viola, Cello, Winds, Percussion, Harp, and Double Bass (1933); *Divertissement* for Bassoon and String Quartet (1944); *Cantate satirique,* after Juvenal, for 4 String Instruments and Piano, 4-hands (1947); *L'Heure de Berger* for Strings and Piano (1947); Wind Quintet (1948); *Variations sans thème* for Cello and Piano (1951); *Sonatine* for Trumpet and Piano (1952); *Ode à la gastronomie* for Chorus (1953); Piano Sonata (1960); Quartet for English Horn, Viola, and Cello (1971).
BIBLIOGRAPHY: M. Lanjean, *Jean Françaix* (Paris, 1961).

Francescatti, Zino, brilliant violinist; b. Marseilles, Aug. 9, 1902. His father, a Frenchman of Italian extraction, was a violin pupil of Paganini; prodded by him, Zino Francescatti appeared in public as a violinist at the age of 5, and played the Beethoven Violin Concerto with an orch. at 10. In 1927 he went to Paris, where he began teaching at the Ecole Normale de Musique; also conducted occasional performances of the Paris symph. organization Concerts Poulet. Between 1931 and 1939 he made several world tours; in 1939 made his home in the U.S., appearing in concert recitals and as a soloist with orchs. He made his U.S. debut on Nov. 1, 1939, with the N.Y. Phil.

Francesch, Homero, Uruguayan pianist; b. Montevideo, June 12, 1947. He studied piano with Santiago Baranda Reyes; then went to Germany and took piano lessons in Munich with Maria Hindemith-Landes and Steurer. Following concerts in West Germany, he began an international career; appeared as soloist with the Berlin Phil., London Symph., Vienna Symph., Orch. National de France of Paris, and other leading orchs.

Franchetti, Alberto, Italian composer; b. Turin, Sept. 18, 1860; d. Viareggio, Aug. 4, 1942. He studied in Turin with Niccolò Coccon and Fortunato Magi; then with Rheinberger in Munich and with Draeseke in Dresden. He devoted his entire life to composition, with the exception of a brief tenure as director of the Cherubini Cons. in Florence (1926–28).
WORKS: Operas: *Asrael* (Reggio Emilia, Feb. 11, 1888); *Cristoforo Colombo* (Genoa, Oct. 6, 1892); *Fior d'Alpe* (Milan, March 15, 1894); *Il Signor di Pourceaugnac* (Milan, April 10, 1897); *Germania* (his most successful opera; produced at La Scala, March 11, 1902; also had repeated perfs. in N.Y., London, Buenos Aires, etc.); *La figlia di Jorio* (Milan, March 29, 1906); *Notte di leggenda* (Milan, Jan. 14, 1915); *Giove a Pompei* (with Umberto Giordano; Rome, June 5, 1921); *Glauco* (Naples, April 8, 1922); Symph. (1886); symph. poems: *Loreley* and *Nella selva nera; Inno* for Soli, Chorus, and Orch. (for the 800th anniversary of the Univ. of Bologna); several pieces of chamber music and songs.

Franchi-Verney, Giuseppe Ippolito, Conte della Valetta, Italian composer and writer; b. Turin, Feb. 17, 1848; d. Rome, May 15, 1911. He studied jurisprudence, but gave up his law career for music. He was one of the founders of the Società del Quartetto (1875); under the pen name of **Ippolito Valetta** he wrote for the *Gazzetta del Popolo;* later for *Il Risorgimento* and other papers. In 1889 he married the violinist **Teresina Tua.** Among his compositions (most of them in a Wagnerian vein) are a "lyric sketch," *Il Valdese* (Turin, 1885), and a ballet, *Il Mulatto* (Naples, 1896).

Franchomme, Auguste-Joseph, famous French cellist; b. Lille, April 10, 1808; d. Paris, Jan. 21, 1884. He studied at the Lille Cons.; then with Levasseur and Norblin at the Paris Cons.; then played cello in various opera houses; in 1828 became solo cellist of the Royal Chapel and was founding member of the Société des Concerts du Conservatoire. In 1846 he was appointed prof. at the Paris Cons. He was an intimate friend of Chopin; established evenings of chamber music in Paris with Hallé and Alard. He wrote cello pieces, mostly in variation form, and operatic potpourris.

Franci, Benvenuto, Italian baritone; b. Pienza, July 1, 1891. He studied in Rome; made his debut there in

1918; from 1923 to 1936 he made regular appearances at La Scala in Milan; then was a member of the Rome Opera (1928–49); also sang at Covent Garden, London; he retired in 1953. He excelled in dramatic roles in Italian operas.

Franci, Carlo, Italian conductor, son of Benvenuto Franci; b. Buenos Aires, July 18, 1927. His family moved to Italy and he studied composition with Turchi and Petrassi at the Rome Cons., and conducting with Previtali at the Santa Cecilia Academy. He went to Ireland, and conducted the Radio Eireann Symph. Orch. in Dublin (1955–57); returning to Rome, he was appointed conductor of the RAI (1961–63). He made his American debut as guest conductor at the Metropolitan Opera in N.Y. in 1969.

Franck, César (-Auguste-Jean-Guillaume-Hubert), great Belgian composer and organist; b. Liège, Dec. 10, 1822; d. Paris, Nov. 8, 1890. He studied first at the Royal Cons. of Liège with Daussoigne and others; at the age of 9 he won first prize for singing, and at 12 first prize for piano. As a child prodigy, he gave concerts in Belgium. In 1835 his family moved to Paris, where he studied privately with Anton Reicha; in 1837 he entered the Paris Cons., studying with Zimmermann (piano), Benoist (organ), and Leborne (theory). A few months after his entrance examinations he received a special award of "grand prix d'honneur" for playing a fugue a third lower at sight; in 1838 he received the first prize for piano; in 1839, a 2nd prize for counterpoint; in 1840, first prize for fugue; and in 1841, 2nd prize for organ. In 1842 he was back in Belgium; in 1843 he returned to Paris, and settled there for the rest of his life. On March 17, 1843, he presented there a concert of his chamber music; on Jan. 4, 1846, his first major work, the oratorio *Ruth,* was given at the Paris Cons. On Feb. 22, 1848, in the midst of the Paris revolution, he married; in 1851 he became organist of the church of St.-Jean-St.-François; in 1853, maître de chapelle and, in 1858, organist at Ste.-Clotilde, which position he held until his death. In 1872 he succeeded his former teacher Benoist as prof. of organ at the Paris Cons. Franck's organ classes became the training school for a whole generation of French composers; among his pupils were d'Indy, Chausson, Bréville, Bordes, Duparc, Ropartz, Pierné, Vidal, Chapuis, Vierne, and a host of others, who eventually formed a school of modern French instrumental music. Until the appearance of Franck in Paris, operatic art dominated the entire musical life of the nation, and the course of instruction at the Paris Cons. was influenced by this tendency. By his emphasis on organ music, based on the contrapuntal art of Bach, Franck swayed the new generation of French musicians toward the ideal of absolute music. The foundation of the famous Schola Cantorum by d'Indy, Bordes, and others in 1894 realized Franck's teachings. After the death of d'Indy in 1931, several members withdrew from the Schola Cantorum and organized the Ecole César Franck (1938).

César Franck was not a prolific composer; but his creative powers rose rather than diminished with advancing age; his only symph. was completed when he was 66; his remarkable Violin Sonata was written at the age of 63; his String Quartet was composed in the last year of his life. Lucidity of contrapuntal design and fullness of harmony are the distinguishing traits of Franck's music; in melodic writing he balanced the diatonic and chromatic elements in fine equilibrium. Although he did not pursue innovation for its own sake, he was not averse to using unorthodox procedures. The novelty of introducing an English horn into the score of his symph. aroused some criticism among academic musicians of the time. Franck was quite alien to the Wagner-Liszt school of composition, which attracted many of his own pupils; the chromatic procedures in Franck's music derive from Bach rather than from Wagner.

WORKS: OPERAS: *Le Valet de Ferme* (1851–53); *Hulda* (1882–85; Monte Carlo, March 8, 1894); *Ghisèle* (unfinished; orchestration completed by d'Indy, Chausson, Bréville, Rousseau, and Coquard; first perf., Monte Carlo, March 30, 1896). ORATORIOS: *Ruth* (1843–46; Paris, Jan. 4, 1846; revised 1871); *La Tour de Babel* (1865); *Les Béatitudes* (1869–79; Dijon, June 15, 1891); *Rédemption* (first version, Paris, April 10, 1873; final version, Paris, March 15, 1875); *Rébecca* (Paris, March 15, 1881; produced as a one-act sacred opera at the Paris Opéra, May 25, 1918). SYMPH. POEMS: *Les Eolides* (Paris, May 13, 1877); *Le Chasseur maudit* (Paris, March 31, 1883); *Les Djinns* (Paris, March 15, 1885); *Psyché* (Paris, March 10, 1888). OTHER WORKS FOR ORCH.: *Variations symphoniques* for Piano and Orch. (Paris, May 1, 1886); *Symph. in D minor* (Paris, Feb. 17, 1889). CHAMBER MUSIC: 4 piano trios (early works; 1841–42); *Andante quietoso* for Piano and Violin (1843); *Duo pour piano et violon concertants,* on themes from Dalayrac's *Gulistan* (1844); Quintet in F minor for Piano and Strings (1879); Violin Sonata (1886); String Quartet (1889). ORGAN WORKS: *6 pièces* (*Fantaisie; Grande pièce symphonique; Prélude, Fugue, et Variations; Pastorale; Prière; Finale*); *3 pièces* (*Fantaisie; Cantabile; Pièce heroïque*); *Andantino; 3 chorales;* an album of 44 *Petites pièces;* an album of 55 pieces, entitled *L'Organiste;* etc. SACRED MUSIC: *Messe solennelle* (1858); *Messe à 3 voix* (1860); *Panis angelicus* for Tenor, Organ, Harp, Cello, and Double Bass; offertories, motets, etc.; 16 songs, among them *La Procession* (also arranged for Voice and Orch.). PIANO PIECES: *4 fantaisies; Prélude, Choral et Fugue; Prélude, Aria et Final; 3 petits riens; Danse lente;* etc.

BIBLIOGRAPHY: A. Coquard, *C. Franck* (Paris, 1890; new ed., 1904); E. Destranges, *L'Œuvre lyrique de C. Franck* (Paris, 1896); G. Servières, *La Musique française moderne* (Paris, 1897); G. Derepas, *C. Franck: Etude sur sa vie, son enseignement, son œuvre* (Paris, 1897); A. Meyer, *Les Critiques de C. Franck* (Orléans, 1898); P. Locard, *Les Maîtres modernes de l'orgue* (Paris, 1900); P.L. Garnier, *L'Héroïsme de C. Franck: Psychologie musicale* (Paris, 1900); F. Baldensperger, *C. Franck, L'Artiste et son œuvre* (Paris, 1901); D.G. Mason, *From Grieg to Brahms* (N.Y., 1904); R. Canudo, *C. Franck e la gio-*

vane scuola musicale francesa (Rome, 1905); Ch. Van den Borren, *L'Œuvre dramatique de C. Franck* (Brussels, 1906); Vincent d'Indy, *C. Franck* (Paris, 1906; in Eng., London, 1910); Romain Rolland, "Le Renouveau," in *Musiciens d'aujourd'hui* (Paris, 1908); O. Séré, *Musiciens français d'aujourd'hui* (Paris, 1911); J. Rivière, *Etudes* (Paris, 1911); J.W. Hinton, *C. Franck, Some Personal Reminiscences* (London, 1912); May de Rudder, *C. Franck* (Paris, 1920); E. Closson, *C. Franck* (Charleroi, 1923); R. Jardillier, *La Musique de chambre de C. Franck* (Paris, 1929); M. Emmanuel, *C. Franck* (Paris, 1930); A. Cortot, *La Musique française de piano* (Paris, 1930); Ch. Tournemire, *C. Franck* (Paris, 1931); Thelma Lynn, *C. Franck: A Bio-bibliography* (N.Y., 1934); H. Haag, *C. Franck als Orgelkomponist* (Kassel, 1936); P. Kreutzer, *Die sinfonische Form César Francks* (Düsseldorf, 1938); M. Kunel, *La Vie de C. Franck* (Paris, 1947); John Horton, *César Franck* (London, 1948); N. Demuth, *C. Franck* (London, 1949); N. Dufourcq, *C. Franck: Le Milieu, l'œuvre, l'art* (Paris, 1949); L. Vallas, *La Véritable Histoire de C. Franck* (Paris, 1950; in Eng., London, 1951); Charlotte Taube, *C. Franck und wir: Eine Biographie* (Berlin, 1951); Nancy van der Elst, *Organist van de Sinte Clotilde* (Tilburg, 1953); E. Buenzod, *César Auguste Franck* (Paris, 1966); W. Mohr, *C. Franck* (Tutzing, 1969); Laurence Davies, *C. Franck and His Circle* (Boston, 1970); S. Roe, "The Manuscripts of C. Franck," *Musical Times* (Nov. 1980); Wilhelm Mohr, in his book *Cäsar Franck: Ein deutscher Musiker* (Stuttgart, 1942), purports to prove that Franck was ethnically German; the same contention is advanced by R. Zimmermann in his similarly titled book, *Cäsar Franck: Ein deutscher Musiker in Paris* (Aachen, 1942). A rebuttal is found in M. Monnikendam's biography, *C. Franck* (Amsterdam, 1949), which presents documentary evidence that Franck was of Flemish and Walloon extraction.

Franck, Eduard, German pianist, pedagogue, and composer; b. Breslau, Oct. 5, 1817; d. Berlin, Dec. 1, 1893. At the age of 17 he studied with Mendelssohn; later he met Schumann and became his friend. These associations were the formative factor in the development of his career; he wrote piano pieces and songs in a Romantic vein, closely adhering to the style of Mendelssohn and, to some extent, of Schumann. As a piano teacher, he enjoyed great renown. He taught in Cologne (1851–58), then in Bern (1859–67) and in Berlin (1867–82). Among his works are 2 piano concertos, 2 violin concertos, much chamber music, and numerous collections of piano pieces.
BIBLIOGRAPHY: R. Franck, *Musikalische und unmusikalische Erinnerungen* (Heidelberg, 1928).

Franck, Johann Wolfgang, German composer; b. Unterschwaningen, June (baptized, June 17) 1644; d. c.1710. He was brought up in Ansbach, and served there as court musician from 1665 till 1679; produced 3 operas at the Ansbach court: *Die unvergleichliche Andromeda* (1675); *Der verliebte Föbus* (1678); and *Die drei Töchter Cecrops* (1679). On Jan.

17, 1679, in a fit of jealousy, he allegedly killed the court musician Ulbrecht, and was forced to flee. He found refuge in Hamburg with his wife, Anna Susanna Wilbel (whom he had married in 1666), and gained a prominent position at the Hamburg Opera; between 1679 and 1686 he wrote and produced 17 operas, the most important of which was *Diokletian* (1682). His private life continued to be stormy; he deserted his wife and their 10 children, and went to London, where he remained from 1690 to about 1702. The exact place and date of his death are unknown. In London he organized (with Robert King) a series of Concerts of Vocal and Instrumental Music; publ. 41 English songs. Other publications are: *Geistliche Lieder* (Hamburg, 1681, 1685, 1687, 1700; republ. in 1856 by D.H. Engel, with new words by Osterwald; newly ed. by W. Krabbe and J. Kromolicki in vol. 45 of Denkmäler Deutscher Tonkunst; 12 arrangements for 4 voices by A. von Dommer, publ. 1859; separate reprints by Riemann, Friedlaender, and others); *Remedium melancholiae* (25 secular solo songs with Basso Continuo; London, 1690); arias; etc.
BIBLIOGRAPHY: F. Zelle, *J.W. Franck, Ein Beitrag zur Geschichte der ältesten deutschen Oper* (Berlin, 1889); A. Werner, "J.W. Francks Flucht aus Ansbach," *Sammelbände der Internationalen Musik-Gesellschaft* (XIV/2); W. Barclay Squire, "J.W. Franck in England," *Musical Antiquary* (July 1912); R. Klages, *J.W. Franck, Untersuchungen zu seiner Lebensgeschichte und zu seinen geistlichen Kompositionen* (Hamburg, 1937); G. Schmidt, *Die Musik am Hofe der Markgrafen von Brandenburg-Ansbach* (Munich, 1953).

Franck, Joseph, Belgian composer and organist, brother of **César Franck;** b. Liège, Oct. 31, 1825; d. Issy, near Paris, Nov. 20, 1891. He studied organ with Benoist at the Paris Cons., obtaining the first prize (1852); then was organist at the church of St. Thomas d'Aquin in Paris. He composed sacred music and piano works, and publ. several manuals on harmony, piano technique, and other pedagogical subjects.

Franck, Melchior, German composer; b. Zittau, c.1579; d. Coburg, June 1, 1639. He went to Nuremberg in 1601 and in 1602 obtained the post of Kapellmeister at Coburg, where he remained to the end of his life. He was an excellent contrapuntist; composed sacred and secular vocal music, and exerted considerable influence on his contemporaries. Selections from his instrumental works, edited by F. Bölsche, constitute vol. XVI of Denkmäler Deutscher Tonkunst; vol. XVII of the *Monatshefte für Musikgeschichte* contains a careful description of his printed works, also of MSS preserved in public libraries. Reprints of his sacred vocal works have been publ. by F. Commer, E. Mauersberger, and F. Jöde; secular works in the *Staatliches Liederbuch, Kaiser-Liederbuch,* and other collections.
BIBLIOGRAPHY: Aloys Obrist, *Melchior Franck* (Berlin, 1892).

Franck, Richard, German pianist, son of **Eduard Franck;** b. Cologne, Jan. 3, 1858; d. Heidelberg, Jan. 22, 1938. He studied with his father in Berlin and also attended the Leipzig Cons. (1878–80). He was in Basel in 1880–83 and again from 1887 till 1900, and was active there as a pianist and teacher. He later lived in Kassel, and finally in Heidelberg. He was highly regarded as an interpreter of Beethoven's sonatas; publ. a book of memoirs, *Musikalische und unmusikalische Erinnerungen* (Heidelberg, 1928).

Franckenstein, Clemens von, German composer; b. Wiesentheid, July 14, 1875; d. Hechendorf, Aug. 19, 1942. He spent his youth in Vienna; then went to Munich, where he studied with Thuille; later took courses with Knorr at the Hoch Cons. in Frankfurt. He traveled with an opera company in the U.S. in 1901; then was engaged as a theater conductor in London (1902–7). In 1912–18 and in 1924–34 was Intendant at the Munich Opera. He wrote several operas, the most successful of which was *Des Kaisers Dichter* (on the life of the Chinese poet Li-Tai Po), performed in Hamburg (Nov. 2, 1920) and elsewhere in Germany. Other operas are *Griselda* (Troppau, 1898), *Fortunatus* (Budapest, 1909), and *Rahab* (Hamburg, 1911). He also wrote several orch. works.
BIBLIOGRAPHY: W. Zentner, "Clemens von Franckenstein," *Zeitschrift für Musik* (1929; pp. 769–75).

Franco of Cologne, medieval theorist and practical musician. His identity is conjectural; there was a learned man known as Magister Franco of Cologne who flourished as early as the 11th century; several reputable scholars regard him as identical with the musical theorist Franco; against this identification is the improbability of the emergence of theories and usages found in Franco's writings at such an early date. The generally accepted period for his activities is the middle of the 13th century (from 1250 to about 1280). The work on which the reputation of Franco of Cologne rests is the famous treatise *Ars cantus mensurabilis.* Its principal significance is not so much the establishment of a new method of mensural notation as the systematization of rules that had been inadequately or vaguely explained by Franco's predecessors. The treatise is valuable also for the explanation of usages governing the employment of concords and discords. It was reprinted, from different MSS, in Gerbert's *Scriptores* (vol. III) and in Coussemaker's *Scriptores* (vol. I). Gerbert attributes it to a Franco of Paris, a shadowy figure who may have been the author of a treatise and 3 summaries, all beginning with the words "Gaudent brevitate moderni." The *Ars cantus mensurabilis* is reproduced in English in O. Strunk's *Source Readings in Music History* (N.Y., 1950).
BIBLIOGRAPHY: O. Koller, "Versuch einer Rekonstruktion der Notenbeispiele zum 11. Kapitel von Francos *Ars cantus mensurabilis,*" *Vierteljahrsschrift für Musikwissenschaft,* VI (pp. 242ff.); J.F.R. Stainer, "The Notation of Mensurable Mu-

sic," *Proceedings of the Musical Association of London,* 26 (1900); Hugo Riemann, *Geschichte der Musiktheorie* (Leipzig, 1898; pp. 114ff.); Johannes Wolf, *Handbuch der Notationskunde* (vol. I, Leipzig, 1913); G. Reese, *Music in the Middle Ages* (N.Y., 1940; pp. 288ff.); W. Apel, *The Notation of Polyphonic Music, 900–1600* (Cambridge, Mass., 1942; pp. 310ff.); Y. Rokseth, *Polyphonies du XIIIe siècle* (Paris, 1948); F. Gennrich, *Franco von Köln, Ars cantus mensurabilis* (Darmstadt, 1955).

Franco, Johan, American composer; b. Zaandam, the Netherlands, July 12, 1908. He studied at the Cons. of Amsterdam (1929–34); in 1936 he emigrated to America; became a U.S. citizen in 1942; served in the U.S. Army during World War II. He wrote 5 symphs. (1933, 1939, 1940, 1950, 1958); symph. poem, *Péripétie* (1935); 5 "concertos liricos": No. 1 for Violin and Chamber Orch. (1937); No. 2 for Cello and Orch. (1962); No. 3 for Piano and Chamber Orch. (1967); No. 4 for Percussion and Chamber Orch. (1970); No. 5 for Guitar and Chamber Orch. (1973); Violin Concerto (Brussels, Dec. 6, 1939); *Serenata concertante* for Piano and Chamber Orch. (N.Y., March 11, 1940); symph. poem, *Baconiana* (1941); Divertimento for Flute and String Quartet (1945); 6 string quartets (1931–60); 6 partitas for Piano (1940–52); 8 toccatas for Carillon (1953–58); *American Suite* for Carillon (1952); *Supplication* for Orch. (1964); Sonata for Violin and Cello (1965); Sonata for Solo Saxophone (1965); *Triumphe* for Orch. (1967); *Ode* for Male Chorus and Wind Orch. (1968); *Saga of the Sea* for Carillon (1970); numerous vocal works with Orch. and Chorus a cappella; many songs. In all his works Franco follows the ideal of cyclic construction, with Classical symmetry governing not only the larger forms but separate sections of each individual work. His instrumental writing is invariably functional.

Francœur, François, French violinist; b. Paris, Sept. 8, 1698; d. there, Aug. 5, 1787. He was a member of the orch. of the Paris Opéra, a chamber musician to the King, and one of the "24 violons du roi" (1730). Conjointly with his inseparable friend François Rebel, he was director of the Opéra (1751) and Superintendent of the King's Music (1760). He wrote 2 books of violin sonatas; produced 10 operas (in collaboration with Rebel).

Francœur, Louis-Joseph, French violinist, nephew of **François Francœur;** b. Paris, Oct. 8, 1738; d. there, March 10, 1804. He entered the orch. of the Paris Opéra at the age of 14; became its conductor at 27. During the Revolution he was imprisoned as a suspect, but was released after the Thermidor coup d'état (1794) and was appointed director of the Paris Opéra. He wrote an act for the opera *Lindor et Ismène* (Paris, Aug. 29, 1766); publ. a treatise, *Diapason général de tous les instruments à vent* (1772). The MS of his *Essai historique sur l'établissement de l'opéra en France* is preserved in the library of the Paris Cons.

François, Samson, French pianist; b. Frankfurt (son of the French consul there), May 18, 1924; d. Paris, Oct. 22, 1970. He received a prize at the Nice Cons. at the age of 11; studied in Paris with Alfred Cortot. He traveled widely as a concert pianist; made his American debut in 1947; played again in N.Y. in 1960 and 1961. In 1964 he made a concert tour of China. He was particularly noted for his interpretations of Debussy.

Frandsen, John, respected Danish conductor; b. Copenhagen, July 10, 1918. He was educated at the Royal Danish Cons. in Copenhagen; then was organist at the Domkirke there (1938–53); also made appearances as a conductor. After serving as conductor with the Danish Radio Symph. (1945–46), he became a conductor at the Royal Danish Theater; also made appearances with the Royal Danish Orch. In 1958 he toured the U.S. with the Danish Radio Symph. He was also active as a teacher, both at the Royal Danish Cons. and the Opera School of the Royal Danish Theater. In 1980 he was named orch. counselor of the Danish Radio. He is particularly noted for his outstanding performances of contemporary Danish music.

Frank, Alan, English music scholar; b. London, Oct. 10, 1910. He studied the clarinet, conducting, and composition. At the age of 17 he joined the staff of the Oxford Univ. Press; during the war was in the Royal Air Force. In 1947 he was appointed music editor of the Oxford Univ. Press; in 1954 became head of its music dept.; retired from there in 1975. In 1935 he married **Phyllis Tate,** the composer. He publ. *The Playing of Chamber Music* (with George Stratton; London, 1935; 2nd ed., 1951) and *Modern British Composers* (London, 1953); he is also co-author (with Frederick Thurston) of *A Comprehensive Tutor for the Boehm Clarinet* (London, 1939). In 1972 he was appointed governor of the British Inst. of Recorded Sound.

Frank, Claude, German-American pianist; b. Nuremberg, Dec. 24, 1925. In 1938 he moved to Paris, and in 1940 went to N.Y.; there he took lessons in piano with Artur Schnabel and in composition with Paul Dessau (1941–44), both of whom were then living in N.Y.; later studied composition with Normand Lockwood (1946–48); also attended classes in conducting under Koussevitzky at Tanglewood (1947). He taught at Bennington College in Vermont (1948–55); eventually joined the staff of the Mannes School of Music in N.Y. A pianist of a grand envergure, he has earned merited encomiums for his sensitive interpretations of the classics.

Frank, Ernst, German conductor and composer; b. Munich, Feb. 7, 1847; d. Oberdöbling, near Vienna, Aug. 17, 1889. He studied with M. de Fontaine (piano) and F. Lachner (composition); in 1868, was conductor at Würzburg; in 1869, chorus master at the Vienna Opera; in 1872–77, conductor at Mannheim; in 1877–79, at Frankfurt; in 1879–87, at the Hannover court opera. He wrote the operas *Adam de la Halle* (Karlsruhe, April 9, 1880), *Hero* (Berlin, Nov. 26, 1884), and *Der Sturm* (after Shakespeare; Hannover, Oct. 14, 1887); completed H. Götz's opera *Francesca da Rimini* and produced it at Mannheim (1877). Frank was a friend of Brahms. Mental illness led to his being committed to an asylum in April 1887.

BIBLIOGRAPHY: A. Einstein, "Briefe von Brahms an E. Frank," *Zeitschrift für Musikwissenschaft* (April 1922).

Frankel, Benjamin, noted English composer; b. London, Jan. 31, 1906; d. there, Feb. 12, 1973. He worked as an apprentice watchmaker in his youth; then went to Germany to study music; returning to London, he earned his living by playing piano or violin in restaurants. It was only then that he began studying composition seriously. In the interim he made arrangements, played in jazz bands, and wrote music for films; some of his film scores, such as that for *The Man in the White Suit,* are notable for their finesse in musical characterization. In 1946 he was appointed to the faculty of the Guildhall School of Music and Drama in London. Frankel also took great interest in social affairs; was for many years a member of the British Communist Party and followed the tenets of socialist realism in some of his compositions.

WORKS: 8 symphs.: No. 1 (1952); No. 2 (Cheltenham, July 13, 1962); No. 3 (1965); No. 4 (London, Dec. 18, 1966); No. 5 (1967); No. 6 (London, March 23, 1969); No. 7 (London, June 4, 1970); No. 8 (1972); *The Aftermath* for Tenor, Trumpet, Harp, and Strings (1947); Violin Concerto (dedicated "to the memory of the 6 million"; Stockholm Festival, June 10, 1956); Bagatelles for 11 Instruments (1959); *Serenata concertante* for Piano Trio and Orch. (1961); Viola Concerto (1966); *A Catalogue of Incidents* for Chamber Orch. (1966); *Overture for a Ceremony* (1970); *Pezzi melodici* for Orch. (Stroud Festival, Oct. 19, 1972); Quintet for Clarinet and String Quartet (1953); 5 string quartets; Piano Quartet; *Pezzi pianissimi* for Clarinet, Cello, and Piano; 2 string trios; 2 sonatas for Solo Violin; *Sonata ebraica* for Cello and Harp; *Elégie juive* for Cello and Piano; Trio for Clarinet, Cello, and Piano; songs.

Frankenstein, Alfred, American writer on music and art; b. Chicago, Oct. 5, 1906; d. San Francisco, June 22, 1981. He played clarinet in the Civic Orch. of Chicago before turning to writing; from 1935 to 1975 he was music critic of the *San Francisco Chronicle;* concurrently served as its principal art critic; from 1937 to 1963 he was program annotator of the San Francisco Symph. He publ., besides innumerable special articles, a book of essays, *Syncopating Saxophones* (Chicago, 1925); *Modern Guide to Symphonic Music* (N.Y., 1966), and several publications dealing with modern American art. He was the first to publ. the sketches of Victor Hartmann that inspired Mussorgsky's *Pictures at an Exhibition* (*Musical Quarterly,* July 1939).

Frankl, Peter, brilliant Hungarian pianist; b. Budapest, Oct. 2, 1935. He studied at the Franz Liszt Academy of Music in Budapest; his teachers included Zoltán Kodály, Leo Weiner, and Lajos Hernadi. In 1957 he won first prize in the Marguerite Long Competition; also won prizes at competitions in Munich and Rio de Janeiro, which catapulted him into an international career. He made his debut in America in a Dallas recital in 1965. Eventually he moved to London and became a British subject in 1967. In England he formed the Frankl-Pauk-Kirshbaum Trio. His repertoire is extensive, ranging from classical music to contemporary works.

Franklin, Aretha, black "soul" singer; b. Memphis, Tenn., March 25, 1942. Her father was a Baptist preacher; the family settled in Detroit, where he established a pastorate; his church became a hearth of gospel songs and evangelical group singing. At 18 Aretha Franklin went to N.Y., where she quickly attracted attention; her singing at the Newport Jazz Festival in 1963 led to numerous important and lucrative engagements; the sales of her recordings skyrocketed to the million mark. In 1967 she toured Europe; in 1968 she made a sensation with her "soul" version of *The Star-Spangled Banner* at the ill-fated Democratic Convention in Chicago.

Franklin, Benjamin, great American statesman; b. Boston, Jan. 17, 1706; d. Philadelphia, April 17, 1790. An amateur musician, he invented (1762) the "armonica," an instrument consisting of a row of glass discs of different sizes, set in vibration by light pressure. A string quartet mistakenly attributed to him came to light in Paris in 1945, and was publ. there (1946); the parts are arranged in an ingenious "scordatura"; only open strings are used, so that the quartet can be played by rank amateurs. Franklin also wrote entertainingly on musical subjects; his letters on Scottish music are found in vol. VI of his collected works.
BIBLIOGRAPHY: O.G. Sonneck, *Suum cuique: Essays in Music* (N.Y., 1916); Lionel de la Laurencie, "Benjamin Franklin and the Claveciniste Brillon de Jouy," *Musical Quarterly* (April 1923); "L'Harmonica de Benjamin Franklin," *Dissonances* (July–Aug. 1944); W. Lichtenwanger, "Benjamin Franklin on Music," in *Church Music and Musical Life in Pennsylvania in the Eighteenth Century,* III/2 (Philadelphia, 1947); K.M. Stolba, "Benjamin Franklin y la musica," *Heterofonia* (July–Aug. 1971); M.E. Granander, "Benjamin Franklin's String Quartet," *Early American Literature* (Fall 1972); W.T. Marrocco, "The String Quartet Attributed to Benjamin Franklin," *Proceedings of the American Philosophical Society* (1972).

Franko, Nahan, American violinist and conductor, brother of **Sam Franko;** b. New Orleans, July 23, 1861; d. Amityville, N.Y., June 7, 1930. As a child prodigy, he toured with Adelina Patti; then studied in Berlin with Joachim and Wilhelmj. Returning to America, he joined the orch. of the Metropolitan Opera; was its concertmaster from 1883 to 1905; made his debut there as a conductor on April 1, 1900;

was the first native-born American to be engaged as conductor there (1904–7).

Franko, Sam, American violinist; b. New Orleans, Jan. 20, 1857; d. New York, May 6, 1937 (from a skull fracture resulting from a fall). He was educated in Germany; studied in Berlin with Joachim, Heinrich de Ahna, and Eduard Rappoldi. Returning to the U.S. in 1880, he joined the Theodore Thomas Orch. in N.Y., and was its concertmaster in 1884–91; in 1883 he toured the U.S. and Canada as a soloist with the Mendelssohn Quintette Club of Boston. In order to prove that prejudice against native orch. players was unfounded, he organized in 1894 the American Symph. Orch., using 65 American-born performers; this orch. he later used for his Concerts of Old Music (1900–9). In 1910 he went to Berlin and taught at the Stern Cons.; he returned to N.Y. in 1915 and remained there for the rest of his life. At the celebration of his 79th birthday (1936), he gave his valuable collection of music MSS to the Music Division of the N.Y. Public Library. He publ. for piano: *Album Leaf* (1889); *Viennese Silhouettes* (a set of 6 waltzes, 1928); etc.; several violin pieces; practical arrangements for violin and piano of works by Bach, Chopin, Mendelssohn, Rimsky-Korsakov, etc.; also edited classical music albums. His memoirs were publ. posthumously under the title *Chords and Discords* (N.Y., 1938).

Frantz, Ferdinand, German bass-baritone; b. Kassel, Feb. 8, 1906; d. Munich, May 26, 1959. He made his debut at the opera in Kassel in 1927 as Ortel in *Die Meistersinger von Nürnberg;* then sang in Halle and Chemnitz; was a leading member of the Hamburg State Opera (1937–43) and the Bavarian State Opera in Munich (1943–59). He made a fine impression at his Metropolitan Opera debut in N.Y. on Dec. 12, 1949, as Wotan in *Die Walküre;* sang there again in 1953; also appeared at Covent Garden in London. He was primarily known as an effective interpreter of Wagnerian roles.

Frantz, Justus, German pianist; b. Hohensalza, May 18, 1944. He studied piano with Eliza Hansen at the Hamburg Hochschule für Musik; later took private courses with Wilhelm Kempff. After winning a prize in the Munich Competition in 1967, he began appearing with the leading European orchs., including the Berlin Phil., the Royal Phil. of London, the Orch. de Paris, and the London Phil. He made his U.S. debut with the N.Y. Phil. in 1975; subsequently appeared with many other American orchs. He also toured with Christoph Eschenbach in duo-piano concerts.

Franz, Paul, French tenor; b. Paris, Nov. 30, 1876; d. there, April 20, 1950. After private voice studies, he made his debut at the Paris Opéra in 1909 as Lohengrin; remained on its roster until 1938. From 1937 he taught voice at the Paris Cons.

Franz, Robert, famous German song composer; b.

Halle, June 28, 1815; d. there, Oct. 24, 1892. His family name was **Knauth;** his father, Christoph Franz Knauth, legally adopted the name Franz in 1847. The parents did not favor music as a profession, but Franz learned to play the organ and participated as an accompanist in performances in his native city. In 1835 he went to Dessau, where he studied with Friedrich Schneider; in 1837 he returned to Halle. He publ. his first set of songs in 1843; they attracted immediate attention and were warmly praised by Schumann. Shortly afterward he received an appointment as organist at the Ulrichskirche in Halle, and also as conductor of the Singakademie there; later he received the post of music director at Halle Univ. (1851–67), which conferred on him the title of Mus.Doc. in 1861. The successful development of his career as a musician was interrupted by a variety of nervous disorders and a growing deafness, which forced him to abandon his musical activities in 1868. Liszt, Joachim, and others organized a concert for his benefit, collecting a large sum of money (about $25,000); admirers in America (Otto Dresel, S.B. Schlesinger, B.J. Lang) also contributed funds for his support.

WORKS: Franz was undoubtedly one of the finest masters of the German lied. He publ. about 350 songs; among the best known are *Schlummerlied, Die Lotosblume, Die Widmung,* and *Wonne der Wehmuth.* He also wrote: *117th Psalm* for Double Chorus a cappella; *Kyrie* for Chorus a cappella and Solo Voices; *Liturgy;* arranged works by Bach (*St. Matthew Passion; Christmas Oratorio;* 10 cantatas; etc.) and Handel (*Messiah; L'Allegro, Il Penseroso, ed Il Moderato;* etc.). He publ. *Mitteilungen über J.S. Bachs Magnificat* (Leipzig, 1863); *Offener Brief an Ed. Hanslick über Bearbeitungen älterer Tonwerke, namentlich Bachscher und Händelscher Vokalwerke* (Leipzig, 1871); both were reprinted by R. Bethge as *Gesammelte Schriften über die Wiederbelebung Bachscher und Händelscher Werke* (Leipzig, 1910).

BIBLIOGRAPHY: F. Liszt, *R. Franz* (Leipzig, 1855; reprinted in *Gesammelte Schriften,* vol. IV, Leipzig, 1882); H.M. Schuster, *R. Franz* (Leipzig, 1874); La Mara, *R. Franz,* in vol. III of *Musikalische Studienköpfe* (Leipzig, 1868–82; publ. separately, 1911); W. Waldmann, *R. Franz: Gespräche aus zehn Jahren* (Leipzig, 1894); R. Procházka, *R. Franz* (Leipzig, 1894); W. Golther, *R. Franz und Arnold Freiherr Senfft von Pilsach: Ein Briefwechsel 1861–89* (Berlin, 1907); R. Bethge, *R. Franz: Ein Lebensbild* (Halle, 1908); H. Kleemann, "R. Franz," *Musical Quarterly* (Oct. 1915); O. Lessmann, "Persönliche Erinnerungen an R. Franz," *Allgemeine musikalische Zeitung* (1915); S.E. Barbak, *Die Lieder von R. Franz* (Vienna, 1922); H. von der Pfordten, *R. Franz* (Leipzig, 1923); J.M. Boonin, *An Index to the Solo Songs of R. Franz* (Hackensack, N.J., 1970).

Fränzl, Ferdinand, German violinist and composer, son of **Ignaz Fränzl;** b. Schwetzingen, May 20, 1770; d. Mannheim, Oct. 27, 1833. He studied with his father; later was a pupil in composition of F.X. Richter and Pleyel at Strasbourg, and of Mattei at Bologna. He entered the Mannheim court orch. at the age of 22; in 1785 began to travel on concert tours with his father. He was appointed conductor of the Munich Opera in 1806, but continued his tours; retired in 1826; finally settled in Mannheim. As a master violinist, he enjoyed great renown. A prolific composer, he wrote 8 violin concertos; Double Concerto for 2 Violins; 6 operas; 9 string quartets; 6 string trios; symphs.; overtures; songs.

BIBLIOGRAPHY: R. Würtz, "Ferdinand Fränzl," *Mannheimer Hefte,* 2 (1967).

Fränzl, Ignaz, German violinist and composer, father of **Ferdinand Fränzl;** b. Mannheim, June 3, 1736; d. there, Sept. 3, 1811. He entered the Mannheim court orch. as a boy of 11; became co-concertmaster in 1774, and was conductor from 1790 to 1803. He made several concert tours with his son; composed symphs. and music for the violin, and also wrote for the stage. His singspiel *Die Luftbälle* was produced in Mannheim with excellent success (April 15, 1787); he also wrote music for Shakespeare's plays.

BIBLIOGRAPHY: R. Würtz, " '. . . ein sehr solider Geiger'. Mozart und Ignaz Fränzl," *Acta Mozartiana* (Nov. 1969); idem, *Ignaz Fränzl* (Mainz, 1970).

Fraschini, Gaetano, noted Italian tenor; b. Pavia, Feb. 16, 1816; d. Naples, May 23, 1887. He studied with F. Moretti; made his debut in Pavia in 1837; subsequently sang in Milan, Venice, Trieste, Rome, and other Italian cities; also appeared in London at Her Majesty's Theatre (1847) and Drury Lane (1868). He created the role of Genaro in Donizetti's *Caterina Cornaro;* much esteemed by Verdi, he sang in the premieres of *Attila, Il Corsaro, La battaglia di Legnano, Alzira, Stiffelio,* and *Un ballo in maschera.* The opera house in his native city of Pavia is named for him.

Fraser, Norman, Chilean-born English pianist; b. Valparaiso, Nov. 26, 1904. He pursued his musical studies in Chile; in 1917 he went to England, and attended classes at the Royal Academy of Music in London; then took piano lessons with Isidor Philipp in Paris. He subsequently made several tours in South America as a representative of various British organizations. From 1954 to 1971 he was engaged as European music supervisor at the BBC; gave numerous joint recitals with his wife, **Janet Fraser,** a British mezzo-soprano (b. Kirkealdy, May 22, 1911). In 1973 he settled at Seaford, England. He composed a number of attractive piano pieces and some chamber music.

Frazzi, Vito, Italian composer; b. San Secondo Parmense, Aug. 1, 1888; d. Florence, July 8, 1975. He studied organ at the Parma Cons.; also took courses in piano and theory. In 1912 he joined the staff of the Florence Cons.; remained until 1958; also taught at the Accademia Chigiana in Siena (1932–63). He wrote a music drama, *Re Lear,* after Shakespeare (Florence, 1939); an opera, *Don Quixote* (Florence, April 27, 1952); several symph. poems; chamber music; orchestrated Monteverdi's stage works.

Freccia, Massimo, Italian conductor; b. Florence, Sept. 19, 1906. He studied at the Florence Cons. and later in Vienna with Franz Schalk. In 1933–35 he conducted the Budapest Symph. Orch.; was guest conductor at the Lewisohn Stadium in N.Y. in 1938–40; then was conductor of the Havana Phil. Orch. (1939–43), the New Orleans Symph. Orch. (1944–52), and the Baltimore Symph. Orch. (1952–59). He returned to Italy in 1959, and conducted the Rome Radio Orch. until 1963.

Frederick II (Frederick the Great) of Prussia; b. Berlin, Jan. 24, 1712; d. Potsdam, Aug. 17, 1786. He was an enlightened patron of music, a flute player of considerable skill, and an amateur composer. He studied flute with Quantz; in 1740, when he ascended to the throne, he established a court orch. and an opera house; Bach's son Carl Philipp Emanuel was his harpsichordist until 1767. In 1747 J.S. Bach himself was invited to Potsdam; the fruit of this visit was Bach's *Musical Offering,* written on a theme by Frederick II. A collection of 25 flute sonatas and 4 concertos by Frederick was publ. by Spitta (3 vols., Leipzig, 1889; reprinted, N.Y., 1967); other works were publ. in vol. XX of *Die Musik am preussischen Hofe.* Selections from different compositions were edited by Barge, G. Lenzewski, E. Schwarz-Reiflingen, H. Osthoff, G. Müller, G. Thouret, and others. Besides instrumental works, Frederick contributed arias to several operas: *Demofoonte* by Graun (1746); *Il Re pastore* (1747; with Quantz and others); *Galatea ed Acide* (1748; with Hasse, Graun, Quantz, and Nichelmann); and *Il trionfo della fedelità* (1753; with Hasse and others).
BIBLIOGRAPHY: K.F. Müller, *Friedrich der Grosse als Kenner und Dilettant auf dem Gebiete der Tonkunst* (Potsdam, 1847); W. Kothe, *Friedrich der Grosse als Musiker* (Leipzig, 1869); G. Thouret, *Friedrichs des Grossen Verhältniss zur Musik* (Berlin, 1895); idem, *Friedrich der Grosse als Musikfreund und Musiker* (Leipzig, 1898); Karl von Forstner, *Friedrich der Grosse, Künstler und König* (Berlin, 1932); G. Müller, *Friedrich der Grosse, Seine Flöten und sein Flötenspiel* (Berlin, 1932); G.M. Fitzgibbon, "Of Flutes and Soft Recorders," *Musical Quarterly* (April 1934); John Bourke, "Frederick the Great as Music Lover and Musician," *Music & Letters* (Jan. 1947); E. Helm, *Music of the Court of Frederick the Great* (Norman, Okla., 1960); C. Wolf, "Überlegungen zum *Thema Regium,*" *Bach-Jahrbuch* (1973). Frederick's correspondence with Algarotti was publ. by F. Förster (Berlin, 1837); correspondence between him and the margravine of Bayreuth is contained in chapter IV of Mary Burrell's *Thoughts for Enthusiasts at Bayreuth* (London, 1891).

Freed, Alan, American disc jockey and passionate popularizer of rock'n'roll; b. Johnstown, Pa., Dec. 15, 1922; d. Palm Springs, Calif., Jan. 20, 1965. His greatest achievement was to desegregate black music by introducing it into white-sponsored radio stations. He was also credited with originating the term rock'n'roll in 1951, although it had been used long before in a musical about a pleasure-boat cruise. He began broadcasting in Cleveland; then went to N.Y. in 1954 to take command of the influential radio station WINS, which became one of the most popular purveyors of rock'n'roll. He also acted in the famous movie *Rock around the Clock.* He began having trouble when stabbings and riots occurred at some of his public concerts in 1958; he was even accused of encouraging such shenanigans for the sake of publicity. Then, with a horrifying peripeteia fit for a Greek tragedy, he suffered a monumental downfall in 1963, when he was convicted of "payola," accepting bribes from commercial record companies for putting their songs on the air. On top of that, he was charged with income-tax evasion. He quit the oppressive city of N.Y. and fled to the more tolerant, laid-back state of California, but he soon died, ignored by enemies and friends alike, in the vacuous spa of Palm Springs.

Freed, Isadore, American composer; b. Brest-Litovsk, Russia, March 26, 1900; d. Rockville Center, Long Island, N.Y., Nov. 10, 1960. He came to the U.S. at an early age; graduated from the Univ. of Pa. in 1918 (Mus.Bac.); then studied with Ernest Bloch and with Vincent d'Indy in Paris; returned to the U.S. in 1934; held various teaching positions; in 1944 was appointed head of the music dept. at Hartt College of Music in Hartford, Conn. WORKS: FOR THE STAGE: *Vibrations,* ballet (Philadelphia, 1928); operas: *Homo Sum* (1930) and *The Princess and the Vagabond* (Hartford, May 13, 1948). FOR ORCH.: *Jeux de timbres* (Paris, 1933); Symph. No. 1 (1941); *Appalachian Symphonic Sketches* (Chautauqua, N.Y., July 31, 1946); *Festival Overture* (San Francisco, Nov. 14, 1946); Rhapsody for Trombone and Orch. (radio premiere, N.Y., Jan. 7, 1951); Symph. No. 2 for Brass (San Francisco, Feb. 8, 1951, composer conducting); Violin Concerto (N.Y., Nov. 13, 1951); Cello Concerto (1952); Concertino for English Horn and Orch. (1953). CHAMBER MUSIC: 3 string quartets (1931, 1932, 1937); Trio for Flute, Viola, and Harp (1940); *Triptych* for Violin, Viola, Cello, and Piano (1943); Passacaglia for Cello and Piano (1947); Quintet for Woodwinds and Horn (Hartford, Dec. 2, 1949); Sonatina for Oboe and Piano (Boston, March 31, 1954); also choral works; piano and organ pieces; songs. He was co-editor of *Masters of Our Day,* contemporary educational material for piano (N.Y., 1936–37).
BIBLIOGRAPHY: E. Steinhauer, *A Jewish Composer by Choice, Isadore Freed: His Life and Work* (N.Y., 1961).

Freed, Richard (Donald), distinguished American music critic; b. Chicago, Dec. 27, 1928. He studied at the Univ. of Chicago; then held various newspaper jobs and subsequently wrote for the *Saturday Review* and the *New York Times* (1965). From 1966 to 1970 he was assistant to the director of the Eastman School of Music in Rochester, N.Y.; in 1973 he joined the staff of *Stereo Review;* other positions were as a record critic for the *Washington Star* (1972–75) and the *Washington Post* (since 1976); program annotator for the St. Louis Symph. Orch. (since 1973), the Philadelphia Orch. (since 1974), the Houston Symph. Orch. (1977–80), and the National Symph. Orch. of Washington, D.C. (since 1977). In 1974 he was appointed executive director of the Music Critics Association. He also contributed reviews and articles to numerous periodicals and served as a consultant to performing and funding organizations.

Freedman, Harry, Polish-born Canadian composer and oboist; b. Lodz, April 5, 1922. He was taken to Canada as an infant, and his family settled in Winnipeg in 1931. He studied composition with Weinzweig and oboe with Perry Bauman at the Toronto Cons. (1945–50); in the summer of 1950 he attended courses of Messiaen and Copland at the Berkshire Music Center in Tanglewood. In the interim he played the English horn in the Toronto Symph. Orch. (1946–70); in 1975 he was elected president of the Canadian League of Composers. His style of composition reflects various influences; he astutely applies serial techniques and electronic sound.
WORKS: Ballets: *Rose Latulippe* (Stratford Festival, Aug. 16, 1966) and *5 over 13* (1969); 2 nocturnes for Orch. (1949, 1975); *Matinée Suite* for Orch. (1951–55); *Fantasia and Dance* for Violin and Orch. (1955; revised 1959); *Images,* symph. suite on 3 Canadian paintings (1957–58); Symph. (1954–60; Washington, D.C., April 23, 1961); *3 poèmes de Jacques Prévert* for Soprano and String Orch. (1962); Chaconne for Orch. (1964); *A Little Symphony* (1966); *Armana* for Orch. (1967); *Tangents,* symph. variations (Montreal, July 21, 1967); *Klee Wych (The Laughing One)* for Orch. (1970; Klee Wych is the Indian name of the artist Emily Carr); *Scenario* for Saxophone, Electric Bass Guitar, and Orch. (Toronto, May 29, 1970); *Graphic I (Out of Silence...)* for Orch. and Tape (1971; Toronto, Oct. 26, 1971); *Preludes for Orchestra,* orchestrated from Debussy (1971); *Tapestry* for Small Orch. (1973); Trio for 2 Oboes and English Horn (1948); Wind Quintet (1962); *The Tokaido* for Chorus and Wind Quintet (1964); *3 Duets* for Basses or Cellos (1965); *Variations* for Oboe, Flute, and Harpsichord (1965); *Graphic II* for String Quartet (1972); Quartet for Trombones, Bassoons, or Cellos (1973); *Vignette* for Clarinet and Piano (1975); *Love and Age* for Soprano, Baritone, Wind Quintet, and Brass Quintet (1975); *5 Rings* for Brass Quintet (1976); *Fragments of Alice* for Soprano, Alto, 8 Instruments, and Percussion (1976); Suite for Piano (1951). He wrote many film scores; of these, *An Act of the Heart* was especially successful.

Freeman, Harry Lawrence, black American composer; b. Cleveland, Oct. 9, 1869; d. New York, March 24, 1954. He studied theory with J.H. Beck and piano with E. Schonert and Carlos Sobrino; taught at Wilberforce Univ. (1902–4) and the Salem School of Music (1910–13); organized and directed the Freeman School of Music (1911–22) and the Freeman School of Grand Opera (from 1923); conducted various theater orchs. and opera companies. In 1920 he organized the Negro Opera Co.; in 1930 received the Har-

mon Gold Award; conducted a pageant, *O Sing a New Song,* at the Chicago World's Fair in 1934. He was the first black composer to conduct a symph. orch. in his own work (Minneapolis, 1907), and the first of his race to write large operatic compositions. All his music is written in folk-song style; his settings are in simple harmonies; his operas are constructed of songs and choruses in simple concatenation of separate numbers.
WORKS: Grand operas (all on Negro, oriental, and Indian themes): *The Martyr* (Denver, 1893); *Valdo* (Cleveland, May 1906); *Zuluki* (1898); *African Kraal* (Wilberforce Univ., Chicago, June 30, 1903, with an all-black cast, composer conducting; revised 1934); *The Octoroon* (1904); *The Tryst* (N.Y., May 1911); *The Prophecy* (N.Y., 1912); *The Plantation* (1914); *Athalia* (1916); *Vendetta* (N.Y., Nov. 12, 1923); *American Romance,* jazz opera (1927); *Voodoo* (N.Y., Sept. 10, 1928); *Leah Kleschna* (1930); *Uzziah* (1931); *Zululand,* a tetralogy of music dramas: *Nada, The Lily* (1941–44; vocal score contains 2,150 pp.), *Allah* (1947), and *The Zulu King* (1934); *The Slave,* ballet for Choral Ensemble and Orch. (Harlem, N.Y., Sept. 22, 1932); songs (*Whither, If thou did'st love,* etc.).
BIBLIOGRAPHY: E.E. Hipsher, *American Opera and Its Composers* (Philadelphia, 1927; 2nd ed., 1934; pp. 189–95).

Freeman, Paul, black American conductor; b. Richmond, Va., Jan. 2, 1936. He studied piano, clarinet, and cello in his youth; continued his musical training at the Eastman School of Music in Rochester, N.Y. (B.Mus., 1956; M.Mus., 1957; Ph.D., 1963); then went to Germany and took music courses at the Berlin Hochschule für Musik (1957–59). Returning to the U.S., he took conducting lessons with Richard Lert and Pierre Monteux. He subsequently held the post of conductor with the Opera Theater of Rochester (1961–66), the San Francisco Cons. Orch. (1966–67), and the San Francisco Little Symph. Orch. (1967–68); then was associate conductor of the Dallas Symph. Orch. (1968–70) and resident conductor of the Detroit Symph. Orch. (1970–79); also served as principal guest conductor of the Helsinki Phil. Orch. (1974–76). In 1979 he became music director of the Victoria (British Columbia) Symph. Orch. In his concert programs he made it a point to include works by black composers.

Freeman, Robert, American oboist, pianist, musicologist, and educator; b. Rochester, N.Y., Aug. 26, 1935. He began his musical studies at the Curtis Inst. in Philadelphia; then studied oboe with Fernand Gillet; piano with Gregory Tucker, Artur Balsam, and Rudolf Serkin; and conducting with Lukas Foss and Leonard Bernstein; he subsequently took courses at Harvard College (1953–57), at Princeton Univ. (1958–60), and at the Univ. of Vienna on a Fulbright grant (1960–62); he received his Ph.D. at Princeton in 1967 with the dissertation *Opera without Drama: Currents of Change in Italian Opera, 1675–1725* (Ann Arbor, 1981). He taught at Princeton Univ. (1963–68) and at the Mass. Inst. of Technology (1968–72). In 1972 he was named director of the Eastman School of Music and prof. of musicology. He served as a contributor to the 6th edition of *The New Grove.*

Freer, Eleanor (née **Everest**), American composer; b. Philadelphia, May 14, 1864; d. Chicago, Dec. 13, 1942. She studied singing in Paris (1883–86) with Mathilde Marchesi; then took a course in composition with Benjamin Godard. Upon her return to the U.S., she taught singing at the National Cons. of Music in N.Y. (1889–91). On April 25, 1891, she married Archibald Freer of Chicago; they lived in Leipzig in 1892–99; then settled in Chicago, where she studied theory with Bernard Ziehn (1902–7). She publ. some light pieces under the name Everest while still a young girl, but most of her larger works were written after 1919.

WORKS: 9 operas, of which the following were performed: *The Legend of the Piper* (South Bend, Ind., Feb. 28, 1924); *The Court Jester* (Lincoln, Nebr., 1926); *A Christmas Tale* (Houston, Dec. 27, 1929); *Frithiof* (Chicago, Feb. 1, 1931; in concert form); *A Legend of Spain* (Milwaukee, June 19, 1931; in concert form); a song cycle (settings of Elizabeth Barrett Browning's entire *Sonnets from the Portuguese*); about 150 songs; piano pieces. She also wrote an autobiography, *Recollections and Reflections of an American Composer* (Chicago, 1929).

BIBLIOGRAPHY: A.G. Foster, *Eleanor Freer and Her Colleagues* (Chicago, 1927); E.E. Hipsher, *American Opera and Its Composers* (Philadelphia, 1927; pp. 196–204).

Freire, Nelson, pianist; b. Boa Esperanza, Brazil, Oct. 18, 1944. After studies in his native country, he went to Vienna to pursue his musical education. He made his concert debut at the age of 15 in 1959. After 1964 he appeared widely in Europe, the U.S., and Japan. He is known for the bravura he brings to the interpretation of the Romantic school of composition.

Freitas, Frederico de, Portuguese composer; b. Lisbon, Nov. 15, 1902; d. there, March 1980. He studied piano, violin, and composition at the Lisbon Cons. In 1935 he began his career as a conductor. In his music he made use of modernistic devices, such as polytonality, under the influence of the French and German schools. Much of his symph. music belongs to the genre of "landscape composition," depicting various scenes of nature. Of the more ambitious kind he wrote an opera, *O eremita* (1957); a ballet, *Imagens de terra e do mar* (1943); Wind Quintet (1950); Flute Concerto (1955); etc. He was also active as a music critic.

Freitas Branco, Luíz de, significant Portuguese composer; b. Lisbon, Oct. 12, 1890; d. there, Nov. 27, 1955. He studied in Lisbon with Tomás Borba; became influenced by the theories of the Belgian modernist Désiré Pâque, who lived in Lisbon at the time. In 1910 Freitas Branco went to Berlin to study with Humperdinck, and then to Paris for studies

with Gabriel Grovlez; returning to Portugal in 1916, he engaged primarily in teaching. His music is cast in an impressionistic vein.

WORKS: *Manfredo,* after Byron's poem, for Soloists, Chorus, Organ, and Orch. (1905); symph. poems: *Depois de uma Leitura de Antero de Quental* (1907–8) and *Paraísos artificiais* (1913); 2 symph. pieces, each entitled *Suite Alentejana* (1910, 1927); *Vathek,* symph. variations on an oriental theme (1914); Violin Concerto (1916); *Balada* for Piano and Orch. (1917); *Cena lírica* for Cello and Orch. (1917); 4 symphs. (1924, 1926, 1943, 1952); 2 violin sonatas (1907, 1928); String Quartet (1911); Cello Sonata (1913); *10 Preludes* for Piano (1918); Piano Sonatina (1930); choruses; songs.

Fremaux, Louis, eminent French conductor; b. Aire-sur-la-Lys, Aug. 13, 1921. He attended the Cons. in Valenciennes, but his education was interrupted by World War II. He served in the Résistance during the Nazi occupation. After the war he studied conducting at the Paris Cons. with Louis Fourestier, graduating in 1952 with the first prize. From 1956 to 1966 he was chief conductor of the Monte Carlo National Opera and Orch. In 1968 he founded the Orch. de Lyon; was its music director until 1971. From 1969 to 1978 he was music director of the City of Birmingham Symph. Orch. In 1979 he became chief conductor of the Sydney (Australia) Symph. Orch.

Fremstad, Olive, famous Swedish-born American dramatic soprano; b. Stockholm, March 14, 1871 (entered into the parish register as the daughter of an unmarried woman, Anna Peterson); d. Irvington-on-Hudson, N.Y., April 21, 1951. She was adopted by an American couple of Scandinavian origin, who took her to Minnesota; she studied piano in Minneapolis; came to N.Y. in 1890 and took singing lessons with E.F. Bristol; then held several church positions; in 1892 she sang for the first time with an orch. (under C. Zerrahn) in Boston. In 1893 she went to Berlin to study with Lilli Lehmann; made her operatic debut in Cologne as Azucena in *Il Trovatore* (1895); sang contralto parts in Wagner's operas at Bayreuth during the summer of 1896; in 1897 made her London debut; also sang in Cologne, Vienna, Amsterdam, and Antwerp. From 1900 to 1903 she was at the Munich Opera. She made her American debut as Sieglinde at the Metropolitan Opera on Nov. 25, 1903. Subsequently she sang soprano parts in Wagnerian operas; at first she was criticized in the press for her lack of true soprano tones; however, she soon triumphed over these difficulties, and became known as a soprano singer to the exclusion of contralto parts. She sang Carmen with great success at the Metropolitan (March 5, 1906), with Caruso; her performance of Isolde under Mahler (Jan. 1, 1908) produced a deep impression; until 1914 she was one of the brightest stars of the Metropolitan Opera, specializing in Wagnerian roles, but she was also successful in *Tosca* and other Italian operas. She sang Salomé at the first American performance of the Strauss opera (N.Y., Jan. 22, 1907) and in Paris (May 8, 1907). After her retirement from the Metropolitan, she appeared with the Manhattan Opera, the Boston Opera, and the Chicago Opera, and in concerts; presented her last song recital in N.Y. on Jan. 19, 1920. In 1906 she married Edson Sutphen of N.Y. (divorced in 1911); in 1916 she married her accompanist, **Harry Lewis Brainard** (divorced in 1925). In Willa Cather's novel *The Song of the Lark,* the principal character was modeled after Olive Fremstad.

French, Jacob, American composer of psalm tunes; b. Stoughton, Mass., July 15, 1754; d. Simsbury, Conn., May 1817. He was co-founder, with William Billings, of the Stoughton Music Society in 1774; fought at the battle of Bunker Hill in the Revolutionary War; was one of the few survivors of the Cherry Valley Massacre. After the war he became a singing teacher, retiring in 1814. He publ. *New American Melody* (1789), *Psalmodist's Companion* (1793), and *Harmony of Harmony* (1802).

BIBLIOGRAPHY: M. Genuchi, *The Life and Music of Jacob French (1754–1817), Colonial American Composer* (Diss., Univ. of Iowa, 1964); J.T. Howard, *Our American Music* (N.Y., 4th ed., 1965).

Freni, Mirella (real last name, **Fregni**), noted Italian soprano; b. Modena, Feb. 27, 1935. Curiously enough, her mother and the mother of the future celebrated tenor Luciano Pavarotti worked for a living in the same cigarette factory; curiouser still, the future opera stars shared the same wet nurse. Mirella Freni studied voice with her uncle, Dante Arcelli; made her first public appearance at the age of 11; her accompanist was a child pianist named Leone Magiera, whom she married in 1955. She later studied voice with Ettore Campogalliani; made her operatic debut in Modena on Feb. 3, 1955, as Micaela in *Carmen;* then sang in provincial Italian opera houses. In 1959 she sang with the Amsterdam Opera Co. at the Holland Festival; then at the Glyndebourne Festival (1960), Covent Garden in London (1961), and La Scala in Milan (1962). She gained acclaim as Mimi in the film version of *La Bohème,* produced at La Scala on Jan. 31, 1963, with Herbert von Karajan conducting; when La Scala toured Russia in 1964, Freni joined the company and sang Mimi at the Bolshoi Theater in Moscow. She also chose the role of Mimi for her American debut with the Metropolitan Opera in N.Y. on Sept. 29, 1965. She subsequently sang with the Vienna State Opera, the Munich Opera, the San Carlo Co. in Naples, and the Rome Opera. In 1976 she traveled with the Paris Opéra during its first American tour. In addition to Mimi, she sang the roles of Susanna in *Le nozze di Figaro,* Zerlina in *Don Giovanni,* Violetta in *La Traviata,* Amelia in *Simon Boccanegra,* and Manon.

Frere, Rudolph Walter Howard, English music scholar; b. Dungate, near Cambridge, Nov. 23, 1863; d. Mirfield, Yorkshire, April 2, 1938. He studied at Trinity College, Cambridge; was ordained curate in 1887; from 1923 to 1934 was bishop of Truro. He specialized in plainsong, and contributed valuable articles on this subject to *Grove's Dictionary of Music and Musicians* and to the *Oxford History of Music.* Among his important publications are *Bibliotheca musica liturgica* (1901) and an introduction to *Hymns, Ancient and Modern* (1909). He edited the *Graduale Sarisburiense* (1893), *The Sarum Gradual,* and the *Gregorian Antiphonale Missarum;* and, with John Stainer and H.B. Briggs, *A Manual of Plainsong* (1902); also *Pars antiphonarii* (1923); *Holy Week Services of the Church of England* (2nd ed., 1933).

Freschi, (Giovanni) Domenico, Italian composer; b. Bassano, Vicenza, c.1625; d. Vicenza, July 2, 1710. He was maestro di cappella at the Cathedral of Vicenza from 1656 until his death; publ. 2 masses and a number of Psalms (1660, 1673). In 1677 he went to Venice, remaining there for 8 years; wrote 15 operas, which were successfully produced there, and a series of short pieces for an opera house in Piazzola, near Padua. He also wrote at least 3 oratorios, including *Giuditta* and *Il Miracolo del mago.*

BIBLIOGRAPHY: Paolo Camerini, *Piazzola* (Milan, 1925).

Frescobaldi, Girolamo, one of the greatest Italian organists and composers of the Renaissance; b. Ferrara (baptized, Sept. 9), 1583; d. Rome, March 1, 1643. He studied with Luzzasco Luzzaschi in Ferrara; by the age of 14 was organist at the Accademia della Morte in Ferrara; in early 1607 became organist of S. Maria in Trastevere; then, in June 1607, traveled to Brussels in the retinue of the Papal Nuncio; publ. his first work, a collection of 5-part madrigals, in Antwerp in 1608, printed by Phalèse. Returning to Rome in the same year, he was appointed organist at St. Peter's as successor to Ercole Pasquini. He retained this all-important post until his death, with the exception of the years 1628 to 1634, when he was court organist in Florence. A significant indication of Frescobaldi's importance among musicians of his time was that Froberger, who was court organist in Vienna, came to Rome especially to study with Frescobaldi (1637–41). Frescobaldi's place in music history is very great; particularly as a keyboard composer, he exercised a decisive influence on the style of the early Baroque; he enlarged the expressive resources of keyboard music so as to include daring chromatic progressions and acrid passing dissonances, "durezze" (literally, "harshnesses"); in Frescobaldi's terminology "toccata di durezza" signified a work using dissonances; he used similar procedures in organ variations on chorale themes, "fiori musicali" ("musical flowers"). His ingenious employment of variations greatly influenced the entire development of Baroque music.

WORKS: *Fantasie a 2, 3 e 4* (Milan, 1608, Book I); *Ricercari e canzoni francese* (Rome, 1615); *Toccate e partite d'intavolatura di cembalo* (Rome, 1615); *Il 2° libro di toccate, canzoni, versi d'inni, magnificat, gagliarde, correnti ed altre partite d'intavolatura di cembalo ed organo* (Rome, 1616); *Capricci sopra diversi soggetti* (Rome, 1624); *Arie musicale a più voci* (Florence, 1630); *Fiori musicali*

di diverse compositioni Toccate, Kirie, Canzoni, Capricci e Recercari in partitura (Venice, 1935); *Canzoni alla francese* was publ. posthumously in Rome, 1945. A complete ed. of organ and other keyboard works by Frescobaldi was issued in 5 vols., ed. by P. Pidoux in Kassel (1950–54); *Keyboard Compositions Preserved in Manuscripts,* No. 30 of Corpus of Early Keyboard Music (3 vols., 1968); selected organ works, in 2 vols., were publ. in Leipzig in 1943–48; *Fiori musicale & Toccate e Partite* in 2 vols. was publ. in Rome in 1936–37; *Fiori musicale* was also brought out by J. Bonnet and A. Guilmant (Paris, 1922); *25 Canzoni, 7 Toccate & Correnti* was ed. by F. Boghen (Milan, 1918); *Toccate, Ricercari, Canzoni,* etc. was issued by Casella in *I classici della musica italiana* (Milan, 1919); numerous other eds. of selected pieces are also available. A "complete works" ed. is now in progress, under the auspices of the Comune di Ferrara and the Società Italiana di Musicologica; the first vol., issued in 1975, is *Due messe a otto voci.*
BIBLIOGRAPHY: The literature is considerable; among the most important essays are N. Bennati, *Ferrara a Girolamo Frescobaldi* (Ferrara, 1908); L. Ronga, *G. Frescobaldi* (Turin, 1930); W. Apel, "Neapolitan Links between Cabezón and Frescobaldi," *Musical Quarterly* (Oct. 1938); A. Machabey, *G. Frescobaldi Ferrarensis (1583–1643)* (Paris, 1952); Roland Jackson, "On Frescobaldi's Chromaticism and Its Background," *Musical Quarterly* (April 1971); F. Hammond, *Girolamo Frescobaldi* (Cambridge, Mass., 1983); J. Harper, "Frescobaldi: New Perspectives after 400 Years," *Musical Times* (Oct. 1983).

Frešo, Tibor, Slovak composer and conductor; b. Štiavnik, Nov. 20, 1918. He studied composition with A. Moyzes and conducting with J. Vincourek at the Bratislava Cons., graduating in 1938; then studied with Pizzetti at the Santa Cecilia Academy in Rome (1939–42). Returning to Czechoslovakia, he served as conductor of the Bratislava Opera (1942–49) and the Košice Opera (1949–52); in 1953 he was appointed director of the Slovak National Opera.
WORKS: Children's opera, *Martin and the Sun* (Bratislava, Jan. 25, 1975); 3 cantatas: *Stabat Mater* (1940); *Mother* (1959); *Hymn to the Fatherland* (1961); *Little Suite* for Orch. (1938); *Concert Overture* (1940); *Symphonic Prolog* (1943); symph. poems: *A New Morning* (1950) and *Liberation* (1955); *Little Concerto* for Piano and Orch.; *Meditation* for Soprano and Orch. (1942); *Song about Woman* for Alto, Narrator, Children's and Mixed Choruses, and Orch. (1975); String Quartet.

Freudenberg, Wilhelm, German composer and conductor; b. Raubacher Hütte, near Neuwied, March 11, 1838; d. Schweidnitz, May 22, 1928. He studied at the Leipzig Cons. with Moscheles and others; in 1870 he went to Wiesbaden, where he was active as a choral conductor; in 1886 he settled in Berlin, where he was a theater conductor and teacher; eventually went to Schweidnitz. He wrote several light operas: *Die Pfahlbauer* (Mainz, 1877); *Die*

Mühle im Wispertale (Magdeburg, 1883); *Das Jahrmarktsfest zu Plundersweilen* (Bremen, 1908); etc.; also choruses, songs, and chamber music.

Freund, John Christian, English-American music journalist; b. London, Nov. 22, 1848; d. Mt. Vernon, N.Y., June 3, 1924. He studied music in London and Oxford; in 1871 arrived in N.Y., where he became the editor of the *Musical and Dramatic Times;* in 1890 began publishing a commercial magazine, *Music Trades.* In 1898 he founded the weekly magazine *Musical America* and was its editor until his death. In his editorials he fulminated against the rival magazine *Musical Courier,* and also wrote sharp polemical articles denouncing composers and music critics who disagreed with his viewpoint; in this respect he was a typical representative of the personal type of musical journalism of the time.

Freund, Marya, remarkable German soprano; b. Breslau, Dec. 12, 1876; d. Paris, May 21, 1966. She first studied violin, taking lessons with Sarasate; then began to study singing; made successful appearances in Europe and America with symph. orchs. and in recital. Her career as a singer was mainly significant, however, not for the excellence of her performances in the standard repertoire, but for her devotion to modern music. She sang the principal vocal works by Schoenberg, Stravinsky, Ravel, Bloch, Milhaud, and many others; eventually settled in Paris as a singing teacher.

Freundt, Cornelius, German composer; b. Plauen, 1535; d. Zwickau, Aug. 26, 1591. He was a cantor at Borna; in 1565, became cantor of St. Marien and a teacher and organist at Zwickau, where he remained until his death. His compositions were designed for use in church and school; most of his sacred works remain in MS. Georg Göhler wrote a dissertation on him (Leipzig, 1896).

Frey, Adolf, German-American pianist; b. Landau, April 4, 1865; d. Syracuse, N.Y., Oct. 4, 1938. He studied with Clara Schumann, and served as court musician to Prince Alexander Friedrich of Hesse (1887–93) before emigrating to the U.S. From 1893 to 1913 he was the head of the piano dept. at the Univ. of Syracuse.

Frey, Emil, eminent Swiss pianist and composer; b. Baden, in the canton of Aargau, April 8, 1889; d. Zürich, May 20, 1946. He studied musical subjects with Otto Barblan at the Geneva Cons.; at the age of 15 was accepted as a student of Louis Diémer in piano and Widor in composition; in 1907 went to Berlin, and later to Bucharest, where he became a court pianist. In 1910 he won the Anton Rubinstein prize for his Piano Trio in St. Petersburg; on the strength of this success he was engaged to teach at the Moscow Cons. (1912–17). Returning to Switzerland after the Russian Revolution, he joined the faculty of the Zürich Cons.; he continued his concert career throughout Europe and also in South

America. He wrote 2 symphs. (the first with a choral finale), Piano Concerto, Violin Concerto, Cello Concerto, Swiss Festival Overture, Piano Quintet, String Quartet, Piano Trio, Violin Sonata, Cello Sonata, several piano sonatas, piano suites, and sets of piano variations; publ. a piano instruction manual, *Bewusst gewordenes Klavierspiel und seine technischen Grundlagen* (Zürich, 1933).

Frey, Walter, Swiss pianist, brother of **Emil Frey;** b. Basel, Jan. 26, 1898. He studied piano with F. Niggli and theory with Andreae. From 1925 to 1958 he was, jointly with his brother, an instructor in piano at the Zürich Cons.; concurrently evolved an active concert career in Germany and Scandinavia; specialized in modern piano music and gave first performances of several piano concertos by contemporary composers. He publ. (with Willi Schuh) a collection, *Schweizerische Klaviermusik aus der Zeit der Klassik und Romantik* (Zürich, 1937).

Fribec, Krešimir, Croatian composer; b. Daruvar, May 24, 1908. He studied in Zagreb; adopted a nationalistic style of composition; wrote mostly vocal music.
WORKS: *Povratak,* poem for Baritone and Orch. (1951); *Bijele noći,* song cycle, with Orch. (1953); *Vibracije,* ballet pantomime (1955); operas: *Sluga Jernej* (Zagreb, Feb. 12, 1952); *Romeo and Juliet* (Zagreb, June 21, 1955); *Krvava svadba* (*Blood Wedding;* 1956). See K. Kovačević, *Hrvatski kompozitori i njihova djela* (Zagreb, 1960).

Fricci, Antonietta, Austrian soprano; b. Vienna, Jan. 8, 1840; d. Turin, Sept. 7, 1912. Her original name was **Antonietta Frietsche,** which she Italianized for professional euphony. She studied with Marchesi in Vienna; made her debut in 1858 in Pisa as Violetta; was a principal singer at La Scala in Milan (1865–73); retired in 1878; then taught voice in Florence and Turin.

Frick, Gottlob, German bass; b. Olbronn, July 28, 1906. He was educated at the Stuttgart Hochschule für Musik; made his debut in Coburg in 1934. In 1938 he became a leading member of the Dresden State Opera. After World War II, he began to appear widely in Europe. He made his Metropolitan Opera debut in N.Y. in 1950. He sang regularly at the Vienna State Opera, La Scala in Milan, the Royal Opera House, Covent Garden, London, and the Bayreuth Festival. He was equally effective in heroic and buffo roles.

Fricker, Herbert Austin, English organist; b. Canterbury, Feb. 12, 1868; d. Toronto, Nov. 11, 1943. He studied organ with W.H. Longhurst, organist of Canterbury Cathedral; composition with Sir Frederick Bridge and Edwin Lemare. After filling posts as organist in Canterbury, Folkstone, and Leeds, he moved to Toronto in 1917, and conducted the Mendelssohn Choir there until 1942. He composed sacred and secular choruses and organ pieces.

Fricker, Peter Racine, significant English composer; b. London, Sept. 5, 1920. He studied at the Royal College of Music and later with Mátyás Seiber. In 1952 he was appointed music director at Morley College in London; taught composition at the Royal College of Music in 1955–64. In 1964 he went to Santa Barbara, Calif., as a visiting prof. at the Univ. of Calif.; in 1970 he became chairman of the music dept. there.
WORKS: *Rondo scherzoso* for Orch. (1948); Symph. No. 1 (1949; Cheltenham Festival, July 5, 1950; awarded the Koussevitzky prize); Symph. No. 2 (Liverpool, July 26, 1951); *Canterbury Prologue,* ballet (London, 1951); Concerto for Viola and Orch. (Edinburgh, Sept. 3, 1953); Piano Concerto (London, March 21, 1954); *Rapsodia concertante* for Violin and Orch. (Cheltenham Festival, July 15, 1954); *Litany* for Double String Orch. (1955); *Concertante* for 3 Pianos, Strings, and Timpani (London, Aug. 10, 1956); *The Death of Vivien,* radio opera (1956); *A Vision of Judgment,* oratorio (Leeds, Oct. 13, 1958); *Comedy Overture* (1958); Toccata for Piano and Orch. (1959); Symph. No. 3 (London, Nov. 8, 1960); *O longs désirs,* song cycle for Soprano and Orch. (1964); Symph. No. 4, "in memoriam Mátyás Seiber" (Cheltenham, Feb. 14, 1967); *3 Scenes* for Orch. (Santa Barbara, Feb. 26, 1967); *7 Counterpoints* for Orch. (Pasadena, Oct. 21, 1967); *Magnificat* for Soloists, Chorus, and Orch. (Santa Barbara, May 27, 1968); *The Roofs* for Coloratura Soprano and Percussion (1970); *Nocturne* for Chamber Orch. (1970); *Introitus* for Orch. (Canterbury, June 24, 1972); Symph. No. 5 (1975). Chamber music: Wind Quintet (1947); *3 Sonnets of Cecco Angiolieri* for Tenor, Wind Quintet, Cello, and Double Bass (1947); String Quartet in One Movement (1948; Brussels Festival, 1950); *Prelude, Elegy and Finale* for Strings (1949); Concerto for Violin and Chamber Orch. (1950); Violin Sonata (1950); *Concertante* for English Horn and Strings (1950); String Quartet No. 2 (1953); Horn Sonata (1955; premiered by Dennis Brain); Suite for Recorders (1956); Cello Sonata (1957); Octet for Wind and String Instruments (1958); *Serenade No. 1* for 6 Instruments (1959); *Serenade No. 2* for Flute, Oboe, and Piano (1959); *4 Dialogues* for Oboe and Piano (1965); *5 Canons* for 2 Flutes and 2 Oboes (1966); Fantasy for Viola and Piano (1966); *Concertante No. 4* for Flute, Oboe, Violin, and Strings (Santa Cruz, Calif., Feb. 25, 1969); *Some Superior Nonsense* for Tenor, Flute, Oboe, and Harpsichord (Santa Barbara, Feb. 26, 1969); *Serenade No. 3* for Saxophone Quartet (1969); *3 Arguments* for Bassoon and Cello (1969); Suite for Harpsichord (1957); *14 Aubades* for Piano (1958); 12 studies for Piano (1961); *Commissary Report* for Men's Voices (1965); *Refrains* for Solo Oboe (1968); *Paseo* for Guitar (1969); *Concertante No. 5* for Piano and String Quartet (Santa Barbara, Jan. 29, 1972); *Come Sleep* for Contralto, Alto, and Bass Clarinet (1972); *The Groves of Dodona* for 6 Flutes (1973); *Spirit Puck* for Clarinet and Percussion (1974); *Trio-Sonata* for Organ (1974); String Quartet No. 3 (1975).

Fricsay, Ferenc, Hungarian conductor; b. Buda-

pest, Aug. 9, 1914; d. Basel, Feb. 20, 1963. He received his early musical training from his father, a military-band leader; he was barely 6 years old when he was accepted as a pupil in the music class for beginners at the Budapest high school; as he grew up he took piano lessons with Bartók and composition with Kodály. He also learned to play almost all orch. instruments. At the age of 15 he conducted a radio performance of his father's military band; in 1934 he became orch. conductor at Szeged, and in 1936 conducted the opera there. In 1944 he returned to Budapest; in 1945 made his debut as conductor at the Budapest Opera. In 1947 he conducted at the Salzburg Festival; subsequently made a European tour as guest conductor; also toured South America. In 1948–52 he was Generalmusikdirektor of the Berlin State Opera; from 1949 to 1954 was artistic director of the radio orch. RIAS in the American sector of divided Berlin, and was regular conductor there until 1961. On Nov. 13, 1953, he made a highly successful American debut with the Boston Symph. Orch.; in 1954 was engaged as conductor of the Houston Symph. Orch., but soon resigned, owing to disagreement on musical policy with the management. He was Generalmusikdirektor of the Bavarian State Opera in Munich from 1956–58. He then settled in Switzerland, continuing to conduct occasional guest engagements, until his illness (leukemia) forced him to abandon all activities.
BIBLIOGRAPHY: Fr. Herzfeld, *Ferenc Fricsay. Ein Gedenkbuch* (Berlin, 1964).

Frid, Géza, Hungarian-born Dutch composer and pianist; b. Máramarossziget, Jan. 25, 1904. He studied composition with Kodály and piano with Bartók at the Budapest Cons. (1912–24); settled in Amsterdam in 1929, becoming a Dutch citizen in 1948. In 1964 he joined the faculty of the Cons. of Utrecht; remained there until 1969.
WORKS: Opera, *De zwarte bruid* (1959; Amsterdam, 1959); 2 ballets: *Luctor et Emergo* (1953) and *Euridice* (1961); *Podium-Suite* for Violin and Orch. (1928); Suite for Orch. (1929); Violin Concerto (1930); *Tempesta d'orchestra* (1931); Divertimento for String Orch. or String Quintet (1932); Symph. (1933); *Romance and Allegro* for Cello and Orch. (1935); *Abel et Cain,* symph. tableau for Low Voice and Orch. (1938); *Schopenhauer Cantata* (1944); Nocturnes for Flute, Harp, and String Orch. or String Quintet (1946); *Paradou,* symph. fantasy (1948); *Variations on a Dutch Folk Song* for Wind Orch., or Chorus and Orch. (1950); *Fête champêtre,* suite of dances for String Orch. and Percussion (1951); *Hymne aan de Arbeid (Hymn to Labor)* for Male Chorus and Orch. (1951); 2-violin Concerto (1952); *Caecilia Ouverture* (1953); *Etudes symphoniques* (1954); *South African Rhapsody* for Orch. or Wind Orch. (1954); *3 Romances* for Soprano and Orch. (1955); *Das Sklavenschiff* for Tenor and Baritone, Male Chorus, Brass, Percussion, and Piano (1956); Serenade for Chamber Orch. (1956); 2-piano Concerto (1957); *Rhythmic Studies* for Chamber Orch. or 2 Pianos (1959); Concertino for Violin, Cello, Piano, and Orch. (1961); *Sinfonietta* for String

Orch. (1963); *7 pauken en een koperorkest,* concerto for 7 Percussionists and Brass Orch. (1964; Amsterdam, May 14, 1965); *Ballade* for Chorus and Wind Orch. (1965; version for Chorus, String Orch., Percussion, and Piano, 4-hands, 1968); *4 Sketches* for Wind Orch. (1966); 3-violin Concerto (The Hague, July 4, 1970); Concerto for 4 different Clarinets (one Soloist) and String Orch. (1972); Toccata for Orch. or 2 Pianos (1973); 4 string quartets (1926, 1939, 1949, 1956); String Trio (1926); Serenade for Wind Instruments (1928); Cello Sonata (1931); Concerto for Piano and Mixed Chorus (1934); Solo Violin Sonata (1936); Viola Sonatina (1946); Piano Trio (1947); *20 Duos* for 2 Violins (1951); *Frühlingsfeier* for Soprano, Alto, Flute, Clarinet, Bassoon, Horn, Violin, Viola, Cello, and Piano (1952); Violin Sonata (1955); *12 Metamorphoses* for 2 Flutes and Percussion (1957); *Fuga* for 3 Harps (1961); Sextet for Wind Quintet and Piano (1965); *Dubbeltrio* for Wind Instruments (1967); *Chemins divers* for Flute, Bassoon, and Piano (1968; also arranged for 2 Violins and Piano); *Paganini Variations* for 2 Violins (1969); *Houdt den Tijd!* for Male Chorus and Percussion (1971); Duo for Violin and Piano (1972) *Caprices roumains* for Oboe and Piano (1975); *Sons roumains* for Flute, Viola, Harp, and Percussion (1975); Little Suite for Saxophone and Piano (1975); *Music* for 2 Violins and Viola (1977); Piano Sonata (1929); *4 Etudes* for Piano (1932); *Foxtrot* for 2 Pianos (1975); songs; choruses.

Friderici, Daniel, German composer and theorist; b. Klein-Eichstedt, near Querfurt, 1584; d. Rostock, Sept. 23, 1638. He served as a choirboy; then studied music in Magdeburg; settled in Rostock, where he was cantor of St. Mary's Church from 1617 till his death. He died of pestilence. He publ. in Rostock a number of sacred and secular songs to German words, and a theoretical work, *Musica Figuralis oder Neue Unterweisung des Singe Kunst* (1618; 6th ed., 1677).
BIBLIOGRAPHY: W. Voll, *Daniel Friderici* (Kassel, 1936).

Fried, Alexej, Czech composer and conductor; b. Brno, Oct. 13, 1922. He studied theory with Theodore Schaefer at the Brno Cons.; then took lessons in composition with Hlobil and Bořkovec at the Prague Academy, graduating in 1953. By that time he had considerable experience in the jazz field; in 1954 organized a dance orch. under his own name. Most of his music is in the "third-stream" manner, fusing jazz with classical styles.
WORKS: 4 musicals: *The Devil Passed through the Town* (1956–67); *A Fete in Harlem* (1959); *Savage River* (1965); *Carnival in San Catarina* (1974); ballet, *Peter and Lucia* (1965); Piano Trio (1951); *For a New Man,* symph. poem (1953); *Corrida,* dance metaphor for Orch. (1965). His symph. jazz works for large jazz band include *Akt (Nude Portrait),* with Solo Trumpet and Flute (1966); Jazz Clarinet Concerto (1970); *Sidonia,* with Solo Trumpet (1970); *Souvenir* (1970); *Jazz Dance Etudes,* with Solo Clarinet, Soprano Saxophone, and Alto Saxophone

(1970); *Moravian Wedding* for Orch. (1972); *Solstice,* concerto for 2 Jazz Bands (1973); Jazz Clarinet Concertino (1974); *Dialogue,* with 2 Solo Alto Saxophones (1974); Concerto for Jazz Band (1976). Jazz works for symph. orch. include a *Triple Concerto* for Flute, Clarinet, Horn, and Orch. (1971); Concerto for Orch. (1974); and Concerto No. 2 for Clarinet and Orch. (1976).

Fried, Miriam, Rumanian violinist; b. Satu Mare, Sept. 9, 1946. She went to Israel while very young; studied at the Rubin Academy of Music in Tel Aviv. She then settled in America, her teachers being Josef Gingold at Indiana Univ. and Ivan Galamian at the Juilliard School of Music in N.Y. She appeared with many orchs. in Europe and America; was also active as a recitalist.

Fried, Oskar, German conductor and composer; b. Berlin, Aug. 10, 1871; d. Moscow, July 5, 1941. He studied with Humperdinck in Frankfurt and P. Scharwenka in Berlin; played the horn in various orchs. until the performance of his choral work with orch. *Das trunkene Lied,* given by Karl Muck in Berlin (April 15, 1904), attracted much favorable attention; he continued to compose prolifically; wrote *Verklärte Nacht* for Solo Voices and Orch.; *Andante und Scherzo* for Wind Instruments, 2 Harps, and Kettledrums; *Präludium und Doppelfuge* for String Orch.; etc. At the same time he began his career as a conductor, achieving considerable renown in Europe; he was conductor of the Stern Choral Society in Berlin (from 1904), of the Gesellschaft der Musikfreunde in Berlin (1907–10), and of the Berlin Symph. Orch. (1925–26); left Berlin in 1934 and went to Russia; became a Soviet citizen in 1940. For several years before his death he was conductor of the Tiflis Opera, in the Caucasus; later was chief conductor of the All-Union Radio Orch. in Moscow. BIBLIOGRAPHY: Paul Bekker, *Oskar Fried* (Berlin, 1907); Paul Stefan, *Oskar Fried* (Berlin, 1911). An important monograph on Fried was publ. in 1971 in Moscow by D.A. Rabinovitz.

Friedberg, Carl, German pianist; b. Bingen, Sept. 18, 1872; d. Merano, Italy, Sept. 8, 1955. He studied piano at the Frankfurt Cons. with Kwast, Knorr, and Clara Schumann; also took a course in composition with Humperdinck; subsequently taught piano at the Frankfurt Cons. (1893–1904) and at the Cologne Cons. (1904–14). In 1914 he made his first American tour, with excellent success; taught piano at the Inst. of Musical Art in N.Y.; was a member of the faculty of the Juilliard School of Music in N.Y. Among his pupils were Percy Grainger, Ethel Leginska, Elly Ney, and other celebrated pianists. BIBLIOGRAPHY: J. Smith, *Master Pianists: The Career and Teaching of Carl Friedberg* (N.Y., 1963).

Friedheim, Arthur, pianist; b. St. Petersburg (of German parents), Oct. 26, 1859; d. New York, Oct. 19, 1932. He was a pupil of Anton Rubinstein and Liszt, and became particularly known as an interpreter of Liszt's works. He made his first American tour in 1891; taught at the Chicago Musical College in 1897; then traveled; lived in London, Munich, and (after 1915) N.Y. as a teacher and pianist; composed a Piano Concerto and many pieces for solo piano, as well as an opera, *Die Tänzerin* (Karlsruhe, 1897). His memoirs, *Life and Liszt: The Recollections of a Concert Pianist,* were publ. posthumously (N.Y., 1961).

Friedhofer, Hugo, American composer of film music; b. San Francisco, May 3, 1901; d. Los Angeles, May 17, 1981. He played cello in theater orchs.; studied composition with Domenico Brescia. In 1929 he went to Hollywood, where he worked as an arranger and composer for early sound films. In 1935 he was engaged as an orchestrator for Warner Brothers, and received valuable instruction from Erich Wolfgang Korngold and Max Steiner. In Los Angeles he attended Schoenberg's seminars and took additional lessons in composition with Ernst Toch and Kanitz; he also had some instruction with Nadia Boulanger during her sojourn in California. He wrote his first complete film score for *The Adventures of Marco Polo* in 1938, and in the following years composed music for about 70 films. His film music for *The Best Years of Our Lives* won the Academy Award in 1946. His other film scores included *Vera Cruz, Violent Saturday, The Sun Also Rises,* and *The Young Lions.* Friedhofer was highly esteemed by the Hollywood theatrical community and by his colleagues in the film studios for his ability to create a congenial musical background, alternatively lyrical and dramatic, for the action on the screen, never sacrificing the purely musical quality for the sake of external effect. He was the only California native of all the famous film composers in Hollywood, the majority of whom were Germans and Austrians. When a Hollywood mogul told Friedhofer to use numerous French horns since the film in question was taking place in France, he acquiesced and, by extension of the dictum, used an English-horn solo to illustrate the approach to the cliffs of Dover of the film characters fleeing the French Revolution. BIBLIOGRAPHY: F.W. Sternfeld, "Music and the Feature Film," *Musical Quarterly* (Oct. 1947); Lawrence Morton, "Film Music Profile: Hugo Friedhofer," *Film Music Notes* (1950).

Friedlaender, Max, eminent German musicologist; b. Brieg, Silesia, Oct. 12, 1852; d. Berlin, May 2, 1934. He was first a bass; studied voice with Manuel García in London and Julius Stockhausen in Frankfurt; appeared at the London Monday Popular Concerts in 1880. He returned to Germany in 1881 and took a course at Berlin Univ. with Spitta; obtained the degree of Dr.Phil. at Rostock with the thesis *Beiträge zur Biographie Franz Schuberts* (1887); then was Privatdozent at Berlin Univ. in 1894, and a prof. and director of music there from 1903. He was exchange prof. at Harvard Univ. in 1911; lectured at many American univs. and received the degree of LL.D. from the Univ. of Wisconsin; retired in 1932. He discovered the MSS of more than 100 lost songs by Schubert and publ. them in his complete edition (7 vols.) of Schubert's songs. Together with Johann Bolte and Johann Meier, he searched for years in every corner of the German Empire in quest of folk songs still to be found among the people; some of these he publ. in a vol. under the title *100 deutsche Volkslieder* in *Goethe Jahrbuch* (1885); was editor of *Volksliederbuch für gemischten Chor* (1912); edited songs of Mozart, Schumann, and Mendelssohn, Beethoven's "Scotch Songs," the first version of Brahms's *Deutsche Volkslieder* (1926), *Volksliederbuch für die deutsche Jugend* (1928), etc.

WRITINGS: *Goethes Gedichte in der Musik* (1896); *Gedichte von Goethe in Kompositionen seiner Zeitgenossen* (1896 and 1916); *Das Deutsche Lied im 18. Jahrhundert* (2 vols., 1902); *Brahms Lieder* (1922; in Eng., London, 1928); *Franz Schubert, Skizze seines Lebens und Wirkens* (1928).

BIBLIOGRAPHY: E.J. Dent, "Max Friedlaender," *Monthly Musical Record* (June 1934).

Friedman, Erick, distinguished American violinist; b. Newark, N.J., Aug. 16, 1939. He first studied violin with his father, an amateur violinist; at the age of 10 he enrolled at the Juilliard School of Music in N.Y., in the class of Ivan Galamian; at 17 he commenced studies with Jascha Heifetz; he also received guidance from Nathan Milstein. His progress was rapid, and he soon garnered prizes in several violin competitions; he then appeared as soloist with the Boston Symph., Chicago Symph., Pittsburgh Symph., N.Y. Phil., Philadelphia Orch., Berlin Phil., Orch. de Paris, and other orchs.; made many extensive concert tours, playing in Europe, the Far East, and South America. Friedman's performances are characterized by a careful regard for the composer's intentions and a technical skill that rank him among the finest violinists of his generation.

Friedman, Ignaz, famous Polish pianist; b. Podgorze, near Cracow, Feb. 14, 1882; d. Sydney, Australia, Jan. 26, 1948. He studied music theory with Hugo Riemann in Leipzig and piano with Leschetizky in Vienna. In 1904 he launched an extensive career as a concert pianist; gave about 2,800 concerts in Europe, America, Australia, Japan, China, and South Africa. In 1941 he settled in Sydney. He was renowned as an interpreter of Chopin; prepared an annotated edition of Chopin's works in 12 vols., publ. by Breitkopf & Härtel; also edited piano compositions of Schumann and Liszt for Universal Edition in Vienna. Friedman was himself a composer; he wrote a hundred or so pieces for piano in an effective salon manner, among them a group of *Fantasiestücke.*

Friedman, Ken, American avant-garde composer; b. New London, Conn., Sept. 19, 1939. He became associated with Richard Maxfield, who initiated him into the arcana of modern music. Friedman developed feverish activities in intellectual and musical fields; edited ephemeral magazines; directed an underground radio program, "Garnisht Kigele," in Mt. Carroll, Ill.; was a founder of the avant-garde group Fluxus. As an avant-garde artist and designer, he exhibited his products in Brno, Nice, Cologne, Copenhagen, Trieste, and San Diego; staged happenings and audiovisual events in California, announcing himself as "The Truly Incredible Friedman." Most of his works are verbal exhortations to existentialist actions, e.g., *Scrub Piece* (scrubbing a statue in a public square), *Riverboat Brawl* (starting a brawl in a riverboat at Disneyland), *Goff Street* (a "theft event," transplanting a street sign), *Come Ze Revolution* (chanting pseudo-Greek songs), *Watermelon* (splitting a watermelon with a karate blow), etc. He also composed a *Quiet Sonata* (1969) for 75 Truncated Guitar Fingerboards with no strings attached; realized for Nam June Paik his alleged *Young Penis Symphony* for 10 ditto, and had it performed at a hidden retreat in San Francisco.

Friedman, Richard, American composer; b. New York, Jan. 6, 1944. He received his formal education in exact sciences, specializing in electronics. He worked at the Intermedia Electronic Music Studio at N.Y. Univ. (1966–68) in collaboration with Morton Subotnick; prepared electronic tape pieces, mostly of scientific inspiration: *Lumia Mix* (1967); *Crescent* (1967); and *To the Star Messenger* (1968), a melodrama depicting the discovery of the moons of Jupiter by Galileo. Another piece of the period was *Alchemical Manuscript* (1968), inspired by the arcane lore of the searchers for the philosopher's stone. In 1968 Friedman moved to California; worked with the music dept. of the radio station KPFA in Berkeley; arranged numerous broadcasts of electronic materials, notably *Serenade* for Viola on Tape and *4-Pole Neuro-Magnet with Double Cross,* composed in 1970. Taking advantage of the techniques of amplification, Friedman was able to create the sound of an orch. of violas with a single viola player. In most of his works he applies the avant-garde philosophy of tonal frugality, limiting his resources to a few notes. Apart from his radio work, he conducted information/media performances at the San Francisco Museum of Art under the general title "Outside/Inside," utilizing closed-circuit television, inflatable structures, and sculptures activated by light beams.

Friedrich, Götz, German opera producer and administrator; b. Naumburg, Aug. 4, 1930. He was educated in Weimar; in 1953 was appointed an assistant to Walter Felsenstein at the East Berlin Komische Oper; became a producer there in 1959 and chief producer from 1968 to 1972; was also active as a producer in West Germany. In 1976 he was named principal producer at Covent Garden, London. In 1981 he became Generalintendant of the Deutsche Oper in West Berlin.

Friedrich, Karl, Austrian tenor; b. Vienna, Jan. 15, 1905; d. there, March 8, 1981. He received his musical education at the Academy of Music in Vienna; sang operatic engagements in Düsseldorf and Hamburg; in 1938 joined the roster of the Vienna State Opera, retiring in 1969.

Friedrich II (der Grosse). See **Frederick II.**

Friemann, Witold, Polish composer; b. Konin, Aug. 20, 1889. He studied composition with Z. Noskowski and piano with A. Michalowski at the Warsaw Cons., graduating in 1910; then went to Germany, where he became a student of Max Reger in Leipzig. Returning to Poland, he taught classes at the Lwow Cons. (1921–29) and at the Katowice Military School of Music (1929–33); was head of the music section of Polish Radio (1934–39); after World War II, taught at a school for the blind in Laski.
WORKS: An exceptionally industrious composer, he wrote nearly a thousand works, including 3 operas (*Gewont, Kasia,* and *Polish Folk Mystery Play*); 6 cantatas; 5 *Mazovia Suites* for Soloists, Chorus, and Orch. (1948, 1949, 1949, 1951, 1956); *Konrad Wallenrod,* symph. poem (1909); 3 symphs.: No. 1, *Slavonic* (1948); No. 2, *Mazovian* (1950); No. 3 (1953); 24 concertos, including 5 for Piano (No. 1, 1911; No. 2, 1951; No. 5, 1960), 3 for Trombone (1969, 1969, 1970), 2 for Viola (1952; with String Orch., 1968), 2 for Clarinet (1954, 1964), and one each for Cello (*Lirico,* 1950), Violin (1953–54), Double Bass (1967), 2 Pianos (1960), Flute (1963), Oboe (*Lirico,* 1961), Bassoon (*Eroico,* 1965–67), 2 Bassoons (with String Orch., 1968), Horn (1966–68), and Trumpet (1967); 600 works for piano; 3 string quartets (1933, 1942, 1953); 80 sonatas, suites, etc., for chamber combinations; songs.

Fries, Wulf (Christian Julius), German-American cellist and teacher; b. Garbeck, Jan. 10, 1825; d. Roxbury, Mass., April 29, 1902. As a cellist, he played in Norway, in the Bergen theater orch. (from 1842), and at Ole Bull's concerts. In 1847 he went to Boston, where he became a founding member of the Mendelssohn Quintette Club, with A. Fries (first violin), Gerloff (2nd violin), Edward Lehmann (first viola), Oscar Greiner (2nd viola), and himself as cellist. He belonged to it for 23 years; also figured in the Musical Fund Society and the Harvard Musical Assoc.; played in trios with Anton Rubinstein, and until 1901 took part in concerts in New England.

Frijsh, Povla (real name, **Paula Frisch**), concert soprano; b. Aarhus, Denmark, Aug. 3, 1881; d. Blue Hill, Maine, July 10, 1960. She first studied piano and theory in Copenhagen with O. Christensen, later voice in Paris with Jean Périer; made her debut in Paris at the age of 19; appeared in concert and recital in Paris and briefly in opera in Copenhagen; made her American debut in 1915; gave many first performances of modern vocal music (Bloch's *Poèmes d'automne,* Loeffler's *Canticle of the Sun,* songs by Griffes, etc.), and made a specialty of modern international song literature. She introduced Negro spirituals to Paris and Copenhagen.

Friml, Rudolf, famous Bohemian-American operetta composer; b. Prague, Dec. 2, 1879; d. Hollywood, Nov. 12, 1972. His original family name was **Frimel.** He was a pupil at the Prague Cons. of Juranek (piano) and Foerster (theory and composition); toured Austria, England, Germany, and Russia as accompanist to Kubelik, the violinist, coming with him to the U.S. in 1900 and again in 1906; remained in the U.S. after the 2nd tour; gave numerous recitals, appeared as soloist with several of the large symph. orchs. (played his Piano Concerto with the N.Y. Symph. Orch.), and composed assiduously; lived in N.Y. and Hollywood, composing for motion pictures.
WORKS: Operettas: *The Firefly* (Syracuse, Oct. 14, 1912); *High Jinks* (Syracuse, Nov. 3, 1913); *Katinka* (Morristown, N.Y., Dec. 2, 1915); *You're in Love,* musical comedy (Stamford, Conn., 1916); *Glorianna* (1918); *Tumble In* (1919); *Sometime* (1919); *Rose Marie* (N.Y., Sept. 2, 1924; very popular); *Vagabond King* (N.Y., Sept. 21, 1925; highly successful); also wrote a great number of piano pieces in a light vein. In 1937 Metro-Goldwyn-Mayer made a film of *The Firefly,* the popular *Donkey Serenade* being added to the original score.

Frimmel, Theodor von, Austrian writer on music; b. Amstetten, Dec. 15, 1853; d. Vienna, Dec. 25, 1928. He first studied medicine in Vienna; then became interested in art and maintained an art gallery; taught the history of art at the Athenäum in Vienna and served as assistant curator of the Hofmuseum from 1884–93. In music his main research concentrated on Beethoven.
PUBLICATIONS: *Beethoven und Goethe: Eine Studie* (Vienna, 1883); *Neue Beethoveniana* (Vienna, 1888; 2nd ed., 1890); *Beethovens Wohnungen in Wien* (Vienna, 1894); "Beethoven," in *Berühmte Musiker* (Berlin, 1901; 6th ed., 1922); *Beethoven Studien* (vol. I, *Beethovens äussere Erscheinung* and vol. II, *Bausteine zu einer Lebensgeschichte des Meisters;* Munich and Leipzig, 1905–06); *Beethoven-Forschung, Lose Blätter* (10 issues, Vienna and Mödling, 1911–25); *Beethoven im zeitgenössischen Bildnis* (Vienna, 1923); *Beethoven-Handbuch* (2 vols., Leipzig, 1926).

Frisch, Paula. See **Frijsh, Povla.**

Frischenschlager, Friedrich, Austrian composer and musicographer; b. Gross Sankt Florian, Styria, Sept. 7, 1885; d. Salzburg, July 15, 1970. He studied music in Graz; in 1909 went to Berlin, where he studied musicology with Johann Wolf and Kretzschmar, and also attended Humperdinck's master classes in composition. In 1918 he was engaged as a music teacher at the Mozarteum in Salzburg; remained there until 1945; also edited the bulletin of the Mozarteum. An industrious composer, he wrote the fairy-tale operas *Der Schweinehirt,* after Hans Christian Andersen (Berlin, May 31, 1913); *Die Prinzessin und der Zwerg* (Salzburg, May 12, 1927); and *Der Kaiser und die Nachtigall,* after Andersen (Salzburg, March 27, 1937); also several choral works; *Symphonische Aphorismen* for Orch.; and teaching materials for voice.

Friskin, James, American pianist and composer; b. Glasgow, March 3, 1886; d. New York, March 16, 1967. He studied with E. Dannreuther (piano) and Stanford (composition) at the Royal College of Music in London; then taught at the Royal Normal College for the Blind (1909–14). In 1914 he came to the U.S. In 1934 he gave 2 recitals in N.Y. consisting of the complete *Wohltemperierte Clavier* of Bach. In 1944 he married Rebecca Clarke. Among his works are *Phantasie* for String Quartet; *Phantasie* for Piano Trio; *Phantasy* for Piano, 2 Violins, Viola, and Cello (1912); Quintet for Piano and Strings; Violin Sonata. He publ. *The Principles of Pianoforte Practice* (London, 1921; new ed., N.Y., 1937); also (with Irwin Freundlich) *Music for the Piano* (N.Y., 1954).

Fritzsch, Ernst Wilhelm, German music publisher; b. Lützen, Aug. 24, 1840; d. Leipzig, Aug. 14, 1902. He was a pupil (1857–62) at the Leipzig Cons.; lived several years in Bern, and in 1866 took over the music publishing firm of Bromnitz in Leipzig, carried on under his own name until 1903, then acquired by C.F.W. Siegel. Fritzsch publ. Wagner's *Gesammelte Schriften,* edited the *Musikalisches Wochenblatt* (from 1870), and in 1875 started the *Musikalische Hausblätter.* By publishing the works of rising composers (Rheinberger, Svendsen, Grieg, Cornelius), he promoted modern musical development.

Frizzell, Lefty (real name, **William Orville Frizzell**), American country-music singer and guitarist; b. Corsicana, Texas, March 31, 1928; d. Nashville, July 19, 1975. He took up the guitar in his youth; later worked the country-music circuits in Texas and New Mexico; eventually gained fame with several hit recordings. He was a regular member of the Grand Ole Opry in Nashville.

Froberger, Johann Jakob, famous German organist and composer; b. Stuttgart, May 18, 1616; d. Héricourt, Haute-Saône, France, May 7, 1667. About 1634 he went to Vienna, where he entered the Inst. of Singer oder Canthoreyknaben; there it was the custom to allow the choirboys, when their voices had changed and when they had attained a certain degree of musical scholarship, to serve as apprentices to famous masters of the time on stipends given by Emperor Ferdinand II. Froberger, however, did not apply for the subvention until late 1636, when it was refused him; thereupon, he held the position of 3rd organist at the court from Jan. 1 to Oct. 30, 1637. He then again applied, with success, and was granted a stipend of 200 gulden; in October of that year he left to study under Frescobaldi in Rome, remaining there for 3½ years. In March 1641 he returned to Vienna, where he again was organist in 1641–45 and 1653–58; after this he made long concert tours (to Paris and London). Stories of his adventures in London, and of his appointment first as organ blower at Westminster Abbey and then as court organist to Charles II (first publ. by Matthe-

son, but not corroborated by any English sources), must be dismissed as apocryphal. He spent his last years in the service of Princess Sybille of Württemberg at her château near Héricourt. Although 2 collections of toccatas, canzoni, and partitas were publ. long after his death (1693 and 1696), there is internal evidence that the majority of these works were written before 1650.

WORKS: Organ toccatas, fantasias, canzoni, fugues, etc., of which 3 MS vols. are in the Vienna Library; in Berlin are 2 printed vols., *Diverse ingegnosissime, rarissime, et non maj più viste curiose partite di toccate, canzoni, ricercari, capricci,* etc. (1693; reprinted at Mainz, 1695) and *Diverse curiose e rare partite musicali,* etc. (1696); also a vol. of suites for clavecin. Froberger's works, ed. by G. Adler, are in Denkmäler der Tonkunst in Österreich (vols. 8, 13, 21; formerly vols. 4.i, 6.ii, 10.ii).

BIBLIOGRAPHY: A monograph on Froberger by F. Beier in Waldersee's *Sammlung musikalischer Vorträge* (Nos. 59 and 60); 2 letters from Princess Sybille to C. Huygens concerning him, publ. by E. Schebek (Prague, 1874); a MS preface to Fuchs's thematic catalogue of Froberger's works (in the Berlin Library; throws some light on his career); A.W. Ambros, *Geschichte der Musik* (vol. IV, pp. 463ff.); E. Schebek, *Zwei Briefe über J.J. Froberger* (Prague, 1874); H. Riemann, *Handbuch der Musikgeschichte* (vol. II, 2; pp. 364ff.); A. Tessier, "Une Pièce inédite de Froberger," *Adler-Festschrift* (1930); K. Seidler, *Untersuchungen über Biographie und Klavierstil Johann Jakob Frobergers* (1930); A. Somer, *The Keyboard Music of J.J. Froberger* (Diss., Univ. of Michigan, 1963); G.B. Sharp, "J.J. Froberger (1616–1667): A Link between the Renaissance and the Baroque," *Musical Times* (Dec. 1967); H.-A. Timmerman, "Johann Jakob Froberger," *De Praestant,* 16/3 (1967); G. Leonhardt, "Johann Jakob Froberger and His Music," *L'Organo* (Jan.–June 1968); U. Scharlau, "Neue Quellenfunde zur Biographie Johann Jakob Frobergers," *Die Musikforschung* (Jan.–March 1969); G. Beechey, "Johann Jakob Froberger," *Consort* (July 1972); D. Starke, *Frobergers Suiten tänze* (Darmstadt, 1972); H. Siedentop, *J.J. Froberger: Leben und Werk* (Stuttgart, 1977); H. Schott, *A Critical Edition of the Works of J.J. Froberger with Commentary* (Diss., Oxford Univ., 1978).

Froidebise, Pierre, important Belgian composer, organist, and teacher; b. Ohey, May 15, 1914; d. Liège, Oct. 28, 1962. He began studies in harmony and organ playing with Camille Jacquemin (1932–35); then entered the classes at the Namur Cons. with René Barbier, and at the Brussels Cons. with Moulaert and Léon Jongen. His chosen specialty was the history of organ music; he publ. in 1958 a monumental *Anthologie de la musique d'orgue des primitifs à la Renaissance.* But he also was deeply interested in the techniques of new music, particularly Schoenberg's method of composition with 12 tones; in 1949 he formed in Liège a progressive society under the name Variation. As a teacher of composition in Liège, he attracted many students of the avant-garde, among them Henri Pousseur.

WORKS: 2 radio operas: *La Bergère et le ramoneur* and *La Lune amère* (both 1957); *De l'aube à la nuit* for Orch. (1934–37); *Antigona* for Soli, Chorus, and Orch. (1936); Violin Sonata (1938); *La Légende de Saint-Julien l'Hospitalier,* symph. poem after Flaubert (1941); *3 poèmes japonais* for Voice and Piano (1942–43); *5 comptines* for Voice and 11 Instruments (1947; International Society for Contemporary Music Festival, Brussels, June 27, 1950); *Amœur,* cantata for Voice, Wind Quintet, and Piano (1948); *Stèle pour sei Shonagon* for Soprano and 19 Instruments (1958; contains aleatory passages); *Justorum animae* and *Puer natus est* for Chorus and Orch.

Frölich, Theodor, Swiss composer; b. Brugg (Aargan), Feb. 20, 1803; d. (suicide) Aarau, Oct. 16, 1836. He studied composition with Zelter in Berlin; returning to Switzerland, was active mainly as an educator. He is remembered chiefly through his colorful songs, *Persische Lieder,* to Rückert's words, and his choruses, *Lieder im Volkston;* one of these choruses, *Wem Gott will rechte Gunst erweisen,* became popular.

Froment, Louis de, French conductor; b. Paris, Dec. 5, 1921. He studied at the Paris Cons.; won the Premier Prix de Direction d'Orchestre there (1948); conducted the orch. of Radiodiffusion Française; was music director at the Casinos in Cannes, Deauville, and Vichy (1950–54); conducted at various festivals in France; toured in Germany, England, Sweden, the Netherlands, Spain, Russia, and South America. In 1958 he was appointed chief conductor of the Radio Luxemberg Orch.

Fromm, Andreas, German composer; b. Plänitz, near Wusterhausen, 1621; d. in the Strahov monastery in Prague, Oct. 16, 1683. A son of a Lutheran pastor, he studied theology; in 1649 became a cantor in Stettin; he was subsequently in Rostock (1651), Wittenberg (1668), and Prague, where he turned to the Roman Catholic Church. His principal musical work was an "actus musicus," *Die Parabel von dem reichen Mann und dem armen Lazarus* (1649); the opinion that it was the first German oratorio (cf. R. Schwartz, "Das erste deutsche Oratorium," *Jahrbuch der Musikbibliothek Peters 1899)* is discounted by later analysts. See Hans Engel's article in *Die Musik in Geschichte und Gegenwart.*

Fromm, Herbert, German-American composer; b. Kitzingen, Germany, Feb. 23, 1905. He studied privately with A. Reuss in Munich; was conductor at the Civic Theater in Bielefeld (1930) and at Würzburg (1931–33). He came to the U.S. in 1937; was organist at Temple Beth Zion in Buffalo (1937–41); in 1941 became music director at Temple Israel in Boston; retired in 1973. He publ. 12 choral works for the Hebrew service; also a Violin Sonata; String Quartet; Flute Concerto; cantatas: *The Stranger* (N.Y., March 12, 1957); *Light Is Sown; Transience; Psalm Cantata* (1962); *Memorial Cantata* (1973);

Festival Cantata (Boston, Oct. 27, 1973).

Frontini, Francesco Paolo, Italian composer; b. Catania, Aug. 6, 1860; d. there, July 26, 1939. He was a pupil of his father, **Martino Frontini,** who was also an opera composer, and of Lauro Rossi at Naples; was director of the Catania Cons. until 1923.

WORKS: Operas: *Nella* (Catania, March 30, 1881); *Malia* (Bologna, May 30, 1893); *Il Falconiere* (Catania, Sept. 15, 1899); oratorio, *Sansone e Dalila* (Catania, Aug. 23, 1882); numerous choral pieces and songs. Ricordi publ. his collection of Sicilian songs, *Eco di Sicilia* (1883), and of Sicilian dances, *Antiche danze di Sicilia* (3 vols., 1936).

BIBLIOGRAPHY: G.C. Balbo, *Note critico-biografiche su F.P. Frontini* (Catania, 1905).

Froschauer, Johann, an Augsburg printer (end of 15th century), once thought to have been the first to print music with movable type, in Michael Keinspeck's *Lilium musicae planae* (1498); however, it is now known that wood blocks were employed for the music illustrations in that work; it also appears fairly certain that music printing with movable type preceded Froschauer's work.

Frost, Charles Joseph, English composer; b. Westbury-on-Trym, June 20, 1848; d. Brockley, Oct. 13, 1918. He was engaged as an organist and choral leader in various provincial towns in England; was active also as a lecturer; he wrote a cantata, *By the Waters of Babylon* (1876); much sacred music; and pieces for organ (55 hymn-tune voluntaries, 40 preludes, a sonata, etc.).

Frost, Henry Frederick, English organist and writer; b. London, March 15, 1848; d. there, May 3, 1901. He was a boy chorister at Windsor; was organist of the Chapel Royal (1865–91); then taught organ at the Guildhall School of Music (1880–88); also wrote for the *Athenaeum* and the *Standard.* He wrote a biography of Schubert for the Great Musicians Series; publ. *Savoy Hymn-tunes and Chants.*

Frotscher, Gotthold, German musicologist; b. Ossa, near Leipzig, Dec. 6, 1897; d. Berlin, Sept. 30, 1967. He studied in Bonn and Leipzig; received his Ph.D. from the Univ. of Leipzig with the dissertation *Die Ästhetik des Berliner Liedes;* was univ. instructor in Danzig (1924–32); completed his Habilitation at the Technische Hochschule there with his *Hauptprobleme der Musikästhetik im 18. Jahrhundert* (1924; publ. in Danzig, 1924); was a prof. at Berlin Univ. (1935–45); from 1950 taught at the Pedagögische Hochschule in Berlin. He wrote a valuable history of organ playing, *Geschichte des Orgelspiels und der Orgelkomposition* (2 vols., Berlin, 1935; 3rd ed., revised, 1966); also publ. *Aufführungspraxis alter Musik* (Wilhelmshaven, 1963; 4th ed., 1977); *Orgeln* (Karlsruhe, 1968).

Frotzler, Carl, Austrian organist and composer; b. Stockerau, April 10, 1873; d. there, July 8, 1960. Of very precocious talent, he wrote a Grand Mass at 14; then entered the Vienna Cons., where he studied with Franz Krenn. He later occupied various posts as organist: at the Pfarrkirche in Stockerau (1887–93); at Tosis, Hungary, as Kapellmeister to Count Nicolaus Esterhazy (1893–97); then lived in Linz; in 1938 was in Vienna; from 1953 lived in retirement in Stockerau.

Frugatta, Giuseppe, Italian pianist and composer; b. Bergamo, May 26, 1860; d. Milan, May 30, 1933. He studied with A. Bazzini (composition) and C. Andreoli (piano) at the Milan Cons., where he became a prof. He composed a number of effective piano pieces (*Polonaise de concert, Moments poétiques*, etc.). He publ. *Preparazione al "Gradus ad Parnassum" di Clementi* (1913).

Frugoni, Orazio, Swiss pianist and pedagogue; b. Davos, Jan. 28, 1921. He studied at the Geneva Cons. and the Verdi Cons. in Milan; his piano teachers included Alfredo Casella and Dinu Lipatti. In 1945 he won the Prix de Virtuosité at the Geneva Cons. He made his American debut at Town Hall in N.Y. in 1947; later joined the faculty of the Eastman School of Music in Rochester, N.Y. (1951–67). He then taught master classes at the Graduate School of Fine Arts in Florence until 1975; also taught at the Cherubini Cons. there.

Früh, Armin Leberecht, German musical inventor; b. Mühlhausen, Thuringia, Sept. 15, 1820; d. Nordhausen, Jan. 8, 1894. He invented, in 1857, the "Semeiomelodicon" (an apparatus for facilitating musical instruction, consisting of a series of note heads which, when pressed by the finger, produced tones of corresponding pitch); he traveled to introduce his invention to prominent musicians, and established a factory in Dresden in 1858, but it soon failed.

Früh, Huldreich Georg, Swiss pianist and composer; b. Zürich, June 16, 1903; d. there, April 25, 1945. He studied piano with Walter Frey and music theory with Andreae at the Zürich Cons.; then became an instructor at the Volksklavierschule, and later joined the group of avant-garde musicians at the cabaret Cornichon. He wrote mainly theatrical pieces and songs on politically oriented radical subjects.

Frühbeck de Burgos, Rafael, Spanish conductor of German parentage; b. Burgos, Sept. 15, 1933. He studied violin and piano at the Bilbao Cons. and later at the Cons. of Madrid and at the Hochschule für Musik in Munich. In 1959 he was appointed music director of the Bilbao Symph. Orch., becoming the youngest musician ever to lead an orch. in Spain. In 1962 he was appointed conductor of the Orquesta Nacional in Madrid; remained at this post until 1977. In the meantime, he toured as a guest conductor in the European music centers. In 1968–70 he was a guest conductor with major orchs. in the U.S.; from 1975 to 1976 he was conductor of the Montreal Symph. Orch.; in 1980 was named principal guest conductor of the National Symph. Orch. in Washington, D.C.

Frumerie, (Per) Gunnar (Fredrik) de, eminent Swedish composer; b. Nacka, near Stockholm, July 20, 1908. He enrolled at the Stockholm Cons., where he studied piano with Lundberg and composition with Ernst Ellberg; was a stipendiary of the Jenny Lind Foundation (1929–32) in Vienna, where he took courses in piano with Emil von Sauer and in composition with Erwin Stein; then went to Paris, where he took piano lessons with Alfred Cortot and composition with Leonid Sabaneyev. After returning to Sweden, he was active as a concert pianist; in 1945 was appointed to the piano faculty at the Stockholm Musikhögskolan; was a prof. there from 1962. As a composer, he adheres to the Scandinavian Romantic tradition.

WORKS: Opera, *Singoalla* (Stockholm, March 16, 1940); ballet, *Johannesnatten* (*The Night of St. John;* 1947); 2 piano concertos (1929, 1932); *Suite in an Ancient Style* for Chamber Orch. (1930); *En moder*, melodrama to a text by Andersen (1932); Variations and Fugue for Piano and Orch. (1932); Violin Concerto (1936); Partita for String Orch. (1937); *Pastoral Suite* for Flute and Piano (1933; revised for Flute, String Orch., and Harp, 1941); *Symphonic Variations* (1941); *Symphonic Ballad* for Piano and Orch. (1943–44); cantata, *Fader vår* (*Our Father;* 1945); Divertimento for Orch. (1951); 2-piano Concerto (1953); *8 Psalms* for Chorus and Orch. (1953–55); Concerto for Clarinet, String Orch., Harp, and Percussion (1958); Trumpet Concerto (1959); Concertino for Oboe, String Orch., Harp, and Percussion (1960); Flute Concerto (1969); Horn Concerto (1971–72); *Ballad* for Orch. (1975); 2 piano trios (1932, 1952); 2 violin sonatas (1934, 1944); 2 piano quartets (1941, 1963); *Elegiac Suite* for Cello and Piano (1946); 2 piano sonatinas (1950); *Ballad* for Piano (1965); *Circulus quintus*, 24 miniatures for Piano (1965); 2 piano sonatas (1968); Suite for Wind Quintet (1973); String Quintet (1974); a cappella choral works; solo songs.

Fry, William Henry, American composer and journalist; b. Philadelphia, Aug. 10, 1813; d. Santa Cruz, West Indies, Sept. 21, 1864. He was one of the most vociferous champions of American music, and particularly of opera on American subjects in the English language. Ironically, his own opera *Leonora* (perf. in Philadelphia, June 4, 1845), for which he claimed the distinction of being the first grand opera by a native American composer, was a feeble imitation of Italian vocal formulas in the manner of Bellini, with a libretto fashioned from a novel by Bulwer-Lytton, *The Lady of Lyons. Leonora* ran for 16 performances before closing; a revival of some numbers in concert form was attempted in N.Y. on Feb. 27, 1929, as a period piece, but was met with puzzled derision. Fry continued his campaign in favor of American opera in English, and composed 3 more operas, one of which, *Notre Dame de Paris,* after Victor Hugo, was produced in Philadelphia on May 3, 1864; 2 other operas, *The Bridal of Dunure* and *Aurelia the Vestal,* were not performed. He also wrote several symphs., including *The Breaking Heart* (1852; not extant); *Santa Claus (Christmas Symphony)* (N.Y., Dec. 24, 1853); *A Day in the Country* (1853?; not extant); *Childe Harold* (N.Y., May 31, 1854; not extant); as well as a symph. poem, *Niagara* (N.Y., May 4, 1854). Fry's various proclamations, manifestos, and prefaces to publ. editions of his works are interesting as illustrations of the patriotic bombast and humbug that agitated American musicians in the mid-19th century.

BIBLIOGRAPHY: W.T. Upton, *The Musical Works of William Henry Fry* (Philadelphia, 1946); idem, *William Henry Fry, American Journalist and Composer-Critic* (N.Y., 1954).

Frye, Walter, English composer of the 15th century. Nothing is known regarding his life, but from indirect indications, it appears that he was attached to the court of Burgundy. Of his 3 masses (in MS at the Royal Library in Brussels), 2 are without a Kyrie, a lack characteristic of the English school; his *Ave Regina* is an early example of the "song motet." His works have been edited by S. Kenney in *Walter Frye: Collected Works,* in Corpus Mensurabilis Musicae, XIX (1960).

BIBLIOGRAPHY: M. Bukofzer, "An Unknown Chansonnier of the 15th Century," *Musical Quarterly* (Jan. 1942; reproduces a chanson by Frye); G. Reese, *Music in the Renaissance* (N.Y., 1954; 2nd ed., revised, 1959, pp. 92–95; contains Frye's *Ave Regina*); D. Plamenac, "A Reconstruction of the French Chansonnier in the Bibl. Colombina, Seville," *Musical Quarterly* (Oct. 1951).

Fryer, George Herbert, English pianist and pedagogue; b. London, May 21, 1877; d. there, Feb. 7, 1957. He studied at the Royal College of Music; then with Matthay in London and Busoni in Weimar. He made his debut as a pianist in London (Nov. 17, 1898); then traveled in Europe; in 1914 he made a tour in the U.S.; in 1915 gave recitals for the British army in France; in 1917 returned to London; taught at the Royal College of Music (1917–47). He wrote miscellaneous pieces for piano; also publ. a book, *Hints on Pianoforte Practice* (N.Y., 1914).

Fryklöf, Harald Leonard, Swedish composer and teacher; b. Uppsala, Sept. 14, 1882; d. Stockholm, March 11, 1919. He studied theory with J. Lindegren at the Stockholm Cons. and piano with P. Scharwenka in Berlin; in 1908 he became a prof. of harmony at the Stockholm Cons. With G. Sandberg, A. Hellerström, and H. Palm, he edited the choral series Musica Sacra (1915); also publ. *Koralharmonisering-Kyrkotonarterna (Choral Harmonizations-Church Modes;* 1915); wrote a concert overture, songs, piano pieces.

Fryklund, Lars Axel Daniel, Swedish musicologist and specialist on musical instruments; b. Västerås, May 4, 1879; d. Hälsingborg, Aug. 25, 1965. He studied Romanic philology at the Univ. at Uppsala; taught at schools in Sundsvall in 1910–21, then at the Univ. of Hölsingborg (1921–44).

WRITINGS: *Swedish Instruments* (Uppsala, 1910); *African Instruments* (1915); *Study on the Pocket Violin* (1917); *Tromba Marina* (1919); *Viola d'Amore* (1921).

Frysinger, J. Frank, American organist; b. Hanover, Pa., April 7, 1878; d. York, Dec. 4, 1954. He studied with F.W. Wolff in Baltimore (1887–95) and with E.S. Kelley (1898–1900); was organist at the First Presbyterian Church at York, Pa., in 1909–11 and again in 1922–53; publ. about 200 works for organ; also piano pieces and songs.

Fuchs, Albert, German composer and pedagogue; b. Basel, Aug. 6, 1858; d. Dresden, Feb. 15, 1910. He studied with Selmar Bagge in Basel, and later at the Leipzig Cons. with Reinecke and Jadassohn (1876–79). He conducted oratorios in Trier (1880–83); then lived in Dresden; was subsequently director of the Wiesbaden Cons. (1889–98). In 1898 he joined the staff of the Dresden Cons.; was also conductor at the Schumann Singakademie (from 1901). He was a prolific composer, and publ. a number of choral works and songs; wrote 2 oratorios *Selig sind, die in dem Herrn sterben* (1906) and *Das tausendjähriges Reich* (1908); several instrumental concertos; publ. *Taxe der Streichinstrumente* (1907; many reprints); edited an album of Italian songs of the early 18th century, and a collection of Italian arias.

BIBLIOGRAPHY: F.A. Seissler, *Albert Fuchs,* in vol. III of *Monographien moderner Musiker* (Leipzig, 1909).

Fuchs, Carl Dorius Johannes, distinguished German music scholar; b. Potsdam, Oct. 22, 1838; d. Danzig, Aug. 27, 1922. He studied piano with Hans von Bülow, thoroughbass with Weitzmann, and composition with Kiel; took the degree of Dr.Phil. at Greifswald, with the dissertation *Präliminarien zu einer Kritik der Tonkunst* (1871). In 1868 he became a teacher at the Kullak Academy in Berlin; then gave piano concerts in Germany. In 1874 he went to Hirschberg; in 1879, to Danzig, where he was organist at the Petrikirche and music critic of the *Danziger Zeitung* (1887–1920); was also organist for many years at the Synagogue in Danzig, and wrote *Andachts-lieder für Tempel und Haus.* Fuchs was a friend of Nietzsche, with whom he corresponded.

WRITINGS: *Betrachtungen mit und gegen Arthur Schopenhauer* (1868); *Ungleiche Verwandte unter den Neudeutschen* (1868); *Virtuos und Dilettant* (Leipzig, 1871); *Die Zukunft des musikalischen Vortrags* (Danzig, 1884); *Die Freiheit des musikalischen Vortrags* (Danzig, 1885); *Praktische Anleitung zum Phrasieren* (Berlin, 1886, with Hugo Riemann; Eng. trans., N.Y., 1892); *Künstler und Kritiker* (1898); *Takt und Rhythmus im Choral* (Berlin, 1911); *Der taktgerechte Choral, Nachweisung seiner 6 Typen* (Berlin, 1923). His letters were publ. by his son, Hans Fuchs, in *Ostdeutsche Monatshefte*

(Sept. 1923).

Fuchs, Johann Nepomuk, Austrian composer and conductor, brother of **Robert Fuchs;** b. Frauenthal, Styria, May 5, 1842; d. Vöslau, near Vienna, Oct. 5, 1899. He studied with Sechter at Vienna; conducted the Pressburg Opera in 1864; held similar positions at Brno, Kassel, Cologne, Hamburg, Leipzig, and (from 1880) at the Vienna Opera. In 1894 he succeeded Hellmesberger as director of the Vienna Cons. He produced the opera *Zingara* (Brünn, 1892) and several others.

Fuchs, Joseph, American violinist; b. New York, April 26, 1900. He studied violin with Franz Kneisel at the Inst. of Musical Art; was concertmaster of the Cleveland Orch. (1926–40); made his N.Y. debut in 1943; joined the faculty of the Juilliard School of Music in 1946; toured Europe in 1954, South America in 1957, and Russia in 1965.

Fuchs, Lillian, American violinist, violist, and teacher; b. New York, Nov. 18, 1903. She studied violin with Svecenski and Kneisel and composition with Goetschius at the Inst. of Musical Art; made her N.Y. debut as a violinist in 1926 but later played viola parts; was a member of the Perolé String Quartet; also appeared in concerts with her brothers Joseph and Harry Fuchs; later taught at the Manhattan School of Music and the Juilliard School of Music. She wrote several works for solo viola.

Fuchs, Lukas. See **Foss, Lukas.**

Fuchs, Marta, German soprano; b. Stuttgart, Jan. 1, 1898; d. there, Sept. 22, 1974. She was educated in Stuttgart, Munich, and Milan; made her operatic debut in Aachen in 1928. In 1930 she became a member of the Dresden State Opera; she was also a fine concert singer.

Fuchs, Peter Paul, Austrian conductor; b. Vienna, Oct. 30, 1916. He studied piano with Leonie Gombrich, composition with Eugene Zador and Karl Weigl, and conducting with Felix Weingartner and Josef Krips. He subsequently had conducting engagements at the Vienna Volksoper and in the German Theater in Brno. In the wake of the Nazi-fomented Anschluss of Austria to the German thousand-year Reich, Fuchs went to the U.S. in 1938; served in the U.S. Army; was accompanist periodically at the San Francisco Opera and at the Metropolitan Opera in N.Y.; organized a small opera company, Opera for Everyone, presenting performances of operas in English at colleges and music schools. From 1950 to 1976 he was on the faculty of Louisiana State Univ. in Baton Rouge as head of the opera workshop there; from 1960 to 1976 also served as conductor of the Baton Rouge Symph. He further made a European tour conducting opera in Rumania, the Netherlands, Greece, West Germany, and Austria. He eventually became music director and conductor of the Greensboro (N.C.) Symph.

Orch. He publ. a manual, *The Psychology of Conducting* (N.Y., 1969) and edited *The Music Theater of Walter Felsenstein* (N.Y., 1975); composed a comic opera, *Serenade at Noon* (Baton Rouge, La., March 22, 1965); *Partita ricercata* for Flute, Oboe, Harpsichord, and Double Bass (1973); *Polyphony* for Orch. (1976); 3 string quartets; choruses.

Fuchs, Robert, renowned Austrian composer and pedagogue, brother of **Johann Nepomuk Fuchs;** b. Frauenthal, Feb. 15, 1847; d. Vienna, Feb. 19, 1927. He studied at the Vienna Cons.; from 1875 till 1912 was a prof. of harmony there, and established himself as a teacher of historical importance; among his students were Gustav Mahler, Hugo Wolf, and Schreker. His own compositions are, however, of no consequence, and there is no evidence that he influenced his famous pupils stylistically or even technically; the only pieces that were at all successful were his 5 serenades for String Orch. He wrote also 5 symphs., Piano Concerto, 2 piano trios, 3 string quartets, 2 piano quartets, Piano Quintet, and numerous pieces for piano solo and for piano, 4-hands. BIBLIOGRAPHY: Anton Mayr, *Erinnerungen an Robert Fuchs* (Graz, 1934).

Fuchs, Viktor, Austrian-American opera singer and teacher; b. Vienna, Jan. 19, 1891; d. Los Angeles, Sept. 14, 1966. He studied voice with Franz Steiner; sang both tenor and baritone parts; made his operatic debut in Breslau in 1912. From 1918 he taught at the Vienna Cons. In 1938 he went to the U.S. and settled in Hollywood as a vocal teacher. He publ. a manual, *The Art of Singing and Voice Technique* (London, 1962).

Fučik, Julius, Czech composer of band music; b. Prague, July 18, 1872; d. Leitmeritz, Sept. 25, 1916. He was a bassoon player at the German Opera in Prague (1893) and later in Zagreb and Budapest; studied composition with Dvořák; was bandmaster of the 86th and 92nd Austrian regiments. He wrote a great number of dances and marches for band, including the immensely popular march *Entrance of the Gladiators.*

Fuenllana, Miguel de, blind Spanish vihuela virtuoso and composer; b. Navalcarnero, Madrid, early in the 16th century; date of death unknown. He was chamber musician to the Marquesa de Tarifa, and later at the court of Philip II, to whom he dedicated (1554) his *Libro de música para vihuela, intitulado Orphenica Lyra.* From 1562 to 1568 he was chamber musician to Queen Isabel de Valois, 3rd wife of Philip II. The *Libro* gives evidence of a high state of musical art in Spain during the 16th century; besides fantasias and other compositions for vihuela by Fuenllana and old Spanish ballads (such as the famous *Ay de mi, Alhama*), it contains arrangements for vihuela of works by Vásquez, Morales, P. and F. Guerrero, Flecha, Bernal, and several Flemish masters. BIBLIOGRAPHY: H. Riemann, in *Monatshefte* *für Musikgeschichte* (1895); G. Morphy, *Les Luthistes espagnols* (Leipzig, 1902); A. Koczirz, "Die Gitarrekompositionen in Miguel de Fuenllana's Orphenica Lyra," *Archiv für Musikwissenschaft* (1922); H. Anglès, "Dades desconegudes sobre Miguel de Fuenllana, vihuelista," *Revista Musical Catalana* (April 1936).

Fuentes, Juan Bautista, Mexican composer; b. Guadalajara, Jalisco, March 16, 1869; d. Leon, Guanajuato, Feb. 11, 1955. He studied in Mexico City; then taught music in various schools there. He publ. the manuals *Teoría de la música* (1899); *Tratado de intervalos y trasposición* (1909); *Método de armonía* (1920); composed a number of piano pieces in a salon style; also some orch. works, among them *Sinfonia mexicana.*

Fuerstner, Carl, German-American pianist, conductor, and composer; b. Strasbourg, June 16, 1912. He attended the Hochschule für Musik in Cologne (1930–34), studying composition and conducting; his teachers there were Hermann Abendroth, Walter Braunfels, Philipp Jarnach, and Ernst Klussmann. While still a student, he composed incidental music for theatrical plays. In 1939 he went to the U.S. as assistant conductor of the San Francisco Opera Co.; served as head coach of the opera dept. at the Eastman School of Music in Rochester, N.Y., and conducted the Rochester Civic Community Orch.; then was engaged as a piano teacher at Brigham Young Univ. in Provo, Utah; toured as piano accompanist to many famous artists, among them the violinists Menuhin, Ricci, and Spivakovsky, the cellist Nelsova, and the singers Martinelli, Kipnis, Traubel, Peerce, Siepi, and Leontyne Price; conducted an impressive repertoire of classical and modern operas with various operatic groups in America and in Europe. In 1963 he was appointed head coach of the opera dept. at Indiana Univ. in Bloomington. In 1973 Fuerstner was elected to the faculty of the International Summer Courses at the Mozarteum in Salzburg. WORKS: *Concerto rapsodico* for Cello and Orch. (Rochester, May 11, 1947); *Metamorphoses on a Chorale Theme,* scored for 20 Trombones, 2 Tubas, and Percussion (Rochester, April 5, 1949); *Symphorama* for Orch. (1960); *Overture,* and many more pieces for concert band, as well as transcriptions for band of various Classical and Romantic works.

Fuga, Sandro, Italian composer; b. Mogliano Veneto, Nov. 26, 1906. He studied piano, organ, and composition at the Verdi Cons.; was a concert pianist until 1940; became a lecturer at the Turin Cons. in 1933, and in 1966 became its director. WORKS: FOR THE STAGE: *La croce deserta* (Bergamo, 1950), *Otto Schnaffs* (Turin, 1950), and *Confessione* (RAI radio, 1962). FOR ORCH.: *Ode in memoria* for Orch. (1945; Turin, March 5, 1948); *Passacaglia* for Orch. (1950); Toccata for Piano and Orch. (1952); Trumpet Concertino (1953); Cello Concerto (1955); Violin Concerto (1959); Concerto for Strings and Percussion (1963); Oboe Concertino (1964); Symph. (1967); Piano Concerto (Rome, Jan. 14, 1970); *Concerto Sacro I* for Chorus and Orch. (1938; Turin, Feb. 3, 1939), *II* for Baritone, Male Chorus, and Orch. (1951), *III* for Orch. (1954), and *IV* for Tenor and Double Chorus (1956). OTHER WORKS: Piano Trio (1943); 4 string quartets (1943, 1945, 1948, 1965); Violin Sonata (1951).

Fugère, Lucien, French baritone; b. Paris, July 22, 1848; d. there, Jan. 15, 1935. He began as a singer in cabarets; then sang in light opera; in 1877 joined the Opéra-Comique, remaining there until 1910; subsequently appeared at the Paris Gaité Lyrique (1910–13); returned to the Opéra-Comique for several appearances after 1919; continued to sing until his 80th year. He acquired a great following as a brilliant performer of the comic parts; his best roles were Leporello, Papageno, Figaro, and Bartolo. He was also well known as a teacher; among his pupils was Mary Garden.
BIBLIOGRAPHY: R. Duhamel, *Lucien Fugère* (Paris, 1929).

Führer, Robert (Johann Nepomuk), composer and organist; b. Prague, June 2, 1807; d. Vienna, Nov. 28, 1861. He studied with Johann Vitásek; was an organist in provincial towns before succeeding his teacher as Kapellmeister at the Prague Cathedral in 1839. He became involved in fraudulent transactions and was dismissed from his post in 1845. He then held various positions as an organist and choral conductor in Vienna, Salzburg, Munich, Augsburg, and Gmunden. A series of embezzlements and other criminal offenses perpetrated by him resulted in his dismissal from several of his positions, but he continued to compose and perform; in 1856 he was Bruckner's competitor for the post of organist in Linz, arousing great admiration for his skill, even though Bruckner was selected. He served a prison term in 1859, but was given full freedom to write music. He publ. numerous sacred works (32 masses, 14 Requiems, 4 litanies, etc.) and many organ pieces; also handbooks on harmony and organ playing. Despite his notoriously dishonest acts and professional untrustworthiness (he publ. one of Schubert's masses under his own name), he enjoyed a fine reputation for his musicianship.

Fujikawa, Mayumi, Japanese violinist; b. Asahigawa, July 27, 1946. She studied at the Toho School of Music in Tokyo and at the Antwerp Cons.; later took lessons with Leonid Kogan in Nice. In 1970 she won second prize in the International Tchaikovsky Competition in Moscow; since then she has appeared as soloist with major orchs. in Europe and America.

Fukai, Shiro, Japanese composer; b. Akita-City, April 4, 1907; d. Kyoto, July 2, 1959. He studied composition in Tokyo with Sugawara. Perhaps his most notable score is a large choral work, *Prayer for Peace* (Tokyo, Aug. 15, 1949). His other works are the ballets *A City* (Tokyo, June 18, 1936) and *Ocean*

(Tokyo, Jan. 30, 1938), and several symph. suites of "landscape music."

Fukushima, Kazuo, Japanese composer; b. Tokyo, April 11, 1930. Autodidact in composition, he became determined to effect an esthetic and idiomatic synthesis between the traditional Japanese style of court music and the serial organization of Western modernism. In 1963 he received a traveling fellowship of the Japan Society of N.Y.

WORKS: *Kadha Hi-Haku (The Flying Spirit)* for Chamber Orch. (1959); *Tsuki-shiro (The Moon Spirit)* for String Orch. and Percussion (1964); *Hi-Kyo* for Flute, Strings, and Percussion (1961; Cologne Radio, Nov. 9, 1962); *3 Pieces from Chu-U* for Flute and Piano; *A Ring of the Wind* for Piano (1968): *Rankei* for Solo Oboe (1970); *Suien* for Piano (1972).

Fuleihan, Anis, American pianist, conductor, and composer; b. Kyrenia, Cyprus, April 2, 1900; d. Palo Alto, Calif., Oct. 11, 1970. He studied at the English School in Kyrenia; came to the U.S. in 1915 and continued his study of the piano in N.Y. with Alberto Jonás; toured the U.S., also the Near East, from 1919 to 1925; then lived in Cairo, returning to the U.S. in 1928; was on the staff of G. Schirmer, Inc. (1932–39); in 1947 became a prof. at Indiana Univ.; in 1953, director of the Beirut Cons. in Lebanon. In 1962 he went to Tunis under the auspices of the State Dept.; in 1963 organized the Orch. Classique de Tunis; remained there until 1965.

WORKS: Opera, *Vasco* (1960); for Orch.: *Mediterranean Suite* (1930; Cincinnati, March 15, 1935); *Preface to a Child's Story Book* (1932); Symph. No. 1 (N.Y. Phil., Dec. 31, 1936); Concerto No. 1 for Piano and String Orch. (Saratoga Springs, N.Y., Sept. 11, 1937, composer soloist); Concerto No. 2 for Piano and Orch. (N.Y., 1938); Fantasy for Viola and Orch. (1938); Violin Concerto (1930); *Fiesta* (Indianapolis Symph. Orch., Dec. 1, 1939); *Symphonie concertante* for String Quartet and Orch. (N.Y. Phil., April 25, 1940); Concerto for 2 Pianos and Orch. (Hempstead, N.Y., Jan. 10, 1941); *Epithalamium* for Piano and Strings (Philadelphia, Feb. 7, 1941); Concerto for Theremin and Orch. (N.Y., Feb. 26, 1945); *Invocation to Isis* (Indianapolis Symph. Orch., Feb. 28, 1941); Concerto for Violin, Piano, and Orch. (1943); Ondes Martinot Concerto (1944); *3 Cyprus Serenades* for Orch. (Philadelphia Orch., Dec. 13, 1946, Ormandy conducting); Rhapsody for Cello and String Orch. (Saratoga Springs, Sept. 12, 1946); *Overture for 5 Winds* (N.Y., May 17, 1947); *The Pyramids of Giza,* symph. poem (1952); Toccata for Piano and Orch. (1960); *Islands,* symph. suite (1961); Flute Concerto (1962); Piano Concerto No. 3 (1963); Cello Concerto (1963); Viola Concerto (1963); Violin Concerto No. 2 (1965); Symph. No. 2 (N.Y., Feb. 16, 1967); Violin Concerto No. 3 (1967); *Le Cors anglais s'amuse,* diversions for English Horn and Strings (1969); Piano Quintet (1967); 5 string quartets (1940–67); 14 piano sonatas (1940–68); Horn Quintet (1959); Clarinet Quintet; Violin Sonata; Viola Sonata; Cello Sonata; choral pieces, songs.

Fulkerson, James, American composer and trombonist; b. Streator, Ill., July 2, 1945. He studied at Wesleyan Univ. (B.M., 1966) and the Univ. of Illinois (M.M., 1968); took lessons in trombone playing from Carmine Caruso and John Silber; studied composition with Gaburo, Hiller, Johnston, and Martinano. He was a creative associate of the Center for the Creative and Performing Arts in Buffalo, N.Y. (1969–72); composer-in-residence at the Deutscher Akademischer Austauschdienst in Berlin (1973) and at the Victorian College of the Arts in Melbourne (since 1978). He is a virtuoso on the trombone, and he makes a specialty of playing the most fantastically difficult modern pieces. His own compositions are no less advanced.

WORKS: *Globs* for Small Orch., Live Electronics, and Tape (1968); *About Time* for Orch. (1969); *Something about Mobiles* for Orch. (1969); *Planes* for 4 Orch. Groups (1969); *Behind Closed Doors* for Violin and Orch. (1971); *Patterns IX* for Orch. (1972); *To See Things Clearly* for Orch. (1972); *For We Don't See Anything Clearly* for Orch. (1972); Guitar Concerto (1972); Trombone Concerto, with Tape (1973); *Orchestra Piece* (1974); *Stations, Regions, and Clouds* for Bass Trombone and Orch. (1977); *Chamber Musics I–V* for Various Chamber Ensembles (1975–77); *Co-ordinative Systems 1–10* for Various Chamber and Solo Instrumental Combinations (1971–76); *Music for Brass* (1975); *Patterns 1–8* and *11* for Various Solo Instruments (1967–77); *Patterns and Processes* for Percussion (1971); *Stations, Regions, Clouds I* for Trombone, Piano, and Tape (1975); *Stations, Regions, Clouds II* for Bass Trombone and Orch. (1977); *Bombs* for Bass Trombone and Prepared Piano (1975); theater pieces.

Fuller, Albert, American harpsichordist; b. Washington, D.C., July 21, 1926. He studied organ with Paul Callaway at the National Cathedral in Washington, D.C.; then attended classes at the Peabody Cons. and at Georgetown and Johns Hopkins univs. He studied harpsichord with Ralph Kirkpatrick at Yale Univ. and also theory there with Hindemith, graduating with a M.Mus. in 1954. He then went to Paris on a Ditson fellowship; upon his return to the U.S., he made his N.Y. recital debut in 1957; his European debut followed in 1959. In 1964 he became a prof. of harpsichord at the Juilliard School of Music in N.Y.

Fuller Maitland, John Alexander, eminent English music scholar; b. London, April 7, 1856; d. Carnforth, Lancashire, March 30, 1936. He studied at Westminster School and Trinity College in Cambridge (M.A., 1882); then took piano lessons with Dannreuther and W.S. Rockstro. He was music critic of the *Pall Mall Gazette* (1882–84) and of the *Manchester Guardian* (1884–89); lectured extensively on the history of English music; appeared as a pianist with the Bach Choir and as a performer on the harpsichord in historical concerts. He contributed to the first edition of *Grove's Dictionary* and edited the Appendix; was editor in chief of the 2nd edition (1904–10); was also editor of *English*

Carols of the 15th Century (1887); *English Country Songs* (1893; with L.E. Broadwood); *Fitzwilliam Virginal Book* (1899; with W. Barclay Squire, his brother-in-law); 12 trio sonatas and the *St. Cecilia Ode* of Purcell in the monumental edition of the Purcell Society, the piano works of Purcell's contemporaries (1921). Together with Clara Bell he translated Spitta's *Bach* (3 vols., 1884; 2nd ed., 1899); compiled the catalogue of the music division of the Fitzwilliam Museum (1893). He is the author of the following books: *Schumann* (1884); *Masters of German Music* (1894); *The Musician's Pilgrimage* (1899); *English Music in the 19th Century* (1902); *The Age of Bach and Handel* (vol. IV of *The Oxford History of Music,* 1902; new ed., 1931); *Joseph Joachim* (1905); *Brahms* (1911; in German, 1912); *The Concert of Music* (1915); *The "48"—Bach's Wohltemperiertes Clavier* (2 vols., 1925); *The Keyboard Suites of J.S. Bach* (1925); *The Spell of Music* (1926); *A Door-Keeper of Music* (1929); *Bach's Brandenburg Concertos* (1929); *Schumann's Concerted Chamber Music* (1929); *The Music of Parry and Stanford* (Cambridge, 1934).

Fulton, (Robert) Norman, English composer; b. London, Jan. 23, 1909. He studied composition with Demuth at the Royal Academy of Music. In 1936 he joined the staff of the BBC; in 1966 he was appointed to the faculty of the Royal Academy of Music.
WORKS: For Orch.: *Sinfonia pastorale* (1950); Symph. No. 2 (1955); Symph. No. 3 (1971–73). Chamber music: Piano Trio (1950); *Scottish Suite* for Recorder and Piano (1954); Sonatina for Oboe and Piano (1962); *Night Music* for Flute and Piano (1969); piano pieces; songs.

Fumagalli, four musical brothers, natives of Inzago, Italy: **Disma,** b. Sept. 8, 1826; d. Milan, March 9, 1893. He was a pupil at, and from 1857 a prof. of, the Milan Cons.; was a prolific composer of piano music (over 250 numbers). **Adolfo,** b. Oct. 19, 1828; d. Florence, May 3, 1856, at the age of 27. He was a pianist, pupil of Gaetano Medaglia, and later of Angeleri and Ray at the Milan Cons.; then undertook tours throughout Italy, France, and Belgium, earning the sobriquet "the Paganini of the pianoforte." During his brief lifetime he publ. about 100 elegant and effective piano pieces, which obtained an extraordinary vogue. Filippo Filippi wrote a sketch, *Della vita e delle opere di Adolfo Fumagalli* (Milan, 1857). **Polibio,** b. Oct. 26, 1830; d. Milan, June 21, 1900. He was a pianist and a composer for piano and for organ. **Luca,** b. May 29, 1837; d. Milan, June 5, 1908. He was a pupil at the Milan Cons.; played with great success in Paris (1860), and publ. salon music for piano; also produced an opera, *Luigi XI* (Florence, 1875).

Fumet, Dynam-Victor, French organist and composer; b. Toulouse, May 4, 1867; d. Paris, Jan. 2, 1949. He studied with César Franck and with Guiraud at the Paris Cons. At an early age he became involved in the political activities of French anarchists and was forced to leave school. For a time he earned his living as a piano player in Paris nightclubs; in 1910 became organist of St. Anne's Church in Paris. His music follows the precepts of French Wagnerism; the influence of Franck is also noticeable. Fumet wrote several orch. works on mystic themes, among them *Magnetisme céleste* for Cello and Orch. (1903); *Trois âmes* (1915); *Transsubstantiation* (1930); *Notre mirage, notre douleur* (1930). During the German occupation he wrote *La Prison glorifiée* (1943).

Fumi, Vinceslao, Italian conductor; b. Montepulciano, Tuscany, Oct. 20, 1823; d. Florence, Nov. 20, 1880. He conducted opera in various Italian cities; also in Istanbul, Montevideo, and Buenos Aires; finally at Florence. His compositions include the opera *Atala* (Buenos Aires, 1862); a Symph.; other orch. works. A collection of folk songs of all times and nations which he undertook remained unfinished.

Furno, Giovanni, Italian composer and pedagogue; b. Capua, Jan. 1, 1748; d. Naples, June 20, 1837. He studied at the Cons. di Saint Onofrio in Naples, and in 1775 became a teacher of theory of composition there; retired in 1835. Among his pupils were Bellini and Mercadante. He wrote 2 operas, sacred choral music, and some instrumental pieces.

Fursch-Madi, Emma, operatic soprano; b. Bayonne, France, 1847; d. Warrenville, N.Y., Sept. 20, 1894. She studied at the Paris Cons.; her first opera engagement was in Paris as Marguerite. She visited America in 1874 with the New Orleans French Opera Co.; sang at Covent Garden (1879–81) and at the Metropolitan Opera, where her final appearance (Feb. 6, 1894) was as Ortrud in *Lohengrin.* She was married 3 times: to **Madi Manjour,** a violinist; to Henry Verié; and to M. Wurst.

Fürstenau, Moritz, German writer on music and flutist; b. Dresden, July 26, 1824; d. there, March 25, 1889. He was a member of the Dresden Court Orch. from 1842; was librarian of the music section of the Royal Library from 1852; from 1858, was a flute teacher at the Cons.
WRITINGS: *Beiträge zur Geschichte der königlich-sächs. musikalischen Kapelle* (1849); *Zur Geschichte der Musik und des Theaters am Hofe zu Dresden* (2 vols., 1861-62; a supplement by Dr. Hans van Brescius, entitled *Die königliche sachs. musikalische Kapelle von Reissiger bis Schuch, 1826–98,* was publ. at Dresden, 1898); *Die Fabrikation musikalischer Instrumente im königlich sächsischen Vogtland* (1876; with Th. Berthold); also essays and articles in musical journals.

Fürstner, Adolph, German publisher; b. Berlin, April 3, 1833; d. Bad Nauheim, June 6, 1908. He was a member of a family of merchants; although lacking in musical education, he showed a keen understanding of the commercial value of good music. He founded a music publishing firm under his own

Furtwängler

name in Berlin in 1868; in 1872 he acquired the catalogue of the Dresden firm of C.F. Meser, which owned several operas by Wagner and some works of Liszt; he subsequently purchased the rights of operas by Massenet, and later demonstrated his business acumen by securing *Pagliacci*. His firm distinguished itself as the earliest publisher of Richard Strauss. Fürstner was succeeded after his death by his son **Otto** (b. Berlin, Oct. 17, 1886; d. London, June 18, 1958); in 1933 Otto Fürstner was compelled to leave Germany; he went to England, where he resumed his business and gradually won back the German rights to the original editions of the firm. After the death of Otto Fürstner his widow, **Ursula Fürstner,** took over the ownership of the firm; in 1970, it was incorporated as Fürstner, London.

Furtwängler, Wilhelm, celebrated German conductor; b. Berlin, Jan. 25, 1886; d. Ebersteinburg, Nov. 30, 1954. His father, Adolf Furtwängler, was a noted archaeologist. He grew up in Munich, where he received a private education; his musical studies were with Schillings, Rheinberger, and Beer-Walbrunn; he also studied piano with Conrad Ansorge. He later served as répétiteur with Mottl in Munich (1908–9). In 1910 he became 3rd conductor at the Strasbourg Opera; then conducted the symph. concerts in Lübeck (1911–15); in 1915 he was engaged as conductor in Mannheim. From 1919 to 1924 he conducted the Vienna Tonkünstler Orch.; concurrently (from 1921) he served as director of the Gesellschaft der Musikfreunde in Vienna. In the interim he led the Berlin Staatskapelle (1920–22); also served as conductor of the Frankfurt Museum concerts. A decisive turn in his career was his appointment in 1922 as chief conductor of the Berlin Phil. as successor to Nikisch; he also assumed the vacant post of Kapellmeister of the Leipzig Gewandhaus Orch., which he held until 1928. On Jan. 3, 1925, he made his American debut with the N.Y. Phil., which was greeted with general acclaim; he conducted this orch. again in 1926 and 1927. In 1927 he was elected conductor of the Vienna Phil. in succession to Weingartner, holding the post of artistic director until 1930, and continuing as guest conductor later on. In 1927 the Univ. of Heidelberg conferred upon him the title of Dr.Phil.; in 1928 the city of Berlin named him Generalmusikdirektor. In 1931 he conducted at the Bayreuth Festival for the first time; on April 17, 1932, he was awarded the prestigious Goethe Gold Medal. In 1933 he was appointed director of the Berlin State Opera and vice-president of the Reichsmusikkammer. He maneuvered adroitly to secure his independence from the increasing encroachment of the Nazi authorities on both his programs and the personnel of the Berlin Phil., and succeeded in retaining several Jewish players. On March 12, 1934, he conducted Hindemith's symph. *Mathis der Maler* and was sharply berated by Goebbels, who called Hindemith a "cultural Bolshevist" and "spiritual non-Aryan" (this with reference to Hindemith's half-Jewish wife). In the face of continued Nazi interference, Furtwängler decided to resign all of his posts on Dec. 4, 1934; however, a few

months later, he made an uneasy peace with the Nazi authorities and agreed to return as a conductor with the Berlin Phil., giving his first concert on April 25, 1935. In 1936 he was offered a contract as permanent conductor of the N.Y. Phil. in succession to Toscanini, but had to decline the prestigious offer to quiet the rising accusations, on the part of American musicians, of his being a Nazi collaborator. In 1937 he went to London to participate in the musical celebrations in honor of the coronation of King George VI; in 1939 he was made a Commander of the Legion of Honor by the French government. After the outbreak of World War II, he confined his activities to Germany and Austria. Continuing to be loyal to Germany but with ambivalent feelings toward the Nazi government, Furtwängler went to Switzerland, where he remained during the last months of the war. He returned to Germany in 1946; faced the Allied Denazification Court, and was absolved from the charges of pro-Nazi activities (Dec. 17, 1946). On May 25, 1947, he conducted the Berlin Phil. for the first time since the end of the war, leading an all-Beethoven concert to great acclaim; he also renewed his close association with the Vienna Phil. and the Salzburg Festival. He was tentatively engaged to conduct the Chicago Symph. in 1949, but the project was canceled when public opinion proved hostile. In Western Europe, however, he took both the Vienna and Berlin phil. orchs. on a number of major tours and was received most enthusiastically; he also became a regular conductor with the Phil. Orch. of London. In 1951 he reinaugurated the Bayreuth Festival by conducting Beethoven's 9th Symph.; in 1952 he resumed his post as chief conductor of the Berlin Phil. His last years of life were clouded by increasing deafness, so that his podium had to be wired for sound. He was to conduct the Berlin Phil. on its first American tour in the spring of 1955, but death intervened, and Herbert von Karajan was elected his successor.

Furtwängler was a perfect embodiment of the great tradition of the German Romantic school of conducting; his interpretations of the music of Beethoven, Schubert, Schumann, Brahms, Bruckner, and Wagner were models of formal purity. He never strove to achieve personal magic with the audience, and never ranked with such charismatic conductors as Stokowski or Koussevitzky in this respect. But to professional musicians he remained a legendary master of the orch. sound and symmetry of formal development of symph. music. Like most German conductors, Furtwängler was himself a composer; quite naturally, the style of his works followed the Romantic tradition, with potential exuberance controlled by a severe sense of propriety. He left behind 3 symphs. (1903, 1947, 1954), a Te Deum (1910), Piano Quintet (1935), Symph. Concert for Piano and Orch. (1937), 2 violin sonatas (1937, 1940), and some minor pieces. He publ. a critical essay, *Johannes Brahms und Anton Bruckner* (Leipzig, 1941; 2nd ed., 1952); *Gespräche über Musik* (Zürich, 1948; in Eng. as *Concerning Music,* London, 1953); *Ton und Wort* (Wiesbaden, 1954); *Der Musiker und sein Publikum* (Zürich, 1954); *Vermächtnis* (Wiesbaden, 1956).

BIBLIOGRAPHY: R. Specht, *Wilhelm Furtwängler* (Vienna, 1922); A. Einstein, "Wilhelm Furtwängler," *Monthly Musical Record* (Jan. 1934); O. Schrenck, *Wilhelm Furtwängler* (Berlin, 1940); F. Herzfeld, *Wilhelm Furtwängler, Weg und Wesen* (Leipzig, 1941); Berta Geissmar, *Two Worlds of Music* (N.Y., 1946); Willy Siebert, *Furtwängler, Mensch und Künstler* (Buenos Aires, 1950); Curt Riess, *Furtwängler; Musik und Politik* (Bern, 1953); Daniel Ellis, ed., *Furtwängler Recalled* (Tuckahoe, N.Y., 1966); Harold Schonberg, *The Great Conductors* (N.Y., 1967; pp. 270–80); Daniel Gillis, *Furtwängler and America* (Woodhaven, N.Y., 1970); Elisabeth Furtwängler, *Über Wilhelm Furtwängler* (Wiesbaden, 1979); Karla Hoecker, *Die nie vergessenen Klänge: Erinnerungen an Wilhelm Furtwängler* (Berlin, 1979); P. Pirie, *Furtwängler and the Art of Conducting* (London, 1980). Newsletters and bulletins are issued by the Wilhelm Furtwängler Society of Los Angeles, the Société Wilhelm Furtwängler of Paris, and the Wilhelm Furtwängler Associates of Urawa City, Japan.

Furuhjelm, Erik Gustaf, Finnish composer; b. Helsinki, July 6, 1883; d. there, June 13, 1964. He studied violin; then took lessons in composition with Sibelius and Wegelius; continued his studies in Vienna with Robert Fuchs. From 1909 to 1935 he lectured on music theory at the Helsinki School of Music, and from 1920 to 1935 served as assistant director there. He founded the magazine *Finsk Musikrevy;* in 1916 he wrote the first book-length biography of Sibelius.
WORKS: Piano Quintet (1906); 2 symphs. (1906–11, 1925–26); *Romantic Overture* (1910); *Konzertstück* for Piano and Orch. (1911); *Intermezzo and Pastorale* for Orch. (1920–24); *Fem bilder (5 Pictures)* for Orch. (1924–25); *Phantasy* for Violin and Orch. (1925–26); *Folklig svit (Rustic Suite)* for Orch. (1939); *Solitude* for Orch. (1940); String Quartet.

Fussan, Werner, German composer; b. Plauen, Dec. 25, 1912. He studied at the Hochschule für Musik in Berlin; served in the German army during World War II; after the war he taught composition at the Cons. of Wiesbaden; in 1948 was appointed to the faculty of the Hochschule für Musik in Mainz.
WORKS: *Capriccio* for Orch. (1949); Suite for Strings (1951); Concertino for Flute and Strings (1957); Concertino for Clarinet, Trumpet, and Strings (1966); Wind Quintet (1948); String Trio (1953); other chamber music; *Tanzlieder,* cantata (1968); choruses and numerous teaching pieces for various instruments.

Fussell, Charles C., American composer; b. Winston-Salem, N.C., Feb. 14, 1938. He studied piano with Clemens Sandresky at the Salem College School of Music; in 1956 enrolled in the Eastman School of Music in Rochester, N.Y., as a student in piano with José Echanis, composition with Thomas Canning, Wayne Barlow, and Bernard Rogers, and conducting with Herman Genhart. In 1962 he received a Fulbright grant and went to Germany, where he studied composition with Boris Blacher at the Hochschule für Musik in Berlin; in the summer of 1963 he attended the Bayreuth Festival Master Class, directed by Wagner's granddaughter, Friedelind Wagner. Returning to the U.S. in 1964, he obtained his M.M. in composition at the Eastman School of Music. In 1966 he joined the faculty of the Univ. of Mass., teaching composition and conducting. In 1976–77 he taught composition at the North Carolina School of the Arts. In 1980 he was appointed prof. of composition at Boston Univ., and was concurrently active as conductor of the Group for New Music (later named Pro Musica Moderna). In his music he adopts a prudent modernistic idiom and favors neo-Romantic but never overladen sonorities, without doctrinaire techniques of the currently prevailing factions.
WORKS: FOR THE STAGE: *Caligula,* opera after Albert Camus (1962); *Julian,* drama for Orch. and Chorus, after Gustave Flaubert (Winston-Salem, N.C., April 15, 1972); *Eurydice,* to a text by Edith Sitwell (Winston-Salem, Jan. 30, 1976); *Cymbeline,* after Shakespeare (Boston, April 2, 1984). FOR ORCH.: 3 symphs.: No. 1 (1963); No. 2 for Soprano and Orch. (Eastman School of Music, May 6, 1969, composer conducting); No. 3, surnamed *Landscapes,* for Chorus and Orch. (1978–81); *Poems* for Chamber Orch. and Voices, after Hart Crane (1965); *3 Processionals* (1972–73; Springfield, April 25, 1974); *Northern Lights,* 2 "portraits" for Chamber Orch., portraying Janáček and Edvard Munch (1977–79); *Virgil Thomson Sleeping,* "portrait" for Chamber Orch. (1981); *4 Fairy Tales,* after Oscar Wilde (1980–81). CHAMBER MUSIC: Piano Trio (1962); *Dance Suite* for Flute, Trumpet, Viola, and 2 Percussionists (1963); *Ballades* for Cello and Piano (1968; revised 1976); String Quartet (1976). FOR VOICES: *Saint Stephen and Herod,* drama for Speaker, Chorus, and Wind Instruments (1964); 3 Choral Pieces (1965; revised 1975); *Voyages,* after Hart Crane, for Soprano, Tenor, Female Chorus, Piano, and Wind Instruments, plus a recorded Speaker (1970; Univ. of Mass., May 4, 1970); *Résumé,* cycle of 9 songs for Soprano, Clarinet, String Bass, and Piano, to texts by Dorothy Parker (1975–76); *A Prophecy* for Chorus and Piano, to texts by Allen Ginsberg (1976); *Song of Return* for Chorus, with Piano, to texts by W.H. Auden (1983); realizations of Sweelinck's *Liedvariationen* (1964) and of Purcell's *Aria for the Blessed Virgin* (1968); also organ pieces; transcriptions for band.

Füssl, Karl Heinz, Czech-born Austrian composer; b. Jablonec, March 21, 1924. He entered the Berlin Hochschule für Musik in 1939; studied with Uhl at the Vienna Academy (1949–50), and had private studies with Polnauer and Ratz. He became co-editor of the Urtext Editions publ. by Universal Edition in Vienna.
WORKS: 2 operas: *Dybuk* (1967–70; Karlsruhe, Sept. 26, 1970) and *Celestina* (1973); *Dialogue in Praise of the Owl and the Cuckoo,* after Shakespeare, for Tenor and 7 Instruments, or for Baritone and 4 Instruments (1948, revised 1961–68); *Divertimento* for Orch. (1948); *Szenen* for String Orch.

(1954); Cello Sonata (1954); *Epitaph und Anti strophe,* 2 movements for Orch. (1956–65); *Concerto rapsodico,* after G.M. Hopkins, for Alto or Mezzo-soprano, and Orch. (1957); *Miorita,* Rumanian folk ballads for Soprano or Tenor, and 5 Instruments (1963); *Refrains* for Piano and Orch. (1972).

Futterer, Carl, Swiss composer; b. Basel, Feb. 21, 1873; d. Ludwigshafen, Nov. 5, 1927. He studied to be a lawyer; then began taking lessons in composition with Hans Huber; wrote operas and other works but kept them hidden until late in life. His comic opera *Don Gil mit den grünen Hosen* (1915) was produced in Freiburg im Breisgau in 1922; another opera, *Der Geiger von Gmünd* (1917), was produced in Basel in 1921. He further wrote a Sinfonietta (1917); Octet (1921); Quartet for Oboe, Clarinet, Horn, and Bassoon (1921); Trio for Clarinet, Cello, and Piano (1924); Piano Trio (1927); Violin Sonata (1927); Piano Concerto (1927).

Fux, Johann Joseph, Austrian composer and learned theorist; b. Hirtenfeld, Styria, 1660; d. Vienna, Feb. 13, 1741. He enrolled at the Jesuit Univ. in Graz as a "grammatista" in 1680; in 1681 entered the Ferdinandum, a Jesuit inst. for gifted music students; also studied at the Jesuit Univ. of Ingolstadt; was organist at St. Moritz there until 1688. In 1696–1702 he was organist at the Schottenkirche in Vienna; in 1698 he was made court composer; in 1705, vice-Kapellmeister at St. Stephen's, and principal Kapellmeister there in 1712–15; was named assistant Kapellmeister to the court in 1713, succeeding Ziani as first Kapellmeister (the highest position attainable for a musician) in 1715. This office he held until his death, under 3 successive emperors, and received many tokens of imperial favor. Over 200 works have been added to the original 405 catalogued works; the greatest and the most enduring is his treatise on counterpoint, *Gradus ad Parnassum,* publ. originally in Latin (Vienna, 1725), since then in German, Italian, French, and Eng. (1791; part of the *Gradus ad Parnassum* was publ. in Eng. as *Steps to Parnassus,* N.Y., 1943; 2nd ed., re-vised, 1965, as *The Study of Counterpoint);* Mozart and Haydn studied it; Cherubini and Albrechtsberger adopted its method, which was sanctioned by Piccinni and Padre Martini. Vogler, however, condemned it (see introduction to Vogler's *Choral-System,* p. 1; Fröhlich's biography of Vogler, p. 18). Fux was well aware of the weakness of contemporary music practice and, in trying to arrive at a satisfactory remedy, disregarded the modern idiom already established when he was writing and chose, as the basis of his theory, the style of Palestrina. Although his presentation of that style is not very strong or even authentic (for, among other things, he could not have been very well acquainted with the main body of Palestrina's works because they were not commonly available at the time), the method is still valuable for its organization and the discipline it affords (cf. K. Jeppesen's *Counterpoint,* 1931; in Eng., N.Y., 1939).

WORKS: 20 operas; 12 oratorios; about 80 partitas and overtures (among them the *Concentus musico-instrumentalis);* much sacred music: about 80 masses (the *Missa canonica* is a contrapuntal masterpiece); 3 Requiems; 2 *Dies irae;* 57 vespers and Psalms; etc.; 38 "sacred sonatas." The Johann Joseph Fux Gesellschaft began issuing the Collected Works in 1959, a series that is still in progress; to date, 11 vols. have been publ.; in addition, a selection from his works is publ. in Denkmäler der Tonkunst in Österreich, vols. 1 (1.i; 4 masses), 3 (2.i; 27 motets), 19 (9.ii; 2 sacred sonatas, 2 overtures), 34/35 (17; the opera *Costanza e fortezza;* later ed. by G.P. Smith, Northampton, Mass., 1936), 47 (23.ii; the *Concentus musico-instrumentalist),* 85 (keyboard works).

BIBLIOGRAPHY: L. von Köchel, *Johann Joseph Fux* (Vienna, 1872; full biography and thematic catalogue of works); C. Schnabl, "Johann Joseph Fux, der österreichische Palestrina," *Jahrbuch der Leo Gesellschaft* (Vienna, 1895); H. Rietsch, "Der Concentus von Johann Joseph Fux," *Studien zur Musikwissenschaft,* 4 (1912); A. Liess, *Johann Joseph Fux* (Vienna, 1948); J.H. Van den Meer, *Johann Josef Fux als Opernkomponist* (3 vols., Bilthoven, 1961); E. Wellesz, *Fux* (London, 1965).

G

Gabichvadze, Revaz, Soviet Georgian composer; b. Tiflis (Tbilisi), June 11, 1913. He graduated in composition from the Tiflis Cons. in 1935; in 1938 joined its faculty.

WORKS: Operas: *Nana* (1949) and *We, Mothers of Peace* (1966); operetta, *Grasshopper* (1953); ballet, *Hamlet* (1971); oratorio, *Knight in a Leopard's Skin* (1938); *3 Monologues about Lenin* for Bass, Women's Chorus, and Orch. (1970); 3 symphs. (1963, 1971, 1972); 2 chamber symphs. (1965, 1968); *9 Variations* for 8 Instruments (1971); Violin Concerto (1947); Cello Concerto (1950); *4 Sketches* for Chamber Orch. (1969); *2 Factures* for Chamber Orch. (1960); Piano Sonata (1964); 3 string quartets; songs; cinema music.

Gabold, Ingolf, German-born Danish composer; b. Heidelberg, March 31, 1942. He studied theory and music history at the Copenhagen Cons., and composition with Nørgaard at the Cons. in Aarhus. His stated goal is to "combine music with Jung's depth psychology."

WORKS: Opera, *Syv scener til Orfeus (Seven Visions to Orpheus)* for 4 Singers, one Actor, Dancers, and Orch. (1969–70; Danish television, Sept. 28, 1970); a television play, *Mod Vandmandens tegn (Toward Aquarius)* for Soprano, Bass, Chorus, and Organ (1971–72; Copenhagen, Nov. 11, 1973); *Für Louise* for Soprano and Chamber Orch. (1966; Copenhagen, Aug. 18, 1967); *Atlantis* for Rock Group and Orch. (1971; Danish Radio, Feb. 4, 1972); *Visione* for 4 Vocal Soloists and Mixed Chorus (1962); *Your Sister's Drown'd* for Soprano and Male Chorus (1968; to a text from *Hamlet*); *Written in Sand* for Chorus a cappella (1973).

Gabriel, Mary Ann Virginia, English composer; b. Banstead, Surrey, Feb. 7, 1825; d. London, Aug. 7, 1877. She studied with Pixis, Döhler, Thalberg, and Molique; married George E. March (1874), who wrote most of her librettos.

WORKS: 3 cantatas: *Evangeline* (Brighton Festival, Feb. 13, 1873); *Dreamland; Graziella;* 6 operettas: *Widows Bewitched* (London, Nov. 13, 1867); *Grass Widows; Shepherd of Cornouailles; Who's the Heir?; Follies of a Night; A Rainy Day;* piano pieces.

Gabrieli, Andrea (also known as **Andrea di Cannaregio**), eminent Italian organist and composer; b. Venice, c.1510; d. there, 1586. He was a pupil of Adrian Willaert at San Marco and chorister there (1536); was organist at S. Geremia in Cannaregio in 1557–58; was in Bavaria in 1562 and went to Frankfurt, to the coronation of Maximilian II, as court organist of Duke Albrecht V of Bavaria. In 1566 he returned to Venice and was appointed 2nd organist at San Marco; became first organist on Jan. 1, 1585, succeeding Merulo. He enjoyed a great reputation as an organist (his concerts with Merulo, on 2 organs, were featured attractions). Among his pupils were his famous nephew, **Giovanni Gabrieli,** and Hans Leo Hassler. A prolific composer, he wrote a large number of works of varied description, many of which were publ. posthumously, edited by his nephew. His versatility is attested by the fact that he was equally adept in sacred music of the loftiest spirit, and in instrumental music, as well as in madrigals, often of a comic nature.

WORKS: *Sacrae cantiones* (37 motets; 1565); *Libro I di madrigali a 5 voci* (30 madrigals; 1566); *Libro II di madrigali a 5 voci* (28 madrigals; 1570); *Greghesche e justiniane* (15 numbers; 1571); *Primus Liber Missarum 6 vocum* (4 masses; 1572); *Libro I di madrigali a 6 voci* (30 madrigals; 1574); *Libro di madrigali a 3 voci* (30 madrigals; 1575); *Ecclesiasticae cantiones a 4 voci* (58 motets; 1576); *Libro II de madrigali a 6 voci* (22 madrigals; 1580); *Psalmi Davidici a 6 voci* (7 Psalms; 1583); *Sonate a 5 strumenti* (lost; 1586); *Concerti di Andrea et di Giovanni Gabrieli* (39 motets; 26 madrigals; 1587); *Edippo Tiranno* (choruses for Sophocles' *Oedipus,* perf. in Vicenza in 1585, 1588); *Libro III di madrigali a 5 voci* (22 madrigals; 1589); *Madrigali et ricercari* (24 madrigals, 7 ricercari; 1589); *Intonazioni d'organo* (12 intonazioni; 1593); *Ricercari di Andrea Gabrieli* (13 ricercari; 1595); *Libro III de ricercari* (6 ricercari, one fantasia, one motet, one canzone, 2 madrigals, one capriccio on the *passamezzo antico*; 1596); *Mascherate di Andrea Gabrieli et altri* (3 mascherate, 3 madrigals; 1601); *Canzoni alla francese et ricercari* (4 canzoni, 7 ricercari; 1605); *Canzoni alla francese* (9 canzoni, one Ricercare; 1605); and a large number of detached works in contemporary and later collections.—Modern eds.: G. Benvenuti, *Istituzioni e monumenti dell' arte musicale italiana* (vols. I and II; vocal and instrumental pieces); L. Torchi, *L'arte musicale in Italia* (vols. II and III; 16 motets and pieces for organ; K. von Winterfeld, in *Joh. Gabrieli und sein Zeitalter* (1834; 2 vols. and a musical supplement); J. von Wasielewski, in *Geschichte der Instrumental-Musik im 16. Jahrhundert* (1878) and in the music supplement of *Die Violine im 17. Jahrhundert* (2nd ed., 1905); A.G. Ritter, *Geschichte des Orgelspiels im 14.–18. Jahrhundert* (1884; revised by Frotscher, 1933); G. d'Alessi, *Classici della musica italiana* (vol. VI); de la Moskowa, *Recueil des morceaux de musique ancienne* (1843); H. Riemann, *Alte Kammermusik* (8-voiced ricercare); O. Kinkeldey in *Orgel und Klavier in der Musik des 16. Jahrhunderts* (organ arrangements by Andrea Gabrieli of Orlando di Lasso's chanson *Susanne un jour*); J. Wolf, in *Sing- und Spielmusik* (a *canzone francese*); H. Bäuerle (*Missa brevis*, 1932); W. Schöllgen (Easter motet, 1932); A. Einstein, in Denkmäler der Tonkunst in Österreich, vol. 77 (41; 3 madrigals in 6, 7, 8 voices, 1934); idem, in the musical supplement (no. 21) of *A Short History of Music* (N.Y., 1938); idem, in *The Golden Age of*

Music (N.Y., 1942); idem, in *The Italian Madrigal* (vol. III; Princeton, 1949); A. Schering, *Geschichte der Musik in Beispielen* (no. 130); Davison and Apel, *Historical Anthology of Music* (vol. I, nos. 135, 136); Parish and Ohl, *Masterpieces of Music before 1750* (no. 21); *Das Chorwerk,* 96 (3 motets). The *Opera Omnia,* ed. by Denis Arnold, is being issued by the American Inst. of Musicology; as of 1977, 6 vols. had appeared.

BIBLIOGRAPHY: G. Benvenuti, "Andrea e Giovanni Gabrieli e la musica strumentale in S. Marco," *Istituzioni e monumenti dell'arte musicale italiana* (vol. II); Ilse Zerr-Becking, *Studien zu Andrea Gabrieli* (Prague, 1933); G. Reese, *Music in the Renaissance* (N.Y., 1954; 2nd ed., revised, 1959); see also bibliography listed under Giovanni Gabrieli.

Gabrieli, Domenico (Gabrielli) (called the "Menghino dal violoncello," Menghino being the diminutive of Domenico), Italian composer; b. Bologna, April 15,1651; d. there, July 10, 1690. He studied composition with Legrenzi in Venice and cello with Petronio Franceschini in Bologna. An excellent cellist, he played in the orch. of San Petronio, Bologna (1680–87); was a member of the Bologna Phil. Academy (1676); then became its president (1683). He was one of the earliest composers for cello solo.

WORKS: He produced 12 operas in Bologna, Venice, Modena, and Turin; his last opera, *Tiberio in Bisanzio,* was perf. posthumously in Lucca (Jan. 20, 1694). Other works: *Ricercari per violoncello solo* (1689; MS at the Liceo in Bologna); *Balletti, gighe, correnti e sarabande* for 2 Violins, Cello, and Basso Continuo (1684; 2nd ed., 1704); *Vexillum pacis* (motets for Contralto, with Instrumental Accompaniment; posthumous, 1695). L. Landshoff ed. 3 *Arie* with Instrumental Obbligato (in *Alte Meister des Bel Canto,* 1912) and 2 cello sonatas (1930); A. Einstein printed a chamber cantata in the music supplement (no. 28) of his *A Short History of Music* (N.Y., 1938).

BIBLIOGRAPHY: E. Albini, "Domenico Gabrieli, Il Corelli del violoncello," *Rivista Musicale Italiana* (1937).

Gabrieli, Giovanni, celebrated Venetian composer, nephew and pupil of **Andrea Gabrieli;** b. Venice, between 1554 and 1557; d. there, Aug. 12, 1612. He lived in Munich from 1575 to 1579. On Nov. 1, 1584, he was engaged to substitute for Merulo as first organist at San Marco in Venice; on Jan. 1, 1585, was permanently appointed as 2nd organist (his uncle meanwhile took charge of the first organ); retained this post until his death. As a composer, he stands at the head of the Venetian school; he was probably the first to write vocal works with parts for instrumental groups in various combinations, partly specified, partly left to the conductor, used as accompaniment as well as interspersed instrumental sinfonie (Sacrae Symphoniae). His role as a composer and teacher is epoch-making; through his innovations and his development of procedures and devices invented by others (free handling of several choirs in the many-voiced vocal works, "concerted" solo parts and duets in the few-voiced vocal works, trio-sonata texture, novel dissonance treatment, speech rhythm, root progressions in fifths, use of tonal and range levels for structural purposes, coloristic effects) and through his numerous German pupils (particularly Schütz) and other transalpine followers. he gave a new direction to the development of music. His instrumental music helped to spark the composition of German instrumental ensemble music, which reached its apex in the symph. and chamber music works of the classical masters. Of interest also is the fact that one of his ricercari, a 4-part work in the 10th tone (1595), is an early example of the "fugue with episodes" (reprinted in Riemann's *Musikgeschichte in Beispielen,* no. 52, Leipzig, 1913).

WORKS: Publications (very few) contain both sacred and secular vocal, as well as instrumental, works: *Concerti di Andrea et di Giovanni Gabrieli* (5 motets, 5 madrigals; 1587); *Intonazioni d'organo di Andrea Gabrieli et di Giovanni suo nepote* (11 *intonazioni;* 1593); *Sacrae Symphoniae Joannis Gabrielii* (42 motets, Mass, 12 instrumental canzoni, 3 sonatas; 1597); *Sacrarum Symphoniarum Continuatio* (9 motets, of which 5 are reprints; 1600); *Canzoni per sonare* (6 canzoni; 1608); *Sacrae Symphoniae Diversorum Autorum* (26 motets; 1613); *Sacrae Symphoniae, Liber II* (26 motets, Mass, 3 Magnificats; 1615); *Canzoni et Sonate* (15 canzoni, 5 sonatas; 1615); *Reliquiae Sacrorum Concentum* (one Magnificat, 19 motets, of which 10 are reprints; 1615). Detached pieces in collections up to 1625: 25 more madrigals, one canticle, Magnificats, motets, ricercari, toccatas, fantasias. Modern publications: G. Benvenuti publ. 3 secular vocal pieces in vol. I (1931), and G. Cesari 13 canzoni and 2 sonatas, (from *Sacrae Symphoniae,* 1597) in vol. II (1932), of the *Istituzioni e monumenti dell'arte musicale italiana (Andrea e Giovanni Gabrieli e la musica strumentale in S. Marco);* K. von Winterfeld, *Johannes Gabrieli und sein Zeitalter* (1834; 2 vols. and a vol. of music supplements); Proske, Griesbacher, Commer, etc. (motets); J. von Wasielewski, *Geschichte der Instrumental-Musik im 16. Jahrhundert* (1878), and in the music supplement of *Die Violine im 17. Jahrhundert* (2nd ed., 1905); Riemann, *Alte Kammermusik (Sonata a 3 violini* and *Canzona a 8);* L. Torchi, *L'arte musicale in Italia* (vols. II, III); H. Besseler, *Das Chorwerk* (vols. 10 and 67; 3 motets in each); A. Schering, *Geschichte der Musik in Beispielen* (nos. 130, 148); G. Tagliapietra *Antologia di musica antica e moderna per piano* (vol. II, 1931); A. Einstein (*Canzoni a 4,* 1933, Schott Antiqua; motet in the music supplement of his *Short History of Music,* no. 19, 1938; madrigal in *The Golden Age of the Madrigal,* 1942, no. 6); W. Danckert (*Sonata a 3 violini,* 1934); Davison and Apel, *Historical Anthology of Music* (vol. I, nos. 157, 173); F. Stein (*Sonata pian e forte,* 1931); J.F. Williamson (motet, 1932); G.W. Woodworth (3 motets; 1950–52); Bongiovanni (5 motets; 1954). Hans David has adapted several of Gabrieli's canzoni for modern use. An *Opera Omnia,* in 10 vols., ed. by Denis Arnold, is being issued by the American Inst. of Musicology in its Corpus Mensurabilis Musicae series.

BIBLIOGRAPHY: A.G. Ritter, *Geschichte des Orgelspiels im 14.–18. Jahrhundert* (1884: revised by Frotscher, 1933): H. Leichtentritt, *Geschichte der Motette* (1908); O. Kinkeldey, *Orgel und Klavier in der Musik des 16. Jahrhunderts* (1910); G.S. Bedbrook, "The Genius of Giovanni Gabrieli," *Music Review* (Jan. 1947); G. Reese, *Music in the Renaissance* (N.Y., 1954); Denis Arnold, *Giovanni Gabrieli* (London, 1977).

Gabrielli, Caterina, famous soprano; b. Rome, Nov. 12, 1730; d. there, Feb. 16, 1796. She was known under the nickname "La Coghetta" (that is, "Little Cook," for her father was a cook in a Roman nobleman's palace). She made her debut at Venice in 1754; then went to Vienna, where she was hailed as a "new star on the musical firmament" and was coached by Gluck and Metastasio; she sang many parts in the Vienna productions of Gluck's operas, up to 1761; made triumphant appearances in Milan, Turin, and Naples; then went to Russia (with Traetta) and sang in St. Petersburg with unfailing acclaim (1772–74). In 1775 she made her first appearance in London, arousing admiration among the cognoscenti; but she was also the object of common gossip related to her notoriously loose morals. She returned to Italy after only one season in London, and eventually settled in Rome.

Gabrielli, Domenico. See **Gabrieli, Domenico.**

Gabrielli, Nicolò, Italian composer; b. Naples, Feb. 21, 1814; d. Paris, June 14, 1891. He was a pupil of Buonamici, Conti, Donizetti, and Zingarelli at the Naples Cons.; from 1854 he lived in Paris. He wrote 22 operas and 60 ballets, produced at Naples, Paris, and Vienna.

Gabrilowitsch, Ossip, notable pianist and conductor; b. St. Petersburg, Feb. 7, 1878; d. Detroit, Sept. 14, 1936. In 1888–94 he was a pupil at the St. Petersburg Cons., studying piano with A. Rubinstein and composition with Navrátil, Liadov, and Glazunov; graduated as winner of the Rubinstein Prize, and then spent 2 years (1894–96) in Vienna studying with Leschetizky; then toured Germany, Austria, Russia, France, and England. His first American tour (debut Carnegie Hall, N.Y., Nov. 12, 1900) was eminently successful, as were his subsequent visits (1901, 1906, 1909, 1914, 1915, 1916). During the season 1912–13 he gave in Europe a series of 6 historical concerts illustrating the development of the piano concerto from Bach to the present day; on his American tour in 1914–15 he repeated the entire series in several of the larger cities, meeting with an enthusiastic reception. On Oct. 6, 1909, he married the contralto **Clara Clemens** (daughter of Mark Twain), with whom he frequently appeared in joint recitals. He conducted his first N.Y. concert on Dec. 13, 1916; was appointed conductor of the Detroit Symph. Orch. in 1918. In 1928 and the following years he also conducted the Philadelphia Orch., sharing the baton with Leopold Stokowski, but still retaining his Detroit position.

BIBLIOGRAPHY: Clara Clemens, *My Husband Gabrilowitsch* (N.Y., 1938).

Gaburo, Kenneth, American composer; b. Somerville, N.J., July 5, 1926. He studied composition with Bernard Rogers at the Eastman School of Music, Rochester, N.Y. (M.M., 1949), and at the Univ. of Illinois, Urbana (D.M.A., 1962); then went to Rome, where he studied with Goffredo Petrassi. Returning to America, he occupied teaching posts at Kent State Univ., Ohio (1949–50); at McNeese State Univ. in Lake Charles, La. (1950–54); and at the Univ. of Illinois, Urbana (1955–68); in 1968 was appointed to the faculty of the Univ. of Calif. at San Diego; remained there until 1975. In 1967 he held a Guggenheim fellowship. He founded and directed the New Music Chorale Ensemble in concerts in the U.S. and Europe. His music is quaquaversal.
WORKS: Operas: *The Snow Queen* (Lake Charles, May 5, 1952) and *The Widow* (Urbana, Feb. 26, 1961); *Bodies,* abstract theater piece (1957); *The Dog-King,* play with music (1959); *On a Quiet Theme* for Orch. (1952); *4 Inventions* for Clarinet and Piano (1953); *Music for 5 Instruments* (1954); set of 3 *Ideas and Transformations* for Strings (1955); String Quartet (1956); *Line Studies* for 4 Instruments (1957); electronic score for the play *The Hydrogen Jukebox; Lingua I–IV,* massive theater play exploring the structural properties of language in a musical context (1965–70); Viola Concerto (1959); *Antiphony I* for 3 String Groups and Electronic Sound; *Antiphony II* for Piano and Electronic Sound; *Antiphony III* for Singers and Electronic Sound; *Antiphony IV* for Piccolo, Double Bass, Trombone, and Electronic Sound; *Antiphony V* for Piano and Electronic Sound; *Shapes and Sounds* for Orch. (1960); *2* for Mezzo-soprano, Alto Flute, and Double Bass (1963); *Circumcision* for 3 Groups of Male Voices (1964); *The Flow of E,* based on a synthesized vowel *e* and its electronic transformations (1965); *Inside,* quartet for a Single Double-bass Player (1969); *Mouthpiece,* sextet for Solo Trumpet and 5 Projection Slides (1970).

Gabussi, Giulio Cesare, Italian composer; b. Bologna, 1555; d. Milan, Sept. 12, 1611. He was a pupil of Costanzo Porta; in 1582 he was called to Milan as singer and composer at the Cathedral, and remained in that post until his death, with the exception of a brief stay in Poland in the service of Sigismund III (1601–2). He publ. 2 books of madrigals for 5 Voices (Venice, 1580 and 1598); motets for 4 and 5 Voices (Venice, 1586); *Te Deum* for 4 Voices (Milan, 1598); etc. He was one of the first composers whose works in the Ambrosian ritual (litanies, etc.) appeared in print.

Gade, Axel Willy, Danish violinist, son of **Niels Gade;** b. Copenhagen, May 28, 1860; d. there, Nov. 9, 1921. He studied with his father and with Joachim; was active in Copenhagen as a theater conductor and teacher. He wrote a Violin Concerto and an opera, *Venezias Nat* (Copenhagen, Jan. 18, 1919).

Gade, Jacob, Danish composer; b. Vejle, Nov. 29, 1879; d. Copenhagen, Feb. 21, 1963. He studied violin; was a member of the N.Y. Symph. Orch. (1919–21); then returned to Copenhagen and was active there as a conductor. Among his light compositions, *Jalousie* (1925) attained great popularity. He also wrote several symph. poems (*Den sidste Viking, Leda and the Swan,* etc.).
BIBLIOGRAPHY: Karl Bjarnjof, *Tango Jalousie* (Copenhagen, 1969).

Gade, Niels (Wilhelm), Danish composer and founder of the modern Scandinavian school of composition; b. Copenhagen, Feb. 22, 1817; d. there, Dec. 21, 1890. He was the only child of an instrument maker; studied violin with a member of the Danish court band, and gave a concert in Copenhagen at the age of 16. He then took composition lessons with A.P. Berggreen; soon he began writing songs to German texts. At the age of 23, he wrote his overture *Nachklänge von Ossian,* for which he was awarded a prize by the Copenhagen Musical Society. The work was performed in Copenhagen on Nov. 19, 1841, and was soon publ.; this early overture remained the most popular work of Gade, and endured in the orch. repertoire for many years. His next important work was Symph. in C minor. Gade sent this to Mendelssohn in Leipzig, and Mendelssohn performed it at a Gewandhaus concert on March 2, 1843. Subsequently, Gade received a government stipend for travel in Germany; he went to Leipzig, where Mendelssohn accepted him as a friend, and let him conduct some of the Gewandhaus concerts. Gade's talent flourished in the congenial atmosphere; an ardent admirer of Mendelssohn and Schumann, he adopted a Romantic style in the prevalent Germanic spirit. After Mendelssohn's death in 1847, Gade assumed the conductorship of the Gewandhaus concerts, but on the outbreak of the Schleswig-Holstein war in the spring of 1848, he returned to Copenhagen. In 1850, he became chief conductor of the Copenhagen Musical Society; also was a co-founder of the Copenhagen Cons. in 1866. He visited Birmingham in 1876 to conduct his cantata *Zion* at the festival there. In the same year, the Danish government granted him a life pension. In Denmark, his position as a prime musician was by then fully established; but he was accepted in Germany, too, as a master composer. Despite his adherence to the Germanic school, he infused elements of national Danish melodies into his works, and so led the way to further development of Scandinavian music.
WORKS: 8 symphs. (1841–71); overtures: *Nachklänge von Ossian* (1840); *Im Hochlande* (1844); *Hamlet* (1861); *Michelangelo* (1861); Violin Concerto (1880); cantatas: *Comala* (1846); *Elverskud* (1853); *The Holy Night* (1861); *At Sunset* (1865); *Kalanus* (1871); *Zion* (1873); *The Crusaders* (1873); *The Mountain Thrall* (1873); *Gefion* (1875); *Psyche* (1882); *Der Strom,* after Goethe's *Mahomet* (1889); chamber music: 2 string quintets, String Octet, Piano Trio, String Quartet, 3 violin sonatas, *Folk Dance* for Violin and Piano, *Pictures of the Orient*

for Violin and Piano; for Piano Solo: *Spring Flowers, Aquarelles* (3 books), *Idylls*, 4 *Fantastic Pieces, Folk Dance*, Sonata in E minor; also 21 vocal works for various combinations, in the style of folk songs; incidental music for a play, *Mariotta;* ballet music; etc.

BIBLIOGRAPHY: Gade's autobiographical *Aufzeichnungen und Briefe*, ed. by Dagmar Gade (German trans., Basel 1893); C. Rubner, "Niels Wilhelm Gade, In Remembrance of the Centenary of His Birth," *Musical Quarterly* (Jan. 1917); C. Kjerulf, *Niels Wilhelm Gade* (Copenhagen, 1917); W. Behrend, *Gade* (Leipzig, 1917); idem, *Minder om Gade* (Copenhagen, 1930).

Gadsby, Henry Robert, English music teacher; b. Hackney, London, Dec. 15, 1842; d. Putney, Nov. 11, 1907. He was a chorister at St. Paul's from 1849 to 1858; organist at St. Peter's, Brockley; in 1884 succeeded Hullah as prof. of harmony at Queen's College, London; was prof. at the Guildhall School of Music from its foundation (1880) until his death. He wrote 3 symphs., several overtures, songs, etc.

Gadski, Johanna (Emilia Agnes), celebrated German soprano; b. Anclam, June 15, 1872; d. Berlin, Feb. 22, 1932, as a result of an automobile accident. She studied voice with Frau Schroeder-Chaloupka at Stettin; made her opera debut at the age of 17 in Berlin with the Kroll Opera; then sang in Mainz, Bremen, and Stettin. On March 1, 1895, she made her American debut with the Damrosch Opera Co. in N.Y. as Elsa in *Lohengrin,* and subsequently sang other Wagnerian roles, including Elisabeth, Eva, and Sieglinde. On Dec. 28, 1899, she made her debut with the Metropolitan Opera on tour, and established herself as a prime interpreter of dramatic parts, excelling in particular as Brünnhilde and Isolde; remained with the Metropolitan until 1904; made her debut at Covent Garden in London on May 15, 1899; in 1904–6 she made 2 transcontinental tours of the U.S., as a concert singer. In 1907 she returned to the Metropolitan Opera, where she continued to appear until her final appearance on April 13, 1917. She left the U.S. for Germany when America entered the war in 1917; returned to the U.S. in 1929, remaining until 1931. On Nov. 11, 1892, she was married to Lieutenant Hans Tauscher.

Gadzhibekov, Uzeir, Azerbaijani composer; b. Agdzhabedy, near Shusha, Sept. 17, 1885; d. Baku, Nov. 23, 1948. He studied in Shusha; then lived in Baku, where he produced his first opera on a native subject, *Leyly and Medzhnun* (Jan. 25, 1908). His comic opera *Arshin Mal Alan* (Baku, Nov. 27, 1913) had numerous performances; another opera, *Kyor-Oglu (A Blind Man's Son),* was produced at the Azerbaijan Festival in Moscow (April 30, 1937).

Gaffurio, Franchino. See **Gaforio, Franchino.**

Gaforio (or **Gafori, Gafuri, Gaffurio**), **Franchino** (Latinized as **Franchinus Gafurius;** often simply

Franchinus), celebrated Italian theorist; b. Lodi, Jan. 14, 1451; d. Milan, June 24, 1522. He studied theology and music; lived in Mantua, Verona, and Genoa (1477); he formed an intimacy with the Doge Prospero Adorno (then in exile) and fled with him to Naples (1478). There he met various distinguished musicians, and held public disputation with Johannes Tinctoris, Guarnier, and Hycart. The plague and the Turkish invasion compelled him to return to Lodi (1480); was a teacher and choirmaster at Monticello for 3 years, made a short visit to Bergamo in 1483, and in 1484 until his death was maestro di cappella at the Milan Cathedral, and first singer in the choir of Duke Lodovico Sforza. In 1485 he also founded a music school at Milan, which prospered.

WRITINGS: *Theoricum opus harmonicae disciplinae* (Naples, 1480; 2nd ed., Milan, 1492, as *Theorica musicae;* facsimile reprint, Rome, 1934); *Practica musicae Franchino Gaforio Laudensis ... in IV libris* (Milan 1496; his magnum opus, with examples of mensural notation in block-print; other eds., 1497, 1502, 1508, 1512, 1522); *Angelicum ac divinum opus musicae materna lingua scriptum* (Milan, 1496); *De harmonia musicorum instrumentorum* (Milan, 1518; with biography of Gaforio by P. Meleguli); *Apologia Franchini Gafurii musici adversus Ioannem Spatarium et complices musicos Bononienses* (Turin, 1520; concerning the controversy between the Milanese and Bolognese schools). A complete ed. of his compositions, edited by Lutz Finscher, was begun in 1955.

BIBLIOGRAPHY: E. Prätorius, *Die Mensuraltheorie des Franchino Gaforio und der folgenden Zeit bis zur Mitte des 16. Jahrhunderts* (Leipzig, 1905); G. Cesari, "Musica e musicisti alla corte Sforzesca," *Rivista Musicale Italiana* (1922; with reprints); P. Hirsch, "Bibliographie der musikalischen Drucke des Franchino Gaforio," *J. Wolf-Festschrift* (1929); G. Zampieri, *Franchino Gaforio* (Milan, 1925); A. Careta, *Franchino Gafurio* (Lodi, 1951).

Gagliano, the name of a family of famous violin makers at Naples. **Alessandro,** who worked from 1695 to 1725, was a pupil of Stradivari, and he, as well as his sons **Nicola** (1695–1758) and **Gennaro** (1700–88), followed largely the Stradivari model. The instruments of **Ferdinando Gagliano** (c.1724–81), a son of Nicola, exhibit less skillful workmanship than those of the older members of the family.

Gagliano, Marco da, Italian opera composer; b. Florence, May 1, 1582; d. there, Feb. 25, 1643. He was a pupil of L. Bati; in 1608, became maestro at S. Lorenzo in Florence, and shortly after at the Medici court as well; was made canon in 1610, and in 1615, Apostolic Protonotary. In 1607 he founded the Accademia degli Elevati. Gagliano was among the first composers to write in the "stile rappresentativo," which he developed further by ornamentation.

WORKS: *Dafne*, "opera in musica" (his most important work; first played at Mantua, 1608; publ. in

Florence, 1608, and reprinted in shortened form by R. Eitner in vol. 10 of the *Publikationen älterer Musikwerke*); *La Flora,* opera (with Peri; Florence, 1628); *Due Messe, a 4, 5* (Florence, 1594); 6 vols. of madrigals *a* 5 (1602–17); *Sacrae cantiones* (*I a* 6, with a Mass, 1614; *II a* 1–6, with Basso Continuo, 1622); *Musiche a 1, 2, e 3 voci* (Venice, 1615, with Continuo).

BIBLIOGRAPHY: L. Piccianti, "Marco da Gagliano," *Gazzetta Musical di Milano* (1843–44); A. Solerti, *Musica alla Corte Medicea* (1905); D. Butchart, *I Madrigali di Marco da Gagliano* (Florence, 1982).

Gagnebin, Henri, Swiss composer and pedagogue; b. Liège (of Swiss parents), March 13, 1886; d. Geneva, June 2, 1977. He studied organ with Vierne and composition with Vincent d'Indy at the Schola Cantorum in Paris; served as a church organist in Paris (1910–16) and in Lausanne (1916–25); was director of the Geneva Cons. from 1925 to 1957. He publ. the books *Entretiens sur la Musique* (Geneva, 1943), *Musique, mon beau souci* (Paris, 1968), and *Orgue, musette et bourbon* (Neuchâtel, 1975).

WORKS: 4 symphs. (1911, 1918–21, 1955, 1970); 3 *Tableaux symphoniques d'après F. Hodler* (1942); *Suite d'orchestre sur des Psaumes huguenots* for Orch. (1950); Piano Concerto (1951); Clarinet Concerto (1971); Concerto for Oboe, Bassoon, and String Orch. (1972); String Trio (1968); Wind Octet (1970); Brass Quintet (1970); Wind Sextet (1971); other chamber music, including several string quartets; many organ pieces.

Gaigerova, Varvara, Russian pianist and composer; b. Oryekhovo-Zuyevo, Oct. 17, 1903; d. Moscow, April 6, 1944. She studied piano at the Moscow Cons. with Neuhaus and composition with Miaskovsky. In most of her compositions she cultivated folk materials of the constituent republics of the U.S.S.R., including those of the Mongol populations of Siberia and Central Asia.

WORKS: 3 symphs. (1928, 1934, 1937); 3 suites for Domra Ensembles on folk themes of Kazakhstan, Turkestan, Uzbekistan, etc. (1932, 1934, 1935); 2 string quartets (1927, 1947); piano pieces; some 150 songs; cantata, *The Sun of Socialism* (1932).

Gailhard, Pierre, French operatic singer; b. Toulouse, August 1, 1848; d. Paris, Oct. 12, 1918. He began his vocal studies in his native city, and entered the Paris Cons. in 1866. After one year of study under Révial he graduated in 1867, winning 3 first prizes. He made his debut at the Opéra-Comique (Dec. 4, 1867) as Falstaff in Thomas's *Songe d'une nuit d'été;* on Nov. 3, 1871, he made his debut at the Opéra as Méphistophélès in Gounod's *Faust.* At the height of his powers and success he gave up the stage when, in 1884, he accepted, jointly with M. Ritt, the management of the famous institution; on the appointment of M. Bertrand as successor to Ritt, in 1892, he retired, but joined Bertrand the following year as co-director; after the latter's death, in 1899, he remained sole director till 1907. His ad-

ministration was remarkably successful, considering both the novelties produced and the engagement of new singers (Melba, Eames, Bréval, Caron, Ackté, Alvarez, Saléza, Renaud, the 2 de Reszkes, etc.). Against violent opposition he introduced, and maintained in the repertoire *Lohengrin* (1895), *Die Walküre* (1893), *Tannhäuser* (1895; the first perf. after the notorious fiasco of 1861), *Meistersinger* (1897), *Siegfried* (1902). His son, **André Gailhard** (b. Paris, June 29, 1885; d. Ermont, Val d'Oise, July 3, 1966), composed the operas *Amaryllis* (Toulouse, 1906), *Le Sortilège* (Paris, 1913), and *La Bataille* (Paris, 1931), and the cantata *La Sirène.*

Gaillard, Marius-François, French composer and conductor; b. Paris, Oct. 13, 1900; d. Evecquemont (Yvelines), July 23, 1973. He studied with Diémer and Leroux at the Paris Cons. He began his career as a pianist; then started a series of symph. concerts in Paris, which he conducted from 1928 till 1949. He traveled all over the world, collecting materials of primitive music. His compositions follow a neo-impressionist trend.

WORKS: *La Danse pendant le festin* (1924) and *Détresse,* ballets (1932); 3 symphs.; *Guyanes,* symph. suite (1925); *Images d'Epinal* for Piano and Orch. (1929); Violin Sonata (1923); String Trio (1935); *Sonate baroque* for Violin and Piano (1950); *Concerto classique* for Cello and Orch. (1950); *Tombeau romantique* for Piano and Orch. (1954); *Concerto leggero* for Violin and Orch. (1954); *Concerto agreste* for Viola and Orch. (1957); Harp Concerto (1960); many songs and piano pieces.

Gaines, Samuel Richards, American vocal teacher; b. Detroit, April 23, 1869; d. Boston, Oct. 8, 1945. He studied composition with Goetschius and Chadwick; lived in Boston and Wellesley, Mass., as a teacher. He won several national and international prizes for his choral compositions.

Gaisser, Dom Ugo Atanasio (Josef Anton), German music scholar; b. Aitrach, Dec. 1, 1853; d. Monastery Ettal, March 26, 1919. He specialized in the study of Byzantine church music, on which he wrote a number of important studies.

WRITINGS: *Guido von Arezzo oder St. Mauro* (Aix-la-Chapelle, 1889); review of Jacobsthal's "Die chromatische Alteration im liturgischen Gesänge der abendländischen Kirche," *Revue Bénédictine de Maredsous* (1897–98); "Le Système musicale de l'Eglise grecque d'après la tradition," *Rassegna Gregoriana* (Rome, 1901); *Les "Hirmoi" de Pâques dans l'office grec* (Rome, 1905).

Gaito, Constantino, Argentine composer; b. Buenos Aires, Aug. 3, 1878; d. there, Dec. 14, 1945. He studied in Naples with Platania; lived in Buenos Aires as a teacher; wrote the operas (all produced at Buenos Aires) *Shafras* (1907), *I Doria* (1915), *I paggi di Sua Maestà* (1918), *Caio Petronio* (Sept. 2, 1919), *Flor de nieve* (Aug. 3, 1922), *Ollantay* (July 23, 1926), *Lázaro* (1929), and *La sangre de las guitarras* (Aug. 17, 1932); the ballet *La flor del Irupé* (Buenos Aires,

July 17, 1929); oratorio, *San Francisco Solano* (1940); symph. poem, *El ombú* (1924); songs; piano pieces.

Gál, Hans, Austrian composer and music scholar; b. Brunn, near Vienna, Aug. 5, 1890. He studied at the Univ. of Vienna with Mandyczewski and Guido Adler; in 1919–29 he lectured at the Vienna Univ.; then went to Germany; was director of the Mainz Cons. in 1929–33; returned to Vienna in 1933; after the advent of the Nazi government, was compelled to leave Vienna in 1938, and settled in Edinburgh, where he became a lecturer on music at the univ. (1945-65) while continuing to compose. WRITINGS: *The Golden Age of Vienna* (London, 1948); *Johannes Brahms* (Frankfurt, 1961; Eng. trans., 1964); *Richard Wagner* (Frankfurt, 1963); *The Musician's World: Great Composers in Their Letters* (London, 1965; German trans., 1966); *Franz Schubert, oder Die Melodie* (Frankfurt, 1970; Eng. trans., 1974). WORKS: Operas: *Der Arzt der Sobeide* (Breslau, 1919); *Die heilige Ente* (Düsseldorf, April 29, 1923); *Das Lied der Nacht* (Breslau, April 24, 1926); *Der Zauberspiegel* (Breslau, 1930; also as an orch. suite); *Die beiden Klaas* (1933); 3 symphs. (1928, 1949, 1952); *A Pickwickian Overture* (1939); Violin Concerto (1931); Cello Concerto (1944); Piano Concerto (1947); *Idyllikon* for Small Orch. (1969); Triptych for Orch. (1970); 2 string quartets (1916, 1929); String Trio (1931); Piano Quartet (1915); Piano Trio (1948); Violin Sonata (1921); numerous choral works, sacred and secular. He publ. a manual, *Anleitung zum Partiturlesen* (Vienna, 1923; in Eng. under the title *Directions for Score-Reading,* 1924). BIBLIOGRAPHY: W. Waldstein, *Hans Gál* (Vienna, 1965).

Galajikian, Florence Grandland, American pianist and composer; b. Maywood, Ill., July 29, 1900; d. River Forest, Ill., Nov. 16, 1970. She studied at Northwestern Univ. and Chicago Musical College; her teachers were Oldberg, Lutkin, Rubin Goldmark, Carl Beecher, and Noelte. She toured as a pianist; composed a number of songs which enjoyed favor among soprano singers; she also wrote orch. pieces; her *Symphonic Intermezzo* was awarded the 4th prize of the National Broadcasting Co., and was performed by the NBC Symph. Orch. on May 8, 1932.

Galamian, Ivan, eminent American violinist and pedagogue; b. Tabriz, Persia, of Armenian parents, Feb. 5, 1903; d. New York, April 14, 1981. He studied violin in Moscow and later in Paris, where he took private lessons with Lucien Capet. In 1930 he settled in the U.S.; was on the staff of the Curtis School of Music in Philadelphia (1944–46); then joined the faculty of the Juilliard School of Music in N.Y. In later years he taught privately in his own apartment, and during the summer at the Meadowmount School in Westport, N.Y. Among his violin pupils were Pinchas Zukerman, Jaime Laredo, Michael Rabin, Paul Zukofsky, and Itzhak Perlman. He publ. *Principles of Violin Playing and Teaching* (Englewood Cliffs, N.J., 1962); *Contemporary Violin Technique* (N.Y., 1966).

Galeffi, Carlo, Italian baritone; b. Malamocco, June 4, 1882; d. Rome, Sept. 22, 1961. After private vocal studies, he made his debut at the Teatro Adriano in Rome in 1904. On Nov. 29, 1910, he made his Metropolitan Opera debut as Germont in *La Traviata;* sang there again in 1920–21; for many years was a member of La Scala in Milan (1912–38); he retired in 1954. He was renowned for his roles of Rigoletto, Boccanegra, and Nabucco in Verdi's operas. BIBLIOGRAPHY: A. Marchetti, *Carlo Galeffi: Una vita per el canto* (Rome, 1973).

Galeotti, Cesare, Italian composer; b. Pietrasanta, June 5, 1872; d. Paris, Feb. 19, 1929. He studied piano with Sgambati and composition with Guiraud at the Paris Cons. Several of his symph. works were performed in Paris; his opera *Anton* was staged at La Scala, Milan (Feb. 17, 1900). Another opera, *Dorisse,* was first given in Brussels (April 18, 1910).

Gales, Weston, American organist and conductor; b. Elizabeth, N.J., Nov. 5, 1877; d. Portsmouth, N.H., Oct. 21, 1939. He studied composition with Horatio Parker at Yale Univ. and organ with Gaston-Marie Déthier in N.Y.; held various posts as church organist in Boston; then took additional instruction with Widor and Vierne in Paris. Returning to America, he was active as a choral conductor. In 1914, he organized the Detroit Symph. Orch.; conducted it until 1917.

Galilei, Vincenzo, celebrated writer on music, father of Galileo Galilei, the astronomer; b. S. Maria a Monte, near Florence, c.1520; d. Florence, June (buried, July 2) 1591. A skillful lutenist and violinist, and student of ancient Greek theory, he was a prominent member of the artistic circle meeting at Count Bardi's house; his compositions for solo voice with lute accompaniment may be regarded as the starting point of the monody successfully cultivated by Peri, Caccini, etc., the founders of the "opera in musica." A zealous advocate of Grecian simplicity, in contrast with contrapuntal complexity, he publ. a *Dialogo ... della musica antica et della moderna* (Florence, 1581; to the 2nd ed. [1602] is appended a polemical *Discorso ... intorno all' opere di messer Gioseffo Zarlino da Chioggia,* which had appeared separately in 1589) and a *Fronimo. Dialogo ...* (in 2 parts: Venice, 1568 and 1569; new ed., 1584), all of considerable historical interest. Vol. IV of *Istituzioni e monumenti dell' arte musicale italiana* (Milan, 1934), edited by F. Fano, is devoted entirely to Galilei; it contains a large selection of music reprints from his *Fronimo. Dialogo* (lute transcriptions by Galilei and original compositions), *Libro d'intavolatura di liuto* (1584), *Il secondo libro de madrigali a 4 et a 5 voci* (1587), and a 4-part *Cantilena,* together with biographical details, list of works, notes about extant MSS, reprints, transcriptions, etc. His *Contrapunti a due* *voci* (1584) was edited by Louise Read (Northampton, Mass., Smith College Music Archives, vol. VIII, 1947).

BIBLIOGRAPHY: Otto Fleissner, *Die Madrigale Vincenzo Galileis und sein Dialogo della musica antica e moderna* (Munich, 1922).

Galin, Pierre, French music pedagogue; b. Samatan, Gers, 1786; d. Bordeaux, Aug. 31, 1821. He was a mathematics teacher at the Lycée in Bordeaux, and conceived the idea of simplifying music instruction by a method which he termed the "Mélo-plaste" and explained in his work *Exposition d'une nouvelle méthode pour l'enseignement de la musique* (1818; 2nd and 3rd eds., 1824 and 1831). The method attracted attention, and was energetically promoted by Chevé.

Galindo (Dimas), Blas, Mexican composer; b. San Gabriel, Jalisco, Feb. 3, 1910. He studied harmony, counterpoint, and fugue with Rolón, musical analysis with Huízar, composition with Chávez, and piano with Rodriguez Vizcarra at the National Cons. in Mexico City (1931–42); had special composition lessons with Aaron Copland at the Berkshire Music Center in Tanglewood, Mass. (1941–42); in 1934 he formed, together with Ayala, Contreras, and Moncayo, the Grupo de los Cuatro for the presentation of modern music (disbanded after a few years). He was a prof. of music and director of the National Cons. in Mexico City from 1942 till 1961; in 1955 became director of the orch. of the Mexican Inst. of Social Security; was pensioned by the government in 1965 and devoted himself mainly to composition thereafter. In his music he stresses native elements, while adhering to classical forms; in his later works he made use of electronic sound. WORKS: 7 BALLETS: *Entre sombras anda el fuego* (*Among Shadows Walks Fire;* Mexico City, March 23, 1940); *Danza de las fuerzas nuevas* (*Dance of the New Forces;* 1940); *El Zanate* (Mexico City, Dec. 6, 1947); *La Manda* (Mexico City, March 31, 1951); *El sueño y la presencia* (Mexico City, Nov. 24, 1951); *La hija del Yori* (Mexico City, 1952); *El maleficio* (Mexico City, Oct. 28, 1954). FOR ORCH.: *Sones de mariachi* (1940); 2 piano concertos: No. 1 (Mexico City, July 24, 1942) and No. 2 (Mexico City, Aug. 17, 1962); *Nocturno* (1945); *Don Quijote* (1947); *Homenaje a Cervantes,* suite (1947); *Astucia* (1948); *Poema de Neruda* for String Orch. (1948); *Pequeñas variaciones* (1951); *Los signos del zodíaco* for Small Orch. (1951); 3 symphs.: No. 1, *Sinfonía breve,* for Strings (Mexico City, Aug. 22, 1952); No. 2 (Caracas, March 19, 1957; shared first prize at the Caracas Festival); No. 3 (Washington, D.C., April 30, 1961); *Obertura mexicana* (1953); Flute Concerto (1960; New Orleans, April 3, 1965); *4 Pieces* (1961; Mexico City, Nov. 15, 1963); *Edipo Rey* (1961; incidental music for Sophocles' *Oedipus Rex*); Violin Concerto (1962; Mexico City, Sept. 13, 1970); *3 Pieces* for Clarinet and Orch. (1962); *Obertura* for Organ and Strings (1963); *3 Pieces* for Horn and Orch. (1963); Concertino for Electric Guitar and Orch. (1973; Mexico City, June 12, 1977); *En busca de un muro* (1973).

FOR VOICE: *Jicarita* for Voice and Orch. (1939); *Primavera,* youth cantata for Wind Orch. and Children's Chorus (1944); *Arrullo* for Voice, and Small Orch. or Piano (1945); *La Montana* for Chorus a cappella (1945); *A la Patria,* cantata (1946); *3 canciones de la Revolución* for Orch. and Chorus (1953); *Homenaje a Juárez,* cantata with Narrator (1957); *A la Independencia,* cantata (Mexico City, Nov. 24, 1960); *Quetzalcoatl* for Orch. and Narrator (1963); *Tríptico Teotihuacán* for Wind Orch., Indigenous Mexican Percussion Instruments, Chorus, and Soloists (Teotihuacán, Sept. 14, 1964); *Letanía erótica para la paz* for Orch., Organ, Chorus, Soloists, Narrator, and Tape (1963–65; Mexico City, May 2, 1969); *La ciudad de los dioses (Luz y Sonido)* for Orch., Chorus, and Narrators (1965); *Homenaje a Rubén Darío* for Narrator and String Orch. (1966); choruses; songs. CHAMBER MUSIC: Suite for Violin and Cello (1933); Quartet for 4 Cellos (1936); *Bosquejos* for Wind Instruments (1937); *2 Preludes* for Oboe, English Horn, and Piano (1938); *Obra para orquesta mexicana* for Indigenous Instruments (1938); Sextet, for Flute, Clarinet, Bassoon, Horn, Trumpet, and Trombone (1941); Violin Sonata (1945); Cello Sonata (1949); Suite for Violin and Piano (1957); Quintet for Piano and String Quartet (1960); *3 sonsonetes* for Wind Quintet and Electronic Sound (1967); String Quartet (1970); *Titoco-tico* for Indigenous Percussion Instruments (1971); *Tríptico* for Strings (1974). FOR PIANO: *Llano Alegre* (1938); *5 preludios* (1945); *7 piezas* (1952); Sonata (1976); numerous small pieces. FOR ORGAN: *Estudio* (1971). A list of his works up to 1965 is found in *Composers of the Americas,* vol. 11 (Washington, 1965).

Galkin, Elliott, American conductor, music critic, and educator; b. Brooklyn, Feb. 22, 1921. He studied at Brooklyn College (B.A., 1943); then served with the U.S. Air Force (1943–46); was stationed in France, and received conducting diplomas from the Paris Cons. and the Ecole Normale de Musique. Returning to the U.S., he studied at Cornell Univ. (M.A., 1950; Ph.D., 1960, with the dissertation *The Theory and Practice of Orchestral Conducting from 1752*). During 1955–56 he was an apprentice conductor with the Vienna State Opera; in 1956 he joined the faculty of Goucher College in Towson, Md.; named prof. there in 1964. In 1957 he joined the faculty of the Peabody Cons. of Music in Baltimore as a conductor; also wrote music criticism for the *Baltimore Sun.* From 1977–82 he served as director of the Peabody Cons. of Music.

Gall, Yvonne, French soprano; b. Paris, March 6, 1885; d. there, Aug. 21, 1972. The spelling of her original name was **Galle.** She studied at the Paris Cons.; made her debut at the Paris Opéra in 1908, and remained on its roster until 1935; also sang at the Opéra-Comique (1921–34). In 1918–21 she was a member of the opera in Chicago, then sang in San Francisco (1931). After her retirement, she taught voice at the Paris Cons. She was highly successful in the French and Italian operatic repertoire. In 1958 she married the French composer and conductor **Henri Paul Busser,** who although much older, outlived her and reached the age of 101.

Galla-Rini, Anthony, American accordionist and composer; b. Manchester, Conn., Jan. 18, 1904. He learned music from his father, a bandmaster; toured the U.S. and Canada from the age of 6, playing accordion, cornet, mandolin, piccolo, oboe, French horn, contrabassoon, euphonium, and sarrusophone, as well as several other instruments. He was the first accordionist to appear with an orch. in a concerto of his own composition (Oklahoma City, Nov. 15, 1941); invented many technical improvements for his instrument; was the first to omit the fifth in the dominant-seventh row. In 1921 he introduced the 160-bass system in an extended left-hand range model. He publ. a number of transcriptions of classical and popular music for accordion.

Gallay, Jules, French cellist and music publisher; b. Saint-Quentin, 1822; d. Paris, Nov. 2, 1897. A wealthy amateur, he became a good cello player and a zealous student of *lutherie* in all its forms; publ. the following valuable pamphlets: *Les Instruments à archet à l'Exposition universelle de 1867* (Paris, 1867); *Les Luthiers italiens aux XVIIᵉ et XVIIIᵉ siècles, nouvelle édition du "Parfait Luthier" (la Chélonomie) de l'abbé Sibire, suivie de notes sur les maîtres des diverses écoles* (Paris, 1869); a reprint of du Manoir's *Le Mariage de la musique avec la danse,* with historical introduction (Paris, 1870); *Les Instruments des écoles italiennes, catalogue précédé d'une introduction et suivi de notes sur les principaux maîtres* (Paris, 1872). As a member of the jury at Vienna, 1873, he edited the *Rapport sur les instruments de musique à archet* (Paris, 1875).

Gallenberg, Wenzel Robert, Austrian composer; b. Vienna, Dec. 28, 1783; d. Rome, March 13, 1839. He studied under Albrechtsberger; in 1803 he married Countess Giulietta Guicciardi (to whom Beethoven dedicated his Sonata No. 2, op. 27). In Naples, shortly thereafter, he made the acquaintance of the impresario Barbaja; wrote numerous successful ballets for him, and in 1821–23 was his partner when Barbaja was director of opera in Vienna. He attempted the management of the Kärnthnertor-Theater in 1829 but failed, and was obliged to return to Italy, rejoining Barbaja. He wrote about 50 ballets; a sonata, marches, fantasies, etc., for piano. On one of his themes Beethoven wrote a set of variations.

Gallès, José, Catalan organist and composer; b. Casteltersol, Catalonia, 1761; d. Vich, 1836. He was for many years organist of the Vich Cathedral; was ordained a priest. J. Nin publ. his Piano Sonata (1800) in the collection *17 sonates et pièces anciennes d'auteurs espagnols* (Paris, 1929).

Galli, Amintore, Italian composer; b. Talamello, near Rimini, Oct. 12, 1845; d. Rimini, Dec. 8, 1919. He

was a pupil of Mazzucato at the Milan Cons. (1862–67); was music editor for the publisher Sonzogno, and critic of *Il Secolo;* later edited *Il Teatro Illustrato* and *Musica Popolare.*
   WORKS: Operas: *Il corno d'oro* (Turin, Aug. 30, 1876) and *David* (Milan, Nov. 12, 1904); oratorios: *Espiazione* (after Moore's *Paradise and Peri*) and *Cristo al Golgota;* Goethe's *Totentanz* for Baritone Solo and Orch.; String Quintet; etc. He publ. *Musica e musicisti dal secolo X sino ai nostri giorni* (1871); *Estetica della musica* (1900); *Storia e teoria del sistema musicale* (1901); *Piccolo lessico di musica* (1902).

Galli, Filippo, celebrated Italian bass; b. Rome, 1783; d. Paris, June 3, 1853. He made his debut as a tenor in Naples in 1801; after an interruption caused by an illness, he returned to the stage as a bass in Venice in 1812, singing in the premiere of Rossini's *L'inganno felice;* his success was so great that Rossini wrote several other roles for him, including Fernando in *La gazza ladra* and the title role in *Maometto II;* Donizetti wrote the role of Henry VIII for him in *Anna Bolena.* He sang in London at the King's Theatre (1827 and subsequent years). His voice began to decline about 1840, and he abandoned the stage; was then active as a chorus master in Lisbon and Madrid; taught voice at the Paris Cons. (1842–48).

Galli-Curci, Amelita, brilliant Italian soprano; b. Milan, Nov. 18, 1882; d. La Jolla, Calif., Nov. 26, 1963. She studied in Milan and intended to be a pianist; graduated in 1903 from the Milan Cons., winning the first prize. She never took regular voice lessons, but acquired an excellent vocal technique by devising a unique method of self-instruction, listening to recordings of her own voice. She received advice from Mascagni and William Thorner. She made her debut in Trani as Gilda (Dec. 26, 1906), then sang in various opera houses in Italy and in South America (1910). She continued her successful career as an opera singer in Europe until 1915; after the entry of Italy into the war, she went to America; made a sensationally successful debut with the Chicago Opera Co. as Gilda (Nov. 18, 1916); she made her first appearance with the Metropolitan Opera as Violetta (Nov. 14, 1921); remained as a member of the Metropolitan until 1930; then gave concert recitals; eventually retired to California. She was married twice: to the painter Luigi Curci (1910; divorced 1920) and to **Homer Samuels,** her accompanist.
   BIBLIOGRAPHY: C. LeMassena, *Galli-Curci's Life of Song* (N.Y., 1945).

Galli-Marié, Célestine (née **Marié de l'Isle**), French dramatic mezzo-soprano; b. Paris, Nov. 1840; d. Vence, near Nice, Sept. 22, 1905. Her father, an opera singer, was her only teacher. She made her debut at Strasbourg (1859); sang in Toulouse (1860) and in Lisbon (1861). She sang *La Bohème* at Rouen (1862) with such success that she was immediately engaged for the Paris Opéra-Comique; made her debut there (1862) as Serpina in *La Serva padrona.*

She created the roles of Mignon (1866) and Carmen (1875).

Galliard, Johann Ernst, German oboist and composer; b. Celle, c.1680; d. London, 1749. He was a pupil of A. Steffani at Hannover. A skillful oboist, he went to London (1706) as chamber musician to Prince George of Denmark; succeeded Draghi as organist at Somerset House; in 1713, played in the Queen's Theatre orch.; in 1717–36, engaged in writing music for the stage productions at Covent Garden and Lincoln's Inn Fields. He last appeared as an oboist probably in 1722.

WORKS: Besides the music to numerous plays, masques, and pantomimes, he wrote cantatas, a Te Deum, a Jubilate, anthems, soli for Flute and Cello, etc.; set to music the *Morning Hymn of Adam and Eve,* from Milton's *Paradise Lost.* He also made some translations.

BIBLIOGRAPHY: *Dictionary of National Biography* (London, 1921–22); S. Lincoln, "J.E. Galliard and *A critical discourse," Musical Quarterly* (July 1967).

Gallico, Paolo, composer and pianist; b. Trieste, May 13, 1868; d. New York, July 6, 1955. At the age of 15, he gave a recital at Trieste; then studied at the Vienna Cons. under Julius Epstein, graduating at 18 with highest honors. After successful concerts in Italy, Austria, Russia, Germany, etc., he settled in N.Y. in 1892 as a concert pianist and teacher; toured the U.S. frequently as pianist in recitals and as a soloist with the principal orchs. He won the prize of the National Federation of Music Clubs in 1921 with his dramatic oratorio *The Apocalypse* (perf. by the N.Y. Oratorio Society, Nov. 22, 1922). His symph. episode, *Euphorion,* was performed in Los Angeles (April 6, 1923), N.Y., and Detroit; his Sextet was performed by the Society of the Friends of Music in N.Y. He also wrote an opera, *Harlekin;* piano pieces; and songs. His son, Paul Gallico, is a well-known writer.

Galliera, Alceo, Italian conductor; b. Milan, May 3, 1910. He was educated there; then appeared as opera conductor throughout Italy. He was artistic director of the Carlo Felice Opera in Genoa (1957–60); also conducted the municipal orch. in Strasbourg.

Gallignani, Giuseppe, Italian composer and writer on music; b. Faenza, Jan. 9, 1851; d. (suicide) Milan, Dec. 14, 1923. He studied at the Milan Cons.; was then choir leader at the Milan Cathedral; edited the periodical *Musica Sacra* (1886–94); was director of the Parma Cons. (1891–97); from 1897, director of the Milan Cons. He produced the operas *Il Grillo del focolare* (Genoa, Jan. 27, 1873), *Atala* (Milan, March 30, 1876), and *Nestorio* (Milan, March 31, 1888), which were unsuccessful; but his church music was greatly appreciated (particularly his Requiem for King Umberto I).

Gallo, Fortune, impresario; b. Torremaggiore, It-aly, May 9, 1878; d. New York, March 28, 1963. He studied the piano in Italy; migrated to the U.S. in 1895; first directed the tours of a number of famous bands (1901–9), then founded the San Carlo Opera Co. (1909); in 1920, brought Anna Pavlova and her Russian Ballet to America; in 1923, organized an opera season in Havana, Cuba; in 1925, was director of the tour of Eleanora Duse; in 1926, built and operated the Gallo Theater; in 1928, made a film version of *Pagliacci;* presented performances of operetta in N.Y. and elsewhere.

Gallois-Montbrun, Raymond, French violinist, composer, and administrator; b. Saigon, Aug. 15, 1918. He studied composition with Büsser, theory with Gallons, and violin with Touche at the Paris Cons.; won the Prix de Rome for his *Louise de la miséricorde* in 1944. He then toured throughout Europe as a violinist, and also played in Japan and Africa. In 1957 he became director of the Versailles Cons.; in 1962 was appointed director of the Paris Cons. His compositions include *Le Rossignol et l'empereur,* a chamber opera after Andersen (1959); *Symphonie japonaise* (1951); Violin Concerto (1957); Cello Concerto (1961); Piano Concerto (1964); chamber music.

Gallon, Jean, French composer and pedagogue; b. Paris, June 25, 1878; d. there, June 23, 1959. He studied piano with Diémer and theory with Lavignac and Lenepveu at the Paris Cons.; was chorus director of the Société des Concerts du Cons. (1906–14) and at the Paris Opéra (1909–14). From 1919 till 1949 he taught harmony at the Paris Cons. Among his pupils were Robert Casadesus, Marcel Delannoy, Henri Dutilleux, Olivier Messiaen, and Jean Rivier. He publ. harmony exercises for use at the Cons.; with his brother **Noël Gallon,** he composed several pieces of theater music, among them a ballet, *Hansli le Bossu* (1914); also composed some chamber music and songs.

Gallon, Noël, French composer, brother of **Jean Gallon;** b. Paris, Sept. 11, 1891; d. there, Dec. 26, 1966. He studied piano with I. Philipp and Risler; theory with Caussade and Lenepveu at the Paris Cons., and also with Rabaud. In 1910 he received the First Prix de Rome. From 1920 he was on the faculty of the Paris Cons. as an instructor in solfège, counterpoint, and fugue. As a composer, he was influenced by his brother, who was his first tutor in music; with him he wrote a ballet, *Hansli le Bossu* (1914); his own works comprise a few symph. pieces; Suite for Flute and Piano (1921); Quintet for Horn and Strings (1953); teaching pieces.

Gallus (also **Gallus Carniolus**), **Jacobus,** important Slovenian composer; b. Carniola (probably in Ribni-ča), between April 15 and July 31, 1550; d. Prague, July 24, 1591. His Slovenian name was **Petelin** (which means "cockerel"); its Germanic equivalent was **Handl,** or **Hähnel** (diminutive of Hahn, "rooster"); he publ. most of his works under the corresponding Latin name Gallus ("rooster"). As a master of polychoral counterpoint, Gallus was highly regarded in his time; he held several important positions as an organist and music director; was Kapellmeister to the Bishop of Olomouc and later was employed at the church St. Johannes in Vado in Prague. A number of his works were publ. during his lifetime. Of these there are several masses: *Selectiores quaedam Missae* (Prague, 1580), containing 4 books of 16 masses, from 4 to 8 voices; a modern edition by Paul A. Pisk was publ. in Denkmäler der Tonkunst in Österreich (Vienna, 1935; reprinted in 1959, 1967, and 1969); 4 books of motets were publ. in Prague in 1586–91 under the title *Opus musicum:* first part (1586) from 4 to 8 voices (exact title, *Tomus primus musici operis harmonium quatuor, quinque, sex, octo et pluribus vocum*); 2nd and 3rd were publ. in 1587, and 4th in 1591; 5 additional motets were printed individually from 1579 to 1614. *Opus musicum* was reprinted in a modern edition by Emil Bezecny and Josef Mantuani in Denkmäler der Tonkunst in Österreich (Vienna, 1899, 1905, 1908, 1913, 1917, 1919; all reprinted again in 1959); *Moralia 5, 6 et 8 vocibus concinnata,* originally publ. in 1596, was reprinted in a modern edition by Dragotin Cvetko (Ljubljana, 1968) and Allen B. Skei (Madison, Wis., 1970). His secular works include *Harmoniae morales* (Prague, 1589–90; modern ed. by Dragotin Cvetko, Ljubljana, 1966) and *Moralia* (Prague, 1596). A motet by Gallus, *Ecce quomodo moritur justus,* was borrowed by Handel for his *Funeral Anthem.*

BIBLIOGRAPHY: Paul A. Pisk, "Die Parodieverfahren in den Messen des Jacobus Gallus," *Studien zur Musikwissenschaft* (1918; pp. 35–48); Allen B. Skei, "Jacob Handl's *Moralia,*" *Musical Quarterly* (Oct. 1966); idem, "Jacob Handl's Polychoral Music," *Music Review* (May 1968); Dragotin Cvetko, *Jacobus Gallus, Sein Leben und Werk* (Munich, 1972).

Gallus, Johannes (Jean le Cocq, Maître Jean, Mestre Jhan), Flemish contrapuntist; d. c.1543. He was maestro di cappella to Duke Ercole of Ferrara in 1534 and 1541. Many of his pieces were publ. in collections and in a vol. of motets printed by Scotto (1543). He was long confused with Jhan Gero.

Galpin, Rev. Francis William, English writer on music; b. Dorchester, Dorset, Dec. 25, 1858; d. Richmond, Surrey, Dec. 30, 1945. He graduated with classical honors from Trinity College, Cambridge (B.A., 1882; M.A., 1885); received his music education from Dr. Garrett and Sterndale Bennett; held various posts as vicar and canon (1891–1921); Hon. Freeman, Worshipful Company of Musicians (1905); wrote many articles on the viola pomposa and other old instruments in *Music & Letters* and *Monthly Musical Record* (1930–33). A Galpin Society was formed in London in 1946 with the object of bringing together all those interested in the history of European instruments and to commemorate the pioneer work of Galpin; it publishes, once a year, the *Galpin Society Journal* (1948—).

WRITINGS: *Descriptive Catalogue of the Euro-*

pean Instruments in the Metropolitan Museum of Art, N.Y. (1902); *The Musical Instruments of the American Indians of the North West Coast* (1903); *Notes on the Roman Hydraulus* (1904); *The Evolution of the Sackbut* (1907); *Old English Instruments of Music* (1910; new ed., London, 1932); *A Textbook of European Musical Instruments* (London, 1937); *The Music of the Sumerians, Babylonians and Assyrians* (1937); *The Music of Electricity* (1938). Galpin was the editor of the revised and augmented ed. of Stainer's *Music of the Bible* (1913).

Galston, Gottfried, Austrian-American pianist; b. Vienna, Aug. 31, 1879; d. St. Louis, April 2, 1950. He was a pupil of Leschetizky in Vienna, and of Jadassohn and Reinecke at the Leipzig Cons.; in 1903–7, he taught at the Stern Cons. in Berlin. On his extended concert tours he proved himself a player of keen analytical powers and intellectual grasp; in 1902, he toured Australia; then Germany, France, and Russia; in 1912–13, he toured in America; toured Russia 11 times (last, in 1926); in 1921–27, lived in Berlin; returned to the U.S. in 1927 and settled in St. Louis. He publ. a *Studienbuch* (1909; 3rd ed., Munich, 1920); analytical notes to a series of 5 historical recitals.

Galuppi, Baldassare, Italian composer, called **Il Buranello** after the island of Burano, near Venice, on which he was born; b. Oct. 18, 1706; d. Venice, Jan. 3, 1785. He studied with his father, a barber and violin player; in 1722 he brought out at Vicenza an opera, *La fede nell'incostanza,* which attracted attention to his talent; he then studied under Lotti in Venice, and in 1729 produced his opera *Dorinda,* with G.B. Pescetti. He cultivated comic opera with such success as to earn the title of "padre dell'opera buffa." He was also a distinguished player on the harpsichord. In 1740 he was appointed maestro del coro at the Ospizio dei Mendicanti; in 1741–43, visited London; in 1748, returned to Venice, where he was 2nd maestro at San Marco; in 1762–64, was principal maestro there. From 1765 to 1768 he acted as maestro to the Russian court; taught many Russian singers and composers; Bortniansky, who later followed him to Venice, was one of his pupils; then he resumed his duties in Venice as maestro del coro. Galuppi wrote a prodigious amount of music: some 112 operas and 20 oratorios; also sacred music and 12 harpsichord sonatas.

BIBLIOGRAPHY: A. Wotquenne, "Baldassare Galuppi," *Rivista Musicale Italiana* (1899); F. Piovano, "Baldassare Galuppi, Note bio-bibliografiche," ibid., XIII/4 (1906), XIV/2 (1907), XV/2 (1908); A. della Corte, *L'opera comica italiana nel 1700* (1923); F. Raabe, *Baldassare Galuppi als Instrumentalkomponist* (Munich, 1926); F. Torrefranca, in *Rivista Musicale Italiana,* XVIII; Ch. Van den Borren, ibid., XXX; W. Bollert, *Die Buffo-Opern Baldassare Galuppis* (Bottrop, 1935); A. della Corte, *Baldassare Galuppi; Profilo critico* (Siena, 1948).

Galvani, Giacomo, noted Italian tenor; b. Bologna,

Nov. 1, 1825; d. Venice, May 7, 1889. He studied in Bologna with Gamberini and Zamboni; made his debut in *I Masnadieri* in Spoleto in 1849; subsequently sang in Bologna, Milan, London, Barcelona, and other cities with great success; after his retirement, he taught voice in Venice. He was acclaimed for his performances in the operas of Rossini and Donizetti.

Galway, James, Irish flute virtuoso; b. Belfast, Dec. 8, 1939. His first instrument was the violin, but he soon began to study the flute. At the age of 14 he went to work in a piano shop in Belfast; a scholarship enabled him to go to London, where he continued to study flute, and also took academic courses in music at the Royal College of Music and the Guildhall School of Music and Drama. He then received a grant to go to Paris to study with the celebrated flutist Jean-Pierre Rampal at the Paris Cons. His first professional job as a flutist was with the wind band at the Royal Shakespeare Theatre in Stratford-upon-Avon. He subsequently played with the Sadler's Wells Opera Co., the Royal Opera House Orch., and the BBC Symph. Orch.; then was appointed principal flutist of the London Symph. Orch., and later with the Royal Phil. As his reputation grew, he was engaged in 1969 by Herbert von Karajan as first flutist in the Berlin Phil., a post he held until 1975. Abandoning his role as an orch. flutist, he devoted himself to a career as a concert artist; in a single season, 1975–76, he appeared as a soloist with all 5 major London orchs.; also toured in the U.S., Australia, and the Orient, as well as in Europe. He became successful on television, playing his 18-karat-gold flute. He publ. *James Galway: An Autobiography* (N.Y., 1979) and *Flute* (London, 1982).
BIBLIOGRAPHY: W. Mann, *James Galway's Music in Time* (London, 1982).

Gamba, Piero, Italian conductor; b. Rome, Sept. 16, 1936. From a musical family (his father was a professional violinist), he was trained in music at home; his precocity was so remarkable that he was reportedly able to read an orch. score at the age of 8, and at 9 was actually allowed to conduct a regular symph. concert in Rome. He also composed. Unlike the talent of so many child musicians, his gift did not evaporate with puberty; he became a professional artist. According to ecstatic press reports, he conducted in 40 countries and 300 cities, so that his name became familiar to uncounted multitudes (including a billion people in China). From 1970 to 1981 he served as conductor and music director of the Winnipeg Symph. Orch., Canada; in 1982 he was appointed principal conductor of the Symph. Orch. of Adelaide, Australia.

Gamucci, Baldassare, Italian music scholar; b. Florence, Dec. 14, 1822; d. there, Jan. 8, 1892. He was a pupil of C. Fortini (piano) and L. Picchianti (composition). In 1849 he founded the Società Corale del Carmine, which later became the Scuola Corale, of the Music Inst. at Florence. He publ. several mono-

graphs on composers, and didactic manuals.

Ganche, Edouard, French writer on music; b. Baulon (Ille-et-Vilaine), Oct. 13, 1880; d. Lyons, May 31, 1945. He studied with Imbert, Henry Expert, and others in Paris. He devoted his life to the study of Chopin and publ. *La Vie de Chopin dans son œuvre* (1909); *Frédéric Chopin, sa vie et ses œuvres* (1913). He was also the editor of the Oxford edition of Chopin's works (1932).

Gandini, Gerardo, Argentinian composer and pianist; b. Buenos Aires, Oct. 16, 1932. He studied with Pía Sebastini, Roberto Caamaño, and Alberto Ginastera in Buenos Aires (1956–59); completed studies in Rome with Petrassi (1966–67). He taught at various schools in Buenos Aires, and in 1970 was appointed to the faculty of the American Opera Center at the Juilliard School of Music in N.Y.; has concertized widely, specializing in contemporary repertoire; founded the Group for Musical Experimentation in Buenos Aires.
WORKS: Piano Concerto (1960); Variations for Orch. (1962); *Concertino I* for Clarinet, String Trio, and Percussion, *II* for Flute and Instruments, and *III* for Harpsichord and Instruments (1962–63); *Música nocturna I* for Flute, Piano, and String Trio (1964), and *II* for Chamber Orch. (1965); *Cadencias I* for Violin and Chamber Orch. (1966), and *II* for Chamber Orch. (1967); *Mutantes I* for Chamber Orch. (1966); *Fuggevole* for Chamber Orch. (1967); *L'Adieu* for Piano, Vibraphone, 3 Percussionists, and Conductor (1967); *A Cow in a Mondrian Painting* for Flute and Instruments (1967); *Soria Moria* for Variable Instrumental Ensemble (1968); *Contrastes* for 2 Pianos and Orch. (1968); *Fases* for Clarinet and Orch. (1969); *Play* for Piano and an Instrument (1969); *Fantasie-Impromptu*, an "imaginary portrait of Chopin," for Piano and Orch. (1970); *Piange e sospira* for Flute, Violin, Clarinet, and Piano (1970); *Il concertino* for Flute and Instruments (1971); Guitar Concerto (1975; Washington, D.C., May 18, 1976).

Gandolfi, Riccardo (Cristoforo Daniele Diomede), Italian composer; b. Voghera, Piedmont, Feb. 16, 1839; d. Florence, Feb. 5, 1920. He was a pupil of Carlo Conti at the Naples Cons., then of Mabellini in Florence; was appointed inspector of studies at the Real Istituto di Musica in Florence (1869); chief librarian in 1889; was pensioned in 1912. He began as a dramatic composer, then turned to the larger instrumental and vocal forms, and finally abandoned composition altogether, devoting himself to historical studies, which won him distinction.
WORKS: Operas: *Aldina* (Milan, 1863); *Il Paggio* (Turin, 1865); *Il Conte di Monreale* (Genoa, 1872); *Caterina di Guisa* (Catania, 1872); *Messa da Requiem;* cantata, *Il Battesimo di S. Cecilia;* several overtures; chamber music.
WRITINGS: *Sulla relazione della poesia colla musica melodrammatica* (1868); *Una riparazione a proposito di Francesco Landino* (1888); *Commemorazioni di W.A. Mozart* (1891); *Illustrazioni*

di alcuni cimeli concernanti l'arte musicale in Firenze (1892); *Appunti di storia musicale* (1893); *Onoranze Fiorentine a G. Rossini* (1902).

Gange, Fraser, distinguished baritone; b. Dundee, Scotland, June 17, 1886; d. Baltimore, July 1, 1962. He studied in Dundee with his father; later was a pupil of Amy Sherwin in London; made his debut as a basso at the age of 16; toured England, Scotland, Australia, and New Zealand twice; taught singing at the Royal Academy of Music in London; in 1923, came to the U.S.; made his American debut in N.Y. (Jan. 18, 1924); from 1932 to 1946 was a prof. of voice at the Juilliard Summer School in N.Y.; from 1931 to 1957 taught at the Peabody Cons. in Baltimore. His repertoire included 40 oratorios and more than 2,000 songs; he presented in Baltimore a concert of songs on his 70th birthday, in 1956.

Ganne, Louis Gaston, French composer; b. Buxières-les-Mines, Allier, April 5, 1862; d. Paris, July 13, 1923. He was a pupil of T. Dubois, Massenet, and César Franck at the Paris Cons. He was conductor of the balls at the Opéra, and at the municipal Casino at Monte Carlo; wrote successful comic operas, ballets, and divertissements.
WORKS: Operas: *Rabelais* (Paris, Oct. 25, 1892); *Les Colles des femmes* (Paris, 1893); *Les Saltimbanques* (Paris, Dec. 30, 1899); *Miss Bouton d'or* (Paris, Oct. 14, 1902); *Hans le joueur de flûte* (his most successful operetta; Monte Carlo, April 14, 1906); *Les Ailes* (Paris, Sept. 1, 1910); ballets: *Au Japon* (1903; very successful) and *Kermesse flamande* (1917); many orch. dances, of which *La Czarine* and *La Tsigane* became favorites; the patriotic tunes *La Marche Lorraine* and *Le Père de la Victoire,* immensely popular in France; about 150 piano pieces.

Gänsbacher, Johann, Austrian composer; b. Sterzing, Tyrol, May 8, 1778; d. Vienna, July 13, 1844. He studied with Abbé Vogler (1803–4) and Albrechtsberger in Vienna (1806); visited Prague, Dresden, and Leipzig; then resumed study under Vogler, at Darmstadt (Weber and Meyerbeer were his fellow pupils). With Weber, he went to Mannheim and Heidelberg, and rejoined him later in Prague. In Vienna Gänsbacher also met Beethoven. He served in the war of 1813, led a roving life for several years, and finally (1823) settled in Vienna as Kapellmeister of the Cathedral. Of his 216 compositions (masses, Requiems, orch. works, piano pieces, songs, etc.), only a small part has been publ.
BIBLIOGRAPHY: C. Fischnaler, *Johann Gänsbacher* (Innsbruck, 1878); J. Woerz, *Johann Gänsbacher* (Innsbruck, 1894).

Gantvoort, Arnold Johann, Dutch musician; b. Amsterdam, Dec. 6, 1857; d. Los Angeles, Calif., May 18, 1937. He came to America in 1876; gave private lessons, and taught in various colleges; in 1894, became head of the dept. for preparing public-school music teachers at the College of Music in Cincinnati. He publ. *Familiar Talks on the History of Music* (N.Y., 1913), and a series of public-school music readers.

Ganz, Rudolph, distinguished pianist and conductor; b. Zürich, Feb. 24, 1877; d. Chicago, Aug. 2, 1972. He studied music assiduously, first as a cellist (with Friedrich Hegar), then as a pianist (with Robert Freund) in Zürich; he continued his piano study with his great-uncle **C. Eschmann-Dumur,** and also took composition lessons with Charles Blanchet at the Cons. of Lausanne; in 1897–98, he studied piano with F. Blumer in Strasbourg; and in 1899 took a course in advanced piano playing with Ferruccio Busoni in Berlin. He made his first public appearance at the age of 12 as a cellist, and at 16 as a pianist. In 1899, he was the soloist in Beethoven's *Emperor Concerto* and Chopin's E-minor Concerto with the Berlin Phil.; and in May 1900 the Berlin Phil. performed his First Symph. In 1901 he went to the U.S. and was engaged as a prof. of piano at the Chicago Musical College; between 1905 and 1908 he made several tours of the U.S. and Canada, and in 1908–11 toured Europe, playing 16 different piano concertos. After 1912 he divided his time touring in Europe and America; in 1921 he added one more profession to his career, that of a symph. conductor; in 1921–27 he was music director and conductor of the St. Louis Symph.; in 1938–49 he conducted a highly successful series of Young People's Concerts with the N.Y. Phil.; concurrently, in 1929–54 he served as director of the Chicago Musical College. He played first performances of many important works by modern composers, including Ravel, Bartók, and Busoni. In July 1900 he married **Mary Forrest,** an American concert singer. He was a highly successful pedagogue, and continued to teach almost to the time of his death, at the age of 95. Besides the early symph., he wrote a lively suite of 20 pieces for Orch., *Animal Pictures* (Detroit, Jan. 19, 1933, composer conducting); Piano Concerto (Chicago Symph. Orch., Feb. 20, 1941, composer soloist); *Laughter—Yet Love, Overture to an Unwritten Comedy* (1950); solo piano pieces; and a couple of hundred songs to words in German, French, Eng., and Swiss and Alsatian dialects. He publ. *Rudolph Ganz Evaluates Modern Piano Music* (N.Y., 1968).

Ganz, Wilhelm, German pianist; b. Mainz, Nov. 6, 1833; d. London, Sept. 12, 1914. He studied music with his father, **Adolf Ganz** (b. Mainz, Oct. 14, 1796; d. London, Jan. 11, 1870), and with Anschütz. He followed his father to London, where he appeared as a pianist; in 1856 he became accompanist to Jenny Lind. In 1879 he organized the Ganz Orch. Concerts in London, and gave first London performances of works by Liszt and Berlioz; many celebrated artists (Saint-Saëns, Pachmann, etc.) made their English debuts at his concerts. After the discontinuance of his enterprise, in 1883, he devoted himself mainly to teaching. He publ. *Memories of a Musician* (London, 1913).

Ganzarolli, Wladimiro, Italian bass-baritone; b. Venice, Jan. 9, 1936. He studied in his native city; made his operatic debut in Spoleto; in 1959 became a member of La Scala, Milan. In 1964 he made his debut at the Vienna State Opera; then sang at Covent Garden in London, in N.Y., and in Buenos Aires. In addition to the Italian repertoire, he gained recognition in the parts of Figaro and Leporello in Mozart's operas.

Garaguly, Carl von, Hungarian-Swedish violinist and conductor; b. Budapest, Dec. 28, 1900. He studied violin with Hubay in Budapest and with Marteau in Lichtenberg. He was then a violinist in the Berlin Phil. Orch.; in 1923 went to Sweden; in 1923–30 he was concertmaster of the Göteborg Orch.; then played the violin in the Stockholm Orch. From 1941 to 1953 he conducted the Stockholm Orch., and from 1953 to 1958 was conductor of the Bergen (Norway) Phil. He was artistic director of the Het Gelders Orch. in Arnhem from 1959 to 1970; from 1965 was conductor of the Sonderborg Symph. Orch.

Garant, Serge, Canadian composer; b. Quebec City, Sept. 22, 1929. He studied piano and clarinet in Sherbrooke and composition in Montreal with Claude Champagne. In 1951 he went to Paris to take a course in musical analysis with Messiaen. Returning to Canada in 1953, he worked as a pianist and music arranger; with the composers Morel and Joachim and the pianist Jeanne Landry he organized in Montreal a modern group, Musique de Notre Temps, dedicated to the presentation of new European and American music; in 1967 he was appointed to the music faculty of the Univ. of Montreal. His music is constructed with formal precision from given thematic, metric, and rhythmic elements, and developed along classical lines.
WORKS: *Musique* for Saxophone and Winds (1948–50); *Pièces* for 4 Saxophones (1948); Piano Sonatina (1948); *2 pièces pour piano* (1953, 1962); Piano Variations (1954); *Musique pour la mort d'un poète* for Piano and Strings (1954); *Nucléogame* for Flute, Oboe, Clarinet, Horn, Trumpet, Trombone, Piano, and Tape (1955); *Canon VI* for 10 Players (1957); a study on chance, *Pièces,* for String Quartet (1958); *Asymétries* No. 1 for Piano (1958) and No. 2 for Clarinet and Piano (1959); *Anerca (The Soul),* cycle for Soprano and 8 Instruments, to words of 2 Eskimo poems (1961; revised 1963); *Ouranos* for Orch. (1963); *Ennéade* for Orch. (1964); *Phrases I* for Mezzo-soprano, Piano, Celesta, and Percussion (1967); *Phrases II* for 2 Orchs. (1968; members of the orch. are instructed to recite texts from proclamations of Ché Guevara); *Amuya* for 20 Musicians (1968); *Jeu à quatre* for 4 Instrumental Groups (1968); a group of 5 works based on mathematical proportions taken from the theme of Bach's *Musical Offering: Offrande I* for 19 Musicians and Prerecorded Voice (1969; alternative title, *Cérémonial du corps;* Montreal, March 6, 1970), *Offrande II* for Orch. (Toronto, July 29, 1970), *Offrande III* for 3 Cellos, 2 Harps, Piano, and 2 Percussionists (1971), *Circuit I* for 6 Percussionists (1972) and *Circuit II* for 14 Players (1972); *Circuit III* for 18 Players (1973); *"... chant d'amours,"* video work with Chorus and Solo Cello (1975); *Rivages* for Baritone

and Chamber Ensemble (1976); songs, including *Cage d'oiseau* for Soprano and Piano (1962).

Garat, Pierre-Jean, famous French concert singer and teacher; b. Ustaritz (Bas-Pyrénées), April 25, 1762; d. Paris, March 1, 1823. His talent was discovered early, and he studied theory and singing with Franz Beck in Bordeaux; his father wished him to become a lawyer, and sent him to the Univ. of Paris in 1782. However, Garat neglected his legal studies, and, aided by the Count d'Artois, he was introduced to Marie Antoinette, whose special favor he enjoyed up to the Revolution. He earned his livelihood as a concert singer; accompanied Rode, in 1792, to Rouen, where he gave numerous concerts before being arrested as a suspect during the Terror; subsequently he went to Hamburg. He returned to Paris in 1794, and sang (1795) at the Feydeau Concerts, where his triumphs speedily procured him a professorship of singing in the newly established Cons.. For 20 years longer, his fine tenor-baritone voice, trained to perfection, made him the foremost singer on the French concert stage. Nourrit, Levasseur, and Ponchard were his pupils.
BIBLIOGRAPHY: Paul Lafond, *Garat* (Paris, 1899); B. Miall, *Pierre Garat, Singer and Exquisite; His Life and His World* (London, 1913); Isidoro de Fagoaga, *Pedro Garat, El Orfeo de Francia* (Buenos Aires, 1948).

Garaudé, Alexis de, French singer and composer; b. Nancy, March 21, 1779; d. Paris, March 23, 1852. He studied theory under Cambini and Reicha, and singing under Crescentini and Garat; was a singer in the royal choir in 1808–30 and prof. of singing in the Cons. in 1816–41. He publ. 3 string quintets; many ensemble pieces for violin, flute, clarinet, and cello; sonatas and variations for piano; a solemn Mass; vocalises, arias, duets, and songs; also a *Méthode de chant* (1809, op. 25; 2nd revised ed. as *Méthode complète de chant,* op. 40); *Solfège, ou Méthode de musique; Méthode complète de piano;* and *L'Harmonie rendue facile, ou Théorie pratique de cette science* (1835). He also arranged the vocal scores of Meyerbeer's *Le Prophète* and other operas.

Garay Narciso, Panamanian violinist, composer, and diplomat; b. Panama, June 12, 1876; d. there, March 27, 1953. He studied at the Brussels Cons., graduating with a Premier Prix; later he attended courses at the Schola Cantorum in Paris. He publ. a Violin Sonata and a valuable treatise on Panamanian folk music, *Tradiciones y cantares de Panama* (1930). He also occupied diplomatic posts and at one time was Minister of Foreign Affairs.

Garbin, Edoardo, Italian tenor; b. Padua, March 12, 1865; d. Brescia, April 12, 1943. He studied with Alberto Selva and Vittorio Orefice in Milan; made his debut in 1891 in Vicenza as Alvaro in *La forza del destino;* also sang in Milan (Teatro dal Verme), Naples, and Genoa; in 1893 he created the role of Fenton in Verdi's *Falstaff* at La Scala in Milan; made guest appearances in Rome, Vienna, Berlin,

London, Russia, and South America. He married the soprano **Adelina Stehle**. He was particularly distinguished in *verismo* roles.

Garbousova, Raya, brilliant Russian cellist; b. Tiflis, Oct. 10, 1905. She studied at the Cons. there, graduating in 1923; later studied with Hugo Becker, Felix Salmond, and Pablo Casals. After many concerts in Europe, she settled in the U.S. (1927); appeared as a soloist with major American orchs. She played the first performance of the Cello Concerto by Samuel Barber (Boston, April 5, 1946) and the Cello Concerto by Rieti (1960).

Garbuzov, Nicolai, eminent Russian musicologist; b. Moscow, July 5, 1880; d. there, May 3, 1955. He studied with Koreshchenko and Kastalsky at the Moscow Phil. Inst.; from 1921 to 1931 was director of the State Inst. for Musicology; from 1923 to 1951 was instructor at the State Academy of the Arts, in the dept. of acoustics; publ. the manual *Musical Acoustics* (Moscow, 1940) and numerous articles in which he derived the laws of harmony from acoustical phenomena.

García Estrada. See **Estrada, García.**

García, Eugénie, French soprano, wife and pupil of **Manuel García;** b. Paris, 1818; d. there, Aug. 12, 1880. She sang for several years in Italian theaters, then at the Opéra-Comique in Paris (1840) and in London (1842); finally, after separating from her husband, she lived as a singing teacher in Paris.

García, Francisco Javier (**Padre García,** called in Rome "lo Spagnoletto"), Spanish composer of church music; b. Nalda, 1731; d. Saragossa, Feb. 26, 1809. He lived for some years in Rome as a student and singing teacher; in 1756 he was appointed maestro at Saragossa Cathedral. His works show a marked contrast to the fugal style prevailing before, being more natural and simple. He wrote an oratorio, *Tobia* (1773); the operas *La finta schiava* (Rome, 1754), *Pompeo Magno in Armenia* (Rome, 1755), *La Pupilla* (Rome, 1755), *Lo Scultore deluso* (Rome, 1756); masses; motets, chiefly in 8 parts. His most noted pupil was Caterina Gabrielli.

Garcia, Jerry, American rock musician; b. San Francisco, Aug. 1, 1942. He was a school dropout, and served in the U.S. Army before associating himself with various rock groups, especially those cultivating the new electronic sound. Garcia's most successful creation was a group bearing the puzzling name "The Grateful Dead." (One theory is that the name was taken from signs on trucks: "Grateful, for proper passing on the left, and Dead, for illegal passing on the right.") He engaged a harmonica player named **"Pig Pen" McKernan** (b. San Bruno, Calif., Sept. 8, 1945; d. of drug-cum-alcohol ingestion, in Marin County, Calif., March 8, 1973), and also brought in a violinist named **Phil Lesh** (b. Berkeley, Calif., March 15, 1940); another acquisi-

tion was a keyboard player who doubled as a vocalist, **Keith Godchaux** (b. San Francisco, July 19, 1948; d. an unnatural death, Ross, Calif., July 23, 1980). The immediate predecessor of The Grateful Dead was a group named the Warlocks. The mortuary connotations of the group continued with such albums as *Workingman's Dead,* but there were also in its repertoire some antonyms, such as *American Beauty.* Garcia's innovative use of electronic amplification established a state of the art for clean, loud, psychedelic rock sound. The Grateful Dead made so much money that they could make a sensational tour to Egypt to play at the foot of the Pyramids for the benefit of the mummified ungrateful dead once buried there, and incidentally contributed funds to the Egyptian Department of Antiquities.

García, Manuel (del Popolo Vicente Rodriguez), famous Spanish tenor, singing teacher, and dramatic composer; b. Seville, Jan. 21, 1775; d. Paris, June 9, 1832. A chorister in the Seville Cathedral at 6, he was taught by Ripa and Almarcha, and at 17 was already well known as a singer, composer, and conductor. After singing in Cadiz, Madrid, and Málaga, he proceeded (1807) to Paris, and sang to enthusiastic audiences at the Théâtre-Italien; in 1809, at his benefit, he sang his own monodrama *El poeta calculista* with extraordinary success. From 1811 to 1816 he was in Italy. On his return to Paris, his disgust at the machinations of Catalani, the manageress of the Théâtre-Italien, caused him to break his engagement and go to London (1817), where his triumphs were repeated. In 1819–24 he was again the idol of the Parisians at the Théâtre-Italien; sang as first tenor at the Royal Opera in London (1824) and in 1825 embarked for N.Y. with his wife, his son Manuel, and his daughter Maria (Malibran), and the distinguished artists Crivelli *fils,* Angrisani, Barbieri, and de Rosich; from Nov. 29, 1825, to Sept. 30, 1826, they gave 79 performances at the Park and Bowery theaters in N.Y.; the troupe then spent 18 months in Mexico. García returned to Paris, and devoted himself to teaching and composition. His operas, all forgotten, comprise 17 in Spanish, 18 in Italian, and 8 in French, besides a number never performed, and numerous ballets. He was a preeminently successful teacher; his 2 daughters, Mme. Malibran and Pauline Viardot-García, as well as Nourrit, Rimbault, and Favelli, were a few of his best pupils.

BIBLIOGRAPHY: G. Malvern, *The Great Garcías* (N.Y., 1958).

García, Manuel Patricio Rodriguez, distinguished Spanish vocal teacher, son of preceding; b. Madrid, March 17, 1805; d. London, July 1, 1906 (aged 101). He was intended to be a stage singer; in 1825 went to N.Y. with his father, but in 1829 adopted the vocation of a singing teacher (in Paris), with conspicuous success. An exponent of his father's method, he also carefully investigated the functions of the vocal organs; invented the laryngoscope, for which the Königsberg Univ. made him a Dr.Phil. In 1840 he sent to the Academy a *Mémoire sur la voix* *humaine,* a statement of the conclusions arrived at by various investigators, with his own comments. He was appointed prof. at the Paris Cons. in 1847, but resigned in 1848 to accept a similar position at the London Royal Academy of Music, where he taught uninterruptedly from Nov. 10, 1848, until 1895. Among García's pupils were his wife, Eugénie, Jenny Lind, Henriette Nissen, and Stockhausen. His *Traité complet de l'art du chant* was publ. in 1847 (Eng. ed., 1870; revised ed. by García's grandson, **Albert García** as *García's Treatise on the Art of Singing,* London, 1924). He also publ. (in Eng.) a manual, *Hints on Singing* (London, 1894).

BIBLIOGRAPHY: M. Sterling Mackinlay, *García, the Centenarian, and His Time* (Edinburgh, 1908); J.M. Levien, *The García Family* (London, 1932); G. Malvern, *The Great Garcías* (N.Y., 1958).

García, Pauline Viardot-. See **Viardot-García, Pauline.**

García Mansilla, Eduardo, American-born French-Argentine composer; b. Washington, D.C., March 7, 1870; d. Paris, May 9, 1930. He was in the diplomatic service, and traveled widely; studied composition with Massenet, Saint-Saëns, and Vincent d'Indy in Paris and with Rimsky-Korsakov in St. Petersburg. His opera *Ivan* was produced in St. Petersburg in 1905, and another opera, *La angelica Manuelite,* in Buenos Aires in 1917. He also wrote choruses.

Gardano, Antonio, one of the earliest and most celebrated Italian music-printers; b. 1509; d. Venice, Oct. 28, 1569. From 1537 he reprinted many current publications as well as important novelties, and compositions of his own, e.g., *Motetti del frutto* (1538) and *Canzoni franzese* (1539). His works also appeared in various collections of the time. After 1569 his sons **Alessandro** and **Angelo** carried on the business till 1575, when they separated; the former later set up for himself in Rome (1582–91), while the latter remained in Venice till his death (1610); his heirs continued publishing under his name till 1677.

Gardel, Carlos, Uruguayan popular singer; b. Tacuarembó, Dec. 11, 1887; d. in an aerial accident, Medellín, Colombia, June 24, 1935. His early years are a matter of conjecture; he apparently was a natural son of Berthe Gardés of Toulouse, France. The identity of his father is concealed in the self-generated mist of fearful illegitimacy; he could have been a Frenchman, or a Uruguayan army colonel named Carlos Escayola; earnest genealogists are at sixes and sevens about this weighty problem. However that might be, Gardel became popular in Argentina as a singer at carnivals around Montevideo and Buenos Aires. In 1912 he formed with Francisco Martino and José Razzano a vocal trio in a repertoire of native songs. Gardel was a pioneer in performances of tangos, which before him were considered unfit for public presentation. He further appeared in Paris, Madrid, and Barcelona. In 1934 and 1935 he sang in the musicals *El Tango en Broadway* and *Tango Bar* in N.Y.

BIBLIOGRAPHY: F.G. Jiménez, *Vida de Carlos Gardel* (Buenos Aires, 1936).

Gardelli, Lamberto, distinguished Italian conductor; b. Venice, Nov. 8, 1915. He studied at the Liceo Musicale Rossini in Pesaro; after a brief career as a concert pianist he went to Stockholm as a guest conductor of symph. concerts there (1946–55). He then conducted concerts of the Danish State Radio Symph. Orch. in Copenhagen (1955–61); in 1973 was appointed a regular conductor of the Royal Opera in Copenhagen.

Garden, Mary, celebrated operatic soprano; b. Aberdeen, Scotland, Feb. 20, 1874; d. Inverurie, Scotland, Jan. 3, 1967. She came to the U.S. as a child; lived in Hartford, Conn., and then in Chicago. She studied violin and piano; in 1893 she began the study of singing with Mrs. Robinson Duff in Chicago; in 1895 she went to Paris, where she studied with many teachers (Sbriglia, Bouhy, Trabadello, Mathilde Marchesi, and Lucien Fugère). Her funds, provided by a wealthy patron, were soon depleted, and Sybil Sanderson, an American soprano living in Paris, came to her aid and introduced her to Albert Carré, director of the Opéra-Comique. Her operatic debut was made under dramatic circumstances on April 10, 1900, when the singer who performed the title role of Charpentier's *Louise* at the Opéra-Comique was taken ill during the performance, and Mary Garden took her place. She revealed herself not only as a singer of exceptional ability, but also as a skillful actress. She subsequently sang in several operas of the general repertoire; also created the role of Diane in Pierné's opera *La Fille de Tabarin* (Opéra-Comique, Feb. 20, 1901). A historic turning point in her career was reached when she was selected to sing Mélisande in the world premiere of Debussy's opera (Opéra-Comique, April 30, 1902); she also became the center of a raging controversy, when Maurice Maeterlinck, the author of the drama, voiced his violent objection to her assignment (his choice for the role was Georgette Leblanc, his common-law wife), and pointedly refused to have anything to do with the production. Mary Garden won warm praise from the critics for her musicianship, despite the handicap of her American-accented French. She remained a member of the Opéra-Comique; also sang at the Grand Opéra, and at Monte Carlo. She made her American debut as *Thaïs* at the Manhattan Opera House, N.Y. (Nov. 25, 1907), and presented there the first American performance of *Pelléas et Mélisande* (Feb. 19, 1908). She also undertook the performance of *Salome* at its 2nd production in N.Y. (Jan. 27, 1909). In 1910 she joined the Chicago Opera Co.; she became its impresario in the season 1921–22, during which the losses mounted to about $1,000,000. She sang in the first American performances of Honegger's *Judith* (Chicago, Jan. 27, 1927), Alfano's *Resurrection* (1930), and Hamilton Forrest's *Camille* (1930), an opera she commissioned specially. After 1930 she made sporadic appearances in opera and concerts;

in 1935, she gave master classes in opera at the Chicago Musical College; acted as technical adviser for opera sequences in motion pictures in Hollywood; in 1939 she returned to Scotland; made a lecture tour in the U.S. in 1947. With Louis Biancolli she wrote a book of memoirs, *Mary Garden's Story* (N.Y., 1951).

Gardes, Roger, French tenor; b. Paris, March 4, 1922. He sang in the chorus of the Opéra-Comique in 1950; in 1954, won first Grand Prix at a contest of tenors in Cannes, and was engaged as soloist at the Opéra-Comique (debut, Aug. 14, 1954, in *La Bohème*); subsequently sang tenor roles in *Lakmé, Eugene Onegin, Les Pêcheurs de perles,* etc.

Gardiner, Henry Balfour, English composer; b. London, Nov. 7, 1877; d. Salisbury, England, June 28, 1950. He was a pupil of Iwan Knorr in Frankfurt; taught singing for a short time in Winchester, but then devoted his whole time to composition. He was also an ardent collector of English folk songs; his own compositions reflect the authentic modalities of the English countryside. He wrote a *Phantasy* for Orch.; *English Dance;* Symph. in D; String Quintet; *News from Wydah* for Soli, Chorus, and Orch.; piano pieces; songs. His most successful piece was *Shepherd Fennel's Dance* for Orch.

Gardiner, John Eliot, English conductor; b. Springhead, Dorset, April 20, 1943. He was educated at King's College, Cambridge; while still a student there, he founded the Monteverdi Choir (1964); then went to France to study with Nadia Boulanger; upon his return to England, took postgraduate courses with Thurston Dart at King's College, London. He made his first major conducting appearance at the Promenade Concerts in London in 1968; also conducted at the Sadler's Wells Opera and at Covent Garden. He continued giving concerts with his Monteverdi Choir; also founded the English Baroque Soloists, a group which played works of the Baroque on original instruments. In 1980 he was appointed principal conductor of the Canadian Broadcasting Corp. Radio Orch. in Vancouver; in 1981 he served as artistic director of the Göttingen Handel Festival. He is credited with the discovery of the manuscript of Rameau's opera *Les Boréades* in Paris in 1971.

Gardiner, William, British writer on music; b. Leicester, March 15, 1770; d. there, Nov. 16, 1853. His father, a hosiery manufacturer, was an amateur musician from whom he acquired the rudiments of music. During his travels on the Continent on his father's business he gathered materials for a collection, *Sacred Melodies* (1812–15), adapted to English words from works by Mozart, Haydn, and Beethoven. His book *The Music of Nature* (London, 1832) enjoyed a certain vogue; he also publ. memoirs, *Music and Friends, or Pleasant Recollections of a Dilettante* (3 vols.; I–II, London, 1838; III, 1853); *Sights in Italy, with some Account of the Present State of Music and the Sister Arts in that Country* (London, 1847).

Gardner, John Linton, English composer; b. Manchester, March 2, 1917. He studied organ at Exeter College, Oxford, with Sir Hugh Allen, Ernest Walker, R.O. Morris, and Thomas Armstrong (Mus.B., 1939). In 1946–52 he was opera coach at Covent Garden; in 1953 was appointed instructor at Morley College; served as its director of music (1965–69); concurrently he was director of music at St. Paul's Girls' School in 1962, and taught at the Royal Academy of Music in London (from 1956); retired in 1975. His style is characteristically fluent and devoid of attempts at experimentation; modernistic devices are used sparingly. He was made a Commander of the Order of the British Empire in 1976.

WORKS: Operas: *The Moon and Sixpence,* after Somerset Maugham (London, May 24, 1957); *The Visitors* (Aldeburgh Festival, June 10, 1972); *Bel and the Dragon* (1973); *The Entertainment of the Senses* (London, Feb. 2, 1974); *Tobermory* (1976); for Orch.: Symph. (Cheltenham, July 5, 1951); *A Scots Overture* (London, Aug. 16, 1954); Piano Concerto No. 1 (1957); *Sinfonia piccola* for Strings (1974); *An English Ballad* (1969); *3 Ridings* (1970); Sonatina for Strings (1974); chamber music: *Rhapsody* for Oboe and String Quartet (1935); Oboe Sonata (1953); *Concerto da camera* for 4 Instruments (1968); *Chamber Concerto* for Organ and 11 Instruments (1969); sacred and secular choruses; piano pieces; songs.

Gardner, Samuel, American violinist and composer; b. Elizavetgrad, Russia, Aug. 25, 1891; d. New York, Jan. 23, 1984. He came early to the U.S. and studied violin with Felix Winternitz and Franz Kneisel; composition with Goetschius, and later with Loeffler in Boston. He was a member of the Kneisel String Quartet (1914); also played violin in American orchs. From 1924 to 1941 he taught violin at the Inst. of Musical Art in N.Y. He wrote a number of pleasant pieces: *Country Moods* for String Orch. (Staten Island Civic Symph., Dec. 10, 1946); a tone poem, *Broadway* (Boston Symph., April 18, 1930, composer conducting); his *From the Canebrake,* op. 5, no. 1, enjoyed popularity; he also publ. *Essays for Advanced Solo Violin* (1960).

Garfunkel, Art, American soft-rock musician, composer and singer; b. Forest Hills, N.Y., Nov. 5, 1941. With his classmate at high school **Paul Simon** he started a song duo and, at the age of 16, they produced together a fairly successful record, *Hey, Schoolgirl.* Their next common effort, *Sounds of Silence,* was a major hit when it was issued in 1966. They demonstrated their dual versatility by writing the soundtrack for the film *The Graduate,* which featured a song, *Mrs. Robinson,* destined to become very popular. Their album *Bridge over Troubled Water* was praised in pop circles; then the two went their separate ways in 1970. Art Garfunkel became interested in acting and appeared in *Catch-22, Carnal Knowledge,* and *Bad Timing/A Sensual Obsession,* giving vent to his latent instability by playing a crazed psychiatrist. Garfunkel was reunited with Simon in 1982, producing a fine album, *The Concert in Central Park*.

Gariel, Edoardo, Mexican music pedagogue; b. Monterrey, Aug. 5, 1860; d. Mexico City, March 15, 1923. He studied with Marmontel in Paris; upon his return to Mexico he occupied various teaching jobs (1887–1908). In 1915 he visited the U.S. From 1916 to his death he was in charge of the School of Theater Arts in Mexico City. He publ. *Nuevo sistema de armoniá basado en cuatro acordes fundamentales* (1916; also in Eng. as *A New System of Harmony Based on Four Fundamental Chords*).

Garlandia, Johannes de (sometimes called **Johannes de Garlandia the Elder** to distinguish him from a hypothetical Joh. Garlandia the Younger, proposed by H. Riemann on rather suppositional grounds), 13th-century writer on mathematics, theology, and alchemy; b. England, c.1195. He studied at Oxford; in 1217 went to Paris; joined the Crusade against the Albigenses; was probably still living in 1272. He is the author of several tracts on music, among them the *De musica mensurabili positio*, a valuable treatise on mensural music, 2 versions of which were printed by Coussemaker in his *Scriptores*, vol. I.; a modern edition was prepared by F. Reimer (Wiesbaden, 1972). There are altogether 4 works printed under his name in Gerbert and Coussemaker.
BIBLIOGRAPHY: H. Riemann, *Geschichte der Musiktheorie im 9.–19. Jahrhundert* (1898); L.J. Paetow, "The Life and Works of John of Garland," in *Memoirs of the Univiversity of California*, IV/2 (1927); R. Rasch, *Johannes de Garlandia en de ontwikkeling van de voor-Franconsiche notatie* (Brooklyn, N.Y., 1969; with summaries in Eng. and German).

Garner, Erroll, black American jazz pianist and composer; b. Pittsburgh, June 15, 1921; d. Los Angeles, Jan. 2, 1977. Completely untutored and unlettered, he composed tunes extemporaneously, singing and accompanying himself at the piano, with an amanuensis to put down the notes. He also played drums and slap-bass. His nervous rubato style won acclaim from the cognoscenti and jazz aficionados. Incredibly precocious, he played regularly over the radio station KDKA in Pittsburgh at the age of 7 with a group called the Candy Kids; as an adolescent, he played piano on riverboats cruising the Allegheny River; then was a featured piano player in nightclubs and restaurants. He went to N.Y. in 1944; formed his own trio in 1946. In 1948 he went to Paris; made further European tours in 1962, 1964, 1966, and 1969. His whimsical piano style especially appealed to French jazz critics, who called him "The Picasso of the Piano" and, alluding to his digital dexterity, "The Man with 40 Fingers." In 1971 the Republic of Mali issued a postage stamp in his honor. Among his own songs, the plangent *Misty* became greatly popular; many of his other songs (he composed about 200 of them) reflect similar wistful moods, exemplified by such titles as *Dreamy, Solitaire,* and *That's My Kick.*
BIBLIOGRAPHY: James Doran, *The Most Happy Piano* (1984).

Garratt, Percival, English composer; b. Little Tew Grange, May 21, 1877; d. London, April 16, 1953. He studied in Vienna, in Berlin, and at Marlborough College; toured Europe and South Africa; was accompanist of Clara Butt and Elman; composed many piano pieces (*Pageant Piece, Rondel, Night Piece, Arabesque, Helston Furry Dance, Mock Antiques,* and others); *Cherry-stones,* a children's musical play; *A Cartload of Villains,* 3-act pantomime.

Garreta, Julio, Catalan composer; b. San Feliu, March 12, 1875; d. there, Dec. 2, 1925. Entirely self-taught, he learned piano and composition. He wrote a great number of "sardanas" (the Catalan national dance); a friendship with Casals stimulated several larger works; his *Impressions symphoniques* for String Orch. was performed in Barcelona on Oct. 29, 1907. His *Suite Empordanesa* for Orch. received first prize at the Catalan Festival in 1920. He also wrote a Cello Sonata, a Piano Sonata, and a Piano Quartet.

Garrett, George Mursell, English composer and organist; b. Winchester, June 8, 1834; d. Cambridge, April 8, 1897. A pupil of Elvey and Wesley, he was assistant organist at Winchester Cathedral (1851–54); organist of Madras Cathedral (1854–56); of St. John's College, Cambridge (1857); organist to the univ., 1873, succeeding Hopkins. He took degrees of Mus.Bac. (1857) and Mus.D. (1867); also received the degree of M.A. *propter merita* (1878). From 1883, he was a univ. lecturer on harmony and counterpoint; also was an examiner in music at Cambridge Univ. He wrote 5 cantatas, 4 services, and other church music.

Garrido, Pablo, Chilean composer and ethnomusicologist; b. Valparaiso, March 26, 1905; d. Santiago, Sept. 14, 1982. He studied in Santiago; conducted concerts of Chilean music and gave lectures; publ. a valuable monograph, *Biografía de la Cueca* (Santiago, 1942). He composed an opera, *La sugestión* (Santiago, Oct. 18, 1961); a ballet, *El Guerrillero* (1963); *Rapsodía chilena* for Piano and Orch. (1938); Piano Concerto (1950); *Fantasía antillana* for Cello and Orch. (1950); *13 & 13* for String Quartet (1951); piano pieces and songs based on Chilean folklore.

Garrido-Lecca, Celso, Peruvian composer; b. Piura, March 9, 1926. He studied music theory with Andrés Sas and Rodolfo Holzmann in Lima; then went to Santiago, Chile, where he took courses in composition with Domingo Santa Cruz. In 1964 he received a Guggenheim fellowship. In 1967 he was appointed to the faculty of the Univ. of Chile.
WORKS: Sinfonia (first perf. at the Inter-American Music Festival in Washington, D.C., April 22,

1961); *Laudes* for Orch. (1963); *Elegía a Machu Picchu* (1965; perf. by the N.Y. Phil., March 23, 1967); *Música* for 6 Instruments and Percussion (1957); Divertimento for Wind Quintet (1965); String Quartet (1963); *Antaras* for String Nonet (1969); choruses; piano pieces; songs.

Garrison, Mabel, American coloratura soprano; b. Baltimore, April 24, 1886; d. New York, Aug. 20, 1963. She was a pupil of W.E. Heimendahl and P. Minetti at the Peabody Cons. (1909–11); then of O. Saenger in N.Y. (1912–14), and of H. Witherspoon (1916). She made her debut as Filina (*Mignon*) in Boston, April 18, 1912; was a member of the Metropolitan Opera from 1914 to 1921; made a world tour; in 1933 she taught singing at Smith College; then retired.

Gaspari, Gaetano, Italian historiographer; b. Bologna, March 15, 1807; d. there, March 31, 1881. He entered the Liceo Musicale in 1820; took first prize in composition in 1827. He served as maestro di cappella at various churches; then devoted himself to historical research.
WRITINGS: *Ricerche, documenti e memorie risguardanti la storia dell'arte musicale in Bologna* (1867); *Ragguagli sulla cappella musicale della Basilica di S. Petronio in Bologna* (1869); *Memorie dell'arte musicale in Bologna al XVI secolo* (1875); etc.
BIBLIOGRAPHY: F. Parisini, *Elogio funebre del professore Gaetano Gaspari* (1882).

Gasparini, Francesco, Italian composer; b. Camaiore, near Lucca, March 5, 1668; d. Rome, March 22, 1727. He was a pupil of Corelli and Pasquini in Rome, where he taught for a time; in 1701–13 was maestro di coro at the Ospedale della Pietà, Venice; became maestro di cappella at S. Lucina in Rome in 1717. In 1725 he was appointed maestro di cappella at the Lateran, Rome. Between 1702 and 1723 he produced about 50 operas at Venice, Rome, and Vienna, with great success; he also wrote masses, motets, cantatas, Psalms, oratorios, etc. His chief work was a method of thorough-bass playing, *L'armonico pratico al cimbalo* (Venice, 1708; 7th ed., 1802), used in Italy for nearly a hundred years. His most famous pupil was Benedetto Marcello.
BIBLIOGRAPHY: E. Celani, "Il primo amore di P. Metastasio," *Rivista Musicale Italiana* (1904).

Gasparo da Salò (family name, **Bertolotti**), Italian instrument maker; b. Polpenazzi (baptized in Salò, May 20), 1540; d. Brescia (buried, April 14), 1609. He came to Brescia in 1562, and settled there as a maker of viols, viole da gamba, and contrabass viols, which gained much celebrity; his violins were less valued. His pupils were his eldest son, **Francesco;** Giovanni Paolo Maggini; and Giacomo Lafranchini. Dragonetti's favorite double bass was an altered "viola contrabassa" of Gasparo's.
BIBLIOGRAPHY: V.M. Rhò-Guerriero, *Gasparo da Salò* (Rome, 1892); P. Bettoni, "Gasparo da Salò e l'invenzione del violino," *Commentari del Ateneo di Brescia* (1901); M. Butturini, *Gasparo da Salò:*

Studio critico (Salò, 1901); G. Bignami, "Gasparo da Salò," *Musica d'Oggi* (Feb. 1940); A.M. Mucchi, *Gasparo da Salò* (Milan, 1940).

Gasperini, Guido, Italian musicologist; b. Florence, June 7, 1865; d. Naples, Feb. 20, 1942. He was a pupil of Tacchinardi (composition) and Sbolci (cello); from 1902 to 1924 was librarian and a teacher of music history at the Parma Cons.; later, librarian at the Naples Cons. (1924–35); in 1908 he founded the Associazione dei Musicologi Italiani, one of the main purposes of which was the examination and cataloguing of all books on music and musical MSS in the Italian libraries; in 1909 it was affiliated with the Internationale Musik-Gesellschaft (as its Italian branch), and began issuing a quarterly *Catalogo delle opere musicali . . . esistenti . . . nelle biblioteche e negli archivi pubblici e privati d'Italia.*
WRITINGS: *Storia della musica* (1899; a series of 10 lectures); *Dell' arte d'interpretare la scrittura della musica vocale del Cinquecento* (1902); *Storia della Semiografia musicale* (1905); *I caratteri peculiari del Melodramma italiano* (1913); *Musicisti alla Corte dei Farnesi;* "L'art italien avant Palestrina," *Mercure Musical,* II, 6–8; *Noterelle su due liutiste al servizio di Casa Farnese* (1923).

Gassmann, Florian Leopold, important Austrian composer; b. Brüx, Bohemia, May 3, 1729; d. Vienna, Jan. 20, 1774. He learned to play the violin and harp from a local chorus master; at the age of 13 ran away from home, and reached Italy; there is no corroboration for the claim that he became a student of Padre Martini in Bologna. After living in Venice in the service of Count Leonardo Veneri, he was asked by the Austrian Emperor Francis I in 1764 to be theater conductor in Vienna. In 1772 he succeeded Reutter as court Kapellmeister, and founded the Tonkünstler-Societät for the relief of the widows and orphans of musicians. He was greatly esteemed as a teacher; among his students was Salieri. Gassmann's 2 daughters, **Maria Anna** (b. Vienna, 1771; d. there, Aug. 27, 1852) and **Therese Maria** (b. Vienna, April 1, 1774; d. there, Sept. 8, 1837), were opera singers. Gassmann was a remarkably prolific opera composer; he wrote about 25 operas, several of which were produced during his travels in Italy: *Achille in Sciro* (Venice, 1766), *Ezio* (Rome, 1770); his "dramma giocoso," *La Contessina,* was one of the earliest comic operas treating the social world of aristocrats and merchants. He further composed many cantatas, some 50 sacred works, numerous trio sonatas and quartets, and about 50 "symphonien" in the concertante manner, some derived from the instrumental portions of his operas. Mozart greatly appreciated some of Gassmann's chamber music. One of the symphs., in B minor, was edited by Karl Geiringer for Universal Edition (1933). *La Contessina* and a selection of Gassmann's sacred music are publ. in Denkmäler der Tonkunst in Österreich, vols. 42–44 and 83 (former nos. 21.i and 45).
BIBLIOGRAPHY: R. Haas and G. Donath, "F.L. Gassmann als Opernkomponist," *Studien zur Mu-*

sikwissenschaft (1914); F. Kosch, "F.L. Gassmann als Kirchenkomponist," ibid. (1927); E. Girach, *F.L. Gassmann* (Reichenberg, 1930); G. Hill, *The Concert Symphonies of Florian Leopold Gassmann (1729–1774)* (Diss., N.Y. Univ., 1975); idem, *A Thematic Catalogue of the Instrumental Music of Florian Leopold Gassmann* (Hackensack, N.J., 1976).

Gassner, Ferdinand Simon, Austrian violinist; b. Vienna, Jan. 6, 1798; d. Karlsruhe, Feb. 25, 1851. In 1816, he was violinist at the National Theater in Mainz; in 1818, he became music director at Giessen Univ., which in 1819 made him Dr.Phil. and lecturer on music. In 1826 he joined the court orch. at Karlsruhe, and afterward became teacher of singing and chorus master at the theater. In 1822–35 he publ. the *Musikalischer Hausfreund* at Mainz; he edited (1841–45) the *Zeitschrift für Deutschlands Musikvereine und Dilettanten.* He wrote *Partiturkenntniss, Ein Leitfaden zum Selbstunterricht* (1838; French ed., 1851, as *Traité de la partition*) and *Dirigent und Ripienist* (1846); contributed to the Supplement of Schilling's *Universallexikon der Tonkunst* (1842) and edited an abridgment of the entire work (1849). He composed 2 operas, several ballets, a cantata, songs, etc.

Gast, Peter. See **Köselitz, Heinrich.**

Gastaldon, Stanislas, Italian composer; b. Turin, April 7, 1861; d. Florence, March 7, 1939. At the age of 17 he began publishing nocturnes, *ballabili,* and other pieces for piano; was, for a number of years, music critic for the *Nuovo Giornale* in Florence. He wrote about 300 songs, some of which have had great vogue (*La musica proibita; Ti vorrei rapire; Frate Anselmo; Donna Clara*); he was fairly successful with his operas *Mala Pasqua* (Rome, 1890), *Il Pater* (Milan, 1894), *Stellina* (Florence, 1905), *Il sonetto di Dante* (Genoa, 1909), *Il Reuccio di Caprilana* (Turin, 1913). He also wrote marches for military band; a piano fantasia, *La dansa delle scimmie;* etc.

Gastinel, Léon-Gustave-Cyprien, French composer; b. Villers, near Auxonne, Aug. 13, 1823; d. Fresnes-les-Rurgis, Oct. 20, 1906. He was a pupil of Halévy at the Paris Cons., taking first Grand Prix de Rome for his cantata *Vélasquez* in 1846. A successful composer of operas, he produced *Le Miroir* (1853), *L'Opéra aux fenêtres* (1857), *Titus et Bérénice* (1860), *Le Buisson vert* (1861), *Le Barde* (Nice, 1896), and the ballet *Le Rêve* (Paris Opéra, 1890), besides other stage works: *La Kermesse, Eutatès, Ourania,* and *La Tulipe bleue;* also 4 oratorios and 3 solemn masses, orch. compositions, chamber music, choruses, etc.
BIBLIOGRAPHY: F. Boisson, *Léon Gastinel* (1893).

Gastoldi, Giovanni Giacomo, Italian composer; b. Caravaggio; d. 1622. In 1581 he was a singer at the court of Mantua; contributed part of the score of *L'Idropica,* produced in Mantua on June 2, 1608. In 1609 he was maestro di cappella in Milan. A number of his works were publ.: 4 books of madrigals (1588, 1589, 1592, 1602); 4 books of canzonette (1592, 1595, 1596, 1597); many individual pieces are reproduced in contemporary collections. His "balletti" (dance songs) are remarkable for their rhythmic vigor in folk-song style.
BIBLIOGRAPHY: A. Einstein, *The Italian Madrigal,* vol. III (Princeton, 1949). See also Denis Arnold's article on Gastoldi in *Die Musik in Geschichte und Gegenwart* and *The New Grove Dictionary of Music and Musicians* (London, 1980).

Gastoué, Amédée, French music scholar; b. Paris, March 19, 1873; d. there, June 1, 1943. He studied piano and harmony with A. Deslandres (1890), harmony with Lavignac (1891), then organ with Guilmant and counterpoint and composition with Magnard. From 1896 to 1905 he was editor of *Revue du Chant Grégorien;* in 1897 began to contribute to the *Tribune de St.-Gervais,* became editor in 1904, and, on the death of C. Bordes (1909), editor in chief and director; he was prof. of Gregorian chant at the Schola Cantorum from its foundation (1896); also music critic of *La Semaine Littéraire* in 1905; he was appointed advisory member of the Pontifical Commission of the Editio Vaticana in 1905. For many years he was organist and maître de chapelle at St.-Jean-Baptiste-de-Belleville, Paris, where he also gave concerts of works in the Palestrina style; was a lecturer at the Catholic Univ. and Ecole des Hautes Etudes Sociales; a laureate of the Académie des Inscriptions et Belles-Lettres; a Commander of the Order of St. Gregory the Great; in 1925, became a member of the Académie des Beaux Arts.
WRITINGS: *Cours théorique et pratique de plain-chant romain grégorien* (1904); *Historie du chant liturgique à Paris* (vol. I: *Des Origines à la fin des temps carolingiens,* 1904); *Les Origines du chant romain, l'antiphonaire grégorien* (1907); *Catalogue des manuscrits de musique byzantine de la Bibliothèque Nationale de Paris et des bibliothèques publiques de France* (1907; with facsimiles); *Nouvelle méthode pratique de chant grégorien* (1908); *Traité d'harmonisation du chant grégorien* (1910); *L'Art grégorien* (1911); *La Musique de l'église* (1911); *Variations sur la musique d'église* (1912); *Musique et liturgie. Le Graduel et l'Antiphonaire romain* (Lyons, 1913); *L'Orgue en France de l'antiquité au début de la période classique* (1921); *Les Primitifs de la musique française* (1922); *Le Cantique populaire en France: Ses sources, son histoire* (Lyons, 1924); *La Vie musicale de l'église* (1929); *La Liturgie et la musique* (1931); *Le Manuscrit de musique polyphonique du trésor d'Apt, XIVe–XVe siècles* (1936); *L'Eglise et la musique* (Paris, 1936). Gastoué ed. several vols. of ecclesiastical music, collected from old sources, and wrote articles on the subject.

Gati, Laszlo, conductor; b. Timisoara, Rumania, Sept. 25, 1925. He received his musical training at the Cons. and the Academy of Music in Budapest. He was a conductor at Hungarian Radio (1954–56); then left Hungary, eventually settling in Canada, where he founded the Montreal Chamber Orch. (1959). In 1967 he was named music director of the Victoria (B.C.) Symph. Orch., a post he held until 1979. In 1979 he became music director of the Windsor (Ontario) Symph. Orch.

Gatlin, Larry, American country-music singer and songwriter; b. Seminole, Texas, May 2, 1948. He was educated at the Univ. of Texas (1966–70); in 1971 he launched his career as a country-music artist, active mainly in Nashville; made numerous appearances as a singer with his brothers in a group dubbed Larry Gatlin and the Gatlin Brothers Band, which for a time enjoyed excellent success.

Gatti, Guido, eminent Italian music critic and writer; b. Chieti, May 30, 1892; d. Grottaferrata, near Rome, May 10, 1973. He was editor of *La Riforma Musicale* (Turin, 1913–15) and *Il Pianoforte* (Turin 1920–27), which changed its name in 1927 to *La Rassegna Musicale.* WRITINGS: *Guida musicale della Giovanna d'Arco di Enrico Bossi; Biografia critica di Bizet* (1914); "Figure di musicisti francesi," *Biblioteca della Riforma Musicale* (Turin, 1915); *Musicisti moderni d'Italia e di fuori* (Bologna, 1920; 2nd ed., 1925); *Le Barbier de Séville de Rossini* (Paris, 1925); *Debora e Jaele di I. Pizzetti* (1922); *Dizionario musicale* (in collaboration with A. della Corte; 1925; 2nd ed., 1930; revised ed., 1952); *Ildebrando Pizzetti* (Turin, 1934; in Eng., London, 1951); *Alfredo Casella* (with F. D'Amico; Milan, 1958); *Victor de Sabata* (Milan, 1958); contributed to *Grove's Dictionary;* wrote numerous articles for music magazines in Europe and America.

Gatti-Casazza, Giulio, Italian impresario; b. Udine, Feb. 3, 1868; d. Ferrara, Sept. 2, 1940. He was educated at the univs. of Ferrara and Bologna, and graduated from the Naval Engineering School at Genoa; when his father, who had been chairman of the board of directors of the Municipal Theater at Ferrara, accepted a position in Rome in 1893, Gatti-Casazza abandoned his career as engineer and became director of the theater. His ability attracted the attention of the Viscount di Modrone and A. Boito, who, in 1898, offered him the directorship of La Scala at Milan. During the 10 years of his administration the institution came to occupy first place among the opera houses of Italy. In 1908–35 he was general director of the Metropolitan Opera, and the period of his administration was, both artistically and financially, the most flourishing in the history of the house; he vastly improved the orch., chorus, and all the mechanical depts.; one of his first suggestions to the board of directors was to offer a $10,000 prize for the encouragement of native operatic composers (won by Horatio Parker with *Mona,* 1912); the doors were opened to American composers (starting with Converse, Damrosch, and Herbert), and eminent foreign composers

gladly accepted invitations to have the world premiere of new works take place at the Metropolitan (Humperdinck's *Königskinder,* Puccini's *Girl of the Golden West,* Granados's *Goyescas,* Giordano's *Madame Sans-Gêne,* etc.); the list of novelties produced is a long one, numbering 110 works; besides, there were noteworthy revivals of older works, e.g., Gluck's *Iphigénie en Tauride* (revised by Richard Strauss), etc. During this period, Giulio Setti was chorus master and set a high standard for the opera chorus. Gatti-Casazza procured the services of the best conductors available, bringing with him from La Scala the master Arturo Toscanini, and such able conductors as Polacco and Panizza. He resigned in 1935, Giulio Setti leaving with him, and went to Italy, where he lived in retirement. On April 3, 1910, Gatti-Casazza married the soprano **Frances Alda;** they were divorced in 1929; in 1930 he married Rosina Galli (d. April 30, 1940), premiere danseuse and ballet mistress.
BIBLIOGRAPHY: I. Kolodin, *The Metropolitan Opera, 1883–1935* (N.Y., 1936); Pitts Sanborn, *Metropolitan Book of the Opera* (N.Y., 1937). Gatti-Casazza's *Memories of the Opera* was posthumously publ. in Eng. in 1941.

Gatty, Nicholas Comyn, English composer; b. Bradfield, Sept. 13, 1874; d. London, Nov. 10, 1946. He was educated at Downing College, Cambridge (B.A., 1896; Mus.B., 1898); then studied with Stanford at the Royal College of Music; was organist to the Duke of York's Royal Military School at Chelsea; music critic of *Pall Mall Gazette,* 1907–14; also acted as assistant conductor at Covent Garden.
WORKS: One-act operas (all produced in London): *Greysteel* (1906); *Duke or Devil* (1909); *The Tempest* (April 17, 1920); *Prince Ferelon* (1921; received the Carnegie Award for this opera); *Macbeth,* 4-act opera (MS); *King Alfred and the Cakes; Ode on Time* for Soli, Chorus, and Orch., after Milton; *3 Short Odes;* Variations for Orch. on *Old King Cole;* Piano Concerto; Piano Trio; String Quartet; waltzes for piano; songs.

Gatz, Felix Maria, German conductor; b. Berlin, May 15, 1892; d. Scranton, Pa., June 20, 1942. He studied at the univs. of Berlin, Heidelberg, and Erlangen (Dr.Phil., 1917), and conducting with Nikisch and Paul Scheinpflug; in 1922–23, he was conductor of the Lübeck Civic Opera; in 1923–33, conductor of the Bruckner Society series with the Berlin Phil.; in 1925–34, was prof. of esthetics at the State Academy of Music, Vienna. In 1934 he settled in the U.S.; in 1934–36, was a prof. at Duquesne Univ., Pittsburgh; in 1936–37, was a visiting prof. at N.Y. Univ.; from 1937 was head of the music and art depts. of the Univ. of Scranton; he was also founder (1938) and conductor (1938–39) of the Scranton Orch.; publ. *Musik-Aesthetik grosser Komponisten* (Stuttgart, 1929), etc.

Gaubert, Philippe, renowned French conductor and composer; b. Cahors, July 3, 1879; d. Paris, July 8, 1941. He studied flute with Taffanel at the Paris

Cons.; in 1905, won the 2nd Prix de Rome; in 1919–38, was conductor of the Paris Cons. concerts; in 1920 was first conductor at the Opéra in Paris.

WORKS: Operas: *Sonia* (Nantes, 1913) and *Naila* (Paris, April 7, 1927); ballet, *Philotis* (Paris, 1914); oratorio, *Josiane* (Paris, Dec. 17, 1921). Symph. works: *Rhapsodie sur des thèmes populaires* (1909); *Poème pastoral* (1911); *Le Cortège d'Amphitrite* (Paris, April 9, 1911); *Fresques,* symph. suite (Paris, Nov. 12, 1923); *Les Chants de la mer,* 3 symph. pictures (Paris, Oct. 12, 1929); Violin Concerto (Paris, Feb. 16, 1930); *Les Chants de la terre* (Paris, Dec. 20, 1931); *Poème romanesque* for Cello and Orch. (Paris, Jan. 30, 1932); *Inscriptions sur les portes de la ville,* 4 symph. tableaux (Paris, Nov. 18, 1934); Symph. in F (Paris, Nov. 8, 1936); *Poème des champs et des villages* (Paris, Feb. 4, 1939); chamber music: *Médailles antiques* for Flute, Violin, and Piano; *Divertissement grec* for Flute and Harp; *Sur l'eau* for Flute and Piano; *Intermède Champêtre* for Oboe and Piano; Violin Sonata; songs; *Méthode complète de flûte* in 8 parts (1923); many transcriptions for flute of works by Mozart, Beethoven, Lully, Rameau, etc.

Gaudimel, Claude. See **Goudimel, Claude.**

Gauk, Alexander, Russian conductor; b. Odessa, Aug. 15, 1893; d. Moscow, March 30, 1963. He studied composition with Kalafati and Vitols, and conducting with N. Tcherepnin, at the Petrograd Cons., where he graduated in 1917; then conducted at the State Opera and Ballet Theater there (1920–31). He was chief conductor of the Leningrad Phil. Orch. (1930–34), the U.S.S.R. State Symph. Orch. of Moscow (1936–41), and the All-Union Radio Symph. Orch. of Moscow (1953–63). He also taught conducting at the conservatories of Leningrad (1927–33), Tiflis (1941–43), and Moscow (1939–63). His pupils included such distinguished conductors as Mravinsky, Melik-Pashayev, Simeonov, and Svetlanov. He championed the music of Russian composers; restored Rachmaninoff's First Symphony to the active Russian repertoire from orch. parts found in the archives of the Moscow Cons. He was also a composer; wrote a symph., a harp concerto, a piano concerto, and songs.

Gaul, Alfred Robert, English composer; b. Norwich, April 30, 1837; d. Worcestershire, Sept. 13, 1913. A chorister in the Cathedral at 9, he was apprenticed to Dr. Buck; was organist at Fakenham, Birmingham, and Edgbaston; graduated (1863) as Mus.Bac., Cantab.; became conductor of the Walsall Phil. in 1887, then teacher and conductor at the Birmingham and Midland Inst., and teacher at King Edward's High School for Girls and at the Blind Asylum.

WORKS: Oratorio, *Hezekiah* (1861); several sacred cantatas, some of which (*Ruth* and *The Holy City*) are popular in the U.S.; Passion music; the 96th Psalm; an ode, *A Song of Life;* glees; vocal trios and duets; songs and part-songs; etc.

Gaul, Harvey Bartlett, American conductor and composer; b. New York, April 11, 1881; d. Pittsburgh, Dec. 1, 1945. He studied harmony, composition, and organ in N.Y. with G.F. Le Jeune and Dudley Buck (1895); later (1906), in England, he studied composition with A.R. Gaul and Dr. Armes. In Paris he attended the Cons. and the Schola Cantorum; studied composition and orchestration with Vincent d'Indy, and organ with Widor, Guilmant, and Decaux (1910). He was conductor of the Pittsburgh Civic String Orch. and a member of the faculty of the Carnegie Inst. in Pittsburgh. He composed many choruses (*Appalachian Mountain Melodies, Prayer of Thanksgiving,* etc.), chamber music, songs, organ pieces, etc.; won prizes in various competitions with his songs.

Gaultier, Denis, famous French lute player and composer; b. Marseilles, c.1600; d. Paris, late Jan. 1672. He was active as a composer from about 1625 or 1630; was a lutenist in Paris in 1626. Much of his work is in the form of dance suites, each selection in the various groups bearing a descriptive title. As a composer, Gaultier developed a type of ornamentation which influenced the keyboard style of Froberger and Chambonnières. Among his pupils were Mouton, DuFaux, and Gallot.

WORKS: *La Rhétorique des Dieux,* a collection of 69 compositions (including some pieces by his cousin) compiled between 1664 and 1672 (facsimile reprint, together with transcription into modern notation, ed. by A. Tessier in *Publications de la Société Française de Musicologie,* vols. VI, 1932, and VII, 1932–33); *Pièces de luth* (publ. 1669; reprinted 1978); *Livre de tablature* (publ. by his widow and Jacques Gaultier, 1672; reprinted 1978); many other MSS in the Berlin, Vienna, and Paris libraries.

BIBLIOGRAPHY: O. Fleischer, "Denis Gaultier," *Vierteljahrsschrift für Musikwissenschaft,* II, 1ff. (with transcription of *La Rhétorique,* 1886; also publ. separately, Leipzig, 1886); L. de La Laurencie, "Le Luthiste Gaultier," *Revue Musicale* (1924).

Gauthier, Eva, soprano; b. Ottawa, Canada, Sept. 20, 1885; d. New York, Dec. 26, 1958. She studied voice in Ottawa and at the Paris Cons. with Frank Buels and Jacques Bouhy, later with Schoen-René in Berlin; in 1909, she made her operatic debut as Micaela in Pavia, Italy; in 1910, appeared at Covent Garden, London (Yniold in *Pelléas et Mélisande*); later devoted herself to a concert career; performed many works of contemporary composers; during her world tours she also made a study of Javanese and Malayan folk songs.

Gauthier-Villars, Henri (called **Willy**), French music critic; b. Villiers-sur-Orge, Aug. 10, 1859; d. Paris, Jan. 12, 1931. He was music critic for the *Revue des Revues* and a writer for the *Revue Internationale de Musique,* the *Echo de Paris* (over the signature "L'Ouvreuse du Cirque"), and other Paris papers. Several vols. of his numerous criticisms have been publ.: *Lettres de l'ouvreuse, Bains de sons, Rhythmes et rires, La Mouche des croches, Entre* *deux airs, Notes sans portées, La Colle aux quintes;* he also wrote a biography of Bizet (1912).

Gautier, Jean-François-Eugène, French composer; b. Vaugirard, near Paris, Feb. 27, 1822; d. Paris, April 1, 1878. He was a pupil of Habeneck (violin) and Halévy (composition) at the Paris Cons.; in 1848, became 3rd conductor at the Théâtre-Italien; also was a prof. of harmony at the Cons. and, in 1872, a prof. of history. He composed 14 comic operas; an oratorio, *La Mort de Jesus;* a cantata, *Le 15 août;* an *Ave Maria;* etc.

Gavazzeni, Gianandrea, Italian composer and conductor; b. Bergamo, July 25, 1909. He studied at the Santa Cecilia Academy in Rome (1921–24); then at the Milan Cons. (1925–31), where his principal teacher was Pizzetti. He then became engaged in musical journalism and in conducting; it was as a conductor that he became mostly known in Italy and abroad; he conducted concerts in England, Moscow, and Canada (1965–67). He was music director of La Scala, Milan, from 1965 to 1972; led the La Scala Opera in Moscow (1965) and in Montreal (1967); on Oct. 11, 1976, made his American debut at the Metropolitan Opera in N.Y.
    WORKS: *Concerto Bergamasco* for Orch. (1931); scenic melodrama, *Paolo e Virginia* (1932); ballet, *Il furioso nell' Isola di San Domingo* (1933); several orch. works and pieces of chamber music. He is also a prolific writer on music; among his publications are *Musicisti d'Europa* (Milan, 1954); *La casa di Arlecchino* (autobiographical; 1957); *Trent'anni di musica* (1958); *Le campane di Bergamo* (Milan, 1963); *I nemici della musica* (1965).

Gaviniès, Pierre, French violinist and composer; b. Bordeaux, May 11, 1728; d. Paris, Sept. 8, 1800. He learned to play the violin as a child in the workshop of his father, who was a lute maker. In 1734, the family moved to Paris. Gaviniès made his first public appearance in a Concert Spirituel at the age of 13; he reappeared at these concerts as a youth of 20; his success with the public was such that Viotti described him as "the French Tartini." From 1773 to 1777 he was director (with Gossec) of the Concert Spirituel. When the Paris Cons. was organized in 1795, he was appointed prof. of violin. His book of technical exercises, *Les 24 Matinées* (violin studies in all the 24 keys), demonstrates by its transcendental difficulty that Gaviniès must have been a virtuoso; he attracted numerous pupils, and is regarded as the founder of the French school of violin pedagogy. His original works are of less importance; he wrote 3 sonatas for violin accompanied by cello (publ. posthumously; the one in F minor is known as *Le Tombeau de Gaviniès);* his most celebrated piece is an air, *Romance de Gaviniès,* which has been publ. in numerous arrangements; he wrote further 6 sonatas for 2 Violins and 6 violin concertos, and produced a comic opera, *Le Prétendu* (Paris, Nov. 6, 1760).
    BIBLIOGRAPHY: C. Pipelet, *Eloge historique de Pierre Gaviniès* (Paris, 1802); L. de La Laurencie,

L'Ecole française du violon (Paris, 1923).

Gavoty, Bernard, French writer on music; b. Paris, April 2, 1908; d. there, Oct. 24, 1981. He took courses in philosophy and literature at the Sorbonne; also studied organ at the Paris Cons. In 1942 he was appointed organist at Saint-Louis des Invalides in Paris; in 1945 he became music critic for *Le Figaro,* under the nom de plume Clarendon, a position he continued to hold until his death. He publ. *Louis Vierne, Le musicien de Notre-Dame* (Paris, 1943); *Jehan Alain, Musicien Français* (Paris, 1945); *Souvenirs de Georges Enesco* (Paris, 1955); *Pour ou contre la musique moderne?* (with Daniel-Lesur, Paris, 1957); *Chopin amoureux* (with Emile Vuillermoz; Paris, 1960); *Vingt grands interprètes* (Lausanne, 1966; also in German); a number of lavishly illustrated monographs about contemporary artists, under the general title *Les Grands Interprètes* (Geneva, 1953, et seq.), containing biographies of Gieseking, Furtwängler, Menuhin, etc.; also made documentary films on famous musicians.

Gawronski, Adalbert, Polish pianist and composer; b. Seimony, near Vilna, April 27, 1868; d. Kowanónak, near Poznan, Aug. 6, 1910. He studied with Noskowski at the Warsaw Music Inst. and later, in Berlin and Vienna; then went to Russia, where he organized a music school in Orel, returning to Warsaw after a few years. He wrote 2 operas, *Marja* and *Pojata;* a Symph.; 3 string quartets; piano pieces; songs; etc.

Gay, John, English librettist of *The Beggar's Opera;* b. Barnstaple, Devon (baptized, Sept. 16), 1685; d. London, Dec. 4, 1732. The opera was brought out in London on Jan. 29, 1728, and was immensely popular for a century, chiefly because of its sharp satire and the English and Scots folk melodies it used. It has had a number of successful revivals. The government disliked *The Beggar's Opera,* and forbade the performance of its sequel, *Polly,* the score of which was printed in 1729. When *Polly* was finally performed in 1777 it was a fiasco, because the conditions satirized no longer prevailed.
    BIBLIOGRAPHY: *Dictionary of National Biography,* VII (reprinted Oxford, 1921–22); C.E. Pearce, *Polly Peachum: The story of "Polly" and "The Beggar's Opera"* (London, 1923); W.E. Schultz, *Gay's Beggar's Opera* (New Haven, Conn., 1923); O. Sherwin, *Mr. Gay; Being a Picture of the Life and Times of the Author of the Beggar's Opera* (N.Y., 1929); Cäcilie Tolksdorf, *John Gay's Beggar's Opera und Bert Brechts Dreigroschenoper* (Rheinberg, 1934); E. Gagey, *Ballad Opera* (N.Y., 1937).

Gay, Maria, Spanish contralto; b. Barcelona, June 13, 1879; d. New York, July 29, 1943. She studied sculpture and the violin, and became a singer almost by chance, when Pugno, traveling in Spain, heard her sing and was impressed by the natural beauty of her voice. She sang in some of his concerts; also with Ysaÿe in Brussels; made her debut there as Carmen (1902), a role that became her finest. She then studied in Paris with Ada Adiny, and when she returned to the operatic stage made an international reputation. After tours in Europe, she made her American debut at the Metropolitan Opera as Carmen on Dec. 3, 1908, with Toscanini conducting. She sang with the Boston Opera Co. in 1910–12 and with the Chicago Opera Co. from 1913 to 1927, when she retired from the stage. She and her husband, the tenor **Giovanni Zenatello,** whom she married in 1913, settled in N.Y.

Gayarre, Julián, famous Spanish tenor; b. Valle de Roncal, Jan. 9, 1844; d. Madrid, Jan. 2, 1890. His original name was Gayarre Sebástian. He studied in Madrid; attracted attention at his appearance at Covent Garden, in London, in 1877; continued to sing there until 1881, and again in 1886–87. He was generally regarded as one of the finest lyrico-dramatic tenors of his time, and was described by enthusiasts as having "the voice of an angel."
BIBLIOGRAPHY: F. Hernandel Girbal, *Julián Gayarre, El tenor de la voz de ángel* (1955).

Gaye, Marvin (Pentz), American black rhythm-and-blues singer; b. Washington, D.C., April 2, 1939; d. murdered by his father, a retired Pentecostal preacher, Los Angeles, April 1, 1984. The family name was **Gay,** but a mute "e" was added to the end to avoid the slang connotation of the original surname. He sang in the choir of his father's church, and also beat the drums at school. In 1956 he sang with the group called Rainbows, which split, and he joined a separate group, The Marquees, which later became the new Moonglows. In 1961 he was recruited by Motown in Detroit; he made duet recordings with Tammi Terrell, including *Ain't No Mountain High Enough* (1967); *Ain't Nothing Like the Real Thing* (1968). Among his early hits was *Heard it through the Grapevine* in 1968: his successful individual albums included *What's Going On* (1970) and *Midnight Love* (1983), on which he also performed almost every instrumental part. His career was broken up by his divorces (he was married thrice) and bouts with cocaine and other narcotics. Although he earned a sizable fortune, he squandered it; he was shot twice in the chest by his father during an altercation about money, and was pronounced D.O.A. at the hospital.

Gayer, Catherine, American soprano; b. Los Angeles, Feb. 11, 1937. She studied at the Univ. of Calif. at Los Angeles and in Berlin; made her operatic debut in Venice in 1961; then joined the Deutsche Oper in West Berlin; also made guest appearances in Vienna, Salzburg, and Milan. She excelled in the modern operatic repertoire.

Gayle, Crystal, American country-music singer; b. Paintsville, Ky., Jan. 9, 1951. Her real name was **Brenda Gail Webb;** her older sister is the country-music singer **Loretta Lynn.** They made concert tours together; later she sequestered herself and produced her first hit, *I'll Get Over You;* she followed it with another hit song, *Don't It Make My Brown*

Eyes Blue, which made the top listing on both country-western and pop charts. Her recordings also sold big.

Gaynor, Mrs. Jessie Smith, American composer of children's songs; b. St. Louis, Feb. 17, 1863; d. Webster Groves, Mo., Feb. 20, 1921. After studying piano with L. Maas and theory with A.J. Goodrich and A. Weidig, she taught in Chicago, St. Louis, and St. Joseph, Mo. Among her publ. works are *Songs of the Child World* (2 books) and *Playtime Songs,* and a children's operetta, *The House That Jack Built.*

Gaztambide, Joaquín, Spanish composer; b. Tudela, Navarre, Feb. 7, 1822; d. Madrid, March 18, 1870. He studied at Pamplona and at the Madrid Cons. with Pedro Albéniz (piano) and Ramón Carnicer (composition). After a stay in Paris, he returned to Madrid as manager of several theaters and as conductor of the Cons. concerts; he became director of the Concert Society in 1868. He was best known, however, for his zarzuelas, the satiric musical productions which are identified with the Madrid stage. Gaztambide wrote 44 zarzuelas, many of which became popular; one, *El juramento,* first produced in 1858, was revived in Madrid in 1933. He took a zarzuela company to Mexico and Havana in 1868–69.

Gazzaniga, Giuseppe, Italian opera composer; b. Verona, Oct. 5, 1743; d. Crema, Feb. 1, 1818. He was a pupil of Porpora in Naples; after the production of his early opera *Il Barone di Trocchia* there (1768), he traveled to Venice and to Vienna; his opera *Don Giovanni Tenorio* (Venice, Feb. 5, 1787) anticipated Mozart's *Don Giovanni;* in all he wrote 50 operas, several of which became quite popular at the time (*La locanda, L'isola di Alcina, La vendemmia, La Moglie capricciosa,* etc.). Mozart's librettist, Lorenzo da Ponte, wrote the libretto of Gazzaniga's opera *Il finto cieco* (Vienna, Feb. 20, 1786).

Gazzelloni, Severino, Italian flutist; b. Roccasecca, Frosinone, Jan. 5, 1919. He studied at the Santa Cecilia Academy in Rome, graduating in 1942; was then employed as an orch. musician; later launched a major career as a concert flutist. His repertoire ranged from the classics to works of the modern school.

Gebel, Georg (Jr.), German composer; b. Brieg, Silesia, Oct. 25, 1709; d. Rudolstadt, Sept. 24, 1753. He studied with his father; was organist at St. Maria Magdalene (1729) in Breslau, and Kapellmeister to the Duke of Oels. In 1735 he joined Count Brühl's orch. at Dresden, where he met Hebenstreit, the inventor of the "Pantaleon," and learned to play that instrument. In 1747 he was appointed Kapellmeister to the Prince of Schwarzburg-Rudolstadt. He was a precocious composer, and wrote a number of light operas (to German rather than Italian librettos, thus upholding the national tradition), and more than 100 symphs., partitas, and concertos.

Gebhard, Heinrich, pianist, composer, and teacher; b. Sobernheim, July 25, 1878; d. North Arlington, N.J., May 5, 1963. As a boy of 8, he came with his parents to Boston, where he studied with Clayton Johns; after a concert debut in Boston (April 24, 1896), he went to Vienna to study with Leschetizky. He gave first American performances of works by Vincent d'Indy; his most notable intepretation was Loeffler's work for Piano and Orch., *A Pagan Poem,* which he played nearly 100 times with U.S. orchs. His own works are also in an impressionistic vein: Fantasy for Piano and Orch. (N.Y. Phil., Nov. 12, 1925, composer soloist); symph. poem, *Across the Hills* (1940); Divertimento for Piano and Chamber Orch. (Boston, Dec. 20, 1927); String Quartet; *Waltz Suite* for 2 Pianos; song cycle, *The Sun, Cloud and the Flower;* many piano pieces. He also arranged Loeffler's *A Pagan Poem* for 2 Pianos. His book *The Art of Pedaling* was publ. posthumously with an introduction by Leonard Bernstein, who was one of his students (N.Y., 1963).

Gédalge, André, eminent French theorist, composer, and pedagogue; b. Paris, Dec. 27, 1856; d. Chessy, Feb. 5, 1926. He began to study music rather late in life, and entered the Paris Cons. at the age of 28. However, he made rapid progress, and obtained the 2nd Prix de Rome after a year of study (under Guiraud). He then elaborated a system of counterpoint, later publ. as *Traité de la fugue* (Paris, 1901; Eng. trans., 1964), which became a standard work. In 1905, Gédalge was engaged as a prof. of counterpoint and fugue at the Paris Cons.; among his students were Ravel, Enesco, Koechlin, Roger-Ducasse, Milhaud, and Honegger. He also publ. *Les Gloires musicales du monde* (1898) and other pedagogic works. As a composer, Gédalge was less significant. Among his works are a pantomime, *Le Petit Savoyard* (Paris, 1891); an opera, *Pris au piège* (Paris, 1895); and 3 operas that were not performed: *Sita, La Farce du Cadi,* and *Hélène;* he also wrote 3 symphs., several concertos, some chamber music, and songs.
BIBLIOGRAPHY: "Hommage à Gédalge," *Revue Musicale* (March 1, 1926), containing articles by Koechlin, F. Schmitt, Honegger, Milhaud, and others.

Gedda, Giulio Cesare, Italian conductor and composer; b. Turin, April 16, 1899; d. Callegno, near Turin, Sept. 7, 1970. He studied composition with Alfano in Turin; played cello and organ; began conducting in 1932; lived mostly in Turin. He wrote an opera, *L'amoroso fantasma* (Turin, 1933); 2 violin concertos (1930, 1954); a Viola Concerto (1940); Cello Concerto; Concerto for 4 Saxophones (1952). He ended his days in a mental institution.

Gedda, Nicolai (real last name, **Ustinov**), noted Swedish tenor; b. Stockholm, July 11, 1925, of Russian-Swedish extraction. Gedda was his mother's name, which he assumed in his professional life. His father was a Russian, Michael Ustinov, who fought in the White Army and emigrated after the

civil war; he then earned his living by singing in the Don Cossack Choir; later he served as chorus master of a Russian Orthodox church in Stockholm; Nicolai Gedda joined him in a children's chorus. In 1950 Gedda entered the opera school at the Stockholm Cons.; on April 8, 1952, he made a successful debut as the leading tenor in Adam's comic opera *Le Postillon de Longjumeau.* In 1953 he made his debut at La Scala in Milan; in 1954 he sang Faust at the Paris Opéra; then had an engagement at Covent Garden in London; in 1957 he sang Don José in *Carmen* at the Vienna State Opera. He made his U.S. debut as Faust with the Pittsburgh Opera on April 4, 1957; his Metropolitan Opera debut followed in N.Y. on Nov. 1, 1957; he created the role of Anatol in Barber's *Vanessa* at the Metropolitan on Jan. 15, 1958. Because of his natural fluency in Russian and his acquired knowledge of German, French, Italian, and English, he was able to sing with total freedom the entire operatic repertoire. In 1980 and in 1981 he made highly successful appearances in Russia, both in opera and on the concert stage, in programs of Russian songs.
BIBLIOGRAPHY: David Ewen, *Musicians since 1900* (N.Y., 1978).

Gedzhadze, Irakly, Georgian composer; b. Mtskheta, Oct. 26, 1925. He studied with Matchavariani at the Cons. of Tiflis; graduated in 1957. His works include the opera *Sunrise* (Tiflis, Nov. 23, 1961); *Lake Palestomi,* symph. poem (1956); piano pieces.

Geehl, Henry Ernest, English composer; b. London, Sept. 28, 1881; d. Beaconsfield, Buckinghamshire, Jan. 14, 1961. A pupil of R.O. Morgan, he was appointed a prof. at Trinity College of Music, London, in 1919. He has written a Symph.; Violin Concerto; Piano Concerto; pieces for brass band, including *Cornwall* and *Cornish Rhapsody;* pedagogic piano pieces; songs.

Gehlhaar, Rolf, Polish-American composer; b. Wroclaw, Dec. 30, 1943. He emigrated to the U.S. in 1953; studied at Yale Univ. (1961–65) and the Univ. of Calif., Berkeley (1965–67); was an assistant to Stockhausen in his course in new music in Cologne (1967–70). In 1974 he began teaching at the annual summer courses in new music in Darmstadt.
WORKS: *Cello Solo* (1966); *Helix* for Saxophone, Trombone, Double Bass, Piano, and Percussion (1967); Piano Pieces *1–1, 1–2* and *2–2* (all 1970); *Wege* for 2 String Instruments, Piano, and Electronics (1971); *Musi-ken* for String Quartet (1971); *Phase* for Orch. (1971–72; Saarbrücken, May 4, 1972); *Der gelbe Klang* for Small Chorus and Chamber Ensemble (1973); *Spektra* for 4 Trumpets and 4 Trombones (1973); *Tachys* for String Instruments (1973); *Solipse* for Solo Cello (1973); *Prototypen* for Orch. (1973); *Liebeslied* for Alto and Orch. (Graz, Austria, Oct. 9, 1974).

Gehot, Jean (also **Joseph**), Belgian violinist and composer; b. Brussels, April 8, 1756; d. in the U.S.

c.1820. He went to London after 1780; there he publ. *A Treatise on the Theory and Practice of Music* (1784), *The Art of Bowing the Violin* (1790), and *Complete Instructions for Every Musical Instrument* (1790). In 1792, he went to America; gave concerts in N.Y., where he presented his work *Overture in 12 movements, expressive of a voyage from England to America.* He then played violin at the City Concerts in Philadelphia, under the management of Reinagle and Capron. However, he failed to prosper in America; most of his works were publ. in London, among them 17 string quartets, 12 string trios, and 24 "military pieces" for 2 Clarinets, 2 Horns, and Bassoon.

BIBLIOGRAPHY: Some information on Gehot's life is found in J.R. Parker's "Musical Reminiscences," *Euterpiad* (Feb. 2, 1822). See also O. Sonneck, *Early Concert Life in America* (1907).

Gehrkens, Karl Wilson, American music educator; b. Kelleys Island, Ohio, April 19, 1882; d. Elk Rapids, Mich., Feb. 28, 1975. After graduation from Oberlin College (B.A., 1905; M.A., 1912), he became a prof. of school music at the Oberlin Cons. of Music in 1907; retired in 1942. He was editor of *School Music* from 1925 to 1934; co-editor, with Walter Damrosch and George Gartlan, of the Universal School Music Series, teachers' manuals for grade and high schools (1923–36); etc.

WRITINGS: *Music Notation and Terminology* (1914); *Essentials in Conducting* (1919); *An Introduction to School Music Teaching* (1919); *Fundamentals of Music* (1924); *Handbook of Musical Terms* (1927); *20 Lessons in Conducting* (1930); *Music in the Grade Schools* (1934); *Music in the Junior High School* (1936); with P.W. Dykema, *The Teaching and Administration of High School Music* (1941).

Geiger-Torel, Herman, German-born Canadian opera producer and administrator; b. Frankfurt, July 13, 1907; d. Toronto, Oct. 6, 1976. He attended Goethe Univ. in Frankfurt; in 1930 became an assistant to Lothar Wallerstein at the Salzburg Festival; then was a stage director in Germany, Austria, Czechoslovakia, and Switzerland (1930–37). In 1948 he settled in Toronto and joined the staff of the Royal Cons. of Music; in 1950 he organized the Canadian Opera Co. from the ranks of his students, and molded it into a professional company; in 1959 he became its general manager, a post he held until his retirement in 1975.

Geiringer, Karl, eminent Austrian-American musicologist; b. Vienna, April 26, 1899. He studied composition with Hans Gál and Richard Stöhr, and musicology with Guido Adler and Wilhelm Fischer in Vienna; continued his musicological studies with Curt Sachs and Johannes Wolf in Berlin; received his Ph.D. from the Univ. of Vienna with the dissertation *Die Flankenwirbelinstrumente in der bildenden Kunst (1300–1550)* in 1923 (publ. in Tutzing, 1979). In 1930 he became librarian and museum curator of the Gesellschaft der Musikfreunde in Vienna. He left Austria after 1938 and went to London, where he worked for the BBC; also taught at the Royal College of Music (1939–40); he then emigrated to the U.S.; was a visiting prof. at Hamilton College, Clinton, N.Y. (1940–41); in 1941 he became a prof. at Boston Univ. and head of graduate studies in music; in 1962 he was made a prof. at the Univ. of Calif., Santa Barbara; he retired in 1972. In 1955–56 he was president of the American Musicological Society. In 1959 he was elected a Fellow of the American Academy of Arts and Sciences; also was an honorary member of the Österreichische Gesellschaft für Musikwissenschaft and of the American chapter of the Neue Bach-Gesellschaft; in addition, was a member of the Joseph Haydn Inst. of Cologne. A music scholar and writer of great erudition, he contributed valuable publications on the Bach family, Haydn, and Brahms. As a member of the editorial board of the Denkmäler der Tonkunst in Österreich, he edited the collected works of Paul Peuerl and the instrumental works of Isaac Posch (vol. 70); also, with E. Mandyczewski, selected works by Antonio Caldara (vol. XXXIX). He edited Gluck's opera *Telemaco, Sämtliche Werke,* I/2; Haydn's opera *Orlando Paladino, Werke,* XXV/11, and 100 arrangements of Scottish folk songs by Haydn, *Werke,* XXXII/1. He was general editor of the Harbrace History of Musical Forms and of the Univ. of Calif., Santa Barbara, Series of Early Music; edited Isaac Posch's *Harmonia concertans 1623.*

WRITINGS: *Führer durch die Joseph Haydn Kollektion im Museum der Gesellschaft der Musikfreunde in Wien* (with H. Kraus; Vienna, 1930); "Joseph Haydn," in Bücken's *Grosse Meister* (Potsdam, 1932); *Wiener Meister um Mozart und Beethoven* (a collection of piano works; Vienna, 1935); *Johannes Brahms: Leben und Schaffen eines deutschen Meisters* (a major study; Vienna, 1935; Eng. trans., London and N.Y., 1936; 3rd ed., revised and enlarged, N.Y., 1981); *Musical Instruments: Their History in Western Culture from the Stone Age to the Present Day* (London, 1943; 3rd ed., revised and enlarged, published as *Instruments in the History of Western Music,* N.Y., 1978); *Haydn: A Creative Life in Music* (N.Y., 1946; 2nd ed., 1963); *A Thematic Catalogue of Haydn's Settings of Folksongs from the British Isles* (Superior, Wis., 1953); *The Bach Family: Seven Generations of Creative Genius* (an important study; N.Y., 1954); *Music of the Bach Family: An Anthology* (a valuable collection; Cambridge, Mass., 1955); *Johann Sebastian Bach: The Culmination of an Era* (an excellent study; N.Y., 1966).

BIBLIOGRAPHY: A. Silver, ed., *Karl Geiringer: A Checklist of His Publications in Musicology* (Santa Barbara, Calif., 1969); H.C. Robbins Landon and R. Chapman, *Studies in 18th Century Music: A Tribute to Karl Geiringer on His 70th Birthday* (N.Y. and London, 1970).

Geiser, Walther, Swiss composer and pedagogue; b. Zofingen, May 16, 1897. He studied violin with Hirt and composition with Suter at the Basel Cons.;

then went to Berlin, where he took lessons with Busoni. After Busoni's death in 1924, he returned to Basel, and taught violin and composition at the Cons. until 1963; was director of the Basel Bach-Chorus (1954–72). He composed 2 symphs. (1953, 1967); a Violin Concerto (1930); Horn Concerto (1934); *Konzertstück* for Organ and Chamber Orch. (1941); *Stabat Mater* for Baritone, Chorus, Orch., and Organ (1938); *Te Deum* for 4 Soloists, Chorus, Orch., and Organ (1960); *Concerto da camera* for 2 Solo Violins, Harpsichord, and String Orch. (1957); Piano Concerto (1959); 2 flute concertos (1921, 1963); several choral works and solo piano pieces.

Geisler, Paul, German conductor and composer; b. Stolp, Aug. 10, 1856; d. Posen, April 3, 1919. He was a pupil of his grandfather, who was a conductor at Marienburg, and also of Constantine Decker. As a conductor, Geisler was associated with the Leipzig musical theater (1881) and A. Neumann's traveling Wagner company (1882); for the following 2 years he was a conductor at Bremen. He lived in Leipzig and Berlin for most of his career before going to Posen, where he became director of the Cons. He wrote much music for the stage; his other work, including 2 cyclic cantatas, symph. poems, and incidental stage music, is mostly in MS.

Geissler, Fritz, East German composer; b. Wurzen, near Leipzig, Sept. 16, 1921; d. Bad Saarow, Jan. 11, 1984. He studied at the Hochschule für Musik in Leipzig with Max Dehnert and Wilhelm Weismann (1948–50); later taught there (1962–70); then joined the faculty of the Dresden Cons.; was named a prof. there in 1974. Geissler's music is dialectical and almost Hegelian in its syllogistic development and climactic synthesis; the ground themes are carefully adumbrated before their integration in a final catharsis; formal dissonances are emancipated by a freely modified application of the Schoenbergian method of composition with 12 tones related only to one another. The human quality of the tightly elaborate polyphonic structure of Geissler's works is expressed with considerable élan by means of variegated rhythmic designs and quasi-aleatory instrumental soliloquies. The formal element remains strictly observed; Geissler favors classical paradigms of symph. and concerto.
WORKS: FOR THE STAGE: *Der verrückte Jourdain,* a "Rossiniada" in 3 acts (1971); *Der Schatten,* fantastic opera (1975); *Die Stadtpfeifer,* opera in 4 scenes (1977); *Das Chagrinleder,* opera in 7 scenes (1978); 3 ballets: *Pigment* (1960); *Sommernachtstraum* (1965); *Der Doppelgänger* (1969). FOR ORCH.: *Italienische Lustspielouvertüre,* after Rossini (1958); *November 1918,* suite in 3 movements, commemorating the 40th anniversary of the German Revolution (1958); 9 symphs.: No. 1 (1961); No. 2, composed in celebration of the 800th anniversary of the city of Leipzig (1963); No. 3 (1965–66); No. 4 for Strings (1968); No. 5, to mark the 20th anniversary of the German Democratic Republic (1969); No. 6, *Sinfonia concertante,* for Wind Quintet and Strings (1971); No. 7 (1973); No. 8 for Soloists, Chorus, and Orch. (1974); No. 9 (1978); 2 chamber symphs. (1954, 1970); *Sinfonietta giocosa* (1963); *The Adventures of the Good Soldier Schweik,* symph. burlesque (1963); *Essay* (1969); *2 Symphonic Scenes* (1970); Piano Concerto (1970); *Beethoven-Variationen* (1971); Cello Concerto (1974); *Offenbach-Metamorphosen* (1977); Concerto for Flute, Strings, Harpsichord, and Percussion (1977); Concerto for Organ, Percussion, and Strings (1979). CHAMBER MUSIC: String Quartet (1951); Suite for Wind Quintet (1957); *Chamber Concerto* for Harpsichord, Flute, and 10 Instruments (1967); *Ode to a Nightingale* for Nonet (1967–68); Viola Sonata (1969); Piano Trio (1970). FOR VOICE: *Gesang vom Menschen,* oratorio (1968); *Nachtelegien,* romance for High Voice and Instruments (1969); *Die Liebenden,* romance for Tenor and 2 Instrumental Groups (1969); *Schöpfer Mensch,* oratorio (1973); *Die Glocke von Buchenwald,* cantata (1974); *Die Flamme von Mansfeld,* oratorio (1978). Also, piano works; choruses; songs.

Geistinger, Maria (Marie) Charlotte Cäcilia, Polish operetta singer; b. Graz, Styria, July 26, 1883; d. Rastenfeld, Sept. 29, 1903. She sang chiefly in Vienna, but also in Prague, Leipzig, Berlin, etc. In 1897 she made a successful appearance in N.Y.

Gelber, Bruno-Leonardo, Argentine pianist; b. Buenos Aries, March 19, 1941. He received his early musical training in Buenos Aires; then went to Paris for advanced training with Marguerite Long; eventually developed a successful career as a pianist, cultivating mainly the Romantic repertoire.

Gelbrun, Artur, Polish-born Israeli composer; b. Warsaw, July 11, 1913. He studied at the Warsaw Cons.; then went to Italy, where he took courses with Molinari and Casella at the Santa Cecilia Academy in Rome; later he studied composition with W. Burkhard and conducting with Scherchen in Zürich. He was an orch. and solo violinist in Warsaw, Lausanne, and Zürich (1936–47). In 1949 he emigrated to Israel and joined the staff of the Academy of Music in Tel Aviv as prof. of conducting and composition.
WORKS: A radiophonic oratorio, *Le Livre du Feu* (1964; Jerusalem, 1966; Prix Italia, 1966); 4 ballets: *Hedva* (1951; concert version, Ein-Gev, May 27, 1951; stage premiere, St. Gallen, Switzerland, 1958); *Miadoux* (1966–67), *Prologue to the Décameron* (1968; Jerusalem, 1968); and *King Solomon and the Hoopoes* (1976); a cantata, *Song of Lamentation* (1952); *Lieder der Maedchen* for Voice and Orch. (1945); *Suite* for Orch. (1947); *Prelude, Passacaglia and Fugue* for Orch. (1954); *Variations* for Piano and Orch. (1955); *Prologue Symphonique* (1956); *5 Capriccios* for Orch. (1957); 3 symphs. (1957–58; 1961; *Jubilee,* 1973); *Song of the River* for Soprano and Orch. (1959); Cello Concerto (1962); *Piccolo Divertimento* for Youth Orch. (1963; has been perf. as a ballet); *4 Pieces* for String Orch. (1963); *Concerto-Fantasia* for Flute, Harp, and String Orch. (1963); *Salmo e Alelujah* for Soprano and Orch. (1968); Concertino for Chamber Orch. (1974); *Adagio* for String

Orch. (1974); Sonatina for 2 Violins (1944); String Trio (1945); *Esquisses* for Narrator, Flute, and Harp (1946); Solo Violin Sonatina (1957); *5 Pieces* for Solo Cello (1962); *5 Pieces* for Solo Viola (1963); String Quartet (1969); *Partita* for Solo Clarinet (1969); *Miniature* for Solo Bassoon (1969); Wind Quintet (1971); Trio for Trumpet, Horn, and Trombone (1972); Piano Trio (1977); Piano Sonatina (1945); *5 Caprices* for Piano (1957); *5 Messages* for Piano (1965); songs.

Gelineau, Joseph, French composer of sacred music and editor; b. Champ-sur-Layon (Maine-et-Loire), Oct. 31, 1920. At the age of 21 he entered the Order of the Jesuits; studied organ and composition at the Ecole César Franck in Paris; also obtained a doctorate in theology. He publ. *Chant et musique dans le culte chrétien* (Paris, 1962); composed *Missa plebs sancta* (1960), Psalms, etc.; trans. and set to music the Psalmody of the Bible of Jerusalem.

Gelinek (properly, **Jelinek**), **Joseph,** composer; b. Seltsch, near Beroun, Bohemia, Dec. 3, 1758; d. Vienna, April 13, 1825. He studied philosophy in Prague and at the same time took lessons in music with Segert; became a good pianist (Mozart praised him); was ordained a priest in 1786, but did not abandon music; went to Vienna and settled there as a piano teacher; c.1810 became music master to Prince Esterhazy. He was a prolific composer; 92 opus numbers are listed in a catalogue issued by André; his fantasias, variations, and dances for piano were quite successful.

Gellman, Steven, Canadian composer; b. Toronto, Sept. 16, 1948. He studied piano and composition with Samuel Dolin at the Royal Cons. in Toronto; then studied with Berio, Sessions, and Persichetti at the Juilliard School of Music in N.Y. (1965–68), with Milhaud at Aspen, Colo. (summers 1965 and 1966), and with Messiaen at the Paris Cons. (1974–76). In 1976 he joined the faculty of the Univ. of Ottawa. He adopted an uncompromisingly modernistic idiom in most of his music, while safeguarding the formal design of classical tradition.

WORKS: Piano Concerto (1964); *Mural* for Orch. (1965); *Movement* for Violin and Orch. (1967); *Symphony in 2 Movements* (Ottawa, July 15, 1971); *Odyssey* for Rock Group, Solo Piano, and Orch. (Hamilton, Ontario, March 9, 1971); *Symphony II* (Toronto, Dec. 2, 1972); *Encore (Mythos I Revisited)* for Orch. (1972); *Overture for Ottawa* (1972); *Chori* for Orch. (1974); *Animus-Anima* for Orch. (Paris, April 28, 1976); *2 Movements* for String Quartet (1963); *Soliloquy* for Solo Cello (1966); *After Bethlehem* for String Quartet (1966); *Quartets: Poems of G.M. Hopkins* for Voice, Flute, Cello, and Harp (1966–67); *Mythos II* for Flute and String Quartet (1968); *Sonate pour sept* for Flute, Clarinet, Cello, Guitar, Piano, and 2 Percussionists (1975); Piano Sonata (1964); Fantasy for Piano (1967); *Melodic Suite* for Piano (1971–72).

Geminiani, Francesco, Italian violinist and writer; b. Lucca (baptized, Dec. 5), 1687; d. Dublin, Sept. 17, 1762. He studied with Carlo Ambrogio Lonati in Milan, and with Corelli in Rome and Alessandro Scarlatti in Naples; in 1706 returned to Lucca and played violin in the town orch. until 1710; in 1711 was concertmaster in the Naples Opera orch. In 1714 he went to London, where he won a reputation as a teacher and performer; in 1731 he presented a series of subscription concerts in London; in 1733 he went to Dublin, where he established a concert hall and gave concerts; in 1734 he returned to London; in 1740 he was briefly in Paris; he was again in Paris for a longer period between 1749 and 1755, when he went back once more to London; in 1759 he settled in Dublin, where he was music master to Charles Coote, later the Earl of Bellamont. Both in London and Dublin he was financially successful; besides music, he was interested in art, and bought and sold pictures. As a virtuoso, Geminiani continued the tradition established by his teacher Corelli, and made further advances in violin technique by the use of frequent shifts of position, and by a free application of double-stops. In his compositions, he adopted the facile method of the Italian school; he excelled particularly in brisk allegro movements. During his years in England and Ireland he made a determined effort to please English tastes; his works are often extremely effective, but his inherent talents fell far short of Corelli's, and in music history he remains but a secondary figure. The claim that Geminiani was the author of the first publ. violin method, *The Art of Playing on the Violin,* which appeared anonymously in vol. V of Prelleur's *The Modern Musick Master* (London, 1730), is erroneous; upon examination it proves to be an edited republication of an earlier anonymous violin method titled *Volens Nolens,* originally publ. in London in 1695; perpetuating the misattribution, this text was later publ. under Geminiani's own name as *The Compleat Tutor for the Violin;* in 1751 a 3rd edition appeared under the original title, *The Art of Playing on the Violin;* it was subsequently trans. into French (Paris, 1752) and German (Vienna, 1785); a facsimile edition of the original, prepared by D.D. Boyden, was issued in 1952. Boyden established the relevant facts in the matter in his paper "Geminiani and the First Violin Tutor" (*Acta Musicologica,* Feb. 1960). Apart from the question of authorship, *The Art of Playing on the Violin* is of historic importance because it sets forth the principles of violin playing as formulated by Corelli, with many of the rules still in common use. Other papers and manuals publ. under Geminiani's name, and assumed to be authentic, are: *Rules for Playing in a true Taste on the Violin, German Flute, Violoncello and Harpsichord* (London, 1745); *A Treatise on good Taste, being the second Part of the Rules* (London, 1749); *Guida Armonica o Dizionario Armonico, being a Sure Guide to Harmony and Modulation* (London, 1742; in French, 1756; in Dutch, 1756); *A Supplement to the Guida Harmonica* (London, 1745); *The Art of Accompaniament* [sic] *or a new and well digested method to learn to perform the Thorough Bass on the Harpsichord* (London, 1775); *The Art of Playing the Guitar* or *Cittra, Containing Several Compositions with a Bass for the Violoncello or Harpsichord* (London, 1760); he also compiled *The Harmonical Miscellany* (London, 1758).

Works (all instrumental): Op. 1, 12 sonatas for Violin and Figured Bass (1716); op. 2, 6 concerti grossi (1732); op. 3, 6 concerti grossi (1733); op. 4, 12 sonatas for Violin and Figured Bass (1739); op. 5, 6 sonatas for Cello and Figured Bass (1739); op. 6, 6 concerti grossi (1741); op. 7, 6 concerti grossi (1746); also 12 string trios and arrangements of Corelli's works for various instrumental combinations. The concerti grossi have been publ. in modern editions by P. Mies (op. 2, no. 2), in *Musik im Haus* (1928); M. Esposito (op. 2, no. 2, arranged for String Orch., London, 1927); H.J. Moser (op. 2, nos. 4, 5, 6, arranged for strings and piano), in *Das Musik-Kränzlein* (Leipzig, 1937); R. Hernried (op. 3, nos. 1–6, Leipzig, 1935). Violin sonatas have been publ. by R.L. Finney (op. 1, nos. 1–12, Northampton, Mass., 1935) and A. Moffat (op. 4, no. 8, Mainz, 1910; op. 4, no. 11, Berlin, 1899).

BIBLIOGRAPHY: W.H. Grattan Flood, "Geminiani in England and Ireland," *Sammelbände der Internationalen Musik-Gesellschaft* (1910–11; pp. 108–12); A. Betti, *La vita e l'arte di Francesco Geminiani* (Lucca, 1933); R. Hernried, "Geminiani's Concerti Grossi, op. 3," *Acta Musicologica* (1937; pp. 22–30).

Gemünder, August Martin Ludwig, violin maker; b. Ingelfingen, Württemberg, Germany, March 22, 1814; d. New York, Sept. 7, 1895. He established a shop at Springfield, Mass., in 1846; then moved to Boston, where he was joined by his brother **Georg** (b. April 13, 1816; d. Jan. 15, 1899), also a violin maker, a pupil of J.B. Vuillaume in Paris. In 1852, the brothers settled in N.Y., where they established themselves as the foremost manufacturers of musical instruments; between 1860 and 1890 they received numerous medals for excellence at expositions in Europe and America. After the death of August Gemünder, the business was continued by 3 of his sons, as August Gemünder & Sons. Georg Gemünder wrote an autobiographical sketch with an account of his work, *Georg Gemünder's Progress in Violin Making* (1880, in German; 1881, in Eng.).

BIBLIOGRAPHY: *Dictionary of American Biography,* VII (N.Y., 1931).

Gencer, Leyla, Turkish soprano; b. Istanbul, Oct. 10, 1924. She studied in Istanbul; made her operatic debut in Ankara in 1950; then continued her musical studies in Italy; sang at the Arena Flegrea in Naples in 1953; became a member of La Scala in Milan in 1956; also made guest appearances in San Francisco, Salzburg, and London.

Gendron, Maurice, eminent French cellist and pedagogue; b. Nice, Dec. 26, 1920. He studied at the Cons. in Nice, and later at the Paris Cons. In 1945 he played in London with the London Phil., creating a favorable impression with his performance of Prokofiev's Cello Concerto; then appeared with major European orchs.

Genée, (Franz Friedrich) Richard, German operetta composer; b. Danzig, Feb. 7, 1823; d. Baden, near Vienna, June 15, 1895. At first a medical student, he took up music, and studied under Stahlknecht at Berlin; was a theater conductor (1848–67) at Riga, Cologne, Düsseldorf, Danzig, Amsterdam, and Prague; in 1868–78, was conductor at the Theater an der Wien in Vienna; then retired to his villa at Pressbaum, near Vienna. He wrote several of his own librettos (some with F. Zell); he also wrote librettos for Strauss, Suppé, and Millöcker.

WORKS: Operettas: *Der Geiger aus Tirol* (1857); *Der Musikfeind* (1862); *Die Generalprobe* (1862); *Rosita* (1864); *Der schwarze Prinz* (1866); *Am Runenstein* (with Fr. von Flotow, 1868); *Der Seekadett* (1876); *Nanon* (1877); *Im Wunderlande der Pyramiden* (1877); *Die letzten Mohikaner* (1878); *Nisida* (1880); *Rosina* (1881); *Die Zwillinge* (1885); *Die Piraten* (1886); *Die Dreizehn* (1887).

Generali (real name, **Mercandetti**), **Pietro,** Italian opera composer; b. Masserano, Oct. 23, 1773; d. Novara, Nov. 3, 1832. He studied in Rome; began to compose sacred music at an early age, but soon turned to opera. He traveled all over Italy as producer of his operas and also went to Vienna and Barcelona. Returning to Italy, he became maestro di cappella at the Cathedral of Novara. He anticipated Rossini in the effective use of dynamics in the instrumental parts of his operas, and was generally praised for his technical knowledge. He wrote about 50 stage works, in both the serious and comic genres, but none survived in the repertoire after his death. The following were successful at their initial performances: *Pamela nubile* (Venice, April 12, 1804); *Le lagrime di una vedova* (Venice, Dec. 26, 1808); *Adelina* (Venice, Sept. 16, 1810); *L'Impostore* (Milan, May 21, 1815); *I Baccanali di Roma* (Venice, Jan. 14, 1816; reputed to be his best work); *Il servo padrone* (Parma, Aug. 12, 1818); *Il divorzio persiano* (Trieste, Jan. 31, 1828).

BIBLIOGRAPHY: Piccoli, *Elogio del maestro Pietro Generali* (1833).

Genetz, Emil, Finnish choral composer; b. Impilahti, Oct. 24, 1852; d. Helsinki, May 1, 1930. He studied at the Dresden Cons. (1875–77); returning to Finland, he devoted himself chiefly to vocal music; many of his male choruses are well known and frequently sung in Finland.

Gennrich, Friedrich, German musicologist; b. Colmar, March 27, 1883; d. Langen (Hessen), Sept. 22, 1967. He studied Roman philology at the Univ. of Strasbourg; took courses in musicology with F. Ludwig. In 1921 he went to Frankfurt, where he taught musicology at the Univ.; retired in 1964. He was regarded as a leading authority on music of the troubadours, trouvères, and Minnesinger.

WRITINGS: *Musikwissenschaft und romanische Philologie* (Halle, 1918); *Der musikalische Vortrag der altfranzösischen Chansons de geste* (Halle, 1923); *Die altfranzösiche Rotrouenge* (Halle, 1925); *Das Formproblem des Minnesangs*

(Halle, 1931); *Grundriss einer Formenlehre des mittelalterlichen Liedes* (Halle, 1932; a comprehensive work); *Die Strassburger Schule für Musikwissenschaft*(Würzburg, 1940); *Abriss der frankonischen Mensuralnotation* (Nieder-Modau, 1946; 2nd ed., Darmstadt, 1956); *Abriss der Mensuralnotation des XIV. und der 1. Hälfte des XV. Jahrhunderts* (Nieder-Modau, 1948); *Melodien altdeutscher Lieder* (Darmstadt, 1954); *Franco von Köln, Ars Cantus Mensurabilis* (Darmstadt, 1955); *Die Wimpfener Fragmente der Hessischen Landesbibliothek* (Darmstadt, 1958); *Der musikalische Nachlass der Troubadours* (Darmstadt, 1960). He further contributed numerous papers to special publications on Romance literature.

Gentele, Goeran, brilliant Swedish opera manager; b. Stockholm, Sept. 20, 1917; killed in an automobile crash near Olbia, Sardinia, July 18, 1972. He studied political science in Stockholm, and art at the Sorbonne in Paris. He was first engaged as an actor, and then was stage director at the Royal Drama Theater in Stockholm (1941–52) and at the Royal Opera (1952–63), where he was appointed director in 1963. In 1970 he became engaged as general manager of the Metropolitan Opera House in N.Y., effective June 1972; great expectations for his innovative directorship in America were thwarted by his untimely death during a vacation in Italy.

Gentry, Bobbie, American country-music singer and guitarist; b. Chickasaw County, Miss., July 27, 1944. She learned to play piano, guitar, banjo, and other instruments; determined to get some real education in classical music, she attended classes at the Univ. of Calif. in Los Angeles and learned to write notes. In 1967 she produced her first hit song, *Ode to Billy Joe.* She made several successful tours across the U.S. and also ventured to give concerts in a few European countries.

Genzmer, Harald, German composer; b. Blumenthal, near Bremen, Feb. 9, 1909. He studied piano and organ in Marburg; then took courses in composition with Hindemith in Berlin. He spent the war years in Berlin; in 1946–57 taught at the Hochschule für Musik in Freiburg im Breisgau; in 1957 he was appointed to the faculty of the Hochschule für Musik in Munich; became a prof. emeritus, 1974. A prolific composer, he writes music in a utilitarian manner, adhering closely to classical forms while allowing for dissonant counterpoint. He took interest in the electronic instrument Trautonium and wrote 2 concertos for it (1939, 1952).
WORKS: *Bremer Sinfonie* (1942); Symph. No. 1 (1957); Symph. No. 2 (1958); Piano Concerto (1948); Cello Concerto (1950); Flute Concerto (1954); Violin Concerto (1959); Viola Concerto (1967); Organ Concerto (1971); Oboe Concerto (1957); Harp Concerto (1965); Trumpet Concerto in memory of the slain brothers Jack and Robert Kennedy (1968); *Symphonic Concerto* for Organ (1974); Sinfonietta for Strings (1955); *Moosbürger Graduale* for Vocal Soloists and Orch. (1971); *3 antike Gesänge* for Chorus

and 5 Woodwinds (1973); much chamber music, including 2 string quartets; Quartet for Violin, Viola, Cello, and Double Bass; 2 piano trios; Trio for Harp, Flute, and Viola; 3 violin sonatas, 2 flute sonatas, Sonata for Viola Solo; several works for piano and for organ; also cantatas and other choral works.

George, Earl, American composer and conductor; b. Milwaukee, May 1, 1924. He studied composition at the Eastman School of Music in Rochester, N.Y., with Howard Hanson and Bernard Rogers (1942–46); in the summer of 1946 he attended seminars of Martinu and Lopatnikoff at the Berkshire Music Center at Tanglewood, and in 1947 studied with Martinu again in N.Y. He subsequently held a teaching position at the Univ. of Minnesota (1948–56). In 1959 he was appointed to the music faculty at Syracuse Univ.; conducted the Syracuse Symph. Orch. there (1973–81). In his music he follows an astute median course of prudent American modernism, embellished by occasional satirical touches.
WORKS: FOR THE STAGE: *Birthdays,* 2 one-act operas, individually titled *Pursuing Happiness* and *Another 4th of July* (Syracuse, April 1976) FOR ORCH.: Concerto for Strings (1948); *A Thanksgiving Overture* (1949); *A Currier and Ives Set* (1953); Violin Concerto (1954); Piano Concerto (1958); *Introducton, Variations, and Finale* (1959); *Declamations* for Wind Instruments and Percussion (1965). FOR VOICE: *Missa Brevis* (1948); *Abraham Lincoln Walks at Midnight,* oratorio (1949); *3 Poems of Wordsworth* for Narrator, Chorus, and Piano (1960); *War Is Kind* for Male Chorus, Percussion, Trumpet, and Piano (1966); *Voyages,* cantata after a poem by Hart Crane (1967); *The Dust of Times,* cantata after Sappho (1969); *Voices* for Soprano, Chorus, 2 Pianos, and Percussion (1974); *Hum-Drum Heaven* for Narrator, Soprano, Chorus, Piano, and Percussion (1978); *Valentines and Graffiti,* after e.e. cummings, for Soprano, Chorus, Clarinet, and Piano (1980). CHAMBER MUSIC: *3 Pieces* for Violin, Cello, and Piano (1949); String Quartet (1961); *Tuckets and Sennets* for Trumpet and Piano (1973); *Lonesome Music* for Solo Clarinet (1973). FOR PIANO: Sonata (1948); *Prelude, Aria and Burlesca* for 2 Pianos (1950); *3 Intermezzi* (1971); *3 Pieces about Marches* (1975).

Georges, Alexandre, French opera composer; b. Arras, Feb. 25, 1850; d. Paris, Jan. 18, 1938. He studied at the Niedermeyer School in Paris, and later became a teacher of harmony there. He occupied various posts as organist in Paris churches, and was a successful organ teacher. As a composer, he was mainly interested in opera; the following operas were produced in Paris: *Le Printemps* (1888); *Poèmes d'amour* (1892); *Charlotte Corday* (March 6, 1901); *Miarka* (Nov. 7, 1905; his most successful work; revived and shortened, 1925); *Myrrha* (1909); *Sangre y sol* (Nice, Feb. 23, 1912). He also wrote the oratorios *Notre Dame de Lourdes, Balthazar,* and *Chemin de Croix;* the symph. poems *Léila, La Naissance de Vénus,* and *Le Paradis perdu.* He wrote some chamber music for unusual combinations: *A* *la Kasbah* for Flute and Clarinet; *Kosaks* for Violin and Clarinet; etc. He is best known, however, for his melodious *Chansons de Miarka* for Voice and Piano (also with Orch.). His arrangement of *Chansons champenoises à la manière ancienne,* by G. Dévignes, is also well known.

Georgescu, Corneliu-Dan, Rumanian composer; b. Craiova, Jan. 1, 1938. He studied at the Popular School for the Arts (1952–56) and with Ion Dumitrescu, Ciortea, Olah, and Mendelsohn at the Bucharest Cons. (1956–61). Since 1962 he has been head of research at the Ethnography and Folklore Inst. of the Rumanian Academy. His music employs folksong motifs in a modern manner.
WORKS: Piano Sonata (1958); Trio for Flute, Clarinet, and Bassoon (1959); *3 Pieces* for Orch. (1959); *Motive maramureşene,* suite for Orch. (1963; Bucharest, Dec. 3, 1967); 4 pieces for Orch.: *Jocuri I* (1963); *II, Dialogue rythmique* (1964); *III, Danses solennelles* (1965); and *IV, Collages* (1966); Partita for Orch. (1966); a cycle of 4 pieces for various orch. groupings: *Alb-negru* (1967), *Zig-Zag* (1967), *Continuo* (1968), and *Rubato* (1969); *Chorals I, II,* and *III* for Flute, Violin, Viola, Cello, and Piano (1970).

Georgescu, Georges, Rumanian conductor; b. Sulina, Sept. 12, 1887; d. Bucharest, Sept. 1, 1964. He studied at the Bucharest Cons.; then took cello lessons with Hugo Becker in Berlin; returning to Rumania, he was a conductor in Bucharest in 1919–38; he founded the George Enesco State Phil. Orch. in 1919, and led it until his death; also conducted guest appearances with European orchs.; during the seasons 1926–27 and 1960–61 he was guest conductor of the N.Y. Phil.

Georgiades, Thrasybulos, Greek musicologist; b. Athens, Jan. 4, 1907; d. Munich, March 15, 1977. He studied piano in Athens; then studied musicology with Rudolf von Ficker at the Univ. of Munich, where he received his Ph.D. in 1935 with the dissertation *Englische Diskanttraktate aus der ersten Hälfte des 15. Jahrhunderts* (published in Würzburg, 1937); he also studied composition with Carl Orff. In 1938 he became a prof. at the Athens Odeon; was its director from 1939 to 1941. He completed his Habilitation at the Univ. of Munich in 1947 with his *Der griechische Rhythmus: Musik, Reigen, Vers und Sprache* (publ. in Hamburg, 1949). In 1948 he joined the faculty of the Univ. of Heidelberg; in 1956 he became a prof. at the Univ. of Munich, retiring in 1972. He contributed valuable papers to German music journals on ancient Greek, Byzantine, and medieval music. His other writings include *Volkslied als Bekenntnis* (Regensburg, 1947); *Musik und Sprache* (Berlin, 1954); *Musik und Rhythmus bei den Griechen; Zum Ursprung der abendländischen Musik* (Hamburg, 1958); *Das musikalische Theater* (Munich, 1965); *Schubert, Musik und Lyrik* (Göttingen, 1967). His book on Greek music was publ. in Eng. under the title *Greek Music, Verse, Dance* (N.Y., 1956).

Georgiadis, Georges, Greek pianist and composer; b. Salonika, Sept. 8, 1912. He studied piano and composition at the Cons. of Athens; in 1943 was appointed prof. of piano there. His music, in a traditional mold, is inspired chiefly by Greek folk resources.
WORKS: Symph. in E minor, surnamed *De la paix* (1960); Concertino for Piano and Orch. (1959); 2 violin sonatas; songs; many piano pieces; incidental music for *Demeter and Persephone, Medea,* etc.

Georgii, Walter, German pianist and pedagogue; b. Stuttgart, Nov. 23, 1887; d. Tübingen, Feb. 23, 1967. He studied piano in Stuttgart and music theory in Leipzig, Berlin, and Halle. From 1914 to 1945 he taught piano in Cologne; then went to Munich. He publ. several valuable books on piano playing: *Weber als Klavierkomponist* (Leipzig, 1914); *Geschichte der Musik für Klavier zu 2 Hände* (Zürich, 1941; revised ed., with added material on piano music for One, 3, 5, and 6 hands, 1950); *Klavierspielerbüchlein* (Zürich, 1953). He also publ. an anthology of piano music, *400 Jahre europäischer Klavier Musik* (Cologne, 1950).

Gérardy, Jean, Belgian cellist; b. Spa, Dec. 6, 1877; d. there, July 4, 1929. At the age of 5 he began to study cello with R. Bellmann; was a pupil of Massau at the Liège Cons. from 1885 to 1889. In 1888 he played as a student in a trio with Ysaÿe and Paderewski; he became noted as an ensemble player; with Ysaÿe and Godowsky, he formed a trio and toured the U.S. in 1913–14. Gérardy's instrument was a Stradivari made in 1710.

Gerber, Ernst Ludwig, celebrated German lexicographer, son and pupil of the organist and composer **Heinrich Nikolaus Gerber;** b. Sondershausen, Sept. 29, 1746; d. there, June 30, 1819. He studied organ and theory with his father; then studied law and music in Leipzig, becoming a skillful cellist and organist, in which latter capacity he became (1769) his father's assistant, and succeeded him in 1775. He was also a chamber musician. He was able to visit Weimar, Kassel, Leipzig, and other cities, and gradually gathered together a large collection of musicians' portraits; to these he appended brief biographical notices, and finally conceived the plan of writing a biographical dictionary of musicians. Though his resources (in a small town without a public library, and having to rely in great measure on material sent him by his publisher, Breitkopf) were hardly adequate to the task he undertook, his *Historisch-biographisches Lexikon der Tonkünstler* (Leipzig, 2 vols., 1790–92; reprinted 1976) was so well received, and brought in such a mass of corrections and fresh material from all quarters, that he prepared a supplementary edition, *Neues historisch-biographisches Lexikon der Tonkünstler* (4 vols., 1812–14; reprinted 1966). Though the former was intended only as a supplement to Walther's dictionary, and both are, of course, out of date, they contain much material still of value, and have been extensively drawn upon by more recent writers. He composed sonatas for piano, chorale preludes for organ, and music for wind band. The Viennese Gesellschaft der Musikfreunde purchased his large library.

Gerber, René, Swiss composer; b. Travers, June 29, 1908. He studied with Andreae in Zürich and with Nadia Boulanger and Paul Dukas in Paris. Upon his return to Switzerland he devoted himself to teaching; in 1947 was appointed director of the Cons. of Neuchâtel, occupying this post until 1951.
WORKS: *3 suites françaises* for Orch. (1933–45); 2 sinfoniettas for String Orch. (1949, 1968); 2 harp concertos (1931, 1969); 2 piano concertos (1933, 1966–70); Clarinet Concerto (1932); Flute Concerto (1934); Bassoon Concerto (1935–39); Trumpet Concerto (1939); Violin Concerto (1941); 3 string quartets (1947–70); opera, *Roméo et Juliette* (1957–61); 3 *Visions espagnoles* for Voice and Small Ensemble (1973).

Gerber, Rudolf, German musicologist; b. Flehingen, Baden, April 15, 1899; d. Göttingen, May 6, 1957. He attended the univs. of Halle and Leipzig, receiving his Dr.Phil. from the latter in 1925. He went as Abert's assistant to the Univ. of Berlin in 1926; in 1928, Gerber joined the faculty at Giessen Univ.; became a prof. there in 1937; he was head of the Music-Historical Inst. there from 1937 to 1943, when he became a prof. at Göttingen Univ. An authority on German music, he publ. *Der Operntypus J.A. Hasses und seine textlichen Grundlagen* (Leipzig, 1925); *Das Passionsrezitativ bei H. Schütz* (Gütersloh, 1929); *Johannes Brahms* (Potsdam, 1938); *Christoph Willibald Ritter von Gluck* (Potsdam, 1941; 2nd ed., revised 1950); *Bachs Brandenburgische Konzerte* (Kassel, 1951). He was editor of the *Mozart-Jahrbuch,* III (1929), as well as of works by Schütz, Bach, Gluck et al.; was a collaborator in F. Blume's collected edition of Praetorius.

Gerbert, Martin, eminent German music scholar; b. Hornau, near Horb am Neckar, Aug. 12, 1720; d. St.-Blasien, May 13, 1793. A student in the Benedictine monastery at St.-Blasien, he joined the order in 1737, became a priest in 1744, then prof. of theology there; in 1759–62, he made trips to Germany, France, and throughout Italy, collecting old MSS, particularly those on music history, of which he later made valuable use in his own works; also visited Padre Martini in Bologna, corresponding with him from 1761 until Martini's death in 1784; in 1764, he was elected Prince-Abbot of the monastery at St.-Blasien. His writings on music are *De cantu et musica sacra* (St.-Blasien, 1774, 2 vols.; from the beginnings of music to the 18th century), *Vetus liturgia alemannica* (1776, 2 vols.), *Monumenta veteris liturgiae alemannicae* (1777, 2 vols.), and *Scriptores ecclesiastici de musica sacra potissimum* (1784, 3 vols.; facsimile ed., Berlin, 1905; also reprinted in *Bolletino bibliografico musicale,* Milan, 1931); the first and last are still among the most valued sources for the study of music history, the last being one of the 2 great collections of treatises

by theorists of the Middle Ages (for the other, see **Coussemaker**).
BIBLIOGRAPHY: J. Bader, *Fürstabt Martin Gerbert* (Freiburg, 1875); Fr. Niecks, "Martin Gerbert: Priest, Prince, Scholar and Musican," *Musical Times* (Nov.–Dec. 1882); A. Lamy, *Martin Gerbert* (Rheims, 1898); A. Brinzinger, "Zu Martin Gerberts ... 200-jährigem Geburtsfest," *Neue Musik-Zeitung* (Sept. 2, 1920); G. Pfeilschifter, *Die Korrespondenz des Fürstabtes Martin Gerbert von St. Blasien* (vol. I, 1752–73; 1931); Eliz. Hegar, *Die Anfänge der neueren Musikgeschichtsschreibung um 1770 bei Gerbert, Burney and Hawkins* (Strasbourg, 1932); G. Pfeilschifter, A. Allgeler, and W. Müller, eds., *Briefe und Akten des Fürstabts Martin II. Gerbert von St. Blasien, 1764–1793* (Karlsruhe, 1957).

Gerelli, Ennio, Italian conductor and composer; b. Cremona, Feb. 12, 1907; d. there, Oct. 5, 1970. He studied at the Cons. of Bologna; conducted ballet and opera in Italy; was on the staff of La Scala in Milan (1935–40); in 1961 he founded the Camerata di Cremona. He also wrote some chamber music.

Gerhard, Roberto, eminent Catalonian composer; b. Valls, near Tarragona (Spain), Sept. 25, 1896; d. Cambridge, England, Jan. 5, 1970. Although of Swiss parentage and nationality, he was prominently associated with the Catalonian musical movement. He studied piano in Barcelona with Granados (1915–16) and was the last composition student of Felipe Pedrell (1916–22). The currents of Central European music were already becoming apparent in his music even before he joined Schoenberg's master classes in Vienna and Berlin (1923–28). Gerhard held a brief professorship in Barcelona and served as head of the music dept. of the Catalan Library there until the defeat of the Republic in the Spanish Civil War; lived in Paris until June 1939, then settled in England and became a British subject. He was a guest prof. of composition at the Univ. of Michigan in the spring of 1960 and at the Berkshire Music Center, Tanglewood, during the summer of 1962. In 1967 he was made a Commander of the Order of the British Empire. In his music written in England, Gerhard makes use of serialistic procedures, extending the dodecaphonic principle into the domain of rhythms (12 different time units in a theme, corresponding to the intervallic distances of the notes in the tone row from the central note).
WORKS: Opera, *The Duenna,* after Sheridan's play (1945–47; perf. in concert form, Wiesbaden, June 27, 1951); 5 ballets: *Ariel* (1934; ballet suite, Barcelona, April 19, 1936); *Soirées de Barcelona* (1936–38); *Don Quixote* (1940–41; London, Feb. 20, 1950); *Alegrías, Divertissement Flamenco* for 2 Pianos (also an orch. suite, BBC Radio, April 4, 1944); *Pandora* for 2 Pianos and Percussion (1943–44; also for Orch., Cambridge, Jan. 26, 1944); 2 cantatas: *L'Alta Naixença del Rei en Jaume* (1931) and *The Plague,* after Camus (London, April 1, 1964). He also wrote *Albade, Interludi i Dansa* for Orch. (1936; London, June 24, 1938); a symph., *Pedrelliana*

(Homenaje a Pedrell), based on themes from Pedrell's opera *La Celestina* (1941); Violin Concerto (1942; revised 1945 and 1949; Florence, Maggio Musicale, June 16, 1950); Concerto for Piano and Strings (1950); 5 numbered symphs.: No. 1 (1952–53; Baden-Baden, June 21, 1955); No. 2 (London, Oct. 28, 1959; revised 1967–68 and retitled *Metamorphoses*); No. 3, *Collages* for Orch. and Tape (London, Feb. 8, 1961); No. 4, *New York* (N.Y., Dec. 14, 1967); No. 5 (1969, unfinished); Concerto for Harpsichord, Strings, and Percussion (1955–56); *Concerto for Orchestra* (Boston, Mass., April 25, 1965); *Epithalamion* for Orch. (Valdagno, Italy, Sept. 17, 1966); *L'Infantament meravellós de Schahrazade,* song cycle for Voice and Piano (1918); Piano Trio (1918); *Dos Apunts* for Piano (1922); *7 Hai-Kai* for Voice, 4 Winds, and Piano (1922–23); *2 Sardanas* for 11 Instruments (1928); *6 cançons populars catalanes* for Soprano and Piano (1928; orchestrated in 1931, and perf. in Vienna, June 16, 1932, Anton von Webern conducting); Wind Quintet (1928); *Cancionero de Pedrell,* 8 songs for Soprano and Chamber Orch. (1941); *Capriccio* for Solo Flute (1949); *Impromptus* for Piano (1950); Viola Sonata (1950); 2 string quartets (1950–55, 1961–62); *The Akond of Swat,* after Edward Lear, for Voice and 2 Percussionists (London, Feb. 7, 1956); Nonet for 4 Woodwinds, 4 Brasses, and Accordion (1956); *Chaconne* for Solo Violin (1958); *Concert for 8* for Flute, Clarinet, Guitar, Mandolin, Double Bass, Accordion, Piano, and Percussion (London, May 17, 1962); *Hymnody* for 7 Winds, Percussion, and 2 Pianos (London, May 23, 1963); Cello Sonata (BBC Radio, Oct. 10, 1964); *Gemini* for Violin and Piano (1966; originally titled *Duo Concertante*); *Libra* for Flute, Clarinet, Violin, Guitar, Piano, and Percussion (BBC Radio, Oct. 26, 1968); *Leo,* chamber symph. (Dartmouth College, Hanover, N.H., Aug. 23, 1969). He wrote an electronic sound track for a medical film, *Audiomobile No. 2 "DNA"* and electronic music to accompany a reading of García Lorca's *Lament for the Death of a Bullfighter;* incidental music to Shakespeare's plays *(Romeo and Juliet, Taming of the Shrew, Midsummer Night's Dream, King Lear);* film music; harmonizations of Catalan melodies; etc.

BIBLIOGRAPHY: Sept. 1956 issue of the *Score,* publ. on the occasion of Gerhard's 60th birthday, with articles by Donald Mitchell, Norman Del Mar, John Gardner, Roman Vlad, David Drew, Laurence Picken, and Roberto Gerhard himself; also the report on Gerhard (pp. 175–87) in Francis Routh's *Contemporary British Music: The Twenty-five Years from 1945 to 1970* (London, 1972); K. Potter, *The Life and Works of Roberto Gerhard* (Diss., Univ. of Birmingham, 1972).

Gerhardt, Elena, celebrated German lieder singer (mezzo-soprano); b. Leipzig, Nov. 11, 1883; d. London, Jan. 11, 1961. She studied at the Leipzig Cons. (1899–1903) with Marie Hedmont; made her public debut on her 20th birthday in a recital, accompanied by Nikisch; toured Europe as a lieder singer with great success; made her English debut in London in 1906, and her American debut in N.Y., Jan. 9,

1912. In 1933 she settled in London, making appearances as a singer, and teaching. She compiled *My Favorite German Songs* (1915), edited a selection of Hugo Wolf's songs (1932), and wrote her autobiography, *Recital* (London, 1953; preface by Dame Myra Hess).

Gericke, Wilhelm, noted Austrian conductor; b. Schwanberg, April 18, 1845; d. Vienna, Oct. 27, 1925. He studied with Dessoff at the Vienna Cons. (1862–65); after a number of engagements as guest conductor in provincial theaters, he became conductor of the municipal theater in Linz. In 1874 he joined the staff of the Vienna Court Opera as an assistant conductor; in 1880 he took charge of the Gesellschaft der Musikfreunde concerts, and also led the Singverein. From 1884 to 1889 he was conductor of the Boston Symph. Orch.; returning to Vienna, he once again served as conductor of the Gesellschaft der Musikfreunde concerts from 1890–95. He was called again to America in 1898 to lead the Boston Symph. Orch., conducting its concerts until 1906; then returned to Vienna. Gericke was the only conductor in the history of the Boston Symph. Orch. to serve two separate terms; as such, he did much to make it a fine ensemble, for he was a remarkably able conductor and a highly efficient drillmaster.

BIBLIOGRAPHY: J.N. Burk, "Wilhelm Gericke: A Centennial Retrospect," *Musical Quarterly* (April 1945).

Gerl, Franz Xaver, German bass and composer; b. Andorf, Nov. 30, 1764; d. Mannheim, March 9, 1827. He sang in the choir at Salzburg; in 1789 became principal bass at the Theater auf der Wieden in Vienna, remaining on its roster until 1793; he created the role of Sarastro in Mozart's *Die Zauberflöte* in 1791; his wife, **Barbara Reisinger** (1770–1806), created the role of Papagena in that production. He composed several works for the stage, collaborating with Bendikt Schack.

Gerlach, Theodor, German conductor and composer; b. Dresden, June 25, 1861; d. Kiel, Dec. 11, 1940. A student of Fr. Wüllner, Gerlach first attracted attention with an effective cantata, *Luthers Lob der Musica.* In 1886, he became conductor of the German Opera in Posen. After several other posts as conductor, he settled in Karlsruhe as director of the Musikbildungsanstalt. He wrote an opera, *Matteo Falcone,* to his own libretto, which was produced with considerable success in Hannover (1898); of greater interest are his experiments with "spoken opera," employing inflected speech; of these, *Liebeswogen* was produced in Bremen on Nov. 7, 1903; later revised and produced under the title *Das Seegespenst* in Altenburg, April 24, 1914; he applied the same principle, using the spoken word over an instrumental accompaniment, in his *Gesprochene Lieder.* Also of interest is his early *Epic Symphony* (1891).

Gerle, Hans, German lutenist; b. Nuremberg, c.1500; d. there, 1570. He was well known in his time

both as a performer on the lute and as a manufacturer of viols and lutes. His works in tablature are of considerable historic value: *Musica Teusch auf die Instrument der grossen unnd kleinen Geygen, auch Lautten* (Nuremberg, 1532; 2nd ed., 1537; 3rd ed., under the title *Musica und Tabulatur*, 1546); *Tabulatur auff die Laudten* (Nuremberg, 1533); *Ein newes sehr künstlichs Lautenbuch* (Nuremberg, 1552; with pieces by Francesco da Milano, Ant. Rotta, Joan da Crema, Rosseto, and Gintzler). Reprints of his works have been edited by W. Tappert in *Sang und Klang aus alter Zeit* (1906) and by H.D. Bruger in *Schule des Lautenspiels*, I/2, and *Alte Lautenkunst I.*
BIBLIOGRAPHY: W. Tappert, "Die Lautenbücher des Hans Gerle," *Monatshefte für Musikgeschichte* (1886).

Gerle, Robert, Hungarian violinist and conductor; b. Abbazia, Italy, April 1, 1924. He was educated at the Franz Liszt Academy of Music and the National Cons. in Budapest; received the Hubay Prize in 1942; he played in recital and with major orchs. in Europe. He eventually settled in the U.S.; he headed the string dept. of the Univ. of Oklahoma (1950–54); then was on the staff of the Peabody Cons. in Baltimore (1955–68), at the Mannes College of Music in N.Y. (1959–70), the Manhattan School of Music (1967–70), and Ohio State Univ. (1968–72). In 1972 he was named head of the Instrumental Program of the Univ. of Maryland, Baltimore County; was conductor of its Community Symph. (from 1972) and Chamber Orch. (from 1973); also continued his career as a violinist.

German, Sir Edward (real name, **Edward German Jones**), English composer; b. Whitchurch, Feb. 17, 1862; d. London, Nov. 11, 1936. He began serious music study in Jan. 1880, under W.C. Hay at Shrewsbury; in Sept. he entered the Royal Academy of Music, studying organ (Steggall), violin (Weist-Hill and Burnett), theory (Banister), and composition and orchestration (Prout), graduating with a symph.; he was elected a Fellow of the Royal Academy of Music in 1895. In 1888–89 he conducted the orch. at the Globe Theatre; here his incidental music to Richard Mansfield's production of *King Richard III* was so successful that Sir Henry Irving commissioned him to write the music to *Henry VIII* (1892). German was then enabled to give up teaching and to devote himself entirely to composition. He was knighted in 1928; awarded the gold medal of the Royal Phil. Society in 1934.
WORKS: FOR ORCH.: *Gypsy Suite* (1892); Suite in D minor (1895); English fantasia, *Commemoration* (1897); symph. poem, *Hamlet* (1897); symph. suite, *The Seasons* (1899); *Rhapsody on March-Themes* (1902); *Funeral March* in D minor for Orch.; *Welsh Rhapsody* (1904); *Coronation March and Hymn* (1911); Theme and 6 Variations (1919); *The Willow Song* (1922); Serenade for Voice, Piano, Oboe, Clarinet, Bassoon, and Horn; *The Guitar; Bolero* for Violin and Orch.; incidental music to *Richard III* (1889), *Henry VIII* (1892), *As You Like It* (1896),

Much Ado about Nothing (1898), *Nell Gwyn* (1900), *The Conqueror* (1905). OPERAS: *The Emerald Isle* (completing the score of Arthur Sullivan, who died in 1900; 1901); *Merrie England* (London, April 2, 1902); *A Princess of Kensington* (1903); *Tom Jones* (London, April 17, 1908); *Fallen Fairies* (1909; the last libretto written by Sir W.S. Gilbert); operetta, *The Rival Poets* (1901). Also, many piano solos (incl. a suite) and duets; chamber music, organ pieces, etc.; Te Deum in F; a patriotic hymn, *Canada;* intercessory hymn, *Father Omnipotent; Three Albums of Lyrics* (with Harold Boulton); *The Just So Song Book* (words by Rudyard Kipling); other songs; etc.
BIBLIOGRAPHY: W.H. Scott, *Sir Edward German* (London, 1932).

Germani, Fernando, Italian organist; b. Rome, April 5, 1906. He studied at the Santa Cecilia Academy; precociously gifted, he was appointed organist in the Augusteo Orch. at the age of 15; in 1927 made an American tour; also taught organ at the Curtis Inst. in Philadelphia. Returning to Italy, he joined the faculty of the Music Academy in Siena in 1932; in 1935 became a prof. at the Rome Cons. and in 1948 was named first organist at St. Peter's Cathedral in the Vatican. In Rome he presented a series of concerts of all the organ works of Bach; he gave a similar series at Westminster Abbey which was broadcast by BBC. In 1961 he gave organ recitals in San Francisco and in 1962 played in N.Y., in varied programs that included, besides Bach's music, works by César Franck and Max Reger. He took part in music festivals in Berlin, Edinburgh, and other cities. He prepared a new complete edition of works by Frescobaldi as *Opere per organo e cembalo* (3 vols., Rome, 1964).

Gernsheim, Friedrich, German composer and conductor; b. Worms, July 17, 1839; d. Berlin, Sept. 11, 1916. He studied at the Leipzig Cons. with Moscheles (piano) and Hauptmann (theory); then was in Paris (1855–61) for further studies. Returning to Germany, he became a prof. at the Cologne Cons. (1865–74); then conducted choral concerts in Rotterdam (1874–80); subsequently taught at the Stern Cons. in Berlin (1890–97). His works are marked by a characteristic Romantic flair, as an epigone of Schumann; he was also influenced by Brahms, who was his friend. He wrote 4 symphs., several overtures, a Piano Concerto, a Violin Concerto, 4 string quartets, 3 piano quartets, 2 piano trios, a String Quintet, 3 violin sonatas, 2 cello sonatas, and numerous choral works, songs, and piano pieces, totaling 92 opus numbers.
BIBLIOGRAPHY: K. Holl, *Friedrich Gernsheim, Leben, Erscheinung und Werk* (Leipzig, 1928).

Gero, Jhan (Jehan), Flemish composer who flourished in the 16th century. He was a fine madrigal writer; publ. 2 books of madrigals for 4 voices (1549), 2 books of madrigals for 3 voices (1553), and a book of madrigals for 2 voices (1541); he also wrote motets. He was at one time confused with **Johannes**

Gallus.
BIBLIOGRAPHY: Alfred Einstein, *The Italian Madrigal*, vol. 1 (Princeton, 1949).

Gérold, Théodore, eminent Alsatian music scholar; b. Strasbourg, Oct. 26, 1866; d. Allenwiller, Feb. 15, 1956. He studied theology at the Univ. of Strasbourg, and musicology with Gustaf Jacobsthal. In 1890 he went to Frankfurt to study singing with Jules Stockhausen; then took courses at the Paris Cons. He received his Dr.Phil. from the German Univ. of Strasbourg with the dissertation *Zur Geschichte der französischen Gesangskunst;* was a lecturer on music at the Univ. of Basel from 1914 to 1918; returned to Strasbourg in 1919 to lecture on music at the new French Univ., from which in 1921 he received the degree of *Dr. ès lettres,* and in 1927, the degree of *Dr. en théologie.* He retired from the univ. in 1937; occupied an ecclesiastical lecturing position in Allenwiller in 1951.
WRITINGS: *Le Manuscrit de Bayeux, Chansons du XVe siècle; Kleine Sängerfibel* (Mainz, 1908); *Chansons populaires des XVe et XVIe siècles* (Strasbourg, 1913); *Les Psaumes de Clément Marot et leurs mélodies* (Strasbourg, 1919); *La Musicologie médiévale* (Paris, 1921); *L'Art du chant en France au XVIIe siècle* (Strasbourg, 1921); *Schubert* (Paris, 1923); *J.S. Bach* (Paris, 1925); *Les Pères de l'église et la musique* (Paris, 1931); *La Musique au moyen âge* (Paris, 1932); *Histoire de la musique des origines à la fin du XIVe siècle* (Paris, 1936). Gérold transcribed into modern notation (with critical notes) the melodies of the 14th-century "drame provençal" *Le Jeu de Ste. Agnès,* ed. by A. Jeanroy (Paris, 1931).

Gerschefski, Edwin, American composer; b. Meriden, Conn., June 10, 1909. He studied piano with Bruce Simons at Yale Univ.; then went to London, where he took a course for a season at the Tobias Matthay Piano School; he further had lessons with Artur Schnabel in Como, Italy. Returning to N.Y. in 1935, he studied the Schillinger system of composition with Schillinger himself (1935–37). From then on he occupied various teaching posts; in 1960 was appointed to the faculty of the Univ. of Georgia; retired in 1972. His works are of a pleasing modernistic type, showing knowledge and ability in handling instrumental and vocal idioms.
WORKS: Piano Quintet (1935); *Discharge in E* and *Streamline* for Band (1935); 8 Variations for String Quartet (1937); Brass Septet (1938); cantata, *Half Moon Mountain,* for Baritone, Women's Chorus, and Orch., after a story in *Time* magazine (Spartanburg, S.C., April 30, 1948); 100 Variations for Solo Violin (1952); Toccata and Fugue for Orch. (1954); Piano Trio (1956); Rhapsody for Violin, Cello, and Piano (1963); 24 Variations for Cello (1963); *Celebration* for Violin and Orch. (1964); *Workout* for 2 Violins and 2 Violas (1970); *Suite* for Horn Solo (1976); choruses.

Gershfeld, David, Moldavian composer; b. Bobrinets, Aug. 28, 1911. He studied French horn and music theory in Odessa; then moved to Kishinev, where he produced 2 operas on Moldavian subjects: *Grozovan* (Kishinev, June 9, 1956) and *Aurelia* (Kishinev, April 26, 1959); also a Violin Concerto (1951) and a ballad for Unaccompanied Chorus, *26 Commissars of Baku* (commemorating the Bolshevik representatives in Azerbaijani martyred by the British expeditionary force). In 1966 he moved to Sochi in the Caucasus.

Gershkovitch, Jacques, Russian conductor; b. Irkutsk, Siberia, Jan. 3, 1884; d. Sandy, Oreg., Aug. 12, 1953. He studied at the St. Petersburg Cons. with Rimsky-Korsakov, Glazunov, and Nicolas Tcherepnin. He graduated with honors, and received a scholarship to study in Germany under Artur Nikisch. Upon his return to Russia, he became director of the Irkutsk Cons.; after the Revolution, he joined the orch. of Pavlova's ballet troupe as a flutist, and traveled with it to the Orient. He settled in Tokyo, where he organized special concerts for young people; after the earthquake of 1923, he went to the U.S.; conducted guest engagements with the San Francisco Symph.; then was in Portland, Oreg., where he founded the Portland Junior Symph.; he conducted it for 30 years, until his death.

Gershwin, George, immensely gifted American composer; b. Brooklyn, N.Y., Sept. 26, 1898; d. Beverly Hills, Calif., July 11, 1937. His real name was **Jacob Gershvin,** according to the birth registry; his father was an immigrant from Russia whose original name was Gershovitz. Gershwin's extraordinary career began when he was 16, playing the piano in music stores to demonstrate new popular songs. His studies were desultory; he took piano lessons with Ernest Hutcheson and Charles Hambitzer in N.Y.; studied harmony with Edward Kilenyi and with Rubin Goldmark; later on, when he was already a famous composer of popular music, he continued to take private lessons; he studied counterpoint with Henry Cowell and with Wallingford Riegger; during the last years of his life, he applied himself with great earnestness to studying with Joseph Schillinger in an attempt to organize his technique in a scientific manner; some of Schillinger's methods he applied in *Porgy and Bess.* But it was his melodic talent and a genius for rhythmic invention, rather than any studies, that made him a genuinely important American composer. As far as worldly success was concerned, there was no period of struggle in Gershwin's life; one of his earliest songs, *Swanee,* written at the age of 19, became enormously popular (more than a million copies sold; 2,250,000 phonograph records). He also took time to write a lyrical *Lullaby* for String Quartet (1920). Possessing phenomenal energy, he produced musical comedies in close succession, using fashionable jazz formulas in original and ingenious ways. A milestone of his career was *Rhapsody in Blue,* for Piano and Jazz Orch., in which he applied the jazz idiom to an essentially classical form. He played the solo part at a special concert conducted by Paul Whiteman at Aeolian Hall in N.Y. on Feb. 12, 1924.

The orchestration was by Ferde Grofé, a circumstance that generated rumors of Gershwin's inability to score for instruments; these rumors, however, were quickly refuted by his production of several orch. works, scored by himself in a brilliant fashion. He played the solo part of his Piano Concerto in F, with Walter Damrosch and the N.Y. Symph. Orch. (Dec. 3, 1925); this work had a certain vogue, but its popularity never equaled that of the *Rhapsody in Blue*. Reverting again to a more popular idiom, Gershwin wrote a symph. work, *An American in Paris* (N.Y. Phil., Dec. 13, 1928, Damrosch conducting). His *Rhapsody No. 2* was performed by Koussevitzky and the Boston Symph. on Jan. 29, 1932, but was unsuccessful; there followed a *Cuban Overture* (N.Y., Aug. 16, 1932) and Variations for Piano and Orch. on his song *I Got Rhythm* (Boston, Jan. 14, 1934, Gershwin soloist). In the meantime, Gershwin became engaged in his most ambitious undertaking: the composition of *Porgy and Bess*, an American opera in a folk manner, for black singers, after the book by Dubose Heyward. It was first staged in Boston on Sept. 30, 1935, and shortly afterward in N.Y. Its reception by the press was not uniformly favorable, but its songs rapidly attained great popularity (*Summertime; I Got Plenty o' Nuthin'; It Ain't Neccessarily So; Bess, You Is My Woman Now*); the opera has been successfully revived in N.Y. and elsewhere; it received international recognition when an American company of black singers toured South America and Europe in 1955, reaching a climax of success with several performances in Russia (Leningrad, Dec. 26, 1955, and also Moscow); it was the first American opera company to visit Russia. Gershwin's death (of a gliomatous cyst in the right temporal lobe of the brain) at the age of 38 was mourned as a great loss to American music; memorial concerts have been held at Lewisohn Stadium in N.Y. on each anniversary of his death, with large attendance. His musical comedies include: numbers for *George White's Scandals* of 1920–24; *Our Nell* (1922); *Sweet Little Devil* (1923); *Lady Be Good* (1924); *Primrose* (1924); *Tip Toes* (1925); *Song of the Flame* (1925); *135th Street* (one act, 1923; produced in concert form Dec. 29, 1925, Paul Whiteman conducting); *Oh Kay!* (1926); *Strike Up the Band* (1927); *Funny Face* (1927); *Rosalie* (1928); *Treasure Girl* (1928); *Show Girl* (1929); *Girl Crazy* (1930); *Of Thee I Sing* (1931; a political satire which was the first musical to win a Pulitzer Prize); *Pardon My English* (1932); *Let 'Em Eat Cake* (1933); for motion pictures: *Shall We Dance, Damsel in Distress, Goldwyn Follies* (left unfinished at his death; completed by Vernon Duke). A collection of his songs and piano transcriptions, *George Gershwin's Song Book*, was publ. in 1932; reprinted as *Gershwin Years in Song* (N.Y., 1973).

BIBLIOGRAPHY: S.N. Behrman, "Troubadour," *New Yorker* (May 1929); I. Goldberg, *George Gershwin, A Study in American Music* (N.Y., 1931); C. Engel, "George Gershwin's Song Book," in "Views and Reviews" of the *Musical Quarterly* (Oct. 1932); V. Thomson, "George Gershwin," *Modern Music* (Nov. 1935); F. Jacobi, "George Gershwin," ibid. (Nov.–Dec. 1937); M. Armitage, ed., *George Gershwin, a collection of articles (N.Y., 1938); O. Levant, A Smattering of Ignorance* (N.Y., 1938); R. Chalupt, *George Gershwin, le musicien de la "Rhapsody in Blue"* (Paris, 1949); M.V. Pugliaro, *Rhapsodia in blu; L'arte e l'amore nella vita di George Gershwin* (Turin, 1951); D. Ewen, *A Journey to Greatness; George Gershwin* (N.Y., 1956; radically revised under the new title *George Gershwin, His Journey to Greatness*, 1970); M. Armitage, *George Gershwin, Man and Legend* (N.Y., 1958); E. Jablonski and L.D. Stewart, *The Gershwin Years* (N.Y., 1958); R. Kimball and A. Simon, *The Gershwins* (N.Y., 1973); C. Schwartz, *Gershwin: His Life and Music* (Indianapolis, 1973); idem, *George Gershwin: A Selective Bibliography and Discography* (Detroit, 1974).

Gershwin, Ira, one of the most talented American librettists and lyricists, brother of **George Gershwin;** b. New York, Dec. 6, 1896; d. Beverly Hills, Calif., Aug. 17, 1983. He attended night classes at the College of the City of N.Y., wrote verses and humorous pieces for the school paper, and served as cashier in a Turkish bath of which his father was part owner. He began writing lyrics for shows in 1918, using the pseudonym **Arthur Francis.** His first fullfledged show as a lyricist was the musical comedy *Be Yourself,* for which he used his own name for the first time. He achieved fame when he wrote the lyrics for his brother's musical comedy *Lady Be Good* (1924). He remained his brother's collaborator until George Gershwin's death in 1937, and his lyrics became an inalienable part of the whole, so that the brothers George and Ira Gershwin became artistic twins, like Gilbert and Sullivan, indissolubly united in some of the greatest productions of the musical theater in America: *Strike Up the Band* (1930), *Of Thee I Sing* (1931), etc., and the culminating product of the brotherly genius, the folk opera *Porgy and Bess* (1935). Ira Gershwin also wrote lyrics for other composers, among them Vernon Duke (*The Ziegfeld Follies of 1936*), Kurt Weill (*Lady in the Dark,* and several motion pictures), and Jerome Kern (the enormously successful song *Long Ago and Far Away* from the film *Cover Girl*).

Gerstberger, Karl, German music scholar and composer; b. Neisse, Feb. 12, 1892; d. Bremen, Oct. 30, 1955. He studied in Cologne with Othegraven and in Munich with Courvoisier. In 1926 he gave a concert of his works in Berlin. In his music he endeavored to revive the spirit of Lutheran polyphony. He wrote choral works, lieder, a String Quartet, 2 string trios, etc.; publ. a collection of essays, *Zum Schicksal der Musik*.

Gerster, Etelka, Hungarian dramatic soprano; b. Kaschau, June 25, 1855; d. Pontecchio, near Bologna, Aug. 20, 1920. She studied with Mathilde Marchesi in Vienna, then made her debut in Venice as Gilda in *Rigoletto,* Jan. 8, 1876. Her great success resulted in engagements in Berlin and Budapest in Italian opera under the direction of Carlo Gardini. She married Gardini on April 16, 1877, and continued her successful career, making her London debut on

June 23, 1877, as Amina in *Sonnambula,* and her U.S. debut in the same role on Nov. 11, 1878, at the N.Y. Academy of Music. She returned to London for 3 more seasons (1878–80), then sang again in N.Y. in 1880–83 and in 1887. After retiring, she taught singing in Berlin, and in N.Y. at the Inst. of Musical Art (1907). She wrote the book *Stimmführer* (1906; 2nd. ed., 1908).

Gerster, Ottmar, eminent German violinist, composer, and pedagogue; b. Braunfels, June 29, 1897; d. Leipzig, Aug. 31, 1969. He studied music theory with Bernhard Sekles at the Frankfurt Cons. (1913–16); then was mobilized during the last years of World War I; after the war, studied violin with Adolf Rebner (1919–21); played the viola in string quartets (1923–27), and concurrently was concertmaster of the Frankfurt Symph. Orch. From 1927 to 1939 he taught violin and theory at the Folkwang-Schule in Essen; in 1940 was again in the army. After that war he was on the faculty of the Hochschule für Musik in Weimar (1947–52) and then in Leipzig (1952–62). His music is marked by melodious polyphony in a neo-Classical vein; in his operas he used folklike thematic material.
WORKS: Operas: *Madame Liselotte* (Essen, 1933); *Enoch Arden* (Düsseldorf, 1936); *Die Hexe von Passau* (Düsseldorf, 1941); *Das Verzauberte Ich* (Wuppertal, 1949); *Der fröhliche Sünder* (Weimar, 1963); ballet, *Der ewige Kreis* (Duisburg, 1939); *Kleine Sinfonie* (1931); *Thüringer Sinfonie* (1952); *Leipziger Sinfonie* (1965); *Oberhessische Bauerntänze* for Orch. (1937); Cello Concerto (1946); Piano Concerto (1956); Horn Concerto (1962); 2 string quartets (1923, 1954); String Trio (1957); *Ballade vom Manne Karl Marx (und der Veränderung der Welt)* for Baritone Solo, Chorus, and Orch. (1961); many other choruses, some to words of political significance; songs.
BIBLIOGRAPHY: O. Goldhammer, *Ottmar Gerster* (Berlin, 1953).

Gerstman, Blanche, South African pianist and composer; b. Cape Town, April 2, 1910; d. there, Aug. 11, 1973. She was of British extraction, but adopted the family name of her adoptive parents. She studied music theory with Hely-Hutchinson and later with William Henry Bell at the South African College of Music. She was subsequently active as a radio pianist; in 1950 she went to London, where she took additional courses at the Royal College of Music with Howard Ferguson. Returning to South Africa in 1952, she was appointed lecturer in harmony at the College of Music in Cape Town. She composed pleasurable piano pieces, singable choruses, and some playable chamber music.

Gertler, André, Hungarian violinist; b. Budapest, July 26, 1907. He studied with Hubay and Kodály; in 1928 settled in Belgium; in 1931 he formed the Quatuor Gertler in Brussels. He later taught at the Brussels Cons.; in 1964 he was appointed prof. of violin at the Hochschule für Musik in Hannover.

Gervaise, Claude, French composer of the 16th century. He was a viol player, and chamber musician to François I and Henri II. He composed many dances and *chansons;* 6 vols. of his *Danceries à 4 et 5 parties* were publ. by Attaignant from about 1545 to 1556, but only 3 vols. remain; a selection of his dances is included in vol. 23 (Danceries) of *Les Maîtres musiciens* edited by H. Expert (1908). Several *chansons* by Gervaise appear in 16th-century collections.

Gerville-Réache, Jeanne, French dramatic contralto; b. Orthez, March 26, 1882; d. New York, Jan. 5, 1915. She spent her childhood in Guadeloupe, French West Indies, where her father was governor. In 1898 she was sent to Paris to study singing with Mme. Viardot-García. she made her debut at the Opéra-Comique in Paris in 1899; continued to sing there until 1903; She created the role of Geneviève in *Pelléas et Mélisande* there on April 30, 1902; went to N.Y., where she became a member of the Manhattan Opera Co. (1907–10); subsequently sang opera in Chicago, Boston, Philadelphia, and Montreal. In 1908 she married Dr. Georges Rambaud, director of the Pasteur Inst. in N.Y.

Gesensway, Louis, American violinist and composer; b. Dvinsk, Latvia, Feb. 19, 1906; d. Philadelphia, March 11, 1976. The family moved to Canada when he was a child; he studied violin; in 1926 joined the Philadelphia Orch., remaining with it until 1971. He was also a prolific composer of some originality; he developed a system of "color harmony" by expanding and contracting the intervals of the diatonic scale into fractions, establishing a difference between enharmonically equal tones; such a scale in Gesensway's projection contained 41 degrees.
WORKS: For Orch.: Flute Concerto (Philadelphia, Nov. 1, 1946); *The 4 Squares of Philadelphia* for Narrator and Orch. (Philadelphia, Feb. 25, 1955); *Ode to Peace* (Philadelphia, April 15, 1960); *Commemoration Symphony* (1966–68; Philadelphia, Feb. 25, 1971); *A Pennsylvania Overture* (1972); Cello Concerto (1973); chamber music: Concerto for 13 Brass Instruments (1942); Quartet for Clarinet and Strings (1950); Quartet for Oboe, Bassoon, Violin, and Viola (1951); Sonata for Solo Bassoon; Duo for Oboe and Guitar (1959); Duo for Viola and Bassoon (1960); Duo for Violin and Cello (1970).

Gesualdo, Don Carlo, Prince of Venosa, lutenist and composer; b. Naples, c.1560; d. there, Sept. 8, 1613. He probably studied with Pomponio Nenna; in 1590, his unfaithful wife and first cousin, Maria d'Avalos, and her lover were murdered at Gesualdo's orders; in 1594, he was at the court of the Estensi in Ferrara, where he married his 2nd wife, Leonora d'Este, in that year; sometime after the death of the Duke of Ferrara, in 1597, Don Carlo returned to Naples, where he remained till death. Living at the epoch when the "new music" (the homophonic style) made its appearance, he was one of the most original musicians of the time. Like Rore, Banchieri, and Vincentino, he was a so-called chromaticist; his later madrigals reveal a distinctly individual style of expression and are characterized by strong contrasts, new (for their time) harmonic progressions, and a skilful use of dissonance; he was a master in producing tone color through the use of different voice registers and in expressing the poetic contents of his texts. He publ. 6 vols. of madrigals *a* 5 (Genoa, 1585, each part separately; an ed. in score was publ. by G. Pavoni, Venice, 1613). A complete edition of his works was begun by the Istituto Italiano per la Storia della Musica (Rome), but only one vol. (2 books of madrigals) appeared (1942); a new edition of the 6 books of madrigals, edited by F. Vatelli and A. Bizzelli, was publ. in 1956–58. A new edition of his works, in 10 vols. (6 books of madrigals, 3 vols. of sacred works, and one vol. of instrumental works, canzonette, and Psalms), edited by W. Weisman and G.E. Watkins, was publ. in 1957–67.

BIBLIOGRAPHY: F. Keiner, *Die Madrigale Gesualdos von Venosa* (Diss., Univ of Leipzig, 1914); Cecil Gray and Philip Heseltine, *Carlo Gesualdo, Prince of Venosa, Musician and Murderer* (London, 1926); F. Vatielli, *Il Principe di Venosa e Leonora d'Este* (Milan, 1941); Glenn Watkins, *Gesualdo, The Man and His Music* (London, 1973).

Geszty, Sylvia, Hungarian soprano; b. Budapest, Feb. 28, 1934. She studied at the Budapest Cons.; made her debut at the National Theater in Budapest in 1959. In 1966 she sang the Queen of the Night in Peter Hall's production of *The Magic Flute* at Covent Garden in London; she repeated the role at the Salzburg Festival in 1967 and also sang Zerbinetta at the Munich Opera Festival; her agile voice and attractive stage presence made her a favorite in this soubrette role, and she chose it for her 1971 debut with the Glyndebourne Festival. She joined the Hamburg Opera in 1970; in the same year she sang at the Teatro Colón in Buenos Aires; then made her North American debut in the same role with the N.Y. City Opera. Her other roles include Olympia in *The Tales of Hoffmann,* and Alcina in Handel's opera.

Getz, Stan(ley), American jazz tenor saxophonist; b. Philadelphia, Feb. 2, 1927. While still a teenager, he joined Jack Teagarden's group; then played with Stan Kenton, Jimmy Dorsy, and Benny Goodman; after a major stint with Woody Herman, he embarked upon a series of recordings with Gerry Mulligan, Dizzy Gillespie, and other noted jazz musicians. He was an impressive exponent of "cool" jazz.

Gevaert, François Auguste, eminent Belgian composer and musicologist; b. Huysse, near Audenarde, July 31, 1828; d. Brussels, Dec. 24, 1908. He was a pupil of De Somère (piano) and Mengal (composition) at the Ghent Cons. (1841–47), taking the Grand Prix de Rome for composition; from 1843 he was also organist at the Jesuit church. He produced 2 operas in 1848, with some success; lived in Paris for a year (1849–50), and was commissioned to write an opera for the Théâtre-Lyrique; then spent a year in Spain, his *Fantasía sobre motivos españoles* winning him the Order of Isabella la Católica; he also wrote a *Rapport sur la situation de la musique en Espagne* (Brussels, 1851). After a short visit to Italy and Germany, he returned to Ghent in 1852, and up to 1861 brought out 9 operas in quick succession. In 1857 his festival cantata *De nationale verjaerdag* won him the Order of Léopold. In 1867 he was appointed music director at the Opéra, Paris; in 1870, the German invasion caused him to return home, and from 1871 he was director of the Brussels Cons., succeeding Fétis. In this position he gave evidence of remarkable talent for organization. As conductor of the "Concerts du Conservatoire," he exerted a far-reaching influence through his historical concerts, producing works of all nations and periods. In 1873 he was elected a member of the Academy, succeeding Mercadante; in 1907 he was made a baron. WORKS: 12 operas; 3 cantatas; a *Missa pro defunctis* and *Super flumina Babylonis* (both for Male Chorus and Orch.); overture, *Flandre au lion;* ballads (*Philipp van Artevelde,* etc.); songs (many in the collection *Nederlandsche Zangstukken*). WRITINGS: Even more important than Gevaert's compositions are his scholarly books: *Leerboek van den Gregoriaenschen Zang* (1856); *Traité d'instrumentation* (1863; revised and enlarged as *Nouveau traité de l'instrumentation,* 1885; German trans. by Riemann, 1887; Spanish trans. by Neuparth, 1896; Russian trans. by Rebikov, 1899); *Histoire et théorie de la musique de l'antiquité* (2 vols., 1875, 1881); *Les Origines du chant liturgique de l'église latine* (1890; German trans. by Riemann; threw new light on the Gregorian tradition); *Cours méthodique d'orchestration* (2 vols., 1890; complement of *Nouveau traité*); *La Mélopée antique dans l'église latine* (1895; a monumental work); *Les Problèmes musicaux d'Aristote* (3 vols., 1899–1902; adopts the theories of Westphal, certain of which were later proved untenable); *Traité d'harmonie théorique et pratique* (2 vols., 1905, 1907). He ed. *Les Gloires de l'Italie* (a collection of vocal numbers from operas, oratorios, cantatas, etc., of the 17th and 18th centuries); *Recueil de chansons du XVe siècle* (transcribed in modern notation); *Vademecum de l'organiste* (classic transcriptions). BIBLIOGRAPHY: F. Dufour, *Le Baron François Auguste Gevaert* (Brussels, 1909); E. Closson, *Gevaert* (Brussels, 1928).

Geyer, Stefi, Swiss violinist of Hungarian descent; b. Budapest, Jan. 28, 1888; d. Zürich, Dec. 11, 1956. She studied violin with Hubay at the Budapest Academy; toured in Europe and the U.S. at an early age. In 1919 she settled in Zürich and married the composer **Walter Schulthess.** She taught at the Zürich Cons. for 30 years (1923–53). She was an object of passion on the part of Béla Bartók, who wrote a violin concerto for her (1907), but she never performed it; it was finally discovered and performed in Basel in 1958. Another composer who was enamored of her was Othmar Schoeck, who also wrote a concerto for her.

Ghedini, Giorgio Federico, Italian composer; b. Cunneo, July 11, 1892; d. Nervi, March 25, 1965. He studied piano and organ with Evasio Lovazzano in Turin, cello with S. Grossi, and composition with G. Cravero; then at the Liceo Musicale in Bologna with M.E. Bossi, graduating in 1911. In 1918 he became an instructor at the Liceo Musicale in Turin; simultaneously taught composition at the Cons. of Parma (1938–41) and in 1941 took a similar post at the Cons. of Milan, where he was later its director (1951–62).
WORKS: FOR THE STAGE: Operas: *Gringoire* (1915); *Maria d'Alessandria* (Bergamo, Sept. 9, 1937); *Re Hassan* (Venice, Jan. 26, 1939); *La pulce d'oro* (Genoa, Feb. 15, 1940); *Le Baccanti* (Milan, Feb. 21, 1948); *Billy Budd* (after the Melville novel; Venice, Sept. 7, 1949); *Lord Inferno,* "harmonious comedy" for radio (after Beerbohm's *The Happy Hypocrite;* Italian radio, Oct. 22, 1952; revised as a stage production, retitled *L'Ipocrita felice,* and presented at La Scala in Milan, March 10, 1956); *La Via della Croce* (Venice, April 9, 1961). Ballet: *Girotondo,* mime play for children (Venice, 1959). FOR ORCH: *Partita* (1926); *Concerto Grosso* for Wind Quintet and Strings (1927); *Pezzo concertante* for 2 Violins, Viola Obbligato, and Orch. (1931); *Marinaresca e baccanale* (1933; Rome, Feb. 2, 1936); Symph. (1938); *Architetture,* concerto for Orch. (1940; Rome, Jan. 19, 1941); *Invenzioni,* concerto for Cello, Strings, Kettledrums, and Cymbals (1940); Piano Concerto (1946); *Musica Notturna* for Chamber Orch. (1947); Concerto for 2 Pianos and Chamber Orch. (1947; Milan, Jan. 24, 1948); *Il Belprato,* concerto for Violin and Strings (1947); *Canzoni* (1948); *L'Alderina,* concerto for Flute, Violin, and Orch. (1951); *L'Olmeneta,* concerto for 2 Cellos and Orch. (1951); *Musica da concerto* for Viola and Strings (1953); *Concentus Basiliensis* for Violin and Chamber Orch. (1954); *Vocalizzo da concerto* for Cello or Baritone Voice, and Orch. (1957); *Composizione* (1958); *Fantasie* for Piano and Strings (1958); *Sonata da concerto* for Flute, Strings, and Percussion (1958); *Divertimento* for Violin and Orch. (1960); *Studi per un affresco di battaglia* (1962); *Contrappunti* for Violin, Viola, Cello, and Strings (1962); *Musica concertante* for Cello and Strings (1962); *Appunti per un credo* for Chamber Orch. (1962); *Concert Overture* (1963). FOR VOICE: *Il pianto della Madonna,* sacred cantata (1921); *Ecco il Re forte,* cantata (1923); *Litanie della Vergine* for Soprano, Women's Chorus, and Orch. (1926); *Le Messa del Venerdì santo (Good Friday Mass),* oratorio (1929; Perugia, Italy, Sept. 27, 1949); *Cantico del sole* for Men's Chorus and Strings (1932); *Antigone,* cantata (1933); *Lectio Libri Sapientiae,* spiritual cantata for Voice, Trumpet, Piano, and Strings (1938); *Concerto spirituale* for 2 Sopranos or Women's Chorus, and 9 Instruments of Chamber Orch. (1943); *Antifona per Luisa* for Soprano Chorus, Boy's Voice, and Organ or Strings (1944); *Concerto dell'Albatro* for Narrator and Small Orch. (Rome, Dec. 11, 1945); *Corona di Sacre Canzoni, o, Laudi Spirituali* for Voice, Chorus, Piano, and Strings (1946); *Concerto funebre per Duccio Galimberti* for Tenor, Bass, 2 Trombones, Strings, and Timpani (1948; Rome, June 8, 1949); *Il Rosero,* concerto for Women's Chorus, Piano, Harp, and Strings (1950); *Lectio Jeremiae prophetae,* cantata da camera for Soprano, Chorus, and Small Orch. (1960); *Credo di Perugia* for Chorus and Orch. (1962); masses and motets; songs. CHAMBER MUSIC: Wind Quintet (1910); Piano Quartet (1917); Double Quartet for 5 Winds, 5 Strings, Harp, and Piano (1921); Violin Sonata (1922); Cello Sonata (1924); 2 string quartets (1927, 1959); *Adagio e allegro da Concerto* for Flute, Clarinet, Horn, Viola, Cello, and Harp (1936); *Concertato* for Flute, Viola, and Harp (1942); *7 Ricercari* for Piano Trio (1943); *Canons* for Violin and Cello (1946); *Concentus* for String Quartet (1948); *Music* for Flute, Cello, and Piano (1963). FOR PIANO: *Pastorale elegiaca* (1926) and *Capriccio* (1934); also several orch. transcriptions for modern performance of works by Bach, Gabrieli, Monteverdi, Schütz, and Frescobaldi. most notably of Frescobaldi's *Quattro Pezzi* (originally for organ) in 1931.

Gheluwe, Leon van, Belgian composer; b. Wanneghem-Lede, Sept. 15, 1837; d. Ghent, July 14, 1914. He studied in Ghent with Gevaert and others; became a prof. at the Ghent Cons. in 1869; later was director of the Ecole de Musique in Bruges. He wrote a Flemish opera, *Philippine van Vlaanderen* (Brussels, 1876), and a number of songs.

Ghent, Emmanuel, American composer; b. Montreal, May 15, 1925. He studied bassoon and music theory at McGill Univ.; also took courses in psychology and psychoanalysis; eventually settled in N.Y. as a practicing psychiatrist. In 1964, with the aid of an engineer, he constructed the Polynome, a device capable of accurate reproduction of multiple rhythms by click signals transmitted to a performer's ear through a tiny earphone; he applied this instrument in several compositions.
WORKS: *Movement* for Wind Quintet (1944); *3 Duos* for Flutes (1944); *Lament* for String Quartet (1958); Quartet for Flute, Oboe, Clarinet, and Bassoon (1960); *2 Duos* for Flute and Clarinet (1962); *Dance Movement* for Trumpet and String Quartet (1962); *Entelechy* for Viola and Piano (1963); *Triality I* and *II* for Violin, Trumpet, and Bassoon, in conjunction with the Polynome (1964); *Dithyrambos* for Brass Quintet (1965); *Hex, an Ellipsis* for Trumpet, 11 Instruments and Synchronized Tape (1966); *Helices* for Violin, Piano, and Tape (1969). Electronic compositions include *Lady Chatterley's Lover* (1969); *L'Après-midi d'un Summit Meeting* (1970); *Our Daily Bread* (1970); *12 Electronic Highlights* (1970).

Gheorghiu, Valentin, Rumanian composer; b. Galatz, March 21, 1928. He studied composition with Jora and Andricu at the Bucharest Cons.; then went to Paris, where he studied piano with Lazare Lévy and harmony at the Paris Cons. (1937–39). His works include 2 symphs. (1949, 1956); a Piano Concerto

(1959); *Imagini din copilărie (Images of Youth),* suite for Orch. (1961); *Burlesca* for Piano and Orch. (1964); String Quartet (1946); Piano Sonata (1946); Cello Sonata (1950); Piano Trio (1950); songs.

Gheyn, Matthias van den, Flemish organist and composer; b. Tirlemont, Brabant, April 7, 1721; d. Louvain, June 22, 1785. From 1741, he was organist at St. Peter's, Louvain, and from 1745, town "carillonneur"; he was celebrated in both capacities. He composed pieces for organ and for carillon.
WRITINGS: *Fondements de la basse continue* (lessons and sonatinas for organ and violin); *6 divertissements pour clavecin* (c.1760).
BIBLIOGRAPHY: S. van Elewyck, *Matthias van den Gheyn* (Louvain, 1862).

Ghezzo, Dinu, Rumanian composer; b. Tusla, July 2, 1941. He studied music at the Bucharest Cons., graduating in 1966; then went to the U.S., where he enrolled at the Univ. of Calif., Los Angeles (Ph.D., 1973). In 1974 he was appointed to the faculty of Queens College. In 1976 he organized in N.Y. the New Repertory Ensemble, for the purpose of presenting programs of new music. His works are of a distinctly modern character, making use of electronic instruments. His compositions include Clarinet Sonata (1967); String Quartet (1967); *Segmenti* for Clarinet, Cello, and Piano (1968); *Music* for Flutes and Tapes (1971); *Kanones* for Flutes, Cello, Harpsichord, and Tapes (1972); *Images* for Bass Flute, Divider, and Echoplex (1972); *Thalla* for Piano, Electric Piano, and 16 Instruments (1974); Concertino for Clarinet and Winds (1975); *Ritualen* for Prepared Piano (1969); *Ritualen II* for Prepared Piano and Tape (1970); *Cantos nuevos,* ballet (1977).

Ghiaurov, Nicolai, Bulgarian bass; b. Lydjene, near Velingrad, Sept. 13, 1929. He studied violin and piano in Bulgaria; then went to Moscow, where he received his vocal training. He made his debut in Sofia as Don Basilio in *The Barber of Seville* in 1955; then appeared in Moscow (1958) and at La Scala in Milan (1959). He soon established himself as a fine singer; his quality of voice is that of basso cantante. He sang Méphistophélès in *Faust* at his debut with the Metropolitan Opera in N.Y. (Nov. 8, 1965).

Ghiglia, Oscar, Italian guitarist; b. Livorno, Aug. 13, 1938. He studied at the Santa Cecilia Academy in Rome; also took lessons with Segovia at the Accademia Chigiana in Siena. After winning a guitar competition in Paris, he received a scholarship to the Schola Cantorum, where he studied music history with Jacques Chailley. He made his American debut in N.Y. in 1966; subsequently toured in America and in Europe.

Ghignone, Giovanni Pietro. See **Guignon, Jean-Pierre.**

Ghione, Franco, Italian conductor; b. Acqui, Aug. 28, 1886; d. Rome, Jan. 19, 1964. He studied violin

with his father; organized a band which he later conducted. After study at the Parma Cons., he became assistant conductor to Toscanini at La Scala (1922–23). From 1937 to 1940 he was associate conductor of the Detroit Symph. Orch.

Ghis, Henri, French pianist and composer; b. Toulon, May 17, 1839; d. Paris, April 24, 1908. He studied at the Paris Cons. with Marmontel (piano); received first prize in 1854; also studied organ with Benoist (graduated in 1855). He became a fashionable piano teacher in Paris; many aristocratic ladies (to whom he dedicated his pieces) were his pupils. He was the first teacher of Ravel. He publ. salon music for piano: waltzes, mazurkas, polonaises, polkas, gavottes, caprices, etc., often with superinduced titles, as *Séduction, Menuet de la petite princesse, La Marquisette,* etc.; but his name is mostly known through his extremely popular arrangement of an old aria, which he publ. for piano as *Air Louis XIII* (1868); the actual melody was definitely not by Louis XIII; its authorship is unknown; in all probability it is an old French folk song.

Ghisi, Federico, Italian musicologist and composer; b. Shanghai, China (of Italian parents), Feb. 25, 1901; d. Luzerna San Giovanni, July 18, 1975. His father was a member of the diplomatic corps in China; the family returned to Italy in 1908, and settled in Milan. Ghisi studied music with Ghedini; in 1937, became instructor at the Univ. of Florence.
WORKS: OPERAS: *Il dono dei Re Magi* (1959); *Il Vagabondo e la guardia* (1960); *L'ultima visione,* oratorio after Plato's *Republic* (1968).
WRITINGS: *I canti carnascialeschi* (Florence, 1937); *Le feste musicali della Firenze Medicea* (Florence, 1939); *Alle Fonti della Monodia* (Milan, 1940).

Ghislanzoni, Antonio, Italian writer and dramatic poet; b. Barco, near Lecco, Nov. 25, 1824; d. Caprino-Bergamasco, July 16, 1893. He was intended for the church, but his fine baritone voice led him to adopt the career of a stage singer (Lodi, 1846), which he speedily abandoned, however, for literary work. He became the manager of *Italia Musicale,* and was for years the editor of the Milan *Gazzetta Musicale,* to which he remained a faithful contributor till his death. He wrote over 60 opera librettos, that of *Aida* being the most famous; publ. *Reminiscenze artistiche* (which contains an episode entitled *La casa di Verdi a Sant' Agata*).
BIBLIOGRAPHY: T. Mantovani, "Librettisti Verdiani, VI: Antonio Ghislanzoni," *Musica d'Oggi* (March–April 1929).

Ghitalla, Armando, American trumpeter; b. Alfa, Ill., June 1, 1925. He studied at the Juilliard School of Music in N.Y. with William Vacchiano; in 1949 he joined the Houston Symph. Orch.; in 1951 he was engaged by the Boston Symph. Orch.; in 1965 became its first trumpet.

Ghys, Joseph, Belgian violinist; b. Ghent, 1801; d.

St. Petersburg, Aug. 22, 1848. A pupil of Lafont at the Brussels Cons., he later taught in Amiens and Nantes, and, beginning in 1832, made concert tours in France, Belgium, Germany, Austria, and northern Europe. He wrote *Le Mouvement perpétuel* for Violin, with String Quartet; a Violin Concerto; and other music for the violin.

Giacomelli, Geminiano, Italian composer; b. Piacenza, c.1692; d. Loreto, Jan. 25, 1740. He studied with Capelli at Parma, and wrote his first opera, *Ipermestra,* in 1724. It was the first of 19 operas which he wrote for Venice, Parma, Naples, and other Italian towns; the most popular was *Cesare in Egitto* (Milan, 1735). He was maestro di cappella at the court of Parma and the Chiesa della Steccata in 1719–27; returned to both posts in 1732–37; was maestro di cappella for the church of San Giovanni in Piacenza from 1727 to 1732; he held a similar post at Santa Casa in Loreto from 1738. His many church compositions include an oratorio, *La conversione di Santa Margherita,* and a setting of Psalm VIII for Two Tenors and Bass.
BIBLIOGRAPHY: G. Tebaldini, *L'Archivio musicale della Cappella Lauretana* (Loreto, 1929); C. Anguissola, *Geminiano Giacomelli e Sebastiano Nasolini, musicisti piacentini* (Piacenza, 1935).

Gialdini, Gialdino, Italian conductor and composer; b. Pescia, Nov. 10, 1843; d. there, March 6, 1919. He was a pupil of T. Mabellini at Florence. His first opera, *Rosamunda* (prize opera in a competition instituted by the Pergola Theater, Florence), given in 1868, was unsuccessful; after producing 2 "opere buffe," *La Secchia rapita* (Florence, 1872) and *L'Idolo cinese* (1874), in collaboration with other musicians, he gave up opera writing, and devoted himself with success to conducting. Later he again turned to dramatic composition, producing the operas *I due soci* (Bologna, Feb. 24, 1892), *La Pupilla* (Trieste, Oct. 23, 1896), and *La Bufera* (Pola, Nov. 26, 1910); these operas were successful. He also publ. *Eco della Lombardia,* a collection of 50 folk songs.

Gianettini (or Zanettini), Antonio, Italian composer; b. Fano, 1648; d. Munich, July 12, 1721. He was organist at San Marco, Venice (1676–86); produced 3 operas in Venice, winning a reputation that led to his appointment as maestro di cappella at the court of Modena; was organist at Modena from 1686 till 1721, except during 1695, when he brought out 3 operas in Hamburg. He moved to Munich with his family in May 1721. He composed 6 operas; 6 oratorios; several cantatas; a Kyrie *a* 5; and Psalms *a* 4, with Instruments (Venice, 1717).
BIBLIOGRAPHY: E.J. Luin, *Antonio Gianettini e la musica a Modena alla fine del secolo 17* (Modena, 1931).

Gianneo, Luis, Argentine composer; b. Buenos Aires, Jan. 9, 1897; d. there, Aug. 15, 1968. He studied composition with Gaito and Drangosch. From 1923 to 1943 he taught at the Inst. Musical in Tucumán; then was a prof. of music at various schools in

Buenos Aires. He was especially interested in the problems of musical education of the very young; in 1945 he organized and conducted the Orquesta Sinfónica Juvenil Argentina; from 1955 to 1960 he was director of the Cons. of Buenos Aires.
WORKS: Ballet, *Blanca nieves* (1939); 3 symphs. (1938, 1945, 1963); *Turay-Turay,* symph. poem (Buenos Aires, Sept. 21, 1929); *Obertura para una comedia infantil* (1939); Piano Concerto (1941); Sinfonietta (Buenos Aires, Sept. 20, 1943); Violin Concerto (Buenos Aires, April 13, 1944); *Cantica Dianae* for Chorus and Orch. (1949); *Variaciones sobre tema de tango* for Orch. (1953); *Angor Dei* for Soprano and Orch. (1962); *Poema de la Saeta* for Soprano and Orch. (1966); 4 string quartets (1936, 1944, 1952, 1958); 2 piano trios; String Trio; Violin Sonata; Cello Sonata; teaching pieces for piano; 3 Piano Sonatas (1917, 1943, 1957); songs.

Giannetti, Giovanni, Italian composer; b. Naples, March 25, 1869; d. Rio de Janeiro, Dec. 10, 1934. He studied in Naples, Trieste, and Vienna; in 1912–13, was director of the Liceo Musicale, Siena; in 1915, was in Rome, where (from 1920) he was music director of the Teatro dei Piccoli, with which he toured Europe and South America.
WORKS: Operas: *L'Erebo* (Naples, April 9, 1891); *Padron Maurizio* (Naples, Sept. 26, 1896); *Milena* (Naples, Nov. 15, 1897); *Il Violinaro di Cremona* (Milan, Nov. 23, 1898); *Don Marzio* (Venice, March 2, 1903); *Il Cristo alla festa di Purim* (Rio de Janeiro, Dec. 16, 1904); *Il Nazareno* (Buenos Aires, Jan. 20, 1911); *La Serenata di Pierrot,* pantomime (Rome, April 18, 1917); *Cuore e baute* (Rome, June 5, 1918); *Il Principe Re,* operetta (Rome, July 7, 1920).

Giannini, Dusolina, American soprano, sister of **Vittorio Giannini;** b. Philadelphia, Dec. 19, 1900. She received her earliest musical education at home; her mother was a violinist; her father, **Ferruccio Giannini** (1869–1948), was an Italian tenor who made one of the earliest phonograph recordings, in 1896. She studied voice with Marcella Sembrich; made her concert debut in N.Y., on March 14, 1920. On Sept. 12, 1925, she made her operatic debut in Hamburg, and subsequently sang in opera in London, Berlin, and Vienna. On Feb. 12, 1936, she appeared with the Metropolitan Opera in the role of Aida, and remained on its staff until 1941. She sang the part of Hester in the first performance of the opera *The Scarlet Letter,* by her brother, Vittorio Giannini (Hamburg, June 2, 1938).

Giannini, Vittorio, American composer, brother of **Dusolina Giannini;** b. Philadelphia, Oct. 19, 1903; d. New York, Nov. 28, 1966. Brought up in a musical family, he showed a precocious talent. He was sent to Italy at the age of 10, and studied at the Cons. of Milan (1913–17). After returning to the U.S., he took private lessons with Martini and Trucco in N.Y.; in 1925 he entered the Juilliard graduate school, where he was a pupil of Rubin Goldmark in composition and Hans Letz in violin; in 1932 he won the

American Prix de Rome; was in Rome for a period of 4 years. Upon his return to N.Y., he was appointed to the faculty of the Juilliard School of Music in 1939 as a teacher of composition and orchestration; in 1941 he also became an instructor in music theory; furthermore, he was appointed prof. of composition at the Curtis Inst. of Music in Philadelphia in 1956. As a composer, Giannini was at his best in opera, writing music of fine emotional éclat, excelling in the art of bel canto and avoiding extreme modernistic usages; in his symph. works he also continued the rich Italian tradition; these qualities endeared him with opera singers, but at the same time left his music out of the mainstream of the modern century. WORKS: Operas: *Lucedia* (Munich, Oct. 20, 1934); *Flora* (1937); *The Scarlet Letter* (Hamburg, June 2, 1938); *Beauty and the Beast* (1938; concert version, CBS Radio, Nov. 24, 1938; stage premiere, Hartford, Conn., Feb. 14, 1946); *Blennerhasset,* radio opera (CBS Radio, Nov. 22, 1939); *The Taming of the Shrew* (his most appreciated opera; in concert form, Cincinnati Symph. Orch., Jan. 31, 1953; in color telecast, NBC opera theater, March 13, 1954); *The Harvest* (Chicago, Nov. 25, 1961); *Rehearsal Call,* opera buffa (N.Y., Feb. 15, 1962); *The Servant of 2 Masters* (posthumous, N.Y., March 9, 1967); for Orch.: Symph., subtitled "In Memoriam Theodore Roosevelt" (1935; N.Y., NBC Orch., Jan. 19, 1936, composer conducting); I.B.M. Symph., commissioned for the N.Y. World's Fair (1939); 4 numbered symphs.: No. 1, *Sinfonia* (Cincinnati, April 6, 1951); No. 2 (St. Louis, April 16, 1956); No. 3 for Band (1958); No. 4 (N.Y., May 26, 1960); 3 divertimentos (1953, 1961, 1964); *Psalm 130,* concerto for Double Bass and Orch. (Brevard, N.C., Aug. 9, 1963); *The Medead,* monodrama for Soprano and Orch. (Atlanta, Ga., Oct. 20, 1960); Piano Concerto (1937); Organ Concerto (1937); Concerto for 2 Pianos (1940); several sacred works for chorus; *Canticle of the Martyrs* (commissioned for the 500th anniversary of the Moravian Church, 1957, at Winston-Salem, N.C.); Concerto Grosso for Strings (1931); Piano Quintet (1931); Woodwind Quintet (1933); Piano Trio (1933); 2 violin sonatas (1926, 1945); Piano Sonata; many songs.

Giarda, Luigi Stefano, Italian cellist and composer; b. Pavia, March 19, 1868; d. Viña del Mar, Chile, Jan. 3, 1953. He was a pupil at the Milan Cons.; a teacher at the Padua music school (1893–97); an instructor at the Royal Cons. in Naples (1897–1910); then went to Santiago, Chile, where he was vicedirector of the Cons. of Santiago; also taught theory there. WORKS: Operas: *Reietto* (Naples, 1898) and *Giorgio Byron* (Santiago, Chile, 1910); symph. poems: *Loreley; La vida; Triptico (Civilization, War, Peace)* for 3 Voices and Orch.; concert pieces for Cello and Orch.; a String Quartet; *Adagio* for 4 Cellos; 2 cello sonatas; Prelude and Scherzo for Violin and Cello.

Giardini, Felice de', Italian violinist and composer; b. Turin, April 12, 1716, d. Moscow, June 8, 1796.

He was a chorister at the Cathedral of Milan; studied singing and harpsichord with Paladini and violin with Somis in Turin. As a young man he played in various theater orchs. in Rome and Naples; often improvised cadenzas at the end of operatic numbers. He acquired popularity in Italy and made a tour in Germany (1748); then went to London (1750), where he made a series of successful appearances as a concert violinist. In 1752 he joined the Italian opera in London as concertmaster and conductor; he became its impresario in 1756, and was connected with the management, with interruptions, for several more seasons, returning to the career of virtuoso and teacher in 1766. He conducted the Three Choirs festival (1770–76) and was concertmaster at the Pantheon Concerts (1774–80); also conducted other theater orchs. In 1784–89 he was in Italy; returned to London in 1789 and led 3 seasons of Italian opera, without financial success. In 1796 he was engaged as a violinist in Russia and gave his initial concert in Moscow, on March 24, 1796, but soon became ill, and died shortly afterward. As a violinist, he was eclipsed in London by Salomon and Cramer, but he left his mark on musical society there. WORKS: Among operas entirely by him were *Rosmira* (April 30, 1757); *Siroe* (Dec. 13, 1763); *Enea e Lavinia* (May 5, 1764); and *Il Re pastore* (March 7, 1765); he also wrote music for various pasticcios; also wrote several overtures, concertos, string quartets, and violin sonatas.

BIBLIOGRAPHY: R.A. Mooser, *Annales de la musique et des musiciens en Russie au XVIIIᵉ siècle* (Lausanne, 1951; vol. 2, pp. 657ff.); S. McVeigh, *The Violinist in London's Concert Life, 1750–1784; Felice Giardini and His Contemporaries* (Diss., Oxford Univ., 1980).

Giazotto, Remo, Italian musicologist; b. Rome, Sept. 4, 1910. He studied piano at the Milan Cons. and later took a course in literature at the Univ. of Genoa; was on the staff of the *Rivista Musicale Italiana* from 1932 to 1949; from 1967 was co-editor of *Nuova Rivista Musicale Italiana;* from 1957, a prof. at the Univ. of Florence; he undertook a detailed study of the musical history of Genoa, and publ. a work of fundamental value, *La musica a Genova nella vita pubblica e privata dal XIII al XVIII secolo* (Genoa, 1952). He is also the author of a biography of Tomaso Albinoni (Milan, 1945), containing newly discovered materials as well as a thematic catalogue. He further publ. a monograph, *Ferruccio Busoni, La vita nell' opera* (Milan, 1948), and biographies on Giovanni Battista Viotti (Milan, 1956) and Vivaldi (Milan, 1965).

Gibbons, Christopher, English organist and composer; b. London (baptized, Aug. 22), 1615; d. there, Oct. 20, 1676. He was the son of **Orlando Gibbons;** was a pupil at the Chapel Royal; in 1638, he became organist at Winchester Cathedral; in 1660, he was appointed organist of the Chapel Royal, private organist to Charles II, and organist at Westminster Abbey. He received the degree of Mus.D. from Oxford in 1663, at the special request of the King. He wrote anthems and many string fantasies, now in MS in the British Library, Christ Church, Oxford; the Royal College of Music; Marsh's Library, Dublin; and Durham and Ely cathedrals; some of his motets are in Playford's "Cantica sacra" (1674). He also collaborated with Matthew Locke in the music for Shirley's masque *Cupid and Death.* C. Rayner prepared the modern edition, *Christopher Gibbons: Keyboard Compositions,* in *Corpus of Early Keyboard Music,* XVIII (1967).

BIBLIOGRAPHY: C. Rayner, *A Little-known 17th-century Composer, Christopher Gibbons* (Diss., Indiana Univ., 1963).

Gibbons, Edward, English musician; b. Cambridge, 1568; d. probably Exeter, c.1650. The eldest living son of **William Gibbons,** who founded this musical family, he was the brother of **Ellis** and **Orlando.** He received a B.Mus. degree from both Oxford and Cambridge; after serving as a lay clerk at King's College, Cambridge, he became master of choristers in 1593, and kept the post until 1598; then he went to the Exeter Cathedral, where he served for many years, with the titles of "priest-vicar" and succentor, though he remained a layman. Little of his music is in existence; a few of his compositions, all for the church, are in the British Library, at Christ Church, Oxford, and in the Bodleian Library.

Gibbons, Ellis, English composer and organist, brother of **Edward** and **Orlando Gibbons;** b. Cambridge, 1573; d. May 1603. The only compositions of his which are known to exist are 2 madrigals included by Morley in his collection *The Triumphes of Oriana (Long live fair Oriana* and *Round about her charret).*

Gibbons, Orlando, celebrated English composer and organist, brother of **Edward** and **Ellis Gibbons;** b. Oxford (baptized, Dec. 25), 1583; d. Canterbury, June 5, 1625. He was taken to Cambridge as a small child; in 1596, he became chorister at King's College there; matriculated in 1598; composed music for various occasions for King's College (1602–3). On March 21, 1605, he was appointed organist of the Chapel Royal, retaining this position until his death. He received the degree of B.Mus. from Cambridge Univ. in 1606, and that of D.Mus. from Oxford in 1622. In 1619 he became chamber musician to the King; in 1623, organist at Westminster Abbey. He conducted the music for the funeral of James I (1625); died of apoplexy 2 months later. His fame as a composer rests chiefly on his church music; he employed the novel technique of the "verse anthem" (a work for chorus and solo voices, the solo passages having independent instrumental accompaniment, for either organ or strings); other works followed the traditional polyphonic style, of which Gibbons became a master. He was also one of the greatest English organists of the time.

WORKS: *Fantasies of 3 Parts ... composed for viols* (1610; described on the title page as "Cut in copper, the like not heretofore extant in England";

ed. by E.F. Rimbault in *Musical Antiquarian Society,* vol. 9; new ed. by E.H. Fellowes, 1924); pieces for the virginal, in *Parthenia* (21 pieces of Gibbons, Byrd, and John Bull; 1611; reprinted in *Musical Antiquarian Society,* vol. 18; new ed. by Margaret H. Glyn, 1927); *The First Set of Madrigals and Mottets of 5 Parts* (London, 1612; reprinted in *Musical Antiquarian Society,* vol. 3; new ed. by E.H. Fellowes in *The English Madrigal School,* vol. 5, 1921); 9 Fancies, appended to *20 konincklijke Fantasien op 3 Fiolen* by T. Lupo, Coperario, and W. Daman (Amsterdam, 1648); 2 anthems in Leighton's *Teares or Lamentacions of a Sorrowfull Soule* (the only sacred works by Gibbons publ. during his lifetime). A "complete" ed. of all extant sacred compositions is in *Tudor Church Music,* 4; Gibbons's entire keyboard works were ed. by Margaret H. Glyn in 5 vols. (London, 1925); also in *Musica Britannica,* 20 (1962). Further new eds. follow: The madrigal *God give you good morrow* (from *The Cryes of London,* an early 17th-century MS [in the Brit. Museum] containing 2 other sets of street cries likewise polyphonically treated by T. Weelkes and R. Deering), ed. by Sir Fred. Bridge (London, 1920); 2 Fantazias for String Quartet or Small String Orch., and a Pavan and Galliard for String Sextet or Small String Orch., ed. by E.H. Fellowes (London, 1925); 10 pieces from the virginal book of B. Cosyn, arranged for modern organ by J.A. Fuller-Maitland (London, 1925); Verse Anthems, in *Early English Church Music,* III (1964).

BIBLIOGRAPHY: E.H. Fellowes, *The English Madrigal Composers* (1921); Margaret H. Glyn, *About Elizabethan Virginal Music and Its Composers* (1924); E.H. Fellowes, *Orlando Gibbons, A Short Account of His Life and Work* (1925); idem, *Orlando Gibbons and His Family* (1925; 2nd ed., 1951).

Gibbs, Cecil Armstrong, English composer; b. Great Baddow, near Chelmsford, Aug. 10, 1889; d. Chelmsford, May 12, 1960. He studied at Trinity College, Cambridge, and at the Royal College of Music in London; later became an instructor there (1921–39); in 1934 he received the Cobbett Gold Medal for his services to British chamber music.

WORKS: Operas: *The Blue Peter* (1924); *Twelfth Night* (1947); *The Great Bell of Burley* (children's opera, 1949); 3 symphs.; *Spring Garland* for Strings; Oboe Concerto; *Peacock Pie,* suite for Piano and Strings; Rhapsody for Violin and Orch.; *Essex Suite* for Strings; several string quartets; Lyric Sonata for Violin and Piano; Piano Trio; cantatas: *La Belle Dame sans merci, The Lady of Shalott, Deborah and Barak, Before Daybreak, Odyssey;* also a Pastoral Suite for Baritone, Chorus, and Orch. (1951). Gibbs wrote more than 100 songs, many of them to poems of Walter de la Mare. His musical style adheres to the Romantic school; the influence of folk melodies and rhythms is also noticeable.

BIBLIOGRAPHY: Cobbett's *Cyclopedic Survey of Chamber Music.*

Gibbs, Terry (real name, **Julius Gubenko**), American jazz percussionist and bandleader; b. New York, Oct. 13, 1924. He began to play the drums and timpani in his youth; won a Major Bowes contest at the age of 12; later played with Tommy Dorsey, Buddy Rich, Woody Herman, Benny Goodman, and other musicians; also was successful as a bandleader.

Gibson, Sir Alexander, distinguished Scottish conductor; b. Motherwell, Feb. 11, 1926. he was educated at Glasgow Univ. and the Royal College of Music in London; also took courses at the Salzburg Mozarteum and in Siena. He made his debut as conductor at the Sadler's Wells Opera in London in 1951; was subsequently conductor of the BBC Scottish Symph. Orch. in Glasgow (1952–54). In 1959 he was appointed principal conductor of the Scottish National Orch. in Glasgow. In 1962 he founded the Scottish Opera, becoming its first music director. In 1977 Queen Elizabeth II knighted him for his services in behalf of the musical life of his native Scotland and Great Britain. In 1981 he became principal guest conductor of the Houston Symph. Orch. He is mainly renowned for his congenial performances of the works of modern Romantic composers, particularly those of the English school.

Gibson, Archer, American organist; b. Baltimore, Dec. 5, 1875; d. Lake Mahopac, N.Y., July 15, 1952. He studied with his father, later with W.G. Owst (composition) and Harold Randolph (organ and piano); held various positions as a church organist; wrote the cantatas *Emancipation* and *A Song to Music;* an opera, *Yzdra;* organ pieces; choral and orch. arrangements.

Gideon, Miriam, American composer; b. Greeley, Colo., Oct. 23, 1906. She studied piano with Hans Barth in N.Y. and with Felix Fox in Boston; then enrolled at Boston Univ. (B.A., 1926) and took courses in musicology at Columbia Univ. (M.A., 1946); studied composition privately with Lazare Saminsky and Roger Sessions. She served on the music faculty of Brooklyn College (1944–54); in 1955 became a prof. of music at the Jewish Theological Center; in 1967 joined the faculty at the Manhattan School of Music; then was a prof. of music at the City Univ. of N.Y. (1971–76); was elected to the American Academy and Inst. of Arts and Letters in 1975. She wrote music in all genres, in a style distinguished by its attractive modernism.

WORKS: Opera, *Fortunato* (1958); *The Adorable Mouse,* French folk tale for Narrator and Chamber Orch. (1960); *Lyric Piece* for String Orch. (1941); *Symphonia brevis* (1953); *Songs of Youth and Madness* for Voice and Orch. on poems of Friedrich Hölderlin (1977); String Quartet (1946); Viola Sonata (1948); *Fantasy on a Javanese Motive* for Cello and Piano (1948); Divertimento for Woodwind Quartet (1948); *Biblical Masks* for Violin and Piano (1960); Cello Sonata (1961); Suite for Clarinet and Piano (1972); *Fantasy on an Irish Folk Motive* for Oboe, Viola, Bassoon, and Vibraphone (1975); *The Hound of Heaven,* to the poem by Francis Thompson, for Voice, Violin, Viola, Cello, and Oboe (1945);

Sonnets from Shakespeare for Voice, Trumpet, and String Quartet (1950); *Sonnets from "Fatal Interview,"* after Edna St. Vincent Millay, for Voice, Violin, Viola, and Cello (1952); *The Condemned Playground* for Soprano and Instruments (1963); *Questions on Nature* for Voice, Oboe, Piano, Tamtam, and Glockenspiel (1965); *Rhymes from the Hill,* after the *Galgenlieder* of Christian Morgenstern, for Voice, Clarinet, Cello, and Marimba (1968); *The Seasons of Time,* after Japanese poetry, for Voice, Flute, Cello, and Piano (1969); Clarinet Sonata (1973); *Nocturnes* for Voice, Flute, Oboe, Violin, Cello, and Vibraphone (1976); *Canzona* for Piano (1945); *6 Cuckoos in Quest of a Composer* for Piano (1953); Piano Sonata (1977); choruses and songs.

Giebel, Agnes, soprano; b. Heerlen, the Netherlands, Aug. 10, 1921. She was educated at the Folkwangschule in Essen; began a career as a concert singer in 1947. She gained wide recognition for her radio broadcasts of the Bach cantatas. At a later period she promoted modern music; her performances of works by Schoenberg, Alban Berg, Hindemith, and Henze were praised by informed critics. She made several tours as a concert artist in the U.S. and Japan.

Gieburowski, Waclaw, eminent Polish musicologist; b. Bydgoszcz, Feb. 6, 1876; d. Warsaw, Sept. 17, 1943. He was a student of theology in Regensburg, where he also took courses in church music with Haberl; then studied in Berlin with Wolf and Kretzschmar and in Breslau with Otto Kinkeldey; obtained a doctorate from the Univ. of Breslau with his dissertation *Die Musica Magistri Szydlowitae, Ein polnischer Choraltraktat des 15. Jahrhunderts* (1913; publ. Poznan, 1915). He settled in Poznan as a prof. of church music at the Univ. (1925–39); in 1916 was appointed choir conductor at the Poznan Cathedral; wrote church music. In 1928 he began the publication of the valuable series Cantica Selecta Musices Sacrae in Polonia; restored to use many sacred works by Polish composers of the Renaissance; publ. several treatises on this subject; also composed several sacred choral works.

Giegling, Franz, Swiss musicologist; b. Buchs, near Aarau, Feb. 27, 1921. He studied piano and theory at the Zürich Cons. with Cherbuliez; received his Ph.D. from the Univ. of Zürich in 1947 with the valuable dissertation *Giuseppe Torelli, Ein Beitrag zur Entwicklungsgeschichte des italienischen Konzerts* (publ. in Kassel, 1949); was music critic of the *Neue Zürcher Zeitung* (1947–53); subsequently worked for Radio Zürich and Radio Basel; was one of the editors of the 6th edition of the Köchel catalogue of Mozart's works; contributed articles to *Die Musik in Geschichte und Gegenwart.*

Gielen, Michael, German conductor; b. Dresden, July 20, 1927. He was a son of Josef Gielen, an opera director who emigrated to Buenos Aires in 1939, and a nephew of the pianist **Eduard Steuermann.** He studied piano and composition in Buenos Aires with Erwin Leuchter; in 1951 went to Vienna; from 1954–60 he served as conductor of the Vienna State Opera. He then was principal conductor of the Royal Swedish Opera in Stockholm (1960–65); also was a conductor with the Cologne Radio Symph. Orch. (1965–69). From 1969–72 he was chief conductor of the Orch. National de Belgique in Brussels; in 1972 was appointed chief conductor of the Netherlands Opera in Amsterdam. In 1977 he became director of the Frankfurt Opera and chief conductor of the Museumgesellschaft Concerts; in 1980 he was appointed music director of the Cincinnati Symph. Orch. He won a solid reputation as a congenial interpreter of contemporary music. He is also a composer in his own right; his works include a Violin Sonata (1946); Trio for Clarinet, Viola, and Bassoon (1948); *Variations* for String Quartet (1949); *Music* for Baritone, Strings, Piano, Trombone, and Percussion (1954); *4 Songs of Stefan George* for Chorus and Instruments (1955); Variations for 40 Instruments (1959); *Pentaphonie* for Piano, 5 Soloists, and 5 Quintets (1960–63).

Gierster, Hans, German conductor; b. Munich, Jan. 12, 1925. He studied at the Hochschule für Musik in Munich and at the Salzburg Mozarteum. He served as a conductor at the Düsseldorf Opera (1945–52); in 1956 became Generalmusikdirektor in Freiburg. In 1965 he was named Generalmusikdirektor at Nuremberg. He appeared as a conductor throughout West Germany; also conducted in England.

Gieseking, Walter, distinguished pianist; b. Lyons, France, of German parents, Nov. 5, 1895; d. London, Oct. 26, 1956. He studied with Karl Leimer at the Hannover Cons., graduating in 1916; then served in the German army during World War I; began his concert career with extensive tours of Europe; made his American debut at Aeolian Hall, N.Y., Feb. 22, 1926, and after that appeared regularly in the U.S. and Europe with orchs. and in solo recitals. He became one of the most brilliant and musicianly pianists of his generation, capable of profound and intimate interpretations of both classical and modern piano music. His dual German-French background enabled him to project with the utmost authenticity the piano masterpieces of both cultures. His playing of Debussy was remarkable; he was an excellent performer of works by Prokofiev and other modernists. He composed some chamber music and made piano transcriptions of songs by Richard Strauss. He became the center of a political controversy when he arrived in the U.S. early in 1949 for a concert tour; he was accused of cultural collaboration with the Nazi regime, and public protests forced the cancellation of his scheduled performances at Carnegie Hall. However, he was later cleared by an Allied court in Germany and was able to resume his career in America. He appeared again at a Carnegie Hall recital on April 22, 1953, and until his death continued to give numerous performances in both hemispheres. His autobiography, *So Wurde ich Pianist,* was publ. posthumously in Wiesbaden (1963).

BIBLIOGRAPHY: B. Gavoty, *Gieseking,* in the series Les Grands Interprètes (Geneva, 1955).

Gigli, Beniamino, famous Italian tenor; b. Recanati, March 20, 1890; d. Rome, Nov. 30, 1957. He studied with Rosati in Rome; made his operatic debut in Rovigo, near Venice, in 1914, as Enzo in *La Gioconda;* then sang in many Italian cities. His first American appearance was as Faust in Boito's *Mefistofele* with the Metropolitan Opera (Nov. 26, 1920); he remained on its staff until 1932, and returned there for one season, 1938–39. He then went back to Italy, where he remained during World War II. He revisited the U.S. in 1955 and gave a series of concerts with considerable success, despite his age. At the height of his career, he ranked among the best tenors in opera; he was particularly impressive in the lyric roles of Verdi's and Puccini's operas; he also sang in the German and French repertoire; his interpretation of Lohengrin was acclaimed. His voice possessed great strength and a variety of expressive powers.

BIBLIOGRAPHY: R. Rosner, *Beniamino Gigli* (Vienna, 1929); R. de Rensis, *Il Cantatore del popolo: Beniamino Gigli* (Rome, 1933; in German, Munich, 1936); D. Silvestrini, *Beniamino Gigli* (Bologna, 1937). Gigli's memoirs were publ. in Eng. in London (1957).

Gigout, Eugène, French organ virtuoso and composer; b. Nancy, March 23, 1844; d. Paris, Dec. 9, 1925. He began music studies in the *maîtrise* of Nancy Cathedral; at 13 he entered the Niedermeyer School at Paris, in which he subsequently taught (1863–85 and 1900–1905); for a time, was a pupil of Saint-Saëns. From 1863, Gigout was organist at the church of St.-Augustin; he won fame as a concert organist in France, England, Germany, Switzerland, Spain, and Italy; he was especially famous for his masterly improvisations. In 1885 he founded at Paris an organ school subsidized by the government, from which many excellent pupils graduated (Boëllmann, Fauré, Messager, A. Georges, A. Roussel, C. Terrasse, etc.); from 1911, he was a prof. of organ and improvisation at the National Cons., Paris. He was also an esteemed writer on music and a critic; he was a Commander of the Order of Isabella la Católica; Officer of Public Instruction (from 1885); and Chevalier of the Legion of Honor (from 1895). As a composer, he followed the severe style. WORKS: For Organ: *100 pièces brèves* (Gregorian); *Album grégorien* (3 vols., each containing 100 pieces exclusively in the church modes); *Rhapsodie sur des Noëls; Toccata; Scherzo; Prélude et Fugue* in B-flat; *Marche de fête; Rhapsodie sur des airs catalans; Rhapsodie sur des airs canadiens; Poèmes mystiques;* Piano Sonata in F; other pieces for piano (2 and 4 hands); sacred choruses; songs. BIBLIOGRAPHY: *Hommage à Eugène Gigout* (Paris, 1923; contains a biographical sketch by Gabriel Fauré and catalogue of works).

Gil-Marchex, Henri, French pianist; b. St. Georges

Gilardi – Gilbert

d'Espérance (Isère), Dec. 16, 1894; d. Paris, Nov. 22, 1970. He studied at the Paris Cons., then with L. Capet and A. Cortot; toured Europe, Russia, and Japan, and performed modern works at various festivals in Europe. In 1956, he was director of the Cons. at Poitiers.

Gilardi, Gilardo, Argentine composer; b. San Fernando, May 25, 1889; d. Buenos Aires, Jan. 16, 1963. He studied with Pablo Berutti, then devoted himself to teaching and composing. Two of his operas were produced at the Teatro Colón in Buenos Aires: *Ilse* (July 13, 1923) and *La leyenda de Urutaú* (Oct. 25, 1934). He also wrote *Sinfonia cíclico* (1961), 3 piano trios, 2 string quartets, *Sonata Popular Argentina* for Violin and Piano (1939), and many dances and songs based on native melodies.

Gilbert, Anthony, English composer; b. London, July 26, 1934. He studied piano at the Trinity College of Music and later at Morley College, where he took composition classes with Milner and Goehr (1959–60); also studied privately with Seiber (1960); then again with Goehr (1960–63). His professional career evolved mainly in teaching; he was on the faculty at Lancaster Univ. (1971–73), at Morley College (from 1971), and at the Royal Northern College of Music in Manchester (from 1973). A modernist by nature, he nevertheless wrote music in classical forms, and was not averse to representational music; on the purely structural side, he adopted various attenuated forms of serial music, and in thematic development used disparate agglutinative blocks. WORKS: Opera, *The Scene-Machine* (1970; Kassel, Germany, April 4, 1971); *Sinfonia* for Chamber Orch. (London, March 30, 1965); *Regions* for 2 Chamber Orchs. (1966); *Peal II* for Jazz or School Orch. (1968); Symph. (Cheltenham Festival, July 12, 1973); *Ghost and Dream Dancing* for Orch. (Birmingham, Sept. 19, 1974); Duo for Violin and Viola (1963); Serenade for 6 Instruments (1963); *Brighton Piece* for 2 Percussionists and Instrumental Ensemble (1967); *9 or 10 Osannas* for Clarinet, Horn, Violin, Cello, and Piano (1967); *The Incredible Flute Music* for Flute and Piano (1968); *Spell Respell* for Electric Bassett Clarinet and Piano (1968); *Mother* for Solo Cello, Clarinet, Flute, Violin or Viola, Keyboard, and Percussion (1969); *A Treatment of Silence* for Violin and Tape (1970); *Love Poems* for Soprano, Clarinet, Cello, and Accordion (1970); *O'Grady Music* for Clarinet, Cello, and Toy Instruments (Los Angeles, Jan. 10, 1972); *String Quartet with Piano Pieces* (1972); *Cantata: A Man Who Tried to Hijack an Airplane* for 3 Voices and Renaissance Instruments (1972); *Canticle* for Wind Ensemble (1973); *Inscapes* for Soprano, Reader, and Instrumental Ensemble (1975); 2 piano sonatas (1962, 1966); *Charm against the Gout* for Chorus (1965); several melodramas for wireless.

Gilbert, Henry Franklin Belknap, remarkable American composer; b. Somerville, Mass., Sept. 26, 1868; d. Cambridge, Mass., May 19, 1928. He studied at the New England Cons. and with E. Mollenhauer;

in 1889–92, was a pupil of MacDowell (composition) in Boston. Rather than do routine music work to earn his livelihood (he had previously been a violinist in theaters, etc.), he took jobs of many descriptions, becoming, in turn, a real estate agent, a factory foreman, a collector of butterflies in Florida, etc., and composed when opportunity afforded. In 1893, at the Chicago World's Fair, he met a Russian prince who knew Rimsky-Korsakov and gave him many details of contemporary Russian composers whose work, as well as that of Bohemian and Scandinavian composers which was based on folk song, influenced Gilbert greatly in his later composition. In 1894 he made his first trip abroad and stayed in Paris, subsequently returning to the U.S.; when he heard of the premiere of Charpentier's *Louise,* he became intensely interested in the work because of its popular character, and, in order to hear it, earned his passage to Paris, in 1901, by working on a cattle boat; the opera impressed him so much that he decided to devote his entire time thereafter to composition. In 1902 he became associated with Arthur Farwell, whose Wa-Wan Press publ. Gilbert's early compositions. During this time (from 1903) he employed Negro tunes and rhythms extensively in his works. The compositions of his mature period (from 1915) reveal an original style, not founded on any particular native American material but infused with elements from many sources, and are an attempt at "un-European" music, expressing the spirit of America and its national characteristics. WORKS: OPERA: *The Fantasy in Delft* (1915). FOR ORCH.: *2 Episodes* (Boston, Jan. 13, 1896); *Humoresque on Negro-Minstrel Tunes* (originally entitled *Americanesque,* 1903; Boston Pops, May 24, 1911); *Comedy Overture on Negro Themes* (1905; perf. at a N.Y. municipal concert, Aug. 17, 1910; Boston Symph., April 13, 1911; also perf. by Glière, in Feodosia, Crimea, July 22, 1914, and in Odessa, Aug. 1, 1914); symph. poem, *The Dance in Place Congo* (1906; perf. as a ballet at the Metropolitan Opera, N.Y., March 23, 1918); *Strife* (1910); *Negro Rhapsody* (Norfolk, [Conn.] Festival, June 5, 1913, composer conducting); symph. prologue for Synge's *Riders to the Sea* (1904; MacDowell Festival, Peterboro, N.H., Aug. 20, 1914; revised version, N.Y. Phil., Nov. 11, 1917); *American Dances* (1915); *Indian Sketches* (Boston Symph., March 4, 1921); Suite from *Music to Pilgrim Tercentenary Pageant* (Boston Symph., March 31, 1922); *Symphonic Piece* (Boston Symph., Feb. 26, 1926); Nocturne, a "symph. mood" after Walt Whitman (Philadelphia, March 16, 1928); Suite for Chamber Orch. (commissioned by the E.S. Coolidge Foundation; first perf., Chamber Orch. of Boston, Slonimsky conducting, April 28, 1928); *To Thee, America,* hymn for Chorus and Orch. (MacDowell Festival, Peterboro, N.H., Jan. 25, 1915); *Salammbô's Invocation to Tänith,* aria for Soprano and Orch. (N.Y., Elise Stevens, with the Russian Symph. Orch., March 10, 1906); an early String Quartet. FOR PIANO: *Negro Episode, Mazurka, Scherzo, 2 Verlaine Moods, The Island of the Fay* (also for Orch.), *Indian Scenes, A Rag Bag, Negro Dances.* SONGS: *Pirate Song,* after Stevenson; *Celtic Studies,* cycle of 4 songs to poems by Irish poets; *The Lament of*

Deirdre; Faery Song; 2 South American Gypsy Songs; Fish Wharf Rhapsody; Give Me the Splendid Sun; The Owl; Orlamonde; Zephyrus; Homesick; Tell Me Where Is Fancy Bred?; Croon of the Dew; 8 Simple Songs; Perdita; The Curl; School Songs; also ed. *100 Folksongs* (Boston, 1910); contributed articles to the *Musical Quarterly* ("The American Composer," April 1915; "The Survival of Music," July 1916; "Originality," Jan. 1919), and to other magazines.

BIBLIOGRAPHY: Arthur Farwell, "*Wanderjahre* of a Revolutionist," *Musical America* (April 10, 1909); "An American Composer's Triumph in Russia," *Current Opinion* (May 1916); E.C. Ranck, "The Mark Twain of American Music," *Theatre Magazine* (Sept. 1917); Olin Downes, "An American Composer," *Musical Quarterly* (Jan. 1918); "Gilbert, Henry," *Dictionary of American Biography* (vol. 7, N.Y., 1931); J.T. Howard, *Our American Music* (N.Y., 1939, and subsequent eds.); Olin Downes, "Henry Gilbert: Nonconformist," in *A Birthday Greeting to Carl Engel* (N.Y., 1943); E. Carter, "American Figure," *Modern Music* (1943); H.G. Sear, "H.F. Gilbert," *Music Review* (1944); Gilbert Chase, *America's Music* (N.Y., 1955; 2nd ed., 1966); K. Longyear, *Henry F. Gilbert: His Life and Works* (Diss., Univ. of Rochester, 1968).

Gilbert, Jean (pen name of **Max Winterfeld**), German operetta composer; b. Hamburg, Feb. 11, 1879; d. Buenos Aires, Dec. 20, 1942. He studied with Scharwenka; was active as a theater conductor in Hamburg and Berlin. In 1933 he left Germany, eventually settling in Buenos Aires.

WORKS: Operettas: *Die keusche Susanne* (1910); *Polnische Wirtschaft* (1910); *Die Kino-Königin* (1911); *Puppchen* (1912); *Die Frau im Hermelin* (1918); *Die Braut des Lucullus* (1920); *Katja, die Tänzerin* (1922); *Das Weib im Purpur* (1923); *In der Johannisnacht* (1926); *Hotel Stadt Lemberg* (1929); *Das Mädel am Steuer* (1930). The song *Puppchen, du bist mein Augenstern,* from the operetta *Puppchen,* achieved immense popularity in Europe.

Gilbert, Kenneth, Canadian harpsichordist, organist, and musicologist; b. Montreal, Dec. 16, 1931. He studied organ in Montreal with Conrad Letendre, piano with Yvonne Hubert, and theory with Gabriel Cusson at the Montreal Cons.; he won the Prix d'Europe for organ in 1953, and subsequently studied in Europe with Nadia Boulanger (theory), Gaston Litaize (organ), and Gustav Leonhardt and Ruggero Gerlin (harpsichord). From 1952–67 he was organist and music director of the Queen Mary Road United Church in Montreal; gave concerts as organist and harpsichordist. He taught at the Montreal Cons. (1957–74), McGill Univ. (1964–72), and Laval Univ. (1969–76). He edited the complete harpsichord works of François Couperin (4 vols., 1969–72); also the complete works of Domenico Scarlatti (11 vols., 1971—).

Gilbert, L. Wolfe, American songwriter; b. Odessa, Russia, Aug. 31, 1886; d. Beverly Hills, Calif., July 12, 1970. His family went to Philadelphia when he was an infant; at the age of 14 he went to N.Y. and sang in vaudeville, burlesque theaters, and nightclubs; he also toured as an entertainer with John L. Sullivan, the prizefighter. In 1912 he wrote his first hit song, *Waitin' for the Robert E. Lee.* He settled in Hollywood in 1929, where he formed his own publishing company. He composed some 250 songs, of which several became perennial favorites: *Ramona* (written for a motion picture in 1927); *Peanut Vendor; Down Yonder;* and *Lucky Lindy,* inspired by Lindbergh's transatlantic flight of 1927.

Gilbert, Timothy, piano maker in Boston. After 1820 he made several innovations of his own invention to improve the action of the piano. He brought out the organ-piano in 1847.

Gilbert, Sir William Schwenck, British playwright, creator, with Sir Arthur Sullivan, of the famous series of comic operas; b. London, Nov. 18, 1836; d. Harrow Weald, Middlesex, May 29, 1911 (of cardiac arrest following a successful attempt to rescue a young woman swimmer from drowning). He was given an excellent education (at Boulogne and at King's College, London) by his father, who was a novelist. After a routine career as a clerk, Gilbert drifted into journalism, contributing drama criticism and humorous verse to London periodicals. His satirical wit was first revealed in a theater piece, *Dulcamara* (1886), in which he ridiculed grand opera. He met Sullivan in 1871, and together they initiated the productions of comic operas which suited them so perfectly. Some plots borrow ludicrous situations from actual Italian and French operas; Gilbert's librettos, in rhymed verse, were nonetheless unmistakably English. This insularity of wit may explain the enormous popularity of the Gilbert & Sullivan operas in English-speaking countries, while they are practically unknown on the Continent. Despite the fact that the targets of Gilbert's ridicule were usually the upper classes of Great Britain, the operas were often performed at court. He was knighted in 1907. After 20 years of fruitful cooperation with Sullivan, a conflict developed, and the 2 severed their relationship for a time. A reconciliation was effected, but the subsequent productions fell short of their greatest successes. The most popular of the Gilbert & Sullivan operettas are *H.M.S. Pinafore* (1878); *The Pirates of Penzance* (1880); *Iolanthe* (1884); *The Mikado* (1885); and *The Gondoliers* (1889). A special theater, the Savoy, was built for the Gilbert & Sullivan productions in London in 1881 by the impresario Richard D'Oyly Carte.

BIBLIOGRAPHY: W.S. Gilbert, *Gilbert before Sullivan; 6 Comic Plays,* ed. by J.W. Stedman (Chicago, 1967); J.W. Stedman, "From Dame to Woman: W.S. Gilbert and Theatrical Transvestism," *Victorian Studies* (Sept. 1970); I. Bradley, ed., *The Annotated Gilbert and Sullivan* (London, 1982); A. Williamson, *Gilbert & Sullivan Opera* (London, 1983); see also entry under Sullivan.

Gilberté, Hallett, American song composer; b.

Winthrop, Maine, March 14, 1872; d. New York, Jan. 5, 1946. He studied piano with J. Orth and C. Barmann and composition with E. Nevin in Boston. He wrote about 250 songs, some of which were quite successful (*Spanish Serenade, Mother's Cradle Song, In Reverie, 2 Roses, Song of the Canoe, Ah, Love But a Day, Spring Serenade, Minuet La Phyllis, Moonlight and Starlight*).

Gilboa, Jacob, Czech-born Israeli composer; b. Košice, May 2, 1920. He grew up in Vienna and went to Palestine in 1938. He studied composition with Josef Tal in Jerusalem and Ben-Haim in Tel Aviv (1944–47); then traveled to Germany and attended courses of new music with Stockhausen, Pousseur, Alois Kontarsky, and Caskel. His music represents a blend of oriental and Eastern Mediterranean idioms, basically lyrical, but technically ultramodern. WORKS: *7 Little Insects,* piano pieces for children (1955); *Wild Flowers,* 4 lyrical pieces for Female Voice, Horn, Harp, and String Orch. (1957); *Passing Clouds* for Female Voice, Clarinet, Cello, and Piano (1958); Violin Sonata (1960); *The 12 Jerusalem Chagall Windows* for Voices and Instruments (1966); *The Beth Alpha Mosaic* for Female Voice, Chamber Ensemble, and Tape (1975; Chicago, Jan. 24, 1976); *Crystals* for Flute, Viola, Cello, Piano, and Percussion (1967); *Horizons in Violet and Blue,* ballet scene for 6 Players (1970); *Pastels* for 2 Prepared Pianos (1970); *Thistles,* theater piece for Singing and Speaking Voices, Horn, Cello, Piano, and Percussion (1970); *Cedars* for Orch. (1971); *From the Dead Sea Scrolls* for Chorus, Children's Chorus, 2 Organs, Tape, and Orch. (1971; Hamburg, Jan. 11, 1972); *14 Epigrams for Oscar Wilde* for Female Voice, Piano, and Tape (1973); *Bedu,* metamorphoses on a Bedouin call, for Male Voice, Cello, Flute, and Piano (1975); *5 Red Sea Impressions* for Violin, Piano, Harp, Electric Guitar, Organ, and Tape (1976).

Gilchrist, William Wallace, American composer; b. Jersey City, N.J., Jan. 8, 1846; d. Easton, Pa., Dec. 20, 1916. He studied organ with H.A. Clarke at the Univ. of Pa., which conferred on him the degree of Mus.D. in 1896. He was a choirmaster at various Philadelphia churches; from 1882, taught at the Philadelphia Music Academy. He formed the Mendelssohn Club and was its conductor later. He wrote cantatas, a Christmas oratorio, 2 symphs., chamber music, church music, and songs. BIBLIOGRAPHY: Sumner Salter, "Early Encouragement to American Composers," *Musical Quarterly* (Jan. 1932).

Gilels, Emil, outstanding Russian pianist; b. Odessa, Oct. 19, 1916. He studied at the Odessa Cons. with Yakov Tkatch and Berthe Ringold; then with Reingbald, graduating in 1935; then went to Moscow for advanced piano studies with Heinrich Neuhaus at the Moscow Cons. (1935–38). He made his first public appearance at the age of 13 in Odessa; in 1933 he received first prize at the Moscow competition; in 1936 he carried 2nd prize at the international piano competition in Vienna, and in 1938 won the first prize at the prestigious international competition in Brussels, which marked the highest point of his career; also in 1938 he was appointed a prof. at the Moscow Cons. He made numerous appearances in concert recitals and as soloist with major orchs. of Europe, America, and the Far East; made his first American tour in 1955, and returned at regular intervals; in 1977 he toured the U.S. for the 12th time. His playing is distinguished by a quality of Romantic intellectuality, with a fine understanding of the special pianistic sonorities. On several of his tours he played all 5 Beethoven piano concertos in succession. BIBLIOGRAPHY: V. Delson, *Emil Gilels* (Moscow, 1959); S. Hentova, *Emil Gilels* (Moscow, 1967).

Giles, Jean, French composer; b. Tarascon, near Avignon, Jan. 8, 1668; d. Toulouse, Feb. 5, 1705. He received his musical training in the choir school of the Cathedral of St. Sauveur at Aix-en-Provence; in 1688 became 2nd instructor and organist there; later he received an appointment as *maître de musique* at St. Etienne at Toulouse. His most famous work was *Messe des morts,* which became part of the regular services at funerals; it was performed at services for Louis XV in 1774. That Giles possessed an excellent technique is proved by the erudite fugue in the final Requiem of his *Messe des morts.* He further wrote 32 choral motets and a number of other sacred works.

Giles, Nathaniel, English organist and composer of church music; b. Worcester, c.1558; d. Windsor, Jan. 24, 1633. A son of **William Giles,** organist of St. Paul's Cathedral, London, he studied at Oxford; was organist at Worcester Cathedral from 1581 to 1585, when he became clerk, organist, and choirmaster at St. George's Chapel, Windsor; in 1597, became Gentleman and Master of the Children there. He wrote 4 services for the church; a great number of anthems; several motets and a 5-part madrigal (incomplete or in MS). Some of his compositions are included in Leighton's *Teares or Lamentacions of a Sorrowfull Soule* (1614); a service and an anthem are in Barnard's *Church Music* (1641); Hawkins's *History of Music* contains Giles's *Lesson of Descant of thirty-eighte Proportions of sundrie Kindes.* BIBLIOGRAPHY: J. Pulver, "Nathaniel Giles," *Monthly Musical Record* (Nov. 1933).

Gilibert, Charles, dramatic baritone; b. Paris, Nov. 29, 1866; d. New York, Oct. 11, 1910. He sang one season at the Opéra-Comique, and then went to the Théâtre de la Monnaie, Brussels, where he became a great favorite; from 1900 to 1903 he was a member of the Metropolitan Opera; at his debut on Dec. 18, 1900, and throughout the entire season, he failed to make a decided impression, but on his appearance in the 2nd season he took the public by storm; in 1906–10, he was at the Manhattan Opera House in N.Y.; he was then reengaged for the Metropolitan, and was to have created Jack Rance in *The Girl of the Golden West,* but died just before the opening of the season. He was also a distinguished concert singer and interpreter of old French songs.

Gille, Jacob Edvard, Swedish composer; b. Stockholm, Aug. 10, 1814; d. there, Nov. 8, 1880. He was a notary public; learned to play the piano and organ; served as choral master at the Catholic church in Stockholm, where he wrote 9 masses. As a composer he acquired a solid technique; his style of composition closely adhered to the German school. His works include 4 operas, 5 symphs., 5 string quartets, 4 piano trios, 2 string trios, 3 piano sonatas, 3 organ sonatas, and numerous minor pieces.

Gillespie, John Birks ("Dizzy"), black American jazz trumpeter and bandleader; b. Cheraw, S.C., Oct. 21, 1917. He picked up the rudiments of music from his father; at the age of 18 he went to Philadelphia, where he joined a local jazz band; in 1939 he became a member of the Cab Calloway orch., and in 1944 he was with the Billy Eckstine band. Soon he emerged as a true innovator in jazz playing, and was one of the founders of the style variously known as bebop, bop, and rebop. He received the nickname "Dizzy" because of his wild manner of playing, making grimaces and gesticulating during his performances. Gillespie is doubtless one of the greatest trumpeters in jazz history and practice, a true virtuoso on his instrument, extending its upper ranges and improvising long passages at breakneck speed.

Gillet, Ernest, French composer; b. Paris, Sept. 13, 1856; d. there, May 6, 1940. He studied cello at the Paris Cons., and was for many years a cellist in the orch. of the Paris Opéra. He publ. a number of melodious pieces, of which *Loin du bal* for Piano became a perennial drawing-room favorite, available also in numerous arrangements.

Gillette, James Robert, American organist and composer; b. Roseboom, N.Y., May 30, 1886; d. Lake Forest, Ill., Nov. 26, 1963. He studied music at Syracuse Univ.; taught at Wesleyan College, Macon, Ga., and at Carleton College, Northfield, Minn.; then was organist of the First Presbyterian Church, Lake Forest, Ill.
WORKS: *Pagan Symphony* for Band; *Cabins,* American rhapsody for Orch.; 3 cantatas: *On Calvary's Cross; The Shepherd and His Lamb; The Resurrection According to Nicodemus;* 42 anthems for church use; 7 overtures for Symph. Band; 40 organ pieces (*Chanson de matin, Toccatina, Pastorale,* etc.). He publ. *The Organist's Handbook* (1928) and *The Modern Band in Theory and Practice* (1936).

Gillis, Don, American composer and arranger; b. Cameron, Mo., June 17, 1912; d. Columbia, S.C., Jan. 10, 1978. He played trumpet and trombone in school bands; graduated from the Christian Univ. at Fort Worth, Texas, in 1936. From 1944 to 1954 he was a producer for the National Broadcasting Co., and became associated with Toscanini, who was then conductor of the NBC Symph. Orch. Gillis acquired a facility for arranging, and also composed music on his own. In 1960 he became chairman of the division of arts at Dallas Baptist College, Texas; later was composer-in-residence at the Univ. of South Carolina.
WORKS: 12 symphs. (2 being unnumbered), supplemented with an intercalatory work which he called *Symphony No. 5½* and subtitled it "Symphony for Fun." It so amused Toscanini that he performed it in 1947 with the NBC Symph.; among Gillis's other orch. works with similarly whimsical titles are *The Panhandle, Thoughts Provoked on Becoming a Prospective Papa,* etc. He also wrote 10 short operas to his own librettos, among them *The Park Avenue Kids* (Elkhart, Ind., May 12, 1957), *Pep Rally* (Interlochen, Mich., Aug. 15, 1957), *The Libretto* (Norman, Okla., Dec. 1, 1961), *The Gift of the Magi* (Fort Worth, Texas, Dec. 7, 1965), *The Legend of the Star Valley Junction* (N.Y., Jan. 7, 1969); patriotic pieces for orch., among them *The Alamo* (1947) and *The Secret History of the Birth of the Nation* with Narrator and Chorus (York, Pa., Nov. 14, 1976); 2 piano concertos; *Rhapsody* for Trumpet and Orch.; 6 string quartets; other chamber music.

Gillock, William L., American pianist and composer; b. Lawrence County, Mo., July 1, 1917. He devoted himself mainly to teaching piano; publ. some 300 piano pieces under such engaging titles as *Autumn Is Here, Happy Holiday,* and *The Prowling Pussy Cat.*

Gilly, Dinh, French baritone; b. Algiers, July 19, 1877; d. London, May 19, 1940. He studied at the Paris Cons.; made his operatic debut as Silvio in *Pagliacci* at the Paris Opéra in 1902; made his first appearance at the Metropolitan Opera in N.Y. on Nov. 24, 1909, as Alfio in *Cavalleria rusticana;* remained on its roster until 1914. On May 15, 1911, he made his London debut at Covent Garden, as Amonasro in *Aida.* In later years he taught voice in London.

Gilman, Lawrence, renowned American music critic; b. Flushing, N.Y., July 5, 1878; d. Franconia, N.H., Sept. 8, 1939. He was self-taught in music; in 1901–13, he was music critic of *Harper's Weekly;* in 1915–23, music, dramatic, and literary critic of the *North American Review;* from 1921, author of the program notes of the N.Y. Phil. and Philadelphia Orch. concerts; from 1923, was music critic of the *N.Y. Herald Tribune;* was a member of the National Inst. of Arts and Letters.
WRITINGS: *Phases of Modern Music* (1904); *Edward MacDowell* (1905, in the Living Masters of Music series; revised and enlarged as *Edward MacDowell: A Study,* 1909); *The Music of To-Morrow* (1906); *Stories of Symphonic Music* (1907); *Aspects of Modern Opera* (1909); *Nature in Music* (1914); *A Christmas Meditation* (1916); "Taste in Music," *Musical Quarterly* (Jan. 1917); *Music and the Cultivated Man* (1929); *Wagner's Operas* (1937); *Toscanini and Great Music* (1938). He set to music 3 poems of W.B. Yeats (*The Heart of the Woman, A*

Dream of Death, and *The Curlew).*
BIBLIOGRAPHY: Carl Engel, "Lawrence Gilman," *Musical Quarterly* (Jan. 1940).

Gilmore, Patrick Sarsfield, American bandmaster; b. County Galway, Ireland, Dec. 25, 1829; d. St. Louis, Sept. 24, 1892. He went to Canada with an English band, but soon settled in Salem, Mass., where he conducted a military band. In 1859 in Boston he organized the famous Gilmore's Band. As bandmaster in the Federal army at New Orleans (1864), he gave a grand music festival with several combined bands, introducing the novel reinforcement of strong accents by cannon shots. He won wide renown through the National Peace Jubilee (1869) and the World's Peace Jubilee (1872), 2 monster music festivals held in Boston; in the former, Gilmore led an orch. of 1,000 and a chorus of 10,000; in the latter, an orch. of 2,000 and a chorus of 20,000; the orch. was reinforced by a powerful organ, cannon fired by electricity, anvils, and chimes of bells. After the 2nd jubilee, Gilmore went to N.Y., and, as a popular bandmaster, traveled with his men throughout the U.S. and Canada, and also (1878) to Europe. He also led bands or orchs. in various resorts in and near N.Y.
WORKS: Military music; dance music; many arrangements for band. Some of his songs were popular. He claimed to be the composer of *When Johnny Comes Marching Home* (1863), a song that remained a favorite long after the Civil War. The song bears the name of Louis Lambert as composer; this may have been one of Gilmore's many aliases—at any rate, he introduced the song and started it on its way to popularity.
BIBLIOGRAPHY: M. Darlington, *Irish Orpheus: The Life of Patrick Gilmore* (Philadelphia, 1950).

Gilse, Jan van, Dutch composer; b. Rotterdam, May 11, 1881; d. Oegstgeest, near Leyden, Sept. 8, 1944. He studied with Wüllner at the Cologne Cons. (1897–1902) and with Humperdinck in Berlin (1902–3). He was a conductor of the Opera at Bremen (1905–8) and of the Dutch Opera at Amsterdam (1908–9); was music director of the City of Utrecht (1917–22). He lived again in Berlin (1922–33); then was director of the Utrecht Cons. (1933–37). His music is heavily imbued with German Romanticism.
WORKS: 2 operas: *Frau Helga von Stavern* (1911) and *Thijl* (1938–40; first complete perf., Amsterdam, Sept. 21, 1976; a symph. extract, *Funeral Music,* is often heard separately); *Concert Overture* (1900); 4 symphs.: No. 1 (1900–1901); No. 2 (1902–3); No. 3, *Erhebung,* with Soprano (1907); No. 4 (1914); No. 5 (1922–23; unfinished sketch only); *Eine Lebensmesse,* oratorio (1904); *Variaties over een St. Nicolaasliedje (Variations on a St. Nicholas Song)* for Orch. or Piano (1909); *3 Songs,* after Tagore's "Gitanjali," for Soprano and Orch. (1915); *3 Songs,* after Tagore's "Der Gartner," for Soprano and Orch. (1923); *3 Tanzkizzen (Dance Sketches)* for Piano and Small Orch. (1926); *Der Kreis des Lebens,* oratorio (1928); *Prologus brevis* for Orch. (1928); *Kleine Vals* for Small Orch. (1936); Nonet (1916);

Trio for Flute, Violin, and Viola (1927); songs.

Gilson, Paul, Belgian composer, critic, and educator; b. Brussels, June 15, 1865; d. there, April 3, 1942. He studied with Auguste Cantillon and Charles Duyck; took lessons from Gevaert; in 1889, he won the Belgian Prix de Rome with his cantata, *Sinai,* performed at Brussels in 1890. His subsequent works, both choral and orch., won him a foremost place among modern Flemish composers. In addition to his composing, he wrote numerous books and articles on music, and taught, beginning in 1899, as a prof. of harmony at the Brussels Cons.; in 1904, he was also on the faculty of the Antwerp Cons.; in 1909, he left both posts to become music inspector in the Belgian schools. He was also an important music critic: for *Soir* from 1906 to 1914, for *Le Diapason* from 1910 to 1914, and later for *Midi.* He was the founder of the *Revue Musicale Belge* (1924). In 1942, he publ. his memoirs, *Notes de musique et souvenirs.* He also publ. *Les Intervalles, Le Tutti orchestral, Quintes et octaves, Traité d'harmonie, Traité d'orchestre militaire.*
WORKS: Choral: *Inaugural Cantata* (for the Brussels Exhibition, 1897); *Francesca da Rimini,* after Dante (Brussels, 1895); *Le Démon,* after Lermontov; *Que la lumière soit; Hymne à l'Art; Ludus pro Patria.* Ballets: *La Captive* (Brussels, 1902); *Les Deux Bossus; Légende rhénane;* also incidental music for E. Hiel's drama, *Alva.* Operas: *Prinses Zonneschijn* (Antwerp, 1903); *Zeevolk* (Antwerp, 1904); *Rooversliefde (Les Aventuriers;* Antwerp, 1906); *Mater Dolorosa.* For Orch.: 3 symph. poems: *La Mer* (Brussels, 1892); *Italia; La Destinée; Variations symphoniques* (1902); 8 suites; *Danses écossaises; Rapsodie écossaise; Andante et presto sur un thème brabançon; Rapsodie canadienne;* 2 string quartets; String Trio; pieces for military band; choruses; piano pieces; instrumental pieces; songs.
BIBLIOGRAPHY: G. Brenta, *Paul Gilson* (Brussels, 1965).

Giltay, Berend, Dutch composer; b. Hilversum, June 15, 1910; d. Utrecht, March 21, 1975. He studied violin and viola with Dick Waleson and composition with Badings; was a violinist with the Hilversum Radio Phil. and with various other Dutch orchs. From 1963 to 1966 he attended courses in electronic music at the Utrecht Univ. and worked in Bilthoven at the Gaudeamus electronic studio.
WORKS: Violin Concerto (1950); *4 Miniatures* for Viola and Piano (1952); *Sonata a tre* for Oboe, Clarinet, and Bassoon (1953); Concerto for Viola and Chamber Orch. (1955); Wind Quintet (1956); Oboe Concerto (1956–57); *Sinfonia* (1956–57); String Quintet (1957); Horn Concerto; Concerto for Orch. (1960); 2 duos for 2 Violins (1962, 1966); Divertimento for 5 Flutes (1963); *Scherzo* for 2 Violins (1963); *6 studi concertante* for Solo Viola (1963); *Phonolieten* for Tape (1965); *Polychromie I* for Tape (1966) and *II* for a Solo Trio of Piccolo, Flute and Alto Flute, 4 Flutes or other Instruments, and Tape (1972); *Kurucz Változatok Zenekarra,* variations for Orch. (1966–67); 2-violin Concerto (1966–67); *Ele-*

gy for Alto Flute and 4 Flutes (1969); *Gossauer Symphonie* (Utrecht, Oct. 3, 1972); Trio for 2 Violins and Cello (1971); *Kosmochromie 1* for 4 Loudspeakers and Orch. (Utrecht, Feb. 22, 1974); *Kosmochromie II* for String Quartet, Chamber Orch., and Tape (1974).

Giménez (Jiménez), Jerónimo, Spanish composer of zarzuelas; b. Seville, Oct. 10, 1854; d. Madrid, Feb. 19, 1923. He studied with Alard, Savard, and A. Thomas at the Paris Cons.; was conductor of the Sociedad de Conciertos in Madrid. He wrote about 60 light operas (*género chico*).

Gimpel, Bronislaw, Austrian-born American violinist, brother of **Jakob Gimpel;** b. Lemberg (Lwow), Jan. 29, 1911; d. Los Angeles, May 1, 1979. He studied with R. Pollack in Vienna (1922–26) and Carl Flesch in Berlin (1928–29). From 1929–31 he was concertmaster at the Radio Orch. in Königsberg; from 1931–36 was in Göteborg, Sweden. In 1937 he emigrated to the U.S.; from 1937–42 he was concertmaster of the Los Angeles Phil.; from 1967–73 was on the faculty of the Univ. of Conn. In 1962 he organized the Warsaw String Quartet and toured with it in the U.S., Europe, and Japan. In 1968 he also became the concertmaster of the New England Quartet. He was to play a joint recital with his brother, Jakob Gimpel, in Los Angeles on May 9, 1979, but died 8 days before the scheduled concert; instead, his brother played a piano recital in his memory.

Gimpel, Jakob, Austrian-born American virtuoso pianist, brother of the violinist **Bronislaw Gimpel;** b. Lemberg (Lwow), April 16, 1906. He received his earliest musical training at home; his father was an excellent musician. After a preliminary study at the Lemberg Cons., he went to Vienna, where he took piano lessons with Eduard Steuermann; also had private instruction in music theory with Alban Berg. He made his concert debut in Vienna in 1923; then engaged in a brilliant concert career; he was especially successful in Germany; in one particular season he gave 80 concerts there, including 5 recitals in Hamburg. He also was a frequent soloist with orchs. His specialty was Romantic music; he infused the works of Beethoven, Schumann, and Chopin with a peculiarly lyrico-dramatic poetry which seemed to recreate the zeitgeist to perfection. When Germany was usurped by the Nazis, he went to Palestine, where he became closely associated with the violinist Bronislaw Huberman, the founder of the Israel Phil. In 1938 he emigrated to America, settling in Los Angeles, where he became active as an artist and a teacher; he also supplied background music to motion pictures, and had several appearances with the Los Angeles Phil. He continued to concertize in Europe; he received the Ben-Gurion Award of the State of Israel and the Order of Merit, First Class, of the Federal Republic of Germany for his "great services as an interpreter of German music," an exquisitely ironic but all the more precious gesture of the country that during its period of darkness closed its doors to Gimpel as a Jew. In 1971 Gimpel joined the music faculty of the Calif. State Univ., Northridge, as Distinguished Professor-in-Residence. He continued to give recitals in programs of Schumann and Chopin. On May 9, 1979, Jakob Gimpel was to give a joint recital in Los Angeles with his brother, the violinist Bronislaw Gimpel, who died suddenly 8 days before the scheduled concert. Instead, Jakob Gimpel played a solo recital in memory of his brother.

Ginastera, Alberto, greatly talented Argentinian composer; b. Buenos Aires, April 11, 1916; d. Geneva, June 25, 1983. His father was of Catalan descent, and Ginastera often preferred to pronounce his name with a soft "g," as in the Catalan language; the standard pronunciation, however, is with a hard "g". His mother was of Italian origin. Ginastera took private lessons in music as a child; then entered the National Cons. of Music in Buenos Aires, where he studied composition with José Gil, Athos Palma, and José André; also took piano lessons with Argenziani. He began to compose in his early youth; in 1934 won first prize of the musical society El Unísono for his *Piezas infantiles* for Piano. His next piece of importance was *Impresiones de la Puna* for Flute and String Quartet, in which he made use of native Argentinian melodies and rhythms; he discarded it, however, as immature; he withdrew a number of his other works, some of them of certain value, for instance, his *Concierto argentino*, which he wrote in 1935, at the age of 19, and *Sinfonía Porteña,* his first symph. (which may be identical in its musical material with *Estancia*). Also withdrawn was his 2nd Symph., the *Sinfonía elegíaca,* written in 1944, even though it was successfully performed. In 1946–47 Ginastera traveled to the U.S. on a Guggenheim fellowship grant. Returning to Argentina, he was appointed to the faculty of his alma mater, the National Cons. in Buenos Aires, where he taught intermittently from 1948 to 1958; he also served as dean of the faculty of musical arts and sciences at the Argentine Catholic Univ. In 1969 he left Argentina and lived mostly in Geneva, Switzerland. From his earliest steps in composition, Ginastera had an almost amorous attachment for the melodic and rhythmic resources of Argentinian folk music, and he evolved a fine harmonic and contrapuntal setting congenial with native patterns. His first significant work in the Argentinian national idiom was *Panambí,* a ballet, composed in 1935 and performed at the Teatro Colón in Buenos Aires on July 12, 1940, conducted by Juan José Castro. There followed a group of *Danzas argentinas* for Piano, written in 1937; in 1938 he wrote 3 songs; the first one, *Canción al árbol del olvido,* is a fine evocation of youthful love; it became quite popular. In 1941 he was commissioned to write a ballet for the American Ballet Caravan, to be called *Estancia;* the music was inspired by the rustic scenes of the pampas; a suite from the score was performed at the Teatro Colón in Buenos Aires on May 12, 1943, and the complete work was brought out there on Aug. 19, 1952. A series of works inspired by native scenes and written for various instrumental combinations followed, all infused with Ginastera's poetic imagination and brought to realization with excellent technical skill. Soon, however, Ginastera began to search for new methods of musical expression, marked by modern and sometimes strikingly dissonant combinations of sound, fermented by asymmetrical rhythms. Of these works, one of the most remarkable is *Cantata para América Mágica,* scored for dramatic soprano and percussion instruments, to apocryphal pre-Columbian texts, freely arranged by Ginastera himself; it was first performed in Washington, D.C., on April 30, 1961, with excellent success. An entirely new development in Ginastera's evolution as composer came with his first opera, *Don Rodrigo* (1964), produced on July 24, 1964, at the Teatro Colón. In it Ginastera followed the general formula of Alban Berg's *Wozzeck,* in its use of classical instrumental forms, such as rondo, suite, scherzo, and canonic progressions; he also introduced a *Sprechstimme.* In 1964 Ginastera wrote the *Cantata Bomarzo* on a commission from the Elizabeth Sprague Coolidge Foundation in Washington, D.C. He used the same libretto by Manuel Mujica Láinez in his opera *Bomarzo,* which created a sensation at its production in Washington on May 19, 1967, by its unrestrained spectacle of sexual violence. It was announced for performance at the Teatro Colón on Aug. 9, 1967, but was taken off at the order of the Argentinian government because of its alleged immoral nature. The score of *Bomarzo* reveals extraordinary innovations in serial techniques, with thematical employment not only of different chromatic sounds, but also of serial progressions of different intervals. Ginastera's last opera, *Beatrix Cenci,* commissioned by the Opera Society of Washington, D.C., and produced there on Sept. 10, 1971, concluded his operatic trilogy. Among instrumental works of Ginastera's last period, the most remarkable was his 2nd Piano Concerto (1972), based on a tone-row derived from the famous dissonant opening of the finale of Beethoven's 9th Symph.; the 2nd movement of the concerto is written for the left hand alone. Ginastera was married to the pianist **Mercedes de Toro** in 1941; they had a son and a daughter. He divorced her in 1965 and married the Argentinian cellist **Aurora Natola,** for whom he wrote the Cello Sonata, which she played in N.Y. on Dec. 13, 1979, and his 2nd Cello Concerto, which she performed for the first time in Buenos Aires on July 6, 1981.

WORKS: Operas: *Don Rodrigo,* in 3 acts and 9 tableaux (Buenos Aires, July 24, 1964); *Bomarzo,* in 2 acts and 15 tableaux, to a libretto from a novel by Manuel Mujica Láinez (Washington, D.C., May 19, 1967); *Beatrix Cenci,* in 2 acts and 14 tableaux (Washington, D.C., Sept. 10, 1971).

BALLETS: *Panambí* (1935; Teatro Colón, July 12, 1940, conducted by Juan José Castro); *Estancia* (Buenos Aires, Aug. 19, 1952).

FOR ORCH.: Suite from the ballet *Panambí* (Buenos Aires, Nov. 27, 1937); *Primer concierto argentino* (Montevideo, July 18, 1941; withdrawn); *Primera sinonía (Porteña)* (1942; withdrawn); *Dances* from the ballet *Estancia* (Buenos Aires, May 12, 1943); *Obertura para el Fausto Criollo* (Santiago, Chile, May 12, 1944); *Sinfonía elegíaca* (2nd Symph.; Buenos Aires, May 31, 1946; withdrawn); *Ollantay,* 3 symph. movements after an Inca poem (Buenos Aires, Oct. 29, 1949); *Variaciones concertantes* for Chamber Orch. (Buenos Aires, June 2, 1953); *Pampeana No. 3,* symph. pastoral (Louisville, Ky., Oct. 20, 1954); Harp Concerto (1956; Philadelphia, Feb. 18, 1965); Piano Concerto No. 1 (Washington, D.C., April 22, 1961); Violin Concerto (N.Y. Phil., Oct. 3, 1963; Ruggiero Ricci, soloist; Leonard Bernstein conducting); Concerto for Strings (Caracas, May 14, 1966); Suite from *Bomarzo* (1967); *Estudios sinfónicos* (Vancouver, March 31, 1968); Cello Concerto No. 1 (1968; Dartmouth College, July 7, 1968; revised 1971–72); Piano Concerto No. 2 (Indianapolis, March 22, 1973; Hilde Somer, soloist); *Popul Vuh* for Orch. (1975–83; unfinished); *Glosses sobre temas de Pau Casals* for String Orch. and String Quintet "in lontano" (San Juan, Puerto Rico, June 14, 1976); Cello Concerto No. 2 (Buenos Aires, July 6, 1981; Aurora Natola, soloist); *Iubilum* (1979–80; Buenos Aires, April 12, 1980).

CHAMBER MUSIC: *Impresiones de la Puna* for Flute and String Quartet (1942; withdrawn); *Dúo* for Flute and Oboe (1945); *Pampeana No. 1* for Violin and Piano (1947); 4 string quartets: No. 1 (1948); No. 2 (1958); No. 3, with Soprano (1973); No. 4, with Baritone, to the text of Beethoven's Heiligenstadt Testament (1974; unfinished); *Pampeana No. 2* for Cello and Piano (1950); Piano Quintet (1963); *Puneña No. 2* for Cello Solo (1976); Guitar Sonata (1976); Cello Sonata (N.Y., Dec. 13, 1979; Aurora Natola, cellist); *Fanfare* for 4 Trumpets in C (1980): *Serenade* for Cello Solo, Flute, Oboe, Clarinet, Bassoon, Horn, Double Bass, Harp, and Percussion (1980).

FOR VOICE: *2 Canciones:* No. 1, *Canción al árbol del ovido;* No. 2, *Canción a la luna lunanca* (1938); *Cantos del Tucumán* for Voice, Flute, Violin, Harp, and 2 Indian Drums (1938); *Psalm 150* for Mixed Choir, Boys' Choir, and Orch. (1938; Buenos Aires, April 7, 1945); *5 Canciones populares argentinas* for Voice and Piano (1943); *Las horas de una estancia* for Voice and Piano (1943); *Hieremiae prophetae lamentatiónes* for Mixed Choir a cappella (1946); *Cantata para América Mágica* for Dramatic Soprano and Percussion, to an apocryphal pre-Columbian text (1960; Washington, D.C., April 30, 1961); *Sinfonía Don Rodrigo* for Soprano and Orch. (Madrid, Oct. 31, 1964); *Cantata Bomarzo* for Speaker, Baritone, and Chamber Orch. (Washington, D.C., Nov. 1, 1964); *Milena,* cantata for Soprano and Orch., to texts from Kafka's letters (Denver, April 16, 1973); *Serenata* for Cello, Baritone, and Chamber Ensemble, to texts of Pablo Neruda (1973); *Turbae ad Passionem Gregorianam* for Tenor, Baritone, and Bass, Boys' Chorus, Mixed Chorus, and Orch. (Philadelphia, March 20, 1975).

FOR PIANO: *Piezas infantiles* (1934); *Danzas argentinas* (1937); *3 Piezas* (1940); *Malambo* (1940); *12 Preludios americanos* (1944); *Suite de Danzas criollas* (1946); *Rondó sobre temas infantiles argentinos* (1947); Sonata No. 1 (1952); *Pequeña danza* from *Estancia* (1955); *Toccata,* arranged from *Toccata per organo* by Domenico Zipoli (1972); Sonata No. 2 (1981); Sonata No. 3 (1982); also *Toccata, Villancico y Fuga* for Organ (1947); *Variazioni e Toc-*

cata for Organ (1980); film music.

BIBLIOGRAPHY: Pola Suárez Urtubey, *Alberto Ginastera* (Buenos Aires, 1967); David Ewen, *Composers since 1900* (N.Y., 1969).

Gingold, Josef, distinguished Russian-born American violinist and pedagogue; b. Brest-Litovsk, Oct. 28, 1909. He came to the U.S. in 1920. He studied violin in N.Y. with Vladimir Graffman, and later in Brussels with Eugène Ysaÿe. He then served as first violinist in the NBC Symph. Orch. under Toscanini (1937–43); was concertmaster of the Detroit Symph. Orch. (1943–46) and the Cleveland Orch. (1947–60). He taught at Case Western Reserve Univ. (1950–60) and was prof. of chamber music at the Meadowmount School of Music (1955–81). In 1960 he was appointed to the faculty of the Indiana Univ. School of Music in Bloomington; was made a distinguished prof. of music there in 1965. He also gave master classes at the Paris Cons. (1970–81), in Tokyo (1970), in Copenhagen (1979), and in Montreal (1980); held the Mischa Elman Chair at the Manhattan School of Music in N.Y. (1980–81). He was a guiding force in establishing the International Violin Competition of Indianapolis; was its first honorary chairman and president of the jury in 1982.

Ginguené, Pierre Louis, French historian of literature and writer on music; b. Rennes, April 25, 1748; d. Paris, Nov. 16, 1816. He studied at Rennes College; then went to Paris; was an original member of the Institut of France; served in government posts, then wrote extensively on the history of French and Italian literature. He was an ardent advocate of Piccini in the Gluck-Piccini controversy; his attacks on Gluck are contained in his *Lettres et articles sur la musique, insérés dans les journaux sous le nom de Mélophile, pendant nos dernières querelles musicales, en 1780, 1781, 1782 et 1783* (Paris, 1783). He also wrote *Notice sur la vie et les ouvrages de Piccini* (Paris, 1800); contributed historical articles to the *Dictionnaire de musique* of the *Encyclopédie méthodique.*

BIBLIOGRAPHY: D.J. Garat, *Notice sur la vie et les ouvrages de P.L. Ginguené* (Paris, 1817).

Ginsburg, Lev, Russian music scholar, cellist, and pedagogue; b. Mogilev, Jan. 28, 1907; d. Moscow, Nov. 21, 1981. He studied cello at the Moscow Cons., graduating in 1931; subsequently was appointed to its faculty, teaching cello and later the methodology of string playing. He publ. a number of valuable works on the subject, among them a basic compendium, *History of the Art of Cello Playing* in 3 vols. (Moscow, 1950, 1957, 1965). He also publ. a number of monographs on cello virtuosos: *Pablo Casals* (Moscow, 1958); *Mstislav Rostropovich* (Moscow, 1963); *Maurice Maréchal* (Moscow, 1972); and contributed numerous articles on string instrumental techniques to Russian and foreign publications.

Ginsburg, Semion, Russian musicologist and pedagogue; b. Kiev, May 23, 1901. He studied art history and musicology in Petrograd; in 1925 was appointed to the faculty of the Leningrad Cons.; in his scientific pursuits, he explored the sociological foundation of national musical resources. He publ. *Fundamentals of Musical Culture* (Leningrad, 1935); *Russian Music on the Threshold of the 20th Century* (Moscow, 1966).

Giordani, Giuseppe (called **Giordanello**), Italian composer; b. Naples, Dec. 9, 1743; d. Fermo, Jan. 4, 1798. He studied with Fenaroli at the San Loreto Cons., Naples; Cimarosa and Zingarelli were fellow students. His first opera, *Epponina,* was given in Florence in 1779. He continued to write operas for various Italian towns, but they were not outstanding, and few of the 30-odd he wrote have survived. He also wrote several oratorios and church music. From 1791 until his death he was maestro di cappella at the Fermo Cathedral. He is sometimes credited with *Il bacio* and other operas and works produced in London by Tommaso Giordani; Giuseppe was not related to Tommaso, and never left Italy. The famous song *Caro mio ben,* popularized in London by Pacchierotti, was probably written by Giuseppe.

Giordani, Tommaso, Italian composer; b. Naples, c.1730; d. Dublin, late Feb. 1806. His family, which included his father, **Giuseppe;** his mother, **Antonia;** his brother, **Francesco;** and his sisters, **Marina** and **Nicolina** (known later as **Spiletta** from one of her opera roles), together formed a strolling opera company, with the father as impresario and singer and the rest of the family, except Tommaso, as singers. Tommaso was probably a member of the orch. and the arranger of music. They left Naples about 1745 and moved northward, appearing in Italian towns, then in Graz (1748), Frankfurt (1750), and Amsterdam (1752). They made their London debut at Covent Garden on Dec. 17, 1753, and returned in 1756, at which time Tommaso first appeared as a composer, with his comic opera *La Comediante fatta cantatrice* (Covent Garden, Jan. 12, 1756). The Giordani company next went to Dublin, appearing there in 1764; Tommaso continued to be active both in Dublin and in London; he was conductor and composer at the King's Theatre, London, in 1769 and many following seasons, and in Dublin, where he lived after 1783, was conductor and composer at the Smock Alley and Crow Street theaters; he also taught piano between operas. In 1794, he was elected president of the Irish music fund. He played an important part in Irish music circles, and wrote altogether more than 50 English and Italian operas, including pasticcios and adaptations.

WORKS: *L'Eroe cinese* (Dublin, 1766); *Il Padre el il figlio rivali* (London, 1770); *Artaserse* (London, 1772); *Il Re pastore* (London, 1778); *Il bacio* (London, 1782). He also wrote several cantatas, including *Aci e Galatea* (London, 1777); an oratorio, *Isaac* (Dublin, 1767); songs for the original production of Sheridan's *The Critic* (Drury Lane, London, Oct. 29, 1779); many Italian and English songs that were popular for a long time; concertos; string quartets; trios; many piano pieces.

Giordano – Giovannelli

Giordano, Umberto, Italian opera composer; b. Foggia, Aug. 28, 1867; d. Milan, Nov. 12, 1948. He studied with Gaetano Briganti at Foggia, and then with Paolo Serrao at the Naples Cons. (1881–90). His first composition performed in public was a symph. poem, *Delizia* (1886); he then wrote some instrumental music. In 1888 he submitted a short opera, *Marina,* for the competition established by the publisher Sonzogno; Mascagni's *Cavalleria rusticana* received first prize, but *Marina* was cited for distinction. Giordano then wrote an opera in 3 acts, *Mala vita,* which was performed in Rome, Feb. 21, 1892; it was only partly successful; was revised and presented under the title *Il voto* in Milan (1897). There followed a 2-act opera, *Regina Diaz* (Rome, Feb. 21, 1894), which obtained a moderate success. Then Giordano set to work on a grand opera, *Andrea Chénier,* to a libretto by Illica. The production of this opera at La Scala (March 28, 1896) was a spectacular success, which established Giordano as one of the best composers of modern Italian opera. The dramatic subject gave Giordano a fine opportunity to display his theatrical talent; but the opera also revealed his gift for lyric expression. *Andrea Chénier* was produced at the N.Y. Academy of Music shortly after its Milan premiere; a performance at the Metropolitan Opera House came considerably later (March 7, 1920). Almost as successful was his next opera, *Fedora* (Teatro Lirico, Milan, Nov. 17, 1898; Metropolitan Opera, Dec. 5, 1906), but it failed to hold a place in the world repertoire after the initial acclaim; there followed *Siberia,* in 3 acts (La Scala, Dec. 19, 1903; revised 1921, and perf. at La Scala, Dec. 5, 1927). Two short operas, *Marcella* (Milan, Nov. 9, 1907) and *Mese Mariano* (Palermo, March 17, 1910), were hardly noticed and seemed to mark a decline in Giordano's dramatic gift; however, he recaptured the attention of the public with *Madame Sans-Gêne,* produced at a gala premiere at the Metropolitan on Jan. 25, 1915, conducted by Toscanini, with Geraldine Farrar singing the title role. With Franchetti, he wrote *Giove a Pompei* (Rome, July 5, 1921); then he produced *La cena delle beffe* in 4 acts, which was his last signal accomplishment; it was staged at La Scala, Dec. 20, 1924, and at the Metropolitan, Jan. 2, 1926. He wrote one more opera, *Il Re,* in one act (La Scala, Jan. 10, 1929). During his lifetime he received many honors, and was elected a member of the Accademia Luigi Cherubini in Florence and of several other institutions. Although not measuring up to Puccini in musical qualities or to Mascagni in dramatic skill, Giordano was a distinguished figure in the Italian opera field.
BIBLIOGRAPHY: G.C. Paribeni, *Madame Sans-Gêne di Umberto Giordano* (Milan, 1923); D. Cellamare, *Umberto Giordano: La vita e le opere* (Milan, 1949); R. Giazotto, *Umberto Giordano* (Milan, 1949); G. Confalonieri, *Umberto Giordano* (Milan, 1958); D. Cellamare, *Umberto Giordano* (Rome, 1967); M. Morini, ed., *Umberto Giordano* (Milan, 1968).

Giorni, Aurelio, pianist and composer; b. Perugia, Italy, Sept. 15, 1895; d. Pittsfield, Mass., Sept. 23, 1938. He studied piano with Sgambati at the Santa Cecilia Cons. in Rome (1909–11); composition with Humperdinck in Berlin (1911–13); in 1915 he came to the U.S., where he remained; taught at Smith College, the Philadelphia Cons. of Music, the Hartford School of Music, and other music schools; in his last years was a teacher in N.Y. He wrote a symph. poem, *Orlando furioso* (1926); *Sinfonia concertante* (1931); Symph. in D minor (1937); 3 trios; 2 string quartets; Cello Sonata; Violin Sonata; Piano Quartet; Piano Quintet; Flute Sonata; Clarinet Sonata; 24 concert études for Piano; songs.

Giornovichi, Giovanni Mane, Italian violinist, probably of Croatian extraction (his real name was **Jarnowick**); b. Raguso or Palermo, c.1735; d. St. Petersburg, Russia, Nov. 23, 1804. He was a pupil of Antonio Lolli in Palermo; gave successful concerts in Europe; on the strength of his reputation, he was engaged as court musician to Catherine II, succeeding his teacher Lolli in that post. He was in Russia in 1789–91; then appeared in London (1791–94), Paris, Hamburg, and Berlin. He returned to Russia in 1803, and died there the following year; was a member of the court orch. in St. Petersburg until his death. In his old age he devoted himself to playing billiards for money. Among his works are 22 violin concertos (17 extant); 3 string quartets; *Fantasia e Rondo* for Piano. He was probably the first to introduce the "romance" into the violin concerto as a slow movement, and he helped to set the rondo as the finale.
BIBLIOGRAPHY: R. Aloys Mooser, *Annales de la musique et des musiciens en Russie au XVIIIe siècle* (Geneva, 1950; vol. II, pp. 379–81); C. White, "The Violin Concertos of Giornovichi," *Musical Quarterly* (Jan. 1972; includes a concordance of editions).

Giorza, Paolo, Italian composer; b. Milan, Nov. 11, 1832; d. Seattle, May 5, 1914. He was especially known for his ballet music; wrote more than 40 ballets. He lived in N.Y., London, and San Francisco; in 1906 settled in Seattle.

Giovaninetti, Reynald, conductor; b. Sétif, Algeria, March 11, 1932. He began his musical studies at the Cons. in Nantes; then entered the Paris Cons., and simultaneously took advanced courses in mathematics at the Sorbonne. He served subsequently as music director of the Opera in Mulhouse (1962–67) and in Marseilles (1968–75); also conducted at the Paris Opéra, La Scala in Milan, the Vienna State Opera, the American Opera Society in N.Y., the Chicago Lyric Opera, and the San Francisco Opera. He also made appearances as a symph. conductor in Europe and the U.S.; led the Chicago Symph. on a tour in the U.S. in 1982.

Giovannelli, Ruggiero, Italian composer; b. Velletri, 1560; d. Rome, Jan. 7, 1625. On Aug. 6, 1583, he was nominated director of the cappella of San Luigi de' Francesi at Rome; later (1591–94) was maestro in the Collegium Germanicum; in 1594 he succeeded Palestrina as maestro at St. Peter's, and in 1599

joined the Pontifical Chapel. He was one of the most famous masters of the Roman School; of his works there have been printed 3 books of madrigals *a* 5 (1586, 1587, 1589; completely reprinted 1600); 2 of *Madrigali sdruccioli a* 4 (1585 [7th ed., 1613], 1589 [5th ed., 1603]); 2 books of motets *a* 5–8 (1589, 1604); *Canzonette* and *Villanelle a* 3 (1592, 1593); also scattered works in collections publ. from 1583 to 1620 (Scotto, Phalèse, Schadaeus, etc.). K. Proske's *Musica divina* contains a Psalm (vol. III, 1859); L. Torchi's *L'arte musicale in Italia* includes a motet and Psalm *a* 8 and a madrigal *a* 5 (vol. II). In the Vatican Library are many sacred works in MS. To Giovannelli was entrusted, by Pope Paul V, the preparation of a new edition of the Gradual (2 vols., 1614, 1615).
BIBLIOGRAPHY: C. Winter, *Ruggiero Giovannelli (c.1560–1625), Nachfolger Palestrinas zu St. Peter in Rom* (Munich, 1935).

Giovanni da Cascia (Johannes de Florentia), Italian 14th-century composer. According to his younger contemporary Filippo Villani, in *Liber de civitatis Florentiae famosis civibus,* he was the initiator of the stylistic reform which spread from Florence shortly after 1300. He was organist and probably chorus master at Santa Maria del Fiore at Florence; lived at the court of Mastino II della Scala, Verona, c.1329–51. His compositions included 16 madrigals, 3 *cacce, ballate,* etc.; MSS may be found in libraries at Florence and Paris, and in the British Museum. In all, 28 works by Giovanni, in 2–3 parts, are known. The madrigal *Agnel son bianco* was edited and publ. by Johannes Wolf in *Sammelbände der Internationalen Musik-Gesellschaft* (1902; ex. 4); 2 other compositions were also edited and publ. by Wolf in his *Geschichte der Mensural-Notation* (pp. 61–64; Leipzig, 1904). For further modern editions of his works, see N. Pirrotta, editor, *The Music of 14th Century Italy,* in Corpus Mensurabilis Musicae, VIII/1 (1954), and W. Marrocco, editor, *Italian Secular Music,* in Polyphonic Music of the Fourteenth Century, VI (1967).
BIBLIOGRAPHY: J. Wolf, "Florenz in der Musikgeschichte des 14. Jahrhunderts," *Sammelbände der Internationalen Musik-Gesellschaft,* III (1901–2; pp. 599–646); H. Riemann, in *Handbuch der Musikgeschichte* (1922; p. 41); A. Morini, "Un celebre musico dimenticato, Giovanni da Cascia," *Bollettino della regia deputazione di storia patria per l'Umbria* (Perugia, 1926; pp. 305ff.); M. Martinez, *Die Musik des frühen Trecento* (Munich, 1963).

Gipps, Ruth, English pianist and composer; b. Bexhill-on-Sea, Sussex, Feb. 20, 1921. She studied at the Royal College of Music in London with Vaughan Williams; studied piano with Matthay. She began to compose very early in life, and at the age of 8 won a prize for a piano piece. Her works include 4 symphs. (1942, 1946, 1965, 1972); Clarinet Concerto (1940); Oboe Concerto (1941); Violin Concerto (1943); Horn Concerto (1968; London, Nov. 15, 1969); Piano Concerto (1948); Double Concerto for Violin, Viola, and Chamber Orch. (1957); Trio for Oboe, Clarinet, and Piano; Quintet for Oboe, Clarinet, Violin, Viola, and Cello; oratorio, *The Cat* (1952); a bizarre piece entitled *Leviathan* for Double Bassoon and Chamber Orch. (London, Feb. 13, 1971). Apart from composition, she conducted the London Repertory Orch. and the Chanticleer Orch. In 1967 she was appointed a prof. at the Royal College of Music in London.

Giraldoni, Eugenio, famous Italian baritone; b. Marseilles, May 20, 1871; d. Helsinki, June 23, 1924. Both his parents were professional singers; his father, **Leone Giraldoni,** was a renowned baritone, and his mother, **Carolina Ferni-Giraldoni,** a famous soprano. He made his debut in Barcelona as Don José in 1891; then sang in Buenos Aires and in Italy (at La Scala and other theaters); made his debut at the Metropolitan Opera in N.Y. as Barnaba in *La Gioconda* on Nov. 28, 1904; remained there only one season (1904–5); eventually settled in Russia.

Giraldoni, Leone, Italian baritone; father of **Eugenio Giraldoni;** b. Paris, 1824; d. Moscow, Oct. 1, 1897. He studied in Florence with Ronzi; made his debut in 1847 in Lodi; created the title roles of *Il Duca d'Alba* by Donizetti, *Simone Boccanegra* by Verdi, and Renato in Verdi's *Un ballo in maschera.* He retired from the stage in 1885; then taught voice in Italy. From 1891 to 1897 he was on the staff of the Moscow Cons. Among his students were Nicolai and Medea Figner. He published *Guida teorico-practico ad uso dell'artista cantante* (Bologna, 1864).

Giraud, Fiorello, Italian tenor; b. Parma, Oct. 22, 1870; d. there, March 29, 1928. He was the son of the tenor **Lodovico Giraud** (1846–82). He studied with Babacini in Parma; made his debut as Lohengrin in 1891 in Vercelli; then sang in Barcelona, Lisbon, and South America, and at La Scala in Milan. He created the role of Canio in Leoncavallo's *Pagliacci;* was a fine interpreter of other *verismo* roles.

Giraudet, Alfred-Auguste, dramatic basso and vocal pedagogue; b. Etampes, March 29, 1845; d. New York, Oct. 17, 1911. He studied with Delsarte; made his operatic debut at the Théâtre-Lyrique in Paris as Méphistophélès (1868); then sang at the Théâtre-Italien, the Opéra-Comique, and the Opéra; in 1883 he retired from the stage and devoted himself to teaching; eventually settled in N.Y.

Girdlestone, Cuthbert (Morton), English music scholar; b. Bovery-Tracey, Sept. 17, 1895; d. St. Cloud, France, Dec. 10, 1975. He was educated at the Sorbonne (licence ès lettres, 1915) and the Schola Cantorum in Paris; then entered Trinity College, Cambridge; became a lecturer at Cambridge in 1922; in 1926 he was appointed prof. of French at the Univ. of Durham, Newcastle division (later the Univ. of Newcastle upon Tyne); retired in 1960 and settled in St. Cloud. He publ. a valuable analysis of Mozart's piano concertos under the title *Mozart et ses concertos pour piano* (Paris, 1939; Eng. trans., 1948; 2nd ed., 1964); also the important monograph *Jean-Phi-*

lippe Rameau: His Life and Work (London, 1957; 2nd ed., revised, 1969). He further wrote *La Tragé-die en musique (1673–1750) considérée comme genre littéraire* (Paris, 1972).

BIBLIOGRAPHY: N. Sucklin, ed., *Essays Present-ed to C.M. Girdlestone* (Newcastle upon Tyne, 1960).

Gitlis, Ivry, Israeli violinist; b. Haifa, Aug. 22, 1922. He began violin lessons at a very early age; he en-tered the Ecole Normale de Musique in Paris at 10 and won the Premier Prix at 13; then studied with Enesco, Thibaud, and Flesch. He subsequently made appearances with the leading London orchs.; won the Thibaud Prize in 1951. He then returned to Israel; also made tours of Europe; made his U.S. debut in 1955. Gitlis has consistently cultivated con-temporary violin music in his recital programs.

Giuffre, Jimmy (James Peter Giuffre), American jazz clarinetist and saxophonist; b. Dallas, April 26, 1921. He studied at North Texas State Teachers Col-lege (B.Mus., 1942); then played in a U.S. Army band; subsequently joined the bands of Jimmy Dorsey, Buddy Rich, and Woody Herman. In 1956 he formed his own jazz trio with the guitarist Jim Hall and the bassist Ralph Pena; his later partners included Paul Bleg on the keyboard and Steve Swallow on the trombone. He was a major figure in progressive jazz circles as a proponent of the free-jazz style.

Giuglini, Antonio, Italian tenor; b. Fano, 1827; d. Pesaro, Oct. 12, 1865. He studied with Cellini; made his debut in Fermo; was highly successful in Lon-don when he sang at Her Majesty's Theatre in 1857; also sang at Drury Lane and the Lyceum there; in 1865 he was in St. Petersburg, where he displayed symptoms of mental aberrations. Upon his return to London, he was committed to an asylum; in the same year he was taken to Pesaro, where he died.

Giuliani, Mauro, Italian guitar virtuoso; b. Bisce-glie, near Bari, July 27, 1781; d. Naples, May 8, 1829. He was entirely self-taught; at the age of 19 under-took a highly successful tour in Europe; settled in Vienna in 1807, where he became associated with Hummel, Moscheles, and Diabelli; Beethoven became interested in him, and wrote some guitar music expressly for his performances. In 1833 he visited London, where he won extraordinary ac-claim; a special publication, named after him *The Giulianiad* and devoted to reports about his activi-ties, was initiated there, but only a few issues ap-peared. Giuliani publ. over 200 works for guitar; he also perfected a new guitar with a shorter finger-board ("la ghitarra di terza").

BIBLIOGRAPHY: *Guitar Review,* 18 (1955), con-taining a biographical sketch of Giuliani by P.J. Bone; Thomas Heck, *The Birth of the Classic Gui-tar and Its Cultivation in Vienna, Reflections in the Career and Compositions of Mauro Giuliani (d. 1829)* (Diss., Yale Univ., 1970); idem, "Mauro Giuliani," *Guitar Review* (1972).

Giulini, Carlo Maria, eminent Italian conductor; b.

Barletta, May 9, 1914. He began to study the violin as a boy; at 16 he entered the Conservatorio di Musi-ca di Santa Cecilia in Rome, where he studied violin and viola with Remy Principe, composition with Alessandro Bustini, and conducting with Bernar-dino Molinari; also received instruction in conduct-ing from Casella at the Chigi Academy in Siena; then joined the Augusteo Orch. in Rome in the viola section, under such great conductors as Richard Strauss, Bruno Walter, Mengelberg, and Furtwäng-ler. He was drafted into the Italian army, but went into hiding as a convinced anti-Fascist; after the liberation of Rome by the Allied troops in 1944, he was engaged to conduct the Augusteo Orch. in a special concert celebrating the occasion. He was then engaged as assistant conductor of the RAI Orch. in Rome, and was made its chief conductor in 1946. In 1950 he helped to organize the RAI Orch. in Milan; in 1952 he conducted at La Scala as an assis-tant to Victor de Sabata; in 1954 he became princi-pal conductor there; his performance of *La Travia-ta,* with Maria Callas in the title role, was particu-larly notable. In 1955 he conducted Verdi's *Falstaff* at the Edinburgh Festival, earning great praise. On Nov. 3, 1955, he was a guest conductor with the Chicago Symph., and returned to it for 5 more ap-pearances in subsequent years. During its Euro-pean tour of 1971 he was joint conductor with Sir Georg Solti. Giulini now became an undisputed master of the art of conducting, in both the operatic and the symph. repertoire; his renown was world-wide. In 1973 he was named principal conductor of the Vienna Symph. Orch., and in 1975 he took it on a world tour, which included the U.S., Canada, and Japan. On Oct. 24, 1975, he led it at a televised con-cert from the United Nations. In 1978 he succeeded Zubin Mehta as chief conductor and music director of the Los Angeles Phil., and succeeded in maintain-ing it at a zenith of orchestral brilliance. In 1983 he took the orchestra to Japan. His conducting style embodies the best traditions of the Italian school as exemplified by Toscanini, but is free from explosive displays of temper. He is above all a Romantic con-ductor who can identify his musical Weltanschau-ung with the musical essence of Beethoven, Verdi, Mahler, and Tchaikovsky; he leads the classics with an almost abstract contemplation. In the music of the 20th century, he gives congenial interpretations of works by Debussy, Ravel, and Stravinsky; the ex-pressionist school of composers lies outside of his deeply felt musicality, but he does not actively pro-mote the experimental school of modern music. His behavior on the podium is free from self-assertive theatrics, and he treats the orchestra as comrades-in-arms, associates in the cause of music, rather than subordinate performers of the task assigned to them. Yet his personal feeling for music is not dis-guised; often he closes his eyes in fervent self-ab-sorption when conducting without score the great Classical and Romantic works.

BIBLIOGRAPHY: *Le Grand Baton* (Sept. 1977; includes articles and discography).

Giulini, Giorgio, Italian composer; b. Milan, 1716;

d. there, 1780. He was the author of several instrumental works of considerable merit.

BIBLIOGRAPHY: G. Cesari, "Giorgio Giulini, musicista," *Rivista Musicale Italiana* (1917).

Giustini, Lodovico, Italian composer; b. Pistova, Dec. 12, 1685; d. Florence, after 1732. He was the first to publ. sonatas for Cristofori's pianoforte (*12 Sonate da Cimbalo di piano e forte,* Florence, 1732).

Gladstone, Francis Edward, noted English organist; b. Summertown, near Oxford, March 2, 1845; d. Hereford, Sept. 6, 1928. He was a pupil of S. Wesley, 1859–64; filled positions as organist at Weston-super-Mare, Llandaff, Chichester, Brighton, London, and Norwich. After embracing the Catholic faith, he was choir director at St. Mary of the Angels, Bayswater, until 1894. In 1876 he took the degree of Mus.Bac. at Cambridge; in 1879, Mus.Doc.; was a prof. of harmony and counterpoint at the Royal College of Music from 1883 to 1910.

WORKS: Oratorio, *Philippi* (1883); much church music; an overture; some chamber music (all in MS); he also publ. organ pieces, *The Organ-Student's Guide* and *A Treatise on Strict Counterpoint* (1906). He wrote an a cappella chorus, *In Paradisium,* for his own funeral and trained 4 monks to sing it.

Glanville-Hicks, Peggy, Australian composer and critic; b. Melbourne, Dec. 29, 1912. She studied composition with Fritz Hart at the Melbourne Cons.; in 1931 went to London, where she took courses in piano with Arthur Benjamin, theory with R.O. Morris and C. Kitson at the Royal College of Music, composition with Ralph Vaughan Williams, orchestration with Gordon Jacob, and conducting with Constant Lambert and Sir Malcolm Sargent. She obtained a traveling scholarship which enabled her to go to Paris for lessons with Nadia Boulanger, and to Vienna, where she took a course in musicology and advanced composition with Egon Wellesz. In 1939 she came to the U.S.; became an American citizen; in 1938–48 was married to the English composer **Stanley Bates;** from 1948 to 1958 she wrote music criticism for the *N.Y. Herald Tribune.* In 1957 she received a Guggenheim fellowship; in 1959 she went to Greece, and made her residence in Athens. There she produced her opera *Nausicaa,* to the text of Robert Graves (Athens, Aug. 19, 1961), which had a modicum of success. Her other operas are *Caedmon* (1934); *The Transposed Heads* (Louisville, March 27, 1954); *The Glittering Gate* (N.Y., May 14, 1959); *Sappho* (1963). She wrote the ballets *Hylas and the Nymphs* (1937); *Postman's Knock* (1940); *The Masque of the Wild Man* (1958); *Saul and the Witch of Endor* (1959); *Triad* (1959); *Tragic Celebration* (1966); *A Season in Hell* (1967); *Dance Cantata* for Soloists, Speaking Chorus, Narrator, and Orch. (1947); *Letters from Morocco* for Voice and Orch. to texts from actual letters she received from the composer Paul Bowles (N.Y., Feb. 22, 1953); *Sinfonia da Pacifica* (1953); *Tapestry* for Orch. (1956); Piano Concerto (1936); Flute Concerto (1937); *Con-*

certino da camera for Flute, Clarinet, Bassoon, and Piano (Amsterdam Festival, June 10, 1948); *3 Gymnopedies* for Harp and Other Instruments (1953); *Etruscan Concerto* for Piano and Chamber Orch. (N.Y., Jan. 25, 1956); *Concerto romantico* for Viola and Orch. (1957); *Drama* for Orch. (1966), *Concertino antico* for Harps and String Quartet; several other works inspired by ancient Greek modalities; choral pieces; songs. As a pragmatic composer of functional music with human connotations, Peggy Glanville-Hicks shuns the monopolistic fashion of mandatory dissonance, but explores attentively the resources of folk music, making use of Greek melos in her opera *Nausicaa,* of Hindu rhythmic modes in the opera *The Transposed Heads,* and of allusions to non-Western modalities in *Letters from Morocco.* She ceased to compose after going blind in 1969.

Glareanus, Henricus (also **Heinrich Glarean;** real name, **Heinrich Loris;** Latinized: **Henricus Loritus**), Swiss musical theorist and writer; b. Mollis, in the canton of Glarus, June 1488; d. Freiburg, Baden, March 28, 1563. He studied with Rubellus at Bern, and later with Cochläus at Cologne, where he was crowned poet laureate by Emperor Maximilian I in 1512, as the result of a poem he composed and sang to the emperor. He first taught mathematics at Basel (1515); in 1517 went to Paris, where he taught philosophy; in 1522 returned to Basel, where he stayed till 1529, when he settled in Freiburg. There he was a prof. of poetry, then of theology. His first important work, *Isagoge in musicen,* publ. at Basel in 1516 (Eng. trans. in the *Journal of Music Theory,* III, 1959; pp. 97–139), dealt with solmization, intervals, modes, and tones. A still more important vol., the *Dodecachordon,* was publ. in 1547; in it, Glareanus advanced the theory that there are 12 church modes, corresponding to the ancient Greek modes, instead of the commonly accepted 8 modes. The 3rd part of the *Dodecachordon* contains many works by 15th- and 16th-century musicians. A copy of the *Dodecachordon,* with corrections in Glareanus's own handwriting, is in the Library of Congress, Washington, D.C. A German trans., with the musical examples in modern notation, publ. by P. Bohn in vol. 16 of *Publikationen der Gesellschaft für Musikforschung* (Leipzig, 1888); Eng. trans. and commentary by C.A. Miller in *Musicological Studies and Documents,* 6 (1965); facsimile edition in *Monuments of Music and Music Literature in Facsimile,* 2/65 (N.Y., 1967). A complete index of Glareanus's works is contained in P. Lichtenthal's *Dizionario e bibliografia della musica,* IV, pp. 274–76 (Milan, 1826). J.L. Wonegger publ. *Musicae epitome ex Glareani Dodekachordo* (1557; 2nd ed., 1559; in German as *Uss Glareani Musik ein Usszug,* 1557).

BIBLIOGRAPHY: Biographies of Glareanus have been written by H. Schreiber (Freiburg, 1837) and O.F. Fritzsche (Frauenfeld, 1890); P. Spitta in *Vierteljahrsschrift für Musik-Wissenschaft* (vol. VII, pp. 123ff.); A. Schering, "Die Notenbeispiele in Glareanus Dodecachordon," *Sammelbände der Internationalen Musik-Gesellschaft* (1912); E. Refardt, *Musikerlexikon der Schweiz* (1928); E.

Glasenapp — Glass

Kirsch, "Studie zum Problem des Heinrich Loriti (Glarean)," *Festschrift A. Schering zum 60.sten Geburtstag* (Berlin, 1937); B. Meier, "Heinrich Loriti Glareanus als Musiktheoritiker," *Aufsätze zur Freiburger Wissenschaft- und Universitätsgeschichte,* XXI (1960); C. Miller, "The *Dodecachordon;* Its Origin and Influence on Renaissance Thought," *Musica Disciplina,* XV (1961).

Glasenapp, Carl Friedrich, music scholar, biographer of Wagner; b. Riga, Oct. 3, 1847; d. there, April 14, 1915. He studied philology at Dorpat; from 1875, was headmaster at Riga. An ardent admirer of Wagner's art, he devoted his entire life to the study of the master's works, and was one of the principal contributors to the *Bayreuther Blätter* from their foundation. His great work is the monumental biography of Wagner *Richard Wagners Leben und Wirken,* of which the first 2 vols. were publ. at Kassel and Leipzig (1876, 1877); after the 2nd enlarged edition (1882) these were rewritten, and the entire work was issued at Leipzig as *Das Leben Richard Wagners* (I, 1813–43 [1894]; II, 1843–53 [1896]; III, 1853–62 [1899]; IV, 1862–72 [1904]; V, 1872–77 [1907]; VI, 1877–83 [1911]). Vols. I, II, and III appeared in Eng. trans. (with amplifications) by W.A. Ellis (London, 1900, 1901, 1903), but after that Ellis continued the biography as an independent work. Though Glasenapp's work was considered the definitive biography in its time, its value is diminished by the fact that he publ. only materials approved by Wagner's family; as a result, it was superseded by later biographies. His other works on Wagner include *Wagner-Lexikon* with H. von Stein (1883); *Wagner-Encyklopädie* (2 vols., 1891); *Siegfried Wagner* (1906); *Siegfried Wagner und seine Kunst* (1911), with sequels, *Schwarzschwanenreich* (1913) and *Sonnenflammen* (1919); he also edited *Bayreuther Briefe, 1871–73* (1907) and *Familienbriefe an Richard Wagner, 1832–74* (1907).

Glaser, Werner Wolf, German-born Swedish composer; b. Cologne, April 14, 1910. He studied composition with Jarnach in Cologne and with Hindemith in Berlin; was then active as a choral conductor. In 1933 he left Germany; from 1934 till 1943 lived in Copenhagen, where he became director, jointly with Lyngby, of a music school. In 1943 he went to Sweden, and in 1945 headed a music school in Västerås. A man of wide interests, he studied modern art and literature; also investigated the potentialities of music therapy. A very prolific composer, he followed the neo-Classical line. WORKS: 3 chamber operas: *Kagekiyo* (1961); *Möten* (Västerås, Dec. 13, 1970); *Cercatori* (1972); opera buffa, *En naken kung (A Naked King),* based on H.C. Andersen (Göteborg, April 6, 1973); ballet for Chamber Orch., *Les Cinq Pas de l'homme* (1973); 7 symphs. (1934, 1935, 1936, 1943, 1949, 1957, 1961); Chamber Symph. (1936); 3 concertos for Orch. (1950–66); Flute Concerto (1934); *Trilogia* for Orch. (1939; Swedish Radio, Sept. 18, 1971); *3 Pieces* for Strings (1947); *Concerto della cappella* for Winds, Percussion, and Piano (1960); *Musica sacra* for

Flute, Clarinet, Organ, and Strings (1960); *Le tre gradi* for Strings (1961); Clarinet Concertino (1962); Concerto for Violin, Winds, and Percussion (1962); *Capriccio III* for Piano and Orch. (1964); Violin Concerto (1964); *ASEA-Musik* for Chorus and Orch. (1965); Concerto for 20 Winds and Percussion (1966); *Transformations* for Piano and Orch. (1966); Oboe Concerto (1966); *Paradosso* for 2 String Orchs. (1967); Horn Concerto (1969); *Canto* for Saxophone and Orch. (1970); *Concerto lirico* for Soprano, Piano, Timpani, and Strings (1971); *Chamber Music* for Winds and Strings (1971). He also wrote 9 string quartets (1934–67); 7 piano sonatas (1933–36); *In memoriam Paul Klee* for Violin (1961); *Capriccio I* for Piano (1963) and *II* for Viola and Piano (1963); *Ordo meatus* for Oboe d'Amore Solo (1968); *Capricci* for Clarinet (1969); *Baroque cantata* for Soprano, Flute, Viola d'Amore, and Cello (1969); *Paysages sonores* for Piano Trio (1973); *Besvärjelser* for Chorus and Chamber Orch. (1974); *3 Symphonic Dances* (1975); piano pieces; children's choruses; incidental music for the theater.

Glass, Louis Christian August, Danish composer; b. Copenhagen, March 23, 1864; d. there, Jan. 22, 1936. He was a pupil of his father, **Christian Hendrik** (1821–93), then at the Brussels Cons. of J. de Zarembski and J. Wieniawski (piano) and of J. Servais (cello); he appeared as both a pianist and a cellist, but was more important as a composer. WORKS: 6 symphs. (the 5th, *Sinfonia svastica,* in C, op. 59); 2 overtures, *Der Volksfeind* and *Dänemark; Sommerliv,* suite for Orch.; dance poem, *Artemis* (Copenhagen, Oct. 27, 1917); *Fantasie* for Piano and Orch.; Concerto for Oboe and Orch.; String Sextet; Piano Quintet; 4 string quartets; Piano Trio; 2 violin sonatas; numerous works for piano.

Glass, Philip, remarkable American composer; b. Baltimore, Jan. 31, 1937. He was the grandchild of Orthodox Jewish immigrants from Russia. His father owned a record store, and Glass worked there from the age of 12; he studied flute at the Peabody Cons. in Baltimore; at the age of 15 he entered the Univ. of Chicago, where he took courses in piano and in wrestling in the featherweight category (1952–56); then moved to N.Y. to study at the Juilliard School of Music, where he was a student of Persichetti in composition, earning his M.S. in 1962. In 1964 he received a Fulbright grant and went to Paris, where, inevitably, he was steered to the "boulangerie," the classroom of Nadia Boulanger, the formidable *nourrice* of 3 generations of American composers; from her he learned a rather abecedarian counterpoint, which gave him a needed discipline. Much more important to his future development was his meeting with the great Indian sitar virtuoso Ravi Shankar, who introduced him to the mysterious world of Hindu ragas. He traveled to Morocco, where he absorbed the arcane modalities of North African melorhythms, which taught him the heterodox art of melodic repetition. He wrote music for a group of traveling American actors and actresses; he married one of them, JoAnne Akalaitis, and traveled with her to the foothills of the Himalayas. Eventually he divorced her and in 1980 married a 29-year-old medical doctor, Luba Burtyk. In 1967 he returned to N.Y. in a state of musical transfiguration; his style of composition became an alternately concave and convex mirror image of Eastern modes, undergoing melodic phases of stationary harmonies in lieu of modulations. In the physical world, he had to take a variety of manual jobs, as a furniture mover, carpenter, and cabdriver. He formed associations with modern painters and sculptors who strove to obtain maximum effects with a minimum of means. Glass began to practice a similar method in music, which soon acquired the factitious sobriquet of Minimalism. Other Americans and some Europeans followed this practice, which was basically Eastern in its catatonic homophony; Steve Reich was a close companion in minimalistic pursuits of maximalistic effects. Glass formed his own phonograph company, Chatham Square, which recorded most of his works. He also organized an ensemble of electrically amplified wind instruments, which became the chief medium of his own compositions. On April 13, 1968, he presented the first concert of the Glass Ensemble at Queens College in N.Y. Between 1969 and 1975 he made altogether 8 European tours. In 1970 and 1973 Glass was again in India.

His productions, both in America and in Europe, became extremely successful among young audiences, who were mesmerized by this mixture of rock realism with alluring mysticism; undeterred by the indeterminability and interminability of his productions, some lasting several hours of merciless, relentless, unremitting homophony, they accepted Glass as a true representative of earthly and unearthly art. The mind-boggling titles of these works added to the tantalizing incomprehensibility of the subjects that Glass selected for his inspiration. The high point of his productions was the "opera" *Einstein on the Beach,* to a text by Robert Wilson, which involved deliberate befuddlement in a surrealistic comminution of thematic ingredients and hypnotic repetition of harmonic subjects. It was first produced at the Festival of Avignon in France, on July 25, 1976, and was subsequently performed in Venice, Belgrade, Brussels, Paris, Hamburg, Rotterdam, and Amsterdam, finally reaching, on Nov. 21, 1976, the stage of the Metropolitan Opera at Lincoln Center in N.Y., where it proved something of a sensation of the season; however, it was not produced as part of the regular subscription series. On Sept. 5, 1980, Glass staged in Rotterdam his opera *Satyagraha,* based on an episode of Gandhi's years in South Africa between 1893 and 1913. "Satyagraha" was Gandhi's slogan, composed of 2 Hindu words: *saty* ("truth") and *agraha* ("firmness"). Another significant production was a film, *Koyaanisquatsi,* a Hopi Indian word meaning "life out of balance." The music represented the ultimate condensation of the basic elements of composition as practiced by Philip Glass; here the pitiless ritualistic repetition of chords arranged in symmetrical sequences becomes hypnotic, particularly since the screen action is devoid of narrative; the effect is enhanced by the deep bass notes of an Indian chant. Other works by Glass consist of the following: *Piece in the Shape of a Square* (N.Y., May 19, 1968); *Music in Fifths* (N.Y., Jan. 16, 1970); *Music with Changing Parts* (N.Y., Nov. 10, 1972); *Music in 12 Parts* (first full perf., N.Y., June 1, 1974); *North Star* for 2 Voices and Instruments (1975). On Oct. 6, 1983, the Brooklyn Academy of Music presented the first American performance of a mixed-media piece by Glass called *The Photographer: Far from the Truth,* based on the life of the 19th-century photographer Eadweard Muybridge; it includes a scene in which he murders his wife's lover. This was followed by the exotic opera *Akhnaton,* set in ancient Egypt, with the singing parts in the ancient Accadian language, in Egyptian, and in Hebrew, with an explanatory narration in English; it was produced in Stuttgart on March 24, 1984.
BIBLIOGRAPHY: A. Kozinn, "Philip Glass," *Ovation* (Feb. 1984).

Glaz, Herta, Austrian contralto; b. Vienna, Sept. 16, 1908. She made her debut at the Breslau Opera in 1931, presaging a successful career, but in 1933 was forced to leave Germany. She toured Austria and Scandinavia as a concert singer; sang at the German Theater in Prague during the season 1935–36; in 1936 she took part in the American tour of the Salzburg Opera Guild; subsequently sang at the Chicago Opera (1940–42); on Dec. 25, 1942, she made her debut with the Metropolitan Opera in N.Y., and remained on its staff until 1956; then taught voice at the Manhattan School of Music, retiring in 1977; settled in Los Angeles.

Glazunov, Alexander, notable Russian composer; b. St. Petersburg, Aug. 10, 1865; d. Neuilly-sur-Seine, March 21, 1936. Of a well-to-do family (his father was a book publisher), he studied at a technical high school in St. Petersburg, and also took lessons in music with a private tutor. As a boy of 15, he was introduced to Rimsky-Korsakov, who gave him weekly lessons in harmony, counterpoint, and orchestration. Glazunov made rapid progress, and at the age of 16 completed his first symph., which was performed by Balakirev on March 29, 1882, in St. Petersburg. So mature was this score that Glazunov was hailed by Stasov, Cui, and others as a rightful heir to the masters of the Russian national school. The music publisher Belaiev arranged for publication of Glazunov's works, and took him to Weimar, where he met Liszt. From that time Glazunov composed assiduously in all genres except opera. He was invited to conduct his symphs. in Paris (1889) and London (1896–97). Returning to St. Petersburg, he conducted concerts of Russian music. In 1899 he was engaged as an instructor in composition and orchestration at the St. Petersburg Cons. He resigned temporarily during the revolutionary turmoil of 1905 in protest against the dismissal of Rimsky-Korsakov by the government authorities, but returned to the staff after full autonomy was granted to the Cons. by the administration. On Dec.

14, 1905, Glazunov was elected director and retained this post until 1928, when he went to Paris. In 1929 he made several appearances as conductor in the U.S.; led his 6th Symph. with the Detroit Symph. Orch. (Nov. 21, 1929) and also conducted the Boston Symph. He was the recipient of honorary degrees of Mus.D. from Cambridge and Oxford univs. (1907). Although he wrote no textbook on composition, his pedagogical methods left a lasting impression on Russian musicians through his many students who preserved his traditions. His music is often regarded as academic, yet there is a flow of rhapsodic eloquence that places Glazunov in the Romantic school. He was for a time greatly swayed by Wagnerian harmonies, but resisted this influence successfully; Lisztian characteristics are more pronounced in his works. Glazunov was one of the greatest masters of counterpoint among Russian composers, but he avoided extreme polyphonic complexity. The national spirit of his music is unmistakable; in many of his descriptive works, the programmatic design is explicitly Russian (*Stenka Razin, The Kremlin,* etc.). His most popular score is the ballet *Raymonda.* The major portion of his music was written before 1906, when he completed his 8th Symph.; after that he wrote mostly for special occasions.

WORKS: Incidental music to Grand Duke Konstantin Romanov's mystery play *The King of the Jews* (1914); ballets: *Raymonda* (1896; St. Petersburg, Jan. 19, 1898); *Ruses d'amour* (1898); *The Seasons* (1899).

FOR ORCH.: Symph. No. 1 (1881; St. Petersburg, March 29, 1882); 2 *Overtures on Greek Themes* (1881–85); 2 serenades (1883); *Stenka Razin,* symph. poem (1884); *A la mémoire d'un héros* (1885); *Suite caractéristique* (1885); *Idyll* and *Rêverie orientale* (1886); Symph. No. 2 (1886; Paris, June 29, 1889, composer conducting); *Une Pensée à Franz Liszt* for String Orch. (1886); *Mazurka* (1887); *The Forest,* symph. poem (1888); *Mélodie* and *Sérénade espagnole* for Cello and Orch. (1888); *Marche des Noces* for Large Orch. (1889); *Une Fête slave,* symph. sketch (1890; from *Quatuor slave*); *The Sea,* symph. fantasy (1890); *Oriental Rhapsody* (1890); *The Kremlin,* symph. picture (1890); Symph. No. 3 (1891); *Printemps,* musical picture (1892); *Triumphal March* on the occasion of the famous Columbian Exposition in Chicago (1893); overture, *Carnaval* (1894); *Chopiniana,* suite on Chopin's themes (1894); 2 *Valses de concert* (1894); Symph. No. 4 (St. Petersburg, Feb. 3, 1894, composer conducting); *Cortège solennel* (1894); *Scènes de ballet* (1894); *Fantaisie* (1895); Symph. No. 5 (1895); suite from the ballet *Raymonda* (1897); Symph. No. 6 (1896; St. Petersburg, Feb. 21, 1897; *Pas de caractère,* on Slavic and Hungarian themes (1900); *Intermezzo romantico* (1901); *Chant du ménestrel* for Cello and Orch. (1901; also for Cello and Piano); *Ouverture solennelle* (1901); *Marche sur un thème russe* (1901); Symph. No. 7 (St. Petersburg, Jan. 3, 1903); *Ballade* (1903); *From the Middle Ages,* suite (1903); Violin Concerto (1904; St. Petersburg, March 4, 1905, Leopold Auer, soloist; first perf. outside Russia, London, Oct. 17, 1905, Mischa Elman, soloist); *Scène dansante* (1905); Symph. No. 8 (Dec. 22, 1906); *Le Chant du destin,* dramatic overture (1907); 2 preludes: No. 1, *In Memory of V. Stasov* (1906), and No. 2, *In Memory of Rimsky-Korsakov* (1908); *In Memory of Gogol* (1909); *Finnish Fantasy* (Helsingfors, Nov. 7, 1910, composer conducting); Piano Concerto No. 1 (1911); *Finnish Sketches* (1912); *Dance of Salomé,* after Oscar Wilde (1912); *Karelian Legend* (1914); Piano Concerto No. 2 (Petrograd, Nov. 11, 1917); *Concerto-Ballata* for Cello and Orch. (Paris, Oct. 14, 1933, composer conducting; Maurice Eisenberg, soloist); Saxophone Concerto (in collaboration with Sigurd Rascher; first perf. by him in Nykoping, Sweden, Nov. 25, 1934).

VOCAL WORKS: *Coronation Cantata* (1894); *Hymn to Pushkin* for Female Chorus (1899); cantata for Women's Chorus with 2 Pianos, 8-hands (1900); *Memorial Cantata* (1901); 21 songs.

CHAMBER MUSIC: 7 string quartets: No. 1, in D (1882); No. 2, in F (1884); No. 3, in G (*Quatuor slave;* 1889); No. 4, in A (1899); No. 5, in D (1900); No. 6, in B-flat (1930); No. 7, in C (1931); *5 Novelettes* for String Quartet (1888); Suite for String Quartet (1894); String Quintet (1895); Suite for String Quartet (1929); *Pensée à Liszt* for Cello and Piano; *Rêverie* for French Horn and Piano; *In modo religioso* for 4 Brass Instruments; *Elegy* for Viola and Piano; *Oberek* for Violin and Piano.

PIANO MUSIC: 2 sonatas (1898, 1899); *Barcarolle; Novelette;* Prelude and 2 mazurkas; 3 études; *Petite valse;* Nocturne; *Grande valse de concert: 3 Miniatures; Valse de salon; 3 morceaux;* 2 *Impromptus;* Prelude and Fugue; Theme and Variations; Suite for 2 Pianos (1920); 4 preludes and fugues (1922). Glazunov also completed and orchestrated the overture to Borodin's *Prince Igor* (from memory, having heard Borodin play it on the piano).

BIBLIOGRAPHY: A.W. Ossovsky, *Glazunov: His Life and Work* (St. Petersburg, 1907); M. Montagu-Nathan, *Contemporary Russian Composers* (N.Y., 1917); V. Belaiev, *Glazunov* (vol. 1, Petrograd, 1921); I. Glebov, *Glazunov* (Leningrad, 1924); M.D. Calvocoressi and G. Abraham, *Masters of Russian Music* (N.Y., 1936); Galina Fedorova, *Glazunov* (Moscow, 1947; 2nd ed., 1961); H. Gunther, *A. Glasunow* (Bonn, 1956); M. Ganina, *Glasunow: Life and Works* (Leningrad, 1961).

Gleason, Frederick Grant, American organist, composer, and critic; b. Middletown, Conn., Dec. 17, 1848; d. Chicago, Dec. 6, 1903. He studied in Hartford with Dudley Buck, later at the Leipzig Cons., in Berlin, and in London. Upon return to the U.S., he was active as a church organist, teacher, and music critic. He wrote 2 operas, *Otho Visconti* (posthumous production; Chicago, June 4, 1907) and *Montezuma;* 4 cantatas; a symph. poem, *Edris;* a Piano Concerto; 3 piano trios; organ and piano pieces; songs; 2 Episcopal church services.

BIBLIOGRAPHY: E.E. Hipsher, *American Opera and Its Composers* (Philadelphia, 1929; 2nd ed., 1934; pp. 216–17).

Gleason, Harold, American organist and musicologist; b. Jefferson, Ohio, April 26, 1892; d. Claremont, Calif., June 27, 1980. He studied organ in Calif. with Lemare, and in Paris with Bonnet; took a course in composition with Herbert Inch at the Eastman School of Music in Rochester, N.Y.; was head of the organ dept. there from 1921 to 1953; also taught musicology. He publ. *Method of Organ Playing* (1937); *Examples of Music before 1400* (1942); *Music in America,* an anthology (in collaboration with W.T. Marrocco; N.Y., 1964).

Glebov, Evgeni, Soviet composer; b. Roslavl, near Smolensk, Sept. 10, 1929. He studied at the Belorussian Cons. in Minsk with Bogatyryov; later was appointed to its faculty. Several of his compositions reflect the events of the war, which devastated Belorussia in 1941.
WORKS: Opera, *Our Spring* (1963); ballet, *A Vision* (1961); cantata, *We Will Fight for Truth* (1956); cantata, *The Communists Lead Us* (1963); *Partisan Symphony* (1958); Concerto for Voice and Orch. (1965); several pieces for native Belorussian instruments.
BIBLIOGRAPHY: L.S. Mukharinskaya, *Evgeny Glebov* (Moscow, 1959); E.Y. Rakova, *Evgeny Glebov* (Minsk, 1971).

Glebov, Igor. Pen name of **Boris Asafiev.**

Glen, John, Scots collector of native music; b. Edinburgh, June 13, 1833; d. there, Nov. 29, 1904. His father, **Thomas** (1804–73), the inventor of the "Serpentcleide," had established himself as a manufacturer of musical instruments, and the son succeeded to the business in 1866; he confined himself to the manufacture of bagpipes, of which he was soon recognized as the foremost manufacturer in Great Britain. He was equally noted for his research in Scottish music; compiled *The Glen Collection of Scottish Dance Music, Strathspeys, Reels and Jigs . . . containing an Introduction on Scottish Dance Music* (2 vols., 1891, 1895); vol. I contains 144 tunes; vol. II, 148. His chief work is *Early Scottish Melodies: including examples from MSS. and early printed works, along with a number of comparative tunes, notes on former annotators, English and other claims, and Biographical Notices, etc.* (1900).
BIBLIOGRAPHY: *Musical Times,* Jan. 1905.

Glick, Srul Irving, Canadian composer; b. Toronto, Sept. 18, 1934. He studied composition with Weinzweig at the Univ. of Toronto (M.M., 1958); then attended classes of Darius Milhaud in Aspen, Colo. (summers 1956, 1957), and later took lessons with him and with Louis Saguer and Max Deutsch in Paris (1959–60). Returning to Canada, he taught theory and composition at the Cons. in Toronto (1963–69). His catalogue of works contains scores of 2 distinct types: those of a traditional Hebraic nature, direct and recognizable, and those that are abstract, written in a highly advanced idiom.
WORKS: *Heritage,* dance symph. (Toronto, Dec. 9, 1967); *2 Essays* for Orch. (1957); Sonata for String

Orch. (1957); *Sinfonietta* (1958); *Sinfonia concertante* No. 1 for String Orch. (1961); *Sinfonia concertante* No. 2, *Lamentations,* for String Quartet and Orch. (1972); *Suite hébraïque* for Orch. (1961); *Dance Concertante No. 1* for Small Orch. (1963); *Symphonic Dialogues* for Piano and Orch. (Toronto, Dec. 20, 1964); *Pan,* sketch for Orch. (1966); Symph. No. 1 for Chamber Orch. (Toronto, April 24, 1966); Symph. No. 2 for Full Orch. (Toronto, Jan. 24, 1969); *Gathering In,* a "symphonic concept" for Strings (Montreal, March 26, 1970); *Psalm* for Orch. (Hamilton, Oct. 17, 1971); *Symphonic Elegy,* with line drawing and funeral march (Toronto, April 20, 1974); Violin Concerto, subtitled *Shir Hamaalot* (*Songs of Ascents;* Victoria, British Columbia, Nov. 14, 1976); *. . . i never saw another butterfly . . . ,* to a text of children's poems written in the Terezin concentration camp, for Alto and Chamber Orch. (1968); *Deborah (Flaming Star)* for Narrator and Brass Quintet (1972); *Divertimento Sextet* for Flute, Clarinet, Bassoon, and String Trio (1958); Trio for Clarinet, Piano, and Cello (1958–59); String Trio (1963); *Dance Concertante No. 2* for Flute, Clarinet, Trumpet, Cello, and Piano (1964); Sonata for Jazz Quintet (1964); Sonatina for Jazz Sextet (1965–66); *Divertissement* for 7 Instruments and Conductor (1968); *Suite hébraïque* No. 2 for Clarinet, Piano, and String Trio (1969); *Suite hébraïque* No. 3 for String Quintet (1975); *Prayer and Dance* for Cello and Piano (1975); a number of piano pieces; songs; liturgical choruses for Hebrew services.

Glière, Reinhold, eminent Russian composer; b. Kiev, Jan. 11, 1875; d. Moscow, June 23, 1956. He studied violin with Hrimaly at the Moscow Cons., where he also took courses with Arensky, Taneyev, and Ippolitov-Ivanov (1894–1900), graduating with a gold medal. In 1905 he went to Berlin, where he remained for 2 years; returning to Russia, he became active as a teacher; was appointed prof. of composition at the Kiev Cons., and was its director in 1914–20; then was appointed to the faculty of the Moscow Cons., a post he retained until 1941. He traveled extensively in European and Asiatic Russia, collecting folk melodies; conducted many concerts of his own works; he made his last tour a month before his death, conducting in Odessa, Kishinev, and other cities. He was an extremely prolific composer, and was particularly distinguished in symph. works, in which he revealed himself as a successor of the Russian national school. He never transgressed the natural borderline of traditional harmony, but he was able to achieve effective results. His most impressive work is his 3rd Symph., surnamed *Ilya Muromets,* an epic description of the exploits of a legendary Russian hero. In his numerous songs Glière showed a fine lyrical talent. He wrote relatively few works of chamber music, most of them early in his career. In his opera *Shah-Senem,* he made use of native Caucasian songs. Glière was the teacher of 2 generations of Russian composers; among his students were Prokofiev and Miaskovsky. He received 2 Stalin prizes, for the String Quartet No. 4 (1948) and for the ballet *The*

Glinka

Bronze Knight (1950).

WORKS: OPERAS: *Shah-Senem* (Baku, May 4, 1934); *Leily and Medzhnun* (Tashkent, July 18, 1940); *Rachel,* one-act opera after Maupassant's *Mademoiselle Fifi* (Moscow, April 19, 1947); *Ghulsara* (Tashkent, Dec. 25, 1949). BALLETS: *Chrysis* (Moscow, Nov. 30, 1912); *Cleopatra* (Moscow, Jan. 11, 1926); *Red Poppy* (Moscow, June 14, 1927); *Comedians* (Moscow, April 5, 1931); *The Bronze Knight* (Leningrad, March 14, 1949). INCIDENTAL MUSIC: *King Oedipus* of Sophocles (1921); *Lysistrata* of Aristophanes (1923); *Marriage of Figaro* of Beaumarchais (1927). FOR ORCH.: Symph. No. 1 (Moscow, Jan. 3, 1903); Symph. No. 2 (Berlin, Jan. 23, 1908, Koussevitzky conducting); *The Sirens,* symph. poem (Moscow, Jan. 30, 1909); Symph. No. 3, *Ilya Muromets* (Moscow, March 23, 1912); *2 Poems* for Soprano and Orch. (1924); *Cossacks of Zaporozh,* symph. poem (1921; Odessa, Dec. 23, 1925); *Trizna,* symph. poem (1915); *For the Festival of the Comintern,* fantasy for Wind Orch. (1924); *March of the Red Army* for Wind Orch. (1924); *Imitation of Jezekiel,* symph. poem for Narrator and Orch. (1919); Concerto for Harp and Orch. (Moscow, Nov. 23, 1938); *Friendship of Nations,* overture (1941); Concerto for Coloratura Soprano and Orch. (Moscow, May 12, 1943); *For the Happiness of the Fatherland,* overture (1942); *25 Years of the Red Army,* overture (1943); *Victory,* overture (Moscow, Oct. 30, 1945); Cello Concerto (Moscow, Feb. 18, 1947); Horn Concerto (Moscow, Jan. 26, 1952, composer conducting); an unfinished Violin Concerto. CHAMBER MUSIC: 5 string quartets (No. 4 won the Stalin Prize, 1948; No. 5 left unfinished at his death); 3 string sextets; String Octet. OTHER MUSIC: 20 pieces for Violin and Piano; 12 duos for 2 Violins; Ballad for Cello and Piano; 4 pieces for Double Bass and Piano; 8 pieces for Violin and Cello; 12 pieces for Cello and Piano; 10 duos for 2 Cellos; miscellaneous pieces for different instruments. He also wrote about 200 songs and 200 piano pieces.

BIBLIOGRAPHY: Igor Boelza, *R.M. Glière* (Moscow, 1955; 2nd ed., 1962). A 2-vol. ed. of articles and memoirs on Glière was publ. in Moscow (1965, 1967).

Glinka, Mikhail, great Russian composer, often called "the father of Russina music" for his pioneering cultivation of Russian folk modalities; b. Novospasskoye, Smolensk district, June 1, 1804; d. Berlin, Feb. 15, 1857. A scion of a fairly rich family of landowners, he was educated at an exclusive school in St. Petersburg (1818–22); he also took private lessons in music; his piano teacher was a resident German musician, Carl Meyer; he also studied violin; when the famous pianist John Field was in St. Petersburg, Glinka had an opportunity to study with him, but he had only 3 lessons before Field departed. He began to compose even before acquiring adequate training in theory. As a boy he traveled in the Caucasus; then stayed for a while at his father's estate; at 20 entered the Ministry of Communications in St. Petersburg; he remained in government employ until 1828; at the same time, he constantly improved his general education by reading; he had friends among the best Russian writers of the time, including the poets Zhukovsky and Pushkin. He also took singing lessons with an Italian teacher, Belloli. In 1830 he went to Italy, where he continued irregular studies in Milan (where he spent most of his Italian years); he also visited Naples, Rome, and Bologna. He met Donizetti and Bellini. He became enamored of Italian music, and his early vocal and instrumental compositions are thoroughly Italian in melodic and harmonic structure. In 1833 he went to Berlin, where he took a course in counterpoint and general composition with the famous German theorist Dehn; thus he was nearly 30 when he completed his theoretical education. In 1834 his father died, and Glinka went back to Russia to take care of the family affairs. In 1835 he was married; but the marriage was unhappy, and he soon became separated from his wife, finally divorcing her in 1846. The return to his native land led him to consider the composition of a truly national opera on a subject (suggested to him by Zhukovsky) depicting a historical episode in Russian history, the saving of the first tsar of the Romanov dynasty by a simple peasant, Ivan Susanin. (The Italian composer Cavos wrote an opera on the same subject 20 years previously, and conducted it in St. Petersburg.) Glinka's opera was produced in St. Petersburg on Dec. 9, 1836, under the title *A Life for the Tsar.* The event was hailed by the literary and artistic circles of Russia as a milestone of Russian culture, and indeed the entire development of Russian national music received its decisive creative impulse from Glinka's patriotic opera. It remained in the repertoire of Russian theaters until the Russian Revolution made it unacceptable, but it was revived, under the original title, *Ivan Susanin,* on Feb. 27, 1939, in Moscow, without alterations in the music, but with the references to the tsar eliminated from the libretto, the idea of saving the country being substituted for that of saving the tsar. Glinka's next opera, *Ruslan and Ludmila,* after Pushkin's fairy tale, was produced on Dec. 9, 1842; this opera, too, became extremely popular in Russia. Glinka introduced into the score many elements of oriental music; one episode contains the earliest use of the whole-tone scale in an opera. Both operas retain the traditional Italian form, with arias, choruses, and orch. episodes clearly separated. In 1844 Glinka was in Paris, where he met Berlioz; he also traveled in Spain, where he collected folk songs; the fruits of his Spanish tour were 2 orch. works, *Jota Aragonesa* and *Night in Madrid.* On his way back to Russia, he stayed in Warsaw for 3 years; the remaining years of his life he spent in St. Petersburg, Paris, and Berlin, where he died.

WORKS: FOR THE STAGE: Operas: *A Life for the Tsar; Ruslan and Ludmila;* sketches for 3 unfinished operas; *Chao-Kang,* ballet (1828–31); incidental music for Kukolnik's tragedy *Prince Kholmsky;* incidental music for the play *The Moldavian Gypsy.* FOR ORCH.: *Andante Cantabile and Rondo; Larghetto;* 2 overtures; Symph. in B-flat; *Trumpet March* (1828); *Overture-Symphony on Russian Themes* (1834; completed in 1938 by V.I. Shebalin);

Valse (1839); *Polonaise* (1839); *Valse-Fantaisie* (1839); *Capriccio brillante* on the *Jota Aragonesa* (1845; afterward renamed *Spanish Overture No. 1*); *Summer Night in Madrid: Spanish Overture No. 2* (1848); *Kamarinskaya* (1848); symph. poem on Gogol's *Taras Bulba* (unfinished, part of first movement only; 1852); *Festival Polonaise* on a bolero melody (1855). CHAMBER MUSIC: Septet in E-flat (1824); 2 string quartets (1824, 1830); *Trio pathétique* (1827); 2 serenades (1832); Sonata for Piano and Viola (1825–28); about 40 piano numbers (5 valses, 7 mazurkas, nocturnes, etc.); much vocal music, including choral works, quartets, duets, arias, and about 85 songs with piano accompaniment, many set to poems by Pushkin and Zhukovsky.

BIBLIOGRAPHY: O. Comettant, *Musique et Musiciens* (Paris, 1862); C. Cui, *La Musique en Russie* (Paris, 1880); O. Fouque, *Glinka* (Paris, 1880); K. Albrecht, *Catalogue of Glinka's Vocal Works* (Moscow, 1891); P. Weimarn, *M.I. Glinka* (Moscow, 1892); L. Shestakova, *Glinka as He Was* (St. Petersburg, 1894); N.F. Findeisen, *M.I. Glinka* (St. Petersburg, 1896); idem, *Glinka in Spain and the Spanish Folk Songs Recorded by Him* (St. Petersburg, 1896); idem, *Catalogue of the Musical Manuscripts, Letters, and Portraits of M.I. Glinka in the Manuscript Section of the Imperial Public Library in St. Petersburg* (St. Petersburg, 1898); V. Avenarius, *Glinka, the Creator of Russian Opera* (St. Petersburg, 1903); A. Pougin, *Essai historique sur la musique en Russie* (Paris, 1904); M.D. Calvocoressi, *Glinka* (Paris, 1913); M. Montagu-Nathan, *Glinka* (London, 1916); K.A. Kuznetzov, *Glinka and His Contemporaries* (1926); M.D. Calvocoressi and G. Abraham, *Glinka* in *Masters of Russian Music* (N.Y., 1936); D. Brook, *Six Great Russian Composers* (London, 1946); I.I. Martinov, *M.I. Glinka* (Moscow, 1947); A. Altayev, *M.I. Glinka* (Moscow, 1947); B. Asafiev, *Glinka* (Moscow, 1947); E. Kann-Novikova, *M.I. Glinka, New Materials and Documents* (Moscow, 1951); A. Orlova, *M.I. Glinka, Chronicle of Life and Work* (Moscow, 1952); P.G. Dippel, *Klingende Einkehr; Glinka und Berlin* (Berlin, 1953); A. Orlova, *Glinka in St. Petersburg* (Leningrad, 1970); D. Brown, *Glinka: A Biographical and Critical Study* (London, 1974). Glinka's autobiographical sketch intended for inclusion in the *Biographie universelle des musiciens* by Fétis was publ. for the first time in *Muzikalnaya Letopis'* in 1926; his collected letters, ed. by N.F. Findeisen, were publ. in 1907.

Glinski, Mateusz, Polish musicologist; b. Warsaw, April 6, 1892; d. Welland, Ontario, Canada, Jan. 3, 1976. He studied at the Warsaw Cons. with Barcewicz (violin) and Statkowski (composition); then took courses in Leipzig with Max Reger, Riemann, and Schering; also had lessons in conducting with Nikisch. He went to St. Petersburg in 1914; studied composition with Glazunov and Steinberg, and conducting with Nicolas Tcherepnin. He conducted several concerts; also contributed articles on music to Russian periodicals. In 1918 he went to Warsaw; from 1924 to 1939 was editor of the Polish periodical *Muzyka.* At the outbreak of World War II he went to Rome, where he engaged in various activities as music critic and editor. In 1949 he established in Rome the Istituto Internazionale Federico Chopin. In 1956 he went to America; from 1959 to 1965 he taught at Assumption Univ. in Windsor, Canada. In 1965 he established the Niagara Symph. Orch., which he conducted. His works include an opera, *Orlotko,* after Rostand's play *L'Aiglon* (1918–27); a symph. poem, *Wagram* (1932); several choral works; songs and piano pieces. He publ., in Polish, a monograph on Scriabin (Warsaw, 1933), and numerous articles in Polish periodicals. He also publ. *Chopin's Letters to Delfina Potocka* (Windsor, Canada, 1961), in which he subscribes to the generally refuted belief that these letters, which came to light in 1945, are indeed genuine.

Globokar, Vinko, French composer of Slovenian descent; b. Anderny, July 7, 1934. He studied trombone in Ljubljana (1949–54) and at the Paris Cons. (1955–59); took composition lessons in Paris with René Leibowitz (1959–63) and with Luciano Berio (1965). He was a trombonist and composer at the Center for Creative Arts at the State Univ. of N.Y. at Buffalo in 1965–66. In 1966 he was appointed trombone instructor at the Cologne Hochschule für Musik. As a composer, he follows the most modern ideas of serial music in aleatory distribution. His works include *Plan* for a Persian Drum and 4 Instruments (1965); *Fluide* for 9 Brasses and 3 Percussion Instruments (1967); *Traumdeutung,* a "psychodrama" (Amsterdam, Sept. 7, 1968); *Etude pour folklore I* for 19 Soloists (1968); *Etude pour folklore II* for Orch. (1968); Concerto Grosso (Cologne, Nov. 6, 1970); *Airs de voyages vers l'interieur* for Ensemble (Stuttgart, Nov. 3, 1972).

Glock, Sir William, English music critic and broadcasting administrator; b. London, May 3, 1908. He studied at Gonville and Caius College, Cambridge; then took piano lessons with Artur Schnabel in Berlin. He made some appearances as a concert pianist, but devoted most of his time and effort to music criticism. In 1934 he joined the staff of the *Observer;* served as its chief music critic from 1939 to 1945. In 1949 he founded *The Score* magazine, and edited it until 1961. In 1948 he established the Summer School of Music at Bryanston, Dorset, which relocated to Dartington Hall, Devon, in 1953; he continued as its music director until 1979. In 1959 he assumed the important post of controller of music of the BBC, retaining it until 1973. In 1964 he was made a Commander of the Order of the British Empire; was knighted in 1970.

Glodeanu, Liviu, Rumanian composer; b. Dirja, Aug. 6, 1938; d. Bucharest, March 31, 1978. He studied first at the Cons. of Cluj, and later at the Bucharest Cons., with Ion Dumitrescu, Martian Negrea, Alfred Mendelsohn, and Tudor Ciortea. He subsequently taught at the School of Arts in Bucharest (1961–63); then was artistic adviser of the Bucharest Phil. Orch. (1963–71).

WORKS: Radio opera, *Zamolxe* (Bucharest, Oct. 8, 1969); 4 cantatas: *The Young Dead Soldiers,* to a text by Archibald MacLeish (1958; Cluj, March 31, 1962); *Inscriptions on the Cradle* (1959); *Bright Horizons* (1960); and *Cantata 1933* (1961); an oratorio, *Un pămint numit România* (1977). Other vocal works: *Suite* for Children's Chorus, Wind Instruments, and Percussion (1961); *2 Madrigals* for Chorus and Percussion (1963); *Incantation* for Chorus, Flute, Clarinet, and Percussion (1965); *Gloire* for Children's Chorus and Percussion (1967); *Ulysses* for Soprano or Tenor, and Orch. or Piano (1967). For Orch.: Concerto for String Orch. and Percussion (1959); Piano Concerto (1960); Symph. Movement (1961); Flute Concerto (1962); Violin Concerto (1966); *Studies* (1967); *Ricercari* (1971); *Symphonies* for Wind Ensemble (1971); *Pintea Vinteazul (Pintea the Brave),* symph. poem (1976); Concerto for Organ and Brass (1978). Chamber music: Clarinet Sonata (1959); 2 string quartets (1959, 1970); *Inventions* for Wind Quintet and Percussion (1963); Violin Sonatina (1963); *Mélopée* for Flute, Clarinet, Violin, and Tape (1971).

Glorieux, François, Belgian pianist and composer; b. Courtrai, Aug. 27, 1932. He studied at the Royal Cons. in Ghent, graduating in 1953; concertized in the U.S., Canada, Latin America, Africa, Spain, and the Middle East. His music, couched in a clear tonal idiom, reflects his preoccupation with exotic rhythms.
WORKS: Ballets: *L'Enigme* and *Ritus paganus* (1970); *Mouvements* for Piano, Brass, and Percussion (Brussels, Nov. 28, 1964); *Effects* for Percussion, Flute, and Piano (1966); *Rites* for 10 Percussionists (1969); *Manhattan* for Orch. (Antwerp, March 28, 1974); Piano Sonata; small piano pieces.

Glossop, Peter, English baritone; b. Sheffield, July 6, 1928. He was educated privately as a singer; was a member of the Sadler's Wells Opera Co. (1953–62). In 1966 he joined the Royal Opera, Covent Garden. His American debut at the Metropolitan Opera took place on Aug. 18, 1967, in *Rigoletto.* He is notable principally for his performances of dramatic roles in Verdi's operas.

Glover, Jane (Alison), English conductor and musicologist; b. Helmsley, Yorkshire, May 13, 1949. She studied at Oxford Univ., obtaining her Ph.D. in 1978 with a dissertation on Cavalli. She made her professional conducting debut in 1975 at the Wexford Festival, where she gave her own performing edition of Cavalli's *Eritrea;* she presented it in London in 1982. In her performing editions, she endeavored to preserve the authenticity of the original; she also made successful presentations on British television programs of Baroque operas. She served as chorus director of the Glyndebourne Festival Opera; conducted *Don Giovanni* at Glyndebourne in 1982.

Glover, John William, Irish composer and conductor; b. Dublin, June 19, 1815; d. there, Dec. 18, 1899.

He studied in Dublin, and was violinist in an orch. there; in 1848, he became a prof. of vocal music in the Normal Training School of the Irish National Education Board and also director of music in the Roman Catholic procathedral. He established the Choral Inst. in 1851, and was noted for his promotion of choral music in Ireland. He edited Moore's *Irish Melodies* (1859).
WORKS: Opera, *The Deserted Village,* after Goldsmith (London, 1880); 2 Italian operas to librettos by Metastasio; cantata, *St. Patrick at Tara* (1870); *Erin's Matin Song* (1873); ode to Thomas Moore, *100 years ago* (1879); also concertos; piano pieces; songs; church music.

Glover, Sarah Anna, English piano pedagogue; b. Norwich, Nov. 13, 1786; d. Malvern, Oct. 20, 1867. She was the originator of the tonic sol-fa system of notation, a method later modified and developed by John Curwen. She wrote *Scheme for rendering Psalmody Congregational* (1835), *Manual of the Norwich Sol-fa System* (1845), and *Manual containing a Development of the Tetrachordal System* (1850). She devised a pictorial chart called the "Norwich Sol-fa Ladder."

Glover, William Howard, English conductor and composer; b. London, June 6, 1819; d. New York, Oct. 28, 1875. He played the violin in the Lyceum Theater orch. in London; conducted opera in Manchester, Liverpool, and London. In 1868 he came to N.Y., where he was conductor at Niblo's Garden until his death.
WORKS: Opera, *Ruy Blas* (London, Oct. 21, 1861); operettas: *Aminta* (London, Jan. 26, 1852); *Once Too Often* (London, Jan. 20, 1862); *Palomita, or The Veiled Songstress* (publ. in N.Y., 1875); cantata, *Tam o' Shanter* (London, July 4, 1855, Berlioz conducting); overtures; piano music; songs.

Gluck, Alma (real name, **Reba Fiersohn**), American soprano; b. Bucharest, Rumania, May 11, 1884; d. New York, Oct. 27, 1938. She was brought to America as a small child and was educated at public schools in N.Y. Her early marriage to Bernard Gluck in 1902 ended in divorce, but they had a talented daughter, Abigail, born in 1903, who became a successful author; in her novel *Of Lena Geyer* (1936) and in her autobiography, *Too Strong for Fantasy* (1967), publ. under her assumed name, Marcia Davenport, she gives many revealing glimpses of her mother's career. From 1906–9 Alma Gluck studied voice with Arturo Buzzi-Peccia, who arranged for her to appear in the role of Sophie in Massenet's opera *Werther* on the stage of the New Theater in N.Y. on Nov. 16, 1909. Shortly afterward, on Nov. 28, 1909, she sang at a Sunday concert at the Metropolitan Opera in N.Y. On Dec. 23, 1909, she appeared in a revival of *Orfeo ed Euridice* at the Metropolitan, with Toscanini conducting. Her success led to further engagements in such diversified roles as Marguerite in *Faust,* Venus in *Tannhäuser,* Gilda in *Rigoletto,* and Mimi in *La Bohème.* On Oct. 10, 1910, she gave a recital in N.Y. Her divorce became final in 1912, and she went to Europe to complete her vocal studies; she coached with Jean de Reszke in Paris and with Marcella Sembrich in Switzerland. Returning to the U.S., she resumed her career, appearing at Sunday concerts under the auspices of the Metropolitan Opera. She rapidly became a favorite with both opera and concert audiences; she also satisfied public demand by recording popular songs such as *Carry Me Back to Old Virginny,* a disc which reportedly sold 2 million copies. On June 15, 1914, she married in London the Russian violinist **Efrem Zimbalist;** their combined artistic genes produced a son, Efrem Zimbalist, Jr., who became a famous actor and whose daughter Stefanie, Alma Gluck's granddaughter, also swam into thespian popularity. Alma Gluck died at the age of 54 of cirrhosis of the liver.

BIBLIOGRAPHY: David Ewen, *Musicians since 1900* (N.Y., 1978).

Gluck, Christoph Willibald (Ritter von), renowned composer; b. Erasbach, near Weidenwang in the Upper Palatinate, July 2, 1714; d. Vienna, Nov. 15, 1787. His father was a forester at Erasbach until his appointment as forester to Prince Lobkowitz of Eisenberg about 1729. Gluck received his elementary instruction in the village schools at Kamnitz and Albersdorf near Komotau, where he also was taught singing and instrumental playing. Some biographers refer to his study at the Jesuit college at Komotau, but there is no documentary evidence to support this contention. In 1732 Gluck went to Prague to complete his education, but it is doubtful that he took any courses at Prague Univ. He earned his living in Prague by playing violin and cello at rural dances in the area; also sang at various churches; there he had an opportunity to meet Bohuslav Černohorsky, who was chapelmaster at St. James' Church from 1735; it is probable that Gluck learned the methods of church music from him. He went to Vienna in 1736, and was chamber musician to young Prince Lobkowitz, son of the patron of Gluck's father. In 1737 he was taken to Milan by Prince Melzi; this Italian sojourn was of the greatest importance to Gluck's musical development. There he became a student of G.B. Sammartini and acquired a solid technique of composition in the Italian style. After 4 years of study, Gluck brought out his first opera, *Artaserse,* to the text of the celebrated Metastasio; it was produced in Milan (Dec. 26, 1741) with such success that Gluck was immediately commissioned to write more operas. There followed *Demetrio* or *Cleonice* (Venice, May 2, 1742); *Demofoonte* (Milan, Jan. 6, 1743); *Il Tigrane* (Crema, Sept. 9, 1743); *La Sofonisba* or *Siface* (Milan, Jan. 13, 1744); *Ipermestra* (Venice, Nov. 21, 1744); *Poro* (Turin, Dec. 26, 1744); *Ippolito* or *Fedra* (Milan, Jan. 31, 1745). He also contributed separate numbers to several other operas produced in Italy. In 1745 Gluck received an invitation to go to London; on his way, he visited Paris and met Rameau. He was commissioned by the Italian Opera of London to write 2 operas for the Haymarket Theatre, as a competitive endeavor to Handel's enterprise. The first of these works was *La Caduta dei giganti,* a tribute to the Duke of Cumberland on the defeat of the Pretender; it was produced on Jan. 28, 1746; the 2nd was a pasticcio, *Artamene,* in which Gluck used material from his previous operas; it was produced March 15, 1746. Ten days later, Gluck appeared with Handel at a public concert, despite the current report in London society that Handel had declared that Gluck knew no more counterpoint than his cook (it should be added that a professional musician, Gustavus Waltz, was Handel's cook and valet at the time). On April 23, 1746, Gluck gave a demonstration in London, playing on the "glass harmonica." He left London late in 1746 when he received an engagement as conductor with Pietro Mingotti's traveling Italian opera company. He conducted in Hamburg, Leipzig, and Dresden; on June 29, 1747, he produced a "serenata," *Le nozze d'Ercole e d'Ebe,* to celebrate a royal wedding; it was performed at the Saxon court, in Pillnitz. Gluck then went to Vienna, where he staged his opera *Semiramide riconosciuta,* after a poem of Metastasio (May 14, 1748). He then traveled to Copenhagen, where he produced a festive opera, *La Contesa dei Numi* (March 9, 1749), on the occasion of the birth of Prince Christian; his next productions (all to Metastasio's words) were *Ezio* (Prague, 1750); *Issipile* (Prague, 1752); *La clemenza di Tito* (Naples, Nov. 4, 1752); *Le Cinesi* (Vienna, Sept. 24, 1754); *La danza* (Vienna, May 5, 1755); *L'innocenza giustificata* (Vienna, Dec. 8, 1755); *Antigono* (Rome, Feb. 9, 1756); *Il Re pastore* (Vienna, Dec. 8, 1756).

In 1750 Gluck married Marianna Pergin, daughter of a Viennese merchant; for several years afterward he conducted operatic performances in Vienna. As French influence increased there, Gluck wrote several entertainments to French texts, containing spoken dialogue, in the style of opéra comique; of these, the most successful were *Le Cadi dupé* (Dec. 1761) and *La Rencontre imprévue* (Jan. 7, 1764; perf. also under the title *Les Pèlerins de la Mecque,* his most popular production in this genre). His greatest work of the Vienna period was *Orfeo ed Euridice,* to a libretto by Calzabigi (in a version for male contralto; Oct. 5, 1762, with the part of Orfeo sung by the famous castrato Gaetano Guadagni). Gluck revised it for a Paris performance, produced in French on Aug. 2, 1774, with Orfeo sung by a tenor. There followed another masterpiece, *Alceste* (Vienna, Dec. 16, 1767), also to Calzabigi's text. In the preface to *Alceste,* Gluck formulated his esthetic credo, which elevated the dramatic meaning of musical stage plays above a mere striving for vocal effects: "I sought to reduce music to its true function, that of seconding poetry in order to strengthen the emotional expression and the impact of the dramatic situations without interrupting the action and without weakening it by superfluous ornaments." Among other productions of the Viennese period were *Il trionfo di Clelia* (Vienna, May 14, 1763); *Il Parnaso confuso* (Schönbrunn Palace, Jan. 24, 1765); *Il Telemacco* (Vienna, Jan. 30, 1765); and *Paride ed Elena* (Vienna, Nov. 30, 1770).

The success of his French operas in Vienna led Gluck to the decision to try his fortunes in Paris,

Gluck

yielding to the persuasion of François du Roullet, an attaché at the French embassy in Vienna, who also supplied Gluck with his first libretto for a serious French opera, an adaptation of Racine's *Iphigénie en Aulide* (Paris, April 19, 1774). Gluck set out for Paris early in 1773, preceded by declarations in the Paris press by du Roullet and Gluck himself, explaining in detail Gluck's ideas of dramatic music. These statements set off an intellectual battle in the Paris press and among musicians in general between the adherents of traditional Italian opera and Gluck's novel French opera. It reached an unprecedented degree of acrimony when the Italian composer Nicola Piccinni was engaged by the French court to write operas to French texts, in open competition with Gluck; intrigues multiplied, even though Marie Antoinette never wavered in her admiration for Gluck, who taught her singing and harpsichord playing. However, Gluck and Piccinni themselves never participated in the bitter polemics unleashed by their literary and musical partisans. The sensational successes of the French version of Gluck's *Orfeo* and of *Alceste* were followed by the production of *Armide* (Sept. 23, 1777), which aroused great admiration. Then followed Gluck's masterpiece, *Iphigénie en Tauride* (May 17, 1779), which established Gluck's superiority to Piccinni, who was commissioned to write an opera on the same subject but failed to complete it in time. Gluck's last opera, *Echo et Narcisse* (Paris, Sept. 24, 1779), did not measure up to the excellence of his previous operas. By that time, Gluck's health had failed; he had several attacks of apoplexy, which resulted in a partial paralysis. In the autumn of 1779 he returned to Vienna, where he lived as an invalid for several more years. His last work was a *De profundis* for Chorus and Orch., written 5 years before his death.

Besides his operas, he wrote several ballets, of which *Don Juan* (Vienna, Oct. 17, 1761) was the most successful; he further wrote a cycle of 7 songs to words by Klopstock, 7 trio sonatas, several overtures, etc. Breitkopf & Härtel publ. several editions of Gluck's most important operas; other operas are included in Denkmäler der Tonkunst in Bayern, vol. 26 (14.ii), and Denkmäler der Tonkunst in Österreich, vols. 44a, 60, and 82 (21.ii, 30.ii, and 44); H. Gál edited a Sinfonia in G, identical with the overture to *Ipermestra;* the trio sonatas are found in Riemann's *Collegium musicum;* songs in Delsarte's *Archives du chant.* Wagner, while in Dresden (1842–49), made a complete revision of the score of *Iphigénie en Aulide;* this arrangement was so extensively used that a Wagnerized version of Gluck's music became the chief text for performances during the 19th century. A complete edition of Gluck's works was begun by the Bärenreiter Verlag in 1951.

BIBLIOGRAPHY: F.J. Riedel, *Über die Musik des Ritters Christoph von Gluck* (Vienna, 1775); C.P. Coqueau, *Entretiens sur l'état actuel de l'opéra de Paris* (Paris, 1779; dialogue on the Gluck-Piccinni controversy); G.M. Leblond, *Mémoires pour servir à l'histoire de la révolution opérée dans la musique par M. le Chevalier Gluck* (Paris, 1781; German trans., 1823; 2nd ed., 1837); J.G. Siegmeyer, *Über den Ritter Gluck und seine Werke* (Berlin, 1837); E. Miel, *Notice sur Gluck* (Paris, 1840); A. Schmid, *Christoph Willibald Ritter von Gluck* (Leipzig, 1854); W. Neumann, *Christoph Willibald Gluck* (Kassel, 1855); J. Baudoin, *L'Alceste de Gluck* (Paris, 1861); A.B. Marx, *Gluck und die Oper* (Berlin, 1863); L. Nohl, *Gluck und Wagner* (Munich, 1870); G. Desnoiresterres, *Gluck et Piccinni* (Paris, 1875); A. Jullien, *La Cour et l'opéra sous Louis XVI* (Paris, 1878); E. Thoinan, *Notes bibliographiques sur la guerre musicale des Gluckistes et Piccinnistes* (Paris, 1878); H. Barbedette, *Gluck* (Paris, 1882); A. Reissmann, *Christoph Willibald von Gluck* (Berlin, 1882); K.H. Bitter, *Die Reform der Oper durch Gluck und Wagner* (Brunswick, 1884); H. Welti, *Gluck* (Leipzig, 1888); E. Newman, *Gluck and the Opera* (London, 1895); J. d'Udine, *Gluck* (Paris, 1906); J. Tiersot, *Gluck* (Paris, 1910); La Mara, *Gluck* (Leipzig, 1912; reprinted from *Musik Studienköpfe*); Ernst Kurth, "Die Jugendopern Gluck," *Studien zur Musikwissenschaft*, I (1913); H. Berlioz, *Gluck and His Operas* (trans. from the French by Edwin Evans, Sr.; London, 1915); S. Wortsmann, *Die deutsche Gluck-Literatur* (Nuremberg, 1914); W.B. Squire, "Gluck's London Operas," *Musical Quarterly* (July 1915); J.-G. Prod'homme, "Gluck's French Collaborators," *Musical Quarterly* (April 1917); J.-G. Prod'homme, "Les Portraits français de Gluck," *Rivista Musicale Italiana*, XXV, 1 (1918); M. Arend, *Gluck* (1921); W. Vetter, "Die Arie bei Gluck," *Zeitschrift für Musikwissenschaft*, III (1921); R. Haas, "Die Wiener Ballet-Pantomime im 18. Jahrhundert und Glucks *Don Juan*," *Studien zur Musikwissenschaft*, X (1923); E.H. Müller, "Zwei unveröffentlichte Briefe Glucks an Carl August," *Die Musik* (Stuttgart, 1923); G. Scuderi, *Christoph Gluck: Orfeo* (Milan, 1924); R. Haas, *Gluck und Durazzo im Burgtheater* (Vienna, 1925); Paul Brück, "Glucks *Orpheus und Eurydike*," *Archiv für Musikwissenschaft*, VIII/4 (1926); Georg Kinsky, "Glucks Reisen nach Paris," *Zeitschrift für Musikwissenschaft*, VIII; idem, *Glucks Briefe an Franz Kruthoffer* (Vienna, 1929); M. Cauchie, "Gluck et ses éditeurs parisiens," *Le Ménestrel* (1927); Th. Veidl, "Neues über Glucks Jugend," *Auftakt*, VIII/3 (1928); Julien Tiersot, "Gluck and the Encyclopaedists," *Musical Quarterly* (July 1930); E. Istel, "Gluck's Dramaturgy," *Musical Quarterly* (April 1931); K. Huschke, "Gluck und seine deutsche Zeitgenossen," *Zeitschrift für Musikwissenschaft* (March 1933); L. de la Laurencie, *Gluck, Orphée: Etude et analyse musicale* (Paris, 1934); D.F. Tovey, "Christoph Willibald Gluck and the Musical Revolution," in H. Foss, *The Heritage of Music*, vol. 2 (London, 1934); M. Cooper, *Gluck* (London, 1935); A. Einstein, *Gluck* (London, 1936); R. Tenschert, *Christoph Willibald Gluck (1714–1787); Sein Leben in Bildern* (Leipzig, 1938); P. Landormy, *Gluck* (Paris, 1941); A. Della Corte, *Gluck* (Turin, 1942); W. Brandl, *Christoph Willibald Ritter von Gluck* (Wiesbaden, 1948); A. Della Corte, *Gluck e i suoi tempi* (Florence, 1948); J.-G. Prod'homme, *Gluck* (Paris, 1948); R. Gerber, *C.W. Ritter von Gluck* (Potsdam, 1950); R. Tenschert, *Christoph Willibald Gluck: Der grosse Reformator der Oper* (Freiburg, 1951); A.A. Abert, *C.W.*

Gluck (Munich, 1959); *The Collected Correspondence and Papers of C.W. Gluck* (London, 1962); Patricia Howard, *Gluck and the Birth of Modern Opera* (N.Y., 1964); W. Vetter, *Christoph Willibald Gluck* (Leipzig, 1964); D. Heartz, "From Garrick to Gluck: The Reform of Theatre and Opera in the Mid-Eighteenth Century," *Proceedings of the Royal Musical Association* (1967–68); G. Croll, "Gluckforschung und Gluck-Gesamtausgabe," in R. Baum and W. Rehm, eds., *Musik und Verlag* (Kassel, 1968); H.C.R. Landon, *Essays on the Viennese Classical Style* (N.Y., 1970); K. Hortschansky, *"Arianna* (1762)— Ein Pasticcio von Gluck," *Die Musikforschung* (Oct.–Dec. 1971). A thematic catalogue was publ. by A. Wotquenne (Leipzig, 1904; German trans. with supplement by J. Liebeskind). See also C. Hopkinson, *A Bibliography of the Printed Works of C.W. von Gluck, 1714–1787* (2nd ed., N.Y., 1967).

Glyn, Margaret Henrietta, English musicologist; b. Ewell, Surrey, Feb. 28, 1865; d. there, June 3, 1946. She studied in London under Henry Frost and Yorke Trotter; became an authority on keyboard music of the Tudor period. She edited organ and virginal music by Byrd, Orlando Gibbons, John Bull, and other composers, and wrote the following books: *The Rhythmic Conception of Music* (1907); *Analysis of the Evolution of Musical Form* (1909); *About Elizabethan Virginal Music and Its Composers* (1924; 2nd ed., 1934); *Theory of Musical Evolution* (1924). She also composed a number of works for organ.

Gnattali, Radamés, Brazilian composer; b. Pôrto Alegre, Jan. 27, 1906. He studied piano, violin, composition, and conducting at the Pôrto Alegre Cons. of Music and the National School of Music in Rio de Janeiro; also appeared as a concert pianist and violist. His music is imbued with indigenous rhythms and harmonies popularized in the 1960s as the "bossa nova sound."
WORKS: 12 *Brasilianas:* 1–3 for Orch. (1945, 1948, 1948); 4 and 5 for Piano (1949, 1950); 6 for Piano and Orch. (1960); 7 for 2 Pianos (1957); 8 for Saxophone and Piano (1957); 9 and 10 for Orch. (1962); 11 for 8 Cellos and Piano (1968; orchestrated 1970); 12 for 2 Pianos and String Orch. (1968); 3 *Sinfonias populares* (1955, 1962, 1969); 4 piano concertos (1934, 1936, 1960, 1967); Cello Concerto (1941); 3 violin concertos (1947, 1962, 1969); 2 *Concêrtos románticos* for Piano and Orch. (1949, 1964); 3 *Concêrtos cariocas* for Various Instrumental Soloists and Orch. (1950–70); 4 guitar concertinos (1952, 1953, 1955, 1968); Harp Concerto (1958); 2 harmonica concertos (1958, 1968); chamber music; 2 piano sonatas (1948, 1963).
BIBLIOGRAPHY: A complete listing of his works to 1970 is found in *Composers of the Americas,* vol. 16 (Washington, D.C., 1970).

Gnazzo, Anthony J., American avant-garde composer; b. New Britain, Conn., April 21, 1936. He studied music theory at Brandeis Univ. (M.F.A., 1965; Ph.D., 1970), mathematics at the Univ. of Hartford (B.A., 1963); served in the U.S. Navy (1957–61); attended 21 navy schools and took courses in technology, data processing, and allied subjects; was instructor in electronic system design at the Univ. of Toronto (1965–66) and a lecturer in music at Mills College (1967–69); in 1969 was appointed design consultant and equipment technician in the electronics laboratory at Calif. State College at Hayward; also worked as a computer programmer. His compositions are notated in the form of geometric graphs with verbal instructions and rhetorical interjections, e.g., " Music, is it? Eh? It IS!!! But! Music? Yes, Music!" His "theater pieces" are graphic scenarios with action indicated by circles, curves, and vectors. His *Canned Music* (1969) is a sticker inscribed, "Caution—Caution—Caution—This Can Has Been Filled with Extremely Loud Sound for 45 Minutes! Open with Care!" He also designed a piece entitled *4-Letter Words* in surrealistically drawn phallic shapes. Among his literary productions are intermittent dialogues and "manifolds" for the theater, e.g., *Inevitably Plastic* (1969) and *Experience Counter Experience* (1970).

Gnecchi, Vittorio, Italian opera composer; b. Milan, July 17, 1876; d. there, Feb. 1, 1954. He studied at the Milan Cons. His opera *Cassandra* was performed at Bologna on Dec. 5, 1905; some years later, after the premiere of Richard Strauss's *Elektra*, there was considerable discussion when the Italian critic Giovanni Tebaldini pointed out the identity of some 50 themes in both *Cassandra* and *Elektra* ("Telepatia Musicale," *Rivista Musicale Italiana,* Feb.–March 1909). Gnecchi also wrote the operas *Virtù d'amore* (1896) and *La rosiera,* after a comedy by Alfred de Musset (given at Gera, Germany, Feb. 12, 1927; in Italian, at Trieste, Jan. 24, 1931).
BIBLIOGRAPHY: F.B. Pratella, *Luci ed ombre: Per un musicista italiano ignorato in Italia* (Rome, 1933).

Gnessin, Mikhail, Russian composer; b. Rostov-on-the-Don, Feb. 2, 1883; d. Moscow, May 5, 1957. He studied at the St. Petersburg Cons. with Rimsky-Korsakov and Liadov in 1901–8; went to Germany in 1911; in 1914 returned to Rostov, where he composed, taught music, and interested himself in various socialist activities. He made a trip to Palestine in 1921 to study Jewish music; some of his subsequent work reflected this visit. After 1923, he composed and taught alternately in Moscow and Leningrad. In addition to his Jewish music, he composed a number of works in the Romantic vein.
WORKS: DRAMATIC MUSIC: *Balagan,* by Blok (1909); *The Rose and the Cross,* by Blok (1914); *Antigone,* by Sophocles (1909–15); *The Phoenician Women,* by Euripides (1912–16); *Oedipus Rex,* by Sophocles (1914–15); *The Story of the Red-Haired Motele,* by Utkin (1926–29); *The Inspector-General,* by Gogol (1926). OPERAS: *Abraham's Youth* (1921–23) and *The Maccabees.* FOR VOICE AND ORCH.: *Ruth* (1909); *Vrubel* (1912); *The Conqueror Worm* (1913); symph. movement for Solo Voices, Chorus, and Orch.: *1905–1917* (1925). FOR ORCH.: Symph. fragment, *After Shelley* (1906–8); *Songs of Adonis* (1919); symph. fantasy, *Songs of the Old Country*

(1919); suite, *Jewish Orchestra at the Town Bailiff's Ball* (1926). CHAMBER MUSIC: Requiem, in memory of Rimsky-Korsakov, for String Quartet and Piano (1913–14); *Variations on a Jewish Theme* for String Quartet (1916); *Azerbaijan Folksongs* for String Quartet (1930); *Adygeya* for Violin, Viola, Cello, Clarinet, Horn, and Piano (1933); *Sonata-Fantasia* for Piano, Violin, Viola, and Cello (1945), *Theme with Variations* for Cello and Piano (1955); several song cycles; piano pieces; arrangements of Jewish folk songs. He publ. *Reflections and Reminiscences of Rimsky-Korsakov* (Moscow, 1956).

BIBLIOGRAPHY: L. Sabaneyev, *Modern Russian Composers* (N.Y., 1927); A. Drozdov, *Gnessin* (Moscow, 1927; in Russian and German).

Gobbaerts, Jean-Louis, Belgian pianist and composer; b. Antwerp, Sept. 28, 1835; d. Saint-Gilles, near Brussels, May 5, 1886. He studied at the Brussels Cons. He wrote more than 1,000 light piano pieces, some quite popular, using the pseudonyms "Streabbog" (Gobbaerts reversed), "Ludovic," and "Lévi." His *Little Fairy Waltz* was a favorite of President Harry S Truman.

Gobbi, Tito, famous Italian baritone; b. Bassano del Grappa, near Venice, Oct. 24, 1913; d. Rome, March 5, 1984. Although he suffered from asthma as a child, he engaged in sports and developed into a fine athlete, an alpinist, and a cyclist. He studied law at the Univ. of Padua; then took singing lessons with Giugio Crimi in Rome. He made his operatic debut as Rodolfo in *La Sonnambula* in Gubbio, near Perugia, in 1935. In 1936 he won first prize in a singing contest in Vienna; in 1937 he sang at the Teatro Adriano in Rome; in 1939 he appeared at the Teatro Costanzi in Rome in the role of Germont *père* in *La Traviata.* In 1942 he sang for the first time at La Scala in Milan as Belcore in *L'elisir d'amore.* In 1948 he made his American debut at the San Francisco Opera; in 1954 he joined the Chicago Opera. On Jan. 13, 1956, he appeared at the Metropolitan Opera in N.Y. in the role that made him famous, the infamous Scarpia in *Tosca.* In subsequent years he toured the whole operatic world, including Covent Garden in London, the Paris Opéra, the Vienna State Opera, the Munich State Opera, Barcelona, Lisbon, the Teatro Colón in Buenos Aires, and Rio de Janeiro; he was also a frequent guest artist at the Maggio Musicale Festival in Florence and at the Salzburg Festival. He gave solo recitals in Scandinavia, Egypt, and Israel. His opera repertoire included about 100 roles; the most notable were Rigoletto, Iago, Falstaff, and Macbeth in Verdi's operas, and the title role in Mozart's *Don Giovanni.* In non-Italian presentations, he gave a congenial rendition of the musically challenging part of Wozzeck in Alban Berg's opera. He retired from the stage in 1979, and devoted himself to his favorite avocation, oil painting. He publ. an entertaining memoir, *Tito Gobbi: My Life* (London, 1979).

Godard, Benjamin (Louis Paul), French composer; b. Paris, Aug. 18, 1849; d. Cannes, Jan. 10, 1895. He studied violin with Richard Hammer and later with Vieuxtemps; composition with Reber of the Paris Cons. He publ. his first work, a Violin Sonata, at the age of 16 and wrote several other chamber music pieces, obtaining the Prix Chartier. In 1878 he received a municipal prize for an orch. work; in the same year he produced his first opera, *Les Bijoux de Jeannette.* His 2nd opera was *Pedro de Zalamea* (Antwerp, Jan. 31, 1884), but it left little impact; then came his masterpiece, *Jocelyn,* after Lamartine's poem (Brussels, Feb. 25, 1888). The famous *Berceuse* from this opera became a perennial favorite, exhibiting Godard's lyric talent at its best. There followed the opera *Dante et Béatrice,* produced at the Opéra-Comique in Paris on May 13, 1890. His opera *La Vivandière* was left unfinished at his death, and the orchestration was completed by Paul Vidal; it was staged posthumously in Paris on April 1, 1895; another posthumous opera, *Les Guelphes,* was produced in Rouen (Jan. 17, 1902). Godard wrote 3 programmatic symphs: *Symphonie gothique* (1883), *Symphonie orientale* (1884), and *Symphonie légendaire* (1886); and a *Concerto Romantique* for Violin and Orch. (1876); he also wrote 3 string quartets, 4 violin sonatas, a Cello Sonata, and 2 piano trios; piano pieces; and more than 100 songs. A 2-vol. collection of Godard's piano works was publ. by G. Schirmer (N.Y., 1895); another collection of piano pieces was edited by Paolo Gallico (N.Y., 1909).

BIBLIOGRAPHY: M. Clerjot, *Benjamin Godard* (Paris, 1902); M. Clavié, *Benjamin Godard* (Paris, 1906).

Goddard, Arabella, English pianist; b. St.-Servan, near Saint-Malo, France, Jan. 12, 1836; d. Boulogne, France, April 6, 1922. She began study with Kalkbrenner in Paris at the age of 6; made her first public appearance at the age of 14, in London, at a Grand National Concert. After 3 years of study with the critic J.W. Davison (whom she married in 1859), she made tours of Germany and Italy (1854–55); later toured the U.S., Australia, and India (1873–76). She wrote some piano pieces and a ballad.

Godfrey, Sir Dan(iel Eyers), English conductor; b. London, June 20, 1868; d. Bournemouth, July 20, 1939. He was the son of **Daniel Godfrey, Sr.;** studied at the Royal College of Music; was conductor of the London Military Band (a civilian group in reality) in 1889–91. In 1893, he settled in Bournemouth as conductor of the Winter Gardens orch.; founded the Symph. Concerts there in 1894; directed them until his retirement in 1934; he brought the concerts to a high level, and used all his efforts to promote the works of British composers. He was knighted in 1922 for his services to orch. music. He wrote his memoirs, *Memories and Music* (London, 1924).

Godfrey, Dan(iel), Sr., English bandmaster; b. Westminster, Sept. 4, 1831; d. Beeston, Nottinghamshire, June 30, 1903. He was a pupil and Fellow of the Royal Academy of Music, in which he was later a prof. of military music. He was also bandmaster of the Grenadier Guards in 1856; traveled with his band in the U.S. in 1872; retired in 1896. He wrote popular waltzes (*Mabel, Guards, Hilda,* etc.), and made many arrangements for military band.

Godfrey, George. See **Müller, Georg Gottfried.**

Godfrey, Isidore, English conductor; b. London, Sept. 27, 1900; d. Sussex, Sept. 12, 1977. He was educated at the Guildhall School of Music in London. In 1925 he joined the D'Oyly Carte Opera Co. as a conductor; from 1929 to 1968 he served as its music director. In 1965 he was named an Officer of the Order of the British Empire.

Godimel, Claude. See **Goudimel, Claude.**

Godowsky, Leopold, famous pianist; b. Soshly, near Vilna, Feb. 13, 1870; d. New York, Nov. 21, 1938. He played in public as a child in Russia; at 14, was sent to Berlin to study at the Hochschule für Musik, but after a few months there, proceeded to N.Y.; gave his first American concert in Boston on Dec. 7, 1884; in 1885, played engagements at the N.Y. Casino; in 1886, toured Canada with the Belgian violinist Ovide Musin. He then went back to Europe; played in society salons in London and Paris, and became a protégé of Saint-Saëns. In 1890 he joined the faculty of the N.Y. College of Music; on May 1, 1891, married Frieda Saxe, and became an American citizen. He taught at the Broad St. Cons. in Philadelphia (1894–95); was head of the piano dept. of the Chicago Cons. (1895–1900); then embarked on a European tour; gave a highly successful concert in Berlin (Dec. 6, 1900), and remained there as a teacher; in 1909–14, conducted a master class at the Vienna Academy of Music; made tours in the U.S. in 1912–14, and settled permanently in the U.S. at the outbreak of World War I. After the war, he traveled in Europe, South America, and Asia as a concert pianist; his career ended in 1930, when he suffered a stroke. Godowsky was one of the outstanding masters of the piano; possessing a scientifically inclined mind, he developed a method of "weight and relaxation"; applying it to his own playing, he became an outstanding technician of his instrument, extending the potentialities of piano technique to the utmost, with particular attention to the left hand. He wrote numerous piano compositions of transcendental difficulty, yet entirely pianistic in style; also arranged works by Weber, Brahms, and Johann Strauss. Particularly remarkable are his 53 studies on Chopin's études, combining Chopin's themes in ingenious counterpoint; among his original works, the most interesting are *Triakontameron* (30 pieces; 1920; no. 11 is the well-known *Alt Wien*) and *Java Suite* (12 pieces). He also wrote simple pedagogical pieces, e.g., a set of 46 *Miniatures* for Piano, 4-hands, in which the pupil is given a part within the compass of 5 notes only (1918); edited piano studies by Czerny, Heller, Köhler, etc.; composed music for the left hand alone (*6 Waltz Poems, Prelude and Fugue,* etc.), and publ. an essay, "Piano Music for the Left Hand," *Musical Quarterly* (July

1935). Maurice Aronson publ. a musical examination paper, providing an analysis of Godowsky's *Miniatures* (N.Y., 1935).

BIBLIOGRAPHY: Leonard S. Saxe, "The Published Music of Leopold Godowsky," *Notes* (March 1957), containing an annotated list of original works, arrangements, and editions.

Godron, Hugo, Dutch composer; b. Amsterdam, Nov. 22, 1900; d. Zoelmond, Dec. 6, 1971. He studied violin at the music school in Bussum, and composition with Sem Dresden in Amsterdam (1921–22). He taught composition and harmony at music schools in Bussum, Hilversum, and Utrecht; from 1939 to 1969 was active as a sound engineer in Hilversum and Amsterdam. His music is generally joyful, almost playful, in character.

WORKS: Radio fairy tale, *Assepoes* (*Cinderella;* 1946–47); Sinfonietta for Small Orch. (1932–33); *7 Miniatures* for Piano and Strings (1933); Piano Concerto (1938–39); *Sérénade occidentale* for Orch. (1942–48); *Amabile Suite* for Clarinet, Piano, and Strings (1943); Concerto Grosso for Clarinet and Small Orch. (1944–45); *Concert Suite* for Piano and String Orch. (1945–47); *Miniatuur symphonie* (1949–50; orchestration of *Gardenia Suite* for Piano); 2 *Polkas* for Orch. (1950–51, 1957–58); Suite for String Orch. and Harpsichord (1950); *Hommage à Chabrier* for Orch. (1950–51); *Hommages classiques* for Flute, Piano, and Strings (1950); Concerto for Orch. (1953–54); *Variations traditionnelles* for Small Orch. (1954); *Promenades,* suite for Orch. (1954–55); *4 impressies* for Chamber Orch. (1956–57); *Aubade Gaudeamus,* suite for Piano, String Orch., and Percussion (1966–68); *Hommage à Bizet* for Small Orch. (1971); String Trio (1937); Serenade for Piano and Wind Quintet (1947); Sonatina for Flute, Violin, Viola, and Piano (1948); Piano Trio (1948); *Sonata facile* for Cello and Piano (1950); Divertimento for 2 Violins and Piano (1956); *Nouvelles* for Piano Trio (1963); *Quatuor bohémien* for Piano Quartet (1970). He wrote several piano works, including *Mon Plaisir* (1937–38); *Suite moderne* for 2 Pianos (1941); Sonata for 2 Pianos (1944–45); *Escapades,* 12 pieces (1944); *Gardenia Suite* (1949); *Pastorale* for 2 Pianos (1953); *3 Nocturnes* (1953); *Introduction and Rondo* (1955); *24 Chansonnettes* (1966).

Goeb, Roger, American composer; b. Cherokee, Iowa, Oct. 9, 1914. He studied agriculture at the Univ. of Wisconsin, graduating in 1936; played in jazz bands; in 1938 went to Paris, where he took lessons with Nadia Boulanger. Returning to America in 1939, he obtained his Ph.D. at the Univ. of Iowa (1945); subsequently occupied teaching posts at the Univ. of Oklahoma (1942–44), the State Univ. of Iowa (1944–45), and the Juilliard School of Music (1947–50). He held 2 Guggenheim fellowships (1950, 1952); taught music at Stanford Univ. (1954–55); then became director of the American Composers' Alliance (1956–62). Personal misfortunes (both his wife and his son died of multiple sclerosis) caused him to interrupt his professional activities in 1964;

but he resumed composition in 1981.

WORKS: FOR ORCH.: 5 symphs.: No. 1 (1942); No. 2 (1945); No. 3 (1950; Columbia Univ., April 3, 1952, Stokowski conducting); No. 4 (1954; Pittsburgh, Feb. 24, 1956); No. 5 (1981); *Lyric Piece* for Trumpet and Orch. (1942); *Fantasy* for Oboe and Strings (1947); 4 *Concertantes:* No. 1 for Flute, Oboe, Clarinet, and Strings (1948); No. 2 for Bassoon or Cello, and Strings (1950); No. 3 for Viola and Orch. (1951); No. 4 for Clarinet, Strings, Piano, and Percussion (1951); *Romanza* for String Orch. (1948); 2 concertinos for Orch.: No. 1 (1949) and No. 2 (1956; Louisville, Ky., Nov. 28, 1956); *5 American Dances* (1952; 1–3 for Strings; 4 and 5 for Orch.); Violin Concerto (1953; N.Y., Feb. 1954); Piano Concerto (1954); 2 *Sinfonias* (1957, 1962); *Iowa Concerto* for Small Orch. (1958); *Encomium* for Woodwinds, Brass, and Percussion (1958); *Fantasy* for 2 Pianos and Strings (1958); *Caprice* (1982); *Memorial* (1982); *Divertissement* (1982).

CHAMBER MUSIC: 3 string quartets (1942, 1948, 1954); Solo Viola Sonata (1942); String Trio (1945); *Suite* for Woodwind Trio (1946); *Prairie Songs* for Wind Quintet (1946; also for Small Orch.); Quartet for 4 Clarinets (1948); Brass Septet (1949); Quintet for Trombone and String Quartet (1949); 4 wind quintets (1949–81); 2 *Divertimenti* for 2 Flutes (1950); *Processionals* for Organ and Brass Quintet (1951); Solo Violin Sonata (1957); *Running Colors* for String Quartet (1961); *Declarations* for Flute, Oboe, Clarinet, Bassoon, Horn, and Cello (1961); Quartet for Oboe and String Trio (1964); *Contrasts,* suite for Solo Cello (1981).

Goedicke, Alexander, Russian pianist and composer; b. Moscow, March 4, 1877; d. there, July 9, 1957. Goedicke was a member of a musical family of German extraction; his father was an organist and a cons. teacher. He entered the Moscow Cons., where he studied piano with Safonov and composition with Arensky; graduated in 1898. In 1900 he won the Rubinstein Prize for his pieces for violin at the international competition in Vienna; in 1909 he was appointed prof. of piano at the Moscow Cons.; he also taught organ playing.

WORKS: 4 operas to his own librettos: *Virineya* (1915); *At the Crossing* (1933); *Jacquerie* (1937); *Macbeth* (1944); 3 symphs. (1903, 1905, 1922); Piano Concerto (1900); Violin Concerto (1951); Horn Concerto; Trumpet Concerto; Piano Quintet; 2 piano trios; String Quartet; numerous teaching pieces for piano; many arrangements of Russian songs. His 80th birthday was celebrated in Moscow at a gala banquet, a few months before his death.

BIBLIOGRAPHY: V. Yakovlev, *A. Goedicke* (Moscow, 1927; in Russian and German); K. Adzhemov, *A. Goedicke* (articles and reminiscences; Moscow, 1960).

Goehr, Alexander, English composer, son of **Walter Goehr;** b. Berlin, Aug. 10, 1932. He studied at the Royal Manchester College of Music (1952–53); then took courses with Messiaen at the Paris Cons. (1955–57). From 1960–67 he was in charge of the prod-

uction of orch. concerts for the BBC. In 1968–69 he was composer-in-residence at the New England Cons. in Boston; in 1969–70 taught at Yale Univ. Returning to England, he joined the faculty of Leeds Univ. (1971–76); from 1975 served as artistic director of the Leeds Festivals. In 1976 he was appointed prof. of music at the Univ. of Cambridge. His compositions are marked with a severe, at times austere, polyphony, tending toward integral serialism.

WORKS: Piano Sonata (1952); *Fantasias* for Clarinet and Piano (1955); *Fantasia* for Orch. (1955); *Narration,* to words of Blake, for Voice and Piano (1955); String Quartet (1958); *The Deluge,* cantata (1958); *Four Seasons from the Japanese* for Soprano and Orch. (1959); *Sutter's Gold,* cantata (1960); *Hecuba's Lament* for Orch. (1960); Suite for Flute, Clarinet, Horn, Violin, Viola, Cello, and Harp (1961); Violin Concerto (1962); *Little Symphony* (1963); *Pastorals* for Orch. (1965); Piano Trio (1966); *Arden muss sterben,* opera (Hamburg, March 5, 1967); String Quartet No. 2 (1967); *Romanza* for Cello and Orch. (1968); *Konzertstück* for Piano and Orch. (1969); *Nonomiya* for Piano (1969); *Symph.* (London, May 9, 1970); *Triptych,* theater piece for Actors, Singers, and Instruments, consisting of *Naboth's Vineyard* (1968), *Shadowplay,* after Plato's *Republic* (1970), and *Sonata about Jerusalem* (1970); Concerto for 11 Instruments (Brussels, Jan. 25, 1971); Piano Concerto (Brighton Festival, May 14, 1972; Daniel Barenboim, soloist); *Chaconne* for Wind Instruments (Leeds, Nov. 3, 1974); *Lyric Pieces* for Chamber Ensemble (London, Nov. 15, 1974); *Metamorphosis/Dance* for Orch. (London, Nov. 17, 1974); String Quartet No. 3 (London, June 28, 1976); *Psalm 4* for Female Soloists, Chorus, Viola, and Organ (London, July 8, 1976, composer conducting); *Fugue on the Fourth Psalm* for Strings (1976); *Babylon the Great Is Fallen* for Chorus and Orch. (1979); *Das Gesetz der Quadrille* for Baritone and Piano, to texts by Kafka (1979); *Sinfonia* for Orch. (1980); 2 *études* for Orch. (1981); *Behold the Sun,* concert aria for Soprano, Vibraphone, and Chamber Ensemble (1981; London, Feb. 9, 1982).

BIBLIOGRAPHY: B. Northcott, ed., *The Music of Alexander Goehr: Interviews and Articles* (London, 1980).

Goehr, Walter, German conductor; b. Berlin, May 28, 1903; d. Sheffield, England, Dec. 4, 1960. He studied theory with Schoenberg in Berlin; then became conductor of Berlin Radio (1925–31). In 1933 he went to England; from 1945 to 1948, was conductor of the BBC Theatre Orch.; was conductor of the Morley College concerts from 1943 until his death.

Goepfart, Karl Eduard, German pianist, conductor, and composer; b. Weimar, March 8, 1859; d. there, Feb. 8, 1942. He studied with his father, **Christian Heinrich Goepfart** (1835–1890); also had lessons with Liszt. He toured as a theater conductor in the U.S. and in Germany; wrote several operas, of which only one, *Der Müller von Sans Souci,* was produced (Weimar, 1907). He further wrote 2 symphs., church music, and many songs.

Goepp, Philip Henry, American organist and writer on music; b. New York, June 23, 1864; d. Philadelphia, Aug. 25, 1936. He studied in Germany (1872–77); graduated from Harvard with honors in music in 1884; while there, he studied composition with J.K. Paine; graduated from the Univ. of Pa. Law School in 1888, and practiced law until 1892. He then devoted himself to music in Philadelphia, as an organist, teacher, and writer; from 1900 to 1921, he wrote the program notes for the Philadelphia Orch.; publ. *Annals of Music in Philadelphia* (1896) and *Symphonies and Their Meaning* (3 vols., 1898, 1902, 1913); and composed pieces for piano and organ, a *Christmas Cantata,* and an operetta, *The Lost Prince.*

Goethals, Lucien, Belgian composer; b. Ghent, June 26, 1931. He was taken to Argentina as a child; returning to Belgium in 1947, he studied with Rosseau at the Royal Cons. in Ghent (1947–56) and took courses at the Ghent Inst. for Psycho-Acoustics and Electronic Music of the Ghent State Univ.; also worked in an electronic studio in Germany; in 1974 became a teacher of analysis at the Ghent Cons. In 1964 he organized the Belgian group Spectra, devoted to the promotion of new music. His own compositions explore the problems of modernistic constructivism.
WORKS: *Vensters,* audio-visual play for 2 Narrators, Cello, Piano, Percussion, Recorded Sounds, and Film Projections (Brussels, Sept. 16, 1967); *Hé,* audio-visual production for 10 Instruments, Tapes, and Film Projections (1971; in collaboration with Herman Sabbe and Karel Goeyvaerts); *5 Impromptus* for Chamber Orch. (1959); *Dialogos* for String Orch., Wind Quintet, 2 String Quintets, Percussion, and Tape (Ghent, Sept. 3, 1963); *Dialogos Suite* for Chamber Orch. (1963); *Sinfonia in Gris Mayor* for 2 Orchs., Percussion, and Tape (Brussels, June 14, 1966); *Enteuxis* for String Orch., Oboe, and Flute (Ghent, Sept. 2, 1968); Concerto for Orch. (1972); *4 Pieces* for Orch. (1976); Violin Sonata (1959); *Rituele Suite* for Wind Quintet (1959); Sonata for Solo Guitar (1961); *Endomorfie I* for Violin, Piano, and Tape (1964); *Endomorfie II* for Flute, Oboe, Clarinet, Bassoon, 2 Trumpets, Trombone, and Tuba (1964); *Cellotape* for Cello, Piano, Tape, and Contact Microphone (1965); *Movimientos y acciones* for Flute, Clarinet, String Quartet, Chromatic Harp, and Percussion (1965); *Lecina* for Mezzo-soprano, Flute, Violin, and Cello (1966); *Mouvement* for String Quartet (1967); *Cascaras,* chamber cantata for Mezzo-soprano, Flute, Clarinet, Violin, Cello, and Piano (1969); *Quebraduras* for Piano Quartet (1969); *Ensimismamientos* for Violin, Cello, Bassoon, Piano, and Tape (1969); *4 Pieces* for Bass Clarinet and Piano (1970); *7 Soliloquies* for Solo Violin (1970); *Superposiciones* for Violin, Cello, Bassoon, and Piano (1970); *Suma* for an undefined number of Instruments, and Tape (1971); *3 paisajes sonores* for Flute, Oboe, Cello, Trombone, Double Bass, and Harpsichord (1973); *Llanto por Salvador Allende* for Solo Trombone (1973); *Difonium* for Bass Clarinet and Tape (1974); *Diferencias* for 10 Instruments (1974); *Fantasia and Humoreske* for 2 Oboes and English Horn (1975); *Triptiek* for Violin and Harpsichord (1975); *Fusion* for Bass Clarinet, Piano, and Tape (1975). For Piano: *Musica dodecafonica* (1957) and *Pentagoon* (1963); for Organ: *Sinfonia* (1959) and *Klankstrukturen* (1962); several works for tape alone.

Goethe, Johann Wolfgang von, illustrious German poet and dramatist; b. Frankfurt am Main, Aug. 28, 1749; d. Weimar, March 22, 1832. Although he could not comprehend Beethoven, and even snubbed him, he had ideas of his own on music (see *Briefwechsel zwischen Goethe und Zelter,* Berlin, 1833); Ferdinand Hiller also shows this in his *Goethes musicalisches Leben* (Cologne, 1883). In recent years Goethe's attitude toward music has been made the subject of investigation by several scholars.
BIBLIOGRAPHY: K. Mendelssohn-Bartholdy, *Goethe und Felix Mendelssohn-Bartholdy* (Leipzig, 1871; in Eng., with additions, London, 2nd ed., 1874); A. Julien, *Goethe et la musique: Ses jugements, son influence, les œuvres qu'il a inspirées* (Paris, 1880); J.W. von Wasielewski, *Goethe's Verhältnis zur Musik* (Leipzig, 1880; in Waldersee's *Sammlung musikalischer Vorträge*); H. Blaze de Bury, *Goethe et Beethoven* (Paris, 1892); W. Nagel, *Goethe und Beethoven* (Langensalza, 1902); idem, *Goethe und Mozart* (Langensalza 1904); J. Chantavoine, *Goethe musicien* (Paris, 1905); J. Simon, *Faust in der Musik* (Berlin, 1906); E. Segnitz, *Goethe und die Oper in Weimar* (Langensalza, 1908); W. Bode, *Die Tonkunst in Goethes Leben* (2 vols., Berlin, 1912); idem, *Goethes Schauspieler und Musiker: Erinnerungen von Eberwein und Lobe* (1912); H. Abert, *Goethe und die Musik* (1922); P. Frenzel, *R. Schumann und Goethe* (1926); H. John, *Goethe und die Musik* (1928); E. Ludwig, *Goethe, The History of a Man* (1928; in Eng.); W. Nohl, *Goethe und Beethoven* (1929); R. Rolland, *Goethe et Beethoven* (Paris, 1930; in Eng., N.Y. and London, 1931); W. Engelsmann, *Goethe und Beethoven* (1931); Goethe issue of *Revue Musicale* (1932); Goethe issue of *Zeitschrift für Musikwissenschaft* (1932); A. Della Corte, *La vita musicale di Goethe* (Turin, 1932); G. Kinsky, *Die Handschriften von Beethovens Egmont-Musik* (Vienna, 1933); F. Küchler, *Goethes Musikverständnis* (Leipzig, 1935); F.W. Sternfeld, *Goethe and Music* (N.Y., 1954); W. Gerstenberg, *Goethes Dichtung und die Musik* (Leipzig, 1966).

Goetschius, Percy, renowned American music teacher and pedagogue; b. Paterson, N.J., Aug. 30, 1853; d. Manchester, N.H., Oct. 29, 1943. He studied at the Stuttgart Cons., and taught various classes there; also wrote music criticism. He returned to the U.S. in 1890; was on the faculty of Syracuse Univ. (1890–92) and at the New England Cons. of Music in Boston (1892–96). In 1905 he was appointed head of the dept. of music at the N.Y. Inst. of Musical Art; retired in 1925. Goetschius was a product of the fossilized Germanic tradition; convinced that the laws of harmony as set by old German pedagogues were unalterable and inviolate, he stood in horror before any vestige of unresolved dissonances.

WRITINGS: He wrote many books on music pedagogy, among them: *The Material Used in Musical Composition* (Stuttgart, 1882; N.Y., 1889; 14th ed., 1913; a valuable contribution to teaching of harmony); *The Theory and Practice of Tone-relations* (Boston, 1892; 17th revised ed., 1917); *Models of Principal Musical Forms* (Boston, 1895); *Syllabus of Music History* (1895); *The Homophonic Forms of Musical Composition* (N.Y., 1898; 10th ed., 1921); *Exercises in Melody Writing* (N.Y., 1900; 9th ed., 1923); *Applied Counterpoint* (N.Y., 1902); *Lessons in Music Form* (Boston, 1904); *Exercises in Elementary Counterpoint* (N.Y., 1910; an attempt to blend the disciplines of harmony and counterpoint); *Essentials in Music History* (N.Y., 1914; jointly with Thomas Tapper); *The Larger Forms of Musical Composition* (N.Y., 1915); *Masters of the Symphony* (Boston, 1929); *The Structure of Music* (Philadelphia, 1934). He composed a number of pieces for piano; was joint ed. of *The School Credit Piano Course* (1918–22).

BIBLIOGRAPHY: Arthur Shepherd, "Papa Goetschius in Retrospect," *Musical Quarterly* (July 1944).

Goetz, Hermann, German composer; b. Königsberg, Prussia, Dec. 7, 1840; d. Hottingen, near Zürich, Dec. 3, 1876. He studied at the Stern Cons. in Berlin in 1860–63, with von Bülow in piano and with H. Ulrich in composition. In 1863, he took the post of organist at Winterthur, Switzerland; then lived in Zürich; gave private lessons; conducted a singing society. His most famous work is the opera *The Taming of the Shrew (Der Widerspenstigen Zähmung),* based on Shakespeare's play, which was given in Mannheim, Oct. 11, 1874; it was then given in Vienna, Berlin, Leipzig, and other German cities, and produced in an Eng. version in London (Drury Lane Theatre, Oct. 12, 1878). His other works include the opera *Francesca da Rimini* (Mannheim, Sept. 30, 1877; unfinished; 3rd act completed by Ernst Frank); incidental music for Widmann's play *Die heiligen drei Könige* (Winterthur, Jan. 6, 1866); Symph. in F; Piano Concerto (Basel, Dec. 1, 1867); String Quartet (1865); chamber music; several pieces for piano; 24 songs.

BIBLIOGRAPHY: A. Steiner, *Hermann Goetz* (Zürich, 1907); E. Kreuzhage, *Hermann Goetz: Sein Leben und seine Werke* (Leipzig, 1916); G.R. Kruse, *Hermann Goetz* (1920); G. Puchelt, "Hermann Goetz (1840–1876)," *Schweizerische Musikzeitung/ Revue Musicale Suisse,* CXVI (1976).

Goetze, Walter W., German composer of light opera; b. Berlin, April 17, 1883; d. there, March 24, 1961. He began as a composer of popular ballads; then produced numerous operettas, among them *Der liebe Pepi* (1913); *Ihre Hoheit, die Tänzerin* (Stettin, May 8, 1919; highly popular; about 700 perfs. in Berlin alone); *Adrienne* (1926); *Der Page des Königs* (1933); *Akrobaten des Glücks* (1933); *Der goldene*

Pierrot (Berlin, March 31, 1934; successful); *Sensation im Trocadero* (1936); *Liebe im Dreiklang* (1951).

Goetzl, Anselm, Bohemian composer; b. Karolinenthal, Aug. 20, 1878; d. Barcelona, Jan. 9, 1923 (while traveling). He studied with Winkler, Fibich, and Dvořák in Prague, and with Schalk and Adler in Vienna; came to the U.S. in 1913 as conductor of Dippel's Light Opera Co. He wrote 3 operettas, a Piano Quartet, 2 string quartets, a Clarinet Quintet, and songs.

Goeyvaerts, Karel, significant Belgian composer; b. Antwerp, June 8, 1923. He studied at the Antwerp Cons. (1943–47), and with Milhaud, Messiaen, and Maurice Martenot in Paris (1947–50); received the Lili Boulanger Award in 1949. He taught music history at the Antwerp Cons. (1950–57); in 1970 he organized the Ghent Inst. of Psycho-Acoustics and Electronic Music (IPEM). Goeyvaerts is one of the pioneers of serialism, spatial music, and electronic techniques. His works bear pointedly abstract titles with structural connotations; he also applies aleatory devices in audio-visual collages.

WORKS: *3 lieder per sonare a venti-sei* for 6 Solo Instruments (1948–49); Sonata for 2 Pianos, op. 1 (1950–51); *Opus 2* for 13 Instruments (1951); *Opus 3 aux sons frappés et frottés (with Striking and Rubbing Sounds)* for 7 Instruments (1952); *Opus 4 aux sons morts (with Dead Sounds)* for Tape (1952); *Opus 5 aux sons purs (with Pure Sounds)* for Tape (1953); *Opus 6* for 180 Sound Objects (1954); *Opus 7 aux niveaux convergents et divergents (with Converging and Diverging Levels)* for Tape (1955); *Diaphonie,* suite for Orch. (1957); *Improperia,* cantata for Good Friday, for Alto, Double Chorus, and 6 Instruments (1958); *Piece for 3* for Flute, Violin, and Piano (1960); *Jeux d'été* for 3 Orch. Groups (1961); *La Passion* for Orch. (1962); *Cataclysme,* ballet for Orch. and ad libitum Narration (1963); *Piece for Piano, with Tape* (1964); *Goathermala* for Mezzo-soprano and Flute (1966); *Parcours* for 2 to 6 Violins (1967); *Mass in Memory of John XXIII* for Chorus and 10 Winds (1968); *Actief-Reactief* for 2 Oboes, 2 Trumpets, and Piano (1968); *Catch à quatre,* verbal composition for 4 Wandering Musicians (1969); *Al naar gelang* for 5 Instrumental Groups (1971); *Hé,* audio-visual production (1971; in collaboration with Herman Sabbe and Lucien Goethals); Piano Quartet, mobile composition for Violin, Viola, Cello, and Tape (1972); *Belise dans un jardin (Belise in the Garden)* for Chorus and 6 Instruments (1972); *Nachklänge aus dem Theater* for Tape (1972); *Op acht paarden wedden (To Bet on 8 Horses),* electronic mobile composition for 8 Sound Tracks (1973); *Landschap,* mobile composition for Harpsichord (1973); *You'll Never Be Alone Anymore* for Bass Clarinet and Electronics (1974); *Mon doux pilote s'endort aussi* for Choral Ensemble (1976).

Gogorza, Emilio Edoardo de, American baritone; b. Brooklyn, May 29, 1874; d. New York, May 10, 1949. After singing as a boy soprano in England, he returned to the U.S. and studied with C. Moderati and E. Agramonte in N.Y.; made his debut in 1897 with Marcella Sembrich in a concert; sang throughout the country in concerts and with leading orchs. Beginning in 1925, was for several years an instructor of voice at the Curtis Inst. of Music in Philadelphia. He married the American soprano **Emma Eames** in 1911.

Goh, Taijiro, Japanese composer; b. Dairen, Manchuria, Feb. 15, 1907; d. Shizuoka, July 1, 1970. He studied in Tokyo, organized the Society of Japanese Composers, and created the Japan Women's Symph. Orch. (1963). In 1961 he founded the Japan Assoc. for Promotion of Student Dormitory Songs; in 1966–68 he resided in the U.S. and Brazil. His music follows the European academic type of harmonic and contrapuntal structure.

WORKS: 3 operas: *Madame Rosaria* (1943); *Tsubaki saku koro* (*When Camellias Blossom;* 1949; unfinished); *Tais* (1959; unfinished); ballet, *Oni-Daiko* (*Devil Drummers;* 1956); 2 choreographic plays, *Koku-sei-Ya* and *Rashōmon* (both 1954); 8 symphs.: No. 1 (1925); No. 2 (1930); No. 3, *Kumo* (*Clouds;* 1938); No. 4 (1938); No. 5, *Nippon* (1939); No. 6, *Asia* (1939); No. 7, *Sokoku* (*Motherland;* 1942); No. 8, *Chô jô Banri* (*The Long Wall;* 1945; only the first movement was completed); 3 violin concertos (1935, 1937, 1962); 2 piano concertos (1936, 1940); *Movement* for Cello, Temple Blocks, and Orch. (1937); Theme and Variations for Orch. (1938); 2 overtures: *Otakebi* (*War Cry;* 1939) and *Over the Tan-Shan Southern Path* (1941); 3 symph. marches: *Eiyū* (*Hero;* 1940); *Taiiku* (*Gymnastics;* 1940); *Akeyuku Azia* (*Asia Dawning;* 1942); *Shimpi-shu* (*Mysteries),* ballet suite (1942); *Nemuri no Serenâde* (*Serenade for Slumber)* for Vocal Solo and Orch. (1944); *The Flow of the River Dalny* for Chorus and Orch. (1950); *Seija to Eiyū* (*The Saint and the Hero),* symph. dance piece (1961); *Brasil,* symph. poem with Narration and Chorus (1967); numerous short symph. works, including *Konchū* (*Insects;* 1941) and *Gekiryū* (*Torrent;* 1952); several pieces for Vocal Soloist or Narrator, and Orch.; Theme and Variations for String Trio (1933); 2 string quartets (1935, 1938); *Imayo* for Cello and Piano (1954); 5 piano sonatas (1915, 1919, 1920, 1927, 1927); *November in Manchuria,* rhapsody for Piano (1926); Fantasy for Piano (1927); Variations for Piano (1931); *8 Chinese Dances* for Piano (1941); *Katyusha,* choreographic poem for Piano (1954); over 100 songs.

Göhler, (Karl) Georg, German conductor and composer; b. Zwickau, June 29, 1874; d. Lübeck, March 4, 1954. He was a pupil of Vollhardt at Zwickau; then studied at the Leipzig Univ. and Cons.; obtained his Dr.Phil. with a dissertation on the 16th-century composer Cornelius Freundt; he then pursued a career as a chorus conductor; in 1913–15 conducted opera at Hamburg; in 1915, succeeded Furtwängler as conductor of symph. concerts in Lübeck; in 1922–27 he was conductor of the State Theater in Altenburg; also conducted symph. concerts in Halle. He wrote 5 symphs.; a Clarinet Concerto; 2 violin

concertos; a Cello Concerto; *Quartetto enimmatico* for Piano and Strings (1940); a String Trio (1942); more than 200 songs; and numerous choral works; also 24 bagatelles for Piano. He edited works by Freundt, Hasse, Handel, Haydn, Schubert, Mozart, etc.; wrote numerous articles on various musical subjects. He was an admirer of Mahler and Bruckner and gave frequent performances of their symphs.

Gold, Arthur, Canadian pianist; b. Toronto, Feb. 6, 1917. He studied with Josef and Rosina Lhévinne at the Juilliard School of Music; upon graduation, formed a piano duo with Robert Fizdale; together they gave numerous concerts in Europe and America, in programs of modern music, including works specially written for them by such celebrated composers as Samuel Barber, Darius Milhaud, Francis Poulenc, Georges Auric, and Virgil Thomson. Gold and Fizdale also pioneered performances of works by John Cage for prepared piano. With Fizdale he publ. a successful book, *Misia* (N.Y., 1979), on the life of Maria Godebska, a literary and musical figure in Paris early in the century.

Gold, Ernest, Austrian-American composer; b. Vienna, July 13, 1921. He studied piano and violin at home (his father was an amateur musician); in 1938 emigrated to the U.S.; studied harmony in N.Y. with Otto Cesana. He began writing songs in a popular vein; of these, *Practice Makes Perfect* became a hit. At the same time he composed in classical forms; to this category belong his *Pan American Symphony,* Piano Concerto, String Quartet, and Piano Sonata. In 1945 he went to Hollywood as an arranger; took lessons with George Antheil (1946–48); then was commissioned to write film scores; among them the following were very successful: *The Defiant Ones; On the Beach; Exodus* (Academy Award, 1960); *Judgment at Nuremberg* (1961); *It's a Mad, Mad, Mad, Mad World* (1963); *The Secret of Santa Vittoria* (1969). In 1950 he married the singer **Marni Nixon;** they were divorced in 1968; in 1975 he married the writer Jeannette Keller Light. In 1975 a star with his name was placed in the pavement of Hollywood's Walk of Fame; he was the first screen composer so honored.

Gold, Julius, American musicologist and teacher; b. St. Joseph, Mo., Feb. 18, 1884; d. Los Angeles, May 29, 1969. He studied at Chicago Musical College; then taught theory and composition at Drake Univ., Des Moines, Iowa (1910–14), and at Dominican College, San Rafael, Calif. (1930–34); later lived in Los Angeles.

Goldbeck, Fred, Dutch-French music critic; b. The Hague, Feb. 13, 1902; d. Paris, Nov. 6, 1981. After study with various teachers in several European countries, he settled in Paris in 1925 as a music critic; contributed numerous articles to the *Revue Musicale* and many other publications; publ. a book, *The Perfect Conductor* (N.Y., 1951); edited the music magazine *Contrepoints* (1946–52).

Goldbeck, Robert, pianist and conductor; b. Potsdam, April 19, 1839; d. St. Louis, May 16, 1908. He studied in Paris; made his concert debut in London; in 1857 came to N.Y., where he remained until 1867, when he founded a cons. in Boston. From 1880 to 1903 he lived variously in N.Y., Germany, St. Louis, Chicago, and London; in 1903 he returned to St. Louis. He publ. a textbook on harmony (1890) and a 3-vol. *Encyclopedia of Music Education* (1903).

Goldberg, Albert, American music critic; b. Shenandoah, Iowa, June 2, 1898. He studied at the Chicago Musical College (1920–22); taught there (1924–26); appeared as pianist and conductor; was music critic of the *Chicago Herald Examiner* (1925–36) and of the *Chicago Tribune* (1943–46). In 1947 he was appointed to the staff of the *Los Angeles Times,* and was still writing for it in 1978.

Goldberg, Johann Gottlieb, remarkable German organist and harpsichord player; b. Danzig (baptized, March 14), 1727; d. Dresden, April 13, 1756. As a child, he was brought to Dresden by his patron, Count Hermann Karl von Keyserlingk; he is reported to have studied with Wilhelm Friedemann Bach, and later with J.S. Bach (1742–43); in 1751 he became musician to Count Heinrich Brühl, a post he held till his death. His name is immortalized through the set of 30 variations written for him by Bach, and generally known as the *Goldberg Variations.* Goldberg's own compositions include 2 concertos; 24 polonaises; a Sonata with Minuet and 12 variations for Clavier; 6 trios for Flute, Violin, and Bass; a Motet; a Cantata; and a Psalm.
BIBLIOGRAPHY: E.A. Dadder, *Johann Gottlieb Goldberg: Leben und Werke* (Bonn, 1923).

Goldberg, Reiner, German tenor; b. Grostau, Oct. 17, 1939. He studied in Dresden with Arno Schellenberg; made his debut there in 1966; in 1973 he joined the Dresden State Opera; in 1980 went with the company to Tokyo, where he sang Max in *Der Freischütz.* On Feb. 22, 1982, he appeared at Covent Garden in London in the role of Walther in *Die Meistersinger von Nürnberg;* he subsequently had guest engagements in Hamburg, Vienna, Madrid, and Leningrad, in the roles of Florestan, Cavaradossi, Bacchus, Siegmund, and Tannhäuser; he also sang the title role in Syberberg's movie version of *Parsifal.* In 1977 he was engaged as a regular member of the State Opera in East Berlin.

Goldberg, Szymon, eminent Polish-born American violinist and conductor; b. Wloclawek, June 1, 1909. He played violin as a child in Warsaw; in 1917 he went to Berlin and took regular violin lessons with Carl Flesch. After a recital in Warsaw in 1921, he was engaged as concertmaster of the Dresden Phil. Orch. (1925–29); in 1929 he was appointed concertmaster of the Berlin Phil. Orch. but was forced to leave in 1934 despite Furtwängler's vigorous attempts to safeguard the Jewish members of the orch.; he then toured Europe. He made his American debut in N.Y. in 1938; while on a tour of Asia, he was interned in Java by the Japanese from 1942–45; eventually he came to the U.S.; became an American citizen in 1953. From 1951–65 he taught at the Aspen Music School; concurrently was active as a conductor. In 1955 he founded the Netherlands Chamber Orch. in Amsterdam, which he led with notable distinction for 22 years; he also took the ensemble on tours.
BIBLIOGRAPHY: B. Gavoty, *Szymon Goldberg* (Geneva, 1961).

Goldberg, Theo, German composer; b. Chemnitz, Sept. 29, 1921. He studied in Berlin (1945–50); in 1954, settled in Canada and taught in Vancouver; received his doctorate in composition from the Univ. of Toronto (1972). He composed the chamber operas *Minotauros; Schwere Zeiten für Engel* (Berlin, Sept. 20, 1952); *Galatea elettronica* (1969); *Jeanne des anges* (1972); a ballet, *Nacht mit Kleopatra* (Karlsruhe, Jan. 20, 1952); *La Femme Cent Têtes* for Orch. (1950); *Variations on a Theme by Strauss* for Orch. (1952); Double Concerto for Oboe, Bassoon, and Orch. (1952); Cantata (1953); Divertissement No. 3 for Orch. (1957); *Sinfonia concertante* for Flute, Clarinet, Trumpet, Violin, Cello, and Orch. (1967); String Quartet (1949); Clarinet Quintet (1952); Quartet for Alto Flute, Viola, Cello, and Harp (1962); *Calliope* for Bassoon, Trombone, Piano, Violin, Tape, and Sound-related Images (1973).

Golde, Walter, American pianist, vocal teacher, and music educator; b. Brooklyn, Jan. 4, 1887; d. Chapel Hill, N.C., Sept. 4, 1963. He studied at Dartmouth College, graduating in 1910; then went to Vienna, where he took vocal lessons as well as academic courses at the Vienna Cons. Returning to the U.S., he became a professional accompanist; played for Casals, Mischa Elman, Mary Garden, and Melchior. From 1944 to 1948 he headed the voice dept. of Columbia Univ.; in 1953 he was appointed director of the Inst. of Opera at the Univ. of North Carolina. He composed a number of attractive songs and piano pieces.

Goldenweiser, Alexander, Russian piano pedagogue; b. Kishinev, March 10, 1875; d. Moscow, Nov. 26, 1961. He studied piano with Pabst and composition with Arensky at the Moscow Cons.; in 1906 became a prof. of piano there, holding this post for 55 years, until his death. Two generations of Russian pianists were his pupils, among them Kabalevsky and Lazar Berman. As a pedagogue, he continued the traditions of the Russian school of piano playing, seeking the inner meaning of the music while achieving technical brilliance. He was a frequent visitor to Tolstoy's house near Moscow, and wrote reminiscences of Tolstoy (Moscow, 1922); publ. several essays on piano teaching; also composed chamber music and piano pieces.

Goldman, Edwin Franko, eminent American bandmaster; b. Louisville, Ky., Jan. 1, 1878; d. New York, Feb. 21, 1956. He was the nephew of **Sam Franko** and **Nahan Franko,** well-known conductors; was brought to N.Y., where he studied composition with Dvořák, and cornet with J. Levy and C. Sohst. He became solo cornetist of the Metropolitan Opera orch. when he was 17, remaining there for 10 years. For the next 13 years he taught cornet and trumpet; he formed his first band in 1911. In 1918, the Goldman Band outdoor concerts were inaugurated. His band was noted not only for its skill and musicianship but for its unusual repertoire, including modern works especially commissioned for the band. Goldman was a founder and first president of the American Bandmasters' Assoc.; he received honorary D.Mus. degrees from Phillips Univ. and Boston Univ., and medals and other honors from governments and associations throughout the world. He wrote more than 100 brilliant marches, of which the best known is *On the Mall;* also other band music; solos for various wind instruments; studies and methods for cornet and other brass instruments; several songs. He was the author of *Foundation to Cornet or Trumpet Playing* (1914); *Band Betterment* (1934); *The Goldman Band System* (1936).

Goldman, Richard Franko (son of **Edwin Franko Goldman**), American bandmaster and composer; b. New York, Dec. 7, 1910; d. Baltimore, Jan. 19, 1980. He graduated from Columbia Univ. in 1931; later studied composition with Nadia Boulanger in Paris. He became an assistant of his father in conducting the Goldman Band in 1937; on his father's death in 1956, he succeeded him as conductor; continued to conduct the band into the summer of 1979, when ill health forced him to retire and allow the band to dissolve. He taught at the Juilliard School of Music (1947–60), was a visiting prof. at Princeton (1952–56), and in 1968 was appointed director of the Peabody Cons. of Music in Baltimore and served as its president (1969–77). He wrote many works for various ensembles: *A Sentimental Journey* for Band (1941); 3 duets for Clarinets (1944); Sonatina for 2 Clarinets (1945); Duo for Tubas (1948); Violin Sonata (1952), etc; many arrangements for band. A progressive musician, Goldman experimented with modern techniques, and his music combines highly advanced harmony with simple procedures accessible to amateurs.
WRITINGS: *The Band's Music* (N.Y., 1938); *The Concert Band* (N.Y., 1946); *The Wind Band: Its Literature and Technique* (Boston, 1961; reprinted, Westport, Conn., 1974); *Harmony in Western Music* (N.Y., 1965). He was co-editor of *Landmarks of Early American Music, 1760–1800* (N.Y., 1943; reprinted, N.Y., 1975; 32 compositions for orch. or band or chorus, with historical and biographical notes and suggestions for performance), was editor of the *Juilliard Review* for the first 6 years after its founding (1953–58), and was N.Y. critic for *Musical Quarterly* (1948–68).
BIBLIOGRAPHY: *Who's Who in America, 1978–79* (for details on honors and awards).

Goldmann, Friedrich, East German composer; b. Siegmar-Schönau, April 27, 1941. He studied composition with Thilman at the Dresden Hochschule für Musik (1959–62); then attended the master classes of Wagner-Régeny at the Akademie der Künste in East Berlin (1962–64); later entered Humboldt Univ. in East Berlin to study musicology (1964–68). In 1973 he received the Hanns Eisler Prize.
WORKS: FOR THE STAGE: *R. Hot bzw. Hitze,* opera fantasy (1976). FOR ORCH.: *Essay I–III* (1963–64, 1968, 1971); 2 symphs. (1972–73, 1976); *Musik für Kammerorchester* (1973); Concerto for Trombone and 3 Instrumental Groups (1977); Violin Concerto (1977); Oboe Concerto (1978); Piano Concerto (1979); *Inclinatio temporum* (1981). CHAMBER MUSIC: Trio for Flute, Percussion, and Piano (1966–67); String Trio (1967); Sonata for Wind Quintet and Piano (1969–70); *So und So* for English Horn, Trombone, and Double Bass (1972); *Cellomusik* (1974); String Quartet (1975); *Zusammenstellung,* music for Wind Instruments (1976); Piano Trio (1978); *Für P.D.* for 15 Strings (1975); Oboe Sonata (1980). FOR VOICE: *Odipus Tyrann: Kommentar* for Chorus and Orch. (1968–69); *Sing' Lessing* for Baritone, Flute, Oboe, Clarinet, Horn, Bassoon, and Piano (1978).
BIBLIOGRAPHY: Ursula Stürzbecher, *Komponisten in der DDR: 17 Gespräche* (Hildesheim, 1979).

Goldmark, Karl, eminent Austro-Hungarian composer; b. Keszthely, Hungary, May 18, 1830; d. Vienna, Jan. 2, 1915. The son of a poor cantor, he studied at the school of the Musical Society of Sopron (1842–44); the talent he showed there as a violinist resulted in his being sent to Vienna, where he studied with L. Jansa (1844–45); later studied at the Vienna Cons., as a pupil of Preyer (harmony) and Böhm (violin). He spent most of his life in Vienna, where the first concert of his compositions was given on March 20, 1857. Landmarks in his career were the first performance of his *Sakuntala* overture by the Vienna Phil. on Dec. 26, 1865, and the premiere of his first opera, *Die Königin von Saba,* at the Vienna Opera on March 10, 1875; both were very successful.
WORKS: Operas (in addition to *Die Königin von Saba*): *Merlin* (Vienna, Nov. 19, 1886); *Das Heimchen am Herd,* based on Dickens's *The Cricket on the Hearth* (Vienna, March 21, 1896); *Die Kriegsgefangene* (Vienna, Jan. 17, 1899); *Götz von Berlichingen,* based on Goethe's play (Budapest, Dec. 16, 1902); *Ein Wintermärchen,* based on Shakespeare's *A Winter's Tale* (Vienna, Jan. 2, 1908). For orch.: 7 overtures: *Sakuntala, Penthesilea, Im Frühling, Der gefesselte Prometheus, Sappho, In Italien, Aus Jugendtagen;* a symph. poem, *Ländliche Hochzeit* (*Rustic Wedding;* Vienna, March 5, 1876); 2 symphs.; symph. poem, *Zrinyi* (1903); Violin Concerto No. 1 (Nuremberg, Oct. 28, 1878); other instrumental concertos. Chamber music: 2 piano trios; Piano Quintet; Cello Sonata; Violin Sonata; piano pieces; songs; choral works. He publ. an autobiography, *Erinnerungen aus meinem Leben* (Vienna, 1922; in Eng. as *Notes from the Life of a Viennese Composer,* N.Y., 1927).
BIBLIOGRAPHY: O. Keller, *Karl Goldmark* (1901); H. Schwarz, *Ignaz Brüll und sein Freundeskreis: Erinnerungen an Brüll, Goldmark und*

Brahms (Vienna, 1922); L. Koch, ed., *Karl Goldmark* (Budapest, 1930, contains full bibliography); biographies in Hungarian by Kálmán (1930), Klempá (1930), and Várnai (1957).

Goldmark, Rubin, American composer and teacher, nephew of **Karl Goldmark;** b. New York, Aug. 15, 1872; d. there, March 6, 1936. He studied at the Vienna Cons. with A. Door (piano) and J.N. Fuchs (composition); in 1891–93 he was a student at the National Cons. in N.Y. with Joseffy (piano) and Dvořák (composition). He went to Colorado Springs for his health in 1894; taught at the College Cons. there (1895–1901). Returning to N.Y. in 1902, for the next 20 years he gave private lessons in piano and theory. In 1924, he was appointed head of the composition dept. of the Juilliard School in N.Y., and remained there until his death; among his pupils were Aaron Copland, Abram Chasins, Frederick Jacobi, and other American composers. He was active in promoting such musical clubs as The Bohemians (of N.Y.), of which he was a founder and president (1907–10), the Beethoven Assoc., and the Society for the Publication of American Music.
WORKS: Overture, *Hiawatha* (Boston, Jan. 13, 1900); tone poem, *Samson* (Boston, March 14, 1914); Requiem, suggested by Lincoln's Gettysburg Address (N.Y., Jan. 30, 1919); *A Negro Rhapsody* (his most popular work; N.Y., Jan. 18, 1923); Piano Quartet (Paderewski Prize, 1909; N.Y., Dec. 13, 1910); Piano Trio; *The Call of the Plains* for Violin and Piano (1915); songs.

Goldovsky, Boris, Russian-American pianist and conductor, son of the violinist **Lea Luboshutz;** b. Moscow, June 7, 1908. He studied piano with his uncle **Pierre Luboshutz;** later in Berlin with Schnabel and Kreutzer, and in Budapest with Dohnányi. He appeared as soloist with the Berlin Phil. at the age of 13 in 1921; came to America in 1930; was director of the Opera Workshop at the Berkshire Music Center, Tanglewood (1942–64); founded the New England Opera Co. in 1946. A versatile musician, he trans. opera librettos into singable English; presented popular radio talks on music; acted as moderator for Metropolitan Opera broadcasts. A collection of his comments was publ. as *Accents on Opera* (N.Y., 1953); he also wrote *Bringing Opera to Life* (N.Y., 1968).

Goldsand, Robert, Austrian pianist; b. Vienna, March 17, 1911. He studied with A. Manhart, M. Rosenthal, Camillo Horn, and Joseph Marx. He played in public at the age of 10; then toured in Europe and South America; made his U.S. debut at Carnegie Hall, March 21, 1927; then was again in Europe, but settled permanently in the U.S. in 1939.

Goldschmidt, Adalbert von, Austrian composer; b. Vienna, May 5, 1848; d. Hacking, near Vienna, Dec. 21, 1906. He studied at the Vienna Cons.; from his earliest efforts in composition, he became an ardent follower of Wagner. At the age of 22, he wrote a cantata, *Die sieben Todsünden* (Berlin,

1875); this was followed by a music drama, *Helianthus* (Leipzig, 1884), for which he wrote both words and music. A dramatic trilogy, *Gaea* (1889), was his most ambitious work along Wagnerian lines. He also brought out a comic opera, *Die fromme Helene* (Hamburg, 1897); wrote about 100 songs and a number of piano pieces.
BIBLIOGRAPHY: E. Friedegg, *Briefe an einen Komponisten: Musikalische Korrespondenz an Adalbert von Goldschmidt* (Berlin, 1909).

Goldschmidt, Berthold, German-born English composer and conductor; b. Hamburg, Jan. 18, 1903. He studied at the Univ. of Hamburg and at the Friedrich Wilhelm Univ. in Berlin; also at the Berlin State Academy of Music with Schreker. He was an assistant conductor at the Berlin State Opera (1926–27) and conductor at the Darmstadt Opera (1927–29); then was a conductor with the Berlin Radio and the Städtische Oper. In 1935 he went to England; became a British citizen in 1947. He made numerous guest appearances in England with various orchs.; also conducted opera. He composed 2 operas: *Der gewaltige Hahnrei* (Mannheim, Feb. 14, 1932) and *Beatrice Cenci* (1949–50); a ballet, *Chronica* (1938); Symphony (1944); Concertino for Violin (1933), Concertino for Cello (1933), Concertino for Harp (1949), and Concertino for Clarinet (1955), as well as miscellaneous works for piano.

Goldschmidt, Hugo, German writer on music; b. Breslau, Sept. 19, 1859; d. Wiesbaden, Dec. 26, 1920. He studied singing under Stockhausen at Frankfurt (1887–90); was co-director of the Klindworth-Scharwenka Cons. in Berlin (1893–1905).
WRITINGS: *Die italienische Gesangsmethode des 17. Jahrhunderts* (1890); *Der Vokalismus des neuhochdeutschen Kunstgesangs und der Bühnensprache* (1892); *Handbuch der deutschen Gegangspädagogik* (1896); *Studien zur Geschichte der italienischen Oper im 17. Jahrhundert* (2 vols., 1901, 1904; the 2nd vol. contains a reprint of Monteverdi's opera *Incoronazione di Poppea;* reprint, 1967); *Die Lehre von der vokalen Ornamentik* (vol. I covers the 17th and 18th centuries to the time of Gluck; 1907); *Die Musikästhetik des 18. Jahrhunderts und ihre Beziehungen zu seinem Kunstschaffen* (Zürich, 1915; reprint, 1968).

Goldschmidt, Otto, German pianist; b. Hamburg, Aug. 21, 1829; d. London, Feb. 24, 1907. He was at first a pupil of Jakob Schmitt and F.W. Grund, then of Mendelssohn at the Leipzig Cons., and of Chopin at Paris (1848). In 1849 he played in London at a concert given by **Jenny Lind;** accompanied her on her American tour (1851) and married her at Boston, Feb. 5, 1852; from 1852 to 1855 they lived in Dresden; from 1858 until her death (1887), in London. He founded the Bach Choir in 1875, and conducted it till 1885. He composed an oratorio, *Ruth* (Hereford, 1867); a choral song, *Music,* for Soprano and Women's Chorus (Leeds, 1898); piano music, including a Concerto, piano studies, 2 duets for 2 Pianos; was co-editor of *The Chorale Book for England,* a collection of hymns (1863).

Goldsmith, Jerry, American composer for films; b. Los Angeles, Feb. 10, 1929. He studied music at the Univ. of Southern Calif.; became a staff composer with the 20th Century-Fox Film Corp.; wrote the scores for *The Sand Pebbles; Freud; Planet of the Apes; 7 Days in May* (1964); *A Patch of Blue* (1966); *Seconds* (1966); *Patton* (1970); *Papillon* (1973); *The Cassandra Crossing* (1976); *Islands in the Stream* (1977); *MacArthur* (1978); etc. He also wrote chamber music and vocal works.

Goldstein, Mikhail, brilliant violinist, composer, and musical investigator; b. Odessa, Nov. 8, 1917. He was a proverbial *wunderkind* who seemed to have been born with an extra limb shaped like a violin; as an infant he began to study with the renowned Odessa violin teacher Pyotr Stoliarsky, known among Russian-Jewish musicians as a "talent manufacturer" (David Oistrakh and Nathan Milstein were his other students). Goldstein played a public concert when he was 5 years old, perched on a table for visibility. At 8 he could play the Mendelssohn Concerto. He was sent to Moscow and at 13 entered the Moscow Cons. as a student of Yampolsky; he studied composition with Miaskovsky and conducting with Saradzhev. During the war of 1941–45 Goldstein was active in the entertainment division of the Red Army; during the battle of Stalingrad he played Bach over a powerful loudspeaker for the benefit of the German soldiers, and the Germans urged him to play some more, promising not to shoot; they did not realize that the Bach player was a lowly Jew. Returning to Odessa in 1946, Goldstein took over Stoliarsky's children's music school. In 1948 he went to Moscow; gave numerous concerts, and began to compose. He won 3 prizes at an anonymous competition; they were, however, canceled when it became known that he was married to a German woman, since international marriages were regarded as inappropriate for a Soviet citizen. In a spirit of witty retaliation, he perpetrated a hoax, claiming the discovery of a symph. allegedly composed in 1810 by a mythical Russian musician named Ovsianiko-Kulikovsky; the work was hailed as a proof that symphs. were written in Russia in Beethoven's time; the score was publ. and recorded, and the Soviet musicologist Valerian Dovzhenko wrote a learned dissertation on the subject. When Goldstein publicly admitted his deception and declared that the symph. was in fact his own composition, he was denounced as an impostor trying to appropriate a historically important Russian work. In eclipse as a result of this episode, Goldstein left Russia in 1964; lived first in East Berlin; in 1967 went to Israel and taught violin at the Musical Academy in Jerusalem. In 1969 he settled in Hamburg, where he resumed his career as a concert violinist and a pedagogue. He also did valuable research in musical biography, establishing important facts about Russian and German composers of the 18th and 19th centuries. In 1969 he was appointed a prof. at the Hamburg Hochschule für

Musik, leading master classes. He also continued to compose prolifically. While still in Russia he had written 4 symphs., a great deal of chamber music, and a variety of violin pieces. One of his most original compositions is a Quartet for 4 Violas, without precedent in instrumental music. Although well versed in modern musical techniques, Goldstein preferred to write music in a style derived from historical practices.
WORKS: For Orch.: 4 symphs.: No. 1 (1934); No. 2, for Strings and Russian Folk Instruments (1936); No. 3 (1944); No. 4 (1945); 2 violin concertos (1936, 1939); Piano Concerto (1940); symph. poem, *Nicolò Paganini* (1963); *Ukrainian Rhapsody* (1965); *Kinderszenen* (1966); *Hamburger Konzert* for Chamber Orch. (1975). Chamber music: *Russian Sonatina* for Violin Solo (1929; written at the age of 12); 3 string quartets (1932, 1940, 1975); Piano Trio (1933); 4 violin sonatas (1935, 1940, 1950, 1975); *Ukrainian Suite* for Violin and Piano (1952); *5 Easy Pieces* for Viola and Piano (1958); *Duo* for Violin and Double Bass (1979); Sonatina for Violin Solo (1980); 2 sonatinas for Flute Solo (1977, 1980); Sonatina for Double-bass Solo (1981); Sonatina for Oboe Solo (1982); Sonatina for Trombone Solo (1982); Quartet for 4 Violas (1982); numerous pieces for various instrumental combinations.

Goléa, Antoine, French music critic of Rumanian origin; b. Vienna, Aug. 30, 1906; d. Paris, Oct. 12, 1980. He studied music at the Cons. of Bucharest; then emigrated to France, where he became active as a journalist, specializing in lively monographs on contemporary composers.
WRITINGS: *Rencontres avec Pierre Boulez* (Paris, 1958); *Georges Auric* (Paris, 1958); *Rencontres avec Olivier Messiaen* (Paris, 1960). Of a more general nature are *Esthétique de la musique contemporaine* (Paris, 1954); *La Musique dans la société européenne depuis le moyen âge jusqu'à nos jours* (Paris, 1960); monographs, *Claude Debussy* (Paris, 1965) and *Richard Strauss* (Paris, 1965); also, *Entretiens avec Wieland Wagner* (Paris, 1967; in German, Salzburg, 1968); *Histoire du ballet* (Lausanne, 1967).

Goleminov, Marin, Bulgarian composer; b. Kjustendil, Sept. 28, 1908. He studied music theory and violin at the Bulgarian State Cons. in Sofia (1927–31); then went to Paris and took courses in composition with Lioncourt and Le Flem (1931–34); from Paris he proceeded to Germany, and enrolled in the class of composition with Joseph Haas at the Akademie der Tonkunst in Munich (1938–39). After World War II he taught at the Bulgarian Cons. in Sofia; was director of the National Opera in 1965–67. His music utilizes folk elements, particularly the asymmetrical rhythms of Bulgarian folk motifs, in a fairly modern but still quite accessible idiom.
WORKS: 2 operas: *Ivailo* (1958; Sofia, Feb. 13, 1959) and *Zahari the Icon Painter* (1971; Sofia, Oct. 17, 1972); operatic fairy tale, *Zlatnata ptica* (*The Golden Bird;* 1961; Sofia, Dec. 20, 1961); 2 ballets: *Nestinarka* (1940; Sofia, Jan. 4, 1942) and *The*

Daughter of Kaloyan (1973; Sofia, Dec. 23, 1973); oratorio, *The Titan* (1972; Sofia, June 25, 1972); cantata, *Father Paissy* (1966); *Night,* symph. poem (1932); Cello Concerto (1949–50); *Prelude, Aria and Toccata* for Piano and Orch. (1947–53); *Poem* for Orch. (1959); Concerto for String Quartet and String Orch. (1963; Moscow, Feb. 11, 1964); 3 symphs.: No. 1, *Detska* (*Children's Symphony;* 1963); No. 2 (1967; Sofia, March 6, 1968); No. 3, *Peace in the World* (1970; Sofia, April 21, 1971); Violin Concerto No. 1 (1968); *Aquarelles* for String Orch. (1973); Piano Concerto (1975); *3 Miniatures* for Soprano and Chamber Orch.; 7 string quartets (1934; 1938; 1944; *Micro-quartet,* 1967; 1969; 1975; 1977); 2 wind quintets (1936, 1946); Trio for Oboe, Clarinet, and Bassoon (1964); Solo Cello Sonata (1969); choruses; songs; incidental music. He publ. several teaching manuals and essays on Bulgarian music: *The Sources of Bulgarian Musical Composition* (Sofia, 1937); *Instrumentation* (Sofia, 1947); *Problems of Orchestration,* (2 vols., Sofia, 1953; 2nd and 3rd eds., 1958, 1966); *Behind the Curtain of the Creative Process* (Sofia, 1971).

Golestan, Stan, Rumanian composer; b. Vaslui, June 7, 1875; d. Paris, April 21, 1956. He studied composition and orchestration with Vincent d'Indy, Albert Roussel, and Paul Dukas at the Schola Cantorum in Paris (1897–1903). Subsequently he wrote music criticism in *Le Figaro.*
WORKS: For Orch.: *La Dembovitza* (1902); *Lăutarul și Cobzarul,* Rumanian dances (1902); Symph. (1910); *Rapsodie roumaine* (1912); *Rapsodie concertante* for Violin and Orch. (1920); *Concerto roumain* for Violin and Orch. (1933); *Concerto moldave* for Cello and Orch. (1936); Piano Concerto, subtitled *Sur les cîmes des Carpathes,* for Piano and Orch. (1935–38). Chamber music: Violin Sonata (1908); 2 string quartets, *Arioso* and *Concert Allegro* for Viola and Piano (1932); Flute Sonatina (1932). For Piano: *Poèmes et paysages* (1922) and *Thème, variations et dances;* vocal pieces.

Golitzin, Nicolai, Russian nobleman, a music amateur; b. St. Petersburg, Dec. 19, 1794; d. Tambov District, Nov. 3, 1866. He was a talented cello player, but his name is remembered mainly because of his connection with Beethoven, who dedicated to Golitzin the overture op. 124 and the string quartets opp. 127, 130, 132. Golitzin was also responsible for the first Russian performance of Beethoven's *Missa solemnis* (1825).
BIBLIOGRAPHY: L. Ginzburg, "Beethoven und Nikolai Golitzin," *Beethoven Jahrbuch* (Bonn, 1962).

Göllerich, August, Austrian writer on music; b. Linz, July 2, 1859; d. there, March 16, 1923. He was a pupil of Liszt; studied composition with Bruckner; acquired Ramann's music school in Nuremberg in 1890, and established branches in Erlangen, Fürth, and Ansbach; from 1896, he was conductor of the Musikverein and director of the Cons. in Linz; his wife, **Gisela Pászthory-Voigt** (also a pupil of Liszt),

supervised the other schools. He publ. *A. Reissmann als Schriftsteller und Komponist* (1884); *Beethoven* (1904); *Franz Liszt* (1908); guides to Liszt's *Graner Festmesse* and Wagner's *Ring des Nibelungen* (1897). His chief work, a biography of Bruckner (who himself selected Göllerich for this task), in 4 vols., was completed by Max Auer (first vol., Regensburg, 1924; 2nd, 1928; remaining vols., 1932 and 1937).

Gollmick, Adolf, German pianist and composer, son of **Karl Gollmick;** b. Frankfurt, Feb. 5, 1825; d. London, March 7, 1883. He studied with his father and other teachers in Frankfurt; in 1844, he settled in London as a pianist and teacher. He composed 3 comic operas: *Dona Constanza, The Oracle, Balthasar;* 2 "operatic cantatas": *The Blind Beggar's Daughter of Bethnal Green* and *The Heir of Lynne;* also several symph. works, piano pieces, and songs.

Gollmick, Karl, German composer and music theorist; b. Dessau, March 19, 1796; d. Frankfurt, Oct. 3, 1866. He was of a musical family; his father, **Friedrich Karl Gollmick** (1774–1852), was an opera tenor. He studied theology in Strasbourg; in 1817, he settled in Frankfurt, where he taught French and served as chorus master. He wrote mostly for piano; publ. potpourris, etc. His writings include *Kritische Terminologie für Musiker und Musikfreunde* (1833; 2nd ed., 1839); *Fétis als Mensch, Kritiker, Theoretiker und Komponist* (1852); *Handlexikon der Tonkunst* (1858); etc. He also wrote an autobiography (1866).

Golovanov, Nicolai, Russian conductor, composer, and pedagogue; b. Moscow, Jan. 21, 1891; d. there, Aug. 28, 1953. He studied choral conducting with Kastalsky at the Synodal School in Moscow, graduating in 1909; then entered the composition classes of Ippolitov-Ivanov and Vassilenko at the Moscow Cons. After graduation in 1914 he was engaged as assistant chorus conductor at the Bolshoi Theater in Moscow; was rapidly promoted, and from 1948 until his death was chief conductor there; he also was director of the theatrical division of Moscow Radio. He was awarded the Order of the Red Banner in 1935, and was 4 times recipient of the First Stalin Prize (1946, 1948, 1950, 1951). He wrote an opera, *Princess Yurata;* a Symph.; a symph. poem, *Salome,* after Oscar Wilde; numerous piano pieces; songs.
BIBLIOGRAPHY: N. Anosov, "Nikolai Golovanov," *Sovetskaya Musyka* (May 1951).

Golschmann, Vladimir, renowned French conductor; b. Paris, Dec. 16, 1893; d. New York, March 1, 1972. He studied violin and piano at the Schola Cantorum; as early as 1919 he organized the Concerts Golschmann in Paris, in programs featuring many first performances of modern works. In 1923 he conducted ballet in the U.S.; then was conductor of the Scottish Orch. in Glasgow (1928–30). In 1931 he was engaged as conductor of the St. Louis Symph. Orch., and held this post for more than a quarter of a century (1931–58); from 1964 to 1970 was conductor of the Denver Symph. Orch.; also appeared as guest conductor with other American orchs.

BIBLIOGRAPHY: "V. Golschmann, Conductor," in *Le Grand Baton* (Sept.–Dec. 1979).

Goltermann, Georg (Eduard), German cellist and composer; b. Hannover, Aug. 19, 1824; d. Frankfurt, Dec. 29, 1898. He studied cello in Munich, where he was also a pupil of Lachner in composition. After concert tours in 1850–52, he became music director at Würzburg; in 1853, he was appointed assistant music director and in 1874 principal music director of the Stadttheater of Frankfurt. He composed a number of works for cello, including 8 concertos; sonatas with piano; *Morceaux caractéristiques; Danses allemandes; Elégie,* etc. He also wrote a Symph., 3 overtures, and songs.

Golther, Wolfgang, German writer; b. Stuttgart, May 25, 1863; d. Rostock, Dec. 14, 1945. He was prof. of Germanic philology at Rostock; besides works on this subject, he wrote several important books on the music of Richard Wagner: *Die Sage von Tristan und Isolde* (1887); *Die sagengeschichtlichen Grundlagen der Ringdichtung Richard Wagners* (1902); *Bayreuth* (1904); *Richard Wagner als Dichter* (1904; Eng. trans., 1907); *Tristan und Isolde in den Dichtungen des Mittelalters und der neueren Zeit* (1907); *Zur deutschen Sage und Dichtung* (1911); *Parsifal und der Gral in deutscher Sage des Mittelalters und der Neuzeit* (1913; new ed., 1925); *Richard Wagner* (1926); edited Wagner's correspondence with the Wesendoncks; *Richard Wagner, 10 Lieder aus den Jahren 1838–58* (1921). He wrote an opera, *Hassan gewinnt* (Rostock, 1929).

Goltz, Christel, German soprano; b. Dortmund, July 8, 1912. She studied in Munich; from 1936 to 1950 she was a member of the Dresden State Opera; also sang with the Berlin State Opera and the Berlin City Opera. From 1951 to 1970 she made many appearances with the Vienna State Opera; in 1952 she was named a Kammersängerin. On Dec. 15, 1954, she made her Metropolitan Opera debut as Salome. She sang in many productions of modern operas.

Golubev, Evgeni, Soviet composer and pedagogue; b. Moscow, Feb. 16, 1910. He studied composition with Miaskovsky at the Moscow Cons., graduating in 1936, and piano with Feinberg. He joined the faculty of his alma mater upon graduation and taught special courses in polyphonic composition. Several well-known Soviet composers were his students, among them Khrennikov, Eshpai, and Schnittke.

WORKS: 7 symphs. (1933, 1937, 1942, 1947, 1960, 1966, 1972); 3 piano concertos (1944, 1948, 1956); Cello Concerto (1958); Viola Concerto (1962); Violin Concerto (1970); 19 string quartets; 2 string quintets; 10 piano sonatas; oratorios: *Return of the Sun* (1936) and *Heroes Are Immortal* (1946); ballet, *Odysseus* (1965); many choruses.

Golyscheff, Jefim (Jef), Russian composer and theorist; b. Kherson, Sept. 20, 1897; d. Paris, Sept. 25, 1970. He studied violin in Odessa and played in public as a child. In 1909, in the wake of anti-Jewish pogroms in Russia, he went to Berlin, where he studied chemistry as well as music theory; at the same time he began to paint in the manner of Abstract Expressionism. Golyscheff played a historic role in the development of the serial methods of composition; his String Trio, written about 1914 and publ. in 1925, contains passages described by him as "Zwölftondauer-Komplexen," in which 12 different tones are given 12 different durations in the main theme. As both a painter and a musician, he was close to the Dada circles in Berlin, and participated in futuristic experiments. On April 30, 1919, he presented at a Dada exhibition in Berlin his *Anti-Symphonie,* subtitled *Musikalische Kreisguillotine (Musical Circular Guillotine),* with characteristic titles of its movements: 1, *Provocational Injections;* 2, *Chaotic Oral Cavity, or Submarine Aircraft;* 3, *Clapping in Hyper F-sharp Major.* On May 24, 1919, he appeared at a Berlin Dada soirée with a piece of his composition entitled *Keuchmaneuver (Cough Maneuver).* All this activity ceased with the advent of the Nazis in 1933. As a Jew, Golyscheff had to flee Germany; he went to Paris, but after the fall of France in 1940 was interned by the Vichy authorities. His life was probably spared because of his expertise as a chemist; he was conscripted as a cement laborer. In 1956 he went to Brazil, where he devoted himself exclusively to painting, and had several successful exhibitions in São Paulo. In 1966 he returned to Paris, where he remained until his death.

BIBLIOGRAPHY: H. Eimert, *Atonale Musiklehre* (Leipzig, 1924; reprinted under the title *Zwölftontechnik,* Wiesbaden, 1954); D. Gojowy, "Jefim Golyscheff, der unbequeme Vorläufer," *Melos* (May–June 1975).

Gombert, Nicolas, Flemish composer; b. southern Flanders, possibly between Lille and St. Omer, c.1490; d. c.1556. He was one of the most eminent pupils of Josquin des Prez, on whose death he composed a funeral dirge. The details of his early life are obscure and uncertain. The physician Jerome Cardan reported that Gombert violated a boy and was sentenced to the galleys on the high seas. He is first positively accounted for in 1526, when his name appears on the list of singers at the court chapel of Charles V that was issued at Granada in that year; the restless Emperor traveled continually throughout his extensive domain—Spain, Germany, and the Netherlands—and his retinue was obliged to follow him in his round of his courts at Vienna, Madrid, and Brussels; Gombert probably was taken into the service of the Emperor on one of the latter's visits to Brussels. He is first mentioned as "maistre des enffans de la chapelle de nostre sr empereur" ("master of the boys of the royal chapel") in a court document dated Jan. 1, 1529; he remained in the Emperor's employ until 1538–40, during which time he took an active part in the various functions of the court, composing assiduously. After his retirement from his post in the royal chapel, he seems to have returned to his native Netherlands (Tournai), and there continued to compose until his death. He held a canonship at Notre Dame, Courtrai, from June 23, 1537, without having to take up residence there, and was also a canon at the Cathedral of Tournai from June 19, 1534. Despite his many trips abroad and the natural influence of the music of other countries, Gombert remained, stylistically, a Netherlander. The chief feature of his sacred works is his use of imitation, a principle which he developed to a high state of perfection. The parts are always in motion, and pauses appear infrequently; when they do occur, they are very short. In his handling of dissonance he may be regarded as a forerunner of Palestrina. His secular works, of which the earliest known printed examples (9 4-part chansons) are included in Attaignant's collection of 1529–49, are characterized by a refreshing simplicity and directness. Gombert's greatest contributions to the development of 16th-century music lay in his recognizing the peculiarities of Netherlandish polyphony and his developing and spreading it abroad. He wrote 11 masses, over 160 motets, and 70 chansons, many of which appeared in contemporary (mostly Spanish) lute and guitar arrangements, a fact which shows the great vogue they had. Reprints have been publ. by F. Commer in Collectio Operum Musicorum Batavorum (1839—), VIII (one motet), and XII (2 chansons); A. Reissmann in *Allgemeine Geschichte der Musik* (1863; one chanson); R.J. v. Maldeghem in Trésor Musical (1865—), II (one motet), XI (3 chansons), XII (one motet), XIV (5 chansons), XVI (one motet of doubtful authorship), XVII (one chanson), XX (2 motets); R. Eitner in Publikationen Älterer Praktischer ... Musikwerke, III (1875; 2 chansons); A.W. Ambros in *Geschichte der Musik*, V (3rd ed., 1911; one motet, revised by O. Kade); E.H. Wooldridge in *The Oxford History of Music*, II (1905; one motet); Th. Kroyer in *Der vollkommene Partiturspieler* (1930; 10 Magnificat selections); A. Schering in *Geschichte der Musik in Beispielen* (1931; no. 102, portion of the Mass *Media vita*); a motet is in Attaignant's *Treize livres de motets* (Book I, pp. 167–75), reprinted by the Lyrebird Press (Paris, 1934). Gombert's *Opera omnia*, edited by J. Schmidt-Görg, was publ. in Corpus Mensurabilis Musicae, VI/1–11 (1951–75). BIBLIOGRAPHY: D. von Bartha, "Probleme der Chansongeschichte im 16. Jahrhundert," *Zeitschrift für Musikwissenschaft* (Aug.–Sept. 1931); H. Eppstein, *Nicolas Gombert als Motettenkomponist* (Würzburg, 1935); J. Schmidt-Görg, "Die acht Magnifikat des Nicolas Gombert," *Gesammelte Aufsätze zur Kulturgeschichte Spaniens,* V (1935; contains a *Magnificat secundi toni* and selections from other Magnificats); J. Schmidt-Görg, *Nicolas Gombert, Leben und Werk* (Bonn, 1938; contains bibliography of works, musical examples, etc.); C.A. Miller, "Jerome Cardan on Gombert, Phinot, and Carpentras," *Musical Quarterly* (July 1972).

Gombosi, Otto, eminent Hungarian musicologist; b. Budapest, Oct. 23, 1902; d. Natick, Mass., Feb. 17, 1955. He studied at the Academy of Music in Budapest; then at the Univ. of Berlin, where he received his Ph.D. in 1925 with the dissertation *Jakob Obrecht: Eine stilkritische Studie* (publ. in Leipzig, 1925); in 1926–28 he edited the progressive Hungarian music periodical *Crescendo.* In 1940 he came to the U.S.; was a lecturer in music at the Univ. of Washington, Seattle (1940–46); then taught at Michigan State College and at the Univ. of Chicago (1949–51); in 1951, was appointed prof. at Harvard Univ. He contributed numerous valuable papers to various periodicals, in Hungarian, German, Italian, and Eng.; among his most important writings are *Jakob Obrecht* (Leipzig, 1925); *Tonarten und Stimmungen der antiken Musik* (Copenhagen, 1939); a treatise on V. Bakfark in *Musicologia Hungarica* (Budapest, 1935; contains Bakfark's 10 fantasias); "Studien zur Tonartenlehre des frühen Mittelalters," *Acta Musicologica* (1938–39). He contributed the chapter on Hungarian music to G. Reese's *Music in the Renaissance* (N.Y., 1954).

Gomes, Antonio Carlos, Brazilian composer; b. (of Portuguese parents) Campinas, Brazil, July 11, 1836; d. Pará (Belém), Sept. 16, 1896. He was a pupil of his father, then of the Cons. in Rio de Janeiro, where he produced 2 operas, *Noite do Castello* (1861) and *Joanna de Flandres* (1863). The success of these works induced Emperor Don Pedro II to grant him a stipend for further study in Milan; there he soon made his mark with a humorous little piece entitled *Se sa minga* (a song from this work, *Del fucile ad ago,* became popular), produced in 1867. After another piece in the same vein (*Nella Luna,* 1868), he made a more serious bid for fame with the opera *Il Guarany,* produced at La Scala on March 19, 1870, with brilliant success; this work, in which Amazon-Indian themes are used, quickly went the round of Italy, and was given in London (Covent Garden) on July 13, 1872. Returning to Rio de Janeiro, Gomes brought out a very popular operetta, *Telegrapho elettrico.* His other operas are *Fosca* (La Scala, Milan, Feb. 16, 1873), *Salvator Rosa* (Genoa, March 21, 1874), *Maria Tudor* (La Scala, Milan, March 27, 1879), *Lo Schiavo* (Rio de Janeiro, Sept. 27, 1889), and *Condor* (La Scala, Milan, Feb. 21, 1891). He wrote the hymn *Il saluto del Brasile* for the centenary of American independence (1876); also the cantata *Colombo,* for the Columbus Festival in 1892. In 1895 he was appointed director of the newly founded Cons. at Pará, but he died soon after arriving there. Besides his operas, he composed songs (3 books), choruses, and piano pieces. BIBLIOGRAPHY: S. Boccanera Júnior, *Um artista brasileiro: In memoriam* (Bahia, 1904); H.P. Vieira, *Carlos Gomes: Sua arte e sua obra* (São Paulo, 1934); I. Gomes Vaz de Carvalho, *A vida de Carlos Gomes* (Rio de Janeiro, 1935; Italian trans., Milan, 1935); R. Seidl, *Carlos Gomes, Brasileiro e patriota* (Rio de Janeiro, 1935); L.F. Vieira Souto, *Antonio Carlos Gomes* (Rio de Janeiro, 1936; centenary issue of *Revista Brasileira de Musica* (1936); J. Prito, *Carlos Gomes* (São Paulo, 1936); R. Almeida, *Carlos Gomes* (Rio de Janeiro, 1937); M. de Andrade, *Car-*

los Gomes (Rio de Janeiro, 1939); P. Cerquera, *Carlos Gomes* (São Paulo, 1944).

Gomes de Araújo, João, Brazilian composer; b. Pindamonhangaba, Aug. 5, 1846; d. São Paulo, Sept. 8, 1942. He studied at São Paulo and Milan; in 1905, became a teacher at the São Paulo Cons., and remained there almost to the end of his long life.

WORKS: 4 operas: *Edmea; Carminosa* (Milan, 1888); *Maria Petrowna* (1904; São Paulo, 1929); *Helena* (São Paulo, 1910); also 6 symphs., 6 masses, and vocal and instrumental works.

Gómez, Calleja. See **Calleja, Gómez Rafael.**

Gomez, Jill, English soprano; b. New Amsterdam, British Guiana, Sept. 21, 1942. She studied at the Royal Academy of Music in London, and also at the Guildhall School of Music; made her debut in 1967 in a Cambridge Univ. opera production; in 1968 she appeared with the Glyndebourne Touring Opera; then sang at Covent Garden (1970). Her other engagements were with the English Opera Group, the Aldeburgh Festival, the Scottish Opera, and the Welsh National Opera.

Gómez, Julio, Spanish composer and musicologist; b. Madrid, Dec. 20, 1886; d. there, Dec. 22, 1973. He studied at the Madrid Cons. In 1911 he became director of the Archeological Museum in Toledo; later head of the music division of the National Library in Madrid, and librarian of the Cons. there. He wrote the comic opera *El Pelele* (1925); also piano pieces; songs.

Gomezanda, Antonio, Mexican pianist and composer; b. Lagos, Jalisco, Sept. 3, 1894. He studied piano with Manuel M. Ponce; then went to Germany, where he took lessons in composition and conducting in Berlin. Returning to Mexico, he taught piano at the National Cons. (1921–29) and at the Univ. of Mexico (1929–32). Among his works are an "Aztec ballet," *Xiuhtzitzquilo,* which was produced in Berlin on Feb. 19, 1928; *Fantasia mexicana* for Piano and Orch. (1923); piano pieces; songs.

Gomez Martínez, Miguel, Spanish conductor; b. Granada, Sept. 17, 1949. He studied piano with his mother; then enrolled at the Granada Cons.; also studied composition, piano, and violin at the Madrid Cons.; later he attended the conducting classes of Sir Adrian Boult and Erich Leinsdorf at Tanglewood; then studied with Igor Markevitch in Madrid and Hans Swarowsky in Vienna. He was music director of the St. Pölten Stadttheater (1971–72) and principal conductor of the Lucerne Stadttheater (1972–74); in 1973 he conducted at the Deutsche Oper in Berlin; was subsequently named its resident conductor (1974–77). In 1976 he was made resident conductor at the Vienna State Opera; also conducted in Berlin, Munich, Hamburg, London (at Covent Garden), Geneva, and Paris; in 1980 he made his U.S. debut, conducting at the Houston Grand

Opera.

Gomólka, Michal, Polish musician, son of **Mikolaj Gomólka;** b. Sandomierz, 1564; d. Jazlowiec, March 9, 1609. He was active as a band conductor at various palaces of Polish noblemen; little is known of his life, except that he enjoyed the favor of Polish aristocratic society.

Gomólka, Mikolaj (Nicolas), Polish composer; b. Sandomierz, c.1535; date of death unknown. He was a chorister at Cracow (1545), and then played trumpet and flute in the court orch. In 1566 he returned to his native town, where he married and served as a judge. His chief work was *Melodiae na psalterz polski* (Cracow, 1580), containing 150 melodies to words from the Psalms trans. by the poet Jan Kochanowski; a new edition was publ. by J.W. Reiss in 1923; several pieces are included in the anthology by Jachimecki and Lissa, *Music of the Polish Renaissance* (Warsaw, 1954).

BIBLIOGRAPHY: J.W. Reiss, *Melodye psalmowe M. Gomolki* (Cracow, 1912); A. Chybinski, *Slownik muzykow dawnej polski* (Cracow, 1949); M. Perez, *Mikolaj Gomólka* (Warsaw, 1969).

Gondimel, Claude. See **Goudimel, Claude.**

Gönnenwein, Wolfgang, German conductor; b. Schwäbisch-Hall, Jan. 29, 1933. He studied music in Stuttgart; in 1959 became conductor of the South German Madrigal Choir; in 1973 he became director of the Hochschule für Musik und darstellende Kunst in Stuttgart. He is best known as a conductor of the choral works of Bach, Haydn, and Mozart.

González-Avila, Jorge, Mexican composer; b. Mérida, Yucatán, Dec. 10, 1925. In 1949 he moved to Mexico City; studied composition with Rodolfo Halffter, harmony with Blas Galindo, piano with Francisco Agea Hermosa, and theory with Hernández Moncada at the National Cons. (1949–53); had a course in musical orientation with Jesús Bal y Gay in 1952, and a year later a similar course with Chávez at the National College. He devoted himself to teaching; in 1972 was appointed director of the Audiotranscription Division of the Centro Nacional de Investigación, Documentación y Información Musical (CENIDIM) of the National Inst. of Fine Arts in Mexico City. He wrote an impressive quantity of piano pieces, and other instrumental music.

WORKS: *3 Inventions* for Solo Violin (1955); *Impromptus* for String Quartet (1960); *Invention* for Soprano, Piano, and Orch. (1964); *Invention interpolar* for Piano and Orch. (1974); 2 sonata trios for Flute, Cello, and Piano (1965, 1977); Solo Violin Sonata (1966); Suite for Solo Guitar (1968); *2 Interludes* for Violin and Piano (1968); *Recitativo* for Violin and Piano (1969); *Inventions quasi Fantasia* for Viola and Piano (1970); *Invention concertante No. 1* for Piano and Orch. (1973); *Impromptu* for Solo Viola (1974); *2 Preludes* for Horn and Piano

(1974); *Invention* for Tuba and Piano (1974); *Fantasia* for Organ (1974); *Invention* for English Horn, Piano, and Orch. (1975); *Prelude and Invention* for String Orch. (1976); Violin Sonata (1977); Duo for Viola and Piano (1977). For Piano: 17 sonatas; 2 sonatinas (1975, 1976); 20 suites (1953–75); 7 partitas (1953–73); 14 fantasias (1956–75); 8 studies (1959–76); 12 impromptus (1960–75); 16 preludes in 3 sets (1969–73); 2 *Symphonic Studies* (1970); 2 ballets (1973, 1975); 8 *Preludes and Inventions* (1974); 5 *Bagatelles* (1975); *24 Inventions* (1959); *5 Variation Studies* (1960); *77 Miniature Studies* (1973); *Prelude and Invention* for 2 Pianos (1975); 2-piano Sonata (1977).

González-Zuleta, Fabio, Colombian composer; b. Bogotá, Nov. 2, 1920. He studied organ and composition at the Bogotá Cons.; after graduation became a member of its faculty; in 1957–72 was its director.
WORKS: Symph. No. 1 (1956); Violin Concerto (1958); Symph. No. 2 (1959); Piano Trio (1955); Trio for Flute, Violin, and Viola (1955); Suite for Wind Quintet (1956); Clarinet Sonata (1958); *Quintetto abstracto* for Wind Instruments (1960); Sonata for Double Bass and Piano (1960).

Goodall, Reginald, English conductor; b. Lincoln, July 13, 1901. He studied piano with Arthur Benjamin and violin with W.H. Reed at the Royal College of Music in London; from 1936 to 1939 was assistant conductor at Covent Garden; then went to Germany, and was engaged as an assistant to Furtwängler at the Berlin Phil.; also led many operatic performances. He is regarded as a foremost interpreter of Wagner's music dramas; in 1973 he conducted the entire cycle of the *Ring of the Nibelung* at Sadler's Wells Opera in London. In 1975 he was made a Commander of the Order of the British Empire.

Goode, Richard, American pianist; b. New York, June 1, 1943. He studied at the Mannes College of Music with Nadia Reisenberg and at the Curtis Inst. of Music with Rudolf Serkin; then made his debut in N.Y. in 1961; subsequently appeared extensively as a chamber music artist. In 1973 he won the Clara Haskil International Competition.

Goodman (real name, **Guttmann**), **Alfred,** German-American composer; b. Berlin, March 1, 1920. He studied at the Berlin Cons.; in 1939 went to England, and in 1940 settled in America; was in the U.S. Army during World War II. In 1946 he was an arranger with several dance bands; at the same time he studied with Henry Cowell and Otto Luening at Columbia Univ., receiving his B.S. in 1952 and his M.A. in 1953. In 1960 he returned to Germany; was active as a composer and broadcaster with Bavarian Radio in Munich; from 1971 was its music adviser. He received his Ph.D. from the Free Univ. of Berlin in 1973; in 1976 was appointed to the faculty of the Hochschule für Musik in Munich.
WORKS: *The Audition,* one-act opera (Athens, Ohio, July 27, 1954); 2 symphs.; choral and chamber music. He publ. a music lexicon, *Musik von A–Z*

(Munich, 1971).

Goodman, Benny (Benjamin David), American clarinetist and jazz-band leader; b. Chicago, May 30, 1909. He acquired a taste for syncopated music as a child by listening to phonographic recordings of ragtime; was playing professionally by the age of 12 (1921), and in 1926 was working with Ben Pollack, one of the leading Chicago jazz musicians of the period. In 1928 he went to N.Y. as a clarinetist in various bands. In 1934 he formed his own band, which became known nationwide from its weekly appearances on the "Let's Dance" radio program. Both as the leader of a large dance band and for his virtuoso performances in various jazz combos, Goodman was the best-known and most successful musician of the swing era; was called the King of Swing. He also played clarinet parts in classical works in concert and for records, appearing as soloist in Mozart's Clarinet Concerto with the N.Y. Phil. (Dec. 12, 1940), and recording works by Copland, Bartók, Stravinsky, Morton Gould, and Leonard Bernstein. His autobiography, *The Kingdom of Swing,* was publ. in 1939; a biographical movie, *The Benny Goodman Story,* was made in 1955.

Goodrich, Alfred John, American music pedagogue; b. Chilo, Ohio, May 8, 1848; d. Paris, April 25, 1920. A self-taught musician, he became a teacher of theory at the Grand Cons., N.Y.; the Fort Wayne Cons. (Ind.); director of the vocal dept. at the Beethoven Cons., St. Louis; member of the music dept., Martha Washington College, Abingdon, Va.; later lived in Chicago, Paris, and St. Louis as a writer and teacher.
WRITINGS: *Music as a Language* (1880); *The Art of Song* (1888); *Complete Musical Analysis* (1889); *Analytical Harmony* (1894); *Theory of Interpretation* (1898; publ. by subscription); *Guide to Memorizing Music* (1904; revised ed., 1906); *Synthetic Counterpoint* (in MS).

Goodrich, (John) Wallace, American organist, conductor, and writer on music; b. Newton, Mass., May 27, 1871; d. Boston, June 6, 1952. He studied at the New England Cons. in Boston (organ with Dunham, composition with Chadwick); then in Munich with Rheinberger (1894–95) and with Widor in Paris. In 1896–97, he was coach at the Leipzig Municipal Theater. In 1897 he returned to Boston and became an instructor at the New England Cons.; he was appointed dean in 1907, and in 1931 director, a post he held until 1942. He was organist of Trinity Church in 1902–9, and for the Boston Symph. Orch. from 1897 to 1909. He founded the Choral Art Society in 1902 and was its conductor until 1907; he was also, at various periods, conductor of the Cecilia Society, the Boston Opera Co., and the Worcester County Choral Assoc. He composed an *Ave Maria* for Chorus and Orch. (Munich, 1895) and other choral music; wrote *The Organ in France* (Boston, 1917); trans. A. Pirro's *J.S. Bach and His Works for the Organ* (1902) and d'Ortigue's *Méthode d'accompagnement du plain-chant* (1905).

Goodson, Katharine, English pianist; b. Watford, Hertfordshire, June 18, 1872; d. London, April 14, 1958. In 1886–92 she was a pupil of O. Beringer at the Royal Academy of Music, and in 1892–96 of Leschetizky in Vienna; made her debut in London at a Saturday Popular Concert, Jan. 16, 1897, with signal success; then made tours of England, France, Austria, and Germany, which established her reputation; her American debut, with the Boston Symph., took place on Jan. 18, 1907; she subsequently made many tours of the U.S., and of the Netherlands, Belgium, and Italy. In 1903 she married the English composer **Arthur Hinton.**

Goossens, Sir Eugene, outstanding English conductor and composer; b. London, May 26, 1893; d. there, June 13, 1962. A scion of a family of musicians of Belgian extraction, he was educated at the Bruges Cons. (1903); returning to England in 1904, he subsequently studied at the Liverpool College of Music (1906); then won a Liverpool scholarship to the Royal College of Music in London (1907); studied violin with Rivarde, piano with Dykes, and composition with Charles Wood and Stanford; won the silver medal of the Worshipful Company of Musicians; in 1912–15 played the violin in the Queen's Hall Orch. He was associated with Sir Thomas Beecham's operatic enterprises (1915–20); conducted a season of concerts with his own orch. in London (1921). In 1923 he was engaged as conductor of the Rochester (N.Y.) Phil. Orch.; in 1931 he was appointed conductor of the Cincinnati Symph. Orch., remaining at that post until 1946. From 1947 to 1956 he was director of the New South Wales Cons. of Music at Sydney and conductor of the Sydney Symph. Orch.; he was knighted in 1955. Goossens belonged to a group of English composers who cultivated exotic themes with modernistic harmonies stemming from Debussy. He conducted his first orch. piece, *Variations on a Chinese Theme,* at the age of 19 at the Royal College of Music in London (June 20, 1912); continued to write prolifically in all genres (opera, ballet, symph., chamber music); his mature style became a blend of impressionistic harmonies and neo-Classical polyphony; while retaining a clear tonal outline, Goossens often resorted to expressive chromatic melos bordering on atonality. WORKS: *Variations on a Chinese Theme* for Orch. (1911); *Miniature Fantasy* for String Orch. (1911); Suite for Flute, Violin, and Harp (1914); *5 Impressions of a Holiday* for Flute, Cello, and Piano (1914); symph. poem, *Perseus* (1914); symph. prelude, *Ossian* (1915); *Phantasy Quartet* for Strings (1915); String Quartet No. 1 (1916); 2 sketches for String Quartet: *By the Tarn* and *Jack o' Lantern* (1916); *Kaleidoscope,* suite of piano pieces in a humorous vein (1917–18); Violin Sonata No. 1 (1918); Prelude to Verhaeren's *Philip II* (1918); *The Eternal Rhythm* for Orch. (London, Oct. 19, 1920); *4 Conceits* for Piano (1918); Piano Quintet (1919); *Lyric Poem* for Violin and Piano (1921; also arranged for Violin and Orch.); ballet, *L'Ecole en crinoline* (1921); *Silence* for Chorus and Piano (1922); incidental music to W. Somerset Maugham's

East of Suez (1922); *Sinfonietta* (London, Feb. 19, 1923); String Sextet (1923); *Pastoral and Harlequinade* for Flute, Oboe, and Piano (1924); Fantasy for Wind Instruments (1924); opera, *Judith* (1925; Covent Garden, June 25, 1929); *Rhythmic Dance* for Orch. (Rochester, March 12, 1927); Concertino for Double String Orch. (1928); Oboe Concerto (London, Oct. 2, 1930; Leon Goossens, soloist); Violin Sonata No. 2 (1930); opera, *Don Juan de Mañara* (1934; Covent Garden, June 24, 1937); Symph. No. 1 (Cincinnati, April 12, 1940); 2nd String Quartet (1942); *Phantasy-Concerto* for Piano and Orch. (Cincinnati, Feb. 25, 1944, composer conducting; Iturbi, soloist); 2nd Symph. (BBC, Nov. 10, 1946); oratorio, *Apocalypse* (1951; Sydney, Nov. 22, 1954, composer conducting). Goossens is the author of *Overture and Beginners; A Musical Autobiography* (London, 1951).

Goossens, Leon, distinguished English oboist, brother of **Sir Eugene Goossens;** b. Liverpool, June 12, 1897. He studied at the Royal College of Music in London (1911–14); then joined the Queen's Hall Orch. (1914–24); subsequently played in the Covent Garden orch., in the Royal Phil. Society's orch., and in the London Phil. (1932–39). From 1924 to 1939 he taught oboe at the Royal College of Music. He commissioned works for oboe to several English composers, among them Elgar and Vaughan Williams. In 1950 he was made a Commander of the Order of the British Empire.

Goovaerts, Alphonse Jean Marie André, Belgian musicologist; b. Antwerp, May 25, 1847; d. Brussels, Dec. 25, 1922. He was a member of a literary family; as a youth he became greatly interested in Flemish literature and in church music. He arranged and publ. a collection of Flemish songs (1868–74); composed several pieces of church music, and performed them with a chorus he established in Antwerp; also made transcriptions for chorus of works by Palestrina and Flemish contrapuntists. He publ. several papers propounding a reform in church music, which aroused opposition from conservative circles (*La Musique de l'église,* 1876; in Flemish as *De kerkmuziek*); also publ. a valuable book, *Histoire et bibliographie de la typographie musicale dans le Pays-Bas* (1880; awarded the gold medal of the Belgian Academy); a monograph on the Belgian music printer Pierre Phalèse; and other studies relating to Flemish music.

Gorchakov, Sergei (real surname, **Zweifel**), Soviet composer and arranger; b. Moscow, Feb. 10, 1905; d. there, July 4, 1976. He studied conducting with Saradzhev at the Moscow Cons., graduating in 1929. From 1939 to 1952 he conducted the orch. of the All-Union Soviet Radio; from 1960 he taught orchestration at the Inst. of Military Band Conducting. He became particularly interested in the problem of orch. arrangements; in 1959 submitted a dissertation, *Specific Problems of Transcribing Piano Music for Wind Orchestra,* for which he received the degree of candidate of arts and sciences. He also publ. *Practical Manual of Orchestration for Wind Orchestra* (Moscow, 1962). He made numerous orch. arrangements of piano music; of these, particularly notable is his orchestration of Mussorgsky's *Pictures at an Exhibition,* which enjoyed a number of performances in Russia and abroad.

Gorczycki, Gregor Gervasius, Polish composer; b. Bytom, Silesia, c.1667; d. Cracow, April 30, 1734. He was a student of theology at the Univ. of Vienna, then at Prague Univ.; was ordained a priest in Cracow in 1692; became chapel master at the Cracow Cathedral in 1698, retaining this position until his death. He was the composer of many excellent motets, hymns, Psalms, and masses in a polyphonic style, a cappella and with instrumental accompaniment, to Latin texts; several of them were reprinted in the Polish collections edited by Cichocki, Surzynski, Sowinski, and Chybinski.

BIBLIOGRAPHY: A. Chybinski, *G.G. Gorczycki* (Posen, 1927); see Chybinski's *Slownik muzykow dawnej polski* (Cracow, 1949) for a complete list of eds. of Gorczycki's sacred works.

Gordeli, Otar, Georgian composer; b. Tiflis, Nov. 18, 1928. He studied composition with Andrei Balanchivadze; later took courses at the Moscow Cons., graduating in 1955. In 1959 he was appointed instructor at the Cons. of Tiflis. In his music he applies resources of native folk songs; his polyphonic structure is considerably advanced.

WORKS: Piano Concerto (1952); cantata, *The Seasons,* for Narrator, Boys' Chorus and Chamber Orch. (1955); Concertino for Flute and Orch. (1958); *Festive Overture* (1959); *Georgian Dance* for Orch. (1961); film music; jazz pieces.

Gordigiani, Luigi, Italian composer; b. Florence, June 21, 1806; d. Modena, May 1, 1860. He is chiefly known for his more than 300 songs for voice and piano; these *canzonette* and *canti populari* were based on Italian folk tunes; Gordigiani wrote the words for many himself. He also publ. a collection of songs based on Tuscan folk poems. Ricordi has publ. 67 songs in 2 vols. in the series Canti Popolari Italiani. Other works by Gordigiani include 10 operas, 3 cantatas, a ballet, and an oratorio.

Gordon, Dexter, black American jazz tenor saxophonist; b. Los Angeles, Feb. 27, 1923. He studied clarinet; took up the alto saxophone at the age of 13; then turned to the tenor saxophone and soon began to play in a local band. He worked with Lionel Hampton (1940–43) and Louis Armstrong (1944); then went to N.Y., where he played in Billy Eckstine's band; after returning to Los Angeles, he appeared with Wardell Gray. In 1962 he moved to Copenhagen, and continued his career in Europe. He is generally acknowledged as a fine tenor saxophonist of the bop period.

Gordon, Gavin Muspratt, Scottish singer and composer; b. Ayr, Nov. 24, 1901; d. London, Nov. 18, 1970. He studied at the Royal College of Music with Vaughan Williams; later was active as a singer, film actor, and composer. He wrote several ballets: *A Toothsome Morsel* (1930); *Regatta* (1931); *The Scorpions of Ysit* (1932); *The Rake's Progress* (London, Sadler's Wells, May 20, 1935).

Gordon, Jacques, Russian violinist; b. Odessa, March 7, 1899; d. Hartford, Conn., Sept. 15, 1948. He studied at the Odessa Cons.; went to the U.S., and took courses at the Inst. of Musical Art, N.Y., with Kneisel (violin) and Goetschius (theory). From 1918 to 1921 he was a member of the Berkshire String Quartet; in 1921, founded the Gordon String Quartet. In 1921–30 he was concertmaster of the Chicago Symph. Orch., and a violin teacher at the American Cons. in Chicago. He publ. some arrangements for violin.

Gordon, James Carel Gerhard, flute maker; b. Cape Town, May 22, 1791; d. (insane) Lausanne, c.1845. He was born of a Dutch captain and a Swiss mother in South Africa. He joined the Swiss Guards of Charles X in Paris in 1814; concurrently, studied flute with Tulou; worked on improvements of its mechanism more or less at the same time as Böhm, so that the priority of the invention became a matter of insoluble controversy. He escaped with his life during the attack on the Swiss Guards in the Revolution of 1830; was pensioned and retired to Switzerland when his mind became deranged.

BIBLIOGRAPHY: C. Welch, *History of the Boehm Flute* (London, 1896); Percival R. Kirby, "Captain Gordon, The Flute Maker," *Music & Letters* (July 1957).

Gordy, Berry Jr., significant black American record producer, creator of the Motown sound (so named after the Motor Town, that is, Detroit); b. Detroit, Nov. 28, 1929. He trained as a featherweight boxer; then was drafted into the U.S. Army; after discharge, he worked on the assembly line for Ford, and began writing songs. However, his significance in popular American music was connected not with songwriting but with his recording enterprise. He attracted a number of talented groups, composers, and singers to record for Motown, among them Smokey Robinson and The Miracles, Mary Wells, Martha and The Vandellas, The Supremes, Jr. Walker and The All Stars, Gladys Knight and The Pips, Diana Ross, Marvin Gaye, The O Jays, Stevie Wonder, and The Jackson Five. He contributed to the final desegregation of the so-called "race music" and its integration into the mainstream of American popular music, which included rhythm-and-blues, soul-and-gospel, and semi-classical pop.

Górecki, Henryk Mikolaj, significant Polish composer; b. Czernica, Dec. 6, 1933. He studied composition with Boleslaw Szabelski at the Cons. of Katowice (1955–60); in 1968 was appointed to its faculty. In his music he makes use of the entire arsenal of modern techniques while preserving traditional formal design.

WORKS: *Toccata* for 2 Pianos (1955); Piano Sonata (1956); *Pieśń o radości i rytmie (Song of Joy and Rhythm)* for Orch. (1956); Sonata for 2 Violins (1957); Concerto for 5 Instruments and String Quartet (1957); *Epitaph* for Chorus and Instrumental Ensemble (1958); *5 Pieces* for 2 Pianos (1959); Symph. No. 1 for String Orch. and Percussion (1959); *3 Diagrams* for Solo Flute (1959); *Monologhi* for Soprano and 3 Instrumental Groups (1960); *Zderzenia (Collisions)* for Orch. (1960); *Genesis,* cycle of 3 works: *Elementi* for String Trio (1962), *Canti strumentali* for 15 Performers (1962), and *Monodram* for Soprano, Metal Percussion, and 6 Double Basses (1963); *Chôros I* for 56 Strings (1964); *Refren (Refrain)* for Orch. (1965); *La Musiquette I* for 2 Trumpets and Guitar (1967), *II* for Brass and Percussion (1967), *III* for Violas (1969), and *IV* for Clarinet, Trombone, Cello, and Piano (1970); *Muzyka staropolska (Old Polish Music),* 3 pieces for Orch. (Warsaw, Sept. 24, 1969); Symph. No. 2, *Copernican Symphony,* for Soprano, Baritone, Chorus, and Orch. (Warsaw, June 22, 1973); *Amen* for Chorus a cappella (1975).

Gorin, Igor, Russian baritone; b. Grodek, Ukraine, Oct. 26, 1908; d. Tucson, Ariz., March 24, 1982. His family moved to Vienna after the Russian Revolution; there he studied medicine and music; entered the Vienna Cons., graduating in 1930; made his professional operatic debut at the Vienna Volksoper in 1930. In 1933 he came to the U.S.; became an American citizen in 1939. He launched a successful career as a radio singer, without forsaking his operatic ambitions. He made his debut at the Metropolitan Opera in N.Y. as Germont *père* in *La Traviata* (Feb. 10, 1964). In 1959 he toured Australia and New Zealand. In his last years of life he taught voice at the Univ. of Arizona in Tucson.

Gorini, Gino, Italian composer and pianist; b. Venice, June 22, 1914. He studied there at the Cons. Benedetto Marcello; received diplomas in piano (1931) and composition (1933); later studied composition with Malipiero; in 1940 was appointed prof. of piano at the Venice Cons.; made many tours in Italy and abroad, including 2-piano team tours in Italy with Sergio Lorenzi.
WORKS: *3 omaggi* for Orch. (1933); suite for Piano and Orch. (1934); Violin Concerto (1934); Symph. (1935); *Introduction and Arioso* for Orch. (1937); *Concertino* for 7 Instruments (1933); *Contrasti* for 5 Instruments (1933); Divertimento for Chamber Orch. (1935); Piano Sonata (1936); String Quartet (1936); Cello Sonata (1939); Quintet for Piano and Strings (1939); Piano Concerto (1948; Rome, March 16, 1952); *5 studi* for 2 Pianos, Strings, and Timpani (1960); *Serenata* for String Orch., Harpsichord or Piano, and Timpani (1966); Concerto for Viola, Orch., and Piano (1968).

Goritz, Otto, German dramatic baritone; b. Berlin, June 8, 1873; d. Hamburg, April 11, 1929. He received his entire musical education from his mother, Olga Nielitz; made his debut, Oct. 1, 1895, as Matteo (*Fra Diavolo*) at Neustrelitz; his success led to an immediate engagement for 3 years; from 1898 to 1900 he was at the Stadttheater in Breslau; from 1900 to 1903, at the Stadttheater in Hamburg. On Dec. 24, 1903, he made his American debut at the Metropolitan Opera as Klingsor in the first production of *Parsifal* outside Bayreuth; remained there until 1917. In 1924 he returned to Germany, where he sang in opera in Berlin and Hamburg.

Gorme, Eydie, American singer of popular music; b. New York, Aug. 16, 1932. She began her professional career as a vocalist with the bands of Tommy Tucker and Tex Beneke; also sang with the orch. of Ray Eberle; then began a solo career as a singer in nightclubs and on radio and television. In 1957 she married the singer **Steve Lawrence.**

Gorney, Jay, American composer; b. Bialystok, Poland, Dec. 12, 1896. He emigrated to the U.S. as a child; studied music at the Univ. of Michigan. Beginning in 1924 he wrote a number of scores and separate songs for Broadway. In 1933 he went to Hollywood. He composed the celebrated song *Brother, Can You Spare a Dime?,* which became a musical symbol of the Depression era.

Gorno, Albino, pianist and composer; b. Casalmorano (Cremona), March 10, 1859; d. Cincinnati, Oct. 29, 1945. He studied at the Milan Cons., where he took 3 gold medals, and where his opera, *Cuore e Patria,* was produced. He was accompanist to Adelina Patti on her American tour (1881–82); stayed in the U.S., and became head of the piano dept. and dean of the faculty at the Cincinnati College of Music. He wrote a cantata, many pieces for piano, and songs.

Gorno, Romeo, pianist and teacher, brother of **Albino Gorno;** b. Cremona, Italy, Jan. 1, 1870; d. Cincinnati, Nov. 28, 1931. He studied in Milan with his father; later was a pupil at the Cons. there; then went to the U.S. and joined his brother as a prof. of piano at the Cincinnati College of Music.

Gorodnitzki, Sascha, Russian pianist; b. Kiev, May 24, 1905. He was brought to the U.S. as an infant; studied at the Inst. of Musical Art and the Juilliard Graduate School in N.Y.; appeared as a child prodigy at 9; toured the U.S. and Canada in recitals; in 1930, won the Schubert Memorial Prize; was appointed prof. of piano at the Juilliard Graduate School in 1932.

Gorr, Rita, Belgian mezzo-soprano; b. Ghent, Feb. 18, 1926. She was educated in Ghent and Brussels. After local appearances in Belgium, she sang in London and Edinburgh. On Oct. 17, 1962, she made her debut at the Metropolitan Opera in N.Y. as Amneris in *Aida.* She excelled in the Wagnerian repertoire, and made several appearances at the Bayreuth Festivals.

Gorter, Albert, German conductor and composer; b. Nuremberg, Nov. 23, 1862; d. Munich, March 14, 1936. He studied at the Royal Music School in Munich and in Italy; became assistant conductor of the Bayreuth Festivals; then conducted in various German cities until 1925, when he settled in Munich. He wrote the text and music of an opera, *Harold;* 3 comic operas: *Der Schatz des Rhampsinit* (Mannheim, 1894), *Das süsse Gift* (Cologne, 1906), and *Der Paria* (Strasbourg, March 31, 1908); 2 symph. poems; piano pieces; songs.

Gosling, John, American conductor; b. Trenton, N.J., May 18, 1928. He was educated at the Juilliard School of Music in N.Y. and at the Catholic Univ. of America; his teachers in conducting included Thor Johnson, Josef Krips, and Antal Dorati. He conducted the Monterey Symph. in Carmel, Calif. (1961–67); then was appointed conductor of the Erie (Pa.) Phil. From 1972 to 1980 he was artistic director and conductor of the North Carolina Symph. in Raleigh; under his direction the orch. played at Carnegie Hall in N.Y., the Kennedy Center in Washington, D.C., and Chicago's Orch. Hall.

Goss, Sir John, English organist and composer; b. Fareham, Hampshire, Dec. 27, 1800; d. London, May 10, 1880. A son of **Joseph Goss,** the Fareham organist, he became a child chorister of the Chapel Royal; then studied under Attwood. He was successively organist of Stockwell Chapel (1821), St. Luke's, Chelsea (1824), and St. Paul's Cathedral (1838–72). In 1856 he was appointed a composer to the Chapel Royal; he was knighted in 1872, and received the degree of Mus.Doc. from Cambridge Univ. in 1876. His music includes church services, anthems, chants, Psalms, etc.; some orch. pieces; songs and glees. He edited a collection of hymns, *Parochial Psalmody* (1827); *Chants, Ancient and Modern* (1841); *Church Psalter and Hymnbook* (1856; with Rev. W. Mercer). He publ. *The Organist's Companion,* 4 vols. of voluntaries and interludes, and *An Introduction to Harmony and Thorough-bass* (1833; many eds.).
BIBLIOGRAPHY: D. Gedge, "John Goss, 1800–1880," *Musical Times* (May and July 1980).

Goss, John, English baritone; b. London, May 10, 1894; d. Birmingham, Feb. 13, 1953. He began to study music relatively late in life, and was active as a singer and a music editor. He gave a number of successful recitals in England and America, in variegated programs of unusual old and new songs. He edited an *Anthology of Song* (London, 1928) and a collection, *Ballads of Britain* (London, 1937); also publ. a novel, *Cockroaches and Diamonds* (1937).

Gossec, François-Joseph, significant Belgian composer; b. Vergnies, Jan. 17, 1734; d. Paris, Feb. 16, 1829. He showed musical inclinations at an early age; as a child, studied at the collegiate church in Walcourt and sang in the chapel of St. Aldegonde in Mauberge; then joined the chapel of St. Pierre there, where he studied violin, harpsichord, harmo-

ny, and composition with Jean Vanderbelen; in 1742 was engaged as a chorister at the Cathedral of Notre Dame in Antwerp; received some instruction with André-Joseph Blavier in violin and organ playing there. In 1751 he went to Paris, and in 1754 joined a private musical ensemble of the rich amateur La Pouplinière. There he wrote chamber music and little symphs., in which he seems to have anticipated Haydn; several works for string quartet followed in 1759. After the death of La Pouplinière in 1762, Gossec became a member of the retinue of the Prince de Condé at Chantilly, and continued to compose for private performances. In 1760 he wrote a Requiem; then turned his attention to stage music; produced a 3-act opéra-comique, *Le Faux Lord* (Paris, June 27, 1765); obtained a decisive success with another short opéra-comique, *Les Pêcheurs* (April 23, 1766); there followed the operas (perf. at the Comédie-Italienne and at the Paris Opéra) *Toinon et Toinette* (June 20, 1767); *Le Double Déguisement* (Sept. 28, 1767); *Sabinus* (Feb. 22, 1774); *Alexis et Daphné* (Sept. 26, 1775); *La Fête du village* (May 26, 1778); *Thésée* (March 1, 1782); *Rosine* (July 14, 1786); several other operas (*Nictocris, La Fédération,* etc.) were not performed. In 1770 he organized a performing society, Concerts des Amateurs; became a director of the Concert Spirituel (1773–77); was also an associate director of the Paris Opéra (1780–85) and manager of the Ecole Royale de Chant (1784–89); when this school became the Cons. in 1795, Gossec became one of the inspectors, and also taught composition there; he publ. a manual, *Exposition des principes de la musique,* for use at the Cons. In 1795 he became a member of the newly founded Académie des Beaux-Arts of the Institut de France. Gossec welcomed the French Revolution with great enthusiasm, and wrote many festive works to celebrate Revolutionary events, among them *L'Offrande à la Liberté* (1792); *Le Triomphe de la République* (1793); *Le Cri de vengeance* (1799); and numerous marches and hymns. During his long life he saw many changes of regime, but retained his position in the musical world and in society throughout the political upheavals. He retired to Passy, then a suburb of Paris, at the age of 80. Gossec's historic role consists in his creation of a French type of symph. composition, in which he expanded the resources of instrumentation so as to provide for dynamic contrasts; he experimented with new sonorities in instrumental and choral writing; his string quartets attained a coherence of style and symmetry of form that laid the foundation of French chamber music. In his choral works, Gossec was a bold innovator, presaging in some respects the usages of Berlioz; his *Te Deum,* written for a Revolutionary festival, is scored for 1,200 singers and 300 wind instruments; in his oratorio, *La Nativité,* he introduced an invisible chorus of angels placed behind the stage; in other works, he separated choral groups in order to produce special antiphonal effects. Among reprints of Gossec's works are a Trio, in Riemann's *Collegium musicum* (Leipzig, 1909); String Quartet, op. 15, no. 2, in *Veröffentlichungen der Musiksammlung W. Höckner* (facsimile reprint; Leipzig,

1932); 2 symphs., edited by S. Beck (N.Y., 1937); a Symph. in Sondheimer's collection *Werke aus dem 18. Jahrhundert* (Berlin, 1922–39); a Symph. for 10 Instruments, in G. Cucuël, *Etudes sur un orchestre de XVIIIᵉ siècle* (Paris, 1913); 3 works edited by Barry Brook (Paris, 1962–63): Symph. in D, op. III/6; Symph. in E-flat, op. VIII/1; Symph. Concertante (from the *Ballet de Mirza*).

BIBLIOGRAPHY: P. Hédouin, *Gossec, Sa vie et ses ouvrages* (Paris, 1852); E.G.J. Gregoir, *Notice bibliographique sur M. Gossë, dit Gossec* (Paris, 1878); F. Hellouin, *Gossec et la musique française à la fin du XVIIIᵉ siècle* (Paris, 1903); L. Dufrane, *Gossec* (Paris, 1927); F. Tonnard, *F.J. Gossec* (Brussels, 1938); J.-G. Prod'homme, *F.-J. Gossec* (Paris, 1949); Barry Brook, *La Symphonie française dans la deuxième moitié du XVIIIᵉ siècle* (3 vols., Paris, 1962); W. Thibaut, *François-Joseph Gossec, Chantre de la Révolution française* (Gilly, 1970).

Gostuski, Dragutin, Serbian composer and musicologist; b. Belgrade, Jan. 3, 1923. He studied art history at the Univ. of Belgrade (Ph.D., 1965); also took courses in composition and conducting at the Belgrade Academy of Music; subsequently was active as a music critic. In 1952 he was engaged as a member of the staff of the Musicological Inst. of the Serbian Academy of Arts and Sciences; in 1974 became its director. His works include a symph. poem, *Belgrade* (Belgrade, June 11, 1951); *Concerto accelerato* for Violin and Orch. (Belgrade, Nov. 14, 1961); a fantastic ballet, *Remis* (1955; first stage perf., Zagreb, May 15, 1963); chamber music; piano pieces; songs.

Gotovac, Jakov, noted Yugoslav composer; b. Split, Oct. 11, 1895; d. Zagreb, Oct. 16, 1982. He studied law at Zagreb Univ., and music with Antun Dobronic in Zagreb and with Joseph Marx in Vienna. In 1923 he was appointed conductor of the Croatian National Opera in Zagreb, retaining this post until 1958. He composed mostly for the theater; his instrumental music is imbued with the folkways of Croatia, enhancing the simple native materials by carefully proportioned modernistic mutations while preserving the impulsive asymmetrical patterns of the original songs. His music was often performed in Yugoslavia and at occasional Central European festivals, but rarely beyond.
WORKS: OPERAS: *Dubravka,* pastoral opera (1928); *Morana* (Brno, Nov. 29, 1930); *Ero s onoga svijeta* (*A Rogue from the World Beyond,* Zagreb, Nov. 2, 1935; also produced in German, under the title *Ero der Schelm,* in Karlsruhe, April 3, 1938); *Kamenik* (*The Quarry;* Zagreb, Dec. 17, 1946); historical music drama, *Mila Gojsalica* (Zagreb, May 18, 1952); *Stanac* (Zagreb, Dec. 6, 1959); *Dalmaro,* opera-legend (Zagreb, Dec. 20, 1964); *Petar Svačiç,* opera-oratorio (1969). FOR ORCH.: *Simfonijsko kolo,* a symph. national dance (Zagreb, Feb. 6, 1927); *Orači* (*Ploughmen,* 1937); *Pjesme i ples za Balkana* (*Balkan Song and Dance)* for String Orch. (1939); *Guslar* (*Gusla Player;* Zagreb, Oct. 7, 1940); *Bunjevačka igra* (1960); *Dalmatinsko pastirče* (*Dalmatian Shepherd)* for Recorders (1962). VOCAL MUSIC:

Anakreontske pjesme (2 Anacreontic Songs) for Baritone and Piano (1918); *Jadovanka za teletom (Elegy for a Dead Calf)* for Chorus (1924); *Koleda,* a peasant dance for Male Chorus, Wind Instruments, and Percussion (1925); *Pjesme Cežnuča (Songs of Desire)* for Mezzo-soprano and Chamber Orch. (1939); *Intima,* 5 songs for Baritone and Piano (1945); *Zvonimirova ladja (Zvonimir's Ship)* for Chorus (1952); *Gjerdam (The Necklace),* play with music (1955).

Gotthelf, Felix, German composer; b. Mönchen-Gladbach, near Düsseldorf, Oct. 3, 1857; d. Dresden, April 21, 1930. He studied music while working for his M.D. degree; became coach at the Stadttheater in Cologne in 1892; in 1893 was conductor in Kolberg; from 1893 to 1898, devoted himself to composition in Bonn; lived in Vienna from 1898 to 1920, when he settled in Dresden.

Gottlieb, Jack, American composer; b. New Rochelle, N.Y., Oct. 12, 1930. He studied with Karol Rathaus at Queens College and with Irving Fine at Brandeis Univ.; at the Berkshire Music Center in Tanglewood with Boris Blacher and Aaron Copland, and at the Univ. of Illinois with Burrill Phillips and Robert Palmer (D.M.A., 1964). He was music director of the Congregation Temple Israel in St. Louis (1970–73), and in 1973 was appointed composer-in-residence at the School of Sacred Music, Hebrew Union College, N.Y. He retired from teaching in 1977; in 1978 he formed his own publishing company.
WORKS: Quartet for 3 Clarinets and Bass Clarinet (1952); String Quartet (1954); *Twilight Crane* for Woodwind Quintet (1961); *Pieces of 7,* overture (Jacksonville, Fla., Oct. 23, 1962); Piano Sonata (1960); *Song of Loneliness,* cycle of 7 songs for Baritone and Piano (1962); *The Silent Flickers,* 12 diversions for Piano, 4-hands (1967); *4 Affirmations* for Chorus and Brass Sextet (N.Y., April 17, 1976).

Gottschalg, Alexander Wilhelm, German organist and editor; b. Mechelrode, Feb. 14, 1827; d. Weimar, May 31, 1908. He studied with G. Töpfer, and succeeded him as court organist upon his death (1870); also publ. a biography of him. Gottschalg's most important publication is the *Repertorium für die Orgel* (issued serially, from 1860), to which Liszt contributed. His memoirs of Liszt were publ. posthumously (1910).

Gottschalk, Louis Moreau, celebrated American pianist and composer; b. New Orleans, May 8, 1829; d. Rio de Janeiro, Dec. 18, 1869. He studied music as a child in New Orleans with François Letellier, organist at the St. Louis Cathedral; then studied in Paris from 1842 to 1846 (piano under Hallé and Stamaty; harmony under Maleden) and became the rage of the salons, winning praise from both Chopin and Berlioz; made his formal debut in the Salle Pleyel on April 17, 1849. He made a successful tour through France, Switzerland, and Spain in 1850–51; returned to the U.S. in 1853 for a grand tour

throughout the country, playing his own piano works and conducting his orch. works at huge festivals; his popularity was phenomenal. The impresario Max Strakosch engaged him for an even more extended tour throughout the U.S. Gottschalk died of yellow fever in Rio de Janeiro during his travels. His compositions are mostly for piano, or piano with other instruments, and are cast in both conventional Romantic idioms and in the more exotic Creole, Afro-Hispanic, and "Americanistic" patterns; about 300 works are currently known, but the existence of additional MSS is suspected.
WORKS: 4 operas: *Charles IX* (1859–60; not extant); *Isaura de Salerno* (1859; never perf.); *Amalia Warden* (1860; Act I libretto extant); *Escenas campestras* for Soprano, Tenor, Baritone, and Orch. (Havana, Feb. 17, 1860); 2 symph. poems, *La Nuit des tropiques* and *Montevideo: Grand Marcha solemne* for Orch. (dedicated to the Emperor of Brazil); *Variations on Dixie's Land; The Dying Poet; Morte!!; The Last Hope* (these last 3 being his most popular works). *The Piano Works of Louis Moreau Gottschalk* (5 vols., N.Y., 1969), ed. by V.L. Brodsky, is a collection of facsimiles of early eds.; it contains a valuable essay by Robert Offergeld. Seven additional, previously unpubl. piano pieces appear in *The Little Book of Louis Moreau Gottschalk*, ed. by Richard Jackson and Neil Ratliff (N.Y., 1976). A list of works compiled by Offergeld is publ. as *The Centennial Catalogue of the Published and Unpublished Compositions of Louis Moreau Gottschalk* (N.Y., 1970). Gottschalk's journals were trans. from French and publ. in Eng. under the title *Notes of a Pianist* (Philadelphia, 1881; reprinted, N.Y., 1964).
BIBLIOGRAPHY: O. Hensel, *Life and Letters of L.M. Gottschalk* (Boston, 1870; unreliable as to facts); L.R. Fors, *Gottschalk* (Havana, 1880); J.T. Howard, "L.M. Gottschalk," *Musical Quarterly* (Jan. 1932); C.F. Lange, "Vida y muerte de Gottschalk, *Revista de Estudios Musicales* (Mendoze, Argentina, Aug. 1950; Dec. 1950; April 1951; Aug. 1951); V. Loggins, *Where the World Ends: The Life of Louis Moreau Gottschalk* (Baton Rouge, 1958); D. Thompson, "Gottschalk in the Virgin Islands," *Yearbook for Inter-American Music Research* (1970); C.F. Lange, "Louis Moreau Gottschalk," *Boletín Interamericano de Musica* (May 1970); L. Rubin, "Louis Moreau Gottschalk and the 1860–61 Opera Season in Cuba," *Inter-American Music Bulletin* (July–Oct. 1970); J. Doyle, *Louis Moreau Gottschalk, 1829–1869: A Bibliographic Study and List of Works* (Detroit, 1893).

Gotze, Emil, German tenor; b. Leipzig, July 19, 1856; d. Charlottenburg, Sept. 28, 1901. He studied in Dresden; then was engaged at the Dresden Opera. Owing to a throat ailment, he was forced to retire temporarily in 1885, but later resumed his career in Berlin.

Götze, Johann Nikolaus Konrad, German violinist; b. Weimar, Feb. 11, 1791; d. there, Feb. 5, 1861. He studied with Kreutzer in Paris; returning to Weimar, he became music director to the Grand Duke (1826–48). He played concerts in Germany and Austria; also wrote operas (some of which he produced in Weimar) and chamber music.

Götze, Karl, German composer; b. Weimar, 1836; d. Magdeburg, Jan. 14, 1887. He was a pupil of Töpfer and Gebhardi, later of Liszt; in 1855, was chorusmaster at the Weimar opera; then theater conductor at Magdeburg, Berlin (1869), Breslau (1872), and Chemnitz (1875).
WORKS: Operas: *Die Korsen* (Weimar, 1866); *Gustav Wasa, Der Held des Nordens* (Weimar, 1868); *Judith* (Magdeburg, 1887); a symph. poem, *Eine Sommernacht;* piano pieces; songs.

Goudimel, Claude (his name was variously spelled in contemporary and later editions as **Gaudimel, Gaudiomel, Godimel, Gondimel, Goudmel, Gudmel,** etc.), celebrated French composer and theorist; b. Besançon, c.1510; killed in the St. Bartholomew massacre at Lyons, Aug. 27, 1572. In 1549 Goudimel studied at the Univ. of Paris; he publ. a book of chansons as a joint publisher with Du Chemin. He lived in Metz between 1557 and 1568; there he became a Huguenot; in 1568 he returned to Besançon, and then lived in Lyons, where he perished. It was long supposed that he lived in Rome, where he founded a school of music, but this assertion is totally lacking in foundation. It seems certain that Goudimel never visited Italy, and it is significant that none of his numerous works appeared in Roman publications. Most of his music was publ. by Du Chemin in Paris; other contemporary publishers were Adrien Le Roy and Robert Ballard, who publ. his complete Huguenot psalter in 1564 under the title *Les CL pseaumes de David, nouvellement mis en musique à quatre parties;* it was publ. in Geneva in 1565 as *Les Pseaumes mis en rime françoise par Clément Marot et Th. de Bèze, mis en musique à 4 parties;* it was reprinted in a facsimile edition in Kassel, 1935; a 1580 edition, also issued in Geneva, was republ. by H. Expert in vols. 2–4 of *Les Maîtres Musiciens de la Renaissance* (1895–97). A German trans. of the Psalms, with Goudimel's musical settings, first appeared in 1573; many reprints followed. Goudimel also composed 5 masses, publ. by Du Chemin (one, 1554) and Le Roy and Ballard (4, 1558), together with other sacred music. Two 4-part motets were included in T. Susato's *Ecclesiasticarum cantionum* (Antwerp, 1553–55). Further reprints have been edited by R.J. v. Maldeghem in *Trésor Musical,* III (1867; 12-part *Salve Regina* and 2 4-part motets) and XI (1875; 3 3-part chansons); C. Bordes in *Anthologie des maîtres religieux primitifs,* II (the mass *Le bien que j'ay*) and III (4-part motet); K. von Winterfeld, A. Ebrard, H. Bellermann, etc. (Psalms). Three masses are in H. Expert's *Monuments de la musique française au temps de la Renaissance,* IX (1928); 9 Psalms in P. Pidoux's *Collection de musique protestante* (1935). Publication of the Complete Works, under the direction of L. Dittmer and P. Pidoux (Inst. of Medieval Music), began in 1967.
BIBLIOGRAPHY: G. Becker, *Goudimel et son*

œuvre (1885); M. Brenet, *Claude Goudimel, Essai bio-bibliographique* (Besançon, 1898); H. Kling, "Les Compositeurs de la musique du Psautier Huguenot Genevois," *Rivista Musicale Italiana* (1899); J. Tiersot, *Ronsard et la musique de son temps* (1901); G.R. Woodward, "The Genevan Psalter of 1562: Set in 4-Part Harmony by Claude Goudimel in 1565," *Proceedings of the Musical Association* (London, 1918; pp. 167–89); E.H. Müller, "Claude Goudimel zum 350. Todestage," *Neue Musikalische Zeitung* (1922; pp. 375–76); C. Schneider, *La Restauration du Psautier huguenot d'après les sources de 1562 et de 1565* (Neuchâtel, 1930); G. Thibault, *Bibliographie des éditions d'Adrien Le Roy et Robert Ballard* (Paris, 1955).

Goudoever, Henri Daniel van, Dutch cellist and composer; b. Utrecht, Nov. 12, 1898; d. The Hague, March 3, 1977. He studied cello privately; then attended classes in composition with Johan Wagenaar at the Utrecht Cons. (1913–16); completed his cello studies with Charles van Isterdael in Utrecht (1916–18) and with Gérard Hekking in Paris (1918–21). He traveled in the winter of 1921–22 to the U.S., where he appeared as soloist in some of his own works with the N.Y. Phil., under Mengelberg; was then first cellist with Mengelberg with the Amsterdam Concertgebouw (1922–24); then served as Kapellmeister in Coburg, Bavaria, at the behest of the exiled King Ferdinand of Bulgaria (1924–32); subsequently conducted the Utrecht Municipal Orch. (1932–37). In 1937 he abandoned music and became a disciple of Rudolf Steiner, founder of the Anthroposophical Society; traveled as a speaker and monitor of anthroposophy until his death. He composed *La Fête bleue*, symph. poem for Cello and Orch. (1917); *Sphynx*, nocturne for Orch. (1919); pieces for cello.

Gould, Glenn Herbert, remarkably individualistic Canadian pianist; b. Toronto, Sept. 25, 1932; d. there, Oct. 4, 1982, as a result of a massive stroke. His parents were musically gifted and gladly fostered his precocious development; he began to play piano, and even compose, in his single-digit years. At the age of 10, he entered the Royal Cons. of Toronto, where he studied piano with Alberto Guerrero, organ with Frederick C. Silvester, and music theory with Leo Smith; he received his diploma as a graduate at 14, in 1946. As he began practicing with total concentration on the mechanism of the keyboard, he developed mannerisms that were to become his artistic signature. He reduced the use of the pedal to a minimum in order to avoid a harmonic haze; he cultivated "horizontality" in his piano posture, bringing his head down almost to the level of the keys. He regarded music as a linear art; this naturally led him to an intense examination of the Baroque stuctures; Bach was the subject of his close study rather than Chopin; he also cultivated performances of early polyphonists, Sweelinck, Gibbons, and others. He played Mozart with emphasis on the early pianoforte techniques; he peremptorily omitted the Romantic composers Chopin, Schumann,

and Liszt from his repertoire. He found the late sonatas of Beethoven more congenial to his temperament, and, remarkably enough, he played the piano works of the modern Vienna school—Schoenberg, Berg, and Webern—perhaps because of their classical avoidance of purely decorative tonal formations. He attracted great attention and evoked unequivocal praise at his American and European concerts, but in 1964 he abruptly terminated his stage career and devoted himself exclusively to recording, which he regarded as a superior art to concertizing. This enabled him to select the best portions of the music he played in the studio, forming a mosaic unblemished by accidental mishaps. A great part of the interest he aroused with the public at large was due to mannerisms that marked his behavior on the stage. He used a 14-inch-high chair that placed his eyes almost at the level of the keyboard; he affected informal dress; he had a rug put under the piano and a glass of distilled water within reach. He was in constant fear of bodily injury; he avoided shaking hands with the conductor after playing a concerto; and he sued the Steinway piano company for a large sum of money when an enthusiastic representative shook his hand too vigorously. But what even his most ardent admirers could not palliate was his unshakable habit of singing along with his performance; he even allowed his voice to be audible on his carefully wrought, lapidary phonograph recordings. Socially, Gould was a recluse; he found a release from his self-imposed isolation in editing a series of radio documentaries for the Canadian Broadcasting Corp. He called three of them a "solitude tragedy." Symbolically, they were devoted to the natural isolation of the Canadian Arctic, the insular life of Newfoundland, and the religious hermetism of the Mennonite sect. He also produced a radio documentary on Arnold Schoenberg, treating him as a musical hermit. Other activities included conducting a chamber orch. without an audience. Needless to add, Gould never married.

Gould, Morton, extraordinarily talented and versatile American composer and conductor; b. Richmond Hill, N.Y., Dec. 10, 1913. His father was an Austrian; his mother came from Russia; both fostered his early addiction to music. If the affectionate family memories are to be accepted as facts (and why not?), Gould composed a piano waltz at the age of 6 (indeed, it was ultimately publ. under the title *Just Six*). Being a prodigy did not harm Gould. He was bent on learning what music really is. He had piano lessons with Joseph Kardos and Abby Whiteside; later he enrolled in the composition class of Vincent Jones at N.Y. Univ.; there, at the age of 16, he presented a concert of his works. To keep body and soul together he played the piano in silent movies and in loud jazz bands, accompanied dancers, and gave demonstrations of musical skill on college circuits. In 1931–32 he served as staff pianist at Radio City Music Hall; in 1934–42 was in charge of the series "Music for Today" on the Mutual Radio network, and in 1943 became music director of the lucrative "Chrysler Hour" on CBS Radio. These contacts gave great impetus to his bursting talent for composing singable, playable, and enjoyable light pieces; he was pregnant with the fertile sperm of musical Americana; his *American Symphonette No. 1* (1933) became a popular success; equally accessible to the musical youth of the day was the *Chorale and Fugue in Jazz* for 2 Pianos and Orch. (1934); no less a musical magus than Stokowski put it on the program of the Philadelphia Orch. (Jan. 2, 1936). Gould then produced 3 more symphonettes (1935, 1938, 1941). No. 3 disgorged the luscious *Pavane;* the misspelling *Pavanne* (sic) was a concession to public illiteracy; the piece cloned several arrangements. There followed the *Latin-American Symphonette* (1940), an engaging tetrad of Latin dances (Rhumba, Tango, Guaracha, Conga). His *Spirituals* for Strings and Orch. (1941) is Gould's interpretation of the religious aspect of the American people. His other works touch on American history, as exemplified by *A Lincoln Legend* (1941), which Toscanini placed on his program with the NBC Symph. on Nov. 1, 1942; there followed the rambunctious orchestral *Cowboy Rhapsody* (1943). In 1945 Gould conducted a whole program of his works with the Boston Symph. Orch. He then turned to ballet in his *Fall River Legend,* based on the story of the notorious New England old maid who may or may not have given her mother 40 whacks and "when she saw what she had done she gave her father 41." Gould's *Symphony of Spirituals,* written for the American bicentennial (1976), was a reverential offering; his other bicentennial work, *American Ballads* (1976), is a symph. florilegium of American songs. Gould wrote the music for the Broadway show *Million Dollar Baby* (1945), several scores for Hollywood films, and also background music for the historical television productions *Verdun* (1963), *World War I* (1964–65), and *Holocaust* (1978). But Gould was not so much seduced by public success as not to test his powers in a field known as absolute music. He studied ways and means of Baroque techniques, and wrote several concertos: one for piano (1937), one for violin (1938), one for viola (1944), *Variations* for 2 Pianos and Orch. (1952), and *Inventions* for 4 Pianos and Orch. (1953); on top of these "classical" works he produced a unique shtick, *Concerto for Tap Dancer,* with Orch. (1953). Gould was a conductor of excellent skills; he toured Australia in 1977, Japan in 1979, Mexico in 1980, and Israel in 1981. In 1983 he received the National Arts Award.

WORKS: Broadway musicals, *Million Dollar Baby* (1945) and *Arms and the Girl* (1950); ballets, *Interplay* (N.Y., Oct. 17, 1945, composer conducting), *Fall River Legend* (N.Y., April 22, 1947), and *Fiesta* (Cannes, France, March 17, 1957); *3 American Symphonettes* (1933, 1935, 1937); *Chorale and Fugue in Jazz* for 2 Pianos and Orch. (Youth Orch., N.Y., Jan. 2, 1936, Stokowski conducting); Piano Concerto (1937; broadcast June 16, 1938, composer soloist); Violin Concerto (1938); *Stephen Foster Gallery* for Orch. (Pittsburgh, Jan. 12, 1940); *Spirituals* for Orch. (N.Y., Feb. 9, 1941, composer conducting); *Latin-American Symphonette* (Brooklyn, Feb. 22,

1941); *Cowboy Rhapsody* (1942); Symph. No. 1 (Pittsburgh, March 5, 1943); *Interplay* for Piano and Orch. (broadcast Aug. 25, 1943); Viola Concerto (1943); *Symphony on Marching Tunes,* No. 2 (N.Y., June 2, 1944); Concerto for Orch. (Cleveland, Feb. 1, 1945); *Harvest* for Harp, Vibraphone, and Strings (St. Louis, Oct. 27, 1945); *Minstrel Show* for Orch. (Indianapolis, Dec. 21, 1946); Symph. No. 3 (Dallas, Feb. 16, 1947, composer conducting); *Symphony* for Band (West Point, April 13, 1952, composer conducting); *Inventions* for 4 Pianos, Brass, and Percussion (N.Y., Oct. 19, 1953); *Dance Variations* for 2 Pianos and Orch. (N.Y., Oct. 24, 1953); *Showpiece* for Orch. (Philadelphia, May 7, 1954); *Derivations* for Clarinet and Band, written for Benny Goodman (Washington, D.C., July 14, 1956, composer conducting); *Declaration* for 2 Speakers, Male Chorus, and Orch.; setting of the Declaration of Independence (Washington, D.C., Jan. 20, 1957); *Jekyll and Hyde Variations* for Orch. (N.Y., Feb. 2, 1957); *Dialogues* for Piano and String Orch. (N.Y., Nov. 3, 1958, composer soloist); *Festive Music* for Orch. (N.Y., Jan. 16, 1965, composer conducting); *Venice* for Double Orch. and Brass Bands (Seattle, May 2, 1967); *Vivaldi Gallery* for Orch. (Seattle, March 25, 1968); *Troubadour Music* for 4 Guitars and Orch. (San Diego, March 1969); *Symphony of Spirituals* (Detroit, April 1, 1976); *American Ballads* for Orch. (Queens, N.Y., April 24, 1976, composer conducting); *Something To Do,* cantata-musical (Washington, D.C., Labor Day, 1976); Music for *Holocaust,* the TV mini-series (broadcast April 1978); *Cheers* for Orch. (Boston, May 1, 1979); *Burchfield Gallery* for Orch. (Cleveland, April 9, 1981); *Celebration '81* (for television; broadcast April 27, 1981); Cello Suite (1982); *Housewarming* for Orch. (Baltimore, Sept. 16, 1982); *American Sing,* commissioned for the opening concert of the Los Angeles Olympic Games (Hollywood Bowl, July 29, 1984).

BIBLIOGRAPHY: David Ewen, *American Composers* (N.Y., 1982).

Goulet, Robert (Gerard), American singer of popular music and actor; b. Lawrence, Mass., Nov. 26, 1933. His family moved to Edmonton, Canada; he then won a scholarship to the opera school of the Royal Cons. of Music in Toronto; made a successful American debut as Lancelot in the Broadway musical *Camelot* in 1960; subsequently appeared in a number of films.

Gounod, Charles François, famous French composer; b. St. Cloud, June 17, 1818; d. Paris, Oct. 18, 1893. His father, Jean François Gounod, was a painter, winner of the 2nd Grand Prix de Rome, who died when Gounod was a small child. His mother, a most accomplished woman, supervised his literary, artistic, and musical education, and taught him piano. He completed his academic studies at the Lycée St. Louis; in 1836, he entered the Paris Cons., studying with Halévy, Lesueur, and Paër. In 1837 he won the 2nd Prix de Rome with his cantata *Marie Stuart et Rizzio;* in 1839 he obtained the Grand Prix with his cantata *Fernand.* In Rome, he studied church music, particularly the works of Palestrina; composed there a Mass for 3 Voices and Orch., which was performed at the church of San Luigi dei Francesi. In 1842, during a visit to Vienna, he conducted a Requiem of his own; upon his return to Paris, he became precentor and organist of the Missions Etrangères; studied theology for 2 years, but decided against taking Holy Orders; yet he was often referred to as l'Abbé Gounod; some religious choruses were publ. in 1846 as composed by Abbé Charles Gounod. Soon Gounod tried his hand at stage music. On April 16, 1851, his first opera, *Sapho*, was produced at the Grand Opéra, with only moderate success; he revised it much later, extending it to 4 acts from the original 3, and it was performed again on April 2, 1884; but even in this revised form it was unsuccessful. Gounod's 2nd opera, *La Nonne sanglante*, in 5 acts, was staged at the Paris Opéra on Oct. 18, 1854; there followed a comic opera, *Le Médecin malgré lui*, after Molière (Jan. 15, 1858), which also failed to realize Gounod's expectations. In the meantime, he was active in other musical ways in Paris; he conducted the choral society Orphéon (1852–60) and composed for it several choruses. Gounod's great success came with the production of *Faust*, after Goethe (Théâtre-Lyrique, March 19, 1859; perf. with additional recitatives and ballet at the Opéra, March 3, 1869); *Faust* remained Gounod's greatest masterpiece, and indeed the most successful French opera of the 19th century, triumphant all over the world without any sign of diminishing effect through a century of changes in musical tastes. However, it was widely criticized for the melodramatic treatment of Goethe's poem by the librettists, Barbier and Carré, and for the somewhat sentimental style of Gounod's music; in Germany, it is usually produced under the title *Margarete* or *Gretchen* to dissociate it from Goethe's work. The succeeding 4 operas, *Philémon et Baucis* (Paris, Feb. 18, 1860), *La Colombe* (Baden-Baden, Aug. 3, 1860), *La Reine de Saba* (Paris, Feb. 29, 1862), and *Mireille* (Paris, March 19, 1864), were only partially successful, but with *Roméo et Juliette* (Paris, April 27, 1867), Gounod recaptured universal acclaim. In 1870, during the Franco-Prussian War, Gounod went to London, where he organized Gounod's Choir, and presented concerts at the Phil. and the Crystal Palace; when Paris fell, he wrote an elegiac cantata, *Gallia*, to words from the Lamentations of Jeremiah, which he conducted in London on May 1, 1871; it was later performed in Paris. He wrote some incidental music for productions in Paris: *Les Deux Reines*, to a drama by Legouvé (Nov. 27, 1872), and *Jeanne d'Arc*, to Barbier's poem (Nov. 8, 1873). In 1874, he returned to Paris; there he produced his operas *Cinq-Mars* (April 5, 1877), *Polyeucte* (Oct. 7, 1878), and *Le Tribut de Zamora* (April 1, 1881), without signal success. The last years of his life were devoted mainly to sacred works, of which the most important was *La Rédemption*, a trilogy, first performed at the Birmingham Festival in 1882; another sacred trilogy, *Mors et vita*, also written for the Birmingham Festival, followed in 1885. Gounod continued to write religious works in close succession, and produced (among many others) the following: *Te Deum* (1886); *La Communion des saints* (1889); *Messe dite le Clovis* (1890); *La Contemplation de Saint François au pied de la croix* (1890); *Tantum ergo* (1892). A Requiem (1893) was left unfinished, and was arranged by Henri Büsser after Gounod's death. One of Gounod's most popular settings to religious words is *Ave Maria*, adapted to the first prelude of Bach's *Well-tempered Clavier*, but its original version was *Méditation sur le premier Prélude de Piano de J.S. Bach* for Violin and Piano (1853); the words were added later (1859). Other works are: 2 symphs. (1855); *Marche funèbre d'une marionnette* for Orch. (1873); *Petite symphonie* for Wind Instruments (1888); 3 string quartets; a number of piano pieces; songs. Among his literary works were *Ascanio de Saint-Saëns* (1889); *Le Don Juan de Mozart* (1890; in Eng., 1895); and an autobiography, *Mémoires d'un artiste* (publ. posthumously, Paris, 1896; in Eng. trans. by W.H. Hutchenson, *Autobiographical Reminiscences with Family Letters and Notes on Music*, N.Y., 1896).

BIBLIOGRAPHY: A. Peña y Goñi, *Impresiones y recuerdos; Charles Gounod* (Madrid, 1879); M.A. de Bovet, *Charles Gounod* (Paris, 1890; in Eng., London, 1891); L. Pagnerre, *Charles Gounod, Sa vie et ses œuvres* (Paris, 1890); C. Saint-Saëns, *Charles Gounod et le Don Juan de Mozart* (Paris, 1893); T. Dubois, *Notice sur Charles Gounod* (Paris, 1894); P. Voss, *Charles Gounod: Ein Lebensbild* (Leipzig, 1895); H. Tolhurst, *Gounod* (London, 1905); P.L. Hillemacher, *Charles Gounod* (Paris, 1906); C. Bellaigue, *Gounod* (Paris, 1910); J.-G. Prod'homme and A. Dandelot, *Gounod: Sa vie et ses œuvres*, in 2 vols., the standard biography (Paris, 1911); H. Soubiès and H. de Curzon, *Documents inédits sur le Faust de Gounod* (Paris, 1912); J. Tiersot, "Charles Gounod, A Centennial Tribute," *Musical Quarterly* (July 1918); J.-G. Prod'homme, "Miscellaneous Letters by Gounod," *Musical Quarterly* (Oct. 1918); J. Tiersot, "Gounod's Letters," *Musical Quarterly* (Jan. 1919); C. Saint-Saëns, "Le Livret de Faust," *Monde Musical* (1914–19); R. d'Ollone, "Gounod et l'opéra comique," *Revue Musicale* (Nov. 1933); M. Cooper, "Charles Gounod and His Influence on French Music," *Music & Letters* (1940); P. Landormy, *Gounod* (Paris, 1942); P. Landormy, *Faust de Gounod: Etude et analyse* (Paris, 1944); H. Wagener, "Die Messen Charles Gounods," *Kirchenmusikaliches Jahrbuch*, 51 (1967; reprinted in *Musica Sacra*, July–Aug. and Sept.–Oct. 1970); idem, "Charles François Gounod. Ein Beitrag zur Kirchenmusik des 19. Jahrhunderts," *Musica Sacra* (Jan. 1968); A. Lebois, "La Reine de Saba ou Amour et Franc-Maçonnerie," *Annales Publiées par la Faculté des Lettres de Toulouse. Littératures* (Oct. 1968); J. Harding, *Gounod* (London, 1973); S. Huebner, "Mireille Revisited," *Musical Times* (Dec. 1983).

Gouvy, Louis Théodore, prolific composer; b. Goffontaine, near Saarbrücken, July 5, 1819; d. Leipzig, April 21, 1898. The son of French parents, he graduated from the college at Metz; went to Paris to study law, but turned to music; presented a concert of his works in Paris in 1847; also made frequent trips to Germany, where his music was received with great favor.

WORKS: About 200 works, including an opera, *Der Cid;* 7 symphs.; Wind Nonet; Wind Octet; Sextet for Flute and Strings; Piano Quintet; String Quintet; 5 string quartets; 5 piano trios; numerous piano pieces in an ingratiating salon manner; songs.

BIBLIOGRAPHY: O. Klauwell, *L.T. Gouvy, Sein Leben und seine Werke* (Berlin, 1902).

Gow, George Coleman, American music pedagogue; b. Ayer Junction, Mass., Nov. 27, 1860; d. Poughkeepsie, N.Y., Jan. 12, 1938. He studied music privately; graduated from Brown Univ. in 1884 and Newton Theological Seminary in 1889; then taught harmony and piano at Smith College for 6 years; from 1895 to 1932, was a prof. of music at Vassar College. He wrote a textbook on notation and harmony, *The Structure of Music* (N.Y., 1895); composed organ pieces and songs.

Gow, Nathaniel, Scottish violinist, arranger, and music publisher; b. Inver, near Dunkeld, May 28, 1763; d. Edinburgh, Jan. 19, 1831. He played the trumpet in Scottish bands; then changed to violin. In 1788 he opened a music shop in Edinburgh; publ. numerous arrangements of Scotch tunes by his father and also his own arrangements of Scottish dances; became a commercial music publisher in 1796, but was bankrupt by 1827. He also led a band for various aristocratic assemblies. Among his original pieces there was an interesting instrumental composition, *Caller Herrin',* based on a street vendor's cry.

BIBLIOGRAPHY: Henry G. Farmer, *History of Music in Scotland* (London, 1947; pp. 343–44).

Gow, Niel, Scottish violinist and composer, father of **Nathaniel Gow;** b. Strathbrand, Perthshire, March 22, 1727; d. Inver, near Dunkeld, March 1, 1807. He played Scottish reels on the violin, and as a young man earned his living by performing at social gatherings in Edinburgh and London. He publ. a number of "Strathspey Reels"; however, many of them were not original compositions but arrangements of old dance tunes.

BIBLIOGRAPHY: John Glen, *The Glen Collection of Scottish Dance Music* (Edinburgh, 1891).

Graben-Hoffmann, Gustav (properly, **Gustav Hoffmann**), German composer; b. Bnin, near Posen, March 7, 1820; d. Potsdam, May 20, 1900. He studied with his father and with other teachers in Posen; then taught music in various localities in eastern Germany; in 1843, settled in Berlin; in 1850, he founded a Musikakademie für Damen; then went to Leipzig, where he studied composition with Moritz Hauptmann; in 1869, returned to Berlin, where he taught singing. In the meantime, he composed industriously; wrote a number of songs, but was compelled to publ. them at his own expense, despite economic hardships; of these, *500,000 Teufel* had a great vogue. He also publ. singing manuals: *Die*

Pflege der Singstimme (1865); *Das Studium des Gesangs* (1872); *Praktische Methode als Grundlage für den Kunstgesang* (1874).

Grabert, Martin, German composer; b. Arnswalde (Neumark), May 15, 1868; d. Berlin, Jan. 23, 1951. He studied with Bellermann and Bargiel. In 1895 he settled in Berlin as a church organist. He wrote some 80 opus numbers, mostly for chorus and for organ; a complete list of his works is in Heinz Becker's article in *Die Musik in Geschichte und Gegenwart.*

Grabner, Hermann, Austrian composer and theorist; b. Graz, May 12, 1886; d. Bolzano, Italy, July 3, 1969. He took his degree in law at Graz Univ. in 1909; then studied music with Reger and Hans Sitt at the Leipzig Cons.; he became a lecturer in theory at Strasbourg Cons. in 1913; served in the German army in World War I; after the Armistice, taught at the Mannheim Cons.; in 1924 was appointed prof. of composition at the Leipzig Cons.; in 1938–46, taught at the Hochschule für Musik in Berlin, and later at the Berlin Cons. (1950–51).

WRITINGS: *Regers Harmonik* in Würz's symposium on Reger (Munich, 1920); *Die Funktionstheorie Hugo Riemanns und ihre Bedeutung für die praktische Analyse* (Munich, 1923); *Allgemeine Musiklehre* (Stuttgart, 1924; 5th ed., 1949); *Lehrbuch der musikalischen Analyse* (Leipzig, 1925); *Der lineare Satz; Ein Lehrbuch des Kontrapunktes* (Stuttgart, 1930; new revised ed., 1950); *Handbuch der Harmonielehre* (Berlin, 1944); several short books of exercises for theory students. He also wrote an opera, *Die Richterin* (Barmen, May 7, 1930); *Perkeo Suite* and *Burgmusik* for Wind Orch.; Concerto for 3 Violins; organ pieces; songs; etc.

Grabovsky, Leonid, Ukrainian composer; b. Kiev, Jan. 28, 1935. He studied at the Kiev Cons. with Revutsky and Liatoshinsky, graduating in 1959. His music is marked by modern tendencies, making use of dissonant counterpoint and asymmetric polyrhythmic combinations.

WORKS: *Intermezzo* for Orch. (1958); String Quartet (1958); *4 Ukrainian Songs* for Chorus and Orch. (1959); Sonata for Unaccompanied Violin (1959); *Symphonic Frescoes* (1961); 2 comic operas, after Chekhov, *The Bear* (1963) and *Marriage Proposal* (1964); Trio for Violin, Double Bass, and Piano (1964); *Microstructures* for Oboe Solo (1964); *Constants* for 4 Pianos, 6 Percussion Groups, and Solo Violin (1964); *From Japanese Haiku* for Tenor, Piccolo, Bassoon, and Xylophone (1964); *La Mer* for Narrator, 2 Choruses, Organ, and Orch. (1964–70; Rotterdam, Sept. 10, 1971); *Pastels* for Female Voice, Violin, Viola, Cello, and Double Bass (1964); *Little Chamber Music* No. 1 for 15 String Instruments (1966); *Homeomorphia I, II,* and *III* for One or 2 Pianos (1968); *Ornaments* for Oboe, Viola, and Harp (1969); *Homeomorphia IV* for Orch. (1970); *Little Chamber Music* No. 2 for Oboe, Harp, and 12 Solo String Instruments (1971); *2 Pieces* for String Orch. (1972); *Concorsuono* for Solo Horn (1974); *St. John's*

Eve, symph. legend for Orch., after Gogol (1976).

Grace, Harvey, English organist and writer on music; b. Romsey, Jan. 25, 1874; d. Bromley, Kent, Feb. 15, 1944. He studied with M. Richardson at Southwark Cathedral, London; was organist at various churches in London; directed the St. Cecilia Festivals; from 1918 to his death, he was editor of the *Musical Times* and wrote editorial articles for it under the name "Feste"; also edited the *New Musical Educator* (London, 1934).
WRITINGS: *French Organ Music, Past and Present* (N.Y., 1919); *The Complete Organist* (London, 1920; 4th ed., 1956; standard teaching manual); *The Organ Works of Bach* (London, 1922); *The Organ Works of Rheinberger* (London, 1925); *Ludwig van Beethoven* (London, 1927); *A Musician at Large* (collection of articles from the *Musical Times;* London, 1928); *A Handbook for Choralists* (London, 1928); also, with Sir Walford Davies, *Music and Worship* (London, 1935); *The Organ Works of César Franck* (London, 1948); composed 20 organ pieces; made 30 transcriptions from Bach, mostly for organ; ed. Rheinberger's 20 sonatas for organ.
BIBLIOGRAPHY: Obituary article, "Harvey Grace," *Musical Times* (March 1944).

Gracis, Ettore, Italian conductor; b. La Spezia, Sept. 24, 1915. He studied violin at the Parma Cons. and piano and composition at the Venice Cons.; also took courses in composition with Gian Francesco Malipiero in Siena. He made his conducting debut in 1942; from that time appeared with many opera houses of Italy. He also conducted symph. concerts. He was active in bringing out contemporary scores; conducted a number of works by Malipiero and other leading Italian composers.

Grad, Gabriel, Lithuanian composer; b. Retovo, near Kovno, July 9, 1890; d. Tel Aviv, Dec. 9, 1950. He studied in Ekaterinoslav and in Berlin; founded a Jewish music school in Kovno (1920–22); went to Palestine in 1924; from 1925 was founder and director of the Benhetov Cons. in Tel Aviv. He wrote an opera, *Judith and Holofernes,* and about 250 other works, including chamber music, piano pieces, choruses, and songs, many of which are based on Jewish folk melodies.

Grädener, Hermann (Theodor Otto), German violinist and composer, son of **Karl Grädener;** b. Kiel, May 8, 1844; d. Vienna, Sept. 18, 1929. He studied at the Vienna Cons.; was violinist in the court orch. in Vienna; then taught theory at the Horaksche Klavierschule in 1873, and at the Cons. of the Gesellschaft der Musikfreunde in Vienna from 1877 to 1913; was also a prof. at the Univ. of Vienna (from 1882); in 1899 succeeded Bruckner there. He wrote 2 operas, *Der Richter von Zalamea* and *Die heilige Zita;* 2 symphs.; concertos for violin, for cello, and for piano; String Octet; String Quintet; Piano Quintet; 2 string quartets; 5 *Impromptus* for Piano and Strings; 5 *Intermezzi* for Violin and Piano; Sonata for 2 Pianos; etc.

Grädener, Karl Georg Peter, German cellist and composer; b. Rostock, Jan. 14, 1812; d. Hamburg, June 10, 1883. He studied cello with Mattstedt; from 1838 was music director at Kiel Univ. for 10 years; in 1851 established an academy for vocal music in Hamburg; after 3 years at the Vienna Cons. (1862–65) he returned to Hamburg, and became a teacher at the Cons. there, until 1873; was also co-founder and a president of the Hamburger Tonkünstlerverein. He wrote *System der Harmonielehre* (Hamburg, 1877); his articles for music periodicals were collected and publ. as *Gesammelte Aufsätze* (Hamburg, 1872).
WORKS: 2 operas, *König Harald* and *Der Mullerin Hochzeit;* oratorio, *Johannes der Täufer;* 2 symphs.; *Fiesco,* overture; Piano Concerto; *Romance* for Violin and Orch.; String Octet; 5 piano quintets; 3 string quartets; String Trio; 2 piano trios; 3 violin sonatas; Cello Sonata; many piano pieces.

Gradenwitz, Peter, German-Israeli musicologist; b. Berlin, Jan. 24, 1910. He studied literature and philosophy at Berlin Univ.; composition with Julius Weismann and Josef Rufer. In 1934 he went to Paris; in 1935, to London; in 1936, settled in Tel Aviv, where he became active as a writer, lecturer, and organizer of concerts; established Israeli Music Publications; he was also active on the radio.
WRITINGS: *Johann Stamitz* (Vienna, 1936); *The Music of Israel* (N.Y., 1949); *Wege zur Musik der Gegenwart* (Stuttgart, 1963); books in Hebrew: *Music History* (Jerusalem, 1939); *The World of the Symphony* (Jerusalem, 1945; 7th ed., 1953); *Music and Musicians in Israel* (Tel Aviv, 1959). He wrote a String Quartet; *Palestinian Landscapes* for Oboe and Piano; songs.

Gradstein, Alfred, Polish composer; b. Czestochowa, Oct. 30, 1904; d. Warsaw, Sept. 9, 1954. He studied at the Warsaw Cons. (1922–25) and at the State Academy of Music in Vienna; from 1928 to 1947 he lived in Paris; then returned to Poland. He wrote mostly for piano; his Piano Concerto was publ. in 1932.

Graener, Paul, significant German composer; b. Berlin, Jan. 11, 1872; d. Salzburg, Nov. 13, 1944. He was a chorister at the Berlin Cathedral; studied composition with Albert Becker at the Veit Cons. in Berlin. He traveled in Germany as a theater conductor; in 1896, went to London, where he taught at the Royal Academy of Music (1897–1902). He was then in Vienna as a teacher at the Neues Konservatorium; subsequently directed the Mozarteum in Salzburg (1910–13); then lived in Munich; in 1920, he succeeded Max Reger as a prof. of composition at the Leipzig Cons. (until 1925); was director of the Stern Cons. in Berlin (1930–33). He wrote music in all genres, and was fairly successful as an opera composer; in his style, he followed the Romantic movement, but also emphasized the folk element.
WORKS: OPERAS: *Don Juans letztes Abenteuer* (Leipzig, June 11, 1914); *Theophano* (Munich, June 5, 1918); *Schirin und Gertraude* (Dresden, April 28,

1920); *Hanneles Himmelfahrt* (Dresden, Feb. 17, 1927); *Friedemann Bach* (Schwerin, Nov. 13, 1931); *Der Prinz von Homburg* (Berlin, March 14, 1935); *Schwanhild* (Cologne, Jan. 4, 1941). FOR ORCH.: Symph.; *Romantische Phantasie; Waldmusik; Gothische Suite;* Piano Concerto; Cello Concerto. CHAMBER MUSIC: 6 string quartets; Piano Quintet; 3 violin sonatas. In several of his chamber music works, Graener attempted to carry out a definite programmatic design while maintaining traditional form, as in his *Kammermusik-Dichtung* for Piano Trio.
BIBLIOGRAPHY: G. Graener, *Paul Graener* (Leipzig, 1922); P. Grümmer, *Verzeichnis der Werke Paul Graeners* (Berlin, 1937).

Graeser, Wolfgang, talented Swiss composer; b. Zürich, Sept. 7, 1906; d. (suicide) Nikolassee, June 13, 1928. He went to Berlin in 1921; studied violin with Karl Klingler, and quickly acquired erudition in general music theory; also made a serious study of various unrelated arts and sciences (mathematics, oriental languages, painting). His signal achievement was an orchestration of Bach's *Kunst der Fuge* (perf. at the Leipzig Thomaskirche by Karl Straube, June 26, 1927). He publ. a book, *Körpersinn* (Munich, 1927).
BIBLIOGRAPHY: A memorial symposium, *Wolfgang Graeser Gedächtnisheft*, publ. in Munich shortly after his tragic death; H. Zurlinden, *Wolfgang Graeser* (Munich, 1935).

Graetzer, Guillermo, Austrian-Argentine composer; b. Vienna, Sept. 5, 1914. He studied in Vienna with Paul A. Pisk; in 1930 moved to Buenos Aires, devoting himself mainly to educational activities; also edited musical anthologies.
WORKS: *Concierto para orquesta* (1939); *La Parábola* for Orch. (1947); *Sinfonía brevis* (1951); Bassoon Concerto (1952); *Concierto de cámara* (1953); *Los burgueses de Calais* for Male Chorus and Orch. (1954–55); Cello Concerto (1957); *Cantos de la eternidad* for Orch. (1958); arrangements of folk dances of Argentina and Brazil for recorder and percussion (1968).

Graf, Herbert, Austrian opera stage director, son of **Max Graf;** b. Vienna, April 10, 1903; d. Geneva, April 5, 1973. He studied at the Univ. of Vienna with Guido Adler; received his Ph.D. in 1925. He then was stage director at the opera houses in Münster, Breslau, Frankfurt, and Basel. In 1934 he came to the U.S.; was associated with the Philadelphia Opera in 1934–35; in 1936 he was appointed stage director of the Metropolitan Opera; in 1949, became head of the opera dept. at the Curtis Inst., Philadelphia. He returned to Europe in 1958. He publ. *The Opera and Its Future in America* (N.Y., 1941) and *Opera for the People* (Minneapolis, 1951).

Graf, Max, Austrian music critic, teacher, and musicologist; father of **Herbert Graf;** b. Vienna, Oct. 1, 1873; d. there, June 24, 1958. He studied at the Univ. of Vienna, where he received his Ph.D. in 1896

with the dissertation *Die Musik der Frau in der Renaissancezeit* (later publ. as *Die Musik im Zeitalter der Renaissance,* Vienna, 1905). From 1900–38 he wrote music criticism for the *Wiener Allgemeine Zeitung;* from 1902–9 lectured on music history at the Cons. of the Gesellschaft der Musikfreunde; then was on the staff of the State Academy of Music (1909–38). In 1938, when Austria was incorporated into the Greater German Reich, he went to the U.S. He returned to Vienna in 1947. A brilliant writer in his homeland, he lapsed into speculative journalism in his books publ. in America, which are rendered worthless because of blatant inaccuracies.
WRITINGS: *Deutsche Musik im 19. Jahrhundert* (Berlin, 1898); *Wagner-Probleme und andere Studien* (Vienna, 1900); *Die innere Werkstatt des Musikers* (Stuttgart, 1910); *Vier Gespräche über deutsche Musik* (Regensburg, 1931); *Legend of a Musical City* (N.Y., 1945; 2nd ed., 1969); *Composer and Critic* (N.Y., 1946; 2nd ed., 1969); *Modern Music* (N.Y., 1946; 2nd ed., 1969; also in German as *Geschichte und Geist der modernen Musik,* Vienna, 1953); *From Beethoven to Shostakovich* (N.Y., 1947; 2nd ed., 1969); *Die Wiener Oper* (Vienna, 1955).

Graffigna, Achille, Italian opera composer; b. S. Martino dall' Argine, near Mantua, May 5, 1816; d. Padua, July 19, 1896. He studied with Alessandro Rolla in Milan; wrote church music and theatrical cantatas; then devoted himself to opera; his *Ildegonda e Rizzardo* (La Scala, Milan, Nov. 3, 1841) was accepted with favor. In 1842 he went to Verona, where he produced *Eleonora di San Bonifacio* (March 11, 1843); there followed *Maria di Brabante* (Trieste, Oct. 16, 1852); *L'assedio di Malta* (Padua, July 30, 1853); *Gli Studenti* (Milan, Feb. 7, 1857); *Veronica Cibo* (Mantua, Feb. 13, 1858; revised and produced at the Théâtre Italien, Paris, March 22, 1865, as *La Duchessa di San Giuliano*); *Il Barbiere di Siviglia* (Padua, May 17, 1879; intended as an homage to Rossini); *Il matrimonio segreto* (Florence, Sept. 8, 1883); *La buona figliuola* (Milan, May 6, 1886).

Graffman, Gary, outstanding American pianist; b. New York, Oct. 14, 1928. He won a scholarship to the Curtis Inst. of Music when he was 8, and studied there with Isabelle Vengerova. He was only 10 years old when he gave a piano recital at Town Hall in N.Y. After graduating from Curtis in 1946, he was a scholarship student at Columbia Univ. (1946–47). In 1946 he won the first regional Rachmaninoff competition, which secured for him his debut with the Philadelphia Orch. in 1947. In 1949 he was honored with the Leventritt Award. Subsequently he received a Fulbright grant to go to Europe (1950–51). Returning to the U.S., he had lessons with Horowitz in N.Y. and Rudolf Serkin in Marlboro, Vt. He was on his way to establishing himself as a pianist of the first rank when disaster struck; about 1979 he began to lose the use of his right hand, a rare ailment, designated by some doctors as a carpal-tunnel syndrome, that attacks instrumentalists. (Leon Fleisher suffered from it but recovered after myotherapy. Schumann had to discontinue his career as a pianist owing to a similar impedimentum, but he applied primitive treatments, such as exercising his weak fingers with a sling and a pulley, which in the end strained the tendons, further weakening the hand.) Happily, the prognosis for Graffman's full recovery remains positive, but he had to cancel his concert appearances pending the process of cure. He brought out an autobiography under the title *I Really Should Be Practicing* (Garden City, N.Y., 1981).

Gräflinger, Franz, Austrian writer on music; b. Linz, Nov. 26, 1876; d. Bad Ischl, Austria, Sept. 9, 1962. He served as municipal accountant in Linz, and at the same time studied music; wrote criticism in local newspapers; then devoted his energies chiefly to Bruckner research; publ. 2 biographies of Bruckner (Munich, 1911; Regensburg, 1921) and *Liebes und Heiteres um Anton Bruckner* (Vienna, 1948); edited vol. I of Bruckner's *Gesammelte Briefe* (1924).

Grahn, Ulf, Swedish composer; b. Solna, Jan. 17, 1942. He studied piano with Herbert Westrell, violin with Rudolf Forsberg, and composition with Gunnar Johanson and Hans Eklund at the Royal College of Music in Stockholm; also took voice lessons and sang bass in various choruses. In 1972 he and his wife, the pianist **Barbro Dahlman,** went to America; he enrolled at the Catholic Univ. (M.M., 1973); with his wife he founded the Contemporary Music Forum, presenting programs of modern music by American and European composers. In his own music he maintains the golden mean of contemporary idioms, without doctrinaire deviations, scrupulously serving the tastes of the general audience.

WORKS: *Musica da camera* for Chamber Orch. (1964); *Serenade* for 2 Oboes (1965); *Fancy* for Orch. (1965); *Elegy* for Oboe, Horn, and Cello (1967); Trio for Flute, Oboe, and Clarinet (1967); Suite for 2 Violins and Viola (1967); *Lamento* for Strings (1967); Symph. No. 1 (1967); *Hommage à Charles Ives* for String Orch. (1968; Trondheim, Norway, Feb. 13, 1969); Chamber Concerto for Double Bass (1968; Santa Barbara, Calif., Feb. 7, 1973); *Dialogue* for Flute and Clarinet (1969); *Joy* for Symphonic Band (1969; Stockholm, Feb. 2, 1970); *Ancient Music* for Piano and Chamber Orch. (1970; Copenhagen, March 20, 1972); *A Dream of a Lost Century* for Chamber Orch. (1971; Stockholm, June 1, 1972); *Lux,* ballet (1972; Stockholm, April 6, 1972); *Alone* for Flute (1972); *This Reminds Me of . . .* for Flute, Clarinet, Horn, Trombone, and Percussion (1972; Washington, D.C., Dec. 15, 1975); Concerto for Orch. (1973; Philadelphia, April 10, 1981); *Soundscapes I* for Flute, Bass Clarinet, English Horn, and Percussion (1973; Washington, D.C., Oct. 28, 1973); *Soundscapes II* for Instruments (1974); *Soundscapes III* for Flute, Clarinet, Percussion, and Tape (1975); *Soundscapes IV* for Soprano, Flute, Bass Clarinet, Percussion, and Piano (1975); Chamber Concerto for Viola d'Amore and 10 Instruments (1975; Washington, D.C., Jan. 17, 1977); *Order-Fragments-Mir-*

ror for Flute, Bass Clarinet, Percussion, and Piano (1975); Flute Sonata (1976); *Magnolias in Snow* for Flute and Piano (1976); Concertino for Piano and Strings (1979; Northern Virginia Symph., Feb. 28, 1981; Barbro Dahlman, soloist); String Quartet No. 2 (1979); *Floating Landscape* for 8 Flutes (1979); Piano Sonata (1980); *Rondeau* for Chamber Orch. (1980); Piano Quartet (1980); *Summer Deviation* for Flute, Violin, Viola, Cello, and Piano (1981); *Images* for Bass Clarinet and Marimba (1981); *Eldorado* for Flute, Violin, Clarinet, Piano, and Baryton (1982); Violin Sonata (1983); Symph. No. 2 (1983).

Grainger, Percy Aldridge, celebrated pianist and composer; b. Melbourne, Australia, July 8, 1882; d. White Plains, N.Y., Feb. 20, 1961. He received his early musical training from his mother; at the age of 10, appeared as pianist at several public concerts; then had lessons with Louis Pabst; in 1894, went to Germany, where he studied with Kwast in Frankfurt; also took a few lessons with Busoni. In 1901 he began his concert career in England; then toured South Africa and Australia. In 1906 he met Grieg, who became enthusiastic about Grainger's talent; Grainger's performances of Grieg's Piano Concerto were famous. In 1914, Grainger settled in the U.S.; made a sensational debut in N.Y., on Feb. 11, 1915; gave summer sessions at the Chicago Musical College from 1919 to 1931; was for one academic year (1932–33) chairman of the music dept. of N.Y. Univ. In 1935 he founded a museum in Melbourne, in which he housed all his MSS and his rich collection of musical souvenirs. After 1940 he lived mostly in White Plains, N.Y. He married Ella Viola Ström in 1928 in a spectacular ceremony staged at the Hollywood Bowl, at which he conducted his work *To a Nordic Princess,* written for his bride. Grainger's philosophy of life and art calls for the widest communion of peoples and opinions; his profound study of folk music underlies the melodic and rhythmic structure of his own music; he made a determined effort to re-create in art music the free flow of instinctive songs of the people; he experimented with "gliding" intervals within the traditional scales and polyrhythmic combinations with independent strong beats in the component parts. In a modest way he was a pioneer of electronic music; as early as 1937 he wrote a quartet for electronic instruments, notating the pitch by zigzags and curves. He introduced individual forms of notation and orch. scoring, rejecting the common Italian designations of tempi and dynamics in favor of colloquial Eng. expressions. An eccentric to the last, he directed that his skeleton, after the removal and destruction of the flesh, be placed for preservation and possible display in the Grainger Museum at the Univ. of Melbourne, but his request was declined and he was buried in an ordinary manner.

WORKS: FOR ORCH.: *Mock Morris* (1911); *Irish Tunes from County Derry* (1909); *Molly on the Shore; Shepherd's Hey; Colonial Song* (1913); *The Warriors* (music to an imaginary ballet; 1916); *English Dance* for Orch. and Organ (1925); *Ye Banks and Braes o' Bonnie Doon* (1932); *Harvest Hymn*

(1933); *Danish Folk-song Suite* (1937). FOR CHAMBER ORCH.: *The Nightingale and the 2 Sisters* (1931). FOR CHORUS AND ORCH.: *Marching Song of Democracy* (1916); *The Merry Wedding* (1916); *Father and Daughter; Sir Eglamore; The Camp; The March of the Men of Harlech; The Hunter in His Career; The Bride's Tragedy; Love Verses from "The Song of Solomon"; Tribute to Foster* (1931). FOR CHORUS AND BRASS BAND: *I'm 17 Come Sunday; We Have Fed Our Seas for a Thousand Years* (1912); *Marching Tune.* FOR A CAPPELLA CHORUS: *Brigg Fair; The Innuit; Morning Song in the Jungle; A Song of Vermland; At Twilight; Tiger-Tiger!; The Immovable Do;* etc. All these are also issued in various arrangements. CHAMBER MUSIC: *Handel in the Strand* (1913); octet, *My Robin Is to the Greenwood Gone; Walking Tune* for Woodwind Quintet; *Green Bushes* (1921); *Hill-Song No. 1* (1923); *Shallow Brown* (1924); *Hill-Song No. 2* (1929); *Spoon River* (1930); *Free Music for Strings* (1935). FOR MILITARY BAND: *Children's March* (1918); march, *The Lads of Wamphrey; Lincolnshire Posy,* 6 folk songs from Lincolnshire, England; settings, in various combinations, of 20 of Kipling's poems (1911–38); 32 settings of British folk songs (1911–38); piano pieces; etc.

BIBLIOGRAPHY: C. Scott, "Percy Grainger, The Music and the Man," *Musical Quarterly* (July 1916); D.C. Parker, *Percy A. Grainger, A Study* (N.Y., 1918); C.W. Hughes, "Percy Grainger, A Cosmopolitan Composer," *Musical Quarterly* (April 1937); R.L. Taylor, *The Running Pianist* (N.Y., 1950); T.C. Slattery, *Percy Grainger: The Inveterate Innovator* (1974); *A Complete Catalogue of Works of Percy Grainger,* ed. by Teresa Balough (Perth, 1975); John Bird, *Percy Grainger* (London, 1976); L. Foreman, ed., *The Percy Grainger Companion* (London, 1981); D. Tall, ed., *Percy Grainger: A Catalogue of the Music* (London, 1982).

Gram, Hans, Danish-born American composer; b. Copenhagen, May 20, 1754; d. Boston, April 28, 1804. He studied philosophy at the Univ. of Copenhagen, and also had some training in music. About 1785 he went to America, and settled in Boston, where he became organist of the Brattle St. Church. He contributed various musical pieces to the *Massachusetts Magazine,* including a curious composition entitled *The Death Song of an Indian Chief* for Voice, 2 Clarinets, 2 Horns, and Strings, which was publ. in the March 1791 issue; it was apparently the first orch. score publ. in the U.S.; he also wrote *Sacred Lines for Thanksgiving Day* (1793) and some other vocal works for the same magazine. He was a co-editor of *The Massachusetts Compiler,* a rather progressive collection on Psalmody, which also contained a music dictionary.

BIBLIOGRAPHY: F.J. Metcalf, *American Writers and Compilers of Sacred Music* (N.Y., 1925).

Gram, Peder, Danish conductor and composer; b. Copenhagen, Nov. 25, 1881; d. there, Feb. 4, 1956. After graduation from the Univ. of Copenhagen, he studied music theory at the Leipzig Cons. with Sitt and Krehl and conducting with Nikisch (1904–7).

Returning to Copenhagen, he was chief conductor of the Danish Concert Society (1918–32) and the Danish Radio Orch. (1937–51). He publ. in Danish the books *Musikens formlaere i grundtraek* (1916), *Moderne musik* (1934) and *Analytisk harmonilaere* (1947).

WORKS: 3 symphs. (1913, 1925, 1954); *Symphonic Fantasy* (1908); *Poème lyrique* (1911); *Romance* for Violin and Orch. (1911); *Festouverture* (1913); *Avalon* for Soprano and Orch. (1916); Violin Concerto (1920); *Prologue to a Shakespearean Drama* (1928); *Ballet Suite* (1944); *Intrada seria* (1946); 3 string quartets (1906, 1927, 1941); Piano Trio (1910); Cello Sonata (1914); Oboe Sonatina (1935); Wind Quintet (1942); piano pieces; songs.

Gramatges, Harold, Cuban composer; b. Santiago de Cuba, Sept. 26, 1918. He studied with José Ardévol and Amadeo Roldán in Havana; in 1942 went to the U.S. and took a summer course in composition with Aaron Copland at the Berkshire Music Center in Tanglewood. Returning to Havana, he founded, with several other modern Cuban composers, the Grupo de Renovación Musical (1943). From 1961 to 1964 he was a member of the Cuban Embassy in Paris. Once again in Havana, he organized the music dept. of the Casa de las Américas. In his own works he pursues the aim of enlightened functionalism in an effective modern style.

WORKS: *Invenciones* for Chamber Orch. (1941); ballet, *Icaro* (1943); *Mensaje al futuro* for Wind Orch. (1944); Symph. (1945); *Móvil* for 7 Instruments (1969); Wind Quintet (1957); *La muerte del guerrillero* for Speaker and Orch. (1969).

Gramm, Donald, American bass-baritone; b. Milwaukee, Feb. 26, 1927; d. New York, June 2, 1983. He was of German ancestry, and his family name was **Grambach;** he abbreviated it to Gramm when he began his career as a singer. He studied piano and organ at the Wisconsin College-Conservatory of Music (1935–44); also studied voice with George Graham. He made his professional debut in Chicago at the age of 17 when he sang the role of Raimondo in Donizetti's opera *Lucia di Lammermoor;* he continued his vocal studies at the Chicago Musical College and at the Music Academy of the West in Santa Barbara, where he was a student of Martial Singher. On Sept. 26, 1952, he made his N.Y. debut at the N.Y. City Opera, as Colline in *La Bohème,* and continued to appear with the company for the rest of his life. He was extremely versatile in his roles; he sang Méphistophélès in *Faust,* Leporello in *Don Giovanni,* Figaro in *Le nozze di Figaro,* Falstaff in Verdi's opera, Baron Ochs in *Der Rosenkavalier,* and Scarpia in *Tosca;* on Jan. 10, 1964, he made his debut at the Metropolitan Opera in N.Y., in the minor role of Truffaldino in *Ariadne auf Naxos;* he also distinguished himself as an interpreter of such difficult parts as Dr. Schön in Berg's *Lulu* and Moses in Schoenberg's *Moses und Aron.*

Grammann, Karl, German composer; b. Lübeck, June 3, 1844; d. Dresden, Jan 30, 1897. He studied at the Leipzig Cons.; spent some years in Vienna; in 1885, settled in Dresden. As a youth, he wrote 2 operas, *Die Schatzgräber* and *Die Eisjungfrau*, which were not produced; the following operas were staged with some success: *Melusine* (Wiesbaden, 1875); *Thusnelda und der Triumphzug des Germanicus* (Dresden, 1881); *Das Andreasfest* (Dresden, 1882); 2 short operas, *Ingrid* and *Das Irrlicht* (Dresden, 1894). His last opera, *Auf neutralem Boden*, was produced posthumously (Hamburg, 1901). He further wrote several cantatas, symphs., string quartets, violin sonatas, and other chamber music works.

BIBLIOGRAPHY: F. Pfohl, *Karl Grammann. Ein Künstlerleben* (Berlin, 1910).

Granados, Eduardo, Spanish composer, son of **Enrique Granados;** b. Barcelona, July 28, 1894; d. Madrid, Oct. 2, 1928. He studied in Barcelona with his father; then at the Madrid Cons. with Conrado del Campo; taught at the Granados Academy in Barcelona; was also active as a conductor; presented many works by his father. He wrote several zarzuelas, of which the first, *Bufon y Hostelero,* was performed with some success in Barcelona (Dec. 7, 1917); other stage works are: *Los Fanfarrones,* comic opera; *La ciudad eterna,* mystery play; *Los Cigarrales,* operatic sketch; also musical comedies (*Cocktails del Nuevo,* etc.).

Granados, Enrique, outstanding Spanish composer; b. Lérida, July 27, 1867; d. at sea, March 24, 1916 (victim of the sinking by a German submarine of the S.S. *Sussex* in the English Channel). He studied piano at the Barcelona Cons. with Jurnet and Pujol, winning first prize (1883); then studied composition there with Pedrell (1884–87); in 1887 went to Paris to study with Charles de Beriot; made his recital debut in Barcelona in 1890. He first supported himself by playing piano in restaurants and giving private concerts. He attracted attention as a composer with an opera, *Maria del Carmen* (Madrid, Nov. 12, 1898); in 1900 he conducted a series of concerts in Barcelona; also established a music school, the Academia Granados. He then wrote 4 operas, which were produced in Barcelona with little success: *Picarol* (Feb. 23, 1901); *Follet* (April 4, 1903); *Gaziel* (Oct. 27, 1906); and *Liliana* (1911). He undertook the composition of a work that was to be his masterpiece, a series of piano pieces entitled *Goyescas,* inspired by the paintings and etchings of Goya; his fame rests securely on these imaginative and effective pieces, together with his brilliant *Danzas españolas.* Later, Fernando Periquet wrote a libretto based on the scenes from Goya's paintings, and Granados used the music of his piano suite for an opera, *Goyescas.* Its premiere took place, in the presence of the composer, at the Metropolitan Opera in N.Y., on Jan. 28, 1916, with excellent success; the score included an orch. *Intermezzo,* one of his most popular compositions. It was during his return voyage to Europe that he lost his life. Other works by Granados include an intermezzo to *Miel de la Alcarría* (1893); symph. poems, *La nit del mort* and

Dante; Suite arabe; Suite gallega; Marcha de los vencidos; Serenata; orch. suites, *Elisenda* and *Navidad;* Piano Trio; String Quartet; *Serenata* for 2 Violins and Piano; *Oriental* for Oboe and Strings; *Trova* for Cello and Piano; *Cant de les Estrelles* for Chorus, Organ, and Piano. Piano works: *Danzas españolas* (4 vols.); *Goyescas:* (Part I) *Los Requiebros, Coloquio en la Reja, El fandango del Candil, Quejas o la Maja y el Ruiseñor;* (Part II) *El Amor y la Muerte (Ballade), Epílogo (Serenade of the Specter), El Pelele (Escena goyesca); Escenas romanticas;* 6 pieces on Spanish popular songs; *Valses poéticos; Cuentos para la juventud; Marche militaire* and *A la Cubana* (also arranged for Orch.); *2 danses caractéristiques: Danza gitana* and *Danza aragonesa.* Songs: *Colección de Tonadillas, escritas en estilo antiguo; Colección de canciones amatorias.* Granados's music is essentially Romantic, with an admixture of specific Spanish rhythms and rather elaborate ornamentation.

BIBLIOGRAPHY: Special Granados number of *Revista Musical Catalana* (June 15, 1916); G. Jean-Aubry, "Enrique Granados," *Musical Times* (Dec. 1916); E. Newman, "The Granados of the *Goyescas,*" ibid. (Aug. 1917); G. Boladeres Ibern, *Enrique Granados, Recuerdos de su vida y estudio crítico de su obra* (Barcelona, 1921); H. Collet, *Albéniz et Granados* (Paris, 1926); J. Subira, *Enrique Granados* (Madrid, 1926); E.L. Mason, "Enrique Granados," *Music & Letters* (1933); A. Livermore, "Granados and the 19th Century in Spain," *Musical Review* (1946); F. Vicens, *Enrique Granados* (Barcelona, 1958).

Grancino, a family of violin makers, active in the 17th and early 18th centuries. **Andrea Grancino** established a workshop in Milan in 1646; his son, **Paolo,** worked in Milan between 1665 and 1692; he belonged to the Amati school, and several violins attributed to Amati are apparently the work of Paolo Grancino. Paolo's son, **Giovanni,** began making violins in 1677; he is reputed to have been the best of the family. His 2 sons, **Giovanni Battista** and **Francesco,** were active between 1715 and 1746; their labels are marked **Fratelli Grancini.**

Grancino (Grancini), Michel Angelo, Italian composer; b. Milan, 1605; d. there, April 17, 1669. He was organist at the Paradiso Church in Milan as a youth of 17; then was appointed organist at San Sepolcro (1624) and later at San Ambrogio (1628). In 1630 he became a maestro di cappella of the Milan Cathedral, and retained this post until his death. During his lifetime he publ. some 20 vols. of his works, which included madrigals, motets, and *concerti sacri,* only a few of which are extant.

Grandert, Johnny, Swedish composer; b. Stockholm, July 11, 1939. He studied under Lidholm at the Royal College of Music in Stockholm (1959–64); also took music courses in Germany, Italy, and America. The titles of his compositions betray a desire to puzzle and tantalize, but the music itself is not forbidding, despite the application of startling effects.

WORKS: *Chamber Music* for Chamber Ensemble (1961); string quartet, *40, 2* (1963); Nonet for Winds, Euphonium, and Cello (1964); *86 T* for Chamber Ensemble (Stockholm, June 4, 1965); *Mirror 25* for Chorus and Orch. (Stockholm, Feb. 11, 1966; the score calls for a machine gun, and the chorus is invited to belch at some points); *10 an' 30* for Chamber Ensemble (1966); Octet for 3 Voices, Flute, Trombone, Viola, Double Bass, and Harp (1966); *The D. of B.* for Orch. (1967); *Barypet,* concerto for Trumpet and Baritone Saxophone, with 16 Flutes, Percussion, and Strings (1968); *Prego I* for Cello and Horn (1968); *Non omesso* for Chamber Ensemble (1969); *Skorogovorka* (Russian for "tongue twister") for Wind Orch. and Percussion (Swedish Radio, April 18, 1971); *Non lo so* (*I do not know it* in Italian) for Flute, Cello, and Piano (1970); wind quintet, *Pour Philippe* (1970); *Pour Pjotr* for Voice, Piano, Cello, Clarinet, and Percussion (1971); 3 symphs.: No. 1 (1971); No. 2 (1972); No. 3, *Sinfonia Calamagrostis* (1972); Quartet for Recorders (1972); *Jerikos murar* for Flute, Slide Flute, 3 Bass Recorders, 3 Clarinets, 15 Trombones, Percussion, Organ, and Strings (Norrtälje, Nov. 25, 1972).

Grandi, Alessandro, Italian composer; b. 1577, place of birth uncertain; d. Bergamo, 1630. He was maestro di cappella in Ferrara, first at the Accademia della Morte (1597–1604), then at the Accademia dello Spirito Santo (1604–16); in 1617 was a singer at San Marco, Venice; in 1620, 2nd maestro di cappella at San Marco; in 1627, he went to Bergamo as maestro di cappella at Santa Maria Maggiore; he and his family died there in 1630 of the plague. He was one of the leading masters of the "stile nuovo" in Italy. His works include 3 books of *Cantade et arie* (Venice, 1620–29); 2 books of *Madrigali concertati* (Venice, 1615–22); several books of motets (Venice, 1610–29); other music in MS is at the Fitzwilliam Museum, Cambridge; Christ Church, Oxford; in Berlin and Vienna.
BIBLIOGRAPHY: Denis Arnold, "Alessandro Grandi, A Disciple of Monteverdi," *Musical Quarterly* (April 1957); M. Seelkopf, *Das geistliche Schaffen von Alessandro Grandi* (Diss., Julius-Maximilian Univ., Würzburg, 1973).

Grandjany, Marcel, French harpist; b. Paris, Sept. 3, 1891; d. New York, Feb. 24, 1975. He studied at the Paris Cons., winning first prize for harp (1905); made his Paris debut on Jan. 24, 1909; his American debut, N.Y., Feb. 7, 1924; taught at the Fontainebleau Cons. (1921–35); in 1936 settled in N.Y.; became an American citizen in 1945. In 1938 he joined the staff of the Juilliard School of Music; remained there until shortly before his death; also taught at the Montreal Cons. from 1943 to 1963. He composed a *Poème symphonique* for Harp, French Horn, and Orch., and several other works for harp; also songs to French texts. He publ. *First Grade Harp Pieces* (N.Y., 1964).

Grandjean, Axel Karl William, Danish composer; b. Copenhagen, March 9, 1847; d. there, Feb. 11, 1932.

He began his career as an opera singer, but gave up the stage for teaching and composition; also conducted several choral societies in Copenhagen. He wrote the operas *Colomba* (Copenhagen, Oct. 15, 1882), *Oluf* (Copenhagen, April 7, 1894), and others; many choral works; also edited (for Holberg's bicentennial in 1884) a collection of incidental music written to Holberg's dramas.

Grandval, Marie Félicie Clémence de Reiset, French composer; b. Saint-Rémy-des-Monts (Sarthe), Jan. 21, 1830; d. Paris, Jan. 15, 1907. She studied composition with Flotow and Saint-Saëns; under various pen names she wrote the operas *Le Sou de Lise* (Paris, 1859); *Les Fiancés de Rose* (Paris, May 1, 1863); *La Comtesse Eva* (Paris, Aug. 7, 1864); *La Pénitente* (Paris, May 13, 1868); *Piccolino* (Paris, Jan. 5, 1869); *Mazeppa* (Bordeaux, 1892); the oratorio *St. Agnès* (Paris, April 13, 1876); *La Forêt,* lyric poem for Soli, Chorus, and Orch. (Paris, March 30, 1875); songs.

Grandi (maiden name, **Garde**), **Margherita,** Australian soprano; b. Hobart, Oct. 4, 1894. She studied with Calvé in Paris; made her debut under the name of **Djema Vécla** (an anagram of Calvé) in 1919 at the Opéra-Comique in *Werther;* after marrying the scenic designer Giovanni Grandi, she used her married name; later sang in Monte Carlo, Milan, Glyndebourne, and London. She was best known for her performances in the Italian repertoire.

Granichstaedten, Bruno, Austrian operetta composer; b. Vienna, Sept. 1, 1879; d. New York, May 20, 1944. He began his career as a cabaret singer; in 1908 he turned to composing light opera; produced 16 stage works before 1930; of these, *Der Orlow* (Vienna, April 3, 1925) was the most successful; other operettas are *Bub oder Mädel, Auf Befehl der Kaiserin, Evelyne, Walzerliebe,* etc. In 1938 Granichstaedten left Austria and settled in the U.S.

Grant, Clifford, Australian bass; b. Randwick, Sept. 11, 1930. He studied at the Sydney Cons.; later had voice lessons with Otakar Kraus in London. In 1951 he made his operatic debut with the New South Wales Opera; in 1966 he became a member of the Sadler's Wells Opera in London; also sang with the San Francisco Opera, the Welsh National Opera, at Covent Garden, and at the Glyndebourne Festival.

Grant, (William) Parks, American composer; b. Cleveland, Jan. 4, 1910. He studied at Capital Univ. in Columbus, Ohio, graduating with a B.Mus. (1932); received a Ph.D. from the Eastman School of Music in Rochester, N.Y. (1948). He retired in 1974, culminating a 40-year teaching career at various institutions. He was an editor for the International Gustav Mahler Society in Vienna (1965–66; 1970; 1972–73), for whose *Critical Collected Edition* he corrected the new editions of Mahler's 2nd, 3rd, 8th, and 9th symphs. and *Das klagende Lied.*
WORKS: *The Dream of the Ballet-Master,* ballet

for Piano Quintet (1934); 3 symphs. (1936, 1947, 1961); *The Masque of the Red Death,* symph. poem (1938); Horn Concerto (1940); 6 overtures; Clarinet Concerto (1944); *Integrated Concerto* for Double Bass and Orch. (1946); *Scherzo* for Flute and Small Orch. (1950); 3 suites for String Orch.; 2 string quartets; *Essay* for Horn and Organ (1948); 3 suites for Brass Quintet (1949, 1951, 1953); *Varied Obstinacy* for 2 Saxophones (1974); *Pensive Monologue* for Solo Cello (1976); choruses; songs.

WRITINGS: *Music for Elementary Teachers* (N.Y., 1951; revised ed., 1960) and *Handbook of Music Terms* (Metuchen, N.J., 1967).

Grant-Schaefer, George Alfred, American composer and teacher; b. Williamstown, Ontario, July 4, 1872; d. Chicago, May 11, 1939. He studied in Montreal, Chicago, and London; from 1896 to 1908 was organist and choirmaster in Chicago; in 1908–20 was head of the vocal dept. of Northwestern Univ., Evanston, Ill. He composed mostly for schools; also publ. a collection of French Canadian songs (Boston, 1925).

Grantham, Donald, American composer; b. Duncan, Okla., Nov. 9, 1947. He studied composition at the Univ. of Oklahoma (B.Mus., 1970). In 1974 he entered the Univ. of Southern Calif. in the composition classes of Robert Linn and Halsey Stevens (M.M., 1974; D.M.A., 1980). In the summers of 1973 and 1974 he studied with Nadia Boulanger at the Cons. Américain in Fontainebleau. WORKS: FOR ORCH.: *Música para "Los desastres de la guerra"* (1974); *5 Variations and Double Fugue on "L'Homme armé"* (1970); *El album de los duendecitos* (1983). CHAMBER MUSIC: Brass Quintet (1970); Piano Trio (1971); *Intrada* for Trumpet, Horn, and Trombone (1973); Chamber Concerto for Harpsichord and String Quartet (1974); *4 caprichos de Francisco Goya* for Solo Violin (1976); *Fanfare festiva* for 2 Trumpets, 2 Trombones, Timpani, and Organ (1978); *Sonata in One Movement* for Bass Trombone and Piano (1979); *Concerto* for Bass Trombone and Wind Ensemble (1979); *Caprichos II* for Solo Cello (1979); *3 Epigrams* for Clarinet, Bassoon, and Piano (1980); *Duendecitos!* for Flute and Piano (1981); *Caprichos III* for Solo Double Bass (1982). FOR VOICES: *The War Prayer,* to words by Mark Twain, for Baritone, and Orch. or Piano (1974); *La noche en la isla* for Baritone, and Chamber Orch. or Piano, to words by Pablo Neruda (1980); *To the King Celestial* for Soprano and Chamber Orch., to a 14th-century Eng. text (1981).

Grappelli (Grappelly), Stéphane, French jazz violinist; b. Paris, Jan. 26, 1908. Trained as a classical musician, he turned to jazz, and in 1934 organized the Quintette du Hot Club de France with the Belgian guitarist Django Reinhardt. He became the foremost jazz violinist in the European style of "Le Jazz hot."

Gräsbeck, Gottfrid, Finnish composer; b. Turku, Feb. 15, 1927. He graduated with a philosophy degree from the Turku Academy; traveled on study trips to West Germany and America. Upon his return to Finland, he taught at Turku; also founded his own concert agency. Among his works are *Toccata dodecafonica* for Orch. (1959); Concerto for Orch. and Tape (1964); *Visan från molnet (Song about the Cloud),* cantata for Female Chorus and Orch. (1967); *Sinfonia da camera* (1969); *Lucia musik* for Solo Voices, Chorus, Organ, and Orch. (1971); Sonata for Guitar (1974).

Grasse, Edwin, American violinist and composer; b. New York, Aug. 13, 1884; d. there, April 8, 1954. Blind from infancy, he dictated his compositions to an accompanist. He studied the violin with Carl Hauser in N.Y.; then went to Brussels for study with César Thomson; in 1899 entered the Brussels Cons., where he won first prize in 1900, and diplôme de capacité in 1901; toured Europe and America. His works include *American Fantasie* for Violin and Orch.; Violin Sonata and other violin pieces; organ pieces.

Grassi, Eugène, composer; b. Bangkok, Siam, July 5, 1881; d. Paris, June 8, 1941. He was born of French parents in Siam; went to France as a youth and studied with Vincent d'Indy; he revisited Siam in 1910–13 to collect materials on indigenous music; his works reflect this study as well as, in harmonic idiom, the influence of Debussy. Among his compositions, all with oriental flavor, are *Le Revéil de Bouddha,* symph. poem (Paris, Feb. 20, 1920); *Poème de l'univers* for Orch. (Paris, April 9, 1922); *Les Sanctuaires* (Paris, March 25, 1926); also songs in the impressionist manner.

Grassini, Josephina (Giuseppina), Italian contralto; b. Varese, April 8, 1773; d. Milan, Jan. 3, 1850. She studied in Varese with Domenico Zucchinetti and in Milan with Antonio Secchi. She made her debut as an opera singer in Parma in 1789 in Guglielmi's *La pastorella nobile;* sang at La Scala in 1790, and soon attained popularity on all the leading Italian stages; in 1800 she sang in Milan before Napoleon, and became his mistress; he took her with him to Paris, where she sang at national celebrations. She was in London in 1804–6; then returned to Paris and sang at the French court; she was noted for her beauty and her acting, as well as her voice.

BIBLIOGRAPHY: P. Cambiasi, "Una famosa cantante varesina," *Gazzetta Musicale di Milano* (Feb. 20, 1902); A. Pougin, *Une Cantatrice "amie" de Napoléon: Giuseppina Grassini* (Paris, 1920); A. Gavoty, *La Grassini* (Paris, 1947).

Grau, Maurice, American operatic impresario; b. Brünn, Moravia, 1849; d. Paris, March 14, 1907. He was taken to the U.S. at the age of 5; studied law at Columbia Univ. In 1872 he was a co-manager of the American tours of Anton Rubinstein; in 1873 he organized the Kellogg Opera Co.; was instrumental in bringing Offenbach to the U.S. In 1890 he presented a special season of 21 performances at the Metropolitan Opera, with such famous artists as Adelina Patti, Emma Albani, Nordica, and Tamagno. From 1891 to 1897 the Metropolitan was leased to the partnership of Abbey, Schoeffel, and Grau, and upon Abbey's death, to the Maurice Grau Opera Co. (1898–1903). In 1903 Grau retired and went to Paris. The secret of Grau's success as an impresario was his perfect understanding of public taste in opera; he frankly subordinated the repertoire to the favorite roles of the great European stars; he did not produce Wagner's operas until Wagnerian cycles presented by Damrosch had shown that American audiences were ripe for them. In fact, the growing popularity of Wagner contributed greatly toward the financial success of Grau's last seasons.

Graudan, Nicolai, Russian-American cellist; b. Libau, Sept. 5, 1896; d. Moscow, Aug. 9, 1964. He studied cello with Abbiate at the St. Petersburg Cons.; subsequently was an instructor there; left Russia in 1922 and went to Germany; was first cellist of the Berlin Phil. (1926–35). In 1935 he went to London, and in 1938 to the U.S.; in 1939–44 was first cellist of the Minneapolis Orch.; in 1944–50 lived in N.Y.; in 1950 settled in Los Angeles; gave duo-recitals with his wife, the pianist **Joanna Freudberg;** was a member of the Festival Quartet; taught at Black Mountain College, Santa Barbara Academy of the West, at Aspen, and at the Univ. of Calif., Los Angeles. In 1964 he went to Moscow for a visit, and died there. He edited 6 Vivaldi cello sonatas with the realization of the keyboard part; arranged several Chopin pieces for cello and piano.

Graun, August Friedrich, German composer, brother of **Carl Heinrich Graun;** b. Wahrenbrück, near Dresden, 1699; d. Merseburg, May 5, 1765. He was active as an organist and cantor at Merseburg, where he settled in 1729. Only one of his works is preserved, *Kyrie et Gloria* for 4 Voices with Instruments.

Graun, Carl Heinrich, German composer; b. Wahrenbrück, near Dresden, May 7, 1704; d. Berlin, Aug. 8, 1759. He received his primary education at the Kreuzschule in Dresden (1713–20), where he studied with Grundig (voice) and Petzold (organ). He sang soprano in the town council choir; then began to study composition with Johann Christoph Schmidt. In 1725 he was engaged as operatic tenor at the Braunschweig court; soon he began to compose operas for production at the court theater: *Sancio und Sinilde* (Feb. 3, 1727), *Iphigenia in Aulis* (Aug. 16, 1728), *Polidorus* (1731), and *Scipio Africanus* (1732), all to German librettos. On June 14, 1733, he staged his first Italian opera, *Lo specchio della fedeltà* (also known under the title *Timareta;* June 13, 1733). In 1735 Graun was invited by Frederick the Great (then Crown Prince of Prussia) to Rheinsberg, as music director; Graun gladly accepted, and followed Frederick to Berlin when he became King (1740). In Rheinsberg, Graun wrote a great number of cantatas, in the Italian style; in Berlin, his chief duty was to establish an Italian opera troupe, for which purpose he traveled to Italy in search of good

singers. Upon his return to Berlin, Graun produced his first opera for his company, *Rodelinda* (Dec. 13, 1741); there followed *Cesare e Cleopatra* (Dec. 7, 1742), staged for the inauguration of the new opera house. He continued to compose operas with unfailing regularity for each season, 28 in all, among them *Artaserse* (Dec. 2, 1743), *Catone in Utica* (Jan. 24, 1744), *Alessandro nell' Indie* (1744), *Adriano in Siria* (Jan. 7, 1746), *Il Mitridate* (Dec. 18, 1750), and *Semiramide* (March 27, 1754). Frederick the Great himself wrote the librettos (in French) for Graun's operas *Montezuma* (Berlin, Jan. 6, 1755; printed in Denkmäler Deutscher Tonkunst, 15) and *La Merope* (March 27, 1756). In those years Graun enjoyed very high renown and royal favor; only Hasse approached him in public esteem. In his operas, Graun adhered to the Italian tradition, and was preoccupied chiefly with the requirements of the singing voice. During the last years of his life he wrote some excellent church music; his *Te Deum* commemorating Frederick's victory at the battle of Prague (1756) is regarded as one of the finest sacred works in Germany; even more renowned is Graun's Passion oratorio, *Der Tod Jesu* (Berlin, March 26, 1755), which was performed annually for a century. Graun's instrumental music displays a high degree of contrapuntal craftsmanship, as well as a facile melodic gift, but despite these qualities, it failed to sustain interest as well as his sacred works did. He wrote a Concerto Grosso for Flute, Violin, Viola da Gamba, Cello, and Strings; about 30 concertos for Harpsichord; 6 flute concertos; 3 quintets for Harpsichord and Strings; about 35 trio sonatas; duets for various instruments; etc.

BIBLIOGRAPHY: A. Mayer-Reinach, *Carl Heinrich Graun als Opernkomponist* (Berlin, 1899); K. Mennicke, "Zur Biographie der Brüder Graun," *Neue Zeitschrift für Musik* (1904); idem, *Hasse und die Brüder Graun als Sinfoniker* (Leipzig, 1906; with biography and complete thematic catalogues); B. Hitzig, "Briefe Carl Heinrich Grauns," *Zeitschrift für Musikwissenschaft* (1926).

Graun, Johann Gottlieb, German composer, brother of **Carl Heinrich Graun;** b. Wahrenbrück, near Dresden, 1703; d. Berlin, Oct. 27, 1771. He studied violin with Pisendel in Dresden and with Tartini in Padua. In 1726 he was appointed Konzertmeister in Merseburg, where he was the teacher of Wilhelm Friedemann Bach. In 1732 he became Konzertmeister for Crown Prince Frederick (later Frederick the Great) at Rheinsberg, and from 1741 held a similar position in the newly founded Royal Opera in Berlin, where his brother, Carl Heinrich, was Kapellmeister. His works include 100 symphs., 60 violin concertos, about 8 string quartets, and a number of sacred works. Only a few are publ.: 6 harpsichord concertos; 8 sonatas for 2 Flutes and Violin. Riemann reprinted 3 trio sonatas in *Collegium musicum* (1906).

Graupner, (Johann) Christoph, German composer; b. Kirchberg, Saxony, Jan. 13, 1683; d. Darmstadt, May 10, 1760. He studied music in Kirchberg with

the cantor Michael Mylius and the organist Nikolaus Kuster, and later at the Thomasschule in Leipzig with Johann Kuhnau and Johann Schelle; he then went to Hamburg, where he became harpsichordist at the Oper-am-Gänsemarkt (1707–9); during this time he composed 5 operas. In 1709 he was called to Darmstadt as Vice-Kapellmeister to the Landgraf Ernst Ludwig; in 1712 he was appointed Kapellmeister, a post he held until his death. Graupner was a highly industrious composer; he wrote 8 operas, some 1,400 church cantatas, 24 secular cantatas, about 100 symphs., 50 concertos, 80 overtures, and many instrumental sonatas and keyboard works. Several of his compositions were publ. during his lifetime, including *8 Partien auf das Clavier ... erster Theil* (Darmstadt, 1718), the *Monatliche Clavier Früchte ... meistenteils für Anfänger* (Darmstadt, 1722), and *Vier Partien auf das Clavier, unter der Benennung der Vier Jahreszeiten* (Darmstadt, 1733); he also brought out a *Neu vermehrtes Darmstädtisches Choralbuch* (Darmstadt, 1728). He was proficient as an engraver, and printed several keyboard pieces in his own workshop. His operas include *Dido, Königin von Carthago* (Hamburg, 1707); *Il fido amico, oder Der getreue Freund Hercules und Theseus* (Hamburg, 1708; not extant); *L'amore ammalato: Die Krankende Liebe, oder Antiochus und Stratonica* (Hamburg, 1708); *Bellerophon, oder Das in die preussisch Krone verwandelte Wagenstirn* (Hamburg, Nov. 28, 1708; not extant); *Der Fall des grossen Richters in Israel, Simson, oder Die abgekühlte Liebesrache der Deborah* (Hamburg, 1709; not extant); *Berenice und Lucilla, oder Das tugendhafte Lieben* (Darmstadt, March 4, 1710; not extant); *Telemach* (Darmstadt, Feb. 16, 1711; not extant); *La constanza vince l'inganno* (Darmstadt, 1715). The Denkmäler Deutscher Tonkunst, vols. 51–52 (1926), contains 17 of his cantatas; an incomplete edition of his works was edited by F. Noack (4 vols., Kassel, 1955–57).
BIBLIOGRAPHY: W. Kleefeld, "Bach und Graupner," *Jahrbuch der Musikbibliothek Peters 1897;* W. Nagel, "Christoph Graupner als Sinfoniker," in *Musikalisches Magazin,* XLIX (Langensalza, 1912); F. Noack, "Bachs und Graupners Kompositionen zur Bewerbung um das Thomaskantorat in Leipzig," *Bach-Jahrbuch 1913;* idem, *Christoph Graupners Kirchenmusiken* (Leipzig, 1916); L. Hoffman-Erbrecht, "Johann Christoph Graupner als Klavierkomponist," *Archiv für Musikwissenschaft,* X (1953); M. Witte, *Die Instrumentalkonzerte von Christoph Graupner* (Diss., Univ. of Göttingen, 1963); A. McCredie, "Christoph Graupner as Opera Composer," *Miscellanea Musicologica,* I (1966); C. Lawson, "J.A. Graupner: Bach's Rival for the Thomaskantorat," *Musical Times* (Jan. 1983).

Graupner, Johann Christian Gottlieb, composer; b. Verden, near Hannover, Germany, Oct. 6, 1767; d. Boston, April 16, 1836. He was the son of the oboist **Johann Georg Graupner,** and became himself an oboist in military bands. In 1788 he was in London, and played in Haydn's orch. in 1791. About 1795, he emigrated to America, settling in Charleston, S.C.; played his Oboe Concerto there on March 21, 1795; early in 1797, he went to Boston; in 1800, he opened a music store; also taught piano, and all orch. instruments, on which he was fairly proficient; publ. works by himself and other composers; he became an American citizen in 1808. In 1810 he organized the Boston Phil. Society, which was the first semiprofessional orch. in Boston; it gave performances of Haydn's symphs., presented the *Messiah* in 1818 and Haydn's *Creation* in 1819; the orch. continued its activity until Nov. 1824. In 1815, Graupner was a co-founder of a musical organization which became the Handel and Haydn Society of Boston, and which greatly influenced the development of choral music in New England. In view of these accomplishments, Graupner is referred to by some writers as the "father of American orchestral music." In 1806, he publ. *Rudiments of the art of playing the piano forte, containing the elements of music* (reprinted 1819, 1825, and 1827). He was married to **Catherine Hillier,** a professional singer (1770–1821); in Boston on Dec. 30, 1799, she sang a Negro ballad; this fact led to erroneous reports that Graupner himself appeared as a blackface minstrel.
BIBLIOGRAPHY: O.G. Sonneck, *Early Concert Life in America* (Leipzig, 1907); J.T. Howard, *Our American Music* (N.Y., 1931; 4th ed., N.Y., 1965); H.E. Johnson, *Musical Interludes in Boston* (N.Y., 1943; chapter VI). Typescript copies of a memoir on Graupner, compiled by his granddaughter, Catherine Graupner Stone (1906), are available in the Library of Congress, the N.Y. Public Library, and the Boston Public Library.

Graveure, Louis (real name, **Wilfred Douthitt**), concert singer; b. London, March 18, 1888; d. Los Angeles, April 27, 1965. He studied voice with Clara Novello-Davies; came to the U.S. and under his real name, Douthitt, sang the baritone part in the operetta *The Lilac Domino,* in N.Y. on Oct. 28, 1914. In 1915 he reappeared in N.Y. as Louis Graveure (after his mother's maiden name) and became a popular concert artist, singing all types of music. On Feb. 5, 1928, he gave a concert in N.Y. as a tenor; from 1931 to 1938 he was in Germany; from 1938 to 1940, in France; from 1940 to 1947, in England; in 1947, returned to the U.S.; taught in various music schools.
BIBLIOGRAPHY: "The Case of a Beardless Baritone," in N. Slonimsky, *A Thing or Two about Music* (N.Y., 1948; pp. 220–21).

Gray, Alan, English organist and composer; b. York, Dec. 23, 1855; d. Cambridge, Sept. 27, 1935. He took degrees in law and music from Trinity College, Cambridge; was music director of Wellington College (1883–92); conductor of the Cambridge Univ. Musical Society (1892–1912); also organist at Trinity College (1892–1930). He wrote 5 cantatas; a *Coronation March;* chamber music; many organ works. He was also an editor for the Purcell Society.

Gray, Cecil, British writer on music; b. Edinburgh, May 19, 1895; d. Worthing, Sept. 9, 1951. He studied music with Healey Willan; in 1920, with Philip Heseltine (Peter Warlock), he edited a new magazine of music criticism, the *Sackbut;* later was music critic for the *Daily Telegraph* and the *Manchester Guardian;* wrote 3 operas (to his own texts) and other music.

WRITINGS: *A Survey of Contemporary Music* (1924); *Carlo Gesualdo, Prince of Venosa; Musician and Murderer* (in collaboration with Philip Heseltine; 1926); *The History of Music* (1928); *Sibelius* (1931); *Peter Warlock* (1934); *Sibelius: The Symphonies* (1935); *Predicaments, or Music and the Future* (1936); *The 48 Preludes and Fugues of Bach* (1938); *Contingencies* (N.Y., 1947); memoirs, *Musical Chairs or Between Two Stools* (London, 1948).

BIBLIOGRAPHY: R. Gorer, "The Music of Cecil Gray," *Musical Review* (Aug. 1947).

Gray, Donald, American publisher; b. New Rochelle, N.Y., May 25, 1903; d. Stamford, Conn., Oct. 21, 1969. He studied at Dartmouth College, graduating in 1924; joined the music publishing house founded by his father, H. Willard Gray; succeeded him as president in 1951. He publ. many works by American composers, among them Aaron Copland, Leo Sowerby, and Philip James.

Gray, Jerry, American bandleader, composer, and arranger; b. Boston, July 3, 1915; d. Dallas, Texas, Aug. 10, 1976. He studied violin with Ondříček in Boston; at the age of 13, was concertmaster of the Boston Junior Symph. Orch.; then became a jazz-band leader. He played in nightclubs and other locales of musical subculture; in 1936 joined the Artie Shaw Orch. as arranger; during World War II was arranger for the fabled Glenn Miller band, which he took over after Miller's death in a plane crash in 1944. He had his own radio show (1946–52); led dance orchs.; also wrote several songs that became popular, among them *Strings of Pearls.*

Gray, Linda Esther, Scottish soprano; b. Greenock, May 29, 1948. She studied at the Scottish Academy of Music and in London with Eva Turner; won the Kathleen Ferrier and John Christie awards in 1973. She made her debut with the Glyndebourne Touring Opera in 1972 as Mimi; sang with the Glyndebourne Festival in 1974 and with the Scottish Opera in 1975 in the roles of Donna Elvira, Ariadne, Eva, and Amelia. Her first role with the English National Opera was Micaela in 1978; she later sang Aida, Tosca, and Isolde there. She also sang Isolde with the Welsh National Opera in 1979 and Sieglinde at Covent Garden. She made her U.S. debut in Dallas as Sieglinde in 1981; then appeared as Beethoven's Leonore with the same company in Mexico.

Graziani, Bonifazio, Italian composer of church music; b. Marino, 1605; d. Rome, June 15, 1664. From 1648 he held a post of maestro di cappella in Rome; composed much sacred music, publ. in 1650–78.

Graziani, Francesco, Italian baritone; brother of **Lodovico Graziani;** b. Fermo, April 26, 1828; d. there, June 30, 1901. He studied with Cellini; made his debut in 1851 in Ascoli Piceno; sang in Paris (1853–61) and the U.S. (1854); made many appearances at Covent Garden in London (1855–80); also sang in St. Petersburg, where he created the role of Don Carlo in Verdi's *La forza del destino* (1862).

Graziani, Lodovico, Italian tenor; brother of **Francesco Graziani;** b. Fermo, Nov. 14, 1820; d. there, May 15, 1885. He studied with Cellini; made his debut in Cambiaggio's *Don Procopio* in Bologna in 1845; created the role of Alfredo in Verdi's *La Traviata* (1853); also sang at La Scala in Milan. He was greatly esteemed for his performances in the operas of Verdi.

Greatorex, Thomas, English organist, singer, and conductor; b. North Wingfield, Derby, Oct. 5, 1758; d. Hampton, near London, July 18, 1831. He was the son of an amateur organist; the family moved to Leicester in 1767. He studied with Dr. B. Cooke (1772); was befriended by Lord Sandwich and became music director of his household for a time. He sang at the Concerts of Antient Music in London (from 1776) and was organist at Carlisle Cathedral (1781–84). He then traveled in the Netherlands, Italy, and France, and took lessons in Strasbourg with Pleyel. Settling in London, he became a highly popular singing teacher (in one week he gave 84 lessons at a guinea each). In 1793 he was appointed conductor of the Concerts of Antient Music, a post which he held until his death, never missing a single concert. He assisted in the revival of the Vocal Concerts in 1801; from 1819 he was organist at Westminster Abbey; he conducted festivals throughout England, and was one of the founders of the Royal Academy of Music in London (1822). He publ. *A Selection of Tunes* (London, 1829); the collection *Parochial Psalmody* (1825); *12 Glees* (1832); anthems; Psalms; and chants; but it was as an organist that Greatorex was best known.

Greef, Arthur de, Belgian pianist and composer; b. Louvain, Oct. 10, 1862; d. Brussels, Aug. 29, 1940. He studied at the Brussels Cons. with L. Brassin (piano) and Gevaert (composition); then traveled as a pianist in Europe; in 1885 he became a prof. of piano at the Brussels Cons., retaining that post until 1930.

WORKS: Opera in Flemish, *De Marketenster* (Louvain, 1879); Symph.; Ballad for Strings; 2 piano concertos; 2 violin sonatas; *4 vieilles chansons flamandes* for Piano; a number of piano études; songs.

BIBLIOGRAPHY: F. Rasse, "Notice sur Arthur de Greef," *Annuaire de l'Académie Royale de Belgique* (1949).

Green, Adolph, American musician, playwright, and lyricist; b. New York, Dec. 2, 1915. After graduating from high school, he sang, danced, and acted with "The Revuers." With the dramatist Betty Comden, he entered a long-standing and highly successful collaboration; their first success came with *On the Town* (1944; music by Leonard Bernstein), which was followed by *Billion Dollar Baby, Two on* *the Aisle, Bells Are Ringing*, etc. He received Tony awards for his contributions to *Applause* (1970) and *On the 20th Century* (1978).

Green, Al, black American rhythm-and-blues singer; b. Forrest City, Ark., April 13, 1946. The family moved to Grand Rapids, Mich., and Al Green sang in local churches with his brothers. He was barely 18 years old when he formed a pop group named The Creations, which scored considerable success. He toured on the "chitlin circuit" in the South, then moved to Memphis and produced his first hit, *Tired of Being Alone*. It was followed by another hit, *Let's Stay Together*. He was also successful as a solo soul singer of gospel songs, which eventually led him to found his own church in Memphis, where he became a regular preacher.

Green, John, American composer and conductor of popular music; b. New York, Oct. 10, 1908. He studied economics at Harvard Univ. (A.B., 1928); music theory with W.R. Spalding; piano with Ignace Hilsberg. He settled in Hollywood in 1942; became arranger for Guy Lombardo; wrote songs, among which *Body and Soul* (1931) and *I Cover the Waterfront* (1933) became popular; conducted many motion picture scores and received Academy Awards for *Easter Parade* (1948), *An American in Paris* (1951), and *West Side Story* (1961); also arranged and conducted music for television. He was conductor of the Los Angeles Phil. Promenade Concerts (1959–63) and guest conductor of other orchs. in the U.S.

Green, L. Dunton (Louis Grein), Dutch music critic; b. Amsterdam, Dec. 22, 1872; d. Ruysselede, Belgium, Dec. 30, 1933. He studied music in Germany and in Paris; lived for many years in London; contributed numerous articles on modern composers to English, Italian, French, and American magazines.

Green, Ray, American composer; b. Cavendish, Mo., Sept. 13, 1909. He studied composition with Ernest Bloch at the San Francisco Cons. (1927–33) and with Albert Elkus at the Univ. of Calif. at Berkeley (1933–35). In 1943 he entered the armed forces; from 1946 to 1948 was chief of music for the Veterans Administration; from 1948 to 1961 served as executive secretary of the American Music Center in N.Y.; from 1961 on he devoted himself to music publishing and electronic music. His own compositions are often modal in harmonic settings; rhythmic animation is much in evidence in his pieces based on American rural music.
WORKS: 2 symphs. (1945–53, 1974–80); *Sunday Sing Symphony* (1946); Violin Concerto (1952); *12 Short Sonatas* for Piano (1949–70); many pieces for band derived thematically from regional American rhythms (*Kentucky Mountain Running Set, Jig Theme, 6 Changes*); madrigals; choruses; rhapsodies; dance scores; hymn tunes; also publ. *Piano Books for Young People* in 6 vols. (1961).

Greenawald, Sheri, American soprano; b. Iowa City, Nov. 12, 1947. After completing her vocal studies, she quickly rose to prominence through her appearances with the Santa Fe Opera, Cincinnati Opera, San Francisco Opera, Houston Grand Opera, Washington Opera, and others; in addition to her roles in the standard Italian and French operatic repertoires, she sang in the world premieres of Pasatieri's *Signor Deluso* (1974) and *Washington Square* (1976) and Bernstein's *A Quiet Place* (1983). She was also a soloist with the Boston Symph., Philadelphia Orch., San Francisco Symph., Cleveland Orch., and St. Louis Symph.

Greenberg, Noah, American conductor; b. New York, April 9, 1919; d. there, Jan. 9, 1966. He studied music privately; served in the U.S. Merchant Marine (1944–49); organized choruses in N.Y. In 1952 he founded the N.Y. Pro Musica Antiqua, an organization specializing in Renaissance and medieval music, performed in authentic styles and on copies of early instruments; revived the medieval liturgical music dramas *The Play of Daniel* (1958) and *The Play of Herod* (1963); traveled with his ensemble in Europe in 1960 and 1963. It was primarily through the efforts of the N.Y. Pro Musica Antiqua (later known as the N.Y. Pro Musica) that early music, formerly known only to musicologists, became a viable idiom available to modern audiences. Greenberg held a Guggenheim fellowship in 1955 and Ford fellowships in 1960 and 1962.

Greene, Harry Plunket, Irish singer; b. near Dublin, June 24, 1865; d. London, Aug. 19, 1936. He studied in Florence with Vannuccini, and in London under J.B. Welsh and A. Blume; made his debut in the *Messiah* at Stepney (Jan. 21, 1888) and soon became a popular concert artist. He made the first of several tours of the U.S. in 1893; also appeared in Canada. He was noted for his interpretations of Schumann and Brahms; publ. a valuable instruction book for singers, *Interpretation in Song* (London, 1912); a biography of Stanford (London, 1935); and a vol. of musical reminiscences, *From Blue Danube to Shannon*.

Greene, Maurice, English organist and composer; b. London, Aug. 12, 1696; d. there, Dec. 1, 1755. He served as a choirboy in St. Paul's Cathedral; became proficient as an organist; was appointed organist of St. Paul's in 1718. In 1727, he succeeded Croft as composer to the Chapel Royal; in 1730, he was Tudway's successor as prof. of music at the Univ. of Cambridge, receiving the title of Mus.Doc. In 1735, he became Master of the King's Musick. Beginning in 1750, he accumulated and collated a great number of English sacred works; he willed this material to Boyce, who made use of it in his monumental collection, *Cathedral Music*.
WORKS: 3 oratorios: *The Song of Deborah and Barak* (1732); *Jephtha* (1737); *The Force of Truth* (1744); 3 dramatic pastorals: *Florimel, or Love's Revenge* (1734); *The Judgment of Hercules* (1740); *Phoebe* (1747); a collection of 12 English songs, *The*

Chaplet; an album of 25 sonnets for Voice, with Harpsichord and Violin, *Spenser's Amoretti;* he collected *40 Select Anthems in Score* (2 vols., 1743); composed numerous catches and canons, organ voluntaries, harpsichord pieces, etc.

BIBLIOGRAPHY: E. Walker, "The Bodleian MSS of Maurice Greene," *Musical Antiquarian* (April–July 1910); E. Janifer, *The English Church Music of Maurice Greene and His Contemporaries: A Study of Traditional and Contemporary Influences* (Diss., Univ. of London, 1959); J. Moore, *The Church Music of Maurice Greene* (Diss., Univ. of Nottingham, 1961); H. Johnstone, *The Life and Works of Maurice Greene (1696–1755)* (Diss., Oxford Univ., 1967).

Greenfield, Edward, English writer on music; b. Westcliff-on-Sea, Essex, July 30, 1928. He studied law at Cambridge Univ. (1949–52); joined the staff of the *Manchester Guardian* as phonograph-record critic in 1955, and became its music critic in 1964. He was a regular broadcaster for the BBC from 1957; contributed to the *Gramophone* and other music journals. He was joint author (with Denis Stevens and Ivan March) of the multi-vol. *Stereo Record Guide.* He publ. a monograph, *Puccini: Keeper of the Seal* (London, 1958).

Greenhouse, Bernard, American cellist; b. Newark, N.J., Jan. 3, 1916. He studied cello with Felix Salmond at the Juilliard School of Music in N.Y.; subsequently took lessons with Feuermann and Casals. He made his debut in N.Y. in a recital in 1946; in 1955 he became a founding member of the Beaux Arts Trio, which gradually acquired a fine reputation in its genre. He was also active as a teacher; taught at the Juilliard School of Music (1950–62), the Manhattan School of Music (1950–72), the Indiana Univ. School of Music (1956–64), the Univ. of Hartford (1962–71), and N.Y. State Univ. (1965–72).

Gregh, Louis, French composer and music publisher; b. Philippeville, Algeria, March 16, 1843; d. St. Mesme (Seine-et-Oise), Jan. 21, 1915. He began his musical career with the production of a light opera, *Un Lycée de jeunes filles* (Paris, 1881), which won a decided success; this was followed by several other operettas, including *Le Présomtif* (1884) and *Le Capitaine Roland* (1895), and ballets. He then turned to publishing; the firm was continued by his son, **Henri Gregh,** who established it as Henri Gregh & Fils (1902); Henri Gregh's son, **André,** succeeded him as director in 1934.

Gregoir, Edouard (Georges Jacques), Belgian composer and writer on music; b. Turnhout, near Antwerp, Nov. 7, 1822; d. Wyneghem, June 28, 1890. He studied piano, and was a professional accompanist; in 1851, he settled in Antwerp.

WORKS: He was a prolific composer; wrote 154 works in all. His Flemish opera, *Willem Beukels,* was produced in Brussels (July 21, 1856); he also wrote incidental music to various patriotic plays: *De Belgen in 1848; La Dernière Nuite du Comte d'Egmont;* etc.; a symph. oratorio, *Le Déluge* (1849); a historical symph., *Les Croisades* (1846).

WRITINGS: *Essai historique sur la musique et les musiciens dans les Pays-Bas* (1861); *Histoire de l'orgue* (1865; with biographical notes on Belgian and Dutch organists and organ builders); *Galerie biographique des artistes-musiciens belges du XVIIIᵉ et du XIXᵉ siècles* (1862; 2nd ed., 1885); *Notice sur l'origine du célèbre compositeur Louis van Beethoven* (1863); *Les Artistes-Musiciens néerlandais* (1864); *Du chant choral et des festivals en Belgique* (1865); *Notice historique sur les sociétés de musique d'Anvers* (1869); *Recherches historiques concernant les journaux de musique depuis les temps les plus reculés jusqu'à nos jours* (1872); *Notice biographique d'Adrian Willaert; Réflexions sur la régénération de l'ancienne école de musique flamande et sur le théâtre flamand; Les Artistes-Musiciens au XIXᵉ siècle; Réponse à un critique de Paris (1984); Documents historiques relatifs à l'art musical et aux artistes-musiciens* (4 vols., 1872–76); *Panthéon musical populaire* (6 vols., 1876–77); *Notice biographique sur F.J. Gossé dit Gossec* (1878); *L'Art musical en Belgique sous les règnes de Léopold I et Léopold II* (1879); *Les Gloires de l'Opéra et la musique à Paris* (4 vols., 1880–3; vol. I embraces the period 1392–1750); *A.-E.-M. Grétry* (1883); *Souvenirs artistiques* (3 vols., 1888–9).

Gregoir, Jacques (Mathieu Joseph), Belgian pianist and composer, brother of **Edouard Gregoir;** b. Antwerp, Jan. 19, 1817; d. Brussels, Oct. 29, 1876. He studied with Henri Herz in Paris and with Rummel in Biebrich. He gave a number of successful piano recitals in Belgium, Germany, and Switzerland; wrote salon pieces for piano and several practical methods of piano playing; publ. duets for violin and piano in collaboration with Vieuxtemps; he also wrote an opera, *Le Gondolier de Venise* (1848).

Gregor, Bohumil, Czech conductor; b. Prague, July 14, 1926. He studied at the Prague Cons.; then conducted in Prague (1947–49), Brno (1949–51), and Ostrava (1958–62). Returning to Prague in 1963, he conducted at the National Theater there. He was also a regular guest conductor at the Royal Opera in Stockholm and at the Hamburg State Opera, where he frequently performed Czech music.

Gregor, Čestmír, Czech composer; b. Brno, May 14, 1926. He studied composition with Kvapil at the Brno Cons.; from 1959 until 1972, was music director of Ostrava Radio.

WORKS: Ballet, *Závrat* (*Vertigo;* 1963; Ostrava, May 9, 1964; ballet version of the *Choreographic Symphony*); *Joyous Overture* (1951); *No One Is Alone,* rhapsody for Piano and Orch. (1955); *Prosím o slovo (May I Speak?),* overture (1956); *Tragic Suite* for Chamber Orch. (1957); *Concerto semplice* for Piano and Orch. (1958); *Polyfonietta* for Orch. (1961); *The Children of Daidalos,* symph. poem (1961); *Choreographic Symphony* (1963); *Prague Walker,* 2 nocturnes for 16 Strings (1963); Violin

Concerto (1965); *Symfonie mého města* (*Symphony of My Town;* 1970); Sinfonietta (1973); Cello Concerto, subtitled *Complimento alla musica di ogni giorno* (1974); *Overture giocosa* (1975); *Sinfonia notturna di Praga* (1976); Trio for Flute, Viola, and Bass Clarinet (1959); String Quartet (1965); *Experiment* for Piano (1946); *Sonata brevis* for Piano (1946); *3 movimenti* for Piano (1966); *Sonata in 3 tempi* for Piano (1966).

Gregor, Christian Friedrich, composer and hymnologist; b. Dirsdorf, Silesia, Jan. 1, 1723; d. Zeist, the Netherlands, Nov. 6, 1801. As an organist, music director, composer, and hymnologist, Gregor was the most important musician of the international Moravian Church (Unitas Fratrum) of the 18th century. Joining the Moravian Brethren in 1742, he soon assumed leading positions in its management: was financial agent of Zinzendorf, member of the Unity Elders Conference (1764–1801), and bishop (1789–1801). He made numerous business trips to Germany, the Netherlands, England, Russia, and North America (Pennsylvania, 1770–72); while in Pennsylvania, he gave instruction in composition to Johann Friedrich Peter. During his stay at Herrnhut, Saxony, as organist, Gregor compiled the first hymnal publ. by the Moravians (*Choral-Buch, enthaltend alle zu dem Gesangbuche der Evangelischen Brüder-Gemeinen vom Jahre 1778 gehörige Melodien;* Leipzig, 1784) and arranged the musical liturgies.
WORKS: 308 hymns (*Gesangbuch zum Gebrauch der evangelischen Brüder-Gemeinen;* Barby, 1778 et seq.), about 100 chorale tunes, and approximately 200 anthems and arias. The last are preserved in MS in the Moravian Church Archives at Bethlehem, Pa., and Winston-Salem, N.C. Several of his anthems were republ. frequently in 19th-century American tune books.
BIBLIOGRAPHY: *Historische Nachricht vom Brüder-Gesangbuche des Jahres 1778, und von dessen Lieder-Verfassern* (Gnadau, 1835); J. Julian, *A Dictionary of Hymnology* (2nd ed., London, 1908; reprinted N.Y., 1957); J. and K. Hamilton, *History of the Moravian Church* (Bethlehem, Pa., 1967).

Gregory I, "the Great"; b. Rome, 540; d. there, March 12, 604. He was Pope from 590 to 604; was celebrated in music history as the reputed reformer of the musical ritual of the Roman Catholic Church. It is traditionally believed that by his order, and under his supervision, a collection was made in 599 of the music employed in the different churches; that various offertories, antiphons, responses, etc., were revised and regularly and suitably distributed over the entire year in an arrangement which came to be known as Gregorian chant. While for centuries the sole credit for the codification, which certainly took place, had been ascribed to Gregory, investigations by such scholars as Gevaert, Riemann, P. Wagner, Frere, Houdard, Gastoué, Mocquereau, and others have demonstrated that some of Gregory's predecessors had begun this reform and even fixed the order of certain portions

of the liturgy, and that the work of reform was definitely completed under some of his immediate successors. Evidence in favor of Gregory's leading part in the reform is marshaled in E.G.P. Wyatt's *Saint Gregory and the Gregorian Music* (1904); evidence against his participation is given in Paul Henry Lang's *Music in Western Civilization* (N.Y., 1941). See also G. Morin, *Les Véritables Origines du Chant grégorien* (Maredsous, 1890); W. Brambach, *Gregorianisch* (Leipzig, 1895); F.H. Duddin, *Gregory the Great* (2 vols., London, 1905); F. Tarducci, *Storia di S. Gregorius e del suo tempo* (Rome, 1909); P.C. Vivell, *Der gregorianische Gesang: Eine Studie über die Echtheit der Tradition* (Graz, 1904).

Grein, Louis. See **Green, L. Dunton.**

Greindl, Josef, German bass; b. Munich, Dec. 23, 1912. He studied in Munich; made his debut in Krefeld (1936); then sang in Düsseldorf, at the Berlin State Opera, the Berlin City Opera, the Vienna State Opera, and in Bayreuth and Salzburg. He made his American debut as Henry in *Lohengrin* at the Metropolitan Opera in N.Y., on Nov. 15, 1952. In 1961 he became a prof. at the Hochschule für Musik in Saarbrücken. He was particularly renowned for his excellent renditions of the heroic bass roles in Wagner's operas.

Greissle, Felix, Austrian music scholar; b. Vienna, Nov. 15, 1899; d. Manhasset, Long Island, N.Y., April 26, 1982. He studied with Guido Adler at the Univ. of Vienna and privately with Schoenberg and Alban Berg; from 1925 to 1937 he conducted the Cantata Association of the Vienna State Opera. After the Anschluss in 1938 he went to the U.S. and worked as an editor and arranger with various publishers in N.Y. In 1925 he contributed an exposition of Schoenberg's method of composition with 12 tones to the Austrian periodical *Anbruch.*

Greiter, Matthaeus, German poet and composer; b. Aichach, Bavaria, c.1490; d. Strasbourg, Dec. 20, 1550. He wrote the texts and melodies of Psalm-Lieder for Lutheran services, and settings, for 4 voices, of German songs. He also wrote a tract, *Elementale musicum inventuti* (Strasbourg, 1544). A modern edition of his works was publ. by H.-C. Müller, *Matthaeus Greiter: Sämtliche Weltliche Lieder,* in *Das Chorwerk,* LXXXVII (1962).
BIBLIOGRAPHY: T. Gérold, *Les Plus Anciennes Melodies de l'église protestante de Strasbourg et leurs auteurs* (Paris, 1928); E.E. Lowinsky, "Matthaeus Greiter's Fortuna; An Experiment in Chromaticism and in Musical Iconography," *Musical Quarterly* (Oct. 1956 and Jan. 1957).

Grell, August Eduard, German organist and composer; b. Berlin, Nov. 6, 1800; d. Steglitz, near Berlin, Aug. 10, 1886. He studied organ with his father and theory with Zelter; at the age of 17, he became a member of the Singakademie and was connected with it for 59 years, until his death; he was director in 1853–76. Grell held the view that only vocal music was true art; consequently, he wrote almost exclusively for voice. His works include a *Missa solemnis* (in 16 parts a cappella); an oratorio, *Die Israelitin in der Wüste;* and other church music.

BIBLIOGRAPHY: H. Bellermann, *Biographie Grells* (Berlin, 1899); Bellermann also ed. Grell's essays, *Aufsätze und Gutachten* (Berlin, 1887).

Grešák, Jozef, Slovak composer; b. Bardejov, Dec. 30, 1907. He had training in piano and organ, but was largely autodidact in composition; after his youthful opera *Prichod Slovákov* (*The Arrival of the Slovaks;* 1925), he had a hiatus in his work as a composer, and did not resume composition until much later, with a ballet, *Radúz and Mahuliena* (1954–55), and an interesting ethnic work, *The Emigrant Songs* for Soloists, Male Chorus, and Orch. (1961). There followed a Piano Concerto (1963); *Concertino-Pastorale* for Oboe, English Horn, Horn, and Orch. (1965); *Zemplin Variations* for Soloists, Chorus, and Orch. (1965); *Morceau I* for Violin and Orch. (1965); *Morceau II* for Violin and Piano (1968); *Rotors I* for Piano (1966); *Rotors II* for Orch. (1969); *Hexody* for Clarinet and Piano (1967); *Workers' Songs* for Soloist, Chorus, and Orch. (1971); *Amoebae,* overture (1971); an opera, *With Rosary* (1970–73); *Zuzanka Hraškovie,* monodrama for Soprano, Organ, and Orch. (1973; Bratislava, Jan. 15, 1975); *Concertant Symfonietta* for Orch. (1975; Košice, May 5, 1976).

Gresnich, Antoine-Frédéric, Belgian composer; b. Liège (baptized, March 2), 1755; d. Paris, Oct. 16, 1799. He was a chorister at the St. Lambert Church in Liège, and studied in Naples under Sala. He made several trips to London, where he produced his operas *Demetrio, Alessandro nell'Indie, Donna di Cattiva Umore,* and *Alceste* with considerable success. He was in Lyons in 1789–93; his opera *L'Amour exilé de Cythère* was produced there in 1793. He returned to Paris in 1794, where he had varying success; he died there in poverty.

BIBLIOGRAPHY: P. Mercier, *A.-F. Gresnich, compositeur liégeois* (Louvain, 1977).

Gretchaninov, Alexander, Russian composer; b. Moscow, Oct. 25, 1864; d. New York, Jan. 3, 1956. He studied at the Moscow Cons. (1881–91) with Safonov (piano) and Arensky (composition); then entered the St. Petersburg Cons. as a pupil of Rimsky-Korsakov (1891–1903); was a prof. of composition at the Moscow Inst. until 1922; then lived in Paris; visited the U.S., where he appeared with considerable success as guest conductor of his own works (1929–31); came to the U.S. again in 1939, settling in N.Y. He became an American citizen on July 25, 1946. He continued to compose until the end of his long life. A concert of his works was presented on his 90th birthday at Town Hall in N.Y. (Oct. 25, 1954) in the presence of the composer. A complete catalogue of his works is appended to his autobiography, *My Life.* His music is rooted in the Russian national tradition; influences of both Tchaikovsky and Rimsky-Korsakov are in evidence in his early works; toward 1910 he attempted to inject some impressionistic elements into his vocal compositions, but without signal success. His masterly sacred works are of historical importance, for he introduced a reform into Russian church singing by using nationally colored melodic patterns; in several of his masses he employed instrumental accompaniment contrary to the prescriptions of the Russian Orthodox faith, a circumstance that precluded the use of these works in Russian churches. His *Missa oecumenica* represents a further expansion toward ecclesiastical universality; in this work he makes use of elements pertaining to other religious music, including non-Christian. His instrumental works are competently written, but show less originality than his vocal music. His early *Lullaby* (1887) and the song *Over the Steppes* still retain their popularity, and have been publ. in numerous arrangements.

WORKS: OPERAS: *Dobrinya Nikititch* (Moscow, Oct. 27, 1903); *Sister Beatrice* (Moscow, Oct. 25, 1912; suppressed after 3 perfs. as being irreverent); *The Dream of a Little Christmas Tree,* children's opera (1911); *The Castle Mouse,* children's opera (1921); *The Cat, the Fox, and the Rooster,* children's opera (1919); *Marriage,* comic opera after Gogol (1945–46; Berkshire Music Festival, Aug. 1, 1948); *Idylle forestière,* ballet divertissement for Orch. (N.Y., 1925); incidental music to Ostrovsky's *Snegurotchka* (Moscow, Nov. 6, 1900), A. Tolstoy's *Tsar Feodor* (Moscow, Oct. 26, 1898), and *Death of Ivan the Terrible* (1899). FOR ORCH.: Concert Overture in D minor (1892; St. Petersburg, March 1893); *Elegy in Memory of Tchaikovsky* (1893; St. Petersburg, Dec. 31, 1898, Rimsky-Korsakov conducting); 5 symphs: No. 1 (1893; St. Petersburg, Jan. 26, 1895); No. 2 (1909; Moscow, March 14, 1909); No. 3 (1920–23; Kiev, May 29, 1924); No. 4 (1923–24; N.Y., April 9, 1942); No. 5 (1936; Philadelphia, April 5, 1939); *Poème élégiaque* (Boston, March 29, 1946); *Festival Overture* (Indianapolis, Nov. 15, 1946); *Poème lyrique* (1948). VOCAL WORKS: *Liturgy of St. John Chrysostom* (Moscow, Oct. 19, 1898); *Laudate Deum* (Moscow, Nov. 24, 1915); *Liturgia domestica* (Moscow, March 30, 1918); *Missa oecumenica* for Soli, Chorus, and Orch. (Boston, Feb. 25, 1944); 84 choruses; 14 vocal quartets; 8 duets; 258 songs (some with orch.). CHAMBER MUSIC: 4 string quartets, 2 trios, Violin Sonata, Cello Sonata, 2 clarinet sonatas, 2 *Miniatures* for Saxophone and Piano. FOR PIANO: 2 sonatas (2nd in 1944); *Petits tableaux musicaux* (1947); etc. After the Revolution, Gretchaninov wrote a new Russian national anthem, *Hymn of Free Russia* (sung in N.Y. at a concert for the benefit of Siberian exiles, May 22, 1917), but it was never adopted by any political Russian faction. He wrote 201 opus numbers in all; op. 201 is a chorus a cappella, *Have Mercy O God.*

BIBLIOGRAPHY: He publ. a book of reminiscences, *My Life* (Paris, in Russian, 1934; in Eng., with additions and introduction by N. Slonimsky, N.Y., 1952; contains a complete catalogue of works). See also M. Montagu-Nathan, *Contemporary Russian Composers* (N.Y., 1917); J. Yasser, "Gretchaninov's 'Heterodox' Compositions," *Musical Quarter-*

ly (July 1942).

Grétry, André Ernest Modeste, greatly significant French opera composer; b. Liège, Feb. 8, 1741; d. Montmorency, near Paris, Sept. 24, 1813. His father was a violinist at the church of St. Martin in Liège; at the age of 9, Grétry was entered as a chorister at the St. Denis Church, but was dismissed 2 years later. At 12, he began to study violin and singing; he learned music under Leclerc and the organist Nicolas Rennekin; studied composition with Moreau. About 1754 an Italian opera company gave a season in Liège, and young Grétry thus received his first impulse toward dramatic music. His early works were instrumental; in 1758, he wrote 6 small symphs.; his next work was a Mass, which interested the ecclesiastical authorities; as a result, he was enabled (through the Canon du Harlez) to go to Rome, where he entered the College de Liège (1761–65), a school founded for the education of natives of Liège. There he studied diligently, and composed several church works, 6 string quartets, a Flute Concerto, and 2 intermezzos, including *Le Vendemmiatrici,* which was produced in Rome in 1765. In 1766, he was in Geneva as a music teacher. He met Voltaire, who advised him to go to Paris; before his departure, he produced in Geneva a stage work, *Isabelle et Gertrude,* to a libretto by Favart, after Voltaire. He arrived in Paris in the autumn of 1767; he sought the patronage of aristocrats and diplomats; the Swedish ambassador, Count de Creutz, gave him the first encouragement by obtaining for him Marmontel's comedy *Le Huron;* it was performed with Grétry's music at the Comédie-Italienne (Aug. 20, 1768). From then on, Grétry produced operas one after another, without interruption, even during the years of the French Revolution.

The merit of Grétry's operas lies in their melodies and dramatic expression. He was not deeply versed in the science of music; yet despite this lack of craftsmanship in harmony and counterpoint, he achieved fine effects of vocal and instrumental writing. His operas suffered temporary eclipse when Méhul and Cherubini entered the field, but public interest was revived by the magnificent tenor Elleviou, in 1801. The changes in operatic music during the next 30 years caused the neglect of Grétry's works. Nevertheless, Grétry—"the Molière of music," as he was called—founded the school of French opéra-comique, of which Boieldieu, Auber, and Adam have been such distinguished alumni. During his lifetime, he was greatly honored: he was elected a member of many artistic and learned institutions in France and abroad; the Prince-Bishop of Liège made him a privy councillor in 1784; a street in Paris was named for him in 1785; he was admitted to the Institut de France in 1795, as one of the first 3 chosen to represent the dept. of musical composition; in 1795 he was also appointed Inspector of the Paris Cons., but resigned in a few months; a bust of him was placed in the Grand Opéra foyer, and a marble statue in the entrance hall of the Opéra-Comique; Napoleon made him a Chevalier of the Legion of Honor in 1802, and granted him a pension of 4,000 francs in compensation for losses during the Revolution. Grétry bought "L'Ermitage," Rousseau's former residence at Montmorency, and lived there in retirement. He was married, and had several children, but survived them all. His daughter, **Lucille** (real name, **Angélique-Dorothée-Lucie;** b. Paris, July 15, 1772; d. there, Aug. 25, 1790), was a gifted musician who died young; at the age of 13, with some assistance from her father, she composed an opera, *Le Mariage d'Antonio,* which was produced at the Opéra-Comique, July 29, 1786; her 2nd opera, *Toinette et Louis,* was produced on March 23, 1787. Grétry's *Mémoires ou Essais sur la musique* was publ. in 1789 (reprinted in 1797 with 2 additional vols. ed. by his friend, Legrand; in German, in 1800 at Leipzig, with critical and historical annotations by K. Spazier; in 3 vols. by Mass in 1829 and an enlarged ed. by P. Magnette, Liège, 1914). In these essays, Grétry set forth his views on the paramount importance of the just declamation of every syllable set to music. He also wrote a *Méthode simple pour apprendre à préluder en peu de temps avec toutes les resources de l'harmonie* (1802) and *De la Vérité,* an ardent avowal of Republican tenets, with remarks on the feelings and the best means of exciting and expressing them by music (1803); his *Réflexions sur l'art,* in 6 vols., was never publ. During the last years of his life he wrote *Réflexions d'un solitaire;* his friends did not think its publication was advisable; the MS was considered lost until C. Malherbe discovered it in 1908; it was publ. in 4 vols., edited by L. Solvay and E. Closson (Brussels and Paris, 1919–22). Besides his dramatic works, Grétry composed a *De Profundis, Confiteor,* a Requiem, an antiphon, motets, and a good deal of instrumental music. Under the auspices of the Belgian government, a complete edition of his works was begun in 1883–97, under the editorship of Gevaert and others.

WORKS: The list of his operas is long; they include *Lucile* (Paris, Jan. 5, 1769); *Le Tableau parlant* (Paris, Sept. 20, 1769; very popular); *Les Deux Avares* (Fontainebleau, Oct. 27, 1770); *Sylvain* (Paris, Feb. 19, 1770); *L'Amitié à l'épreuve* (Fontainebleau, Nov. 13, 1770); *L'Ami de la maison* (Fontainebleau, Oct. 26, 1771); *Zémire et Azor* (Fontainebleau, Nov. 9, 1771); *Le Magnifique* (Paris, March 4, 1773); *La Rosière de Salency* (Fontainebleau, Oct. 23, 1773); *Céphale et Procris, ou L'Amour conjugal* (Versailles, Dec. 30, 1773); *La Fausse Magie* (Paris, Feb. 1, 1775); *Les Mariages samnites* (3 acts, from the one-act opera of 1768; Paris, June 12, 1776); *Amour pour amour* (Versailles, March 10, 1777); *Matroco* (Chantilly, Nov. 12, 1777); *Le Jugement de Midas* (Paris, March 28, 1778); *Les Fausses Apparences, ou L'Amant jaloux* (Versailles, Nov. 20, 1778); *Les Événements imprévus* (Versailles, Nov. 11, 1779); *Aucassin et Nicolette, ou Les Mœurs du bon vieux temps* (Versailles, Dec. 30, 1779); *Andromaque* (Paris, June 6, 1780); *Emilie* (Paris, Feb. 22, 1781); *La Double Epreuve, ou Colinette à la Cour* (Paris, Jan. 1, 1782); *Le Sage dans sa retraite* (The Hague, Sept. 19, 1782); *L'Embarras de richesses* (Nov. 26, 1782); *La Caravane du Caire* (Fontainebleau, Oct. 30, 1783); *Théodore et Paulin* (Versailles,

March 5, 1784); *Richard Cœur de Lion* (his greatest masterpiece; Paris, Oct. 21, 1784); *Panurge dans l'isle des lanternes* (Paris, Jan. 25, 1785); *Amphitrion* (Versailles, March 15, 1786); *Les Méprises par ressemblance* (Fontainebleau, Nov. 7, 1786); *Le Comte d'Albert* (Fontainebleau, Nov. 13, 1786); *Le Prisonnier anglois* (Paris, Dec. 26, 1787; with alterations in 1793 as *Clarice et Belton*); *Le Rival confident* (Paris, June 26, 1788); *Raoul Barbe-Bleue* (Paris, March 2, 1789); *Aspasie* (Paris, March 17, 1789); *Pierre le grand* (Paris, Jan. 13, 1790); *Guillaume Tell* (Paris, April 9, 1791); *Cécile et Ermancé, ou Les Deux Couvents* (Paris, Jan. 16, 1792); *A Trompeur, trompeur et demi* (Paris, Sept. 24, 1792); *Joseph Barra* (Paris, June 5, 1794); *Denys le tyran, maître d'école à Corinthe* (Paris, Aug. 23, 1794); *La Rosière républicaine, ou La Fête de la vertu* (Paris, Sept. 3, 1794); *Callias, ou Nature et patrie* (Paris, Sept. 18, 1794); *Lisbeth* (Paris, Jan. 10, 1797); *Anacréon chez Polycrate* (Paris, Jan. 17, 1797); *Le Barbier de village, ou Le Revenant* (Paris, May 6, 1797); *Elisca, ou L'Amour maternel* (Paris, Jan. 1, 1799); *Le Casque et les colombes* (Paris, Nov. 7, 1801); *Delphis et Mopsa* (Paris, Feb. 15, 1803).

BIBLIOGRAPHY: Comte de Livry, *Recueil de lettres écrites à Grétry, ou à son sujet* (Paris, 1809); A.J. Grétry (the composer's nephew), *Grétry en famille* (Paris, 1815); Gerlache, *Essai sur Grétry* (Liège, 1821); F. van Hulst, *Grétry* (Liège, 1842); L. de Saegher, *Notice biographique sur André Grétry* (Brussels, 1869); E. Gregoir, *André E.M. Grétry* (1883); M. Brenet, *Grétry* (Paris, 1884); C. Gheude, *Grétry* (Liège, 1906); H. de Curzon, *Grétry* (Paris, 1907); E. Closson, *Grétry* (Turnhout, 1907); P. Long des Clavières, *La Jeunesse de Grétry et ses débuts à Paris* (Besançon, 1921); idem, "Les Ancêtres de Grétry," *Revue Musicale,* IV, 3 (1923); O.G. Sonneck, "Grétry," *Scheurleer-Festschrift* (1925); H. Wichmann, *Grétry und das musikalische Theater in Frankreich* (Halle, 1929); Romain Rolland, "Grétry," *Musiciens d'autrefois* (Paris, 1908; 2nd ed., 1925; Eng. trans., London, 1915); J.E. Bruyr, *Grétry* (Paris, 1931); P. Lasserre, *Essay en "Philosophie du gout musical"* (Paris, 1931); J. Sauvenier, *André Grétry* (Brussels, 1934); G. de Froidcourt, ed., *43 lettres inédites de Grétry à A. Rousselin, 1806–12* (Liège, 1937); Gérard-Gailly, *Grétry à Honfleur* (Paris, 1938); S. Clercx, *Grétry* (Brussels, 1944); G. de Froidcourt, *Grétry, Rouget de Lisle et la Marseillaise* (Liège, 1945); *La Correspondance générale de Grétry* (Brussels, 1962); R. Jobe, *The Operas of André-Ernest-Modeste-Grétry* (Diss., Univ. of Michigan, 1965); D. Charlton, "The Appeal of the Beast; A Note on Grétry and 'Zémire et Azor,'" *Musical Times* (March 1980).

Grevillius, Nils, Swedish conductor; b. Stockholm, March 7, 1893; d. Mariefred, Sweden, Aug. 15, 1970. He studied at the Stockholm Academy of Music (1905–11), receiving first prize for violin and the Prix Marteau; in 1911–14 was leader of the Royal Opera orch.; conducted the Swedish ballet season in Paris in 1922–23; then returned to Stockholm to conduct the Radio Orch. (1927–39).

Grey, Madeleine, French soprano; b. Villaines-la-Juhel, Mayenne, June 11, 1896. She made her debut in Paris in 1919 in the first performance of Fauré's *Mirages;* thereafter she was identified with modern French music; was chosen to present French art songs at 3 international festivals (Venice, 1930; Siena, 1932; Florence, 1934); also toured South America. She abandoned her career in 1952.

Grider, Rufus, American Moravian musician and historian; b. Bethlehem, Pa., 1817; date and place of death unknown (sometime after 1873 he wandered away from home and was never heard from again). Raised in the exceedingly rich musical culture of the American Moravians, Grider was a flutist in the Bethlehem orch. and a leading tenor; he was also a poet, artist, and antiquarian. His claim to remembrance stems from his unique and detailed portrayal of Moravian musical life in *Historical Notes on Music in Bethlehem, Pennyslvania, from 1741 to 1871* (Bethlehem, 1873; reprinted as Moravian Music Foundation Publication No. 4, Winston-Salem, N.C., 1957).

Griebling, Karen Jean, American singer, bassoon player, and composer; b. Akron, Ohio, Dec. 31, 1957. She studied at the Eastman School of Music in Rochester, N.Y., majoring in composition; subsequently studied voice and bassoon at the Cleveland Inst. of Music. During her student days she succeeded in capturing a number of educational honors and more than 20 prizes in competitions, 2 Gold Cups, and various fellowship awards. Besides singing, she learned to play the viola. Her works include 4 string quartets (1970–73); a Trio for 2 Violins and Viola (1973); a Trio for Flute, Clarinet, and Bassoon (1976); a Viola Sonata (1976); and a number of songs.

Grieg, Edvard Hagerup, celebrated Norwegian composer; b. Bergen, June 15, 1843; d. there, Sept. 4, 1907. The original form of the name was **Greig.** His great-grandfather, Alexander Greig, of Scotland, emigrated to Norway about 1765, and changed his name to Grieg (see J. Russell Greig, "Grieg and His Scottish Ancestry," in Hinrichsen's *Music Year Book,* 1952). Grieg received his first instruction in music from his mother, an amateur pianist. At the suggestion of the Norwegian violinist Ole Bull, young Grieg was sent to the Leipzig Cons. (1858), where he studied piano with Plaidy and Wenzel, and later with Moscheles; and theory with E.F. Richter, Robert Papperitz, Moritz Hauptmann, and Reinecke. He became immersed in the atmosphere of German Romanticism, with the esthetic legacy of Mendelssohn and Schumann; Grieg's early works are permeated with lyric moods related to these influences. In 1863 he went to Copenhagen, where he took a brief course of study with Niels Gade. In Copenhagen, he also met the young Norwegian composer Rikard Nordraak, with whom he organized the Euterpe Society for the promotion of national Scandinavian music, in opposition to the German influences dominating Scandinavian music. The premature death of Nordraak at the age of 23

(1866) left Grieg alone to carry on the project. After traveling in Italy, he returned to Norway, where he opened a Norwegian Academy of Music (1867), and gave concerts of Norwegian music; he was also engaged as conductor of the Harmonic Society in Christiania (Oslo). In 1867 he married his cousin, the singer **Nina Hagerup.** At that time he had already composed his 2 violin sonatas and the first set of his *Lyric Pieces* for Piano, which used Norwegian motifs. On April 3, 1869, Grieg played the solo part in the world premiere of his Piano Concerto, which took place in Copenhagen. Thus, at the age of 25, he established himself as a major composer of his time. In 1874–75 he wrote incidental music to Ibsen's *Peer Gynt;* the 2 orch. suites arranged from this music became extremely popular. The Norwegian government granted him an annuity of 1,600 crowns, which enabled him to devote most of his time to composition. Performances of his works were given in Germany with increasing frequency; soon his fame spread all over Europe. On May 3, 1888, he gave a concert of his works in London; he also prepared recitals of his songs with his wife. He revisited England frequently; received the honorary degree of Mus.Doc. from Cambridge (1894) and Oxford (1906). Other honors were membership in the Swedish Academy (1872), the French Academy (1890), etc. Despite his successes, Grieg was of a retiring disposition, and spent most of his later years in his house at Troldhaugen, near Bergen, avoiding visitors and shunning public acclaim. However, he continued to compose at a steady rate. His death, of heart disease, was mourned by all Norway; he was given a state funeral and his remains were cremated, at his own request, and sealed in the side of a cliff projecting over the fjord at Troldhaugen.
_. Grieg's importance as a composer lies in the strongly pronounced nationalism of his music; without resorting to literal quotation from Norwegian folk songs, he succeeded in re-creating their melodic and rhythmic flavor. In his harmony, he remained well within the bounds of tradition; the lyric expressiveness of his best works and the contagious rhythm of his dancelike pieces imparted a charm and individuality which contributed to the lasting success of his art. His unassuming personality made friends for him among his colleagues; he was admired by Brahms and Tchaikovsky. The combination of lyricism and nationalism in Grieg's music led some critics to describe him as "the Chopin of the North." He excelled in miniatures, in which the perfection of form and the clarity of the musical line are remarkable; the unifying purpose of Grieg's entire creative life is exemplified by his lyric pieces for piano. He composed 10 sets of these pieces in 34 years, between 1867 and 1901. His songs, which he wrote for his wife, are distinguished by the same blend of Romantic and characteristically national inflections. In orch. composition, Grieg limited himself to symph. suites, and arrangements of his piano pieces; in chamber music, his 3 violin sonatas, a Cello Sonata, and a String Quartet are examples of fine instrumental writing. Publication of a complete list of his works began in Frankfurt in 1977.

WORKS: FOR ORCH.: Symph. in C (1864; Grieg withdrew it after several early perfs.; it was revived at the Bergen Festival on May 30, 1981); *In Autumn,* concert overture (op. 11, 1865); *2 Elegiac Melodies* for String Orch. (op. 34, based on songs from op. 33: *The Wounded One* and *The Last Spring*); Concerto in A minor for Piano and Orch. (op. 16, 1868); *Norwegian Dances* (op. 35, 1881); *Holberg Suite* for String Orch. (op. 40, 1884–85); *Peer Gynt Suite* No. 1 (op. 46, 1876; includes *Morning, Aase's Death, Anitra's Dance, In the Hall of the Mountain King*); *2 Melodies* for String Orch. (op. 53, 1891; based on songs from op. 21 and op. 23: *Norwegian* and *First Meeting*); *Peer Gynt Suite* No. 2 (op. 55, 1876; includes *The Abduction and Ingrid's Lament, Arab Dance, Peer Gynt's Homecoming, Solveig's Song*); *Sigurd Jorsalfar Suite* (op. 56, 1872); *2 Norwegian Melodies* for String Orch. (op. 63, 1894–95; based on melodies from op. 17: *In the Style of a Folk Song* and *Cowkeeper's Tune and Peasant Dance*); *Symphonic Dances* (1898); *Evening in the Mountains* for Oboe, Horn, and Strings (arranged from op. 68, no. 4; 1898); *At the Cradle* for String Orch. (arranged from op. 68, no. 5; 1898); *Funeral March in Memory of Rikard Nordraak* for Military Band (arranged from the Piano Solo written in 1866); *Lyric Suite* (arranged from piano solos, op. 54, 1891; includes *Shepherd Boy, Norwegian March, Nocturne, March of the Dwarfs*). CHAMBER MUSIC: Sonata in F for Violin and Piano (op. 8, 1865); Sonata in G minor for Violin and Piano (op. 13, 1867); String Quartet in G minor (op. 27, 1877–78); Sonata in A minor for Cello and Piano (op. 36, 1883); Sonata in C minor for Violin and Piano (op. 45, 1886–87); String Quartet in F (2 movements only; 1892). CHORAL WORKS: *At a Southern Convent's Gate* (op. 20, 1871); 2 songs from *Sigurd Jorsalfar* (op. 22, 1870); *Album for Male Voices* (op. 30, 1877); *Landsighting* (op. 31, 1872); *Scenes from "Olav Trygvason"* (op. 50, 1873); *Ave Maris Stella* (no opus number); *4 Psalms* (op. 74, 1906); he also wrote *The Bewitched One* for Baritone, with Strings and 2 Horns (op. 32, 1878), and the ballad *Bergliot* for Declamation and Orch. (op. 42, 1870–71). He wrote the incidental music for Björnson's *Sigurd Jorsalfar* (Christiania, April 10, 1872) and Ibsen's *Peer Gynt* (Christiania, Feb. 24, 1876), from which the suites so named were taken. FOR PIANO: Piano solos: 4 pieces (op. 1, 1862); *Poetic Tone-Pictures* (op. 3, 1863); *Humoresker* (op. 6, 1865); Sonata in E minor (op. 7, 1865); *Funeral March in Memory of Rikard Nordraak* (1866); 10 sets of *Lyric Pieces* (Book 1, op. 12, 1867; Book 2, op. 38, 1883; Book 3, op. 43, 1884; Book 4, op. 47, 1888; Book 5, op. 54, 1891; Book 6, op. 57, 1893; Book 7, op. 62, 1895; Book 8, op. 65, 1896; Book 9, op. 68, 1898; Book 10, op. 71, 1901; among the most famous individual numbers of the *Lyric Pieces* are: *Butterfly, Erotik,* and *To Spring* in Book 3; *March of the Dwarfs* in Book 5); *Norwegian Dances and Songs* (op. 17, 1870); *Scenes from Peasant Life* (op. 19, 1872); *Ballad in the Form of Variations on a Norwegian Folk Song* (op. 24, 1875); *Album Leaves* (op. 28, 1864, 1874, 1876, 1878); *Improvisations on Norwegian Folk Songs* (op. 29, 1878); *Holberg Suite* (op. 40, 1884); *Norwegian Folk Melodies* (op. 66, 1896); *Norwegian Peas-*

ant Dances (op. 72, 1902); *Moods* (op. 73, 1906); *6 Norwegian Mountain Tunes* (no opus number); 3 piano pieces (no opus number; nos. 2 and 3 written in 1898 and 1891); arrangements for piano solo of a number of his songs and orch. works; original piano duets: *Norwegian Dances for 4 Hands* (op. 35, 1881); *Valses-Caprices* (op. 37, 1883); 2nd piano parts to 4 piano sonatas by Mozart (1877). SONGS: 25 sets of songs to German and Norwegian words; of these, *I Love Thee* attained enormous popularity; song cycle, *Haugtussa* (*A Child of the Mountains* op. 67, 1895). An ed. of his works, in 20 vols., is projected by the Edvard Grieg Committee, in Oslo.

BIBLIOGRAPHY: E. Closson, *Grieg et la musique scandinave* (Paris, 1892); D.G. Mason, *From Grieg to Brahms* (N.Y., 1902); G. Schjelderup, *Edvard Grieg, ghans vaerker* (Copenhagen, 1903); H.T. Finck, *Edvard Grieg* (N.Y., 1905; considerably enlarged and publ. as *Grieg and His Music,* 1909; new ed., 1929); E.M. Lee, *Edvard Grieg* (London, 1908); G. Schjelderup and W. Niemann, *Edvard Grieg: Biographie und Würdigung seiner Werke* (Leipzig, 1908); R.H. Stein, *Grieg* (Berlin, 1921); M. Beyer, *Edvard Grieg: Breve til Frants Beyer 1872–1907* (Christiania, 1923); P. de Stoecklin, *Edvard Grieg* (Paris, 1926); J. Röntgen, *Grieg* (The Hague, 1930); E. von Zschinsky-Troxler, *Edvard Grieg: Briefe an die Verleger der Edition Peters 1866–1907* (Leipzig, 1932); Y. Rokseth, *Grieg* (Paris, 1933); D. Monrad Johansen, *Edvard Grieg* (Oslo, 1934; in Eng., Princeton, N.J., 1938); K.G. Fellerer, *Edvard Grieg* (Potsdam, 1942); G. Abraham, ed., *Grieg, A Symposium* (London, 1948); J. Horton, *Edward Grieg* (London, 1950); K. Dale, "Grieg Discoveries," *Monthly Musical Record* (Dec. 1954); H.J. Hurum, *I Edvard Griegs verden* (Oslo, 1960); J. Horton, *Grieg* (London, 1974).

Grieg, Nina (née **Hagerup**), Norwegian singer, wife of **Edvard Grieg**; b. near Bergen, Nov. 24, 1845; d. Copenhagen, Dec. 9, 1935. Her father, Herman Hagerup, was a brother of Grieg's mother. She studied singing with Helsted; she met Grieg in Copenhagen, and married him on June 11, 1867. Her interpretations of Grieg's songs elicited much praise from the critics.

Griend, Koos van de, Dutch composer; b. Kampen, near Zwolle, Dec. 11, 1905; d. Amsterdam, Jan. 12, 1950. He studied in Amsterdam and in Berlin. Returning to Amsterdam in 1933, he developed energetic activities as a pianist, conductor, and music critic. He wrote 2 symphs., a Cello Concerto, and 3 string quartets; also a Quartet for 4 Horns.

Griepenkerl, Wolfgang Robert, German music theorist, son of **Friedrich Konrad Griepenkerl;** b. Hofwyl, May 4, 1810; d. Braunschweig, Oct. 16, 1868. He studied philosophy and literature at Berlin Univ.; taught art history at the Carolinum, Braunschweig (1839), and at the Braunschweig Cadet School (1840–47). He wrote the tragedies *Robespierre* (which inspired Litolff's well-known overture) and *Girondistes.* He also publ. *Das Musikfest, oder Die Beethovener* (a novel, 1838; 2nd ed., 1841); *Ritter*

Berlioz in Braunschweig (1843); *Die Oper der Gegenwart* (1847); and papers in *Neue Zeitschrift für Musik.*

BIBLIOGRAPHY: O. Sievers, *Robert Griepenkerl* (Braunschweig, 1879); Th.W. Werner, "Wolfgang Robert Griepenkerls Schriften über Musik," *Zeitschrift für Musikwissenschaft,* II (1920).

Griesbach, John Henry, English composer; b. Windsor, June 20, 1798; d. London, Jan. 9, 1875. He was of German descent; he studied cello with his father, and played in the court band. His major work was an oratorio, *Belshazzar's Feast* (1835; revised and perf. as *Daniel,* London, June 30, 1854); also wrote a number of overtures and cantatas. He was an amateur scientist and wrote several papers dealing with acoustics which remained in MS.

Griesbacher, Peter, German theorist and church music composer; b. Egglham, March 25, 1864; d. Regensburg, Jan. 28, 1933. He studied theology; was ordained a priest in 1886; was an instructor at the Franciscan church in Regensburg (from 1894); edited various publications for Catholic church music; wrote 40 masses, secular cantatas, and songs (about 250 opus numbers). He began as a composer in the strict style of contrapuntal writing; his later works, in which he applied modern harmonies to Gregorian melodies, aroused considerable opposition. He publ. several manuals: *Lehrbuch des Kontrapunkts* (1910); *Kirchenmusikalische Stilistik und Formenlehre* (3 vols., 1912–13); *Glockenmusik* (1926).

BIBLIOGRAPHY: M. Tremmel, *Peter Griesbacher* (Passau, 1935).

Griffes, Charles Tomlinson, outstanding American composer; b. Elmira, N.Y., Sept. 17, 1884; d. New York, April 8, 1920. He studied piano with a local teacher, Mary S. Broughton; also took organ lessons. In 1903, he went to Berlin, where he was a pupil of Gottfried Galston (piano) and of Rüfer and Humperdinck (composition). To eke out his living, he gave private lessons; also played his own compositions in public recitals. In 1907, he returned to the U.S., and took a music teacher's job at the Hackley School for Boys at Tarrytown, N.Y.; at the same time he continued to study music by himself; he was fascinated by the exotic art of the French Impressionists, and investigated the potentialities of oriental scales. He also was strongly influenced by the Russian school, particularly Mussorgsky and Scriabin. A combination of natural talent and determination to acquire a high degree of craftsmanship elevated Griffes to the position of a foremost American composer in the impressionist genre; despite changes of taste, his works retain an enduring place in American music.

WORKS: His best are *The White Peacock* for Piano (1917; also for Orch., Philadelphia, Stokowski conducting, Dec. 19, 1919) and the tone poem *The Pleasure Dome of Kubla Khan,* after Coleridge (Boston Symph. Orch., Nov. 28, 1919); others are *The Kairn of Koridwen,* dance drama for 5 Woodwinds, Celesta, Harp, and Piano (N.Y., Feb. 10, 1917); *Shojo,*

Japanese pantomimic drama for 4 Woodwinds, 4 Muted Strings, Harp, and Percussion (1917); *Poem for Flute and Orch.* (N.Y., Nov. 16, 1919); *2 Sketches on Indian Themes* for String Quartet (1922); for Piano: *3 Tone Pictures* (*The Lake at Evening, The Vale of Dreams,* and *The Night Winds;* 1915); *Fantasy Pieces* (*Barcarolle, Notturno,* and *Scherzo;* 1915); *Roman Sketches* (*White Peacock, Nightfall, The Fountain of Acqua Paola,* and *Clouds;* 1917); Sonata in F (Feb. 26, 1918); vocal works: *These Things Shall Be* for Unison Chorus (1917); songs to German texts (*Auf geheimen Waldespfade, Auf dem Teich,* etc.); songs to Eng. words: *The First Snowfall, The Half-ring Moon, Evening Song; Tone Images* (*La Fuite de la lune, Symphony in Yellow,* and *We'll to the Woods, and Gather May;* 1915); *2 Rondels* (*Come, love, across the sunlit land* and *This book of hours;* 1915); *3 Poems* (*In a Myrtle Shade, Waikiki,* and *Phantoms;* 1916); *5 Poems of Ancient China and Japan* (*So-Fei gathering flowers, Landscape, The Old Temple, Tears,* and *A Feast of Lanterns;* 1917); *3 Poems* (*The Lament of Ian the Proud, Thy Dark Eyes to Mine,* and *The Rose of the Night;* 1918); *An Old Song Re-sung* (1920).
BIBLIOGRAPHY: W.T. Upton, "The Songs of Charles T. Griffes," *Musical Quarterly* (July 1923); M. Bauer, "Charles T. Griffes as I Remember Him," *ibid.* (July 1943); E.M. Maisel, *Charles Tomlinson Griffes* (N.Y., 1943; reprinted with new preface by D.K. Anderson, N.Y., 1972); D. Boda, *The Music of Charles Griffes* (Diss., Florida State Univ., 1962); D.K. Anderson, *The Works of Charles Tomlinson Griffes: A Descriptive Catalogue* (Diss., Indiana Univ., 1966).

Griffis, Elliot, American pianist and composer; b. Boston, Jan. 28, 1893; d. Los Angeles, June 8, 1967. He studied at the Yale School of Music with Horatio Parker and at the New England Cons. with Chadwick; held numerous educational posts as a teacher of piano and theory; appeared in recitals; eventually settled in Los Angeles. His music is set in ingratiatingly Romantic colors. He also publ. several vols. of verse.
WORKS: *Paul Bunyan; Colossus,* symph. poem (1926–34); *Fantastic Pursuit* for Strings (1941); *Port of Pleasure,* one-act opera (Los Angeles, June 29, 1963); semiclassical piano pieces.

Grignon, Ricard Lamote de. See **Lamote de Grignon, Ricard.**

Grigoriu, Theodor, Rumanian composer; b. Galatz, July 25, 1926. He studied violin with Enacovici at the Bucharest Cons. and composition with Jora; then went to Moscow, where he had lessons with Khatchaturian and Golubev (1954–55).
WORKS: 2 cantatas: *Cantată pentru 23 August* (1951) and *Odă orașului meu* (*Ode to My City,* 1963; revised 1971); *Sinfonia cantabile* (1950; revised 1966); *Dans tătar,* choreographic piece for Orch. (1953); *Theatrical Suite in the Classical Style* for Chamber Orch. (1956); *Symphonic Variations,* on a melody by Anton Pann, for Orch. (1955; Bucharest,

Jan. 21, 1956); Concerto for Double Chamber Orch. and Solo Oboe (1957); *Vis cosmic* (*Cosmic Dream),* symph. poem, with Vocalizing Tenor or Electronic Instrument (1959; Bucharest, Oct. 28, 1965); *Hommage to Enesco* for 4 groups of Violins (1960); *Melodic infinitā* for Chamber String Orch. (1969); *Elegie pontică,* to verses by Ovid, for Bass-Baritone, Female Chorus, and Chamber Orch. (Bucharest, June 24, 1969); String Quartet (1943); Piano Trio (1943); *Pe Argeș în sus* (*The River Arges Flows On),* suite for String Quartet (1953); choral music; songs; film music.

Grimm, Carl Hugo, American organist and composer; b. Zanesville, Ohio, Oct. 31, 1890; d. Cincinnati, Oct. 25, 1978. He studied music with his father; subsequently held positions as organist in Cincinnati; taught composition at the Cincinnati Cons. (1907–31).
WORKS: *Erotic Poem* for Orch. (1927); *Thanatopsis* for Orch. (1928); *Abraham Lincoln,* "character portrait" for Orch. (1930); *Montana,* symph. poem (Cincinnati, March 26, 1943); *An American Overture* (Cincinnati, Feb. 15, 1946); Trumpet Concerto (1948); Symph. in F minor (1950); *Pennsylvania Overture* (1954); Gothic Mass (1970); *Byzantine Suite* for 10 Instruments (1930); *Little Serenade* for Wind Quintet (1934); Cello Sonata (1945); many anthems, songs, and organ pieces; also works for multiple flutes (ensembles of 4, 8, and 12 flutes).

Grimm, Friedrich Melchior (Baron von), German writer; b. Regensburg, Sept. 25, 1723; d. Gotha, Dec. 19, 1807. He went to Paris in 1750 and remained there till the Revolution, frequenting literary and musical circles and taking an active part in all controversies; his "Lettre sur Omphale" in the *Mercure de France* (1752) took the side of Italian opera in the "guerre des bouffons," but some years later he upheld Gluck against the Italian faction supporting Piccinni. He edited the *Correspondance littéraire, philosophique et critique,* which offers important data on French opera (standard ed. in 16 vols., Paris, 1877–82). He befriended the Mozarts on their first visit to Paris (see the many references to him in E. Anderson, *Letters of Mozart and His Family,* London, 1938; 2nd ed., revised, 1966, by A. Hyatt King and M. Carolan). He also wrote a satire on J. Stamitz, *Le Petit Prophète de Boehmisch-Broda;* reproduced in Eng. in O. Strunk's *Source Readings in Music History* (N.Y., 1950).
BIBLIOGRAPHY: Carlez, *Grimm et la musique de son temps* (1872); Jullien, *La Musique et les philosophes* (1873); E. Schérer, *Melchior Grimm* (1887); E. Hirschberg, *Die Encyklopädisten und die französische Oper im 18. Jahrhundert* (1903); H. Kretzschmar, "Die *Correspondance littéraire* als musikgeschichtliche Quelle," *Jahrbuch Peters* (1903); P. Nettl, *Der kleine Prophète de Boehmisch-Broda* (Esslingen, 1951).

Grimm, Heinrich, German composer; b. Holzminden, c.1593; d. Braunschweig, July 10, 1637. He studied with Michael Praetorius; then studied theology at the Univ. of Helmstedt; in 1619, became rector of the Magdeburg town school; in 1631, when the town was destroyed, he fled with his family to Braunschweig, where he became a cantor at the church of St. Catherine; subsequently was a cantor at St. Andreas's church (1632–37). He was an exponent of the concerted style, with thorough-bass, at that time still a novel technique in Germany. His extant works include masses, Psalms, Passions, and several pedagogical works; he publ. *Unterricht, wie ein Knabe nach der alten Guidonischen Art zu solmisieren leicht angeführt werden kann* (Magdeburg, 1624) and *Instrumentum Instrumentorum* (1629); prepared a combined edition of *Melopoeia seu melodiae condendae ratio* by Calvisius and *Pleiades Musicae* by Baryphonus (Magdeburg, 1630).

BIBLIOGRAPHY: B. Engelke, *Magdeburgische Musikgeschichte* (1914); H. Lorenzen, *Der Cantor Heinrich Grimm; Sein Leben und seine Werke mit Beitrag zur Musikgeschichte Magdeburgs und Braunschweigs* (Hamburg, 1940).

Grimm, Julius Otto, German composer; b. Pernau, Latvia, March 6, 1827; d. Münster, Dec. 7, 1903. He studied philosophy at the Univ. of Dorpat; then lived in St. Petersburg; in 1851, he went to Leipzig, where he studied with Moscheles and Hauptmann; there he formed close friendships with Brahms and Joachim. In 1855, he went to Göttingen; in 1860, obtained a position as conductor in Münster. During the 40 years of his life there, he presented some 1,500 orch. works, ranging from Bach to the modern Russian school. He wrote a Symph. (1874); a Suite for String Orch. in canon form; several cycles of songs; albums of piano pieces.

BIBLIOGRAPHY: F. Ludwig, *Julius Otto Grimm* (Leipzig, 1925); *Brahms im Briefwechsel mit J.O. Grimm* (Berlin, 1912).

Grimm, Karl, German cellist; b. Hildburghausen, April 28, 1819; d. Freiburg, Jan. 9, 1888. He was for half a century the first cellist at the Wiesbaden Opera; composed many cello pieces, some of which attained considerable popularity.

Grimm, Karl Konstantin Ludwig, German harpist; b. Berlin, Feb. 17, 1820; d. there, May 23, 1882. He enjoyed a considerable reputation as a harp soloist; also wrote various pieces for his instrument.

Grinblat, Romuald, Soviet composer; b. Tver, April 11, 1930. He studied at the Latvian Cons. in Riga; after graduation in 1955, he devoted himself to composition and teaching. His works include 4 symphs. (1955, 1957, 1964, 1967); *Youth Overture* (1958); Piano Concerto (1963); Flute Concerto (1970); Piano Quintet (1954); Nocturne for 17 Strings (1966); a ballet, *Rigonda* (1959); a children's opera, *Barber's Daughter* (1972); piano pieces; a curious work for voices, *Exercises in Phonetics* (1969).

Grisar, Albert, Belgian dramatic composer; b. Antwerp (of German-Belgian parentage), Dec. 26, 1808; d. Asnières, near Paris, June 15, 1869. He studied for a short time (1830) with Reicha in Paris. Returning to Antwerp, he brought out his opera *Le Mariage impossible* (Brussels, March 4, 1833), and obtained a government subsidy for further study in Paris. On April 26, 1836, he produced *Sarah* at the Opéra-Comique; then *L'An mille* (June 23, 1837), *La Suisse à Trianon* (March 8, 1838), *Lady Melvil* (Nov. 15, 1838, with Flotow), *L'Eau merveilleuse* (Jan. 31, 1839, with Flotow), *Le Naufrage de la Méduse* (May 31, 1839, with Flotow and Pilati), *Les Travestissements* (Nov. 16, 1839), and *L'Opéra à la cour* (July 16, 1840, with Boieldieu, Jr.). In 1840 he went to Naples for further serious study under Mercadante; returning to Paris in 1848, he brought out *Gilles ravisseur* (Feb. 21, 1848), *Les Porcherons* (Jan. 12, 1850), *Bonsoir, M. Pantalon* (Feb. 19, 1851), *Le Carillonneur de Bruges* (Feb. 20, 1852), *Les Amours du diable* (March 11, 1853), *Le Chien du jardinier* (Jan. 16, 1855), *Voyage autour de ma chambre* (Aug. 12, 1859), *Le Joaillier de St. James* (revision of *Lady Melvil;* Feb. 17, 1862), *La Chatte merveilleuse* (March 18, 1862), *Bégaiements d'amour* (Dec. 8, 1864), and *Douze innocentes* (Oct. 19, 1865). He left, besides, 12 finished and unfinished operas; also dramatic scenes, over 50 romances, etc. His statue (by Brackeleer) was placed in the vestibule of the Antwerp Theater in 1870.

BIBLIOGRAPHY: A. Pougin, *Albert Grisar* (Paris, 1870).

Grisart, Charles Jean Baptiste, French composer; b. Paris, Sept. 29, 1837; d. Compiègne, March 11, 1904. He is known for his light operas, the most popular of which were *La Quenouille de verre* (1873), *Les Trois Margots* (1877), *Le Pont d'Avignon* (1878), *Les Poupées de l'Infante* (1881), *Le Bossu* (1888), *Le Petit Bois* (1893), and *Voilà le roi!* (1894). He also wrote many piano pieces, masses, *mélodies,* etc., and a quantity of transcriptions.

Griselle, Thomas, American composer; b. Upper Sandusky, Ohio, Jan. 10, 1891; d. Hollywood, Dec. 27, 1955. He studied at the Cincinnati College of Music; later took courses in Europe with Nadia Boulanger and Arnold Schoenberg; toured as accompanist of Alice Nielsen and other singers; in 1928, won the $10,000 prize of the Victor contest for American composers with his *2 American Sketches.* In 1939, he settled in Hollywood. He wrote a number of semipopular pieces, often with humorous intent, such as *A Keyboard Symphony* for 6 Pianos (Providence, March 27, 1928); *Tutti-Frutti* and *Czerny Pilots a Flying Saucer* for Piano; etc.

Grishkat, Hans, German choral conductor; b. Hamburg, Aug. 29, 1903; d. Stuttgart, Jan. 10, 1977. He studied at the Univ. of Tübingen and at the Hochschule für Musik in Stuttgart. In 1924 he organized the Reutlingen Chorale; in 1931 he formed the Swabian Chorale, and in 1936 the Grishkat Chorale in Stuttgart; gained a fine reputation as a choral conductor in Germany. From 1945–50 he led the

Swabian Symph. Orch. in Reutlingen. In 1946 he was appointed instructor of choral conducting at the Hochschule für Musik in Stuttgart; from 1968 until his death he led the orch. conducting classes there.

Grisi, Giuditta, Italian mezzo-soprano; b. Milan, July 28, 1805; d. Robecco d'Oglio, near Cremona, May 1, 1840. She was a niece of the famous contralto **Josephina Grassini;** a cousin of the dancer Carlotta Grisi; and the elder sister of the celebrated soprano **Giulia Grisi.** She studied at the Milan Cons.; made her first appearance in Vienna in 1826; afterward sang with success in Italy and in Paris at the Théâtre-Italien under Rossini's management; retired in 1838, after her marriage to Count Barni. Bellini wrote for her the part of Romeo in *I Capuleti ed i Montecchi* (Venice, March 11, 1830); her sister sang Juliet.

Grisi, Giulia, celebrated Italian soprano; b. Milan, July 28, 1811; d. Berlin, Nov. 29, 1869. She studied with her sister, **Giuditta Grisi,** and with Filippo Celli and Pietro Guglielmi, son of the composer; also with Marliani in Milan and with Giacomelli in Bologna; made her first appearance at 17 as Emma in Rossini's *Zelmira;* won the admiration of Bellini, who wrote for her the part of Juliet in *I Capuleti ed i Montecchi* (Venice, March 11, 1830); she sang in Milan until 1832; dissatisfied with her contract and unable to break it legally, she fled to Paris, where she joined her sister at the Théâtre-Italien; she made her Paris debut in the title role of Rossini's *Semiramide* (Oct. 16, 1832); her success was phenomenal, and for the next 16 years she sang during the winter seasons at the Théâtre-Italien. She made her London debut in Rossini's *La gazza ladra* (April 8, 1834), and continued to visit London annually for 27 years. With Rubini, Tamburini, and Lablache, she appeared in Bellini's *I Puritani* and other operas; when the tenor **Giovanni Mario** replaced Rubini, Grisi sang with him and Tamburini; she married Mario (her 2nd husband) in 1844; toured the U.S. with him in 1854; retired in 1861, and lived mostly in London, making occasional visits to the Continent; on one visit to Berlin, she died of pneumonia.

Grist, Reri, black American soprano; b. New York, 1932. She studied at the High School of Music and Art and at Queens College; began her professional career on Broadway, appearing in *West Side Story* (1957); made her operatic debut with the Santa Fe Opera as Blonde in *Die Entführung aus dem Serail* in 1959; in 1960 sang at the Cologne Opera as the Queen of the Night. She made her Metropolitan Opera debut in N.Y. on Feb. 25, 1966, as Rosina in *Il Barbiere di Siviglia.* She held several teaching posts; was for several years on the faculty of the Indiana Univ. School of Music in Bloomington.

Griswold, Putnam, American bass; b. Minneapolis, Dec. 23, 1875; d. New York, Feb. 26, 1914. He studied with A. Randegger in London, Bouhy in Paris, Stockhausen in Frankfurt, and Emerich in Berlin; sang at the Berlin Opera in 1904; in 1904–5 toured the U.S. with Savage's company, appearing in the Eng. version of *Parsifal;* from 1906 to 1911 was a popular singer at the Berlin Opera; made his Metropolitan Opera debut on Nov. 23, 1911, in the role of Hagen in *Götterdämmerung.* He was identified with the bass parts in Wagner's works until his death; German critics pronounced him the greatest foreign interpreter of these roles, and he was twice decorated by the Kaiser.

Grob-Prandl, Gertrud, Austrian soprano; b. Vienna, Nov. 11, 1917. She was educated in Vienna; made her debut at the Volksoper in 1938. In 1947 she became a member of the Vienna State Opera, remaining on its roster until 1964. She then toured Europe and South America. She was particularly effective in Wagnerian roles.

Grocheo, Johannes de (active in Paris about 1280), author of the treatise *Theoria* (c.1300), important as a source of information on secular music of the Middle Ages. It is printed in the original Latin with German trans. by J. Wolf in *Sammelbände der Internationalen Musik-Gesellschaft* (1899–1900; vol. I, pp. 69–130); emendations were provided by H. Müller (op. cit., vol. IV, pp. 361–68).
    BIBLIOGRAPHY: Ernst Rohloff, *Studien zum Musiktraktat des Johannes de Grocheo* (Leipzig, 1930); also J.A. Westrup, *Medieval Song,* in *New Oxford History of Music* (London, 1954; vol. II, pp. 223–29); J.E. Maddrell, "*Mensura* and the Rhythm of Medieval Monodic Song," *Current Musicology,* 10 (1970); H. Vanderwerf, "Concerning the Measurability of Medieval Music," ibid.; J.E. Maddrell, "Grocheo and the Measurability of Medieval Music," ibid., 11 (1971); E. Rohloff, *Die Quellenhandschriften zum Musiktraktat des Johannes de Grocheo* (Leipzig, 1972).

Grofé, Ferde (Ferdinand Rudolph von), American composer, pianist, and arranger; b. New York, March 27, 1892; d. Santa Monica, Calif., April 3, 1972. He attended N.Y. and California public schools; studied music with Pietro Floridia; then was engaged as viola player in the Los Angeles Symph. Orch., at the same time working as popular pianist and conductor in theaters and cafés; joined Paul Whiteman's band in 1920 as pianist and arranger; it was his scoring of Gershwin's *Rhapsody in Blue* (1924) that won him fame. In his own works, Grofé successfully applied jazz rhythms, interwoven with simple ballad-like tunes; his *Grand Canyon Suite* (Chicago, Nov. 22, 1931, Paul Whiteman conducting) has become very popular. Other light pieces in a modern vein include a Piano Concerto (1932–59); *Broadway at Night; Mississippi Suite; 3 Shades of Blue; Tabloid Suite* (N.Y., Jan. 25, 1933); *Symphony in Steel* (N.Y., Jan. 19, 1937); *Hollywood Suite; Wheels Suite; New England Suite; Metropolis; Aviation Suite; San Francisco Suite* for Orch. (San Francisco, April 23, 1960); *Niagara Falls Suite* for Orch. (Buffalo, Feb., 1961); *World's Fair Suite* for Orch. (N.Y., April 22, 1964); *Virginia City: Requiem* *for a Ghost Town,* symph. poem (Virginia City, Nev., Aug. 10, 1968).

Gröndahl, Launy, Danish conductor and composer; b. Ordrup, near Copenhagen, June 30, 1886; d. Copenhagen, Jan. 21, 1960. He studied violin with Anton Bloch and Axel Gade, and theory with Ludolf Nielsen; later took music courses in Paris, Italy, Vienna, and elsewhere. Returning to Denmark, he became president of the Society of Young Musicians; then was appointed conductor of the Danish State Radio Orch., giving his first concert on Oct. 28, 1925.

WORKS: Symph. (1919); Violin Concerto (1917); Trombone Concerto (1924); Bassoon Concerto (1943); 2 string quartets; Violin Sonata; numerous piano pieces and songs.

Groningen, Stefan van, Dutch pianist and pedagogue; b. Deventer, June 23, 1851; d. Laren, March 25, 1926. He studied with Kiel in Berlin; gave concerts as a pianist; taught in various music schools in The Hague, Utrecht, and Leiden. He wrote mostly piano music, also a Piano Quartet.

Groot, Cor de, Dutch pianist and composer; b. Amsterdam, July 7, 1914. He studied composition with Sem Dresden at the Amsterdam Cons.; in 1936 won the international piano contest in Vienna; then gave concerts in Europe and America and made numerous recordings. He taught piano in The Hague; also served as librarian and archivist in Hilversum.

WORKS: Piano concerto (1931); *Concerto classico* for Piano and Orch. (1932); 2-piano Concerto (1939); 2-oboe Concerto (1939); Piano Concertino (1939); Clarinet Concerto (1940); Flute Concerto (1940); Violin Concerto (1940); Divertimento for Orch. (1949); *Wilhelmus ouverture* (1950); *Minuten Concerto* for Piano and Orch. (1950); *Ouverture energico* (1951); *Capriccio* for Piano and Orch. (1955); *Variations imaginaires* for Piano, left-hand, and Orch. (1960–62); Concertino for Clarinet and Small Orch. (1971); *"Bis" (Evocation)* for Piano and Orch. (1972); String Quartet (1947); Serenade for Oboe and Bassoon (1949); *Apparition* for Violin and Piano (1960); *2 Figures* for Oboe and Piano (1968); *Solitude* for Cello and Piano (1968); *Invocation* for Cello and Piano (1974); Piano Sonatina (1940); *Cloches dans le matin* for One or 2 Pianos (1972).

Grosbayne, Benjamin, American conductor; b. Boston, April 7, 1893; d. Brookline, Mass., Jan. 24, 1976. He studied at Harvard Univ. (B.A., 1917) and at the New England Cons.; studied conducting with Monteux and Weingartner; was engaged as violinist and conductor with various opera companies in the U.S.; in 1931–38 was head of the music dept. of Brooklyn College. He publ. *Techniques of Modern Orchestral Conducting* (Cambridge, Mass., 1956).

Grosheim, Georg Christoph, German composer; b. Kassel, July 1, 1764; d. there, Nov. 18, 1841. He played viola in the court orch. at Kassel; edited the music magazine *Euterpe* in 1797–98; wrote biographical articles on composers, and corresponded with Beethoven. He composed 3 operas: *Titania* (1792); *Das heilige Kleeblatt* (1793; Oct. 1794); and *Les Esclaves d'Alger* (Kassel, Oct. 14, 1808; not extant); also set the Ten Commandments for voices. His autobiography was publ. by G. Heinrichs (1926).

Grosjean, Ernest, French organist and composer, nephew of **Jean Romary Grosjean;** b. Vagney, Dec. 18, 1844; d. Versailles, Dec. 28, 1936. He studied in Paris with Boëly and Stamaty; was organist at Verdun Cathedral from 1868 to 1916; then organist at St. Antoine, Versailles; from 1888 to 1914 was editor of the *Journal des Organistes.* He wrote many works for organ and a *Théorie et pratique de l'accompagnement du plainchant.*

Grosjean, Jean Romary, French organist and composer; b. Epinal, Jan. 12, 1815; d. St. Dié, Feb. 13, 1888. He was organist at the St. Dié Cathedral from 1839; he publ. a 2-vol. collection of organ works, *Album d'un organiste catholique,* which included some of his own compositions; also edited a complete collection of noëls and folk songs of Lorraine.

Grosskopf, Erhard, German composer; b. Berlin, March 17, 1934. He studied with Repping at the Berlin Church Music School (1957–59) and then with Blacher and others at the Berlin Hochschule für Musik (1959–64); afterward he engaged in teaching. In his compositions he explores highly complex abstract constructivism.

WORKS: 3 sonatas: No. 1 for Piano Trio (1965); No. 2 for Solo Violin (1965); No. 3 for Flute, Violin, Viola, and Cello (1967); *Sonata concertante No. 1* for Small Orch. (1966) and *No. 2* for Violin and Orch. (1967); *Konzertante Aspekte II* for Flute, Cello, Piano, and Orch. (1967); *Nexus* for Flute, Percussion, and Chamber Ensemble or Tape (1968); *Konzert: Flecktreue Raritätenkunst P* for Clarinet and Instrumental Ensemble (1969); *Dialectics 1969* for 3 Instruments and Tape (1969); *Stop* for 5 Choral Groups (1971); *Hörmusik* for Cello, 5 Orch. Groups, and Electronics (1970–71); West Berlin, Sept. 30, 1971); *Sun Music* for 3 Instrumental Groups (West Berlin, July 16, 1972); *Balance JENC* for Violin and Tape (1972); *Looping* for 5 Performers and Tape, *Looping III* for 5–7 Performers and Tape, and *Looping IV* for 5 Performers (all 1973); *Arbeiter und Bauer müssen sich erheben . . . (Looping II)* for Ensemble (1974).

Grossmann, Ferdinand, Austrian conductor; b. Tulln, July 4, 1887; d. Vienna, Dec. 5, 1970. He studied music in Linz; later took a course in conducting with Weingartner in Vienna. In 1923 he founded a Volkskonservatorium in Vienna; in 1946 organized the Chamber Chorus of the Vienna Academy of Music and toured with it in Europe and America. He was also a composer; wrote a *German Mass* a cappella (1952) and some chamber music.

Grosvenor, Ralph L., American organist and

teacher; b. Grosvenor's Corners, N.Y., Dec. 5, 1893. He studied organ with Huntington Woodman in N.Y., and composition with Ernest Bloch. He served in World War I, and remained in France after service, taking lessons in organ with Poillot and Moissenet. Upon his return to the U.S., he occupied various organ positions in and around N.Y.; also took vocal lessons, and appeared as tenor in local opera companies. He wrote a number of sacred choruses and semipopular songs (*My Desire, Wishing,* etc.).

Grosz, Wilhelm (Will), Austrian composer; b. Vienna, Aug. 11, 1894; d. New York, Dec. 10, 1939. He studied composition with Franz Schreker in Vienna; then lived in Berlin (1928–33). In 1933 he went to London; in 1938 went to N.Y. He wrote an opera, *Sganarell,* after Molière (Dessau, Nov. 21, 1925); *Der arme Reinhold,* a "danced fable" (Berlin, Dec. 22, 1928); a modern musical comedy, *Achtung, Aufnahme!* (Frankfurt, March 23, 1930); *Jazzband* for Violin and Piano (1924); Violin Sonata (1925); a song cycle, *Liebeslieder.* As Will Grosz, he wrote light songs.

Grout, Donald Jay, eminent American musicologist; b. Rock Rapids, Iowa, Sept. 28, 1902. He studied philosophy at Syracuse Univ. (A.B., 1923) and musicology at Harvard Univ. (A.M., 1932; Ph.D., 1939). He studied piano in Boston, and gave a solo recital there in 1932. In the interim he went to Europe, where he took a course in French music of the Baroque period in Strasbourg and in the history of opera in Vienna. In 1935–36 he was a visiting lecturer in music history at Mills College in Calif.; from 1936 to 1942 he was on the staff of the music dept. at Harvard Univ.; from 1942 to 1945 was at the Univ. of Texas in Austin; from 1945 to 1970 was a prof. of musicology at Cornell Univ. He held a Guggenheim Foundation grant in 1951. He served as president of the American Musicological Society (1961–63); in 1966 became curator of the Accademia Monteverdiana in N.Y. He is the author of the valuable publications *A Short History of Opera* (2 vols., N.Y., 1948; revised ed., 1965); *A History of Western Music* (N.Y., 1960; 3rd ed., 1980); *Mozart in the History of Opera* (Washington, D.C., 1972); and *Alessandro Scarlatti: An Introduction to His Operas* (Berkeley, 1979). He is a member of the Editorial Board of *The New Grove Dictionary of Music and Musicians* (London, 1980). In his honor a Festschrift was issued, W.W. Austin, edition, *New Looks at Italian Opera: Essays in Honor of Donald J. Grout* (Ithaca, N.Y., 1968).

Grove, Sir George, eminent English musicographer; b. Clapham, in South London, Aug. 13, 1820; d. Sydenham, May 28, 1900. He studied civil engineering; graduated in 1839 from the Institution of Civil Engineers, and worked in various shops in Glasgow, and then in Jamaica and Bermuda. He returned to England in 1846, and became interested in music; without abandoning his engineering profession, he entered the Society of Arts, of which he was appointed secretary in 1850; this position placed him in contact with the organizers of the 1851 Exhibition; in 1852 he became secretary of the Crystal Palace. He then turned to literary work; was an editor, with William Smith, of the *Dictionary of the Bible;* traveled to Palestine in 1858 and 1861 in connection with his research; in 1865 he became director of the Palestine Exploration Fund. In the meantime, he accumulated a private music library; began writing analytical programs for Crystal Palace concerts; these analyses, contributed by Grove during the period 1856–96, established a new standard of excellence in musical exegesis. Grove's enthusiasm for music led to many important associations; with Arthur Sullivan he went to Vienna in 1867 in search of unknown music by Schubert, and discovered the score of Schubert's *Rosamunde.* In 1868 he became editor of *Macmillan's Magazine;* remained on its staff for 15 years; in 1878 he visited America; he received many honors for his literary and musical achievements, among them the D.C.L., Univ. of Durham (1875), and LL.D., Univ. of Glasgow (1885). In 1883 he was knighted by Queen Victoria. When the Royal College of Music was formed in London (1882), Grove was appointed director, and retained this post until 1894. His chief work, which gave him enduring fame, was the monumental *Dictionary of Music and Musicians,* which Macmillan began to publ. in 1879. It was first planned in 2 vols., but as the material grew, it was expanded to 4 vols., with an appendix, its publication being completed in 1889. Grove himself contributed voluminous articles on his favorite composers, Beethoven, Schubert, and Mendelssohn; he gathered a distinguished group of specialists to write the assorted entries. The 2nd edition of Grove's *Dictionary* (1904–10), in 5 vols., was edited by Fuller-Maitland; the 3rd edition (1927–28), by H.C. Colles; an American supplement, first publ. in 1920, edited by W.S. Pratt and C.H.N. Boyd, was expanded and republ. in 1928; the 4th edition, also edited by H.C. Colles, was publ. in 5 vols., with a supplementary vol. in 1940. Eric Blom was entrusted with the preparation of an entirely revised and greatly enlarged 5th edition, which was publ. in 9 vols. in 1954; it became the largest music reference book in the Eng. language; Grove's original articles on Beethoven, Schubert, and Mendelssohn were publ. separately in 1951, since their bulk was out of proportion even in this edition; revised articles on these composers were included instead. A new, 6th edition, under the editorship of Stanley Sadie, in 20 vols., numbering some 15,000 pages, containing about 22,500 articles and over 3,000 illustrations, reflecting the contributions of some 2,400 scholars from all over the world, was publ. in London in 1980, under the title *The New Grove Dictionary of Music and Musicians.* Grove further publ. *Beethoven and His 9 Symphonies* (London, 1896; 3rd ed., 1898; reprint, 1962); contributed prefaces to Otto Jahn's *Life of Mozart* and Novello's *Short History of Cheap Music;* also numerous articles to the musical press.

BIBLIOGRAPHY: C.L. Graves, *The Life and Letters of Sir George Grove* (London, 1904); idem, "George Grove: A Centenary Study," *Music & Letters* (1920); P. Young, *George Grove, 1820–1900* (London, 1980).

Grové, Stefans, South African composer; b. Bethlehem, Orange Free State, July 23, 1922. He studied piano with his mother and his uncle; later took courses with Cameron Taylor at the South African College of Music, with W.H. Bell in Cape Town, and with Walter Piston at Harvard Univ. (1953–55), where he received his M.A. In 1956 he was appointed instructor at the Peabody Cons., Baltimore, where he founded the Pro Musica Rara group for performance of Baroque music; in 1972 he was appointed senior lecturer in composition at the Univ. of Cape Town and in 1972 took a similar post at the Univ. of Pretoria. He edited the orch. score of the newly discovered (1971) Concerto for 2 Pianos and Orch. of Max Bruch. Grové's music is distinguished by clarity of formal presentation and a free flow of melodic line; the contrapuntal structure is often complex, but it is invariably cast within clearly outlined harmonies.
    WORKS: Clarinet Sonata (1947); String Trio (1948); *Elegy* for String Orch. (Cape Town, July 9, 1948); Duo for Violin and Cello (1950); *Die Dieper Reg,* ballet (1950); Piano Trio (1952); Trio for Oboe, Clarinet, and Bassoon (1952); Quintet for Flute, Oboe, Viola, Bass Clarinet, and Harp (1952); *Tower Music* for Brass Ensemble (1954); Flute Sonata (1955); Sinfonia Concertante (Johannesburg, Oct. 23, 1956); Quartet for Flute, Oboe, Clarinet, and Bassoon (1956); Violin Concerto (1959); *Alice in Wonderland* for Viola, Piccolo, Alto Flute, Wind Ensemble, and Percussion (1959); *Symphony 1962;* Partita for Orch. (1964); *Ritual,* fantasy for Organ (1969); *An Experience in Style,* 14 imitative pieces for Harpsichord and Piano (1971); *Kaapse Draaie* for Chorus, Piano, Guitar, Marimba, Flute, Clarinet, and Saxophone (1974); Concerto Grosso for Violin, Cello, Piano, and Youth Orch. (1974); *Maya,* concerto for Violin, Piano, and Youth String Orch. (1976); *Warata,* ballet for Young Dancers (1976); *For a Winter Day,* fantasy for Bassoon and Piano (1977); *Chain Rows* for Orch. with Instrumental Soloists (1978); *Rendezvous* for Piccolo and Tuba (1978).

Groven, Eivind, Norwegian composer and musicologist; b. Lårdal, Telemark, Oct. 8, 1901. He studied at the Oslo Cons. (1923–25) and later in Berlin. In 1932 he was appointed a consultant on folk music for Norwegian Radio; remained there until 1946; in 1940 he received a state composer's pension. He collected about 1,800 Norwegian folk tunes, several of which he used as thematic foundation for his own compositions. In 1965 he patented an electronic organ, with special attachments for the production of non-tempered intervals.
    WORKS: Symph. poems: *Renaissance* (1935), *Historiske syner (Historical Visions,* 1936), *Fjelltonar (Tunes from the Hills;* 1938), *Skjebner (The Fates;* 1938), and *Bryllup i skogen (Wedding in the Wood;* 1939); 2 symphs.: No. 1, *Innover viddene (Toward the Mountains;* 1937; revised 1951), and No. 2, *Midnattstimen (The Midnight Hour;* 1946); *Hjalarljod,* overture (1950); Piano Concerto (1950); *Symfoniske slåtter (Norwegian Folk Dances),* 2 sets: No. 1 (1956) and No. 2, *Faldafeykir* (1967). Vocal music: *Brud-*

gommen (The Bridegroom) for Soprano, 2 Altos, Tenor, Chorus, and Orch. (1928–31); *Naturens tempel (The Temple of Nature)* for Chorus and Orch. (1945); *Ivar Aasen,* suite for Soprano, Bass, Chorus, and Orch. (1946); *Soga om ein by (The Story of a Town)* for Soprano, Tenor, Bass, Chorus, and Orch. (1956); *Margjit Hjukse* for Chorus and Hardanger Fiddle (1963); *Draumkaede* for Soprano, Tenor, Baritone, Chorus, and Orch. (1965); *Ved foss og fjord (By Falls and Fjord)* for Male Chorus and Orch. (1966); among his many songs for solo voice, most scored with piano and later rescored with orch., are: *Moen (The Heath;* 1926; orchestrated 1934); *Neslandskyrkja (The Nesland Church;* 1929; orchestrated 1942); *Moderens korstegn (The Mother's Sign of the Cross;* 1930; orchestrated 1942); *På hospitalet om natten (In the Hospital at Night;* 1930; orchestrated 1946); *Høstsanger (The Autumn Song;* orchestrated 1946). Chamber music: *Solstemning (Sun Mood)* for Solo Flute, or Flute and Piano (1946); *Balladetone* for 2 Hardanger Fiddles (1962); *Regnbogen (The Rainbow)* for 2 Hardanger Fiddles (1962). His many theoretical studies include *Naturskalaen (The Natural Scale;* Skein, 1927); *Temperering og renstemning (Temperament and Non-tempered Tuning,* dealing with a new system of piano tuning according to natural intervals; Oslo, 1948; Eng. trans., 1970); *Eskimomelodier fra Alaska (Eskimo Melodies from Alaska;* Oslo, 1955).

Groves, Sir Charles, distinguished English conductor; b. London, March 10, 1915. He was educated at the Royal College of Music in London. In 1941 he joined the BBC as a choral conductor. He then was music director of the Bournemouth Symph. Orch. (1951–63) and the Welsh National Opera (1961–63). From 1967 to 1977 he was music director of the Royal Liverpool Phil. Orch. In 1978 he became music director of the English National Opera in London, resigning in 1979. He was knighted by Queen Elizabeth II in 1973. He was especially fond of the music of Elgar and Delius, which he performed with great élan, and was also noted for his sensitive readings of the symphs. of Sibelius. He was instrumental in launching the careers of several English conductors of the younger generation, especially in his sponsorship of the Liverpool International Conductors' Competition.

Grovlez, Gabriel (Marie), French conductor, writer, and composer; b. Lille, April 4, 1879; d. Paris, Oct. 20, 1944. He studied at the Paris Cons. under Diémer, Lavignac, Gédalge, and Fauré; won first prize in piano there (1899); was then taught piano at the Schola Cantorum (from 1908); was appointed conductor at the Paris Opéra in 1914; also conducted the Chicago Opera Co. (1921–22 and 1925–26).
    WORKS: Operas: *La Princesse au jardin* (Monte Carlo, 1920); *Psyché; Cœur de rubis* (Nice, 1922); opéra-bouffe, *Le Marquis de Carabas* (1925); 2 ballets: *Maïmouna* (Paris Opéra, April 25, 1921) and *Le Vrai Arbre de Robinson* (Chicago, 1921); symph. poems: *Madrigal lyrique; La Vengeance des fleurs; Le Reposoir des amants; Dans le jardin* for Soprano,

Women's Chorus, and Orch.; Violin Sonata; Cello Sonata; more than 50 songs, and many piano pieces, including *Recuerdos, 2 études, A Child's Garden, Nocturne, Le Royaume puéril, 2 impressions,* and the sets *Almanach aux images* and *London Voluntaries.* He was an ed. of Rameau's works; ed. the collection *Les Plus Beaux Airs de l'opéra français* (8 vols., Paris, 1924); publ. a book, *L'Initiation à l'orchestration* (Paris, 1944).

Grozăvescu, Trajan, Rumanian tenor; b. Lugoj, Nov. 21, 1895; d. (murdered) Vienna, Feb. 15, 1927. He studied in Bucharest and Cluj; made his debut in Cluj as Pinkerton in *Madama Butterfly* in 1920; continued his vocal studies in Vienna with F. Steiner; made appearances with the Vienna Volksoper, the Prague National Theater, and the Vienna State Opera. He was shot to death by his wife.
BIBLIOGRAPHY: M. Demeter-Grozăvescu and I. Voledi, *Trajan Grozăvescu* (1965).

Grua, Carlo Luigi Pietro, Italian composer; b. Florence, c.1665; date of death unknown. He was in Dresden from 1691 to 1694, first as singer in the electoral chapel, then as assistant Kapellmeister; his opera *Camillo generoso* was produced in Dresden in 1693; he next went to the Palatine court at Düsseldorf as assistant Kapellmeister; his opera *Telegono* was given there during the 1697 Carnival; he remained in Düsseldorf for a number of years; then went to Venice, where he produced 2 operas: *Il Pastor fido* (1721) and *Romolo e Tazio* (1722).

Grua, Carlo Pietro, Italian composer; b. c.1695; place of birth uncertain; d. Mannheim (buried, April 11), 1773. He may have been a son or relative of **Carlo Luigi Pietro Grua.** He was Kapellmeister at Mannheim from about 1734 until his death; during this time, wrote 2 operas, *Meride* (1742) and *La clemenza di Tito* (1748); also 5 oratorios; a *Miserere.*

Grua, Francesco de Paula (or **Paolo**), Italian composer, son of **Carlo Pietro Grua;** b. Mannheim (baptized, Feb. 1), 1753; d. Munich, July 5, 1833. He studied with Holzbauer at Mannheim; then went to Bologna, where he was a pupil of Padre Martini, and to Parma, where he studied with Traetta. Returning to Mannheim, he became a member of the electoral orch.; in 1778, accompanied the court to Munich; became court conductor there in 1784. He wrote one opera, *Telemaco,* given at the Munich Carnival in 1780; also much church music, including 31 orch. masses.

Gruber, Franz Xaver, Austrian composer and organist; b. Unterweizburg, Nov. 25, 1787; d. Hallein, near Salzburg, June 7, 1863. He acquired fame as the composer of the Christmas carol *Stille Nacht, Heilige Nacht.* Of a poor family, Gruber had to do manual work as a youth, but managed to study organ; by dint of perseverance he obtained, at the age of 28, his first position, as church organist and schoolmaster at Oberndorf. It was there, on Christmas Eve of 1818, that a young curate, Joseph Mohr, brought him a Christmas poem to be set to music, and Gruber wrote the celebrated song.
BIBLIOGRAPHY: K. Weinmann, *Stille Nacht, Heilige Nacht* (Regensburg, 1918); J. Mühlmann, *Franz Xaver Gruber* (Salzburg, 1966); A. Schmaus and L. Kriss-Rettenbeck, *Stille Nacht, Heilige Nacht* (Innsbruck, 1967).

Gruber, Georg, Austrian conductor; b. Vienna, July 27, 1904. He studied music at the Univ. of Vienna; received his Ph.D. in 1928. In 1930, he became conductor of the famous Vienna Choirboys, and toured with them throughout Europe, South America, and the U.S. He also arranged for his choir folk songs and choral works of the Renaissance period. In 1953 he was appointed prof. of music at Rhodes Univ. in Grahamstown, South Africa.

Gruber, H(einz) K(arl), Austrian composer; b. Vienna, Jan. 3, 1943. He was a member of the famous Vienna Boys' Choir (1953–57); studied composition with Uhl and Jelinek; also played double bass and French horn; took courses in film music at the Hochschule für Musik in Vienna (1957–63); in 1963–64 attended master classes there held by Einem. He played principal double bass in the Tonkünstler Orch. in Vienna (1963–69); was a co-founder, with Schwertsik and Zukan, of an avant-garde group, MOB art & tone ART (1968). In 1961 he joined the Vienna ensemble *die reihe* as a double-bass player; in 1969 was engaged as double-bass player in the ORF (Austrian Symph. Orch.), where he also performed as an actor. In his own music Gruber maintains a wide amplitude of styles, idioms, and techniques, applying the dodecaphonic method of composition in works of a jazz and pop nature. His "pandemonium," *Frankenstein!!,* which is a mega-multimedia affair, with children's verses recited in a bizarre and mock-scary manner, became quite popular.
WORKS: FOR THE STAGE: Melodrama in 5 scenes, *Die Vertreibung aus dem Paradies (The Expulsion from Paradise)* for Speakers and 6 Solo Instruments (1966); musical spectacle, *Gomorrah* (1970–72); "pandemonium," *Frankenstein!!,* after H.C. Artmann, for Baritone Chansonnier and Orch. (1976–77; London, Nov. 25, 1978; U.S. premiere, Berkshire Music Center, Tanglewood, Aug. 13, 1980; version for Vocalist and 12-player Ensemble, Berlin Festival, Sept. 30, 1979).
FOR ORCH.: Concerto for Orch. (1960–64); *Manhattan Broadcasts* for Light Orch. (1962–64); *fürbass,* concerto for Double Bass and Orch. (1965); *Revue* for Chamber Orch. (1968); *Vergrösserung (Magnification,* 1970); *Arien* for Violin and Orch. (1974–75); *Phantom-Bilder (Photo-Fit Pictures)* for Chamber Ensemble (1977); *. . . aus Schatten duft gewebt (. . . of shadow fragrance woven)* for Violin and Orch. (1977–78; Berlin Festival, Sept. 29, 1979); *Entmilitärisierte Zonen (Demilitarized Zones),* march-paraphrases (1979); *Charivari,* subtitled *An Austrian Journal* (1981); *Rough Music,* concerto for Percussion and Orch. (1982–83).

CHAMBER MUSIC: *Suite* for 2 Pianos, Wind Instruments, and Percussion (1960); *Improvisation* for Wind Quintet (1961); Concerto No. 1 for Flute, Vibraphone, Xylophone and Percussion (1961); Concerto No. 2 for Tenor Saxophone, Double Bass, and Percussion (1961); *4 Pieces* for Solo Violin (1963); *Gioco a tre* for Piano Trio (1963); *Spiel* for Wind Quintet (1967); *3 "MOB" Pieces* for 7 interchangeable Instruments and Percussion (1968, revised 1977); *Bossa Nova* for Ensemble (1968); *Die wirkliche Wut über den verlorenen Groschen (A Real Rage over a Lost Penny)* for 5 Players (1972).
FOR VOICE: Mass for Mixed Chorus, 2 Trumpets, English Horn, Double Bass, and Percussion (1960); *Drei Lieder* for Baritone, Ensemble, and Tape (1961); *Frankenstein-Suite* for Voice and Ensemble (1970; incorporated into *Frankenstein!!*); *Reportage aus Gomorrah* for 5 Singers and 8 Players (1975–76).
FOR PIANO: *Episodes* for 2 Pianos (1961); *6 Episodes from a Discontinued Chronicle* (1967); *Luftschlösser (Castles in the Air)*, cycle in 4 movements (1981).

Gruberová, Edita, Czech coloratura soprano; b. Bratislava, Dec. 23, 1946. She received her musical education in Prague and Vienna; made her debut with the Slovak National Theater in Bratislava in 1968; in 1972 she made a successful appearance at the Vienna State Opera; she also sang at the Bayreuth Festivals, the Hamburg State Opera, the Frankfurt Opera, the Bavarian State Opera in Munich, and other major opera houses, establishing herself as one of the finest coloratura sopranos of her generation.

Gruenberg, Erich, Austrian-born English violinist; b. Vienna, Oct. 12, 1924. After studying in Vienna, he was awarded a scholarship to enroll in the Jerusalem Cons. in 1938; subsequently was engaged as concertmaster of the radio orch. there. In 1946 he went to London; became an English citizen in 1950. He served as concertmaster of the Boyd Neel Orch.; then went to Sweden and was appointed concertmaster of the Stockholm Phil. (1956–58); returning to England, he became concertmaster of the London Symph. Orch. (1962–65), and of the Royal Phil. (from 1972); also made appearances as a soloist.

Gruenberg, Eugene, Austrian-American violinist; b. Lemberg, Oct. 30, 1854; d. Boston, Nov. 11, 1928. He studied violin with Heissler and ensemble playing with Hellmesberger at the Vienna Cons.; took a course in composition with Bruckner. He went to Leipzig, where he played the violin in the Gewandhaus Orch. In 1891 he emigrated to America and taught at the New England Cons. He publ. *The Violinist's Manual* (N.Y., 1897; revised ed., 1919, as *Violin Teaching and Violin Studies,* with a preface by Fritz Kreisler). Gruenberg composed a Symph. and a Violin Sonata, and wrote a cadenza for Brahms's Violin Concerto.

Gruenberg, Louis, eminent American composer; b. near Brest Litovsk, Poland, Aug. 3, 1884; d. Los Angeles, June 9, 1964. He was brought to the U.S. as an infant; studied piano with Adele Margulies in N.Y.; then went to Berlin, where he studied with Busoni (piano and composition); in 1912 made his debut as a pianist with the Berlin Phil.; intermittently took courses at the Vienna Cons., where he also was a tutor. In 1919 he returned to the U.S. and devoted himself to composing. He was one of the organizers and active members of the League of Composers (1923); became a champion of modern music, and one of the earliest American composers to incorporate jazz rhythms in works of symph. dimensions (*Daniel Jazz, Jazzettes,* etc.); from 1933 to 1936 he taught composition at the Chicago Music College; then settled in Santa Monica, Calif.
WORKS: His opera *The Emperor Jones,* to O'Neill's play (Metropolitan Opera, N.Y., Jan. 7, 1933), attracted a great deal of attention by its dramatic effects and novel devices, particularly in the use of percussion; it received the David Bispham Medal. OTHER STAGE WORKS: *The Witch of Brocken* (1912); *The Bride of the Gods* (1913); *Dumb Wife* (1921); *Jack and the Beanstalk* (libretto by John Erskine; N.Y., Nov. 19, 1931); *Queen Helena* (1936); *Green Mansions,* radio opera (CBS, Oct. 17, 1937); *Volpone,* opera (1945); *The Miracle of Flanders,* mystery play (1950); *Anthony and Cleopatra,* opera (1940–60). FOR ORCH.: 5 symphs.: No. 1 (1919; revised in 1929; won the $5,000 RCA Victor prize in 1930; perf. by Koussevitzky and the Boston Symph., Feb. 10, 1934); Nos. 2–5 (1942–48); *Vagabondia* (1920); *The Hill of Dreams,* symph. poem (won the Flagler prize; N.Y., Oct. 23, 1921); *Jazz Suite* (Cincinnati, March 22, 1929); *The Enchanted Isle,* symph. poem (Worcester Festival, Oct. 3, 1929); *9 Moods* (1929); *Music for an Imaginary Ballet,* 2 sets (1929, 1944); *Serenade to a Beauteous Lady* (Chicago, April 4, 1935); 2 piano concertos (1947; 1938, revised 1961); Violin Concerto (Philadelphia Orch., Dec. 1, 1944, Heifetz, soloist); *Americana,* suite for Orch. (1945). VOCAL WORKS: *Daniel Jazz* for Tenor and 8 Instruments (N.Y., Feb. 22, 1925); *Creation* for Baritone and 8 Instruments (N.Y., Nov. 27, 1926); *Animals and Insects* for Voice and Piano; *4 Contrasting Songs; A Song of Faith,* spiritual rhapsody for Speaker, Voices, Chorus, Orch., and a Dance Group, dedicated to the memory of Mahatma Gandhi (1952–62; brought out in a posthumous perf. for the first time in Los Angeles on Nov. 1, 1981); also publ. 4 vols. of Negro spirituals. CHAMBER MUSIC: Suite for Violin and Piano (1914); 3 violin sonatas (1912, 1919, 1950); *Indiscretions* for String Quartet (1922); *Diversions* for String Quartet (1930); 2 string quartets (1937, 1938); *Jazzettes* for Violin and Piano (1926); 2 piano quintets (1929, 1937); *Poem in Form of a Sonatina* for Cello and Piano (1925); *4 Whimsicalities* for String Quartet (1923). PIANO WORKS: *Jazzberries, Polychromatics, Jazz Masks, 6 Jazz Epigrams, 3 Jazz Dances,* etc.

Gruhn, Nora, English soprano; b. London, March 6, 1905. She was a daughter of the German conductor **Hermann Grünebaum,** and abbreviated her name for professional reasons to Gruhn. She studied at the

Royal College of Music; also took voice lessons with Hermine Bosetti in Munich. She made her debut in Kaiserslautern in 1928; sang for a season with the Cologne Opera (1929–30); then appeared at Covent Garden in London (1929–33 and again in 1936–37) and at Sadler's Wells (1946–48). She sang the part of Gretel in an English production of Humperdinck's opera *Hänsel und Gretel* reportedly more than 400 times.

Grumiaux, Arthur, eminent Belgian violinist; b. Villers-Perwin, March 21, 1921. He studied violin and piano with Fernand Quinet at the Charleroi Cons. and violin with Alfred Dubois at the Royal Cons. in Brussels; also took private lessons in composition with Enesco in Paris. In 1939 he received the Vieuxtemps Prize; in 1940 was awarded the Prix de Virtuosité from the Belgian government. In 1949 he was appointed prof. of violin at the Royal Cons. In 1973 he was knighted by King Baudouin for his services to music; he thus shared the title of baron with Paganini. His performances are characterized by a studied fidelity to the composer's intentions, assured technical command, and a discerning delineation of the inner structure of the music.

Grümmer, Elisabeth, famous German soprano; b. Niederjeutz, March 31, 1911. She first pursued a career as an actress. In 1941 Herbert von Karajan invited her to sing at the Aachen Opera, which marked the beginning of a successful career. In 1951 she appeared at Covent Garden; in 1957 at Bayreuth. In 1959 she became a prof. at the Hochschule für Musik in West Berlin. In 1961 she toured South America; in 1964 she gave concerts in Korea and Japan. It was not until April 20, 1967, at the age of 56, that she sang for the first time at the Metropolitan Opera in N.Y., as Elsa in *Lohengrin.* Her acting ability greatly redounded to her success in opera.

Grümmer, Paul, German cellist; b. Gera, Feb. 26, 1879; d. Zug, Switzerland, Oct. 30, 1965. He studied in Leipzig and Berlin; in 1899 went to London as cellist at Covent Garden and member of the Jan Kubelik String Quartet; in 1913, he joined the Adolf Busch Quartet; in 1926–33 he taught at the Hochschule für Musik in Cologne; in 1933–40, was a prof. at the Hochschule für Musik in Berlin; in 1940–45, at the Vienna Academy of Music; retired to Zürich in 1945. He wrote pedagogic works for the cello and edited Bach's unaccompanied cello suites. His autobiography, *Begegnungen,* was publ. in Munich in 1963.

Grün, Jakob, violinist and teacher; b. Budapest, March 13, 1837; d. Baden, near Vienna, Oct. 1, 1916. He was a pupil of J. Böhm in Vienna and M. Hauptmann in Leipzig; in 1858 he became a member of the Weimar Court Orch.; went to Vienna in 1868, as concertmaster at the court opera; from 1877 till he retired in 1909 he was a prof. at the Vienna Cons.

Grünbaum, Therese, famous Austrian soprano; b. Vienna, Aug. 24, 1791; d. Berlin, Jan. 30, 1876. She studied with her father, **Wenzel Müller,** the composer and conductor; appeared on stage while still a child; in 1807 she went to Prague; in 1816 she joined the Kärnthnertortheater in Vienna, remaining as a principal member there until 1826; while in Vienna, she gained fame for her Rossini roles; also created the role of Eglantine in Weber's *Euryanthe;* after appearances in Berlin (1828–30), she taught voice. She married the tenor **Johann Christoff** (b. Haslau, Oct. 28, 1785; d. Berlin, Oct. 10, 1870); a daughter, **Caroline** (b. Prague, March 18, 1814; d. Braunschweig, May 26, 1868), was also a soprano.

Grund, Friedrich Wilhelm, German conductor and composer; b. Hamburg, Oct. 7, 1791; d. there, Nov. 24, 1874. He was brought up in a musical family, his father having been a theater conductor. He studied cello, but after a brief concert career devoted himself mainly to conducting. In 1819, he founded in Hamburg the Gesellschaft der Freunde des Religiösen Gesanges, which later became the Hamburg Singakademie. In 1828, was engaged to lead the newly established Phil. Concerts, a post he held until 1862. In 1867 he organized (with Karl Grädener) the Hamburg Tonkünstlerverein. He wrote several operas, which were not performed; a cantata, *Die Auferstehung und Himmelfahrt Christi;* some chamber music (Octet for Wind Instruments and Piano; Quintet for Oboe, Clarinet, Horn, Bassoon, and Piano; *Trio de Salon* for Piano, 4-hands, and Cello); many piano pieces, which enjoyed considerable success and were praised by Schumann.

Grunenwald, Jean-Jacques, French organist and composer of Swiss parentage; b. Cran-Gevrier, near Annecy, Feb. 2, 1911; d. Paris, Dec. 19, 1982. He studied organ with Dupré at the Paris Cons.; received first prize in 1935; studied composition with Henri Busser, obtaining another first prize in 1937. From 1936 to 1945 he was the assistant of Dupré at St.-Sulpice in Paris; in 1955–70 was organist at St.-Pierre-de-Montrouge. He was a prof. at the Schola Cantorum in Paris from 1958 to 1961, and from 1961 to 1966 was on the faculty of the Cons. of Geneva. Through the years he played more than 1,500 concerts, presenting the complete organ works of Bach and César Franck. He also became famous for the excellence of his masterly improvisations, which rivaled those of his teacher Marcel Dupré. His compositions include *Fêtes de la lumière* for Orch. (1937); Piano Concerto (1940); *Concert d'été* for Piano and String Orch. (1944); lyric drama, *Sardanapale,* after Byron (1945–50); *Ouverture pour un Drame sacre* for Orch. (1954); *Cantate pour le Vendredi Saint* (1955); *Psalm 129 (De profundis)* for Chorus and Orch. (1959); *Fantaisie en dialogue* for Organ and Orch. (1964); Sonata for Organ (1964); piano pieces; etc.
BIBLIOGRAPHY: A. Machabey, *Portraits de 30 musiciens français* (Paris, 1949, pp. 93–96).

Grüner-Hegge, Odd, Norwegian pianist, conductor and composer; b. Oslo, Sept. 23, 1899; d. there, May 11, 1973. He studied piano and compostion in

Oslo; then took courses in conducting with Wein-gartner. He was conductor of the Olso Phil. (1931–61) and of the Norwegian Opera there (1932–61); was a member of the board of the Society of Norwegian Composers (1923–64). In 1945 he was named artistic director of the Oslo Phil.; was choirmaster of the National Theater in Oslo (1934–47); was manager of the Norwegian Opera (1961–69). He composed a Violin Sonata (1915); a Piano Trio (1918, revised 1959); piano pieces.

Grünfeld, Alfred, Austrian pianist and composer; b. Prague, July 4, 1852; d. Vienna, Jan. 4, 1924. He studied in Prague, and later at Kullak's Academy in Berlin; settled in Vienna in 1873, and established himself there as a popular concert pianist and teacher; he also made tours in other European countries, including Russia. He composed an operetta, *Der Lebemann* (Vienna, Jan. 16, 1903) and the comic opera, *Die Schönen von Fogaras* (Dresden, 1907); made brilliant arrangements for piano of waltzes by Johann Strauss; also publ. piano studies and various other pieces (*Spanish Serenade, Hungarian Fantasy, Barcarolle, Impromptu,* etc.).

Grünfeld, Heinrich, renowned cellist, brother of **Alfred Grünfeld;** b. Prague, April 21, 1855; d. Berlin, Aug. 26, 1931. He studied at the Prague Cons.; went to Berlin in 1876, and taught cello at Kullak's Academy; also played chamber music with X. Scharwenka and G. Hollander. He publ. a book of memoirs, *In Dur und Moll* (Berlin, 1924).

Grunn, John Homer, American pianist and composer; b. West Salem, Wis., May 5, 1880; d. Los Angeles, June 6, 1944. He studied piano with E. Liebling in Chicago and then at Stern's Cons. in Berlin; taught piano at the Chicago Music College (1903–7), then was in Phoenix, Ariz.; in 1910, he settled in Los Angeles as a piano teacher. He became especially interested in Indian music, and wrote a number of pieces based on Indian motifs: the ballets *Xochitl* and *The Flower Goddess* (both on Aztec subjects); *Hopi Indian Dance* for Orch.; *Zuni Indian Suite* for Orch.; many songs (*From Desert and Pueblo,* etc.).

Grunsky, Karl, German music critic; b. Schornbach, March 5, 1871; d. Vaihingen, near Stuttgart, Aug. 2, 1943. He studied political science at the Univ. of Stuttgart; obtained his Ph.D. in 1893, and began a career as a political journalist; also studied music; wrote music criticism in Stuttgart and Munich papers.
WRITINGS: *Musikgeschichte des 19. Jahrhunderts* (Leipzig, 1902; 4th ed., in 2 vols., 1923); *Musikgeschichte des 17. Jahrhunderts* (Leipzig, 1905; 3rd ed., 1925); *Musikgeschichte des 18. Jahrhunderts* (Leipzig, 1905; 2nd ed., 1914); *Musikästhetik* (Leipzig, 1907; 4th ed., 1923); *Anton Bruckner* (Stuttgart, 1922); *Franz Liszt* (Leipzig, 1925); *Hugo Wolf* (Leipzig, 1928); *Der Kampf um deutsche Musik* (Stuttgart, 1933); *Richard Wagner* (Stuttgart, 1933); *Volkstum und Musik* (Esslingen, 1934). He publ.

transcriptions for 2 pianos, 8-hands, of all the Bruckner symphs.; wrote program notes for the Bayreuth Festivals (1924); commentaries to performances of Bruckner's works, etc.; also *Die Technik des Klavierauszuges, entwickelt am dritten Akt von Wagners Tristan* (Leipzig, 1911; contains technical discussion of arranging).

Grunwald, Hugo, German-American pianist and teacher; b. Stuttgart, March 17, 1869; d. New York, Oct. 2, 1956. He studied music at the Stuttgart Cons.; emigrated in 1893 to the U.S., where he taught at the N.Y. College of Music. He was one of the founders, in 1905, of the Bohemian Club of N.Y.

Gruppe, Paulo Mesdag, American cellist; b. Rochester, N.Y., Sept. 1. 1891. He studied at The Hague Cons., then in Paris with J. Salomon; won a scholarship at the Paris Cons., where he studied with Casals; made his debut at The Hague in 1907, then toured Europe; in 1909 made his first appearance in the U.S.; was a member of the Letz Quartet and the Tollefsen Trio; in 1953 lived in New Haven; then in Mexico City. He publ. *A Reasonable and Practical Approach to the Cello* (Urbana, Ill., 1964).

Grützmacher, Friedrich (Wilhelm Ludwig), renowned German cellist; b. Dessau, March 1, 1832; d. Dresden, Feb. 23, 1903. He received his musical training from his father, a chamber musician at Dessau; at the age of 16 he went to Leipzig, and produced such a fine impression that Ferdinand David secured for him the post of first cellist of the Gewandhaus Orch. (1849). In 1860 he went to Dresden, where he remained for more than 40 years, until his death, as a teacher and chamber music player. Among his pupils were Hugo Becker and several other well-known cellists. He wrote a Cello Concerto; *Hohe Schule des Violoncellspiels* (Leipzig, 1891); several books of cello studies, and numerous arrangements for cello of works by classical composers; also edited cello works by Beethoven, Mendelssohn, Chopin, and Schumann. His brother, **Leopold Grützmacher** (b. Dessau, Sept. 4, 1835; d. Weimar, Feb. 26, 1900), was also a cellist; he studied in Dessau, and later joined the Gewandhaus Orch. in Leipzig; after occupying various posts in theater orchs., he settled in Weimar as a teacher at the court chapel. He wrote 2 cello concertos and a number of salon pieces for his instrument. Leopold's son, **Friedrich** (b. Meiningen, July 20, 1866; d. Cologne, July 25, 1919), carried on the family tradition of cello playing; was a pupil of his father as well as of his uncle; was a member of various theater orchs. in Budapest and elsewhere; finally settled in Cologne as a teacher at the Cons. there. He publ. a number of valuable cello collections and transcriptions.

Guadagni, Gaetano, famous male contralto; b. Lodi, c.1725; d. Padua, Nov., 1792. He began his career in Parma (1746); in 1748, went to London, where he attracted the attention of Handel, who gave him contralto parts in *Messiah* and *Samson;*

after many successful appearances in London, he sang in Dublin (1751–52); then went to Paris (1754) and to Lisbon (1755), where he studied with Gizziello. He then returned to Italy; in 1762, Gluck secured an engagement for him in Vienna to sing Orfeo in Gluck's opera. In 1769, Guadagni was again in London. In 1770 he sang in Munich; in 1772, he appeared in Venice; in 1776, he was summoned by Frederick the Great to Potsdam, receiving great acclaim; in 1777, he settled in Padua, where he continued to sing at churches. He was not only a fine singer but an excellent actor; also wrote various arias, one of which, *Pensa a serbarmi,* is preserved in the Bologna library.

Guadagnini, family of famous violin makers of Piacenza, Italy. **Lorenzo** (1695–1748) used the label "Laurentius Guadagnini, alumnus Antonius Stradivarius," and he may have studied with Stradivarius in Cremona shortly before the latter's death in 1737; certainly he followed Stradivarius's models in his violin making. Lorenzo's son, **Giovanni Battista** (b. Cremona, 1711; d. Turin, Sept. 18, 1786), received his training presumably from his father, and may have been with him at the shop of Stradivarius; he followed his father from Cremona to Piacenza in 1737; worked in Milan (1749–58); was in Parma (1759–71); then settled in Turin. His violins are regarded as the finest of the Guadagninis. His two sons, **Giuseppe** (1736–1805) and **Gaetano** (1745–1817), continued the family tradition and manufactured some good instruments, but failed to approach the excellence of their father's creations. Violin-making remained the family's occupation through 4 more generations in Turin; the last representative, **Paolo Guadagnini,** perished in the torpedoing of an Italian ship, on Dec. 28, 1942.
BIBLIOGRAPHY: W.L. von Lütgendorff, *Die Geigen- und Lautenmacher vom Mittelalter bis zur Gegenwart* (Frankfurt, 1904); E.N. Doring, *The Guadagnini Family of Violin Makers* (Chicago, 1949).

Guadagno, Anton, Italian conductor; b. Castellammare del Golfo, Grapani, May 2, 1925. He studied at the Santa Cecilia Academy in Rome and at the Salzburg Mozarteum. His teachers in conducting were Franco Ferrara, Bernardino Molinari, Carlo Zecchi, and Herbert von Karajan. He appeared in many of the regional opera houses of Italy; then served as an assistant conductor at the Metropolitan Opera in N.Y. (1958–59) and as music administrator of the Philadelphia Lyric Opera (1966–72). Returning to Europe, he was named chief conductor of the Vienna Volksoper.

Gualdo, Giovanni (John), Italian musician and wine merchant. He arrived in Philadelphia from London in 1767 and opened a store there; among other things, he sold instruments, taught violin, flute, guitar, and other instruments; also arranged music; presented concerts; the first of these, given in Philadelphia on Nov. 16, 1769, was devoted largely to Gualdo's own compositions, and may well be regarded as the earliest "composer's concert" in America. He died insane at the Pennsylvania Hospital, Philadelphia, Dec. 20, 1771. His *6 easy evening entertainments for 2 mandolins or 2 violins with a thorough bass for the harpsichord or violincello* are in MS in the Library of Congress, Washington, D.C.; the printed op. 2, *6 Sonates for 2 German flutes with a thorough bass* (his name appears here as **Giovanni Gualdo da Vandero**) is in the British Museum. Copies of both sets are owned by the N.Y. Public Library.
BIBLIOGRAPHY: O.G. Sonneck, *Early Concert-Life in America* (Leipzig, 1907; pp. 70–74).

Guami, Francesco, Italian musician, brother of **Gioseffo Guami;** b. Lucca, c.1544; d. there, Jan. 30, 1602. He was trombonist at the court chapel in Munich (1568–80), and maestro di cappella at Baden-Baden (1580–88), at Venice (1593), and at Lucca (1598–1601). He wrote madrigals on the Venetian model, and some church music.
BIBLIOGRAPHY: L. Nerici, *Storia della musica in Lucca* (1879).

Guami, Gioseffo (Giuseppe), Italian organist and composer; brother of **Francesco Guami;** b. Lucca, c.1540; d. there, 1612. He was organist at the court in Munich (1568–79), maestro di cappella at the court in Genoa (1585). From 1588–91 he was first organist at San Marco in Venice (while Giovanni Gabrieli was second organist); in 1591 he returned to Lucca as church organist. His surviving compositions include madrigals, motets, and toccatas; in his madrigals, he followed the Venetian school. Some of his masses are reprinted in F. Commer's *Musica sacra* (vols. 17 and 18); a toccata is included in L. Torchi's *L'arte musicale in Italia* (vol. 3).
BIBLIOGRAPHY: L. Nerici, *Storia della musica in Lucca* (1879); G. Benvenuti (editor), *Istituzioni e monumenti dell'arte musicale italiana,* vol. 1 (1931).

Guarino, Carmine, Italian composer; b. Rovigo, Oct. 1, 1893; d. Genoa, June 5, 1965. He studied violin and composition at the Cons. of Naples. His first opera *Madama di Challant,* set in a Verdian tradition, was produced there on March 9, 1927, attracting favorable comments. He was also the composer of the first Italian radio opera, *Cuore di Wanda* (Radio Italiano, Dec. 20, 1931). Other works for the stage comprise an operetta, *Gaby* (San Remo, March 20, 1924); a musical fable, *Tabarano alla Corte di Nonesiste* (1931); the one-act opera *Balilla* (Rome, March 7, 1935); the one-act opera *Sogno di un mattino d'autunno* (Cluj, Rumania, March 30, 1936); and a ballet, *El Samet, il silenzioso* (1958).

Guarino, Piero, Italian conductor and composer; b. Alexandria, Egypt, June 20, 1919. He studied at the Athens Cons. and the Santa Cecilia Academy in Rome. He made his debut as a conductor in 1946; then conducted opera and symph. throughout Italy. In 1960 he returned to Alexandria as director of the Cons.; also taught at the Salzburg Mozarteum. In

1962 he was named chief conductor of the Orch. of the Academy of Music in Naples, with which he toured in Europe and the U.S. In 1969 he was appointed director of the Cons. at Sassari in Sardinia. He is also a competent composer of Italianate music of considerable sophistication. Among his works are *Chamber Music*, to words of James Joyce, set for Middle Strings and Piano (1963), and a one-act opera, *Vettura-Letto*, after Thornton Wilder (1969).

Guarneri, famous family of violin makers in Cremona. The Italian form of the name was **Guarnieri**; Guarneri was derived from the Latin spelling, **Guarnerius;** the labels invariably used the Latin form. **Andrea,** head of the family (b. Cremona, c.1625; d. there, Dec. 7, 1698), was a pupil of Nicolo Amati; he lived in Amati's house from 1641 to 1646, and again from 1650 to 1654, when, with his wife, he moved to his own house in Cremona and began making his own violins, labeling them as "alumnus" of Amati and, after 1655, "ex alumnis," often with the additional words of "sub titolo Sanctae Theresiae." Andrea's son **Pietro Giovanni,** known as **Peter of Mantua** (b. Cremona, Feb. 18, 1655; d. Mantua, March 26, 1720), worked first at Cremona; then went to Mantua, where he settled; he also used the device "sub titolo Sanctae Theresiae." Another son of Andrea, **Giuseppe** (b. Cremona, Nov. 25, 1666; d. there, c.1740), worked in his father's shop, which he eventually inherited; in his own manufactures, he departed from his father's model and followed the models of Stradivarius. Giuseppe's son, **Pietro** (b. Cremona, April 14, 1695; d. Venice, April 7, 1762), became known as **Peter of Venice;** he settled in Venice in 1725, and adopted some features of the Venetian masters, Montagnana and Serafin. **(Bartolomeo) Giuseppe Antonio,** known as **Giuseppe del Gesù,** from the initials IHS often appearing on his labels (b. Cremona, Aug. 21, 1698; d. there, Oct. 17, 1744), was a son of Giuseppe. He became the most celebrated member of the family; some of his instruments bear the label "Joseph Guarnerius Andreae Nepos Cremonae," which establishes his lineage as a grandson of Andrea. His violins are greatly prized; only Stradivarius excelled him in the perfection of instrumental craftsmanship; he experimented with a variety of wood materials, and also made changes in the shapes of his instruments during different periods of his work. Paganini used one of his instruments.

BIBLIOGRAPHY: G. de Piccolellis, *Liutai antichi e moderni, genealogia degli Amati et dei Guarnieri* (Florence, 1886); Lütgendorff, *Die Geigen- und Lautenmacher vom Mittelalter bis zur Gegenwart* (Frankfurt, 1904; 4th ed., 1922, in dictionary form); H. Petherick, *Joseph Guarnerius, His Work and His Master* (London, 1906); A. Pougin, *Une Famille de grands luthiers italiens;* H. Wenstenberg, *Joseph Guarnerius del Gesù Abbildungen und Beschreibungen seiner Instrumente aus seinen drei Perioden* (Berlin, 1921); W. H. Hill, *Violin Makers of the Guarneri Family, 1626–1762: Their Life and Work* (London, 1931).

Guarnieri, Antonio, Italian conductor; b. Venice, Feb. 1, 1880; d. Milan, Nov. 25, 1952. He studied cello; was a member of the Martucci Quartet. In 1922 he conducted at La Scala; in 1929 he became one of its regular conductors, remaining there until his death. He excelled in the Italian repertoire.

Guarnieri, (Mozart) Camargo, outstanding Brazilian composer; b. Tiété, state of São Paulo, Feb. 1, 1907. He studied piano and composition in São Paulo before going, in 1938, to Paris, where he took a course in composition with Charles Koechlin and one in conducting with Rühlmann. In 1942 and 1946 he visited the U.S. as a conductor of his own works. He later returned to Brazil, where he taught at various institutions. His music is permeated with "Brasilidad," a syndrome that is Brazilian in its melody and rhythm; his *Dansa brasileira* is typical in its national quality.

WORKS: *Pedro Malazarte,* one-act comic opera (1931); opera, *Um homem só* (1960); 4 symphs. (1944, 1946, 1952, 1963); 5 piano concertos (1936, 1946, 1964, 1967, 1970); 2 violin concertos (1940, 1953); *Overture concertante* (1943); *Dansa brasileira* for Orch. (São Paulo, March 7, 1941; originally for Piano, 1931); *Dansa negra* for Orch. (1947); *Chôro* for Violin and Orch. (1951); *Variations on a Northeast Brazilian Theme* for Piano and Orch. (1953); *Suite IV Centenário* for Orch. (1954; Louisville Orch., Jan. 15, 1955); *Chôro* for Clarinet and Orch. (1956); *Chôro* for Piano and Orch. (1957); *Sêca,* cantata (1957); *Suite Vila Rica* for Orch. (1958); *Chôro* for Cello and Orch. (1961); Piano Concertino (1961); *Seresta* for Piano and Chamber Orch. (1965); *Guaná bará,* cantata (1965); *Homage to Villa-Lobos* for Wind Orch. (1966); *Següencia, Coral e Ricercare* for Chamber Orch. (1966); 3 string quartets (1932, 1944, 1962); 5 violin sonatas (1930, 1933, 1950, 1959, 1962); many songs and piano pieces.

Guarrera, Frank, American baritone; b. Philadelphia, Dec. 3, 1923. He studied voice with Richard Bonelli in Philadelphia. On Dec. 14, 1948, he made his Metropolitan Opera debut as Escamillo in *Carmen;* was invited by Toscanini to sing at La Scala in Milan; also made guest appearances in San Francisco, Chicago, Paris, and London. He was best known for his performances of Italian roles.

Guastavino, Carlos, Argentine composer; b. Santa Fé, Argentina, April 5, 1912. He studied chemistry; then turned to music, and took a course in composition with Athos Palma. He cultivates miniature forms, mostly for piano; of these, the suites *10 cantilenas argentinas* (1958) and *Las presencias* (1961) radiate a certain melorhythmic charm. He also wrote a ballet, *Fué una vez* (1942); *Romance de Santa Fé* for Piano and Orch. (1952); Violin Sonata (1952); choruses on Argentine themes; many songs. A complete catalogue of his works through 1961 is found in *Composers of the Americas,* vol. 1 (Washington, D.C., 1955; new ed., 1962).

Guba, Vladimir, Ukrainian composer; b. Kiev, Dec.

22, 1938. He studied at the Kiev Cons. with Liatoshinsky; became interested in modern techniques of composition; applied the 12-tone method in his piano pieces *Deformation* and *Echo* (1961); also wrote a series of 30 piano pieces, *In the World of Childhood*, and a cycle of 24 piano pieces, *Sonorous Exhibits.*

Gubaidulina, Sofia, Soviet composer of the extreme avant-garde; b. Chistopol, Oct. 24, 1931. She studied at the Cons. of Kazan; graduated in 1954; then enrolled at the Moscow Cons. to study composition with Peiko and Shebalin. Her music follows vectorially divergent paths, without adhering to a prearranged doctrine of modern composition. Perhaps her most astounding work is the Concerto for Bassoon and Low String Instruments, in 5 movements (1975), in which the bassoon is embedded in a net of 4 cellos and 3 double basses, creating a claustrophobic syndrome of ingrown low sonorities, while the solo instrument is forced to perform acrobatic feats to escape constriction, such as labial glissandos and rapid repetitions of a single note. WORKS: Symph. (1958); Piano Concerto (1959); String Quintet (1957); *Intermezzo* for 16 Harps, 8 Trumpets, and Drums (1961); *Allegro rustico* for Flute and Piano (1963); 5 Etudes for Harp, Double Bass, and Percussion (1966); Sonata for Percussion (1966); *Pantomimes* for Double Bass and Piano (1966); *Detto No. 1* for Organ (1969); *Detto No. 2* for Chamber Ensemble; electronic work, *Vivant-non-Vivant* (1970); String Quartet (1971); *Concordanza* for Chamber Group (1971); *Rumore e Silenzio* for Harpsichord, Celesta, and Percussion (1974); Concerto for Bassoon and Low String Instruments (1975); Concerto for Piano and String Orch. (1978); *In croce* for Cello and Organ (1979); *Percussio di Pekarsky* (1979; Pekarsky is a top percussionist in the U.S.S.R.); *Garden of Joy and Sorrow* for Flute, Viola, and Harp (1980); Violin Concerto (Moscow, April 15, 1982); piano pieces; songs.

Gudehus, Heinrich, German tenor; b. Altenhagen, near Celle, March 30, 1845; d. Dresden, Oct. 9, 1909. He first studied organ, and also taught school; then took up singing; made his debut in Berlin in Spohr's *Jessonda* (Jan. 7, 1871). After several engagements in various German towns, he sang Parsifal in Bayreuth (July 28, 1882) with excellent success; was with the Dresden Opera from 1880–90; appeared in London (1884) in Wagnerian roles; was with the Metropolitan Opera in N.Y. (1890–91); then returned to Germany.

Gudmel, Claude. See **Goudimel, Claude.**

Gudmundsen-Holmgreen, Pelle, Danish composer; b. Copenhagen, Nov. 21, 1932. He studied theory and composition with Finn Höffding and Svend Westergaard at the Royal Danish Cons. in Copenhagen (1953–58); served as stage manager of the Royal Theater there (1959–64); taught composition at the Jutland Academy of Music in Aarhus (1967–73). He followed serial techniques; then experimented with

a "new simplicity" achieved through persistent repetition of notes and patterns; employed optical notation, in which the distance between notes in a score equals the "time span" between the playing of those notes. WORKS: *Ouverture* for Strings (1955); *Improvisations* for 10 Instruments (1960); *Chronos* for 22 Instrumentalists (1962); *Collegium Musicum Concerto* for Chamber Orch. (1964); *Mester Jakob (Frère Jacques)* for Chamber Orch. (1964); *Reprises (Recapitulations)* for 15 Instrumentalists (1965); Symph. (1962–65; Danish Radio, Jan. 11, 1968); *5 Pieces* for Orch. (1966); *Je ne me tairai jamais, jamais!* for 12 Voices and 9 Instruments (1966); *Rerepriser (Rerecapitulations)* for 13 Instruments (1967); *Variations for Aunt Rix* for Chamber Orch. (1968); *Stykke for stykke (Piece by Piece)* for Chamber Orch. (1968); *3 Movements* for String Orch. and Cowbells (1968); *Tricolore IV* for Orch. (Copenhagen, Sept. 11, 1969; 3 previous *Tricolores* are unfinished); *5 Movements* for Concert Band (1969); *Catalogue and Coda* for Concert Band (1969); *Prelude and Fugue* for Brass Band (1969); *Spejl II (Mirror II)* for Orch. (Copenhagen, Feb. 24, 1974); *Antiphony* for Orch. (1974–77); 4 string quartets (1958; 1959; 1960; 1967); *In terra pax* for Clarinet, Piano, and 2 Percussionists (1961); *Canon* for 9 Instruments ad lib. (1967); *Plateaux pour 2* for Cello and Percussion (1970); *Terrace,* in 6 stages, for Wind Quintet (1970); *Solo* for Electric Guitar (1972); *Spejl I* for Violins and Tape (1971–73); Septet (1975); *The Old Man* for 2 Flutes, Harp, Viola, and Cello (1976); *Ritual Dances* for 6 Percussionists, or 5 Percussionists and Electric Guitar (1976); Variations for Piano (1959); *Udstillingsbilleder (Pictures at an Exhibition)* for Piano (1968); *Spejl III* for Organ (1974); *5 Songs* for Soprano, Flute, Violin, and Cello (1958); *3 Songs to Texts from Politiken* (a Danish newspaper) for Contralto, Violin, Viola, Cello, Guitar, and Percussion (1967); *Songs Without* for Mezzo-soprano and Piano (1976); a cappella choruses, including *Examples* (1975).

Gueden, Hilde, Austrian soprano; b. Vienna, Sept. 15, 1917. Both her parents were musicians. She made her debut in operetta at the age of 16; in 1939 the family moved to Switzerland; in 1941 she sang Zerlina in Munich; in 1942, made her debut in Rome. In 1947 Gueden became a member of the Vienna State Opera; also appeared at La Scala, Milan. She made her American debut at the Metropolitan Opera in N.Y., on Nov. 15, 1951, as Gilda, and sang there until 1961; then continued her career in Europe, mainly appearing with the Vienna State Opera.

Guédron, Pierre, French composer; b. Châteaudun, 1565; d. Paris, 1621. He was a choirboy in the chapel of Cardinal de Guise and later sang in the royal chapel (1588). In 1601 he was appointed Composer of the King's Music. He wrote ballets for the court, which included solo songs. Some of his airs are included in *Airs de Cour* (1615–18), and other contemporary collections. He is regarded as a precursor of Lully in the creation of French ballet music.

BIBLIOGRAPHY: H. Quittard, "L'Air de cour: Pierre Guédron," *Revue Musicale* (1905); H. Prunières, *Le Ballet de cour en France avant Benserade et Lully* (Paris, 1914); L. de La Laurencie, "Un Musicien dramatique du XVIIᵉ siècle français; Pierre Guédron," *Rivista Musicale Italiana* (1922); D. Royster, *Pierre Guédron and the Air de Cour, 1600–1620* (Diss., Yale Univ., 1972).

Guelfi, Giangiacomo, Italian baritone; b. Rome, Dec. 21, 1924. He studied law in Florence; then began voice studies with Titta Ruffo; made his debut in Spoleto in 1950 as Rigoletto; in 1952 joined La Scala in Milan; also sang in Chicago and in London. On Feb. 5, 1970, he made his Metropolitan Opera debut as Scarpia in *Tosca*.

Guénin, (Marie) Alexandre, French violinist and composer; b. Maubeuge, Feb. 20, 1744; d. Etampes, Jan. 22, 1835. He showed a precocious talent, and was sent to Paris for study with Gaviniès (violin) and Gossec (composition). In 1771 he joined the orch. of the Paris Opéra; later was active as a conductor in the Paris society called Concert Spirituel; taught at the Ecole Royale de Chant. Several of his works were publ. in his lifetime: 6 symphs.; 6 violin duos; 6 string trios.

BIBLIOGRAPHY: L. de La Laurencie, *L'Ecole française du violon* (Paris, 1922).

Guenther, Felix, pianist and writer on music; b. Trautenau, Austria, Dec. 5, 1886; d. New York, May 6, 1951. He studied at the Vienna Cons.; then at the Univ. of Berlin, obtaining his Ph.D. there in 1913. He emigrated to the U.S. in 1937; was connected with various music publishers in N.Y.; made arrangements and edited classical anthologies. He publ. *Weingartner* (Berlin, 1918), *Schuberts Lied* (Stuttgart, 1928), and *Mein Freund Schubert* (Hamburg, 1928).

Guéranger, Dom Prosper Louis Pascal, French ecclesiastic scholar; b. Sable-sur-Sarthe, April 4, 1805; d. Solesmes, Jan. 30, 1875. As abbot of the Benedictine monastery at Solesmes, his research and writings gave the impetus to and laid the foundations for scholarly investigations leading to the restoration of Gregorian melodies. Dom Guéranger and the Benedictines of Solesmes played a role of prime importance in the accomplishment of this work. He wrote *Institutions liturgiques* (3 vols., 1840–53; 2nd ed., 4 vols., 1878–85); *L'Année liturgique* (15 parts, 1840–1901; continued by Fromage); *Ste. Cécile et la Société Romaine* (1873; 8th ed., 1898).

BIBLIOGRAPHY: G. Guépin, *Prosper Guéranger* (Le Mans, 1876); *Bibliographie des Bénédictins de la Congrégation de France* (Solesmes, 1889); Chamard, *Gué ranger et l'abbé Bernier* (Angers, 1901); P. Delatte, *Dom Guéranger, abbé de Solesmes* (2 vols., Paris, 1909).

Guerra-Peixe, César, Brazilian composer; b. Petropolis, March 18, 1914. He studied composition with H.J. Koellreuther; played violin in theater orchs.; arranged music for radio. As a composer, he plunged headlong into the torrent of dodecaphony, but about 1949 changed his orientation and returned to his Brazilian roots, nurtured by melorhythmic folk-song resources. He wrote 2 symphs. (1946, 1960); Nonet (1945); 2 string quartets (1947, 1958); Violin Sonata (1950); Piano Trio (1960); Guitar Sonata (1969); *Duo* for Clarinet and Bassoon (1970). A complete catalogue of his works to 1970 is found in *Composers of the Americas*, vol. 16 (Washington, D.C., 1970); pieces for guitar.

BIBLIOGRAPHY: Vasco Mariz, "César Guerra-Peixe," in the compendium *Mésica brasileña contemporánea* (Rosario, Argentina, 1952).

Guerrero, Francisco, Spanish composer; b. Seville, 1528 (probably on St. Francis Day, Oct. 4); d. there, Nov. 8, 1599. He was a pupil of his brother, **Pedro,** and for a short time of Morales. In 1546, he became maestro di cappella of Jaén Cathedral; in 1549, he went to Seville as cantor at the Cathedral there. In both 1551 and 1554, he was offered a similar post at the Cathedral of Malaga, but declined it. In 1556, he was in Lisbon; in 1567, in Cordova; in 1570, in Santander; in 1581–82 he went to Rome; in 1588, he was in Venice, whence he undertook a pilgrimage to Palestine. His account of his journey, *El viaje de Jerusalem que hizo Francisco Guerrero,* was publ. in 1611, and went through numerous editions. As a composer he was greatly appreciated by his contemporaries, but the comparisons with Morales or Victoria overestimate his importance.

WORKS: *Sacrae cantiones vulgo moteta* (1555); *Psalmorum, Liber I, accedit Missa defunctorum* (1559; 2nd ed., with Italian title, 1584); *Canticum beatae Mariae quod Magnificat nuncupatur, per octo musicae modos variatum* (1563); *Liber I missarum* (1566; contains 9 masses for 4–5 voices and 3 motets for 4–8 voices); *Motteta* (1570); *Missarum Liber II* (1582; contains 7 masses and a *Missa pro defunctis*); *Liber vesperarum* (1584; includes 7 Psalms, 24 hymns, 8 Magnificats, Te Deum, etc.); *Passio...secundum Matthaeum et Joannem more Hispano* (1585); *Canciones y villanescas espirituales* (1589); *Mottecta* (1589); *Missa Saeculorum Amen* (1597), etc. Reprints have been made by Eslava (2 *Passiones)* in *Lira sacro-hispana* and by Pedrell in *Hispaniae schola musica sacra* (in vol. II: *Magnificat, Officium defunctorum,* Passions, antiphonals, etc.; in vol. VI: a *Falso bordone).* The *Libro de música para vihuela, intitulado Orphénica Lyra* of Miguel de Fuenllana contains some works by Guerrero arranged for vihuela. Two vols. of Guerrero's *Opera omnia* (unfinished), ed. by V. Garcia and M.Q. Garalda (1955–57), containing *Canciones y villanescas espirituales,* comprise vols. 16 and 19 of *Monumentos de la Música Española.*

BIBLIOGRAPHY: R. Mitjana, *Francisco Guerrero, estudio crítico-biográfico* (Madrid, 1922); R. Stevenson, *Spanish Cathedral Music in the Golden*

Age (Cal., 1961).

Guerrini, Guido, Italian composer; b. Faenza, Sept. 12, 1890; d. Rome, June 13, 1965. He was a pupil of Consolini (violin), and Toschi and Busoni (composition) at the Liceo Musicale at Bologna; was prof. of harmony there (1919–23); prof. of composition at Parma Cons. (1924–28); director of the Cherubini Cons. in Florence (1928–44); director of the Bologna Cons. (1944–50); in 1951 was appointed director of the Santa Cecilia Cons. in Rome; retired in 1960. WORKS: Operas: *Zalebi* (1915), *Nemici* (Bologna, Jan. 19, 1921), *La vigna* (Rome, March 7, 1935), *Enea,* after Virgil (Rome, Feb. 11, 1953); *Missa pro defunctis,* in memory of Marconi, for Solo Voices, Chorus, and Orch. (1939); *La città perduta,* biblical cantata (1942); *Tre liriche* for Voice and Orch. (1947); Cello Concerto (1914); *Canzonetta* for 4 Saxophones (1938); *Arcadia* for Oboe and Piano; piano quintet; 3 string quartets; *Le Suore,* 3 pieces for Harp; vocal works, *Le fiamme su l'altare* for Voice, Double String Quartet, and 2 Harps; songs. He also wrote the books *Trattato di armonia complementare* (1922); *Origine, evoluzione e caratteri degli strumenti musicali* (1926); *Prontuario dei tempi e colori musicali* (1939); *F. Busoni, La vita, la figura, l'opera* (Florence, 1944); *Appunti d'orchestrazione* (1945); *A. Vivaldi,* (Florence, 1951); A catalogue of his works and an appreciation were publ. for his 70th birthday in Rome (1960).

Guerrini, Paolo, Italian music historian; b. Bagnolo Mella, near Brescia, Nov. 18, 1880; d. Brescia, Nov. 19, 1960. He specialized in Italian sacred music; edited the periodical *Brixia Sacra* (1910–25); in 1930, he began publication of the historical studies *Memorie storiche della Diocesi di Brescia;* served further as archivist and librarian in Brescia. In 1936, he was appointed canon of the Brescia Cathedral. He revived and translated into Italian the music books of Cardinal Katschthaler *(Storia della musica sacra);* publ. *Storia della cappella musicale del Duomo di Brescia e del Duomo di Salò* and *Storia della musica sacra in Italia nei secolo XIX e XX.*

Guézec, Jean-Pierre, French composer; b. Dijon, Aug. 29, 1934; d. Paris, March 9, 1971. He enrolled at the Paris Cons. where he attended classes of Olivier Messiaen, Darius Milhaud, and Jean Rivier; received the Premier Prix in 1963; joined the faculty of the Paris Cons. in 1969. WORKS: Concerto for Violin and 14 Instruments (1960); *Concert en Trois Parties* for 11 Instruments (1961); *Suite pour Mondrian* for Orch. (1962); *Architectures colorées* for 15 Instruments (1964); *Ensemble multicolore 65* for 18 Instruments (1965); *Formes* for Orch. (1966); *Textures enchaînées* for 13 Wind Instruments (1967); *Assemblages* for 28 Instruments (1967); String Trio (1968); *Reliefs polychromés* for Chorus (1969); *Couleurs juxtaposées* for 2 Percussion Groups (1969); *Onze pour Cinz* for Percussionists (1970).

Guglielmi, Pietro Alessandro, Italian composer; b. Massa di Carrara, Dec. 9, 1728; d. Rome, Nov. 18, 1804. He studied with his father, **Jacob Guglielmi,** and with Durante at the Cons. Santa Maria di Loreto at Naples. His first comic opera, *Lo solachianello 'mbroglione,* was performed at Naples in 1757; during the next 10 years he wrote 24 operas, including *Il ratto della sposa* (Venice, 1765) and *La sposa fedele* (Venice, 1767), which were played all over Europe and became highly popular. He went to London in 1767; during his 5 years there, conducted and wrote several operas, among them *Ezio* (Jan. 13, 1770), in which his wife, **Lelia Achiapati,** sang. He returned to Italy in 1772; in 1793 was appointed maestro di cappella of San Pietro in Vaticano by Pope Pius VI and turned to church music; composed several oratorios, of which *Debora e Sisara* (Naples, Feb. 13, 1789) was regarded as his masterpiece. A detailed list of Guglielmi's operas is found in F. Piovano's articles on him and his son in the *Rivista Musicale Italiana* (1905, 1910).
BIBLIOGRAPHY: G. Bustico, *Pietro Guglielmi* (Massa, 1899); A. Della Corte, *L'opera comica italiana nel settecento* (Bari, 1923).

Guglielmi, Pietro Carlo, Italian composer, son of **Pietro Alessandro Guglielmi;** b. Naples, c.1763; d. there, Feb. 28, 1817. After study at the Cons. di Santa Maria di Loreto at Naples, he went to Spain; his first operas were performed at Madrid in 1793 and 1794; then lived in Italy, producing operas in Naples, Florence, and Rome. He went to London in 1809; presented several operas at the King's Theatre; returned to Italy in 1810, and was appointed maestro di cappella to the Duchess Beatrice at Massa di Carrara. A list of his works, including some 40 operas, oratorios, and cantatas, was publ. by Francesco Piovano in the *Rivista Musicale Italiana* (1909–10).

Gui, Vittorio, Italian composer and conductor; b. Rome, Sept. 14, 1885; d. Florence, Oct. 16, 1975. He studied at the Liceo Musicale di Santa Cecilia in Rome; began his career as an opera conductor; then conducted in Parma, Naples, and at La Scala in Milan (1923); eventually settled in Florence; was founder of the Maggio Musicale Fiorentino in 1933. From 1947 to 1965 he conducted opera in England; was counsellor of Glyndebourne Festival Opera (1960–65). WORKS: Opera, *Fata Malerba* (Turin, May 15, 1927); symph. works *Giulietta e Romeo* (1902), *Il tempo che fu* (1910), *Scherzo fantastico* (1913), *Fantasia bianca* (1919; an orch. experiment making use of films), *Giornata di festa* (1921); he publ. a vol. of critical essays, *Battute d'aspetto* (Florence, 1944).

Guidetti, Giovanni Domenico, Italian ecclesiastic scholar; b. Bologna, 1530 (baptized, Jan. 1, 1531); d. Rome, Nov. 30, 1592. After taking holy orders, he went to Rome, where he became Palestrina's pupil and in 1575 was appointed "cappellano" (a clerical beneficiary) and chorister in the papal choir. From 1576 to 1581, he worked with Palestrina on a revised edition of the Gradual and Antiphonary, but this work being forestalled by the publ. of Leichtenstein's edition (Venice, 1580), he obtained permission to publ. the services for everyday use: *Directorium chori ad usum sacro-sanctae basilicae Vaticanae* (Rome, 1582, and several reprints); *Cantus ecclesiaticus passionis Domini Nostri Jesu Christi* (Rome, 1586); *Cantus ecclesiasticus officii majoris* (Rome, 1587; new ed., 1619); he also publ. *Praefationes in cantu firmo* (Rome, 1588).

Guido d'Arezzo (known also as **Guido Aretinus**), famous reformer of musical notation and vocal instruction; b. c.997; d. Pomposa; date of death uncertain; May 17, 1050, often cited, is unfortunately without foundation. He received his education at the Benedictine abbey at Pomposa, near Ferrara. He left the monastery in 1025, as a result of disagreements with his fellow monks, who were envious of his superiority in vocal teaching; he was then summoned by Bishop Theobald of Arezzo to the cathedral school there; it was because of this association that he became known as Guido d'Arezzo. The assertions that he traveled in France and spent several years at the monastery of Saint-Maur des Fossés, near Paris (see, for example, Dom G. Morin in *Revue de l'art chrétien,* 1888) are not borne out by documentary evidence. Still more uncertain are the claims of his travels in Germany, and even in England. However this may be, his fame spread and reached the ears of Pope John XIX, who called him to Rome to demonstrate his system of teaching (1028). In his last years, he was a prior of the Camaldolite fraternity at Avellano. Guido's fame rests on his system of solmization, by which he established the nomenclature of the major hexachord Ut, Re, Mi, Fa, So, La, from syllables in the initial lines of the Hymn of St. John:

Ut queant laxis *Re*sonare fibris
*Mi*ra gestorum *Fa*muli tuorum,
*Sol*ve polluti *La*bii reatum,
Sancte Joannes.

No less epoch-making was Guido's introduction of the music staff of 4 lines, retaining the red *f*-line and the yellow *c*-line of his predecessors, and drawing between them a black *a*-line, above them a black *e*-line, and writing the plainsong notes (which he did *not* invent) in regular order on these lines and in the spaces:

New black line e_____
Old yellow line c_____
New black line a_____
Old red line   f_____

He also added new lines above or below these, as occasion required; thus, Guido's system did away with all uncertainty of pitch. Another invention credited to Guido is the so-called Guidonian hand, relating the degrees of the overlapping hexachords to various places on the palm of the left hand, a device helpful in directing a chorus by indicating manually the corresponding positions of the notes. Opinions differ widely as to the attribution to Guido of all these innovations; some scholars maintain that he merely popularized the already-established ideas and that solmization, in particular, was intro-

duced by a German abbot, Poncius Teutonicus, at the abbey of Saint-Maur des Fossés. Guido's treatises are *Micrologus de disciplina artis musicae* (publ. by A. Amelli, Rome, 1904; ed. by J. Smits van Waesberghe, 1955); *Regulae de ignoto cantu; Epistola de ignoto cantu* (publ. in Eng. in Strunk's *Source Readings in Music History,* N.Y., 1950).

BIBLIOGRAPHY: L. Angeloni, *Sopra la vita, le opere ed il sapere di Guido d'Arezzo* (Paris, 1811); R. G. Kiesewetter, *Guido von Arezzo* (1840); G. Ristori, *Biografia di Guido Monaco d'Arezzo* (2nd ed., 1868); M. Falchi, *Studi su Guido Monaco di San Benedetto* (1882); J. Wolf, *Handbuch der Notationskunde* (vol. I); H. Wolking, *Guidos Micrologus de disciplina artis musicae und seine Quellen* (Emsdetten, 1930); J. Smits van Waesberghe, *De musicopaedogogico et theoretico Guidone Aretino eiusque vita et moribus* (in Latin; Florence, 1953); H. Oesch, *Guido von Arezzo* (Bern, 1954); J. Smits van Waesberghe, *Musikerziehung. Lehre und Theorie der Musik im Mittelalter.* Musikgeschichte in Bildern 3/3 (Leipzig, 1969); M. Huglo, "L'Auteur du *Dialogue sur la musique* attribué à Odon," *Revue de Musicologie* LV/2 (1969); D. Harbinson, "The Hymn *Ut queant laxis,*" *Music & Letters* (Jan. 1971).

Guignon, Jean-Pierre (Giovanni Pietro Ghignone), violinist and composer; b. Turin, Feb. 10, 1702; d. Versailles, Jan. 30, 1774. He went to Paris from Italy in his youth; was engaged as music tutor to the Dauphin, and persuaded the King to revive and bestow on him the title of Roi des Violons et Ménétriers, which had last been used in 1695; every professional musician in France was required to join a guild and to pay a fee to Guignon as holder of the title; so much opposition was aroused by this requirement that Parliament considered the case and deprived Guignon of this prerogative. He wrote several books of concertos, sonatas, and duos for violin.

Guilbert, Yvette, famous French *diseuse* and folksong singer; b. Paris, Jan. 20, 1865; d. Aix-en-Provence, Feb. 2, 1944. She made her debut in Paris as an actress in 1885; in 1890 she began her career as a café singer; at first she sang popular songs in Paris; later, as she toured Europe and the U.S., where she first appeared in 1896, she became noted for her interpretations of French folk songs; she regarded herself as primarily an actress, rather than a singer. She wrote her memoirs, *La Chanson de ma vie* (Paris, 1927) and *Autres temps, autres chants* (Paris, 1946).

Guillemain, (Louis-) Gabriel, French violinist and composer; b. Paris, Nov. 7, 1705; d. there (suicide), Oct. 1, 1770. He was a member of the King's orch. and gave concerts as a virtuoso. He was one of the first French composers to write violin sonatas with a developed clavichord accompaniment. He also wrote several ballets, and instrumental music for various combinations.

BIBLIOGRAPHY: L. de La Laurencie, *L'Ecole française de violon,* vol. II.

Guillou, Jean, French organist, pianist and composer; b. Angers, April 4, 1930. He began playing the piano and organ as a child; in 1952 he went to study with Dupré and Duruflé at the Paris Cons.; upon graduation, he taught organ playing in Lisbon (1955–58); then moved to Berlin, where he was active as a concert pianist and organist (1958–63). Returning to France, he was appointed organist of the St. Eustache Church in Paris; since 1972 he has conducted annual master classes in Zürich. As a solo organist he has given concerts in Poland, Russia, Japan, and the U.S.; he often concludes his concerts with improvisations on themes proposed by members of the audience. He has made numerous effective transcriptions for organ of works by Bach, Vivaldi, Mozart, and other classical composers; also a transcription of Stravinsky's *Petrouchka.* His own compositions, especially those before 1960, are written in a neo-Baroque idiom.

WORKS: Oratorio *Le Jugement dernier* (1958; Cracow, June 16, 1968); 3 concertos for Organ and Orch.: *Inventions,* No. 1 (1956), No. 2 (1966; Leningrad, Oct. 10, 1972) and No. 3 (1967; Rouen, France, Jan. 16, 1972); *Triptyque* for Strings (1957); 3 symphs.: *Judith* (No. 1), with Soprano (1968; Paris, Feb. 25, 1971); No. 2 for Strings (1971; Paris, Nov. 30, 1972); No. 3 (1974); Piano Concerto (1970); 5 *Colloques:* No. 1 for Flute, Oboe, Violin, and Piano (1954); No. 2 for Piano and Organ (1960); No. 3 for Oboe, Harp, Celesta, Vibraphone, Xylophone, Timpani, Percussion, 4 Cellos, and 2 Double Basses (1961); No. 4 for Piano, Organ, and Percussion (1965); No. 5 for Piano and Organ (1975); *Cantilia* for Piano, Harp, Timpani, and 4 Cellos (1961); Oboe Quartet (1975); 2 piano sonatas (1967, 1975). For organ: 18 Variations (1954); Sinfonietta (1958); *Fantaisie* (1962); Toccata (1963); *Pour le Tombeau de Colbert* (1963); *Symphonie initiatique* for 3 Organs (1965; 1 live, 2 on tape); *Allen* (1966); *6 Sagas* (1973); *La Chapelle des Abîmes* (1973); *Scènes d'énfants* (1973).

Guilmant, (Félix) Alexandre, eminent French organist and composer; b. Boulogne, March 12, 1837; d. Meudon, near Paris, March 29, 1911. He studied organ with his father, Jean-Baptiste Guilmant (1793–1890); took harmony lessons with Gustave Carulli in Boulogne. In 1860, he took an advanced course in organ playing with Lemmens in Brussels. When still a child, he substituted for his father at the Church of St.-Nicolas in Boulogne; at 20, he taught at the Boulogne Cons. and conducted choral concerts. He then played organ in various churches in Paris, including St.-Sulpice (1863) and Notre Dame (1868); in 1871, he was appointed organist of Ste. Trinité, remaining at this post for 30 years. He was one of the founders of the Schola Cantorum (1894); in 1896, he was appointed prof. of organ at the Paris Cons.; also appeared as organ soloist with Paris orchs. and subsequently all over Europe and in the U.S. (1893–97). He was not only a virtuoso of the first rank, but a master in the art of improvisation; he formed a great school of students, among whom were René Vierné, Joseph Bonnet, Nadia Boulanger, Marcel Dupré, and the American organist William Carl. He was a prolific composer of works for organ, which include 8 sonatas, 2 symphs. for Organ and Orch., 25 books of organ pieces, 10 books of *L'Organiste liturgiste;* there are also 3 masses, Psalms, vespers, motets, etc. Of greater importance than these are Guilmant's monumental editions of old masters: *Archives des maîtres de l'orgue* (Paris, 1898–1914; 10 vols.) and *Ecole classique de l'orgue* (1898–1903); he also edited selected works of French composers performed at his historical concerts (1902–06); made numerous arrangements for organ of various classical works.

BIBLIOGRAPHY: *A la mémoire de Alexandre Guilmant,* by his friends of the Schola (Paris, 1911); A. Eaglefield-Hull, "The Organ Works of Guilmant," *Monthly Musical Record* (Oct.-Nov. 1914); N. Dufourcq, *La Musique d'orgue française* (Paris, 1949).

Guion, David (Wendell Fentress), American composer; b. Ballinger, Texas, Dec. 15, 1892; d. Dallas, Oct. 17, 1981. He studied piano with Leopold Godowsky in Vienna; returning to the U.S. in 1915, he occupied various teaching posts in Texas; then lived in N.Y., while continuing to gravitate toward Texas; was commissioned to write a musical panorama, *Cavalcade of America,* for the 1936 Texas centennial; his *Texas Suite* for band followed in 1952. Guion devoted many years to collecting and arranging American folk songs for various folk ensembles. Of these arrangements, the most famous were *Turkey in the Straw, Arkansas Traveler,* and *Home on the Range.* He also wrote an African ballet suite, *Shingandi;* several orch. suites, among them *Southern Nights Suite; Sheep and Goat Walking to the Pasture; Alley Tunes;* and *Mother Goose Suite.*

Guiraud, Ernest, French composer; b. New Orleans, June 23, 1837; d. Paris, May 6, 1892. He studied with his father, Jean Baptiste Guiraud; produced his first opera *Le Roi David,* in New Orleans at the age of 15. He then went to Paris, which was his home for the rest of his life; studied at the Paris Cons., with Marmontel (piano) and Halévy (composition); won the Grand Prix de Rome in 1859 with his cantata *Bajazet et le joueur de flûte.* He stayed in Rome for 4 years; then returned to Paris, where his one-act opera, *Sylvie,* was produced at the Opéra-Comique (May 11, 1864). He was appointed a prof. at the Cons. in 1876; among his students were Debussy, Gédalge, and Loeffler. He wrote the recitatives to Bizet's *Carmen* and completed the orchestration of Offenbach's *Contes d'Hoffmann.* His operas (all first perf. in Paris) include *En prison* (March 5, 1869); *Le Kobold* (July 2, 1870); *Madame Turlupin* (1872); *Piccolino* (April 11, 1876, his most popular stage work); *Galante aventure* (March 23, 1882); *Frédégonde* (completed by Saint-Saëns; Dec. 18, 1895). He also wrote a ballet, *Gretna Green* (1873); 2 suites for Orch.; *Arteveld,* an overture; *Caprice* for Violin and Orch.; and a treatise on instrumentation.

Gulak-Artemovsky, Semyon, Ukrainian singer and composer; b. Gorodishche, Feb. 16, 1813; d. Moscow, April 17, 1873. He studied voice in Italy; sang at the Imperial Opera of St. Petersburg (1842–64); then lived in Moscow. His opera *Zaporozhets za Dunayem (A Cossack beyond the Danube)* was produced in St. Petersburg on April 26, 1863, and subsequently acquired considerable popularity in Russia.

BIBLIOGRAPHY: L. Kaufman, *Semyon Gulak-Artemovsky* (Kiev, 1962; in Ukrainian).

Gulbins, Max, German organist and composer; b. Kammetschen, East Prussia, July 18, 1862; d. Breslau, Feb. 19, 1932. He studied at the Hochschule für Musik in Berlin; was organist at Elbing in 1900–1908, then went to St. Elizabeth's in Breslau. He wrote, for men's chorus and orch., *Sturmlied, An das Vaterland,* and *Burggraf Friedrich von Nürnberg;* also organ pieces.

Gulbranson, Ellen (née **Norgren**), Swedish soprano; b. Stockholm, March 4, 1863; d. Oslo, Jan. 2, 1947. She studied at the Stockholm Cons., then with Mathilde Marchesi in Paris; returning to Stockholm, she made her concert debut in 1886; in 1896 she sang the part of Brünnhilde at Bayreuth, with great success; she also sang in Berlin, Paris, Moscow, Amsterdam, and London.

Gulda, Friedrich, Austrian pianist; b. Vienna, May 16, 1930. He studied piano in early childhood (1937–42) with Felix Pazofsky; then enrolled at the Vienna Music Academy as a piano student of Bruno Seidlhofer. At the age of 16 he won first prize at the International Pianists' Contest in Geneva, and immediately embarked on a concert career, giving recitals in Europe (1947–48), South America (1949), and the U.S., making a brilliant American debut in Carnegie Hall, N.Y., on Oct. 11, 1950. He was praised by critics for his intellectual penetration of the music of Bach, Beethoven, and Mozart; about 1955 he became intensely fascinated by jazz, particularly in its improvisatory aspect, which he construed as corresponding to the freedom of melodic ornamentation in Baroque music. He often included jazz numbers (with drums and slap bass) at the end of his recitals; he learned to play the saxophone, began to compose for jazz, and organized the Eurojazz Orch. As a further symptom of his estrangement from musical puritanism he returned the Beethoven Bicentennial ring given to him by the Vienna Music Academy (his old alma mater) in appreciation of his excellence in playing Beethoven's music, and gave a speech explaining the reasons for his action. He composed and performed jazz pieces, among them *Music* Nos. 1 and 2 for Piano and Big Band (1962, 1963); *Music* for 3 Jazz Soloists and Band (1962); Symph. in F for Jazz Band and Orch.; *The Veiled Old Land* for Jazz Band (1964); *The Excursion* for Jazz Orch. (1965, celebrating the flight of the American spaceship Gemini 4); *Concertino for Players and Singers* (1972). He further made a bold arrangement of Vienna waltzes in the manner of the blues; also composed a jazz musical, *Drop-out oder Gustav der Letzte* (1970), freely after Shakespeare's *Measure for Measure;* publ. a book of essays, *Worte zur Musik* (Munich, 1971). He eventually made his home in Munich.

BIBLIOGRAPHY: Erich Jantsch, *Friedrich Gulda* (Vienna, 1953); K. Geitel, *Fragen an Friedrich Gulda* (Berlin, 1973).

Gulli, Franco, distinguished Italian violinist; b. Trieste, Sept. 1, 1926. He studied violin with his father; then went to the Trieste Cons.; also studied in Siena and Paris; his teachers included Arrigo Serato and Joseph Szigeti. He married the pianist **Enrica Cavallo;** in 1947 they formed the noted Gulli-Cavallo Duo, which made several successful tours. In 1968 he was soloist with the Dallas Symph.; subsequently played with several American orchs. In 1972 he was appointed prof. at the Indiana Univ. School of Music. An artist of integrity, he secures fine performances of classical and modern music faithful to the style of the period.

Gumbert, Ferdinand, German composer; b. Berlin, April 22, 1818; d. there, April 6, 1896. He was first trained by his father for book selling, but he pursued his musical studies, developing a particular interest in opera. After a short study of singing, he appeared at the Cologne Opera (1840–42); in 1842 he settled in Berlin as a voice teacher and also began to compose. His songs, written in a facile, eclectic style, enjoyed a considerable vogue; the song *An des Rheines grünen Ufern* is used as an insert in Lortzing's opera *Undine.* He produced several operettas in Berlin: *Der kleine Ziegenhirt* (Jan. 21, 1854), *Bis der Rechte kommt* (Nov. 20, 1856), etc.; publ. *Musik, Gelesenes und Gesammeltes* (Berlin, 1860).

BIBLIOGRAPHY: W. Neumann, *Ferdinand Gumbert* (Kassel, 1856).

Gumpelzhaimer, Adam, German composer; b. Trostberg, c.1559; d. Augsburg, Nov. 3, 1625. He studied music with Father Jodocus Entzenmüller at the monastery of St. Ulric in Augsburg; from 1581 to his death he was cantor at St. Anna, Augsburg.

WORKS: *Erster (zweiter) Teil des Lustgärtleins teutsch und lateinischer Lieder mit drei Stimmen* (1591 and 1611); *Erster (zweiter) Teil des Wirtzgärtleins 4 stimmiger geistlicher Lieder* (1594 and 1619); *Psalmus LI octo vocum* (1604); *Sacri concentus octonis vocibus modulandi cum duplici basso in organorum usum* (1601 and 1614; 2 parts); *10 geistliche Lieder mit 4 Stimmen* (1617); *2 geistliche Lieder mit 4 Stimmen; 5 geistliche Lieder mit 4 Stimmen von der Himmelfahrt Jesu Christi; Newe teutsche geistliche Lieder mit 3 und 4 Stimmen* (1591 and 1594); *Das Inventar der Kantorei St. Anna in Augsburg* (compiled 1620–22; publ. in the ed. of R. Schaal; Kassel, 1965). A number of Gumpelzhaimer's motets have been reprinted in Bodenschatz's *Florilegium Portense,* Schadaeus's *Promptuarium,* and Vintzius's *Missae.* O. Mayr ed. a selection of his works in Denkmäler der Tonkunst in Bayern, 19 (10.ii).

BIBLIOGRAPHY: O. Mayr, *Adam Gumpeltzhai-*

mer (Munich, 1908).

Gumpert, Friedrich Adolf, German horn player; b. Lichtenau, April 27, 1841; d. Leipzig, Dec. 31, 1906. He studied with Hammann in Jena; from 1864, played first horn in the Gewandhaus Orch., Leipzig. He publ. valuable manuals for horn and other instruments: *Praktische Hornschule;* a *Solobuch* for horn (difficult passages from operas, symphs., etc.); *Hornquartette* (2 books); *Hornstudien;* and orch. studies for clarinet, oboe, bassoon, trumpet, and cello.

Gumprecht, Armand J., American organist and composer; b. Boston, Mass., June 26, 1861; d. Washington, D.C., March 13, 1943. He studied violin with C. Eichler, and organ with J. Singenberger and S.B. Whitney; from 1891 to 1918, was prof. of music and organist at Georgetown Univ. He wrote 4 masses; piano pieces; songs.

Gumprecht, Otto, German music critic; b. Erfurt, April 4, 1823; d. Meran, Feb. 6, 1900. He studied law in Halle and Berlin, but developed an interest in music, and began writing music criticism in 1849, continuing until 1889, when he suffered a stroke of paralysis.
WRITINGS: *Musikalische Charakterbilder* (1869); *Neue Charakterbilder* (1876); *Richard Wagner und der Ring des Nibelungen* (1873); *Unsere klassischen Meister* (2 vols., 1883–85) and *Neuere Meister* (2 vols., 1883); the last two are continuations of the *Charakterbilder;* he also edited 5 vols. of *Erlesene musikalische Meisterwerke.*

Gundry, Inglis, English composer; b. London, May 8, 1905. He studied law at Oxford Univ.; 1935 entered the Royal College of Music in London, where he took a music course with Vaughan Williams. In 1942 he was appointed Royal Marines Schoolmaster; then taught music history at London Univ. In 1960 he became music director of the Sacred Music Drama Society. He wrote the operas (all to his own librettos) *Naaman, The Leprosy of War* (1938); *The Return of Odysseus* (1941; revised 1957); *The Partisans* (London, May 28, 1946); *Avon* (London, April 11, 1949); *The Logan Rock* (Portchurno, Aug. 15, 1956); *The Prince of the Coxcombs* (London, Feb. 3, 1965); *The Three Wise Men* (London, Jan. 11, 1968); *The Prisoner Paul* (1969); a ballet, *Sleep* (1943); *Symphonic Fantasy* for Orch. (1948); the song cycles *The Black Mountains* (1956) and *The Year of the Firebird* (1957); he also arranged several old English music dramas.

Gungl, Joseph, famous Hungarian bandmaster and popular composer; b. Zsámbék, Dec. 1, 1810; d. Weimar, Jan. 31, 1889. He played the oboe in an artillery regiment in the Austrian army, and later became that band's conductor; he wrote a number of marches and dances, which became extremely popular; traveled with his band all over Germany. In 1843, he established his own band in Berlin; made

an American tour in 1849; then returned to Europe and lived mostly in Munich and Frankfurt.

Gunn, Glenn Dillard, American pianist and music critic; b. Topeka, Kans., Oct. 2, 1874; d. Washington, D.C., Nov. 22, 1963. He studied at the Leipzig Cons. with Carl Reinecke (piano); appeared as a pianist in German cities; returning to the U.S. in 1900, he taught at the Chicago Music College (1901–5). In 1915 he founded the American Symph. Orch. of Chicago, the object of which was the performance of American works and the engagement of American soloists. He was music critic for the *Chicago Tribune* (1910–14) and the *Chicago Herald and Examiner* (1922–36); in 1940, was appointed music critic of the *Washington Times-Herald.* He publ. *A Course of Lessons on the History and Esthetics of Music* (1912) and *Music, Its History and Enjoyment* (1930).

Gunn, John, Scottish cellist and writer on music; b. Edinburgh, c.1765; d. there, c.1824. He went to London in 1790, where he taught cello and flute; returned to Edinburgh in 1795.
WRITINGS: *40 Scotch Airs arranged as trios for flute, violin and violoncello; The Art of Playing the German Flute on New Principles; The Theory and Practice of Fingering the Violoncello* (London, 1793); *An Essay, Theoretical and Practical, on the Application of Harmony, Thorough-Bass, and Modulation to the Violoncello* (Edinburgh, 1801). He also wrote a valuable work, commissioned by the National Society of Scotland, *An Historical Inquiry respecting the Performance on the Harp in the Highlands of Scotland from the earliest Times until it was discontinued about the year 1734* (Edinburgh, 1807).

Gunsbourg, Raoul, Rumanian-French impresario; b. Bucharest, Dec. 25, 1859; d. Monte Carlo, May 31, 1955. After directing opera companies in Russia, he became the director of the Grand Theatre in Lille (1888–89); of the Nice Opera (1889–91); then of the Monte Carlo Opera (1893–1950); his first important production there was the stage version of *The Damnation of Faust* by Berlioz (Feb. 18, 1893). He produced at Monte Carlo several of his own operas (he wrote the piano scores, and the orchestration was done by L. Jehin); of these, *Le Vieil Aigle,* after Maxim Gorky's fable (Monte Carlo, Feb. 13, 1909), had a modicum of success.

Gura, Eugen, operatic baritone; b. Pressern, near Saatz, Bohemia, Nov. 8, 1842; d. Aufkirchen, Bavaria, Aug. 26, 1906. He studied in Vienna and in Munich; sang in Munich (1865–67), Breslau (1867–70), and Leipzig (1870–76), obtaining extraordinary success; then was in Hamburg (1876–83) and Munich (1883–96). He was particularly impressive in Wagnerian roles; his performance of Hans Sachs was greatly praised. He publ. *Erinnerungen aus meinem Leben* (Leipzig, 1905). His son, **Hermann Gura** (b. Breslau, April 5, 1870; d. Bad Wiessee, Bavaria, Sept. 13, 1944), was also a baritone; like his father, he specialized in Wagnerian roles; after a successful career as an opera singer in Germany, he settled in Berlin as voice teacher.

Guridi, Jesús, Spanish composer; b. Vitoria, Basque province of Álava, Sept. 25, 1886; d. Madrid, April 7, 1961. He studied in Madrid, at the Schola Cantorum in Paris, in Brussels (with Jongen), and in Cologne. He returned to Spain in 1909; became an organist at Bilbao, where he remained until 1939; then moved to Madrid; was appointed prof. of organ at the Madrid Cons. in 1944. During his 30 years in Bilbao, he promoted the cause of Basque folk music; publ. an album of 22 Basque songs. His zarzuelas make frequent use of Basque folk music; of these, *El caserío* (Madrid, 1926) attained enormous success in Spain; other stage works are *Amaya*, lyric drama in 3 acts (Bilbao, 1920), *La meiga* (Madrid, 1928), and *Mirentxu*, idyll in 2 acts; he further wrote a symph. poem, *An Adventure of Don Quixote; Sinfonia pirenáica; Basque Sketches* for Chorus and Orch.; an orch. suite, *10 Basque Melodies* (very popular in Spain); a number of choral works a cappella on Basque themes; 4 string quartets; pieces for piano; various songs.

BIBLIOGRAPHY: J.M. de Arozamena, *Jesús Guridi* (Madrid, 1967).

Gurlitt, Cornelius, German composer; b. Altona, Feb. 10, 1820; d. there, June 17, 1901. He was a member of an artistic family; his brother, Louis Gurlitt, was a well-known landscape painter. He studied piano with Johann Peter Reinecke in Altona, and with Weyse in Copenhagen, where he went in 1840. In 1845, he made a journey through Europe; he met Schumann, Lortzing, Franz, and other eminent composers. In 1864 he was appointed organist of the Altona Cathedral, retaining this post until 1898; also taught at the Hamburg Cons. (1879–87). He wrote an opera, *Die römische Mauer* (Altona, 1860); another opera, *Scheik Hassan*, was not performed. He further composed 3 violin sonatas, 3 cello sonatas, several cycles of songs, etc. He is chiefly remembered, however, by his numerous piano miniatures, in Schumann's style; a collection of these was publ. by W. Rehberg, under the title *Der neue Gurlitt* (2 vols.; Mainz, 1931).

BIBLIOGRAPHY: Paul T. Hoffman, *Neues Altona* (Jena, 1929; vol. II).

Gurlitt, Manfred, German conductor and composer; b. Berlin, Sept. 6, 1890; d. Tokyo, April 29, 1972. He was of an artistic family; his grandfather was the well-known landscape painter Louis Gurlitt, whose brother was the composer **Cornelius Gurlitt.** He studied in Berlin with Humperdinck (composition) and Karl Muck (conducting); rapidly progressed as a professional conductor; was a coach at the Berlin Opera (1908) and at the Bayreuth Festival (1911); was theater conductor in Essen and Augsburg; conductor and music director at the Bremen Opera (1914–27); then at the Berlin Opera and on the German radio. After 1933, he was deprived of his position by the Nazi regime; in 1939 he settled in Japan

as a teacher and conductor; organized the Gurlitt Opera Co. in Tokyo.

WORKS: Operas: *Die Heilige* (Bremen, Jan. 27, 1920); *Wozzeck* (Bremen, April 22, 1926; written almost at the same time as Alban Berg's *Wozzeck*); *Soldaten* (1929); *Nana* (1933); *Seguidilla Bolero* (1937); *Nordische Ballade;* and *Wir schreiten aus; 3 politische Reden* for Baritone, Men's Chorus, and Orch.; *Goya Symphony* (1950); *Shakespeare Symphony* (1954) for 5 Solo Voices and Orch.; songs with Orch.; concertos for Piano, for Violin, for Cello; Piano Quartet; songs.

Gurlitt, Wilibald, eminent German musicologist and editor; b. Dresden, March 1, 1889; d. Freiburg im Breisgau, Dec. 15, 1963. He was a grandnephew of the composer **Cornelius Gurlitt,** and a cousin of **Manfred Gurlitt.** He studied musicology at the Univ. of Heidelberg with Philipp Wolfrum; also at the Univ. of Leipzig with Hugo Riemann and Arnold Schering, where he received his Ph.D. in 1914 with the dissertation *Michael Praetorius (Creuzbergensis): Sein Leben und seine Werke* (publ. in Leipzig, 1915); subsequently was an assistant to Riemann. He served in World War I, and was taken prisoner in France. After the Armistice, he became a lecturer at the Univ. of Freiburg; directed its dept. of musicology from 1920; was made a full prof. in 1929, but was removed from his position by the Nazi regime in 1937; resumed his professorship in 1945; retired in 1958. Gurlitt's investigations of the organ music of Praetorius led him to construct (in collaboration with Oscar Walcker) a "Praetorius organ," which was to reproduce the tuning of the period. This gave impetus in Germany to performance of historic works on authentic or reconstructed instruments. Gurlitt's other interests included the problem of musical terminology, resulting in the publ. of his *Handwörterbuch der musikalischen Terminologie.* In 1952 he revived the moribund *Archiv für Musikwissenschaft.* He ed. the first two vols. of the 12th ed. of Riemann's *Musik-Lexikon* (Mainz, 1959 and 1961). He also publ. *Johann Sebastian Bach: Der Meister und sein Werk* (Berlin, 1936; 4th ed., 1959; in Eng., St. Louis, 1957). For a complete list of his writings and scholarly eds., see his autobiographical article in *Die Musik in Geschichte und Gegenwart;* also A. Schmitz, "Wilibald Gurlitt," in *Jahrbuch der Akademie der Wissenschaften und der Literatur* (Mainz, 1964).

Gurney, Ivor, English song composer; b. Gloucester, Aug. 28, 1890; d. Dartford, Kent, Dec. 26, 1937. He was a chorister at Gloucester Cathedral; studied at the Royal College of Music in London with Stanford and Vaughan Williams; served in World War I, was wounded and gassed, and never recovered his physical and mental health; the 2 vols. of his war poems illustrate the turmoil of his inner life. After the Armistice, Gurney began to compose songs; 27 were publ. before his death, and several more were included in a 2-vol. edition of his melodies publ. posthumously. Gurney's gift was not for larger forms; he was at his best in his songs; he also wrote

5 Western Watercolors, 5 preludes for piano, and some violin pieces. A memorial Gurney issue of *Music & Letters,* with articles by Vaughan Williams, Walter de la Mare, and others, was publ. in 1938.

BIBLIOGRAPHY: Charles W. Moore, *Maker and Lover of Beauty: Ivor Gurney, Poet and Songwriter* (London, 1976).

Gürsching, Albrecht, German oboist and composer; b. Nuremberg, Sept. 9, 1934. He studied composition in Stuttgart with Karl Marx and in Munich with Günter Bialas; was engaged as oboist in various ensembles. His works include a Concerto for Oboe, Viola and Strings (1961); *Rondo* for Violin and String Quartet (1963); 3 string quartets (1964, 1965, 1968); Quartet for Oboe and String Trio (1964); Symph. for Small Orch. (1964); Piano Concerto (1967); Violin Concerto (1968); *Fantasy* for Chamber Orch. (1969).

Guschlbauer, Theodor, Austrian conductor; b. Vienna, April 14, 1939. He was educated at the Vienna Academy of Music; then was conductor of the Vienna Baroque Ensemble (1961–69); subsequently served as chief conductor of the Salzburg Landestheater (1966–68); then went to Lyons as conductor of the Opera. In 1975 he was appointed chief conductor of the Landestheater in Linz; concurrently assumed the post of chief conductor of the Linz-Bruckner Symph. Orch. and director of the annual Bruckner Festival. In 1983 he became chief conductor of the Strasbourg Phil. and also of the Oper am Rhein in Düsseldorf.

Gusikoff, Michel, American violinist and composer; b. New York, May 15, 1893; d. there, July 10, 1978. He was of a musical family; his father was a violin maker and his great-grandfather, **Michal Jozef Guzikov,** was a famous performer on the xylophone. He studied violin with Franz Kneisel and composition with Percy Goetschius; served as concertmaster with the Russian Symph. Orch. in N.Y., the N.Y. Symph. Orch., the Philadelphia Orch., and the NBC Symph. Orch. He subsequently became concertmaster and associate conductor of the Pittsburgh Symph. He made violin arrangements of songs by Gershwin; also wrote an *American Concerto* for Violin and Orch.

Gutchë, Gene (real name, **Romeo E. Gutsche**), American composer; b. Berlin, July 3, 1907. He studied in Germany, then went to the U.S., where he undertook additional academic work at the Univ. of Minnesota with Donald Ferguson and at the Univ. of Iowa with Philip Greeley Clapp (Ph.D., 1953); held two Guggenheim fellowships (1961, 1964). His music is marked by a fairly advanced idiom and a neo-Romantic treatment of programmatic subject matter. In some of his orch. works he applies fractional tones by dividing the strings into two groups tuned at slightly differing pitches.

WORKS: Symph. No. 1 (Minneapolis, April 11, 1950); Symph. No. 2 (1950–54); Symph. No. 3 (1952); *Rondo Capriccioso* (1953; N.Y., Feb. 19, 1960; with the application of fractional tones); Piano Concerto (Minneapolis, June 19, 1956); Cello Concerto (1957); Symph. No. 4 (1960; Albuquerque, March 8, 1962); Symph. No. 5 for Strings (Chautauqua, July 29, 1962); *Bongo Divertimento* for Solo Percussionist and Orch. (1962); *Timpani Concertante* (Oakland, Calif., Feb. 14, 1962); Violin Concerto (1962); *Genghis Khan,* symph. poem (Minneapolis, Dec. 6, 1963); *Rites in Tenochtitlán* for Small Orch. (St. Paul, Jan. 26, 1965); *Gemini* for Orch., with microtones (Minneapolis, July 26, 1966); *Classic Concerto* for Orch. (St. Paul, Nov. 11, 1967); Symph. No. 6 (1968); *Epimetheus USA* for Orch. (Detroit, Nov. 13, 1969); *Icarus,* suite for Orch. (1975); *Bi-Centurion* for Orch. (1975; Rochester, N.Y., Jan. 8, 1976); *Perseus and Andromeda XX* for Orch. (1976; Cincinnati, Feb. 25, 1977); *Akhenaten* for Chorus and Orch. (St. Louis, Sept. 23, 1983). 4 string quartets; 3 piano sonatas; choruses.

BIBLIOGRAPHY: *Composers of the Americas,* vol. 15 (Washington, 1969).

Gutheil-Schoder, Marie, German mezzo-soprano; b. Weimar, Feb. 10, 1874; d. Ilmenau, Oct. 4, 1935. She studied in Weimar, made her debut there in 1891; sang with the court opera until 1900, when she went to the Vienna Opera, becoming an outstanding singer-actress in such roles as Carmen, Elektra, Salome; in 1926 she was appointed stage director of the opera. She married the composer and conductor **Gustav Gutheil.**

BIBLIOGRAPHY: L. Andro, *Marie Gutheil-Schoder* (1923).

Guthrie, Woody (full name, **Woodrow Wilson Guthrie**), American folk singer; b. Okemah, Okla., July 14, 1912; d. New York, Oct. 3, 1967. His father was a prizefighter and a professional guitar player. The family suffered adversity during the Depression; Woody Guthrie took to the road; performed in saloons and at labor meetings, improvising songs of social significance. Later he joined Pete Seeger and others in a group known as Almanac Singers; publ. the books *Bound for Glory* and *American Folksong.* Although not a trained singer, Guthrie acquired fame as an impassionate balladeer of disadvantaged Americans. Ignoring for the moment his freely professed radical convictions, the U.S. government bestowed upon him in 1966 an award of merit as "a poet of the American landscape." His career was cut short in 1957 when he contracted Huntington's chorea, which incapacitated him. His son **Arlo Guthrie** (b. New York, July 10, 1947) carried on Woody Guthrie's tradition as a folk singer; became famous for his ballad *Alice's Restaurant,* which is also the title of a motion picture in which he starred as himself, getting busted.

Gutiérrez, Gonzalo, Spanish organist and composer; b. about 1540; d. Granada, 1605. He was appointed organist at the Cathedral of Granada in 1569, and held this post until his death.

BIBLIOGRAPHY: José Lopez Calo, *La música en la catedral de Granada en el siglo XVI* (Granada,

1963; vol. I, pp. 205–10; vol. II includes several of his works).

Gutiérrez, Horacio, brilliant Cuban pianist; b. Havana, Aug. 28, 1948. He studied in Havana; made his concert debut there as a young child; continued his studies in Los Angeles and at the Juilliard School in N.Y. He gained fame in 1970, after winning 2nd prize in the world's most prestigious musical arena, the International Tchaikovsky Competition in Moscow. Since then, he has appeared with major American and European orchs.

Gutiérrez Heras, Joaquín, Mexican composer; b. Tehuacán, Sept. 28, 1927. He attended classes in architecture at the National Univ. of Mexico and then studied composition with Blas Galindo and Rodolfo Halffter at the National Cons. of Mexico (1950–52). A scholarship from the French Inst. of Mexico enabled him to go to Paris, where he took courses in composition with Messiaen, Rivier and Georges Dandelot at the Paris Cons. (1952–53); on a Rockefeller Foundation scholarship, he studied composition with Bergsma and Persichetti at the Juilliard School of Music in N.Y. (1960–61). Upon his return to Mexico, he gave radio lectures and taught music theory. As a composer, he professes a "voluntary lack of complexity."
WORKS: Divertimento for Piano and Orch. (1949); satirical ballet, *El deportista* (1957); *Variations on a French Song* for Piano or Harpsichord (1958–60); *Chamber Cantata on Poems by Emilio Prados* for Soprano, 2 Flutes, Harp, and 4 Strings (1961); a symph. scene, *Los Cazadores* (*The Hunters,* 1962); Duo for Alto Flute and Cello (1964); *Sonata simple* for Flute and Piano (1965); Trio for Oboe, Clarinet, and Bassoon (1965); *2 Pieces for 3 Brasses* (1967); *Night and Day Music* for Wind Symph. Orch. (1973); *De profundis* for a cappella Chorus (1977); several scores for theater and film.

Gutman, Robert W., American writer on music; b. New York, Sept. 11, 1925. He studied at N.Y. Univ. (B.A., 1945; M.A., 1948); his principal teacher in musicology was Curt Sachs. In 1957 he was appointed to the faculty of the State Univ. of N.Y. He contributed essays to music magazines; publ. a searching and original biographical analysis of Wagner, *Richard Wagner: The Man, His Mind and His Music* (N.Y., 1968; German trans., Munich, 1970; French trans., 1971).

Gutmann, Adolph, German pianist; b. Heidelberg, Jan. 12, 1819; d. Spezia, Oct. 27, 1882. He lived mostly in Paris, where he studied with Chopin, and became a close friend of his. He publ. an album of *Etudes caractéristiques* which were quite popular in the 19th century, and much salon music for piano. He was also a successful performer whose virtuoso technique made him popular with audiences.

Gutsche, Romeo E. See **Gutché, Gene.**

Guy-Ropartz. See **Ropartz, Guy.**

Guyonnet, Jacques, Swiss composer; b. Geneva, March 20, 1933. He studied at the Geneva Cons. (1950–58); had courses in new music with Boulez at the summer sessions held in Darmstadt (1958–61); in 1959 he founded the Studio de Musique Contemporaine in Geneva; in 1965 was elected president of the Swiss section of the International Society for Contemporary Music.
WORKS: *Monades I* for Chamber Ensemble (1958); *Monades II-III* for Orch. (1960, 1961); *Polyphonie I* for Flute and Piano (1961); *Polyphonie II* for 2 Pianos (1959); *Polyphonie III* for Flute, Viola, and 2 Pianos (1964); *Chronicles* for Piano (1964–71); *En 3 Eclats!* for Piano and Chamber Orch. (1964); *Stèle in memoriam J.F. Kennedy* for Chamber Orch. and Tape (1964); *The Approach to the Hidden Man I* for Solo Cello and 6 Instruments (1966), and *II* for Mezzo-soprano, Chamber Orch., and Electronic Sound (1967); *7 Portes du Temps* for Orch. (1966–69); *Entremonde,* ballet for Flute, Piano, 4 Percussionists, and Tape (1967); *Let There Be Events!* for 17 Instrumental Soloists (1968-71); *Good Grief Jerry!* for Soprano and Chamber Orch. (1970–71); *Modèles I–II* for any number of Instrumental Soloists (1970); *A Single R* for Viola and Chamber Orch. (1971); *Le Chant remémoré* for 4 Vocal Soloists and Orch. (1972); *Die Wandlung* for Orch. (1973); *Les Enfants du Désert* for String Orch. (1974); *Mémorial* for 4 Trumpets and 4 Trombones (1974).

Guyot, Jean, Flemish musician, also known under the names of **Jean de Chatelet** and **Johannes Castileti;** b. Chatelet (Hainaut) in 1512; d. Liège, March 11, 1588. He studied at the Univ. of Louvain, and received the degree of licencié-ès-arts on March 22, 1537; in 1546 he was chaplain at St. Paul's in Liège; publ. his first motets in Antwerp that year; about 1557 assumed the duties of maître de chapelle at the Cathedral of St. Lambert in Liège; on Nov. 1, 1563, was appointed music master at the Imperial Court in Vienna; he returned to Liège in Aug., 1564, and remained maître de chapelle at the Cathedral of St. Lambert to his death.
BIBLIOGRAPHY: C. Lyon, *Jean Guyot* (Charleroi, 1876); B. Even, *Jean Guyot de Châtelet et son œuvre* (Diss., Univ. of Liège, 1974).

Guzikov, Michal Jozef, famous performer on the xylophone; b. Szklow, Poland, Sept. 14, 1806; d. Aachen, Oct. 21, 1837. Of a Jewish musical family, he showed precocious talent; with four relatives he traveled all over Europe; his virtuosity on the xylophone was extraordinary, and elicited praise from the public as well as from celebrated musicians, among them Mendelssohn. Guzikov's programs consisted of arrangements of well-known works and also his own pieces; his most successful number was a transcription of Paganini's *La Campanella.*
BIBLIOGRAPHY: S. Schlesinger, *Josef Guzikov* (Vienna, 1936).

Gyrowetz, Adalbert, notable Austrian composer;

b. Budweis, Bohemia, Feb. 19, 1763; d. Vienna, March 19, 1850. He studied piano, violin, and composition with his father, a local choirmaster; then went to Prague, where he studied law; at the same time, began to compose band pieces and waltzes; he was befriended by Count Franz von Fünfkirchen, who was a music lover, and whose secretary he became. For the private orch. of Count von Fünfkirchen, Gyrowetz wrote 6 symphs. in Haydn's style; later, when he was in Vienna, he showed these works to Mozart, who encouraged him and arranged for a performance of one of Gyrowetz's symphs. From Vienna, he traveled through Italy; in Naples, he studied with Sala and Paisiello. In 1789, he went to Milan, Genoa, and finally to Paris, where several of his works were accepted by publishers. He then moved to London, where one of his pieces was performed at a Haydn concert (March 23, 1792). He was commissioned to write an opera, *Semiramide,* for the Pantheon Theatre, but before the announced performance the opera building burned down, and with it perished the MS of *Semiramide.* After 3 years in London, he returned to the Continent, eventually settling in Vienna (1793), where he became Kapellmeister at the Vienna Opera (1804–31). In Vienna, he enjoyed a great reputation as composer, and his name was often coupled with Beethoven's in public prints.

WORKS: He composed a number of operas, which were performed, one after another, at the Vienna Opera: *Selico* (Oct. 15, 1804); *Agnes Sorel* (Dec. 4, 1806); *Die Junggesellen-Wirtschaft* (June 18, 1807); *Die Pagen des Hertzogs von Vendome* (Aug. 5, 1808); *Der betrogene Betrüger* (Feb. 17, 1810); *Der Augenartz* (his most successful opera; Oct. 1, 1811); *Das Winterquartier in Amerika* (Oct. 30, 1812); *Robert* (July 15, 1813); *Helene* (Feb. 16, 1816); *Aladin* (Feb. 7, 1819); *Der blinde Harfner* (Dec. 19, 1827); *Der Geburtstag* (Feb. 11, 1828); *Felix und Adele* (Aug. 10, 1831); also several operettas and singspiels. In 1834, he produced in Dresden an opera, *Hans Sachs,* using essentially the same literary material as Wagner's *Meistersinger.* He further wrote a number of ballets; much church music; some 60 symphs.; about 60 string quartets; 30 trios; about 40 violin sonatas, as well as piano pieces and songs. The historical reasons for the rapid decline of Gyrowetz's repute as a composer after his death are not easy to explain; attempted revivals of his music proved futile.

BIBLIOGRAPHY: Gyrowetz publ. his autobiography (Vienna, 1848); it was brought out in an annotated ed. by Alfred Einstein (Leipzig, 1915); numerous references to Gyrowetz are found in the Haydn literature; see also K. Mey, "A. Gyrowetz und seine neu aufgefundene Hans Sachs-Oper," *Die Musik* (May 1903); E. Doernberg, "Adalbert Gyrowetz," *Music & Letters,* XLIV (1963).

Gysi, Fritz, Swiss musicologist; b. Zofingen, Feb. 18, 1888; d. Zürich, March 5, 1967. He studied at the Basel Cons., at Zürich Univ., and at Berlin Univ.; in 1921 became lecturer in music at the Univ. of Zürich. He publ. *Mozart in seinen Briefen* (1921); *Max Bruch* (1922); *Claude Debussy* (1926); *Richard Wagner und die Schweiz* (1929); *Richard Strauss* (1934); *Hans Georg Nägeli* (1936).

H

Haan, Willem de, Dutch composer; b. Rotterdam, Sept. 24, 1849; d. Berlin, Sept. 26, 1930. He studied at the Leipzig Cons.; in 1876 became a conductor in Darmstadt; in 1923 moved to Berlin. He wrote an opera, *Die Kaiserstochter* (Darmstadt, Feb. 1, 1885), and much choral music.

Haapanen, Toivo, Finnish musicologist and conductor; b. Karvia, May 15, 1889; d. Asikkala, July 22, 1950. He studied violin and music theory in Helsinki, Berlin, and Paris; he studied musicology with I. Krohn at the Univ. of Helsinki (M.A., 1918; Ph.D., 1925, with the dissertation *Die Neumenfragmente der Universitätsbibliothek Helsingfors*). In 1925 he became a lecturer at the Univ. of Helsinki; was a prof. there from 1946. From 1929–46 he was head of the music division of the Finnish Broadcasting Co.; was chief conductor of its Radio Symph. Orch. from 1929 until his death. He publ. a valuable *Verzeichnis der mittelalterlichen Handschriftenfragmente in der Universitätsbibliothek zu Helsingfors* (3 vols., Helsinki, 1922; 1925; 1932). He further publ. *Suomen säveltaide* (*The Art of Music in Finland;* Helsinki, 1940) and edited a dictionary of music (Helsinki, 1948).

Haarklou, Johannes, Norwegian composer; b. Söndfjord, near Bergen, May 13, 1847; d. Oslo, Nov. 26, 1925. He studied at the Leipzig Cons.; then in Berlin with Haupt, Kiel, and Bungert; for 40 years (1880–1920) he was organist at the old Akers Church in Oslo; also conducted symph. concerts there for 3 seasons. His 5 operas have not made their way beyond Norway, but among the works more generally known is an oratorio, *Skapelsen* (*The Creation;* 1891; Oslo, 1924). He further wrote 4 symphs. and *Olafs-Legende* for Orch.; a Violin Sonata; piano pieces; choruses; organ works.

BIBLIOGRAPHY: F. Benestad, *Johannes Haarklou, Mannen og verket* (Oslo, 1961).

Haas, Joseph, eminent German composer and pedagogue; b. Maihingen, March 19, 1879; d. Munich, March 30, 1960. He studied with Max Reger in Munich and with Karl Straube in Leipzig (organ). In 1911 he was appointed composition teacher at the Stuttgart Cons.; in 1921 became a prof. in the Catholic church music dept. at the Akademie der Tonkunst in Munich. From 1945 to 1950 he was president of the Hochschule für Musik in Munich. Through the long years of his pedagogical activities, Haas established himself as one of the most reputable teachers in Germany. As a composer, Haas is equally estimable, but his music has failed to gain popularity outside his circle. He wrote more than 100 opus numbers. At the time of his retirement in 1950, a Joseph Haas Society was organized in Munich, with the aim of issuing bulletins regarding his works.

WORKS: Operas: *Tobias Wunderlich* (Kassel, Nov. 24, 1937) and *Die Hochzeit des Jobs* (Dresden, July 2, 1944); oratorios: *Die heilige Elisabeth* (1931); *Christnacht* (1932); *Das Lebensbuch Gottes* (1934); *Das Lied von der Mutter* (1939); *Das Jahr in Lied* (1952); *Die Seligen* (Kassel, April 12, 1957); *Deutsche Kindermesse* (1958); *Marienkantate* (1959); *Variations on a Rococo Theme* for Orch.; *Ouvertüre zu einem frohen Spiel* (1943); 2 string quartets (1908, 1919); Trio for 2 Violins and Piano (1912); many song cycles. He publ. a biography of Max Reger (Bonn, 1949); contributed articles to various publications.

BIBLIOGRAPHY: *Festgabe J. Haas* (a collection of articles by his students and colleagues on his 60th birthday; Mainz, 1939); a catalogue of works compiled by K.G. Fellerer (issued by the Haas Society, 1950; 2nd ed., 1953); K. Laux, *J. Haas* (Mainz, 1931; 2nd ed., 1954); special issue of the *Zeitschrift für Musik* on his 75th birthday, March 1954). A collection of his speeches and articles was publ. posthumously, as *Reden und Aufsätze* (Mainz, 1964).

Haas, Karl, German conductor and musicologist; b. Karlsruhe, Dec. 27, 1900; d. London, July 7, 1970. He studied at the univs. of Munich and Heidelberg; then worked for the Karlsruhe and Stuttgart radios; was active as a collector of valuable old instruments; made microfilms of old music. In 1939 he emigrated to England; in 1943 he organized the London Baroque Ensemble; led it until 1966 in performances of little-known Baroque music. He also edited works by Haydn, Boccherini, and Cherubini.

Haas, Monique, French pianist; b. Paris, Oct. 20, 1906. She studied at the Paris Cons. with Lazare Lévy; became greatly interested in modern music, and gave numerous concerts all over Europe in programs of 20th-century composers; also appeared with orchs. in modern concertos. She is married to the composer **Marcel Mihalovici.**

Haas, Pavel, Czech composer; b. Brno, June 21, 1899; put to death in the concentration camp at Auschwitz (Oswiecim), Poland, Oct. 17, 1944. He studied piano and composition in Brno; was a soldier in the Austrian army in World War I; after the Armistice, continued his study with Petřzelka at the Brno Cons. (1919–21) and at the master class there with Janáček (1921–22). He tried to leave Czechoslovakia after its occupation by the Nazi hordes, but the outbreak of World War II made this impossible; in 1941 he was placed in a concentration camp in Terezín, where he continued to compose until, in Oct. 1944, he was sent to Auschwitz and put to death there.

WORKS: Opera, *Šarlatán (The Charlatan),* to his own libretto (1936; Brno, April 2, 1938); *Zesmutnělé Scherzo (Mournful Scherzo)* for Orch. (1921); *Předehra pro rozhlas (Overture for Radio)* for Orch., Male Chorus, and Narrator (1930); Symph. (1941; unfinished); *Studie* for String Orch. (1943); Variations for Piano and Orch. (1944); cantata, *Introduction and Psalm XXIX* (1931); 3 string quartets (1920, 1925, 1938); *Fata morgana,* piano quintet, with Tenor Solo (1923); Wind Quintet (1929); Suite for Oboe and Piano (1939); Suite for Piano (1935); songs. His extant MSS are preserved in the Moravian Museum in Brno.

Haas, Robert (Maria), distinguished Austrian musicologist; b. Prague, Aug. 15, 1886, d. Vienna, Oct. 4, 1960. He received his primary education in Prague; then studied music history at the univs. of Prague, Berlin, and Vienna; obtained his Ph.D. in 1908 from the Univ. of Prague with his dissertation *Das Wiener Singspiel.* He then was an assistant to Guido Adler at the Inst. for Music History in Vienna (1908–09). During World War I he was in the Austrian army; then joined the staff of the Nationalbibliothek in Vienna, becoming chief of the music division in 1920. He completed his Habilitation at the Univ. of Vienna in 1923 with his *Eberlins Schuldramen und Oratorien;* then became a lecturer there; also devoted much of his time to the music of the Baroque and Classical eras. After the founding of the International Bruckner Society, he became editor of the critical edition of Bruckner's works; he also edited works for Denkmäler der Tonkunst in Österreich. He retired in 1945.

WRITINGS: *Gluck und Durazzo im Burgtheater* (Vienna, 1925); *Die estensischen Musikalien: Thematisches Verzeichnis mit Einleitung* (Regensburg, 1925); *Die Wiener Oper* (Vienna, 1926); *Wiener Musiker vor und um Beethoven* (Vienna, 1927); *Die Musik des Barocks* (Potsdam, 1928); *Aufführungspraxis der Musik* (Potsdam, 1931); *W.A. Mozart* (Potsdam, 1933; 2nd ed., 1950); *Anton Bruckner* (Potsdam, 1934); *Bach und Mozart in Wien* (Vienna, 1951); *Ein unbekanntes Mozart-Bildnis* (Vienna, 1955).

BIBLIOGRAPHY: G. Reichert, "Robert Haas," *Österreichische Musikzeitschrift,* XIII (1958); H. Federhofer, "In memoriam Robert Haas," *Acta Musicologica,* XXXII (1960).

Haas, Werner, talented German pianist; b. Stuttgart, March 3, 1931; d. Nancy, Oct. 13, 1976. He studied at the Hochschule für Musik in Stuttgart and at the Saarbrücken Cons. Following the example of Walter Gieseking, whose master courses he had attended, Haas developed a particular interest in French music, and became a fine interpreter of works of Debussy and Ravel.

Haase, Hans, German musicologist; b. Neumünster (Schleswig-Holstein), May 12, 1929. He studied with Friedrich Blume and Albrecht at the Univ. of Kiel (1950–55); from 1954–58 was editorial contributor to *Die Musik in Geschichte und Gegenwart;* then did valuable work in various archives and libraries; also wrote music criticism for newspapers. He publ. the monographs *Jobst vom Brandt* (Kassel, 1967) and *Heinrich Schütz* (Wolfenbüttel, 1972), and numerous valuable articles on German composers of the Reformation. He also became interested in applied psychology; lectured on this subject in Zürich and Vienna; publ. *Die harmonikalen Wurzeln der Musik* (Vienna, 1969) and *Aufsätze zur harmonikalen Naturphilosophie* (Graz, 1974).

Hába, Alois, notable Czech composer of microtonal music; b. Vizovice, Moravia, June 21, 1893; d. Prague, Nov. 18, 1973. He studied with Novák at the Prague Cons. (1914–15); then privately with Schreker in Berlin (1918–22); returned to Prague in 1923; taught there from 1924 to 1951. He became interested in the folk music of the Orient, which led him to consider writing in smaller intervals than the semitone. His first work in the quarter-tone system was the 2nd String Quartet (op. 7, 1920); in his 5th String Quartet (op. 15, 1923) he first applied the sixth-tones; in his 16th String Quartet (op. 98, 1967) he introduced the fifth-tones. He notated these fractional intervals by signs in modified or inverted sharps and flats. The piano manufacturing firm A. Förster constructed for him a quarter-tone piano (1925) and a sixth-tone harmonium (1927); other firms manufactured at his request a quarter-tone clarinet (1924) and trumpet (1931). From 1923–53 Hába led a class of composition in fractional tones at the State Cons. in Prague, attracting a large number of students, among them his brother, **Karel,** the conductors Ančerl and Susskind, and the composers Dobiáš, Ježek, Kowalski, Kubín, Lucký, Ponc, Karel Reiner (who, along with E. Schulhoff, specialized in quarter-tone piano playing and premiered 10 of Hába's works), Seidel, Srnka, Constantin Iliev of Bulgaria, Slavko Osterc of Yugoslavia, and Necil Kâzim Akses of Turkey. Hába publ. an important manual of modern harmony, *Neue Harmonielehre des diatonischen, chromatischen, Viertel-, Drittel-, Sechstel-, und Zwölfteltonsystems* (*New Principles of Harmony of the Diatonic, Chromatic, Fourth-, Third-, Sixth-, and Twelfth-Tone Systems;* Leipzig, 1927), detailing new usages introduced by him in his classes; he further publ. *Harmonické základy čtvrttónové soustavy* (*Harmonic Foundation of the Quarter-Tone System;* Prague, 1922) and *Von der Psychologie der musikalischen Gestaltung, Gesetzmässigkeit der Tonbewegung und Grundlagen eines neuen Musikstils* (*On the Psychology of Musical Composition; Rules of Tonal Structure and Foundation of New Musical Style;* Vienna, 1925); also *Mein Weg zur Viertel- und Sechstetonmusik* (Düsseldorf, 1971). As a composer, he cultivated a "non-thematic" method of writing, without repetition of patterns and devoid of development.

WORKS: OPERAS: *Matka* (*Mother;* 1927–29), in quarter-tones, to his own text; it was first perf. in Munich in a German version as *Die Mutter* on May 17, 1931, and subsequently produced in Czech (Prague, May 27, 1947); *Nová Země* (*The New Land;* 1934–36), written in the traditional tempered scale; never perf., except for the overture, played in Prague on April 8, 1936; *Přijd království Tvé* (*Thy Kingdom Come*), in fractional tones, to Hába's own text (1937–40; unperf.); cantata, *Za mír* (*For Peace;* Prague, Nov. 1, 1950). FOR ORCH.: Overture (Berlin, Dec. 9, 1920); *Symphonic Fantasy* for Piano and Orch. (1921); *Cesta života* (*The Path of Life;* Winterthur, Switzerland, March 15, 1934); *Valašská suita* (Prague, Oct. 29, 1953); Violin Concerto (1955; Prague, Feb. 17, 1963); Viola Concerto (1955–57). CHAMBER MUSIC: The following are in the tempered scale: 4 nonets for Wind and String Instruments (1931, based on a 12-tone row; 1932, based on a 7-tone row; 1953; 1963); string quartets Nos. 1, 7, 8, 9, 13, and 15 (1919; 1951; 1951; 1952; Astronautic, 1961; 1964); Violin Sonata (1915); Fantasy for Flute or Violin, and Piano, op. 34, (1928; op. 34a, version for Bass Clarinet and Piano, 1967); Sonata for Guitar Solo (1943); Sonata for Chromatic Harp, op. 59 (1944); Sonata for Diatonic Harp, op. 60 (1944); *Intermezzo and Preludium* for Diatonic Harp (1945); Suite for Solo Bassoon (1950; op. 69a, version for Bass Clarinet, 1968); Suite, quartet for Bassoons (1951); *Fantasy* and *Fantasy and Fugue* for Organ (both 1951); Solo Clarinet Sonata (1952); Suite for Solo Violin, op. 81a (1955); Suite for Solo Cello, op. 81b (1955); Suite for Solo Cymbalom (1960); Suite for Solo Bass Clarinet, op. 96 (1964); Suite for Solo Saxophone (1968); Suite for Bass Clarinet and Piano (1969); *Observations from a Journal* for Narrator and String Quartet (1970); Suite for Violin and Piano, op. 103 (1972; his last work); *Fugue Suite* for Piano (1918); *Variations on a Canon by Schumann* for Piano (1918); *2 morceaux* for Piano (1917–18; arranged for String Orch. by R. Kubín, 1930); Piano Sonata, op. 3 (1918); *6 Pieces* for Piano (1920); *4 Modern Dances* for Piano (1927); *Toccata quasi una Fantasia* for Piano (1931); *6 Moods* for Piano (1971). Works in quarter-tones: string quartets Nos. 2, 3, 4, 6, 12, and 14 (1920, 1922, 1922, 1950, 1960, 1963); Fantasy for Solo Violin (1921); *Music* for Solo Violin (1922); Fantasy for Solo Cello (1924); Fantasy for Violin and Piano, op. 21 (1925); Suite No. 1 for Clarinet and Piano (1925); Fantasy for Viola and Piano (1926); Fantasy for Cello and Piano (1927); 2 suites for Solo Guitar (1943, 1947); Suite No. 2 for Solo Clarinet (1943–44); Suite for Trumpet and Trombone (1944); Suite for 4 Trombones (1950); Suite for Solo Violin, op. 93 (1961–62); 6 suites for Piano (1922, revised 1932; 1922, revised 1932; 1923; 1924; 1925; 1959); 11 fantasies for Piano (Nos. 1–10, 1923–26; No. 11, 1959); Piano Sonata, op. 62 (1947). Works in fifth-tones: String Quartet No. 16 (1967). Works in sixth-tones: string quartets Nos. 5, 10, and 11 (1923, 1952, 1958); Duo for 2 Violins (1937); Suite for Solo Violin, op. 85a (1955); Suite for Solo Cello, op. 85b (1955); *6 Pieces* for Harmonium (1928). He also wrote songs and choral pieces, many of them in the quarter-tone system.

BIBLIOGRAPHY: Jiří Vysloužil, *Alois Hába: Život a dílo* (Prague, 1974).

Hába, Karel, Czech composer, brother of **Alois Hába;** b. Vizovice, Moravia, May 21, 1898; d. Prague, Nov. 21, 1972. He studied violin with Karel Hoffmann and Jan Mařák and music theory with V. Novák, J. Křička, and J.B. Foerster at the Prague Cons.; also attended his brother's class in quarter-tone music (1925–27). He wrote only 3 pieces in quarter-tones, but he faithfully followed the athematic method of composing that was the cornerstone of Alois Hába's esthetics. Karel Hába was employed as a violinist in the orch. of Prague Radio (1929–36); was later a music critic and lecturer in music education at Charles Univ. (1951–63). He wrote *Violin Manual in the Quarter-tone System* (MS, 1927) and *Modern Violin Technique,* in 2 vols. (Prague, 1928).

WORKS: 4 operas: *Jánošík* (1929–32; Prague, Feb. 23, 1934; first operatic treatment of this famous historical Czech figure); *Stará historia (The Old Story;* 1934–37; unperf.); *Smoliček,* children's radio opera (Prague, Sept. 28, 1950); *Kalibův zločin (Kaliba's Crime;* 1957–61; Košice, May 16, 1968); cantata, *To Those Who Build Up Ostrava* (1950–51); Overture (1922); Violin Concerto (Prague, March 6, 1927); *Scherzo* for Orch. (1928); Cello Concerto (Prague, Sept. 1, 1935); 2 symphs. (1947–48, 1953–54); *Brigand's Suite* for Orch. (1955); Suite for Orch. (1963); 4 string quartets (1922, 1924, 1943, 1969); Trio for Violin, Cello, and Quarter-tone Piano (1926); *3 Pieces* for Violin and Piano in quarter-tones (1927); Flute Sonatina (1927); Septet for Violin, Clarinet, Viola, Horn, Cello, Bassoon, and Piano (1928–29); Duo for Violin and Cello (1935); Piano Trio (1940); Wind Quintet (1944); *3 Inventions* for Harp (1945); Nonet (1950); Trio for 2 Violins and Viola (1952); *15 Concert Etudes* for Violin (1956); Sonatina for 3 Violins (1960); Sonatina for 3 Clarinets (1960); *3 Instructive Duos* for 2 Violins (1968); 2 Suites for Piano (1920, 1929); Suite for Quarter-tone Piano (1925); Piano Sonata (1942); choral pieces; songs.

Habeneck, François-Antoine, eminent French conductor; b. Mézières, Jan. 22, 1781; d. Paris, Feb. 8, 1849. His father, a native of Mannheim and a member of a regimental band, taught him the violin. In 1800 Habeneck entered the Paris Cons., studying violin with Baillot. In 1804 he became a violinist in the orch. of the Opéra-Comique; shortly thereafter he joined the orch. of the Paris Opéra, becoming principal violin in 1817. From 1806–15 he conducted the student orch. at the Paris Cons., and also taught violin there (1808–16; 1825–48). From 1824–31 he was *premier chef* (with Valentino) of the Paris Opéra, holding that post alone from 1831–46; during his tenure there he conducted the premieres of *Guillaume Tell, La Juive, Les Huguenots,* and *Benvenuto Cellini.* In 1828 he founded the Société des Concerts du Conservatoire de Paris, which initially consisted of an orch. of 86 musicians and a chorus of 79 singers (the average complement of orch. members was 60). At his first concert on March 9, 1828, he conducted Beethoven's *Eroica* Symph.; he subsequently championed Beethoven's symphs. in his concerts, giving the first Paris perf. of the 9th Symph. on March 27, 1831. Under his guidance the orch. became the finest in its day, gaining the praise of such musicians as Mendelssohn and Wagner. He led it for 20 years, conducting his last concert on April 16, 1848. A pioneering figure among conductors, Habeneck retained many of the characteris-

tics of the earlier violin-leader type of conductor (for instance, he used the violin part, with other instruments cued in, instead of a full score; directed with a violin bow; and, at the beginning of his career, played along with his musicians); nevertheless, he assumed a foremost place among the conductors of his era. He was also a composer, but his works are not significant. With Isouard and Benincori he wrote an opera, *Aladin ou La Lampe merveilleuse* (Paris Opéra, Feb. 6, 1822); he composed 2 violin concertos and other violin music; also publ. a *Méthode théorique et pratique de violon* (Paris, 1835).

BIBLIOGRAPHY: H. Schonberg, *The Great Conductors* (N.Y., 1967; pp. 99–106).

Haberbier, Ernst, German pianist; b. Königsberg, Oct. 5, 1813; d. Bergen, Norway, March 12, 1869. He studied with his father, an organist; left home in 1832; went to Russia and became a court pianist in St. Petersburg in 1847; gave concerts in London in 1850; in 1852 appeared in Paris, where he scored a sensational success; in 1866 he settled in Bergen. He perfected what he considered a novel system of piano technique, dividing difficult passages between the 2 hands (however, this had been done by Scarlatti and Bach long before). He wrote a number of effective piano pieces, of which *Etudes-Poésies* (op. 53) are the best known.

Haberl, Franz Xaver, eminent German theorist, music editor, and historiographer; b. Oberellenbach, Lower Bavaria, April 12, 1840; d. Regensburg, Sept. 5, 1910. He studied in the Boys' Seminary at Passau, and took Holy Orders in 1862; in 1862–67 was Cathedral Kapellmeister and music director at the Seminary; in 1867–70 was organist at S. Maria dell' Anima in Rome; in 1871–82 was Cathedral Kapellmeister at Regensburg, where he founded, in 1875, a world-renowned school for church music. He was an authority on Catholic church music, past and present. In 1872 he assumed the editorship of the collection *Musica divina,* and edited the periodical *Musica Sacra* in 1888. In 1876 he began to publ. the *Cäcilienkalender,* the scope of which was greatly widened until, after 1885, it was issued under the more appropriate name of *Kirchenmusikalisches Jahrbuch;* as such it has become one of the most important publications for historical studies concerning the church music of the 15th, 16th, and 17th centuries; Haberl continued as editor until 1907, when he resigned and was succeeded by Karl Weinmann. He founded the Palestrina Society in 1879, and (beginning with vol. X) was editor in chief of Breitkopf & Härtel's complete edition of Palestrina's works (33 vols., completed on the tercentenary of Palestrina's death, 1894), which he aided not only by his experience and learning, but also by rare MSS from his private collection. In 1899 he was elected president of the Allgemeiner Cäcilienverein, and became editor of its official organ, *Fliegende Blätter für Katholische Kirchenmusik.* In 1889 he was made Dr.Theol. (*honoris causa*) by the Univ. of Würzburg; in 1908, "Monsignore." Under his general supervision, a new edition of the *Editio Medicea* (1614) of the plainchant melodies was issued, with papal sanction, at Regensburg (1871–81). When modern scholarship had proved that the original edition had not been publ. with papal sanction and had not been revised by Palestrina; that, in fact, it contained the old melodies in badly distorted and mutilated form, the papal sanction was withdrawn, and the edition suppressed and replaced by a new *Editio Vaticana* in 1904. The result of this was that Haberl's books dealing with plainchant (which had been held in the highest esteem, and had passed through many editions) fell into desuetude. The books thus affected are: *Praktische Anweisung zum harmonischen Kirchengesang* (1864), *Magister Choralis* (1865; 12th ed., 1899; trans. into Eng., French, Italian, Spanish, Polish, and Hungarian), *Officium hebdomadae sanctae* (1887, in German), and *Psalterium vespertinum* (1888). His other writings, the value of which remains unimpaired, are *Bertalotti's Solfeggien* (1880), *Wilhelm Dufay* (1885), *Die römische "Schola Cantorum" und die päpstlichen Kapellsänger bis zur Mitte des 16. Jahrhunderts* (1887), and *Bibliographischer und thematischer Musikkatalog des päpstlichen Kapellarchivs im Vatikan zu Rom* (1888).

Habert, Johannes Evangelista, Bohemian organist, composer, and writer; b. Oberplan, Bohemia, Oct. 18, 1833; d. Gmunden, Sept. 1, 1896. He was organist at Gmunden from 1861; wrote sacred music and organ pieces; a complete edition of his works was publ. by Breitkopf & Härtel. He was founder and editor of the *Zeitschrift für katholische Kirchenmusik* (1868–83); also publ. *Beiträge zur Lehre von der musikalischen Komposition* (4 vols.; 1889 et seq.).
 BIBLIOGRAPHY: A. Hartl, *Johannes Evangelista Habert, Organist in Gmunden* (Vienna, 1900).

Habich, Eduard, German baritone; b. Kassel, Sept. 3, 1880; d. Berlin, March 15, 1960. He studied in Frankfurt; made his debut in Koblenz in 1904; then sang in Posen, Halle, and Düsseldorf at the Berlin Royal (later State) Opera (1910–30) and at the Bayreuth Festivals (1911–31). He made his Metropolitan Opera debut in N.Y. on Dec. 20, 1935, as Peter in *Hänsel und Gretel;* returned to Germany in 1937; then taught voice.

Hackett, Charles, American tenor; b. Worcester, Mass., Nov. 4, 1889; d. New York, Jan. 1, 1942. He studied voice first in Boston, and then in Florence; made his opera debut in Genoa; then sang at La Scala in Milan; subsequently appeared in South America, London, Paris, etc. On Jan. 31, 1919, he made his American debut as the Count in *Il Barbiere di Siviglia* with the Metropolitan Opera Co., remaining until 1921; was a member of the Chicago Civic Opera (1923–33); in 1934 rejoined the Metropolitan, and remained on its staff until 1939.

Hackett, Robert Leo (Bobby), American jazz cornetist and guitarist; b. Providence, Jan. 31, 1915; d.

West Chatham, Mass., June 7, 1976. He started playing guitar at the age of 8, and later picked up the violin. After playing in a Chinese restaurant as a youth, he changed to the trumpet and earned a living working in speakeasies and other dives in Boston and N.Y. He hit the big time when he appeared with Benny Goodman in Carnegie Hall, N.Y., in 1938, but dental trouble forced him to give up trumpet playing. Luck seemed to smile at him again when he was hired as a guitarist by Glenn Miller, in 1941, but Miller perished in the war. His teeth repaired by a skillful orthodontist, Hackett resumed trumpet playing, excelling in hot, cool, lukewarm, and tepid jazz. He became a favorite with young enthusiasts of jazz and pop music, but grew inexorably old and died peacefully in bed, of an irrelevant heart failure.

Hackh, Otto (Christoph), German-American music teacher and composer; b. Stuttgart, Sept. 30, 1852; d. Brooklyn, Sept. 21, 1917. He studied at the Stuttgart Cons.; traveled as a concert pianist in Europe; in 1880 settled in N.Y.; was head of the Grand Cons. there (1880–89); then taught piano privately. He publ. some 200 pieces for piano, in a modern salon style, and also many songs, some of which became extremely popular.

Hadden, James Cuthbert, Scottish writer on music; b. Banchory-Ternan, near Aberdeen, Sept. 9, 1861; d. Edinburgh, May 1, 1914. He studied organ in London; was an organist in Aberdeen and Edinburgh; edited the *Scottish Musical Monthly* (1893–96); publ. several biographies: *Handel* (1888; new ed., 1904); *Mendelssohn* (1888; new ed., 1904); *George Thomson, The Friend of Burns* (1898); *Haydn* (1902); *Chopin* (1903); also *The Operas of Wagner; Their Plots, Music and History* (1908); *Master Musicians* (1909); *Favorite Operas* (1910); *Composers in Love and Marriage* (1913); *Modern Musicians* (1914); edited *The Lays of Caledonia,* a collection of Scottish airs (Glasgow, 1883).

Hadley, Henry (Kimball), eminent American composer and conductor; b. Somerville, Mass., Dec. 20, 1871; d. New York, Sept. 6, 1937. He studied piano and violin with his father and then with S. Emery and G.W. Chadwick at the New England Cons. in Boston; in 1894, studied theory with Mandyczewski in Vienna. Returning to America, he became director of music at St. Paul's School in Garden City, N.Y. (1895–1902); toured various cities in Germany, conducting his own works (1905–9); conducted at the Stadttheater in Mainz (1908–9) and brought out there his one-act opera *Safié.* In 1909 he was engaged as conductor of the Seattle Symph. Orch.; from 1911–15 he was conductor of the San Francisco Symph. Orch., and from 1920–27, associate conductor of the N.Y. Phil. Orch. In 1924 he again toured Europe; conducted symph. concerts in Buenos Aires in 1927; was conductor of the Manhattan Symph. Orch. (1929–32), producing many American works. He was conductor at the opening concert of the Berkshire Festival at Stockbridge, Mass., in 1933. He traveled extensively; conducted his own works in Japan and Argentina; spent his last years mostly in N.Y. He received a Mus.D. from Tufts College (1925); was a member of the National Inst. of Arts and Letters and the American Academy of Arts and Letters; received the Order of Merit from the French government. Hadley occupied a position of prominence among American composers. In his style, he frankly adhered to programmatic writing. Although he shunned the unresolved dissonances of the ultramodern school, he was not averse to using fairly advanced harmonies in an impressionist vein; he often applied exotic colors when the subject matter justified it. He was an excellent craftsman, both as composer and conductor, and contributed much to the growth of American music culture.

WORKS: Comic opera, *Nancy Brown;* grand operas: *Safié* (Mainz, April 4, 1909); *Azora, the Daughter of Montezuma* (Chicago, Dec. 26, 1917); *Bianca* (N.Y., Oct. 15, 1918, composer conducting); *The Fire-Prince,* operetta (1917); *Cleopatra's Night* (N.Y., Jan. 31, 1920); *A Night in Old Paris* (N.Y., Feb. 22, 1933); festival play, *The Atonement of Pan* (San Francisco, Aug. 10, 1912); 5 symphs.: No. 1, *Youth and Life* (N.Y. Phil., Dec. 2, 1897); No. 2, *The 4 Seasons* (N.Y. Phil., Dec. 20, 1901; won the Paderewski prize and one offered by the New England Cons.); No. 3 (Berlin Phil., Dec. 27, 1907, composer conducting); No. 4, *North, East, South, West* (Norfolk [Conn.] Festival, Jan. 6, 1911, composer conducting); No. 5, *Connecticut* (Norfolk [Conn.] Festival, 1935); overtures: *Hector and Andromache; In Bohemia* (Boston Symph., Dec. 16, 1901); *Herod; Othello* (Philadelphia Orch., Dec. 26, 1919); *Youth Triumphant; Aurora Borealis* (1931); *Academic Overture; Alma Mater* (1932); *The Enchanted Castle* (1933); tone poems: *Salome* (composed in 1905, before the production of *Salome* by Richard Strauss; publ. in 1906; perf. by Muck and the Boston Symph., April 12, 1907); *Lucifer* (Norfolk [Conn.] Festival, June 2, 1914, composer conducting); *The Ocean* (N.Y. Phil., Nov. 17, 1921, composer conducting); orch. rhapsody, *The Culprit Fay* (Chicago Symph. at Grand Rapids, Mich., May 28, 1909, composer conducting; won a $1,000 prize of the National Federation of Music Clubs); orch. suites: *Oriental* (1903); *Ballet of the Flowers* (1925); *Suite ancienne* (1926); *Silhouettes, San Francisco* in 3 movements (Robin Hood Dell, July 17, 1932, composer conducting); *Streets of Pekin* (Tokyo, Sept. 24, 1930, composer conducting); *Scherzo diabolique* for Orch., "to recall a harrowing personal experience during a terrifying automobile ride at night, exceeding all speed limits" (Century of Progress Exposition, Chicago, Aug. 1934, composer conducting); incidental music to *The Daughter of Hamilcar* and *Audrey; Konzertstück* for Cello and Orch. (1937); Piano Quintet (1920); 2 string quartets; 2 piano trios; Violin Sonata; Elegy for Cello and Piano; choral works with Orch.: *In Music's Praise* (1899; won the Oliver Ditson Prize); *Merlin and Vivien; The Fate of Princess Kiyo; The Nightingale and the Rose; The Golden Prince; The Fairy Thorn; Ode to Music* (1917); *The New Earth* (1919); *Resurgam* (Cincinnati Music Festival, May 1923); *Mirtil in Arcadia* (Harrisburg [Pa.] Festival, May 17, 1928); *Belshazzar* (1932); 6 ballads (*The Fairies; In Arcady; Jabberwocky; Lelawala, a Legend of Niagara; The Princess of Ys; A Legend of Granada*); many anthems; piano pieces; over 150 songs to German and Eng. words. A Henry Hadley Foundation for the Advancement of American Music was organized in 1938.

BIBLIOGRAPHY: H.R. Boardman, *Henry Hadley, Ambassador of Harmony* (Diss., Emory Univ., 1932); P. Berthoud, *The Musical Works of Dr. Henry Hadley* (N.Y., 1942).

Hadley, Patrick Arthur Sheldon, British composer; b. Cambridge, March 5, 1899; d. King's Lynn, Norfolk, Dec. 17, 1973. He studied at the Royal College of Music in London with Vaughan Williams and others (1922–25); then taught there in 1925–38; in 1938–46 held a fellowship at Gonville and Caius College in Cambridge; held a chair of music at Cambridge from 1946 to 1962. He composed mostly vocal music; among his works are the cantatas *The Trees So High* (1931); *La Belle Dame sans merci* (1935); *Travelers* (1940); *The Hills* (1946); *Fen and Flood* (1956); *Connemara* (1958); *Cantata for Lent* (1960).

BIBLIOGRAPHY: W. Todds, *Patrick Hadley; A Memoir,* with a catalogue of works (London, 1974).

Hadow, Sir William Henry, English music educator; b. Ebrington, Gloucestershire, Dec. 27, 1859; d. London, April 8, 1937. He studied at Malvern College (1871–78) and Worcester College, Oxford (1878–82); received the degrees of M.A. (1888) and Mus.B. (1890). He held various positions in English univs. from 1885–1919; was knighted in 1918. He wrote a cantata, *The Soul's Pilgrimage;* a String Quartet; 2 violin sonatas; a Viola Sonata; and a number of anthems. These, however, are of little significance; Hadow's importance lies in his books, written in a lively journalistic style. His book on Haydn, *A Croatian Composer* (London, 1897), claiming that Haydn was of Slavonic origin, aroused considerable controversy; modern research proves the claim fanciful and devoid of foundation. Of more solid substance are his other writings: *Studies in Modern Music* (2 vols., 1892–95; 10th ed., 1921); *Sonata Form* (1896); *The Viennese Period* (vol. 5 of the *Oxford History of Music,* 1904); *Beethoven* (1917); *William Byrd* (1923); *Music* (in the Home Univ. Library, 1924; 3rd revised ed., by Sir George Dyson, 1949); *Church Music* (1926); *A Comparison of Poetry and Music* (1926); *Collected Essays* (1928); *English Music* (1931); *The Place of Music among the Arts* (1933); *Richard Wagner* (1934). He edited songs of the British Isles (1903); was editor in chief of the *Oxford History of Music* (1901–5 and 1929); contributed articles to various British magazines and to the *Musical Quarterly* (Jan. 1915).

Hadzidakis, Manos, Greek composer; b. Xanthi, Macedonia, Oct. 23, 1925. He wrote piano pieces in an advanced idiom, recalling Prokofiev; then turned to film music. He is the composer of the famous theme song in the film released in America under the title *Never on Sunday.*

Haebler, Ingrid, Austrian pianist; b. Vienna, June 20, 1926. She was educated in Vienna, Salzburg, and Geneva. After winning first prize in the International Competition in Munich and the Schubert Competition in Geneva, she developed a fine career as a soloist with orchs. and as a concert artist. She excels in the music of Haydn, Mozart, Schubert, and Schumann. In 1969 she was appointed to the faculty of the Salzburg Mozarteum.

Haeffner, Johann Christian Friedrich, German composer; b. Oberschönau, near Suhl, March 2, 1759; d. Uppsala, Sweden, May 28, 1833. He was a pupil of Vierling at Schmalkalden; studied at the Univ. of Leipzig, and served as proofreader for Breitkopf; then became conductor of a traveling opera troupe; in 1781 he arrived in Stockholm, where he became an organist at a German church. He produced at Stockholm several operas in the style of Gluck which had a favorable reception: *Electra* (July 22, 1787), *Alcides inträde i Världen* (Nov. 11, 1793), and *Renaud* (Jan. 29, 1801). In 1792 he was appointed court conductor; in 1808 he went to Uppsala, where he remained for the rest of his life, acting as organist of the Cathedral and music director of the univ. He took great interest in Swedish national music; publ. Swedish folk songs with accompaniment, and revised the melodies of the Geijer-Afzelius collection; edited a *Svenska Choralbok* (2 parts, 1819–21), in which he restored the choral melodies of the 17th century, and added preludes (1822); also arranged a collection of old Swedish songs in 4 parts (1832–33; he finished only 2 books).

Haefliger, Ernst, Swiss tenor; b. Davos, July 6, 1919. He studied at the Univ. of Zürich; also in Prague and Munich. His appearance at the Salzburg Festival (1949) catapulted him onto an international career. He made many concert appearances with the leading orchs. of Europe; was also a fine lieder singer in solo recitals. His repertoire is most extensive; he is best known for his Mozart interpretations.

Haendel, Ida, violinist; b. Chelm, Poland, Dec. 15, 1924. She studied at the Warsaw Cons., receiving its gold medal; made a remarkable London debut when she was only 10 years old by appearing with Sir Henry Wood at a Proms concert in the Brahms Violin Concerto. She then continued her studies with Carl Flesch and Georges Enesco. She settled in England and became a British subject. She was a soloist with the London Phil. on its tour of China in 1973. A facile writer, she publ. an interesting account of her life and career in *Woman with Violin* (London, 1970).

Haesche, William Edwin, American music educator; b. New Haven, Conn., April 11, 1867; d. Roanoke, Va., Jan. 26, 1929. He studied violin with Bernhard Listemann and piano with Perabo, then composition with Horatio Parker at Yale Univ. (Mus.Bac., 1897); taught orchestration at Yale Univ. (1903–22); in 1923 was appointed violin teacher at Hollins College in Va., a post he held until his death. He was one of the organizers of the New Haven Symph. Orch., and was its concertmaster for 20 years. He wrote a symph. poem, *Fridthjof and Ingeborg* (1897); *The Haunted Oak of Nannau* for Chorus and Orch. (1902); many violin pieces.

Hafez, Abdel Halim (Abdel Halim Shabana), Egyptian singer; b. Halawat, 1930; d. London, March 30, 1977. He rose to prominence in Egypt, and the Arab world in general, as the foremost interpreter of romantic and nationalistic songs; won renown for his renditions of *Safini Marra* and *Ala Kad el Shouk.* He used Western instruments in his performances, and even utilized the Moog synthesizer. So widespread was his fame at the time of his death, that 100,000 Egyptians lined the streets of the funeral procession in Cairo.

Hafgren, Lily, Swedish soprano; b. Stockholm, Oct. 7, 1884; d. Berlin, Feb. 27, 1965. She was educated in Frankfurt; began her career as a pianist; Siegfried Wagner encouraged her to consider an operatic career, and she studied voice in Stuttgart with Max Fleisch; made her debut at the Bayreuth Festival in 1908; then sang in Mannheim (1908–12) and at the Royal (later State) Opera in Berlin (1912–21); also appeared in Paris, Rome, and Milan. She retired in 1934. In later years she used her married names, **Hafgren-Waag** and **Hafgren-Dinkela.**

Hagegård, Håkan, Swedish baritone; b. Karlstad, Nov. 25, 1945. He studied at the Royal Academy of Music in Stockholm; also took lessons with Tito Gobbi in Rome, Gerald Moore in London, and Erik Werba in Vienna. He made his operatic debut as Papageno in Mozart's *Die Zauberflöte* at the Royal Opera in Stockholm in 1968; subsequently appeared throughout Europe, following his successful portrayal of Papageno in the film by Ingmar Bergman. He is particularly distinguished as an interpreter of baritone parts in the operas of Mozart, Rossini, Verdi, and Donizetti.

Hagel, Richard, German conductor; b. Erfurt, July 7, 1872; d. Berlin, May 1, 1941. He studied with his father; was an orch. violinist in Abo, Finland (1889), Koburg (1890), Meiningen (1892), and Sondershausen (1893); later undertook serious study at the Leipzig Cons. (1898–1900); conducted at the Leipzig Stadttheater (1900–9) and at Braunschweig (1911–14). From 1919–25 he was a conductor of the Berlin Phil.; subsequently taught at various schools. He publ. *Die Lehre vom Partiturspiel* (Berlin, 1937).

Hageman, Maurits Leonard, Dutch violinist and composer; b. Zutfen, Sept. 25, 1829; d. Nijmegen, April 16, 1906. He studied with Bériot and Fétis at the Brussels Cons., graduating in 1852. After playing violin in the Italian Opera orch. at Brussels, he became a conductor at Groningen; then was director of the Cons. of Batavia, Java (1865–75), and conductor of the orch. there. Returning to the Netherlands, he founded a music school in Leeuwarden. He wrote an oratorio, *Daniel;* several other choral works; piano pieces; songs.

Hageman, Richard, distinguished American pianist, conductor, and composer; b. Leeuwarden, the Netherlands, July 9, 1882; d. Beverly Hills, March 6, 1966. He studied music with his father, **Maurits Hageman;** then took courses at the Brussels Cons. with Gevaert and Arthur de Greef. He held an auxiliary position as conductor at the Royal Opera in Amsterdam (1899–1903). After playing accompaniments for Mathilde Marchesi in Paris (1904–5), he came to the U.S. as accompanist for Yvette Guilbert in 1906; from 1913–21 and again in 1936 was on the conducting staff of the Metropolitan Opera; also conducted the summer opera at Ravinia Park in Chicago and taught voice at the Chicago Musical College. In 1938 he settled in Hollywood, where he was engaged as a composer of film music. He wrote 2 operas: *Caponsacchi* (1931; produced in Freiburg, Germany, as *Tragödie in Arezzo,* Feb. 18, 1932; at the Metropolitan Opera House, N.Y., Feb. 4, 1937; received the David Bispham Memorial Medal) and *The Crucible* (Los Angeles, Feb. 4, 1943). He achieved a lasting reputation mainly through his solo songs, of which *Do Not Go My Love* (to words by Rabindranath Tagore) and *At the Well* became extremely popular.

Hagen, Francis Florentine, American Moravian minister and composer; b. Salem, N.C., Oct. 30, 1815; d. Lititz, Pa., July 7, 1907. He served as a teacher and minister in various Moravian congregations; edited and compiled the *Church and Home Organist's Companion* (several vols.). He wrote a number of anthems, in which a definite sense for distinguished popular melody is noticeable; also a cantata and an overture. His *Morning Star,* a Christmas carol, which in Moravian communities stood in continuous favor for almost a century, was reprinted in 1939. Another anthem is included in the series Music of the Moravians in America, publ. by the N.Y. Public Library.
BIBLIOGRAPHY: A.G. Rau and H.T. David, *A Catalogue of Music by American Moravians* (Bethlehem, Pa., 1938).

Hagen, Friedrich Heinrich von der, German scholar; b. in the Ukraine, Feb. 19, 1780; d. Berlin, June 11, 1856, as a prof. of German literature at the univ. He publ. the valuable collection *Minnesinger* (1838–56, in 5 vols.; in vol. III are *Minnegesänge* in notation according to the Jena Codex and other sources, with a treatise on the music of the Minnesinger); *Melodien zu der Sammlung deutscher, vlämischer und französicher Volkslieder* (1807; with Büsching).

Hagen, Theodor, writer on music; b. Hamburg, April 15, 1823; d. New York, Dec. 21, 1871. He lived in N.Y. from 1854 as a teacher and critic; edited the *New York Weekly Review.* Under the nom de plume **Joachim Fels** he publ. *Civilisation und Musik* (1845).

Hagen-Groll, Walter, German choral conductor; b. Chemnitz, April 15, 1927. He was educated at the Hochschule für Musik in Stuttgart; in 1952 he became conductor of the choir at the Stuttgart Opera; obtained a similar position at the Heidelberg Opera in 1957. In 1961 he was appointed conductor of the Deutsche Oper Chorus in West Berlin; also became director of the choir of the Berlin Phil. Orch. concerts. Furthermore, he served as chorus leader at Bayreuth and Salzburg; appeared in London as conductor of the Philharmonia Orch. Chorus.

Hager, Leopold, Austrian conductor; b. Salzburg, Oct. 6, 1935. He was educated at the Mozarteum; then served as an assistant conductor in Mainz (1957–62) and Linz (1962–64). He was first conductor of the Cologne Opera (1964–66) and Generalmusikdirektor in Freiburg im Breisgau (1965–69); then returned to Salzburg as chief conductor of the Mozarteum Orch.; left this post in 1981. He was a regular conductor at the Bavarian State Opera in Munich; also conducted opera in America.

Hagerup Bull, Edvard, Norwegian composer; b. Bergen, June 10, 1922. He studied composition in Norway with Bjarne Brustad and Ludvig Irgens Jensen; in 1947 went to Paris, where he took courses with Koechlin, Rivier, Messiaen, and Milhaud; continued his studies in Berlin with Boris Blacher. His music bears a pleasing neo-Classical stamp.
WORKS: *Le Soldat de plomb,* ballet suite (1948–49); Serenade for Orch. (1950); *Morceaux rapsodiques,* divertimento for Orch. (1950); 2 trumpet concertos (1950, 1960); *Sinfonia di teatro,* symph. prelude (1950–51); *Petite suite symphonique* for Small Orch. (1951); *Escapades,* suite for Orch. (1952); Divertimento for Piano and Orch. (1954); 5 symphs.: No. 1, *3 mouvements symphoniques* (1955); No. 2, *In modo d'una sinfonia* (1958–59); No. 3, *Sinfonia espressiva* (1964); No. 4, *Sinfonia humana* (1968); No. 5, *Sinfonia in memoriam* (1971–72); *3 morceaux brefs* for Saxophone and Orch. (1955); *Cassation* for Chamber Orch. (1959); *Münchhausen,* ballet (1961); *Epilogue* for Strings (1961); *Undecim Sumus* for Chamber Orch. of Soloists (1962); *Dialogue* for Flute, Strings, and Piano (1965); *6 épigrammes* for Chamber Ensemble (1969); Concerto for Flute and Chamber Orch. (1969); *Air solennel,* symph. movement (1972); Clarinet Sonata (1951); *3 bucoliques* for Oboe, Clarinet, and Bassoon (1953); Duo for Violin and Piano (1956); *Ad usum amicorum* for Flute, Violin, Cello, and Piano (1957); *Marionnettes sérieuses* for Wind Quintet (1960); *Quadrige* for 4 Clarinets (1963); Sextet for Saxophone and Wind Quintet (1965); *Sonata cantabile* for Flute, Violin, Cello, and Piano (1966); *Concert* for Trumpet, Horn, and Trombone (1966); *Accents* for Piano (1968); *Sonata con spirito* for Piano Quartet (1970).

Hägg – Hahn

Hägg, Gustaf Wilhelm, eminent Swedish organist and composer; b. Visby, Nov. 28, 1867; d. Stockholm, Feb. 7, 1925. Hägg was his mother's name, which he legally adopted; his father's name was Peterson. Hägg was a remote relative of **Jacob Adolf Hägg.** He studied organ at the Stockholm Cons.; in 1893 he was appointed organist at the Klara Church in Stockholm, retaining this position for the rest of his life. In the interim he traveled for further study purposes in Germany and France (1897–1900). In 1904 he joined the staff of the Stockholm Cons., as a teacher of harmony and organ playing. He enjoyed a distinguished reputation in Sweden as an organist, and gave numerous recitals in which he played the works of César Franck and other organ composers. He also composed 5 organ concertos and other organ pieces; several cantatas; songs. He arranged and publ. collections of Swedish songs (Stockholm, 1908), and an album, *Songs of Sweden* (N.Y., 1909).

Hägg, Jacob Adolf, Swedish composer; b. Oestergarn, June 27, 1850; d. Hudiksvall, March 1, 1928. He was a remote relative of **Gustaf Wilhelm Hägg.** He studied at the Stockholm Cons.; then received a stipend to take courses in Denmark with Gade, who exercised a decisive influence on his style of composition; he further studied piano with Anton Door in Vienna and music theory with Kiel in Berlin. Ambition to learn and relentless diligence in his studies upset his mental equilibrium so that he had to spend 15 years in a sanatorium (1880–95). He recovered but retired to the country, reducing his activity to a minimum. Despite this misadventure he was able to leave a considerable legacy of works, among them 5 symphs., of which *Nordische Symphonie* (1870; revised 1890) was the best known; 3 overtures; Cello Sonata, Piano Trio, String Quartet, and other chamber music; piano pieces; songs.
BIBLIOGRAPHY: *Jacob Adolf Hägg* (Leipzig, 1903).

Haggard, Merle, American country-western singer, fiddler, and guitarist; b. Checotah, Okla., April 6, 1937. His impoverished family moved to California, where they lived in an abandoned boxcar near Bakersfield. He started early on a criminal career; escaped 7 times from reform schools, stole cars and held up a bar, and finally ended up at San Quentin as prisoner No. 845,200. There he met the notorious "red-light bandit" Caryl Chessman, eventually executed for a series of brutal rapes; Chessman exercised a profound intellectual influence on Haggard, who began improvising songs of destitution, despair, and crime, exemplified by such an autobiographical ballad as "Did you ever steal a quarter when you was 10 years old?" In due time he completed his term and in 1972 was pardoned by Ronald Reagan, then governor of California. No longer did he have to steal money, for he commanded a fee of $15,000 per concert, sold millions of record albums to his own lyrics and music, and won awards galore in the city of Nashville. He married 3 times and made more successful recordings, gradually reaching the topnotch rank as a country-western singer with such hits as *Okie from Muskogee, Workin' Man Blues, Daddy Frank (the Guitar Man),* and *Hungry Eyes.* He authored an autobiography (ghost-written for him by Peggy Russell) titled *Sing Me Back Home.* And—supreme reward—he made the *Time* magazine cover story (March 11, 1977).

Haggin, Bernard H., American music critic; b. New York, Dec. 29, 1900. He was music critic of the *Brooklyn Daily Eagle* (1934–37) and of the *Nation* (1936–57). An aggressive writer who held unalterable opinions on musical matters, he adopted a polemical manner of personal journalism, disregarding all conventional amenities. He collected many of his articles in book form. He publ. *A Book of the Symphony* (N.Y., 1937); *Music on Records* (N.Y., 1938; 4th ed., 1946); *Music for the Man Who Enjoys Hamlet* (N.Y., 1944); *Music in The Nation* (N.Y., 1949; a collection of articles from the *Nation*); *The Listener's Musical Companion* (New Brunswick, N.J., 1956); *Conversations with Toscanini* (N.Y., 1959; 2nd ed., enlarged, 1979); *Music Observed* (N.Y., 1964; reprinted 1974 under the title *35 Years of Music*); *The New Listener's Companion and Record Guide* (N.Y., 1967; new eds., 1968, 1971); *The Toscanini Musicians Knew* (N.Y., 1967); *A Decade of Music* (N.Y., 1973).

Hahn, Carl, American conductor; b. Indianapolis, Oct. 23, 1874; d. Cincinnati, May 13, 1929. A member of a musical family (his father played the flute; his brother was a violinist), he studied piano and cello. From 1909–12 he conducted the Beethoven Society, a male chorus, in San Antonio, Texas; then lived in N.Y. and Cincinnati. He wrote a number of choruses and songs, some of which are quite singable.

Hahn, Georg, remarkable Austrian bass; b. Vienna, Jan. 30, 1897; d. Munich, Dec. 9, 1950. He enlisted in the Austrian army in World War I; after demobilization began to study singing with Theodor Lierhammer at the Vienna Academy of Music. In 1927 he joined the Bavarian State Opera in Munich; made guest appearances in Brussels, Berlin, Paris, and London; also sang at La Scala, Milan. He was equally successful in such dramatic roles as Pizarro in *Fidelio,* Sarastro in *Die Zauberflöte,* and Rigoletto, as well as in buffo parts such as Falstaff and Leporello. He performed all his roles in German, even in the Italian repertoire, and continued to sing and record to the very last months of the war, in 1943 and 1944.

Hahn, Reynaldo, Venezuelan-born French composer; b. Caracas, Aug. 9, 1874; d. Paris, Jan. 28, 1947. His father, a merchant from Hamburg, settled in Venezuela c.1850; the family moved to Paris when Reynaldo Hahn was 5 years old. He studied singing and apparently had an excellent voice; a professional recording he made in 1910 testifies to that. He studied music theory at the Paris Cons. with Dubois and Lavignac and composition with Massenet, who exercised the most important influence on Hahn's own music. He also studied conducting, achieving a high professional standard as an opera conductor. In 1906 he was invited to conduct at the Mozart Sesquicentennial Festival in Salzburg (other conductors were Mahler and Richard Strauss). In 1934 he became music critic of *Le Figaro.* He remained in France during the Nazi occupation at a considerable risk to his life, since he was Jewish on his father's side. In 1945 he was named a member of the Inst. de France and music director of the Paris Opéra. Hahn's music is distinguished by a facile, melodious flow and a fine Romantic flair. Socially, he was known in Paris for his brilliant wit. He maintained a passionate youthful friendship with Marcel Proust, who portrayed him as a poetic genius in his novel *Jean Santeuil;* their intimate correspondence was publ. in 1946.

WORKS: OPERAS: *L'île du rêve,* "Polynesian idyll," after Pierre Loti (Opéra-Comique, Paris, March 23, 1898); *La Carmélite* (Opéra-Comique, Paris, Dec. 16, 1902); *Nausicaa* (Monte Carlo, April 10, 1919); *Fête triomphale* (Paris Opéra, July 14, 1919); *La Colombe de Bouddah* (Cannes, March 21, 1921); *Ciboulette,* light opera (Théâtre des Variétés, Paris, April 7, 1923); *Le Marchand de Venise,* after Shakespeare (Paris Opéra, March 25, 1935). OPERETTAS: *Miousic* (Paris, March 22, 1914); *Mozart,* after a play by Sascha Guitry (Paris, Dec. 2, 1925); *Brummel* (Paris, Jan. 20, 1931); *O mon bel inconnu* (Paris, Oct. 5, 1933); *Malvina* (Gaîté Lyrique, Paris, March 25, 1935). INCIDENTAL MUSIC: To Daudet's *L'Obstacle* (1890); Croisset's *Deux courtisanes* (1902); Racine's *Esther* (1905); Hugo's *Angelo* (1905) and Lucrèce Borgia (1911); Wolff and Duvernois's *Le Temps d'aimer* (1926). BALLETS: *Fin d'amour* (1892); *Le Bal de Béatrice d'Este* (Paris, April 11, 1907); *La Fête chez Thérèse* (Paris, Feb. 16, 1910); *Medusa* (Monte Carlo, Dec. 24, 1911); *Le Dieu bleu* (Diaghilev's Ballets Russes, Paris, May 14, 1912); *Le Bois sacré* (1912); 2 symph. poems: *Nuit d'amour bergamasque* (1897) and *Promethée triomphant* (1911); Christmas mystery, *La Pastorale de Noël* (1908). A lyric comedy, *Le Oui des jeunes filles,* left unfinished at Hahn's death, was completed and orchestrated by Henri Busser and perf. posthumously at the Opéra-Comique in Paris on June 21, 1949. Hahn further wrote a Violin Concerto (Paris, Feb. 26, 1928); Piano Concerto (Paris, Feb. 4, 1931); Cello Concerto; Piano Quintet; String Quartet; and a number of piano pieces, among them a suite, *Portraits des peintres,* inspired by poems of Marcel Proust. But his most signal accomplishment lies in his songs, such as *Les Chansons grises* (1891–92, written when he was still a cons. student), *L'Heure exquise,* and *Si mes vers avaient des ailes.* Hahn was a brilliant journalist. His articles were collected in the following publications: *Du Chant* (Paris, 1920); *Notes. Journal d'un musicien* (Paris, 1933); *L'Oreille au guet* (Paris, 1937); and *Thèmes variés* (Paris, 1946).

BIBLIOGRAPHY: Daniel Bendahan, *Reynaldo Hahn. Su vida y su obra* (Caracas, 1973; profusely illustrated with photographs and musical examples); Bernard Gavoty, *Reynaldo Hahn: Le Musicien de la belle époque* (Paris, 1976).

Hahn, Ulrich. See **Han, Ulrich.**

Haibel, (Johann Petrus) Jakob, Austrian composer; b. Graz, July 20, 1762; d. Djakovar, March 24, 1826. He was engaged in Vienna as a tenor; in 1806 settled in Djakovar; there he married Sophie Weber, sister of Mozart's widow. He produced several stage works in Vienna, among them the ballet *Le nozze disturbate* (May 18, 1795) and a singspiel, *Der Tyroler Wastl* (May 14, 1796), which became very popular. Other productions were *Der Papagei und die Gans* (May 25, 1799); *Tsching, Tsching, Tsching* (Feb. 6, 1802); *Der kleine Cesar* (July 25, 1804); etc.

Haieff, Alexei, Russian-American composer; b. Blagoveshchensk, Siberia, Aug. 25, 1914. He received his primary education at Harbin, Manchuria; in 1931 came to the U.S.; studied with Rubin Goldmark and Frederick Jacobi at the Juilliard School of Music in N.Y.; during 1938–39 he studied with Nadia Boulanger in Cambridge, Mass. He held a Guggenheim fellowship in 1946 and again in 1949; was a Fellow at the American Academy in Rome (1947–48), a prof. at the Univ. of Buffalo (1962–68), and composer-in-residence at the Univ. of Utah (1968–70). In his music Haieff follows Stravinsky's type of neo-Classical writing, observing an austere economy of means, but achieving modernistic effects by a display of rhythmic agitation, often with jazzy undertones.

WORKS: Ballets: *The Princess Zondilda and Her Entourage* (1946) and *Beauty and the Beast* (1947); 3 symphs.: No. 1 (1942); No. 2 (Boston, April 11, 1958); received the American International Music Fund Award); No. 3 (New Haven, Conn., April 11, 1961); Divertimento for Orch. (N.Y., April 5, 1946); Violin Concerto (1948); Piano Concerto (N.Y., April 27, 1952; received the Award of the N.Y. Music Critics Circle); Sonatina for String Quartet (1937); 3 *Bagatelles* for Oboe and Bassoon (1939); Serenade for Oboe, Clarinet, Bassoon, and Piano (1942); *Eclogue* for Cello and Piano (1947); *La Nouvelle Héloïse* for Harp and String Quartet (1963); Cello Sonata (1963); *Eloge* for Chamber Orch. (1967); *Caligula* for Baritone and Orch., after Robert Lowell (N.Y., Nov. 5, 1971); Sonata for 2 Pianos (1945); Piano Sonata (1955); songs.

Haig, Al(lan Warren), American jazz pianist; b. Newark, N.J., July 22, 1924; d. New York, Nov. 16, 1982. He served in the U.S. Coast Guard in World War II; in 1945 he joined the band of Dizzy Gillespie, and also was a member of the Charlie Parker Quintet. His piano style was influenced by the popular bebop technique. He was a colorful figure in the new jazz world, but his career was interrupted when he had to stand trial on the charge of having murdered his first wife, Bonnie. Fortunately, he was acquitted and was able to resume piano playing; he also found another woman to marry.

Haile, Eugen, German-American composer; b. Ulm, Feb. 21, 1873; d. Woodstock, N.Y., Aug. 14, 1933. He studied at the Stuttgart Cons.; emigrated to

America in 1903. He wrote about 200 songs to German texts, some of them of excellent quality (*Herbst, Der Todesengel singt, Teufelslied, Soldaten kommen,* etc.). His musical setting to a spoken drama ("gesprochene Oper"), *The Happy Ending,* produced in N.Y. on Aug. 21, 1916, is an interesting attempt to combine spoken words in the play with pitch inflections in the vocal parts, in the manner of *Sprechtstimme.* His other opera, *Harold's Dream,* was produced in Woodstock on June 30, 1933. His wife, **Elise Haile,** was a singer; together they presented several concerts of his German songs in N.Y. A Eugen Haile Society was formed in N.Y. in 1914 to organize further performances of his music.

Hainl, François, French cellist and conductor; b. Issoire, Nov. 16, 1807; d. Paris, June 2, 1873. After graduating as a cellist from the Paris Cons. with a first prize (1830), he went to Lyons, where he conducted theater music (1841–63); then conducted at the Paris Opéra (1863–72). He wrote an orch. fantasy on Rossini's *William Tell;* publ. a valuable account, *De la musique à Lyon depuis 1713 jusqu'à 1852.*

Haitink, Bernard, eminent Dutch conductor; b. Amsterdam, March 4, 1929. He studied violin at the Amsterdam Cons.; then played in the Radio Phil. Orch. in Hilversum. In 1954–55 he attended the conducting course of Ferdinand Leitner, sponsored by the Netherlands Radio; in 1955 he was appointed to the post of second conductor of the Radio Phil. Orch. in Hilversum, becoming its principal conductor in 1957. In 1956 he made his first appearance as a guest conductor with the Concertgebouw Orch. of Amsterdam. He made his U.S. debut with the Los Angeles Phil. Orch. on Jan. 2, 1958. In 1959 he conducted the Concertgebouw Orch. in England. In 1961 he became co-principal conductor of the Concertgebouw Orch., sharing his duties with Eugen Jochum; that same year he led it on a tour of the U.S., followed by one to Japan in 1962. In 1964 he became chief conductor of the Concertgebouw Orch. In 1967 he also assumed the post of principal conductor and artistic adviser of the London Phil. Orch., becoming its artistic director in 1969; he resigned from this post in 1978. He made his first appearance at the Glyndebourne Festival in 1972, and in 1978 was named its music director. He also acted as a guest conductor with the Berlin Phil., Vienna Phil., N.Y. Phil., Chicago Symph., Boston Symph., and Cleveland Orch. In 1982 he led the Concertgebouw Orch. on a transcontinental tour of the U.S. In his interpretations Haitink avoids personal rhetoric, allowing the music to speak for itself. Yet he achieves eloquent and colorful effect; especially fine are his performances of the symphs. of Bruckner and Mahler; equally congenial are his projections of the Classical repertoire. He has received numerous international honors, including the Netherlands' Royal Order of Orange-Nassau (1969), the Medal of Honor of the Bruckner Society of America (1970), and the Gustav Mahler Society Gold Medal (1971); he was named a Chevalier de l'Ordre des Arts et des Lettres of France (1972). He received the rare distinction of being made an Honorary Knight Commander of the Order of the British Empire by Queen Elizabeth II in 1977.

Haitzinger, Anton, Austrian tenor; b. Wilfersdorf, Liechtenstein, March 14, 1796; d. Vienna, Dec. 31, 1869. He studied in Vienna; made his opera debut in 1821; then sang in Prague, Frankfurt, Paris, and London; retired in 1850, and returned to Vienna. In his prime he enjoyed an excellent reputation, and was equally successful in the Italian and German repertoires. He publ. a song, *Vergiss mein nicht,* and a manual of singing.

Hajdú, André, Hungarian-born Israeli composer; b. Budapest, March 5, 1932. He studied with Kodály, Szabó, Szervánszky, and Kosá at the Budapest Music Academy; then took seminars in Paris with Milhaud and Messiaen (1956). For 2 years he taught at the Cons. in Tunis (1959–61); emigrated to Israel in 1966, and in 1967 became a teacher at the Tel Aviv Academy of Music. His music is folkloristic in its sources of inspiration, while the harmonic idiom is fairly advanced.

WORKS: *Gypsy Cantata* (1956); *A Little Hell* for Orch. (1960); *Babeliana* for Orch. (1964); Piano Concerto (1968); *Ludus Paschalis* for 8 Soloists, Children's Chorus, and 9 Instruments (1970); *Terouath Melech,* Jewish rhapsody for Clarinet and String Orch. (1973); *Military Diary (The Art of the Canon),* 50 canons for different instrumental combinations (1976); *Stories about Mischievous Boys* for Orch. (1976); *5 Sketches in a Sentimental Mood* for Piano Quartet (1976); *The Prophet of Truth and the Prophet of Deceit* for Narrator and String Orch. (1977).

Hajdú, Lóránt, Rumanian-born Hungarian composer; b. Bucharest, Aug. 12, 1937. He was brought to Budapest as an infant; he studied music with István Szelényi; also studied horn playing at the Budapest Cons.; later took courses in composition with Endre Szervánszky at the Academy of Music, graduating in 1965. He subsequently devoted himself to teaching. Among his works are Bagatelles for Piano (1955); Elegy for Horn and Piano (1958); Cello Sonata (1958); Piano Sonatina (1959); Horn Quartet (1960); Suite for 2 Horns and Piano (1962); 2 wind quintets (1965, 1973); Piano Concerto (1966); Violin Concerto (1967); Symph. No. 1 (1968); *10 Miniatures,* trio for Winds (1970); Trumpet Sonata (1971); Piano Concertino (1972); *Oscillazione* for Clarinet and Piano (1972); Toccata for Piano (1972); *Scherzo-capriccio* for Piano (1972).

Hajdú, Mihály, Hungarian composer; b. Orosháza, Jan. 30, 1909. He studied composition with Kodály at the Academy of Music in Budapest; in 1961 was appointed to its faculty.

WORKS: Opera, *Kádár Kata* (1957; Budapest, 1959); *2 scherzi* for Piano (1931); Suite for Orch. (1934); 2 string quartets (1936, 1970); Piano Sonata (1940); Piano Sonatina (1952); Violin Sonata (1953);

Variations and Rondo for Cello and Piano (1955); Piano Trio (1957); *A munka dicsérete (In Praise of Work),* symph. poem (1958); Trio for Winds (1958); Concertino for Cello and Strings (1966); Piano Concerto (1968); Cello Sonatina (1969); *Capriccio all'ongarese* for Clarinet and Orch. (1969); *8 Etudes* for String Orch. (1970); *3 Pieces* for 2 Pianos (1971); *30 Little Pieces* for Cello and Piano, or 2 Cellos (1973).

Hakansson, Knut Algot, Swedish composer; b. Kinna, Nov. 4, 1887; d. Göteborg, Dec. 13, 1929. He studied philosophy and philology at the Univ. of Uppsala; later traveled to Germany. He wrote a ballet, *Mylitta* (1918); several orch. suites on Swedish themes; a String Quartet, a String Trio, and other chamber music. His most significant works are for chorus, many of them derived from the melodic patterns of Swedish folk songs.

Hakim, Talib Rasul, black American composer; b. Asheville, N.C., Feb. 8, 1940. His original name was **Stephen A. Chambers;** he changed it to Hakim in 1973 after conversion to Sufism, a precursory philosophy of Islam. He studied music at the Manhattan School of Music, the N.Y. College of Music, and the New School for Social Research (1958–65), where his teachers included Starer, Sydeman, Overton, Feldman, Chou Wen-Chung, Whittenberg, and the jazz saxophonist Ornette Coleman. He taught at Pace College in N.Y. (1970–72) and, beginning in 1972, at Adelphi Univ. Hakim received a National Endowment for the Arts grant for 1973–74 and for 1975; received the ASCAP Composers' Award 3 times and the Bennington Composers' Conference Fellowship 4 times. He employs in his music a series of dissonant blocks of sound moving along in asymmetrical progressions.
    WORKS: *Mutations* for Bass Clarinet, Trumpet, Horn, Viola, and Cello (1964); *Peace-Mobile* for Wind Quintet (1964); *Ode to Silence* for Soprano and Piano (1964); *Encounter* for Wind Quintet, Trumpet, and Trombone (1965); *4* for Clarinet, Trumpet, Trombone, and Piano (1965); *A Piano Piece* (1965); *Shapes* for Chamber Orch. (1965); *Portraits* for Flute, Bass, Clarinet, Piano, and 3 Percussionists (1965); *Titles* for Wind Quartet (1965); *Contours* for Oboe, Bassoon, Horn, Trumpet, Cello, and Double Bass (1966); *Inner-Sections* for Flute, Clarinet, Trombone, Piano, and Percussion (1967); *Roots and Other-things* for Flute, Oboe, Clarinet, Horn, Trumpet, Trombone, Viola, Cello, and Double Bass (1967); *Sound-Gone,* "philosophical sketch" for Piano (1967); *Currents* for String Quartet (1967); *Quote-Unquote* for Baritone, Oboe, Trumpet, and 2 Percussionists (1967); *Sound-Image* for Female Voices, Brass, Strings, and Percussion (1969); *Placements* for Piano and 5 Percussionists (1970); *Set-3* for Soprano, Cello, and Piano (1970); *Visions of Ishwara* for Orch. (N.Y., Oct. 10, 1970); *Reflections on the 5th Ray* for Narrator and Chamber Orch. (1972); *Sketchy Blue-bop* for Jazz-band Ensemble (1973); *Tone-Prayers* for Chorus, Piano, and Percussion (1973); *Re/Currences* for Orch. (Washington, D.C., June 7, 1975); *Concepts* for Orch. (1976); *Music for

Soprano and 9 Players (1977).

Halász, László, Hungarian-American conductor; b. Debrecen, June 6, 1905. He studied piano, theory, and conducting at the Budapest Cons., graduating in 1929; toured Europe as a concert pianist (1928–31), but devoted himself mainly to conducting. After numerous conducting engagements in Budapest, Prague, and Vienna, he emigrated to America in 1936; became a naturalized American citizen in 1943. He was conductor of the St. Louis Grand Opera (1939–42); in 1943 was appointed conductor and music director of the N.Y. City Opera Co., where he established an audacious policy of producing modern operas, but became embroiled in personal difficulties with the management, and resigned in 1951. He then filled engagements as an opera conductor in America, Spain, and Brazil. From 1965–68 he conducted the Eastman Philharmonia Orch. in Rochester, N.Y.; then was director of the Music College at the Old Westbury campus of the State Univ. of N.Y. (1968–71); in 1971 was appointed program director of music at the State Univ. of N.Y. at Stony Brook.

Hale, Adam de la. See **Adam de la Halle.**

Hale, Philip, eminent American music critic; b. Norwich, Vt., March 5, 1854; d. Boston, Nov. 30, 1934. He took music lessons in his early youth, and as a boy played the organ in the Unitarian Church at Northampton, Mass.; went to Yale Univ. to study law, and was admitted to the bar in 1880. He then took organ lessons with Dudley Buck; subsequently went to Europe (1882–87), where he studied organ with Haupt in Berlin, and composition with Rheinberger in Munich and with Guilmant in Paris. Returning to America, he served as a church organist in Albany and Troy, N.Y., and in Boston, but soon abandoned this employment for his true vocation, that of drama and music criticism. He was a forceful and brilliant writer; his articles were often tinged with caustic wit directed against incompetent performers and, regrettably, against many modern composers; he also disliked Brahms, and was credited with the celebrated but possibly apocryphal quip that the exits in the newly opened Symph. Hall in Boston should have been marked not "Exit in Case of Fire," but "Exit in Case of Brahms." Another verbal dart attributed to Philip Hale was his dismissal of a singer with the concluding sentence "Valuable time was consumed." Hale was the music critic for the *Boston Home Journal* (1889–91), the *Boston Post* (1890–91), the *Boston Journal* (1891–1903), and the *Boston Herald,* of which he was also drama editor (1904–33). He was also editor of the *Boston Musical Record* (1897–1901). From 1901–33 he compiled the program books of the Boston Symph. Orch., setting a standard of erudition and informative annotation. He edited *Modern French Songs* for The Musician's Library (1904); was joint author, with Louis C. Elson, of *Famous Composers and Their Works* (1900). Hale was succeeded as the program annotator of the Boston Symph. by John N. Burk, who publ. a selection of

Hale's articles under the title *Philip Hale's Boston Symphony Programme Notes* (N.Y., 1935; revised ed., 1939). Hale's voluminous archives and collections of newspaper articles are preserved in the Music Division of the Boston Public Library.

Hales, Hubert (James), English composer; b. Bradford, April 29, 1902; d. Cromer, July 13, 1965. He studied at Eton College and at King's College in Cambridge; subsequently devoted himself to teaching; occupied various posts as director of music in British schools and colleges. He wrote several works for orch., a String Quartet, and a number of piano pieces.

Halévy, Jacques-François-Fromental-Elie, celebrated French opera composer; b. Paris, May 27, 1799; d. Nice, March 17, 1862. He was a child prodigy. At 10 he entered the Paris Cons. as an elementary pupil of Cazot. In 1810 he studied piano with Lambert; in 1811, harmony with Berton; and counterpoint for 5 years with Cherubini. At 17 he competed for the Prix de Rome, winning the 2nd prize with his cantata *Les Derniers Moments du Tasse;* in 1817 he again won the 2nd prize, with *La Mort d'Adonis;* in 1819 he gained the Grand Prix de Rome with his *Herminie.* He had previously composed an opera, *Les Bohémiennes* (never perf.), publ. a Piano Sonata for 4-hands, and set to music the 130th Psalm in Hebrew, the De Profundis. During his stay in Italy he wrote another opera. In 1822, on his return to Paris, he made vain attempts to produce his grand opera *Pygmalion* and *Les Deux Pavillons,* a comedy-opera. It was not until 1827 that he brought out a one-act comedy-opera, *L'Artisan,* at the Théâtre Feydeau, though with little success. The same year he succeeded Daussoigne as prof. of harmony and accompaniment at the Cons., following Fétis as prof. of counterpoint and fugue in 1833, and taking a class of advanced composition in 1840. In 1827 he was engaged as the harpsichordist at the Italian Opera. In 1828, with Rifaut, he composed *Le Roi et le bâtelier* in honor of Charles X. On Dec. 9 of the same year, *Clari* (with Malibran as prima donna) was a success at the Théâtre Italien; *Le Dilettante d'Avignon* was produced on Nov. 7, 1829; and on May 3, 1830, the grand ballet *Manon Lescaut.* Halévy was now appointed "chef du chant" at the Opéra, a post he retained for 16 years. In 1831 *La Langue musicale* was produced at the Opéra-Comique; then *La Tentation* (Paris, June 20, 1832; ballet-opera, with Gide), at the Opéra; *Les Souvenirs de Lafleur,* at the Opéra-Comique (March 4, 1833); and on May 16 of 1933, a completion of Hérold's unfinished *Ludovic,* which proved very successful. On Feb. 23, 1835, the Paris Opéra produced Halévy's masterpiece, *La Juive,* which soon became one of the most spectacular successes in opera theaters throughout Europe and America. A few months later appeared *L'Eclair* (Dec. 16, 1835), a sparkling comedy-opera. To add to his growing reputation, Halévy was created a Chevalier of the Legion of Honor. On the death of Reicha (1836), Halévy succeeded him as one of the 3 musical members of the Académie; and in 1854 he was appointed Secretary for life. With *La Juive* Halévy attained not only the zenith of his powers, but also of his triumphs. *La Juive* was followed by *Guido et Ginevra* (March 5, 1838); *Les Treize* (April 15, 1839); *Le Shérif* (Sept. 2, 1839); *Le Drapier* (Jan. 6, 1840); *Le Guitarrero* (Jan. 21, 1841); *La Reine de Chypre* (Dec. 22, 1841); *Charles VI* (Feb. 3, 1843); *Le Lazzarone* (March 23, 1844); and *Les Mousquetaires de la reine* (March 15, 1846). He collaborated with Adam, Auber, and Carafa in *Les Premiers Pas* for the inauguration of the National Opera (1847). His next productions were: *Le Val d'Andorre* (Nov. 11, 1848); *La Fée aux roses* (Oct. 1, 1849); *La Dame de pique* (Dec. 28, 1850). On June 8, 1850, Halévy conducted in London an Italian opera, *La Tempesta.* He then produced in Paris *Le Juif errant* (April 23, 1852); *Le Nabab* (Sept. 1, 1853); *jaguarita* (May 14, 1855); *L'Inconsolable* (under the nom de plume **Albert;** 1855); *Valentine d'Aubigny* (1856); *La Magicienne* (March 17, 1858). Besides his operas, Halévy wrote a Piano Sonata for 4-hands; romances; nocturnes; part-songs for men's voices; scenes from *Prometheus Unbound* (Paris, March 18, 1849); and the cantatas *Italie* (1849) and *Les Plagues due Nil* (1959); he also left the almost-finished scores of 2 operas, *Vanina d'Ornano* and *Le Déluge* (originally *Noé,* completed by Bizet; perf. April 5, 1885). In the Paris schools his *Leçons de lecture musicale* (Paris, 1857) was adopted as the textbook for singing. *Souvenirs et portraits* (1861) and *Derniers souvenirs et portraits* (1863) were collections of the funeral orations that, as secretary of the Académie, he had delivered at the obsequies of deceased members. At the Paris Cons. he had many distinguished pupils, among them Gounod and Bizet (who married Halévy's daughter).

BIBLIOGRAPHY: Short biographies of Halévy were publ. by his brother Léon (1862), E. Monnais (1863), A. Catelin (1863), and A. Pougin (1865); see also Mina Curtiss, "F. Halévy," *Musical Quarterly* (April 1953).

Haley, Bill (real name, **William John Clifton Haley, Jr.**), popular American singer, guitarist, and bandleader; b. Highland Park, Mich., July 6, 1925; d. Harlingen, Texas, Feb. 9, 1981. He began to play guitar as a youth, and at the age of 15 embarked on a tour with country and western groups; soon he formed his own band, The Saddlemen; in 1952 it was renamed The Comets, to impart a more cosmological beat to the music. Haley precipitated the rock-'n-roll era with his rendition of *Crazy Man Crazy* in 1953; there followed his hit version of Joe Turner's *Shake, Rattle and Roll,* which combined the elements of the blues, country music, and urban pop. His fame skyrocketed in 1955 with his strident projection of *Rock around the Clock.* Immortalized in the motion picture *Blackboard Jungle,* it became the banner of the rising generation of long-haired, wide-eyed, loose-eared, spaced-out, stoned American youth; 22 million albums of this song were sold. But like so many instinctual musicians of the period, Haley gradually sank into a state of oblivious torpor, and his once-agile style gave way to the irresistible ascent of the more sexually explicit art of Elvis Presley.

Halffter, Cristóbal, significant Spanish composer and conductor, nephew of **Ernesto** and **Rodolfo Halffter;** b. Madrid, March 24, 1930. He studied composition with Conrado del Campo at the Cons. in Madrid (1947–51); then had private lessons with Alexandre Tansman in Paris. He taught at the Madrid Cons. (1960–67) and was associated with the Radio Nacional de España; traveled as a conductor and lecturer in Europe; visited the U.S. in 1966. In his music he adopted a radical modern idiom; evolved a modified technique of dodecaphonic writing, and explored electronic sound.

WORKS: FOR THE STAGE: Opera, *Don Quichotte* (Düsseldorf, 1970); ballet, *Saeta* (Madrid, Oct. 28, 1955). FOR ORCH.: *Scherzo* for Orch. (1951); Piano Concerto (Madrid, March 13, 1954); *2 Movements for Timpani and Strings* (Madrid, June 26, 1957); Concertino for String Orch. (1956; expanded version of his First String Quartet); *5 Microformas* for Orch. (1960); *Rhapsodia española de Albeniz* for Piano and Orch. (1960); Sinfonia for 3 Instrumental Groups (1963); *Sequencias* for Orch. (1964; Madrid, June 16, 1964); *Lineas y puntos* for 20 Winds and Tape (1967; Donaueschingen, Oct. 22, 1967); *Anillos* for Orch. (1967–68; perf. as a ballet, Lyons, April 13, 1971); *Fibonaciana,* concerto for Flute and String Orch. (Lisbon, May 30, 1970); *Planto por las victimas de la violencia (Plaint for the Victims of Violence)* for Chamber Ensemble and Tape (Donaueschingen, Oct. 17, 1971); *Requiem por la libertad imaginada* for Orch. (1971); *Pinturas negras* for Orch. and Concertante Organ (1972); *Procesional* for 2 Pianos, Winds, and Percussion (Strasbourg, June 8, 1974); *Tiempo para espacios* for Harpsichord and 12 Strings (1974); Cello Concerto (1974; Granada, June 24, 1975); *Elegias a la muerte de tres poetas españoles* for Orch. (1974–75); *Pourquoi* for 12 Strings (1974–75); *Officium defunctorum* (Paris, 1979); Violin Concerto. FOR VOICE: *Antifona Pascual a la Virgen (Regina coeli)* for Soprano, Contralto, and Orch. (1951); *Misa ducal* for Chorus and Orch. (Madrid, May 14, 1956); *In exspectatione resurrectionis Domini,* cantata (1962); *Brecht-Lieder* for Voice and Orch. (1967); *In memoriam Anaick* for Child Narrator, Children's Chorus, and ad lib. Instruments (1967); *Symposion* for Baritone, Chorus, and Orch. (1968); *Yes Speak Out Yes,* cantata, after a text by Norman Corwin, in honor of the 20th anniversary of the UN's declaration of human rights (N.Y., Dec. 12, 1968); *Noche pasiva del sentido* for Soprano, 2 Percussionists, and Tapes (1971); *Gaudium et Spes* for 32 Voices and Tapes (1972); *Oración a Platero* for Narrator, Chorus, Children's Chorus, and 5 Percussionists (1975). CHAMBER MUSIC: 2 string quartets: No. 1, *3 Pieces* (1955), and No. 2, *Memories, 1970* (1970); *3 Pieces* for Solo Flute (1959); Solo Violin Sonata (1959); *Codex* for Guitar (1963); *Espejos (Mirrors)* for 4 Percussionists and Tape (1963); *Antiphonismoi* for 7 Players (1967); *Oda* for 8 Players (1969); *Noche activa del espiritu* for 2 Pianos and

Electronics (1973); *Mijar* for 2 Flutes and Electronic Ensemble (Basel, June 1, 1980). FOR PIANO: Sonata (1951), and *Formantes* for 2 Pianos (1961).

Halffter, Ernesto, important Spanish composer, brother of **Rodolfo Halffter;** b. Madrid, Jan. 16, 1905. He studied composition with Manuel de Falla and Adolfo Salazar; as a young man he organized a chamber ensemble in Seville, with which he presented works by contemporary Spanish composers. He first attracted the attention of the music world with his *Sinfonietta,* which was included in the program of the Oxford Festival of the International Society for Contemporary Music (July 23, 1931). At the outbreak of the Spanish Civil War in 1936, he went to Lisbon; returned to Madrid in 1960. In his music he continued the tradition of Spanish modern nationalism, following the stylistic and melorhythmic formations of his teacher Manuel de Falla; he also completed and orchestrated Falla's unfinished scenic cantata, *Atlántida,* which was first performed at La Scala in Milan on June 18, 1962. His other significant works are *Fantaisie portugaise* for Orch. (Paris, March 23, 1941); *Automne malade* for Voice and Orch.; *Suite ancienne* for Wind Instruments; chamber opera, *Entr'acte* (1964); ballets: *Sonatina* (1928); *Dulcinea* (1940); *Cojo enamorado* (1954); *Fantasía galaica* (1955; Milan, 1967); *Rapsodia portuguesa* for Piano and Orch. (1962); *Canticum in memoriam P.P. Johannem XXIII* for Soprano, Baritone, Chorus, and Orch. (1964); *Psalmen* for Soloist, Chorus, and Orch. (1967); Guitar Concerto (1968).

BIBLIOGRAPHY: A. Salazar, *La música contemporanea en España* (Madrid, 1930).

Halffter, Rodolfo, eminent Spanish-Mexican composer, brother of **Ernesto** and uncle of **Cristóbal;** b. Madrid, Oct. 30, 1900. He acquired a considerable technique of composition, mainly by the study of classical works; received some instruction and advice from Manuel de Falla in Granada (1929). As a young man he was a member of a group of Spanish composers promoting national Spanish music in a modern idiom. From 1934–36 he was a music critic of *La Voz.* During the Spanish Civil War, he occupied important positions in the cultural sections of the Loyalist government; was chief of the Music Section of the Ministry of Propaganda (1936) and then became a member of the Central Music Council of the Spanish Republic (1937); after the Loyalist defeat, he fled to France and then to Mexico, where he settled in 1939 and became a naturalized citizen. In 1940 he founded the first Mexican company for contemporary ballet, La Paloma Azul; founded the publishing house Ediciones Mexicanas de Música in 1946 and remains its manager; edited the journal *Nuestra Música* (1946–52); was director of the music dept. of the National Inst. of Fine Arts (1959–64). WORKS: His early music is influenced by Manuel de Falla and is imbued with Spanish melorhythms; he experimented with dodecaphonic structures; his *3 hojas de álbum* (1953) were the earliest pieces of 12-tone music publ. in Mexico. The scores of his opera buffa *Clavileño* (1934–36) and an *Impromptu for Orch.* (1931–32) were lost when a bomb hit the house where he stayed on the Spanish border during the Civil War. His other works include 3 ballets: *Don Lindo de Almería* (1935; Mexico City, Jan. 9, 1940); *La madrugada del Panadero (The Baker's Morning;* Mexico City, Sept. 20, 1940); *Elena la Traicionera* (Mexico City, Nov. 23, 1945); Suite for Orch. (1924–28; Madrid, Nov. 5, 1930); *Obertura concertante* for Piano and Orch. (1932; Valencia, May 23, 1937); Divertimento for 9 Instruments (1935; Mexico City, Nov. 18, 1943); Violin Concerto (1939–40; Mexico City, June 26, 1942); an orch. scoring of *3 sonatas* of Antonio Soler (1951); *Obertura festiva* (Mexico City, May 25, 1953); *3 piezas* for String Orch. (Mexico City, Aug. 10, 1955); *Tripartita* for Orch. (Mexico City, July 15, 1960); *Diferencias* for Orch. (Mexico City, Sept. 13, 1970); *Alborada* for Orch. (Mexico City, May 9, 1976); *Giga* for Solo Guitar (1930); *Pastorale* for Violin and Piano (1940); *3 piezas breves* for Solo Harp (1944); String Quartet (1957–58); Cello Sonata (1960); *3 movimientos* for String Quartet (1962); *8 tientos (Fantasias)* for String Quartet (1973). FOR PIANO: *2 sonatas de El Escorial* (1928); *Preludio y fuga* (1932); *Danza de Ávila* (1936); *Pequeñas variaciones elegiacas* (1937); *Homenaje a Antonio Machado* (1944); 3 sonatas (1947, 1951, 1967); *11 bagatelles* (1949); *3 hojas de álbum* (1953); *Música* for 2 Pianos (1965); *Laberinto: Cuatro intentos de acertar con la salida (Labyrinth: 4 Attempts to Locate the Exit;* 1971–72); *Homenaje a Arturo Rubinstein* (1973); *Facetas* (1976). FOR VOICE: *La nuez* for Children's Chorus (1944); *3 epitafios* for Chorus a cappella (1947–53); *Pregón para una Pascua pobre* for Chorus, 3 Trumpets, 2 Tenor Trombones, Bass Trombone, and Percussion (Mexico City, April, 6, 1969); 3 song cycles: *Marinero en tierra* (1925); *2 sonetos* (1940–46); *Desterro* (1967).

Halíř, Carl, distinguished violinist; b. Hohenelbe, Bohemia, Feb. 1, 1859; d. Berlin, Dec. 21, 1909. He was a pupil of Bennewitz at the Prague Cons., and of Joachim in Berlin. In 1884 he was appointed concertmaster of the court orch. at Weimar; in 1893 he obtained a similar post in Berlin; was also appointed prof. at the Hochschule für Musik there; for a time he was a member of the Joachim Quartet, but later formed his own quartet (with Exner, Müller, and Dechert), which became famous. His tour of the U.S. (1896–97) was very successful. His pedagogic exercises for the violin, *Tonleiterstudien,* are still in use. In 1888 he married **Theresa Zerbst,** a fine soprano.

Hall, Charles King, English composer and writer; b. London, 1845; d. there, Sept. 1, 1895. He was an organist at various London churches; publ. *A School for Harmonium,* and produced a number of operettas, some of which were successful in their day (*Foster Brothers, Doubleday's Will, A Tremendous Mystery, The Artful Automaton, A Strange House, A Christmas Stocking,* etc.).

Hall, David, American writer on music; b. New Rochelle, N.Y., Dec. 16, 1916. He was educated at Yale Univ. (B.A., 1939) and Columbia Univ. (graduate study in psychology, 1939–40); then worked for Columbia Records and NBC; from 1948 to 1956 he was music director of the classics division of the Mercury Record Corp., where he pioneered in the development of high-fidelity recordings; then was music editor of *Stereo Review* (1957–62); later was named president of Composers Recordings, Inc. (1963–66). From 1967 to 1980 he was head of the Rodgers and Hammerstein Archives of Recorded Sound at the N.Y. Public Library, and from 1980 its curator. He publ. several annotated guides to recordings; also contributed countless articles and record reviews to leading publications.

Hall, John, English songwriter; b. c.1529; d. c.1566. He was a surgeon by profession and a musician by avocation. A collection consisting of 30 melodies and one song in 4 parts has been preserved, entitled *The Court of Vertu* (London, 1565; modern ed. publ. by R. Fraser, London, 1961).

Hall, Marie (Mary Paulina), English violinist; b. Newcastle upon Tyne, April 8, 1884; d. Cheltenham, Nov. 11, 1956. As a small child she gave performances in the homes of music-lovers in Newcastle, Malvern, and Bristol with her father, an amateur harp player; her uncle (violin); her brother (violin); and her sister (harp). Elgar heard her, and was impressed by her talent; he sent her to Wilhelmj in London for regular study; she also studied with Johann Kruse. At the age of 15 she won the first Wessely Exhibition at the Royal Academy of Music. She was recommended by Jan Kubelik to Ševčik in Prague (1901), from whom she received a rigorous training; she made her professional debut in Prague (1902); then played in Vienna. After a highly successful London concert (Feb. 16, 1903), she made her American debut as soloist with the N.Y. Symph., Walter Damrosch conducting (Nov. 8, 1905); toured Australia (1907) and India (1913). On Jan. 27, 1911, she married her manager, Edward Baring, and settled in Cheltenham; she continued to appear in concerts in England until 1955, with her daughter, **Pauline Baring,** as her accompanist.

BIBLIOGRAPHY: J. Cuthbert Hadden, "Marie Hall," in *Modern Musicians* (Edinburgh, 1913; pp. 176–83).

Hall, Pauline, Norwegian composer; b. Hamar, Aug. 2, 1890; d. Oslo, Jan. 24, 1969. She studied composition with Catharinus Elling in Oslo (1910–12) and later in Paris (1912–14) and Dresden. From 1934 to 1964 she served as music critic of *Dagbladet.* In her music, Pauline Hall follows the modern French ideal of classical clarity, seasoned with euphonious dissonance.

WORKS: *Verlaine Suite* for Orch. (1929); *Circus Sketches,* orch. suite (1933); Suite for Wind Quintet (1945); *Little Dance Suite* for Oboe, Clarinet, and Bassoon (1958); *4 tosserier* for Soprano, Clarinet, Bassoon, Horn, and Trumpet (1961); *Variations on a Classical Theme* for Solo Flute (1961); *Markisen*

(The Marquise), ballet (1964).

Hall, Sir Peter, noted English theater and opera producer; b. Bury St. Edmunds, Nov. 22, 1930. He was educated at St. Catharine's College, Cambridge. In 1955–56 he was director of the Arts Theatre, London. He was managing director of the Royal Shakespeare Theatre from 1960 to 1968; from 1973 he was director of the National Theatre; worked also at the Royal Opera House, Covent Garden. In 1970 he began a long and fruitful association as an opera producer at Glyndebourne. He was knighted in 1977. He is known for his versatility, having produced operas by Cavalli, Mozart, Wagner, Tchaikovsky, Schoenberg, and Tippett. In 1983 he produced the new *Ring* cycle at Bayreuth for the 100th anniversary of Wagner's death, with Solti conducting.

Hall, Tom T., American country-music singer and songwriter; b. Olive Hill, Ky., May 25, 1936. He sang on a local radio station as a youth; then served in the army. He made many appearances on television, often giving vent to his liberal views in the form of social commentary. Of his songs, *Harper Valley P.T.A.* achieved popular success.

Hall, Walter Henry, English-American organist and choral conductor; b. London, April 25, 1862; d. New York, Dec. 11, 1935. He studied at the Royal Academy of Music; settled in America in 1883; was organist at various churches in Pennsylvania before settling in N.Y.; was organist at St. James' (1896–1913). In 1893 he founded the Brooklyn Oratorio Society, which he led until his death; also conducted the Musurgia Society (1889–1906); was a lecturer in music at Columbia Univ. (1909–30).

Hallberg, Björn Wilho, Norwegian-born Swedish composer; b. Oslo, July 9, 1938. He studied with Bjarre Brustad and Finn Mortensen; in 1962 came to Sweden, where he studied with Lidholm, Bo Wallner, and Blomdahl at the Royal College of Music in Stockholm; also took sporadic lessons with Ligeti. His own compositions are exploratory in techniques.
WORKS: Opera, *Evakueringen (The Evacuation;* 1969; Stockholm, Dec. 9, 1969); *Felder* for Flute and Percussion (Vienna Festival, June 17, 1961); String Quartet (1963); *Ur dagboken (From the Diary)* for Percussion Ensemble (1964); Etudes for Chamber Ensemble (1966); *Missa pro defunctis,* in memory of Dag Hammarskjöld, for Soprano, Chorus, Tape, and Orch. (Stockholm, May 17, 1968); *Conversation/ Vide* for 5 Singers, 5 Woodwinds, Tape, and Loudspeakers (1968); *Etats* for Soprano, Flute, Double Bass, Piano, and Percussion (1970); *Aspiration* for Orch. (Östersund, July 11, 1971); *Novelletten* for Orch. (1973); *Die Drohung,* ballet music for Wind Orch. (1973).

Halle, Adam de la. See **Adam de la Halle.**

Hallé, Sir Charles (real name, **Carl Hallé**), renowned pianist and conductor; b. Hagen, Westphalia, April 11, 1819; d. Manchester, Oct. 25, 1895. The son of a local church organist, he revealed a musical talent as a child, and performed in public at the age of 4; at 16 he was sent to study music seriously with Rinck at Darmstadt; in 1836 he went to Paris, where he entered the friendly circle of Chopin, Liszt, and others. In 1846 he gave concerts of his own as a pianist in chamber music. After the Revolution of 1848, he went to England, settling in Manchester, where he conducted an orch., choruses, and opera. In 1857 he established subscription concerts with an orch. ensemble of his own, which became famous as Charles Hallé's Orch. (debut, Jan. 30, 1858); he conducted it until his death; it endured for 125 years as one of the finest orchs. of Europe, eventually becoming known as the Hallé Orch. Although his chief activities were connected with Manchester, he also conducted the London Popular Concerts; gave piano recitals; in 1861 he presented all of Beethoven's sonatas in 8 concerts, repeating this cycle in 2 successive seasons. From 1873 till 1893 he conducted the Bristol Festivals; in 1883 he became conductor of the Liverpool Phil. Society, as successor to Max Bruch; in 1893 was appointed the first principal of the Royal Manchester College of Music. He was a champion of Berlioz in England, and gave several complete performances of Berlioz's *Damnation de Faust.* His first wife was Désirée Smith de Rilieu; with his 2nd wife, the violinist **Wilma Neruda,** he made 2 Australian tours (1890 and 1891). He was knighted in 1888. He established a very high standard of excellence in orch. performance, which greatly influenced musical life in England. He publ. a *Pianoforte School* (1873) and edited a *Musical Library* (1876). M. Kennedy edited *The Autobiography of Charles Hallé* (London, 1972).
BIBLIOGRAPHY: L. Engel, *From Handel to Hallé* (London, 1890); C.E. and M. Hallé, *Life and Letters of Sir Charles Hallé* (London, 1896); C. Rigby, *Sir Charles Hallé* (Manchester, 1952); C.B. Rees, *100 Years of the Hallé* (London, 1957); M. Kennedy, *Hallé Orchestra* (Manchester, 1968; revised ed., 1976); idem, *The Hallé, 1858–1983* (Manchester, 1983).

Hallén, (Johannes) Andreas, notable Swedish composer; b. Göteborg, Dec. 22, 1846; d. Stockholm, March 11, 1925. He studied with Reinecke in Leipzig, Rheinberger in Munich, and Rietz in Dresden; upon his return to Sweden, conducted in Göteborg (1872–78 and 1883–84); then was conductor of the Phil. Concerts in Stockholm (1884–92) and of the Royal Opera (1892–97). From 1908–19 he was a prof. of composition at the Stockholm Cons.
WORKS: Operas: *Harald der Viking* (Leipzig, Oct. 16, 1881); *Hexfällan* (Stockholm, March 16, 1896); *The Treasure of Waldemar* (Stockholm, April 8, 1899); *Walpurgis Night* (revised version of *Hexfällan;* Stockholm, March 15, 1902); choral works, with Orch.: *The Page and the King's Daughter; Dream-King and His Love; Goblin's Fate; Christmas Eve; Peace; Missa solemnis* (Stockholm, 1923);

symph. poems: *En Sommarsaga; Die Toteninsel; Sphärenklänge;* overtures.
BIBLIOGRAPHY: P. Vretblad, *Andreas Hallén* (Stockholm, 1918).

Haller, Michael, German church composer; b. Neusaat, Jan. 13, 1840; d. Regensburg, Jan. 4, 1915. He was educated at Matten monastery; took Holy Orders in 1864; was appointed prefect of the Regensburg Cathedral Choristers' Inst.
WORKS: 14 masses; Psalms; litanies; a Te Deum; melodramas; string quartets; etc. He completed the 3rd-choir parts of 6 compositions *a* 12 of Palestrina, which had been lost (vol. XXVI of the complete ed.).
WRITINGS: *Vademecum für den Gesangsunterricht* (1876; 12th ed., 1910); *Kompositionslehre für den polyphonen Kirchengesang* (1891); *Modulation in den Kirchentonarten; Exempla polyphoniae ecclesiasticae* (in modern notation, with explanatory notes).

Hallgrimsson, Haflidi Magnus, Icelandic composer and cellist; b. Akureyri, Sept. 18, 1941. He graduated from the Icelandic Music Cons. in 1962; then studied at the Santa Cecilia Academy in Rome and the Royal Academy in London; also took private lessons with Alan Bush and P.M. Davies. Returning to Iceland, he was active as a cello player.
WORKS: 2 string quartets (1962, 1964); Fantasia for Solo Cello (1969); *Elegy* for Mezzo-soprano, Piano, Celesta, Flute, and 2 Cellos (1971); Duo for Viola and Cello (1972); *Hoa-Haka-Nana-Ia* for Clarinet, Strings, and Percussion (1972); *7 Icelandic Folk Songs* for Cello and Piano (1973); Divertimento for Harpsichord and String Trio (1974); *2 Icelandic Folk Songs* for Mezzo-soprano, Clarinet, Flute, Cello, and Piano (1974).

Hallnäs, Hilding, Swedish composer and organist; b. Halmstad, May 24, 1903. He studied at the Royal Academy of Music in Stockholm (1924–29); subsequently served as church organist in Göteborg, where he was also active as a teacher. His works reflect the prevalent Romantic style of Scandinavian music; in later compositions he applies modified serial techniques.
WORKS: He wrote 9 symphs., but withdrew the first 2 and renumbered the others: No. 1, *Sinfonia pastorale* (1944; Göteborg, March 22, 1945); No. 2, *Sinfonia notturna* (Göteborg, March 4, 1948); No. 3, *Little Symphony,* for Strings and Percussion (Göteborg, Oct. 3, 1948); No. 4, *Metamorfose sinfonische* (Göteborg, April 17, 1952; revised 1960); No. 5, *Sinfonia aforistica* (Göteborg, Jan. 24, 1963); No. 6, *Musica intima,* for Strings and Percussion (Malmö, Nov. 7, 1967); No. 7, *A Quite Small Symphony,* for Chamber Orch. (Minneapolis, June 12, 1974). He further wrote 2 ballets, *Kärlekens ringdans (Love's Dance in the Round;* 1955–56) and *Ifigenia* (1961–63; also a suite); Divertimento for Orch. (1937); 2 violin concertos (1945, 1965); *Symphonic Ballet Suite* (1955–56); Piano Concerto (1956); *Cantica lyrica* for Tenor, Chorus, and Orch. (1957); 2 concertos for Flute, Strings, and Percussion (1957, 1962);

Concerto for String Orch. and Percussion (1959); *Epitaph* for Strings (1963); *Rapsodie* for Chamber Orch. and Soprano (1963); *En grekisk saga (A Greek Saga)* for Orch. (1967–68; dedicated to Melina Mercouri, Mikis Theodorakis, and the Greek people); *Momenti bucolichi* for Oboe and Orch. (1969); *Horisont och linjespel* for String Orch. (1969); *Triple Concerto* for Violin, Clarinet, Piano, and Orch. (1972–73); 2 string quartets (1949, 1967); Quintet for Flute, Oboe, Viola, Cello, and Piano (1954); *Cantata* for Soprano, Flute, Clarinet, Cello, and Piano (1955); 2 violin sonatas (1957, 1975); piano trio, *Stanze sensitive* (1959); 3 piano sonatas (1963–75); organ sonata, *De Profundis* (1965); *24 Preludes* for Guitar (1967); *Passionsmusik,* 15 pieces for Organ (1968); *3 momenti musicali* for Violin, Horn, and Piano (1971); *Invocatio* for Chorus and String Quartet (1971); *Confessio,* trio for Clarinet, Cello, and Piano (1973); *Triptykon* for Violin, Clarinet, and Piano (1973).

Hallström, Ivar, significant Swedish composer; b. Stockholm, June 5, 1826; d. there, April 11, 1901. He studied jurisprudence at the Univ. of Uppsala; there he became a friend of Prince Gustaf, who was himself a musical amateur; on April 9, 1847, jointly with Gustaf, he produced in Stockholm an opera, *The White Lady of Drottningholm;* in 1853 he became librarian to Prince Oscar; in 1861–72 he was director of Lindblad's music school in Stockholm. His 2nd opera, *Hertig Magnus,* was produced at the Royal Opera in Stockholm on Jan. 28, 1867, but had only 6 performances in all, purportedly because it contained more arias in minor keys (10, to be exact) than those in major (only 8). He then produced another opera, *The Enchanted Cat* (Stockholm, April 20, 1869), which was more successful. With his next opera, *Den Bergtagna (The Bewitched One),* produced in Stockholm on May 24, 1874, he achieved his greatest success; it had repeated performances not only in Sweden, but also in Germany and Denmark. In this work Hallström made use of Swedish folk motifs, a pioneer attempt in Scandinavian operatic art. His next opera, *Vikingarna* (Stockholm, June 6, 1877), was but moderately successful; there followed *Neaga* (Stockholm, Feb. 24, 1885), to a libretto by Carmen Sylva (Queen Elisabeth of Rumania). He also wrote several ballets, cantatas, and arrangements of Swedish folk songs for piano.

Halm, August, German composer and writer; b. Gross-Altdorf, Württemberg, Oct. 26, 1869; d. Saalfeld, Feb. 1, 1929. A member of a family of scholars, he received an excellent general education; then studied theology at Tübingen. In 1892 he went to Munich, where he took courses with Rheinberger. Subsequently he devoted himself mainly to musical pedagogy; taught in various schools in Thuringia; conducted choral societies and also wrote music criticism. An August Halm Society was organized after his death. He was a prolific composer, but his music failed to take hold. He wrote 2 symphs., which were performed in Ulm and Stuttgart; a Piano Concerto; 8 string quartets; 2 suites for String

Trio; and a number of piano studies. He publ. *Harmonielehre* (Berlin, 1905); *Von zwei Kulturen der Musik* (Munich, 1913; 3rd ed., 1947); *Die Symphonien A. Bruckners* (Munich, 1914; 2nd ed., 1923); *Von Grenzen und Ländern der Musik* (Munich, 1916); *Einführung in die Musik* (Berlin, 1926); *Beethoven* (Berlin, 1927).

Halvorsen, Johan, Norwegian violinist and composer; b. Drammen, March 15, 1864; d. Oslo, Dec. 4, 1935. He studied violin with Lindberg at the Stockholm Cons.; was concertmaster of the Bergen Orch.; then went to Leipzig to study with Brodsky; subsequently studied with César Thomson in Belgium; returning to Norway in 1892, he became conductor of a theater orch. in Bergen; in 1899 was appointed conductor at the National Theater in Oslo. He was married to a niece of Grieg; this association was symbolic of his devotion to Grieg's art; his music reflects Grieg's influence very strongly. He wrote incidental music to Björnson's *Vasantasena* and *The King,* Drachmann's *Gurre,* Eldegard's *Fossegrimen* and *Dronning Tamara,* and to other works. He further wrote 3 symphs., a Violin Concerto, 2 Norwegian rhapsodies, and several orch. suites on Norwegian themes. His most popular works are the march *Triumphant Entry of the Boyars* and an arrangement of Handel's Passacaglia for Violin, and Viola or Cello.

Halvorsen, Leif, Norwegian violinist and composer; b. Oslo, July 26, 1887; d. there, Dec. 28, 1959. He studied violin with local teachers; then went to St. Petersburg, where he became a pupil of Leopold Auer. Upon his return to Norway, he served as concertmaster in the National Theater Orch. of Oslo (1915–17), then was an opera conductor (1918–21); also led the Fredrikstad Singing Society (1925–47). He wrote much incidental music for theatrical plays; an orch. suite, *Peasant's Legend;* piano pieces; songs.

Ham, Albert, English organist; b. Bath, June 7, 1858; d. Brighton, Feb. 4, 1940. He studied music in Dublin; in 1897 went to Canada, where he taught at the Toronto Cons. and served as a cathedral organist there. He wrote a number of choral works; his choral arrangements of the tune *Little Jack Horner* became very popular.

Hamal, Henri-Guillaume, Belgian organist and composer; b. Liège, Dec. 3, 1685; d. there, Dec. 3, 1752. As a youth he excelled in the various capacities of harpsichord player, singer, and cellist; was also a versatile composer of songs to texts in many languages. However, none of his works is preserved, and his reputation was transmitted mainly by members of his family. His son, **Jean-Noël Hamal** (b. Liège, Dec. 23, 1709; d. there, Nov. 26, 1778), studied with his father and later served as chorus master at the Liège Cathedral; he also traveled in Italy, where he acquired additional knowledge of composition. He wrote a great number of church works: 56 masses, 32 cantatas, 5 oratorios, 179 motets; also

operas, overtures, and numerous pieces for the harpsichord. **Henri Hamal** (b. Liège, July 20, 1744; d. there, Sept. 17, 1820), a nephew of Jean-Noël Hamal, studied with him, and later in Italy. He was a chorus master at the Liège Cathedral for some time. He wrote much church music, of which 3 vols. are preserved in the Royal Library at Brussels.
  BIBLIOGRAPHY: Louis de Lavalleye, *Les Hamal de Liège* (Liège, 1860); M. de Smet, *Jean-Noël Hamal, chanoine impérial et Directeur de la Musique de la Cathédrale Saint-Lambert de Liège: Vie et œuvre* (Brussels, 1959).

Hamari, Julia, Hungarian mezzo-soprano; b. Budapest, Nov. 21, 1942. She was educated at the Academy of Music in Budapest and at the Stuttgart Hochschule für Musik. She then appeared in concerts and lieder recitals, to great acclaim; also made appearances in opera, singing in Stuttgart, Düsseldorf, and at the Salzburg and Holland festivals.

Hambourg a family of musicians of Russian extraction. **Michael Hambourg,** pianist and teacher; b. Yaroslavl, July 12, 1855; d. Toronto, Canada, June 18, 1916. He went to England in 1890; in 1911 moved to Toronto, where he established, with his son Boris, the Hambourg Cons. of Music. **Boris Hambourg,** cellist, son of Michael Hambourg; b. Voronezh, Jan. 8, 1885; d. Toronto, Nov. 24, 1954. He studied cello with Hugo Becker in Frankfurt (1898–1903); in 1910 made an American tour, and in the following year went to Toronto, where he established, with his father, the Hambourg Cons. **Jan Hambourg,** violinist; b. Voronezh, Aug. 27, 1882; d. Tours, France, Sept. 29, 1947. He studied violin with Sauret and Wilhelmj in London, with Sevčik in Prague, and with Eugène Ysaÿe in Brussels. With his brothers Boris and Mark he established the Hambourg Trio; he died during a concert tour in France. **Mark Hambourg,** pianist; b. Bogutchar, June 12, 1879; d. Cambridge, England, Aug. 26, 1960. He studied piano with his father, Michael Hambourg, and made his debut in Moscow at the age of 9; then went to Vienna to study with Leschetizky. He was highly successful as a concert pianist; traveled all over the world; played his 1,000th concert on June 16, 1906. He toured with his brothers Boris and Jan in the U.S. in 1935; then returned to England. He publ. 2 piano manuals, *How to Play the Piano* (Philadelphia, 1922) and *From Piano to Forte; A Thousand and One Notes* (London, 1931); and a book of memoirs, *The Eighth Octave* (London, 1951).

Hamboys, John. See **Hanboys, John.**

Hambraeus, Bengt, prominent Swedish composer, organist, and musicologist; b. Stockholm, Jan. 29, 1928. He took organ lessons with Alf Linder (1944–48); then entered Uppsala Univ. (M.A., 1956); also attended the summer courses in modern music at Darmstadt (1951–55). In 1957 he joined the music staff of the Swedish Broadcasting Corp.; in 1972 was appointed to the faculty of McGill Univ. in Montreal. His style of composition oscillates between modernistic constructivism based on strong dissonant polyphony and sonoristic experimentalism; he is regarded as a leader of the Swedish musical avant-garde.

WORKS: 2 chamber operas: *Experiment X*, making use of Electronic Sound (Stockholm, March 9, 1971), and a church opera, *Se människan* (Stockholm, May 15, 1972); 3 string quartets (1948–64); Concerto for Organ and Harpsichord (1947–51); *Diptychon* for Flute, Oboe, Viola, Celesta, and Harpsichord (1952); *Spectogram* for Soprano and Instrumental Ensemble (1953); *Giuoco del cambio (Play of Changes)* for 5 Instruments and Percussion (1952–54); *Antiphones en rondes* for Soprano and 24 Instruments (1953); *Crystal Sequence* for Soprano Choir and Instrumental Ensemble (1954); *Cercles* for Piano (1955); a 5-work cycle of compositions: *Rota I* for 3 orchs. (Stockholm, May 27, 1964); *Rota II* for Electronically Modulated Organ and Bell Sounds (1963); *Transit I* for Tape (1963); *Transit II* for Horn, Piano, Trombone, and Electric Guitar (1963); *Transfiguration* for Orch. (1962–63; Swedish Radio, Feb. 20, 1965); *Constellations I–III: I* for Organ (1958); *II* for Taped Organ Sounds (1959); *III* includes tape from *II*, plus new, superimposed live organ score (1961); *Introduzione—Sequenze—Coda* for 3 Flutes, 6 Percussion, and Amplifier (1958–59); *Segnali* for 7 String Instruments (1956–60); *Notazioni* for Harpsichord, 10 Wind Instruments, Celesta, and Percussion (1961); *Mikrogram* for Alto Flute, Viola, Harp, and Vibraphone (1961); *Interferences* for Organ (1962); *Responsorier* for Tenor, Chorus, 2 Organs, and Church Bells (1964); *Tetragon (Homenaje a Pablo Picasso)* for Electronically Modulated Soprano and Chamber Ensemble (1965); *Klassiskt spel (Classical Play)*, electronic ballet (1965); *Praeludium, Kyrie, Sanctus* for Solo Voice, 2 Choruses, 2 Organs, and Church Bells (1966); *Motetum Archangeli Michaelis* for Chorus and Organ (1967); *Movimento—Monodia—Shogaku* for Organ (1967); *Fresque sonore* for Electronically Modulated Soprano and Chamber Ensemble (1965–67); *Inventions II* for Piano (1967–68); *Rencontres* for Orch. (Swedish Radio, Aug. 8, 1971); *Pianissimo in due tempi* for 20 String Instruments (1970–72); *Récit de deux* for Soprano (vocalizing and playing percussion), Flute, and Piano (1973); *Ricercare* for Organ (1974); *Carillon (Le Récital oublié)* for 2 Pianos (1974); *Icons* for Organ (1974–75); *Advent* for Organ and 10 Brasses (1975); *Continuo—A partire da Pachelbel* for Organ and Orch. without Violins (1975; Nuremberg, June 5, 1976); *Ricordanza* for Orch. (1976). He publ. a book, *Om notskifter (On Notation;* Stockholm, 1970).

Hamel, Fred, German musicologist; b. Paris, Feb. 19, 1903; d. Hamburg, Dec. 9, 1957. He studied chemistry in Bonn and Berlin and musicology in Berlin and Giessen; in 1930 received his Ph.D. from the Univ. of Giessen with the dissertation *Form und Stilprinzipien in der Vokalmusik Johann Rosenmüllers;* also publ. a monograph on J.S. Bach, *Geistige Welt* (Göttingen, 1951) and contributed numerous articles to German music journals. From 1948 he served as production manager for Deutsche Grammophon Gesellschaft; founded its prestigious Archiv-Produktion of recordings of early music in authentic performances.

Hamel, Marie-Pierre, French organ builder; b. Auneuil, Oise, Feb. 24, 1786; d. Beauvais, July 25, 1879. He was from a family of jurists, and himself pursued a legal career; in 1817 he became a judge at Beauvais. Apart from his professional activities, he was from his childhood interested in music; he manufactured a small organ of 3 octaves at the age of 13, and successfully repaired an old organ in a neighboring village to the satisfaction of the church wardens. He later rebuilt the grand organ of the Cathedral of Beauvais (1826). He publ. several manuals and descriptions of organs in various French cities. His principal writings were *Rapport sur les travaux du grand orgue de l'Eglise de la Madeleine à Paris* (Paris, 1846); *Nouveau manuel complet du facteur d'orgues* (3 vols., Paris, 1849; new ed. by Guédon, 1903; contains a history of organ building).

Hamelle, Jacques, French music publisher; in 1877 he acquired the publishing firm established by J. Maho in 1855. After Hamelle's death in 1917, the business was taken over by his sons. Among the principal composers represented in the catalogue are Franck, Saint-Saëns, Fauré, and Vincent d'Indy.

Hamerik (real name, **Hammerich**), **Asger,** Danish composer; b. Copenhagen, April 8, 1843; d. Frederiksborg, July 13, 1923. He was a son of a prof. of divinity, who discouraged his musical interests; despite this opposition, he studied with Gade in Copenhagen and with Hans von Bülow in Berlin. He met Berlioz in Paris in 1864, and accompanied him to Vienna in 1866, studying orchestration. Hamerik was probably the only pupil that Berlioz had. He received a gold medal for his work *Hymne de la paix,* at the contest for the Paris Exposition. His opera *Tovelille* was performed in Paris in concert form (May 6, 1865); another opera, *Hjalmar and Ingeborg,* was not performed in its entirety. In 1870 he visited Italy and produced his Italian-language opera, *La vendetta* (Milan, Dec. 23, 1870). He then received an invitation to become director of the newly organized Peabody Cons. in Baltimore. He accepted, and remained in Baltimore for 26 years, until 1898, when he returned to Copenhagen. In Baltimore he wrote a number of symph. works, which he conducted with the cons. orch.

WORKS: *5 Nordic Suites* (1872–78); *Symphonie poétique* (1879); *Symphonie tragique* (1881); *Symphonie lyrique* (1885); *Symphonie majestueuse* (1888); *Symphonie sérieuse* (1892); *Symphonie spirituelle* for String Orch. (1895); Choral Symph. (No. 7).

Hamerik, Ebbe, Danish composer, son of **Asger Hamerik;** b. Copenhagen, Sept. 5, 1898; d. there, Aug. 11, 1951 (drowned in the Kattegat). He studied music with his father; was active mainly as a conductor. He composed the operas *Stepan* (Mainz, Nov. 30, 1924); *Leonardo da Vinci* (Antwerp, 1939); *Marie Grubbe* (Copenhagen, May 17, 1940); *Rejsekammeraten,* after Andersen (Copenhagen, Jan. 5, 1946); also 5 symphs., subtitled *Ur cantus firmus I–V* (1937, 1947, 1947–48, 1949, 1950); Wind Quintet (1942); 2 string quartets; piano pieces; songs.

Hamilton, Clarence Grant, American organist and music educator; b. Providence, R.I., June 9, 1865; d. Wellesley, Mass., Feb. 14, 1935. He studied piano with Arthur Foote in Boston and Matthay in London; composition with Chadwick. He occupied various positions as an organist in and around Boston; taught at Wellesley College for many years (1904–34); wrote piano pieces and songs. WRITINGS: *Outlines of Music History* (1908; new ed., 1924); *Piano Teaching* (1910); *Sound and Its Relation to Music* (1911); *Music Appreciation, Based upon Methods of Literary Criticism* (1920); *Piano Music, Its Composers and Characteristics* (1925); *Epochs in Musical Progress* (1926); *Touch and Expression in Piano Playing* (1927); *What Every Piano Pupil Should Know* (1928); *Ornaments in Classical and Modern Music* (1929).

Hamilton, David, American music critic; b. New York, Jan. 18, 1935. He was educated at Princeton Univ. (1952–56; A.B., 1956; M.F.A., music history, 1960); then was music and record librarian at Princeton Univ. (1961–65); in 1965 he became assistant music editor of W.W. Norton & Co. in N.Y.; was music editor from 1968 to 1974. In 1967 he became a contributing editor of *High Fideltiy,* and in 1968, music critic of the *Nation;* also served as N.Y. music correspondent for the *Financial Times* of London (1969–74) and associate editor of the *Musical Newsletter* (1971–77). He wrote *The Listener's Guide to Great Instrumentalists* (N.Y., 1981).

Hamilton, George, IV, American country-music singer; b. Winston-Salem, N.C., July 19, 1937. He was educated at the Univ. of North Carolina and at the American Univ.; while still in college, he began to make appearances as a singer of popular music; made several tours abroad; sang many of his songs in German, Japanese, and other languages for his appearances overseas.

Hamilton, Iain, remarkable Scottish composer; b. Glasgow, June 6, 1922. He was taken to London at the age of 7, and attended Mill Hill School; after graduation he became an apprentice engineer, but studied music in his leisure time. He was 25 years old when he decidedly turned to music as his career; entered the Royal Academy of Music, where he was a piano student of Harold Craxton and a composition student of William Alwyn; concurrently he attended the Univ. of London, obtaining his B.Mus. in 1950. He made astonishing progress as a composer, and upon graduation from the Royal Academy received the prestigious Dove Prize; other awards followed, among them the Royal Phil. Society Prize for his Clarinet Concerto, the Koussevitzky Foundation Award for his 2nd Symph., the Edwin Evans Prize, the Butterworth Award, and the Arnold Bax Gold Medal. From 1952 to 1960 he taught composition at Morley College in London, and during the same period conducted classes in musical analysis at the Univ. of London. In 1962 he received an appointment to the faculty at Duke Univ. in North Carolina; became a prof. there in 1966–67; was resident composer and teacher at Tanglewood in the summer of 1962, and also taught at the Summer School of Music at Dartington Hall in England. In 1970 he received the honorary degree of D.Mus. from Glasgow Univ.; in 1971 he received a professorship at Lehman College, City Univ. of N.Y., but resigned precipitously after a single day because of unacceptable teaching conditions. Apart from his regular pedagogic activities, he has served as a music consultant on various committees, including the Music Advisory Panel of the BBC and the National Music Council. During the first 2 decades of his work as a composer he wrote mainly instrumental music, but beginning in 1966 he devoted himself primarily to the composition of operas, completing 5 opera scores within 10 years; of these, *The Catiline Conspiracy* is acknowledged as his masterpiece. Hamilton's style of composition is marked by terse melodic lines animated by a vibrant rhythmic pulse, creating the impression of kinetic lyricism; his harmonies are built on a set of peculiarly euphonious dissonances, which repose on emphatic tonal centers. For a period of several years he pursued a sui generis serial method, but soon abandoned it in favor of a free modern manner; in his operas he makes use of thematic chords depicting specific dramatic situations. WORKS: OPERAS: *The Royal Hunt of the Sun,* to his own libretto from a play by Peter Shaffer (1966–68; orchestration completed 1975; produced by the English National Opera in London, Feb. 2, 1977); *Agamemnon,* after Aeschylus (1967–69); *Pharsalia,* dramatic commentary with a libretto by the composer from Lucan (1968); *The Catiline Conspiracy,* to a text by the composer, based on Ben Jonson's play (Stirling, Scotland, March 16, 1974); radio opera, *Tamburlaine* (BBC, London, Feb. 14, 1977); *Anna Karenina* (1977–78; London, May 7, 1981). FOR ORCH.: *Variations on an Original Theme* for String Orch. (1948); Symph. No. 1 (1948); Clarinet Concerto (1950); Symph. No. 2 (1951); Violin Concerto (1952); *Bartholomew Fair,* overture (1952); *Symphonic Variations* (1953); *Scottish Dances* (1956); *Sonata* for Chamber Orch. (1957); *Overture: 1912* (1957); Concerto for Jazz Trumpet and Orch. (1957); *Sinfonia for 2 Orchestras* (1958); *Ecossaise* (1959); Piano Concerto (1960); *Arias* for Small Orch. (1962); *The Chaining of Prometheus* for Wind Instruments and Percussion (1963); *Cantos* (1964); Concerto for Organ and Small Orch. (1964); *Circus* for 2 Trumpets and Orch. (1969); *Alastor* (1970); *Voyage* for Horn and Chamber Orch. (1970); *Amphion* (2nd Violin Concerto) for Violin and Orch. (1971); *Commedia,* concerto for Orch. (London, May 4, 1973); *Aurora* (N.Y., Nov. 21, 1975). CHAMBER MUSIC: Quintet No. 1 for Clarinet and String Quartet (1948); String Quartet (1950); Quartet for Flute and String

Trio (1951); *Variations* for Unaccompanied Violin (1951); *3 Nocturnes* for Clarinet and Piano (1951); Viola Sonata (1951); *Capriccio* for Trumpet and Piano (1951); Clarinet Sonata (1954); Octet for Strings (1954); *Songs of Summer* for Soprano, Clarinet, Cello, and Piano (1954); *Serenata* for Violin and Clarinet (1955); Piano Trio (1955); Cello Sonata No. 1 (1959); Sextet for Flute, 2 Clarinets, Violin, Cello, and Piano (1962); *Sonatas and Variants* for 10 Wind Instruments (1963); Brass Quintet (1964); *Sonata notturna* for Horn and Piano (1965); String Quartet No. 2 (1965); *Sonata for 5* for Wind Quintet (1966); Flute Sonata (1966); *Sea Music* (Quintet No. 2) for Clarinet and String Quartet (1971); *5 Scenes* for Trumpet and Piano (1971); Violin Sonata (1974); Cello Sonata No. 2 (1974); *The Alexandrian Sequence* for 12 Instruments (1976). VOCAL WORKS: *The Bermudas* for Baritone, Chorus, and Orch. (1956); Cantata for Tenor and Piano (1957); *5 Love Songs* for Voice and Orch. (1957); *Nocturnal* for 11 Solo Voices (1959); *A Testament of War* for Baritone and Small Ensemble (1961); *Dialogues* for Coloratura Soprano and Small Ensemble (1965); *Epitaph for This World and Time* for 3 Choruses and 2 Organs (1970); *Te Deum* for Mixed Chorus, Wind Instruments, and Percussion (1972); *To Columbus,* a setting of Walt Whitman's poem, for Mixed Chorus, 3 Trumpets, 3 Trombones, and Percussion, written for the U.S. Bicentennial (1976). FOR KEYBOARD: Organ pieces; 2 piano sonatas (1951, 1970); *Nocturnes with Cadenzas* for Piano (1963); *Palinodes* for Piano (1972); *A Vision of Canopus* for Organ (1975).

Hamilton, James Alexander, English musician; b. London, 1785; d. there, Aug. 2, 1845. He was a son of a bookseller; his voluminous reading gave him a fine literary education. He developed a knack of transmitting knowledge acquired from music books to the public in an easy and attractive form; his numerous manuals went through several editions, but because of his intemperate habits, he was always in penury. WRITINGS: *Modern Instructions for the Piano; Catechism of Singing; Catechism of the Rudiments of Harmony and Thoroughbass; Catechism of Counterpoint, Melody and Composition; A New Theoretical and Practical Musical Grammar;* a dictionary of musical terms; trans. Cherubini's *Counterpoint and Fugue.*

Hamlin, George, American tenor; b. Elgin, Ill., Sept. 20, 1868; d. New York, Jan. 20, 1923. He studied irregularly with various teachers; sang in oratorios; made his operatic debut in Victor Herbert's *Natoma* (Philadelphia, Dec. 15, 1911); among his chief parts were Cavaradossi in *Tosca* and Don José in *Carmen.*

Hamlisch, Marvin, American composer of popular music; b. New York, June 2, 1944. His father, an accordionist, trained him in music; he studied piano at the Juilliard School of Music and at Queens College; began writing songs at the age of 15. His first signal success came in 1974, when he won 3 Academy Awards for the music scores for the movies *The Way We Were* and *The Sting.* (For the latter, his award was won for a score written mostly by others: the piano music was by Scott Joplin, composed 60–70 years earlier, and the orchestrations were by Gunther Schuller, adapted from 60-year-old stock arrangements.) In 1975 he wrote the score for the musical *A Chorus Line,* which received the Pulitzer Prize for the play and a Tony award for the best musical score; Universal Pictures bought the cinema rights for $5.5 million. The Broadway production opened on July 25, 1975, to a chorus line of hosannas from otherwise sober-sided critics; a 2nd Broadway production followed in 1976; an international touring company was started in Toronto in May 1976, and a national company began its cross-country tour a few days later.

BIBLIOGRAPHY: *Current Biography* (May 1976).

Hamm, Adolf, church organist and choral conductor; b. Strasbourg, March 9, 1882; d. Basel, Oct. 15, 1938. He studied with Straube in Leipzig; in 1906 settled in Basel, where he became chief organist at the Cathedral; also organized the Bach Choir there; taught at the Basel Cons. Paul Sacher edited a memorial vol., *Adolf Hamm: Erinnerungsschrift* (Basel, 1942).

Hamm, Charles (Edward), American musicologist; b. Charlottesville, Va., April 2, 1925. He studied at the Univ. of Virginia (B.A., 1947) and Princeton Univ. (M.F.A., 1950; Ph.D., 1960, with the dissertation *A Chronology of the Works of Guillaume Dufay,* publ. in Princeton, 1964). He taught at Princeton Univ. (1948–50 and 1958), at the Cincinnati Cons. of Music (1950–57), and at Tulane Univ. (1959–63). In 1963 he was appointed prof. of musicology at the Univ. of Illinois; in 1976 joined the faculty of Dartmouth College. He served as president of the American Musicological Society from 1972–74. A versatile scholar, he publ. books on a variety of subjects; these include *Opera* (Boston, 1966); *Yesterdays: Popular Song in America* (N.Y., 1979); *Music in the New World* (N.Y., 1983).

Hammelboe, Arne, Danish conductor; b. Copenhagen, June 24, 1916. He studied privately, making his conducting debut in 1936. He was a conductor of the Danish State Radio (1943–44); also with the Royal Danish Theater (1945–46). In 1948–49 he was conductor of the orch. and theater in Odense. He then returned to Copenhagen; appeared with many of the Danish orchs. and theaters. In 1957 he was appointed to the faculty of the Royal Danish Cons. of Music.

Hammer, Heinrich Albert Eduard, German-American violinist, conductor, and composer; b. Erfurt, Germany, Oct. 27, 1862; d. Phoenix, Ariz., Oct. 28, 1954. He studied violin with A. Pott and theory with H. Ritter; also took singing lessons with Mme. Viardot-Garcia in Paris. He then lived in the Netherlands (1893–96) and Bochum, Germany (1897–

1901); conducted the Lausanne Symph. Orch. (1901–5); in 1905 he organized a symph. orch. in Göteborg, Sweden. In 1908 he settled in America; conducted his own orch. in Washington, D.C., until 1921, when he went to California; lived mostly in Pasadena. He continued to compose until the end of his long life; at the age of 90, married his pupil Arlene Hammer, who helped him to edit his autobiography. Among his works are a Symph.; 3 American Indian rhapsodies for Orch.; a symph. poem, *Sunset at Sea;* an orch. ode, *Columbia Triumphant in Peace* (1915); and much church music.

Hammerich, Angul, Danish writer on music, brother of **Asger Hamerik** (whose real name was Hammerich); b. Copenhagen, Nov. 25, 1848; d. there, April 26, 1931. He studied cello; at the same time, occupied a post in the Dept. of Finance; wrote music criticism; taught musicology at the Univ. of Copenhagen. In 1898 he founded the Collection of Ancient Musical Instruments; was a founder of the Danish Musicological Society (1921).
WRITINGS: *Studies in Old Icelandic Music* (1900; in Danish and German); *The Conservatory of Music at Copenhagen* (1892; in Danish); *Essay on the Music at the Court of Christian IV* (1892; in German, 1893); *On the Old Norse Lurs* (1893; in German, 1894); *Descriptive Illustrated Catalogue of the Historical Musical Museum of Copenhagen* (1909; in Danish; German trans. by E. Bobé, 1911); *Medieval Musical Relics of Denmark* (1912; in Danish; Eng. trans. by Margaret Williams-Hamerik, 1912); *J.P.E. Hartmann, Biographical Essays* (1916); a history of Danish music to c.1700 (1921).

Hammerschlag, János, music critic and composer; b. Prague, Dec. 10, 1885; d. Budapest, May 21, 1954. He was taken to Budapest as a child and studied music and literature; as a young man, became a newspaper critic; also taught music history and conducted choral concerts at the Budapest Cons. (1919–47); led the Madrigal Society; publ. a book on Bach (Budapest, 1926); numerous other writings (in Hungarian and German) are listed in J.S. Weissmann's article on Hammerschlag in *Die Musik in Geschichte und Gegenwart.*

Hammerschmidt, Andreas, important composer of sacred music; b. Brüx, Bohemia, 1612; d. Zittau, Nov. 8, 1675. In 1626 his father took him to Freiberg, Saxony, and it was there that he received his education; he was appointed organist at Freiberg in 1634, and in 1639 at Zittau, retaining this post until his death. A statue was erected to his memory there. His works for the Lutheran services are of great significance. He was one of the earliest composers to adopt the new Italian style of writing elaborate instrumental accompaniments to polyphonic vocal works.
WORKS: *Musikalische Andachten* (subtitled *Geistliche Concerten*), in 5 parts (1638, 1641, 1642, 1646, 1652); *Dialogi oder Gespräche zwischen Gott und einer gläubigen Seelen,* in 2 parts (Dresden, 1645; first part reprinted in Denkmäler der Tonkunst in Österreich, 16 [8.i]); *Weltliche Oden oder Liebesgesänge,* in 2 parts (1642–43); *Musicalische Gespräche über die Sonntags- und Fest-Evangelia* (Dresden, 1655–56). Reprints by H.J. Moser in *Alte Meister des deutschen Liedes* and A. Schering in *Geschichte der Musik in Beispielen* (no. 194). Hugo Leichtentritt publ. a selection in vol. 40 of the Denkmäler Deutscher Tonkunst; other reprints by Commer in *Musica Sacra* (nos. 25/26), Oppenheimer, Sulzbach, etc.
BIBLIOGRAPHY: E. Steinhard, *Zum 300. Geburtstage Andreas Hammerschmidts* (Prague, 1914); G. Schünemann, "Beiträge zur Biographie Hammerschmidts," *Sammelbände der Internationalen Musik-Gesellschaft,* XII; F. Blume, *Das monodische Prinzip in der protestantischen Kirchenmusik* (Leipzig, 1925).

Hammerstein, Oscar, celebrated impresario; b. Stettin, Germany, May 8, 1846; d. New York, Aug. 1, 1919. At the age of 16 he ran away from home; spent some time in England; then went to America, where he worked in a N.Y. cigar factory. Possessing an inventive mind, he patented a machine for shaping tobacco leaves by suction; later edited a tobacco trade journal. At the same time, he practiced the violin; learned to write music, and dabbled in playwriting; in 1868 he produced in N.Y. a comedy in German; also wrote the libretto and music of an operetta, *The Kohinoor* (N.Y., Oct. 24, 1893). His main activity, however, was in management. He built the Harlem Opera House (1888), the Olympia Music Hall (1895), and the Republic Theater (1900), and presented brief seasons of plays and operas there. In 1906 he announced plans for the Manhattan Opera House in N.Y., his crowning achievement. The enterprise was originally planned as a theater for opera in English, but it opened with an Italian company in Bellini's *Puritani* (Dec. 3, 1906). Hammerstein entered into bold competition with the Metropolitan Opera, and engaged celebrated singers, among them Melba, Nordica, Tetrazzini, and Mary Garden; among the spectacular events presented by him were the first American performances of 5 operas by Massenet, Charpentier's *Louise,* and Debussy's *Pelléas et Mélisande.* The new venture held its own for 4 seasons, but in the end Hammerstein was compelled to yield; in April 1910, he sold the Manhattan Opera House to the management of the Metropolitan for $1.2 million, and agreed not to produce grand opera in N.Y. for 10 years. He also sold to the Metropolitan (for $100,000) his interests in the Philadelphia Opera House, built by him in 1908. (The texts of these agreements were publ. in full in the *Musical Courier* of March 29, 1911.) Defeated in his main ambition in America, Hammerstein transferred his activities to England. There he built the London Opera House, which opened with a lavish production of *Quo Vadis* by Nougès (Nov. 17, 1911). However, he failed to establish himself in London, and after a season there, returned to N.Y. In contravention of his agreement with the Metropolitan, he announced a season at the newly organized American Opera House in

N.Y., but the Metropolitan secured an injunction against him, and he was forced to give up his operatic venture.

BIBLIOGRAPHY: Vincent Sheean, *Oscar Hammerstein, I: The Life and Exploits of an Impresario* (with a preface by Oscar Hammerstein II; N.Y., 1956); J.F. Cone, *Oscar Hammerstein's Manhattan Opera Company* (Norman, Okla., 1966).

Hammerstein, Oscar, II, American lyricist, grandson of the preceding; b. New York, July 12, 1895; d. Highland Farms, Doylestown, Pa., Aug. 23, 1960. He studied law at Columbia Univ., graduating in 1917; then became interested in the theater. He collaborated on the librettos for Friml's *Rose Marie* (1924) and Romberg's *The Desert Song* (1926); his greatest success as a lyricist came with the production of Jerome Kern's *Show Boat* (1926), including the celebrated song *Ol' Man River*. In 1943 he joined hands with the composer Richard Rodgers, and together they produced several brilliant musical comedies, with spectacular success: *Oklahoma!* (1943; Pulitzer Prize); *Carousel* (1945); *Allegro* (1947); *South Pacific* (1949; Pulitzer Prize, 1950); *The King and I* (1951); *Me and Juliet* (1953); *Pipe Dream* (1955); etc. His lyrics are characterized by a combination of appealing sentiment and sophisticated nostalgia, making them particularly well suited to the modern theater.

BIBLIOGRAPHY: Deems Taylor, *Some Enchanted Evenings: The Story of Rodgers and Hammerstein* (N.Y., 1953); David Ewen, *Richard Rodgers* (N.Y., 1957); Max Wilk, *They're Playing Our Song* (N.Y., 1973); Hugh Fordin, *Getting to Know Him, A Biography of Oscar Hammerstein II* (N.Y., 1977).

Hammond, Dame Joan, New Zealand soprano; b. Christchurch, May 24, 1912. She studied at the Sydney Cons.; made her operatic debut in Sydney in 1929; then went to London, where she continued vocal studies with Dino Borgioli; also studied in Vienna. She made her London debut in 1938; then sang with the Vienna State Opera; was a member of the Carl Rosa Opera Co. (1942–45). She made her Covent Garden debut in 1948; also sang with the Sadler's Wells Opera; appeared in the U.S. with the N.Y. City Center Opera in 1949; she retired in 1965. In 1974 she was made a Dame of the British Empire. She wrote an autobiography, *A Voice, a Life* (London, 1970).

Hammond, John Hays, Jr., American organist and manufacturer of organs; b. San Francisco, April 13, 1888; d. New York, Feb. 12, 1965. He studied at Yale Univ. (B.S., 1910); devoted himself to the task of improving pipe organ mechanisms; invented a new type of reflecting modulator for pianos and a dynamic multiplicator for electrical recording; he also patented a gadget named the Pirafon, designed to combine in one unit a piano, a phonograph, and a radio.

Hammond, Laurens, American manufacturer of keyboard instruments; b. Evanston, Ill., Jan. 11, 1895; d. Cornwall, Conn., July 1, 1973. He studied engineering at Cornell Univ.; then went to Detroit to work on the synchronization of electrical motor impulses, a principle which he later applied to the Hammond Organ, an electronic keyboard instrument, resembling a spinet piano, which suggests the sound of the pipe organ. Still later, he developed a newfangled electrical device which he called the Novachord and which was designed to simulate the sound of any known or hypothetical musical instrument; he gave the first demonstration of the Novachord in the Commerce Dept. auditorium in Washington, D.C., on Feb. 2, 1939. In 1940 he introduced the Solovox, an attachment to the piano keyboard which enables an amateur player to project the melody in organlike tones. A further invention that proved attractive to dilettantes was the "chord organ," which he introduced in 1950, and which is capable of supplying basic harmonies when a special button is pressed by the performer.

Hammond-Stroud, Derek, English baritone; b. London, Jan. 10, 1929. He studied with Elena Gerhardt in London and Gerhard Hüsch in Vienna and Munich. He made his debut in London in 1955; in 1962 he joined the Sadler's Wells Opera; was a leading member of the Royal Opera, Covent Garden, from 1971. He made his American debut with the Houston Grand Opera in 1975, and on Dec. 5, 1977, his Metropolitan Opera debut as Faninal in *Der Rosenkavalier*. He was known for his vivid portrayals of the Wagnerian roles of Alberich and Beckmesser; was also a distinguished concert singer.

Hampton, Lionel, American jazz vibraphonist, drummer, pianist, and bandleader; b. Louisville, Ky., April 12, 1909. He played drums in Chicago nightclubs; then moved to Los Angeles, where he formed a band of his own. He was a pioneer in introducing to jazz the vibraphone, on which he is a virtuoso performer; he gained nationwide prominence as a member of the Benny Goodman Quartet from 1936–40. From then on he usually led his own bands, most often playing vibes, but occasionally performing on other instruments; he is the originator of the "trigger-finger" method of piano playing (2 forefingers drumming upon a single note *prestissimo*). Beginning in 1956, he made several successful European tours. In 1965 he gave up his big band and founded a sextet called the Jazz Inner Circle.

Han (Hahn), Ulrich (Udalricus Gallus), German music printer; b. Ingolstadt, c.1425; d. Rome, after 1478. He is believed to be the first to print music with movable type, in his *Missale secundum consuetudinem curie romane* (Rome, 1476). In this work the double-process method was employed, i.e., 2 impressions were made; first, the lines of the staff were printed, following which the note forms (mostly square black heads with a stem at the right side) were superimposed over them.

BIBLIOGRAPHY: O. Kinkeldey, "Music and Music Printing in Incunabula," *Papers of the Bibliographic Society of America* (1932).

Hanboys (or **Hamboys**), **John,** English music theorist of the 15th century. He was one of the first Englishmen on whom the degree of Mus.D. was conferred. He also held an ecclesiastic rank. His Latin treatise *Summa super musicam continuam et discretam,* which describes the musical notation of his time, was printed by Coussemaker in his *Scriptores* (vol. 1, p. 416).

BIBLIOGRAPHY: J. Bale, *Illustrium Maioris Britanniae Scriptorum Catalogus* (1559; p. 617); J. Pulver, *Biographical Dictionary of Old English Music* (1923); idem, "The English Theorists, VI; John Hanboys," *Musical Times* (March 1934).

Hanchett, Henry Granger, American music pedagogue and inventor; b. Syracuse, N.Y., Aug. 29, 1853; d. Siasconset, Mass., Aug. 19, 1918. He studied at the N.Y. Homeopathic Medical College (M.D., 1884); at the same time he pursued pianistic studies with various teachers; held teaching positions in music schools in N.Y. and elsewhere; also was organist at many churches (1884–98). In 1874 he obtained a patent for the sustaining piano pedal, now in use on all grand pianofortes. He publ. *Teaching as a Science* (1882), *The Art of the Musician* (1905), and *An Introduction to the Theory of Music* (1918); also wrote several church services and anthems.

Hancock, Herbie (Herbert Jeffrey Hancock), black American jazz pianist; b. Chicago, April 12, 1940. A precocious musician, he made an appearance with the Chicago Symph. Orch. at 12; growing to maturity, he studied engineering at Grinnell (Iowa) College (1956–60); then took courses at the Manhattan School of Music and The New School for Social Research in N.Y. While still in school, he led his own band; also made appearances with such jazz artists as Coleman Hawkins, Donald Byrd, and Miles Davis. In 1968 he organized the Herbie Hancock Sextet, which later was reduced to the Herbie Hancock Quartet; with it he appeared in pop concerts. In addition to jazz piano he became adept as a player on an electric piano. In 1972 he went to Los Angeles, and in 1973 he became converted to a Californian brand of Buddhism.

Handel, George Frideric (the Anglicized form of the name, adopted by Handel in England; the original German spelling was **Georg Friedrich Händel;** other forms used in various branches of the family were Hendel, Hendeler, Händler, and Hendtler; the early spelling in England was Hendel; in France it is spelled Haendler; the Russian transliteration of the name from the Cyrillic alphabet, which lacks the aspirate, is Ghendel), great German-born English composer; b. Halle, Feb. 23, 1685; d. London, April 14, 1759. His father was a barber-surgeon and valet to the Prince of Saxe-Magdeburg; at the age of 61 he took a second wife, Dorothea Taust, daughter of the pastor of Giebichenstein, near Halle; Handel was the 2nd son of this marriage. As a child, he was taken by his father on a visit to Saxe-Weissenfels, where he had a chance to try out the organ of the court chapel. The Duke, Johann Adolf, noticing his interest in music, advised that he be sent to Halle for organ lessons with Friedrich Wilhelm Zachau, the organist of the Liebfrauenkirche there. Zachau gave him instruction in harpsichord and organ playing and also introduced him to the rudiments of composition. Handel proved to be an apt student, and was able to substitute for Zachau as organist whenever necessary; he also composed trio sonatas and motets for church services on Sundays. After the death of Handel's father in 1697, he entered the Univ. of Halle in 1702, and was named probationary organist at the Domkirche there. In 1703 he went to Hamburg, where he was engaged as "violino di ripieno" by Reinhard Keiser, the famous composer and director of the Hamburg Opera. There he met Johann Mattheson; in 1703 the two undertook a journey to Lübeck together, with the intention of applying for the post of organist in succession to Buxtehude, who was chief organist there. It was the custom for an incoming organist to marry a daughter of the incumbent as a condition of appointment; apparently neither Mattheson nor Handel availed themselves of this opportunity. (Bach made the same journey in 1704, and also returned without obtaining the succession.) There was apparently a quarrel between Mattheson and Handel at a performance of Mattheson's opera *Cleopatra,* in which he sang the leading male role of Antonio, while Handel conducted from the keyboard as maestro al cembalo. When Mattheson completed his stage role he asked Handel to yield his place at the keyboard to him; Handel declined, and an altercation ensued, resulting in a duel with swords, which was called off when Mattheson broke his sword on a metal button of Handel's coat. There is no independent confirmation of this episode, however, and the two apparently reconciled.

Handel's first opera, *Almira,* was produced at the Hamburg Opera on Jan. 8, 1705; his next opera, *Nero,* was staged there on Feb. 25, 1705. He was then commissioned to write 2 other operas, *Florindo* and *Daphne,* originally planned as a single opera combining both subjects. In 1706 Handel undertook a long voyage to Italy, where he visited Florence, Rome, Naples and Venice. The first opera he wrote in Italy was *Rodrigo,* presented in Florence in 1707. Then followed *Agrippina,* produced in Venice on Dec. 26, 1709; it obtained an excellent success, being given 27 performances. In Rome, Handel composed the serenata *Il trionfo del tempo e del disinganno,* which was performed there in the spring of 1707. Handel's oratorio *La Resurrezione* was given in Rome on April 8, 1708. On July 19, 1708, he brought out in Naples his serenata *Aci, Galatea, e Polifemo;* its score was remarkable for a bass solo that required a compass of 2 octaves and a fifth. During his Italian sojourn Handel met Alessandro and Domenico Scarlatti. In 1710 he returned to Germany and was named Kapellmeister to the Elector of Hannover, as successor to the Italian musician Agostino Steffani. Later that year he visited England, where he produced his opera *Rinaldo* at the Queen's Theatre in London on Feb. 24, 1711; it received 15 performances in all. After a brief return to Hannover in June 1711, he made another visit to

Handel

London, where he produced his operas *Il pastor fido* (Nov. 22, 1712) and *Teseo* (Jan. 10, 1713). He also wrote an ode for Queen Anne's birthday, which was presented at Windsor Palace on Feb. 6, 1713; it was followed by 2 sacred works, *Te Deum* and *Jubilate,* performed on July 7, 1713, to celebrate the Peace of Utrecht; these performances won him royal favor and an annuity of 200 pounds sterling.

An extraordinary concurrence of events persuaded Handel to remain in London, when Queen Anne died in 1714 and Handel's protector, the Elector of Hannover, became King George I of England. The King bestowed many favors upon Handel and augmented his annuity to 400 pounds sterling. He became a British subject in 1727, and Anglicized his name to George Frideric Handel, dropping the original German umlaut. He continued to produce operas, invariably to Italian librettos, for the London stage. His opera *Silla* was produced in London on June 2, 1713; it was followed by *Amadigi di Gaula* on May 25, 1715. In 1716 Handel wrote *Der für die Sünden der Welt gemarterte und sterbende Jesus,* to the text of the poet Heinrich Brockes. In 1717 Handel produced one of his most famous works, written expressly for King George I, his *Water Music.* On July 17, 1717, an aquatic fête on the Thames River was held by royal order; the King's boat was followed by a barge on which an orch. of 50 musicians played Handel's score, or at least a major portion of it. The final version of *Water Music* combines 2 instrumental suites composed at different times; one was written for the barge party, the other is of an earlier provenance. In 1717 Handel became resident composer to the Duke of Chandos, for whom he wrote the 11 so-called *Chandos Anthems* (1717–18), the secular oratorio *Acis and Galatea* (1718), and the oratorio *Esther* (1718). He also served as music master to the daughters of the Prince of Wales; for Princess Anne he composed his first collection of *Suites de pièces pour le clavecin* (1720), also known as *The Lessons,* which includes the famous air with variations nicknamed *The Harmonious Blacksmith;* the appellation is gratuitous, and the story that Handel was inspired to compose it after he visited a blacksmith shop, where he was impressed by the steady beat of the artisan's hammer, was a persistent figment of anonymous imagination. In 1719 Handel was made Master of Musick of a new business venture under the name of the Royal Academy of Music, established for the purpose of presenting opera at the King's Theatre. The first opera he composed for it was *Radamisto* (April 27, 1720). In the fall of 1720 the Italian composer Giovanni Bononcini joined the company. A rivalry soon developed between him and Handel which was made famous by a piece of doggerel by the poet John Byrom ("Some say, compar'd to Bononcini, that Mynheer Handel's but a ninny. Others aver that he to Handel is scarcely fit to hold a candle. Strange all this difference should be twixt tweedledum and tweedledee."). Handel won a Pyrrhic victory when Bononcini had the unfortunate idea of submitting to the London Academy of Music a madrigal which he had appropriated *in extenso* from a choral piece by the Italian composer Antonio Lotti; Lotti discovered it, and an embarrassing controversy ensued, resulting in Bononcini's disgrace and expulsion from London (he died in obscurity in Vienna, where he sought refuge). The irony of the whole episode is that Handel was no less guilty of plagiarism. An article on Handel in the 1880 edition of the *Encyclopædia Britannica* spares no words condemning Handel's conduct: "The system of wholesale plagiarism carried on by Handel is perhaps unprecedented in the history of music. He pilfered not only single melodies but frequently entire movements from the works of other masters, with few or no alterations, and without a word of acknowledgment." Between 1721 and 1728 Handel produced the following operas at the King's Theatre: *Florindante, Ottone, Flavio, Giulio Cesare, Tamerlano, Rodelinda Scipione, Alessandro, Admeto, Riccardo Primo, Siroe,* and *Tolomeo;* of these, *Giulio Cesare* and *Rodelinda* became firmly established in the operatic repertoire and had numerous revivals. In 1727 he composed 4 grand anthems for the coronation of King George II and Queen Caroline. In the spring of 1728 the Royal Academy of Music ceased operations, and Handel became associated with the management of the King's Theatre. The following year, he went to Italy to recruit singers for a new Royal Academy of Music. Returning to London, he brought out the operas *Lotario, Partenope, Poro, Ezio, Sosarme,* and *Orlando;* only *Orlando* proved to be a lasting success. On May 2, 1732, Handel gave a special production of a revised version of his oratorio *Esther* at the King's Theatre; it was followed by the revised version of *Acis and Galatea* (June 10, 1732) and the oratorio *Deborah* (March 17, 1733). On July 10, 1733, he produced his oratorio *Athalia* at Oxford, where he also appeared as an organist; he was offered the degree of Mus.Doc. (*honoris causa*), but declined the honor. Discouraged by the poor reception of his operas at the King's Theatre, Handel decided to open a new season under a different management. But he quarreled with the principal singer, the famous castrato Senesino, who was popular with audiences, and thus lost the support of a substantial number of his subscribers, who then formed a rival opera company, called The Opera of the Nobility. It engaged the famous Italian composer Porpora as director, and opened its first season at Lincoln's Inns Fields on Dec. 29, 1733. Handel's opera *Arianna in Creta* had its premiere at the King's Theatre on Jan. 26, 1734, but in July of that year both Handel's company and the rival enterprise were forced to suspend operations. Handel set up his own opera company at Covent Garden, inaugurating his new season with a revised version of *Il pastor fido* (Nov. 9, 1734); this was followed by *Ariodante, Alcina, Atalanta, Arminio, Giustino,* and *Berenice,* all staged between 1735 and 1737; only *Alcina* sustained a success; Handel's other operas met with an indifferent reception. On Feb. 19, 1736, Handel presented his ode *Alexander's Feast* at Covent Garden, and on March 23, 1737, he brought out a revised version of his oratorio *Il trionfo del tempo e della verità.* His fortunes improved when he was confirmed by the Queen as music master to Princesses Amelia and

Caroline. He continued to maintain connections with Germany; he traveled to Aachen in 1737. Upon his return to London he suffered from attacks of gout, an endemic illness of British society at the time, but he managed to resume his work. On Jan. 3, 1738, he produced his opera *Faramondo,* and on April 15, 1738, presented his opera *Serse* (a famous aria from this opera, *Ombra mai fu,* became even more famous in an instrumental arrangement made by parties unknown, under the title "Handel's Celebrated Largo"). There followed a pasticcio, *Giove in Argo* (May 1, 1739), and *Imenea* (Nov. 22, 1740). On Jan. 10, 1741, he produced his last opera, *Deidamia,* which marked the end of his operatic enterprise. In historical perspective, Handel's failure as an operatic entrepreneur was a happy turn of events, for he then directed his energy toward the composition of oratorios, in which he achieved greatness. For inspiration he turned to biblical themes, using English texts. On Jan. 16, 1739, he presented the oratorio *Saul;* on April 4, 1739, there followed *Israel in Egypt.* He also wrote an *Ode for St. Cecilia's Day,* after Dryden (Nov. 22, 1739), and his great set of 12 *Concerti grossi,* op. 6. Milton's *L'Allegro* and *Il Penseroso* inspired him to write *L'Allegro, il Penseroso, ed il Moderato* (Feb. 27, 1740). In 1741 Handel was invited to visit Ireland, and there he produced his greatest masterpiece, *Messiah;* working with tremendous concentration of willpower, and imagination, he completed Part I in 6 days, Part II in 9 days, and Part III in 6 days. The work on orchestration took him only a few more days; he signed the score on Sept. 14, 1741. The first performance of *Messiah* was given in Dublin on April 13, 1742, and its London premiere was presented on March 23, 1743. If contemporary reports can be trusted, King George II rose to his feet at the closing chords of "Hallelujah," and the entire audience followed his example. This established a tradition, at least in England; since then every performance of *Messiah* moved the listeners to rise during this celebratory chorus. Handel's oratorio *Samson,* produced in London on Feb. 18, 1743, was also successful, but his next oratorio, *Semele* (Feb. 10, 1744), failed to arouse public admiration. Continuing to work, and alternating between mythological subjects and religious themes, he produced *Joseph and His Brethren* (March 2, 1744), *Hercules* (Jan. 5, 1745), and *Belshazzar* (March 27, 1745). His subsequent works, composed between 1746 and 1752, were a pasticcio under the titles *Occasional Oratorio, Judas Maccabaeus, Joshua, Alexander Balus, Susanna, Solomon, Theodora, The Choice of Hercules,* and *Jephtha.* Of these, *Judas Maccabaeus, Solomon,* and *Jephtha* became favorites with the public. Besides oratorios, mundane events also occupied Handel's attention. To celebrate the Peace of Aachen, he composed the remarkable *Music for the Royal Fireworks,* which was heard for the first time in Green Park in London on April 27, 1749. In 1750 he revisited Germany. But soon he had to limit his activities on account of failing eyesight, which required the removal of cataracts; the operation proved unsuccessful, but he still continued to appear in performances of his music, with the assis-

tance of his pupil John Christopher Smith. Handel's last appearance in public was at the London performance of *Messiah* on April 6, 1759; 8 days later, on April 14, the Saturday between Good Friday and Easter, he died. He was buried at Westminster Abbey; a monument by Roubiliac marks his grave. (It should be noted that the year of birth on Handel's gravestone is marked as 1684 rather than 1685; this discrepancy is explained by the fact that the calendar year in England and other European countries began in March, and not in January.)

A parallel between 2 great German contemporaries, Bach and Handel, is often drawn. Born a few months apart, Bach in Eisenach, Handel in Halle, at a distance of about 130 kilometers, they never met. Bach visited Halle at least twice, but Handel was then away, in London. The difference between their life's destinies was profound. Bach was a master of the Baroque organ who produced religious works for church use, a schoolmaster who regarded his instrumental music as a textbook for study; he never composed for the stage, and traveled but little. By contrast, Handel was a man of the world who dedicated himself mainly to public spectacles, and who became a British subject. Bach's life was that of a German burgher; his genius was inconspicuous; Handel shone in the light of public admiration. Bach was married twice; survivors among his 20 children became important musicians in their own right. Handel remained celibate, but he was not a recluse. Physically, he tended toward healthy corpulence; he enjoyed the company of friends, but had a choleric temperament, and could not brook adverse argument. Like Bach, he was deeply religious, and there was no ostentation in his service to his God. Handel's music possessed grandeur of design, majestic eloquence, and lusciousness of harmony. Music lovers did not have to study Handel's style to discover its beauty, while the sublime art of Bach could be fully understood only after knowledgeable penetration into the contrapuntal and fugal complexities of its structure.

Handel bequeathed the bulk of his MSS to his amanuensis, John Christopher Smith, whose son presented them in turn to King George III. They eventually became a part of the King's Music Library; they comprise 32 vols. of operas, 21 vols. of oratorios, 7 vols. of odes and serenatas, 12 vols. of sacred music, 11 vols. of cantatas, and 5 vols. of instrumental music. Seven vols. containing sketches for various works are in the Fitzwilliam Collection at Cambridge. An edition of Handel's works in 36 vols., edited by Arnold, was publ. by command of George III between 1787 and 1797. A monumental edition in 100 vols. was issued by the German Handel Society under the editorship of F.R. Chrysander between 1856 and 1894. J.M. Coopersmith collected and edited 10 vols. of publ. material to complete Chrysander's edition, and brought out an authentic version of *Messiah* in vocal score. In 1955 a new edition, the Hallische Handel Ausgabe, was begun by Max Schneider and Rudolf Steglich for the Handel Gesellschaft in Halle. A thematic catalog was compiled by A.C. Bell in 1969.

BIBLIOGRAPHY: COLLECTED EDITIONS, SOURCE MA-

TERIAL: The first ed. of Handel's collected works was ed. by S. Arnold in 180 installments in 54 vols. (1787–97). It was superseded by the monumental ed. prepared by F. Chrysander under the title *G.F. H.s Werke: Ausgabe der deutschen Händelgesellschaft* (100 vols., Leipzig and Bergedorf bei Hamburg, 1858–94; 6 supplementary vols., 1888–1902). In 1955 the *Hallische H.-Ausgabe* was begun as a supplement to the Chrysander ed.; however, it soon became a new critical ed. in its own right, being ed. by M. Schneider and R. Steglich as the *Hallische H.-Ausgabe im Auftrage der Georg Friedrich H.-Gesellschaft*, and publ. in Kassel. A. Bell ed. a *Chronological Catalogue of H.'s Work* (Greenock, Scotland, 1969).

Other sources include the following: R. Streatfeild, "The Granville Collection of H. Manuscripts," *Musical Antiquary*, II (1910–11); N. Flower, *Catalogue of a H. Collection Formed by Newman Flower* (Sevenoaks, 1920); W. Squire, *Catalogue of the King's Music Library, I: The H. Manuscripts* (London, 1927); F. Zobeley, "Werke H.s in der Gräfl. von Schönbornschen Musikbibliothek," *H.-Jahrbuch 1931;* K. Taut, "Verzeichnis des Schriftums über G.F. H.," *H.-Jahrbuch 1933;* J. Coopersmith, "Handelian Lacunae: A Project," *Musical Quarterly* (April 1935); idem, "The First Gesamtausgabe: Dr. Arnold's Edition of H.'s Works," *Notes*, IV (1946–47); P. Hirsch, "Dr. Arnold's H. Edition," *Music Review*, VIII (1947); W. Smith, "Verzeichnis der Werke G.F. H.s," *H.-Jahrbuch 1956;* F. Hudson, "Concerning the Watermarks in the Manuscripts and Early Prints of G.F. H.," *Music Review*, XX (1959); H. Shaw, *A First List of Word-books of H.'s "Messiah," 1742–83* (Worcester, 1959); R. Ewerhart, "Die H.-Handschriften der Santini-Bibliothek in Münster," *H.-Jahrbuch 1960;* W. Smith and C. Humphries, *H.: A Descriptive Catalogue of the Early Editions* (London, 1960; 2nd ed., revised, 1970); H. Federhofer, *Unbekannte Kopien von Werken G.F. H.s* (Kassel, 1963); K. Sasse, *H.-Bibliographie* (Leipzig, 1963; new ed., 1967; with supplement, 1969); L. Duck, "The Aylesford H. Manuscripts," *Manchester Review*, X (1965); M. Picker, "Handeliana in the Rutgers University Library," *Journal of the Rutgers University Library*, XXIX (1965); W. Smith, *A Handelian's Notebook* (London, 1965); P. Krause, *Handschriften und altere Drucke der Werke G.F. H.s in der Musikbibliothek der Stadt Leipzig* (Leipzig, 1966); J. Hall, "The Importance of the Aylesford H. Manuscripts," *Brio*, IV/1 (1967); A. Hyatt King, *H. and His Autographs* (London, 1967); H. Lenneberg and L. Libin, "Unknown H. Sources in Chicago," *Journal of the American Musicological Society*, XXII (1969); A. Mann and J. Knapp, "The Present State of H. Research," *Acta Musicologica*, XLI (1969); W. Meyerhoff, ed., *50 Jahre Göttinger H.-Festspiele. Festschrift* (Kassel, 1970); H. Clausen, *H.s Direktionspartituren ("Handexemplare")* (Hamburg, 1972); A. Walker, *G.F. H.: The Newman Flower Collection in the Henry Watson Music Library* (Manchester, 1972); J. Knapp, "The Hall H. Collection," *Princeton University Library Chronicle*, XXXVI (1974); F. Hudson, "The Earliest Paper Made by James Whatman the Elder (1702–1759) and Its Significance in Relation to G.F. H. and John Walsh," *Music Review*, XXXVIII (1977).

BIOGRAPHICAL: J. Mattheson, *Grundlage einer Ehren-Pforte . . .* (contains 8 pages on Handel; Hamburg, 1740; reprint ed. by M. Schneider, Berlin, 1910); J. Mainwaring, *Memoirs of the Late G.F. H.* (London, 1760; reprint, 1967); J. Mattheson, *G.F. H.s Lebensbeschreibung* (based almost entirely on Mainwaring's biography; Hamburg, 1761; reprint, 1976); C. Burney, *An Account of the Musical Performances in Westminster Abbey and the Pantheon May 26th, 27th, 29th; and June the 3rd and 5th, 1784: In Commemoration of H.* (London, 1785; reprint, 1965); W. Coxe, *Anecdotes of G.F. H. and John Christopher Smith* (London, 1799; reprint, 1980); R. Clark, *Reminiscences of H.* (London, 1836); K. Förstemann, *G.F. H.s Stammbaum* (Leipzig, 1844); W. Callcott, *A Few Facts in the Life of H.* (London, 1850); H. Townsend, *An Account of H.'s Visit to Dublin: With Incidental Notices of His Life and Character* (Dublin, 1852); V. Schoelcher, *The Life of H.* (London, 1857); A. Stothard, *H.: His Life, Personal and Professional* (London, 1857); F. Chrysander, *G.F. H.* (an important source in its day; incomplete, bringing the life down only to 1740; 3 vols., Leipzig, 1858–67; reprint, 1966); M. Delany, *Autobiography and Correspondence of Mary Granville, Mrs. Delany* (contains a detailed account of Handel's death; London, 1861–62); F. van Kempen, *G.F. H.: Een Leven* (Leyden, 1868); J. Marshall, *H.* (London, 1881; 3rd ed., 1912); W. Rockstro, *The Life of G.F. H.* (London, 1883); J. Opel, *Mitteilungen zur Geschichte der Familie des Tonkünstlers H.* (Leipzig, 1885); A. Ademollo, *G.F. H. in Italia* (Milan, 1889); F. Volbach, *G.F. H.* (Berlin, 1897; 3rd ed., 1914); W. Cummings, *H.* (London, 1904); F. Williams, *H.* (London, 1904); J. Hadden, *Life of H.* (London, 1905); R. Streatfeild, *H.* (London, 1909; reprint, 1964); idem, "H. in Italy," *Musical Antiquary*, I (1909–10); R. Rolland, *H.* (Paris, 1910; 2nd ed., 1974; Eng. trans., 1916; reprint, 1975); M. Brenet, *H.* (Paris, 1912); H. Davey, *H.* (London, 1912); G. Thormälius, *G.F. H.* (Stuttgart, 1912); R. Streatfeild, *H., Canons and the Duke of Chandos* (London, 1916); N. Flower, *G.F. H.: His Personality and His Times* (London, 1923; 3rd ed., revised, 1959); H. Leichtentritt, *H.* (Stuttgart, 1924); H. Moser, *Der junge H. und seine Vorgänger in Halle* (Halle, 1929); J. Coopersmith, "A List of Portraits, Sculptures, etc., of H.," *Music & Letters*, XII (1932); J. Müller-Blattau, *G.F. H.* (Potsdam, 1933); E. Dent, *H.* (London, 1934); L. Liebeman, *G.F. H. und Halle* (Halle, 1935); E. Müller, ed., *The Letters and Writings of G.F. H.* (London, 1935); C. Williams, *H.* (London, 1935); H. Weinstock, *H.* (a perceptive study; N.Y., 1946; 2nd ed., revised, 1959); P. Young, *H.* (a good introduction to Handel and his music; London, 1946; 3rd ed., revised, 1975); W. Smith, *Concerning H., His Life and Works* (London, 1948); A.-E. Cherbuliez, *G.F. H.: Leben und Werk* (Olten, 1949); H. and E.H. Müller von Asow, *G.F. H.: Briefe und Schriften* (Lindau, 1949); W. Smith, "Handeliana," *Music & Letters*, XXXI (1950) and XXXIV (1953); O. Deutsch, *H., A Documentary Biography* (most valuable; reproduces in chronological order pertinent contemporary documents and notices in the press;

N.Y., 1954, and London, 1955); W. Siegmund-Schultze, *G.F. H.: Leben und Werk* (Leipzig, 1954; 3rd ed., revised, 1962); W. Serauky, *G.F. H.: Sein Leben, sein Werk* (only vols. III–V publ.; Kassel, 1956–58); E. Flessa, *Ombra mai fu: Die H. Chronik des Christopher Smith* (Biberbach, 1958); P. Nettl, *G.F. H.* (Berlin, 1958); R. Friedenthal, *G.F. H. in Selbstzeugnissen und Bilddokumenten* (Hamburg, 1959; 3rd ed., Reinbeck, 1967); B. Matthews, "Unpublished Letters Concerning H.," *Music & Letters* (July 1959); J. Müller-Blattau, *G.F. H.: Der Wille zur Vollendung* (Mainz, 1959); M. Nicolescu, *H.* (Bucharest, 1959); B. Matthews, "H.: More Unpublished Letters," *Music & Letters* (April 1961); W. Rackwitz and H. Steffens, *G.F. H., Persönlichkeit, Umwelt, Vermächtnis* (Leipzig, 1962); S. Sadie, *H.* (London, 1962); P. Lang, *G.F. H.* (an exhaustive and scholarly study, both biographically and historically invaluable; N.Y., 1966); K. Sasse, *Bildsammlung; Hogarth-Grafik; Darstellung zur Geschichte, H.-pfege und Musikkunde* (Halle, 1967); M. Szentkuthy, *H.* (Budapest, 1967); W. Ober, "Bach, H., and 'Chevalier' John Taylor, M.D., Opthalmiater," *New York State Journal of Medicine* (June 1969); M. Foss, *The Age of Patronage: The Arts in England 1660–1750* (Ithaca, N.Y., 1971); C. Timms, "H. and Steffani," *Musical Times* (April 1973); R. Strohm, "H. in Italia: Nuovi contributi," *Rivista Italiana di Musicologia*, IX (1974); W. Siegmund-Schultze, ed., *G.F. H.: Beiträge zu seiner Biographie aus dem 18. Jahrhundert* (Leipzig, 1977); M. Keynes, "H. and His Illnesses," *Musical Times* (Sept. 1982).

CRITICAL, ANALYTICAL: In addition to the writings listed below, important articles may also be found in the *H.-Jahrbuch* (1928–33; 1955—). J. Weissebeck, *Der grosse Musikus H. im Universalruhme* (Nuremberg, 1809); H. Chorley, *H.-Studies* (2 vols., London, 1859); G. Gervinus, *H. und Shakespeare: Zur Ästhetik der Tonkunst* (Leipzig, 1868); R. Franz, *Über Bearbeitungen älterer Tonwerke, namenlich Bachscher und Händelscher Vokalmusik* (Leipzig, 1871; reprinted by R. Bethge as *Gesammelte Schriften uber die Wiederbelebung Bachscher und Händelscher Werke*, Leipzig, 1910); E. Frommel, *H. und Bach* (Berlin, 1878); F. Chrysander, *H.s biblische Oratorien in geschichtlicher Betrachtung* (Hamburg, 1897); F. Volbach, *Die Praxis der H.-Aufführung* (Charlottenburg, 1900); J. Shedlock, "H.'s Borrowings," *Musical Times*, XLII (1901); G. Vernier, *L'Oratorio biblique de H.* (Cahors, 1901); J. Garat, *La Sonate de H.* (Paris, 1905); E. Bernoulli, *Quellen zum Studium Händelscher Chorwerke* (Leipzig, 1906); S. Taylor, *The Indebtedness of H. to Works by Other Composers* (Cambridge, 1906); P. Robinson, *H. and His Orbit* (London, 1908); A. Schering, *Geschichte des Oratoriums* (Leipzig, 1911); H. Abert, *H. als Dramatiker* (Göttingen, 1921); J. Benson, *H.'s "Messiah": the Oratorio and Its History* (London, 1923); E. Bairstow, *The Messiah* (London, 1928); F. Kahle, *H.s Cembalo-Suiten* (Berlin, 1928); E. Bredenfoerder, *Die Texte der H.-Oratorien* (Leipzig, 1934); F. Ehrlinger, *H.s Orgelkonzerte* (Erlangen, 1934); G. Abraham, "H.'s Clavier Music," *Music & Letters* (Oct. 1935); E. Dent, "H. on the Stage," *Music & Letters* (July 1935); H. Leichtentritt, "H.'s Har-monic Art," *Musical Quarterly* (April 1935); V. Redway, "H. in Colonial and Post-Colonial America," *Musical Quarterly* (April 1935); E. Völsing, *G.F. H.s englische Kirchenmusik* (Leipzig, 1940); J. Eisenschmidt, *Die szenische Darstellung der Opern H.s auf der Londoner Bühne seiner Zeit* (Wolfenbüttel, 1940–41); J. Herbage, *Messiah* (London, 1948); R. Myers, *H.'s Messiah, A Touchstone of Taste* (N.Y., 1948); P. Young, *The Oratorios of H.* (London, 1949); G. Cuming, "The Text of 'Messiah,'" *Music & Letters* (July 1950); W. Dean, "The Dramatic Element in H.'s Oratorios," *Proceedings of the Royal Musical Association*, LXXIX (1952–53); G. Abraham, ed., *H.: A Symposium* (London, 1954); R. Myers, *H., Dryden and Milton* (London, 1956); J. Larsen, *H.'s Messiah: Origins, Composition, Sources* (London, 1957; 2nd ed., revised, 1972); H. Wolff, *Die H.-Oper auf der modernen Bühne* (Leipzig, 1957); W. Dean, *H.'s Dramatic Oratorios and Masques* (London, 1959); J. Knapp, "H., the Royal Academy of Music, and Its First Opera Season in London (1720)," *Musical Quarterly* (April 1959); H. Dietz, *Die Chorfuge bei G.F. H.* (Tutzing, 1961); B. Trowell, "H. as a Man of the Theatre," *Proceedings of the Royal Musical Association*, XXXVIII (1961–62); H. Shaw, *The Story of H.'s Messiah* (London, 1963); J. Tobin, *H. at Work* (London, 1964); H. Shaw, *A Textual and Historical Companion to H.'s Messiah* (London, 1965); D. Kimbell, *A Critical Study of H.'s Early Operas* (Diss., Oxford Univ., 1968); W. Dean *H. and the Opera Seria* (Berkeley, Calif., 1969); J. Tobin, *H.'s Messiah* (London, 1969); T. Best, "H.'s Keyboard Music," *Musical Times* (Sept. 1971); S. Sadie, *H. Concertos* (London, 1972); D. Burrows, "H.'s Performances of 'Messiah': The Evidence of the Conducting Score," *Music & Letters* (July–Oct. 1975); H. Friedrichs, *Das Verhältnis von Text und Musik in den Brockespassionen Keisers, H.s, Telemanns und Matthesons* (Munich and Salzburg, 1975); A. Hicks, "H.'s Early Musical Development," *Proceedings of the Royal Musical Association*, CIII (1976–77); G. Beeks, *The Chandos Anthems and Te Deum of G.F. H.* (Diss., Univ. of Calif., Berkeley, 1977); D. Burrows, "H. and the Foundling Hospital," *Music & Letters* (July 1977); E. Harris, *H. and the Pastoral Tradition* (London, 1980); D. Burrows, "H. and 'Alexander's Feast,'" *Musical Times* (April 1982); J. Knapp, 'H.'s Second Song on the London Stage," *Musical Times* (April 1982).

Handford, Maurice, English conductor; b. Salisbury, April 29, 1929. He studied at the Royal Academy of Music in London; then went to Manchester as principal horn player in the Hallé Orch. He made his conducting debut with that ensemble in 1960; in 1964 was named its assistant conductor; in 1966 its associate conductor; he resigned in 1971. From 1971 to 1975 he was music director of the Calgary (Alberta) Phil.

Handl, Jacob. See **Gallus, Jacob Handl.**

Handley, Vernon, English conductor; b. Enfield, Nov. 11, 1930. He was educated at Balliol College,

Oxford, and the Guildhall School of Music. He made his debut with the Bournemouth Symph. in 1961. In 1962 he became principal conductor of the Guildford Phil.; was also a prof. at the Royal College of Music in London (1966–72). In 1982 he was appointed associate conductor of the London Phil.; in 1983 he became principal guest conductor of the BBC Scottish Symph. in Glasgow.

Handrock, Julius, German piano pedagogue and composer; b. Naumburg, June 22, 1830; d. Halle, Jan. 5, 1894. He publ. several collections of piano studies which have retained their popularity among teachers and students for many years (*Moderne Schule der Geläufigkeit; 50 Melodisch-technische Klavier-Etuden*, etc.).

Handschin, Jacques, eminent Swiss musicologist; b. Moscow, April 5, 1886; d. Basel, Nov. 25, 1955. He studied organ in Moscow; in 1905 he studied mathematics and history at the Univ. of Basel; then went to Munich to pursue his academic studies; also studied organ and theory with Max Reger; he later attended some of the lectures in musicology given in Leipzig by Riemann and in Berlin by Hornbostel; took additional courses in organ playing with Karl Straube in Leipzig and with Widor in Paris. Returning to Russia, he taught organ at the St. Petersburg Cons. (1909–20); gave numerous organ recitals in Russia, and promoted contemporary organ works by Russian composers, among them Glazunov and Taneyev; included these works in his anthology *Les Maîtres contemporains de l'orgue* (Paris, 1913–14). In 1920 he returned to Switzerland; in 1921 he received his Ph.D. from the Univ. of Basel with the dissertation *Choralbearbeitungen und Kompositionen mit rhythmischem Text in der mehrstimmigen Musik des 13. Jahrhunderts;* he completed his Habilitation there in 1924 with his tract *Über die mehrstimmige Musik der St. Martial-Epoche sowie die Zusammenhänge zwischen Notre Dame und St. Martial und die Zusammenhänge zwischen einem dritten Stil und Notre Dame und St. Martial.* In 1924 he became Privatdozent at the Univ. of Basel; was a prof. of musicology there from 1935–55. He also served as a church organist in Zürich and Basel. He was greatly esteemed for his ample erudition and the soundness of his analytical theories; he evolved philosophical principles of musical esthetics seeking the rational foundations of the art. His most important work is *Der Toncharakter: Eine Einführung in die Tonpsychologie* (Zürich, 1948), which sets down his principles of musical esthetics; other works include *La Musique de l'antiquité* (Paris, 1946) and *Musikgeschichte im Überblick* (Lucerne, 1948).
BIBLIOGRAPHY: A memorial vol. edited by Dr. Hans Oesch, *Gedenkschrift Jacques Handschin: Aufsätze und Bibliographie* (Bern and Stuttgart, 1957), contains reprints of some 50 articles by Handschin; see also H. Anglés et al., eds., *In memoriam Jacques Handschin* (Strasbourg, 1962).

Handy, W(illiam) C(hristopher), black American composer, "father of the blues"; b. Florence, Ala., Nov. 16, 1873; d. New York, March 28, 1958. His father and grandfather were ministers. In 1892 he was graduated from the Teachers' Agricultural and Mechanical College in Huntsville, Ala.; became a schoolteacher and also worked in iron mills; learned to play the cornet and was a soloist at the Chicago World's Fair (1893); became bandmaster of Mahara's Minstrels. From 1900–2 he taught at the Agricultural and Mechanical College; then from 1903–21, conducted his own orch. and toured the South. He received the award of the National Assoc. for Negro Music, St. Louis (1937). On Jan. 1, 1954, he married his secretary, Irma Louise Logan. His famous song *Memphis Blues* (publ. 1912; the 2nd piece to be publ. as a "blues," and the first blues to achieve popularity) was originally written as a campaign song for the mayor of Memphis, E.H. Crump (1909); this song, along with his more celebrated *St. Louis Blues* (1914), opened an era in popular music, turning the theretofore prevalent spirit of ragtime gaiety to ballad-like nostalgia, with the lowered third, fifth, and seventh degrees ("blue notes") as distinctive melodic traits. He followed these with more blues: *Yellow Dog; Beale Street; Joe Turner;* the march *Hail to the Spirit of Freedom* (1915); *Ole Miss* for Piano (1916); the songs *Aunt Hagar's Children* (1920); *Loveless Love* (1921); *Aframerican Hymn;* etc. He publ. the anthologies *Blues: An Anthology* (also publ. as *A Treasury of the Blues;* N.Y., 1926; 2nd ed., 1949; 3rd ed., revised by J. Silverman, 1972); *Book of Negro Spirituals* (N.Y., 1938); *Negro Music and Musicians* (N.Y., 1944); also *Negro Authors and Composers of the U.S.* (N.Y., 1936); wrote an autobiography, *Father of the Blues* (N.Y., 1941). A commemorative stamp showing Handy playing the trumpet was issued on May 17, 1969, in Memphis, Tenn., the birthplace of his "blues."

Handy, Will, pseudonym for the songwriting team Cole and Johnson Bros.; See **Johnson, J. Rosamond** and **Johnson, James Weldon.**

Hanff, Johann Nikolaus, German organist and composer; b. Wechmar, near Mühlhausen, 1665; d. Schleswig, 1711. He was organist in Eupin; later in Hamburg (1706–11). A few months before his death, he was appointed organist at the Cathedral of Schleswig. He was a master of the chorale prelude, and his works considerably influenced J.S. Bach's style in this form. Only 6 of his chorale preludes are extant (publ. 1907 by K. Straube in his *45 Choralvorspiele alter Meister;* reprinted by E. White in *Masterpieces of Organ Music,* N.Y., 1949).
BIBLIOGRAPHY: Hans Schillings, *Tobias Eniccelius, Friedrich Meister, Nikolaus Hanff: Ein Beitrag zur Geschichte der evangelischen Frühkantate in Schleswig-Holstein* (Kiel, 1934); H.J. Moser, *Die evangelische Kirchenmusik in Deutschland* (Berlin, 1954).

Hanfstängel, Marie, German soprano; b. Breslau, April 30, 1846; d. Munich, Sept. 5, 1917. She studied at Baden-Baden with Mme. Viardot-García; made her debut as Agathe in *Der Freischütz* at the Théâtre Lyrique in Paris (Feb. 27, 1867). On the declaration of the Franco-Prussian War, she returned to Germany, and was engaged at the Stuttgart Opera. She publ. *Meine Lehrweise der Gesangskunst* (1902).

Hanisch, Joseph, German organist and composer; b. Regensburg, March 24, 1812; d. there, Oct. 9, 1892. He studied with his father, and with Proske, with whom he went to Italy as an assistant (1834). In 1839 he became organist at the Regensburg Cathedral. He wrote *Missa auxilium Christianorum and Quatuor hymni pro festo corporis Christi;* contributed organ accompaniments to the *Graduale* and *Vesperale Romanum* (with Haberl); also composed pieces for organ solo. He was a master of improvisation, and was regarded as one of the greatest in this field in his time.

Hanke, Karl, German composer; b. Rosswalde, Silesia, c.1750; d. Flensburg, June 10, 1803. As a young man he was sent to Vienna to pursue his music studies; there he briefly associated himself with Gluck, and profited by the master's advice. He then held the post of music director in Brünn (1778–81), Warsaw (1781–83), and Hamburg (1784–86); was in Schleswig in 1786–92. In 1792 he settled in Flensburg, where he remained until the end of his life. He composed several pieces for the stage; his singspiel *Der Wunsch mancher Mädchen* (1781), dedicated to Gluck, was performed on various occasions with some success; 2 albums of his songs were publ. in 1796–97.
BIBLIOGRAPHY: Alfred Einstein, "Ein Schüler Glucks," *Acta Musicologica* (1938).

Hann, George, Austrian bass-baritone; b. Vienna, Jan. 30, 1897; d. Munich, Dec. 9, 1950. He was educated in Vienna; in 1927 he became a member of the Bavarian State Opera in Munich, remaining there until his death. He also made regular appearances with the Vienna State Opera and at the Salzburg Festival. He was best known for his buffo roles.

Hannay, Roger, talented American composer; b. Plattsburg, N.Y., Sept. 22, 1930. He studied composition with F. Morris and Dika Newlin at Syracuse Univ. (1948–52), H. Norden at Boston Univ. (1952–53), Bernard Rogers and Howard Hanson at the Eastman School of Music in Rochester, N.Y. (1954–56; Ph.D., 1956), and Lukas Foss and Aaron Copland at the Berkshire Music Center (1959); had sessions with Sessions and attended lectures by Elliott Carter at the Princeton Seminar for Advanced Studies (1960). He taught at various colleges; in 1966 joined the music faculty of the Univ. of North Carolina at Chapel Hill; was founder and director of the New Music Ensemble (1967–82), and also served as chairman of the Division of Fine Arts there in 1979–82. An unprejudiced and liberal music-maker, he makes use of varied functional resources, from neo-Classical pandiatonism to dodecaphony; resorts also to the device of "objets trouvés," borrowing thematic materials from other composers.

WORKS: 2 chamber operas: *2 Tickets to Omaha, The Swindlers* (1960) and *The Fortune of St. Macabre* (1964); *Requiem,* after Whitman's "When Lilacs Last in the Dooryard Bloom'd" (1961); Cantata (1952); *The Inter-Planetary Aleatoric Serial Factory* for Soprano Solo, String Quartet, Rock Band, Actors, Dancers, Tapes, Film, and Slides (1969); 4 symphs.: No. 1 (1953; revised 1973); No. 2 (1956); No. 3, "The Great American Novel," with Chorus and Tape-recorded Sound (1976–77); No. 4, "American Classic" (1977); *Dramatic Overture,* an homage to Schoenberg (1955); *Lament* for Oboe and Strings (1957); Symph. for Band (1963); *Sonorous Image* for Orch. (1968); *Sayings for Our Time,* to a text from the "current news media," for Chorus and Orch. (Winston-Salem, N.C., Aug. 2, 1968); *Fragmentation* for Orch. or Chamber Orch. (1969); *Listen* for Orch. (1971; Guilford College, N.C., July 7, 1973); *Celebration* for Tape and Orch. (N.Y., May 19, 1975); *Suite-Billings* for Youth Orch. (1975); *Rhapsody* for Flute and Piano (1952); Sonata for Brass Ensemble (1957); Divertimento for Wind Quintet (1958); *Concerto da camera* for Recorder, Violin, Viola, Cello, Harpsichord, and Soprano (1958; revised 1975); 4 string quartets: No. 1 (1962); No. 2, *Lyric* (1962); No. 3, *Designs* (1963); No. 4, *Quartet of Solos* (1974; comprising the simultaneous perfs. of the 4 solo pieces *Grande Concerte, Second Fiddle, O Solo Viola,* and *Concert Music*); *The Fruit of Love,* after St. Vincent Millay, for Soprano, and Piano or Chamber Orch. (1964, 1969); *Spectrum* for Brass Quintet (1964); *Structure* for Percussion Ensemble (1965; revised 1974); *Marshall's Medium Message* for Mod-Girl Announcer and Percussion Quartet (1967); *America Sing!* for Tape and Visuals (1967); *Fantome* for Viola, Clarinet, and Piano (1967); *Live and in Color!* for Mod Girl Announcer, Percussion Quartet, 2 Action Painters, Tape, Films, and Slides (1967); *Confrontation* for Tape and Percussion (1969); *Squeeze Me* for Chamber Ensemble and Film (1970); *Tuonelan Joutsen,* vocalise for Soprano, English Horn, and Film (1972, after Sibelius's *Swan of Tuonela*); *Prophecy of Despair* for Male Chorus and Percussion (1972); *Grande Concerte* for Solo Violin (1972); *Concert Music* for Solo Cello (1973); *Sphinx* for Tape and Trumpet (1973); *4 for 5* for Brass Quintet (1973); *O Solo Viola* for Solo Viola (1974); *2nd Fiddle* for Solo Violin (1974); *Phantom of the Opera* for Organ and Soprano (1975); *Pied Piper* for Tape and Clarinet (1975); *Oh Friends!* for Chamber Wind Ensemble and Pitch Percussion (1976); Suite for Piano (1954); *Abstractions* for Piano (1962); Piano Sonata (1964); *Sonorities* for Piano (1966); *The Episodic Refraction* for Tape and Piano (1971); choruses; songs.

Hannikainen, Ilmari, Finnish pianist and composer; b. Jyväskylä, Oct. 19, 1892; d. Kuhmoinen, July 25, 1955. A scion of a musical family (his father, **Pekka Hannikainen,** was a conductor and composer), he studied in Helsinki; then took lessons with Alexander Siloti in St. Petersburg and with Alfred Cortot in Paris. Returning to Finland, he was active as a piano teacher; with his brothers **Tauno** and **Arvo**

Hannikainen, he organized a concert trio. He composed a folk play, *Talkoottanssit* (1930); a Piano Concerto; a Piano Quartet; and many solo piano pieces.

Hannikainen, Pekka, Finnish conductor; b. Nurmes, Dec. 9, 1854; d. Helsinki, Sept. 13, 1924. He was the founding member of a musically important family in Finland; his sons **Ilmari, Tauno, Arvo,** and **Väinö** were respectively a pianist, a cellist, a violinist, and a harpist.

Hannikainen, Tauno, Finnish cellist and conductor; b. Jyväskylä, Feb. 26, 1896; d. Helsinki, Oct. 12, 1968. A member of a prominent musical family in Finland (his father, **Pekka Hannikainen,** was a conductor and composer; his brother **Ilmari Hannikainen** was a pianist and composer), he studied in Helsinki, and took some cello lessons with Pablo Casals in Paris. Returning to Finland, he organized a trio with his brothers **Arvo,** a violinist, and Ilmari. He conducted the Symph. Orch. of Turku (1927–40); then went to America, where he was the principal conductor of the Symph. Orch. of Duluth, Minn. (1942–46), and conductor of the Chicago Civic Symph. Orch. (1947–50); at the same time was assistant conductor of the Chicago Symph. Orch. (1947–49), then its associate conductor (1949–50); he then returned to Finland, where he was conductor of the City Orch. in Helsinki; he retired in 1963, but continued as a guest conductor. He was active in promoting works by contemporary Finnish composers. He was married to the Finnish soprano **Anne Niskanen.**

Hannikainen, Väinö, Finnish harpist and composer, son of **Pekka Hannikainen;** b. Jyväskylä, Jan. 12, 1900; d. Kuhmoinen, Aug. 7, 1960. He studied in Helsinki and Berlin; from 1923–57 was first harpist of the Helsinki Orch. He wrote several symph. poems, a Harp Concerto, a Harp Sonata, some theater music, and songs.

Hanon, Charles-Louis, French pianist and pedagogue; b. Renescure, near Dunkerque, July 2, 1819; d. Boulogne-sur-Mer, March 19, 1900. Next to Czerny, Hanon was the most illustrious composer of piano exercises, embodied in his chef d'œuvre, *Le Pianiste-virtuose,* which for over a century was the vademecum for many millions of diligent piano students all over the face of the musical globe; its validity as a book of exercises remains solid well into the 21st century. He further wrote a collection of 50 instructive piano pieces under the title *Méthode élémentaire de piano;* a useful compilation, *Extraits des chefs-d'œuvres des grands maîtres;* as well as a selection of 50 ecclesiastical chants, *50 cantiques choisis parmi les plus populaires.* He also attempted to instruct uneducated musicians in the art of accompanying plainchant in a curious didactic publication, *Système nouveau pour apprendre à accompagner tout plainchant sans savoir la musique.*

Hansen, (Emil) Robert, Danish cellist; b. Copenhagen, Feb. 25, 1860; d. Aarhus, July 18, 1926. He received his first instruction from his father, then studied with F. Neruda at the Copenhagen Cons., and with Friedrich Grützmacher in Dresden; from 1877–89, was a member of the court orch. in Copenhagen. After a stay in London, he settled in 1891 in Leipzig, where he joined the Gewandhaus Orch. and became a prof. at the Cons. From 1918 he was conductor of the Symph. Orch. of Aarhus, Denmark.

WORKS: Opera, *Frauenlist* (Sondershausen, 1911); operetta, *Die wilde Komtesse* (Eisenach, 1913); Symph.; Symph. Suite for Strings and 2 Horns; Piano Concerto; Cello Concerto; Piano Quintet; String Quartet.

Hansen, Wilhelm, Danish music publishing firm founded in Copenhagen by Jens Wilhelm Hansen (1821–1904). His sons, **Jonas W. Hansen** (1850–1919) and **Alfred W. Hansen** (1854–1922), also played an active part in the business, which was eventually entrusted to the sons of Alfred, **Asger** (b. 1889) and **Svend** (b. 1890). A large proportion of publ. Scandinavian (Danish, Swedish, Norwegian) music is brought out by this firm; it has also bought other smaller firms, and publ. some of the works of Arnold Schoenberg. Branches have been established in Oslo, Stockholm, Frankfurt, and London.

Hanslick, Eduard, greatly renowned music critic; b. Prague, Sept. 11, 1825; d. Baden, near Vienna, Aug. 6, 1904. He studied law at Prague and Vienna; took the degree of Dr.Jur. in 1849, qualifying himself for an official position. But he had already studied music under Tomaschek at Prague; in 1848–49 was music critic for the *Wiener Zeitung,* and soon adopted a literary career. His first work, *Vom Musikalisch-Schönen: Ein Beitrag zur Revision der Aesthetik der Tonkunst* (Leipzig, 1854; in French, 1877; Spanish, 1879; Italian, 1884; Eng., 1891; Russian, 1895), brought him worldwide fame. Its leading idea is that the beauty of a musical composition lies wholly and specifically in the music itself; i.e., it is immanent in the relations of the tones, without any reference whatever to extraneous (non-musical) ideas, and can express no others. Such being his point of view through life, it follows logically that he could not entertain sympathy for Wagner's art; his violent opposition to the music-drama was a matter of profound conviction, not personal spite; he in fact wrote a moving tribute after Wagner's death. On the other hand, he was one of the very first and most influential champions of Brahms. From 1855–64 Hanslick was music editor of the *Presse;* thereafter of the *Neue Freie Presse;* he became a lecturer on music history and esthetics at Vienna Univ., prof. extraordinary in 1861, and full prof. in 1870, retiring in 1895 (succeeded by Guido Adler). At the Paris Expositions of 1867 and 1878, and the Vienna Exposition of 1873, Hanslick was a juror in the dept. of music. What gives his writings permanent value is the sound musicianship underlying their brilliant, masterly style. Yet in music history he is chiefly known as a captious and intemperate reviler of genius; Wagner caricatured him in the part of Beckmesser (in an early version of *Die Meistersinger* the name was to be Hans Lick).

WRITINGS: *Geschichte des Concertwesens in Wien* (1869); *Aus dem Concertsaal* (1870); a series begun with *Die moderne Oper* (1875) and followed by 8 more vols., giving a fairly comprehensive view of the development of opera from Gluck to 1900: II, *Musikalische Stationen* (1880); III, *Aus dem Opernleben der Gegenwart* (1884); IV, *Musikalisches Skizzenbuch* (1888); V, *Musikalisches und Litterarisches* (1889); VI, *Aus dem Tagebuch eines Musikers* (1892); VII, *Fünf Jahre Musik* (1896); VIII, *Am Ende des Jahrhunderts* (1899); IX, *Aus neuer und neuester Zeit* (1900); *Suite, Aufsätze über Musik und Musiker* (1885); *Konzerte, Komponisten und Virtuosen der letzten fünfzehn Jahre* (1886); *Aus meinem Leben* (2 vols., 1894). All these books passed through several eds. He also ed. T. Billroth's posthumous essay *Wer ist musikalisch?* (1895; 4th ed., 1912), and wrote the commentary for the illustrated *Galerie deutscher Tondichter* (1873) and *Galerie französischer und italienischer Tondichter* (1874). A collection of Hanslick's articles in the *Neue Freie Presse* was publ. in Eng. trans. under the title *Vienna's Golden Years of Music, 1850–1900* (N.Y., 1950).

BIBLIOGRAPHY: R. Schafke, *Eduard Hanslick und die Musikästhetik* (1922); S. Deas, *In Defense of Hanslick* (London, 1940); A. Wilhemer, *Der junge Hanslick* (Klagenfurt, 1959); D. Glatt, *Zur geschichtlichen Bedeutung der Musikästhetik Eduard Hanslicks* (Munich, 1972); W. Abegg, *Musikästhetik und Musikkritik bei Eduard Hanslick* (Regensburg, 1974).

Hanson, Howard, important American composer and educator; b. Wahoo, Nebr., Oct. 28, 1896; d. Rochester, N.Y., Feb. 16, 1981. His parents emigrated from Sweden to America and made their home in Nebraska, which had a large population of Scandinavian settlers; Hanson's northern ancestry played an important part in his spiritual outlook and his own music. His mother taught him piano; he began to compose very early in life; he also learned to play the cello. He attended the Luther College in Wahoo and played piano and organ in local churches; in 1912 he enrolled in the Univ. of Nebraska; in 1913 he went to N.Y. where he took piano lessons with James Friskin and studied composition with Percy Goetschius at the Inst. of Musical Art. In 1915 he enrolled at Northwestern Univ. in Evanston, Ill., where his teachers in composition were Arne Oldberg and P.C. Lutkin; he graduated in 1916 with a B.A. degree. He progressed rapidly as a composer; his *Symphonic Prelude* was performed by the Chicago Symph.; he also wrote a Piano Quintet and some other works. In 1916, at the age of 20, he received an appointment to teach music at the College of the Pacific in San Jose, Calif.; was named its dean in 1919. In 1921 he became the first American to win the prestigious Prix de Rome, which enabled him to spend 3 years at the American Academy there. He composed copiously; the major part of his works reflected his profound sentiment for his ancestral land; his *Scandinavian Suite* for Piano (1919) exemplified this devotion. He believed in music as a function of the natural environment. During his stay in the west, he wrote the score for a *California Forest Play* (1920). The work that gained him admission to Rome was a symph. poem, *Before the Dawn;* in 1923 he completed a piece for chorus and orch. entitled *North and West.* All these works clearly indicated his future path as a composer; they were permeated with the spirit of the northern country, inspired by both Scandinavia and the American West. There followed his first important work, Symph. No. 1, subtitled *Nordic;* he conducted its first performance in Rome on May 30, 1923. In it he expressed, as he himself said, "the solemnity, austerity, and grandeur of the North, of its restless surging and strife, and of its somberness and melancholy." Hanson was often described as an American Sibelius; indeed, he professed profound admiration for the great Finn, with whom he shared an affinity for slowly progressing lyrical modalities and somber harmonies anchored in deep organ points. In 1923 he conducted the American premiere of his *Nordic Symphony* in Rochester, and met George Eastman, the inventor of Kodak film. Eastman, who knew next to nothing about music, had nonetheless a keen appreciation of ability among artists and composers; in 1924 he offered Hanson the position of director of the Eastman School of Music; Hanson was not quite 28 years old at that time. Eastman's insight was justified; Hanson elevated the Eastman School of Music from a provincial conservatory to one of the most important musical institutions in America. He retained his post as director for 40 years; apart from his teaching, he inaugurated annual festivals of American music in Rochester; as director and conductor of these festivals, he showed an extraordinary measure of liberal choice, programming not only musical compositions that were naturally congenial to him, but also modern works in dissonant harmonies; and he maintained a friendly attitude toward his students even when they veered away into the field of cosmopolitan abstractions. All told, during his tenure in Rochester Hanson presented works by 700 composers and something like 1,500 different compositions. In 1925 he completed one of the most significant works, *The Lament of Beowulf,* for chorus and orch., based on an Old English saga. In 1930 he wrote his 2nd symph., entitled *Romantic,* on commission from Koussevitzky and the Boston Symph. on its 50th anniversary; Koussevitzky conducted its first performance on Nov. 28, 1930. Hanson's 3rd symph. (1936–37) glorified the pioneer spirit of Swedish immigrants; it was presented over the NBC Radio network on March 26, 1938, with Hanson himself conducting. In his Symph. No. 4, subtitled *The Requiem,* written in 1943, Hanson paid a tribute to the memory of his father; he conducted its first performance with the Boston Symph. on Dec. 3, 1943; in 1944 the work received the Pulitzer Prize in music. There followed the 5th symph. *Sinfonia Sacra,* in a single movement (1954); in it Hanson invoked his deep-rooted Christian faith; it was first performed by the Philadelphia Orch. on Feb. 18,

1955. Hanson wrote his 6th symph. to commemorate the 125th anniversary of the N.Y. Phil.; Leonard Bernstein conducted it on leap-year day of 1968. Hanson's 7th symph., *A Sea Symphony,* with chorus, derived from Walt Whitman's poem, was first performed on Aug. 7, 1977, at the National Music Camp at Interlochen. Whitman's poetry was close to Hanson's creative imagination; he wrote several other works based on Walt Whitman's poems, among them *3 Songs from "Drum Taps"* (1935); *Song of Democracy,* which Hanson conducted in Philadelphia on April 9, 1957; and *The Mystic Trumpeter,* performed in Kansas City on April 26, 1970. Hanson remained faithful to his musical and philosophical convictions throughout his long career. Like Sibelius, he wrote music of profound personal feeling, set in an idiom which reflected the triumphs and laments of his life and of his double inheritance. In 1933 he composed his opera, *The Maypole of Merry Mount,* based on *The Maypole Lovers of Merry Mount* by Nathaniel Hawthorne. Hanson dedicated the work to the memory of George Eastman, who had committed suicide 2 years before. Hanson conducted its first performance in concert form in Ann Arbor on May 20, 1933; on Feb. 10, 1934, it was produced by the Metropolitan Opera in N.Y., conducted by Tullio Serafin. It was one of the few operas by an American composer staged at the Metropolitan, and the production was very successful; according to reports, there was a total of 50 curtain calls for Hanson and the singers after its 4 acts. Despite this popular reception and favorable critical reviews, the opera had only 4 performances, and was not retained in the repertoire, a fate not unlike that of other American operas produced at the Metropolitan. A symph. suite drawn from the score enjoyed frequent performances at summer symph. concerts and on the radio.

In the meantime, Hanson continued an active career as conductor. In 1932 he led several concerts of American music in major cities of Europe. During the season 1961–62 he took the Eastman School Phil. Orch. on a grand European tour, under the auspices of the State Dept.; the itinerary included Portugal, Spain, Switzerland, France, Luxembourg, Belgium, Sweden, Greece, Cyprus, Syria, Egypt, Lebanon, Turkey, Germany, Poland, and Russia; in each of these countries Hanson received a most gratifying success; he was praised as both composer and able conductor; his school orch. also received its share of appreciation. As an educator, Hanson enjoyed a great prestige; many talented American composers studied under him. He received numerous honorary degrees. In 1935 he was elected a member of the National Inst. of Arts and Letters; in 1938 he became a fellow of the Royal Academy of Music in Sweden. He held, at various times, a presidency of the National Association of Schools of Music; served also as president of the Music Teachers National Association and of the National Music Council. He was awarded 19 honorary doctorates in music, among them from Syracuse Univ., Univ. of Nebraska, Northwestern Univ., New England Cons. of Music, and Univ. of Michigan. In 1945 he received the Ditson Award and in 1946 was given the George Foster Peabody Award. But with the radical changes in contemporary composition, Hanson's own music seemed to recede into an old-fashioned irrelevance; the number of performances of his music dwindled; only occasionally were his symphs. broadcast from old recordings. Hanson never tried to conceal his bitterness at this loss of appreciation in his country for whose artistic progress he labored so mightily. Yet Hanson's music cannot in all fairness be judged as unredeemingly obsolete. His array of sonorous harmonies, often in modulations at a tritone's distance of their respective tonics, reaches the borderline of pungent bitonality; his bold asymmetrical rhythms retain their vitality; his orchestration is masterly in its instrumental treatment. True, Hanson never accepted the modern techniques of serialism or a total emancipation of dissonance; yet he maintained a liberal attitude toward these new developments. Many of his conservative conservatory admirers were surprised by the publ. of his book, *Harmonic Materials of Modern Music,* in which he presented an exhaustive inventory of advanced harmonic formulas, tabulating them according to their combinatory potentialities.

WORKS: FOR THE STAGE: *California Forest Play of 1920,* ballet, with Solo Voices, Chorus, and Orch. (1919; Calif. State Redwood Park, 1920); *Merry Mount,* opera in 3 acts (1933, commissioned by the Metropolitan Opera; concert perf., Ann Arbor, May 20, 1933; first stage perf., Metropolitan Opera, Feb. 10, 1934); *Nymph and Satyr,* ballet (1978; Chautauqua, N.Y., Aug. 9, 1979). FOR ORCH: *Symph. Prelude* (1916); *Symph. Legend* (San Francisco, 1917); *Symph. Rhapsody* (1920; Los Angeles, May 26, 1921); *Before the Dawn,* symph. poem (Los Angeles, 1920); *Exultation,* symph. poem with Piano obbligato (San Francisco, 1920); Concerto for Organ, Strings, and Harp (1921); 7 symphs.: No. 1, *Nordic Symphony* (1922; Rome, May 30, 1923, composer conducting; first American perf., Rochester, March 19, 1924); No. 2, *Romantic Symphony* (1928–30; commissioned for the 50th anniversary of the Boston Symph. Orch., Koussevitzky conducting, Nov. 28, 1930); No. 3 (1937–38; first complete perf., NBC studio with NBC Symph., March 26, 1938, composer conducting; first public perf., Boston Symph., Nov. 3, 1939, composer conducting); No. 4, *Requiem* (1943; Boston Symph., Dec. 3, 1943, composer conducting; won Pulitzer Prize of 1944); No. 5, *Sinfonia Sacra* (1954; Philadelphia Orch., Feb. 18, 1955); No. 6 (1967; N.Y. Phil. Orch., Feb. 29, 1968); No. 7, *A Sea Symphony,* after Whitman, for Chorus and Orch. (1977; Interlochen, Mich., Aug. 7, 1977; for the 50th anniversary of the National Music Camp there); *North and West,* symph. peom with Choral Obbligato (1923; N.Y., 1924); *Lux Aeterna,* symph. poem with Viola Obbligato (1923); *Pan and the Priest,* symph. poem with Piano Obbligato (1925–26; London, Oct. 26); Concerto for Organ and Orch. (1926; Rochester, Jan. 6, 1927; uses themes from *North and West*); *Merry Mount Suite* (1937; from the opera); *Fantasy* for String Orch. (1939; based on the String Quartet of 1923); *Serenade* for Flute,

Harp, and Strings (1945; also arranged for Flute and Piano); Piano Concerto (Boston Symph., Dec. 31, 1948, composer conducting); *Pastorale* for Oboe, Harp, and Strings (1949; also arranged for Oboe and Piano); *Fantasy-Variations on a Theme of Youth* for Piano and Strings (for the Northwestern Univ. Centennial, Feb. 18, 1951); *Elegy in Memory of My Friend, Serge Koussevitzky* (Boston Symph., Jan. 20, 1956, Munch conducting); *Mosaics* (1957; Cleveland Orch., Jan. 23, 1958); *Summer Seascape I* for Orch. (New Orleans, March 10, 1959); *Summer Seascape II* for Strings (1965); *Bold Island Suite* (1959–61; Cleveland Orch., Jan. 25, 1962); *For the First Time* (Rochester Univ., 1963); *Dies natalis I* (1967); *Young Composer's Guide to the 6-tone Scale*, suite for Piano, Winds, and Percussion (1971–72).

FOR BAND: *March Carillon* (1920; arranged for Band by Erik Leidzen); *Chorale and Alleluia* (1953); *Centennial March* (1968); *Dies Natalis II* (1972); *Laude* (1974).

FOR VOICE: *The Lament for Beowulf*, for Chorus and Orch. (1923–25; Ann Arbor Festival, 1926); *Heroic Elegy* for Orch. and Chorus without words (for the Beethoven centenary, 1927); *3 Songs from "Drum Taps,"* after Whitman, for Baritone, Chorus, and Orch. (1935); *Hymn to the Pioneers* for Men's Voices a cappella (1938); *The Cherubic Hymn* for Chorus and Orch. (1948–49); *Centennial Ode* for Narrator, Baritone, Chorus, and Orch. (1950); *How Excellent Thy Name* for Chorus and Piano (1952); *The Song of Democracy* for Chorus and Orch. (1956; Philadelphia, April 9, 1957); *The Song of Human Rights*, cantata for Speaking Chorus and Orch., to the Universal Declaration of Human Rights (Washington, D.C., Dec. 10, 1963); *4 Psalms* for Baritone, Solo Cello, and String Sextet (Washington, D.C., Oct. 31, 1964); *2 Psalms: Psalm 150 (A Jubilant Song)* for Chorus and Orch. (1965) and *Psalm 121* for Chorus and Orch. (1968); *Streams in the Desert* for Chorus and Orch. (1969); *The Mystic Trumpeter* for Narrator, Chorus, and Orch. (1969; Kansas City, Mo., April 26, 1970); *New Land, New Covenant* for Soloist, Children's Chorus, Mixed Chorus, and Orch.; to words by Isaac Watts, T. S. Eliot, and John Newton, and from the Bible and the Declaration of Independence (1976; Byrn Mawr, Pa., May 2, 1976); *Prayer for the Middle Ages* for Chorus a cappella (1976); songs.

CHAMBER MUSIC: Piano Quintet (1916); *Concerto da Camera* for Piano and String Quartet (1916–17; version for Strings Alone, Rome, March 20, 1922); String Quartet (1923).

FOR PIANO: *Prelude and Double Concert Fugue* for 2 Pianos (1915); *4 Poems* (1917–18); Sonata (1918); *3 Miniatures* (1918–19); *Scandinavian Suite* (1919); *3 Etudes* (1920); *2 Yule-Tide Pieces* (1920).

PUBLICATIONS: *Harmonic Materials of Modern Music: Resources of the Tempered Scale* (N.Y., 1960).

BIBLIOGRAPHY: E. Royce, "Howard Hanson," in Henry Cowell's symposium *American Composers on American Music* (Stanford, 1933); E. E. Hipsher, *American Opera and Its Composers* (Philadelphia, 1934; pp. 241–44); B.C. Tuthill, "Howard Hanson," *Musical Quarterly* (April 1936); M. Al-ter, "Howard Hanson," *Modern Music* (Jan.–Feb. 1941); R. Watanabe, "Howard Hanson's Manuscript Scores," *The University of Rochester Library Bulletin* (vol. V, no. 2, Winter 1950); M. Goss, *Modern Music-Makers* (N.Y., 1952; pp. 223–36); *Composers of the Americas*, vol. 5 (Washington, D.C., 1959); *High Fidelity* (Dec. 1966); *Current Biography Yearbook 1966* (N.Y., 1967; pp. 152–54); V. Thomson, *American Music since 1900* (N.Y., 1970) B. Wehrung, "A Life in American Music," *Le Grand Baton* (March 1981; with discography compiled by N. Brown); *The Obituary Annual 1981* (N.Y., 1982; pp. 136–39).

Hanssens, Charles-Louis, Belgian cellist, conductor, and composer; b. Ghent, July 12, 1802; d. Brussels, April 8, 1871. As a child of 10 he played in the orch. of the National Theater in Amsterdam; was first cellist of the orch. in the Brussels theater (1824–27); then taught harmony at the Brussels Cons.; subsequently conducted French opera at The Hague and at Ghent. From 1848 to 1869 he was conductor at the Théâtre de la Monnaie in Brussels.

WORKS: 8 operas; ballets; symphs.; overtures; orch. fantasies; Violin Concerto; Cello Concerto; Clarinet Concerto; several piano concertos; string quartets; *Symphonie concertante* for Clarinet and Violin; masses; cantatas; a cappella choruses.

BIBLIOGRAPHY: L. de Burbure, *Notice sur Charles-Louis Hanssens* (Antwerp, 1872); L. Bäwolf, *Charles-Louis Hanssens* (Brussels, 1895).

Hanuš, Jan, Czech composer; b. Prague, May 2, 1915. He studied composition privately with Jeremiáš, and conducting with Pavel Dědeček at the Prague Cons. He then devoted himself to editorial work in music publishing houses; was an assistant in preparing the complete critical edition of Dvořák's collected works; also completed the instrumentations of the unfinished operas *Tkalci* by Nejedlý and *Balada o lásce* by Doubrava. His own music is marked by lyrical Romanticism, not without stringent dissonant textures.

WORKS: 4 operas: *Plameny (Flames;* 1942–44; Pilsen, 1956); *Sluha dvou pánů (Servant of 2 Masters;* 1958; Pilsen, 1959); *Pochodeň Prometheova (The Torch of Prometheus;* 1961–63; Prague, 1965); *Pohádka jedné noci (The Story of One Night;* 1965–68); 2 ballets: *Sůl nad zlato (Salt Is Worth More Than Gold;* 1953) and *Othello* (1956); 2 cantatas: *The Country Speaks* (1940) and *The Song of Hope* (1945–48); *Rondo capriccio* for Orch. (1937); 5 symphs. (with Solo Alto, 1942; 1951; 1957; 1960; 1965); *The Eulogy*, sinfonietta for Soprano and Orch. (1945); *Concertante Symphony* for Organ, Harp, Timpani, and Strings (1954); *Petr a Lucie (Peter and Lucia),* symph. fantasy (1955); *Overture*, after Walt Whitman's "The Bugler's Secret" (1961); Double Concerto for Oboe, Harp, and Orch. (1965); *Relay Race*, symph. allegro (1968); *Pražská nokturna (Prague Nocturne)* for Chamber Orch. (1972–73); Fantasy for String Quartet (1939); *Sonata-Rhapsody* for Cello and Piano (1941); *Suite to Paintings by Mánes* for Violin and Piano (1948); *A Year in Bohemia* for Children's Chorus, and Piano or

Chamber Orch. (1949–52); Serenade for Nonet (1953); Viola Sonatina (1958); *Suita dramatica* for String Quartet (1959); *3 Portraits from "Othello"* for Violin and Piano (1960); *Frescoes,* piano trio (1961); *Suita domestica* for Wind Quintet (1964); *Poselství (The Message),* tryptich for Baritone, Chorus, 2 Prepared Pianos, Electric Guitar, Percussion, and Tape (1969); *Musica concertante* for Cello, Piano, Winds, and Percussion (1969–70); Concertino for 2 Percussionists and Tape (1972); *The Swallow,* concerto piccolo for Chorus, Flute, and Cello (1973); *Meditations* for Piano (1938–39); Preludes for Piano (1949); *Suita lyrica* for Organ (1957); *Contemplazioni* for Organ (1969); Canons for Children's Chorus (1971–72); other choral works; songs.

Harasiewicz, Adam, Polish pianist; b. Chodziez, western Poland, July 1, 1932. He studied with Kazimierz Mirski until 1950; then at the State School of Music in Cracow. He entered the Chopin Contest in 1949, but failed to win a prize. In March 1955 he competed again, at the 5th International Chopin Contest in Warsaw, in which pianists of 27 countries took part, and won the first prize of 30,000 zlotys.

Harasowski, Adam, Polish pianist and writer on music; b. Delatyn, district of Stanisławów, Sept. 16, 1904. He was brought up in a musical family. He studied at the Lwow Cons. with Adam Soltys (1923–29); also took private lessons in composition with Szymanowski during his frequent visits at Lwow. Concurrently he studied mechanical engineering, graduating from the Lwow Polytechnic in 1931, and subsequently earned his living mainly as an engineering draftsman. At the outbreak of World War II he went to England with the Polish Air Force, and remained with the Royal Air Force of Great Britain as a flight lieutenant (1943–58); he retired in 1958 and devoted himself to journalism, both in Polish and in Eng.; publ. *The Skein of Legends around Chopin* (Glasgow, 1967); also compiled collections of Polish songs.

Haraszti, Emile, Hungarian musicologist; b. Nagyvárad, Nov. 1, 1885; d. Paris, Dec. 27, 1958. He studied composition and musicology in Vienna, Munich, Leipzig, Berlin, and Paris. Returning to Budapest, he served as the music critic of the *Budapest Hirlap* (1908–30); then lectured on music at the Univ. of Budapest. In 1945 he went to Paris. WRITINGS: *Wagner et la Hongrie* (Budapest, 1916); *La Musique hongroise* (Paris, 1933); *Béla Bartók, His Life and Works* (Oxford, 1938); *Un Centenaire romantique: Berlioz et la Marche Hongroise d'après des documents inédits* (Paris, 1946); also contributed valuable studies to various magazines. His monograph on Liszt was publ. posthumously in Paris in 1967. A complete list of his writings is found in his autobiographical notice in *Die Musik in Geschichte und Gegenwart.*

Harbison, John (Harris), American composer; b. Orange, N.J., Dec. 20, 1938. He grew up in an intellectual environment; his father was a prof. of history at Princeton Univ.; his mother was a magazine writer; both were musical. Exceptionally versatile, he studied violin, viola, piano, voice, and tuba at Princeton High School; also took theory lessons and won an award at a BMI contest at the age of 16. In 1956 he entered Harvard Univ. as a composition student (B.A., 1960); got a bundle of prestigious prizes, not only for music but even for poetry. He also received a Paine Traveling Fellowship from Harvard for a season of study in Berlin; there he took composition lessons with Boris Blacher, and also sang in a choir. Returning to the U.S., he studied composition with Roger Sessions and Earl Kim at Princeton Univ. (M.F.A., 1963). From 1963 to 1968 he was a member of the Society of Fellows at Harvard; from 1969 to 1982 he taught at the Mass. Inst. of Technology; then was composer-in-residence of the Pittsburgh Symph. Orch. (1982–84). He also made appearances as a conductor; led the Cantata Singers from 1969 to 1973 and again from 1980 to 1982. In 1977 he held a Guggenheim fellowship. In his music Harbison has freely adopted quaquaversal methods of composition, *sine ira et studio,* without doctrinaire pedestrianism; he makes use of dodecaphonic techniques when they suit his structural design; in his Shakespearean opera, *The Winter's Tale,* he introduces innovative "dumbshows" acted by pantomime, and also uses recordings; in his opera *Full Moon in March* he includes "prepared piano."

WORKS: For the Stage: Operas: *The Winter's Tale,* after Shakespeare (1974; San Francisco, Aug. 20, 1979), and *Full Moon in March,* after Yeats (1977; Cambridge, Mass., April 30, 1979); 2 ballets after Homer: *Ulysses' Raft* (1983) and *Ulysses' Bow* (1983; Pittsburgh, May 11, 1984). For Orch.: *Sinfonia* for Violin and Double Orch. (1963); *Confinement* for Chamber Ensemble (1965); *Elegiac Songs* for Mezzo-soprano and Chamber Orch., to poems by Emily Dickinson (N.Y., Jan. 12, 1974); *Descant-Nocturne* (1976); *Diotima* (1976; Boston, March 10, 1977); Piano Concerto (1978; N.Y., May 12, 1980); *Snow Country* for Oboe and String Orch. (1979); Violin Concerto (1980); Symph. No. 1 (1981; Boston, March 22, 1984). Chamber music: *Serenade* for 6 Players (1968); *Bermuda Triangle* for Tenor Saxophone, Cello, and Electric Organ (1970); *Book of Hours and Seasons* for Mezzo-soprano, Flute, Cello, and Piano (1975); Wind Quintet (1978); Piano Quintet (1981); *Variations* for Violin, Cello, and Piano (1982); also *The Flower-Fed Buffaloes* for Baritone and Chorus (1976) and other choral music; songs.
BIBLIOGRAPHY: David Ewen, *American Composers* (N.Y., 1982).

Harburg, E.Y. (Edgar "Yip" Harburg), American lyricist; b. New York, April 8, 1898; d. Los Angeles (in a car accident), March 5, 1981. He graduated from the City College of N.Y. in 1921; then was co-proprietor of an electrical appliance company, which failed during the Depression; he then began to write lyrics for Broadway; with Jay Gorney he produced the famous song *Brother, Can You Spare a Dime.* In

1939 he won an Academy Award for *Over the Rainbow* from *The Wizard of Oz;* his other lyrics included *We're Off to See the Wizard, It's Only a Paper Moon,* and *April in Paris* (to music by Vernon Duke). He was lyricist and co-author, with Burton Lane and Fred Saidy, of *Finian's Rainbow.*

d'Harcourt, Eugène, French conductor and composer; b. Paris, May 2, 1859; d. Locarno, Switzerland, March 4, 1918. He studied at the Paris Cons. with Massenet, Durand, and Savard (1882–86); then took courses in Berlin with Bargiel. In 1892 he built the "Salle d'Harcourt" in Paris, where he presented 3 seasons of Concerts Eclectiques Populaires. He wrote an unsuccessful opera, *Le Tasse* (Monte Carlo, 1903), in addition to 3 unnecessary symphs. and some passable chamber music.

d'Harcourt, Marguerite, French folk-song collector and composer; b. Paris, Feb. 24, 1884; d. there, Aug. 2, 1964. She studied composition with Vincent d'Indy and Maurice Emmanuel; composed 2 symphs.; *Rapsodie péruvienne* for Oboe, Clarinet, and Bassoon; and many songs. With her husband, **Raoul d'Harcourt,** she publ. a valuable treatise, *Musique des Incas et ses survivances* (2 vols., Paris, 1925), based on materials gathered during their journeys in Peru; another valuable publication which she compiled was a collection of 240 songs, *Chansons folkloriques françaises au Canada* (Quebec, 1956).

Hardegg, Grad, Austrian pianist; b. Vienna, April 24, 1834; d. there, March 22, 1867. He was a piano pupil of Czerny, and composed a number of pieces of salon music which became popular.

d'Hardelot, Guy (Mrs. W.I. Rhodes, née **Helen Guy),** French song composer; b. 1858 at the Château d'Hardelot, Boulogne-sur-Mer; d. London, Jan. 7, 1936. She studied at the Paris Cons.; traveled with Emma Calvé in the U.S. in 1896; then married, and settled in London. She wrote many melodious songs: *Sans toi; Because* (very popular); *Tristesse;* etc.

Harding, A(lbert) A(ustin), American college bandmaster; b. Georgetown, Ill., Feb. 10, 1880; d. Champaign, Ill., Dec. 3, 1958. At 14 he began to play cornet, and then trombone and other wind instruments. After graduation from high school in Paris, Ill., he conducted the local concert band. In 1902 he enrolled as an engineering student at the Univ. of Illinois, acquiring his bachelor's degree in 1906. At the same time he developed many campus music contacts, and in 1905 was made acting leader of the Univ. Band; in 1907 he was appointed director, a post he held until 1948. Harding was the first to succeed in raising college bands to a "symphonic" level in which oboes, saxophones, and other reed instruments supplied variety to the common brass-heavy contingent; thanks to this sonic enhancement, he was able to arrange orch. works of the general repertoire and perform them in a satisfac-tory musical manner; he was credited with 147 such transcriptions. John Philip Sousa, who greatly admired Harding, bequeathed to him and his band his own entire music library. Harding was a charter founder of the American Bandmasters' Assoc. in 1929 and was its president in 1937–38; was honorary life president from 1956 until his death. He also was active in founding the College Band Directors' Assoc., of which he was honorary life president from its founding in 1941.

BIBLIOGRAPHY: Calvin E. Weber, "Albert Austin Harding: Pioneer College Bandmaster," *Journal of Band Research* (Autumn 1966).

Harewood, 7th Earl of, George Hubert Lascelles, British music editor and organizer; b. London, Feb. 7, 1923. He was educated at Eton and King's College, Cambridge; served as captain in the Grenadier Guards in World War II; was wounded and taken prisoner in 1944. He was founder and editor of the magazine *Opera* (1950–53); was a member of the board of directors of the Royal Opera at Covent Garden (1951–53; 1969–72); from 1956–66 served as chairman of the Music Advisory Committee of the British Council; from 1961–65 was artistic director of the Edinburgh International Festival; from 1962–67 was chancellor of the Univ. of York. In 1972 he was appointed managing director of the Sadler's Wells Opera (known after 1974 as the English National Opera). He edited Kobbé's *Complete Opera Book* in 1954, 1963, and 1972; it was finally publ. as *The New Kobbé's Complete Opera Book* in 1976.

Harker, F. Flaxington, organist and composer; b. Aberdeen, Scotland, Sept. 4, 1876; d. Richmond, Va., Oct. 23, 1936. While acting as assistant organist at the York Minster, he studied with T. Tertius Noble, who was organist there. In 1901 he came to the U.S. and served as organist in churches in Biltmore, N.C., and Richmond, Va. He wrote 2 cantatas, *The Star of Bethlehem* and *The Cross;* publ. *Harker's Organ Collection* (2 vols.; 27 works by modern masters of the organ).

Harline, Leigh, American composer; b. Salt Lake City, March 26, 1907; d. Long Beach, Calif., Dec. 10, 1969. He studied music at the Univ. of Utah; went to Los Angeles in 1928, when he became arranger for Walt Disney (1931–42); then worked as a film-music composer in Hollywood; his song *When You Wish upon a Star* received an Academy Award in 1940.

Harling, William Franke, American composer; b. London, Jan. 18, 1887; d. Sierra Madre, Calif., Nov. 22, 1958. He was brought to the U.S. in his infancy; filled various jobs as a church organist. Eventually he settled in Hollywood. He wrote a one-act opera, *A Light from St. Agnes* (Chicago, Dec. 26, 1925); a "native opera with jazz," *Deep River* (Lancaster, Pa., Sept. 18, 1926; N.Y., Oct. 4, 1926); some instrumental music; and more than 100 songs. He was also the composer of the march *West Point Forever.*

BIBLIOGRAPHY: E.E. Hipsher, *American Opera*

and Its Composers (Philadelphia, 1927; pp. 250–56).

Harman, Carter, American music critic, recording-firm executive, and composer; b. Brooklyn, June 14, 1918. He studied with Roger Sessions at Princeton Univ. (1936–40); was a pilot in the U.S. Army Air Corps in the Burma-Indochina theater in World War II (1942–45); then returned for further study at Columbia Univ. (1945–48). From 1947–52 he was a music critic for the *N.Y. Times* and later music editor of *Time* magazine (1952–57); from 1958–67 he lived in Puerto Rico, where he became president of the West Indies Recording Corp.; was location sound engineer for the film *Lord of the Flies* and others. In 1967 Harman became producer and executive vice-president of Composers Recordings, Inc., in N.Y., devoted mainly to recording contemporary American music.

WORKS: Ballet, *Blackface* (N.Y., May 18, 1947); children's operas: *Circus at the Opera* (1951) and *Castles in the Sand* (1952); a group of 34 songs for children. In 1974 he began experiments with the total electronic synthesizing of nursery rhymes (with vocal parts accomplished by using a Sonovox and "artificial larynx") for an "entertainment" called *Alex and the Singing Synthesizer*, completed in 1977. He publ. *A Popular History of Music from Gregorian Chant to Jazz* (N.Y., 1956; revised 1968).

Harmat, Artur, Hungarian composer; b. Nyitrabajna (now Bojna, Czechoslovakia), June 27, 1885; d. Budapest, April 20, 1962. He studied at the Budapest Academy of Music and later took courses in Prague and Berlin. From 1920 to 1946 he was an inspector of singing in the Budapest schools; from 1924 to 1959 he was a prof. of religious music at the Budapest Academy. He wrote 2 valuable manuals on counterpoint (1947, 1956) and composed a great quantity of church music, based on the lines of Palestrina's polyphony.

WORKS: *Te Deum* for Chorus and Organ (1912–29); *Tu es Petrus* for Chorus and Orch. (1929); *Psalm 150* for Chorus and Instruments (1929); *De Profundis* for a cappella Chorus (1932); *Szép Ilonka (Fair Helen),* cantata (1954); Organ Sonata (1956).

Harmati, Sándor, Hungarian-American violinist; b. Budapest, July 9, 1892; d. Flemington, N.J., April 4, 1936. He studied at the Budapest Academy of Music; came to the U.S. in 1914 and became a member of the Letz Quartet (1917–21), then of the Lennox Quartet (1922–25); from 1925–30 he was conductor of the Omaha Symph. Orch. He composed a Symph. Poem, a String Quartet, and several works for violin, as well as piano pieces and songs; his song *Bluebird of Happiness* became popular.

Harnoncourt, Nikolaus, noted cellist, conductor, and musicologist; b. Berlin, Dec. 6, 1929. He was educated at the Vienna Academy of Music; then played in the Vienna Symph. In 1952 he founded the Vienna Concentus Musicus, an ensemble devoted to original performances in the Baroque style. He made many tours with this group.

Harper, Heather, distinguished English soprano; b. Belfast, May 8, 1930. She studied piano and voice at the Trinity College of Music; also took voice lessons with Helene Isepp and Frederic Husler; made her operatic debut in 1954 with the Oxford Univ. Opera; then appeared at the Glyndebourne Festival and with the English Opera Group. She made her Covent Garden debut in 1962; also sang at the Bayreuth Festivals, the Teatro Colón in Buenos Aires, the San Francisco Opera, and the Metropolitan Opera in N.Y. In 1965 she was made a Commander of the Order of the British Empire.

Harraden, Samuel, English music scholar; b. Cambridge, 1821; d. Hampstead, July 17, 1897. He studied with Walmisley; in 1841 became organist at St. Luke's in Manchester; in 1846 went to India and settled in Calcutta, where he became organist at the Old Mission Church. He greatly influenced the musical life of Calcutta; founded the first glee club there; became an enthusiastic student of Hindu music; was on the staff of the Hindu College of Music. In appreciation of his contribution to native art, he was made a Mus.D. by the Bengal Royal Academy of Music.

Harrell, Lynn, outstanding American cellist; b. New York, Jan. 30, 1944. His father was the baritone **Mack Harrell**; his mother was a violinist. He studied at the Juilliard School of Music in N.Y. with Leonard Rose and at the Curtis Inst. of Music in Philadelphia with Orlando Cole; also attended master classes with Piatigorsky in Dallas (1962) and Casals in Marlboro, Vt. (1963). He made his debut at a young people's concert of the N.Y. Phil. in 1961; then was first cellist of the Cleveland Orch. (1965–71). In 1975 he was named co-recipient (with the pianist Murray Perahia) of the first Avery Fisher Prize. He taught at the Univ. of Cincinnati College-Cons. of Music from 1971 to 1976; then joined the faculty of the Juilliard School of Music, while continuing his concert career. His playing is marked by ingratiating tonal mellowness and a facile, unforced technical display.

Harrell, Mack, American baritone; b. Celeste, Texas, Oct. 8, 1909; d. Dallas, Jan. 29, 1960. He studied violin and voice at the Juilliard School of Music in N.Y.; after some concerts as a soloist he joined the staff of the Metropolitan Opera (1939–45) and continued to make appearances there between 1947 and 1954; also taught voice at the Juilliard School (1945–56). He publ. a book, *The Sacred Hour of Song* (N.Y., 1938).

Harris, Sir Augustus, celebrated English impresario; b. Paris, 1852; d. Folkestone, England, June 22, 1896. An actor by profession, he became a stage manager and producer (with his brother Charles) with the Mapleson Co. in Manchester in 1873. In 1879 he leased the Drury Lane Theatre in London; in 1887 took up the promotion of Italian opera and secured control of Her Majesty's Theatre, Covent Garden, the Olympia, and various provincial stages.

He introduced to the English public many of the most famous singers of his time, among them Melba, Maurel, and the de Reszkes. He was knighted in 1891.

Harris, Charles K(assell), American song composer; b. Poughkeepsie, N.Y., May 1, 1865; d. New York, Dec. 22, 1930. He played banjo and piano as a child, and soon began to write songs; went into business for himself at 18 and put out the shingle "Banjoist and song writer/Songs written to order." He established his own publishing firms in Milwaukee and N.Y. His most spectacular success was the song *After the Ball* (1892); characteristically, he entitled his autobiography *After the Ball: 40 Years of Melody* (N.Y., 1926).

Harris, Donald, American composer and educator; b. St. Paul, Minn., April 7, 1931. He studied composition with Ross Lee Finney at the Univ. of Michigan (B.M., 1952; M.M., 1954); also took lessons with Boris Blacher and Lukas Foss at the Berkshire Music Center in Tanglewood (1954–55) and with Nadia Boulanger in Paris; later took courses with André Jolivet at Aix-en-Provence (1960). From 1954 to 1968 he lived in Paris; then returned to the U.S. In 1968 he joined the administrative staff of the New England Cons. of Music, where he was vice-president for academic affairs (1971–74) and executive vice-president (1974–77); concurrently he taught composition and music literature there (1970–77). In 1977 he became a prof. and chairman of the composition and theory dept. of the Hartt School of Music, and in 1980 was appointed its dean. With C. Hailey and J. Brand, he edited *The Correspondence between Alban Berg and Arnold Schoenberg* (N.Y., 1985). In his music he follows the trends of the cosmopolitan avant-garde.

WORKS: *The Legend of John Henry,* ballet for Orch. (1954; revised 1979); *The Golden Deer,* ballet for Orch. (1955); Piano Sonata (1957); Fantasy for Violin and Piano (1957); *Intervals,* dance work for Chamber Ensemble (1959); Symph. in 2 movements (1958–61); String Quartet (1965); *Ludus* for 10 Instruments (1966); *Ludus II* for 5 Instruments (1973); *On Variations* for Chamber Orch. (1976); *For the Night to Wear* for Mezzo-soprano and Chamber Ensemble (1978); *A Fanfare for the Seventies,* march for Band (1978); *Balladen* for Piano (1979); *Charmes* for Soprano and Orch. (1971–80); *Prelude to a Concert in Connecticut* for Orch. (1981); *Meditations* for Organ (1983); songs; incidental music.

Harris, Emmylou, American singer of country-music and pop songs; b. Birmingham, Ala., April 12, 1947. She studied drama at the Univ. of North Carolina; then made appearances as a successful singer of folk music, extending her repertoire in the kindred genres of country and pop music.

Harris, Roy, significant American composer; b. Chandler, Lincoln County, Okla., Feb. 12, 1898; d. Santa Monica, Calif., Oct. 1, 1979. His parents, of Irish and Scottish descent, settled in Oklahoma; in 1903 the family moved to California, where Roy Harris had private music lessons with Henry Schoenfeld and Arthur Farwell. In 1926 he went to Paris, where he studied composition with Nadia Boulanger; was able to continue his stay in Paris thanks to 2 consecutive Guggenheim fellowship awards (1927, 1928). Upon return to the U.S. he lived in California and in N.Y.; several of his works were performed and attracted favorable attention; his former teacher Arthur Farwell publ. an article in the *Musical Quarterly* (Jan. 1932) in which he enthusiastically welcomed Harris as an American genius. In his compositions, Harris showed a talent of great originality, with a strong melodic and rhythmic speech that is indigenously American. He developed a type of modal symbolism akin to Greek ethos, with each particular mode related to a certain emotional state. Instrumental music is the genre in which Harris particularly excelled. He never wrote an opera or an oratorio, but made astute use of choral masses in some of his works. He held the following teaching positions: Westminster Choir School, Princeton (1934–35); Cornell Univ. (1941–43); Colorado College (1943–48); Utah State Agricultural College in Logan (1948–49); Peabody College for Teachers at Nashville (1949–51); Sewanee, Tenn. (1951); Pa. College for Women (1951–56); Univ. of Southern Illinois (1956–57); Indiana Univ. (1957–60); Inter-American Univ., San Germán, Puerto Rico (1960–61); Univ. of Calif., Los Angeles (1961–73). In 1973 he was appointed composer-in-residence at Calif. State Univ., Los Angeles, a post he held until his death. He received honorary D.Mus. degrees from Rutgers Univ. and the Univ. of Rochester in N.Y.; in 1942 he was awarded the Elizabeth Sprague Coolidge Medal "for eminent services to chamber music." In 1936 he married the pianist **Johana Harris** (née **Beula Duffey;** b. Ottawa, Canada, Jan. 1, 1913); she assumed her professional name Johana in honor of J.S. Bach; the single *n* is used owing to some esoteric numerologic considerations to which Roy Harris was partial. After Roy Harris's death, she married, on Dec. 17, 1982, her 21-year-old piano student John Hegge.

WORKS: FOR ORCH.: 13 symphs.: No. 1 (Boston, Jan. 26, 1934); No. 2 (Boston, Feb. 28, 1936); No. 3 (Boston, Feb. 24, 1939; his best-known and most frequently performed work; it was the first American symph. to be played in China, during the 1973 tour of the Philadelphia Orch. under the direction of Eugene Ormandy); No. 4, *Folksong Symphony,* with Chorus (Cleveland, Dec. 26, 1940); No. 5 (Boston, Feb. 26, 1943); No. 6, *Gettysburg Address* (Boston, April 14, 1944); No. 7 (Chicago, Nov. 20, 1952); No. 8 (San Francisco, Jan. 17, 1962); No. 9 (Philadelphia, Jan. 18, 1963); No. 10, *Abraham Lincoln Symphony* for Chorus, Brass, 2 Amplified Pianos, and Percussion (Long Beach, Calif., April 14, 1965); No. 11 (N.Y., Feb. 8, 1968); No. 12 (partial perf., Milwaukee, Feb. 24, 1968); No. 13 for Chorus and Orch. (1969; Washington, D.C., Feb. 10, 1976); Symph. for Band (West Point, N.Y., May 30, 1952); *When Johnny Comes Marching Home,* symph. overture (Minneapolis, Jan. 13, 1935); *Farewell to Pioneers,* symph. elegy (Philadelphia, March 27, 1936); Concerto for 2

Pianos and Orch. (Denver, Jan. 21, 1947); *Kentucky Spring* (Louisville, Ky., April 5, 1949); Piano Concerto (Louisville, Dec. 9, 1953); *Fantasy* for Piano and Orch. (Hartford, Conn., Nov. 17, 1954); *Epilogue to Profiles in Courage: J.F.K.* (Los Angeles, May 10, 1964); *These Times* for Orch., with Piano (1962); Concerto for Amplified Piano, Wind Instruments, and Percussion (1968). VOCAL WORKS: *Whitman Triptych* for Women's Voice and Piano (1927); *A Song for Occupations,* after Whitman, for Chorus a cappella (1934); *Symphony for Voices,* after Walt Whitman, for Chorus a cappella (Princeton, May 20, 1936); *American Creed* for Chorus and Orch. (Chicago, Oct. 30, 1940); Mass for Men's Voices and Organ (N.Y., May 13, 1948); *Canticle to the Sun* for Coloratura Soprano and Chamber Orch., after St. Francis (Washington, Sept. 12, 1961); *Jubilation* for Chorus, Brasses, and Piano (San Francisco, May 16, 1964). CHAMBER MUSIC: Concerto for Clarinet, Piano, and String Quartet (Paris, May 8, 1927); 3 string quartets (1930, 1933, 1939); String Sextet (1932); Fantasy for Piano, Flute, Oboe, Clarinet, Bassoon, and Horn (Pasadena, Calif., April 10, 1932); Piano Trio (1934); Quintet for Piano and Strings (1936); *Soliloquy and Dance* for Viola and Piano (1939); String Quintet (1940). FOR PIANO: Sonata (1929); *Variations on an Irish Theme* (1938); *Little Suite* (1938); *American Ballads* (1942).
BIBLIOGRAPHY: Arthur Farwell, "Roy Harris," *Musical Quarterly* (Jan. 1932); Henry Cowell, "Roy Harris," *American Composers on American Music* (Stanford, Calif., 1933); Walter Piston, "Roy Harris," *Modern Music* (Jan.–Feb. 1934); Nicolas Slonimsky, "Roy Harris," *Musical Quarterly* (Jan. 1947); David Ewen, *American Composers* (N.Y., 1982).

Harris, Victor, American song composer; b. New York, April 27, 1869; d. there, Feb. 15, 1943. He studied voice and organ; music theory with Fred K. Schilling, and conducting with Anton Seidl. He subsequently served as organist at various churches in N.Y., and was vocal coach at the Metropolitan Opera (1892–95); from 1902–36 was conductor of the St. Cecilia Club in N.Y. He publ. about 150 songs, some of which enjoyed considerable popularity.

Harrison, Beatrice, English cellist; b. Roorke, India, Dec. 9, 1892; d. Smallfield, Surrey, March 10, 1965. She was brought to England in infancy; entered the Royal College of Music in London; won a prize at the age of 10; she was 14 when she made her first public appearance as a soloist with an orch. (London, May 29, 1907); then went to Berlin, where she took lessons with Hugo Becker; was the winner of the prestigious Mendelssohn Prize. She made several European tours, most of them in company with her sister, **May,** the violinist; toured the U.S. in 1913 and 1932.

Harrison, George, English rock singer, member of the celebrated group The Beatles; b. Liverpool, Feb. 25, 1943. Like his co-Beatles, he had no formal musical education, and learned to play the guitar by osmosis and acclimatization. Not as extraverted as John Lennon, not as exhibitionistic as Paul McCartney, and not as histrionic as Ringo Starr, he was not as conspicuously projected into public consciousness as his comrades-in-rock. Yet he exercised a distinct influence on the character of the songs that The Beatles sang. He became infatuated with the mystical lore of India; sat at the feet of a hirsute guru; introduced the sitar into his rock arrangements. He is the author of *Something,* one of the greatest successes of The Beatles. When the group broke up in 1970, Harrison proved sufficiently talented to impress his individual image in his own music; he also collaborated on songs of social consciousness with Bob Dylan.
BIBLIOGRAPHY: Hunter Davies, *The Beatles: The Authorized Biography* (N.Y., 1968); Ned Rorem, "The Beatles," *N.Y. Review of Books* (Jan. 18, 1968); G. Geppert, *Songs der Beatles. Texte und Interpretationen* (2nd ed., Munich, 1968); E. Davies, "The Psychological Characteristics of Beatle Mania," *Journal of the History of Ideas* (April–June 1969); P. McCabe and R.D. Schonfeld, *Apple to the Core: The Unmaking of the Beatles* (N.Y., 1972); F. Seleron, *Les Beatles* (Paris, 1972); W. Mellers, *Twilight of the Gods: The Music of the Beatles* (N.Y., 1973).

Harrison, Guy Fraser, American conductor; b. Guildford, Surrey, England, Nov. 6, 1894. He studied at the Royal College of Music, where he won an organ scholarship; served as an organist of the Episcopal Cathedral in Manila (1914–20); then emigrated to America; was organist of St. Paul's Cathedral in Rochester, N.Y. (1920–24); then was conductor of the Eastman Theater Orch. in Rochester (1924–49). In 1951 he was appointed conductor of the Oklahoma City Orch.; retired in 1973.
BIBLIOGRAPHY: Hope Stoddard, *Symphony Conductors of the U.S.A.* (N.Y., 1957).

Harrison, Jay, American music critic and editor; b. New York, Jan. 25, 1927; d. there, Sept. 12, 1974. He studied music with Philip James at N.Y. Univ. (A.B., 1948); was subsequently active mainly as a music critic; was on the staff of the *N.Y. Herald-Tribune* (1948–61); contributed articles to various music magazines. He collected a large number of valuable autograph letters by famous musicians, which he bequeathed to the Music Division of the Library of Congress.

Harrison, Julius Allan Greenway, English conductor and composer; b. Stourport, Worcestershire, March 26, 1885; d. Harpenden, Hertfordshire, April 5, 1963. He studied music with Granville Bantock; subsequently was active mainly as a conductor; filled in engagements with the Beecham Opera Co., the Scottish Symph. Orch., the Handel Society, the Hastings Orch. (1930–40), etc. In his music he makes competent use of English folk songs. He wrote an opera, *The Canterbury Pilgrims;* an orch. suite, *Worcestershire Pieces;* cantatas; some chamber music; many songs.

Harrison, Lou, American composer of the avant-garde; b. Portland, Oreg., May 14, 1917. After a period of study with Henry Cowell at San Francisco State College, he plunged headlong into the crosscurrents of modern music. In 1941 he attended the classes of Schoenberg at the Univ. of Calif. at Los Angeles; in 1943 moved to N.Y., where he worked as a music critic for the *N.Y. Herald-Tribune* (1945–48); for a while taught at the progressive Black Mt. College in North Carolina. He held 2 Guggenheim Foundation awards (1952 and 1954); eked out his finances by accompanying modern dancers, and also performing himself as a dancer; at one time he was employed as a florist. He tried his luck as an instrument maker; invented 2 new principles of clavichord construction; built a Phrygian aulos; developed a process for direct composing on a phonograph disc; in 1938 proposed a theory in interval control, and in 1942 supplemented it by a device for rhythm control; also wrote plays and versified poematically. He was one of the earliest adherents of an initially small group of American musicians who promoted the music of Charles Ives, Carl Ruggles, Varèse, and Cowell; he prepared for publication the 3rd Symph. of Charles Ives, which he conducted in its first performance, in 1947. He visited the Orient in 1961, and fortified his immanent belief in the multiform nature of music by studying Japanese and Korean modalities and rhythmic structures. Returning to California, he taught at San Jose State College. Seeking new sources of sound production, he organized a percussion ensemble of multitudinous drums and such homely sound makers as coffee cans and flowerpots. He wrote texts in Esperanto for his vocal works.

WORKS: Opera, *Rapunzel* (N.Y., May 14, 1959); *Young Caesar,* puppet opera (Aptos, Calif., Aug. 21, 1971); ballet scores: *Marriage at the Eiffel Tower* (1948); *Perilous Chapel* (1949); *Solstice* (1950); other works for dance: *Changing World, Johnny Appleseed, Almanac of the Seasons, Changing Moment, Omnipotent Chair, Praises for Hummingbirds and Hawks, Something to Please Everybody,* etc.; *Jephthah's Daughter,* "a theater kit" (Cabrillo College, March 9, 1963); for Orch.: *Elegiac Symphony* (1942–75); *Symphony on G* (1947–53; Oakland, Calif., Feb. 8, 1966); Suite for Solo Violin, Solo Piano, and Orch. (N.Y., Jan. 11, 1952, composer conducting); *Simfony from Simfonies* in free style for Orch. (1956); *Koncerto por la Violono kun perkuta orkestro* (title in Esperanto; N.Y., Nov. 19, 1959); *Suite for Simfoniaj Kordoj* (Esperanto for "Suite for String Orch."; 1960); *Concerto in Slendro* for Violin, Celesta, and Percussion (1961); *Nova Odo* for Chorus and Oriental Instruments (Seoul, Korea, 1963); 14 or more sinfonias for Percussion Orch.; *Recording Piece* for Concert Boobams, Talking Drums, and Percussion (1955); Mass, and other sacred works for chorus.

Harrison, May, British violinist, sister of **Beatrice Harrison;** b. Roorke, India, March 1891; d. South Nutfield, Surrey, June 8, 1959. She attended the Royal College of Music in London; like her sister, she was a precocious talent; at the age of 10 she won a gold medal of the Royal College of Music, competing against some 3,000 contestants. She then went to St. Petersburg, where she took lessons with Leopold Auer; returning to England, she made several concert tours, often in the company of her sister.

Harrison, William, English tenor and operatic impresario; b. London, June 15, 1813; d. there, Nov. 9, 1868. He studied at the Royal Academy of Music in London; made his debut in 1839 at Covent Garden; then made many appearances at Drury Lane. With the soprano Louisa Pyne, he organized an opera company in 1856; presented seasons of opera at Covent Garden (1858–64), producing works by Wallace, Balfe, Benedict, and other British composers.

Harriss, Charles Albert Edwin, English composer and organist; b. London, Dec. 15, 1862; d. Ottawa, Ontario, Aug. 1, 1929. As a boy he sang in a church choir at Wrexham, where his father was organist; in 1883 the family went to Montreal, where Harriss became a church organist. He wrote an opera, *Torquil* (Montreal, 1896); a cantata, *Daniel before the King* (1890); organ music; songs.

Harsányi, Tibor, Hungarian composer; b. Magyarkanizsa, Hungary, June 27, 1898; d. Paris, Sept. 19, 1954. He studied at the Budapest Academy of Music with Kodály; in 1923 he settled in Paris, where he devoted himself to composition. The melodic material of his music stems from Hungarian folk melos; his harmonic idiom is largely polytonal; the rhythms are sharp, often with jazz-like syncopation; the form remains classical.

WORKS: FOR THE STAGE: Chamber opera, *Les Invités* (Gera, Germany, 1930); radio opera, *Illusion* (Paris, June 28, 1949); 4 ballets: *Le Dernier Songe* (Budapest, Jan. 27, 1920); *Pantins* (Paris, 1938); *Chota Roustaveli* (in collaboration with Honegger and A. Tcherepnin; Monte Carlo, 1945); *L'Amour et la vie* (1951); puppet show, *L'Histoire du petit tailleur* for 7 Instruments and Percussion (1939). FOR ORCH.: *La Joie de vivre* (Paris, March 11, 1934, composer conducting); 2 divertissements (1940–41, 1943); Violin Concerto (Paris Radio, Jan. 16, 1947); *Figures et rythmes* (Geneva, Nov. 19, 1947, composer conducting); *Danses variées* (Basel, Feb. 14, 1950, composer conducting); Symph. (Salzburg Festival, June 26, 1952). CHAMBER MUSIC: Sonatina for Violin and Piano (1918); *3 Pieces* for Flute and Piano (1924); 2 string quartets (1918, 1935); Cello Sonata (1928); Nonet for String and Wind Instruments (Vienna Festival, June 21, 1932); Rhapsody for Cello and Piano (1939); *Picnic* for 2 Violins, Cello, Double Bass, and Percussion (1951); many piano pieces, among them *5 études rythmiques* (1934), *3 pièces lyriques,* and albums for children. He also wrote several choral works, including *Cantate de Noël* for Voices, Flute, and Strings (Paris, Dec. 24, 1945).

BIBLIOGRAPHY: J.S. Weissmann, "Tibor Harsányi," *Chesterian* (1952).

Harshaw, Margaret, outstanding American opera

singer; b. Narberth, Pa., May 12, 1909. She began her career as a contralto; later expanded her voice to mezzo-soprano and soprano, while retaining her capacity as a contralto. She was a scholarship student at the Juilliard Graduate School of Music in N.Y., where she studied voice with Anna Schoen-René, graduating in 1942. Shortly after graduation, she won the Metropolitan Opera Auditions of the Air and made her debut with the company in N.Y. as a mezzo-soprano in the role of the Second Norn in *Götterdämmerung* on Nov. 25, 1942; subsequently sang contralto and mezzo-soprano roles in German, Italian, and French operas; she also acquitted herself brilliantly as a dramatic soprano in her appearance as Senta in *Der fliegende Holländer* at the Metropolitan Opera on Nov. 22, 1950; was particularly successful in Wagnerian roles; she sang Isolde, Sieglinde, Kundry, Elisabeth, and all 3 parts of Brünnhilde. She also excelled as Donna Anna in *Don Giovanni* and Leonore in Beethoven's *Fidelio.* She was a guest soloist with the opera companies of Philadelphia, Cincinnati, San Francisco, and Covent Garden in London, and at the Glyndebourne Festivals. In 1962 she joined the faculty of the Indiana Univ. School of Music in Bloomington; she retired from the Metropolitan Opera in 1963.

Hart, Frederic Patton, American composer; b. Aberdeen, Wash., Sept. 5, 1894. He studied at the American Cons. in Chicago and at the Art Inst. there; later took courses with Rubin Goldmark, with Ernest Hutcheson, and at the Diller-Quaile School in N.Y. He taught at Sarah Lawrence College (1929–47) and at the Juilliard School of Music (1947–60); then settled in Los Angeles.

WORKS: Opera, *The Wheel of Fortune* (1943); opera-ballet, *The Romance of Robot* (1937); chamber music; piano pieces; songs.

Hart, Fritz, English conductor and composer; b. Brockley, Kent, Feb. 11, 1874; d. Honolulu, July 9, 1949. He studied at the Royal College of Music in London in 1893–96; in 1908 he went to Australia and settled there; in 1915 he became director of the Melbourne Cons.; in 1928 was appointed joint artistic director of the Melbourne Symph. Orch.; conducted both the Manila Symph. and the Honolulu Orch. (1932 until his death); settled in Honolulu in 1936 when appointed prof. of music at the Univ. of Hawaii; retired in 1942. He wrote operas, operettas, orch. works, chamber music, choruses, and songs.

Hart, James, English bass singer and composer; b. York, 1647; d. London, May 8, 1718. He was a singer in York Minster until 1670; was then appointed Gentleman of the Chapel Royal and lay-vicar of Westminster Abbey; settled in London and composed songs, publ. in *Choice Ayres, Songs and Dialogues* (1676–84), *The Theater of Musick* (1685–87), *Banquet of Musick* (1688–92), and other collections. He wrote *Adieu to the pleasures and follies of love* for Shadwell's operatic adaptation of *The Tempest* (1674), publ. as one of 6 "Ariel's Songs."

Hart, Lorenz, American lyricist; b. New York, May 2, 1895; d. there, Nov. 22, 1943. He began as a student of journalism at Columbia Univ. (1914–17); then turned to highly successful theatrical writing. During his 18-year collaboration with Richard Rodgers, he wrote the lyrics for *Connecticut Yankee* (1927); *On Your Toes* (1936); *Babes in Arms* (1937); *The Boys from Syracuse* (1938); *I Married an Angel* (1938); *Too Many Girls* (1939); *Pal Joey* (1940); *By Jupiter* (1942). Some of their best songs (*Manhattan, Here in My Arms, My Heart Stood Still, Small Hotel, Blue Moon, Where or When, I Married an Angel*) are publ. in the album *Rodgers & Hart Songs* (N.Y., 1951).

BIBLIOGRAPHY: S. Marx and J. Clayton, *Rodgers and Hart* (N.Y., 1976); D. Hart, *Thou Swell, Thou Witty: The Life and Lyrics of Lorenz Hart* (N.Y., 1976).

Hart, Philip, English organist; date and place of birth unknown; d. London, July 17, 1749. He composed anthems, organ fugues, and music for Hughes's *Old in Praise of Musick* (1703) and for *The Morning Hymn* from Milton's *Paradise Lost*, Book V (1729).

Hart & Sons, a firm of London violin makers, founded in 1825 by **John Hart.** His son, **John Thomas Hart** (b. Dec. 17, 1805; d. London, Jan. 1, 1874), a pupil of Gilkes, made a complete study of Cremonese and other violins of Italian make, establishing a reputation as an expert in his field. John Thomas's son, **George Hart** (b. London, March 23, 1839; d. near Newhaven, April 25, 1891), succeeded him. He was a good violinist himself; publ. valuable books, *The Violin: Its Famous Makers and Their Imitators* (London, 1875; French ed., Paris, 1886) and *The Violin and Its Music* (London, 1881). His sons, **George** and **Herbert Hart,** inherited the business.

Hart, Weldon, American composer; b. Place-Bear Spring, Tenn., Sept. 19, 1911; d. East Lansing, Mich., Nov. 20, 1957 (suicide). He studied music in Nashville, at the Univ. of Michigan, and at the Eastman School in Rochester, N.Y., with Howard Hanson and Bernard Rogers, receiving his Ph.D. in 1946. He was head of the music dept. of Western Kentucky State College (1946–49) and director of the School of Music of the Univ. of West Virginia (1949–57). In 1957 he was engaged as head of the music dept. of Michigan State Univ. at East Lansing; upon arrival there he became despondent over his inability to produce an impression with a concert of his works, and killed himself with carbon monoxide exhaust in his car. Yet his music, although not innovative, is well crafted. He wrote a *Sinfonietta* (1944); a symph. poem, *The Dark Hills* (1939); Symph. (1945); Violin Concerto (1951); *3 West Virginia Folk Songs* for Chorus and Orch. (1954); several violin pieces and choruses.

Harth, Sidney, American violinist, conductor, and pedagogue; b. Cleveland, Oct. 5, 1929. He studied at the Cleveland Inst. of Music (Mus.B., 1947); then took lessons with Joseph Fuchs and Georges Enesco; was a recipient of the Naumburg prize in 1948; made his debut at Carnegie Hall in N.Y. in 1949. He later served as concertmaster and assistant conductor of the Louisville Orch. (1953–58), and taught at the Univ. of Louisville. For 3 seasons he was concertmaster of the Chicago Symph. Orch. (1959–62) and concurrently taught at De Paul Univ.; was also concertmaster of the Casals Festival Orch. in San Juan (1959–65; 1972). From 1963–73 he was a prof. of music and chairman of the music dept. at Carnegie-Mellon Univ. in Pittsburgh. He then went to California and served as concertmaster and associate conductor of the Los Angeles Phil. (1973–79); was interim concertmaster of the N.Y. Phil. in 1980; also served as music director of the Puerto Rico Symph. Orch. (1977–79). In 1981 he became orch. director at the Mannes College of Music and a prof. of violin at the State Univ. of N.Y. at Stony Brook. With his wife, **Teresa Testa Harth,** he gave duo violin concerts.

Harthan, Hans, German composer and pianist; b. Bavaria, Feb. 23, 1855; d. Glendale, Calif., March 14, 1936. He studied with Lachner and Rheinberger in Germany. In 1883 he obtained a post of prof. of music in Odessa, Russia; in 1896 he went to Chile, where he became director of the National Cons. of Music in Santiago. In 1903 he emigrated to the U.S., eventually settling in California, the final destination of so many retiring European musicians. During his extended lifetime he wrote and publ. an astounding number of vocal and instrumental compositions, particularly for piano, expertly imitating the models of Schumann and Mendelssohn.

Hartig, Heinz, German composer; b. Kassel, Sept. 10, 1907; d. Berlin, Sept. 16, 1969. He studied piano at the Kassel Cons., and musicology at the Univ. of Vienna. Unable to hold a teaching post under the Nazi regime, he occupied himself with performances as a harpsichord player; in 1948 he joined the Hochschule für Musik in Berlin. In his compositions he applies varied techniques of modern music, from neo-Classicism to serialism, with formal unity achieved by the principle of free variations. He wrote a ballet, *Schwarze Sonne* (1958); chamber opera, *Escorial* (1961); Violin Concerto (1952); *Concertante Suite* for Guitar and Orch. (1954); Piano Concerto (1959); *Mass after a Holocaust,* after Dylan Thomas, for Baritone, Chorus, and Orch. (1960); *Wohin,* oratorio (1965); *Immediate* for Flute, Clarinet, Piano, and 2 Cellos (1966); *Concerto strumentale* for Violin and Orch. (1969); *Komposition in 5 Phasen* for Cello, Orch., Chorus, and Tape (1969).
BIBLIOGRAPHY: Wolfgang Burde, *Heinz Hartig* (Berlin, 1967).

Hartley, Walter S., American composer; b. Washington, D.C., Feb. 21, 1927. He studied with Bernard Rogers and Howard Hanson at the Eastman School of Music in Rochester, N.Y.; served in the U.S. Army during World War II. He taught at the National Music Camp in Interlochen in 1956–60; was chairman of the music dept. at Davis Elkins College beginning in 1960. In his works he cultivates the wind instruments; he wrote a Concerto for Alto Saxophone, Tuba, and Wind Octet (1969); Octet for Saxophones (1975); Sonatina for Tuba; band music.

Hartmann, Arthur, Hungarian-American violinist; b. Maté Szalka, Hungary, July 23, 1881; d. New York, March 30, 1956. He was brought to Philadelphia as a child and first studied with his father; then was a pupil of Loeffler (violin) and Homer Norris (composition). He made his debut in Philadelphia (1887) as a child prodigy; by the time he was 12, he had played practically the entire modern violin repertoire. He toured the U.S., Canada, and Scandinavia; played in Paris in recitals with Debussy, and became his intimate friend. In 1939 he settled in N.Y.; retired in 1954. He made numerous transcriptions and arrangements; discovered and edited 6 sonatas of Felice de' Giardini; wrote an essay on Bach's Chaconne which has been translated into 14 languages.

Hartmann, August Wilhelm, Danish organist and composer, son of **Johann Ernst Hartmann;** b. Copenhagen, Nov. 6, 1775; d. there, Nov. 15, 1850. He studied with his father; was first violinist in the Royal Chapel (1796–1817); then was appointed organist at the Garrison Church in Copenhagen. His organ works and other compositions are found in the Royal Library.

Hartmann, Carl, German tenor; b. Solingen, May 2, 1895; d. Munich, May 30, 1969. He studied in Cologne and Düsseldorf; made a successful debut in Elberfeld as Tannhäuser (1928), and then sang all over Germany, in Vienna, in Paris, and in Stockholm. In 1930 he toured the U.S. with Gadski's Opera Co., appearing in Wagnerian tenor roles; from 1937–40 was a member of the Metropolitan Opera Co. in N.Y.; then returned to Germany and lived mostly in Munich.

Hartmann, Eduard von, German writer on musical esthetics; b. Berlin, Feb. 23, 1842; d. Grosslichterfelde, near Berlin, June 5, 1906. He studied philosophy; music was his avocation; he wrote numerous songs, and even began writing an opera. In his philosophical essays he proposed some plausible theories concerning the laws of musical esthetics; of chief importance in this respect are his publications *Deutsche Ästhetik seit Kant* (Berlin, 1886) and *Philosophie des Schönen* (Berlin, 1887), which contains the chapter "Idealismus und Formalismus in der Musikästhetik."

Hartmann, Emil, Danish composer, son of **Johan Peter Emilius Hartmann;** b. Copenhagen, Feb. 21, 1836; d. there, July 18, 1898. He received his early education from his father and from **Niels Gade** (who was his brother-in-law); from 1861 till his death was organist in various churches in Denmark. After Gade's death, Hartmann conducted a season of the Musical Society at Copenhagen (1891–

92).

WORKS: Operas: *Elverpigen* (Copenhagen, Nov. 5, 1867); *Korsikaneren* (Copenhagen, April 7, 1873); *Ragnhild* (1896); *Det store Lod* (1897); ballet, *Fjeldstuen* (Copenhagen, May 13, 1859); 7 symphs.; other instrumental works.

Hartmann, Georg, German opera producer and administrator; b. Nuremberg, Feb. 19, 1891; d. Munich, Jan. 9, 1972. He was educated in Marburg and Munich; then was an opera producer in Hannover (1919–20) and in Dresden (1920–23). Later he served as Intendant at the opera houses of Lübeck (1923), Dessau (1925), Breslau (1929), Dortmund (1934), and Duisburg (1937). From 1947 to 1952 he was Intendant of the Bavarian State Opera, Munich, gaining distinction as one of the most important opera producers in Germany.

Hartmann, Johan Peter Emilius, celebrated Danish composer; b. Copenhagen, May 14, 1805; d. there, March 10, 1900. He was the most famous of the Hartmann family in Denmark; was grandson of **Johann Ernst Hartmann** and son of **August Wilhelm Hartmann.** He studied law at the Univ. of Copenhagen, and for many years occupied a public position as a jurist (1828–70), but he was also profoundly interested in music; studied with his father and became his assistant as organist at the Copenhagen Cathedral (1843), remaining in that capacity until his death. He also taught at the Cons. of Copenhagen (from 1827). In 1836 he was one of the organizers of the Danish Music Society; in 1868 was appointed its director. He was also co-director (with **Niels Gade,** his son-in-law) of the new Copenhagen Cons., established in 1867. He spent almost his entire life in Denmark; the only extensive traveling he undertook was in 1836, when he visited Germany and France. He was greatly esteemed in Denmark. A Hartmann Scholarship was founded on the occasion of his 50th jubilee, and he received the Daneborg order.

WORKS: Operas: *The Raven* (Copenhagen, Oct. 29, 1832); *The Corsairs* (Copenhagen, April 23, 1835); *Little Christina* (Copenhagen, May 12, 1846); ballets: *Valkyrien* (Copenhagen, Sept. 13, 1861) and *Thrymskviden* (Copenhagen, Feb. 21, 1868); melodrama, *The Golden Horns* (1834); 2 symphs.: in G minor (1835) and in E major (1848); overtures; Violin Concerto; Flute Sonata; Violin Sonata; pieces for piano; songs.

BIBLIOGRAPHY: W. Behrend, *J.P.E. Hartmann* (Copenhagen, 1895); A. Hammerich, *J.P.E. Hartmann, Biographical Essays* (Copenhagen, 1916); R. Hove, *J.P.E. Hartmann* (Copenhagen, 1934).

Hartmann, Johann Ernst, German-Danish composer and violinist, founder of the "Hartmann dynasty" of musicians active in Denmark; b. Glogau, Silesia, Dec. 24, 1726; d. Copenhagen, Oct. 21, 1793. He studied violin in Silesia, and held various posts as a band violinist. In 1766 he settled in Copenhagen; became conductor of the Royal Orch. in 1768. Most of his MSS were lost in a fire (1794), but his

violin method and a few instrumental works are extant. His chief claim to fame is the fact that the melody of the present national anthem of Denmark, *Kong Christian stod ved hojen Mast,* was used in the score he wrote for the melodrama *Fiskerne* (Copenhagen, Jan. 31, 1780), and was for a long time regarded as his own composition, although it may have been borrowed from some unknown source of folk origin. A study of this melody is included in Angul Hammerich's book *J.P.E. Hartmann, Biographical Essays* (Copenhagen, 1916).

Hartmann, Karl Amadeus, outstanding German composer; b. Munich, Aug. 2, 1905; d. there, Dec. 5, 1963. He studied with Joseph Haas at the Music Academy in Munich (1923–27) and later with Scherchen. He began to compose rather late in life; his first major work was a Trumpet Concerto, which was performed in Strasbourg in 1933. During the war he studied advanced musical composition and analysis with Anton von Webern in Vienna (1941–42). After the war he organized in Munich the society Musica Viva. He received a prize from the city of Munich in 1948; in 1952 was elected a member of the German Academy of Fine Arts, and soon after became president of the German section of the International Society for Contemporary Music. Despite his acceptance of a highly chromatic, atonal idiom and his experimentation in the domain of rhythm (patterned after Boris Blacher's "variable meters"), Hartmann retained the orthodox form and structural cohesion of basic Classicism. He was excessively critical of his early works, and discarded many of them, but some have been retrieved and performed after his death.

WORKS: Chamber opera, *Des Simplicius Simplicissimus Jugend* (1934–35; Cologne, Oct. 20, 1949; a revised, reduced scoring of the work was made in 1955 and retitled *Simplicius Simplicissimus*); 8 symphs.: No. 1, *Versuch eines Requiems (Attempt at a Requiem),* to words by Walt Whitman, for Soprano and Orch. (1936–40; Vienna, June 22, 1957); No. 2, *Adagio* (1941–46; Donaueschingen, Sept. 10, 1950); No. 3 (1948–49; Munich, Feb. 10, 1950); No. 4 for String Orch. (1946–47; Munich, April 2, 1948); No. 5, *Symphonie concertante,* for Wind Instruments, Cellos, and Double Basses (1950; Stuttgart, April 21, 1951; based on "variable meters"); No. 6 (1951–53; Munich, April 24, 1953); No. 7 (1958; Hamburg, March 15, 1959); No. 8 (1960–62; Cologne, Jan. 25, 1963); *Miserae* (Prague, Sept. 1, 1935); *Concerto funebre* for Violin and String Orch. (1939; revised 1959; Braunschweig, Nov. 12, 1959); *Symphonischen Hymnen* (1942; Munich, Oct. 9, 1975); symph. overture, *China kämpft* (*China at War;* 1942; Darmstadt, July 1947); Concerto for Piano, Winds, and Percussion (Donaueschingen, Oct. 10, 1953); Concerto for Viola, Piano, Winds, and Percussion (Frankfurt, May 25, 1956); *Gesangsszene,* on German texts of Jean Giraudoux's "Sodome et Gomorrhe," for Baritone and Orch. (1962–63; unfinished; Frankfurt, Nov. 12, 1964); *Kammerkonzert* for Clarinet, String Quartet, and String Orch. (Zürich, June 17, 1969); *Jazz-Toccata und -Fugue* for

Piano (1928); *Tanzsuite* for Wind Quintet (1931; Frankfurt, April 20, 1975); Piano Sonatina (1931); 2 string quartets (*Carillon,* 1933; 1945–46); *Burleske Musik* for 6 Winds, Percussion, and Piano (c.1933; Rotterdam, June 30, 1967); *Friede Anno 48,* after Gryphius, for Soprano, Chorus, and Piano (1937; Cologne, Oct. 22, 1968; the sections for soprano and piano also exist as a separate piece called *Lamento,* a cantata for Soprano and Piano); *Kleines Konzert* for String Quartet and Percussion (version for String Orch. and Percussion, Braunschweig, Nov. 29, 1974).

BIBLIOGRAPHY: R. Wagner, ed., *Karl Amadeus Hartmann und die Musica Viva* (Munich, 1980).

Hartmann, Pater (real name, **Paul Eugen Josef von An der Lan-Hochbrunn**), German conductor and composer; b. Salurn, near Bozen, Dec. 21, 1863; d. Munich, Dec. 5, 1914. He entered the Franciscan order at the age of 16; studied theology and music in various monasteries; then completed his musical studies with Josef Pembaur in Innsbruck; was ordained a priest in 1886; was appointed organist at the Church of the Redeemer in Jerusalem (1893) and at the Church of the Holy Sepulchre (1894); in 1895 he was transferred to Rome as organist of the monastery Ara Coeli and director of the Scuola Musicale Cooperativa. From 1906 till his death he lived in the Franciscan monastery of St. Anna at Munich. During the season of 1906–7 he visited the U.S., conducting some of his oratorios. His sacred music retains its importance in Germany.

WORKS: Oratorios: *Petrus* (1900); *Franziskus* (1902); *Das letzte Abendmahl* (1904); *Der Tod des Herrn* (1905); *Septem ultima verba Christi in Cruce* (1908); *Te Deum* (1913); masses; organ works.

Hartmann, Rudolf, German opera producer and administrator; b. Ingolstadt, Oct. 11, 1900. He studied in Munich; then became an opera producer successively in Altenburg (1924–27), in Nuremberg (1928–34), and at the State Opera in Berlin (1934–37). From 1937 to 1944 he worked at the Bavarian State Opera in Munich; then was Intendant of the Bavarian State Opera (1952–67). His productions were noteworthy for their fusion of traditional and contemporary stage practices. He publ. a book, *Richard Strauss: The Staging of His Operas and Ballets* (Oxford, 1982).

Hartmann, Thomas de, Russian composer; b. Khoruzhevka, Ukraine, Sept. 21, 1885; d. Princeton, N.J., March 26, 1956. He studied piano with Anna Essipova at the St. Petersburg Cons.; composition with Taneyev and Arensky. His first important work, the ballet *The Little Crimson Flower,* was produced at the Imperial Theater in St. Petersburg in 1907 with Pavlova, Karsavina, Nijinsky, and Fokine. After the Revolution he went to the Caucasus; taught at the Tiflis Cons. (1919); then went to Paris, where he remained until 1951, when he settled in N.Y. His early music is in the Russian national style, influenced particularly by Mussorgsky; from about 1925, he made a radical change in his style of composition, adopting many devices of outspoken modernism (polytonality, etc.).

WORKS: *The Little Crimson Flower,* ballet (St. Petersburg, Dec. 16, 1907); *Babette,* ballet (Nice, March 10, 1935); opera, *Esther* (not perf.); 4 symphs. (1915; 1944; 1953; 1955, unfinished); Cello Concerto (1935; Boston, April 14, 1938); Piano Concerto (1940; Paris, Nov. 8, 1942); Double-bass Concerto (1943; Paris, Jan. 26, 1945); Harp Concerto (1944); Violin Concerto (Paris, March 16, 1947); Flute Concerto (Paris, Sept. 27, 1950); *12 Russian Fairy Tales* for Orch. (Houston, April 4, 1955, Stokowski conducting); Violin Sonata (1937); Cello Sonata (1942); Trio for Flute, Violin, and Piano (1946); 3 song cycles to words by Verlaine, Proust, and James Joyce; other songs; piano pieces. His music to Kandinsky's spectacle *The Yellow Sound,* arranged by Gunther Schuller from Hartmann's sketches, was played in N.Y. in a series of performances beginning Feb. 9, 1982.

Hartog, Edouard de, Dutch composer; b. Amsterdam, Aug. 15, 1829; d. The Hague, Nov. 8, 1909. He studied in Germany with Hoch and Mme. Dulcken, and in Paris with Elwart. He lived many years in Paris, where he produced the opera *Le Mariage de Don Lope* (1865); another opera by him, *L'Amour et son Hôte,* was produced in Brussels (1873). He also wrote several symph. works, chamber music, and piano pieces.

Hartog, Jacques, Dutch composer and writer; b. Zalt-Bommel, Oct. 24, 1837; d. Amsterdam, Oct. 3, 1917. He studied with Ferdinand Hiller at Cologne; upon his return to the Netherlands, he was appointed a prof. at the Amsterdam School of Music, and held this post for many years (1886–1913). He publ. monographs (in Dutch) on Beethoven (1904), Mozart (1904), Haydn (1905), Mendelssohn (1909), Schumann (1910), Bach (1911), and Wagner (1913); trans. into Dutch several German theory books; also wrote some orch. and chamber music.

Härtwig, Dieter, German musicologist; b. Dresden, July 18, 1934. He studied musicology at the Univ. of Leipzig (Ph.D., 1963, with the dissertation *Der Opernkomponist Rudolf Wagner-Régeny: Leben und Werke;* publ. in Berlin in an enlarged ed. as *Rudolf Wagner-Régeny: Der Opernkomponist*); then completed his Habilitation there in 1970 with *Fidelio F. Finke: Leben und Werk.* He was a dramaturge at the Schwerin State Theater (1959–60); then at the Radebeul Theater in Dresden (1960–65); lectured in music history at the Dresden Hochschule für Musik from 1960 to 1962, and then again from 1973. In 1965 he also assumed the positions of chief dramaturge and deputy artistic director of the Dresden Phil. Orch. He publ. a valuable history of the Dresden Phil., *Die Dresdner Philharmonie: Eine Chronik des Orchesters 1870 bis 1970* (Leipzig, 1970).

Harty, Sir Hamilton, eminent conductor and composer; b. Hillsborough, County Down, Ireland, Dec.

4, 1879; d. Brighton, England, Feb. 19, 1941. He received his entire education from his father, an organist; so well grounded was he as a performer that on Feb. 12, 1894, at the age of 14, he was formally appointed as organist at Magheragall Church, in County Antrim; later he also filled positions as church organist in Belfast and in Bray, outside Dublin. In 1901 he went to London, where he began to compose; his Piano Quintet, String Quartet, and *Irish Symphony* won prizes; in London he also began to conduct. On July 15, 1904, he married the singer **Agnes Nicholls.** In 1920 he was appointed conductor of the renowned Hallé Orch. in Manchester, remaining at that post for 13 seasons. In 1932 he became conductor of the London Symph. Orch. In 1931 he made his first American tour, during which he conducted in Boston, Chicago, and Cleveland, and at the Hollywood Bowl. In 1934 he conducted in Australia. He was knighted in 1925. Harty's arrangements of Handel's *Water Music* and *Royal Fireworks Music* for large orch. became standard repertoire pieces; of his original works, only his *Irish Symphony,* first performed under his direction in Manchester on Nov. 13, 1924, received praise; he also wrote *Comedy Overture* (1906); *Ode to a Nightingale,* after Keats, for Soprano and Orch. (1907); Violin Concerto (1908–9); *With the Wild Geese,* symph. poem (1910); *The Mystic Trumpeter* for Baritone, Chorus, and Orch. (1913); *The Children of Lir,* symph. poem (London, March 1, 1939). He arranged *A John Field Suite* for Orch., based on piano pieces by Field.

BIBLIOGRAPHY: D. Greer, ed., *Hamilton Harty: His Life and Music* (Belfast, 1978).

Harvey, Jonathan, significant British composer; b. Sutton, Goldfield, May 3, 1939. He served as a chorister at St. Michael's College, Tenbury (1948–52); won a scholarship to St. John's College, Cambridge; studied music there with Erwin Stein and Hans Keller; gained his Ph.D. from Glasgow Univ. in 1964; then joined the music faculty of Southampton Univ. In 1969–70 he lectured at Princeton Univ.; in 1980 became prof. of music at Sussex Univ. As a composer, Harvey absorbed and astutely synthesized a number of quaquaversal idioms and techniques ranging from medieval modalities to ultra-modern procedures; he also made use of electronic resources.

WORKS: FOR ORCH.: Symph. (1966); Chaconne on *Iam dulcis amica* (1967); *Benedictus* (1970); *Persephone's Dream* (London, Jan. 18, 1973); *Inner Light* (London, March 3, 1976); *Smiling Immortal* for Chamber Orch. (London, July 11, 1977); *Whom ye adore* (Glasgow, Sept. 19, 1981). CHAMBER MUSIC: Variations for Violin and Piano (1965); *Studies* for 2 Clarinets (1970); Trio for Violin, Cello, and Piano (1971); *Inner Light I* for 7 Players (London, Nov. 26, 1973); *Quantumplation* for Instrumental Ensemble (1973); *Meditation* for Cello and Quadrophonic Tape (1976); String Quartet (1977); *Album,* 7 miniatures for Wind Quintet (1978); *Be(com)ing* for Clarinet and Piano (1979); *Concelebration* for Instrumental Ensemble (London, Jan. 6, 1980); *Mortuos*

plango, vivos, voco for Computerized Concrete Sounds (1980; Lille, Nov. 30, 1980); *Modernsky Music* for 2 Oboes, Bassoon, and Harpsichord (Sounthorpe, Sept. 19, 1981). VOCAL MUSIC: 4 songs of Yeats for Bass and Piano (1965); Cantata I for Soloists, Chorus, Organ, and Strings (1965); Cantata II, *Three Lovescapes* for Soprano and Piano (1967); Cantata III for Soprano and 6 Players (1968); Cantata IV, *Ludus Amoris,* for Soloists, Speaker, Chorus, and Orch. (1969); Cantata V for Soloists and Wind Quintet (1970); Cantata VI, *On Faith,* for Chorus and Strings (1970); Cantata VII, *On Vision* (1971); Cantata VIII (1971); Cantata IX (1973); Cantata X, *Spirit Music,* for Soprano, 3 Clarinets, and Piano (Sheffield, Feb. 20, 1976); *Inner Light II* for Soloists, Instruments, and Tape (Cheltenham, July 8, 1977); *Hymn* for Chorus and Orch. (1979, for the 900th anniversary of Winchester Cathedral, July 12, 1979); *Passion and Resurrection,* church opera (Winchester Cathedral, March 21, 1981); *Resurrection* for Double Chorus and Organ (Worcester, Aug. 28, 1981).

Harwood, Basil, English organist and composer; b. Woodhouse, Gloucestershire, April 11, 1859; d. London, April 3, 1949. He studied piano with J.L. Roeckel and organ with George Risely; also studied with Reinecke and Jadassohn at the Leipzig Cons. Returning to England, he occupied various posts as an organist: at St. Barnabas Church, Pimlico (1883–87); Ely Cathedral (1887–92); and Christ Church Cathedral, Oxford (1892–1909). He edited the *Oxford Hymn Book* (1908); wrote a number of sacred works for chorus; organ pieces (2 sonatas, Organ Concerto, Christmastide, *Dithyramb,* etc.); a cantata, *Ode on May Morning*, after Milton (Leeds Festival, 1913).

Harwood, Elizabeth, English soprano; b. Kettering, May 27, 1938. She studied at the Royal Manchester College of Music; won the Kathleen Ferrier Memorial Prize in 1960. In 1961 she joined the Sadler's Wells Opera; was a winner of the Verdi Sesquicentennial Competition in Busetto in 1963; subsequently sang with the Scottish Opera, Covent Garden, and the English Opera Group; also made guest appearances at La Scala in Milan and at the Salzburg Festival. She made her Metropolitan Opera debut in N.Y. on Oct. 15, 1975, as Fiordiligi in *Così fan tutte.*

Häser, August Ferdinand, German composer; b. Leipzig, Oct. 15, 1779; d. Weimar, Nov. 1, 1844. He was a member of a musical family; his 3 brothers and a sister were musicians. He was educated at the Thomasschule in Leipzig, and studied theology at Leipzig Univ. In 1797 he went to Lemgo, Westphalia, where he taught mathematics in high school. He traveled in Italy from 1806–13; then returned to Lemgo. In 1817 he was engaged in Weimar as music teacher to Princess Augusta (the future German empress); also conducted the chorus at the Court Opera there; was a church organist and a teacher of Italian.

WORKS: 3 operas, which were performed in Weimar; an oratorio, *Die Kraft des Glaubens;* many sacred choruses; 4 overtures; several instrumental works in salon style. He publ. *Versuch einer systematischen Übersicht der Gesanglehre* (Leipzig, 1822); *Chorgesangschule für Schul- und Theaterchöre* (Mainz, 1831; in French as *Méthode pour apprendre à chanter en chœur à l'usage des écoles, des théâtres*).

Häser, Charlotte, German soprano; b. Leipzig, June 24, 1784; d. Rome, May 1, 1871. She studied with her father, **Johann Georg Häser,** a composer; then sang in Dresden; she went to Italy in 1806, where she enjoyed tremendous success; she was also one of the first women to sing male roles. After she left the stage, she settled in Rome. Her brother, **August Ferdinand Häser,** was a composer.

Haskil, Clara, brilliant Rumanian pianist; b. Bucharest, Jan. 7, 1895; d. Brussels, Dec. 7, 1960. A precocious musician, she played in public at the age of 7; then entered the Paris Cons., where she studied piano with Cortot and won a first prize at the age of 14. Busoni heard her in Basel and invited her to study with him in Berlin. She played programs of Beethoven sonatas with Enesco, Ysaÿe, and Casals; subsequently gave piano recitals and appeared as a soloist with major symph. orchs. in Europe and America. A muscular deficiency severely impeded her concert career; however, she continued playing concerts during periods of remission of her ailment. Music critics praised her fine musicianship and her penetrating interpretation of classical piano music.
BIBLIOGRAPHY: R. Wolfensberger, *Clara Haskil* (Bern, 1961); J. Spycket, *Clara Haskil,* with a preface by Herbert von Karajan (Paris, 1975).

Haslinger, Tobias, Austrian music publisher; b. Zell, March 1, 1787; d. Vienna, June 18, 1842. He went to Vienna in 1810 after studying music in Linz; was bookkeeper in Steiner's music establishment; later became a partner and, after Steiner's retirement in 1826, sole proprietor. A gregarious and affable person, he made friends with many musicians, and was on excellent terms with Beethoven, who seemed to enjoy Haslinger's company; many letters to him from Beethoven are extant, among them the humorous canon *O Tobias Dominus Haslinger.* He was succeeded by his son **Carl Haslinger** (b. Vienna, June 11, 1816; d. there, Dec. 26, 1868). The latter studied with Czerny and became a brilliant pianist as well as an industrious composer; he publ. more than 100 works of various kinds. Continuing the tradition of his father, he publ. several symphs., piano concertos, overtures, and other works by Beethoven, and later Liszt's Piano Concerto in E-flat; he was also the publisher of many Strauss waltzes. In 1875 the firm was bought from his widow by Schlesinger of Berlin (subsequently, R. & W. Lienau).

Hassard, John Rose Green, American journalist and music critic; b. New York, Sept. 4, 1836; d. there, April 18, 1888. He studied at St. John's College, Fordham; served as music critic of the *N.Y. Tribune* (1868–84). His account of the Festival at Bayreuth in 1876 (later publ. as a pamphlet) was the fullest to appear in any American newspaper.

Hasse (née **Bordoni**), **Faustina,** famous Italian mezzo-soprano, wife of **Johann Adolf Hasse;** b. Venice, c.1700; d. there, Nov. 4, 1781. She studied with Gasparini and Benedetto Marcello. She made her debut in 1716 in Pollarolo's opera *Ariodante,* and obtained such success that soon she was called the "New Siren." When she sang in Florence a few years later (1722), a special medal was issued in her honor; she was equally successful in Naples. She became a member of the court theater in Vienna in 1724, at a high salary. Handel heard her there, and engaged her for his opera enterprise in London, where she made her debut on May 5, 1726, winning high praise. She remained in London for 2 seasons; her quarrel with Francesca Cuzzoni in a competition for public attention resulted in her departure from England. She went back to Venice; in 1730 she married Hasse, and devoted her life thenceforth to his success, without abondoning her own career. From 1731 till 1763 they lived in Dresden; then in Vienna (until 1773), finally settling in Venice. According to Burney, she could sustain a note longer than any other singer; her trills were strong and rapid; her intonation, perfect. Burney also praised her physical qualities.
BIBLIOGRAPHY: A. Niggli, "Faustina Bordoni-Hasse," in Waldersee's *Sammlung musikalischer Vorträge* (1880); G.M. Urbani de Gheltof, *"La Nuova Sirena" ed il "Caro Sassone"* (Venice, 1890); Margarete Högg, *Die Gesangskunst der Faustina Hasse und das Sängerinnenwesen ihrer Zeit in Deutschland* (Berlin, 1931). An interesting fictional biography is Elise Polko's *Faustina Hasse* (Leipzig, 1860; new ed., 1895).

Hasse, Johann Adolf, important German composer; b. Bergedorf, near Hamburg, March 25, 1699; d. Venice, Dec. 16, 1783. He received his first instruction in music from his father, a schoolmaster and organist. In 1714–17 he studied in Hamburg; then, in 1718, at the recommendation of J. Ulrich von König, the poet, he was engaged by Keiser, director of the Hamburg Opera, as a tenor; he sang there 4 seasons, and from 1719 was tenor at the Braunschweig theater; it was there that Hasse first appeared as a composer, with his opera *Antioco* (Aug. 11, 1721). He then went to Naples to study the craft of composition more thoroughly; there he was a pupil of Porpora and later of Alessandro Scarlatti. In 1725 he wrote a serenade for 2 voices which was performed by Farinelli and Vittoria Tesi, and this further promoted Hasse's career in Italy; there followed a successful production of his new opera, *Sesostrate* (Naples, May 13, 1726). In 1727 he was appointed to the staff of the Scuola degl'Incurabili in Venice; there he wrote his *Miserere,* which enjoyed excellent success throughout Italy for many years afterward. His ability to ingratiate himself with society, his affable manners, and his handsome appearance contributed to his artistic success; he was often referred to as "il caro Sassone" (even though he was not a Saxon). In 1729 he met the famous singer **Faustina Bordoni,** and married her in Venice the following year. She sang the leading roles in many of his operas, and together they attained the highest positions in the operatic world. He wrote 2 operas for her, *Artaserse* and *Dalisa,* produced in Venice shortly after their marriage; he also brought out his 11th opera, *Tigrane* (Nov. 4, 1729). In 1731 Hasse received an appointment as music director of the Dresden Opera, with Faustina Hasse as prima donna; his first operatic production in Dresden was *Cleofide,* on Sept. 13, 1731, in which his wife scored a brilliant success. During frequent leaves of absence they traveled in Italy, where Hasse produced the following operas: *Catone in Utica* (Turin, Dec. 26, 1731); *Caio Fabrizio* (Rome, Jan. 12, 1732); *Siroe, re di Persia* (Bologna, May 2, 1733); and *Tito Vespasiano* (Pesaro, Sept. 24, 1735). In Dresden he produced *Senocrita* (Feb. 27, 1737); *Atalanta* (July 26, 1737); *Asteria* (Aug. 3, 1737); *Alfonso* (May 11, 1738); *Numa Pompilio* (Oct. 7, 1741); *Arminio* (Oct. 7, 1745); *La Spartana generosa* (June 14, 1747); *Demofoonte* (Feb. 9, 1748); *Attilio Regolo* (Jan. 12, 1750); *Ciro riconosciuto* (Jan. 20, 1751); *Adriano in Siria* (Jan. 17, 1752); *Solimano* (Feb. 5, 1753); *Artemisia* (Feb. 6, 1754); *L'Olimpiade* (Feb. 16, 1756); etc. Among other capital cities he visited during this period was Warsaw, where he produced *Il sogno di Scipione* (Oct. 7, 1738; not extant). His productions in Vienna were *Ipermestra* (Jan. 8, 1744); *Alcide al Bivio* (Oct. 8, 1760); *Zenobia* (Oct. 7, 1761); *Il trionfo di Clelia* (April 27, 1762); *Egeria* (April 24, 1764); *Partenope* (Sept. 9, 1767); and *Piramo e Tisbe* (Nov. 1768). His last opera was *Ruggerio,* produced in Milan on Oct. 16, 1771.

Although Hasse was fortunate in his artistic life and never lacked the support of the public, he had to face strong rivalry on the part of the Italian composer Porpora, who was engaged by the Dresden court in 1747. Furthermore, Porpora's pupil, a young singer named Regina Mingotti, became a formidable competitor to Faustina Hasse, no longer in her prime. Hasse succeeded in maintaining his firm position in Dresden, and Porpora departed for Vienna in 1752. In 1760, during the siege of Dresden in the course of the Seven Years' War, Hasse's house was set afire by gunfire, and nearly all of his MSS perished. Hasse's vitality and determination overcame these challenges, and he never ceased to produce new works with astounding facility. His music did not break new paths in operatic art, but he was a master of singing melody in the Italian style, and a fine craftsman in harmony and instrumentation. *Pallido è il sole* and *Per questo dolce amplesso,* from his opera *Artaserse,* were the 2 airs that Farinelli sang every evening for 10 years to soothe the melancholy of the ailing Spanish King Philip. In addition to his operas, Hasse wrote 11 oratorios, many masses, 3 Requiems, 23 Psalms, 5 litanies, 22 motets, a Te Deum, and a *Salve regina* (publ. in London in 1740, under the title *The Famous Salve Regina Composed by Signor Hasse*); he also wrote instrumental concertos, string trios, sonatas, etc. An important collection of Hasse's MSS is in the Dresden Library. A selection of his works was publ. by A. Schering in Denkmäler Deutscher Tonkunst (vols. 20, 29/30) and by Otto Schmid in *Musik am sächsischen Hofe* (vols. 1, 2, 6, 7, 8); G. Göhler edited *10 ausgewählte Orchesterstücke* (1904). Other reprints are by Christian I. Latrobe in his *Selection of Sacred Music* (6 vols., 1806–26), by B. Engländer (keyboard sonatas; Leipzig, 1930), etc.; cantatas for solo female and orch. are in Le Pupitre, 11. S.H. Hansell's *Works for Solo Voice of Johann Adolph Hasse* (Detroit, 1968) is a thematic index of 132 solo vocal works with orch. or continuo accompaniment: cantatas, motets, and antiphons.

BIBLIOGRAPHY: W.H. Riehl, *Musikalische Charakterköpfe,* vol. 1 (6th ed., Stuttgart, 1879); K. Mennicke, "J.A. Hasse," *Sammelbände der Internationalen Musik-Gesellschaft* (1904); K. Mennicke, *Hasse und die Brüder Graun als Symphoniker* (Leipzig, 1906; with a thematic catalogue); W. Müller, *J.A. Hasse als Kirchenkomponist* (Leipzig, 1911; with a thematic catalogue of Hasse's sacred works); L. Kamiensky, *Die Oratorien von J.A. Hasse* (Berlin, 1911); B. Zeller, *Das Recitativo accompagnato in den Opern Hasses* (Halle, 1911); Rudolf Gerber, *Der Operntypus J.A. Hasses und seine textlichen Grundlagen* (Leipzig, 1925); F. Millner, *The Operas of Johann Adolf Hasse* (Ann Arbor, Mich., 1979).

Hasse, Karl, German composer and musicologist; b. Dohna, near Dresden, March 20, 1883; d. Cologne, July 31, 1960. He studied with Kretzschmar and Riemann at the Univ. of Leipzig and with Straube and Nikisch at the Leipzig Cons.; later took courses at the Munich Academy with Reger and Mottl. He was music director and a prof. at Tübingen Univ. from 1919; in 1923 received his Ph.D. there. He also held posts as a choral conductor and organist in Heidelberg, Chemnitz, and Osnabrück, and taught music in Cologne; was director of the Staatliche Musikhochschule there from 1935–45. He wrote a number of works for orch., chamber groups, organ, and voice, aggregating 120 opus numbers; publ. several books on Max Reger (Leipzig, 1921; Berlin, 1936; Leipzig, 1948; Dortmund, 1951); 3 books on Bach (Leipzig, 1925; Cologne, 1938; Leipzig, 1949); contributed numerous articles to German music magazines.

Hasse, Max, German musicologist; b. Buttelstedt, near Weimar, Nov. 24, 1859; d. Magdeburg, Oct. 20, 1935. He was music critic of the *Magdeburger Zeitung* from 1894 to 1927; publ. the basic works on Cornelius, *Peter Cornelius und sein Barbier von Bagdad* (1904) and *Der Dichter-Musiker Peter Cornelius* (2 vols., 1922–23); edited the complete works of Cornelius, in 5 vols.

Hassell, Jon, American composer of the avantgarde; b. Memphis, Tenn., March 22, 1937. He was trained as a trumpet player; studied composition with Bernard Rogers at the Eastman School of Music in Rochester, N.Y. (B.M., 1969; M.M., 1970). Progressing away from traditional arts, he took courses in advanced electronic techniques with Karlheinz Stockhausen and Henri Pousseur in Cologne (1965–67); returning to the U.S., was composer-in-residence and a performer at the Center for Creative and Performing Arts in Buffalo (1967–69). In 1969 he moved to N.Y. to pursue independent activities in music and in sculpture.

WORKS: *Music for Vibraphones* (1965); *Blackboard Piece with Girls and Loops* for 2 Girls and 2 Pitch-producing Blackboards (N.Y., March 26, 1968); *Superball* for 4 Players, with Hand-held Magnetic Tape Heads (Ithaca, Oct. 29, 1969); *Goodbye Music* for Mixed Media (Buffalo, May 4, 1969); also sound sculptures: *Map 1* and *Map 2* for Hand-held Magnetic Playback Heads, designed to explore potential sounds (exhibited in Buffalo as sculptures, 1969); and *Elemental Warnings* (1969).

Hasselmans, Louis, French cellist and conductor; b. Paris, July 25, 1878; d. San Juan, Puerto Rico, Dec. 27, 1957. He was the son of a harpist and grandson of a conductor. He studied the cello with Jules Delsart at the Paris Cons., winning first prize at the age of 15, and theory with Lavignac and B. Godard. From 1893 to 1909 he was cellist in the Capet Quartet; made his debut as a conductor in Paris in 1905; then conducted at the Opéra-Comique (1909–11) and in Montreal (1911–13); was conductor of the Chicago Opera (1918–20) and was engaged as conductor of French operas at the Metropolitan Opera in N.Y. (1921–36); then taught at Louisiana State Univ. in Baton Rouge (1936–48).

Hassler, Caspar, German composer, brother of **Hans Leo Hassler;** b. Nuremberg (baptized, July 17), 1562; d. there, Aug. 19, 1618. In 1586 he was appointed organist at the Lorenz-Kirche; also supervised the building of the organ in the Würzburg Cathedral. He wrote a number of organ pieces; edited several collections of sacred works by various authors.

Hassler, Hans Leo, celebrated German composer; b. Nuremberg, Oct. 25, 1564; d. Frankfurt, June 8, 1612. He studied with his father, Isaak Hassler (1530–91), and from his earliest years became extremely proficient on the organ. In 1584 he went to Venice to study with Andrea Gabrieli. Hassler was the first notable German composer to go to Italy for musical study; however, he did not remain long in Venice; after 18 months there, he was recalled to Germany, where he obtained the post of chamber musician to Count Octavianus Fugger in Augsburg (1586); following the latter's death in 1600, Hassler became director of town music in Nuremberg and also organist at the Frauenkirche there. On Jan. 1, 1602, he received the post of chamber organist to the Court of Rudolf II at Prague; this was an honorary position rather than an actual occupation, and Hassler appeared but infrequently, if at all, at the imperial court in Prague. At the time he was busily engaged in the manufacture and installation of musical clocks; his commercial pursuits led to numerous litigations with business rivals. In 1604 he took a leave of absence from Nuremberg and went to Ulm; in 1608 he became organist to the Elector of Saxony in Dresden, and in 1612 accompanied him to Frankfurt; but Hassler was weakened by tuberculosis and died shortly after his arrival there. The style of Hassler's music is greatly influenced by his teacher Andrea Gabrieli, and by the latter's nephew, Giovanni Gabrieli, with whom Hassler became friendly in Venice. Having absorbed the Italian techniques, Hassler applied his knowledge to the composition of strongly national German songs, and became one of the founders of national musical art in Germany.

WORKS: *Canzonette a* 4 (Nuremberg, 1590); *Cantiones sacrae a* 4–12 (Augsburg, 1591); *Neue teutsche Gesäng nach Art der welschen Madrigalien und Canzonetten a* 4–8 (Augsburg, 1596); *Madrigali a* 5–8 (Augsburg, 1596); 8 masses *a* 4–8 (Nuremberg, 1599); *Sacri concentus a* 4–12 (Augsburg, 1601; 2nd ed., 1612); *Lustgarten neuer teutscher Gesäng, Balletti, Gailliarden und Intraden a* 4–8 (Nuremberg, 1601; later eds., 1605, 1610; reprints in Eitner's *Publikationen älterer praktischer und theoretischer Musikwerke*, vol. 15); *Psalmen und christliche Gesäng mit vier Stimmen auf die Melodien fugweis componirt* (Nuremberg, 1607); *Kirchengesänge, Psalmen und geistliche Lieder, auf die gemeinen Melodien mit vier Stimmen simpliciter gesetzt* (Nuremberg, 1608; 2nd and enlarged ed., 1637); *Venusgarten oder Neue lustige liebliche Tänz a* 4–6 (with V. Haussmann; Nuremberg, 1615); numerous motets, litanies, and organ works in various contemporary collections. Reprints are in Denkmäler Deutscher Tonkunst, vols. 2, 7, 24/25; Denkmäler der Tonkunst in Bayern, vols. 7, 9, 20 (4.ii, 5.ii, 11.i); Riemann's *Illustrationen zur Musikgeschichte* and *Musikgeschichte in Beispielen;* Schering's *Geschichte der Musik in Beispielen;* Leichtentritt's *Meisterwerke deutscher Tonkunst;* etc. R. von Saalfeld ed. the Psalms and sacred songs (1925); H. Bäuerle ed. 2 masses. A chronological list of Hassler's printed works was publ. by Eitner in the *Monatshefte für Musik-Geschichte* (1874). Publication of the *Collected Works,* ed. by C. Russell Crosby, was begun in 1961 (Wiesbaden).

BIBLIOGRAPHY: R. Schwartz, "Hans Leo Hassler unter dem italienischen Madrigalisten," *Vierteljahrsschrift für Musikwissenschaft* (1893); A. Sandberger, "Bemerkungen zur Biographie Hans Leo Hasslers und seiner Brüder," Denkmäler der Tonkunst in Bayern, 8 (5.i); Hugo Leichtentritt, *Geschichte der Motette* (Leipzig, 1908; pp. 293ff.); P. Wagner, *Geschichte der Messe* (1914; pp. 342ff.); M. Seiffert, *Geschichte der Klaviermusik* (1899; pp. 95ff.); H.J. Moser, *Geschichte der deutschen Musik* (vol. I, pp. 493–504; 5th ed., 1930).

Hassler, Jakob, German organist and composer, brother of **Hans Leo Hassler;** b. Nuremberg, (baptized, Dec. 18) 1569; d. Eger, between April and Sept. 1622. Like his famous brother, he enjoyed the patronage of the Fugger family; was enabled to go to Italy in 1590 to improve his musical education; upon his return to Germany, on his brother's recommendation, he received the honorary post of organist to

Emperor Rudolf II in Prague. In 1611 he settled in Eger. He publ. a collection of Italian madrigals (Nuremberg, 1600) and a book of sacred works (Nuremberg, 1601). E. von Werra publ. several keyboard pieces by Jakob Hassler in Denkmäler der Tonkunst in Bayern, 7 (4.ii).

Hässler, Johann Wilhelm, German composer and pianist; b. Erfurt, March 29, 1747; d. Moscow, March 29, 1822. His father was a maker of men's headwear; he followed his father's trade while studying organ with his uncle, Johann Christian Kittel. At the age of 14, he was able to earn his living as organist at an Erfurt church. After his father's death, in 1769, he maintained for some years a manufactory of fur muffs. A meeting in Hamburg with Carl Philipp Emanuel Bach gave him a fresh impetus toward continuing his musical activities. He gave concerts as a pianist, and publ. several piano sonatas. On Feb. 8, 1779, he married his pupil Sophie Kiel. In 1780 he opened public winter concerts in Erfurt; his wife appeared there as a singer and choral director. In 1789 he played in Berlin and Potsdam; in Dresden he took part in a contest with Mozart, as organist and pianist, without producing much impression either on Mozart himself or on the listeners. In 1790 he went to London, where he performed piano concertos under the direction of Haydn. In 1792 he went to Russia, where he remained for 30 years, until his death. In Moscow he became greatly renowned as a pianist, as a composer, and particularly as a teacher. Most of his works were publ. in Russia; these included sonatas, preludes, variations, fantasies, etc., and also pieces for piano, 4-hands. His style represents a transition between Bach and Beethoven, without attaining a degree of the imagination or craftsmanship of either. However, his piano pieces in the lighter vein have undeniable charm. His Gigue in D minor was well known. His autobiography is included in Willi Kahl, *Selbstbiographien deutscher Musiker* (Cologne, 1948). See also W. Georgii, *Klavier-Musik* (Zürich, 1950); R.-A. Mooser, *Annales de la musique et des musiciens en Russie au XVIIIe siècle* (Geneva, 1951; vol. II, pp. 659–61).

Hastings, Thomas, American composer of hymn tunes; b. Washington, Litchfield County, Conn., Oct. 15, 1784; d. New York, May 15, 1872. The family moved to Clinton, N.Y., when Hastings was 12; he became interested in practical music and was a leader of a village chorus. He collected hymns, which were later publ. in a collection, *Musica Sacra* (Utica, N.Y., 1815; 2nd ed., 1816); it was later combined with S. Warriner's *Springfield Collection* (Boston, 1813) as *Musica Sacra: or, Springfield and Utica Collection* (Utica, 1818; 9 subsequent eds. to 1830). He moved to Utica in 1823 and was a member of a Handel and Haydn society there; he also edited a religious weekly publication, *The Western Recorder.* In 1832 he settled in N.Y., where he was connected with the Normal Inst., in association with Lowell Mason. He received the honorary degree of D.Mus. from N.Y. Univ. (1858).
WRITINGS: Among his many publications were *Musical Reader* (1817); *Dissertation on Musical Taste* (in which he discourses on the superiority of German music; Albany, 1822; 2nd enlarged ed., 1853); *The Union Minstrel* (1830); *Spiritual Songs for Social Worship* (with Lowell Mason; 1831); *Devotional Hymns and Religious Poems* (1850); *History of Forty Choirs* (1854); and *Sacred Praise* (1856). His own hymn tunes have been estimated to number more than 1,000, and, next to those of Lowell Mason, are regarded as the finest of his time in America. These include the tune to which the celebrated hymn *Rock of Ages* is sung; the words are by Augustus Toplady, and Hastings entitled his tune simply *Toplady* to honor the author of the words. Other well-known hymn tunes are *Retreat, Zion,* and *Ortonville.* He publ. many of his melodies under foreign-sounding names, and it is not always possible to ascertain their authorship.
BIBLIOGRAPHY: F.J. Metcalf, *American Writers and Compilers of Sacred Music* (N.Y., 1925); J.T. Howard, *Our American Music* (N.Y., 1939, and subsequent eds.); M.B. Scanlon, "Thomas Hastings," *Musical Quarterly* (April 1946); also the article on Hastings in *Dictionary of American Biography.*

Hastreiter, Helene, American dramatic contralto; b. Louisville, Ky., Nov. 14, 1858; d. Varese, Italy, Aug. 6, 1922. She sang as a child in a Chicago church; at the age of 22 went to Italy, where she studied with the Lampertis (father and son) in Milan. She made her operatic debut there, and after several successful appearances in Italy was engaged by Col. Mapleson for his London season (1885). She then sang mostly in Italy; married Dr. Burgunzio there and lived in Genoa. Some of her leading operatic parts were Orfeo, Euridice, Dalila, Senta, and Ortrud.

Hathaway, Donny, black American jazz singer and composer; b. Chicago, Oct. 1, 1945; d. New York, Jan. 13, 1979. He played piano and sang gospel songs as a youth; studied at Howard Univ. in Washington, D.C.; while in college, he played organ in churches and acted as an entertainer in nightclubs; also arranged music. He composed for films and television; his best-known songs were *The Ghetto* and *You've Got a Friend.* His early death was a grievous loss to black music.

Hatrík, Juraj, Slovak composer; b. Orkučany, May 1, 1941. He studied with Alexander Moyzes at the Bratislava Music Academy (1958–62); then taught esthetics and psychology of music there.
WORKS: Sinfonietta (1962); *Contrasts* for Violin and Piano (1963); *Canto responsoriale* for Double Chorus and 4 Kettledrums (1964); *Čakanie (Waiting)* for Narrator, Flute, Harp, Strings, and Percussion (1965); *Monumento malincolico* for Organ and Orch. (1965); *Concertino in modo classico* for Piano and Orch. (1968); *Introspection* for Soprano, Flute, Violin, Cello, Clarinet, Horn, and Vibraphone (1968); *Domov sú ruky,* cantata (1968); *Sonata ciacona* for Piano (1970); *Da capo al fine,* symph. poem (1975; Bratislava, Feb. 19, 1976); *Choral Fantasia* for Accordion and Chamber Ensemble (1976).

Hatton, John Liptrot, British composer of light music; b. Liverpool, Oct. 12, 1809; d. Margate, Sept. 20, 1886. He acquired facility as a pianist and singer, and appeared on the vaudeville stage as a musical comedian. He publ. a great number of songs, among which *Anthea* and *Good-bye, sweetheart, good-bye* became extremely popular. In 1832 he went to London; produced his operetta, *The Queen of the Thames,* there (Feb. 25, 1843). He then went to Vienna, where he staged his opera *Pascal Bruno* (March 2, 1844). For some of his numbers he used the punning pseudonym **Czapek** (genitive plural of the Hungarian word for "hat"). In 1848–50 he made an extensive American tour. Returning to England, he was music director at the Princess's Theatre (1853–59); wrote music for several Shakespeare plays there; wrote a cantata, *Robin Hood* (Bradford Festival, Aug. 26, 1856); a grand opera, *Rose, or Love's Ransom* (London, Nov. 26, 1864); and a sacred drama, *Hezekiah* (Dec. 15, 1877); edited collections of old English songs.

Hattstaedt, John James, American pianist and pedagogue; b. Monroe, Mich., Dec. 29, 1851; d. Chicago, Nov. 30, 1931. He studied in Germany; then taught piano in Detroit (1870–72), St. Louis (1872–73), and Chicago (1875–86). In 1886 he founded the American Cons. of Music in Chicago. He publ. a *Manual of Musical History.*

Hatze, Josip, Croatian composer; b. Split, March 21, 1879; d. there, Jan. 30, 1959. He studied with Mascagni in Italy. He belongs to a generation of Croatian composers entirely influenced by Italian music. He wrote the operas *Povratak (The Return;* Zagreb, March 21, 1911) and *Adel i Mara* (Zagreb, March 1, 1933); many songs.

Haubenstock-Ramati, Roman, Polish composer of experimental music; b. Cracow, Nov. 27, 1919. He studied philosophy at the Univ. of Cracow; also took music lessons with Arthur Malawski and Josef Koffler. From 1947 to 1950 he was music director of Radio Cracow; then went to Israel, where he was director of the State Music Library in Tel Aviv (1950–56). In 1957 he settled in Vienna, where he was for a time employed by Universal Edition as reader and adviser for publications of new music. In 1959 he organized in Donaueschingen the first exhibition of musical scores in graphic notation; he himself evolved an imaginative type of modern particella in which the right-hand page gives the outline of musical action for the conductor while the left-hand page is devoted to instrumental and vocal details. This type of notation combined the most advanced type of visual guidance with an aide-mémoire of traditional theater arrangements. In 1967 he inaugurated a weekly seminar for avant-garde music in Bilthoven, the Netherlands. In 1968 he gave lectures in Buenos Aires, and in 1969 he conducted a seminar in Stockholm. Several of his works bear the subtitle "Mobile" to indicate the flexibility of their architectonics.
WORKS: *Ricercari* for String Trio (1950); *Bless-*

ings for Voice and 9 Players (1952); *Recitativo ed Aria* for Harpsichord and Orch. (1954); *Papageno's Pocket-Size Concerto* for Glockenspiel and Orch. (1955); *Les Symphonies des timbres* for Orch. (1957); *Chants et Prismes* for Orch. (1957, revised 1967); *Séquences* for Violin and Orch. in 4 groups (1957–58); *Interpolation,* a "mobile" for Solo Flute (1958); *Liaisons,* a "mobile" for Vibraphone and Marimbaphone (1958); *Petite musique de nuit,* a "mobile" for Orch. (1958); *Mobile for Shakespeare* for Voice and 6 Players (1960); *Credentials or "Think, Think Lucky,"* after Beckett, for Speech-voice and 8 Players (1960); *Decisions,* 10 pieces of musical graphics for Variable Instrumentation (1960–68); *Jeux 6,* "mobile" for 6 Percussionists (1960); opera, *Amerika,* after Kafka's novel (1962–64; Berlin, Oct. 8, 1966); *Vermutungen über ein dunkles Haus,* 3 pieces for 3 Orchs., 2 of which are on tape (1963; material from the opera); *Klavierstücke I* for Piano (1963–65); *Jeux 2* and *4,* "mobiles" for 2 and 4 Percussionists (1965, 1966); *Hotel Occidental* for Speech-chorus, after Kafka (in 3 versions, 1967); an anti-opera, *La Comédie,* after Beckett, for One Male and 2 Female Speech-singers, and 3 Percussionists (St. Paul-de-Vence, Alpes-Maritimes, France, July 21, 1969; German version as *Spiel,* Munich, 1970; Eng. version as *Play*); *Tableau I, II,* and *III* for Orch. (1967, 1968, 1970); *Symphonie "K"* (1967; material from the opera *Amerika*); *Psalm* for Orch. (1967); *Divertimento,* text collage for Actors, Dancer, and/ or Mime, and 2 Percussionists (1968; after *Jeux 2*); *Catch I* for Harpsichord (1969), *II* for One or 2 Pianos (1970), and *III* for Organ (1971); *Multiple I–VI* for various instrumental combinations (1969); *Alone* for Trombone and Mime (1969); *Describe* for Voice and Piano (1969); *Hexachord I* and *II* for 2 Guitars (1972); *Concerto a tre* for Piano, Trombone, and Percussion (1973); 2 string quartets (1973, 1978); *Shapes (in Memory of Stravinsky) I* for Organ and Tape, and *II* for Organ, Piano, Harpsichord, and Celesta (both 1973); *Endless,* endless "mobile" for 7 Players and Conductor (1974); Solo Cello Sonata (1975); *Musik* for 12 Instruments (1976); *Ulysses,* ballet (1977); *Concerto per archi* (1977; Graz, Oct. 11, 1977); *Symphonien* (1977; Baden-Baden, May 10, 1978); *Self* for Bass Clarinet and 3 Tapes (1978).

Haubiel, Charles, American composer; b. Delta, Ohio, Jan. 30, 1892; d. Los Angeles, Aug. 26, 1978. He practiced piano; then went to Europe and studied composition with Alexander von Fielitz in Leipzig. Returning to the U.S., he enlisted in the army. After his service he taught piano at the Inst. of Musical Art in N.Y.; then was on the faculty of N.Y. Univ. (1923–47). In 1935 he founded the Composer's Press, with the aim of publishing American works. His technically expert music was marked by a fine Romantic flair, not without a winsome infusion of coloristic harmonies, but his pieces had few performances.
WORKS: Mexican folk opera, *Sunday Costs Five Pesos* (Charlotte, N.C., Nov. 6, 1950); *Rittrati (Portraits)* for Orch. (Chicago, Dec. 12, 1935); *Cryptics* for Bassoon and Piano (1932); *Nuances* for Flute

and Piano (1947); many songs and choral pieces.

Haubiel, Charles Trowbridge (original name, **Charles Trowbridge Pratt**), American composer; b. Delta, Ohio, Jan. 30, 1892; d. Los Angeles, Aug. 26, 1978. His father's last name was Pratt, but he adopted his mother's maiden name, Haubiel, as his own. He had piano lessons with his sister **Florence Pratt,** an accomplished pianist. In 1911 he went to Europe, where he studied piano with Rudolf Ganz in Berlin; also took composition lessons with Alexander von Fielitz in Leipzig. Returning to the U.S. in 1913, he taught music at various schools in Oklahoma. When the U.S. entered the war in 1917, he enlisted in the field artillery and served in France. After the Armistice he resumed a serious study of composition with Rosario Scalero at the David Mannes Music School in N.Y. (1919–24), while continuing taking piano lessons with Rosina and Josef Lhévinne. Intermittently he taught musical subjects at the Inst. of Musical Art in N.Y. (1921–31) and at N.Y. Univ. (1923–47). In 1935 he organized Composers Press, Inc., with the purpose of promoting the publication of American music, and served as its president until 1966. He was a recipient of numerous awards of merit for outstanding contributions to music. His own compositions reveal an excellent theoretical and practical grasp of harmony, counterpoint, instrumentation, and formal design. In his idiom he followed the models of the Romantic school of composition, but he embroidered the basic patterns of traditional music with winsome coloristic touches, approaching the usage of French Impressionism. He was extremely prolific; many of his works underwent multiple transformations from a modest original, usually for solo piano or a chamber group, to a piece for full orch.; in all these forms his compositions remain eminently playable. WORKS: Mexican folk opera, *Sunday Costs 5 Pesos* (Charlotte, N.C., Nov. 6, 1950). FOR ORCH.: *Gothic Variations* (originally for Violin and Piano, 1919; revised 1942; adapted for Full Orch., perf. in Los Angeles, June 9, 1970); *Vox Cathedralis* (originally for Organ, 1925; arranged for 2 Pianos, 1928; finally transcribed for Orch., 1934, and perf. in N.Y. May 6, 1938); *Rittrati (Portraits;* originally for Piano, 1919; orch. transcription first perf., Chicago Symph., Dec. 12, 1935); *Karma,* symph. variations (1928; received first prize at the Schubert Centennial in a contest by Columbia Records; revised in 1968 and retitled *Of Human Destiny*); *Suite Passacaglia* (Los Angeles, Jan. 31, 1936; originally for 2 Pianos); *Symphony in Variation Form* (1937); *Miniatures* for String Orch. (N.Y., April 23, 1939); *American Rhapsody* (1948); *Pioneers,* symphonic saga of Ohio (1946; revised 1956; perf. in Los Angeles, Feb. 19, 1960); *Metamorphosis* (1926; set of 29 variations on Stephen Foster's *Swanee River;* filmed as a short subject and produced under the title *Swanee River Goes Hi-Hat*); *1865 A.D.* (1943; revised 1958, under the title *Mississippi Story;* first perf. Los Angeles, April 24, 1959). CHAMBER MUSIC: *Ecchi classici* for String Quartet (1924); *Duo Forms* for Cello and Piano (1929–31); *Cryptics* for Bassoon and Piano

(1932); *Lodando la danza* for Oboe, Violin, Cello, and Piano (1932); *Nuances,* suite for Flute and Piano (1938); Cello Sonata (1941); *In the French Manner* for Flute, Cello, and Piano (1942); String Trio (1943); Violin Sonata (1945); *Shadows* for Violin and Piano (1947); *Pastoral Trio* for Flute, Cello, and Piano (1949); *Epochs* for Violin and Piano (1954–55); *Threnody for Love* for 6 Instruments (1965); *Ohioana,* cycle for Violin and Piano (1966); Trio for Clarinet, Cello, and Piano (1969). Also numerous choral works: *Vision of Saint Joan* (1941); *Jungle Tale* (1943); *Father Abraham* (1944), etc.; piano suite, *Solari* (1932–34); other pieces for piano solo.
BIBLIOGRAPHY: David Ewen, *American Composers, A Biographical Dictionary* (N.Y., 1982).

Haudebert, Lucien, French composer; b. Fougères, April 10, 1877; d. Paris, Feb. 24, 1963. He studied organ; then went to Paris, where he took lessons in composition with Fauré. He followed in his music the traditions of César Franck, preferring large sonorities and clear tonal harmonies. He stood aloof from modern developments in France and had little recognition even among traditional musicians, despite praise from Romain Rolland. His most effective work is the oratorio *Dieu Vainqueur* (1916–22); other significant works are the oratorio *Moïse* (1928); *Symphonie bretonne* (1936); *Symphonie française* (1941); *Voyage en Bretagne* for Orch. (1953); *Chants de la mer* for Voices and Orch. (1950); also chamber music, including a Quartet for Saxophones.

Hauer, Josef Matthias, significant Austrian composer and original theorist; b. Wiener-Neustadt, near Vienna, March 19, 1883; d. Vienna, Sept. 22, 1959. After attending a college for teachers, he became a public-school instructor; at the same time he studied music. An experimenter by nature, with a penchant for mathematical constructions, he developed a system of composition based on "tropes," or patterns, which aggregated to thematic formations of 12 different notes. As early as 1912 he publ. a piano piece, entitled *Nomos (Law),* which contained the germinal principles of 12-tone music; in his theoretical publications he elaborated his system in greater detail. These were *Vom Wesen des Musikalischen* (Berlin, 1922); *Deutung des Melos* (Vienna, 1923); *Vom Melos zur Pauke* (Vienna, 1925), and finally *Zwölftontechnik* (Vienna, 1926), in which the method of composing in the 12-tone technique was illustrated with practical examples. Hauer vehemently asserted his priority in 12-tone composition; he even used a rubber stamp on his personal stationery proclaiming himself the true founder of the 12-tone method. This claim was countered, with equal vehemence but with more justification, by Schoenberg; indeed, the functional basis of 12-tone composition in which the contrapuntal and harmonic structures are derived from the unifying tone row did not appear until Schoenberg formulated it and put it into practice in 1924. Hauer lived his entire life in Vienna, working as a composer, conductor, and teacher. Despite its forbidding character, his music attracted much attention.

WORKS: 2 operas: *Salammbô,* after Flaubert (1930; unperf.) and *Die schwarze Spinne* (1932; posthumous, Vienna, May 23, 1966); an oratorio, *Wandlungen,* for 6 Soloists, Chorus, and Chamber Orch. (1927; Baden-Baden, April 16, 1928); 2 cantatas: *Emilie vor ihrem Brauttag* for Alto and Orch. (1928) and *Der Menschen Weg,* in 7 sections, to poems by Hölderlin, for 4 Soloists, Chorus, and Orch. (1934; reduced in 1952 to 5 sections; Vienna, June 1953); *Lateinische Messe* for Chorus, Chamber Orch., and Organ (1926, unfinished; posthumous, Vienna, June 18, 1972); *Vom Leben,* after Hölderlin, for Narrator, Small Chorus, and Small Orch. (1928). OTHER WORKS: *Nomos* (Symph. No. 1), in 7 parts, for 1 or 2 Pianos, or Orch. (1912–13; version for 2 Pianos, Sankt Pölten, June 7, 1913); *Nomos* (Symph. No. 2), in 5 parts, for Piano or Small Orch. (1913); *Nomos,* 7 little piano pieces (1913); *Apokalyptische Phantasie* (Symph. No. 3) for 2 Pianos or Orch. (1913; version for 2 Pianos, Wiener-Neustadt, May 9, 1914; version for Orch., posthumous, Styrian Autumn Festival, Graz, Austria, Oct. 21, 1969); *Oriental Tale* for Piano (1916); *Nomos* for Piano and String Ensemble (1919); Quintet for Clarinet, Violin, Viola, Cello, and Piano (1924); 6 string quartets (1924–26); 8 suites for Orch. (1924; 1924; 1925, with Baritone Solo; 1926; 1926; 1926, also for String Quartet; 1926; 1927); *Romantische Fantasie* for Small Orch. (1925); *7 Variations* for Flute, Clarinet, Violin, Viola, Cello, and Double Bass (1925); *Symphonische Stücke (Kammerstücke)* for String Orch., Piano, and Harmonium (1926); Sinfonietta (1927; Berlin, Dec. 13, 1928); Violin Concerto (1928; Berlin, Nov. 12, 1929); Piano Concerto (1928); *Divertimento* for Small Orch. (1930); *Konzertstücke* for Orch. (1932; from *Die schwarze Spinne*); *Tanzphantasien* Nos. 1 and 2 for 4 Soloists and Orch. (1933) and Nos. 3–7 for Chamber Orch. (1934); *2 Tanzsuiten* for 9 Solo Instruments (1936); *Labyrinthischer Tanz* for Piano, 4-Hands (1952); *Langsamer Walzer* for Orch. (1953); *Chinesisches Streichquartet* (1953); *Hausmusik* for Piano, 4-Hands (1958). After 1940, Hauer was primarily concerned with composing a series of pieces, each ostentatiously bearing the subtitle *Zwölftonspiel,* for orch. and chamber combinations of all descriptions—their total number exceeding 100—with each one designated by the month and year composed, as, for example, his *Zwölftonspiel* for Orch. (August 1940), *Zwölftonspiel* for Violin and Harpsichord (July 1948), *Zwölftonspiel* for Orch. (September 1957), and *Zwölftonspiel* for String Sextet (May 1958).

BIBLIOGRAPHY: Willi Reich, "J.M. Hauer," *Die Musik* (May 1931); H. Picht, *J.M. Hauer, Ein Vorkämpfer geistiger Musikauffassung* (Stuttgart, 1934); Monika Lichtenfeld, *Untersuchungen zur Theorie der Zwölftontechnik bei J.M. Hauer* (Regensburg, 1964); Walter Szmolyan, *Josef Matthias Hauer* (Vienna, 1965); J. Sengstschmid, "Anatomie eines Zwölftonspiele, Ein Blick in die Werkstatt Josef Matthias Hauers," *Zeitschrift für Musiktheorie* (April 1971); H. Schöny, "Die Vorfahren des Komponisten Josef Matthias Hauer," *Genealogie* (Aug. 1971).

Haug, Gustav, Swiss composer; b. Strasbourg, Nov. 30, 1871; d. St. Gallen, April 22, 1956. He studied at the Cons. of Strasbourg; then went to Switzerland and settled in St. Gallen, where he was active as a church organist and voice teacher. As a composer, he produced a number of singable choral anthems, several works for solo voice with orch. accompaniment, and many songs to German texts.

Haug, Hans, Swiss composer; b. Basel, July 27, 1900; d. Lausanne, Sept. 15, 1967. He studied piano with Egon Petri and Ernst Levy in Basel, and later with Busoni at the Munich Academy of Music. Returning to Switzerland, he became choral conductor at the Municipal Theater in Basel (1928–34); from 1935–38 he conducted the orch. of the Radio Suisse Romande and also taught at the Cons. of Lausanne, where he finally settled. As a composer, he was most successful in writing for the theater.

WORKS: Operas: *Don Juan in der Fremde* (Basel, Jan. 15, 1930); *Madrisa* (Basel, Jan. 15, 1934); *Tartuffe* (Basel, May 24, 1937); *Le Malade imaginaire,* after Molière (Zürich, Feb. 8, 1947); *Der Spiegel der Agrippina* (1954); *Justice du roi* (1963); radio operas: *Gardien vigilant* (1967) and *Le Souper de Venise* (1967); oratorio, *Michelangelo* (Solothurn, Feb. 28, 1943); operettas: *Barbara* (1938); *Gilberte de Courgenay* (1939); several radio operettas; ballets: *L'Indifférent* and *Pan und Apollo;* incidental music for theatrical plays; numerous cantatas, including a humorous *Cantate gastronomique* for Soli, Chorus, and Orch.; Symph. (1948); *Capriccio* for Wind Instruments and Piano (1957); Concertino for Flute and Small Orch. (1943); Concertino for Oboe, Viola, and Small Orch.; Concertino for Piano and Orch.; Guitar Concerto (1952); 2 piano concertos (1938, 1962); Double Concerto for Oboe and Viola (1953); 3 string quartets; Wind Quartet; Wind Quintet; *Kurze Musik* for Cello and Orch.; etc.; also a curious symph. poem entitled *Charlie Chaplin* (1930).

Haugland, Aage, Danish bass-baritone; b. Copenhagen, Feb. 1, 1944. He studied voice in Copenhagen; made his operatic debut with the Norwegian Opera in Oslo in 1968; then sang in Copenhagen, at Covent Garden in London, and at the Florence May Festival. He was mainly renowned for his Wagnerian roles, but he also excelled in buffo parts, such as that of Leporello.

Hauk, Minnie (real name, **Amalia Mignon Hauck**), celebrated American soprano; b. New York, Nov. 16, 1851; d. Triebschen, near Lucerne, Switzerland, Feb. 6, 1929. Her father was a German carpenter who became involved in the political events of 1848, emigrated to America, and married an American woman; he named his daughter Mignon after the character in Goethe's *Wilhelm Meister.* The family moved to Atchison, Kans., when Minnie was very young; her mother maintained a boarding house at a steamboat landing on the Missouri. In 1860 they moved to New Orleans; there Minnie Hauk began to

sing popular ballads for entertainment. She made her operatic debut at the age of 14 in Brooklyn, in *La Sonnambula* (Oct. 13, 1866); then took lessons with Achille Errani of N.Y. On Nov. 15, 1867, she sang Juliette at the American premiere of Gounod's opera in N.Y. She attracted the attention of the rich industrialist Leonard Jerome and the music publisher Gustave Schirmer, who financed her trip to Europe. She sang in opera in Paris during the summer of 1868; made her London debut at Covent Garden on Oct. 26, 1868; in 1870 she sang in Vienna. She sang the title roles in the first American performances of *Carmen* (N.Y. Academy of Music, Oct. 23, 1878) and Massenet's *Manon* (Dec. 23, 1885); made her debut at the Metropolitan Opera in N.Y. as Selika in *L'Africaine* on Feb. 10, 1891; continued to appear there for that season, but following a disagreement with the management, decided to organize her own opera group; with it, she gave the first Chicago performance of *Cavalleria rusticana* (Sept. 28, 1891). She then settled in Switzerland with her husband, Baron Ernst von Hesse-Wartegg, whom she had married in 1881; after his death she lived mostly in Berlin; lost her fortune in the depreciation of her holdings in Germany. In 1919, Geraldine Farrar launched an appeal to raise funds for her in America. Hauk's autobiography, collated by E.B. Hitchcock, was publ. as *Memories of a Singer* (London, 1925).
BIBLIOGRAPHY: Oscar Thompson, *The American Singer* (N.Y., 1937; pp. 93–118).

Haupt, Karl August, German organist; b. Kuhnau, Silesia, Aug. 25, 1810; d. Berlin, July 4, 1891. He studied with Dehn and others in Berlin; played in various Berlin churches and became famous for his masterly improvisations in the style of Bach. He was one of the experts consulted for the specifications in building the grand organ at the Crystal Palace in London. He had many distinguished pupils, including about 40 American organists. He publ. a valuable *Choralbuch* (1869); many other compositions for organ remain in MS.

Hauptmann, Moritz, eminent German theorist and composer; b. Dresden, Oct. 13, 1792; d. Leipzig, Jan. 3, 1868. His father was an architect and hoped to bring up his son in that profession; however, there was no parental opposition to music studies; Hauptmann took lessons with Scholz (violin), Grose (piano and harmony), and Morlacchi (composition) in Dresden; later studied with Weinlig; in 1811 he went to Gotha to study violin and composition with Spohr and became his lifelong friend; went to Vienna in 1813 as a violinist in Spohr's orch. at the Theater an der Wien. In 1812 he joined the Dresden Court Orch. as violinist; in 1815 he became music teacher in the family of the Russian military governor of Dresden, Prince Repnin, and went with them to Russia, where he remained for 5 years. In 1820 he returned to Dresden; in 1822, Spohr engaged him as violinist in the court orch. at Kassel. In 1842, at Mendelssohn's recommendation, he was appointed cantor at the Thomasschule and prof. of composition at

the Leipzig Cons., retaining these posts until his death. He became greatly renowned as a teacher of violin and composition. Among his pupils were Ferdinand David, Joachim, Hans von Bülow, Jadassohn, and Arthur Sullivan. A master of classical form, he was a polished composer, in the tradition of Spohr and Mendelssohn; the architectonic symmetry of his instrumental works and the purity of part-writing in his vocal music aroused admiration among his contemporaries; yet his music failed to endure, and rapidly went into decline after his death. He publ. about 60 works, among them 3 violin sonatas, 4 violin sonatinas, 2 string quartets, piano pieces, sacred works, and a number of lieder, a genre in which he excelled. His theoretical work *Die Natur der Harmonik und Metrik* (Leipzig, 1853; 2nd ed., 1873; Eng. trans., London, 1888) is an attempt to apply Hegel's dialectical philosophy to the realm of music. It exercised considerable influence on the later development of German theory of harmony; among other German scholars, Riemann was influenced by it. Hauptmann's other writings are: *Erläuterungen zu J.S. Bachs Kunst der Fuge* (Leipzig, 1841; 2nd ed., 1861); *Die Lehre von der Harmonik* (ed. by Oscar Paul; Leipzig, 1868); *Opuscula* (miscellaneous writings, ed. by E. Hauptmann; Leipzig, 1874). His letters to Spohr and others were edited by F. Hiller (Leipzig, 1876). A.D. Coleridge publ. a selection, in Eng., of Hauptmann's correspondence as *Letters of a Leipzig Cantor* (1892).
BIBLIOGRAPHY: O. Paul, *Moritz Hauptmann, Eine Denkschrift zur Feier seines Siebzigjährigen Geburtstages am 13. Oktober 1862* (Leipzig, 1862); Stephan Krehl, *Moritz Hauptmann; Ein Dank- und Gedenkwort* (Leipzig, 1918); P. Rummenhöller, *Moritz Hauptmann als Theoretiker* (Wiesbaden, 1963).

Hauschka, Vincenz, gifted cellist and composer; b. Mies, Bohemia, Jan. 21, 1766; d. Vienna, Sept. 13, 1840. He was a pupil of his father, a schoolteacher; became chorister in the Prague Cathedral; studied composition with Zöger and cello with Christ. He was appointed cellist to Count Joseph von Thun in Prague (1782); made successful concert tours through Germany performing not only on the cello, but also on the baryton (a popular instrument at the time; Haydn wrote numerous works for it). He publ. 9 sonatas for cello and a book of vocal canons; in MS are several pieces for the baryton.

Hausegger, Friedrich von, Austrian musicologist; b. St. Andrä, Carinthia, April 26, 1837; d. Graz, Feb. 23, 1899. He was a pupil of Salzmann and Otto Desoff; also studied law and became a barrister at Graz. In 1872 he became a teacher of history and theory of music at the Univ. of Graz. He contributed to music periodicals.
WRITINGS: His *Musik als Ausdruck* (Vienna, 1885) is a valuable essay on musical esthetics. He also wrote *Richard Wagner und Schopenhauer* (1890); *Vom Jenseits des Künstlers* (1893); *Die künstlerische Persönlichkeit* (1897). After his death, his book *Unsere deutschen Meister* was ed.

by R. Louis (1901); his *Gesammelte Schriften* was brought out by his son in 1939.

Hausegger, Siegmund von, Austrian conductor and composer; b. Graz, Aug. 16, 1872; d. Munich, Oct. 10, 1948. He was trained musically by his father, Friedrich von Hausegger. At the age of 16 he composed a grand Mass, which he himself conducted; at 18 he brought out in Graz an opera, *Helfrid.* Richard Strauss thought well enough of Hausegger as a composer to accept for performance his comic opera *Zinnober,* which he conducted in Munich on June 19, 1898. Hausegger began his own conducting career in Graz as a theater conductor in 1895; in 1897 he was guest conductor in Bayreuth; was conductor of the Volk-Symphonie-Konzerte in Munich (1899–1902) and of the Museum Concerts in Frankfurt (1903–6). In 1910 he was appointed conductor of the Phil. Concerts in Hamburg. From 1918 to 1934 he was director of the Academy of Musical Art in Munich; in 1920 was named Generalmusikdirektor of the Munich Konzertverein, which became the Munich Phil. in 1928; remained there until his retirement in 1938. WORKS: *Dionysische Fantasie* for Orch. (1899); symph. poems: *Barbarossa* (1900) and *Wieland der Schmied* (1904); *Natursymphonie,* with a choral finale (1911); several works for chorus and orch.; symph. variations on a children's song, *Aufklänge* (1919); etc. He publ. a monograph, *Alexander Ritter, Ein Bild seines Charakters und Schaffens* (Berlin, 1907); ed. *R. Wagners Briefe an Frau Julie Ritter* (Munich, 1920) and his father's correspondence with Peter Rosegger (Leipzig, 1924). His collected articles appeared under the title *Betrachtungen zur Kunst* (Leipzig, 1921).

Hauser, Miska, Austrian violinist; b. Pressburg (Bratislava), 1822; d. Vienna, Dec. 8, 1887. He studied with Kreutzer in Vienna, and traveled as a child prodigy in Europe; in 1853–58 made a grand tour of America and Australia. He wrote an operetta, *Der blinde Leiermann;* numerous violin pieces, of which his meretricious *Rapsodie hongroise* and *Lieder ohne Worte* enjoyed undeserved popularity; and *American Rhapsody* for Violin and Piano (1855). During his American tour he sent correspondence to the *Ostdeutsche Post* which was collected and publ. in 2 vols., *Aus dem Wanderbuch eines österreichischen Virtuosen* (Leipzig, 1858–59). *History of Music in San Francisco* (San Francisco, 1939) contains Eng. translations of some of these reports, which are not devoid of interest.

Hausmann, Robert, German cellist; b. Rottleberode, Harz, Aug. 13, 1852; d. Vienna, Jan. 18, 1909. He studied cello with Theodore Müller in Berlin; was the cellist of the Hochberg quartet in Dresden (1872–76); then joined the Joachim quartet (1879), with which he remained until its dissolution after Joachim's death (1907).

Haussermann, John, American composer; b. Manila, Philippines, Aug. 21, 1909. He was taken to New Richmond, Ohio, as a child and studied piano with local teachers; returned to Manila in 1922 and studied music theory with Dr. Ebeneezer Cook there. In 1924 he enrolled in the Cincinnati Cons. of Music, studying organ with Parvin Titus and music theory with George Leighton. In 1930 he went to Paris, where he studied organ with Marcel Dupré and composition with Paul Le Flem. In 1934 he was again in Manila, where he was active as an organist; then lived in Cincinnati; dedicated himself mainly to composing. His music is marked by a pragmatic sense of formal cohesion, which does not exclude a flair for innovation, as exemplified by his Concerto for Voice and Orch. WORKS: FOR ORCH.: Symphs.: No. 1 (1938; partial perf., N.Y., May 28, 1939); No. 2 (1941; Cincinnati, March 31, 1944, Eugene Goossens conducting); No. 3 (1947; Cincinnati, April 1, 1949, Thor Johnson conducting); *Rhapsodic Overture* for Piano and Chamber Orch. (1938); *The After Christmas Suite* for Orch. (Cincinnati, March 22, 1938); Concerto for Voice and Orch. (Cincinnati, April 24, 1942); *Ronde carnavalesque* for Orch. (N.Y., Feb. 6, 1949); *Stanza* for Violin and Orch. (Mallorca, Spain, Feb. 22, 1956); *Sacred Cantata* for Baritone and Orch. (Cincinnati, Jan. 31, 1965). CHAMBER MUSIC: Quintet for Flute, Oboe, Clarinet, Bassoon, and Harpsichord (1935); Piano Quintet (1935); String Quartet (1937); *Suite rustique* for Flute, Cello, and Piano (1937); *Divertissements* for String Quartet (1940); *Serenade* for Theremin and Strings (1945); *Poème et Clair de lune* for Violin and Piano (1940); Violin Sonata (1941). FOR PIANO: *24 préludes symphoniques* (1932–33); *Sonatine fantastique* (1932); *Pastoral fantasie* for 2 Pianos, 4-hands (1933); *Sonatine romantique* (1933); *Ballade, Burlesque, et Légende* (1936); *7 Bagatelles* (1948); *9 Impromptus* (1958); *5 Harmonic Etudes* (1968); a great number of organ pieces; songs.

Haussmann, Valentin. Five German musicians in direct lineal descent bore this name: **Valentin Haussmann I,** the eldest, b. Nuremberg, 1484, composed chorales, and was a friend of Luther. His son, **Valentin Haussmann II,** was organist at Gerbstädt, and an industrious composer of motets, canzonets, and dances. A selection of his instrumental works was publ. by F. Bölsche in Denkmäler Deutscher Tonkunst (vol. 16). **Valentin Haussmann III,** son of the preceding, was organist at Löbejün, and an expert in organ construction. His son, **Valentin Haussmann IV,** b. Löbejün, c.1647, occupied the post of chapel musician to the Köthen court. **Valentin Bartholomäus Haussmann V,** son of the preceding, b. Löbejün, 1678, became cathedral organist at Merseburg and Halle, and burgomaster at Lauchstadt.

Hausswald, Günter, distinguished German musicologist; b. Rochlitz, March 11, 1908; d. Stuttgart, April 23, 1974. He studied piano with Max Pauer and composition with Karg-Elert in Leipzig; he studied theory with Grabner at the Leipzig Hochschule für Musik; also musicology with Kroyer and others at the Univ. of Leipzig, where he took his Ph.D. in 1937 with the dissertation *Johann David Heinichens Instrumentalwerke* (publ. in Wolfenbüttel and Berlin, 1937); he completed his Habilitation in 1949 at the Dresden Technical College with his *Mozarts Serenaden* (publ. in Leipzig, 1951). From 1933–45 he taught school in Dresden; then was dramaturge at the Dresden State Opera (1947–53); he also lectured at the Dresden Hochschule für Musik and at the Univ. of Jena from 1950–53. He then settled in West Germany, where he edited the monthly *Musica* (1958–70); was also program director for the South German Radio at Stuttgart (1960–68). His important monographs include *Heinrich Marschner* (Dresden, 1938); *Die deutsche Oper* (Cologne, 1941); *Die Bauten des Staatstheater Dresden* (Dresden, 1948); *Das neue Opernbuch* (Dresden, 1951; 5th ed., 1956); *Richard Strauss* (Dresden, 1953); *Dirigenten: Bild und Schrift* (Berlin, 1966). He also contributed exemplary editions to the complete works of Telemann, Gluck, Bach, and Mozart.

Hautzig, Walter, pianist; b. Vienna, Sept. 28, 1921. He studied at the Vienna Academy of Music; left Austria after the rise of the Nazis to power, and went to Jerusalem; studied at the Cons. there. He eventually settled in America; continued his musical education at the Curtis Inst. in Philadelphia with Harry Kaufmann and Mieczyslaw Munz; also in N.Y. with Artur Schnabel. He became an American citizen in 1945. In 1979 he represented the U.S. in the first visit of an American pianist to the People's Republic of China since the Cultural Revolution. He taught at the Peabody Cons. in Baltimore from 1960; also gave master classes at the Hartt College of Music in Providence beginning in 1969.

Havelka, Svatopluk, Czech composer; b. Vrbice, Silesia, May 2, 1925. He began composing as a child; studied violin, piano, and harmony; took courses in history and philosophy at the Univ. of Prague; studied privately with K.B. Jirák; later was active as director of music programs at the Ostrava Radio (1949–51) and with the Army Artistic Ensemble in Prague (1951–54). His music follows folkloric trends, with some sonoristic and generally modernistic deflections from the nationalistic formulae. WORKS: *Mort et Redemption* for Orch. (1944); *4 Baroque Songs* for Medium Voice and Piano (1944; retitled *Růže ran [Rose of Wounds]* and scored with instrumental accompaniment, 1974); Suite for Small Orch. (1947); *2 Pastorales* for Orch. (1948, 1951); *4 Suites to Moravian Folk Texts* for Narrator, Soli, Chorus, and Chamber Orch. (1948, 1949, 1949, 1951); cantata, *Spring* (1949); Symph. No. 1 (Prague, Nov. 5, 1956); cantata, *Chvála světla (In Praise of Light;* Prague, May 4, 1960); *Heptameron,* subtitled *A Poem of Nature and Love,* for Narrator, 4 Soli, and Orch. (Prague, March 25, 1964); *Pěna (Foam),* to the poem of the same title by H.M. Enzensberger, for Orch. (1965; Olomouc, Feb. 9, 1966); *Ernesto Ché Guevara,* symph. poem in memory of the fallen Cuban revolutionary (1969); ballet, *Pyrrhos* (1970); *Hommage à Hieronymus Bosch,* symph. fantasy (1974); Nonet (1976); songs; film music.

Havemann, Gustav, German violinist; b. Güstrow, March 15, 1882; d. Schöneiche, near Berlin, Jan. 2, 1960. He studied with his father; then enrolled at the Berlin Hochschule für Musik, where he was a pupil of Joachim. As a youth he played in the Court Orch. in Schwerin; then was concertmaster in Lübeck, Darmstadt, and Hamburg. In 1911 he joined the faculty of the Leipzig Cons.; subsequently was concertmaster at the Dresden State Opera (1915–20); from 1920 to 1945 was a prof. at the Berlin Hochschule für Musik. He was first violinist in the prestigious Havemann String Quartet, which performed much modern music. He himself composed a Violin Concerto (1938) and a useful manual, *Die Violintechnik bis zur Vollendung* (1928).

Havingha, Gerhardus, Dutch organist and theorist; b. Groningen, Nov. 15, 1696; d. Alkmaar, March 6, 1753. He studied with his father, a church organist at Groningen; then became an organist at various churches in the Netherlands; publ. *Oorspronk en Voortgang der orgelen* (Alkmaar, 1727; reprinted 1973), an important source of organ history and practice in the Netherlands. His Suite for Harpsichord (Amsterdam, 1725) was republ. by J. Watelet in 1951.

Hawel, Jan, Polish composer; b. Pszow, July 10, 1936. He studied composition and conducting at the Katowice State College of Music, graduating in 1967; then became a member of its faculty. WORKS: *Profiles* for Male Chorus and Orch. (1962); Symph. for Strings (1962); *Contrasts* for Orch. (1964); *Constructions* for Orch. (1965); Divertimento for Trombone, Piano, and Percussion (1968); *Woodland Impressions* for Narrator, Chorus, and Orch. (1969); *Sinfonia concertante* for Organ and Orch. (1972); String Quartet (1971–72); *Stained Glass Windows* for Piano (1972).

Hawes, William, English composer and conductor; b. London, June 21, 1785; d. there, Feb. 18, 1846. As a boy he was a chorister at the Chapel Royal (1793–1801); then violinist at Covent Garden (1802); became Gentleman of the Chapel Royal in 1805; vicar-choral and master of choristers at St. Paul's Cathedral (1812); master of the children of the Chapel Royal (1817); and lay-vicar of Westminster Abbey (1817–20). He was director of English opera at the Lyceum; it was at his suggestion that Weber's *Der Freischütz* was given for the first time in England (July 22, 1824); he contributed some airs of his own composition to this production. Subsequently, he adapted and produced many Italian, French, and German operas for the English stage; he wrote and staged several light operas, among them *Broken Promises* (1825), *The Quartette, or Interrupted Harmony* (1828), *The Sister of Charity* (1829), etc. Some of his glees were popular. He edited the publication (in score) of the *Triumphes of Oriana* (1818), various collections of glees, etc.

Hawkins, Coleman (nicknamed **Bean** and **Hawk**), black American jazz tenor saxophonist; b. St. Jo-

seph, Mo., Nov. 21, 1904; d. New York, May 19, 1969. He joined the Kansas City group Jazz Hounds in 1921; from 1923–34 was a member of Fletcher Henderson's band in N.Y.; his full tone and heavy vibrato became the standard for tenor saxophone, and he was considered the foremost performer on the instrument. In 1934–39 he worked in Europe; upon his return to the U.S. in 1939 he made his most influential recording, *Body and Soul;* departing from the usual paraphrase approach of swing improvisation, his extemporized solo became an inspiration to the new generation of jazz musicians and paved the way for the bebop of the 1940s.
BIBLIOGRAPHY: A. McCarthy, *Coleman Hawkins* (London, 1963).

Hawkins, John, Canadian composer and pianist; b. Montreal, July 26, 1944. He studied piano at the Montreal Cons. (Premier Prix, 1967) and composition with Anhalt at McGill Univ.; then attended a course in modern music given by Boulez in Basel, Switzerland (1969). Returning to Canada in 1970, he taught music theory at the Univ. of Toronto.
WORKS: *8 Movements* for Flute and Clarinet (1966); *3 Cavatinas* for Soprano, Violin, Cello, Vibraphone, and Celesta (1967); *Sequences for 2 Groups* for 18 Instruments, (1968); *Remembrances* for Piano, Harp, Horn, Trumpet, and Trombone (1968); Variations for Orch. (1969–70; Montreal, June 4, 1975); *Waves* for Soprano and Piano (1971); *Etudes* for 2 Pianos (1974).

Hawkins, Sir John, eminent English music historian; b. London, March 29, 1719; d. there, May 21, 1789. He studied law while serving as a clerk, and soon was able to act as an attorney. An ardent devotee of music, he entered the musical society of the time and was on friendly terms with Handel; he also participated in literary clubs, and knew Samuel Johnson, Goldsmith, and others. A wealthy marriage (1753) enabled him to devote his leisure to literature and music. In the meantime, he progressed on the ladder of success in the legal profession. In 1761 he became a magistrate; in 1763, chairman of the Quarter Sessions; he was knighted in 1772. His first publication dealing with music was brought out anonymously: *An Account of the Institution and Progress of the Academy of Ancient Music* (1770). The culmination of 16 years of labor was his monumental *General History of the Science and Practice of Music,* publ. in 1776 in 5 vols. (quarto), containing 58 portraits of musicians; it was reprinted in 1853 (2 vols.) and 1875 (3 vols.) by Novello (octavo); the 1875 edition was reprinted again, with posthumous notes by Hawkins, in 2 vols., edited by O. Wessely, in Graz, 1969. The first vol. of Burney's *General History of Music* appeared at the same time as the 5 vols. of Hawkins; thus, Hawkins undoubtedly held priority for the first general history of music publ. in England; however, its reception was rather hostile; Burney himself derided Hawkins in an unpubl. poem. Yet the Hawkins work contained reliable information, particularly dealing with musical life in London in the 18th century.

Hawkins died of a paralytic stroke and was buried in Westminster Abbey.
BIBLIOGRAPHY: R. Stevenson, "'The Rivals'— Hawkins, Burney, and Boswell," *Musical Quarterly* (Jan. 1950); Percy A. Scholes, *Sir John Hawkins: Musician, Magistrate, and Friend of Johnson* (London, 1953; a definitive biography); B. Davis, *A Proof of Eminence: The Life of Sir John Hawkins* (Bloomington, Ind., and London, 1973).

Hawley, Charles Beach, American organist; b. Brookfield, Mass., Feb. 14, 1858; d. Red Bank, N.J., Dec. 29, 1915. He studied organ at the Cheshire Military Academy; took composition lessons in N.Y. with Dudley Buck; then served as organist in various churches; publ. some songs, showing a facile melodic invention.

Hay, Edward Norman, Irish composer and organist; b. Faversham, April 19, 1889; d. Belfast, Sept. 10, 1943. He studied organ with Koeller and Eaglefield-Hull; was organist of various churches in Ireland. He won the Feis Ceoil Prize in 1916 with his Cello Sonata on Irish folk tunes, the Cobbett Prize (1917) with his *Folksong Phantasy* for String Quartet, and the Carnegie Award (1918) with his String Quartet in A. He also wrote the orch. compositions *The Gilly of Christ, Dunluce* (1921), etc.; organ works; songs.

Hay, Frederick Charles, Swiss composer; b. Basel, Sept. 18, 1888; d. Langau, July 18, 1945. He was a medical student; then studied with Huber in Basel, Widor in Paris, and F. Schalk in Vienna; conducted the Univ. of Bern orch. (1912) and oratorio concerts in Geneva (1920–25); taught musicology at the Univ. of Geneva. He wrote the orch. works *Heaven and Earth* and *Der Dom;* concertos for oboe, violin, piano, and viola; *Notturno, intermezzo e capriccio* for Piano and Woodwind Orch.; choral works; hymns; piano pieces.

Hayasaka, Fumio, Japanese composer, b. Sendai-City, Aug. 19, 1914; d. Tokyo, Oct. 15, 1955. He studied in Tokyo with Alexander Tcherepnin; won the Weingartner Prize (1938). He was particularly successful in writing for Japanese motion pictures; wrote the score for the film *Rashomon,* which received first prize at the International Festival in Venice (1952).
WORKS: Overture in D major (Tokyo, March 17, 1940); Piano Concerto No. 1 (Tokyo, June 22, 1948); *The Ancient Dance* (Tokyo, May 15, 1939); *Yukara,* suite (Tokyo, June 9, 1955).

Hayashi, Hikaru, Japanese composer; b. Tokyo, Oct. 22, 1931. He studied at the Tokyo Music Academy with H. Otaka and T. Ikenouchi.
WORKS: *Variations* for Orch. (1955; Tokyo, Nov. 17, 1955); radio opera, *The Naked King* (1955); television opera, *Amanjaku and Urikohime* (1958); 2-act opera, *The Wife in the Picture* (1961); ballet, *White-haired Woman* (1961); oratorio, *Beggar's Song* (1962); *Movement* for Orch. (1953); Symph. in

Haydn

G (1953); *Allegro* for Strings (1954); *The Humid Area* for Orch. (1960); *Music* for Orch. (1965); *Etude* for 2 Guitars (1960); *Rhapsody* for Violin and Piano (1965); *Contrasts* for 2 Marimbas (1965); Flute Sonata (1967); *Duo* for Violin and Piano (1968); *Winter on 72nd Street (Rhapsody No. 2)* for Violin and Piano (1968); *AYA* for Flute and Harp (1970) and *AYA II* for Solo Harp (1972); *Play I* for 10 Players (1971) and *II* for Voice, Violin, and Piano (1971–72); *Wonderland I* for Flute, Violin, and Piano (1972); *Shirabe* for 3 Flutes (1974); Piano Sonata (1965); Piano Sonatina (1966); choruses; songs.

Haydn, (Franz) Joseph, illustrious Austrian composer; b. Rohrau, Lower Austria, probably March 31, 1732 (baptized, April 1, 1732); d. Vienna, May 31, 1809. He was the 2nd of 12 children born to Mathias Haydn, a wheelwright, who served as village sexton, and Anna Maria Koller, daughter of the market inspector and a former cook in the household of Count Harrach, lord of the village. Their 2nd son, **Michael,** also became a musician. On Sundays and holidays music was performed at home, the father accompanying the voices on the harp, which he had learned to play by ear. When Haydn was a small child his paternal cousin Johann Mathias Franck, a choral director, took him to Hainburg, where he gave him instruction in reading, writing, arithmetic, and instrumental playing. When Haydn was 8 years old, Karl Georg Reutter, Kapellmeister at St. Stephen's Cathedral in Vienna, engaged him as a soprano singer in the chorus. After Haydn's voice began to break, he moved to the household of Johann Michael Spangler, a music teacher. He obtained a loan of 150 florins from Anton Buchholz, a friend of his father, and was able to rent an attic room where he could use a harpsichord. In the same house lived the famous Italian poet and opera librettist Pietro Metastasio, who recommended Haydn to a resident Spanish family as a music tutor. He was also engaged as accompanist to students of Nicolò Porpora, for whom he performed various menial tasks in exchange for composition lessons. He made a diligent study of *Gradus ad Parnassum* by Fux and *Der volkommene Kapellmeister* by Mattheson. Soon he began to compose keyboard music. In 1751 he wrote the singspiel *Der krumme Teufel.* A noblewoman, Countess Thun, engaged Haydn as harpsichordist and singing teacher; he met Karl Joseph von Fürnburg, for whom he wrote his first string quartets. In 1759 Haydn was engaged by Count Ferdinand Maximilian von Morzin as Kapellmeister at his estate in Lukaveč. On Nov. 26, 1760, Haydn married Maria Anna Keller, the eldest daughter of his early benefactor, a Viennese wigmaker.

A decided turn in Haydn's life was his meeting with Prince Paul Anton Esterházy. Esterházy had heard one of Haydn's symphs. during a visit to Lukaveč, and engaged him to enter his service as 2nd Kapellmeister at his estate in Eisenstadt; Haydn signed his contract with Esterházy on May 1, 1761. Prince Paul Anton died in 1762, and his brother, Prince Nikolaus Esterházy, known as the "Mag-

nificent," succeeded him. He took Haydn to his new palace at Esterház, where Haydn was to provide 2 weekly operatic performances and 2 formal concerts. Haydn's service at Esterház was long-lasting, secure, and fruitful; there he composed music of all descriptions, including most of his known 83 string quartets, about 80 of his 104 symphs., a number of keyboard works, and nearly all his operas; in 1766 he was elevated to the rank of first Kapellmeister. Prince Nikolaus Esterházy was a cultural patron of the arts, but he was also a stern taskmaster in his relationship to his employees. His contract with Haydn stipulated that each commissioned work had to be performed without delay, and that such a work should not be copied for use by others. Haydn was to present himself in the "antichambre" of the palace each morning and afternoon to receive the Prince's orders, and he was obliged to wear formal clothes, with white hose and a powdered wig with a pigtail or a hairbag; he was to have his meals with the other musicians and house servants. In particular, Haydn was obligated to write pieces that could be performed on the viola da gamba, an instrument which the Prince could play; in consequence, Haydn wrote 175 separate numbers for the viola da gamba. He also wrote 3 sets of 6 string quartets each (opp. 9, 17, and 20), which were brought out in 1771–72. His noteworthy symphs. included No. 49 in F minor, *La passione;* No. 44 in E minor, known as the *Trauersinfonie;* No. 45 in F-sharp minor; and the famous *Abschiedsinfonie* (the *Farewell* Symph.), performed by Haydn at Esterház in 1772. The last movement of the *Farewell* Symph. ends in a long slow section during which one musician after another ceases to play and leaves the stage, until only the conductor and a single violinist remain to complete the work. The traditional explanation is that Haydn used the charade to suggest to the Prince that his musicians deserved a vacation after their arduous labors, but another and much more plausible version, found in *Anedotti piacevoli ed interessanti,* publ. in 1830 by G.G. Ferrari, who personally knew Haydn, is that the Prince had decided to disband the orch. and that Haydn wished to impress on him the sadness of such a decision; the known result was that the orch. was retained. In 1780 Haydn was elected a member of the Modena Phil. Society; in 1784 Prince Henry of Prussia sent him a gold medal; in 1785 he was commissioned to write a "passione istrumentale," *The Seven Last Words,* for the Cathedral of Cádiz; in 1787 King Friedrich Wilhelm II gave him a diamond ring; many other distinctions were conferred upon him. During his visits to Vienna he formed a close friendship with Mozart, who was nearly a quarter of a century younger, and for whose genius Haydn had great admiration. If the words of Mozart's father can be taken literally, Haydn told him that Mozart was "the greatest composer known to me either in person or by name." Mozart reciprocated Haydn's regard for him by dedicating to him a set of 6 string quartets. Prince Nikolaus Esterházy died in 1790, and his son Paul Anton (named after his uncle) inherited the estate. Haydn was granted an annuity of 1,000 florins; nominally he remained in the service of the new Prince as Kapellmeister, but he took up permanent residence in Vienna.

In 1790 Johann Peter Salomon, the enterprising London impresario, visited Haydn and persuaded him to travel to London for a series of concerts. Haydn accepted the offer, arriving in London on Jan. 1, 1791. On March 11 of that year he appeared in his first London concert in the Hanover Square Rooms, presiding at the keyboard. Haydn was greatly feted in London by the nobility; the King himself expressed his admiration for Haydn's art. In July 1791 he went to Oxford to receive the honorary degree of Mus.D. For this occasion, he submitted his Symph. No. 92 in G major, which became known as the *Oxford* Symph.; he composed in a 3-part canon, *Thy Voice, O Harmony, Is Divine,* as his exercise piece. It was also in England that he wrote his Symph. No. 94 in G major, the *Surprise* Symph. The surprise of the title was provided by the loud drum strokes at the end of the main theme in the slow movement; the story went that Haydn introduced the drum strokes with the sly intention of awakening the London dowagers, who were apt to doze off at a concert. On his journey back to Vienna in the summer of 1792 Haydn stopped in Bonn, where young Beethoven showed him some of his works, and Haydn agreed to accept him later as his student in Vienna. In 1794 Haydn went to London once more. His first concert, on Feb. 10, 1794, met with great success. His *London* symphs., also known as the *Salomon* symphs., because Haydn wrote them at Salomon's request, were 12 in number, and they included No. 99 in E-flat major; No. 100 in G major, known as the *Military* Symph.; No. 101 in D major, nicknamed *The Clock* because of its pendulum-like rhythmic accompanying figure; No. 102 in B-flat major; No. 103 in E-flat major, known as the *Drum Roll* Symph.; and No. 104 in D major.

Returning to Vienna, Haydn resumed his contact with the Esterházy family. In 1794 Prince Paul Anton had died and was succeeded by his son Nikolaus; the new Prince has plans to revive the Haydn orch. at Eisenstadt, with Haydn again as Kapellmeister. Conforming to the new requirements of Prince Nikolaus, Haydn turned to works for the church, including 6 masses. His Mass in C major was entitled *Missa in tempore belli* (1796), for it was composed during Napoleon's drive toward Vienna. The 2nd Mass, in B-flat major, the *Heiligmesse,* also dates from 1796. In 1798 Haydn composed the 3rd Mass, in D minor, which is often called the *Nelsonmesse,* with reference to Lord Nelson's defeat of Napoleon's army at the Battle of the Nile. The 4th Mass, in B-flat major (1799), is called the *Theresienmesse,* in honor of the Austrian Empress Maria Theresa. The 5th Mass, in B-flat major, written in 1801, is known as the *Schöpfungsmesse,* for it contains a theme from the oratorio *Die Schöpfung (The Creation).* The 6th Mass, in B-flat major (1802), is referred to as the *Harmoniemesse,* for its extensive use of wind instruments; the word "harmonie" is here used in the French meaning, as the wind instrument section. Between 1796 and 1798 Haydn composed his great oratorio *Die Schöpfung,* which was first performed at a private concert for the no-

bility at the Schwarzenburg Palace in Vienna on April 29, 1798. In 1796 he wrote the Concerto in E-flat major for trumpet, which became a standard piece for trumpet players. In 1797 Haydn was instructed by the Court to compose a hymn-tune of a solemn nature that could be used as the national Austrian anthem. Haydn succeeded triumphantly in this task; he made use of this tune as a theme of a set of variations in his String Quartet in C major, op. 76, no. 3, which itself became known as the *Emperor* Quartet. The original text for the hymn, written by Lorenz Leopold Haschka, began "Gott erhalte Franz den Kaiser." This hymn had a curious history: a new set of words was written by August Heinrich Hoffmann during a period of revolutionary disturbances in Germany preceding the general European revolution of 1848; its first line, "Deutschland, Deutschland über alles," later assumed the significance of German imperialism; in its original it meant merely, "Germany above all (in our hearts). Between 1799 and 1801 Haydn completed the oratorio *Die Jahreszeiten;* its text was trans. into German from James Thomson's poem *The Seasons.* It was first performed at the Schwarzenburg Palace in Vienna on April 24, 1801. In 1802, beset by illness, Haydn resigned as Kapellmeister to Prince Nikolaus. Despite his gradually increasing debility, Haydn preserved the saving grace of his natural humor; in response to the many salutations of his friends, he sent around a quotation from his old song, *Der Alte,* confessing his bodily weakness. Another amusing musical jest was Haydn's reply to a society lady who identified herself at a Vienna party as a person to whom Haydn had dedicated a lively tune ascending on the major scale; she sang it for him, and he replied wistfully that the tune was now more appropriate in an inversion. Haydn made his last public appearance at a concert given in his honor in the Great Hall of the Univ. of Vienna on March 27, 1808, with Salieri conducting *Die Schöpfung.* When Vienna capitulated to Napoleon, he ordered a guard of honor to be placed at Haydn's residence. Haydn died on May 31, 1809, and was buried at the Hundsturm Cemetery. In consequence of some fantastic events, his skull became separated from his body before his reinterment at Eisenstadt in 1820; it was actually exhibited under glass in the hall of the Gesellschaft der Musikfreunde in Vienna for a number of years, before being reunited with his body in the Bergkirche in Eisenstadt on June 5, 1954, in a solemn official ceremony.

Haydn was often called "Papa Haydn" by his intimates in appreciation of his invariable good humor and amiable disposition. Ironically, he never became a papa in the actual sense of the word. His marriage was unsuccessful; his wife was a veritable termagant; indeed, Haydn was separated from her for most his life. Still, he corresponded with her and sent her money, even though, according to a contemporary report, he never opened her letters.

In schoolbooks Haydn is usually described as "father of the symphony," the creator of the classical form of the symph. and string quartet. Historically, this absolute formulation cannot be sustained; the symphonic form was established by Stamitz and his associates at the Mannheim School; the string quartet, an outgrowth of the string trio-sonata, was of an even earlier provenance. But Haydn's music was not limited to formal novelty; its greatness was revealed in the variety of moods, the excellence of variations, and the contrast among the constituent movements of a symph.; string quartets, as conceived by Haydn, were diminutions of the symph.; both were set in sonata form, consisting in 3 contrasting movements, *Allegro, Andante, Allegro,* with a *Minuet* interpolated between the last 2 movements. It is the quality of invention that places Haydn above his contemporaries and makes his music a model of classical composition. A theory has been put forward that Haydn's themes were derived from the folk melodies of Croatian origin that he had heard in the rural environment of his childhood, but no such adumbrations or similarities can be convincingly proved. Genius is a gift bestowed on a musician or poet without external urgencies.

The intimate *Volkstümlichkeit,* a popular impressiveness of Haydn's music, naturally lent itself to imaginative nicknames of individual compositions. There are among his symphs. such appellations as *Der Philosoph* and *Der Schulmeister;* some were titled after animals: *L'Ours* and *La Poule;* others derived their names from the character of the main theme, as in *Die Uhr (The Clock),* the *Paukenschlag (Surprise),* and the *Paukenwirbel (Drum Roll).* Among Haydn's string quartets there are *La Chasse,* so named because of the hunting horn fanfares; the *Vogelquartett,* in which one hears an imitation of bird calls; the *Froschquartett,* which seems to invoke a similarity with frog calls in the finale; the *Lerchenquartett,* containing a suggestion of a lark call; and the *Farmyard* string quartet. The famous *Toy* Symph., scored for an ensemble which includes the rattle, the triangle, and instruments imitating the quail, cuckoo, and nightingale, was long attributed to Haydn but is actually a movement of a work by Leopold Mozart.

Haydn played a historic roll in the evolution of functional harmony by adopting 4-part writing as a fundamental principle of composition, particularly in his string quartets. This practice has also exercised a profound influence on the teaching of music theory.

WORKS: The precise extent of Haydn's vast output will probably never be known. Many works are lost; others, listed in various catalogues, may never have existed or were duplications of extant works; some are of doubtful authenticity, and some are definitely spurious. The following list of his works attempts to be comprehensive in scope, but it is not an exhaustive compilation.

SYMPHS.: The generally accepted list of Haydn's authentic symphs. numbers 104. For detailed information, consult the monumental study by H.C. Robbins Landon, *The Symphonies of Joseph Haydn* (London, 1955; supplement, 1961); see also his exhaustive biography *Haydn: Chronicle and Works* (5 vols., Bloomington, Ind., and London, 1976–80). The numbering follows the thematic catalogue prepared by Anthony van Hoboken. Also included are the descriptive titles, whether authorized by Hadyn or not. No. 1, in D major (1759); No. 2, in C major (1761); No. 3, in G major (1762); No. 4, in D major (1760); No. 5, in A major (1760); No. 6, in D major, *Le Matin* (1761); No. 7, in C major, *Le Midi* (1761); No. 8, in G major, *Le Soir* (1761); No. 9, in C major (1762); No. 10, in D major (1761); No. 11, in E-flat major (1760); No. 12, in E major (1763); No. 13, in D major (1763); No. 14, in A major (1764); No. 15, in D major (1761); No. 16, in B-flat major (1763); No. 17, in F major (1762); No. 18, in G major (1764); No. 19, in D major (1760); No. 20, in C major (1763); No. 21, in A major (1764); No. 22, in E-flat major, *The Philosopher* (1764); No. 23, in G major (1764); No. 24, in D major (1764); No. 25, in C major (1761); No. 26, in D minor, *Lamentatione* (1770); No. 27, in G major (1761); No. 28, in A major (1765); No. 29, in E major (1765); No. 30, in C major, *Alleluja* (1765); No. 31, in D major, *Hornsignal* (1765); No. 32, in C major (1760); No. 33, in C major (1760); No. 34, in D minor/ D major (1767); No. 35, in B-flat major (1767); No. 36, in E-flat major (1765); No. 37, in C major (1758); No. 38, in C major (1769); No. 39, in G minor (1765); No. 40, in F major (1763); No. 41, in C major (1770); No. 42, in D major (1771); No. 43, in E-flat major, *Mercury* (1772); No. 44, in E minor, *Trauersinfonie* (1772); No. 45, in F-sharp minor, *Abschiedsinfonie* (1772); No. 46, in B major (1772); No. 47, in G major (1772); No. 48, in C major, *Maria Theresia* (1769); No. 49, in F minor, *La Passione* (1768); No. 50, in C major (1773); No. 51, in B-flat major (1774); No. 52, in C minor (1774); No. 53, in D major, *Imperial* or *Festino* (1778); No. 54, in G major (1774); No. 55, in E-flat major, *The Schoolmaster* (1774); No. 56, in C major (1774); No. 57, in D major (1774); No. 58, in F major (1768); No. 59, in A major, *Fire* (1769); No. 60, in C major, *Il Distratto* (1774); No. 61, in D major (1776); No. 62, in D major (1780); No. 63, in C major, *La Roxelane* or *Roxolana* (1779); No. 64, in A major, *Tempora mutantur* (1773); No. 65, in A major (1773); No. 66, in B-flat major (1776); No. 67, in F major (1776); No. 68, in B-flat major (1774); No. 69, in C major, *Laudon* or *Loudon* (1776); No. 70, in D major (1779); No. 71, in B-flat major (1779); No. 72, in D major (1765); No. 73, in D major, *La Chasse* (1782); No. 74, in E-flat major (1781); No. 75, in D major (1781); No. 76, in E-flat major (1782); No. 77, in B-flat major (1782); No. 78, in C minor (1782); No. 79, in F major (1784); No. 80, in D minor (1784); No. 81, in G major (1784); *Paris* symphs.: No. 82, in C major, *L'Ours* or *The Bear* (1786), No. 83, in G minor, *La Poule* or *The Hen* (1785), No. 84, in E-flat major (1786), No. 85, in B-flat major, *La Reine* or *The Queen* (1785); No. 86, in D major (1786), and No. 87, in A major (1785); No. 88, in G major (1787); No. 89, in F major (1787); No. 90, in C major (1788); No. 91, in E-flat major (1788); No. 92, in G major, *Oxford* (1789); *London* or *Salomon* symphs.: No. 93, in D major (1791; London, Feb. 17, 1792), No. 94, in G major, *Mit dem Paukenschlag* or *The Surprise* (1791; London, March 23, 1792), No. 95, in C minor (1791; London, 1791), No. 96, in D major, *The Miracle* (1791; London, 1791), No. 97, in C major (1792; London, May 3 or 4, 1792), No. 98, in B-flat major (1792; London, March 2, 1792), No. 99, in E-flat major (1793;

London, Feb. 10, 1794), No. 100, in G major, *Militär* or *Military* (1793–94; London, March 31, 1794), No. 101 in D major, *Die Uhr* or *The Clock* (1793–94; London, March 3, 1794), No. 102, in B-flat major (1794; London, Feb. 2, 1795), No. 103, in E-flat major, *Paukenwirbel* or *Drum Roll* (1795; London, March 2, 1795), and No. 104, in D major, *London* or *Salomon* (1795; London, May 4, 1795); also the Concertante (now called Sinfonia Concertante) in B-flat major, listed in the Hoboken catalogue as No. 105 (1792; London, March 9, 1792). Hoboken also lists No. 106, in D major (1769; only first movement extant; may have been composed as the overture to *Le Pescatrici*); No. 107, in B-flat major (1761; may be by Wagenseil); and No. 108, in B-flat major (1761).

CONCERTOS: 4 for Violin: No. 1, in C major (1765); No. 2, in D major (1765; not extant); No. 3, in A major (1770); No. 4, in G major (1769); 2 for Cello: No. 1, in C major (1765), and No. 2, in D major (1783); another cello concerto may be lost or has been confused with No. 1; 2 for Organ or Harpsichord: C major (1756) and D major (1767); also most likely by Haydn are 3 others for Organ or Harpsichord, all in C major (1763, 1766, 1771); one for Violin, and Harpsichord or Organ, in F major (1766); 3 for Harpsichord: F major (1771); G major (1770; also for Piano); D major (1784; also for Piano); one for Trumpet, in E-flat major (1796); 5 for 2 Lire Organizzate: C major (1787); F major (1786); G major (1787); F major (1787); G major (1787); also divertimenti, notturni, etc. Several other concertos for oboe, flute, horn, and bassoon are either lost or spurious.

Haydn also composed several miscellaneous orch. works, including overtures to his dramatic pieces: G minor (to *L'isola disabitata*); D major (to *L'incontro improvviso*); G major (to *Lo speziale*); B-flat major (to *La vera costanza*); C major (to *L'infedeltà delusa*); C minor/C major (to *Il ritorno di Tobia*); also the *Musica instrumentale sopra le 7 ultime parole del nostro Redentore in croce ossiano 7 sonate con un'introduzione ed al fine un terremoto* (1786; for Cadiz).

DRAMATIC WORKS: *Der krumme Teufel*, singspiel (1751?; first confirmed perf., Vienna, May 29, 1753; not extant); *Der neue krumme Teufel (Asmodeus, der krumme Teufel)*, singspiel (1758?; music not extant); *Acide*, festa teatrale (1762; Eisenstadt, Jan. 11, 1763; only fragment and libretto extant; revised version, 1773; only fragment extant); *Marchese (La Marchesa Nespola)*, comedia (1762?; only fragment extant; dialogues not extant); *Il Dottore*, comedia (1765?; not extant); *La Vedova*, comedia (1765?; not extant); *Il scanarello*, comedia (1765?; not extant); *La Canterina*, intermezzo in musica (1766; Bratislava, Sept. 11?, 1766); *Lo speziale (Der Apotheker)*, dramma giocoso (1768; Esterháza, Autumn 1768); *Le Pescatrici (Die Fischerinnen)*, dramma giocoso (1769; Esterháza, Sept. 16?, 1770); *L'infedeltà delusa (Liebe macht erfinderisch; Untreue lohnt sich nicht; Deceit Outwitted)*, burletta per musica (1773; Esterháza, July 26, 1773); *Philemon und Baucis oder Jupiters Reise auf die Erde*, singspiel/marionette opera (1773; Esterháza, Sept. 2, 1773); *Hexenschabbas*, marionette opera (1773?; not extant);

L'incontro improvviso (Die unverhoffte Zusammenkunft; Unverhofftes Begegnen), dramma giocoso (1775; Esterháza, Aug. 29, 1775); *Dido*, singspiel/marionette opera (1776?; Esterháza, March?, 1776; music not extant); *Opéra comique vom abgebrannten Haus* (not extant; may be identical with the following work); *Die Feuerbrunst*, singspiel/marionette opera (1775?–78?; may be by Haydn; dialogues not extant); *Il mondo della luna (Die Welt auf dem Monde)*, dramma giocoso (1777; Esterháza, Aug. 3, 1777); *Die bestrafte Rachbegierde*, singspiel/marionette opera (1779?; Esterháza, 1779; music not extant); *La vera costanza*, dramma giocoso (1778?; Esterháza, April 25, 1779; only music extant appears in the revised version of 1785, known as *Der flatterhafte Liebhaber; Der Sieg der Beständigkeit; Die wahre Beständigkeit; List und Liebe*; etc.); *L'isola disabitata (Die wüste Insel)*, azione teatrale (1779; Esterháza, Dec. 6, 1779; revised 1802); *La fedeltà premiata (Die belohnte Treue)*, dramma pastorale giocoso (1780; Esterháza, Feb. 25, 1781); *Orlando paladino (Der Ritter Roland)*, dramma eroicomico (1782; Esterháza, Dec. 6, 1782); *Armida*, dramma eroico (1783; Esterháza, Feb. 26, 1784); *L'anima del filosofo ossia Orfeo ed Euridice*, dramma per musica (1791; composed for London but not perf.; first confirmed perf., Florence, June 10, 1951, with Callas and Christoff in the principal roles); *Alfred, König der Angelsachsen, oder Der patriotische König* (1796; perf. as the incidental music to *Haldane, König der Dänen*, Eisenstadt, Sept. 1796).

MASSES: *Missa Rorate coeli desuper* in G major (date unknown; not extant, or identical with the following); Mass in G major (date unknown; composed by G. Reutter, Jr., Arbesser, and Haydn; publ. in London, 1957); *Missa brevis* in F major (1749?); *Missa Cellensis in honorem Beata Maria Virgine* in C major, *Cäcilienmesse* (1766); *Missa Sunt bona mixta malis* in D minor (1769?; not extant); *Missa in honorem Beata Maria Virgine* in E-flat major, *Missa Sancti Josephi; Grosse Orgelmesse* (1769?); *Missa Sancti Nicolai* in G major, *Nicolaimesse; 6/4-Takt-Messe* (1772); *Missa brevis Sancti Joannis de Deo* in B-flat major, *Kleine Orgelmesse* (1775?); *Missa Cellensis* in C major, *Mariazeller Messe* (1782); *Missa Sancti Bernardi von Offida* in B-flat major, *Heiligmesse* (1796); *Missa in tempore belli* in C major, *Kriegsmesse; Paukenmesse* (1796; Vienna, Dec. 26, 1796?); *Missa in D minor, Nelsonmesse; Imperial Mass; Coronation Mass* (1798; Eisenstadt, Sept. 23, 1798?); *Missa in B-flat major, Theresienmesse* (1799); *Missa in B-flat major, Schöpfungsmesse* (1801; Eisenstadt, Sept. 13, 1801); *Missa in B-flat major, Harmoniemesse* (1802; Eisenstadt, Sept. 8, 1802).

ORATORIOS: Stabat Mater (1767); *Applausus (Jubilaeum virtutis Palatium)*, allegorical oratorio/cantata (1768; Zwettl, April 17, 1768); *Il ritorno di Tobia* (1774–75; Vienna, April 2 and 4, 1775, in 2 parts; revised 1784); *Die sieben letzten Worte unseres Erlösers am Kreuze* (1795–96; Vienna, 1796); *Die Schöpfung (The Creation;* 1796–98; first private perf., Schwarzenburg Palace, Vienna, April 29, 1798; first public perf., Kärnthnertortheater, Vienna, March 19, 1799); *Die Jahreszeiten (The Seasons;*

Haydn

1799–1801; Schwarzenburg Palace, Vienna, April 24, 1801).

Haydn's other vocal works include 2 Te Deums (both in C major); offertories; secular cantatas; secular vocal works for orch.; more than 50 songs with keyboard accompaniment; vocal duets, trios, and quartets with keyboard accompaniment; more than 50 canons; arrangements of Scottish and other songs; and *Gott erhalte Franz den Kaiser* (*God Save the Emperor Franz;* 1797; was the Austrian national anthem until 1918).

STRING QUARTETS: Op. 1 (c.1757–59): No. 1, in B-flat major, *La Chasse;* No. 2, in E-flat major; No. 3, in D major; No. 4, in G major; No. 5, in E-flat major; No. 6, in C major; op. 2 (c.1760–62): No. 1, in A major; No. 2, in E major; No. 4, in F major; No. 6, in B-flat major; op. 9 (1771): No. 1, in C major; No. 2, in E-flat major; No. 3, in G major; No. 4, in D minor; No. 5, in B-flat major; No. 6, in A major; op. 17 (1771): No. 1, in E major; No. 2, in F major; No. 3, in E-flat major; No. 4, in C minor; No. 5, in G major, *Recitative;* No. 6, in D major; *Sun Quartets,* op. 20 (1772): No. 1, in E-flat major; No. 2, in C major; No. 3, in G minor; No. 4, in D major; No. 5, in F minor; No. 6, in A major; *Russian Quartets; Jungfernquartette,* op. 33 (1781): No. 1, in B minor; No. 2, in E-flat major, *The Joke;* No. 3, in C major, *The Bird;* No. 4, in B-flat major; No. 5, in G major, *How do you do?;* No. 6, in B-flat major; op. 42, in D minor (1785); *Prussian Quartets,* op. 50 (1787): No. 1, in B-flat major; No. 2, in C major; No. 3, in E-flat major; No. 4, in F-sharp minor; No. 5, in F major, *Ein Traum;* No. 6, in D major, *The Frog;* *Tost Quartets,* op. 54 (1788): No. 1, in G major; No. 2, in C major; No. 3, in E major; *Tost Quartets,* op. 55 (1788): No. 1, in A major; No. 2, in F minor, *The Razor;* No. 3, in B-flat major; *Tost Quartets,* op. 64 (1790): No. 1, in C major; No. 2, in B minor; No. 3, in B-flat major; No. 4, in G major; No. 5, in D major, *The Lark;* No. 6, in E-flat major; *Apponyi Quartets,* op. 71 (1793): No. 1, in B-flat major; No. 2, in D major; No. 3, in E-flat major; *Apponyi Quartets,* op. 74 (1793): No. 1, in C major; No. 2, in F major; No. 3, in G minor, *The Rider; Erdödy Quartets,* op. 76 (1797): No. 1, in G major; No. 2, in D minor, *Fifths;* No. 3, in C major, *Emperor;* No. 4, in B-flat major, *Sunrise;* No. 5, in D major; No. 6, in E-flat major; *Lobkowitz Quartets,* op. 77 (1799): No. 1, in G major; No. 2, in F major; op. 103, in D minor (1803?; unfinished; only movements 2 and 3 finished).—Haydn also arranged the orch. version of the *Musica instrumentale sopra le 7 ultime parole del nostro Redentore in croce . . .* for String Quartet (1787), as well as pieces from the operas *La vera costanza* and *Armida.*

Other works by Haydn include 21 string trios (3 not extant); a great number of works for baryton, written for Prince Esterházy, who was an avid baryton player: about 125 baryton trios (divertimentos), various works for one or 2 barytons, etc.; 29 keyboard sonatas (3 listed as trios), most of them for harpsichord or piano, with violin and cello; 47 solo keyboard sonatas (7 not extant, one not complete), almost all of them for harpsichord; etc.

BIBLIOGRAPHY: COLLECTED EDITIONS, SOURCE MATERIAL: The first attempt to publish a complete ed. was made by Breitkopf & Härtel; *Joseph Haydns Werke,* ed. by G. Adler, H. Kretzschmar, E. Mandyczewski, M. Seiffert, and others, reached only 10 vols. in its coverage (Leipzig, 1907–33). An attempt to continue it after World War II as *Joseph Haydn: Kritische Gesamtausgabe,* under the editorship of Jens Peter Larsen and the sponsorship of the Haydn Society of Boston, also failed; only 4 vols. were issued (Boston, Leipzig, and Vienna, 1950–51). Finally, in 1955, through the efforts of Friedrich Blume and the publisher Günter Henle, the Joseph Haydn-Institut of Cologne was founded to sponsor a monumental critical ed. The new ed., *Joseph Haydn: Werke,* also includes accompanying Kritische Berichte. Jens Peter Larsen ed. the first series of vols. (Munich, 1958–61); he was succeeded as ed. by Georg Feder. Expected to be completed by the year 2000, this exhaustive ed. will contain more than 100 vols. H.C. Robbins Landon has ed. all of the symphs. in a separate series, issued in miniature score as *Joseph Haydn: Kritische Ausgabe sämtlicher Symphonien* (I–XII, Vienna, 1965–68). A. van Hoboken has prepared a thematic catalogue, *Joseph Haydn: Thematisch-bibliographisches Werkverzeichnis* (2 vols., Mainz, 1957 and 1971).

Invaluable articles may be found in the *Haydn Yearbook* (1962—) and *Haydn Studien* (Joseph Haydn-Institut, Cologne, 1965—).

Other sources include the following: A. Csatkai, *J. H.: Katalog der Gedächtnisausstellung in Eisenstadt 1932* (Eisenstadt, 1932); R. Lachmann, "Die H.-Autographen der Staatsbibliothek zu Berlin," *Zeitschrift für Musikwissenschaft,* XIV (1932); A. Orel, *Katalog der H.-Gedächtnisausstellung Wien 1932* (Vienna, 1932); G. de Saint-Foix, "Les Manuscrits et les copies d'œuvres de J. H. à la Bibliothèque du Conservatoire (Fonds Malherbe)," *Revue de Musicologie,* XIII (1932; supplement by Y. Rokseth in *Revue de Musicologie,* XIV, 1933); J. Larsen, *Die H.-Überlieferung* (Copenhagen, 1939); J. Larsen, ed., *Drei H. Kataloge in Faksimile: Mit Einleitung und ergänzenden Themenverzeichnissen* (Copenhagen, 1941; 2nd ed., revised, 1979); R. Feuchtmüller, F. Hadamowsky, and L. Nowak, *J. H. und seine Zeit: Ausstellung Schloss Petronell (N. Ö.) Mai bis Oktober 1959* (Vienna, 1959); H.C. Robbins Landon, "Survey of the H. Sources in Czechoslovakia," *Internationale Konferenz zum Andenken J. H.s: Budapest 1959;* L. Nowak, ed., *J. H.: Ausstellung Ausstellung zum 150. Todestag: Vom 29. Mai bis 30. September 1959* (Vienna, 1959); A. Brown, C. Brown, and J. Berkenstock, "J. H. in Literature: A Bibliography," *H.-Studien* (July 1974, Bd. III, Heft 3/4, pp. 173–352; an alphabetical list, chiefly by author, of 2,285 books, monographs, periodical and *Festschrift* articles, and some unpubl. dissertations, with full bibliographical information and indexes by name, topic, and work); see also their "J. H. in Literature: A Survey," *Notes* (March 1975).

CORRESPONDENCE: H.C. Robbins Landon, ed., *The Collected Correspondence and London Notebooks of J. H.* (London, 1959); D. Bartha, ed., *J. H.: Gesammelte Briefe und Aufzeichnungen: Unter Benützung der Quellensammlung von H.C. Robbins Landon* (Kassel, 1965).

BIOGRAPHY: G. Griesinger, "Biographische Notizen über J. H.," *Allgemeine Musikalische Zeitung,* XI (Leipzig, 1809; also publ. separately, Leipzig, 1810; 2nd ed., 1819; modern ed. by F. Grasberger, Vienna, 1954; Eng. trans. in V. Gotwals, ed., *J. H.: Eighteenth-century Gentleman and Genius,* Madison, Wis., 1963; 2nd ed., 1968, as *H.: Two Contemporary Portraits,* including Eng. trans. of Dies); S. Mayr, *Brevi notizie istoriche della vita e delle opere di H.* (Bergamo, 1809); A. Dies, *Biographische Nachrichten von J. H.: Nach mündlichen Erzählungen desselben entworfen und herausgegeben von Albert Christoph Dies, Landschaftmahler* (Vienna, 1810; modern ed. by H. Seeger, Berlin, 1959; 4th ed., 1976; Eng. trans. in V. Gotwals, ed., *J. H.: Eighteenth-century Gentleman and Genius,* Madison, 1963; 2nd ed., 1968, as *H.: Two Contemporary Portraits,* including Eng. trans. of Griesinger); G. Carpani, *Le Haydine, ovvero Lettere su la vita e le opere del celebre maestro Giuseppe H.* (Milan, 1812; 2nd ed., 1823; Eng. trans. as *The Life of H. in Letters,* 1839); T. von Karajan, *J. H. in London, 1791 und 1792* (Vienna, 1861); C. von Wurzbach, *J. H. und sein Bruder Michael: Zwei bio-bibliographische Künstler-Skizzen* (Vienna, 1861); C. Pohl, *Mozart und H. in London:* Vol. II, *H. in London* (Vienna, 1867); idem, *J. H.* (incomplete; 2 vols.; Vol. I, Berlin, 1875; 2nd ed., 1878; Vol. II, Leipzig, 1882; Vol. III, completed by H. Botstiber, Leipzig, 1927); J. Hadden, *H.* (London and N.Y., 1902; 2nd ed., revised, 1934); F. Artaria and H. Botstiber, *J. H. und das Verlagshaus Artaria: Nach den Briefen des Meisters an das Haus Artaria & Compagnie dargestellt* (Vienna, 1909); M. Brenet, *H.* (Paris, 1909; 2nd ed., 1910; Eng. trans., 1926); H. von Hase, *J. H. und Breitkopf & Härtel* (Leipzig, 1909); F. Scherber, "J. H.s Tod," *Neue Musik-Zeitung,* XXX (1909); A. Schnerich, *J. H. und seine Sendung* (Zürich, 1922; 2nd ed., 1926, with supplement by W. Fischer); O. Deutsch, "H. und Nelson," *Die Musik,* XXIV (1931–32); H. Botstiber, "H. and Luigia Polzelli," *Musical Quarterly* (April 1932); K. Geiringer, *J. H.* (Potsdam, 1932); J. Muller, "H. Portraits," *Musical Quarterly* (April 1932); E. Schmid, "J. H. in Eisenstadt: Ein Beitrag zur Biographie des Meisters," *Burgenländische Heimatblätter,* I (Eisenstadt, 1932); M. Scott, "H. in England," *Musical Quarterly* (April 1932); E. Schmid, *J. H.: Ein Buch von Vorfahren und Heimat des Meisters* (Kassel, 1934); D. Bartha, "Zur Abstammung J. H.s," *Acta Musicologica,* VII (1935); K. Geiringer, *H.: A Creative Life in Music* (N.Y., 1946; 2nd ed., revised, 1963); R. Hughes, *H.* (London, 1950; 5th ed., revised, 1975); L. Nowak, *J. H.: Leben, Bedeutung und Werk* (Zürich, 1951; 3rd ed., revised, 1966); R. Sondheimer, *H., A Historical and Psychological Study Based on His Quartets* (London, 1951); E. Schmid, "J. H.s Jugendliebe," in *Festschrift Wilhelm Fischer* (Innsbruck, 1956); J. Larsen, "H. und Mozart," *Österreichische Musikzeitschrift,* XIV (1959); D. Bartha and L. Somfai, *H. als Opernkapellmeister: Die H.-Dokumente der Esterházy-Opernsammlung* (Budapest, 1960; revised ed. in *New Looks at Italian Opera: Essays in Honor of Donald J. Grout,* Ithaca, N.Y., 1968); H. Seeger, *J. H.* (Leipzig, 1961); A. van Hoboken, *Discrepancies in H. Biographies* (Washington, D.C., 1962); L. Somfai, *J.*

H.: Sein Leben in zeitgenössischen Bildern (Budapest and Kassel, 1966; Eng. trans., 1969); J. Chailley, "J. H. and the Freemasons," in *Studies in Eighteenth-century Music: A Tribute to Karl Geiringer* (N.Y., 1970); G. Feder, "J. H. als Mensch und Musiker," *Jahrbuch für österreichische Kulturgeschichte, ½: Beiträge zur Musikgeschichte des 18. Jahrhunderts,* II (1972); H.C. Robbins Landon, *H.* (London, 1972); B. Redfern, *H.: A Biography, with a Survey of Books, Editions and Recordings* (London, 1972); H.C. Robbins Landon, *H.: Chronicle and Works* (a monumental study of his life and music; 5 vols., Bloomington, Ind., and London; Vol. I, *H.: The Early Years, 1732–1765* [1980]; Vol. II, *H. at Esterháza, 1776–1790* [1978]; Vol. III, *H. in England, 1791–1795* [1976]; Vol. IV, *H.: The Years of "The Creation," 1796–1800* [1977]; Vol. V, *H.: The Late Years, 1801–1809* [1977]); idem, *H.: A Documentary Study* (London, 1981); J. Webster, "Prospects for H. Biography," *Musical Times* (March 1982).

CRITICISM, ANALYSIS: L. Wendschuh, *Über J. H.'s Opern* (Halle, 1896); A. Sandberger, "Zur Geschichte des Haydnschen Streichquartetts," *Altbayerische Monatshefte* (1900; revised ed. in *Ausgewählte Aufsätze zur Musikgeschichte,* I, Munich, 1921); H. Abert, "J. H.s Klavierwerke," *Zeitschrift für Musikwissenschaft,* II (1919–20); F. Blume, "J. H.s künstlerische Persönlichkeit in seinen Streichquartetten," *Jahrbuch der Musikbibliothek Peters 1931;* G. Adler, "H. and the Viennese Classical School," *Musical Quarterly* (April 1932); K. Geiringer, "H.'s Sketches for 'The Creation,' " ibid. (April 1932); M. Herter Norton, "H. in America (before 1820)," ibid. (April 1932); O. Strunk, "H.'s Divertimenti for Baryton, Viola, and Bass," ibid. (April 1932); C. Smith, "H.'s Chamber Music and the Flute," ibid. (July and Oct. 1933); B. Rywosch, *Beiträge zur Entwicklung in J. H.'s Symphonik, 1759–1780* (Turbenthal, 1934); O. Strunk, "Notes on a H. Autograph," *Musical Quarterly* (April 1934); J. Larsen, "H. und das 'kleine Quartbuch,' " *Acta Musicologica,* VII (1935; for reply, see A. Sandberger in the *Zeitschrift für Musik,* 1935); H. Wirth, *J. H. als Dramatiker: Sein Bühnenschaffen als Beitrag zur Geschichte der deutschen Oper* (Wolfenbüttel and Berlin, 1940); C. Brand, *Die Messen von J. H.* (Würzburg, 1941); H. Therstappen, *J. H.s sinfonisches Vermächtnis* (Wolfenbüttel, 1941); M. Scott, "H.: Fresh Facts and Old Fancies," *Proceedings of the Royal Musical Association,* LXVIII (1941–42); P. Radcliffe, "The Piano Sonatas of J. H.," *Music Review,* VII (1946); M. Scott, "The Opera Concerts of 1795," ibid., XII (1951); H. Wirth, *J. H.: Orfeo ed Euridice; Analytical Notes* (Boston, 1951); H.C. Robbins Landon, "H. and Authenticity: Some New Facts," *Music Review,* XVI (1955); idem, *The Symphonies of J. H.* (includes a thematic catalogue, with exhaustive commentaries on their authenticity, chronology, and availability; London, 1955; supplement, 1961; for additional information, consult his *H.: Chronicle and Works,* Bloomington, Ind., and London, 5 vols., 1976–80); J. Larsen, "Zu H.s künstlerischer Entwicklung," in *Festschrift Wilhelm Fischer* (Innsbruck, 1956); D. Arnold, "H.'s Counterpoint and Fux's *Gradus,*" *Monthly Musical Record,*

LXXXVII (1957); H.C. Robbins Landon, "Doubtful and Spurious Quartets and Quintets Attributed to H.," *Music Review*, XVIII (1957); H. Keller, "The Interpretation of the H. Quartets," *Score*, no. 23 (1958); E. Schenk, "Das Weltbild J. H.s'," *Österreichische Akademie der Wissenschaften: Almanach*, CIX (1959); J. Larsen, "Probleme der chronologischen Ordnung von H.s Sinfonien," in *Festschrift Otto Erich Deutsch* (Kassel, 1963); A. Tyson and H.C. Robbins Landon, "Who Composed H.'s Op. 3?," *Musical Times* (July 1964); R. Hughes, *H. String Quartets* (London, 1966); H.C. Robbins Landon, *H. Symphonies* (London, 1966); I. Saslav, *Tempos in the String Quartets of J. H.* (Diss., Indiana Univ., 1969); A. Brown, *The Solo and Ensemble Keyboard Sonatas of J. H.: A Study of Structure and Style* (Diss., Northwestern Univ., 1970); D. Cushman, *J. H.'s Melodic Materials: An Exploratory Introduction to the Primary and Secondary Sources Together with an Analytical Catalogue and Tables of Proposed Melodic Correspondence and/or Variance* (Diss., Boston Univ., 1972); H.C. Robbins Landon, "The Operas of H.," in *The New Oxford History of Music* (vol. VII, London, 1973); W. Steinbeck, *Das Menuett in der Instrumentalmusik J. H.s* (Munich, 1973); J. Webster, *The Bass Part in H.'s Early String Quartets and in Austrian Chamber Music, 1756–1780* (Diss., Princeton Univ., 1973); L. Somfai, "The London Revision of H.'s Instrumental Style," *Proceedings of the Royal Musical Association*, C (1973–74); R. Barrett-Ayres, *J. H. and the String Quartet* (London and N.Y., 1974); L. Finscher, *Studien zur Geschichte des Streichquartetts, Vol. I: Die Entstehung des klassischen Streichquartetts: Von den Vorformen zur Grundlegung durch J. H.* (Kassel, 1974); O. Moe, "Texture in H.'s Early Quartets," *Music Review*, XXV (1974); J. Drury, *H.'s Seven Last Words: An Historical and Critical Study* (Diss., Univ. of Illinois, 1975); G. Feder, "Opera seria, opera buffa und opera semiseria bei H.," in *Opernstudien: Anna Amalie Abert zum 65. Geburtstag* (Tutzing, 1975); W. Koller, *Aus der Werkstatt der Wiener Klassiker: Bearbeitung H.s* (Tutzing, 1975); B. Wackernagel, *J. H.s frühe Klaviersonaten: Ihre Beziehungen zur Klaviermusik um die Mitte des 18. Jahrhunderts* (Tutzing, 1975); J. Webster, "The Chronology of H.'s String Quartets," *Musical Quarterly* (Jan. 1975); A. Brown, "Critical Years for H.'s Instrumental Music: 1787-90," ibid. (July 1976); I. Lowens, *H. in America* (Detroit, 1979); C. Wolff, ed., *The String Quartets of H., Mozart, and Beethoven: Studies of the Autograph Manuscripts* (a valuable investigation; Cambridge, Mass., 1981); G. Feder, "From the Workshop of the H. Edition," *Musical Times* (March 1982); J. Larsen, "H.: Repertory, Interpretation, Image," ibid. (March 1982); D. McCaldin, "H. as Self-Borrower," ibid. (March 1982). MISCELLANEOUS: W. Hadow, *A Croatian Composer: Notes toward the Study of J. H.* (London, 1897; an attempt to prove H.'s Slavic origin; modern research has disproved Hadow's theory); J. Tandler, "Über den Schädel H.s'," *Mitteilungen der Anthropologischen Gesellschaft*, XXXIX (1909); V. Gotwals, "J. H.'s Last Will and Testament," *Musical Quarterly* (July 1961).

Haydn, (Johann) Michael, Austrian composer, brother of **Franz Joseph Haydn;** b. Rohrau (baptized, Sept. 14, 1737) d. Salzburg, Aug. 10, 1806. He served as a boy soprano at St. Stephen's Cathedral in Vienna (1745–55); his voice was remarkable for its wide range, reaching 3 octaves. He replaced his brother in solo parts when a younger voice was required. He studied composition mainly by reading books on counterpoint, particularly *Gradus ad Parnassum* by Fux. In 1757 he became chapel master at Grosswardein; in 1762, music director to Archbishop Sigismund at Salzburg. In 1768 he married the daughter of the organist Lipp, Maria Magdalena, an excellent soprano singer who was praised by Mozart. The French occupation of Salzburg in 1800 deprived him of his property, but he was aided by his brother. His fortunes were mended somewhat by the handsomely rewarded commission of a mass which he received from the Empress Teresa, wife of the Emperor Franz I, and which was performed at the Luxemburg Palace on Oct. 4, 1801. He opened a school of composition, and educated many distinguished pupils, including Carl Maria von Weber. In 1833, Martin Bischofsreiter, a Benedictine monk, publ. *Partitur-Fundamente*, a collection of thoroughbass exercises written by Michael Haydn for his scholars. He composed a mass and vespers for Prince Esterházy, who twice offered to make him assistant chapel master; but Haydn declined, hoping that the Salzburg chapel would be reorganized. A prolific composer, his best works were his sacred compositions, which his brother held in high esteem. Although he had advantageous offers for publ. from Breitkopf & Härtel, he was reluctant to accept, so that most of his music remained in MS at the time of his death. WORKS: DRAMATIC: Singspiels, *Rebekka als Braut* (Salzburg, April 10, 1766); *Die Hochzeit auf der Alm* (Salzburg, May 6, 1768); *Die Warheit der Natur* (Salzburg, July 7, 1869); *Der englische Patriot* (1779); *Die Ahrenleserin* (Salzburg, July 2, 1788); the oratorios *Die Schuldigkeit des ersten Gebots,* parts 2 (1767; collaborated with Mozart); *Der Kampf der Busse und Bekehrung* (Salzburg, Feb. 21, 1768); *Der remutige Petrus* (Salzburg, March 11, 1770); *Der büssender Sünder* (Salzburg, Feb. 15, 1771); *Oratorium de Passione Domini nostri Jesu Christi* (1775); several operas, including the opera seria *Andromeda e Perseo* (Salzburg, March 14, 1787); incidental music to Voltaire's *Zaïre* (Salzburg, Sept. 29, 1777). SACRED MUSIC: Over 400 works, including 38 masses, 2 of which are *Missa Hispanica* (Salzburg, Aug. 4, 1786) and *Pro defunctor Archiepscopo Sigismundo* (Salzburg, Dec. 31, 1771; known as Requiem in C minor, which influenced Mozart's Requiem); cantatas, Requiems, settings of the Te Deum, *Litaniae laurentanae*, vespers, responsories, graduals and offertories; also 2 collections of 4-part songs. INSTRUMENTAL MUSIC: About 40 symphs.; 30 divertimenti (1760–95); serenades (1760–85); marches; minuets; partitas; cassations; nocturnes; concertos for flute, violin, and harpsichord; Double Concerto for Viola, Organ, and Strings; string quartets and quintets; a Sextet. A selection of his masses and other church works was edited by A.M. Klafsky in

Denkmäler der Tonkunst in Österreich, vols. 45 and 62 (formerly 22 and 32.i); a selection of his instrumental works, edited and partly reorchestrated by L.H. Perger, in vol. 29 (formerly 14.ii), including a Symph. in E-flat (1783), a Symph. in C major (1788), a Turkish March, etc.; additional recent publications are in *Accademia Musicale* (Mainz), vols. 7, 8, 9; *Musica Rinata* (Budapest), vols. 3, 4, 7; and by the Haydn-Mozart Press in Salzburg.

BIBLIOGRAPHY: F.J. Schinn and G. Otter, *Biographische Skizze von J.M. Haydn* (Salzburg, 1808); C. Wurzbach, *Joseph Haydn und sein Bruder Michael* (Vienna, 1862); J.E. Engl, *Zum Gedenken J.M. Haydns* (Salzburg, 1906); O. Schmid, *J.M. Haydn: Sein Leben und Wirken* (Vienna, 1906); K.M. Klob, *Drei musikalische Biedermänner* (Ulm, 1911); F. Martin, *Kleine Beiträge zur Musikgeschichte Salzburgs,* (Salzburg, 1913); A.M. Klafsky, "Michael Haydn als Kirchenkomponist," in Adler's *Studien zur Musikwissenschaft* (1915); G. de Saint-Foix, "Histoire de deux trios de Michael Haydn," *Revue de Musicologie,* 38; H. Jancik, *Michael Haydn, Ein vergessener Meister* (Zürich, 1952); H.C. Robbins Landon, "An Introduction to Michael Haydn," *Essays on the Viennese Classical Style* (N.Y., 1970).

Haydon, Glen, eminent American musicologist; b. Inman, Kans., Dec. 9, 1896; d. Chapel Hill, N.C., May 8, 1966. He studied at the Univ. of Calif., Berkeley (B.A., 1918; M.A., 1921); he then went to Paris, where he studied clarinet playing and composition; then enrolled at the Univ. of Vienna, where he obtained his Ph.D. in 1932 with the dissertation *Zur Entwicklungsgeschichte des Quartsertakkordes; The Evolution of the Six-Four Chord: A Chapter in the History of Dissonance Treatment* (publ. in Berkeley, 1933). Returning to America, he became head of the dept. of music at the Univ. of North Carolina at Chapel Hill (1934), and held this post until his death. A Festschrift in his honor, planned for his 70th birthday, was publ. posthumously in Chapel Hill (1969) under the title *Studies in Musicology. Essays in the History, Style and Bibliography of Music in Memory of Glen Haydon,* edited by J.W. Pruett. Among Haydon's theoretical publications are the valuable books *The Evolution of the Six-Four Chord* and *Introduction to Musicology* (N.Y., 1941; reprinted 1959); he also publ. a *Graded Course of Clarinet Playing* (N.Y., 1927), and trans. into Eng. Jeppesen's *Counterpoint: The Polyphonic Vocal Style of the 16th Century* (N.Y., 1939). Haydon wrote a ballet, *The Druids Weed* (1929), and several pieces of sacred choral music.

Hayes, Gerald Ravenscourt, English writer; b. London, April 18, 1889; d. there, Sept. 13, 1955. He entered the Hydrographic Dept. of the Admiralty in 1911; became chief cartographer in 1934; then transferred to the Secretary's Dept. (1946–53). Apart from his writings on cartography, he became interested in musical instruments; was one of the founders of the Dolmetsch Foundation; publ. *The Treatment of Instrumental Music* (1928); *The Viols and Other Bowed Instruments* (1930); *King's Musick,* an anthology (1937); numerous articles on instruments in various publications.

Hayes, Isaac, black American rhythm-and-blues singer and songwriter; b. Covington, Tenn.; Aug. 6, 1938. He learned to play saxophone and piano; in 1962 he formed a duo with David Porter, with whom he arranged songs such as *Hot Buttered Soul* which became immediately successful in the Sunbelt. Other successful songs were *B-A-B-Y, Soul Man, Walk On By,* and *By the Time I Get to Phoenix.* He also arranged and performed the sound track for the movie *Shaft.*

Hayes, Philip, English organist and composer, son of **William Hayes;** b. Oxford, (baptized, April 17) 1738; d. London, March 19, 1797. He studied mainly with his father; received a Mus.B. from Oxford (May 18, 1763); became a Gentleman of the Chapel Royal in 1767; organist of New College, Oxford (1776); succeeded his father as organist of Magdalen College and prof. of music at the univ. (1777); also received his Mus.D. the same year; became organist of St. John's College (1790).

WORKS: Oratorio, *Prophecy* (Oxford, 1781); masque, *Telemachus;* odes; anthems; services; Psalms; glees; 6 concertos for Organ, Harpsichord, or Piano (1769); also some numbers in Dibdin's *The 2 Misers* and Dr. Arnold's *2 to One.* He ed. *Harmonia Wiccamica* (London, 1780).

Hayes, Roland, distinguished black tenor; b. Curryville, Ga., June 3, 1887; d. Boston, Jan. 1, 1977. His parents were former slaves. He studied singing with A. Calhoun in Chattanooga, Tenn., and later at Fisk Univ. in Nashville; subsequently continued vocal studies in Boston and in Europe. He made his concert debut in Boston on Nov. 15, 1917, in a program of German lieder and arias by Mozart; then made a successful tour in the U.S. In 1920 he went to London, where he studied the German repertoire with Sir George Henschel. A grand European tour followed, with appearances in Paris, Vienna, Leipzig, Munich, Amsterdam, Madrid, and Copenhagen. In 1924 he gave more than 80 concerts in the U.S., obtaining a veritable triumph for his interpretation of lyrical German and French songs, and most particularly for his poignant rendition of Negro spirituals. In 1925 he was awarded the Spingarn Medal for "most outstanding achievement among colored people," and in 1939 he received the honorary degree of Mus.D. from Wesleyan Univ. in Delaware, Ohio. He publ. expert arrangements of 30 Negro spirituals, *My Songs* (N.Y., 1948).

BIBLIOGRAPHY: Mackinley Helm, *Angel Mo' and Her Son, Roland Hayes* (N.Y., 1942); F.W. Woolsey, "Conversation with Roland Hayes," and W. Marr, II, "Roland Hayes," both in *Black Perspectives in Music* (Fall 1977).

Hayes, William, English organist and composer; b. Gloucester, Dec. 1707 (baptized, Jan. 26, 1708); d. Oxford, July 27, 1777. He was a chorister at Gloucester Cathedral; was organist of St. Mary's, Shrewsbury

(1729–31); then of Worcester Cathedral (1731–34). In 1734 he became organist of Magdalen College, Oxford; received a Mus.Bac. (Oxford, 1735); was univ. prof. of music (1742); in 1749 received a Mus.D. He conducted the Gloucester music festival in 1757, 1760, and 1763.

WORKS: His canons *Allelujah* and *Miserere nobis* and his glee *Melting airs soft joys inspire* won prizes offered by the Catch Club in 1763; also a masque, *Circe;* Psalms; odes; glees; canons; ballads; cantatas. He also wrote *Remarks on Mr. Avison's Essay on Musical Expression* (1762); *Anecdotes of the Five Music-Meetings* (1768); and was co-editor of Boyce's *Cathedral Music.*

Haym (Haim), Nicola Francesco, Italian cellist, composer, and librettist of German descent; b. Rome, July 6, 1678; d. London, Aug. 11, 1729. He was a violone player in the private orch. of Cardinal Ottoboni in Rome under Corelli (1694–1700); then went to London, where he was composer and cellist to the 2nd Duke of Bedford (1701–11); later was a bass player in the employ of the Duke of Chandos. He was a major figure in organizing performances of Italian opera in London. In 1722 he became the official librettist and Italian secretary of the Royal Academy of Music, the business venture responsible for presenting Italian opera in London. His works include 2 oratorios, *David sponsae restitutus* (1699) and *Santa Costanza* (1700); a serenata, *Il reciproco amore di Tirsi e Clori* (1699); a secular cantata, *Lontan del idol mio* (1704); and instrumental pieces, including *12 Sonate e tre* (1703) and a second set of *12 Sonate a tre* (1704).

Hayman, Richard, American composer of the extreme avant-garde; b. Sandia, N.Mex., July 29, 1951. He studied humanities and philosophy at Columbia Univ.; attended classes of Vladimir Ussachevsky in electronic music; also studied flute with Eleanor Laurence at the Manhattan School of Music and had sessions on Indian vocal music with Ravi Shankar; consulted with Philip Corner and John Cage on the problems of ultramodern music; attended Pierre Boulez's conducting seminars at the Juilliard School of Music. He eked out a meager living by intermittent employment as a construction worker, gardener, operating-room assistant in a hospital, and church pipe organ renovator; earned an occasional few dollars as a subject in sleep-laboratory experiments; as a last resort, boldly peddled earplugs in the N.Y. subway. He arranged exhibitions of his graffiti at the Univ. of Buffalo; organized assemblages of objects and sounds at the Avant-Garde Festival at Shea Stadium in N.Y.; wrote provocatively titled articles. In 1975 he was appointed an editor of *Ear* magazine. Perhaps his most mind-boggling musical work is *Dali,* composed at the command of Salvador Dali, scored for large orch., and notated on a toothpick, with instructions to "ascend chromatically in slow pulse." It was "performed" on March 23, 1974. Another work is *it is not here,* a light-and-sound piece, realized in Morse code at the Museum of Modern Art in N.Y. on June 14, 1974.

Other pieces are *heartwhistle,* with the audience beating their collective pulses and whistling continuous tones (Aug. 3, 1975); *sleep whistle,* with the composer whistling while asleep in a store window during a paid sleep exhibition (Dec. 7, 1975); *roll,* with the composer rolling, lying down, in the street, covered with bells as a token of Hindu devotion (April 9, 1975); *dreamsound,* a sleep event in which the composer makes various sounds for the benefit of slumbering participants (Berkeley, Calif., Feb. 20, 1976); *home* for a Telephone; *Boo Boo* for Piano; *Buff Her Blind* for Musical Toys and Electronic Instruments; *spirits* for Transduced Piano.

Hayman, Richard (Warren Joseph), American composer, arranger, and conductor; b. Cambridge, Mass., March 27, 1920. He studied composition with Alfred Newman and Max Steiner and conducting with Arthur Fiedler; then pursued a highly successful career as a composer and arranger of light musical fare; also appeared extensively as a guest conductor throughout North America. He led the pop concerts of the Detroit Symph. Orch. (from 1970) and the St. Louis Symph. Orch. (from 1976).

Haynes, John C., American music publisher; b. Brighton, Mass., Sept. 9, 1829; d. Boston, May 3, 1907. He entered the employ of Oliver Ditson in 1845; was given an interest in the business in 1851, and on Jan. 1, 1857, became a co-partner, the firm name being changed to O. Ditson & Co. In 1889, after the death of O. Ditson, Haynes became president on the firm's incorporation.
BIBLIOGRAPHY: *Musician* (June 1907).

Haynes, Roy, black American jazz drummer; b. Roxbury, Mass., March 13, 1926. After taking up the drums in Boston, he went to N.Y., where he worked with Lester Young, Miles Davis, and Charlie Parker. He had a particularly successful association with Stan Getz and Gary Burton, and also led his own group, the Hip Ensemble. He is regarded as one of the most gifted jazz drummers of his generation.

Haynes, Walter Battison, English organist and composer; b. Kempsey, near Worcester, Nov. 21, 1859; d. London, Feb. 4, 1900. He studied first with his uncle, an organist, then with F. Taylor and E. Prout; also studied with C. Reinecke and S. Jadassohn at the Leipzig Cons., where he won the Mozart scholarship. In 1884 he was appointed organist at St. Philip's Church, Sydenham; from 1890, also taught at the Royal Academy of Music.
WORKS: Symph.; Concert Overture; *Idyll* for Violin and Orch.; Piano Trio; organ pieces; 2 cantatas for Women's Voices: *Fairies' Isle* and *A Sea Dream.*

Hays, Doris, American pianist and composer of the avant-garde; b. Memphis, Tenn., Aug. 6, 1941. She attended the Cadek Cons. of Chattanooga, and studied with Richard Hervig at the Univ. of Iowa and later with Paul Badura-Skoda at the Univ. of Wisconsin; then traveled to Europe, where she took courses at the Hochschule für Musik in Munich. In 1971 she won first prize at the International Competition for Interpreters of New Music in Rotterdam. Returning to the U.S., she took lessons in advanced piano playing with Hilde Somer in N.Y.; gave numerous piano recitals in programs of ultramodern music; taught music at Queens College in N.Y. and at the Univ. of Wisconsin; made records of piano works by contemporary American and European composers. In her own compositions she endeavors to unite auditory, visual, and tactile elements; several of her works employ rhythmic patterns of lights and motorized sculptures designed by herself and programmed through computers. Typical of these multimedia works is *SensEvents* (1971–77), scored for a group of instruments instructed to play simultaneously but non-synchronously, of an indeterminate duration, with beams of colored light directed at individual musicians to indicate clues. Other works are: *Scheveningen Beach* (1973) for Piccolo, Several Ordinary Flutes, and Alto Flute; *Duet for Pianist and Audience* (1971); *Chartres Red* (1972) for Piano; *Pieces from Last Year* (1974) for 16 Instruments Playing Non-synchronously; *Breathless* (1975) for Bass Flute; *Sunday Nights* (1976) and *Sunday Mornings* (1980) for Piano; *Southern Voices* for Orch. (Chattanooga, April 6, 1982); numerous pieces for modernistic children.

Hays, Lee, American folk singer; b. Little Rock, Ark., 1914; d. Tarrytown, N.Y., Aug. 26, 1981. He was a co-founder, with Pete Seeger, of the folk-song group The Weavers, with which he sang bass; made appearances with this group from 1949 to 1963. He collaborated on writing such successful songs as *Kisses Sweeter than Wine* and *If I Had a Hammer.*

Hays, William Shakespeare, American song composer; b. Louisville, Ky., July 19, 1837; d. there, July 22, 1907. He wrote his first song at 16 years of age; publ. nearly 300, having enormous sales, totaling several million. The most widely known were *Evangeline, My Southern Sunny Home, Write Me a Letter from Home, Driven from Home,* and *Mollie Darling.*

Hayton, Leonard George (Lennie), American jazz pianist, arranger, and conductor; b. New York, Feb. 13, 1908; d. Palm Springs, Calif., April 24, 1971. He played piano in various jazz groups in N.Y.; then went to California, where he was music director for Metro-Goldwyn-Mayer and for the 20th Century-Fox Film Corp. He composed several semi-classic instrumental numbers and orchestrated scores for films. He married the black singer **Lena Horne** in 1948, and acted as song arranger for her.

Haywood, Charles, American musicologist; b. Grodno, Russia, Jan. 2, 1905. He came to the U.S. in 1916; studied singing at the Inst. of Musical Art in N.Y. and at the Juilliard School of Music; received his B.S. at City College in N.Y. in 1926; completed his musical education at Columbia Univ. (M.A., 1940; Ph.D., 1949). His first profession was that of an op-

era singer; he was a member of the Chautauqua Opera Co. and the Philadelphia Opera Co., and taught singing at the Juilliard School. In 1939 he joined the faculty at Queens College in N.Y. as a lecturer on opera, folk music, and American music; he retired in 1973. He publ. a valuable compendium, *A Bibliography of North American Folklore and Folksong* (N.Y., 1951; new enlarged ed., N.Y., 1961); edited *The Art Song in Soviet Russia* (N.Y., 1947); brought out *A Treasury of World Folksongs* (N.Y., 1965); and contributed numerous articles dealing with folk music of various nations.

Head, Michael, English singer, pianist, and composer; b. Eastbourne, Jan. 28, 1900; d. Cape Town, South Africa, Aug. 24, 1976. He studied with Frederick Corder at the Royal Academy of Music in London, and in 1927 joined its faculty as a piano instructor. In 1947 he made a grand tour through Asia, Canada, and Australia, performing both as singer and pianist. He publ. several collections of English songs; also wrote 2 children's operas, *The Bachelor Mouse* (1954) and *Key Money* (1966); Trio for Oboe, Bassoon, and Piano (1966); Suite for Recorders (1968); cantata, *Daphne and Apollo* (1964).

Headington, Christopher, English composer and pianist; b. London, April 28, 1930. He studied piano and composition at the Royal Academy of Music in London; also took private lessons with Benjamin Britten. He publ. the *Bodley Head History of Western Music* (London, 1974).
WORKS: Variations for Piano and Orch. (1950); Cello Sonata (1950); *Introduction and Allegro* for Chamber Orch. (1951); String Quartet (1953); Piano Sonata (1956); *Chanson de l'éternelle tristesse,* ballet (1957); Violin Concerto (1959); Sonatina for Oboe and Piano (1960); Sonatina for Unaccompanied Flute (1960); Toccata for Piano (1962); *Towards a Pindaric Ode* for Soprano, Mezzo-soprano, and Piano (1965).

Healey, Derek, English-born Canadian composer; b. Wargrave, May 2, 1936. He studied music theory (with Howells); flute, organ, and piano at the Royal College of Music in London; then went to Italy; took courses in composition with Petrassi and conducting with Celibadache at the Accademia Chigiana in Siena (summers of 1961–63 and 1966) and composition with Porena in Rome (1962–66); then settled in Canada; taught at the Univ. of Victoria, British Columbia (1969–71), and at the Univ. of Toronto (1971–72); in 1972 was appointed to the faculty of the College of Arts at the Univ. of Guelph. His style of composition was influenced at first by Britten and Hindemith; later he began to experiment with large and discordant blocks of sonorities.
WORKS: Opera, *Seabird Island* (Guelph, May 7, 1977); children's opera, *Mr. Punch* (1969); 2 ballets: *Il Carcerato* (1965) and *The 3 Thieves* (1967); *The Willow Pattern Plate* for Orch. (1957); Concerto for Organ, Strings, and Timpani (1960); *Ruba'i* for Orch. (1968); *Butterflies* for Mezzo-soprano and Small Orch. (Victoria, July 20, 1970); *Arctic Images*

for Orch. (Vancouver, Sept. 21, 1971); *Noh,* triple concerto for Flute, Piano, Synthesizer, and Orch. (1974); *Primrose in Paradise,* fantasy on a shape-note hymn, for Chamber Orch. (1975; last movement of a projected symph.); *Tribulation* for Orch. (1977; first movement of a projected symph.); String Quartet (1961); Cello Sonata (1961); *Partita bizzara* for Oboe and Piano (1962); *Divisions* for Brass Quintet (1963); *Mobile* for Flute, Vibraphone, Celesta, Harp, 2 Percussionists, and Cello (1963); *6 Epigrams* for Violin and Piano (1963); *Movement* for Flute, Oboe, Clarinet, and String Trio (1965); *Laudes* for Flute, Horn, Percussion, Harp, 2 Violins, and Cello (1966); *Maschere* for Violin and Piano (1967); *Stinging* for Alto Recorder, Cello, Harpsichord, and Tape (1971). For Piano: *October's Dream* (1957); *Partita moderna* (1959); *12 Preludes* (1960); *Lieber Robert,* with musical phrases quoting from Schumann (1974); for Organ: *Voluntaries 1–6* (1956–62), Sonata (1961), *Variants* (1964), and *The Lost Traveler's Dream* (1970); also songs.

Heap, Charles Swinnerton, English pianist and choral conductor; b. Birmingham, April 10, 1847; d. there, June 11, 1900. He studied at the Leipzig Cons.; returning to England, took courses at Cambridge; obtained the degree of Mus.D. in 1872. He was then engaged in conducting choral societies in Birmingham; also led the Birmingham Phil. He wrote several cantatas and orch. overtures and a number of works of chamber music, as well as organ pieces and songs.

Heartz, Daniel, American musicologist; b. Exeter, N.H., Oct. 5, 1928. He studied at the Univ. of New Hampshire in Durham (A.B., 1950) and at Harvard Univ. (A.M., 1951; Ph.D., 1957, with the dissertation *Sources and Forms of the French Instrumental Dance in the Sixteenth Century*). In 1957–60 he was on the faculty of the Univ. of Chicago; in 1960 he was appointed to the music faculty of the Univ. of Calif., Berkeley. He publ. a valuable monograph, *Pierre Attaingnant, Royal Printer of Music: A Historical Study and Bibliographical Catalogue* (Berkeley, 1969); edited *Preludes, Chansons, and Dances for Lute, Published by P. Attaingnant, Paris (1529–1530)* (Neuilly-sur-Seine, 1964) and *Keyboard Dances of the Earlier Sixteenth Century,* in *Corpus of Early Keyboard Music,* VIII (1965); also contributed numerous articles on Renaissance music to various music journals.

Hebenstreit, Pantaleon, German musician; b. Eisleben, 1667; d. Dresden, Nov. 15, 1750. In his early years, he was engaged variously as a violinist and a dancing master in Leipzig, but fled from his creditors to Merseburg. There the idea of improving the dulcimer was suggested to him, and he invented the instrument with which he made long and brilliant concert tours, and which Louis XIV named the Pantaleon, after its originator's Christian name. As a precursor of the piano, it has disappeared in the process of evolution. In 1706, Hebenstreit was appointed Kapellmeister and dancing master to the court at Eisenach; in 1714, "pantaleon chamber musician" at the Dresden court.

Heckel, Emil, German music publisher and piano manufacturer; b. Mannheim, May 22, 1831; d. there, March 28, 1908. He was trained by his father, **Karl Ferdinand Heckel** (1800–70), in piano manufacturing. He was a great admirer of Wagner, was one of the most important supporters of the Bayreuth Festivals, and maintained a voluminous correspondence with Wagner himself, which was publ. by his son Karl Heckel under the title *Briefe Richard Wagners an Emil Heckel* (Berlin, 1899; Eng. trans. by W.A. Ellis, London, 1899). Emil Heckel had an enormous bust of Wagner, sculpted by J. Hoffart, installed in his palatial residence at Mannheim, but the bust was busted during the anti-Wagnerian air bombardment in World War II.

Heckel, Johann Adam, German manufacturer of musical instruments; b. Adorf, July 14, 1812; d. Biebrich, April 13, 1877. From 1824–35 he worked with the bassoonist Carl Almenräder on experiments for improving the clarinet and the bassoon. His son and successor, **Wilhelm** (b. Biebrich, Jan. 25, 1856; d. there, Jan. 13, 1909), continued his experiments with success and constructed the "Heckelphone" (a baritone oboe; used by Strauss in the score of *Salome*) in 1904; also made various changes in the construction of other woodwind instruments. He wrote *Der Fagott. Kurzgefasste Abhandlung über seine historische Entwicklung, seinen Bau und seine Spielweise* (1899; new ed., 1931).

Heckel, Wolf, German lutenist at Strasbourg in the 16th century; b. Munich, c.1515. He publ. a *Lautenbuch* (Strasbourg, 1556, 1562), a valuable and interesting collection of old German, French, and Italian songs, dances, fantasias, ricercari, pavanes, and saltarelli, arranged for 2 lutes; a copy of it is in the Hamburg town library. Reprints from it have been publ. by J. Wolf and L. Nowak in Denkmäler der Tonkunst in Österreich, 28 (14.i) and 72 (37.ii), respectively; by H.D. Bruger in his *Lautenschule;* and by W. Tappert in *Sang und Klang aus alter Zeit.*

Heckscher, Céleste de Longpré (née **Massey**), American composer; b. Philadelphia, Feb. 23, 1860; d. there, Feb. 18, 1928. Of an artistic family (her grandfather was the artist Louis de Longpré), she studied piano and participated in the musical affairs of her native city; was for many years president of the Philadelphia Operatic Society. She began to compose about 1890; wrote the operas *The Flight of Time* and *Rose of Destiny* (Philadelphia, May 2, 1918); *Dances of the Pyrenees,* an orch. suite (Philadelphia, Feb. 17, 1911); a fantasy, *To the Forest,* for Violin and Piano (1902); songs; and piano pieces. Her style, melodious and without pretensions, is akin to Chaminade's.
BIBLIOGRAPHY: E.E. Hipsher, *American Opera and Its Composers* (Philadelphia, 1927; pp. 256–58).

Hedges, Anthony, English composer; b. Bicester,

March 5, 1931. He studied at Keble College, Oxford, graduating in 1953; taught at the Royal Scottish Academy of Music (1957–63) and in 1968 was appointed senior lecturer at the Univ. of Hull; has written on music for various journals and has held executive positions in the Northern Branch of the Composers' Guild of Great Britain and been a council member of the Society for Promotion of New Music.

WORKS: Opera, *Shadows in the Sun* (1976); *The Birth of Freedom,* ballet (1961); Sinfonietta (1955); *Comedy Overture* (1962, revised 1967); *Sinfonia Semplice* (1963); *Expressions* for Orch. (1964); *Concertante Music* for Piano and Orch. (1965); *Variations on a Theme of Rameau* for Orch. (1969); *4 Diversions* for Strings (1971); Symph. (1972–73); *Celebrations* for Orch. (1973); *Cantiones Festivals* for Chorus and Orch. (1960); *Epithalamium* for Chorus and Orch. (1969); *To Music* for Chorus and Orch. (1972); *A Manchester Mass* for Chorus, Brass Band, and Orch. (1974); *Rondo Concertante* for Clarinet, Horn, Violin, and Cello (1967); Sonata for Violin and Harpsichord (1967); String Quartet (1970); Piano Sonata (1974); choruses; songs.

Hedley, Arthur, English musicologist; b. Dudley, Northumberland, Nov. 12, 1905; d. Birmingham, Nov. 8, 1969. He studied French literature at the Federal Univ. of Durham (1923–27), and music with W.G. Whittaker at Newcastle. An ardent Chopinist, he learned the Polish language to be able to study Chopin documentation in the original; publ. a biography, *Chopin* (London, 1947; 3rd ed., revised 1974, by M.J.E. Brown); edited and trans. *Selected Correspondence of Fryderyk Chopin* (London, 1962); helped to dispel cumulative misconceptions and deceptions relating to Chopin's life; was instrumental in exposing the falsity of the notorious Potocka-Chopin correspondence produced by Mme. Czernicka (who killed herself in 1949 on the 100th anniversary of Chopin's death, after the fraudulence of her claims was irrefutably demonstrated by Hedley at the Chopin Inst. in Warsaw). Hedley's Chopinolatry was carried to the point of fetishism; he acquired Chopin's cuff links and a lead pencil; proved the authenticity of Chopin's silk waistcoat, which came to light in Paris.

Hédouin, Pierre, French lawyer and littérateur; b. Boulogne, July 28, 1789; d. Paris, Dec. 20, 1868. He studied law in Paris from 1809; became an attorney, and for 30 years practiced in Boulogne. He settled in Paris in 1842, when he was appointed head of the Ministry of Public Works. His relationship with Monsigny fostered a predilection for music and the arts, and he occupied his leisure moments with literature, especially that of music, and in composition. He wrote novels, contributed to the *Annales archéologiques, Annales romantiques,* and several musical periodicals; composed nocturnes, romances, and songs, also writing the words; furnished the librettos of several operas.

WRITINGS: *Notice historique de Monsigny* (1821); *Gossec, Sa vie et ses ouvrages* (1852); *De l'a-*bandon des anciens compositeurs; Ma première visite à Grétry; "Richard Cœur de Lion" de Grétry; Lesueur; Meyerbeer à Boulogne-sur-Mer; Paganini; Joseph Dessauer; "Trois anecdotes musicales" (on Lesueur, Mlle. Dugazon, and Gluck) in his *Mosaïque* (1856; a collection of his miscellaneous articles); *Gluck, Son arrivée en France* (1859); etc.

Hedwall, Lennart, Swedish conductor and composer; b. Göteborg, Sept. 16, 1932. He studied composition with Bäck and Blomdahl; in 1957 attended the Darmstadt composition courses. Returning to Sweden, he became active as a theater conductor and pedagogue. The idiom of his music ranges from the traditional to the audaciously dissonant.

WORKS: 4 pieces for String Orch., noncommittally entitled *Music* (1950–69); *Metamorphoses* for Chamber Ensemble (1955); Oboe Concerto (1956; Swedish Radio, Dec. 21, 1961); *Variazioni piccoli* for Orch. (1958); *Lyric Music* for Soprano and Orch. (1959); *Canzona* for Strings (1965); Concerto for Cello and String Orch. (1970); *Fantasia on Veni redemptor gentium* for String Orch. (1972); 2 string trios (1952, 1960); Solo Flute Sonata (1954); Trio for Flute, Viola, and Cello (1955); Duo for Clarinet and Bassoon (1955); Solo Violin Sonata (1957); 2 suites for Organ (1958–59, 1970); Piano Sonata (1960); Partita for 13 Winds (1961); Trio for Flute, Clarinet, and Bassoon (1962); Wind Quintet (1965); String Quartet (1965); *6 Monologues* for Solo Oboe (1965); *3 Dialogues* for Clarinet and Cello (1969); Organ Sonata (1971); liturgical cantatas; a cappella choral pieces; songs; theater music.

Heermann, Hugo, distinguished German violinist; b. Heilbronn, Württemberg, March 3, 1844; d. Merano, Italy, Nov. 6, 1935. As a boy he was taken to Rossini in Paris for advice; then went to Brussels, where he studied with Bériot and Meerts at the Brussels Cons., graduating in 1861; subsequently took lessons with Joachim. In 1865 he became first violinist of the famous Frankfurt String Quartet; also taught at the Hoch Cons. In 1904 he founded his own violin school; made extended tours as a concert violinist in Europe, the U.S., and Australia; from 1906–9 he taught violin at the Chicago Musical College; returning to Europe, he taught at the Stern Cons. in Berlin, and at the Geneva Cons. (1911–22). He had the distinction of having been the first to play the Violin Concerto of Brahms in Paris, N.Y., and Australia. He publ. a book of memoirs, *Meine Lebenserinnerungen* (Leipzig, 1935).

Hegar, Friedrich, Swiss composer and conductor; b. Basel, Oct. 11, 1841; d. Zürich, June 2, 1927. He studied at the Leipzig Cons. with Hauptmann, Richter, Ferdinand David, Rietz, and Plaidy. In 1860 he played violin in a Warsaw orch.; then taught music in Gebweiler, Alsace. In 1863 he established himself in Zürich, where he was active as a violinist, conductor, and pedagogue. He conducted the Choral Society of Zürich for 37 years (1864–1901), and the concerts of the Tonhalle Orch. for 41 years (1865–1906); also led various other choral organizations. He was a founder of the Zürich Music School (later the Zürich Cons.) in 1876, and its director until 1914. He received many honors, including membership in the Berlin Academy of Arts in 1917. As a composer, he contributed a great deal to Swiss choral music, particularly in the field of romantic ballads. His most successful work is *Manasse* for Soli, Mixed Chorus, and Orch. (Zürich, Oct. 25, 1885; revised version, Jan. 10, 1888); other works are *Hymne an die Musik* for Chorus and Orch. (1870); *Das Herz von Douglas* for Soli, Male Chorus, and Orch. (1905); *Festival Overture* (1895); Cello Concerto (1919); Ballade for Violin and Orch. (1922); String Quartet; Violin Sonata; 16 songs; etc.

BIBLIOGRAPHY: A. Steiner, *Friedrich Hegar, Sein Leben und Wirken* (Zürich, 1928); W. Jerg, *Hegar, Ein Meister des Männerchorliedes* (Lachen, 1946).

Hegedüs, Ferencz, celebrated Hungarian violinist; b. Fünfkirchen, Feb. 26, 1881; d. London, Dec. 12, 1944. His precocious talent was carefully fostered by his father, a professional cellist; his mother (of Spanish origin) was also a musician; he then studied at the Budapest Cons. with Hubay. His style of playing had the manner of the Hungarian school, but his performances of Beethoven and other classics were entirely traditional. He lived in Switzerland after 1930; then went to London.

Heger, Robert, Alsatian-born German conductor and composer; b. Strasbourg, Aug. 19, 1886; d. Munich, Jan. 14, 1978. He studied composition with Max Schillings in Munich; then engaged in opera conducting. He conducted at Nuremberg from 1913 to 1921; was subsequently engaged at the State Opera in Vienna (1925–33); was at the Berlin State Opera (1933–45), and after the war at the Berlin City Opera (1945–50); he subsequently led the Bavarian State Opera in Munich.

WORKS: Several operas, among them *Ein Fest auf Haderslev* (Nuremberg, Nov. 12, 1919); *Der Bettler Namenlos* (Munich, April 8, 1932); *Der verlorene Sohn* (Dresden, March 11, 1936); *Lady Hamilton* (Nuremberg, Feb. 11, 1951); 3 symphs.; symph. poem, *Hero und Leander;* Violin Concerto; Cello Concerto; Piano Trio; String Quartet; other pieces of chamber music; also choral works and songs.

Hegner, Anton, Danish cellist and composer; b. Copenhagen, March 2, 1861; d. New York, Dec. 4, 1915. He studied at the Copenhagen Cons.; in 1899 went to N.Y., where he became active mainly as a cello teacher. He composed 4 string quartets; a Piano Trio; 2 cello concertos; a number of pieces for cello solo; and about 60 songs.

Hegner, Otto, Swiss pianist; b. Basel, Nov. 18, 1876; d. Hamburg, Feb. 22, 1907. He studied piano with Eugene d'Albert; at the age of 12 made an American tour and was hailed as one of the most phenomenal young pianists. His early death, at the age of 30, cut short his brilliant career. His sister **Anna Hegner** (b.

Basel, March 1, 1881; d. there, Feb. 3, 1963) was an excellent violinist.

Hegyesi (real name, **Spitzer**), **Louis,** noted Hungarian cellist; b. Arpad, Nov. 3, 1853; d. Cologne, Feb. 27, 1894. He studied with Demis in Vienna and with Franchomme in Paris. In 1888 he was appointed to the faculty of the Cologne Cons. He publ. several brilliant cello pieces and a valuable theoretical manual, *Neue rhythmische Tonleiter- und Akkordstudien.*

Heiden, Bernhard, German-born American composer; b. Frankfurt am Main, Aug. 24, 1910. He studied piano, clarinet, and violin; also theory and harmony; then (1929–33) studied at the Hochschule für Musik in Berlin, where his principal teacher was Paul Hindemith. In 1935 he emigrated to the U.S.; taught at the Art Center Music School in Detroit; was also conductor of the Detroit Chamber Orch., as well as pianist, harpsichordist, and chamber music artist. He served in the U.S. Army (1943–45); then studied musicology with Donald Grout at Cornell Univ. (A.M., 1946). In 1946 he joined the faculty of the Indiana Univ. School of Music in Bloomington; retired in 1981. His music is neo-Classical in its formal structure, and strongly polyphonic in texture; it is distinguished also by its impeccable sonorous balance and effective instrumentation.

WORKS: FOR THE STAGE: Incidental music to *Henry IV* (1940) and *The Tempest* (1942); *Dreamers on a Slack Wire,* dance drama for 2 Pianos and Percussion (1953); *The Darkened City,* opera (1962; Indiana Univ., Bloomington, Feb. 23, 1963). FOR ORCH.: Symph. No. 1 (1938); *Euphorion: Scene for Orch.* (1949); Concerto for Small Orch. (1949); Symph. No. 2 (1954); *Memorial* (1955); Concerto for Piano, Violin, Cello, and Orch. (1956); *Philharmonic Fanfare* (1958); *Variations* for Orch. (1960); *Envoy* for Orch. (1963); Concerto for Cello and Orch. (1967); Concertino for String Orch. (1967); Concerto for Horn and Orch. (1969); *Partita* for Orch. (1970); Concerto for Tuba and Orch. (1976); Concerto for Trumpet and Wind Orch. (1981). CHAMBER MUSIC: 5 Short Pieces for Flute and Piano (1933); Sonata for Alto Saxophone and Piano (1937); Sonata for Horn and Piano (1939); String Quartet No. 1 (1947); Sinfonia for Woodwind Quintet (1949); String Quartet No. 2 (1951); Quintet for Horn and String Quartet (1952); Sonata for Violin and Piano (1954); Sonatina for Clarinet and Piano (1955); Quintet for Clarinet and Strings (1955); Serenade for Bassoon, Violin, Viola, and Cello (1955); Trio for Violin, Cello, and Piano (1956); Sonatina for Violin (in first position) and Piano (1956); Sonata for Cello and Piano (1958); Sonatina for Flute and Piano (1958); Sonata for Viola and Piano (1959); *Siena* for Cello and Piano (1961); Quintet for Oboe and Strings (1962); *Intrada* for String Quartet (1962); 7 Pieces for String Quartet (1964); Woodwind Quintet (1965); 4 Dances for Brass Quintet (1967); Inventions for 2 Cellos (1967); Solo for Alto Saxophone and Piano (1969); *Intrada* for Woodwind Quintet and Saxophone (1970); *Aria con due variazione* for Viola or Cello (1970); 5 Canons for 2 Horns (1971); *Conversations* for Violin and Cello (1971); Variations for Tuba and 9 Horns (1974); Quintet for Flute, Violin, Viola, Bassoon, and Contrabass (1975); 4 Movements for Saxophone Quartet and Timpani (1976); variations on *Lilliburlero* for Cello Solo (1976); Terzetto for 2 Flutes and Cello (1979); Quartet for Horns (1981). KEYBOARD MUSIC: Piano Sonata No. 1 (1941); Sonata for Piano, 4-hands (1946); Variations on *The Cruel Ship's Carpenter* for Organ (1950); Piano Sonata No. 2 (1952); Variations for Piano (1959); Fantasia for 2 Pianos (1971); *Hommage à Scarlatti* for Piano (1971). VOCAL MUSIC: *4 Songs after Sappho* for Mezzo-soprano and Piano (1939); *2 Songs of Spring* for Women's Chorus (1947); *4 Songs from the Song of Songs* for Soprano and Orch. or Piano (1948); *Divine Poems* for Mixed Chorus, after John Donne (1949); *In Memoriam* for Mixed Chorus (1964); *Advent Song* for Mixed Chorus (1965); *7 Fragments of Sappho* for Soprano and Piano (1965); *Riddles of Jonathan Swift* for Women's Chorus (1975); *Sonnets of Louise Labe* for Soprano and String Quartet (1977); *Triptych* for Baritone and Orch. (1982).

Heider, Werner, German composer; b. Fürth, Jan. 1, 1930. He studied in Nuremberg and Munich, and became active as a pianist, conductor, and composer. In 1963 he organized a modern ensemble named Kammermusik + Jazz, and in 1968 formed Ars Nova Ensemble in Nuremberg. Structurally, his music presents an empirical surface in which thematic elements are organized in hidden serial progressions.
WORKS: *Glimpses* for Soprano, Piano, and Orch. (1958); *Choreographie* for Clarinet and Jazz Band (1961); *Konturen* for Violin and Orch. (1962); *Konflikte* for Percussion and Orch. (1963); *Picasso-Musik* for Voice and 3 Instruments (1966); *Passatempo per 7 Solisti* (1967); *Kunst-Stoff* for Electrified Clarinet, Prepared Piano, and Tape (1971).

Heidingsfeld, Ludwig, German composer; b. Jauer, March 24, 1854; d. Danzig, Sept. 14, 1920. He studied at the Stern Cons. in Berlin, and later taught there. He subsequently settled in Danzig, and founded a cons. there (1899). He wrote 2 operettas, *Der neue Dirigent* (Danzig, 1907) and *Alle Burchenherrlichkeit* (Danzig, 1911); the symph. poems *King Lear* and *Der Totentanz;* piano pieces; songs.

Heifetz, Jascha, celebrated violinist; b. Vilna, Feb. 2, 1901. His father, Ruben Heifetz, an able musician, taught him the rudiments of violin playing at a very early age; he then studied with Elias Malkin at the Vilna Music School, and played in public before he was 5 years old; at the age of 6, he played Mendelssohn's Concerto in Kovno. In 1910 he was taken by his father to St. Petersburg, and entered the Cons. there in the class of Nalbandian; after a few months, he was accepted as a pupil by Leopold Auer. He gave his first public concert in St. Petersburg on April 30, 1911. The following year, with a letter of recommendation from Auer, he went to Berlin; his first concert there (May 24, 1912), in the large hall of the Hochschule für Musik, attracted great attention: Artur Nikisch engaged him to play the Tchaikovsky Concerto with the Berlin Phil. (Oct. 28, 1912), and Heifetz obtained sensational success as a child prodigy of extraordinary gifts. He then played in Austria and Scandinavia. After the Russian Revolution of 1917, he went to America, by way of Siberia and the Orient. His debut at Carnegie Hall in N.Y. (Oct. 27, 1917) won for him the highest expression of enthusiasm from the public and in the press; veritable triumphs followed during his tour of the U.S., and soon his fame spread all over the world. He made his first London appearance on May 5, 1920; toured Australia (1921), the Orient (1923), Palestine (1926), and South America. He revisited Russia in 1934, and was welcomed enthusiastically. He became a naturalized American citizen in 1925, and made his home in Beverly Hills, Calif.; in subsequent years he continued to travel as a concert violinist, visiting virtually every country in the world, but about 1970 ceased to appear in public as a soloist; he participated in a trio (with Piatigorsky and Pennario) and also taught classes of exceptionally talented pupils at the Univ. of Southern Calif., Los Angeles.

The quality of his playing is unique in luminous transparency of texture, tonal perfection, and formal equilibrium of phrasing; he never allowed his artistic temperament to superimpose extraneous elements on the music; this inspired tranquillity led some critics to characterize his interpretations as impersonal and detached. Heifetz made numerous arrangements for violin of works by Bach, Vivaldi, and contemporary composers; his most famous transcription is *Hora Staccato* by the Rumanian composer Grigoraş Dinicu (1889–1949), made into a virtuoso piece by adroit ornamentation and rhythmic elaboration. In his desire to promote modern music, Heifetz commissioned a number of composers (Walton, Gruenberg, Castelnuovo-Tedesco, and others) to write violin concertos for him, and performed several of them. Herbert R. Axelrod edited and publ. an "unauthorized pictorial biography" of Heifetz (1977); Heifetz filed a lawsuit for $7.5 million against the publisher and compiler, claiming invasion of privacy.

Heiller, Anton, significant Austrian organist and composer; b. Vienna, Sept. 15, 1923; d. there, March 25, 1979. He studied piano and organ at the Vienna Cons.; in 1952 won first prize at the International Organ Contest in Haarlem, the Netherlands; in 1969 he received the Austrian Grand Prize for Music; in 1971 he was appointed prof. at the Hochschule für Musik in Vienna. His own music is rooted deeply in the tradition of the Renaissance, while his contrapuntal technique adopts modern procedures. He particularly excelled in sacred works, to Latin texts; in these he occasionally made use of the 12-tone method of composition.
WORKS: Chamber oratorio, *Tentatio Jesu* (1952); *Psalmenkantate* (1955); Concerto for Organ and Orch. (1963); cantata, *In principio erat verbum* (1965); *Stabat mater* for Chorus and Orch. (1968);

several masses, including *Kleine Messe über Zwolf-tonmodelle*, a cappella (1962); *English Mass* (1965); *Adventsmusik* for Chorus and Organ (1971).

Heilman, William Clifford, American composer; b. Williamsport, Pa., Sept. 27, 1877; d. there, Dec. 20, 1946. He studied at Harvard Univ. (B.A., 1900) and in Europe with Rheinberger and Widor. He was a member of the music dept. of Harvard Univ. from 1905 till 1930. Among his works are a symph. poem, *By the Porta Catania* (1916); Piano Trio; Romance for Cello and Piano; a number of character pieces for piano; choruses. He also made arrangements of Negro spirituals.

Hein, Carl, German-American cellist and choral conductor; b. Rendsburg, Feb. 2, 1864; d. New York, Feb. 27, 1945. He studied at the Hamburg Cons.; played cello in the Hamburg Phil. Orch.; in 1890 he emigrated to America, and lived in N.Y., where he became the leader of several German choral societies, among them the Mozart-Verein and Schubert-Chor. Later he was active mainly as a vocal coach. He composed a number of male choruses.

Heinefetter, 6 sisters, all well known as opera singers. **Sabina** (b. Mainz, Aug. 19, 1809; d. Illemau, Nov. 18, 1872) was an itinerant harpist as a child; at the age of 16, she went to Kassel to study with Spohr; then sang with brilliant success in Vienna, Berlin, and Milan. One of her outstanding roles was Donna Anna in *Don Giovanni*. She died insane. **Maria** (**Mme. Stöckel;** b. Mainz, Feb. 16, 1816; d. Vienna, Feb. 23, 1857) achieved during her short career several notable successes; she also died insane. **Katinka** (1820–58), **Fatima, Eva,** and **Nanette** were the other sisters who appeared professionally on the opera stage.

Heinemann, Alfred, German composer; b. Bückeburg, April 10, 1908. He played piano as a child, and began to compose at the age of 10. In 1936 he left Germany and went to Johannesburg, South Africa. In 1944 he moved to Cape Town; was active mainly as a teacher. In 1949 he settled in the U.S.; in 1967 joined the staff of Broadcast Music Inc. His music follows the tenets of enlightened functionalism, without transgressing the natural capacities of the instruments.
WORKS: Opera, *Torso* (1958); ballets: *Galaxy* (1941); *Roulette* (1946); *La Manie des titres et des abbréviations* (1953); *Kobold* (1963); Piano Concerto (1941); Violin Concerto (1942); *March of the Neanderthal Men* (Cape Town, April 7, 1946); Symph. (1959–64).

Heinemeyer, Ernst Wilhelm, outstanding German flutist; b. Hannover, Feb. 25, 1827; d. Vienna, Feb. 12, 1869. He studied with his father, **Christian Heinemeyer** (1796–1872), who was the chamber flutist at Hannover. In 1847 he went to Russia, where he played the flute in the Imperial Orch. at St. Petersburg; in 1859 he returned to Hannover; in 1866

he went to Vienna. He wrote several concertos for the flute.

Heinichen, Johann David, notable German composer and theorist; b. Krössuln, near Weissenfels, April 17, 1683; d. Dresden, July 16, 1729. He was educated at the Thomasschule in Leipzig, studying with Schell and Kuhnau; at the same time, he studied law, and practiced as a lawyer in Weissenfels. His first opera, *Der Karneval von Venedig, oder Der angenehme Betrug,* was performed in Leipzig in 1709; he then held a position as conductor at Zeitz. Councillor Buchta of Zeitz supplied the funds for Heinichen to accompany him to Italy (1710–16), where he produced several operas. In Venice, he joined the Elector of Saxony, Frederick Augustus, and followed him to Dresden as Kapellmeister of the Italian opera company there (1717). However, as a result of confusion brought about by a violent quarrel between Heinichen and the celebrated singer Senesino the Dresden opera was dissolved. Heinichen remained in Dresden as director of church and chamber music. He was a prolific composer; a thematic catalogue of his works is found in G.A. Seibel, *Das Leben des J.D. Heinichen* (Leipzig, 1913), listing, besides his operas, 2 oratorios, 16 masses, 63 cantatas, more than 100 other sacred works, 4 symphs., 2 overtures, 30 concertos, 17 sonatas, 7 pieces for Flute, many separate airs, etc. Most of them were preserved in the Dresden library, but unfortunately many perished in the fire-bombing of Dresden in 1945. Few of his works have been publ. Heinichen's importance lies not so much in his compositions as in his basic theoretical work, *Neu erfundene und gründliche Answeisung zu vollkommener Erlernung des General-Basses* (Hamburg, 1711; new revised ed. as *Der General-Bass in der Composition,* Dresden, 1728).
BIBLIOGRAPHY: R. Tanner, *J.D. Heinichen als dramatischer Komponist* (Leipzig, 1916); G. Hausswald, *J.D. Heinichens Instrumentalwerke* (Berlin, 1937); G. Buelow, *Thorough-Bass Accompaniment According to Johann David Heinichen* (Berkeley, Calif., 1966).

Heininen, Paavo, Finnish composer; b. Järvenpää, Jan. 13, 1938. He studied at the Univ. of Helsinki and at the Sibelius Academy, graduating in 1960; later studied with Bernd Alois Zimmermann at the Hochschule für Musik in Cologne; then went to America and took courses in composition with Vincent Persichetti at the Juilliard School of Music in N.Y. Returning to Finland, he occupied teaching posts in Turku and, since 1966, at the Sibelius Academy of Music in Helsinki.
WORKS: *The Silken Drum,* chamber opera after a Japanese Noh play (1976); 4 symphs.: No. 1 (1958; revised 1960; Helsinki, March 24, 1964); No. 2, *Petite symphonie joyeuse* (Helsinki, Dec. 7, 1962); No. 3 (1969); No. 4 (Oslo, Sept. 4, 1972); 2 piano concertos: No. 1 (Turku, Jan. 23, 1965) and No. 2 (Turku, Dec. 1, 1966); *Preambulo* for Orch. (1959); *Tripartita* for Orch. (1959); Concerto for Strings (1959); *Soggetto* for 14 Solo Strings and Orch. (1963); *Adagio* for

Orch., "concerto in the form of variations" (1963; revised 1966; London, Feb. 19, 1967); *Arioso* for Strings (1967); *Cantico delle creature* for Baritone, and Orch., Piano, or Organ (1968); *2 chansons* for Cello and Orch. (1976); *Tritopos* for Orch. (1977); *Dia* for Small Orch. (1979); Quintet for Flute, Saxophone, Piano, Vibraphone, and Percussion (1961); *Musique d'été* for Flute, Clarinet, Harpsichord, Violin, Cello, Vibraphone, and Percussion (1963); *Discantus I* for Alto Flute (1965); *Discantus II* for Solo Clarinet (1969); *Discantus III* for Solo Saxophone (1976); *Cantilena I* for Solo Viola (1970); *Cantilena II* for Solo Cello (1970); *Cantilena III* for Solo Violin (1976); Violin Sonata (1970); *2 chansons* for Cello and Piano (1974); String Quartet (1974); *Jeu I* for Flute and Piano (1980) and *II* for Violin and Piano (1980); Toccata for Piano (1956); Piano Sonatina (1957); *Oculus aquilae*, triptych for Organ (1968); *Libretto della primavera* for Piano (1971); *Poesia squillante ed incandescente*, piano sonata (1974); *Préludes-Etudes-Poèmes* for Piano (1974); String Quartet (1975); songs.

Heiniö, Mikko, Finnish composer; b. Tampere, May 5, 1948. He studied musicology at the Univ. of Helsinki; took courses in composition with Joonas Kokkonen and in piano with Liisa Pohjola at the Sibelius Academy (1971–75); in 1975–77 studied composition with Witold Szalonek at the Hochschule der Künste in West Berlin; also took lessons in piano with Martin Krause and in conducting with Hans Hildorf. In 1977 he joined the musicology dept. of the Univ. of Helsinki.

WORKS: String Quartet No. 1 (1971); Trio for Flute, Violin, and Guitar (1971); Piano Concerto No. 1 (Tampere, Nov. 17, 1972); *Luominen (The Creation)* for Soprano, Baritone, Chorus, and Orch. (1972); Suite for Flute and 2 Guitars (1974); *4 romantische Lieder* for Soprano and Orch. (1974); Piano Concerto No. 2 (Helsinki, Feb. 26, 1975); *Tredicia* for Orch. (1976); Bassoon Concerto (1977); Horn Concerto (1978); Concerto for Orch. (Turku, Nov. 11, 1982); Piano Concerto No. 3 (1982).

Heinitz, Wilhelm, German musicologist; b. Altona, Dec. 9, 1883; d. Hamburg, March 31, 1963. He studied the bassoon, and played in various orchs.; then became interested in phonetics; studied primitive music and the languages of Africa and Polynesia; became a member of the Phonetic Laboratory at the Univ. of Hamburg, and led a seminar in comparative musicology until his retirement in 1949. He wrote a number of valuable papers on the structural problems of speech, which he publ. in specialized journals; also the books *Klangprobleme im Rundfunk* (Berlin, 1926); *Strukturprobleme in primitiver Musik* (Hamburg, 1931); *Neue Wege der Volksmusikforschung* (Hamburg, 1937); *Physiologische Reaktion und Pulsationsmessung* (Hamburg, 1958).

Heinrich, Anthony Philip (Anton Philipp), American violinist and composer of Bohemian birth; b. Schönbüchel, March 11, 1781; d. in extreme poverty in New York, May 3, 1861. As a boy he acquired proficiency on the piano and violin, but began adult life as a wholesale merchant and banker; in 1810 he emigrated to America, settling in Philadelphia as a merchant and as unpaid music director of the Southwark Theatre. After business reverses in 1817 he moved to the wilds of Kentucky, first to Bardstown and then to nearby Lexington, where he managed to find enough musicians to conduct in a performance of a Beethoven symph. Without any knowledge of harmony, he began to compose in 1818; these first songs and choral and instrumental pieces he publ. later as op. 1, *The Dawning of Music in Kentucky, or The Pleasures of Harmony in the Solitudes of Nature,* and op. 2, *The Western Minstrel* (both 1820; reprinted N.Y., 1972). He became music director at the Southwark Theatre in Philadelphia; later, in Louisville, Ky. The year 1827 found him in London, playing violin in a small orch.; there he also studied theory, and about 1830 began to write for orch.; returned to the U.S. in 1832. In 1834 he again visited England, as well as Germany and Austria (1835), and had some of his works produced at Dresden, Prague, Budapest, and Graz (his symph. *The Combat of the Condor* was perf. at Graz in 1836; also in France); in Vienna he entered a competition with a symph., but the prize was awarded to Franz Lachner; disappointed, he returned to America and settled in N.Y., where he soon gained immense popularity, and was generally known as "Father Heinrich." He was a commanding figure in the musical affairs of the U.S., publishing many of his piano pieces and songs; grand festivals of his works being arranged in N.Y., Philadelphia, and Boston; and the critics speaking of him as the "Beethoven of America." But a tour of Germany in 1857–58 was a dismal failure. The quality of his works is dubious at best; he wrote for an enormous orch., *à la* Berlioz, and his musical ideas, out of all proportion to the means employed, recall the style of Haydn's imitators; nevertheless, he is historically important, being the first to employ American Indian themes in works of large dimensions and to show decided nationalist aspirations. In 1917 the Library of Congress acquired Heinrich's "Memoranda" (letters, programs, newspaper clippings, etc.), many publ. works, and almost all the orch. scores, enumerated in a list made by Heinrich himself in 1857. A perusal of the titles is amusing and instructive: *Grand American Chivalrous Symphony; The Columbiad, or Migration of American Wild Passenger Pigeons; The Ornithological Combat of Kings, or The Condor of the Andes and the Eagle of the Cordilleras; Pocahontas, the Royal Indian Maid and the Heroine of Virginia, the Pride of the Wilderness; The Wild-wood Spirit's Chant or Scintillations of "Yankee Doodle," forming a Grand National Heroic Fantasia scored for a Powerful Orch. in 44 Parts; Manitou Mysteries, or The Voice of the Great Spirit; Gran Sinfonia Misteriosa-Indiana* (U.S. perf., N.Y., Dec. 2, 1975). Reprints (in addition to opp. 1 and 2): *Songs without Words,* vol. I of Piano Music in Nineteenth Century America (Chapel Hill, N.C., 1975); *Yankeedoodle* (for Piano) in W.T. Marrocco and H. Gleason, *Music in America* (N.Y.,

1964); *The Maiden's Dirge,* in E. Gold, *The Bicentennial Collection of American Music* (Dayton, Ohio, 1975).

BIBLIOGRAPHY: F.A. Mussik, *Skizzen aus dem Leben des . . . A.Ph. Heinrich* (Leipzig, 1843); O.G. Sonneck, "Musical Landmarks in New York," *Musical Quarterly* (April 1920); *Dictionary of American Biography* (1932); W.T. Upton, *A.P. Heinrich* (N.Y., 1939); D.M. Barron, *The Early Vocal Works of Anthony Philip Heinrich* (Diss., Univ. of Illinois, 1972); L.H. Filbeck, *The Choral Works of Anthony Philip Heinrich* (Diss., Univ. of Illinois, 1973); W.R. Maust, *The Symphonies of Anthony Philip Heinrich Based on American Themes* (Diss., Indiana Univ., 1973).

Heinrich, Max, German-American baritone; b. Chemnitz, June 14, 1853; d. New York, Aug. 9, 1916. He studied at the Dresden Cons.; in 1873, came to America; taught at Marion, Ala. (1876–82), then moved to N.Y., where he appeared in oratorio with various orchs. From 1888–93, he taught singing at the Royal Academy of Music in London; then lived in Chicago (1894–1903) and in Boston (1903–10). He gave numerous recitals of German lieder, the last of them shortly before his death.

Heinroth, Charles, American organist; b. New York, Jan. 2, 1874; d. Southampton, Long Island, N.Y., Jan. 8, 1963. He studied organ with John White and composition with Victor Herbert in N.Y.; subsequently took theory lessons with Rheinberger in Munich. Returning to America, he occupied various posts as a church organist in N.Y. and Brooklyn; from 1907–32 he was organist at the Carnegie Inst. in Pittsburgh; from 1932–42 was head of the music dept. at the City College of N.Y.

Heinroth, Johann August Günther, German composer and writer; b. Nordhausen, June 19, 1780; d. Göttingen, June 2, 1846. He studied with his father, Christoph Gottlieb Heinroth, an able organist. He then attended the univs. of Leipzig and Halle. In 1804 he became attached to the School of Jewish Studies organized by Israel Jacobson. This was the beginning of a lifelong study of the Jewish liturgy, which he reorganized, adding numerous original melodies that became part of the Jewish service. He also attempted to introduce a simplified musical notation by figures. From 1818 he served as music director of the Univ. of Göttingen, in succession to Forkel.

WRITINGS: (all publ. at Göttingen): *Gesangunterrichts-Methode für höhere und niedere Schulen* (1821–23; 3 parts); *Volksnoten oder vereinfachte Tonschrift* (1828); *Kurze Anleitung, das Klavier oder Forte-Piano spielen zu lehren* (1828); *Musikalisches Hilfsbuch für Prediger, Kantoren und Organisten* (1833).

BIBLIOGRAPHY: A monograph on Heinroth is included in W. Boetticher's book *Die Musik an der Georgia Augusta-Univ. zu Göttingen* (1958).

Heinsheimer, Hans (Walter), American publishing executive and writer on music; b. Karlsruhe, Sept. 25, 1900. He studied law in Heidelberg, Munich, and Freiburg im Breisgau (Juris Dr., 1923); then joined Universal Edition in Vienna, where he was in charge of its opera dept. (1924–38), and supervised the publication of such important stage works as Alban Berg's *Wozzeck*, Krenek's *Jonny spielt auf,* Weinberger's *Schwanda,* Kurt Weill's *Aufstieg und Fall der Stadt Mahagonny,* and George Antheil's *Transatlantic.* He came to the U.S. in 1938 and was associated with the N.Y. branch of Boosey & Hawkes. In 1947 he was appointed director of the symph. and operatic repertoire of G. Schirmer, Inc.; in 1957 became director of publications and in 1972 vice-president of the firm; in these capacities he promoted the works of Samuel Barber, Gian Carlo Menotti, Leonard Bernstein, and Elliott Carter. He retired in 1974 and has devoted himself mainly to writing. A brilliant stylist in both German and English, he has contributed numerous informative articles to *Melos, Musical Quarterly, Holiday, Reader's Digest,* etc. He publ. the entertaining books *Menagerie in F-sharp* (N.Y., 1947) and *Fanfare for Two Pigeons* (1952); the 2 works were publ. in German in a single vol. entitled *Menagerie in Fis-dur* (Zürich, 1953); he also wrote *Best Regards to Aida* (publ. in German as *Schönste Grüsse an Aida;* Munich, 1968).

Heintze, Gustaf Hjalmar, Swedish pianist and composer; b. Jönköping, July 22, 1879; d. Saltsjöbaden, March 4, 1946. He was of a musical family; his father, **Georg Wilhelm Heintze** (1849–95), was a well-known organist, as was his grandfather, **Gustaf Wilhelm Heintze** (1825–1909). He studied at the Stockholm Cons.; in 1910 was appointed organist at a Stockholm church, a post he held until his death. He wrote cantatas, 2 violin concertos, chamber music, and organ pieces.

Heinze, Sir Bernard Thomas, eminent Australian conductor; b. Shepparton, near Melbourne, July 1, 1894; d. Sydney, June 9, 1982. He studied at the Univ. of Melbourne and the Royal College of Music in London, and attended classes of Vincent d'Indy at the Schola Cantorum in Paris. He also took violin lessons in Berlin with Willy Hess. Returning to Australia after service in the Royal Artillery during World War I, he became a teacher at the Melbourne Conservatorium in 1924; was named a prof. in 1925 and remained on its faculty until 1956. He also served as director of the New South Wales Cons. (1956–66). In 1938 he made a European tour as conductor; from 1933 until 1949 he was also conductor of the Melbourne Symph. Orch. He was knighted in 1949.

Heinze, Gustav Adolph, German composer and conductor; b. Leipzig, Oct. 1, 1820; d. Muiderberg, near Amsterdam, Feb. 20, 1904. He received his early musical education from his father, a clarinetist in the Gewandhaus Orch. in Leipzig, and joined that orch. as clarinetist at the age of 16. He then conducted at the Breslau Opera, and also produced 2 operas there. In 1850 he went to Amsterdam as conductor of the German Opera, and remained in the Netherlands till the end of his life. He composed, besides his operas, several oratorios and other choral works.

Heise, Peter Arnold, Danish composer; b. Copenhagen, Feb. 11, 1830; d. Stockkerup, Sept. 12, 1879. He studied music with Niels Gade and Berggreen in Copenhagen and with Hauptmann at the Leipzig Cons. Returning to Denmark, he became a music teacher and organist at Sorö, where he remained until 1865. He then settled in Copenhagen; produced 2 successful operas, *The Pasha's Daughter* (Sept. 30, 1869) and *King and Marshal* (Sept. 25, 1878). He also wrote a Symph., chamber music, etc., which remain mostly unpubl. It was in his many lieder to Danish texts that Heise achieved enduring fame.
BIBLIOGRAPHY: G. Hetsch, *Peter Heise* (Copenhagen, 1926).

Hekking, André, French cellist; b. Bordeaux, July 30, 1866; d. Paris, Dec. 14, 1925. He was the son of the Dutch cellist **Robert Gérard Hekking** (1820–75), who settled in France; received his training from him. From 1909 he lived in Paris; in 1919 was appointed prof. at the Paris Cons.; also taught at the American Cons. in Fontainebleau. He publ. a practice book for cellists, *Violoncelle, Exercices quotidiens* (Paris, 1927).

Hekking, Anton, notable cellist, brother of **André Hekking;** b. The Hague, Sept. 7, 1856; d. Berlin, Nov. 18, 1935. He studied at the Paris Cons. with Joseph Giese; then undertook an American tour with the pianist Mme. Essipova. Returning to Europe, he was first cellist of the Berlin Phil. (1884–88, 1898–1902). After another American tour, he became first cellist of the Boston Symph. (1889–91) and later of the N.Y. Symph. (1895–98). He returned to Berlin in 1898; taught at the Stern Cons. there, and became a member of a trio with Schnabel and Wittenberg (1902).

Hekking, Gérard, French cellist, cousin of **André** and **Anton Hekking;** b. Nancy, Aug. 22, 1879; d. Paris, June 5, 1942. He studied at the Paris Cons., winning first prize (1899). He was first cellist of the Concertgebouw Orch. in Amsterdam (1903–14) and taught at the Amsterdam Cons.; also made tours in Russia, Spain, Germany, and France. He was in the French army during World War I; from 1921–27, was again in the Netherlands; in 1927 became a prof. at the Paris Cons. He wrote several cello pieces; also revised *Principes de la technique du violoncelle* of François Gervais (Paris, 1930).

Hekster, Walter, Dutch composer; b. Amsterdam, March 29, 1937. He studied composition and clarinet at the Amsterdam Cons., graduating in 1961; then went to the U.S., where he was engaged as clarinetist with the Conn. Symph. Orch. (1962–65); attended classes of Roger Sessions at Tanglewood in the summer of 1966; from 1965–71 he taught clarinet and composition at Brandon Univ. in Canada; then returned to the Netherlands and assumed teaching posts at the Utrecht Cons. and the Arnhem Cons.
WORKS: *Epitaphium (In Memoriam Eduard van Beinum)* for Strings (1959); *Foci* for Violin and Chamber Ensemble (1965–66); *Facets* for Orch. (1967–68); *Branches* for 15 Strings (1969); *Nocturnal Conversation* for Orch. in 4 groups (1970–71); *Early One Morning* for 15 Winds (1972); *Mobiles* for Orch. in 4 groups (1973); *The Auroras of Autumn* for Oboes and Orch. (1975); *Pentagram* for Wind Quintet (1961); *Reflections* for Clarinet, Horn, Cello, Vibraphone, Celesta, and Percussion (1964); *Dialogues* for Flute and Clarinet (1965); *Music for Bassoon and Piano* (1965); 2 sonatas: No. 1 for Piano (1966) and No. 2 for Solo Cello (1967); *Interpolations* for Violin and Piano (1967); *Fluxus* for Solo Flute (1968); *Fluxions* for Clarinet and Piano (1968); 5 *Reliefs* scored for Various Instrumental Combinations (1968–69); *The Snow Man* for Soprano, Percussion, and Bass Clarinet (1969); *Windsong* for Trumpet, Flute, and Saxophone (1970); *Reedmusic* for Oboe, Clarinet, and Bassoon (1970); *Incenter* for Flute, Oboe, and Cello (1970); *Fresco* for Clarinet and String Trio (1970); *Diversities* for Flute, Clarinet, Horn, Bassoon, and Piano (1970); *Ambage* for String Quartet (1970); *Credences of Summer* for Violin, Clarinet, and Piano (1974); *Tropos* for Flute, Oboe, Violin, Viola, Cello, and Piano (1974–75); *Map* for Solo Ondes Martenot (1975); *Epicycle I* for Flute, Guitar, and Double Bass (1975); *Epicycle II* for Trumpet, Bass Clarinet, Accordion, and Percussion (1975); *Echoes of Summer* for Oboe, Clarinet, and Bassoon (1975); *Graffiti* for Ondes Martenot, Percussion, and Piano (1975); *Derivations* for Piano (1965); *Studies in Spatial Notation* for Piano (1970).

Helder, Bartholomäus, German composer; b. Gotha, 1585; d. Remstedt, near Gotha, Oct. 28, 1635. He studied theology in Leipzig; was a schoolteacher at a village near Gotha (1607–16); then was for 20 years a pastor at Remstedt. He died of the plague. He publ. a collection of Christmas and New Year's songs, *Cymbalum genethliacum* (1614), and a book of psalm tunes, *Cymbalum Davidicum;* many of his secular songs are included in contemporary anthologies. His New Year's song *Das alte Jahr vergangen ist* became very popular.

Helfer, Walter, American composer; b. Lawrence, Mass., Sept. 30, 1896; d. New Rochelle, N.Y., April 16, 1959. He studied at Harvard Univ.; then took courses in composition with Caussade in Paris and with Respighi in Rome. Returning to the U.S., he joined the staff of Hunter College in N.Y. He wrote an orch. *Fantasy on Children's Tunes* (1935); *Symphony on Canadian Airs* (1937); Concertino for Piano and Chamber Orch. (1947); *Soliloquy* for Cello and Piano; String Quartet; String Trio; *Elegiac Sonata* for Piano; various minor piano pieces and songs.

Helfert, Vladimír, Czech musicologist; b. Plánice,

Bohemia, March 24, 1886; d. Prague, May 18, 1945. He studied with Hostinsky in Prague and with Kretzschmar and Wolf at Berlin Univ., receiving the degree of Mus.D. in 1908 with the dissertation *G. Benda und J.J. Rousseau;* in 1921 was an instructor, and in 1926 prof. of musicology, at the Univ. of Brno; was director of the Czech Orch. Society there; from 1924, was editor of the paper *Hudebni Rozhledy.* In 1940 he was arrested by the Nazis and held in Breslau; was released in 1943, then rearrested in 1945 and taken to the Terezin concentration camp. He died a few days after his liberation.

WRITINGS: (mostly in Czech): *History of the Melodrama* (1908); *Jaroměřice and the Count J.A. Questenberg* (Prague, 1917); *The Music of the Jaroměřice Castle: A Critical Analysis of the Works of the Composer Franz Míča* (Prague, 1924); *Contribution to the Development of the History of the Marseillaise* (in Italian; Turin, 1922); *The Creative Development of Smetana* (Prague, 1924); "Zur Entwicklungsgeschichte der Sonatenform," *Archiv für Musikwissenschaft* (1925); *Histoire de la musique dans la république tchécoslovaque* (in collaboration with Erich Steinhardt; Prague, 1936); other essays, mostly about Czech music in the 18th century; joint author of O. Pazdirek's *Dictionary of Music* (in Czech; vol. I, 1929; vol. II, 1937).

Helfman, Max, American choral conductor and composer; b. Radzin, Poland, May 25, 1901; d. Dallas, Texas, Aug. 9, 1963. He was taken to the U.S. in 1909; studied at the David Mannes Music College in N.Y. and at the Curtis Inst. in Philadelphia, where his teachers were Rosario Scalero in composition and Fritz Reiner in conducting. He subsequently was active mainly as a conductor of Jewish choral groups; was in charge of choral singing at Temple Emanuel in Paterson, N.J. (1926–39); then at Temple B'nai Abraham in Newark (1940–53); at Temple Sinai in Los Angeles (1954–57); and of the Washington Hebrew Congregation (1958–62). He wrote a dramatic cantata, *New Hagadah* (1949); several pieces of Jewish liturgical music; and edited a series of choral works for the Jewish Music Alliance.

Helfritz, Hans, German ethnomusicologist and composer; b. Hilbersdorf, July 25, 1902. He studied with Hindemith at the Hochschule für Musik in Berlin, and with Egon Wellesz in Vienna. In 1936 he went to South America; lived mostly in Chile, where he worked on problems of musical folklore. In 1956 he undertook a journey along the west coast of Africa and made recordings of native songs. In 1962 he settled in Ibiza in the Balearic Islands. He composed 2 string quartets, a Violin Sonata, a Saxophone Concerto, and various short orch. pieces; in some of them he makes use of South American and African motifs.

WRITINGS: Books on ethnic subjects: *Amerika, Land der Inka, Maya und Azteken* (Vienna, 1965); *Die Götterburgen Mexikos* (Cologne, 1968); *Mexiko, Land der drei Kulturen* (Berlin, 1968).

Hellendaal, Pieter, organist and composer; b. Rotterdam, March (baptized, April 1) 1721; d. Cambridge, England, April 26, 1799. In 1760 he went to England, and on June 12, 1760, was appointed successor to Charles Burney as organist at St. Margaret's, King's Lynn in Norfolk.

WORKS: 12 sonatas for Violin (Amsterdam, 1744); 6 concertos for Violin (London, 1760); 6 solos for Violin, with Thorough-bass (London, 1761); 8 solos for Cello, with Thorough-bass (London, 1770); *Celebrated Rondo* for Violin, with Instrumental Accompaniment; *A Collection of Psalms for the Use of Parish Churches;* 2 glees for 4 Voices.

BIBLIOGRAPHY: G.A.C. De Graaf, "Pieter Hellendaal, Musiquant (1721–1799)," *Mens en Melodie* (Aug. 1950).

Heller, Hans Ewald, German-American composer; b. Vienna, April 17, 1894; d. New York, Oct. 1, 1966. He studied with J.B. Foerster and Camillo Horn; was engaged in Vienna as a music critic and teacher. In 1938 he settled in the U.S. Among his compositions are the light operas *Satan* (Vienna, 1927), *Messalina* (Prague, 1928), and *Der Liebling von London* (Vienna, 1930); an overture, *Carnival in New Orleans* (1940); a cantata, *Ode to Our Women* (1942); 2 string quartets; Suite for Clarinet and Piano; about 150 songs.

Heller, James G., American composer; b. New Orleans, Jan. 4, 1892; d. Cincinnati, Dec. 19, 1971. He studied at Tulane Univ. in New Orleans (B.A., 1912), the Univ. of Cincinnati (M.A., 1914), the Hebrew Union College (Rabbi, 1916), and the Cincinnati Cons. (Mus.D., 1934); for 12 years wrote the program notes for the Cincinnati Symph. Orch.; then taught musicology at the Cincinnati Cons. Among his works are *Elegy and Pastorale* for Voice and String Orch. (Cincinnati, Dec. 30, 1934); String Quartet; Violin Sonata; Jewish services (New Union Hymnal, 1930–32).

Heller, Stephen, celebrated Hungarian pianist and composer; b. Pest, May 15, 1813; d. Paris, Jan. 14, 1888. He was of a Jewish family, but was converted to Christianity as a youth. He studied piano with F. Brauer and showed such extraordinary ability that he was sent to Vienna to continue his studies; there he studied briefly with Czerny before he took lessons with Anton Halm. In 1828 he began a tour through Austria and Germany. However, the exertion of travel proved too much for him; in Augsburg he became ill, and decided to remain there for a time; financial means were provided by a wealthy family. In 1838 he went to Paris, where he became friendly with Berlioz, Chopin, and Liszt. Soon he became very successful as a pianist; some critics even judged him as superior to Chopin. In Paris, Heller began to compose piano pieces somewhat akin to Schumann's: brilliant salon dances, studies, and character pieces that became exceedingly popular. In 1849 he visited London, where his concerts charmed a large circle of music-lovers. A nervous ailment forced him to curtail his appearances; in 1862 he revisited England and played with

Hallé at the Crystal Palace. He then returned to Paris, where he remained for the rest of his life.

WORKS: He wrote in all several hundred piano pieces, arranged in groups in 158 opus numbers; of these, the most effective are *Traumbilder; Promenades d'un solitaire; Nuits blanches; Dans les bois; Voyage autour de ma chambre; Tablettes d'un solitaire; Tarentelles;* admirable études; ballades (notably *La Chasse*); 4 sonatas; 3 sonatinas; waltzes; mazurkas; caprices; nocturnes; variations; etc.

BIBLIOGRAPHY: M. Hartmann, "Stephen Heller," *Monatshefte* (1859); H. Barbedette, *Stephen Heller* (Paris, 1876; Eng. trans., London, 1877); R. Schütz, *Stephen Heller* (Leipzig, 1911; standard biography); Isidor Philipp, "Some Recollections of Stephen Heller," *Musical Quarterly* (Oct. 1935); R. Booth, *The Life and Music of Stephen Heller* (Diss., Univ. of Iowa, 1969); J.-J. Eigeldinger, ed., *Stephen Heller: Lettres d'un musicien romantique à Paris* (Paris, 1981).

Hellmesberger, Georg, Sr., renowned Austrian violinist and conductor; b. Vienna, April 24, 1800; d. Neuwaldegg, near Vienna, Aug. 16, 1873. His father, a country schoolmaster, gave him his first musical instruction; he succeeded Schubert as soprano chorister in the Imperial Chapel; in 1820 became a pupil of the Vienna Cons. under Böhm (violin) and E. Förster (composition); in 1821 became an assistant instructor there; in 1833, a prof. In 1830 he succeeded Schuppanzigh as conductor of the Imperial Opera; also in 1830, became a member of the court chapel; was pensioned in 1867; conducted the Vienna Phil. from 1847 to 1848. He had many distinguished pupils, including Ernst, Hauser, Auer, Joachim, and his own sons, **Georg** and **Joseph.**

Hellmesberger, Georg, Jr., Austrian violinist, son of the preceding; b. Vienna, Jan. 27, 1830; d. Hannover, Nov. 12, 1852. He studied violin with his father and composition with Rotter; made a successful concert tour through Germany and England. At the age of 20, he was appointed concertmaster of the Hannover Royal Orch., and produced there 2 operas, *Die Bürgschaft* and *Die beiden Königinnen* (1851), when his career, so brilliantly begun, was cut short by tuberculosis, to which he succumbed at the age of 22.

Hellmesberger, Joseph, Jr., Austrian violinist, conductor, and dramatic composer, son of the preceding; b. Vienna, April 9, 1855; d. there, April 26, 1907. He studied with his father; from 1870–84 was concertmaster of the Vienna Phil.; in 1884 became ballet conductor at the Vienna court opera, and was engaged as opera conductor there in 1890. In 1887 he succeeded his father as leader of the Hellmesberger Quartet. He also conducted the Vienna Phil. (1901–3) and the Stuttgart Opera (1904–5).

WORKS: 10 operettas, produced in Vienna, Munich, and Hamburg between 1880 and 1906: *Kapitän Ahlström; Der Graf von Gleichen; Der schöne Kurfürst; Rikiki, oder Nelly, das Blumenmädchen; Das Orakel; Der bleiche Gast; Das Veilchenmädel; Die drei Engel; Mutzi;* and *Der Triumph des Weibes.* Also, ballets: *Fata Morgana; Die verwandelte Katze; Das Licht; Die fünf Sinne;* etc.

Hellmesberger, Joseph, Sr., Austrian conductor and violinist; b. Vienna, Nov. 3, 1828; d. there, Oct. 24, 1893. He studied violin with his father, **Georg Hellmesberger, Sr.,** at the Vienna Cons. In 1851 he was appointed conductor of the Gesellschaftskonzerte; also served as director of the Gesellschaft der Musikfreunde in Vienna (1851–59). Concurrently he taught violin at the Vienna Cons. (1851–77) and was concertmaster of the Vienna Phil. (1855–77). He further occupied the post of the concertmaster at the Imperial Austrian Opera (1860), and in 1877 became conductor of the court orch. From 1849 to 1887 he played the first violin in the famous string quartet bearing his name.

BIBLIOGRAPHY: A. Barthlmé, *Vom alten Hellmesberger* (Vienna, 1908); R.M. Prose, *Die Hellmesberger: Hundert Jahre aus dem Leben einer Wiener Musikerfamilie* (Vienna, 1947).

Hellouin, Frédéric, French writer on music; b. Paris, April 18, 1864; d. St. Germain-en-Laye, March 26, 1924. He was a pupil of Massenet at the Paris Cons.; from 1902, was a lecturer at the Ecole des Hautes Etudes Sociales. He publ. *Feuillets d'histoire musicale française* (1902); *Gossec et la musique française à la fin du XVIIIe siècle* (1903); *Essai de critique de la critique musicale* (1906); *Le Noël musical français* (1906); *Un Musicien oublié: Catel* (1910).

Hellwig, Karl Friedrich Ludwig, German composer; b. Kunersdorf, near Wrietzen, July 23, 1773; d Berlin, Nov. 24, 1838. He learned to play all the string instruments and piano; then studied theory with Zelter and others; at the same time, he was engaged in the manufacture of paint, which enabled him to pursue his musical studies as an avocation. In 1813 he became organist at the Berlin court. He wrote 2 operas, *Die Bergknappen* (Dresden, April 27, 1820) and *Don Sylvio di Rosalbo* (unperf.); much church music; and a number of German lieder, which show a certain poetic sensitivity and a ballad-like quality in the manner of Zelter and other early German Romanticists.

Helm, Anny, Austrian soprano; b. Vienna, July 20, 1903. She studied in Vienna and Berlin; made her debut in Magdeburg in 1924. She sang at the Berlin State Opera (1926–33); also at Bayreuth. In 1933 she settled in Italy; subsequently made her professional appearances under her married name, **Anny Helm-Sbisa** (her husband, **Giuseppe Sbisa,** was the director of the Teatro Giuseppe Verdi in Trieste).

Helm, Everett, American composer and musicologist; b. Minneapolis, July 17, 1913. He studied at Harvard Univ., graduating in 1935; then went to Europe, where he took courses with Malipiero in Italy and Vaughan Williams in London. Returning to the U.S., he taught at Western College in Oxford, Ohio (1943–44); then toured South America (1944–46). From 1948–50 he was a music officer under the U.S. Military Government in Germany; then lived mostly in Germany, Austria, and Italy. In 1963 he made his home in Asolo, near Venice. A linguist, he contributed articles to various music magazines in several languages; he made a specialty of the music of Yugoslavia and was a guest lecturer at the Univ. of Ljubljana (1966–68).

WORKS: Piano Concerto (N.Y., April 24, 1954); *Adam and Eve*, an adaptation of a medieval mystery play (Wiesbaden, Oct. 28, 1951, composer conducting); Concerto for 5 Instruments, Percussion, and String Orch. (Donaueschingen, Oct. 10, 1953); *The Siege of Tottenburg*, radio opera (1956); *Le Roy fait battre tambour*, ballet (1956); *500 Dragon-Thalers*, singspiel (1956); Piano Concerto No. 2 (Louisville, Ky., Feb. 25, 1956); Divertimento for Flutes (1957); *Sinfonia da camera* (1961); Concerto for Double Bass and String Orch. (1968); 2 string quartets; Woodwind Quintet (1967); numerous piano pieces and songs.

WRITINGS: *Béla Bartók in Selbstzeugnissen und Bilddokumenten* (Reinbek-bei-Hamburg, 1965; a reduction and Eng. trans. was publ. in N.Y., 1972); *Composer, Performer, Public: A Study in Communication* (Florence, 1970; in Eng.).

Helm, Theodor, Austrian music critic; b. Vienna, April 9, 1843; d. there, Dec. 23, 1920. He was the son of a physician; studied jurisprudence in Vienna and became a government employee; in 1867 he began writing music criticism for various Viennese publications; in 1874 became a music teacher at Horák's music school; from 1875 till 1901 he was editor of Fromme's *Kalender für die Musikalische Welt*; publ. *Beethovens Streichquartette: Versuch einer technischen Analyse im Zusammenhang mit ihrem geistigen Gehalt* (Leipzig, 1885; 2nd ed., 1910).

Helmholtz, Hermann (Ludwig Ferdinand) von, celebrated German scientist and acoustician; b. Potsdam, Aug. 31, 1821; d. Berlin, Sept. 8, 1894. His father was a schoolteacher in Potsdam, and Helmholtz received his education there. His mother, Caroline Penn, was of English extraction. He studied medicine at the Military Inst. of Berlin; received his M.D. and became a member of the staff of the Charité Hospital there (1842); in 1843 he was appointed a military surgeon at Potsdam; was then recalled to Berlin as a teacher of anatomy (for artists) at the Academy of Fine Arts (1848). In 1849 he obtained a position as prof. of physiology at the Univ. of Königsberg; in 1855 was a prof. at Bonn; in 1858, at Heidelberg. In 1871, abandoning the teaching of physiology and anatomy, he accepted the position of prof. of physics at the Univ. of Berlin; publ. various scientific studies. The work of most interest to musicians, and indispensable for students of acoustics, is his *Lehre von den Tonempfindungen als physiologische Grundlage für die Theorie der Musik* (Braunschweig, 1863); it was trans. by Alexander John Ellis and publ. in London under the title

On the Sensations of Tone as a Physiological Basis for the Theory of Music (London, 1875; new ed., N.Y., 1948). By a long series of experiments, Helmholtz established a sure physical foundation for the phenomena manifested by musical tones, either single or combined. He supplemented and amplified the theories of Rameau, Tartini, Wheatstone, Corti, and others, furnishing impregnable formulae for all classes of consonant and dissonant tone effects, and proving with scientific precision what Hauptmann and his school sought to establish by laborious dialectic processes. Helmholtz's labors resulted primarily in instituting the laws governing the differences in quality of tone (tone color) in different instruments and voices, covering the whole field of harmonic, differential, and summational tones; and those governing the nature and limits of musical perception by the human ear.

BIBLIOGRAPHY: S. Epstein, *Hermann von Helmholtz als Mensch und Gelehrter* (Stuttgart, 1896); L. Königsberger, *Hermann von Helmholtz* (3 vols., Braunschweig, 1902–3; one vol., 1911); E. Waetzman, *Zur Helmholtzschen Resonanztheorie* (Breslau, 1907); L.S. Lloyd, "Helmholtz and the Musical Ear," *Musical Quarterly* (April 1939); H. Ebert, *Hermann von Helmholtz* (Stuttgart, 1949).

Helms, Hans G., German composer; b. Teterow, Mecklenburg, June 8, 1932. He studied literature and comparative philology; in 1957 settled in Cologne; worked on various speech problems; also supervised numerous recordings of modern music. His compositions exploit the musical possibilities of the speaking voice; of these, *Golem*, "polemics for 9 vocal soloists," has been widely performed at modern music festivals in Germany. Other works are *Daidalos* for 4 Solo Singers, and a group of speaking and listening pieces, *Geschichte von Yahud* (1963).

Helps, Robert, American pianist and composer; b. Passaic, N.J., Sept. 23, 1928. He studied at the Juilliard School of Music in N.Y. with Abby Whiteside (piano) and Roger Sessions (composition). He occupied teaching posts at Princeton Univ., the San Francisco Cons. of Music (1968–70), Stanford Univ., and the Univ. of Calif. at Berkeley. In 1970–72 he was on the staff of the New England Cons. of Music; then taught at the Manhattan School of Music (1973–76) and, from 1978, at the Univ. of Southern Florida. His natural pianism helps Helps to write idiomatically for his instrument.

WORKS: Fantasy for Piano (1952); Symph. No. 1 (1955); Piano Trio (1957); *Image* for Piano (1958); *Recollections* for Piano (1959); *Portrait* for Piano (1960); *Cortège* for Orch. (1963); Serenade in 3 parts: (1) Fantasy for Violin and Piano; (2) Nocturne for String Quartet; (3) *Postlude* for Piano, Violin, and Horn (1964); Piano Concerto (1966); *Saccade* for Piano, 4-hands (1967); *Quartet* for Piano Solo, divided into 4 equal parts, each numbering 22 keys (1971).

Helsted, Gustaf, Danish composer; b. Copenhagen, Jan. 30, 1857; d. there, March 1, 1924. He was a pupil of Hartmann and Gade; from 1892 was a prof. of theory, and from 1904 also a prof. of organ, at the Copenhagen Cons.; from 1915 was organist of the Frauenkirche. He wrote 2 symphs.; a Decimet for Woodwinds and Strings; a String Sextet; 3 string quartets; a Piano Trio; 2 violin sonatas; 2 cantatas: *Gurresänge* (Copenhagen, April 18, 1904) and *Vort Land* (Copenhagen, April 19, 1909).

Hemberg, Eskil, Swedish conductor and composer; b. Stockholm, Jan. 19, 1938. He studied at the Royal College of Music in Stockholm; took lessons in conducting from Herbert Blomstedt. He conducted the chorus of Stockholm Univ. on an extensive tour in Europe and America. Most of his works are for vocal groups; he maintains the main lines of classical polyphony in sacred music, while in his instrumental writing he ventures into modern harmony.

WORKS: A cappella opera, *Love,* after Robert Graves (1969–70; first stage perf., Stockholm, Oct. 30, 1973); *3 Jerusalem Choruses* (1958); *2 Evangelical Motets* (1960); *Zoo,* 5 nonsense songs for Chorus (1965); *Paradise,* cantata (1965); *En natt som lyste,* cantata (1966); *18 Movements,* choreographic choral suite (Stockholm, April 30, 1968); *Signposts,* to the texts of Dag Hammarskjöld, for Chorus (1968); *The Gallery,* after E.A. Robinson, for Bass and Male Chorus (1969); *Messa d'oggi* for 5 Solo Voices and Chorus (1968–70); *Jesu lidande, död och uppständelse,* a St. Mark Passion for Soli, Chorus, and Orch. (Stockholm, March 26, 1972); *Cantica* for Soli, Chorus, and Orch. (Bergen, Norway, Nov. 29, 1973); *En gammal saga (An Old Tale),* cantata for Soprano, Harp, and Harpsichord (1973); *Migraine* for Orch. (1973); *Zona rosa* for String Quartet (1973); *Epitaffio* for Organ (1974); *Pietà,* to texts by Hammarskjöld, for Alto Voice and Piano (1974); many choruses and songs.

Hemel, Oscar van, Dutch composer; b. Antwerp, Aug. 3, 1892; d. Hilversum, July 9, 1981. He studied with Lodewijk Mortelmans at the Royal Flemish Cons. in Antwerp; settled in the Netherlands in 1914; took lessons in composition with Pijper in Rotterdam, but did not begin to write music until late in life; he compensated for this delay by composing prolifically. His style oscillates between the Romantic trends of German and Austrian music of the early 20th century and the more complex technical structures favored by Dutch modernists.

WORKS: Radio opera, *Viviane* (Hilversum Radio, 1950); *Maria Magdalena,* sacred cantata (1941); *De bruid (The Bride)* for Soprano, Male Chorus, and Orch. (1946); *Dat liet van Alianora* for Soprano, Male Chorus, and Orch. (1947); *Hart van Nederland (Heart of Holland)* for Male Chorus, Winds, and Percussion (1952); *Ballade van Brabant* for Narrator, Boys' Chorus, Male Chorus, and Orch. (1952); *Le Tombeau de Kathleen Ferrier* for Alto and Orch. (1954); *Herdenkingshymne 1940–1945 (Memorial Hymn 1940–1945)* for Mixed Chorus, Children's Chorus, Brass, and Percussion (1955; for Full Orch., 1970); *Les Mysteres du Christ,* 5 psalms for Alto, Baritone, Male Chorus, and Orch. (1958); *Te Deum*

for 4 Soloists, Chorus, and Orch. (1958); *Tuin van Holland* for Soprano, Baritone, Chorus, and Orch. (1958); *Ballade van Kapitein Joos de Decker* for Alto, Bass, Chorus, and Orch. (1943–59); *Trittico liturgico* for Soprano and Strings (1959); *Huwelijks Cantata* (1966); *Song of Freedom* for Speaking Chorus, Mixed Chorus, and Orch. (1968–69); 5 Symphs.: No. 1 (1935); No. 2 (1948); No. 3, *Sinfonietta* for Small Orch. (1952); No. 4 (1962); No. 5 (1963–64, revised 1967); Suite for Chamber Orch. (1936); Suite for Flute, and Chamber Orch. or Piano (1937); Piano Concerto (1941–42); Ballade for Orch. (1942); 3 violin concertos (1945, 1968, 1977); *De stad (The City),* symph. poem (1949); *Divertimento Ballet* for Orch. (1950; drawn from his opera *Viviane*); Viola Concerto (1951); *Feestelijke ouverture* (1952); *Olof Suite* for Orch. (1953); *Entrada festante* (1953); *Tema con variazioni* for Orch. (1953); Oboe Concerto (1955); Concerto for Wind Orch. (1960); *Concerto da camera* for Flute and String Orch. (1962); Violin Concertino (1963); Cello Concerto (1963); *3 Contrasts* for Winds and Percussion (1963); Divertimento for Strings (1964); *Entrada* for Orch. (1964); Serenade for 3 Solo Winds and String Orch. (1965); Polonaise for Orch. (1966); Concerto for 2 Violins and String Orch. (1970–71); Divertimento for Orch. and Piano (1974); 2 violin sonatas (1933, 1945); 6 string quartets (Nos. 3-6: 1946–47, 1953, 1956, 1961); Piano Trio (1937); Piano Quartet (1938); Viola Sonata (1942); String Trio (1951); Concertino for Trumpet and Piano (1953); *Canticum psalmorum* for Contralto, Chorus, 2 Pianos, and Percussion (1954); *4 Koperkwartetten* for Horn, 2 Trumpets, and Trombone (1955); Clarinet Quintet (1958); *Divertimento II* for 12 Winds and Piano (1959); Trio for Flute, Oboe and Bassoon (1959); *Rondeau et Ballade* for Female Chorus, Flute, String Quartet, and Harp (1959); *Capriccio* for Clarinet and Piano (1960); Sextet for Piano and Wind Quintet (1962); *Donquichotterie* for 4 Trombones (1962); Suite for 2 Violins (1966); *About Commedia dell'arte* for Oboe Quartet (1967); Wind Quintet (1972).

Hemke, Frederick, American saxophone player; b. Milwaukee, July 11, 1935. He studied at the Univ. of Wisconsin (1953–58) and at the Eastman School of Music in Rochester, N.Y. (1960–62); also took lessons (1955–56) with Marcel Mule in Paris, where he became the first American to win the Premier Prix in saxophone (1956). In 1964 he joined the Chicago Symph. Orch.; from 1962 was on the faculty of Northwestern Univ. In 1966 he made a tour of 11 countries in the Orient under the auspices of the State Dept. On Feb. 24, 1983, in Stockholm, he gave the first performance of the last work of Allan Pettersson, Symph. No. 16 for Alto Saxophone and Orch., commissioned by Hemke in 1979.

Hemmer, Eugene, American pianist and composer; b. Cincinnati, March 23, 1929; d. Lomita, Calif., Sept. 17, 1977. He studied piano at the College of Music in Cincinnati with Albino Gorno, and composition with Felix Labunski. He then devoted himself mainly to teaching; was instructor in music for the dance at the Univ. of Cincinnati (1950–58); taught music appreciation at El Camino College in Torrance, Calif. He composed a number of affable and amiable piano pieces with pleasant titles such as *Fantastic Creatures, Gnu Music, Autumn Trails,* etc. His concert career was fatally handicapped by his excessive weight (c.300 lbs.).

Hempel, Frieda, brilliant German coloratura soprano; b. Leipzig, June 26, 1885; d. Berlin, Oct. 7, 1955. In 1900 she entered the Leipzig Cons. as a piano pupil; in 1902–5 she studied singing with Frau Nicklass-Kempner in Berlin; made her debut in Breslau; made her Berlin Opera debut in Nicolai's *Merry Wives of Windsor* (Aug. 22, 1905); in 1905–7 was at the Court Opera in Schwerin; in 1907–12 was a member of the Royal Opera in Berlin; in 1912–19 was one of the foremost members of the Metropolitan Opera, where she made her debut as the Queen in *Les Huguenots* on Dec. 27, 1912. In 1920 she impersonated Jenny Lind in the Lind centenary celebrations in N.Y. and throughout the U.S. (70 concerts). She was married to William B. Kahn in 1918 (divorced in 1926). From 1940 till 1955 she lived in N.Y. A few months before her death, knowing that she was incurably ill, she returned to Berlin. Her memoirs, *Mein Leben dem Gesang,* were publ. posthumously (Berlin, 1955).

Hemsi, Alberto, composer; b. Cassaba, Turkey, Dec. 23, 1896; d. Paris, Oct. 7, 1975. He was of Italian-Jewish extraction. After preliminary study in Turkey, he went to Italy and enlisted in the Italian army in World War I. In 1928 he went to Alexandria, Egypt, where he served as director of the Israeli Music School; also taught at the Alexandria Cons. In 1929 he founded the Edition Orientale de Musique. As was to be expected, his works were of an oriental flavor; the most characteristic of them was a symph. suite, *Croquis égyptiens* (1951). Other pieces in an oriental genre were *Poème biblique* for Voice and Orch; *Suite Séfardie* for Violin and Piano; *6 danses turques* for Piano; and a number of songs.

Hemsley, Thomas, English baritone; b. Coalville, April 12, 1927. He studied voice with Lucie Manen; then made his professional debut in London (1951). He then sang at Aachen (1953–56) and Düsseldorf (1953–63). From 1953 he made regular appearances at Glyndebourne; also sang at Bayreuth, where he distinguished himself as one of the few English singers in the Wagnerian repertoire.

Henderson, Alva, American opera composer; b. San Luis Obispo, Calif., April 8, 1940. He studied voice and music theory at the San Francisco State College; devoted himself mainly to vocal works. His first opera, *Medea,* based on the play by Robinson Jeffers, was produced with a modicum of critical favor in San Diego, on Nov. 29, 1972; his 2nd opera was adapted from Shakespeare's play *The Tempest.* He obtained his most decisive success with his 3rd opera, *The Last of the Mohicans,* after the novel of James Fenimore Cooper, produced by the Wilmington Opera Society on June 12, 1976, in Wilmington, Del.

Henderson, (James) Fletcher "Smack," black American jazz bandleader; b. Cuthbert, Ga., Dec. 18, 1897; d. New York, Dec. 28, 1952. He studied piano as a child and chemistry as a youth; received a degree in chemistry from Atlanta Univ. College. In 1920 he went to N.Y.; abandoning chemical science, he formed the Fletcher Henderson band, which rapidly advanced into the front ranks of jazzdom; a number of famous jazz figures played in it. He made arrangements for other jazz bands as well as for his own.

Henderson, Ray, American composer of popular songs; b. Buffalo, Dec. 1, 1896; d. Greenwich, Conn., Dec. 31, 1970. He studied music at the Univ. of Southern Calif.; played the organ in churches and piano in jazz groups in Buffalo; then went to N.Y. as a song plugger in Tin Pan Alley, and soon began writing songs of his own. His first success was *Georgette* (1922); this was followed by *Sonny Boy,* which he wrote for Al Jolson's early talkie *The Singing Fool;* subsequent hits were *You're the Cream in My Coffee, Button Up Your Overcoat, Alabamy Bound, Hold Everything, 3 Cheers,* etc.; some of these songs were written in collaboration with B.G. DeSylva. Unlike most Broadway composers, Henderson could read and write music; he even took private lessons with Benjamin Britten. His film biography, *The Best Things in Life Are Free,* was made in 1966.

Henderson, Roy, Scottish baritone; b. Edinburgh, July 4, 1899. He studied at the Royal Academy of Music in London (1920–25); made his London debut as Zarathustra in *A Mass of Life* by Delius in 1925; his operatic debut followed in 1929 as Donner in Wagner's *Das Rheingold* at Covent Garden; he also sang at the Glyndebourne Festivals (1934–39). He was founder and conductor of the Nottingham Oriana Choir (1936–52); was a prof. of singing at the Royal Academy of Music (1940–74). He was made a Commander of the Order of the British Empire in 1970.

Henderson, "Skitch" (Lyle Russell Cedric Henderson), English-born American conductor; b. Birmingham, England, Jan. 27, 1918. He came to the U.S. in his youth; took up the organ and piano, and then played on a radio station in North Dakota; moving to Hollywood, he was accompanist to Judy Garland and worked at MGM. During World War II he served as a fighter pilot in the Royal Air Force and the U.S. Air Force; after the war, he returned to Hollywood as a conductor for radio and films; also studied with Ernst Toch. In 1949 he joined the music staff of NBC; later was music director for several television shows; also had guest engagements with provincial orchs. In 1983 he organized his own N.Y. Pops Orch., which made its first appearance at Carnegie Hall.

Henderson, William James, American music critic; b. Newark, N.J., Dec. 4, 1855; d. (suicide) New York, June 5, 1937. He was a graduate (1876) of Princeton (M.A., 1886); studied piano with Carl Langlotz (1868–73) and voice with Torriani (1876–77); was chiefly self-taught in theory. He wrote many librettos of light operas, and also *Cyrano de Bergerac* for Walter Damrosch (1913). He was first a reporter (1883), then music critic of the *N.Y. Times* (1887–1902) and, for 35 years, until his death, for the *N.Y. Sun* (1902–37); lectured on music history at the N.Y. College of Music (1899–1902); from 1904, lectured on the development of vocal art at the Inst. of Musical Art in N.Y. A brilliant writer, Henderson was an irreconcilable and often venomous critic of modern music; he loved Wagner, but savagely attacked Debussy and Richard Strauss. Henderson, in turn, was the butt of some of Charles Ives's caustic wit.

WRITINGS: *The Story of Music* (1889; 12th enlarged ed., 1912); *Preludes and Studies* (1891); *How Music Developed* (1898); *What Is Good Music?* (1898; 3rd ed., 1905); *The Orchestra and Orchestral Music* (1899); *Richard Wagner, His Life and His Dramas* (1901); *Modern Musical Drift* (1904); *The Art of the Singer* (1906); *Some Forerunners of Italian Opera* (1911); *Early History of Singing* (1921); "The Function of Musical Criticism," *Musical Quarterly* (Jan. 1915); "Beethoven after a Hundred Years," ibid. (April 1927); many other articles in various journals. In the series Famous Composers and Their Works, Henderson wrote the biographies of Goldmark, Tchaikovsky, and Wagner, as well as the chapter on Dutch composers.

BIBLIOGRAPHY: O. Thompson, "An American School of Criticism: The Legacy Left by W.J. Henderson, R. Aldrich and Their Colleagues of the Old Guard," *Musical Quarterly* (Oct. 1937); O. Thompson also ed. excerpts from Henderson's scrapbook, publ. as *The Art of Singing* (N.Y., 1938); *Charles E. Ives: Memos,* ed. by J. Kirkpatrick (N.Y., 1972).

Hendl, Walter, American conductor; b. West New York, N.J., Jan. 12, 1917. He studied conducting with Fritz Reiner at the Curtis Inst. of Music in Philadelphia. He was associate conductor of the N.Y. Phil. from 1945–49 and music director of the Dallas Symph. from 1949–58. From 1964–72 he was director of the Eastman School of Music in Rochester, N.Y.; in 1976 he was appointed music director of the Erie (Pa.) Phil. He composed some incidental music for theatrical plays.

Hendricks, Barbara, black American soprano; b. Stephen, Ariz., Nov. 20, 1948. She studied voice with Jennie Tourel; made her debut at the San Francisco Opera in 1974; in Europe, she appeared at the Glyndebourne Festival and at the Netherlands Opera in Amsterdam. In America, she had several engagements with leading orchs.; also gave recitals.

Hendrix, Jimi (James Marshall), black American rock-'n'-roll musician; b. Seattle, Nov. 27, 1942; d. London, Sept. 18, 1970, as a result of asphyxiation from vomiting while unconscious after taking an overdose of barbiturates. He rose to fame as a singer-guitarist whose erotic body movements underscored the sexual implications of his lyrics. He produced a sensation by his performance of an electronically amplified version of *The Star-Spangled Banner* at the Woodstock Festival in August 1969. His popularity in England was enhanced by his appearance at the Isle of Wight Festival in August 1970.

BIBLIOGRAPHY: Curtis Knight, *Jimi; An Intimate Biography of Jimi Hendrix* (N.Y., 1974).

Hengeveld, Gerard, Dutch pianist and composer; b. Kampen, Dec. 7, 1910. He studied piano with Carl Friedberg; appeared as a soloist with European orchs. and in recital; then was appointed to the piano faculty at The Hague Cons. He composed a Violin Sonata (1944); Concertino for Piano and Orch. (1946); Piano Concerto (1947); Cello Sonata (1965); *Musica concertante* for Oboe and Chamber Orch. (1968); numerous teaching pieces for piano.

Henkel, Heinrich, German pianist, son of **Michael Henkel;** b. Fulda, Feb. 17, 1822; d. Frankfurt, April 10, 1899. He was a pupil of his father; also studied with Aloys Schmitt. He settled in Frankfurt in 1849, as a teacher. He publ. a piano method, *Vorschule des Klavierspiels,* an abridged edition of A. André's *Lehrbuch der Tonsetzkunst* (1875); *Mitteilungen aus der musikalischen Vergangenheit Fuldas* (1882); piano pieces and songs.

Henkel, Michael, German composer of church music; b. Fulda, June 18, 1780; d. there, March 4, 1851. He studied with Vierling; then served as a local music teacher. He wrote a great number of sacred works, organ pieces, and instrumental works.

Henkemans, Hans, Dutch composer and pianist; b. The Hague, Dec. 23, 1913. He took lessons in piano and composition with Bernhard van den Sigtenhorst-Meyer and Willem Pijper (1930–36); made his debut as a pianist in his own Piano Concerto at 19. Concurrently he studied medicine at the Univ. of Utrecht, and was active as a practicing psychiatrist. As a composer, he follows the stylistic manner of the modern French school, cultivating sonorous harmonies supporting melodic lines of a modal character.

WORKS: 2 piano concertos (1932, 1936); Symph. (1934); *Voorspel (Prelude)* for Orch. (1935–36); *Ballade* for Alto and Chamber Orch. (1936); *Driehonderd waren wij (300 Were We . . .),* cantata (1933–40); *Passacaglia and Gigue* for Piano and Orch. (1941–42; Amsterdam, Dec. 2, 1945); *Primavera* for 12 Instruments (1944; revised 1959); Flute Concerto (1945–46); Violin Concerto (1948–50); Viola Concerto (1954); Harp Concerto (1955); Partita for Orch. (1960; Scheveningen, Dec. 8, 1960); *Barcarola fantastica* for Orch. (Groningen, Nov. 13, 1962); *Dona Montana,* 3 pieces for Orch. (1964); *Bericht aan de Levenden (Message to the Living)* for Chorus, Narration, and Orch. (1964; Amsterdam, May 4, 1965); *Villonnerie* for Baritone and Orch., after Villon's poems (1965); *Elégies* for 4 Flutes and Orch. (Utrecht, Oct. 18, 1967); *Tre aspetti d'amore* for Chorus and Orch. (1967–68; Amsterdam, July 5, 1971); *Canzoni amorose* for Soprano, Baritone, Piano, and Orch. (1972–73); 2 wind quintets (1934, 1962); 3 string quartets; Cello Sonata (1936); Violin Sonata (1944); *Épilogue* for Flute and Piano (1947); *4 Pieces* for Harp and Flute (1963); *Aere festivo* for 3 Trumpets and 2 Trombones (1965); 2 Etudes for Piano (1937); 2-piano Sonata (1943); Piano Sonata (1958); songs, including *De Tooverfluit* (*The Magic Flute;* 1946) and *3 Liederen* (1964); choruses. In 1971 he orchestrated 12 of Debussy's preludes (Amsterdam, July 5, 1971).

BIBLIOGRAPHY: M. Flothuis, "Hans Henkemans," *Sonorum Speculum* (1963).

Henneberg, Albert, Swedish composer, son of **Richard Henneberg;** b. Stockholm, March 27, 1901. He studied composition in Stockholm (1920–24) and later in Vienna and Paris (1926–30). Returning to Stockholm in 1931, he became active as a conductor.

WORKS: 5 operas: *Inka* (1935–36); *Det jäser i Småland* (1937–38); *Den lyckliga staden* (1940–41); *Bolla och Badin* (1942–44); *I madonnans skugga* (1946); Chamber Symph. (1927); 6 symphs.: No. 1, *På ledungsfärd* (1925); No. 2, with Baritone Solo (1927); No. 3, *Vårvindar* (1927); No. 4, *Pathétique* (1930–31); No. 5 (1935); No. 6, *Vinterskärgård* (1953–54); Piano Concerto (1925); *Valborgsmässonatt,* symph. poem (1928); Serenade for String Orch. (1931; also for String Quartet); *Sommar,* suite for Orch. (1932); *Det ljusa landet* for Soloists, Chorus, and Orch. (1933); Trumpet Concerto (1934); Trombone Concerto (1935); *I brytningstider,* symph. suite (1943); *Gustavianska kapriser* for Orch. (1943); Concertino for Flute and Strings (1944); Cello Concerto (1948); Concertino for Bassoon and Strings (1956); Concertino for Clarinet, Strings, Piano, and Percussion (1960); 2 string quartets (1931); *Little Quartet* for Flute, Oboe, Bassoon, and Horn; Violin Sonata.

Henneberg, Johann Baptist, Austrian conductor and composer; b. Vienna, Dec. 6, 1768; d. there, Nov. 26, 1822. He conducted at Vienna theaters (1790–1803); then became a member of the orch. of Count Esterházy; in 1818, returned to Vienna. He wrote a great number of singspiels, of which the most successful were *Die Waldmänner* (Vienna, Oct. 14, 1793) and *Liebe macht kurzen Prozess* (Leipzig, 1799).

Henneberg, Richard, German conductor and composer; b. Berlin, Aug. 5, 1853; d. Malmö, Oct. 19, 1925. He studied piano with Liszt; then traveled as accompanist with various artists, including Wieniawski; held posts as operatic coach at the Italian Opera in London, and at various theaters in Berlin and Stockholm; from 1885–1907 conducted at the Stockholm Opera; from 1914–20 was conductor of the Malmö Orch. Henneberg gave the first performance of *Tannhäuser* in Stockholm (1876) and the

first complete production of the *Ring of the Nibelung* in Sweden (1907), and was an ardent propagandist of Wagner's music. He wrote a comic opera, *Drottningens Vallfart* (Stockholm, 1882); incidental music to Ibsen's *Brand;* various Shakespearean pieces; a ballet, *Undine;* some choral works and songs (all in a Wagnerian vein).

Hennerberg, Carl Fredrik, Swedish musicologist; b. Algaras, Jan. 24, 1871; d. Stockholm, Sept. 17, 1932. As a young man he was an organist at Varola; then went to Stockholm, where he studied at the Cons. (1899–1903) and remained on the faculty as a harmony teacher. In 1909 he was appointed organist at the Royal Chapel; also served as librarian of the Music Academy. He specialized in the study of organ manufacture; traveled in European countries to collect information; publ. *Die schwedischen Orgeln des Mittelalters* (Vienna, 1909); *Orgelns byggnad och vard* (a treatise on organ building; Uppsala, 1912; 2nd ed., 1928); contributed numerous bibliographical papers to musicological journals.

Hennes, Aloys, German pianist; b. Aachen, Sept. 8, 1827; d. Berlin, June 8, 1889. He studied with Hiller and Reinecke in Cologne; then taught piano in various provincial towns; in 1872 settled in Berlin. He publ. *Klavierunterrichtsbriefe,* containing ingenious teaching pieces. His daughter, **Therese,** was a child prodigy, who made an exceptionally successful tour in England in 1877.

Hennessy, Swan, American composer; b. Rockford, Ill., Nov. 24, 1866; d. Paris, Oct. 26, 1929. He was the son of an Irish-American settler; studied general subjects in Oxford, and music in Germany; then traveled in Italy, France, and Ireland, eventually settling in Paris.

WORKS: About 70 compositions, several of which are derived from Irish folk melos; his technical equipment was thorough; his idiom, impressionistic. Among his Irish-inspired works are *Petit trio celtique* for Violin, Viola, and Cello; *Rapsodie celtique* for Violin and Piano; *Rapsodie gaëlique* for Cello and Piano; *Sonata in Irish Style* for Violin and Piano; several piano albums "*à la manière de . . .*"; characteristic piano pieces in a humorous vein, such as *Epigrammes d'un solitaire, Impressions humoristiques,* etc.; 4 string quartets.

Hennig, Carl, German organist and composer; b. Berlin, April 23, 1819; d. there, April 18, 1873. A precocious musician, he brought out a Psalm for Soli, Chorus, and Orch. at the age of 14; began to conduct choral groups at an early age; then became a church organist at the Sophienkirche in Berlin; also was conductor of the Lyra Choral Society. He wrote a great number of miscellaneous pieces, sacred works, and cantatas, as well as popular dances for piano.

Hennig, Carl Rafael, German music theorist and composer; son of **Carl Hennig;** b. Berlin, Jan. 4, 1845;

d. Posen, Feb. 6, 1914. He studied music with his father; then with Richter in Leipzig and Kiel in Berlin; at the same time, studied law. After a brief period of teaching in Berlin, he went to Posen, where he founded the Hennig Vocal Society; he also served as a church organist. He composed several cantatas, choruses, songs, and instrumental pieces, but it is as a writer on theoretical subjects that he is mainly remembered.

WRITINGS: *Die Methodik des Schulgesang-Unterrichts* (Leipzig, 1885); *Die Unterscheidung der Gesangregister auf physiologischer Grundlage* (Leipzig, 1892); *Beitrag zur Wagner-Sache* (Leipzig, 1893); *Asthetik der Tonkunst* (Leipzig, 1896); *Über die Entstehung der "hohen Resonanz"* (Leipzig, 1902); *Musiktheoretisches Hilfsbuch* (Leipzig, 1903; 2nd ed., 1906); *Einführung in das Wesen der Musik* (Leipzig, 1906); excellent analyses of Beethoven's 9th Symph. and *Missa Solemnis.*

Hennig, Ervin Arthur, American composer; b. Marion, S.Dak., Nov. 22, 1910, of German immigrant parents. He studied music in Chicago with **Roslyn Brogue,** whom he subsequently married. In 1944 he entered the New England Cons. in Boston, graduating in 1946. He writes mostly for chamber music combinations; in his later works he adopted the 12-tone method of composition.

WORKS: Quintet for Flute, Horn, Violin, Viola, and Cello (1946); Partita for String Quartet (1948); Suite for Viola Concertante, 2 Violins, and Cello (1950); Divertimento for Unaccompanied Bassoon (1950); Trio for Clarinet, Viola, and Piano (1959); Piano Sonata (1959); pieces for recorders; arrangements of Bach for various woodwind ensembles.

Henriot, Nicole, French pianist; b. Paris, Nov. 23, 1925. She studied with Marguerite Long; entered the Paris Cons. at the age of 12, graduating with a first prize 2 years later. She toured Europe (1946–49), appearing with major orchs.; made her American debut on Jan. 29, 1948; toured Canada and South America (1949–50).

Henriques, Fini Valdemar, Danish composer; b. Copenhagen, Dec. 20, 1867; d. there, Oct. 27, 1940. He studied violin with Valdemar Tofte in Copenhagen, and with Joachim at the Hochschule für Musik in Berlin; studied composition with Svendsen; returning to Copenhagen, he was a violinist in the court orch. (1892–96); also appeared as a soloist. He organized his own string quartet, and traveled with it in Europe; also conducted orchs.

WORKS: As a composer, he followed the Romantic school; he possessed a facile gift of melody; his *Danish Lullaby* became a celebrated song in Denmark. He also wrote an opera, *Staersstikkeren* (Copenhagen, May 20, 1922); several ballets (*The Little Mermaid,* after Hans Andersen; *Tata,* etc.); *Hans Andersen Overture;* 2 symphs.; String Quartet; Quartet for Flute, Violin, Cello, and Piano; Violin Sonata; a number of piano pieces (several cycles, *Lyrik, Erotik,* etc.).

BIBLIOGRAPHY: S. Berg, *F.V. Henriques* (Copenhagen, 1943).

Henriques, Robert, Danish cellist, conductor, and composer; b. Copenhagen, Dec. 14, 1858; d. there, Dec. 29, 1914. He studied cello with Popper, and composition with Kretschmer in Dresden. Upon his return to Copenhagen, he conducted orch. concerts; wrote music criticism; composed an overture, *Olaf Trygvason;* a symph. sketch, *Aquarellen;* a number of pieces for the cello.

Henry, Harold, American pianist; b. Neodesha, Kans., March 20, 1884; d. Orangeburg, N.Y., Oct. 15, 1956. He studied in Kansas; then went to Berlin, where he took lessons with Leopold Godowsky; also studied with Moszkowski in Paris. He made his American debut in Chicago on Jan. 30, 1906, and then launched a moderately successful concert career before settling in N.Y. as a piano teacher. He wrote a number of character pieces for piano (*Heroic Rhapsody, Dancing Marionette, Night Sounds),* and some singable songs.

Henry, Hugh Thomas, American Roman Catholic priest, and writer on church music; b. Philadelphia, 1862; d. there, March 12, 1946. He taught church music at Overbrook Seminary from 1889 to 1917; was a prof. of homiletics at Catholic Univ. in Washington, D.C., in 1919–37. Besides his many religious and literary writings, he contributed the following articles to the *Musical Quarterly:* "Music Reform in the Catholic Church" (Jan. 1915), "Choir-Boys in Catholic Churches" (July 1917), and "Music in Lowell's Prose and Verse" (Oct. 1924).

Henry, Leigh Vaughan, English writer and conductor; b. Liverpool, Sept. 23, 1889; d. London, March 8, 1958. He received his earliest training from his father, John Henry, a singer and composer; then studied with Granville Bantock in London, Ricardo Viñes in France, and Buonamici in Italy; taught music at Gordon Craig's Theatrical School in Florence (1912); then was in Germany, where he was interned during World War I. Returning to England, he edited a modern-music journal, *Fanfare* (1921–22); also was active in various organizations promoting modern music; in 1930 he went to the U.S.; lectured at various colleges. He was music director of the Shakespeare Festival Week in London in 1938, 1945, and 1946; organized and conducted orch. concerts of British music, and the National Welsh Festival Concerts; also at the BBC.

WRITINGS: *Music: What It Means and How to Understand It* (London, 1920); *The Growth of Music in Form and Significance* (1921); *The Story of Music* (1935); *Dr. John Bull* (largely fictional; London, 1937); *My Surging World,* autobiography (with R. Hale; 1937). Among his compositions are *The Moon Robber,* opera; *Llyn-y-Fan,* symph. poem; various pieces on Welsh themes.

Henry, Michel, a member of the 24 "violons du roi" under Henry IV and Louis XIII; b. Paris, Feb.

1555; date of death unknown. He wrote ballets for the court. His younger brother, known as Le Jeune, also in the "violons du roi," composed some very interesting instrumental music: a *Fantaisie* for 5 Violins; another *Fantaisie,* for 5 *cornetti; Pavane* for 6 Oboes; some of this is reproduced by P. Mersenne in his *Harmonie universelle* (vol. 3, pp. 186–277). Dolmetsch made a modern arrangement of the *Fantaisie* for 5 Violins.

BIBLIOGRAPHY: F. Lesure, "Le Recueil de ballets de Michel Henry," in *Les Fêtes de la Renaissance* (Paris, 1956).

Henry, Pierre, French composer and acoustical inventor; b. Paris, Dec. 9, 1927. He studied with Messiaen at the Paris Cons.; also took courses with Nadia Boulanger; in 1950 was a founder of the Groupe de Recherche de Musique Concrète with Pierre Schaeffer, but in 1958 separated from the group to experiment on his own projects in the field of electro-acoustical music and electronic synthesis of musical sounds. In virtually all of his independent works he applied electronic effects, often with the insertion of pre-recorded patches of concrete music and sometimes "objets trouvés" borrowed partially or in their entirety from pre-existent compositions.

WORKS: In collaboration with Pierre Schaeffer he wrote *Symphonie pour un homme seul* (1950) and the experimental opera *Orphée 53* (1953); independently he wrote *Microphone bien tempéré* (1952); *Musique sans titre* (1951); *Concerto des ambiguités* (1951); *Astrologie* (1953); *Spatiodynamisme* (1955); 4 ballets: *Haut voltage* (1956); *Coexistence* (1959); *Investigations* (1959); *Le Voyage* (1962); also *Messe de Liverpool* (1967); *Ceremony* (1970); *Futuristie 1,* "electro-acoustical musical spectacle," with the reconstruction of the "bruiteurs" introduced by the Italian futurist Luigi Russolo in 1909 (Paris, Oct. 16, 1975).

Henry V, English king; b. Monmouth, Sept. 1387; d. Bois de Vincennes, Aug. 31, 1422. During his reign (1413–22), he established a flourishing musical service at the Chapel Royal; was a musician himself; probably was the author of a Gloria and a Sanctus for 3 Voices in the Old Hall MS (transcribed into modern notation, and publ. by the Plainsong and Medieval Music Society, 1933–38, vols. I and III; in that edition, these works are ascribed to Henry VI).

Henry VI, English king; b. Windsor, Dec. 6, 1421; d. London, May 21, 1471. He reigned from 1422 till 1471. For a long time, he was regarded as the "Roy Henry" who was the author of a Gloria and a Sanctus in the Old Hall MS; however, research by M. Bukofzer tends to indicate that the works may actually be by Henry V.

BIBLIOGRAPHY: W. Barclay Squire, "Henry VI," *Sammelbände der Internationalen Musik-Gesellschaft* (1900–1, p. 342); G.R. Hayes, *King's Music,* an anthology (London, 1937).

Henry VIII, English king; b. Greenwich, June 28,

1491; d. Windsor, Jan. 28, 1547. He reigned from 1509 to 1547. He received regular instruction in music; his compositions include 2 masses (lost); a Latin motet for 3 Voices (publ. in the *Baldwin Collection,* 1591); the anthem *O Lord, the Maker of All Things;* a secular ballad, *Passe tyme with good cumpanye,* for 3 Voices (publ. in Chappell's *Popular Music of the Olden Time*); 5 4-part songs and 12 3-part songs; also several pieces for 3 and 4 viols; 35 pieces are printed in *Music at the Court of Henry VIII,* vol. 18 of *Musica Britannica.*

BIBLIOGRAPHY: Lady Mary Trefusis, *Music Composed by Henry VIII* (Roxburghe Club, 1912; privately printed); G.R. Hayes, *King's Music* (London, 1937).

Henschel, Sir George (full name, **Isador Georg Henschel**), German conductor, composer, and singer; b. Breslau, Feb. 18, 1850; d. Aviemore, Scotland, Sept. 10, 1934. Both his parents were of Polish-Jewish descent, but he was converted to Christianity when young. He studied with Julius Shäffer at Breslau, and with Moscheles (piano), Götze (singing), and Reinecke (theory) at the Leipzig Cons. (1867–70); then with Friedrich Kiel (composition) and Adolf Schulze (singing) in Berlin. He was a boy soprano; when his voice broke he gave concerts as a tenor; made his debut in Leipzig (1868) as Hans Sachs (baritone) in a concert performance of *Die Meistersinger;* he then toured throughout Europe; later gave recitals as a bass, and in 1914 appeared in London singing as a basso profondo. At the age of 78 he sang a group of Schubert lieder in London (at the Schubert centennial, 1928). An important turning point in his career came when he was selected as the first conductor of the Boston Symph., which he led for 3 seasons (1881–84); he also gave concerts in Boston and N.Y. as a singer. Settling in England, he founded the London Symph. Concerts (inaugural concert, Nov. 17, 1886), and conducted them until the series was concluded in 1897. He was a vocal teacher at the Royal College of Music (1886–88) and conductor of the Scottish Symph. Orch. (1893–95). In 1905–8 he was a prof. of singing at the Inst. of Musical Art in N.Y. In 1931, at the age of 81, he was engaged to conduct a commemorative concert on the 50th anniversary of the Boston Symph. Orch., identical (except for one number) with his inaugural Boston concert of 1881. In 1881 Henschel married the American singer **Lillian Bailey,** with whom he gave concerts; she died in 1901. In 1907 he was married, for a 2nd time, to Amy Louis. He was knighted in 1914.

WORKS: His musical compositions (mostly vocal) are in the German Romantic tradition. They include the opera *Nubia* (Dresden, Dec. 9, 1899); *Stabat Mater* (Birmingham, Oct. 4, 1894); *Requiem,* in memory of his first wife (Boston, Dec. 2, 1902); Mass for 8 Voices (London, June 1, 1916); String Quartet; about 200 songs (almost all publ.). He was the author of *Personal Recollections of Johannes Brahms* (Boston, 1907) and the autobiographical *Musings and Memories of a Musician* (1918).

BIBLIOGRAPHY: Mark Antony de Wolfe Howe,

The Boston Symphony Orchestra, 1881–1931 (Boston, 1931); H. Earle Johnson, *Symphony Hall* (Boston, 1950).

Henschel, Lillian June (née **Bailey**), American soprano; b. Columbus, Ohio, Jan. 17, 1860; d. London, Nov. 4, 1901. She made her professional debut in Boston at 16; then went to Paris to study with Mme. Viardot-García. On April 30, 1879, she appeared in London, at a Phil. concert, when she sang, besides her solo number, a duet with **George Henschel.** She then studied with him and on March 9, 1881, married him. When Henschel was appointed first conductor of the Boston Symph. Orch., she appeared as a soloist with him accompanying her at the piano, also in duets at Boston Symph. concerts. Until her untimely death, the Henschels were constantly associated with American artistic life. Her well-trained voice and fine musical feeling won her many admirers.
BIBLIOGRAPHY: Helen Henschel, *When Soft Voices Die. A Musical Biography* (London, 1944).

Hensel, Fanny Cäcilia, pianist and composer; sister of **Felix Mendelssohn;** b. Hamburg, Nov. 14, 1805; d. Berlin, May 14, 1847. Brought up in the cultured atmosphere of the Mendelssohn family, she received an excellent musical education at home. She married the painter W. Hensel on Oct. 3, 1829, but remained very close to her brother, who constantly asked her advice in musical matters; her death, which occurred suddenly, was a great shock to Mendelssohn, who died a few months afterward. She had a talent for composing; publ. 4 books of songs; a collection of part-songs, *Gartenlieder* (reprinted, London, 1878); also *Lieder ohne Worte* for Piano.
BIBLIOGRAPHY: Jack Werner, "Felix and Fanny Mendelssohn," *Music & Letters* (1947); S. Hensel, *Die Familie Mendelssohn* (Berlin, 1879). See also bibliography for Felix Mendelssohn.

Hensel, Heinrich, German dramatic tenor; b. Neustadt, Oct. 29, 1874; d. Hamburg, Feb. 23, 1935. He studied in Vienna and Milan; was a member of the Frankfurt Opera (1900–6), then at Wiesbaden (1906–11), where Siegfried Wagner heard him and engaged him to create the chief tenor part in his opera *Banadietrich* (Karlsruhe, 1910) and also to sing Parsifal at the Bayreuth Festival. He obtained excellent success; subsequently sang at Covent Garden, London (1911). He made his American debut at the Metropolitan Opera House in N.Y. as Lohengrin (Dec. 22, 1911) and was hailed by the press as one of the finest Wagnerian tenors; he also appeared with the Chicago Opera; returned to Germany and sang at the Hamburg Opera (1912–29).

Hensel, Octavia (real name, **Mary Alice Ives Seymour**), American writer on music; b. 1837; d. near Louisville, Ky., May 12, 1897. She publ. *Life and Letters of Louis Moreau Gottschalk,* a regrettably unreliable vol. (Boston, 1870); also *The Rheingold Trilogy* (Boston, 1884).

Hensel, Walther (real name, **Julius Janiczek**), music educator; b. Moravska Trebova, Bohemia, Sept. 8, 1887; d. Munich, Sept. 5, 1956. He studied in Vienna, Prague, and Freiburg, Switzerland, where he obtained his Dr.Phil. (1911); taught languages in Prague (1912–18). He traveled in Europe (1918–25) as an organizer of folk-song activities, with the aim of raising the standards of choral music for the young. From 1925–29, he was the head of the Jugendmusik School at the Dortmund Cons. In 1930 he went to Stuttgart, where he organized an educational program for the promotion of folk music. In 1938 he returned to Prague; taught at the German Univ. there. After 1945, he went to Munich. He edited a number of folk-song collections (*Der singende Quell,* etc.); edited the periodicals *Finkensteiner Blätter, Lied und Volk,* etc.; publ. *Lied und Volk, Eine Streitschrift wider das falsche deutsche Lied* (1921); "Über die gesamte Musikpflege in Schule und Haus," in H.J. Moser's *Grundfragen der Schulmusik* (1931); *Im Zeichen des Volksliedes* (1922; 2nd ed., 1936); *Musikalische Grundlehre* (Kassel, 1937); *Auf den Spuren des Volksliedes* (Kassel, 1944; reprint, 1964).

Henselt, Adolph von, distinguished German pianist and composer; b. Schwabach, May 9, 1814; d. Warmbrunn, Silesia, Oct. 10, 1889. The family moved to Munich when he was still an infant, and he studied piano there with Mme. von Fladt. In 1831, an allowance from King Ludwig I enabled him to continue piano study with Hummel at Weimar; he then took a course of theory under Sechter in Vienna. After a highly successful tour in Germany (1837), he went to St. Petersburg (1838), where he established himself as a piano teacher; was appointed chamber pianist to the Empress, and inspector of music at Imperial Institutes for girls in principal Russian cities. He remained in Russia for 40 years; a generation of Russian pianists studied under him. He was a virtuoso of the first rank; like Liszt (whose intimate friend he became), he developed an individual manner of playing, designed to express a personal feeling for the music. His technical specialty was the artful execution, in legato, of widely extended chords and arpeggios, for the achievement of which he composed extremely difficult extension studies. As a composer of piano pieces, he was praised by Schumann and Liszt. His principal works are a Piano Concerto, 2 sets of études, and a number of effective piano pieces (*Frühlingslied, La gondola,* etc.); altogether, he publ. 54 works. He publ. a long-winded but historically and didactically interesting paper entitled *Instructions for Teaching of Playing the Fortepiano, Based on Experience of Many Years, a Manual for the Teachers and Pupils of the Educational Institutions Entrusted to Him by the Government* (in Russian; St. Petersburg, 1868).
BIBLIOGRAPHY: W. von Lenz, *Die grossen Pianoforte Virtuosen unserer Zeit* (Berlin, 1872; Eng. ed., N.Y., 1899, revised 1971; includes a sympathetic character sketch of Henselt); La Mara, *Adolph Henselt,* in *Musikalische Studienköpfe*

(vol. III, 1909; reprinted separately, 1911); H.C. Schonberg, *The Great Pianists* (N. Y., 1963).

Hentschel, Ernst Julius, German music educator; b. Zudel, near Görlitz, July 26, 1804; d. Weissenfels, Aug. 14, 1875. He was taken as a child to Langenwaldau, where he taught violin and piano; later he learned to play all the wind instruments also. He devoted himself mainly to musical education, and won the highest regard in this field. He compiled several collections of school songs; was co-founder and editor of the musical journal *Euterpe.*

Hentschel, Franz, German conductor and composer; b. Berlin, Nov. 6, 1814; d. there, May 11, 1889. He studied with A.W. Bach; after conducting theater orchs. in provincial towns, he settled in Berlin as music teacher. He wrote an opera, *Die Hexenreise,* and numerous marches for military bands.

Hentschel, Theodor, German conductor and composer; b. Schirgiswalde, March 28, 1830; d. Hamburg, Dec. 19, 1892. He studied with Reissiger and Ciccarelli in Dresden; was active as a theater conductor in Bremen (1860–90), and then at Hamburg. He wrote the operas *Matrose und Sänger* (Leipzig, 1857); *Der Königspage* (Bremen, 1874); *Die Braut von Lusignan, oder Die schöne Melusine* (Bremen, 1875); *Lancelot* (Bremen, 1878); *Des Königs Schwerdt* (Hamburg, 1891); overtures and symph. marches for orch.; piano music; songs; Mass for Double Chorus; etc.

Henze, Hans Werner, outstanding German composer of the modern school; b. Gütersloh, Westphalia, July 1, 1926. His early studies at the Braunschweig School of Music were interrupted by military service, and for a year he was in the German army on the Russian front. After the war he took music courses at the Kirchenmusikalisches Inst. in Heidelberg; at the same time he studied privately with Wolfgang Fortner. Early in his career as a composer he became fascinated with the disciplinary aspects of Schoenberg's method of composition with 12 tones, and attended the seminars on the subject given by René Leibowitz at Darmstadt. A musician of restless temperament, he joined a radical political group and proclaimed the necessity of writing music without stylistic restrictions in order to serve the masses. In search of natural musical resources, he moved to Italy; lived in Ischia from 1953 to 1956; then stayed in Naples and finally settled in Marino. He successfully attempted to integrate musical idioms and mannerisms of seemingly incompatible techniques; in his vocal works he freely adopted such humanoid effects as screaming, bellowing, and snorting; he even specified that long sustained tones were to be sung by inhaling as well as exhaling. Nonetheless, Henze manages to compose music that is feasible for human performance. But political considerations continued to play a decisive role in his career. In 1967 he, in company with the German radical composer Paul Dessau, withdrew from the membership of the Academy of the Arts of West Berlin, in a gesture of protest against its artistic policies. He defiantly placed the red flag on the stage at the first performance of his oratorio *Das Floss der Medusa* in Hamburg on Dec. 9, 1968; when the chorus refused to sing under such circumstances, Henze canceled the performance, and declared that revolutionary action was more important than any world première. During his stay in Italy he became a member of the Italian Communist Party.

WORKS: FOR THE STAGE: *Das Wundertheater,* opera for Actors, after Cervantes (1948; Heidelberg, May 7, 1949; revised for Singers, 1964; Frankfurt, Nov. 30, 1965); *Ballet Variations* (concert premiere, Düsseldorf, Oct. 3, 1949; stage premiere, Wuppertal, Dec. 21, 1958); *Jack Pudding,* ballet (1949; Wiesbaden, Jan. 1, 1951); *Rosa Silber,* ballet (1950; concert premiere, Berlin, May 8, 1951; stage premiere, Cologne, Oct. 15, 1958); *Labyrinth,* choreographic fantasy (1951; concert perf., Darmstadt, May 29, 1952); *Die schlafende Prinzessin,* ballet after Tchaikovsky (1951; Essen, June 5, 1954); *Ein Landarzt,* radio opera after the story by Kafka (Hamburg, Nov. 19, 1951; broadcast, Nov. 29, 1951; revised as a monodrama for Baritone and Orch., 1964; first perf., Berlin, Oct. 12, 1965, Dietrich Fischer-Dieskau, soloist; radio opera revised for the stage, 1964; first perf., Frankfurt, Nov. 30, 1965); *Boulevard Solitude,* opera (1951; Hannover, Feb. 17, 1952); *Der Idiot,* ballet pantomime after Dostoyevsky (Berlin, Sept. 1, 1952); *Pas d'action,* ballet (Munich, 1952; withdrawn by the composer and revised as *Tancredi,* 1964; Vienna, May 14, 1966); *Das Ende einer Welt,* radio opera (Hamburg, Dec. 4, 1953; revised for the stage, 1964; Frankfurt, Nov. 30, 1965); *König Hirsch,* opera (1952–55; Berlin, Sept. 23, 1956; revised as *Il Re cervo,* 1962; Kassel, March 10, 1963); *Maratona,* ballet (1956; Berlin, Sept. 24, 1957); *Ondine,* ballet (1956–57; London, Oct. 27, 1958); *Der Prinz von Homburg,* opera (1958; Hamburg, May 22, 1960); *L'Usignolo dell'Imperatore,* pantomime after Andersen (Venice, Sept. 16, 1959); *Elegy for Young Lovers,* chamber opera (1959–61; in German, Schwetzingen, May 20, 1961; first perf. to Auden's original Eng. libretto, Glyndebourne, July 13, 1961); *Der junge Lord,* comic opera (1964; Berlin, April 7, 1965); *The Bassarids,* opera seria (1965; in German, Salzburg, Aug. 6, 1966; first perf. to the original Eng. libretto by Auden and Kallman, Santa Fe, Aug. 7, 1968); *Moralities,* scenic cantatas after Aesop, to texts by Auden (1967; Cincinnati, May 18, 1968); *Der langwierige Weg in die Wohnung der Natascha Ungeheuer,* show (RAI, Rome, May 17, 1971); *La cubana, oder Ein Leben für die Kunst,* vaudeville (1973; NET Opera Theater, N.Y., March 4, 1974; stage premiere, Munich, May 28, 1975); *We Come to the River,* actions for music (1974–76; London, July 12, 1976); *Don Chisciotte,* opera, arrangement of Paisiello (Montepulciano, Aug. 1, 1976); *Orpheus,* ballet in 2 acts by Edward Bond (Stuttgart, March 17, 1979); *Pollicino,* fairy-tale opera (Montepulciano, Aug. 2, 1980); *The English Cat,* chamber opera (Schwetzingen, June 2, 1983).

FOR ORCH: Chamber Concerto for Piano, Flute, and Strings (Darmstadt, Sept. 27, 1946); Concertino for Piano and Winds, with Percussion (Baden-Baden, Oct. 5, 1947, Werner Egk conducting); Symph. No. 1 (Bad Pyrmont, Aug. 25, 1948, Wolfgang Fortner conducting; revised version, Berlin, April 9, 1964, composer conducting); Violin Concerto No. 1 (Baden-Baden, Dec. 12, 1948); Symph. No. 2 (Stuttgart, Dec. 1, 1949); Symph. Variations (1950); Piano Concerto No. 1 (1950; Düsseldorf, Sept. 14, 1952, composer conducting); Symph. No. 3 (Donaueschingen, Oct. 7, 1951); *Ode to the West Wind* for Cello and Orch., to the poem by Shelley (Bielefeld, April 30, 1954); *4 poemi* (Frankfurt, May 31, 1955, Stokowski conducting); Symph. No. 4, in one movement (1955; Berlin, Oct. 9, 1963, composer conducting); Sonata for Strings (Zürich, March 21, 1958, Paul Sacher conducting); *3 Symphonic Studies* (1955–64; first version perf. as *Symphonic Studies*, Hamburg, Feb. 14, 1956); *3 Dithyrambs* for Chamber Orch. (Cologne, Nov. 27, 1958); *Jeux des Tritons,* divertimento from the ballet *Ondine,* for Piano and Orch. (Zürich, March 28, 1960); *Antifone* (1960; Berlin, Jan. 20, 1962, Karajan conducting); Symph. No. 5 (1962; N.Y., May 16, 1963, Bernstein conducting); *Los Caprichos,* fantasia for Orch. (1963; Duisburg, April 6, 1967); *Doppio Concerto* for Oboe, Harp, and Strings (Zürich, Dec. 2, 1966, Paul Sacher conducting); *Telemanniana* (Berlin, April 4, 1967); Fantasia for Strings, from the film *Junge Torless* (Berlin, April 1, 1967); Concerto for Double Bass and Orch. (Chicago, Nov. 2, 1967); Piano Concerto No. 2, in one movement (1967; Bielefeld, Sept. 29, 1968); Symph. No. 6 (Havana, Nov. 24, 1969); *Compases para Preguntas Ensimismadas* (Basel, Feb. 11, 1971, Paul Sacher conducting); *Heliogabalus Imperator,* "allegoria per musica" (Chicago, Nov. 16, 1972, Solti conducting); *Tristan* for Piano, Tape, and Mixed Orch. (1973; London, Oct. 20, 1974, Colin Davis conducting); *Ragtimes and Habaneras* for Brass Instruments (London, Sept. 13, 1975); Concert Suite from the film *Katharina Blum* (Brighton, May 6, 1976, composer conducting); *Aria de la folia española* for Chamber Orch. (St. Paul, Sept. 17, 1977); *Il Vitalino raddoppiato* for Violin Concertante and Chamber Orch. (Salzburg, Aug. 2, 1978); *Barcorola* (1979; Zürich, April 22, 1980); *Apollo triofante,* suite from *Orpheus* (Gelsenkirchen, Sept. 1, 1980); dramatic scenes from *Orpheus* (1979; Zürich, Jan. 6, 1981, composer conducting); *I sentimenti di Carl Philip Emmanuel Bach,* transcriptions for Flute, Harp, and Strings (Rome, April 14, 1982); *Le Miracle de la rose* for Clarinet and 13 Players (London, May 26, 1982); Symph. No. 7 (Berlin, Dec. 1, 1984).

CHAMBER MUSIC: Violin Sonata (1946); Sonatina for Flute and Piano (1947); String Quartet No. 1 (1947); Serenade for Solo Cello (1949); Variations for Piano (1949); Chamber Sonata for Piano, Violin, and Cello (1948; Cologne, March 16, 1950; revised 1963); *Apollo et Hyazinthus* for Harpsichord, Alto, and 8 Instruments (Frankfurt, June 26, 1949); String Quartet No. 2 (Baden-Baden, Dec. 16, 1952); Wind Quintet (1952; Bremen, Feb. 15, 1953); *Concerto per il Marigny* for Piano and 7 Instruments (Paris, March 9, 1956); Sonata for Piano (1959); *Chamber Music 1958* for Tenor, Guitar, and 8 Instruments (Hamburg, Nov. 26, 1958); *Lucy Escott Variations* for Piano (1963; Berlin, March 21, 1965); Divertimento for 2 Pianos

(N.Y., Nov. 30, 1964); *Royal Winter Music,* 2 sonatas on Shakespearean characters, for Guitar (1975–79); String Quartet No. 3 (Berlin, Sept. 12, 1976); *Amicizia* for Clarinet, Cello, and Percussion Instruments (Montepulciano, Aug. 6, 1976); String Quartets Nos. 4 and 5 (Schwetzingen, May 25, 1977); Sonata for Violin Solo (Montepulciano, Aug. 10, 1977); *L'autunno* for Wind Instruments (London, Feb. 28, 1979); Sonata for Viola and Piano (Witten, April 20, 1980).

VOCAL MUSIC: 5 madrigals, to poems by François Villon, for Mixed Chorus and 2 Solo Instruments (1947; Frankfurt, April 25, 1950); *Chorus of the Captured Trojans,* from *Faust,* Part 2, for Mixed Chorus and Large Orch. (1948; Bielefeld, Feb. 6, 1949; revised 1964); *Whispers from Heavenly Death,* cantata from the poem by Walt Whitman, for High Voice and 8 Solo Instruments (1948); *Der Vorwurf (The Reproach),* concert aria to words by Franz Werfel, for Baritone, Trumpet, and Strings (Darmstadt, July 29, 1948); 5 Neapolitan songs for Baritone and Orch. (Frankfurt, May 26, 1956, Dietrich Fischer-Dieskau, soloist); *Nocturnes and Arias* for Soprano and Orch. (Donaueschingen, Oct. 20, 1957); *Novae de Infinito Laudes,* cantata to text by Giordano Bruno (1962; Venice, April 24, 1963); *Ariosi,* to poems by Tasso, for Soprano, Violin, and Orch. (1963; Edinburgh Festival, Aug. 23, 1964); *Being Beauteous,* cantata from the poem by Arthur Rimbaud, for Soprano, Harp, and 4 Cellos (1963; Berlin, April 12, 1964); *Cantata della Fiaba Estrema* for Soprano, Small Chorus, and 13 Instruments (1963; Zürich, Feb. 26, 1965); Choral Fantasy for Small Chorus, 5 Instruments, and Percussion (1964; Berlin, Jan. 23, 1967); *Muses of Sicily* for Chorus, 2 Pianos, Winds, and Timpani (Berlin, Sept. 20, 1966); *Versuch über Schweine (Essay on Pigs)* for Baritone and Chamber Orch. (London, Feb. 14, 1969; the title is an ironic reference to certain revolting students, active during the 1960s); *Das Floss der Medusa (The Raft of the Medusa),* popular and military oratorio to the memory of Ché Guevara (1968; the projected premiere in Hamburg on Dec. 9, 1968, had to be canceled as a result of left-wing political action; concert premiere, Vienna, Jan. 29, 1971; stage premiere, Nuremberg, April 15, 1972); *El Cimarrón* for Baritone, Flute, Guitar, and Percussion, to texts from *The Autobiography of a Runaway Slave* by Esteban Montejo (Aldeburgh Festival, June 22, 1970); *Voices* for Mezzo- soprano, Tenor, and Instrumental Group, to 22 revolutionary texts (London, Jan. 4, 1974, composer conducting); *Jephtha,* oratorio by Carissimi, realized by Henze (London, July 14, 1976, composer conducting); *The King of Harlem* for Mezzo-soprano and Instrumental Ensemble, to a text by Federico García Lorca (Witten, April 20, 1980); *3 Auden Pieces* for Voice and Piano (Aldeburgh, June 15, 1983).

WRITINGS: *Musik und Politik: Schriften und Gespräche, 1955–1975* (Munich, 1976; also in Eng., as *Music and Politics: Collected Writings, 1953–81,* London and Ithaca, N.Y., 1982).

BIBLIOGRAPHY: Klaus Geitel, *H.W. Henze* (Berlin, 1968); H.H. Stuckenschmidt, "Hans Werner Henze und die Musik unserer Zeit," *Universitas,*

XXVII/2 (1972).

Heppener, Robert, Dutch composer; b. Amsterdam, Aug. 9, 1925. He took piano lessons with Jan Ode and Johan van den Boogert at the Amsterdam Cons.; later studied composition with Bertus van Lier. He then engaged in teaching; joined the staff of the Cons. of the Music Lyceum Society in Amsterdam. In his own compositions he observes the rational boundaries of modern harmony.
WORKS: *Cantico delle creature di S. Francesco d'Assisi* for Soprano, Harp, and Strings (1952; revised 1954); Nocturne for Piano (1953); Symph. (1957); Septet (1958); *Derivazioni* for String Orch. (1958); *Arcadian Sonatina* for 2 Recorders and Violin (1959); *A fond de fleurettes* for String Quartet (1961); Sinfonietta for Small Orch. (1961); *Het derde land (The 3rd Country),* 3 songs for Chorus and Chamber Orch. (1962); *Cavalcade,* overture and rondo for Orch. (1963); *Eglogues* for Orch. (1963); *Scherzi* for Strings (1965); *Canti carnascialeschi (Carnival Songs),* 5-movement cycle for a cappella Chorus (1966); *Fanfare trionfale* for Chorus, Winds, Timpani, and Piano (1967); Quartet for Alto Flute, Violin, Viola, and Cello (1967); *Air et sonneries* for Orch. (1969); *Canzona* for Saxophone Quartet (1969); *Hymns and Conversations* for 28 Harps (1969; Amsterdam, July 8, 1969); *4 Songs,* after Pound, for Middle Voice and Piano (1968–70); *Muziek voor straten en pleinen (Music for Streets and Squares)* for Orch. (Amsterdam, Oct. 31, 1970); *Del iubilo del core che esce in voce* for a cappella Chorus (1974); *Pas de quatre-mains* for Piano, 4-hands (1975); *Nachklänge* for Chamber Chorus (1977); *Sweelinck Fanfare* for Orch. (1978); Viola Concerto (Amsterdam, Oct. 6, 1979).
BIBLIOGRAPHY: W. Paap, "Robert Heppener," *Sonorum Speculum,* 39 (1969).

Herbage, Julian, English musicologist; b. Woking, Sept. 4, 1904; d. London, Jan. 15, 1976. He studied harmony and counterpoint with Charles Wood at St. John's College, Cambridge. In 1927 he became a member of the music staff of the BBC; from 1940–46 was assistant director of music there. With his wife, Anna Instone, he edited the BBC "Music Magazine" radio program from 1944–73. He also made appearances as a conductor of music by Baroque composers. He wrote the book *Handel's Messiah* (London, 1948).

Herbart, Johann Friedrich, eminent German philosopher and musician; b. Oldenburg, May 4, 1776; d. Göttingen, Aug. 14, 1841. He studied at Jena with Fichte. In 1805, he was appointed prof. of philosophy at Göttingen; in 1809–35, he was at Königsberg; from 1835 to his death he was again at Göttingen. Of importance to music theory are his *Psychologische Bemerkungen zur Tonlehre* (1811), treating of intervals, and the chapter "Von den schönen Künsten," in his *Kurze Enzyklopädie der Philosophie* (1931). He composed a Piano Sonata, which was publ. (Leipzig, 1808), and several other works.

BIBLIOGRAPHY: W. Kahl, *Herbart als Musiker* (Langensalza, 1926).

Herbeck, Johann (Franz) von, Austrian conductor and composer; b. Vienna, Dec. 25, 1831; d. there, Oct. 28, 1877. He was a boy chorister at the Heiligenkreuz monastery, where he had instruction in piano; then studied composition with Ludwig Rotter in Vienna; he also studied philosophy and law at the Univ. of Vienna; from 1859 to 1870, and from 1875 to his death, he was conductor of the Gesellschaft der Musikfreunde; in 1866 he was named first Hofkapellmeister and in 1869 first Kapellmeister of the court opera; in 1870 was named its director as well, remaining there until 1875. He was particularly successful as conductor and organizer of several choral societies in Vienna. Herbeck publ. numerous choral works of considerable worth, if not of any originality. His son, Ludwig Herbeck, publ. a biography, *Johann Herbeck, ein Lebensbild* (Vienna, 1885), which contains a complete catalogue of his works. See also the sketch on Herbeck in Hanslick's *Suite* (Vienna, 1885).
BIBLIOGRAPHY: J. Braun, *Johann Ritter von Herbeck und das Wiener Hofoperntheater* (Diss., Univ. of Vienna, 1949).

Herberigs, Robert, Belgian composer; b. Ghent, June 19, 1886; d. Oudenaarde, Sept. 20, 1974. He studied singing at the Ghent Cons. and made his debut as a baritone at the Flemish Opera in Antwerp (1908), but soon abandoned his operatic aspirations and began an assiduous study of composition. He succeeded swiftly, and won the Belgian Grand Prix in 1909 with his cantata, *La Legénde de St. Hubert.* But he also pursued an interest in literature, and publ. several novels. His music reflects the manner of French Romanticism.
WORKS: 2 comic operas: *Le Mariage de Rosine,* after Beaumarchais (1919; Ghent, Feb. 13, 1925) and *L'Amour médecin,* after Molière (1920); radio play, *Antoine et Cleopatra,* after Shakespeare, for 6 Speakers, Chorus, and Orch. (1949); open-air play, *Lam Godsspel* or *Jeu de l'Agneau Mystique (Pageant of the Mystic Lamb,* 1948; Ghent, 1949); a play of "light and sound in stereorama," *Le Château des comtes de Gand* (1960); 2 piano concertos (1932, 1952); 2 suites for Brass Ensemble (1946); *Sinfonia breve* (1947; 2 earlier symphs. were withdrawn); Organ Concerto (1957); numerous symph. poems and orch. suites: *Cyrano de Bergerac,* with Solo Horn, in the form of a concerto (Brussels, April 12, 1912); *Le Chant d'Hiawatha,* after Longfellow (1921); *Vlaanderen, O Welig Huis (Flanders, the Well-Beloved,* 1949); *De Vrolijke Vrouwtjes van Windsor (The Merry Wives of Windsor,* 1950); *Rapsodia alla Zingara* (1952); *A la Fontaine Bellerie* (1954; originally for Piano, 1923); *Echos et mirages* (1954); *Esquisses et impromptus* (1954); *La Chanson d'Eve,* 2 suites (1955, 1959; originally a cycle of 40 songs, 1922–24); *4 ballades* (1955); *La Petite Sirène,* after Hans Christian Andersen (1955); *Odes aux Muses* (1955); *4 saisons,* after Breughel (1956); *4 odes à Botticelli* (1958); *Commedia dell'arte* (1958); *De Nach-*

telijke *Wapenschouw* (*Nocturnal Parade,* 1961); *Hamlet* (1962); *Roméo et Juliette* (1963); *Reinaut et Armida* (1967); *Cantata* to the memory of Jan Willems (1946); *Te Deum laudamus* for Chorus and Organ (1912); *Missa pro defunctis* for Chorus a cappella (1926); 7 other masses for Chorus and Organ, including *Messe in nativitate* (1926) and *Messe pour la Paix* (1938); String Quartet (1921); *Poème* for Piano Trio (1923); Violin Sonata (1932); *Concert champêtre* for Wind Quintet (1938); Clarinet Sonatina (1939); Piano Quartet (1939); *Suite Miniature* and Sonatine for Flute and String Trio (both 1954); 21 piano sonatas and sonatinas (1941–45); piano pieces; songs.

Herbert, Victor, famous composer of light music; b. Dublin, Feb. 1, 1859; d. New York, May 26, 1924. He was a grandson of Samuel Lover, the Irish novelist; his father died when he was an infant; soon his mother married a German physician and settled in Stuttgart (1867), taking the boy with her. He entered the Stuttgart high school, but did not graduate; his musical ability was definitely pronounced by then, and he selected the cello as his instrument, taking lessons from the celebrated cellist Bernhard Cossmann in Baden-Baden. He soon acquired a degree of technical proficiency that enabled him to take a position as cellist in various orchs. in Germany, France, Italy, and Switzerland; in 1880 he became a cellist of the Eduard Strauss waltz band in Vienna; in 1881, returned to Stuttgart, where he joined the court orch., and studied composition with Max Seifritz at the Cons. His earliest works were for the cello with orch.; he performed his Suite with the Stuttgart orch. on Oct. 23, 1883, and his First Cello Concerto on Dec. 8, 1885. On Aug. 14, 1886, he married the Viennese opera singer **Therese Förster** (1861–1927); in the same year she received an offer to join the Metropolitan Opera in N.Y., and Herbert was engaged as an orch. cellist there, appearing in N.Y. also as soloist (played his own Cello Concerto with the N.Y. Phil., Dec. 10, 1887). In his early years in N.Y., Herbert was overshadowed by the celebrity of his wife, but soon he developed energetic activities on his own, forming an entertainment orch. which he conducted in a repertoire of light music; he also participated in chamber music concerts; was soloist with the Theodore Thomas and Seidl orchs. He was the conductor of the Boston Festival Orch. in 1891; Tchaikovsky conducted this orch. in Philadelphia in a miscellaneous program, and Herbert played a solo. He was associate conductor of the Worcester Festival (1889–91), for which he wrote a dramatic cantata, *The Captive* (Sept. 24, 1891). In 1893 he became bandmaster of the famous 22nd Regiment Band, succeeding P.S. Gilmore. On March 10, 1894, he was soloist with the N.Y. Phil. in his 2nd Cello Concerto. In the same year, at the suggestion of William MacDonald, the manager of the Boston Ideal Opera Co., Herbert wrote a light opera, *Prince Ananias,* which was produced with encouraging success in N.Y. (Nov. 20, 1894). From 1898 to 1904, Herbert was conductor of the Pittsburgh Symph. Orch., presenting some of his own

compositions: *Episodes amoureuses* (Feb. 2, 1900); *Hero and Leander* (Jan. 18, 1901); *Woodland Fancies* (Dec. 6, 1901); *Columbus* (Jan. 2, 1903). In 1900 he directed at Madison Square Garden, N.Y., an orch. of 420 performers for the benefit of the sufferers in the Galveston flood. On April 29, 1906, he led a similar monster concert at the Hippodrome for the victims of the San Francisco earthquake. In 1904 he organized the Victor Herbert N.Y. Orch., and gave concerts in N.Y. and neighboring communities.

But it is as a composer of light operas that Herbert became chiefly known. In the best of these he unites spontaneous melody, sparkling rhythm, and simple but tasteful harmony; his experience as a symph. composer and conductor imparted a solidity of texture to his writing that placed him far above the many gifted amateurs in this field. Furthermore, he possessed a natural communicative power in his music, which made his operettas spectacularly successful with the public. In the domain of grand opera, he was not so fortunate. When the production of his first grand opera, *Natoma,* took place at Philadelphia on Feb. 25, 1911, it aroused great expectations; but the opera failed to sustain lasting interest. Still less effective was his 2nd opera, *Madeleine,* staged by the Metropolitan Opera Co. in N.Y. on Jan. 24, 1914. Herbert was one of the founders of the American Society of Composers, Authors and Publishers (ASCAP) in 1914, and was vice-president from that date until his death. In 1916 he wrote a special score for the motion picture, *The Fall of a Nation,* in synchronization with the screen play.

WORKS: Operettas: *Prince Ananias* (N.Y., Nov. 20, 1894); *The Wizard of the Nile* (Chicago, Sept. 26, 1895); *The Gold Bug* (N.Y., Sept. 21, 1896); *The Serenade* (Cleveland, Feb. 17, 1897); *The Idol's Eye* (Troy, N.Y., Sept. 20, 1897); *The Fortune Teller* (Toronto, Sept. 14, 1898); *Cyrano de Bergerac* (Montreal, Sept. 11, 1899); *The Singing Girl* (Montreal, Oct. 2, 1899); *The Ameer* (Scranton, Pa., Oct. 9, 1899); *The Viceroy* (San Francisco, Feb. 12, 1900); *Babes in Toyland* (Chicago, June 17, 1903); *Babette* (Washington, D.C., Nov. 9, 1903); *It Happened in Nordland* (Harrisburg, Pa., Nov. 21, 1904); *Miss Dolly Dollars* (Rochester, N.Y., Aug. 31, 1905); *Wonderland* (Buffalo, Sept. 14, 1905); *Mlle. Modiste* (Trenton, Oct. 7, 1905; Herbert's most popular work); *The Red Mill* (Buffalo, Sept. 3, 1906); *Dream City* (N.Y., Dec. 25, 1906); *The Tattooed Man* (Baltimore, Feb. 11, 1907); *The Rose of Algeria* (Wilkes-Barre, Sept. 11, 1909); *Little Nemo* (Philadelphia, Sept. 28, 1908); *The Prima Donna* (Chicago, Oct. 5, 1908); *Old Dutch* (Wilkes-Barre, Nov. 6, 1909); *Naughty Marietta* (Syracuse, Oct. 24, 1910; highly successful); *When Sweet Sixteen* (Springfield, Mass., Dec. 5, 1910); *Mlle. Rosita* (later called *The Duchess,* Boston, March 27, 1911); *The Enchantress* (Washington, Oct. 9, 1911); *The Lady of the Slipper* (Philadelphia, Oct. 8, 1912); *The Madcap Duchess* (Rochester, N.Y., Oct. 13, 1913); *Sweethearts* (Baltimore, March 24, 1913); *The Débutante* (Atlantic City, Sept. 21, 1914); *The Only Girl* (Atlantic City, Oct. 1, 1914); *Princess Pat* (Atlantic City, Aug. 23, 1915); *Eileen* (Cleveland, Jan. 1, 1917, as *Hearts of Erin*); *Her Regiment*

(Springfield, Mass., Oct. 22, 1917); *The Velvet Lady* (Philadelphia, Dec. 23, 1918); *My Golden Girl* (Stamford, Conn., Dec. 19, 1919); *The Girl in the Spotlight* (Stamford, Conn., July 7, 1920); *Oui, Madame* (Philadelphia, March 22, 1920); *Orange Blossoms* (Philadelphia, Sept. 4, 1922); *The Dream Girl* (New Haven, April 22, 1924). Other stage productions: *Cinderella Man* (1915), *The Century Girl* (1916), *Ziegfeld Follies* (1917, 1920–23), *The Willow Plate* (marionette play by Tony Sarg, 1924). Nonstage works: Serenade, op. 12; First Cello Concerto (Dec. 8, 1885); 2nd Concerto for Cello, op. 30 (N.Y. March 10, 1894); *Pan-Americana*; *Suite of Serenades* (composed for Paul Whiteman's orch.; perf. 1924); *Golden Days*; *Dramatic Overture*; orch. arrangements; men's choruses; songs; many pieces for piano, violin and piano, and cello and piano.
BIBLIOGRAPHY: J. Kaye, *Victor Herbert* (N.Y., 1931); Edward N. Waters, *Victor Herbert* (exhaustive biography, with a full list of works; N.Y., 1955).

Herbig, Günther, German conductor; b. Usti-nad-Labem, Czechoslovakia, Nov. 30, 1931. He studied conducting with H. Abendroth at the Franz Liszt Hochschule in Weimar; then worked with Scherchen, Yansons, and Karajan. In 1956 he conducted at the City Theater in Erfurt; from 1957–62 was conductor at the German National Theater in Weimar; then held the position of music director of the Hans Otto Theater in Potsdam (1962–66). From 1966–72 he was conductor of the East Berlin Symph. Orch.; in 1970 became also Generalmusikdirektor of the Dresden Phil., and in 1972 its chief conductor. In 1977 he was appointed chief conductor of the East Berlin Symph.; later made worldwide tours in the Orient and South America. From 1979–81 he served as principal guest conductor of the Dallas Symph. Orch. In 1983 he was appointed music director-designate of the Detroit Symph. Orch., and in Sept. 1984 was named its music director.

Herbst, Johannes, American Moravian minister and composer; b. Kempten, Swabia, July 23, 1735; d. Salem, N.C., Jan. 15, 1812. Herbst came to the U.S. in 1786 to serve as minister at Lancaster, Pa., and later at Lititz. In 1811 Herbst was elevated to the episcopate and transferred to the Southern Province of the Moravian Church at Salem, where he died the following year. When he emigrated to the U.S. he brought with him a large number of musical MSS, this being the practice of those traveling to the American Moravian settlements. During the following years, in which he was a performing musician, composer, and teacher, he added to his collection, copying MSS brought from Europe by other Moravians, and music composed by American Moravians; altogether there are almost 12,000 pages in his hand, constituting the most extensive individual collection of 18th- and 19th-century Moravian (and non-Moravian) music in the U.S. The Herbst Collection is in the Archives of the Moravian Music Foundation in Winston-Salem, N.C., and is available complete on either microfiche or roll microfilm: A. 493 MS scores of about 1,000 vocal-instrumental pieces (Congregation Music); B. 45 MS scores or parts of larger vocal works by C.P.E. Bach, Mozart, Haydn, and others, including Herbst and other Moravians; C. 6 miscellaneous vols. of keyboard works, texts, etc.; the entire collection totals 11,676 pages. An itemized *Catalog of the Johannes Herbst Collection,* prepared by Marilyn Gombosi, was publ. in Chapel Hill, N.C., in 1970 and includes a biographical sketch of Herbst and a short history of the collection. Herbst was the most prolific of all the American Moravian composers, having to his credit some 127 choral anthems and songs (all included in the above collection; a few pieces were publ. by H.W. Gray, Peters, and Boosey & Hawkes). Many of his works show him to have been a highly skilled musical craftsman. His music collection is particularly important as the principal source of music by American and European Moravian composers.
BIBLIOGRAPHY: A.G. Rau and H.T. David, *A Catalogue of Music by American Moravians* (Bethlehem, Pa., 1938); H.T. David, "Background for Bethlehem: Moravian Music in Pennsylvania," *Magazine of Art* (April 1939); idem, "Musical Life in the Pennsylvania Settlements of the Unitas Fratrum," *Transactions of the Moravian Historical Society* (1942; reprinted as Moravian Music Foundation Publication No. 6, 1959); Donald M. McCorkle, *Moravian Music in Salem: A German-American Heritage* (Diss., Indiana Univ., 1958); Joan O. Falconer, *Bishop Johannes Herbst (1735–1812), An American Moravian Musician, Collector and Composer* (Diss., Columbia Univ., 1969; 2 vols.).

Hercigonja, Nikola, Croatian composer; b. Vinkovcim, Feb. 19, 1911. He studied in Zagreb; in 1950 became a prof. of the Music Academy in Belgrade. In his music he follows a general trend of realistic composition, inspired by national folk songs.
WORKS: *Vječni Žid u Zagrebu (The Wandering Jew in Zagreb),* musical burlesque (1942); *Gorski vijenac (Mountain Wreath),* opera-oratorio (Belgrade, Oct. 19, 1957); *Planetarium,* scenic action for Voices, Speaking Chorus, and Orch. (1960); numerous choruses.

Herford, Julius, American musician and pedagogue; b. Berlin, Feb. 21, 1901; d. Bloomington, Ind., Sept. 17, 1981. He studied at Stern's Cons. in Berlin; then pursued a rather successful career as a choral conductor and concert pianist. He emigrated to the U.S. in 1939 and devoted himself mainly to teaching; was at various times on the faculty of Columbia Univ., the Juilliard School of Music, and Westminster Choir College. In 1964 he was appointed prof. of music at Indiana Univ. Among his students were Lukas Foss, Robert Shaw, Robert Wagner, and John Nelson.

Herincx, Raimund, English bass-baritone; b. London, Aug. 23, 1927, of Belgian parentage. He studied voice in Belgium and Italy; made his operatic debut in 1950 with the Welsh National Opera; then sang at the Sadler's Wells Opera (1957–66), and at Covent

Garden (from 1968). He also made guest appearances in America.

Hering, Karl (Friedrich August), German violinist; b. Berlin, Sept. 2, 1819; d. Burg, near Magdeburg, Feb. 2, 1889. He studied with Rungenhagen in Berlin and Tomaschek in Prague; established a music school in Berlin (1851); publ. *Methodischer Leitfaden für Violinlehrer* (1857) and an elementary violin method; also wrote a monograph on Kreutzer's studies (1858).

Hering, Karl Gottlieb, German music pedagogue; b. Bad Schandau, Oct. 25, 1765; d. Zittau, Jan. 4, 1853. He studied academic subjects at Leipzig Univ.; studied music with J.G. Schicht. In 1811 he was appointed music teacher at the Zittau seminary, and remained there until 1836, when he retired. He publ. a number of manuals on practical music study: *Praktisches Handbuch zur leichten Erlernung des Klavier-Spielens* (Halberstadt, 1796); *Praktische Violin-Schule* (Leipzig, 1810), etc.; also compiled *Zittauer Choralbuch* (Leipzig, 1822) and other collections, including original compositions. Some of his pieces for children became celebrated in Germany and elsewhere, particularly *Steckenpferd* ("Hopp, hopp, hopp, Pferdchen lauf Galopp"), *Weihnachtsfreude* ("Morgen, Kinder, wird's was geben"), and (most famous of them all) *Grossvaterlied,* which was used by Schumann in his *Carnaval.*
BIBLIOGRAPHY: Lucy Gelber, "Karl Gottlieb Hering," in *Die Liederkomponisten* (Berlin, 1936).

Héritte-Viardot, Louise-Pauline-Marie, vocal teacher; daughter of **Pauline Viardot-García;** b. Paris, Dec. 14, 1841; d. Heidelberg, Jan. 17, 1918. She was for many years a singing teacher at the St. Petersburg Cons.; then taught in Frankfurt, Berlin, and Heidelberg. She was married to a French consular official, Héritte. She was also a composer; her opera *Lindoro* was performed in Weimar (1879); she further wrote the cantatas *Das Bacchusfest* (Stockholm, 1880) and *Le Feu de ciel;* some chamber music; and vocal exercises. Her memoirs (trans. from the original German) were publ. in Eng. as *Memories and Adventures* (London, 1913), in French as *Mémoires de Louise Héritte-Viardot* (Paris, 1923).

Herman, Jerry, American composer of popular music; b. New York, July 10, 1933. He played piano by ear but never learned to read music. He studied drama at the Univ. of Miami; then became a scriptwriter for television in N.Y. Later he devoted himself entirely to musical comedies, for which he wrote both lyrics and music. His shows *Parade* (1960) and *Milk and Honey* (1961) were fairly successful; but he made his greatest hit with the production of *Hello, Dolly!* (N.Y., Jan. 16, 1964), which had the longest run in the history of Broadway shows, closing on Dec. 26, 1970. A comparable success was achieved by his next musical, *Mame,* which opened in N.Y. on May 24, 1966.

Herman, Reinhold (Ludwig), conductor and composer; b. Prenzlau, Germany, Sept. 21, 1849; d. probably in New York, c.1920. He studied at the Stern Cons. in Berlin; came to the U.S. in 1871 as a singing teacher; from 1884, conducted the choral society Liederkranz; from 1898–1900, conducted the Handel and Haydn Society in Boston; then lived in Italy; returned to N.Y. in 1917. He publ. *An Open Door for Singers* (N.Y., 1912); wrote 3 operas, of which *Wulfrin* was performed in Kassel (Oct. 11, 1898); also several choral works.

Herman, Vasile, Rumanian composer; b. Satu-Mare, June 10, 1929. He studied piano in his home-town and composition with Demian, Toduţă, and Comes at the Cluj Cons. (1949–57); subsequently was appointed to its staff. His music is cautiously modernistic, with occasional overflow into aleatory indeterminacy.
WORKS: Oratorio, *Balada lui Pintea Viteazul* (1957); 2 piano sonatas (*Sonata da ricercar,* 1958; 1967); *8 Small Pieces* for Piano (1959); Partita for Piano (1961); *Sonata-Baladă* for Oboe and Piano (1961); *Variante* for 2 Clarinets, Piano, and Percussion (1963–64); *4 Ritornele* for Orch. (1964; Cluj, Dec. 18, 1966); *3 Pieces* for Solo Violin (1964); *Microforme* for Piano (1965); *Cantilaţii (Cantillations)* for Orch. (Cluj, March 23, 1968); Flute Sonata (1967); *Episodes* for Flute, Marimba, Vibraphone, and Percussion (1968); *Melopee* for Solo Flute (1968); *Polifonie* for 7 Instrumental Groups (1968); *Strofe* for Chorus, Brass, and Percussion (1968); *Graphie musicale* for One or 2 Pianos (1969; of variable duration); 2 cantatas (1969, 1970); *Postlude* for Orch. (1970); String Quartet (1971); choruses; songs.

Herman, Woody (real given names, **Woodrow Charles**), American clarinetist and bandleader; b. Milwaukee, May 16, 1913. He studied there and at Marquette Univ. In 1931 he joined a jazz band as a clarinet player, and in 1937 formed his first band; has had several since then, most being called "Herds"; i.e., the First Herd, Second Herd, etc. In the mid-1940s Herman's was the first prominent big band to make the transition from swing to a more advanced, bebop-influenced idiom characterized by "progressive" harmonies; it became known as "progressive jazz." On March 25, 1946, he presented in Carnegie Hall the first performance of Stravinsky's *Ebony Concerto,* written specially for him. He is also the composer of numerous popular songs.
BIBLIOGRAPHY: E. Edwards, *Woody Herman and the Swinging Herd, 1959–1966* (Los Angeles, 1966).

Hermann, Hans, German composer; b. Leipzig, Aug. 17, 1870; d. Berlin, May 18, 1931. He studied with W. Rust in Leipzig, E. Kretschmer in Dresden, and H. von Herzogenberg in Berlin; from the age of 18, played the double bass in various European orchs.; then taught at the Klindworth-Scharwenka Cons. in Berlin (1901–7). From 1907–27, he lived in Dresden; then returned to Berlin. He publ. some 100 songs, of which several became fairly well known (*Drei Wanderer, Alte Landsknechte,* etc.); he had a flair for imitating the simple style of the folk ballad; he further wrote a Symph., subtitled *Lebensepisoden;* a stage work, *Der rote Pimpernell;* pieces for clarinet with piano, etc.

Hermann, Robert, Swiss composer; b. Bern, April 29, 1869; d. Ambach, Bavaria, Oct. 22, 1912. He studied in Frankfurt; as a youth, developed an original approach to composition; he met Grieg, who encouraged him; studied briefly with Humperdinck; his Symph. was performed by the Berlin Phil. Orch. (Nov. 7, 1895), and other works followed.
  BIBLIOGRAPHY: W. Niemann, "Robert Hermann," in *Monographien moderner Musiker,* III (Leipzig, 1909).

Hermannus (surnamed **Contractus** on account of his paralyzed limbs), Swabian theoretician and composer; b. Saulgau, July 18, 1013; d. Altshausen, near Biberach, Sept. 24, 1054. He was the son of Hermann, Count of Vehringen. He was a student in the Reichenau monastery; under the guidance of his tutor, Abbot Berno, he acquired wide learning. In 1043 he entered the Benedictine order. His best-known work (containing valuable historical notices on music) is a chronology from the time of Christ to 1054. It has been republ. several times, and is to be found in Peres's (Pertz's) *Monumenta* (vol. V). Hermannus was the author of *Opuscula musica,* in which he gives a thorough discussion of the church modes and criticizes the Daseian notation used in the 10th-century tract *Musica enchiriadis.* He proposed his own notation by Greek and Latin letters. In the indication of a change in pitch, it had an advantage over neume notation. Hermannus's notation is written above the neume notation in some MSS of the 11th and 12th centuries in the Munich Library. He was the composer of the Gregorian Marian antiphons *Salve Regina* and *Alma Redemptoris Mater.* A transcription (into modern notation) of his *Versus ad discernendum cantum* is to be found in A. Schering's *Geschichte der Musik in Beispielen* (no. 7).
  BIBLIOGRAPHY: W. Brambach, *Hermanni Contracti Musica* (Leipzig, 1884); Leonard Ellinwood, *Musica Hermanni Contracti* (Rochester, N.Y., 1936), gives the Latin text, ed. after both the Vienna MS and an 11th-century MS now at the Eastman School, Rochester, N.Y., an Eng. trans., and commentary; H. Oesch, *Berno und Hermann von Reichenau als Musiktheoretiker* (Bern, 1961); R. Crocker, "Hermann's Major Sixth," *Journal of the American Musicological Society* (Spring 1972).

Hermanson, Åke, Swedish composer; b. Mollösund, June 16, 1923. He studied piano and organ in Göteborg and Stockholm; took courses in composition with Hilding Rosenberg (1950–52). In his music he follows a type of concentrated brevity marked by an alternation of short contrasting motifs; Hermanson defines this usage as "pendulum dynamics."
  WORKS: *Lyrical Metamorphoses* for String Quartet (1957–58); *A due voci* for Flute and Viola (1957–58); *Invoco* for Strings (Norrköping, May 24,

1961); *Stadier* for Soprano, Flute, Bass Clarinet, Viola, and Percussion (1960–61); *Suoni d'un flauto* for Solo Alto Flute (1961); *In nuce* (*In a Nutshell*) for Orch. (1962–63; the title is justified, for the piece takes barely 3 minutes to play; first perf., Stockholm, Oct. 9, 1964); *Nenia bahusiensis* for Children's Chorus a cappella (1963); Symph. No. 1 (1964–67; Stockholm, Oct. 29, 1967); *Appel I–IV* for Orch. (1968–69; first complete perf., Swedish Radio, Dec. 12, 1970); *Alarme* for Solo Horn (1969); *In sono* for Flute, Oboe, or English Horn, Viola, and Cello (1970); *Ultima* for Orch. (Swedish Radio, Nov. 18, 1972); *Flauto d'inverno* for Bass Flute Solo (1976); Symph. No. 2 (Stockholm, Sept. 26, 1976). *Ars lineae* for 6 Wind Instruments (1976); *Thrice* for Oboe, Clarinet, and Trombone (1976–79); *Bild* for Tenor and Trombone (1978–79); *Äggjakten* for Narrator, Tenor Saxophone, Guitar, and Percussion (1979); Symph. No. 3 (1980); *La Strada* for Horn and Organ (1980).

Hermesdorff, Michael, German musicologist; b. Trier (Trèves), March 4, 1833; d. there, Jan. 1885. He entered the priesthood, and was appointed organist of Trier Cathedral. He founded the Choral Society, chiefly for the exposition of Gregorian plainchant, on which he was an authority by virtue of his study of original sources. He edited the *Graduale ad usum Romanum cantus S. Gregorii* (Leipzig, 1876–82, 10 nos.) in the monthly supplements of the *Cäcilia* journal, but died before its completion. He revised the 2nd edition of Lück's collection of sacred compositions (4 vols.); publ. a German trans. of the *Micrologus* and *Epistola* of Guido d'Arezzo; a *Kyriale; Harmonica cantus choralis a* 4; a *Graduale;* several anthems and *Praefatio* (prayers used in the Trier diocese); and 3 masses of his own composition.

Hermstedt, (Johann) Simon, famous German clarinetist; b. Langensalza, Dec. 29, 1778; d. Sondershausen, Aug. 10, 1846. He was educated at the Annaberg school for soldiers' children; studied with Knoblauch and Baer; became a clarinetist in the Langensalza regiment; then conducted a military band in Langensalza. He made improvements in his instrument; composed concertos, variations, and other pieces for clarinet. Spohr wrote a Clarinet Concerto for him.

Hernández, Hermilio, Mexican composer; b. Autlán, Jalisco, Feb. 2, 1931. He studied music with José Valadez and Domingo Lobato at the Escuela Superior Diocesana de Música Sagrada in Guadalajara, graduating in 1956; then studied in Italy and Paris.
  WORKS: *Cantata Adviento* (1953); *5 Pieces* for Orch. (1955); Violin Concerto (1960); *Sonata* for Chamber Orch. (1964); *Suite* for Violin and Piano (1952); String Quartet (1954); Piano Trio (1955); Cello Sonata (1962); Wind Quintet (1965); *Poliédros* for Oboe, Bassoon, and Piano (1969); *Music for 4 Instruments* for Flute, Violin, Cello, and Piano (1970); 2 piano sonatinas (1955, 1971); *Tema transfigurado* for Piano (1962); *6 Inventions* for Piano (1968);

Piano Sonata (1970); *Diálogos* for 2 Pianos (1970); *Fantasia* for Organ (1970); songs.

Hernández, Pablo, Spanish composer; b. Saragossa, Jan. 25, 1834; d. Madrid, Dec. 10, 1910. He was first a church chorister; at 14 played organ at the San Gil church in Saragossa. At 22 he went to Madrid to study with Eslava at the Madrid Cons.; graduated with a gold medal (1861), and joined the faculty in 1863 as a singing teacher. He wrote 2 zarzuelas: *Gimnasio higienico* and *Un Sevillano en la Habana;* also many sacred works.

Hernández-López, Rhazés, Venezuelan composer and musicologist; b. Petare, June 30, 1918. He studied in Caracas with Vicente Emilio Sojo and Juan Bautista Plaza. Apart from composition, he engaged in teaching and radio work.
WORKS: In his series of piano pieces under the title *Casualismo* he applies the 12-tone method of composition. Other works include *Las Torres desprevenidas,* symph. poem (1951); *Sonorritmo* for Orch. (1953); *Mérida, geografía celeste,* symph. suite (1958); *Expansión tres* for Orch. (1965); *Tres dimensiones* for Strings (1967); *Cuadros* for Flute, Violin, Viola, Cello, and Harp (1950); Viola Sonata (1952); *Tres espacios* for Violin, Cello, and Piano (1965); *Horizontal* for Flute and Strings (1966); piano pieces; songs.

Hernández Moncada, Eduardo, Mexican composer; b. Jalapa, Sept. 24, 1899. He studied with Rafael Tello at the National Cons. in Mexico City. He conducted theater orchs.; in 1936 became assistant conductor of the Orquesta Sinfónica in Mexico. As a composer he made an impression with his Symph., first performed in Mexico City (July 31, 1942). His ballet *Ixtepec* (1945) employs Mexican rhythms.

Hernándo (y Palomar), Rafael (José María), Spanish composer; b. Madrid, May 31, 1822; d. there, July 10, 1888. He studied with Carnicer and Saldoni at the Madrid Cons. (1837–43); then went to Paris, where he took lessons with Auber. His *Stabat Mater* was performed there, and a grand opera, *Romilda,* was accepted for performance at the Théâtre des Italiens, but the revolutionary upheaval of 1848 prevented its production. Hernándo returned to Madrid, where he produced a number of zarzuelas, of which the most successful was *El duende* (June 6, 1849); others were *Palo de ciego* (Feb. 15, 1849); *Colegialas y soldados* (March 21, 1849); *Bertoldo y Comparsa* (May 23, 1850); *Cosas de Juan* (Sept. 9, 1854); *El tambor* (April 28, 1860); *Aurora;* etc.; he also collaborated with Barbieri, Oudrid, and Gaztambide in *Escenas de Chamberi* (Nov. 19, 1850) and *Don Simplicio Bobadilla* (May 7, 1853). In 1852 he became secretary of the Madrid Cons.; later taught harmony there.

Hernried, Robert, writer on music and composer; b. Vienna, Sept. 22, 1883; d. Detroit, Sept. 3, 1951. He studied at the Univ. of Vienna; for some years conducted opera at provincial theaters (1908–14); taught theory at the Mannheim Academy of Music (1919–22), at the Cons. of Heidelberg (1923), in Erfurt, and in Berlin. In 1934 he went to Vienna; in 1939, to the U.S.; he taught in N.Y.; Davenport, Iowa; Dickinson, N.Dak.; and Fort Wayne, Ind. In 1946 he became a prof. of music at the Detroit Inst. of Musical Art. He wrote 2 operas, *Francesca da Rimini* and *Die Bäuerin;* about 75 choral works; a Mass; some characteristic pieces for orch., etc.; publ. a monograph on Jaques-Dalcroze (Geneva, 1929); a biography of Brahms (Leipzig, 1934); and 2 theoretical works, *Allgemeine Musiklehre* (Berlin, 1932) and *Systematische Modulationslehre* (Berlin, 1935; 2nd ed., 1948).

Herold, (Louis-Joseph) Ferdinand, celebrated French composer; b. Paris, Jan. 28, 1791; d. Thernes, near Paris, Jan. 19, 1833. His father, **François-Joseph Hérold** (pupil of C.P.E. Bach), a piano teacher and composer, did not desire his son to become a musician, and sent him to the Hix school, where his aptitude for music was noticed by Fétis, then assistant teacher there. After his father's death (1802), Herold began to study music seriously; in 1806 he entered the Paris Cons., taking piano lessons with Louis Adam, and winning first prize for piano playing in 1810. He studied harmony under Catel, and (from 1811) composition under Méhul; in 1812 his cantata *Mlle. de la Vallière* won the Prix de Rome (the MS score is in the Cons. library, with works composed during his 3 years' study in Rome). From Rome he went to Naples, where he became pianist to Queen Caroline; here he produced his first opera, *La gioventù di Enrico Quinto* (Jan. 5, 1815), which was well received. From Naples he went to Vienna, and after a few months' stay returned to Paris, where he finished the score of Boieldieu's *Charles de France,* an "opéra d'occasion" (Opéra-Comique, June 18, 1816), and where all the rest of his operas were produced. The flattering reception of *Charles de France* led to the successful production of *Les Rosières* (Jan. 27, 1817), *La Clochette* (Oct. 18, 1817), *Le Premier Venu* (Sept. 28, 1818), *Les Troqueurs* (Feb. 18, 1819), and *L'Auteur mort et vivant* (Dec. 18, 1820); the failure of the last-named opera caused him to distrust his natural talent, and to imitate, in several succeeding stage works, the style then in vogue—that of Rossini. With the comic opera *Marie* (Aug. 12, 1826) Herold returned, however, to his true element, and won instant and brilliant success. Meantime he had obtained the post of chorus master at the Italian Opera (1824); during this period he brought out *Le Muletier* (May 12, 1823), *Lasthénie* (Sept. 8, 1823), *Vendôme en Espagne* (Dec. 5, 1823), *Le Roi René* (Aug. 24, 1824), and *Le Lapin blanc* (May 21, 1825). In 1826 he was appointed to the staff of the Grand Opéra, for which he wrote several melodious and elegant ballets: *Astolphe et Jaconde* (Jan. 29, 1827); *La Somnambule* (Sept. 19, 1827); *Lydie* (July 2, 1828); *La Fille mal gardée* (Nov. 17, 1828); *La Belle au bois dormant* (April 27, 1829); *La Noce de village* (Feb. 11, 1830). *La Somnambule* furnished Bellini with the subject of his popular opera. On July 18, 1829, Herold produced *L'Illusion,* a one-act opera full of charming numbers. *Emmeline,* a grand opera (Nov. 28, 1829), was a failure, but his next opera, *Zampa* (May 3, 1831), was sensationally successful and placed Herold in the first rank of French composers. He then wrote *L'Auberge d'Aurey* (May 11, 1830) jointly with Carafa; *La Marquise de Brinvilliers* (Oct. 31, 1831) in collaboration with Auber, Batton, Berton, Blangini, Boieldieu, Carafa, Cherubini, and Paër; also produced *La Médecine sans médecin* (Oct. 15, 1832). His last work publ. in his lifetime, *Le Pré aux clercs* (Dec. 15, 1832), had a remarkable vogue. He died of consumption shortly before his 42nd birthday. His unfinished opera *Ludovic* was completed by Halévy and produced posthumously at the Opéra-Comique on May 16, 1833. Herold's piano music (55 opus numbers) consists of sonatas, caprices, rondos, divertissements, fantasies, variations, and potpourris.

BIBLIOGRAPHY: B. Jouvin, *Herold, sa vie et ses œuvres* (Paris, 1868); Hector Berlioz, *Les Musiciens et la musique* (Paris, 1903); A. Pougin, *Herold* (Paris, 1906).

Herold, Vilhelm, Danish tenor; b. Hasle, March 19, 1865; d. Copenhagen, Dec. 15, 1937. He studied in Copenhagen and Paris; made his debut at the Royal Danish Theater in Copenhagen in 1893 as Faust; was a member of the Royal Theater in Stockholm (1901–3; 1907–9); also made guest appearances in London, Berlin, Dresden, and Hamburg. He served as director of the Royal Danish Theater (1922–24).

Heron-Allen, Edward, English writer on the violin; b. London, Dec. 17, 1861; d. Selsey, Sussex, March 28, 1943. He was the author of a standard manual on the history of violin manufacture: *Violin-Making, As It Was and Is* (London, 1884).

Herrera, Luis de la Fuente, Mexican conductor and composer; b. Mexico City, April 26, 1916. He studied piano and violin; took composition lessons with Rodolfo Halffter. From 1954 to 1972 he served as principal conductor of the National Symph. Orch. in Mexico City; in the interim he led the National Symph. Orch. of Peru (1965–71); was guest conductor of orchs. in the U.S., Canada, Europe, and New Zealand; in 1978 was appointed music director of the Oklahoma Symph. Orch. in Oklahoma City.

WORKS: Opera, *Cuauhtemoc;* ballets, *La Estrella y la Sirena* and *Fronteras;* he also composed chamber music.

Herriot, Edouard, French statesman and writer on music; b. Troyes, July 5, 1872; d. Lyons, March 26, 1957. He entered politics as a member of the Radical Party; was premier of France 3 times between 1924 and 1932; then became president of the Chamber of Deputies. He was arrested in 1942 for refusing to cooperate with the Vichy Government, deported to Germany, and held in a castle near Potsdam until the end of the war. Returning to France, he resumed his activities; in 1946, he was elected to the French Academy. He was the author of a popular biography, *La Vie de Beethoven* (Paris, 1929; many eds.), publ. in Eng. as *The Life and Times of Beethoven* (N.Y., 1935).

Herrmann, Bernard, American conductor and outstanding composer for films; b. New York, June 29, 1911; d. Los Angeles, Dec. 24, 1975. He won a composition prize at the age of 13; then enrolled at N.Y. Univ., where he studied with Philip James and Percy Grainger; later took courses with Wagenaar in composition and Albert Stoessel in conducting at the Juilliard Graduate School of Music. In 1934 he was appointed to the staff of the Columbia Broadcasting System as a composer of background music for radio programs and conductor of the CBS Symph. Orch. summer radio series; from 1940 till 1955 he was chief conductor of the CBS Symph. Orch. in boldly progressive programs of modern works, including those by Charles Ives. He became associated with Orson Welles and wrote several film scores for the radio broadcasts of the Mercury Theater. His music for *Citizen Kane* (1940), the first of his 61 film scores, is still regarded as a classic of the genre. His use of an electric violin and electric bass in the score for *The Day the Earth Stood Still* (1951) is an example of early application of electronic music in films. He subsequently wrote film scores for the thrillers of Alfred Hitchcock, succeeding in capturing the eerie spirit of Hitchcock's peculiar art by the use of atonal devices; of these, the score for *Psycho* (1960), for strings only, was particularly apt. Among Herrmann's other film scores were *The Devil and Daniel Webster* (1941; also known as *All that Money Can Buy;* received an Academy Award); *Jane Eyre* (1942); *Anna and the King of Siam* (1946); *The Ghost and Mrs. Muir* (1948); *Snows of Kilimanjaro* (1952); *Garden of Evil* (1954); *The Trouble with Harry* (1955); *The Man Who Knew Too Much* (1956); *The Wrong Man* (1957); *Vertigo* (1958); *North by Northwest* (1959); *The Man in the Gray Flannel Suit* (1956); *The 7th Voyage of Sinbad* (1958); *Journey to the Center of the Earth* (1959); *The Birds* (1963); *Fahrenheit 451* (1966); *La Mariée était en noir* (*The Bride Wore Black,* 1967); *Sisters* (1973); and *Obsession* (1975). Herrmann spent the last 10 years of his life in England, but was in Los Angeles in Dec. 1975 to conduct the score for his last film, *Taxi Driver;* he died in his sleep shortly after completing the final recording session. His concert works include the 4-act opera *Wuthering Heights* (1948–50; recorded in England in 1966; first complete stage perf., Portland, Oreg., Nov. 6, 1982); 2 Christmas operas for television: *A Christmas Carol* (CBS Television, N.Y., Dec. 23, 1954) and *A Child Is Born;* 2 cantatas: *Moby Dick* (N.Y., April 11, 1940) and *Johnny Appleseed* (1940). For Orch.: *The City of Brass,* symph. poem (1934); *Sinfonietta* for Strings (1935); *Currier and Ives,* suite (1935); *Nocturne and Scherzo* (1936); *Fiddle Concerto* (1940); Symph. No. 1 (1940; N.Y. Phil., Nov. 12, 1942); *For the Fallen* (N.Y. Phil., Dec. 16, 1943, composer conducting); *The Fantasticks* for Vocal Quartet and Orch. (1944). He also wrote a String

Quartet (1932); *Aubade* for 14 Instruments (1933); *Echoes* for String Quartet (1966); clarinet quintet, *Souvenirs de Voyage* (1967).

Herrmann, Eduard, conductor and composer; b. Oberrotweil, Germany, Dec. 18, 1850; d. Miami, Fla., April 24, 1937. He studied violin with Joachim in Berlin; played in various German orchs.; in 1878–81 he was concertmaster of the Imperial Orch. in St. Petersburg. In 1881 he settled in N.Y.; formed a quartet with Schenck, Lilienthal, and Hauser, which enjoyed an excellent reputation; one of their features was the annual performance of all of Beethoven's quartets. He wrote a Violin Concerto; String Quintet; String Quartet; Sextet for Oboe, Clarinet, and Strings; etc.

Herrmann, Hugo, German composer; b. Ravensburg, April 19, 1896; d. Stuttgart, Sept. 7, 1967. He acquired primary knowledge of music without systematic study; was drafted into the German army during World War I and severely wounded in 1918. After the Armistice he took courses in composition with Schreker in Berlin. In 1923 he went to the U.S. and was employed as a church organist; in 1925 he returned to Germany; from 1935 to 1962 he was director of a music school in Trossingen. A believer in practical art, he promoted community music; took especial interest in the accordion and wrote several works for this instrument; he also composed pieces for the mouth organ. He also wrote several operas: *Gazellenhorn; Picknick; Vasantasena; Das Wunder; Paracelsus; Der Rekord; Der Überfall; Die Heinzelmännchen;* 5 symphs.; 5 string quartets, etc. He publ. a manual, *Einführung in die Satztechnik für Mundharmonika-Instrumente* (Trossingen, 1958), containing instructions for performance on the mouth organ.
BIBLIOGRAPHY: A Festschrift, *Hugo Herrmann, Leben und Werk,* was publ. for his 60th birthday (Trossingen, 1956; ed. by Armin Fett).

Herschel, Friedrich Wilhelm, eminent astronomer; b. Hannover, Nov. 15, 1738; d. Slough, near Windsor, Aug. 25, 1822. The son of a military musician, he was brought up as a musician, like his 3 brothers. At 14 years of age he entered the band of the Hannoverian Guards as an oboist, and was stationed at Durham when that regiment went to England (1755). He later played organ at the Halifax parish church. In 1766 he was employed at the Octagon Chapel in Bath. He devoted his leisure to astronomy, constructed the great "Herschel" telescope, discovered the planet Uranus, was appointed "Astronomer Royal" (1781), and abandoned the musical profession. He received the honor of knighthood (1816) and an Oxford degree. He composed a Symph. and 2 concertos for Wind Instruments.

Herseth Adolph, outstanding American trumpeter; b. Lake Park, Minn., July 25, 1921. He studied with Marcel LaFosse and Georges Mager in Boston (1946–48); in 1948 he was appointed first trumpeter

of the Chicago Symph. Orch., a position he held with distinction for more than a quarter of a century. He also made many appearances as a soloist.

Hertog, Johannes den, Dutch conductor and composer; b. Amsterdam, Jan. 20, 1904. He studied with his father, Herman Johannes den Hertog; then with Cornelis Dopper. He occupied various posts as an operatic coach; was director and conductor of the Wagner Society in Amsterdam; in 1938–41 was assistant conductor of the Concertgebouw; also conducted at The Hague; in 1948 he was appointed conductor of the Flemish Opera in Antwerp, and in 1960 he became artistic director of the Netherlands Opera in Amsterdam. He wrote an opera, *Pygmalion* (1957); a musical play, *Pandora* (1968); a number of songs; and some orch. pieces.

Hertz, Alfred, eminent German-American conductor; b. Frankfurt, July 15, 1872; d. San Francisco, April 17, 1942. After completing his academic studies he entered the Raff Cons., where he studied with Anton Urspruch; then held positions as an opera conductor in Altenburg (1892–95), Barmen-Elberfeld (1895–99), and Breslau (1899–1902). In 1902 he was engaged as conductor of the German repertoire at the Metropolitan Opera; he conducted the first American performance of *Parsifal* (Dec. 24, 1903), which took place against the wishes of the Wagner family; consequently, Hertz could no longer obtain permission to conduct Wagner in Germany. He made his Covent Garden debut in 1910. In 1915 he was engaged to lead the San Francisco Symph. Orch.; he retained that post until 1930. He also organized the summer series of concerts at the Hollywood Bowl (1922), and conducted more than 100 concerts there; he was affectionately known as the "Father of the Hollywood Bowl."

Hertzka, Emil, Austrian music publisher; b. Budapest, Aug. 3, 1869; d. Vienna, May 9, 1932. He studied chemistry at the Univ. of Vienna; also took courses in music. He was engaged on the staff of the music publisher Weinberger in Vienna (1893); then joined Universal Edition, organized in 1901. In 1907 he became its director, and remained in that capacity until his death. He purchased the catalogues of other music publishing firms: the Wiener Philharmonischer Verlag and the Albert J. Gutmann Co. (which publ. Bruckner and Mahler), and acquired the rights of publication to works by many celebrated modern composers (Bartók, Schoenberg, Alban Berg, Kurt Weill, Krenek); also represented Soviet composers. An impassioned believer in the eventual worth of experimental music, he encouraged young composers, took active part in the organization of concerts of modern music, etc. An Emil Hertzka Foundation was established by his family after his death, for the purpose of helping unknown composers secure performances and publication of their works.

Hertzmann, Erich, German-American musicologist; b. Krefeld, Germany, Dec. 14, 1902; d. Berkeley,

Calif., March 3, 1963. He studied music at the Hoch Cons. in Frankfurt; then took courses with several eminent teachers (J. Wolf, Abert, Schering, Sachs, Hornbostel, and Friedrich Blume) at the Univ. of Berlin, where he obtained his doctorate with a dissertation on Willaert (1931). In 1938 he emigrated to the U.S., and joined the faculty of Columbia Univ.; also lectured at Princeton Univ. (1946–49). In 1949 he held a Guggenheim fellowship; in 1955 received a stipend from Columbia Univ. to study the creative processes of Beethoven. Apart from his dissertation on Willaert, he publ. numerous articles in German and American music journals, mostly dealing with structural analysis of classical scores.

Hervé (properly, **Florimond Ronger**), French dramatic composer, the creator of French operetta; b. Houdain, near Arras, June 30, 1825; d. Paris, Nov. 3, 1892. He was a chorister and scholar of St.-Roch; became organist at various churches in Paris. With his friend Kelm, in 1848, he sang in *Don Quichotte et Sancho Pansa,* an interlude of his own composition, at the Opéra National. In 1851 he conducted the orch. at the Palais Royal; in 1855 he opened the Folies-Concertantes, a small theater for the production of pantomimes, *saynètes* (musical comediettas for 2 persons), etc., and, with phenomenal activity, developed the light French operetta from these diminutive and frivolous pieces, writing both librettos and music, conducting the orch., and often appearing as an actor on the stage. From 1856 to 1869 he led this feverish life in Paris, producing his works at various theaters, and responding to failures by doubling his efforts. In 1870–71, when the Franco-Prussian War and the Commune stopped theatrical activities in Paris, he went to London, where he produced several of his light operas; he revisited London many times afterward. In all, he wrote about 50 operettas, of which only one became a universal success, *Mam'zelle Nitouche* (Paris, Jan. 26, 1883, followed by numerous productions in European cities); other fairly successful works were *L'Œil crevé* (Paris, Oct. 12, 1867) and *Le Petit Faust* (Paris, April 28, 1869). He also wrote a grand opera, *Les Chevaliers de la table ronde* (Paris, Nov. 17, 1866); the ballets *Sport, La Rose d'Amour, Les Bagatelles,* etc.
BIBLIOGRAPHY: L. Schneider, *Les Maîtres de l'opérette française, Hervé et Charles Lecocq* (Paris, 1924).

Hervey, Arthur, composer and writer; b. (of Irish parentage) Paris, Jan. 26, 1855; d. London, March 10, 1922. At first intended for the diplomatic service, he embraced a musical career in 1880; was a critic for *Vanity Fair* (1889–92); in 1892–1908, was on the staff of the London *Morning Post.*
WRITINGS: *Masters of French Music* (London, 1894); *French Music in the XIXth Century* (1904); *Alfred Bruneau* (1907); *Franz Liszt and His Music* (1911); *Meyerbeer* (1913); *Rubinstein* (1913); *Saint-Saëns* (1921); etc.

Hervig, Richard, American composer and teacher; b. Story City, Iowa, Nov. 24, 1917. He studied with Philip Greeley Clapp at the Univ. of Iowa; in 1955 was appointed to its faculty. He wrote 2 symphs., 2 clarinet sonatas, choral music, and piano pieces.

Herz, Henri, brilliant Austrian pianist; b. Vienna, Jan. 6, 1803; d. Paris, Jan. 5, 1888. He was taught by his father, and by Hünten at Coblenz; later (1816) by Pradher, Reicha, and Dourlen at the Paris Cons.; he won first piano prize; improved himself in Moscheles's style after that virtuoso's visit in 1821; was in high repute as a fashionable teacher and composer, his compositions realizing 3 and 4 times the price of those of his superior contemporaries. In 1831 he made a tour of Germany with the violinist Lafont; visited London in 1834, where at his first concert Moscheles and Cramer played duets with him. In 1842, he was appointed a piano prof. at the Paris Cons. He suffered financial losses through partnership with a piano manufacturer, Klepfer, and thereupon undertook a concert tour through the U.S., Mexico, and the West Indies (1845–51). Returning, he established a successful piano factory, his instruments receiving first prize at the Paris Exhibition of 1855. He resigned his professorship at the Cons. in 1874. Herz acknowledged that he courted the popular taste; his numerous works (over 200) include piano concertos, variations, sonatas, rondos, violin sonatas, nocturnes, dances, marches, fantasias, etc. He publ. an interesting and vivid book, *Mes voyages en Amérique* (1866), a reprint of his letters to the *Moniteur Universel.*
BIBLIOGRAPHY: A. Loesser, *Men, Women, and Pianos* (N.Y., 1954); H.C. Schonberg, *The Great Pianists* (N.Y., 1963).

Herz, Joachim, German opera producer and administrator; b. Dresden, June 15, 1924. He was educated at the Hochschule für Musik in Dresden; also studied in Berlin. From 1953 to 1956 he was assistant producer to Walter Felsenstein at the East Berlin Komische Oper. In 1957 he joined the Leipzig Opera as producer; from 1959 to 1976 was its director. In 1976 he was named director of the Komische Oper in Berlin. He has also served as an opera producer in many of the major European music centers. With Walter Felsenstein, he wrote the book *Musiktheater: Beiträge zur Methodik und zu Inszenierungskonzeptionen* (Leipzig, 1976).
BIBLIOGRAPHY: H.-J. Irmer and W. Stein, *Joachim Herz, Regisseur im Musiktheater* (Berlin, 1977).

Herzog, Emilie, Swiss soprano; b. Ermatingen, Switzerland, Dec. 17, 1859; d. Aarburg, Switzerland, Sept. 16, 1923. She studied voice in Zürich and Munich; made a debut in a minor role at the Munich Opera in 1880, and afterward sang in other German opera houses, including Bayreuth. In 1889 she was engaged at the Berlin Opera, where she became one of the best interpreters of soubrette roles; she also gave recitals in Germany as a lieder singer. She made guest appearances in the opera houses of London, Paris, Vienna, and Brussels, and in 1896 sang at the Bolshoi Theater in Moscow; she also sang for a season at the Metropolitan Opera in N.Y. (1899–1900). Returning to Europe, she continued to sing at the Berlin Opera (until 1910); then taught at the Zürich Cons. (1910–22).

Herzog, George, Hungarian-born American ethnomusicologist; b. Budapest, Dec. 11, 1901. He studied musicology and anthropology in Budapest and Berlin; in 1925 he went to America; became a research associate in anthropology at the Univ. of Chicago in 1929; was a member (1930–31) of its expedition to Liberia, where he made a thorough study of West African music; then was on the faculty of Yale Univ. (1932–35); was a visiting lecturer at Columbia Univ. in 1936–37, and took his Ph.D. there in 1937 with the dissertation *A Comparison of Pueblo and Pima Musical Styles;* subsequently was a visiting assistant prof. there (1937–38), and then an assistant prof. of anthropology (1939–48). In 1948 he was appointed prof. of anthropology and folk music at Indiana Univ. in Bloomington; was made prof. emeritus in 1962. He publ. numerous informative papers on the folk music of American Indian tribes. The most important of these is *Research in Primitive and Folk Music in the United States: A Survey* (Washington, D.C., 1936).
BIBLIOGRAPHY: B. Krader, "George Herzog: A Bibliography," *Ethnomusicology Newsletter,* 1 (1956).

Herzog, Johann Georg, German organist and composer; b. Hummendorf, near Kronach, Aug. 5, 1822; d. Munich, Feb. 3, 1909. He studied at the music school in Schmölz, in Bavaria, and at the age of 11 began to earn a living playing the organ. In 1843 he went to Munich, where he was a church organist, and later (1850) a prof. at the Munich Cons.; among his pupils was Rheinberger. In 1854, he went to Erlangen; established a series of historical organ concerts there (1861–65); he then returned to Munich. He wrote a great number of organ works; also practical manuals.

Herzog, Sigmund, pianist; b. Budapest, June 13, 1868; d. New York, Aug. 28, 1932. He studied with Julius Epstein at the Vienna Cons., graduating in 1885; later with Rafael Joseffy in N.Y., where he then taught at the Inst. of Musical Art. He publ. *The Art of Octave-Playing* and various piano pieces.

Herzogenberg, Heinrich von, Austrian pianist and composer; b. Graz, June 10, 1843; d. Wiesbaden, Oct. 9, 1900. He studied with Dessoff at the Vienna Cons.; then lived in Graz; went to Leipzig in 1872; with Spitta, Holstein, and Volkland, he founded the Bach-Verein there (1874); was its conductor from 1875–85; then was a prof. of composition at the Hochschule für Musik in Berlin (1885–88); was director of the Meisterschule (1889–92 and 1897–1900). He was a very prolific composer; his chief influences were Brahms and Bruch.
WORKS: Oratorios: *Die Geburt Christi; Die Passion; Erntefeier;* choral works with Orch.: *Der Stern*
des Liedes; Die Weihe der Nacht; Nannas Klage; Totenfeier; and several Psalms and motets; cantata, *Columbus;* symph. poem, *Odysseus;* 2 symphs.; Piano Quintet; String Quintet; 5 string quartets; Quartet for Piano, Horn, Clarinet, and Bassoon; 2 piano quartets; 2 piano trios; 2 string trios; Trio for Piano, Oboe, and Horn; 3 violin sonatas; 3 cello sonatas; several works for piano, 4-hands; fantasies for organ. Herzogenberg's wife, **Elisabet,** née **von Stockhausen** (b. Paris, April 13, 1847; d. San Remo, Jan. 7, 1892), was an excellent pianist. They were great friends of Brahms, with whom they maintained a long correspondence (see M. Kalbeck, *Johannes Brahms im Briefwechsel mit Heinrich und Elisabet von Herzogenberg,* 1907).
BIBLIOGRAPHY: J.H. Spengel, *Heinrich von Herzogenberg in seinen Vokalwerken* (Leipzig, 1893); W. Altmann, *Heinrich von Herzogenberg, Sein Leben und Schaffen* (Leipzig, 1903). J. Rieter-Biedermann publ. a complete catalogue of Herzogenberg's works (1900).

Hesch, Wilhelm (real name, **Vilém Heš**), Bohemian bass; b. Týnec nad Labem, July 3, 1860; d. Vienna, Jan. 3, 1908. He made his debut in Brno in 1880; then sang in Prague and Hamburg (1893); was a principal member of the Vienna Court Opera (1895–1908). He gained distinction for his outstanding performances of Wagnerian roles.

Heseltine, Philip (pen name, **Peter Warlock**), brilliant English composer and writer; b. London, Oct. 30, 1894; d. there, Dec. 17, 1930. He studied at Eton with Colin Taylor (1908–10); a meeting with Delius in France in 1910 influenced him profoundly in the direction of composition; he adopted a style that was intimately connected with English traditions of the Elizabethan period and yet revealed impressionistic undertones in harmonic writing. Another influence was that of Bernard van Dieren, from whom he absorbed an austerely contrapuntal technique. He publ. all his musical works under the name Peter Warlock. He was a conscientious objector during World War I; in 1917 was in Ireland; after the Armistice returned to London; in 1920 he founded the progressive journal of musical opinion *The Sackbut;* wrote criticism; made transcriptions of old English music; participated in organizing the Delius Festival in 1929. Suffering from depression, he committed suicide by gas in his London flat.
WRITINGS: (under the name Philip Heseltine): *Frederick Delius* (London, 1923; revised ed. by Hubert Foss, London, 1952); *Carlo Gesualdo, Prince of Venosa, Musician and Murderer* (in collaboration with Cecil Gray; London, 1926); a pamphlet of 8 pages, *Thomas Whythorne: An Unknown Elizabethan Composer* (Oxford, 1927); as Peter Warlock, publ. a monograph, *The English Ayre* (London, 1926); ed. (with P. Wilson) 300 old songs (*English Ayres, Elizabethan and Jacobean; French Ayres*); was co-editor of *Oxford Choral Songs* and the *Oxford Orchestral Series,* a collection of old English and Italian dances; transcribed for piano some lute music of John Dowland, *Forlorne Hope;* many other

transcriptions. Musical compositions: song cycle *The Curlew* (with Flute, English Horn, and String Quartet); *Saudades* (3 songs); *Lilligay* (5 songs); *Peterisms* (2 sets of 3 songs each); *Candlelight* (12 nursery songs), and many separate songs; *Capriol Suite* (on tunes from Arbeau's *Orchésographie*, in 2 versions: for String Orch. and Full Orch.); *Corpus Christi* (2 versions, for Chorus a cappella and for Soprano and Tenor Soli, with String Quartet); numerous other vocal works.

BIBLIOGRAPHY: Cecil Gray, *Peter Warlock: A Memoir of Philip Heseltine* (London, 1934); G. Cockshott, "A Note on Warlock's Capriol Suite," *Monthly Musical Record* (1940); idem, "Some Notes on the Songs of Peter Warlock," *Music & Letters* (July 1940); K. Avery, "The Chronology of Warlock's Songs," ibid. (Oct. 1948); F. Tomlinson, *A Peter Warlock Handbook* (2 vols., Rickmansworth, 1974, 1977); I. Copley, *The Music of Peter Warlock: A Critical Survey* (London, 1979).

Hess, Ludwig, German tenor; b. Marburg, March 23, 1877; d. Berlin, Feb. 5, 1944. He studied singing with Vidal in Milan; gave concerts of German lieder throughout Europe, specializing in the modern repertoire; made a successful tour of the U.S. and Canada in 1911; conducted a choral society in Königsberg (1917–20); then settled in Berlin. He was also a composer; wrote the operas *Abu und Nu* (Danzig, 1919) and *Vor Edens Pforte* (after Byron); *Kranion* (Erfurt, 1933); a Symph.; symph. poem, *Himmelskönig mit musizierenden Engeln* (after Hans Memling); *Ariadne*, a cantata; many choral works, and numerous songs. He publ. *Die Behandlung der Stimme vor, während und nach der Mutation* (Marburg, 1927).

Hess, Dame Myra, distinguished English pianist; b. London, Feb. 25, 1890; d. there, Nov. 25, 1965. She studied at the Royal Academy of Music with Tobias Matthay; made her concert debut in London on Nov. 14, 1907, at the age of 17, playing Beethoven's G-major Concerto with Thomas Beecham, and producing a highly favorable impression. She then embarked on a successful and steady career; made several tours in Germany and France; played recitals in America in 1922, repeating her American tours at regular intervals. She organized the National Gallery Concerts in 1939, continuing them through the war and the blitz. It was mainly for her work during this period that she was created a Dame of the British Empire by King George IV in 1941. Her playing was marked by classical precision and poetic imagination; although she was never attracted by the modern repertoire of her time, she occasionally performed piano music by contemporary British composers.

BIBLIOGRAPHY: D. Lassimonne and H. Ferguson, eds., *Myra Hess, By Her Friends* (London, 1966); M. McKenna, *Myra Hess: A Portrait* (London, 1976).

Hess, Willy, noted Swiss musicologist; b. Winterthur, Oct. 12, 1906. He studied piano and music theory at the Zürich Cons. and musicology at the Univ. of Zürich. He was also a professional bassoon player; from 1942–71 he played bassoon in the Winterthur Stadtorchester. As a musicologist, he devoted most of his effort to the compilation of a Beethoven catalogue. He edited a valuable *Verzeichnis der nicht der Gesamtausgabe veröffentlichen Werke Ludwig van Beethovens* (Wiesbaden, 1957); also edited the extensive supplement *Ludwig van Beethoven: Sämtliche Werke: Supplement zur Gesamtausgabe* (14 vols., Wiesbaden, 1959–71). His other important writings include *Ludwig van Beethoven* (Geneva, 1946); *Beethovens Oper Fidelio und ihre drei Fassungen* (Zürich, 1953); *Beethoven* (Zürich, 1956; 2nd ed., revised, 1976); *Die Harmonie der Künste* (Vienna, 1960); *Die Dynamik der musikalischen Formbildung* (2 vols., Vienna, 1960; 1964); *Vom Doppelantlitz des Bösen in der Kunst, dargestellt am Beispiel der Musik* (Munich, 1963); *Vom Metaphysischen im Künstlerischen* (Winterthur, 1963); *Parteilose Kunst, parteilose Wissenschaft* (Tutzing, 1967); *Beethoven-Studien* (Munich, 1972); also an autobiography, *Aus meinem Leben: Erlebnisse, Bekenntnisse, Betrachtungen* (Zürich, 1976). He was also a prolific composer; he wrote several fairy-tale operas, a Symph., a Sonata for Bassoon and Small Orch., a Horn Concerto, and numerous pieces of chamber music, including a curious work for double bassoon and string quartet.

Hess, Willy, German violinist; b. Mannheim, July 14, 1859; d. Berlin, Feb. 17, 1939. His first teacher was his father, who was a pupil of Spohr. As a child, he was taken to the U.S.; at the age of 9, he played with the Thomas Orch. He then studied with Joachim in Berlin; later occupied posts as concertmaster in Frankfurt (1878–86), Rotterdam, where he taught at the Cons. (1886–88), and in Manchester, England, with the Hallé Orch. (1888–95). From 1895 to 1903, he was a prof. of violin at the Cons. of Cologne; then taught at the Royal Academy of Music in London (1903–4); in 1904, he was engaged as concertmaster of the Boston Symph. Orch., and remained in that position until 1910; also organized the Hess Quartet in Boston. From 1910–28 he taught at the Hochschule für Musik in Berlin; he remained there until his death.

BIBLIOGRAPHY: F. Bonavia, "Willy Hess as Teacher," *Monthly Musical Record,* LXI (1931).

Hesse, Adolph (Friedrich), German organist and composer; b. Breslau, Aug. 30, 1808; d. there, Aug. 5, 1863. His father was an organ builder, and Hesse received his first instruction from him; he further profited by the advice of Hummel and Spohr. He was church organist at Breslau; visited Paris in 1844 for the inauguration of the new organ at St.-Eustache; his virtuoso handling of the pedal evoked praise. In 1851 he gave demonstrations of organ playing in London; then returned to Breslau; there he enjoyed a great reputation, not only as an organist, but also as conductor of the Breslau Symph. He publ. a collection, *Practical Organist*; his organ works were brought out by Steggall in a complete edition.

Hesse, Ernst Christian, German composer; b. Grossgottern, April 14, 1676; d. Darmstadt, May 16, 1762. He studied the viola da gamba, first at Darmstadt, then in Paris; gave successful demonstrations of his virtuosity in various European towns. In 1713, he married the opera singer **Johanna Döbricht.** He wrote 2 operas and many works for viola da gamba.

Hesse, Julius, German pianist; b. Hamburg, March 2, 1823; d. Berlin, April 5, 1881. He originated and successfully introduced a new measurement for piano keys; publ. *System des Klavierspiels.*

Hesse, Max, German music publisher; b. Sondershausen, Feb. 18, 1858; d. Leipzig, Nov. 24, 1907. In 1880 he founded under his name a publishing house, with headquarters in Leipzig; in 1915 the firm moved to Berlin. Among its most important publications were the 3rd through 11th editions of Riemann's *Musik Lexikon* (1887–1929) and H.J. Moser's *Musik-Lexikon.* Great devastation was wreaked on the physical materials of the firm by air bombardment during World War II. After the war the firm was re-established in Berlin.
BIBLIOGRAPHY: *80 Jahre Max Hesses Verlag* (Berlin, 1960).

Hesse-Bukowska, Barbara, Polish pianist; b. Lodz, June 1, 1930. She studied piano with Margerita Trombini-Kazuro; continued her musical education at the Warsaw Academy of Music. In 1949 she won 2nd prize in the Chopin Competition in Warsaw; in 1953 she was awarded the Chopin Prize at the Long-Thibaud Competition. From that time she made regular appearances in London, Paris, Moscow, Vienna, and Rome; also made extensive tours of India, Egypt, and Japan. In 1963 she became a member of the faculty of the State Academy of Music in Wroclaw; in 1973 she joined the Academy of Music in Warsaw. She is regarded as a fine interpreter of Chopin and also a leading champion of contemporary Polish music.

Hesselberg, Edouard Gregory, pianist and teacher; b. Riga, May 3, 1870; d. Los Angeles, June 12, 1935. He studied at the Cons. of the Moscow Phil. Society (1888–92); later was a private pupil of Anton Rubinstein. In 1892 he came to the U.S.; taught at the Ithaca Cons. (1895–96), the Music Academy in Denver (1896–1900), the Cons. of Music at Wesleyan College (1900–5), Belmont College in Nashville (1905–12), and the Toronto Cons. (1912–18). He wrote *Russian Suite* and *Russian Rhapsody* for Orch.; also piano pieces; made arrangements for 2 pianos of works by Bach, Chopin, and Schubert.

Hessen, Alexander Friedrich, Landgraf von, German musician; b. Copenhagen, Jan. 25, 1863; d. Fronhausen, March 26, 1945. In 1888 he became landgrave of the House of Hessen. Although blind from childhood, he studied music with admirable diligence; took violin lessons in Berlin with Joachim and Bruch; studied composition with Draeseke in Dresden and with Fauré in Paris. By an extraordinary effort he managed to compose a number of works, mostly chamber music and lieder.
BIBLIOGRAPHY: P. Hiller, *Der Liederzyklus von Alexander Friedrich von Hessen* (1910).

Hessenberg, Kurt, German composer; b. Frankfurt, Aug. 17, 1908. He studied in Leipzig with Raphael (composition) and Reichmüller (piano). In 1933 he was appointed to the faculty of the Hoch Cons. in Frankfurt. Possessing great facility in composition, Hessenberg evolved an effective idiom, fundamentally Classical, but containing Wagnerian elements in dramatic passages, with occasional infusion of prudential modernistic devices.
WORKS: His most successful work was *Struwwelpeter,* a suite for Small Orch. based on a well-known German children's tale. He further wrote 3 symphs. (1936, 1943, 1954); Concerto for Orch. (1958); Piano Concerto (1940); Concerto for 2 Pianos and Orch. (1950); 2 flute sonatas (1932); Cello Sonata (1941); Violin Sonata (1942); String Trio (1949); Piano Trio (1950); 5 string quartets (1934–67); numerous piano pieces; a number of cantatas; and a multitude of lieder.
BIBLIOGRAPHY: Karl Laux, *Kurt Hessenberg* (Essen, 1949).

Hetsch, (Karl) Ludwig Friedrich, German conductor; b. Stuttgart, April 26, 1806; d. Mannheim, June 28, 1872. He studied with Abeille; was attached to the court of the King of Württemberg; then conducted in Heidelberg (from 1846) and in Mannheim (from 1856 until his death). He wrote an opera, *Ryno* (Stuttgart, 1833); orch. works; and chamber music.

Hétu, Jacques, Canadian composer; b. Trois Rivières, Quebec, Aug. 8, 1938. He studied composition with Clermont Pépin at the Montreal Cons. (1956–61). A Canadian Council scholarship enabled him to go to Paris, where he took lessons with Dutilleux and Messiaen; upon his return to Canada in 1963, he was appointed to the staff of the Laval Univ. in Quebec. In his music he makes use of permissible modern devices, while hewing to Classical formal conventions.
WORKS: 3 symphs.: No. 1 for String Orch. (1959), No. 2 (1961), and No. 3 for Chamber Orch. (1971); *Adagio and Rondo* for String Quartet (1960); Trio for Flute, Oboe, and Harpsichord (1960); 2-piano Sonata (1961); *Petite suite* for Piano (1962); Variations for Piano (1964); Rondo for Cello and String Orch. (1965); *4 Pieces* for Flute and Piano (1965); Variations for Solo Violin, or Viola, or Cello (1967); Double Concerto for Violin, Piano, and Chamber Orch. (1967); *L'Apocalypse,* symph. poem (1967); Piano Concerto (1969); *Cycle* for Piano and Wind Instruments (1969); Passacaille for Orch. (1970); String Quartet (1972); *Fantaisie* for Piano and Orch. (1973).

Hétu, Pierre, Canadian conductor; b. Montreal, April 22, 1936. He studied piano at the Montreal

Cons.; continued his education at the Univ. of Montreal. He then studied conducting at the Paris Cons. with Louis Fourestier and in Siena with Sergiu Celibidache. In 1961 he won first prize in the International Competition held in Besançon, France. Later he took conducting courses at the Vienna Academy of Music with Hans Swarowsky, in Düsseldorf with Jean Marinon, and at Tanglewood with Charles Munch; then was assistant conductor of the Montreal Symph. Orch. In 1968 he became music director of the Kalamazoo (Mich.) Symph. Orch., a post he held until 1973; concurrently he served as associate conductor of the Detroit Symph. Orch. (1970–73). In 1973 he became conductor of the Edmonton (Alberta) Symph. Orch., resigning this post in 1979. As a guest conductor, he was active in Canada and Europe.

Heuberger, Richard (Franz Joseph), Austrian conductor and composer; b. Graz, June 28, 1850; d. Vienna, Oct. 27, 1914. By profession a civil engineer, in 1876 he turned his full attention to music; became choral master of the Vienna Gesangverein and conductor of the Singakademie (1878); in 1902–9, was conductor of the Männergesangverein; was appointed a prof. at the Vienna Cons. (1902). In 1881 he became music critic of the *Wiener Tageblatt,* then of *Neue Freie Presse* (1896–1901); after 1904, of *Neue Musikalische Presse,* and editor of *Musikbuch aus Österreich* (1904–6).

WORKS: Operas: *Abenteuer einer Neujahrsnacht* (Leipzig, 1886); *Manuel Venegas* (Leipzig, March 27, 1889), remodeled as the 3-act grand opera *Mirjam, oder Das Maifest* (Vienna, Jan. 20, 1894); *Barfüssele* (Dresden, 1905); operettas (all first perf. at Vienna): *Der Opernball* (Jan. 5, 1898; exceptionally successful; in N.Y., May 24, 1909); *Ihre Excellenz* (1899; new version as *Eine entzückende Frau*); *Der Sechsuhrzug* (1900); *Das Baby* (1902); *Der Fürst von Düsterstein* (1909); *Don Quixote* (1910); ballet, *Struwwelpeter* (Dresden, 1897); cantata, *Geht es dir wohl, so denk' an mich,* from *Des Knaben Wunderhorn;* overture to Byron's *Cain;* and songs. He publ. a selection of his critiques as *Musikalische Skizzen* (Leipzig, 1901); a biography, *Franz Schubert* (Berlin, 1902; 3rd ed., revised, 1920, by H. von der Pfordeten); *Anleitung zum Modulieren* (Vienna, 1910).

Heubner, Konrad, German composer; b. Dresden, April 8, 1860; d. Coblenz, June 6, 1905. He studied with Riemann in Leipzig, Nottebohm in Vienna, and Nicodé in Dresden. In 1890 he was appointed director of the Coblenz Cons. He wrote a Symph.; a cantata, *Das Geheimnis der Sehnsucht;* several overtures; and a Violin Concerto.

Heugel, Henry, Swiss-French music theorist; b. Neuchâtel, Switzerland, Sept. 26, 1789; d. Nantes, France, May 2, 1841. He studied in Paris with Galin and Reicha; developed a "méthode de méloplaste" along the lines of Galin's system; publ. *Nouvelle méthode pour l'enseignement de la musique inventée par H. Heugel et developpée par lui de manière à permettre d'apprendre sans maître* (1832).

Heugel, Jacques-Léopold, French music publisher; son of **Henry Heugel;** b. La Rochelle, March 1; 1811; d. Paris, Nov. 12, 1883. In 1839 he joined a music publishing establishment founded in Paris by J.A. Meissonnier (1812), and became its director; the name was changed to "Heugel et Cie." After his death his nephew, **Paul Chevalier Heugel** (1861–1931), became its owner. The firm is now managed by **Philippe** and **François Heugel,** successors to their father, **Jacques-Paul Heugel,** who was the grandson of Jacques-Léopold Heugel. The list of publications includes the famous Paris Cons. methods, in all branches of music, and the works of celebrated composers (Bizet, Bruneau, Charpentier, Delibes, Fauré, Franck, Honegger, Ibert, d'Indy, Lalo, Massenet, Milhaud, Offenbach, Poulenc, Ravel, Roussel, Florent Schmitt, Widor, etc.). The firm also publ. the important weekly *Le Ménestrel* (founded in 1833; suspended publication during the Franco-Prussian War, 1870–71, and during World War I; ceased publishing in 1940).

Heuss, Alfred Valentin, Swiss musicologist; b. Chur, Jan. 27, 1877; d. Gaschwitz, Germany, July 9, 1934. He studied at the Stuttgart Cons. (1896–98), then at the Akademie der Tonkunst in Munich, attending the Univ. of Munich simultaneously (1898–99); in 1899–1902, he studied musicology with Kretzschmar at the Univ. of Leipzig (Dr.Phil., 1903, with the dissertation *Die Instrumentalstücke des "Orfeo" und die venezianischen Opernsinfonien*). He was music critic of the *Signale* (1902–5); of the *Leipziger Volkszeitung* (1905–12); of the *Leipziger Zeitung* (1912–18); editor of the *Zeitschrift der Internationalen Musik-Gesellschaft* (1904–14), to which he contributed valuable articles; editor in chief of the *Zeitschrift für Musik* (1921–29); wrote analyses of works by Bach, Beethoven, Liszt, Bruckner, etc., for Breitkopf & Härtel's *Kleiner Konzertführer.* Of special value are his program books of the Bach Festivals at Leipzig (1904–27); he also publ. *Bachs Matthäuspassion* (1909). Other writings include "Über die Dynamik der Mannheimer Schule," in the *Riemann-Festschrift* (1909); *Kammermusikabende* (1919); *Beethoven: Eine Charakteristik* (1921); *Beethovens Orch.-Crescendo* (Basel, 1924); etc.

Heward, Leslie, English conductor; b. Littletown, Liversedge, Yorkshire, Dec. 8, 1897; d. Birmingham, May 3, 1943. He was a pupil of his father, an organist; then studied with Stanford and Vaughan Williams at the Royal College of Music in London. He began his conducting career with the British National Opera Co. From 1924–27 he was music director of the South African Broadcasting Corp. and conductor of the Cape Town Symph. Orch. In 1930 he was appointed conductor of the City of Birmingham Orch., a position he held until his death. He was also a composer; he wrote several orch. suites, choruses, and songs, as well as chamber music. A memorial volume was publ. in his honor under the editorship of Eric Blom (London, 1944), and a discography was compiled by William Holmes in *Le*

Grand Baton (Dec. 1980, pp. 17–21).

Hewitt, Harry Donald, unimaginably fecund American composer; b. Detroit, March 4, 1921. His paternal grandmother was an authentic Winnebago Indian. He was completely autodidact in music, and achieved such mastery of composition in quaquaversal directions without stylistic prejudice, that in some 40 years of writing music he produced 3,300 works in every conceivable manner, using every speculative idiom, from jazz to pop, couched in every available tonal, atonal, polytonal, and incommensurate oriental scale. Entirely free from supercilious elitism, he was not ashamed to admit the authorship of a *Hymn to Mickey Mouse* or an *Homage to Bugs Bunny.* None of his 30 symphs. were ever performed. The brute weight of his collected MSS is one and a half tons.

WORKS: 8 operas: *The Shadowy Waters, Moby Dick, The Song of Kawas, The Happy Hymadrayad, Doctor Too-Big, Clara's Friend, Remember George, Pierre;* 30 symphs., 2 of which are unnumbered, *Amerindian Symphony* and *War Symphony;* over 300 works for Orch., including 19 symph. poems: *Kabir, The Manchild, The Night, Fairyland, The Mysterious Sea, The Seasons, In the Shade of the Upas Tree, New Year's Eclogue, The House of Sleep, Raggedy Ann, Wa-Kon-Da, The Happy Garden, In a Green Shade, Seven, Selene, The Wheel, Aldebaran, Angkor, Anglesley Abbey;* 2 piano concertos; Trombone Concerto; Guitar Concerto; 18 piano sonatas; 23 string quartets; and more than 100 other works for diverse chamber ensembles, e.g., Preludes for Flute and Marimba, Fantasia for Flute and Horn, *Leaf in the Stream* for Oboe and Tuba, etc.; uncountable songs and choruses.

Hewitt, Helen, American musicologist; b. Granville, N.Y., May 2, 1900; d. Denton, Texas, March 19, 1977. She studied at the Eastman School of Music in Rochester, N.Y.; then traveled to Paris, and took a course in theory with Nadia Boulanger and organ lessons with Widor. Returning to America, she enrolled in the musicology class of Paul Henry Lang at Columbia Univ. (M.A., 1933); further supplemented her studies at Heidelberg Univ., where she was a student of Besseler. She obtained her Ph.D. from Radcliffe College in 1938, with the dissertation *O. Petrucci: Harmonice Musices Odhecaton A* (publ. in Cambridge, Mass., 1942); received a Guggenheim fellowship grant in 1947. From 1942 until 1969 she was on the music faculty of North Texas State Univ. in Denton. She edited the valuable compilation *Doctoral Dissertations in Musicology* (Denton, 1952; 4th ed., 1965); contributed valuable articles on the music of the Renaissance to various periodicals.

Hewitt, James, American composer, publisher, organist, and violinist; b. Dartmoor, England, June 4, 1770; d. Boston, Aug. 1, 1827. He played in the court orch. in London as a youth. In 1792 he went to America and settled in N.Y., where he was described as one of the "professors of music from the Opera House, Hanover Square, and Professional Concerts under the direction of Haydn, Pleyel, etc., London." On Sept. 21, 1792, he gave a benefit concert with the violinists J. Gehot and B. Bergmann, the flutist W. Young, and a cellist named Phillips, which included Hewitt's *Overture in 9 Movements, expressive of a battle.* Subsequently, Young and Gehot went to Philadelphia, and in 1793 Hewitt, Bergmann, and Phillips gave a series of 6 subscription concerts; at their 5th concert (March 25, 1793) they presented for the first time in America, Haydn's *Passion of Our Saviour* (i.e., *The Seven Last Words*); in 1794 Henri Capron joined Hewitt in promoting his "City Concerts"; meanwhile, Hewitt became the leader of the Old American Co. Orch., and in 1795 gave up his activities in connection with the subscription concerts. In 1798 he bought out the N.Y. branch of Carr's "Musical Repository" and established a publishing business of his own. In 1811 he went to Boston, where he played organ at Trinity Church and was in charge of the music presented at the Federal Street Theatre. In 1816 he returned to N.Y.; also traveled in the South. In N.Y. he was director of the Park Theatre.

WORKS: Ballad operas: *Tammany* (produced in N.Y., 1794, under the auspices of the Tammany Society; only one song, "The Death Song of the Cherokee Indians," survives; reprinted in W.T. Marrocco and H. Gleason, *Music in America*); *The Patriot or Liberty Asserted* (1794); *The Mysterious Marriage* (1799); *Columbus* (1799); *Pizarro, or The Spaniards in Peru* (1800); *Robin Hood* (1800); *The Spanish Castle* (N.Y., Dec. 5, 1800); *The Wild Goose Chase* (1800); overture, *Demophon;* set of 3 piano sonatas; *Battle of Trenton* for Piano (reprinted in the collection *Music from the Days of George Washington,* ed. by Carl Engel and Oliver Strunk); *The 4th of July—A Grand Military Sonata for the Pianoforte;* some other music, much of it extant in the Library of Congress, Washington, D.C.; the N.Y. Public Library; and the Boston Public Library. In 1816 Hewitt publ. a new setting of the *Star-Spangled Banner* to Key's poem, but it never took root. His *Nahant Waltz* is reprinted in J.T. Howard's *A Program of Early American Piano Music* (N.Y., 1931). **John Hill Hewitt** (b. New York, July 12, 1801; d. Baltimore, Oct. 7, 1890), eldest son of James Hewitt, studied at West Point Academy; was a theatrical manager, a newspaper man, and drillmaster of Confederate recruits in the Civil War; wrote poems and plays; about 300 songs (*The Minstrel's Return from the War, All Quiet along the Potomac, Our Native Land, The Mountain Bugle,* etc.); cantatas (*Flora's Festival, The Fairy Bridal, The Revelers,* and *The Musical Enthusiast*); ballad operas (*Rip Van Winkle, The Vivandiere, The Prisoner of Monterey, The Artist's Wife*). His admirers dubbed him the "father of the American ballad," but the ballad form existed in America long before him. He wrote a book of memoirs, *Shadows on the Wall* (1877; reprinted 1971). **James Lang Hewitt** (1807–53), another son of James, was associated with the publishing firm of J.A. Dickson in Boston (1825); after his father's death he returned to N.Y. and continued his father's publishing business.

BIBLIOGRAPHY: *Sammelbände der Interna-*

tionalen Musik-Gesellschaft (p. 459); J.T. Howard, "The Hewitt Family in American Music," *Musical Quarterly* (Jan. 1931); idem, *Our American Music* (N.Y., 1939, and subsequent eds.); C.E. Huggins, *John Hill Hewitt: Bard of the Confederacy* (Diss., Florida State Univ., 1964); J.W. Wagner, *James Hewitt: His Life and Works* (Diss., Indiana Univ., 1969); W.C. Winden, *The Life and Music Theater Works of John Hill Hewitt* (Diss., Univ. of Illinois, 1972); Frank W. Hoogerwerf, *John Hill Hewitt: Sources and Bibliography* (Atlanta, 1982).

Hewitt, Maurice, French violinist; b. Asnières (Seine), Oct. 6, 1884; d. Paris, Nov. 7, 1971. He studied at the Paris Cons.; was a violinist in the Capet Quartet (1908–28); taught at the Cleveland Inst. of Music (1930–34); from 1934, was a teacher at the American Cons. of Fontainebleau; was at the Paris Cons. from 1938 (chamber music class); in 1928, organized in Paris the Quatuor Hewitt; in 1939, founded the Orch. de Chambre Hewitt.

Hey, Julius, German singing teacher; b. Irmelshausen, April 29, 1832; d. Munich, April 22, 1909. He first studied painting, but turned to music. He became an ardent Wagnerian after his introduction to the master by King Ludwig II, and worked under the direction of Hans von Bülow at the Munich School of Music (established by the King in accordance with Wagner's plans). After Bülow's departure (1869), Hey vainly tried to effect a reform from a German national standpoint in the cultivation of singing, but met with so many obstacles that he resigned when Wagner died (1883), and devoted himself to finishing his method of singing, *Deutscher Gesangsunterricht* (4 parts; 1886). It contains a complete and logical exposition of Wagner's views on vocal training. His book *Richard Wagner als Vortragsmeister* was publ. posthumously by his son Hans.

Heyden, Hans, German organist; son of **Sebald Heyden;** b. Nuremberg, Jan. 19, 1536; d. there, Oct. (buried, Oct. 22) 1613. He was his father's successor as organist at St. Sebald Church, and was the inventor of the unique "Geigen-Clavicymbel" ("Nürnbergisch Geigenwerk"), which he described in *Musicale instrumentum reformatum* (1605).
BIBLIOGRAPHY: G. Kinsky, "Hans Heyden," *Zeitschrift für Musikwissenschaft* (1924).

Heyden (Heiden, Haiden), Sebald, German composer; b. Bruck, near Erlangen, Dec. 8, 1499; d. Nuremberg, July 9, 1561. In 1521 he was appointed cantor at the Spitalkirche and rector of its school in Nuremberg; in 1525 became rector of the school at St. Sebald. He was the author of the important theoretical work *Musicae, id est, artis canendi libri duo* (1537; 2nd ed. as *De arte canendi*, etc., 1540; trans. into Eng. by C. Miller in *Musicological Studies and Documents*, XXVI, 1972). The famous Passion song *O Mensch, bewein dein Sünde gross* has been ascribed to him.
BIBLIOGRAPHY: A. Kosel, *Sebald Heyden* (Würzburg, 1940).

Heyer, Wilhelm, German patron of music; b. Cologne, March 30, 1849; d. there, March 20, 1913. A wealthy co-owner of the wholesale paper manufacturing firm Poensgen & Heyer, he was an enthusiastic amateur and was active in the musical affairs of Cologne in advisory capacities. In 1906 he established a historical musical museum in Cologne, in which he assembled more than 2,600 instruments with accessories, about 20,000 autographs of musicians, 3,500 portraits, and a library of books about music, containing many rare editions. Georg Kinsky, curator of the museum from 1909, publ. an illustrated catalogue of the Heyer collections. The museum was dissolved in 1927, and the instruments were acquired by the Musicological Inst. of Leipzig Univ.; the books were dispersed by auction sales.

Heyman, Katherine Ruth Willoughby, American pianist; b. Sacramento, Calif., 1877; d. Sharon, Conn., Sept. 28, 1944. She made her debut as soloist with the Boston Symph. Orch. in 1899; from 1905 till 1915 toured the U.S. and Europe with Schumann-Heink, Marcella Sembrich, and others. She became greatly interested in the works of Scriabin, and played recitals of his works in Europe and America; also publ. many articles on Scriabin's theosophic ideas. In 1928 she founded in Paris the Groupe Estival pour la Musique Moderne. She publ. *The Relation of Ultra-Modern to Archaic Music* (Boston, 1921); composed *Studies in Modern Idiom* for the piano, and songs.

Heymann, Werner Richard, German-American composer; b. Königsberg, Feb. 14, 1896; d. Munich, May 30, 1961. He studied violin and composition; wrote a number of scores of incidental music for theatrical plays; spent several years in Hollywood, where he wrote the music score for the highly successful film *Ninotchka.*

Hickman, Hans Robert Hermann, German musicologist; b. Rosslau, May 19, 1908; d. Blandford Forum, Dorset, England, Sept. 4, 1968. He studied in Halle and Berlin, where he took courses in musicology with Sachs, Schering, Schünemann, and Wolf. In 1933 he went to Egypt, where he collected materials dealing with ancient Egyptian music. In 1957 he joined the faculty of the Univ. of Hamburg; then lived in England. His principal works include the books *Das Portativ* (Ph.D diss. at the Univ. of Berlin, 1934; publ. in Kassel, 1936); *La Trompette dans l'Egypte ancienne* (Cairo, 1946); *Terminologie arabe des instruments de musique* (Cairo, 1947); *Musikgeschichte in Bildern,* vol. 2, on Egypt (Leipzig, 1962). For other details see his autobiographical notice in *Die Musik in Geschichte und Gegenwart.*

Hickox, Richard, English conductor; b. Stokenchurch, Buckinghamshire, March 5, 1948. He studied at the Royal Academy of Music in London; was also an organ scholar at Queen's College, Cambridge. He then founded the Richard Hickox Singers and Orch., with which he presented programs ranging from the 14th to 20th centuries. He also served as music director of the City of London Sinfonia and artistic director of the Northern Sinfonia of Newcastle upon Tyne. In 1983 he became associate conductor of the San Diego Symph. Orch. while continuing his various activities in England.

Hidalgo, Juan, one of the earliest and most notable Spanish opera composers; b. c.1600; d. Madrid, March 30, 1685. In 1631 he became a member of the Royal Chapel in Madrid as harpist and also as player of the "clavi-harpa," an instrument he is said to have invented. A document of 1677 attests that he was "of superior skill, and had merited the highest honors from Their Majesties at all times." So great was his reputation that the Duke of Infantado called him "unique in the faculty of music." He composed the opera *Celos aun del aire matan,* to a text by Calderón de la Barca (perf. Madrid, Dec. 5, 1660); the music of Act I (voices and basso continuo) was discovered by J. Subirá and publ. by him in 1933 (this is the longest extant specimen of Spanish operatic music from the 17th century). Hidalgo also wrote music for Calderón's comedies *Ni amor se libra de amor* (1662) and *Hado y divisa de Leónido y de Marfisa* (1680), and for *Los celos hacen estrellas* by Juan Vélez (c.1662). It is very probable that he also composed the opera *La púrpura de la rosa* (1660), text by Calderón. He was likewise known as a composer of sacred and secular songs (some preserved in the National Library, Madrid). Music by Hidalgo is reprinted in Pedrell's *Cancionero* (IV) and *Teatro lírico* (vols. III, IV, and V).
BIBLIOGRAPHY: J. Subirá, *Celos aun del aire matan, Opera del siglo XVII* (Barcelona, 1933); idem, "El operista español Don Juan Hidalgo," *Las Ciencias* I/3 (Madrid, 1934); O. Ursprung, "Die älteste erhaltene spanische Oper," in the *Schering-Festschrift* (Berlin, 1937); G. Chase, "Origins of the Lyric Theater in Spain," *Musical Quarterly* (July 1939); J. Moll, "Nuevos datos para la biografía de Juan Hidalgo" in the Festschrift for H. Anglés (Barcelona, 1958–61).

Hidas, Frigyes, Hungarian composer; b. Budapest, May 25, 1928. He studied composition with Viski at the Budapest Academy of Music (1947–52); served as music director and conductor of the National Theater in Budapest (1952–66); in 1974 was appointed director of the Budapest Operetta Theater. His music derives from national Hungarian modalities, which are dressed up in modernistic harmonies.
WORKS: FOR THE STAGE: 3 operas: *Asszony és az igazság* (*The Woman and the Truth;* 1965); *Tökéletes alattvaló* (*The Perfect Subject;* 1973); *Bösendorfer* (1977); operetta, *Riviera* (1963); 2 ballets: *Színek* (*Colors;* 1966) and *Cédrus* (*Cedar;* 1975).
FOR ORCH.: Oboe Concerto (1951); Violin Concertino (1957); Viola Concerto (1959); Symph. (1960); Concertino for Strings (1960); Flute Concerto (1967); Horn Concerto (1968); Concertino for Winds and Strings (1969); Piano Concerto (1972); *Concerto sem-*

plice for Clarinet and Orch. (1977); *Adagio,* 2 dances (1977; from the ballet *Cédrus*); *Merry Music* for Wind Band (1981); *Ballet Music* for Wind Band (Manchester, England, July 26, 1981); *Rhapsody* for Bass Trombone and Small Wind Orch. (1982).
CHAMBER MUSIC: 2 string quartets (1954, 1963); Oboe Sonata (1954); 2 wind quintets (1961, 1969); *Fantasy* for Clarinet and Piano (1965); Brass Sextet (1972); Brass Quintet (1973); Brass Quartet (1973); Horn Quartet (1974); *Fantasy* for Solo Trombone (1977); *Introduction and Fugue* for 2 Trombones (1977); *Interludio* for 3 Trombones (1977); *Scherzo e chorale* for 4 Trombones (1977); *Meditation* for Bass Trombone (1979); *7 Bagatelles* for 10 Tenor Trombones and 2 Bass Trombones (1980); *3 Sketches* for 15 Clarinets (1981); also organ music; songs.

Hier, Ethel Glenn, American pianist and composer; b. Cincinnati, June 25, 1889; d. New York, Jan. 14, 1971. She studied at the Cincinnati Cons. of Music and at the Inst. of Musical Art, N.Y., where she was a pupil of Goetschius; also took lessons with Ernest Bloch. She lived mostly in N.Y. Among her compositions are *Asolo Bells* for Orch. (Rochester, N.Y., Oct. 25, 1939); a cantata, *Mountain Preacher* (N.Y., Dec. 5, 1941); numerous pieces of chamber music; also piano works.

Higginbotham, J.C., black American jazz trombonist; b. Social Circle, Ga., May 11, 1906; d. New York, May 26, 1973. He acquired mastery of the trombone in his youth; in 1928 moved to N.Y., where he played with Chick Webb, Fletcher Henderson, and Benny Carter; later worked with Louis Armstrong (1937–40) and Henry "Red" Allen (1940–47); subsequently led his own groups.

Higgins, Richard C. (Dick), American avant-garde composer; b. Cambridge, England, March 15, 1938. He was taken to America as a child; studied piano in Worcester, Mass.; composition and mycology with John Cage in N.Y. Eventually he moved to California; became active in the mushrooming avant-garde groups; participated in staging "happenings" across the country; joined the ultramodern group Fluxus in 1961; organized the Something Else Press (1964) with the aim of publishing something else. Not averse to academic activities, he joined the faculty of the Calif. Inst. of the Arts in Los Angeles. In his productions he pursues the objective of total involvement, in which music is verbalized in conceptual designs without reification, or expressed in physical action; the ultimate in this direction is achieved by his work *The Thousand Symphonies* (1968), in which the composer shoots machine-gun bullets through MS paper; his Symph. No. 585, shot by a sergeant of the army at the composer's behest, was distributed in holographs in No. 6 of the avant-garde magazine *Source* (1969) under the subtitle "The Creative Use of Police Resources." Other major compositions include: *Graphis,* 146 works for Varying Groups (1958); *A Loud Symphony* (1958); Symph. No. 3½ (duration, 50 seconds; 1959); *In the Context of Shoes,* a happening for

Tape, Vacuum Cleaners, Drills, Gardener's Shears, Piano, and Anti-Dancers (1960); *In Memoriam,* 164-part canon (1960); *Musical Processes,* cycle of 5 pieces for Indeterminate Ensembles (1960); *Constellations and Contributions* for Multimedia (1959–60); *Symphoniae sacrae,* conceptual works without a definite realization (1961); *The Peaceable Kingdom,* spoken opera with Bells (1961); *Danger Musics,* a cycle of 43 conceptual pieces (1961–63); *Litany* for 5 Pianos and Tape Recorder (1962–68); *Requiem for Wagner the Criminal Mayor* for Tape Recorder (1962); *Lavender Blue,* opera (1963); *Egg* for Magnetic Tape (1967); *Sophocles I and II,* fatal pieces for Piano (1970). He publ. *foew&ombwhnw,* "a grammar of the mind and a phenomenology of love and a science of the arts as seen by a stalker of the wild mushroom" (N.Y., 1969). His zodiac parameter is Aries, with the sun in Pisces.

Higginson, Henry Lee, founder of the Boston Symph. Orch.; b. New York, Nov. 18, 1834; d. Boston, Nov. 15, 1919. He studied at Boston's Latin School, and attended Harvard in 1951; in 1852–53 was in Europe; in 1856–60 studied voice, piano, composition, and theory in Vienna; in 1868 he became a partner in his father's brokerage firm in Boston (Lee, Higginson & Co.). In 1881, in order to found the Boston Symph. Orch., he assumed the responsibility of providing for about $50,000 yearly of the annual budget of some $115,000, thus clearing the estimated deficit and assuring the organization's successful continuance; the orch., consisting of 67 performers, gave its first concert at the old Music Hall on Oct. 22, 1881; in the summer of 1885, the series of concerts of lighter music, famous as the 'Pops,' were instituted; on Oct. 15, 1900, the Boston Symph. Orch. inaugurated its own permanent home, Symph. Hall; in 1903 the Pension Fund was established, for the benefit of which a special concert is given annually. A firm believer in the superiority of German musicians, Higginson engaged George Henschel as the first conductor of the orch. (1881–84); there followed a line of German conductors: Wilhelm Gericke (1884–89), Artur Nikisch (1889–93), Emil Paur (1893–98), Gericke again (1898–1906), Karl Muck (1906–8), Max Fiedler (1908–12), and again Karl Muck, from 1912 till 1918, when he submitted to arrest to avoid prosecution under the Mann Act as an enemy alien when the U.S. entered World War I. Higginson, distraught over Muck's arrest, resigned his position shortly after and selected a board of directors to control the orch.. He died the following year.

BIBLIOGRAPHY: M.A. de Wolfe Howe, *The Boston Symphony Orchestra* (Boston, 1914; new augmented ed., 1931); H. Earle Johnson, *Symphony Hall* (Boston, 1950); J. Baker-Carr, *Evening at Symphony: A Portrait of the Boston Symphony Orchestra* (Boston, 1977; pp.1–16).

Hignard, (Jean-Louis) Aristide, French composer; b. Nantes, May 20, 1822; d. Vernon, March 20, 1898. He studied with Halévy at the Paris Cons., taking the 2nd Grand Prix de Rome. He was an earnest composer of lofty aims, but brought out operas and other works of secondary importance; his best opera, *Hamlet,* composed in 1868, was to be performed in Paris; unluckily for him, *Hamlet* by Ambroise Thomas was produced that same year, with such spectacular success that Hignard could not compete with it; accordingly, he had to be content with a provincial production in his native city (Nantes, April 21, 1888). His other operas that reached the stage include *Le Visionnaire* (Nantes, 1851); *Le Colin-Maillard* (Paris, 1853); *Les Compagnons de la Marjolaine* (Paris, 1855); *M. de Chimpanzé* (Paris, 1858); *Le Nouveau Pourceaugnac* (Paris, 1860); *L'Auberge des Ardennes* (Paris, 1860); *Les Musiciens de l'orchestre* (Paris, 1861)

Hijman, Julius, Dutch composer and pianist; b. Almelo, Jan. 25, 1901; d. New York, Jan. 6, 1969. He studied piano privately with Dirk Schaefer, then with Paul Weingartner in Vienna; theory and composition with Sem Dresden in the Netherlands. He went to the U.S. in 1940; was an instructor at the Houston Cons. in Texas (1940–42) and at the Kansas City Cons. (1945–49); then taught composition at the Philadelphia Music Academy and the N.Y. College of Music. He composed mostly chamber music; sonatas for violin, cello, saxophone, oboe, and flute, with piano; 4 string quartets; a Sonata for 2 Violins and Piano; publ. a study, *New Austrian Music* (in Dutch; Amsterdam, 1937).

Hildach, Eugen, German baritone; b. Wittenberge-on-the-Elbe, Nov. 20, 1849; d. Zehlendorf, near Berlin, July 29, 1924. He began to study voice at the age of 24; married **Anna Schubert,** a singer, and went to Dresden, where they both taught at the Cons.; they also toured together in Germany. In 1904, they established their own singing school in Frankfurt. He publ. a number of songs, several of which became well known; particularly popular was *Der Lenz.*

Hiles, Henry, English composer and pedagogue; b. Shrewsbury, Dec. 31, 1826; d. Worthing, near London, Oct. 20, 1904. He filled various positions as organist and harmony teacher for nearly 60 years (1846–1904); was editor of the *Quarterly Musical Review* (1885–88). He composed several oratorios, glees, and part-songs; publ. the manuals *Harmony of Sounds* (1871); *Grammar of Music* (2 vols., 1879); *First Lessons in Singing* (1881); *Part-Writing or Modern Counterpoint* (1884); *Harmony or Counterpoint?* (1889); *Harmony, Choral or Contrapuntal* (1894).

Hill, Alfred, Australian composer; b. Melbourne, Nov. 16, 1870; d. Sydney, Oct. 30, 1960. He went to study music in Germany; took violin lessons at the Leipzig Cons., and played violin for 2 years in the Gewandhaus Orch., which was conducted by Brahms, Grieg, and Tchaikovsky, among others. He then went to New Zealand, where he became interested in the study of the aboriginal music of the Maori. From 1916 to 1934 he was a prof. at the Sydney Cons.

WORKS: Operas: *The Weird Flute; Tapu; The Rajah of Shivapore; Giovanni the Sculptor; The Ship of Heaven; Lady Dolly; The Whipping Boy;* cantatas: *Hinemoa* and *Tawhaki;* 12 symphs.; 17 string quartets; other pieces of chamber music; many songs. Several of his works are based on Maori themes. He publ. a manual, *Harmony and Melody* (Sydney, 1927).

BIBLIOGRAPHY: A.D. McCredie, "Alfred Hill (1870–1960): Some Background and Perspectives for an Historical Edition," *Miscellanea Musicologica* (1968); J. Thomson, *A Distant Music: The Life and Times of Alfred Hill, 1870–1960* (Oxford, 1982).

Hill, Bertha ("Chippie"), black American blues singer; b. Charleston, S.C., March 15, 1905; d. (struck and killed by an automobile) New York, May 7, 1950. She was an offspring of a large family, which included 16 children. She made her way to N.Y., where she first appeared as a dancer in Harlem; then toured as a dancer and singer with Ma Rainey; subsequently made tours and recordings with Louis Armstrong and others. She was active in Chicago as a singer in nightclubs; in 1948 she appeared at Carnegie Hall in N.Y.

Hill, Edward Burlingame, eminent American composer; b. Cambridge, Mass., Sept. 9, 1872; d. Francestown, N.H., July 9, 1960. A member of a distinguished family of educators (his father was a prof. of chemistry at Harvard, and his grandfather, president of Harvard), he pursued regular courses at Harvard Univ.; studied music with J.K. Paine; graduated in 1894 summa cum laude; took lessons in piano with B.J. Lang and A. Whiting, in composition with Chadwick and Bullard; also (for one summer) studied with Widor in Paris. He became greatly interested in the new tonal resources of the impressionist school of composers; wrote articles in the *Boston Evening Transcript,* and other publications dealing with French music; publ. a book, *Modern French Music* (Boston, 1924). In 1908 he joined the faculty of Harvard Univ. as an instructor in music; became associate prof. in 1918; prof. in 1928–37; then James E. Ditson Prof. (1937–40); retired in 1940, and lived mostly in New Hampshire; was a member of the National Inst. of Arts and Letters, American Academy of Arts and Sciences; was a Chevalier of the Légion d'Honneur; lectured at the univs. of Strasbourg and Lyons (1921). In his music, Hill reveals himself as a follower of the French school; clarity of design and elegance of expression are his chief characteristics. His best works are for orch.; but he also composed some fine chamber and choral music.

WORKS: FOR ORCH.: symph. poem, *The Parting of Lancelot and Guinevere* (St. Louis, Dec. 31, 1915); *Stevensoniana Suite No. 1* (N.Y., Jan. 27, 1918); symph. poem, *The Fall of the House of Usher,* after Poe (Boston, Oct. 29, 1920); *Stevensoniana Suite No. 2* (N.Y., March 25, 1923). The following were perf. for the first time by the Boston Symph. Orch: *Waltzes* (Feb. 24, 1922); *Scherzo* for 2 Pianos and Orch. (Dec. 19, 1924); symph. poem, *Lilacs* (his best

work in the impressionist manner; Cambridge, March 31, 1927; many subsequent perfs.); Symph. No. 1 (March 30, 1928); *An Ode* (for the 50th anniversary of the Boston Symph. Orch.; Oct. 17, 1930); Symph. No. 2 (Feb. 27, 1931); Concertino for Piano and Orch. (Boston, April 25, 1932); Sinfonietta for String Orch. (Brooklyn, April 3, 1936; also in Boston); Symph. No. 3 (Dec. 3, 1937); Violin Concerto (Nov. 11, 1938); Concertino for String Orch. (April 19, 1940); *Music for English Horn and Orch.* (March 2, 1945); *Prelude* for Orch. (N.Y., March 29, 1953). *Diversion* for Small Ensemble was performed at the Saratoga Festival (Sept. 6, 1947). CHAMBER MUSIC: Flute Sonata (1926); Clarinet Sonata (1927); Sextet for Flute, Oboe, Clarinet, Bassoon, Horn, and Piano (1934); String Quartet (1935); Piano Quartet (1937); Sonata for 2 Clarinets (1938); Quintet for Clarinet and String Quartet (1945); Sonata for Bassoon and Piano (1948); Sonatina for Cello and Piano (1949); Sonatina for Violin and Piano (1951). VOCAL WORKS: *Nuns of the Perpetual Adoration,* cantata for Women's Voices, with Orch. or Piano (1908); *Autumn Twilight* for Soprano and Orch.; *The Wilderness Shall Rejoice,* anthem for Mixed Chorus (1915); 2 pantomimes (with orch. accompaniment): *Jack Frost in Midsummer* (1908) and *Pan and the Star* (1914). FOR PIANO: *Poetical Sketches* (1902); *Country Idyls,* a set of 6 pieces; *Jazz Study* for 2 Pianos (1924).

Hill, Granville, English organist and music critic; b. Manchester, March 9, 1878; d. there, Dec. 26, 1953. As a youth he was a church organist in Manchester; later began to study piano, achieving a commendable degree of proficiency; in 1936 he was appointed a prof. of piano at the Leeds College of Music; also became music critic of the *Manchester Guardian,* leaving that position shortly before his death.

Hill, Junius Welch, American organist and music editor; b. Hingham, Mass., Nov. 18, 1840; d. Hollywood, Sept. 7, 1916. After studying in Boston with J.C.D. Parker, he went to Germany, where he took courses in piano and composition with Moscheles, Plaidy, Richter, and Reinecke. Returning to Boston in 1863, he was organist at various churches; taught at Wellesley College (1884–97); then settled in California. He publ. a number of choral works for women's voices; edited several collections of music, among them *Treasures of Lyric Art; Arabesques; Mozaïques; Characteristic Piano Pieces;* etc.

Hill, Ralph, English writer on music; b. Watford, Oct. 8, 1900; d. London, Oct. 19, 1950. He was first active in music publishing (1920–29); was music editor of the *Radio Times* (1933–45); also wrote for the *Daily Mail* (1933–39 and 1945–50); publ. the following works, all in London: *An Outline of Musical History* (1929); *Brahms: A Study in Musical Biography* (1933); *Liszt* (1936; 2nd ed., 1949); *Challenges: A Series of Controversial Essays* (1943); *Music without Fears* (1945); *Prelude to Music* (1951); also edited *The Symphony* (London, 1949) and *The Concerto* (London, 1952).

Hill, Richard S., American music librarian; b. Chicago, Sept. 25, 1901; d. Naples, Fla., Feb. 7, 1961. He was educated at Phillips Exeter Academy; then studied at Cornell Univ. (B.A., 1924) and did postgraduate work at Oxford Univ. (1924–26); held a research fellowship in psychology with Kurt Koffka at Smith College (1927–29); returned to Cornell Univ. for further study in psychology and musicology, the latter under Otto Kinkeldey. He joined the staff of the Music Division, Library of Congress, Washington, D.C. in 1939; served as editor of *Notes,* the quarterly journal of the Music Library Association, from 1943 to the time of his death; concurrently was president of the International Association of Music Libraries (1951–55). In 1946 he was sent by the Library of Congress to Germany and Austria to investigate the conditions of music libraries there and estimate the losses inflicted by the war; publ. an important account, *The Former Prussian State Library,* listing MSS of Mozart, Beethoven, and Haydn which were missing in the aftermath of the war (*Notes,* Sept. 1946). He contributed several important articles to music magazines, one of the most notable being "Schoenberg's Tone Rows and the Tonal System of the Future" (*Musical Quarterly,* Jan. 1936). In collaboration with Kurtz Myers, he edited a new type of discography, publ. under the title *Record Ratings* (N.Y., 1956).

Hill, Ureli Corelli, American violinist and conductor; b. New York, c.1802; d. Paterson, N.J., Sept. 2, 1875. His father, Uri K. Hill, was a teacher of music in Boston and N.Y., and author of a manual, *Solfeggio Americano, A System of Singing* (N.Y., 1820). An admirer of Corelli, he named his son after him; the first name (Ureli) is a combination of the father's name, Uri, and a friend's name, Eli. Ureli Corelli Hill played violin in various theaters in N.Y. as a boy; was a violinist in the orch. of Garcia's opera company in 1825; then joined the N.Y. Sacred Musical Society, and conducted it in the first American performance, with orch. accompaniment, of Handel's *Messiah* (1831). In 1835–37 he was in Germany, where he studied a year with Spohr. Returning to N.Y., he became a founder and first president of the N.Y. Phil. (1842–48); then went West in quest of fortune, which, however, failed to materialize. In N.Y. he exhibited a pianoforte of his own invention, in which he used small bell tuning forks in place of strings, so as to secure perfect intonation; the attempt to promote this instrument met with failure. He played the violin in the N.Y. Phil. from 1850 until 1873, when he retired because of age; continued to play engagements in various theater orchs. throughout his life; then moved to Paterson, N.J., where he engaged (unsuccessfully) in real-estate schemes. Depressed on account of constant setbacks in his ventures of promotion in music and in business, he committed suicide by swallowing morphine.
BIBLIOGRAPHY: H. Shanet, *Philharmonic: A History of New York's Orchestra* (Garden City, N.Y., 1975).

Hill, W.E. & Sons, a firm of violin makers and music dealers in London. It is claimed that "Mr. Hill, the instrument maker," mentioned in Pepys's Diary (1660), was an ancestor of the present owners. The founder of the firm was **Joseph Hill** (1715–84); he was an apprentice to Peter Wamsley; established his business in 1750. He had 5 sons, who were good violinists. **William Ebsworth Hill,** a great-grandson of the founder (b. London, Oct. 20, 1817; d. Hanley, April 2, 1895), adopted the present name of the firm; his instruments took first prize at the expositions in London (1851) and Paris (1867). His sons, **William Henry Hill** (b. London, June 3, 1857; d. there, Jan. 20, 1927), **Arthur Frederick Hill** (b. London, Jan. 24, 1860; d. there, Feb. 5, 1939), and **Alfred Ebsworth Hill** (b. London, Feb. 11, 1862; d. there, April 21, 1940), collaborated in the writing of *Antonio Stradivari, His Life and Work* (London, 1902), a standard work. From material also gathered by them, Lady M.L. Huggins previously wrote *Giovanni Paolo Maggini: His Life and Work* (London, 1892). William Henry, Arthur F., and Alfred Ebsworth Hill are the joint authors of *The Violin-Makers of the Guarneri Family* (with introductory note by E.J. Dent; London, 1931). The Ashmolean Museum at Oxford contains a valuable collection of stringed instruments, including a 1716 Stradivari violin with a bow dated 1694, presented by Arthur F. Hill. The firm continues to exist in the second half of the 20th century, under the direction of the descendants of the founder, **Andrew Hill** (b. London, July 3, 1942) and **David Hill** (b. London, Feb. 28, 1952).

Hill, Wilhelm, German pianist and composer; b. Fulda, March 28, 1838; d. Homburg, June 6, 1902. He studied in Frankfurt, and received a prize for his opera *Alona* in the competition for the opening of a new opera house. He was a prolific composer; publ. violin sonatas; a Piano Quartet; piano pieces. His song *Es liegt eine Krone im tiefen Rhein* achieved immense popularity.
BIBLIOGRAPHY: K. Schmidt, *Wilhelm Hill, Leben und Werke* (Leipzig, 1910).

Hille, Eduard, German composer and conductor; b. Wahlhausen, May 16, 1822; d. Göttingen, Dec. 18, 1891. He studied music with Heinroth. In 1855 he founded a Singakademie in Göttingen, and gave many concerts of choral music. He wrote an opera, *Der neue Oberst* (Hanover, 1849), and a number of part-songs.

Hillemacher, two brothers, French composers; **Paul** (b. Paris, Nov. 29, 1852; d. Versailles, Aug. 13, 1933) and **Lucien** (b. Paris, June 10, 1860; d. there, June 2, 1909). They both studied at the Paris Cons.; Paul Hillemacher won the 2nd Prix de Rome in 1875, and the first in 1876, with the cantata *Judith;* Lucien Hillemacher obtained the 2nd Prix de Rome in 1879, and the first in 1880. After graduation, they decided to write music in collaboration, and adopted a common signature—P.L. Hillemacher.
WORKS: Together they produced the following stage works: *Saint-Mégrin,* opera (Brussels, March

2, 1886); *Une Aventure d'Arlequin,* opéra-comique (Brussels, March 22, 1888); *Le Régiment qui passe* (Royan, Sept. 11, 1894); *Le Drac,* lyric drama (perf. at Karlsruhe in German as *Der Flutgeist,* Nov. 14, 1896); *Orsola,* lyric drama (Paris, May 21, 1902); *Circé,* lyric drama (Paris, April 17, 1907). Paul Hillemacher, who survived his brother by 24 years, wrote a short "tableau musical," *Fra Angelico,* which was produced at the Paris Opéra-Comique on June 10, 1924. In addition to their operas, the brothers wrote a symph. legend, *Loreley,* which won the prize of the City of Paris (1882); 2 orch. suites, *La Cinquantaine* and *Les Solitudes;* an oratorio, *La Légende de Sainte Geneviève* (1886); songs. They also brought out a biography of Gounod (Paris, 1905).

Hiller, Ferdinand, distinguished German conductor and composer; b. Frankfurt, Oct. 24, 1811; d. Cologne, May 10, 1885. He was a member of a wealthy Jewish family; received a fine education; studied piano with Aloys Schmitt, and appeared in public at the age of 10. In 1825 he went to Weimar to study with Hummel, whom he accompanied to Vienna in 1827, and visited Beethoven. He lived in Paris from 1828–35 and became a friend of Chopin, Liszt, Berlioz, and many other celebrated musicians. When his father died in 1836, he went back to Frankfurt, where he conducted the concerts of the Cäcilien-Verein. He went then to Italy, where he produced an opera, *Romilda* (Milan, 1839). It was unsuccessful, but an oratorio, *Die Zerstörung Jerusalems,* which he wrote in the following year, aroused the interest of Mendelssohn, who invited Hiller to Leipzig, where it was performed by the Gewandhaus Orch. (April 2, 1840). In 1841 he went to Italy, where he studied church music. His subsequent activities consisted mainly of conducting in Germany; he led the Gewandhaus concerts in Leipzig during the 1843–44 season; then conducted in Dresden, where he staged his operas *Der Traum in der Christnacht* (1845) and *Konradin* (Oct. 13, 1847); he was municipal conductor at Düsseldorf (1847–50), then at Cologne. He established the Cologne Cons., and was its first director until his death; also conducted the Lower Rhine Festival, which further enhanced his reputation. His other engagements were at the Italian Opera in Paris (1851–52) and in St. Petersburg, Russia, where he led a group of symph. concerts (1870); he also visited London several times between 1852 and 1872. He never ceased to compose works in large forms, despite their indifferent success; wrote 3 more operas: *Der Advokat* (Cologne, 1854); *Die Katakomben* (Wiesbaden, Feb. 15, 1862); and *Der Deserteur* (Cologne, Feb. 17, 1865); an oratorio, *Saul;* cantatas: *Lorelei; Nal und Damajanti; Israels Siegesgesang; Prometheus; Rebecca; Prinz Papagei;* a ballad, *Richard Löwenherz,* for Soli, Chorus, and Orch.; 3 symphs.; 3 overtures; 3 piano concertos; 5 string quartets; 5 piano quartets; 5 piano trios; many choral works; more than 100 songs; piano music. In his musical leanings, he was a conservative, and violently attacked Wagner. His classical training and friendly association with Spohr, and especially Mendelssohn, naturally influenced his style. Gifted in many fields of artistic endeavor, he was also a brilliant critic; his writings were publ. in collected form as *Die Musik und das Publikum* (1864); *Beethoven* (1871); *Aus dem Tonleben unserer Zeit* (2 vols.; 1868, 1871); *Musikalisches und Persönliches* (1876); *Briefe von M. Hauptmann an Spohr und andere Komponisten* (1876); *Felix Mendelssohn-Bartholdy, Briefe und Erinnerungen* (1874); *Briefe an eine Ungenannte* (1877); *Künstlerleben* (1880); *Wie hören wir Musik?* (1881); *Goethes musikalisches Leben* (1883); and *Erinnerungsblätter* (1884).

BIBLIOGRAPHY: W. Neumann, *W. Taubert und Ferdinand Hiller* (Kassel, 1857); H. Hering, *Die Klavier Kompositionen F. Hillers* (Cologne, 1927); R. Sietz, ed., *Aus Ferdinand Hillers Briefwechsel,* in 7 vols. (Cologne, 1958, 1961, 1964, 1965, 1967, 1968, 1970—the final vol. with M. Sietz); R. Sietz, "Felix Mendelssohn and Ferdinand Hiller. I: Ihre persönlichen Beziehungen," *Jahr-Buch des Kölnischen Geschichtsvereins,* 16 (1967); idem, ". . . II: Ihre künstlerischen Beziehungen," ibid., 43 (1971).

Hiller, Friedrich Adam, German composer; son of **Johann Adam Hiller;** b. Leipzig, 1768; d. Königsberg, Nov. 23, 1812. He studied music with his father; was a conductor at various provincial theaters in Germany, and wrote a number of light operas: *Biondetta* (Schwerin, 1792); *Das Schmuckkästchen* (Königsberg, 1804); *Die drei Sultaninen* (Königsberg, 1809); etc.; also chamber music.

Hiller (Hüller), Johann Adam, significant German composer; b. Wendisch-Ossig, near Görlitz, Dec. 25, 1728; d. Leipzig, June 16, 1804. After completing his primary education in his native town, he went to Dresden, where he studied music with Homilius. In 1751 he entered the Univ. of Leipzig, where he studied law; at the same time he was forced to earn his living by performing at popular concerts as a singer and flute player. In 1754 he became tutor to a nephew of Count Brühl at Dresden, whom he accompanied in 1758 to Leipzig; there he finally settled, and devoted himself to a revival of the Subscription Concerts, known as the Liebhaberkonzerte, in 1763, a concert series originally organized by Johann Doles in 1743; these developed into the famous Gewandhaus concerts, of which he was appointed conductor and led until 1785. In 1771 he founded a singing school, and from 1789 to 1801 was cantor and music director of the Thomasschule as successor of Doles. Hiller was one of the originators of the singspiel; in order to stress the disparity of characters in his operas, he assigned arias in a grand manner to the gentry, while persons of low degree were given simple songs.

WORKS: Singspiels: *Lisuart und Dariolette, oder Die Frage und die Antwort* (Leipzig, Nov. 25, 1766); *Lottchen am Hofe* (Leipzig, April 24, 1767); *Die Liebe auf dem Lande* (Leipzig, May 18, 1768); *Die Jagd* (Weimar, Jan. 29, 1770; his best-known work); *Der Krieg* (Berlin, Aug. 17, 1772); *Die Jubelhochzeit* (Berlin, April 5, 1773); *Das Grab des Mufti, oder Die zwey Geizigen* (Leipzig, Jan. 17, 1779). Several remained unperf. (*Das Orakel, Poltis, Die Friedensfeyer,* etc.). He further wrote many instrumental works, church music, and lieder, in which he excelled; particularly fine are his *Lieder für Kinder,* to words by C.F. Weisse (1769; new ed., 1865); also *Lieder mit Melodien an meinen Canarienvogel* (1759); *Letztes Opfer, in einigen Lieder-Melodien* (1790); setting of Horace's *Carmen ad Aelium Lamian;* 3 string quartets (1796); a Symph.; keyboard compositions. He edited many classical works, and also brought out numerous collections of contemporary pieces by German and Italian composers; publ. *Allgemeines Choral-Melodienbuch für Kirchen und Schulen* (1793). He brought out a weekly publication on music, *Wöchentliche Nachrichten und Anmerkungen, die Musik betreffend* (1766–70; reprinted in 4 vols., Hildesheim, 1970), the first music periodical in Germany to report news regularly. His writings include *Lebensbeschreibungen berühmter Musikgelehrten und Tonkünstler* (1784); *Über Metastasio und seine Werke* (1786); *Anweisung zum musikalisch-richtigen Gesang* (1774); *Anweisung zum musikalisch-zierlichen Gesang* (1780); *Anweisung zum Violinspiel* (1792). His autobiography, *Lebensläufe deutscher Musiker,* was reprinted in an edition by A. Einstein (Leipzig, 1914).

BIBLIOGRAPHY: K. Peiser, *Johann Adam Hiller* (Leipzig, 1894); M. Friedländer, *Das deutsche Lied im 18. Jahrhundert* (1902); G. Calmus, *Die ersten deutschen Singspiele von Standfuss und Hiller* (Berlin, 1908); H. von Hase, "Johann Adam Hiller und Breitkopf," *Zeitschrift für Musikwissenschaft* (Oct. 1919); A. Schering, *Das Zeitalter J.S. Bachs und Johann Adam Hillers* (Leipzig, 1940); V. Duckles, "Johann Adam Hiller's *Critical Prospectus for a Music Library,*" in H.C.R. Landon and R. Chapman, eds., *Studies in Eighteenth-Century Music* [Geiringer Festschrift] (London, 1970).

Hiller, Lejaren A., American composer and theorist of computer music; b. New York, Feb. 23, 1924. He studied chemistry at Princeton Univ. (Ph.D., 1947) and music at the Univ. of Illinois (M.Mus., 1958); began his career as a chemist; was assistant prof. of chemistry at the Univ. of Illinois (1953–58), and subsequently taught music there, until 1968; then became Slee Prof. of Composition at the State Univ. of N.Y. at Buffalo.

WORKS: 2 symphs. (1953, 1960); Piano Concerto (1949); 5 string quartets (1949, 1951, 1953, 1962, 1972); 5 piano sonatas, etc.; achieved notoriety with his computer composition *Illiac Suite* for String Quartet (in collaboration with Leonard M. Isaacson; 1957), the name being an abbreviation of *Illinois Accumulator;* the result is a programmed, i.e., dictated, production which includes vast stretches of cadential C-major chords. Encouraged by publicity, Hiller wrote a *Computer Cantata* for Soprano, Magnetic Tape, and Chamber Ensemble (1963); other works are *Man with the Oboe* (1962); *Machine Music* for Piano, Percussion, and Tape (1964); *An Avalanche for Pitchmen, Prima Donna, Player Piano, Percussion and Pre-recorded Playback* (1968). He publ. (with Isaacson) a manual, *Experimental Music* (N.Y., 1959), and numerous articles on the application of computers to musical composition; also some really valuable writings on chemistry.

Hillis, Margaret, American conductor; b. Kokomo, Ind., Oct. 1, 1921. She studied piano as a child; also played the tuba and double bass in school bands. An energetic person, she became a junior golf champion and, fantastically, was a civilian flying instructor for the U.S. Navy during World War II. She then enrolled as a music student at Indiana Univ. (B.A., 1947), and studied choral conducting at the Juilliard School of Music in N.Y. (1947–49). Her teacher, Robert Shaw, engaged her as his assistant. She became conductor of the chorus of the American Opera Society in N.Y. in 1952, remaining in this post until 1968. In 1957, at Fritz Reiner's behest, she organized the Chicago Symph. Orch. Chorus, which soon developed into an outstanding choral aggregation. Her various, often synchronous, employments included the following: instructor in choral conducting at the Juilliard School of Music (1951–53); music director of the Kenosha (Wis.) Orch. (1961–68); director of the Cleveland Orch. Chorus (1969–71); resident conductor of the Chicago Civic Orch. (from 1967); director of choral activities at Northwestern Univ. in Chicago (1970–77); music director of the Elgin (Ill.) Symph. Orch. (from 1971). In 1978 she became a visiting professor of conducting at the Indiana Univ. School of Music in Bloomington. In 1981 she was named music director of the Concert Society, Libertyville, Ill.; in 1982 she was appointed director of choral activities for the San Francisco Symph. She had numerous engagements as a guest conductor. On Oct. 31, 1977, in a sort of coup de théâtre, she substituted on short notice for the temporarily incapacitated Sir Georg Solti to conduct a performance of Mahler's monumental Symph. No. 8 at Carnegie Hall in N.Y. She received many awards of merit from various organizations; she is also the recipient of honorary degrees of Mus.D. from Temple Univ. (1967) and Indiana Univ. (1972).

Hilsberg (real name, **Hillersberg**), **Alexander,** violinist and conductor; b. Warsaw, April 24, 1897; d. Camden, Maine, Aug. 10, 1961. He studied violin with Auer at the St. Petersburg Cons. In 1918 he went on a concert tour in Siberia, eventually reaching Harbin in Manchuria; in 1923 he went to the U.S. via Japan. In 1926 he joined the violin section of the Philadelphia Orch.; became its concertmaster in 1931, and associate conductor in 1945. He was also on the staff of the Curtis Inst. of Music in the ensemble department (1927–51). The great success that Hilsberg achieved conducting the Philadelphia Orch. at a Carnegie Hall concert in 1950 led to his engagement as permanent conductor of the New Orleans Symph. Orch. (1952); in the spring of 1956 he took this orch. on a tour of Latin America.

BIBLIOGRAPHY: Hope Stoddard, *Symphony Conductors of the U.S.A.* (N.Y., 1957; pp. 89–95).

Hilsberg, Ignace, Russian-American pianist; b. Warsaw, July 20, 1894; d. San Diego, Calif., July 6, 1973. He studied at the St. Petersburg Cons. with Isabelle Vengerova, Essipova, and Dubassov, graduating in 1917. After the Revolution he went to China, where he gave a series of concerts, including a command performance for Sun Yat-sen in Peking. In 1922 he taught at the Cons. of Athens, Greece. In 1923 he went to America; in 1936 he settled in Hollywood; played piano for sound films. In 1969 he moved to San Diego. As a pianist, Hilsberg represented the time-honored Russian tradition, combining Romantic expressiveness with technical virtuosity.

Hilton, John (the Elder), English organist and composer; d. Cambridge, March, 1608. He was appointed organist at Trinity College, Cambridge, on Jan. 26, 1594. He was probably the composer of the anthem *Lord, for Thy tender mercies' sake;* another anthem, *Call to Remembrance* (modern reprint by the Oxford Univ. Press), is also most likely by him. To distinguish him from a younger John Hilton, who may have been his son, he is referred to as John Hilton the Elder.

Hilton, John (the Younger), English composer; b. Oxford, 1599; d. London, March (buried, March 21) 1657. He may have been the son of **John Hilton the Elder;** obtained his degree of Mus.B. from Trinity College at Cambridge (1626); in 1628 he was appointed organist at St. Margaret's, Westminster. WORKS: *Ayres, or Fa-las for 3 voyces* (London, 1627; reprinted by the Musical Antiquarian Society, XIII, London, 1844); the following works are attributed to him: *Catch that catch can, or, a Choice collection of catches, rounds, and canons for 3 or 4 voyces* (1625); 2 services; *Elegy;* anthems. The British Museum has further MSS. Other compositions are to be found in F. Keel's collection *Elizabethan Love-Songs* (N.Y., 1913), C.K. Scott's *Euterpe* (vol. 12, London, 1910), and E.H. Meyer's *Spielmusik des Barock* (vol. 1, Kassel, 1934). Six pieces for string trio have been arranged by Peter Warlock (London, 1930). BIBLIOGRAPHY: W.H.G. Flood, "New Light on Late Tudor Composers: John Hilton," *Musical Times* (1927).

Himmel, Friedrich Heinrich, German opera composer; b. Treuenbrietzen, Brandenburg, Nov. 20, 1765; d. Berlin, June 8, 1814. He studied theology at the Univ. of Halle; at the same time, he cultivated music. He received a stipend from Friedrich Wilhelm II to study with Naumann in Dresden; subsequently he went to Italy, where he acquired skill in stage music. His cantata *Il primo navigatore* was performed in Venice (March 1, 1794), and his opera *La morte di Semiramide,* in Naples (Jan. 12, 1795). He then returned to Berlin and was appointed court conductor. In 1798 he went to St. Petersburg, where he produced his opera *Alessandro* (Jan. 1799). In 1800 he returned from Russia by way of Sweden and Denmark; in Berlin he produced his Italian opera

Vasco di Gama (Jan. 12, 1801). His subsequent operas, staged in Berlin, were in the nature of singspiels, to German words: *Frohsinn und Schwärmerei* (March 9, 1801); *Fanchon das Leiermädchen* (May 15, 1804; his most successful work; many revivals); *Die Sylphen* (April 14, 1806); etc. His last opera, Der Kobold, was produced in Vienna (May 22, 1813). Many of his songs had great vogue (*An Alexis, Es kann ja nicht immer so bleiben,* etc.). He also composed an oratorio, *Isacco figura del Redentore* (Berlin, 1792); several works of sacred music; a Piano Concerto; Piano Sextet; Piano Quartet; pieces for piano solo. BIBLIOGRAPHY: L.O. Odendahl, *Fr.H. Himmel; Bemerkungen zur Geschichte der Berliner Oper um die Wende des 18. und 19. Jahrhunderts* (Bonn, 1917).

Hinckley, Allen (Carter), American bass; b. Gloucester, Mass., Oct. 11, 1877; d. Yonkers, N.Y., Jan. 28, 1954. He studied for the ministry at Amherst College and the Univ. of Pa.; then took up singing and studied with Oscar Saenger in N.Y. He then proceeded to Germany, where he made a successful debut at the Hamburg State Opera as the King in *Lohengrin* (1903), and remained on the staff until 1908. Returning to America, he made his debut at the Metropolitan Opera in the part of Hunding in *Die Walküre* (Nov. 18, 1908), and was on the staff until 1911, then again in 1913–14; then devoted himself to vocal teaching in N.Y.

Hindemith, Paul, eminent German composer, one of the leading masters of 20th-century music; b. Hanau, near Frankfurt, Nov. 16, 1895; d. Frankfurt, Dec. 28, 1963. He began studying violin music at the age of 9; at 14 he entered the Hoch Cons. in Frankfurt, where he studied violin with A. Rebner, and composition with Arnold Mendelssohn and Sekles. His father was killed in World War I, and Hindemith was compelled to rely on his own resources to make a living. He became concertmaster of the orch. of the Frankfurt Opera House (1915–23), and later played the viola in the string quartet of his teacher Rebner; from 1922–29 he was the viola player in the Amar String Quartet; also appeared as soloist on the viola and viola d'amore; later also was engaged as a conductor, mainly in his own works. As a composer, he joined the modern movement and was an active participant in the contemporary music concerts at Donaueschingen, and later in Baden-Baden. In 1927 he was appointed instructor in composition at the Berlin Hochschule für Musik. With the advent of the Hitler regime in 1933, Hindemith began to experience increasing difficulties, both artistically and politically. Although his own ethnic purity was never questioned, he was married to Gertrud Rottenberg, daughter of the Jewish conductor Ludwig Rottenberg, and he stubbornly refused to cease ensemble playing with undeniable Jews. Hitler's propaganda minister, Dr. Goebbels, accused Hindemith of cultural Bolshevism, and his music fell into an official desuetude. Unwilling to compromise with the barbarous regime, Hindemith accepted engagements abroad. Beginning in 1934, he made 3 visits to Ankara at the invitation of the Turkish government, and helped to organize the music curriculum at the Ankara Cons. He made his first American appearance at the Coolidge Festival at the Library of Congress, Washington, D.C., in a performance of his Unaccompanied Viola Sonata (April 10, 1937); after a brief sojourn in Switzerland, he emigrated to the U.S.; was instructor at the Berkshire Music Center in Tanglewood in the summer of 1940; in 1940–53 he was a prof. at Yale Univ.; he was elected a member of the National Inst. of Arts and Letters; and during the academic year 1950–51 he was Charles Eliot Norton Lecturer at Harvard Univ. He became an American citizen in 1946. He conducted concerts in the Netherlands, Italy, and England during the summer of 1947; in 1949, revisited Germany for the first time since the war, and conducted the Berlin Phil. in a program of his own works (Feb. 14, 1949). In 1953 he went to Switzerland; gave courses at the Univ. of Zürich; also conducted orchs. in Germany and Austria. In 1954 he received the prestigious Sibelius Award of $35,000, offered annually to distinguished composers and scientists by a Finnish shipowner. In 1959–61, he conducted guest appearances in the U.S.; in 1963 he visited America for the last time; then went to Italy, Vienna, and finally to Frankfurt, where he died. Hindemith's early music reflects rebellious opposition to all tradition; this is noted in such works as the opera *Mörder, Hoffnung der Frauen* (op. 12, 1921) and *Suite 1922* for Piano (op. 26); at the same time, he cultivated the techniques of constructivism, evident in such a work as his theatrical sketch *Hin und Zurück* (op. 45a, 1927), in which *Krebsgang* (retrograde movement) is applied to the action on the stage, so that events are reversed; in a work of a much later period, *Ludus Tonalis* (1943), the postlude is the upside-down version of the prelude. Along constructive lines is Hindemith's cultivation of so-called *Gebrauchsmusik*, that is, music for use; he was also an ardent champion of *Hausmusik*, to be played or sung by amateurs at home; the score of his *Frau Musica* (as revised in 1944) has an obbligato part for the audience to sing. A neo-Classical trend is shown in a series of works, entitled *Kammermusik*, for various instrumental combinations, polyphonically conceived, and Baroque in style. Although Hindemith made free use of atonal melodies, he was never tempted to adopt an integral 12-tone method, which he opposed on esthetic grounds. Having made a thorough study of old music, he artfully assimilated its polyphony in his works; his masterpiece of this genre was the opera *Mathis der Maler.* An exceptionally prolific composer, Hindemith wrote music of all types for all instrumental combinations, including a series of sonatas for each orch. instrument with piano. Hindemith's style may be described as a synthesis of modern, Romantic, Classical, Baroque, and other styles, a combination saved from the stigma of eclecticism only by Hindemith's superlative mastery of technical means. As a theorist and pedagogue, Hindemith developed a self-consistent method of presentation derived from the acoustical nature of harmonies.

WORKS: OPERAS: *Mörder, Hoffnung der Frauen (Murderer, Hope of Women),* op. 12, in one act (1919; Stuttgart, June 4, 1921); *Das Nusch-Nuschi,* op. 20, marionette opera (1920; Stuttgart, June 4, 1921; revised version, Königsberg, Jan. 22, 1931); *Sancta Susanna,* op. 21, in one act (1921; Frankfurt, March 26, 1922); *Cardillac,* op. 39, 3 acts (Dresden, Nov. 9, 1926; revised version, Zürich, June 20, 1952); *Hin und Zurück,* op. 45a, one-act sketch (Baden-Baden, July 15, 1927); *Neues vom Tage (News of the Day),* in 3 parts (1928–29, revised 1953; Berlin, June 8, 1929; revised version in 2 acts, Naples, April 7, 1954, composer conducting); *Mathis der Maler (Matthias the Painter),* in 7 scenes (1934–35; Zürich, May 28, 1938; U.S. premiere, Boston, Feb. 17, 1956; Hindemith's best stage work); *Orfeo,* realization of Monteverdi's opera (1943); *Die Harmonie der Welt (The Harmony of the Universe),* 5 acts (1950–57; Munich, Aug. 11, 1957, composer conducting); *Das lange Weihnachtsmahl (The Long Christmas Dinner;* 1960; Mannheim, Dec. 17, 1961; U.S. premiere, N.Y., March 13, 1963); *Tuttifäntchen,* incidental music for a Christmas fairy tale (1922; Darmstadt, Dec. 13, 1922).

BALLETS: *Der Dämon (The Demon),* op. 28, a pantomime (1922; Darmstadt, Dec. 1, 1923); *Nobilissima Visione,* dance legend in 6 scenes (perf. under the title *St. Francis* by the Ballets Russes de Monte Carlo, in London, July 21, 1938, composer conducting); *Theme and Variations: The 4 Temperaments* for String Orch. and Piano (1940; N.Y. City Ballet, Nov. 20, 1946; most often perf. as a concert piece); *Hérodiade,* with recitation, after Mallarmé (produced as *Mirror before Me,* by the Martha Graham Dance Group, Washington, D.C., Oct. 30, 1944; also as a concert piece, with optional narration).

FOR ORCH.: Cello Concerto, op. 3 (1916); *Lustige Sinfonietta,* op. 4 (1916); Piano Concerto, op. 29 (1924); Concerto for Orch., with Oboe, Bassoon, and Violin Soli, op. 38 (Duisburg, July 25, 1925); *Konzertmusik* for Wind Orch., op. 41 (Donaueschingen, July 1926); *Konzertmusik* for Viola and Orch., op. 48 (Hamburg, March 28, 1930, composer soloist); *Konzertmusik* for Piano, Brass, and 2 Harps, op. 49 (Chicago, Oct. 12, 1930); *Konzertmusik* for Strings and Brass, op. 50 (for 50th anniversary of the Boston Symph. Orch.; perf. there, April 3, 1931); *Konzertstück* for Trautonium and Strings (1931); *Philharmonisches Konzert,* variations (Berlin, April 14, 1932); *Mathis der Maler,* symph. from the opera (Berlin, March 12, 1934, Furtwängler conducting); *Der Schwanendreher,* concerto for Viola and Small Orch. (Amsterdam, Nov. 14, 1935, composer soloist); *Trauermusik* for Solo Viola or Violin or Cello, and String Orch. (written for a memorial broadcast for King George V, who died on Jan. 20, 1936; London, Jan. 22, 1936, composer soloist); *Symphonic Dances* (London, Dec. 5, 1937); *Nobilissima Visione,* suite from the ballet (Venice, Sept. 13, 1938); Violin Concerto (1939; Amsterdam, March 14, 1940); *Theme and Variations: The 4 Temperaments* for String Orch. and Piano (Boston, Sept. 3, 1940, Foss, soloist; premiered in 1946 as a ballet); Cello Concerto (1940; Boston, Feb. 7, 1941, Piatigorsky, soloist); Symph. in

E-flat (1940; Minneapolis, Nov. 21, 1941), Mitropoulos conducting); *Cupid and Psyche,* overture for a ballet (1943; Philadelphia, Oct. 29, 1943); *Symphonic Metamorphosis on Themes of Carl Maria von Weber* (1943; N.Y., Jan. 20, 1944); Piano Concerto (1945; Cleveland, Feb. 27, 1947, Sanromá, soloist); *Symphonia Serena* (1946; Dallas, Feb. 2, 1947, Dorati conducting); Clarinet Concerto (1947; Philadelphia, Dec. 11, 1950, Benny Goodman, soloist); Concerto for 4 Winds, Harp, and Small Orch. (N.Y., May 15, 1949); Concerto for Trumpet, Bassoon, and String Orch., in 2 movements (New Haven, Conn., Nov. 4, 1949; 3rd movement added in 1952); Sinfonietta (1949; Louisville, March 1, 1950, composer conducting); Horn Concerto (1949; Baden-Baden, June 8, 1950, Dennis Brain, soloist); Symph. in B-flat for Concert Band (Washington, April 5, 1951, composer conducting); *Die Harmonie der Welt,* symph. from the opera (1951; Basel, Jan. 24, 1952); *Pittsburgh Symphony* (1958; Pittsburgh, Jan. 30, 1959, composer conducting); Organ Concerto (1962–63; N.Y., April 25, 1963, composer conducting; Heiller, soloist).

CHAMBER MUSIC: *Andante and Scherzo,* op. 1, trio for Clarinet, Horn, and Piano (1914); unnumbered String Quartet in C, op. 2 (1915); Piano Quintet, op. 7 (1917); *3 Stücke* for Cello and Piano, op. 8 (1917); First String Quartet, in F minor, op. 10 (Frankfurt, June 2, 1919; a set of 6 sonatas, opp. 11/1–6, of which 2 are for Violin and Piano (1918); one for Cello and Piano (1919); one for Viola and Piano (1919); one for Solo Viola (1919); one for Solo Violin (1919); 2nd String Quartet, in C, op. 16 (Donaueschingen, Aug. 1, 1921); 3rd String Quartet, op. 22 (Donaueschingen, Nov. 4, 1922); *Kleine Kammermusik,* op. 24/2, for Wind Quintet (1922); a set of 4 sonatas, opp. 25/1–4: for Solo Viola (1922); for Viola d'Amore and Piano (1923); for Solo Cello (1923); for Viola and Piano (1924; publ. 1977); *"Minimax"—Reportorium für Militärmusik,* parody for String Quartet (1923; publ. 1978); Quintet for Clarinet and String Quartet, op. 30 (Salzburg Festival, Aug. 7, 1923); 4th String Quartet, op. 32 (Vienna, Nov. 5, 1923); a set of 4 sonatas, opp. 31/1–4, of which 2 are for Solo Violin (1924); one, a *Canonic Sonatina,* for 2 Flutes (1924); one for Solo Viola (1924); First Trio for Violin, Viola, and Cello, op. 34 (Salzburg, Aug. 6, 1924); *Rondo* for 3 Guitars (1925); *3 Stücke* for 5 Instruments (1925); 7 numbered pieces titled *Kammermusik: No. 1,* op. 24/1 (Donaueschingen Festival, July 31, 1922); *No. 2,* op. 36/1, for Piano and 12 Instruments (Frankfurt, Oct. 31, 1924); *No. 3,* op. 36/2, for Cello and 10 Instruments (Bochum, April 30, 1925, composer's brother, Rudolf, soloist); *No. 4,* op. 36/3, for Violin and Large Chamber Orch. (Dessau, Sept. 25, 1925); *No. 5,* op. 36/4, for Viola and Large Chamber Orch. (Berlin, Nov. 3, 1927) *No. 6,* op. 46/1, for Viola d'Amore and Chamber Orch. (1927; Cologne, March 29, 1928); *No. 7,* op. 46/2, for Organ and Chamber Ensemble (1927; Frankfurt, Jan. 8, 1928); *8 Pieces* for Solo Flute (1927); Trio for Viola, Heckelphone or Saxophone, and Piano, op. 47 (1928); *2 Canonic Duets* for 2 Violins (1929); *14 Easy Duets* for 2 Violins (1931); 2nd Trio for Violin, Viola, and Cello (Antwerp, March 17, 1933); *Konzertstück* for 2 Saxophones (1933);

Duet for Viola and Cello (1934); Violin Sonata in E (1935); Flute Sonata (1936); Sonata for Solo Viola (1937); *Meditation* for Violin or Viola or Cello, and Piano (1938); Quartet for Clarinet, Violin, Cello, and Piano (1938); Oboe Sonata (1938); Bassoon Sonata (1938; transcribed for Bass Clarinet in 1959 for Josef Horák); Clarinet Sonata (1939); Horn Sonata (1939); Trumpet Sonata (1939); Solo Harp Sonata (1939); Violin Sonata in C (1939); Viola Sonata in C (1939); English Horn Sonata (1941); Trombone Sonata (1941); *A Frog He Went a-Courting,* variations for Cello and Piano (1941); *Echo* for Flute and Piano (1942); 5th String Quartet, in E-flat (Washington, Nov. 7, 1943); Sonata for Saxophone (or Alto Horn or French Horn) and Piano (1943); 6th String Quartet (Washington, March 21, 1946); Cello Sonata (1948); Septet for Winds (1948); Double-bass Sonata (1949); Sonata for 4 Horns (1952); Tuba Sonata (1955); Octet for Clarinet, Bassoon, Horn, and String Quintet (Berlin, Sept. 23, 1958).

VOCAL WORKS: *3 Songs* for Soprano and Orch., op. 9 (1917); *Melancholie* for Contralto and String Quartet, op. 13 (1918); *Des Todes Tod,* op. 23/1, 3 songs for Female Voice, 2 Violas, and 2 Cellos (1922); *Die junge Magd,* op. 23/2, 6 poems for Contralto, Flute, Clarinet, and String Quartet (1922); *Lieder nach alten Texten* for Mixed Chorus a cappella, op. 33 (1923); *Die Serenaden,* op. 35, little cantata on romantic poems, for Soprano, Oboe, Viola, and Cello (1925); *Der Lindenbergflug* for Soloists and Orch. (1929); *Das Unaufhörliche,* oratorio (Berlin, Nov. 21, 1931); *5 Songs on Old Texts* for Mixed Chorus a cappella (c.1938; includes revisions of some songs of op. 33); *6 Chansons,* after Rilke, for Mixed Chorus a cappella (1939); *3 Choruses* for Male Chorus a cappella (1939); *The Demon of the Gibbet* for Male Chorus a cappella (1939); *When Lilacs Last in the Dooryard Bloom'd,* an American requiem after Walt Whitman, for Mezzo-soprano, Baritone, Chorus, and Orch. (N.Y., May 14, 1946); *Apparebit Repentina Dies* for Chorus and Brass (Harvard Symposium, Cambridge, Mass., May 2, 1947); *Das Marienleben,* after Rilke, for Soprano and Orch. (1938–48; revised, shortened, and orchestrated version of songs originally for Voice and Piano, 1923); *Ite, angeli veloces,* cantata trilogy: *Chant de triomphe du roi David, Custos quid de nocte,* and *Cantique de l'espérance* (1953-55; first complete perf., Wuppertal, June 4, 1955); *12 Madrigals* for 5-part Mixed Chorus a cappella (1958); *Der Mainzer Umzug* for Soprano, Tenor, Baritone, Mixed Chorus, and Orch.; (Mainz, June 23, 1962); Mass for Mixed Chorus a cappella (Vienna, Nov. 12, 1963; his last work).

FOR VOICE AND PIANO: *3 Hymnen,* op. 14, after Whitman (1919); *8 Songs* for Soprano, op. 18 (1920); *Das Marienleben,* op. 27, a cycle of songs after Rilke (Donaueschingen, June 17, 1923; revised radically and perf. in Hannover, Nov. 3, 1948); *6 Lieder* for Tenor and Piano (1933–35); *9 English Songs* (1942–44); *13 Motets* (1941–60).

FOR PIANO: *7 Waltzes,* op. 6, for 4-hands (1916); *In einer Nacht,* op. 15, a set of 15 pieces (1920); Sonata, op. 17 (1917); *Tanzstücke,* op. 19 (1922); *Suite "1922,"* op. 26 (1922); *Klaviermusik,* op. 37, incorporating *Übung in drei Stücken,* op. 37/1 (1925) and *Reihe kleiner Stücke,* op. 37/2 (1927); 3 numbered sonatas (1936); Sonata for 4-hands (1938); Sonata for 2 Pianos (1942); *Ludus Tonalis,* studies (Chicago, Feb. 15, 1943).

GEBRAUCHSMUSIK: Music for Mechanical Instruments, op. 40: Toccata for Player Piano, and Music for Mechanical Organ (both 1926–27); Music for the film *Felix the Cat* for Mechanical Organ, op. 42 (1927); *Spielmusik (Music to Play)* for Strings, Flutes, and Oboes, op. 43/1 (1927); *Lieder für Singkreise (Songs for Singing Groups)* for a cappella Voices, op. 43/2 (1927); *Schulwerk für Instrumental-Zusammenspiel (Educational Music for Instrumental Ensembles),* op. 44, including the often-performed *5 Pieces* for String Orch., op. 44/4 (1927); *Sing- und Spielmusiken für Liebhaber und Musikfreunde (Music to Sing and Play for Amateurs and Music Lovers),* including: *Frau Musica* for Soli, Chorus, and String Orch., op. 45/1 (1928; revised as *In Praise of Music,* 1943), *8 Canons* for 2 Voices and Instruments, op. 45/2 (1928), *Ein Jäger aus Kurpfalz (The Hunter of Kurpfalz),* for Strings and Winds, op. 45/3 (1928), *Kleine Klaviermusik,* op. 45/4 (1929), and *Martinslied* for Unison Chorus and 3 Instruments, op. 45/5 (1929); *Lehrstück (Lesson Piece),* after Brecht, for Male Soli, Narrator, Chorus, Orch., Dance Group, Clowns, and Community Singing (Baden-Baden, July 28, 1929); *Wir bauen eine Stadt (Let's Build a Town),* play for Children's Soli and Chorus, and Instruments (Berlin, June 21, 1930); *Plöner Musiktag (Music for a Daylong Festival in Plön),* in 4 sections: *Morgenmusik (Morning Music)* for Brass Quintet, *Tafelmusik (Table Music)* for Strings and Brass, *Kantate* for Soli, Children's Chorus, Narrator, Strings, Winds, and Percussion, and *Abendkonzert (Evening Concert),* 6 individual pieces for Chamber and Orch. Grouping (all 1932; Plön, June 1932); *Wer sich die Musik erkiest (The One Who Chooses Music)* for Voices and Instruments (1952). The Auftrag der Hindemith-Stiftung is issuing a Collected Works edition (begun in 1975). Thematic indexes have been compiled by Kurt Stone (for the Associated Music Publishers, N.Y., 1954; verified by the composer) and H. Rösner, *Paul Hindemith—Katalog seiner Werke, Diskographie, Bibliographie, Einführung in das Schaffen* (Frankfurt am Main, 1970).

WRITINGS: *Unterweisung im Tonsatz* (2 vols., 1937, 1939; in Eng. as *The Craft of Musical Composition,* N.Y., 1941; revised, 1945); *A Concentrated Course in Traditional Harmony* (2 vols., N.Y., 1943, 1953); *Elementary Training for Musicians* (N.Y., 1946); *J.S. Bach: Heritage and Obligation* (New Haven, Conn., 1952; German ed., *J.S. Bach: Ein verpflichtendes Erbe,* Wiesbaden, 1953); *A Composer's World: Horizons and Limitations* (Cambridge, Mass., 1952).

BIBLIOGRAPHY: Franz Willms, "Paul Hindemith," in *Von neuer Musik* (Cologne, 1925); W. Altmann, "Paul Hindemith," ibid.; Hans Kleemann, "Das Kompositionsprinzip Paul Hindemiths," in *Gedenkschrift für Hermann Abert* (Halle, 1928); Heinrich Strobel, *Paul Hindemith* (the basic biography; Mainz, 1928; 2nd enlarged ed., 1931; 3rd amplified ed., 1948); Edwin Evans, "Hindemith," in *Cobbett's Cyclopedic Survey of Chamber Music* (1929); A. Machabey, "Paul Hindemith, musicien allemand," *Revue Musicale* (1930); Willi Reich, "Paul Hindemith," *Musical Quarterly* (Oct. 1931); Paul Rosenfeld, "Neo-Classicism and Hindemith," in *Discoveries of a Music Critic* (N.Y., 1936); H.H. Stuckenschmidt, "Hindemith Today," *Modern Music* (1937); Frani B. Muser, "The Recent Works of Paul Hindemith," *Musical Quarterly* (Jan. 1944); N. Cazden, "Hindemith and Nature," *Music Review* (Nov. 1954); R. Stephan, "Hindemith's Marienleben, An Assessment of Its Two Versions," *Music Review* (Nov. 1954); *Paul Hindemith, Zeugnis in Bildern,* brought out by Schott (Mainz, 1955; updated ed., *Paul Hindemith: Die letzten Jahre; ein Zeugnis in Bildern,* Mainz, 1965); i.L. Schilling, *Paul Hindemith's Cardillac* (Würzburg, 1962); H. Boatwright, "Paul Hindemith as a Teacher," *Musical Quarterly* (July 1964); H. Tischler, "Remarks on Hindemith's Contrapuntal Technique," in *Essays in Musicology* (Apel Festschrift; Bloomington, Ind., 1968); A. Briner, *Paul Hindemith* (Zürich, 1970); I. Kemp, *Hindemith* (London, 1970); A. Lanza, "Libertà e determinazione formale nel giovane Hindemith," *Rivista Italiana di Musicologia* V/1 (1970); Eberhard Zwink, *Paul Hindemiths Unterweisung im Tonsatz* (Göppingen, 1974); G. Skelton, *Paul Hindemith: The Man behind the Music* (London, 1975); Günther Metz, *Melodische Polyphonie in der Zwölftonordnung: Studien zum Kontrapunkt Paul Hindemiths* (Baden-Baden, 1976). The Hindemith Stiftung began publication of the *Hindemith-Jahrbuch* in 1971.

Hinderas, Natalie (real last name, **Henderson**) black American pianist; b. Oberlin, Ohio, June 15, 1927. Her father was a jazz musician, and her mother was a trained music teacher. She herself was a child prodigy and was accepted at the Oberlin School of Music at the age of 8; graduated at 18 (B.Mus., 1945). She subsequently took lessons with Olga Samaroff at the Juilliard School of Music in N.Y.; then studied piano with Eduard Steuermann and composition with Vincent Persichetti. She made her N.Y. debut in 1954; later toured in Europe and the Far East. In addition to the standard piano repertoire, she included in her concert programs pieces by black composers.

Hindle, John, English composer; b. London, 1761; d. there, 1796. He was mainly known as a composer of glees, one of which, *Queen of the Silver Bow,* became extremely popular.

Hine, William, English composer and organist; b. Brightwell, 1687; d. Gloucester, Aug. 28, 1730. He studied with Jeremiah Clarke; then served as organist at Gloucester Cathedral. A collection of his anthems under the title *Harmonia sacra Glocestriensis* was publ. posthumously by his widow.

Hines, Earl (Kenneth) "Fatha," black American

jazz pianist; b. Duquesne, Pa., Dec. 28, 1905; d. Oakland, Calif., April 22, 1983. His father was a professional trumpet player and his mother played piano and organ. He took piano lessons as a child, but became interested mainly in jazz piano. He played with big bands as a young man, and in 1927 joined a quintet led by Louis Armstrong in Chicago. He began recording with Armstrong and under his influence evolved a special type of "trumpet piano style" characterized by sharp accents, octave tremolos in the treble, and insistently repeated melodic notes. In 1928 he organized his own big band in Chicago, and toured with it in the U.S., including the Southern states; his was one of the first black big bands to play in the South; its theme song, *Deep Forest,* became popular. A radio announcer used to introduce him as "Fatha Hines coming through deep forest with his children," and the nickname "Fatha" stuck. After a hiatus of several years, Hines reappeared on the jazz horizon as a solo pianist and made a hit wherever he appeared. In 1957 he toured Europe; played in Berlin in 1965 and in Russia in 1966; he also played in Japan. During his last years he made his residence in San Francisco, where he played his last engagement just a week before his death. He was described by jazz critics as "the last of the great masters."
BIBLIOGRAPHY: Stanley Dance, *The World of Earl Hines* (N.Y., 1977).

Hines, Jerome, American singer; b. Hollywood, Calif., Nov. 8, 1921. His real name was **Heinz,** but he changed it to its Anglo-Saxon homonym when he began to sing professionally. He studied mathematics and chemistry at the Univ. of Calif. in Los Angeles, graduating in 1943; at the same time took vocal lessons with Gennaro Curci in Los Angeles, and later with Samuel Margolis in N.Y. After a few performances in light opera, he sang the part of Biterolf in *Tannhäuser* with the San Francisco Opera, on Oct. 24, 1941. In 1944 he sang Méphistophélès in *Faust* with the New Orleans Opera Co. He was not drafted into the U.S. Army during the war because of his excessive height (6 feet 6 inches), but instead was employed as a chemist in war-related work. On Nov. 21, 1946, he made his debut at the Metropolitan Opera in N.Y. in a minor role, as the Sergeant in *Boris Godunov,* and on Feb. 18, 1954, sang its title role. He made numerous guest appearances with European opera houses, the Edinburgh Festival in 1953, at La Scala in Milan in 1958, and at the Bayreuth Festival in 1958. On Sept. 23, 1962, he made history when he sang the role of Boris Godunov, in Russian, at the Bolshoi Theater in Moscow, with the Soviet Premier, Khrushchev, in attendance. He repeated his feat a month later at the Bolshoi Theater, and also performed in Leningrad, Kiev, and Tiflis. On his return to the U.S., he sang the part of Boris Godunov in the original Mussorgsky version with the Metropolitan Opera in N.Y. on Oct. 14, 1975. His other roles included Don Giovanni, Don Basilio, Sarastro, Des Grieux, Wotan, and Rodolfo. His 30th anniversary with the Metropolitan was observed in a special ceremony on Jan. 8, 1976. Altogether, he

had sung 454 times with the company. He publ. an autobiography, *This Is My Story, This My Song* (Westwood, N.J., 1968), and a book, *Great Singers on Great Singing* (London, 1983). He also composed an opera, *I Am the Way,* based on the life of Christ.
BIBLIOGRAPHY: David Ewen, *Musicians since 1900* (N.Y., 1978).

Hingston, John, English composer and organist; date of birth unknown; d. London, Dec. (buried, Dec. 16) 1683. He studied with Orlando Gibbons; was in the service of Oliver Cromwell and taught music to his daughter. He was a member of the Chapel Royal from 1661 to 1666. After the Restoration, he was engaged as Keeper of the Organs at the Court. Six vols. of his works are preserved in Oxford.

Hinrichs, Gustav, German-American conductor; b. Ludwigslust, Germany, Dec. 10, 1850; d. Mountain Lake, N.J., March 26, 1942. He studied violin and piano with his father; composition with E. Marxsen in Hamburg. In 1870 he settled in America; was in San Francisco until 1885; then went to Philadelphia, where he organized his own opera company; gave the American premieres of *Cavalleria rusticana* (Philadelphia, Sept. 9, 1891) and *Pagliacci* (N.Y., June 15, 1893). In 1903–4, he conducted at the Metropolitan Opera House; then retired. He was the composer of an opera, *Onti-Ora* (Indian name of the Catskill Mountains; Philadelphia, July 28, 1890).

Hinrichsen, Max, German music publisher; b. Leipzig, July 6, 1901; d. London, Dec. 17, 1965. He worked with his father, **Heinrich Hinrichsen** (1868–1942), at Peters Edition, Leipzig, until 1937, when he went to London, becoming a British subject in 1947. There he established Hinrichsen Edition, Ltd.; in 1944 he began publishing *Hinrichsen's Musical Year Book,* which appeared irregularly until 1961.

Hinrichsen, Walter, music publisher; brother of **Max Hinrichsen;** b. Leipzig, Sept. 23, 1907; d. New York, July 21, 1969. He studied at the Univ. of Leipzig; then was connected with Peters Edition there, headed by his father, **Heinrich Hinrichsen** (1868–1942; see **Peters, Carl Friedrich**). In 1936 Walter Hinrichsen came to America; was in the U.S. Army (1942–45); after the war became a government employee in the U.S. Zone in Germany (1945–47). He then returned to America and in 1948 opened the new offices of the C.F. Peters Corp. in N.Y. After his death the firm has continued with his widow, Evelyn Hinrichsen, as president.

Hinshaw, William Wade, American baritone; b. Union, Iowa, Nov. 3, 1867; d. Washington, D.C., Nov. 27, 1947. He studied voice with L.G. Gottschalk in Chicago; was choir director at various churches; made his operatic debut as Méphistophélès in Gounod's *Faust* with the H.W. Savage Co. (St. Louis, Nov. 6, 1899); in 1903, opened the Hinshaw School of Opera in Chicago, which was later incorporated into the Chicago Cons.; Hinshaw became president of the combined institutions (1903–7). In 1909 he organized the International Grand Opera Co. of Chicago. He made his debut at the Metropolitan Opera House, N.Y., on Nov. 16, 1910, remaining on its roster until 1913; in 1912 he sang in the Wagner festival at Graz, and in 1914, in the special *Ring* festival at Berlin; then returned to America. In 1916 he offered a prize of $1,000 for the best one-act opera by an American composer (awarded to Hadley for his opera *Bianca*). From 1920 to 1926 he produced Mozart's operas in Eng. with his own company in the U.S., Canada, and Cuba (about 800 perfs. in all). He then settled in Washington, D.C.

Hinton, Arthur, English composer; b. Beckenham, Nov. 20, 1869; d. Rottingdean, Aug. 11, 1941. He studied at the Royal Academy of Music in London; then taught violin there; subsequently went to Munich for further study with Rheinberger. There he composed a Symph., which he conducted at one of the concerts of the Munich Cons.; traveled in Italy; returned to London in 1896. He continued to compose; his 2nd Symph. was performed in London in 1903. He married the pianist **Katharine Goodson,** who gave many performances of his piano works, including a concerto. He wrote the children's operettas *The Disagreeable Princess* and *St. Elizabeth's Rose;* also a number of songs.

Hinze-Reinhold, Bruno, German pianist; b. Danzig, Oct. 20, 1877; d. Weimar, Dec. 26, 1964. He studied at the Leipzig Cons.; taught piano at the Stern Cons. in Berlin (1901–13). In 1913 he moved to Weimar; was director of the State Music School (1916–49); then retired, but continued his activity as a private piano teacher. He publ. a pedagogical manual, *Technische Grundbegriffe eines natürlichen neuzeitlichen Klavierspiels.*

Hipkins, Alfred James, English authority on musical instruments; b. London, June 17, 1826; d. there, June 3, 1903. He was connected with the Broadwood piano manufacturers; acquired an excellent knowledge of the piano and was Chopin's favorite tuner on his last visit to England. He himself learned to play the piano well enough to give recitals. He publ. standard works on instruments, among them *Musical Instruments, Historic, Rare, and Unique* (Edinburgh, 1888; contains numerous colored plates; reprinted, London, 1921) and *A Description and History of the Pianoforte, and of the Older Keyboard Stringed Instruments* (London, 1896).

Hirai, Kozaburo, Japanese composer; b. Kochi, Sept. 10, 1910. He studied violin with Robert Pollak and composition and conducting with Klaus Pringsheim at the Tokyo Imperial Academy of Music (1929–34); taught at the Academy (1937–47); in 1966 he organized the Association of Composers and Authors (ACA).
WORKS: Operetta, *Taketori-Monogatari* (1949); ballet, *Spirit of the Snow,* for String Orch. (1942; revised 1968); several contatas; *Festival of Insects,* suite for Orch. (1941; Tokyo, Sept. 15, 1941); *Pastoral*

for Clarinet and String Orch. (1943); *On the Grass,* suite for Orch. (1947); Koto Concerto (1950; Tokyo, Nov. 12, 1950); *Festival,* concerto grosso for 3 Koto Soli and Koto Orch. (1962); *Symphonic Ballad* (1963); *Seaside Sketch* for Chamber Orch. (1967); *Marriage of the Whale,* symph. chorus for 3 Voices, Chorus, and Orch. (1969; Tokyo, Nov. 27, 1969); *Hakusan* for Shakuhachi, Solo Koto, Chorus, Percussion, and Koto Ensemble (1970); Trio for Flute, Viola, and Guitar (1942); String Quartet No. 1, *Japanese Suite* (1943); String Trio (1946); *Fantasy* for Strings (1954); Cello Sonata (1956); Sonata for Koto and Oboe (1956); *Duet* for Violin and Trombone (1966); *3 Capriccios* for Solo Violin (1971); *Sakura Sakura,* fantasy for Piano (1971).

Hirao, Kishio, Japanese composer; b. Tokyo, July 8, 1907; d. there, Dec. 15, 1953. He graduated from Keio Univ. in 1930; studied composition with Guy de Lioncourt at the Schola Cantorum in Paris (1931–34); became a prof. at the Tokyo Music Academy.
WORKS: Choreographic drama in 3 acts, *Histoire de Wanasa—Otome* (1943); *Cantilène antique* for Orch. (1937); *Variations on a Japanese Theme* for Orch. (1938); *Suite* for Flute and Orch. (1940); *Kinuta,* symph. poem (1942); *La Paix,* overture (1951); String Quartet (1940); Flute Sonatina (1941); Octet (1944); Piano Quintet (1945); Trio for Flute, Violin, and Piano (1949); Wind Quintet (1950); Violin Sonata (1947); Oboe Sonata (1951); Piano Sonata (1948).

Hirayoshi, Takekuni, Japanese composer; b. Kobe, July 10, 1936. He studied with Yoshio Hasegawa at the Tokyo Univ. of Arts (1955–61), later attended the graduate school there (1963–67). In 1970 he was appointed an instructor at the Toho Girls' High School.
WORKS: String Quartet (1960); *Composition* for Orch. (Tokyo, Nov. 5, 1962); Ballade for Orch. (1966); *Dialog* for Marimba, Flute, Clarinet, and Cello (1968); Symphonic Variations (Tokyo, Oct. 23, 1969; winner of the 1969 Odaka Prize); Prelude and Fantasia for Solo Guitar (1970); *Monodrama* for Piano (1970); *Impromptu* for Flute, Violin, and Piano (1970); *Epitaph* for Solo Cello (1971); Octet for 4 Japanese Instruments and String Quartet (1972); *Epitaph* for 2 Flutes (1973); *Song of the Wind* for 2 Marimbas (1973); Ballade for Organ and Orch. (1974); *Requiem* for Violin and Orch. (1975).

Hirsch, Paul Adolf, German bibliographer and collector; b. Frankfurt, Feb. 24, 1881; d. Cambridge, England, Nov. 23, 1951. He began collecting rare musical editions as a young man, and publ. successive catalogues of his rapidly growing library. In 1936 he left Germany and was able to transport his entire collection to England; it was purchased by the British Museum in 1946; the total number of items was about 20,000. In 1922 he began the publication of new editions (several in facsimile, and with commentaries) of rare works; these are Francesco Caza, *Tractato vulgare de canto figurato* (Milan, 1492; ed. J. Wolf, 1922); Giovanni Luca Conforto, *Breve et fac-*

ile maniera d'essercitarsi a far passaggi (Rome, 1593; ed. J. Wolf, 1922); *Neujahrsgrüsse Seelen; Eine Sammlung von Liedern mit Melodien und Bilderschmuck aus den Jahren 1770–1800* (ed. M. Friedlaender, 1922); Georg Philipp Telemann, *Fantaisies pour le clavessin: 3 douzaines* (ed. Max Seiffert, 1923); Hercole Bottrigari, *Il desiderio, overo de' concerti di varii strumenti musicali* (Venice, 1594; ed. Kathi Meyer, 1924); Karl Friedrich Zelter, *Fünfzehn ausgewählte Lieder* (ed. Moritz Bauer, 1924); Giovanni Spataro, *Dilucide et probatissime demonstratione* (Bologna, 1521; ed. J. Wolf, 1925); Nicolaus Listenius, *Musica, ab authore denuo recognita* (Nuremberg, 1549; ed. Georg Schünemann, 1927); Carl Philipp Emanuel Bach, *Zwölf zwei- und dreistimmige kleine Stücke für die Flöte oder Violine und das Klavier* (1770; ed. Richard Hohenemser, 1928); Christoph Schultze, *Lukas-Passion* (Leipzig, 1653; ed. Peter Epstein, 1930); Martin Luther, *Deutsche Messe* (1526; ed. J. Wolf, 1934); Wolfgang Amadeus Mozart, *The Ten Celebrated String Quartets,* first authentic ed. in score (ed. Alfred Einstein, 1945).

BIBLIOGRAPHY: P.H. Muir, "The Hirsch Catalogue," *Music Review* (1948); a list of editions is found in the Jan. 1951 issue of *Music Review.*

Hirschfeld, Robert, writer on music; b. Brünn, Moravia, Sept. 17, 1857; d. there, April 2, 1914. He studied at the univs. of Breslau and Vienna; in 1884, took his degree of Dr.Phil. at the Univ. of Vienna, with a dissertation on Johannes de Muris; made arrangements of several stage works by Haydn, Mozart, etc., for modern performances.

Hirt, Al(ois Maxwell), popular American trumpet player; b. New Orleans, Nov. 7, 1922. He studied with Frank Simon at the Cincinnati Cons. of Music (1940–42); then served in the U.S. Army, and played in the 82nd Army Air Force Band; after his discharge in 1946, he played with various bands; in 1956 he formed his own band, and began touring with it in 1960. His first major recording, in 1961, was the album *The Greatest Horn in the World.* A versatile musician, he came to espouse the "Nashville sound," being equally at ease in the country-western, jazz, and popular music genres.

Hirt, Franz Josef, Swiss pianist; b. Lucerne, Feb. 7, 1899. He studied with Hans Huber and Ernst Lévy at the Cons. of Basel; later took lessons with Egon Petri and Alfred Cortot. In 1919 he became a teacher at the Cons. of Bern; also gave numerous piano recitals in Europe. He publ. *Meisterwerke des Klavierbaues* (1955; issued in Eng. under the title *Stringed Keyboard Instruments, 1440–1880;* Boston, 1968).

Hirt, Fritz, Swiss violinist; b. Lucerne, Aug. 9, 1888; d. Chigny-sur-Morges, Switzerland, Jan. 5, 1970. He studied in Zürich and had an extended career as a concert violinist in Europe; was also a member of the Basel String Quartet.

Hitchcock, H(ugh) Wiley, eminent American musicologist and editor; b. Detroit, Sept. 28, 1923. He was educated at Dartmouth College (A.B., 1943) and the Univ. of Michigan (M.Mus., 1948; Ph.D., 1954, with the dissertation *The Latin Oratorios of Marc-Antoine Charpentier*); taught music at the Univ. of Michigan (1947–61); then was prof. of music at Hunter College (1961–71); in 1971 became prof. of music at Brooklyn College (named Distinguished Prof. of Music in 1980), where he also served as director of the Inst. for Studies in American Music. A recipient of numerous grants, including Fulbright senior research fellowships in 1954–55 (Italy) and 1968–69 (France), and a Guggenheim fellowship in 1968–69, he also served on the boards of the Music Library Association (1965–72) and the American Musicological Society (1966–78, in various capacities), and as president of the Charles Ives Society (since 1973); was also editor of The Prentice-Hall History of Music Series (Englewood Cliffs, N.J., 1965—), *Earlier American Music* (reprints of music; N.Y., 1972), and Recent Researches in American Music (Madison, Wis., 1976—). He was a member of the executive committee and area editor for the Americas of *The New Grove Dictionary of Music and Musicians* (1969–79; publ. in London, 1980); was co-editor, with Stanley Sadie, of *The New Grove Dictionary of Music in the United States* (scheduled for publ. in 1984). His research interests are wide and meritorious, covering French Baroque and American music; his editorial contributions include the works of Caccini, Leonardo Leo, Charpentier, and Lully.

WRITINGS: *Music in the United States: A Historical Introduction* (Englewood Cliffs, N.J., 1969; 2nd ed., revised and enlarged, 1974); *Charles Ives Centennial Festival-Conference 1974* (program book; N.Y., 1974); *Ives* (London, 1977); co-editor, with V. Perlis, of *An Ives Celebration: Papers and Panels of the Charles Ives Centennial Festival-Conference* (Urbana, Ill., 1977); *The Phonograph and Our Musical Life* (Brooklyn, 1980); co-author, with L. Inserra, of *The Music of Ainsworth's Psalter (1612)* (Brooklyn, 1981); *The Works of Marc-Antoine Charpentier: A Catalogue Raisonné* (Paris, 1982).

Hjort Albertsen, Per. See **Albertsen, Per Hjort.**

Hlobil, Emil, Czech composer; b. Veselí nad Lužnici, Oct. 11, 1901. He studied with Křička at the Prague Cons. (1921–23) and Suk at the Master School there (1924–30); taught at the Cons. (1941–58) and afterward at the Academy of Music and Dramatic Arts in Prague. He followed the national tradition of the modern Czech school, and also cautiously experimented with serial methods of composition.

WORKS: 2 operas: *Anna Karenina,* after Tolstoy (1962; České Budějovice, April 16, 1972) and *Le Bourgeois gentilhomme,* after Molière (1965); *Weekend,* symph. suite (1933); Divertimento for Small Orch. (1935); *The Song of Youth,* symph. poem (1942); *Commemoration of the Martyrs,* symph. fresco (1944–45); 7 symphs.: No. 1 (1949); No.

2, *The Day of Victory* (1951); No. 3 (1957); No. 4 (1959); No. 5 (1969); No. 6, for Strings (1972); No. 7 (1973); symph. suites: *Summer in the Giant Mountains* (1950); *Folk Merry-Making* (1950); *Spring in the Gardens of Prague* (1951–53); *In the Valachian Village* (1952); cantata, *On the Gift of Coal* (1952); Serenade for Small Orch. (1955); Violin Concerto (1955); Rhapsody for Clarinet and Orch. (1955); Accordion Concerto (1956); *Labor Holiday* for Orch. (1960); Concerto for String Orch. (1963); Organ Concerto (1963); *Concerto filharmonico* for Orch. (1965); Sonata for Chamber String Orch. (1965); *Invocazioni* for Orch. (1967); Double-bass Concerto (1968); *Contemplation* for Viola and String Orch. (1968); *The Path of the Living* for Orch. (1974); String Quintet (1925); 4 string quartets (1931, 1936, 1955, 1969); Violin Sonatina (1935); Piano Trio (1938); Wind Quintet (1940); Horn Sonata (1942, revised 1948); Quartet for Harpsichord, Violin, Viola, and Cello (1943); Nonet (1946); Serenade for String Quartet (1956); Wind Octet (1956); Violin Sonata (1959); Quartet for Flute, Oboe, Clarinet, and Bassoon (1964); *Chamber Music* for 2 Clarinets, Basset Horn, and Bass Clarinet (1965); Flute Sonata (1966); Trio for Clarinet, Horn, and Double Bass (1967); Trumpet Sonata (1967); Bass-clarinet Sonata (1970); *Dialogue* for 2 Bassoons (1971); Trombone Sonata (1973); Sonata for 2 Cellos (1973); 2-piano Sonata (1958); 2 piano sonatas (both 1968); *Aria and Toccata* for Organ (1963); songs; choruses.

Hoboken, Anthony van, eminent Dutch music bibliographer; b. Rotterdam, March 23, 1887; d. Zürich, Nov. 1, 1983. He studied with Iwan Knorr at the Hoch Cons. in Frankfurt and with Schenker in Vienna. In 1927 he founded the Archive for Photographs of Musical Manuscripts in the National Library at Vienna; he then began to collect first editions of classical works; his Haydn collection is particularly rich. He publ. the complete thematic catalogue of Haydn's work in 2 vols. (1957, 1971). He also contributed a number of articles on Haydn to music journals. A Festschrift in his honor was publ. on his 75th birthday, edited by J. Schmidt-Görg (Mainz, 1962). His archive of early music publications was purchased by the Austrian government in 1974, and officially opened at the Austrian National Library in Vienna on Hoboken's 90th birthday, March 23, 1977, as a tribute to his signal accomplishments in musical bibliography; although frail, Hoboken was present on this occasion.

Hochberg, Count Bolko von (pseudonym, **J.H. Franz**), German composer; b. Fürstenstein Castle, Silesia, Jan. 23, 1843; d. near Salzbrunn, Dec. 1, 1926. He established and for several years maintained the Hochberg Quartet; also founded the Silesian music festivals (1876); was general intendant of the Berlin Royal Theaters (1886–1903). His works include the operas *Claudine von Villabella* (Schwerin, 1864) and *Die Falkensteiner* (Hannover, 1876; rewritten and produced as *Der Wärwolf*, Dresden, 1881); 3 symphs.; 3 string quartets; 2 piano trios; a Concerto for Piano; songs; and choruses.

Hochreiter, Emil, Austrian composer; b. Debrecen, Hungary, Dec. 27, 1871; d. Vienna, Aug. 3, 1938. He studied jurisprudence and music; composed mainly sacred choruses; also some symph. overtures in a traditional Romantic manner. During his sojourn of many years in Novo Mesto he collected Slovenian eucharistic songs, some of which he publ. in anthologies.

Hoddinott, Alun, Welsh composer; b. Bargoed, Aug. 11, 1929. He studied music at the Univ. College of South Wales in Cardiff; also took private instruction with Arthur Benjamin. In 1951 he was appointed lecturer in music at Cardiff College of Music and Drama; in 1959 joined the music faculty of the Univ. College of South Wales. He also serves as organizer of the annual Cardiff Music Festival. His music follows the judicious line of humanitarian modernism, without blundering into musical chaos. WORKS: 5 OPERAS: *The Beach of Falesá* (Cardiff, March 26, 1974); *Murder, the Magician* (Welsh Television, Feb. 11, 1976); *What the Old Man Does Is Always Right* (1975); *The Rajah's Diamond* (1979); *The Trumpet Major* (Manchester, England, April 1, 1981). FOR ORCH.: Symph. No. 1 (National Eisteddfod of Wales; Pwillheli, Aug. 5, 1955, composer conducting); Symph. No. 2 (Cheltenham Festival, July 11, 1962); Symph. No. 3 (Manchester, Dec. 5, 1968); Symph. No. 4 (Manchester, Dec. 4, 1969); Symph. No. 5 (London, March 6, 1973); Concerto No. 1 for Piano, Wind Instruments, and Percussion (London, Feb. 22, 1960); Concerto No. 2 for Piano and Orch. (National Eisteddfod of Wales, Cardiff, Aug. 5, 1969, composer conducting); Concertino for Viola and Chamber Orch. (Llandaff Festival, June 25, 1958); Harp Concerto (Cheltenham Festival, July 16, 1958); Concerto for Clarinet and String Orch. (Cheltenham Festival, July 16, 1954); Concerto for Organ and Orch. (Llandaff Festival, June 19, 1967); Horn Concerto (Llandaff Festival, June 3, 1969); Concertino for Viola and Small Orch. (Llandaff Festival, June 25, 1958); Violin Concerto (Birmingham, March 30, 1961); Concertino for Trumpet, Horn, and Orch. (Llangefni, April 8, 1971); Concerto Grosso No. 1 (Caerphilly Festival, June 11, 1965); Concerto Grosso No. 2 (1966); *Variants* for Orch. (London, Nov. 2, 1966); *Fioriture* (London, Nov. 24, 1968); Divertimento for Orch. (Llandaff, Nov. 14, 1969); *4 Welsh Dances* (London, June 28, 1958); *Investiture Dances* (commissioned to celebrate the investiture of the Prince of Wales; London, June 22, 1969); *Night Music* (Aberystwyth, Jan. 30, 1967); *Sinfonia* for String Orch. (Bromsgrove Festival, April 19, 1964); *Sinfonietta No. 1* (Cardiff Festival, 1968); *Sinfonietta No. 2* (Cheltenham Festival, July 4, 1969); *Sinfonietta No. 3* (Swansea, March 10, 1970); *Sinfonietta No. 4* (Wales, July 30, 1971); *The Sun, the Great Luminary of the Universe* (Swansea, Oct. 8, 1970); *Sinfonia Fidei* for Soprano, Tenor, Chorus, and Orch. (1977); *The Heaventree of Stars* for Violin and Orch. (1980). CHAMBER MUSIC: 4 violin sonatas (1969, 1970, 1971, 1976); Cello Sonata (1970); Clarinet Sonata (1967); Sonata for Harp (1964); Horn Sonata (1971); Divertimenti for 8 Instruments

(1968); Divertimento for Oboe, Clarinet, Horn, and Bassoon (1963); Piano Quintet (1972); Septet for Wind Instruments, Strings, and Piano (1956); Sextet for Flute, Clarinet, Bassoon, Violin, Viola, and Cello (1960); String Quartet (1966); Variations for Flute, Clarinet, Harp, and String Quartet (1962); 6 piano sonatas (1959–72); *Ritornelli* for Trombone, Wind Instruments, and Percussion (1974); *A Contemplation Upon Flowers* for Soprano and Orch. (1976); organ music; choruses; songs.

BIBLIOGRAPHY: Basil Deane, *Alun Hoddinott* (Cardiff, 1977).

Hodeir, André, French music critic and jazz enthusiast; b. Paris, Jan. 22, 1921. He studied at the Paris Cons. with Messiaen and others; in 1954 founded the Jazz Group of Paris, which he led until 1960. He edited the periodical *Jazz Hot* (1947–50); publ. *Introduction à la musique de jazz* (Paris, 1948); *Les Formes de la musique* (Paris, 1951; 5th ed., 1969; in Eng., N.Y., 1966); *Hommes et problèmes du jazz* (Paris, 1954; in Eng. as *Jazz, Its Evolution and Essence,* N.Y. 1956); *La Musique étrangère contemporaine* (Paris, 1954; 3rd ed., 1971); *La Musique depuis Debussy* (Paris, 1961; in Eng. as *Since Debussy,* N.Y., 1961); *Toward Jazz* (N.Y., 1963); *Les Mondes du jazz* (Paris, 1970; in Eng. as *The Worlds of Jazz,* N.Y., 1972).

Hodges, Edward, English organist and composer; b. Bristol, July 20, 1796; d. Clifton, England, Sept. 1, 1867. He was an organist at Bristol; received his Mus.Doc. at Cambridge (1825); in 1838, went to America, where he became an organist in Toronto and then in N.Y. (1839). He returned to England in 1863. He publ. *An Essay on the Cultivation of Church Music* (N.Y., 1841). The Library of Congress acquired the bulk of his music library (743 vols.), including his own works in MS, in 1919. His daughter, **Faustina Hasse Hodges** (b. Malmesbury, Aug. 7, 1823; d. Philadelphia, Feb. 4, 1895), was also an organist in the U.S. She composed songs and instrumental pieces and publ. a biography of her father (N.Y., 1896). His son, **Rev. John Sebastian Bach Hodges** (b. Bristol, 1830: d. Baltimore, May 1, 1915), an accomplished organist, composed many anthems and services.

BIBLIOGRAPHY: A.H. Messiter, *History of the Choir and Music of Trinity Church* (N.Y., 1906).

Hodges, John Cornelius (a.k.a. **"Johnny"** or **"Rabbit"**), black American jazz alto and soprano saxophonist; b. Cambridge, Mass., July 25, 1906; d. New York, May 11, 1970. After playing drums and piano, he studied the saxophone with Sidney Bechet; then played with Willie "the Lion" Smith, Bechet, and Chick Webb; from 1928 to 1951 he was a member of Duke Ellington's band; subsequently led his own band and septet for several years; then rejoined Ellington in 1955, remaining with him until his death.

Hodkinson, Sydney P., Canadian composer; b. Winnipeg, Jan. 17, 1934. He played the clarinet in bands; studied composition at the Eastman School of Music in Rochester, N.Y., with Louis Mennini and Bernard Rogers (1953–58); then had sessions with Sessions, Carter, and Babbitt at Princeton Univ. (1960); in 1967 enrolled at the Univ. of Michigan as a student of Leslie Bassett and Ross Lee Finney (Mus.D., 1968). He was on the faculty of the Univ. of Virginia (1958–63), Ohio Univ. (1963–68), and the Univ. of Michigan (1968–73); in 1973 was appointed to the staff of the Eastman School of Music. He held a Guggenheim fellowship in 1978–79; received numerous awards for specific compositions. In his music he explores with pragmatic coherence all resources of modern techniques.

WORKS: *Lyric Impressions* for Orch. (1956); *Threnody* for Orch. (1957); *Diversions on a Chorale* for Orch. (1958); *2 Studies* for String Quartet (1958); *Structure* for Percussion Ensemble (1958); *Stanzas* for Piano Trio (1959); *Litigo* for Winds and Percussion (1959); *Dynamics,* 5 miniatures for Orch. (1960); *Lament for Guitar and 2 Lovers,* theatrical action for Actors, Dancers, and Musicians (1962); *Dialogue,* concertino for Piano and Wind Band (1963); *5 Absurdities from Lewis Carroll* for 5 Trombones (1964); *Mosaic* for Brass Quintet (1964); *Taiwa,* myth for Actors, Dancers, and Musicians (Athens, Ohio, April 28, 1965); *Caricatures* for Orch. (1966; Dallas, April 5, 1969); *Armistice,* truce for Dancers and Musicians (1966); *Interplay,* histrionic controversy for 4 Musicians on Flute and Piccolo, Clarinet and Saxophone, Percussion, and Double Bass (Montreal, July 17, 1967); *Scissors,* electronic film score (1967); *Dissolution of the Serial* for Piano and One Instrument (1967; Ann Arbor, Mich., Dec. 10, 1967); *Funks,* improvisations for 7 Jazz Musicians (1967); *Imagin'd Quarter,* "an incentive" for 4 Percussionists (1967); *Shifting Trek* for 11 Instruments (1967); *Fresco,* mural for Orch. (1968); *Organasm,* scenario for Organ Soloist and Assistants (1968); *Flux* for Chamber Orch. (1968); *Arc,* aria with interludes for Soprano, Fute, Piccolo, Piano, and 2 Percussionists (1969); *Valence* for Chamber Orch. (1970); *Stabile* for Youth Orch. (1970); *One Man's Meat* for Live and Recorded Double-bass Solo (1970); *Another Man's Poison* for Brass Quintet (1970); *Epigrams* for Orch. (1971); *Trinity* for Solo Treble Instrument (2972); *Incentus* for Orch. (1972); *Blocks* for Symph. Band (1972); *Contemporary Primer* for Symph. Band (1972); *Vox Populous,* chamber oratorio (1972); *The Edge of the Olde One* for Electrified English Horn, Strings, and Percussion (N.Y., May 13, 1977); *Bumberboom: Scherzo diabolique* for Orch. (Montreal, Nov. 9, 1982); 8 pieces for various ensembles under the generic title *Megaliths;* 8 ensembles under the title *Drawings.*

Höeberg, Georg, Danish composer, conductor, and violinist; b. Copenhagen, Dec. 27, 1872; d. Vedboek, Aug. 3, 1950. He studied at the Cons. of Copenhagen, and later in Berlin; taught at the Copenhagen Cons. in 1900–14; in 1914–30, was conductor at the Royal Opera; in 1915–49 he appeared as a guest conductor in Scandinavia and Germany. He wrote the opera *Bryllup i Katakomberne* (*The Wedding in the Catacombs*; Copenhagen, March 6, 1909); the ballet *The Paris Cathedral* (Copenhagen, Oct. 25, 1912); several pieces for violin and orch.; a Symph.; choral works; and songs.

Hoelscher, Ludwig, noted German cellist; b. Solingen, Aug. 23, 1907. He studied cello in Leipzig with Julius Klengel and in Berlin with Hugo Becker. In 1930 he won the Mendelssohn Prize; in 1936 was appointed prof. at the Berlin Hochschule für Musik; later gave master classes in cello playing at the Mozarteum in Salzburg and at the summer courses at the International Academy there. In 1931 he engaged in far-flung tours in Europe and in the Far East; gave duo-recitals with the pianist Elly Ney. A musician of great culture, he arranged his programs covering both the classical and the modern literature, ranging from Bach to the works of Pfitzner, Krenek, Fortner, and Henze. In 1953 he was named an honorary prof. of the Univ. of Tokyo.
BIBLIOGRAPHY: E. Valentin, *Cello, Das Instrument und sein Meister Ludwig Hoelscher* (Pfullingen, 1955); M. Kaindl-Hönig, *Ludwig Hoelscher* (Geneva, 1962); W.-E. von Lewinski, *Ludwig Hoelscher* (Tutzing, 1967).

Hoelscher, Ulf, talented German violinist; b. Kitzingen, Jan. 17, 1942. After study in Germany he received a grant which enabled him to go to America and enroll in the classes of Ivan Galamian at the Curtis Inst. of Music in Philadelphia and of Josef Gingold at the Indiana Univ. School of Music in Bloomington. He then developed an international career, touring Europe, Australia, and the Far East, as well as the U.S. His repertoire was commendably large, encompassing works of the Baroque era, the Romantic school, and the contemporary avant-garde.

Hoérée, Arthur, Belgian music critic and composer; b. Saint Gilles, near Brussels, April 16, 1897. He studied organ and music theory at the Brussels Cons. In 1919 he went to Paris, where he studied composition with Paul Vidal and orchestration with Vincent d'Indy. He then devoted himself mainly to music criticism, without abandoning composition. He gave several courses in composition at the Ecole Normale Supérieure de Musique in Paris and at the French Radio Center. In 1972 he was appointed instructor in musicology at the Sorbonne. His compositions include several ballets and scores of incidental music for theatrical plays; *Pastorale et danse* for String Quartet (1923); Septet (1923); *Pour le premier jour du printemps* for Piano (1949); *Crève-Coeur, le Magicien* for Soli, Chorus, and Orch. (1961). He publ. a monograph, *Albert Roussel* (Paris, 1938); a later major study, *Roussel* (Paris 1969); and *La Musique française au XXᵉ siècle* (Paris, 1974).

Hoesick, Ferdinand, Polish musicologist; b. Warsaw, Oct. 16, 1867; d. there, April 13, 1941. He received an excellent European education; studied at the univs. of Heidelberg, Cracow, and Paris, returning to Warsaw in 1891; was editor and writer on literature; his writings on music deal exclusively

with Chopin; publ. (in Polish) the basic biography, *Chopin's Life and Works* (3 vols.; Warsaw, 1910–11; 2nd ed., in 2 vols., 1926); a brief preliminary biography, *Chopin* (Warsaw, 1898); *Selection from J. Elsner's Memoirs* (Warsaw, 1901); *Chopiniana* (letters, etc.; Warsaw, 1912); *Slowacki and Chopin, Historic-Literary Parallels and Sketches* (Warsaw, 1928).

Hoesslin, Franz von, German conductor; b. Munich, Dec. 31, 1885; d. (in a plane crash in southern France) Sept. 28, 1946. He studied general subjects at the Univ. of Munich; conducting with Felix Mottl, composition with Max Reger. He held the post of conductor at the Municipal Theater of St. Gall, Switzerland (1908–11); then conducted in Riga (1912–14); was in the German army during World War I; then in Lübeck (1919–20), Mannheim (1920–22), and at the Berlin Volksoper (1922–23); was Generalmusikdirektor in Dessau (1923–26); opera conductor in Barmen-Elberfeld (1926–27); later was engaged as conductor for the Bayreuth Festival; conducted opera in France and Spain. He was also a composer; wrote some orch. works, a Clarinet Quintet, and choruses.

Høffding, Finn, Danish composer; b. Copenhagen, March 10, 1899. He studied violin with K. Sandby (1911–21), organ with R.S. Rung-Keller (1919–21), composition and harmony with Knud Jeppesen (1918–21), and music history with Thomas Laub (1920–23); then went to Vienna, where he took lessons with Joseph Marx (1921–22). He subsequently was for 38 years on the faculty of the Royal Academy of Music in Copenhagen (1931–69), during the last 15 of which he acted as director there. His style of composition is influenced by linear counterpoint as practiced by Carl Nielsen.
WORKS: 3 operas: *Kejserens nye Klaeder* (*The Emperor's New Clothes*), after Hans Christian Andersen (1926; Copenhagen, Dec. 29, 1928); *Kilderejsen* (*The Healing Spring*), after Holberg (1931; Copenhagen, Jan. 13, 1942); a school opera, *Pasteur* (1935; Copenhagen, March 9, 1938); 4 symphs.: No. 1, *Sinfonia impetuosa* (1923; Copenhagen, Aug. 22, 1925); No. 2, *Il Canto de Liberato*, to a phonic text devised by the composer, for Coloratura Soprano, Chorus, and Orch. (1924); No. 3 for 2 Pianos and Orch. (1928); No. 4, *Sinfonia concertante*, for Chamber Orch. (1934); 4 symph. fantasies: No. 1, *Evolution* (1939; Copenhagen, Sept. 4, 1940); No. 2, *Det er ganske vist* (*It Is Perfectly True*), after Hans Christian Andersen (1940; Copenhagen, March 6, 1944; as a pantomime, Tivoli Gardens, July 1, 1948); No. 3, *Vår-Höst* (*Spring-Autumn*) for Baritone and Orch. (1944; Copenhagen Radio, Jan. 24, 1946); No. 4, *The Arsenal at Springfield,* after Longfellow's poem, for 3 Soloists, Chorus, and Orch. (1953; Copenhagen Radio, Sept. 22, 1955); *Overture* for Small Orch. (1930); Concerto for Oboe and String Orch. (1933); *Fanfare,* concert piece for Orch. (1939); *Fire Minespil,* suite for Small Orch. (1944); *Majfest,* fantasy on a Danish folk dance, for Orch. (1945); *Fantasia concertante* for Orch. (Copenhagen Radio, April 1, 1965); *Karlsvognen* for Soloists,

Chorus, and Orch. (1924); *Fem Svaner* (*The 5 Swans*) for Soloists, Chorus, and Orch. (1937; Copenhagen, Sept. 9, 1938); *Christofer Columbus,* chaconne for Male Chorus, Baritone Solo, and Orch. (1937; Copenhagen, March 5, 1941); *Giordano Bruno* for Baritone Solo, Male Chorus, Winds, and Percussion (Univ. of Copenhagen, Dec. 8, 1968); several works for school performance, including *Da solen blev forkølet* (*When the Sun Caught a Cold*) for Children's Chorus and School Orch. (1977); *Kammermusik* for Soprano, Oboe, and Piano (1927); *Das Eisenbahngleichnis* for Chorus, Piano, and 3 Saxophones (1934); *Fire Satser* for Chorus and Instruments (1965); *Vintersolhverv* for Chorus and Instruments (1965); *Arets kredsgang,* cycle for Chorus and Instruments (1965); *Davids 18 og 23,* 2 Psalms for Voice and Organ (1966); several a cappella choruses, including *Agent* (1969), *2 Songs* (1977), and *4 Songs* (1977). Chamber music: 2 string quartets (1920, 1925); *Dialogues* for Oboe and Clarinet (1927); 2 wind quintets (1940; *Familien Vind,* 1954); Oboe Sonata (1943). For Piano: Sonatina (1951); Canon (1959); several sets of pieces. He publ. the teaching manuals *Harmonilaere* (Copenhagen, 1933; enlarged ed., 1970; harmonic analysis); *Den Elementaere Horelaere* (*Elementary Ear-Training,* Copenhagen, 1935; 2nd ed., 1964); *Indforelse i Palestrinastil* (*Introduction to the Style of Palestrina,* Copenhagen, 1969; a textbook on counterpoint); *Textbook on Harmony* (Copenhagen, 1976).
BIBLIOGRAPHY: S. Bruhns and D. Fog, *Finn Høffdings Kompositionen* (Copenhagen, 1969).

Höffer, Paul, German composer; b. Barmen, Dec. 21, 1895; d. Berlin, Aug. 31, 1949. He studied piano with Walter Georgii in Cologne; then took courses in composition with Franz Schreker in Berlin. In 1923 he became piano teacher at the Hochschule für Musik in Berlin, and in 1948 became director there. In his compositions he adopted a fairly radical idiom, making free use of the modern techniques of polytonality and atonality. However, most of his works preserve the formal unity of the Romantic school; the influence of his teacher Schreker is discernible.
WORKS: Operas: *Borgia* (1931) and *Der Falsche Waldmar* (1934); oratorios: *Der reiche Tag* (1938); *Von edlen Leben* (1941); *Mysterium der Liebe* (1942); *Sinfonie der grossen Stadt* (1937); Piano Concerto (1939); Oboe Concerto (1946); 3 string quartets; Clarinet Quintet; Wind Sextet.
BIBLIOGRAPHY: Karl Laux, *Musik und Musiker der Gegenwart* (Essen, 1949; pp.127–35).

Höffgen, Marga, German contralto; b. Mülheim, April 26, 1921. She made her concert debut in Berlin in 1952; in 1953 she made a highly successful appearance in Vienna in a concert conducted by Herbert von Karajan; from that time on she was active as an oratorio singer in Europe; also appeared in opera, at Covent Garden in London, at the Vienna State Opera, and at the Bayreuth Festival.

Hoffman, Grace, American mezzo-soprano; b.

Cleveland, Jan. 14, 1925. She was educated at Western Reserve Univ. in Cleveland; then studied voice with Friedrich Schorr in N.Y. and Mario Basiola in Milan; after appearances in the U.S., she went to Europe, where she sang in Florence and Zürich; in 1955 became a member of the Württemberg State Theater in Stuttgart. On March 27, 1958, she made her Metropolitan Opera debut in N.Y. as Brangäne in *Tristan und Isolde.* She made many appearances at La Scala in Milan, Covent Garden in London, Bayreuth, and the Vienna State Opera. In 1978 she became a prof. of voice at the Hochschule für Musik in Stuttgart. She was noted for her performances of the music of Wagner and Verdi, particularly for her roles of Brangäne, Kundry, and Eboli; also sang widely in concerts.

Hoffman, Irwin, American conductor; b. New York, Nov. 26, 1924. He studied violin at the Juilliard School of Music; then was music director of the Vancouver Symph. Orch. (1952–64). Later he served as associate conductor of the Chicago Symph. Orch. (1964–70), and for a season was its acting music director (1968–69). In 1968 he became music director of the Florida Gulf Coast Symph. Orch. in St. Petersburg. He also served as chief conductor of the Orch. of Belgian Radio and Television in Brussels (1972–76).

Hoffman, Richard, pianist and composer; b. Manchester, England, May 24, 1831; d. Mt. Kisco, N.Y., Aug. 17, 1909. He received his first instruction from his father and then studied with Leopold de Meyer, Pleyel, Moscheles, Rubinstein, Döhler, and Liszt. He spent most of his life in the U.S. and was a major figure in American musical life, but chose to retain his British citizenship. (Perhaps this was due to his having the same birthdate as Queen Victoria; on their joint birthday he would place a British flag on the mantel and play *God Save the Queen* on the piano.) He came to N.Y. in 1847; traveled with Jenny Lind on her American tour (1850–52) as joint artist; appeared often with Louis Moreau Gottschalk for duo–piano recitals. He was a prolific composer, mainly of salon music for piano; wrote about 100 opus numbers; also songs, anthems, etc. He publ. *Some Musical Recollections of Fifty Years* (with biographical sketch by his wife; posthumous, 1910).

Hoffmann, Bruno, German player on the glass harmonica; b. Stuttgart, Sept. 15, 1913. He studied piano, organ, and voice. In 1929 he became interested in building a modern "glass harp" and eventually expanded its range to 4 octaves, covering a full chromatic scale. With this instrument he gave several concert tours: in Europe (from 1949), in Asia (from 1962), in the U.S. and Canada (from 1964), and in South America (from 1969); he also composed a number of works for the glass harp.

Hoffmann, Ernst Theodor Amadeus (his third Christian name was Wilhelm, but he replaced it by Amadeus, from love of Mozart), famous German writer, who was also a composer; b. Königsberg, Jan.

24, 1776; d. Berlin, June 25, 1822. He was a student of law, and served as assessor at Poznan; also studied music with the organist Podbielski. He acquired considerable proficiency in music; served as music director at the theater in Bamberg; then conducted opera performances in Leipzig and Dresden (1813–14). In 1814 he settled in Berlin, where he remained. He used the pen name of **Kapellmeister Johannes Kreisler** (subsequently made famous in Schumann's *Kreisleriana*); his series of articles in the *Allgemeine Musikalische Zeitung* under that name were reprinted as *Phantasiestücke in Callot's Manier* (1814). As a writer of fantastic tales, he made a profound impression on his period, and influenced the entire Romantic school of literature; indirectly, he was also a formative factor in the evolution of the German school of composition. His own compositions are passable from the technical viewpoint, but strangely enough, for a man of his imaginative power, they lack the inventiveness that characterizes his literary productions. If his music is occasionally performed, it is only as a curiosity.

WORKS: Operas: *Die Maske* (1799); *Scherz, List und Rache* (Poznan, 1801); *Der Renegat* (Plozk, 1803); *Faustine* (Plozk, 1804); *Die ungeladenen Gäste, oder Der Canonicus von Mailand* (Warsaw, 1805); *Lustige Musikanten* (Warsaw, 1805); *Liebe aus Eifersucht* (Warsaw, 1807); *Der Trank der Unsterblichkeit* (Bamberg, 1808); *Das Gespenst* (Warsaw, 1809); *Aurora* (perf. planned in Bamberg, 1811, when Hoffmann conducted the theater there, but production failed to materialize; the opera was revised by L. Böttcher, and produced in a new version in Bamberg, Nov. 5, 1933); *Undine* (Berlin, Aug. 3, 1816; his best work; vocal score ed. by Hans Pfitzner, 1907); *Julius Sabinus* (unfinished); also a ballet, *Harlekin;* some sacred works; Symph.; Piano Trio; 4 piano sonatas. Two vols. of Hoffmann's collected musical works were publ. in 1922–23, ed. by Gustav Becking. His writings on music were publ. separately by Hans von Ende (Cologne, 1896).

BIBLIOGRAPHY: There is a large literature on Hoffmann as a writer; books and articles on Hoffmann as a musician include E. Istel, "E.T.A. Hoffmann als Musikschriftsteller," *Neue Zeitschrift für Musik* (1903); Hans von Müller, *Das Kreislerbuch* (Leipzig, 1903); Hans von Wolzogen, *E.T.A. Hoffmann und R. Wagner* (Berlin, 1906); E. Kroll, *E.T.A. Hoffmanns musikalische Anschauungen* (Königsberg, 1909); Hans Ehinger, *E.T.A. Hoffmann als Musiker und Musik-Schriftsteller* (Cologne, 1954); H. Dechant, *E.T.A. Hoffmanns Oper Aurora* (1975); R. Murray Schafer, *E.T.A. Hoffmann and Music* (Toronto, 1975).

Hoffmann, Hans, German music scholar; b. Neustadt, Silesia, Jan. 26, 1902; d. Bielefeld, Aug. 8, 1949. He studied musicology at the Univ. of Breslau, and later in Leipzig, Berlin, and Kiel. Concurrently he took instruction in singing and for several years sang in numerous oratorio performances in Germany. In 1933 he became choral conductor in Hamburg, and taught music theory at Hamburg Univ. He was also active as a symph. and opera conductor, and in 1940 was appointed music director of the Bielefeld Opera. Among his publications the most important are *H. Schütz und J.S. Bach* (Kassel, 1940) and *Vom Wesen der zeitgenössischen Kirchenmusik* (Kassel, 1949).

Hoffmann, Heinrich August (called **Hoffmann von Fallersleben**), German writer; b. Fallersleben, Hannover, April 2, 1798; d. at Castle Korvei, Jan. 29, 1874. He received his education at the Univ. of Göttingen; in 1835 he was appointed prof. at Breslau Univ. For some years (1842–48) he was not allowed to teach or reside in Prussia, on account of his dissenting political views; after 1848 he was librarian to Prince Lippe at Korvei. He wrote several important books dealing with music, *Geschichte des deutschen Kirchenlieds* (1832; 2nd ed., 1854); *Schlesische Volkslieder mit Melodien* (1842); etc., but his chief claim to fame is the text of *Deutschland, Deutschland, über alles,* which he wrote to Haydn's hymn *Gott erhalte Franz den Kaiser.*

Hoffmann, Richard, Austrian-American composer; b. Vienna, April 20, 1925. He studied violin and harmony in Vienna as a child; was in New Zealand in 1935–47; graduated from Auckland Univ. College in 1945. He settled in the U.S. in 1947; studied composition with Arnold Schoenberg, and subsequently became his amanuensis and secretary. In 1954 he joined the faculty of the Oberlin Cons. of Music. He developed a sui generis serial technique, in which intervals, meters, rhythms, timbres, and dynamics are systematically organized, while the tone row is not necessarily dodecaphonic.

WORKS: String Quartet (1947); Trio for Piano, Violin, and Bass Clarinet (1948); Piano Quartet (1950); *Fantasy and Fugue, in Memoriam Arnold Schoenberg* for Orch., in which the subject is a single reiterated note in 5 different dynamics (1951); Piano Concerto (1954); Cello Concerto (1956–59); String Trio (1961–63); *Memento mori* for Double Male Chorus, Tape, and Orch. (1966–69); choruses; songs.

Hoffmeister, Franz Anton, German composer and publisher; b. Rothenburg, May 12, 1754; d. Vienna, Feb. 9, 1812. He went to Vienna as a law student, but became greatly interested in music, and in 1783 established his publishing firm, of historic significance owing to its publications of Mozart and Beethoven. In 1800 he went to Leipzig, where he organized (with Kühnel) a "Bureau de Musique," which eventually became incorporated into the celebrated firm of C.F. Peters. In 1805 he returned to Vienna, where he devoted himself mostly to composition. Amazingly prolific, he composed 9 operas, 66 symphs. and overtures, 42 string quartets, 5 piano quartets, 11 piano trios, 18 string trios, and 12 piano sonatas; in addition to these he wrote a very great number of compositions for flute with various instruments. Hoffmeister's craftsmanship was of sufficient excellence to lead to confusion of his music with Haydn's. Regarding this, see E.F. Schmid, "F.A. Hoffmeister und die *Göttweiger Sonaten*,"

Zeitschrift für Musik (1937), and A. Weinmann, *Die Wiener Verlagswerke von Franz Anton Hoffmeister* (Vienna, 1969).

Hofhaimer (Hofheimer), Paul, celebrated organist and composer; b. Radstadt, Jan. 25, 1459; d. Salzburg, 1537. Cuspinianus and Luscinius both wrote of him as an unrivaled organist and lutenist. He was greatly appreciated at the various courts where he served. He was court organist to the Archduke Sigismund of Tyrol from 1480, residing at Innsbruck, and from 1490, at the court of the Emperor Maximilian I there. He was ennobled by the Emperor in 1515, when he played in St. Stephen's Cathedral in Vienna; he was also made Knight of the Golden Spur by King Ladislas of Hungary. Little of his organ music survives; some is preserved in the Berlin State Library. Extant works are *Harmoniae poeticae* (odes of Horace set for 4 Voices; 35 by Hofhaimer and 9 by Senfl; Nuremberg, 1539; republ. by Achtleitner, 1868); 4-part German songs in contemporary collections (5 in Oeglin's *Liederbuch*, 1512; others in Forster's *Liederbuch*, 1539); etc.

BIBLIOGRAPHY: H.J. Moser, *Paul Hofhaimer* (Stuttgart, 1929), containing transcriptions of Hofhaimer's surviving works.

Hofman, Shlomo, Polish-Israeli composer and musicologist; b. Warsaw, April 24, 1909. He studied at the Warsaw Cons., graduating in 1934; then went to Paris, where he studied composition with Roger-Ducasse, Charles Koechlin, and Darius Milhaud (1937–38). He subsequently settled in Palestine; in 1954 became a lecturer in musicology at the Israel Academy of Music in Tel Aviv. Among his works are Oboe Concerto (1950); Hebrew cantata, *Tawashih* (1960); Quintet for Clarinet and Strings (1945); several song titles. He publ. a valuable thesis, *L'Œuvre de clavecin de François Couperin Le Grand* (Paris, 1961); a polyglot *Dictionary of Musical Terms* (Jerusalem, 1955); *The Music of Israel* (1959); *La Musique arabe en Israël* (1963), etc.

Hofmann, Casimir, Polish pianist; father of **Josef Hofmann**; b. Cracow, 1842; d. Berlin, July 6, 1911. He studied at the Vienna Cons.; then conducted opera in Cracow. In 1878 he moved to Warsaw, where he taught and conducted. After the spectacular success of his young son, he followed him on his extended tours throughout Europe and America. From 1886, he lived mainly in Berlin. He wrote numerous works in various genres.

Hofmann, Heinrich (Karl Johann), German pianist and composer; b. Berlin, Jan. 13, 1842; d. Gross-Tabarz, Thuringia, July 16, 1902. He studied in Berlin with Grell, Dehn, and Wüerst. He became a concert pianist, then turned to composition. Exceptionally productive, he wrote a great deal of operatic, symph., and chamber music; choral works; and solo piano pieces; all of which were publ. and frequently performed. His popularity declined precipitously toward the end of his life; his music vanished from concert programs after his death. His style reflected

Wagnerian procedures, particularly in heroic moods; he possessed complete mastery of technique, but his music lacked originality or distinction.

WORKS: Stage works: comic opera, *Cartouche* (Berlin, 1869); heroic drama, *Armin* (Dresden, Oct. 14, 1877); pastoral opera, *Aennchen von Tharau* (Hamburg, Nov. 6, 1878); historic opera, *Wilhelm von Oranien* (1882); comic opera, *Donna Diana* (Berlin, Nov. 15, 1886). His *Frithjof Symphony* (1874) was enormously popular, having had 43 perfs. during the 1874–75 season in German cities alone; it was also perf. in England and America. Similarly successful was his orchestral *Hungarian Suite* (1873). He also wrote a great number of choral works and songs; characteristic piano pieces; chamber music.

Hofmann, Josef, celebrated pianist; b. Podgorze, near Cracow, Jan. 20, 1876; d. Los Angeles, Feb. 16, 1957. He was the son of the pianist **Casimir Hofmann;** his mother was a professional opera singer. At the age of 4 he began to play the piano, tutored by an older sister and an aunt; at 5, his father began giving him regular lessons. He was barely 6 when he first appeared in public in Ciechocinek; at the age of 10 he played Beethoven's Concerto No. 1 with the Berlin Phil., under Hans von Bülow. He also made a tour of Scandinavia; played in France and England; his concerts as a child prodigy became a European sensation; soon an American offer of a concert tour came from the impresarios Abbey, Schoeffel & Grau. On Nov. 29, 1887, Hofmann appeared at the Metropolitan Opera House, as a soloist in Beethoven's Concerto No. 1, with an orch. conducted by Adolf Neuendorff, and played works by Chopin and some of his own little pieces. He electrified the audience, and hardheaded critics hailed his performance as a marvel. He appeared throughout the U.S., giving 42 concerts in all; then agitation was started by the Society for the Prevention of Cruelty to Children against the exploitation of his talent. Alfred Corning Clark of N.Y. offered $50,000 to the family for his continued education. The offer was accepted, and young Hofmann began serious study with Moszkowski (piano) and Urban (composition) in Berlin. Then Anton Rubinstein accepted him as a pupil in Dresden, where Hofmann traveled twice a week for piano lessons. At the age of 18 he resumed his career, giving recitals in Dresden and elsewhere in Germany with enormous success; made his first tour of Russia in 1896, attaining huge popularity there; he reappeared in Russia frequently. In 1898 he again played in the U.S.; from then on, he appeared in American cities almost every year. At the peak of his career, he came to be regarded as one of the greatest pianists of the century. He possessed the secret of the singing tone, which enabled him to interpret Chopin with extraordinary delicacy and intimacy. He was also capable of summoning tremendous power playing Liszt and other works of the virtuoso school. His technique knew no difficulties; but in his interpretations, he subordinated technical effects to the larger design of the work. When the Curtis Inst. of Music was founded in Philadelphia (1924), Hofmann was engaged to head the piano dept.; in 1926–38 he was director of the Curtis Inst. On Nov. 28, 1937, his golden jubilee in the U.S. was celebrated with a concert at the Metropolitan Opera House, where he had first played as a child 50 years before. He performed the D-minor Concerto of Anton Rubinstein, and his own *Chromaticon* for Piano and Orch. From 1938 to his death he lived mostly in California. He became an American citizen in 1926. Hofmann was also a composer, under the pen name **Michel Dvorsky** (a transliteration of the literal translation into Polish of his German name, meaning "courtyard man"). Among his works are several piano concertos; some symph. works; *Chromaticon* for Piano and Orch. (first played by him with the Cincinnati Symph. Orch., Nov. 24, 1916); numerous piano pieces. He publ. a practical manual, *Piano-Playing with Piano-Questions Answered* (1915).

BIBLIOGRAPHY: A. Chasins, *Speaking of Pianists* (N.Y., 1957; 2nd ed., 1961); H. Schonberg, *The Great Pianists* (N.Y., 1961).

Hofmann, Leopold, Austrian composer; b. Vienna, Aug. 14, 1738; d. there, March 17, 1793. He studied piano and violin; held posts as choirmaster in Vienna churches; also served as a court organist. He wrote much church music and a number of instrumental concertos and chamber works, highly competent technically but lacking in invention and polyphonic strength. The article by Hermine Prohaszka in *Die Musik in Geschichte und Gegenwart* gives a detailed list of his publ. and unpubl. works.

Hofmann, Peter, outstanding German tenor; b. Marienbad, Aug. 12, 1944. He studied at the Hochschule für Musik in Karlsruhe; made his operatic debut in 1972 in Lübeck as Tamino; in 1973 joined the Württemberg State Theater in Stuttgart. He came to prominence in his performance of the role of Siegmund in the centennial Bayreuth productions of *Der Ring des Nibelungen;* later he appeared as Parsifal at Covent Garden in London. He made his U.S. debut as Siegmund with the San Francisco Opera in 1977; sang Lohengrin with the Metropolitan Opera in N.Y. in 1980. His other roles included Max, Florestan, Alfred in *Die Fledermaus,* Loge, and Bacchus.

Hofmann, Richard, German violinist; b. Delitzsch, April 30, 1844; d. Leipzig, Nov. 13, 1918. He studied with Dreyschock and Jadassohn in Leipzig; later settled there as music teacher. He publ. instructive pieces for various instruments, and a valuable manual, *Praktische Instrumentationsschule* (Leipzig, 1893; 3rd ed., 1907; in Eng., 1898); *Katechismus der Musikinstrumente* (many eds.); *Neuer Führer durch die Violin- und Viola-Litteratur* (1909); "Die F-Trompete im 2. Brandenburgischen Konzert von J.S. Bach," *Bach-Jahrbuch* (1916).

Hofmeister, Friedrich, German music publisher; b. Strehlen, Jan. 24, 1782; d. Reudnitz, near Leipzig, Sept. 30, 1864. In 1807 he established in Leipzig the music firm that bears his name; beginning in 1829, he publ. a valuable monthly catalogue, the *Musikalisch-litterarischer Monatsbericht.* His son and successor, **Adolf Hofmeister** (b. c.1802; d. Leipzig, May 26, 1870), publ. a 3rd and enlarged edition of Whistling's *Handbuch der musikalischen Litteratur* (1845), with supplementary vols. filled from issues of Hofmeister's *Monatsbericht.* After 1852, the 12 *Monatsberichte* for each complete year were arranged in alphabetical order and issued as a *Jahresbericht.* All these valuable editions were continued by the firm under the proprietorship of Albert Röthing (b. Leipzig, Jan. 4, 1845; d. there, Aug. 11, 1907). In 1905, Karl Günther became the head of the firm; he was succeeded by Karl Ganzenmüller. In 1935 the firm acquired the catalogue of Merseburger (Leipzig); after World War II the firm had offices both in Frankfurt and Leipzig.

Hofstetter, Romanus, German cleric and composer; b. Laudenbach (Württemberg), April 24, 1742; d. Miltenberg, May 21, 1815. He publ. 12 string quartets under his own name and, more importantly, is the true author of 6 string quartets commonly attributed to Haydn as his op. 3.

BIBLIOGRAPHY: Alan Tyson and H.C. Robbins Landon, "Who Composed Haydn's Op. 3?" *Musical Times* (July 1964).

Hogarth, George, Scottish writer on music; b. Carfrae Mill, near Oxton, Berwickshire, 1783; d. London, Feb. 12, 1870. He was a practicing lawyer in Edinburgh, and an amateur musician. He settled in London in 1830; contributed articles to the *Harmonicon;* also wrote reviews for the *Morning Chronicle.* His daughter married Charles Dickens in 1836; when Dickens became editor of the *Daily News* (1846), Hogarth began writing music criticisms for it; also wrote for other papers. In 1850–64 he was secretary to the Phil. Society of London.

WRITINGS: *Musical History, Biography, and Criticism* (1835); *Memoirs of the Musical Drama* (1838; 2nd ed., 1851, as *Memoirs of the Opera*); *The Birmingham Festival* (1855); *The Philharmonic Society of London* (1862); *The Life of Beethoven.*

Hogwood, Christopher, English harpsichordist, musicologist, and conductor; b. Nottingham, Sept. 10, 1941. He studied at Cambridge Univ. and at the Charles Univ. in Prague. In 1967 he and David Munrow organized the Early Music Consort, an ensemble devoted to the performance of medieval music. In 1973 he founded the Academy of Ancient Music with the aim of giving authentic renditions of music of the Baroque period; he made an intensive study of the works of Mozart, recording all of the symphs. on instruments of Mozart's time. He made a tour of the U.S. in 1974. In 1979 he became a professor-in-residence at Sydney (Australia) Univ. He edited works by J.C. Bach, Purcell, and Croft; was also a contributor to the 6th edition of *The New Grove Dictionary of Music and Musicians* (1980).

Hoiby, Lee, American composer; b. Madison, Wis., Feb. 17, 1926. After a preliminary music study in his hometown he took piano lessons with Egon Petri at Mills College, where he received his M.A. in 1952; intermittently he studied with Menotti at the Curtis Inst. in Philadelphia, and then attended various courses in Rome and Salzburg. In 1957 he received an award of $1,000 from the National Inst. of Arts and Letters. He is at his best in composing operas on contemporary subjects in a manner reminiscent of Menotti—concise, dramatic, and aurally pleasing, and sometimes stimulating.
WORKS: Operas: *The Scarf,* after Chekhov's story *The Witch* (Spoleto, June 20, 1958); *Beatrice,* after Maeterlinck (Louisville, Ky., Oct. 23, 1959); *Natalia Petrovna,* after Turgenev (N.Y., Oct. 8, 1964); *Summer and Smoke,* after a play by Tennessee Williams (St. Paul, Minn., June 19, 1971); also incidental music to the play *The Duchess of Malfi* (N.Y., March 19, 1957). Other works are *Noctambulation* for Orch. (N.Y., Oct. 4, 1952); *Hearts, Meadows & Flags* for Orch. (Rochester, N.Y., Nov. 6, 1952); *Pastoral Dances* for Flute and Orch. (New Orleans, Nov. 6, 1956); *Violin Sonata;* 5 *Preludes* for Piano; *Design for Strings; Diversions* for Woodwind Quintet; *Songs of the Fool* for Mixed Chorus; etc.

Hol, Richard, Dutch composer, conductor, pianist, and organist; b. Amsterdam, July 23, 1825; d. Utrecht, May 14, 1904. He studied organ with Martens and theory with Bertelmann. After traveling in Germany, he taught music in Amsterdam; in 1862, became city music director at Utrecht, succeeding Kufferath; then cathedral organist (1869) and director of the School of Music (1875); conducted concerts in The Hague and Amsterdam.
WORKS: A prolific composer, he wrote the operas *Floris V* (Amsterdam, April 9, 1892), *Uit de branding* (Amsterdam, 1894), and *De schoone schaapster;* the oratorio *David* (1880); 4 symphs.; choral and orch. works; chamber music; and songs. In 1886–1900 he was editor of *Het Orgel;* wrote a monograph on Sweelinck (1860).
BIBLIOGRAPHY: H. Nolthenius, *Richard Hol, Levensschets* (Haarlem, 1904).

Holbrooke, Josef, English composer; b. Croydon, July 5, 1878; d. London, Aug. 5, 1958. He received his primary education from his father; then studied at the Royal Academy of Music in London with F. Corder. After graduation, he conducted ballet and various summer orchs. Although he composed prolifically, and had many ardent admirers of his music, he never succeeded in establishing himself as a representative British composer. Perhaps this was owing to the fact that he stood aloof from modernistic developments of European music, and preferred to write for a hypothetical mass audience, which, however, failed to materialize at the infrequent performances of his music.
WORKS: OPERAS: *Pierrot and Pierrette* (London, Nov. 11, 1909); a trilogy (his main dramatic work), *The Cauldron of Anwyn:* I. *The Children of Don* (London, June 15, 1912), II. *Dylan, Son of the Wave* (London, July 4, 1913), III. *Bronwen, Daughter of Llyr* (Huddersfield, Feb. 1, 1929); *The Enchanter* (Chicago, 1915); *The Snob,* one-act comic opera. BALLETS: *The Red Masque; The Moth; The Enchanted Garden.* ORCH. WORKS: Symph. poems, *The Raven* (London, 1900); *The Viking; Ulalume* (1904); *Byron,* with Chorus; *Queen Mab,* with Chorus (Leeds Festival, 1904); *Homage to E.A. Poe,* with Chorus; *The Bells,* with Chorus (Birmingham, 1906); *The Skeleton in Armor; The Masque the Red Death;* 5 symphs.; variations on *3 Blind Mice, The Girl I Left behind Me,* and *Auld Lang Syne; Dreamland Suite; Les Hommages,* suite; *The Haunted Palace,* fantasy; *The New Renaissance,* overture. CHAMBER MUSIC: 5 string quartets; 4 string sextets; 3 violin sonatas; 2 piano quartets; 2 clarinet quintets; Piano Quintet; Trio for Violin, Horn, and Piano. He wrote many piano pieces, songs, and clarinet pieces; also a book, *Contemporary British Composers* (1925).
BIBLIOGRAPHY: George Lowe, *Josef Holbrooke and His Work* (1920); a symposium, *Josef Holbrooke: Various Appreciations by Many Authors* (London, 1937).

Holde, Artur, German music critic; b. Rendsburg, Oct. 16, 1885; d. New York, June 23, 1962. He studied musicology at the Univ. of Berlin; from 1910 to 1936 was music director of the Frankfurt Synagogue; also was active as a music critic. In 1937 he emigrated to the U.S.; was choirmaster at the Hebrew Tabernacle in N.Y. (1937–43) and music critic of the German periodical *Aufbau* in N.Y. He publ. the books *Jews in Music* (N.Y., 1959); *A Treasury of Great Operas* (N.Y., 1965); contributed articles to the *Musical Quarterly* and other American publications.

Holden, Oliver, American musician, carpenter, and minister; b. Shirley, Mass., Sept. 18, 1765; d. Charlestown, Mass., Sept. 4, 1844. After serving as a marine in the navy, he settled in Charlestown in 1787 and was active there as a justice of the peace and carpenter; then abandoned carpentry and established a music store (about 1790); also offered music lessons; officiated as preacher of the Puritan Church; served as Charlestown representative in the State House of Representatives (1818–33). He composed psalm tunes and odes; at least 21 hymns are known to be of his authorship, his best being *Coronation* (set to the words of *All Hail the Power of Jesus' Name*), first publ. in vol. I of his *Union Harmony* (1793); it has retained its popularity until modern times. His *From Vernon's mount behold the hero rise,* one of the many works written in commemoration of George Washington's death, was sung at the Old South Meeting House, Boston, in Jan. 1800. Other publications are *The American Harmony* (1792); *The Massachusetts Compiler* (1795; with H. Gram and S. Holyoke); *The Worcester Collection* (1797; ed. and revised by Holden); *Sacred Dirges, Hymns and Anthems* (1800); *Modern Collection of Sacred Music* (1800); *Plain Psalmody* (1800); *Charlestown Collection of Sacred Songs* (1803); *Vocal Companion* (1807); and *Occasional Pieces.*

BIBLIOGRAPHY: F.J. Metcalf, *American Psalmody* (1917); idem, *American Writers and Compilers of Sacred Music* (1925); *Dictionary of American Biography*, IX (1932); D.W. McCormick, *Oliver Holden, Composer and Anthologist* (Union Theological Seminary, 1963); R. Patterson, *Three American "Primitives": A Study of the Musical Styles of Samuel Holyoke, Oliver Holden, and Hans Gram* (Diss., Washington Univ., 1963); G. Chase, *America's Music* (2nd ed., N.Y., 1966).

Holewa, Hans, Austrian-born Swedish composer; b. Vienna, May 26, 1905. He studied music in Vienna; in 1938 went to Stockholm, where he established himself as a pianist and pedagogue. He was the first composer living in Sweden to adopt Schoenberg's method of composing with 12 tones related only to one another. In 1949–70 he served on the staff of the Swedish Broadcasting Corp.

WORKS: Opera, *Apollos förvandling* (1967–71); 2 string quartets (1939, 1965); Piano Sonata (1940); 12 *Pieces* for Piano (1945); 13 *Pieces* for String Quartet (1948); 4 symphs.: No. 1 (1948); No. 2 (1976); No. 3, with Soprano (1977); and No. 4 (1980); *Music* for 2 Pianos (1949); Sonata for Cello Solo (1952); *Och vilar inom oss,* cantata (1953); String Trio (1959); Solo Violin Sonata (1960); *Concertino I* for Clarinet, Horn, Viola, Piano, Harp, and Percussion (1960); *Miniatures* for String Quartet (1961); Quintet for Clarinet, Cello, Trombone, Percussion, and Piano (1962); Violin Concerto (Swedish Radio, Feb. 7, 1965); *Concertino II* for Octet and Percussion (1964); *Kammermusik I* and *II* for Cello and Piano (1964, 1973); *Composition* for Orch. (Swedish Radio, Oct. 8, 1966); *Chamber Concerto* for Viola and 11 Strings (1966); *4 Cadenze* for Cello and Orch. (Swedish Radio, April 12, 1970); *Movimento espressivo* for Orch. (1971); 2 piano concertos: No. 1 (1972) and No. 2, with Strings (1975); *Concertino III* for Chamber Ensemble (1974); Concerto for 2 Pianos and String Orch. (1975); *Concertino IV* for 14 Instruments (1978); *Concertino V* for 14 Instruments (1979).

Holguín, Guillermo. See **Uribe-Holguín, Guillermo.**

Holiday, Billie (called **Lady Day**), black American jazz singer; b. Baltimore, April 7, 1915; d. New York, July 17, 1959. She began singing professionally in Harlem nightclubs at age 15; was discovered by impresario John Hammond and bandleader Benny Goodman in 1933 and appeared with his band; also with Count Basie, Artie Shaw, and others; toured Europe (1954, 1958). Her otherwise brilliant career was marred by personal tragedies and, above all, addiction to narcotics and alcohol. Despite the oft-quoted phrase "Lady Day sings the blues," Billie Holiday rarely sang classic blues; with her unique vocal endowments she managed to make everything she performed—mostly popular tunes of the day—sound "bluesy." She publ. (with some professional journalistic help) an autobiography, *Lady Sings the Blues* (N.Y., 1956).

Hollaender, Alexis, German pianist; b. Ratibor, Silesia, Feb. 25, 1840; d. Berlin, Feb. 5, 1924. He studied at the Berlin Royal Academy with Grell and others; became an instructor at the Kullak Academy (1861); conducted choral groups (1864) and the Cäcilienverein (1870). He composed piano works, choruses, songs, etc.; publ. an instructive edition of Schumann's piano music and *Methodische Übungen fürs Halten einer tieferen Stimme.*

Hollaender, Gustav, German violinist; b. Leobschütz, Silesia, Feb. 15, 1855; d. Berlin, Dec. 4, 1915. He was taught the violin by his father; appeared in public at an early age; then studied at the Leipzig Cons. with Ferdinand David, and in Berlin with Joachim. At the age of 20 he embarked on a concert career; gave concerts of chamber music with Scharwenka and Grünfeld in Berlin (1878–81); in 1881 he was appointed a teacher at the Cologne Cons.; in 1894 became director of the Stern Cons. in Berlin, which post he filled until his death. He wrote numerous pieces for violin, in an effective virtuoso style.

Hollaender, Viktor (pen name, **Arricha del Tolveno**), German composer, brother of **Gustav Hollaender;** b. Leobschütz, April 20, 1866; d. Hollywood, Oct. 24, 1940. He studied with Kullak; was a theater conductor in Berlin for a number of years; also a theater conductor in London. He lived mostly in Berlin until 1933, when he went to America and settled in Los Angeles. His works include the light operas *San Lin, Trilby, The Bey of Morocco, Schwan von Siam, Die dumme Liebe, Der rote Kosak, Der Regimentspapa,* etc.; songs and piano pieces.

Holland, Dulcie, Australian pianist and composer; b. Sydney, Jan. 5, 1913. She studied at the Sydney Cons. with Alfred Hill, Frank Hutchens, and Roy Agnew. She then went to London, where she took courses with John Ireland at the Royal College of Music. Returning to Australia, she was active as a radio lecturer and concert pianist. Among her works are *Symphony for Pleasure* (1974), some theater music, and songs for children. She also publ. several school manuals.

Holland, Theodore, English composer; b. London, April 25, 1878; d. there, Oct. 29, 1947. He studied with Frederick Corder at the Royal Academy of Music and with Joachim at the Hochschule für Musik in Berlin. In 1927 he became prof. of composition at the Royal Academy of Music. Although his career was mainly that of a teacher, he was an estimable composer, particularly proficient in writing for the theater. Among his works is a children's operetta, *King Goldemar;* a musical play, *Santa Claus; Evening on a Lake* for Chamber Orch. (1924); *Cortège* for an ensemble of Cellos (1939); *Spring Sinfonietta* (1943); 2 string quartets; 2 piano trios; Suite for Viola and Piano; several song cycles.

Hollander, Lorin, American pianist; b. New York,

July 19, 1944. He received his early musical training from his father, the violinist **Max Hollander,** and studied violin before tackling the piano. He earned the reputation of an aggressive pianist to whom technical difficulties, whether in Bach or Prokofiev, did not exist. His principal piano teacher was Steuermann at the Juilliard School of Music in N.Y.

Holle, Hugo, German writer on music; b. Mehlis, Thuringia, Jan. 25, 1890; d. Stuttgart, Dec. 12, 1942. He was a pupil of Max Reger; in 1919–21, was director of the Heilbronn Cons.; in 1921–25, editor of the *Neue Musikzeitung* in Stuttgart; from 1925, was a teacher of music theory at the Hochschule für Musik, Stuttgart; was conductor of the famous Holle's Madrigal Choir, with which he toured Central Europe; was a member of the board of the Max Reger Society; also co-editor of the Musikalische Volksbücher.
WRITINGS: *Goethes Lyrik in Weisen deutscher Tonsetzer bis zur Gegenwart* (1914); *Die Chorwerke Max Regers* (Munich, 1922); and numerous articles in music periodicals. He revised Storck's *Mozartbiographie* in 1923, and has ed. old choral music for the Schott publishing firm (*Die hohen Feste, Motetten alter Meister,* etc.).

Höller, Karl, German composer; b. Bamberg, July 25, 1907. He received a good musical training as a chorister at the Cathedral of Bamberg; pursued his formal studies at the Cons. of Würzburg; later took courses at the Academy of Music in Munich, where he studied composition with Joseph Haas. He subsequently was engaged as an instructor there (1933–37); then taught at the Hochschule für Musik in Frankfurt until 1946; in 1949 he succeeded Haas as composition teacher at the Hochschule für Musik in Munich; remained there until 1972.
WORKS: Symph. (1953); Chamber Concerto for Violin and Orch. (1931); *Hymnen* for Orch. (1933); *Symphonic Fantasy on a Theme of Frescobaldi* for Orch. (1934); Chamber Concerto for Harpsichord and Small Orch. (1934); 2 violin concertos (1938, 1948); 2 cello concertos (1941, 1949); *Srveelnick Variations* for Orch. (1951); 6 string quartets; Clarinet Quintet; Piano Quartet; Piano Trio; 8 violin sonatas; Cello Sonata; 2 flute sonatas; Viola Sonata ("in memoriam Hindemith," 1967); a multitude of piano pieces; and some vocal works.

Holliger, Heinz, Swiss oboe player and composer; b. Langenthal, May 21, 1939. He studied oboe with Cassagnaud and composition with Veress at the Cons. of Bern; then oboe with Pierlot and piano with Lefebure in Paris and with Boulez in Basel. In 1959 he obtained the first prize for oboe playing in the international competition held in Geneva, and won first prize again in Munich in 1961. He embarked on a career as a concert oboist with his wife, the harpist **Ursula Hänggi,** touring in Europe and in the U.S. Several modern composers wrote special works for him, among them Penderecki, Henze, Stockhausen, Krenek, Berio, and Jolivet. He composes mostly chamber music works, several of them scored, un-

derstandably, for oboe and harp.
WORKS: Sonata for Unaccompanied Oboe (1956); 3 *Liebeslieder* for Voice and Orch. (1960); *Erde und Himmel* for Tenor and 5 Instruments (1961); *Studie* for Soprano, Oboe, Cello, and Harpsichord (1962); *Improvisationen* for Oboe, Harp, and 12 Instruments (1963); Trio for Oboe, Viola, and Harp (1968); *Der magische Tänzer,* chamber opera for 2 Men and 2 Marionettes (Basel, April 26, 1970); *Pneuma* for Winds, Percussion, and Organ (Donaueschingen, Oct. 18, 1970); *Cardiophonic* for a Wind Instrument and 3 Magnetophones (1971); String Quartet (1973); *Atenbogen* for Orch. (1975); *Komposition* for Organ and Tape (Baden-Baden, Oct. 18, 1980).

Hollingsworth, John, English conductor; b. Enfield, Middlesex, March 20, 1916; d. London, Dec. 29, 1963. He studied music at the Guildhall School in London; during World War II conducted a band of the Royal Air Force; after the war, he was active primarily as a conductor in film studios in London.

Hollingsworth, Stanley, American composer; b. Berkeley, Calif., Aug. 27, 1924. He studied at San Jose State College; then with Darius Milhaud at Mills College and with Gian Carlo Menotti at the Curtis Inst. of Music in Philadelphia; subsequently was at the American Academy in Rome (1955–56). He received a Guggenheim fellowship in 1958; also was awarded several grants from the National Endowment for the Arts. From 1961 to 1963 he taught at San Jose State College; in 1963 joined the faculty of Oakland Univ. in Rochester, Mich. His music follows the principles of practical modernism; in this respect he emulates Menotti. He used the pseudonym **Stanley Hollier** in some of his works.
WORKS: 4 operas: *The Mother,* after Andersen (1949; Philadelphia, March 29, 1954); *La Grande Bretèche,* after Balzac (1954; NBC TV, Feb. 10, 1957); *The Selfish Giant* (1981); *Harrison Loved His Umbrella* (1981); *Dumbarton Oaks Mass* for Chorus and String Orch.; *Stabat Mater* for Chorus and Orch. (San Jose, May 1, 1957); *Psalm of David* for Tenor, Chorus, and Orch. (1962); Piano Concerto (1980); Divertimento for Orch. (1982); *3 Ladies beside the Sea* for Narrator and Orch. (1983); chamber music: Sonata for Oboe and Piano; 3 impromptus for Flute and Piano (1975); *Ricordanza* for Oboe and String Trio (in memory of Samuel Barber; 1981); *Reflections and Diversions* for Clarinet and Piano (1984).

Hollins, Alfred, blind English pianist; b. Hull, Sept. 11, 1865; d. Edinburgh, May 17, 1942. He studied piano at several schools for the blind; then studied with Hans von Bülow in Berlin. In 1886 he made a tour of the U.S. playing in an ensemble with other blind musicians; in 1888, appeared in America once more, as soloist with several orchs. Returning to England, he became a church organist in Edinburgh (1897–1904). Then followed tours in Australia (1904), South Africa (1907, 1909, and 1916), and the U.S. (1925). He also composed some music. He publ. an autobiography, *A Blind Musician Looks Back*

(London, 1936).

Hollmann, Joseph, Dutch cellist; b. Maastricht, Oct. 16, 1852; d. Paris, Jan. 1, 1927. He studied with Servais at the Brussels Cons., winning first prize (1870); then at the Paris Cons. with Jacquard; played many concerts in Europe and America; lived mostly in Paris. Saint-Saëns wrote his 2nd Cello Concerto for Hollmann.

Holloway, Robin, English composer; b. Leamington Spa, Oct. 19, 1943. He took lessons in composition with Alexander Goehr. In 1974 he was appointed music lecturer at Cambridge Univ. His music is deeply rooted in Englishry; he resists the procrustean deformation of fashionable dodecaphony, preferring the relatively liberal discipline of neo-medieval counterpoint, clinging resolutely to basic tonality and modality. Yet on occasion he audaciously piles tonal Pelion on modal Ossa in his effort to achieve mountainous polyharmony; he also makes use of occasional *objets trouvés* from the music of Brahms, Debussy, and Schoenberg, treating such objects as legitimate flotsam and jetsam. His dramatizations, intensifications, and amplifications of Schumann's lieder are notable.
WORKS: *Garden Music* for 6 Players (1962); 3 Concertinos for Chamber Orch. (1964–69, 1967, 1975); Concerto for Organ and Wind Instruments (1966); Concerto No. 1 for Orch. (1966–72); *Divertimento* No. 1 for Piano and Orch. (1968); *Souvenirs de Schumann* for Orch. (1970); *The Wind Shifts* for High Voice and Strings, to 8 poems of Wallace Stevens (1970); *Fantasy-Pieces* on Schumann's *Liederkreis* (1971); *Clarissa,* opera after the novel by Richardson (1971–77); *Divertimento* No. 2 for Wind Nonet (1972); *Evening with Angels* for 16 Players (1972); *The Death of God,* melodramatic cantata (1973); *Domination of Black* (1974); *Sea Surface Full of Clouds,* cantata to poems by Wallace Stevens (1974–75); *Romanza* for Violin and Chamber Orch. (1976); *The Rivers of Hell* for Chamber Ensemble (1977); Concerto No. 2 for Orch. (1979); *Serenade* for Octet (1979); *Ode* for Chamber Orch. (1980); *The Dark Air* for Chamber Orch. (1980); *Clarissa Symphony* (Birmingham, Dec. 9, 1982); *Sound Idyll* for Chamber Orch. (London, Oct. 10, 1983).

Hollreiser, Heinrich, German conductor; b. Munich, June 24, 1913. He studied at the Munich State Academy of Music; took lessons in conducting with Karl Elmendorff. He subsequently was engaged as an opera conductor in Wiesbaden, Darmstadt, Mannheim, and Duisburg. From 1945 to 1952 he was Generalmusikdirektor in Düsseldorf. He then was a conductor at the Vienna State Opera (1952–61) and chief conductor of the Deutsche Oper in West Berlin (1961–64); also served as a regular conductor at Bayreuth for several seasons. In 1978 he was engaged as a guest conductor with the Cleveland Orch.

Hollweg, Ilse, German soprano; b. Solingen, Feb. 23, 1922. She was educated at the Cologne Hochschule für Musik; made her debut at the Opera in Saarbrücken in 1943. In 1946 she sang in Düsseldorf; later in Berlin and Hamburg; in 1952 at the Vienna State Opera; in 1955 she was appointed to the Düsseldorf Opera. She has also made appearances at Salzburg, at Bayreuth, and in England.

Hollweg, Werner, German tenor; b. Solingen, Sept. 13, 1936. He studied at Detmold; made his professional debut with the Vienna Chamber Opera in 1962; then sang in Bonn and Düsseldorf. He made his first American appearance in 1968 as a soloist with the N.Y. Phil.; subsequently sang at the Salzburg Festival, the Berlin Deutsche Oper, the Bavarian State Opera, and the Hamburg State Opera.

Holly, Buddy, greatly talented American rock musician; b. Lubbock, Texas, Sept. 7, 1936; d. in a plane crash, following a concert at Clear Lake, Iowa, Feb. 2, 1959. His real name was **Charles Hardin Holley.** He played the fiddle as a small boy, then switched to guitar. He joined a friend playing western and bop music on a local radio station; then teamed with a guitarist, a drummer, and a bass player to record his first song, *That'll Be the Day;* it soon became a hit and after Holly's death was included in an album significantly named *The Great Buddy Holly.* Stylistically, he was distinguished as one of the first white performers who used a characteristic "backbeat" of rhythm-and-blues in country-western music. In the last years of his short career he organized a group called The Crickets; in 1958 he toured in the U.S. and Australia as a guitarist in a trio with two other members of The Crickets. His songs have been reissued in record albums many times after his death. A motion picture, *The Buddy Holly Story,* was issued in 1978.

Holm, Mogens Winkel, Danish composer; b. Copenhagen, Oct. 1, 1936. He studied composition and oboe at the Cons. of Copenhagen (1955–61); then became music critic on the foremost Danish daily newspaper, *Politiken.*
WORKS: Chamber opera, *Aslak* (1962; Copenhagen, Jan. 27, 1963); textless chamber opera, *Sonata for 4 Opera Singers,* with Jazz Instruments and Electronics (Copenhagen, April 19, 1968); 5 ballets: *Tropismer II* (Copenhagen, May 24, 1964); *Kontradans* (Danish Radio, July 16, 1965); *Chronicle* (Swedish Radio, May 5, 1969); *Galgarien* (Malmö, Sweden, Nov. 27, 1970); *Rapport* (Danish Radio, March 19, 1972); *Chamber Concertante* for Bassoon, String Quartet, and String Orch. (1959); *Concerto piccolo* for Orch. (1961); *A Ghost Story* for Soloists, Chorus, and Orch. (1964); *Cumulus* for Orch. (Danish Radio, Aug. 17, 1965); *Alios,* symph. for 4 Instrumental Groups (Danish Radio, March 24, 1972; symph. version of the ballet *Rapport*); Trio for Oboe, Clarinet, and Bassoon (1956); Wind Quintet (1957); *Little Chamber Concerto* for 5 Wind Instruments, Violin, and Cello (1958); String Quartet (1959); *ABRACADABRA* for Flute, Trumpet, Cello, and 4 Timpani (1960); *Tropismer I* for Oboe, Bassoon, Horn, and Piano (1961); *Annonce* for Soprano

and Chamber Group (1965; to a text from a marriage advertisement in *Politiken*); *Ricercare* for Oboe and 4 Continuo Groups (1967); *Sonata* for Wind Quintet (1968); *Overtoninger I* for Soprano, Cymbalom, and Cello (1971); *Overtoninger II* for Flute, Piano, and Cello (1972); choruses.

Holm, Peder, Danish composer; b. Copenhagen, Sept. 30, 1926. He studied violin with Thorval Nielsen and counterpoint with Jeppesen at the Royal Cons. in Copenhagen (1945–47); became a lecturer at the Cons. in Esbjerg in 1949 and in 1964 was named its director; conducted the West Jutland Symph. Orch.; was a member of the program committee of Radio Denmark (1963–67).
WORKS: Ballad opera, *Ingen mad i dag, men i morgen* (*No Food Today but Tomorrow,* 1962); Violin Concerto (1952); Piano Concerto (1953); *Fantasy for Viola and Orch.* (1954); Concerto for Orch. (1955); Symph. No. 1 (1955); *Preludio, Scherzo, and Fantasia* for Orch. (1956); *Symphonic Dance* (1957); *Capriccio* for Orch. (1959); 2 concertos for Piano and Strings (1963, 1967); *Pezzo concertante* for Orch. (1964); *2 Sketches* for Trumpet, Trombone, and Orch. (1966); *3 Pieces* for Orch. (1966); String Quartet (1967); *VYL* for Orch. (1967; Esbjerg, May 2, 1968); *2 Pieces* for Wind Quintet (1968); *KHEBEB* for 2 Pianos and Orch. (1968); Trumpet Concertino (1970); Clarinet Concertino (1970).

Holm, Renate, German soprano; b. Berlin, August 10, 1931. She studied with Maria Ivogün; made a successful debut at the Vienna Volksoper in the operetta *Waltz Dream* by Oskar Strauss. In 1961 she joined the roster of the Vienna State Opera; received acclaim for her performances in the operas of Mozart, Rossini, and Richard Strauss. She also continued to appear in operettas, especially those by Johann Strauss and Franz Lehár.

Holm, Richard, German tenor; b. Stuttgart, Aug. 3, 1912. He studied in Stuttgart; in 1937 he became a member of the Kiel Opera; also made guest appearances at other German opera houses; in 1948 he joined the Bavarian State Opera in Munich. On March 15, 1952, he made his Metropolitan Opera debut in N.Y. as David in *Die Meistersinger von Nürnberg;* was on its roster until 1953. He also made successful appearances in London, Vienna, Salzburg, and Bayreuth. In 1967 he became a prof. of voice at the Hochschule für Musik in Munich.

Holmboe, Vagn, eminent Danish composer; b. Horsens, Jutland, Dec. 20, 1909. He studied composition with Knud Jeppesen and Høffding at the Royal Cons. in Copenhagen (1927–29); then took intermittent courses in Berlin (1930–33); traveled in Transylvania (1933–34), where he gained first-hand knowledge of Balkan folk music. Upon return to Copenhagen, he taught at the Royal Danish Inst. for the Blind (1940–49), wrote music criticism for the newspaper *Politiken* (1947–55), and taught at the Copenhagen Cons. (1950–65). A recipient of a government lifetime grant, and remarkably productive, he

wrote 22 symphs. (of which he withdrew 3 early ones); 13 chamber concertos for different solo instruments; and 14 extant string quartets (after he withdrew 10 previous ones). His music evolved from the legacy of Sibelius and Carl Nielsen; he then developed a method of composition with "germ themes," that grow metamorphically; his symph. works give an impression of grandeur, with long, dynamic crescendos in expanded tonality.
WORKS: 3-act opera, *Lave og Jon* (*Lave and Jon,* 1946–48); one-act chamber opera, *Kniven* (*The Knife,* 1959–60); symph. fairy play, *Fanden og borgemesteren* (*The Devil and the Mayor,* 1940); radio play, *Fløjten* (1946); ballet, *Den galsindede tyrk* (1942–44). FOR ORCH.: 11 numbered symphs.: No. 1, for Chamber Orch. (1935; Aarhus, Feb. 21, 1938); No. 2 (Copenhagen, Dec. 5, 1939); No. 3, *Sinfonia rustica* (1941; Copenhagen, June 12, 1948); No. 4, *Sinfonia sacra,* with Chorus (1941, revised 1945; Copenhagen, Sept. 2, 1945); No. 5 (1944; Copenhagen, June 16, 1945); No. 6 (1947; Copenhagen, Jan. 8, 1948); No. 7 (1950; Copenhagen, Oct. 18, 1951); No. 8, *Sinfonia boreale* (1951–52; Copenhagen, March 5, 1953); No. 9 (Copenhagen, Dec. 19, 1968); No. 10 (1970–71; Detroit, Jan. 27, 1972); No. 11 (Copenhagen, Feb. 17, 1983); *Sinfonia in memoriam* (1954–55); 4 sinfonias for String Orch., known collectively as *Kairos* (1957, 1957, 1958–59, 1962); 3 chamber symphs.: No. 1, *Collegium musicum concerto No. 1* (1951); No. 2 (1968); No. 3, *Frise* (1969–70); 3 works representing symph. metamorphoses: *Epitaph* (1956); *Monolith* (1960); *Epilogue* (1961–62); *Tempo variabile* (1971–72); Concerto for Orch. (1929); Concerto for Chamber Orch. (1931); Concerto for String Orch. (1933); *Rapsodi* for Flute and Chamber Orch. (1935); Violin Concerto (1938); Cello Concerto (1974); Concerto for Recorder, Celeste, Vibraphone, and Strings (1974); Flute Concerto (1976); Tuba Concerto (1976); 13 chamber concertos: No. 1 for Piano, Strings, and Percussion (1939); No. 2 for Flute, Violin, Celesta, Percussion, and String Orch. (1940); No. 3 for Clarinet, 2 Trumpets, 2 Horns, and Strings (1940); No. 4, *Triple Concerto,* for Violin, Cello, Piano, and Chamber Orch. (1942); No. 5 for Viola and Chamber Orch. (1943); No. 6 for Violin and Chamber Orch. (1943); No. 7 for Oboe and Chamber Orch. (1944–45); No. 8, *Sinfonia concertante,* for Chamber Orch. (1945); No. 9 for Violin, Viola, and Chamber Orch. (1945–46); No. 10, *Træ-messing-tarm,* for Chamber Orch. (1945–46); No. 11 for Trumpet, 2 Horns, and String Orch. (1948); No. 12 for Trombone and Chamber Orch. (1950); and No. 13, *Collegium musicum concerto No. 2,* for Oboe, Viola, and Chamber Orch. (1955–56); Concertino No. 1 for Violin, Viola, and String Orch. (1940) and No. 2 for Violin and String Orch. (1940); *Symphonic Overture* for Percussion, Piano, and Strings (1941). CHAMBER MUSIC: 14 string quartets: No. 1 (1948–49); No. 2 (1949); No. 3 (1949–50); No. 4 (1953–54, revised 1956); No. 5 (1955); No. 6 (1961); No. 7 (1964–65); No. 8 (1965); No. 9 (1965–66, revised 1969); No. 10 (1969); No. 11, *Quartetto rustico* (1972); No. 12 (1973); No. 14 (1975); *Musik for fugle og frøer* for 2 Flutes and 16 Bassoons (1971); Sextet for Flute, Clarinet, Bassoon, Violin, Viola, and Cello (1972–73); Wind Quintet (1933);

Quintet for Flute, Oboe, Clarinet, Violin, and Viola (1936); *Notturno* for Wind Quintet (1940); *Aspekter* for Wind Quintet (1957); *Tropos* for String Quintet (1960); Brass Quintet (1961–62); *Musik til Morten* for Oboe and String Quartet (1970); Serenade for Flute, Piano, Violin, and Cello (1940); *Primavera* for Flute, Piano, Violin, and Cello (1951); *Quartetto medico* for Flute, Oboe, Clarinet, and Piano (1956); Quartet for Flute, Violin, Viola, and Cello (1966); *Fanden løs i Voldmosen* for Clarinet, 2 Violins, and Double Bass (1971); *Ondata* for Percussion (1972); *Firefir,* quartet for 4 Flutes (1977); *Rhapsody Intermezzo* for Violin, Clarinet, and Piano (1954); *Isomeric* for 2 Violins and Piano (1950); Piano Trio (1954); Trio for Flute, Piano, and Cello (1968); *Nuigen,* piano trio (1976); an unnumbered Violin Sonata (1929); 3 numbered violin sonatas (1935, 1939, 1965); *Sonatina capricciosa* for Flute and Piano (1942); sonata for Violin and Viola (1963); Oboe Sonatina (1966); *Triade* for Trumpet and Organ (1975). FOR SOLO INSTRUMENTS: Violin Sonata (1953); Flute Sonata (1957); Double-bass Sonata (1962); Cello Sonata (1968–69). For Piano: *Choral Fantasy* (1929); 2 sonatas (1929, 1930); *Allegro affettuoso* (1931); 4 suites (1930–33); *Julen 1931* (1931); *6 Sketches* (1934); *Rumaensk Suite* (1937–38); *6 Pieces* (1939); *Sonatina briosa* (1941); *Suono da bardo* (1949–50); *Moto austero* (1965); *I venti* (1972). For Organ: *Fabula I* (1972); *Fabula II* (1973); *Contrasti* (1972). FOR VOICE: *Requiem for Nietzsche* for Tenor, Baritone, Mixed Chorus, and Orch. (1963–64); *Skoven (The Forest)* for Mixed Chorus, Children's Chorus, and Instruments (1960); *3 Inuit sange (3 Eskimo Songs)* for Baritone, Male Chorus, and Percussion (1956); *Beatus parvo* for Chorus and Chamber Orch. (1973); *Edward* for Baritone and Orch. (1971); *The wee-wee man* for Tenor and Orch. (1971); *Zeit* for Alto and String Quartet (1966–67); a cappella choruses, including *Solhymne* (1960) and the Latin motets *Liber Canticorum I* (1951–52), *II* (1952–53), *III* (1953), *IV* (1953), and *V, Beatus vir* (1967); numerous cantatas for ceremonial events; songs. He wrote a book on contemporary music, *Mellemspil (Interlude;* Copenhagen, 1966).
BIBLIOGRAPHY: "Tre symfonier" in *Modern nordisk musik* (Stockholm, 1957; pp. 152–66); P. Rapoport, *Vagn Holmboe: A Catalogue of His Music, Discography, Bibliography, Essays* (London, 1974; 2nd ed., revised and enlarged, issued in honor of his 70th birthday, Copenhagen, 1979); idem, *Vagn Holmboe's Symphonic Metamorphoses* (Diss., Univ. of Illinois, 1975); idem, *Opus Est* (1979).

Holmes, Alfred, English violinist; b. London, Nov. 9, 1837; d. Paris, March 4, 1876. His only teacher was his father, an amateur violinist; he sang at the Oratory in London as a soprano chorister; appeared as a violinist at the age of 9, playing a duet with his brother, Henry. The 2 brothers then went on a European tour, playing in Belgium, Germany, Sweden, Denmark, and the Netherlands (1855–61). Alfred Holmes then lived in Paris (1861–64); visited Russia in 1867; then returned to Paris, making occasional visits to London. He composed several programmat-

ic symphs., entitled *Robinhood, The Siege of Paris, Charles XII,* and *Romeo and Juliet;* also overtures, *The Cid* and *The Muses.* His brother, **Henry Holmes** (b. London, Nov. 7, 1839; d. San Francisco, Dec. 9, 1905), was also a precocious violinist; after 1865 he settled in London, where he taught at the Royal College of Music. In 1894 he went to San Francisco, where he remained until his death. He wrote 4 symphs.; 2 cantatas; a Violin Concerto (London, Dec. 11, 1875); also some chamber music.

Holmès, Augusta (Mary Anne), French composer; b. Paris (of Irish parents), Dec. 16, 1847; d. there, Jan. 28, 1903. She progressed very rapidly as a child pianist, and gave public concerts; also composed songs, under the pen name **Hermann Zenta.** She studied harmony with H. Lambert, an organist; later became a pupil of César Franck. She then began to compose works in large forms, arousing considerable attention, mixed with curiosity, for she was undoubtedly one of the very few professional women composers of the time. Her music, impartially considered, lacks individuality or strength; at best, it represents a conventional by-product of French Romanticism, with an admixture of fashionable exotic elements.
WORKS: Operas: *La Montagne noire* (Paris Opéra, Feb. 8, 1895); *Héro et Léandre; Astarte; Lancelot du lac;* for Orch.: *Andante pastoral* (Paris, Jan. 14, 1877); *Lutèce* (Angers, Nov. 30, 1884); *Les Argonautes* (Paris, April 24, 1881); *Irlande* (Paris, March 2, 1882); *Ode triomphale* (Paris, March 4, 1888); *Pologne; Andromède; Hymne à Apollon;* etc.; cantatas: *La Vision de la Reine; La Chanson de la caravane; La Fleur de Neflier;* some piano pieces; 117 songs, some of which have remained in the active repertoire of French singers.
BIBLIOGRAPHY: P. Barillon-Bauché, *Augusta Holmès et la femme compositeur* (Paris, 1912); R. Pichard du Page, *Augusta Holmès; Une Musicienne versaillaise* (Paris, 1921); R. Myers, "Augusta Holmès: A Meteoric Career," *Musical Quarterly* (July 1967).

Holmes, Edward, English pianist and author; b. London, 1797; d. there, Aug. 28, 1859. He received a fine education; was a friend of Keats at Enfield. He studied music with Vincent Novello. In 1826 he became a contributor to a literary journal, *Atlas.* He publ. *A Ramble among the Musicians of Germany* (1828; reprint, with a new introduction and indexes by Charles Cudworth, N.Y., 1969); *The Life of Mozart* (his most important work; 1845; 2nd ed., 1878); *Life of Purcell; Analytical and Thematic Index of Mozart's Piano Works;* also articles in the *Musical Times* and other journals.

Holoubek, Ladislav, Slovak conductor and composer; b. Prague, Aug. 13, 1913. He studied music theory with Alexander Moyzes at the Bratislava Academy of Music (1926–33) and with Vítěslav Novák at the Prague Cons. (1934–36). He was on the staff of the Slovak National Theater in Bratislava (1933–52 and 1959–66), and at the State Theater in

Košice (1955–58 and again from 1966).

WORKS: 5 operas, all brought out in Bratislava: *Stella* (March 18, 1939); *Svitanie* (*Dawn*, March 14, 1941); *Túžba* (*Yearning*, Feb. 12, 1944), *Rodina* (*Fatherland*, 1956–60); *Professor Mamlock* (May 21, 1966); Symph. (1946); Sinfonietta (1950); *10 Variations on an Original Theme* for Orch. (1950); *Defiances and Hopes*, symph. poem (1973); 2 cantatas: *Mesačná noc* (*Moonlight Night*, 1951) and *The Promise* (1952); Violin Sonata (1933); 3 string quartets (1936, 1948, 1962); Wind Quintet (1938); Trio for Flute, Violin, and Harp (1939); 2 piano sonatas (1931, 1947); songs.

Holst, Edvard, composer of light music; b. Copenhagen, 1843; d. New York, Feb. 4, 1899. He emigrated to America in 1874, and was active in N.Y. as an actor, dancing master, etc.; also wrote numerous pieces for military band (*Marine Band March, Battle of Manila*, etc.); a number of songs; and a comic opera, *Our Flats* (N.Y., 1897); in all, more than 2,000 numbers.

Holst, Gustav (full baptismal name, **Gustavus Theodore von Holst),** significant British composer; b. Cheltenham, Sept. 21, 1874; d. London, May 25, 1934. He was of Swedish stock; his paternal great-grandfather settled in England in 1807. Holst's father was an organist; his mother, a piano teacher; Holst received his primary musical education from his parents. He played the organ in Wyck Rissington, Gloucestershire; in 1893 enrolled at the Royal College of Music in London, where he took piano lessons with Herbert Sharpe, and also learned to play the trombone; in composition he studied with Charles Villiers Stanford and Rockstro. For some years he earned his living as trombonist in various orchs. in London. In 1905 he was appointed music master at St. Paul's Girls' School, and in 1907 was engaged as music director at Morley College in London, retaining both positions throughout his whole life. Plagued by suspicions of his German sympathies at the outbreak of World War I in 1914, Holst removed the Germanic-looking (but actually Swedish) nobiliary particle "von" from his last name (his early works were publ. under the name **Gustav von Holst**). Upon the advice of Percy A. Scholes, Holst traveled during the later period of the war to Salonika and Constantinople to organize musical activities among British troops, which further enhanced his reputation as a patriot. In 1919 he was appointed teacher of composition at the Royal College of London; from 1919–23 he also was on the faculty of Reading College. Early in his life he became deeply interested in Hindu philosophy, religion, and music; his music of the period reveals his fascination with Sanskrit epics. His most famous work, the symph. suite *The Planets,* is inspired by the astrological significance of the planets. There are 7 movements, each bearing a mythological subtitle: *Mars, the Bringer of War; Venus, the Bringer of Peace; Mercury, the Winged Messenger; Jupiter, the Bringer of Jollity; Saturn, the Bringer of Old Age; Uranus, the Magician;* and *Neptune, the Mys-*

tic, with an epilogue of female voices singing wordless syllables. The suite had a private performance in London on Sept. 29, 1918; 5 movements were played in public on Feb. 15, 1920; the entire work was first given in its entirety on Nov. 15, 1920. Its success was immediate and lasting in England and America; it was featured by some American orchs. at special concerts in celebration of space travel, and was even given in connection with the production of the science-fiction film *2001: A Space Odyssey.* The melodic and harmonic style of *The Planets* epitomizes Holst's musical convictions, in which lyrical, dramatic, and triumphant motifs are alternately presented in coruscatingly effective orch. dress. Holst also contributed greatly to the national style based on English folk songs. He was a master of choral writing, and several of his vocal compositions retain their validity. Some of his orientally inspired pieces also enjoy occasional performances. He was a highly successful teacher and an able conductor. In 1923 and again in 1932 he visited the U.S. as a lecturer and conductor; chronic ill health limited his activities. His daughter Imogen Holst described his mind in the last year of his life as "closed in gray isolation."

WORKS: FOR THE STAGE: *Lansdown Castle,* operetta (Cheltenham, Feb. 7, 1893); *The Revoke* (one act; 1895); *The Youth's Choice* (1902); *Sita* (1899–1906); *Savitai,* chamber opera after the Hindu epic *Mahabharata* (1908; London, Dec. 5, 1916); *The Perfect Fool* (Covent Garden, London, May 14, 1923); *At the Boar's Head* (Manchester, April 3, 1925); *The Wandering Scholar* (1929; Liverpool, Jan. 31, 1934); choral ballet, *The Golden Goose* (BBC, London, Sept. 21, 1926, composer conducting); choral ballet, *The Morning of the Year* (London, March 17, 1927, composer conducting); *The Coming of Christ,* mystery play for Chorus, Piano, Strings, and Trumpet (1927; Canterbury, May 28, 1928, composer conducting).

FOR ORCH.: *A Winter Idyll* (1897); overture, *Walt Whitman* (1899); *Suite de Ballet* (1899; London, May 20, 1904); Symph. in F, *The Cotswolds* (1900; Bournemouth, April 24, 1902); symph. poem, *Indra* (1903); *Song of the Night* for Violin and Orch. (1905); *Marching Song* and *Country Song* for Chamber Orch. (1906); *Songs of the West* (1906); 2 *Songs without Words* for Chamber Orch. (1906); *Somerset Rhapsody* (London, April 6, 1910); incidental music to the masque *The Vision of Dame Christian* (London, July 22, 1909); music for the Stepney Pageant (1909); Suite No. 1 for Military Band (1909); oriental suite, *Beni Mora* (1910; London, May 1, 1912); *Invocation* for Cello and Orch. (1911); Suite No. 2 for Military Band (1911); *Phantastic Suite* (1911); *St. Paul's Suite* for String Orch. (1913); *The Planets,* suite for Large Orch. and Voices (1914–16; London, Nov. 15, 1920; Holst's most famous work); *Japanese Suite* (1915; London, Oct. 19, 1919); *Fugal Concerto* for Flute, Oboe, and Strings (London, Oct. 11, 1923); *First Choral Symphony* for Soprano and Mixed Voices (Leeds Festival, Oct. 7, 1925); symph. poem, *Egdon Heath,* after Thomas Hardy (N.Y., Feb. 12, 1928); *Moorside Suite* for Brass Band (London, Sept. 29, 1928); *Double Concerto* for 2 Violins (London, April 3, 1930); *Hammersmith,* prelude and scherzo

(London, Nov. 25, 1931); *Capriccio* for Jazz Band (edited by Imogen Holst; 1932; London, Jan. 16, 1968); *Brook Green Suite* for Strings and Woodwinds (1933); *Lyric Movement* for Viola and Chamber Orch. (1933; London, March 18, 1934).

CHAMBER MUSIC: *Fantasy Pieces,* 3 pieces for Oboe and String Quartet (1896; revised 1910); Piano Quintet for Piano and Wind Instruments (1896); Woodwind Quintet (1903; London, Sept. 15, 1982).

VOCAL WORKS: *Clear and Cool* for Chorus and Orch. (1897); *Ornulf's Drapa,* scena for Baritone and Orch. (1898); *Ave Maria* for 8-part Women's Chorus (1900); *5 Partsongs* (1903); *6 Songs* for Baritone and Piano; *6 Songs* for Soprano and Piano; *King Estmere,* ballade for Chorus and Orch. (1903; London, April 4, 1908); *The Mystic Trumpeter,* after Walt Whitman (1904; London, June 29, 1905); *5 Songs* for Female Chorus, after *The Princess* by Tennyson (1905); *Hymns* from the *Rig Veda* for Voice and Piano (1908); *10 Choral Hymns* from the *Rig Veda* (1908–10); *The Cloud Messenger,* ode for Chorus and Orch. (1910); *Christmas Day* (1910); 4 part-songs for Children, Women's Chorus, and Harp (1911); *Hecuba's Lament* for Contralto, Female Chorus, and Orch. (1911); 2 Psalms for Chorus, Strings, and Organ (1912); *Hymn to Dionysus* (1913); *Dirge for 2 Veterans* for Men's Chorus and Brass Band (1914); part-songs for Mixed Chorus (1916); 3 hymns for Chorus and Orch. (1916); 6 folk songs for Chorus (1916); *Hymn of Jesus* for 2 Choruses, Orch., Piano, and Organ (1917; London, March 25, 1920); *Ode to Death,* with Orch., after Walt Whitman (1919; Leeds Festival, Oct. 6, 1922); choruses to *Alcestis* for Women's Chorus, Harp, and Flutes (1920); motet, *The Evening Watch* (1924); *Choral Fantasia* for Soprano, Chorus, Organ, and Orch. (1930; Gloucester, Sept. 8, 1931); 12 Welsh folk songs for Mixed Chorus (1930–31); *6 Choruses* for Male Voice and Strings (1932); *6 Canons* for Chorus a cappella (1932); songs.

FOR PIANO: *Toccata* on the Northumbrian pipe tune *Newburn Lads* (1924); *Chrissemas Day in the Morning* (1926); *Nocturne* (1930); *Jig* (1932).

BIBLIOGRAPHY: Louise B.M. Dyer, *Gustav Holst* (London, 1931); E. Rubbra, *Gustav Holst* (Monaco, 1947); Imogen Holst, *Gustav Holst* (London, 1938); Imogen Holst, *The Music of Gustav Holst* (London, 1951); A.E.F. Dickinson, *Gustav Holst,* ed. by A.L. Bacharach (London, 1954); Imogen Holst, *A Thematic Catalogue of Gustav Holst's Music* (London, 1974); Michael Short, *Gustav Holst: A Centenary Documentation* (London, 1974).

Holst, Henry, Danish violinist of English parentage; b. Copenhagen, July 25, 1899. He studied at the Copenhagen Cons.; then went to Berlin, where he took violin lessons with Willy Hess; subsequently was engaged as concertmaster of the Berlin Phil. (1923–31); then taught at the Royal College of Music in Manchester, England (1931–45); from 1945 to 1954 he was prof. of violin at the Royal College of Music in London; from 1961 to 1963 taught violin classes at the Univ. of Arts in Tokyo, Japan; in 1963 returned to Denmark and was appointed a prof. of violin at

the Cons. of Copenhagen.

Holst, Imogen Clare, English musician, daughter of **Gustav Holst;** b. Richmond, Surrey, April 12, 1907; d. Aldeburgh, March 9, 1984. She was a faithful keeper of her father's musical materials and writings. From 1952 to 1964 she was musical assistant to Benjamin Britten; she also conducted the ensemble of the Purcell Singers (1953–67) and served as artistic director of the Aldeburgh Festival (1956–77). She was one of the first women in Britain to conduct brass and military bands. In 1975 she was named by Queen Elizabeth II a Commander of the Order of the British Empire.

WORKS: *Gustav Holst* (London, 1938); *The Music of Gustav Holst* (London, 1951); *A Thematic Catalogue of Gustav Holst's Music* (London, 1974).

Holstein, Franz (Friedrich) von, German composer; b. Braunschweig, Feb. 16, 1826; d. Leipzig, May 22, 1878. His father was an army officer; at his behest, Holstein entered the Cadet School; there he had an opportunity to study musical theory. While a lieutenant, he privately produced his operetta, *Zwei Nächte in Venedig* (1845). He fought in the Schleswig-Holstein campaign; returning to Braunschweig, he wrote a grand opera, *Waverley,* after Walter Scott. He sent the score to Hauptmann at the Leipzig Cons.; the latter expressed his willingness to accept Holstein as a student. Accordingly, he resigned from the army (1853) and studied with Hauptmann until 1856. He then undertook some travels in Italy, finally returning to Leipzig, where he settled. He was also a poet, and wrote his own librettos. The musical style of his operas was close to the French type, popularized by Auber. He was a man of means, and left a valuable legacy for the benefit of indigent music students.

WORKS: Operas: *Der Haideschacht* (Dresden, Oct. 22, 1868); *Der Erbe von Morley* (Leipzig, Jan. 23, 1872); *Die Hochländer* (Mannheim, Jan. 16, 1876); another opera, *Marino Faliero,* remained unfinished; overture, *Frau Aventiure* (left in sketches only; orchestrated by Albert Dietrich; perf. posthumously, Leipzig, Nov. 13, 1879); *Beatrice,* scene for Soprano Solo with Orch.; Piano Trio; other chamber music; part-songs for Mixed and Men's Voices; etc.

BIBLIOGRAPHY: G. Glaser, *Franz von Holstein: Ein Dichterkomponist des 19. Jahrhunderts* (Leipzig, 1930).

Holt, Henry, Austrian-born American conductor and operatic administrator; b. Vienna, April 11, 1934. He studied with Hugo Strelitzer at Los Angeles City College and with Ingolf Dahl at the Univ. of Southern Calif.; made his conducting debut in *Rigoletto* with the American Opera Co. in Los Angeles in 1961; then was general director of the Portland (Oreg.) Opera (1964–66). In 1966 he was appointed general director of the Seattle Opera; conducted its highly acclaimed Wagner Festivals. In 1983 he became music director of the Univ. of Southern Calif. Opera; also continued to lead the Wagner Festivals in Seattle.

Holt, Simeon ten, Dutch composer; b. Bergen, North Holland, Jan. 24, 1923. He studied piano with Jacob van Domselaer; later took composition lessons with Honegger in Paris. From 1960 to 1970 he was connected with the Inst. for Sonologie in Utrecht; in 1970 opened his own electronic-music studio.

WORKS: Suite for String Quartet (1954); *Diagonal Music* for String Orch. (1956); Divertimento for 3 Flutes (1957); *Epigenese* for Orch. (1964); *Triptichon* for 6 Percussionists (1965); *Sandpipers* for Percussion (1965); String Quartet (1965); *Atalon* for Mezzo-soprano and 36 Playing and Talking Instrumentalists (1967–68); *Differenties* for 3 Clarinets, Piano, and Vibraphone (1969); *Scenario X* for Brass Quintet (1970); for Piano: *Compositions I–IV* (1942–45); Suite (1953); 2 sonatas (1953, 1959); *20 Bagatelles* (1954); *Allegro ex machina* (1955); *Diagonal Suite* (1957); *Journal* (1957); *Music for Peter,* 7 little pieces (1958); *20 Epigrams* (1959); *5 Etudes* (1961); electronic compositions: *Sevenplay* (1970); *Inferno I* and *II* (1970, 1971); *Modules I–IV* (1971); *I am Sylvia* (1973); *Recital I* and *II* (1972–74).

Holter, Iver (Paul Fredrik), Norwegian composer; b. Gausdal, Dec. 13, 1850; d. Oslo, Jan. 25, 1941. He entered the Univ. of Christiania (Oslo) as a student of medicine, but devoted much more time to music, which he studied under Svendsen; then was a pupil of Jadassohn, Richter, and Reinecke at the Leipzig Cons. (1876–78); lived in Berlin (1879–81); became Grieg's successor as conductor of the Harmonie in Bergen (1882); from 1886 to 1911 he was conductor of Musikföreningen in Oslo, and from 1890–1905, also of Handvaerkersångföreningen; in 1907, founded (and conducted until 1921) Holters Korförening, a society devoted to the production of large choral works (sacred and secular); was conductor of several of the great Scandinavian festivals; in 1900 he conducted with Svendsen the Northern Concerts in Paris. In 1919 the Norwegian government granted him an artist's stipend. He was editor of the *Nordisk Musik Revue* (1900–6). His compositions include a Symph. (1885); a Violin Concerto; and several cantatas: for the 300-year jubilee of Christiania (1924); for the 900-year Olavs-jubilee (1930); also choruses; chamber music; songs.

Holtzner, Anton, German organist and composer of the early 17th century; d. 1635. He was educated in Italy. His keyboard canzonas make use of free rhythmic transformation of themes in the manner of Frescobaldi's "variation canzonas"; one of them is reprinted in A.G. Ritter's *Geschichte des Orgelspiels im 14.–18. Jahrhundert* (1884).

Holy, Alfred, harpist; b. Oporto, Portugal, Aug. 5, 1866; d. Vienna, May 8, 1948. He studied violin and piano; then took harp lessons with Stanek at the Prague Cons. (1882–85). He subsequently was engaged as first harpist at the German Opera in Prague (1885–96), the Berlin State Opera (1896–1903), and the Vienna Court Opera (1903–13). In 1913 he became first harpist of the Boston Symph. Orch.;

he retired in 1928, and returned to Vienna. He publ. studies for harp, arranged from the symph. works of Richard Strauss, and various other harp transcriptions.

Holyoke, Samuel, American composer; b. Boxford, Mass., Oct. 15, 1762; d. East Concord, N.H., Feb. 7, 1820. His father was a clergyman, and Holyoke was naturally drawn to composing hymns. Although he received no formal training in music, he began to compose early, following his innate musical instinct. He wrote his most popular hymn tune, *Arnheim,* when he was only 16. He attended Harvard College, graduating in 1789; in 1793 he organized a school of higher education, known as the Groton Academy (later Lawrence Academy). In 1800 he went to Salem, where he was active as a teacher; was also a member of the Essex Musical Assoc. in Salem. Holyoke was among those who did not favor the application of "fuging" tunes in sacred music, as advocated by Billings, and generally omitted that style of composition from his collections; in the preface to his *Harmonia Americana* he states his reason for this as being because of "the trifling effect produced by that sort of music; for the parts . . . confound the sense and render the performance a mere jargon of words." His first collection was the *Harmonia Americana* (Boston, 1791); then followed *The Massachusetts Compiler* (co-ed. with Hans Gram and Oliver Holden; Boston, 1795); *The Columbian Repository of Sacred Harmony* (publ. Exeter, N.H., and dedicated to the Essex Musical Association; copyright entry dated April 7, 1802; contains 734 tunes, many of his own composition); *The Christian Harmonist* (Salem, 1804); and *The Instrumental Assistant* (Exeter; 2 vols., 1800–7; includes instructions for violin, German flute, clarinet, bass viol, and hautboy). He also publ. the song *Washington* (1790), and *Hark from the Tombs* (music for the funeral of Washington; 1800), etc.

BIBLIOGRAPHY: F.J. Metcalf, *American Psalmody* (N.Y., 1917); idem, *American Writers and Compilers of Sacred Music* (Cincinnati, 1925); J.L. Willhide, *Samuel Holyoke, American Music-Educator* (Diss., Univ. of Southern Calif., 1954); R. Patterson, *Three American "Primitives." A Study of the Musical Styles of Samuel Holyoke, Oliver Holden, and Hans Gram* (Diss., Washington Univ., 1963).

Holzbauer, Ignaz (Jakob), noted Austrian composer; b. Vienna, Sept. 17, 1711; d. Mannheim, April 7, 1783. He studied law and at the same time received instruction in music from members of the choir at St. Stephen's in Vienna; he also perused *Gradus ad Parnassum* by Fux, whom he met later and who advised him to go to Italy for further studies. He then proceeded to Venice, but soon returned home. For a brief period he served as Kapellmeister to Count Rottal of Holešov in Moravia; in 1737 he married Rosalie Andreides, a singer; shortly thereafter they moved to Vienna, where he became a conductor and she a singer at the court theater; they also spent several years in Italy. In 1751 he was named Oberkapellmeister in Stuttgart. In 1753 he became Kapellmeister at the court of the elector Karl Theodor in Mannheim, a post he held until the court moved to Munich in 1778. He visited Rome in 1756, Turin in 1758, and Milan in 1759; during these visits he produced several of his operas. Holzbauer was greatly respected as a composer, especially for his church music; Mozart heard one of his masses in Mannheim in 1777 and found it excellent. Holzbauer was an important figure among symph. composers of the Mannheim school; he wrote some 65 works for orch. Of his operas, *Günther von Schwarzburg* (Mannheim, Jan. 5, 1777) is historically significant for its departure from Italian convention; it is thoroughly German in subject and treatment, and is noteworthy for the inclusion of accompanied recitative in place of the dialogue of the singspiel. It was publ. in Mannheim in 1776; reprinted in *Denkmäler deutscher Tonkunst*, VIII–IX (1902). His other operas include *Il figlio delle selve* (Schwetzingen, 1753); *L'isola disabitata* (Schwetzingen, 1754); *L'issipile* (Mannheim, Nov. 4, 1754); *Don Chisciotte* (Schwetzingen, 1755); *I cinesi* (Mannheim, 1756); *Le nozze d'Arianna* (Mannheim, 1756); *Il filosofo di campagna* (Mannheim, 1756); *La clemenza di Tito* (Mannheim, Nov. 4, 1757); *Nitteti* (Turin, 1758); *Alessandro nell'Indie* (Milan, 1759); *Ippolito ed Aricia* (Mannheim, Nov. 4, 1759); *Adriano in Siria* (Mannheim, Nov. 4, 1768); *Tancredi* (Munich, Jan. 1783). He also wrote ballet music for operas by J.A. Hasse: *L'Ipermestra* (Vienna, Jan. 8, 1744) and *Arminio* (Vienna, May 13, 1747). In addition, he composed 4 oratorios, 21 masses (also a *Deutsche Messe*), 37 motets, a Miserere, and other church music. His instrumental works, in addition to the symphs., include concertos, divertimentos, string quartets, string quintets, etc.

BIBLIOGRAPHY: U. Lehmann, ed., *Ignaz Holzbauer: Instrumentale Kammermusik*, in *Das Erbe deutscher Musik*, first series, XXIV (1953); H. Werner, *Die Sinfonien von Ignaz Holzbauer* (Diss., Univ. of Munich, 1942).

Homer, Louise (née **Louise Dilworth Beatty**), American contralto; b. Shadyside, near Pittsburgh, April 28, 1871; d. Winter Park, Fla., May 6, 1947. She studied in Philadelphia, and later in Boston, where her teacher in harmony was **Sidney Homer**, whom she married in 1895. With him she went to Paris, and there continued her study of voice with Fidèle Koenig; she also took lessons with Paul Lhérie in dramatic action. She made her debut in opera as Leonora in *La Favorita* (Vichy, 1898). In 1899 she was engaged at the Théâtre de la Monnaie in Brussels, singing various parts of the French and Italian repertoires. She subsequently sang Wagnerian contralto roles in German at Covent Garden, London. She made her American debut in opera as Amneris with the Metropolitan Opera Co. (then on tour) at San Francisco (Nov. 14, 1900); sang the same part in N.Y. (Dec. 22, 1900); continued on the staff of the Metropolitan from 1900 to 1919, the 1914–15 season excepted; was then with the Chicago Opera Co. (1920–25); with the San Francisco and Los Angeles Opera companies (1926), and again with the Met-

ropolitan, reappearing there on Dec. 14, 1927. Her classic interpretation of Orfeo at the Paris revival of Gluck's opera (1909) and subsequently in N.Y. (Dec. 23, 1909, under Toscanini) produced a great impression. One of her greatest operatic triumphs was her performance of Dalila, with Caruso singing Samson. She gave her last appearance on Nov. 28, 1929. After retiring from the opera stage, she gave recitals with her daughter, **Louise Homer Stires,** a soprano. Her husband wrote a book of memoirs, *My Wife and I* (N.Y., 1939).

BIBLIOGRAPHY: Anne Homer, *Louise Homer and the Golden Age of Opera* (N.Y., 1973).

Homer, Sidney, American composer; b. Boston, Dec. 9, 1864; d. Winter Park, Fla., July 10, 1953. He studied in Boston, with Chadwick; then in Leipzig and Munich. In 1895 he married **Louise Dilworth Beatty,** his pupil, and went with her to Paris. He retired in 1940 and settled in Winter Park. He publ. about 100 songs, many of which won great favor, particularly *A Banjo Song;* also *Dearest, Requiem, Prospice, Bandanna ballads, It was the time of roses, General William Booth enters into Heaven, The song of the shirt, Sheep and Lambs, Sing me a song of a lad that is gone, The pauper's drive;* also 17 lyrics from Christina Rossetti's *Sing-song*. Other works include Sonata for Organ (1922); Quintet for Piano and Strings (1932); Violin Sonata (1936); String Quartet (1937); Piano Trio (1937). He publ. a book of memoirs, *My Wife and I* (1939).

BIBLIOGRAPHY: H.C. Thorpe, "The Songs of Sidney Homer," *Musical Quarterly* (Jan. 1931).

Homilius, Gottfried August, eminent German organist and composer; b. Rosenthal, Feb. 2, 1714; d. Dresden, June 5, 1785. He studied composition and keyboard playing with J.S. Bach; completed his education at the Univ. of Leipzig in 1735; in 1742 became organist of the Frauenkirche in Dresden; then was appointed music director of 3 main churches there (1755). His publ. works are: a Passion (1775); a Christmas oratorio, *Die Freude der Hirten über die Geburt Jesu* (1777); *6 deutsche Arien* (1786); in MS in the Berlin State Library and in the Dresden Kreuzchor archives: Passion according to St. Mark; church music for each Sunday and Feast day in the year; motets, cantatas, fugued chorales, a thorough-bass method, 2 chorus books, etc.

BIBLIOGRAPHY: R. Steglich, "Ph.Em. Bach und G.A. Homilius im Musikleben ihrer Zeit" (*Bach-Jahrbuch,* 1915); R. Fricke, "Gottfried August Homilius," *Zeitschrift für Kirchenmusiker,* XVII (1935); H. John, *Gottfried August Homilius und die evangelische Kirchenmusik Dresdens im 18. Jahrhundert* (Diss., Univ. of Halle, 1973). For a complete list of works, see Georg Feder's detailed article in *Die Musik in Geschichte und Gegenwart.*

Homs, Joaquín, Catalan composer; b. Barcelona, Aug. 22, 1906. He studied cello; began to compose late in life. He took lessons in music theory with Roberto Gerhard (1931–37); formed a constructivist style with thematic contents derived from Catalan melos.

WORKS: 7 string quartets (1938–68); Duo for Flute and Clarinet (1936); Wind Quintet (1940); Concertino for Piano and Strings (1946); Sextet (1959); String Trio (1968); *Impromtu for Ten* (1970).

Honegger, Arthur (Oscar), remarkable French composer; b. Le Havre (of Swiss parents), March 10, 1892; d. Paris, Nov. 27, 1955. He studied violin in Paris with Lucien Capet; then went to Switzerland, where he took courses with L. Kempter and F. Hegar at the Zürich Cons. (1909–11). Returning to France in 1912, he entered the Paris Cons., in the classes of Gedalge and Widor; also took lessons with Vincent d'Indy. His name first attracted attention when he took part in a concert of Les Nouveaux Jeunes in Paris on Jan. 15, 1918. In 1920 the Paris critic Henri Collet publ. an article in *Comoedia* in which he drew a fortuitous parallel between the Russian Five and a group of young French composers whom he designated as Les Six. These Six were Honegger, Milhaud, Poulenc, Auric, Durey, and Tailleferre. The label persisted, even though the 6 composers went their separate ways and rarely gave concerts together. Indeed, only Honegger, Milhaud, and Poulenc became generally known; Auric limited his activities mainly to the theater and the cinema, while Germaine Tailleferre produced some musical plays and concert pieces; as to Durey, he was known more as a dedicated member of the French Communist Party than as a composer.

In the early years of his career, Honegger embraced the fashionable type of urban music, with an emphasis on machinelike rhythms and curt, pert melodies. In 1921 he wrote a sport ballet, *Skating Rink,* and a mock-militaristic ballet, *Sousmarine.* In 1923 he composed the most famous of such machine pieces, *Mouvement symphonique No. 1,* subtitled *Pacific 231.* The score was intended to be a realistic tonal portrayal of a powerful American locomotive, bearing the serial number 231. The music progressed in accelerating rhythmic pulses toward a powerful climax, then gradually slackening its pace until the final abrupt stop; there was a simulacrum of a lyrical song in the middle section of the piece. *Pacific 231* enjoyed great popularity and became in the minds of modern-minded listeners a perfect symbol of the machine age. Honegger's 2nd *Mouvement symphonique,* composed in 1928, was a musical rendering of the popular British sport rugby. His *Mouvement symphonique No. 3,* however, bore no identifying subtitle. This abandonment of allusion to urban life coincided chronologically with a general trend away from literal representation and toward absolute music in classical forms, often of historical or religious character. Among his most important works in that genre were *Le Roi David,* to a biblical subject, and *Jeanne d'Arc au bûcher,* glorifying the French patriot saint on the semimillennium of her martyrdom. Honegger's symphs. were equally free from contemporary allusions; the first 2 lacked descriptive titles; his 3rd symph. was entitled *Liturgique,* with a clear reference to an ecclesiastical ritual; the 4th symph. was

named *Deliciae Basilienses,* because it was written to honor the city of Basel; the somewhat mysterious title of the 5th symph., *Di tre re,* signified nothing more arcane than the fact that each of its movements ended on the thrice-repeated note D. Honegger spent almost all of his life in France, but he retained his dual Swiss citizenship, a fact that caused some biographers to refer to him as a Swiss composer. In 1926 he married the pianist-composer **Andrée Vaurabourg** (1894–1980), who often played piano parts in his works. In 1929 he paid a visit to the U.S.; he returned to America in 1947 to teach summer classes at the Berkshire Music Center at Tanglewood, but soon after his arrival was stricken with a heart ailment and was unable to complete his term; he returned to Paris and remained there until his death.

WORKS: FOR THE THEATER: *Le Roi David,* dramatic psalm in 3 parts for Narrator, Soloists, Chorus, and 15 Instruments (1921; Mézières, Switzerland, June 11, 1921; revised as an oratorio with Full Orch. in 1923 and produced in Winterthur, Switzerland, Dec. 2, 1923); *Antigone,* opera in 3 acts (1924–27; Brussels, Dec. 28, 1927); *Judith,* biblical drama in 13 scenes (1925; Mézières, June 11, 1925; expanded to a 3-act opera and presented at Monte Carlo Opera, Feb. 13, 1926); *Amphion,* melodrama (1929; Paris, June 23, 1931); *Les Aventures du Roi Pausole,* operetta (1929–30; Paris, Dec. 12, 1930); *Cris du Monde,* stage oratorio for Soprano, Contralto, Baritone, Chorus, and Orch. (1930; Solothurn, Switzerland, May 3, 1931); *La Belle de Moudon,* operetta in 5 acts (1931; Mézières, May 30, 1931); *Jeanne d'Arc au bûcher,* dramatic oratorio in a Prologue and 11 scenes (1934–35; concert version, without Prologue, Basel, May 12, 1938; stage premiere, in German, Zürich, June 13, 1942); *L'Aiglon,* opera in collaboration with Jacques Ibert (1935; Monte Carlo Opera, March 11, 1937); *Les Mille et Une Nuits,* spectacle for Soprano, Tenor, Chorus, and Orch. (1937; Paris Exhibition, 1937); *Les Petites Cardinal,* operetta in collaboration with Jacques Ibert (1937; Paris, Feb. 20, 1938); *Nicolas de Flue,* dramatic legend for Narrator, Mixed Choir, Children's Choir, and Orch. (1939; concert premiere, Solothurn, Oct. 26, 1940; stage production, Neuchâtel, Switzerland, May 31, 1941).

BALLETS: *Vérité-Mensonge,* marionette ballet (1920; Paris, Nov. 1920); *Skating Rink* (1921; Paris, Jan. 20, 1922); *Sousmarine* (1924; Paris, June 27, 1925); *Roses de métal* (Paris, 1928); *Sémiramis,* ballet-melodrama (1931; Paris, May 11, 1934); *Un Oiseau blanc s'est envolé* (1937; Paris, June 1937); *Le Cantique des cantiques* (1937; Paris, Feb. 2, 1938); *La Naissance des couleurs* (1940; Paris, 1949); *Le Mangeur de rêves* (1941; Paris, 1941); *L'Appel de la montagne* (1943; Paris, July 9, 1945); scenes one and 4 of *Chota Roustaveli,* in 4 scenes (also known as *L'Homme à la peau de léopard;* 1945; Monte Carlo Opera, May 5, 1946; scenes 2 and 3 composed by Harsányi and Alexandre Tcherepnin); *De la musique* (1950).

INCIDENTAL MUSIC: *Les Dit des jeux du monde,* in the form of 10 dances, 2 interludes, and epilogue, for Flute, Trumpet, Percussion, and Strings (1918; as a ballet, Paris, Dec. 2, 1918); *La Mort de Sainte Al-*

méenne (1918); *La Danse macabre* (1919); *Saül* (Paris, June 16, 1922); *Fantasio* (1922); *Antigone* (1922); *La Tempête* (1923); *Liluli* (1923); *Le Miracle de Notre-Dame* (1925); *L'Impératrice aux rochers* (1925; Paris, Feb. 17, 1927); *Phaedre* (1926); *800 mètres* (1941); *Le Soulier de satin* for Soprano, Baritone, and Orch. (Paris, Nov. 17, 1943); *Charles le Téméraire* for Choir, 2 Trumpets, 2 Trombones, and Percussion (1943–44; Mézières, May 27, 1944); *Hamlet* for Narrator, Chorus, and Orch. (Paris, Oct. 17, 1946); *Prométhée* (1946); *L'Etat de siège* (Paris, Oct. 27, 1948); *Tête d'or* (1948); *Œdipe-Roi* (1948).

FOR ORCH.: *Prélude pour "Aglavaine et Sélysette"* by Maeterlinck (1916–17; Paris Cons. orch. class, April 3, 1917, composer conducting); *Le Chant de Nigamon* (1917; Paris, Jan. 3, 1920); *Entrée, Nocturne et Berceuse* for Piano and Chamber Orch. (1919; Paris, 1919); *Pastorale d'été* (1920; Paris, Feb. 12, 1921); *Horace Victorieux*, "mimed symph." (1920–21; concert premiere, Lausanne, Oct. 30, 1921; mimed premiere, Essen, Germany, Dec. 28, 1927); *Marche funèbre* (one section of *Les Mariés de la Tour Eiffel*, with other individual sections by Les Six members Auric, Milhaud, Poulenc, and Tailleferre, 1921; Paris, June 18, 1921); *Chant de joie* (1923; Paris, April 7, 1923); *Prélude pour "La Tempête*," after Shakespeare (1923; Paris, May 1, 1923); *Pacific 231* (designated as *Mouvement symphonique No. 1;* 1923; Serge Koussevitzky's concert, Paris, May 8, 1924); Concertino for Piano and Orch. (1924; Paris, May 23, 1925; Andrée Vaurabourg, soloist); Suite from incidental music to *L'Impératrice aux rochers* (1925); Suite from incidental music to *Phèdre* (1926); *Rugby* (*Mouvement symphonique No. 2;* 1928; Paris, Oct. 19, 1928; inaugural concert of L'Orchestre Symphonique of Paris, Ernest Ansermet conducting); *Prélude, Fugue et Postlude,* from the melodrama *Amphion* (1929; Geneva, Nov. 3, 1948); Cello Concerto (1929; Boston, Feb. 17, 1930); 5 symphs.: No. 1 (1929–30; Boston, Feb. 13, 1931); No. 2 for String Orch. and optional Trumpet (1941; Zürich, May 18, 1942); No. 3, *Liturgique* (1945–46; Zürich, Aug. 17, 1946); No. 4, *Deliciae Basilienses* (1946; Basel, Jan. 21, 1947); No. 5, *Di tre re* (1950; Boston, March, 9, 1951); *Mouvement symphonique No. 3* (1932–33; Berlin, March 26, 1933); Suite from the film *Les Misérables* (1934; Paris, Jan. 19, 1935); *Prélude, Arioso et Fughetta sur le nom de BACH* for String Orch. (arranged by A. Hoérée, 1936; Paris, Dec. 5, 1936; originally for Piano); *Nocturne* (1936; Brussels, April 30, 1936); *La Marche sur la Bastille* for Band, from incidental music for Romain Rolland's pageant *Le Quatorze Juillet* (1936; Paris, July 14, 1936); *La Grande Barrage,* an "image musicale" (1942); *Jour de fête suisse,* suite from music to the ballet *L'Appel de la montagne* (1943; Winterthur, Nov. 14, 1945); 2 extracts from the film *Mermoz* (1943); *Sérénade à Angélique* for Small Orch. (1945; Zürich Radio, Nov. 19, 1945); *Concerto da camera* for Flute, English Horn, and Strings (1949; Zürich, May 6, 1949); *Toccata* (one section of *La Guirlande de Campra,* with other individual sections by Lesur, Manuel, Tailleferre, Poulenc, Sauguet, and Auric, 1950; complete work, Aix-en-Provence Festival, July 31, 1952); *Suite archaïque* (1950–51; Louisville,

Ky., Feb. 28, 1951); *Monopartita* (1951; Zürich, June 12, 1951).

VOCAL MUSIC: *Cantique de Pâques* for 3 Women's Voices, Women's Chorus, and Orch. (1918; Toulouse, March 27, 1923); *Pâques à New York* for Voice and String Quartet (1920); *Chanson de Ronsard* for Voice, Flute, and String Quartet (1924); *3 chansons de la petite sirène* for Voice, Flute, and Strings or String Quartet (1926); *La Danse des morts,* oratorio for Narrator, Soloists, Chorus, Organ, and Orch. (1938; Basel, March 1, 1940); *Chant de libération* for Baritone, Unison Chorus, and Orch. (1942; Paris, Oct. 22, 1944); *Une Cantate de Noël* for Baritone, Mixed Chorus, Children's Chorus, Organ, and Orch. (sketched 1941, completed 1953; Basel, Dec. 18, 1953).

CHAMBER MUSIC: 2 violin sonatas (1916–18, 1919); 3 string quartets (1916–17, 1934–36, 1936–37); *Rapsodie* for 2 Flutes, Clarinet (or 2 Violins, Viola), and Piano (1917); *Danse de la chèvre* for Solo Flute (1919); Sonatina for 2 Violins (1920); Viola Sonata (1920); Cello Sonata (1920); *Hymn* for 10 String Instruments (1920); Sonatina for Clarinet or Cello, and Piano (1921–22); *3 contrepoints* for Flute, English Horn, Violin, and Cello (1923); *Prélude et Blues* for Quartet of Chromatic Harps (1925); Sonatina for Violin and Cello (1932); *Petite suite* for any 2 Treble Instruments and Piano (1934); Solo Violin Sonata (1940); *Sortilèges* for Ondes Martenot (1946); *Intrada* for Trumpet and Piano (1947); *Romance* for Flute and Piano (1953).

RADIO MUSIC: *Les Douze Coups de minuit,* a "radio-mystère" for Chorus and Chamber Orch. (1933; Paris Radio, Dec. 27, 1933); *Radio panoramique* for Tenor, Soprano, Organ, String Quintet, Wind Instruments, and Percussion (1935; Geneva Radio, March 4, 1935; concert premiere, Paris, Oct. 19, 1935); *Christophe Colomb,* radio oratorio for 2 Tenors, Chorus, and Orch. (1940; Lausanne Radio, April 17, 1940); *Les Battements du monde* for Woman's Voice, Child's Voice, Chorus, and Orch. (Lausanne Radio, May 18, 1944); *Saint François d'Assise* for Narrator, Baritone, Chorus, and Orch. (Lausanne Radio, Dec. 3, 1949).

FILM MUSIC: *Les Misérables* (1934); *Mayerling* (1935); *Regain* (1937); *Mlle. Doctor* (1937); *Pygmalion,* after G.B. Shaw's play (1938); *Mermoz* (1943); *Bourdelle* (1950); 36 others.

PIANO MUSIC: *3 pièces (Scherzo, Humoresque,* and *Adagio espressivo;* 1910); *3 pièces: Hommage à Ravel* (1915); *Prélude et Danse* (1919); *Toccata et Variations* (1916); *7 pièces brèves* (1919–20); *Sarabande* (1920); *Le Cahier Romand,* 5 pieces (1921–23); *Hommage à Albert Roussel* (1928); Suite for 2 Pianos (1928); *Prélude, Arioso et Fughetta sur le nom de BACH* (1932; arranged for Strings by A. Hoérée in 1936); *Scenic-Railway* (1937); *Partita* for 2 Pianos (1940; arranged from *3 contrepoints*); *2 esquisses,* in Nicolas Obouhov's simplified notation (1943–44); *Souvenir de Chopin* (1947).

SONGS: *4 poèmes* (1914–16); *6 poèmes de Apollinaire* (1915–17; Nos. 1 and 3–6 orchestrated as *5 poèmes de Apollinaire,* 1916–17); *3 poèmes de Paul Fort* (1916); *6 poésies de Jean Cocteau* (1920–23); *2 chants d'Ariel* (1923; also arranged for Orch.); *3 po-*

èmes de Claudel (1939–40); 3 psalms (1940–41); 5 mélodies-minute (1941); 4 Songs for Low Voice and Piano (1944–45). Honegger publ. a book, Je suis compositeur (Paris, 1951; in Eng. as I Am a Composer, London, 1966).

BIBLIOGRAPHY: R. Chalupt, "Arthur Honegger," Revue Musicale (1922); E.B. Hill, Modern French Composers (N.Y., 1924); Roland-Manuel, Arthur Honegger (Paris, 1925); A. George, Arthur Honegger (Paris, 1926); Willy Tappolet, Arthur Honegger (in German, Zürich, 1933; 2nd German ed., Zürich, 1954; French ed., Neuchâtel, 1938; 2nd French ed., Neuchâtel, 1957); Claude Gérard, Arthur Honegger: Catalogue succinct des œuvres (Brussels, 1945); José Bruyr, Honegger et son œuvre (Paris, 1947); J. Matter, Honegger ou La Quête de joie (Lausanne, 1956); A. Gauthier, Arthur Honegger (London, 1957); M. Landowski, Honegger (Paris, 1957); W. Reich, ed., Arthur Honegger, Nachklang: Schriften, Photos, Dokumente (Zürich, 1957); Jacques Feschotte, Arthur Honegger: L'Homme et son œuvre (Paris, 1966); P. Meylan, Arthur Honegger, Humanitäre Botschaft der Musik (Frauenfeld, 1970); K. Thompson, St. Martin's Dictionary of Twentieth-Century Composers (N.Y., 1973); J.H.O. Maillard and J. Nahoum, Les Symphonies d'Arthur Honegger (Paris, 1974); Editions Salabert brochure, Honegger (Paris and N.Y., 1974).

Honegger, Henri, Swiss cellist; b. Geneva, June 10, 1904. He studied with Ami Briquet in Geneva; then went to Germany, where he took lessons with Julius Klengel at the Leipzig Cons.; from there he traveled to Paris, where he took lessons with Casals; returning to Switzerland, he became first cellist in the Orch. de la Suisse Romande, but also continued his tours as a soloist; in 1950 he presented a series of concerts in N.Y., performing all of Bach's cello suites. In 1964 he resigned from the Orch. de la Suisse Romande in order to devote himself exclusively to concert activities.

Honegger, Marc, French musicologist; b. Paris, June 17, 1926. He studied music history and theory at the Sorbonne with Chailley and P.-M. Masson; in 1954 was appointed to the faculty of the musicological dept. of the Univ. of Paris. In 1958 he joined the staff of the Univ. of Strasbourg; in 1970 received the degree of Docteur-ès-lettres. He publ. several valuable papers on French music of the late Renaissance; also a historical survey, La Musique française de 1830 à 1914 (1962). He is the editor of the valuable 4-vol. encyclopedia Dictionnaire de la musique (Strasbourg, 1970–77).

Höngen, Elisabeth, German mezzo-soprano; b. Gevelsberg, Dec. 7, 1906. She was educated at the Hochschule für Musik in Berlin; also studied voice with Herman Weissenborn. She made her debut at the Wuppertal Opera in 1933, remaining there until she joined the Düsseldorf Opera in 1935; then sang at the Dresden State Opera (1940–43). In 1943 she became a member of the Vienna State Opera. On Jan. 10, 1952, she made her debut at the Metropoli-

tan Opera in N.Y. as Hérodias in Salome; then continued her career in Europe. In 1947 she was named an Austrian Kammersängerin.

Hood, Helen, American song composer; b. Chelsea, Mass., June 28, 1863; d. Brookline, Mass., Jan. 22, 1949. She studied piano with B.J. Lang and composition with Chadwick; also took a piano course with Moszkowski in Berlin; lived most of her life in Boston. Among her publ. pieces are The Robin (partsong); 5 Pieces for Violin and Piano; Song Etchings (a set of 6 songs); she also wrote some chamber music.

Hood, Mantle, American ethnomusicologist; b. Springfield, Ill., June 24, 1918. He studied composition privately with Ernst Toch (1945–50); was enrolled at the Univ. of Calif., Los Angeles (B.A., 1951; M.A. in composition, 1951); continued his studies at the Univ. of Amsterdam, receiving his Ph.D. in 1954 with the dissertation The Nuclear Theme as a Determinant of Patet in Javanese Music (publ. in Groningen, 1954). In 1954 he joined the faculty at the Univ. of Calif., Los Angeles, becoming a full prof. there in 1962; in 1961 he was appointed director of the Inst. of Ethnomusicology there. In 1956–57 he traveled to Indonesia on a Ford Foundation fellowship, and in 1976 received a Fulbright fellowship for study in India. In 1976 he became an adjunct prof. at the Univ. of Maryland; in 1977 was a visiting prof. at Yale Univ. and at Wesleyan Univ. He publ. The Ethnomusicologist (N.Y., 1971); contributed numerous valuable articles on oriental music to various learned journals and musical encyclopedias; also made arrangements of Indonesian melodies. His compositions include a symph. poem, Vernal Equinox (1955); Woodwind Trio (1950); 6 duets for Soprano and Alto Recorder (1954); piano pieces.

Hoof, Jef van, Belgian composer; b. Antwerp, May 8, 1886; d. there, April 24, 1959. He studied composition at the Antwerp Cons. with Gilson, Mortelmas, and Huybrechts; composed 3 operas: Tycho-Brahe (1911), Meivuur (1916), and Jonker Lichthart (1928); 5 symphs. (1938, 1941, 1945, 1951, 1956); choruses; lieder; piano pieces. His style of composition is neo-Romantic, with a penchant for expansive sonorities.

Hoogstraten, Willem van, Dutch conductor; b. Utrecht, March 18, 1884; d. Tutzing, Germany, Sept. 11, 1965. He studied violin with Alexander Schmuller; then with Bram Eldering at the Cons. of Cologne and with Ševčik in Prague; played concerts with the pianist **Elly Ney,** whom he married in 1911 (divorced in 1927). In 1914–18 he conducted the municipal orch. in Krefeld; in 1922 he was engaged as conductor of the summer concerts of the N.Y. Phil. (until 1938); was its associate conductor (1923–25). He was regular conductor of the Portland (Oreg.) Symph. Orch. in 1925–37. During World War II he was in charge of the Mozarteum Orch. in Salzburg (1939–45). In 1949 he settled in Stuttgart; conducted the Stuttgart Phil.

Hook, James, English organist and composer; b. Norwich, June 3, 1746; d. Boulogne, 1827. He exhibited a precocious talent as a boy; took lessons with Garland, organist of the Norwich Cathedral. In 1764 he went to London, where he played organ at various entertainment places. In 1765 he won a prize for his *Parting Catch.* He was subsequently organist and music director at Marylebone Gardens, London (1769–73) and at Vauxhall Gardens (1774–1820); his last position was at St. John's, Horsleydown.
WORKS: He was a highly industrious composer of songs; he may have written as many as 2,000 numbers; of these, only a few escaped oblivion (*Within a mile of Edinboro' Town; Sweet Lass of Richmond Hill,* etc.); many oratorios and odes; concertos for harpsichord; 117 sonatas, sonatinas, and divertimentos for piano; about 30 theater scores, all produced in London: *Cupid's Revenge* (June 12, 1772); *The Lady of the Manor* (Nov. 23, 1778); *The Fair Peruvian* (March 8, 1786); *Jack of Newbury* (May 6, 1795); *Wilmore Castle* (Oct. 21, 1800); *The Soldier's Return* (April 23, 1805); *The Invisible Girl* (April 28, 1806); *The Fortress* (July 16, 1807); *Safe and Sound* (August 28, 1809); etc. He publ. a manual, *Guida di musica,* in 2 parts (1785; 1794); some of the musical examples from it were reprinted by H. Wall in *Leaves from an Old Harpsichord Book.*
BIBLIOGRAPHY: C. Cudworth, "James Hook," *Norwich Journal* (Aug. 24, 1946).

Hope-Jones, Robert, English organ manufacturer; b. Hooton Grange, Cheshire, Feb. 9, 1859; d. (suicide) Rochester, N.Y., Sept. 13, 1914. As a boy, he entered the employ of Laird Bros., engineers at Birkenhead; then became chief electrician of the National Telephone Co.; at the same time, was engaged as a church organist. In 1889 he set up his own business as an organ builder. In 1903 he settled in America; was connected with the E.M. Skinner Co. of Boston; in 1907, founded the Hope-Jones Organ Co. at Tonawanda, N.Y., but sold the plant and his patents in 1910 to the Rudolph Wurlitzer Co. of N.Y. He introduced many innovations into the building of electrical organs; the development of the modern organ in the U.S. owes much to his inventive genius. One of the finest of his organs is in the Auditorium at Ocean Grove, N.J.
BIBLIOGRAPHY: G.L. Miller, *The Recent Revolution in Organ Building* (N.Y., 1913).

Hopekirk, Helen, Scottish pianist; b. Edinburgh, May 20, 1856; d. Cambridge, Mass., Nov. 19, 1945. She studied with A.C. Mackenzie; then went to Germany; made her debut with the Gewandhaus Orch., Leipzig (Nov. 28, 1878); also took lessons with Leschetizky in Vienna. She married William Wilson, a businessman, in 1882; lived in Vienna; in 1897, settled in Boston; taught at the New England Cons. In her recitals she featured many works of the modern French school (Debussy, Fauré, etc.). She was also a composer; played her own Piano Concerto with the Boston Symph. Orch. (Dec. 27, 1900); publ. a collection of Scottish folk songs.
BIBLIOGRAPHY: Constance Hall, *Helen Hopekirk* (Cambridge, Mass., 1954).

Hopf, Hans, German tenor; b. Nuremberg, Aug. 2, 1916. He studied in Munich, making his debut there in 1936. He then was engaged with the Opera in Augsburg (1939–42). In 1946 he sang at the Berlin State Opera and, after 1949, was a leading member of the Bavarian State Opera in Munich. He made his debut at the Metropolitan Opera in N.Y. as Walther in *Die Meistersinger von Nürnberg,* on March 15, 1952.

Hopkins, Charles Jerome (first name is sometimes erroneously given as **Edward**), American composer and musical journalist; b. Burlington, Vt., April 4, 1836; d. Athenia, N.J., Nov. 4, 1898. Self-taught in music (he took only 6 lessons in harmony), he learned to play piano sufficiently well to attain professional status. He studied chemistry at the N.Y. Medical College; played organ in N.Y. churches, and was active in various educational enterprises; in 1856 he founded the American Music Assoc., which promoted concerts of music by Gottschalk, Bristow, and other American composers. In 1868 he founded the *N.Y. Philharmonic Journal,* and was its editor until 1885. In 1886 he organized several "Free Singing and Opera Schools," for which he claimed nearly 1,000 pupils. In 1889 he went to England on a lecture tour, announcing himself as "the first American Operatic Oratorio composer and Pianist who has ever ventured to invade England with New World Musical theories and practices." Throughout his versatile career, he was a strong advocate of American music; his sensational methods and eccentric professional conduct brought him repeatedly into public controversy; in England he was sued for libel. Hopkins claimed a priority in writing the first "musicianly and scientific Kinder-Oper" (*Taffy and Old Munch,* a children's fairy tale, 1880). He further wrote an operatic oratorio, *Samuel,* and a great number of choruses and songs, few of which were publ. He compiled 2 collections of church music and an *Orpheon Class-Book.*
BIBLIOGRAPHY: N. Slonimsky, "The Flamboyant Pioneer," in *A Thing or Two about Music* (N.Y., 1947, pp. 250-61).

Hopkins, Claude, black jazz pianist; b. Alexandria, Va., Aug. 24, 1903; d. Riverdale, N.Y., Feb. 19, 1984. He studied piano; then enrolled at Howard Univ. in Washington, D.C. (B.A., 1923). He then went to Paris, where he acted as music director for Josephine Baker, and led a band that featured the famous saxophone player Sidney Bechet. Returning to the U.S., he presided over bands at the Coconut Grove in Harlem, also filling engagements at the top clubs in N.Y. In his own playing he followed the uninhibited insouciant manner of the famous Harlem jazz pianist "Fats" Waller. Hopkins fell sick in his later years and died in a nursing home.

Hopkins, Edward John, English organist and composer; b. London, June 30, 1818; d. there, Feb. 4, 1901. He was a chorister at the Chapel Royal (1826–33); then studied theory with T.F. Walmisley. In 1834 he became organist at Mitcham Church; from 1838, was at St. Peter's Islington; from 1841, at St. Luke's; and from 1843, at the Temple Church, London. There he remained for 55 years, retiring in 1898; Walford Davies was his successor. Several of his many anthems have become established in the church repertoire (*Out of the Deep, God is Gone Up, Thou Shalt Cause the Trumpet of the Jubilee to Sound,* etc.). His book, *The Organ: Its History and Construction* (in collaboration with Rimbault, London, 1855; 5th ed., 1887), is a standard work. He contributed articles to *Grove's Dictionary of Music and Musicians* and to various musical publications.

BIBLIOGRAPHY: Charles W. Pearce, *The Life and Works of Edward John Hopkins* (London, 1910).

Hopkins, John Henry, American clergyman and writer of hymn tunes; b. Pittsburgh, Oct. 28, 1820; d. Hudson, N.Y., Aug. 13, 1891. He studied at schools of divinity and served as a deacon in several churches. His Christmas carol *We Three Kings of Orient Are* is a perennial favorite. He publ. a collection, *Carols, Hymns and Songs* (1862).

BIBLIOGRAPHY: R.G. McCutchan, *Our Hymnody* (N.Y., 1937).

Hopkins, Sam (a.k.a. **Lightnin'**), black country-blues singer and guitarist; b. Centerville, Texas, March 15, 1912; d. Houston, Jan. 30, 1982. He worked on a farm in Texas; learned to play the guitar; accompanied the singer **Texas Alexander,** a cousin, and developed a style of his own, with deep organ points in the bass and irregular rhythms in the melody. He was responsive to world events; composed *Happy Blues for John Glenn* after the astronaut's orbital flight. He was a popular singer at the Village Gate in N.Y. and took part in a hootenanny with Joan Baez and Pete Seeger.

Hopkinson, Francis, American statesman, writer, and composer; signer of the Declaration of Independence; b. Philadelphia, Sept. 21, 1737; d. there, May 9, 1791. By profession a lawyer, he was deeply interested in music; learned to play the harpsichord; studied music theory with James Bremner; was a member of an amateur group in Philadelphia who met regularly in their homes to play music, and also gave public concerts by subscription. He was the composer of the first piece of music written by a native American, *Ode to Music,* which he wrote in 1754, and of the first original American song, *My days have been so wondrous free* (1759). At least, this is the claim he makes in the preface to his *7 Songs* (actually 8, the last having been added after the title page was engraved) *for the harpsichord or forte piano,* dated Philadelphia, Nov. 20, 1788, and dedicated to George Washington: "I cannot, I believe, be refused the Credit of being the first Native of the United States who has produced a Musical

Composition." Other works: *Ode in Memory of James Bremner* (1780); a dramatic cantata, *The Temple of Minerva* (1781); there are also some songs. Hopkinson's music was couched in the conventional English style, modeled after pieces by T.A. Arne, but he undoubtedly possessed a genuine melodic gift. He also provided Benjamin Franklin's glass harmonica with a keyboard, introduced improvements in the quilling of the harpsichord, and invented the Bellarmonic, an instrument consisting of a set of steel bells. He was probably, but not certainly, the compiler of *A Collection of Psalm Tunes with a Few Anthems,* etc. A MS book of songs in Hopkinson's handwriting is in the possession of the Library of Congress. Hopkinson's son, **Joseph Hopkinson,** wrote the words to *Hail Columbia.*

BIBLIOGRAPHY: O.G. Sonneck, *Francis Hopkinson, The First American Poet Composer . . .* (Washington, D.C., 1905; reprinted, N.Y., 1969); H.V. Milligan, *The First American Composer: 6 Songs by Francis Hopkinson* (Boston, 1918); G.E. Hastings, *The Life and Works of Francis Hopkinson* (Chicago, 1926); O.E. Albrecht, "Francis Hopkinson, Musician, Poet and Patriot," *Univ. of Pa. Library Chronicle* (1933, 1937, 1938); J.T. Howard, *Our American Music* (N.Y., 1939, and subsequent eds.).

Hoppin, Richard Hallowell, American musicologist; b. Northfield, Minn., Feb. 22, 1913. He studied piano at the Ecole Normale de Musique in Paris (1933–35); musicology at Harvard Univ. (M.A., 1938; Ph.D., 1952). He was on the music faculty of the Univ. of Texas, Austin (1949–61); in 1961, was appointed a prof. of music at Ohio State Univ. In 1959–60 he was the recipient of a Guggenheim fellowship. He edited the important collection *The Cypriot-French Repertory of the Manuscript Torino* (4 vols., Rome, 1960–63); publ. *An Introduction to Medieval Music* (N.Y., 1978); contributed numerous articles to scholarly musical publications.

Horák, Adolph, pianist and teacher; b. Jankovic, Bohemia, Feb. 15, 1850; d. Vienna, Jan. 14, 1921. With his brother **Eduard** he established the Horák Pianoforte School in Vienna; in collaboration, they publ. a valuable *Klavierschule;* Adolph alone wrote *Die technische Grundlage des Klavierspiels.*

Horák, Antonin, Czech composer; b. Prague, July 2, 1875; d. Belgrade, March 12, 1910. He was engaged as an opera conductor in Prague and Belgrade; his own opera, *Babička (Grandmother),* was fairly successful at its first production, in Prague (March 3, 1900); he also wrote cantatas and other choral works.

Horák, Eduard, pianist and teacher; b. Holitz, Bohemia, April 22, 1838; d. Riva, Lake of Garda, Dec. 16, 1892. With his brother **Adolph** he founded in Vienna the Horák Pianoforte School, which soon acquired a European reputation. In collaboration with F. Spigl, who succeeded him as director of the Horák School, he publ. *Der Klavierunterricht in neue, natürliche Bahnen gelenkt* (2 vols., Vienna, 1892), and with his brother, a practical manual, *Kla-*

vierschule.

Horák, Josef, Czech bass clarinetist; b. Znojmo, March 24, 1931. He attended the State High School for Musical and Dramatic Arts in Prague; was a clarinetist in the Brno State Phil. and Czech Radio Orch. On Oct. 20, 1955, he made his debut as a performer on the bass clarinet, and began a unique career as a virtuoso on that instrument; along with the Dutch bass clarinetist Harry Sparnaay, Horák is responsible for the revival of interest in the bass clarinet. Hindemith transcribed for Horák his Bassoon Sonata. In 1963 Horák and the pianist Emma Kovárnová formed the chamber duo Due Boemi di Praga, and performed nearly 300 specially commissioned works by Alois Hába, André Jolivet, Frank Martin, Messiaen, Stockhausen, and many, many others. In 1972 Horák was appointed to the faculty of the Prague Cons.

Horák, Wenzel Emanuel, Bohemian composer and organist; b. Mscheno-Lobes, Bohemia, Jan. 1, 1800; d. Prague, Sept. 3, 1871. He studied theory by himself, with the aid of the standard manuals of Vogler, Cherubini, etc.; also played organ, and was an organist at various churches in Prague; wrote 10 masses, motets, and a theoretical work, *Die Mehrdeutigkeit der Harmonien* (1846).

Horenstein, Jascha, renowned Russian conductor; b. Kiev, May 6, 1898; d. London, April 2, 1973. His family moved to Germany when he was a child; he studied with Max Brode in Königsberg and Adolf Busch in Vienna; also took courses in composition with Franz Schreker in Berlin, where he became an assistant to Wilhelm Furtwängler. He made his conducting debut with the Vienna Symph. Orch. in 1923; then was a guest conductor with the Berlin Phil. Orch.; from 1925 to 1928 was conductor of the Berlin Symph. Orch.; in 1929 he became chief conductor of the Düsseldorf Opera, a post he held until forced to leave in 1933. In 1940 he came to the U.S.; after the war he returned to Europe. He was especially noted for his authoritative interpretations of the symphs. of Bruckner and Mahler.
BIBLIOGRAPHY: *Le Grand Baton* (June 1976).

Horký, Karel, Czech composer; b. Štěmechy, near Třebíč, Sept. 4, 1909. He played in a military band as a boy; studied bassoon; took private lessons in composition with V. Polívka and Pavel Haas; then entered the Prague Cons. as a student of Křička, graduating in 1944. He taught harmony at the Brno Cons. (1945–52) and in 1964 was appointed its director.
WORKS: 4 operas: *Jan Hus* (Brno, May 27, 1950); *Hejtman Šarovec* (Brno, 1953); *Jed z Elsinoru (The Poison from Elsinor),* freely after Shakespeare's *Hamlet* (Brno, Nov. 11, 1969); *Dawn* (Brno, July 4, 1975); 2 ballets: *Lastura (The Shell;* Brno, Oct. 23, 1945) and *Král Ječmínek (King Ječmínek;* Brno, Sept. 21, 1951); cantata, *Český sen (The Czech Dream;* 1961–62); *Klythia,* symph. poem (1941); *Romantic Sinfonietta* (1944); Cello Concerto (1953); Violin Concerto (1955); 5 symphs. (1959, 1964, 1971,

1974, 1977); Serenade for String Orch. (1963); Bassoon Concerto (1966); Horn Concerto (1971); *Fateful Preludes* for Piano and Orch. (1972); *Dimitrov,* symph. poem with Narrator and Chorus, honoring the memory of the chairman of the Bulgarian Communist Party (1972); 4 string quartets (1938, 1954, 1955, 1963); String Trio (1940); Violin Sonata (1943); Suite for Wind Quintet (1943); Oboe Sonatina (1958); Nonet (1958); Clarinet Quintet (1960); Double-bass Sonatina (1961); Clarinet Sonatina (1965); *3 Compositions* for Piano (1971); *3 Compositions* for Cello and Piano (1972); choruses; songs; film music.

Horn, August, German composer and arranger; b. Freiberg, Sept. 1, 1825; d. Leipzig, March 25, 1893. He was a pupil of Mendelssohn at the Leipzig Cons.; wrote overtures and light music; but became principally known as an arranger of symphs., operas, etc., for piano, 2- and 4-hands. His comic opera *Die Nachbarn* was produced in Leipzig in 1875.

Horn, Camillo, composer; b. Reichenberg, Bohemia, Dec. 29, 1860; d. Vienna, Sept. 3, 1941. He was a pupil of Bruckner at the Vienna Cons.; conducted choruses there, and was also active as a music critic. Many of his works have been publ.; he wrote a Symph.; a cantata, *Bundeslied der Deutschen in Böhmen; Deutsches Lied* for Chorus and Orch.; many choruses a cappella; a number of piano pieces.

Horn, Charles Edward, composer and conductor, son of **Karl Friedrich Horn;** b. London, June 21, 1786; d. Boston, Oct. 21, 1849. He studied with his father, and practiced voice under the guidance of Rauzzini. He made his debut as a singer in a light opera (June 26, 1809); sang Kaspar in the Eng. production of *Der Freischütz.* In 1827 he went to N.Y., where he staged several of his operas; returned to London in 1830; in 1832 he emigrated to America; there he wrote several oratorios, including *The Remission of Sin* (later named *Satan*). In 1847 he became conductor of the Handel and Haydn Society in Boston. In the U.S., he was notable primarily as a singer and composer of ballads.

Horn, Karl Friedrich, German composer; b. Nordhausen, April 13, 1762; d. Windsor, England, Aug. 5, 1830. He settled in England at the age of 20, and with the patronage of Count Brühl, Saxon ambassador in London, became a fashionable teacher. In 1823 he became organist of St. George's Chapel at Windsor. With Wesley he prepared an Eng. edition of Bach's *Wohltemperierte Clavier;* also wrote a treatise on thoroughbass; composed 12 sets of piano variations, with flute obbligato; 6 piano sonatas; *Military Divertimentos.*

Hornbostel, Erich Moritz von, eminent musicologist; b. Vienna, Feb. 25, 1877; d. Cambridge, England, Nov. 28, 1935. He studied philosophy in Vienna and Heidelberg; received a Ph.D. in chemistry from the Univ. of Vienna (1900); in 1905–6 was the assistant of Stumpf in Berlin; in 1906, came to the U.S. to record and study Indian music (Pawnee); in 1906–33, was director of the Phonogramm-Archiv in Berlin, and concurrently a prof. at the Univ. of Berlin (1917–33); then went to the U.S. In 1934 he went to England. He was a specialist in Asian, African, and other non-European music; also investigated the problems of tone psychology; contributed hundreds of articles to scholarly publications on these subjects. He edited a collection of records, *Musik des Orients* (Lindström, 1932); from 1922 until his death was co-editor, with C. Stumpf, of the *Sammelbände für vergleichende Musikwissenschaft*. Hornbostel's writings are being prepared for reissue, edited by K.P. Wachsmann et al. (The Hague, 1975—).

Horne, Lena, black American singer; b. Brooklyn, June 30, 1917. She sang in supper clubs in N.Y. and in Las Vegas; became popular in café society, and invited praise by her earthy and husky voice, capable of considerable depth of expression. She publ. an autobiography, *In Person, Lena Horne* (N.Y., 1950).

Horne, Marilyn, outstanding American mezzo-soprano; b. Bradford, Pa., Jan. 16, 1934. In 1945 the family moved to Long Beach, Calif.; she enrolled as a vocal student of William Vennard at the Univ. of Southern Calif., in Los Angeles; also attended master classes given by Lotte Lehmann. In 1952 she joined the Roger Wagner Chorale and traveled to Europe with it. Returning to California, she gave a recital at the Hollywood Bowl in 1954. She went to Europe again in 1956; spent a year in Vienna, and joined the staff of the Municipal Opera at Gelsenkirchen, where she sang a variety of roles, including Mimi in *La Bohème*, Tatiana in *Eugene Onegin*, Minnie in *The Girl of the Golden West*, and the demanding role of Marie in *Wozzeck*. In 1960 she returned to California, where she married the conductor **Henry Lewis,** who became the first black conductor of a standard American symph. orch. when he was appointed to the post of music director of the New Jersey Symph. Orch. in 1968. Their interracial marriage prospered; a daughter was born to them, but their psychological incompatibility led to a separation in 1976. Marilyn Horne's career progressed with excellent allure; she impressed her audience with her performance of Marie in *Wozzeck* at the San Francisco Opera on Oct. 4, 1960. On March 3, 1970, she made her debut at the Metropolitan Opera in N.Y. in the role of Adalgisa in *Norma;* she subsequently sang there the roles of Rosina in *The Barber of Seville* (Jan. 23, 1971), Carmen (Sept. 19, 1972), Isabella in *L'Italiana in Algeri* (Nov. 10, 1973), and Fides in *Le Prophète* (Jan. 18, 1977). On Oct. 16, 1975, she appeared in the title role of Handel's *Rinaldo* at the Houston Opera; on Oct. 13, 1977, she sang with the Houston Grand Opera the title role of Rossini's *Tancredi*. She wrote (with assistance) an autobiography, *My Life* (N.Y., 1983).
BIBLIOGRAPHY: David Ewen, *Musicians since 1900* (N.Y., 1978).

Horneman, Christian Frederik Emil, Danish composer, son of **Johan Ole Horneman;** b. Copenhagen, Dec. 17, 1840; d. there, June 8, 1906. He studied at the Leipzig Cons. (1858–60), where he became a friend of Grieg. He composed light music under various pseudonyms; returning to Copenhagen, he organized a concert society there; produced an opera, *Aladdin* (Nov. 18, 1888); also was active as a choral conductor and teacher. He wrote, in addition, 2 string quartets and numerous songs.

Horneman, Johan Ole, Danish composer; b. Copenhagen, May 13, 1809; d. there, May 29, 1870. He composed music in a popular vein; in 1844 established a publishing firm with Emil Erslev. His collection of piano pieces, *Nordiske sange uden tekst (Nordic Songs without Text),* enjoyed some popularity; he further publ. a piano manual, *Ny praktisk Pianoforteskole* (new ed. by L. Schytte).

Horner, Ralph Joseph, English conductor and composer; b. Newport, Monmouthshire, April 28, 1848; d. Winnipeg, Canada, April 7, 1926. He studied at the Leipzig Cons. (1864–67) with Moscheles, Reinecke, and Plaidy. On his return to England, he was active as a choral conductor; also conducted light opera. From 1906–9 he was in N.Y.; then settled in Winnipeg, where he became director of the Imperial Academy of Music and Arts and conductor of the Oratorio Society (1909–12). He wrote the operas *Confucius, Amy Rosbart,* and *The Belles of Barcelona;* the oratorios *St. Peter* and *David's First Victory; Torch Dance* for Orch.; many sacred cantatas, anthems, piano pieces, songs.

Hornstein, Robert von, German composer; b. Donaueschingen, Dec. 6, 1833; d. Munich, July 19, 1890. He studied at the Leipzig Cons.; then went to Munich, where he became a teacher at the municipal school of music. He was a close friend of Wagner; composed operas in a Romantic vein; one of these, *Adam und Eva,* was produced in Munich in 1870; other works are a ballet, *Der Blumen Rache;* incidental music to Shakespeare's *As You Like It;* many songs.

Horovitz, Joseph, Austrian-born British composer; b. Vienna, May 26, 1926. He was taken to England after the Anschluss in 1938, and studied music at Oxford, gaining his degree of B.Mus. there; then went to Paris to take a course with Nadia Boulanger. He developed a series of mannerisms that, when synthesized, became a recognizable style, modernistic without solemnity, appealing without crudity, and often cachinnogenic.
WORKS: Operas: *Gentleman's Island* (Cheltenham, July 9, 1959); *The Dumb Wife* (Antwerp, Jan. 10, 1972). Ballets: *Les Femmes d'Alger* (London, 1952); *Alice in Wonderland* (London, 1953); *Let's Make a Ballet* (London, 1965). For Orch.: *Fantasia on a Theme of Couperin* for Strings (1962); Trumpet Concerto (1965); *Horizon Overture* (1972); *Toy Symphony* (1977); 5 string quartets; Cello Sonata (1951); Oboe Quartet (1956); *Horrortorio* (a horror

oratorio; 1959); *Jazz Harpsichord Concerto;* other synthetic pieces.

Horowitz, Vladimir, fabulous Russian-born American pianist; b. Berdichev, Oct. 1, 1904. He began to study piano with his mother, who was herself an excellent pianist, a pupil of Vladimir Puchalsky, who later became Horowitz's own teacher at the Kiev Cons. His other teachers were Sergei Tarnowsky and Felix Blumenfeld. He made his public debut in a recital in Kiev on May 30, 1920, which was the beginning of a remarkable career. He made his first appearance outside Russia in a recital in Berlin on Jan. 2, 1926; then gave concerts throughout Europe. In Paris in 1928 he took a few lessons with Alfred Cortot, confined mostly to suggestions about style and interpretation. On Jan. 12, 1928, he made his American debut, performing Tchaikovsky's First Piano Concerto, with the N.Y. Phil. conducted by Sir Thomas Beecham, who was also making his American debut; he then appeared as a soloist with other American orchs., earning the reputation of a piano virtuoso of the highest caliber, so that his very name became synonymous with pianistic greatness. In 1931 he played at the White House for President Hoover, his family, and guests. In 1933 he married Wanda Toscanini, daughter of Arturo Toscanini. He became an American citizen in 1942. He celebrated the 25th anniversary of his American debut with a recital at Carnegie Hall in N.Y. on Feb. 25, 1953. Horowitz seemed to possess every gift of public success; he was universally admired; his concerts sold out without fail whenever and wherever he chose to play. His idol, Rachmaninoff, became his friend. But amidst all these artistic blessings he developed a nervous ailment that made it impossible for him to play in public; there were anxious moments before his scheduled appearances when his managers and his family were not sure whether he would be able or willing to play. For a period of 12 years, between 1953 and 1965, he withdrew from the stage; public confrontation seemed to lead to physiological impediments. However, he enjoyed making recordings when he was free to change his successive versions in the sanctuary of a studio. He also accepted a few private pupils. On May 9, 1965, he finally returned to the stage in a recital at Carnegie Hall, but another hiatus in his concert activity occurred from 1969–74; once again he had to overcome his reluctance to face an audience; he would announce a concert, only to cancel it at the crucial moment. On Jan. 8, 1978, he performed Rachmaninoff's 3rd Piano Concerto with Eugene Ormandy and the N.Y. Phil.; on Feb. 26, 1978, he played at the White House at the invitation of President Carter; this coincided with the 50th anniversary of his American debut. On May 22, 1982, at the behest of the Prince of Wales, he gave a recital in the Royal Festival Hall in London, marking his first appearance in Europe in 31 years. Through his recordings he formed a large following in Japan; in June 1983 he decided to give a series of concerts in Tokyo and other Japanese cities, which became an event of the season. Horowitz's tastes lie with Romantic music;

his performances of works by Chopin, Liszt, Tchaikovsky, and Rachmaninoff are incomparable. He also excels in congenial renditions of Scriabin's music. Among contemporary composers Horowitz prefers those of a lyrical nature. He gave the world premiere of Samuel Barber's Piano Sonata in Havana on Dec. 9, 1949. He himself composed a sparkling piano paraphrase of themes from *Carmen* and made a vertiginous transcription for piano of Sousa's march *Stars and Stripes Forever,* a veritable tour de force of pianistic pyrotechnics, which he performed for years as an encore, to the delight of his audiences.

BIBLIOGRAPHY: A. Chasins, *Speaking of Pianists* (N.Y., 1957; 2nd ed., 1961); H. Schonberg, *The Great Pianists* (N.Y., 1963); G. Plaskin, *Horowitz: A Biography* (N.Y., 1983).

Horsley, Charles Edward, English organist and composer; b. London, Dec. 16, 1822; d. New York, Feb. 28, 1876. He was a pupil of his father, **William Horsley;** then studied with Moscheles. In Leipzig he became friendly with Mendelssohn, who instructed him in composition. Upon his return to London, he obtained a post as organist of St. John's; wrote the oratorios *David, Joseph,* and *Gideon;* incidental music to Milton's *Comus.* In 1862 he went to Australia, and served as organist in Melbourne. There he wrote an ode, *Euterpe,* for the opening of the Town Hall (1870). He eventually settled in N.Y. His *Text Book of Harmony* was publ. posthumously (1876).

Horsley, William, English organist and composer, father of **Charles Edward Horsley;** b. London, Nov. 15, 1774; d. there, June 12, 1858. He had little formal study, but his friendly association with John Callcott, the composer of glees, led him to try his hand at the composition of light vocal pieces. He married Callcott's daughter in 1813. He was instrumental in the establishment of the choral society Concentores Sodales (1798–1847), for which he wrote many anthems, catches, and glees; was also a founder of the Phil. Society of London (1813); occupied various posts as church organist. Many of his songs (*See the Chariot at Hand, O Nightingale,* etc.) were frequently sung. He further publ. 5 albums of glees (1801–07), hymn tunes (1820), canons, piano pieces, etc.; also *An Explanation of Musical Intervals and of the Major and Minor Scales* (1825); *Introduction to Harmony and Modulation* (1847); edited Callcott's glees, with a biography and analysis; brought out the first book of Byrd's *Cantiones sacrae.*

Horst, Anthon van der, Dutch composer, conductor, and organist; b. Amsterdam, June 20, 1899; d. Hilversum, March 7, 1965. He studied composition with Bernard Zweers, and piano and organ with de Pauw at the Amsterdam Cons.; won the Prix d'Excellence for organ in 1917. He then served as an organist of the English Reformed Church in Amsterdam (1918–41) and of the Netherlands Protestant League in Hilversum; in 1936 he was appointed prof. of organ and conducting at the Amsterdam

Cons. In some of his organ and piano works he adopted the scale of alternating tones and semitones known in the Netherlands as "Pijper's scales," which he called "modus conjunctus."

WORKS: 3 symphs.: No. 1 (1935–37); No. 2, *Divertimento pittorale* (1954); No. 3, with Chorus (1959); *Choros I–VIII,* 8 separate works for Soloists, Chorus, and Orch., based on various texts (1931–58); *Rembrandt Cantata* (1956); *Nocturne funèbre* for Orch. (1950–51); *Concerto per organo romantico* for Organ and Orch. (1952); *Concerto spagnuolo* for Violin and Orch. (1953; perf. posthumously in Groningen, May 26, 1965); *3 études symphoniques* (1954); *Concerto in Baroque Style* for Organ and Strings (1960); *Reflexions sonores* for Orch. (1962); *Ricercar svelato* for Brass, Organ, and Strings (1963); *Salutation joyeuse* for Orch. (1964); *Hymn* for Solo Soprano (1935); Suite for Solo Cello (1941); *Suite in modo conjuncto* for Organ (1943); *Partita diverse sopra Psalm 8* for Organ (1947); *Tema con variazioni in modo conjuncto* for Piano (1950); *Sonata in modo conjuncto* for 2 Pianos (1951); Suite for 31-tone Organ (1953); *Theme, Variations, and Fugue* for Flute, Violin, and Viola (1957); Sextet for Flute and Strings; songs; choruses.

Horszowski, Mieczyslaw, Polish pianist; b. Lemberg (Lwow), June 23, 1892. He was a certified child prodigy; made his first public appearance at the age of 10, playing Beethoven's First Piano Concerto with the Warsaw Phil. He studied piano with Henryk Melcer in Lemberg; was then sent to Vienna, where Leschetizky accepted him as a private pupil. On Feb. 16, 1906, he played a solo recital at La Scala in Milan. He also played for Pope Pius X in Rome; then gave a command performance for Queen Alexandra at Buckingham Palace in England. He played for Granados in Barcelona; then undertook an extensive concert tour in Europe; also played joint recitals with Casals. In 1954 he gave a series of piano recitals in N.Y. in programs including the piano works of Beethoven. On Nov 13, 1961, he played for President John F. Kennedy at the White House with Alexander Schneider and Casals. In 1942 he joined the faculty of the Curtis Inst. in Philadelphia. In 1981, at the age of 89, he married his longtime companion, the Italian pianist **Bice Costa** of Genoa, whom he had met 26 years before. At the age of 90 he played a Mozart concerto at the Metropolitan Museum of Art in N.Y. His name is pronounced Mee-eh-chee-sláv Hor-shóv-skee.

Horton, Austin Asadata Dafora, Nigerian composer; b. Freetown, Sierra Leone, West Africa, Aug. 4, 1890; d. New York, March 4, 1965. As a youth, he became deeply interested in African folk dance festivals and studied the culture of many African tribes. He then went to Europe and organized a dance group in Germany. He settled in the U.S. in 1921, devoting himself to the propagation of African art, coaching singers, dancers, and drummers for performance of African dances. He utilized authentic African melorhythms in several of his stage spectacles, for which he also arranged the musical scores. Of these, *Kykunkor, the Witch,* produced at the Unity Theater Studio in N.Y. on May 7, 1934, attracted considerable attention. He also produced a dance drama, *Tunguru.*

Horvat, Milan, Yugoslav conductor; b. Pakrac, July 28, 1919. He studied piano and conducting at the Zagreb Academy of Music. In 1946 he became a conductor of the Zagreb Phil. From 1958 to 1969 he was chief conductor of the Belgrade Phil.; later directed the Austrian Radio Symph. Orch. in Vienna; also made guest appearances in Europe, conducting both orch. and operatic performances.

Horvat, Stanko, Croatian composer; b. Zagreb, March 12, 1930. He studied composition with Šulek at the Zagreb Academy of Music, graduating in 1956; then took a course with Tony Aubin at the Paris Cons. and private composition lessons with René Leibowitz (1958–59); returning to Yugoslavia, he was appointed to the music faculty of the Zagreb Academy in 1961. In his style of composition he traversed successively a period of neo-Classical mannerisms, serialism in its dodecaphonic aspect, aleatory expressionism, and sonorism; eventually he returned to a median technique of pragmatic modernism.

WORKS: Television opera, *3 Legends* (Salzburg, 1971); ballet, *Izabranik (The Chosen One;* 1961); Sinfonietta (1954); Symph. (1956); *Concerto rustico* for Strings (1958); Piano Concerto (1966; Zagreb, April 3, 1967); *Choral* for Strings (1967); *Taches* for Piano and Chamber Orch. (1968; Graz, Sept. 26, 1968); *Hymnus* for Orch. (1969); *Perpetuum mobile* for String Orch. (1971; Zagreb, May 9, 1971); *Krik (The Cry),* after García Lorca, for Mezzo-soprano and Orch. (1968; Zagreb, March 19, 1969); cantata, *Jama (The Pit;* 1971; Zagreb, Dec. 18, 1971); *Choral Variations* for String Quartet (1953); *Contrasts* for String Quartet (1963); *Rondo* for String Quartet (1967); *Variants* for Piano (1965); *Sonnant* for Piano (1970).

Horvath, Josef Maria, Austrian composer of Hungarian descent; b. Pécs, Dec. 20, 1931. He studied piano and composition at the Liszt Academy in Budapest; in 1956 he went to Salzburg, where he studied composition and took instruction in electronic music. Subsequently he became a composition teacher at the Salzburg Mozarteum.

WORKS: *Entropia,* symph. in 5 movements (1961); Trio for Violin, Horn, and Piano (1963); a group of works under the generic title *Redundance,* for Wind Octet and/or String Quartet (1970); *Origines* for Chamber Group (1975).

Horwitz, Karl, Austrian composer; b. Vienna, Jan. 1, 1884; d. Salzburg, Aug. 18, 1925. He studied with Arnold Schoenberg, and adopted an atonal idiom. He was active in organizing the Donaueschingen Festivals (from 1921) and in other societies devoted to modern music; among his works are a symph. poem, *Vom Tode;* 2 string quartets; several song cycles. In 1924 he suffered a loss of hearing, as a result of disease, and died shortly afterward.

Hosmer, Elmer Samuel, American organist and composer; b. Clinton, Mass., March 21, 1862; d. Pawtucket, R.I., April 25, 1945. He studied music in Boston with George Whiting, Percy Goetschius, and others; occupied various positions as an organist; composed cantatas (*Pilgrims of 1620, The Man without a Country,* etc.) and many anthems.

Hosmer, Lucius, American composer; b. South Acton, Mass., Aug. 14, 1870; d. Jefferson, N.H., May 9, 1935. He studied with Chadwick at the New England Cons.; lived mostly in Boston; wrote a "romantic comic opera," *The Rose of the Alhambra* (Rochester, N.Y., 1905; N.Y., Feb. 4, 1907); a comic opera, *The Walking Delegate* (revised and produced under the title *The Koreans*); various light pieces for Orch.: *On Tiptoe, Chinese Wedding Procession, Southern Rhapsody, Northern Rhapsody, Ethiopian Rhapsody,* etc.; also songs.

Hostinský, Otakar, Czech writer on music; b. Martinoves, Jan. 2, 1847; d. Prague, Jan. 19, 1910. He studied at the Univ. of Prague and later in Munich; became an instructor of esthetics and history of music at Charles Univ. in Prague (1877); was made a prof. in 1892.
WRITINGS: *Das Musikalisch-Schöne und das Gesammtkunstwerk vom Standpunkt der formalen Ästhetik* (1877), as a philosophical reply to Hanslick's famous book (in Czech as *Hostinského esthetika,* Prague, 1921); *Die Lehre von den musikalischen Klängen* (1879); *Über die Entwicklung und den jetzigen Stand der tschechischen Oper* (1880); *Über die Bedeutung der praktischen Ideen Herbarts für die allgemeine Ästhetik* (1883); his articles on Smetana were collected and publ. in 1901 (new ed., 1941); he wrote numerous articles on Czech folk songs, etc. A jubilee pamphlet was publ. in Prague on the occasion of his 60th birthday (1907).

Hothby, John, English music theorist; b. c.1415; d. probably in England, Nov. 6, 1487. He was a student at Oxford; was a member of the Carmelite order; lived in Florence, Italy, about 1440, and was known there under the Italianized name **Ottobi;** was then in Lucca (1468–86), where he taught in canonic schools. In 1486 he was recalled to England by Henry VII. A. Seay edited *The Musical Works of John Hothby* in Corpus Mensurabilis Musicae, XXXIII (1964). An edition of his theoretical works is in progress.
WRITINGS: About 12 treatises: *Ars musica; Regulae super proportionem; De cantu figurato; Regulae de monochordo manuali; Quid est proportio; Tractatus quarundam regularum artis musices;* etc. His *La Calliopea legale* was publ. by Coussemaker in *Histoire de l'harmonie au moyen-âge; Regulae super proportionem, De cantu figurato* and *Regulae super contrapunctum* in Coussemaker's *Scriptores de musica* (vol. 3).

BIBLIOGRAPHY: U. Kornmüller, "Johann Hothby . . . ," *Kirchenmusikalisches Jahrbuch* (1893); A.W. Schmidt, *Die "Calliopea legale" des J. Hothby* (Leipzig, 1897).

Hotter, Hans, greatly esteemed German bass-baritone; b. Offenbach, Jan. 19, 1909. He studied voice in Munich; in 1920 made his debut at Troppau; sang there from 1930; subsequently was a member at the German Theater in Prague (1932–34). He then sang at the Hamburg State Opera (1934–45), the Bavarian State Opera in Munich (1937–42), the Berlin State Opera (1939–42), and the Vienna State Opera (1939–42). He also made appearances with La Scala in Milan, Covent Garden in London, the Teatro Colón in Buenos Aires, the Paris Opéra, and the Chicago Opera. He made his Metropolitan Opera debut on Nov. 9, 1950, as the Dutchman in *Der fliegende Holländer,* and remained on its roster until 1954. From 1977 he taught at the Vienna Hochschule für Musik. He was particularly acclaimed for his Wagnerian roles; he was ranked as the foremost Wotan at the Bayreuth Festivals.
BIBLIOGRAPHY: B.W. Wessling, *Hans Hotter* (Bremen, 1966).

Hotteterre, a family of French musicians: **Nicolas Hotteterre** (b. 1637; d. Paris, May 10, 1694), a hurdy-gurdy player; his brother **Martin** (d. 1712), also a hurdy-gurdy player and a performer at the court ballets; **Louis Hotteterre** (d. 1719), son of Nicolas, who played the flute at the French court for 50 years (1664–1714); his brother **Nicolas Hotteterre** (d. Paris, Dec. 4, 1727), who (like his brother) played flute and oboe in Lully's orch. at the court of Louis XIV; **Jacques Hotteterre** (b. Sept. 29, 1674; d. Paris, July 16, 1762), surnamed "le Romain," evidently owing to his long sojourns in Rome, popularized the transverse (German) flute at the French court and publ. several manuals on that instrument and others: *Principes de la flûte traversière, de la flûte d'Allemagne, de la flûte à bec ou flûte douce et du hautbois* (Paris, 1707; sometimes attributed to his cousin Louis; the 1728 ed. was reprinted in facsimile, Kassel, 1941); *Méthode pour la musette* (1738); *L'Art de préluder sur la flûte traversière, sur la flûte à bec, etc.* (Paris, 1712; 2nd ed. under the title *Méthode pour apprendre . . . ,* c.1765); he also wrote sonatas, duos, trios, suites, *rondes (chansons à danser),* and minuets for flute.
BIBLIOGRAPHY: J.A. Carlez, *Les Hotteterre* (Caen, 1877); E. Thoinan, *Les Hotteterre et les Chédeville* (Paris, 1894); N. Mauger, *Les Hotteterre, Nouvelles recherches* (Paris, 1912); H.M. Fitzgibbon, "Of Flutes and Soft Recorders," *Musical Quarterly* (April 1934).

Houdard, Georges, French authority on Gregorian chant; b. Neuilly-sur-Seine, March 30, 1860; d. Paris, Feb. 28, 1913. He studied with L. Hillemacher and with Massenet at the Paris Cons.; then devoted himself exclusively to old church music; publ. valuable treatises.
WRITINGS: *L'Art dit grégorien d'après la nota-*

tion neumatique (1897); *L'Evolution de l'art musical et l'art grégorien* (1902); *Aristoxène de Tarente* (1905); *La Rythmique intuitive* (1906); *Textes théoriques; Vademecum de la rythmique grégorienne des Xe et XIe siècles* (1912); also wrote some sacred music (a Requiem, offertories, elevations, etc.).

Houdoy (Hudoy), Jules François Aristide, French writer on music; b. Lille, Dec. 12, 1818; d. there, Jan. 28, 1883. He was president of the Société des Sciences et des Arts at Lille; author of *Histoire artistique de la cathédrale de Cambrai* (Lille, 1880), a very valuable work as regards the music of the 15th century.

Houseley, Henry, organist and composer; b. Sutton-in-Ashfield, England, Sept. 20, 1852; d. Denver, Colo., March 13, 1925. He studied at the Royal College of Organists in London; then filled various posts as church organist. In 1888 he emigrated to the U.S., settling in Denver, where he was active in many musical and cultural fields; produced there several light operas: *The Juggler* (May 23, 1895); *Pygmalion* (Jan. 30, 1912); *Narcissus and Echo* (Jan. 30, 1912); also wrote a cantata, *Omar Khayyâm,* which was performed in Denver on June 1, 1916.

BIBLIOGRAPHY: E.E. Hipsher, *American Opera and Its Composers* (Philadelphia, 1934; pp. 268–69).

Housman, Rosalie, American composer; b. San Francisco, June 25, 1888; d. New York, Oct. 28, 1949. She studied with Arthur Foote in Boston; also took lessons in N.Y. with Ernest Bloch; composed *Color Sequence* for Soprano and Small Orch.; women's choruses; children's pieces; songs.

Houtmann, Jacques, French conductor; b. Mirecourt, March 27, 1935. He studied at the Cons. of Nancy, and later at the Ecole Normale de Musique in Paris with Jean Fournet and Henri Dutilleux; then took courses in conducting with Franco Ferrara in Rome. He won first prize in the conductors' competition in Besançon (1961) and the Mitropoulos Competition in N.Y. (1964); was for a season an assistant conductor of the N.Y. Phil. (1965–66). He then returned to France, and served as conductor with the Rhône-Alpes Phil. in Lyons (1967–71). In 1971 he went again to the U.S., and was appointed music director of the Richmond (Va.) Symph. Orch.

Hovhaness, Alan (Vaness) Scott, prolific and proficient American composer of Armenian-Scottish descent; b. Somerville, Mass., March 8, 1911. His family name was **Chakmakjian.** He took piano lessons with Adelaide Proctor and with Heinrich Gebhard in Boston; his academic studies were at Tufts Univ.; in 1932 he enrolled in the New England Cons. as a student of Frederick S. Converse. From his earliest attempts at composition, he took great interest in the musical roots of his paternal ancestry, studying the folk songs assembled by the Armenian musician Komitas, and gradually came to believe that music must reflect the natural monody embodied in

national songs and ancient church hymns. In his own music he adopted modal melodies and triadic harmonies. This *parti pris* had the dual effect of alienating him from the milieu of modern composers while exercising great attraction for the music consumer at large. By dint of ceaseless repetition of melodic patterns and relentless dynamic tension, he succeeded in creating a sui generis type of impressionistic monody, flowing on the shimmering surfaces of euphony, free from the upsetting intrusion of heterogeneous dissonance; an air of mysticism pervades his music, aided by the programmatic titles which he often assigns to his compositions. After completion of his studies, he served on the faculty of the New England Cons. of Music (1948–51); then moved to N.Y. He was awarded two Guggenheim fellowships (1954 and 1958). In 1959 he received a Fulbright fellowship and traveled to India and Japan, where he collected native folk songs for future use and presented his own works, as pianist and conductor, receiving tremendous acclaim. In 1962 he was engaged as composer-in-residence at the Univ. of Hawaii; he then traveled to Korea. He eventually settled in Seattle. A composer of relentless fecundity, he produced 51 symphs., several operas, quasi-operas, and pseudo-operas, as well as an enormous amount of choral music. The totality of his output is in excess of 370 opus numbers. In a laudable spirit of self-criticism, he destroyed 7 of his early symphs. and began numbering them anew so that his first numbered symph. (subtitled *Exile*) was chronologically his 8th. He performed a similar auto-da-fé on other dispensable pieces. Among his more original compositions is a symph. score *And God Created Great Whales,* in which the voices of humpback whales recorded on tape were used a solo with the orch.; the work was performed to great effect in the campaign to save the whale from destruction by human (and inhuman) predators.

WORKS: OPERAS (each one to the composer's own libretto): *Etchmiadzin* (1946); *The Blue Flame* (San Antonio, Texas, Dec. 13, 1959); *Spirit of the Avalanche* (Tokyo, Feb. 15, 1963); *Wind Drum* and *The Burning House* (both at Gatlinburg, Tenn., Aug. 23, 1964); *Pilate* (Los Angeles, June 26, 1966); *The Travelers* (Foothill College, Los Altos Hills, Calif., April 22, 1967); *Pericles,* grand opera (1975); *Tale of the Sun Goddess Going into the Stone House* (1979). Operetta, *Afton Water,* on the play of William Saroyan (1951).

SYMPHS. (the numbering does not always coincide with the chronological order of composition): No. 1, *Exile* (BBC, London, May 26, 1939); No. 2, *Mysterious Mountain* (Houston, Oct. 31, 1955, Stokowski conducting); No. 3 (N.Y., Oct. 14, 1956); No. 4 for Concert Band (Pittsburgh, June 28, 1959); No. 5, *Short Symphony* (1959); No. 6, *Celestial Gate* (1959); No. 7, *Nanga Parvat,* for Band (1959); No. 8, *Arjuna* (1947; Madras, India, Feb. 1, 1960); No. 9, *St. Vartan* (N.Y., March 11, 1951); No. 10 (1959); No. 11, *All Men Are Brothers* (1960, New Orleans, March 21, 1961; revised, New Orleans, March 31, 1970); No. 12, with Chorus (1960); No. 13 (1953); No. 14, *Ararat* (1960); No. 15, *Silver Pilgrimage* (N.Y., March 28, 1963); No. 16, *Korean Kayageum,* for Strings and Korean Per-

Hovhaness

cussion Instruments (Seoul, Jan. 26, 1963); No. 17 for Metal Orch., commissioned by the Amercian Metallurgical Congress (Cleveland, Oct. 23, 1963); No. 18, *Circe* (1964); No. 19, *Vishnu* (N.Y., June 2, 1967); No. 20, *3 Journeys to a Holy Mountain,* for Concert Band (1968); No. 21, *Etchmiadzin* (1968); No. 22, *City of Light* (1970); No. 23, *Ani,* for Band (1972); No. 24, *Majnun,* with Chorus (1973; Lubbock, Texas, Jan. 25, 1974); No. 25, *Odysseus,* for Chamber Orch. (1973; London, April 10, 1974); No. 26, *Consolation* (San Jose, Calif., Oct. 24, 1975); No. 27 (1975); No. 28 (1976); No. 29 for Horn and Orch. (Minneapolis, May 4, 1977); No. 30 (1976); No. 31 for Strings (Seattle, Dec. 7, 1977); No. 32 for Chamber Orch. (1977); No. 33 for Chamber Orch. (1978); No. 34 (1977); No. 35 for Korean Instruments and Orch. (Seoul, June 9, 1978); No. 36 for Flute and Orch., op. 312 (Washington, D.C., Jan. 16, 1979; Rampal, soloist; Rostropovich conducting); No. 37 (1978); No. 38 for Soprano and Orch. (1978); No. 39 for Guitar and Orch. (1978); No. 40 for Brass, Timpani, and Orch. (1979; Interlochen, April 9, 1982); No. 41, *Mountain Sunset* (1979); No. 42 (1979); No. 43 (1979; Aptos, Calif., Aug. 20, 1981); No. 44 (1980); No. 45 (1979); No. 46, *To the Green Mountains* (Burlington, Vt., May 2, 1981); No. 47, *Walla Walla, Land of Many Waters,* for Soprano and Orch. (Walla Walla, Wash., Nov. 24, 1981); No. 48, *Vision of Andromeda* (Miami, Fla., June 21, 1982, by the visiting Minneapolis Symph. Orch.); No. 49, *Christmas,* for Strings (1981); No. 50, *Mount St. Helens* (1982); No. 51 (1982). **23 CONCERTOS:** Concerto for Cello and Orch. (1936); *Lousadzak (Coming of Light)* for Piano and Strings (1944; Boston, Feb. 4, 1945); *Return and Rebuild the Desolate Places,* concerto for Trumpet and Strings (N.Y., June 17, 1945); *Asori,* concerto for Flute, Cornet, Bassoon, Trumpet, Timpani, and Strings (1946); *Sosi,* concerto for Violin, Piano, Percussion, and Strings (1948; N.Y., March 6, 1949); *Artik,* concerto for Horn and Orch. (1948; Rochester, N.Y., May 7, 1954); *Zertik Parkim,* concerto for Piano and Chamber Orch. (1948); *Elibris (God of Dawn),* concerto for Flute and Strings (1949; San Francisco, Jan. 26, 1950); *Khaldis,* concerto for 4 Trumpets, Piano, and Percussion (1951); *Talin,* concerto for Viola and String Orch. (1952); Accordion Concerto (1959); Concerto for Harp and Strings (1973); Concerto for Euphonium and Orch. (1977); Concerto for Guitar and Orch. (1979); Concerto for Soprano Saxophone and Orch. (1980); 8 numbered concertos: No. 1, *Arevakal (Season of the Sun),* for Orch. (1951; N.Y., Feb. 18, 1952); No. 2 for Violin and Strings (1951–57); No. 3, *Diran,* for Baritone Horn or Trombone, and Strings (1948); No. 4 for Orch. (1952; Louisville, Ky., Feb. 20, 1954); No. 5 for Piano and Strings (1952); No. 6 for Harmonica and Strings (1953); No. 7 for Orch (1953); No. 8 for Orch. (1953). **OTHER WORKS FOR ORCH.:** *Storm on Mt. Wildcat* (1931); *Celestial Fantasy* (1944); 3 *Armenian Rhapsodies* (1944); *Khiriam Hairis* for Trumpet and Strings (1944); *Tzaikerk (Evening Song)* for Orch. (1945); *Kohar* for Orch. (1946); *Forest of Prophetic Sounds* for Orch. (1948); *Overture* for Trombone and Strings (1948); *Janabar,* 5 hymns for Violin, Trumpet, Piano, and Strings (1949; N.Y., March 11,

1951); Prelude and Quadruple Fugue for Orch. (1955); *Meditation on Orpheus* for Orch. (1957–58); *Copernicus,* tone poem (1960); *Mountain of Prophecy* for Orch. (1960); *Meditation on Zeami,* symph. poem (1963; N.Y., Oct. 5, 1964); *Ukiyo, Floating World,* tone poem (1964; Salt Lake City, Jan. 30, 1965); *Fantasy on Japanese Wood Prints* for Xylophone and Orch. (Chicago, July 4, 1964); *The Holy City* for Orch. (Portland, Oreg., April 11, 1967); *Fra Angelico,* symph. poem (Detroit, March 21, 1968); *Mountain and Rivers without End* for 10 Instruments (1968); *And God Created Great Whales* for Orch., with Voices of Humpback Whales recorded on Tape (1969; N.Y., June 11, 1970); *A Rose for Emily,* ballet for Orch. (1970); *Dawn on Mt. Tahoma* for Orch. (1973); *Fanfare to the New Atlantis* for Orch. (1975); *Ode to Freedom* for Violin and Orch. (Wolf Trap Farm Park, near Washington, D.C., July 3, 1976; Yehudi Menuhin, soloist); *Rubáiyát* for Narrator, Accordion, and Orch. (1975; N.Y., May 20, 1977).

CHAMBER MUSIC: Piano Quintet No. 1 (1926; revised 1962); Piano Trio (1935); String Quartet No. 1 (1936); Violin Sonata (1937); Suite for English Horn and Bassoon (1938); *Varak* for Violin and Piano (1944); *Anahid* for Flute, English Horn, Trumpet, Timpani, Percussion, and Strings (1944); *Saris* for Violin and Piano (1946); *Haroutiun (Resurrection),* aria and fugue for Trumpet and Strings (1948); *Sosi (Forest of Prophetic Sounds)* for Violin, Piano, Horn, Timpani, Giant Tam-tam, and Strings (1948), String Quartet No. 2 (1950); *Khirgiz Suite* for Violin and Piano (1951); *Orbit No. 1* for Flute, Harp, Celesta, and Tam-tam (1952); *Orbit No. 2* for Alto Recorder and Piano (1952); *Koke No Kiwa (Moss Garden)* for English Horn, Clarinet, Harp, and Percussion (1954); Wind Quintet (1960); *Nagooran* for an Ensemble of South Indian Instruments (1962); String Trio (1962); Piano Quintet No. 2 (1964); Sextet for Violin and 5 Percussionists (1966); *6 Dances* for Brass Quintet (1967); *Spirit of Ink,* 9 pieces for 3 Flutes (1968); String Quartet No. 3 (1968); *Vibration Painting* for 13 String Instruments (1969); String Quartet No. 4 (1970); *The Garden of Adonis* for Flute and Harp (1971); Sonata for 2 Bassoons (1973); Clarinet Quartet (1973); *Night of a White Cat* for Clarinet and Piano (1973); *Fantasy* for Double Bass and Piano (1974); String Quartet No. 5 (1976); Suite for 4 Trumpets and Trombone (1976); Suite for Alto Saxophone and Guitar (1976); Septet for Flute, Clarinet, Bass Clarinet, Trumpet, Trombone, Double Bass, and Percussion (1976); Sonata for 2 Clarinets (1977); *Sunset on Mt. Tahoma* for 2 Trumpets, Trombone, and Organ (1978); Sonata for Clarinet and Harpsichord (1978); Saxophone Trio (1979); 2 Sonatas for 3 Trumpets and 2 Trombones (1979).

PIANO MUSIC: *Mountain Lullaby* (1931); *3 Preludes and Fugues* (1935); *Sonata Ricercare* (1935); *Macedonian Mountain Dance* (1937); *Do you remember the last silence?* (1957); *Poseidon Sonata* (1957); *Child of the Garden,* for Piano, 4-hands (1958); *Madras Sonata* (1947; final revision, 1959); *Bardo Sonata* (1959); *Love Song Vanishing into Sounds of Crickets* (1979); *Sonata Catamount* (1980); *Sonata, Journey to Arcturus* (1981); *Hiro-*

shige's Cat (1982); *Sonata on the Long Total Eclipse of the Moon, July 6, 1982* (1982); *Tsugouharu Fujita's Cat* (1982); *Lake Sammamish* (1983).

VOCAL WORKS: *Ad Lyram* for Solo Voices, Double Chorus, and Chamber Orch. (Houston, Texas, March 12, 1957); *To the God Who Is in the Fire,* cantata (Urbana, Ill., April 13, 1957); *Magnificat* for Solo Voices, Chorus, and Chamber Orch. (1957); *Fuji,* cantata for Female Voices, Flute, Harp, and String Orch. (1960); *In the Beginning Was the Word* for Vocal Soloists, Chorus, and Orch. (1963); *Lady of Light* for Solo Voices, Chorus, and Chamber Orch. (1969); *Saturn,* 12 pieces for Soprano, Clarinet, and Piano (1971); *The Way of Jesus,* folk oratorio (St. Patrick's Cathedral, N.Y., Feb. 23, 1975); *Revelations of St. Paul,* cantata (1980; N.Y., Jan. 28, 1981); innumerable hymns, anthems, sacred and secular choruses; songs.

BIBLIOGRAPHY: David Ewen, *American Composers* (N.Y., 1982).

Hovland, Egil, Norwegian composer; b. Mysen, Oct. 18, 1924. He studied organ and composition at the Oslo Cons. (1946–49), later studying privately with Bjarne Brustad (1951–52, in Oslo), Vagn Holmboe (1954, in Copenhagen), Aaron Copland (1957, at Tanglewood), and Dallapiccola (1959, in Florence). In Norway he was active as a music critic and as an organist at a church in Fredrikstad. He cultivates a peculiarly Scandinavian type of neo-Classical polyphony, but is apt to use serial techniques.

WORKS: Church opera, *Brunnen (The Well;* 1971–72); Passacaglia and Fugue for String Orch. (1949); *Festival Overture* (1951); 3 symphs.: No. 1, *Symphonia Veris (Symphony of Spring;* 1952–53); No. 2 (1954–55); No. 3, for Narrator, Chorus, and Orch. (1969–70); Suite for Orch. (1954); Concertino for 3 Trumpets and Strings (1954–55); *Music for 10 Instruments* (1957); Suite for Flute and Strings (1959); *Festival Overture* for Wind Orch. (1962); *Lamenti* for Orch. (Oslo, April 24, 1964); *Rorate* for 5 Sopranos, Organ, Chamber Orch., and Tape (1966–67); *Missa vigilate* for Soprano, Baritone, Chorus, 2 Female Dancers, Organ, and Tape (1967); *Mass to the Risen Christ* for Chorus and Instruments (1968); *Rapsodi 69* for Orch. (1969); *All Saints' Mass* for Soprano, Chorus, Organ, and Instruments (1970); *Den vakreste rosen (The Most Beautiful Rose),* after Hans Christian Andersen, for Narrator, 4 Sopranos, Organ, and Orch. (1970); Trombone Concerto (1972); *Missa verbi* for Chorus, Organ, and Instruments (1972–73); Violin Concerto (1974); *Noël-Variations* for Orch. (1975); Piano Concerto (1976–77); *Tombeau de Bach* for Orch. (1977–78); *Pilgrim's Mass* for Choir, Organ, Congregation, and 9 Brasses (1982); Suite for Flute and Piano (1950); *Motus* for Solo Flute (1961); *Song of Songs* for Soprano, Violin, Percussion, and Piano (1962–63); *Magnificat* for Alto, Flute, and Harp (1964); *Varianti* for 2 Pianos (1964); Piano Trio (1965); Wind Quintet (1965); *Elemento* for Organist and 2 Assistants (1965; revised 1966); Variations for Oboe and Piano (1968–69); *I DAG* for Chorus and Instruments (1974); String

Quartet (1981); numerous sacred works and organ pieces.

Howard, Ann, English mezzo-soprano; b. Norwood, July 22, 1936. She studied in London; won a Royal Opera House grant to study with Modesti in Paris; made her operatic debut at the Sadler's Wells Opera in 1964 as Czipra in *Der Zigeunerbaron;* also sang at Covent Garden, at the Scottish Opera, at the Welsh National Opera, and at the Santa Fe Opera.

Howard, John Tasker, eminent American writer on music; b. Brooklyn, Nov. 30, 1890; d. West Orange, N.Y., Nov. 20, 1964. He attended Williams College in Williamstown, Mass.; then studied composition with Howard Brockway and Mortimer Wilson. He then devoted himself primarily to musical journalism; was managing editor of the *Musician* (1919–22); served as educational director of the Ampico Corp. (1922–28); then edited the music section of *McCall's Magazine* (1928–30) and *Cue* (1936–38); taught at Columbia Univ. in 1950–54. From 1940 to 1956 he was the curator of the Americana Music Collection at the N.Y. Public Library, which he enriched to a great extent. His major achievement was the publication of several books and monographs on American music and musicians.

WRITINGS: *Our American Music* (N.Y., 1931; 4 eds., the last one posthumous, 1965); *Stephen Foster, America's Troubadour* (N.Y., 1934; revised 1953); *Ethelbert Nevin* (N.Y., 1935); *Our Contemporary Composers, American Music in the 20th Century* (1941); *This Modern Music* (N.Y., 1942; new ed. by James Lyons, 1957, under the title *Modern Music*); *The World's Great Operas* (N.Y., 1948); *A Short History of Music in America* (N.Y., 1957; with G.K. Bellows). He was also a composer of modest, but respectable, attainments. He wrote a piece for Piano and Orch., entitled *Fantasy on a Choral Theme* (New Jersey Orch., Orange, N.J., Feb. 20, 1929); also *Foster Sonatina* for Violin and Piano; piano pieces; and some songs.

BIBLIOGRAPHY: G.K. Bellows, "John Tasker Howard," *Notes* (Sept. 1957; with a complete list of his publ. writings).

Howard, Kathleen, contralto; b. Niagara Falls, Canada, July 17, 1884; d. Hollywood, Aug. 15, 1956. She studied in N.Y. with Bouhy and in Paris with Jean de Reszke; sang at the Metz Opera (1907–9); at Darmstadt (1909–12); at Covent Garden in London (1913); with the Century Opera in N.Y. (1914–15). She made her first appearance with the Metropolitan Opera in N.Y. in *The Magic Flute* (Nov. 20, 1916); remained on the staff until 1928. After her retirement from the stage, she was engaged in magazine work; was fashion editor of *Harper's Bazaar* (1928–33); publ. an autobiography, *Confessions of an Opera Singer* (N.Y., 1918). She married Edward Kelley Baird on June 27, 1916.

Howarth, Elgar, English trumpeter and conductor; b. Cannock, Staffordshire, Nov. 4, 1935. He studied at the Univ. of Manchester and the Royal Manchester College of Music; then played trumpet in the orch. of the Royal Opera House, Covent Garden, with the Royal Phil. Orch., and with other London ensembles. In 1969 he began his career as a conductor with the London Sinfonietta; became its director in 1973.

Howe, Mary, American composer; b. Richmond, Va., April 4, 1882; d. Washington, D.C., Sept. 14, 1964. She studied at the Peabody Cons. in Baltimore; was a pupil of Gustav Strube (composition) and Ernest Hutcheson (piano); in 1915, settled in Washington, where she played a prominent part in musical organizations. She was a vice-president of the Friends of Music of the Library of Congress; was a member of the board of directors of the National Symph. Orch.
WORKS: Violin Sonata (1922); Suite for String Quartet and Piano (1923); *Sand* for Orch. (1928); *Dirge* for Orch. (1931); *Castellana* for 2 Pianos and Orch. (1935); *Spring Pastoral* for Solo Violin and 13 Instruments (1936); *Stars and Whimsy* for 15 Instruments (1937); *Potomac,* orch. suite (1940); *Agreeable Overture* (1949); *Rock,* symph. poem (Vienna, Feb. 15, 1955); choral works: *Chain Gang Song* (1925) and *Prophecy, 1792* (1943).
BIBLIOGRAPHY: M. Goss, "Mary Howe," in *Modern Music Makers* (N.Y., 1952).

Howell, Dorothy, English pianist and composer; b. Handsworth, Feb. 25, 1898; d. London, Jan. 12, 1982. She studied composition with McEwen and piano with Tobias Matthay at the Royal Academy of Music in London; from 1924 to 1970 she taught music theory there. Among her works are a ballet, *Koong Shee;* a symph. poem, *Lamia* (after Keats); an overture, *The Rock;* a Piano Concerto; and some chamber music.

Howell, Gwynne, Welsh bass; b. Gorseinon, June 13, 1938. He began his career as a town planner; concurrently studied at the Royal Manchester College of Music and later with Otakar Kraus in London. He made his professional operatic debut as Monterone in *Rigoletto* at the Sadler's Wells Opera in 1968; subsequently sang at Covent Garden, the English National Opera, Aix-en-Provence, and Barcelona. He also continued his career as a concert and oratorio singer in England and America.

Howells, Anne, English mezzo-soprano; b. Southport, Lancashire, Jan. 12, 1941. She studied at the Royal Manchester College of Music; made her operatic debut as Flora in *La Traviata* with the Welsh National Opera in 1966; first sang at Covent Garden in 1967. She made her American debut in Chicago in 1972; her Metropolitan Opera debut in N.Y. followed on Oct. 15, 1975, as Dorabella in *Così fan tutte.* She also sang in Paris, Geneva, Lyons, and other opera centers. She married the tenor **Ryland Davies.**

Howells, Herbert, distinguished English composer; b. Lydney, Gloucestershire, Oct. 17, 1892; d. Oxford, Feb. 24, 1983. In 1912 he entered the Royal College of Music in London, where he studied composition with Stanford and counterpoint with Charles Wood; in 1920 he was appointed an instructor in composition there, a position he held for more than 40 years. In 1936 he succeeded Holst as music director at St. Paul's Girls' School, remaining there until 1962; he also was a prof. of music at the Univ. of London (1954–64). In 1953 he was made a Commander of the Order of the British Empire and in 1972 a Companion of Honour. The music Howells wrote during his long life was nobly British, in its national references, its melodic outspokenness, and its harmonic opulence; in this it was a worthy continuation of the fine tradition of Elgar and Vaughan Williams.
WORKS: FOR ORCH.: Piano Concerto No. 1 in C major (1913; London, July 10, 1914); 3 dances for Violin and Orch. (1915); "The B's," suite (1915); *Puck's Minuet* and *Merry-eye* (1917–20); *Procession* (1922); *Pastoral Rhapsody* (1923); Piano Concerto No. 2 in C minor (1924); *Paradise Rondel* (1925); *Pageantry* for Brass Band (1934); *Fantasia* for Cello and Orch. (1937); Concerto for Strings (1939); Suite for Strings (1944); *Music for a Prince,* suite (1949); *Triptych* for Brass Band (1960).
CHORAL MUSIC: *Sine nomine* for 2 Soloists, Chorus, and Orch. (1922); *A Kent Yeoman's Wooing Song* for Soloists, Chorus, and Orch. (1933); *Requiem* for Unaccompanied Chorus (1936); *Hymnus Paradisi* for Soprano, Tenor, Chorus, and Orch. (1938); *A Maid Peerless* for Women's Voices and Strings, or Piano (1949); *Missa Sabrinensis* for Soloists, Chorus, and Orch. (1954; Worcester Festival, Sept. 7, 1954); *An English Mass* (1956); *Stabat Mater* for Tenor, Chorus, and Orch. (1963); *Take him, earth, for cherishing* (Motet on the Death of President Kennedy) (1964); *The Coventry Mass* for Choir and Organ (1968).
CHAMBER MUSIC: Piano Quartet (1916); *Rhapsodic Quintet* for Clarinet and Strings (1917); *Phantasy String Quartet* (1918); *In Gloucestershire,* string quartet (1923); 3 Sonatas for Violin and Piano (1918, 1918, 1923); Sonata for Oboe and Piano (1943); Sonata for Clarinet and Piano (1949).
FOR KEYBOARD: Organ Sonata No. 1 (1911); Organ Sonata No. 2 (1933); *Prelude—De profundis* for Organ (1958); *Partita* for Organ (1971); 2 sets of pieces for Clavichord: *Lambert's Clavichord* (1926–27) and *Howells' Clavichord* (1951–56); *Sonatina* for Piano (1971).
BIBLIOGRAPHY: R. Spearing, *H.H.: A Tribute to Herbert Howells on his Eightieth Birthday* (London, 1972); C. Palmer, *Herbert Howells: A Study* (London, 1978); M. Dreyer, "Herbert Howells at 90: The Cello Fantasia and Its Orchestral Predecessors," *The Musical Times* (Oct. 1982).

Howes, Frank (Stewart), English music critic, writer, and editor; b. Oxford, April 2, 1891; d. Standlake, Oxfordshire, Sept. 28, 1974. He studied at St. John's College, Oxford. In 1925 he joined the staff of the *Times* of London as music critic, and from 1943–60 was its chief music critic. He also served as editor of the *Folk Song Journal* (later known as the

Journal of the English Folk Dance and Song Society) from 1927–45; taught music history and appreciation at the Royal College of Music in London from 1938–70; and was Cramb Lecturer at the Univ. of Glasgow (1947 and 1952). In 1954 he was made a Commander of the Order of the British Empire.

WRITINGS: *The Borderland of Music and Psychology* (London, 1926); *The Appreciation of Music* (London, 1928); *William Byrd* (London, 1928); *A Key to the Art of Music* (London, 1935); *A Key to Opera* (in collaboration with P. Hope-Wallace; London, 1939); *Full Orchestra* (London, 1942; 2nd ed., revised and enlarged, 1976); *The Music of William Walton* (2 vols., London, 1942–43; new ed., 1965); *Man, Mind and Music* (London, 1948); *Music: 1945–50* (London, 1951); *The Music of Ralph Vaughan Williams* (London, 1954); *Music and Its Meanings* (London, 1958); *The Cheltenham Festival* (London, 1965); *The English Musical Renaissance* (London, 1966); *Oxford Concerts: A Jubilee Record* (Oxford, 1969); *Folk Music of Britain—and Beyond* (London, 1970).

Howland, William Legrand, American composer; b. Asbury Park, N.J., 1873; d. at his cottage, Douglas Manor, Long Island, N.Y., July 26, 1915. He studied with Philip Scharwenka in Berlin, and lived most of his life in Europe. His one-act opera, *Sarrona,* to his own libretto, was produced in Italian in Bruges, Belgium (Aug. 3, 1903), and subsequently had a number of performances in Italy; it was staged in N.Y. (in Eng.) on Feb. 8, 1910; in Philadelphia (in German) on March 23, 1911. He wrote another opera, *Nita;* 2 oratorios: *The Resurrection* and *Ecce Homo;* and some choral works.

Hoyer, Karl, German organist and composer; b. Weissenfels, Saale, Jan. 9, 1891; d. Leipzig, June 12, 1936. He studied at the Leipzig Cons. with Reger, Straube, and Krehl; was organist in Reval (1911), in Chemnitz (1912–26), and at the St. Nicholas Church in Leipzig (from 1926); also taught organ and theory at the Leipzig Cons. He wrote about 50 valuable organ works; also selections for organ and string orch.; chamber music; choral works; songs.

Hřimalý, Adalbert (Vojtech), Czech violinist and composer; b. Pilsen, July 30, 1842; d. Vienna, June 15, 1908. A member of an exceptionally musical family (his father was an organist; his 3 brothers were violinists), he received an early training at home; then studied with Mildner at the Prague Cons. (1855–61); was subsequently active as a conductor, composer, and teacher in various towns in the Netherlands, Sweden, and Rumania. He wrote a great number of works, including an opera, *Zaklety princ* (*The Enchanted Prince;* Prague, May 13, 1872).

Hřimalý, Johann (Jan), celebrated violinist and teacher; b. Pilsen, April 13, 1844; d. Moscow, Jan. 24, 1915. Like his older brother **Adalbert,** he studied at the Prague Cons. At the age of 24 he went to Moscow, where he became a prof. of violin at the Cons. (1874). He remained in Moscow for 40 years until his death, and was regarded there as a great teacher; 2

generations of Russian violinists studied under him. He also organized a string quartet in Moscow; publ. *Tonleiterstudien und Übungen in Doppelgriffen für die Violine* (Prague, 1895).

Hřimalý, Otakar, Czech violinist, son of **Adalbert Hřimalý;** b. Cernauti, Rumania, Dec. 20, 1883; d. Prague, July 10, 1945. He studied at the Vienna Cons. In 1909 he went to Moscow upon the recommendation of his uncle, **Johann Hřimalý;** became a prof. at the Moscow Cons., and remained there until 1922; then lived in Rumania; in 1939, went to Prague. He was known not only as a violin teacher but also as a composer; wrote an opera; 2 symphs.; the symph. poems *Ganymed* and *Der goldene Topf;* also chamber music and violin pieces.

Hrisanidis (Hrisanide), Alexandre, Rumanian-born composer and pianist of Greek citizenship, living in the Netherlands; b. Petrila, June 15, 1936. He studied at the Bucharest Cons. with Paul Constantinescu, Tudor Ciortea, Zeno Vancea, Mihail Jora, and Alfred Mendelsohn (1953–64); continued his studies at the American Cons. in Fontainebleau, France, with Nadia Boulanger (1965); attended the Darmstadt summer courses in new music (1966–67); then taught at the Bucharest Academy (1959–62) and at the Bucharest Cons. (1962–72); in 1972 he left Rumania; was a visiting prof. of music at the Univ. of Oregon (1972–73); in 1974 settled in the Netherlands. To reassert his Greek ancestry, he changed the Rumanian spelling of his last name to Hrisanidis. His music follows constructivist tendencies, with the application of modified serial techniques. In 1965 he won the annual award of the Lili Boulanger Memorial Fund, Boston, for his *Volumes—Inventions* and his Clarinet Sonata.

WORKS: 2 cantatas: *C'était issu stellaire* for Male Chorus, Organ, 3 Trumpets, 4 Trombones, and Percussion (1965; Zagreb, May 16, 1967) and *Les Lumières de la patrie* (1965); *Poem* for Orch. (1958; Bucharest, Feb. 8, 1963); Passacaglia for Orch. (1959; Cluj, Nov. 25, 1962); *"Vers-Antiqua" (Hommage à Euripide)* for Chamber Orch. (1960; Hannover, Jan. 28, 1966); Concerto for Orch. (1964); *Ad perpetuam rei memoriam,* 3 pieces for Orch. (1966; Bucharest, Dec. 22, 1967); *RO* for Orch. (1968); *I-RO-LA-HAI* for Voice and Orch. (Nuremberg, June 8, 1971); *Sonnets,* concerto for Harpsichord and Orch. (Hilversum, March 26, 1973); 3 flute sonatas (1956, 1960–62, 1956); Violin Sonata (1957; its 3 movements can be played as separate pieces: *Hommages à Bartók, Enesco,* and *Schoenberg*); Trio for Violin, Viola, and Bassoon (1958); String Quartet (1958); Clarinet Sonata (1960–62); *Mers-Tefs* for Solo Violin (1960–68); *Volumes—Inventions* for Cello and Piano (1963); *Music* for Viola and Piano (1965); *A la recherche de la verticale* for Solo Oboe (1965); *M. P.5 (Musique pour 5)* for Violin, Viola, Cello, Saxophone (or Clarinet), and Piano (1966); *Directions* for Wind Quintet (1967–69); *Première musique pour RA* for Piano and Tape (1968–69); *Seconde musique pour RA* for Piano and Tape (1969); *Troisième musique pour RA* for Piano, Varying Percussion Instruments, and Tape, divided into 3 separate pieces: *Das Finale der Unendlichkeit, Vergangenheit schauende Stunde,* and *glorreich ist alles* (all composed in 1970); *Quatrième musique pour RA* for Piano and Tape, in 2 separate pieces: *Maister Manole* and *Blaga* (both written in 1970); *Cinquième musique pour RA* for Piano, Celesta, Harpsichord, and Tape (1973); *Sixième musique pour RA* for Piano, Varying Instruments, and Tape, in 3 separate pieces: *Là où ça passe, "ZED-UE,"* and *Mnemosyne* (all 1970); *Soliloquium × 11* for String Quartet (1970); *Music for 1 to 4 Violins,* quartet for Violins (1970); *Chanson sous les étoiles,* duet for Flute and Oboe (1973); *Du soir venant* for Solo Bass Clarinet (1974–75); *Suite classique* for Piano (1954); *Piano Pieces 1–13* (1955–56); 3 piano sonatas: No. 1 (1955–56; movements can be played independently: *Flames, Duality,* and *Study No. 4*); No. 2, *Sonata piccola* (1959); No. 3, *Picasso Sonata* (1956–64); *Desseins espagnols* for Prepared Piano (1971); *Unda* for Organ (1965); songs.

Hristić, Stevan, Serbian composer; b. Belgrade, June 19, 1885; d. there, Aug. 21, 1958. He studied in Leipzig, Rome, Paris, and Moscow. Returning to Belgrade, he became conductor of the National Opera Theater; also taught at the Music Academy there. He composed a music drama, *Suton (Sunset,* 1925); a ballet, *Legend of Okhrid* (1947); and many choral works, of which *Jesen (Autumn)* became fairly popular.

Hrušovský, Ivan, Slovak composer; b. Bratislava, Feb. 23, 1927. In 1947 he began studies of composition with A. Moyzes at the Bratislava Cons.; continued composition studies with Moyzes at the Academy of Musical Arts, graduating in 1957; then joined its faculty. His music represents the common denominator of Central European trends. WORKS: *Suite pastorale* for Orch. (1955); Piano Concerto (1957); Sinfonietta for 2 String Orchs. (1959); *The Tatra Poem,* symph. poem (1960); *Hirošima,* cantata (1961–62); *Concertante Overture* for String Orch. (1963); *Combinazioni sonorische* for 9 Instruments (1963); *Sen o člevěku (A Dream about a Man),* cantata (1964); *Passacaglia eroica* for Orch. (1964); *Musica nocturna* for String Orch. (1971); 2 piano sonatas (1965, 1970); Sonata for Solo Violin (1969); *Sonata in modo classico* for Solo Cymbalom (1976); electronic tape pieces: *Invocation* (1974) and *Idée fixe* (1975); choruses.

Hubay, Jenö, celebrated Hungarian violinist; b. Budapest, Sept. 15, 1858; d. Vienna, March 12, 1937. He received his initial training from his father, Karl Hubay, prof. of violin at the Budapest Cons.; gave his first public concert at the age of 11; then studied with Joachim in Berlin (1873–76). His appearance in Paris, at a Pasdeloup concert, attracted the attention of Vieuxtemps, of whom he became a favorite pupil; in 1882 he succeeded Vieuxtemps as prof. at the Brussels Cons. In 1886 he became a prof. at the Budapest Cons. (succeeding his father); from 1919 to 1934 he was its director. In Budapest he formed the celebrated Hubay String Quartet. In 1894 he married the Countess Rosa Cebrain. Among his pupils were Vecsey, Szigeti, Telmányi, Eddy Brown, and other renowned violinists. Hubay was also a prolific composer. WORKS: Operas (all produced in Budapest): *Alienor* (Dec. 5, 1891); *Le Luthier de Crémone* (Nov. 10, 1894); *A Falu Rossza (The Village Vagabond;* March 20, 1896); *Moosröschen* (Feb. 21, 1903); *Anna Karenina* (Nov. 10, 1923); *Az álarc (The Mask;* Feb. 26, 1931); 4 symphs.: No. 1 (1885); No. 2, *1914–15* (1915); No. 3, *Vita nuova,* for Soli, Chorus, and Organ; No. 4, *Petöfi-Sinfonie,* for Soli, Chorus, and Orch.; also *Biedermeyer Suite* for Orch. (1913); 4 violin concertos; 14 pieces for Violin and Orch., in the Hungarian manner; *Scènes de la Csárda; Sonate romantique* for Violin and Piano; he also ed. the violin études of Kreutzer (1908), Rode, Mayseder, and Saint Lubin (1910).

Hubbard, "Freddie" (Frederick De Wayne), black American jazz trumpeter, pianist, and bandleader; b. Indianapolis, April 7, 1938. After playing with local jazz musicians, including Wes Montgomery, he worked with Art Blakey, Max Roach, Quincy Jones, and others; also played with Friedrich Gulda in Europe.

Hubbell, Frank Allen, American conductor, arranger, and composer; b. Denver, Colo., May 9, 1907; d. Kirkland, Wash., April 21, 1971. He was taken to California as a child and was reared on an orange grove. He learned to play the cornet and also began to compose music. In 1936 he arranged a native Hawaiian tune and launched it with a band as *The Hawaiian War Chant;* it became his most popular creation. His reputation was further enhanced by his arrangement of old California songs for band, under the title *California El Dorado Suite.* His later band pieces, all in the "landscape music" genre, included *The San Diego Story* (1957), *The Oregon Story* (1959), and *The Kansas Story* (1961). He was also active on the pageant stage, and was music director of the International Beauty Congress, for which he wrote 2 theme songs, *World of Beauty* and *Sound the Trumpets.*

Hubeau, Jean, French composer and pianist; b. Paris, June 22, 1917. He entered the Paris Cons. at the age of 9; studied piano with Lazare Lévy; composition with Jean and Noël Gallon and Paul Dukas. He won first prize for piano at 13, and for composition at 16; in 1934, at the age of 17, he received the 2nd Grand Prix de Rome with his cantata *La Légende de Roukmani.* He made several European tours as a pianist; from 1942 to 1957 he was director of the Cons. of Versailles; afterward joined the staff of the Paris Cons., teaching a class of chamber music. WORKS: Ballets: *Trois fables de La Fontaine* (Paris, March 2, 1945); *La Fiancée du diable* (Paris, Dec. 8, 1945); *Un Cœur de diamant ou L'Infante* (Monte Carlo, April 7, 1949); for Orch.: *Tableaux hindous* (Paris, Oct. 18, 1936); Violin Concerto (Par-

is, March 30, 1941); Cello Concerto (Paris, Nov. 28, 1942); *Concerto héroïque* for Piano and Orch. (Paris, Dec. 22, 1946); chamber music: Violin Sonata (1941); *Sonatine-Humoresque* for Horn, Flute, Clarinet, and Piano (1942); Sonata for Trumpet and Piano (1943); *Sonate-Caprice* for 2 Violins (1944); *Air varié* for Clarinet and Piano (1961); *Idylle* for Flute and Piano (1966); Piano Sonata; other piano pieces; songs; choral works.
BIBLIOGRAPHY: A. Machabey, *Portraits de trente musiciens français* (Paris, 1949; pp. 97–100).

Huber, Hans, Swiss composer; b. Eppenberg, near Olten, June 28, 1852; d. Locarno, Dec. 25, 1921. He studied at the Leipzig Cons. with Richter, Reinecke, and Wenzel (1870–74); then taught music at Wesserling, at Thann (Alsace), and at Basel; received an honorary degree of Dr.Phil. from Basel Univ. (1892). In 1896 he became director of the Basel Cons., a post that he held until his death. Huber composed prolifically in all genres; his style combined the rhapsodic form typical of Lisztian technique with simple ballad-like writing. He often used Swiss songs for thematic material. In Switzerland his reputation is very great and his works are frequently performed, but they are virtually unknown elsewhere.
WORKS: Operas: *Weltfrühling* (Basel, March 28, 1894); *Kudrun* (Basel, Jan. 29, 1896); *Der Simplicius* (Basel, Feb. 22, 1912); *Die schöne Bellinda* (Bern, April 2, 1916); *Frutta di mare* (Basel, Nov. 24, 1918); 8 symphs. (all except No. 2 perf. first in Basel): No. 1, *William Tell* (April 26, 1881); No. 2, *Böcklinsinfonie* (Zürich, July 2, 1900); No. 3, *Heroische* (Nov. 9, 1917); No. 4, *Akademische* (May 23, 1909); No. 5, *Romantische* (Feb. 11, 1906); No. 6 (Nov. 19, 1911); No. 7, *Swiss* (June 9, 1917); No. 8 (Oct. 29, 1921); 4 piano concertos (Basel, 1878, 1891, 1899, 1910); Violin Concerto (1878); Sextet for Piano and Wind Instruments (1900); Quintet for Piano and Wind Instruments (1914); 2 string quintets (1890, 1907); String Quartet; 2 piano quartets; 5 piano trios; 10 violin sonatas; 5 cello sonatas; a number of piano works, among them 48 preludes and fugues for piano, 4-hands.
BIBLIOGRAPHY: E. Refardt, *Hans Huber* (Leipzig, 1906); idem, *Hans Huber, Beiträge zu einer Biographie* (1922); idem, *Hans Huber* (Zürich, 1944; supersedes his previous monographs; contains a complete list of works and full bibliography); Gian Bundi, *Hans Huber, Die Persönlichkeit nach Briefen und Erinnerungen* (1925).

Huber, Klaus, Swiss composer; b. Bern, Nov. 30, 1924. He studied violin with Stefi Geyer and composition with Willy Burkhard at the Zürich Cons. (1947–49); later took courses in composition with Boris Blacher in Berlin (1955–56). He taught violin at the Zürich Cons. in 1950; from 1960–63 he lectured on music history at the Lucerne Cons.; in 1961 joined the faculty of the Basel Musical Academy.
WORKS: *Oratio Mechtildis* for Contralto and Chamber Orch. (Strasbourg Festival, June 9, 1958); *Des Engels Anredung an die Seele,* cantata for Voice and 4 Instruments (Rome, June 13, 1959); *Al-*

veare vernat for Flute and 12 Solo Strings (1965); *Tenebrae* for Orch. (1966–67); *James Joyce Music* for Harp, Horn, and Chamber Orch. (1966–67); *Tempora,* violin concerto (1969–70); *Im Paradies oder Der Alte vom Berge* (1974–75).

Huber, Kurt, eminent Swiss musicologist; b. Chur, Oct. 24, 1893; executed by the Gestapo in Munich, July 13, 1943, for participation in student protests against the Nazi government. He studied with Sandberger and Kroyer in Munich (Dr.Phil., 1917, with the dissertation *Ivo de Vento: Ein Beitrag zur Musikgeschichte des 16. Jahrhunderts,* 1, publ. in Lindenberg, 1918); from 1920, he taught at the Univ. of Munich; publ. *Die Doppelmeister des 16. Jahrhunderts* (Munich, 1920); *Der Ausdruck musikalischer Elementarmotive: Eine experimental psychologische Untersuchung* (Leipzig, 1923). From 1925 he devoted himself to collecting and recording old Bavarian folk songs, and publ. them (with Paul Klem).
BIBLIOGRAPHY: W.H. Rubsamen, "Kurt Huber of Munich," *Musical Quarterly* (April 1944); Clara Huber, *Kurt Huber zum Gedächtnis* (Regensburg, 1947). Huber's lectures on musical esthetics were reconstructed, ed. by Otto Ursprung, and publ. as *Musikästhetik* (1954); E. Grave, *Die ästhetischen Kategorien in Kurt Hubers Ästhetik* (Diss., Univ. of Munich, 1957).

Huberman, Bronislaw, famous Polish violinist; b. Częstochowa, Dec. 19, 1882; d. Corsier-sur-Vevey, Switzerland, June 15, 1947. At a very early age he began to study the violin with Michalowicz, a teacher at the Warsaw Cons.; he then studied with Isidor Lotto; in 1892 he was taken to Berlin, where he studied with Joachim. He made public appearances at the age of 11 in Amsterdam, Brussels, and Paris. Adelina Patti heard him in London and engaged him to appear with her at her farewell concert in Vienna (Jan. 12, 1895); on Jan. 29, 1896, he played Brahms's Violin Concerto in Vienna; Brahms, who was present, commended him warmly. Huberman toured the U.S. in 1896–97; many world tours followed; he gave a series of 14 concerts in Paris (1920), 10 in Vienna (1924), 8 in Berlin (1926); toured America again in 1937. At a concert arranged on May 16, 1909, by the city of Genoa for the victims of the Messina earthquake, Huberman was honored by an invitation to play upon Paganini's Guarneri violin (preserved in the Museum of Genoa). He taught a master class at the Vienna State Academy (1934–36); in 1936 organized a new Palestine Symph. Orch., consisting chiefly of Jewish musicians who had lost their positions in Europe. He came to the U.S. in 1940; returned to Europe after the war. He publ. *Aus der Werkstatt des Virtuosen* (Vienna, 1912); *Mein Weg zu Paneuropa* (1925).
BIBLIOGRAPHY: *An Orchestra Is Born. The Founding of the Palestine Orchestra as Reflected in Bronislaw Huberman's Letters, Speeches, and Articles* (Tel Aviv, 1969); H. Goetz, *Bronislaw Huberman and the Unity of Europe* (Rome, 1967).

Hubert, Nicolai, Russian conductor and pedagogue; b. St. Petersburg, March 19, 1840; d. Moscow, Oct. 8, 1888. He studied with his father; then at the St. Petersburg Cons. (1863) with Zaremba and Rubinstein. In 1869 he was in Odessa as an opera conductor; in 1870 was engaged as a prof. of music theory at the Moscow Cons.; he succeeded Nicholas Rubinstein as its director in 1881, resigning in 1883. Hubert also wrote music criticism in Moscow newspapers.

Huberti, Gustave-Léon, Belgian composer; b. Brussels, April 14, 1843; d. Schaerbeek, June 28, 1910. He studied at the Brussels Cons., where he won the Prix de Rome in 1865 for his cantata *La Fille de Jephté.* He was director of the Mons Cons. (1874–78); then a conductor in Antwerp and Brussels; in 1899, was appointed a prof. at the Brussels Cons.; was also director of the Music School of St.-Josse-ten-Noodle-Schaerbeek. In 1891 he was elected a member of the Belgian Academy. WORKS: 3 oratorios: *Een Laatste Zonnestraal* (1874); *Bloemardinne; Willem van Oranjes dood;* dramatic poem, *Verlichting (Fiat lux),* for Soli, Chorus, Organ, and Orch.; symph. poem, *Kinderlust en Leed,* for Chorus and Orch.; *Symphonie funèbre; Suite romantique; In den Garade; Triomffeest,* with Organ; also various festival marches, etc.; vocal soli, with orch. accompaniment; numerous French, Flemish, and German songs, with piano; *Andante et intermezzo* for 4 Flutes and Orch.; Piano Concerto; compositions for piano (*Etude, Conte d'enfant, Tarentelle, Impromptu, Historiette, Etude rythmique, Valse lente);* men's chorus, *Van Maerlantszang.* He also publ. a book, *Histoire de la musique religieuse des Italiens et des Néerlandais* (Brussels, 1873).

Huberty, Albert, Belgian operatic bass; b. Seraing-sur-Meuse, Feb. 2, 1879; d. Nieuport-les-Bains, March 10, 1955. He studied in Brussels; sang in Belgium, the Netherlands, and England; then in Montreal (1909–13). He made his Paris debut at the Opéra-Comique on May 20, 1915, as Roméo; thereafter, sang 62 different roles there.

Hucbald (Hugbaldus, Ubaldus, Uchubaldus), Flemish monk and musical theorist; b. at or near Tournai, c.840; d. Saint-Amand, near Tournai, June 20, 930. He was a pupil of his uncle Milo, director of the singing school at Saint-Amand; then was himself director of a similar school at Nevers (860); subsequently returned to Saint-Amand and succeeded his uncle. The following works are printed under his name in Gerbert's *Scriptores* (vol. I): *De Harmonica institutione; Musica enchiriadis* (gives the earliest detailed account of the beginnings of polyphonic music and of the Daseian notation, in which the Greek aspirate sign is used in various combinations and positions to produce 18 symbols indicating that many pitches); *Scholia enchiriadis;* fragments entitled *Alia musica;* and *Commemoratio brevis de tonis et psalmis modulandis.* However, it has been established (by W.

Mühlmann, in *Die "Alia Musica";* Leipzig, 1914) that Hucbald was not the author of *Musica enchiriadis.*

BIBLIOGRAPHY: C.E.H. de Coussemaker, *Memoire sur Hucbald et sur ses traités de musique* (1814); J.F. Rowbotham, *History of Music* (vol. III, pp. 366ff.); P. Spitta, "Die Musica enchiriadis und ihr Zeitalter," *Vierteljahrsschrift für Musikwissenschaft* (vol. 5, pp. 443–82, and vol. 6, pp. 293–309); R. Schlecht, German trans. of the *Musica enchiriadis,* in *Monatshefte für Musikgeschichte* (1874–76); H. Riemann, *Geschichte der Musiktheorie* (Leipzig, 1898); E.J. Grutchfield, "Hucbald, A Millenary Commemoration," *Musical Times* (1930; 2 installments); A.H. Fox-Strangways, "A Tenth Century Manual," *Music & Letters* (1932); J. Handschin, "Etwas Greifbares über Hucbald," *Acta Musicologica,* 7; R. Weakland, "Hucbald as Musician and Theorist," *Musical Quarterly* (Jan. 1956); C. Palisca, ed., and W. Babb, trans., *Hucbald, Guido, and John on Music: Three Medieval Treatises* (New Haven, 1979).

Hudson, Frederick, English musicologist; b. Gateshead, Durham, Jan. 16, 1913. He studied with Edward Bairstow at the Univ. of Durham and with Gordon Slater at Lincoln Cathedral; specialized as an organist; received the degree of B.Mus. at the Univ. of Durham in 1941, and of D.Mus. in 1950. He served as organist and choirmaster at Alnwick (1941–48); was a lecturer in music at King's College, Univ. of Durham; at the Univ. of Newcastle upon Tyne (1949–70); was subsequently a reader in music there. He edited works by Bach, Handel, Giovanni Gabrieli, William Byrd, and others for the new editions of their works; contributed important papers dealing with watermarks of undated MSS and prints, making use of beta-radiography with Carbon-14 sources; also compiled a catalogue of the works of Charles Villiers Stanford (*Music Review,* May 1976); contributed to *The New Grove.*

Hüe, Georges-Adolphe, French composer; b. Versailles, May 6, 1858; d. Paris, June 7, 1948. He was a pupil at the Paris Cons. of Reber and Paladilhe; took first Grand Prix de Rome in 1879, and the Prix Crescent in 1881; lived in Paris as a teacher and composer; was a member (succeeding Saint-Saëns) of the Académie des Beaux-Arts (1922). WORKS: Operas: *Les Pantins* (Opéra-Comique, Dec. 28, 1881); *Le Roi de Paris* (Paris Opéra, April 26, 1901); *Titania,* after Shakespeare (Opéra-Comique, Jan. 20, 1903); *Le Miracle* (Paris Opéra, Dec. 30, 1910); *Dans l'ombre de la cathédrale,* after Blasco Ibañez (Opéra-Comique, Dec. 7, 1921); *Riquet à la houppe,* after Perrault (Opéra-Comique, Dec. 21, 1928); ballet, *Cœur brisé* (Paris, 1890); pantomime, *Siang Sin* (Paris Opéra, March 19, 1924); *Rübezahl,* symph. legend in 3 parts (Concerts Colonne, 1886); "féerie dramatique," *La Belle au bois dormant* (Paris, 1894); *Résurrection,* "épisode sacré" (1892); *Le Berger,* ballade and fantaisie for Violin and Orch. (1893); Symph.; *Rêverie* and *Sérénade* for Small Orch.; *Romance* for Violin and Orch.; choral works; songs of more than average merit (6 songs from Heine's *Lyrisches Intermezzo; Croquis d'Orient; Chansons printanières; Berceuse pour les gueux; 2 chansons;* etc.).

Hueffer, Francis, English author and music critic; b. Münster, May 22, 1843; d. London, Jan. 19, 1889. He studied philology and music in London, Paris, Berlin, and Leipzig; received a Dr.Phil. degree from Göttingen Univ. for his first publication (1869), a critical edition of the works of Guillem de Cabestant, troubadour of the 12th century. In 1869 he settled in London as a writer on music, and from 1878 was music critic of the *Times.* He publ. *Richard Wagner and the Music of the Future* (1874); *The Troubadours: A History of Provençal Life and Literature in the Middle Ages* (1878); *Musical Studies* (1880; reprints of his articles from the *Times* and *Fortnightly Review;* Italian trans., Milan, 1883); *Italian and Other Studies* (1883); *Half a Century of Music in England* (1889; 2nd ed., 1898); he also trans. the correspondence of Wagner and Liszt into Eng., and was editor of Novello's Great Musicians series of biographies, for which he wrote *Wagner* (1881).

Huehn, Julius, American baritone; b. Revere, Mass., Jan. 12, 1904; d. Rochester, N.Y., June 8, 1971. He studied engineering at the Carnegie Inst. of Technology; later took voice lessons with Anna Schoen-René at the Juilliard School in N.Y. He made his operatic debut with the Metropolitan Opera as the herald in *Lohengrin* on Dec. 21, 1935, singing there until 1944; then served in the U.S. Air Force and carried out missions in Europe as a bombardier. He sang again at the Metropolitan after the war (1945–46). He was particularly noted for his performances of heroic baritone parts in Wagner's operas.

Hughes, Arwel, Welsh conductor and composer; b. Rhosllanerchrugog, Aug. 25, 1909. He studied with Kitson and Vaughan Williams at the Royal College of Music in London; then returned to Wales, where he became a member of the music dept. of the BBC in 1935; from 1965–71 was head of music there. He was made an Officer of the Order of the British Empire in 1969. He wrote the operas *Menna* (1950–51) and *Serch yw'r doctor (Love's the Doctor),* after Molière (1959); also a Symph. (1971), choral works, and chamber music.

Hughes, Dom Anselm, eminent English musicologist; b. London, April 15, 1889; d. Nashdom Abbey, Burnham, Buckinghamshire, Oct. 8, 1974. He studied at Oxford (B.A., 1911; M.A., 1915); lectured on medieval church music in univs. and colleges in the U.S. and Canada (1932, 1934, 1939, and 1940); contributed articles to *Grove's Dictionary of Music and Musicians;* edited (with others) the *Old Hall Manuscript* (1933–38).
WRITINGS: *Early English Harmony* (vol. II; London, 1912); *Latin Hymnody* (London, 1923); *Worcester Mediaeval Harmony* (Burnham, 1928); *The House of My Pilgrimage* (London, 1929); *Anglo-*

French Sequelae (London, 1934); *Index to the Facsimile Edition of MS Wolfenbüttel 677* (Oxford, 1939); *Liturgical Terms for Music Students* (Boston, 1940); *Medieval Polyphony in the Bodleian Library* (Oxford, 1951); *Catalogue of the Musical Manuscripts at Peterhouse, Cambridge* (Cambridge, 1953). He also composed *Missa Sancti Benedicti* (London, 1918) and various small pieces of church music.

Hughes, Edwin, American pianist; b. Washington, D.C., Aug. 15, 1884; d. New York, July 17, 1965. He studied with S.M. Fabian in Washington, with Rafael Joseffy in N.Y. (1906–7), and with T. Leschetizky in Vienna (1907–10); taught at the Ganapol School of Musical Art in Detroit (1910–12), the Volpe Inst. of Music in N.Y. (1916–17), and the Inst. of Musical Art in N.Y. (1918–23); lectured at various schools. From 1920–26 he was special editor of piano music for G. Schirmer, Inc.; edited Bach's *Well-Tempered Clavier* for Schirmer's Library of Musical Classics (with a preface in Eng. and Spanish); publ. piano transcriptions of Strauss's waltzes; wrote songs; etc.

Hughes, Herbert, Irish critic and composer; b. Belfast, March 16, 1882; d. Brighton, England, May 1, 1937. He studied at the Royal College of Music in London. He was one of the founders of the Irish Folksong Society and co-editor of its early journals; was music critic of the *Daily Telegraph.* He collected and edited many folk songs, including the collections Boosey's *Modern Festival Series; Irish Country Songs* (in 4 vols.); *Old Irish Melodies* (3 vols.); *Historical Songs and Ballads of Ireland; Songs from Connacht; Songs of Uladh.* He composed incidental music to the comedy *And So to Bed;* the film *Irish Hearts; Nursery Rhymes,* studies in imitation (2 vols.); *Parodies* for Voice and Orch. (2 vols.); *Brian Boru's March* for Piano; *3 Satirical Songs* for Violin, Flute, Clarinet, and Bassoon; *Shockheaded Peter,* cycle for Soprano, Baritone, and Piano; etc.

Hughes, Owain Arwel, Welsh conductor, son of **Arwel Hughes;** b. Cardiff, March 21, 1942. He first studied at Univ. College in Cardiff; then (1964–66) at the Royal College of Music in London, where his teachers included Sir Adrian Boult and Harvey Philips; subsequently studied with Kempe in London and Haitink in Amsterdam. He made his London debut in 1968; then appeared as a guest conductor with leading English orchs.; also conducted at the Welsh National Opera and the English National Opera. In 1977 he became music director of the Royal National Eisteddfod of Wales.

Hughes, Robert, Scottish-born Australian composer; b. Leven, Fyfeshire, March 27, 1912. He emigrated to Australia in 1930; worked as a music librarian at the Australian Broadcasting Commission in Melbourne. He withdrew most of his early compositions; his extant works include *Festival Overture* (1948); *Farrago,* suite for Orch. (1949); *Serenade* for Small Orch. (1952); Symph. No. 1 (1952); *Essay* for Orch. (1953); ballet, *Xanadu* (1954); *Masquerade*

Overture (1956); Sinfonietta (1957; Manchester, England, Nov. 10, 1957); television ballet, *The Forbidden Rite* (1962); *Synthesis* for Orch. (1969); *5 Indian Poems* for Chorus, Woodwind Instruments, and Percussion (1971); *Sea Spell* for Orch. (1973).

BIBLIOGRAPHY: James Murdoch, *Australia's Contemporary Composers* (Melbourne, 1972).

Hughes, Rupert, American writer on music; b. Lancaster, Mo., Jan. 31, 1872; d. Los Angeles, Sept. 9, 1956. He studied with W.G. Smith in Cleveland (1890–92), E.S. Kelley in N.Y. (1899), and C. Pearce in London (1900–1). His publications include: *American Composers* (Boston, 1900; revised 1914); *The Musical Guide* (2 vols., N.Y., 1903; republ. as *Music Lovers' Encyclopedia,* in one vol., 1912; revised and newly ed. by Deems Taylor and Russell Kerr as *Music Lover's Encyclopedia,* 1939; revised 1954); edited *Thirty Songs by American Composers* (1904). He composed a dramatic monologue for Baritone and Piano, *Cain* (1919); piano pieces; songs. He was principally known, however, as a successful novelist.

Hugo, John Adam, American pianist and composer; b. Bridgeport, Conn., Jan. 5, 1873; d. there, Dec. 29, 1945. In 1888–97 he studied at the Stuttgart Cons. with Speidel, Faiszt, Doppler, and Zumpe; appeared as a concert pianist in Germany, England, and Italy; returned to the U.S. in 1899. His one-act opera, *The Temple Dancer,* was one of the few operas by American composers presented by the Metropolitan Opera in N.Y. (March 12, 1919); it was also produced in Honolulu (Feb. 19, 1925). His other works are the operas *The Hero of Byzanz* (written while studying at the Stuttgart Cons.) and *The Sun God;* Symph.; 2 piano concertos; Piano Trio; pieces for violin; pieces for cello; piano pieces; and songs.

BIBLIOGRAPHY: E.E. Hipsher, *American Opera and Its Composers* (Philadelphia, 1927; pp. 270–74).

Hugon, Georges, French composer; b. Paris, July 23, 1904; d. Blauvac, Vaucluse, July 19, 1980. He studied at the Paris Cons.; received the Prix Bizet (1926). He was director of the Cons. of Boulogne-sur-Mer (1934–41); in 1941, became a prof. at the Cons. of Paris.

WORKS: Oratorio, *Chants de deuil et d'espérance* (1947); 2 symphs. (1941, 1949); symph. poems: *Au nord* (1930) and *La Reine de Saba* (1933); Piano Concerto (1962); Flute Sonata (1965); Piano Trio; String Quartet; various pieces for piano; songs.

BIBLIOGRAPHY: A. Machabey, *Portraits de trente musiciens français* (Paris, 1949; pp. 101–4).

Huhn, Bruno, song composer; b. London, Aug. 1, 1871; d. New York, May 13, 1950. He studied piano in London and N.Y.; toured in Egypt, India, and Australia (1889–91). In 1891 he settled in N.Y., where he made a successful debut as a pianist (April 17, 1896). Subsequently he held various positions as a conductor of suburban choral groups and also as an accompanist to singers. He wrote many sacred choruses and solo songs, of which his setting of Henley's *Invictus* (1910) attained great popularity.

Huízar, Candelario, Mexican composer; b. Jerez, Feb. 2, 1883; d. Mexico City, May 3, 1970. He studied violin and composition; in 1917 settled in Mexico City, where he continued his studies with Gustavo Campa. He was a copyist in various music schools (1920–25), and in 1931 became librarian of the Cons. Nacional. His compositions reflect Mexican folklore, and often contain authentic Mexican themes.

WORKS: For Orch. (all first perf. in Mexico City): *Imágenes,* symph. poem (Dec. 13, 1929); Symph. No. 1 (Nov. 14, 1930); *Pueblerinas,* symph. poem (Nov. 6, 1931); *Surco,* symph. poem (Oct. 25, 1935); Symph. No. 2 (Sept. 4, 1936); Symph. No. 3 (July 29, 1938); Symph. No. 4 (Aug. 7, 1942); Sonata for Clarinet and Bassoon (1931); String Quartet (1938); choral works; and songs.

BIBLIOGRAPHY: J.C. Romero, "Candelario Huízar," *Nuestra Música* (Jan. 1952).

Hull, Anne, American pianist and composer; b. Brookland, Pa., Jan. 25, 1888. She studied at the Peabody Cons. in Baltimore, and upon graduation became active as a piano teacher; made numerous appearances with Mary Howe in duo-piano recitals. Her work for 2 Pianos, *Ancient Ballad,* attained considerable popularity.

Hull, Arthur Eaglefield, English writer on music; b. Market Harborough, March 10, 1876; d. London, Nov. 4, 1928. He studied privately with Matthay and Charles Pearce in London; served as organist at Huddersfield Parish Church; was (from 1912) editor of the *Monthly Musical Record.* In 1918 he founded the British Music Society; was its honorary director until 1921; received his Mus.Doc. from Queen's College, Oxford. In 1906 he married **Constance Barratt,** an accomplished violinist. A man of broad culture, he was an enthusiast for new music; was an early champion of Scriabin in England. In 1924 he brought out a *Dictionary of Modern Music and Musicians.* This was a pioneer vol. and, despite an overabundance of egregious errors and misconceptions, is of service as a guide; a German trans. was made by Alfred Einstein, with numerous errors corrected (1926); another vol. which still retains its value is *Modern Harmony: Its Explanation and Application* (London, 1914; 3rd ed., 1923; reprinted 1934). In 1927 he publ. a book, *Music: Classical, Romantic and Modern,* which proved to be a pasticcio of borrowings from various English and American writers; this was pointed out by many reviewers, and the book was withdrawn by the publishers in 1928; this episode led directly to Hull's suicide; he threw himself under a moving train at the Huddersfield Railway Station, suffered grave injuries and loss of memory, and died a few weeks later. The list of his publications also includes *Organ Playing, Its Technique and Expression* (1911); *The Sonata in Music* (1916); *Scriabin* (1916); *Modern Musical Styles* (1916); *Design or Construction in Music* (1917); *Cyril Scott* (1918); he made Eng. translations of Romain Rolland's *Handel* (1916) and *Vie de Beethoven;* edited the complete organ works of Bach and Mendelssohn (with annotations for students);

was also editor of the series Music Lovers' Library and Library of Music and Musicians (in which his book on Scriabin appeared); other books by him in the same series were *Bach* and *Three English Composers*.

Hullah, John Pyke, English composer and organist; b. Worcester, June 27, 1812; d. London, Feb. 21, 1884. He was a pupil of William Horsley; in 1833 he studied singing with Crivelli at the Royal Academy of Music; as a composer he was entirely self-taught. At the age of 24 he produced an opera to a story by Charles Dickens, *The Village Coquette* (London, Dec. 6, 1836); 2 other operas followed: *The Barber of Bassora* (London, Nov. 11, 1837) and *The Outpost* (May 17, 1838). In the meantime, he obtained the post of church organist at Croydon. He made several trips to Paris, where he became interested in the new system of vocal teaching established by Wilhem; he modified it to suit English requirements, and, with the sanction of the National Education Committee, he opened his Singing School for Schoolmasters at Exeter Hall (1841). The school became the target of bitter criticism; nonetheless, it prospered; thousands of students enrolled; his wealthy supporters helped him build St. Martin's Hall for performances of vocal music by his students; the hall was inaugurated in 1850; it was destroyed by fire in 1860. From 1844 to 1874 Hullah taught singing at King's College, and later at Queen's College and Bedford College in London. He conducted the student concerts of the Royal Academy of Music (1870–73); in 1872 he became an inspector of training schools. He held the honorary degree of LL.D. from Edinburgh Univ. (1876); was also a member of the Cecilia Society in Rome and of the Academy of Music in Florence. He edited Wilhem's *Method of Teaching Singing Adapted to English Use* (1841); publ. *A Grammar of Vocal Music* (1843); *A Grammar of Harmony* (1852); *A Grammar of Counterpoint* (1864); *The History of Modern Music* (1862); *The Third or Transition Period of Musical History* (1865); *The Cultivation of the Speaking Voice* (1870); *Music in the House* (1877); also brought out useful collections of vocal music: *The Psalter; The Book of Praise Hymnal;* the *Whole Book of Psalms with Chants.* He was the composer of the celebrated song *O that we two were Maying;* other popular songs are *The Storm* and *3 Fishers.* A *Life of John Hullah* was publ. by his wife (London, 1886).

Hüller, Johann Adam. See **Hiller, Johann Adam.**

Hüllmandel, Nicolas-Joseph, Alsatian musician; b. Strasbourg, May 23, 1756; d. London, Dec. 19, 1823. He was an illegitimate son of **Michel Hüllmandel,** organist at the Strasbourg Cathedral and nephew of the French-horn player Jean-Joseph Rodolphe. He studied with Carl Philip Emmanuel Bach in Hamburg; in 1776 he went to Paris, where he taught piano and the glass harmonica; among his pupils in composition were Onslow and Aubert. After the French Revolution he went to London, where he remained until his death. There he publ. a manual, *Principles of Music, Chiefly Calculated for the Pianoforte* (1795).
WORKS: 17 sonatas for Piano; 34 sonatas for Piano with Violin obbligato; 54 Airs for Piano; 12 Suites for Piano; 2 books of divertissements for Piano. He composed in a typical manner of his time; Mozart, in one of his letters to his father, expressed appreciation of Hüllmandel's sonatas.
BIBLIOGRAPHY: Rita Benton, "N.-J. Hüllmandel," *Revue de Musicologie* (Dec. 1961).

Humbert, Georges, Swiss organist and writer on music; b. St. Croix, Aug. 10, 1870; d. Neuchâtel, Jan. 1, 1936. He studied with Huberti at the Brussels Cons. and with Bargiel in Berlin. In 1892 he became a prof. of music history at the Geneva Cons., retaining this post until 1912; in 1898–1918 he was an organist at Morges. In 1918 he established the Neuchâtel Cons., and was its director until his death; also conducted various performing societies in Switzerland. He was editor of *Gazette Musicale de la Suisse Romande* (1894–96) and *La Vie Musicale* (1918–24); publ. *Notes pour servir à l'étude de l'histoire de la musique* (1904). He was the translator into French of Riemann's *Musiklexikon* (1899; 3rd ed., 1931).

Humble, Keith, Australian composer; b. Geelong, Sept. 6, 1927. He studied at the Melbourne Cons. (1945–51); then went to Paris, where he took lessons with René Leibowitz. He returned to Australia in 1956 to teach piano and music theory at the Melbourne Cons.; the following year he went again to Paris, where he organized a modernistic workshop, Le Centre de Musique. Once more in Australia, in 1966 he resumed his post at the Melbourne Cons., where he formed a studio for electronic music. In the interim he made several visits to the U.S., where he lectured at the Univ. of Calif. at La Jolla, and also spent some time at Princeton Univ., working with Milton Babbitt. His own compositions reflect the avant-garde tendencies of British, French, and American modern music.
WORKS: *L'Armée des saluts* for Singers, Instrumentalists, and Actors (1965); *Music for Monuments* for Instruments and Voices (1967); 5 pieces for Various Ensembles under the generic category *Arcade* (1968–69); *Après la légende* for Piano and Orch. (1969); 6 pieces titled *Nunique* (1968–71; *Nunique V* is an opera entitled *La Rountala,* which was commissioned by the Australian Opera Co., 1971).
BIBLIOGRAPHY: James Murdoch, *Australia's Contemporary Composers* (Melbourne, 1975; pp. 120–132).

Hume, Paul, American music critic; b. Chicago, Dec. 13, 1915. He studied at the Univ. of Chicago; took private lessons in piano, organ, and voice; was organist, choirmaster, and baritone soloist at various churches in Chicago and Washington, D.C.; gave song recitals in Boston and in the Midwest; taught voice at Catholic Univ. in Washington; in

1946, became music editor and critic of the *Washington Post* (until 1982); was an instructor in music history at Georgetown Univ. (1950–77); was also a visiting prof. at Yale Univ.; has contributed to the *Saturday Review* (N.Y.); was active as a lecturer and radio commentator on music; publ. *Catholic Church Music* (N.Y., 1956) and *Our Music, Our Schools, and Our Culture* (National Catholic Education Assoc., 1957). Paul Hume leaped to national fame in 1950, when President Truman, outraged by Hume's unenthusiastic review of Margaret Truman's song recital, wrote him a personal letter threatening him with bodily injury. Hume sold the letter to a Connecticut industrialist for an undisclosed sum of money.

Humel, Gerald, American composer; b. Cleveland, Nov. 7, 1931. He studied at Hofstra Univ., N.Y. (B.A., 1954), the Royal College of Music in London (A.R.C.M., 1956), Oberlin Cons. (M.M., 1958), and the Univ. of Michigan in Ann Arbor (1958–60); in 1960 went to Berlin, where he took private lessons with Boris Blacher and Rufer; remained in Berlin as a permanent resident. His music at first maintained a median line of cosmopolitan modernism, in a neo-Classical direction, but gradually he became oriented toward dodecaphonic techniques.
WORKS: Operas: *The Proposal* (1949) and *The Triangle* (Oberlin, Nov. 14, 1958); ballets: *Devil's Dice* (1957); *First Love* (1965); *Herodias* (1967); Flute Concerto (1964); Chamber Concerto for Horn, Piano, and Strings (1966); Concerto for Wind Orch. (1968); *Flashes* for Chamber Ensemble (1968); *Fantasie* for 2 Flutes, Cello, and Piano (1968); *Lepini* for Orch. (1977); *Duo* for Viola and Cello (1964); Cello Sonata (1967); Clarinet Sonata (1968); 2 sonatas for Solo Viola (1967, 1968).

Humes, Helen, American jazz and blues singer; b. Louisville, Ky., June, 23, 1913; d. Santa Monica, Calif., Sept. 9, 1981. She first gained prominence as a singer with Count Basie's orch. (1938–42). Among her most successful renditions were the songs *If Papa Has Outside Lovin', Do What You Did Last Night, Everybody Does It Now, Sub-Deb Blues,* and *He May Be Your Man but He Comes to See Me Sometimes;* her greatest hit was *Be-Baba-Leba.*

Humfrey, Pelham, English composer; b. 1647; d. Windsor, July 14, 1674. He was among the first children appointed to the restored Chapel Royal in 1660, and (together with fellow-choristers John Blow and William Turner) he wrote the famous *Club Anthem.* In 1664 King Charles II sent him to study in France and Italy under the Secret Service Funds; that he worked under Lully remains unverified, nor can it be proved that he got to Italy. He returned to England in 1667 and was appointed Gentleman of the Chapel Royal on Oct. 26, 1667. An entry in Pepys's diary for Nov. 15, 1667, described him as being "full of form, and confidence, and vanity" and disparaging "everything, and everybody's skill but his own." Humfrey's justification of his self-confidence lay in his undoubted mastery of the Italian declamatory style, greater than anyone had yet achieved in England. On July 15, 1672, he was appointed Master of the Children of the Chapel Royal. Two years later he died, at the early age of 27. One of his wards was the young Henry Purcell, whose style clearly shows Humfrey's influence.
WORKS: 24 secular songs; 4 sacred songs; a dialogue, composed with John Blow; songs and vocal ensembles for Shadwell's version of Shakespeare's *The Tempest;* 3 odes, all to Charles II; 26 anthems, of which 19 are extant (one composed with John Blow and William Turner); *Have Mercy upon Me, O God,* in MS in the British Museum; *O Praise God in His Holyness,* in MS at the Durham Cathedral Library; and *Hear My Prayer, O God* (in the Egerton MSS of the British Museum); etc.; one complete Service for the Anglican Church (Morning Prayer, Communion, and Evening Prayer); *The Grand Chant,* a widely used Anglican chant. Seven anthems by Humfrey are included in Boyce's *Cathedral Music;* 3 sacred songs in *Harmonia Sacra* (1714); a number of secular songs in the following collections: Playford's *Choice Songs* (1673) and *Choice Ayres, Songs and Dialogues* (1676–84); J.S. Smith's *Musica Antiqua* (1812); Humfrey's *Complete Church Music* is publ. in *Musica Britannica,* 34–35.
BIBLIOGRAPHY: W. Barclay Squire, "The Music of Shadwell's Tempest," *Musical Quarterly* (Oct. 1921); P. Dennison, *The Life and Works of Pelham Humfrey* (Diss., Oxford Univ., 1970; includes an ed. and catalogue of complete works); idem, "The Will of Pelham Humfrey," *R.M.A. Research Chronicle,* 7 (1970); idem, "The Church Music of Pelham Humfrey," *Proceedings of the Royal Music Association,* 98 (1971–72).

Humiston, William Henry, American organist; b. Marietta, Ohio, April 27, 1869; d. New York, Dec. 5, 1923. He studied organ with C. Eddy in Chicago (1885–94); held various positions in and around Chicago as a church organist. In 1896 he moved to N.Y., where he became a pupil of MacDowell (1896–99); served as organist at suburban churches until 1909; conducted traveling opera companies (1909–12). He wrote *Southern Fantasy* for Orch. (1906); some overtures; songs.

Hummel, Ferdinand, German composer and harpist; b. Berlin, Sept. 6, 1855; d. there, April 24, 1928. He gave concerts as a child harpist (1864–67); then studied music at Kullak's Academy in Berlin and later at the Hochschule für Musik there. He established himself as a teacher in Berlin, and also became a prolific composer. Much impressed by the realistic school of Italian opera (Mascagni), he wrote several short operas in the same genre: *Mara* (Berlin, 1893); *Angla* (Berlin, 1894); *Assarpai* (Gotha, 1898); *Sophie von Brabant* (Darmstadt, 1899); *Die Beichte* (Berlin, 1900); *Ein treuer Schelm; Die Gefilde der Seligen* (Altenburg, 1917). He also wrote a Symph., a Piano Concerto, chamber music, and choral works, aggregating to about 120 opus numbers.

Hummel, Johann Nepomuk, celebrated German pianist and composer; b. Pressburg, Nov. 14, 1778; d. Weimar, Oct. 17, 1837. He studied with his father, **Johannes Hummel,** who was music master of the Imperial School for Military Music. In 1786 the father was appointed conductor at Schikaneder's Theater in Vienna; there Mozart interested himself in young Hummel, took him into his house, and for 2 years instructed him. Hummel made his debut in 1787 at a concert given by Mozart in Vienna; in 1788–93 he accompanied his father on professional concert tours as a pianist, visiting Bohemia, Germany, Denmark, Scotland, England, and the Netherlands. In London he studied briefly with Clementi; in Oxford he presented his String Quartet. In 1793 he returned to Vienna and began a course of studies with Albrechtsberger, and also profited by the counsel of Haydn and Salieri in composition; became a friend of Beethoven and of Goethe. In 1804–11 he acted as deputy Kapellmeister for Haydn, in Prince Esterházy's service. In the meantime, he had his opera *Mathilde von Guise* produced in Vienna (March 26, 1810). He settled in Vienna in 1811 as a teacher; in 1816–18 was court Kapellmeister at Stuttgart, and in 1819, at Weimar, a post he held until his death. His duties were not too rigorous, and he was allowed to make frequent professional tours. He traveled to St. Petersburg in 1822; in 1825 he was in Paris, where he was made a Chevalier of the Legion of Honor; in 1826, visited Belgium and the Netherlands; in 1827, was in Vienna; in 1828, in Warsaw; and in 1829, again in France. He conducted a season of German opera at the King's Theatre in London in 1833. The last years of his life were marred by ill health and much suffering. At the peak of his career as a pianist, he was regarded as one of the greatest virtuosos of his time; both as pianist and composer, he was often declared to be the equal of Beethoven. His compositions were marked by excellent craftsmanship; his writing for instruments, particularly for piano, was impeccable; his melodic invention was rich, and his harmonic and contrapuntal skill was of the highest caliber. Yet, with his death, his music went into an immediate eclipse; performances of his works became increasingly rare, until the name of Hummel all but vanished from active musical programs. However, some of his compositions were revived by various musical societies in Europe and America, and, as a result, at least his chamber music was saved from oblivion. He wrote 124 opus numbers; these include 9 operas; several ballets; cantatas; 3 masses for 4 Voices and Organ; *Missa solemnis* (1826); a Graduale and Offertorium, still in use in Austrian churches; 7 concertos and concertinos for Piano and Orch.; many works for piano solo; 6 piano trios; Piano Quintet; Quintet for Violin, Viola, Cello, Double Bass, and Piano; Septet in D minor (his most outstanding work) for Flute, Oboe, Viola, Horn, Cello, Double Bass, and Piano; cadenzas to the Mozart concertos. He also publ. *Anweisung zum Pianofortespiel* (1828), an elaborate instruction book and one of the first to give a sensible method of fingering. His wife, **Elisabeth Hummel-Röckl** (1793–1883), was an opera singer; they had 2 sons, a pianist and a painter. Hummel's great-great-grandson Mike Hummel, an industrialist in Los Angeles, son of Wilhelm Hummel, who came to the U.S. in 1922, sought to restore interest in Hummel and collected his memorabilia, which were kept in Mike's grandfather's place in Florence, and in 1975 shipped everything to Los Angeles. In 1978 Hummel's bicentennial was celebrated in Weimar.

BIBLIOGRAPHY: G. Sporck, *L'Interprétation des sonates de J.N. Hummel* (Paris, 1933); K. Benyovszky, *J.N. Hummel, Der Mensch und Künstler* (Bratislava, 1934); Dieter Zimmerschied, *Thematisches Verzeichnis der Werke von Johann Nepomuk Hummel* (1971); J. Sachs, "Authentic English and French Editions of J.N. Hummel," *Journal of the American Musicological Society* (Summer 1972); idem, "Hummel and the Pirates: The Struggle for Musical Copyright," *Musical Quarterly* (Jan. 1973); idem, "A Checklist of the Works of Johann Nepomuk Hummel," *Notes* (June 1974; corrects and complements Zimmerschied's *Thematisches Verzeichnis*); idem, *Kapellmeister Hummel in England and France* (Detroit, 1977).

Humperdinck, Engelbert, celebrated German composer; b. Siegburg, near Bonn, Sept. 1, 1854; d. Neustrelitz, Sept. 27, 1921. He first studied architecture in Cologne; there he met Ferdinand Hiller, who discovered his musical talent and took him as a student at the Cologne Cons.; his other teachers there were Gernsheim and Jensen (composition), Seiss and Mertke (piano), Rensberg and Ehlert (cello). In 1876 he won a Mozart scholarship at Frankfurt; studied in Munich with Franz Lachner and Rheinberger; there he publ. his first works, *Humoreske* for Orch. (1880) and *Die Wallfahrt nach Kevelaar* for Chorus, which won the Mendelssohn Prize (1879); he also won the Meyerbeer prize of 7,600 marks (1881), which enabled him to visit Italy and France. In Italy he met Wagner, who invited him to be his guest at Bayreuth. Here Humperdinck assisted in preparing the score of *Parsifal* for publication; from then on the relations between Humperdinck and the Wagner family were most cordial; Siegfried Wagner became Humperdinck's pupil and received his entire musical education from him. In 1885–87 Humperdinck was a prof. at the Cons. in Barcelona; after his return to Germany he taught for a short time in Cologne, and then went to Mainz in the employ of the Schott publishing firm; in 1890 he became a prof. at the Hoch Cons. in Frankfurt, and music critic for the *Frankfurter Zeitung.* On Dec. 23, 1893, in Weimar, he produced the fairy-opera *Hänsel und Gretel* (text by his sister, Adelheid Wette). The work, aside from its intrinsic merit, appeared at the right psychological moment. The German public, weary of the bombast of the Wagner-imitators, were almost willing to accept the blunt realism of the Italian *verismo* as a relief from the labored dullness of pseudo-Wagnerian music dramas. And now a new composer, drawing inspiration from folk music, found musical expression for a thoroughly German subject, and the public was delighted. Before a year had passed, the work was in the repertoire of every German opera house; abroad as well its success was extraordinary and lasting (London, Dec. 26, 1894; N.Y., Oct. 8, 1895). A host of imitators ransacked German fairy-lore, but with ill success. Since Humperdinck's health had never been robust, he determined after this success to give up teaching, and after production of his next work, *Die sieben Geislein* (Berlin, Dec. 19, 1895), a fairy play for children written for voice and piano, he retired (in 1896) to Boppard on the Rhine to devote himself entirely to composition. In 1898 he wrote incidental music to Rosmer's *Königskinder* (Munich, Jan. 23, 1897); in this music Humperdinck made a bold attempt to prescribe definite rhythmic and pitch inflections ("sprechnoten") to the actors in the drama; he later recast the score into an opera, which was produced at the Metropolitan Opera House in N.Y. (Dec. 28, 1910). In 1900 he became director (with practically nominal duties) of the Akademische Meisterschule in Berlin. His other operas are *Dornröschen* (Frankfurt, Nov. 12, 1902); *Die Heirat wider Willen* (Berlin, April 14, 1905); *Die Marketenderin* (Cologne, May 10, 1914); and *Gaudeamus* (Darmstadt, March 18, 1919); he wrote incidental music for Berlin productions of 5 plays of Shakespeare: *The Merchant of Venice* (Nov. 9, 1905); *The Winter's Tale* (Sept. 15, 1906); *Romeo and Juliet* (Jan. 29, 1907); *Twelfth Night* (Oct. 17, 1907);. *The Tempest* (Oct. 8, 1915); also to *Lysistrata,* by Aristophanes (Berlin, Feb. 27, 1908), and to *The Blue Bird,* by Maeterlinck (Berlin, Dec. 23, 1912). He contributed music to Max Reinhardt's production of *The Miracle* (London, Dec. 23, 1911). He further wrote a choral ballade, *Das Glück von Edenhall* (1884); *Maurische Rhapsodie* for Orch. (1898); and a Symph. Among his songs, the cycle *Kinderlieder* is particularly fine. Humperdinck's lasting fame still rests, however, upon one opera, *Hänsel und Gretel,* which succeeded thanks to Humperdinck's ability to write melodies of ingenuous felicity, despite the almost incompatible Wagnerian instrumental and dramatic design.

BIBLIOGRAPHY: G. Münzer, *E. Humperdinck* (Leipzig, 1906); E. Istel, "German Opera since Richard Wagner," *Musical Quarterly* (April 1915); O. Besch, *E. Humperdinck* (Leipzig, 1915); H. Kühlmann, *Stil und Form in Humperdincks "Hänsel und Gretel"* (Marburg, 1930); K.G. Fellerer, "Engelbert Humperdinck und seine Stellung im deutschen Musikleben," *Heimatbuch der Stadt Siegburg,* 2 (1967).

Humperdinck, Engelbert (real name, **Arnold George Dorsey**), Indian-born rock singer; b. Madras, May 3, 1936; his family moved to England. As a youth, he showed innate aptitude for raucous sentimentality and unmitigated schmaltz; these propensities attracted the attention of a hustler in search of potential rock singers; dissatisfied with the lackluster name of his chosen candidate for lucre and glory, he brazenly picked up the name Engelbert Humperdinck from a music dictionary, and conferred it on Dorsey. As luck would have it, the rechristened rock singer (and his manager) pros-

pered, making a quantum leap from his early beginnings as a hapless entertainer in British pubs to a successful crowd-pleaser in England and America. His voice is bland and colorless, but his stance is sincere, and his records sell prodigiously among the low classes of British-American music fans. *Chacun à son goût.*

Humpert, Hans, German composer; b. Paderborn, April 19, 1901; killed in battle at Salerno, Sept. 15, 1943. He studied at the Frankfurt Cons. and in Berlin; then taught at Paderborn until he was called into the army. His music is marked by a neo-Romantic quality, with a strong contrapuntal structure.

WORKS: 2 symphs. (1937, 1942); 3 string quartets; String Trio; Violin Sonata; Viola Sonata; Sonata for Flute Solo; 5 cantatas; 4 masses; 3 motets; 7 Psalms; many choral and organ works.

BIBLIOGRAPHY: G. Hoffmann, "Hans Humpert," *Musica* (Sept. 1953).

Huneker, James Gibbons, brilliant American journalist and writer on music; b. Philadelphia, Jan. 31, 1857; d. Brooklyn, Feb. 9, 1921. He studied piano with Michael Cross in Philadelphia, and in 1878 in Paris with Théodore Ritter; later with Joseffy at the National Cons. in N.Y.; then taught piano there (1888–98). He was music and drama critic of the *N.Y. Recorder* (1891–95) and the *Morning Advertiser* (1895–97); music, drama, and art critic for the *N.Y. Sun* (1900–12). In 1917 he was music critic of the *Philadelphia Press;* after one season (1918–19) with the *N.Y. Times* he became music critic for the *N.Y. World,* a position he held until his death; also wrote for various journals in N.Y., London, Paris, Berlin, and Vienna. He publ. a novel dealing with artistic life in N.Y., *Painted Veils* (1921), but devoted most of his uncommon gifts to musical journalism. He was capable of rising to true poetic style when writing about Chopin and other composers whom he loved; but he also possessed a talent for caustic invective; his attacks on Debussy were particularly sharp. He had a fine sense of humor, and candidly described himself as an "old fogy." In addition to his literary publications, he furnished introductory essays for Joseffy's edition of Chopin's works.

WRITINGS: *Mezzotints in Modern Music* (1899); *Chopin: The Man and His Music* (1900; in German, 1914); *Melomaniacs* (1902); *Overtones, A Book of Temperaments* (1904); *Iconoclasts: A Book for Dramatists* (1905); *Visionaries: Fantasies and Fiction* (1905); *Egoists: A Book of Supermen* (1909); *Promenades of an Impressionist: Studies in Art* (1910); *Franz Liszt: A Study* (1911; in German, 1922); *The Pathos of Distance* (1913); *Old Fogy, His Musical Opinions and Grotesques* (1913); *New Cosmopolis* (1915); *Ivory Apes and Peacocks* (1915); *Unicorns* (1917); *The Philharmonic Society of New York and Its 75th Anniversary* (1917); *Bedouins* (1920); *Steeplejack* (his memoirs; 1920); *Variations* (1921). A selection of his letters was publ. posthumously by Josephine Huneker (1922); a collection of essays, with an introduction by Mencken, in 1929.

BIBLIOGRAPHY: B. De Casseres, *James Gibbons Huneker* (N.Y., 1925); A.T. Schwab, *James Gibbons Huneker: Critic of the Seven Arts* (Stanford, Calif., 1963).

Hungerford, Bruce, Australian pianist; b. Korumburra, Victoria, Nov. 24, 1922; d. in an automobile accident in the Bronx, N.Y., Jan. 26, 1977. He received his education in Melbourne; studied piano with Ignaz Friedman in Sydney (1944), and later with Ernest Hutcheson at the Juilliard School of Music in N.Y. (1945–47); took private lessons with Myra Hess in N.Y. between 1948 and 1958, and also with Carl Friedberg in 1948–55. He gave his first piano recital in N.Y. in 1951; from then until 1965 he appeared under the name **Leonard Hungerford.** Apart from his virtuoso technique, he possessed an extraordinary mastery of dynamic gradations and self-consistent musical phraseology. He also gained recognition as a color photographer and archeologist, specializing in Egyptology; he recorded a 17-part audiovisual lecture entitled "The Heritage of Ancient Egypt" (1971).

Hüni-Mihacsek, Felice, Hungarian soprano; b. Pécs, April 3, 1891; d. Munich, March 26, 1976. She studied in Vienna with Rosa Papier; made her debut with the Vienna State Opera in 1919, remaining there until 1926; was then a member of the Bavarian State Opera, Munich (1926–44); she retired from the stage in 1953. She particularly excelled in Mozart's operas.

Hunt, Jerry, American composer; b. Waco, Texas, Nov. 30, 1943. He studied piano at North Texas State Univ.; developed a successful career as a performer of modern music; was on the faculty of Southern Methodist Univ. in Texas (1967–73) and concurrently was artist-in-residence at the Video Research Center in Dallas.

WORKS: The titles of his works indicate a preoccupation with mathematical and abstract concepts, as exemplified by his 8 pieces for varying instrumental groups bearing the generic title *Helix* (1961–71); other works are *Sur Dr. John Dee,* scored for "zero to 11 performers" (1963); *Tabulatura Soyga,* for zero to 11 Instruments (1965); *Preparallel* for Orch. Groups (1965); *Unit,* a "solo situation" (1967); *Infrasolo* for 10 Cymbals "or something else" (1970); *Autotransform glissando* (1970); *Symphony* for Electronics (1971); *Haramand Playing: Recursive/Regenerative* for Electronic Audio and Video Generating Systems (1972); *Quaquaversal Transmission,* a theater work (1973); *21 Segments* for varying numbers of Instruments (1973–77).

Hünten, Franz, German pianist and composer; b. Coblenz, Dec. 26, 1793; d. there, Feb. 22, 1878. He studied with his father, an organist; at the age of 26 he went to Paris and took courses at the Cons. with Pradher (piano) and Cherubini (composition); composed salon music for piano (fantasies, variations on opera themes, waltzes, etc.), some 250 opus numbers in all, most of which he succeeded in publishing; also brought out a *Méthode nouvelle pour le piano,* and other didactic compilations which became popular among teachers and students; Hünten was very much in demand as a piano teacher in Paris. Having accumulated considerable capital from his enterprises, he returned to Coblenz in 1848, and remained there until his death.

BIBLIOGRAPHY: Gerd Zöllner, *Franz Hünten: Sein Leben und sein Werk* (Cologne, 1959).

Hunter, Alberta, black American blues singer; b. Memphis, Tenn., April 1, 1895; d. New York, Oct. 17, 1984. She went to Chicago; began her career there with appearances in nightclubs; subsequently gained fame as an outstanding blues singer; also worked in Europe as a singer and actress. She retired in 1956; after a silence of 21 years, she resumed her career in 1977 and astonished her auditors as one of the last of the great blues singers. She continued to make public appearances in her 89th year.

Hunter, Rita, English soprano; b. Wallasey, Aug. 15, 1933. She studied voice in Liverpool; later took lessons with Dame Eva Turner; then joined the Sadler's Wells Chorus; also sang with the Carl Rosa Opera Co. In 1959 she joined the Sadler's Wells Opera; obtained success with her interpretation of Brünnhilde (in English) in performances of Wagner's operas. On Dec. 19, 1972, she made her American debut with the Metropolitan Opera in N.Y. as Brünnhilde; in 1975 sang with the San Francisco Opera. In 1980 she was named a Commander of the Order of the British Empire.

Hupfeld, Herman, American composer of popular music, singer, pianist, and lyricist; b. Montclair, N.J., Feb. 1, 1894; d. there, June 8, 1951. He served in the U.S. Navy in World War I. While in the service he wrote and performed his songs to his own words. Possessing a natural flair for sentimental melodies and nostalgic lyrics, he contributed successfully to Broadway shows; occasionally employed jazz rhythms, as in his song *When Yuba Plays the Rhumba on the Tuba.* He achieved fame with the theme song for the movie *Casablanca* (with Ingrid Bergman and Humphrey Bogart), *As Times Goes By,* a tune that indelibly impinged on the hearts of millions.

Hupperts, Paul, Dutch conductor; b. Gulpen, Jan. 1, 1919. He studied music in Utrecht; then appeared as a guest conductor in the Netherlands. In 1945 he was appointed conductor of the Limburg Orch. in Maastricht. From 1949 to 1977 he was chief conductor of the Utrecht Symph. Orch.; in his programs he often included works by modern Dutch composers.

Huré, Jean, French composer and writer on music; b. Gien, Loiret, Sept. 17, 1877; d. Paris, Jan. 27, 1930. He received his musical education at a monastery in Angers; went to Paris in 1895; there he founded the Ecole Normale pour Pianistes (1912) and the monthly magazine *L'Orgue et les Organistes* (1923); in 1925 he became church organist at St. Augustin; in 1926 he won the Prix Chartier for composition.

WORKS: His ballet, *Le Bois sacré*, was produced at the Opéra-Comique in Paris on June 28, 1921; he further wrote incidental music to Musset's *Fantasio;* 3 symphs.; Violin Concerto; *Andante* for Saxophone and Orch.; 2 string quartets; Piano Quintet; Violin Sonata; 3 cello sonatas; etc.; he publ. the manuals *La Technique du piano* (1908); *La Technique de l'orgue* (1918); also *L'Esthétique de l'orgue* (1923) and *Saint Augustin, musicien* (1924).

BIBLIOGRAPHY: G. Migot, *Jean Huré* (1926).

Hurford, Peter, noted English organist; b. Minehead, Somerset, Nov. 22, 1930. He studied law and music at Jesus College, Cambridge; later took organ lessons with André Marchal in Paris. In 1958 he was named Master of the Music at St. Albans Abbey; in 1963 he founded the International Organ Festival there. He left St. Albans in 1979 to pursue his international career as a leading interpreter of the music of the Baroque period. In 1984 he was made an officer of the Order of the British Empire.

Hurley, Laurel, American coloratura soprano; b. Allentown, Pa., Feb. 14, 1927. Of a musical family, she studied with her mother, a church organist; at 16, appeared on Broadway (Aug. 21, 1943) as Kathie in Romberg's operetta *The Student Prince;* then toured with the company that produced it. She was the winner of the Walter W. Naumburg Foundation Award, which enabled her to give a song recital in N.Y. (Nov. 6, 1952). She made her debut at the Metropolitan Opera on Feb. 8, 1955, in a minor role; on Jan. 11, 1957, she appeared in the title role of *La Périchole.* On May 6, 1949, she married John Peter Butz; she remained at the Metropolitan until 1967.

Hurlstone, William Yeates, English composer and pianist; b. London, Jan. 7, 1876; d. there, May 30, 1906. A precocious musician, he composed waltzes as a young child; studied at the Royal College of Music with Stanford (composition) and Edward Dannreuther (piano); performed his own Piano Concerto in 1896. In 1905 he was appointed a prof. at the Royal College of Music but died in the following year; his early death was much regretted.

WORKS: *The Magic Mirror,* fairy suite for Orch.; *Variations on a Hungarian Air* and *Variations on a Swedish Air* for Orch.; Quartet for Flute, Oboe, Horn, and Bassoon; Quintet for Flute, Oboe, Horn, Bassoon, and Piano; Piano Trio; Trio for Clarinet, Bassoon, and Piano; Clarinet Sonata; Bassoon Sonata; several song cycles.

BIBLIOGRAPHY: H.G. Newell, *W.Y. Hurlstone: Musician and Man* (London, 1936); Katharine Hurlstone, *William Hurlstone, Musician: Memories and Records by His Friends* (London, 1949).

Hurník, Ilja, Czech composer; b. Poruba, near Svinov, Nov. 25, 1922. He moved to Prague in 1938; studied composition with Řídký and was the last pupil of Novák (1941–44); studied piano at the Prague Academy of Music (1945–51); then made several concert tours in Czechoslovakia. His own works are marked with impressionistic flavor, while retaining a classical format.

WORKS: 3 operas: *Dáma a lupiči (The Lady and the Gangster),* after the film *The Ladykillers* (1966); *Mudrci a bloudi (The Wise and the Foolish;* 1968); *Diogenes* (1974); ballet, *Ondráš* (1950); oratorio, *Noe (Noah;* 1959); 2 cantatas: *Maryka* (1948; revised 1955) and *Ezop (Aesop;* 1964); *Sulamit,* cycle of songs after the Old Testament, for Female Voice and Orch. (1963); Flute Concerto (1953); Serenade for Strings (1954); Concerto for Winds and Percussion (1956); Concerto for Oboe, String Orch., and Piano (1959); *Musikanti (The Musicians)* for 20 Instruments (1962); *Chamber Music* for Strings (1962); *Kyklopes (Cyclops)* for Orch. (Prague, June 4, 1965); Concerto for Piano and Small Orch. (1972); Wind Quintet (1944); 2 string quartets (1949; 2nd, with Baritone Solo, to Old Testament texts, 1961); Viola Sonata (1952); *Die vier Jahreszeiten (The 4 Seasons of the Year)* for 12 Solo Instruments (1952); *Sonata da camera* for Flute, Oboe, Cello, and Harpsichord (1953); Piano Quintet (1953); *Ballet* for 9 Instruments (1954); *Esercizi* for Flute, Oboe, Clarinet, and Bassoon (1958); *Moments musicaux* for 11 Winds (1962); *Gloria di flauti* for 2 Flutes (1973); Preludes for Piano (1943); Piano Sonatina (1952); 3 organ sonatas (1956); Etude for Piano (1972).

Hurok, Sol, Russian-American impresario; b. Pogar, April 9, 1888; d. New York, March 5, 1974. Fleeing the political iniquities of the Czarist regime in regard to Jews, he emigrated to the U.S. in 1905, and became a naturalized citizen in 1914. In 1913 he inaugurated a series of weekly concerts announced as "Music for the Masses" at the Hippodrome in N.Y.; then became an exclusive manager for famous Russian artists, among them Anna Pavlova, Feodor Chaliapin, Artur Rubinstein, Mischa Elman, and Gregor Piatigorsky, as well as numerous other celebrities in the field of the ballet and opera. He negotiated the difficult arrangements with the Soviet government for American appearances of the Bolshoi Ballet, the Ukrainian dance company, and the Leningrad Kirov Ballet; made frequent trips to Russia, helped by his fluency in the language. Ironically, his N.Y. office became the target of a bomb attack by a militant Jewish organization which objected to Hurok's importation of Soviet artists, even though many of the artists were themselves Jewish.

Hurst, George, English conductor; b. Edinburgh, May 20, 1926, of Rumanian-Russian parentage. He first studied piano with Isserlis; then took courses in conducting and composition at the Royal Cons. of Music in Toronto; also studied conducting with Monteux. He was a teacher and conductor at the Peabody Cons. of Music in Baltimore (1947–55); then was assistant conductor of the London Phil. Orch. (1955–57) and of the BBC Northern Symph. Orch. at Manchester (1958–68); subsequently served as artistic director of the Bournemouth Sinfonietta; after

1978 he made guest appearances with various orchs. in Europe.

Hurum, Alf, Norwegian-born composer and painter; b. Oslo, Sept. 21, 1882; d. Honolulu, Aug. 15, 1972. He studied with Max Bruch at the Hochschule für Musik in Berlin (1905–09); later took additional courses in Paris and in Russia. He was a co-founder of the Society of Norwegian Composers in 1917. After touring as a concert pianist, he settled in Hawaii, where he established the Honolulu Symph. Orch. and was its conductor briefly (1924–26). His 2nd career was that of a silk painter in the Japanese manner, which preoccupied him during his later years. In his music he cultivates coloristic harmonies, somewhat in an impressionist mode.
WORKS: 2 violin sonatas (1911, 1916); *3 Aquarelles* for Piano (1912); String Quartet (1913); *Exotic Suite* for Violin and Piano (1916); *Pastels,* 4 pieces for Piano (1916); *Eventyrland (Fairy Land),* suite for Orch. or Piano (1920); *Gotiske bilder,* 6 pieces for Piano (1920); *Norse Suite* for Orch. (1920); *Bendik and Aarolilja,* symph. poem (1923); Symph. (Bergen, 1927); piano pieces; songs; motets.

Hurwitz, Emanuel, English violinist; b. London, May 7, 1919. He received a scholarship from Bronislaw Huberman which allowed him to study at the Royal Academy of Music. In 1948 he became concertmaster of the Goldsborough (later English) Chamber Orch., a position he held until 1968; was then concertmaster of the New Philharmonia Orch. (1969–71). He was also active as a chamber music artist; was first violinist of the Hurwitz String Quartet (1946–51), the Melos Ensemble (1956–72), and the Aeolian Quartet (from 1970). In 1968 he founded the Hurwitz Chamber Orch. (from 1972 known as the Serenata of London), a conductorless ensemble. He was made a Commander of the Order of the British Empire in 1978.

Hus-Desforges, Pierre Louis, French cellist and composer; b. Toulon, March 14, 1773; d. Pont-le-Voy, near Blois, Jan. 20, 1838. He studied at the Paris Cons.; played the cello in various orchs.; held numerous posts as a theatrical conductor and teacher. He was conductor at the Théâtre-Français in St. Petersburg early in the 19th century; returning to France, was cellist at the Théâtre Saint-Martin in Paris; from 1819 –22 taught at Metz; in 1823 was in Bordeaux; from 1824, again in Paris. His name as composer appears for the first time as **Citoyen Desforges,** on a song entitled *L'Autel de sa patrie* (Paris, 1798); he was the author of *Méthode de violoncelle à l'usage des commençants* (Paris, 1828); a String Quartet; and a "Sinfonia concertante" with Violin and Cello obbligato; he also publ. a historical novel, *Sapho à Leucade* (Paris, 1818).

Husa, Karel, distinguished Czech-born American composer, conductor, and pedagogue; b. Prague, Aug. 7, 1921. He studied violin and piano in his youth; concurrently took courses in engineering; in 1941 he entered the Prague Cons., studying composition with Jaroslav Řídký; in 1945–46 he attended the Academy of Music; in 1946 was awarded a French government grant to continue his studies in Paris at the Ecole Normale de Musique and the Paris Cons.; his teachers included Arthur Honegger and Nadia Boulanger; he also studied conducting with Jean Fournet and André Cluytens. In 1954 he emigrated to the U.S., and joined the music dept. of Cornell Univ. as teacher of composition and conductor of the student orch. He became an American citizen in 1959. He appeared widely as a guest conductor, frequently including his own music in his programs. In his early works he followed the modern Czech school of composition, making thematic use of folk tunes; later he enlarged his musical resources to include atonal, polytonal, microtonal, and even occasional aleatory procedures, without following doctrinaire prescriptions to the letter. His music is oxygenated by humanistic Romanticism; as a result, it gains numerous performances. In 1969 Husa received the Pulitzer Prize for his 3rd String Quartet.
WORKS: FOR ORCH.: Overture for Large Orch. (first public perf., Prague, June 18, 1946); Sinfonietta for Orch. (Prague, April 25, 1947); *3 Fresques* for Orch. (Prague, April 27, 1949; revised as *Fresque* for Orch., Syracuse, N.Y., May 5, 1963); Divertimento for String Orch. (Paris, Oct. 30, 1949); Concertino for Piano and Orch. (Brussels, June 6, 1952); *Musique d'Amateurs,* 4 Easy Pieces for Oboe, Trumpet, Percussion, and Strings (1953); *Portrait* for String Orch. (Donaueschingen, Oct. 10, 1953); Symph. No. 1 (Brussels, March 4, 1954); 4 Little Pieces for Strings (Fürsteneck, Germany, March 17, 1957); *Fantasies for Orch.* (Ithaca, N.Y., April 28, 1957); Divertimento for Brass and Percussion (Ithaca, N. Y., Feb. 17, 1960); Poem for Viola and Chamber Orch. (Cologne, June 12, 1960); *Mosaiques for Orchestra* (Hamburg, Nov. 7, 1961); *Elegie et Rondeau* for Alto Saxophone and Orch. (Ithaca, N.Y., May 6, 1962); Serenade for Woodwind Quintet Solo with String Orch., Xylophone, and Harp (Baltimore, Jan. 7, 1964); *Festive Ode* for Chorus and Orch. (1965); Concerto for Brass Quintet and String Orch. (Buffalo, Feb. 15, 1970); Concerto for Alto Saxophone and Concert Band (Ithaca, N.Y., March 17, 1968); *Music for Prague 1968* (2 versions; for Band: Washington, D.C., Jan. 31, 1969; for Orch.: Munich, Jan. 31, 1970); Concerto for Percussion and Wind Instruments (Waco, Texas, Feb. 7, 1972); *Apotheosis of This Earth* for Wind Instruments (Ann Arbor, Mich., April 1, 1971; 2nd version for Chorus and Orch.: Ithaca, N.Y., April 12, 1973); *2 Sonnets from Michelangelo* for Orch. (Evanston, Ill., April 28, 1972); Trumpet Concerto (Storrs, Conn., Aug. 9, 1974); *The Steadfast Tin Soldier* for Narrator and Orch. (Boulder, Colo., May 10, 1975); *Monodrama,* ballet for Orch. (Indianapolis, March 26, 1976); *An American Te Deum* for Baritone, Chorus, and Wind Ensemble (Cedar Rapids, Iowa, Dec. 4, 1976; 2nd version for Baritone, Chorus, and Orch.: Washington, D.C., May 10, 1978); Fanfare for Brass Ensemble (1980); Pastoral for Strings (Miami Beach, April 12, 1980); *The Trojan Women,* ballet for Orch. (Louisville, March 28, 1981); Concerto for Wind Ensemble (Lansing,

Mich., Dec. 3, 1982); Cantata for Men's Chorus and Brass Quintet (Crawfordsville, Ind., April 20, 1983).
CHAMBER MUSIC: Sonatina for Piano (1943); String Quartet (1942–43); Suite for Viola and Piano (1945); Sonatina for Violin and Piano (1945); String Quartet No. 1 (Prague, May 23, 1948); Piano Sonata No. 1 (1950); *Evocations of Slovakia* for Clarinet, Viola, and Cello (Paris, May 4, 1952); String Quartet No. 2 (Paris, Oct. 23, 1954); *2 Preludes* for Flute, Clarinet, and Bassoon (Ithaca, N.Y., April 21, 1966); Divertiment for Brass Quintet (Ithaca, N.Y., Nov. 20, 1968); String Quartet No. 3 (Chicago, Oct. 14, 1968); Studies for Percussion (1968); Sonata for Violin and Piano (N.Y., March 31, 1974); Piano Sonata No. 2 (1975); *Landscapes* for Brass Quintet (Kalamazoo, Mich., Oct. 17, 1977); *3 Dance Sketches* for Percussion (Miami Beach, April 12, 1980); *Intradas and Interludes* for 7 Trumpets and Timpani (Columbus, Ohio, June 20, 1980); *3 Moravian Songs* for Chorus a cappella (1981); *Every Day* for Chorus a cappella (1981); *Sonata a tre* for Violin, Clarinet, and Piano (Hong Kong, March 23, 1982); *Recollections* for Woodwind Quintet and Piano (Washington, D.C., Oct. 28, 1982); *12 Moravian Songs* for Voice and Piano (1956); other vocal pieces.
BIBLIOGRAPHY: L. Hartzell, "Karel Husa: The Man and the Music," *Musical Quarterly* (May 1976).

Hüsch, Gerhard, noted German baritone; b. Hannover, Feb. 2, 1901. He made his debut in Osnabrück in 1923; then sang in Bremen. From 1927 to 1930 he was a member of the Cologne Opera; then went to Berlin, appearing with the Berlin Opera and State Opera (1930–44); also sang at Bayreuth. In later years he became known as a lieder singer.

Husmann, Heinrich, distinguished German musicologist; b. Cologne, Dec. 16, 1908. He studied musicology with Ludwig at the Univ. of Göttingen and with Hornbostel, Schering, Wolf, and Blume at the Humboldt Univ. in Berlin; received his Ph.D. there in 1932 with the dissertation *Die dreistimmige Organa der Notre-Dame-Schule.* In 1933 he was appointed assistant lecturer at the musicological institute at the Univ. of Leipzig; completed his Habilitation there in 1941, and then was made its acting director in 1944. He completed a second Habilitation at the Univ. of Hamburg in 1948; then organized its musicological institute in 1949; was a reader there from 1956 and a prof. from 1958. In 1960 he became a prof. of musicology at the Univ. of Göttingen. His books include *Fünf- und siebenstellige Centstafeln zur Berechnung musikalischer Intervalle* (Leiden, 1951); *Vom Wesen der Konsonanz* (Heidelberg, 1953); *Einführung in die Musikwissenschaft* (Heidelberg, 1958); *Grundlagen der antiken und orientalischen Musikkultur* (Berlin, 1961).
BIBLIOGRAPHY: H. Becker and R. Gerlach, eds., *Speculum musicae artis: Festgabe für Heinrich Husmann* (Munich, 1970).

Huss, Henry Holden, American composer and pianist; b. Newark, N.J., June 21, 1862; d. New York,

Sept. 17, 1953. He was a descendant of Leonhard Huss, brother of the Bohemian martyr John Huss. His mother, Sophia Ruckle Holden Huss, was a granddaughter of Levi Holden, a member of Washington's staff. Huss studied piano and theory with his father and with Otis B. Boise. In 1882 he went to Germany, and studied organ and composition with Rheinberger at the Munich Cons.; graduated with a *Rhapsody* for Piano and Orch. (1885), which he subsequently performed with several American orchs.; he also played his Piano Concerto in B with the N.Y. Phil., the Boston Symph., etc. In 1904 he married **Hildegard Hoffmann,** a concert singer; they appeared frequently in joint recitals. He continued to compose almost to the very end of his long life.
WORKS: Symph. poems: *Life's Conflicts* (1921) and *La Nuit* (originally for Piano Solo, 1902; orchestrated 1939; first perf., Washington, D.C., March 12, 1942); 4 string quartets; Violin Sonata; Cello Sonata; Viola Sonata; choral works: *The 23rd Psalm; Mankind's Own Song; Winged Messengers of Peace; The Flag; The Fool's Prayer; Captain, Oh My Captain; Lord, Make My Heart a Place Where Angels Sing;* etc.

Huston, Scott, American composer; b. Tacoma, Wash., Oct. 10, 1916. He studied with Burrill Phillips, Bernard Rogers, and Howard Hanson at the Eastman School of Music in Rochester, N.Y. (B.M., 1941; M.M., 1942; Ph.D., 1952); in 1952 he was appointed to the faculty of the College-Cons. of Music in Cincinnati. Huston leans toward a modern concept of Romanticism, not without an admixture of decidedly advanced techniques.
WORKS: Toccata for Piano and Orch. (Rochester, May 30, 1951); *Abstract* for Orch. (Cincinnati, Nov. 20, 1955); *The 8th Word of Christ,* cantata (1959); Organ Sonata (1960); *Intensity I* for Wind Ensemble (1962); Concerto for Trumpet, String Orch., Harp, and Timpani (1963); Symph. No. 3, *Phantasms* (Cincinnati, Feb. 2, 1968); *Pro vita* for Piano and Brass Quintet (1965); *The Wisdom of Patriotism* for Chorus, Band, and Orch. (1966); *Penta-Tholoi* for Piano (1966); *Phenomena* for Flute, Oboe, Double Bass, and Harpsichord (1967); *Idioms* for Violin, Clarinet, and Horn (1968); *Love and Marriage,* chamber cantata (1969); *The Oratorio of Understanding* (1969); *The Song of Deborah,* cantata (1969); *Orthographics* for 4 Trombones (1970); *Divinely Superfluous Beauty and Natural Music,* song cycle for Soprano and Chamber Ensemble (1971); *A Game of Circles* for Clarinet, Celesta, and Piano (1971); *Sounds at Night* for Brass Choir (1971); *Life-Styles I* and *II* for Piano Trio, or Clarinet, Cello, and Piano (1972); Symph. No. 4 for String Orch. (Cincinnati, Aug. 10, 1972); *Suite: For Our Times* for Brass Sextet (1973); *Tamar,* monodrama for Soprano and Piano (1974); *Eleatron* for Viola and Piano (1975); *Impressions from Life* for Small Chamber Orch. (1977); *Ecstasies of Janus* for Countertenor and Small Ensemble (1978); *Time/Reflections,* cantata enigmatica for Chorus and Chamber Orch. (1978); *Blind Girl,* opera (1981); Symph. No. 6, *The Human Condition* (1982); many liturgical set-

tings for chorus; songs; chamber pieces.

Hutchens, Frank, pianist and composer; b. Christchurch, New Zealand, Jan. 15, 1892; d. Sydney, Australia, Oct. 18, 1965. He studied at the Royal Academy of Music in London with Matthay (piano) and Corder (composition); taught there in 1908–14; in 1915 was appointed a prof. at the New South Wales State Cons. in Sydney. His compositions include *Ballade* for Orch. (1938); Concerto for 2 Pianos and Orch. (1940); *Air Mail Palestine* for Voice and Orch. (1942); also piano pieces.

Hutcheson, Ernest, Australian pianist and teacher; b. Melbourne, July 20, 1871; d. New York, Feb. 9, 1951. He studied piano in Australia with Max Vogrich; played concerts as a very young child; then was sent to the Leipzig Cons. to study with Reinecke, graduating in 1890. In 1898 he performed his own Piano Concerto with the Berlin Phil. In 1900 he arrived in the U.S.; was head of the piano dept. at the Peabody Cons. in Baltimore (1900–12). In 1915 he created a sensation in N.Y. by playing 3 concertos (Tchaikovsky, Liszt, and MacDowell) in a single evening; in 1919 he repeated his feat, playing 3 Beethoven concertos in one evening; during 1924–45 he was dean of the Juilliard School. Among his compositions are several symph. works and numerous piano pieces. He publ. *Elements of Piano Technique* (N.Y., 1907); *Elektra by Richard Strauss: A Guide to the Opera* (N.Y., 1910); *A Musical Guide to the Richard Wagner Ring of the Nibelung* (N.Y., 1940); *The Literature of the Piano* (N.Y., 1948; 2nd ed., revised, 1964).

Hutchings, Arthur, English musicologist; b. Sunbury-on-Thames, July 14, 1906. He studied violin and piano; then was engaged in teaching music and composing; became prof. of music at Durham Univ. in 1947; was prof. of music at Exeter Univ. from 1968–71. His books include *Schubert* (London, 1945; 4th ed., 1973); *Delius* (London, 1948); *A Companion to Mozart's Piano Concertos* (London, 1948; 3rd ed., 1980); *The Invention and Composition of Music* (London, 1958); *The Baroque Concerto* (London, 1961; 3rd ed., revised, 1973); *Church Music in the Nineteenth Century* (London, 1967); *Mozart: The Man, the Musician* (London, 1976); *Purcell* (London, 1982).

Hutschenruyter, Wouter, Dutch composer; b. Rotterdam, Dec. 28, 1796; d. there, Nov. 18, 1878. He was a pupil of Hummel; also studied trumpet, and became a famous trumpet player. An energetic promoter of band music, he organized a music corps of the Civic Guard (1821); established a choral society called Eruditio Musica; also led various other music societies. He wrote an opera, *Le Roi de Bohème;* 4 symphs.; more than 150 works for military band; *Konzertstück* for 8 Kettledrums, with Orch.; cantatas; songs.

Hutschenruyter, Wouter, Dutch conductor and musicologist, grandson of the identically named Dutch composer; b. Rotterdam, Aug. 15, 1859; d. The Hague, Nov. 14, 1943. After diligent study he became a choral conductor; in 1890, was appointed assistant conductor of the Concertgebouw Orch. in Amsterdam; from 1894 to 1917 he conducted the municipal band in Utrecht, which he brought to a high degree of excellence; performed many works by Dutch composers. In 1917–25 he taught at Rotterdam; then lived in The Hague. He wrote a number of symph. and chamber works; publ. many books and manuals: *Orkest en orkestspel na 1600* (1903); *Mozart* (1905; new ed., 1927); *De geschiedenis der toonkunst* (1919); *Geschiedenis van het orkest en van den instrumenten* (1926); *De symphonieën van Beethoven geanalyseerd en toegelicht* (1928); *Chopin* (1926); *Mahler* (1927); *Wagner* (1928); *Brahms* (1929); *Richard Strauss* (1929); *De sonates van Beethoven toegelicht* (1930); *De Antwikkeling der Symphonie door Haydn, Mozart en Beethoven* (1931); *De Programma-Muziek* (1933); also a vol. of personal memoirs (1930).

Hüttenbrenner, Anselm, Austrian composer; b. Graz, Oct. 13, 1794; d. Ober-Andritz, near Graz, June 5, 1868. At the age of 7 he studied with the organist Gell; studied law at the Univ. of Graz; in 1815 he went to Vienna to study with Salieri. Schubert was his fellow student, and they became close friends. Hüttenbrenner also knew Beethoven intimately, and was present at his death. He was an excellent pianist and a prolific composer; Schubert praised his works. He wrote 6 operas; an operetta; 8 symphs.; many overtures; 10 masses; 4 Requiems; 3 funeral marches; 2 string quartets; a String Quintet; piano sonatas; 24 fugues; other piano pieces; some 300 male quartets; 200 songs. One of his songs, *Erlkönig,* was included in the collection *12 Lieder der deutschen Romantik,* ed. by H.H. Rosenwald (1929). His reminiscences of Schubert were publ. by Otto Deutsch in 1906. It was Hüttenbrenner who came into the possession of many Schubert MSS after Schubert's death, among them that of the "Unfinished Symph.," which he held until 1865. It has been suggested that Hüttenbrenner had lost the 3rd and 4th movements of Schubert's work, and for that reason was reluctant to part with the incomplete MS, but the extant sketches for the Scherzo make that unlikely.

BIBLIOGRAPHY: K. Kurth, *Anselm Hüttenbrenner als Liederkomponist* (Cologne, 1932); T.C.L. Pritchard, "The Unfinished Symphony," *Music Review* (Jan. 1942); F. Hüttenbrenner, "Anselm Hüttenbrenner und Schuberts H-moll Symphonie," *Zeitschrift des Historischen Vereines für Steiermark,* LII (1961). This article defends his custodianship of the MS of the Unfinished Symph.

Huybrechts, Albert, Belgian composer; b. Dinant, Feb. 12, 1899; d. Woluwe-St.-Pierre, near Brussels, Feb. 21, 1938. He studied at the Brussels Cons. with Martin Lunssens, Paulin Marchand, Léon Dubois, and Joseph Jongen. In 1926 he gained international recognition by winning 2 U.S. prizes, the Elizabeth

Sprague Coolidge Prize of the Library of Congress for his Violin Sonata, and the Ojai Valley Prize in California for his String Quartet. In 1937 he was appointed a prof. at the Brussels Cons., but a severe attack of uremia led to his premature death. He wrote in a judiciously modern idiom, seasoned with prudential dissonance.

WORKS: 2 symph. poems: *David* (1923) and *Poème feerique* (1923); *Chant funèbre* for Cello and Orch. (1926); *Sérénade* for Orch. (1929); *Chant d'angoisse* for Orch. (1930; his most distinctive work); Nocturne for Orch. (1931); *Divertissement* for Brass and Percussion (1931); Cello Concertino (1932); 2 string quartets (1924, 1927); Violin Sonata (1925); Trio for Flute, Viola, and Piano (1926); Sextet for Wind Quintet, with 2nd Flute (1927); Suite for Flute, Oboe, Clarinet, Bassoon, and Piano (1929); *Choral* for Organ (1930); *Sicilienne* for Piano (1934); *Pastourelle* for Cello and Piano (1934); Sonatine for Flute and Viola (1934); String Trio (1935); Wind Quintet (1936); songs, of which the best known is *Horoscopes* (1926). A catalogue of his works was publ. by the Centre Belge de Documentation Musicale (1954).

Huybrechts, François, Belgian conductor; b. Antwerp, June 15, 1946. He studied in Belgium, in France, and at the Salzburg Mozarteum; took courses with Bruno Maderna. In 1968 he won first prize in the Mitropoulos Competition in N.Y.; then was assistant conductor of the N.Y. Phil. From 1972 to 1977 he was music director of the Wichita Symph. Orch.; served for a season as music director of the San Antonio Symph. (1979–80).

Hvoslef, Ketil, Norwegian composer, son of **Harald Saeverud;** b. Fana, near Bergen, July 19, 1939. His original name was **Ketil Saeverud;** he took his mother's maiden name in 1980. He studied organ and viola at the Cons. in Bergen, graduating in 1962; took composition with Blomdahl and Lidholm in Stockholm and with Jersild in Copenhagen. From 1963 to 1979 he was on the faculty of the Cons. in Bergen. After a period of hesitant serialism he evolved a "motivic assimilation technique," wherein a central motif influences all the other thematic material in the manner of a theme with variations.

WORKS: FOR THE STAGE: Choral opera, *The Ballad of Narcissus and Echo,* for Mixed Chorus a cappella (1981). FOR ORCH.: Sinfonietta (1963); Piano Concertino (1964); Trumpet Concerto (1968–69; Bergen, April 22, 1972); *Mi-Fi-Li,* symph. poem (Oslo, Sept. 4, 1972); Double-bass Concerto (1973); Cello Concerto (1976); *Variations* for Chamber Orch. (1976); Double Concerto for Flute, Guitar, and String Orch. (1977); Concertino for Orch. (Trondheim, Sept. 20, 1979); Concerto for Bassoon and Strings (1979); *Suite* for School Orch. (1980); *Antigone,* symph. variations (1981–82). CHAMBER MUSIC: Clarinet Quartet (1962); Wind Quintet (1964); *Suite* for Guitar (1966); *Ariseturo,* concerto for Percussion and 8 Wind Instruments (1966); *Duets* for Bassoons (1966); 2 string quartets (1969, 1973); *Flauto Solo* (1970); *Tromba Solo* (1971); *Kim* for 4 Crum-

horns, 4 Recorders, Bass Gamba, and Percussion (1975); Trio for Oboe, Violin, and Percussion (1978); Octet for Flutes (1978); *Brass* for 13 Brass Instruments (1978); *Violino Solo* (1980); *Post,* sextet (1980); *Duodu* for Violin and Viola (1982); *Erkejubel* for 2 Trumpets, 2 Trombones, Synthesizer, and Percussion (1982). FOR VOICE: *So einsam ist der Mensch,* after Nelly Sachs, for Chorus or Vocal Quartet (1970); *Or "Håvamål" (Sayings of the High One),* cantata for Chorus and Orch. (1971; revised 1974); *Kvartoni* for Voice, Recorder, Guitar, and Piano (1974); Trio for Soprano, Alto, and Piano (1974); *Collage in Black/White with Red* for Baritone Narration, Violin, Guitar, Clarinet, and Percussion (1975); Concerto for Choir and Orch. (1977); *Spillemaend (Fiddlers)* for Chorus, Hardanger Fiddle, and Organ (1980). FOR PIANO: *Rondo con variazioni* (1970); *Beethoven Fantasy* (1982). FOR ORGAN: *Organ Variations* (1972); *Organo Solo* (1974).

Hyde, Walter, English tenor; b. Birmingham, Feb. 6, 1875; d. London, Nov. 11, 1951. He studied with Gustave Garcia; sang in light opera before he undertook Wagnerian roles, which became his specialty. He sang Siegmund at Covent Garden in 1908; his other roles included Walter in *Die Meistersinger* and also Parsifal. He made his Metropolitan Opera debut on March 28, 1910, as Siegmund in *Die Walküre;* then returned to England and made regular appearances at Covent Garden; later sang with the Beecham Opera Co. and the British National Opera Co., serving as a director of the latter. He was a frequent participant at many musical festivals in England.

Hye-Knudsen, Johan, distinguished Danish conductor; b. Nyborg, May 24, 1896; d. Copenhagen, Sept. 28, 1975. He studied cello at the Royal Danish Cons. of Music in Copenhagen with Rudinger; also in Paris with André Hekking; studied conducting in Dresden with Fritz Busch. In 1925 he was named conductor of the Royal Danish Theatre in Copenhagen; concurrently led concerts of the Royal Danish Orch. He was also a composer; wrote a number of orch. works and 2 operas: *Orfeus i underverdenen* (Copenhagen, Jan. 1, 1934) and *Kirke og orgel* (Copenhagen, Nov. 8, 1947).

Hyllested, August, Swedish pianist and composer; b. Stockholm, June 17, 1856; d. Blairmore, Scotland, April 5, 1946. He played in public as a child; then studied at the Copenhagen Cons. with Niels Gade, and subsequently with Theodor Kullak (piano) and Friedrich Kiel (composition) in Berlin; then had some lessons from Liszt. He gave concerts as pianist in England (1883) and in America (1885). In 1886–91 he was a prof. and assistant director of the Chicago Musical College; in 1891–94, taught piano at the Gottschalk Lyric School in Chicago. After a concert tour in Europe, he returned to Chicago in 1897; he was in Glasgow in 1903–14; then again in the U.S. (1916–19); in Denmark and Sweden (1919–21); in 1923, retired to Blairmore, where he died shortly before his 90th birthday. He publ. numerous piano pieces in a Romantic style (*Album Leaf, Valse sentimentale, Suite romantique,* etc.); a suite of Scandinavian dances; a fantasia on Scotch tunes; choral pieces; a symph. poem, *Elizabeth,* with Double Chorus (London, 1897, composer conducting).

Hynninen, Jorma, distinguished Finnish baritone and operatic administrator; b. Leppävirta, April 3, 1941. He studied at the Sibelius Academy in Helsinki (1966–70); also took courses in Rome with Luigi Ricci and in Salzburg with Kurt Overhoff. He won first prize at the singing competition in Lappeenranta in 1969, and in the Finnish division of the Scandinavian singing competition in Helsinki in 1971. In 1970 he made his concert debut in Helsinki, as well as his operatic debut as Silvio in *Pagliacci* with the Finnish National Opera there, and subsequently sang leading roles with the company. He also made guest appearances at La Scala in Milan (1977), at the Vienna State Opera (1977, 1982, 1983), at the Hamburg State Opera (1977, 1978), at the Bavarian State Opera (1979, 1980, 1981), and at the Paris Opéra (1980); gave recitals throughout Europe and the U.S. He made his N.Y. debut in a recital in 1980; his operatic debut followed in 1983, when he sang with the Finnish National Opera during its visit to America; made his Metropolitan Opera debut as Posa in 1984. He was appointed artistic director of the Finnish National Opera in 1984. In addition to such traditional operatic roles as Pelléas, Wolfram, Orpheus, and Valentin in *Faust,* he has sung parts in contemporary Finnish operas; he created the role of the King in *The King Goes Forth to France* by Aulis Sallinen, first performed at the Savonlinna Opera Festival on July 7, 1984.

I

Iannaccone, Anthony, American composer; b. Brooklyn, Oct. 14, 1943. He studied composition with Giannini, Diamond, and Flagello at the Manhattan School of Music (1961–68), and with Adler and Benson at the Eastman School of Music in Rochester, N.Y. (1968–71). In 1971 he was appointed to the music faculty of Eastern Michigan Univ.; he founded there an Electronic Music Studio. In his own music he applies serial methods with a certain liberality toward unintentional occurences of tonal, and even explicitly triadic, elements. In his band music he openly exploits pop devices.

WORKS: For Orch.: *Suite* (1962); 2 symphs. (1965, 1966); Concertino for Violin and Orch. (1967); *Lysistrata,* overture (1968); *Variations* for Violin and Orch. (1969); *Interlude* for Wind Instruments (1970); *Antiphonies* for Wind Instruments (1973); *Scherzo* for Band (1976); *Of Fire and Ice* for Band (1977); *After a Gentle Rain* for Band (1980); *Images of Songs & Dance:* No. 1, *Orpheus,* for Wind Instruments (1982); No. 2, *Terpsichore,* for Wind Instruments (1981); *Plymouth Trilogy* for Wind Instruments (1981); *Divertimento* (1983). Chamber music: Piano Trio (1959); Viola Sonata (1961); 2 violin sonatas (1964, 1971); String Quartet (1965); *Remembrance* for Viola and Piano (1968); *Hades* for Brass Quartet (1968); *3 Mythical Sketches* for Brass Quintet (1971); *Anamorphoses* for 2 Trumpets, Trombone, and Percussion (1972); *Rituals* for Violin and Piano (1973); *Parodies* for Wind Quintet (1974); *Bicinia* for Flute and Saxophone (1975); Sonatina for Trumpet and Tuba (1975); *Night Song* for Bassoon and Piano (1975); *Aria Concertante* for Cello and Piano (1976); *Invention* for 2 Saxophones (1978); Trio for Flute, Clarinet, and Piano (1979). For Piano: *Retail Rags* (1959); *Partita* (1967); *Keyboard Essays* (1972). For Voice: *The Prince of Peace,* cantata (1970); *Walt Whitman Song* for Soloists, Chorus, and Wind Instruments (1981); numerous choruses.

Ibach, Johannes Adolf, German piano maker; b. Barmen, Oct. 17, 1766; d. there, Sept. 14, l848. In 1794, he founded a piano factory at Barmen; also manufactured organs from 1834, with his son **C. Rudolf Ibach;** then traded under the name of Adolf Ibach & Sohn; from 1839, as Rudolf & Söhne, when his son **Richard** joined the firm. From 1862 the firm was known as C. Rudolf & Richard Ibach, to distinguish it from another business founded by a third son, **Gustav J.** The same year C. Rudolf died, and in 1869 his son **Rudolf** (d. Herrenalb, Black Forest, July 31, 1892) continued the piano factory alone as Rudolf Ibach Sohn; he established a branch at Cologne, gained medals for the excellence of his pianos, and became purveyor to the Prussian court. **Richard Ibach** continued the organ factory.

BIBLIOGRAPHY: *Das Haus Ibach 1794–1894* (1895).

Ibert, Jacques, French composer; b. Paris, Aug. 15, 1890; d. there, Feb. 5, 1962. He studied at the Paris Cons. with Gédalge and Fauré (1911–14); during World War I served in the French navy; returned to the Paris Cons. after the Armistice and studied with Paul Vidal; received the Prix de Rome in 1919 for his cantata *Le Poète et la fée;* while in Rome, he wrote his most successful work, the symph. suite *Escales (Ports of Call),* inspired by a Mediterranean cruise while serving in the navy. In 1937 he was appointed director of the Academy of Rome, and held this post until 1955, when he became director of the united management of the Paris Opéra and Opéra-Comique (until 1957). In his music, Ibert combines the most felicitous moods and techniques of Impressionism and neo-Classicism; his harmonies are opulent; his instrumentation is coloristic; there is an element of humor in lighter works, such as his popular orch. *Divertissement* and an even more popular piece, *Le Petit Ane blanc,* from the piano suite *Histoires.* His craftsmanship is excellent; an experimenter in tested values, he never fails to produce the intended effect.

WORKS: OPERAS: *Angélique* (Paris, Jan. 28, 1927); *Persée et Andromède* (Paris, May 15, 1929); *Le Roi d'Yvetot* (Paris, Jan. 15, 1930); *Gonzague* (Monte Carlo, 1935); *L'Aiglon,* after Edmond Rostand, in collaboration with Honegger (Monte Carlo, March 11, 1937); *Les Petites Cardinal,* with Honegger (Paris, 1938); *Barbebleue,* radio opera (Lausanne Radio, Oct. 10, 1943). BALLETS (all first perf. in Paris): *Les Rencontres* (Nov. 21, 1925); *Diane de Poitiers* (April 30, 1934, produced by Ida Rubinstein); *Les Amours de Jupiter* (March 9, 1946); *Le Chevalier errant* (May 5, 1950); *Tropismes pour des Amours Imaginaires* (1957). FOR ORCH.: Symph. poem, *Noël en Picardie* (1914); *Ballade du la geôle de Reading,* after Oscar Wilde (Paris, Oct. 22, 1922); *Escales,* 3 symph. pictures (Paris, Jan. 6, 1924); *Féerique,* symph. scherzo (Paris, Dec. 12, 1925); Concerto for Cello and Wind Instruments (Paris, Feb. 28, 1926); *Divertissement,* suite (Paris, Nov. 30, 1930; from incidental music to *Le Chapeau de paille d'Italie); Paris,* suite for Chamber Orch. (Venice, Sept. 15, 1932; from incidental music to *Donogoo,* play by Jules Romains); Flute Concerto (Paris, Feb. 25, 1934); *Concertino da Camera* for Saxophone and Chamber Orch. (Paris, May 2, 1935); *Capriccio* (1938); *Ouverture de fête* (Paris, Jan. 18, 1942); *Suite élisabéthaine* (1944); *Symphonie concertante* for Oboe and String Orch. (Basel, Feb. 11, 1949); *Louisville Concerto* (Louisville, Feb. 17, 1954); *Hommage à Mozart* for Orch. (1957); *Bacchanale* for Orch. (1958); *Bostoniana* for Orch. (1956–61). VOCAL WORKS: *Le Poète et la fée,* cantata (1919); *Chant de folie* for Solo Voices, Chorus, and Orch. (Boston, April 23, 1926); *3 chansons* for Voice, and Orch. or Piano; *La Verdure dorée* for Voice and Piano; *Chanson du rien* for Voice and Piano; *Quintette de la peur* for Chorus and Piano

(1946). CHAMBER MUSIC: *2 mouvements* for 2 Flutes, Clarinet, and Bassoon (1923); *Jeux,* sonatina for Flute and Piano (1924); *3 pièces brèves* for Flute, Oboe, Clarinet, Horn, and Bassoon (1930); *Pastoral* for 4 Fifes (in *Pipeaux,* by various composers, 1934); *Entr'acte* for Flute and Guitar (1935); String Quartet (1944); Trio for Violin, Cello, and Harp (1944); *2 Interludes* for Violin and Harpsichord (1949); also 6 pieces for Harp (1917); a piece for Unaccompanied Flute (1936). FOR PIANO: *Histoires* (10 pieces); *Les Rencontres,* arranged from the ballet (5 pieces); *Petite suite en 15 images* (1943).

BIBLIOGRAPHY: A. Hoerée, "J. Ibert," *Revue Musicale* (July 1929); G. Samazeuilh, *Musiciens de mon temps* (Paris, 1947); J. Feschotte, *Jacques Ibert* (Paris, 1959); G. Michel, *Jacques Ibert, L'Homme et son œuvre* (Paris, 1968).

Idelsohn, Abraham Zevi, eminent Jewish musicologist; b. Pfilsburg, near Libau (Latvia), July 13, 1882; d. Johannesburg, South Africa, Aug. 14, 1938. He studied in Königsberg, in Berlin, and with Jadassohn and Kretzschmar at the Leipzig Cons. He possessed a powerful baritone voice and for a time was cantor of the synagogue at Regensburg (1903); then went to Johannesburg and later (1906–21) was in Jerusalem, where he founded an Inst. for Jewish Music (1910) and a Jewish music School (1919). In 1921, he returned to Germany; then went to the U.S.; lectured at the Hebrew Union College in Cincinnati (1924–34). In 1934 he suffered a paralytic stroke; was taken to Miami, and in 1937 to Johannesburg, where he finally succumbed. Idelsohn was one of the greatest authorities on Jewish music and contributed much towards its establishment on a scientific basis.

WRITINGS: He publ. a quantity of studies in English, German, and Hebrew on oriental and Hebrew music, of which the most important are: *History of Jewish Music* (in Hebrew; 2nd ed., 1928, also publ. in English); *The Ceremonies of Judaism* (1923 –30); *Diwan of Hebrew and Arabic Poetry of the Yemenite Jews* (in Hebrew; 1930); *Jewish Liturgy and Its Development* (1932; reprint issued by the Hebrew Union College, N.Y., 1956); "Musical Characteristics of East European Jewish Folk-Songs," in the *Musical Quarterly* (Oct. 1932). His most important contribution to the study of Jewish music is the monumental *Thesaurus of Hebrew-Oriental Melodies* (10 vols.; 1914–32), in which are collected, with the aid of phonograph recordings, Jewish melodies of North Africa, Asia Minor, Palestine, and other parts of the world. He also composed and publ. 6 synagogue services; Hebrew songs (1929); a music drama, *Jephtah* (1922); and a *Jewish Song Book for Synagogue, Home and School* (1929).

Ifukube, Akira, Japanese composer; b. Kushiro (Hokkaido), March 7, 1914. As a young man he was trained in forestry; then turned to music and took lessons from Alexander Tcherepnin, who was in Japan at the time. Ifukube has written several ballets based on Japanese melodies. His music is rooted in Japanese modalities, but he adorns them with impressionistic harmonies.

WORKS: Ballets: *Salome* (1948); *Enchanted Citadel* (Tokyo, Dec. 20, 1949); *Fire of Prometheus* (1950); *Drums of Japan* (Tokyo, Dec. 29, 1951); *The Martyrs of Japan* (1972; Tokyo, March 30, 1972). For Orch.: *Japanese Rhapsody* (1935; Boston, April 5, 1936); *Triptyque aborigène* (1937); Piano Concerto (1941; Tokyo, March 3, 1942; music destroyed in an air raid); *Ballade symphonique* (1943; Tokyo, Nov. 20, 1943); *Arctic Forest* (Changchun, Manchuria, April 26, 1944); Violin Concerto (Tokyo, June 22, 1948); *Bascana* (1949); *Rhapsody* for Violin and Orch. (1951); *Buddha* (1953); *Tapkoara* (1954); *Ostinato sinfonica* for Piano and Orch. (1961); *Rondo in Burlesque* for Concert Band (1972); *Okhotsk*, choral ode for Chorus and Orch. (1958); several pieces for solo guitar.

Igumnov, Konstantin, Russian pianist and pedagogue; b. Lebedyan, near Tambov, May 1, 1873; d. Moscow, March 24, 1948. He studied piano with Zverev and Siloti, and theory with Taneyev, Arensky, and Ippolitov-Ivanov at the Moscow Cons., graduating as a pianist in the class of Pabst (1894). He gave numerous concerts, specializing in Romantic music, and was regarded as an artist of impeccable taste who worked out every detail of the music to the utmost perfection. But great as his artistic reputation was in Russia (he rarely, if ever, played abroad), his main accomplishment was as a piano pedagogue. He was appointed a prof. of the Moscow Cons. in 1899, and remained on its staff for nearly half a century, until his death. Among his students were Nicolai Orlov, Dobrowen, and Oborin.

BIBLIOGRAPHY: Yakov Milstein, *K.N. Igumnov* (Moscow, 1975).

Ikebe, Shin-Ichiro, Japanese composer; b. Tokyo, Sept. 15, 1943. He studied with Ikenouchi, Yashiro, and Miyoshi at the Tokyo Univ. of Arts, graduating in 1967.

WORKS: Opera, *The Death Goddess* (1971; NHK-TV, July 25, 1971; winner of the 1971 Salzburg Opera Prize); Piano Sonatina (1964); *Movement* for Orch. (1965); Sonata for Solo Violin (1965); *Crepa in sette capitoli* for Solo Violin, 3 Violas, Cello, and Double Bass (1966); *Construction,* 2 movements for Orch. (1966); Trio for Oboe, Clarinet, and Bassoon (1966); Piano Concerto (1966–67); *Raccontino* for Violin and Piano (1967); Symph. (1967; Tokyo, March 30, 1968); *Petite symphonie pour enfants* for Small Orch. (1969); *Lion* for Brass Ensemble (1969); *Un-en* for 2 Kotos, Ju-shichi-gen, Violin, Viola, Cello, and Double Bass (1970); *Energia* for 60 Players (1970); *Clipper by 9* for Nonet (1971); *Trivalence I* for Flute, Violin, and Piano or Organ (1971) and *II* for Harpsichord, Clarinet, and Cello (1973); *Flash!* for Flute Ensemble (1972); *Kusabi* for 11 Players, Female Chorus, and Dance (1972); *Monovalence I* for Marimba (1972) and *III* for Voice (1973); *Dimorphism* for Organ and Orch. (1974); *Quadrants* for Japanese Instruments and Orch. (1974); choruses; songs.

Ikenouchi, Tomojirô, Japanese composer; b. Tokyo, Oct. 21, 1906. In 1927 he became the first Japanese student at the Paris Cons., where he studied with Paul Fauchey, Henri Busser, and Georges Caussade; returned to Japan in 1936 and became a prof. of composition at Tokyo Univ. (1938–48); from 1946, taught at the Univ. of Arts in Tokyo. He stopped composing in 1958.

WORKS: *Yuya,* music for a Noh drama (Tokyo, Feb. 1, 1943); *3 Pieces* for Orch. (1937); *4 Seasons* for Orch. (1938); *Umaki-Uta* for Orch. (1938); Symph. in 2 movements (1951; Tokyo, Nov. 4, 1951); 3 string quartets (1937, 1945, 1946); *Fantasy* for Cello and Piano (1940); Flute Sonata (1946); Violin Sonata (1946); Cello Sonatina (1946); Piano Sonatina (1946); *Ceremonial Music* for Piano Duet (1958).

Ikonen, Lauri, Finnish musicologist and composer; b. Mikkeli, Aug. 10, 1888; d. Helsinki, March 21, 1966. He studied at Helsinki Univ. and with Paul Juon in Berlin (1910–13); was editor of the Finnish music magazine *Suomen Musikkilehti* (1923–29). His music follows the Romantic tradition of Sibelius.

WORKS: 6 symphs.; No 1, *Sinfonia inornata* (1922); No. 2 (1937); No. 3, *Lemmin poika (Son of Lemmi,* 1941, revised 1959); No. 4, *Sinfonia concentrata* (1942); No. 5, *Sinfonia aperta* (1943); No. 6 (1956); *Koulemaantuomitun mielialoja (Thoughts of a Condemned Man)* for Baritone and Orch. (1936); Violin Concerto (1939); Piano Trio (1941); *Concerto Meditativo* for Cello and Orch. (1942); *Concerto Intimo* for Piano (1956); *Elaman lahja (The Gift of Life)* for Soloists, Chorus, and Orch. (1956); 2 violin sonatas; Piano Sonata; choral works; songs.

Ikonomov, Boyan, Bulgarian composer; b. Nikopol, Dec. 14, 1900; d. Sofia, March 27, 1973. He studied music in Sofia (1920–26); then went to Paris, where he attended classes of Vincent d'Indy and Guy de Lioncourt at the Schola Cantorum in Paris (1928–32); also took a course in conducting with Weingartner in Basel (1934). Returning to Bulgaria, he was music director of Sofia Radio (1937–48) and of the Bulgarian film center (1948–56). His music is rooted in Bulgarian folk songs, with an emphasis on modal melodic progressions and asymmetric rhythms.

WORKS: *Indje Voivoda* (1960); children's operetta, *The Young Artful Boys* (1960); 3 ballets: *The 7 Mortal Sins* (1933), *The Tragedy of Othello* (1946), and *The Light Floods Everything* (1967); 2 oratorios: *The Legend of Shipka* (1968) and *Vassil Levsky* (1972); 2 cantatas: *George Dimitrov* (1954) and *Poem about Lenin* (1969); *Haidouk Rhapsody* for Orch. (1932); Sinfonietta (1934); *Kaliakra,* symph. poem (1935); *Pastorale* for Chamber Orch. (1937); 4 symphs. (1937, 1947, 1955, 1971); *Pastorale and Dance* for Orch. (1939); *Shar Planina,* symph. poem (1942); Violin Concerto (1951); Divertimento for String Quartet and Orch. (1956); Piano Concertino (1958); 6 string quartets (1933, 1937, 1941, 1944, 1945, 1949); 2 trios for Oboe, Clarinet, and Bassoon (1935, 1968); Cello Sonata; choral and solo songs; incidental music.

Ilerici, Kemal, Turkish composer; b. Kastamonu, Oct. 15, 1910. He studied composition with Ferit Alnar. Among his works are a symph. suite, *In My Village* (1945), *Pastoral Fantasy* for Orch. (1951), String Quartet, Suite for Oboe and Piano, and choral works. He wrote a book on Turkish music, *Türk musikisi tonal sistemi ve armonisi* (1948).

Iliev, Konstantin, Bulgarian composer and conductor; b. Sofia, March 9, 1924. He studied composition with Khadzhiev and Vladigerov, and conducting with Goleminov, at the Sofia Music Academy (1942–46); later took courses in composition with Řídký and Alois Hába, and in conducting with Talich, at the Prague Cons. (1946–48). Returning to Bulgaria, he devoted himself mainly to conducting; was a conductor at the State Opera in Sofia (1947–56); then conducted the Sofia Phil. Orch. (1956–72). In 1964 he was appointed to the faculty of the State Cons. in Sofia. As a composer, he has evolved a rather stimulating idiom, adroitly exploring the asymmetric Balkan rhythms and oriental melismas to create an aura of folkloric authenticity; in non-ethnic pieces he often applies serial principles of melodic formations.
WORKS: Opera, *The Master of Boyana* (Sofia, Oct. 3, 1962); oratorio, *Eulogy to Constantin the Philosopher* (1971); 5 symphs. (1947, 1951, 1954, 1958, 1959); *Concerto Grosso* for String Orch., Piano, and Percussion (1949); *Symphonic Variations* (1951); *Tempi concertanti I* for String Orch. (1967); *Tempi concertanti II* for Flute, Harpsichord, and 12 Instruments (1969); Violin Concerto (1971); 4 string quartets (1949, 1952, 1953, 1956); Piano Trio (1976); choruses.

Iliffe, Frederick, English composer; b. Smeet-on-Westerby, Leicester, Feb. 21, 1847; d. Oxford, Feb. 2, 1928. He was organist at St. John's College in Oxford; wrote an oratorio, *The Visions of St. John the Divine* (1880); a cantata, *Lara* (1885); organ music; publ. *Critical Analysis of Bach's Well-tempered Clavichord* (London, 1869).

Ilitsch, Daniza, Serbian soprano; b. Belgrade, Feb. 21, 1914; d. Vienna, Jan. 15, 1965. She studied at the Stankovic Cons. there; made her debut as Nedda in *Pagliacci* with the Berlin State Opera (Nov. 6, 1936); was on its staff for 2 seasons; then became a member of the Vienna State Opera (1938–41). The German army of occupation put her in a concentration camp in 1944, and she spent 4 months there until the liberation of Vienna. In 1947 she came to America; made her debut with the Metropolitan Opera as Desdemona (March 12, 1947).

Illica, Luigi, Italian librettist; b. Castell' Arquato, Piacenza, May 9, 1857; d. Colombarone, Piacenza, Dec. 16, 1919. He was engaged as a journalist in Milan; after 1892 devoted himself to writing librettos. He was the author (in collaboration with Giacosa) of librettos for Puccini's operas *La Bohème, Tosca,* and *Madama Butterfly,* and the sole writer of the text for Giordano's *Andrea Chenier* and Mas-

cagni's *Le Maschere.*

Ilyinsky, Alexander, Russian composer; b. Tsarskoye Selo, Jan. 24, 1859; d. Moscow, Feb. 23, 1920. He studied in Berlin with Kullak (piano) and Bargiel (composition); upon returning to Moscow in 1885, was a teacher at the Philharmonica Inst. there. He wrote an opera, *The Fountain of Bakhchisaray;* publ. *3 valses brillantes* for Piano, etc.

Imai, Nobuko, Japanese violist; b. Tokyo, March 18, 1943. She studied at the Toho School of Music in Tokyo and at the Juilliard School of Music in N.Y.; won first prize at viola competitions in Munich and Geneva; subsequently played in several chamber music groups.

Imbert, Hugues, French music critic and essayist; b. Moulins-Engilbert, Nièvre, Jan. 11, 1842; d. Paris, Jan. 15, 1905. He studied violin; was on the editorial staff of *Le Guide Musical.* He publ. *Profils des Musiciens* (in 3 series: 1888, 1892, 1897); *Symphonie* (1891); *Portraits et Etudes* (1894); *Rembrandt et Wagner* (1897); *Charles Gounod, L'Autobiographie et les Mémoires* (1897); *Bizet* (1899); *La Symphonie après Beethoven* (1900); *Médaillons contemporains* (1902); *J. Brahms: Sa vie et son œuvre* (publ. posthumously, 1906).

Imbrie, Andrew (Welsh), notable American composer; b. New York, April 6, 1921. He studied piano with Leo Ornstein (1930–42); then served in the Signal Corps of the U.S. Army during World War II; spent a summer studying composition with Nadia Boulanger at Fontainebleau; intermittently had fruitful sessions with Sessions, first privately, then at Princeton Univ. and at the Univ. of Calif. at Berkeley (M.A., 1947). In 1947 he was awarded the American Prix de Rome; after a sojourn in Italy, was appointed a prof. of music at Berkeley, in 1960. He held 2 Guggenheim grants (1953–54, 1960–61). His style of composition is marked by a sharp and expressive melodic line, while the polyphony is vigorously motile; harmonic confluence is dissonant but euphoniously tonal. Imbrie's natural propensity is toward instrumental writing; even his choral pieces possess the texture of chamber music.
WORKS: FOR ORCH.: *Ballad in D* (1947; Florence, June 20, 1949); Violin Concerto (1954; San Francisco, April 22, 1958); *Little Concerto* for Piano, 4-hands, and Orch. (1956); *Legend,* symph. poem (San Francisco, Dec. 9, 1959); Symph. No. 1 (San Francisco, May 11, 1966); Symph. No. 2 (1969); Symph. No. 3 (1970); Cello Concerto (1972); Piano Concerto No. 1 (1973); Piano Concerto No. 2 (1974); Flute Concerto (N.Y., Oct. 13, 1977). CHAMBER MUSIC: 4 string quartets (1942, 1953, 1957, 1969); Piano Trio (1946); *Divertimento* for 6 Instruments (1948); *Serenade* for Flute, Viola, and Piano (1952); *Impromptu* for Violin and Piano (1960); Cello Sonata (1966); Chamber Symph. (1968); Piano Sonata (1947). VOCAL WORKS: *On the Beach at Night,* to words by Walt Whitman (1948); *Drum Taps,* cantata to words by Walt Whitman (1961); 2 operas: *Christmas in Peeples Town*

(Berkeley, Dec. 3, 1964) and *Angle of Repose,* after the novel of Wallace Stegner (San Francisco, Nov. 6, 1976).

Inbal, Eliahu, Israeli conductor; b. Jerusalem, Feb. 16, 1936. He was educated at the Academy of Music in Jerusalem; then studied conducting with Franco Ferrara in Rome, Louis Fourestier in Paris, and Sergiu Celibidache. In 1963 he won first prize in the Guido Cantelli International Competition for Conductors; he then appeared widely in Europe as a guest conductor. In 1974 he became chief conductor of the Frankfurt Radio Symph. Orch.; in 1980 brought this orch. to the U.S. for the first time.

Inch, Herbert Reynolds, American composer; b. Missoula, Mont., Nov. 25, 1904. He studied at the State Univ. of Montana and then at the Eastman School of Music in Rochester, N.Y., with Howard Hanson (Mus. Bac., 1925; M.M., 1928); he was a fellow of the American Academy in Rome in 1931. After teaching for several years at the Eastman School, he became a member of the faculty at Hunter College, N.Y. (1937–65); in 1965 moved to La Jolla, Calif.

WORKS: *Variations on a Modal Theme* (Rochester, April 29, 1927); *3 Pieces* for Small Orch. (Rochester, Oct. 24, 1930); Symph. No. 1 (Rochester, May 5, 1932); Serenade for Small Orch. (Rochester, Oct. 24, 1939); Piano Concerto (1940); *Answers to a Questionnaire* for Orch. (1942); *Northwest Overture* (1943); Violin Concerto (Rochester, May 1, 1947); *Return to Zion* for Women's Chorus (1945); Piano Quintet (1930); *Mediterranean Sketches* for String Quartet (1933); Divertimento for Brass (1934); String Quartet (1936); Cello Sonata (1941); *3 Conversations* for String Quartet (1944); 3 symphoniettas (1948, 1950, 1955); Piano Trio (1963); 3 piano sonatas (1935, 1946, 1966).

d'India, Sigismondo, Italian madrigal composer; b. c.1580, probably in Palermo; d. 1629, possibly in Modena. He traveled throughout Italy between 1601 and 1610, visiting various courts. From 1611–23 he was director of chamber music at the court of Carlo Emanuele I, Duke of Savoy, in Turin; then was in the service of Cardinal Maurizio of Savoy, in Rome, and with the Este court in Modena. He publ. 8 books of madrigals in 5 parts; 5 books of arias and cantatas in the monodic style, which was then coming into fashion, entitled simply *Musiche* (possibly by association with Caccini's *Le nuove musiche*); and, in the polyphonic style, 2 books of *Sacri Concentus* (1610) and a book of motets (1627). D'India is reputed for the comparative boldness of his harmonic progressions in the otherwise static monody affected by his Florentine contemporaries. His opera (in recitative), *Zalizura,* is extant. There is an edition of his works edited by J. Joyce and G. Watkins in *Musiche rinascimentali siciliane* (1980—).

BIBLIOGRAPHY: N. Fortune, "Sigismondo d'India: An Introduction to His Life and Works," *Proceedings of the Royal Musical Association,* LXXXI (1954–55); F. Mompellio, *Sigismondo d'India, Musicista palermitano* (Milan, 1956); G. Watkins, "The Polyphonic Madrigals of Sigismondo d'India," *Abstracts of Papers Read at the 38th Annual Meeting of the American Musicological Society* (1972); J. Joyce, *The Monodies of Sigismondo d'India* (Diss., Tulane Univ., 1975).

d'Indy, (Paul-Marie-Théodore-) Vincent, eminent French composer; b. Paris, March 27, 1851; d. there, Dec. 2, 1931. Owing to the death of his mother at his birth, his education was directed entirely by his grandmother, a woman of culture and refinement who had known Grétry and Monsigny, and who had shown a remarkable appreciation of the works of Beethoven when that master was still living. From 1862–65 he studied piano with Diémer, and later harmony and theory with Marmontel and Lavignac. In 1869 he made the acquaintance of Henri Duparc, and with him spent much time studying the masterpieces of Bach, Beethoven, Berlioz, and Wagner; at that time, he wrote his opp. 1 and 2, and contemplated an opera on Victor Hugo's *Les Burgraves* (1869–72; unfinished). During the Franco-Prussian War he served in the Garde Mobile, and wrote of his experiences in *Histoire du 105e bataillon de la Garde nationale de Paris en l'année 1870–71* (1872). He then began to study composition with César Franck (1872–80); when the latter was appointed prof. of organ at the Cons. (1873), he joined the class, winning a 2nd *accessit* in 1874 and the first, the following year. On his first visit to Germany in 1873 he met Liszt and Wagner, and was introduced to Brahms; in 1876, he heard the first performances of the *Ring* dramas at Bayreuth, and for several years thereafter made regular trips to Munich to hear all the works of Wagner; he also attended the première of *Parsifal* in 1882. In 1872–76, he was organist at St.-Leu; in 1873–78, chorus master and timpanist with the Colonne Orch.; for the Paris première of *Lohengrin* in 1887 he drilled the chorus and was Lamoureux's assistant. In 1871 he joined the Société Nationale de Musique as a junior member, and was its secretary from 1876 till 1890, when, after Franck's death, he became president. In 1894 he founded, with Bordes and Guilmant, the famous Schola Cantorum (opened 1896), primarily as a school for plainchant and the Palestrina style. Gradually the scope of instruction was enlarged to include all musical disciplines, and the inst. became one of the world's foremost music schools. D'Indy's fame as a composer began with the performance of *Le Chant de la cloche* at a Lamoureux concert in 1886; the work itself had won the City of Paris Prize in the competition of the preceding year. As early as 1874, Pasdeloup had played the overture *Les Piccolomini* (later embodied as the second part in the *Wallenstein* trilogy), and in 1882 the one-act opera *Attendez-moi sous l'orme* had been produced at the Opéra-Comique; but the prize work attracted general attention, and d'Indy was recognized as one of the most important of modern French masters. Although he never held an official position as a conductor, he frequently, and with marked success, appeared in that capacity (chiefly upon invitation to direct his own works); thus, he visited Spain in 1897, Russia in 1903 and 1907, and the U.S. in 1905, when he conducted the regular subscription concerts of Dec. 1 and 2 of the Boston Symph. Orch. In 1892 he was a member of the commission appointed to revise the curriculum of the Cons., and refused a proffered professorship of composition; but in 1912 accepted an appointment as prof. of the ensemble class. Besides his other duties, he was, from 1899, inspector of musical instruction in Paris; made his last U.S. visit in 1921. He was made a Chevalier of the Legion of Honor in 1892, an Officer in 1912; was also a member of many academies and artistic associations (in Belgium, the Netherlands, Spain, Italy, Sweden, etc.). Both as teacher and creative artist, d'Indy continued the traditions of César Franck. Although he cultivated almost every form of composition, his special talent seemed to be in the field of the larger instrumental forms. Some French critics assign to him a position in French music analogous to that of Brahms in German music. His style rests on Bach and Beethoven; however, his deep study of Gregorian chant and the early contrapuntal style added an element of severity, and not rarely of complexity, that renders his approach somewhat difficult, and has prompted the charge that his music is lacking in emotional force.

WRITINGS: In addition to composition, d'Indy did some important editing and wrote several books. For the edition of Rameau's complete works (ed. by Saint-Saëns and Malherbe) he revised *Dardanus, Hippolyte et Aricie,* and *Zaïs;* also ed. Monteverdi's *Orfeo* and *Incoronazione di Poppea;* he also made piano arrangements of orch. works by Chausson, Duparc, and other composers. His numerous articles in various journals are remarkable for their critical acumen and literary finish. He publ. an important manual, *Cours de Composition musicale* (Book I, 1903; Book II: Part 1, 1909, Part 2, 1933); *César Franck* (1906; in Eng., 1910, reprinted, N.Y., 1965); *Beethoven: Biographie critique* (1911; Eng. trans. by T. Baker, Boston, 1913; reprint, N.Y., 1970); *La Schola Cantorum en 1925* (1927); *Wagner et son influence sur l'art musical français* (1930); *Introduction à l'étude de Parsifal* (1937; posthumous).

WORKS: FOR THE STAGE: *Attendez-moi sous l'orme,* op. 14, one-act comic opera (Opéra-Comique, Feb. 11, 1882); *Le Chant de la cloche,* op. 18, dramatic legend (Brussels, Théâtre de la Monnaie, Nov. 21, 1912); *Fervaal,* op. 40, lyric drama (Brussels, March 12, 1897); *L'Etranger,* op. 53, lyric drama (Brussels, Jan. 7, 1903); *La Légende de Saint-Christophe,* op. 67, lyric drama (Paris Opéra, June 9, 1920); *Le Rêve de Cynias,* op. 80, lyric comedy (Paris, June 10, 1927).

FOR ORCH.: *Jean Hunyade,* op. 5, symph. (Paris, May 15, 1875); *Antoine et Cléopâtre,* op. 6, overture (Paris, Feb. 4, 1877); *La Forêt enchantée,* op. 8, symph. legend (Paris, March 24, 1878); *Wallenstein,* op. 12, symph. trilogy: a) *Le Camp de Wallenstein* (April 12, 1880), b) *Max et Thécla* (Jan. 25, 1874; originally *Les Piccolomini*), c) *La Mort de Wallenstein* (April 11, 1884); *Lied,* op. 19, for Cello and

Orch. (Paris, April 18, 1885); *Saugefleurie,* op. 21, legend (Paris, Jan. 25, 1885); *Symphonie Cévenole (sur un chant montagnard français),* op. 25, for Orch. and Piano (Paris, March 20, 1887); *Sérénade et Valse,* op. 28 (from op. 16 and 17), for Small Orch. (1887); *Fantaisie,* op. 31, for Oboe and Orch. (Paris, Dec. 23, 1888); incidental music to Alexandre's *Karadec,* op. 34 (Paris, May 2, 1891); *Tableaux de Voyage,* op. 36 (Le Havre, Jan. 17, 1892); *Istar,* op. 42, symph. variations (Brussels, Jan. 10, 1897); incidental music to Mendès's *Medée,* op. 47 (1898); *Choral varié,* op. 55, for Saxophone and Orch. (Paris, May 17, 1904); 2nd Symph., op. 57, in B-flat (Paris, Feb. 28, 1904); *Jour d'été à la montagne,* op. 61 (Paris, Feb. 18, 1906); *Souvenirs,* op. 62, tone poem (Paris, April 20, 1907); *La Queste de Dieu,* op. 67, descriptive symph. (from *La Légende de Saint-Christophe;* 1917); 3rd Symph., op. 70: *Sinfonia brevis de bello Gallico* (1916–18; Paris, Dec. 14, 1919); *Le Poème des rivages,* op. 77 (N.Y., Dec. 1, 1921); *Diptyque méditerranéen,* op. 87 (Paris, Dec. 5, 1926); Concerto for Piano, Flute, Cello, and String Orch., op. 89 (Paris, April 2, 1927).

CHAMBER MUSIC: Piano Quartet in A minor, op. 7 (1878); Suite in D, op. 24, for Trumpet, 2 Flutes, and String Orch. (Paris, March 5, 1887); Trio for Piano, Clarinet, and Cello, op. 29 (1888); String Quartet No. 1, op. 35 (1891); String Quartet No. 2, op. 45 (1898); *Chansons et Danses,* op. 50, *divertissement* for 7 Wind Instruments (Paris, March 7, 1899); Violin Sonata, op. 59 (1905); Piano Quintet in G minor, op. 81 (1925); Cello Sonata, op. 84 (1926); *Suite en 4 parties,* op. 91, for Flute, Strings, and Harp (Paris, May 17, 1930); String Sextet, op. 92 (1928); String Quartet No. 3, op. 96 (1929); Trio No. 2, op. 98, for Piano, Violin, and Cello (1929).

VOCAL WORKS: *Chanson des aventuriers de la mer,* op. 2, for Baritone Solo and Men's Chorus (1870); *La Chevauchée du Cid,* op. 11, for Baritone, Chorus, and Orch. (1879); *Cantate Domino,* op. 22 (1885); *Ste. Marie-Magdeleine,* op. 23, cantata (1885); *Sur la mer,* op. 32, for Women's Voices and Piano (1888); *Pour l'inauguration d'une statue,* op. 37, cantata (1893); *L'Art et le peuple,* op. 39, for Men's Chorus (1894); *Deus Israël,* op. 41, motet (1896); *Ode à Valence,* op. 44, for Soprano and Chorus (1897); *Les Noces d'or du sacerdoce,* op. 46 (1898); *Sancta Maria,* op. 49, motet (1898); 6 *Chants populaires français,* opp. 90 and 100, for a cappella Chorus (1928, 1931); *Le Bouquet de printemps,* op. 93, for Women's Chorus (1929); songs (opp. 3, 4, 10, 13, 20, 43, 48, 52, 56, 58, 64).

FOR PIANO: *3 romances sans paroles,* op. 1 (1870); *Petite sonate,* op. 9 (1880); *Poème des montagnes,* op. 15: *Le Chant des bruyères, Danses rythmiques, Plein-air* (1881); *4 pièces,* op. 16 (1882); *Helvetia,* op. 17, 3 waltzes (1882); *Saugefleurie,* op. 21 (1884; also arranged for Orch.); Nocturne, op. 26 (1886); *Promenade,* op. 27 (1887); *Schumanniana,* op. 30, 3 pieces (1887); *Tableaux de voyage,* op. 33, 13 pieces (1889); *Petite chanson grégorienne,* op. 60, for Piano, 4-hands (1904); Sonata, op. 63 (1907); *Menuet sur le nom de Haydn,* op. 65 (1909); *13 Short Pieces,* op. 68; *12 petites pièces faciles,* op. 69, in old style; *7 chants de terroir,* op. 73, for Piano, 4-hands; *Pour les en-*

fants de tous les âges, op. 74, 24 pieces; *Thème varié, fugue et chanson,* op. 85; *Conte de fées,* op. 86, suite (1926); 6 paraphrases on French children's songs, op. 95; *Fantaisie sur un vieil air de ronde française,* op. 99 (1931).

FOR ORGAN: *Prélude et Petit Canon,* op. 38 (1893); *Vêpres du Commun d'un Martyr,* op. 51 (1889); *Prélude,* op. 66 (1913).

WITHOUT OPUS NUMBER: O *gai Soleil,* canon *a* 2 (1909); incidental music to *Veronica* (1920); *3 chansons anciennes du Vivarais* (1926); *La Vengeance du mari,* for 3 Soli, Chorus, and Orch. (1931).

BIBLIOGRAPHY: E. Deniau, *Vincent d'Indy* (Toulouse, 1903); A. Hervey, *French Music in the 19th Century* (London, 1903); F. Starczewski, *La Schola Cantorum de Paris, ou Vincent d'Indy considéré comme professeur* (Warsaw, 1905); O. Séré, *Musiciens français d'aujourd'hui* (2nd ed., Paris, 1911); L. Borgex, *Vincent d'Indy: Sa vie et son œuvre* (Paris, 1913); A. Sérieyx, *Vincent d'Indy* (Paris, 1913); Romain Rolland, *Musiciens d'aujourd'hui* (Paris, 1914); E.B. Hill, "Vincent d'Indy, an Estimate," *Musical Quarterly* (April 1915); Paul Landormy, "Vincent d'Indy," *Musical Quarterly* (July 1932); M.M. de Fraguier, *Vincent d'Indy* (Paris, 1933); L. Vallas, "The Discovery of Musical Germany by Vincent d'Indy in 1873," *Musical Quarterly* (April 1939); idem, *Vincent d'Indy: I. La Jeunesse. II. La Maturité, La Vieillesse* (Paris, I., 1946; II., 1950; the basic biography); J. Canteloube, *Vincent d'Indy* (Paris, 1949); Norman Demuth, *Vincent d'Indy* (London, 1951); J. Guy-Ropartz, ed., *Le Centenaire de Vincent d'Indy, 1851–1951* (Paris, 1952); L. Davies, *Cesar Franck and His Circle* (Boston, 1970); C.B. Paul, "Rameau, d'Indy, and French Nationalism," *Musical Quarterly* (Jan. 1972).

Infantas, Fernando de las, Spanish musician and theologian; b. Córdoba, 1534; d. after 1609. He belonged to a noble family and enjoyed the protection of the Emperor Charles V and later of Philip II, who employed him on diplomatic missions in Italy. He went to Venice, and then to Rome, where he lived for 25 years (1572–97). He exerted a decisive influence upon the course of Catholic church music by opposing the plan for the reform of the Roman Gradual undertaken by Palestrina in 1578 at the request of Pope Gregory XIII. Backed by the authority of Philip II of Spain, he succeeded in having the project abandoned. He publ. *Sacrarum varii styli cantionum tituli Spiritus Sancti,* a collection of motets in 3 books: I for 4 voices, II for 5 voices (both publ. in Venice, 1578), III for 6–8 voices (Venice, 1579), and *Plura modulationum genera quae vulgo contrapuncta appellantur super excelso gregoriano cantu* (Venice, 1579; contains 100 contrapuntal exercises for 2–8 voices based on one plainsong theme; it pointed the way to a new freedom and elasticity in polyphonic writing); separate compositions were also publ. in various collections of the time. A Sequence for 6 voices, *Victimae paschali,* was publ. by W. Dehn in *Sammlung älterer Musik aus dem 16. und 17. Jahrhundert,* vol. V, pp. 6–11 (Berlin, 1837–40).

BIBLIOGRAPHY: R.F. Molitor, *Die nachtridentinische Choralreform* (vol. I); R. Mitjana, *Don Fernando de las Infantas, teólogo y músico* (Madrid, 1918); R. Stevenson, *Spanish Cathedral Music in the Golden Age* (Berkeley, Calif., 1961).

Infante, Manuel, Spanish composer; b. Osuna, near Seville, July 29, 1883; d. Paris, April 21, 1958. He studied piano and composition with Enrique Morera; in 1909 he settled in Paris; gave concerts of Spanish music; wrote numerous pieces for piano, mostly on Spanish themes: *Gitanerias; Pochades andalouses; Sevillana,* fantasy (1922); *El Vito* (variations on a popular theme); also an opera, *Almanza.*

Ingegneri, Marco Antonio, Italian composer; b. Verona, c.1545; d. Cremona, July 1, 1592. He was a pupil of Vincenzo Ruffo, organist of the Verona Cathedral. He went to Cremona about 1568 and became maestro di cappella at the Cathedral there (1579). Monteverdi was his pupil.

WORKS: A book of masses *a* 5–8 (1573); a 2nd, *a* 5 (1587); 4 of madrigals *a* 4–5 (1578, 1579, 1580, 1584); *Sacrae cantiones a* 5 (1576); *Sacrae cantiones a* 7–16 (1589). The 27 celebrated Responses, formerly attributed to Palestrina, are by Ingegneri. They had been printed in Breitkopf & Härtel's edition of Palestrina's works (vol. 32) as of doubtful authenticity, but were eliminated when Haberl, in 1897, discovered a copy (printed in Venice, 1588) with the full name of Ingegneri. Many other motets and madrigals appeared in collections of the time. A reprint of one of his motets is in Johannes Wolf's *Sing- und Spielmusik aus älterer Zeit.*

BIBLIOGRAPHY: F. Haberl, "M.A. Ingegneri," *Kirchenmusikalisches Jahrbuch* (1898); R. Casimiri, in *Note d'Archivio* (1926); Ellinor Dohrn, *Marc Antonio Ingegneri als Madrigalkomponist* (Hannover, 1936); G. Cesari, "La musica in Cremona," in *Istituzioni e monumenti dell'arte musicale italiana* (vol. 6).

Ingenhoven, Jan, Dutch composer; b. Breda, May 29, 1876; d. Hoenderlo, May 20, 1951. He studied with L. Brandts-Buys in Rotterdam and Mottl in Munich; lived in Germany and Switzerland; conducted a madrigal choir in Munich (1909–12); then devoted himself mainly to composition. His works are influenced by Debussy, but he preserves an element of peculiarly native melos. Among his works are a symph. fantasy, *Brabant and Holland;* 3 symph. poems (*Lyric; Dramatic; Romantic*); 4 string quartets; Woodwind Quintet; Trio for Violin, Cello, and Harp; Trio for Flute, Clarinet, and Harp; Trio for Piano, Violin, and Cello; several choral works in the classical tradition; songs.

BIBLIOGRAPHY: D. Ruyneman, *De komponist Jan Ingenhoven* (Amsterdam, 1938).

Inghelbrecht, Désiré Emile, French conductor and composer; b. Paris, Sept. 17, 1880; d. there, Feb. 14, 1965. He studied at the Paris Cons.; after graduation, conducted at various theaters in Paris; toured as conductor of the Ballets Suédois (1919–22); was director of the Opéra-Comique (1924–25 and 1932–33), of the Pasdeloup Orch. (1928–32), and of the Algiers Opera (1929–30). In 1945–50 he was conductor of the Paris Opéra; also conducted abroad. He was the founder of the Orch. National de la Radiodiffusion in Paris in 1934. He publ. several books and pamphlets on conducting: *Comment on ne doit pas interpréter Carmen, Faust et Pelléas* (1932); *Diabolus in musica* (1933); *Mouvement contraire: Souvenirs d'un musicien* (1947); and *Le Chef d'orchestre et son équipe* (1948; Eng. trans. as *The Conductor's World*, 1953).

WORKS: *La Nuit vénitienne,* opera in 3 acts after Musset (1908). BALLETS: *La Bonne Aventure* (1912); *El Greco* (Ballets Suédois, Paris, Nov. 18, 1920); *Le Diable dans le beffroi* (after Edgar Allan Poe; Paris Opéra, June 1, 1927); *Jeux de Couleurs* (Opéra-Comique, Feb. 21, 1933); *Le chêne et le tilleul,* opera-ballet (Paris, 1961). FOR ORCH.: *Automne* (1905); *Pour le jour de la première neige au vieux Japon* (1908); *Rapsodie de printemps* (1910); *3 poèmes dansés* (1925); *La Métamorphose d'Eve* (1925); *La Légende du grand St. Nicolas* (1925); *Iberiana* for Violin and Orch. (1948); *Vézelay, évocation symphonique* (1952). CHAMBER MUSIC: *2 esquisses antiques* for Flute and Harp (1902); *Poème sylvestre* for Woodwinds (1905); Quintet for Strings and Harp (1918); pieces for cello and piano, and for viola and piano. CHORAL WORKS: *Le Cantique des créatures de Saint François d'Assise* for Chorus and Orch. (1919); Requiem (1940); *4 chansons populaires françaises* for Mixed Chorus. PIANO WORKS: *La Nursery,* 4-hand pieces for children, 3 vols. (1905 and 1911); *Suite petite-russienne* (1908); *Paysages* (1918); etc.; also songs (*Mélodies sur des poésies russes,* 1905; *Au jardin de l'infante,* 1910; etc.).

Inghilleri, Giovanni, Italian baritone; b. Porto Empedocle, March 9, 1894; d. Milan, Dec. 10, 1959. He made his debut in Milan at the Teatro Carcano in 1919; then made regular appearances in Italy; he also sang in London and Chicago. Following his retirement from the stage in 1953, he taught voice.

Insanguine, Giacomo (Antonio Francesco Paolo Michele), called **Monopoli,** Italian composer; b. Monopoli, March 22, 1728; d. Naples, Feb. 1, 1795. He studied with Cotumacci at the Cons. of San Onofrio in Naples; then became his master's assistant (1767) and 2nd teacher (1774); after Cotumacci's death (1785), first teacher. He concurrently was 2nd organist at the Cappella del Tesoro di San Gennaro (1774), first organist (1776), and maestro di cappella there (1781).

WORKS: Some 15 operas, among them: *Lo Fumaco revotato* (1756); *Didone abbandonata* (1772); *Arianna e Teseo* (1773); *Adriano in Siria* (1773); *Le astuzie per amore* (1777); *Medonte* (1779); *Calipso* (1782). His best work is the 71st Psalm for 3-part Chorus and Orch.; he also composed other Psalms, hymns, masses, etc.

Inten, Ferdinand, German-American pianist and teacher; b. Leipzig, Feb. 23, 1848; d. New York, Jan. 16, 1918. He studied at the Leipzig Cons. (1862–66) with Moscheles, Plaidy, Hauptmann, and Reinecke; in 1868, came to the U.S. and settled in N.Y.; made his American debut as piano soloist in N.Y., on Dec. 12, 1868. He organized concerts of chamber music, which became famous. As a teacher, he also achieved success; among his pupils were Frank and Walter Damrosch.

Inzenga, José, Spanish writer on music; b. Madrid, June 3, 1828; d. there, June 28, 1891. He first studied with his father, then at the Madrid Cons. and the Paris Cons.; became a prof. at the Madrid Cons. (1860). He was commissioned by the Minister of Public Instruction to make a collection of Spanish folk songs, which he publ. as *Cantos y bailes populares de España* (4 vols., 1888); also wrote a treatise on accompaniment, and *Impresiones de un artista en Italia.* He was very successful as a composer of zarzuelas: *Para seguir una mujer* (1851); *Don Simplicio Bobadilla* (1853); *Un día de reino* (1854); *El campamento* (1861); *Si yo fuera rey* (1862); etc.

Ioannidis, Yannis, Greek composer; b. Athens, June 8, 1930. He studied piano in Athens (1946–55), then music theory at the Cons. there; and organ, composition, and conducting at the Vienna Musical Academy (1955–63); taught at Pierce College in Athens (1963–68); in 1968 went to live in Caracas (his family was from Venezuela), where he served as artistic director of the chamber orch. of the National Inst. of Culture and Fine Arts; he was a prof. there from 1969, and at the Caracas Cons. and Univ. from 1971. As a composer, he follows the precepts of the 2nd Vienna School, with a firm foundation of classical forms.

WORKS: 2 string quartets (1961, 1971); *Triptych* for Orch. (1962); Duo for Violin and Piano (1962); *Peristrophe* for String Octet (1964); *Versi* for Solo Clarinet (1967); *Arioso* for String Nonet (1960); *Tropic* for Orch. (1968); *Schemata (Figures)* for String Ensemble (1968); *Projections* for Strings, Winds, and Piano (1968); *Fragments I* for Cello and Piano (1969) and *Fragments II* for Solo Flute (1970); *Metaplassis A* and *B* for Orch. (1969, 1970); *Actinia* for Wind Quintet (1969); *Transiciones* for Orch. (1971); *Estudio I, II,* and *III* for Piano (1971–73); *Fancy for 6* for 4 Winds, Cello, and Percussion (1972); *Nocturno* for Piano Quartet (1972); transcriptions of Greek folk songs for chorus.

Iparraguirre y Balerdí, José María de, Spanish-Basque composer and poet; b. Villarreal de Urrechu, Aug. 12, 1820; d. Zozobastro de Isacho, April 6, 1881. He led a wandering life; improvised songs, accompanying himself on the guitar; one of his songs, *Guernikako arbola,* a hymn to the sacred tree of Guernica, became the national anthem of the Basques. As a result of the unrest in the Basque country, and his own participation in it, he was compelled to leave Spain; spent many years in South America; was enabled to return to Spain in 1877, and even obtained an official pension.

Ipavec, Benjamin, Slovenian composer; b. St. Jurij, Dec. 24, 1829; d. Graz, Dec. 20, 1909. He studied medicine in Vienna and became a professional physician, with music as an avocation, but he was the first to cultivate national Slovenian motifs systematically, and therefore became historically important. He wrote a national Slovenian opera, *Teharski plemiči* (*The Nobles of Teharje;* Ljubljana, 1892); numerous songs in a Romantic vein; also brought out collections of Slovenian folk songs.

Ippolitov-Ivanov, Mikhail (real name **Ivanov,** but he assumed his mother's name to distinguish himself from Michael Ivanov, the music critic; the name is pronounced Ippolítov-Ivánov); important Russian composer and pedagogue; b. Gatchina, Nov. 19, 1859; d. Moscow, Jan. 28, 1935. He entered the St. Petersburg Cons. in 1875; studied composition with Rimsky-Korsakov, graduating in 1882. He then received the post of teacher and director of the Music School in Tiflis, in the Caucasus, where he remained until 1893; he became deeply interested in Caucasian folk music; many of his works were colored by the semi-oriental melodic and rhythmic inflections of that region. Upon Tchaikovsky's recommendation, he was appointed in 1893 prof. of composition at the Moscow Cons.; in 1906 became its director, retiring in 1922. Among his pupils were the composers Glière and Vasilenko. From 1899 on, he was conductor of the Mamontov Opera in Moscow; in 1925, he became conductor of the Bolshoi Theater in Moscow. Outside Russia, he is known mainly for his effective symph. suite *Caucasian Sketches* (1895).
WORKS: OPERAS: *Ruth* (Tiflis, Feb. 8, 1887); *Azra* (Tiflis, Nov. 28, 1890); *Asya* (Moscow, Sept. 28, 1900); *Treason* (1909); *Ole from Nordland* (Moscow, Nov. 21, 1916); *The Last Barricade* (1934); also completed Mussorgsky's unfinished opera *Marriage* (1931). FOR ORCH.: *Symphonic Scherzo* (St. Petersburg, May 20, 1882); *Yar-Khmel,* spring overture (St. Petersburg, Jan. 23, 1883, composer conducting); *Caucasian Sketches* (Moscow, Feb. 5, 1895, composer conducting); *Iveria* (2nd series of *Caucasian Sketches;* Moscow, 1906); Symph. No. 1 (Moscow, 1908); *Armenian Rhapsody* (Moscow, 1909); *On the Volga* (Moscow, 1910); *Mtzyri,* symph. poem (Moscow, 1922); *Turkish March* (Baku, 1929); *From the Songs of Ossian,* 3 musical pictures (Moscow, 1927); *Episodes of the Life of Schubert* (1929); *In the Steppes of Turkmenistan; Voroshilov March; Musical Scenes of Uzbekistan;* symph. poem, *Year 1917; Catalan Suite* (1934); suite on Finnish themes, *Karelia* (1935, last work; only the Finale was orchestrated). CHAMBER MUSIC: Violin Sonata; 2 string quartets; *An Evening in Georgia* for Harp, Flute, Oboe, Clarinet, and Bassoon. VOCAL WORKS: *Alsatian Ballad* for a cappella Mixed Chorus; *5 Characteristic Pieces* for Chorus, and Orch. or Piano; *The Legend of a White Swan* for a cappella Mixed Chorus; *Cantata in Memory of Pushkin* for Children's Chorus and Piano; *Cantata in Memory of Zhukovsky* for Mixed Chorus and Piano; *Pythagorean Hymn to the Rising Sun* for Mixed Chorus, 10 Flutes, 2 Harps, and Tuba; *Cantata in Memory of Gogol* for Children's Chorus and Piano; *Hymn to Labor* for Mixed Chorus and Orch.; 116 songs. He publ. *The Science of the Formation and Resolution of Chords* (1897, in Russian) and *50 Years of Russian Music in My Memories* (Moscow, 1934; in Eng. in *Musical Mercury,* N.Y., 1937).
BIBLIOGRAPHY: Sergei Boguslavsky, *Ippolitov-Ivanov* (Moscow, 1936); L. Podzemskaya, *M.M. Ippolitov-Ivanov and Georgian Musical Culture* (Tiflis, 1963).

Ipuche-Riva, Pedro, Uruguayan composer; b. Montevideo, Oct. 26, 1924. He studied at the Cons. of Montevideo, and later in Paris with Jean Rivier and Nöel Gallon. Returning to Uruguay, he unfolded energetic activities as a music critic, lecturer, teacher, and radio commentator.
WORKS: Symph. poem, *El Arbol solo* (1961); 3 symphs. (1962, 1965, 1968); Cello Concerto (1962); *Fantasía concertante* for Trumpet and String Orch. (1963); String Quartet (1962); Quartet for Flute, Violin, Cello, and Piano (1963); *Espejo roto* for Violin, Horn, and Piano (1966); Concerto for Small Orch. (1966); *Sinfonietta-Concertino* for Piano and Orch. (1967); *Animales ilustres,* suite for Wind Quintet (1967); *Pieza* for Oboe and Piano (1969); *Variaciones antipianísticas* for Piano (1969); other piano pieces; choruses; songs.

Ireland, John, eminent English composer; b. Inglewood, Bowdon, Cheshire, Aug. 13, 1879; d. Rock Mill, Washington, Sussex, June 12, 1962. A member of a literary family (both his parents were writers), he received a fine general education. As his musical inclinations became evident, he entered the Royal College of Music in 1893, studying piano with Frederick Cliffe and composition with Stanford. His parents died while he was still a student; he obtained positions as organist in various churches; the longest of these was at St. Luke's, Chelsea (1904–26). In 1905 he received the degree of Bac.Mus. at the Univ. of Durham; was awarded an honorary Mus.Doc. there in 1932. He taught at the Royal College of Music for a number of years; Benjamin Britten, Alan Bush, E.J. Moeran, and other British composers were his pupils. He began to compose early in life; during his student years, he wrote a number of works for orch., chamber groups, and voices, but destroyed most of them. His creative catalogue, therefore, begins in 1903 (with the song cycle *Songs of a Wayfarer*). His early compositions were influenced by the German Romantic school; soon he felt the impact of modern musical ideas; he adopted many devices of the French impressionist school; his rhythmic concepts were enlivened by the new Russian music presented by the Diaghilev Ballet. At the same time, he never wavered in his dedication to the English spirit of simple melody; his music re-creates the plainsong and the usages of Tudor music in terms of plagal modalities and freely modulating triadic harmonies.
WORKS: FOR ORCH.: *The Forgotten Rite,* symph. prelude (1913); *Mai-Dun,* symph. rhapsody (1921); *A*

London Overture (1936); *Concertino pastorale* for Strings (1939); *Epic March* (1942); *Satyricon* (1946); Piano Concerto (London, Oct. 2, 1930). CHORAL WORKS: *Morning Service* for Voices with Organ (1907–20); motet, *Greater love hath no man* (1912); *Communion Service* (1913); *Evening Service* (1915); *These things shall be* for Baritone Solo, Chorus, and Orch. (1937); a number of 4-part songs a cappella; 2-part songs with piano accompaniment; unison choral songs with piano accompaniment. CHAMBER MUSIC: *Fantasy Trio* for Piano, Violin, and Cello (1906); Trio for Violin, Clarinet, and Piano (1913; rewritten for Violin, Cello, and Piano, 1915, and revised again in 1938); Trio No. 2 for Violin, Cello, and Piano (1917); Violin Sonata No. 1 (1909; revised twice, 1917, 1944); Violin Sonata No. 2 (1917); Cello Sonata (1923); *Fantasy Sonata* for Clarinet and Piano (1943). FOR PIANO: *The Daydream* and *Meridian* (1895; revised 1941); *Decorations* (1913); *The Almond Trees* (1913); Rhapsody (1915); *London Pieces* (1917–20); *Leaves from a Child's Sketchbook* (1918); *Summer Evening* (1919); Sonata (1920); *On a Birthday Morning* (1922); *Soliloquy* (1922); Sonatina (1927); Ballade (1929); *Indian Summer* (1932); *Green Ways* (1937); *Sarnia*, "An Island Sequence" (1941); *3 Pastels* (1941); organ works; about 100 songs, to words by D.G. Rossetti, Christina Rossetti, Thomas Hardy, A.E. Housman, Ernest Dowson, etc.

BIBLIOGRAPHY: A miniature essay on Ireland was publ. by J. & W. Chester, Ltd., in 1923; see also Edwin Evans's article on Ireland in Cobbett's *Cyclopedic Survey of Chamber Music;* Josef Holbrooke, *Contemporary British Composers* (London, 1925); Nigel Townshend, "The Achievement of John Ireland," *Music & Letters* (April 1943); John Longmire, *John Ireland: Portrait of a Friend* (London, 1969); M. Searle, *John Ireland: The Man and His Music* (Tunbridge Wells, 1979).

Irgens Jensen, Ludwig, Norwegian composer; b. Oslo, April 13, 1894; d. Enna, Sicily, April 11, 1969. He studied philosophy, music theory, and piano in Oslo, but was mainly self-taught in composition; from 1946 was a recipient of the Norwegian State Salary of Art, which is a government life pension. His output was relatively small; his compositions are influenced mainly by German Romanticism.
WORKS: *Japanischer Frühling* for Voice and Piano (1918–19); *Der Gott und die Bajadere,* cantata (1921–32); Violin Sonata (1924); *Tema con variazioni* for Orch. (1925); Passacaglia for Orch. (1926); Piano Quintet (1927); *Heimferd (The Return),* dramatic symph. for Soloists, Chorus, and Orch., commemorating the 900th anniversary of the death of St. Olav (1929; Oslo, 1930; recast as an opera and produced in Oslo, Aug. 27, 1947); *Partita sinfonica* (1937); Symph. (1942); *Canto d'omaggio,* festival overture (Oslo, 1950); choruses; songs.

Irino, Yoshirō, Japanese composer; b. Vladivostok, Siberia, Nov. 13, 1921; d. Tokyo, June 28, 1980. Although of pure Japanese ancestry, he was baptized in the Greek Orthodox faith, which he retained throughout his life. He was sent to Tokyo as a child, and studied economics at Tokyo Univ.; at the same time he took composition lessons with Saburo Moroi. In 1954 he was appointed to the faculty of the Tokyo Music School. A prolific composer, he wrote music of all categories, adopting a style decidedly modern in character, marked by fine instrumental coloration, with a complete mastery of contemporary techniques. Most of his vocal and stage music is imbued with a pronounced Japanese sensibility, with touches that are almost calligraphic in their rhythmic precision.
WORKS: An operetta, *The Man in Fear of God* (Tokyo, May 25, 1954); a television opera, *Drum of Silk* (1962); a ballet, *Woman-Mask* (1959); *Adagietto and Allegro vivace* for Orch. (1949); Sinfonietta for Chamber Orch. (1953); Ricercari for Chamber Orch. (1954); Double Concerto for Violin, Piano, and Orch. (1955); *Concerto Grosso* (1957); Sinfonia (1959); Concerto for String Orch. (1960); Suite for Jazz Ensemble (1960); *Music* for Harpsichord, Percussion, and 19 String Instruments (1963); Symph. No. 2 (1964); 2 *Fantasies* for 17 and 20 kotos (1969); *Sai-un (Colorful Clouds)* for 15 String Instruments (1972); *Wandlungen* for 2 Shakuhachi and Orch. (1973); 2 string quartets (1945, 1957); Flute Sonatina (1946); Piano Trio (1948); String Sextet (1950); *Chamber Concerto* for 7 Instruments (1951); *Music* for Violin and Piano (1957); Quintet for Clarinet, Saxophone, Trumpet, Cello, and Piano (1958); Divertimento for 7 Winds (1958); *Music* for Violin and Cello (1959); *Music* for Vibraphone and Piano (1961); Partita for Wind Quintet (1962); String Trio (1965); 3 *Movements* for 2 Kotos and Jushichi-gen (1966); 7 *Inventions* for Guitar and 6 Players (1967); Violin Sonata (1967); 3 *Movements* for Solo Cello (1969); Sonata for Piano, Violin, Clarinet, and Percussion (1970); Trio for Flute, Violin, and Piano (1970); *A Demon's Bride* for Chorus, Oboe, Horn, Piano, and Percussion (1970); *Globus I* for Horn and Percussion (1970); *Globus II* for Marimba, Double Bass, and Percussion (1971); *Globus III* for Violin, Cello, Piano, Harp, Shō, and 2 Dancers (1975); Suite for Solo Viola (1971); *Cloudscape* for String Ensemble (1972); 3 *Improvisations* for Solo Flute (1972); 5 *Days* for Violin and Viola (1972); 3 *Scenes* for 3 Kotos (1972); *Strömung* for Flute, Harp, and Percussion (1973); Shō-yō for Japanese Instruments (1973); *Gafu* for Flute, Shō, and Double Bass (1976); *Klänge* for Piano and Percussion (1976); *Movements* for Solo Marimba (1977); *Cosmos* for Shakuhachi, Violin, Piano, 2 Kotos, and Percussion (1978); *Shi-dai* for Shakuhachi, 20-gen, 17-gen, and Shamisen (1979); Duo Concertante for Alto Saxophone and Koto (1979).

Irrgang, Heinrich Bernhard, German organist; b. Zduny, July 23, 1869; d. Berlin, April 8, 1916. He was a church organist and teacher in Berlin; composed organ music and songs.

Irving, Robert, English conductor; b., Winchester, Aug. 28, 1913. He studied at Winchester College, at New College, Oxford, and at the Royal College of Music, London. In 1936 he became a répétiteur at the Royal Opera House, Covent Garden, and also music master of Winchester College. At the outbreak of World War II in 1939 he joined the Royal Air Force. From 1945–48 he was associate conductor of the BBC Scottish Orch.; from 1949–58 he conducted the Royal Ballet at Covent Garden. In 1958 he was appointed conductor of the N.Y. City Ballet. He made guest conducting appearances with orchs. in Europe and the U.S., but it was as a highly efficient ballet conductor that he gained distinction.

Isaac, Adèle, French soprano; b. Calais, Jan. 8, 1854; d. Paris, Oct. 22, 1915. She studied with Duprez in Paris; made her debut at the Théâtre Montmartre in Paris in 1870, in *Noces de Jeannette;* then sang at the Opéra-Comique (1873; 1878–88) and the Paris Opéra (1883–85); retired from the stage in 1894. She was noted for her performances of French operatic roles.

Isaac, Heinrich (or **Isaak, Izak, Yzac, Ysack;** in Italy, **Arrigo Tedesco** [Henry the German]; Low Latin, **Arrighus**), Netherlandish polyphonist (the Italian term "Tedesco" was used at the time for Netherlanders as well as Germans); b. Brabant, c.1450; d. Florence, March 26, 1517. From 1485 to 1492 he was in the service of Lorenzo de' Medici, in the capacities of organist, maestro di cappella, and teacher to Lorenzo's children. He afterward spent several years in Rome, and finally was called to the court of Maximilian I, at Vienna, as "Symphonista regis"; from 1514 until his death he lived in Florence. He was greatly influenced by the music of the countries in which he lived, writing with equal facility in the Netherlandish, Italian, and German styles as they flourished in his day.
WORKS: 23 masses *a* 4–6 (of which 10 were publ. between 1506–39); those in MS are in libraries in Vienna (8), Munich (4), and Brussels (1). Motets and psalms by Isaac were printed in some 40 collections from 1501–64 (see Eitner, *Bibliographie der Musiksammelwerke;* Berlin, 1877). One of the most beautiful of German chorales, *Nun ruhen alle Wälder,* is sung to Isaac's melody *Inspruk, ich muss dich lassen.* A voluminous collection of motets, *Choralis Constantinus,* was ed. by his pupil Ludwig Senfl, in 1550 (3 parts). Parts I and II were republ. in Denkmäler der Tonkunst in Österreich, 10 and 32 (5.i and 16.i); part III, by the Univ. of Michigan Press (1950; ed. by Louise Cuyler). Isaac's secular works were ed. by Joh. Wolf and also republ. in Denkmäler der Tonkunst in Österreich, 28 and 32 (14.i and 16.i). The *Missa carminum* and other works are publ. in F. Blume's *Das Chorwerk,* 7, 81, and 100. Other reprints are in Eitner's *Publikation älterer Musikwerke* I (5 4-voiced vocal works), and A. Schering's *Geschichte der Musik in Beispielen* (a Kyrie and a canzona). Five polyphonic masses from Isaac's *Choralis Constantinus* were transcribed and ed. by Louise Cuyler (Univ. of Michigan, 1956).
BIBLIOGRAPHY: H. Rietsch, "Heinrich Isaac und das Innsbrucklied," *Jahrbuch der Musikbibliothek Peters* (1917); Peter Wagner, *Geschichte der Messe* (pp. 281–317); P. Blaschke, "Heinrich Isaaks Choralis Constantinus," *Kirchenmusikalisches Jahrbuch* (1931); Frank A. d'Accone, "Heinrich Isaac in Florence: New and Unpublished Documents," *Musical Quarterly* (Oct. 1963); F. Ghisi, "Arrigo il Tedesco, musicista fiorentino," *Chigiana,* 24 (1967); S. Novack, "Fusion of Design and Tonal Order in Mass and Motet: Josquin Desprez and Heinrich Isaac," *Music Forum,* 2 (1970); Martin Stähelin, *Die Messen Heinrich Isaacs,* 3 vols. (Bern, 1977).

Isamitt, Carlos, Chilean composer; b. Rengo, Colchagua, March 13, 1887; d. Santiago, July 2, 1974. He studied both music and painting in Chile; then in Italy, Spain, France, and the Netherlands. As a composer, he became interested in the folk music of the Araucanian Indians, and made use of these authentic materials in several of his works. Among them are *4 movimientos sinfonicos* (1960), *Te kuduam mapuche* for Voice, Bassoon, and the Araucanian Drum Kultrún (1958), Harp Concerto (1957), and Sonata for Flute Solo (1954). A catalogue of his works is found in *Compositores de América,* vol. XIII (Washington, D.C., 1967).

Iseler, Elmer, Canadian choral conductor; b. Port Colborne, near Niagara Falls, Ontario, Oct. 14, 1927. He studied piano and organ; then studied church music at Waterloo Lutheran Univ.; subsequently enrolled at the Univ. of Toronto (B.Mus., 1950). He taught music in high schools in Toronto (1952–64); in 1964 he became conductor of the Toronto Mendelssohn Choir; taught choral music at the Univ. of Toronto (1965–68); edited the Festival Singers of Canada Choral Series. Iseler is generally acknowledged as one of Canada's leading choral conductors.

Isepp, Martin, Austrian pianist and harpsichordist; b. Vienna, Sept. 30, 1930. He went to England; studied at Lincoln College, Oxford, and at the Royal Academy of Music in London; in 1957 he joined the music staff of the Glyndebourne Festival. From 1973–76 he was on the faculty of the Juilliard School of Music in N.Y. He became best known as an accompanist to many of the foremost singers of the day, including Dame Janet Baker, Hans Hotter, Elisabeth Schwarzkopf, and John Shirley-Quirk.

Ishii, Kan, Japanese composer, brother of **Maki Ishii;** b. Tokyo, March 30, 1921. He is one of two sons of Baku Ishii, a renowned scholar of modern dance. He studied in Tokyo at the Musashino Music School with Goh, Ikenouchi, and Odaka (1939–43); in 1952 went to Germany and took lessons in composition with Carl Orff at the Hochschule für Musik in Munich. Returning to Japan, he taught at the Toho Music Univ. and at the Aichi-Prefectural Arts Univ.; in 1970 was elected president of the All-Japan Chorus League.
WORKS: 4 operas: *Mermaid and Red Candle* (1961); *Kaguyahime* (*Prince Kaguya,* 1963); *En-no-Gyojia* (Tokyo, 1964); *Lady Kesa and Morito* (Tokyo, Nov. 24, 1968); 9 ballets: *God and the Bayadere* (Tokyo, Nov. 6, 1950); *Birth of a Human* (Tokyo, Nov. 27, 1954); *Frökln Julie* (1955); *Shakuntara*

(1961); *Marimo* (Tokyo, 1963); *Biruma no tategoto* (*Harp of Burma,* 1963); *Haniwa* (1963); *Hakai* (1965); *Ichiyo Higuchi* (1966); symph. poem, *Yama* (*Mountain,* Tokyo, Oct. 7, 1954); *Kappa's Penny* for Youth Orch. (1956); *Sinfonia Ainu* for Soprano, Chorus, and Orch. (1958–59); *The Reef,* cantata for Baritone, Chorus, 4 Pianos, and Percussion (1967); *Akita the Great* for Chorus and Brass (1968); *Music for Percussion* for 8 Players (1970); Viola Sonata (1960); Music for Solo Flute (1972); *Footsteps to Tomorrow,* cantata for Solo Soprano (1972); folk songs; choruses, etc. He compiled a valuable collection of Japanese folk songs, publ. in 6 vols.

Ishii, Maki, Japanese composer, brother of **Kan Ishii;** b. Tokyo, May 28, 1936. He received an early training in music from his father, a renowned promoter of modern dance; studied composition with Akira Ifukube and Tomojiro Ikenouchi, and conducting with Akeo Watanabe, in Tokyo (1952–58); then went to Germany, where he took courses at the Berlin Hochschule für Musik with Boris Blacher and Josef Rufer (1958–61); after a brief return to Japan he went back to Germany, where he decided to remain. In his works he attempts to combine the coloristic effects of Japanese instruments with European techniques of serial music and electronic sounds.

WORKS: Prelude and Variations for 9 Players (1959–60); *7 Stücke* for Small Orch. (1960–61); *4 Bagatelles* for Violin and Piano (1961); *Transition* for Small Orch. (1962); *Aphorismen I* for String Trio, Percussion, and Piano (1963); *Galgenlieder* for Baritone, Male Chorus, and 13 Players (1964); *Characters* for Flute, Oboe, Piano, Guitar, and Percussion (1965); *Hamon* for Violin, Chamber Ensemble, and Tape (1965); *Expressions* for String Orch. (Tokyo, Jan. 11, 1968); *5 Elements* for Guitar and 6 Players (1967); *Piano Piece* for Pianist and Percussionist (1968); *Kyō-ō* for Piano, Orch., and Tape (Tokyo, Feb. 22, 1969); *Kyō-so* for Percussion and Orch. (Tokyo, Feb. 7, 1969); *La-sen I* for 7 Players and Tape (1969); *La-sen II* for Solo Cello (1970); *Sō-gū I* for Shakuhachi and Piano (1970); *Music for Gagaku* (1970); *Dipol* for Orch. (1971); *Sō-gū II* for Gagaku and Symph. Orch. (Tokyo, June 23, 1971; work resulting from simultaneous perf. of *Music for Gagaku* and *Dipol*); *Sen-ten* for Percussion Player and Tape (1971); *Aphorismen II* for a Pianist (1972); *Chō-etsu* for Chamber Group and Tape (1973); *Polaritäten* for Soloists and Orch. (1973; work exists in 3 versions, each having different soloists: *I* for Biwa and Harp; *II* for Biwa, Shakuhachi, and Flute; *III* for Shakuhachi and Flute); *Synkretismen* for Marimba, 7 Soloists, Strings, and 3 Percussionists (1973); *Anime Amare* for Harp and Tape (1974); *Jo* for Orch. (1975); *Translucent Vision* for Orch. (1981–82).

Isidore of Seville, Spanish cleric; b. Cartagena, c.560; d. Seville, April 4, 636. He was brought to Seville as a child; in 599 became archbishop there. Between 622 and 633, compiled a treatise on the arts, *Etymologiarum sive originum libri XX;* he ex-pressed the conviction that music can only be preserved through memory, for musical sounds could never be notated (*scribi non possunt*). The text was publ. in Oxford (1911); an Eng. trans. of the pertinent parts is included in Strunk's *Source Readings in Music History* (N.Y., 1950).

BIBLIOGRAPHY: Karl Schmidt, *Quaestiones de musicis scriptoribus romanis imprimis Cassiodoro et Isidoro* (Leipzig, 1898); J. Fontaine, *Isidore de Séville et la culture classique dans l'Espagne wisigothique* (Paris, 1959); J. Madoz, *San Isidoro de Sevilla* (Madrid, 1960).

Isler, Ernst, Swiss organist and music critic; b. Zürich, Sept. 30, 1879; d. there, Sept. 26, 1944. He studied in Zürich and Berlin; served as an organist in Zürich, and taught organ there. He became music critic of the influential daily paper *Neue Zürcher Zeitung* in 1902, and held this position until his death; from 1910 to 1927 he was editor of the *Schweizerische Musikzeitung.* He publ. monographs on Hans Huber, Max Reger, etc.; also a valuable compendium, *Das Züricherische Konzertleben 1895–1914* (Zürich, 1935), and its sequel, covering the years 1914–31 (Zürich, 1936).

Ísólfsson, Páll, Icelandic organist and composer; b. Stokkseyri, Oct. 12, 1893; d. Reykjavik, Nov. 23, 1974. He studied organ at the Leipzig Cons. with Straube, and later in Paris with Bonnet. Returning to Iceland, he served as organist at the Reykjavik Cathedral (1939–68) and director of the Reykjavik Cons. and of Icelandic Radio. He wrote a number of attractive piano pieces in the manner of Grieg (humoresques, intermezzi, capriccios, etc.), choruses, and a cantata on the millennial anniversary of the Icelandic Parliament (1930); also compiled (with S. Einarsson) a collection of choral pieces by various composers. In 1963–64 he publ. his autobiography in 2 vols. (in Icelandic).

BIBLIOGRAPHY: J. Thorarinsson, *Páll Ísólfsson* (Reykjavik, 1963).

Isouard, Nicolo, important French opera composer; b. Malta, Dec. 6, 1775; d. Paris, March 23, 1818. A son of a prosperous merchant, he was sent to Paris to study engineering; afterward, he served as a clerk in Malta, in Palermo, and in Naples, where he took lessons with Sala and Guglielmi. In the spring of 1794 he produced his first opera, *L'avviso ai maritati,* in Florence; from that time on he abandoned business pursuits, dedicating himself to operatic composition. In order not to embarrass his family, and particularly his father, who was against his career as a musician, he adopted the name **Nicolo de Malte,** or simply **Nicolo.** He served as organist of St. John of Jerusalem at Malta (1795–98); in 1799, went to Paris, where he became increasingly successful as an opera composer; he was also popular as a pianist. In Paris he had to undergo strong competition with Boieldieu; but the lengthy list of productions of his operas up to 1816 shows that he had never relaxed his industry. The music of his operas demonstrates a facile melodic gift in

the French manner, as well as sound craftsmanship. Besides operas, he wrote church music. The best known of his operas are *Cendrillon, Joconde,* and *Jeannot et Colin.* A list of his operas, produced in Paris, includes: *Le Petit Page* (with R. Kreutzer; Feb. 14, 1800); *La Statue* (April 26, 1802); *L'Intrigue au sérail* (April 25, 1809); *Cendrillon* (Feb. 22, 1810); *La Victime des arts* (Feb. 27, 1811); *La Fête du village* (March 31, 1811); *Le Billet de loterie* (Sept. 14, 1811); *Le Magicien sans magie* (Nov. 4, 1811); *Lully et Quinault* (Feb. 27, 1812); *Le Prince de Catane* (March 4, 1813); *Les Français à Venise* (June 14, 1813); *Joconde* (Feb. 28, 1814); *Michel-Ange* (Dec. 11, 1802); *Les Confidences* (March 31, 1803); *Le Baiser et la quittance* (June 18, 1803); *Le Médecin turc* (Nov. 19, 1803); *L'Intrigue aux fenêtres* (Feb. 26, 1805); *Le Déjeuner de garçons* (April 24, 1805); *La Ruse inutile* (May 30, 1805); *Léonce* (Nov. 18, 1805); *La Prise de Passaw* (Feb. 8, 1806); *Idala* (July 30, 1806); *Les Rendezvous bourgeois* (May 9, 1807); *Les Créanciers* (Dec. 10, 1807); *Un Jour à Paris* (May 24, 1808); *Cimarosa* (June 28, 1808); *Jeannot et Colin* (Oct. 17, 1814); *Les deux Maris* (March 18, 1816); *L'Une pour l'autre* (May 11, 1816); *Aladin* (Feb. 6, 1822; posthumous work, completed by Benincori and Habeneck).
BIBLIOGRAPHY: E. Wahl, *Nicolo Isouard* (Munich, 1906).

Isserlis, Julius, Russian pianist; b. Kishinev, Nov. 7, 1888; d. London, July 23, 1968. He studied with Puchalski at the Kiev Cons.; then with Safonov and Taneyev at the Moscow Cons. He taught at the Moscow Phil. Inst. of Music (1913–23); then in Vienna (1923–28); in 1928, he settled in London. He wrote a number of character pieces for piano.

Istel, Edgar, eminent German musicologist; b. Mainz, Feb. 23, 1880; d. Miami, Fla., Dec. 17, 1948. He studied in Munich with Thuille and Sandberger; received his Dr.Phil. with the dissertation *J.J. Rousseau als Komponist seiner lyrischen Scene "Pygmalion"* (1900; publ. in *Publikationen der Internationa Musikgesellschaft,* I/i, Leipzig, 1901); then settled in Munich as a teacher; in 1919, taught in Berlin; in 1920 he moved to Madrid, where he remained until the outbreak of the civil war in 1936; then went to England, and eventually to the U.S. (1938). WRITINGS: *Das deutsche Weihnachtsspiel und seine Wiedergeburt aus dem Geiste der Musik* (Langensalza, 1901); *Richard Wagner im Lichte eines zeitgenössischen Briefwechsels* (1902); *Peter Cornelius* (1906); *Die Entstehung des deutschen Melodramas* (1906); *Die komische Oper* (1906); *Die Blütezeit der musikalischen Romantik in Deutschland* (1909); *Das Kunstwerk Richard Wagners* (1910); *Das Libretto* (1914; Eng. ed. as *The Art of Writing Opera Librettos,* N.Y., 1922); *Die moderne Oper vom Tode Wagners bis zum Weltkrieg* (Leipzig, 1915); *Niccolo Paganini* (Leipzig, 1919); *Revolution und Oper* (1919); *Das Buch der Oper; Die deutschen Meister von Gluck bis Wagner* (Berlin, 1919); *Bizet und Carmen* (Stuttgart, 1927). Between 1915 and 1934, he contributed a number of

articles on various composers to the *Musical Quarterly;* ed. the musical writings of E.T.A. Hoffmann, the collected essays of Cornelius, and Dittersdorf's autobiography; publ. analytical brochures on works of Mahler, Humperdinck, and others. Istel was also a composer; he wrote several operas, oratorios, and smaller pieces.

Istomin, Eugene, American pianist; b. New York, Nov. 26, 1925, of Russian parents. He studied with Rudolf Serkin at the Curtis Inst. in Philadelphia; in 1943 he won the Leventritt Award for an appearance as soloist with the N.Y. Phil. Orch. (Nov. 21, 1943), playing the 2nd Piano Concerto of Brahms. After that he developed a highly successful concert career; appeared with a number of American orchs., and also gave recitals in America and in Europe. On Feb. 15, 1975, he married Martita Casals, widow of Pablo Casals.

Istrate, Mircea, Rumanian pianist and composer; b. Cluj, Sept. 27, 1929. He studied piano and composition at the Cons. of Cluj (1945–53) and in Bucharest (1954–57); subsequently taught piano in Bucharest. He composed a Flute Sonata (1954); *Burlesca,* chamber concerto for Violin, Oboe, Clarinet, Bassoon, and Double Bass (1955); *Muzică stereofonică* for 2 String Orchs. (1955–57); *Evocare* for Mezzo-soprano, Female Chorus, and Orch. (1960); *Pe o plajă japoneză (On a Japanese Beach),* sequences for Female Chorus, Orch., and Tape (1961); Oboe Sonata (1962); *Algoritm* for Orch. (1964); *Interferente (Interferences)* for Orch. and Electronics (1965); *Evenimente I–II–III,* etc., for Prepared Piano, Percussion within a Piano, Electric Guitar, Double Bass, Vibraphone, Horn, Marimba, and Tape (1966; of variable duration); *Pulsations* for Orch. (1973); songs.

Ištvan, Miloslav, Czech composer; b. Olomouc, Sept. 2, 1928. He studied music at the Janáček Academy in Brno with Jaroslav Kvapil (1948–52); subsequently was active mainly as a music teacher. Like many of his compatriots he cultivated a national style of composition, thematically derived from folk music, but later adopted the *modus operandi* of the cosmopolitan avant-garde. In 1963 he joined the Creative Group A of Brno, dedicated to free musical experimentation "uninhibited by puritanically limited didactical regulations." He also worked in the electronic music studio of Brno Radio. WORKS: Concerto for Horn, String Orch., and Piano (1949); Symph. (1952); *Winter Suite* for Strings, Piano, and Percussion (1956); *Concerto-Symphony* for Piano and Orch. (1957); *Balada o Jihu (Ballad of the South),* 3 symph. frescoes after Lewis Allan's satirical view of the American South (Brno, Dec. 8, 1960); Concertino for Violin and Chamber Orch. (1961); *6 Studies* for Chamber Ensemble (1964; revised for Chamber Orch. and perf. at the International Society for Contemporary Music Festival, Prague, Oct. 9, 1967); *Zaklínání času (Conjuration of Time)* for Orch. and 2 Narrators (1967; Ostrava, Jan. 23, 1969); *Ja, Jakob (I, Jacob),* chamber oratorio, with Tape (1968); Sonata for Violin and Chamber Orch. (1970); *In memoriam Josef Berg* for Orch. (1971); *Hymn to the Sun,* small cantata (1971); *The Beauty and the Animal,* chamber oratorio (1974); *Shakespearean Variations* for Orch. (1975); Rondos for Viola and Piano (1950); Trio for Clarinet, Cello, and Piano (1950); Clarinet Sonata (1954); Suite for Horn and Piano (1955); Piano Trio (1958); *Rhapsody* for Cello and Piano (1961); String Quartet (1963); *Dodekameron* for 12 Players (1962–64); *Refrains* for String Trio (1965); *Ritmi ed antiritmi* for 2 Pianos and 2 Percussionists (1966); *Lamentations,* 5 songs for Alto, Piano, and Tape (1970); Cello Sonata (1970); *5 framenti* for Solo Salterio (1971); *Omaggio a J.S. Bach* for Wind Quintet (1971); *Psalmus niger* for 6 Percussionists (1971); *Blacked-Out Landscape,* in memory of those fallen in World War II, for String Quartet (1975); *Ad fontes intimas* for Double Bass or Trumpet, and Percussion (1975); 2 piano sonatas (1954, 1959); *Impromptus* for Piano (1956); *Odyssey of a Child from Lidice* for Piano (1963); *Musica aspera* for Organ (1964); Variations for 2 Pianos (1972); 2 scores of "musique concrète," *Island of Toys* (1968) and *A vete morituri* (1970); many choruses and songs.

Ito, Ryûta, Japanese composer; b. Kure City, in the Hiroshima Prefecture, March 4, 1922. He graduated from the faculty of medicine of the Univ. of Tokyo in 1946 (Doctor of Medical Science, 1955); then turned to music and studied composition with S. Takata, S. Moroi, T. Ikenouchi, and S. Fukai. Subsequently he divided his interests between music and medicine and became a prof. of pharmacy at the school of medicine of Toho Univ.; also served as secretary and a member of the committee of the Japanese Society for Contemporary Music (1952–61). Several of his works received prizes awarded by the Tokyo newspaper *Mainichi.*
WORKS: Chamber opera, *The Court of Judgment* (1954); *Allemand and Aria* for Orch. (1945; Tokyo, May 19, 1950); *2 Moments* for Orch. (1947; Tokyo, Oct. 29, 1947); *Divertissement* for Orch. (1950); *Festival Music* for Orch. (1953); *Suite* for String Orch. (1954); *Ostinato concertanto* for Piano and Orch. (1957; Tokyo, Oct. 18, 1957); *Temariuta (Handball Song)* for Orch. (1958); Concerto for Japanese Flute and Orch. (1958; Tokyo, Nov. 28, 1958); *Suzuka,* suite for Orch. (1959); *Suite* for Chamber Orch. (1959); *Suite* for Orch. (1961); *Les Cloches,* symph. suite for Japanese Instruments, Celesta, Percussion, Male Chorus, Viola, Cello, and Double Bass (1971; Tokyo, Nov. 9, 1971); several works for Japanese instruments alone.

Iturbi, José, celebrated Spanish pianist; b. Valencia, Nov. 28, 1895; d. Hollywood, June 28, 1980. He took piano lessons with Malats in Barcelona; while still a very young boy he earned a living by playing in street cafés. A local group of music lovers collected a sum of money to send him to Paris for further study; he was accepted as a student at the Paris Cons., and graduated in 1912. After a while he developed a brilliant concert career; his performances of Spanish music were acclaimed for their authentic rhythmic spirit. He made a tour of South America; in 1928 he appeared as soloist in the U.S.; during his second American tour in 1930 he gave 67 concerts. In 1936 he turned to conducting; led the Rochester Phil. until 1944. He wrote a number of pleasing piano pieces in a typical Spanish vein; of these, *Pequeña danza española* exercised considerable attraction. His sister, **Amparo Iturbi** (b. Valencia, March 12, 1898; d. Beverly Hills, Calif., April 21, 1969), was also a talented pianist; she played piano duos with José Iturbi on numerous occasions in Europe and America.
BIBLIOGRAPHY: David Ewen, *Musicians since 1900* (N.Y., 1978; pp. 363–65).

Iturriberry, Juan José, Uruguayan composer; b. Pando, Oct. 24, 1936. He studied in Montevideo with Carlos Estrada and Héctor Tosar, and also took a course in electro-acoustical techniques. His works are quaquaversal; some require electronic applications. His *Meditation in F* (1975) is concentrated on the single note F, which is repeated ad nauseam.

Ivanov, Georgi, Bulgarian composer; b. Sofia, Aug. 23, 1924. He studied with Lubomir Pipkov and Veselin Stoyanov in Sofia; then went to Moscow, where he studied with Shaporin (1946–50). Returning to Bulgaria, he became conductor of the National Youth Theater in Sofia.
WORKS: 2 symph. poems: *Legend of the Lopian Forest* (Sofia, Feb. 15, 1951) and *The Mutiny on the S.S. Nadezhda* (1955); Symph. (Sofia, June 22, 1960); Divertimento for Clarinet, Violin, Harpsichord, and Chamber Orch. (1962); *Metamorphosis* for Strings (1967); *Timbres in Rhythm* for Orch. (1968); Variations for Orch. (1969); *Musica concertante* for Orch. (1970).

Ivanov, Konstantin, Russian conductor, b. Efremov, May 21, 1907. He played trumpet in Soviet cavalry orchs.; then enrolled in the conducting class at the Moscow Cons.; after graduation in 1937, served as assistant conductor at various operatic and symph. posts. In 1941–46 he was conductor of the Bolshoi Radio Orch.; in 1946–75 acted as conductor of the State Symph. Orch. of the U.S.S.R.; made world tours with it, which included the U.S. and Japan, as well as countries of Western Europe. He was also a composer; among his works are several symph. poems and a Double-bass Concerto.

Ivanov, Mikhail, Russian music critic and composer; b. Moscow, Sept. 23, 1849; d. Rome, Oct. 20, 1927. He studied mechanical sciences at the Technological Inst. in St. Petersburg, graduating in 1869; then went to Moscow, where he took private harmony lessons with Tchaikovsky; from 1870 to 1875 he lived in Italy, where he took music lessons with Sgambati. In 1875 he returned to St. Petersburg, where he obtained the position of music critic on the influential daily newspaper *Novoye Vremya,* which he held from 1880 to 1917. After the Revolution he emigrated to Italy, where he remained until his death. A critic of reactionary tendencies, he assailed the composers of the Russian national school; endowed with a lively literary style, he made use of irony against any new musical developments; this in turn earned him the enmity of liberal musicians. He was also a composer of sorts; wrote a ballet, *Vestal Virgin* (St. Petersburg, Feb. 29, 1888); the operas *Zabava Putiatishna* (Moscow, Jan. 15, 1899) and *Potemkin Holiday* (St. Petersburg, Dec. 16, 1902); and a number of songs; publ. *Pushkin in Music* (St. Petersburg, 1899); *The Historical Development of Music in Russia* (2 vols., St. Petersburg, 1910–12); trans. into Russian Hanslick's *Von Musikalisch-Schönen.*

Ivanov, Nicolai, Russian tenor; b. Voronezh, Oct. 22, 1810; d. Bologna, July 19, 1880. He sang as a child in the Imperial Court Chapel in St. Petersburg, where he attracted the attention of Glinka, who took him to Italy in 1830; there he studied singing with Bianchi in Milan and with Joséphine Fodor-Mainvielle and Nozzari in Naples. He made his debut at the Teatro San Carlo in Naples in 1832 as Percy in Donizetti's opera *Anna Bolena;* subsequently sang in Paris at the Théâtre-Italien (1833–37); concurrently appeared in London. Later he was a member of La Scala in Milan. He retired in 1852. He was reputed to be one of the best representatives of the Italian school of *bel canto,* and enjoyed the friendship of Rossini and other famous contemporaries.
BIBLIOGRAPHY: S. Smolensky, *The Tenor Ivanov, Companion of Glinka in Italy* (St. Petersburg, 1904).

Ivanov-Boretzky, Mikhail, Russian musicologist; b. Moscow, June 16, 1874; d. there, April 1, 1936. He studied jurisprudence at the Univ. of Moscow, graduating in 1896; at the same time he took music lessons; in 1898 he went to St. Petersburg and became a student of composition of Rimsky-Korsakov; his own music was mainly imitative of Rimsky-Korsakov's works. He wrote the operas *Adolfina* (Moscow, Dec. 10, 1908) and *The Witch* (Moscow, Aug. 14, 1918); a Symph.; piano music; choruses; songs. His importance to Russian music, however, lies in his writings. He publ. monographs on Palestrina, Handel, Schumann, Mendelssohn, and Beethoven; also a useful anthology of music history, with a synoptic table of 18th-century music (Moscow, 1934), and numerous articles on Russian music. From 1921 to 1936 he taught various academic subjects at the Moscow Cons. A collection of his articles was publ. in Moscow in 1972.

Ivanov-Radkevitch, Nicolai, Russian composer; b. Krasnoyarsk, Siberia, Feb. 10, 1904; d. Moscow, Feb. 4, 1962. He studied composition with Glière and orchestration with Vasilenko at the Moscow Cons., graduating in 1928; subsequently joined its staff (1929–48). In 1952 he was appointed instructor in orchestration at the Inst. of Military Bandleaders of the Soviet Army. He was particularly successful in writing popular marches for band, of which *Our*

Own Moscow and *Victory March* received the State Prize. He also composed 4 symphs. (1928, 1932, 1937, 1945); 12 symph. suites on folk motifs; Violin Sonata; various pieces for other instruments; film music.

Ivanovici, Ion, Rumanian bandleader and composer of light music; b. Banat, 1845; d. Bucharest, Sept. 29, 1902. He played the flute and clarinet in a military band in Galatz, and in 1880 conducted his own band there. In the same year he wrote the waltz *Valurile Dunării (The Waves of the Danube),* which became a perennial favorite all over the world. He took part in the Paris Exposition of 1889, and conducted there a band of 116 musicians. In 1900 he was appointed Inspector of Military Music in Rumania. He publ. about 150 pieces for piano and dances for band.
BIBLIOGRAPHY: Viorel Cosma, *Ivanovici* (Bucharest, 1958).

Ivanovs, Janis, prolific Latvian composer; b. Preili, Oct. 9, 1906. He studied composition with Wihtol, piano with Dauge, and conducting with Schneevoigt at the Latvian Cons. in Riga, graduating in 1931; then worked at Latvian Radio; in 1949 was appointed to the composition faculty at the Latvian Cons. An exceptionally fecund composer, he wrote 20 symphs., several of a programmatic nature descriptive of the Latvian countryside: No. 1, *Symphonie-Poème* (1933); No. 2, *Atlantida* (1941); No. 6, *Latgales* (*Latvian,* 1949); No. 12, *Sinfonia energica* (1967); No. 13, *Symphonia humana* (1969). His symph. peoms also reflect nature scenes; e.g., *Varaviksne (Rainbow,* 1938) and *Padebešu Kalns (Mountain under the Sky,* 1939). He further wrote 3 string quartets (1933, 1946, 1961); a Cello Concerto (1938); Violin Concerto (1951); Piano Concerto (1959); choruses; songs; piano pieces; film music.
BIBLIOGRAPHY: N. Grünfeld, *Janis Ivanovs* (Moscow, 1959); V. Berzina, *Dzives simfonija Jana Ivanovs* (Riga, 1964; in Latvian).

Ives, Burl, American folksinger; b. Hunt Township, Jasper County, Ill., June 14, 1909. He studied briefly at N.Y. Univ.; traveled through the U.S. and Canada as an itinerant handyman, supplementing his earnings by singing and playing the banjo. He then became a dramatic actor and appeared on the stage and in films, and gave concerts of folk ballads, accompanying himself on the guitar. He publ. an autobiography, *Wayfaring Stranger* (N.Y., 1948), and the anthologies *The Burl Ives Songbook* (1953) and *The Burl Ives Book of Irish Songs* (1958).

Ives, Charles Edward, one of the most remarkable American composers, whose individual genius created music so original, so universal, and yet so deeply national in its sources of inspiration, that it profoundly changed the direction of American music; b. Danbury, Conn., Oct. 20, 1874; d. New York, May 19, 1954. His father, **George Ives,** was a bandleader of the First Connecticut Heavy Artillery during the Civil War, and the early development of Charles Ives was, according to his own testimony, deeply influenced by his father. At the age of 12, he played the drums in the band and also received from his father rudimentary musical training in piano and cornet playing. At the age of 13 he played organ at the Danbury Church; soon he began to improvise freely at the piano, without any dependence on school rules; as a result of his experimentation in melody and harmony, encouraged by his father, Charles Ives began to combine several keys, partly as a spoof, but eventually as a legitimate alternative to traditional music; at 17 he composed his *Variations on America* for organ in a polytonal setting; still earlier he wrote a band piece, *Holiday Quick Step*, which was performed by the Danbury Band in 1888. He attended the Danbury High School; in 1894 he entered Yale Univ., where he took regular academic courses and studied organ with Dudley Buck and composition with Horatio Parker; from Horatio Parker he received a fine classical training; while still in college he composed 2 full-fledged symphs., written in an entirely traditional manner demonstrating great skill in formal structure, fluent melodic development, and smooth harmonic modulations. After his graduation from Yale Univ., in 1898, Ives joined an insurance company; also played organ at the Central Presbyterian Church in N.Y. (1899–1902). In 1907 he formed an insurance partnership with Julian Myrick of N.Y.; he proved himself to be an exceptionally able businessman; the firm of Ives & Myrick prospered, and Ives continued to compose music as an avocation. In 1908 he married Harmony Twichell. In 1918 he suffered a massive heart attack, complicated by a diabetic condition, and was compelled to curtail his work both in business and in music to a minimum because his illness made it difficult to handle a pen. He retired from business in 1930, and by that time had virtually stopped composing. In 1919 Ives publ. at his own expense his great masterpiece, *Concord Sonata*, for piano, inspired by the writings of Emerson, Hawthorne, the Alcotts, and Thoreau. Although written early in the century, its idiom is so extraordinary, and its technical difficulties so formidable, that the work did not receive a performance in its entirety until John Kirkpatrick played it in N.Y. in 1939. In 1922 Ives brought out, also at his expense, a volume of *114 Songs*, written between 1888 and 1921 and marked by great diversity of style, ranging from lyrical Romanticism to powerful and dissonant modern invocations. Both the *Concord Sonata* and the *114 Songs* were distributed gratis by Ives himself to anyone wishing to receive copies. His orch. masterpiece, *Three Places in New England*, also had to wait nearly 2 decades before its first performance; of the monumental 4th Symph., only the 2nd movement was performed in 1927, and its complete performance was given posthumously in 1965. In 1947 Ives received the Pulitzer Prize for his 3rd Symph., written in 1911. The slow realization of the greatness of Ives and the belated triumphant recognition of his music were phenomena without precedent in music history. Because of his chronic ailment, and also on account of his personal disposition, Ives lived as a recluse, away from the mainstream of American musical life; he never went to concerts and did not own a record player or a radio; while he was well versed in the musical classics, and studied the scores of Beethoven, Schumann, and Brahms, he took little interest in sanctioned works of modern composers; yet he anticipated many technical innovations, such as polytonality, atonality, and even 12-tone formations, as well as polymetric and polyrhythmic configurations, which were prophetic for his time. In the 2nd movement of the *Concord Sonata* he specified the application of a strip of wood on the white and the black keys of the piano to produce an echo-like sonority; in his unfinished *Universe Symphony* he planned an antiphonal representation of the heavens in chordal counterpoint and the earth in contrasting orch. groups. He also composed pieces of quarter-tone piano music. A unique quality of his music was the combination of simple motifs, often derived from American church hymns and popular ballads, with an extremely complex dissonant counterpoint which formed the supporting network for the melodic lines. A curious idiosyncrasy is the frequent quotation of the "fate motive" of Beethoven's 5th Symph. in many of his works. Materials of his instrumental and vocal works often overlap, and the titles are often changed during the process of composition. In his orchestrations he often indicated interchangeable and optional parts, as in the last movement of the *Concord Sonata*, which has a part for flute obbligato; thus he reworked the original score for large orch. of his *3 Places in New England* for a smaller ensemble to fit the requirements of Slonimsky's Chamber Orch. of Boston, which gave its first performance, and it was in this version that the work was first publ. and widely performed until the restoration of the large score was made in 1974. Ives possessed an uncommon gift for literary expression; his annotations to his works are both trenchant and humorous; he publ. in 1920 *Essays before a Sonata* as a literary companion vol. to the *Concord Sonata;* his *Memos* in the form of a diary, publ. after his death, reveal an extraordinary power of aphoristic utterance. He was acutely conscious of his civic duties as an American, and once circulated a proposal to have federal laws enacted by popular referendum. His centennial in 1974 was celebrated by a series of conferences at his alma mater at Yale Univ., in N.Y., in Miami and many other American cities, and in Europe, including Russia. While during his lifetime he and a small group of devoted friends and admirers had great difficulties in having his works performed, recorded, or publ., a veritable Ives cult emerged after his death; eminent conductors gave repeated performances of his orch. works, and modern pianists were willing to cope with the forbidding difficulties of his works. In the number of orch. performances, in 1976 Ives stood highest among modern composers on American programs, and the influence of his music on the new generation of composers reached a high mark, so that the adjective "Ivesian" became common in music criticism to describe certain acoustical and coloristic effects characteristic of his music. America's youth expressed especial enthusiasm for Ives, which received its most unusual tribute in the commercial marketing of a T-shirt with Ives's portrait. All of the Ives MSS and his correspondence were deposited by Mrs. Ives at Yale Univ., forming a basic Ives archive.

WORKS: FOR ORCH.: 4 symphs.: No. 1 (1896–98); No. 2 (1897–1902; N.Y., Feb. 22, 1951); No. 3 (1901–4; N.Y., April 5, 1946); No. 4 (1910–16; 2nd movement only perf., N.Y., Jan. 29, 1927; first perf. in its entirety was given in N.Y. on April 26, 1965, Leopold Stokowski conducting the American Symph. Orch.); also incomplete fragments of a *Universe Symphony* (1911–16); *3 Places in New England* (*Orchestral Set No. 1: The "St. Gaudens" in Boston Common; Putnam's Camp, Redding, Connecticut; The Housatonic at Stockbridge;* 1903–14; N.Y., Jan. 10, 1931, Chamber Orch. of Boston, Nicolas Slonimsky conducting); *Calcium Light Night* for Chamber Orch. (1898–1907); *Central Park in the Dark* (1898–1907; Columbia Univ., N.Y., May 11, 1946); *The Unanswered Question* (1908); *Theater Orchestra Set: In the Cage, In the Inn, In the Night* (1904–11); *The Pond* (1906); *Browning Overture* (1911); *The Gong on the Hook and Ladder, or Firemen's Parade on Main Street* for Chamber Orch. (1911); *Lincoln, the Great Commoner* for Chorus and Orch. (1912); *A Symphony: Holidays,* in 4 parts, also perf. separately: *Washington's Birthday* (1913), *Decoration Day* (1912), *4th of July* (1913), *Thanksgiving and/or Forefathers' Day* (1904); *Over the Pavements* for Chamber Orch. (1913); *Orchestral Set No. 2* (1915); *Tone Roads* for Chamber Orch. (1911–15); *Orchestral Set No. 3* (1919–27). CHAMBER MUSIC: String Quartet No. 1, subtitled *A Revival Service* (1896); *Prelude,* from "Pre-First Sonata," for Violin and Piano (1900); Trio for Violin, Clarinet, and Piano (1902); "Pre-Second String Quartet" (1905); *Space and Duration* for String Quartet and a very mechanical Piano (1907); *All the Way Around and Back* for Piano, Violin, Flute, Bugle, and Bells (1907); *The Innate* for String Quartet and Piano (1908); *Adagio Sostenuto* for English Horn, Flute, Strings, and Piano (1910); Violin Sonata No. 1 (1908); Violin Sonata No. 2 (1910); Trio for Violin, Cello, and Piano (1911); String Quartet No. 2 (1913); Violin Sonata No. 3 (1914); *Set for String Quartet and Piano* (1914); Violin Sonata No. 4, subtitled *Children's Day at the Camp Meeting* (1915). VOCAL WORKS: *Psalm 67* (1898); *The Celestial Country,* cantata (1899); *3 Harvest Home Chorales* for Mixed Chorus, Brass, Double Bass, and Organ (1898–1912); *General William Booth Enters into Heaven* for Chorus with Brass Band (1914); *114 Songs* (1884–1921). PIANO PIECES: *3-page Sonata* (1905); *Some Southpaw Pitching* (1908); *The Anti-Abolitionist Riots* (1908); Sonata No. 1 (1909); *22* (1912); *3 Protests for Piano* (1914); Sonata No. 2 for Piano, subtitled *Concord, Mass., 1840–1860,* in 4 movements: *Emerson, Hawthorne, The Alcotts, Thoreau* (1909–15; publ. 1919; first perf. in its entirety by John Kirkpatrick, N.Y., Jan. 20, 1939; the 2nd movement requires the application of a strip of wood on the keys to produce tone-clusters; *3 Quartertone Piano Pieces* (1903–24).

WRITINGS: As a companion piece to his "Concord Sonata" (Piano Sonata No. 2), Ives wrote *Essays before a Sonata* (publ. N.Y., 1920), commentaries on the Concord writers who inspired his work, and on various musical and philosophical matters; this has been reprinted as *Essays before a Sonata and Other Writings,* ed. by Howard Boatwright (N.Y., 1961). Most of his other expository writings are publ. as *Memos,* ed. by John Kirkpatrick (N.Y., 1972), composed of autobiography, explanation, and criticism.

BIBLIOGRAPHY: Henry Bellamann, "Charles Ives, The Man and His Music," *Musical Quarterly* (Jan. 1933); Henry Cowell, "Charles Ives," in *American Composers on American Music* (Stanford Univ., 1933); Paul Rosenfeld, *Discoveries of a Music Critic* (N.Y., 1936); Paul Rosenfeld, "Ives' Concord Sonata," *Modern Music* (Jan.–Feb. 1939); Madeleine Goss, *Modern Music Makers* (N.Y., 1952); N. Slonimsky, "Charles Ives, America's Musical Prophet," *Musical America* (Feb. 15, 1954); Henry and Sidney Cowell, *Charles Ives and His Music* (the basic biography; N.Y., 1955; reprinted with additional material, 1969); Gilbert Chase, *America's Music* (N.Y., 1955); J. Kirkpatrick, *A Temporary Mimeographed Catalogue of the Music Manuscripts and Related Materials of Charles Edward Ives* (New Haven, 1960); S.R. Charles, "The Use of Borrowed Materials in Ives' Second Symphony," *Music Review* (May 1967); D. Marshall, "Charles Ives' Quotations: Manner or Substance?" *Perspectives of New Music* (Spring–Summer 1968); J. Bernlef and R. de Leeuw, *Charles Ives* (Amsterdam, 1969); Dominique-René de Lerma, *Charles Edward Ives, 1874–1954: A Bibliography of His Music* (Kent, Ohio, 1970); Richard Warren Jr., compiler, *Charles E. Ives: Discography* (Yale Univ. Library, New Haven, 1972); H. Wiley Hitchcock, *Music in the United States: A Historical Introduction* (Englewood Cliffs, N.J., 1969; 2nd ed., 1974); V. Perlis, *Charles Ives Remembered: An Oral History* (New Haven, Conn., 1974; won the 1974 Kinkeldey Award); Rosalie Sandra Perry, *Charles Ives and the American Mind* (Kent, Ohio, 1974); David Wooldridge, *From the Steeples and Mountains: A Study of Charles Ives* (N.Y., 1974); Frank R. Rossiter, *Charles Ives and His America* (N.Y., 1975); H. Wiley Hitchcock, *Charles Ives* (London, 1977); H. Wiley Hitchcock and Vivian Perlis, *An Ives Celebration: Papers and Panels of the Charles Ives Centennial Festival-Conference* (Urbana, Ill., 1977); Helen Sive, *Music's Connecticut Yankee* (N.Y., 1977); Betty E. Chmaj, *Sonata for American Studies: Perspectives on Charles Ives* (Sacramento, 1978); H. Wiley Hitchcock, *Ives: A Survey of the Music* (N.Y., 1983). The Charles Ives Society, in N.Y., promotes research and publications. Letters from Charles Ives to Nicolas Slonimsky are reproduced in the latter's book *Music since 1900* (4th ed., N.Y., 1971). A television movie, "A Good Dissonance Like a Man," produced and directed by Theodor W. Timreck in 1977, with the supervision of Vivian Perlis, depicts the life of Ives with fine dramatic impact. See also *Modern Music . . . Analytical Index,* compiled by Wayne Shirley and ed. by William and Carolyn Lichtenwanger (N.Y., 1976; pp. 107–8).

Ives (Ive), Simon, English composer; b. Ware

(baptized, July 20), 1600; d. London, July 1, 1662. He was organist in Newgate and a choral master at St. Paul's Cathedral in London; wrote music for masques at the court; in 1633 contributed material to Shirley's masque *The Triumph of Peace*. His songs, catches, and rounds were publ. in several 17th-century collections: Playford's *Select Ayres and Dialogues* (1669) and *Musical Companion* (1672), Hilton's *Catch that Catch can* (1652), etc. He also wrote instrumental music, some of which was included in *Musick's Recreation* (1652 and 1661).

Ivogün, Maria, Hungarian soprano; b. Budapest, Nov. 18, 1891. Her real name was **Ilse von Günther,** which she histrionically compressed into I(lse)vo(n)gün(ther) = Ivogün. Her father was an officer, her mother an operetta singer. She went to Vienna to study with Irene Schlemmer-Ambros; then moved to Munich, where she took lessons with Hanny Schöner. She made a successful operatic debut at the Bavarian State Opera in Munich in 1913, as Mimi in *La Bohème;* in 1925 she joined the Städtische Oper in Berlin, remaining on its roster until 1934. In 1922 she went on a concert tour in the U.S. She also appeared at Covent Garden in London, at La Scala in Milan, and at the Salzburg Festivals. She retired from the stage in 1932, and became active as a voice teacher; from 1948–50 she taught at the Vienna Academy of Music, and from 1950–58 was on the faculty of the Berlin Hochschule für Musik. She was married twice: to the tenor **Karl Erb** from 1921–32 and to her accompanist **Michael Raucheisen** in 1933.

Ivry, Richard d', French opera composer; b. Beaune, Feb. 4, 1829; d. Hyères, Dec. 18, 1903. He studied music as an avocation; wrote mostly for the stage; also wrote songs and hymns; composed several grand operas: *Les Amants de Vérone,* after *Romeo and Juliet* (Paris, Oct. 12, 1878); *Fatma, Omphale et Pénélope,* etc. He used the anagram **Yrvid** as a nom de plume.

Iwaki, Hiroyuki, distinguished Japanese conductor; b. Tokyo, Sept. 6, 1932. He was educated in Tokyo; then conducted many of the major Japanese orchs. In 1969 he assumed the post of chief conductor of the NHK (Japan Broadcasting Corp.) Symph. Orch.; in 1974 he also became chief conductor of the Melbourne (Australia) Symph.; in addition, was principal guest conductor of the Atlanta Symph. In Europe, he received encomiums for his appearances with the Berlin and Vienna Phil. orchs.

Iwamoto, Marito, Japanese violinist; b. Tokyo, Jan. 19, 1926. She studied at the Music Academy in Tokyo; played at 14 with the Tokyo Symph. Orch. She made her American debut in N.Y. on June 14, 1950, with considerable success, and remained in the U.S.

J

Jacchia, Agide, Italian conductor; b. Lugo, Jan. 5, 1875; d. Siena, Nov. 29, 1932. He studied at the Cons. of Parma and at the Liceo Musicale in Pesaro; won prizes as a flute player (1896), as apprentice conductor (1897), and as composer (1898). He made his conducting debut in Brescia on Dec. 26, 1898; then filled in numerous engagements as a theater conductor in Italy. In 1902 he accompanied Mascagni on his American tour; also conducted the Milan Opera Co. on its American tour in 1907–9. He was conductor of the Montreal Opera Co. (1910–13) and of the Boston National Opera (1915–16). From 1918 to 1926 he conducted the Boston Pops concerts; then returned to Italy.

Jachet di Mantua (Jaquet Collebaud de Vitré), French-born Italian composer; b. Vitré, 1483; d. Mantua, Oct. 2, 1559. He went to Mantua about 1526, and became its citizen in 1534. He was titular maestro di cappella at the Cathedral of Peter and Paul from 1534–59. His publ. works include 4-part motets (Venice, 1539); 5-part motets (Venice, 1540); a Mass in 4 parts (Paris, 1554); masses in 5 parts (Venice, 1555); *Messe dei Fiore* in 5 parts (Venice, 1555); Passions in 5 parts (Venice, 1567); and other sacred pieces. A complete edition of his works began publication in 1970 under the editorship of P. Jackson and G. Nugent in Corpus Mensurabilis Musicae.

BIBLIOGRAPHY: G. Reese, *Music in the Renaissance* (N.Y., 1954; 2nd ed., revised, 1959); P. Jackson, *The Vesper Hymns of Jachet di Mantua* (Diss., Univ. of North Carolina, 1965); idem, *The Masses of Jachet di Mantua* (Diss., Univ. of North Carolina, 1968); G. Nugent, *The Jacquet Motets and Their Authors* (Diss., Princeton Univ., 1973).

Jachimecki, Zdzislaw, eminent Polish musicologist; b. Lwow, July 7, 1882; d. Cracow, Oct. 27, 1953. He studied in Lwow with S. Niewiadomski and H. Jarecki, and in Vienna with Adler (musicology) and Schoenberg (composition); received a Dr.Phil. with the dissertation *150 Psalms by Mikolaj Gomolka* (1906). He then became a member of the faculty at the Univ. of Cracow. Jachimecki was one of the most renowned Polish musicologists; he was also a composer of choral works; was a conductor of symph. concerts in Cracow from 1908–24. Most of his writings were publ. in Polish, in Cracow. They include *The Influence of Italian Music on Polish Music* (1911); *Organ Tablature of the Holy Ghost Cloister in Cracow, 1548* (1913); *Music of the Royal Court of King Wladyslaw Jagiello* (1915); *Outlines of Polish History of Music* (Warsaw, 1919); *Moniuszko* (Warsaw, 1921); *Chopin* (1926; in French as *F.*

Chopin et son œuvre, Paris, 1930); monographs on Mozart, Haydn, Wagner, Szymanowski, etc.; he also contributed an article on Moniuszko to the *Musical Quarterly* (Jan. 1928); publ. *Muzyka Polska* (2 vols., 1948, 1951).

Jachino, Carlo, Italian composer; b. San Remo, Feb. 3, 1887; d. Rome, Dec. 23, 1971. He studied with Luporini in Lucca and with Riemann in Leipzig; then taught at the Parma Cons. (until 1936), at Naples (1936–38), and at the Santa Cecilia Academy in Rome (1938–50). He then went to South America; was director of the National Cons. in Bogotá, Colombia (1953–57); returning to Italy, he served as artistic director of the Teatro San Carlo in Naples (1961–69). His opera *Giocondo e il suo rè* was produced in Milan (June 24, 1924). He also wrote several works of chamber music; a treatise on the 12-tone method of composition, *Tecnica dodecafonica* (Milan, 1948); and *Gli strumenti d'orchestra* (Milan, 1950). In his early compositions he followed the Romantic Italian style; later he adopted a modified 12-tone method.

Jackson, George K., English-American organist and theorist; b. Oxford (baptized, April 15), 1757; d. Boston, Mass., Nov. 18, 1822. He was a pupil of Dr. James Narer; became a surplice boy at the Chapel Royal, London; was among the tenor singers at the Handel Commemoration in 1784; in 1791, received a Mus.Doc. from St. Andrew's College. In 1796 he came to Norfolk, Va., then to Elizabeth, N.J., and N.Y. (in 1804, became music director at St. George's Chapel). By 1812 he was in Boston, where he remained as an organist at various churches; also gave a series of oratorios with Graupner and Mallet. A collection of his music is in the library of the Harvard Music Association, Boston. He publ. *First Principles, or a Treatise on Practical Thorough Bass* (London, 1795); *David's Psalms* (1804); *A Choice Collection of Chants* (1816); *The Choral Companion* (1817); *Watt's Divine Hymns set to music.*
BIBLIOGRAPHY: F.J. Metcalf, *American Writers and Compilers of Sacred Music* (1925); H.E. Johnson, "George K. Jackson, Doctor of Music (1745–1822)," *Musical Quarterly* (Jan. 1943).

Jackson, George Pullen, American folklorist and writer; b. Monson, Maine, Aug. 20, 1874; d. Nashville, Tenn., Jan. 19, 1953. He studied philology in Dresden and at the Univ. of Chicago (Ph.B., 1904; Ph.D., 1911); was a teacher of German at Vanderbilt Univ. (1918–43); founder of the Tennessee State Sacred Harp Singing Association; was elected president of the Tennessee Folklore Society (1942).
WRITINGS: *The Rhythmic Form of the German Folk Songs* (1917); *White Spirituals in the Southern Uplands* (1933); *Spiritual Folksongs of Early America* (1937; 2nd ed., 1953); *White and Negro Spirituals* (1943); *Story of the Sacred Harp* (1944); *Another Sheaf of White Spirituals* (1952).

Jackson, Mahalia, black American singer; b. New Orleans, Oct. 26, 1911; d. Evergreen Park, Ill., Jan. 27, 1972. She went to Chicago and was employed as a hotel maid; sang in Baptist churches; operated a beauty salon; owned a flower shop. She revealed an innate talent for expressive hymn singing, and soon was in demand for conventions and political meetings. She steadfastly refused to appear in nightclubs. In 1952 she made a triumphant European tour; other successful appearances followed. She publ. her autobiography as a "soul singer" under the title *Movin' On Up* (N.Y., 1966).

Jackson, Michael, black American rock superstar; b. Gary, Ind., Aug. 29, 1958. He began his career as a ryhthm-and-blues singer; then joined his 4 brothers in a group billed as The Jackson Five, which scored immediate success. But Michael Jackson soon outshone his brothers and was accorded superstar status in the field of popular music with his lycanthropic album *Thriller* (1983), also issued in videocassette, in which Jackson turns into a werewolf, scaring his sweet girl friend out of her wits. The album sold some 30 million copies universewide, certified in the *Guinness Book of World Records* in 1984 as the largest sale ever of a single album. According to one enthusiast, Jackson could count on an audience of one-quarter of the entire earth's population (c.2,000,000,000). In 1984 he won a record number of 8 Grammys for his assorted talents. Jackson's androgynous appearance and his penchant for outlandish apparel (he wore a sequined naval commodore's costume at the Grammy show) seem to act like a stream of powerful pheromones on squealing admiring youths of both sexes. Jackson suffered a minor catastrophe when his hair caught fire during the filming of a TV commercial, and he had to be outfitted with an inconspicuous hairpiece to cover the burned spot.
BIBLIOGRAPHY: *Current Biography* (Nov. 1983); *Rolling Stone* (March 15, 1984); N. George, *The Michael Jackson Story* (N.Y., 1984).

Jackson, Milt(on) ("Bags"), black American jazz vibraphonist, pianist, and guitarist; b. Detroit, Jan. 1, 1923. He began his career in 1945 with Dizzy Gillespie; after working with several other musicians, he organized the Milt Jackson Quartet in 1951, with John Lewis, Ray Brown, and Kenny Clarke; in 1952 it was renamed the Modern Jazz Quartet, a group that was crucial in the synthesis of "cool" jazz with "classical" jazz which eventually came to be known as Third Stream. The Modern Jazz Quartet disbanded in 1974.

Jackson, Samuel P., American organist; b. Manchester, England, Feb. 5, 1818; d. Brooklyn, N.Y., July 27, 1885. Son of the organ builder James Jackson, he was taken to America in 1825, and learned his father's trade. He filled in positions at various churches as an organist; for many years was music proofreader for G. Schirmer, Inc., in N.Y. He publ. a variety of vocal sacred works, the collection *Gems for the Organ*, and 4 books of *Organ-Voluntaries.*

Jackson, William (I), English organist and composer; b. Exeter, May 29, 1730; d. there, July 5, 1803. He was a pupil of Sylvester, organist of Exeter Cathedral, and of J. Travers in London. After teaching for years at Exeter, he became (1777) organist and choirmaster at the Cathedral. Besides the operas *The Lord of the Manor* (London, Dec. 27, 1780) and *Metamorphoses* (London, Dec. 5, 1783), he composed odes (Warton's *Ode to Fancy;* Pope's *The Dying Christian to his Soul;* etc.) and a large number of songs, canzonets, madrigals, pastorals, hymns, anthems, church services, etc.; also sonatas for harpsichord.

WRITINGS: *30 Letters on Various Subjects* (London, 1782); *Observations on the Present State of Music in London* (1791); *The Four Ages, together with Essays on Various Subjects* (1798).

Jackson, William (II), English organist and composer; b. Masham, Yorkshire, Jan. 9, 1815; d. Bradford, April 15, 1866. A self-taught musician, he became organist at Masham in 1832; won first prize, offered by the Huddersfield Glee Club, in 1840; in 1852 established a music business and became organist of St. John's Church at Bradford; later was conductor of Bradford Choral Union.

Jacob, Benjamin, English organist; b. London, May 15, 1778; d. there, Aug. 24, 1829. He was a pupil of Willoughby, Shrubsole, and Arnold (1796); served as organist at various churches, finally at Surrey Chapel (1794–1825). With Wesley and Crotch, he gave organ recitals (1808–14), which were attended by large crowds; conducted a series of oratorios in 1800, and the Lenten Oratorios at Covent Garden in 1818. Jacob was very active in spreading the Bach cult in London (see O.A. Mansfield, "J.S. Bach's First English Apostles," *Musical Quarterly,* April 1935). He publ. *National Psalmody* (London, 1819) and other collections; also glees and catches.

Jacob, Gordon, English composer and pedagogue; b. London, July 5, 1895; d. Saffron Walden, England, June 8, 1984. He studied music theory with Stanford at the Royal College of Music, and from 1926 to 1966 was on its faculty; also served as examiner of other music schools. In 1968 he was named a Commander of the Order of the British Empire.

WORKS: 2 symphs. (1929, 1944); 3 sinfoniettas (1942, 1951, 1953); *Variations on an Air by Purcell* for Strings (1930); Viola Concerto (1925); Concerto for Piano and String Orch. (1927); Concerto for Oboe and Strings (1933); Concerto for Bassoon, Strings, and Percussion (1947); *Rhapsody* for English Horn and Strings (1948); Concerto for Horn and Orch. (1951); Concerto for Violin and String Orch. (1953); Violin Concerto (1954); Cello Concerto (1955); Trombone Concerto (1952); Divertimento for Harmonica and Strings (1954); 2nd Piano Concerto (1956); 2nd Oboe Concerto (1956); Concerto for Woodwind Instruments (1971); also a considerable amount of chamber music: Quartet for Oboe and Strings (1938); Quintet for Clarinet and Strings (1942); Suite for 4 Trombones (1968); Piano Trio

(1955); Cello Sonata (1957); piano works; arrangements of Schumann's *Carnaval* and suites from works by William Byrd, Orlando Gibbons, Liszt, Chopin, etc., suitable for ballet performances; choral pieces, both secular and sacred; the books *Orchestral Technique: A Manual for Students* (Oxford, 1931), *How to Read a Score* (Oxford, 1944), *The Composer and His Art* (London, 1955), and *The Elements of Orchestration* (London, 1962).

Jacob, Maxime, French composer; b. Bordeaux, Jan. 13, 1906; d. at the Benedictine Abbey at En-Calcat (Tarn), Feb. 26, 1977. He studied music in Paris with Gédalge, Koechlin, and Darius Milhaud. Pursuing a whimsical mode, he became associated with the so-called Ecole d'Arcueil, named after a modest Paris suburb where Erik Satie presided over his group of disciples; then made a 180° turn toward established religion, and in 1930 entered the Benedictine Order, where he served mainly as an organist. He continued to compose prolifically; between 1929 and 1949 he wrote 15 piano sonatas, 3 violin sonatas, 2 cello sonatas, etc.; then produced 8 string quartets (1961–69); a curious *Messe syncopée* (1968); 500 or more songs.

BIBLIOGRAPHY: Jean Roy, "Maxime Jacob," *Revue Musicale* (July 1939).

Jacobi, Erwin, Swiss musicologist; b. Strasbourg, Sept. 21, 1909; d. Zürich, Feb. 27, 1979. He studied economics in Berlin, obtaining a diploma of engineering in 1933; from 1934 to 1952 he lived in Israel; there he studied harpsichord with Pelleg and composition with Ben-Haim; in 1952 he went to America, where he took lessons in harpsichord playing with Wanda Landowska, composition with Hindemith, and music history with Curt Sachs. In 1953 he went to Switzerland to work at the Univ. of Zürich as a graduate student, in 1961 he became an assistant lecturer there. In 1970 he was a visiting prof. at the Univ. of Iowa, and in 1971 was active in the same capacity at Indiana Univ. He contributed a great number of valuable papers on Baroque composers to various musicological journals; of these the most important was a dissertation on the evolution of music theory in England (publ. in Strasbourg, 1957–60; new ed., Baden-Baden, 1971).

Jacobi, Frederick, American composer; b. San Francisco, May 4, 1891; d. New York, Oct. 24, 1952. He studied piano with Paolo Gallico and Rafael Joseffy, and composition with Rubin Goldmark; then took private lessons with Ernest Bloch. Subsequently he was on the faculty of the Juilliard School of Music in N.Y. (1936–50), and served as a member of the executive board of the League of Composers. In his own music he often made use of authentic American Indian themes; also drew from jazz, black music, folk songs, and even some Hebraisms. WORKS: Opera, *The Prodigal Son* (1944); for Orch.: *The Pied Piper,* symph. poem (1915); *A California Suite* (San Francisco, Dec. 6, 1917); 2 symphs.: No. 1, *Assyrian* (San Francisco, Nov. 14, 1924); No. 2 (San Francisco, April 1, 1948); *Ode for*

Orchestra (San Francisco, Feb. 12, 1943); Concertino for Piano and String Orch. (Saratoga Springs, Sept. 3, 1946); *2 Assyrian Prayers* for Voice and Orch. (1923); *The Poet in the Desert* for Baritone Solo, Chorus, and Orch. (1925); *Sabbath Evening Service* for Baritone Solo and Mixed Chorus (1931); 3 string quartets (1924, 1933, 1945); *Impressions from the Odyssey* for Violin and Piano (1947); *Meditation* for Trombone and Piano (1947); miscellaneous piano pieces and songs.

BIBLIOGRAPHY: David Diamond, "Frederick Jacobi," *Modern Music* (March–April 1937).

Jacobi, George, violinist and composer; b. Berlin, Feb. 13, 1840; d. London, Sept. 13, 1906. He studied in Brussels with Bériot and in Paris with Massart and Gevaert; won first prize (violin) at the Paris Cons. in 1861; became first violinist at the Paris Opéra and also conducted concerts in Paris. In 1871 he became conductor at the Alhambra Theatre in London; from 1896, taught at the Royal College of Music. He wrote about 100 ballets and a comic opera, *The Black Crook,* which attained temporary popularity.

Jacobs, Arthur, English music critic, lexicographer, opera librettist and translator; b. Manchester, June 14, 1922. He studied at Oxford Univ. From 1947 to 1952 he was music critic for the *Daily Express* and has since then written articles for a number of publications. From 1960 to 1971 he was an associate editor of the London monthly *Opera.* In 1952 he publ. a book on Gilbert and Sullivan. He then became deeply involved in musical lexicography; compiled an uncommonly intelligent, compact reference work, *A New Dictionary of Music* (London, 1958; 2nd ed., 1967; reprints with revisions, 1968, 1970; completely revised in 1977). In 1964 Jacobs was appointed a lecturer in music history at the Royal Academy of Music, London; was visiting prof. at the Univ. of Illinois (1967), at the Univ. of Calif., Santa Barbara (1969), and at Temple Univ. in Philadelphia (1970, 1971); he also toured Australia and Russia. In 1979 he became head of music at Huddersfield Polytechnic. An accomplished linguist, he mastered Russian, German, French, and Italian; trans., with admirable fidelity to the syllabic and musical values of the originals, some 20 operas, among them Tchaikovsky's *The Queen of Spades,* Schoenberg's *Erwartung,* and Alban Berg's *Lulu;* wrote the libretto of Nicholas Maw's opera *One Man Show* (London, 1964). Several of these translations have been adopted by the Royal Opera, Covent Garden, and Sadler's Wells Opera (from 1974 the English National Opera) in London. In 1971 he was appointed editor of the *Music Yearbook,* publ. in London.

Jacobs, Paul, American pianist; b. New York, June 22, 1930; d. there, a victim of AIDS (Acquired Immune Deficiency Syndrome), Sept. 25, 1983. He was a prototypical child prodigy, but overcame his musical precocity by an extraordinary intellectual endeavor, specializing in the twin aspects of structural composition, Baroque and avant-garde; he played the former on the harpsichord; by disposition and natural selection he eschewed Romantic music. He studied piano with Ernest Hutcheson; from 1951–60 he was in Europe; gave an unprecedented recital in Paris of a complete cycle of piano music of Schoenberg; became associated with the European centers of avant-garde music, at the Domaine Musical in Paris, at the contemporary music festivals in Darmstadt, and in various other localities. Returning to the U.S., he was appointed official pianist of the N.Y. Phil. in 1962; also taught at the Manhattan School of Music and at Brooklyn College, remaining on its faculty until his death. He recorded the piano works of Debussy, Schoenberg, Stravinsky, Elliot Carter, and others.

Jacobs-Bond, Carrie. See **Bond, Carrie Jacobs.**

Jacobson, Maurice, English publisher and composer; b. London, Jan. 1, 1896; d. Brighton, Feb. 1, 1976. He studied at the Royal College of Music in London with Stanford and Holst; wrote stage music for Shakespeare productions for the Old Vic Theatre. In 1923 he joined the music publishing house J. Curwen & Sons, Ltd., and in 1950 was elected its president. Among his compositions are the ballet *David* (1935); the cantatas *The Lady of Shalott* (1940) and *The Hound of Heaven* (1953); many short instrumental pieces and songs.

Jacobsthal, Gustav, German music theorist; b. Pyritz, Pomerania, March 14, 1845; d. Berlin, Nov. 9, 1912. He studied at the Univ. of Strasbourg (1863–70); from 1872, taught music there; publ. the valuable treatises *Die Mensuralnotenschrift des 12. und 13. Jahrhunderts* (1871) and *Die chromatische Alteration im liturgischen Gesange der abendländischen Kirche* (1897). F. Ludwig and E. Schmidt publ. a tribute to him, *Trauerfeier für Gustav Jacobsthal* (Berlin, 1912).

BIBLIOGRAPHY: Friedrich Gennrich, *Die Strassburger Schule für Musikwissenschaft* (1940).

Jacoby, Hanoch, Israeli composer and violist; b. Königsberg, March 2, 1909. He studied composition with Hindemith at the Hochschule für Musik in Berlin (1927–30); was a member of the radio orch. in Frankfurt (1930–33); in 1934 emigrated to Jerusalem; taught at the Jerusalem Music Academy until 1958, when he joined the Israel Phil. Orch. as a violist.

WORKS: 3 symphs. (1940, 1951, 1960); Viola Concerto (1939); Violin Concerto (1942); *King David's Lyre* for Small Orch. (1948); *7 Miniatures* for Small Orch. (1945); *Capriccio Israélien* for Orch. (1951); Sinfonietta (1960); *Serio Giocoso* for Orch. (1964); *Partita concertata* for Orch. (1970–71); *Mutatio* for Orch. (1975); *Variations* for Orch. (1976); *Jewish Oriental Folklore,* suite for String Orch. (1977); Concertino for String Trio (1932); 2 string quartets (1937, 1938); *Theme, Variations and Finale* for Piano Trio (1940); Wind Quintet (1946); *Canzona* for Solo Harp (1960); *2 Suites of Jewish Oriental Folklore* for Brass Quintet (1975); *Mutatio II* for Oboe,

Bassoon, 2 Trumpets, 2 Trombones, 2 Violas, and Double Bass (1976).

Jacopo da Bologna (Jacobus de Bononia), 14th-century composer, one of the earliest representatives of the Florentine "Ars nova". He wrote madrigals, *ballate,* etc.; his MSS are in the libraries of Florence and Paris and at the British Museum in London. His complete works are publ. in W.T. Marrocco, *The Music of Jacopo da Bologna* (Berkeley and Los Angeles, 1954). Johannes Wolf publ. 3 madrigals in his *Geschichte der Mensuralnotation* (nos. 40–42); one madrigal is in G. Reese's *Music in the Middle Ages* (N.Y., 1940; p. 363), and another in A.T. Davison and W. Apel, *Historical Anthology of Music* (Cambridge, Mass., 1947).
 BIBLIOGRAPHY: J. Wolf, "L'arte del biscanto misurato secondo el maestro Jacopo da Bologna," *Kroyer-Festschrift* (1933); K. von Fischer, " 'Portraits' von Piero, Giovanni da Firenze, und Jacopo da Bologna in einer Bologneser Handschrift des 14. Jahrhunderts?" *Musica Disciplina,* 27 (1973).

Jacotin (real name, **Jacques Godebrie**), Flemish composer; b. Antwerp, c.1445; d. there, March 23, 1529. He was for nearly half a century "chapelain" in the choir of Notre Dame in Antwerp (1479–1528). His vocal works were publ. in collections by Attaignant (1529, 1530–35) and Rhaw (1545), in Le Roy's & Ballard's *Chansons nouvellement composées* (1556), etc. He excelled especially in French chansons; of these *Trop dure m'est ta longue demeure* is reproduced in H. Expert's reprint of Attaignant's collection of 1529; and *Mon triste cœur* in Eitner's *Selection of 60 Chansons* (1899). Several motets attributed to Jacotin and publ. by Petrucci are of doubtful authenticity. His *Sancta Divinitas unus Deus* for 8 voices appeared in Uhlhardt's collection of 1546.

Jacques de Liège (Jacobus Leoniensis), Belgian music theorist; b. Liège, c.1260; d. there, after 1330. He studied in Paris; then was a cleric in Liège. About 1330, already at an advanced age, he wrote the important compendium *Speculum musicae* in 7 parts and 293 folios (586 pages; approximating some 2,000 pages in modern typography); it was formerly attributed to Johannes de Muris, but the authorship of Jacques de Liège is proved by the specific indication in the MS (Paris, Bibliothèque Nationale) that the initial letters of the 7 chapters form the name of the author; these letters are I-A-C-O-B-U-S. W. Grossmann, in *Die einleitenden Kapitel des Speculum Musicae von J. Muris* (Leipzig, 1924), overlooks this indication.
 BIBLIOGRAPHY: For detailed discussion of the problem, see R. Bragard, "Le Speculum Musicae du compilateur Jacques de Liège," *Musica Disciplina* (1953–54; also printed separately); H. Besseler, "Studien zur Musik des Mittelalters," *Archiv für Musikwissenschaft* (1925–27). Selections from the *Speculum musicae* are given in Eng. trans. in O. Strunk's *Source Readings in Music History* (N.Y., 1950); the complete Latin text, ed. by R. Bragard,

was publ. in the *Corpus Scriptorum de Musica* of the American Inst. of Musicology (1956).

Jacquet, (Jean Baptiste) Illinois, black American tenor saxophonist; b. Broussard, La., Oct. 31, 1922. He learned to play the soprano saxophone, then the alto saxophone; after working in local jazz circles, he joined Lionel Hampton's band; later played with Cab Calloway and Count Basie; then led his own groups on tours.

Jacquillat, Jean-Pierre, French conductor; b. Versailles, July 13, 1935. He was educated at the Paris Cons.; was awarded first prizes in harmony, percussion, and piano. In 1967 he was named assistant conductor at the Orch. de Paris; in 1968, associate conductor. With this ensemble, he toured the Soviet Union, Canada, the U.S., and Mexico. In 1970 he was named resident conductor and music director of the Angers Phil. Orch.; in 1971 he became permanent conductor of the Lyons Opera and the Rhône-Alpes Phil. In 1975 he became resident conductor and music adviser to the Orch. Lamoureux in Paris, leaving this post in 1978. He also appeared at leading opera houses and festivals.

Jadassohn, Salomon, noted German pedagogue; b. Breslau, Aug. 13, 1831; d. Leipzig, Feb. 1, 1902. He studied piano and violin in Breslau; in 1848 took courses at the Leipzig Cons.; in 1849 he was in Weimar, where Liszt accepted him as a student; then he returned to Leipzig, and studied privately with Hauptmann. He remained in Leipzig during his entire life; organized a choral society, Psalterion (1866); conducted the concerts of the Euterpe Society. In 1871 he was appointed instructor at the Leipzig Cons.; in 1887 was made Dr.Phil. (honoris causa); in 1893 he became Royal Professor. A scholar of the highest integrity and of great industry, he codified the traditional views of harmony, counterpoint, and form in his celebrated manuals, which have been trans. into many languages. He was a firm believer in the immutability of harmonic laws, and became the Rock of Gibraltar of conservatism in musical teaching; through his many students, who in turn became influential teachers in Germany and other European countries, the cause of orthodox music theory was propagated far and wide. He was also a composer: wrote 4 symphs.; a Piano Concerto; 3 piano quintets; a Piano Quartet; 4 piano trios; 2 string quartets; a Serenade for Flute and String Orch.; a Cavatina for Cello with Orch.; choral works; many piano pieces and songs. He was a master of contrapuntal forms, and wrote a number of vocal duets in canon; other contrapuntal devices are illustrated in many of his works. His music is totally forgotten; but his importance as a theorist cannot be doubted.
 WRITINGS: His manuals, covering a wide range of musical subjects, are: *Harmonielehre* (Leipzig, 1883; 7th ed., 1903; Eng. ed., N.Y., 1893, under the title *A Manual of Harmony,* trans. by T. Baker); *Kontrapunkt* (1884; 5th ed., 1909); *Kanon und Fuge* (1884; 3rd ed., 1909); *Die Formen in den Werken der*

Tonkunst (1889; 4th ed., 1910); *Lehrbuch der Instrumentation* (1889; 2nd ed., 1907); *Die Kunst zu Modulieren und Präludieren* (1890); *Allgemeine Musiklehre* (1892); *Elementar-Harmonielehre* (1895); *Methodik des musiktheoretischen Unterrichts* (1898); *Das Wesen der Melodie in der Tonkunst* (1899); *Das Tonbewusstsein; die Lehre vom musikalischen Hören* (1899); *Erläuterung der in Bachs "Kunst der Fuge" enthaltenen Fugen und Kanons* (1899); *Der Generalbass* (1901).

Jadin, Louis Emmanuel, French composer and conductor; b. Versailles, Sept. 21, 1768; d. Paris, April 11, 1853. He was at first a page in the household of Louis XVI; after the Revolution, he was on the staff of the Théâtre de Monsieur; there he produced his comic opera, *Joconde* (Sept. 14, 1790). He then wrote all kinds of festive compositions to be performed on special occasions during the revolutionary years. In 1802 he became prof. of piano at the newly established Paris Cons., succeeding his brother, **Hyacinthe Jadin** (1769–1802). During the Napoleonic wars he continued to write patriotic pieces; his orch. overture, *La Bataille d'Austerlitz,* enjoyed great popularity for a while. He also wrote pieces for piano, and piano duets.
BIBLIOGRAPHY: G. de Saint-Foix, "Les Frères Jadin," *Revue Musicale* (1925).

Jadlowker, Hermann, tenor; b. Riga, July 17, 1877; d. Tel Aviv, May 13, 1953. He left home as a boy to escape a commercial career, and entered the Vienna Cons. He made his debut as operatic tenor in Cologne (1897); then sang at the Royal Opera in Berlin, and later when it became the Berlin State Opera; also at the Vienna Opera. He made his American debut at the Metropolitan Opera House in *Faust* (Jan. 22, 1910); in 1913, went again to Berlin; from 1929 until 1938 he was cantor at the synagogue of his native town, Riga; then went to Palestine, where he settled as a teacher.

Jaëll, Alfred, noted French pianist; b. Trieste, March 5, 1832; d. Paris, Feb. 27, 1882. He studied with his father, Eduard Jaëll; appeared as a child prodigy in Venice in 1843; continual concert tours earned him the nickname of "le pianiste voyageur." He traveled in America in 1852–54; after this, lived in Paris, Brussels, and Leipzig. In 1866 he married **Marie Trautmann;** made piano transcriptions from works of Wagner, Schumann, and Mendelssohn.

Jaëll-Trautmann, Marie, French pianist, wife of **Alfred Jaëll;** b. Steinseltz, Alsace, Aug. 17, 1846; d. Paris, Feb. 4, 1925. She studied with Henri Herz at the Paris Cons., where she won first prize. After her marriage, she accompanied her husband on his travels. She wrote many characteristic pieces for piano, and publ. pedagogical works: *La Musique et la psycho-physiologie* (1895); *Le Mécanisme du toucher* (1896); *Le Toucher* (1899); *L'Intelligence et le rythme dans les mouvements artistiques* (1905); *Le Rythme du regard et la dissociation des doigts* (1906); *La Coloration des sensations tactiles* (1910);

La Résonance du toucher et la topographie des pulpes (1912); *La Main et la pensée musicale* (posthumous, 1925).
BIBLIOGRAPHY: H. Kiener, *Marie Jaëll* (1952).

Jaffee, Michael, American instrumentalist; b. Brooklyn, N.Y., April 21, 1938. He studied music at N.Y. Univ. (B.A., 1959; M.A., 1963); while still a student, he married **Kay Jaffee** (née Cross; b. Lansing, Mich., Dec. 31, 1937) in 1961; with her he founded the Waverly Consort, an early-music group dedicated to authentic performances using period instruments and costumes; it obtained considerable success on the concert circuit. His wife played recorder in the Waverly Consort.
BIBLIOGRAPHY: H. Waleson, "The Waverly Consort," *Ovation* (Nov. 1983).

Jagel, Frederick, American tenor; b. Brooklyn, N.Y., June 10, 1897; d. San Francisco, July 5, 1982. His parents were both pianists. He studied singing with William Brady in N.Y.; then went to Milan for further study; made his operatic debut in Livorno in 1924; returning to the U.S., he appeared with the Metropolitan Opera in N.Y. as Radames (Nov. 8, 1927). He subsequently sang at the San Francisco Opera Co. and at the Teatro Colón in Buenos Aires. In 1948 he sang the title role in the first American performance of Britten's opera *Peter Grimes.* On June 12, 1928, he married **Nancy Weir,** an opera singer. From 1949 to 1970 he taught voice at the New England Cons. in Boston.

Jagger, Mick (Michael Philip Jagger), English rock singer and songwriter, the demonic protagonist of the fantastically popular rock group The Rolling Stones. b. Dartford, Kent, July 26, 1944. He studied at the London School of Economics (1962–64); at the same time, pursued his interest in music, forming The Rolling Stones in 1962; his first success came with *Satisfaction* (1965), a song of candid sexual expression composed by Keith Richard with lyrics by Jagger. With this frontal assault upon the social sensibilities of the Establishment, the group earned a reputation as the outlaws of rock; Jagger assumed the role of high priest at their "concerts," which often degenerated into mad orgies among the audience, incited by the plenary obscenity of the words and metaphorical gestures of Jagger and his celebrants. He is responsible for such hallucinogenic psychedelic hits as *Midnight Rambler, Jumpin' Jack Flash,* and *Sympathy for the Devil.*

Jahn, Otto, learned German philologist and musicographer; b. Kiel, June 16, 1813; d. Göttingen, Sept. 9, 1869. He studied languages and antiquities at Kiel, Leipzig, and Berlin; then traveled in France and Italy; in 1839 he settled in Kiel as a lecturer on philology; in 1842 became prof. of archeology at Greifswald; was director of the Archeological Museum in Leipzig (1847); he lost this position in the wake of the political upheaval of 1848. In 1855 he was appointed prof. of archeology at Bonn Univ. He went to Göttingen shortly before his death. In the field of music, his magnum opus was the biography of Mozart (Leipzig, 1856–59, in 4 vols.; 2nd ed., 1867, in 2 vols.; 3rd ed., 1889–91, revised by H. Deiters; 4th ed., also revised by Deiters, 1905–7; exhaustively rewritten and revised by Hermann Abert as *Wolfgang Amadeus Mozart: Neu bearbeitete und erweiterte Ausgabe von Otto Jahns "Mozart,"* 2 vols., Leipzig, 1919–21, rendering it the standard biography; further revision by A.A. Abert, 2 vols., Leipzig, 1955–56). The Eng. trans. (by P. Townsend) appeared in 3 vols. in London (1882). Jahn's biography was the first musical life written according to the comparative critical method; it reviews the state of music during the period immediately preceding Mozart; this comprehensive exposition has become a model for subsequent musical biographies. Jahn intended to write a biography of Beethoven according to a similar plan, but could not complete the task; Thayer utilized the data accumulated by Jahn in his own work on Beethoven; Pohl used Jahn's notes in his biography of Haydn. Numerous essays by Jahn were publ. in his *Gesammelte Aufsätze über Musik* (1866). He composed songs, of which 32 were publ. in 4 books; he also brought out a vol. of songs for mixed voices; edited the vocal score of Beethoven's *Fidelio.*

BIBLIOGRAPHY: J. Vahlen, *Otto Jahn* (Vienna, 1870); E. Petersen, *Otto Jahn in seinen Briefen* (Leipzig, 1912); J. Pulver, "Otto Jahn," *Musical Times* (April 1913).

Jahn, Wilhelm, Austrian conductor and opera adminstrator; b. Hof, Moravia, Nov. 24, 1834; d. Vienna, April 21, 1900. At the age of 20 he became a theater conductor in Budapest; then occupied similar posts in Agram, Amsterdam, and Prague. He spent a number of years in Wiesbaden (1864–80); finally settled in Vienna, where he became music director of the Vienna Opera in 1880; for one season was conductor of the Vienna Phil. (1882–83). He retired in 1897, and was succeeded by Mahler.

Jähns, Friedrich Wilhelm, German vocal pedagogue and writer on music; b. Berlin, Jan. 2, 1809; d. there, Aug. 8, 1888. He studied singing with Grell; sang at the Berlin Opera as a boy soprano in the chorus. In 1845 he founded a singing society, which he conducted until 1870; in 1881 he became instructor of rhetoric at Scharwenka's Cons. He was very successful as a vocal teacher in Berlin; had some 1,000 pupils. His admiration for Weber impelled him to collect all the available materials pertaining to Weber's life and works; his unique library, containing 300 autograph letters and many other documents, pamphlets, essays, and first editions, was acquired in 1883 by the Berlin Royal Library. He publ. a treatise on Weber, with a thematic catalogue, *Carl Maria von Weber in seinen Werken* (Berlin, 1871). Apart from exhaustive biographical data, this book is historically interesting because in the preface the author introduced, for the first time in print, the Wagnerian term "Leitmotiv"; this was later popularized by Wolzogen and others. He was also a composer; his works include a *Grand Sonata* for Violin and Piano, a Piano Trio, a book of *Schottische Lieder,* and many other vocal pieces.

Jalas (real name, **Blomstedt**), **Jussi,** Finnish conductor; b. Jyväskylä, June 23, 1908. He studied with Krohn in Helsinki, and later in Paris with Rhené-Baton and Monteux. Since 1945 he has conducted at the Helsinki Opera. He has appeared as guest conductor in Scandinavia, Germany, France, and England; also in the U.S. (1950 and 1955). Jalas is regarded as one of the most authentic interpreters of the music of **Sibelius,** whose son-in-law he was.

James, Dorothy, American composer and pedagogue; b. Chicago, Dec. 1, 1901; d. St. Petersburg, Fla., Dec. 1, 1982. She studied with Louis Gruenberg and Adolf Weidig at the Chicago Musical College and at the American Cons. of Music in Chicago (M.M., 1927); also took composition courses with Howard Hanson at the Eastman School of Music in Rochester, N.Y., with Healey Willan in Toronto, and with Ernst Krenek at the Univ. of Michigan. For 41 years (1927–68) she valiantly taught music appreciation at Eastern Michigan Univ. at Ypsilanti, before retiring to Florida. She publ. a valuable brochure, *Music of Living Michigan Composers* (1976). She composed an opera, *Paolo and Francesca* (partial perf. in concert form, Rochester, April 2, 1931, on the same program with her *3 Symphonic Fragments*); *The Jumblies,* children's cantata, to a text by Edward Lear (1935); *Paul Bunyan,* children's cantata (1938); a piano suite, *Tone-Row* (1962); and a number of pieces of chamber music.

James, Harry (Haag), greatly popular American jazz trumpeter and bandleader; b. Albany, Ga., March 15, 1916; d. of lymphatic cancer, Las Vegas, July 5, 1983. His father was the director and trumpeter in the Mighty Haag Circus, and his mother was a trapeze artist there; Harry James got his middle name from the circus. He was trained to be a contortionist, but revealed greater talent in blowing the trumpet. He played in his father's band and in dance bands around Texas, where the family moved. In 1937 he joined Benny Goodman's band; in 1939 organized a group of his own. His trumpet playing had a virtuoso quality; he could blow it *dolce* and even *dolcissimo* but when needed he blew it with deafening *fortissimo.* He also could perform ultra-chromatic glissando. Apart from his brilliance as a trumpeter he also possessed an intuitive entrepreneurial sense; after hearing Frank Sinatra sing on the radio, he hired him as a soloist with his band. The popularity of Harry James reached its peak during the era of big bands; his recording albums, some of them bearing such self-proclamatory titles as "*Wild about Harry,*" sold into the millions, even in wartime, when shellac, from which disks were manufactured, was rationed. In 1943 he married Betty Grable, the pin-up girl of the G.I.s in World War II, famous for the lissome beauty of her nether limbs. She was his second wife, out of the total of four. They were divorced in 1965; she died in 1973. Faithful to the slogan that the show must go

on, Harry James, wracked with cancerous pain, continued to perform; he played in Denver on June 10 and 11, 1983; he played his last gig in Los Angeles, on June 26, nine days before his death. He observed, as he was dying, "Let it just be said that I went up to do a one-nighter with Archangel Gabriel."
BIBLIOGRAPHY: F. Stacy, *Harry James's Pin-Up Life Story* (N.Y., 1944).

James, Philip (Frederick Wright), notable American composer and conductor; b. Jersey City, N.J., May 17, 1890; d. Southampton, Long Island, N.Y., Nov. 1, 1975. His older sister gave him the rudiments of music; he served also as a choirboy in New Jersey Episcopalian churches. He later studied composition with Rubin Goldmark and Rosario Scalero, and organ with J. Warren Andrews. He was in the army during World War I; after the Armistice, was appointed bandmaster of the American Expeditionary Force General Headquarters Band; he also took organ lessons with Joseph Bonnet and Alexandre Guilmant in Paris. Returning to the U.S., he held various posts as organist and choirmaster in several churches in N.Y., and also conducted numerous theatrical and symph. organizations, among them the Victor Herbert Opera Co. (1919–22), New Jersey Symph. Orch. (1922–29), Brooklyn Orch. Society (1927–30), Bamberger Little Symph. (Station WOR; 1929–36). In 1933 he was elected a member of the National Inst. of Arts and Letters; won numerous prizes, among them one for his orch. suite *Station WGZBX,* awarded by the National Broadcasting Co. In 1923 he joined the faculty of N.Y. Univ.; became chairman of the music dept. in 1933; retired in 1955.
WORKS: FOR THE STAGE: *Judith,* dramatic reading with Ballet and Chamber Orch. (1927; N.Y., Feb. 18, 1933). FOR ORCH.: *Overture in Olden Style on French Noëls* (1926; revised 1929; N.Y., Feb. 23, 1930); *Sea Symphony* for Bass-baritone and Orch. (1928; Frankfurt, July 14, 1960); *Song of the Night,* symph. poem (1931; N.Y., March 15, 1938); *Station WGZBX,* satirical suite (NBC Symph. Orch., May 1, 1932); Suite for Strings (N.Y. Univ., April 28, 1934); *Gwalia, a Welsh Rhapsody* (N.Y., Nov. 14, 1935); *Bret Harte Overture No. 3* (N.Y., Dec. 20, 1936); *Brennan on the Moor* for Chamber Orch. (N.Y., Nov. 28, 1939); Sinfonietta (N.Y., Nov. 10, 1941; revised 1943); Symph. No. 1 (1943; revised 1961); 2nd Suite for Strings (1943; Saratoga Springs, Sept. 5, 1946); Symph. No. 2 (1946; Rochester, N.Y., May 7, 1966); *Miniver Cheevy* and *Richard Cory* for Narrator and Orch. (Saratoga, N.Y., Sept. 9, 1947); *Chaumont,* symph. poem for Chamber Orch. (1948; N.Y., May 2, 1951). CHAMBER MUSIC: String Quartet (1924; revised 1939); Suite for Woodwind Quintet (1936); Piano Quartet (1937; revised 1948). CHORAL WORKS: *The Nightingale of Bethlehem,* cantata (1920; revised 1923); *Shirat Ha-Yam,* cantata (1920; revised 1933–58); *Song of the Future* for Mixed Chorus a cappella (1922); *Missa Imaginum* for Mixed Chorus and Orch. (1929); *General William Booth Enters into Heaven* for Tenor, Male Voices, and Chamber Orch. (1932); *World of Tomorrow* for Mixed Chorus

and Orch. (1938); *Psalm 150* for Mixed Chorus and Orch. (1940; revised 1956); *Chorus of Shepherds and Angels,* cantata (1956); *To Cecilia,* cantata for Chorus and Chamber Orch. (1966); choruses; hymns; songs. FOR BAND: *Perstare et Perstare,* festal march (N.Y., June 10, 1942; arranged for Orch. 1946); *E.F.G. Overture* (1944; N.Y., June 13, 1945); *Fanfare and Ceremonial* (1955; N.Y., June 20, 1956; revised 1962). FOR ORGAN: *Méditation à Sainte Clotilde* (1915); *Dithyramb* (1921); *Fête* (1921); Sonata No. 1 (1929); *Pantomime* (1941); *Galarnad* (1946); *Novelette* (1946); *Solemn Prelude* (1948); *Alleluia-Toccata* (1949); *Pastorale* (1949); *Requiescat in pace* (1949; revised 1955); *Passacaglia on an Old Cambrian Bass* (1951; arranged for Orch., 1956; for Band, 1957); *Sortie* (1973); piano pieces.
BIBLIOGRAPHY: Helga James, *A Catalog of the Musical Works of Philip James (1890–1975)* (N.Y., 1980); David Ewen, *American Composers* (N.Y., 1982).

Jan, Karl von, German writer on music; b. Schweinfurt, May 22, 1836; d. Adelboden, Switzerland, Sept. 4, 1899. He took the degree of Dr.Phil. at Berlin (1859) with the thesis *De fidibus Graecorum;* publ. several essays on ancient Greek music. An important work is his critical edition of the Greek writers on music: *Musici scriptores graeci; Aristoteles, Euclides, Bacchius, Cleonides, Nichomachus, Gaudentius, Alypius* (1895), with an appendix, *Melodiarum reliquiae,* containing all the vocal music known in his day to be extant (this also in a separate ed., augmented and revised, 1899).

Janáček, Leoš, greatly renowned Czech composer; b. Hukvaldy, Moravia, July 3, 1854; d. Ostrava, Aug. 12, 1928. At the age of 10 he was placed at the Augustine monastery in Brno as a chorister; then studied at the Brno Teachers' Training College (1872–74) and at the Organ School (College of Music) in Prague, where he studied organ with Skuherský (1874–75); later took lessons in composition with L. Grill at the Leipzig Cons. and with Franz Krenn at the Vienna Cons. (1879–80). Returning to Brno, he was active as a teacher; from 1881 to 1888 he conducted the Czech Phil. there; from 1919 to 1925 he taught at the Cons. of Brno; many Czech composers of the younger generation were his students. Although he began to compose early in life, it was not until 1916, with the production of his opera *Její pastorkyňa* (commonly known under its German title, *Jenufa*), that his importance as a national composer was realized in the music world; the work was widely performed in Austria, Germany, and Russia, and was eventually produced in America. In the field of religious music, he created a unique score, *Glagolitic Mass* (also known as *Slavonic Mass* or *Festival Mass*), to a text in old Slavonic, with an instrumental accompaniment. Janáček took great interest in Russian literature and music; he visited Russia 3 times; his operas *Kát'a Kabanová* and *From the House of the Dead* and several other works are based on Russian literary works. There is an affinity between Janáček's method of dramatic

1103

prosody and Mussorgsky's ideas of realistic musical speech, but Janáček never consciously imitated the Russian models. He was a firm believer in the artistic importance of folk songs, and collected a number of them in his native Moravia; contributed a paper on the musical structure of national songs to the Prague Academy (1901). During the last 2 decades of his life, Janáček was strongly influenced by the French school; the idiom of his instrumental works of that period clearly reflects impressionist usages.

WORKS: FOR THE STAGE: 9 operas: *Šárka* (1887, revised in 1918; instrumentation of the 3rd act and final revision of the first and 2nd acts accomplished by Janáček's student Oswald Chlubna in 1918–19 and 1924; Brno, Nov. 11, 1925); *Počátek románu (Beginning of a Romance,* 1891; Brno, Feb. 10, 1894); *Její pastorkyňa (Her Foster Daughter;* German title, *Jenufa;* 1894–1903; Brno, Jan. 21, 1904; revised 1906, 1911, and 1916; final version first perf., Prague, May 26, 1916); *Osud (Fate,* 1903–4; Brno Radio, Sept. 18, 1934; first stage perf., Brno, Oct. 25, 1958); the satiric opera *Výlety páně Broučkovy (The Excursions of Mr. Brouček),* made up of 2 separately performable scenes, *Výlet pana Broučka do Měsíce (Mr. Brouček's Flight to the Moon,* 1908–17) and *Výlet pana Broučka do XV století (Mr. Brouček's Trip to the 15th Century,* 1917; both in Prague, April 23, 1920); *Káťa Kabanová* (after Ostrovsky's play *The Storm,* 1919–21; Brno, Nov. 23, 1921); *Příhody lišky Bystroušky (The Cunning Little Vixen,* 1921–23; Brno, Nov. 6, 1924); *Věc Makropulos,* after Čapek (*The Makropulos Affair,* 1923–25; Brno, Dec. 18, 1926); *Z mrtvého domu,* after Dostoyevsky (*From the House of the Dead,* 1927–28; produced posthumously, Brno, April 12, 1930); and a ballet, *Rákocz Rákoczy* (1891; Prague, July 24, 1891). CHORAL WORKS: 6 cantatas: *Hospodine pomiluj ny (Lord, Have Mercy Upon Us)* for Solo Quartet and Double Chorus, with Organ, Harp, 3 Trumpets, 3 Trombones, and 2 Tubas (1896); *Amarus* for Solo Trio, Chorus, Harp, and Orch. (1897; revised 1901 and 1906); *Otčenáš (The Lord's Prayer)* for Tenor, Chorus, Harp, and Organ (1901; revised 1906); *Elegie* for Tenor, Mixed Chorus, and Piano (1903–4; Brno, Dec. 20, 1930; written on the death of Janáček's daughter); *Mass in E-flat major,* unfinished, for Mixed Choir and Organ (1908; Brno, March 7, 1943); *Na Soláni Čarták (At the Inn of Solan)* for Male Chorus and Orch. (1911); *Věčné evangelium (The Eternal Gospel),* cantata-legend for Soprano, Tenor, Chorus, and Orch. (1914) and *Glagolská mše (Glagolitic Mass* or *Slavonic Mass* or *Festival Mass)* for Soli, Chorus, and Orch. (1926; Brno, Dec. 5, 1927); a cappella choruses. CHAMBER VOCAL WORKS: *Zápisník zmizelého (The Diary of One Who Vanished)* for Tenor, Alto, 3 Female Voices, and Piano (1917–19, revised 1924) and *Říkadla (Nursery Rhyme)* for 9 Singers and Chamber Ensemble (1925–27); numerous folk-song arrangements. FOR ORCH.: Suite for String Orch. (Brno, Dec. 2, 1877); *Idyll* for String Orch. (Brno, Dec. 15, 1878); *Moravian Dances* (1888–91); *6 Lašske tance (6 Lachian Dances,* 1889–90; as a ballet, Brno, Feb. 19, 1925); *Suite* (1891); *Žárlivost (Jealousy),* symph. poem (1894); *Šumařovo dítě (The Fiddler's Child),* ballad (1912; Prague, Nov. 14, 1917), *Taras Bulba,* rhapsody after Gogol (1915–18; Brno, Oct. 9, 1921); *Balada blanická (The Ballad of Blaník),* symph. poem (1920; Brno, March 21, 1920); Sinfonietta (1926; Prague, June 29, 1926; his most popular instrumental work); *Dunaj (The Danube),* symph. poem (1923–28; completed by Chlubna, 1948); Violin Concerto (1927–28; only a fragment was completed). CHAMBER MUSIC: 2 string quartets: No. 1 (inspired by Tolstoy's *Kreutzer Sonata,* 1923) and No. 2, *Intimate Letters* (1928); *Dumka* for Violin and Piano (1880); *Pohádka (Fairytale)* for Cello and Piano (1910); Violin Sonata (1913); *Mládí (Youth)* for Wind Sextet (1924); Concertino for Piano and Ensemble of Clarinet, Bassoon, Horn, 2 Violins, and Viola (1925; Brno, Feb. 16, 1926); *Capriccio* for Piano, left-hand, and Flute, Piccolo, 2 Trumpets, 3 Trombones, and Tuba (1926; Prague, March 2, 1928). FOR PIANO: *Tema con variazioni* (known as the *Zdeňka Variations,* 1880); *3 Moravian Dances* (1892, 1904); *Po zarostlém chodníčku (On an Overgrown Path),* cycle in 2 series (1901–8); sonata, *1. X. 1905* (also known as *From the Street,* 1905); *V mlhách (In the Mist),* 4 pieces (1912); *Memory* (1928). A complete list of works with exact dates of composition and performance is found in Gr. Černušák and Vlad. Helfert, *Pazdírkuv Hudebni Slovník Naučny,* vol. 2 (Prague, 1937), and in Kenneth Thompson, *Dictionary of Twentieth-Century Composers 1911–1971* (N.Y., 1973). A complete critical edition of his works began publication in 1979 in Prague and Kassel.

BIBLIOGRAPHY: Max Brod, *Leoš Janáček* (Prague, 1924; in German, Vienna 1925); H. Hollander, "Leoš Janáček and His Operas," *Musical Quarterly* (Jan. 1929); Daniel Muller, *Leoš Janáček* (Paris, 1930); J. Procházka, *Lašske Kořeny života i díla Loeše Janáčka* (Prague, 1948); B. Štědroň, *Leoš Janáček: Letters and Reminiscences* (Prague, 1946; in Eng., 1955); H. Hollander, "The Music of Leoš Janáček—Its Origin in Folklore," *Musical Quarterly* (April 1955); J. Seda, *Leoš Janáček* (Prague, 1956, in Czech and Eng.); H. Richter, *Leoš Janáček* (Leipzig, 1958); J. Vogel, *Leoš Janáček: Leben und Werk* (Prague, 1958; in Eng., London, 1962); B. Štědroň, *The Works of Leoš Janáček* (Prague, 1959); J. Rocek, *Leoš Janáček* (Leipzig, 1962); Hans Hollander, *Leoš Janáček: His Life and Work* (N.Y., 1963); Erik Chisholm, *The Operas of Leoš Janáček* (N.Y., 1971); T. Kneif, *Die Bühnenwerke von Leoš Janáček* (1974); Michael Ewens, *Janáček's Tragic Operas* (London, 1977); *Janáček: Leaves from His Life,* edited and trans. from the Czech by Villem and Margaret Tausky (N.Y., 1982). A collection of documents and studies pertaining to Janáček's work was publ. in Prague under the title *O lidové písne a lidové hudbě* (1955).

Janeček, Karel, Czech composer and theorist; b. Czestochowa, Poland, Feb. 20, 1903; d. Prague, Jan. 4, 1974. He spent his boyhood in Kiev. After completing his secondary education at an industrial school, he went to Prague, where he took courses in composition with Křička and Novák (1924–27). From 1929 to 1941 he taught at the Pilsen Music School; then was prof. of composition at the Prague Cons. (1941–46) and later at the Prague Academy. In his early works Janeček adopted a traditional national style; later he occasionally employed a personalized dodecaphonic scheme.

WORKS: *Overture* (1926–27); 2 symphs. (1935–40, 1954–55); *Lenin,* symph. triptych (1953); *Legend of Prague,* overture for String Orch. (1956); *Fantasy for Orch.* (1962–63); Sinfonietta (1967); *Large Symposium* for 15 Soloists (1967); 3 string quartets (1924, 1927, 1934); Divertimento for 8 Instruments (1925–26); String Trio (1930); Trio for Flute, Clarinet, and Bassoon (1931); Duo for Violin and Viola (1938); Violin Sonata (1939); Divertimento for Oboe, Clarinet, and Bassoon (1949); Cello Sonata (1958); *Little Symposium,* chamber suite for Flute, Clarinet, Bassoon, and Piano (1959); Duo for Violin and Cello (1960); *Chamber Overture* for Nonet (1960); Quartet for Flute, Oboe, Clarinet, and Bassoon (1966); *Trifles and Abbreviations* for Piano (1926); *Tema con variazioni* for Piano, inspired by the tragedy of the village of Lidice, destroyed by the Nazis (1942); several choral works, including *To the Fallen* (1950–51), *To the Living* (1951), and *My Dream* (1972); songs.

WRITINGS: *Základy moderní harmonie* (*The Basis of Modern Harmony;* written 1942–49; publ. in Prague, 1965), *Hudební formy* (*Musical Forms;* Prague, 1955), *Melodika* (Prague, 1956), *Harmonie rozborem* (*Harmony Through Analysis;* Prague, 1963; originally known as *Analytical Introduction to Harmony*), *Tektonika* (*Tectonics, the Science of Construction of Compositions;* Prague, 1968), and *Tvorba a tvůrci* (*Creativity and Creations;* Prague, 1968).

Janequin, Clément, creator and chief representative of the new 16th-century French polyphonic chanson; b. Châtellerault, c. 1485; d. Paris, 1558. He was a pupil of Josquin. In his youth he may have been in the service of Louis Ronsard, father of the poet Pierre Ronsard, and may have accompanied his master during the Italian campaigns, from 1507 to the battle of Marignano, 1515. About 1520 he was in Paris, and later perhaps in Spain. There is evidence that in 1529 he was in Bordeaux, was subsequently in the service of the Cardinal of Lorraine (d. 1550), then was chaplain of the Duke de Guise, whose victories he celebrated by extended chansons. From 1545 to 1558 he was curate at Unverre. In a 1559 dedication in verse, he bemoans his old age and poverty.

WORKS: Besides many detached pieces in collections of the time (Attaignant's, Gardane's, etc.), and chansons in special editions, there were publ. 2 masses (1532, 1554), *Sacræ cantiones seu motectæ 4 voc.* (1533), *Proverbs de Salomon mis en cantiques et ryme françoise* (1554); *Octante deux psaumes de David* (1559); etc. Among the most interesting "Inventions" (chansons) in 4–5 parts are *La Bataille* (portraying the battle of Marignano; Verdelot added a 5th part to the original 4), *La Prise de Boulogne,* *Le Chant des oiseaux,* etc. Some of Janequin's

works are ambitious examples of program music. Reprints have been made by Henri Expert in his *Maîtres Musiciens de la Renaissance Française* (chansons; vol. 7) and by Maurice Cauchie in *Les Concerts de la Renaissance,* Part 2 (a collection of 30 3- and 4-voiced chansons by Janequin; 1928). Cauchie also edited 2 5-voiced chansons (*Le Caquet des femmes* and *La Jalouzie*). His complete chansons are publ. in 6 vols. as *Chansons polyphoniques,* ed. by T. Merritt and F. Lesure (Monaco, 1965–71).

BIBLIOGRAPHY: M. Cauchie, "Clément Janequin: Recherches sur sa famille et sur lui-même," *Revue de Musicologie* (Feb. 1923); M. Cauchie, "Clément Janequin, chapelain du duc de Guise," *Le Ménestrel* (Jan. 21, 1927); M. Cauchie, *Les Psaumes de Janequin* (Liège, 1930); J. Levron, *Clément Janequin, Musicien de la Renaissance* (Paris, 1948); F. Lesure, "Clément Janequin, Recherches sur sa vie et son œuvre," *Musica Disciplina* (1951); G. Reese, *Music in the Renaissance* (N.Y., 1954; pp. 295–99 and 340).

Janigro, Antonio, Italian cellist and conductor; b. Milan, Jan. 21, 1918. He studied at the Cons. of Milan and in Paris; pursued a successful career as a solo cellist but later turned mostly to conducting. In 1950 he founded the group I Solisti di Zagreb and toured with this small ensemble extensively. In 1968 he was appointed conductor of the Radio Chamber Orch. in Saarland, and toured with it in Europe and America (1969 and 1971). In 1965 he was appointed prof. of cello playing at the Schumann Cons. in Düsseldorf.

Janis (real name, **Yanks,** abbreviated from **Yankelevitch**), **Byron,** noted American pianist; b. McKeesport, Pa., March 24, 1928. He began to study piano with a local teacher; at the age of 8 he was taken to N.Y., where he became a pupil of Adele Marcus. Progressing rapidly, he made his important debut in 1943, playing Rachmaninoff's 2nd Piano Concerto with the NBC Symph. Orch.; he played it again with the Pittsburgh Symph. Orch. on Feb. 20, 1944, with the 13-year-old Lorin Maazel on the podium; Vladimir Horowitz happened to be present at the concert and told Janis that he would be willing to take him as a private pupil; these private lessons with Horowitz continued for several years, leaving an indelible mark on Janis's pianism. In 1948 he toured South America, obtaining a particularly resounding success in Buenos Aires. On Oct. 29, 1948, he played in Carnegie Hall, N.Y., with exceptionally favorable reviews in the press. In 1952 he made a tour of Europe. In 1960 he made his first tour of Russia, under the auspices of the U.S. State Dept.; he played in Moscow, Leningrad, Odessa, Minsk, and Kiev; the Soviet critics praised him for his poetic performances of Romantic music; he played again in Russia in 1962. In 1961, on the occasion of the sesquicentennial of the birth of Liszt, he played both of Liszt's piano concertos with the Boston Symph. Orch. During a visit to France in 1967, Janis discovered the autograph MSS of 2 waltzes by Chopin, the G-flat major, op. 70, no. 1, and the E-flat major, op. 18; in 1973 he located 2 variants of these waltzes in the library of Yale Univ. In 1975 he made the film *Frédéric Chopin: A Voyage with Byron Janis,* which was produced by the Public Broadcasting Service. In 1953 he was married, in London, to June Dickinson Wright; they were divorced in 1965, and in 1966 he married Maria Veronica Cooper, the daughter of the movie star Gary Cooper. At the climax of his highly successful career, Byron Janis was stricken with the dreaded amyotrophic lateral sclerosis, which affects the motor neuron cells, gradually depriving the victim of command of his bodily movements.

BIBLIOGRAPHY: David Ewen, *Musicians since 1900* (N.Y., 1978).

Janitsch, Johann Gottlieb, Silesian composer and bass viol player; b. Schweidnitz, June 19, 1708; d. Berlin, c.1763. He studied music in Breslau and law at the Univ. of Frankfurt an der Oder (1729–33). In 1733 he became secretary to Franz Wilhelm von Happe, a minister of state. In 1736 Crown Prince Friedrich (later Frederick the Great) made him a member of his personal orch. in Ruppin; he followed Friedrich to Rheinsberg, where he organized a series of famous concerts known as the "Friday Academies." In 1740 he was named "contraviolinist" in Frederick the Great's orch. in Berlin, and continued his "Friday Academies" there. His *Sonata da camera* for Flute, Oboe, Violin, Viola, Cello, and Harpsichord, entitled *Echo,* composed in 1757, is reprinted in *Collegium musicum,* LXVIII (Leipzig, 1938); another work in this genre was publ. in 1970. A collection of his compositions has been assembled from the available MSS by Josef Marx of the McGinnis & Marx firm of music publishers in N.Y.

Jankélévitch, Vladimir, French philosopher and writer on music; b. Bourges, Aug. 31, 1903. He was educated in Paris at the School of Oriental Languages and at the Ecole Normale Supérieure; received a degree in philosophy in 1925 and the doctorat ès lettres in 1933. He was a prof. of philosophy at the Institut de Prague (1927–33); then at the univs. of Lille (1933–39; 1945–52) and Toulouse (1939–45); in 1952 he became a prof. of ethics and moral philosophy at the Sorbonne. His writings on music reflect his philosophical bent; these include *Gabriel Fauré et ses mélodies* (Paris, 1938; 2nd ed., augmented, 1951, as *Gabriel Fauré, Ses mélodies, son esthétique*); *Maurice Ravel* (Paris, 1939; 2nd ed., augmented, 1956, as *Ravel*); *Debussy et le mystère* (Neuchâtel, 1949); *La Rhapsodie, verve et improvisation musicale* (Paris, 1955); *Le Nocturne: Fauré: Chopin et la nuit: Satie et le matin* (Paris, 1957); *La Musique et l'ineffable* (Paris, 1961); *La Vie et la mort dans la musique de Debussy* (Neuchâtel, 1968); *Fauré et l'inexprimable* (Paris, 1974); *Debussy et le mystère de l'instant* (Paris, 1976).

BIBLIOGRAPHY: L. Jerphagnon, *Jankélévitch* (Paris, 1969).

Jankó, Paul von, Hungarian pianist and inventor; b. Totis, June 2, 1856; d. Constantinople, March 17, 1919. He studied at the Polytechnic in Vienna, and at the Cons. (under Hans Schmitt, Krenn, and Bruckner); then (1881–82) at Berlin Univ. (mathematics), and with Ehrlich (piano); from 1892 lived in Constantinople (now Istanbul). His keyboard, invented in 1882, is a new departure in piano mechanics, though standing in distant relationship to the older "chromatic" keyboard advocated by the Chroma society. It has 6 rows of keys; each pair of rows consists of 2 mutually exclusive whole-tone scales; the fingering of all diatonic scales is alike; chromatic scales are played by striking alternative keys in any 2 adjoining rows. A full description of the keyboard was publ. in pamphlet form by its inventor (1886). The "Jankó keyboard" was espoused by quite a few enthusiastic souls, but like many similar "inventions" it soon lapsed into innocuous desuetude.

BIBLIOGRAPHY: F.B. Boyes, *Das Jankó-Klavier* (Vienna, 1904); H.F. Münnich, *Materialen für die Jankó-Klaviatur* (1905).

Janků, Hana, Czech soprano; b. Brno, Oct. 25, 1940. She studied at the Brno Cons.; made her debut in Brno in 1959; later sang with the Prague National Theater Opera; in 1967 she appeared at La Scala in Milan; also sang at the Deutsche Oper in West Berlin (1970) and at Covent Garden in London (1973).

Jannaconi, Giuseppe, one of the last composers in "Palestrina-style"; b. Rome, 1741; d. there, March 16, 1816. A pupil of S. Rinaldini and G. Carpani, he succeeded Zingarelli in 1811 as maestro di cappella at St. Peter's. He is noted for his scoring of many of Palestrina's works, aided by his friend Pisari. His works remain in MS in the Santini College, now at Münster; they include a Mass, a Te Deum, a Magnificat, a *Dixit Dominus,* and a *Tu es Petrus,* all *a* 16; 16 masses in 4–8 parts, with Organ; 14 other masses; 32 Psalms in 4–8 parts; 10 masses with orch.; 16 motets in 2–6 parts; 57 offertories and anthems *a* 3–8; a canon *a* 64; 2 canons *a* 16; an *Ecce terrae motus* for 6 Basses; an oratorio for 2 Tenors and one Bass, *L'agonia di Gesù Christo;* etc.

Janowitz, Gundula, Austrian soprano; b. Berlin, Aug. 2, 1937. She studied at the Graz Cons.; made her professional debut in 1959 at the Vienna State Opera. She soon came to the attention of Herbert von Karajan, who featured her in a number of his concert and operatic ventures in Berlin and elsewhere. She then became a member of the Vienna State Opera and the Deutsche Oper in West Berlin.

Janowka, Thomas Balthasar (Janovka, Tomáš Baltazar), Bohemian organist; b. Kuttenberg (baptized, Jan. 6), 1669; d. (buried, June 13) 1741. He received a Jesuit education at the St. Wenceslas seminary in Prague; earned his M.Phil. from Charles Univ. there in 1689. In 1691 he was appointed organist at Tyne Church in Prague, remaining in his post for half a century until his death. He compiled the *Clavis ad thesaurum magnae artis musicae* (Prague, 1701), which was the 2nd (after Tinctoris) music dictionary ever publ. Only a few copies of the original edition are extant, but the book was reprinted in 1973.

Janowski, Marek, Polish conductor; b. Warsaw, Feb. 18, 1939. He was taken to Germany while young; studied mathematics and music at the Univ. of Cologne; continued his musical studies in Vienna. He conducted opera in Aachen and Cologne; was first conductor of the Düsseldorf Opera (1964–69); then was with the Hamburg State Opera. From 1975 to 1979 he was Generalmusikdirektor in Dortmund. He also conducted opera in Berlin, Munich, London, Paris, and Buenos Aires; in addition, he had engagements with the Berlin Phil., Dresden State Orch., Residentie Orch. in The Hague, and the Bavarian Radio Symph.

Jansa, Leopold, Bohemian violinist and composer; b. Wildenschwert, March 23, 1795; d. Vienna, Jan. 24, 1875. He studied in Vienna; then taught violin there; was dismissed in 1849 after he took part in a concert in London for the benefit of the Hungarian revolutionists. He remained in England as a teacher for several years until the amnesty of 1868, when he returned to Vienna and received a pension. He was greatly esteemed as a violinist; he composed much violin music, including 4 concertos and 36 violin duets; other works are 8 string quartets, 3 string trios, and some church music.

Janson, Alfred, Norwegian composer; b. Oslo, March 10, 1937. His mother gave him piano lessons, but he soon turned to the accordion as his favorite musical instrument, and as a youth earned a living by playing in cafés and restaurants, mostly in jazz groups. He then took some composition lessons with Finn Mortensen. His own music is a cross-section of a variety of modern techniques.
WORKS: Opera, *Fjeldeventyret (A Mountain Adventure,* 1970–73; Oslo, April 9, 1973); *Vuggesang (Cradle Song)* for 48 Strings and Piano (1963); *Konstruksjon og hymne (Construction and Hymn)* for Orch. (1963); *Canon* for Saxophone, Percussion, Piano, Hammond Organ, Double Bass, Voice, and Tape (1964); *Tema* for Chorus, Organ, Percussion, and Piano (1966); *Nocturne,* after Nietzsche, for 2 Choruses, 2 Cellos, 2 Percussion Groups, and Harp (1967); *Mot solen (Toward the Sun),* ballet with 2 Solo Saxophones, Chorus, and Orch. Ensemble (1968); *I dag død, imorgen rosenrød (Candy and Balloons),* ballet (1969); *Röster i mänskligt landskap (Voices in Human Landscape),* Mass for 3 Actors, Chorus, and 10 Instruments (1969); *Valse triste* for Jazz Quintet and Tape (1970); *Aberte,* music for a television play (1972); Violin Concerto (1973–75); String Quartet (1978); *Vinger (Wings)* for Chorus and Jazz Orch. (1982–83).

Janson, Arvid. See **Yansons, Arvid.**

Jansons, Mariss, conductor; b. Riga, Latvia, Jan. 14, 1943. He was a son of the noted conductor **Arvid Yansons.** He studied at the Leningrad Cons., where he took courses in violin, viola, piano, and conducting. He profited from initial conducting studies with his father; then studied with Swarowsky in Vienna, Karajan in Salzburg, and Mravinsky in Leningrad. In 1971 he won 2nd prize in the Karajan Competition in West Berlin; then made appearances with major orchs. and opera houses in the Soviet Union and Eastern Europe; also conducted in Western Europe and America. In 1979 he was named chief conductor of the Oslo Phil. Orch.

Janssen, Herbert, German baritone; b. Cologne, Sept. 22, 1895; d. New York, June 3, 1965. He studied in Cologne and Berlin; gave recitals; then became a member of the Berlin State Opera. He made his American debut with the Metropolitan Opera Co. (Philadelphia, Jan. 24, 1939) as Wotan in *Siegfried;* then sang in other Wagnerian roles; remained on the Metropolitan's roster until 1952.

Janssen, Werner, American composer and conductor; b. New York, June 1, 1899. He studied music theory with Frederick Converse in Boston and conducting with Felix Weingartner in Basel and Hermann Scherchen in Strasbourg (1921–25); won the Prix de Rome of the American Academy (1930) and made his debut as a conductor in Rome; he gave a concert of music by Sibelius in Helsinki in 1934 and was praised by Sibelius himself; received the Finnish Order of the White Rose. He made his American debut with the N.Y. Phil. on Nov. 8, 1934; served as regular conductor of the Baltimore Symph. (1937–39); then went to Hollywood, where he organized the Janssen Symph. (1940–52) and commissioned American composers to write special works. He was subsequently conductor of the Utah Symph. Orch., Salt Lake City (1946–47), of the Portland (Oreg.) Orch. (1947–49), and of the San Diego Symph. (1952–54). In 1937 he married the famous motion picture actress Ann Harding; they were divorced in 1963. As a composer, Janssen cultivates the art of literal pictorialism; his most successful work of this nature was *New Year's Eve in New York* (Rochester, May 9, 1929), a symph. poem for Large Orch. and Jazz Instruments; the orch. players were instructed to shout at the end "Happy New Year!" Other works are: *Obsequies of a Saxophone* for 6 Wind Instruments and a Snare Drum (Washington, D.C., Oct. 17, 1929); *Louisiana Suite* for Orch. (1930); *Dixie Fugue* (extracted from the *Louisiana Suite;* Rome, Nov. 27, 1932); *Foster Suite* for Orch., on Stephen Foster's tunes (1937); 2 string quartets.

Janssens, Jean-François-Joseph, Belgian composer; b. Antwerp, Jan. 29, 1801; d. there, Feb. 3, 1835. He studied with his father and later with Lesueur in Paris. Returning to Antwerp, he became a lawyer; was a notary public until the siege of Antwerp (1832); composed in his leisure hours. Going to Cologne, he lost his MSS and other possessions in a fire on the night of his arrival; this misfortune so affected him that he became insane. He wrote 4 operas, 2 cantatas, 2 symphs., 5 masses; a number of motets, anthems, and hymns; also songs.

BIBLIOGRAPHY: Hendricks, *Simple histoire. Boutades biographiques à l'occasion du 25ᵉ anniversaire de la mort de J.-F.-J. Janssens* (Antwerp, 1860); E. van der Straeten, *J.-F.-J. Janssens, Compositeur de musique* (Brussels, 1866; contains a list of his works).

Jaques-Dalcroze, Emile, composer and creator of "Eurhythmics"; b. (of French parents) Vienna, July 6, 1865; d. Geneva, July 1, 1950. In 1873 his parents moved to Geneva; having completed his course at the Univ. and also at the Cons. there, he went to Vienna for further study under R. Fuchs and A. Bruckner, and then to Paris, where he studied orchestration at the Cons. with Delibes; in 1892 he returned to Geneva as instructor of theory at the Cons. Since he laid special stress on rhythm, he insisted that all his pupils beat time with their hands, and this led him, step by step, to devise a series of movements affecting the entire body. Together with the French psychologist Edouard Claparide, he worked out a special terminology and reduced his practice to a regular system, which he called "Eurhythmics." When his application to have his method introduced as a regular course at the Cons. was refused, he resigned, and in 1910 established his own school at Hellerau, near Dresden. Even before that time the new system had attracted wide attention, and the school flourished from the beginning; within 3 years branches were opened in France, Russia, Germany, England, and the U.S. (Bryn Mawr College, N.Y., and Chicago). Conditions resulting from the war brought about the closing of the school at Hellerau in 1915. After that he founded another school at Geneva, the headquarters of which was later moved to Paris. In 1925 the Hellerau School was established in Laxenburg, near Vienna. Jaques-Dalcroze himself also taught in London; in his later years he lived in Geneva. Without question, the results obtained by Jaques-Dalcroze have contributed toward the recent development of the ballet. Aside from his rhythmical innovations, he also commanded respect as a composer of marked originality and fecundity of invention; many of his works show how thoroughly he was imbued with the spirit of Swiss folk music.

WORKS: Operas: *Le Violon maudit* (Geneva, 1893); *Janie* (Geneva, March 13, 1894); *Sancho Panza* (Geneva, 1897); *Onkel Dazumal* (Cologne, 1905; as *Le Bonhomme Jadis,* Paris, 1906); *Les Jumeaux de Bergame* (Brussels, 1908); *Fête de la jeunesse et de la joie* (Geneva, 1932); operetta, *Respect pour nous* (Geneva, 1898); pantomime, *Echo et Narcisse* (Hellerau, 1912); *Festival vaudois* for Soli, Chorus, and Orch.; *La Veillée* for Soli, Chorus, and Orch.; *Dance Suite in A* for Orch.; *Suite de ballet;* 2 violin concertos; String Quartet; Suite for Cello and Piano; *Fantasia appassionata* for Violin and Piano; *Images* (1928); *Dialogues* (1931); *Ariettes* (1931); *Rondeaux* for Piano (1933); several collections of songs (*Chansons romandes et enfantines, Chansons populaires et enfantines, Idylles et chansons, Volkskinderlieder, Tanzlieder für Kinder, Chansons religieuses, Chansons de la gosse,* etc.). He publ. *Le Cœur chante; Impressions d'un musicien* (Geneva, 1900); *L'Education par le rhythme,* a series of lectures (1907); a comprehensive *Méthode Jaques-Dalcroze* (5 parts, 1907–14); *Rhythm, Music and Education* (Basel, 1922; in German, French, and Eng.); *Souvenirs* (Neuchâtel and Paris, 1942); *La Musique et nous* (Geneva, 1945); also "The Child and the Pianoforte," *Musical Quarterly* (April 1928); "Eurhythmics and Its Implications," in the *Musical Quarterly* (July 1930); "L'Improvisation au piano," *Rhythm* (1932).

BIBLIOGRAPHY: A. Seidl, *Die Hellerauer Schulfeste und die Bildungsanstalt Jaques-Dalcroze* (Regensburg, 1912); K. Storck, *Emile Jaques-Dalcroze: Seine Stellung und Aufgabe in unserer Zeit* (Stuttgart, 1912); M.E. Sadler, *Eurhythmics* (London, 1912); *Dalcroze Kongress-Bericht* (Geneva, 1926); H. Brunet-Lecomte, *Jaques-Dalcroze, Sa vie, son œuvre* (Geneva, 1950).

Járdányi, Pál, Hungarian composer; b. Budapest, Jan. 30, 1920; d. there, July 27, 1966. He studied piano and violin as a child; in 1938 became a composition student of Kodály at the Academy of Music in Budapest, where he later joined the faculty. He was awarded the Erkel Prize in 1952 and the Kossuth Prize in 1954. His works follow the style of modern Hungarian music, based on national folk songs.

WORKS: Sinfonietta (1940); *Divertimento concertante* for Orch. (1942–49); *Dance Music* for Orch. (1950); *Tisza mentén (Along the Tisza),* symph. poem (1951); *Vörösmarty Symphony* (1953); *Rhapsody from Borsod* for Orch. (1953); *Symphonic March* (1953); Harp Concerto (1959); *Vivente e moriente* for Orch. (1963); Concertino for Violin and String Orch. (1964); *Székely rapszódia* for Orch. (1965); violin duets (1934–37); Rondo for Piano (1939); Piano Sonata (1940); 2-piano Sonata (1942); 2 string quartets (1947, 1953–54); Flute Sonata (1952); *Fantasy and Variations on a Hungarian Folk Song* for Wind Quintet (1955); *Bulgarian Rhythm* for Piano Duet (1956); Quartet for 3 Violins and Cello (1958); String Trio (1959).

Jarecki, Henryk, Polish conductor and composer; b. Warsaw, Dec. 6, 1846; d. Lwow, Dec. 18, 1918. He studied with Moniuszko; from 1877 to 1900 he was conductor at the Lwow Opera; wrote 7 operas on subjects from Polish literature; also a *Polish Mass* and a number of songs.

Jarecki, Tadeusz, Polish conductor and composer; b. Lwow, Dec. 31, 1888; d. New York, April 29, 1955. He studied with his father, **Henryk Jarecki;** then went to Moscow, where he studied with Taneyev at the Moscow Cons., graduating in 1913. During World War I he lived in N.Y.; then went back to Poland and conducted opera in Stanislawow (1932–37); after a brief sojourn in Paris and in London he returned to N.Y., where he remained until his death. He composed a symph. suite, *Chimère* (1926); *Sinfonia breve* (which he conducted in Lwow, Jan. 15, 1932); 3 string quartets; songs. On Feb. 23, 1921, he married the American lyric soprano **Louise Llew-ellyn** (b. New York, Dec. 10, 1889; d. there, March 6, 1954).

Jarnach, Philipp, composer; b. Noisy, France, July 26, 1892; d. Bornsen, near Bergedorf, Dec. 17, 1982. He was a son of the Catalonian sculptor E. Jarnach and a German mother. He studied at the Paris Cons. with Risler (piano) and Lavignac (theory). At the outbreak of World War I he went to Zürich, where he met Busoni; this meeting was a decisive influence on his musical development; he became an ardent disciple of Busoni; after Busoni's death, he completed Busoni's last opera, *Doktor Faust,* which was produced in Jarnach's version in Dresden on May 21, 1925. During the years 1922–27 Jarnach wrote music criticism in Berlin. In 1927 he was appointed prof. of composition at the Cologne Cons., and remained at that post until 1949; from 1949 to 1970 he taught at the Hamburg Cons. Jarnach's own music is determined by his devotion to Busoni's ideals; it is distinguished by impeccable craftsmanship, but it lacks individuality. He participated in the modern movement in Germany between the two world wars, and many of his works were performed at music festivals during that period. Among his works are a *Sinfonie brevis* (1923); String Quintet (1920); String Quartet (1924); *Musik zum Gedächtnis des Einsamen* for String Quartet (1952); Sonatina for Flute and Piano; Cello Sonatina; etc.
BIBLIOGRAPHY: Hans Mersmann and E.G. Klussmann, *Philipp Jarnach zum 60. Geburtstag* (Hamburg, l952); also references in E.J. Dent's *Ferruccio Busoni* (Oxford, 1933).

Järnefelt, Armas, Finnish conductor and composer; b. Vyborg, Aug. 14, 1869; d. Stockholm, June 23, 1958. He studied with Wegelius at the Helsinki Cons. and also with Busoni, who taught there at the time; he then went to Berlin (1890) and to Paris (1892), where he studied with Massenet. He began his career as an opera coach in Magdeburg (1896); then was at Düsseldorf (1897). Returning to Finland in 1898, he was a conductor in his native town; in 1903 he received a government stipend for travel; was for 25 years conductor of the Stockholm Opera (1907–32);was conductor of the Helsinki Opera (1932–36), and of the Helsinki Municipal Orch. (1942–43). He was married to the Finnish singer **Maikki Pakarinen** (1893; divorced in 1908), then to another singer, **Liva Edström.** He wrote several works for orch., in a national Finnish style: *Korsholm, Suomen synty, Laulu Vuokselle, Abo slott,* etc.; his *Berceuse* and *Praeludium* for Small Orch. became extremely popular.
BIBLIOGRAPHY: Väinö Pesola, "Armas Järnefelt," *Suomen Säveltäjiä,* ed. by Sulho Ranta (Helsinki, 1945; pp. 300–306).

Järnefelt, Maikki (née **Pakarinen**), Finnish soprano, wife of **Armas Järnefelt;** b. Joensuu, Aug. 26, 1871; d. Turku, July 4, 1929. She studied with Mme. Marchesi in Paris; became a well-known opera

singer in Europe; also lived in America for several years. She was married to Järnefelt in 1893 and divorced in 1908; then was married to **Selim Palmgren** (1910).

Jarno, Georg, composer; b. Budapest, June 3, 1868; d. Breslau, May 20, 1920. He conducted opera in Breslau; produced his own operas there: *Die schwarze Kaschka* (May 12, 1895; his most successful opera), *Der Richter von Zalamea* (1899), and *Der Goldfisch* (1907); in Vienna he produced *Die Förster-Christel* (1907), *Das Musikantenmädel* (1910), and *Die Marine-Gustel* (1912). Another opera, *Das Farmermädchen,* was produced in Berlin (1913).

Jarnowick, Giovanni. See **Giornovichi, Giovanni Mare.**

Jarnowick, Pierre Louis Hus-Desforges. See **Hus-Desforges, Pierre Louis.**

Jaroch, Jiří, Czech composer; b. Smilkov, Sept. 23, 1920. He studied composition with Řídký at the Prague Cons.; played violin in theater orchs.; then was engaged as a program editor of musical broadcasts. As a composer, he takes a median line in Central European music, within the pragmatic limits of modernistic permissiveness.
WORKS: *Scherzo* for Orch. (1947); *Burlesque* for Orch. (1951); *Symphonic Dance* (1953); *Smuteční fantasie (Mourning Fantasy)* for Orch. (1954); 4 symphs.: No. 1 (1954–56), No. 2 (1958–60), No. 3, *Concertante,* for Violin and Orch. (1968–69), and No. 4 (1975); *Shakuntala,* suite for Orch. (1957); *Stařec a moře (The Old Man and the Sea),* symph. poem based on the Hemingway novel (1961); *Summer Festival,* tarantella for Orch. (1964); *Fantasy* for Viola and Orch. (1966); 2 string quartets (1949–50; 1970); *Children's Suite* for Nonet (1952); Nonet No. 2 (1963); *Metamorphosis* for 12 Winds (1967–68); Sonata for Solo Violin (1973).

Jarov, Sergei, Russian choral conductor; b. Moscow, March 20, 1896. He studied at the Academy for Church Singing at the Imperial Synod; then became a Cossack officer. After the Revolution and the defeat of the White Army, he left Russia and established the Don Cossack Chorus, with which he made successful tours in Europe; he eventually settled in America. The repertoire of his chorus includes popular Russian songs in artful arrangements, emphasizing dynamic contrasts, and also sacred works by Russian composers.

Jarre, Maurice, French composer for films; b. Lyons, Sept. 13, 1924. He studied electrical engineering at Lyons; in 1944 went to Paris and began to study music. He became a successful film composer; won the Academy Award for his emotional score to *Dr. Zhivago* (1966).
WORKS: *Mouvements en relief* for Orch.; *Polyphonies concertantes* for Piano, Trumpet, Percus-

sion, and Orch.; *Passacaille,* in memory of Honegger (Strasbourg Festival, June 15, 1956); *Mobiles* for Violin and Orch. (Strasbourg Festival, June 20, 1961).

Jarrett, Keith, American jazz pianist; b. Allentown, Pa., May 8, 1945. He studied in Boston; then began his career in 1965 with Art Blakey; from 1966 he played with Charles Lloyd's group, and subsequently toured with it. At the height of his career as a jazz virtuoso he bagan giving piano recitals of classical modern music, specializing in performances of Béla Bartók. He also composed several works in a somewhat improvisatory manner.

Järvi, Neeme, conductor; b. Tallinn, Estonia, June 7, 1937. He studied at the Tallinn Music School, graduating with degrees in percussion and choral conducting; then studied conducting at the Leningrad Cons. with Mravinsky. In 1963 he became conductor of the Estonian Radio and Television Orch. and chief conductor of the Estonian Opera Theater. In 1971 he won first prize at the international conducting competition sponsored by the Santa Cecilia Academy in Rome, which resulted in his appointment as chief conductor of the Estonian State Symph. Orch. He made guest appearances throughout the Soviet Union, Europe, and Japan. In 1980 he emigrated to the U.S.; subsequently was a guest conductor with the N.Y. Phil., Boston Symph., Philadelphia Orch., San Francisco Symph., National Symph., and Indianapolis Symph. In 1984 he became music director and principal conductor of the Scottish National Orch. in Glasgow.

Jaubert, Maurice, French composer; b. Nice, Jan. 3, 1900; killed in action in France, June 19, 1940. He studied law and took lessons in piano and composition at the Cons. of Nice. He abandoned the legal profession in 1923, when he went to Paris. He obtained considerable success with the score for the French film *Carnet de bal* (1938). His works include: *Suite française* for Orch. (St. Louis, Nov. 10, 1933); *Sonata a due* for Violin, Cello, and String Orch. (Boston, Dec. 27, 1946); *Jeanne d'Arc,* symph. poem (1937); etc.

Jausions, Dom Paul, French writer on church music; b. Rennes, Nov. 15, 1834; d. Vincennes, Ind., Sept. 9, 1870. He entered the order of St. Benedict at Solesmes in 1856, and under the direction of Dom Guéranger began to study Gregorian chant; continued his investigations together with Dom Pothier, whose *Mélodies grégoriennes* are the result of their joint labors. In 1869 he was sent to the U.S. to collect data for a biography of Bruté de Rémut, bishop of Vincennes (an uncle of Dom Guéranger), and died as he was about to return. His interpretation of the Gregorian melodies according to the tonic accent has become one of the guiding principles in the publications of the Benedictines of Solesmes. A complete list of his writings is found in the *Bibliographie des Bénédictins de la congrégation de France* (1907).

Jean-Aubry, Georges, French writer on music; b. Le Havre, Aug. 13, 1882; d. Weldon, Northamptonshire, Nov. 14, 1949. He was a journalist; became interested in music; traveled in Europe and South America (1908–15); then lived in London, where he edited the *Chesterian* (1919–30), house organ of the publishing firm J. & W. Chester; then returned to Paris. He publ. *La Musique française d'aujourd'hui* (1910; 2nd ed., 1916; in Eng., London, 1919) and *La Musique et les nations* (1922; in Eng., London, 1923).

Jeanneret, Albert, Swiss violinist, composer, and educator; b. La Chaux-de-Fonds, Feb. 7, 1886. He studied violin with Andreas Moser at the Hochschule für Musik in Berlin and with Henri Marteau at the Geneva Cons., graduating with the Premier Prix de Virtuosité in 1909; subsequently joined the staff of the Jaques-Dalcroze Institute of Eurhythmics in Hellerau. In 1919 he went to Paris, where he founded a school of rhythmic gymnastics and organized a children's orch. In 1939 he returned to Switzerland and settled in Vevey, where he led a children's orch. similar to the one he had in Paris. About the same time, he became a follower of the Moral Rearmament Movement. On July 21, 1968, he received (and subsequently publ.) a telepathic message from his brother, the architect Le Corbusier (Charles Edouard Jeanneret), who had died 3 years before, urging him to continue his pursuits of functional art. In accordance with these ideas, which he shared with his brother, Jeanneret wrote some 25 "symphonies enfantines" for children's orch., employing "bruits humanisés" produced by graduated bottles partially filled with water at different levels, metal pipes, wooden boxes, etc.; a *Suite pittoresque* for 3 Violins; and choruses for Moral Rearmament meetings.
BIBLIOGRAPHY: Pierre Meylan, "Albert Jeanneret et les 'bruits humanisés,'" *Revue Musicale de la Suisse Romande* (March 1971).

Jeannin, Dom Jules Cécilien, French musicologist, specialist on Gregorian chant; b. Marseilles, Feb. 6, 1866; d. Hautecombe, Feb. 15, 1933. He studied in Marseilles; later traveled extensively in Syria and Mesopotamia, gathering material for his collection *Mélodies liturgiques syriennes et chaldéennes* (in 3 vols.: I, 1925; II, 1928; III, not publ.). Other works: *Etudes sur le rythme grégorien* (Lyons, 1926); *Nuove osservazioni sulla ritmica gregoriana* (Turin, 1930); "La Question rythmique grégorienne," *Revue Musicale* (1930). As a scholar he was an opponent of Dom Mocquereau, and wrote a book, *Rythme grégorien: Réponse à Dom Mocquereau* (Lyons, 1928), disputing his theories. He spent the last years of his life as organist in the Hautecombe monastery.
BIBLIOGRAPHY: L. Bonvin, "Jules Cécilien Jeannin," *Kirchenmusikalisches Jahrbuch* (1930).

Jeanson, Bo Gunnar, Swedish musicologist; b. Göteborg, Oct. 10, 1898; d. Stockholm, Jan. 20, 1939. He studied at the Stockholm Cons. with L. Lundberg (piano) and T. Norlind (musicology); then took courses in Vienna with Wellesz, and in Freiburg, Switzerland, with Peter Wagner. In 1926 he received the degree of Dr.Phil., with a dissertation on August Söderman; in 1927 he became editor of the musicological publication *Svensk Tidskrift för Musikforskning.* He publ. a music history, *Musiken genom tiderna* (2 vols.; Stockholm, 1927 and 1931; revised by J. Rabe, 1945).

Jedliczka, Ernst, Russian pianist; b. Poltava, June 5, 1855; d. Berlin, Aug. 3, 1904. He studied at the Moscow Cons. with Tchaikovsky and Nicolai Rubinstein; then taught there (1881–88). In 1888 he settled in Berlin; was first a prof. of the Klindworth Inst. (1888–97); then at the Stern Cons. (from 1897).

Jeep, Johannes, German composer; b. Dransfeld, 1581; d. Hanau, Nov. 19, 1644. He studied in Göttingen and Celle; traveled in Italy; was Kapellmeister in Weickersheim (1613–33); cathedral organist in Frankfurt (1633–40); from 1640 was in Hanau. He publ. a book of songs for 3, 4, 5, and 6 Voices, *Studentengärtlein* (2 vols., 1607 and 1609; many subsequent reprints; included in H.J. Moser, *Studentenlust,* 1930); sacred songs (1607); secular songs, *Tricinia* (1610).
BIBLIOGRAPHY: W. Jeep, *Die Familie Jeep, 1540–1940* (Bremen, 1940); W. Brennecke, "Die Leichenpredigt auf Johann Jeep: Neues zur Biographie," *Archiv für Musikwissenschaft,* XV (1958).

Jefferson, "Blind Lemon," black American blues singer and guitarist; b. Couchman, Texas, July 1897; d. Chicago, Dec. 1929. He was afflicted by poor eyesight from childhood; as a youth he supported himself by singing in the streets of Texas towns and cities. In Dallas he met Huddie Ledbetter and formed a blues duo with him. In 1925 he settled in Chicago. His playing represented a Texas blues style akin to that of Leadbelly.

Jeffries (Jeffreys), George, English composer; b. c.1610; d. Weldon, July 1, 1685. He served as organist to King Charles I at the Chapel Royal; from 1646 was steward to Sir Christopher (later Lord) Hatton at Kirkby, Northamptonshire. Among his works (preserved in the British Library) are some 190 motets and anthems and several church services (in Latin); also madrigals, masques, and stage pieces.
BIBLIOGRAPHY: P. Aston, *George Jeffreys and the English Baroque* (Diss., Univ. of York, 1970; includes performing eds. of several of his works).

Jehin, François, celebrated Belgian violinist; b. Spa, Belgium, April 18, 1839; d. Montreal, Canada, May 29, 1899. As a child he studied with Servais and with his uncle, **François Prume,** whose name he added to his own, often performing as **Jehin-Prume;** then took lessons with Bériot at the Brussels Cons.; studied harmony with Fétis; won first prize in violin and in theory; at the age of 16, after completing advanced studies with Vieuxtemps and Wieniawski, he undertook a European tour; appeared with

Anton and Nicholas Rubinstein, Jenny Lind, and other celebrities; formed a famous trio with Kontski and Monsigny. In 1863 he traveled through Mexico, Cuba, and N.Y. to Montreal; met and married the singer **Rosita del Vecchio.** Thenceforth, his time was divided between Europe and America; he eventually settled in Montreal. Among his pupils was Eugène Ysaÿe. He wrote 2 violin concertos and many brilliant solo pieces for his instrument. He publ. in Montreal a book of memoirs, *Une Vie d'artiste* (contains a list of his works from op. 1 to op. 88).

Jelich, Vincenz, Austrian composer; b. Fiume, 1596; d. Zabern, Alsace, c.1636. His original name was **Jeličić,** indicating Croatian extraction. From 1606–9 he served as a choirboy in Graz; there he studied music with Matthia Ferrabosco; then was at the Jesuit Univ. (1610–15). In 1618 he went to Zabern in Alsace as a court musician. He publ. *Parnassia militia* (1622), 2 books of sacred songs under the title *Arion* (1628), and a number of motets.
BIBLIOGRAPHY: H. Federhofer, "Vincenz Jelich," *Archiv für Musikwissenschaft* (1955).

Jelinek, Hanns, Austrian composer; b. Vienna, Dec. 5, 1901; d. there, Jan. 27, 1969. He considered himself self-taught in composition, though he studied briefly with F. Schmidt and Berg in Vienna (1918–19) and had studies with Schoenberg and adopted the 12-tone method. In 1958 Jelinek was appointed a lecturer at the Academy of Music in Vienna, becoming a full prof. in 1965.
WORKS: Operetta, *Bubi Caligula* (1947; from this, the orch. pieces *Ballettmusik* and *Suite*). For orch.: 6 symphs.: No. 1 in D (1926–30; Breslau, June 13, 1932; revised in 1940 and in 1945–46); No. 2, *Sinfonia ritmica,* for Jazz Band and Orch. (1929; Vienna, March 14, 1931; revised in 1949); No. 3, *Heitere Symphonie,* for Brass and Percussion (1930–31; Vienna Festival of the International Society for Contemporary Music, June 20, 1932); No. 4, *Sinfonia concertante,* for String Quartet and Orch. (1931; revised 1953; Vienna, May 2, 1958); No. 5, *Symphonie brevis* (1948–50; Vienna, Dec. 19, 1950); No. 6, *Sinfonia concertante* (1953; Venice, Sept. 15, 1953; revised 1957); *Praeludium, Passacaglia und Fuge* for Flute, Clarinet, Bassoon, Horn, and Strings (1922; Wuppertal, March 12, 1954); *Sonata ritmica* for Jazz Band and Orch. (1928; revised 1960; Vienna, Nov. 26, 1960); *Rather Fast,* rondo for Jazz Band and Orch. (1929); Suite for String Orch. (1931); Concertino for String Quartet and String Orch. (1951); *Phantasie* for Clarinet, Piano, and Orch. (1951; Salzburg Festival of the ISCM, June 21, 1952); *Preludio solenne* for Orch. (1956); *Perergon* for Small Orch. (1957); *Rai buba,* étude for Piano and Orch. (1956–61). For voice: *Prometheus,* after Goethe, for Baritone and Orch. (1936); *Die Heimkehr,* radio cantata for Soloists, Chorus, Orch., and Tape (1954); *Unterwegs,* chamber cantata for Soprano, Vibraphone, and Double Bass (1957); *Begegnung,* dance scene for Chorus and Orch. (1965); songs. Chamber music: *6 Aphorismen* for 2 Clarinets and Bassoon (1923–30);

Jellinek – Jeney

Suite for Solo Cello (1930); 2 string quartets (1931, 1935); *Das Zwölftonwerk*, a collection of 9 individually titled chamber pieces in 2 series: Series one of 6 works for Piano (1947–49) and Series 2 of 3 works for Various Instruments (1950–52); *3 Blue Sketches* for 9 Jazz Soloists (1956); Sonata for Solo Violin (1956); *Ollapotrida*, suite for Flute and Guitar (1957); *2 Blue O's* for 7 Jazz Performers (1959); *10 Zahme Xenien* for Violin and Piano (1960). FOR PIANO: Sonatina (1923–30); *4 Structuren* (1952); *Zwölftonfibel* (1953–54).
WRITINGS: The manual *Anleitung zur Zwölftonkomposition* (2 vols., Vienna, 1952; 2nd ed., 1967).

Jellinek, George, writer on music; b. Budapest, Dec. 22, 1919. He studied violin in Hungary (1925–37); in 1941 he came to the U.S.; was naturalized as an American citizen in 1943; served in the U.S. Army; was active in broadcasting; in 1968 was named music director of radio station WQXR in N.Y., where he produced such popular programs as "The Vocal Scene" and "Music at First Hearing." From 1958 he was a contributing editor of *Stereo Review;* also wrote articles for the *Saturday Review, Opera News,* and other publications. In 1976 he became an associate prof. of music at N.Y. Univ. He received an honorary doctorate from Long Island Univ. in 1984. He wrote librettos for Eugene Zador's operas *The Magic Chair* and *The Scarlett Mill.* His study of Maria Callas, *Portrait of a Prima Donna,* was publ. in 1960.

Jelmoli, Hans, Swiss pianist and composer; b. Zürich, Jan. 17, 1877; d. there, May 6, 1936. He studied with Humperdinck and Iwan Knorr at Frankfurt; then conducted operatic productions in Mainz and Würzburg. Upon his return to Zürich, he was mainly active as a teacher and writer; wrote music criticism for the *Schweizerische Musikzeitung.* He composed the operas *Die Schweizer, Sein Vermächtnis,* and *Die Badener Fahrt;* incidental music to various plays; also 26 Swiss songs in the Zürich dialect. He publ. *Ferruccio Busonis Zürcher Jahre* (1928) and other pamphlets concerning musical life in Zürich.

Jemnitz, Sándor (Alexander), Hungarian composer; b. Budapest, Aug. 9, 1890; d. Balatonföldvár, Aug. 8, 1963. He studied with Koessler at the Budapest Academy (1912–16); then briefly with Max Reger in Leipzig. From 1917 to 1921 he occupied various posts as assistant conductor at German opera theaters; from 1921 to 1924, attended Schoenberg's classes at the Prussian Academy of Music in Berlin. In 1924 he returned to Budapest; was engaged as a music critic. As a composer, he followed the median line of Middle European modernism of the period between the 2 world wars, representing a curious compromise between the intricate contrapuntal idiom of Max Reger and the radical language of atonality modeled after Schoenberg's early works. He wrote mostly instrumental music.
WORKS: Concerto for Chamber Orch. (1931); *Pre-*

lude and Fugue for Orch. (1933); *7 Miniatures* for Orch. (1948); *Overture for a Peace Festival* (1951); Concerto for String Orch. (1954); Fantasy for Orch. (1956); 3 violin sonatas (1921, 1923, 1925); Cello Sonata (1922); 3 solo violin sonatas (1922, 1932, 1938); Flute Trio (1924); 2 wind trios (1925); Trumpet Quartet (1925); 2 string trios (1925, 1929); Flute Sonata (1931); Partita for 2 Violins (1932); Guitar Trio (1932); Solo Cello Sonata (1933); Solo Harp Sonata (1933); *Duet Sonata* for Saxophone and Banjo (1934); Solo Double-bass Sonata (1935); Solo Trumpet Sonata (1938); Solo Flute Sonata (1941); Solo Viola Sonata (1941); String Quartet (1950); 2 suites for Violin and Piano (1952, 1953); Trio for Flute, Oboe, and Clarinet (1958); *3 Pieces* for Piano (1915); 2 piano sonatinas (1919); *17 Bagatelles* for Piano (1919); 5 piano sonatas (1914, 1927, 1929, 1933, 1954); *Recueil* for Piano (1938–45); Sonata for Pedal Organ (1941); *8 Pieces for Piano* (1951); 2 organ sonatas (1959); songs. His ballet, *Divertimento,* written in 1921, was not produced until 26 years later (Budapest, April 23, 1947). He also publ. brief monographs on Mozart, Beethoven, Mendelssohn, Schumann, and Chopin.

Jencks, Gardner, American pianist and composer; b. New York, Jan. 7, 1907. He studied piano with Heinrich Gebhard in Boston in the summer of 1923; in 1927 began taking piano lessons with Josef and Rosina Lhévinne in N.Y.; later took courses at the Diller-Quaile School (1930–34); concurrently took private lessons in composition with Franklin Robinson; in 1934 he went to Baltimore, where he enrolled in the Peabody Inst. of Music in the composition class of Gustav Strube, receiving his "artist's diploma" in 1940. On Feb. 24, 1941, he made his debut in N.Y. as a pianist to excellent critical acclaim; he combined his concert career with continued studies in composition; in 1956 he took courses at Columbia Univ. with Roger Goeb and Henry Cowell; as a practicing composer, he set for himself a rigid regimen, with a minimum yearly output of 30 pieces, all of them for piano. His idiom of composition was derived from the considerations of relative sonorous masses in chordal structures and interactive rhythmic patterns; the general effect may be likened to neo-Classical concepts; indeed, most of his works bear formal designations, such as sonata; tonality and atonality are applied without prejudice in his melodic lines, as are concords and discords in contrapuntal combinations.

Jeney, Zoltán, Hungarian composer; b. Szolnok, March 4, 1943. He studied piano as a child; took courses in music theory with Zoltán Pongrácz at the Kodály Vocational Music School at Debrecen; then became a student of Farkas at the Academy of Music in Budapest (1961–66); subsequently went to Rome and attended a seminar in composition with Goffredo Petrassi at the Santa Cecilia Academy (1967–69). His music is constructivist, derived from the acoustical agglutination of kindred sounds.
WORKS: *5 Songs* for Soprano, Clarinet, Cello, and Harp (1963); *Statue of Streaming* for Vocal Quintet

(1965); *Omaggio* for Soprano and Orch. (1966); *Aritmie—Ritmiche* for Flute and Cello (1967); *Soliloquium* No. 1 for Flute (1967); *Wei wu wei* for Flute, Clarinet, Viola, Cello, Double Bass, Harp, Piano, Celesta, and Percussion (1968); *Alef (Hommage à Schönberg)* for Orch. (1971–72; Budapest, June 19, 1972); *Mandala* for 3 Hammond Organs (1972); *Yanta* for any number of Electric Organs (1972); *Round* for Piano, Harp, and Harpsichord (1972); *4 Sounds* for 3 to 11 Instruments (1972); *Movements of the Eye I* for Piano, *II* for 2 Prepared Pianos, and *III* for 3 Pianos (all 1973); *For Quartet (Wei wu wei* No. 2) for String Quartet (1973).

Jenkins, David, Welsh composer; b. Trecastle, Dec. 30, 1848; d. Aberystwyth, Dec. 10, 1915. He studied at the Univ. of Wales; then taught there; became widely known as a choral conductor; wrote oratorios and other choral works for Welsh festivals; his cantata, *The Ark of the Covenant,* was performed at the Caernarvon Festival in 1876. He was editor of the Welsh music periodical *Y Cerddor.*

Jenkins, Gordon, American pianist, composer, and arranger; b. Webster Groves, Mo., May 12, 1910; d. Malibu, Calif., April 24, 1984, of amyotrophic lateral sclerosis (Lou Gehrig's disease). He played "relief" organ at a Chicago movie theater, where his father was a regular organist; was a pianist at a St. Louis speakeasy during Prohibition; then was employed in various capacities at a St. Louis radio station. He was hired by Isham Jones as pianist and arranger in his band; in 1936 the band was taken over by Woody Herman, and Jenkins continued to arrange for him. He also wrote for Paul Whiteman, Benny Goodman, and André Kostelanetz. In 1938 he moved to California, where he took charge of the West Coast outlet of NBC. In 1945 he became conductor of Decca Records, and made records himself; his performing hits were *I Wanna Be Loved* and *Bewitched;* the identifiable characteristic of his music was extreme sentimentality, with throbbing violins and sobbing female voices. In 1945 he composed the score for *Manhattan Tower,* and in 1949 wrote the Broadway musical *Along Fifth Avenue.* Among his hit songs were *P.S. I Love You* and *When a Woman Loves a Man.*

Jenkins, John, English composer; b. Maidstone, 1592; d. Kimberley, Norfolk, Oct. 26, 1678. His father was a carpenter by trade but was apparently musical, for upon his death, in 1617, an inventory of his possessions included "Seven Vialls and Violyns, One Bandora and a Cytherne." In John's early years he was a domestic tutor and lute player to various aristocrats; also played at the courts of Charles I and Charles II. He wrote many *Fancies* for viols or organ, and light pieces which he called *Rants;* of these, *Mitter Rant* was included in Playford's *Musick's Handmaid* (1678); *The Fleece Tavern Rant* and *The Peterborough Rant,* both in Playford's *Apollo's Banquet* (1690); his popular air *The Lady Katherine Audley's Bells* or *The Five Bell Consort* appeared in Playford's *Courtly Masquing Ayres*

(1662). He wrote some music for violin; an edition entitled *12 Sonatas for 2 Violins and a Base, with a Thorough Base for the Organ or Theorbo* attributed to Jenkins, and supposedly publ. in London in 1660, is not extant; the claim made by some historians that Jenkins was the first English composer of violin sonatas cannot be sustained inasmuch as William Young had anticipated him by publishing 11 violin sonatas in 1653. Reprints: *John Jenkins, Fancies and Ayres,* ed. by Helen Joy Sleeper (Wellesley, 1950); *J. J. 3 Part Fancy and Ayre Divisions* (Wellesley Ed. 10, 1966); *J. J. Consort Music of 4 Parts,* ed. by Andrew Ashbee (*Musica Britannica,* 26, 1969).

BIBLIOGRAPHY: J.T. Johnson, "How to 'Humor' John Jenkins' 3-Part Dances," *Journal of the American Musicological Society* (Summer 1967); A. Ashbee, "John Jenkins's Fantasia-Suites for Treble, 2 Basses and Organ," *Chelys,* 1, 2 (1969, 1970); G. Dodd, "Provisional Index of the Works of J. J.," *Chelys,* 1 (1969); A. Ashbee, "The 4-Part Consort Music of J. J.," *Proceedings of the Royal Music Association* (1969–70); A.C. Coxon, "A Handlist of the Sources of John Jenkins' Vocal and Instrumental Music," *R.M.A. Research Chronicle,* 9 (1971).

Jenkins, Newall, American conductor and musicologist; b. New Haven, Conn., Feb. 8, 1915. He studied at the Orchesterschule der Sachsischen Staatskapelle in Dresden, and later in Freiburg at the Städtische Musikseminar; also took courses with Willibald Gurlitt in Freiburg and with Carl Orff in Munich. Upon his return to the U.S., he worked with Leon Barzin at the National Orch. Assoc. in N.Y. Following army service in World War II, he received a Fulbright grant to study in Italy. In 1957 he founded the Clarion Music Society of N.Y.; with it he presented a stimulating series of annual concerts of rarely performed works of the Baroque period. He also appeared as a guest conductor in London, Hilversum, Milan, Naples, Turin, Florence, Stuttgart, and Stockholm. In 1975 he founded the Festival of Venetian Music of the 17th and 18th Centuries at Castelfranco Veneto. From 1964 to 1974 he taught at N.Y. Univ.; from 1971 to 1979 he was a lecturer at the Univ. of Calif. at Irvine. He edited (with B. Churgin) *Thematic Catalogue of the Works of G.B. Sammartini* (1976); also edited the symphs. of Brunetti (1979).

Jenko, Davorin, Slovenian composer; b. Dvorje, Nov. 9, 1835; d. Ljubljana, Nov. 25, 1914. He studied jurisprudence and music in Trieste and Vienna; was a choral conductor in Belgrade (1871–1902); then settled in Ljubljana. He was the composer of the first Serbian operetta, *Vračara (The Fortune Teller;* Belgrade, May 3, 1882), a musical comedy, *Dido* (Belgrade, June 19, 1892), and many choral works. The melody of the royal Serbian national anthem was taken from one of Jenko's choruses.

Jenks, Alden Ferriss, American composer; b. Harbor Beach, Mich., Aug. 10, 1940. He studied at Yale Univ. (B.A., 1962) and at the Univ. of Calif. at Berkeley (M.A., 1968); also attended seminars with Karlheinz Stockhausen at the Univ. of Calif., at Davis (1966–67). In 1968 he organized in Berkeley a group called Deus ex Machina, which gave performances of acoustical and electronic music with human and mechanical participants. His productions fall into three categories: (1) written scores that can be performed by untutored players; (2) electronic music on magnetic tape; and (3) conceptual composition that exists only in verbalized instructions. Inventory: *Expedition* for Orch. (1964); *The Exterminator* for Double Chorus and Individual Speaking, Shouting, Laughing, and occasionally Singing Voices (1965); *Quasar* for Brass and Percussion (1966); *Chez Elle* for Magnetic Tape (1968); *Q.E.D.* for Amplified Autoharp, Amplified Metal Wastebasket, Modulated Spoken Material, and Slide Projector (1969); *Emissions,* duet for 3 World War II Shortwave Receivers and a Gesticulating Lecturer whose discourse is inaudible (1969); *The Magic Pillow Show* for Mixed Media (1970); music for experimental films.

Jenner, Gustav, German composer and writer; b. Keitum, Dec. 3, 1865; d. Marburg, Aug. 29, 1920. He studied with Mandyczewski, and also took some lessons with Brahms; in 1895, became music director at Marburg. He composed fine lieder, choral works, several violin sonatas, a Trio for Piano, Clarinet, and Horn; transcribed old German songs, etc.; publ. *Johannes Brahms als Mensch, Lehrer und Künstler* (1905; 2nd ed., 1930).
   BIBLIOGRAPHY: W. Kohleick, *Gustav Jenner* (1943).

Jennings, Waylon (Arnold), American country-music singer, guitarist, and songwriter; b. Littlefield, Texas, June 15, 1937. Taking up the guitar in his youth, he dropped out of school at 14; then played bass in Buddy Holly's band (1958–59); subsequently formed his own band, The Waylors; in 1965 he went to Nashville, where he became a leading figure in the promotion of "outlaw" country music, or redneck rock, and a traditional country-blues style; he won a wide following with such recordings as *Lonesome, On'ry and Mean* (1973), *Honky Tonk Heroes* (1973), *This Time* (1974), *Waylon, the Ramblin' Man* (1974), and *Dreamin' My Dreams* (1975). His album *Wanted: The Outlaws* (1976) garnered a platinum album award.

Jensen, Adolf, German composer; b. Königsberg, Jan. 12, 1837; d. Baden-Baden, Jan. 23, 1879. He stemmed from a family of musicians in Königsberg; studied with Ehlert and Köhler; began to compose as a boy; at 19, went to Russia as a music tutor; then was theater conductor in Posen (1857); was in Copenhagen (1858–60), where he studied with Gade; then returned to Königsberg. He subsequently taught at Tausig's school in Berlin (1866–68); then lived in Dresden, Graz, and finally at Baden-Baden, where he died of consumption. A great admirer of Schumann, he closely imitated him in his songs, of which about 160 were publ. He also wrote an opera,

Die Erbin von Montfort (1864–65); it was revised by Kienzl, to a new libretto by Jensen's daughter, under the title *Turandot*. Other works are the cantatas *Jephthas Tochter, Der Gang der Jünger nach Emmäus, Adonisfeier,* etc., and many characteristic piano pieces.
   BIBLIOGRAPHY: A. Niggli, *Adolph Jensen* (Zürich, 1895); another biography, also by Niggli, was publ. in Heinrich Reimann's *Berühmte Musiker* (Berlin, 1900); G. Schweizer, *Das Liedschaffen A. Jensens* (Frankfurt, 1933). Jensen's letters were publ. by P. Kuczynski (1879).

Jensen, Gustav, German violinist and composer, brother of **Adolf Jensen;** b. Königsberg, Dec. 25, 1843; d. Cologne, Nov. 26, 1895. He studied with his brother; then with Dehn in Berlin (theory) and with Joachim (violin). In 1872 he became prof. of composition at the Cologne Cons., and held that position until his death. He wrote a Symph.; String Quartet; Violin Sonata; Cello Sonata; *Ländliche Serenade* for String Orch.; various violin pieces; publ. the series Klassische Violinmusik; trans. into German Cherubini's *Manual of Counterpoint.*

Jensen, Ludvig Irgens. See **Irgens Jensen, Ludwig.**

Jensen, Niels Peter, Danish organist and composer; b. Copenhagen, July 23, 1802; d. there, Oct. 19, 1846. He was blind from childhood, but learned to play the flute and organ; was organist at St. Peter's Church in Copenhagen from 1828. He wrote 2 sonatas and other pieces for the flute.

Jenson, Dylana, talented American violinist; b. Los Angeles, May 14, 1960. Her mother gave her early instruction in violin playing; later she took lessons with Manuel Compinsky. She was a soloist with the N.Y. Phil. at the age of 12, in the Mendelssohn Concerto; at 13 she began studies with Nathan Milstein in Zürich; at 14 she made her European debut there. In 1978 she won second prize in the Tchaikovsky Competition in Moscow, which automatically launched her on a successful career; she played with the Philadelphia Orch., the Chicago Symph., the Cleveland Orch., the San Francisco Symph., the Minneapolis Orch., and the Los Angeles Phil.; also toured in recital in Germany, the Soviet Union, and Latin America.

Jeppesen, Knud, eminent Danish musicologist and composer; b. Copenhagen, Aug. 15, 1892; d. Aarhus, Denmark, June 14, 1974. He studied at the Univ. of Copenhagen with Laub and Nielsen, and at the Univ. of Vienna with G. Adler and R. Lach (Dr.Phil., 1922, with the dissertation *Die Dissonanzbehandlung in den Werken Palestrinas;* Eng. trans. by Margaret W. Hamerik, as *The Style of Palestrina and the Dissonance,* with introduction by E.J. Dent, Copenhagen, 1927; 2nd ed., 1946; very valuable). From 1920 to 1946, he taught at the Cons. in Copenhagen; in 1946–57 was a prof. of musicology at the

Univ. of Aarhus; from 1931 to 1954, editor of *Acta Musicologica*. He edited *Der Kopenhagener Chansonnier* (1927). Other writings: *Kontrapunkt* (1930; Eng. trans., with introduction by Glen Haydon, N.Y., 1939; 2nd German ed., Leipzig, 1956); *Die mehrstimmige italienische Laude um 1500* (1935); *Die italienische Orgelmusik am Anfang des Cinquecento* (Copenhagen, 1943); etc. In his compositions Jeppesen lives up to his reputation as a profound student of polyphonic masterpieces of the Renaissance; his music is the product of his erudition: precise in its counterpoint, unfailingly lucid in its harmonic structure, and set in impeccable classical forms.

WORKS: Opera, *Rosaura* (1946; Copenhagen, Sept. 20, 1950); Symph. (1939); Horn Concerto (1941); *Little Summer Trio* for Flute, Cello, and Piano (1941); *Te Deum Danicum* (1942; Copenhagen, 1945; London, Oct. 27, 1948); *Tvesang (Twin Song)* for Tenor, Bass, Double Chorus, Orch., Piano, and Organ (1965; Danish Radio, Copenhagen, Jan. 12, 1967).

BIBLIOGRAPHY: A Festschrift, *Natalicia musicologica: Knud Jeppesen, septuagenario collegis oblata*, co-ed. by Søren Sørensen and Bjørn Hjelmborg (Copenhagen, 1962).

Jepson, Harry Benjamin, American organist; b. New Haven, Conn., Aug. 16, 1870; d. Noank, Conn., Aug. 23, 1952. He studied organ with Stoeckel, and composition with Horatio Parker; in 1895, was appointed instructor of organ at Yale Univ., and served in that capacity until 1950. He edited *Yale University Hymns* and publ. a number of works for organ.

Jepson, Helen, American soprano; b. Titusville, Pa., Nov. 28, 1904. Of a musical family, she sang in church choirs at 13 in Akron, Ohio, where she went to school; worked as a corset fitter and salesgirl; then was enabled to go to Philadelphia to study at the Curtis Inst. (1923–28); in 1936, went to Paris to study with Mary Garden; also took lessons with Queena Mario; then became a member of the Philadelphia Grand Opera Co. She made her debut with the Metropolitan Opera Co. on Jan. 24, 1935, and remained on the staff until 1943; also sang with the Chicago Civic Opera Co. She was married to George Rosco Possell (1931); divorced, and married Walter Dellera (1942).

Jeremiáš, Jaroslav, Czech composer, son of the organist and composer **Bohuslav Jeremiáš** (1859–1918); b. Písek, Aug. 14, 1889; d. Budějovice, Jan. 16, 1919. He studied at the Prague Cons.; also took lessons with Novák. He was engaged as an opera conductor at Ljubljana, then returned to Prague. Although he died at the age of 29, he left several significant works: the opera *Starý král (The Old King;* produced posthumously, Prague, April 13, 1919); the oratorio *Jan Hus* (also posthumous; Prague, June 13, 1919); a Viola Sonata; songs.

BIBLIOGRAPHY: B. Bělohlávek, *Jaroslav Jeremiáš* (Prague, 1935).

Jeremiáš, Otakar, Czech conductor and composer, brother of **Jaroslav Jeremiáš;** b. Písek, Oct. 17, 1892; d. Prague, March 5, 1962. He studied composition, as did his brother, with Vítězslav Novák at the Prague Cons.; also took lessons in cello playing; was a cellist in the Czech Phil. He subsequently directed a music school at Budějovice (1918–28); conducted the orch. of the Prague Radio (1929–45); was director of the Prague Opera (1945–51) and the first chairman of the Czech Composers Guild. His music continues the traditions of the Czech national school, with a pronounced affinity to the style of Smetana, Foerster, and Ostrčil.

WORKS: 2 operas: *Bratři Karamazovi (The Brothers Karamazov,* after Dostoyevsky, 1922–27; Prague, Oct. 8, 1928) and *Enšpígl (Til Eulenspiegel,* 1940–44; Prague, May 13, 1949); 2 cantatas: *Mohamedův zpěv* (1932) and *Písně o rodné zemi (Song of the Native Land,* 1940–41); *Písně jara (Spring Song)* for Orch. (1907–8); *Podzimní suita (Autumn Suite)* for Orch. (1907–8); 2 symphs. (1910–11, 1914–15); *Jarní předehra (Spring Overture,* 1912); *Fantasie* for Orch. and 2 Mixed Choruses (1915; Prague Radio, Oct. 27, 1942); *Romance o Karlu IV,* melodrama with Orch. (1917); *Láska,* 5 songs with Orch. (1921); Piano Trio (1909–10); String Quartet (1910); Piano Quartet (1911); String Quintet (1911); *Fantasie na staročeské chorály (Fantasy on Old Czech Chorales)* for Nonet (1938); 2 piano sonatas (1909, 1913); songs; film music.

BIBLIOGRAPHY: J. Plavec, *Otakar Jeremiáš* (Prague, 1943; contains a list of works with dates of perf.).

Jerger, Alfred, Austrian bass-baritone; b. Brno, June 9, 1889; d. Vienna, Nov. 18, 1976. He was educated in Vienna; made his formal debut with the Munich Opera in 1919; from 1921 till 1953 was a member of the Vienna State Opera. In 1947 he joined the faculty of the Vienna Academy of Music. Among his many outstanding roles was that of Mandryka in *Arabella* by Richard Strauss in its first performance in Dresden, on July 1, 1933.

Jeritza (real name, **Jedlitzka**), **Maria,** dramatic soprano; b. Brünn, Oct. 6, 1887; d. Orange, N.J., July 10, 1982. She studied voice privately as a young girl, then joined the chorus at the Brünn Opera. She made her professional debut in Olmütz, as Elsa in *Lohengrin* in 1910; later sang at the Vienna Volksoper, where she made her debut in 1911, as Elisabeth in *Tannhäuser.* Emperor Franz Josef heard her sing the part of Rosalinda in *Die Fledermaus* at the summer spa in Bad Ischl, and was so impressed by her physical appearance, as well as her voice, that he decreed that she should be engaged at the Vienna Opera. This was the beginning of a glorious career. On Oct. 25, 1912, she created the title role in the opera *Ariadne auf Naxos* by Richard Strauss at the Stuttgart Opera Theater. She also created the role of the Empress in the first performance of *Die Frau ohne Schatten* by Richard Strauss, in Vienna on Oct. 10, 1919. One of her most impressive subsequent appearances was that of Marietta in Korngold's opera *Die tote Stadt,* which she sang in Hamburg on Dec. 4, 1920. She also sang this role in the American premiere of Korngold's opera, on Nov. 19, 1921, in her American debut at the Metropolitan Opera in N.Y. Her appearance in the title role of *Tosca* at the Metropolitan Opera on Dec. 1, 1921, established her as a prima donna beyond the reach of any female rival; N.Y. critics praised not only her exquisite voice and dramatic power, but also her blonde beauty and other undeniable feminine attractions. She was equally impressive in such diverse roles as Sieglinde, Thaïs, Minnie in *The Girl of the Golden West,* and the title role of *Turandot.* Faithful to the developing talent of Erich Korngold, she sang the title role in the American premiere of his *Violanta* at the Metropolitan Opera, on Nov. 5, 1927. By turning the musical clock around, she sang operettas by Suppé with extraordinary effect; she also toured the U.S. in Rudolf Friml's operetta *Music Hath Charms* in 1934. She was married 3 times: to Baron Leopold Popper de Podhurgen in 1919 (divorced in 1935); to the motion picture executive Winfield Sheehan; and, after Sheehan's death in 1945, to Irving P. Seery, a New Jersey businessman, who died in 1966. A convivial person, she maintained many friends; her 90th birthday was celebrated at her estate in October 1977; she was 94 when she died. She publ. *Sunlight and Song,* an autobiography (N.Y., 1924); a monograph on her life and career by Ernst Decsey was publ. in Vienna in 1931.

Jersild, Jørgen, Danish composer and music pedagogue; b. Copenhagen, Sept. 17, 1913. He studied musicology at the Univ. of Copenhagen, obtaining his Magister Artis degree in 1940; then went to Paris, where he studied with Albert Roussel; returning to Denmark, he taught music history and theory at the Copenhagen Cons. His works are written in an effective neo-Classical manner with an impressionistic flavor. He composes mostly in small forms; among his works are *Pastorale* for Strings (1945); Serenade for Wind Instruments (1947); a group of *Quartetti piccoli* for String Quartet (1950); a ballet, *Lunefulde Lucinda* (1954); Harp Concerto (Aldeburg, June 9, 1972). He publ. a number of informative articles dealing with Danish music history; also several useful singing manuals, among them a book on solfeggio (Copenhagen, 1948; also in Eng., N.Y., 1966).

Jerusalem, Siegfried, German tenor; b. Oberhausen, April 17, 1940. He studied violin and piano at the Folkwang Hochschule in Essen; then played bassoon in German orchs., including the Stuttgart Radio Symph.; at the same time he studied voice, finally deciding to turn to singing as a career; appeared in opera in Stuttgart, Hamburg, and Zürich.

Jervis-Read, Harold Vincent, English composer; b. Powyke, Worcestershire, March 14, 1883; d. Salisbury, Dec. 15, 1945. He studied at the Royal Academy of Music, and later taught there. He wrote for chorus *The Hound of Heaven, Dream Tryst, That Land, To the Daughter of Earth, High Tide,* etc.;

String Sextet; 2 piano sonatas; *5 Caprices* for Piano; songs; etc.

Jesinghaus, Walter, Swiss violinist and composer; b. Genoa, July 13, 1902; d. Ticino, Sept. 17, 1966. He studied violin in Milan and Lugano; gave concerts as a child virtuoso. In 1918 he went to Zürich to study academic music subjects with Andreae and Jarnach; later enrolled at the Basel Cons.; in 1921–25 was active as a theater conductor in Germany; in 1925 he settled in Lugano. He wrote several operas (*Tartuffe, Sœur Béatrice, Belinda e il mostro, La luna e la città*); also a *Symphonia choralis* and much chamber music, including a number of pieces for viola d'amore.
  BIBLIOGRAPHY: D. Poli, *Walter Jesinghaus* (Bologna, 1929).

Jessel, Léon, German operetta composer; b. Stettin, Jan. 22, 1871; d. Berlin, Jan. 4, 1942. He began his career as a theater conductor in Germany; then produced numerous operettas, some of which enjoyed considerable popular success, among them *Die beiden Husaren* (Berlin, 1913), *Schwarzwaldmädel* (1917), *Verliebte Frauen* (1920), *Die Postmeisterin* (1921), *Schwalbenhochzeit* (1921), *Des Königs Nachbarin* (1924), *Die Luxuskabine* (1929), *Junger Wein* (1933), and *Die goldene Mühle* (1940). His piano piece *Die Parade der Zinnsoldaten (The Parade of Tin Soldiers),* composed in 1905, achieved perennial popularity.

Ježek, Jaroslav, Czech composer; b. Prague, Sept. 25, 1906; d. New York, Jan. 1, 1942. He studied composition with Jirák and Josef Suk; also experimented with quarter-tone techniques under the direction of Alois Hába. In 1928 he became resident composer for the "Liberated Theater," a Prague satirical revue; produced the scenic music for 20 of its plays. In 1939, shortly before the occupation of Czechoslovakia by the Nazis, he emigrated to America.
  WORKS: For Orch.: Piano Concerto (Prague, June 23, 1927); *Nerves,* ballet (1928); Fantasy for Piano and Orch. (Prague, June 24, 1930); Concerto for Violin and Wind Orch. (Prague, Sept. 26, 1930); *Symphonic Poem* (Prague, March 25, 1936). Chamber music: Wind Quartet (1929); Wind Quintet (1931); String Quartet No. 1 (1932); Violin Sonata (1933); Duo for 2 Violins (1934); String Quartet No. 2 (1941). For Piano: Suite for Quarter-tone Piano (1927); *Capriccio* (1932); *Bagatelles* (1933); *Rhapsody* (1938); *Toccata* (1939); Sonata (1941).

Jílek, František, Czech conductor; b. Brno, May 22, 1913. He took courses in conducting with Zdenek Chalabala; then engaged in a professional career; conducted opera in Ostrava (1939–48) and Brno (1948–52). From 1952 to 1978 he was chief conductor of the Brno Opera. In 1978 he became chief conductor of the Brno State Phil. Orch. In addition, he taught at the Janáček Academy of Music in Brno.

Jiménez-Mabarak, Carlos, Mexican composer; b.

Tacuba, Jan. 31, 1916. He studied piano with Jesús Castillo in Guatemala; attended classes in humanities in Santiago, Chile (1930–33); then studied musicology with Charles Van den Borren in Brussels (1933–36); returned to Mexico in 1937 and studied conducting with Revueltas. After more travel in Europe, he taught music theory at the National Cons. in Mexico (1942–65) and at the School of Arts in Villahermosa (1965–68). He draws his thematic materials from the folk songs of Mexico; his predilection is for the theater; he was one of the first to use electronic music and "musique concrète" in Mexico.

WORKS: Opera, *Misa de seis* (Mexico City, June 21, 1962); incidental music to *Calígula*, after Camus (1947); ballets: *Perifonema* (Mexico City, March 9, 1940); *El amor del agua* (Mexico City, 1950); *El Ratón Pérez* (1955); *El Paraíso de los Ahogados*, "música magnetofónica" (1960); *Pitágoras dijo ...* for Small Ensemble (1966); several cantatas; Piano Concerto (1944); 2 symphs. (1945, 1962); *Sinfonia Concertante* for Piano and Orch. (1966; Mexico City, March 11, 1977); *Concierto del abuelo* for Piano and String Quartet (1938); Concerto for Timpani, Bells, Xylophone, and Percussion (1961); *La ronda junto a la fuente* for Flute, Oboe, Violin, Viola, and Cello (1965); piano pieces; songs.

Jirák, Karel Boleslav, eminent Czech composer and conductor; b. Prague, Jan. 28, 1891; d. Chicago, Jan. 30, 1972. He studied privately with Vítězslav Novák and with J.B. Foerster. In 1915 he was appointed conductor of the Hamburg City Opera; in 1918 went to Brno, where he was conductor at the National Theater for a season (1918–19). He then was choral conductor and prof. of composition at the Prague Cons. (1920–30); from 1930 to 1945, was music director of the Czechoslovak Radio. In 1947 he went to the U.S.; in 1948 became chairman of the theory dept. at Roosevelt College (later Univ.) in Chicago; held the same position also at Chicago Cons. College, from 1967 to 1971. His music represents the finest traditions of Middle-European 20th-century Romanticism.

WORKS: Opera, *A Woman and God* (1911–14; Brno, March 10, 1928); 6 symphs.: No. 1 (1915–16); No. 2 (1924); No. 3 (1929–38; Prague, March 8, 1939); No. 4, *Episode from an Artist's Life* (1945; Prague, April 16, 1947); No. 5 (1949; Edinburgh Festival, Aug. 26, 1951; winner of the Edinburgh International Festival prize); No. 6 (1957–70; Prague, Feb. 17, 1972); *Overture to a Shakespearean Comedy* (1917–21; Prague, Feb. 24, 1927); Serenade for Strings (1939); *Symphonic Variations* (Prague, March 26, 1941); *Overture "The Youth"* (1940–41); Rhapsody for Violin and Orch. (1942); *Symphonietta* for Small Orch. (1943–44); Piano Concerto (1946; Prague, Dec. 12, 1968); *Symphonic Scherzo* for Band or Orch. (1950; orch. version, Chicago, April 25, 1953); Serenade for Small Orch. (1952; first complete perf., Santa Barbara, Calif., March 24, 1965); *Legend* for Small Orch. (1954; Chicago, March 20, 1962); Concertino for Violin and Chamber Orch. (1957; Chicago, May 18, 1963). CHAMBER MUSIC: 7 string quartets (1915, 1927,

1937–40, 1949, 1951, 1957–58, 1960); String Sextet, with Alto Voice (1916–17); Cello Sonata (1918); *Night Music* for Violin and Piano (1918; orchestrated, 1928); Violin Sonata (1919); Viola Sonata (1925); Divertimento for String Trio (1925); Flute Sonata (1927); Wind Quintet (1928); *3 Pieces* for Violin and Piano (1929); *Variations, Scherzo and Finale,* nonet (1943); Serenade for Winds (1944); Piano Quintet (1945); Violin Sonatina (1946); *Mourning Music* for Viola and Organ (1946; also orchestrated); Clarinet Sonata (1947); *Introduction and Rondo* for Horn and Piano (1951); *3 Pieces* for Cello and Piano (1952); Horn Sonata (1952); Oboe Sonata (1953); Trio for Oboe, Clarinet, and Bassoon (1956); *4 Essays* for Violin and Piano (1959–62); Suite for Solo Violin (1964); Piano Trio (1966–67); Bass Clarinet Sonatina (1968–69). VOCAL WORKS: *Psalm 23* for Chorus and Orch. (1919); *Requiem* for Solo Quartet, Chorus, Organ, and Orch. (1952; Prague, Nov. 17, 1971); several a cappella works for male chorus; song cycles (many also with orch.): *Lyric Intermezzo* (1913); *Tragicomedy,* 5 songs (1913); *Fugitive Happiness,* 7 songs (1915–16); *13 Simple Songs* (1917); *3 Songs of the Homeland* (1919); *Evening and Soul* (1921); *Awakening* (1925); *The Rainbow* (1925–26); *The Year* (1941); *7 Songs of Loneliness* (1945–46); *Pilgrim's Songs* (1962–63); *The Spring* (1965). FOR PIANO: *Summer Nights,* 4 pieces (1914); *Suite in Olden Style* (1920); *The Turning Point* (1923); 2 sonatas (1926, 1950); *Epigrams and Epitaphs* (1928–29); *4 Caprices in Polka Form* (1945); *5 Miniatures* (1954); *4 Pieces for the Right Hand* (1968–69). FOR ORGAN: *5 Little Preludes and Fugues* (1957); Suite (1958–64); Passacaglia and Fugue (1971); also incidental music for plays. He is the author of a textbook on musical form (in Czech, 5 eds., 1924–45).

BIBLIOGRAPHY: M. Očadlík, *Karel Boleslav Jirák* (Prague, 1941).

Jiránek, Josef, Bohemian violinist and pedagogue; b. Ledeč, March 24, 1855; d. Prague, Jan. 5, 1940. He studied music with Smetana, who legally adopted him; then took violin lessons with A. Hřímalý and harp lessons with Stanek; also became proficient as a pianist. From 1877 to 1891 he was in Russia, where he held teaching posts; brought out a teaching guide, *Musical Grammar,* publ. in Russian. Upon his return to Prague, he taught piano at the Prague Cons. (1891–1923). He publ. a number of useful piano manuals (all in German): *Schule des Akkordspiels und der Akkordzerlegungen; Theoretischpraktische Schule der wesentlichen Verzierungen im Pianofortespiel; Anschlagübungen zur Erreichung gleichzeitig verschiedener Tongebung im mehrstimmigen Spiel; Tonleitern in Doppelgriffen; Technische Übungen in Verbindung mit praktischen Fingersatzstudien; Neue Schule der Technik und des musikalischen Vortags;* composed *Scherzo fantastique* for Orch.; Piano Quintet; 2 piano sonatas; other pieces.

Jirásek, Ivo, Czech composer and conductor; b. Prague, July 16, 1920. He studied conducting with Dědeček and composition with Alois Hába, Řídký,

M. Krejčí, and Šin at the Prague Cons. (1938–45); conducted opera in Opava (1946–55); then was engaged as a music editor with the Copyright Union in Prague.

WORKS: 5 operas: *Pan Johanes* (*Mr. Johanes,* 1951–52; Opava, 1956); *Svítání nad vodami* (*Daybreak over the Waters,* 1960; Pilsen, 1963); *Medvěd* (*The Bear,* after Chekhov, 1964; Prague, 1965); *The Key* (1968); *And It Was Evening and It Was Morning* (on the theme of Bergman's film *The Seventh Seal,* 1971–72); *Ciaconna* for Orch. (1944); *Concertant Symphony* for Violin and Orch. (1958); *Little Suite* for Orch. (1964); Variations for Orch. (Prague, April 15, 1965); *Festive Prelude* for Orch. (1971); Partita for Wind Orch. (Prague, June 2, 1973); Symph. for Baritone and Orch. (1973–74; Prague, March 16, 1974); oratorio, *Stabat Mater,* for 4 Soloists, Children's and Mixed Choruses, Organ, Winds, and Percussion (1968; Prague, March 3, 1969); 3 cantatas: *Ballad from Hospital* (1944); *Love* (1960); *Zpěv o planetě Jménem země* (*Song of the Planet Called Earth,* 1976; Prague, April 2, 1977); *Riddles* for Children's Choir, Wind Quintet, and Percussion (1962); Violin Sonata (1946); *4 Studies* for String Quartet (1963–66); *Sonata da camera* for 13 Strings (1966); *Music* for Soprano, Flute, and Harp (1967); *Serenades* for Flute, Bass Clarinet, and Percussion (1967); *3 Pieces* for Flute, Violin, Viola, and Cello (1971); *Hudba k odpolední kávě* (*Music for Afternoon Coffee*) for 4 Clarinets (1972); Piano Sonata (1940); Suite for Piano (1943); choruses; songs.

Jirko, Ivan, Czech composer; b. Prague, Oct. 7, 1926; d. there, Aug. 20, 1978. After a period of musical study with K. Janeček and Bořkovec at the Prague Cons. he pursued the career of psychiatry; but double activity in such different fields of endeavor did not seem to hamper his development as either a practicing psychiatrist or a composer.

WORKS: 5 operas: *The Twelfth Night* (after Shakespeare, 1963–64; Liberec, Feb. 25, 1967); *The Strange Story of Arthur Rowe* (after Graham Greene's novel *Ministry of Fear,* 1967–68; Liberec, Oct. 25, 1969); *The Millionairess,* operatic divertimento (1969–71); *The Strumpet* (1970; Olomouc, June 23, 1974); *The Way Back* (1974); 4 piano concertos (1949, 1951, 1958, 1966); *Serenade* for Small Orch. (1951); Clarinet Concerto (1955); 3 symphs.: No. 1 (1957); No. 2, *The Year 1945* (1962, withdrawn); No. 3 (1977); *Macbeth,* symph. fantasy (1962); *Elegy on the Death of a Friend* for Orch. (1965); *Divertimento* for Horn and Orch. (1965); *Symphonic Variations* (1966); *Serenata giocosa* for Chamber String Orch. (1967; alternate version for Violin and Guitar); Sonata for 14 Winds and Kettledrums (1967); *Capriccio all'antico* for Orch. (1971); *Prague Seconds,* symph. sketches (1972); Trumpet Concerto (1972); Flute Concerto (1973); *Prague Annals,* symph. triptych (1973); *At the Turning Point,* symph. fantasy (1972–73; uses material from the 2nd symph.); *Double Concerto* for Violin, Piano, and Orch. (1976; Charleroi, Belgium, Nov. 18, 1976); *The Most Beautiful Land,* cantata (1950–51); *The Day,* cycle for Baritone and Orch. (1960–62); *Requiem* (1971); *Song of These Days,* 4 episodes for Baritone, Chorus, and Orch. (1973–74); *Štěstí (Happiness),* musical panorama for Narrator, Soprano, Baritone, and Orch. (1975–76); Wind Quintet (1947); 6 string quartets (1954, 1962, 1966, 1969, 1972, 1974); Cello Sonata (1954–55); Suite for Wind Quintet (1956); Violin Sonata (1959); *Kaleidoscope* for Violin and Piano (1965); *Serenata in due tempi* for Nonet or Oboe Quartet (1970); *Guiocchi per tre* for String Trio (1972); Partita for Solo Violin (1974); Piano Quintet (1977–78); 2 piano sonatas (1956; *Elégie disharmonique,* 1970); *Preludio, Canzone e Toccata* for Piano (1977).

Joachim, Amalie (née **Weiss**), German concert singer, wife of **Joseph Joachim;** b. Marburg, May 10, 1839; d. Berlin, Feb. 3, 1899. Her real maiden name was **Schneeweiss,** but she abridged it to Weiss in 1854 when she appeared as a singer in Vienna. She began her career as a soprano; after her marriage to Joachim (1863) she abandoned the stage but continued to give recitals as a lieder singer; her interpretations of Schumann's songs were particularly fine.

BIBLIOGRAPHY: Olga Plaschke, *Amalie Joachim* (Berlin, 1899).

Joachim, Joseph, one of the greatest masters of the violin; b. Kittsee, near Pressburg, June 28, 1831; d. Berlin, Aug. 15, 1907. He began to study the violin at the age of 5; his first teacher was Szervaczinski, with whom he appeared in public at the age of 7, playing a violin duet. At the age of 10 he was sent to the Vienna Cons., where he studied with Böhm; in 1843 he played in Leipzig at a concert presented by Pauline Viardot; Mendelssohn did him the honor of accompanying him on the piano. He appeared with the Gewandhaus Orch. (Nov. 16, 1843); then made his first tour in England (1844), arousing admiration for his mature musicianship and remarkable technique. Returning to Leipzig, he studied with Ferdinand David; also played as concertmaster of the Gewandhaus Orch. in David's absence. From 1849 till 1854 Joachim served as concertmaster of the court orch. in Weimar. Liszt, who reigned supreme in Weimar, did not favor young Joachim, and in 1854 Joachim went to Hannover as solo violinist at the court; in 1863 he married the singer **Amalie Weiss.** In 1868 he was appointed director of the Hochschule für Ausübende Tonkunst in Berlin. His fame as a teacher spread far and wide, and aspiring violinists from all over Europe flocked there to study with him. He did not, however, abandon his career as a virtuoso; he was particularly popular in England, which he visited annually after 1862; he received an honorary degree of D.Mus. from Cambridge Univ. (1877), and also from Oxford and Glasgow. His style of playing, nurtured on the best Classical models, was remarkable for masterful repose, dignity, and flawless technique. It was his unswerving determination to interpret the music in accordance with the intentions of the composer; this noble objectivity made him an authentic exponent of the best of violin literature. As a player of chamber music he was unexcelled in his day. The famous Joachim Quartet, organized in 1869, attained great and merited celebrity in Europe; the Joachim tradition of excellence and faithful interpretation of classical works influenced the subsequent generations of German violinists. From 1882 to 1887 Joachim also served as one of the principal conductors of the Berlin Phil.

WORKS: His compositions for the violin are virtuoso pieces that have never ceased to attract performers; of these, the most famous is the Concerto in D minor, op. 11, known as the *Hungarian Concerto* (marked "in ungarischer Weise"), which he wrote in Hannover in the summer of 1857, and first performed there on March 24, 1860; another Concerto, in G major (Hannover, Nov. 5, 1864, composer soloist), was revised in 1889. Other works are: Variations for Violin and Orch. (Berlin, Feb. 15, 1881, composer soloist); *Andantino* and *Allegro scherzoso* for Violin and Orch.; *3 Stücke (Romanze, Fantasiestück, Frühlingsfantasie)* for Violin and Piano; *3 Stücke (Lindenrauschen, Abendglocken, Ballade)* for Violin and Piano; *Hebrew Melodies* for Viola and Piano; *Variations on an Original Theme* for Viola and Piano; *Notturno* for Violin and Orch.; several overtures; cadenzas for violin concertos by Beethoven and Brahms; songs.

BIBLIOGRAPHY: A. Moser, *J. Joachim, Ein Lebensbild* (Berlin, 1898; 2nd enlarged ed., 2 vols., 1908, 1910; Eng. trans. from 2nd German ed., London, 1900); K. Storck, *J. Joachim, Eine Studie* (Leipzig, 1902); J.A. Fuller-Maitland, *J. Joachim* (London, 1905); L. Brieger-Wasservogel, *Joachim-Gedenkbüchlein* (Dresden, 1907); H.J. Moser, *J. Joachim* (Zürich, 1908); G. Schünemann, "Aus Joachims Nachlass," in *Bericht der Hochschule* (vol. 53); S. Joachim-Chaigneau, "3 épisodes de la vie de Joachim," *Revue Musicale* (Jan. 1940); G. Maas, *The Instrumental Music of Joseph Joachim* (Diss., Univ. of North Carolina, 1973). Joachim's letters were publ. by A. Moser, *Johannes Brahms im Briefwechsel mit J. Joachim* (Berlin, 1908; vols. V and VI); Johannes Joachim and A. Moser, *Briefe an und von J. Joachim* (3 vols., Berlin, 1911–13).

Joachim, Otto, German-born Canadian composer and violinist; b. Düsseldorf, Oct. 13, 1910. He took violin lessons with his father; later studied violin in Cologne (1928–31). He fled Germany in 1934 and spent the next 15 years in the Far East, mainly in Singapore and Shanghai. In 1949 he emigrated to Canada; played the viola in the Montreal Symph. Orch.; in 1956 he joined the staff of the Cons. of Montreal. His music is quaquaversal, but its favorite direction is asymptotic.

WORKS: *Asia,* symph. poem (1928–39); *3 Bagatelles* for Piano (1939); *Music for Violin and Viola* (1954); *L'Eclosion* for Piano (1954); Cello Sonata (1954); *Concertante No. 1* for Violin, String Orch., and Percussion (1955, revised 1958; Paris, Sept. 9, 1958) and *No. 2* for String Quartet and String Orch. (1961; Montreal, March 12, 1962); String Quartet (1956); *Psalm* for Chorus (1960); *Interlude* for 4 Saxophones (1960); Nonet for Strings, Winds, and Piano

(1960); *12 12-Tone Pieces for the Young* for Piano (1961); *Expansion* for Flute and Piano (1962); Divertimento for Wind Quintet (1962); *Music for 4 Viols* (1962); *Dialogue* for Viola and Piano (1964); *Illuminations I* and *II*—aleatory works of indeterminate duration, wherein performers are cued in by a light-triggering system operated by a "conductor": *I* for Live Narrator and 4 Instrumentalists (1965) and *II* for 10 Performers and 4-track Taped Reading of a Scientific Text (1969; Grand Prix Paul Gilson, 1969); *Contrastes* for Orch. (Montreal, May 6, 1967); *Katimavik* for Tape (1966–67); *Kinderspiel,* aleatory music for children, for Narrator, Violin, Cello, and Piano (1969; variable duration); *12 12-Tone Pieces for the Young* for Violin and Piano (1970); *Mankind,* multimedia work for 4 Synthesizers, Pianist, Timpanist, Slides, Burning Incense, and 4 Readers who are to be ordained clerics of 4 major world religions (1972).

João IV, King of Portugal; b. Villa-Vicosa, March 19, 1604; d. Lisbon, Nov. 6, 1656. As a prince he received a fine musical training at the court chapel. He began collecting church music, gradually accumulating a magnificent library, which was totally destroyed in the earthquake of 1755. However, its contents are known, for a catalogue of it was issued in Lisbon in 1649, and reprinted by Vasconcellos in 1873. João IV was a true music scholar, well acquainted with the flow of conflicting opinions regarding musical theory. He publ. (anonymously) the pamphlets *Defensa de la musica moderna contra la errada opinion del obispo Cyrillo Franco* (in Spanish; 1649); *Respuesta a las dudas que se pusieron a la missa "Panis quem ego dabo" de Palestrina* (1654); Italian translations were made of both. He composed a considerable quantity of church music; his motets *Crux fidelis* and *Adjuva nos* are reprinted in S. Lück's *Sammlung ausgezeichneter Kompositionen für die Kirche* (1884–85).

BIBLIOGRAPHY: J. Freitas Branco, *D. João IV, Músico* (Lisbon, 1956).

Jobert, Jean, French music publisher; b. Lyons, Oct. 11, 1883; d. Paris, Nov. 27, 1957. He was an employee of the publishing firm of Fromont in Paris; he purchased the business in 1922, including the valuable catalogue of Debussy's early works (*L'Après-midi d'un faune, Clair de lune,* etc.). In 1945 he was elected president of the Syndicated Society of Music Publishers in France.

Jochum, Eugen, German conductor, brother of **Georg Ludwig** and **Otto Jochum;** b. Babenhausen, Bavaria, Nov. 1, 1902. He studied organ and piano at the Augsburg Cons. (1914–22), composition with Waltershausen at the Munich Academy of Music (1922–24), and conducting with Sigmund von Hausegger. He subsequently occupied various posts as opera coach and assistant conductor in Munich, Kiel, Mannheim, and Duisburg. From 1934 to 1949 he was Generalmusikdirektor of the Hamburg Phil.; simultaneously (1934–45) he served as music director of the Hamburg State Opera; then conducted the Radio Orch. in Munich (1949–60); in 1961 he became conductor of the Concertgebouw Orch. in Amsterdam; later was conductor and artistic director of the Bamberg Symph. (1969–73); then held the title of laureate conductor of the London Symph. Orch. from 1977 to 1979. He is reputed as one of the best conductors of the symph. works of Bruckner and Mahler.

Jochum, Georg Ludwig, German conductor, brother of **Eugen** and **Otto Jochum;** b. Babenhausen, Dec. 10, 1909; d. Mülheim an der Ruhr, Nov. 1, 1970. He studied in Munich with Hausegger and Pembaur; occupied numerous posts as conductor: at the Frankfurt Opera (1937–40); in Linz (1940–45); etc. From 1946 to 1958 he was director of the Duisburg Cons.; also filled in numerous appearances as guest conductor in Europe, Japan, and South America.

Jochum, Otto, prolific German composer, brother of **Eugen** and **Georg Ludwig Jochum;** b. Babenhausen, March 18, 1898; d. Bad Reichenhall, Nov. 24, 1969. He studied at the Augsburg Cons. and at the Munich Academy of Music with Heinrich Kasper Schmid, Gustav Geierhaas, and Joseph Haas (1922–31). In 1933 he was appointed director of the Municipal Singing School in Augsburg; in 1949, became director of the Augsburg Cons.; retired in 1952. He composed about 150 opus numbers, among them 2 oratorios (*Der jüngste Tag* and *Ein Weihnachtssingen*); 12 masses; a great number of works for chorus, both accompanied and a cappella; arrangements of folk songs; a *Goethe-Sinfonie* (1941); *Florianer-Sinfonie* (1946); songs.

Jodál, Gábor, Rumanian composer of Hungarian parentage; b. Odorhei, April 25, 1913. He studied law and music in Cluj (1930–37); then enrolled as a student of composition at the Liszt Academy in Budapest with Kodály, Kósa, and J. Adám (1939–42). After graduation, he devoted himself to choral coaching and teaching; in 1950 he was appointed to the faculty of the Cons. in Cluj; was its director from 1965 to 1973. As a composer, he continues an amiable but rhythmically incisive tradition of the ethnically variegated music of Transylvania.
WORKS: 2 cantatas: *Revoluția* (1964) and *Slăvite zile* for Chorus, Winds, Percussion, and 2 Pianos (1967); 2 violin sonatas (1946, 1953); *3 Pieces* for Viola and Piano (1946); Suite for Flute and Piano (1955); String Quartet (1955); *3 Pieces* for Wind Quintet (1959); *Introduction and Scherzo* for Bassoon and Piano (1964); Suite for Wind Quintet (1966); *3 Nocturnes* for Flute, Clarinet, Viola, Cello, and Piano (1967); Viola Sonata (1974); Piano Sonatina (1954); *3 Pieces* for 2 Pianos (1970); choruses; songs.

Jöde, Fritz, German music educator; b. Hamburg, Aug. 2, 1887; d. there, Oct. 19, 1970. He began his career as a provincial school teacher; was in the German army during World War I; then undertook a serious study of music at the Univ. of Leipzig. He organized societies for the propagation of folk music, and was very active in various youth movements in Germany. In 1939 he became an instructor at the Hochschule für Musik in Salzburg and leader of the seminar at the Mozarteum (1939–45); then was an instructor on school music in Hamburg (1947–52). He publ. a number of books on music education and collected German folk songs. Among his anthologies are *Ringel-Rangel-Rosen* (children's songs; 1913; enlarged ed., 1927); *Der Rosengarten* (1917); *Der Musikant* (1923; new ed., 1942); *Der Kanon* (in 3 parts; 1925); *Chorbuch* (6 vols., 1927–31); *Die Singstunde* (1929); *Lasst uns singen* (1930); *Frau Musika* (songs for home; 1929); *Die Weihnachtsnachtigall* (1939); *Unser Mutterlied* (1940).
WRITINGS: *Musikalische Jugendkultur* (1918); *Musik und Erziehung* (1920); *Die Lebensfrage der neuen Schule* (1921); *Unser Musikleben Absage und Beginn* (1923); *Musikschulen für Jugend und Volk* (1924); *Die Kunst Bachs* (1926); *Elementarlehre der Musik* (1927); *Musikdienst am Volk* (1927); *Das schaffende Kind in der Musik* (1928); *Musik in der Volksschule* (1929); *Kind und Musik* (1930); *Deutsche Jugendmusik* (1934); *Vom Wesen und Werden der Jugendmusik* (1954). From 1940 to 1952 he was editor of the *Zeitschrift für Spielmusik.*
BIBLIOGRAPHY: R. Stapelberg, ed., *Fritz Jöde: Leben und Werk* (Wolfenbüttel, 1957).

Joel, Billy, top-seeded American pop pianist and song composer; b. Hicksville, Long Island, N.Y., May 9, 1949. To exorcise the image implicit in the name of his hometown, he undertook an assiduous study of classical piano playing as a raw youth. Prematurely sophisticated, he joined the rock band The Echoes, which was later metamorphosed into a more belligerent group called The Hassles. When The Hassles disintegrated after internecine hassles, Joel teamed up with drummer Jon Small to form a duo named Attila after the murderous King of the Huns popularly known in Western Europe as "the scourge of God." They recorded an album, which did not sell. Joel then organized a band of his own and recorded his first original ballad, *Cold Spring Harbor,* for the label Family Productions. It did not sell either, and after a family feud with Family Productions, Billy Joel went over to Columbia Records, moved to Los Angeles, and thereafter marched on the gold-paved road to neon-lighted success. He composed a balled called, autobiographically, *Piano Man,* which made a hit. He soon progressed on the periodic table of elements from gold to platinum, and received a certified platinum award for his song *The Stranger* in 1978. Other smash album hits followed: *52nd Street, Glass House,* etc.; the single songs *My Life, Big Shot,* and *Honesty;* and his big hit, *Just the Way You Are.* His ballad *You May Be Right* produced an impressive thud, if not quite a smash. He signified his gratitude to his generating force in the top hit *It's Still Rock and Roll to Me.* By 1984 he could demand, and get, million-dollar advances from royalty distributors.

Johannes Chrysorrhoas (John of Damascus), Christian saint; b. Damascus, c.700; d. at the monastery of St. Sabas, near Jerusalem, 754. He was canonized by both the Greek and Roman Church; was the earliest dogmatist of the Greek Church; wrote many examples of the *kanon,* a special type of Byzantine hymn that usually used a pre-existent melody. John is credited, by what may be a legend, with having arranged the Byzantine Oktoechos and having improved Byzantine notation.

BIBLIOGRAPHY: H.J.W. Tillyard, *Byzantine Music and Hymnography* (1923; pp. 20ff.); E. Wellesz, *Byzantinische Musik* (1927; pp. 33ff.); K. Wachsmann, *Untersuchungen zum vorgregorianischen Gesang* (1935; pp. 78ff.).

Johannesen, Grant, eminent American pianist and pedagogue; b. Salt Lake City, July 30, 1921. He studied piano with Robert Casadesus at Princeton Univ. (1941–46) and with Egon Petri at Cornell Univ.; also took courses in composition with Roger Sessions and Nadia Boulanger. He made his concert debut in N.Y. in 1944. In 1949 he won first prize at the Ostend Concours International, which was the beginning of his international career. He toured Europe with Mitropoulos and the N.Y. Phil. in 1956 and 1957; made a European tour, including Russia, with Szell and the Cleveland Orch. in 1968; also played at leading music festivals in France, the Netherlands, and Norway. From 1960 to 1966 he taught at the Aspen Music School; in 1973 he became music consultant and adviser of the Cleveland Inst. of Music; was named its music director in 1974, and finally president in 1977. Johannesen acquired a reputation as a pianist of fine musicianly stature, subordinating his virtuoso technique to the higher considerations of intellectual fidelity to the composer's intentions; he was particularly esteemed for his performances of French and American music. He also composed some piano works. He was married to the Canadian cellist **Zara Nelsova** from 1963 to 1973.

Jóhannsson, Magnús Blöndal, Icelandic composer; b. Skálar, Sept. 8, 1925. He was taken to Reykjavík as an infant, and showed a precocious musical talent; at the age of 10, was admitted to the Reykjavík School of Music, where he studied under F. Mixa and V. Urbantschitsch (1935–37 and 1939–45); then was sent to America and took courses in composition at the Juilliard School of Music in N.Y. (1947–53). He returned to Iceland in 1954 and became a staff member of the Iceland State Broadcasting Service (1956–76); was also conductor for the National Theater in Reykjavík (1965–72). As a composer, he was attracted to the novel resources of electronic music; his *Study* for Magnetic Tape and Wind Quintet (1957) was the first Icelandic work employing electronic sound. His other works include *4 Abstractions* for Piano (1955); *Ionization* for Organ (1956); *Samstirni* for Tape (1960); *Punktar (Points)* for Tape and Small Orch. (1961); *15 Minigrams* for Flute, Oboe, Clarinet, and Double Bass (1961); *Dimensions* for Solo Violin (1961); *Sonorities I–III* for Piano (1961–68); *Birth of an Island,* tape music for the film depicting the volcanic creation of an island near Iceland (1964); *Sequence,* ballet for Dancers, Instruments, and Lights (1968); *The Other Iceland,* music from the film (1973).

Johanos, Donald, American conductor; b. Cedar Rapids, Iowa, Feb. 10, 1928. He studied violin with André de Ribaupierre and Cecil Burleigh at the Eastman School of Music, Rochester, N.Y.; conducting with Eugene Ormandy, George Szell, Eduard van Beinum, and Otto Klemperer (1955–57). From 1963 to 1970 he was principal conductor and music director of the Dallas Symph. Orch., achieving estimable results. Subsequently he was guest conductor with numerous American and European orchs. In 1970 he was appointed associate conductor of the Pittsburgh Symph.; concurrently, he was also conductor of the Honolulu Symph. Orch. and artistic director of the Hawaii Opera Theatre.

Johansen, David Monrad, Norwegian composer; b. Vefsn, Nov. 8, 1888; d. Sandvika, Feb. 20, 1974. He studied piano with Karl Nissen and music theory with Iver Holter; in 1915 he went to Berlin, where he took lessons with Humperdinck; by this time in middle age, he continued his studies in composition in Paris (1927) and in Leipzig (1933–35), where he took a special course in counterpoint with Grabner. In the meantime he pursued an active career as a concert pianist and composer; gave a recital of his own works in Oslo in 1915. He also wrote music criticism in *Aftenposten* (1925–45). His music continued the national Norwegian tradition, in the lyric manner of Grieg; as time went by, Johansen experienced a mild influence of Russian and French music, gradually forming an innocuous modern style with sporadic audacious incursions into the domain of sharp dissonance.

WORKS: *Symphonic Fantasy* (1936); symph. poem, *Pan* (1939); Piano Concerto (1955); Violin Sonata (1912); Piano Quartet (1947); Quintet for Flute and String Quartet (1967); String Quartet (1969); oratorio, *Voluspa* (1926); *Sigvat Skald* for Baritone and Orch. (1928); several choruses and a group of songs; piano pieces. He publ. a monograph on Grieg (Oslo, 1934; in Eng., Princeton, 1938).

BIBLIOGRAPHY: O.M. Sandvik and O. Gaukstad, *David Monrad Johansen* (Oslo, 1968).

Johansen, Gunnar, Danish-American pianist; b. Copenhagen, Jan. 21, 1906. He studied piano with Victor Schiøler; later in Berlin with Frederic Lamond, Edwin Fischer, and Egon Petri. From 1924 to 1929 he toured Europe as a concert pianist; then lived in California. In 1939 he joined the faculty of the Univ. of Wisconsin in Madison as artist-in-residence, a title that was specially created for him. An early admirer of Busoni, he devoted himself to propagandizing his music. In March 1966 he presented a Busoni Centennial Commemorative program at the Univ. of Wisconsin, including Busoni's formidable *Fantasia Contrappuntistica.* He recorded for Artist Direct Records the complete piano works of Busoni and his Bach transcriptions, the complete piano works of Liszt, and the complete clavier works of Bach. Johansen produced a sensation of seismic proportions on Jan. 14, 1969, when he played with the Philadelphia Orch. in N.Y. the piano version of Beethoven's Violin Concerto at 30½ hours' notice. Johansen is also a composer of truly fantastic fecundity. He wrote 2 piano concertos (1930, 1970); *East-West,* cantata for Wordless Women's Voices, Piano, 3 Woodwinds, and Percussion (1944); 31 piano sonatas (1941–51); and 246 piano sonatas improvised directly on the keyboard and recorded on tape (1952–70). A scholar as well as a musician, Johansen trans. from Danish into Eng. George Brandes's biography of Kierkegaard.

Johanson, Sven-Eric, Swedish organist and composer; b. Västervik, Dec. 10, 1919. He studied composition with H.M. Melchers and Hilding Rosenberg in Stockholm; was a church organist in Uppsala (1944–50) and Göteborg (1950–54). In 1954 he became a teacher of organ playing and harmony at the Göteborg Cons. His early works show the marked influence of Max Reger and Hindemith; later he adopted some atonal usages.
WORKS: Saga-opera, *Bortbytingarna* (*The Changelings,* 1953); chamber opera, *Kunskapens vin* (*The Wine of Knowledge,* in 2 acts; 1959–68); micro-drama, *Rivalerna* (*The Rivals,* 1967); operabuffa, *Tjuvens pekfinger* (*The Forefinger Thieves,* 1966–68); Concerto for Organ and Strings (1946); *Aff Sancto Christofforo,* chamber oratorio (1948); *Sinfonietta concertante* for Violin and Chamber Orch. (1951); 4 symphs.: No. 1, *Sinfonia ostinata* (1949); No. 2, *Duinoelegi,* for Solo Voices, Chorus, and Orch. (1954; transcribed for String Orch. under the title *Sinfonia elegiaca,* 1955; Göteborg, Feb. 8, 1956); No. 3 (1956; Göteborg, Sept. 23, 1959); No. 4, *Sånger i Förvandlingens Natt (Songs in the Night of Transformation)* for a cappella Chorus (Stockholm, April 3, 1959); *Concerto de camera* for Cello and Orch. (1958); *Maskarad-Divertissement* for Orch. (1958); *Variations on a Värmland Folk Tune* for Small Orch. (1963); *Vagues* for Orch. (1965); *Fotia* for Orch. (1966); *Vienti* for Orch. (1967); *Terra* for Large Orch. and Orch. (Göteborg, Sept. 12, 1968); *Fantyr* for Orch. (1969); *Concerto Göteborg* for Piano and Orch. (1970); Concerto for Nyckel Harp and Strings (1971; a nyckel harp is a keyed fiddle); *Sinfonietta pastorella* for Orch. (1972); 5 string quartets (1947; 1948; 1950; *Séquences variables,* 1961; 1964); *The Haze Trees,* song cycle for Soprano, Clarinet, Violin, Viola, Piano, and Tape (1961); Wind Quintet (1964); *Ave Crax, Ave Crux* for Soprano, Baritone, Chorus, Organ, and Tape (1967); *Don Quixote* for Flute, Clarinet, Cello, and Double Bass (1971); *Purpurgreven* for Flute, Trumpet, Violin, Cello, and Piano (1971); 3 piano sonatas (1949, 1956, 1959); motets; organ and piano pieces; songs.

Johansson, Bengt, Finnish composer; b. Helsinki, Oct. 2, 1914. He studied composition with Sulho Ranta and Selim Palmgren; also cello at the Sibelius Academy in Helsinki, graduating in 1947; made study trips to Europe, Italy, and America; upon his return to Finland, he became director of music broadcasting for Finnish Radio (1952); was a teacher at the Helsinki Academy from 1960; in 1965 he became a lecturer in music history at the Sibelius Academy. His music makes use of a wide variety of resources, including electronic sound.
WORKS: FOR ORCH.: Serenade for Strings (1945); *Petite suite de ballet* (1948); *Aquarelles* (1948); Piano Concerto (1951); Suite for Violin, Strings, Piano, and Timpani (1952); *Festivo,* overture (1952); *Expressions* for Strings (1954); *Tema con 7 variazioni in modo antico* for Cello and Orch. (1954). VOCAL WORKS: *Stabat Mater* for Chorus a cappella (1951); *It's Perfectly True,* "musical fairy tale" for Narrator, Solo Voices, Female Chorus, and Orch. (1957); *Missa Sacra* for Tenor, Chorus, and Orch. (1960); *12 Passages from the Bible* for Male Chorus and Organ (1960); *The Tomb at Akr Çaar,* to a text by Ezra Pound, for Baritone and Chamber Chorus (1964); *Triptych* for Soprano, Baritone, and Chorus (1965); *Requiem* for Baritone, 2 Choruses, 2 String Orchs., and Timpani (1966); *3 Classic Madrigals* for Chorus (1967); *Cantata humana,* to words of Dag Hammarskjöld, for Baritone, 4 Narrators on Tape, Chorus, and Orch. (Helsinki, April 9, 1970); *The Song of the Bride* for Soprano and Orch. (1972). CHAMBER MUSIC: *Sonata piccola* for Cello and Piano (1945); *Dialogues* for Cello and String Quintet (1970); pieces for violin; also *3 Electronic Etudes* (1960).

John, Elton, English rock songwriter, singer, and piano player; b. Pinner, Middlesex, March 25, 1947. His real name was **Reginald Kenneth Dwight;** he attended classes at the Royal Academy in London, and actually managed to learn how to read music; he earned his living as a jazz pianist in various London clubs and pubs; then joined a rock group bearing the pretentious appellation Bluesology; it was from the sax player Elton Dean, of whom he was inordinately fond, that he annexed his first name, while his last name he took from the first name of the leader of the band, John Baldry. For all his low aspirations, Elton John is capable of forming lines of communication with kindred souls on a comparable level of intelligence among his audiences. He affects bizarre behavior, wearing multicolored attires and psychedelic eyeglasses of which he has collected several hundred. In 1971 he flew across the ocean and captivated American rock audiences with his strangulated voice and uninhibited conduct. He wrote most of his songs with lyricist Bernie Taupin. In May 1979 he gave 4 concerts in Leningrad and 4 in Moscow before thousands of young Soviet fans screaming with delight.

Johner, Dominicus (Franz), prior of the Beuron monastery, authority on ecclesiastical music; b. Waldsee, Dec. 1, 1874; d. Beuron, Jan. 4, 1955. He studied theology and music in Prague and also in Portugal; entered the Benedictine order in Beuron in 1894; was ordained a priest in Lisbon in 1898. In 1900 he went back to Beuron; taught Gregorian chant there, and at the Hochschule für Musik in Cologne (from 1925). He composed a cycle, *Neue*

Marienlieder, for Chorus in unison with Organ (2 books; 1916 and 1918), and *Neue Kommunionslieder* (1916).

WRITINGS: His writings, of great importance to students of Gregorian chant, include *Neue Schule des gregorianischen Choralgesanges* (Regensburg, 1906; 6th ed., 1929); *Cantus ecclesiastici* (1909; 7th ed., 1925); *Die Psalmodie nach der Vaticana* (1911); *Litaniae Lauretanae octo modis accomodatae* (1921; 2nd ed., 1927); *Der gregorianische Choral* (1924; in Danish, Copenhagen, 1931); *Die Sonn- und Festtagslieder des vatikanischen Graduale* (1928); *Wie gelangen wir zu einem würdigen des gregorianischen Chorals?* (1928); *Erklärung des Kyriale* (1933); *Wort und Ton im gregorianischen Choral* (Leipzig, 1940). A collection of articles, *Der kultische Gesang der abendländischen Kirche*, ed. by F. Tack, was publ. in his honor on his 75th birthday (Cologne, 1950).

Johns, Clayton, American pianist and composer; b. New Castle, Del., Nov. 24, 1857; d. Boston, March 5, 1932. He studied architecture in Philadelphia (1875–79); then turned to music, studying in Boston with J.K. Paine (theory) and W.H. Sherwood (piano), and in Berlin (1882–83) with Kiel (composition) and Rummel (piano); he settled in Boston. His works include a *Berceuse* and *Scherzino* for String Orch.; several piano pieces; music for violin and piano; about 100 songs; he also publ. *The Essentials of Pianoforte Playing* (1909), *From Bach to Chopin* (1911), and *Reminiscences of a Musician* (1929).

Johns, Emile, American pianist and publisher; b. in Austria c.1800; d. Paris, Aug. 10, 1860. He settled in New Orleans in 1822 and opened a music store; publ. *Album Louisiannais: Hommage aux dames de la Nouvelle Orléans*, containing 8 piano pieces. He eventually went to Paris, where he became friendly with Chopin and other musicians; Chopin dedicated to him his 5 mazurkas, op. 7.

BIBLIOGRAPHY: J.S. Kendall, "The Friend of Chopin and Some Other New Orleans Musical Celebrities," *Louisiana Historical Quarterly* (Oct. 1948).

Johnsen, Hallvard, Norwegian composer; b. Hamburg, Germany, June 27, 1916, to Norwegian parents. He went to Norway as a youth; studied music theory with Bjarne Brustad (1937–41) and Karl Andersen (1943–45) in Oslo and with Vagn Holmboe in Denmark. He also learned to play the flute and was employed as a flutist in Norwegian military bands.

WORKS: Opera, *The Legend of Svein and Maria* (1971; Oslo, Sept. 9, 1973); 13 symphs.: No. 1 (1949); No. 2, *Pastorale* (1954); No. 3 (1957); No. 4 (1959); No. 5 (1960); No. 6 (1961); No. 7 (1962); No. 8 (1964); No. 9 (1968); No. 10 (1973); No. 11 (1975); No. 12 (1976); No. 13 (1983); cantata, *Norwegian Nature* (1952); 2 *Overtures* (1954, 1968); 2 flute concertos with String Orch. (1939, 1955); 2 violin concertos with Chamber Orch. (1955, 1967); Trumpet Concerto (1966); *Canzona* for Wind Orch. (1968); Cello Concerto (1977); Trio for Flute, Violin, and Viola (1938); Quartet for

Flute and String Trio (1945); *Tema con variazioni* for Piano (1957); 3 string quartets (1962, 1966, 1972); Serenade for Wind Quintet (1962); Suite for Flute and Horn (1964); Quintet for Winds, with Vibraphone (1965); Sextet (1974); *Trio Serenade* for Flute, Viola, and Cello (1974); Quartet for 4 Saxophones (1974); *Divertimento* for 2 Cornets, Horn, Baritone Horn, and Tuba (1974); Duet for 2 Flutes (1975); Quintet for 2 Trumpets, Horn, Trombone, and Bass Trombone (1978); Trio for Trumpet, Trombone, and Vibraphone (1980); *Pastoral* for Flute, Violin, and Vibraphone (1981); choral pieces.

Johnson, Bengt-Emil, Swedish composer and poet; b. Ludvika, Dec. 12, 1936. He studied composition with Knut Wiggen; at the same time pursued his abiding interest in modernistic poetry; publ. 4 collections of poems (1963–66) in a "concrete" idiom polyphonically elaborated in the technique of recited "text-sound compositions," a process electronically combining semantic and abstract sounds. Most of his works are of this nature; in emulation of computer-type identification (also used by Xenakis), he includes the year of composition in the title: *Semikolon; Äventyr på vägen (Semicolon; Adventure on the Way;* 1965); *1/1966: Släpkoppel (Dragleash . . .); 1/1967: Nya släpkoppel med vida världen (New drag-leashes with the wide world); 2/1967: (Meden) (While); "from any point to any other point,"* a ballet in collaboration with Lars-Gunnar Bodin and Margaretha Åsberg (1968); *1/1969: Genom törstspegeln (första passeringen) (Through the mirror of thirst—first passage); 2/1969: För Abraham Jakobsson, på vägen (For Abraham Jakobsson, on the way,* after C.J.L. Almquist; *3/1969: Through the mirror of thirst (second passage); 1/1970: (bland) (among); 2/1970: (among) II; 3/1970: (among) III; 4/1970: Jakter (Hunts),* after C.F. Hills; *6/1970: Hyllning till Mr. Miller (Homage to Mr. Miller),* based on Henry Miller; *1/1971: under publikens jubel (Under the cheers of the people); 1/1972: (among) IV; 2/1972: (While) II; 3/1972: Släpkoppel (uppsläpp); 4/1972: Släpkoppel (Weltanschauung) (Drag-leash—World Outlook)* for a cappella Chorus; *5/1972: Mimicry (Erik Rosenberg in memoriam)* for Voice, Cello, Trombone, Piano, and Percussion; *1/1973: Pierrot på rygg* for Soprano, Cello, Piano, and Percussion; *2/1973: Subsong II; 3/1973: Ej blir det natt* for Chorus; *Disappearances* for Piano and Tape (1974).

Johnson, "Bunk" (real Christian names, **William Geary**), black American jazz trumpeter; b. New Orleans, Dec. 27, 1879; d. New Iberia, La., July 7, 1949. As a youth he played trumpet with Dixieland bands; toured with minstrel shows, circus troupes, and numerous jazz aggregations. He lost all his teeth due to the ravages of pyorrhea and had to stop playing. After many years of musical inactivity he was "rediscovered" in 1937, working in sugar-cane fields, by "hot jazz" aficionados; fitted with dentures, he resumed his career and enjoyed belated fame in a revival of Dixieland music.

Johnson, Edward, Canadian tenor and operatic impresario; b. Guelph, Ontario, Aug. 22, 1878; d. there, April 20, 1959. He studied at the Univ. of Toronto; in 1900, went to N.Y., where he sang in light opera; then went to Italy for further study; appeared there in opera under the name of **Eduardo di Giovanni.** In 1919 he returned to the U.S.; was a member of the Chicago Opera Co.; then joined the Metropolitan Opera Co. (debut, Nov. 16, 1922); in 1935 he was appointed general manager of the Metropolitan, succeeding Herbert Witherspoon. He resigned in 1950. He eventually moved to Toronto, where he taught voice at the Univ. of Toronto.

Johnson, Hall, black American choral leader, composer, and arranger; b. Athens, Ga., June 2, 1887; d. New York, April 30, 1970. He studied at the Univ. of Atlanta and at the Univ. of Southern Calif. in Los Angeles; also took courses with Percy Goetschius in N.Y. In 1925 he formed the Hall Johnson Choir, with which he gave numerous concerts; in 1936 he organized the Negro Chorus of Los Angeles. In 1951 he toured Germany and Austria with his chorus under the auspices of the U.S. State Department. He composed choral music and made arrangements for the films and television.

Johnson, Horace, American composer and journalist; b. Waltham, Mass., Oct. 5, 1893; d. Tucson, Ariz., May 30, 1964. He studied with Bainbridge Crist. He wrote several popular pieces for orch., among them *Astarte* (Richmond, Jan. 2, 1936) and *Streets of Florence* (Mexico, July 9, 1937); also songs (*The Pirate, When Pierrot Sings, The Three Cherry Trees,* and *Thy Dark Hair*).

Johnson, Hunter, American composer; b. Benson, N.C., April 14, 1906. He studied at the Univ. of North Carolina (1924–26), and at the Eastman School of Music in Rochester, N.Y., graduating in 1929; subsequently occupied various teaching posts: at the Univ. of Michigan (1929–33), the Univ. of Manitoba (1944–47), Cornell Univ. (1948–53), the Univ. of Illinois (1959–65), and the Univ. of Texas (1966–71). WORKS: For the stage: 4 ballets: *In Time of Armament* (1939), *Letter to the World* (1940), *Deaths and Entrances* (1942), and *The Scarlet Letter* (1975). For Orch.: Symph. (1931); Concerto for Piano and Chamber Orch. (1935); *Elegy* for Clarinet and Strings (1937); *Music* for Strings (1939); Concerto for Orch. (1944); *North State,* to commemorate the tricentennial of Carolina Charter (1963); *Past the Evening Sun* (1964). Chamber music: Violin Sonatina (1937); Trio for Flute, Oboe, and Piano (1954); piano pieces.

Johnson, James P(rice), black American jazz pianist and composer; b. Brunswick, N.J., Feb. 1, 1891; d. New York, Nov. 17, 1955. He studied piano with his mother; began his career as a pianist in N.Y. and Atlantic City nightclubs; later led his own orch. and appeared as soloist. Among his most popular songs were *Charleston, If I Could Be with You, Carolina Shout, One Hour,* and *Runnin' Wild.*

Johnson, James Weldon, black American lyricist, librettist, anthologist, and writer on music (also a poet, novelist, newspaper editor, lawyer, and international diplomat); b. Jacksonville, Fla., June 17, 1871; d. in an automobile accident at Wiscasset, Maine, June 26, 1938. He studied literature at Atlanta University; then returned to Jacksonville, becoming a teacher and school principal; after self-study, became a lawyer (1898; the first black to pass the Florida bar examinations). A poem written for school use in 1900 to commemorate Abraham Lincoln's birthday, *Lift Every Voice and Sing,* was set to music by his brother, the composer **J. Rosamond Johnson,** and performed in Jacksonville the same year; though its beginnings were inauspicious, the song gradually acquired popularity, and in 15 years became known as "the Negro National Anthem." In the summer of 1899 the brothers visited N.Y. in an attempt to find a producer for their collaborative Gilbert and Sullivan–styled operetta, *Tolosa, or The Royal Document;* while their effort failed, they became acquainted with Oscar Hammerstein and many figures in the black musical life of N.Y. They returned to N.Y. in subsequent summers, selling some 30 songs to various musical reviews, and moved there permanently in 1902, forming, with Bob Cole, an enormously successful songwriting team of Cole and Johnson Bros.; among their hit songs, mostly in black dialect, were *Under the Bamboo Tree* (1902), which was parodied by T.S. Eliot in "Fragment of the Agon," *Congo Love Song* (1903), and, under the pseudonym **Will Handy,** *Oh, Didn't He Ramble* (1902), which was to become a jazz standard; the team's success was such that they became known as "Those Ebony Offenbachs." In 1906 James Weldon Johnson was consul to Venezuela, and later, to Nicaragua. During this period he wrote his only novel, *The Autobiography of an Ex-Colored Man* (publ. anonymously, as if it were a true confession; Boston, 1912), in which he gives vivid descriptions of the "ragtime" musical life in N.Y. during the first decade of the century; soon afterward, his trans. of Granados's *Goyescas* was used for the Metropolitan Opera's first performance of this work. In 1926 he compiled (with a lengthy and valuable introduction) *The Book of American Negro Spirituals* (N.Y.), with arrangements by his brother, and, in 1927, *The 2nd Book of American Negro Spirituals;* his book *Black Manhattan* (N.Y., 1930), a historical study of blacks in N.Y., also draws together considerable information on black musical life. He also wrote an autobiography, *Along This Way* (1931). His papers are on deposit at Yale Univ.
BIBLIOGRAPHY: E. Levy, *James Weldon Johnson* (Chicago, 1973).

Johnson, J.J. (James Louis Johnson), black American jazz trombonist and composer; b. Indianapolis, Jan. 22, 1924. He began to play the piano at the age of 11 and the trombone at 14. Influenced by Tommy Dorsey and Jack Teagarden, he went to play with Benny Carter's band in 1942; in 1945 he joined Count Basie's orch., then worked with Illinois Jacquet (1947–49); subsequently appeared with Woody Herman, Dizzy Gillespie, and others. After a hiatus away from the jazz scene (1952–54), he resumed his career, touring with Kai Winding (1954–56); then formed his own quintet, with which he went to Europe. He was acknowledged as one of the pioneer figures of the bop era.

Johnson, J(ohn) Rosamond, black American composer and bass, brother of **James Weldon Johnson;** b. Jacksonville, Fla., Aug. 11, 1873; d. New York, Nov. 11, 1954. He studied at Atlanta Univ. and at the New England Cons. of Music; took voice lessons with David Bispham. He set his brother's poem *Lift Every Voice and Sing* (1900) to music, this later becoming known as "the Negro National Anthem"; the brothers collaborated on many other songs at this time, selling them to various musical reviews in N.Y.; in 1902 they formed, with Bob Cole, the songwriting team of Cole and Johnson Bros., meeting with tremendous success; in addition to popular black-dialect songs, Johnson wrote some songs that were accepted on the concert stage, such as *Li'l Gal* and *Since You Went Away.* In 1912–13 he was music director of Hammerstein's Opera House in London; he also sang in opera; subsequently toured America and Europe in programs of Negro spirituals; with his brother he compiled two vols. of Negro spirituals (1926, 1927), adding piano accompaniments; wrote a ballet, *African Drum Dance,* and many vocal works; also *Rolling Along in Song* (a history of black music with 85 song arrangements). He sang the role of Lawyer Frazier in the early performances of Gershwin's *Porgy and Bess.*

Johnson, Lockrem, American composer; b. Davenport, Iowa, March 15, 1924; d. Seattle, March 5, 1977. He studied at the Cornish School of Music in Seattle (1931–38) and at the Univ. of Washington (1939–42); subsequently was a member of its faculty (1947–49); concurrently served as pianist in the Seattle Symph. (1948–51). In 1952 he held a Guggenheim fellowship; lived in N.Y., where he served as head of the Orch. Dept. of C.F. Peters Corp. for several years. Returning to Seattle, he became head of the music dept. at the Cornish School (1962–69). In 1970 he founded Puget Music Publications, devoted to publishing works by composers of the Northwest. Among his own works, the most popular was the chamber opera *A Letter to Emily* (N.Y., Jan. 25, 1955), which was performed nearly 100 times in various cities. He further wrote a ballet, *She;* a Symphony (Seattle, Dec. 2, 1966); 6 piano sonatas; 3 violin sonatas; 2 cello sonatas; and *Suite of Noëls* for Mixed Voices and Organ.

Johnson, Robert Sherlaw, English composer; b. Sunderland, May 21, 1932. He was educated at King's College at the Univ. of Durham; after graduation he enrolled in the Royal Academy of Music in London; in 1957 he went to Paris, where he studied piano with Jacques Février and composition with Nadia Boulanger; also attended classes of Olivier Messiaen at the Paris Cons.; returning to England, he gave piano recitals in programs of 20th-century music. In 1961 he became a member of the faculty of Leeds Univ., and later was lecturer in music at the Univ. of York (1965–70). In 1970 he was appointed to the staff of Oxford Univ. In his music he recreates Renaissance forms and mannerisms in a modern modal idiom. He composes mainly for chamber ensembles and vocal groups.

WORKS: Opera, *The Lampton Worm* (1976); 2 string quartets (1966, 1969); *Triptych* for Flute, Clarinet, Violin, Cello, Piano, and Percussion (1973); Quintet for Clarinet, Violin, Viola, Cello, and Piano (1974); Sonata for Alto Flute and Cello (1976); *The Praises of Heaven and Earth* for Soprano, Electronic Tape, and Piano (1969); *Incarnatio* for Chorus a cappella (1970); *Green Whispers of Gold* for Voice, Electronic Tape, and Piano (1971); *Carmina vernalia* for Soprano and Instruments (1972); *Christus resurgens* for Chorus a cappella (1972); *Festival Mass of the Resurrection* for Choir and Chamber Orch. (1974); *Anglorum feriae* for Soprano, Tenor, Chorus, and Orch. (1976); *Veritas veritatus* for 6 Voices (1980); 3 piano sonatas (1963, 1967, 1976); *Asterogenesis* for 8-octave Piano (manufactured by Bösendorfer of Vienna), extending the range to the C below the lowest C on an ordinary piano (1973); *Nymphaea ("Projections")* for Piano (1976).

BIBLIOGRAPHY: R. Harris, "Robert Sherlaw Johnson at 50," *Musical Times* (May 1982).

Johnson, Thor, American conductor; b. Wisconsin Rapids, Wis., June 10, 1913 (of Norwegian parentage); d. Nashville, Tenn., Jan. 16, 1975. He studied at the Univ. of North Carolina and later at the Univ. of Michigan (M.A., 1935); organized the Univ. of Michigan Little Symph., with which he toured in the U.S. in 1935–36 and in 1937–41. In 1936 he won the Huntington Beebe Fellowship. This enabled him to study conducting in Europe during 1936–37. His principal teachers were Malko, Abendroth, Weingartner, and Bruno Walter. Returning to America, he attended Koussevitzky's conducting courses at the Berkshire Music Center; conducted the Grand Rapids (Mich.) Symph. Orch. (1940–42), and was guest conductor of the Philadelphia Orch. at Ann Arbor. He enlisted in the U.S. Army in 1942; from 1947 to 1958 he was principal conductor of the Cincinnati Symph. Orch., one of the few Americans to hold the conductorship of a major American orch. for such a length of time. From 1958 to 1964 he was director of conducting activities at Northwestern Univ., Chicago, and from 1967 till his death, directed the Nashville (Tenn.) Orch. Assoc.; also filled in guest engagements in Europe; in 1971 he conducted in Italy and Rumania. He also traveled as a guest conductor in the Orient.

BIBLIOGRAPHY: Hope Stoddard, *Symphony Conductors of the U.S.A.,* chap. XII (N.Y., 1957).

Johnson, Tom, American composer and music critic; b. Greeley, Colo., Nov. 18, 1939. He studied at Yale Univ. (B.A., 1961; M.Mus., 1967). Subsequently he was employed as instructor of the 52nd Army Band Training Unit at Fort Ord, Calif. (1963–65), and in

1967 was a dance accompanist at N.Y. Univ. In 1971 he became music critic of the radical Greenwich Village paper *The Village Voice,* and pugnaciously proceeded to preach the gospel of asymptotic modernity. In his own compositions he aims to displease, but much to his chagrin, often fails in his design to shock. The most beguiling of his productions is *The 4-Note Opera* for Soloists, Chorus, Piano, and Tape, to his own libretto, produced at The Cubiculo in N.Y. on May 11, 1972; the score actually makes use of only 4 notes, A, B, D, and E, but employs them with quaquaversal expertise. Among his other works are *Pendulum* for Orch. (1965); *Fission* for Orch. (1966); *4 Violins* for 4 Violins and Percussion (1966); Trio for Flute, Cello, and Piano (1967); *5 Americans* for Orch. (1969); *411 Lines,* theater piece (1970); and several pieces of "Action Music" for dancers and piano. Apart from his activities as a composer and writer, Tom Johnson has also appeared as a singer, even though he grievously lacks the *bel canto* quality in his throaty voice; on June 11, 1976, in the summer gardens of the Museum of Modern Art in N.Y., he gave a rendition of a group of 18 "Secret Songs" of his composition, set to nonsense syllables; after singing each of the songs he burned the MS in a specially provided white bowl in which an eternal flame burns—sustained by alcohol.

Johnston, Benjamin, American avant-garde composer; b. Macon, Ga., March 15, 1926. He was educated at the College of William and Mary (A.B., 1949), at the Cincinnati Cons. of Music (M.Mus., 1950), and at Mills College (M.A., 1952). In 1951 he joined the faculty of the Univ. of Illinois at Urbana. In 1959 he received a Guggenheim fellowship. His works include *Celebration* for Solo Piano; Duo for Flute and String Bass; *9 Variations for String Quartet; Knocking Piece* for Percussion; *Night,* cantata (1955); *Gambit* for Dancers and Orch. (1959); *Sonata for Microtonal Piano* (1965); *Quintet for Groups* (1966) and a "tombstone" piece, *Ci gît Satie,* for the Swingle Singers (1966); also an opera, *Carmilla* (1970).

Johnstone, Arthur Edward, composer and teacher; b. London, May 13, 1860; d. Wilkes-Barre, Pa., Jan. 23, 1944. He was brought to N.Y. as a child and studied there with Leopold Damrosch (composition), William Scharfenberg and William Mason (piano), and S.P. Warren (organ). He was a lecturer at Washington Univ. in St. Louis (summer sessions) for many years; composed an overture; piano works; songs; etc.; publ. a useful book, *Instruments of the Modern Symphony Orchestra and Band* (N.Y., 1917; revised ed., 1948).

Johnstone, John Alfred, Shakespearean scholar and writer on music; b. Cork, Ireland, July 6, 1861; d. Sidmouth, England, March 21, 1941. After studying literature and music in Dublin, he went to Australia in 1882; spent many years in Melbourne, where he was director of the music school of the Atheneum; returning to England, he continued to publ. books and articles on the English theater and on music. In addition to his writings, he taught piano; publ. numerous manuals (*The Art of Expression in Piano Playing; The Royal Method for Scales and Arpeggios; The Simplicity Piano Tutor; Muscular Relaxation, Weight, Touch and Rotary Movement;* etc.).

Jokinen, Erikki, Finnish composer; b. Janakkala, Oct. 16, 1941. He studied with Kokkonen and Bergman at the Sibelius Academy in Helsinki; subsequently held various teaching posts. Among his works are: Cello Concerto (Helsinki, Oct. 21, 1971) and String Quartet (1972).

Jokl, Georg, composer, brother of **Otto Jokl;** b. Vienna, July 31, 1896; d. New York, July 29, 1954. He studied with Schreker; was active as an accompanist and teacher in Vienna; in 1938, settled in N.Y. Among his works are a Symph.; a symph. poem, *Heldensang* (Königsberg, 1923); *Burletta piccola* for Wind Instruments (1952); music works.

Jokl, Otto, composer, brother of **Georg Jokl;** b. Vienna, Jan. 18, 1891; d. New York, Nov. 13, 1963. He studied with Hermann Grädener and Alban Berg (1926–30). His Suite for Orch. (1934) won the Hertzka Prize in Vienna; other works are *Sinfonietta seria* (1935); 2 string quartets; etc. In 1940 he emigrated to America and settled in N.Y.

Jolas, Betsy, French composer of American parentage; b. Paris, Aug. 5, 1926. She went to America in 1939; studied at Bennington College (B.A., 1946); returned to Paris in 1946 and took courses with Olivier Messiaen at the Paris Cons. In her music she applies constructive methods in neo-Baroque forms and quasi-serial techniques.
WORKS: *Figures* for 9 Instruments (1956); *Mots* for 5 Voices and 8 Instruments (1963); *Quatuor* for Coloratura Soprano, Violin, Viola, and Cello (1964); *J.D.E.* for 14 Instruments (1966); *D'un opéra de voyage* for 22 Instruments (1967); *Quatre plages* for String Orch. (1968); *Etats* for Violin and Percussion (1969); *Winter Music* for Organ and Chamber Orch. (1970); *Le Pavillon au bord de la rivière,* musical spectacle after a medieval Chinese play (Avignon, July 25, 1975); *O Wall,* a "mini-opera" as an instrumental counterpart to a line from Shakespeare's *A Midsummer Night's Dream,* for Woodwind Quintet (N.Y., Nov. 5, 1976).

Jolivet, André, prominent French composer; b. Paris, Aug. 8, 1905; d. there, Dec. 20, 1974. A son of artistically inclined parents, he took an interest in the fine arts, wrote poetry, and improvised at the piano; studied cello with Louis Feuillard and music theory with Aimé Théodas at Notre Dame de Clignancourt. At the age of 15 he wrote a ballet and designed a set for it; in 1928 he undertook a prolonged study of musical techniques with Paul Le Flem. Of decisive importance to the maturation of his creative consciousness was his meeting in 1930 with Varèse, then living in Paris, who gave him a sense of direction in composition. In 1935 Jolivet organized in Paris the progressive group La Spirale. In 1936, in association with Yves Baudrier, Olivier Messiaen, and Daniel Lesur, he founded La Jeune France, dedicated to the promotion of new music in a national French style. Jolivet was also active as conductor of his own works, and traveled all around the world, including America, Russia, Egypt, and Japan, in this capacity. He served as conductor and music director of the Comédie Française (1943–59); was technical adviser of the Direction Générale des Artes et des Lettres (1959–62), and president of the Concerts Lamoureux (1963–68); he also was prof. of composition at the Paris Cons. (1965–70). Jolivet injected an empiric spirit into his music, making free use of modernistic technical resources, including the electronic sounds of the Ondes Martenot. Despite these esoteric preoccupations, and even a peripheral deployment of serialism, Jolivet's music is designed mainly to provide aural stimulation and esthetic satisfaction.

WORKS: Opera buffa, *Dolorès*, subtitled *Le Miracle de la femme laide* (1942; Paris Radio, May 4, 1947); 3 ballets: *Guignol et Pandore* for Piano or Orch. (1943; Paris, April 29, 1944); *L'Inconnue* (1950; Paris Opéra, April 19, 1950); *Ariadne* (1964; Paris, March 12, 1965); oratorio, *La Vérité de Jeanne* (1956; Domrémy Festival, May 20, 1956; 3 orch. interludes drawn from it are often played separately); 2 cantatas: *La Tentation dernière* (1941; Paris, May 16, 1941) and *Le Cœur de la matière* (1965; Paris, April 9, 1965); scenic music for radio legends and other productions such as *La Queste de Lancelot* (1943; Paris, Jan. 21, 1944); *Le Livre de Christophe Colomb* (1946; Paris, Feb. 21, 1947); *Hélène et Faust*, after Goethe (1949); 2 productions of *Antigone* (1951; 1960); *Empereur Jones* (1953); *L'Amour médecin* (1955); and *L'Eunuque* (1959). He also wrote *Andante* for String Orch. (1935); *Danse incantatoire* for Orch. with 2 Ondes Martenot (1936); *3 chants des hommes* for Baritone and Orch. (1937); *Poèmes pour l'enfant* for Voice and 11 Instruments (1937; Paris, May 12, 1938); *Cosmogonie*, prelude for Orch. (1938; Paris, Nov. 17, 1947; also for Piano); *5 danses rituelles* (1939; Paris, June 15, 1942); *3 complaintes du soldat* for Voice, and Orch. or Piano (1940); *Symphonie de danses* (1940; Paris, Nov. 24, 1943); *Suite delphique* for Wind Instruments, Harp, Ondes Martenot, and Percussion (1943; Vienna, Oct. 22, 1948); *Psyché* for Orch. (1946; Paris, March 5, 1947); *Fanfares pour Britannicus* for Brass and Percussion (1946); Concerto for Ondes Martenot and Orch. (1947; Vienna, April 23, 1948); 2 trumpet concertos: Concertino (Concerto No. 1) for Trumpet, String Orch., and Piano (1948) and No. 2 (1954); 2 flute concertos: No. 1, with String Orch. (1949) and No. 2, *Suite en concert*, for Flute and Percussionists (1965); Piano Concerto (1949–50; Strasbourg Music Festival, June 19, 1951); Concerto for Harp and Chamber Orch. (1952); 3 numbered symphs.: No. 1 (1953; International Society for Contemporary Music Festival, Haifa, May 30, 1954), No. 2 (1959; Berlin Festival Oct. 3, 1959), and No. 3 (1964; Mexico City, Aug. 7, 1964, composer conducting); Concerto for Bassoon, String Orch., Harp, and Piano (1954; Paris Radio, Nov. 30, 1954); *Suite transocéane* (1955; Louisville, Ky., Sept. 24, 1955); *Suite française* for Orch. (1957); Percussion Concerto (1958; Paris, Feb. 17, 1959); *Adagio* for Strings (1960); *Les Amants magnifiques* for Orch. (1961; Lyons, April 24, 1961); Symph. for Strings (1961; Paris, Jan. 9, 1962); 2 cello concertos: No. 1 (1962; Paris, Nov. 20, 1962) and No. 2, with String Orch. (1966; Moscow, Jan. 6, 1967); *12 Inventions* for 12 Instruments (1966; Paris, Jan. 23, 1967); *Songe à nouveau rêvé* for Soprano and Orch. (1970); Violin Concerto (1972; Paris, Feb. 28, 1973); *La Flèche du temps* for 12 Solo Strings (1973); *Yin-Yang* for 11 Solo Strings (1974). His chamber and solo instrumental works include *3 Temps* for Piano (1930); Suite for String Trio (1930); String Quartet (1934); *Mana* for Piano (1935); *3 poèmes* for Ondes Martenot and Piano (1935); *5 incantations* for Solo Flute (1936); *Messe pour le jour de la paix* for Voice, Organ, and Tambourine (1940); *Ballet des étoiles* for 9 Instruments (1941); *Suite liturgique* for Voice, Oboe, Cello, and Harp (1942); Nocturne for Cello and Piano (1943); *Pastorales de Noël* for Flute or Violin, Bassoon or Viola, and Harp (1943); *Chant des Linos* for Flute and Piano, or Flute, Violin, Viola, Cello, and Harp (1944); *Sérénade* for Oboe and Piano, or Wind Quintet (1945); 2 piano sonatas (1945, 1957); *Hopi Snake Dance* for 2 Pianos (1948); *Epithalame* for 12-part Vocal "Orch." (1953; Venice, Sept. 16, 1956); *Sérénade* for 2 Guitars (1956); *Rhapsodie à 7* for Clarinet, Bassoon, Trumpet, Trombone, Percussion, Violin, and Double Bass (1957); Flute Sonata (1958); Sonatina for Flute and Clarinet (1961); *Hymne à l'univers* for Organ (1961); *Messe "Uxor tua"* for 5 Voices, and 5 Instruments or Organ (1962); Sonatina for Oboe and Bassoon (1963); *Madrigal* for 4 Voices and 4 Instruments (1963); *Alla rustica* for Flute and Harp (1963); *Suite rhapsodique* for Solo Violin (1965); *Suite en concert* for Solo Cello (1965); *5 églogues* for Solo Viola (1967); *Ascèses*, 5 pieces for Solo Flute or Clarinet (1967); *Cérémonial en hommage à Varèse* for 6 Percussionists (1968); *Controversia* for Oboe and Harp (1968); *Mandala* for Organ (1969); *Arioso barocco* for Trumpet and Organ (1969); *Patchinko* for 2 Pianos (1970); *Heptade* for Trumpet and Percussion (1971–72).

BIBLIOGRAPHY: V. Fédorov and P. Guinard, compilers, *André Jolivet: Catalogue des œuvres* (Paris, 1969); Hilda Jolivet, *Avec André Jolivet* (Paris, 1978).

Jommelli, Niccolò, greatly significant Italian composer; b. Aversa, near Naples, Sept. 10, 1714; d. Naples, Aug. 25, 1774. He began his musical studies with Canon Muzzillo, the director of the Cathedral choir in Aversa; in 1725 he entered the Cons. S. Onofrio in Naples, where he studied with Prota and Feo; in 1728 he enrolled in the Cons. Pietà dei Turchini in Naples, where he continued his studies with Fago, Sarcuni, and Basso. In 1737 he composed a comic opera, *L'errore amoroso,* for Naples; this was followed by a 2nd comic opera, *Odoardo* (Naples, 1738). On Jan. 16, 1740, his first serious opera,

Jommelli

Ricimero rè de' Goti, was produced in Rome. After composing *Astianatte* (Rome, Feb. 4, 1741), he went to Bologna for the premiere of his *Ezio* (April 29, 1741); there he studied with Padre Martini; was also elected to membership in the Accademia Filarmonica. He then proceeded to Venice, where his opera *Merope* was given on Dec. 26, 1741; in 1743 he became music director of the Ospedale degli Incurabili there; during this time he composed several notable sacred works, including the oratorios *Isacco figura del Redentore* and *La Betulia liberata.* In 1747 he left Venice for Rome; in 1749 he went to Vienna, where his opera *Achille in Sciro* was successfully staged on Aug. 30, 1749. Several of his operas had been performed in Stuttgart, resulting in a commission for a new opera from Karl Eugen, the Duke of Württemberg. *Fetonte* was premiered in Stuttgart on the duke's birthday on Feb. 11, 1753. On Jan. 1, 1754, Jommelli became Ober-Kapellmeister in Stuttgart. Among the operas he composed for Stuttgart were *Pelope* (Feb. 11, 1755), *Nitteti* (Feb. 11, 1759), and *L'Olimpiade* (Feb. 11, 1761); he also composed sacred music, including a *Miserere* and a *Te Deum,* both of which were widely performed. In 1768 Jommelli accepted an offer from King José of Portugal to compose operas and sacred music for the court of Lisbon. He left Stuttgart in 1769 and returned to Italy; for Naples he composed the operas *Armida abbandonata* (May 30, 1770) and *Ifigenia in Tauride* (May 30, 1771); also the serenata *Cerere placata* (Sept. 14, 1772). His opera *Il trionfo di Clelia* was produced in Lisbon with great success on June 6, 1774. His last work for Naples was a *Miserere* on Psalm 50, which was heard during Holy Week 1774.

The historical significance of Jommelli lies in his being a mediator between the German and Italian styles of composition, especially in opera. He introduced into Italian opera the German solidity of harmonic texture and also the expressive dynamics associated with the "Mannheim" school of composition; he also abandoned the formal Neapolitan convention of the da capo aria, thus contributing to a more progressive and realistic operatic form; this earned him the sobriquet "the Italian Gluck." On the other hand, he influenced the development, during his long stay in Stuttgart, of German opera in the direction of simple melodiousness and natural rhythmic flow without dependence on contrapuntal techniques. Thus his influence was beneficial both for his native art and for the most austere German operatic traditions.

WORKS: OPERAS: *L'errore amoroso,* comic opera (Naples, 1737; not extant); *Odoardo,* comic opera (Naples, 1738; not extant); *Ricimero rè de' Goti* (Rome, Jan. 16, 1740); *Astianatte* (Rome, Feb. 4, 1741; also known as *Andromaca*); *Ezio* (Bologna, April 29, 1741; 2nd version, Naples, Nov. 4, 1748; 3rd version, Stuttgart, Feb. 11, 1758, not extant; 4th version, 1771; revised by da Silva, Lisbon, April 20, 1772); *Merope* (Venice, Dec. 26, 1741); *Semiramide riconosiuta* (Turin, Dec. 26, 1741; 2nd version, Piacenza, 1753; 3rd version, Stuttgart, Feb. 11, 1762); *Don Chichibio,* intermezzi (Rome, 1742); *Eumene* (Bologna, May 5, 1742; 2nd version, as *Artemisia,*

Naples, May 30, 1747); *Semiramide* (Venice, Dec. 26, 1742); *Tito Manlio* (Turin, 1743; 2nd version, Venice, 1746, not extant; 3rd version, Stuttgart, Jan. 6, 1758, not extant); *Demofoonte* (Padua, June 13, 1743; 2nd version, Milan, 1753; 3rd version, Stuttgart, Feb. 11, 1764; revised, Ludwigsburg, Feb. 11, 1765; revised by da Silva, Lisbon, June 6, 1775; 4th version, Naples, Nov. 4, 1770); *Alessandro nell'Indie* (Ferrara, 1744, not extant; 2nd version, Stuttgart, Feb. 11, 1760, not extant; revised by da Silva, Lisbon, June 6, 1776); *Ciro riconosciuto* (Bologna, May 4, 1744; 2nd version, 1747?; 3rd version, Venice, 1749; completely new version, 1751 or 1758); *Sofonisba* (Venice, 1746; not extant); *Cajo Mario* (Rome, Feb. 6, 1746; 2nd version, Bologna, 1751); *Antigono* (Lucca, Aug. 24, 1746); *Didone abbandonata* (Rome, Jan. 28, 1747; 2nd version, Vienna, Dec. 8, 1749; 3rd version, Stuttgart, Feb. 11, 1763); *L'amore in maschera,* comic opera (Naples, 1748; not extant); *La cantata e disfida di Don Trastullo,* intermezzi (Rome, 1749; 2nd version, Lucca, 1762); *Artaserse* (Rome, Feb. 4, 1749; 2nd version, Stuttgart, Aug. 30, 1756); *Demetrio* (Parma, 1749); *Achille in Sciro* (Vienna, Aug. 30, 1749; 2nd version, Rome, Jan. 26, 1771); *Cesare in Egitto* (Rome, 1751; not extant); *La Villana nobile,* comic opera (Palermo, 1751; not extant); *Ifigenia in Aulide* (Rome, Feb. 9, 1751; revised with arias by Traetta, Naples, Dec. 18, 1753); *L'Uccellatrice,* intermezzi (Venice, May 6, 1751; 2nd version as *Il paratajo [ovvero] La Pipée,* Paris, Sept. 25, 1753); *Ipermestra* (Spoleto, Oct. 1751); *Talestri* (Rome, Dec. 28, 1751; *I Rivali delusi,* intermezzi (Rome, 1752); *Attilio Regolo* (Rome, Jan. 8, 1753); *Fetonte* (Stuttgart, Feb. 11, 1753, not extant; 2nd version, Ludwigsburg, Feb. 11, 1768); *La clemenza di Tito* (Stuttgart, Aug. 30, 1753, not extant; 2nd version, Ludwigsburg, Jan. 6, 1765, not extant; revised by da Silva, Lisbon, June 6, 1771); *Bajazette* (Turin, Dec. 26, 1753); *Don Falcone,* intermezzi (Bologna, Jan. 22, 1754); *Lucio Vero* (Milan, 1754); *Catone in Utica* (Stuttgart, Aug. 30, 1754; not extant); *Pelope* (Stuttgart, Feb. 11, 1755; revised by da Silva, Salvaterra, 1768); *Enea nel Lazio* (Stuttgart, Aug. 30, 1755, not extant; revised by da Silva, Salvaterra, 1767); *Creso* (Rome, Feb. 5, 1757); *Temistocle* (Naples, Dec. 18, 1757; 2nd version, Ludwigsburg, Nov. 4, 1765); *Nitteti* (Stuttgart, Feb. 11, 1759, not extant; revised by da Silva, Lisbon, June 6, 1770); *Endimione ovvero Il trionfo d'amore,* pastorale (Stuttgart, 1759, not extant; 2nd version, Queluz, June 29, 1780); *Cajo Fabrizio* (Mannheim, Nov. 4, 1760; includes arias by G. Cola); *L'Olimpiade* (Stuttgart, Feb. 11, 1761; revised by da Silva, Lisbon, March 31, 1774); *L'isola disabitata,* pastorale (Ludwigsburg, Nov. 4, 1761, not extant; 2nd version, Queluz, March 31, 1780); *Il trionfo d'amore,* pastorale (Ludwigsburg, Feb. 16, 1763; not extant); *La pastorella illustre,* pastorale (Stuttgart, Nov. 4, 1763, not extant; revised by da Silva, Salvaterra, 1773); *Il Re pastore* (Ludwigsburg, Nov. 4, 1764, not extant; revised by da Silva, Salvaterra, 1770); *Imeneo in Atene,* pastorale (Ludwigsburg, Nov. 4, 1765; revised by da Silva, Lisbon, March 19, 1773); *La Critica,* comic opera (Ludwigsburg, 1766; revised as *Il giuoco di picchetto,* Koblenz, 1772; revised as *La conversazione [e] L'accademia di musica,* Salvaterra, 1775); *Vologeso* (Ludwigsburg, Feb. 11, 1766; revised by da Silva, Salvaterra, 1769); *Il matrimonio per concorso,* comic opera (Ludwigsburg, Nov. 4, 1766, not extant; revised by da Silva, Salvaterra, 1770); *Il Cacciatore deluso [ovvero] La Semiramide in bernesco,* serious-comic opera (Tübingen, Nov. 4, 1767; revised by da Silva, Salvaterra, 1771); *La Schiava liberata,* serious-comic opera (Ludwigsburg, Dec. 18, 1768; revised by da Silva, Lisbon, March 31, 1770); *Armida abbandonata* (Naples, May 30, 1770; revised by da Silva, Lisbon, March 31, 1773); *L'amante cacciatore,* intermezzi (Rome, 1771; not extant); *Le avventure di Cleomede,* serious-comic opera (Naples, 1771?; revised by da Silva, Lisbon, June 6, 1772); *Ifigenia in Tauride* (Naples, May 30, 1771; revised by da Silva, Salvaterra, 1776); *Il trionfo di Clelia* (Naples, 1774?); etc. His opera *Fetonte* was publ. in Denkmäler Deutscher Tonkunst, vols. 22–23 (1907).

OTHER STAGE WORKS: *Componimento drammatico* (Rome, Feb. 9, 1747; not extant); *Componimento drammatico* (Ronciglione, Feb. 28, 1751; not extant); *La reggia de' Fati* (with G.B. Sammartini; Milan, March 13, 1753); *La pastorale offerta* (with G.B. Sammartini; Milan, March 19, 1753); *Il giardino incanto* (Stuttgart, 1755; not extant); *L'asilo d'amore* (Stuttgart, Feb. 11, 1758; not extant); *Le Cinesi* (Ludwigsburg, 1765; not extant); *L'unione coronata* (Solitude, Sept. 22, 1768; not extant); *Cerere placata* (Naples, Sept. 14, 1772); etc.; also, serenatas, several secular cantatas and other vocal pieces; he also contributed to a number of pasticcios.

ORATORIOS, PASSIONS, AND SACRED CANTATAS: *Che impetuoso è questo torrente* for 2 Sopranos, Tenor, and Orch. (Naples, 1740); *Isacco figura del Redentore* for 2 Sopranos, Alto, Tenor, Bass, 4-part Chorus, and Orch. (Venice, 1742); *La Betulia liberata* for Soprano, Alto, Tenor, Bass, 4-part Chorus, and Orch. (Venice, 1743); *Gioas* for 3 Sopranos, 3 Altos, 4-part Chorus, and Strings (Venice, 1945); *Juda proditor* for 3 Sopranos, 3 Altos, and Chorus (Venice, 1746?; not extant); *Ove son? Chi mi guida?* for Soprano, Alto, Tenor, and Orch. (Naples, 1747); *La passione di Gesù Cristo* for Soprano, Alto, Tenor, Bass, 4-part Chorus, and Orch. (Rome, 1749); *Giuseppe glorificato in Egitto* for 2 Sopranos, Tenor, and Orch. (Rome, 1749); *Le Spose di Elcana* for 4-part Chorus (Palermo, 1750; not extant); *In questa incolte riva* for 2 Sopranos and Orch. (Rome, May 20, 1751); *Non più: L'atteso istante* for Soprano, Alto, Tenor, and Orch. (Rome, 1752); *Il sacrifizio di Gefte* for 4-part Chorus and Strings (Palermo, 1753; not extant); *La reconciliazione della Virtù e della Gloria* for 2-part Chorus (Pistoia, 1754; not extant); *Gerusalemme convertita* (Palermo, 1755; not extant); *Il sogno di Nabucco* (Palermo, 1755; not extant); etc. Additional sacred works include many masses, as well as graduals, offertories, antiphones, Psalms, motets, hymns, etc. His instrumental works include harpsichord concertos, quartets, divertimenti, and sonatas.

BIBLIOGRAPHY: S. Mattei, *Elogio del Jommelli* (Colle, 1785); P. Alfieri, *Notizie biografiche di Niccolò Jommelli* (Rome, 1845); H. Abert, *Niccolò Jommelli als Opernkomponist* (Halle, 1908); idem, "Die Stuttgarter Oper unter Jommelli," *Neue Musikzeitung,* XLVI/24 (1925); F. Abbiati, "D'umor concettoso l'inedito Jommelli," *La Scala,* no. 6 (1950); idem, "Qui buongustaio l'inedito Jommelli," *La Scala,* no. 7 (1950); R. Pattengale, *The Cantatas of Niccolò Jommelli* (Diss., Univ. of Michigan, 1973); H. Brofsky, "Jommelli e Padre Martini," *Rivista Italiana di Musicologia,* VIII (1973); J. Carlson, *Selected Masses of Niccolò Jommelli* (Diss., Univ. of Illinois, 1974); L. Tolkoff, *The Stuttgart Operas of Niccolò Jommelli* (Diss., Yale Univ., 1974); M. McClymonds, *Niccolò Jommelli: The Last Years, 1769–1774* (Ann Arbor, Mich., 1980).

Jonák, Zdeněk, Czech composer; b. Prague, Feb. 25, 1917. He studied composition with Řídký at the Prague Cons.; devoted himself mainly to pragmatic musical tasks, such as making arrangements of folk songs and writing music for the theater.

WORKS: String Quartet No. 1 (1941); *Prelude* for Orch. (1944); *Passacaglia* for Orch. (1947); String Quartet No. 2 (1951); Cello Sonata (1951); Wind Quintet (1953); *Serenade* for Chamber Orch. (1955); Concerto for Wind Orch. (1963); *Chamber Symphony* (1964); *Mim* for Flute and Harp (1965); *Epigrams,* song cycle for Chorus a cappella (1970); Trumpet Concerto (1974).

Jonás, Alberto, Spanish-American pianist; b. Madrid, June 8, 1868; d. Philadelphia, Nov. 9, 1943. He received primary music training in Madrid; then studied piano and theory of composition at the Brussels Cons. In 1890 he went to St. Petersburg, Russia, where he had some lessons with Anton Rubinstein. After a brief concert career in Europe, he went to the U.S., where he taught piano at the Univ. of Michigan (1894–98) and the Cons. of Detroit (1898–1904). From 1904 to 1914 he lived in Berlin; after the outbreak of World War I he came back to America, settling in N.Y., where he established a fine reputation as a piano pedagogue. In collaboration with 16 pianists, he publ. *Master School of Modern Piano Playing and Virtuosity* (N.Y., 1922), which went through 5 editions, and also brought out several books of piano exercises for beginners. He wrote a number of attractive piano pieces in a salon manner, among them *Northern Dances, Humoresque, Nocturne,* and *Evening Song.*

Jonas, Emile, French composer; b. Paris, March 5, 1827; d. St.-Germain-en-Laye, May 21, 1905. He studied at the Paris Cons.; received the 2nd Grand Prix de Rome for his cantata *Antonio* (1849). After graduation, he became an instructor at the Paris Cons. (until 1865); also was music director at the Portuguese Synagogue, and a bandmaster.

WORKS: Light operas (all produced in Paris): *Le Duel de Benjamin* (1855); *La Parade* (Aug. 2, 1856); *Le Roi boit* (April 1857); *Les Petits Prodiges* (Nov. 19, 1857); *Job et son chien* (Feb. 6, 1863); *Le Manoir de La Renardière* (Sept. 29, 1864); *Avant la noce* (March 24, 1865); *Les Deux Arlequins* (Dec. 29, 1865); *Le Canard à trois becs* (Feb. 6, 1869); *Désiré, sire de*

Champigny (April 11, 1869); operetta to an Eng. libretto, *Cinderella the Younger* (London, Sept. 25, 1871; in French as *Javotte*, Paris, Dec. 22, 1871). He publ. a valuable *Receuil de chants hébraïques* (1854) for the Portuguese Synagogue.

Jonas, Maryla, Polish pianist; b. Warsaw, May 31, 1911; d. New York, July 3, 1959. She was a precocious child pianist, and appeared in public at the age of 9; took lessons with Turczynski and was commended by Paderewski. She began her professional career as a concert pianist at the age of 15; after the invasion of Poland in 1939, she made her way to Rio de Janeiro, and gave a series of concerts in South America; then went to N.Y., where she made an exceptionally successful debut in Carnegie Hall (Feb. 25, 1946); her auspicious career was thwarted by an irremediable illness and early death.

Jonas, Oswald, Austrian musicologist; b. Vienna, Jan. 10, 1897; d. Riverside, Calif., March 19, 1978. He studied law at the Univ.; was a student of Schenker in musicology; subsequently taught at the Schenker Inst. in Vienna (1935–38). After the annexation of Austria by the Nazis he went to America; was on the faculty of the Roosevelt Univ. in Chicago (1945–63). In 1966 he was appointed a prof. of music at the Univ. of Calif. at Riverside. He publ. *Das Wesen des musikalischen Kunstwerks* (Vienna, 1934) and numerous articles dealing with Schenker's theories; also prepared for publication Schenker's posthumous work, *Kunst des Vortrags*.

Joncières, Victorin de (real name, **Felix Ludger Rossignol**), French composer; b. Paris, April 12, 1839; d. there, Oct. 26, 1903. He was first a student of painting; music was his avocation. At the age of 20 he produced a light opera for a student performance; encouraged by its success with the critics, he began to study music seriously, first with Elwart, then with Leborne at the Paris Cons. He was a great admirer of Wagner, and when Leborne expressed his opposition to Wagner, Joncières impulsively left his class. WORKS: Operas (all produced in Paris): *Sardanapale* (Feb. 8, 1867); *Le Dernier Jour de Pompei* (Sept. 21, 1869); *Dimitri* (May 5, 1876; his most successful work); *La Reine Berthe* (Dec. 27, 1878); *Le Chevalier Jean* (March 11, 1885; successful in Germany under the title *Johann von Lothringen*); *Lancelot du lac* (Feb. 7, 1900); he further wrote music to *Hamlet* (Nantes, Sept. 21, 1867); *Symphonie romantique* (Paris, March 9, 1873); Violin Concerto (Paris, Dec. 12, 1869); a symph. ode, *La Mer;* etc.

Jones, Alton, American pianist; b. Fairfield, Nebr., Aug. 3, 1899; d. New York, Jan. 2, 1971. He studied at Drake Univ. (B.M., 1919) and at the Inst. of Musical Art in N.Y., where his teachers were Edwin Hughes and Richard Buhlig; he graduated in 1921; made his concert debut in N.Y. in 1924; was a soloist with the N.Y. Phil. in 1949; gave his last N.Y. recital in 1955. He taught at the Juilliard School of Music from 1921 until his death; his reputation as a pedagogue was high; many American pianists were his pupils.

Jones, Booker T., founder of the instrumental American group called Booker T. and the MGs (for Memphis Group), noted for its "Memphis sound"; b. Memphis, Sept. 12, 1944. The group lit the rock firmament in 1962 with their smash hit *Green Onions.* In 1965 Jones authored a blues song with the pseudo-astrological title *Born under a Bad Sign.* Seized by a peculiar yen for musical culture, he received a degree in applied music from the respectable Indiana Univ. Fortunately, this academic distinction did not kill off his natural gift for pleasing the public. His records sold well; among his greatest hits were *Soul Limbo, Hip Hug-Her,* and *Uptight.*

Jones, Brian, British rock musician; b. Cheltenham, Feb. 28, 1942; d. San Francisco, July 3, 1969 (found inanimate in a swimming pool). His real name was **Lewis Brian Hopkins-Jones.** He joined Mick Jagger and others to form The Rolling Stones, who rapidly ascended the ladder of success on both sides of the Atlantic, finally graduating in the immensity of a cult. Brian Jones went through the customary drug period, but managed to learn to play the Hindu sitar and the plebeian dulcimer, making him the group's most versatile instrumentalist. In 1967 and again in 1968 he was busted for illicit drug possession; in 1969 he left The Rolling Stones and soon died an unnatural death.

Jones, Charles, American composer; b. Tamworth, Canada, June 12, 1910. He settled in the U.S. in 1928; then studied violin at the Inst. of Musical Art in N.Y. (diploma, 1932) and composition with Bernard Wagenaar at the Juilliard School of Music (diploma, 1939). He taught at Mills College in Oakland, Calif. (1939–44); joined the faculty of the Juilliard School in 1954 and of the Mannes College of Music in N.Y. in 1972; also taught at the Aspen School of Music from 1951. WORKS: BALLET: *Down with Drink* for Female Voices, Piano, and Percussion (1943). FOR ORCH.: 4 symphs.: No. 1 (1939); No. 2 (1957); No. 3 (1962); No. 4, in 5 short movements (1965); *Little Symphony for the New Year* (1953); Suite for Strings (1937); *Galop* (1940); *Pastorale* for Chamber Orch. (1940); *Cowboy Song* for Oboe and Strings (1941); *Overture* (1942); *5 Melodies* (1945); *Cassation* (1948); *Introduction and Rondo* for Strings (1957); *Suite after a Notebook of 1762* for Chamber Orch. (1957); Concerto for 4 Violins and Orch. (1963); *Allegory* (1970). CHAMBER MUSIC: 8 string quartets (1936–84); Sonatina for Solo Violin (1938); Sonatina for Violin and Piano (1942); Suite for Violin and Piano (1945); Duo for Violin and Piano (1947); *Threnody* for Solo Viola (1947); *Lyric Waltz Suite* for Wind Quartet (1948); *Sonata a tre* for Piano Trio (1952); Duo for Violin and Viola (1956); Sonata for Violin and Piano (1958); *Sonata piccola* for Piccolo and Harpsichord (1961); Sonata for Oboe and Harpsichord (1965); *Music for 2 Violinists* (1966); String Trio (1968); *In Nomine* for Violin and Piano (1972); Serenade for Flute, Violin, Cello, and Harpsichord (1973); *Triptychon* for Violin, Viola, and Piano (1975); *Triptychon II* for Violin and Piano (1981); Trio for Violin, Cello, and Piano (1982); *Meditation* for Bass Clarinet and Piano (1982); *Capriccio* for Cello and Piano (1983). VOCAL MUSIC: 3 songs for Voice and Piano (1952–53); *The Seasons,* cantata (1959); *I Am a Mynstrel* for Tenor, Violin, Harpsichord, Piano, and Percussion (1967); *Masque,* after Pope's "Rape of the Lock," for Speaker and 12 Players (1968); *The Fond Observer* for Voice and Piano, after Henry James (1977); 4 scenes for Voice and Piano, after Pope (1982). FOR PIANO: 2 sonatas for 2 Pianos (1946, 1950); Sonata for 2 Pianos (1947); *Toccata* (1955); *Psalm* (1976); *Book of the Hours* (1979—); Sonata for Piano, 4-hands (1983); also *Keyboard Book* for Harpsichord (1953); *Noël* for Organ (1983).

Jones, Daniel, remarkable Welsh composer; b. Pembroke, Dec. 7, 1912. Both his parents were musicians, and he absorbed the natural rudiments of music instinctively at home. He attended the Swansea Univ. College; then entered the Royal Academy of Music in London, where he studied a variety of theoretical and practical aspects of music: composition with Farjeon, conducting with Sir Henry Wood, viola with Lockyear, and French horn with Aubrey Brain; in 1935 he was awarded the Mendelssohn Scholarship; received his M.A. for a thesis on Elizabethan lyric poetry and its relations with music; obtained his D.Mus. at the Univ. of Wales in 1951; received an honorary D.Litt. in 1970. During World War II he served in the British Intelligence Corps; continued his interests in literature and was editor of the collected poems of Dylan Thomas (1971). An exceptionally prolific composer, he wrote 9 symphs. within 30 years, between 1945 and 1974; several oratorios; 2 operas; much chamber music. In 1936 he promulgated a system of "complex metres," in which the numerator in the time signature indicates the succession of changing meters in a clear numerical progression, e.g. 32-322-3222-322-32, followed by 332-3332, 332, etc.; his other innovation is a category of "continuous modes," with the final note of the mode (non-octaval) serving as the initial note of a transposed mode. WORKS: Symphs.: No. 1 (1944); No. 2 (1950); No. 3 (1951); No. 4 (1954); No. 5 (1958); No. 6 (1964); No. 7 (1971); No. 8 (1972); No. 9 (1974); operas: *The Knife* (London, Dec. 2, 1963) and *Orestes* (1967); oratorios and cantatas: *The Country beyond the Stars* (1958), *St. Peter* (1962), *The 3 Hermits* (1969), *The Ballad of the Standard-Bearer* (1969), *The Witnesses* (1971); *Capriccio* for Flute, Harp, and Strings (1965); Violin Concerto (1966); Sinfonietta (1972); several concert overtures and symph. suites; a "miscellany" for Small Orch. (1947), etc.; 8 string quartets; 5 string trios; String Quintet; Sonata for Unaccompanied Cello (1946); Sonata for Cello and Piano (1972); Kettledrum Sonata (1947); 8 Pieces for Violin and Viola (1948); Wind Septet (1949); Wind Nonet (1950); Sonata for 4 Trombones (1955); 24 bagatelles for Piano Solo (1943–55); 6 piano sonatas; 3 piano sonatinas. He is the author of numerous articles expounding

his philosophy of music, some of them incorporated in a book, *Music and Esthetic* (1954).

Jones, Edward, Welsh musician and writer ("Barrd y Brenin"); b. Llanderfel, Merionethshire, March 29, 1752; d. London, April 18, 1824. He was taught by his father, and the family organized a Welsh ensemble, consisting of harps and string instruments. In 1775 he went to London; in 1783, was appointed Welsh bard to the Prince of Wales. He publ. several anthologies of Welsh music, including *Musical and Poetical Relicks of the Welsh Bards* (1784; 2nd ed., 1794; an additional vol. appeared under the title *The Bardic Museum*, 1802; 3rd vol., 1824; a supplementary vol. was publ. posthumously; the entire work contains 225 Welsh melodies); in addition to these, he publ. collections of melodies by other nations; also *Musical Trifles Calculated for Beginners on the Harp.*
BIBLIOGRAPHY: T. Ellis, *Edward Jones, Barrd y Brenin* (Cardiff, 1957).

Jones, Elvin (Ray), black American jazz drummer; b. Pontiac, Mich., Sept. 9, 1927. He grew up in a musical family; his father played guitar, and his mother was proficient on the piano. He was inducted into the armed forces (1946–49) and played in a military band; in 1956 moved to N.Y., where he played in several professional bands; in 1960–66 he played with John Coltrane's group and attracted favorable notice by his imaginative drumming. In 1973 and 1975 he traveled to Europe, South America, and the Orient with his own trio under the auspices of the U.S. State Dept.

Jones, George, American country-music singer; b. Saratoga, Texas, Sept. 12, 1931. He began to play the guitar when he was 9; made some appearances locally before serving in the Korean War; then worked as a house painter. In 1955 he recorded his first hit song, *Why, Baby, Why;* subsequently gained fame with such songs as *Window Up Above* (1961), *She Thinks I Still Care* (1962), *We Must Have Been Out of Our Minds* (1963), and others. He was temporarily married to the country-music star Tammy Wynette; after their divorce he took to drink; his alcoholism did not prevent the Country Music Assoc., however, from naming him the male vocalist of the year in 1981.

Jones, Geraint, Welsh organist, harpsichordist, and conductor; b. Porth, May 16, 1917. He studied at the Royal Academy of Music in London; made his debut as harpsichordist at the National Gallery in 1940; subsequently gave numerous recitals as organist, often on historical instruments of Europe; in 1951 he founded the Geraint Jones Singers and Orch., which he led in many performances of Baroque music.

Jones, Gwyneth, Welsh soprano; b. Pontnewyndd, Nov. 7, 1936. She was educated at the Royal College of Music in London; also studied in Siena and Geneva. She started her career in Zürich in 1962. In 1963 she joined the Royal Opera at Covent Garden; subsequently sang in Vienna, Bayreuth, Munich, and at La Scala, Milan. On Nov. 24, 1972, she made her American debut at the Metropolitan Opera in N.Y. as Sieglinde in *Die Walküre.*

Jones, Jo(nathan), black American jazz drummer; b. Chicago, Oct. 7, 1911. He was reared in Alabama; studied saxophone, trumpet, and piano before mastering the drums; joined Count Basie's band in 1935 and remained with his group, off and on, until 1948; in 1957 he traveled to Europe with Ella Fitzgerald and Oscar Peterson; in N.Y. he led his own groups; in 1973 he acted in a movie, *Born to Swing.* He established his own distinctive rhythmic style stressing all four beats of the bar, diversifying it with a wire-brush technique on the high-hat cymbal.

Jones, Kelsey, American-born Canadian composer; b. South Norwalk, Conn., June 17, 1922. He went to Canada in 1939; studied with Sir Ernest MacMillan, Healey Willan, and Leo Smith at the Univ. of Toronto (Mus.D., 1951), and with Nadia Boulanger in Paris. Returning to Canada, he was appointed to the faculty of the Univ. of Montreal in 1954. In his compositions he follows traditional Baroque forms. WORKS: Chamber opera, *Sam Slick* (Halifax, Sept. 5, 1967); *Miramichi Ballad,* suite for Orch. (1954); Suite for Flute and Strings (1954); *4 Pieces* for Recorder Quartet (1955); *Songs of Time* for Chorus and Piano, 4-hands (1955); *Sonata da camera* for Flute, Oboe, and Harpsichord (1957); *Introduction and Fugue* for Violin and Piano (1959); *Songs of Innocence,* after Blake, for Soprano and Chamber Orch. (1961); *Prelude, Fughetta and Finale* for Violin, Cello, and Harpsichord (1963); *Rondo* for Solo Flute (1963); *Prophecy of Micah* for Chorus and Orch. (Montreal, Feb. 5, 1964); *Sonata da chiesa* for Flute, Oboe, and Harpsichord (1967); Wind Quintet (1968); *Hymn to Bacchus* for Chorus and Piano, 4-hands (1972); *Adagio, Presto and Fugue* for String Quartet and String Orch. (1973); *Songs of Winter* for Soprano, Contralto, and Piano (1973); *Passacaglia and Fugue* for Brass Quintet (1975).

Jones, Parry, Welsh operatic tenor; b. Blaina, Monmouthshire, Feb. 14, 1891; d. London, Dec. 26, 1963. He studied in London, in Italy, and in Germany; made his debut in London in 1914. He sang in America; survived the German submarine attack on the S.S. *Lusitania* on his return trip to England. In London he sang with the Beecham and D'Oyly Carte opera companies, with the Carl Rosa Opera Co. (1919–22), and with the British National Opera Co. (1922–28). He first sang at Covent Garden in 1920–21; then again in 1925–26, 1930–32, 1935, and 1937. In 1949 he became a principal tenor at Covent Garden and remained on its roster until 1955. Subsequently, he taught voice at the Guildhall School of Music.

Jones, Philip, outstanding English trumpet player;

b. Bath, March 12, 1928. He studied at the Royal College of Music in London with Ernest Hall; then served as principal trumpet player in the Royal Phil. (1956–60), Philharmonia Orch. (1960–64), London Phil. (1964–65), New Philharmonia (1965–67), and BBC Symph. (1968–71). In 1957 he founded the Philip Jones Brass Ensemble; he commissioned many composers to write works for his ensemble. He was made an Officer of the Order of the British Empire in 1977.

Jones, "Philly Joe" (Joseph Rudolph Jones), American jazz drummer; b. Philadelphia, July 15, 1923. He studied piano with his mother; then played drums in local groups. Making his way to N.Y., he played with Zoot Sims, Lee Konitz, and Miles Davis. In 1967 he went to Europe, remaining there until 1972; eventually led a jazz-rock group, with which he toured the U.S.

Jones, Quincy Delight, Jr., American pianist, trumpeter, bandleader, and composer; b. Chicago, March 14, 1933. He studied hot trumpet in Seattle and in Boston; joined Lionel Hampton's band; toured with Dizzy Gillespie in the Near East; traveled in Europe (1957–60). His songs and arrangements (*Kingfish, Stockholm Sweetnin', Evening in Paris,* etc.) are sophisticated realizations of swing patterns.

Jones, Robert (I), English composer; b. c.1485; d. London, c.1536. He served as a chorister in the Chapel Royal; traveled with Henry VIII in France (1513); held a royal patent in England (1514–19); in 1520 was in France again; then returned to England, remaining in London until his death. Some of his sacred works are preserved in MS.
BIBLIOGRAPHY: W.H. Grattan Flood, *Early Tudor Composers* (London, 1925).

Jones, Robert (II), English lutenist and composer; flourished in the late 16th and the early 17th century. He obtained a Mus.Bac. degree from Oxford in 1597; held grants to establish a school for children in London in 1610 and in 1615. He publ. *The First Book of Ayres* (1600), followed by 4 other books (1601, 1605, 1607, 1611); a book of madrigals, *First Set of Madrigals of 3, 4, 5, 6, 7 and 8 Parts, for viols and voices or for voices alone; or as you please;* also a madrigal in 6 parts, *Oriana, seeming to wink at Folly,* in *The Triumphes of Oriana* (1601), and 3 pieces in Leighton's *Teares or Lamentacions* (1614). The 5 books of Ayres were republ. with the original accompaniment of each song transcribed into modern notation, by E.H. Fellowes (London, 1925–27).
BIBLIOGRAPHY: E.H. Fellowes, *The English Madrigal Composers* (Oxford, 1921; 2nd ed., 1948); P. Heseltine, "Robert Jones and His Prefaces," *Musical Times* (1923; pp. 99–101 and 168–71); E.H. Fellowes, *The English Madrigal* (London, 1925); idem, *The English Madrigal School* (London, 1926); P. Heseltine, *The English Ayre* (London, 1926); E.H. Fellowes, "The Text of the Songbooks of Robert Jones," *Music & Letters* (1927).

Jones, Sidney, English composer of light music; b. London, June 17, 1861; d. there, Jan. 29, 1946. At an early age he became conductor of a military band; then toured the English provinces and Australia as conductor of various light opera companies; in 1905 he was appointed conductor at the London Empire Theatre. He owes his fame mainly to his enormously successful operetta *Geisha* (London, April 25, 1896), which was for decades performed all over the world. His other operettas are: *The Gayety Girl* (London, 1893); *An Artist's Model* (London, 1895); *A Greek's Slave* (Vienna, 1899); *San Toy* (Vienna, 1899); *My Lady Molly* (London, 1903); *The Medal and the Maid* (London, 1903); *See See* (London, 1906); *The King of Cadonia* (London, 1908); *The Persian Princess* (London, 1909); *Spring Maid* (London, 1911); *The Girl from Utah* (London, 1913); *The Happy Day* (London, 1916).

Jones, Sissieretta (real name, **Matilda S. Joyner**), black American soprano, known as "the Black Patti" (with reference to Adelina Patti); b. Portsmouth, Va., Jan. 5, 1868; d. Providence, R.I., June 24, 1933. She studied voice at the New England Conservatory of Music; began singing professionally in 1888. Her first success was in 1892 at a Cakewalk Jubilee held in Madison Square Garden in N.Y.; afterward she gave recitals at the Academy of Music; the Metropolitan Opera considered her for African roles in *Aida* and *L'Africaine,* but racial attitudes and conservative management policies would not permit such parts to be taken by Afro-Americans. She subsequently toured the U.S., including a command performance before President Harrison at the White House. From 1893 to 1910 she led the Black Patti's Troubadours, with which she toured and sang operatic arias.
BIBLIOGRAPHY: William Lichtenwanger, in *Notable American Women* (Cambridge, Mass., 1971).

Jones, "Spike" (Lindley Armstrong), American bandleader; b. Long Beach, Calif., Dec. 14, 1911; d. Los Angeles, May 1, 1965. He played drums as a boy; then led a school band. On July 30, 1942, he made a recording of a satirical song, *Der Führer's Face,* featuring a Bronx-cheer razzer; toured the U.S. with his band, The City Slickers, which included a washboard, a Smith and Wesson pistol, anti-bug Flit guns in E-flat, doorbells, anvils, hammers to break glass, and a live goat trained to bleat rhythmically. Climactically, he introduced the Latrinophone (a toilet seat strung with catgut). With this ensemble, he launched a Musical Depreciation Revue. He retired in 1963, when the wave of extravaganza that had carried him to the crest of commercial success subsided.

Jones, Thad(deus Joseph), black American jazz trumpeter, cornetist, and bandleader; b. Pontiac, Mich., March 28, 1923. While still in school, he formed a jazz combo with his brothers; then served in the U.S. Army (1943–46); resuming his career, he was a featured member of Count Basie's orch. from 1954 to 1963. In 1965 he formed a band with Mel Lewis, which subsequently gained fame through its many tours of the U.S. and Europe, including a visit to the Soviet Union in 1972.

Jones, Tom (real name, **Thomas Jones Woodward**), English singer and drummer; b. Pontypridd, South Wales, June 7, 1940. He sang, as most Welshmen do, with a natural feeling for melody; dropped out of school at 16 and began to play drums and sing in British pubs; his big chance at success came when he was heard by the famed manager Gordon Mills, a Welshman himself, who decided to propel him into fame; but first he had to abbreviate his name to plain Tom Jones. His greatest asset was lung power; he could outscream anyone in the rock field; he wore extremely tight "sexy" pants, whose protuberances excited middle-aged women; with these assets he successfully invaded America.

Jones, Sir William, English orientalist; b. London, Sept. 28, 1746; d. Calcutta, April 27, 1794. He was a magistrate in India, where he lived from 1783; publ. *On the Musical Modes of the Hindus* (1784), which was included in vol. 6 of his collected works (1799).
BIBLIOGRAPHY: *Dictionary of National Biography* (vol. 10).

Jones, William, known as **Jones of Nayland,** English minister and musician; b. Lowick, Northamptonshire, July 30, 1726; d. Nayland, Jan. 6, 1800. He studied at Oxford; was a vicar at Bethersden, Kent; then was a curate of Nayland. He publ. *A Treatise on the Art of Music* (1784; 2nd ed., 1827).

Jong, Marinus de, Dutch-born Belgian pianist and composer; b. Osterhout, Aug. 14, 1891. He studied composition with Mortelmans and piano with Bosquet at the Antwerp Cons. After several tours as pianist in Europe and America (he played a recital in N.Y. on Feb. 7, 1921), he settled in Belgium in 1926, and in 1931 became a prof. of piano at the Antwerp Cons. He developed a neo-impressionistic style, with polytonal counterpoint as its mainstay.
WORKS: 3 operas: *Mitsanoboe* (1962); *Die häslichen Mädchen von Bagdad* (*The Hateful Maidens of Baghdad;* Antwerp, Jan. 7, 1967); and *Esmoreit* (Antwerp, Sept. 11, 1970); 5 ballets: *De vrouwen van Zalongo* (1951); *De kleine haven* (1952); *De kringloop* (1955); *Carrefour* (1956); and *De Reiskameraad* (1959); 4 oratorios: *Hiawatha's Lied* (1947); *Imitatio Christi* (1956); *Kerkhofblommen* (1957); and *Proverbia Bruegeliana* (1961); the cantata *Summum bonum* (1955); *Ode aan Peter Benoit* for Baritone, Chorus, and Orch. (1946); *Hymnus "Civitas Dei"* for Soloists, Chorus, Children's Chorus, and Orch. (1957); *Hymne aan de Schoonheid* for Soprano, Baritone, Chorus, and Orch. (1961); 3 piano concertos (1924, 1952, 1956–57); concertos for Trumpet (1937), Cello (1946; revised 1969), Violin (1954), Viola (1958), Oboe (1966–67), Horn (1966–67), Bassoon (1967), Flute (1967), Clarinet (1967), and Organ (1974); 3 symphs. (1932, 1965–66, 1976); 3 *Flemish Rhapsodies:* No. 1 for Orch. (1955), No. 2 for Orch.

(1971), and No. 3 for Piano and Orch. (1971); *Rhapsodie No. 4* for Wind Orch. (1974); *Heidestemmingen (Impressions de Bruyère)* for Orch. (1937); *Hiawatha,* symph. poem (1945); *Aphoristische tryptiek* for Orch. or Wind Quintet (1952); *Boublitschky Suite* for Orch. (1956); *Ruimteraket, Atlas (Fusée interplanétaire),* symph. poem (1964); 6 string quartets (1923, 1926, 1947, 1956, 1956, 1962); *Pacis, Doloris et Amoris,* violin sonata (1927); Quartet for 4 Cellos (1936); Nonet (1939); 3 wind quintets (1952, 1965, 1971); Suite for 4 Trombones (1958); Trio for Oboe, Clarinet, and Bassoon (1961); Wind Quartet (1968); Fantasia for Saxophone and Piano (1968); Piano Quartet (1971); Sextet for Piano and Wind Quintet (1972); 3 piano sonatas (1926, 1933, 1934); *Fantaisie-Walsen* for Piano (1960); *12 Preludes* for Piano (1975); Concerto for Solo Organ (1964); numerous organ pieces, choruses, and songs.

Jongen, (Marie-Alphonse-Nicolas-) Joseph, eminent Belgian composer; brother of **Léon Jongen;** b. Liège, Dec. 14, 1873; d. Sart-lez-Spa, July 12, 1953. He studied at the Liège Cons.; received a premier prix for each of the academic subjects and also for piano and organ. In 1891 he joined the staff of the Liège Cons. as a teacher of harmony and counterpoint. In 1894 he gained attention as a composer when he won 2 national prizes; in 1897 he won the Belgian Prix de Rome. He then went abroad; received advice from Richard Strauss in Berlin and Vincent d'Indy in Paris. After returning to Brussels, he taught at a music academy; from 1898, also held the position of *professeur adjoint* at the Liège Cons., where he became a prof. in 1911. After the outbreak of the war in 1914, he went to London; made appearances as a pianist and organist there, and with Defauw, Tertis, and Doehaerd, organized a piano quartet which became known as the Belgian Quartet. In 1919 he returned to Belgium; in 1920 he became a prof. of counterpoint and fugue at the Brussels Cons.; from 1925–39 he was its director; was succeeded by his brother, Léon. During World War II, he lived in France; then returned to his country estate at Sart-lez-Spa, where he remained until his death. He was a prolific composer and continued to write music to the end of his life; the total of his works aggregates to 137 opus numbers. While not pursuing extreme modern effects, Jongen succeeded in imparting an original touch to his harmonic style.
WORKS: For orch.: Symph. (1899); Violin Concerto (1899); Cello Concerto (1900); *Fantasie sur deux Noëls populaires wallons* (1902); *Lalla-Roukh,* symph. poem after Thomas Moore (1904); *Prélude et Danse* (1907); *2 Rondes wallones* (1912; also for Piano); Trumpet Concertino (1913); *Impressions d'Ardennes* (1913); Suite for Violin and Orch. (1915); *Epithalame et Scherzo* for 3 Violins, and Orch. or Piano (1917); *Tableaux pittoresques* (1917); *Poème héroïque* for Violin and Orch. (1919); *Prélude élégiaque et Scherzo* (1920); *Fantasie rhapsodique* for Cello and Orch. (1924); *Hymne* for Organ and Strings (1924); *Symphonie concertante* for Organ and Orch. (1926), his finest work, popularized

by the organist Virgil Fox in his appearances with American orchs.; *Pièce symphonique* for Piano and Orch. (1928); *Passacaille et Gigue* (1929); *Suite No. 3, dans le style ancien* (1930); *10 Pièces* (1932); *Triptyque* (1935); *Ouverture Fanfare* (1939); *Alleluia* for Organ and Orch. (1940); *Ouverture de fête* (1941); Piano Concerto (1943); *Bourrée* (1944); Harp Concerto (1944); Mass for Organ, Chorus, and Orch. (1946); *In memoriam* (1947); *Ballade, Hommage à Chopin* (1949); *3 Mouvements symphoniques* (1951). Chamber music: 3 string quartets (1893, 1916, 1921); Piano Trio (1897); Piano Quartet (1901); 2 violin sonatas (1902, 1909); Trio for Piano, Violin, and Viola (1907); Cello Sonata (1912); *2 Serenades* for String Quartet (1918); *2 Pièces* for Flute, Cello, and Harp (1924); *2 Pièces* for 4 Cellos (1929); *Sonata eroica* for Organ (1930); Wind Quintet (1933); Quintet for Harp, Flute, Violin, Viola, and Cello (1940); Concerto for Wind Quintet (1942); Quartet for 4 Saxophones (1942); String Trio (1948); a number of piano pieces, including 24 preludes in all keys (1941); solo pieces for various instruments with piano; many songs with instrumental accompaniment; choral works.
BIBLIOGRAPHY: J. Whiteley, "Jongen and His Organ Music," *Musical Times* (March 1983; includes a biographical profile); a catalogue of his works was publ. by the Centre Belge de Documentation Musicale (Brussels, 1954).

Jongen, Léon, important Belgian composer, brother of **Joseph Jongen;** b. Liège, March 2, 1884; d. Brussels, Nov. 18, 1969. He studied organ and served as a church organist in Liège; received the Belgian Grand Prix de Rome for his cantata *Les Fiancés de Noël* (1913); was in the Belgian army during World War I; after the war traveled to the Far East and became the first conductor of the Opéra Français in Hanoi. Returning to Belgium in 1934, he became an instructor at the Brussels Cons.; from 1939 to 1949 was successor to his brother as its director.
WORKS: Operas: *L'Ardennaise* (1909) and *Thomas l'Agnelet* (1922-23; Brussels, Feb. 14, 1924); musical fairy tale, *Le Rêve d'une nuit de Noël* (1917; Paris, March 18, 1918); ballet, *Le Masque de la Mort rouge,* after Poe (1956). Also 2 lyric scenes for Chorus and Orch.: *Geneviève de Brabant* (1907) and *La Légende de St. Hubert* (1909; first public perf., St. Hubert, July 21, 1968); *Campéador* for Orch. (1932); *Malaisie,* suite for Orch. (1935); *In Memoriam Regis* for Orch. (1935); *Prélude, Divertissement et Final* for Piano and Orch. (1937); *Trilogie de Psaumes* for Chorus and Orch. (1937–39); *Rhapsodia belgica* for Violin and Orch. (1948); *Musique for a Ballet* (1954); *Divertissement en forme de variations sur un thème de Haydn* for Orch. (1956); Violin Concerto (1962; compulsory work for the 12 finalists of the 1963 Queen Elisabeth violin contest held in Brussels). He further wrote a String Quartet (1919); Fantasia for Piano (1930); *Divertissement* for 4 Saxophones (1937); Trio for Oboe, Clarinet, and Bassoon (1937); Trio for Flute, Violin, and Viola (1937); Piano Quartet (1955); Quintet for Piano, Flute, Clarinet, Horn, and Bassoon (1958); songs.

Jonsson, Josef Petrus, Swedish composer; b. Enköping, June 21, 1887; d. Norrköping, May 9, 1969. He studied piano, but soon turned to musical journalism. He wrote 3 symphs. (*Nordland,* 1919–22; 1931; 1947); *Chamber Symphony* (1949); several orch. overtures and suites; Violin Concerto (Norrköping, April 10, 1960); *Festival Prelude* for Orch. (1961); *Korallrevet,* symph. poem for Baritone, Chorus, and Orch. (1916); *Missa solemnis* for Chorus, Orch., and Organ (1934); Cantata for Speaking Chorus, Female Chorus, Soli, 2 Flutes, and Piano (Norrköping, May 5, 1962); chamber music; piano pieces; songs.

Jooss, Kurt, German choreographer; b. Wasseralfingen, near Stuttgart, Jan. 12, 1901; d. Heilbronn, West Germany, May 22, 1979. His father brewed beer on a farm; Jooss received his education in Stuttgart, and organized a group of dance enthusiasts. His group became very successful in its production of satirical modern dances; particularly arresting was his creation under the title *The Green Table,* which won first prize in Paris in 1932 at a choreographic competition sponsored by Les Archives Internationales de la Danse. In 1933 Jooss fled Germany and went to England. He named his group Ballets Jooss, and made several successful tours with it. Their American debut took place in N.Y. on Oct. 31, 1933.

Joplin, Janis, American rock and blues singer; b. Port Arthur, Texas, Jan. 19, 1943; d. Hollywood, Oct. 4, 1970, of an overdose of heroin. After several attempts at formal education, she held sporadic jobs as a barroom singer in Austin and Los Angeles. In 1966 she joined the band of Travis Rivers in San Francisco; made a profound impression by her passionate wailing in a raspy voice; her appearances in such esoteric emporia as the Psychedelic Supermarket in Boston, Kinetic Playground in Chicago, Whisky A-Go-Go in Los Angeles, and Fillmore East in N.Y. established her reputation as an uninhibited representative of the young generation. She was arrested in Tampa, Fla., in 1969 for having hurled porcine epithets at a policeman, which further endeared her to her public. On the more positive side, the Southern Comfort Distillery Co. presented her with a fur coat in recognition of the publicity she gave the firm by her habitual consumption of a quart of Southern Comfort at each of her appearances, brandishing the bottle conspicuously so as to display the brand name on its label. Her extraordinary ability to inject religious passion even into a commercial theme is illustrated by a song she composed, *Oh Lord, Won't You Buy Me a Mercedes-Benz?*

Joplin, Scott, black American pianist and composer; b. Texarkana, Nov. 24, 1868; d. New York, April 1, 1917. He learned to play the piano at home, and later studied music seriously with a local German musician. He left home at 17 and went to St. Louis, earning his living by playing piano in local emporia. In 1893 he moved to Chicago (drawn by the prospect of music-making and other gaiety of the World's Fair), and in the following year went to Sedalia, Mo., where he took music courses at George Smith College, a segregated school for blacks. His first music publications were in 1895, of genteel, maudlin songs and marches, typical of the period. His success as a ragtime composer came with the *Maple Leaf Rag* (1899; the most famous of all piano rags), which he named after a local dance hall, the Maple Leaf Club. The sheet-music edition sold so well that Joplin was able to settle in St. Louis and devote himself exclusively to composition; he even tried to write a ragtime ballet (*The Ragtime Dance,* 1902) and a ragtime opera, *A Guest of Honor* (copyright 1903, but the music is lost; newspaper notices indicate it was probably perf. by the Scott Joplin Opera Co. in 1903). In 1907 he went to N.Y., where he continued his career as a composer and teacher. Still intent on ambitious plans, he wrote an opera, *Treemonisha,* to his own libretto (the title deals with a black baby girl found under a tree by a woman named Monisha); he completed the score in 1911 and produced it in concert form in 1915 without any success. Interest in the opera was revived almost 60 years later; T.J. Anderson orchestrated it from the piano score, and it received its first complete performance at the Atlanta Symph. Hall on Jan. 28, 1972. Despite Joplin's ambitious attempts to make ragtime "respectable" by applying its principles to European forms, it was with the small, indigenous dance form of the piano rag that he achieved his greatest artistic success. As one noted historian phrased it, these pieces are "the precise American equivalent, in terms of a native dance music, of minuets by Mozart, mazurkas by Chopin, or waltzes by Brahms." Altogether, he wrote about 50 piano rags, in addition to the 2 operas, and a few songs, waltzes, and marches. The titles of some of these rags reflect his desire to transcend the trivial and create music on a more serious plane: *Sycamore,* "A Concert Rag" (1904); *Chrysanthemum,* "An Afro-American Intermezzo" (1904); *Sugar Cane,* "A Ragtime Classic 2 Step" (1908); *Fig Leaf Rag,* "A High Class Rag" (1908); *Reflection Rag,* "Syncopated Musings" (1917). In his last years he lamented at having failed to achieve the recognition he felt his music merited. Suffering from syphilis, he became insane and died shortly afterward in a state hospital. More than 50 years later, in the early 1970s, an extraordinary sequence of events—new recordings of his music and its use in an award-winning film, *The Sting* (1974)—brought Joplin unprecedented popularity and acclaim: among pop recordings, *The Entertainer* (1902) was one of the best-selling discs for 1974; among classical recordings, Joplin albums represented 74 percent of the best sellers of the year. In 1976 he was awarded exceptional posthumous recognition by the Pulitzer Prize Committee. Among the numerous collections of his music, the best is the 2-vol. set, facsimiles of the original eds., issued by the N.Y. Public Library, *The Collected Works of Scott Joplin,* ed. by Vera Brodsky Lawrence (N.Y., 1971; lacks 3 rags, for which reprint permission was denied, and 2 song collaborations, discovered subsequent to publication).

BIBLIOGRAPHY: R. Blesh and H. Janis, *They All*

Played Ragtime (N.Y., 1950; 4th ed., 1971; the basic biographical study); A. Reed, "Scott Joplin, Pioneer," *Black Perspective in Music* (Spring 1975; Fall 1975; corrects some biographical details); T. Waldo, *This Is Ragtime* (N.Y., 1976; treats the Joplin revival).

Jora, Mihail, Rumanian composer; b. Roman, Aug. 14, 1891; d. Bucharest, May 10, 1971. He studied piano privately in Iaşi (1901–12) and theory at the Cons. there (1909–11); then went to Germany, where he became a student of Max Reger at the Leipzig Cons. (1912–14); after World War I he went to Paris, where he studied with Florent Schmitt (1919–20). Returning to Rumania, he held the professorship in composition at the Bucharest Cons. (1929–62). He was a founding member of the Society of Rumanian Composers in 1920, and was consultant to the Bucharest Opera (1931–45). He was also a music critic. WORKS: 6 ballets: *La piaţă (At the Market Place,* 1928; Bucharest, 1931); *Demoazela Măriuţa (Damoiselle Mariutza,* 1940; Bucharest, 1942); *Curtea veche (The Old Court,* 1948); *Cînd strugurii se coc (When the Grapes Ripen,* Bucharest, 1954); *Întoarcerea din adîncuri (Return to the Abyss,* 1959; Bucharest, 1965); *Hanul Dulcinea (The Inn Dulcinea;* Bucharest, 1967); Suite for Orch. (1915); *Poveste indică (Hindu Tale),* symph. poem with Vocalizing Tenor (1920); *Privelişti moldoveneşti (Moldavian Landscapes),* suite for Orch. (1924); *Şase cîntece şi-o rumbă (6 Songs and a Rumba)* for Orch. (1932); Symph. (1937); *Burlesca* for Orch. (1949); *Baladă* for Baritone, Chorus, and Orch. (1955); *Small Suite* for Violin and Piano (1917); 2 string quartets (1926, 1966); Viola Sonata (1951); Violin Sonata (1962); choruses; several song cycles. For piano he wrote *Joujoux pour ma dame* (1925); *Cortegiu (Marche juive,* 1925); Sonata (1942); *Variations on a Theme of Schumann* (1943); *Poze şi pozne (Portraits and Jokes),* miniatures in 3 sets (1948, 1959, 1963); *13 Preludes* (1960); Sonatina (1961). He publ. the book *Momente muzicale* (Bucharest, 1968). Jora is regarded in Rumania as one of the finest composers of the Romantic national school, with a strongly pronounced lyric inspiration. Many composers of the younger generations were his students.

Jordá, Enrique, Spanish conductor; b. San Sebastian, March 24, 1911. He was a chorister in the parochial school and played organ at his parish church in Madrid; in 1929 he went to Paris as a medical student, but then turned decidedly to music, studying organ with Marcel Dupré, composition with Paul Le Flem, and conducting with Frans Rühlmann. He made his debut as an orch. conductor in Paris in 1938; then became the regular conductor of the Madrid Symph. Orch.; subsequently was principal conductor of the Cape Town Symph. Orch. in South Africa (1947–51). From 1954 to 1963 he was conductor of the San Francisco Symph. Orch.; in 1970 he became conductor of the Phil. Orch. at Antwerp, Belgium, remaining there until 1976. He publ. a popular book, *El director de orquesta ante la partitura* (Madrid, 1969).

Jordan, Irene, American soprano; b. Birmingham, Ala., April 25, 1919. Both her parents were professional music teachers, and she began playing piano at the age of 5; then studied voice at Judson College in Marion, Ala. (A.B., 1939); in 1940 she went to N.Y., where she continued her vocal studies; in 1946 she took up operatic coaching with Boris Goldovsky. She then filled in engagements in Broadway shows and on the radio; made her operatic debut in a minor role at the Metropolitan Opera in 1946; sang there in 1947, 1948, and 1957; in 1954 was engaged at the Chicago Lyric Opera; in 1956 sang the Queen of the Night in Mozart's opera *The Magic Flute,* at Covent Garden, London; subsequently sang as a soprano soloist with the Boston Symph. and other American orchs., and appeared at the St. Louis Municipal Opera. Possessing a diversified vocal technique, she was able to sing both dramatic and lyric soprano parts. In 1962 she was engaged as a prof. of voice at Northwestern Univ.

Jordan, Jules, American singer and composer; b. Willimantic, Conn., Nov. 10, 1850; d. Providence, R.I., March 5, 1927. He moved to Providence in 1870 and established himself as a singer, choral conductor, and teacher; for 40 years (1880–1920), conducted the Arion Club (250 voices). He was a successful composer of school operettas (*The Alphabet, Cloud and Sunshine,* etc.); wrote 6 light operas: *Star of the Sea; An Eventful Holiday; The Buccaneers; Princess of the Blood; Her Crown of Glory; A Leap Year Furlough;* the vaudeville sketches *Cobbler or King* and *Managerial Tactics;* etc. His romantic comedy opera, *Rip Van Winkle,* was produced at the Providence Opera House (May 25, 1897); another opera, *Nisiea,* remained unperformed. He wrote his own librettos for his stage works as well as for his cantatas *The Night Service, Barbara Fritchie,* etc.
BIBLIOGRAPHY: E.E. Hipsher, *American Opera and Its Composers* (Philadelphia, 1934, pp. 280–81).

Jordan, Louis, American jazz alto saxophonist and singer; b. Brinkley, Ark., July 8, 1908; d. Los Angeles, Feb. 4, 1975. He took up the clarinet and the alto saxophone; from 1929 played with various bands; formed his own band in N.Y., the Tympany Five. As a soloist, he recorded with Louis Armstrong, Ella Fitzgerald, and other jazz luminaries; in later years he toured with his own combo, visiting England (1962) and Asia (1967 and 1968).

Jordan, Mary, American contralto; b. Cardiff, Wales, Nov. 27, 1879; d. San Antonio, Texas, May 15, 1961. She entered St. Cecilia's Convent, in Scranton, Pa.; then studied with various teachers in Seattle, San Francisco, and N.Y. She made her operatic debut as Amneris with the Boston Opera Co. (March 28, 1911); also sang in churches in Brooklyn and N.Y.; toured in the Orient, and was for some years a prof. at the Manila Cons.; then settled in San Antonio, Texas, as a vocal teacher.

Jordan, Sverre, Norwegian composer; b. Bergen, May 25, 1889; d. there, Jan. 10, 1972. He studied piano; then traveled to Germany, where he took courses in piano and composition in Berlin with Ansorge and Klatte (1907–14). In 1914 he returned to Bergen; was active as music director of the National Theater (1932–57). In his works he made liberal use of national folk songs, which met the tastes of the general public. Typical of these nationally oriented works are *Suite in Old Style* for Small Orch. (1911); *Norvegiani* for Orch. (1921); *Smeden (The Smith)* for Baritone, Chorus, and Orch. (1924); *Norge i vare hjerter,* cantata for the opening of the Bergen Exhibition (1928); *Suite on Norwegian Folk Tunes and Dances* for Orch. (1936); *Holberg-silhuetter* for Orch. (1938); *Norwegian Rhapsody* for Orch. (1950); *Suite in Old Style on Holberg Themes* for Orch. (1954); *Concerto romantico* for Horn and Orch. (1956); and *Kongen (The King),* orch. melodrama with narration and choral finale (1957). Other works are a Piano Concerto (1945); Cello Concerto (1947); *Concerto piccolo* for Piano and Orch. (1963); Violin Concerto (1966); 2 violin sonatas (1917, 1943); Flute Sonatina (1955); 2 piano trios (1958, 1963); Piano Sonata (1963); incidental music for many plays; over 200 songs, often with orch. accompaniment.

Jørgensen, Erik, Danish composer; b. Copenhagen, May 10, 1912. He studied theory of music with Knud Jeppesen in Copenhagen (1928–31); then took private lessons with Finn Høffding; in 1936 he took conducting courses with Scherchen in Geneva. He evolved an individual idiom of composition, marked by an abundance of asymmetrical rhythmic configurations in the neo-Baroque manner; he later experimented with dodecaphony; eventually adopted a technique of "controlled coincidences." WORKS: Concerto Grosso for Flute, Clarinet, Bassoon, and String Orch. (1933–34); *3 Antiphonies* for Soprano, Tenor, and Chamber Orch. (1934–35); Concerto for Solo Violin, String Orch., and Piano (1937); Concertino for Flute, Clarinet, Violin, and Piano (1938); *Rhapsodies* for Violin and Piano (1939–40); Sonatina for Clarinet and Bassoon (1942); *Modello per archi* for String Orch. or String Quartet (1957); *Figure in Tempo* for Cello and Piano (1960–61); Quintet for 2 Pianos, 2 Percussionists, and Double Bass (1962); *Modello 2* for 4 Vocal Soloists and 12 Instruments (1963); *Astrolabium,* chamber concerto for 11 Instruments (1964); String Quartet (1964–65); *Notturno* for 24 Solo Instruments (1965); Variations for Piano (1966); *Confrontations* for Orch. (1967–68); chamber opera, *The Shadow of a Dream* (1969); *Improvisations* for Wind Quintet (1971); *Moods and States,* quartet for Flute, Horn, Violin, and Cello (1973); madrigal comedy for children and grown-ups, *The Fairytale* (1973–77).

Jørgensen, Poul, Danish conductor; b. Copenhagen, Oct. 26, 1934. He was educated at the Univ. of Copenhagen and the Royal Academy of Music. In 1961 he became a conductor at the Royal Theater in Copenhagen; in 1966 was appointed Royal Conductor; was also active in Sweden as a conductor of the Radio Symph. Orch. in Stockholm. From 1972 to 1976 he was a member of the State Music Council in Copenhagen; from 1976 served as its president. In his concert programs he steadfastly cultivated symph. works by Danish, Norwegian, Swedish, and Finnish composers.

Jörn, Karl, tenor; b. Riga, Latvia, Jan. 5, 1876; d. Denver, Dec. 19, 1947. He studied in Riga and Berlin; then sang in provincial German towns; was on the staff of the Hamburg City Theater (1899–1902); then at the Berlin Opera; sang in London (1908) and in N.Y. (1908–11); was particularly successful in Wagnerian roles; toured the U.S. with the German Grand Opera Co. (1931); then taught in Denver, where he remained until his death.

Joseffy, Rafael, eminent Hungarian-American pianist and teacher; b. Hunfalu, July 3, 1852; d. New York, June 25, 1915. At the age of 8 he began to study piano with a local teacher at Miskolcz, and later at Budapest. In 1866 he entered the Leipzig Cons., where his principal teacher was E.F. Wenzel, though he also had some lessons with Moscheles. From 1868 to 1870 he studied with Karl Tausig in Berlin, and the summers of 1870 and 1871 he spent with Liszt in Weimar. He made his debut at Berlin in 1870; his excellent technique and tonal variety elicited much praise; his career was then securely launched. He made his American debut in 1879, playing at a symph. concert of Leopold Damrosch in N.Y., where he settled permanently; he taught at the National Cons. from 1888 till 1906. In America he gained appreciation both as a virtuoso and as a musician of fine interpretative qualities; his programs featured many works of Brahms at a time when Brahms was not yet recognized in America as a great master. As a pedagogue, Joseffy was eminently successful; many American concert pianists were his pupils. He brought out an authoritative edition of Chopin's works in 15 vols. (with critico-historical annotations by Huneker); also ed. studies by Czerny, Henselt, Moscheles, Schumann, and others. His *School of Advanced Piano Playing* (1902; in German as *Meisterschule des Klavierspiels*) is a valuable practical method. Joseffy was also a composer; he publ. a number of characteristic piano pieces (*Die Mühle, Romance sans paroles, Souvenir d'Amérique, Mazurka-Fantasie, Spinnlied,* etc.) and arrangements of works by Schumann, Bach, Boccherini, Gluck, and Delibes. BIBLIOGRAPHY: E. Hughes, "Rafael Joseffy's Contribution to Piano Technique," *Musical Quarterly* (July 1916).

Joselson, Tedd, talented American pianist; b. Antwerp, Belgium, of American parents, Oct. 4, 1954. He studied piano with Adele Marcus at the Juilliard School of Music in N.Y.; in 1974 he was a soloist with the Philadelphia Orch.; then made a coast-to-coast recital tour of the U.S. in 1976–77; subsequently appeared as soloist with the Chicago Symph., the Cleveland Orch., the N.Y. Phil., the Pittsburgh Symph., and the Los Angeles Phil. His forte is Russian music, but he also has a natural affinity with the masters of the Classical period.

Josephs, Wilfred, English composer; b. Newcastle upon Tyne, July 24, 1927. He studied harmony and dentistry; gained a degree in dental surgery in 1951, and was a military orthodontist in the British army. In 1954 he entered the Guildhall School of Music in London, where he studied with Alfred Nieman; then went to Paris, where he took private lessons with Max Deutsch (1958–59). About that time he turned passionately toward the ideals of his ancestral Judaism; in memory of Jews who perished during World War II, he wrote a Requiem, to the text of the Hebrew prayer, Kaddish, containing 9 slow sections and a single faster movement; it won first prize at the International Competition of La Scala in Milan in 1963. In his instrumental music he adopted the dodecaphonic method of composition without doctrinaire adherence to the idiom; he described his music as "atonal with tonal implications." A highly prolific composer, he wrote music of all genres.

WORKS: For THE STAGE: Opera-entertainment, *Pathelin* (1963); television opera, *The Appointment* (1968); children's opera, *Through the Looking Glass and What Alice Found There* (1977–78); 3-act opera, *Rebecca* (1982–83); 3 ballets: *The Magic Being* (1961); *La Répétition de Phèdre* (1964–65); *Equus* (1978; produced in Baltimore, March 21, 1979); children's musical, *The King of the Coast* (1967); *A Child of the Universe* for Narrator, Soloists, Actors, Dancers, Mimes, Ballet, Choruses, Band, and Orch. (1971). For ORCH.: *The Ants,* comedy overture (1955); 9 symphs.: No. 1 (1955; revised 1957–58 and 1974–75); No. 2 (1963–64); No. 3, *Philadelphia,* for Chamber Orch. (1967); No. 4 (1967–70); No. 5, *Pastoral* (1970–71); No. 6, with Solo Singer and Chorus (1972–74); No. 7, *Winter,* for Chamber Orch. (1976); No. 8, *The 4 Elements,* for Symph. Band (1975–77); No. 9, *Sinfonia Concertante,* for Chamber Orch. (1979–80); *Elegy* for Strings (1957); *Concerto da Camera* for Solo Piano, Solo Violin, and Chamber Orch. (1959); *A Tyneside Overture* (1960); *Meditatio de Boernmundo* for Viola and Orch. (1960–61); *Cantus Natalis,* cello concerto (1961–62); *Aelian Dances,* 5 dances based on Newcastle tunes (1961); *Monkchester Dances,* 6 dances on Newcastle tunes (1961); Piano Concerto No. 1 (1965); *Canzonas on a Theme of Rameau* for Strings (1965); Concerto for Light Orch. (1966); *Polemic* for Strings (1967); *Rail,* symph. picture (1967); Oboe Concerto (1967–68); *Serenade* for Chamber Orch. (1968); *Variations on a Theme of Beethoven* (1969); Double Violin Concerto (1969); Piano Concerto No. 2 (1971); *Saratoga Concerto,* triple concerto for Guitar, Harp, Harpsichord, and Chamber Orch. (1972); *The 4 Horsemen of the Apocalypse,* overture (1973–74); Concerto for Brass Band (1974); Clarinet Concerto (1975); *Eve (d'après Rodin),* symph. poem (1977–78); *Divertimento* for 2 Oboes, 2 Horns, and Strings (1979); *Concerto d'Amore* for 2 Violins and Orch. (1979); Double-bass Concerto (1980); *The Brontës,* overture (1981); *High Spirits,* overture (1981–82); Percussion Concerto (1982); Concerto for Viola and Chamber Orch. (1983).

CHAMBER MUSIC: 4 string quartets (1954, 1958, 1971, 1981); Sonata for Solo Violin (1957); *Requiescant pro defunctis iudaeis* for String Quintet, in memory of the Jews (1961); *Chaconne* for Violin and Piano (1962–63); Octet (1964); 2 violin sonatas (1965, 1975); Trio for Flute, Violin, and Cello (1966); String Trio (1966); Sonata for Solo Cello (1970); Trio for Horn, Violin, and Piano (1971); *Solo Oboe Piece* (1973); Piano Quintet (1974–76); Sonata for Brass Quintet (1974; revised 1981); Piano Trio (1974; revised 1981); Flute Sonata (1976–77); Wind Quintet (1977); Concerto for 4 Pianos and 6 Percussionists (1978); Quartet for Oboe, Violin, Viola, and Cello (1979); *Piano Piece* for Clarinet and Piano (1979–80); Double-bass Sonata (1980); *8 Aphorisms* for 8 Trombones (1981).

For VOICE: *12 Letters,* after Belloc, for Narrator, Clarinet, String Trio, and Piano (1957); *Requiem* (1962–63; Milan, Oct. 28, 1965); *Adam and Eve,* entertainment for Narrator and Ensemble (1967); *Mortales,* oratorio (1967–69; Cincinnati, May 23, 1970); *Nightmusic* for Voice and Orch. (1969–70); *Aeroplanes and Angels,* after 12 poems by Günter Grass, for Soloists and Piano Duo (1977–78); choruses, songs.

For PIANO: *29 Preludes* (1969); *Doubles* for 2 Pianos (1970–73); *Sonata Duo* for 2 Pianos (1976); *Byrdsong* for Piano and Organ (1981).

For ORGAN: *Fantasia on 3 Notes* (1978); *Tombeau* (1980); *Testimony,* toccata in memoriam DSCH (1981; DSCH are Shostakovich's initials in German nomenclature).

Josephson, Jacob Axel, Swedish composer and conductor; b. Stockholm, March 27, 1818; d. Uppsala, March 29, 1880. He studied music in Uppsala; then taught at the Cathedral School there (1841–43); in 1844 he went to Germany; studied with Hauptmann and Niels Gade in Leipzig. After further study in Rome (1845–46), he returned to Uppsala, where he became conductor of the Phil. Society; he became music director at Uppsala Univ. in 1849; in 1864, was appointed organist at the Cathedral there. He wrote mostly choral works (Psalms, cantatas); edited a series of articles on sacred songs, "Zion" (1867–70).

BIBLIOGRAPHY: K. Nyblom, *J.A. Josephson* (Stockholm, 1926).

Josif, Enriko, Serbian composer; b. Belgrade, May 1, 1924. He studied music theory with Milenko Živković at the Belgrade Music Academy (1947–50); then went to Italy and took a course in composition with Petrassi at the Santa Cecilia Academy in Rome (1961–62); returning to Belgrade, he was appointed to the faculty of the Serbian Music Academy.

WORKS: Ballet, *Ptico, ne sklapaj svoja krila (Bird, Don't Break Your Wings,* 1970; Belgrade, Oct. 7, 1970); Sinfonietta (1954); *Sonata antica* for Orch. (1955); *Lyrical Symphony* for 4 Flutes, Harp, and

String Orch. (1956); Piano Concerto (1959); *Symphony in One Movement* (1964; Belgrade, Jan. 24, 1966); *Sinfonietta di tre re* (1968); *Oratorio profano da camera* for Narrator, Soprano, Celesta, Piano, and Percussion (1956); *Smrt Stefana Dečanskog (The Death of Stefan of Decane),* chamber motets for Narrator, Soloists, Chorus, and 16 Instruments (1956; enlarged and orchestrated as a dramatic epic in 1970 under the title *Stefan Dečanski;* Belgrade, Oct. 7, 1970); *Rustikon,* cantata (1962); *Improvisations on a Folk Theme* for 14 Winds (1949); String Quartet (1953); *Snovidenja (Dream Visions)* for Flute, Harp, and Piano (1964); *Divertimento* for Wind Quintet (1964); *Epigram I* for Chamber Ensemble and *Epigram II* for Piano Trio (1967); *Zapisi (Chronicles)* for Wind Quintet (1971); *Vatrenja* for Piano Trio (1972); *Sonata brevis* for Piano (1949); *4 Priče (Stories)* for Piano (1957); *4 Skice (Sketches)* for Piano (1957); *3 Psalms* for Piano (1963).

Josten, Werner, American composer; b. Elberfeld, Germany, June 12, 1885; d. New York, Feb. 6, 1963. He studied music theory in Munich; then took courses with Jaques-Dalcroze in Geneva; he lived in Paris from 1912 to 1914; at the outbreak of World War I, he returned to Germany; in 1918 was appointed assistant conductor at the Munich Opera. In 1920 he went to the U.S. and appeared as composer-accompanist with several singers; in 1933 he became an American citizen. He taught at Smith College in Northampton, Mass., from 1923 to 1949; also conducted the Smith College Orch., with which he presented performances of works by Monteverdi and Handel. His own compositions are couched in the lyrical manner of German Romantic music, with a strong undercurrent of euphonious counterpoint within the network of luscious harmonies. During his American period, he became interested in exotic art, and introduced impressionistic devices in his works.
WORKS: FOR ORCH.: *Jungle,* symph. movement, inspired by Henri Rousseau's painting *Forêt exotique* (Boston Symph., Oct. 25, 1929); *Batouala,* choreographic poem, also arranged as an African ballet (1931; a symph. suite drawn from it was first perf. at Smith College, Nov. 10, 1963, under the title *Suite nègre); Concerto sacro I–II* for Piano and String Orch. (1925; N.Y., March 27, 1929); *Joseph and His Brethren,* ballet (1932; N.Y., March 9, 1936; as a symph. suite, Philadelphia, May 15, 1939); *Endymion,* ballet (1933; as a symph. suite, N.Y., Oct. 28, 1936); Serenade for Small Orch. (1934); Symph. in F (Boston Symph., Nov. 13, 1936, composer conducting); *Symphony for Strings* (Saratoga Springs, N.Y., Sept. 3, 1946). CHAMBER MUSIC: String Quartet (1934); Violin Sonata (1936); Cello Sonata (1938); Sonatina for Violin and Piano (1939); Trio for Flute, Clarinet, and Bassoon (1941); Trio for Violin, Viola, and Cello (1942); Trio for Flute, Cello, and Piano (1943); Sonata for Horn and Piano (1944); *Canzona seria* for Flute, Oboe, Clarinet, Bassoon, and Piano (N.Y., Nov. 23, 1957). VOCAL WORKS: *Crucifixion* for Bass Solo and Mixed Chorus a cappella (1915); *Hymnus to the Quene of Paradys* for Women's Voices, Strings, and Organ (1921); *Indian Serenade* for Tenor with Orch. (1922); *Ode for St. Cecilia's Day* for Voices and Orch. (1925); *A une Madone* for Solo Tenor and Orch., after Baudelaire (1929); about 50 songs.
BIBLIOGRAPHY: *Werner Josten, 1885–1963. A Summary of His Compositions with Press Reviews* (N.Y., 1964).

Joteyko, Tadeusz, Polish composer; b. Poczuiki, April 1, 1872; d. Teschen, Aug. 19, 1932. He studied in Brussels with Gevaert and in Warsaw with Noskowski; held positions as head of music societies in Kalisz and Lodz; conducted the Warsaw Phil. from 1914 to 1918; taught at the Warsaw Cons. He wrote the operas *Grajek (The Player;* Warsaw, Nov. 23, 1919); *Zygmund August* (his most successful work; Warsaw, Aug. 29, 1925); *Królowa Jadwiga (Queen Jadwiga;* Warsaw, Sept. 7, 1928); chamber music; numerous songs and piano pieces.

Joubert, John, significant South African composer; b. Cape Town, March 20, 1927. After preliminary studies in South Africa, he traveled to Great Britain with a Performing Right Scholarship in 1946 and took music courses with Howard Ferguson at the Royal Academy of Music in London (1946–50). He was a lecturer in music at the Univ. of Hull (1950–62); then at the Univ. of Birmingham. In his music he cultivates the pragmatic goal of pleasurability, wherein harmony and counterpoint serve the functional role of support for a flowing melody; in several works he makes use of primitive elements derived from Hottentot rites, transmuting the primitive vocalizations into modern polytonal and polyrhythmic formations. His carols *Torches* and *There Is No Rose* enjoy wide popularity.
WORKS: FOR THE STAGE: *Antigone,* radio opera (BBC, London, July 21, 1954); *In the Drought,* chamber opera (Johannesburg, Oct. 20, 1956); *Silas Marner,* after the novel by George Eliot (Cape Town, May 20, 1961); *The Quarry,* opera for young people (Wembley, March 26, 1965); *Under Western Eyes,* after the novel by Joseph Conrad (Camden, England, May 29, 1969); *The Prisoner,* opera for schools (Barnet, March 14, 1973); *Legend of Princess Vlei,* ballet (Cape Town, Feb. 21, 1952). CANTATAS: *The Burghers of Calais* (1954); *Leaves of Life* (1963); *Urbs beata* (first perf. at St. George's Cathedral, Cape Town, Nov. 26, 1963); *The Choir Invisible* (Halifax, May 18, 1968); *The Martyrdom of St. Alban* (London, June 7, 1969); *The Raising of Lazarus* (Birmingham, Sept. 30, 1971). VARIOUS CHORAL WORKS: *Pro Pace,* cycle of 3 motets for Unaccompanied Chorus (1960); *The Holy Mountain,* canticle for Chorus and 2 Pianos (1963); numerous sacred works, anthems, and carols, including *Torches, There Is No Rose, Great Lord of Lords, Welcome Yule, Christ Is Risen, The Beatitudes, Te Deum;* secular part-songs, among them *The God Pan* and *Sweet Content;* also *African Sketchbook (Hottentot Animal Songs)* for Vocal Quartet and Wind Instruments (1970); *3 Hymns to St. Oswald* for Vocal Quartet and Organ (1972); *Crabbed Age and Youth*

for Countertenor and Ensemble (London, Nov. 9, 1974); *The Magus* for Soloists, Chorus, and Orch. (Sheffield, Oct. 29, 1977); *Herefordshire Canticles* for Soprano, Baritone, Chorus, and Orch. (Hereford, Aug. 23, 1979); *The Turning Wheel* for Soprano and Piano (Ounedin, New Zealand, Oct. 1, 1980). FOR ORCH.: Overture (Cheltenham Festival, June 12, 1953); *Symphonic Prelude* (Durban Centenary Festival, May 15, 1954); Violin Concerto (York, June 17, 1954); Symph. No. 1 (Hull, April 12, 1956); *North Country Overture* (1958); Piano Concerto (Manchester, Jan. 11, 1959); Sinfonietta for Chamber Orch. (1962); *In Memoriam, 1820* (1962); Symph. No. 2 (London, March 24, 1971, composer conducting); Concerto for Bassoon and Chamber Orch. (1974); *Deploration* for Chamber Orch. (Birmingham, Dec. 28, 1978). CHAMBER MUSIC: String Quartet No. 1 (1950); *Miniature String Quartet* (1953); Viola Sonata (1952); String Trio (1958); Octet for Clarinet, Bassoon, Horn, String Quartet, and Double Bass (1960); *Sonata a cinque* for Recorder, 2 Violins, Cello, and Harpsichord (1963); 2 piano sonatas (1956, 1971); Duo for Violin and Cello (1971); *Kontakion* for Cello and Piano (1974); *Threnos* for Harpsichord and Strings (1974); String Quartet No. 2 (1977); organ pieces; songs.

Jouret, Léon, Belgian composer; b. Ath, Oct. 17, 1828; d. Brussels, June 6, 1905. He studied at the Brussels Cons.; in 1874, was appointed prof. of singing there. His 2 operas, *Quentin Metsys* and *Le Tricorne enchanté,* were produced semi-privately in Brussels (1865 and 1868); of more importance is his collection of folk melodies of his native region, *Chants populaires du pays d'Ath.*

Journet, Marcel, French bass; b. Grasse, Alpes Maritimes, July 25, 1867; d. Vittel, Sept. 5, 1933. He made his operatic debut at Bezières (1891); performed at summer seasons at Covent Garden, London (1893–1900); sang at the Théâtre de la Monnaie in Brussels (1894–1900); made his American debut at the Metropolitan Opera, N.Y., in 1900 and remained on the staff for 8 seasons; in 1908–14, was in Europe; at the outbreak of World War I in 1914, he joined the Chicago Opera Co., leaving it in 1916; later, returned to France. His repertoire included 8 Wagner operas, and 27 Italian and 65 French operas.

Jousse, Jean, French music pedagogue; b. Orleans, 1760; d. London, Jan. 19, 1837. A scion of an aristocratic family, he was compelled to flee France during the Revolution; he settled in London, where he became a successful teacher of singing and piano. He publ. several textbooks, among them *Lectures on Thoroughbass* (1819; new revised and augmented ed., N.Y., 1894, under the title *A Catechism of Music*).

Joy, Geneviève, French pianist; b. Bernaville, Oct. 4, 1919. She studied at the Paris Cons. with Yves Nat (piano) and Jean and Noël Gallon (theory); received the Premier Prix in piano in 1941. In 1945 she married the composer **Henri Dutilleux.** She specialized in modern music; gave numerous first performances of piano works by French composers, some of them written especially for her.

Juch, Emma (Antonia Joanna), American operatic soprano; b. Vienna, July 4, 1863 (of American parents); d. New York, March 6, 1939. She was brought to the U.S. at the age of 4, and studied in N.Y. with Murio Celli; made her debut in the old Chickering Hall in 1881; made her stage debut in London (June, 1881); sang 3 seasons under Mapleson's management in England and in the U.S.; in 1886–87 she was principal soprano of the American Opera Co., and with the National Opera Co. (1887–88); in 1889 she organized the Emma Juch Grand Opera Co., which presented opera in the U.S. and Mexico (until 1891); after that, she confined herself chiefly to concert appearances. On June 26, 1894, she married District Attorney Francis L. Wellman, but they were divorced in 1911.
BIBLIOGRAPHY: N.S. Putnam, in *Notable American Women* (Cambridge, Mass., 1971).

Juchelka, Miroslav, Czech composer; b. Velká Polom, March 29, 1922. He studied composition with Řídký and Hlobil at the Prague Cons. (1939–43) and then with Albín Šíma at the Master School there (1943–47); in 1952 was appointed music director of the Czech Radio in Prague.
WORKS: *Symphonic Fantasy* for Orch. (1952); Accordion Concerto (1954); *Burlesque* for Piano and Orch. (1958); Suite for String Orch. (1961); *Burlesque* for Clarinet and Promenade Orch. (1970); *From the Beskyds,* suite for Orch. (1972); Clarinet Concerto (1974); *Miniatures* for Cello and Piano (1951); Suite for Nonet (1962); Clarinet Sonatina (1964); *5 Compositions for Due Boemi* for Bass Clarinet and Piano (1972; Due Boemi is a Czech chamber duo, led by Josef Horák).

Judge, Jack, English composer of popular songs; b. 1878; d. West Bromwich, July 28, 1938. His song *It's a long, long way to Tipperary,* written in 1912, attained enormous popularity in England and elsewhere as a wartime song during World War I.

Judson, Arthur, American concert manager; b. Dayton, Ohio, Feb. 17, 1881; d. Rye, N.Y., Jan. 28, 1975. He took violin lessons with Max Bendix; played in orchs., and himself conducted summer resort orchs. In 1900 he was appointed dean of the Cons. of Music of Denison Univ., Granville, Ohio. In 1907 he was in N.Y.; was connected with the editorial and advertising depts. of *Musical America.* From 1915 to 1935 he was manager of the Philadelphia Orch.; in 1922 he was appointed manager of the N.Y. Phil. Orch., and held this position for 34 years, resigning in 1956. In 1928 his concert management took over the Wolfsohn Musical Bureau; in 1930, these organizations merged into the Columbia Concerts Corp., with Judson as president.

Juhan, Alexander, American violinist, conductor,

and composer, probably the son of **James Juhan;** b. Halifax, 1765; d. 1845. He was brought to Boston in 1768; was a violinist in Philadelphia in 1783; later went to Charleston, S.C., where he was active from 1790 to 1792; returned to Philadelphia in 1792. He composed 6 piano sonatas, of which 3 are accompanied by a flute (or a violin); also a book of 12 songs, with instrumental accompaniment.

Juhan, James, French musician active in Boston (1768–70), in Charleston, S.C. (1771), and later in Philadelphia, where he exhibited the "great North American Forte Piano" (1786).
BIBLIOGRAPHY: O.G. Sonneck, *Early Concert Life in America* (1907).

Juilliard, Augustus D., American music patron; b. at sea, during his parents' voyage on a sailing vessel from Burgundy to America, April 19, 1836; d. New York, April 25, 1919. He was a prominent industrialist; left the residue of his estate for the creation of the Juilliard Musical Foundation (established in 1920). The objects of his foundation are to aid worthy students of music in securing a complete musical education, and to arrange and give concerts for the education of the general public in the musical arts. The Juilliard School of Music was founded and has been maintained by the foundation.
BIBLIOGRAPHY: *Dictionary of American Biography,* vol. X (N.Y., 1933).

Jullien, Gilles, French organist; b. c.1650; d. Chartres, Sept. 14, 1703. He became organist at the Chartres Cathedral in 1667, and held this post until his death. His *Premier livre d'orgue* was publ. by Lesclop in Chartres (1680); a modern reprint, with annotations and an introduction by Norbert Dufourcq, was issued in Paris (1952).

Jullien, Jean-Lucien-Adolphe, French writer on music, son of **Marcel-Bernard Jullien;** b. Paris, June 1, 1845; d. Chaintreauville, Seine-et-Marne, Aug. 30, 1932. He studied law in Paris and took private lessons with Bienaimé, a former prof. of the Paris Cons. He became a music journalist; contributed to various magazines, and took a strong position in favor of the new music of Berlioz and Wagner.
WRITINGS: *L'Opéra en 1788* (1873); *La Musique et les philosophes au XVIIIe siècle* (1873); *La Comédie à la cour de Louis XVI, Le Théâtre de la reine à Trianon* (1873); *Histoire du théâtre de Mme. Pompadour, dit Théâtre des petits cabinets* (1874); *Les Spectateurs sur Le Théâtre* (1875); *Le Théâtre des demoiselles Verrières* (1875); *Les Grandes Nuits de Sceaux, Le Théâtre de la duchesse du Maine* (1876); *Un Potentat musical* (1876); *Weber à Paris* (1877); *Airs variés; Histoire, critique, biographie musicales et dramatiques* (1877); *La Cour et l'opéra sous Louis XVI; Marie-Antoinette et Sacchini; Salieri; Favart et Gluck* (1878); *Goethe et la musique* (1880); *L'Opéra secret au XVIIIe siècle* (1880); *Richard Wagner, sa vie et ses œuvres* (1886; also in Eng. trans., Boston, 1892); *Hector Berlioz* (1888); Musici-ens d'Aujourd'hui (first series, 1891; 2nd series, 1894); *Musique* (1895); *Le Romantisme et l'éditeur Renduel* (1897); *Amours d'opéra au XVIIIe siècle* (1908); *Ernest Reyer* (1909).
BIBLIOGRAPHY: F. Delhasse, *A. Jullien* (Paris, 1884).

Jullien, Louis Antoine, French conductor; b. Sisteron, April 23, 1812; d. Paris, March 14, 1860. The son of a bandmaster, he went to Paris in 1833 and studied composition with Le Carpentier and Halévy, but could not maintain the discipline of learning music, and began to compose light dances instead; of these, the waltz *Rosita* attained enormous, though transitory, popularity in Paris. He left the Cons. in 1836 without taking a degree, and became engaged as conductor of dance music at the Jardin Turc. He also attempted to launch a musical journal, but an accumulation of carelessly contracted debts compelled him to leave France (1838). He went to London, where he conducted summer concerts at the Drury Lane Theatre (1840) and winter concerts with an enlarged ensemble of instrumentalists and singers (1841). He then opened a series of "society concerts," at which he presented large choral works, such as Rossini's *Stabat Mater,* as well as movements from Beethoven's symphs. In 1847 he engaged Berlioz to conduct at the Drury Lane Theatre, which he had leased. He became insolvent in 1848, but attempted to recoup his fortune by organizing a "concert monstre" with 400 players, 3 choruses, and 3 military bands. He succeeded in giving 3 such concerts in London in 1849. He then essayed the composition of an opera, *Pietro il Grande,* which he produced at his own expense at Covent Garden, on Aug. 17, 1852. He used the pseudonym **Roch Albert** for his spectacular pieces, such as *Destruction of Pompeii;* publ. some dance music (*Royal Irish Quadrille,* etc.) under his own name. In 1853 he was engaged by P.T. Barnum for a series of concerts in the U.S. For his exhibition at the Crystal Palace in N.Y. (June 15, 1854), attended by a great crowd, he staged a simulated conflagration for his *Fireman's Quadrille.* Despite his eccentricities, however, Jullien possessed a true interest in musical progress. At his American concerts he made a point of including several works by American composers: *Santa Claus Symphony* by William Henry Fry and some chamber music by George Frederick Bristow. In 1854 he returned to London; his managerial ventures resulted in another failure. In 1859 he went to Paris, but was promptly arrested for debt, and spent several weeks in prison. He died a few months later in an insane asylum to which he had been confined.
BIBLIOGRAPHY: J.W. Davison, *Memoirs* (London, 1912); J.T. Howard, *Our American Music* (4th ed., 1965); N. Slonimsky, *A Thing or Two about Music* (N.Y., 1948); pp. 226–35); A. Carse, *The Life of Jullien: Adventurer, Showman-Conductor and Establisher of the Promenade Concerts in England* (Cambridge, 1951); H. Schonberg, *The Great Conductors* (N.Y., 1967; pp. 149–55).

Jullien, Marcel-Bernard, French music scholar; b. Paris, Feb. 2, 1798; d. there, Oct. 15, 1881. He was secretary-general to the Société des Méthodes d'Enseignement and a learned grammarian.

WRITINGS: *De l'étude de la musique instrumentale dans les pensions des demoiselles* (1848); *De quelques points des sciences dans l'antiquité (Physique, métrique, musique)* (1854); *Thèses supplémentaires de métrique et de musique ancienne* (1861).

Jumilhac, Dom Pierre-Bênoit de, Benedictine monk, specialist in Gregorian chant; b. Château St. Jean-de-Ligourre, near Limoges, 1611; d. St. Germain-des-Prés, March 21, 1682. He wrote *La Science et la pratique du plain-chant* (Paris, 1673; ed. by Nisard and Leclerq and republ. in 1847), an erudite work containing many musical examples.

Junck, Benedetto, Italian composer; b. Turin, Aug. 21, 1852; d. San Vigilio, near Bergamo, Oct. 3, 1903. He was of Alsatian-Italian extraction; was trained for a commercial career but practiced the piano in his free time; then entered the Milan Cons. for serious study, and developed a fine lyric talent for songwriting; his youthful ballad *La Simona* became very popular; *Dolce sera,* from his album *8 romanze,* also was well known. In addition to songs, he wrote a String Quartet and 2 violin sonatas.

Jung, Manfred, German tenor; b. Oberhausen, July 9, 1945. He studied with Hilde Wesselmann at the Folkwang Hochschule in Essen; then was a member of the Bayreuth Festival chorus (1970–73); he made his debut as a soloist in Dortmund in 1974, and subsequently sang in Kaiserslautern, Saarbrücken, and Karlsruhe. In 1977 he became a member of the Deutsche Oper am Rhein in Düsseldorf; also in 1977 he made his debut at the Bayreuth Festival as Siegfried in *Götterdämmerung,* and then appeared in the televised version of that role in *Der Ring des Nibelungen.* From 1980 he also sang at the Metropolitan Opera, where he appeared in the leading Wagnerian roles. He returned to the Bayreuth Festival in 1983 to sing Siegfried in the centenary anniversary season production of *Der Ring des Nibelungen* (commemorating Wagner's death in 1883), staged by Sir Peter Hall and conducted by Sir Georg Solti. He was also active in recitals; gave concerts throughout Europe and in N.Y., Chicago, Montreal, Toronto, and Toyko.

Jüngst, Hugo, German conductor; b. Dresden, Feb. 26, 1853; d. there, March 3, 1923. He studied at the Dresden Cons.; was conductor of the Dresden Male Choral Society, which he founded in 1876, and of numerous festivals; composed many men's choruses, including the well-known *Scissors Grinder.*

Jungwirth, Manfred, Austrian bass; b. St. Pölten, June 4, 1919. He was educated in St. Pölten, Vienna, Bucharest, Munich, and Berlin; received his doctorate in Vienna in 1948. Conscripted into the German army in World War II, he was nevertheless able to continue his singing career. In 1948 he won the voice competition held in Geneva; then sang in Zürich, Berlin, Hamburg, and London; from 1967 he made regular appearances at the Vienna State Opera. On Feb. 16, 1974, he made his debut at the Metropolitan Opera in N.Y. as Baron Ochs in *Der Rosenkavalier* by Richard Strauss.

Juon, Paul, Russian composer; b. Moscow, March 6, 1872; d. Vevey, Switzerland, Aug. 21, 1940. He was a pupil of Hřimaly (violin) and of Taneyev and Arensky (composition) in Moscow; in Berlin, of Bargiel (1894–96); he lived in Berlin, and was appointed professor of composition at the Hochschule für Musik in 1906.

WORKS: For Orch.: Symph. in A; *Vaegtevise,* fantasy on Danish folk songs; *Aus einem Tagebuch,* suite; Serenade; 3 violin concertos; *Episodes Concertantes,* triple concerto for Violin, Cello, and Piano with Orch. Chamber music: 4 string quartets; Sextet for 2 Violins, Viola, 2 Cellos, and Piano; Octet for Piano, Violin, Viola, Cello, Oboe, Clarinet, Horn, and Bassoon; 2 quintets for Piano and Strings; Divertimento for Piano and Woodwinds; *Rhapsodie* for Piano Quartet; other piano quartets; 3 piano trios; *Caprice, Legende,* and *Litaniae* for Trio; 6 *Silhouettes* for 2 Violins and Piano; sonatas for violin, viola, cello, flute, and clarinet (with piano); pieces for violin, cello, and piano (*Satyre und Nymphen, Intime Harmonien,* etc.); compositions for piano, 4-hands; songs. He publ. *Praktische Harmonielehre* (1901); *Handbuch für Harmonielehre* (1920); *Anleitung zum Modulieren* (1929); *Der Kontrapunkt* (1932).

Juozapaitis, Jurgis, Lithuanian composer; b. near Šiauliai, June 29, 1942. He studied with Juzeliunas at the Lithuanian State Cons. in Vilnius, graduating in 1968. His music is rooted in native folk modes, which are enhanced by a modernistic harmonic investiture and a rich employment of polyrhythmic percussion.

WORKS: For the stage: Opera, *Sea Bird* (1976). For Orch.: Concerto for Organ, Strings, and Kettledrums (1970); *Vitrages,* symph. poem (1971); *Rex,* symph. in memory of M.K. Čiurlionis (1973); *Festive Poem* (1976); *Zodiacus* (1977). Chamber music: Wind Quintet (1970); *Music* for Flute, Percussion, Piano, Viola, and Cello (1970); Concerto for 4 Percussionists (1971); Sonata for Solo Violin (1972); *Jūrate and Kastytis,* chamber symph. for Flute, Oboe, Viola, Cello, Piano, Percussion, and Electronic Tape (1974); *Diptych* for Wind Quintet (1977); 2 string quartets (1978, 1980); organ pieces; songs; choruses.

Jupin, Charles-François, French violinist and composer; b. Chambéry, Nov. 30, 1805; d. Paris, June 12, 1839. He studied with Baillot at the Paris Cons., taking first prize in 1823; wrote an opera, *La Vengeance italienne* (1834); numerous pieces for violin.

Jürgens, Fritz, German composer; b. Düsseldorf,

April 22, 1888; killed in action in Champagne, Sept. 25, 1915. He studied music largely by himself; wrote some fine lieder; set to music 45 poems by Gustav Falke, and 35 by Martin Greif.

Jürgens, Jürgen, German conductor; b. Frankfurt, Oct. 5, 1925. He studied conducting with Kurt Thomas in Frankfurt. In 1955 he became conductor of the Hamburg Monteverdi Choir; toured with it throughout Europe, America, and the Far East. In 1960 he was named director of the Akademische Musikpflege and lecturer at Hamburg Univ. He also edited works of Monteverdi and Alessandro Scarlatti. As a conductor he cultivated works of the Baroque period, while not neglecting modern music of a polyphonic nature.

Jurgenson, Pyotr, Russian music publisher; b. Reval, July 17, 1836; d. Moscow, Jan. 2, 1904. The youngest son of indigent parents, he learned the music trade with M. Bernard, owner of a music store in St. Petersburg; Jurgenson served in 3 other music-selling houses there, before opening a business of his own in 1861, in Moscow. With a small investment, he gradually expanded his firm until it became one of the largest in Russia. Through Nicolai Rubinstein he met the leading musicians of Russia, and had enough shrewdness of judgment to undertake the publication of works of Tchaikovsky, beginning with his op. 1. He became Tchaikovsky's close friend, and, while making a handsome profit out of Tchaikovsky's music, he demonstrated a generous regard for Tchaikovsky's welfare; he publ. full scores of Tchaikovsky's symphs. and operas, as well as his songs and piano works. His voluminous correspondence with Tchaikovsky, from 1877 to Tchaikovsky's death, was publ. in 2 vols. in Moscow (1938 and 1952). Jurgenson also publ. many works by other Russian composers; issued vocal scores of Glinka's operas; also publ. the first Russian eds. of the collected works of Chopin, Schumann, and Mendelssohn, and the scores of Wagner's operas. His catalogue contained some 20,000 numbers. After his death, his son **Boris Jurgenson** succeeded to the business; it was nationalized after the Russian Revolution.

Jurinac, Sena, famous Yugoslav soprano; b. Travnik, Oct. 24, 1921. Her father was a Croatian physician; her mother was Viennese. She studied in Zagreb; made her formal debut there as Mimi in *La Bohème;* for her professional appearances she changed her original Slavic first name, **Srebrenka** (literally, the Silver One), to a more mellifluous Sena. She made her debut with the Vienna State Opera on May 1, 1945; subsequently sang in Salzburg, Edinburgh, Glyndebourne, Florence, London, at La Scala in Milan, and at the Teatro Colón in Buenos Aires. She made her American debut with the San Francisco Opera in 1959. In 1953 she married the singer **Sesto Bruscantini.**
BIBLIOGRAPHY: U. Tamussino, *Sena Jurinac* (Augsburg, 1971).

Jurjāns, Andrejs, Latvian composer; b. Erlaa, Sept. 30, 1856; d. Zehsis, Sept. 28, 1922. He studied with Rimsky-Korsakov (1875–82) in St. Petersburg. In 1882, he was appointed a prof. at the Cons. of Kharkov, where he taught for 34 years, until 1916. In 1917 he went to Riga. He wrote a Symph. Poem, a Cello Concerto, some chamber music, and a number of orch. arrangements of Latvian folk melodies, which he employed also in his original works.
BIBLIOGRAPHY: Jahnis Straumes, *Our Musicians* (in Latvian; Riga, 1922).

Jurovský, Šimon, Slovak composer; b. Ulmanka, Feb. 8, 1912; d. Prague, Nov. 8, 1963. He attended the Bratislava Academy of Music (1931–36); then took courses in composition with Josef Marx at the Vienna Academy of Music (1943–44). He held various posts in Slovakia; was manager of the Bratislava Opera, director of the Slovak Folk Art Ensemble, etc. In his music he followed the broad tenets of national Romanticism, with frequent references to folk themes.
WORKS: Opera, *Dcery Abelovy (The Daughters of Abel,* 1961); ballet, *Rytierska balada (The Song of Chivalry;* Bratislava, 1960); 2 orch. suites (1939; 1943); Serenade for String Orch. (1940); *Začatá cesta (The Journey Begun),* symph. poem (1948); *Radostné súženie (A Joyous Competition),* symph. scherzo (1949); 2 symphs.: No. 1, *Mírová (Peace),* for Piano and Strings (1950), and No. 2, *Heroická (Heroic),* for Organ and Orch. (1960); Cello Concerto (1953); Concertino for Piano and String Orch. (1962); *3 uspávanky (Lullabies)* for Soprano, Piano, Harp, and Strings (1947); Quartet for Winds (1936); *Melodies and Dialogues,* string quartet (1944); String Trio (1948); *Concert Dance* for Piano (1960); much film music; choral pieces; songs (including arrangements of folk songs).
BIBLIOGRAPHY: Zdenka Bokesová, *Šimon Jurovský* (Bratislava, 1955).

Juzeliunas, Julius, Lithuanian composer; b. Čepales, in the Žeimelis district, Feb. 20, 1916. He studied with Gruodis at the Kaunas Cons., graduating in 1948; then entered the Leningrad Cons., in the class of Voloshinov. Returning to Lithuania, he taught at the Lithuanian State Cons. in Vilnius. His compositions follow the spirit of socialist realism, treating heroic themes in stage productions and romantic subjects in instrumental music; on occasion, he uses modern techniques, including dodecaphony.
WORKS: For the stage: 2 operas: *Sukiléliai (The Rebels)* (1957; Vilna, 1960); *Žaidimas (The Game;* 1968). For Orch.: 4 symphs.: No. 1 (1948); No. 2 (1949); No. 3, *Žmogaus lyra (Man's Lyre)* for Baritone, Chorus, and Orch. (1965); No. 4 (1974); *Heroic Poem* (1956); *African Sketches,* suite (1961); *Poem-Concerto* for String Orch. (1961); *Passacaglia* (1962); Concerto for Violin, Organ, and String Orch. (1963); *Concerto Grosso* for String Orch., Wind Quintet, and Piano (1966). For Voice: Concerto for Tenor and Orch. (1955); *Pelenu lopšine (Lullaby to the Ashes),* symph. poem for Mezzo-soprano, Chorus, and Orch. (1963); *Melika,* sonata for Voice and Organ (1973).

Jyrkiäinen

Chamber music: 4 string quartets (1962, 1966, 1969, 1980); Sonata for Oboe and Clarinet (1971); Violin Sonata (1972); Sonata for Horn Solo (1975); Sonata for Violin and Cello (1977); *Diptych* for Violin and Organ (1981); *Radamalika* for Wind Quintet (1982).

Jyrkiäinen, Reijo, Finnish composer; b. Suistamo, April 6, 1934. He studied composition with Nils-Eric Fougstedt and Joonas Kokkonen at the Sibelius Academy in Helsinki (1956–63), and theory at the Univ. of Helsinki (1958–63); later attended modern-music courses at Darmstadt (1962–63) and the electronic sessions at the Bilthoven Radio Studio in the Netherlands (1963). From 1957 to 1966 he was librarian of music recordings at the Finnish Broadcasting Co.; then taught at the Sibelius Academy (1966–67). In 1972 he became managing director of the Helsinki Phil. Orch. In his own works, he has pursued advanced experimentation, ranging from classical Schoenbergian dodecaphony to electronics.

WORKS: *5 Dodecaphonic Etudes* for Piano (1961); *Frammenti per il septetto d'archi* for 3 Violins, 2 Violas, Cello, and Double Bass (1962); *Sounds I, II,* and *III,* concrete music on Tape (1963–66); *Mesto* for Flute, Clarinet, Guitar, and Percussion (1963); *For 4* for Violin, Clarinet, Guitar, and Percussion (1963); *Contradictions* for Flute, Clarinet, Piano, Guitar, and String Quartet (1965); *5 Piano Pieces for Children* (1966); *Idiopostic I* and *II,* electronic music (1963, 1966); *Varianti* for Viola and Piano (1967).

K

Kàan-Albest, Heinrich, Polish pianist and composer; b. Tarnopol, May 29, 1852; d. Roudná, Bohemia, March 7, 1926. He studied in Prague with Blodek and Skuherský; went with Dvořák to London in 1884; from 1889, taught piano at the Prague Cons.; was its director from 1907 to 1918. He wrote 2 operas: *Escape* (1895) and *Germinal,* after Zola (1908); 2 ballets: *Bajaja* and *Olim;* a symph. poem, *Sakuntala; Frühlings-Eklogen* for Orch.; many piano pieces and arrangements.

Kabaivanska, Raina, Bulgarian soprano; b. Burgas, Dec. 15, 1934. She studied at the Sofia Cons.; made her debut with the National Opera in Sofia in 1957. She then went to Milan for further studies, and in 1961 made her appearance at La Scala; in 1962 she sang in Covent Garden in London. On Oct. 27, 1962, she made her American debut at the Metropolitan Opera in N.Y. in the role of Nedda in *Pagliacci.* She is at her best in the Italian repertoire.

Kabalevsky, Dmitri, noted Russian composer; b. St. Petersburg, Dec. 30, 1904. When he was 14 years old, his family moved to Moscow; there he received his primary musical education at the Scriabin Music School (1919–25); also studied music theory privately with Gregory Catoire; in 1925 he entered the Moscow Cons. as a student of Miaskovsky in composition and Goldenweiser in piano; in 1932 he was appointed instructor in composition there; in 1939 became a full prof. As a pedagogue, he developed effective methods of musical education; in 1962 he was elected head of the Commission of Musical Esthetic Education of Children; in 1969 became president of the Scientific Council of Educational Esthetics in the Academy of Pedagogical Sciences of the U.S.S.R.; in 1972 he received the honorary degree of president of the International Society of Musical Education. As a pianist, composer, and conductor, he made guest appearances in Europe and America. Kabalevsky's music represents a paradigm of the Russian school of composition in its Soviet period; his melodic writing is marked by broad diatonic lines invigorated by an energetic rhythmic pulse; while adhering to basic tonality, his harmony is apt to be rich in euphonious dissonances. A prolific composer, he writes in all musical genres; in his operas he successfully reflects both the lyrical and the dramatic aspects of the librettos, several of which are based on Soviet subjects faithful to the tenets of socialist realism. His instrumental writing is functional, taking into consideration the idiomatic capacities of the instruments.

Kabasta – Kačinkas

WORKS: OPERAS: *Colas Breugnon,* after Romain Rolland (Leningrad, Feb. 22, 1938); *At Moscow* (Moscow, Nov. 28, 1943; revised and produced under the title *In the Fire* in Moscow, Nov. 7, 1947); *The Family of Taras* (Leningrad, Nov. 7, 1950); *Nikita Vershinin* (Moscow, Nov. 26, 1955); *The Sisters* (1969). FOR ORCH.: 4 symphs.: No. 1 (Moscow, Nov. 9, 1932); No. 2 (Moscow, Dec. 25, 1934); No. 3, subtitled *Requiem for Lenin,* with a choral ending (Moscow, Jan. 21, 1934); No. 4 (Moscow, Oct. 17, 1956); *The Comedians,* orch. suite, from incidental music to a play (1940); *Spring,* symph. poem (1960); *Pathetic Overture* (1960); 3 piano concertos: No. 1 (Moscow, Dec. 11, 1931, composer soloist); No. 2 (Moscow, May 12, 1936); No. 3 (Moscow, Feb. 1, 1953, composer conducting; Vladimir Ashkenazy, soloist); Violin Concerto (Leningrad, Oct. 29, 1948); 2 cello concertos: No. 1 (Moscow, March 15, 1949) and No. 2 (1964). CHAMBER MUSIC: 2 string quartets (1928, 1945); *20 Simple Pieces* for Violin and Piano (1965). FOR PIANO: 3 piano sonatas (1928, 1945, 1946); 24 preludes (1943); many other piano pieces, including 30 children's pieces (1938); *24 Simple Pieces* for children (1944). VOCAL WORKS: *7 Merry Songs* for Voice and Piano (1945); numerous school songs and choruses; *Requiem* for Voices and Orch. (Moscow, Feb. 9, 1963); oratorio, *A Letter to the 30th Century* (1970); also incidental music for plays; film scores.
BIBLIOGRAPHY: L. Danilevich, *Dmitri Kabalevsky* (Moscow, 1954); G. Abramovsky, *Dmitri Kabalevsky* (Moscow, 1960); L. Danilevich, *Creative Work of D.B. Kabalevsky* (Moscow, 1963); R.V. Glezer, *Kabalevsky* (Moscow, 1969); Y. Korev, *Kabalevsky* (Moscow, 1970).

Kabasta, Oswald, Austrian conductor; b. Mistelbach, Dec. 29, 1896; d. (suicide) Kufstein, Austria, Feb. 6, 1946. He studied at the Vienna Academy of Music and in Klosterneuburg; was a choir director in Florisdorf, and a teacher of singing in Viennese high schools. In 1924 he was appointed music director to the Municipal Theater of Baden near Vienna; in 1926, conductor of opera and concert in Graz and guest conductor of the Gesellschaft der Musikfreunde in Vienna; in 1931–37 was music director of the Austrian Radio. In 1935 he was appointed director of the Gesellschaft der Musikfreunde. As conductor of the Vienna Radio Orch., he toured with it in London (1936), Berlin, Warsaw, Budapest, Amsterdam, etc. He was conductor of the Bruckner Festivals in Linz in 1936 and 1937; in 1938 he succeeded Von Hausegger as conductor of the Munich Phil. Having compromised himself by a close association with the Austrian Nazis, he committed suicide a few months after the conclusion of World War II.

Kabeláč, Miloslav, Czech composer; b. Prague, Aug. 1, 1908; d. there, Sept. 17, 1979. He studied composition with K.B. Jirák and conducting with Pavel Dědeček at the Prague Cons. (1928–31); also took piano lessons with Vilém Kurz there (1931–34). He then served as conductor and music director at the Czech Radio in Prague (1932–39, 1945–54); taught

composition at the Prague Cons. from 1958 to 1962. From 1968 to 1970 he lectured on electronic music at the Czech Radio in Plzeň. In his music he followed a fairly advanced modern idiom, occasionally applying dodecaphonic devices, but hewing close to the fundamentals of tonality.
WORKS: FOR ORCH. AND VOCAL: Sinfonietta (1931); *Fantasy* for Piano and Orch. (1934); *Little Christmas Cantata* for Soprano, Men's Chorus, and Chamber Ensemble (1937); a resistance cantata, *Neustupujte (Do Not Yield)* for Men's Chorus, Band, and Percussion, to words urging Czechoslovakia to resist the Nazis (1939; Prague, Oct. 28, 1945); 2 overtures (1939, 1947); 8 symphs.: No. 1, for Strings and Percussion (1941–42); No. 2 (1942–46); No. 3, for Organ, Brass, and Timpani (1948–57); No. 4, for Chamber Orch. (1954–58); No. 5, *Dramatica,* for Soprano and Orch. (1959–60); No. 6, *Concertante,* for Clarinet and Orch. (1961–62); No. 7, on Old Testament texts, for Narrator and Orch. (1967–68); No. 8, *Antiphonies,* for Soprano, Chorus, Percussion, and Organ (1970); *Moravian Lullabies* for Soprano and Chamber Orch. (1951); *Dětem (For Children),* suite for Orch. (1955); 6 lullabies for Alto, Women's Chorus, and Orch. (1955); *Mysterium času (Mystery of Time)* for Orch. (Prague, Oct. 23, 1957); *3 Melodramas* for Narrators and Orch. (1957); *Hamletovská improvizace (Hamlet Improvisations),* commemorating the Shakespeare quadricentennial (1962–63; Prague, May 26, 1964); *Zrcadlení (Reflections),* 9 miniatures (1963–64; Prague, Feb. 2, 1965); *Tajemství ticha (Euphemias Mysterion)* for Soprano and Chamber Orch. (1964–65; Warsaw Autumn Festival, Sept. 30, 1965); Variations on the chorale *Hospodine, pomiluj ny (Our Lord, Forgive Us)* II for Piano and Orch. (1978).
CHAMBER MUSIC: Wind Sextet (1940); *3 Pieces* for Cello and Piano (1941); Oboe Sonatina (1955); *Ballade* for Violin and Piano (1956); *Suite* for Saxophone and Piano (1959); *8 Inventions* for Percussion (1963; in the form of a ballet, Strasbourg, April 22, 1965); *8 Ricercari* for Percussion (1966–67; revised 1971); *Laments and Smiles,* 8 bagatelles for Flute and Harp (1969; revised 1976); *Fated Dramas of Man,* sonata for Narrator, Trumpet, Percussion, and Piano (1975–76); Variations on the chorale *Piano Hospodine, pomiluj ny (Our Lord, Forgive Us)* I for Female Speaker, Baritone, Men's Chorus, and Mixed Chorus (1977).
FOR PIANO: *8 Preludes* (1955–56); *Motifs,* cycle (1959); *Small Suite* for Piano, 4-hands (1960).
FOR ORGAN: *Fantasy* (1957); *4 Preludes* (1963); also *E fontibus Bohemicis (From Bohemian Sources,* an anthology*).*

Kačinkas, Jeronimas, Lithuanian composer and conductor; b. Viduklé, April 17, 1907. He studied with his father, a church organist; then at the State Music School in Klaipeda and at the Prague Cons. with Jaroslav Křička and Alois Hába. Returning to Lithuania, he became conductor of the Klaipeda Symph. Orch. (1932–38); in 1938 was appointed music director for the Lithuanian Radio in Kaunas; during World War II, conducted the Vilna Phil.; left

Lithuania in 1944; from 1945 to 1949 lived in a displaced-persons camp in Augsburg, Germany. In 1949 he settled in the U.S.; he lives mostly in Boston. His music reflects the influences of Scriabin and French Impressionists. Among his works are a Trumpet Concerto; 2 string quartets; sacred choruses; piano pieces.

Kade, Otto, German musicologist; b. Dresden, May 6, 1819; d. Bad Doberan, near Rostock, July 19, 1900. He studied composition with J. Otto Schneider; also took courses in choral conducting. In 1848 he established in Dresden the singing society Cäcilia for the promotion of old church music. In 1860 he became conductor of the court choir in Schwerin. He publ. a number of useful papers dealing with German choral music, among them an *Offizielles Melodienbuch,* and a *Choralbuch* for the Mecklenburg Landeskirche; edited the musical supplements to vol. 1 of Ambros's *Geschichte der Musik* (1881, publ. as vol. 5) and the revised edition of its vol. 3 (1893). His major accomplishment in musical bibliography was the compilation of *Die Musikalien-Sammlung des grossherzoglich Mecklenburg-Schweriner Fürstenhauses aus den letzten zwei Jahrhunderten* (2 vols., Schwerin, 1893; a supplement, *Der Musikalische Nachlass der Frau Erbgrossherzogin Auguste von Mecklenburg-Schwerin,* appeared in 1899). Some of his own compositions are collected in the *Cantional* which he publ. for the Mecklenburg Landeskirche.

Kadosa, Pál, talented Hungarian composer and pianist; b. Léva (now Levice, Czechoslovakia), Sept. 6, 1903; d. Budapest, March 30, 1983. He studied piano with Arnold Székely and composition with Kodály at the Budapest Academy of Music (1921–27); had a brief career as a concert pianist; then taught piano at the Fodor Music School in Budapest (1927–43). In 1945 he was appointed to the piano faculty at the Budapest Academy of Music. He won the Kossuth Prize for composition in 1950 and the Erkel Prize twice, in 1955 and 1962. In his music he combined the elements of the cosmopolitan modern idiom with strong Hungarian rhythms and folklike melodies; in his treatment of these materials, and particularly in the energetic asymmetrical passages, he was closer to the idiom of Béla Bartók than to that of his teacher Kodály. The lyrical element in modal interludes adds to the Hungarian charm of his music.
    WORKS: Opera, *A huszti kaland (The Adventure of Huszt;* 1949–50; Budapest, Dec. 22, 1951); 5 cantatas: *De amore fatale* (1939–40); *Terjed a fény (Light Is Spreading;* 1949); *Sztálin esküje (Stalin's Oath;* 1949); *A béke katonai (The Soldiers of Peace;* 1950); *Március fia (Son of March;* 1950); Chamber Symph. (1926); 2 divertimentos for Orch. (1933; 1933–34, revised 1960); 8 symphs.: No. 1 (1941–42; Budapest, 1965); No. 2, *Capriccio* (Budapest, 1948); No. 3 (1953–55; Budapest, 1957); No. 4 for String Orch. (1958–59; Budapest, 1961); No. 5 (1960–61; Hungarian Radio, 1962); No. 6 (1966; Hungarian Radio, Aug. 19, 1966); No. 7 (1967; Budapest, 1968); No. 8

(1968; Hungarian Radio, 1969); *Partita* for Orch. (1943–44); *Morning Ode* for Orch. (1945); March, overture (1945); *Honor and Glory,* suite (1951); Suite for Orch. (1954); *Pian e forte,* sonata for Orch. (1962); Suite for Small Orch. (1962); Sinfonietta (1974); 4 piano concertos: No. 1 (1931; Amsterdam International Society for Contemporary Music Festival, June 9, 1933, composer soloist); No. 2, concertino (1938); No. 3 (1953); No. 4 (1966); 2 violin concertos (1932, revised 1969–70; 1940–41, revised 1956); Concerto for String Quartet and Chamber Orch. (1936); Viola Concertino (1937); 3 string quartets (1934–35, 1936, 1957); Serenade for 10 Instruments (1967); solo sonatinas for Violin (1923) and Cello (1924); Sonatina for Violin and Cello (1923); 2 violin sonatas (1925, revised 1969–70; 1963); Suite for Violin and Piano (1926; revised 1970); 2 string trios (1929–30, 1955); *Partita* for Violin and Piano (1931); Suite for Solo Violin (1931); Wind Quintet (1954); Piano Trio (1956); *Improvisation* for Cello and Piano (1957); Flute Sonatina (1961); Violin Sonatina (1962); 3 suites for Piano (1921; 1921–23; 1923, revised 1970); several piano cycles: *7 Bagatelles* (1923), *8 Epigrams* (1923–24), *5 Sketches* (1931), *6 Hungarian Folksongs* (1934–35), *6 Little Preludes* (1944), *10 Bagatelles* (1956–57), *4 Caprichos* (1961), *Kaleidoscope* (8 pieces, 1966), *Snapshots* (1971); 4 piano sonatas (1926, revised 1970; 1926–27; 1930; 1959 –60); Piano Sonatina (1927); 2-piano Sonata (1947); Suite for Piano Duet (1955); *3 Radnóti Songs* (1961); *7 Attila József Songs* (1964); folk-song arrangements; piano albums for children.

Kaempfert, Bert, German composer and bandleader; b. Hamburg, Oct. 16, 1923; d. on the island of Majorca, Jan. 20, 1980. He studied clarinet, saxophone, and accordion; was drafted into the German army as a member of a music corps; taken prisoner of war in 1945, he conducted a band in the camp. He returned to Hamburg in 1947; in 1949 he became director of North German Radio, for which he composed numerous songs which attained great popularity, among them *Spanish Eyes, Swinging Safari, Blue Midnight,* and *Strangers in the Night,* which was catapulted to the top of the song hits by Frank Sinatra.

Kaempfert, Max, German violinist and composer; b. Berlin, Jan. 3, 1871; d. Solothurn, June 2, 1941. He studied violin in Paris and Munich; was a member of the Kaim Orch. in Munich (1893–98); in 1899 went to Frankfurt, where he remained most of his life. He wrote an opera, *Der Schatz des Sultans,* in a folk style; a grand opera, *Der tote Gast;* 3 rhapsodies for Orch.; chamber music and songs.

Kaffka, Johann Christoph (real name, **J.C. Engelmann**), German composer and singer; b. Regensburg, 1754; d. Riga, Jan. 29, 1815. He studied with Riepel; appeared on the stage as a singer and actor in Berlin (1778), Breslau, and Dessau (1800); in 1803, settled in Riga as a bookseller. He wrote a dozen operas, several ballets, 2 oratorios, masses, vespers, etc.

Kafka, Johann Nepomuk, Bohemian composer; b. Neustadt, May 17, 1819; d. Vienna, Oct. 23, 1886. He composed numerous popular salon pieces (many based on Austrian themes) for the piano.

Kagel, Mauricio, leading composer of the cosmopolitan avant-garde; b. Buenos Aires, Dec. 24, 1931. He studied in Buenos Aires with Juan Carlos Paz and Alfredo Schiuma; also attended courses in philosophy and literature at the Univ. of Buenos Aires. In 1949 he became associated with the Agrupación Nueva Música. From 1949 to 1956 he was choral director at the Teatro Colón. In 1957 he obtained a stipend of the Academic Cultural Exchange with West Germany and went to Cologne, which he made his permanent home. From 1960 to 1966 he was a guest lecturer at the International Festival Courses for New Music in Darmstadt; in 1961 and 1963 he gave lectures and demonstrations of modern music in the U.S., and in 1965 was a prof. of composition at the State Univ. of N.Y. in Buffalo; in 1967 he was a guest lecturer at the Academy for Film and Television in Berlin; in 1968 he presented a course in new music in Göteborg, Sweden; in 1969, returned to Cologne as director of the Inst. for New Music at the Musikschule in Cologne; was named prof. there in 1974. As a composer, Kagel evolved an extremely complex system in which a fantastically intricate and yet wholly rational serial organization of notes, intervals, and durations is supplemented by aleatory techniques; some of these techniques are derived from linguistic permutations, random patterns of lights and shadows on exposed photographic film, and other seemingly arcane processes. In his hyper-serial constructions, Kagel endeavors to unite all elements of human expression, ultimately aiming at the creation of a universe of theatrical arts in their visual, aural, and societal aspects. WORKS: *Palimpsestos* for Chorus a cappella (1950); String Sextet (1953); *Traummusik* for Instruments and Musique Concrète (1954); *Anagrama* for Speaking Chorus, 4 Vocalists, and Chamber Ensemble (1958); *Transición I* for Electronic Sounds (1958); *Transición II* for Piano, Percussion, and 2 Magnetic Tapes (1959); *Pandora's Box* for Magnetic Tape (1961); *Sonant* for Electric Guitar, Harp, Double Bass, and 20 Instruments (1961); *Sur scène* for 6 Participants in mixed media, with Musicians instructed to interfere with Actors and Singers (concert perf., Radio Bremen, May 6, 1962); *Heterophonie* for Optional Ensemble, in 5 sections, optionally played or unplayed, with the conductor given an option to regard all instructions in the score as binding or not binding (Cologne, May 22, 1962, optionally conducted by the composer with the oboe giving A-sharp for tuning); *Phonophonie,* 4 melodramas for 2 Voices and Sound Sources (1963); *Composition & Decomposition,* a reading piece (1963); *Diaphonie* for Chorus, Orch., and Slide Projections (1964); *Music for Renaissance Instruments* for 23 Performers (1966); String Quartet (1967); *Montage* for different Sound Sources (1967); *Ornithologica multiplicata* for Exotic Birds (1968); *Ludwig van,* a surrealistic film score bestrewed with thematic fragments from Beethoven's works (1970; a bicentennial homage to Beethoven); *Staatstheater,* a "scenic composition" involving a ballet for "non-dancers" and orchestrated for a number of household objects, including a chamber pot and medical appurtenances such as a large clyster filled with water held in readiness to administer a rectal enema (Hamburg Staatsoper, April 25, 1971); *Variations ohne Fuge* for Orch. (1972); *Con voce* for 3 Mute Actors (1972); *Mare nostrum,* scenic play (1975); *Kantrimiusik* (phonetic rendition into German of "country music"; 1975); *Variété,* "concert-spectacle for Artists and Musicians" (Metz Festival, Fall 1977); opera, *Die Erschöpfung der Welt* (Stuttgart, Feb. 8, 1980).
BIBLIOGRAPHY: Dieter Schnebel, *Mauricio Kagel: Musik, Theater, Film* (Cologne, 1970); Karl Heinz Zarius, *Staatstheater von Mauricio Kagel* (Vienna, 1977).

Kagen, Sergius, Russian-American pianist and composer; b. St. Petersburg, Aug. 22, 1909; d. New York, March 1, 1964. He went to Berlin in 1921; emigrated to the U.S. in 1925; studied at the Juilliard School of Music in N.Y., graduating in 1930; later joined its faculty. He wrote an opera, *Hamlet* (Baltimore, Nov. 9, 1962); piano pieces and vocal works; edited *40 French Songs* (2 vols., N.Y., 1952).

Kahl, Willi, German musicologist; b. Zabern, Alsace, July 18, 1893; d. Cologne, Oct. 3, 1962. He first studied in Freiburg and Munich; received his Ph.D. in 1919 from the Univ. of Bonn with the dissertation *Das lyrische Klavierstück zu Beginn des 19. Jahrhunderts (1800 bis 1830) und seine Vorgeschichte im 17. und 18. Jahrhundert;* subsequently completed his Habilitation in 1923 at the Univ. of Cologne with his *Studien zur Geschichte der Klaviermusik des 18. Jahrhunderts.* In 1928 he became Bibliotheksrat of the Univ. of Cologne and of the city library; was also a reader at the Univ. from 1928; he retired in 1958. His writings include *Musik und Musikleben im Rheinland* (Cologne, 1923); *Herbart als Musiker* (Langensalza, 1936); *Verzeichnis des Schrifttums über Franz Schubert, 1828–1928* (Regensburg, 1938). He also edited various works and compiled the important documentary vol. *Selbstbiographien deutscher Musiker des XVIII. Jahrhunderts* (Cologne, 1948).

Kähler, Willibald, German conductor and composer; b. Berlin, Jan. 2, 1866; d. Klein-Machnow, Oct. 17, 1938. He was a pupil of Kiel and Herzogenberg at the Hochschule für Musik in Berlin; then occupied various posts as a conductor: from 1891 he was in Mannheim, and from 1906 was court conductor at Schwerin; after 1931 he lived in retirement at Gauting, near Munich. He wrote music for Goethe's *Faust;* a symph. prologue to Kleist's *Der Prinz von Homburg;* choral works; piano pieces; etc.; publ. a guide to Bruckner's 8th Symph. and Te Deum; revised the unfinished orch. scores of some lieder by Hugo Wolf and Weber's *Silvana* (1928).

Kahlert, August Karl Timotheus, German writer on music and composer; b. Breslau, March 5, 1807; d. there, March 29, 1864. He taught at Breslau Univ.; wrote *Blätter aus der Brieftasche eines Musikers* (1832); *Tonleben* (1838); contributed articles to the *Allgemeine Musikalische Zeitung* and Dehn's *Caecilia;* also composed songs.

Kahn, Erich Itor, German-American pianist and composer; b. Rimbach, July 23, 1905; d. New York, March 5, 1956. He studied at the Hoch Cons. in Frankfurt; went to France in 1933; in 1938–39 toured as accompanist to Casals in France and North Africa; in 1941 emigrated to America; organized the Albeneri Trio (the name being derived from assorted syllables of the first names of the participants: Alexander Schneider, violin; Benar Heifetz, cello; and Erich Kahn, piano). In 1948 he was awarded the Coolidge Medal for eminent service to chamber music. He was held in high esteem as a composer of inventive intellect.
WORKS: Suite for Violin and Piano (1937); *Ciaccona dei tempi di guerra* for Piano (40 variations on a 12-tone theme in the bass; 1943); String Quartet (1953); 4 Nocturnes for Voice and Piano (1954); *Symphonies bretonnes* for Orch. (1955); *Actus tragicus* for 10 Instruments (Baden-Baden Festival, June 18, 1955).
BIBLIOGRAPHY: Dika Newlin, "In Memoriam: Erich Itor Kahn, Retrospect and Prospect," *American Composers Alliance Bulletin,* 3 (1957); R. Leibowitz and K. Wolff, *Erich Itor Kahn, un grand représentant de la musique contemporaine* (Paris, 1958).

Kahn, Otto Hermann, American patron of music; b. Mannheim, Feb. 21, 1867; d. New York, March 29, 1934. He was engaged in the banking profession in London (1888–93); settled in N.Y. in 1893; was a member of the firm Kahn, Loeb & Co.; became interested in the musical affairs of N.Y. City; from 1907 to his death, was on the board of the Metropolitan Opera Co.; was vice-president of the N.Y. Phil. He was a brother of **Robert Kahn,** the composer.
BIBLIOGRAPHY: M.J. Matz, *The Many Lives of Otto Kahn* (N.Y., 1963).

Kahn, Robert, German pianist and composer; b. Mannheim, July 21, 1865; d. Biddenden, Kent, May 29, 1951. He studied music with Lachner in Mannheim and with Rheinberger in Munich. In 1885 he went to Berlin, and in 1890 moved to Leipzig, where he organized a Ladies' Choral Union, which he conducted; in 1893 he was appointed instructor of piano at the Berlin Hochschule für Musik, retiring in 1931. After the advent of the Nazi government in Germany, he went to England, where he remained until his death. He composed a considerable amount of respectable chamber music and many singable choruses. He was a brother of the banker **Otto Kahn.**
BIBLIOGRAPHY: E. Radecke, *Robert Kahn* (Leipzig, 1894).

Kahnt, Christian Friedrich, German music pub-

lisher; b. Leipzig, May 10, 1823; d. there, June 5, 1897. He was the founder and, till 1886, head of the music publishing firm of C.F. Kahnt at Leipzig and Zwickau; from 1857 was publisher, and after 1868 titular editor, of Schumann's *Neue Zeitschrift für Musik.* The firm and the magazine were acquired by Oscar Schwalm ("C.F. Kahnt Nachfolger") in 1886, by Dr. Paul Simon in 1888, and by Alfred Hoffmann in 1903. After Hoffmann's death in 1926, his wife, Maria, directed the business; when she died, in 1959, the firm was taken over by her son.

Kahowez, Günter, Austrian composer; b. Vöcklabruck, Dec. 4, 1940. He studied at the Bruckner Cons. in Linz and later at the Vienna Music Academy with Karl Schiske. With neo-Classical precepts as points of departure, he rapidly progressed in the direction of modern serialism.
WORKS: Wind Quintet (1959); String Quartet (1960); *Klangrhythmen* for Piano (1962); *Flächengitter* for Flute Solo (1962); *Megalyse* for Electronic Instruments (1962); *Duale* for Clarinet and Guitar (1963); *Schichtungen* for Orch. (1963); *Ouverture & Pantomime* for Orch. (1964); *Elementalichemie* for Cello and Percussion (1975).

Kaim, Franz, German impresario; b. Kirchheim unter Tech, near Stuttgart, May 13, 1856; d. Munich, Nov. 17, 1935. Having built a concert hall and organized an orch. in Munich, he established there (1893) the celebrated series of concerts bearing his name, the "Kaimkonzerte," which presented classical works and also new compositions by German composers; the successive conductors were Hans Winderstein (1893), Zumpe (1895), Löwe (1897), Hausegger (making guest appearances in 1898), Weingartner (1898–1905), and Schneevoigt (from 1905 until the dissolution of the orch. in 1908). Besides the regular symph. concerts, a series of Volkssinfoniekonzerte was given. Immediately after the orch. broke up, its members formed the Konzertverein under the direction of Löwe (later under Pfitzner and Hausegger). In 1928 the Kaim orch. became the Munich Phil.

Kaiser, Alfred, Belgian-born British composer; b. Brussels, Feb. 29, 1872; d. Bournemouth, Oct. 1, 1917. He studied composition with Bruckner in Vienna and with Foerster in Prague; went to London to live. During World War I he changed his name to **De Keyser** to escape the odium attached to the Kaiser of Germany. Among his works are the operas *Le Billet de Joséphine* (Paris, 1902), *Die schwarze Nina* (Elberfeld, 1905), and *Stella Maris* (Düsseldorf, 1910). He also wrote a Symph., a Piano Concerto, and chamber music.

Kajanus, Robert, outstanding Finnish conductor; b. Helsingfors, Dec. 2, 1856; d. there, July 6, 1933. He studied at the Helsingfors Cons., and later at the Leipzig Cons., with Reinecke, Richter, and Jadassohn (1877–79); then went to Paris, where he studied with Svendsen (1879–80); he then lived for some time in Dresden. In 1882 he returned to Helsingfors, and founded an orch. society which sponsored concerts by the newly organized Helsingfors Phil., an ensemble he led until his death; from 1897–1926 he was music director at the Univ. of Helsingfors. Kajanus was the earliest champion of the music of Sibelius; he made the first recordings of the first and 2nd symphs. of Sibelius with the London Symph. Orch. In 1900 he was engaged by the French government to present a concert of Finnish music with the Helsingfors Phil. at the World Exposition in Paris; he was also awarded the French Legion of Honor. He composed some orch. and choral pieces on Finnish themes, among them the symph. poems *Kullerro* and *Aino;* an orch. suite, *Sommarminnen;* 2 Finnish rhapsodies; piano pieces; songs.

BIBLIOGRAPHY: K. Flodin, *Finska musiker* (in Swedish; Helsingfors, 1900); Yrjö Suomalainen, *Robert Kajanus* (Helsingfors, 1952).

Kalabis, Viktor, Czech composer; b. Červený Kostelec, Feb. 27, 1923. He studied music theory with J. Řídký at the Academy of Arts in Prague; after the end of the war, in 1945, attended classes of E. Hlobil at the Prague Cons.; from 1953 to 1972 he served as music programmer for Radio Prague. In his early works he adhered to traditional methods of composition, but later adopted modified serial procedures.

WORKS: Cello Concerto (1951); Piano Concerto (1954); Symph. No. 1 (1957); Violin Concerto (1958); Symph. No. 2 (*Sinfonia Pacis;* 1960); *Symphonic Variations* (1964); *Concerto for Orchestra* (1966); Symph. No. 3 (1971); Symph. No. 4 (1972); Trumpet Concerto (1973); Concerto for Harpsichord and String Orch. (1975); Divertimento for Flute, Oboe, Clarinet, Horn, and Bassoon (1952); *Classical Nonet* (1956); 2 string quartets (1949, 1962); Wind Quintet (1952); Cello Sonata (1968); Sonata for Clarinet and Piano (1969); Variations for Horn and Piano (1969); Sonata for Trombone and Piano (1970); Nonet No. 2 (1977).

Kalafati, Vasili, Russian composer and pedagogue of Greek extraction; b. Eupatoria, Crimea, Feb. 10, 1869; d. Leningrad, during the siege, Jan. 30, 1942. He studied at the St. Petersburg Cons. with Rimsky-Korsakov, graduating in 1899; subsequently was appointed to the teaching staff. A musician of thorough knowledge of every aspect of music theory, he was held in great esteem by his colleagues and students; Rimsky-Korsakov sent Stravinsky to Kalafati for additional training in harmony. As a composer, Kalafati faithfully continued the traditions of the Russian national school; many of his works were publ. by Belaieff; he wrote a Symph., a Piano Quintet, 2 piano sonatas, and a number of songs, all set in impeccably euphonious harmonies.

Kalbeck, Max, German music historian, biographer of Brahms; b. Breslau, Jan. 4, 1850; d. Vienna, May 4, 1921. He studied at Munich Univ.; in 1875 went to Breslau, where he wrote music criticism; his collected articles were publ. as *Wiener Opernabende* (1881), *Gereimtes und Ungereimtes* (1885), and *Opernabende* (2 vols., 1898); also *Humoresken und Phantasien* (1896). His most important publication was the monumental biography *Johannes Brahms* (8 vols., 1904–14). He also edited Brahms's correspondence with Hanslick and E. von Herzogenberg (2 vols., 1906), with P.J. and Fritz Simrock, and with Joseph Widmann; and the correspondence of Keller-Heyse (1918).

Kalhauge, Sophus Viggo Harald, Danish composer and teacher; b. Copenhagen, Aug. 12, 1840; d. there, Feb. 19, 1905. He studied with P. Heise, C. Rongsted, and J.C. Gebauer; also studied in Germany, Switzerland, and Italy; returned to Copenhagen as a teacher of piano and singing.

WORKS: Operas: *Zouavens Hjemkomst* (1868); *Paa Krigsfod* (1880); *Mantillen* (1889); *An den Frühling* for Soli, Chorus, and Orch.; piano pieces and songs.

Kalichstein, Joseph, Israeli pianist; b. Tel Aviv, Jan. 15, 1946. He studied at the Juilliard School of Music in N.Y. with Ilona Kabos and Eduard Steuermann. In 1969 he won first prize in the Leventritt Competition. Since that time he has appeared with major orchs. in America and Europe.

Kálik, Václav, Czech composer; b. Opava, Oct. 18, 1891; d. Prague, Nov. 18, 1951. He studied with J. Novotný and V. Novák at the Charles Univ. in Prague; later with J. Suk at the Master School there; was active as a choral conductor and concert pianist. Among his works are 3 operas: *A Spring Morning* (1933; Olomouc, 1943); *Lásky div* (*Love's Miracle;* 1942–43; Liberec, Nov. 20, 1950); *Consecration of Youth* (1946–48); *Fantazie* for Orch. (1915); *Moře (The Sea),* symph. poem (1924); 2 symphs.: No. 1, *Mírová (Peace),* for Soprano and Orch. (1927) and No. 2 (1941–43); Prelude for Orch. (1931); *Venezia* for String Orch. (1932); *Intermezzo* for Tenor, Violin, and Piano (1913); *Evil Love* for Soprano, Violin, and Piano (1919); Violin Sonata (1919); *Pražské obrazy (Prague Pictures)* for Male Chorus (1949–50); several piano pieces.

Kalinnikov, Vasili, Russian composer; b. Voin, near Mtzensk, Jan. 13, 1866; d. Yalta, Crimea, Jan. 11, 1901. He studied in Orel; in 1884 he enrolled at the Moscow Cons., but had to leave it a year later because of inability to pay; he then studied the bassoon at the Music School of the Moscow Phil. Society, which provided free tuition. He earned his living by playing bassoon in theater orchs.; also studied composition with A. Ilyinsky and Blaramberg. While still a student, he composed his first work, the symph. poem *The Nymphs* (Moscow, Dec. 28, 1889); later wrote another symph. poem, *The Cedar and the Palm;* the overture and entr'actes for *Tsar Boris;* and a prelude to the opera *In the Year 1812.* In 1895 he completed his most successful work, Symph. in G minor (Kiev, Feb. 20, 1897); a 2nd symph., in A (Kiev, March 12, 1898), was not as successful; he also wrote a cantata, *John of Damascus; Ballade* for Women's Chorus and Orch.; songs and piano pieces. Owing to his irregular habits and undernourishment, he contracted tuberculosis, and was sent to Yalta for treatment; there he died a few months later. Kalinnikov possessed a fine lyric talent; there is a definite trend in Russia toward greater recognition of his music. Several of his works in MS (Serenade for Strings; the overture *Bylina;* etc.) were publ. on the 50th anniversary of his death (1951).

BIBLIOGRAPHY: V. Paskhalov, *V.S. Kalinnikov, Life and Works* (Moscow, 1938; greatly enlarged ed., 1951); a collection of his letters and other materials was publ. in Moscow, in 2 vols., in 1959.

Kalisch, Paul, German tenor; b. Berlin, Nov. 6, 1855; d. St. Lorenz am Mondsee, Salzkammergut, Austria, Jan. 27, 1946. He studied architecture; then went to Milan, where he took voice lessons with Leoni and Lamperti; he sang with considerable success in Italy (Milan, Rome, Florence), then at the Munich Opera and in Berlin; in 1889 he sang the Wagner roles at the Metropolitan Opera House with **Lilli Lehmann,** whom he married in N.Y. the following year. At the first Paris performance of *Tristan und Isolde* (1904) he and his wife sang the title roles; they were later separated (though not legally divorced); after Lilli Lehmann's death in 1929, he lived on her estate in Salzkammergut, remaining there until his death at the age of 90.

Kalischer, Alfred, German writer on music; b. Thorn, March 4, 1842; d. Berlin, Oct. 8, 1909. After taking the degree of Dr.Phil. at Leipzig, he studied music with Burgel and Bohmer at Berlin, where he edited the *Neue Berliner Musikzeitung* (from 1873). Of special value are his writings about Beethoven; he also publ. philosophical works, poems, and dramas.

WRITINGS: *Lessing als Musikästhetiker* (1889); *Die "Unsterbliche Geliebte" Beethovens* (1891); *Die Macht Beethovens* (1903); *Beethoven und seine Zeitgenossen* (4 vols., 1908: I, *Beethoven und Berlin;* II and III, *Beethovens Frauenkreis;* IV, *Beethoven und Wien*). He also edited *Neue Beethovenbriefe* (1902); *Beethovens sämtliche Briefe* (5 vols., 1906–8; in Eng., 1909).

Kalish, Gilbert, American pianist; b. Brooklyn, July 2, 1935. He studied at Columbia College (1952–56; B.A., 1956); also attended the Graduate School of Arts and Sciences at Columbia Univ. (1956–58). In addition, he took piano lessons with Isabelle Vengerova, Leonard Shure, and Julius Hereford. He was a pianist with both the Contemporary Chamber Ensemble and the Boston Symph. Chamber Players; as a soloist, he toured widely in the U.S., Europe, and Australia, in programs including works by Stravinsky, Charles Ives, and others. He also was a regular accompanist with the American mezzo-soprano Jan DeGaetani. He served as artist-in-residence at the State Univ. of N.Y. at Stony Brook and head of keyboard activities at the Berkshire Music Center at Tanglewood.

Kalkbrenner, Christian, German composer and writer, father of **Friedrich W.M. Kalkbrenner;** b. Minden, Hannover, Sept. 22, 1755; d. Paris, Aug. 10, 1806. He studied piano with Becker and violin with Rodewald in Kassel; was choirmaster at the court of the Queen in Berlin (1788), then in the court of Prince Heinrich at Rheinsberg (1790–96); in 1797, went to Naples; in 1798 he became choirmaster at the Paris Opéra. There he produced his opera *Olimpie* (Dec. 18, 1798); also some pasticcios from music by Mozart and Haydn; he further wrote 2 symphs., a Piano Concerto, and several piano sonatas; publ. *Theorie der Tonkunst* (1789) and *Kurzer Abriss der Geschichte der Tonkunst* (1792).

Kalkbrenner, Friedrich Wilhelm Michael, celebrated German pianist; b. near Kassel, between Nov. 2 and Nov. 8, 1785; d. Deuil, Seine-et-Oise, June 10, 1849. He was taught by his father, **Christian Kalkbrenner.** In 1799–1801 he was enrolled at the Paris Cons., where he studied with Adam and Nicodami (piano) and Catel (harmony), taking first prizes in 1801. From 1803 he studied counterpoint with Albrechtsberger in Vienna; appeared as a concert pianist in Berlin, Munich (1805), and Stuttgart; also in Paris, with great success, in 1806. As a teacher, too, he was in great vogue. The years 1814–23 he spent in London; in 1818 he took up Logier's newly invented Chiroplast, simplified it, and applied it practically. After a German tour in 1823 with the harpist Dizi, Kalkbrenner settled (1824) in Paris as a partner in the Pleyel piano factory (the future Mme. Camilla Pleyel was one of his pupils). He revisited Germany in 1833 and Belgium in 1836. Kalkbrenner was inordinately vain of the success of his method of teaching, which aimed at the independent development of the fingers and wrist; his practical method of octave playing became a standard of modern piano teaching. He also developed left-hand technique, and a proper management of the pedals. As for his playing, his technique was smooth and well-rounded, his fingers supple and of equal strength, and his tone full and rich; his style, while fluent and graceful, lacked emotional power. His numerous études (among them several for left hand alone) are interesting and valuable. Chopin took some advice from him in Paris, but did not become his pupil despite Kalkbrenner's urging.

WORKS: 4 piano concertos (the last, op. 125, for 2 Pianos); Piano Septet, with Strings and 2 Horns; Quintet for Piano, Clarinet, Horn, Bassoon, and Double Bass; 2 piano sextets; piano quintets; 3 piano quartets; 7 piano trios; 15 sonatas; also rondos, fantasies, variations, caprices, etc., of a light character.

WRITINGS: *Méthode pour apprendre le pianoforte à l'aide du guide-mains* (1830); *Traité d'harmonie du pianiste* (1849).

BIBLIOGRAPHY: "Memoir of Mr. Frederick Kalkbrenner," *Quarterly Music Magazine and Review* (1824); L. Boivin, *Kalkbrenner* (Paris, 1840).

Kallenberg, Siegfried Garibaldi, German composer; b. Schachen, near Lindau, Nov. 3, 1867; d. Munich, Feb. 9, 1944. He studied at the Cons. of Stuttgart with Faisst; from 1892, taught at Stettin,

Königsberg, and Hannover. In 1910 he settled in Munich; a Kallenberg Society was established there in 1921 to promote his creative output. As a composer, Kallenberg was inspired by neo-Romanticism; in some of his works there are touches of Impressionism; his absorption in symbolic subjects brought him into a kinship with the Expressionist school in Germany. Apart from works on exotic subjects, he wrote music in a traditional style; he was particularly strong in choral polyphony.

WORKS: Operas: *Sun Liao, Das goldene Tor,* and *Die lustigen Musikanten;* choral works: *90th Psalm, Germania an ihre Kinder,* Requiem, *Den Gefallenen, Eine kleine Passionmusik, Eine Pfingstmusik;* 3 symphs.; *Impressionen* for Orch.; *Konzertante Fantasie* for Piano and Orch.; about 10 chamber works; 3 piano sonatas; a set of *Miniaturen* for Piano; some 300 songs. He wrote monographs on Richard Strauss (Leipzig, 1926) and Max Reger (Leipzig, 1930).

Kalliwoda, Johann Wenzel, famous Bohemian violinist and composer; b. Prague, Feb. 21, 1801; d. Karlsruhe, Dec. 3, 1866. He studied at the Prague Cons. (1811–16) with Pixis (violin) and D. Weber (composition); played in the Prague Orch. (1817–21). In 1822 he became conductor of Prince Fürstenberg's orch. in Donaueschingen; there he spent 30 years, eventually retiring to Karlsruhe. He enjoyed an enviable reputation; some of his music was highly praised by Schumann.

WORKS: 2 operas: *Blanda* (Prague, Nov. 29, 1827) and *Prinzessin Christine* (1827); 10 masses; 7 symphs.; 14 overtures and 13 fantasias for Orch.; Violin Concerto; Concerto for 2 Violins; 7 concertinos; 3 string quartets; 3 string trios; a variety of solos for violin; also choruses, duets, and songs.

BIBLIOGRAPHY: K. Strunz, *J. W. Kalliwoda* (Vienna, 1910).

Kalliwoda, Wilhelm, German pianist and composer, son of **Johann Wenzel Kalliwoda;** b. Donaueschingen, July 19, 1827; d. Karlsruhe, Sept. 8, 1893. He studied with Hauptmann in Leipzig; also took some lessons from Mendelssohn; wrote piano pieces and songs; was also a reputable conductor.

Kallmann, Helmut, Canadian librarian and musicologist; b. Berlin, Aug. 7, 1922. He studied music with his father; left Germany in 1939 for London. In 1940 he was sent to Canada; was interned in refugee camps; upon release, took music courses at the Univ. of Toronto, graduating in 1949. In 1951 he became music librarian for the Canadian Broadcasting Corp. In 1970 he was appointed chief of the music division of the National Library of Canada in Ottawa. He publ. a valuable *Catalogue of Canadian Composers* (Toronto, 1952); *A History of Music in Canada 1534–1914* (Toronto, 1960); and *Encyclopedia of Music in Canada* (Toronto, 1981); collaborated in various other publications dealing with Canadian composers.

Kallstenius, Edvin, Swedish composer; b. Filipstad, Aug. 29, 1881; d. Stockholm, Nov. 22, 1967. He first studied science at Lund Univ. (1898–1903); then took courses in music at the Leipzig Cons. (1903–7); returning to Stockholm, he became music critic of the *Svenska Dagbladet;* was a music librarian at Radio Sweden (1928–46) and a board member of the Society of Swedish Composers (1932–61). In his early works he followed the Romantic traditions of Scandinavian music; but later turned to advanced modern techniques, including explicit application of dodecaphonic configurations.

WORKS: FOR ORCH.: *Scherzo fugato* for Small Orch. (1907; revised 1923); *Sista Striden,* dramatic overture (1908); *En serenad i sommarnatten (A Serenade in the Summer Night;* 1918); *Sinfonia concertata* for Piano and Orch. (1922); 4 sinfoniettas (1923; 1946; *Dodicitonica,* 1956; *Semi-seriale,* 1958); 5 symphs. (1926, revised 1941; 1935; 1948; 1954; *Sinfonia su temi 12-tonici,* 1960); *Dalarapsodi* (1931); *Dalslandsrapsodi* (1936); *Romantico,* overture (1938); *Högtid och fest,* trilogy (1940); *Musica gioconda* for Strings (1942); *Cavatina* for Viola and Orch. (1943); *Passacaglia enarmonica* (1943); *Kraus-variationer* (1947); *Sonata concertate* for Cello and Orch. (1951); *Musica sinfonica* for Strings (1953; full orch. version, 1959); *Nytt vin i gamla läglar (New Wine in Old Bottles)* for Small Orch. (1954); *Choreographic Suite* (1957); *Prologo seriale* (1966). VOCAL WORKS: *När vi dö (When Mankind Perishes),* Requiem for Chorus and Orch. (1919); *Sångoffer (Song Offering),* cantata for Baritone and Orch. (1944); *Stjärntändningen* for Chorus and Orch. (1949); *Hymen, o, Hymenaios* for Soli, Chorus, and Orch. (1955). CHAMBER MUSIC: 8 string quartets (1904; 1905; 1913; *Divertimento alla serenata,* 1925; 1945; 1953; *Dodecatonica,* 1957; 1961); Cello Sonata (1908); Violin Sonata (1909); Clarinet Quintet (1930); Suite for Winds and Percussion (1938); Wind Quartet (1943); *Trio divertente* for Flute, Violin, and Viola (1950); *Piccolo trio seriale* for Flute, English Horn, and Clarinet (1956); *Trio svagante* for Clarinet, Horn, and Cello (1959); solo sonatas for Cello (1961), Flute (1962), and Violin (1965); *Lyric Suite* for Flute, Saxophone, and Cello (1962); String Trio (1965).

Kálmán, Emmerich (Imre), Hungarian composer of light opera; b. Siófok, Oct. 24, 1882; d. Paris, Oct. 30, 1953. He studied with Kössler in Budapest; won the Imperial Composition Prize (1907). Settling in Vienna, he produced a great number of tuneful and successful operettas; in 1938 he left Vienna; was in Paris until 1940; then came to America; lived in N.Y. and Hollywood; in 1949 went again to Europe.

WORKS: He made his debut as a composer with the symph. scherzo *Saturnalia,* perf. by the Budapest Phil. Orch. (Feb. 29, 1904); later dedicated himself exclusively to the composition of operettas in the Viennese style. His first success was with *Ein Herbstmanöver* (first perf. in Hungarian, Budapest, Feb. 22, 1908; perf. in N.Y. in the same year as *The Gay Hussars).* His other popular operettas were *Gold gab ich für Eisen* (Vienna, Oct. 16, 1914; N.Y., Dec. 6, 1916, as *Her Soldier Boy); Fräulein Susi*

(Budapest, Feb. 23, 1915; Eng. and American productions as *Miss Springtime*); *Die Csardasfürstin* (Vienna, Nov. 17, 1915; in England as *Gypsy Princess;* in America as *The Riviera Girl*); *Gräfin Mariza* (Vienna, Feb. 28, 1924); *Die Zirkusprinzessin* (*The Circus Princess;* Vienna, March 26, 1926). The following were moderately successful: *Der gute Kamerad* (first version of *Gold gab ich für Eisen;* Vienna, Oct. 10, 1911); *Der kleine König* (Vienna, Nov. 27, 1912); *Die Faschingsfee* (Vienna, Jan. 31, 1917); *Die Bajadere* (Vienna, Dec. 23, 1921); *Golden Dawn* (N.Y., Nov. 30, 1927); *Die Herzogin von Chicago* (Vienna, April 6, 1928); *Ronny* (Berlin, Dec. 22, 1931); *Kaiserin Josephine* (Zürich, Jan. 18, 1936); *Marinka* (N.Y., July 18, 1945). His last work, *Arizona Lady*, was perf. posthumously in Bern in 1954.

BIBLIOGRAPHY: J. Bistron, *Emmerich Kálmán* (Vienna, 1932); R. Oesterreicher, *Emmerich Kálmán* (Vienna, 1954); V. Kálmán, *Mein Leben mit Emmerich Kálmán* (Bayreuth, 1966).

Kalmár, László, Hungarian composer and music editor; b. Budapest, Oct. 19, 1931. He studied composition with Ervin Major and Farkas; in 1957 was appointed editor of the Editio Musica Budapest.

WORKS: Cantata, *Soldiers Weep at Night,* after Quasimodo (1962); *4 Canons* for Piano (1966); *Symmetriae* for String Orch. (1966); Trio for Flute, Marimba, and Guitar (1968); *3 Monologos:* No. 1 for Solo Guitar (1968), No. 2 for Solo Violin (1973), and No. 3 for Solo Flute (1973); *Toccata concertante* for Piano and String Orch. (1968–70); Flute Sonata (1970–71); *Triangoli* for Clarinet, Horn, Harp, Violin, and Cello (1970–71); *Distichon* for Piano, Harp, and Percussion (1970–71); *Memoriale* for Chorus, Percussion, and String Orch. (1969–71); *Cicli* for 18 Strings (1971); *Cantus* for 2 Contraltos, Clarinet, Cello, and Harp (1969–72); *2 Duets* for 2 Trumpets (1972); Quartet for English Horn, Viola, Vibraphone, and Harpsichord (1972); String Trio (1972); *Combo* for Guitar, Conga, and Double Bass (1971–73); *Sotto voce* for Harmonium, Vibraphone, and Harp (1973); *Sereno* for Cello and Harp (1974–75).

Kalninš, Alfreds, Latvian composer; b. Zehsis, Aug. 23, 1879; d. Riga, Dec. 23, 1951. He studied at the St. Petersburg Cons. with Homilius (organ) and Liadov (composition); was organist at various Lutheran churches in Dorpat, Libau, and Riga; also played organ recitals in Russia. While in Riga, he was active as a teacher and composer. From 1927 till 1933 he lived in N.Y.; then returned to Latvia and settled in Riga.

WORKS: Operas: *Banuta* (first national Latvian opera; Riga, May 29, 1920); *Salinieki* (*The Islanders;* Riga, 1925); *Dzimtenes atmoda* (*The Nation's Awakening;* Riga, Sept. 9, 1933); symph. poem, *Latvia;* piano pieces; some 100 choruses; about 200 songs; arrangements of Latvian folk songs (publ. in Riga).

BIBLIOGRAPHY: J. Vitolinš, *Alfreds Kalninš* (in Latvian; Riga, 1968).

Kalninš, Janis, Latvian composer and conductor, son of **Alfreds Kalninš;** b. Pernav (Pärnu), Nov. 2, 1904. He studied in Riga with Vitols and in Leipzig with H. Abendroth; was conductor at the Latvian National Theater in Riga (1924–33), then at the Riga Opera House (1933–44). In 1948 he settled in Canada. From 1962 to 1968 he conducted the New Brunswick Symph.

WORKS: *Hamlet,* opera (Riga, Feb. 17, 1936); 3 symphs.: No. 1 (1939–44); No. 2, *Symphony of the Beatitudes,* with Chorus (1953); No. 3 (1972–73); Violin Concerto (1945–46); *Theme and Variations* for Clarinet, Horn, and Orch. (1963); String Quartet (1948); choruses; songs.

Kalomiris, Manolis, distinguished Greek composer; b. Smyrna, Turkey, Dec. 26, 1883; d. Athens, April 3, 1962. He studied piano with A. Sturm and composition with Herman Grädener at the Vienna Cons. (1901–6); then went to Russia, where he taught piano at a private school in Kharkov. In 1910 he settled in Greece; was instructor of the Athens School of Music (1911–19) and founder of the Hellenic Cons. of Athens (1919–26). In 1926 he founded the Cons. of Athens; was its director until 1948. As a music educator, he was greatly esteemed in Greece; 2 generations of Greek composers were his pupils. Kalomiris was the protagonist of Greek nationalism in music; almost all his works are based on Greek folk-song patterns, and many are inspired by Hellenic subjects. In his harmonies and instrumentation he followed the Russian school of composition, with a considerable influx of lush Wagnerian sonorities. His catalogue of works, publ. in Athens in 1964, lists 222 opus numbers; he also brought out several textbooks on harmony, counterpoint, and orchestration.

WORKS: OPERAS: *O Protomastoras (The Master-Builder),* to a libretto by Nikos Kazantzakis, the first opera by a Greek composer on a native subject (Athens, March 24, 1916); *Mother's Ring,* music drama (1917); *Anatoli* (*The Orient*), musical fairy tale, to a libretto by Kalomiris, after Cambyssis (1945–48); *The Shadowy Waters,* opera to a libretto after Yeats (1950–52); *Constantin Palaeologus,* music legend after a story by Kazantzakis (Athens, Aug. 12, 1962). FOR ORCH.: *Greek Suite* (1907); *The Olive Tree* for Women's Chorus and Orch. (1909); *Iambs and Anapests,* suite (1914); *Valor Symphony* for Chorus and Orch. (1920); *Greek Rhapsody* for Piano and Orch. (orchestrated by Gabriel Pierné and conducted by him for the first time in Paris, April 3, 1926); *Island Pictures* for Violin and Orch. (1928); *Symphony of the Kind People* for Mezzo-soprano, Chorus, and Orch. (1931); *3 Greek Dances* (1934); Piano Concerto (1935); *At the Ossios Loukas Monastery* for Narrator and Orch. (1937); *Triptych* (1940); *Minas the Rebel,* tone poem (1940); *The Death of the Courageous Woman,* tone poem (1945); Concertino for Violin and Orch. (1955); *Palamas Symphony* for Chorus and Orch., to texts by the Greek poet Palamas (Athens, Jan. 22, 1956). CHAMBER MUSIC: Piano Quintet, with Soprano (1912); String Trio (1921); *Quartet quasi fantasia* for Harp, Flute, English Horn, and Viola (1921); Violin Sonata

1153

(1948). For piano: *Sunrise* (1902); *3 Ballads* (1906); *For Greek Children* (1910); *2 Rhapsodies* (1921); 5 preludes (1939); choruses; songs.

Kalter, Sabine, mezzo-soprano; b. Jaroslaw, Poland, March 28, 1889; d. London, Sept. 1, 1957. She studied at the Vienna Academy of Music; made her debut at the Vienna Volksoper in 1911; was a principal member of the Hamburg Opera (1915–35); compelled to leave Germany, she settled in London, where she sang at Covent Garden until 1939; in later years she appeared in concerts. She was distinguished in her Wagnerian roles.

Kamburov, Ivan, Bulgarian writer on music; b. Leskovec, Oct. 8, 1883; d. Sofia, Jan. 23, 1955. He studied music with Max Reger and Krehl at the Leipzig Cons.; in 1910–14 was a high school teacher at Plovdiv, Bulgaria; in 1922–24 and 1929–30, traveled for scientific-research purposes.
WRITINGS (in Bulgarian): *Bulgarian Music* (1926); *Operatic Art* (1926); *Music and Nation* (1932); *Illustrated Music Dictionary; Music for All* (Sofia, 1934); *Polish Music* (Sofia, 1939); *Yugoslav Music* (Sofia, 1940); *Bulgarian Folk Songs* (Sofia, 1941); *Dvořák* (Sofia, 1941).

Kamensky, Alexander, Russian pianist; b. Geneva (of Russian parentage), Dec. 12, 1900; d. Leningrad, Nov. 7, 1952. The family returned to Russia early in the century, and Kamensky studied piano at the Petrograd Cons., graduating in 1923. He developed an energetic career as a concert pianist; did not interrupt his activities even during the siege of Leningrad in 1941–42, when he played almost 500 recitals under the most dangerous conditions. In his programs he featured many works by Soviet composers and also by modern Western music masters, including Schoenberg and Stravinsky. In 1934 he was appointed prof. of piano of the Leningrad Cons. He made a number of transcriptions for piano of selections from Russian operas.
BIBLIOGRAPHY: A. Bushen, "A Pianist's Heroism," in his book *Music on the Fronts of the Great Patriotic Wars* (Moscow, 1970; pp. 217–32).

Kamieński, Lucian, Polish composer; b. Gniezno, Jan. 7, 1885; d. Thorn, July 27, 1964. He studied composition with Max Bruch in Berlin, musicology with Kretzschmar and Johannes Wolf; received his Dr.Phil. with the dissertation *Die Oratorien von J.A. Hasse* (1910). He then was music critic at Königsberg (until 1919); in 1920 was appointed instructor at the Music Academy in Poznan; taught musicology at the Univ. of Poznan. In 1939 he was forced to leave his post; returning to Poznan after 1945, he established himself as a private teacher.
WORKS: 2 comic operas: *Tabu* (Königsberg, April 9, 1917) and *Dami i huzary* (Poznan, Oct. 2, 1938); *Sinfonia paschalis* (1928); *Silesia sings,* symph. sketch (1929); Violin Sonata; several piano suites on Polish themes; an album of 60 workers' songs to his own words (Berlin, 1905–10), which he issued under the name **Dolega-Kamieński.**

Kamieński, Mathias, earliest composer of Polish opera; b. Ödenburg, Hungary, Oct. 13, 1734; d. Warsaw, Jan. 25, 1821. He studied composition in Vienna, and settled in Warsaw as a teacher. On May 11, 1778, his first opera, *Nędza uszczęśliwiona (Poverty Made Happy),* was produced in Warsaw and enthusiastically received; he produced 4 more Polish operas, and also wrote a ballad opera, *Zośka* (Warsaw, Jan. 21, 1781); a cantata for the unveiling of the Sobieski monument (1788); masses, offertories, and polonaises.

Kaminski, Heinrich, eminent German composer; b. Tiengen, Baden, July 4, 1886; d. Ried, Bavaria, June 21, 1946. He studied at Heidelberg Univ. with Wolfrum and in Berlin with Kaun, Klatte, and Juon; taught a master class at the Berlin Academy of Music (1930–32). In 1933 he settled in Ried, where he remained to the end of his life. His writing is strictly polyphonic and almost rigid in form; the religious and mystic character of his sacred music stems from his family origins (he was the son of a clergyman of Polish extraction); the chief influences in his work were Bach and Bruckner. Interest in his music was enhanced after his death by posthumous editions of his unpubl. works.
WORKS: For the stage: Opera, *Jürg Jenatsch* (Dresden, April 27, 1929); music drama for Narrator and Orch., *Das Spiel vom König Aphelius* (his last work, completed in 1946; produced posthumously, Göttingen, Jan. 29, 1950); a Passion, after an old French mystery play (1920). Choral works: *69th Psalm* (1914); *Introitus und Hymnus* (1919); *Magnificat* (1925); *Der Mensch,* motet (1926); *Die Erde,* motet (1928); etc. For orch.: Concerto Grosso for Double Orch. (1922); *Dorische Musik* (1933); Piano Concerto (Berlin, 1937); *In Memoriam Gabrielae* for Orch., Contralto, and Solo Violin (1940); *Tanzdrama* (1942). Chamber music: Quartet for Clarinet, Viola, Cello, and Piano (1912); 2 string quartets (1913, 1916); Quintet for Clarinet, Horn, Violin, Viola, and Cello (1924); *Music for 2 Violins and Harpsichord* (1931); *Hauskonzert* (1941); *Ballade* for Horn and Piano (1943). For organ: Toccata (1923); *Chorale-Sonata* (1926); 3 chorale preludes (1928); Toccata and Fugue (1939). For piano: *Klavierbuch* (1934); *10 kleine Übungen für das polyphone Klavierspiel* (1935). Songs: *Brautlied* for Soprano and Organ (1911); *Cantiques bretons* (1923); *3 geistliche Lieder* for Soprano, Violin, and Clarinet (1924); *Triptychon* for Alto and Organ (1930); *Lied eines Gefangenen* (1936); *Weihnachtsspruch* (1938); *Hochzeitsspruch* for 2 Altos and Organ (1940); *Dem Gedächtnis eines verwundeten Soldaten* for 2 Sopranos and Piano (1941); folk-song arrangements.
BIBLIOGRAPHY: S. Günther, "Heinrich Kaminski," *Die Musik,* XXII/7; E. Krieger, "Heinrich Kaminski," *Zeitschrift für Musik* (1933); K. Schleifer, *Heinrich Kaminski* (Kassel, 1945); K. Schleifer and R. Schwarz-Stilling, *Heinrich Kaminski: Werkverzeichnis* (Kassel, 1947); I. Samson, *Das Vokalschaffen von Heinrich Kaminski, mit Ausnahme der Opern* (Frankfurt, 1956).

Kaminski, Joseph, Russian-born Israeli violinist and composer; b. Odessa, Nov. 17, 1903; d. Gedera, Israel, Oct. 14, 1972. He studied in Warsaw, Berlin, and Vienna; was concertmaster of the Warsaw Radio Orch. In 1935 he emigrated to Palestine and settled in Tel Aviv; was concertmaster of the Israel Phil. Orch. (1937–69).
WORKS: Trumpet Concertino (1940–41; Tel Aviv, May 5, 1941); *Ha'Alijah,* variations for Orch. (1942); *Comedy Overture* (1944); String Quartet (1945); *Ballade* for Harp and Chamber Orch. (Tel Aviv, Feb. 2, 1946); Violin Concerto (1947–49; Tel Aviv, 1954); *3 Israeli Sketches* for Orch. (1955); *Triptych* for Piano (1958); *Variations* for English Horn and String Orch. (1958); *Symphonic Overture* (1960).

Kamionsky, Oscar, Russian baritone; b. Kiev, 1869; d. Yalta, Aug. 15, 1917. He studied with Everard in St. Petersburg and Rossi in Naples; made his debut in Naples in 1891; sang in Kharkov (1893–94, 1898–99), Kiev (1894–95), and Tiflis (1896–98, 1899–1901); also appeared in St. Petersburg, Moscow, and other cities as a guest artist. He later sang in Moscow at the Zimin Theater (1905–8, 1913–14); retired from the stage in 1915. As a singer, he followed the precepts of the Italian school of *bel canto;* was famous for his roles as Valentin in *Faust,* Rigoletto, Wolfram in *Tannhäuser,* and other lyrico-dramatic parts.

Kämpf, Karl, German organist and composer; b. Berlin, Aug. 31, 1874; d. Mönchengladbach, Nov. 4, 1950. He was a pupil of F.E. Koch; became a professional performer on the harmonium; in 1925, was appointed conductor of the choral society Liedertafel in Mönchengladbach. He wrote several symph. marches on literary subjects: *Hiawatha, Aus baltischen Landen, Andersens Märchen,* etc.; also a choral symph. in 6 movements, *Die Macht des Liedes;* piano works; various pieces for the harmonium; etc.
BIBLIOGRAPHY: J. Hagemann-Bonn, *Karl Kämpf* (Leipzig, 1907).

Kamu, Okko, Finnish violinist and conductor; b. Helsinki, March 7, 1946. He studied violin at the Sibelius Academy in Helsinki under Onni Suhonen; at the age of 23 he won the international competition for conductors arranged by the Herbert von Karajan Foundation; in 1971 was appointed conductor with the Finnish Radio Symph. Orch.; from 1976 to 1979 was chief conductor of the Oslo Phil. Orch.; in 1979 was appointed chief conductor of the Helsinki Phil.

Kancheli, Giya, Soviet Georgian composer; b. Tiflis, Aug. 10, 1935. He studied composition at the Tiflis Cons. (1959–63); in 1970 was appointed to its faculty. His sources of inspiration are nourished by Caucasian melos, with its quasi-oriental fiorituras and deflected chromatics which impart a peculiar aura of lyric introspection to the music; but his treatment of these materials is covertly modernistic and overtly optimistic, especially in sonoristic effects. He wrote 6 symphs. (1967, 1970, 1973, 1975, 1977, 1981); his 4th Symph., commemorating the semimillennium of the death of Michelangelo, was given its American premiere by the Philadelphia Orch. on Jan. 13, 1978. He also wrote a musical comedy, *The Pranks of Hanum* (1973); *Largo and Allegro* for Strings, Piano, and Timpani (1963); and several film scores.

Kandler, Franz Sales, Austrian writer on music; b. Klosterneuburg, Aug. 23, 1792; d. Baden, near Vienna, Sept. 26, 1831. As a boy he sang in the court choir in Vienna; studied with Albrechtsberger, Salieri, and Gyrowetz. He was an Imperial military draughtsman; when ordered to Italy (1815–26), he pursued the study of Italian music and its history as an avocation. He publ. *Cenni storico-critici intorno alla vita ed alle opere del celebre compositore Giovanni Adolfo Hasse, detto il Sassone* (1820); *Über das Leben und die Werke des G. Pierluigi da Palestrina, genannt der Fürst der Musik* (1834); and *Cenni storico-critici sulle vicende e lo stato attuale della musica in Italia* (1836).
BIBLIOGRAPHY: L. Schiedermair, "Venezianer Briefe F.S. Kandlers," in *Riemann-Festschrift* (Leipzig, 1909).

Kanitz, Ernst, Austrian-American composer; b. Vienna, April 9, 1894; d. Menlo Park, Calif., April 7, 1978. He changed his first name to **Ernest** in order to distinguish himself from a homonymous concert manager in Vienna. He studied with Richard Heuberger (1912–14) and with Franz Schreker (1914–20). In 1922 he joined the staff of the Neues Konservatorium in Vienna; after the Anschluss of Austria in 1938 he emigrated to the U.S.; he taught music theory in various American colleges, among them the Univ. of Southern Calif. (1945–59) and Marymount College in Palos Verdes, Calif. (1960–64).
WORKS: *Heitere Ouvertüre* (1918); an oratorio, *Das Hohelied* (1921); radio cantata, *Zeitmusik* (1931); *Dance Sonata* for Flute, Clarinet, Trumpet, Bassoon, and Piano (1932); Concertino for Theremin and Orch. (1938); *Quintettino* for Piano and Wind Instruments (1945); Sonata for Violin and Cello (1947); *Intermezzo concertante* for Saxophone and Orch. (1948); *Divertimento* for Viola and Cello (1949); Concerto Grosso (1949); *Notturno* for Flute, Violin, and Viola (1950); String Trio (1951); *Sonata breve* for Violin, Cello, and Piano (1952); *Sonata Californiana* for Alto Saxophone and Piano (1952); one-act opera, *Kumana* (1953); Sonata for Unaccompanied Cello (1956); *Room No. 12* and *Royal Auction,* a pair of one-act operas (Los Angeles, Feb. 26, 1958); Sonatina for Viola and Piano (1958); *The Lucky Dollar,* opera (1959); Suite for Brass Quintet (1960); *Perpetual,* opera (Los Angeles, April 26, 1961); *Cantata 1961* for Mixed Chorus and 2 Pianos (1961); *Visions at Midnight,* opera-cantata (Los Angeles, Feb. 26, 1964); Bassoon Concerto (San Francisco, April 8, 1964); *Sinfonia seria* (St. Louis, Oct. 17, 1964); Symph. No. 2 (1965; San Francisco, Dec. 11, 1968); *Little Concerto* for Unaccompanied Saxophone (Chicago, Dec. 15, 1970). He also publ. *A*

Counterpoint Manual: Fundamental Techniques of Polyphonic Music Writing (Boston, 1948).

Kann, Hans, Austrian pianist and composer; b. Vienna, Feb. 14, 1927. He studied piano with A. Göllner; composition with Pollnaur. After World War II, he gave a series of piano recitals in Europe; won prizes at piano competitions in Geneva, Munich, and Vienna. He taught at the Academy of Music in Vienna (1950–52); then taught piano at the Univ. of Arts in Tokyo (1955–58). Returning to Europe, he gave courses in advanced piano techniques at the Inst. of New Music in Darmstadt (1963–69); publ. several collections of piano exercises.

Kanner, Jerome Herbert, American violinist, composer, and arranger; b. New York, Nov. 17, 1903. He made his debut as a violinist in N.Y. at the age of 8; studied violin with Kneisel, Stoeving, and Auer; conducting with Walter Damrosch and Albert Stoessel; composition with Edward Kilenyi; also took lessons with Ravel in Paris. After 1925 he gave up the violin and devoted himself mainly to composing and conducting for radio and motion pictures. He composed 2 symphs.; a symph. poem, *The Rubayat;* and songs in the light vein.

Kanner-Rosenthal, Hedwig, piano pedagogue; b. Budapest, June 3, 1882; d. Asheville, N.C., Sept. 5, 1959. She studied with Leschetizky and **Moriz Rosenthal,** whom she married; appeared with him in duo recitals; taught in Vienna; in 1939 settled in N.Y. as a teacher.

Kantner, Paul, American pop musician and songwriter; b. San Francisco, March 12, 1942. He was a founding member of The Jefferson Airplane and contributed to its first album, *Jefferson Airplane Takes Off.* His own songs form a bridge between hippie ballads and psychedelic rock; later he was preoccupied with science fiction and expansion of consciousness, as expressed in *Wooden Ships* (co-authored with David Crosby and Steve Stills) and *We Can Be Together;* he also was an eager participant in militant politics. In another avatar, he gave voice to the themes of unrequited love, as in his songs *Won't You Try* and *Saturday Afternoon.* He remained the constant member of the original Jefferson Airplane throughout its late psychedelic era.

Kapell, William, brilliant American pianist; b. New York, Sept. 20, 1922, of Russian and Polish parents; d. in an airplane crash at King's Mountain, near San Francisco, Oct. 29, 1953. He studied with Olga Samaroff at the Philadelphia Cons. of Music; made his N.Y. debut on Oct. 28, 1941; subsequently appeared as a soloist with all major American orchs. and also in Europe, specializing in modern music. He met his death returning from an Australian concert tour.

Kaper, Bronislaw, Polish-born American songwriter; b. Warsaw, Feb. 5, 1902; d. (of cancer) Beverly Hills, Calif., April 26, 1983. He received his academic education in music at the Warsaw Cons.; left Poland in the 1920s, and proceeded to Hollywood via Berlin and Paris. An adept and intelligent musician who understood the requirements of the popular idiom, he composed background music for numerous films, among them *San Francisco, Gaslight,* 2 versions of *Mutiny on the Bounty* (with Clark Gable in 1935 and Marlon Brando in 1962), and *Lili* (for which he received an Academy Award in 1953).

Kaplan, Mark, outstanding American violinist; b. Cambridge, Mass., Dec. 30, 1953. He was brought up in Syracuse, N.Y.; began violin lessons as a small child; at the age of 8 he won a local violin competition, and enrolled as a student of Dorothy DeLay at the Juilliard School of Music in N.Y.; received its Fritz Kreisler Memorial Award. In 1973 he was awarded the prestigious Award of Special Distinction at the Leventritt Competition in N.Y.; subsequently was a soloist with the N.Y. Phil., Philadelphia Orch., Cleveland Orch., Los Angeles Phil., and Minnesota Orch.; also played in Europe with the Berlin Phil., Stockholm Phil., North German Radio Symph. Orch. of Hamburg, and the Scottish National Orch. of Glasgow, meriting praise for his fine musicianship and virtuoso technique.

Kapp, Arthur, Estonian composer; b. Suure-Iani, Feb. 28, 1875; d. Tallinn (Reval), Jan. 14, 1952. He studied at the St. Petersburg Cons. with Rimsky-Korsakov. From 1904 to 1920 he was director of the Cons. of Astrakhan, on the Volga; from 1920 to 1943, director of the Reval (Tallinn) Cons. in Estonia. In his capacity as a prof. of composition there he was the teacher of a generation of Estonian musicians. WORKS: 4 symphs., concertos (for piano, violin, cello, clarinet, and french horn), and a String Sextet. His Symph. No. 4, subtitled *Youth Symphony* (1949), was awarded the State Prize in 1949, and the First Stalin Prize in 1950; he also wrote a cantata, *For Peace* (1951).

Kapp, Eugen, notable Estonian composer, son of **Arthur Kapp;** b. Astrakhan, May 26, 1908. He studied with his father, who was director of the Astrakhan Cons.; followed him to Estonia in 1920, and graduated from the Tallinn Cons. there in 1931; succeeded his father as prof. of composition at the Tallinn Cons. and served as its director until 1965. WORKS: His operas, *Flames of Vengeance* (Tallinn, July 21, 1945) and *Freedom's Singer* (Tallinn, July 20, 1950), were awarded Stalin prizes. Other works: ballet, *Kalevipoeg* (1949); *Patriotic Symphony;* cantata, *Power of the People;* 2 violin sonatas; piano pieces; choral works. BIBLIOGRAPHY: G.A. Polyanovsky, *Eugen Kapp* (Moscow, 1951); H. Kyrvits, *Eugen Kapp* (Moscow, 1959).

Kapp, Julius, German writer on music; b. Seelbach in Baden, Oct. 1, 1883; d. Sonthofen, March 18, 1962. He studied in Marburg, Berlin, and Munich; received his Dr.Phil. in 1906. From 1904 to 1907 he was editor of *Literarischer Anzeiger,* which he founded in 1904; in 1923–45 was stage director of the Berlin State Opera and edited its bulletin, *Blätter der Staatsoper;* in 1948–54 held a similar post at the Berlin Municipal Opera.

WRITINGS: *Wagner und Liszt* (1908); *Franz Liszt* (1909; went through 20 printings before 1924); *Register zu Liszts Gesammelten Schriften* (1909); *Liszt-Brevier* (1910); *Liszt und die Frauen* (1911); *Wagner und die Frauen* (1912; 16th printing, 1929; completely rewritten and publ. in Eng. trans. as *The Loves of Richard Wagner,* London, 1951); *Paganini* (1913; many eds.; 15th ed., 1969); *Berlioz* (1914); *Das Dreigestirn: Berlioz—Liszt—Wagner* (1920); *Meyerbeer* (1920; 8th printing, 1932); *Franz Schreker* (1921); *Das Opernbuch* (1922; 16th printing, 1928); *Die Oper der Gegenwart* (1922); *Weber* (1922; 5th revised ed., 1931); *Die Staatsoper 1919 bis 1925* (1925); *Wagner und seine erste Elisabeth* (with H. Jachmann, 1926); *185 Jahre Staatsoper* (1928); *Wagner und die Berliner Staatsoper* (1933); *Wagner in Bildern* (1933); *Geschichte der Staatsoper Berlin* (1937); *200 Jahre Staatsoper in Bild* (1942). He ed. Liszt's *Gesammelte Schriften* (4 vols., 1910) and Wagner's *Gesammelte Schriften und Briefe* (24 vols., 1914).

Kapp, Richard, American conductor; b. Chicago, Oct. 9, 1936. He studied at Johns Hopkins Univ. (B.A., 1957); then took courses in conducting, composition, and piano at the Staatliche Hochschule für Musik in Stuttgart, Germany. Returning to the U.S., he studied jurisprudence at N.Y. Univ. (J.D., 1966) and had private lessons with Rosbaud and Halasz in conducting, with Simon in piano, and with Marlowe in harpsichord. He began his musical career as a répétiteur at the Stadttheater in Basel, Switzerland (1960–62); then was music director of the Opera Theater of the Manhattan School of Music in N.Y. (1963–65). In 1968 he led a concert in N.Y. with a specially assembled group billed as the Philharmonia Virtuosi; later toured with it in programs of varied repertoire, from Baroque to jazz.

Kapp, Villem, Estonian composer, nephew of **Arthur Kapp,** first cousin of **Eugen Kapp;** b. Suure-Jõani, Sept. 7, 1913; d. Tallinn, March 24, 1964. He studied music at the Tallinn Cons.; from 1944 was a prof. of composition there. He wrote in an expansive Romantic style rooted in folk song; his opera, *Lembitu* (Tallinn, Aug. 23, 1961), glorifies Estes Lembitu, the leader of the Estonian struggle against the invading Teutonic crusaders in 1217. He also wrote 2 symphs., chamber music, and choral pieces.

BIBLIOGRAPHY: Helga Tönson, *Villem Kapp* (Tallinn, 1967).

Kappel, Gertrude, German soprano; b. Halle, Sept. 1, 1884; d. Pullach, April 3, 1971. She studied with Nikisch and Noe at the Leipzig Cons.; made her debut in 1903 at the Hannover Opera, after which she was engaged in Munich, Berlin, and Vienna for the leading Wagnerian roles; appeared also in Amsterdam, Brussels, Madrid, London, and Paris; made her first American appearance as Isolde with the Metropolitan Opera on Jan. 16, 1928, and remained a member until 1936; in 1932, sang the title part in *Elektra* at its first Metropolitan performance; in 1933 she joined the roster of the San Francisco Opera Co.; retired in 1937 and returned to Germany.

Kapr, Jan, Czech composer; b. Prague, March 12, 1914. He studied first with his father, who was a professional musician; then took courses at the Prague Cons. with Řídký and later with J. Křička (1933–40). He was music producer with the Czech Radio (1939–46), a music critic (1946–49), and an editor in music publishing (1950–54); from 1961 to 1970 he taught at the Janáček Academy of Musical Arts in Brno. His style of composition is derived from the Czech national school; in his later works he audaciously introduced modernistic serial procedures.

WORKS: Opera, *Muzikantská pohádka (Musicians' Fairy Tale;* 1962); 2 piano concertos (1938, 1953); *Marathon,* symph. scherzo (1939); Sinfonietta for Small Orch. (1940); 8 symphs.: No. 1 (1943); No. 2 (1946); No. 3 for Small Orch. (1946); No. 4 (1957); No. 5, *Olympijská (Olympic;* 1959); No. 6 (1960; revised 1964); No. 7, *Krajina dětství (Country of Childhood),* for Children's Chorus and Orch. (1968); No. 8, *Campanae Pragenses (The Bells of Prague),* for Chorus, Orch., and Bell Sounds on Tape (1970); 2 cantatas: *A Song to the Native Land* (1950) and *In the Soviet Land* (1950); *Harvested,* symph. rhapsody (1950); *Zitra (Tomorrow),* symph. picture (1953); *Léto (Summer)* for Chamber Orch. (1954); *Allegretto* for Violin and Orch. (1955); Violin Concerto (1955); Variations for Flute and String Orch. (1958); Concertino for Viola and Wind Orch. (1965); *Omaggio alla tromba* for 2 Solo Trumpets, Wind Orch., Piano, and Timpani (1967–68; Prague, March 6, 1970); *Anachron* for Chamber Orch. (1974); Concertino for Clarinet and Chamber Ensemble (1975); 7 string quartets (1937; 1941; 1954; 1957; 1961; with Solo Baritone, 1963; 1965); Nonet (1943); Fantasy for Violin and Piano (1958); *4 Moods* for Nonet (1959); *Contrario romana* for Baritone and Piano (1965); *Dialogues* for Flute and Harp (1965); *Šifry (Ciphers)* for Piano, Percussion, and Tape (1966); *Oscilace (Oscillation)* for Violin, Clarinet, Trumpet, Piano, Cello, and Percussion (1965); *Rotation 9* for Piano Quartet (1967); *Shadow Play and Dreambook* for Soprano, Flute, and Harp (1968); Sonata for Solo Cimbalom (1968); *Testimonies* for Cello, Bass Clarinet, Piano, and Light Source (1969); *Woodcuts* for 8 Brass (1973); *Colors of Silence* for 8 Instruments (1973); *Circuli* for Violin and Accordion (1974); *Vendanges* for Soprano, Baritone, and Piano (1974); *Molto vivo* for Solo Flute (1974); *Signals* for Trumpet and Piano (1976); Sonata for Flute, Horn, and Piano (1976); 3 piano sonatas (1945, 1947, 1958); *Home,* cycle for Piano (1953–55); *Bagatelles* for Piano (1957); *Momente* for Piano (1957); Variations for Piano (1961); *Chess Sonata* for 2 Pianos, one live and one on tape (1972); *Příležitosti (Opportunities)* for Piano (1976); choruses; film music. He publ. a vol. on new music: *Konstanty (The Constants;*

Prague, 1967).

Kaprál, Václav, Czech composer, father of **Vítěz-slava Kaprálová;** b. Určice, near Prostějova, Moravia, March 26, 1889; d. Brno, April 6, 1947. He studied composition with Janáček in Brno (1907–10) and with Novák in Prague (1919–20); then took piano lessons with Alfred Cortot in Paris (1923–24). He established his own music school in Brno in 1911; lectured at the Univ. of Brno (1927–36); then taught at the Brno Cons. from 1936 until his 3-year internment in a concentration camp in Svatobořice during World War II; in 1946, became a prof. at the Music Academy in Brno. In his works he shows a fine eclectic talent.

WORKS: He wrote mostly for piano: 4 sonatas (1912, 1921, 1924, 1939); Nocturne (1915); *Spring Lullabies* (1916–17); *Suita romantica* (1918); the highly modern *Miniatures* (1924); *Con duolo* for Left Hand Alone (1926); 3 sonatinas (1930; *Sonatina bucolica,* 1936; 1943); Fantasy (1934); also *Wedding March* for Orch. (1923); 2 string quartets (1925, 1927); *Pizeň podzimu (Song of Autumn)* for Voice and String Quartet (1929); *5 uspávanky (5 Lullabies)* for Voice and Small Orch. (1932–33; perf. at the International Society for Contemporary Music Festival, Barcelona, April 20, 1936); *Ballad* for Cello and Piano (1946).

Kaprálová, Vítězslava, Czech composer, daughter of **Václav Kaprál** (family names in Slavic languages assume adjectival gender endings); b. Brno, Jan. 24, 1915; d. Montpellier, France, June 16, 1940. She received her early education from her father; then (1930–35) studied at the Brno Cons. under Vilém Petrželka (conducting and composition); later at the Prague Cons. with Novák (composition) and Talich (conducting). In 1937 she received a scholarship to Paris, where she took lessons in conducting with Munch and composition with Martinu. Her early death, from tuberculosis, cut short a remarkable career.

WORKS: *Suite en miniature* for Orch. (1932–35); Piano Concerto (Brno, June 17, 1935); *Military Sinfonietta* (Prague, Nov. 26, 1937); *Suita rustica* (Brno, April 16, 1939); *Partita* for String Orch. and Piano (perf. posthumously, Brno, Nov. 12, 1941); *Christmas Prelude* for Chamber Orch. (1939); Concertino for Violin, Clarinet, and Orch. (1940; unfinished); *Legenda a Burleska* for Violin and Piano (1932); *Sonata appassionata* for Piano (1933); String Quartet (1936); *6 Variations on the Bells of the Church of Saint Etienne in Paris* for Piano (1938); *2 Ritournelles* for Cello and Piano (1940).

Kapsberger, Johann Hieronymus von, 17th-century composer of a noble German family (known in Italy as **Giovanni Geronimo Tedesco della Tiorba,** because of his ability as a player); b. Venice, c.1580; d. Rome, 1651. He was a noted virtuoso on the theorbo, chitarrone, lute, and trumpet. He lived in Venice about 1604, and then in Rome, enjoying the favor of Pope Urban VIII. His compositions are in the then "modern" Florentine style; those for lute are written in a much simplified lute tablature.

WORKS: *Intavolatura di chitarrone* (3 books: 1604, 1616, 1626); *Villanelle a 1, 2 e 3 voci* (4 books: 1610, 1619, 1619, 1623); *Arie passeggiate* (2 books: 1612, 1623); *Intavolatura di lauto* (2 books: 1611, 1623); *Motetti passeggiati* (1612); *Balli, gagliarde e correnti* (1615); *Sinfonie a 4 con il basso continuo* (1615); *Capricci a due stromenti, tiorba e tiorbino* (1617); *Missae Urbanae,* 4–8 voices (1631); *Apotheosis of St. Ignatius de Loyola;* musical drama, *Fetonte* (1630); wedding cantatas; etc.

BIBLIOGRAPHY: J. Wolf, *Handbuch der Notationskunde* (vol. 2, pp. 194ff.).

Karabits, Ivan, Soviet composer; b. Yalta, Jan. 17, 1945. He studied at the Kiev Cons. with Boris Liatoshynsky, graduating in 1971.

WORKS: *Little Symphony* for String Orch. (1967); 2 piano concertos (1968, 1972); 2 symphs. (1974, in 5 movements; 1975, in 3 movements); *Little Concerto* for Chamber Orch. (1970); *The Garden of Divine Songs* for Soloists, Chorus, and Orch. (1971); 2 cello sonatas (1968, 1972); String Quartet (1973); *Divertimento concertante* for 6 Performers (1975); *Impromptu* for Viola and Piano (1976); 24 Preludes for Piano (1976); numerous vocal cycles to Ukrainian words.

Karabtchevsky, Isaac, Brazilian conductor; b. São Paulo, Dec. 27, 1934. He studied in Brazil; then went to Germany to continue his education at the Hochschule für Musik in Freiburg. Upon his return to Brazil, in 1969, he became music director of the Brazil Symph. Orch. in Rio de Janeiro; also was a guest conductor in the U.S. His conducting is marked by an expansively Romantic quality, much in the vein of the old Russian school of interpretation.

Karajan, Herbert von, great conductor in the grand Germanic tradition; b. Salzburg, April 5, 1908. He was a scion of a cultured musical family; his great-grandfather **Theodore von Karajan** was a learned music scholar. His parentage was partly Serbian and partly Greek; his father, Ernst von Karajan, was a medical officer; his mother's maiden name was Martha Cosmâc. His father played the clarinet; his brother was a child pianist; and he too began taking piano lessons at a very early age. He attended the Mozarteum in Salzburg, where he studied piano and also took conducting lessons with the director of the Mozarteum, Bernard Paumgartner; later he went to Vienna, where he studied conducting with Franz Schalk at the Vienna Academy of Music. He made his debut as a conductor there on Dec. 17, 1928, with a student orch. In 1929 he received his first appointment as a conductor, at the Ulm Staatheater. From Ulm he went to Aachen, where he was engaged to conduct opera and symph. concerts (1934). In 1936 he conducted *Tristan und Isolde* at the Vienna State Opera; in 1937 he conducted a concert of the Berlin Phil., and in 1938 was engaged to conduct *Fidelio* at the Berlin Städtische Oper (Sept. 30, 1938). His reputation as an impeccable technician and disciplinarian was firmly established during his tenure at the Berlin Opera, so that the *Berliner Tageblatt* once referred to him as "das Wunder Karajan." His capacity of absorbing the music at hand and transmitting its essence to the public became his most signal characteristic; he conducted all his scores from memory, including Wagner's *Ring*. He also began to accept engagements abroad; in 1938 he conducted at La Scala in Milan and also made guest appearances in Belgium, the Netherlands, and Scandinavia. He continued to conduct in Berlin throughout the devastation of the war. There was a dark side to Karajan's character, revealing his lack of human sensitivity and even a failure to act in his own interests. He became fascinated with the organizing solidity of the National Socialist Party in Germany; on April 9, 1933, he registered in the Salzburg office of the Austrian National Socialist Party; his party number was 607525. A month later he joined the German Nazi organization in Ulm under No. 3430914. He lived to regret these actions after the Nazi *Götterdämmerung,* but he was denazified by the Allies' army of occupation in 1946. On June 15, 1932, Karajan married **Elmy Holgerloef,** an operetta soprano; he divorced her in 1942 and married Anita Gutermann; he divorced her, too, after he found out that her ancestry was partly Jewish. He retired to Salzburg to await his political clearance, and on Jan. 12, 1946, he was permitted to lead the Vienna Phil. He was also allowed to make recordings with the Vienna Phil. for the British division of Columbia Gramophone Co. In 1948 he was appointed artistic director of the Gesellschaft der Musikfreunde in Vienna, and was also named music director of the Vienna Symph. In 1950 he was engaged as music director at La Scala in Milan; later he led the Bach Festival in Vienna. In 1951 he conducted the complete cycle of *Der Ring des Nibelungen,* and in 1952 conducted in Bayreuth a new production of *Tristan und Isolde.* He was also engaged as music director of the London Phil. Orch., with which he gave concerts in Germany, Austria, France, and Switzerland. In 1954 he became principal conductor of the Berlin Phil. When Furtwängler died in Nov. 1954, on the eve of an announced tour of the Berlin Phil. in the U.S., Karajan took the orch. over and gave a series of memorable performances with it in American cities. Ironically, there were no organized protests of Karajan's employment, even though Furtwängler's engagement with the N.Y. Phil. some years before were canceled because of his alleged toleration of Nazi philosophy; yet Furtwängler never joined the Nazi party, while Karajan joined it twice. On his 47th birthday, April 5, 1955, the members of the Berlin Phil. elected him artistic director and conductor. He became to all intents and purposes an absolute dictator of the affairs of the Berlin Phil., brooking no insubordination whatsoever; a minor scandal erupted in 1982 when Karajan insisted on engaging a young lady clarinetist as the principal of the clarinet section of the orch., threatening to discontinue the highly lucrative recording activities should his request be refused; a compromise was reached in which she was allowed to play with the orch. on

probation; apart from her apparent lack of orch. experience, her engagement would have broken the established tradition of the Berlin Phil. in excluding women from membership. His association with the Berlin Phil. made it impossible for him to continue his formal contract as chief conductor of the Vienna Symph., and he resigned his Vienna position in 1960. His American connections grew stronger when he brought the Berlin Phil. to the U.S. in 1976, and again in 1982, when he conducted a triumphant series of concerts in N.Y. and Los Angeles. About that time he was named permanent conductor and music director of the Berlin Phil. for life. He made an operatic debut in America conducting *Die Walküre* at the Metropolitan Opera in N.Y. on Nov. 21, 1967. He was popular in France, and served as artistic adviser of the Orch. de Paris from 1969–71. In 1968 he established the Karajan Foundation for the purpose of promoting biennial international competitions for young conductors. As his fame spread, he conducted all over the world; in 1962 he took the Vienna Phil. Orch. to Russia; he took the La Scala Orch. to Russia in 1964, and the Berlin Phil. in 1969. He was the recipient of numerous honorary titles; he received the Mozart Ring in Vienna in 1957 and the Prix France-Allemagne in 1970. Finland awarded him the Order of the White Rose. In 1973 he was elevated to the rank of Honorary Citizen of West Berlin. The great reputation that Karajan earned despite political disadvantages is explained by his extraordinary capacity for systematic work, his emotional strength, and his justified self-assurance; both in opera and in symph. he is capable of achieving superlative performances. His cycles of Beethoven symphs. are recognized as exemplary in fidelity to style and excellence of execution.

BIBLIOGRAPHY: Harold Schonberg, *The Great Conductors* (N.Y., 1967; pp. 324–26); Ernst Haeussermann, *Herbert von Karajan* (Gütersloh, 1968); Christian Spiel, ed., *Anekdoten um Herbert von Karajan* (Munich, 1968); P. Robinson, *Karajan* (Toronto, 1975); W. Stresemann, *The Berlin Philharmonic from Bülow to Karajan* (in German and Eng., Berlin, 1979; pp. 90–106).

Karajan, Theodor Georg von, Austrian writer on music, great-grandfather of **Herbert von Karajan;** b. Vienna, Jan. 22, 1810; d. there, April 28, 1873. He studied history, philology, and law; after holding various minor posts, he became president of the Austrian Academy of Science (1866–69). His important monograph *J. Haydn in London, 1791 und 1792* (Vienna, 1861) contains Haydn's correspondence with Maria Anna von Genzinger; he also publ. *Aus Metastasios Hofleben* (Vienna, 1861).

Karasowski, Moritz, Polish writer on music; b. Warsaw, Sept. 22, 1823; d. Dresden, April 20, 1892. He was a cellist in the opera orch. in Warsaw from 1851, and later court cellist at Dresden. He publ. (in Polish) *History of Polish Opera* (Warsaw, 1859) and *Life of Mozart* (1868), but his most important contribution was his book *Chopin's Youth* (1862), and particularly the first comprehensive biography of

Chopin, publ. in German as *F. Chopin, Sein Leben, seine Werke und Briefe* (Dresden, 1877; in Eng., N.Y., 1878).

Karastoyanov, Assen, Bulgarian composer; b. Samokov, June 3, 1893; d. Sofia, Sept. 8, 1976. He studied flute at the Sofia State Music School (1914–18); then went to Germany, where he took lessons in music theory with Paul Juon at the Berlin Hochschule für Musik (1921–22); later took a course in composition with Paul Dukas at the Ecole Normale de Musique in Paris (1930–31); went again to Germany and enrolled at the Leipzig State Cons. as a composition student of Günther Raphael. Returning to Bulgaria, he taught for 25 years at the State Cons. in Sofia (1933–58).
WORKS: 7 operettas, including *Michel Strogoff*, after Jules Verne (1937–40); 7 patriotic cantatas; *A Balkan Suite* for Orch. (1928); 4 symphs.: No. 1, *Miner's Symphony* (1940); No. 2, *Danubian*, for Brass Orch. (1960); No. 3, *Rhodopean* (1973); No. 4, *Proto-Bulgarian* (1975); Flute Concerto (1959); *A Bogomil Legend* for String Orch. (1973); 2 string quartets (1937, 1970); 2 suites for Flute and Piano (1955, 1968); *Capriccio* for Violin and Piano (1970); *Scherzino* for Piano (1933); Piano Sonata (1938); songs.

Karatygin, Vyacheslav, Russian writer on music; b. Pavlovsk, Sept. 17, 1875; d. Leningrad, Oct. 23, 1925. He learned to play the piano from his mother, who was a professional pianist, but he entered the Univ. of St. Petersburg as a student of chemistry; from 1898 to 1907 he worked in a chemical factory in St. Petersburg; at the same time took lessons in composition with Sokolov; from 1907 until 1917 he served as a music critic on various publications and gave courses at several conservatories and music schools. A broad-minded musician, he welcomed the music of Scriabin, Stravinsky, and Prokofiev at a time when most Russian critics regarded them as unacceptable, and he enunciated the idea of a "musical revolution." He publ. monographs on Mussorgsky, Chaliapin, and Scriabin, and he himself composed some piano pieces and songs. A memorial collection of articles, *V.G. Karatygin, His Life and Work,* was publ. by the Russian Inst. for the History of Art (Leningrad, 1927).

Karayev, Kara, Soviet composer; b. Baku, Feb. 5, 1918; d. Moscow, May 13, 1982. He studied piano and theory in Baku; then took courses in composition with Shostakovich at the Moscow Cons., graduating in 1946. From 1949 to 1953 he was director of the Azerbaijani Cons. in Baku. His music is derived mainly from his semi-oriental environment, comprising not only the native Tartar motifs, but also other Asian resources; particularly effective are his theatrical spectacles featuring native dances and choral ensembles.
WORKS: Opera, *Fatherland* (1945); ballets: *Seven Beauties* (1952) and *On the Track of Thunder* (1958); cantatas: *The Song of the Heart* (1938) and *The Song of Happiness* (1947); oratorio, *Hymn of Friendship* (1972); for Orch.: 3 symphs. (1944, 1946, 1965); *Leyly and Medzhnun,* symph. poem (1947); *Albanian Rhapsody* (1952); *Don Quixote,* symph. sketches (1960); *Poem of Joy* for Piano and Orch. (1937); Violin Concerto (1967); numerous pieces for folk instruments; 2 string quartets; a series of piano pieces, including 24 preludes; choruses; film music.
BIBLIOGRAPHY: L. Karagicheva, *Kara Karayev* (Baku, 1956).

Kardoš, Dezider, Slovak composer; b. Nadlice, Dec. 23, 1914. He studied composition with Alexander Moyzes at the Bratislava Academy of Music and Drama (1932–37), and with Vítězslav Novák at the Prague Cons. (1937–39). He worked at the Czech Radio in Prešov (1939–45) and Košice (1945–51) in eastern Slovakia. In 1961 he was appointed prof. of composition at the Academy of Music in Bratislava. The thematic sources of his musical inspiration are found in eastern Slovak folklore.
WORKS: *Peace Cantata* (1951); 6 symphs.: No. 1 (1942); No. 2, *Of Native Land* (1955); No. 3 (1961); No. 4, *Piccola* (1962); No. 5 (1965); No. 6 (1974–75); 3 overtures: *My Home* (1946); *East Slovak Overture* (1950); *Res philharmonica* (1970); Concerto for Orch. (1957); *Heroic Ballad* for String Orch. (1959); Concerto for String Orch. (1963); Piano Concerto (1969); *Partita* for 12 Strings (1972); *Songs about Life,* cycle of 4 microdramas for Soprano, Tenor, and Orch. (1973–74); *Slovakophonia,* variations on a folk theme for Orch. (1975–76); 2 string quartets (1935, 1966); 2 suites for Piano (1937); Wind Quintet (1938); *Preludium quasi una fantasia* for Organ (1940); *Bagatelles* for Piano (1948); *3 Compositions for Violin and Piano* (1966); *Elevazioni* for Organ (1967); choruses and songs.

Kardos, István, Hungarian composer; b. Debrecen, June 6, 1891; d. Budapest, Dec. 22, 1975. He studied composition at the Academy of Music in Budapest. From 1917 to 1946 he conducted musical plays in Hungary, Germany, and Switzerland; taught at the Budapest Academy of Music (1948–59).
WORKS: *Dance* for Orch. (1918); 4 symphs. (1919, 1958, 1967, 1968); *Hungarian Scherzo* for Orch. (1936); Violin Concertino (1947); *Aprilisi hajnal (Dawn in April),* cantata (1950); *Janus* for Orch. (1950); 2 piano concertos (1956, 1963); Concertino for Double Bass and Orch. (1959); Double Concerto for Viola, Double Bass, and Orch. (1964); *Alliage* for Violin and Chamber Orch. (1966); *intrada* for Orch. (1968); *Visitation* for Orch. (1969); 6 string quartets (1917, 1925, 1951, 1960, 1967, 1971); Viola Sonata (1942); Double-bass Sonata (1949); Flute Sonata (1957); Wind Quintet (1959); String Trio (1960); *Bipartitum* for Bassoon and Piano (1963); Sonata for Solo Clarinet (1965); *Poem and Burlesque* for Double Bass and Piano (1969); 2 sextets for Clarinet, String Quartet, and Piano (1971); *Grotesque* for Octave Flute, Cello, and Double Bass (1971); *Notturno* for Horn, Flute, Violin, and Harp (1971); Piano Sonata (1916); piano pieces: *Dickens Suite* (1957); *Toccata* (1960); *Variations and Fugue* (1969); songs.

Karel, Rudolf, Czech composer; b. Pilsen, Nov. 9, 1880; d. at the Terezín concentration camp, March 6, 1945. He was the last student of Dvořák, with whom he studied in Prague for one year during Karel's term at the Prague Cons. (1901–4). In 1914 he went to Russia as a teacher, and remained there during World War I. After the Revolution he made his way to Irkutsk, Siberia; during the Russian civil war he became a member of the Czechoslovak Legion and conducted an orch. organized by the legionnaires. He returned to Prague in 1920; from 1923 to 1941 taught at the Prague Cons. As a member of the Czech resistance in World War II, he was arrested by the Nazis in March 1943; was transferred to Terezín in Feb. 1945, and died there of dysentery shortly before liberation. His music reflects the Romantic concepts; he had a predilection for programmatic writing; the national element is manifested by his treatment of old modal progressions; his instrumental writing is rich in sonority; the polyphonic structure is equally strong.
WORKS: Lyric comedy, *Ilseino srdce* (*Ilsea's Heart;* 1906–9; Prague, Oct. 11, 1924); 2 musical fairy tales: *Smrt Kmotřička* (*Godmother Death;* 1928–33; Brno, Feb. 3, 1933) and *Tři vlasy děda Vševěda* (*3 Hairs of the Wise Old Man;* 1944–45; his last work, written in camp, left as a draft only, arranged by his student Zbyněk Vostřák, and perf. posthumously in Prague, Oct. 28, 1948); Suite for Orch. (1903–4); *Comedy Overture* (1904–5); Fantasy for Orch. (1905); *Ideály* (*The Ideals)*, symph. epic from an artist's life (1906–9); 2 symphs.: *Renaissance* (1910–11) and *Spring* (1935–38); 2 other symphs., of 1904 and 1917, are lost; *Vzkříšení* (*Resurrection)*, symph. for Soli, Chorus, and Orch. (1923–27; Prague, April 9, 1928); *Capriccio* for Violin and Orch. (1924); *4 Slavonic Dance Moods* for Orch. (1912); *The Demon,* symph. poem (1918–20); *Revolutionary Overture* (1938–41); *Sladká balada dětská* (*Sweet Ballad for a Child)* for Soprano, Chorus, and Orch. (1928–30); *Černoch* (*A Negro)*, exotic ballad for Baritone, and Orch. or Piano (1934); 3 string quartets (1902–3, 1907–13, 1935–36); Piano Trio (1903–4); Violin Sonata (1912); Nonet for Wind Quintet and String Quartet (1945; left in draft form and completed by F. Hertl); Piano Sonata (1910); other piano pieces: *5 Pieces* (1902); *Notturno* (1906–7); *Thema con variazioni* (1910); *3 Waltzes* (1913); *Burlesques* (1913–14); also, choruses; songs; incidental music.
BIBLIOGRAPHY: O. Šourek, *Rudolf Karel* (Prague, 1947).

Karg-Elert, Sigfrid, distinguished German organist and composer; b. Oberndorf, Württemberg, Nov. 21, 1877; d. Leipzig, April 9, 1933. He studied with Reinecke and Jadassohn at the Leipzig Cons.; in 1919 was appointed to its staff. Concurrently with his teaching activities, he began to give organ recitals, and soon became known as one of the greatest virtuosos on the instrument; he also played on the Kunstharmonium, for which he wrote many original compositions. His real name, **Karg,** sounded unattractive to his audiences (it means "avaricious"), and he changed it to Karg-Elert. As a com-

poser, he developed a brilliant style, inspired by the music of the Baroque, but he embellished this austere and ornamental idiom with impressionistic devices; the result was an ingratiating type of music with an aura of originality. In 1932 he undertook a concert tour in the U.S.
WORKS: For Kunstharmonium: sets of pieces: *Skizzen* (1903); *Aquarellen* (1906); *Miniaturen* (1908); *Intarsien* (1911); *Impressions* (1914); *Idyllen* (1915); *Innere Stimmen* (1918); fundamental technical works: *Die Kunst des Registrierens; Die ersten grundlegenden Studien; Hohe Schule des Legatospiels; Die Harmoniumtechnik (Gradus ad Parnassum); Theoretische-praktische Elementarschule.* For Organ: 66 chorale improvisations (1908–10); 20 chorale preludes and postludes (1912); 10 *Poetic Tone Pictures;* 3 *Pastels, Cathedral Windows* (on Gregorian themes); Wind Quintet; 2 clarinet sonatas; Sonata for Flute Unaccompanied; *Trio bucolico* for Violin, Flute, and Piano; a number of lieder. He publ. *Akustische Ton-, Klang-, und Funktionsbestimmung* (1930) and *Polaristiche Klang- und Tonalitätslehre* (1931).
BIBLIOGRAPHY: Hans Avril publ. a catalogue of Karg-Elert's works: *Kompositions-verzeichnis mit einer monographischen Skizze* (Berlin, 1928). See also A. Eaglefield Hull, "Karg-Elert," *Musical Times* (Feb.–March 1913); H.B. Gaul, "Bonnet, Bossi, Karg-Elert," *Musical Quarterly* (July 1918); Paul Schenk, *Sigfrid Karg-Elert* (Berlin, 1927); Godfrey Sceats, *The Organ Works of Karg-Elert* (Orpington, 1940; revised ed., London, 1950); Walter Kwasnik, *S. Karg-Elert: Sein Leben und Werk in Heutiger Sicht* (1971).

Karjalainen, Ahti, Finnish composer; b. Oulu (Uleaborg), March 20, 1907. He studied composition at the Helsinki Cons., the Viipuri (Vyborg) Inst., and the Sibelius Academy; played violin and trombone in various orchs.; later conducted the Jyväskylä City Orch.
WORKS: *Polonaise* for Trombone and Orch. (1935); *Scherzo* for Trumpet, Trombone, and Orch. (1940); Trombone Concerto (1942); *Summer Scenes* for Oboe and Orch. (1944); *Winter Scenes* for Orch. (1948); Symph. No. 1 (1948); *Concert Suite* for Bassoon and Orch. (1949); Duo for 2 Trumpets and Orch. (1950); Violin Concerto (1952); *Ostinato* for Cello and Orch. (1954); 2 cello concertos (1956, 1966); *The Eagle's Way* for Chorus and Orch. (1965); *Setting Out* for Narrator, Baritone, Mixed Chorus, Male Chorus, and Orch. (1968); *The Song of Wood,* cantata (1971); 6 partitas for various instrumental combinations (1936, 1940, 1945, 1961, 1964, 1965); Wind Sextet (1945); other chamber music; songs; solo pieces.

Karkoff, Maurice Ingvar, prominent Swedish composer; b. Stockholm, March 17, 1927. He studied piano and conducting at the Royal Academy of Music in Stockholm (1948–53); composition with Blomdahl, Lars-Erik Larsson, Erland von Koch in Stockholm, with Holmboe in Copenhagen, and later with Nadia Boulanger and André Jolivet in Paris (1957),

Wladimir Vogel in Switzerland (1959–61), and Alexander Boscovich in Tel Aviv (1963). Returning to Sweden in 1965, he devoted himself principally to teaching. In his music he absorbed many cultures; these are reflected in his style of composition, which may be described as romantic modernism; thematically he is sensitive to exotic resources and coloristic instrumental timbres.

WORKS: FOR ORCH.: *Serenade* for Strings (1953); *Short Variations* for String Quartet (1953; revised 1956); Sinfonietta (1954); Saxophone Concertino (1955); 8 symphs.: No. 1 (1955–56; Bergen, Norway, Oct. 22, 1956); No. 2 (1957; Swedish Radio, Jan. 5, 1959); No. 3, *Sinfonia breve* (1958–59; Gävle, Jan. 10, 1960); No. 4 (1963; Stockholm, April 4, 1964); No. 5, *Sinfonia da camera* (1964–65; Gävle, Nov. 11, 1965); No. 6 (1972–73; Stockholm, Oct. 12, 1974); No. 7, *Sinfonia da camera* (1975); No. 8 (1979–80); *Short Symphony* for Symph. Band (Stockholm, Sept. 27, 1982); Violin Concerto (1956); Piano Concerto (1957); Cello Concerto (1957–58); *Lyric Suites I* and *II* for Chamber Orch. (1958); Trombone Concerto (1958); Horn Concerto (1959); *9 Aphoristic Variations* (1959); Clarinet Concerto (1959); Variations (1961); *Serenata* for Chamber Orch. (1961); *7 pezzi* (1963); *Oriental Pictures* (1965–66; also for Piano); Suite for Harpsichord and Strings (1962); *Concerto da camera* for Balalaika and Orch. (1962–63); Concerto for Orch. (1963); *Transfigurate mutate* (1966); *Tripartita* (1966–67); *Textum* for Strings (1967); *Metamorphoses* (1967); *Sinfonietta grave* (1968–69); *Epitaphium* for Small Chamber Orch. (1968; also for Nonet); *5 Summer Scenes* (1969); *Triptyk* (1970); *Partes caracteris* (1971); *Symphonic Reflexions* (1971); *Passacaglia* for Strings (1971); Trumpet Concerto (1977); *Texture* (1978). VOCAL MUSIC: *6 Allvarliga Songs* for High Voice and Orch. (1955); *Det Svenska Landet*, festival cantata (1956); *Livet*, songs and recitation for Low Voice and Orch. (1959); *Gesang des Abgeschiedenen*, 5 songs for Baritone, and Orch. or Piano (1959–60); *10 Japanese Songs* for High Voice, and Orch. or Piano (1959); *Himmel och Jord*, cantata (1960); *Sieben Rosen später*, cantata (1964); *Das ist sein Erlauten*, cantata (1965); *Landscape of Screams*, after Nelly Sachs, for Soprano, Narrator, and Instruments (1967); *6 Chinese Impressions* for High Voice and Instrumental Ensemble (1973); songs. CHAMBER MUSIC: Flute Sonata (1953); Cello Sonata (1954–55); Violin Sonata (1956); Wind Quintet (1956–57); String Quartet (1957); Quartet for 2 Trumpets, Horn, and Trombone (1958); String Trio (1960); *Chamber Concerto* for 14 Winds, Timpani, Percussion, and String Basses (1961); *Metamorphoses* for 4 Horns (1966); *Terzetto* for Flute, Cello, and Piano (1967); *3 Episodes* for Clarinet, Cello, and Piano (1968); *4 parte* for 13 Brasses and Percussion (1968); *4 momenti* for Violin and Piano (1970); *Epitaphium* for Accordion, Electric Guitar, and Percussion (1970); *6 pezzi breve* for Oboe Solo (1972); minor chamber pieces. PIANO MUSIC: Piano Sonata (1956); *Partita piccola* (1958); *Capriccio on Football* (1961; musical report on a football game); *Monopartita* (1969); *3 Expressions* for 2 Pianos (1971); other pieces for piano. Under the impression of his travels to Israel, he wrote a chamber opera, *The Boundary Kibbutz* (1972–73).

Karkoschka, Erhard, German composer; b. Ostrava, Bohemia, March 6, 1923. He studied music in Stuttgart and in Tübingen; in 1958 was appointed to the staff of the Hochschule für Musik in Stuttgart. He adopted the serial method of composition, following the example of Anton Webern; often incorporated electronics in his works; also resorted to graphic notation in order to achieve greater freedom of resulting sonorities. He wrote *Symphonische Evolutionen* (1953); *Kleines Konzert* for Violin and Chamber Orch. (1955); *Undarum continuum* for Orch. (1960); *Antinomie* for Wind Quintet (1968); *Quattrologe* for String Quartet (1966); *Tempora mutantur* for String Quartet (1971); electronic works; much choral music and stage melodramas. He publ. *Zur rhythmischen Struktur in der Musik von heute* (Kassel, 1962); *Das Schriftbild der neuen Musik* (Celle, 1966; in Eng. as *Notation in New Music*, London, 1972); and many magazine articles dealing with problems of new music.

Karl, Tom, Irish tenor; b. Dublin, Jan. 19, 1846; d. Rochester, N.Y., March 19, 1916. He studied in England with Henry Phillips, and in Italy with Sangiovanni. He sang in Italy for many years, then settled in N.Y. His remarkable success as Ralph in *Pinafore* (1879) made him resolve to abandon grand opera; some years later he organized (with H.C. Barnabee and W.H. MacDonald) the famous light opera company The Bostonians. He had a repertoire of about 150 operas and operettas. He retired in 1896; had an operatic school in N.Y.; then went to Rochester, where he taught singing.

Karlins, M. William, American composer; b. New York, Feb. 25, 1932. He studied composition in N.Y. with Frederick Piket (1954–57); then took courses with Vittorio Gianinni at the Manhattan School of Music (1958–61); later enrolled at the Univ. of Iowa (Ph.D., 1965). He taught at Western Illinois Univ. (1965–67); in 1967 joined the faculty at Northwestern Univ.; became a prof. there in 1973.

WORKS: *Concert Music I* for Orch. (1959); 3 piano sonatas (1959, 1962, 1965); *Concerto Grosso I* for 9 Instruments (1959–60); String Quartet, with Soprano (1960); *Concert Music II* for Chorus and Orch. (1960; Milwaukee, Feb. 14, 1971); *Concerto Grosso II* for 7 Solo Instruments (1961); *Outgrowths-Variations* for Piano (1961); *Birthday Music I* for Flute, Bass Clarinet, and Double Bass (1962); *Birthday Music II* for Flute and Double Bass (1962); String Trio (1962–63); *Concert Music III* for Winds, Brass, Piano, and Percussion (Urbana, Ill., April 17, 1964); *Solo Piece with Passacaglia* for Clarinet (1964); *Concert Music IV* for Orch. (Evanston, Ill., May 14, 1965); *Variations on "Obiter Dictum"* for Cello, Piano, and Percussion (1965); *Music for Solo Cello* (1966); *Music for Oboe, Bass Clarinet and Piano* (1966); Quartet No. 1 for Saxophones (1966–67); *Lamentations—In Memoriam* for Narrator and Chamber Group (1968); *Music for Alto Saxophone and Piano* (1968); *Music for Tenor Saxophones and*

Piano (1969); *Graphic Mobile* for any 3 or multiple of 3 Instruments (1969); Wind Quintet No. 1 (1970); *Reflux*, concerto for Double Bass and Wind Ensemble (Chicago, April 8, 1972); *Concert Music V* for Orch. (Chicago, Dec. 20, 1973); Quintet for Saxophone and String Quartet (1973–74); *4 Etudes* for Double Bass and Tape, or 3 Double Basses (1974); Quartet No. 2 for Saxophones (*Variations and Cadenzas*) (1975); *"and all our world is dew,"* Woodwind Quintet No. 2 (1977–78); *Infinity* for Oboe d'Amore, Clarinet, Viola, and Female Voice (1978); *Fantasia* for Tenor Saxophone and Percussion (1978–79); Symph. No. 1 (1979–80; Chicago, May 10, 1980); *Catena I* for Chamber Orch., with Clarinet obbligato (1980–81); *Fanfare with Fugato* for Cello, 2 Trumpets, and 2 Trombones (1981); Concerto for Alto Saxophone and Orch. (1981–82; Nuremberg, July 8, 1982); *Catena II* for Soprano Saxophone and Brass Quintet (1982); *Catena III,* concerto for Horn and Orch. (1983; Appleton, Wis., April 29, 1984).

Karlowicz, Jan, Polish music scholar, father of **Mieczyslaw Karlowicz;** b. Subortowicze, near Troki, May 28, 1836; d. Warsaw, June 14, 1903. He studied music in Wilno, Moscow, Paris, Brussels, and Berlin. Settling in Warsaw, he publ. translations of several German textbooks on harmony; also publ. (in Eng., German, and French) a pamphlet, *Project of a New Way of Writing Musical Notes* (Warsaw, 1876); composed some songs.
BIBLIOGRAPHY: F. Starczewski, *The Musical Activities of Jan Karlowicz* (Warsaw, 1904).

Karlowicz, Mieczyslaw, Polish composer, son of the theorist **Jan Karlowicz;** b. Wiszniewo, Dec. 11, 1876; d. Zakopane, Galicia, Feb. 8, 1909. He was sent to Germany to study violin as a child. In 1887 he began composition studies in Warsaw with Noskowski, Roguski, and Maszynski; violin with Barcewicz; later he continued his studies in Berlin with H. Urban (1895–1900). Returning to Warsaw, he devoted himself to composition and teaching; was director of the Warsaw Music Society (1904–6); after a sojourn in Germany (where he studied conducting with Nikisch in Leipzig), he settled in Zakopane; also traveled to France, Austria, and Germany. An enthusiastic mountain climber, he was killed in an accident, under an avalanche. Essentially a Romantic composer, he succeeded in blending the national elements of Polish folk music with the general European genre of mild modernism; there is an influence of Richard Strauss in his expansive tone painting. The appreciation of his music in Poland rose rather than declined after his death; some of his piano pieces and songs have been established in the concert repertoire.
WORKS: Serenade for String Orch. (1898); Symph. in E minor, subtitled *Renaissance* (1900); symph. poem, *Returning Waves* (1904); symph. trilogy, *Eternal Songs* (1907); *Lithuanian Rhapsody* for Orch. (1908); *Stanislaw and Anna of Oswiecim,* symph. poem (1908); *Sad Story,* symph. poem (1908); *Episode at the Masquerade,* symph. poem (1908–9; unfinished; completed by G. Fitel-

berg). He publ. some previously unknown letters of Chopin (Warsaw, 1904; in French as *Souvenirs inédits de F. Chopin,* Paris, 1904).
BIBLIOGRAPHY: F. Kecki, *Karlowicz* (Warsaw, 1934); A. Chybinski, *Karlowicz* (Cracow, 1947); Igor Boelza, *Karlowicz* (Moscow, 1951).

Karow, Karl, German composer; b. Alt-Stettin, Nov. 15, 1790; d. Bunzlau, Dec. 20, 1863. He taught music at Bunzlau; publ. a *Choralbuch,* a *Leitfaden für den Schulgesang-Unterricht,* motets, piano pieces, etc.

Karpath, Ludwig, Austrian singer and music critic; b. Budapest, April 27, 1866; d. Vienna, Sept. 8, 1936. He was a pupil at the Cons. in Budapest; studied singing in Vienna; was a member of the National Opera Co. in the U.S. (singing minor bass roles) for 3 seasons (1886–88); returning to Vienna, he became an influential music critic; for many years (1894–1921) wrote for the *Neues Wiener Tageblatt.* He publ. *Siegfried Wagner als Mensch und Künstler* (1902), *Zu den Briefen Wagners an eine Putzmacherin* (1906), *R. Wagner, der Schuldenmacher* (1914), and *Wagners Briefe an Hans Richter* (1924).

Kárpáti, János, Hungarian musicologist; b. Budapest, July 11, 1932. He studied musicology with Kodály, Szabolcsi, and Bartha at the Franz Liszt Academy of Music in Budapest; then was an editor with the music dept. of the Hungarian Radio (1957–59) and music producer with the Hungaroton Record Co. (1959–61); in 1961 he was named chief librarian of the Liszt Academy; he obtained his degree of Candidate of Sciences in 1968 and his Ph.D. in 1969 with the dissertation *Bartók vonósnegyesi* (publ. in Budapest, 1967; Eng. trans., augmented, Budapest, 1975). His books include *Domenico Scarlatti* (Budapest, 1959); *Arnold Schönberg* (Budapest, 1963); *Bartók kamarazenéje* (Budapest, 1976); *Kelet zenéje* (*Music of the Orient;* Budapest, 1981). He compiled the 2nd and 4th vols. for an encyclopedic edition, *Muzsikáló zenetörténet (History of Music).* In 1981 he was guest lecturer at Harvard Univ.; in 1982 he was a delegate at the Bartók Memorial Conference in Bloomington, Ind., and in 1983 was a guest lecturer at the Univ. of Calif. at Los Angeles, at North Texas Univ. in Denton, and at the Univ. of Texas in Austin.

Karpeles Maud, English ethnomusicologist; b. London, Nov. 12, 1885; d. there Oct. 1, 1976. She became an associate with Cecil Sharp in collecting and organizing English folk songs; in 1915 she went to the U.S., where she assembled American songs of English origin, publ. in 2 vols., *English Folk Songs from the Southern Appalachians* (London, 1917; 1932); she further publ. *Songs from Newfoundland* (London, 1934; 2nd ed., 1970). From 1949 to 1963 she edited the annual *Journal of the International Folk Music Council.* In 1961 she was made a Dame Commander of the Order of the British Empire. Among her many publications were *Cecil Sharp* (London, 1933; reprinted 1955, in collaboration with

A.H. Fox Strangways); *Folk Songs of Europe* (London, 1956; N.Y., 1964); *An Introduction to English Folk Song* (London, 1973).

BIBLIOGRAPHY: Willard Rhodes, "Memorial Obituary: Maud Karpeles 1885–1976," *Ethnomusicology* (May 1977).

Karr, Gary, American virtuoso double-bass player; b. Los Angeles, Nov. 20, 1941. He was a scion of a family of musicians which numbered 7 bass players (his father, grandfather, 2 uncles, and 3 cousins). He absorbed the technique of manipulating this mastodon of string instruments by natural selection: studied with a cellist, a pianist, and a singer (Jennie Tourel) before taking lessons with Herman Reinshagen, former first double-bass player of the N.Y. Phil. He then took an additional course with the cellist Gabor Rejto at the Univ. of Southern Calif.; subsequently studied at the Aspen Music School and finally at the Juilliard School of Music in N.Y. He launched his spectacular career as a soloist with major American orchs., and then played with the London Phil. and the Oslo Phil. His solo recitals attracted a great deal of curiosity and elicited astounded praise from even the most skeptical of music critics. To expand the meager repertoire for the instrument, he commissioned Hans Werner Henze, Gunther Schuller, Alec Wilder, Malcolm Arnold, and other modern composers to write special works for him. He also introduced some works in the jazz manner. As an instructor, he gave courses at several music schools in the U.S. and Canada.

Kartzev, Alexander, Russian composer; b. Moscow, July 19, 1883; d. there, July 3, 1953. He was a pupil of Juon in Berlin, and Taneyev and Glière in Moscow. He wrote an opera, *Undine;* Symph.; Violin Concerto; String Quartet; Piano Quintet; Violin Sonata; etc.

Karyotakis, Theodore, Greek composer; b. Argos, July 21, 1903; d. Athens, June 14, 1978. He studied composition in Athens with Mitropoulos and Varvoglis; concurrently was enrolled in the law dept. of the Univ. of Athens. He wrote music in a neo-Romantic vein, permeated with euphonious dissonances; several of his works are inspired by Greek folk modes. WORKS: Opera, *Moon Flower* (1953–55); *Rhapsody* for Violin and Orch. (1940); *Epic Song* for Orch. (1944); *Serenities,* 10 songs for Voice, Clarinet, Celesta, Strings, and Percussion (1962); Concerto for Orch. (1967); Symph. (1974); much chamber music, including 2 violin sonatas (1945, 1955); *6 Erotic Songs* for Voice, Flute, and Harp (1948); String Trio (1949); String Quartet, with Voice (1963); *11 Sketches* for Flute and Viola (1963); *9 Inventions* for Violin and Piano (1966); Trio for Clarinet, Viola, and Piano (1969); Duo for Flute and Clarinet (1969); *Music for Flute, Clarinet, Horn, and Bassoon* (1973); numerous piano pieces; also a dramatic scene from *The Iliad* (1964) and songs.

Kasemets, Udo, Estonian-born Canadian composer; b. Tallinn, Nov. 16, 1919. He studied at the Tallinn Cons. and the Stuttgart State Academy of Music, and attended a Darmstadt summer course in new music under Krenek (1950). He emigrated to Canada in 1951 and became an organist, accompanist, and teacher; later became music critic for the Toronto *Daily Star;* was also lecturer on mixed-media music at the Ontario College of Arts in Toronto. In 1966 he became editor of *Canavangard,* an annotated catalogue of avant-garde Canadian composers. His early music is set in peaceful Romantic modalities with Estonian undertones, but soon he espoused serialism and the pantheatricalism of the most uninhibited avant-garde. WORKS: *Estonian Suite* for Chamber Orch. (1950); *Sonata da camera* for Solo Cello (1955); Violin Concerto (1956); String Quartet (1957); *Logos* for Flute and Piano (1960); *Haiku* for Voice, Flute, Cello, and Piano (1961); *Squares* for Piano, 4-hands (1962); *5* for 2 Performers on 2 Pianos and Percussion (1962–63); *Trigon* for One, 3, 9, or 27 Performers, a multidimensional score in which thematic information is provided by a deoxyribonucleic matrix (1963; 11 subsequent versions, 1964–66); *Communications, a noncomposition to words by e.e. cummings,* a cybernetic manifestation for singular or plural singers, speakers, instrumentalists, or dancers, of an indeterminate duration (1963); *Cumulus* for any Solo Instrument or Ensemble, and 2 Tape Recorders, the score consisting of 9 segments to be played in any order (1963–64; 2 later versions, 1966, 1968); *Calceolaria,* time/space variations on a floral theme, for any number of Performers (1966; version for 4-channel Tape, 1967); *Contactics,* a choreography for Musicians and Audience (1966); *Variations on Variations on Variations* for Singers, Instrumentalists, and 4 Loudspeakers (1966); *Quartets of Quartets,* 4 separate works for varying ensembles of Readers, Tape, Calibrators, Wind-bells, Wind Generators, Opaque Projectors, and any other sound-producing media: *Music for Nothing, Music for Anything (Wordmusic), Music for Something (Windmusic),* and *Music for Everything* (all 1971–72); *Music(s) for John Cage,* incorporating *Guitarmusic for John Cage* for any number of Guitars, Projections, and Dimmers, *Voicemusic for John Cage* for any number of Voices, *Saladmusic for John Cage* for any number of Salad Makers, and *Walking/Talking* for any number of Walkers/Talkers (all 1972); *Time-Space Interface* for any number of participants and any media, in both indoor and outdoor versions (1971–73); *Quadraphony (Music of the Quarter of the Moon of the Lunar Year),* an acoustical/architectural time/space exploration project (1972–73); *La Crasse du Tympan* for Record/Tape Mix (1973); *WATEARTHUNDAIR: Music of the 10th Moon of the Year of the Dragon,* a nature-sound-mix with verbal and visual commentary (1976); *KANADA-NAK,* a "celebration of our land and its people ..." for Readers, Drummers, and Audience participation (1976–77). *Counterbomb Renga,* a spectacle by about 100 poets and musicians, protesting against the proliferation of nuclear weapons, was conceived and coordinated by Kasemets (Canadian

Broadcasting Corp., April 3, 1983).

Kashin, Daniil, Russian composer; b. Moscow, 1769; d. there, Dec. 22, 1841. He was a serf, property of an aristocratic landowner, Gavril Bibikov. His master engaged Sarti, who was in Russia at the time, to teach Kashin; when Sarti accompanied Potemkin to southern Russia, Kashin went along. Returning to Moscow, he demonstrated his ability by presenting a piano concerto and an overture of his own composition (March 17, 1790). Bibikov sent him to Italy for further study; there Kashin spent 7 years; upon his return in 1798, he was given his liberty. On April 10, 1799, he gave in Moscow a monster concert with the participation of 200 executants, including an ensemble of Russian horns; at this concert he presented several of his Russian songs, which later became popular. He wrote 3 operas: *Natalia, the Boyard's Daughter* (Moscow, Oct. 21, 1801); *Fair Olga* (Moscow, Jan. 14, 1809); *The One-day Reign of Nourmahal,* after Thomas Moore's *Lalla Rookh* (1817; not produced); also collections of "patriotic songs" and an album of Russian folk songs. In 1806 he publ. 6 issues of a periodical, *Musical Journal of Russia.* BIBLIOGRAPHY: R.A. Mooser, *Annales de la musique et des musiciens en Russie au XVIIIe siècle* (vol. 2, Geneva, 1950, pp. 491–93).

Kashkin, Nicolai, Russian music critic; b. Voronezh, Dec. 9, 1839; d. Kazan, March 15, 1920. After receiving rudimentary instruction in music from his father, an amateur, Kashkin became a private tutor in elementary music in his native town. In 1860 he settled in Moscow, where he studied piano; in 1866 he joined the staff of the Moscow Cons., where he taught for 30 years. He became music critic of 2 Moscow papers, and his opinions exercised considerable influence in the musical life of Moscow in the last quarter of the 19th century. He was an intimate friend of Tchaikovsky; his little pamphlet *Reminiscences of Tchaikovsky* (Moscow, 1896) is valuable for authentic biographical and psychological data. A selection of his articles was publ. in Moscow (1953).

Kashperov, Vladimir, Russian composer; b. Tchufarovo, Simbirsk region, Sept. 6, 1826; d. Romantsevo, near Mozhaisk, July 8, 1894. He studied with Voigt and Henselt in St. Petersburg and with Dehn in Berlin (1856); went to Italy to study singing (1858), and remained there until 1864; he wrote several operas in the Italian style which were produced in Italy: *Maria Tudor* (Milan, 1859); *Rienzi* (Florence, 1863); *Consuelo* (Venice, 1865). In 1865 he returned to Russia and taught voice at the Moscow Cons. (1866–72); in 1872 opened his own school of singing. In Moscow he produced 2 operas with Russian librettos: *The Storm,* after Ostrovsky (1867), and *Taras Bulba,* after Gogol (1893). Even in his Russian works, Kashperov remained faithful to the Italian style of composition, taking Donizetti as a model.

Kasianov, Alexandr, Russian composer; b.

Bolobonovo, near Nizhny-Novgorod (Gorky), Aug. 29, 1891; d. Gorky, Feb. 13, 1982. He studied at the Petrograd Cons., graduating in 1917 in the class of Sokolov in composition; also studied piano with Liapunov. In 1918 he went to Nizhny-Novgorod; there he was active in organizing radio broadcasts; in 1951 joined the faculty of the local Cons. In his compositions he continued the tradition of old Russian music; his many choral works are quite effective. WORKS: Operas: *Stepan Razin* (Gorky, Oct. 29, 1939; revised, Gorky, Nov. 14, 1953); *A Partisan Girl* (1941); *On Far North* (1947); *Ermak* (1957); for Orch., *Overture on Russian Themes* (1943); 7 piano sonatas; 24 preludes for Piano; numerous choruses and songs. BIBLIOGRAPHY: N. Ugrumov, *Alexandr Kasianov* (Moscow, 1957).

Kaskel, Karl von, German composer; b. Dresden, Oct. 10, 1866; d. Berlin, Nov. 22, 1943. While a law student at Leipzig, he studied music in the Cons. under Reinecke and Jadassohn (1886–87); later at Cologne under Wüllner and Jensen. He lived many years in Dresden; later in Munich. He was a fairly successful composer. WORKS: Operas: *Hochzeitsmorgen* (Hamburg, 1893); *Sjula* (Cologne, 1895); *Die Bettlerin vom Pont des Arts* (Kassel, 1899); *Der Dusle und das Babeli* (Munich, 1903); *Der Gefangene der Zarin* (Dresden, 1910); *Die Nachtigall* (Stuttgart, 1910); *Die Schmiedin von Kent* (Dresden, 1916). For Orch.: *Lustspielouvertüre; Humoresque; Ballade.* Piano pieces; songs. BIBLIOGRAPHY: E. Schmitz, "Karl von Kaskel," *Monographien moderner Musiker* (Leipzig, 1909).

Kašlík, Václav, Czech conductor and opera producer; b. Poličná, Sept. 28, 1917. He studied conducting with Václav Talich in Prague; also took courses in music theory at the Univ. of Prague. He was chief conductor of the Brno State Theater (1943–45); then conducted the 5th of May Theater in Prague (1945–48); subsequently served as chief producer of the Prague National Theater. His productions are noteworthy for their use of film, experimental lighting, stereophonic sound, and other modern innovations.

Kassern, Tadeusz Zygfrid, Polish composer; b. Lwow, March 19, 1904; d. New York, May 2, 1957. He studied with M. Soltys at the Lwow Cons. and with Opieński in Poznan. He also took a course in law; in 1931, went to Paris. In 1945 he was appointed cultural attaché at the Polish Consulate in N.Y. However, he broke with the Communist government in Poland, and remained in N.Y.; became an American citizen in 1956. Among Polish composers, he pursued a cosmopolitan trend; although many of his works are inspired by Polish folk music, the idiom and the method are of a general European modern character. WORKS: 2 operas: *The Anointed* (1951) and *Sun-Up* (1952; N.Y., Nov. 10, 1954); *Dies irae,* symph. poem in memory of Marshal Pilsudski (1935); Concerto for Soprano (1928); Concerto for Double Bass and Orch. (1937); Concerto for String Orch. (1944); Concertino for Oboe and String Orch. (1946); Concertino for Flute, String Orch., Xylophone, and Celesta (1948); *Teen-Age Concerto* for Piano and Orch. (N.Y., May 1956); choruses; chamber music; piano pieces; songs.

Kässmayer, Moritz, Austrian violinist and composer; b. Vienna, March 20, 1831; d. there, Nov. 9, 1884. He studied with Sechter at the Vienna Cons.; then played violin in the orch. of the Vienna Opera; later became ballet conductor there. He wrote a comic opera, *Das Landhaus zu Meudon* (1869); symphs.; masses and other church music; 5 string quartets; songs. His *Mesalliansen* for String Quartet, with Piano, 4-hands, and *Volksweisen und Lieder* for String Quartet "humoristisch und kontrapunktisch bearbeitet" are amusing specimens of old-fashioned humor.

Kastalsky, Alexander, Russian choral conductor and composer; b. Moscow, Nov. 28, 1856; d. there, Dec. 17, 1926. He was a pupil of Tchaikovsky, Taneyev, and Hubert at the Moscow Cons. (1875–82). In 1887 he became instructor of piano at the Synodal School in Moscow; in 1891, assistant conductor of the Synodal Chorus; in 1910, was appointed director of the school and principal conductor of the choir. In 1911 he took the choir on an extended European tour. In 1918 the Synodal School became a choral academy; in 1923 it merged with the Moscow Cons. Kastalsky was also a teacher of conducting at the Moscow Phil. Inst. (1912–22); in 1923, was appointed prof. of choral singing at the Moscow Cons. He was a notable composer of Russian sacred music, into which he introduced modern elements, combining them with the ancient church modes.
WORKS: Opera, *Clara Militch,* after Turgenev (Moscow, 1916); oratorio, *The Furnace of Nabucho* (1909); Requiem (1916; in memory of Allied soldiers fallen in World War I; in 12 sections, based on the modes of the Greek Orthodox, Roman Catholic, and Anglican churches); *Rustic Symphony* (Moscow, Dec. 13, 1925); incidental music to *Stenka Rasin* (Moscow, 1918), to Shakespeare's *King Lear* (Moscow, 1919), and to Hauptmann's *Hannele* (Moscow, 1920); cantata, *1812;* symph. suite, *Pictures of Russian Festivities* (1912); *A Marketplace in Ancient Russia* (completed 1924); 5 choruses on patriotic texts; about 80 sacred choruses a cappella; *In Georgia,* suite for Piano; *Ancient Times* (4 vols. of restorations of ancient music, for Piano: I. China, India, Egypt; II. Greece, Judea, Islam; III. Early Christianity; IV. Ancient Russia). He publ. a valuable paper, *Peculiarities of the National Russian Musical System* (Moscow, 1923), greatly expanded by him during the last 3 years of his life, and publ. posthumously as *Foundations of National Polyphony,* ed. by Victor Belaiev (Moscow, 1948).
BIBLIOGRAPHY: His autobiographical sketch, *My Musical Career and My Thoughts on Church Music,* was publ. in the *Musical Quarterly* (April 1925). See also W.S. Pring, "Kastalsky and Russian Folk Polyphony," *Music & Letters* (1929).

Kastendieck, Miles Merwin, American music critic; b. Brooklyn, April 16, 1905. He studied at Yale Univ. with D.S. Smith. He became critic of the *New Haven Journal-Courier* (1929–38), of the *Brooklyn Eagle* (1938–46), the *N.Y. Journal-American* (from 1946), and N.Y. correspondent for the *Christian Science Monitor* (1945–72). He wrote *England's Musical Poet, Thomas Campion* (N.Y., 1938).

Kastle, Leonard, American composer; b. New York, Feb. 11, 1929. He studied composition with George Szell and piano with Frank Sheridan and Paul Wittgenstein. In 1945 he entered the Curtis Inst. and studied with Isabelle Vengerova (piano) and Rosario Scalero (composition); continued his studies with Gian Carlo Menotti and Carl Bamberger (conducting); graduated in 1950. Among his works are a Piano Sonata (1950); one-act opera for television, *The Swing* (NBC television network, June 11, 1956); choral work, *Whispers of Heavenly Death* (1956); *Deseret* (NBC Opera Co., N.Y., Jan. 1, 1961).

Kastner, Alfred, Austrian harpist; b. Vienna, March 10, 1870; d. Hollywood, May 24, 1948. He studied with Zamara at the Vienna Cons.; then played first harp in the orchs. of the Dresden Opera and Warsaw Opera; later taught harp in Budapest (1892–98); was in the U.S. (1898–1900); then in Switzerland. From 1904 to 1919 he was harpist in the Queen's Hall Orch. in London; also taught at the Royal Academy of Music there. In 1919 he was engaged as first harpist of the Los Angeles Phil. He publ. several concert pieces for the harp and various arrangements.

Kastner, Emmerich, Austrian writer on music; b. Vienna, March 29, 1847; d. there, Dec. 5, 1916. He publ. several valuable works dealing with Wagner: *Richard Wagner-Katalog* (1878); *Wagneriana* (1885); *Briefe R. Wagners an seine Zeitgenossen 1830–38* (1885); *Die dramatischen Werke R. Wagners* (1899). Other writings are *Bayreuth* (1884) and *Neuestes und vollständigstes Tonkünstler- und Opern-Lexikon* (1889; only A–Azzoni printed); edited *Beethovens sämmtliche Briefe* (Leipzig, 1911). He was editor of the *Wiener Musikalische Zeitung.*

Kastner, Georg Friedrich, Alsatian acoustician, son of **Johann Georg Kastner;** b. Strasbourg, Aug. 10, 1852; d. Bonn, April 6, 1882. He followed his father's ideas of music as a science; at the age of 20, read a paper before the Académie des Sciences in Paris, *Pyrophone: Flammes chantantes,* which was subsequently publ.; constructed the Pyrophone, an organ of 3 octaves on which the sound was produced by burning gas jets. A description and picture of the Pyrophone are in vol. 3 of H. Ludwig von Jan's biography of Kastner's father.

Kastner, Jean Georges (Johann Georg), Alsatian composer and theorist; b. Strasbourg, March 9, 1810; d. Paris, Dec. 19, 1867. He studied organ as a child; later entered the Strasbourg Lutheran Seminary. He then gave up his theological studies and went to Paris. There he resumed his musical education, taking lessons with Berton and Reicha. An industrious scholar, Kastner acquired enormous erudition in various arts and sciences. He pursued the study of acoustics and formulated a theory of the cosmic unity of the arts. At the same time he took great interest in practical applications of music; he was active in organizing the contest of bands of 9 nations held at the Paris Exposition of 1867. He was a founder and vice-president of the Assoc. des Artistes-Musiciens. He was elected a member of the Institut and an Officer of the Legion of Honor. Among the grandiose projects that he carried out were several vols. of "Livres-Partitions," that is, symph.-cantatas illustrating musico-historical subjects, preceded by essays upon them. Of these the following were publ.: *Les Danses des morts; dissertations et recherches historiques, philosophiques, littéraires et musicales sur les divers monuments de ce genre qui existent tant en France qu'à l'étranger* and *Danse macabre, grande ronde vocale et instrumentale* (Paris, 1852; 310 pp.); *La Harpe d'Eole, et la musique cosmique* and *Stéphen, ou La Harpe d'Eole, grand monologue avec chœurs* (1856); *Les Sirènes* and *Le Rêve d'Oswald ou Les Sirènes, grande symphonie dramatique vocale et instrumentale* (1858); *Parémiologie musicale de la langue française* and *La Saint-Julien de ménétriers, symphonie-cantate à grand orchestre, avec solos et chœurs* (1862; 659 pages); *Les Voix de Paris* and *Les Cris de Paris, grande symphonie humoristique vocale et instrumentale,* making use of vendors' cries with orch. accompaniment (1875). Kastner wrote several operas, 4 of which were produced in Strasbourg: *Gustav Wasa* (1832); *Oskars Tod* (1833); comic opera, *Der Sarazene* (1834); *Die Königin der Sarmaten* (1835). In Paris he produced 2 operas: *La Maschera* (June 17, 1841) and *Le Dernier Roi de Juda* (1844). He also wrote 5 overtures, Sextet for Saxophones, and 2 collections of men's choruses (*Les Chants de la vie,* 1854; *Chants de l'armée française,* 1855); publ. a useful and highly practical *Manuel général de musique militaire à l'usage des armées françaises* (Paris, 1848). His great project, *Encyclopédie de la musique,* was left uncompleted at his death.

BIBLIOGRAPHY: H. Ludwig (real name, H. Ludwig von Jan), *J.G. Kastner, Ein elsässischer Tondichter, Theoretiker und Musikforscher* (Leipzig, 1886; 3 parts in 2 vols.).

Kastner, (Macario) Santiago, musicologist; b. London, Oct. 15, 1908. He studied at Amsterdam, Leipzig, Berlin, and Barcelona; settled in Lisbon in 1933; lectured throughout Europe; made many appearances as a concert pianist and harpsichordist. His writings include *Música hispanica* (Madrid, 1936); *Contribución al estudio de la música española y portuguesa* (Lisbon, 1941); *Federico Mompou* (Madrid, 1947); *Carlos de Seixas* (Coimbra,

1947); *Francisco Correa de Arauxo* (Barcelona, 1948). He edited 80 keyboard sonatas by Seixas (1965) and several other works by Portuguese and Spanish composers.

Kastorsky, Vladimir, Russian bass; b. Bolshive Soly, in Yaroslavl district, March 14, 1871; d. Leningrad, July 2, 1948. He studied with Cotogni and Gabel; then sang with a touring opera company throughout Russia; in 1899 he became a member of the Maryinsky Theater in St. Petersburg; also appeared in Diaghilev's *Russian Seasons* in Paris and London (1907–8); concurrently formed a vocal quartet specializing in Russian folk songs, with which he toured abroad. He remained on the stage for nearly 45 years and appeared at concerts to the end of his long life.

Katchen, Julius, American pianist; b. Long Branch, N.J., Aug. 15, 1926; d. Paris, April 29, 1969. He studied in N.Y. with David Saperton; made his debut with the Philadelphia Orch. on Oct. 21, 1937. He studied academic subjects at Haverford College, graduating in 1945. In 1948 he toured Palestine; then settled in Paris; gave a series of successful concerts in Europe.

Kate, André ten, Dutch composer and cellist; b. Amsterdam, May 22, 1796; d. Haarlem, July 27, 1858. He studied cello with Bertelmann. He wrote the operas *Seid e Palmira* (1831) and *Constantia* (1835); also other operas; chamber music; part-songs; etc.

Kates, Stephen, American cellist; b. New York, May 7, 1943. He studied at the Juilliard School of Music; in 1963 won an honorable mention and a medal of merit at the International Cello Competition in Budapest; appeared at the Young People's Concerts with the N.Y. Phil. under Leonard Bernstein; in 1964 toured Europe with the Pittsburgh Symph. Orch.; then went to study with Gregor Piatigorsky in Los Angeles. In 1965 he won a debut grant of the Young Musicians Foundation in California. In 1966 he won the 2nd prize in the Tchaikovsky Competition in Moscow.

Katims, Milton, American conductor and violist; b. New York, June 24, 1909. He attended Columbia Univ.; studied viola and conducting with L. Barzin. In 1935–43 he was a viola player and assistant conductor at station WOR in N.Y.; in 1943, joined the NBC Symph. Orch. as first violist, and subsequently became assistant conductor under Toscanini. From 1954 to 1974 he was conductor and music director of the Seattle Symph. Orch. In 1976 he was appointed artistic director of the School of Music at the Univ. of Houston; he resigned in 1983.

Katin, Peter, English pianist; b. London, Nov. 14, 1930. He studied at the Royal College of Music in London; made his debut there in 1948. His appearances as a soloist with orchs. were mainly in England; in his own concerts he ardently cultivated the works of contemporary English composers.

Katlewicz, Jerzy, Polish conductor; b. Bochnia, April 2, 1927. He studied at the State Academy of Music in Cracow. In 1952 he became artistic director of the Cracow Opera and conductor of the Phil. Orch. there. In 1955 he won first prize at the conducting competition in Besançon, France. In 1958 he was appointed artistic director of the Poznan Phil.; in 1961 he took the post of music director of the Phil. Orch. and Opera in Gdansk. From 1968 he served in the same capacity with the Cracow Phil. Orch.; made tours in Europe with it. In 1972 he was named prof. of conducting at the State Academy of Music in Cracow; in 1979 he became conductor of the Noordhollands Philo. Orkest in Haarlem, while remaining in charge of the Cracow Philo. Orch.

Katwijk, Paul van, pianist and composer; b. Rotterdam, Dec. 7, 1885; d. Dallas, Texas, Dec. 11, 1974. He studied at the Cons. of The Hague; then in Berlin with Klatte and in Vienna with Godowsky; then devoted himself chiefly to conducting and teaching. In 1912 he settled in the U.S.; taught at Drake Univ. in Des Moines, Iowa (1914–18), and also conducted the Des Moines Symph. Orch.; in 1919, he was appointed dean of music at Southern Methodist Univ. in Dallas; resigned in 1949, but continued to teach piano there until 1955. He was conductor of the Dallas Municipal Opera (1922–25), then of the Dallas Symph. Orch. (1925–36). He composed several symph. works; his orch. suite *Hollandia* was performed by the Dallas Symph. Orch. on March 15, 1931.

Katz, Israel J., American musicologist; b. New York, July 21, 1930. He studied at the Univ. of Calif., Los Angeles, with Klaus Wachsmann and Boris Kremenliev, earning his B.A. in 1956 and his Ph.D. in 1967 with the dissertation *Judeo-Spanish Traditional Ballads from Jerusalem: An Ethnomusicological Study* (publ. in N.Y., 1972; 1975). He taught at McGill Univ. (1968–69); in 1969 joined the faculty of Columbia Univ. He contributed scholarly articles to the *Encyclopedia Judaica, Ethnomusicology,* and other publications.

Katz, Mindru, pianist; b. Bucharest, June 3, 1925; d. during a recital in Istanbul, Jan. 30, 1978. He received his musical training in Rumania; eventually made his home in Israel; gave many concerts there and in England.

Katzer, Georg, East German composer; b. Habelschwerdt, Silesia, Jan. 10, 1935. He studied piano and composition with Rudolf Wagner-Régeny and Ruth Zechlin at the Hochschule für Musik in East Berlin (1954–59); then entered the classes of Hanns Eisler and Leo Spies at the Akademie der Künste there (1960–63). In 1979 he was elected to the membership of the Akademie der Künste. In his music Katzer is a universalist, applying constructivist principles with lapidary precision. Under the influence of Hanns Eisler he adopted a broad variety of methods, including 12-tone techniques, using his materials for specific purposes accessible to mass audiences. WORKS: FOR THE STAGE: *Das Land Bum-Bum,* opera for children (1974); *Schwarze Vögel,* ballet (1975); *Ein neuer Sommernachtstraum,* ballet (1979–80). FOR ORCH.: 3 sonatas for Orch. (1968, 1969, 1970); *Baukasten* (1972); Concerto for Orch. (1973); *D-Dur Musikmaschine* (1973); Concerto for Jazz Group and Orch. (1975); *Empfindsame Musik* for 58 String Instruments and 3 Percussion Groups (1976); *Dramatische Musik* (1977); *Sound-Hous* for Orch., 3 Instrumental Groups, and Tape (1979); Piano Concerto (1980); Double Concerto for Cello, Harp, and Orch. (1980). CHAMBER MUSIC: String Quartet No. 1 (1966); String Quartet No. 2, with Soprano (1967); *Streichmusik I* for 14 Solo Strings (1971); *Streichmusik II* for 18 Solo Strings (1972); Piano Quintet (1972); *Scene* for Chamber Ensemble (1975); Concerto for Harpsichord and Wind Quintet (1977); Trio for Oboe, Cello, and Piano, with Tape (1979); choruses; songs.
BIBLIOGRAPHY: Ursula Stürzbecher, *Komponisten in der DDR: 17 Gespräche* (Hildesheim, 1979).

Kauder, Hugo, Austrian composer; b. Tobitschau, Moravia, June 9, 1888; d. Bussum, the Netherlands, July 22, 1972. He studied violin; was a member of the Konzertverein Orch. in Vienna. In 1938 he came to America and settled in N.Y. His music is contrapuntal, with canonic devices much used in free and often asymmetric rhythm, while the and settled in N.Y. His music is contrapuntal, with canonic devices much used in free and often asymmetric rhythm, while the and settled in N.Y. His music is contrapuntal, with canonic devices much used in free and often asymmetric rhythm, while the harmonies are conservative. He wrote 4 symphs., a Cello Concerto, and a great number of works for chamber music combinations. He publ. *Entwurf einer neuen Melodie- und Harmonielehre* (Vienna, 1932) and *Counterpoint* (N.Y., 1960).

Kauer, Ferdinand, Austrian composer; baptized at Klein-Tajax (Znaim), Moravia, Jan. 18, 1751; d. Vienna, April 13, 1831. As a boy he played organ in a Jesuit church at Znaim; in 1784 he played violin in a Vienna theater, and also supplied music for a number of plays performed there. He wrote some 100 operettas and other stage works; of these, *Das Donauweibchen* (Vienna, Jan. 11, 1798) was sensationally successful and was performed all over Europe for many years; other works (an oratorio, *Die Sündflut;* a quantity of church music; symphs.; concertos; etc.) also enjoyed favor. Most of his MSS were lost in the flood of 1830; a list of extant works is given by Eitner in his *Quellen-Lexikon.* Kauer publ. *Singschule nach dem neuesten System der Tonkunst* (1790) and *Kurzgefasste Generalbass-Schule für Anfänger* (1800).
BIBLIOGRAPHY: Th. Haas, "Ferdinand Kauer," *Neue Musik Zeitung* (1925); K. Manschinger, *Ferdi-*

nand Kauer (Vienna, 1929).

Kauffmann, Emil, German composer and writer on music, son of **Ernst Friedrich Kauffmann;** b. Ludwigsburg, Nov. 23, 1836; d. Tübingen, June 17, 1909. He studied at the Stuttgart Cons. with Keller, Faiszt, Jung, and Singer; joined the court orch. in 1863 as a violinist; was a teacher in the music school at Basel (1868–77) and music director at Tübingen Univ. (Dr.Phil., 1885). He wrote *Die Nacht;* over 60 lieder; male choruses; sonatas and other piano pieces; also the essays *Entwickelung der Tonkunst von der Mitte des 18. Jahrhunderts bis zur Gegenwart* (1884) and *Justinus Heinrich Knecht: Ein schwäbischer Tonsetzer* (1892); contributed articles to the Leipzig *Musikalisches Wochenblatt.*

Kauffmann, Ernst Friedrich, German composer, father of **Emil Kauffmann;** b. Ludwigsburg, Nov. 27, 1803; d. Stuttgart, Feb. 11, 1856. He studied at Tübingen Univ. (1825–27); became principal of the Realschule at Ludwigsburg, but because of his connection with revolutionists he lost his position in 1835; was imprisoned in Asperg (1838–42), where he wrote 6 sets of songs, which became popular.

Kauffmann, Fritz, German composer; b. Berlin, June 17, 1855; d. Magdeburg, Sept. 29, 1934. He was an apothecary; began to study music seriously at 23, with Kiel in Berlin; 3 years later, won the Mendelssohn Prize for composition. After a sojourn in Vienna, he lived mostly in Berlin; in 1889 became choral conductor in Magdeburg; from 1897 till 1920 he conducted the Kirchengesangverein there. He wrote a comic opera, *Die Herzkrankheit;* Symph.; 2 violin concertos; Piano Concerto; Cello Concerto; 2 piano sonatas; *Tanz-Improvisationen* for Piano; choruses; songs.

Kauffmann, Leo Justinus, Alsatian composer; b. Dammerkirch, Sept. 20, 1901; killed in an air raid, Strasbourg, Sept. 25, 1944. He studied with Marie Joseph Erb in Strasbourg and with Jarnach and Abendroth in Cologne; in 1932–40 was active in radio work in Cologne; then taught at the Strasbourg Cons.; served as its director until he was killed. He wrote the opera *Die Geschichte vom schönen Annerl* (Strasbourg, June 20, 1942); a Mass; a Symph.; Concertino for Double Bass, with Chamber Orch.

Kaufman, Harry, American pianist; b. New York, Sept. 6, 1894; d. Beverly Hills, Calif., Aug. 22, 1961. He studied at the Inst. of Musical Art with Stojowski; later was a pupil of Josef Hofmann; in 1924 he was appointed teacher of the art of accompanying at the Curtis Inst. in Philadelphia. Though principally known as an excellent accompanist, he also appeared as soloist with the N.Y. Phil., the Philadelphia Orch., etc., and as a member of several chamber music groups.

Kaufman, Louis, distinguished American violinist; b. Portland, Oreg., May 10, 1905. He studied with

Kneisel; won the Loeb Prize in 1927 and the Naumburg Award in 1928. In 1950 he regularly gave concerts in Europe. On Oct. 21, 1950, he presented in Paris, as violinist and conductor, the 12 concertos by Vivaldi, op. 8; in 1954 he played 12 concertos by Torelli, op. 8, in London; also performed Vivaldi's concertos in Rio de Janeiro and Buenos Aires (1952). He gave numerous first performances of works by contemporary composers, among them a violin concerto by Dag Wiren (Stockholm, Oct. 25, 1953), and first American performances of violin works by Darius Milhaud, Lev Knipper, Bohuslav Martinů, and others; also played American works in Europe; gave the first performance in England of Walter Piston's Violin Concerto (London, April 6, 1956). He edited 6 sonatas for violin by G.P. Telemann and *Sonata concertante* by L. Spohr; publ. *Warming Up Scales and Arpeggios* for violinists (1957).

Kaufmann, Armin, Rumanian composer, b. Itzkany, Bukovina, Oct. 30, 1902; d. Vienna, June 30, 1980. In 1914 his family settled in Vienna, where he enrolled at the Vienna Academy of Music, studying music theory with Joseph Marx. From 1938 to 1966 he played the viola in the Vienna Symph. Orch. As a composer, he wrote mostly instrumental music.
   WORKS: 4 symphs. (1929, 1962, 1966, 1968); Piano Concerto (1970); Quintet for Piano, Violin, Viola, Cello, and Double Bass (1965); 7 string quartets; Trio for Violin, Zither, and Guitar (1962); Trio for Flute, Viola, and Harp (1967); Rhapsody for Solo Guitar (1970); a curious Concerto for Tárogató and Orch. (1967).

Kaufmann, Friedrich, German inventor; b. Dresden, Feb. 5, 1785; d. there, Dec. 1, 1866. He invented a trumpet automaton (1808), the Belloneon, the Klaviatur-Harmonichord, the Chordaulodion, and the Symphonion. In 1851 his son, **Friedrich Theodor Kaufmann** (b. Dresden, April 9, 1823; d. there, Feb. 5, 1872), made an Orchestrion from the Symphonion.

Kaufmann, Helen, American writer on music; b. New York, Feb. 2, 1887; d. there, Sept. 17, 1978. She was educated at Barnard College; upon graduation, devoted herself to educational work. She publ. a number of popular books on music appreciation, among them *Home Book of Music Appreciation* (1942); *Little Guide of Music Appreciation* (1948); *The Story of Music through the Ages* (1949); also concise biographies of Mozart, Prokofiev, and other composers.

Kaufmann, Walter, German-born American conductor, composer, and musicologist; b. Karlsbad, April 1, 1907; d. Bloomington, Ind., Setp. 9, 1984. He studied composition with Schreker in Berlin; also studied musicology in Prague. In 1935 he traveled to India, where he remained for 10 years; devoted much time to the study of the Hindu systems of composition; also appeared as conductor, serving as music director of the Bombay Radio. In 1947 he moved to Nova Scotia and taught piano at the Halifax Cons. there; from 1949–57 he was music director of the Winnipeg Symph. Orch. In 1957 he settled in the U.S., where he joined the faculty of the Indiana Univ. School of Music in Bloomington. He became an American citizen in 1964. He was awarded a D.Mus. *honoris causa* by the Spokane (Wash.) Cons. in 1946. He wrote *Musical Notations of the Orient* (Bloomington, 1967); *The Ragas of North India* (Bloomington, 1968); *Tibetan Buddhist Chant* (with translations by T. Norbu; Bloomington, 1975); *Involvement with Music: The Music of India* (N.Y., 1976); *Musical References in the Chinese Classics* (Detroit, 1976); *The Ragas of South India* (Bloomington, 1976); *Altinden* (Leipzig, 1981); also valuable articles on Eastern music for American music journals.

WORKS: OPERAS: *Der grosse Dorin* (1932); *Der Hammel bringt es an den Tag* (1932); *Esther* (1931–32); *Die weisse Göttin* (1933); *Anasuya*, radio opera (Bombay, Oct. 1, 1938); *The Cloak,* after Gogol (1933–50); *A Parfait for Irene* (Bloomington, Feb. 21, 1952); *The Research* (1951); *The Golden Touch,* short opera for children (1953); *Christmas Slippers,* television opera (1955); *Sganarelle* (1955); *George from Paradise* (1958); *Paracelsus* (1958); *The Scarlet Letter,* after Hawthorne (Bloomington, May 6, 1961); *A Hoosier Tale* (Bloomington, July 30, 1966); *Rip van Winkle,* short opera for children (1966). BALLETS: *Visages* (1950); *The Rose and the Ring* (1950); *Wang* (1956). FOR ORCH.: Symph. No. 1 for Strings (1931); *Prag,* suite (1932); Concerto No. 1 for Piano and Orch. (1934); Symph. No. 2 (1935); Symph. No. 3 (1936); Symph. No. 4 (1938); *2 Bohemian Dances* (1942); Concerto No. 1 for Violin and Orch. (1943); *6 Indian Miniatures* (1943); Concerto No. 2 for Violin and Orch. (1944); *Navaratnam,* suite for Piano and Chamber Orch. (1945); *Phantasmagoria* (1946); Variations for Strings (1947); Concertino for Piano and Strings (1947); *Dirge* (1947); *Madras Express* (Boston Pops, June 23, 1948); *Fleet Street Overture* (1948); *Strange Town at Night* (1948); *Faces in the Dark* (1948); *Andhera* for Piano and Orch. (1942–49); Sinfonietta No. 1 (Symph. No. 5; 1949); Divertimento for Strings (1949); Concerto No. 2 for Piano and Orch. (1949); Concerto for Violoncello and Orch. (1950); *Chivaree Overture* (1950); *Main Street* for Strings (1950); *Kalif Storch,* fairy tale for Speaker and Orch. (1951); *Arabesques* for 2 Pianos and Orch. (1952); *Vaudeville Overture* (1952); *Sewanee River Variations* (1952); *Short Suite* for Small Orch. (1953); *Nocturne* (1953); *Pembina Highway* (1953); *4 Skies* (1953); *3 Dances to an Indian Play* (1956); Symph. No. 6 (1956); *4 Essays* for Small Orch. (1956); Sinfonietta No. 2 (1959); Concerto for Timpani and Orch.-1963); *Festival Overture* (1968); Concertino for Violin and Orch. (1977). CHAMBER MUSIC: 10 string quartets (1935–46); 3 piano trios (1942–46); 6 Pieces for Piano Trio (1957); String Quartet (1961); Partita for Woodwind Quintet (1963); *Arabesques* for Flute, Oboe, Harpsichord, and Bass (1963); 8 Pieces for 12 Instruments (1967); *Passacaglia and Capriccio* for Brass Sextet (1967); Sonatina for Piccolo or Flute Solo (1968). FOR PIANO: Concertino (1932); Sonatina No. 1 (1948); Sonata (1948–51); *Arabesques* for 2 Pianos (1952); Sonatina No. 2 (1956); Suite (1957). He

further wrote the cantatas *Galizische Bäume* for Chorus and Orch. (1932), *Coronation Cantata* for Soloists, Chorus, and Orch. (1953), and *Rubayyat* for Soloist and Orch. (1954); also songs.

BIBLIOGRAPHY: T. Noblitt, ed., *Music East and West: Essays in Honor of Walter Kaufmann* (N.Y., 1981).

Kaul, Oskar, German musicologist; b. Heufeld, Oct. 11, 1885; d. Unterwössen, July 17, 1968. He studied music at the Cologne Cons.; then took courses in musicology with Sandberger in Munich; obtained his degree of Dr.Phil. at the Univ. of Munich in 1911. He was in the army during World War I; in 1922, became Privatdozent in Würzburg; in 1930, prof.; also was director of the State Cons. there. He retired in 1945; lived in Unterwössen, Bavaria. He edited 5 symphs. and chamber music by Rosetti for Denkmäler der Tonkunst in Bayern (vols. 12 and 25) and publ. a dissertation, *Die Vokalwerke Anton Rosettis* (Cologne, 1911); other writings include *Geschichte der Würzburger Hofmusik im 18. Jahrhundert* (Würzburg, 1924), *Athanasius Kircher als Musikgelehrter* (Würzburg, 1932), and many valuable papers on the music history of Bavaria.

Kaun, Hugo, German composer; b. Berlin, March 21, 1863; d. there, April 2, 1932. He studied piano with Oskar Raif and composition with Friedrich Kiel in Berlin; composed industriously as a very young man. In 1887 he went to live in America, settling in Milwaukee, where he remained for 14 years (1887–1901); was a successful teacher, and continued to compose. In 1902 he returned to Berlin to teach privately; in 1922, became a prof. at the Klindworth-Scharwenka Cons.; publ. an autobiography, *Aus meinem Leben* (Berlin, 1932); also a manual for students, *Harmonielehre und Aufgabenbuch.* A cultured composer, thoroughly versed in the craft, he wrote a great number of works, and enjoyed recognition among large groups of friends; his musical style contained elements of both Brahmsian and Wagnerian idioms.

WORKS: Operas: *Sappho* (Leipzig, Oct. 27, 1917); *Der Fremde* (Dresden, Feb. 23, 1920); *Menandra* (staged in Kiel and several other German opera houses simultaneously, Oct. 29, 1925). For Orch.: 3 symphs.; 2 piano concertos; *Der Sternenbanner,* a festival march on the *Star-Spangled Banner;* overture, *Der Maler von Antwerpen* (Chicago, Feb. 3, 1899); *Im Urwald,* 2 symph. poems, after Longfellow's *Minnehaha* and *Hiawatha* (Chicago, Feb. 7, 1903); etc.; *Auf dem Meere* for Baritone, Chorus, and Orch.; several settings of Psalms; a Requiem; other church music. Chamber music: Octet for Wind and String Instruments; String Quintet; 4 string quartets; Piano Trio; Violin Sonata; numerous piano pieces.

BIBLIOGRAPHY: W. Altmann, *Hugo Kaun* (Leipzig, 1906); G.R. Kruse, "Hugo Kaun," *Die Musik* (1909–10); R. Schaal, *Hugo Kaun, Leben und Werk* (Regensburg, 1946).

Kay, Hershy, American composer, arranger, and

orchestrator; b. Philadelphia, Nov. 17, 1919; d. Danbury, Conn., Dec. 2, 1981. He studied cello with Felix Salmond and orchestration with Randall Thompson at the Curtis Inst. of Music in Philadelphia (1936–40); then went to N.Y., and began a fruitful career as an arranger of Broadway musicals and ballets. He orchestrated a number of Leonard Bernstein's theater works: *On the Town* (1944), *Peter Pan* (1951), *Candide* (1956; revival, 1973), *Mass* (1971), and the Bicentennial pageant *1600 Pennsylvania Avenue* (1976). His last arrangement for Bernstein was *Olympic Hymn*, performed at the opening of the Olympic Congress in Baden-Baden (Sept. 23, 1981). His other orchestrations for Broadway include Kurt Weill's *A Flag Is Born* (1947), Latouche's *The Golden Apple* (1954), Mary Rogers's *Once upon a Mattress* (1958), Blitzstein's *Juno* (1958), *Sand Hog* (1958), *Livin' the Life* (1958), *Milk and Honey* (1961), *The Happiest Girl in the World* (1961), *110 in the Shade* (1963), *Coco* (1969), *A Chorus Line* (1975), *American Musical Jubilee* (1976), *Music Is* (1976), *On the Twentieth Century* (1977), *Evita* (1979), *Carmelina* (1979), and *Barnum* (1980). He further made numerous arrangements for the N.Y. City Ballet, among them *Cakewalk* (1951, after Gottschalk), *Western Symphony* (1954, after cowboy songs and fiddle tunes; produced by Balanchine on Sept. 7, 1954, and included in his company's Russian tour in 1962), *The Concert* (1956, after Chopin), *Stars and Stripes* (1958, after Sousa's marches), *Who Cares?* (1970, after Gershwin), and *Union Jack* (1976, after popular British music). His ballet arrangements for other companies include *The Thief Who Loved a Ghost* (1950, after Weber), *L'Inconnue* (1965), *The Clowns* (1968; a rare 12-tone arrangement), *Meadowlark and Cortège Burlesque* (1969), *Grand Tour* (1971, after Noel Coward), and *Winter's Court* (1972). He also orchestrated a Gottschalk piano piece, *Grand Tarantella*, for Piano and Orch. (1957) and completed orchestration of Robert Kurka's opera *The Good Soldier Schweik* (N.Y. City Center, April 23, 1958).

BIBLIOGRAPHY: Michael Sonino, "Hershy Kay," *Musical America* (Oct. 1961); *Current Biography* (1962); *The Annual Obituary 1981* (N.Y., 1982; pp. 726–27).

Kay, Ulysses Simpson, eminent black American composer; b. Tucson, Ariz., Jan. 7, 1917. He received his early music training at home; on the advice of his mother's uncle **"King" Oliver,** a leading jazz cornetist, he studied piano. In 1934 he enrolled at the Univ. of Arizona at Tucson (Mus.B., 1938); he then went to study at the Eastman School in Rochester, N.Y., where he was a student of Bernard Rogers and Howard Hanson (M.M., 1940); later attended the classes of Paul Hindemith at the Berkshire Music Center in Tanglewood (1941–42). He served in the U.S. Navy (1942–45); went to Rome as winner of the American Rome Prize, and was attached there to the American Academy (1949–52). From 1953 to 1968 he was employed as a consultant by Broadcast Music Inc. in N.Y.; was on the faculty of Boston Univ. (1965) and of the Univ. of Calif., Los Angeles (1966–

67); in 1968 was appointed prof. of music at the Herbert H. Lehman College in N.Y.; was made Distinguished Prof. there in 1972. In 1964 he held a Guggenheim fellowship; in 1969 he was awarded an honorary doctorate in music by the Univ. of Arizona. Kay's music follows a distinctly American idiom, particularly in its rhythmic intensity, while avoiding ostentatious ethnic elements; in harmony and counterpoint, he pursues a moderately advanced idiom, marked by prudentially euphonious dissonances; his instrumentation is masterly.

WORKS: Operas: *The Boor,* after Chekhov (1955; Louisville, April 3, 1968); *The Juggler of Our Lady* (1956; New Orleans, Feb. 3, 1962); *The Capitoline Venus* (Quincy, Ill., March 12, 1971); *Jubilee* (Jackson, Miss., April 12, 1976); Oboe Concerto (Rochester, N.Y., April 16, 1940); *5 Mosaics* for Chamber Orch. (Cleveland, Dec. 28, 1940); ballet. *Dance Calinda* (Rochester, N.Y., April 23, 1941); *Of New Horizons,* overture (N.Y., July 29, 1944); *A Short Overture* (N.Y., March 31, 1947); Suite for Strings (Baltimore, April 8, 1949); *Sinfonia in E* (Rochester, N.Y., May 2, 1951); *6 Dances* for Strings (1954); Concerto for Orch. (N.Y., 1954); *Song of Jeremiah,* cantata (Nashville, April 23, 1954); Serenade for Orch. (Louisville, Sept. 18, 1954); *3 Pieces after Blake* for Soprano and Orch. (1952; N.Y., March 27, 1955); *Fantasy Variations* for Orch. (1963); *Umbrian Scene* for Orch. (New Orleans, March 31, 1964); *Markings,* symph. essay, dedicated to the memory of Dag Hammarskjöld (Rochester, Mich., Aug. 8, 1966; television perf., with scenes from Hammarskjöld's life, on "The Black Composer," shown on educational TV in N.Y. on June 19, 1972); *Theater Set* for Orch. (1968); *Scherzi musicali* for Chamber Orch. (1971); *Aulos* for Flute and Chamber Orch. (Bloomington, Ind., Feb. 21, 1971); *Quintet Concerto* for 5 Brass Soli and Orch. (N.Y., March 14, 1975); *Southern Harmony* for Orch. (North Carolina Symph., Feb. 10, 1976); 2 string quartets (1953, 1956); Quintet for Flute and Strings (1947); Piano Quintet (1949); Piano Sonata (1940); film score for *The Quiet One* (1948); many choral pieces and songs.

BIBLIOGRAPHY: N. Slonimsky, "Ulysses Kay," *American Composers Alliance Bulletin* (Fall 1957); L.M. Hayes, *The Music of Ulysses Kay, 1939–1963* (Univ. of Wisconsin, 1971); R.T. Hadley, *The Published Choral Music of Ulysses Simpson Kay, 1943–1968* (Diss., Univ. of Iowa, 1972); C. Dower, "Ulysses Kay: Distinguished American Composer," *Musart* (Jan.–Feb. 1972); L.R. Wyatt, "Ulysses Kay's *Fantasy Variations:* An Analysis," *Black Perspective in Music* (Spring 1977).

Kayser, Heinrich Ernst, German violinist; b. Altona, April 16, 1815; d. Hamburg, Jan. 17, 1888. He was a theater violinist in Hamburg (1840–57); then became a violin teacher there; wrote numerous violin studies that became standard exercises, and a violin method.

Kayser, Leif, Danish composer; b. Copenhagen, June 13, 1919. He studied at the Copenhagen Cons., and later took courses with Rosenberg in Stockholm; then went to Rome, where he studied theology (1942–49), and was ordained a priest of the Catholic Church. Returning to Copenhagen, he served as chaplain of the Catholic church of St. Ansgar (1949–64); in 1964 was appointed to the faculty of the Copenhagen Cons. He wrote 4 symphs. (1939, 1940, 1956, 1963); *Christmas Oratorio* (1943); Sinfonietta for Amateur Orch. (1967); Divertimento for 4 Recorders (1968); Organ Sonata; several sacred choruses; 4 Psalms for Women's Chorus; etc.

Kayser, Philipp Christoph, German composer and pianist; b. Frankfurt, March 10, 1755; d. Zürich, Dec. 23, 1823. In 1775 he settled in Zürich as a teacher. From Goethe's correspondence with him it appears that he wrote music to several of Goethe's singspiels, but only one, *Scherz, Liszt und Rache,* is preserved, in MS. He publ. *Weihnachtskantate: 2 Sonates en symphonie* for Piano and 2 Horns; and songs.
BIBLIOGRAPHY: C.A. Burkhardt, *Goethe und der Komponist Philipp Christoph Kayser* (Leipzig, 1879); E. Refardt, *Historisches-biographisches Musik-Lexikon der Schweiz* (1928).

Kazachenko, Grigori, Russian composer; b. St. Petersburg, May 3, 1858; d. Leningrad, May 18, 1938. He studied piano and composition at the St. Petersburg Cons.; then was chorus master at the Imperial Opera and appeared as conductor. In 1924 he became a prof. of choral singing at the Leningrad Cons. He wrote 2 operas, *Prince Serebryanny* (St. Petersburg, 1892) and *Pan Sotnik* (St. Petersburg, Sept. 17, 1902); Symph.; *An Armenian Overture; Fantasia on Russian Themes* for Viola and Orch.; several choral works, songs, and piano pieces.

Kazandjiev, Vasil, Bulgarian composer and conductor; b. Ruse, Sept. 10, 1934. He studied composition with Vladigerov and conducting with Simeonov at the Bulgarian State Cons., graduating in 1957; in 1964 was appointed to its faculty. In 1979 he became principal conductor of the Bulgarian Radio Symph. Orch. In his music he applies modern techniques, including modified serialism, to modalities of Bulgarian folk music.
WORKS: FOR ORCH.: Concerto for String Orch. (1951); Sinfonietta (1954); Trumpet Concerto (1955); *Divertimento* (1957); Concerto for Piano, Saxophone, and Orch. (1957–60); Violin Concerto (1961); *Complexi sonori* for Strings (1965); *Symphony of Timbres* (1968); *The Living Icons* for Chamber Orch. (1970; Sofia, Jan. 26, 1972); *Pictures from Bulgaria* for String Orch. and Percussion (1971); *Festive Music* (1972); *Capriccio* (1974); *Apocalypse* (1978); *Illuminations* (1980); Symph. No. 3 (1981). CHAMBER MUSIC: Wind Quintet (1951); *Variations* for Oboe, Clarinet, Violin, Viola, Cello, and Piano (1954); Horn Sonata (1955); Clarinet Sonata (1956); Sonata for Solo Violin (1957); 2 string quartets (1965, 1970); *Concert Improvisations* for Flute, Viola, Harp, and Harpsichord (1974); *Poco a poco* for Percussion and Organ (1979); Piano Quintet (1981). FOR PIANO: Sonata (1957); *The Triumph of the Bells*

(1974); also choruses; songs.

Kazanly, Nicolai, Russian composer; b. Tiraspol, Dec. 17, 1869; d. St. Petersburg, Aug. 5, 1916. He received his primary education in music in Odessa (1879–83); then went to St. Petersburg, where he entered the class in composition of Rimsky-Korsakov at the St. Petersburg Cons., graduating in 1894. In 1897 he traveled to Germany, where he conducted symph. concerts in Munich; returning to Russia, he supervised music education in military schools. He wrote an opera, *Miranda* (1910); Symph.; several symph. poems, among them *La Nuit du Carnaval;* cantatas and songs, all in the traditional Russian style. Under the general title of "Philharmonica" he publ. over 100 classical pieces in arrangement for small orch.

Kazuro, Stanislaw, Polish composer; b. Teklinapol, near Wilno, Aug. 1, 1881; d. Warsaw, Nov. 30, 1961. He studied in Warsaw, Paris, and Rome; after his return to Warsaw he was active mainly as a pedagogue and chorus conductor; he also publ. several school manuals. His compositions, in an academic style, were chiefly designed for pedagogic purposes; among them are 2 folk operas, several choral works, albums of pieces for piano, etc.

Każyński, Wiktor, Polish composer; b. Wilno, Dec. 30, 1812; d. St. Petersburg, March 18, 1867. He studied jurisprudence in Wilno; was mostly self-taught in music. From 1836 to 1840 he was a church organist; then went to Warsaw, where he took lessons with Chopin's teacher Elsner. In 1843 he went to St. Petersburg; in 1845 he conducted the orch. of the Alexandrinsky Theater there. He was one of the first pianists to play Chopin's works in Russia. His own compositions are of little importance, but they are of historical interest as early examples of Polish Romanticism. He wrote an opera to a Polish libretto, *Zyd wieczny tulacz (The Wandering Jew),* which was produced in Wilno in 1840, and an opera to a French libretto, *Mari et femme* (St. Petersburg, 1848); he also publ. *History of Italian Opera* (St. Petersburg, 1851; in Polish and in a Russian trans.).

Keats, Donald, significant American composer; b. New York, May 27, 1929. He studied piano at the Manhattan School of Music; then enrolled in Yale Univ., where he attended classes with Quincy Porter and Paul Hindemith in composition (Mus.B., 1949) and musicology with Alfred Einstein and Leo Schrade; then attended classes in composition at Columbia Univ. with Otto Luening, Douglas Moore, and Henry Cowell (M.A., 1953), and took a course in musicology with Paul Henry Lang. Subsequently he joined the Graduate School of Music at the Univ. of Minnesota, where he studied composition with Paul Felter and Dominick Argento and musicology with Johannes Riedel (Ph.D., 1962). In 1954 he received a Fulbright traveling grant and went to Germany, where he became a student of Philipp Jarnach at the Hochschule für Musik in Hamburg. In 1964–65 he received his first Guggenheim fellowship grant

to continue his studies in Paris, Florence, and Vienna; in 1972–73 he obtained a second Guggenheim grant and traveled to France and England. Other awards and prizes were from the National Endowment for the Arts, from Yale Univ., from the Rockefeller Foundation, and from the Ford Foundation. In 1948–49 he served as a teaching fellow at Yale Univ. School of Music; was then called to the army and was an instructor at the U.S. Naval School of Music at Washington, D.C., (1953–54); later was a member of the faculty of Antioch College in Yellow Springs, Ohio (1957–76); in 1969–70 he was visiting prof. of music at the School of Music, Univ. of Washington, in Seattle. In 1976 he was appointed prof. of music and composer-in-residence at the Univ. of Denver School of Music. In the meantime he gave guest performances in various parts of the world as a pianist in his own works; he gave concerts of his own music in Tel Aviv and Jerusalem in 1973; performed at a concert of his music in N.Y. in 1975, under the auspices of the U.S. Dept. of the Interior; and accompanied singers in programs of American songs, including his own. In his own compositions Keats appears as a classical lyricist; his music is sparse in texture but opulent in sonorous substance, frugal in diction but expansive in elaborate developments; its expressive power is a musical equivalent of "Ockham's razor," a medieval law of parsimony which proclaims the principle of *multa paucis,* multitude by paucity, abundance in concision. The titles of his works often indicate this economic precision of design: *Musica Instrumentalis; Polarities; Diptych; Branchings.* In his *Elegiac Symphony* he gives full expression to the lyric nature of his talent; it is an outgrowth of an orchestral *Elegy* inspired by the sadness upon the death of his infant son.
WORKS: For Orch.: Symph. No. 1 (1954); Symph. No. 2, *Elegiac Symph.* (Dayton, Ohio, Jan. 20, 1966; numerous subsequent hearings); *The New Work,* ballet (1967); *Concert Piece* (Columbus, Ohio, Feb. 3, 1968); *Branchings* for Orch. (1976). Chamber music: Sonata for Clarinet and Piano (1948); Piano Trio (1948); *Divertimento* for Wind and String Instruments (1949); 2 string quartets (1951, 1965); String Trio (1951); *Polarities* for Violin and Piano (1968); *Dialogue* for Piano and Wind Instruments (1973); *Diptych* for Cello and Piano (1973); *Epithalamium* for Violin, Cello, and Piano (1977); *Musica Instrumentalis* for 9 Instruments (1980). For Piano: *Theme and Variations* (1954); Sonata (1966). For Voices: *The Hollow Men* for Chorus, Clarinet, 3 Trombones, and Piano, to words by T.S. Eliot (Hamburg, July 12, 1955); *The Naming of Cats* for Vocal Quarter and Piano, to words by T.S. Eliot (1962); *A Love Triptych,* song cycle to poems by Yeats (1970); *Tierras del alma* for Soprano, Flute, and Guitar (Denver, May 23, 1979).

Kee, Cor, Dutch organist and composer, father of **Piet Kee;** b. Zaandam, Nov. 24, 1900. He studied the organ in the Netherlands; was especially praised for his talent in improvisation; in 1951 began a class in organ improvising in connection with the annual International Organ Improvisation Competition in Haarlem. He publ. 3 collections of Psalms for organ, which treat old Psalm tunes contrapuntally. In some of his own compositions (almost exclusively for organ) he applies polyphonic devices of the classical Flemish school in a modern way, including serial procedures.
WORKS: *Reeksveranderingen (Serial Permutations;* 1966); *Phases* for Organ (1966); *Phases* for Organ (1969); *Blijde Incomste (Joyful Entry),* variations on a traditional song, for Brass, Percussion, and Piano (1969); *Sweelinck Variations* for Horn, 2 Trumpets, 2 Trombones, and Organ (1973); numerous teaching pieces for organ.

Kee, Piet, Dutch organist and composer, son of **Cor Kee;** b. Zaandam, Aug. 30, 1927. He studied organ with his father and with Horst at the Amsterdam Cons., graduating in 1948; won the International Organ Improvisation Competition for 3 consecutive years (1953–55); in 1956 became organist of the St. Bavo Church in Haarlem, where the annual contest is held; from 1954 was a prof. of organ at the Muzieklyceum in Amsterdam; traveled as a concert organist in Europe and the U.S. Like his father, he has written music almost exclusively for organ: *Triptych on Psalm 86* (1960); *Variations on a Carol* (1952–60); *Music and Space,* rondo for 2 Organs, 3 Trumpets, and 2 Trombones (1969). He also has made arrangements of hymns and folk songs.

Keene, Christopher, American conductor; b. Berkeley, Calif., Dec. 21, 1946. He studied piano and cello; took courses at the Univ. of Calif., Berkeley, majoring in history in 1963. While still a student he organized an opera company, with which he staged several modern works, including the West Coast premiere of Henze's *Elegy for Young Lovers;* was a guest conductor of the Spoleto Festivals in the summers of 1968, 1969, and 1971. Concurrently, he was music director of the American Ballet Co., for which he wrote a ballet of his own, *The Consort* (1970). In 1970 he joined the conducting staff of the N.Y. City Opera as the winner of the Julius Rudel Award; made a brilliant debut in Ginastera's opera *Don Rodrigo;* on March 12, 1971, conducted the world premiere of Menotti's opera *The Most Important Man;* on Aug. 12, 1971, he conducted the posthumous world premiere of the opera *Yerma* by Villa-Lobos, with the Santa Fe Opera Co. At his N.Y. appearances he was enthusiastically acclaimed by the critics as one of the brightest precocious talents in the profession. In April 1971 he distinguished himself with the N.Y. City Opera by a highly competent performance of *La Traviata,* and later conducted also at the Metropolitan Opera. These accomplishments are all the more remarkable since he never took a regular course in conducting, but learned to lead orchs. by instinctual instrumental navigation. In 1975 he was appointed music director of the Syracuse (N.Y.) Symph. Orch. While retaining this position he also assumed the posts of music director of the Spoleto Festival in Charleston, S.C. (1977), and of the Long Island Phil. (1979). In 1982 he was appointed artistic supervisor of the N.Y. City Opera.

Kéfer, Paul, French cellist; b. Rouen, Dec. 30, 1875; d. Rochester, N.Y., May 22, 1941. He studied cello at the Paris Cons. with Delsart; won first prize in 1900. After coming to the U.S. in 1913, he formed, in N.Y., the Trio de Lutèce with Barrère (flute) and Salzedo (harp); was also founder and a member of the Franco-American Quartet. In 1923 he became a prof. of cello at the Eastman School of Music in Rochester, N.Y.

Kegel, Herbert, distinguished German conductor; b. Dresden, July 29, 1920. He studied at the Dresden Cons. In 1946 he became conductor of the Rostock Opera; in 1949 was engaged as a regular conductor of the Leipzig Radio Orch.; in 1960 he was named its chief conductor. From 1975 to 1978 he was a prof. at the Hochschule für Musik in Leipzig, and in 1978 became a prof. at the Dresden Hochschule für Musik. In 1977 was appointed to the prestigious post of chief conductor of the Dresden Phil. He was regarded as one of the most competent conductors of East Germany, combining a thorough knowledge of his repertoire with a fine sense of effective presentation of the music.

Kehr, Günter, German violinist and conductor; b. Darmstadt, March 16, 1920. He studied violin in Frankfurt and Cologne; then took univ. courses in Berlin and Cologne, receiving a Ph.D. with the dissertation *Untersuchungen zur Violintechnik um die Wende des 18. Jahrhunderts* (1941). As a violinist, he gave the first German performances of the concertos of Hindemith and Bartók; also played in a string trio. He then pursued a career as a conductor; in 1955 he founded the Mainz Chamber Orch., with which he made numerous tours. From 1953 to 1961 he was director of the Peter-Cornelius-Konservatorium in Mainz; from 1959 he taught at the Hochschule für Musik in Cologne, becoming a prof. there in 1961. He edited Urtext editions of the violin sonatas of Bach and Brahms; also supervised new editions of the orch. works of Albinoni, Rameau, Telemann, and other composers.

Keil, Alfredo, Portuguese composer; b. Lisbon, July 3, 1850; d. Hamburg, Oct. 4, 1907. He was of German extraction and received his education in Germany. Returning to Portugal, he devoted his energies to the furtherance of national music, and was the first to produce an opera on a Portuguese subject in the Portuguese language. His song *Herois do mar* (1890) was adopted as the national anthem of the Republic of Portugal in 1910.
WORKS: Operas: *Donna Bianca* (Lisbon, March 10, 1888); *Irene* (Turin, March 22, 1893); *Serrana* (the first grand opera in Portuguese; Lisbon, March 13, 1899); 2 symph. sketches: *India* and *Simao;* songs.
BIBLIOGRAPHY: Lavignac's *Encyclopédie de la musique* (vol. 4, p. 2,453).

Keilberth, Joseph, German conductor; b. Karlsruhe, April 19, 1908; d. Munich, July 20, 1968. He served as a conductor at the Karlsruhe State Opera (1935–40), of the Berlin Phil. Orch. (1940–45), and at the Dresden Opera (1945–51). He assumed the post of chief conductor of the Bamberg Symph. in 1949, retaining this position until his death in 1968; concurrently he served as Generalmusikdirektor of the Hamburg Phil. (1950–59); from 1959 until his death he also held the post of Generalmusikdirektor of the Bavarian State Opera in Munich. In 1951 he toured with the Bamberg Symph. in Switzerland, the Netherlands, France, Spain, and Portugal. In 1953 he conducted the Wagner Festival in Bayreuth; in 1954 toured with the Bamberg Symph. in Cuba and Mexico. He made his U.S. conducting debut at Carnegie Hall in N.Y. on April 4, 1954.

Keiser, Reinhard, important German opera composer; b. Teuchern, near Weissenfels, Jan. 9, 1674; d. Hamburg, Sept. 12, 1739. He received his early musical training from his father, **Gottfried Keiser,** an organist; was then sent to Leipzig, where he studied at the renowned Thomasschule directed by Johann Schelle. In 1693 he was in Braunschweig, where he began his career as a composer for the stage. His first opera-pastorale, *Der königliche Schäfer oder Basilius in Arcadien,* was performed shortly after his arrival in Braunschweig; in 1894 he produced a singspiel, *Procris und Cephalus;* there followed another pastorale, *Die wiedergefundenen Verliebten,* in 1695; it was revived in Hamburg in 1699 under the title *Die beständige und getreue Ismene.* In 1694 he was named Cammer-Componist in Braunschweig. In 1695 he went to Hamburg, which became his permanent residence. In 1696 he was engaged as Kapellmeister with the Hamburg Opera; in 1702 he became its co-director, retaining this position until 1707. Hamburg was then the main center of opera productions in Germany, and Keiser worked industriously producing not only his own operas there, but also the stage works of Handel and Mattheson. The number of Keiser's stage works was never calculated with credible precision; the best estimate is that he wrote in Hamburg at least 77 operas and 39 singspiels and theatrical intermezzi. The subjects of his operas are still predominantly taken from Greek and Roman mythology, as was customary in the Baroque era, but he introduced a decisive innovation by using the German language in his dramatic works; he further made use of popular local themes; he made a concession, however, in resorting to the Italian language in arias. Thus his last opera, *Circe,* produced in Hamburg on March 1, 1734, contains 21 German arias and 23 Italian arias. Keiser also continued the common tradition of having other composers contribute to the music. In his ballets he followed the French *style galant* and effectively used Rococo devices. In so doing he formed a German Baroque idiom national in essence and cosmopolitan in treatment; this aspect of his work influenced his younger contemporaries Bach and Handel. In 1718 Keiser became a guest Kapellmeister to the Duke of Württemberg in Stuttgart. In 1721 he went to Copenhagen to supervise the productions of his operas *Die unvergleichliche Psyche, Ulysses,* and *Der Armenier.* In 1723 he returned to Hamburg, and in 1725 composed 2 operas on subjects connected with Hamburg history and society: *Der Hamburger Jahrmarkt* and *Die Hamburger Schlachtzeit.* In 1728 he became Canonicus minor and Cantor of the Katharinenkirche in Hamburg. Apart from operas, he wrote many sacred works (oratorios, cantatas, Psalms, Passions), of which several were publ. in the collections *R. Keisers Gemüths-Ergötzung bestehend in einigen Sing-Gedichten mit einer Stimme und unterschiedlichen Instrumenten* (1698); *Divertimenti serenissimi* (airs with harpsichord accompaniment, 1714); *Kaiserliche Friedenpost* (songs and duets with harpsichord, 1715); etc. Several excerpts from his operas were publ. in Denkmäler Deutscher Tonkunst and other collections.

WORKS: FOR THE STAGE: *Der königliche Schäfer oder Basilius in Arcadien* (Braunschweig, 1693); *Procris und Cephalus,* singspiel (Braunschweig, 1694); *Die wiedergefundenen Verliebten,* Schäferspiel (Braunschweig, 1695; revised as *Die beständige und getreue Ismene,* Hamburg, 1699); *Mahumet II,* Trauerspiel (Hamburg, 1696); *Der geliebte Adonis* (Hamburg, 1697); *Die durch Wilhelm den Grossen in Britannien wieder eingeführte Treue* (Hamburg, 1698); *Allerunterthäbigster Gehorsam,* Tantzspiel and singspiel (Hamburg, Nov. 15, 1698); *Der aus Hyperboreen nach Cymbrien überbrachte güldene Apfel zu Ehren Friedrichs und Hedwig Sophiens zu Holstein* (Hamburg, 1698); *Der bey dem allgemeinen Welt-Friede und dem Grossen Augustus geschlossene Tempel des Janus* (Hamburg, 1699); *Die wunderbahr-errettete Iphigenia* (Hamburg, 1699); *Die Verbindung des grossen Hercules mit der schönen Hebe,* singspiel (Hamburg, 1699); *Die Wiederkehr der güldnen Zeit* (Hamburg, 1699); *La forza della virtù, oder Die Macht der Tugend* (Hamburg, 1700); *Das höchstpreissliche Crönungsfest Ihrer Kgl. Majestät zu Preussen,* ballet opera (Hamburg, 1701); *Störtebecker und Jödge Michaels* (2 versions; Hamburg, 1701); *Die wunderschöne Psyche,* singspiel (Hamburg, Oct. 20, 1701); *Circe oder Des Ulisses erster Theil* (Hamburg, 1702); *Penelope oder Des Ulysses ander Theil* (Hamburg, 1702); *Sieg der fruchtbaren Pomona* (Hamburg, Oct. 18, 1702); *Die sterbende Eurydice oder Orpheus erster Theil* (Hamburg, 1702); *Orpheus ander Theil* (Hamburg, 1702); *Neues preussisches Ballet* (Hamburg, 1702); *Die verdammte Staat-Sucht, oder Der verführte Claudius* (Hamburg, 1703); *Die Geburt der Minerva* (Hamburg, 1703); *Die über die Liebe triumphierende Weissheit oder Salomon* (Hamburg, 1703); *Der gestürzte und wieder erhöhte Nebucadnezar, König zu Babylon* (Hamburg, 1704); *Die römische Unruhe oder Die edelmüthige Octavia* (Hamburg, Aug. 5, 1705); *Die kleinmüthige Selbstmörderinn Lucretia oder Die Staats-Thorheit des Brutus,* Trauerspiel (Hamburg, Nov. 29, 1705); *La fedeltà coronata oder Die gekrönte Treue* (Hamburg, 1706); *Masaniello furioso, oder Die Neapolitanische Fischer-Empörung* (Hamburg, June 1706); *La costanza sforzata, Die gezwungene Beständigkeit oder Die listige Rache des Sueno*

(Hamburg, Oct. 11, 1706); *Il genio d'Holsatia* (Hamburg, 1706; used as prologue to succeeding work); *Der durchlauchtige Secretarius, oder Almira, Königin von Castilien* (Hamburg, 1706); *Der angenehme Betrug oder Der Carneval von Venedig* (Hamburg, 1707; includes arias by C. Graupner); *La forza dell'amore oder Die von Paris entführte Helena* (Hamburg, 1709); *Die blutdürstige Rache oder Heliates und Olympia* (Hamburg, 1709; with C. Graupner); *Desiderius, König der Langobarden* (Hamburg, July 26, 1709); *Die bis und nach dem Todt unerhörte Treue des Orpheus* (Hamburg, 1709; based on *Die sterbende Eurydice oder Orpheus erster Theil* and *Orpheus ander Theil*); *La grandezza d'animo oder Arsinoe* (Hamburg, 1710); *Le Bon Vivant oder Die Leipziger Messe* (Hamburg, 1710); *Der Morgen des europäischen Glückes oder Aurora,* Schäferspiel (Hamburg, July 26?, 1710); *Der durch den Fall des grossen Pompejus erhöhte Julius Caesar* (Hamburg, Nov. 1710); *Der hochmüthige, gestürzte und wieder erhabene Croesus,* dramma musicale (Hamburg, 1710); *Die oesterreichische Grossmuth oder Carolus V* (Hamburg, June 1712); *Die entdeckte Verstellung oder Die geheime Liebe der Diana,* Schäferspiel (Hamburg, April 1712; revised 1724); *Die wiederhergestellte Ruh oder Die gecrönte Tapferkeit des Heraclius* (Hamburg, June 1712); *L'inganno fedele oder Der getreue Betrug* (Hamburg, Oct. 1714); *Die gecrönte Tugend* (Hamburg, Nov. 15, 1714); *Triumph des Friedens,* serenata (Hamburg, March 1, 1715); *Fredegunda* (Hamburg, March 1715); *L'amore verso la patria oder Der sterbende Cato* (Hamburg, 1715); *Artemisia* (Hamburg, 1715); *Das römische Aprilfest,* Lust- and Tantz-spiel (Hamburg, June 1716); *Das verewigte und triumphirende Ertz-Haus Oesterreich,* serenata (Hamburg, 1716); *Das zerstörte Troja oder Der durch den Tod Helenen versöhnte Achilles* (Hamburg, Nov. 1716); *Die durch Verstellung und Grossmuth über die Grausamkeit siegende Liebe oder Julia* (Hamburg, Feb. 1717); *Die grossmüthige Tomyris* (Hamburg, Feb. 1717); *Der die Festung Siebenbürgisch-Weissenburg eroberude und über Dacier triumphirende Kayser Trajanus* (Hamburg, Nov. 1717); *Das bey seiner Ruh und Gebuhrt eines Printzen frolockende Lycien unter der Regierung des Königs Jacobates und Bellerophon* (Hamburg, Dec. 28, 1717); *Die unvergleichliche Psyche* (Copenhagen, April 16, 1722); *Ulysses* (Copenhagen, Oct. 1722); *Der Armenier* (Copenhagen, Nov. 1722); *Die betrogene und nochmahls vergötterte Ariadne* (Hamburg, Nov. 25, 1722; based on the opera by Conradi of 1691); *Sancio oder Die siegende Grossmuth* (1723?); *Das wegen Verbannung der Laudplagen am Geburthstage Herrn Friedrich IV zu Dennemark jauchzende Cimbrien,* serenata (Copenhagen, 1724); *Das frohlockende Gross Britannien,* serenata (Hamburg, June 8, 1724); *Der sich rächende Cupido,* Schäferspiel (Hamburg, 1724; based on *Die entdeckte Verstellung oder Die geheime Liebe der Diana*); *Bretislaus oder Die siegende Beständigkeit* (Hamburg, Jan. 27, 1725); *Der Hamburger Jahrmarkt oder Der glückliche Betrug* (Hamburg, June 27, 1725); *Die Hamburger Schlachtzeit oder Der misslungene Betrug* (Hamburg, Oct. 22, 1725); *Prologus beim Geburths Feste Friderici Ludovici von Hannover,* serenata (Hamburg, Jan. 31, 1726); *Mistevojus König der Obotriten oder Wenden* (Hamburg, 1726); *Der lächerliche Printz Jodelet* (Hamburg, 1726); *Buchhofer der stumme Printz Atis,* intermezzo (Hamburg, 1726); *Barbacola,* intermezzo (Hamburg, 1726; includes music by Lully); *Lucius Verus oder Die siegende Treue* (Hamburg, Oct. 18, 1728; based on *Berenice* by Bronner of 1702); *Der hochmüthige, gestürtzte und wieder erhabene Croesus,* singspiel (Hamburg, 1730; based on the dramma musicale of 1710); *Jauchzen der Kunste* (1733); *Circe* (Hamburg, March 1, 1734; with arias by other composers). Of these, *Die römische Unruhe oder Die edelmüthige Octavia* was ed. by M. Schneider in the supplement to the Handel *Gesamtausgabe* (Leipzig, 1902); *Der lächerliche Printz Jodelet* was ed. by F. Zelle in the *Publikationen der Gesellschaft für Musikforschung* (1892); the 1730 version of *Der hochmüthige, gesturtzte und wieder erhabene Croesus* was ed. by M. Schneider in the Denkmäler Deutscher Tonkunst, vol. 37 (1912).

Keiser also composed several secular cantatas and other pieces, including *Gemüths-Ergötzung,* cantata (Hamburg, 1698); *Componimenti musicali, oder Teutsche und italiänische Arien, nebst unterschiedlichen Recitativen aus Almira und Octavia* (Hamburg, 1706); *Divertimenti serenissima delle cantate, duette ed arie diverse senza stromenti oder Durchlauchtige Ergötzung* (Hamburg, 1713); *Musikalische Land-Lust, bestehend in verschiedenen moralischen Cantaten* (Hamburg, 1714); *Kayserliche Friedenspost, nebst verschiedenen moralischen Singgedichten und Arien* (Hamburg, 1715).

Sacred works by Keiser include *Der blutige und sterbende Jesus* (Hamburg, Holy Week, 1704); *Der für die Sünde der Welt gemartete und sterbende Heiland Jesus* (Hamburg, 1712); *Der zum Tode verurtheilte und gecreutzigte Jesus* (Hamburg, 1715); *Passions Oratorium* (Hamburg, 1717?); *Die über den Triumph ihres Heylandes Jesu jubilirende gläubige Seele* (Hamburg, Nov. 2, 1717; not extant); *Die durch Grossmuth und Glauben triumphirende Unschuld oder Der siegende David* (Hamburg, Aug. 9, 1721); etc. The *Passions Oratorium* has been publ. in a modern ed. in the *Geistliche Chormusik,* vol. X (Stuttgart, 1963).

BIBLIOGRAPHY: J. Mattheson, *Das neu-eröffnete Orchester . . .* (Hamburg, 1713); idem, *Grundlage einer Ehren-Pforte . . .* (Hamburg, 1740; new ed., by M. Schneider, Berlin, 1910); J. Sittard, "Reinhard Keiser in Württemberg," *Monatshefte für Musikgeschichte,* XVIII (1886); F. Voigt, "Reinhard Keiser," *Vierteljahrsschrift für Musikwissenschaft* (1890); H. Leichtentritt, *Reinhard Keiser in seinen Opern* (Diss., Univ. of Berlin, 1901); T. Krogh, "Reinhard Keiser in Kopenhagen," in *Musikwissenschaftliche Beiträge: Festschrift für Johannes Wolf* (Berlin, 1929); R. Petzold, *Die Kirchen-Kompositionen und weltliche Kantaten Reinhard Keisers* (Berlin, 1934); J. Rudolph, "Reinhard Keiser und *Masaniello*," *Musik und Gesellschaft* (Oct. 1967); R. Brenner, *The Operas of Reinhard Keiser in Their Relationship to the Affektenlehre* (Diss.,

Brandeis Univ., 1968); D. Moe, *The St. Mark Passion of Reinhard Keiser* (Diss., Univ. of Iowa, 1968); M. Peckham, "First Performances of Reinhard Keiser's *Croesus,*" *Current Musicology,* 6 (1968); W. Paap, "De *Markus Passion* van Reinhard Keiser," *Mens en Melodie* (March 1970); J. Rudolph, "Probleme der Hamburger deutschen Frühoper," *Händel-Jahrbuch 1969–70;* R. Brenner, "Emotional Expression in Keiser's Operas," *Music Review* (Aug. 1972); B. Deane, "Reinhard Keiser: An Interim Assessment," *Soundings,* IV (1974); K. Zelm, *Die Opern Reinhard Keisers* (Munich, 1975); J. Wenzel, *Geschichte der Hamburger Oper, 1678–1978* (Hamburg, 1978).

Kelbe, Theodore, German conductor; b. Braunschweig, Oct. 6, 1862; d. Milwaukee, Oct. 12, 1922. He studied violin in his native town; from 1879 to 1882, was a member of the court orch. there; in 1882, joined the opera orch. in Cologne. In 1901 he came to America as concertmaster of the Milwaukee Symph. Orch.; in 1904, became conductor of the Sängerbund des Nordwestens there; was in charge of its festivals in Milwaukee (1904), St. Paul (1906 and 1912), Omaha (1910), and Kansas City (1917).

Kelberine, Alexander, pianist; b. Kiev, Feb. 22, 1903; d. (suicide) New York, Jan. 30, 1940. He studied at the Kiev Cons., then at the Univ. of Vienna; took lessons from Busoni in Berlin; in 1923, came to America and studied at the Juilliard Graduate School in N.Y. with Siloti (piano) and Rubin Goldmark (composition); later also studied with Ernst Toch. A victim of acute depression, he programmed his last recital for pieces in minor keys and of funereal connotations, concluding with Liszt's *Todtentanz;* he then went home and took an overdose of sleeping pills. His body was discovered on Jan. 30, 1940. He was married to the pianist **Jeanne Behrend,** but was estranged from her.

Keldorfer, Robert, Austrian composer and conductor, son of **Viktor Keldorfer;** b. Vienna, Aug. 10, 1901; d. Klagenfurt, Sept. 13, 1980. He received his early musical training from his father; then took courses at the Vienna Academy of Music with Carl Prohaska and Max Springer, graduating in 1930. From 1941 to 1966 he was director of the Klagenfurt Cons. Among his works are an opera, *Verena* (1951); Oboe Concerto (1965); *Sonata ritmica* for Alto Recorder and Piano (1964); Viola Sonata (1964); Sonata for Recorder and Guitar (1967); and a considerable number of choral works and solo songs. In his music he followed the dramatic lines of Richard Strauss.

Keldorfer, Viktor, Austrian conductor and composer, father of **Robert Keldorfer;** b. Salzburg, April 14, 1873; d. Vienna, Jan. 28, 1959. He was a student at the Mozarteum in Salzburg; then conducted choruses in Vienna; in 1922–38, and again in 1945–54, he was director of the Vienna Schubertbund; also was conductor of the Ostdeutscher Sängerbund, which became a model for many Austrian male choruses. He publ. 150 opus numbers; a *Missa solemnis,* 2 vols.

of *Lieder für grosse und kleine Kinder,* many men's choruses, and arrangements of Strauss waltzes for men's chorus and orch. He also edited a complete collection of Schubert's men's choruses.

BIBLIOGRAPHY: O. Dobrowolny, *Viktor Keldorfer: Leben und Wirken* (Vienna, 1947).

Kelemen, Milko, significant Croatian composer; b. Podrawska Slatina, March 30, 1924. He was taught to play piano by his grandmother; in 1945 entered the Zagreb Academy of Music, where he studied theory with Šulek; then went to Paris, where he took courses with Messiaen and Aubin at the Paris Cons. (1954–55); supplemented his studies at Freiburg with Fortner (1958–60); then worked on electronic music at the Siemens studio in Munich (1966–68); in the interim he taught composition at the Zagreb Cons. (1955–58, 1960–65). He was co-founder of the Zagreb Biennial Festival of New Music, and became its president in 1961. In 1969 he was appointed to the faculty of the Schumann Cons. in Düsseldorf; in 1973 he became a prof. of composition at the Hochschule für Musik in Stuttgart. As a composer, Kelemen began his career following the trend of European modernism well within academically acceptable lines, but changed his style radically about 1956 in the direction of the cosmopolitan avant-garde, adopting successively or concurrently the techniques of serialism, abstract expressionism, constructivism, and sonorism, making use of electronic sound; he further writes alternatively valid versions for a single piece. WORKS: FOR THE STAGE: A "theater-of-the-absurd" musical scene, *Novi stanar (The New Tenant),* after Ionesco (1964; Münster, Sept. 20, 1964); 2 operas: *König Ubu* (1965; Hamburg, 1965) and *Der Belagerungszustand (State of Siege),* after Camus's novel *The Plague* (1968–69; Hamburg, Jan. 10, 1970); a "scenic action," *Opera bestial* (1973–74); 2 ballets: *Le Héros et son miroir* (*The Hero and His Mirror;* 1959; Paris, May 10, 1961) and *Napuštene* (*Abandoned;* 1964; Lübeck, Nov. 4, 1964). FOR ORCH.: *Prelude, Aria and Finale* for String Orch. (1948); Sinfonietta (1950); Symph. (1951; Zagreb, Feb. 18, 1952); Piano Concerto (1952; Zagreb, Dec. 22, 1953); Violin Concerto (1953; Zagreb, April 19, 1957); *Koncertantne improvizacije* for Strings (1955); *Adagio and Allegro* for Strings (1955); *Concerto giocosa* for Chamber Orch. (1956; Zagreb, Jan. 4, 1957); Concerto for Bassoon and Strings (1956; Zagreb, April 11, 1957); *Simfonijska muzika 1957* (Zagreb, June 4, 1958); *3 Dances* for Viola and Strings (1957); *Konstelacije* for Chamber Orch. (1958; Zagreb, April 27, 1960); Concertino for Double Bass and Strings (1958); *Skolion* (1958); *5 Essays* for Strings (1959); *Ekvilibri* for 2 Orchs. (1961); *Transfiguracije* for Piano and Orch. (1961; Hamburg, April 6, 1962); *Sub Rosa* (1964; Zagreb, May 23, 1965); *Surprise* for Chamber String Orch. (1967; Zagreb, May 13, 1967); *Composé* for 2 Pianos and Orch. Groups (1967; Donaueschingen, Oct. 22, 1967); *Changeant* for Cello and Orch. (1967–68); *Floreal,* in 3 versions (1969–70; Coolidge Festival, Washington, D.C., Oct. 30, 1970); *Oliphant* for 5 Winds and Chamber Ensemble

(1971); *Sonabile* for Piano, with Ring Modulator and Orch. (1972); *Abecedarium* for Chamber String Orch. (1973; Graz, Oct. 13, 1974); *Mirabilia II* for Piano, with Ring Modulator and 2 Orch. Groups (Graz, Oct. 12, 1977). FOR VOICE: *Igre (Games),* song cycle for Baritone and Strings (1955; Zagreb, Sept. 29, 1956); *Epitaph* for Mezzo-soprano and Chamber Orch. (1961); *O Primavera,* cantata for Tenor and Strings (1964); *Hommage à Heinrich Schütz* for Chorus a cappella (1964); *Le Mot* for Mezzo-soprano and 2 Orchs. (1964–65); *Musik für Heinssenbüttel* for Voice and Chamber Ensemble (1967); *Passionato* for Flute and Choral Group (1971); *Yebell* for Narrator, Pantomime, and Chamber Ensemble (1972; Munich, Sept. 1, 1972); *For You* for Voice and Ring Modulator (1972); *Gassho* for 4 Choruses (1974). CHAMBER MUSIC: *Musika* for Solo Violin (1957); *Etudes contrapunctiques* for Wind Quintet (1959); Oboe Sonata (1960); *Studija* for Solo Flute (1961); *Radiant* for Flute, Viola, Piano or Celesta, Harpsichord, and Percussion (1961); *Entrances* for Wind Quintet (1966); *Motion* for String Quartet (1968); *Varia melodia* for String Quartet (1972); *Fabliau* for Solo Flute (1972); *Tantana,* 5 movements of instrumental "happening," with Voices in one movement (1972). FOR PIANO: *Theme and Variations* (1949); Sonata (1954); *5 Studies* (1958); *Dessins commentées* (1963).

Kelemen, Zoltán, Hungarian bass; b. Budapest, March 12, 1926; d. Zürich, May 9, 1979. He was educated at the Franz Liszt Academy of Music in Budapest and at the Santa Cecilia Academy in Rome; then sang in Augsburg, Cologne, Düsseldorf, Hamburg, and Munich; also appeared in Bayreuth and Salzburg. On Nov. 22, 1968, he made his Metropolitan Opera debut in N.Y. as Alberich in *Das Rheingold;* also sang at Covent Garden in London. He was at his best in portentous tragicomic roles; especially memorable were his interpretations of Falstaff and Leporello.

Kéler-Béla (real name, **Albert von Keler**), Hungarian violinist, band conductor, and composer of light music; b. Bartfeld, Feb. 13, 1820; d. Wiesbaden, Nov. 20, 1882. He was a law student; then became a farmer; finally took up music in 1845, studying under Sechter and Schlesinger in Vienna, and playing the violin at the Theater-an-der-Wien, where he developed his specialty, the composition of dance music. In 1854 he went to Berlin for a time to conduct the Gungl Orch.; the following year he succeeded Lanner as the conductor of his band in Vienna. In 1856–63 he conducted an army band; then the Spa Orch. at Wiesbaden, resigning in 1873 owing to ill health. He wrote a great number of dances and other light pieces, some of which attained enormous popularity, such as the waltz *Hoffnungssterne,* the galop *Hurrah-Sturm,* and particularly his *Lustspiel Ouvertüre.*

BIBLIOGRAPHY: Z. Sztehlo, *Kéler-Béla* (Budapest, 1930).

Kell, Reginald, English clarinet virtuoso; b. York,

June 8, 1906; d. Frankfort, Ky., Aug. 5, 1981. He studied violin at an early age, but later took up the clarinet, and earned a living by playing in silent-movie houses; in 1927 he enrolled at the Royal Academy of Music in London with Haydn Draper; upon Draper's death in 1934 he succeeded him as clarinet teacher at the Royal Academy of Music, a post he held until 1939. He subsequently occupied positions as principal clarinet player at the Royal Phil. (1931–32), London Phil. (1932–36), Covent Garden Opera (1932–36), London Symph. Orch. (1936–39), Liverpool Phil. (1942–45), and the Philharmonia (1945–48). In 1948 he went to the U.S., where he became active as a performer in chamber music ensembles and as a teacher; he was back in London in 1958; retired in 1966, and took up watercolor painting; in 1978 he exhibited his paintings at the Aspen Music Festival.
BIBLIOGRAPHY: R. Gelatt, *Music Makers* (N.Y., 1953; pp. 189–94).

Keller, Gottfried (called **Godfrey**), German harpsichord teacher who was active in England late in the 17th century; d. London, 1704. He publ. *A Compleat Method for Attaining to Play a Thoroughbass upon either Organ, Harpsichord, or Theorbolute* (London, 1705; posthumous; reprinted in W. Holder's *A Treatise of the Natural Grounds, and Principles of Harmony*, London, 1731); 6 sonatas for 2 Violins, Trumpet or Oboe, Viola, and Continuo; 6 suites for 2 Flutes, with Continuo.

Keller, Hans, Austrian-British musicologist; b. Vienna, March 11, 1919. He emigrated to England in 1938; studied violin and viola, and played in orchs. and string quartets; mastered the English language to an extraordinary degree, and soon began pointing out solecisms and other infractions on the purity of the tongue to native journalists; wrote articles on film music, and boldly invaded the sports columns in British newspapers, flaunting his mastery of the lingo. In 1947 he founded (with Donald Mitchell) the periodical *Music Survey;* joined the music division of the BBC in 1959. He launched a system of "functional analysis," applying symbolic logic and pseudo-Babbagean taxonomy to render esthetic judgment on the value of a given musical work. He publ. several articles expounding the virtues of his ratiocination, among them the fundamental essay "Functional Analysis: Its Pure Application," *Music Review* (1957).
BIBLIOGRAPHY: H. Raynor, "Hans Keller and Pontius Pilate," *Music Review,* 1957.

Keller, Harrison, American violinist and music educator; b. Delphos, Kans., Oct. 8, 1888; d. Wellesley, Mass., March 13, 1979. He studied violin at Bethany College in Lindsborg, Kans. (B.M., 1907; honorary D.M., 1954); then in Germany, at the Stern Cons. in Berlin (1907–11); in Prague, with Anton Witek (1912); and in St. Petersburg, with Leopold Auer (1913–14). He served in the U.S. Army in World War I; received the French Legion of Honor. Returning to the U.S., he organized a string quartet in Boston; was head of the string dept. at the New England

Cons. (1922–46); then became its director (1947–52) and president (1952–58).

Keller, Hermann, German organist and musicologist; b. Stuttgart, Nov. 20, 1885; d. Freiburg im Breisgau, Aug. 17, 1967, in an automobile accident. He studied with Max Reger (composition), Straube (organ), and Teichmüller (piano); filled various posts as organist in Weimar, Stuttgart, etc.; from 1920 till 1950 taught at the Württemberg Hochschule für Musik.
WRITINGS: *Reger und die Orgel* (1923); *Schule des Generalbassspiels* (1931); *Schule der Choralimprovisation* (1939); *Die Kunst des Orgelspiels* (1941); *Bachs Orgelwerke* (1948); *Bachs Klavierwerke* (1950); *Phrasierung und Artikulation* (Kassel, 1955; in Eng., N.Y., 1965); *Domenico Scarlatti* (Leipzig, 1957); *Das wohltemperierte Klavier von J.S. Bach* (Kassel, 1965).

Keller, Homer, American composer; b. Oxnard, Calif., Feb. 17, 1915. He studied at the Eastman School of Music in Rochester, N.Y. with Howard Hanson and Bernard Rogers (B.M., 1937; M.M., 1938); received a Fulbright grant to go to Paris, where he took lessons with Honegger and Boulanger (1950–51). He filled a number of teaching posts, including those at the Univ. of Michigan (1947–54) and at the Univ. of Oregon (1958–77).
WORKS: 3 symphs.: No. 1 (N.Y. Phil., Nov. 2, 1940); No. 2 (Ann Arbor, Mich., April 1, 1948); No. 3 (Honolulu, Dec. 9, 1950); Concerto for Piano and Orch. (Ojai, Calif., May 29, 1949); *Sonorities* for Orch. (Eugene, Oreg., Feb. 23, 1971); many pieces of chamber music and works for voice.

Keller, Karl, German composer and flutist; b. Dessau, Oct. 16, 1784; d. Schaffhausen, July 19, 1855. His father was a court organist and chamber musician. Keller was a flute virtuoso; he was court musician at Berlin (until 1806), Kassel (until 1814), Stuttgart (until 1816), and Donaueschingen (1817), where he later became chorus master. He married the opera singer **Wilhelmine Meierhofer.** In 1849 he received a pension and retired to Switzerland. He wrote 3 flute concertos; 4 polonaises, with Orch.; 2 divertissements, with Orch.; 6 part-songs for Male Chorus; duos and solos for flute; songs.

Keller, Matthias, German violinist and composer; b. Ulm, March 20, 1813; d. Boston, Oct. 12, 1875. He studied music in Stuttgart and Vienna; at 16 became first violinist of the Royal Chapel in Vienna (for 5 years); then was bandmaster in the army (for 7 years); in 1846, went to America and played in theater orchs. in Philadelphia; became interested in violin making and founded Keller's Patent Steam Violin Manufactory (1857). He then went to N.Y. and won a $500 prize for his *American Hymn* (*Speed our Republic, O Father on high*), for which he wrote both words and music; composed over 100 songs, including some patriotic songs for the Civil War; also *Ravel Polka* (1846). He also publ. *A Collection of Poems* (1874).

BIBLIOGRAPHY: F.J. Metcalf, *American Writers and Compilers of Sacred Music* (1925); *Dictionary of American Biography* (1933).

Keller, Max, Bavarian composer and organist; b. Trostberg, Oct. 7, 1770; d. Altötting, Sept. 16, 1855. He was organist at Altötting; publ. 6 Latin and 6 German masses; other sacred works and organ music.

Keller, Otto, Austrian writer on music; b. Vienna, June 5, 1861; d. Salzburg, Oct. 25, 1928. He studied music history with Hanslick and theory with Bruckner; publ. biographies of Beethoven (1885), Goldmark (1900), von Suppé (1905), Tchaikovsky (1914), and Mozart (2 vols., 1926–27); also an illustrated history of music (5th ed., 1926) and *Die Operette* (1926); compiled a valuable collection of source material relating to music and the theater.

Keller, Walter, American organist; b. Chicago, Feb. 23, 1873; d. there, July 7, 1940. He studied at the American Cons. of Music in Chicago (1891–94) and at the Leipzig Cons. (1894–96). Returning to America, he occupied various teaching posts; also was a church organist in Chicago from 1903. He wrote a comic opera, *The Crumpled Isle;* a melodrama, *Alaric's Death; Synchronous Prelude and Fugue* for Orch. (Chicago, 1924); also a number of works for organ; sacred choruses; songs.

Kellermann, Christian, Danish cellist; b. Randers, Jutland, Jan. 27, 1815; d. Copenhagen, Dec. 3, 1866. He studied with Merk in Vienna; made many concert tours; in 1847, was appointed soloist in the royal orch. at Copenhagen. He publ. solos for cello.

Kelley, Edgar Stillman, important American composer and writer; b. Sparta, Wis., April 14, 1857; d. New York, Nov. 12, 1944. He studied first with F.W. Merriam (1870–74), then with Clarence Eddy and N. Ledochowsky in Chicago (1874–76). In 1876 he went to Germany, where he took courses at the Stuttgart Cons. (until 1880) with Seifritz (composition), Krüger and Speidel (piano), and Friedrich Finck (organ). Returning to the U.S., he served as an organist in Oakland and San Francisco; conducted performances of light opera companies in N.Y.; taught piano and theory at various schools and at the N.Y. College of Music (1891–92); was music critic for the *San Francisco Examiner* (1893–95); lecturer on music for the Univ. Extension of N.Y. Univ. (1896–97); then acting prof. at Yale Univ. (1901–2). In 1902 he went to Berlin, where he taught piano and theory (until 1910). In 1910 he was appointed dean of the dept. of composition at the Cincinnati Cons., retaining this post until 1934, at the same time holding a fellowship in composition at Western College in Oxford, Ohio. He received an honorary Litt.D. from Miami Univ. (1916) and an honorary LL.D. from the Univ. of Cincinnati (1917). He contributed articles to various music journals; also publ. correspondence from Germany during his stay there. With his wife, **Jessie Stillman Kelley,** he organized the Kelley

Stillman Publishing Co., which publ. several of his scores. Although his stage works and his symph. pieces were quite successful when first performed (some critics described him as a natural successor to MacDowell in American creative work), little of his music survived the test of time.

WORKS: Theme and Variations for String Quartet (c.1880); *Wedding Ode* for Tenor Solo, Men's Chorus, and Orch. (c.1882); incidental music to *Macbeth*, for Orch. and Chorus (San Francisco, Feb. 12, 1885); comic opera, *Puritania* (Boston, June 9, 1892; 100 consecutive perfs.; publ. in vocal score); *Aladdin*, Chinese suite for Orch. (San Francisco, April 1894); incidental music to *Ben Hur*, for Soli, Chorus, and Orch. (N.Y., Oct. 1, 1900; highly successful, used for perfs. of that popular play some 6,000 times up to 1918); music to Fernald's play *The Cat and the Cherub* (N.Y., June 15, 1901); *Alice in Wonderland*, suite for Orch. (Norfolk [Conn.] Festival, June 5, 1919, composer conducting); First Symph., *Gulliver* (Cincinnati, April 9, 1937); 2nd Symph., *New England* (Norfolk Festival, June 3, 1913, composer conducting); *The Pilgrim's Progress,* musical miracle play for Soli, Chorus, Children's Chorus, Organ, and Orch. (Cincinnati May Festival, May 10, 1918); *A California Idyll* for Orch. (N.Y., Nov. 14, 1918); *The Pit and the Pendulum,* symph. suite, after Poe (1925); *Israfel* and *Eldorado,* for Voice and Orch.; Piano Quintet; 2 piano quartets; many choral works, of which the best known are *My Captain,* after Whitman, and *The Sleeper,* after Poe; 3 pieces for Piano: *The Flower Seekers; Confluentia* (also arranged for String Orch., 1913); *The Headless Horseman;* a song, *The Lady Picking Mulberries* (1888); song cycle, *Phases of Love* (1890). He also publ. *Chopin the Composer* (N.Y., 1913); *Musical Instruments* (Boston, 1925).

Kelley, Jessie Stillman, American piano pedagogue; b. Chippewa Falls, Wis., 1866; d. Dallas, April 3, 1949. She studied piano with William Mason and theory with **Edgar Stillman Kelley** (whom she later married); received an L.H.D. from Western College in Oxford, Ohio, and a Litt.D. from Miami Univ. For many years she taught piano in San Francisco, N.Y., and Berlin; in 1910–34, was director of music at Western College; was active in music clubs.

Kellie, Lawrence, English tenor and song composer; b. London, April 3, 1862; d. there, Aug. 20, 1932. He was apprenticed to a solicitor; began to study music in 1884 at the Royal Academy of Music; appeared in a minor operatic role at Covent Garden in 1886; made his American debut in a vocal recital in N.Y. (May 23, 1887). His songs have had a great vogue; among them, the most popular were *Is It Too Late?, Sleeping Tide, All for Thee, This Heart of Mine,* and *Douglas Gordon.*

Kellner, Ernst August, English pianist and singer; b. Windsor, Jan. 26, 1792; d. London, July 18, 1839. He began to study piano at the age of 2; at 5 he played a Handel concerto before the court; also studied voice in England with W. Parsons, and in Italy with

Nozzari, Casella, and Crescentini in Naples in 1815. Returning to England in 1820, he won acclaim as a pianist and baritone; sang in Venice (1824); sang and played in St. Petersburg (1828) and Paris (1833); in 1834, became organist at the Bavarian Chapel in London.

BIBLIOGRAPHY: A biographical sketch by Richard Cull, *Case of Precocious Musical Talent,* was publ. in London (1839).

Kellogg, Clara Louise, famous American soprano; b. Sumterville, S.C., July 9, 1842; d. New Hartford, Conn., May 13, 1916. She received her vocal training in N.Y., from Manzocchi, Errani, and Muzio; made her professional debut at the Academy of Music in N.Y. (Feb. 27, 1861); then sang in Boston. She sang Marguerite in the N.Y. premiere of *Faust* (Nov. 25, 1863); made her London debut as Marguerite on Nov. 2, 1867. In 1872 she organized an opera company with Pauline Lucca, but the rivalry between them precluded its success. In 1873 she launched an opera enterprise of her own, known as the English Opera Co.; she extended her supervision to the translations of the librettos, the stage settings, and the training of the soloists and chorus. She herself sang 125 performances in the winter of 1874–75. After that, she divided her time between Europe and America. In 1887 she married her manager, Karl Strakosch, nephew of Maurice and Max Strakosch, and retired from the stage. She wrote *Memoirs of an American Prima Donna* (N.Y., 1913).

Kelly, Michael, Irish singer and composer; b. Dublin, Dec. 25, 1762; d. Margate, Oct. 9, 1826. He studied singing under Rauzzini, and in Naples (1779) under Fenaroli and Aprile. He then sang in Palermo, Livorno, Florence, Bologna, and Venice. Visiting Vienna, he was engaged at the court opera for 4 years, becoming the friend of Mozart, and taking the role of Basilio in the production of *Figaro.* In 1787 he appeared for the first time at Drury Lane in London, and sang leading tenor roles there until his retirement. In 1789 his debut as a composer was made with *False Appearances* and *Fashionable Friends;* up to 1820 he wrote the music for 62 stage pieces, also many songs. He had a music shop from 1802 to 1811; when it failed, he went into the wine trade; it was Sheridan who said, considering the quality of his music and wines, that he was "a composer of wines and an importer of music." His *Reminiscences,* publ. in the year of his death (1826), were written by Theodore Hook from material supplied by Kelly (reprinted with a new introduction by A.H. King, N.Y., 1968); the vol. is replete with amusing musical anecdotes.

BIBLIOGRAPHY: S. Ellis, *The Life of Michael Kelly, Musician, Actor and Bon Viveur* (London, 1930).

Kelly, Robert, American composer; b. Clarksburg, W.Va., Sept. 26, 1916. He studied composition with Scalero at the Curtis Inst. in Philadelphia and violin with Samuel Gardner. After service in the U.S. Army, he joined the faculty of the Univ. of Illinois at Urbana, retiring in 1976.

WORKS: *Adirondack Suite* for Orch. (1941); *A Miniature Symphony* (Austin, Texas, Oct. 15, 1950); *The White Gods,* opera in 3 acts on the Aztec impression of the conquistadores (Urbana, July 3, 1966); Symph. No. 2 (1958); Concerto for Violin, Cello, and Orch. (Urbana, March 8, 1961); Symph. No. 3, *Emancipation Symphony* (Washington, D.C., Feb. 5, 1963); *An American Diptych* for Orch. (Austin, April 26, 1963); *Colloquy* for Chamber Orch. (Chicago, April 17, 1965); Violin Concerto (1968); 2 string quartets (1944, 1952); Viola Sonata (1950); Violin Sonata (1952); Sonata for Trombone and Piano (1952); Sonata for Oboe and Harp (1955); Quintet for Clarinet and Strings (1956); Cello Sonata (1958); *Toccata* for Marimba and Percussion (1959); *Triptych* for Cello and Piano (1962); *Tod's Gal,* opera (Norfolk, Va., Jan. 8, 1971); *Mosaic* for String Quartet (1975); choruses; songs; band music.

Kelterborn, Rudolf, Swiss composer; b. Basel, Sept. 3, 1931. He studied piano and rudimentary music theory in high school; then entered the Univ. of Basel and studied musicology with Jacques Handschin; later took a course in composition with Willy Burkhard in Zürich and Boris Blacher in Salzburg; for one semester he studied in Detmold with Wolfgang Fortner (1955). In 1960 he was engaged as a teacher of composition at the Music Academy in Detmold; in 1968 he became a prof. at the Hochschule für Musik in Zürich. In 1975 he was appointed music director of the Basel Radio. He was also active as a conductor, mostly of his own music. In his music, Kelterborn applies a precisely coordinated serial organization wherein quantitative values of duration form a recurrent series; the changes of tempo are also subjected to serialization. Both melody and harmony are derived from a tone row in which the dissonant intervals of major seventh and minor second are the mainstays.

WORKS: OPERAS: *Die Errettung Thebens* (Zürich, June 23, 1963) and *Kaiser Jovian* (Karlsruhe, March 4, 1967). FOR ORCH.: Suite for Woodwinds, Percussion, and Strings (1954); Concertino for Violin and Chamber Orch. (1954); Sonata for 16 Solo Strings (1955); *Canto appassionato* (1959); Concertino for Piano, Percussion, and Strings (1959); *Metamorphosen* (1960); Cello Concerto (1962); *Phantasmen* (1966); Symph. No. 1 (Vienna, April 26, 1968); Symph. No. 2 (1969); *Musik* for Piano and 8 Wind Instruments (1970); *Traummusik* for Small Orch. (1971); *Kommunikationen* for 6 Instrumental Groups (1972); *Changements* (1973); *Tableaux encadrés* (1974). CHAMBER MUSIC: 4 string quartets (1954, 1956, 1962, 1970); *5 Fantasien* for Wind Quintet (1958); *Esquisses* for Harpsichord and Percussion (1962); *Meditationen* for 6 Wind Instruments (1962); *Kammersonate* for Flute, Oboe, String Trio, and Harpsichord (1963); *Fantasia a tre* for Piano, Violin, and Cello (1967); *4 Stücke* for Clarinet and Piano (1970); *9 Momente* for Viola and Piano (1973); *Reaktionen* for Violin and Piano (1974). VOCAL WORKS: *Cantata profana* (1960); *Ewige Wiederkehr,* chamber cantata (1960); *Musica spei* for Soprano,

Chorus, and Orch. (1968); *Dies unus* for Voices and Orch. (1971); *3 Fragmente* for Chorus and Orch. (1968); *Dies unus* for Voices and Orch. (1971); *3 Fragmente* for Chorus a cappella (1973).
BIBLIOGRAPHY: D. Larese and F. Goébels, *Rudolf Kelterborn* (Amriswil, 1970).

Kemble, Adelaide, English soprano; b. London, 1814; d. Warsash House, Hampshire, Aug. 4, 1879. She first sang in concerts; then studied with Pasta in Italy; made her debut as Norma in 1838 in Venice. In 1841 she appeared at Covent Garden in London. She retired from the stage following her marriage in 1843. Her life is recounted in *Record of a Girlhood,* written by her sister, the famous actress Fanny Kemble.

Kemp, Barbara, German dramatic soprano; b. Cochem, Dec. 12, 1881; d. Berlin, April 17, 1959. She sang in opera in Rostock and Breslau before being engaged as a member of the Berlin State Opera in 1914. She married the composer **Max von Schillings** in 1923; in the same year (on March 1) she sang the title role in his opera *Mona Lisa* at the Metropolitan Opera in N.Y. She returned to Germany in 1924; sang Wagnerian roles at Bayreuth; continued on the roster of the Berlin State Opera until 1932, when she retired, but continued to produce opera in Berlin for several years.
BIBLIOGRAPHY: Oscar Bie, *Barbara Kemp* (Berlin, 1921).

Kemp, Joseph, English composer and pedagogue; b. Exeter, 1778; d. London, May 22, 1824. He studied organ with W. Jackson; was organist of Bristol Cathedral (1802); received a Mus.Bac. from Cambridge (1808) and a Mus.Doc. (1809); then taught in London. As one of the earliest promoters of music instruction by classes, he publ. the pamphlet *New System of Musical Education* (1819). He composed *The Jubilee,* an "occasional piece" (1809); *The Siege of Isca,* melodrama (1810); *Musical Illustrations of the Beauties of Shakespeare; Musical Illustrations of The Lady of the Lake;* Psalms; anthems; songs; etc.

Kemp, Robert, known as **"Father Kemp";** b. Wellfleet, Mass., June 6, 1820; d. Boston, May 14, 1897. He was a shoe dealer but loved music; in 1854 organized the Old Folks Concerts in Boston. His book, *Father Kemp and His Old Folks* (Boston, 1868), contains his autobiography.

Kempe, Rudolf, eminent German conductor; b. Niederpoyritz, near Dresden, June 14, 1910; d. Zürich, May 11, 1976. He studied oboe at the Orchestral School of the Dresden Staatskapelle; in 1929 became first oboist of the Gewandhaus Orch. in Leipzig. He made his conducting debut at the Leipzig Opera in 1936. He served in the German army during World War II; then conducted in Chemnitz; was director of the Opera there (1945–48) and at the Weimar National Theater (1948–49). From 1949 to 1953 he was Generalmusikdirektor of the Dresden Staatskapelle; then served in an identical capacity with the Bavarian State Opera in Munich (1952–54); also made appearances in opera in Vienna, in London (Covent Garden), and at the the Bavarian State Opera in Munich (1952–54); also made appearances in opera in Vienna, in London (Covent Garden), and at the Metropolitan in N.Y. In 1960 Sir Thomas Beecham named him associate conductor of the Royal Phil. Orch. of London; upon Beecham's death in 1961, he became its principal conductor; from 1963 till 1975 was artistic director as well. He was chief conductor of the Tonhalle Orch. in Zürich (1965–72) and of the Munich Phil. (from 1967); from 1975 he conducted the BBC Symph. He was a distinguished interpreter of Beethoven, Brahms, Wagner, Bruckner, and Richard Strauss; also conducted light opera.
BIBLIOGRAPHY: C. Kempe-Oettinger, *Rudolf Kempe: Pictures of a Life* (Munich, 1977; in Eng., London, 1979); a Kempe memorial issue was publ. in *Le Grand Baton* (March/June 1978).

Kemper, Paul van, Dutch conductor; b. Zoeterwoude, May 16, 1893; d. Hilversum, Dec. 8, 1955. He first studied violin, eventually becoming concertmaster of the Concertgebouw Orch. under Willem Mengelberg. In 1934 he went to Germany as chief conductor of the Dresden Phil. Orch., remaining there until 1942, when he succeeded Herbert von Karajan as Generalmusikdirektor in Aachen. After World War II he returned to the Netherlands; in 1949 became chief conductor of the Radio Phil. Orch. His appearances with the Concertgebouw Orch. provoked protests from musicians and audiences, owing to his alleged collaboration with the Nazis during the occupation. However, several prominent Dutch musicians testified in his favor, and the turmoil subsided.

Kempff, Wilhelm, distinguished German pianist; b. Juterbog, Nov. 25, 1895. He studied piano with his father, also named **Wilhelm Kempff;** at the age of 9 he entered the Berlin Hochschule für Musik, where he studied composition with Robert Kahn and piano with Heinrich Barth; also attended the Univ. of Berlin. He began his concert career in 1916; in 1918 he made the first of many appearances with the Berlin Phil.; from that time he toured throughout Europe, South America, and Japan, featuring improvisation as part of his programs. From 1924 to 1929 he was director of the Stuttgart Hochschule für Musik; from 1957 he gave annual courses in Positano, Italy. He made his London debut in 1951 and his American debut in N.Y. in 1964. He continued to appear in concerts well past his octogenarian milestone; in 1979 he was a soloist with the Berlin Phil., after having had an association with it for more than 50 years. Kempff epitomized the old tradition of German pianism; he eschewed flamboyance in his performances of Mozart, Beethoven, Schubert, and other classics. He publ. a book of memoirs, *Unter dem Zimbelstern* (Stuttgart, 1951). He was also a composer.

WORKS: Operas: *König Midas* (Königsberg, 1930); *Die Fasnacht von Rottweil* (Hannover, 1937); *Familie Gozzi* (Stettin, 1934); 2 symphs.; Piano Concerto No. 1 (1915); Piano Concerto No. 2, with Chorus (1931); Violin Concerto (1932); *Arkadische Suite* for Chamber Orch. (1939); *Legende* for Piano and Orch. (1947); *Epitaph*, suite for String Orch. (1946); 2 string quartets (1942); a number of piano pieces.

Kempter, Karl, German organist and composer; b. Limbach, Jan. 17, 1819; d. Augsburg, March 11, 1871. He was choirmaster at Augsburg Cathedral. He wrote 4 oratorios, numerous masses and graduals; also publ. *Der Landchorregent,* a collection for use in small churches.

Keneman, Feodor, Russian pianist and composer of German descent; b. Moscow, April 20, 1873; d. there, March 29, 1937. He was a piano student of Safonov at the Moscow Cons. (graduated in 1895) and a student of composition of Ippolitov-Ivanov there (graduated in 1897); also attended counterpoint classes of Taneyev. From 1899 to 1932 he taught music theory at the Moscow Cons. He gave piano recitals and was the favorite accompanist of Chaliapin, for whom he composed the popular Russian ballad "As the King Went to War" and arranged the folk song "Ei ukhnem!" which became one of the greatest successes at Chaliapin's concerts. Keneman made an American tour with Chaliapin in 1923–24. He also composed a number of military marches and band pieces.

Kenessey, Jenö, Hungarian composer; b. Budapest, Sept. 23, 1906; d. there, Aug. 19, 1976. He studied with Lajtha and Siklós in Budapest and attended Franz Shalk's conducting course in Salzburg; in 1932 he was appointed a member of the conducting staff at the Budapest Opera House; conducted his opera *Gold and the Woman* (1942) there on May 8, 1943, and his ballet *May Festival* (1948) on Nov. 29, 1948. His other works include 5 more ballets: *Montmartre* (1930); *Johnny in Boots* (1935); *Mine Is the Bridegroom* (1938); *The Kerchief* (1951); *Bihari's Song* (1954); also, *Dance Impressions* for Orch. (1933); Divertimento for Orch. (1945); *Dances from Sárköz* for Orch. (1953); *Beams of Light,* cantata (1960); *Canzonetta* for Flute and Chamber Orch. (1970); *Dawn at Balaton,* symph. poem, with Narrator and Female Voices (1972); Piano Quartet (1928–29); Sonata for Harp and Flute (1940); Sonata for Harp, Flute, and Viola (1940); Divertimento for Viola and Harp (1963); Trio for Violin, Viola, and Harp (1972); *Elegy and Scherzo* for Piano (1973); songs and choruses.

Kenins, Talivaldis, Latvian-born Canadian composer; b. Liepaja, April 23, 1919. He studied composition with Wihtol at the State Cons. in Riga (1940–44); during the final years of the Nazi-Soviet War he was conscripted as a laborer in Germany. After the war he traveled to France and studied with Aubin, Plé-Caussade, and Messiaen at the Paris Cons. (1945–

50), winning a first prize in composition. In 1951 he emigrated to Canada; settled in Toronto, where he served as music director of the Latvian Lutheran Church; in 1952 joined the music faculty of the Univ. of Toronto; in 1956 received Canadian citizenship. In his music he maintains a rigorous formality of Classical design; his thematic material draws on folk-song resources of his native Latvia and the pentatonic Indian melos of his adoptive country; he also applies cosmopolitan modern techniques.

WORKS: Piano Concerto (1946); Duo for Piano and Orch. (1951); *Scherzo concertante* for Orch. (1953); 5 symphs.: No. 1 for Chamber Orch. (1959); No. 2, *Sinfonia concertante,* for Flute, Oboe, Clarinet, and Orch. (1967); No. 3 for Orch. (1970); No. 4 for Chamber Orch. (1972); No. 5 for Full Orch. (1975); *Nocturne and Dance* for String Orch. (1963); *Folk Dance, Variations and Fugue* for School Orch. (1964); Concerto for Violin, Cello, and String Orch. (1964); *Fantaisies concertantes* for Piano and Orch. (1971; Toronto, June 20, 1973); Violin Concerto (1974); *Naačnaača (Trance),* symph. poem (1975); Sinfonietta (1976); *Beatae voces tenebrae* for Orch. (1977); *To a Soldier,* cantata for 2 Soloists, Chorus, and Organ (1953); *Daniel,* biblical scene after the 2nd Book of Daniel, for 2 Soloists, Chorus, and Organ (1956); *Lyrical Suite* for 2 Soloists, Chorus, and Organ (1953); *Gloria (Chants of Glory and Mercy)* for 4 Soloists, Chorus, and Orch. (Guelph, May 3, 1970); *Lagalai: Legend of the Stone,* chamber drama for Chorus, Flute, Horn, and Percussion (1970); *Sawan-Oong (The Spirit of the Winds)* for Narrator, Solo Bass, Chorus, and Small Orch. (1973); *Baltica,* cantata for Solo Bass or Alto, Chorus, 2 Trumpets, Timpani, and Organ (1974); a cappella choruses; String Quartet (1948); *Prelude and Scherzo* for Flute, Clarinet, and Bassoon (1947); Septet (1949); Cello Sonata (1950); Piano Trio (1952); Violin Sonata (1955); *Suite concertante* for Cello and Piano (1955); *Diversions on a Gypsy Song* for Cello and Piano (1958); Piano Quartet (1958); Divertimento for Clarinet and Piano (1960); *Little Suite* for String Quartet (1966); *Concertante* for Flute and Piano (1966); *Fantasy-Variations* for Flute and Viola (1967); *Concertino à cinque* for Flute, Oboe, Viola, Cello, and Piano (1968); *2 Dialogues* for Cello and Piano (1968); *Partita brève* for Viola and Piano (1971); Serenade for Oboe and Cello (1973); *Concerto-Fantasy* for Organ and Percussion (1976); Concertino for 2 Pianos (1956); Piano Sonata (1961); other piano pieces; songs.

Kennan, Kent Wheeler, American composer and teacher; b. Milwaukee, Wis., April 18, 1913. He studied composition with Hunter Johnson at the Univ. of Michigan (1930–32); then took courses with Howard Hanson and Bernard Rogers at the Eastman School of Music in Rochester, N.Y. (M.B., 1934; M.M., 1936); spent 3 years in Europe after winning the American Prix de Rome, and took some lessons with Pizzetti in Rome. Returning to the U.S., he taught at Kent State Univ. in Ohio (1939–40) and at the Univ. of Texas at Austin (1940–42); during World War II, served as bandleader in the U.S. Army (1942–

45); then taught again at the Univ. of Texas (1945–46) and at Ohio State Univ. (1947–49). In 1949 he joined the staff of the Univ. of Texas on a permanent basis, and in 1964 was appointed chairman of the music dept. there; retired in 1983. His music is so conducive to listening pleasure that Toscanini himself chose one of Kennan's innocent little symph. pieces, *Night Soliloquy* for Flute and Orch., to conduct with the NBC Symph. Orch. (Feb. 26, 1943), a rare distinction for an American composer. Kennan's other works are *Il campo dei fiori* for Trumpet and Orch. (1937); *Nocturne* for Viola and Orch. (1937); *Promenade* for Orch. (1938); *Symph.* (1938); *Blessed Are They That Mourn* for Chorus and Orch. (1939); *Andante* for Oboe and Orch. (Philadelphia, March 7, 1947); *Trumpet Sonata* (1956). A protracted hiatus in composition that followed was filled by the publication of useful teaching manuals: *The Technique of Orchestration* (N.Y., 1952; revised ed., 1970); *Counterpoint Based on 18th-Century Practice* (N.Y., 1959); 2 workbooks on orchestration (1952, 1969) and a counterpoint workbook (1959).

Kennedy, Daisy, Australian violinist; b. Burra, 1893; d. London, July 30, 1981. She studied at the Univ. Conservatorium in Adelaide; in 1908 she went to Prague and took violin lessons with Otakar Sevčík; gave concerts in London in 1914; toured the U.S. in 1920 and 1925.

Kennedy, Michael, English writer on music; b. Manchester, Feb. 19, 1926. He received his education in Manchester; then joined the staff of the *Daily Telegraph* there in 1941, becoming its northern editor in 1960.
WRITINGS: *The Hallé Tradition: A Century of Music* (Manchester, 1960); *The Works of Ralph Vaughan Williams* (London, 1964; revised ed., 1980); *Portrait of Elgar* (London, 1968; revised ed., 1982); *Elgar: Orchestral Music* (London, 1969); *Portrait of Manchester* (Manchester, 1970); *A History of the Royal Manchester College of Music* (Manchester, 1971); *Barbirolli: Conductor Laureate* (London, 1971); *Mahler* (London, 1974); *Richard Strauss* (London, 1976). He also ed. *The Autobiography of Charles Hallé, with Correspondence and Diaries* (London, 1976) and *The Concise Oxford Dictionary of Music* (London, 3rd revised ed., 1980).

Kennedy-Fraser, Marjory, Scottish singer, pianist, and folk-song collector; b. Perth, Oct. 1, 1857; d. Edinburgh, Nov. 22, 1930. She was the daughter of the famous Scottish singer **David Kennedy** (1825–86) and traveled with him as his accompanist from the age of 12. She then studied with Mathilde Marchesi in Paris; also took courses in piano with Matthay and in music history with Niecks. Inspired by the example of her father, she became a dedicated collector of folk songs. In 1905 she went to the Outer Hebridean Isles, after which she made a specialty of research in Celtic music, including the adaptation and arranging of Gaelic folk material into art forms; publ. the famous collection *Songs of the Hebrides,* with texts in Gaelic and Eng., in 3 vols. (1909, 1917, 1921); also wrote a *Hebridean Suite* for Cello and Piano (1922), several collections of folk music for schools, piano pieces based on Hebridean folk songs, etc. She publ. the important handbook *Hebridean Song and the Laws of Interpretation* (Glasgow, 1922); a similar vol. for Lowland Scots songs; *From the Hebrides* (London, 1925); an autobiography, *A Life of Song* (London, 1928); wrote the libretto for Bantock's opera *The Seal Woman,* and sang the title role in it. She was married to A.J. Fraser, a schoolteacher in Glasgow.

Kent, James, English organist and composer; b. Winchester, March 13, 1700; d. there, May 6, 1776. He was chorister in Winchester Cathedral and in the Chapel Royal; organist of Trinity College, Cambridge (1731–37), then of Winchester Cathedral (1737–74). He wrote 2 services; also *Kent's Anthems* (2nd ed., 2 vols.; London, 1844).

Kentner, Louis, Hungarian pianist; b. Karwin, Silesia, July 19, 1905. He studied piano in Budapest with Arnold Szekely and composition with Kodály. As a youth he gave a series of concerts in Budapest, performing all of Beethoven's sonatas. In 1935 he settled in England; toured India with Yehudi Menuhin in 1954; made his American debut in N.Y., Nov. 28, 1956. He publ. some valuable articles on Liszt. In 1978 he was made a Commander of the Order of the British Empire.

Kenton (real name, **Kornstein**), **Egon F.,** Hungarian-American musicologist; b. Nagyszalonta, Hungary, May 22, 1891. He studied violin with Hubay at the Budapest Academy of Music, graduating in 1911; was violist in the Hungarian String Quartet (1911–23); then emigrated to the U.S.; in 1947 received his M.A. in musicology from N.Y. Univ.; subsequently taught musicology at the Univ. of Conn. in Storrs (1950–61); from 1961 to 1971 served as librarian of the Mannes College of Music in N.Y.; in 1975 went to Paris to live. He publ. a valuable biography of Giovanni Gabrieli (Rome, 1967; publ. in Eng. by the American Inst. of Musicology in Rome).

Kenton, Stan (Stanley Newcomb), American jazz bandleader; b. Wichita, Kans., Feb. 19, 1912; d. Hollywood, Aug. 25, 1979. He spent his youth in California; earned a living playing piano in local saloons and speakeasies and at the same time began experimenting with new sounds in jazz. A volatile but talented musician, he constantly invented slogans to describe his arrangements and his manner of conducting, such as "progressive jazz," "artistry in rhythm," and "innovations in modern music," but above all he believed that music must be loud to overwhelm and subjugate the public. He kept discovering modernistic devices, such as already obsolescent progressions of whole-tone scales and consecutive major ninth-chords. He was ecstatic when he stumbled upon the Schillinger System of Composition, which professed to impart the power of creativity to untutored musicians. Although commercially successful, Kenton suffered mandatory nervous breakdowns, and at one time decided to abandon music and become a psychiatrist; he gave up the idea when he realized that he would have to learn Greek-derived words and unpronounceable German terms. He married frequently; one of his sons was indicted for conspiracy to commit murder (he put a snake in the mailbox of a bothersome attorney).

Kepler, Johannes, illustrious German astronomer; b. Weil, Württemberg, Dec. 27, 1571; d. Regensburg, Nov. 15, 1630. He explored Pythagorean concepts of harmony and relationships among music, mathematics, and physics in books 3 and 5 of his *Harmonices mundi.*
BIBLIOGRAPHY: D.P. Walker, "Kepler's Celestial Music," *Journal of the Warburg and Courtland Institutes,* 20 (1967); R. Haase, "Keplers harmonikale Denkweise," *Musikerziehung* (Nov. 1969); idem, "Johannes Keplers wahre Bedeutung," *Kunstjahrbuch der Studt Linz 1970* (1971); R. Hannas, "Johann Kepler's Excursion into Political Proportions," *Diapason* (April 1972); R. Haase, "Fortsetzungen der Keplerschen Weltharmonik," *Johannes Kepler, Werk und Leistung* (1971).

Keppard, Freddie, black American jazz cornetist; b. New Orleans, Feb. 15, 1889; d. Chicago, July 15, 1933. He learned to play the mandolin, violin, and accordion before mastering the cornet; organized his own group, The Olympia Orch.; later became co-leader of The Original Creole Orch., playing with it in Los Angeles, Chicago, and N.Y.; after moving to Chicago, he played with King Oliver, Jimmie Noone, and others. Although forgotten in the last years of his life, he was one of the pioneer jazz figures; he had few equals as a cornetist in his time.

Kerle, Jacobus de, Flemish organist and composer; b. Ypres, 1531 or 1532; d. Prague, Jan. 7, 1591. He served as church organist at the Cathedral of Orvieto (1555–61); then was ordained a priest and in 1561 went to Venice, where he supervised the publ. of his *Liber Psalmorum.* He then proceeded to Rome, where he met Cardinal Otto Truchsess, Lord High Steward and Bishop of Augsburg, who commissioned Kerle to write his *Preces speciales pro salubri generalis concilii successu* for the Council of Trent. In 1563–64 he traveled throughout northern Italy to Barcelona, and later was in Dillingen, Bavaria (1564). He returned to Ypres in 1565; traveled to Rome once more; in 1568 went to Augsburg, where he became vicar-choral and organist at the Cathedral; later held a prebend in Cambrai (1575–87). Early in 1582 he became Kapellmeister to Elector Gebhard Truchsess of Waldburg in Cologne; in Sept. 1582 became chaplain at the imperial court in Augsburg under Rudolph II; in Oct. 1582 he joined the court chapel in Vienna; in 1583 settled in Prague. He exerted a considerable influence on the musical culture of his time.
WORKS: *Preces speciales pro salubri generalis*

concilii successu, for the Council of Trent (Venice, 1562); masses (Venice, 1562; Munich, 1572, with the *Cantio de sacro foedere contra Turcas*); also hymns, Psalms, madrigals, and various works in MS. The *Preces* were transcribed by O. Ursprung in Denkmäler der Tonkunst in Bayern, 34 (26; 1926), together with a list of Kerle's publ. works, extant MSS, reprints, etc.
BIBLIOGRAPHY: O. Ursprung, *Jacobus de Kerle* (Munich, 1913); Glen Haydon, "The Hymns of Jacobus de Kerle," in the *Festschrift for Gustav Reese* (N.Y., 1966).

Kerll (or **Kerl, Kherl, Cherl**), **Johann Kaspar,** German organist and composer; b. Adorf, Saxony, April 9, 1627; d. Munich, Feb. 13, 1693. He served a musical apprenticeship with his father, an organist and organ manufacturer; in his youth, was court organist in Vienna, where he studied with the imperial court Kapellmeister, Giovanni Valentini; then went to Rome; he converted to Catholicism and received instruction from Carissimi; it is possible that he also met Frescobaldi. He was subsequently court organist in Brussels. On Sept. 22, 1656, he was appointed Kapellmeister in Munich; he resigned this post in 1673. From 1674–77 he served as organist at St. Stephen's Cathedral in Vienna; on March 16, 1677, he was named imperial court organist in Vienna. He was ennobled in 1664.
WORKS: Preludes, interludes, and postludes for Organ; toccatas and suites for Harpsichord; a number of masses; sacred concertos; etc. In Munich he produced several operas to Italian librettos (none of which are extant), among them *Applausi festivi* (Aug. 28, 1658); *Antiopa giustificata* (Sept. 26, 1662); *Atalanta* (Jan. 30, 1667); *Le pretensioni del sole* (Nov. 6, 1667); *Amor tiranno* (Oct. 31, 1672). Of importance is his organ work *Modulatio organica super Magnificat octo tonis* (1689). Modern editions of his works are found in Denkmäler der Tonkunst in Österreich, 49 and 59, and Denkmäler der Tonkunst in Bayern, 3 (2.ii.).
BIBLIOGRAPHY: K. Weitzmann-Seiffert, *Geschichte der Klaviermusik* (vol. 1, pp. 185ff.); A. Giebler, *The Masses of Johann Kaspar Kerll* (Diss., Univ. of Michigan, 1956); Fr. W. Riedel, "Eine unbekannte Quelle zu Johann Kaspar Kerlls Musik für Tasteninstrumente," *Die Musikforschung* (1960).

Kerman, Joseph, American musicologist; b. London (of American parents), April 3, 1924. He studied at the Univ. College School in London; then went to the U.S.; enrolled at N.Y. Univ. (A.B., 1943); subsequently studied musicology at Princeton Univ. with Strunk, receiving his Ph.D. there in 1950 with the dissertation *The Elizabethan Madrigal: A Comparative Study* (publ. in the series American Musicological Society Studies and Documents, N.Y., 1962). He taught at Westminster Choir College (1949–51); in 1951 he joined the faculty of the Univ. of Calif. at Berkeley; was named associate prof. there in 1955, and prof. in 1960; from 1960 to 1963 served as chairman of its music dept. From 1971 to 1974 he was Heather Prof. of Music at Oxford Univ.;

then resumed his professorship at Berkeley. His books include *Opera as Drama* (N.Y., 1956); *The Beethoven Quartets* (N.Y., 1967); with H. Janson, *A History of Art and Music* (N.Y., 1968); with V. Kerman, *Listen* (N.Y., 1972).

Kern, Adele, German soprano; b. Munich, Nov. 25, 1901; d. there, May 6, 1980. She studied in Munich; made her debut there in 1924; then sang in various German opera houses; made appearances at the Bavarian State Opera, Munich (1927–46); also sang at Salzburg; retired in 1947. She was best known for her soubrette roles in the operas of Mozart.

Kern, Jerome (David), famous American composer; b. New York, Jan. 27, 1885; d. there, Nov. 11, 1945. He was educated in N.Y. public schools; studied music with his mother; then with Paolo Gallico and Alexander Lambert (piano) and Austin Pearce and Albert von Doenhoff (theory); went to Germany, where he continued to study composition; returned to N.Y. in 1904; became a pianist and a salesman for a publishing firm; publ. his first song, *How'd You Like to Spoon with Me,* in 1905, and it became famous; in 1906 he was in London, where he was connected with a theatrical production. In 1911 he obtained his first success as a composer for the stage with his musical comedy *The Red Petticoat* (Nov. 13, 1912). After that he continued to produce musical comedies in rapid succession; in 1917 alone he produced 7 shows on Broadway; altogether he composed more than 60 works for the stage, including several motion picture scores. His most important productions include *Very Good, Eddie* (N.Y., Dec. 23, 1915); *Have a Heart* (N.Y., Jan. 11, 1917); *Head over Heels* (N.Y., April 29, 1918); *Sally* (N.Y., Dec. 21, 1920; extremely successful); *Stepping Stones* (N.Y., Nov. 6, 1923); *Sunny* (N.Y., Sept. 22, 1925); *Show Boat* (Washington, D.C., Nov. 15, 1927; N.Y., Dec. 27, 1927; his most remarkable score, one of the finest American works of its genre; includes the famous bass aria *Ol' Man River*); *The Cat and the Fiddle* (N.Y., Oct. 15, 1931); *Music in the Air* (N.Y., Nov. 8, 1932); *Roberta* (N.Y., Nov. 18, 1933); *The 3 Sisters* (London, April 9, 1934); *Gentlemen Unafraid* (St. Louis, June 3, 1938); *Very Warm for May* (N.Y., Nov. 17, 1939). He also composed an orch. work, *Portrait of Mark Twain* (Cincinnati, May 14, 1942). A motion picture on his life, *As the Clouds Roll By,* was produced posthumously (1946). A selection of his songs are in *The Jerome Kern Song Book,* with an introduction by Oscar Hammerstein II (N.Y., 1955).
BIBLIOGRAPHY: Robert Simon, "Jerome Kern," *Modern Music* (Jan. 1929); David Ewen, *The Story of Jerome Kern* (N.Y., 1953); A. Wilder, *American Popular Song* (N.Y., 1972); H. Fordin, *Jerome Kern: The Man and His Music* (Santa Monica, Calif., 1975).

Kern, Patricia, Welsh mezzo-soprano; b. Swansea, July 4, 1927. She studied with Parry Jones at the Guildhall School of Music in London; made her debut in London with the Opera for All group in 1952; then sang with the Welsh National Opera. In 1959 she joined the Sadler's Wells Opera in London; also sang at Covent Garden (from 1967); made guest appearances in the U.S. with the Dallas Opera, the N.Y. City Opera, etc. She was highly successful in soubrette roles.

Kerr, Harrison, American composer; b. Cleveland, Oct. 13, 1897; d. Norman, Okla., Aug. 16, 1978. He completed his general studies in Cleveland; in 1921 he went to France, where he took courses with Nadia Boulanger at the American Cons. Upon returning to America, he became active mainly as a pedagogue; also organized musical exchange agencies in Europe and the Far East. He was dean of the College of Fine Arts at the Univ. of Oklahoma (1949–60), continuing there as composer-in-residence until 1968.
WORKS: Opera, *The Tower of Kel* (1958–60); 3 symphs.: No. 1 (1927–29; revised 1938); No. 2 (1943–45); No. 3 (1953–54); Violin Concerto (1950–51); *Sinfonietta da Camera* (Norman, Okla., April 25, 1968); *Episodes from "The Tower of Kel"* for Orch. (1974); Trio for Clarinet, Cello, and Piano (1936); 3 string quartets (1937–73); Piano Trio (1938); *Overture, Arioso, and Finale* for Cello and Piano (1944–51); Solo Violin Sonata (1954); Sonata for Violin and Piano (1956); *Quasi Quodlibet* for 8 Trombones (1974); 2 piano sonatas (1929, 1943); *Dance Suite* for 2 Pianos and Percussion (1938); songs.
BIBLIOGRAPHY: Alexander Ringer, "Harrison Kerr: Composer and Educator," *American Composers Alliance Bulletin* (vol. 8, No. 2, 1959).

Kersjes, Anton, Dutch conductor; b. Arnhem, Aug. 17, 1923. He studied conducting with Felix Hupka in Amsterdam and Eugène Bigot in Paris. In 1953 he became co-founder and conductor of the Kunstmaand Chamber Orch. in Amsterdam, which became the Kunstmaand Orch. in 1955 and the Amsterdam Phil. in 1969. He took this orch. to the Soviet Union in 1972, making it the first Dutch ensemble to give concerts there. From 1969 to 1979 he led the conducting class at the Sweelinck Cons. in Amsterdam. He received numerous honors, including the Royal Order of Orange-Nassau.

Kersters, Willem, Belgian composer; b. Antwerp, Feb. 9, 1929. He studied at the conservatories of Antwerp and Brussels with Jean Louel, Jean Absil, Marcel Quinet, and Marcel Poot; then taught music at various schools; in 1968 was appointed prof. at the Cons. in Maastricht, the Netherlands. His music reveals traits of the classical Flemish school of composition, with lucidly sonorous contrapuntal lines in which tonality is ingeniously intertwined with atonal melodic progressions. Most of his works are written for instruments.
WORKS: Sinfonietta (1955); *Sinfonia concertante* for Flute, Clarinet, Bassoon, and String Orch. (1957); *Sinfonia piccola* (1958); Divertimento for String Orch. (1958); 4 symphs. (1962; 1963; 1967; *De Apocalypsis,* 1968); *Suite in the Form of a French Overture* for 4 Clarinets and String Orch. (1964);

Sinfonietta for Wind Orch. (1967); *Contrasts* for Percussion, and Orch. or Piano (1969); *Anaglyphos* for 10 Percussion Players (1969); *Capriccio* for Orch. (1972); *Laudes* for Brass and Percussion (1973); Wind Quintet (1954); Viola Sonata (1954); *Berceuse and Humoresque* for Oboe, Clarinet, and Bassoon (1956); *Partita* for Violin and Piano (1956); 2 string quartets (1962, 1964); Solo Violin Sonata (1965); *De drie tamboers*, septet for 4 Clarinets, Percussion, Timpani, and Piano (1966); *Variations on a Theme of Giles Farnaby* for 4 Clarinets (1967); *Notturno* for Solo Guitar (1968); *3 Rondos* for Brass Quintet (1969); Variations for Flute, Oboe, Clarinet, and Bassoon (1969); *Ballade* for Violin and Piano (1970); Piano Quartet (1970); Quartet for Clarinet, Violin, Viola, and Cello (1971); Oboe Sonatina (1974); organ pieces; oratorio, *Marianna Alcoforado* (1961); ballets: *Parwati* (1956); *Le Triomphe de l'Esprit* (1961); *Halewijn* (1973).

Kertész, István, Hungarian conductor; b. Budapest, Aug. 28, 1929; d. Kfar Saba, Israel, April 16, 1973 (drowned while swimming in the Mediterranean). He studied at the Academy of Music in Budapest and at the Santa Cecilia Academy in Rome (1958); was conductor at Györ (1953–55) and at the Budapest Opera (1953–57); from 1958–64 served as music director in Augsburg; then went to the Cologne Opera. From 1965–68 he was principal conductor of the London Symph. Orch. He made his U.S. debut in 1961 with the Detroit Symph.; his accidental death was deplored.

Kes, Willem, violinist, composer, and conductor; b. Dordrecht, the Netherlands, Feb. 16, 1856; d. Munich, Feb. 21, 1934. He studied with various teachers in the Netherlands; in 1871 went to Germany, where he took lessons with Ferdinand David at the Leipzig Cons.; also studied with Wieniawski in Brussels and Joachim in Berlin. However, he did not pursue the career of a virtuoso, but turned to conducting. In 1876 he became conductor of the Park Orch. in Amsterdam, and in 1888 assumed the conductorship of the Concertgebouw Orch. In 1895 he succeeded Henschel as conductor of the Scottish Orch. in Glasgow. In 1898 he went to Russia, where he conducted the Moscow Phil. Society. In 1905 he became director of the Cons. of Coblenz; retired in 1926, and settled in Munich. Among his works are a Symph.; several overtures; Violin Concerto; Cello Concerto; choral work with Orch., *Der Taucher;* Violin Sonata; piano pieces; songs.

Kessler, Ferdinand, German composer, violinist, and teacher; b. Frankfurt, Jan. 1793; d. there, Oct. 28, 1856. He studied with his father and Vollweiler. One of his pupils was Franz Wüllner. He publ. sonatas, rondos, etc., for piano.

Kessler (real name, **Kötzler**), **Joseph Christoph,** German pianist and pedagogue; b. Augsburg, Aug. 26, 1800; d. Vienna, Jan. 14, 1872. He studied with the organist Bilek in Feldsberg; then was tutor with the family of Count Potocki in Lemberg; there he spent 20 years; from 1855 lived in Vienna. He publ. a series of practical studies for piano; Moscheles used them in his teaching, and Liszt recommended them. Pyllemann publ. his reminiscences of Kessler in the *Allgemeine Musikalische Zeitung* (1872).

Kessler, Thomas, Swiss composer; b. Zürich, Sept. 25, 1937. He studied literature in Zürich and Paris; in 1962 moved to Berlin, where he enrolled at the Hochschule für Musik, graduating in 1968. His works include the ballets *Countdown for Orpheus* (1967) and *Revolutionsmusik* (1968); Trombone Concerto (1968); String Trio (1969); *Drumphony* for Percussion, Computer, and Orch. (Cologne, Sept. 19, 1981); several other pieces of chamber music.

Kessner, Daniel, American composer; b. Los Angeles, June 3, 1946. He studied composition with Henri Lazarof at the Univ. of Calif. in Los Angeles, where he received his Ph.D. in 1971. In 1970 he was appointed to the faculty of the California State Univ. in Northridge.
WORKS: Chamber opera, *The Telltale Heart*, after Edgar Allan Poe (Utrecht, the Netherlands, March 12, 1982). For Orch.: *Strata* (Los Angeles, Oct. 12, 1971); *The Masque of the Red Death*, after Poe (Pasadena, Calif., Nov. 6, 1979). Chamber music: Six pieces under the title *Equali* for various groupings (1970–83); *Interactions* for Flute, Cello, Piano, and Electronic Tape (1971); *Array*, pieces for Several Guitars (1973); *Solennité* for Bass Flute, Viola, and Percussion (1975); Trio for Violin, Guitar, and Cello (1976); *Triform*, Variations for Clarinet, Cello, and Piano (1976); *The Bells of Poe* for 4 Percussion Players (1978); *Ancient Song* for Alto Recorder, Viola, and Prepared Guitar (1980); also *Intercurrence I* for Harp and Tape (1972); *Intercurrence II* for Piano and Tape (1974); *Intercurrence III* for Percussion and Tape (1975); *Continuum* for Solo Marimba (1982).

Kestenberg, Leo, eminent Hungarian music educator and writer; b. Rosenberg, Nov. 27, 1882; d. Tel Aviv, Jan. 14, 1962. In Berlin he studied piano with Franz Kullak and Busoni, and composition with Draeseke; then taught at the Klindworth-Scharwenka Cons. and played piano recitals, distinguishing himself as a fine interpreter of Liszt's works. In 1918 he was appointed chairman of the music dept. of the Prussian Ministry of Art; in 1929, councilor in the ministry. In that capacity, he reorganized the system of musical education in Prussia, along the lines set forth in 3 pamphlets which he prepared in collaboration with W. Günther: *Prüfung, Ausbildung und Anstellung der Musiklehrer an den höheren Lehranstalten in Preussen* (1925); *Schulmusikunterricht in Preussen* (1925); *Privatunterricht in der Musik* (1929). In 1933 he was compelled to leave Germany; he settled temporarily in Prague, where he was active in music education. After the occupation of Czechoslovakia by the Nazis in 1939, he went to Palestine; from 1939 to 1945 he was general manager of the Palestine Symph. Orch.; then lived in Tel Aviv as a teacher. In 1957 Kestenberg received from the West German government a large sum compensating him for his unlawful removal from his position in the Prussian Ministry of Art by the Nazi government.

WRITINGS: *Musikerziehung und Musikpflege* (Berlin, 1921); ed. of *Jahrbuch der deutschen Musikorganisation* (with Beidler; 1929; 2nd ed., 1931) and the magazines *Die Musikpflege* (with E. Preussner) and *Musik und Technik* (1930); general ed. of a series of books, Musikpädagogische Bibliothek. He also wrote a book of memoirs, *Bewegte Zeiten; Musisch-musikantische Lebenserinnerungen* (Zürich, 1961).

BIBLIOGRAPHY: P. Bekker, *Briefe an zeitgenössische Musiker* (Berlin, 1932; pp. 44ff.).

Ketèlbey, Albert William, English composer of light music; b. Aston, Aug. 9, 1875; d. Cowes, Isle of Wight, Nov. 26, 1959. He was of remote Danish origin. Precociously gifted in music, he wrote a piano sonata at the age of 11, and played it at the Worcester Town Hall; Elgar heard it and praised it. At the age of 13, he competed for a Trinity College scholarship, and was installed as Queen Victoria Scholar; at 16 he obtained the post of organist at St. John's Church at Wimbledon; at 20 began tours as the conductor of a musical comedy troupe. For some years he was music director of Columbia Gramophone Co. and music editor at Chappell's Music Publishing Co. Among his works are: Quintet for Woodwinds and Piano; String Quartet; *Caprice* for Piano and Orch.; comic opera, *The Wonder Worker;* etc. He achieved fame with a series of remarkably popular instrumental pieces on exotic subjects (*In a Persian Market, In a Monastery Garden, Sanctuary of the Heart, In a Chinese Temple Garden,* etc.). He also publ. many small pieces under various pseudonyms.

Ketten, Henri, Hungarian pianist; b. Baja, March 25, 1848; d. Paris, April 1, 1883. He studied at the Paris Cons. with Halévy and Marmontel; wrote a number of ingratiating and successful piano pieces in the salon genre, also suitable as teaching material (*Chasse au papillon, Romance sans paroles, Tranquillité, Mélancolie,* etc.).

Kettenus, Aloys, Belgian violinist and composer; b. Verviers, Feb. 22, 1823; d. London, Oct. 3, 1896. He studied at the Liège Cons. and in Germany; in 1845, became leader of the Mannheim orch.; in 1855, a member of the Hallé Orch. in London, and later of the Royal Italian Orch. He wrote an opera, *Stella Monti* (1862); Violin Concerto; Concertino for 4 Violins and Orch.; Duet for Violin and Piano; etc.

Ketterer, Eugène, French pianist and composer; b. Rouen, 1831; d. Paris, Dec. 18, 1870. He studied at the Paris Cons. He publ. 290 piano pieces in drawing-room style, many of which became popular (*Grand caprice hongrois, L'Argentine, La Châtelaine, Gaëtana, Rondo oriental,* etc.).

Ketting, Otto, Dutch composer, son of **Piet Ketting;**

b. Amsterdam, Sept. 3, 1935. He studied composition at The Hague Cons. (1952–58); played trumpet in various orchs. (1955–61); taught composition at the Rotterdam Cons. (1967–71) and at the Royal Cons. in The Hague (1971–74). In 1983 he was appointed artistic adviser to the Utrecht Symph. Orch. His music represents a valiant effort to adapt Classical modalities to the esthetics of the 20th century.

WORKS: 2 operas: *Dummies* (The Hague, Nov. 14, 1974) and *O, Thou Rhinoceros* (Holland Festival, June 2, 1977); 6 ballets: *Het laatste bericht* (*The Last Message;* 1962); *Intérieur* (1963); *Barrière* (1963); *The Golden Key* (1964); *Choreostruction* (1963); *Theater Piece* (1973); *Kerstliederen* (*Christmas Songs)* for Chorus and Small Orch. (1953); Sinfonietta (1954); *2 canzoni* for Orch. (1957); Passacaglia for Orch. (1957); Concertino for 2 Solo Trumpets, String Orch., 3 Horns, and Piano (1958); Symph. (1957–59); Concertino for Jazz Quintet and Orch. (1960); Variations for Wind Orch., Harp, and Percussion (1960); *Pas de deux,* choreographic commentary for Orch. (1961); a series of "collages," among which the most uninhibited is *Collage No. 9* for 22 Musicians (Conductor, 16 Brass, and 5 Percussionists; 1963; Amsterdam, Jan. 26, 1966; audience reaction, hopefully that of outrage, is part of the perf.: the conductor is instructed to treat his environment with disdain and contempt, to arrive late, leave early, and refuse to acknowledge social amenities); *In Memoriam Igor Stravinsky* for Orch. (1971); *Time Machine* for Winds and Percussion (Rotterdam, May 5, 1972); *For Moonlight Nights* for Flutist (alternating on Piccolo and Alto Flute) and 26 Players (1973; Hilversum, April 17, 1975); *Adagio* for Chamber Orch. (1977); *Symphony* for Saxophones and Orch. (1978); Concerto for Solo Organ (1953); Sonata for Brass Quartet (1955); Piano Sonatina (1956); Serenade for Cello and Piano (1957); *A Set of Pieces* for Flute and Piano (1967); *A Set of Pieces* for Wind Quintet (1968); *Minimal Music* for 28 Toy Instruments (1970).

Ketting, Piet, Dutch composer, conductor, and pianist, father of **Otto Ketting;** b. Haarlem, Nov. 29, 1904. He studied singing and choral conducting at the Utrecht Cons.; then took lessons in composition with Willem Pijper. As a pianist, he formed a duo with the flutist Johan Feltkamp (1927), and a unique trio with Feltkamp and oboist Jaap Stotijn (1935) that toured the Dutch East Indies in 1939; from 1949 to 1960 he conducted the Rotterdam Chamber Orch.; was also founder and conductor of the Rotterdam Chamber Choir (1937–60). From 1960 till 1974 he immersed himself in the numerical symbolism of J.S. Bach's works, with some startling, though unpubl., results. In his own music he pursues a modern Baroque system of composition, with a discreet application of euphonious dissonance. He allowed himself a 20-year hiatus in composition between 1942 and 1962, partly on account of the war, but then resumed production with renewed vigor.

WORKS: 2 symphs. (1929, 1975); Sinfonia for Cello and Orch. (1963; radio perf., Dec. 1, 1965); *De minnedeuntjes (The Love Songs)* for Chorus and Orch.

(1966–67; Dutch Radio, May 9, 1968); Bassoon Concertino (1968); Clarinet Concertino (1973); String Trio (1925); 3 string quartets (1927–28); Cello Sonata (1928); Trio for Flute, Clarinet, and Bassoon (1929); Flute Sonata (1930); Sonata for Flute, Oboe, and Piano (1936); *Partita* for 2 Flutes (1936); *Fantasia No. 1* for Harpsichord, Descant, and Treble Recorders and Flute (1969); *Fantasia No. 2* for Harpsichord (1972); *Preludium e Fughetta* for Alto Flute and Piano (1969); 4 piano sonatinas (1926, 1926, 1927, 1929); *Prelude, Interlude and Postlude* for 2 Pianos (1971); *Jazon and Medea,* dramatic scene for Chorus, Piano, Flute, and Clarinet (1975).

Keuris, Tristan, Dutch composer; b. Amersfoort, Oct. 3, 1946. He studied music theory and composition first with Jan van Vlijmen, then with Ton de Leeuw; also took piano lessons at the Utrecht Cons. He subsequently became an instructor in 20th-century music at the Amsterdam Cons. His music is austerely structural.
WORKS: *Quartet* for Orch. in 4 groups (1966–67); *Play* for Clarinet and Piano (1967); *Choral Music I* for Orch. (1969); Quartet for 4 Saxophones (1970); Piano Sonata (1970); *Soundings* for Orch. (1970); Saxophone Concerto (1971); *Concertante Music* for Clarinet, Oboe, Bassoon, Piano, and 5 Strings (1972–73); *Music* for Violin, Clarinet, and Piano (1973); Sinfonia (1972–74; Amsterdam Radio, Jan. 31, 1976); *Fantasia* for Solo Flute (1976); Serenade for Oboe and Orch. (1974–76); Concertino for Bass Clarinet and String Quartet (1977); *Tweede symfonie* (Amsterdam, Oct. 25, 1981).

Keurvels, Edward H.J., Belgian conductor and composer; b. Antwerp, March 8, 1853; d. Eckeren (Hogblom), Jan. 29, 1916. He studied with Peter Benoit; was choirmaster and later conductor at the National Flemish Theater in Antwerp. In 1896 he established a series of symph. concerts at the Antwerp Zoological Gardens, which assumed considerable importance in Antwerp's musical life. He wrote an opera, *Parisina* (Antwerp, 1890); also numerous songs.

Keussler, Gerhard von, German composer and conductor; b. Schwanenburg, Latvia, July 5, 1874; d. Niederwartha, near Dresden, Aug. 21, 1949. He studied biology in St. Petersburg; then went to Leipzig, where he took courses in music theory with Riemann and Kretzschmar at Leipzig Univ. and with Reinecke and Jadassohn at the Cons. From 1906 to 1910 he conducted a German chorus in Prague; then went to Hamburg, where he conducted the Phil. Orch. until 1920 and led the Singakademie. In 1931 he toured in Australia as a conductor; returning to Germany in 1934, he taught at the Prussian Academy of Arts in Berlin; in 1941 he settled in Niederwartha, near Dresden, where he remained until his death. He wrote operas in a Wagnerian vein, of which several were performed: *Wandlungen* (1904); *Gefängnisse* (Prague, April 22, 1914); and *Die Gesselfahrt* (Hamburg, 1923); he further composed 2 symphs. and a symph. poem, *Australia* (1936).

Kewitsch, Theodor, German composer and writer on music; b. Posilge, Feb. 3, 1834; d. Berlin, July 18, 1903. He studied organ with his father; was a teacher and organist in various towns; received a pension in 1887 and went to Berlin; edited the *Musikkorps* (1891–92), the *Hannoverische Musikzeitung* (1893–97), and the *Deutsche Militärmusiker-Zeitung;* also wrote articles for other music journals. He publ. a *Vade-mecum* for organists; much church music; 4-part songs for mixed and male chorus; piano pieces; etc.; also wrote *Vermächtnis an die deutschen Militärmusikmeister* (1901).

Key, Francis Scott, a Baltimore lawyer, author of the words of the American national anthem; b. Carroll County, Md., Aug. 1, 1779; d. Baltimore, Jan. 11, 1843. He wrote the text of the anthem aboard a British ship (where he was taken as a civilian emissary to intercede for release of a Maryland physician) on the morning of Sept. 14, 1814, setting it to the tune of the British drinking song *To Anacreon in Heaven,* popular at the time, written by John Stafford Smith. The text and the tune did not become an official national anthem until March 3, 1931, when the bill establishing it as such was passed by Congress and signed by President Herbert Hoover.
BIBLIOGRAPHY: O.G. Sonneck, *Report on the Star Spangled Banner, Hail Columbia, Yankee Doodle* (1909); idem, *The Star Spangled Banner* (1914); J. Muller, *The Star Spangled Banner* (N.Y., 1935); J.A. Kouwenhoven and L.M. Patten, "New Light on *The Star Spangled Banner,*" *Musical Quarterly* (April 1937); W. Lichtenwanger, "The Music of *The Star-Spangled Banner,*" *Quarterly Journal of the Library of Congress* (Washington, D.C., July 1977).

Key, Pierre van Rensselaer, American music lexicographer; b. Grand Haven, Mich., Aug. 28, 1872; d. New York, Nov. 28, 1945. He was educated at the Chicago Musical College; then held positions as music critic of the *Chicago Times-Herald, Chicago American, Chicago Examiner,* and the *N.Y. World* (1907–19). He was the editor of valuable compilations: *Pierre Key's Musical Who's Who* (1931); *Pierre Key's Music Year Book; Pierre Key's Radio Annual;* and the periodical *Music Digest;* publ. *John McCormack: His Own Life Story* (1919); *Enrico Caruso* (with Bruno Zirato; 1922); *This Business of Singing* (1936).

Khachaturian, Aram, brilliant Russian composer of Armenian extraction; b. Kodzhori, suburb of Tiflis, June 6, 1903; d. Moscow, May 1, 1978 (buried in Erevan). His father was a bookbinder. The family stayed in Tiflis until 1920; Khachaturian played the tuba in the school band, and also studied biology. He then went to Moscow and entered the Gnessin School to study cello; later studied composition with Gnessin himself. In 1929 he became a student at the Moscow Cons., graduating in 1934 in the class of Miaskovsky. Although he started to compose rather late in life, he developed rapidly, and soon progressed to the first rank of Soviet composers. His music is in the tradition of Russian Orientalism; he applies the characteristic scale progressions of Caucasian melos, without quoting actual folk songs. His *Sabre Dance* from his ballet *Gayane* became popular all over the world. In 1948 Khachaturian was severely criticized by the Central Committee of the Communist Party, along with Prokofiev, Shostakovich, and others, for modernistic tendencies; although he admitted his deviations in this respect, he continued to compose essentially in his typical manner, not shunning highly dissonant harmonic combinations. As a conductor of his own works, he gave a concert in Reykjavik, Iceland, in 1951; conducted in Bulgaria in 1952, in Finland in 1955, in London in 1955 and again in 1977, in Japan in 1963, and in Greece in 1965. He made his American debut in Washington, D.C., on Jan. 23, 1968, conducting the National Symph. Orch. in a program of his works; on Jan. 28, 1968, he conducted in N.Y. to a rousing audience reception. In 1933 he married the composer **Nina Makarova** (1908–76). Khachaturian's name is to be properly pronounced Hachaturyán, with a stress on the palatalized last syllable, and with the initial consonant "H" ("Kh") pronounced as the German "ch."

WORKS: FOR THE STAGE: 3 ballets: *Happiness* (1939; Erevan, 1939; Moscow, Oct. 24, 1939); *Gayane* (1940–42; Perm, Dec. 9, 1942; revised 1952 and 1957; extracted 3 symph. suites, 1943; includes the immensely popular *Sabre Dance*); *Spartak* (*Spartacus;* 1950–56; Leningrad, Dec. 26, 1956; revised 1957–58; 4 symph. suites extracted: Nos. 1–3, 1955, and No. 4, 1966).

FOR ORCH.: *Dance Suite* (1932–33); 3 symphs.: No. 1 (1932–33; Moscow, April 23, 1935); No. 2 (1943; Moscow, Dec. 30, 1943; revised, Moscow, March 6, 1944); No. 3 for 15 Solo Trumpets, Orch., and Organ (1947; Leningrad, Dec. 13, 1947); Piano Concerto (1936; Leningrad, July 5, 1937); *The Widow of Valencia,* incidental music (1939–40; orch. suite, 1953); *Masquerade,* incidental music to Lermontov's play (1940; orch. suite, 1944); Violin Concerto (1940; Moscow, Nov. 16, 1940; transcribed for Flute in 1968 by Jean-Pierre Rampal); *2 Armenian Dances* for Cavalry Band (1943); *Solemn Overture* (1945); *Russian Fantasy* (1946); Cello Concerto (1945–46; Moscow, Oct. 30, 1946); *Ode in Memory of Lenin* (1948; Moscow, Dec. 26, 1948); *Battle of Stalingrad,* music for film (screened in Moscow, Dec. 9, 1949); *Concerto-Rhapsody* for Piano and Orch. (1955–68); overture, *Salutation* (1958–59); *Concerto-Rhapsody* for Violin and Orch. (1961–62; Yaroslavl, Oct. 7, 1962; Moscow, Nov. 3. 1962); *Concerto-Rhapsody* for Cello and Orch. (1963; Gorky, Jan. 4, 1964).

CHAMBER MUSIC: *Song-Poem* for Violin and Piano (1929); Violin Sonata (1932); String Quartet (1932); Trio for Clarinet, Violin, and Piano (1932); *Jazz Composition* for Solo Clarinet (1966; written for Benny Goodman); *Sonata-Monologue* for Solo Cello (1974); *Sonata-Fantasia* for Solo Violin (1975).

FOR VOICE: *Poem about Stalin* for Orch., with choral ending (1938; Moscow, Nov. 29, 1938); *3 Concert Arias* for Soprano and Orch. (1946); *Ode to Joy* for Mezzo-soprano, Chorus, 10 Harps, Unison Violins, Band, and Orch. (1955); *Ballade about the Father-*

land for Bass and Orch. (1961); *In Memory of the Heroes,* cantata for Soprano, Male Chorus, and Orch. (1976; a reworking of *Battle of Stalingrad*); songs.

FOR PIANO: 2 albums of children's pieces (1926–47, 1965); *Poem* (1927); *Suite* (1932); *Toccata* (1932); *Suite,* 3 pieces for 2 Pianos (1945); Sonatina (1952); Sonata (1961); *7 Fugues with Recitatives* (1928–66); music for films; numerous marches for band.

BIBLIOGRAPHY: I. Martynov, *Aram Khachaturian* (Moscow, 1956); G. Schneerson, *Aram Khachaturian* (Moscow, 1958); G. Khubov, *Aram Khachaturian* (Moscow, 1962).

Khachaturian, Karen, Soviet composer; nephew of **Aram Khachaturian;** b. Moscow, Sept. 19, 1920. He studied at the Moscow Cons. with Litinsky; during World War II he served in the entertainment division of the Red Army. He resumed studies in 1945 at the Moscow Cons. with Shebalin, Shostakovich, and Miaskovsky, graduating in 1949; in 1952 he was appointed to the faculty of the Moscow Cons. His music follows the general line of socialist realism, nationalist or ethnic in thematic resources and realistic in harmonic and contrapuntal treatment. He wrote a number of effective scores for films. His name, like the name of his uncle, is stressed on the last syllable.

WORKS: For the stage: Operetta, *An Ordinary Girl* (1959); ballet, *Cipollino,* after Rodari's fairy tale (1973). For Orch.: Sinfonietta (1949); Overture (1949); *New-Year Tree,* suite (1951); *Youth Overture* (1951); *In Mongolia,* suite (1951); *Oriental Suite* (1952); *Sports Suite* (1954); 2 symphs.: No. 1 (Moscow, March 12, 1955) and No. 2 (1968); *Friendship Overture* (1959); *At the Circus,* suite (1968). For Voice: *At the Lone Willow,* cantata (1950); *A Moment of History,* oratorio, to documented texts of the Soviet Revolution of 1917 (1971); choruses, songs. Chamber music: Violin Sonata (1947); Cello Sonata (1966); String Quartet (1969).

BIBLIOGRAPHY: M. Uspenskaya, *Karen Khachaturian* (Moscow, 1956); E. Dolinskaya, *Karen Khachaturian* (Moscow, 1975).

Khadzhiev, Parashkev, Bulgarian composer; b. Sofia, April 14, 1912. He studied composition with Vladigerov and piano with Stoyanov at the Bulgarian State Cons. in Sofia, graduating in 1936; then went to Vienna, where he studied composition with Joseph Marx (1937), and to Berlin, where he took a course in composition with Thiessen at the Hochschule für Musik in Berlin (1938–40). Returning to Bulgaria, he occupied various teaching positions.

WORKS: 9 operas: *Imalo edno vreme* (*Once upon a Time;* 1957; Sofia, April 11, 1957); *Lud gidiya* (*Madcap;* 1959; Sofia, Nov. 15, 1959); *Albena* (1962; Varna, Nov. 2, 1962); *Jukka nosht* (*July Night;* 1964; Plovdiv, Feb. 16, 1965); *The Millionaire* (1964; Sofia, March 14, 1965); *Master Woodcarvers* (1966; Sofia, Oct. 9, 1966); *The Knight* (1969; Varna, 1969); *The 3 Brothers and the Golden Apple* (1970; Sofia, Jan. 28, 1971); *The Year 893* (1972; Ruse, March 26, 1973); 4 operettas: *Delyana* (1952); *Aika* (1955); *Madame*

Sans-Gêne (1958); *King Midas Has Ass's Ears* (1976); musical, *Job Hunters* (1972); ballet, *Srebarnite pantofki* (*The Silver Slippers*; 1961; Varna, March 20, 1962); *Skici (Sketches)* for Orch. (1940); Violin Concertino (1941); Flute Concertino (1945); *Capriccio* for Orch. (1951); *Small Dance Suite* for Orch. (1952); *Rondino* for Orch. (1969); 2 violin sonatas (1940, 1946); *3 Pieces* for Wind Quintet (1942); 2 string quartets (1948, 1953); piano pieces; choruses; arrangements of Bulgarian folk songs. He has publ. 4 theoretical texts: *Harmonia* (Sofia, 1959; 2nd ed., 1973); *Textbook on Harmony* (Sofia, 1962; 2nd ed., 1964); *Short Practical Course in Harmony* (Sofia, 1974); *Elementary Theory of Music* (Sofia, 1974).

Khaikin, Boris, eminent Russian conductor; b. Minsk, Oct. 26, 1904; d. Moscow, May 10, 1978. He studied piano with Goedicke, and conducting with Saradzhev at the Moscow Cons.; then became a conductor at the Stanislavsky Theater (1928–35). From 1936 to 1943 he served as principal conductor of the Malyi Theater in Leningrad; from 1944 to 1953 conducted at the Leningrad Theater of Opera and Ballet. From 1954 till his death in 1978 he was on the staff of the Bolshoi Theater in Moscow; he performed for the first time a number of Soviet operas. Khaikin was greatly valued in Russia for his fine professionalism.

Khandoshkin Ivan, Russian violinist and composer; b. 1747; d. St. Petersburg, March 28, 1804. He was the first Russian violin virtuoso, and the first to write instrumental music on Russian folk themes. He studied in St. Petersburg with an Italian musician, Tito Porta; then was sent to Italy, where he was a student at the Tartini school in Padua; it is probable that he took lessons from Tartini himself. Returning to Russia in 1765, he became a violinist in the Imperial Chapel; was concertmaster of the Court Orch. in 1773; also taught violin at the Academy of Arts in St. Petersburg, and later in Moscow and in Ekaterinoslav. These appointments were highly unusual honors to one of Khandoshkin's origin (he was a liberated serf). The following pieces were publ. during his lifetime: *6 sonates pour deux violons* (Amsterdam, 1781); *Chansons russes variées pour violon et basse* (Amsterdam, 1781); *Nouvelles variations sur des chansons russes* for Violin (St. Petersburg, 1784). A set of Russian songs for unaccompanied violin was publ. in 1820; a number of works by Khandoshkin came to light in Russian archives in recent times; his Concerto for Viola and String Orch. was publ. in 1947; *Sentimental Aria* for Unaccompanied Violin was publ. in 1949.
BIBLIOGRAPHY: G. Fesetchko, "Ivan Khandoshkin," *Sovietskaya Musica* (Dec. 1950); R. Aloys Mooser, *Annales de la musique et des musiciens en Russie au XVIIIᵉ siècle* (Geneva, 1950; vol. II, pp. 386–92); I. Yampolsky, *Russian Violin Art* (Moscow, 1951; vol. I, pp. 76–121; contains musical examples from Khandoshkin's works).

Khodzha-Einatov, Leon, Russian composer; b. Tiflis, March 23, 1904; d. Leningrad, Nov. 1, 1954. He studied with Spendiarov; in 1927, went to Leningrad, where he wrote music for the stage. He wrote the opera *Rebellion* (Leningrad, May 16, 1938); 3 Armenian operas: *Arshak* (1945); *David Bek* (1951); *Namus* (1952); *Symphonic Dances* (16 numbers); Symph. (1953).

Khokhlov, Pavel, noted Russian baritone; b. Spassky, Aug. 2, 1854; d. Moscow, Sept. 20, 1919. He studied in Moscow; made his debut with the Bolshoi Theater there in the role of Valentin in *Faust* in 1879; was on its roster until he retired in 1900; also appeared at the Maryinsky Theater in St. Petersburg (1881, 1887–88). He sang the title role in *Eugene Onegin* at the first professional performance of the opera in Moscow in 1881, was also noted for other roles in the Russian repertoire.
BIBLIOGRAPHY: B. Yakovlev, *P.A. Khokhlov* (1950).

Khrennikov, Tikhon, important Soviet composer socially active in music administration; b. Elets, June 10, 1913. He was the 10th child in the family of a provincial clerk, but his parents, his brothers, and sisters were musical, played the Russian guitar and the mandolin, and sang peasant songs. He took piano lessons with a local musician; in 1927 he went to Moscow, where he was introduced to Gniessin, who accepted him as a student in his newly founded musical Technicum; there he studied counterpoint with Litinsky and piano with Ephraim Hellman. After graduation from Gniessin's school, he entered the Moscow Cons., where he studied composition with Shebalin and piano with Neuhaus. At the age of 19 he composed his first important work, a Piano Concerto, which he performed as soloist in Moscow in 1933. He also wrote a piece for a children's theater directed by Natalie Satz, about the time that Prokofiev presented *Peter and the Wolf* at the same theater. In addition, he wrote a number of lyrical ballads and patriotic mass songs. Khrennikov graduated from the Moscow Cons. in 1936; later continued his postgraduate work with Shebalin. In 1961 he joined the faculty of the Moscow Cons., and was named a prof. in 1966. In the meantime he became engaged in the political life of the country. He was attached to the music corps of the Red Army and accompanied it during the last months of the war, entering Berlin in May 1945. In 1947 he joined the Communist party; was also a deputy of the Supreme Soviet; in 1948 he was appointed secretary-general of the Union of Soviet Composers, and in 1949 became president of the music section of the All-Union Society for Cultural Exchange with Europe and America. In 1973 he was named a Hero of Socialist Labor. He further served as head of the organizing committee for the International Festivals and the Tchaikovsky Competitions in Moscow. He held numerous honors, including the Lenin Prize in 1974. Amid all this work he never slackened the tempo of his main preoccupation, that of composition. He wrote operas, ballets, symphs., and concertos, and appeared as a piano soloist. He was a member of the Soviet delegation to the U.S. in 1959.

Khrennikov was named a Hero of Socialist Labor in 1973. During his entire career he was a stout spokesman for the Soviet musical policy along the lines of socialist realism, and his own works express forcefully the desirable qualities of Soviet music, a flowing melody suggesting the broad modalities of Russian folk songs, a vibrant and expressive lyricism, and effective instrumental formation.

WORKS: FOR THE STAGE: Operas: *Brothers* (later renamed *In the Storm;* Moscow, May 31, 1939); *Frol Skobeyev* (Moscow, Feb. 24, 1950; 2nd version renamed *Unrelated Son-in-Law*); *Mother,* after the novel by Maxim Gorky (Moscow, Oct. 26, 1957); fairy-tale opera for children, *Boy Giant* (1969); comic opera, *Much Ado about . . . Hearts,* a parody on Shakespeare's play *Much Ado about Nothing* (1976); operettas: *100 Devils and a Single Girl* (Moscow, May 16, 1963); *White Nights* (Moscow, Nov. 3, 1967); ballet, *Happy Childhood* (1970). FOR ORCH.: 3 symphs.: No. 1 (Moscow, Oct. 10, 1955); No. 2, expressing "the irresistible will to defeat the Fascist foe" (Moscow, Jan. 10, 1943); No. 3 (1973); 3 piano concertos (1933, 1970, 1982); 2 violin concertos (1959, 1975); Cello Concerto (Moscow, May 13, 1964). INCIDENTAL MUSIC: *A Soldier Returns from the Front* (1938); *Don Quixote* (1941). FILM MUSIC: *Shepherdess and Shepherd* (1941); *At Six o'Clock after the War* (1944); *The Balladeer Goes West* (1947); *Hussar's Ballad* (1962); *We Need Not a Password* (1964). Also chamber music; piano pieces; many songs and choruses.

BIBLIOGRAPHY: L. Kaltat, *Tikhon Khrennikov* (Moscow, 1946); V. Kukharsky, *Tikhon Khrennikov* (Moscow, 1957); Y. Kremlev, *Tikhon Khrennikov* (Moscow, 1963); I. Martinov, *Tikhon Khrennikov* (Moscow, 1967).

Khubov, Georgi, Soviet writer on music; b. Kars, Turkey, May 9, 1902; d. Moscow, Nov. 5, 1981. He was born in Turkey, but went to the U.S.S.R. shortly after the Revolution; studied piano at the Odessa Cons. (1920); later took courses in composition with Paliashvili at the Cons. of Tiflis. In 1922 he entered the Moscow Cons., graduating as a pianist in 1930. In Moscow he organized the first school of mass music; also edited musical publications. During the war (1941–45) he was in charge of the musical broadcasts over the Soviet Radio; in 1943 he joined the Communist Party. From 1934–38 he taught music history at the Moscow Cons., and for the first time in Soviet pedagogy introduced a special course in Soviet music. He also publ. informative monographs: *Borodin* (Moscow, 1933); *J.S. Bach* (Moscow, 1936); *Aram Khachaturian* (Moscow, 1962; Armenian trans., Erevan, 1977); *Mussorgsky* (Moscow, 1969).

Kidson, Frank, English musical folklorist and bibliographer; b. Leeds, Nov. 15, 1855; d. there, Nov. 7, 1926. Originally a landscape painter, he became interested in historical studies and began to collect English, Scottish, and Irish folk songs and dance melodies; subsequently became one of the founders of the Folksong Society in England. He publ. *Old English Country Dances* (1890); *Traditional Tunes* (1891); *British Music Publishers, Printers and Engravers . . .* (1900); *English Folksong and Dance* (1915); *The Beggar's Opera, Its Predecessors and Successors* (1922); contributed valuable articles to the *Musical Antiquary* and the *Musical Quarterly;* with A. Moffat, he edited *The Minstrelsy of England; Songs of the Georgian Period; British Nursery Rhymes; Children's Songs of Long Ago; 80 Singing Games for Children;* etc.

Kiel, Friedrich, German music pedagogue and composer; b. Puderbach, near Siegen, Oct. 7, 1821; d. Berlin, Sept. 13, 1885. He studied the rudiments of music with his father, a schoolmaster. One of his youthful works, a set of variations (1832–34), attracted the attention of Prince Karl von Wittgenstein, who gave him violin lessons in 1835, and took him into his orch. Kiel further studied with Kaspar Kummer at Coburg, becoming leader of the ducal orch. there (1840); then moved to Berlin, and studied with Dehn (1842–44). He received a stipend from King Friedrich Wilhelm IV; in 1865, was elected to the Prussian Academy of Fine Arts. From 1866 to 1870 he taught composition at the Stern Cons. in Berlin. He wrote the oratorios *Christus* and *Der Stern von Bethlehem; Stabat Mater; Requiem; Te Deum;* 4 piano sonatas. He was a prolific composer, but it was as a pedagogue that he gained distinction. W. Altmann publ. a complete list of his works in *Die Musik,* 1 (1901).

Kielland, Olav, Norwegian conductor and composer; b. Trondheim, Aug. 16, 1901. He studied music theory at the Leipzig Cons. (1921–23) and took Weingartner's conducting class in Basel (1929). He conducted in Göteborg (1925–31), Oslo (1931–45), Trondheim (1946–48), and Bergen (1948–55), and filled some conducting engagements in London and N.Y. In 1952 he organized, in Reykjavik, Iceland's first symph. orch.

WORKS: 4 sinfonias: *I* (1935); *II* (1961); *III* (1966); *IV* (1976); Violin Concerto (1939–40); *Overtura tragica* (1941); *Mot blåsnøhøgdom (The White-capped Mountains),* symph. suite for High Voice and Orch. (1945–46); *Concerto grosso norvegese* for 2 Horns and String Orch. (1952); *Tvileikar* for 4 Instruments (1954); String Quartet (1964); *Marcia del Coraggio* for Orch. (1968); *Ouverture solenne* (1974); Piano Concerto (1977).

BIBLIOGRAPHY: Bjarne Kortsen, *Contemporary Norwegian Orchestral Music* (Bergen, 1969; pp. 244–82).

Kienle, Ambrosius, authority on Gregorian chant; b. Sigmaringen, May 8, 1852; d. in the monastery at Beuron, June 18, 1905. He entered the monastery in 1873, and devoted himself to the study of Gregorian chant. He publ. *Choralschule* (1884; 3rd ed., 1899); *Kleines kirchenmusikalisches Handbuch* (1892); *Mass und Milde in kirchenmusikalischen Dingen* (1901); essays in periodicals.

Kienzl, Wilhelm, Austrian composer; b. Waizenkirchen, Jan. 17, 1857; d. Vienna, Oct. 3, 1941. He studied music at the Graz Gymnasium with Ignaz Uhl, and with W.A. Remy (composition); later with Josef Krejči at Prague, Rheinberger in Munich, and Liszt at Weimar, at length receiving his Ph.D. in Vienna in 1879 for the dissertation *Die musikalische Deklamation* (Leipzig, 1880). A 2nd work, *Miscellen* (Leipzig, 1885), concerning impressions received in Bayreuth (1879), created a stir by its bold criticism. During 1880 he lectured on music in Munich; in 1881–82, made a pianistic tour in Hungary, Rumania, and Germany; in 1883, was appointed conductor of the German opera in Amsterdam. Shortly thereafter, he went to Krefeld to take up a similar position; in 1886 he married the concert singer **Lili Hoke.** In 1886–90 he was artistic director of the Styrian Musikverein at Graz and directed the symph. concerts and the programs of the provincial vocal and instrumental schools. In 1890–92 he held the position of first conductor at the Hamburg Opera; in 1892–94 was court conductor at Munich, before returning to Graz. In 1917, he received the honorary degree of Doc.Mus. from the Univ. of Graz; later, in Vienna, was music critic for various papers. His early operas include *Urvasi* (Dresden, Feb. 20, 1886; rewritten 1909); *Heilmar, der Narr* (Munich, March 8, 1892; very successful); *Der Evangelimann* (Berlin, May 4, 1895; his most famous work). Then followed *Don Quichote,* a "musical tragi-comedy" (Berlin, Nov. 18, 1898); *In Knecht Rupprechts Werkstatt,* a "Märchenspiel" (Graz, 1906); *Der Kuhreigen (Ranz des Vaches)* (Vienna, Nov. 23, 1911); *Das Testament* (Vienna, Dec. 6, 1916); *Hassan der Schwarmer* (Chemnitz, 1925); *Sanctissimum* (Vienna, 1925); *Hans Kipfel,* singspiel (Vienna, 1928). Kienzl finished Adolf Jensen's opera *Turandot,* and edited Mozart's *Titus.* His own publ. compositions include about 120 songs; much light piano music; incidental music to *Die Brautfahrt; Septuaginta* (1937); 3 *Phantasiestücke* for Piano and Violin; Piano Trio; 2 string quartets; choral music. He also composed the new Austrian national anthem, with a text by the future president of Austria, Karl Renner, to replace that written by Haydn in 1797; its adoption was announced by the Republican government on June 6, 1920, but on Dec. 13, 1929, the Haydn melody was once more adopted as a national anthem (with a different set of words). Kienzl edited Brendel's *Grundzüge der Geschichte der Musik* (Leipzig, 1886) and *Geschichte der Musik in Italien, Deutschland und Frankreich* (7th ed., Leipzig, 1889). In addition, he wrote *Richard Wagner* (1904; 2nd ed., 1908); *Aus Kunst und Leben* (1904); *Im Konzert* (1908); *Betrachtungen und Erinnerungen* (1909); *Meine Lebenswanderung,* an autobiography (1926); *Hans Richter* (1930). BIBLIOGRAPHY: M. Morold, *Wilhelm Kienzl* (Leipzig, 1909); *Festschrift zum 60. Geburtstag von Wilhelm Kienzl* (1917); *Festschrift zum 80. Geburtstag von Wilhelm Kienzl* (Vienna, 1937); Hans Sittner, ed., Wilhelm Kienzl's *Lebenswanderung* (Vienna, 1953; includes Kienzl's correspondence with Peter Rosegger).

Kiepura, Jan, Polish tenor; b. Sosnowiec, May 16, 1902; d. Rye, N.Y., Aug. 15, 1966. He studied in Warsaw, where he made his first public appearance in 1923; was then engaged as an opera singer by a number of European opera houses (Vienna, Berlin, Milan, etc.). He made his American debut in Chicago in 1931; appeared at the Metropolitan Opera in N.Y. as Rodolfo in *La Bohème* (Feb. 10, 1938); sang there until 1939; appeared again in 1942. He settled in the U.S., making frequent tours in Europe as well. He was married to the Austrian singer **Martha Eggerth.**

Kiesewetter, Raphael Georg, Edler von Wiesenbrunn, Austrian scholar and writer on musical subjects; b. Holleschau, Moravia, Aug. 29, 1773; d. Baden, near Vienna, Jan. 1, 1850. He was educated for an official career as an Austrian functionary; was connected with the War Ministry; traveled in various European countries; in 1801 settled in Vienna. His musical interests impelled him to undertake serious study with Albrechtsberger, who instructed him in counterpoint. He was an indefatigable collector of old musical MSS, and archeological research became his specialty. He received the rank of nobility in 1845. **A.W. Ambros** was his nephew.

WRITINGS: *Die Verdienste der Niederländer um die Tonkunst* (received the prize of the Netherlands Academy in 1826; Dutch trans., 1829); *Geschichte der europäisch-abendländischen, das ist unserer heutigen Musik* (Leipzig, 1834; Eng. trans., 1846); *Über die Musik der neuern Griechen, nebst freien Gedanken über altägyptische und altgriechische Musik* (1838); *Guido von Arezzo, Sein Leben und Wirken* (1840); *Schicksale und Beschaffenheit des weltlichen Gesangs vom frühen Mittelalter bis zur Erfindung der dramatischen Styles und den Anfangen der Oper* (1841); *Die Musik der Araber nach Originalquellen* (1842); *Der neuen Aristoxener; zerstreute Aufsätze* (1846); *Über die Oktave des Pythagoras* (1847); *Galerie der alten Kontrapunktisten* (1847; a catalogue of his old scores, bequeathed to the Vienna Library); also essays on old music and on Gregorian notation in German periodicals.

Kiesewetter, Tomasz, Polish composer and conductor; b. Sosnowka, Sept. 8, 1911. He studied composition with Rytel and conducting with Berdiayev at the Warsaw Cons.; during the German occupation in World War II, he was active in resistance groups; after the war, taught at the State College of Music in Lodz. WORKS: Operetta, *The Lonely Ones* (1963); ballet, *King's Jester* (1954); *Polish Dances* for Orch. (1947, 1950); 3 symphs. (1949, 1952, 1958); Viola Concerto (1950).

Kijima, Kiyohiko, Japanese composer; b. Tokyo, Feb. 19, 1917. He studied composition with Ikenouchi at Nihon Univ.; later joined its faculty. He received 2 prizes given by the Tokyo newspaper *Mainichi* (1938, 1948). His works include *Satsukino,* poem for Soprano and Small Orch. (1940); *Symphonic Overture* (1942); *Prelude and Fugue* for Orch. (1948); String Quartet (1950); Violin Sonata

(1951); *5 Meditations* for Orch. (1956); *Trio* for Flute, Violin, and Piano (1958; revised 1970); *Divertimento* for Orch. (1963); *Mi-Chi-No-Ku* for Chorus, Flute, Piano, and Percussion (1963); Piano Quintet (1965); *2 Legends* for Piano (1969); songs.

Kiladze, Grigori, Soviet Georgian composer; b. Batum, Oct. 25, 1902; d. Tiflis, April 3, 1962. He studied at the Tiflis Cons. with Ippolitov-Ivanov (1924–27); then at the Leningrad Cons. with Vladimir Shcherbachev (1927–29). Kiladze was one of the most active proponents of ethnic Georgian music in a modern idiom derived thematically from folk melorhythms. He wrote operas on subjects from Caucasian revolutionary history: *Bakhtrioni* (1936) and *Lado Ketzkhoveli* (1941); a ballet, *Sinatle* (1947); *Poem about Stalin* for Chorus and Orch. (1935); *Heroic Symphony* (1944); oratorio, *Childhood and Adolescence of the Leader* (1951); overture, *Triumph* (1957).

Kilar, Wojciech, Polish composer; b. Lwow, July 17, 1932. He studied piano and composition with Woytowicz at the State College of Music in Katowice (1950–55); later took courses at the Cracow Academy (1955–58); then went to Paris, where he took private lessons with Nadia Boulanger (1959–60). Returning to Poland, he became a teacher at the College of Music in Katowice. Of an experimental turn of mind, he makes use of a variety of modern techniques while retaining essential Classical forms.
WORKS: *The Mask of the Red Death,* ballet after Poe (1962); *Little Overture* (1955); 2 symphs.: No. 1 for Strings (1955) and No. 2, *Sinfonia concertante,* for Piano and Orch. (1956); *Béla Bartók in Memoriam* for Solo Violin, Winds, and 2 Percussion Groups (1957); Concerto for 2 Pianos and Percussion (1958); *Herbsttag,* after Rilke, for Soprano and String Quartet (1960); *Riff 62* for Orch. (1962); *Générique* for Orch. (1963); *Diphthongs* for Chorus, 6 Percussionists, 2 Pianos, and Strings (1964); *Springfield Sonnet* for Orch. (1965); *Solenne* for Soprano, Strings, and Brasses (1967); *Training 68* for Clarinet, Trombone, Cello, and Piano (1968); *Upstairs-Downstairs* for 2 Children's Choruses (without words) and Orch. (Warsaw, Sept. 25, 1971); *Prelude and a Carol* for 4 Oboes and String Orch. (1972); *Bogurodzica (Mother of God)* for Chorus and Orch. (1975); incidental music for theatrical plays; film scores.

Kilburn, Nicholas, English choral conductor and composer; b. Bishop Auckland, Durham, Feb. 7, 1843; d. there, Dec. 4, 1923. He studied in Cambridge, then conducted a musical society in his native town and the Phil. Society of Sunderland (from 1885); these posts he filled until his death. He publ. *Notes and Notions on Music; How to Manage a Choral Society; Wagner, A Sketch; Parsifal and Bayreuth; The Story of Chamber Music;* etc.; also wrote some choral works.

Kilenyi, Edward, Jr., American pianist, son of **Edward Kilenyi, Sr.;** b. Philadelphia, May 7, 1911. In 1927 he went to Budapest to study with Dohnányi at the Cons. there; after graduating (1930), he traveled in Europe, giving concerts; returning to America, he continued his career as a concert pianist; his American debut was in N.Y., Oct. 21, 1940, in a recital.

Kilenyi, Edward, Sr., Hungarian composer and pedagogue; b. Bekes, Jan. 25, 1884; d. Tallahassee, Fla., Aug. 15, 1968. He studied in Budapest, at the Cons. of Cologne, and in Italy (with Mascagni). In 1908 he settled in the U.S.; took courses at Columbia Univ. with Rybner and Daniel Gregory Mason (M.A., 1915). In 1930 he went to Hollywood, where he remained as a pedagogue and a composer for the films. He was for 5 years the teacher of George Gershwin.

Killebrew, Gwendolyn, black American mezzo-soprano; b. Philadelphia, Aug. 26, 1941. She studied at Temple Univ. in Philadelphia; also at the Juilliard School of Music in N.Y. She sang with the N.Y. City Opera; on Nov. 21, 1967, she made her Metropolitan Opera debut; in Europe she sang at the Salzburg Festival. In addition to opera, she has made many appearances as a concert singer.

Killmayer, Wilhelm, German composer; b. Munich, Aug. 21, 1927. He studied in Munich with H.W. von Waltershausen (1945–50); then at the Univ. of Munich (1950–52), and later with Carl Orff; was engaged as conductor of the Marionette Theater of Munich. He has written mostly for choral groups, in a modern madrigal manner, with rapidly altering rhythmic patterns and massive harmonies; the influence of Carl Orff is decidedly apparent. Among his works are *Missa brevis; Chansons* for Tenor, Flute, Strings, and Percussion; *Canti amorosi* for 6 Voices a cappella; *Lauda* for Chorus (1968); *Sinfonie "Folgi"* (Hannover, Feb. 9, 1971); music for marionettes.

Kilpatrick, Jack Frederick, American composer of Cherokee origin; b. Stillwater, Okla., Sept. 23, 1915; d. Muskogee, Okla., Feb. 22, 1967. He studied at the Univ. of Redlands, Calif., and at the Catholic Univ. of America in Washington, D.C. A prolific composer, he composed more than 200 works of various types. His opera *The Blessed Wilderness* was performed in Finland; other works were played in Rome, Munich, Berlin, Copenhagen, Stockholm, Manila, Tokyo, Melbourne, and London. His historical drama with music, *The Golden Crucible,* was commissioned by the city of Pittsburgh for its bicentennial. Virtually all of his music is derived from Indian folklore, with the pentatonic scale at its foundation.
WORKS: Music dramas: *Unto These Hills* (Cherokee, N.C., July 1, 1950); *The Golden Crucible* (Pittsburgh, 1959); *The Blessed Wilderness* (Dallas, April 18, 1959); 8 symphs., of which No. 4 is scored for Voices and Orch. (Dallas, Jan. 17, 1951); No. 5 (Honolulu, Feb. 19, 1957); No. 6 (San Antonio, March 2, 1957); No. 7, subtitled "The Republic of Texas" (San Antonio, 1957); No. 8, subtitled "Oklahoma,"

for Narrator, Dancers, and Orch. (Oklahoma City, Nov. 17, 1957); numerous other instrumental works, most of them based on Indian legends.

WRITINGS: *Friends of Thunder* (1964); *Walk in Your Soul* (1965); *Sequoyah* (1965).

Kilpinen, Yrjö, Finnish song composer; b. Helsingfors, Feb. 4, 1892; d. Helsinki, March 2, 1959. He had very little academic education in music; took a few courses at the Helsingfors Cons., in Berlin, and in Vienna. His chosen form was that of lyric song; possessing an exceptional talent for expressing poetic lines in finely balanced melodies, he attained great renown in Finland, and has been called the Finnish Hugo Wolf. He composed about 800 lieder to words in German, Finnish, and Swedish, by classical and modern poets. In 1948 he was appointed a member of the Academy of Finland. About 300 of his songs are publ.; other works are *Pastoral Suite* for Orch. (1944); *Totentanz* for Orch. (1945); 6 piano sonatas; Cello Sonata; Suite for Viola da Gamba, with Piano; etc.

BIBLIOGRAPHY: M. Pulkkinen, *Yrjö Kilpinen: Gedruckte Kompositionen* (Helsinki, 1960).

Kim, Earl, American composer; b. Dinuba, Calif., Jan. 6, 1920. He studied at the Univ. of Calif., Berkeley (M.A. 1952); was an associate prof. at Princeton Univ. (1952–67) and subsequently on the staff of Harvard Univ. His works include *Dialogues* for Piano and Orch. (1959); *They Are Far Out* for Soprano, Violin, Cello, and Percussion (1966); *Gooseberries, She Said* for Soprano, 5 Instruments, and Percussion (1968); *Letter Found near a Suicide,* song cycle; *Exercises en route,* multimedia composition. He received in 1971 the Brandeis Univ. Creative Arts Award.

Kim, Young-Uck, South Korean violinist; b. Seoul, Sept. 1, 1947. A typical child prodigy, he began to fiddle with astounding precocity on a minuscule violin. He was sent to the U.S. when he was 11 and accepted as a student of Ivan Galamian at the Curtis Inst. of Music in Philadelphia. On May 10, 1963, he made an auspicious appearance with Ormandy and the Philadelphia Orch. in a nationally televised concert; then toured with them in South America. This was the beginning of a brilliant career; he made a European tour as a soloist with the Berlin Phil., the Concertgebouw Orch. of Amsterdam, the Vienna Phil., and the London Symph. He also organized the Ax-Ma-Kim Trio, with the Polish-born American pianist Emanuel Ax and the Chinese cello virtuoso Yo-Yo Ma.

Kimball, Jacob, Jr., American composer; b. Topsfield, Mass., Feb. 22, 1761; d. in the almshouse there, Feb. 6, 1826. In 1775 he was a drummer in the Massachusetts militia; then entered Harvard Univ. (graduated 1780); subsequently studied law and was admitted to the bar, but soon gave up that profession for music, teaching in various New England towns. He wrote hymns, psalm tunes, and "fuguing pieces," in the style of Billings; compiled *The Rural Harmony* (71 original compositions for 3 and 4 voices; Boston, 1793). Another collection, *The Essex Harmony* (44 tunes and 2 anthems), is also attributed to him; it was publ. in Exeter, N.H., in 1800, and dedicated to the Essex (Mass.) Music Assoc.; the Boston Public Library possesses an imperfect copy.

BIBLIOGRAPHY: F.J. Metcalf, *American Psalmody* (1917); idem, *American Writers and Compilers of Sacred Music* (1925); G. Wilcox, *Jacob Kimball, Jr. (1761–1826): His Life and Works* (Diss., Univ. of Southern Calif., Los Angeles, 1957).

Kincaid, W. Bradley, American folk-song collector and singer; b. Garrard County, Ky., July 13, 1895. He began to sing and play the guitar as a child; after serving in the U.S. Army in World War I, he went to Chicago and studied at the YMCA College. He made his first appearances as a singer on the "National Barn Dance" radio program; subsequently sang on the "Grand Ole Opry" in Nashville, Tenn.; he also owned his own radio station in Springfield, Ohio (1949–53). As a folk-song collector, he publ. 13 songbooks containing material from traditional sources, as well as some compositions of his own.

Kincaid, William, outstanding American flutist and pedagogue; b. Minneapolis, April 26, 1895; d. Philadelphia, March 27, 1967. He studied flute with Georges Barrère at the Inst. of Musical Art in N.Y.; then played in the N.Y. Symph. Orch. (1914–21). In 1921 Stokowski engaged him as first flutist of the Philadelphia Orch., a position he held with great distinction until his retirement in 1960; he also was a distinguished teacher at the Curtis Inst. of Music, where he taught a number of noted flute players. He maintained a valuable collection of historic flutes; his own instrument was a specially made platinum flute.

BIBLIOGRAPHY: J. Krell, *Kincaidiana: A Flute Player's Notebook* (Culver City, Calif., 1973).

Kinder, Ralph, American organist; b. Stalybridge, near Manchester, England, Jan. 27, 1876; d. Bala, suburb of Philadelphia, Nov. 14, 1952. He was taken to the U.S. at the age of 5; was a chorister in Bristol, R.I.; studied in America, and then in London with E.H. Lemare. He held various posts as a church organist in Bristol (1890–98), Providence (1898), and Philadelphia (from 1899). He wrote numerous organ pieces of considerable charm; of these the following are publ.: *Arietta, Berceuse, Caprice, Festival March, Jour de printemps, Moonlight, Souvenir, In Springtime.*

Kindermann, August, German bass-baritone; b. Potsdam, Feb. 6, 1817; d. Munich, March 6, 1891. He sang in the chorus of the Berlin Court Opera; then went to Leipzig, where he appeared at the theater (1839–46); in 1846 he became a member of the Munich Court Opera, and remained on its roster until his death; he also sang at Bayreuth, where he created the role of Titurel in *Parsifal* (1882).

Kindermann, Johann Erasmus, German organist

and composer; b. Nuremberg, March 29, 1616; d. there, April 14, 1655. He was a student of J. Staden; in 1634, went to Venice, where he took lessons with Cavalli; returning to Nuremberg in 1636, he became 2nd organist at the Frauenkirche; was organist in Schwäbisch-Hall in 1640; then returned to Nuremberg as organist at the Egidienkirche until his death.

WORKS: *Cantiones pathetikai* (1639); *Friedensklag* (1640); *Opitianischer Orpheus* (1642); *Concentus Salomonis* (1642); *Musica catechetica* (1643); *Deliciae studiosorum* (1640–48; many reprints); *Intermedium musico-politicum*, a collection of quodlibets (1643); *Harmonia organica* (in tablature; 1645; 2nd ed., 1665); *Göttliche Liebesflamme*, 20 sacred songs (1640–75); also various instrumental works.

BIBLIOGRAPHY: F. Schreiber, *Der Nürnberger Organist Johannes Erasmus Kindermann (1616–1655)* (Leipzig, 1913); H.J. Moser, *Corydon* (1933; vol. 1, pp. 31–42; vol. 2, pp. 77–88).

Kindler, Hans, Dutch-American cellist and conductor; b. Rotterdam, Jan. 8, 1892; d. Watch Hill, R.I., Aug. 30, 1949. He studied at the Rotterdam Cons., receiving first prize for piano and cello in 1906. In 1911 he was appointed prof. at the Scharwenka Cons. in Berlin, and first cellist at the Berlin Opera. In 1912–13 he made a successful tour of Europe; in 1914, came to the U.S. to become first cellist of the Philadelphia Orch., a post he held until 1920. In 1927 he made his debut as a conductor in Philadelphia; in 1928 he conducted the world premiere of Stravinsky's ballet *Apollon Musagète* at the Library of Congress Festival in Washington, D.C.; in 1929 he appeared as a cellist in 110 concerts throughout the U.S. and Europe, also touring as far as Java and India. In 1931 he organized the National Symph. Orch. in Washington, of which he was permanent conductor until his resignation on Nov. 30, 1948.

King, Alec (Alexander) Hyatt, English bibliographer and musicologist; b. Beckenham, Kent, July 18, 1911. He was educated at Culwich College and King's College, Cambridge (B.A., 1933); in 1934 he joined the Dept. of Printed Books of the British Museum; became head of the music division in 1944; retired in 1976. He publ. a number of valuable textual and bibliographical studies.

WRITINGS: *Chamber Music* (London, 1948); *Handel's Messiah* (the exhibition catalogue of the British Museum; London, 1951); *Mozart in Retrospect: Studies in Criticism and Bibliography* (London, 1955; 3rd ed., 1970); *Mozart in the British Museum* (London, 1956; 2nd ed., 1966); *Henry Purcell 1659–1695; George Frideric Handel 1685–1759* (the exhibition catalogue of the British Museum; London, 1959); *Some British Collectors of Music c.1600–1960* (Cambridge, 1963); *Four Hundred Years of Music Printing* (London, 1964; 2nd ed., 1968); *Handel and His Autographs* (London, 1967); *Mozart Chamber Music* (London, 1968; 2nd ed., 1969); *Mozart: A Biography, with a Survey of Books, Editions and Recordings* (London, 1970); *Mozart Wind and String Concertos* (London, 1978); *Printed Music in the British Museum: An Account of the Collections, the Catalogues, and their Formation, up to 1920* (London, 1979).

BIBLIOGRAPHY: O. Neighbour, ed., *Music and Bibliography: Essays in Honour of Alec Hyatt King* (London, 1980).

King, "B.B." (Riley B. King), black American blues singer and guitarist; b. Itta Bena, Miss., Sept. 16, 1925. While working on a farm he learned to play the guitar. In 1950 he scored his first hit with his recording of *Three O'Clock Blues;* in the late 1960s he assumed a prominent place among the great blues singers and guitarists; in 1968 he made his first tour of Europe, and then headed an all-blues concert at Carnegie Hall in N.Y. in 1970. Utilizing an electric guitar, he is regarded as one of the most innovative blues artists of his era.

King, Carole, American pop songwriter; b. Brooklyn, Feb. 9, 1941. Her real name was **Carole Klein.** She took regular piano lessons as a child; an intellectually precocious teenager, she started a female vocal ensemble in school under a trigonometrical name, Co-Sines. At 17, she met the songwriter Gerry Goflin, whom she soon married. Together, they produced a hit song *Will You Love Me Tomorrow.* Several other hits followed, among them *Some Kind of Wonderful, When My Little Girl Is Smiling, Up on the Roof, Take Good Care of My Baby, The Loco-Motion,* and *It Might As Well Rain until September.* On her own, she produced the smash hits *You've Got a Friend, It's Too Late,* and *I Feel the Earth,* which had a direct appeal to folk-rockers of all ages. In the meantime, she divorced Goflin and temporarily married Charles Larkey; then divorced him and married the songwriter Rick Evers, who died of a cocaine overdose in Los Angeles, on March 21, 1978, leaving her a widow.

King, Harold Charles, Swiss-born Dutch composer; b. Winterthur, Dec. 30, 1895. He came to the Netherlands to study engineering at the Delft Technical Univ.; served as a management consultant with a municipal corporation in Amsterdam; while thus occupied, he took composition lessons with Cornelis Dopper and Henk Badings.

WORKS: Serenade for String Orch. (1934); *Per Ardua,* symph. suite (1946–49); *Concerto da camera* for Flute and Strings (1962); *Triptyque symphonique* (1964); Sinfonietta (1965); Organ Concerto (1966); Cello Sonata (1940); *Trio patetico* for Violin, Viola, and Cello (1942); *3 Impressions* for Solo Cello (1948); Wind Quintet (1949); 2 string quartets (1953, 1962); *A fleur d'eau* for Flute, Violin, Spinet, and Viola da Gamba (1964); Sonata for Solo Cello (1966); Duo for 2 Cellos (1966); *Piccolo quartetto* for String Quartet (1976); *Little Laddie,* piano sonatina (1966); *King David's Dance* for 4-octave Carillon (1975).

King, James, American tenor; b. Dodge City, Kans., May 22, 1925. He studied at Kansas State Univ. and Louisiana State Univ. He then went to Europe;

made his professional debut in Florence in 1961. In 1962 he became a member of the Deutsche Oper in West Berlin; also sang at Salzburg (1962), Munich (1963), Bayreuth (1965), and at Covent Garden in London (1966). On June 8, 1966, he made his Metropolitan Opera debut in N.Y. as Florestan in *Fidelio.*

King, Karl L(awrence), American Midwestern bandmaster and composer of band music; b. Painterville, Ohio, Feb. 21, 1891; d. Fort Dodge, Iowa, March 31, 1971. After 8 grades of public schools in Cleveland and Canton, Ohio, during which he began to play brass instruments (primarily the baritone horn) under the tutelage of local musicians, he quit school to learn the printing trade, but soon began to play in and compose for local bands. In 1910 he initiated his short career as a circus bandsman, bandmaster, and composer, ending it in 1917–18 as bandmaster of the Barnum & Bailey Circus Band (for which he had already written what was to remain his most famous march, *Barnum & Bailey's Favorite*). On Sept. 13, 1920, he conducted his first concert with the Fort Dodge Military Band, with which he was to be associated for half a century. It was a time when the small-town band in the U.S. was passing its heyday; but King took a group of only 18 bandsmen, added to them, and in a very few years had created a notable institution, not only in Iowa but in the whole Midwestern rural culture (and this over a period when most town bands were disappearing under the competition of radio, recordings, the school-band movement, and faster transportation and communications). In 1922 the band began to receive municipal tax support under the Iowa Band Law (for which one of King's marches is named), and its name was changed to the Fort Dodge Municipal Band, although it was known commonly as Karl L. King's Band. For 40 years it toured widely over its region, especially to play at county fairs, and King himself traveled even more widely to conduct or judge at band contests, conventions, massed band celebrations, and all manner of band events. He was one of the founders, in 1930, of the American Bandmasters Assoc.; he served as president of that group in 1939, and in 1967 was named Honorary Life President. Among his 260-odd works for band (most publ. the firm of C.L. Barnhouse in Oskaloosa, Iowa) are concert works, novelties, waltzes, and all manner of dance forms; but marches predominate, from the circus marches of his early days to sophisticated marches for univ. bands (such as *Pride of the Illini* for Illinois and *Purple Pageant* for Northwestern) and especially to easy but tuneful and well-written marches for the less-accomplished school bands. The musical *The Music Man* (1957) was inspired in part by King's music, according to its composer and fellow Iowan, **Meredith Willson.**

BIBLIOGRAPHY: T.J. Hatton, *Karl L. King, An American Bandmaster* (Evanston, Ill., 1975).

King, Matthew Peter, English composer; b. London, 1773; d. there, Jan. 1823. He composed 10 or 12 operas for the Lyceum Theatre; an oratorio, *The Intercession;* Quintet for Piano, Flute, and Strings; piano sonatas; etc.; also publ. *A General Treatise on Music* (London, 1800) and an *Introduction* to sight singing (1806).

King, Oliver A., English pianist; b. London, July 6, 1855; d. there, Aug. 23, 1923. He was a pupil of J. Barnby; later studied piano with Reinecke at the Leipzig Cons. (1874–77). In 1880–83 he toured Canada, giving recitals, and visited N.Y. In 1893 he was appointed prof. of piano at the Royal Academy of Music in London.
WORKS: 3 cantatas: *The Romance of the Roses; Proserpina; The Naiades; 137th Psalm* (Chester Festival, 1888); symph. poem, *Night;* 2 overtures; Piano Concerto; Violin Concerto; pieces for piano solo and for organ.

King, Pete, American composer, arranger, and conductor; b. Greenville, Ohio, Aug. 8, 1914; d. Newport Beach, Calif., Sept. 20, 1982. He attended a prep school in Newport, R.I., the Univ. of Michigan, and the Cincinnati Cons. of Music; then went to N.Y., where he began a successful career as conductor and arranger for Broadway productions. In 1952 he moved to Los Angeles, where he led popular ensembles advertised as the Pete King Chorale and the Pete King Orch. He became a favorite conductor-arranger for many Hollywood stars and television personalities, among them Bing Crosby, Frank Sinatra, and Lawrence Welk. He earned a credit line as music director for such famous motion pictures as *South Pacific* and *The Godfather.* Unhappily, he was stricken in 1974 with meningitis, which caused total deafness and forced him to retire.

Kinkel, Johanna (née **Mockel**), German composer; b. Bonn, July 8, 1810; d. London, Nov. 15, 1858. She studied music in Berlin with Karl Böhmer, and married the poet, in 1843. She wrote *Die Vogel-Cantate;* the operetta *Otto der Schutz;* and the well-known song *The Soldier's Farewell;* also publ. *Acht Briefe an eine Freundin über Klavierunterricht* (1852).

Kinkeldey, Otto, eminent American musicologist; b. New York, Nov. 27, 1878; d. Orange, N.J., Sept. 19, 1966. He graduated from the College of the City of N.Y. in 1898 (B.A.) and from N.Y. Univ. in 1900 (M.A.); then took lessons with MacDowell at Columbia Univ. (until 1902). After that he went to Germany, where he undertook a course of study with Radecke, Egidi, and Thiel at the Akademisches Inst. für Kirchenmusik in Berlin; studied musicology at the Univ. of Berlin with Fleischer, Friedlaender, Kretzschmar, and J. Wolf (1902–6); received his Ph.D. from the Univ. of Berlin in 1909. He was organist and choirmaster at the Chapel of the Incarnation in N.Y. (1898–1902); organist and music director of the American Church in Berlin (1903–5); instructor in organ and theory, lecturer on musicology, and music director at the Univ. of Breslau (1909–14); was named Royal Prussian Prof. in 1910.

Returning to the U.S. at the outbreak of World War I, he became organist and choirmaster at All-Souls Church in N.Y. (1915–17); was an infantry captain in the U.S. Army (1917–19); in 1915–23, and again in 1927–30, was chief of the Music Division of the N.Y. Public Library; in 1923–27 he was a prof. of music at Cornell Univ.; in 1930–46, a prof. of musicology and librarian there; prof. emeritus, 1946. He was a guest prof. at Harvard Univ. (1946–48), the Univ. of Texas (1948–50), Princeton Univ. (1950–51), North Texas State College (1952–53), the Univ. of Illinois (1953–54), the Univ. of Calif., Berkeley (1954–55), Boston Univ. (1957), and the Univ. of Washington, Seattle (1958). He was elected president of the American Musicological Society for 1934–36, and reelected for 1940–42; was also nominated an honorary member of the Musical Assoc. in London. In 1947 he received a Litt.D. *honoris causa* from Princeton Univ. He publ. the valuable book *Orgel und Klavier in der Musik des 16. Jahrhunderts* (Ph.D. dissertation, 1909; publ. in Leipzig, 1910); many articles in the *Musical Quarterly,* the *Proceedings* of the Music Teachers' National Assoc., etc.; edited Erlebach's *Harmonische Freude musikalischer Freunde* for vols. 46 and 47 of Denkmäler Deutscher Tonkunst (1914). Later publications include *A Jewish Dancing Master of the Renaissance, Guglielmo Ebreo* (reprinted in 1929 from A.S. Freidus Memorial Volume) and *Music and Music Printing in Incunabula* (reprinted in 1932 from the *Papers of the Bibliographical Society of America,* vol. 26).

BIBLIOGRAPHY: Articles by E.J. Dent and G.S. Dickinson in the *Musical Quarterly* (Oct. 1938); Carleton Sprague Smith, "Otto Kinkeldey," *Notes* (Dec. 1948); C. Seeger, ed., *A Musicological Offering to Otto Kinkeldey upon the Occasion of His 80th Birthday* (Philadelphia, 1960).

Kinsky, Georg, German musicologist; b. Marienwerder, Sept. 29, 1882; d. Berlin, April 7, 1951. He was self-taught in music; after working under Klopfermann for some months at the Royal Library in Berlin, he was appointed curator of the private museum of W. Heyer in Cologne (1909). The Heyer Library was dissolved in 1927. In 1921–32 Kinsky lectured at the Univ. of Cologne; in 1925, received his Ph.D. there. In 1944 his home and his private library and collection were confiscated by the Nazi government; he then served a year at hard labor until the Allied victory. He publ. a very valuable illustrated catalogue of the Heyer collections: vol. I, Keyed Instruments (1910); vol. II, Stringed Instruments (1912); vol. III, Wind and Percussion Instruments (remains in MS); vol. IV (in MS, 1916). He also publ. a condensed *Handkatalog,* containing valuable historical notes (1913); *Briefe Glucks an Kruthoffer* (Vienna, 1927); *Geschichte der Musik in Bildern* (Leipzig and Paris, 1929; London, N.Y., and Milan, 1930; new ed. with introduction by Eric Blom, London, 1937); *Die Originalausgaben der Werke J.S. Bachs* (Vienna, 1937); *Manuscripte-Briefe-Dokumente von Scarlatti bis Stravinsky,* catalogue of autographs in the Louis Koch Collection (Stuttgart, 1953; posthumous); a thematic catalogue of Beethoven's works (completed by H. Halm and publ. 1955).

Kipnis, Alexander, eminent Russian-born American bass; b. Zhitomir, Feb. 13, 1891; d. Westport, Conn., May 14, 1978. He learned to play trombone and double bass; enrolled in the Warsaw Cons. and graduated in 1912 in conducting; subsequently served in the Russian army as a military bandmaster. Later he decided to study singing and went to Berlin, where he took voice lessons with Ernst Grenzebach at the Klindworth-Scharwenka Cons. In 1913 he sang at Monti's Operetten Theater and in 1914 at the Filmzauber operetta theater. At the outbreak of the war in 1914 he was interned as an enemy alien, but was soon released and made his operatic debut in Hamburg in 1915; then was a member of the Wiesbaden Opera (1917–22). He made his American debut as Pogner in *Die Meistersinger von Nürnberg* with the visiting German Opera Co. in Baltimore on Jan. 31, 1923; he then was a member of the Chicago Civic Opera (1923–32). He also sang regularly at the Deutsches Opernhaus in Berlin (from 1919), at the Berlin State Opera (1932–35), and at the Vienna State Opera (until 1938). He became an American citizen in 1931. During these years he made guest appearances at the Bayreuth, Salzburg, and Glyndebourne festivals, as well as at Covent Garden in London and the Teatro Colón in Buenos Aires. On Jan. 5, 1940, he made his Metropolitan Opera debut in N.Y. as Gernemanz in *Parsifal,* and continued to sing there until 1946; he then devoted himself mainly to teaching. Through the years he appeared as a soloist with Richard Strauss, Siegfried Wagner, and Toscanini. His son, **Igor Kipnis,** is a well-known harpsichordist.

BIBLIOGRAPHY: David Ewen, *Musicians since 1900* (N.Y., 1978).

Kipnis, Igor, distinguished American harpsichordist, son of the famous singer **Alexander Kipnis;** b. Berlin, Sept. 27, 1930. In 1938 the family moved to the U.S., where he took piano lessons with his maternal grandfather, the noted musician **Heniot Levy.** Kipnis first studied at the Westport (Conn.) School of Music; for several years served as an accompanist for his father's pupils. He then entered Harvard Univ., where his instructors were Randall Thompson and the visiting British musicologist Thurston Dart. He also took harpsichord lessons with Fernando Valenti. After graduation from Harvard (B.A., 1952), Kipnis served abroad in the Signal Corps of the U.S. Army. Returning to the U.S., he eked out his living as a bookstore salesman in N.Y.; later was employed as an editorial adviser to Westminster Records Co. He made his concert debut as a harpsichordist in N.Y. in 1961. During the summers of 1964, 1965, 1966, and 1967 he was instructor in Baroque performances at the Berkshire Music Center in Tanglewood. In 1967 he made his first European tour; in 1968 he gave concerts in South America; then traveled to Israel in 1969, and in Australia in 1971. He served as an associate prof. of fine arts at Fairfield Univ., Conn. (1971–75), and artist-in-residence there (1975–77); also taught and played at the Festival Music Society in Indianapolis and at its Early-Music Inst. In 1982 he became visiting tutor in Harpsichord and Baroque Music Studies at the Royal Northern College of Music in Manchester, England. He did much to revive the fortepiano, a keyboard instrument that succeeded the harpsichord as the favorite medium of composers in the early 19th century. He also promoted interest in modern music. Several contemporary composers, among them Ned Rorem, George Rochberg, Richard Rodney Bennet, Barbara Kolb, and John McCabe, wrote special works for him.

BIBLIOGRAPHY: David Ewen, *Musicians since 1900* (N.Y., 1978).

Kipper, Hermann, German composer; b. Koblenz, Aug. 27, 1826; d. Cologne, Oct. 25, 1910. He studied with Anschütz and H. Dorn. He was a music teacher and critic in Cologne. He wrote the comic operettas *Der Quacksalber, oder Doktor Sägebein und sein Famulus; Incognito, oder Der Fürst wider Willen; Kellner und Lord; Der Haifisch;* etc.

Kirby, John, black American jazz string-bass player and combo leader; b. Baltimore, Dec. 31, 1908; d. Los Angeles, June 14, 1952. He first played trombone, then tuba; after joining Fletcher Henderson's band in 1930, he took up the string bass; later played with Chick Webb and again with Henderson; then led his own sextet and band.

Kircher, Athanasius, highly significant Jesuit scholar; b. Geisa, near Fulda, Germany, May 2, 1601; d. Rome, Nov. 27, 1680. He attended the Jesuit Seminary in Fulda (1612–18), and was ordained in Paderborn in 1618. He subsequently studied philosophy and theology in Cologne (1622), Koblenz (1623), and Mainz (1624–28); from 1629 to 1631 he taught theology and philosophy at the Univ. of Würzburg; in 1631 he went to Lyons, then to Avignon, and in 1633 to Rome, where he taught at the Collegio Romano; he remained in Rome until the end of his life. His *Oedipus aegiptiacus* contains a curious chapter on hieroglyphic music; in his treatise *De arte magnetica* he gives examples of musical airs which were popularly regarded as a cure for tarantism (a nervous condition supposedly induced by the bite of a tarantula). Indeed, his writings present a curious mixture of scientific speculation and puerile credulity. His principal work is the Latin compendium *Musurgia universalis sive ars magna consoni et dissoni* (Rome, 1650; in German, 1662; a facsimile ed. was issued in 1969).

BIBLIOGRAPHY: U. Scharlau, *Athanasius Kircher (1601–1680) als Musikschriftsteller* (Kassel, 1969).

Kirchner, Fritz, German pianist and composer; b. Potsdam, Nov. 3, 1840; d. there, May 14, 1907. He studied piano with Theodor Kullak, and with Wüerst and Seyffert (theory) at Kullak's Academy; taught there (1864–89), then at the Mädchenheim school in Berlin. He wrote educational pieces and other piano works (*Ball-Scenes; 24 Preludes*), and

songs.

Kirchner, Leon, significant American composer; b. Brooklyn, Jan. 24, 1919, of Russian-Jewish parents. In 1928 the family moved to Los Angeles; there he studied piano with Richard Buhlig; in 1938 he entered the Univ. of Calif., Berkeley, where he took courses in music theory with Albert Elkus and Edward Strickland (B.A., 1940); he also took lessons with Ernest Bloch in San Francisco. In 1942 he went to N.Y., where he had some fruitful private sessions with Sessions; in 1943 he entered military service in the U.S. Army; after demobilization in 1946 he was appointed to the faculty of the San Francisco Cons., concurrently teaching at the Univ. of Calif., Berkeley; in 1948 he received a Guggenheim fellowship; in 1950 he became associate prof. at the Univ. of Southern Calif., Los Angeles; from 1954 to 1961 he taught at Mills College in Oakland, Calif., and in 1961 was named prof. of music at Harvard Univ.; during the academic year 1970–71 he was a guest prof. at the Univ. of Calif., Los Angeles. He received the N.Y. Music Critics Award in 1950 and 1960, and in 1967 was awarded the Pulitzer Prize. In his music Kirchner takes the prudential median course, cultivating a distinct modern idiom without espousing any particular modernistic technique, but making ample and effective use of euphonious dissonance; the contrapuntal fabric in his works is tense but invariably coherent. Through his natural inclinations toward Classical order, he prefers formal types of composition, often following the established Baroque style.

WORKS: Opera, *Lily*, after Saul Bellow's novel *Henderson, The Rain King* (N.Y., April 14, 1977); Sinfonia (N.Y., Jan. 31, 1952); *Toccata* for Strings, Wind Instruments, and Percussion (San Francisco, Feb. 16, 1956); Piano Concerto No. 1 (N.Y., Feb. 23, 1956, composer soloist); Piano Concerto No. 2 (Seattle, Oct. 28, 1963); *Music for Orchestra* (1969); chamber music: Duo for Violin and Piano (1947); String Quartet No. 1 (1949); *Sonata concertante* for Violin and Piano (1952); Piano Trio (1954); String Quartet No. 2 (1958); Concerto for Violin, Cello, 10 Instruments, and Percussion (1960); String Quartet No. 3, with Electronic Sound (1966; awarded the Pulitzer Prize for 1967); *Lily* for Violin, Viola, Cello, Woodwind Quintet, Piano, Percussion, and Voice (1973; material from this work was used in his opera, *Lily*); vocal works: *Letter* (1943); *The Times Are Nightfall* for Soprano and Piano (1943); *Dawn* for Chorus and Organ (1946); *Of Obedience and the Runner,* after Walt Whitman, for Soprano and Piano (1950); *Words from Wordsworth* for Chorus (1966); Piano Sonata (1948); *Little Suite* for Piano (1949).

BIBLIOGRAPHY: A.L. Ringer, "Leon Kirchner," *Musical Quarterly* (Jan. 1957).

Kirchner, Theodor, distinguished German composer; b. Neukirchen, near Chemnitz, Dec. 10, 1823; d. Hamburg, Sept. 18, 1903. On Mendelssohn's advice, he studied in Leipzig with K.F. Becker (theory) and J. Knorr (piano), and, in the summer of 1842,

with Johann Schneider in Dresden. He was engaged as organist at Winterthur (1843–62) and then taught at the Zürich Music School (1862–72); later held the post of director of the Würzburg Cons. (1873–75). He then returned to Leipzig; finally went to Hamburg in 1890. As a youth he enjoyed the friendship of Mendelssohn and Schumann, who encouraged and aided him with their advice. He wrote about 90 piano works, in the style of Schumann; some of his miniatures are of very high quality; he also made numerous transcriptions for piano solo and piano duet (*Alte Bekannte in neuem Gewande*); *Kinder-Trios* for Piano, Violin, and Cello; Piano Quartet; String Quartet; 8 pieces for Piano and Cello; etc.
BIBLIOGRAPHY: A. Niggli, *Theodor Kirchner* (Leipzig, 1880); Otto Klauwell, *Theodor Kirchner* (Langensalza, 1909); *Theodor Kirchner, Briefe aus den Jahren 1860–1868,* ed. by P.O. Schneider (Zürich, 1949).

Kirchoff, Walther, German tenor; b. Berlin, March 17, 1879; d. Wiesbaden, March 26, 1951. He studied in Berlin with Lilli Lehmann; made his debut at the Berlin Court Opera in 1906 as Faust; continued on its roster until 1920 after it became the Berlin State Opera; sang there again in 1923–24, 1928–29, and 1932; also appeared at Covent Garden in London in 1913 and 1924. He made an acclaimed Metropolitan Opera debut in N.Y. as Loge in *Das Rheingold* on Jan. 28, 1927; remained on the roster until 1931. He was particularly successful in Wagnerian roles.

Kiriac-Georgescu, Dumitru, Rumanian musician; b. Bucharest, March 18, 1866; d. there, Jan. 8, 1928. As a young man he went to Paris and studied with Vincent d'Indy at the Schola Cantorum; returning to Rumania in 1900, he was appointed prof. at the Bucharest Cons. In 1901 he founded the Choral Society Carmen in Bucharest. His chief work is a collection of sacred choruses in 5 vols. He was a noted folklorist, and also contributed to a resurgence of interest in the church music of the Orthodox faith.

Kirigin, Ivo, Croatian composer and music critic; b. Zadar, Feb. 2, 1914; d. Zagreb, Oct. 21, 1964. He studied in Italy with Pizzetti; was active as a theater conductor in Zagreb; among his works are Concertino for Piano and Orch.; Symph. (1950); cantata, *Pjesma o zemliji* (*Song of the Land;* 1952); *Kameni horizonti* (*Stone Horizons;* Zagreb, March 16, 1955); *5 Movements* for Strings (1958); numerous songs.

Kirk, "Andy" (Andrew Dewey Kirk), black American jazz saxophonist and bandleader; b. Newport, Ky., May 28, 1898. He studied piano, alto saxophone, and music theory with Wilberforce Whiteman in Denver; then joined the George Morrison orch. in 1918; after moving to Dallas in 1925 he played in Terence Holder's Dark Clouds of Joy orch., becoming its conductor in 1929 and making a notable reputation in Kansas City; it was one of the leading big bands until its demise in 1948. His wife, **Mary Lou Williams,** was a composer-arranger for Kirk's band.

Kirk, Roland, black American jazz musician; b. Columbus, Ohio, Aug. 7, 1936; d. Bloomington, Ind., Dec. 5, 1977. He lost his sight in infancy and was brought up at the Ohio State School for the Blind; learned to play trumpet, tenor saxophone, flute, clarinet, manzello (a saxophone hybrid), strichophone (an abortion of a French horn), and nose flute. He had an uncanny ability to play 2 or 3 wind instruments simultaneously. In 1963 he organized his own band, with which he toured Europe, Australia, and New Zealand. He composed many songs of the pop variety; typical titles are *Here Comes the Whistleman; I Talk with the Spirits; Rip, Rig and Panic; Funk Underneath.* A converted Muslim, he changed his first name to **Rahsaan.**

Kirkby, Emma, English soprano; b. Camberley, Feb. 26, 1949. She made her debut in London in 1974; specialized in early music; was a member of the Academy of Ancient Music, the London Baroque, and the Consort of Musicke. In 1978 she toured the U.S.; then gave concerts in the Middle East with the lutenist Anthony Rooley. Her repertoire ranges from the Italian quattrocento to arias by Handel, Mozart, and Haydn. The careful attention she paid to the purity of intonation free from intrusive vibrato was praised.

Kirkby-Lunn, Louise, English dramatic contralto; b. Manchester, Nov. 8, 1873; d. London, Feb. 17, 1930. She studied voice in Manchester and at the Royal College of Music in London; appeared as an opera singer at various London theaters, making her debut at Drury Lane in 1893; then toured with Sir Augustus Harris's company, and with the Carl Rosa Opera Co. from 1897 until 1899, when she married W.J. Pearson, and retired from the stage for 2 years. In 1901 she reappeared as a member of the Royal Opera at Covent Garden, where she soon became one of the popular favorites. On Dec. 26, 1902, she sang for the first time at the Metropolitan Opera in N.Y., where her interpretations of Wagnerian roles (Ortrud and Brangäne) made a deep impression; in 1904 she sang Kundry in Savage's production of *Parsifal* in English. In 1906–8 she was again with the Metropolitan Opera; sang with the British National Opera Co. in 1919–22; toured in Australia.

Kirkman (real name, **Kirchmann**), **Jakob,** founder of the firm of Kirkman and Sons, the London harpsichord makers; b. Bischweiler, near Strasbourg, March 4, 1710; d. Greenwich, June (buried, June 9) 1792. He settled in London about 1730; there he was associated with a Flemish harpsichord maker, Hermann Tabel. After Tabel's death, Kirkman married his widow and acquired Tabel's tools. In 1755 he was naturalized as a British subject. In 1773 Kirkman, who was childless, formed a partnership with his nephew, **Abraham Kirkman** (1737–94). The descendants of Abraham Kirkman continued the business until 1896, when the firm was merged with Collard; it was eventually absorbed by Chappell. For details and a list of surviving instruments, see the exhaustive article on Kirkman in Donald Boalch, *Makers* *of the Harpsichord and Clavichord* (London, 1956).

Kirkpatrick, John, eminent American pianist and pedagogue; b. New York, March 18, 1905. He studied at Princeton Univ.; then took courses in Paris with I. Philipp, C. Decreus, and Nadia Boulanger; returning to America in 1931, he became an energetic promoter of the cause of American music. His signal achievement was the first performance of the *Concord Sonata* by Charles Ives, which he gave in N.Y. on Jan. 20, 1939, playing it from memory, an extraordinary feat for the time; this performance, which earned enthusiastic reviews for both Ives and Kirkpatrick, played an important role in the public recognition of Ives. As a pedagogue, Kirkpatrick taught at Mount Holyoke College (1943–46) and at Cornell Univ. (1946–68); later joined the faculty of Yale Univ. (1968–75), where he was also curator of the Charles Ives Collection. His compendia *A Temporary Mimeographed Catalogue of the Music Manuscripts and Related Materials of Charles Edward Ives* (New Haven, 1960; reprinted 1973) and *Charles E. Ives: Memos* (N.Y., 1972) are primary sources of the Ives studies.

Kirkpatrick, Ralph, eminent American harpsichordist and music editor; b. Leominster, Mass., June 10, 1911; d. Guilford, Conn., April 13, 1984. He studied at Harvard Univ. (A.B., 1931); then went to Paris to study theory with Nadia Boulanger, and also took lessons in harpsichord playing with Wanda Landowska. He subsequently worked with Arnold Dolmetsch at Haslemere, England, in order to acquaint himself with the technical problems of performing on old keyboard instruments and on their modern replicas. He also studied with Günther Ramin and Heinz Tiessen in Berlin. In 1937 he was awarded a Guggenheim fellowship for research in Baroque performing practices; he undertook an extensive tour of Europe, studying private collections of MSS. His research was particularly fruitful in Spain; he consulted the Madrid telephone book for descendants of Domenico Scarlatti (who spent his last years of life in Spain) and was fortunate enough to discover that several Scarlattis listed in the directory were indeed related to the family; the MSS he was able to find there became the foundation of his standard biography, *Domenico Scarlatti* (Princeton and London, 1953; 3rd ed., revised, 1968). In 1940 he was appointed to the staff of Yale Univ., remaining on its staff until his retirement in 1978. Kirkpatrick was highly selective in his evaluation of Baroque music; while emphasizing the importance of William Byrd, François Couperin, and Domenico Scarlatti, he regarded Vivaldi and Telemann as minor composers serving the temporary tastes of the general public. He. edited 60 sonatas by Scarlatti (1953) and recorded them; he also edited Bach's *Goldberg Variations* and prepared a vol. on Bach's *Well-tempered Clavier* (1984). His interpretations as a harpsichordist were of the highest degree of fidelity to the Baroque style; but he also gave brilliant performances of modern piano works, including those of Stravinsky, Darius Milhaud, Henry Cowell, Walter Piston, and Elliott Carter.
BIBLIOGRAPHY: David Ewen, *Musicians since 1900* (N.Y., 1978).

Kirnberger, Johann Philipp, noted German theorist; b. Saalfeld, April 24, 1721; d. Berlin, July 27, 1783. He first studied violin and harpsichord at home; then. took organ lessons with P. Kellner at Gräfenroda, and with H.N. Gerber at Sondershausen; also studied violin with Meil there. By 1741 he was a pupil of Bach in Leipzig, and spent 2 years with him. He then traveled in Poland (1741–50) as a tutor in various noble Polish families; in 1751 he became violinist to Frederick the Great, and in 1758, Kapellmeister to Princess Amalie. He was greatly renowned as a teacher; among his pupils were Schulz, Fasch, and Zelter. As a theoretical writer, he was regarded as one of the greatest authorities of his time. In his own compositions he displayed an amazing contrapuntal technique, and seriously strove to establish a scientific method of writing music according to basic rules of combination and permutation; his *Der allezeit fertige Polonaisen- und Menuetten-componist* (1757) expounded the automatic method of composition. Other works are: *Die Konstruction der gleichschwebenden Temperatur* (1760); *Die Kunst des reinen Satzes in der Musik aus sicheren Grundsätzen hergeleitet und mit deutlichen Beispielen versehen* (2 vols., 1771, 1779; his magnum opus); *Grundsätze des Generalbasses, als erste Linien zur Komposition* (1781; often republ.); *Gedanken über die verschiedenen Lehrarten in der Komposition, als Vorbereitung zur Fugenkenntniss* (1782). *Die wahren Grundsätze zum Gebrauch der Harmonie* (1773) was claimed by a pupil of Kirnberger's, J.A.P. Schulz, as his work.
BIBLIOGRAPHY: H. Riemann, *Geschichte der Musiktheorie* (Leipzig, 1898; pp. 478ff.); A. Schering, "Kirnberger als Herausgeber Bachscher Choräle," *Bach Jahrbuch* (1918); S. Borris, *Kirnbergers Leben und Werk* (Berlin, 1933).

Kirshbaum, Ralph, American cellist; b. Denton, Texas, March 4, 1946. He studied music at Yale Univ. (B.A., 1968). In 1971 he went to London to pursue his career; in 1972 he joined the pianist Peter Frankl and the violinist Gyorgy Pauk in organizing a trio for chamber music performances; the trio acquired a fine reputation in England.

Kirsten, Dorothy, American soprano; b. Montclair, N.J., July 6, 1915. She studied singing at the Juilliard School of Music in N.Y.; Grace Moore took an interest in her and enabled her to go to Italy for further voice training. She studied in Rome with Astolfo Pescia; the outbreak of war in 1939 forced her to return to the U.S. She became a member of the Chicago Opera Co. (debut, Nov. 9, 1940); made her first appearance in N.Y. as Mimi with the San Carlo Opera Co. (May 10, 1942); appeared with the Metropolitan Opera in the same role on Dec. 1, 1945; she sang there in 1945–52, 1954–57, and 1960–75. In 1947 she went to Paris, where she sang Louise in Charpentier's opera, coached by Charpentier himself. On New Year's Eve of 1975 she made her farewell appearance at the Metropolitan Opera, in the role of Tosca, in celebration of the 30th anniversary of her debut with the company. She publ. an autobiography, *A Time to Sing* (Garden City, N.Y., 1982).

Kisielewski, Stefan, Polish composer; b. Warsaw, March 7, 1911. He studied piano and composition at the Warsaw Cons. (1927–37); was also active as a music journalist and teacher.

WORKS: Musical, *Terrible Manor House* (1963); 3 ballets: *Polish Devils* (1957); *System of Doctor Tar,* after Poe (1962); *Amusement Grounds* (1966); Concerto for Chamber Orch. (1948); *Rustic Rhapsody* for Orch. (1950); Symph. No. 2 (1951); *Little Overture* (1953); *Perpetuum mobile* for Orch. (1955); Chamber Symph. (1956); Symph. for 15 Performers (1961); Divertimento for Flute and Chamber Orch. (1964); *Journey in Time* for String Orch. (1965); *Sport Signals,* overture (1966); *Rencontres dans un désert* for 10 Performers (1969); *Intermezzo* for Clarinet and Piano (1942); Suite for Oboe and Piano (1957); *Capriccio energico* for Violin and Piano (1960); Clarinet Sonata (1972); *Toccata* for Piano (1945); 2 piano sonatas; songs.

Kiss, Janos, Hungarian-American composer; b. Hosszupalyi, Hungary, March 21, 1920. He studied at the Béla Bartók Cons. of Music in Budapest, receiving a teaching diploma in 1954. In 1956, in the wake of the Soviet invasion of Hungary, he emigrated to the U.S., becoming a naturalized citizen in 1973. In America he took courses in music education at Case Western Reserve Univ. in Cleveland. He subsequently taught at the Cleveland Music School Settlement (1964–79) and concurrently at Western Reserve Academy in Hudson, Ohio (1967–72), at Holy Family School in Parma, Ohio (1974–80), and at other educational institutions. In 1982 he became choir director and composer-in-residence at the West Side Hungarian Reformed Church in Cleveland. A prolific composer, he wrote numerous orch. and choral works which are distinguished by a facility of execution reflecting his experience as a teacher.

WORKS: *Spring—At Last!* for Harp Ensemble (1970); Flute Concerto (1970); Trombone Concerto (1972); *Josepha* for 5 Alto Recorders, Violin, Viola, Cello, and Harp (1973); Cello Concerto (1975); Divertimento for Solo Violin, Solo Viola, Solo Double Bass, Harp, and Chamber Ensemble (1977); *Salute—in Retrospect* for Cimbalom Solo and Orch. (1970); *Suite in stilo antico* for Orch. (1978); *Episode* for French Horn, Oboe, Bassoon, and Harp (1978); *Via Lactea,* symph. fantasy (1978); *Sinfonia Atlantis* for Orch. (1979); *Las Vegas* for Cimbalom Solo and Orch. (1980); *Benedictus Dominus* for Chorus and Orch. (1981); *Mount of Atlantis* for Clarinet, Synthesizer, and Orch. (1981); *Quo Vadis,* symph. poem (1982); *Rainbow at the Sea* for Flute and Chamber Orch. (1982).

Kist, Florentius Cornelis, Dutch writer on music

and teacher; b. Arnhem, Jan. 28, 1796; d. Utrecht, March 23, 1863. He was a physician, practicing in The Hague (1818–25); as a youth, he played the flute and horn. In 1821 he gave up medicine and founded the Diligentia music society; in 1841, settled in Utrecht, where he edited the *Nederlandsch Muzikaal Tijdschrift* (1841–44). In Utrecht he also established amateur concerts and the singing society Duce Apolline. He publ. *De toestand van het protestantsche kerkgezang in Nederland* (1840) and *Levensgeschiedenis van Orlando de Lassus* (1841); trans. Brendel's *Grundzüge der Geschichte der Musik* (1851); contributed articles to German musical journals; also wrote vocal music and pieces for the flute.

Kistler, Cyrill, German composer; b. Gross-Aitingen, near Augsburg, March 12, 1848; d. Kissingen, Jan. 1, 1907. He was a schoolteacher (1867–76); then studied music at Munich under Wüllner, Rheinberger, and Franz Lachner (1876–80). In 1883 he was called to the Sondershausen Cons.; from 1885 he lived in Bad Kissingen as principal of a music school and music publisher; he also edited the *Musikalische Tagesfragen.* An enthusiastic admirer of Wagner, he unsuccessfully attempted to employ the master's forms and principles in his 10 operas, among them *Kanhild* and *Eulenspiegel.* Besides these, he wrote 104 works (festive marches, funeral marches for orch., choruses, songs, pieces for organ and harmonium), a *Harmonielehre* (1879; based on Wagner's innovations; 2nd augmented ed., 1903); *Musikalische Elementarlehre* (1880); *Der Gesang- und Musikunterricht an den Volksschulen* (1881); *Volksschullehrer-Tonkünstlerlexikon* (3rd ed., 1887); *Jenseits des Musikdramas* (1888); *Franz Witt* (1888); *Über Originalität in der Tonkunst* (1894; 2nd ed., 1907); *Der einfache Kontrapunkt und die einfache Fuge* (1904); *Der drei- und mehrfache Kontrapunkt* (1908).

BIBLIOGRAPHY: A. Eccarius-Sieber, *Cyrill Kistler* (Leipzig, 1906).

Kistner, Karl Friedrich, German music publisher; b. Leipzig, March 3, 1797; d. there, Dec. 21, 1844. In 1831 he took over Probst's music publishing business, which he carried on from 1836 under the firm name of Friedrich Kistner. He acquired many works by Mendelssohn, Schumann, and Chopin for his catalogue. His son, **Julius Kistner,** succeeded him; in 1866 he sold his business to Karl Friedrich Ludwig Gurckhaus (1821–84). In 1919 it was bought by Linnemann, and in 1923 merged with C.F.W. Siegel, and operated under the name Fr. Kistner & C.F.W. Siegel.

Kitayenko, Dimitri, Russian conductor; b. Leningrad, Aug. 18, 1940. He studied choral conducting at the Leningrad Cons. and the Moscow Cons. He then went to Vienna to study conducting at the Academy of Music (1966–67). Upon his return to Moscow, he became a conductor at the Nemirovich-Danchenko Music Theater; in 1970 became chief conductor there. He also appeared as a guest conductor in

Western Europe, usually in programs of Russian music; in 1975 he served as assistant conductor during the U.S. tour of the Moscow Phil. (1975). In 1976 he was appointed its chief conductor.

Kitson, Charles Herbert, notable English theorist and music pedagogue; b. Leyburn, Yorkshire, Nov. 13, 1874; d. London, May 13, 1944. He studied for an ecclesiastical career, but also took a D.Mus. degree at Oxford (1902). He was organist of Christ Church Cathedral in Dublin (1913–20); also taught at the Royal Irish Academy of Music. In 1915 he was appointed prof. of music at Univ. College in Dublin. Returning to London, he was appointed prof. of harmony and counterpoint at the Royal College of Music (1920); was also a prof. of music at Trinity College in Dublin in 1920–35, a non-resident position. He publ. a number of valuable manuals, distinguished by their clarity of presentation and didactic logic. The most important of these are: *The Art of Counterpoint* (1907); *Studies in Fugue* (1909); *Evolution of Harmony* (1914); *Applied Strict Counterpoint* (1916); *Elementary Harmony* (1920); *Invertible Counterpoint and Canon* (1927); *Rudiments of Music* (1927); *Elements of Fugal Construction* (1929); *Contrapuntal Harmony for Beginners* (1931); *The Elements of Musical Composition* (1936). He also wrote some church music.

Kitt, Eartha, black American singer of popular songs; b. in the town named North, S.C., Jan. 26, 1928. She moved to Brooklyn and sang at various emporia around town. In 1948 she went to Paris, where she attracted attention as an exotic chanteuse. She excelled particularly in earthy, passion-laden songs delivered in a low-key monotone. She publ. an autobiography, *Thursday's Child* (N.Y., 1956; her date of birth indeed fell on a Thursday).

Kittel, Bruno, German violinist and conductor; b. Entenbruch, near Posen, May 26, 1870; d. Wassersberg, near Cologne, March 10, 1948. He studied in Berlin; played in theater orchs. there. From 1901 till 1907 he was conductor of the Royal Theater Orch. in Brandenburg; also was director of the Brandenburg Cons. (until 1914). In 1902 he established the Kittelsche Chor, which soon developed into one of the finest choral societies of Europe, and with which he made many tours. In 1935 he was appointed director of the Stern Cons. in Berlin, where he remained until 1945.

Kittel, Hermine, Austrian contralto; b. Vienna, Dec. 2, 1879; d. there, April 7, 1948. She began her career as an actress; then studied voice with Amalie Materna in Vienna; in 1900 she joined the Vienna Opera, and remained on its roster for 30 years; also sang at Bayreuth (1902, 1908) and Salzburg (1922, 1925); made guest appearances in Paris, Budapest, and other cities; following her retirement, she taught voice in Vienna.

Kittel, Johann Christian, German organist and composer; b. Erfurt, Feb. 18, 1732; d. there, April 17, 1809. He studied at the Thomasschule in Leipzig, and was one of Bach's last students there. After Bach's death, he became organist at Langensalza (1751); then at the Barfüsserkirche in Erfurt (from 1756) and in 1762 at the Predigerkirche there. Despite the meager remuneration, he remained in Erfurt almost all his life; in search of betterment, he undertook several tours in nearby towns; even as an old man, in his late 60s, he traveled as an organist, giving concerts in Göttingen, Hannover, Hamburg, and Altona. He stayed in Altona for a few years; publ. a book of church melodies, *Neues Choralbuch,* there in 1803. In his last years he obtained a small stipend from Prince Primas of Dalberg. Among his other works are *Der angehende praktische Organist* (3 books; Erfurt, 1801–8; 3rd ed., 1831); 6 sonatas and a Fantasia for Clavichord; *Grosse Präludien, Hymne an das Jahrhundert* (1801); smaller organ pieces. The famous organist C.H. Rinck was one of his pupils.
BIBLIOGRAPHY: A. Dreetz, *J.C. Kittel, der letzte Bach-Schüler* (Leipzig, 1932); G. Fock, "Zur Biographie des Bachschülers Johann Christian Kittel," *Bach-Jahrbuch,* XLIX (1962).

Kittl, Johann Friedrich (Jan Bedřich), Bohemian composer; b. Castle Worlik, May 8, 1806; d. Lissa, in German Poland, July 20, 1868. He studied jurisprudence at Prague Univ.; took private lessons in piano with Zavora and in composition with Tomášek; at the age of 19 brought out his opera *Daphnis Grab* (1825). In 1837 he wrote a *Jagdsinfonie,* which was performed by the Gewandhaus Orch. in Leipzig on Jan. 9, 1840, at Mendelssohn's behest, and subsequently enjoyed considerable vogue in Germany. In 1843 Kittl was appointed director of the Prague Cons., resigning in 1865. He was a friend of Wagner, who wrote for him a libretto, *Bianca und Giuseppe,* which Kittl set to music and produced as *Die Franzosen vor Nizza* (Prague, Feb. 19, 1848). He further wrote the operas *Waldblume* (1852) and *Die Bilderstürmer* (1854), produced in Prague; some symph. and chamber music.
BIBLIOGRAPHY: W. Neumann, *J.F. Kittl* (Kassel, 1857); E. Rychnovsky, *J.F. Kittl* (2 vols., Prague, 1904–5); Jan Branberger, *Das Konservatorium für Musik in Prag* (Prague, 1911); M. Tarantová, *J.F. Kittl* (Prague, 1948).

Kitzinger, Fritz, German conductor; b. Munich, Jan. 27, 1904; d. New York, May 23, 1947. He studied at the Munich Cons. and the Univ. of Munich, graduating in 1924; served as conductor of the Dortmund Opera (1925–27), Berlin State Opera (1927–30), and Chemnitz Opera (1930); toured China and Japan as a symph. conductor. In 1934 he came to the U.S. and subsequently settled in N.Y.

Kitzler, Otto, German conductor and cellist; b. Dresden, March 16, 1834; d. Graz, Sept. 6, 1915. He studied with Johann Schneider, J. Otto, and Kummer (cello); then at the Brussels Cons. with Servais and Fétis; was cellist in the opera orchs. at Strasbourg and Lyons; chorus master at theaters in Troyes, Linz, Königsberg, Temesvar, Hermannstadt, and Brünn. In 1868 he became director of the Brünn Music Society and of the Brünn Music School; also conductor of the Männergesangverein; retired in 1898. His reputation was very high; Bruckner, 10 years his senior, took orchestration lessons from him in 1861–63. Kitzler wrote orch. music, piano pieces, songs, etc.; also *Musikalische Erinnerungen* (1904; containing letters from Wagner, Brahms, and Bruckner).

Kiurina, Berta, Austrian soprano; b. Linz, Feb. 19, 1882; d. Vienna, May 3, 1933. She studied voice with Geiringer at the Vienna Cons.; made her debut in Linz in 1904; then sang at the Vienna Opera (1905–22, 1926–27); made guest appearances in Salzburg, Berlin, and Buenos Aires. A fine coloratura, she excelled in such roles as the Queen of the Night, Desdemona, and Gilda.

Kiurkchiysky, Krasimir, Bulgarian composer; b. Troyan, June 22, 1936. He studied composition with Vladigerov at the Bulgarian State Cons. in Sofia, graduating in 1962; went to Moscow and took some lessons with Shostakovich. His own music reflects Shostakovich's influence in its rhapsodic compactness.
WORKS: Opera, *Yula* (1969; Zagora, 1969); Piano Concerto (1958); Trio for Violin, Clarinet, and Piano (1959); String Quartet (1959); *Adagio* for String Orch. (1959); Cello Sonata (1960); *Symphony Concertante* for Cello and Orch. (1960); Violin Sonata (1961); *Symphony-Requiem* (1966); *Diaphonous Study* for Orch. (1967); Concerto for Orch. (1975); choruses; incidental music.

Kiyose, Yasuji, Japanese composer; b. Oita, Jan. 13, 1900; d. Tokyo, Sept. 14, 1981. He studied with Yamada, Pringsheim, and Alexander Tcherepnin; was president of the Japanese section of the International Society for Contemporary Music (1951–56).
WORKS: *Japanese Festival Dance* for Orch. (1940); Piano Concerto (Tokyo, March 10, 1955); *Sketch of Japan* for Orch. (1963); *Unknown Soldier,* requiem (1963); 2 piano trios (1938, 1955); 3 violin sonatas (1941, 1948, 1950); String Trio (1949); String Quartet (1952); Quintet for Harp and Woodwinds (1957); *2 Movements* for Violin and Piano (1960); Quartet for 4 Recorders (1969); *Duet* for Flute and Clarinet (1970); *2 Movements* for Solo Cello (1973).

Kjellsby, Erling, Norwegian composer and conductor; b. Oslo, July 7, 1901; d. there, Feb. 18, 1976. He studied composition with Brustad and Valen; became a lecturer at Oslo Teacher's College in 1923. He wrote *Norwegian Rhapsody* for Small Orch. (1937); *Melody* for Orch. (1938); 4 string quartets (1940–57); piano pieces; choruses.

Kjellström, Sven, Swedish violinist; b. Lulea, March 30, 1875; d. Stockholm, Dec. 5, 1950. He studied in Stockholm and later in Paris. Returning to Sweden in 1909, he was active in chamber music societies; was director of the Stockholm Cons. (1929–40). He also formed a string quartet, with which he traveled to remote communities in Scandinavia, including Lapland; he was an ardent collector of Swedish folk songs.
BIBLIOGRAPHY: O. Ottelin, *Sven Kjellström och folkets musikliv* (1945).

Kjerulf, Halfdan, Norwegian song composer; b. Christiania, Sept. 15, 1815; d. Grefsen, near Christiania, Aug. 11, 1868. He was a member of a family of artists and scholars; studied piano as a child; then took up law, subsequently working as a journalist. In 1848–49 he took lessons with a resident German musician, Carl Arnold; then studied with Gade in Copenhagen (1849–50); in 1850–51 he enrolled in the Leipzig Cons.; in 1851 he returned to Norway, where he taught piano. He limited himself to composition in small forms; although he followed the German model, he injected melodic and rhythmic elements of a national Norwegian character into his songs. Grieg was deeply influenced by his example and frequently expressed admiration for his music; many celebrated singers (Jenny Lind, Christine Nilsson, and Henriette Sontag among them) included his songs in their programs, and thus made them known. He wrote about 130 songs in all, among which the most popular are *Last Night, Tell Me, The Nightingale,* and *Synnöve's Song;* he also composed some 30 works for men's chorus and 10 albums of piano pieces marked by a strong Scandinavian cast (*Elfin Dance, Shepherd's Song, Cradle Song, Spring Song, Album-leaf, Capriccio, Scherzo, Scherzino,* etc.); also publ. the album *25 Selected Norwegian Folk Dances* for Piano (1861) and *Norwegian Folk Songs* for Piano (1867); these are arrangements of Norwegian melodies from collections by Lindeman and others. In 1874 a monument was erected to him in Christiania.
BIBLIOGRAPHY: A. Grønvold, "Halfdan Kjerulf," in *Norske Musikere,* I (Christiania, 1883); K. Nyblom, *Halfdan Kjerulf* (1926); Dag Schjelderup-Erbe, "Modality in Halfdan Kjerulf's Music," *Music & Letters* (July 1957).

Klafsky, Anton Maria, Austrian musicologist and composer, nephew of **Katharina Klafsky;** b. Winden, Burgenland, July 8, 1877; d. Baden, near Vienna, Jan. 1, 1965. He studied at the Univ. of Vienna; took lessons in composition with Hermann Grädener. He composed much church music, 3 symphs., piano pieces, and songs; edited sacred choral works of Michael Haydn for Denkmäler der Tonkunst in Österreich, vols. 44 and 62 (22 and 32.i).

Klafsky, Katharina, Hungarian soprano; b. St. Johann, Sept. 19, 1855; d. Hamburg, Sept. 22, 1896. She studied with Mme. Marchesi in Vienna; began her career as a chorus singer in various opera houses; in 1881 she attracted attention as a Wagnerian singer; appeared in Hamburg (1885), in London (1892, 1894), and in the U.S. (1895–96). She was one of the most spectacular prima donnas of her day, and her early death was mourned by opera-lovers as a great loss.

BIBLIOGRAPHY: L. Ordemann, *Aus dem Leben und Wirken von Katharina Klafsky* (Hameln, 1903).

Klami, Uuno, Finnish composer; b. Virolahti, Sept. 20, 1900; d. Helsinki, May 29, 1961. He studied the rudiments of music in Helsinki schools; then traveled to Paris and Vienna for further advancement as a composer. In 1938 he received from the Finnish government a life pension. In 1959 he was elected to the Academy of Finland. His music was influenced by the folk modalities of the Karelian region, which was his birthplace; the impact of the profundities of the idiom of Sibelius was considerable, but Klami ornamented it with impressionistic detail. WORKS: For Orch.: *Sérénades espagnoles* (1924; revised 1944); *Karelian Rhapsody* (1927); *Rhapsody* (1927); *Merikuvia (Sea Pictures;* 1928–30); 3 symphs.: *Symphonie enfantine* (1928); No. 1 (1937); No. 2 (1944); *Opernredoute* (1929); *Kuvia maalaiselämästä (Rustic Scenes;* 1930); *Helsinki March* (1930); *Kalevala Suite* (1932; revised 1943); *Sérénades joyeuses* (1933); *Lemminkäinen* (1934); *Karelian Dances* (1935); *Suomenlinna (Fortress of Finland;* 1940); *Revontulet (Aurora Borealis;* 1946); *Pyöräilijä (The Cyclist),* orch. rondo (1946); *Karjalainen tori (Karelian Market Place;* 1947); 2 piano concertos: No. 1, *Night in Montmartre* (1924) and No. 2 (1950); *4 Folk Songs* for Piano and Strings (1930); *Cheremissian Fantasy* for Cello and Orch. (1930); Violin Concerto (1942); *Theme and Variations* for Cello and Orch. (1950). Vocal and choral works: *Psalmus* for Soloists, Chorus, and Orch. (1935–36); *Vipusessa käynti (In the Belly of Vipunen)* for Baritone, Male Chorus, and Orch. (1938); *Laulu Kuujärvestä (The Song of Kuujarvi)* for Baritone and Orch. (1956); *Kultasauvalliset (The People with the Golden Staffs),* festive cantata (1961). Chamber music: String Quartet, *Nain tragédie* (1920); Piano Quartet (1921); Piano Quintet (1923). At his death, Klami left over a thousand pages of an unfinished ballet score.

Klatte, Wilhelm, German music critic and writer; b. Bremen, Feb. 13, 1870; d. Berlin, Sept. 12, 1930. He studied music in Leipzig, and took lessons with Richard Strauss in Weimar. For some time he held various positions as a conductor and a music critic; from 1904 he taught at the Stern Cons. in Berlin; in 1925 he was appointed prof. at the Academy for Church and School Music in Berlin. He publ. (in collaboration with A. Seidl) *Richard Strauss, Eine Charakterskizze* (1895); "Zur Geschichte der Programm-Musik," in the collection of monographs founded by Richard Strauss, *Die Musik* (1905); *Franz Schubert* (1907); *Grundlagen des mehrstimmigen Satzes* (1922; 3rd ed., 1930).

Klatzow, Peter, South African composer; b. Springs, Transvaal, July 14, 1945. He studied piano in his hometown (1951–57), then in Johannesburg (1958–62); studied composition (with Bernard Stevens and Gordon Jacob) and piano at the Royal College of Music in London (1964–65) and had brief studies with Nadia Boulanger in Paris in 1966. Klatzow returned to South Africa in 1966 and was a lecturer in composition and piano at the Rhodesian College of Music in Salisbury (1966–68), a music producer at the South African Broadcasting Corp. (1968–73), and in 1973 was appointed a lecturer in composition at the Univ. of Cape Town. WORKS: *Variations* for Orch. (1965; Royal College of Music, London, Feb. 10, 1966); *Nagstuk* for Orch. (1966); Violin Sonata (1967); *Interactions I* for Piano, Percussion, and Chamber Orch. (1971) and *II* for Solo Piano (1972); *The Temptation of St. Anthony* for Cello and Orch. (1972; Barcelona, May 14, 1977); *The World of Paul Klee* for Flute, Viola, and Harp (1972); *Symphony 1972, Phoenix* (1972; first public perf., Cape Town, Oct. 21, 1975); *Time Structure I* for Piano (1973) and *II* for Orch. and Tape (1974; version in 1976 for Orch. and Organ); *Still Life, with Moonbeams* for Orch. (1975; Johannesburg, July 13, 1975); *The Garden of Memories and Discoveries* for Soprano, Ensemble, and Tape (1975); *Night Magic I* for Soprano and Chamber Orch. (1976) and *II,* trio for Violin, Horn, and Piano (1977); *Contours and Transformations* for Guitar and 5 Instrumentalists (1977); String Quartet (1977); Horn Concerto (1978; Cape Town, June 16, 1978); Chamber Concerto (1978–79); Horn Sonata (1979).

Klaus, Kenneth Blanchard, American violist, composer, and conductor; b. Earlville, Iowa, Nov. 11, 1923; d. Baton Rouge, La., Aug. 4, 1980. He studied violin with Cecil Burleigh and Louis Krasner, and composition with Philip Greeley Clapp at the Univ. of Iowa (Ph.D., 1950); also studied meteorology at the Univ. of Chicago and served as a meteorologist in the Army Air Corps during World War II; in 1950 joined the faculty at Louisiana State Univ. In his own works he applied a sui generis synthesis of expanded tonality verging on serialism. In his vocal compositions he modernized the medieval device of "sogetto cavato" by deriving a theme from the vowels of letter names. He publ. *The Romantic Period in Music* (Boston, 1970). WORKS: Operas: *Tennis Anyone?* (1957) and *Crimson Stones; Moira* for Female Singer; *Deidra* for Female Singer; incidental music for *Death of a Salesman* (1954); 6 symphs.; several symph. poems; 2 violin concertos; Flute Concerto; Cello Concerto; Clarinet Concerto; *Concerto brevis* for Percussion and Orch. (1955); Concerto for Piano, right-hand, and Orch.; 4 string quartets (1947, 1951, 1957, 1963); Woodwind Quintet; Woodwind Sextet; sonatas for various instruments; vocal works.

Klauser, Julius, American writer on music; b. New York, July 5, 1854; d. Milwaukee, April 23, 1907. He studied with his father, **Karl Klauser;** also took courses at the Leipzig Cons. (1871–74); returning to America, he settled in Milwaukee as a music teacher. He wrote a book on harmony according to his own system, *The Septonate and the Centralization of the Tonal System* (1890); also *The Nature of Music* (1909).

Klauser, Karl, music editor and arranger; b. St. Petersburg, Russia, Aug. 24, 1823 (of Swiss parents); d. Farmington, Conn., Jan. 5, 1905. He studied music in Germany; went to N.Y. in 1850, and settled in Farmington as a music teacher in 1856. He edited *Half-hours with the Best Composers* and (with Theodore Thomas and J.K. Paine) *Famous Composers.*

Klauwell, Adolf, German music pedagogue; b. Langensalza, Dec. 31, 1818; d. Leipzig, Nov. 21, 1879. He publ. elementary class books, and instructive piano pieces (*Goldnes Melodien-Album*).

Klauwell, Otto, German writer on music; b. Langensalza, April 7, 1851; d. Cologne, May 11, 1917. He served in the Franco-Prussian War; then entered Leipzig Univ., where he studied mathematics and music; obtained his degree of Dr.Phil. with the dissertation *Die historische Entwickelung des musikalischen Canons* (1874). In 1875 he was appointed a prof. at the Cologne Cons. He was also a composer; wrote 2 Romantic operas, *Das Mädchem vom See* (Cologne, 1899) and *Die heimlichen Richter* (Elberfeld, 1902); overtures; chamber music; piano pieces; songs.
WRITINGS: *Musikalische Gesichtspunkte* (1881; 2nd ed., 1892, as *Musikalische Bekenntnisse*); *Der Vortrag in der Musik* (1883; in Eng., N.Y., 1890); *Die Formen der Instrumentalmusik* (1894; 2nd ed., 1918); *Geschichte der Sonate* (1899); *Beethoven und die Variationenform* (1901); *Studien und Erinnerungen* (1904); *Geschichte der Programm-Musik* (1910).

Klebe, Giselher, German composer; b. Mannheim, June 28, 1925. He studied at the Berlin Cons. with Kurt von Wolfurt (1942–43), with Josef Rufer, and with Boris Blacher (1946–51). He worked in the program division of the Berlin Radio (1946–49); in 1957 was appointed to the faculty of the Nordwestdeutsche Musik Akademie in Detmold; was elected member of the Academy of Arts in Berlin. An experimenter by nature, he writes music in widely ranging forms, from classically conceived instrumental pieces to highly modernistic inventions; his technique is basically dodecaphonic; coloristic and sonoristic schemes also play an important role.
WORKS: OPERAS: *Die Räuber,* after Schiller (1951–56; Düsseldorf, June 3, 1957; revised 1962); *Die tödlichen Wünsche,* after Balzac (1957–59; Düsseldorf, June 14, 1959); *Die Ermordung Cäsars,* after Shakespeare (1958–59; Essen, Sept. 20, 1959); *Alkmene,* after Kleist (1961; Berlin, Sept. 25, 1961); *Figaro lässt sich scheiden,* opera buffa after von Horváth (1962–63; Hamburg, June 28, 1963); *Jakobowsky und der Oberst,* comic opera after Werfel (1965; Hamburg, Nov. 2, 1965); *Das Märchen von der schönen Lilie,* fairy-tale opera after Goethe (1967–68; Schwetzingen, May 15, 1969); *Ein wahrer Held,* after Synge's *Playboy of the Western World,* adapted by Boll (1972–73; Zürich Festival, Jan. 18, 1975); *Das Mädchen aus Domremy,* after Schiller (1975–76; Stuttgart, June 19, 1976); *Das Rendez-vous* (Hannover, Oct. 7, 1977). BALLETS: *Pas de trois* (1951;

Wiesbaden, 1951); *Signale* (1955; Berlin, 1955); *Fleurenville* (1956; Berlin, 1956); *Menagerie* (1958); *Das Testament* (Symph. No. 4; 1970). FOR ORCH.: *Con moto* (1948; Bremen, Feb. 23, 1953); *Divertissement joyeux* for Chamber Orch. (1949; Darmstadt, July 8, 1949); *Die Zwitschermaschine (The Twittering Machine),* metamorphosis on Klee's famous painting (1950; Donaueschingen, Sept. 10, 1950); *2 Nocturnes* (1951; Darmstadt, July 20, 1952); 4 symphs.: No. 1 for 42 Strings (1951; Hamburg, Jan. 7, 1953); No. 2 (1953); No. 3 (1967); No. 4, *Das Testament,* ballet-symph. for Orch. and 2 Pianos tuned a quarter-tone apart (1970–71; Wiesbaden, April 30, 1971); *Rhapsody* (1953); *Double Concerto* for Violin, Cello, and Orch. (1954; Frankfurt, June 19, 1954); *Moments musicaux* (1955); Cello Concerto (1957); *Omaggio* (1960); *Adagio and Fugue,* on a motif from Wagner's *Die Walküre* (1962); *Herzschläge,* 3 symph. scenes for Beat Band and Orch. (1969); Concerto for Electronically Altered Harpsichord and Small Orch. (1971–72); *Orpheus,* dramatic scenes (1976). VOCAL MUSIC: *Geschichte vom lustigen Musikanten* for Tenor, Chorus, and 5 Instruments (1946–47); *5 Römische Elegien,* after Goethe, for Narrator, Piano, Harpsichord, and Double Bass (1952; Donaueschingen, Oct. 10, 1953); *Raskolnikows Traum,* dramatic scene after Dostoyevsky, for Soprano, Clarinet, and Orch. (1956); *5 Lieder* for Alto and Orch. (1962); *Stabat Mater* for Soprano, Mezzo-soprano, Alto, Chorus, and Orch. (1964); *Gebet einer armen Seele (The Prayer of a Poor Soul),* dodecaphonic Mass for Chorus and Organ (1966); choruses; songs. CHAMBER MUSIC: Wind Quintet (1948); 2 string quartets (1949, 1963); Viola Sonata (1949); 2 solo violin sonatas (1952, 1955); 2 violin sonatas (1953, 1972); *Elegia appasionata,* piano trio (1955); *Dithyrambe* for String Quartet (1957); *7 Bagatelles* for Basset Horn, Trombone, Harp, and Tubular Bells (1961); *9 Duettini* for Flute and Piano (1962); *Missa "Miserere nobis"* for 18 Wind Instruments (1965); *Concerto a 5* for Piano, Harpsichord, Harp, Percussion, and Double Bass (1965); *Quasi una fantasia,* piano quintet (1967); *Scene and Aria* for 3 Trumpets, 3 Trombones, 2 Pianos, and 8 Cellos (1967–68); *Variations on a Theme of Berlioz* for Organ and 3 Drummers (1970); Double-bass Sonata (1971); *Nenia* for Solo Violin (1975). FOR PIANO: *Nocturnes* (1949); 2-piano Sonata (1949); *4 Inventions* (1956).

Kleber, Leonhard, German organist; b. Göppingen, Württemberg, c.1490; d. Pforzheim, March 4, 1556. He studied at the Univ. of Heidelberg; was vicar-choral and organist in Horb (1516–17); then organist in Esslingen (1517–21). From 1521 he was organist at the collegiate and parish church in Pforzheim. Between 1521 and 1524 he oversaw the compilation of a book of 112 pieces by Hofhaimer, Josquin, Obrecht, and others, arranged in keyboard tablature. Modern transcriptions of his books are to be found in: A. Ritter, *Zur Geschichte des Orgelspiels, vornehmlich des deutschen, im 14. bis zum Anfang des 18. Jahrhunderts,* II (Leipzig, 1884); R. Eitner, *Monatshefte für Musikgeschichte,* XX (1888); H.J. Moser, *Paul Hofhaimer* (Stuttgart and

Berlin, 1929); W. Apel, *Musik aus früher Zeit* (Mainz, 1934); W. Apel and A.T. Davison, *Historical Anthology of Music*, vol. I (Cambridge, Mass., 1946).
  BIBLIOGRAPHY: H. Löwenfeld, *Leonhard Kleber und sein Orgeltabulaturbuch als Beitrag zur Geschichte der Orgelmusik im beginnenden XVI. Jahrhundert* (Berlin, 1897; reprint, Hilversum, 1968).

Klecki, Paul. See **Kletzki, Paul.**

Klee, Bernhard, German conductor: b. Schleiz, April 19, 1936. He studied piano and conducting at the Leipzig Cons.; then conducted opera in Cologne and Bern; in 1966 became Generalmusikdirektor in Lübeck; from 1976 to 1979 was chief conductor of the Hannover Radio Orch. In 1977 he became Generalmusikdirektor of the Düsseldorf Symph. In 1974 he made a successful American debut as a guest conductor with the N.Y. Phil.

Klee, Eugen, German choral conductor; b. Kaiserslautern, Dec. 15, 1869; d. Philadelphia, Dec. 18, 1929. He studied with his father, Jacob Klee, and later with Thuille in Munich. In 1894 he emigrated to America and settled in Philadelphia, where he was active as a leader of German choral societies; also trained similar societies in Brooklyn.

Klee, Ludwig, German pianist and pedagogue; b. Schwerin, April 13, 1846; d. Berlin, April 14, 1920. He was a pupil at the Kullak Academy in Berlin, and then taught there until he established a music school of his own. He publ. *Die Ornamentik der klassichen Klaviermusik*, treating ornamentation from Bach to Beethoven; also edited 2 vols. of *Klassische Vortragsstücke*.

Kleefeld, Wilhelm, German writer on music; b. Mainz, April 2, 1868; d. Berlin, April 2, 1933, on his 65th birthday. He was a pupil of Spitta in Berlin; took his degree of Dr.Phil. at Berlin Univ. with the dissertation *Das Orchester der ersten deutschen Oper, Hamburg, 1678–1738* (publ. 1898); in 1898 he became a teacher at the Klindworth-Scharwenka Cons.; from 1904 taught at Berlin Univ. He wrote numerous valuable articles on opera; under the title *Opernrenaissance* he edited a number of early operas; publ. a monograph on Clara Schumann (1910). He wrote many songs and piano pieces (for 2 and 4 hands).

Kleffel, Arno, German composer and conductor; b. Pössneck, Sept. 4, 1840; d. Nikolassee, near Berlin, July 15, 1913. He studied with Hauptmann in Leipzig; then conducted theater orchs. and opera in Riga, Cologne, Amsterdam, Berlin, Augsburg, Magdeburg, etc. In 1904 he became conductor of Stern's Gesangverein in Berlin; in 1910, head of the operatic dept. at the Hochschule für Musik there. He wrote an opera, *Des Meermanns Harfe* (Riga, 1865); music to Goethe's *Faust;* many characteristic piano pieces (*Ritornelles, Jungbrunnen,* etc.); teaching

pieces; *Fête d'enfants; Nuits italiennes* for Piano, 4-hands; also songs.

Klega, Miroslav, Slovak composer; b. Ostrava, March 6, 1929. He studied composition with Křička in Prague and with Suchoň and Cikker at the Bratislava Cons. (1946–50); taught at the Ostrava Cons. (1955–73); was its director in 1967–73. In 1973 he became music director of Czech Radio in Ostraya.
  WORKS: *Suite Bagatelle* for Piano (1948); *Černá země (Black Soil),* symph. variations (1951); Symph. (1959); Concertino for 4 String Instruments (1961); *Pantomima,* suite for Orch. (1963); *Concerto-Partita* for Violin and Orch. (1965); *Confessions of the Lonely Infantryman* for Narrator and Orch. (1968).

Kleiber, Carlos, outstanding German conductor, son of **Erich Kleiber;** b. Berlin, July 3, 1930. He accompanied his parents to South America in 1935, and received his musical education in Buenos Aires. He studied chemistry in Zürich before deciding upon a conducting career. He conducted at the Theater am Gärtnerplatz in Munich in 1953, and subsequently in Potsdam (1954); then at the Deutsche Oper am Rhein in Düsseldorf (1956–64) and at the Zürich Opera (1964–66); after 1966 he was on the staff of the Württemberg State Theater in Stuttgart; later conducted at the Bavarian State Opera in Munich (from 1968), and at the Vienna State Opera (from 1973); in 1974 was engaged at the Bayreuth Festival and also at Covent Garden in London. He had guest appearances as an orch. conductor with the Berlin Phil. and the Vienna Phil. On Sept. 8, 1977, he made his American debut conducting Verdi's *Otello* with the San Francisco Opera; in 1979 conducted a guest engagement with the Chicago Symph. Orch. Following in his father's tradition of astutely eloquent interpretation of both operatic and symph. repertoire, Carlos Kleiber advanced securely into the foremost ranks of modern conductors.

Kleiber, Erich, eminent Austrian conductor; b. Vienna, Aug. 5, 1890; d. Zürich, Jan. 27, 1956. He studied at the Prague Cons. and the Univ. of Prague; in 1911, was conductor at the Prague National Theater; then conducted opera in Darmstadt (1912–19), Barmen-Elberfeld (1919–21), Düsseldorf (1921–22), and Mannheim (1922–23). In 1923 he was appointed Generalmusikdirektor of the Berlin State Opera; conducted the world premiere of Berg's opera *Wozzeck* (Dec. 14, 1925). In 1935, in protest against the German National Socialist government, he emigrated to South America, where he toured as a guest conductor; also appeared in Mexico, Cuba, and the U.S.; in 1936–49, conducted German opera at the Teatro Colón in Buenos Aires. He conducted the Havana Phil. Orch. (1944–47); appeared as guest conductor of the NBC Symph. Orch. (1945–46); was engaged as chief conductor of the Berlin State Opera in 1954, but resigned in March 1955, before the opening of the season, because of difficulties with the officials of the German Democratic Republic. He wrote: Violin Concerto; Piano Concerto; orch. variations; *Capriccio* for Orch.; Overture; numer-

ous chamber music works, piano pieces, and songs.
BIBLIOGRAPHY: J. Russell, *Erich Kleiber: A Memoir* (London, 1957).

Klein, Bernhard, German composer; b. Cologne, March 6, 1793; d. Berlin, Sept. 9, 1832. He went to Paris in 1812 to study with Cherubini at the Paris Cons.; returning to Cologne, he was appointed music director of the Cathedral. In 1818 he settled in Berlin; from 1820 taught at the Royal Inst. for Church Music. During his lifetime he was greatly praised for his contrapuntal craftsmanship in sacred works, and was even described by some as "the Berlin Palestrina." WORKS: 2 operas: *Dido* (Berlin, Oct. 15, 1823) and *Ariadne* (1825; unperf.); another opera, *Irene*, remained unfinished; 3 oratorios: *Job* (Leipzig, 1820); *Jephtha* (Cologne, 1828); *David* (Halle, 1830); cantata, *Worte des Glaubens* (1817); 8-part *Pater noster;* 6-part Magnificat; 6-part responses; 8 books of Psalms, hymns, motets for men's voices, etc.; sonatas and variations for piano; songs. His younger brother, **Joseph Klein** (1801–62), was also a composer; he lived mostly in Berlin.
BIBLIOGRAPHY: C. Koch, *Bernhard Klein* (Rostock, 1902).

Klein, Bruno Oscar, composer, pianist, and pedagogue; b. Osnabrück, Germany, June 6, 1858; d. New York, June 22, 1911. He studied with his father, Karl Klein (organist of the Osnabrück Cathedral), and later at the Munich Cons. In 1878 he settled in America. From 1884 till his death in 1911 he was head of the piano dept. at the Convent School of the Sacred Heart in N.Y.; also served as organist in various churches. His opera, *Kenilworth,* was performed in Hamburg (Feb. 13, 1895); he also wrote: Piano Concerto; Violin Concerto; *American Dances* for Orch.; choral music; chamber music; piano pieces.

Klein, Elisabeth, Hungarian-born Danish pianist; b. Trenčín (now in Czechoslovakia), July 23, 1911. She studied piano at the Liszt Academy in Budapest, graduating in 1934; then had private lessons with Bartók; married a Danish citizen and moved to Denmark. She taught piano at the Royal Danish Academy of Music in Copenhagen and at the Music Academy in Oslo. In 1980 she moved to Norway. In her concert programs she included many works by contemporary Scandinavian composers.

Klein, Fritz Heinrich, Austrian composer and theorist of an original bent; b. Budapest, Feb. 2, 1892; d. Linz, July 11, 1977. He took piano lessons with his father; then went to Vienna, where he studied composition with Schoenberg and Alban Berg, and became their devoted disciple. From 1932 to 1957 he taught music theory at the Bruckner Cons. in Linz. His most ingenious composition is *Die Maschine* (1921; first perf. N.Y., Nov. 24, 1924), subtitled "Eine extonale Selbstsatire" and publ. under the pseudonym "Heautontimorumenos" (i.e., self-tormentor); this work features instances of all kinds of tonal combinations, including a "Mutterakkord," which consists of all 12 different chromatic tones and all 11 different intervals, the first time such an arrangement was proposed. He also publ. an important essay bearing on serial techniques then still in the process of formulation, "Die Grenze der Halbtonwelt," in *Die Musik* (Jan. 1925). He made the vocal score of Alban Berg's opera *Wozzeck.* Among his own works are *Partita* for 6 Instruments (1953); Divertimento for String Orch. (1954); *Ein musikalisches Fliessband* for Orch. (1960); *Musikalisches Tagebuch* for Orch. (1970); he further wrote several stage works, among them a mystery opera, *Nostradamus.*

Klein, Herman, English music journalist; b. Norwich, July 23, 1856; d. London, March 10, 1934. He studied voice with Manuel Garcia; then taught singing; at the same time wrote music criticism; was critic of the *Sunday Times* from 1881 to 1901; from 1902 till 1909 he was in America as critic of the *N.Y. Herald.* He then returned to London as critic of the *Saturday Review* (1917–21).
WRITINGS: *30 Years of Musical Life in London* (N.Y., 1903); *Unmusical New York* (London, 1910); *The Reign of Patti* (N.Y., 1920); *The Art of the Bel Canto* (London, 1923); *Musicians and Mummers* (London, 1925); *Great Women Singers of My Time* (London, 1931); *The Golden Age of Opera* (London, 1933). He was co-ed. of Manuel Garcia's *Hints on Singing* (London, 1894); ed. *Musical Notes 1886–89; Lieder in English* (a collection of about 60 translations of songs of Schubert, Schumann, Brahms, etc.). He also made a trans. of *Carmen.*

Klein, Ivy Frances (née **Salaman**), English song composer; b. London, Dec. 23, 1895. She wrote a number of songs to texts by English poets and appeared in concerts singing and accompanying herself. In 1924 she married Daryl Klein. Among her songs are *Ode on Solitude* (after Pope) and *Music When Soft Voices Die* (Shelley). Her choral work *She Walked in Beauty* (Byron) was performed at Queen Elizabeth's coronation (1953).

Klein, John, American organist and composer; b. Rahns, Pa., Feb. 21, 1915; d. there, April 30, 1981. He studied at the Philadelphia Musical Academy; then went to Salzburg, where he took courses at the Mozarteum, and later to Paris, where he had lessons with Nadia Boulanger in composition and with Marcel Dupré in organ. Returning to America, he was employed as organist at the Presbyterian Church in Columbus, Ohio (1937–42); then was engaged in radio shows as a pianist (1944–57); played carillon in recitals and at carillon festivals in Cobb, Ireland, and at the World Fair in Brussels. He publ. *The Art of Playing the Modern Carillon* and *The First 4 Centuries of Music;* composed a Violin Concerto and a number of songs and marches, including the U.S. Army radio show theme, *Sound Off.*

Klein, Kenneth, talented American conductor; b. Los Angeles, Sept. 5, 1939. He studied violin at the

Univ. of Southern Calif. School of Music with Eudice Shapiro, Vera Barstow, and Peter Meremblum; took piano lessons with Gerhard Albersheim; studied conducting with Fritz Zweig in Los Angeles, Izler Solomon at the Aspen School of Music, and Richard Lert in Asilomar, Calif. Klein played violin under the direction of Lert in the Pasadena Symph. Orch., and in the All-State Symph. of Calif. In 1963 he organized the Westside Symph. Orch. in Los Angeles, and conducted it until 1968; then was engaged as music director of the Symph. Orch. of Guadalajara, Mexico (1968–78). He also conducted in Austria, Germany, Switzerland, and Scandinavia, and in Russia. In 1983 he was appointed conductor of the South Dakota Symph.

Klein, Lothar, German-born Canadian composer; b. Hannover, Jan. 27, 1932. He moved to England in 1939 and to the U.S. in 1941; studied composition with Paul Fetler at the Univ. of Minnesota, graduating in 1954, and orchestration with Dorati (1956–58); took courses in composition with Josef Rufer at the Free Univ. of Berlin and with Blacher at the Hochschule für Musik there (1958–60). Returning to the U.S., he taught at the Univ. of Minnesota (1962–64) and the Univ. of Texas at Austin (1964–68); in 1968 was appointed to the faculty of the Univ. of Toronto, where he became chairman of the graduate music dept. (1971–76). His early music is essentially tonal, esthetically derived from neo-Romantic procedures; he then experimented with various branches of serialism; also wrote collage pieces embodying elements of all historical periods through linkage of stylistic similarities. WORKS: 2 *Cantatas: I* for Soli, Chorus, Harp, and Wind Ensemble (1957) and *II (On Epigrams of Sappho)* for Actress and 6 Solo Instruments (1958); 3 ballets: *Charades, Lost Love,* and *La Ronde* (all 1950–56); dance drama, *The Prodigal Son* (1966); Divertimento for Band (1953); Piano Concerto (1954); *Eclogues* for Horn and Strings (1954); 3 symphs. (1955, 1965, 1972); Concerto for Wind Quartet, Brass, Timpani, and Strings (1956); *Symmetries* for Orch. (1958); *Appasionato* for Orch. (1958); *Trio Concertante* for String Trio and Orch. (1961; New Orleans, April 4, 1965); *Épitaphs,* dedicated to the memory of Hemingway, Camus, and President Kennedy, for Orch. (1963; New Orleans, April 4, 1965); *Janizary Music* for Winds, Percussion, and Cellos (1970); *Prelude, Madrigal, and Fantastic Sprites,* suite for Orch. (1971); *Passacaglia of the Zodiac* for 14 Solo Strings (1971); *Music for Violin and Orchestra* (1972); *Le Trésor des dieux,* suite for Guitar or Harpsichord, and Orch. (1972); *Slices of Time* for Trumpet and String Orch. (1973); *The Philosopher in the Kitchen,* "gastronomic meditation" for Contralto and Orch. (1974; Toronto, July 8, 1975); *Invention, Blues, and Chase* for Free-bass Accordion and Strings (1975); *Musica antiqua,* allegory for Consort and Orch. (1975; performers also sing); *Orpheus: A Lyrical Essay* for Narrator, Chorus, Winds, and Piano (1976); Wind Quintet (1952); Piano Quintet (1953); *Music for Violin and Piano* (1963); *Hommage à Satie* for Piano (1966); Piano Sonata (1968);

Trio Sonata, "third-stream music" for Clarinet, Cello, Piano, and Jazz Drums (1969); *4 for 1,* suite for Solo Double Bass (1970); *6 Exchanges* for Solo Saxophone (1972); songs; choral works; incidental music for 10 plays.

Klein, Manuel, English-American conductor and composer; b. London, Dec. 6, 1876; d. New York, June 1, 1919. He studied in London; in 1904 settled in N.Y., where he was music director of the N.Y. Hippodrome and composer of the music for a great many of the productions there.

Klein, Peter, German tenor; b. Zündorf, near Cologne, Jan. 25, 1907. He studied at the Cologne Cons.; then made appearances in Düsseldorf, Kaiserslautern, and Zürich; was a member of the Hamburg State Opera (1937–41); also appeared at the Salzburg Festival. He made his Metropolitan Opera debut on Nov. 21, 1949, as Valzacchi in *Der Rosenkavalier,* returning to Europe at the close of the season. In 1956 he joined the faculty of the Vienna Cons.

Kleinheinz, Franz Xaver, German composer and conductor; b. Mindelheim, June (baptized, June 26) 1765; d. Budapest, Jan. 26, 1832. He played in the Munich Orch.; in 1803 he went to Vienna to study with Albrechtsberger; then was active in Brünn; subsequently in Budapest (1814–23). He made transcriptions for string quartet of Beethoven's early piano sonatas; wrote the operas *Harald* (Budapest, March 22, 1814) and *Der Käfig* (Budapest, 1816); much chamber music; sacred choral works; Piano Concerto; etc.
BIBLIOGRAPHY: Emil Haraszti, "Les Compositions inconnues de F.X. Kleinheinz," *Revue Musicale* (March 1930).

Kleinknecht, Jakob Friedrich, German flutist, violinist, and composer; b. Ulm, April (baptized, April 8) 1722; d. Ansbach, Aug. 14, 1794. In 1743 he was engaged as flutist in the Margrave's orch. in Bayreuth, and in 1756 was appointed its Kapellmeister. He wrote a number of pieces of chamber music, almost all of them including solo parts for the flute.

Kleinmichel, Richard, German pianist and composer; b. Posen, Dec. 31, 1846; d. Charlottenburg, Aug. 18, 1901. He studied with his father, Friedrich Kleinmichel (1827–94), a bandmaster; subsequently took courses at the Leipzig Cons.; taught music in Hamburg for some years; returned to Leipzig in 1876, and in 1882 became music director of the Municipal Theater there; then was active in similar positions in Danzig and Magdeburg. He married **Clara Monhaupt,** a soprano. He wrote 2 operas, *Der Pfeiffer von Dusenbach* (Hamburg, 1881) and *Manon* (Hamburg, 1883); 2 symphs.; many characteristic pieces for piano; 4 books of piano études "für kleine und grosse Leute" and other pedagogical studies. He arranged for piano several of Wagner's scores, including the entire *Ring* cycle.

Kleinsinger, George, American composer; b. San Bernardino, Calif., Feb. 13, 1914; d. New York, July 28, 1982. He was apprenticed to study dentistry; then turned to music; studied with Philip James at N.Y. Univ. and later at the Juilliard Graduate School with Jacobi and Wagenaar. From his earliest attempts at composition he adopted a hedonistic regard toward music as a medium of education and entertainment. In this vein he wrote in 1942 a Broadway musical for children entitled *Tubby the Tuba,* which was highly successful; other works in a similarly whimsical manner were *Pee-Wee the Piccolo* (1946); *Street Corner Concerto* for Harmonica and Orch. (1946); and *Brooklyn Baseball Cantata* (1948). His crowning work was the chamber opera *Archy and Mehitabel,* based on the popular comic strip featuring a garrulous cockroach and an emotional cat; it was first performed in N.Y. on Dec. 6, 1954, and later metamorphosed into a Broadway musical under the title *Shinbone Alley.* Kleinsinger's private life reflected the eccentricity of his musical talents; he inhabited the famous bohemian Hotel Chelsea in N.Y., where he maintained a running waterfall, a turtle, a skunk, an iguana, 40 fish, a dog, a python, and a cat. He used to play the piano with a boa constrictor wrapped around him. How he maintained his menagerie in peace was his guarded secret.

Klementyev, Lev, Russian tenor; b. St. Petersburg, April 1, 1868; d. Tiflis, Oct. 26, 1910. He appeared in operetta in Kharkov and St. Petersburg; then became a member of the Kiev Opera (1888–89) and the Tiflis Opera (1889–90); went to Moscow, where he sang at the Bolshoi Theater from 1892 until his death. He was noted for his faithful rendition of Russian operatic roles.

Klemetti, Heikki, Finnish composer and choral conductor; b. Kuortane, Feb. 14, 1876; d. Helsinki, Aug. 26, 1953. He studied philosophy, and then music at the Stern Cons. in Berlin. In 1900 he founded the famous men's choir Suomen Laulu (became a mixed choir in 1907), with which he toured Scandinavia and Europe (1901–25); also the U.S. (1939). He publ. a history of music (in Finnish; several vols. since 1916), a textbook of choral singing (1917), and a textbook of voice production (1920); composed numerous choruses, masses, and antiphons (collected and officially approved as the hymnal of the State Church of Finland in 1924); also arranged songs for school and home (3 vols., 1927–28) and some early church music.

Klemm, Johann Gottlob. See **Clemm, Johann Gottlob.**

Klemperer, Otto, celebrated German conductor; b. Breslau, May 14, 1885; d. Zürich, July 6, 1973. He received early musical training from his mother; in 1901 he entered the Hoch Cons. in Frankfurt, where he studied piano with Kwast and music theory with Knorr; later went to Berlin to study composition and conducting with Pfitzner. At the age of 21 he was engaged to conduct Max Reinhardt's production of *Orpheus in the Underworld* in Berlin. He was later appointed chorus master, and subsequently conductor, at the German Theater in Prague. In 1910 he assisted Mahler in his preparations for the Munich premiere of the *Symphony of a Thousand;* also conducted at the Hamburg Opera (1910–12). He subsequently had engagements in the provinces; in 1917 he received the prestigious appointment of music director of the Cologne Opera, where he conducted the first German performance of Janáček's *Kát'a Kabanová.* In 1924 he became music director of the Wiesbaden Opera. On Jan. 24, 1926, he made his U.S. debut as a guest conductor with the N.Y. Symph. Orch. In 1927 he became music director of the Kroll Opera in Berlin; there he presented the first German performances of Stravinsky's *Oedipus Rex* and Schoenberg's *Erwartung.* In 1933 he was forced to leave Germany and he emigrated to the U.S. In 1933 he became music director of the Los Angeles Phil. Orch., and also appeared as a guest conductor in N.Y., Philadelphia, and Pittsburgh. A disaster nearly put an end to his career in 1939 when he had to undergo an operation for a brain tumor. Still, during a period of remission, he accepted the post of conductor with the Budapest Opera, which he led from 1947–50. In 1951 he made a guest appearance with the Philharmonia Orch. However, he could never regain complete control of his body and mind, and on several occasions lost the memory of his own identity, and was found wandering in the streets. In his active years he distinguished himself by a series of Beethoven's symphs. which he presented at the Royal Festival Hall in London. His interpretations of Mahler's symphs. were notable for their Classical restraint without loss of their fervor. In 1970 he conducted in Jerusalem and accepted Israeli citizenship. He retired in 1972, and then lived in Switzerland until his death. Klemperer was also a composer; in his works he was mainly influenced by the Romantic style of his early teacher Hans Pfitzner. He wrote an opera, *Das Ziel* (1915; revised 1970); *Missa sacra* (1916); 6 symphs. (from 1960); 9 string quartets (1968–70); 17 pieces for Voice and Orch. (1967–70); and about 100 lieder. He publ. *Meine Errinerungen an Gustav Mahler* (Zürich, 1960; in Eng. as *Minor Recollections,* London, 1964).
BIBLIOGRAPHY: P. Heyworth, *Conversations with Klemperer* (London, 1973); C. Osborne and K. Thomson, eds., *Klemperer Stories: Anecdotes, Sayings and Impressions of Otto Klemperer* (London, 1980); P. Heyworth, *Otto Klemperer: His Life and Times,* vol. I, 1885–1933 (London, 1983).

Klenau, Paul (August) von, Danish conductor and composer; b. Copenhagen, Feb. 11, 1883; d. there, Aug. 31, 1946. He studied violin with Hillmer and composition with Malling in Copenhagen; then took lessons in violin with Halir and in composition with Max Bruch at the Berlin Hochschule für Musik (1902). In 1904 he went to Munich, where he studied composition privately with Thuille; in 1908 moved to Stuttgart, where he became a student of Max von Schilling. He began his conducting career at the

Freiburg Opera during the season of 1907–8; in 1909 was conductor at the Court Opera Theater there; in 1912 was conductor of the Bach Society in Frankfurt; then returned to the Freiburg Opera (1913). After World War I he studied with Schoenberg. From 1920 to 1926 he was conductor of the Danish Phil. Society; concurrently conducted the Vienna Konzerthausgesellschaft (1922–30). He returned to Copenhagen in 1940.

WORKS: 6 operas: *Sulamith,* after Song of Songs (Munich, Nov. 16, 1913); *Kjartan und Gudrun* (Mannheim, April 4, 1918; revised version as *Gudrun auf Island,* Hagen, Nov. 27, 1924); *Die Lästerschule (The School for Scandal,* after Sheridan; Frankfurt, Dec. 25, 1926); *Michael Kolhaas* (after Kleist; Stuttgart, Nov. 4, 1933; new version, Berlin, March 7, 1934); *Rembrandt van Rijn,* libretto by Klenau (simultaneous premiere, Berlin and Stuttgart, Jan. 23, 1937); *Elisabeth von England* (Kassel, March 29, 1939; title changed to *Die Königen* after the outbreak of World War II to avoid mentioning England; produced in Berlin, April 1940); 7 symphs.; *Inferno,* 3 fantasies for Orch. (after Dante); chamber music; piano pieces; songs. His most successful work was a ballet after Han Christian Andersen, *Kleine Idas Blumen* (Stuttgart, 1916).

Klengel, August Alexander, German pianist and composer; b. Dresden, Jan. 27, 1783; d. there, Nov. 22, 1852. He studied with Milchmayer, and from 1803, with Clementi, with whom he traveled through Germany and, in 1805, to St. Petersburg, where he remained as a private tutor to aristocratic families until 1811. He then lived in Paris; visited London in 1815; returned to Dresden in 1816, and was appointed organist at the Roman Catholic Court Church. He was a fine organist and pianist, particularly distinguished by his *legato* piano style; as a composer, he was a master of contrapuntal forms; his canons were so ingenious that he was known under the sobriquet "Kanon-Klengel."

WORKS: His piano canons were publ. under the title *Les Avantcoureurs* (Dresden, 1841); he also wrote 48 canons and 48 fugues, taking Bach's *Well-Tempered Clavier* as the model (publ. posthumously, 1854). His other publ. piano works include 2 concertos; a 4-hand fantasia; a rondo; *Promenade sur mer, interrompue par une tempête;* and other salon music.

BIBLIOGRAPHY: R. Jäger, *A.A. Klengel, und seine Kanons und Fugen* (Leipzig, 1928).

Klengel, Julius, German cellist, brother of **Paul Klengel;** b. Leipzig, Sept. 24, 1859; d. there, Oct. 27, 1933. Brought up in a musical atmosphere (virtually all members of his family were professional or amateur musicians), he developed rapidly; studied cello with Emil Hegar and theory with Jadassohn. He joined the Gewandhaus Orch. in Leipzig when he was 15; in 1881 he became first cellist, and remained at that post until his resignation in 1924. He also taught at the Leipzig Cons. He traveled widely in Europe as a soloist; composed a number of works for his instrument, among them 4 concertos; *Kon-*zertstück for Cello with Piano; *Hymnus* for 12 Cellos; Double Concerto for Violin and Cello; 2 string quartets; Piano Trio; also edited a number of cello works and publ. cello exercises.

Klengel, Paul, German conductor and composer, brother of **Julius Klengel;** b. Leipzig, May 13, 1854; d. there, April 24, 1935. He studied at the Leipzig Cons. and at Leipzig Univ.; took the degree of Dr.Phil. with the dissertation *Zur Ästhetik der Tonkunst.* In 1881–86 he conducted the Leipzig Euterpe Concerts; in 1888–93, was 2nd court conductor at Stuttgart; then was again in Leipzig. From 1898 to 1902 he conducted German choral societies in N.Y.; then went back to Germany. He was a versatile musician and was proficient as a violinist as well as a pianist, although he did not engage in a concert career. He wrote numerous works for violin, and also publ. many skillful arrangements for various combinations.

BIBLIOGRAPHY: Eva Klengel, *Stammtafel der Familie Klengel* (Leipzig, 1929).

Klenovsky, Nicolai, Russian composer; b. Odessa, 1853; d. St. Petersburg, July 6, 1915. He studied violin with Hřimalý and harmony with Tchaikovsky at the Moscow Cons. In 1893 he was appointed director of the Cons. of Tiflis in the Caucasus, and in 1902 was engaged as conductor of the Court Chapel in St. Petersburg. He composed 3 ballets: *Hashish* (Moscow, 1885); *Svetlana* (Moscow, 1886); *Salanga* (St. Petersburg, 1900); orch. suite, *Fata Morgana;* a number of choruses. Some of his songs had merit.

Klenovsky, Paul. Pseudonym of **Wood, Sir Henry.**

Klerk, Albert de, Dutch organist and composer; b. Haarlem, Oct. 4, 1917. He served as assistant organist in a Haarlem church as a boy; then studied at the Amsterdam Cons.; in 1964 became a prof. of organ and improvisation there. He has also been active as a choral conductor. He has written much music for the church and made arrangements of old Flemish songs.

WORKS: Concerto for Organ and Orch. (1941); *Jam lucis orto sidere* for High Voice and Orch. (1942–43); *Cantabile* for Orch. (1952); *Stabat Mater* for Alto, Tenor, Chorus, and Chamber Orch. (1952); *Super omnia,* sacred cantata for Alto, Chorus, and Organ (1960); *Adagium-Suite* for School Chorus and Orch. (1960); *5 noëls français* for Alto and 10 Wind Instruments (1963); Concerto for Organ-positive and String Orch. (1964); Concerto for Solo Organ, 2 Horns, 2 Trumpets, and 2 Trombones (1967); *Laudate Dominum (Psalm 150)* for Chorus and Orch. (1968); *Suite Concertante* for Organ and String Orch. (1976); a number of sacred works, including *Mater Sanctus Laelitiae (Mother of Blessed Happiness)* for Female Chorus, Flute, English Horn, and Bassoon (1957) and *Ad modum tubae* for Chorus, Wind Quartet, and Organ; Sonatina for Violin and Cello (1937); *Aria met variaties* for Piano, 4-hands (1944); *Fantasy* for Violin and Piano (1949–50); numerous organ pieces, including Prelude and

Fugue (1940); Sonata (1942); *6 Inventions* (1945); *Ricercare (Hommage à Sweelinck)* (1950); *8 Fantasies on a Gregorian Theme* (1954); *Images.*

Kletzki (originally spelled **Klecki**), **Paul,** Polish conductor; b. Lodz, March 21, 1900; d. Liverpool, March 5, 1973. He studied violin with Emil Mlynarski; during World War I was a member of the Lodz Phil.; then lived in Berlin (1921–33) and in Italy. After World War II he occupied various conducting posts; appeared as a guest conductor with the Liverpool Phil. (1954–55). From 1958 to 1962 he conducted the Dallas Symph.; then went to Switzerland, where he conducted the Bern Orch. (1964–66) and the Orch. de la Suisse Romande (1967–70); also was a guest conductor in South America and Australia. He wrote about 50 compositions for various combinations, including 2 symphs.

Kleven, Arvid, Norwegian composer and flutist; b. Drontheim, Nov. 29, 1899; d. Oslo, Nov. 23, 1929. He studied in Oslo, Paris, and Berlin; from 1919, played flute in the National Theater Orch. in Oslo, and in the Phil. Orch. there. He wrote a tone poem, *Lotusland* (Oslo, 1922); 2 *Aquarelles* for Orch. (1923); *Sinfonia libera* (1927); several works for violin; piano pieces; songs.

Klička, Josef, Bohemian organist and composer; b. Klattau, Dec. 15, 1855; d. there, March 28, 1937. He studied with Skuherský in Prague; then conducted various choral societies there; in 1906–20 he was inspector of music in Bohemia. He was appointed prof. of organ at the Prague Cons. in 1885 and taught until his retirement in 1924. He wrote an opera, *The Miller's Beautiful Wife* (Prague, 1886); 9 masses; 2 oratorios; many organ works, including a fantasia on the chorale melody *St. Wenzeslaus,* and *Legend* (both publ. in *Les Maîtres contemporains d'orgue,* Paris); chamber music; also pieces for harp.
BIBLIOGRAPHY: K. Hoffmeister, *Josef Klička* (Prague, 1944).

Klien, Walter, Austrian pianist; b. Graz, Nov. 27, 1928. He studied at the Vienna Academy of Music with Joseph Dichler, and later with Arturo Benedetti Michelangeli; also took composition lessons with Hindemith. In 1951 and 1952 he won the Busoni prize. In 1963 he formed a duo-piano team with Wolfgang Schneiderhan.

Klima, Alois, Czech conductor; b. Klatovy, Dec. 21, 1905; d. Prague, June 11, 1980. His father was a choral conductor who taught him to play different orch. instruments. Later Klima studied composition with Křička and Řídký at the Prague Cons.; then began to conduct radio concerts in Ostrava and Brno. In 1950 he was appointed principal conductor of the Prague Radio Orch.

Klimov, Mikhail, Russian choral conductor and pedagogue; b. Moscow, Oct. 21, 1881; d. Zavidovo, near Tver, Feb. 20, 1937. He studied composition with Rimsky-Korsakov and conducting with Nicolas Tcherepnin at the St. Petersburg Cons., graduating in 1908. In 1919 he was called upon to reorganize the former Imperial Church Choir as a secular group, and toured with it in Europe in 1928. He also taught choral singing at the St. Petersburg Cons. He publ. a textbook of solfeggio (1929).
BIBLIOGRAPHY: V. Muzalevsky, *M.G. Klimov* (Leningrad, 1960).

Klimov, Valery, Russian violinist; b. Kiev, Oct. 16, 1931. His father was a professional conductor and a pedagogue. Klimov studied violin in Moscow and Odessa; then studied with Oistrakh at the Moscow Cons., graduating in 1956. That year he won first prize at the Prague Competition and in 1958 received first prize at the important International Tchaikovsky Competition, which opened for him great opportunities for world tours; he played with much success in Europe, the U.S., and Australia.

Klindworth, Karl, eminent German pianist, pedagogue, and editor; b. Hannover, Sept. 25, 1830; d. Stolpe, near Potsdam, July 27, 1916. He learned to play violin and piano as a child; obtained work as conductor of a traveling opera company when he was only 17; also traveled in Germany as a concert pianist; then went to Weimar to study with Liszt. In 1854 he went to London, where he remained until 1868, establishing himself as a popular piano teacher. When Wagner was in London in 1855, they became friends; as a result of his admiration for Wagner, Klindworth undertook the most important work of his life, the arrangement in vocal scores of Wagner's tetralogy *Der Ring des Nibelungen.* In 1868, he was engaged as a prof. at the newly founded Moscow Cons. at the invitation of its director, Nicolai Rubinstein; after Rubinstein's death in 1881 Klindworth returned to Germany; in 1882–87 was one of the principal conductors of the Berlin Phil. In 1884 he established in Berlin his own Klavierschule; in 1893 it was merged with the Scharwenka Cons. of Music in Berlin, as Konservatorium der Musik Klindworth-Scharwenka, which became one of the most famous music schools in Germany. Klindworth was an exceptionally competent arranger and music editor; apart from his masterly transcriptions of Wagner's operas, he made an arrangement for 2 pianos of Schubert's C major Symph. He also wrote a number of virtuoso pieces for piano, of which the brilliant *Polonaise-Fantaisie* and 24 grand études in all keys enjoyed some vogue among pianists.
BIBLIOGRAPHY: Hugo Leichtentritt, *Das Konservatorium der Musik Klindworth-Scharwenka, 1881–1931* (Berlin, 1931).

Klingenberg, Friedrich Wilhelm, German pedagogue; b. Sulau, June 6, 1809; d. Görlitz, April 2, 1888. He was director of the Music Academy at Breslau (1830–37); in 1840–85, cantor at the Peterskirche in Görlitz. He wrote a Symph., overtures, piano pieces, vocal church music, and songs.

Klitzsch – Klusák

Klitzsch, Karl Emanuel, German conductor and composer; b. Schönhaide, Oct. 30, 1812; d. Zwickau, March 5, 1889. He lived most of his life in Zwickau; was co-founder and conductor of the Music Society there. Under the pen name of **Emanuel Kronach** he composed the opera *Juana, oder Ein Tag auf St. Domingo;* the 96th Psalm for Soli, Chorus, and Orch.; also songs.

Klobučar, Berislav, conductor; b. Zagreb, Aug. 28, 1924. He was educated at the Zagreb Academy of Music; studied conducting with Lovro von Matacic and Clemens Krauss. He was conductor at the Zagreb National Theater (1941–51); in 1953 he appeared at the Vienna State Opera; became a regular conductor there. In 1961 he became chief conductor of the Phil. Orch. and Opera in Graz.

Klose, Friedrich, Swiss composer; b. Karlsruhe (of Swiss parents), Nov. 29, 1862; d. Ruvigliana, Lugano, Dec. 24, 1942. He studied in Karlsruhe and Geneva; in 1886 he went to Vienna, where he took a course with Bruckner. He traveled in Germany, Austria, and Switzerland, occupying teaching posts for a year or two in various places, until 1907, when he was appointed prof. of composition at the Akademie der Tonkunst in Munich. In 1920 he went to Switzerland. He wrote several large works that reveal the influence of Bruckner and Wagner; of these, the most important is *Ilsebill,* described as a "dramatic symphony" (Munich, Oct. 29, 1905); another important work is an oratorio, *Der Sonne-Geist* (Basel, 1918); he further wrote a symph. poem, *Das Leben ein Traum;* organ works; String Quartet; songs. He publ. the books *Meine Lehrjahre bei Bruckner* (Regensburg, 1927) and *Bayreuth* (1929). BIBLIOGRAPHY: R. Louis, *Friedrich Klose* (Munich, 1905); H. Knappe, *Friedrich Klose* (1921). A symposium of articles, *Friedrich Klose, zum 80. Geburtstag,* was publ. at Lugano (1942).

Klosé, Hyacinthe-Eléonore, noted clarinetist and pedagogue; b. on the island of Corfu, Oct. 11, 1808; d. Paris, Aug. 29, 1880. He studied at the Paris Cons.; then taught there for nearly 30 years (1839–68). In 1843 he introduced an important innovation into Böhm's system of ring-keys, which was widely adopted; publ. *Grande méthode pour la clarinette à anneaux mobiles* (1844) based on that system; also studies and exercises. He did much to promote the then-novel saxophone, and wrote some music for it.

Klose, Margarete, German contralto; b. Berlin, Aug. 6, 1902; d. there, Dec. 14, 1968. She studied music at the Klindworth-Scharwenka Cons. in Berlin; made her debut in Ulm in 1927; then sang in Mannheim (1928–31) and at the Berlin State Opera, where she obtained a decisive popular and musical success; she remained there until 1949; then sang at the Berlin City Opera until 1958, returning to the Berlin State Opera until her retirement in 1961; also sang in Italy, England, and the U.S. She was particularly praised for her Wagnerian contralto roles.

Kloss, Erich, German writer on music; b. Görlitz, Feb. 19, 1863; d. (in an automobile accident) Berlin, Nov. 1, 1910. He began his career as a teacher, but because of deafness he was obliged to give it up; directed his attention to writing.
WRITINGS: *20 Jahre Bayreuth* (1896); *Wagner, wie er war und ward* (1901); *Ein Wagner-Lesebuch* (1904); *Wagner-Anekdoten* (1908); *R. Wagner in seinen Briefen* (1908); *R. Wagner an siene Künstler* (1909); *R. Wagner im Liede* (1910); *R. Wagner über Die Meistersinger* (1910); *R. Wagner über den Ring des Nibelungen* (1913; publ. posthumously); also ed. *Richard Wagner an Freunde und Zeitgenossen* (1909), and the 3rd augmented ed. of the Wagner-Liszt correspondence (1910).

Klotz, a family of Bavarian violin makers at Mittenwald. Their instruments were brought into repute by **Matthias Klotz** (b. Mittenwald, June 11, 1653; d. there, Aug. 16, 1743), the son of Ägidius Klotz; he is believed to have learned the art of violin making from Nicola Amati, during his travels in Italy; he manufactured his best instruments between 1670 and 1696. His son **Sebastian Klotz** (b. Mittenwald, Jan. 18, 1696; d. there, Jan. 20, 1775) is regarded as even superior to him in making violins after Italian models. There followed, in the 18th century, several other violin makers named Klotz, but their relationship to the family cannot be established.

Klughardt, August (Friedrich Martin), German composer; b. Cöthen, Nov. 30, 1847; d. Rosslau, near Dresden, Aug. 3, 1902. He was a pupil of Blassmann and Reichel at Dresden. In 1867 he was appointed theater conductor at Posen; had similar posts in Lübeck (1868) and Weimar (1869–73); he then was active in Neustrelitz (1873–82) and Dessau (from 1883).
WORKS: 4 operas: *Miriam* (Weimar, 1871); *Iwein* (Neustrelitz, 1879); *Gudrun* (Neustrelitz, 1882); *Die Hochzeit Mönchs* (Dessau, Nov. 10, 1886; given in Prague as *Astorre,* 1888); 5 symphs.; chamber music; songs; piano pieces.
BIBLIOGRAPHY: L. Gerlach, *August Klughardt, Sein Leben und seine Werke* (Leipzig, 1902).

Klusák, Jan, Czech composer; b. Prague, April 18, 1934. He studied music theory with Řídký and Bořkovec at the Prague Academy of Music (1953–57), obtaining a thorough technique in the traditional Central European style of composition, and wrote a number of works in a neo-Baroque idiom, set in tolerably dissonant counterpoint; also paid tribute to the ethnic resources of Czech music. He soon succumbed, however, to the Circean lure of cosmopolitan formalism and total serialism, with a well-nigh monastic exercise of tonal egalitarianism.
WORKS: FOR THE STAGE: Opera, *Proces (The Trial),* after Kafka (1966). FOR ORCH.: Concertino for Flute and Strings (1955); *Partita* for Strings (1955); 3 symphs. (1956, 1959, 1960); Concerto Grosso for Wind Quintet and Strings (1957); *Inventions I, II, III, IV, VII, VIII* for Chamber Orch.: *I* (1961); *II*

(1962); *III* (1962); *IV* (1964); *VII* (1973); *VIII,* surnamed *Quadratura orbis (Squaring of the circle,* 1973); *Variations on a Theme of Mahler* (1960–62; based on a theme from Mahler's 5th Symph.); *2 Czech Dances* for Wind Orch. (1964); *Lyric Fantasy,* subtitled *Hommage à Grieg* (1965); *Le Forgeron harmonieux,* after Handel's so-called *Harmonious Blacksmith* (1966); *Pasticcio olandese per orchestra,* subtitled *A Friesland Friday* (1969–70); *Hamburger Doppelinvention* (1974); *Kleine Farbenlehre,* subtitled *Hommage à Goethe* (1974–75). CHAMBER MUSIC: *Music to the Fountain* for Wind Quintet (1954); 3 string quartets (1956, 1961–62, 1975); *Přislovi (Proverbs)* for Low Voice and Wind Instruments (1959); *Obrazy (Pictures)* for 12 Wind Instruments (1960); *Monoinvention* for Solo Cello (1962); *Risposte* for Solo Violin (1963); Sonata for Violin and Wind Instruments (1964–65); *Invention V, Hra v šachy (Game of Chess)* for Wind Quintet (1965); *1-4-3-2-5-6-7-10-9-8-11* (invertible all-interval 12-tone series) for Flute Solo (1965); *Invention VI* for Wind Quintet and String Quartet (1969); *Contrapunto fiorito* for 8 Instruments (1966); *Short John* for Cimbalom (1971); *Jupiter-Duo* for Clarinet and Cello (1973); Sonata for Percussion (1974); *Solo* for Trumpet (1975–76); *Die heilige Zahl (The Holy Number),* duo for Violin and Percussion (1975–76); *Tango-Polka* for Clarinet, Trumpet, Cello, and Piano (1980). FOR VOICE: *4 Small Vocal Exercises,* on texts by Kafka, for Narrator and 11 Wind Instruments (1960); *Radix nativitatis I. S.* (memorial for Igor Stravinsky) for Voice, Flute, Clarinet, Viola, and Piano (1972); *Bridal Cantata 1979* for Male Chorus and Orch. (1979); *The Moon in Zenith,* to words by Anna Akhmatova, for Mezzo-soprano, Clarinet, Viola, and Piano (1981); piano pieces.

Kmentt, Waldemar, Austrian tenor; b. Vienna, Feb. 2, 1929. He studied at the Vienna Academy of Music; made his concert debut in 1950 in Vienna, singing in Beethoven's 9th Symph. with Karl Böhm conducting; in 1951 was engaged at the State Opera in Vienna; in 1958 became a regular lyric tenor at the Düsseldorf Opera; subsequently sang at the Salzburg and Bayreuth festivals, at La Scala in Milan, and at Covent Garden in London, as well as in Rome, Munich, and Stuttgart.

Knab, Armin, German composer; b. Neu-Schleichach, Feb. 19, 1881; d. Bad Wörishofen, June 23, 1951. He studied piano in Würzburg; in 1934–43, taught at the Hochschule für Musik-Erziehung in Berlin. Knab was particularly esteemed in Germany as a composer of lieder. He followed the Romantic tradition, but tended toward a more severe modal style in his larger works.
WORKS: Sacred cantatas: *Mariae Geburt* (1928); *Vanitas mundi* (1946); *Engelsgruss* (1950); etc.; musical fairy tales: *Sneewittchen* and *Rumpelstilzchen;* folk-song cantatas: *Singt und klingt* (1934); *Grüss Gott, du schöner Maien* (1935); *Glück auf, ihr Bergleute* (1946); a great number of choral works; many instrumental pieces for school use.
BIBLIOGRAPHY: O. Lang, *Armin Knab, Ein*

Meister deutscher Liedkunst (Munich, 1937).

Knabe, William (Valentine Wilhelm Ludwig), founder of the celebrated piano manufacturing firm of Baltimore; b. Kreuzberg, near Oppeln, Prussia, June 3, 1803; d. Baltimore, May 21, 1864. He opened his business in 1839 with Henry Gaehle; in 1854 the partnership was dissolved. His successors were his sons **William Knabe** (1841–89) and **Ernest Knabe** (1827–94), joined later by Charles Keidel, and Knabe's grandsons **Ernest J. Knabe** and **William Knabe** (1872–1939). The firm was later amalgamated with the American Piano Corp.

Knaifel, Alexander, Russian composer; b. Tashkent, Nov. 28, 1943. He studied cello with Rostropovich at the Moscow Cons.; took a course in composition with Arapov at the Leningrad Cons., graduating in 1967. He edited the progressive publication *Soviet Composer* (1970–73). His music uses a variety of modern techniques, without venturing into unintelligibility.
WORKS: FOR THE STAGE: Ballet, *Striving* (1964); chamber opera, *The Canterville Ghost,* after Oscar Wilde (1965–66); choreographic scene, *The Penitent Magdalene* (1967); ballet, *Medea* (1968). FOR ORCH.: *Dream Fantasy* (1963); *Burlesque* for Trombone and Strings (1963); Concerto for Viola, Double Bass, and 23 Wind and Percussion Instruments (1964). CHAMBER MUSIC: *2 Pieces* for Flute, Viola, Piano, and Percussion (1962); *Ostinati* for Violin and Cello (1964); *Tournament Music* for Horn and Piano (1967); *Lamento* for Solo Cello (1967); *Constanta* for Horn and 6 Percussion Groups (1969–71); *A prima vista* for 4 Players on 5 Percussion Sets (1972); *Anna Akhmatova: Midnight Poems,* a commentary for 4 Performers (1973); *Joan of Arc,* choreography for 13 groups of Instruments (1970–78); *Da,* composition for Ensemble of Soloists (1980). FOR PIANO: *Short Sonata* (1961); *Classic Suite* (1963); *Musique militaire* (1964). VOCAL MUSIC: *150,000,000,* dithyramb after the poem of Mayakovsky, for Chorus, 6 Piccolos, 6 Trumpets, 6 Trombones, a few Violas and Double Basses, and Kettledrums (1966); *The Petrograd Sparrows,* phantasmagoria for Boys' Chorus and Chamber Orch. (1967); *Funeral Music* for Soprano and Orch. (1967); *Monody* for Solo Female Voice (1968); *Lenin: A Letter to the Central Committee Members* for Bass Voices in unison (1969); *Status nascendi* for 3 groups of Voices and Instruments (1973–75); *Ainana,* 17 variations for Chamber Choir, Percussion, and Electronic Tape (1978); *Stupid Horse,* 15 stories for Female Singer and Piano (1981); *Ordinary* for Chorus, Strings, Organ, and Female Soloist (1982).

Knap, Rolf, Dutch composer; b. Amsterdam, Oct. 17, 1937. He studied oboe at the Amsterdam Cons.; took private composition lessons with Karel Mengelberg; then studied electronic music at the Inst. of Sonology of the Univ. of Utrecht. He was an orch. oboist (1960–67); taught oboe at several schools of music in the Netherlands (1967–74).
WORKS: *(Sym)phonic Piece* for Orch. (1971); *Le*

Couple(t) for Voice, Piano, and Electronics (1971); *Dilemmaniana for Marrie* for Narrator, Cello, and Live Electronics (1972); *Zelomanniana* for Oboe and Piano (1974); 2 song cycles: *Liederen van Doofstommen (Songs of Deaf-Mutes;* 1974, 1976).

Knape, Walter, German musicologist, conductor, and composer; b. Bernburg, Jan. 14, 1906. He studied at the Univ. of Leipzig, receiving his Ph.D. there in 1934 with the dissertation *Die Sinfonien von Karl Friedrich Abel;* then joined its faculty. From 1948–57 he was conductor of the Leipzig Sing-Akademie and the Phil. Choir; he also taught at the Berlin Hochschule für Musik (1954–57), and subsequently at the univs. of Hamburg, Hannover, and Cuxhaven. He devoted much time to the study of the life and works of Abel; he edited a complete edition of his works (16 vols., Cuxhaven, 1958–74) and a bibliographic-thematic catalogue (Cuxhaven, 1971); also wrote *Karl Friedrich Abel: Leben und Werk eines frühklassischen Komponisten* (Bremen, 1973). As a composer, he wrote several symph. and choral works, as well as chamber music and a considerable number of piano pieces.

Knapp, Phoebe Palmer, American hymn-tune writer; b. New York, 1839; d. Poland Springs, Maine, July 10, 1908. She and her husband, the founder of the Metropolitan Life Insurance Co., supported much philanthropic work as members of the Methodist Episcopal Church. She wrote both verse and music for church hymns; her most popular hymn is *Assurance* (1873).
BIBLIOGRAPHY: R.G. McCutchan, *Our Hymnody* (N.Y., 1937).

Knappertsbusch, Hans, eminent German conductor; b. Elberfeld, March 12, 1888; d. Munich, Oct. 25, 1965. He studied with Steinbach and Lohse at the Cologne Cons. (1908–12); served as an assistant to Siegfried Wagner and Richter at Bayreuth. He conducted opera in Elberfeld (1913–18), Leipzig (1918–19), and Dessau (1919–22). From 1922 to 1936 he was Generalmusikdirektor of the Bavarian State Opera in Munich, a post he held with great distinction. He then conducted at the Vienna State Opera (1936–45); was also a conductor with the Vienna Phil. (1937–44). After World War II, he returned to Germany, making his home in Munich. He conducted at the Salzburg Festivals (1947–50, 1954–55); from 1951 he conducted at the Bayreuth Festivals; from 1947 to 1964 he was a regular guest conductor with the Vienna Phil. Knappertsbusch was one of the best exponents of the German school of conducting, in which fidelity to the music was the paramount virtue, over and above the pursuits of personal success.
BIBLIOGRAPHY: R. Betz and W. Panofsky, *Knappertsbusch* (Ingolstadt, 1958).

Knecht, Justin Heinrich, German composer and organist; b. Biberach, Sept. 30, 1752; d. there, Dec. 1, 1817. He was an organist and music director in Biberach from 1771 to the end of his life, traveling only briefly to Stuttgart, where he was court conductor from 1807 till 1809. Despite his provincial field of activity he attained considerable repute in Germany through his compositions and theoretical writings. He was a follower of the Vogler system of harmony; taught chord building by thirds up to chords of the eleventh on all degrees of the scale. His publications include: *Erklärung einiger missverstandenen Grundsätze aus der Vogler' schen Theorie* (Ulm, 1785); *Gemeinnützliches Elementarwerk der Harmonie und des Generalbasses* (4 parts, 1792–98); *Kleines alphabetisches Wörterbuch der vornehmsten und interessantesten Artikel aus der musikalischen Theorie* (1795); *Vollständige Orgelschule für Anfänger und Geübtere* (3 parts, 1795–98); *Theoretisch-praktische Generalbass-Schule; Kleine Klavierschule für die ersten Anfänger* (republ. as *Bewährtes Methodenbuch beim ersten Klavierunterricht*); *Allgemeiner musikalischer Katechismus* (Biberach, 1803); *Luthers Verdienst um Musik und Poesie* (1817). He wrote about 15 operas, several sacred works, and a piece for 15 instruments, *Tongemälde der Natur,* to which he supplied a programmatic description, seemingly anticipating Beethoven's "Pastoral" Symph. However, the resemblance is superficial, and there is no reason to believe that Beethoven was influenced by Knecht in this "tone painting" of nature.
BIBLIOGRAPHY: E. Kauffmann, *J.H. Knecht* (Tübingen, 1892); A. Bopp, *J.H. Knecht* (Kassel, 1930).

Kneisel, Franz, violin virtuoso; b. Bucharest (of German parentage), Jan. 26, 1865; d. New York, March 26, 1926. He studied at the Cons. of Bucharest, graduating at the age of 14; in 1879 went to Vienna, where he became a pupil of Grün and Hellmesberger at the Vienna Cons.; made his debut on Dec. 31, 1882, in Vienna; in 1884 he went to Berlin, where he was concertmaster of the Bilse Orch. (1884–85). In 1885 he was engaged as concertmaster of the Boston Symph. Orch.; made his debut as a soloist in Boston on Oct. 31, 1885, playing the Beethoven Concerto. In 1886 he organized the celebrated Kneisel Quartet (with Emmanuel Fiedler as 2nd violin; Louis Svecenski, viola; Fritz Giese, cello), which gave performances of high quality in Boston, N.Y., and other American cities, and also in Europe, obtaining world fame before dissolving in 1917. Kneisel was admirable in ensemble playing; his service to the cause of chamber music in America was very great. He was made honorary Mus.Doc. by Yale Univ. (1911) and by Princeton Univ. (1915). In 1903 he resigned his post as concertmaster of the Boston Symph.; from 1905 he taught violin at the Inst. of Musical Art in N.Y. He composed *Grand Concert Etude* for Violin; publ. *Advanced Exercises* for the violin (1900); edited a collection of violin pieces (3 vols., 1900).

Kniese, Julius, German conductor; b. Roda, near Jena, Dec. 21, 1848; d. Dresden, April 22, 1905. He was a pianist and organist; studied with W. Stade in Altenburg, then in Leipzig with Brendel and C. Riedel (1868–70). In 1871–76 he was director of the Singing Academy at Glogau; then conducted the singing society at Rühl and the Wagnerverein at Frankfurt; was music director at Aix (1884–89); from 1882 he was also chorus master for the festival operas at Bayreuth, where he settled in 1889; became director of the Preparatory School for Stage Singers (1890). He wrote an opera, *Jery und Bätely* (Bayreuth, 1890); publ. 4 albums of songs.

Knight, Gladys, black American rhythm-and-blues singer; b. Atlanta, Ga., May 28, 1944. Her parents sang gospel hymns, and she herself joined a church choir as a mere tot; at 8 she won a television contest; a little later she got together a group consisting of her sisters and cousins and named it The Pips. Unusual for a family act, they continued to perform professionally for over 25 years. Their repertoire reflected a religious background, under such titles as *Every Beat of My Heart, Everybody Needs Love, Bless This House, About Love,* and *Touch;* on a more secular side, they scored smash hits with *I Heard It through the Grapevine, Neither One of Us, I've Got to Use My Imagination,* and *On and On.* Their acts were choreographed with precision routines, which gave them a ready audience on the nightclub circuit.

Knight, Joseph Philip, English song composer and clergyman; b. Bradford-on-Avon, July 26, 1812; d. Great Yarmouth, June 2, 1887. He studied organ with Corfe at Bristol. He began to compose songs at the age of 20, and from the very first revealed an exceptional knack of contriving a melody with suitable harmony that was memorable and conveyed a sincere sentiment. While in the U.S. in 1839–41 he brought out his most celebrated song, *Rocked in the Cradle of the Deep;* another successful song was *Why Chime the Bells so Merrily?* After 2 years as vicar and organist at St. Agnes in the Scilly Islands, he married, lived abroad for a time, and then returned to England. Among his songs written in England are: *Venice, Say What Shall My Song Be Tonight?, The Dream, All on the Summer Sea, She Wore a Wreath of Roses, Of What Is the Old Man Thinking?*

Knipper, Lev, important Russian composer; b. Tiflis, Dec. 3, 1898; d. Moscow, July 30, 1974. He studied piano, and took lessons in composition with Glière in Moscow; traveled to Germany and took private lessons with Jarnach in Berlin and Julius Weissmann in Freiburg. Under the influence of western European trends he wrote music in a fairly advanced style of composition, but soon abandoned these experiments and devoted himself to the study of folk music of different nationalities of the Soviet Union; notated folk songs of Turkestan, Kirghiziya, etc.
    WORKS: An extraordinarily prolific composer, he wrote 20 symphs.; the choral finale of his 4th symph. was arranged as a song, which became extremely popular, not only in Russia, but in the U.S. (as *Meadowland*); several ballets and orch. suites

on ethnic motives; overtures; 3 violin concertos (1944, 1965, 1967); 2 cello concertos (1962, 1972); Clarinet Concerto (1966); Oboe Concerto (1967); Bassoon Concerto (1969); 3 string quartets and other chamber music; piano pieces; songs; operas: *The North Wind* (Moscow, March 30, 1930) and *On the Baikal Lake* (1948), making use of Mongol themes.

Knittl, Karl, Bohemian conductor and composer; b. Polna, Oct. 4, 1853; d. Prague, March 17, 1907. He was a pupil of Skuhersky at the Prague School for Organists; later studied singing with Pivoda and conducting with Smetana. In 1877–90, and again in 1897–1901, he conducted the choral society Hlahol in Prague; in 1890 he was appointed prof. at the Prague Cons.; in 1902 became its administrative director. He composed cantatas; choruses; songs; piano pieces; also *Beispiele zur allgemeinen Musiklehre* and *Lehre vom homophonen Satze.*

Knoch, Ernst, German conductor; b. Karlsruhe, Aug. 1, 1875; d. New York, March 20, 1959. He studied at the Karlsruhe Cons., and later took a course in conducting with Felix Mottl, whose assistant he became at the Karlsruhe Opera (1898–1901). He made his professional debut as a conductor in 1901 in Strasbourg, where he remained till 1907; conducted at Bayreuth (1904–7), Essen (1907–9), and Cologne (1909–12). He then made a world tour in the Thomas Quinlan Co. as conductor of Wagner's operas; gave the first Australian performance of *Tristan und Isolde* (Melbourne, July 14, 1912). In 1913–14 he conducted 20 performances of *Parsifal* in Elberfeld. In 1914 he went to America; conducted opera in N.Y., Chicago, and Cleveland; settled in N.Y. as an opera coach and teacher in 1938.

Knorr, Ernst Lothar von, German composer; b. Eitorf, near Cologne, Jan. 2, 1896; d. Heidelberg, Oct. 30, 1973. He studied at the Cologne Cons. with Bram Eldering (violin), Franz Bölsche (composition), and Fritz Steinbach (conducting). After graduation he played violin in various provincial orchs.; in 1925 he moved to Berlin and taught violin at the Hochschule für Musik. During the air raid on Frankfurt in 1944 almost all of his MS works were destroyed; among extant scores are several cantatas; Concerto for 2 Orchs.; Chamber Concerto for Piano, Saxophone, Chorus, and Small Orch.; some choral works. After the war he composed a Wind Quintet (1958); *Diaphonia* for 2 Pianos (1971); some chamber music. He served as director of the Academy of Music in Hannover (1952–61); then was in charge of the Hochschule für Musik in Heidelberg (until 1969). He was principally known for his educational work; his school cantatas are well adapted to performance.

Knorr, Iwan, eminent German music pedagogue and composer; b. Mewe, Jan. 3, 1853; d. Frankfurt, Jan. 22, 1916. His family went to Russia when he was 3 years old, returning to Germany in 1868; he then entered the Leipzig Cons., where he studied piano with Moscheles and theory with Richter and

Reinecke. In 1874 he went back to Russia, where he taught at the Kharkov Cons., and also at the Imperial Inst. for Noble Ladies in St. Petersburg. He finally settled in Frankfurt in 1883 as a teacher at the Hoch Cons.; in 1908, became its director. He had many distinguished pupils, among them Cyril Scott, Pfitzner, Braunfels, and Ernst Toch. He wrote music in a Romantic vein; several of his works are inspired by Ukrainian folk songs, which he had heard in Russia.

WORKS: Operas: *Dunja* (Coblenz, March 23, 1904) and *Durchs Fenster* (Karlsruhe, Oct. 4, 1908); *Ukrainische Liebeslieder* for Vocal Quartet and Piano, op. 6 (1890); *Variationen* (on a Ukrainian folk song), op. 7 (1891); Variations for Piano, Violin, and Cello, op. 1; Piano Quartet, op. 3; Variations for Piano and Cello, op. 4; etc. He wrote a biography of Tchaikovsky for the series Berühmte Musiker (1900) and several pedagogic works: *Aufgaben für den Unterricht in der Harmonielehre* (1903); *Lehrbuch der Fugenkomposition* (1911); *Fugen des Wohltemperirten Klaviers in bildlicher Darstellung* (1912; 2nd ed., 1926); also a number of analyses for Schlesinger's *Musikführer.*

BIBLIOGRAPHY: Moritz Bauer, *Iwan Knorr* (Frankfurt, 1916; contains a complete list of works).

Knorr, Julius, eminent German pianist and pedagogue; b. Leipzig, Sept. 22, 1807; d. there, June 17, 1861. He made his debut as a pianist at the Gewandhaus, in Leipzig, in 1831; was an intimate friend of Schumann and an editor of the *Neue Zeitschrift für Musik* during its first year. Knorr introduced the preparatory technical exercises that have become the groundwork of technical study on the piano.

WRITINGS: *Neue Pianoforteschule in 184 Übungen* (1835; 2nd ed., 1841, as *Die Pianoforteschule der neuesten Zeit; Ein Supplement zu den Werken von Cramer, Czerny, Herz, Hummel, Hünten, Kalkbrenner, Moscheles*); *Das Klavierspiel in 280 Übungen; Materialien für das mechanische Klavierspiel* (1844); *Methodischer Leitfaden für Klavierlehrer* (1849); *Ausführliche Klaviermethode,* in 2 parts: *Methode* (1859) and *Schule der Mechanik* (1860); *Erklärendes Verzeichniss der hauptsächlichsten Musikkunstwörter* (1854).

Knote, Heinrich, German tenor; b. Munich, Nov. 26, 1870; d. Garmisch, Jan. 12, 1953. He studied with Kirchner; was appointed to the staff of the Munich Opera in 1892; from 1904 to 1906, and again in 1907–8, he sang at the Metropolitan Opera in N.Y.; in 1908 he joined the roster of the Hamburg Opera; also sang in Wiesbaden, Berlin, and Würzburg. In 1923–24 he made a North American tour; then returned to Munich, singing in the Bavarian State Opera until 1932. He was particularly noted for his interpretations of Wagnerian roles.

BIBLIOGRAPHY: J.H. Wagenmann, *Der 60-jährige deutsche Meistersänger Heinrich Knote* (Munich, 1930).

Knüpfer, Paul, German bass; b. Halle, June 21, 1865; d. Berlin. Nov. 4, 1920. He studied in Sonders-

hausen; made his debut there in 1885; then sang at the Leipzig Opera (1888–98). In 1898 he joined the Berlin Court (later State) Opera, remaining on its roster until his death; also sang at Bayreuth (1901–12) and Covent Garden in London (1909–14).

Knussen, Oliver, English composer; b. Glasgow, June 12, 1952. Remarkably precocious, he began playing piano as a very small boy and showed unusual diligence also in his studies of music theory, mostly with John Lambert. On April 7, 1968, he made musical headlines when, at the age of 15, he conducted the London Symph. Orch. in the first performance of his own First Symph., written in an eclectic, but astoundingly effective, modern style. He was awarded fellowships for 3 years (1970, 1971, 1973) at Tanglewood, where he studied advanced composition with Gunther Schuller.

WORKS: 3 symphs.: No. 1 (1966–67; London, April 7, 1968); No. 2 for Soprano and Orch. (1970–71; Tanglewood, Aug. 18, 1971); No. 3 (1973–76; revised 1979; first complete perf., London, Sept. 6, 1979); *Pantomime* for Chamber Ensemble (1968; revised 1971); Concerto for Orch. (1968–69; London, Feb. 1, 1970; revised 1974); *Masks* for Solo Flute (1969); *Fire-Capriccio* for Flute and String Trio (1969); *Tributum,* overture (1969); *Vocalise with Songs of Winnie-the-Pooh* for Soprano and 6 Instruments (1970; revised without text, 1974–75); *Choral* for Wind Orch. (1970–72; Boston, Nov. 8, 1973); *Rosary Songs* for Soprano, Clarinet, Viola, and Piano (1972); *Océan de terre* for Soprano and Chamber Ensemble (1972–73; revised 1975); *Puzzle Music,* 4 pieces after puzzle canons by John Lloyd, for Flute, Clarinet, 2 Percussionists, Harp, Guitar or Mandolin, and Celesta (1972–73); *Chiara* for Soprano, Female Chorus, and Small Orch. (1971–75); *Ophelia Dances,* Book I, for Ensemble (1975); *Coursing* for Chamber Ensemble (1979); *Max and the Maximonsters,* a children's opera (Brussels, Nov. 28, 1980).

Knyvett, Charles, Jr., English vocalist and organist, son of **Charles Knyvett, Sr.,** and brother of **William Knyvett;** b. London, 1773; d. there, Nov. 2, 1859. He studied organ with Samuel Webbe; in 1801 he participated in the Vocal Concerts in London; in 1802 he became organist at St. George's; also was active as a teacher. He publ. a *Selection of Psalm Tunes* (1823).

Knyvett, Charles, Sr., English organist and tenor, father of **Charles** and **William Knyvett;** b. Norfolk, Feb. 22, 1752; d. London, Jan. 19, 1822. He was a chorister in London; in 1786, was appointed a Gentleman of the Chapel Royal, and in 1796, an organist there. In 1791–94 he led the Vocal Concerts (with S. Harrison).

Knyvett, William, English singer, conductor, and composer, son of **Charles Knyvett, Sr.,** and brother of **Charles Knyvett, Jr.;** b. London, April 21, 1779; d. Ryde, Isle of Wight, Nov. 17, 1856. He sang alto at the Concerts of Ancient Music; in 1797, became a Gentleman of the Chapel Royal, and in 1802, a composer there. He participated in concerts in London as a singer for many years; also composed a number of glees, of which one, *When the Fair Rose,* won a prize of the Harmonic Society in 1800.

Kobald, Karl, Austrian writer on music; b. Brno, Aug. 28, 1876; d. Vienna, Oct. 12, 1957. He studied at Vienna Univ. with Guido Adler, Hellmesberger, and Hans Richter; also took lessons with Bruckner. In 1918 he became music adviser in the Austrian Ministry of Education; in 1932–38, and again in 1945–46, was president of the State Academy; then retired. WRITINGS: *Alt-Wiener Musikstätten* (1919; 2nd ed., 1923); *Schubert und Schwind* (1920); *Franz Schubert* (1922); *In Memoriam Anton Bruckner* (1924); *Johann Strauss* (1925); *Beethoven* (1927; new eds., 1936, 1946, and 1952); *Franz Schubert und seine Zeit* (1927); *Klassische Musikstätten* (1929); *Joseph Haydn* (1929); *Wo unsterbliche Musik entstand* (1950).

Kobbé, Gustav, American writer on music; b. New York, March 4, 1857; killed in his sailboat by a Navy seaplane maneuvering in the bay near Babylon, Long Island, July 27, 1918. He studied piano and composition with Adolf Hagen in Wiesbaden (1867–72), and with Joseph Mosenthal in N.Y. He attended Columbia College (School of Arts, 1877; School of Law, 1879). He was a frequent contributor, on musical and other subjects, to the daily press and to magazines. WRITINGS: *Wagner's Life and Works* (N.Y., 1890; 2 vols., containing analyses, with the *Leitmotive* of the music dramas); *The Ring of the Nibelung* (1899; part of the preceding, printed separately); *Opera Singers* (1901); a novel, *Signora, A Child of the Opera House* (1902); *Loves of the Great Composers* (1905); *How to Appreciate Music* (1906); *Wagner and His Isolde* (1906); *Famous American Songs* (1906). Shortly before his accidental death, he finished his *Complete Opera Book,* which was publ. posthumously (N.Y., 1919) and proved so successful that 20 printings were issued before 1950; a revised and enlarged ed., *Kobbé's Complete Opera Book,* compiled by the Earl of Harewood (1,246 pages; includes stories of many operas by modern composers), was publ. in 1963 and 1972; in 1976 an ed. appeared as *The New Kobbé's Complete Opera Book.*

Koch, Caspar Petrus, German-American organist and pedagogue; b. Carnap, Nov. 25, 1872; d. Pittsburgh, April 3, 1970. He was taken to the U.S. as a child and was employed as a church organist in Pittsburgh and elsewhere. From 1914 to 1941 he taught organ playing at the Carnegie Inst. of Technology in Pittsburgh. He edited several collections of Bach's organ pieces and composed some organ music.

Koch, Eduard Emil, German scholar and authority on Lutheran church music; b. Schloss Solitude, near Stuttgart, Jan. 20, 1809; d. Stuttgart, April 27, 1871. He became pastor at Gross-Anspach (1837), then at Heilbronn (1847); was superintendent there (1853–64). He wrote the valuable work *Geschichte des Kirchenliedes und Kirchengesanges, insbesondere der deutschen evangelischen Kirche* (1847; 3rd ed. in 8 vols., 1866–77).

Koch, Erland von (full Christian name, **Sigurd Christian Erland**), Swedish composer, son of **Sigurd von Koch;** b. Stockholm, April 26, 1910. He studied music with his father, then at the Stockholm Cons. (1931–35); went to Germany, where he studied composition with Paul Höffer and conducting with Clemens Krauss (1936–38). He returned to Stockholm in 1939. He conducted the Swedish Radio Orch. (1943–45); in 1953 was appointed to the staff of the Royal College of Music. In some of his later works he endeavors to create a curious amalgam of folk motifs with 12-tone rows ("12-tone and folktone"). WORKS: FOR THE STAGE: Children's opera, *Pelle svanslös (Tailless Peter;* 1948; revised 1966); 2 ballets: *Askungen (Cinderella;* 1942; also an orch. suite) and *Samson and Delila* (1963; orch. suite, 1964); music for the radio play *Bjälbojarlen,* after Strindberg (Swedish Radio, Jan. 25, 1968). FOR ORCH.: *Little Suite* for Chamber or String Orch. (1933); 3 piano concertos: No. 1 (1936); No. 2 (1962); No. 3, with Wind Orch. (1970; version with Full Orch., 1972); 2 violin concertos (1937, 1979–80); Concertino for Strings (1938); 4 symphs.: No. 1 (1938); No. 2, *Sinfonia Dalecarlia* (1944); No. 3 (1948); No. 4, *Sinfonia seria* (1952–53; revised 1962); *Nordic Capriccio* (1943); *Rural Suite* for Strings (1945); Viola Concerto (1945; revised 1966); *Concertino pastorale* for Flute and Strings (1947; revised 1963); Sinfonietta (1949); *Triptychon* for Violin and Orch. (1949); *Arkipelag* (1950); *Musica intima* for Strings (1950; revised 1965); Cello Concerto (1951); *Musica malinconica* for Strings (1952); *Concert Music* (1955); Concerto for Small Orch. (1955); the Oxberg trilogy: *Oxberg Variations* (1956), *Lapland Metamorphoses* (1957), and *Dance-Rhapsody* (1957); *Dalecarlia Suite* (1957); Concerto for Saxophone and String Orch. (1958); *12 Scandinavian Dances* (1958–60); *Concerto lirico* for Strings (1959; revised version of 4th String Quartet); *Concerto piccolo* for 2 Saxophones (Soprano and Alto) and Strings (1962); *Fantasia concertante* for Violin and Orch. (1964); the Impulsi trilogy: *Impulsi* (1964), *Echi* (1965), and *Ritmi* (1966); *Arioso e Furioso* for Strings (1967); *Polska svedese* (1968); *Musica concertante* for 8 Winds, Strings, and Percussion (1969); Double Concerto for Flute, Clarinet, and Strings (1971); *A Swede in New York* (1973); Concerto for Oboe and String Orch. (1978); Tuba Concerto (1978); *4 Symphonic Myths* (Stockholm, Oct. 9, 1982); Guitar Concerto (Göteborg, Feb. 3, 1983). CHAMBER MUSIC: 6 string quartets: No. 1 (1934); No. 2 (1944); No. 3, *Musica intima* (1950); No. 4 (1956; revised 1959); No. 5 (1961); No. 6, *Serenata espressiva* (1963); *Larghetto* for Cello or Viola, and Piano (1937; revised 1965); *Berceuse* for Violin and Piano (1953); *Sonatina semplice* for Violin and Piano (1960); *Varianti virtuosi II* for Violin and Piano (1968); *Quattro tempi* for Wind Quintet (1968); *Miniatures* for Saxophone Quartet (1970). VOCAL MUSIC: *Midsommar-dalen (Midsummer Valley)* for Baritone, Chorus, and Orch. (1960–61); *Sångarkväll (Evening Song)* for Baritone, Male Chorus, and Wind Orch. (1972). FOR PIANO: *Rhythmic Bagatelles* (1957); *Intermezzi concertanti* (1963); *Varianti virtuosi* (1965); songs.

Koch, Friedrich E., German composer and teacher; b. Berlin, July 3, 1862; d. there, Jan. 30, 1927. He studied cello with Hausmann and theory with Bargiel; played cello in the Court Orch. in Berlin (1883–91); then taught privately; in 1901 was elected a member of the Academy. As a composer, he cultivated almost exclusively the large forms; his style was somewhat severe in its elevation.

WORKS: Opera, *Die Halliger* (Cologne, 1897); oratorios: *Von den Tageszeiten* and *Die Sündflut;* 2 symphs.; *Deutsche Rhapsodie* for Violin and Orch.; String Trio; Piano Trio; many choral works.

BIBLIOGRAPHY: K. Kämpf, *F.E. Koch* (Leipzig, 1907).

Koch, Heinrich Christoph, German music theorist; b. Rudolstadt, Oct. 10, 1749; d. there, March 19, 1816. He studied with Göpfert at Weimar; was violinist in the orch. at Rudolstadt (1768), then leader of chamber music there (1777). He publ. *Musikalisches Lexikon* (1802); *Versuch einer Anleitung zur Composition* (3 vols., 1782–93); *Handbuch bei dem Studium der Harmonie* (1811); a manual of enharmonic modulation (1812); also contributed articles to periodicals. He also wrote a *Choralbuch* for Wind Band, and cantatas. He started the *Journal der Tonkunst* in 1795, but it was unsuccessful.

Koch, Helmut, German conductor; b. Wuppertal-Barmen, April 5, 1908; d. East Berlin, Jan. 26, 1975. He studied conducting with Scherchen; was for many years leader of workers' choruses; after 1945 was chorus director of the East Berlin Radio; in 1963 became director of the East Berlin Singakademie. He made numerous arrangements of German folk songs for various groups.

Koch, Karl, Austrian organist and composer of sacred music; b. Biberwier, Tyrol, Jan. 29, 1887; d. Innsbruck, Sept. 20, 1971. He studied religion and music at a theological seminary in Brixen (1905–9); took courses in conducting with Max Springer and composition with Joseph Marx at the Academy of Music in Vienna (1920–21). In 1924 he settled in Innsbruck as a choral conductor, retiring in 1967.

WORKS: *Jubilate Deo* for Chorus and Orch. (1916); *Festmesse zu Ehren der Geburt unseres Herren Jesu Christi* for Soloists, Chorus, and Orch. (1916; Bozen, Jan. 6, 1917); *Requiem* in C minor for Chorus and Organ (1916); *Missa "In medio vitae"* for Soloists, Chorus, and Orch. (1925); *Missa "Super flumina Babylonis"* for Soloists, Chorus, and Orch. (1932; Innsbruck, Nov. 20, 1932); *Sinfonie "Aus den Bergen"* (1942; Innsbruck, Feb. 17, 1947); *Missa in honorem Papae Pii X,* in 2 versions (1953); *Psalmkantate,* vocal symph. for Solo, Vocal Quartet, Female Chorus, Mixed Chorus, and Orch. (1958;

Wattens, Austria, Oct. 26, 1958); *Requiem* for Soloists, Chorus, and Orch. (1955–58; Innsbruck, Feb. 20, 1960); *Brixner—Dom—Messe* for Soloists, Boys' Chorus, Mixed Chorus, Organ, and Orch. (1958; Brixen, Sept. 10, 1958); *Hubertus-Messe* for Unison Chorus, and Wind Septet or Organ (1967); String Quartet (1948); 2 piano sonatas; sacred choruses; and much organ music.

WRITINGS: The theoretical works *Harmonielehre* (Vienna, 1948) and *Ergänzungsbuch zur Harmonielehre* (Vienna, 1957).

BIBLIOGRAPHY: Wilhelm Isser, *Karl Koch: Das Bild eines zeitgenössischen Komponisten* (Innsbruck, 1969).

Koch, Sigurd von (full Christian name, **Richard Sigurd Valdemar**), Swedish composer; b. Agnö, near Stockholm, June 28, 1879; d. Stockholm, March 16, 1919. He studied piano in Germany; composed several symph. works, instrumental concertos, and much chamber music; his Violin Sonata has been publ.

Kochan, Günter, East German composer; b. Luckau, Oct. 2, 1930. He studied composition with Boris Blacher, Konrad Friedrich Noetel, and Hermann Wunsch in Berlin-Charlottenburg and then with Hanns Eisler at the Akademie der Künste of the German Democratic Republic in East Berlin (1946–50). In 1950 he became an instructor in music theory at the Hochschule für Musik in East Berlin; in 1965 was elected to the Akademie der Künste. His music is eminently functional, and in it the formal design is paramount; main subjects are stated repeatedly with utmost clarity; the rhythmic formulas are explicit; there is a distinct affinity with the symph. processes used by Eisler; polymodal themes abound within starkly dissonant harmonies.

WORKS: FOR THE STAGE: *Karin Lenz,* opera depicting the tragic conflict between enlightened socialist ideals and ingrained capitalistic habits in the life of a German woman (1968–70). FOR ORCH.: Violin Concerto (1951–52); *Kleine Suite* (1956); Piano Concerto (1958); Sinfonietta (1960); *Fröhliche Ouvertüre* for Chamber Orch. (1960); Concerto for Orch. (1961–62); Flute Concertino (1964); 3 symphs.: No. 1, with Chorus (1963–64); No. 2 (1968); No. 3, with Solo Soprano (1972); *Divertimento,* variations on a theme of C.M. von Weber (1964); *Variationen über eine venezianische Canzonetta* for Piano and Chamber Orch. (1966); *4 Movements* for String Orch. (1966); 2 cello concertos (1967, 1976); *Mendelssohn-Variationen* for Piano and Orch. (1972); Viola Concerto (1974); Concerto for Wind Quintet and 2 String Groups (1975–77); *7 Orchesterstücke* (1976–77). FOR VOICE: *Die Welt ist jung,* cantata (1952); *Ernst Thälmann,* cantata in memory of the leader of the German Communist Party who died in a concentration camp (1959); *3 Shakespeare-Lieder* for Alto, Flute, and Strings (1964); *Asche von Birkenau,* cantata for Alto and Orch. (1965); *Aurora* for Women's Voices, Chorus, and Orch. (1966; a tribute to the sailors of the Russian ship *Aurora,* which bombarded the Winter Palace in Petrograd on the day of the

Soviet Revolution in 1917); *Wir, unaufhaltsam,* "symphonic demonstration" for Baritone, Speaker, Chorus, and Orch. (1970); *Das Testament von Ho Chi-Minh* for Speaker, Chamber Orch., and 9 Solo Instruments (1971); *Die Hände der Genossen,* cantata for Baritone and Orch. (1974); *3 Epitaphe* for Baritone and Instruments (1975); *Das Friedensfest oder Die Teilhabe,* oratorio (1978); choruses; songs. CHAMBER MUSIC: Piano Trio (1953–54); *Divertimento* for Flute, Clarinet, and Bassoon (1956); Cello Sonata (1960); *5 Movements* for String Quartet (1961); *Short String Quartet* (1965); String Quartet (1973–74); *7 Miniaturen* for 4 Tubas (1977). FOR PIANO: *Suite* (1952); *Präludien, Intermezzi und Fugen* (1954); *11 Short Pieces* for 4-hands (1958); *5 Piano Pieces* (1971); *7 Short Piano Pieces* (1971); Sonata (1981).
BIBLIOGRAPHY: Ursula Stürzbecher, *Komponisten in der DDR: 17 Gespräche* (Hildesheim, 1979).

Kochanski, Paul, Polish violinist; b. Odessa, Sept. 14, 1887; d. New York, Jan. 12, 1934. He studied with Mlynarski in Warsaw; in 1901 became concertmaster of the Warsaw Phil.; in 1903 went to Brussels to study with César Thomson; in 1907 was appointed prof. at the Warsaw Cons. From 1916 to 1918 he taught violin at the Petrograd Cons.; then joined the staff of the Cons. of Kiev (1919–20); in 1920 he left Russia, reaching America in 1921; made his American debut with the N.Y. Symph. Orch., Feb. 14, 1921. From 1924 he taught at the Juilliard School. He excelled in the performance of modern works; did a great service in promoting the violin music of Szymanowski; publ. several transcriptions for violin and piano, among them a *Spanish Popular Suite* (after *7 Spanish Popular Songs* of Manuel de Falla).

Köchel, Ludwig von, Austrian musicographer, compiler of the famous Mozart catalogue; b. Stein, near Krems, Jan. 14, 1800; d. Vienna, June 3, 1877. He studied natural sciences and law at the Univ. of Vienna, and attained distinction in botany and mineralogy; music was his hobby; his love for Mozart's art moved him to compile a Mozart catalogue as methodically as he would a descriptive index of minerals; the result of this task of devotion was the monumental *Chronologisch-thematisches Verzeichnis sämmtlicher Tonwerke Wolfgang Amade Mozarts* (Leipzig, 1862; 2nd ed., prepared by Waldersee, 1905; 3rd ed., extensively revised by A. Einstein, who supplemented the "K numbers" used to identify Mozart's works by secondary numbers, 1937; reprinted, with further alterations and corrections and supplement, Ann Arbor, 1947; 6th ed., a major revision, by F. Giegling, A. Weinmann, and G. Sievers, Wiesbaden, 1964; further supplementary material in the *Mozart-Jahrbuch 1971–72,* pp. 342–401, as prepared by P. van Reijen). Köchel himself publ. some supplementary matter in the *Allgemeine Musikalische Zeitung* (1864). His writings on music include further *Über den Umfang der musikalischen Produktivität W.A. Mozarts* (1862),

which preceded the publication of the catalogue; *Die kaiserliche Hofmusikkapelle in Wien von 1543 bis 1867* (1869); and *Johann Josef Fux* (1872); he also edited *83 neuaufgefundene Originalbriefe L. van Beethovens an den Erzherzog Rudolph* (1865).

Kocher, Conrad, German composer; b. Ditzingen, near Stuttgart, Dec. 16, 1786; d. Stuttgart, March 12, 1872. In 1803 he went to St. Petersburg, where he studied piano with Klengel and Berger, and composition with J.H. Müller; traveled in Italy (1819). Returning to Germany in 1820, he settled in Stuttgart and devoted himself to composition; received the honorary degree of Dr.Phil. from Tübingen Univ. in 1827. He wrote 2 operas, an oratorio, etc.; also publ. a piano method; a manual of composition, *Die Tonkunst in der Kirche* (1823); and *Zionsharfe* (ancient and modern chorales).

Kocián, Jaroslav, Czech violinist; b. Ústí nad Orlicí, Feb. 22, 1883; d. Prague, March 9, 1950. He studied violin with Ševčik at the Prague Cons., and also took lessons in composition with Dvořák. After his graduation in 1901 he traveled widely as a concert violinist, almost rivaling the success of his famous compatriot Jan Kubelik. He made 4 American tours; also appeared in Asia and Africa. After 1920 he confined himself mainly to teaching; became a prof. at the Master School of the Prague Cons. in 1929; retired in 1943. He composed several effective violin pieces (2 *Humoresques, Sérénade, Intermezzo pittoresque, Hymne au printemps, Dumka, Berceuse,* etc.).
BIBLIOGRAPHY: A memorial vol., *Jaroslav Kocián: Sborník statí a vzpomínek,* was publ. at Prague in 1953.

Kocsár, Miklós, Hungarian composer; b. Debrecen, Dec. 21, 1933. He studied with Farkas at the Budapest Academy of Music; upon graduation he devoted himself to theater conducting and teaching. In 1973 he won the National Erkel Prize.
WORKS: Cantata, *Hegyi legények (Mountain Lads;* 1957); Horn Concerto (1957); *Serenata* for String Quartet (1959; revised for String Orch., 1971); *Capriccio* for Orch. (1961); *Magányos ének (Lonely Song),* a song cycle for Soprano and Chamber Ensemble (1969); 2 wind quintets (1956, 1959); Piano Sonatina (1956); Violin Sonata (1957); Trio for 2 Trombones and Trumpet (1958); *Movimento* for Violin (1961–62); *Dialoghi* for Bassoon and Piano (1964–65); Variations for Wind Quintet (1968); *Repliche* for Flute, and Cimbalom or Harpsichord (1971); *Improvisazioni* for Piano (1972); Brass Septet (1972); choruses; many songs.

Kocsis, Zoltán, brilliant Hungarian pianist; b. Budapest, May 30, 1952. He studied at the Franz Liszt Academy of Music with Pál Kadosa, Ferenc Rados, and Gyorgy Kurtág, receiving his diploma there in 1973. In 1970 he won the Hungarian Radio Beethoven Competition, which launched him on an international career; in 1971 he made his first tour of the U.S.; played again in the U.S. in 1982. A pianist of extraordinary versatility, he can deliver authentic performances of works ranging from Bach through Beethoven and Rachmaninoff to the avant-garde music of the present day.

Koczalski, Raoul (Armand Georg), Polish pianist; b. Warsaw, Jan. 3, 1884; d. Poznan, Nov. 24, 1948. He was trained by his mother; at the age of 4 he played at a charity concert in Warsaw and was at once proclaimed an "infant phenomenon"; his progress was watched by psychologists, and a detailed biography of him was publ. by B. Vogel when he was only 12. He gave concerts in Vienna (1892), Russia, Paris, and London (1893); made nearly 1,000 public appearances before 1896. His sensational success diminished as he grew out of the prodigy age, but he was appreciated as a mature pianist for his sensitive playing of Chopin. He lived mostly in France, Germany, and Sweden; after World War II he returned to Poland and taught in Posnan; shortly before his death he was appointed to a state teaching post in Warsaw. He was precocious not only as a pianist but also as a composer; wrote some 50 opus numbers before he was 10. His opera *Rymond,* written at the age of 17, was produced at Elberfeld, Oct. 14, 1902; he wrote another opera, *Die Sühne* (Mühlhausen, 1909); many piano pieces.

Koczirz, Adolf, Austrian music scholar; b. Wierowan, Moravia, April 2, 1870; d. Vienna, Feb. 22, 1941. He was a government functionary; studied musicology with Guido Adler in Vienna (Dr.Phil., 1903); edited vols. 37 and 50 (18.ii and 25.ii) of Denkmäler der Tonkunst in Österreich (lute music of the 16th and 17th centuries); contributed many essays on old instrumental music to various publications.

Kodalli, Nevit, Turkish composer; b. Mersin, Jan. 12, 1924. He studied with Necil Kazim Akses at the Ankara Cons., graduating in 1948; then went to Paris, where he took lessons with Honegger. His music preserves the traits of Turkish folk melos, but the harmonic and contrapuntal treatment is in the manner of the French modern school. Among his works are a Symph. (Ankara, May 20, 1950); oratorio, *Ataturk* (Ankara, Nov. 9, 1953); opera, *Gilgamesch* (Ankara, 1962); 2 string quartets (1947, 1966).

Kodály, Zoltán, illustrious Hungarian composer; b. Kecskemét, Dec. 16, 1882; d. Budapest, March 6, 1967. He was brought up in a musical family; received general education at the Archiex Episcopal Grammar School in Nagyszombat; at the same time, he took lessons in piano, violin, viola, and cello; soon began to compose; wrote a Mass at the age of 16. He then enrolled at the Univ. of Budapest, and also studied composition with Hans Koessler at the Budapest Academy of Music. His early works were mostly sacred choral compositions and chamber music; his doctoral thesis, *Strophic Structure in the Hungarian Folk Song* (1906), indicates his growing interest in folk music. He became associat-

ed with Béla Bartók in collecting, organizing, and editing the vast wealth of national folk songs; he also made use of these melodies in his own works. He publ. his findings in the bulletins of the Hungarian Ethnographic Society. In Dec. 1906 he went to Berlin, and in April 1907 proceeded to Paris, where he took some lessons with Widor; in 1907 he was appointed instructor at the Budapest Academy of Music; wrote music criticism for several newspapers in Budapest; also contributed correspondence to the *Revue Musicale,* the *Musical Courier,* and other journals. In 1913 he issued, with Bartók, a detailed paper dealing with the subject of collecting national songs. During World War I he continued to teach and compose, but his activity in collecting and publishing Hungarian folk songs was inevitably curtailed. In 1919 Kodály was appointed assistant director of the Academy of Music in Budapest; for political reasons he was relieved of this post; however, he resumed his teaching in 1922. In 1923 he was commissioned to write a commemorative work in celebration of the half-century of the union of Buda and Pest; for this occasion he wrote *Psalmus Hungaricus,* which proved to be one of his most significant works. The initial performance in Budapest was followed by numerous productions all over Europe, and also in America. Another signal success was the presentation of Kodály's national opera, in a comic style, *Háry János* (1926); an orch. suite from this work is widely played. Two suites of folk dances, arranged in a modern manner, *Dances of Marosszék* and *Dances of Galánta,* won for Kodály a worldwide popularity. His reputation as one of the most significant national composers was firmly established with the repeated performances of these works. During the turbulent events of 1939–45, Kodály remained in Budapest, working on his compilations of folk songs. In 1946–47 he visited the U.S. and conducted concerts of his works. His first wife, Emma, whom he married in 1910, died in 1958; on Dec. 18, 1959, he married Sarolta Péczely, a student (b. 1940). In 1965 he visited the U.S. as a lecturer. Kodály's musical style is not as radical as that of Bartók; he never departs from basic tonality, and his experiments in rhythm do not reach the primitivistic power of Bartók's percussive idiom. Kodály prefers a Romantic treatment of his melodic and harmonic materials; there is also a decided tinge of Impressionism in his orchestration. But there is no mistaking his ability to present nationally colored melorhythms in a pleasing and stimulating manner.

WORKS: FOR THE STAGE: Incidental music, *Notre Dame de Paris* (Budapest, Feb. 1902); *Le Cid* (Budapest, Feb. 1903); *A nagybacsi (The Uncle;* Budapest, Feb. 1904); *Pacsirtaszo (Lark Song;* Budapest, Sept. 14, 1917); singspiel, *Háry János* (Budapest, Oct. 16, 1926; U.S. premiere, N.Y., March 18, 1960; Kodály's most popular work); *Székelyfonó (The Transylvanian Spinning Room),* lyric scenes based on Hungarian folk songs and dances (Budapest, April 24, 1932); singspiel, *Czinka Panna* (Budapest, March 15, 1948); ballet, *Kuruc mese (Kuruc Tale;* 1935; from the music to *Dances of Marosszék* and *Dances of Galánta).*

FOR ORCH.: *Nyári este (Summer Evening),* tone poem (Budapest, Oct. 22, 1906; reorchestrated 1929–30; N.Y. Phil., April 3, 1930, Toscanini conducting); *Hungarian Rondo, on Old Hungarian Soldiers' Songs* for Cello and Orch. (1917; Vienna, Jan. 12, 1918); *Ballet Music* (1925; Budapest, Oct. 16, 1926; originally intended for *Háry János*); orch. suite from *Háry János* (N.Y., Dec. 15, 1927; version for Brass Band, not arranged by Kodály, Barcelona, March 24, 1927); *Theater Overture* (1927; Budapest, Jan. 10, 1928; from *Háry János*); *Dances of Marosszék* (1930; Dresden, Nov. 28, 1930); *Dances of Galánta* (Budapest, Oct. 23, 1933, for the 80th anniversary of the Budapest Phil. Society; Philadelphia, Dec. 11, 1936); *Variations on a Hungarian Folk Song,* known as *Peacock Variations* (1938–39; Amsterdam, Nov. 23, 1939); Concerto for Orch. (1939–40; Chicago Symph., Feb. 6, 1941); *Minuetto serio* (1953; from *Czinka Panna*); Symph. in C (1957–61; Lucerne, Aug. 16, 1961).

CHAMBER MUSIC: Trio for 2 Violins and Viola (1899); *Intermezzo* for String Trio (1905); *Adagio* for Violin or Cello, and Piano (1905); 2 string quartets (1908–9, 1916–18); Cello Sonata (1909); *Duo* for Violin and Cello (1914); Solo Cello Sonata (1915; very popular); *Capriccio* for Solo Cello (1915); *Hungarian Rondo* for Cello and Piano (1917); *Serenade* for 2 Violins and Viola (1919–20); Cello Sonatina (1921–22); *Invitation to the Campfire* for Solo Clarinet (1930); *Epigrams* for Instrument or Voice, and Piano (1954); several transcriptions for Cello or Violin, and Piano, of pieces by J.S. Bach.

FOR VOICE: *Stabat Mater* for Male Chorus a cappella (pre-1900); *Assumpta est* for Chorus and Orch. (1902); *20 Hungarian Folk Songs* for Voice and Piano (with Bartók; 1906); *2 Songs* for Bass and Orch. (1913–16); *Psalmus hungaricus,* based on the 55th Psalm, for Tenor, Chorus, and Orch. (Budapest, Nov. 19, 1923; U.S. premiere, N.Y. Phil., Dec. 19, 1927; his most important work); *Magyar nepzene (Hungarian Folk Music),* 57 arrangements of folk songs for Voice and Piano (publ. in Eng., N.Y., 1960); *Pange lingua* for Chorus and Organ (1929); *Te Deum Budavár* for 4 Soloists, Chorus, and Orch. (for the 250th anniversary of the delivery of Buda from the Turks; perf. in the Budapest Cathedral, Sept. 11, 1936); *Molnár Anna* for Chorus and Chamber Orch. (1942; revised 1959); *Kádár Kata* (Transylvanian folk ballad) for Contralto and Chamber Orch. (1943); *Missa brevis* for Chorus, and Organ or Orch. (1942–44; Budapest, Feb. 11, 1945); *Vértanúk sírjánál (At the Graves of the Martyrs)* for Chorus and Orch. (1945); *Kállai kettös (Double Dances of Kálló)* for Chorus, 3 Clarinets, 2 Cimbaloms, and Strings (1950; Budapest, April 4, 1951); *An Ode: The Music Makers,* after O'Shaughnessy, for Chorus, 2 Trumpets, 3 Trombones, and Strings (1964); *Laudes organi* for Chorus and Organ (1966); numerous songs and choruses for children and music students: *Bicinia hungarica* (1937–42); *333 Reading Exercises* (1943); *441 Melodies,* collected in 4 books, subtitled *Pentatonic Music* (1945–48); etc.; also song collections for general use.

FOR PIANO: *Meditation* (1907); *9 Pieces* (1910); *Marosszék Dances* (1930); *24 Little Canons on the Black Keys* (1945); *Children's Dances* (1946).

He publ. numerous articles in ethnographic and musical publications. He ed. the periodical *Studia Musicologica Academiae Scientiarum Hungaricae;* wrote the book *Die ungarische Volkmusik* (Budapest, 1962). His collected writings were publ. as *Kodály Zoltán: Visszatekintés,* ed. by F. Bónis (Budapest, 1964).

BIBLIOGRAPHY: M.D. Calvocoressi, "Zoltán Kodály," *Monthly Musical Record* (April 1922); A. Toth, "Zoltán Kodály," *Revue Musicale* (Sept.–Oct. 1929); Imre Waldbauer, "Kodály," in Cobbett's *Cyclopedic Survey of Chamber Music* (London, 1930); H. Mersmann, *Kodály,* in *Kammermusik* (vol. IV, pp. 186ff.); E. Haraszti, "Zoltán Kodály et la musique hongroise," *Revue Musicale* (Feb. 1947); *Emlékkönyv Kodály Zoltán* (on the occasion of his 70th birthday; 1953); L. Eösze, *Zoltán Kodály: His Life and Work* (in Eng., Budapest, 1962); Percy M. Young, *Zoltán Kodály* (London, 1964); C. Jolly, "Kodály—A Personal View," *Tempo,* 83 (Winter 1967); H. Stevens, "The Choral Music of Zoltán Kodály," *Musical Quarterly* (April 1968); C. Kokas, "Kodály's Concept of Music Education," *Council for Research in Music Education Bulletin* (Fall 1970); L. Eösze, *Zoltán Kodály: His Life in Pictures* (N.Y., 1971); L. Wheeler and L. Raebeck, *Orff and Kodály Adapted for the Elementary School* (Dubuque, Iowa, 1972). The Kodály Musical Training Inst. in Wellesley, Mass., issues a newsletter.

Koeberg, Frits Ehrhardt Adriaan, Dutch composer; b. The Hague, July 15, 1876; d. there, Nov. 9, 1961. He studied with H. Viotta in the Netherlands and with Xaver Scharwenka in Berlin; returned to The Hague in 1902; taught at the Cons. and conducted the Musica orch. there.

WORKS: Opera, *Bloemenkind* (1917); 3 symphs.; symph. poems: *Zeelandia* (1920) and *Chimères* (1941); *Suite de Lage Landen* for Orch. (1946); *Dances in the Village* for Orch. (1948); *Hollandia* for Band (1933); chamber music; songs.

Koechlin, Charles, notable French composer; b. Paris, Nov. 27, 1867; d. Canadel, Var, Dec. 31, 1950. He studied at the Paris Cons. with Gedalge, Massenet, and Fauré, graduating in 1897. He lived mostly in Paris, where he was active as a composer, teacher, and lecturer; made 3 visits to the U.S. (1918, 1928, 1937), lecturing on French music (in Eng.); contributed to various journals (*Gazette des Beaux Arts, Chronique des Arts,* etc.) and to Lavignac's *Encyclopédie* (valuable and comprehensive essays on modern music). He also participated in modern-music societies, and worked in various social organizations for the promotion of worldwide music culture. In his own compositions he created a style that is unmistakably French in its clarity and subtlety of nuance and dynamics; although highly sympathetic to all innovation, he stopped short of crossing the borders of perceptible tonality and coherent rhythmic patterns; he was a master of orchestration. As a pedagogue, he possessed a clear insight into the problems of musical technique; publ. several manuals of fundamental value: *Traité d'harmonie* (3 vols., 1927–30); *Etude sur les notes de passage* (1922); *Etude sur l'écriture de la fugue d'école* (1933); *Précis des règles du contrepoint* (1927; also in Eng. as *A Summary of the Rules of Counterpoint*); *Traité d'orchestration* (4 vols.); *Théorie de la musique* (1935); also an advanced paper, *Essai sur la musique polytonale et atonale.* A *Traité de polyphonie modale* is in MS. He also publ. monographs on Gabriel Fauré (1927) and Debussy (1927).

WORKS: *Jacob chez Laban*, biblical pastoral (1896–1908; Paris, May 19, 1925); ballets: *La Forêt païenne* (Paris, June 17, 1925) and *L'Ame heureuse* (1947); *La Forêt*, symph. poem (1896–1907); *En mer, la nuit*, symph. poem (1899–1904); *L'Automne*, symph. suite (1896–1909); *Nuit de Walpurgis classique*, symph. poem (1901–7); *Etudes antiques*, symph. suite (1908–14); symph. poems: *Le Printemps, L'Hiver, Nuit de juin, Midi en août* (1910–12); *Suite légendaire* (1915–20); *Rapsodie sur des chansons françaises* (1916); *La Course de printemps*, symph. poem after Kipling's *Jungle Book* (1925–27); *The 7 Stars Symphony*, symph. suite (1933); *Symphonie d'hymnes* (1936); *La Loi de la jungle*, after Kipling (1939); Partita for Chamber Orch. (1945); also 2 symphs. arranged mostly from earlier works; *Ballade* for Piano and Orch. (1919); *20 chansons bretonnes* for Cello and Chamber Orch. (1934); *Offrande musicale sur le nom de B.A.C.H.*, 15 pieces for Organ and Orch. (1942); *Silhouettes comiques*, 12 pieces for Bassoon and Orch. (1943); 3 string quartets; several fugues for String Quartet; *Suite en quatuor* for Flute, Violin, Viola, and Piano; Sonata for 2 Flutes; Piano Quintet; *Divertissement* for 2 Flutes and Bass Flute; Trio for Flute, Clarinet, and Bassoon; Modal Sonatina for Flute and Clarinet; *Primavera* for Flute, Violin, Viola, Cello, and Harp; Septet for Flute, Oboe, English Horn, Clarinet, Bassoon, Horn, and Saxophone; Flute Sonata; Viola Sonata; Oboe Sonata; Violin Sonata; Cello Sonata; Horn Sonata; Bassoon Sonata; 2 clarinet sonatas; several suites of pieces for Unaccompanied Flute; several sets of piano pieces (*Paysages et marines, Les Heures persanes, 12 pastorales, L'Ancienne Maison de campagne, 12 petites pièces très facile*, etc.); organ music; vocal duets, trios, and quartets; several cycles of songs.

BIBLIOGRAPHY: M.D. Calvocoressi, "Charles Koechlin's Instrumental Works," *Music & Letters* (1924); W.H. Mellers, "A Plea for Koechlin," *Music Review* (1942); Pierre Renaudin, *Charles Koechlin* (Paris, 1952); Henri Sauguet, *L'Œuvre de Charles Koechlin* (Paris, 1975).

Koellreutter, Hans Joachim, German composer; b. Freiburg im Breisgau, Sept. 2, 1915. He studied flute, piano, and composition in Berlin and in Geneva. In 1937 he went to Brazil and unfolded an energetic program of performances of modern music. In 1939 he formed in São Paulo the group Música Viva Brasil and also publ. a magazine of the same name. He was a prof. at the Inst. Musical in São Paulo (1942–44) and directed an international course on new music in Teresópolis. In 1952 he founded an orch. in Bahia, which he conducted until 1962; then was in charge of the music programs of the Goethe Inst. in Munich (1963–65); the years 1965–69 he spent in New Delhi, India, where he founded a music school. From 1969 to 1975 he was music instructor and director of performances at the Goethe Inst. in Tokyo; then returned to Brazil. His music follows Classical forms, while the thematic materials are modeled after the 12-tone method of composition; in several of his works he makes use of exotic motives of South America, India, and Japan.

WORKS: *American Psalm* for Chorus and Orch. (1945); *Proletarian Psalm* (1946); *Konzertmusik* for Piano and Chamber Orch. (1946); *Systatica* for Flute, Percussion, and Dancing (1955); *Concretion* for Orch. (1960); *Constructio ad synesin* for Orch. (1962); *8 Haikai* for Voice, Flute, Guitar, Piano, and Percussion (1963); *Indiaⁱ Report* for Voices, Chamber Orch., and a group of Indian Instruments (1969); *Sunyata* for Flute and Instrumental Ensemble, including Indian Percussion Instruments (1969); Concerto for Sitar and Orch. (1969); *Tanka* for Koto (1971). He publ. *Three Lectures on Music* (Mysore, 1968) and *Attitudes of Consciousness in Indian and Western Music* (New Delhi, 1966).

Koemmenich, Louis, German-American conductor; b. Elberfeld, Germany, Oct. 4, 1866; d. New York, Aug. 14, 1922. He studied at Kullak's Academy in Berlin; in 1890 emigrated to the U.S., settling in N.Y., where he became active as a choral conductor and a singing teacher; founded the Oratorio Society of Brooklyn for the production of new works (1898) and the New Choral Society of N.Y., which gave its first concert on April 4, 1918 (Verdi's *Requiem*). He wrote many choruses for men's voices, including *Lockung* and *Wer weiss wo*, which received prizes in 1894 and 1900.

Koenemann, Theodore. See **Keneman, Feodor.**

Koenen, Friedrich, German composer; b. Rheinbach, near Bonn, April 30, 1829; d. Cologne, July 6, 1887. He studied piano and organ with his father, and cello with Biermann; in 1854, was ordained priest; in 1862–63, studied church music at Regensburg with Haberl, Schrems, and Witt; went to Cologne, where he was appointed choirmaster of the Cathedral; also taught music at the Seminary for Priests; in 1869, founded the Cäcilienverein. Among his 58 compositions are 7 masses, 2 church cantatas, a Te Deum, motets, Psalms, organ preludes, and songs.

Koenen, Tilly (Mathilde Caroline), Dutch mezzo-soprano; b. Salatiga, Java, Dec. 25, 1873; d. The Hague, Jan. 4, 1941. She studied piano, on which she became a proficient performer; then took up voice with Cornelia van Zanten. She toured Germany and Austria from 1900 with excellent success; visited America in 1909–10 and in 1915–16. She was particularly impressive in her interpretations of German Romantic songs; also performed some songs by her compatriots.

Koenig, Gottfried Michael, German composer; b. Magdeburg, Oct. 5, 1926. He studied in Braunschweig, Detmold, Cologne, and Bonn. In 1954 he became a member of the studio for electronic music at the Cologne Radio; in 1964 was appointed artistic director of the studios of electronic music at the Univ. of Utrecht. His philosophical attitude toward music is that it should represent the past, present, and future; accordingly he is apt to give abstract and scientific titles to his works, particularly for electronic music, such as *Terminus I* (1963); *Terminus II* (1967); *Funktion Grün* (1968); *Funktion Gelb* (1968); *Funktion Orange* (1968); *Funktion Rot* (1968). He also wrote 2 quintets for Wind Instruments (1959, 1965); String Quartet (1962); piano pieces; publ. a number of papers dealing with the application of serial and aleatory procedures to electronic music.

Koering, René, French composer; b. Andlau, Alsace, May 27, 1940. He studied piano; in 1960 went to Darmstadt, where he absorbed some modernistic notions at a festival for new music. He then began to compose experimentally in every conceivable classical and popular genre. The denouement was his decision to write understandable music with a minimum of feasible modernities.
WORKS: *Triple et trajectoires* for Piano and 2 Orchs. (1963); *Combat T 3 N* for Piano and Orch. (1970); Symph. No. 1 (Royan, March 23, 1974).

Koessler, Hans, German organist and composer; b. Waldeck, Jan. 1, 1853; d. Ansbach, May 23, 1926. He studied with Rheinberger in Munich; then taught at the Dresden Cons.; in 1882, went to Budapest to teach organ and, later, composition at the Academy of Music, remaining on the staff until 1908. In 1918 he retired to Ansbach. In his music he follows the tradition of Brahms; although his technical achievements inspire respect, his works lack any durable quality that would distinguish them from the mass of other competent compositions by German composers of his generation.
WORKS: Opera, *Der Münzenfranz* (Strasbourg, 1903); oratorio, *Triumph der Liebe; Silvesterglocken* for Voices and Orch.; *Hymne an die Schönheit* for Men's Chorus and Orch.; 2 symphs.; Violin Concerto; Cello Concerto; 2 string quartets; String Quintet; String Sextet; Violin Sonata; Cello Sonata; songs.

Koetsier, Jan, Dutch conductor and composer; b. Amsterdam, Aug. 14, 1911. He studied in Berlin at the Stern Cons. (1924–26) and at the Hochschule für Musik there (1927–34); was a conductor in Lübeck and Berlin; returned to the Netherlands and conducted in The Hague (1941–42); was 2nd conductor of the Concertgebouw Orch. in Amsterdam (1942–49), then again conducted in The Hague (1949–50). In 1950 he moved to Germany and became permanent conductor of the Bavarian Radio Symph. Orch. in Munich. In 1966 he became a prof. of the Staatliche Hochschule für Musik in Munich. In his music he explores the modern applications of the Baroque techniques.
WORKS: Opera, *Frans Hals* (1951); *Symphony "Demeter"* (1943); *Variations on a Children's Song* for Orch. (1932; revised 1967); 3 Baroque suites: for Orch., for Violin and String Orch., and for Cello and 12 Woodwinds (all 1935); *Adagietto e Scherzino* for Orch. (1933); *Serenata serena* for String Orch. (1935); Oboe Concertino (1936); Piano Concertino (1936); *Duo concertante* for Flute, Violin, and Orch. (1936); *Vision pastorale* for English Horn and String Orch. (1937); Cello Concerto (1938); *Symphonische Musik* (1939); Viola Concerto (1940); *Valerius Overture* (1942; revised 1966); *Siciliano e Rondino* for 2 Oboes and Orch. (1942); *Music* for 2 String Orchs., 3 Trumpets, 3 Trombones, and Timpani (1943); *Symphonietta* (1943); Divertimento for Orch. (1944); *Music* for 4 Orchs. (1944); 3 symphs.: No. 1 (1945); No. 2 for Chorus and Orch. (1946); No. 3 (1954); *Music* for Chamber Orch. (1948); *Trauermusik* for Flute, Clarinet, and Strings (1954); *Musical Sketch,* fantasia for Piano and Orch. (1956); *De Mann Lot* for Narrator, Baritone, Male Chorus, and Orch. (1940–62); Concerto for Trumpet, Trombone, and Orch. (1965); *Kreisleriana,* concertino for 2 Pianos and Orch. (1965); *Valerius Suite* for Orch. (1966); *Valerius Rhapsody* for Orch. (1967); *Symphonia concertante* for Oboe, Clarinet, Bassoon, Horn, and Strings (1967); *Concertino lirico* for Violin, Cello, and String Orch. (1968); *Homage to Gershwin* for Orch. (1966–69); *Intrada classica* for Wind Orch., Timpani, and Harp (1971); *March of Twins,* scherzo for 2 Solo Percussionists and Orch. (1971); *Hymnus monaciensis* for Orch. (1971); *Müldorfer Serenade* for Orch. (1971); *Concerto capriccioso* for Piano and Orch. (1975); much chamber music, including Quintet for Flute, Oboe, Violin, Viola, and Cello (1932; revised 1964); Septet (1932; revised 1957); Violin Sonatina (1933); 2 divertimentos for Wind Quintet (1937, 1947); *Gesang der Geister über Wassern* for Chorus and 7 Instruments (1939; revised 1973); *Von Gottes und des Menschen Wesen,* 7 madrigals for Chorus and 7 Instruments (1940; revised 1968); *Amsterdam,* chamber cantata for Soprano or Tenor, and 7 Instruments; *Choral-fantasy* for Organ, with ad libitum 3 Trumpets, and 3 Trombones (1955; revised 1974); *Introduction and 8 Etudes* for String Quartet (1956); Octet for 2 Oboes, 2 Clarinets, 2 Horns, and 2 Bassoons (1968); *Bamberger Promenade* for 2 Trumpets and 3 Trombones (1970); *5 Impromptus* for 4 Trombones (1970); sonatinas: for Trumpet, for Trombone, and for Tuba (all 1970); Trio for Alto Flute, Viola da Gamba, and Harpsichord (1971); *5 Miniatures* for 4 Horns (1971); Sonatina for Trumpet and Organ (1971; revised 1974); Sonata for Cello and Harp (1972); *Colloquy* for 12 Horns (1972); Horn Sonatina (1972); Brass Quintet (1974); piano and organ pieces.

Koffler, Jósef, Polish composer; b. Stryj, Nov. 28, 1896; killed, with his wife and child, in Wieliczka, near Cracow, during a street roundup of Jews in 1943. He was a pupil of Schoenberg and Guido Adler; graduated from the Univ. of Vienna in 1923; then went to Lwow, where he taught at the Cons., edited the Polish monthly review *Orchestra,* and contributed to other music magazines. He was the first Polish composer to use the method of composition with 12 tones according to Schoenberg's principles; his *15 Variations* for String Orch. (Amsterdam Festival, June 9, 1933) are derived from a 12-tone row. He composed 3 symphs.; his 3rd Symph. was performed at the London Festival on June 17, 1938; other works are String Trio (Oxford Festival, July 23, 1931); Divertimento for Oboe, Clarinet, and Bassoon; String Quartet; *40 Polish Folk Songs* for Piano; *Quasi una sonata;* a cycle of piano pieces; *Love Cantata; 4 Poems* for Voice and Piano.

Kofler, Leo, Austrian organist and singing teacher; b. Brixen, March 13, 1837; d. New Orleans, Nov. 29, 1908. He studied at the Stern Cons. in Berlin; in 1866, came to America, and held various positions as organist in St. Louis, Cincinnati, Brooklyn, and N.Y. He publ. *The Act of Breathing as the Basis of Tone Production* (7th ed., N.Y., 1897) and *Take Care of Your Voice, or, The Golden Rule of Health;* also edited *Selected Hymn-tunes and Hymn-anthems.*

Kogan, Leonid, Soviet virtuoso of the violin; b. Dnepropetrovsk, Nov. 14, 1924; d. on the train, at the Mytishcha railroad station on his way to a concert engagement, Dec. 17, 1982. His father was a photographer who played the violin; when Kogan was 10 years old the family moved to Moscow, and he became a pupil of Abram Yampolsky at the Moscow Cons., graduating in 1948. He was obviously a *wunderkind,* but was prudently spared harmful exploitation. In 1947 he won a prize in Prague at the Youth Festival. In 1951 he went to Brussels to take part in the competition sponsored by the Belgian Queen, and received first prize. His career was instantly assured; he played recitals in Europe to unanimous acclaim. He made an auspicious American debut in 1958, playing the Brahms Violin Concerto with the Boston Symph. In 1965 he received the Lenin Prize. In 1952 he joined the faculty of the Moscow Cons.; was named prof. in 1963 and head of the violin dept. in 1969. his playing exemplified the finest qualities of the Russian School: an emotionally romantic élan and melodious filigree of technical detail. In addition to the standard repertoire, in which he excelled, he also played modern violin works, particularly those by Soviet composers. He was married to Elizabeth Gilels, sister of the Soviet pianist Emil Gilels, who was herself an accomplished violinist. Following the violinistic genetic code, their 2 children were also musical: a girl played the piano, and a boy, **Pavel Kogan** (b. Moscow, June 6, 1952), was so good on the violin that in 1970 he won the Sibelius contest in Finland. On Oct. 16, 1975, Pavel Kogan was soloist with the Philadelphia Orch. The family shunned politics, and Leonid Kogan resolutely declined to participate in any protests, domestic or foreign, against the presumed anti-Semitism in Russian politics, even though he himself was patently Jewish.
   BIBLIOGRAPHY: M. Zazovsky, *Leonid Kogan* (Moscow, 1956); David Ewen, *Musicians since 1900*

(N.Y., 1976).

Kogel, Gustav Friedrich, German conductor; b. Leipzig, Jan. 16, 1849; d. Frankfurt, Nov. 13, 1921. He studied at the Leipzig Cons.; was editor for C.F. Peters (1870–74); then was active as a conductor in various provincial theaters; conducted the Berlin Phil. in 1888; was conductor of the Museum Concerts in Frankfurt from 1891 till 1903; also filled engagements as a guest conductor in Russia, Spain, etc.; was guest conductor at the N.Y. Phil. in 1906. He edited full scores and piano scores of several operas; wrote piano pieces.

Köhler, Ernesto, Italian flutist; b. Modena, Dec. 4, 1849; d. St. Petersburg, May 17, 1907. He studied flute with his father; became first flutist of the court orch. at Modena, then at the Karltheater in Vienna; in 1871, became first flutist of the Imperial Orch. in St. Petersburg. He wrote numerous compositions for the flute; also an opera, *Ben Achmed,* and several ballets.

Köhler, Ernst, German organist and pianist; b. Langenbielau, May 28, 1799; d. Breslau, May 26, 1847. He was first organist of the Elisabethkirche in Breslau from 1827 until his death. He wrote 2 symphs., 9 overtures, 12 church cantatas, 12 large vocal works with orch., organ works, and piano pieces.

Kohler, Franz, American violinist and conductor; b. Clinton, Iowa, Feb. 20, 1877; d. Erie, Pa., Dec. 22, 1918. He studied with Karl Halir (violin) in Weimar and Berlin; returning to America in 1898, he joined the Pittsburgh Symph. Orch. as a violinist; was concertmaster briefly in 1910; in 1911–13 taught violin at Oberlin College; from 1913 till his death, conducted the Erie Symph. Orch.

Köhler, Louis, German composer of celebrated piano studies; b. Braunschweig, Sept. 5, 1820; d. Königsberg, Feb. 16, 1886. He studied piano in Braunschweig with Sonnemann; then took courses in composition in Vienna (1839–43) with Sechter and Seyfried; also studied piano there with Bocklet. After a season of theater conducting, he settled in Königsberg (1847) and established there a successful school for piano playing. He wrote 3 operas, a ballet, a Symph., overtures, cantatas, and other works, but he is remembered exclusively for his albums of piano studies, which have been adopted in music schools all over the world; next to Czerny, he is the most popular purveyor of didactic piano literature; it must be observed that while his studies are of great instructive value, they are also worthwhile from a purely musical standpoint. His chief work, in which he laid the foundation of methodical piano pedagogy, is *Systematische Lehrmethode für Klavierspiel und Musik,* in 2 vols.: I. *Die Mechanik als Grundlage der Technik* (1856; 3rd ed., revised by Riemann, 1888) and II. *Tonschriftwesen, Harmonik, Metrik* (1858); other publications are *Führer durch den Klavierunterricht* (6th ed., 1879); *Der*

Klavierfingersatz (1862); *Der Klavierunterricht, oder Studien, Erfahrungen und Ratschläge* (4th ed., 1877); *Die neue Richtung in der Musik* (1864); *Leichtfassliche Harmonie- und Generalbasslehre* (a valuable manual of harmony; 3rd ed., 1880); *Brahms und seine Stellung in der neueren Klavierliteratur* (1880); *Der Klavierpedalung* (1882); *Allgemeine Musiklehre* (1883).

Kohn, Karl, American pianist and composer; b. Vienna, Aug. 1, 1926. After the Nazi absorption of Austria in 1938, his family emigrated to the U.S.; he studied piano with Carl V. Werschinger and conducting with Prüwer at N.Y. College of Music (1940–44); then took courses in music theory and composition at Harvard Univ. with Walter Piston, Irving Fine, and Randall Thompson (B.A., 1950; M.A., 1955). In 1956 he traveled to Finland on a Fulbright grant; upon return to the U.S. he taught piano and music theory at Pomona College in Claremont, Calif., and at the Claremont Graduate School of Music. He also taught several summers at the Berkshire Music Center at Tanglewood, Mass.; held a Guggenheim fellowship in 1961–62; in 1975 was awarded a grant by the National Endowment for the Arts. As a pianist, he specializes in modern music, deploying a virtuoso technique in tackling the most formidable piano works; also gave duo-piano concerts with his wife, **Margaret Kohn.** In his compositions he tends toward prudential serialism but also explores diatonic modalities, applying the power of pervicacious iteration of pandiatonic chordal complexes; he successfully adapts medieval polyphonic devices to contemporary usages, such as the integration of the precomposed thematic fragments, a technique anciently known as "centone" (literally, "patchwork quilt"). He makes use of topological rearrangements of classical pieces, as in *Son of Prophet Bird,* dislocated and paraphrased from Schumann's *Bird as a Prophet.* WORKS: FOR ORCH.: *Sinfonia concertante* for Piano and Orch. (1951); *Overture* for String Orch. (Helsinki, April 17, 1956); *Castles and Kings,* symph. suite for children (1958); *3 Scenes* for Orch. (1958–60); *Concerto mutabile* for Piano and Orch. (1962); *Interlude* for Orch. (1964); *Episodes* for Piano and Orch. (1966); *Interlude I* for Flute and String Orch. (1969); *Interlude II* for Piano and String Orch. (1969); *Esdras* for Flute, Piano, Chorus, and Orch. (1969–70); *Centone per orchestra* (1973; Claremont Music Festival, June 27, 1973, composer conducting); *Innocent Psaltery,* "colonial music" for Orch. (1976); *The Prophet Bird I* (a metamorphosis of Schumann's *Bird as a Prophet;* 1976); *The Prophet Bird II* for Piano and Chamber Orch., in 3 movements (Los Angeles, March 9, 1982, composer conducting; Margaret Kohn, soloist). CHAMBER MUSIC: *Fanfare* for Brass and Percussion (1952); *Motets* for 8 Horns (1953); *Song* for Violin or Clarinet, and Piano (1956); *Concert Music* for 12 Wind Instruments (1956); *Quartet* for Horns (1957); *3 Pieces* for Flute and Piano (1958); Divertimento for Flute, Oboe, Clarinet, and Bassoon (1959); *Capriccio* for Flute, Clarinet, Cello, Harp, and Piano (1962); Sere-

nade for Wind Quintet and Piano (1962); *Little Suite* for Wind Quintet (1963); *Kaleidoscope* for String Quartet (1964); *Sonata da camera* for Alto Flute, Clarinet, and Piano (1964); *Encounters I* for Flute, Piccolo, and Piano (1965); *Encounters II* for Horn and Piano (1967); *Introduction and Parodies* for Clarinet, Horn, Bassoon, String Quartet, and Piano (1967); *4 Musical Pictures* for Violin and Piano (1967); *Rhapsodies* for Marimba, Vibraphone, and Percussion (1968); *Impromptu* for 8 Wind Instruments (1969); *Reflections* for Clarinet and Piano (1970); Variations for Horn and Piano (1971); *Souvenirs* for Violin and Piano (1971); *Encounters III* for Violin and Piano (1971); Trio for Violin, Horn, and Piano (1972); *Encounters IV* for Oboe and Piano (1972); *Romanza* for Flute and Piano (1972); *Encounters V* for Bassoon and Piano (1973); *3 Duets* for 2 Violins (1973); *Paronyms* for Flutes and Piano (1974); Concerto for Horn and Piano (1974); *Son of Prophet Bird* for Harp Solo (1977). FOR PIANO SOLO: *3 Rhapsodies* (1960, 1971, 1977); *5 Bagatelles* (1961); *Partita* (1963); *Recreations* for Piano, 4-hands (1968); *Bits and Pieces* (1973); sacred choruses; songs.

Kohoutek, Ctirad, Czech composer; b. Zábřeh, March 18, 1929. He studied composition with Petrželka at the Brno Cons., then with Kvapil at the Janáček Academy of Music there (1949–53); joined the Academy's faculty after graduation. His music follows the traditions of Central European modernism, well contained within classical forms but diversified by serial procedures and glamorized by electronic sound. WORKS: Oboe Sonatina (1950); *Ukolébavka černošské mámy (The Lullaby of the Negro Mother),* cantata (1952); *Munich,* symph. poem (1953); *Festival Overture* (1954); Suite for Viola and Piano (1957); Violin Concerto (1958); Suite for Wind Quintet (1959); String Quartet (1959); *Velký přelom (The Great Revolution),* symph. (1960); *Ballads from the Rebellion,* 2 cantatas (1960); *Symphonic Dances* (1961); *Pátý živel (The 5th Element),* melodrama for Narrator and Orch. (1962); Symphonietta (1963); *Rapsodia eroica* for Organ (1963); Concertino for Cello and Chamber Orch. (1964); *Preludes* for Chamber Orch. (1965); *Inventions* for Piano (1965); *Miniatures* for 4 Horns (1965; version for String Orch., 1966); *Memento 1967,* concerto for Percussion and Winds (1966); *Panychida letní noci (Panychide of the Summer Night),* music for 2 sound layers of 2 Violas, 2 Pianos, Percussion, and Tape (1968); *Teatro del mondo,* symph. rotation in 4 movements (1968–69); *Loutkové scény (Puppet Scenes),* piano pieces for children (1969); *Pantheon,* sound picture for Orch. (1970); *Sluneční zaře (Sunshine),* symph. poem (1975); several children's choruses. He publ. 2 books: *Novodobé skladebné teorie západoevropské hudby (Modern Composing Theories of West European Music;* Prague, 1962; 2nd ed., revised and retitled *Novodobé skladebné směry v hudbě [Modern Composing Trends in Music],* Prague, 1965) and *Projektová hudební kompozice (Project Musical Composition;* Brno, 1968).

Kohs, Ellis Bonoff, notable American composer; b. Chicago, May 12, 1916. His mother was a good violinist, and when Kohs learned to play the piano he often accompanied her at home. In 1928 the family moved from San Francisco (following his early musical studies there at the Cons.) to Brooklyn, and Kohs studied with Adelaide Belser at the Inst. of Musical Art in N.Y. In 1933 he returned to Chicago and enrolled at the Univ. of Chicago as a student in composition with Carl Bricken (M.A., 1938). Upon graduation he proceeded to N.Y., where he entered the Juilliard School of Music, studying composition with Bernard Wagenaar and musical pedagogy with Olga Samaroff Stokowski. He continued his musical studies at Harvard Univ., with Walter Piston in composition and with Hugo Leichtentritt and Willi Apel in musicology (1939–41); he also attended a seminar given by Stravinsky at Harvard in 1940–41. During the summer of 1940 he was a lecturer in music at the Univ. of Wisconsin in Madison. From 1941 to 1946 he served in the U.S. Army as a chaplain's assistant and organist, and in the U.S. Air Force as a bandleader. After his discharge from service, he engaged in pedagogical work and in active composition; his teaching posts included Wesleyan Univ. (1946–48), the Kansas City Cons. of Music (summers of 1946 and 1947), the College of the Pacific at Stockton, Calif. (1948–50), Stanford Univ. (summer of 1950), and, from 1950, the Univ. of Southern Calif., Los Angeles. In his music he pursues the aim of classical clarity; he is particularly adept in variation structures; the rhythmic patterns in his works are often asymmetrical, and the contrapuntal fabric highly dissonant; in some of his works he makes use of a unifying 12-tone row, subjecting it to ingenious metamorphoses, as revealed in his opera *Amerika,* after the novel by Franz Kafka. A humorous streak is shown in his choral piece *The Automatic Pistol,* to words from the U.S. Army weapons manual, which he composed during his military service. As a pedagogue, he wrote there useful manuals: *Music Theory, a Syllabus for Teacher and Student* (2 vols., N.Y. 1961); *Musical Form: Studies in Analysis and Synthesis* (Boston, 1976); and *Musical Composition: Projects in Ways and Means* (Metuchen, N.J., 1980). WORKS: FOR THE STAGE: Opera, *Amerika,* after Kafka (1969; abridged concert version produced in Los Angeles, May 19, 1970); incidental music to Shakespeare's *Macbeth* (1947). FOR ORCH.: Concerto for Orch. (Berkeley, Calif., Aug. 9, 1942); *Passacaglia* for Organ and String Orch. (1946); *Legend* for Oboe and String Orch. (Columbus, Ohio, Feb. 27, 1947); Cello Concerto (1947); Chamber Concerto for Viola and String Nonet (1949); Symph. No. 1 (1950); Symph. No. 2, with Chorus (Univ. of Illinois, Urbana, April 13, 1957); Violin Concerto (1980; Los Angeles, April 24, 1981). CHAMBER MUSIC: String Quartet (1942); *Night Watch* for Flute, Horn, and Timpani (1943); Sonatina for Bassoon and Piano (1944); *Short Concert* for String Quartet (1948); Clarinet Sonata (1951); *Variations* for Recorder (1956); Brass Trio (1957); *Studies in Variation* in 4 parts: for Woodwind Quintet, for Piano Quartet, for Piano Solo, for Violin Solo (1962); Sonata for Snare Drum and Piano (1966); *Duo* for Violin and Cello, after Kafka's *Amerika* (1971); Concerto for Percussion Quartet (1978). FOR VOICE: *The Automatic Pistol* for Male Voices a cappella (Washington, D.C., Army Music Chorus, Sept. 5, 1943); *25th Psalm* (1947); *Fatal Interview,* song cycle (text by Edna St. Vincent Millay) 1951); *Lord of the Ascendant* (based on the Gilgamesh legend) for Chorus, Soloists, Dancers, and Orch. (1956); *3 Songs* from the Navajo, for Mixed Chorus (1957); *3 Greek Choruses* for Women's Chorus (1957); *23rd Psalm* for Soloists and Chorus a cappella (1957); *Men* for Narrator and 3 Percussionists, text by Gertrude Stein (1982; Los Angeles, March 15, 1984); *Subject Cases* for Narrator and Percussionist, text by Gertrude Stein (Los Angeles, Feb. 14, 1983). FOR PIANO: *Etude in Memory of Bartók* (1946); *Variations* (1946); *Variations on L'Homme armé* (1947); *Toccata* for Harpsichord or Piano (1948); *Fantasy on La, Sol, Fa, Re, Mi* (1949); *10 Inventions* (1950). FOR ORGAN: *Capriccio* (1948); 3 Chorale-Variations on Hebrew Hymns (1952).

BIBLIOGRAPHY: Autobiographical sketch, "Thoughts from the Workbench," in *American Composers Alliance Bulletin* (Autumn 1956); *Composers of the Americas,* vol. 15 (Washington, D.C., 1969); David Ewen, *American Composers* (N.Y., 1982).

Kohut, Adolf, German writer on music; b. Mindszent, Hungary, Nov. 10, 1847; d. Berlin, Sept. 21, 1917. He publ. *Moses Mendelssohn und seine Familie* (1886); *Weber-Gedenkbuch* (1887); *Friedrich Wieck* (1888); *Das Dresdener Hoftheater in der Gegenwart* (1888); *Die grössten deutschen Soubretten im 19. Jahrhundert* (1890); *Joseph Joachim* (1891); *Bilder aus der Musikwelt* (1891); *Aus dem Zauberlande Polyhymnias* (1892); *Dur- und Mollakkorde* (1894); *Schiller in seinen Beziehungen zur Musik* (1905); *Die Gesangsköniginnen in den letzten drei Jahrhunderten* (1906); also wrote biographies of Auber, Meyerbeer, and Rossini for Reclam's *Universalbibliothek.*

Koizumi, Kazuhiro, Japanese conductor; b. Kyoto, Oct. 16, 1949. He studied at the Tokyo Univ. of the Arts, and later at the Hochschule für Musik in Berlin. In 1970 he won first prize in a conducting competition in Japan and was named an assistant conductor to Ozawa and the Japan Phil. Orch. In 1973 he won first prize in the Karajan International Conductors' Competition and in 1975 was appointed music director of the New Japan Phil. Orch. He also filled many engagements as a guest conductor in Europe and America.

Kojian, Varujan, violinist and conductor; b. Beirut, Lebanon, of Armenian parentage, March 12, 1945. He was taken to France as a child and studied violin at the Paris Cons.; then went to the U.S. and took violin lessons with Ivan Galamian and Jascha Heifetz. He subsequently became assistant concertmaster of the Los Angeles Phil., and also served for a while as assistant conductor. Then he went to Vienna for additional conducting studies with Hans

Swarowsky. In 1972 he won first prize in the conducting competition in Sorrento, Italy; from 1973 to 1976 he acted as principal guest conductor with the Seattle Symph. From 1980 to 1983 he served as music director of the Utah Symph. Orch. in Salt Lake City.

Kókai, Rezső, Hungarian composer; b. Budapest, Jan. 15, 1906; d. there, March 6, 1962. He studied composition with János Koessler and piano with Emanuel Hegyi at the Budapest Academy (1919–26); he received his doctorate from the Univ. of Freiburg (1933) with a dissertation on Liszt's early piano music. In 1929 he joined the faculty of the National Academy of Music in Budapest.
WORKS: Oratorio, *István király* (*King Stephen;* 1942); ballet, *A rossz feleség* (*The Bad Wife;* 1946); *2 Rondos* for Small Orch. (1947); *Recruiting Suite* for Orch. (1950); Violin Concerto (1952); *Dances from Szék* for Orch. (1952); *Concerto all'Ungherese* for Orch. (1957); *Hungarian Dance* for Youth Orch. (1960); *Toccata* for Piano (1927); Serenade for String Trio (1949–50); 2-piano Sonata (1949); *4 Improvisations* for Piano (1949–50); Quartet for Clarinet and String Trio (1952); *Capriccio* for Violin and Piano (1952); music for radio plays and films; songs. He wrote 2 books, *Methodical Aesthetics of Music* (Budapest, 1938) and *The Music of Our Century* (Budapest, 1961).

Kokkonen, Joonas, prominent Finnish composer; b. Iisalmi, Nov. 13, 1921. He studied composition with Selim Palmgren at the Sibelius Academy in Helsinki, and later taught there. In 1963 he was elected to membership of the Finnish Academy; in 1965 he became chairman of the Union of Finnish Composers. In 1973 he was awarded the Sibelius Prize. Like all composers of his generation in Finland, he experienced the inevitable influence of Sibelius, but he soon abandoned the characteristic diatonic modalities of Finnish folk music and formed an individual style of composition marked by a curiously anfractuous chromaticism and involuted counterpoint, freely dissonant but hewing to clearly identifiable tonal centers. For a period he dabbled in dodecaphonic writing, but found its doctrinaire discipline uncongenial. He derives his techniques from the contrapuntal procedures of Bach and, among the moderns, from Bartók. Thematically, he adopts an objective method of formal structure, in which a free succession of formative motives determines the content.
WORKS: Opera, *Viimeiset Kiusaukset (The Last Temptations),* on the subject of the life of a 19th-century Finnish evangelist (Helsinki, Sept. 2, 1975); 5 symphs.: No. 1 (1960); No. 2 (1961); No. 3 (Helsinki, Sept. 12, 1967); No. 4 (1970; Helsinki, Nov. 7, 1971); No. 5 (1982; Helsinki, Jan. 12, 1983); *Lintujen Tuonela (The Hades of the Birds)* for Mezzo-soprano and Orch. (1959); *Sinfonia da camera* for String Orch. (1962); *Opus sonorum* for Orch. (1964); Cello Concerto (1969); *Inauguratio,* suite for Orch. (1971); *... durch einen Spiegel* for 12 Strings and Harpsichord (1977); *Requiem* (1981); Piano Trio (1948);

Piano Quintet (1953); Duo for Violin and Piano (1955); 3 string quartets (1959, 1966, 1976); Wind Quintet (1973); *Improvvisazione* for Violin and Piano (1982); several sacred choruses; also piano pieces and songs.

Kolar, Victor, American conductor; b. (of Bohemian parentage) Budapest, Feb. 12, 1888; d. Detroit, June 16, 1957. He studied violin with Ševčik and composition with Dvořák at the Prague Cons. In 1900 he emigrated to America; played violin in the Pittsburgh Orch. (1905–8) and in the N.Y. Symph. Orch. (1908–20). In 1920 he became associate conductor at the Detroit Symph. Orch., and later was appointed principal conductor there, until 1941. As assistant conductor of the N.Y. Symph. Orch. he brought out several of his own works, among them his Symph. (Jan. 28, 1916); his other works were *Hiawatha,* a symph. poem (Pittsburgh, Jan. 31, 1908); *3 Humoresques* for Violin and Piano; numerous songs; 7 marches.

Kolb, Barbara, talented American composer; b. Hartford, Conn., Feb. 10, 1939. She was of a musical family; her father was a song composer. She studied the visual arts; also took up clarinet. She enrolled at the Hartt College of Music in Hartford, where she studied composition with Arnold Franchetti (B.A., 1961; M.M., 1964). During the summers of 1960, 1964, and 1968 she attended the classes of Lukas Foss and Gunther Schuller at the Berkshire Music Center in Tanglewood. In 1969 she became the first American woman to win the U.S. Prix de Rome in composition, and spent the years 1969–71 at the American Academy in Rome. In 1971 she received a Guggenheim fellowship; in 1976 she was awarded a 2nd Guggenheim fellowship; she was also the recipient of the award by the National Inst. of Arts and Letters; in 1975 and 1977 she was given the Creative Artists Public Service awards. From 1973 to 1975 she was on the music faculty at Brooklyn College; she further received grants from the National Endowment for the Arts in 1972, 1974, 1977, and 1979. In her music she builds a sui generis melodic, harmonic, and rhythmic environment, making use of variegated techniques; a factor in several of her works is a persistent iteration and emphatic reiteration of thematic materials, creating an aura of quaquaversal melorhythmic rotation invariably reverting to the thematic exordium, while constantly changing the timbres. The most remarkable of her compositions in this manner of flowing recurrence is *Soundings,* of which she made 3 different versions.
WORKS: *Rebuttal* for 2 Clarinets (1964); *Chansons bas* for Voice, Harp, and Percussion (1965); *Fragments* for Flute and Piano (1966); *Three Place Settings* for Narrator, Clarinet, Violin, Double Bass, and Percussion (1968); *Trobar clus* for 13 Instruments, representing wordlessly the ancient Provençal verse form of the rondeau type (Tanglewood, Aug. 29, 1970); *Soundings* for 11 Instruments and Electronic Tape; her most successful work (Lincoln Center, N.Y., Oct. 27, 1972; revised for Full Orch.

and perf. by the N.Y. Phil., Pierre Boulez conducting, Dec. 11, 1975; a 2nd revision made in 1977 was first perf. by the Boston Symph. Orch., Seiji Ozawa conducting, Feb. 16, 1978; also conducted by him during the tour of the Boston Symph. in Japan in March 1978, with the tape replaced by a supernumerary orch. group); *Frailties* for Tenor, 4-channel Electronic Tape, and Orch. (1972); *Spring, River, Flowers, Moon, Night* for 2 Pianos and Electronic Tape (1974); *Looking for Claudio* for Guitar and Electronic Tape (1975); *Appello* for Piano Solo (1976); *Musique pour un vernissage* for Flute, Violin, Viola, and Guitar, originally intended as "furniture music" or "music to walk by" à la Satie, to be played at the opening of a Paris art exhibition (1977; first perf. as such in Paris, composer conducting, then arranged as a concert piece and presented at the Kennedy Center for the Performing Arts in Washington, D.C., Feb. 3, 1979, Leon Fleisher conducting); *Songs before an Adieu* for Flute, Guitar, and Voice (1977–79); *Chromatic Fantasy* for Narrator and Chamber Ensemble (1979); *3 Lullabies* for Solo Guitar (1980); *Related Characters* for Viola and Piano (1980); *The Point that Divides the Wind* for Organ and 4 Percussionists (1981).

BIBLIOGRAPHY: David Ewen, *American Composers* (N.Y., 1982).

Kolbe, Oskar, German music theorist; b. Berlin, Aug. 10, 1836; d. there, Jan. 2, 1878. He studied with Grell and Löschhorn in Berlin; taught theory at the Stern Cons. (1859–75). He publ. a *Kurzgefasstes Handbuch der Generalbasslehre* (1862) and a *Handbuch der Harmonielehre* (1873); also wrote an oratorio, *Johannes der Täufer;* an overture to *Wallensteins Tod;* piano music; songs.

Kolberg, Oskar, Polish composer and song collector; b. Przysucha, near Radom, Feb. 22, 1814; d. Cracow, June 3, 1890. He studied at the Warsaw Cons. with Chopin's teacher Elsner, then in Berlin; returned to Warsaw in 1840. He devoted a major part of his life to traveling in the country in order to collect folk songs, while earning his living as an employee of the Warsaw-Vienna Railroad. He started a series of publications on Polish folklore, including folk music, in 1860; 23 vols. were issued before his death, and publication of the materials assembled by him was continued later by the Polish Academy. He also wrote a number of Polish dances for piano, and composed an opera, *Krol Pasterzy* (*The Shepherd's Inn;* Warsaw, March 2, 1859).

Kolchinskaya, Camilla, Russian conductor; b. Moscow, 1940. She studied violin, and was accepted at the age of 6 at a Moscow school for musically gifted children, where she conducted choral rehearsals. She played the violin in the orch. of Moscow film studios; then ventured to compete for the post of conductor of the orch. of the city of Yaroslavl; she won the contest and conducted a season of classical and modern programs there. She also was guest conductor of orchs. in Siberia; in 1975, after 8 years of conducting in provincial cities, she re-turned to Moscow, where she became guest conductor of the U.S.S.R. National Symph. Orch. In 1976 she applied for an exit visa to Israel; conducted her first concert there with the Israel Phil. in Tel Aviv on Jan. 12, 1977.

Kolessa, Filaret, Ukrainian ethnomusicologist; b. Chodowitschi, near Lwow, July 17, 1871; d. Lwow, March 3, 1947. He studied in Vienna with Bruckner (composition) and with Guido Adler (musicology); in 1898 was appointed to the faculty of the state high school in Lwow; in 1939 he became a prof. at Lwow Univ. and director of the Ethnographic Museum there. He publ. a number of important papers dealing with Ukrainian folk songs: *Rhythmics of Ukrainian Folk Songs* (1906–7); *Melodies of Ukrainian Historical Dumas* (1910–13; reprint, Kiev, 1969); *Genesis of Ukrainian Historical Dumas* (1921); *Folk Songs of the South Carpathians* (1923); *Recitative Forms in Ukrainian Folk Poetry* (1927); *Folk Songs of Galician Lemko Region* (1929).

Kolff, J. van Santen, Dutch-born German writer on music; b. Rotterdam, April 19, 1848; d. Berlin, Nov. 29, 1896. A polyglot, he contributed hundreds of articles and essays on music to publications in German, French, and Dutch; of value is his historical analysis of the Leitmotiv, publ. in vols. VIII and IX of *Bayreuther Blätter,* under the title "Geschichtliches und Ästhetisches über das Erinnerungsmotiv." He was the first to use the term "reminiscence motif" in reference to Wagner's works.

Kolinski, Mieczyslaw, Polish-born Canadian composer, ethnomusicologist, and music theorist; b. Warsaw, Sept. 5, 1901. He studied piano and composition at the Hochschule für Musik in Berlin; then took courses in musicology, psychology, and anthropology at Berlin Univ. (Ph.D., 1930); concurrently assisted Hornbostel at the Staatliches Phonogramm-Archiv in Berlin (1926–33); then moved to Prague; in 1938 went to Belgium to avoid the Nazis; then settled in N.Y. in 1951. In 1955 he was co-founder, and in 1958–59, president, of the Society for Ethnomusicology; in 1966–76 taught at Toronto Univ.; became a Canadian citizen in 1974. As an ethnomusicologist, he transcribed over 200 works from Samoa, New Guinea, Surinam, West Africa, and Haiti; also edited numerous folk-song editions. As a music theorist, he publ. *Konsonanz als Grundlage einer neuen Akkordlehre* (Prague, 1936).

WORKS: Ballet, *Expresszug-Phantasie* (Salzburg, 1935); 2 piano sonatas (1919; 1946, revised 1966); Violin Sonata (1924); Cello Sonata (1926); *Lyric Sextet* for Soprano, Flute, and String Quartet (1929); 4 *Suites* for Piano (1929–46); String Quartet (1931); *Dahomey Suite* for Flute, and Piano or String Orch. (1951); *Katikvah Variations* for String Quartet (1960); *Dance Fantasy* for String Orch. (1969); songs; folk-song arrangements.

BIBLIOGRAPHY: R. Kennedy, "A Bibliography of the Writings of Mieczyslaw Kolinski," *Current Musicology* (1966).

Kolisch, Rudolf, Austrian violinist; b. Klamm, July 20, 1896; d. Watertown, Mass., Aug. 1, 1978. He studied violin with Ševčik at the Univ. of Vienna; also took private lessons in composition with Schoenberg. In 1922 he organized the Kolisch Quartet, which systematically presented works by modern composers. His was the first string quartet to perform its programs from memory. In 1935 he went to the U.S.; in 1942 he became the leader of the Pro Arte Quartet; taught at the Univ. of Wisconsin until 1967, and then was artist-in-residence at the New England Cons. of Music in Boston. He was one of the few professional left-handed violinists.

Kollmann, August Friedrich Christoph, German composer; b. Engelbostel, March 21, 1756; d. London, March 21, 1829. He was organist in the German Chapel, St. James', London. Among his works are a symph., *The Shipwreck;* 100 Psalms harmonized in 100 ways; Rondo for Piano on the chord of the diminished seventh; etc.; also publ. *Essays on Practical Harmony* (1796); *First Beginning on the Pianoforte;* etc.

Kollo, René, German tenor; b. Berlin, Nov. 20, 1937. He was educated in Berlin; made his operatic debut in 1965 in Braunschweig. He then sang at the Opera in Düsseldorf (1967–71); appeared at Bayreuth in 1969 and at the Vienna State Opera in 1971. He made his American debut at the Metropolitan Opera in N.Y. on Nov. 4, 1976, as Lohengrin. He also sang at La Scala in Milan.

Kollo, Walter, German operetta composer; b. Neidenburg, Jan. 28, 1878; d. Berlin, Sept. 30, 1940. He studied in Sondershausen and Königsberg. In 1901 he settled in Berlin and was active as a theater conductor; wrote songs that became popular favorites. Among his most successful operettas are *Drei alte Schachteln* (Berlin, Oct. 6, 1917) and *Die Frau ohne Kuss* (Berlin, July 6, 1924).

Kolman, Petr, Slovak composer; b. Bratislava, May 29, 1937. He studied theory with Očenáš and Cikker at the Bratislava Cons. (1951–56) and advanced composition with Alexander Moyzes at the High School for Musical Arts in Bratislava (1956–60); was editor of symph. music at the Bratislava Radio (1961–65) and later worked in an electronic music studio. He adopted the serial method of composition, according to Schoenberg's practice. WORKS: *Romeo and Juliet,* symph. poem (1956); String Trio (1957); Violin Concerto (1959–60); *3 Piano Pieces in Memory of Schoenberg* (1960); *Participazioni* for 12 Instruments (1962); *Sonata canonica* for Clarinet and Bass Clarinet (1963); *Panegyrikos* for 16 Instruments (1964); *Homage to Kandinsky* for String Quartet (1964); *Monumento per 6,000,000* for Orch. (1964); *Mollisation mobile* for Flute and Vibraphone (1965).

Kolneder, Walter, Austrian musicologist; b. Wels, July 1, 1910. He studied composition privately with Johann Nepomuk David (1927–29); also took courses at the Mozarteum in Salzburg (1925–35), studying conducting with Paumgartner and viola with Strub. He taught at the Graz Cons. (1936–39) and the Staatliche Hochschule für Musikerziehung in Graz-Eggenberg (1936–45); received his Ph.D. in 1949 from the Univ. of Innsbruck with the dissertation *Die vokale Mehrstimmigkeit in der Volksmusik der österreichischen Alpenländer;* completed his Habilitation at the Univ. of Saarbrücken with his *Antonio Vivaldi: Neue Studien zur Biographie und Stilistik seiner Werke.* He became Privatdozent at the Univ. of Saarbrücken in 1956; was also director of the Cons. of the city of Luxemburg from 1953 to 1959; then taught in Darmstadt from 1959 to 1965. He was director of the Hochschule für Musik in Karlsruhe from 1966 to 1972; served as Ausserplanmässiger Prof. of musicology at the Univ. of Karlsruhe from 1966. His writings include *Aufführungspraxis bei Vivaldi* (Leipzig, 1955; 2nd ed., 1973; includes extracts from his Habilitationsschrift); *Anton Webern: Einführung in Werk und Stil* (Rodenkirchen, 1961; in Eng. as *Anton Webern: An Introduction to His Works,* Los Angeles, 1968); *Geschichte der Musik: Ein Studien- und Prüfungshelfer* (Heidelberg, 1963; 3rd ed., 1972); *Antonio Vivaldi: Leben und Werk* (Wiesbaden, 1965; in Eng., Berkeley, Calif., 1970); *Anton Webern: Genesis und Metamorphosen seines Stils* (Vienna, 1973); *Melodietypen bei Vivaldi* (Zürich, 1973).

Kolodin, Irving, American music critic; b. New York, Feb. 22, 1908. He studied at the Inst. of Musical Art in N.Y.; was music critic on the *N.Y. Sun* (1932–50); in 1947 he became editor of the music section of the *Saturday Review.* He publ. a number of valuable reference works and monographs: *The Metropolitan Opera 1883–1935* (N.Y., 1936; new revised ed., as *The Story of the Metropolitan Opera, 1883–1950,* N.Y., 1953; 4th ed., N.Y., 1966); *The Kingdom of Swing* (with Benny Goodman; N.Y., 1939); *A Guide to Recorded Music* (N.Y., 1941; new ed., as *New Guide to Recorded Music,* Garden City, N.Y., 1946; 3rd revised ed., 1950); *Mozart on Records* (N.Y., 1942); *Orchestral Music,* in the series The Guide to Long-Playing Records (N.Y., 1955); editor, *The Saturday Review Home Book of Recorded Music and Sound Reproduction* (N.Y., 1956); *Musical Life* (N.Y., 1958); *The Continuity of Music: A History of Influence* (N.Y., 1969); *The Interior Beethoven: A Biography of the Music* (N.Y., 1975); *The Opera Omnibus: Four Centuries of Critical Give and Take* (N.Y., 1976); *In Quest of Music* (N.Y., 1980).

Komitas, Sogomon, Armenian composer, pioneer of national folk music; b. Kutina, Turkey, Oct. 8, 1869; d. Paris, Oct. 22, 1935. His family name was **Sogomian;** orphaned at the age of 11, he was sent to study singing at a seminary in Etchmiatsin; upon graduation in 1893, he was given the name Komitas, after a 7th-century Armenian hymn writer. In 1895 he went to Tiflis, where he studied music theory; then lived in Berlin (1896–99), where he took courses in composition and choral conducting. During all these years he studiously collected materials pertaining to Armenian folk music, and publ. numerous papers in German dealing with the subject; also composed original music based on Armenian motifs. In 1910 he moved to Constantinople; the massacre of Armenian populations in Turkey in 1915 so affected him that he became incurably psychotic. He lived afterwards in Paris. Komitas is regarded as the founder of scientific Armenian musicology; his works were publ. in a collected edition on the centennial of his birth; his body was reverently transferred from Paris for reburial in Erevan, capital of Soviet Armenia. There is a considerable body of biographical and bibliographical publications, mostly in the Russian language; the basic biographies are A. Shaverdian, *Komitas and Armenian Music* (Erevan, 1956), and G. Geodakian, *Komitas* (Erevan, 1969).

Komorous, Rudolf, Czech composer of avant-garde tendencies; b. Prague, Dec. 8, 1931. He studied bassoon at the Prague Cons. (1946–52) and composition with Pavel Bořkovec at the Academy of Musical Arts in Prague (1952–59); concurrently served as first bassoonist at the Prague Opera. From 1959 to 1961 he was in China as a teacher of bassoon at the Cons. of Peking. Returning to Prague, he took an active part in the modern music movement; in 1961 he was one of the organizers of the progressive group Musica Viva Pragensis. After the Soviet occupation of Czechoslovakia in 1968, Komorous left Prague and went with his family to Canada. In 1971 he was appointed prof. of composition at the Univ. of Victoria in British Columbia. In his works he explores the ultramodern potentialities of composition, often resorting to graphic music notation.

WORKS: *Lady Whiterose,* chamber opera for Voices a cappella (1964–66); *Chamber Music* for Bassoon and Small Orch. (1959); *The Green Twig* for Basset Horn, Triangle, Harmonium, Piano, Viola, and Cello (1960); *Still Life with Florets* for 2 Clarinets, Bassoon, Cymbal, and 3 Violas (1961); *The Sweet Queen* for Mouth Harmonica, Bass Drum, and Piano (1962–63); *Venus* for Strings and Percussion (1963); *Olympia* for Flexatone, Harmonica, Nightingale, Acolyte Bells, Sleigh Bells, and Rattle (1964); *Piccolomini* for 4 Piccolos (1964); *The Devil's Trills* for Piano (1964); *Mignon* for 4 Four-string Instruments (1965); *Chanson* for Guitar, Spirale, and Viola (1965); *York* for Flute, Oboe or Trumpet, Bassoon, Triangle, Piano, Mandolin, and Double Bass (1967); *The Gloomy Grace* for 11 Instruments and Nightingale (1968); *Bare and Dainty* for Orch. (1970); *Lethe* for Orch. and Tape (1971); *Dingy Yellow* for Soprano Saxophone, Piano, and Tape (1972); *Untitled 1* for Tape (1973), *2* for Solo Trumpet (1973), *3* for 10 Instruments (1974), *4* for 4 Oboes, 2 Trumpets, and Violin (1974), and *5* for Flute, Horn, Viola, and Double Bass (1974); *Preludes* for 13 Early Instruments (1974); *The Grand Chopper* for Tape (1974); *Anatomy of Melancholy* for Tape (1974); *Rossi* for Small Orch. (1975); *At Your Memory the Transparent Tears Are Like Molten Lead* for Viola da Gamba and Harpsichord (1976); *The Gentle Touch (In Answer to Assistant Magistrate Chang)* for 5 Flutes, 4 Violas, 3 Cellos, and Piano (1977).

Komorzynski, Egon, Austrian musicologist; b. Vienna, May 7, 1878; d. there, March 16, 1963. He studied musicology with Guido Adler at the Univ. of Vienna and with Riemann at the Univ. of Leipzig. He devoted himself to the study of Mozart; publ. a fundamental work on Mozart's librettist Schikaneder (Vienna, 1901; revised ed., 1951); a monograph on Mozart (Berlin, 1941; 2nd ed., 1955); a novel about Schubert, *Genius zwischen 2 Welten* (Berlin, 1944).

Kondorossy, Leslie, Hungarian-American composer; b. Pressburg, June 25, 1915. He studied at the Academy of Music in Budapest; after World War II he emigrated to America and settled in Cleveland; there he evolved fruitful activity as a teacher, conductor, and composer. He is especially proficient in producing short operas; among them are *Night in the Puszta* (Cleveland, June 28, 1953); *The Voice* (Cleveland, May 15, 1954); *The Pumpkin* (Cleveland, May 15, 1954); *Unexpected Visitor* and *The 2 Imposters* (Cleveland, Oct. 21, 1956); *The Fox* (Cleveland, Jan. 28, 1961); *The Baksis* (1964); *Nathan the Wise* (1964); radio operas: *The Midnight Duel* (Cleveland Radio, March 20, 1955) and *The String Quartet* (Cleveland Radio, May 8, 1955); children's operas: *The Poorest Suitor* (Cleveland, May 24, 1967); *Shizuka's Dance* (Cleveland, April 22, 1969; also perf. on Tokyo Television, Japan, July 31, 1974); *Kalamona and the 4 Winds* (Cleveland Radio, Sept. 12, 1971); church opera, *Ruth and Naomi* (Cleveland, April 28, 1974); *Kossuth Cantata* (Cleveland, March 16, 1952); *David, a Son of Jesse,* oratorio (Cleveland, June 4, 1967); Trombone Concerto (1958); Trumpet Concerto (1959); Harp Concerto (1961); *Jazz Mass* for Voices and Jazz Band (1968); Harpsichord Concerto (1972); numerous organ pieces.

Kondracki, Michal, Russian-born composer; b. Poltava, Oct. 5, 1902. He studied with Statkowski and Melcer at the Warsaw State Cons., graduating in 1926 with honors; then went to Paris, where he was a pupil of Paul Dukas; later also studied with Szymanowski; in 1928–33 lived in Paris; in 1933 returned to Warsaw as a music critic; left Poland after the outbreak of war in 1939 and reached Brazil; stayed in Rio de Janeiro from 1940 till 1943; then settled in N.Y.

WORKS: Opera, *Popieliny* (Warsaw, May 3, 1934); ballet, *Metropolis* (1929); *Cantata ecclesiastica* (1937); *Partita* for Chamber Orch. (1928); Symph. (1942); a set of Brazilian dances for Orch. (1944).

Kondrashin, Kirill, noted Russian conductor; b. Moscow, March 6, 1914; d. Amsterdam, March 7, 1981. He studied piano and music theory at the Musical Technicum in Moscow; then took a course in conducting with Khaikin at the Moscow Cons.

While still a student he began conducting light opera (1934–37); then conducted at the Malyi Opera Theater in Leningrad (1937–41). In 1943 he received the prestigious appointment to the staff of the Bolshoi Theater in Moscow, where he conducted a wide repertoire emphasizing Russian operas. He received Stalin prizes in 1948 and 1949. In 1969 he was named People's Artist of the U.S.S.R. Kondrashin was the first Soviet conductor to appear in the U.S. (1958), and held numerous subsequent engagements in America, the last being a concert he conducted at the Hollywood Bowl in February 1981. In 1960 he was appointed chief conductor of the Moscow Phil., with which he performed numerous new Soviet works, including Shostakovich's controversial 13th Symph. In 1950–53 and 1972–75 he also taught at the Moscow Cons. After 1975 he increased his guest engagements outside Russia, and in 1978 decided to emigrate; in 1979 he assumed the post of permanent conductor of the Concertgebouw Orch. in Amsterdam; in 1981 he died suddenly of a heart attack after a concert. His conducting style was marked by an effective blend of lyrical melodiousness and dramatic romanticism, without deviating from the prevalent Russian traditions. He publ. a book, *On the Art of Conducting* (Leningrad, 1970).

BIBLIOGRAPHY: D. McIntire, "Kirill Kondrashin (1914–1981)," in *Le Grand Baton* (Sept./Dec. 1981).

Konetzni, Anny, Austrian soprano, sister of **Hilde Konetzni;** b. Vienna, Feb. 12, 1902; d. there, Sept. 6, 1968. She studied at the Vienna Cons. and later in Berlin with Jacques Stuckgold; made her debut as a contralto at the Vienna Volksoper in 1925; then sang in Augsburg, Elberfeld, and Chemnitz; joined the Berlin State Opera in 1931, and also appeared with the Vienna State Opera, La Scala in Milan, the Paris Opéra, and London's Covent Garden. She made her Metropolitan Opera debut in N.Y. as Brünnhilde in *Die Walküre* on Dec. 26, 1934; remained on the roster until the close of the season. After World War II, she taught voice in Vienna. She was particularly successful as an interpreter of heroic roles in Wagner's operas.

Konetzni, Hilde, famous Austrian soprano, sister of **Anny Konetzni;** b. Vienna, March 21, 1905; d. there, April 20, 1980. She studied at the Vienna Cons., and later in Prague with Prochaska-Neumann; made her debut as Sieglinde in *Die Walküre* in Chemnitz in 1929; then sang at the German Theater in Prague (1932–36). In 1936 she became a member of the Vienna State Opera; also appeared at Salzburg, La Scala in Milan, Covent Garden in London, South America, and the U.S. In 1954 she joined the faculty of the Vienna Academy of Music. She was an outstanding interpreter of the soprano parts in the operas of Wagner and Richard Strauss.

König, Gustav, German conductor; b. Schwabach, Aug. 12, 1910. He received his musical training in Munich; then conducted opera in Osnabrück (1932–34) and Stettin (1934–36). He subsequently was conductor at the Berlin Volksoper (1938–41); then in Aachen (1941–43). In 1943 he was appointed Generalmusikdirektor of Essen, a post he held until 1975. He gave first performances of Reutter's *Die Brücke von San Luis Rey* (1954), Fortner's *Der Wald* (1954), and Klebe's *Die Ermördung Cäsars* (1959).

Königslöw, Johann Wilhelm Cornelius, German organist and composer; b. Hamburg, March 16, 1745; d. Lübeck, May 14, 1833. He was organist at the Marienkirche in Lübeck from 1773 until his death. He composed many "Abendmusiken," following Buxtehude's example.

Königslöw, Otto Friedrich von, German violinist and conductor; b. Hamburg, Nov. 13, 1824; d. Bonn, Oct. 6, 1898. He studied at the Leipzig Cons. with David (violin) and Hauptmann (theory); following 12 years of concert tours, he became conductor of the Gürzenich Orch. at Cologne (1858–81); also was a member of the staff of the Cologne Cons. In 1884 he settled in Bonn.

Koning, David, Dutch pianist and composer; b. Rotterdam, March 19, 1820; d. Amsterdam, Oct. 6, 1876. He studied with Aloys Schmitt in Frankfurt; from 1840, was conductor of the choral society Felix Meritis in Amsterdam; was a member of various music organizations in Europe; was active mainly as a piano teacher. He wrote a comic opera, *The Fishermaiden; Elegy on the Death of an Artist* for Soli, Chorus, and Orch.; much vocal music; many piano pieces and studies.

Konitz, Lee, American jazz alto saxophone player; b. Chicago, Oct. 13, 1927, of Russian-Polish-Jewish parentage. He took up the clarinet at 11 years of age; growing up, he practiced on the saxophone, which eventually became his chosen instrument. He gained early experience playing with the Gay Claridge band in Chicago; then appeared with Claude Thornhill (1947–48) and Miles Davis (1948–50); subsequently became associated with the blind jazz pianist Lennie Tristano, from whom he began taking lessons in jazz harmony and rhythm. He developed a sui generis variations style related to bebop, with the melody notes patterned after the available ingredients in piano harmonies. In 1952–53 he worked with Stan Kenton; in 1954 he organized his own combo.

Konius, Georgi. See **Conus, Georgi.**

Konjović, Petar, eminent Serbian composer; b. Sombor, May 6, 1882; d. Belgrade, Oct. 1, 1970. He studied at the Prague Cons. with Novák; was choral director and teacher in Zemun and Belgrade (1906–14). In 1920 he toured Europe as a pianist; in 1921–26 was music director of the Zagreb Opera. In 1927–33 he was director of national theaters in Osijek, Split, and Novi Sad; in 1933–39, intendant of the national theater in Zagreb. In 1939 he settled in Belgrade as rector and prof. of the Academy of Music.

WORKS: Operas: *Vilin Veo* or *Ženidba Miloševa* (*The Wedding of Milos;* Zagreb, April 25, 1917); *Koštana* (Zagreb, April 16, 1931); *Knez od Zete* (*The Duke of Zeta;* Belgrade, May 25, 1929); *Seljaci* (*The Peasants;* Belgrade, March 3, 1952); Symph. in C (1908); *Capriccio adriatico* for Violin and Orch. (1920); *Makar Chudra,* symph. poem after Maxim Gorky (1944); 2 string quartets; solo pieces for violin, cello, and piano; 24 songs; *Moja zemlja,* 100 Yugoslav folk songs, of which 25 are arranged for voice and small orch. He publ. a book of essays, *Ličnosti* (*Personalities;* Zagreb, 1920), and a monograph on Miloje Milojević (Belgrade, 1954).

Kono, Kristo, Albanian composer; b. Tirana, July 17, 1907. He studied at the Milan Cons.; wrote the first national Albanian operetta, *The Dawn* (1954); also an opera, *Flowers of Memories* (1959), and many choruses.

Konoye, Hidemarō, Japanese composer and conductor; b. Tokyo, Nov. 18, 1898; d. there, June 2, 1973. A member of an aristocratic Japanese family, he received his education in Japan and in Europe; attended classes in composition of Vincent d'Indy at the Schola Cantorum in Paris; then took courses with Franz Schreker and Georg Schumann at the Berlin Cons. He made his European debut as a conductor with the Berlin Phil., on Jan. 18, 1924. Returning to Japan, he was principal conductor of the New Symph. Orch. in Tokyo (1926–34), specializing in new works of Japanese, European, and American composers. He conducted in the U.S. in 1937 and 1957. He is the composer of several orch. pieces based on Japanese subjects; also orchestrated old Japanese court music for the modern Western orch.; arranged the music of *Madama Butterfly* for the films (inserting many Japanese folk melodies).

Kont, Paul, Austrian composer; b. Vienna, Aug. 19, 1920. He studied violin and piano in his early youth; then took courses in conducting with Krips and Swarowsky at the Vienna Academy of Music. In 1948 he went to Paris, where he studied composition with Milhaud, Honegger, and Messiaen. Returning to Vienna, he adopted a serial method applying the statistical principles of valid recurrences of all musical parameters, including pitch, rhythm, and dynamics. Typical of this idiom are his *Celestina* for "total theater" (1966) and *Inzwischen,* a "mystery play for our time" (Vienna Television, Jan. 5, 1967). His other works are: *Indische Legende,* radio cantata (1951); *Peter und Susanne* (Vienna Television, June 26, 1959); chamber ballets: *Annoncen* (1956); *Die traurigen Jäger* (1958); *Italia passata* (1967); a choreographic symph. (1970); 2 wind quartets; Trio for Flute, Cello, and Harp; piano pieces; film music. He publ. *Antianorganikum,* essays on new music (Vienna, 1967).

Kontarsky, Alfons, German pianist, brother of **Aloys** and **Bernhard Kontarsky;** b. Iserlohn, Westphalia, Oct. 9, 1932. He studied piano with Else Schmitz-Gohr at the Hochschule für Musik in Co-

logne (1953–55) and with Erdmann in Hamburg (1955–57); in 1955 received, along with his older brother, Aloys, the first prize for duo-piano playing at the International Competition of the Bavarian Radio in Munich; with Aloys, made a concert tour of duo recitals through the U.S., South America, South Africa, and Japan; in 1967 was appointed prof. of piano at the Hochschule für Musik in Cologne.

Kontarsky, Aloys, German pianist, brother of **Alfons** and **Bernhard Kontarsky;** b. Iserlohn, Westphalia, May 14, 1931. He studied piano with Else Schmitz-Gohr at the Hochschule für Musik in Cologne and with Erdmann in Hamburg; in 1955 he received, along with his younger brother Alfons, the first prize for duo-piano playing at the International Competition of the Bavarian Radio in Munich; then embarked with him on a worldwide tour of duo-piano recitals in the U.S., South America, South Africa, and Japan. He specialized in ultramodern music; gave premiere performances of works by Stockhausen, Berio, Earle Brown, Pousseur, Bussotti, and B.A. Zimmermann. In 1960 he joined the faculty of the International Festival Series of New Music in Darmstadt.

Kontarsky, Bernhard, German pianist and conductor, brother of **Alfons** and **Aloys Kontarsky;** b. Iserlohn, Westphalia, April 26, 1937. He studied at the Hochschule für Musik in Cologne and at the Univ. of Cologne. In 1964 he received the Mendelssohn Prize in Chamber Music. He was conductor of the Stuttgart State Opera; was also active as a concert pianist, both as a soloist and in ensemble with his brothers.

Kontski, Antoine de, Polish pianist, brother of **Apollinaire** and **Charles de Kontski;** b. Cracow, Oct. 27, 1817; d. Ivanichi, near Okulova, Novgorod district, Russia, Dec. 7, 1889. He was the most famous member of the Kontski family of precocious musicians. He studied with John Field in Moscow (1830); went to Paris in 1851; then was in Berlin (1853); in 1854–67 he was in St. Petersburg; then he lived in London as a piano teacher. He toured the U.S. in 1883 and again in 1885; lived for a time in Buffalo, N.Y. At the age of nearly 80, he undertook a world tour (1896–98), giving concerts in Australia, Japan, and Siberia. He died at the estate of friends near St. Petersburg.

WORKS: He was a composer of effective salon music and virtuoso pieces for piano; his picturesque *Réveil du lion* was enormously successful for many years; it was an epitome of Romantic exuberance to the point of being ludicrous; he also wrote 2 piano concertos, the waltzes *La Victorieuse* and *Souvenir de Biarritz; Grande Polonaise;* a characteristic piece, *La Nuit sur la mer;* and several orch. overtures; also 2 light operas: *Les Deux Distraits* (London, 1872) and *Le Sultan de Zanzibar* (N.Y., May 8, 1886).

Kontski, Apollinaire de, Polish violinist, brother of **Antoine** and **Charles de Kontski;** b. Cracow, Oct.

23, 1825; d. Warsaw, June 29, 1879. He studied with his elder brother Charles; he appeared with his brothers as a small child in Russia and later in Germany, frankly exploited by his family for sensational publicity and gain. In 1837 he played for Paganini in Paris; in 1861 he became director of the Warsaw Cons., of which he was a founder, and remained in that post until his death. He publ. some violin music.

Kontski, Charles de, Polish pianist, brother of **Antoine** and **Apollinaire de Kontski;** b. Cracow, Sept. 6, 1815; d. Paris, Aug. 27, 1867. Like his brothers, he was a child prodigy, and made appearances with them at various public exhibitions and concerts. He studied in Warsaw and in Paris, eventually settling in Paris as a private piano teacher, enjoying considerable success in society.

Konwitschny, Franz, German conductor; b. Fulnek, Czechoslovakia, Aug. 14, 1901; d. Belgrade, July 28, 1962. He studied violin at the German Musikverein School in Brünn (Brno) before enrolling at the Leipzig Cons. (1923–25); while still a student he played violin at the Gewandhaus Orch. in Leipzig. In 1927 he became a conductor at the opera in Stuttgart. In 1933 he went to Freiburg as Generalmusikdirektor; then held the same post with the operas in Frankfurt (1938) and Hannover (1945). In 1949 he became chief conductor of the Gewandhaus Orch. in Leipzig, and succeeded in restoring its prestige and competence of performance to its former standard, before World War II. He also served as Generalmusikdirektor of the Dresden State Opera (1953–55); then went to East Berlin as chief conductor of the State Opera. He died in Belgrade during a tour.

Konya, Sándor, Hungarian tenor; b. Sarkad, Sept. 23, 1923. He was educated at the Franz Liszt Academy of Music in Budapest; also studied in Detmold, Rome, and Milan. He made his first professional appearance at the Bielefeld Opera in 1951; in 1958 sang for the first time at the Bayreuth Festival. On Oct. 28, 1961, he made his American debut at the Metropolitan Opera as Lohengrin; also had engagements with the San Francisco Opera.

Koole, Arend, Dutch musicologist; b. Amsterdam, April 22, 1908. He studied at the Amsterdam Cons. (1925–30) and later at Utrecht; his doctoral dissertation is a valuable monograph on Locatelli (Amsterdam, 1949). He also took lessons in conducting with Pierre Monteux; made appearances as a guest conductor in the Netherlands and Belgium. In 1949 he went to South Africa, where he served as senior lecturer in musicology at the Univ. of Bloemfontein; from 1964 to 1973 he was a prof. of music history at the Univ. of Southern Calif. in Los Angeles; in 1974 he returned to South Africa. Besides his book on Locatelli, he publ. a monograph on Mendelssohn (1953); contributed numerous articles to music periodicals and encyclopedias.

Kooper, Al, keyboard player, vocalist and founder of the American rock group Blood, Sweat and Tears; b. Brooklyn, Feb. 5, 1944. He got together with Steve Katz (b. Brooklyn, May 9, 1945) and Bobby Colomby (b. New York, Dec. 20, 1944) and with them put together a synthetic group of rock, pop, and jazz music, with the title patently derived from Winston Churchill's famous wartime speech promising his people nothing but hemorrhage, perspiration, and copious discharge from lacrimal glands. The individual songs hurled by the group at the defenseless populace expressed similar sentiments, as in *My Days Are Numbered.* However, in 1968 Kooper left the group for the more lucrative role of a producer. Without Kooper, the group fell into desuetude; hopeful zombies dropping in and out did not stop the deterioration of the group. On Jan. 31, 1971, one such extraterrestrial, named Gregory Herbert, a member of Blood, Sweat and Tears, justified the title by being found dead in a dingy hotel room in Amsterdam, Holland, during the group's European tour.

Kopelent, Marek, Czech composer; b. Prague, April 28, 1932. He studied composition with Řídký at the Academy of Musical Arts in Prague (1951–55); was editor for contemporary music at Supraphon, the state music publishing house (1956–71). In his music he experiments with a wide variety of musical resources of the multimedia avant-garde.
WORKS: 4 string quartets (1954, 1955, 1963, 1967); *3 Movements* for String Orch. (1958); *Nénie s flétnou (Nenie with Flute)* for Flute, 9 Female Voices, and Chamber Ensemble (1961); *Small Pantomime* for Wind Quintet (1961); Trio for Flute, Clarinet, and Bassoon (1962); Trio for Flute, Bass Clarinet, and Piano (1962); *Reflexe* for Flute, Violin, Viola, and Cello (1962); oratorio, *Chléb a ptáci (Bread and Birds;* 1957–62); *Canto intimo* for Flute and Vibraphone (1963); *Matka (The Mother),* fresco for Chorus and Flute (1964); *Hudba pro pět (Music for 5)* for Oboe, Clarinet, Bassoon, Viola, and Piano (1964); *Modlitba kamene (Prayer of Stones)* for Narrator, 2 Small Choruses, 3 Gongs, and Tam-tam (1965); *Rozjímání (Contemplation)* for Chamber Orch. (1966); *Game,* a happening for String Quartet (1965–66); *Snehah* (Sanskrit for "love") for Soprano and Chamber Ensemble (1967); *Bijoux de Bohème* for Harpsichord (1967); *Sváry (Quarrels)* for 12 Solo Instruments and Orch. (1967–68; Prague, March 7, 1969); *Zátiší (Seclusion)* for Viola and Chamber Orch. (1968); *Žaloby (Complaints)* for 2 Choruses, Trumpet, Percussion, and ad libitum Tape (1969); *Bludný hlas (The Wandering Voice)* for Actress, Chamber Ensemble, Tape, and ad libitum Film and Light Projection (1969–70); *Appassionato* for Piano and Orch. (1970–71); *Secret Signals from Outer Space,* piece for Young Pianist (1971); *Intimissimo* for Chamber Ensemble (1971); *Musique piquante* for Violin and Cimbalom (1971); *A Few Minutes with an Oboist* for Oboe and Chamber Orch. (1972); Wind Quintet (1972); *Black and White Tears* for Solo Voices (1972); *Syllabes mouvementées* for Vocal Soloists (1972); *Veroničina rouška (Veronika's*

Veil), sonata for 11 Strings (1972–73); *Rondo* for 5 Percussionists (1973); *T'ukáta (Taps)* for Harp, Harpsichord, Cimbalom, and Guitar (1974); *Hrátky (A Cozy Chat)* for Saxophone and Orch. (1974–75); *Il canto degli augei* for Soprano and Orch. (Baden-Baden, March 22, 1980).

Koppel, Herman David, Danish composer, father of **Thomas Herman Koppel;** b. Copenhagen, Oct. 1, 1908. He studied piano and composition at the Royal Academy of Music in Copenhagen (1926–29); made his debut in 1930 as a concert pianist; toured widely in Europe and the Soviet Union; upon return to Denmark, was appointed to the staff of the Copenhagen Cons. (1949). In his piano recitals he emphasized modern Danish music, especially that of Carl Nielsen; his own compositions are, in turn, influenced by Nielsen's works.
WORKS: Koppel is a prolific composer; he wrote 7 symphs.: No. 1 (1930); No. 2 (1943); No. 3 (1944–45); No. 4 (1946); No. 5 (1955); No. 6, *Sinfonia breve* (1957); No. 7 (1960–61; Copenhagen, May 16, 1961); Violin Concerto (1929); *Music for Strings* (1930); 4 piano concertos (1931–32, 1936–37, 1948, 1960–63); *Music for Jazz Orchestra* (1932); *Capriccio* for Violin and Orch. (1934); Variations for Small Orch. (1935); 2 concertinos for Strings (1937–38, 1957); Clarinet Concerto (1941); Sinfonietta (1945); Concerto for Violin, Viola, and Orch. (1947); *3 Psalms of David* for Tenor, Chorus, and Orch. (1949); Cello Concerto (1952); *Immortalis mortalium* for Baritone, Boys' Chorus, and Orch. (1954); *2 Biblical Songs* for Soprano, and Orch. or Piano (1955); *The Song of the Sun* for Children's Chorus, Strings, and Piano (1958); *Moses,* oratorio (1963–64; Copenhagen, Oct. 21, 1965); *Requiem* (1965–66); Oboe Concerto (1970); Chamber Concerto for Violin and Strings (1970); Flute Concerto (1971); *Hymns of Thanksgiving* for Soli, Chorus, and Orch. (1974); 5 string quartets (1928–29, 1939, 1944–45, 1964, 1975); Duo for Violin and Piano (1930); Trio for Clarinet, Violin, and Piano (1931); Duo for Clarinet and Bassoon (1932); Sextet for Winds and Piano (1942); *Fantasy* for Solo Clarinet (1947); Piano Sonata (1950); *Ternio I* for Cello or Violin, and Piano (1951); Piano Quintet (1953); Cello Sonata (1956); Variations for Clarinet and Piano (1961); *Capriccio* for Flute and Piano (1961); *Macbeth,* opera after Shakespeare (1968; Copenhagen, 1970); *9 Variations* for Piano Trio (1969); Suite for Solo Cello (1971); Piano Trio (1971); *8 Variations and Epilogue* for Piano and 13 Players (1972); Divertimento for String Trio (1972); *Ternio II* for Solo Saxophone (1973); *Pastorale Variations* for Flute, Violin, Viola, and Cello (1975); incidental music for plays; music to 29 films; songs.

Koppel, Thomas Herman, Danish composer, son of **Herman David Koppel;** b. Orebro, Sweden, April 27, 1944. He studied piano and theory with his father at the Royal Danish Cons. in Copenhagen (1963–67). In 1968 he organized in Copenhagen the pop group Savage Rose, and joined the Danish avant-garde in other venturesome activities.
WORKS: Operas: *Historien om en moder (The Story of a Mother),* after H.C. Andersen (Copenhagen, Oct. 17, 1965), and *Bérénice* (1968); 3 string quartets (1963, 1964, 1966); *Cloches* for Voice, Clarinet, Horn, Celesta, Piano, Cello, and Percussion (1964); *Phrases,* cantata for 2 Sopranos, 12 Mezzo-sopranos, 4 Solo Instruments, and Orch. (Danish Radio, April 6, 1967); *Visions fugitives* for Piano and Orch. (1965); *Concert héroïque* for 3 Pianos, Orch., Chorus, and Wind Machine (Copenhagen, Jan. 9, 1967); *Petit air* for Soprano and 4 Instruments (1966); *Ouverture solennelle* (1967); *Impressions lyriques* for Percussion (1968); music for the ballet *Dødens triumf (Triumph of Death;* Danish Radio, May 23, 1971).

Kopylov, Alexander, Russian composer; b. St. Petersburg, July 14, 1854; d. Strelna, near St. Petersburg, Feb. 20, 1911. He studied violin and piano at the Court Chapel (1862–72); upon graduation, took lessons in composition with Rimsky-Korsakov and Liadov. From 1872 till 1896 he taught at the Court Chapel. He wrote a Symph.; a concert overture; 5 string quartets; *Souvenir de Peterhof* for Violin and Piano; 2 albums of *Tableaux musicaux de la vie enfantine* for Piano; other piano pieces, most of them publ. by Belaieff. He was an epigone of the Romantic school of minor Russian composers, emulating Tchaikovsky. A complete list of his publ. works is found in the *Verzeichnis russischer Komponisten* publ. by Fr. Hofmeister (Leipzig, 1949).

Kopytman, Mark, Ukrainian-born Israeli composer; b. Kamenets-Podolski, Dec. 6, 1929. He had piano studies at an early age, but graduated as a doctor of medicine in Chernovtsy in 1952; while a practicing physician, he studied composition; received his master's degree in music from the Lwow Academy of Music in 1955 and a doctorate from the Moscow Academy of Music in 1958. He taught in various Soviet music institutes from 1955 to 1972; then emigrated to Israel, where he taught at the Rubin Academy in Jerusalem.
WORKS: Oratorio, *Songs of Kodr* (1965); opera, *Kasa Mare* (1966); Piano Concerto (1970); *Voices* for Soprano and Orch. (1974–75); ballet, *Monodrama* (1975); Concerto for Orch. (1976); *Rotations* for Orch. (1979); 3 string quartets; *Lamentation* for Solo Flute (1973).

Korbay, Francis Alexander, Hungarian tenor and composer; b. Budapest, May 8, 1846; d. London, March 9, 1913. He was a pupil of Gustave Roger; sang at the Hungarian Opera in Budapest (1865–68); at the same time he pursued piano study, profiting by advice from Liszt, who was his godfather; made a rather successful tour as a pianist in Europe (1869–71), and then went to the U.S., settling in N.Y. in 1871 as a teacher of voice and piano. In 1894 he went to London; was a prof. of singing at the Royal Academy of Music (1894–1903); remained in London until his death. He wrote an orch. work, *Nuptiale; Hungarian Overture; Le Matin* for Solo Voice and Piano, which was arranged by Liszt for Orch.; also numerous lieder and piano pieces.

Korchmarev, Klimenti, Russian composer; b. Verkhnedneprovsk, July 3, 1899; d. Moscow, April 7, 1958. He studied at the Odessa Cons. with Maliszewski; then went to Moscow. He was one of the first Soviet composers to write on revolutionary themes; in 1923 he wrote *March on the Left,* to words by Mayakovsky. In 1927 he produced an operatic fairy tale, *Ivan the Soldier,* and a ballet, *The Serf Ballerina* (Leningrad, Dec. 11, 1927). His other works of social significance and revolutionary content were the choral symphs. *October* (1931) and *The Peoples of the Soviet Land* (1935). In 1939 he went to Turkmenistan, where he collected native songs; he also composed the first Turkmenian ballet, *The Merry Deceiver.* In 1950 he wrote a cantata, *Free China,* for which he received a Stalin Prize.

Kord, Kazimierz, Polish conductor; b. Pogórze, Nov. 18, 1930. He studied piano at the Leningrad Cons.; then took courses in composition and conducting at the Cracow Academy of Music. He conducted at the Warsaw Opera (1960–62); in 1962 became artistic director of the Cracow Opera; from 1968 to 1973 he was artistic director and chief conductor of the Symph. Orch. of Polish Radio and Television in Katowice. In 1972 he made his Metropolitan Opera debut in N.Y.; also conducted opera in San Francisco, London, Amsterdam, and Copenhagen. In addition, he conducted orchs. in Moscow, Leningrad, N.Y., Chicago, Cleveland, and London. In 1977 he became artistic director and chief conductor of the National Phil. Orch. in Warsaw. In 1980 he was appointed chief conductor of the symph. orch. of Southwest Radio in Baden-Baden; also served as principal guest conductor of the Cincinnati Symph. Orch. (1980–82).

Koreshchenko, Arseni, Russian composer; b. Moscow, Dec. 18, 1870; d. Kharkov, Jan. 3, 1921. He studied piano with Taneyev and composition with Arensky at the Moscow Cons.; later was an instructor in music theory there; from 1906 to 1919 he taught composition at the Moscow Phil. Inst.; then went to Kharkov, where he taught piano and composition at the local Music Academy until his death. He wrote music imitative of Tchaikovsky and Arensky; his songs have a certain obsolete charm. He composed 3 operas: *Belshazzar's Feast* (Moscow, 1892); *The Angel of Death* (1893); *The House of Ice* (Moscow, Nov. 19, 1900); ballet, *The Magic Mirror* (Moscow, 1902); several orch. pieces, including *Armenian Suite* for Orch. and *Concerto Fantasy* for Piano and Orch.; String Quartet; choruses; piano pieces; songs.

Korganov, Genari, Armenian pianist and composer; b. Kvarely, May 12, 1858; d. Rostov-on-the-Don, March 7, 1890. He studied with Reinecke at the Leipzig Cons. and with L. Brassin in St. Petersburg. In 1879 he settled in Tiflis. In his works he often used authentic Caucasian motifs, while his harmonic treatment was modeled after Rimsky-Korsakov's oriental pieces. His fantasia for piano on Caucasian themes, *Bayati,* presents a certain interest.

Kořínek, Miroslav, Slovak composer; b. Brno, Jan. 29, 1925. He studied composition with Alexander Moyzes at the Bratislava Cons.; in 1950 joined its staff as a lecturer in music.
WORKS: Concertino for Viola and Orch. (1951); Accordion Concerto (1956); *Divertimento concertato* for String Orch. (1962); Flute Concerto (1964); *Chamber Concerto* for Clarinet and Orch. (1966); Horn Concerto (1968); *Atlantide,* cantata (1972); 2 string quartets (1951, 1963); Trio for 2 Oboes and English Horn (1961); Piano Quintet (1967); Wind Quintet (1970); *2 Capriccios* for Trombone and Piano (1973); *Concertante Fantasy* for Flute and Guitar (1974); *Apocryphas* for Piano (1968); numerous instructive pieces for schools.

Korn, Clara Anna, German composer and teacher; b. Berlin, Jan. 30, 1866; d. New York, July 14, 1940. She was brought to America at an early age; studied with Horatio Parker and Bruno Oscar Klein; taught at the National Cons. in N.Y. (1893–98); afterward, settled in Brooklyn as a private teacher. She wrote an opera, *Their Last War;* Symph.; symph. poem, *Morpheus;* orch. suite, *Rural Snapshots;* Piano Concerto; Violin Concerto; piano pieces; songs.

Korn, Peter Jona, German-American composer; b. Berlin, March 30, 1922. He left Germany as a child in 1933; studied in England (1934–36); lived in Jerusalem (1936–39); in 1941 emigrated to the U.S., settling in Los Angeles. His teachers in composition were Edmund Rubbra in London, Stefan Wolpe in Jerusalem, Hanns Eisler and Ernst Toch in Los Angeles; he also attended Schoenberg's classes at the Univ. of Calif., Los Angeles (1942), and studied the technique of composition for films with Ingolf Dahl and Miklós Rózsa. The resulting style ultimately adopted by Korn is that of pragmatic Romanticism marked by polycentric tonality in the framework of strong rhythmic counterpoint. In 1965 he returned to Germany; in 1967 he was appointed director of the Richard Strauss Konservatorium in Munich.
WORKS: Opera, *Heidi* (1961–63); 3 symphs. (1946, 1952, 1956); Variations on a tune from *Beggar's Opera,* for Orch. (Louisville, Oct. 1, 1955); *Tom Paine Overture* (1950; Malmö, Sweden, Dec. 8, 1959, composer conducting); *In medias res,* symph. overture (1953); *Rhapsody* for Oboe and Strings (1952); Concertino for Horn and Double String Orch. (1952); Saxophone Concerto (1956); Cello Sonata (1949); Oboe Sonata (1949); Horn Sonata (1953); String Quartet No. 1 (1950); Serenade for 4 Horns (1957); Passacaglia and Fugue for 8 Horns (1952); String Quartet No. 2 (1963); *Quintettino* for Flute, Clarinet, Bassoon, Cello, and Piano (1964); Violin Concerto (1965); *Semi-Symphony* (1966); Wind Quintet (1966). He wrote a polemical book of essays, *Musikalische Umwelt Verschmutzung* (Wiesbaden, 1975).

Kornauth, Egon, Austrian composer; b. Olmütz (Olomouc), May 14, 1891; d. Vienna, Oct. 28, 1959. He studied in Vienna with Fuchs, Schreker, and Schmidt; took a course in musicology with Guido

Adler at the Univ. (Ph.D., 1915). In 1926 he was engaged to organize an orch. in Medan, Sumatra; despite the difficulties of such an undertaking, he maintained this orch. for 2 seasons; later he toured through Java, Celebes, and Ceylon with the Vienna Trio, which he founded. Kornauth's music is marked by considerable contrapuntal skill; his instrumental pieces and songs are mostly in a Romantic vein.

WORKS: 4 symph. suites (1913–39); Symph. Overture (1914; revised 1925); *Ballade* for Orch., with Cello obbligato (Vienna, Feb. 20, 1919); Nonet for various Instruments; String Sextet; String Quintet; Piano Quintet; Clarinet Quintet; String Quartet; Piano Quartet; Piano Trio; Violin Sonata, Viola Sonata, Cello Sonata, Clarinet Sonata; various choral works and several song cycles.

BIBLIOGRAPHY: E.H. Müller von Asow, *Egon Kornauth* (Vienna, 1941; includes a complete list of works).

Korndorf, Nicolai, Russian composer; b. Moscow, Jan. 23, 1947. He studied composition with Balasanian at the Moscow Cons., graduating in 1970. In 1973 he was appointed to the staff of the Moscow Cons.

WORKS: Opera, *Feast during the Plague* (1973); *Cantata of Lenin* (1970; on Lenin's centennial); Concerto for Organ, Piano, and Strings (1969); Viola Concerto (1970); *Concerto-Pastorale* for Bassoon and Orch. (1972); Concerto for Double Bass and 12 Wind Instruments (1973); Concerto for Harp and 10 Brass Instruments (1974); 2 symphs. (1975, 1980); *Confessions,* chamber symph. (1979); *Yarilo* (old Slavic name for "Sun"), chamber symph. (1979); Concerto for Violin, Cello, Piano, and Orch. (1980); Piano Trio (1971); Sonata for 3 Violins and Piano, in memory of Stravinsky (1971); *Polyphonic Suite* for Saxophone and Piano (1972); 6 Songs for Voice and Wind Quintet, to words by Alexander Blok (1968).

Körner, Christian Gottfried, German music theorist; b. Leipzig, July 2, 1756; d. Berlin, May 13, 1831. He was the father of Theodor Körner, the poet. He publ. an essay, "Über den Charakter der Töne oder über Charakterdarstellung in der Musik," in the *Horen* (1775); also composed songs, etc.

BIBLIOGRAPHY: W. Seifert, *C.G. Körner: Ein Musikästhetiker der deutschen Klassik* (Regensburg, 1960).

Körner, Gotthilf Wilhelm, German music publisher; b. Teicha, near Halle, June 3, 1809; d. Erfurt, Jan. 3, 1865. He founded his music-publishing firm in 1838 and publ. many organ works; in 1886 the company merged with C.F. Peters.

Kornerup, Thorwald Otto, Danish writer on musical subjects; b. Copenhagen, March 11, 1864; d. there, Dec. 20, 1938. His publications, which deal mostly with the problems of acoustics and various special tone systems, include *The 19-tone and 31-tone Precursors of the Well-tempered Systems; The Acoustical Theory of Atonality; From the Original Prototype of the 5-tone Scales to the Golden Tones of Electrical Musical Instruments; The Indian Tone System with Its 22 Srutis* (all in Danish).

Korngold, Erich Wolfgang, Austrian composer of remarkable and precocious gifts; b. Brno, May 29, 1897; d. Hollywood, Nov. 29, 1957. He received his earliest musical education from his father, **Julius Korngold;** he then studied with Fuchs, Zemlinsky, and Grädener in Vienna. His progress was astounding; at the age of 12 he composed a Piano Trio, which was soon publ., revealing a competent technique and an ability to write in a modern style (strongly influenced by Richard Strauss). About the same time he wrote (in piano score) a pantomime, *Der Schneemann;* it was orchestrated by his teacher Zemlinsky, and performed at the Vienna Court Opera (Oct. 4, 1910), creating a sensation. In 1911 Nikisch played Korngold's *Schauspiel-Ouvertüre* in a concert of the Gewandhaus Orch. at Leipzig; in the same year the youthful composer gave a concert of his works in Berlin, appearing also as a pianist; his Sinfonietta was given by Felix Weingartner and the Vienna Phil. in 1913. Korngold was not quite 19 when his 2 short operas, *Der Ring des Polykrates* and *Violanta,* were produced in Munich. His first lasting success came with the opera *Die tote Stadt,* produced first in Hamburg (1920) and then on many opera stages all over the world. In 1929 he entered a fruitful collaboration with the famous director Max Reinhardt; in 1934 he went to Hollywood to arrange Mendelssohn's music for the Reinhardt film production of *A Midsummer Night's Dream.* He was intermittently in Europe; taught at the Vienna Academy of Music (1930–34) before settling in Hollywood; composed a number of film scores; conducted light opera with the N.Y. Opera Co. in 1942 and 1944. He became an American citizen in 1943; after 1945 he divided his time between the U.S. and Europe; lived for some time in Vienna.

Korngold's music represents the last breath of the Romantic spirit of Vienna; it is marvelously consistent with the melodic, rhythmic, and harmonic style of the judicious modernity of the nascent 20th century. When Mahler heard him play some of his music as a young boy, he kept repeating: "Ein Genie! Ein Genie!" Korngold never altered his established idiom of composition, and was never tempted to borrow modernistic devices, except for some transitory passages in major seconds or an occasional whole-tone scale. After the early outbursts of incautious enthusiasms on the part of some otherwise circumspect critics nominating Korngold as a new Mozart, his star, his erupting nova, began to sink rapidly, until it became a melancholy consensus to dismiss his operas at their tardy revivals as derivative products of an era that had itself little to exhibit that was worthwhile. Ironically, his film scores, in the form of orchestrated suites, experienced long after his death a spontaneous renascence, particularly on records, and especially among the unprejudiced and unopinionated American musical youth, who found in Korngold's music the stuff of their own new dreams.

WORKS: OPERAS: *Der Ring des Polykrates* and

Violanta (Munich, March 28, 1916); *Die tote Stadt* (Hamburg, Dec. 4, 1920; Metropolitan Opera, N.Y., Nov. 19, 1921); *Das Wunder der Heliane* (Hamburg, Oct. 7, 1927); *Kathrin* (Stockholm, Oct. 7, 1939); *Die stumme Serenade* (Dortmund, Dec. 5, 1954); pantomime, *Der Schneemann* (Vienna, Oct. 4, 1910). FOR ORCH.: *Schauspiel-Ouvertüre* (Leipzig, 1911); Sinfonietta (Vienna, Nov. 28, 1913); Suite from the music to Shakespeare's *Much Ado about Nothing*, for Chamber Orch. (Vienna, 1919); *Sursum Corda,* symph. overture (1919); Piano Concerto for Left Hand Alone (1923; written for Paul Wittgenstein); Cello Concerto (1946); Violin Concerto (Jascha Heifetz with the St. Louis Symph. Orch., Feb. 15, 1947); *Symphonic Serenade* for String Orch. (1949); Symph. in F-sharp (1950; first public perf., Munich, Nov. 27, 1972); *Theme and Variations* for Orch. (1953). CHAMBER MUSIC: Piano Trio (1910); Violin Sonata; String Sextet; Piano Quintet; 3 string quartets (1922, 1935, 1945); 3 piano sonatas (1908, 1910, 1932).

BIBLIOGRAPHY: R.S. Hoffmann, *Erich Wolfgang Korngold* (Vienna, 1923); L. Korngold, *Erich Wolfgang Korngold. Ein Lebensbild* (Vienna, 1967); B. Carroll, "Korngold's 'Violanta,' " *Musical Times* (Nov. 1980).

Korngold, Julius, noted Austrian music critic; b. Brno, Dec. 24, 1860; d. Hollywood, Sept. 25, 1945. He was a law student; at the same time he studied music with Franz Krenn at the Vienna Cons. In 1902 he became music critic of the influential *Neue Freie Presse.* He was much in the limelight when his son **Erich** began his spectacular career at the age of 13 as a child composer, and an unfounded suspicion was voiced that Korngold was using his position to further his son's career. He publ. a book on a contemporary German opera, *Deutsches Opernschaffen der Gegenwart* (1922). In 1938 he joined his son in the U.S., settling in Hollywood, where he remained until his death.

Kornmüller, Utto, German writer on church music; b. Straubing, Jan. 5, 1824; d. Metten, Feb. 13, 1907. He was ordained to the priesthood in 1847; became choirmaster of the Benedictine monastery at Metten (1858); also president of the Regensburg branch of the Cäcilienverein until 1903. He publ. *Lexikon der kirchlichen Tonkunst* (1870); *Der katholische Kirchenchor* (1868); *Die Musik beim liturgischen Hochamt* (1871); contributed articles to the *Kirchenmusikalisches Jahrbuch* and *Monatshefte für Musikgeschichte;* wrote a number of masses and motets.

Kórodi, András, Hungarian conductor; b. Budapest, May 24, 1922. He studied at the Franz Liszt Academy of Music in Budapest with Ferencsik in conducting and with Lajtha in composition. He joined the staff of the Budapest Opera in 1946; in 1963 he became principal conductor there. In 1967 he became chief conductor of the Budapest Phil. Orch.; also taught conducting at the Liszt Academy.

Korte, Karl, American composer; b. Ossining, N.Y., Aug. 25, 1928. He studied at Illinois Wesleyan Univ. (1948–49); attained professional skill as a trumpet player; then took composition courses with Peter Mennin and William Bergsma at the Juilliard School of Music in N.Y. (B.S., 1953); in 1953 he went to Italy on a Fulbright grant and studied with Goffredo Petrassi at the Santa Cecilia Academy. From 1954 to 1956 he was again a student at Juilliard, in the composition class of Vincent Persichetti (M.S., 1956); later took private lessons with Otto Luening (1956–59); attended the seminar of Aaron Copland in Tanglewood in the summers of 1960 and 1961. He composed industriously and had the satisfaction of having his works performed, praised, published, and recorded. He was awarded two Guggenheim Foundation grants, in 1960 and in 1970. His music is quaquaversal in an attractively scientific manner, with the stylistic spectrum ranging from infrared, so to speak, in his archaically impressed works through the mandatory neo-Baroque essays to the ultra-violet rarefaction of mathematical conceits, abstractions, serialism, and electronics. His teaching posts included Arizona State Univ. (1963–64); State Univ. of N.Y. at Binghamton (1964–71); Univ. of Texas in Austin, beginning in 1971.

WORKS: For Orch.: Concertato on a Choral Theme (1955); *For a Young Audience* (1959); Symph. No. 2 (1961); *Southwest,* dance overture (1963); Symph. No. 3 (1968); Concerto for Piano and Wind Instruments (1976). Chamber music: 2 string quartets (1948, 1965); *Fantasy* for Violin and Piano (1959); Quintet for Oboe and Strings (1960); *Matrix* (1968); *Facets* (1969); *Rembembrances* for Solo Flute and Tape (1971); *Symmetrics* (1974); Trio for Piano, Violin, and Cello (1977); *Sonata 1955* for Piano (1955). Choral music: *Mass for Youth* (1963); *Aspects of Love* (1965); *May the Sun Bless Us* (1968); *Pale Is This Good Prince* (1973); *Libera Me* (1974); *Time and Season* (1975); *Sappho Says* (1979); *Music for a New Easter* (1980); *Music for a New Christmas* (1980).

Korte, Oldřich František, Czech composer; b. Šala-on-Váh, April 26, 1926. He studied with Pícha at the Prague Cons. (1943–49); then toured as a pianist and an actor with the modernistic group Laterna Magica and also worked as a photographer. His music is similarly quaquaversal and quite uninhibited in its methods and resources.

WORKS: *Iniuria* for Piano (1942–44); *The Drinker's Transformations,* variations for Piano (1945); Sinfonietta (1945–47); *In Praise of Death* for Piccolo and Glockenspiel (1948); *Příběh fléten (The Story of the Flutes)* for Orch. (1949–51; Prague Radio, Oct. 23, 1953); *Concerto grosso* for Strings, Trumpets, and Piano (1954–62; revised 1968); *Philosophical Dialogues* for Violin and Piano (1964–68); 2-act musical, *The Pirates of the Fortune* (Vienna, April 15, 1974).

Korte, Werner, German musicologist; b. Münster, May 29, 1906; d. there, Nov. 26, 1982. He studied science at the univs. of Münster and Freiburg (1924–26); then took a course in musicology with Johannes

Wolf at the Univ. of Berlin (1926–28), receiving his Ph.D. there in 1928 with the dissertation *Die Harmonik des frühen 15. Jahrhunderts in ihrem Zusammenhang mit der Formtechnik;* completed his Habilitation in 1932 at the Univ. of Münster with his dissertation *Studien zur Geschichte der Musik in Italien im ersten Viertel des 15. Jahrhunderts* (publ. in Kassel, 1933). He was an assistant in musicology at the Univ. of Heidelberg (1928–31); in 1932 became director of the musicology dept. at the Univ. of Münster. His books include *Bach* (Berlin, 1935); *Ludwig van Beethoven* (Berlin, 1936); *Robert Schumann* (Potsdam, 1937); *Musik und Weltbild* (Leipzig, 1940); *Händel und der deutsche Geist* (Leipzig, 1942); *Bruckner und Brahms* (Tutzing, 1963).

Kortschak, Hugo, Austrian violinist and conductor; b. Graz, Feb. 24, 1884; d. Honolulu, Sept. 20, 1957. He studied violin with Ševčík at the Prague Cons.; went to America and in 1913 organized in Chicago the Kortschak Quartet, later renamed Berkshire String Quartet. He helped organize the Coolidge Chamber Music Festival at Pittsfield, Mass., in 1918, and in 1938 received the Coolidge Medal for "distinguished services to chamber music."

Kortsen, Bjarne, Norwegian musicologist; b. Haugesund, July 4, 1930. He studied music and electrical engineering; was employed by the Norwegian railways for 3 years while studying musicology at the Univ. of Oslo (M.A., 1962); later studied at the Univ. of Glasgow (Ph.D., 1964), at the Univ. of Cologne, and at the Hochschule für Musik in Berlin. He publ. a number of valuable books in Norwegian, German, and Eng.: *Fartein Valen, Life and Music* (3 vols., Oslo, 1965); *Modern Norwegian Chamber Music* (Haugesund, 1965); *Contemporary Norwegian Orchestral Music* (West Berlin, 1969); *Chamber Music Works by Johan Svendsen* (Bergen, 1971).

Kósa, György, Hungarian composer and pianist; b. Budapest, April 24, 1897; d. Budapest, Aug. 16, 1984. He exhibited a precocious talent for music, and when he was 7 years old Béla Bartók accepted him as a piano student. At 13 he entered the Budapest Academy of Music, where he studied with Kodály, Siklós, and Victor Herzfeld; he continued his piano studies in the class of Dohnányi and received his diploma in 1917. He then traveled as an accompanist with violinists and other artists in Germany, Austria, and Italy; returned to Budapest in 1921 and in 1927 became prof. of piano at the Budapest Academy of Music. He remained in Budapest during World War II and was compelled to serve as a manual laborer in a war camp; after 1945 he resumed his teaching at the Academy, where he stayed until retirement in 1962. The primary influence in his music is that of Bartók, but he also experienced the attraction of impressionist techniques.
WORKS: 7 operas: *The King's Robe* (1926–27); *The 2 Knights,* opera buffa (1934; Budapest, 1936); *Cenodoxus,* mystery opera (1941–42); *The Scholar Ansel-*

mus (1944–45); *Tartuffe* (1950); *Knight Pázmány* (1962–63); *The Wedding of Mihály Kocsonya,* opera buffa (1971); 7 biblical oratorios; 6 secular oratorios, including *Villon* (1960–61) and *Manole* (1965); 3 biblical cantatas; 6 secular cantatas, including *Orpheus, Eurydike, Hermes* (1967), *Cantata humana* (1967), and *Susanna* (1971); 3 masses (1946, 1949, 1951); 2 Requiems (1949, 1966); ballets and pantomimes, including *White Pierrot* (Budapest, 1920), *Laterna Magica* (with Voices, 1922; Budapest, Feb. 23, 1927), *The 3 Miracles of Joe the Orphan* (1932; Budapest, Feb. 26, 1933; *Mohács,* 1957; 1959; 1969); *Fairy Tale Suite* (1931); *Fantasy on 3 Hungarian Folk Songs* (1948); *Ballad and Rondo* for Violin and Wind Orch. (1961). Chamber music: 8 string quartets (1920, 1929, 1933, 1937, 1956, 1959–60, 1963, 1965); Duet for Violin and Double Bass (1928); *Music for 17 Instruments* (1928); Quintet for Harp and Winds (1938); Trio for Flute, Violin, and Cello (1941); Trio for 2 Violins and Viola (1946); Trio for Wordless Soprano, Violin, and Clarinet (1947); 2 wind quintets (1955, 1960); *Cello Cantata* for Cello, Organ, Piano, and Percussion (1963); Duet for Violin and Cello (1964). He also wrote 3 piano sonatas (1941, 1947, 1956); Solo Cello Sonata (1928); Variations for Piano (1933); Violin Sonata (1937); *Gaby Sonata* for Violin and Piano (1958); *Concerto patetico* for Violin and Piano (1960); *Elegy* for Solo Violin (1964); Cello Sonata (1965); many songs, often with string quartet and other ensemble accompaniment; choruses.

Kosakoff, Reuven, American pianist and composer; b. New Haven, Conn., Jan. 8, 1898. He studied at Yale Univ. and at the Juilliard School of Music in N.Y.; then went to Berlin as a private piano student of Artur Schnabel. He has written several biblical cantatas; 2 Sabbath services; Piano Concerto on Hebrew themes (Pittsburgh, March 24, 1941); *Jack and the Beanstalk* for Narrator and Orch. (New Haven, April 22, 1944).

Koschat, Thomas, Austrian bass singer and composer; b. Viktring, near Klagenfurt, Aug. 8, 1845; d. Vienna, May 19, 1914. He sang in the chorus at various churches; then turned to composition; publ. his first vocal quartets in the Carinthian dialect in 1871; they became so successful that he publ. some 100 more. In 1875 he organized the famous Kärnthner Quintett with 4 other singers; their performances were exceedingly popular. His "Liederspiel" *Am Wörthersee* (Vienna, March 22, 1880), containing many of his favorite vocal numbers, had great vogue; he also produced a 4-act "Volksstück mit Gesang," *Die Rosenthaler Nachtigall,* and the singspiel *Der Bürgermeister von St. Anna* (Vienna, May 1, 1884; given in Italian as *Un colpo di fuoco*).
BIBLIOGRAPHY: Karl Krobath, *Thomas Koschat, der Sänger Kärnthners* (Leipzig, 1912).

Köselitz, Heinrich (pen name, **Peter Gast**), German

writer and composer; b. Annaberg, Jan. 10, 1854; d. there, Aug. 15, 1918. He studied with Richter at the Leipzig Cons. While in Basel, he formed an intimate friendship with Nietzsche, from whom he also took lessons in composition; after Nietzsche's death, Köselitz became his literary executor; edited Nietzsche's letters. As a composer, he elaborated the Wagnerian system of *Leitmotive;* he used the pen name of Peter Gast for his musical productions, among them the operas *Wilbram und Siegeheer* (1879); *Scherz, List und Rache* (1881); *Die heimliche Ehe* (Danzig, 1891; publ. in 1901 as *Der Löwe von Venedig*); *König Wenzel* (not produced); and *Orpheus und Dionysos* (not produced); a festival play, *Walpurgisnacht* (1903); a symph. poem, *Helle Nächte;* choruses; songs.
    BIBLIOGRAPHY: L. Brieger-Wasservogel, *Peter Gast* (Leipzig, 1906); F. Götz, *Peter Gast* (Annaberg, 1934); F. Tutenberg, "Peters Gasts Löwe von Venedig," *Zeitschrift für Musik* (Feb. 1940).

Koshetz, Nina, Russian soprano; b. Kiev, Dec. 30, 1894; d. Santa Ana, Calif., May 14, 1965. She studied piano as a child; then began to study singing. She toured Russia with Rachmaninoff, of whose songs she was a congenial interpreter. After the Revolution she went to the U.S.; appeared as a soloist with major American orchs. and also sang recitals of Russian songs. In 1941 she went to California and devoted herself to teaching.

Kosleck, Julius, German trumpet and cornet virtuoso; b. Neugard, Dec. 3, 1825; d. Berlin, Nov. 5, 1904. He was a trumpeter in the court orch. in Berlin; in 1871 he founded the Kaiser Cornett Quartett; also a wind band, Patriotischer Bläserbund; from 1873 taught at the Hochschule für Musik in Berlin. He was influential in reviving the historic art of the fanfare; publ. a method for the trumpet and cornet à pistons. In 1884 he introduced a trumpet with a broad, funnel-shaped mouthpiece, which was regarded as a "Bach trumpet," capable of playing high florid parts.

Košler, Zdeněk, Czech conductor; b. Prague, March 3, 1928. He studied at the Prague Academy; made his debut at the Prague National Theater in 1951. In 1966 he became chief conductor of the Prague Symph.; concurrently served as Generalmusikdirektor of the Komische Oper in East Berlin (1965–68). In 1971 he was appointed chief conductor of the Slovak National Theater in Bratislava. In 1980 he became chief conductor of the Prague National Theater.

Kosma, Joseph, Hungarian-French composer; b. Budapest, Oct. 22, 1905; d. La Roche-Guyon, near Paris, Aug. 7, 1969. He studied at the Music Academy in Budapest; in 1933 he went to Paris and settled there as a composer of ballet and film music.
    WORKS: Ballets: *Le Rendez-vous* (Paris, June 15, 1945); *Baptiste* (1946); *L'Ecuyère* (1948); *Le Pierrot de Montmartre* (1952); film scores to *La Grande Illusion, Les Enfants du paradis,* etc.; comic operas:

Les Chansons de Bilitis (1954); *Un Amour électronique* (Paris, 1962); *La Révolte des canuts* (Lyons, 1964); *Les Hussards* (Lyons, Oct. 21, 1969). He also wrote an oratorio, *Les Ponts de Paris* (1947); a number of characteristic piano pieces (*Danse des automates,* etc.); songs.

Kössler, Hans. See **Koessler, Hans.**

Kossmaly, Carl, German writer on music and conductor; b. Breslau, July 27, 1812; d. Stettin, Dec. 1, 1893. He studied in Berlin with Berger, Zelter, and Klein; then was chorus master at theaters in Wiesbaden, Mainz, Amsterdam, Bremen, Detmold, and Stettin, where he settled as a teacher and concert conductor. He publ. *Schlesisches Tonkünstler-Lexikon* (1846–47); *Mozarts Opern* (1848); *Über die Anwendung des Programmes zur Erklärung musikalischer Compositionen* (1858); *Über Richard Wagner* (1873; anti-Wagnerian); contributed articles to music periodicals; also wrote symphs., overtures, instrumental and vocal works, songs, etc.

Kostelanetz, André, Russian-American conductor; b. St. Petersburg, Dec. 22, 1901; d. Port-au-Prince, Haiti, Jan. 13, 1980. He studied at the St. Petersburg Cons. In 1922 he left Russia and went to America. He was employed as a rehearsal accompanist at the Metropolitan Opera in N.Y.; in 1930 was engaged to conduct the CBS Symph. Orch. On June 2, 1938, he married the famous soprano **Lily Pons;** they were divorced some years later. During World War II he organized concerts for the U.S. Armed Forces; subsequently conducted numerous popular concerts in America and in Europe, particularly summer concerts. He also made successful arrangements of light music; his technique of massive concentration of instrumental sonorities and of harmonic saturation by means of filling in harmonies with inner thirds and sixths influenced film music. An intelligent musician, he commissioned special works from American composers, of which the most successful was Copland's *Lincoln Portrait.*
    BIBLIOGRAPHY: André Kostelanetz with Gloria Hammond, *Echoes: Memoirs of André Kostelanetz* (N.Y., 1981).

Kostić, Dušan, Croatian composer; b. Zagreb, Jan. 23, 1925. He studied at the Music Academy in Belgrade; later took a course in conducting with Scherchen. He incorporated neo-Classical, impressionistic, and serial techniques in his music; also wrote occasional pieces on national folk themes.
    WORKS: 2 symphs. (1957, 1961); symph. poem, *Contrasts* (1954); *Crnogorska suita* for Orch. (1957); *Sonata amorosa* for Violin and Piano (1957); opera buffa, *Majstori su prvi ljudi* (Belgrade, April 23, 1962); *Kragujevac,* symph. poem for Voices and Orch., commemorating the execution of the schoolboys at Kragujevac in 1941 by the Nazi occupation forces (Belgrade, Feb. 5, 1962); choruses; songs; piano pieces.

Kostić, Vojislav, Serbian composer; b. Belgrade, Sept. 21, 1931. He studied in his native city; adopted a sophisticated style of utilitarian music. His *Karakteri* for Clarinet, Piano, and 18 Percussion Instruments (1958) had numerous performances in Yugoslavia. He also wrote a Divertimento for Wind Quintet; Suite for Bassoon and Piano; *Ciganska priča (Gypsy Tale)* for Male Chorus and Chamber Orch., to Gypsy texts (1964).

Köstlin, Heinrich Adolf, theologian and organizer of church festivals; b. Tübingen, Oct. 4, 1846; d. Cannstadt, June 4, 1907. He was the son of **Josephine Lang-Köstlin,** the song composer (1815–80). In 1875 he united the choirs of 3 towns (Sulz, Kalw, Nagold) for church music performances, which became the nucleus of the Württemberg Evangelical "Kirchengesangverein," organized by him in 1877, the festivals of which he also conducted. In 1883 he organized, with L. Hallwachs, a similar society for all Germany, with annual meetings in different cities; this led to the establishment of more choral branches for sacred music (more than 2,000 choirs in 1916). Köstlin publ. *Geschichte der Musik im Umriss* (1873; 6th ed., revised by W. Nagel, 1910); *Die Tonkunst: Einführung in die Asthetik der Musik* (1878); *Luther als Vater des evangelischen Kirchenliedes* (1882); *Geschichte des christlichen Gottesdienstes* (1886); also a biographical sketch of his mother (Leipzig, 1881).

Köstlin, Karl Reinhold, German music theorist; b. Urach, Sept. 28, 1819; d. Tübingen, April 12, 1894. He taught esthetics and art history at Tübingen Univ. He publ. *Asthetik* (2 vols., 1863–69); an essay on musical esthetics in Vischer's *Asthetik* (vol. 3); and a pamphlet on Wagner.

Kostov, Georgi, Bulgarian composer; b. Sofia, Jan. 21, 1941. He studied composition with Pantcho Vladigerov and Peter Stoyanov at the Bulgarian State Cons., graduating in 1966; pursued his studies at the Moscow Cons. (1972); returning to Bulgaria, he became an instructor at his alma mater.
WORKS: Ballet, *The Broadside of "Avrora"* (1967); 2 oratorios: *Glorious Days* (1969) and *Alive He Is* (1976); 2 cantatas: *The Communist Man* (1964) and *We Are Proud of You, Our Party* (1975); Clarinet Concerto (1958); Viola Concertino (1965); Concerto for Horn, String Orch., and Timpani (1966); *Youth Overture* (1967); *3 Diaphonous Dances* for Orch. (1972); *Poem* for Trumpet, Percussion, and String Orch. (1973); *Prelude, Chorale, and Fugue* for Orch. (1974); *Rhythmic Movements* for Orch. (1974); *Antiphonous Dialogues* for Orch. (1974); *September Ballad* for Orch. (1974); chamber music; choral songs; popular music.

Kotek, Joseph, Russian violinist; b. Kamenetz-Podolsk, Oct. 25, 1855; d. Davos, Switzerland, Jan. 4, 1885. He studied violin with Ferdinand Laub and composition with Tchaikovsky at the Moscow Cons.; later took violin lessons with Joachim in Berlin. He was an intimate friend of Tchaikovsky, and often served as mediator in financial matters between him and Nadezhda von Meck; also worked over the solo part of Tchaikovsky's Violin Concerto, and played it with the composer at the piano, privately, at Clarens, Switzerland (April 3, 1878); however, he was reluctant to try it out in public performance despite Tchaikovsky's urgings. In 1878–82 he taught violin at the Hochschule für Musik in Berlin. He died of tuberculosis at the age of 29; Tchaikovsky made a special trip to Davos to see him before his death.

Köth, Erika, German soprano; b. Darmstadt, Sept. 15, 1927. After winning a prize sponsored by the Hessische Radio in 1947, she made her debut in a radio performance in Darmstadt; then sang with the Karlsruhe Opera (1950–53); also appeared with the Bavarian State Opera in Munich and with the Vienna State Opera.

Kothe, Aloys, German music teacher, brother of **Bernhard** and **Wilhelm Kothe;** b. Gröbnig, Oct. 3, 1828; d. Breslau, Nov. 13, 1868. He studied with Grell in Berlin; taught at the Teachers' Seminary in Breslau. He publ. a Mass for Men's Voices; piano pieces; songs, etc.

Kothe, Bernhard, German writer on music, brother of **Aloys** and **Wilhelm Kothe;** b. Gröbnig, May 12, 1821; d. Breslau, July 25, 1897. He studied in Berlin with A.B. Marx; in 1851, became church music director and teacher at Oppeln; then succeeded his brother Aloys Kothe as music teacher at the Teachers' Seminary in Breslau, where he founded the Cäcilien-Verein for Catholic church music. He publ. *Musica Sacra;* 2 pamphlets: *Die Musik in der katholischen Kirche* (1862) and *Abriss der Musikgeschichte für Lehrerseminare und Dilettanten* (1874); also edited the 4th edition of Seidel's *Die Orgel und ihr Bau* (1887) and, with Forchhammer, *Führer durch die Orgellitteratur* (1890). He also publ. a book of organ preludes; other organ pieces; motets.

Kothe, Robert, German singer and folk-song arranger; b. Straubing, Feb. 6, 1869; d. Gräfelfing, near Munich, May 24, 1944. He appeared as a singer, accompanying himself on the lute; established a school for lutenists in Gelsenkirchen; publ. 12 albums of folk-song arrangements; also a method of lute playing (1929).
BIBLIOGRAPHY: Fritz Jöde, *Robert Kothe* (1916).

Kothe, Wilhelm, German music teacher, brother of **Aloys** and **Bernhard Kothe;** b. Gröbnig, Jan. 8, 1831; d. Habelschwerdt, Dec. 31, 1897. He studied organ in Berlin; from 1871 until his death he was music teacher at the Teachers' Seminary in Habelschwerdt. He publ. the pamphlet *Friedrich der Grosse als Musiker;* also methods for violin and voice; songs; piano music.

Kothen, Karl Axel, Finnish singer and composer; b. Frederikshamm, Aug. 15, 1871; d. Helsinki, July 7, 1927. He studied in Helsinki, Rome, St. Petersburg, Vienna, Paris, and Munich; returning to Helsinki in 1908, he became a prof. of singing at the Helsinki Cons. He wrote several choral works, among them *Vagorna sjunga* and *Finlands namm* (both for the Finland Jubilee of 1920); also a cantata for the festival of the tercentenary of Vasa; incidental music to *Kristina Vasa;* piano pieces and songs.

Kotík, Petr, Czech flutist and composer; b. Prague, Jan. 27, 1942. He studied in Prague and later at the Vienna Academy of Music with Schiske and Jelinek; in 1966 formed there an experimental music ensemble, Quax. His works, which tend to embrace all manner of contemporary techniques, include *Spontano* for Piano and 10 Wind Instruments (1964); *Contrabandt* for Several Players and Electronic Music (1967); *6 švestek (6 Plums)* for 24 Instruments (1968).

Kotilainen, Otto, Finnish composer; b. Heinävesi, Feb. 5, 1868; d. Helsinki, Aug. 9, 1936. He studied with Wegelius and Sibelius at the Helsingfors Cons., and in Berlin. He wrote a cantata, *Cygneus; Festsang* for Chorus and Horns; Orch. Suite; *Legend* for String Orch.; incidental music for plays; pieces for violin and piano; choruses; songs.

Kotoński, Wlodzimierz, Polish composer of the avant-garde; b. Warsaw, Aug. 23, 1925. He studied theory with Piotr Rytel at the Warsaw Cons. (1945–51) and also took private lessons with Tadeusz Szeligowski in Poznan. He became a research worker in Polish folk music at the State Inst. of Art, and simultaneously began experimenting with alteration of sound by electronic means; produced an *Etude concrète* in which a single stroke of cymbals was electronically metamorphosed and expanded into a work of considerable length (1949). In 1959–60 he attended the summer sessions of new music at Darmstadt; then went to Paris, where he researched the problems of musique concrète with Pierre Schaeffer; in 1966–67 he worked at the Electronic Music Studio of the West German Radio in Cologne; in 1978 lectured at the State Univ. of N.Y. at Buffalo; in 1981 he again visited the U.S. to attend the world premiere of his *Sirocco.* WORKS: *Etude concrète* for a single stroke of Cymbals electronically metamorphosed (1949; Darmstadt, July 9, 1960); *Poème* for Orch. (1949); *Quartettino* for 4 Horns (1950); *Danses montagnardes* for Orch. (1950); *Prelude and Passacaglia* for Orch. (1953); *6 Miniatures* for Clarinet and Piano (1957); *Chamber Music* for 21 Instruments and Percussion (1958; Warsaw Festival, Oct. 2, 1958); *Musique en relief,* cycle of 5 miniatures for 6 Orch. Groups (1959; Darmstadt, Sept. 5, 1959); Trio for Flute, Guitar, and Percussion (1960); *Concerto per quattro* for Harp, Harpsichord, Guitar, Piano, and Chamber Orch. (1960); *Canto* for 18 Instruments (1961); *Selection I* for 4 Jazz Players (1962); *Pezzo* for Flute and Piano (1962); *Musica per fiati e* timpani (1964); 2 wind quintets (1964, 1967); *Monochromie* for Solo Oboe (1964); *A battere* for Guitar, Viola, Cello, Harpsichord, and Percussion (1966); *Pour quatre* for Clarinet, Trombone, Cello, and Piano (1968); *Action* for Electronic Sound (Cracow, June 5, 1969); *Music* for 16 Cymbals and Strings (1969; Warsaw, Sept. 20, 1969); *Multiplay,* instrumental theater for Brass Quintet (1971); *Musical Games,* instrumental theater for 5 Players (1972); Oboe Concerto (1972); *Aeolian Harp* for Soprano and 4 Instruments (1972–73); *Promenade* for Clarinet, Trombone, and Cello, all electronically amplified, and 2 Synthesizers (1973); *Wind Rose* for Orch. (1976); *Spring Music* for Flute, Oboe, Violin, and Synthesizer (1978); *Bora* for Orch. (1979); *Sirocco* for Orch. (1981). He publ. a book, *Instrumenty perkusyjne we współczesnej orkiestrze (Percussion Instruments in the Modern Orchestra;* Cracow, 1963).

Kotter, Hans, Alsatian organist and composer; b. Strasbourg, c.1480; d. Bern, 1541. He studied organ with Paul Hofhaimer; was organist at the electoral court in Torgau; then served as organist at the collegiate church of St. Nikolaus in Fribourg, Switzerland (1514–30) until he was banished for espousing the doctrines of the reformer Zwingli. In 1534 Kotter was able to return to Switzerland, and he took up residence in Bern as a schoolmaster. He compiled a collection of keyboard pieces in tablature (1513), including preambles, fantasies, dances, transcriptions of vocal music, and settings of plainchant. There is also in existence a setting of a *Nobis post hoc* by Kotter interpolated in a *Salve Regina* by Hofhaimer.
BIBLIOGRAPHY: W. Merian, *Die Tabulaturen des Organisten Hans Kotter* (Leipzig, 1916); W. Apel, "Early German Keyboard Music," *Musical Quarterly* (April 1937); G. Reese, *Music in the Renaissance* (N.Y., 1954; 2nd ed., revised, 1959).

Kottlitz, Adolf, German violinist; b. Trier, Sept. 27, 1820; killed while hunting in Uralsk, Russia, Oct. 26, 1860. He began his career as a child prodigy; gave public concerts at the age of 10; spent 3 years in Paris, where he was a protégé of Liszt; then played violin in the orch. of the Königsberg Opera (1848–56). In 1856 he undertook a long tour in Russia, and finally settled in Uralsk as a violin teacher. He publ. 2 string quartets. His wife, **Clothilde** (née **Ellendt;** 1822–67), was a singing teacher in Königsberg.

Kotzeluch, Leopold Anton. See **Koželuch, Leopold Anton.**

Kotzolt, Heinrich, German vocal teacher; b. Schnellewalde, Aug. 26, 1814; d. Berlin, July 2, 1881. He first studied philology in Breslau, but turned to music, studying in Berlin with Dehn and Rungenhagen (1836–38); then sang at the Danzig Opera (1838–42). Returning to Berlin, he founded a singing society there in 1849. He publ. a method for a cappella singing; also composed a setting of the 54th Psalm for Double Chorus a cappella; *Lobet den Herrn alle*

Heiden for 8-part Chorus; etc.

Kotzschmar, Hermann, organist; b. Finsterwalde, Germany, July 4, 1829; d. Portland, Maine, April 12, 1909. As a child, he learned to play the organ and virtually all orch. instruments; then studied seriously in Dresden. In 1848 he came to America with the Saxonia Band and settled in Portland, Maine, as a teacher; was for 47 years organist at the First Unitarian Church there. He publ. many vocal quartets, songs, and piano pieces. His Te Deum in F was often sung in American churches. He was also esteemed as a teacher; J.K. Paine was his pupil.
BIBLIOGRAPHY: G.T. Edwards, *Music and Musicians of Maine* (Portland, 1928; pp. 167–69).

Kotzwara (*recte* **Kočvara**), **Franz,** Bohemian composer; b. Prague, 1730; d. (by hanging himself) London, Sept. 2, 1791. He traveled in Europe; then settled in London toward the end of the 18th century. In 1790 he went to Dublin as a viola player in the orch. at the King's Theatre; returning to London the same year, he played in the orch. at the Handel Commemoration in May. He is remembered solely for his piano piece *The Battle of Prague,* which attained tremendous popularity in the 19th century.

Kouguell, Arkadie, Russian-American pianist and composer; b. Simferopol, Dec. 25, 1898. He studied at the St. Petersburg Cons. From 1928 to 1948 he lived in Beirut; then in Paris. In 1952 he settled in N.Y. as a piano teacher.
WORKS: *Impressions of Damascus* for Orch. (1930); *Rapsodi tartare* for Orch. (1947); Piano Concerto (1930); Piano Concerto for Left Hand (1934); Cello Concerto (1950); Concertino for Trombone and Piano (1956); *Bédouin Dance* for an ensemble of 60 Cellos (1932); 2 string quartets; 3 piano sonatas; Violin Sonata; 2 cello sonatas; suites for various chamber groups.

Kounadis, Arghyris, Greek composer; b. Constantinople, Feb. 14, 1924. He moved to Athens in his infancy; studied piano at home and jurisprudence at the Univ. of Athens; at the same time began to compose. In 1958 he went to Freiburg, Germany, where he studied composition with Wolfgang Fortner; became interested in the theater; wrote incidental music for Greek plays produced at Epidaurus (1958, 1960, 1961). In his instrumental works he follows the dodecaphonic technique. Of these, his *Chorikon* for Orch. was performed by the Berlin Phil. on May 15, 1962. This was followed by other symph. works in the same manner: *Triptychon* (1964) and *Heterophonika Idiomela* (1967).

Kountz, Richard, American composer; b. Pittsburgh, July 8, 1896; d. New York, Oct. 14, 1950. In 1927–39 he was manager of the Standard and Educational Publications dept. of M. Witmark & Sons in N.Y. He wrote *The Sleigh* and other songs; a *Pastorale* for Organ; etc.; also made arrangements for various choral combinations.

Koussevitzky, Serge, celebrated Russian conductor; b. Vishny-Volochok, July 26, 1874; d. Boston, June 4, 1951. His father and his 3 brothers were all amateur musicians. Koussevitzky learned to play the trumpet and took part, with his brothers, in a small wind ensemble, numbering 8 members in all; they earned their living by playing at balls and weddings and occasionally at village fairs. At the age of 14 he went to Moscow; since Jews were not allowed to live there, he became baptized. He then received a fellowship with free tuition at the Musico-Dramatic Inst. of the Moscow Phil., in the class of the double bass; his teacher was the famous double-bass player Ramboušek; he also studied music theory with Blaramberg and Kruglikov. In 1894 he joined the orch. of the Bolshoi Opera Theater, where Ramboušek held the first chair in the double-bass section. Upon Ramboušek's death in 1901, Koussevitzky succeeded him at his post. Koussevitzky before long became known as a soloist of the first magnitude on the double bass who was able to achieve high artistic performance on this supposedly unwieldy instrument. On March 25, 1901, he gave his first public concert in Moscow in a program which included an adaptation of Handel's Cello Concerto; on subsequent occasions he performed his own arrangement for double bass of Mozart's Bassoon Concerto and of Bruch's *Kol Nidrei.* On March 27, 1903, he gave a double-bass recital in Berlin, attracting great attention. To supplement the meager repertoire, he wrote several pieces for the double bass and performed them at his concerts; with some aid from Glière, he composed a Double-bass Concerto, which he performed for the first time in Moscow on Feb. 25, 1905. On Sept. 8, 1905, he married Natalie Ushkov, of a wealthy tea-merchant family. He soon resigned from the orch. of the Bolshoi Opera Theater; in an open letter to the Russian publication *Musical Gazette,* explained the reason for his resignation as the economic and artistic difficulties in the orch. He then went to Germany, where he continued to give double-bass recitals; played the First Cello Concerto by Saint-Saëns on the double bass. In 1907 he conducted a student orch. at the Berlin Hochschule für Musik; his first public appearance as a conductor took place on Jan. 23, 1908, with the Berlin Phil. In 1909 he established a publishing house, Editions Russes de Musique; in 1915 he purchased the catalogue of the Gutheil Co.; among composers with whom he signed contracts were Scriabin, Stravinsky, Prokofiev, Medtner, and Rachmaninoff; the association with Scriabin was particularly fruitful, and in subsequent years Koussevitzky became the greatest champion of Scriabin's music. In 1909 he organized his own symph. orch. in Moscow, featuring works by Russian composers, but also including classical masterpieces; played many Russian works for the first time, among them Scriabin's *Prometheus.* In the summer of 1910 he took his orch. to the towns along the Volga River in a specially chartered steamboat. He repeated the Volga tour in 1912 and 1914. The outbreak of World War I made it necessary to curtail his activities; however, he continued to give his concerts in Moscow; in 1915 he presented a memorial Scriabin program. After the Revolution of 1917, Koussevitzky was offered the directorship of the State Symph. Orch. (former Court Orch.) in Petrograd; he conducted it until 1920; also presented concerts in Moscow despite the hardships of the revolutionary times. In 1920 he left Russia; went first to Berlin, then to Rome, and finally to Paris, where he settled for several years. There he organized the Concerts Koussevitzky with a specially assembled orch.; presented many new scores by French and Russian composers, among them Ravel's orchestration of Mussorgsky's *Pictures at an Exhibition,* Honegger's *Pacific 231,* and several works by Prokofiev and Stravinsky. In 1924 Koussevitzky was engaged as permanent conductor of the Boston Symph. Orch., a post that he was to hold for 25 years, the longest tenure of any conductor of that organization; until 1928 he continued his Paris series (during the summer months). Just as in Russia he championed Russian composers, in France the French, so in the U.S. he encouraged American composers to write works for the Boston Symph. Orch. Symphonic compositions by Aaron Copland, Roy Harris, Walter Piston, Samuel Barber, Howard Hanson, Edward Burlingame Hill, William Schuman, and others were performed by Koussevitzky for the first time. For the 50th anniversary of the Boston Symph. Orch. (1931) Koussevitzky commissioned works from Stravinsky (*Symphony of Psalms*), Hindemith, Honegger, Prokofiev, Albert Roussel, Ravel (piano concerto), Copland, Gershwin, etc. In 1950 he conducted in Rio de Janeiro, Israel, and in Europe; also was guest conductor at several concerts of the Boston Symph. after his successor, Charles Munch, became principal conductor. A highly important development in Koussevitzky's American career was the establishment of the Berkshire Music Center at Tanglewood, Mass. This was an outgrowth of the Berkshire Symph. Festival, organized in 1934 by Henry Hadley; Koussevitzky and the Boston Symph. Orch. presented summer concerts at the Berkshire Festival in 1935 for the first time; since then, the concerts have become an annual institution. The Berkshire Music Center was opened on July 8, 1940, with Koussevitzky as director and Copland as assistant director; among the distinguished guest instructors were Hindemith, Honegger, and Messiaen; Koussevitzky himself taught conducting; he was succeeded after his death by his former student Leonard Bernstein. Koussevitzky held many honorary degrees: Mus.Doc. from Brown Univ. (1926), Rutgers Univ. (1937), Yale Univ. (1938), Rochester Univ. (1940), Williams College (1943), and Boston Univ. (1945); LL.D. from Harvard Univ. (1929) and from Princeton Univ. (1947). He was a member of the French Legion of Honor; held the Cross of Commander of the Finnish Order of the White Rose (1936). Besides his Double-bass Concerto, he wrote *Humoresque, Valse miniature, Chanson triste,* and other small pieces for his instrument; and an orch. work, *Passacaglia on a Russian Theme* (Boston Symph., Oct. 12, 1934). Koussevitzky became an American citizen on April 16, 1941. In 1942 his wife died; he established the Koussevitzky Foundation as a memorial

to her, the funds to be used for commissioning works by composers of all nationalities. He married Olga Naoumoff (1901–78), a niece of Natalie Koussevitzky, on Aug. 15, 1947.

As a conductor, Koussevitzky possessed an extraordinary emotional power; in Russian music, and particularly in Tchaikovsky's symphs., he was unexcelled; he was capable of achieving the subtlest nuances in the works of the French school; his interpretations of Debussy were notable. As a champion of modern music, he introduced a great number of compositions for the first time anywhere; his ardor in projecting unfamiliar music before new audiences in different countries served to carry conviction among the listeners and the professional music critics. He was often criticized for the liberties he allowed himself in the treatment of classical masterpieces; undoubtedly his performances of Bach, Beethoven, Brahms, and Schubert were untraditional; but they were nonetheless musicianly in the sincere artistry that animated his interpretations.

BIBLIOGRAPHY: A. Lourié, *S.A. Koussevitzky and His Epoch* (N.Y., 1931); Hugo Leichtentritt, *Serge Koussevitzky, The Boston Symphony Orchestra and the New American Music* (Cambridge, Mass., 1946); M.A. DeWolfe Howe, *The Boston Symphony Orchestra 1881–1931* (Boston, 1931); idem, *The Tale of Tanglewood* (Boston, 1946); Moses Smith, *Koussevitzky* (N.Y., 1947; a controversial biography; Koussevitzky instituted a suit against the author and publisher for invasion of his right of privacy, but lost his case in court).

Koutzen, Boris, Russian-American violinist and composer; b. Uman, near Kiev, April 1, 1901; d. Mount Kisco, N.Y., Dec. 10, 1966. He studied violin with Leo Zetlin and composition with Glière at the Moscow Cons. (1918–22). In 1922 he went to the U.S. and joined the violin section of the Philadelphia Orch.; also taught violin at the Philadelphia Cons. His music possesses an attractive Romantic flavor in an old Russian manner. He composed a number of orch. pieces, among them *Solitude* (Philadelphia, April 1, 1927, composer conducting); *Valley Forge,* symph. poem (N.Y., Feb. 19, 1940); Concerto for 5 Solo Instruments (Boston, Feb. 23, 1940); Violin Concerto (Philadelphia, Feb. 22, 1952, **Nadia Koutzen,** composer's daughter, soloist); Piano Concertino (1959); opera, *You Never Know* (1962); *Concertante* for 2 Flutes and Orch. (1965).

Koval, Marian, Russian composer; b. Pristan Voznesenya, Olonets district, Aug. 17, 1907; d. Moscow, Feb. 15, 1971. He studied composition with Gnessin and Miaskovsky at the Moscow Cons. (1925–30). Inspired by the revolutionary ideas of a new collective society, he organized with others a group named Procoll ("Productive Collective"), dedicated to the propaganda of music in its sociological aspects; in 1929–31 he was also a member of the Russian Assoc. of Proletarian Musicians until it was disbanded by the Soviet government as being counterproductive. He became known mainly through his choruses and solo songs on socialist subjects; all of his music is derived from modalities of Russian folk songs and those of the ethnic group of the Urals, to which he belonged. He wrote the operas *Emelian Pugatchev* (Moscow, Nov. 25, 1939) and *Sevastopoltzy* (Perm, Nov. 28, 1946); cantatas: *The People's Sacred War* (1941); *Valery Tchkalov* (1942); *The Kremlin Stars* (1947); children's opera, *The Wolf and 7 Little Goats* (1939); 2 cycles of songs about Lenin; etc.

BIBLIOGRAPHY: G. Polyanovsky, *Marian Koval* (Moscow, 1968).

Kovalev, Pavel, Russian composer; b. Nikolayev, Jan. 6, 1890; d. Paris, Nov. 16, 1951. He studied at the Cons. of Odessa; then took courses at the Leipzig Cons. with Teichmüller and Max Reger. Returning to Russia, he taught at the Odessa Cons. (1919–22). In 1927 he left Russia via China and Japan and settled in Paris, where he remained until his death. He wrote an opera, *Ariane et Barbe-bleue;* some ballet scores; a number of chamber music pieces and songs.

Kovaříček, František, Czech composer; b. Litětiny, near Pardubice, May 17, 1924. He studied with Řídký at the Prague Academy of Music, graduating in 1952; was music director of Czech Radio (1953–57); in 1966 joined the staff of the Prague Cons.

WORKS: Comic opera, *The Stolen Moon* (1966); Cello Sonata (1958); *Serenade* for 9 Instruments (1958); *Divertimento* for Strings (1960); *Larghetto* for Clarinet and Piano (1963); Clarinet Concerto (1964); *Capriccio* for Chamber Orch. (1970–71); 2 piano sonatas; songs.

Kovařovic, Karel, noted Czech conductor and composer; b. Prague, Dec. 9, 1862; d. there, Dec. 6, 1920. He studied clarinet, harp, and piano at the Prague Cons., and composition with Fibich. In 1900 he was appointed opera conductor of the National Theater in Prague, and held this post until his death; he also led symph. concerts in Prague. As a conductor, he demonstrated great craftsmanship and established a high standard of excellence in his operatic productions; his interpretations of Dvořák and Smetana were particularly notable; an ardent believer in the cause of Czech music, he promoted national compositions. In his own music, he also made use of national materials, but his treatment was mostly imitative of the French models; the influences of Gounod and Massenet are particularly noticeable. He publ. some of his lighter works under a series of humorously misspelled names of French opera composers (C. Biset, J. Héral, etc.).

WORKS: Operas (all produced in Prague): *Ženichové* (*The Bridegrooms;* May 13, 1884); *Cesta oknem* (*Through the Window;* Feb. 11, 1886); *Noc Šimona a Judy* (*The Night of Simon and Jude;* original title, *Frasquita;* Nov. 5, 1892); *Psohlavci* (*The Dog-Heads;* April 24, 1898; his most famous opera); *Na starém bělidle* (*At the Old Bleaching-House;* Nov. 22, 1901); ballets: *Hashish* (June 19, 1884); *Pohádka o nalezeném štěstí* (*A Tale of Found Happiness;* Dec. 21, 1886); *Na zaletech* (*Flirtation;* Oct. 24, 1909); symph. works; Piano Concerto; 2 string quartets; etc.

Koven, Reginald de. See **De Koven, Reginald.**

Kowalski, Henri, French pianist and composer; b. Paris, 1841; d. Bordeaux, July 8, 1916. He studied piano with Marmontel and composition with Reber; wrote characteristic piano pieces (*Marche hongroise, 12 caprices en forme d'études, Barcarolle chinoise, Sérénade japonaise,* etc.). He described his American tour in a book, *A travers l'Amérique: Impressions d'un musicien* (Paris, 1872; contains a list of his compositions).

Kowalski, Július, Slovak composer; b. Ostrava, Feb. 24, 1912. He studied composition with Rudolf Karel and Alois Hába at the Prague Cons. (1929–33); subsequently took courses in composition with Suk and conducting with Talich at the Master School there (1933–34); then went to Vienna, where he studied conducting with Clemens Krauss (1939). After the war he occupied administrative and managerial positions in Bratislava. In 1971 he became concert manager of the Music and Arts Center. As a student of Alois Hába he wrote some microtonal pieces, e.g., Suite for Violin and Viola in the sixth-tone system (1936) and Duo for Violin and Cello in the quarter-tone system (1937), but later composed in a more or less traditional style.

WORKS: Chamber opera, *Lampionová slávnost* (*The Chinese Lantern Celebration;* 1961; Ostrava, 1963); *Russian Rhapsody* for Orch. (1933–34); *Serbian Fantasy* for Orch. (1934); 5 symphs. (1954, 1957, 1959, 1970, 1974); Concertino for Violin and Chamber Orch. (1955); *Impressions* for Orch. (1965); Concerto for Cello and String Orch. (1970); Concerto for String Quartet and Orch. (1973–74; Bratislava, Nov. 14, 1974); *Concertante Symphonietta* for Wind Quintet and Orch. (1976; Bratislava, Feb. 7, 1977); 2 piano trios (1931, 1975); 4 string quartets (1932, 1954, 1965, 1975); *Divertimento* for Flute, Oboe, and Bassoon (1966); Violin Sonatina (1966); *Little Fantasy* for Flute and Piano (1969); *Grimaces* for Flute, Clarinet, Trombone, and Tuba (1970).

Kowalski, Max, German composer and pedagogue; b. Kowal, Poland, Aug. 10, 1882; d. London, June 4, 1956. He was taken to Frankfurt as an infant, and received his primary education there; studied law, obtaining his Dr.Juris. at Marburg Univ.; returning to Frankfurt, he studied music with Bernhard Sekles; in 1912 wrote a cycle of songs to Guiraud's *Pierrot Lunaire* (independently from Schoenberg's work of the same year) and during the following 20 years composed a number of lieder, which were widely performed in Germany. After 1933 he was put in the Buchenwald concentration camp, but was released in 1939, and went to England; settled in London as a teacher and a synagogal cantor; eked out his existence by also tuning pianos.

Kox, Hans, Dutch composer; b. Arnhem, May 19,

1930. He studied at the Utrecht Cons., then became a private student of Henk Badings; subsequently taught at the Doetinchem Music School (1956–70); then was appointed prof. of composition at the Utrecht Cons. He became fascinated with mathematical properties of music, both in formal structure and in the intervallic divisions; in some of his works he applies a scale of 31 equal intervals, invented by the Dutch physicist Adriaan Fokker. In his series of *Cyclophonies (Sound Cycles)* he experimented with "open-end" forms.

WORKS: He wrote 2 operas: *Dorian Gray,* after Wilde (1972–73; Scheveningen, March 30, 1974), and *Lord Rochester* (1978); *Little Lethe Symphony* (1956); *Concertante Music* for Horn, Trumpet, Trombone, and Orch. (1956); Flute Concerto (1957); *Macbeth,* overture (1958); Concerto for Orch. (1959); 2 symphs.: No. 1 for String Orch. (1959) and No. 2 (1960–66; incorporates the orch. pieces *Ballade* and *Paráklesis*); *Ballet "Spleen"* for Orch. (1960); Piano Concerto (1961); *De Kantate van St. Juttemis* for Baritone, Tenor, Chorus, and Piano (1962); 2 violin concertos (1963, 1978); 2-violin Concerto (1964); 12 *Cyclophonies:* No. 1 for Cello and Small Orch. (1964); No. 2 for 3 Orch. Groups (1964); No. 3 for Piano and Tape (1964); No. 4 for Treble Recorder and 9 Strings (1965); No. 5 for Oboe, Clarinet, Bassoon, and 19 Strings (1966); No. 6 for Violin, Trumpet, Piano, Vibraphone, and 16 Strings (1967); No. 7 for Violin, Piano, and 6 Percussionists (1971); No. 8 for Wind Quintet, Violin, Viola, Cello, and Double Bass (1971); No. 9 for Solo Percussion and Small Orch. (1974); No. 10 for Mixed Choir and Strings (1975); No. 11 for Big Band (1978); No. 12 for 8 Cellos (1979); *Zoo,* cantata (1964); *Litania* for Female Chorus, Percussion, and Strings (1965); *Music for Status Seekers* for Orch. (1966); *L'Allegria* for Soprano and Orch. (1967); Cello Concerto (1969); *In Those Days* for Chorus and Orch. (1969; Prix Italia, 1970); *Phobos* for Orch. (1970); *Puer natus est,* European carols for Chorus and Orch. (1971); *Requiem for Europe* for 4 Choruses and Orch. (1971); *6 One-act Plays* for 29 Musicians (1971); *Gedächtnislieder* for Voice and Orch. (1972); *Concerto bandistico* for Orch. (1973); *Gothic Concerto* for Harp and Chamber Orch. (1975); *Sinfonia concertante* for Violin, Cello, and Orch. (1976); *Vangoghiana* for Brass Band, Strings, and Percussion (1977); Concerto for Alto Saxophone and Orch. (1978); 4 violin sonatas (1952, 1955, 1961, 1966); 2 trios for 2 Violins and Viola (1952, 1954); 4 sextets of varying instrumental combinations (1957, 1957, 1959, 1961); String Quartet (1955); Trio No. 3A for Violin, Viola, and Cello (1955); String Quintet (1957); *Amphion* for 2 Narrators, Brass, and Percussion (1958); *3 Pieces* for Solo Violin, in the 31-tone system (1958); 2 piano quartets (1959, 1968); Sonata for Solo Cello (1959); *4 Pieces* for String Quartet, in the 31-tone system (1961); the 31-tone *4 Pieces* for 2 Trumpets and Trombone (1964); Serenade for 3 Violins (1968); *Préludes* for Violin (1971); *De Vierde Kraai oftewel De Kraaiende Vier* for Male Chorus, Brass Quartet, and Percussion (1972); *Capriccio* for 2 Violins and Piano (1974); *The Jealous Guy Plays His Tune* for Violin and Piano (1975); Piano Trio (1976); *Suite* for Cello Solo (1976);

Suite for Guitar Trio (1977); 2 piano sonatas (1954, 1955); *3 Etudes* for Piano (1961); *Melancholies* for Piano (1975); Prelude and Fugue for Organ (1954); the 31-tone Passacaglia and Chorale for Organ (1960).

Koyama, Kiyoshige, Japanese composer; b. Nagano, Jan. 15, 1914. He studied composition with Komei Abe; wrote a number of works in a Japanese national style, among them *Shina no Bayashi* for Orch. (Tokyo, June 3, 1946); *Kobiki-Uta* for Orch. (Tokyo, Oct. 3, 1957); symph. suite, *Nomen,* for a Noh play (Tokyo, Dec. 5, 1959); *Ubusuna* for Koto and other Japanese Instruments (1962); *Ainu no Uta* for String Orch. (Tokyo, May 23, 1964); opera, *Sansho Dayu* (Tokyo, March 29, 1972); several pieces for Japanese instruments.

Koželuh (Kozeluch; Koscheluch), Johann Antonín (Jan Evangelista Antonín Tomáš), Bohemian composer, cousin of **Leopold Koželuh;** b. Welvarn, Dec. 14, 1738; d. Prague, Feb. 3, 1814. He began music studies at school in Welwarn; was then a chorister at the Jesuit College in Breznice; subsequently, studied with J.F.N. Seger in Prague; then went to Vienna, where he had instruction from Gluck, Gassmann, and Hasse. Upon his return to Prague, he established himself as a music teacher; in 1784 he became Kapellmeister at St. Vitus' Metropolitan Cathedral, where he remained until his death. His cousin was one of his pupils. He composed 2 operas: *Alessandro nell'Indie* (Prague, 1769) and *Il Demofoonte* (Prague, 1771); much sacred music, including 2 oratorios, about 45 masses, 5 requiems, etc.; 4 symphs.; an oboe concerto; 2 bassoon concertos; and many other instrumental works.

BIBLIOGRAPHY: R. Fikrle, *Jan Evangelista Antonín Koželuh: Život, dilo a osobnost svatovitsheho kapelnika* (a study of his life and music with a list of works; Prague, 1946).

Koželuh (Kozeluch; Kotzeluch), Leopold (Jan Antonín), Bohemian composer, pianist, and teacher, cousin of **Johann Antonín Koželuh;** b. Welvarn, June 26, 1747; d. Vienna, May 7, 1818. He began his musical studies in Welwarn; then had instruction with his cousin and with F.X. Dušek in Prague. He also studied law but turned to a career in music after the success he attained with his ballets and pantomimes. In 1778 he went to Vienna, where he established himself as a pianist, teacher, and composer; also was active as a music publisher. In 1792 he was appointed Kammer Kapellmeister and Hofmusik Compositor, succeeding Mozart; he held this position until his death. Although Beethoven referred to him contemptuously in a letter of 1812 as "miserabilis," Koželuh was an excellent pianist; he composed about 50 solo sonatas, 22 piano concertos, 28 symphs., about 80 piano trios, and other pieces of chamber music. His stage works included operas, ballets, and pantomimes, but little of this music is extant; his only extant opera is *Gustav Wasa* (c.1792).

BIBLIOGRAPHY: G. Löbl, *Die Klaviersonate bei*

Leopold Kozeluch (Diss., Univ. of Vienna, 1937); O. Deutsch, "Kozeluch ritrovato," *Music & Letters,* XXVI (1945); M. Poštolka, *Leopold Koželuh: Život a dílo* (a study of his life and music with summary in Eng. and German; Prague, 1964); C. Flamm, *Leopold Koželuh: Biographie und stilkritische Untersuchung der Sonaten für Klavier, Violine und Violoncello* (Diss., Univ. of Vienna, 1968).

Kozina, Marjan, Slovenian composer; b. Novo Mesto, June 4, 1907; d. there, June 19, 1966. He studied at the Cons. of Ljubljana; later took courses with Joseph Marx at the Vienna Academy of Music and with Josef Suk at the Prague Cons. During the occupation of Yugoslavia by the Nazi armies, Kozina took part in the armed resistance movement; after the liberation he taught at the Musical Academy of Ljubljana. He wrote music in a fine, unaffected manner, making circumspect use of modern harmonies, while deriving his melorhythmic essence from native Slovenian folk-song patterns. His most important work is the music drama *Equinox* (Ljubljana, May 2, 1946), which had numerous revivals in Yugoslavia and was also performed in Prague and Moscow. Other works are the ballet *Diptihon* (1952) and a cantata, *Lepa Vida* (*Beautiful Vida;* 1939).

Kozlovsky, Ivan, Russian tenor; b. Maryanovka, near Kiev, March 24, 1900. He studied at the Kiev Cons. with Lysenko and Muravyova; made his debut as Faust in Poltava in 1920; then sang in Kharkov (1924) and Sverdlovsk (1925); in 1926 he joined the Bolshoi Theater in Moscow, where he was one of its leading singers until 1954. An artist of imaginative power, Kozlovsky expanded his activities into stage direction, striving to synthesize dramatic action with its musical realization. Apart from operatic performances, he gave recitals in programs of the classical repertoire as well as Russian and Ukrainian songs.
BIBLIOGRAPHY: G. Polinovsky, *Ivan Kozlovsky* (Moscow, 1945); V. Sletov, *Ivan Kozlovsky* (Moscow, 1951); A. Kuznetzova, *Ivan Kozlovsky* (Moscow, 1964).

Kozma, Matei, Rumanian composer and organist; b. Tîrgu-Mureș, July 23, 1929. He acquired the rudiments of music from his father, **Géza Kozma,** a Rumanian composer and cellist; then studied at the Cluj Cons. (1947–54), where his teachers were Jodál and Demian. He served as organ soloist (1955–57) and director (1959–66) of the Tîrgu-Mureș Phil.; then became an instructor at the Music Inst. there.
WORKS: *Rondo* for Piano (1954); 2 ballets: *Balada lacului Sf. Ana* (1957) and *Balada celui care cînta in cătușe* (1963); Organ Concerto (1961; revised 1965); *Trandafirii roșii,* poem for Chorus and Orch. (1962); *Theme and Variations* for Organ (1963); Trio for Solo Clarinet (1965); *Omagiu eroilor,* overture (1967); *Toccata, Trio, and Ricercari* for Organ (1968); choruses; songs.

Kraft, Anton, Austrian cello virtuoso, father of

Nicolaus Kraft; b. Rokitzán, near Pilsen, Dec. 30, 1749; d. Vienna, Aug. 28, 1820. He began to study at an early age with his father, an amateur cellist; then went to Prague, and later to Vienna; there he enjoyed the friendship of Haydn, who recommended him for a post as cellist in the chapel of Prince Esterházy (1778); he was subsequently in the employ of Prince Grassalkowicz; in 1795 entered the service of Prince Lobkowitz in Vienna. Among Kraft's works are 3 sonatas; 3 grand duos for Violin and Cello; several grand duos for 2 Cellos; Divertissement for Cello and Double Bass; etc. For a time it was thought that Haydn's famous Cello Concerto in D was actually written by Kraft, but it is now generally agreed by specialists that it is an authentic work by Haydn. Since it was written for Kraft, he may have made technical suggestions that were adopted by Haydn.

Kraft, Leo, American composer and pedagogue; b. New York, July 24, 1922. He studied composition with Karol Rathaus at Queens College in N.Y. (B.A., 1945), with Randall Thompson at Princeton Univ. (M.A., 1947), and with Nadia Boulanger in Paris (1954–55). In 1947 he was appointed prof. at Queens College. Kraft's craftsmanship preserves formal ties with the revered past, along with a salute to the turbulent present and a wink at an ominous future.
WORKS: *Let Me Laugh* for Chorus and Piano (1954); *Two's Company* for 2 Clarinets (1957); 4 partitas: No. 1 for Piano; No. 2 for Violin and Viola; No. 3 for Wind Quintet (1958); No. 4 (1968); *Statements and Commentaries* for Piano (1965); *5 Pieces* for Clarinet and Piano (1969); *Toccata* for Band (1970); *Fantasy* for Flute and Piano (1971); *Dualities* for 2 Trumpets (1971); *Line Drawings* for Flute and Percussion (1974); *10 Short Pieces* for Piano (1976); *Trios and Interludes* for Flute, Viola, and Piano (1977); *Diaphonies* for Oboe and Piano (1978). He also publ. textbooks: *A New Approach to Sight Singing* (with S. Berkowitz and G. Fontrier; N.Y., 1960); *A New Approach to Ear Training* (N.Y., 1967); *Gradus: An Integrated Approach to Harmony, Counterpoint, and Analysis* (N.Y., 1976).

Kraft, Nicolaus, Hungarian cellist and composer, son of **Anton Kraft;** b. Esterház, Dec. 14, 1778; d. Eger, May 18, 1853. He studied cello with his father, and went with him on concert tours while quite young; he and his father played chamber music with Mozart at the Dresden court (1789); when the Krafts went to Vienna in 1790, Nicolaus became a member of the famous Schuppanzigh Quartet. He was subsequently chamber musician to Prince Lobkowitz, who sent him to Berlin in 1791 to study for a year with Duport. After concerts in Germany, he returned to Vienna, and joined the court orch. (1809); then entered the court orch. at Stuttgart in 1814. He retired after an accident to his hand, in 1834. He wrote 5 cello concertos; 6 cello duos; 3 divertissements for 2 Cellos; Cello Fantasia, with String Quartet; *Polonaise* and *Bolero* for Cello, with Orch.; other cello music. His son, **Friedrich Kraft** (b. Vienna, Feb. 13, 1807; d. Stuttgart, Dec. 4, 1874), was also a cellist, and played in the Stuttgart Court Orch. for many years.

Kraft, Walter, noted German organist; b. Cologne, June 9, 1905. He studied piano with Rebbert and organ with Hannemann in Hamburg, and composition with Hindemith in Berlin. In 1924 he became organist of the Markuskirche in Hamburg; from 1927–29 he was organist at the Lutherkirche in Altona-Bahrenfeld. From 1929 he was organist of the Marienkirche in Lübeck; the church was destroyed in 1942, but he resumed his post there after the church was restored. He was also a prof. of organ in Freiburg; in addition, served as director of the Schleswig-Holstein Music Academy (1950–55). He gained wide distinction as an improviser; was particularly noteworthy for his performances of Baroque music.

Kraft, William, American virtuoso percussionist, composer and conductor; b. Chicago, Sept. 6, 1923. His parental name was **Kashereffsky,** which his parents Americanized to Kraft. The family moved to California and Kraft began to study piano. He took music courses at San Diego State College and at the Univ. of Calif. in Los Angeles, where he also had professional percussion instruction with Murray Spivack. In 1943 he was called to arms, and served in the U.S. forces as pianist, arranger, and drummer in military bands; while in Europe with the army he took time out to attend music courses at Cambridge Univ. Returning to the U.S. after discharge from military duty, he earned a living as percussionist in jazz bands. In the summer of 1948 he enrolled in the Berkshire Music Center in Tanglewood, where he studied composition with Irving Fine and conducting with Leonard Bernstein. In 1949 he entered Columbia Univ., where his instructors in composition were Jack Beeson, Otto Luening, Seth Bingham, Vladimir Ussachevsky, and Henry Cowell; he also attended classes in musicology with Erich Hertzmann and Paul Henry Lang (B.S., 1951; M.A., 1954). He continued to perfect his technique as a percussion player; and took lessons with Morris Goldenberg and Saul Goodman; he attained a high degree of virtuosity as a percussion player, both in the classical tradition and in jazz. In 1955 he was named chief of the percussion section of the Los Angeles Phil. Orch., retaining this position until 1981. In the meantime he developed his natural gift for conducting; from 1969 to 1972 he served as assistant conductor of the Los Angeles Phil.; in a parallel development, he composed assiduously and successfully. In 1981 he was appointed composer-in-residence of the Los Angeles Phil.; then founded the Los Angeles Phil. New Music Group, presenting programs of modern works for chamber orch. combinations. He held 2 Guggenheim fellowship grants (1967, 1972). As a composer, he explores without prejudice a variety of quaquaversal techniques, including serial procedures; naturally, his music coruscates with a rainbow spectrum of asymmetrical rhythms. There is a tendency in the very titles of his works toward tex-

tured constructivism, e.g. *Momentum, Configurations, Collage, Encounters, Translucences, Triangles, Mobiles,* but there are also concrete representations of contemporary events, as in *Riots—Decade '60.*
WORKS: Nonet for Brass and Percussion (Los Angeles, Oct. 13, 1958); *3 Miniatures* for Percussion and Orch. (Los Angeles, Feb. 14, 1959); *Variations on a Folksong* for Orch. (Los Angeles, March 26, 1960); *Symphony* for Strings and Percussion (N.Y., Aug. 21, 1961); *Concerto Grosso* (San Diego, March 22, 1963); *Silent Boughs,* song cycle (1963); *6 Pieces* for String Trio (1963); Concerto for 4 Percussion Soloists and Orch. (Los Angeles, March 10, 1966); Double Trio for Piano, Prepared Piano, Amplified Guitar, Tuba, and Percussion (Los Angeles, Oct. 31, 1966); *Configurations* for 4 Percussion Soloists and Jazz Orch. (Los Angeles, Nov. 13, 1966); *Contextures: Riots—Decade '60* (Los Angeles, April 4, 1969); *Games: Collage No. 1* for Brass and Percussion (Pasadena, Calif., Nov. 21, 1969); *Triangles,* concerto for Percussion and 10 Instruments (Los Angeles, Dec. 8, 1969); *Mobiles* for 10 Instruments (Berkeley, Calif., Oct. 18, 1970); *Cadenze* for 7 Instruments (1972); *In Memoriam Igor Stravinsky* for Violin and Piano (1972–74); Piano Concerto (Los Angeles, Nov. 21, 1973); *Des Imagistes* for 2 Readers and Percussion (1974); *Requiescat* for Electric Piano (1975); *Translucences* for Piano (1975); *Encounters I (Soliliquy)* for Percussion (1975); *Encounters II* for Unaccompanied Tuba (1975); *Encounters IV,* a Duel for Trombone and Percussion (1975); *Encounters V (In the Morning of the Winter Sea)* (1975); *The Innocents: The Witch Trial at Salem* for Voices, Percussion, and Celesta (Los Angeles, Oct. 18, 1976); *Andirivieni (Coming and Going)* for Tuba and Orch. (Los Angeles, Jan. 26, 1978); *The Sublime and the Beautiful* for Orch. (1979); *Luminescences* for Piano (1979); *Dialogues and Entertainments* for Wind Ensemble (1980); *Solo Piece* for Horn (1981); *Triple Play* for Orch. (1982); Double Concerto No. 2 for Violin, Piano, and Chamber Orch. (1982); music for the film *Fire and Ice* (1983); Timpani Concerto (Indianapolis, March 9, 1984); *Study for Contextures II: The Final Beast* (Los Angeles, April 2, 1984, composer conducting).
BIBLIOGRAPHY: David Ewen, *American Composers* (N.Y., 1982).

Kramer, A. Walter, American music critic and composer; b. New York, Sept. 23, 1890; d. there, April 8, 1969. He studied music with his father, Maximilian Kramer, and took violin lessons with Carl Hauser and Richard Arnold. After graduating from the College of the City of N.Y. in 1910, he joined the staff of *Musical America* (1910–22) and served as its editor in chief from 1929 till 1936. His music criticism was journalistically voluble and knowledgeable. He wrote many pleasant and entirely singable songs and also essayed an ambitious *Symphonic Rhapsody* for Violin and Orch. (1912).
BIBLIOGRAPHY: J.T. Howard, *A. Walter Kramer* (N.Y., 1926); W.T. Upton, *Art-Song in America* (N.Y., 1930; pp. 225–35).

Kranich & Bach, well-known firm of piano makers founded in N.Y. in 1864 by **Helmuth Kranich, Sr.** (b. Grossbreitenbach, Germany, Aug. 22, 1833; d. New York, Jan. 29, 1902), and **Jacques Bach** (b. Lorentzen, Alsace, June 22, 1833; d. New York, Oct. 29, 1894). The business, incorporated in 1890, has been continued by the founders' descendants: **Frederick Kranich** served as president from 1902 to 1920, and was succeeded by **Louis P. Bach** from 1920 to 1930. In 1930 **Jacques Bach Schlosser** (grandson of Jacques Bach) was elected president. **Helmuth Kranich,** son of Helmuth Sr., was appointed a member of the board of directors in 1894, secretary of the firm in 1902, and president in 1946; retired in 1950; died in N.Y. on Oct. 24, 1956. Other members of the board of directors included **Philip Schlosser** (grandson of Jacques Bach), **Victor Kranich** (son of Helmuth Kranich, Sr.), **Lucy Bach** (daughter of Jacques Bach), and **John J. Kuhn** (grandnephew of Jacques Bach). Frederick Kranich invented the "Isotonic" pedal, doing away with the shifting keyboard in grand pianos, and the "Violyn" plate for upright pianos, and perfected various improvements in piano construction.

BIBLIOGRAPHY: A. Dolge, *Pianos and Their Makers,* vol. II (Covina, Calif., 1913).

Krantz, Eugen, German pianist; b. Dresden, Sept. 13, 1844; d. Gohrisch, near Königstein, May 26, 1898. He studied at the Dresden Cons.; was chorus master at the court opera there (1869–84); taught at the Dresden Cons., becoming director in 1890, when he bought the institution. He publ. some songs and a *Lehrgang im Klavierunterricht* (1882); was also critic for the Dresden *Presse* and the *Nachrichten.*

Krapf, Gerhard, German-American organist and composer; b. Meissenheim-bei-Lahr, Dec. 12, 1924. He studied piano and organ in Karlsruhe; was church organist in Offenburg, Germany (1939–42); was drafted into the German army and taken prisoner of war in Russia; upon his release he returned to Karlsruhe, where he continued to study organ, choral conducting, and composition (1950). In 1951 he went to America, where he studied organ at the Univ. of Redlands in Calif., and took a course in composition with Paul A. Pisk. He then taught music at Albion, Mich. (1953–54), at the Northwest Missouri State College in Maryville (1954–58), and at the Univ. of Wyoming in Laramie (1958–61). In 1961 he joined the faculty of the Univ. of Iowa, where he was appointed head of the organ dept. He composed a great number of organ pieces and sacred choral works; publ. a manual, *Liturgical Organ Playing* (Minneapolis, 1964), and *Organ Improvisation: A Practical Approach to Chorale Elaborations for the Service* (Minneapolis, 1967).

Krapp, Edgar, distinguished German organist and pedagogue; b. Bamberg, June 3, 1947. He studied the organ at the Hochschule für Musik in Munich, where he was a pupil of Franz Lehrndorfer; subsequently took organ lessons with Marie-Claire Alain in Paris. In 1970 he won first prize in the Competition of the German Academies in Munich, and in 1971 the prize of the Mendelssohn Competition in Berlin. In 1974 he was named successor to Helmut Walcha as prof. of organ at the Hochschule für Musik in Frankfurt; from 1982 was a visiting prof. at the Salzburg Mozarteum. He is particularly noted for his performance of the organ music of Bach.

Krása, Hans, Czech composer; b. Prague, Nov. 30, 1899; d. Auschwitz, Oct. 16, 1944. He was of Czech-German (Jewish) extraction; studied in a German high school in Prague; took lessons in music with Zemlinsky and Keussler in Prague. He made rapid progress, and had his first orch. piece, *Grotesques,* performed in Prague on May 20, 1921; also successful were his beginnings as a conductor; he was engaged as chorus master at the German Theater in Prague; then went to Berlin, where he conducted at the Kroll Opera. He returned to Prague in 1928, and in 1942 was interned at the Theresienstadt concentration camp; nevertheless he continued to compose, and produced an opera, *Brundibár,* which had several performances arranged by an opera group of the Jewish inmates. On Oct. 16, 1944, he was transported to Auschwitz and put to death. He was a composer of some interesting works in a "hedonistic" manner, aiming at sophisticated entertainment; his idiom was mildly atonal. So promising was his career as a composer that his *Pastorale* and *March* (originally first and 2nd movements from a symph.) were performed in Paris (April 24, 1923) and also by the Boston Symph. Orch. (Nov. 19, 1926). His String Trio was performed posthumously at the Aspen (Colo.) Festival (Oct. 22, 1951). He also wrote incidental music to *Lysistrata,* and the cantata *Die Erde ist des Herrn.* Other works were *Theme with Variations* for String Quartet (1942); a group of songs to words by Rimbaud; some piano pieces.

Krasnapolsky, Yuri, American conductor; b. New York, Nov. 24, 1934. He studied piano with Isabelle Vengerova at the Curtis Inst. of Music in Philadelphia; subsequently took courses in conducting with Leonard Bernstein, and also with Jean Morel at the Juilliard School of Music in N.Y. He began his career as an assistant conductor to Bernstein at the N.Y. Phil. (1962–63); then was guest conductor-in-residence of the Florida Symph. Orch. and music director of the Omaha Symph. Orch. In 1974 he became music director of the Des Moines Symph. Orch.; also appeared as guest conductor with the Philadelphia Orch., Detroit Symph., Baltimore Symph., and New Jersey Symph.; in addition, he conducted in Europe, and made 3 tours of the Soviet Union.

Krasner, Louis, American violinist; b. Cherkassy, Russia, June 21, 1903. He was taken to the U.S. as a small child; studied at the New England Cons. in Boston, graduating in 1923; then went abroad, where he studied violin with Carl Flesch, Lucien Capet, and Ševčik. From 1944 to 1949 he was concertmaster of the Minneapolis Symph. Orch.; then became prof. of violin and chamber music at Syracuse Univ. In 1974 he joined the staff of the New

England Cons. He commissioned Alban Berg in 1934 to write a violin concerto for him; gave its world premiere at the Barcelona Festival of the International Society for Contemporary Music (April 19, 1936); also gave the world premiere of Schoenberg's Violin Concerto (Philadelphia, Dec. 6, 1940, Stokowski conducting).

Krásová, Marta, Czech contralto; b. Protivin, March 16, 1901; d. Vráz, near Beroun, Feb. 20, 1970. She studied voice in Prague and Vienna; made her debut in Bratislava in 1924; subsequently joined the National Theater in Prague; made highly successful guest appearances in Hamburg, Dresden, Madrid, Paris, Moscow, and Warsaw; toured the U.S. in 1938–39. In 1935 she married the Czech composer **Karel Boleslav Jirák;** they divorced in 1946. She achieved distinction in the principal parts in national Czech operas; was also notable as a Wagnerian singer.

Kraus, Alessandro, German collector of musical instruments; b. Frankfurt, Aug. 6, 1820; d. Florence, Sept. 22, 1904. He was noted for his extensive and valuable collection of musical instruments; was cofounder of the Tonkünstlerhilfsverein in Frankfurt and of the Florentine Società del Quartetto.

Kraus, Alfredo, noted tenor; b. Las Palmas, Canary Islands, Sept. 24, 1927. He studied in Barcelona, Valencia, and Milan; made his operatic debut in Cairo in 1956; then sang in Rome, London, Milan, Chicago, and San Francisco. He made his debut at the Metropolitan Opera in N.Y. on Feb. 16, 1966, as the Duke in *Rigoletto;* in subsequent years he became its regular member. He is considered to be the finest *tenore di grazia* since Schipa.

Kraus, Detlef, distinguished German pianist; b. Hamburg, Nov. 30, 1919. He made a notable debut at the age of 16, performing the complete *Well-tempered Clavier* in 2 successive recitals in Hamburg; then continued his studies with Edwin Fischer and later with Wilhelm Kempff in Berlin and Potsdam. In 1958 he performed a cycle of Beethoven piano sonatas in London; in 1970 he gave Beethoven cycles in Tokyo, Valencia, and Pittsburgh; in 1980 he played all of the solo piano works of Brahms in N.Y. He also taught classes at the Folkwang Hochschule für Musik in Essen. His playing is remarkable for its freedom from pedantry; his interpretations are notable for their spontaneity.

Kraus, Ernst, German tenor; b. Erlangen, June 8, 1863; d. Wörthsee, Sept. 6, 1941. He studied in Milan with Cesare Galliera and in Munich with Frau Schimon-Regan; made his debut as a concert singer at a Kaim Concert in Munich (Jan. 18, 1893); made his opera debut in Mannheim on March 26, 1893, as Tamino in *Die Zauberflöte;* then remained there as a member of the opera (1893–96); from 1896 to 1923, was engaged at the court opera in Berlin; made his debut at the Metropolitan Opera in N.Y. on Nov. 25, 1903, as Siegmund in *Die Walküre;* in 1924, returned to Munich as a singing teacher.

Kraus, Felix von, Austrian bass singer; b. Vienna, Oct. 3, 1870; d. Munich, Oct. 30, 1937. He first studied musicology at the Univ. of Vienna (Dr.Phil., 1894), then singing with Stockhausen. In 1899, after a European tour as a concert singer, he appeared at the Wagner Festival in Bayreuth as Hagen, and subsequently participated in the festivals every summer for many years; established himself as one of the finest interpreters of Wagnerian bass roles. He also taught dramatic singing at the Akademie der Tonkunst in Munich from 1908 to 1935. In 1899 he married the American singer **Adrienne Osborne.**

Kraus, Joseph Martin, important German-born Swedish composer; b. Miltenberg-am-Main, June 20, 1756; d. Stockholm, Dec. 15, 1792. He attended the Jesuit School in Mannheim; subsequently studied law at the univs. of Mainz (1773–74), Erfurt (1775–76), and Göttingen (1777–78). In 1778 he went to Sweden, making his home in Stockholm; in 1780 was elected a member of the Swedish Academy of Music; in 1781 was appointed deputy conductor of the court orch. His great interest in Swedish culture prompted King Gustavus III to send him to Germany, Austria, Italy, France, and England for study purposes between the years 1782 and 1787. During his travels he met Gluck and Haydn, both of whom warmly praised his music. In 1788 he was appointed Hovkapellmästare in Stockholm, holding this position until his untimely death from tuberculosis. During his short life (he was almost an exact contemporary of Mozart), he composed several distinguished works for the stage; his operas (to Swedish texts) are estimable achievements, especially *Aeneas i Carthago (Dido och Aeneas),* which was premiered posthumously in Stockholm on Nov. 18, 1799. He also composed a *Symphonie funèbre* and *Begravingskantata* for the assassinated Gustavus III. After Kraus's death, his MSS and letters were deposited in the library of the Univ. of Uppsala. In recent years, a number of his works have been publ. His own writings include *Versuch von Schäfergedichten* (Mainz, 1773) and *Etwas von und über Musik fürs Jahr 1777* (Frankfurt, 1778).

WORKS: FOR THE STAGE: *Azire,* opera (1778; only fragments extant); *Proserpina,* opera (Ulriksdal Castle, June 1781); *Fintbergs Bröllop (Fintberg's Wedding),* comic play with music (Stockholm, Jan. 1788); *Soliman II, eller De tre sultaninnorna,* comic opera (Stockholm, Sept. 22, 1789); *Afventyraren (The Adventurer),* comic play with music (Stockholm, Jan. 30, 1791); *Aeneas i Carthago (Dido och Aeneas),* opera (Stockholm, Nov. 18, 1799); etc. FOR VOICE: *Cantata for the King's Birthday* (1782–83); *Begravningskantata* (1792); songs; sacred music. FOR ORCH.: *Wiener Sinfonie* (1783); *Pariser Sinfonie* (1784); *Symphonie funèbre* (1792); Violin Concerto (1777); Sinfonia Concertante (1780); overtures, etc. CHAMBER MUSIC: 9 string quartets, 4 violin sonatas, pieces for solo piano.
BIBLIOGRAPHY: F. Silverstolpe, *Biographie af*

Kraus – Krause

Kraus (Stockholm, 1833); B. Anrep-Nordin, "Studier över Joseph Martin Kraus," *Svensk tidskrift för musikforskning*, V (1923) and VI (1924); K. Schreiber, "Verzeichnis der musikalischen Werke von Joseph Kraus," *Archiv für Musikwissenschaft*, VII (1925; not complete); K. Schreiber, *Biographie über den Odenwälder Komponisten Joseph Martin Kraus* (Buchen, 1928); R. Engländer, *Joseph Martin Kraus und die Gustavianische Oper* (Uppsala and Leipzig, 1943); H.C. Robbins Landon, "Joseph Martin Kraus," *The Musical Times*, CIII (1972); V. Bungardt, *Joseph Martin Kraus ... ein Meister des klassischen Klavierliedes* (Regensburg, 1973); I. Leux-Henschen, *Joseph Martin Kraus in seinen Briefen* (Stockholm, 1978).

Kraus, Lili, Hungarian pianist; b. Budapest, April 3, 1905. Her father was a stonecutter of Czech descent, but her mother sang. Lili Kraus studied piano, and was accepted as a student of Bartók and Kodály at the Academy of Music in Budapest, graduating at the age of 17. She then went to Vienna, where she studied piano with Eduard Steuermann at the Vienna Cons.; in 1926 she received her diploma; from 1930 to 1934 she attended master classes in piano study with Artur Schnabel in Berlin. She became known in Europe as a congenial Chopin player, but after a series of concerts and duo recitals with the violinist Szymon Goldberg in Beethoven programs she was hailed as a true Beethovenian; then she played Mozart and was extolled as an authentic Mozartian. But she also gave performances of piano works by Béla Bartók. Thus equipped, she toured Europe, Japan, Australia, and South Africa. She married the German philosopher Otto Mandl and settled in London. Recklessly, she engaged in a world tour through the Orient in 1942 and was caught in Java when the Japanese captured the island; fortunately she was helped by a Japanese conductor with whom she played in Tokyo, and he made her life tolerable. After the war she acquired New Zealand citizenship, which exorcised her former Austrian affiliation. In 1948 she went to South Africa and taught piano at the Univ. of Cape Town. In 1949 she arrived in the U.S., where she gave a series of highly lauded concerts; she played in London in 1960. In 1967 she was engaged as artist-in-residence at Texas Christian Univ. in Austin; she retired in 1983. A widow since 1956, she eventually settled on her farm in North Carolina, where she engaged in her artistic hobbies, such as dressmaking, painting, and yoga. She continued in her religion as a Roman Catholic. On March 4, 1978, she was awarded by her native Austria the Cross of Honor for Science and Art.
BIBLIOGRAPHY: David Ewen, *Musicians since 1900* (N.Y., 1978).

Kraus, Otakar, Czech baritone; b. Prague, Dec. 10, 1909; d. London, July 28, 1980. He was educated in Prague and Milan; made his debut in Brno in 1935; then sang in Bratislava. At the outbreak of World War II, he went to England, where he joined the staff of the Carl Rosa Opera Co. From 1951 until 1973 he sang at the Royal Opera House, Covent Garden; also made guest appearances at Bayreuth (1960–62). He was particularly distinguished in the German repertoire.

Krause, Anton, German pianist and conductor; b. Geithain, Nov. 9, 1834; d. Dresden, Jan. 31, 1907. He began to study piano at an early age; then studied at Dresden; from 1850 to 1853 studied at the Leipzig Cons. with Wenzel, Moscheles, Hauptmann, Richter, Rietz, and David; taught music and also conducted in Leipzig. In 1859 he succeeded Reinecke at Barmen as director of the Singverein and the Konzertgesellschaft, retiring in 1897. He wrote *Prinzessin Ilse* for Soli, Female Chorus, Piano, and Declamation; choral works; songs; also instructive piano pieces. He publ. a collection of classical sonatinas and *Library for Two Pianofortes* (18 vols.).

Krause, Eduard, German pianist and teacher; b. Swinemünde, March 15, 1837; d. Berlin, March 28, 1892. He studied with Kroll in Berlin and Hauptmann in Leipzig; then went to Stettin as a pianist and teacher. He publ. characteristic pieces for the piano (*Berceuse, Impromptu, Grosse Sonate, Ungarische Rhapsodie, Konzertfantasie über schwedische Volkslieder*, etc.).

Krause, Emil, German piano pedagogue and music critic; b. Hamburg, July 30, 1840; d. there, Sept. 5, 1916. He was a pupil of Hauptmann, Richter, Rietz, Moscheles, and Plaidy at the Leipzig Cons. In 1860 he went to Hamburg, where he taught piano and wrote music criticism for the *Fremdenblatt* from 1864 until 1907. He publ. *Beiträge zur Technik des Klavierspiels*, with supplementary matter in *Ergänzungen; Aufgabenbuch für die Harmonielehre* (1869; 8th ed., 1908); *Praktische Klavierschule* (1892); *Neuer "Gradus ad Parnassum"* (100 études); and *Anleitung zum Studium der Musikgeschichte* (1906); *Johannes Brahms in seinen Werken* (Hamburg, 1892; contains a catalogue of works); *Kurzgefasste Darstellung der Passion, des Oratoriums und modernen Konzertwerkes für Chor, Soli und Orchester* (Langensalza, 1902). His compositions include an oratorio, *Den Heimgegangenen; Trio non difficile* for Piano, Violin, and Cello (1863); songs; piano pieces.

Krause, Karl Christian Friedrich, German writer on music; b. Eisenberg, May 6, 1781; d. Munich, Sept. 27, 1832. He publ. many philosophical works; also *Darstellungen aus der Geschichte der Musik* (1827); *Vollständige Anweisung* (1808); *Anfangsgründe der allgemeinen Theorie der Musik* (1838).

Krause, Martin, German pianist and pedagogue; b. Lobstadt, near Leipzig, June 17, 1853; d. Plattling, Bavaria, Aug. 2, 1918. He was a pupil of his father, a cantor, and of Wenzel and Reinecke at the Leipzig Cons. After successful tours in the Netherlands and Germany (1878–80), he was prostrated by nervous exhaustion for 2 years. He played before Liszt in

1883, and for 3 years, until Liszt's death, was in constant communication with the master and his pupils. In 1885 Krause, Siloti, Frau Moran-Olden, and others gave 2 grand concerts in Leipzig, which marked the establishment of the Lisztverein, of which Krause was the chief promoter, chairman, and manager till 1900, when it was discontinued. After 1900 he taught in Leipzig, Dresden, and at the Stern Cons. in Berlin.

Krause, Theodor, German choir conductor and teacher; b. Halle, May 1, 1833; d. Berlin, Dec. 12, 1910. He was a theological student; studied music with Hentschel, Hauptmann, and Grell. He organized church choirs in Berlin; was conductor of the Seiffert a cappella society; taught sight-singing by use of the "Wandernote" (movable "do"). He wrote church music, part-songs, and songs; was music critic for several Berlin papers; publ. *Die Wandernote* (1888) and *Deutsche Singschule* (1888).

Krause, Tom, Finnish baritone; b. Helsinki, July 5, 1934. He studied in Helsinki, Vienna, and Hamburg; made his concert debut in Helsinki in 1957, his operatic debut at the Berlin Städtische Oper in 1958. In 1962 he joined the Hamburg State Opera; also sang at Bayreuth, Covent Garden in London, Glyndebourne, and the Vienna State Opera. On Oct. 11, 1967, he made his American debut at the Metropolitan Opera in N.Y. as Count Almaviva in *Le nozze di Figaro.*

Kraushaar, Otto, German writer on music; b. Kassel, May 31, 1812; d. there, Nov. 23, 1866. He studied with Hauptmann, whose idea of the opposition of the major and minor modes he developed in a treatise on *Der accordliche Gegensatz und die Bergründung der Scala* (1852), prior to Hauptmann's *Natur der Harmonik.* He also publ. *Die Construktion der gleichschwebenden Temperatur ohne Scheiblerische Stimmgabeln* (1838); contributed essays to periodicals; wrote songs.

Krauss, Clemens, eminent Austrian conductor; b. Vienna, March 31, 1893; d. Mexico City, May 16, 1954. He served as a chorister at the Imperial Chapel in Vienna; then studied at the Vienna Cons. with Reinhold (piano), Grädener (composition), and Heuberger (theory), graduating in 1912. He was then choral director at the State Theater in Brünn; subsequently conducted opera in Riga (1913–14), Nuremberg (1915–16), Stettin (1916–21), and Graz (1921–22). In 1922 he became an assistant to Franz Schalk at the Vienna State Opera; also taught conducting at the Vienna Academy of Music and was conductor of the Vienna Tonkünstlerkonzerte (1923–27). In 1924–29 he was director of the Frankfurt Opera and conductor of the Museum Concerts; from 1929 to 1934 he was director of the Vienna State Opera; was also conductor of the Vienna Phil. (1930–33). In 1929 he undertook an American tour, and had a signal success as guest conductor with the N.Y. Phil. and the Philadelphia Orch. Returning to Germany in 1934, he served as director of the Berlin State Opera; in 1937 he assumed the post of Generalmusikdirektor of the Bavarian State Opera in Munich, a position he held until 1944; was also a conductor at the Salzburg Festivals and at the Mozarteum; during the last months of the devastating war (1944–45) he conducted concerts of the Vienna Phil. He was compromised by his mute acquiescence in the Nazi barbarism, but as an artist, he tried to protect Jewish musicians who worked under his direction. Unlike his more tainted colleagues, he was not called to account for his dubious political attitudes, however, and after the war he continued to serve as conductor of the Vienna State Opera; led concerts of the Vienna Phil. from 1947, including its famous New Year's Day Concerts. He was married to the singer **Viorica Ursuleac,** whom he often accompanied at the piano in her recitals. Krauss was a close friend and collaborator of Richard Strauss; he conducted the premieres of his operas *Arabella, Friedenstag, Capriccio* (for which he wrote the libretto), and *Die Liebe der Danae.* He was regarded as one of the foremost operatic and symph. conductors in Austria and Germany; he was particularly praised for his interpretations of the operas of Wagner and Strauss. He died suddenly on a tour of Mexico.

BIBLIOGRAPHY: A. Berger, *Clemens Krauss* (Graz, 1924; 3rd ed., 1929); J. Gregor, *Clemens Krauss, Eine musikalische Sendung* (Vienna, 1953); Oscar von Pander, *Clemens Krauss in München* (Munich, 1955).

Krauss, Gabrielle, Austrian soprano; b. Vienna, March 24, 1842; d. Paris, Jan. 6, 1906. She studied general music subjects at the Vienna Cons.; voice with Mathilde Marchesi. She made her first important appearance at the Vienna Opera on July 20, 1860, in Rossini's *Wilhelm Tell;* remained on the roster until 1867; then went to Paris; sang Leonora in *Il Trovatore* at the Théâtre-Italien (April 6, 1867) and became a favorite. The Franco-Prussian War of 1870 compelled her to leave Paris; she sang in Italy and in Russia. When the new building of the Paris Grand Opéra was opened in 1875, she sang *La Juive* (Jan. 5, 1875); remained with the Opéra until 1888, when she retired.

Krauze, Zygmunt, Polish composer and pianist; b. Warsaw, Sept. 19, 1938. He studied composition with Sikorski and piano with Maria Wilkomirska at the Warsaw Cons., graduating in 1962 (M.A., 1964); completed studies with Nadia Boulanger in Paris (1966–67). He is an inventive composer, cultivating with equal devotion primitive rustic instruments and electronic sounds. As a pianist, he specializes in new music; he taught piano at Cleveland State Univ. (1970–71).

WORKS: *3 Malay Pantuns,* to Indonesian texts, for 3 Flutes and Contralto (1961); *5 Unitary Piano Pieces* (1963); *Triptych* for Piano (1964); *Voices* for 5–15 Optional Instruments (1968); *Polychrony* for Clarinet, Trombone, Cello, and Piano (1968); 2 string quartets (1960, 1969); *Piece for Orchestra No. 1* (1969); *Piece for Orchestra No. 2* (1970); *Folk Music* for Orch. (1971–72); *Aus aller Welt stammende* for 10 Strings (1973); *Vibrations* for Piano, 8-hands (1973); *Song* for Flute, Clarinet, Bassoon, Violin, Cello, Double Bass, and 3 Automatophones (1974); *Automatophone* for 15 Musical Boxes and 15 Plucked Instruments (1974); *Fête galante et pastorale*, space music for a castle, for 13 Tapes and 6 Instrumental Groups (1974; Graz, Austria, Oct. 12, 1974); *Idyll* for Tape, 4 Hurdy-gurdies, 4 Bagpipes, 4 Zlobcoki, 8 Fifes, 16 Bells, and 4 Whistles (1974).

Krebs, Carl, German music scholar and critic; b. Hanseberg, Feb. 5, 1857; d. Berlin, Feb. 9, 1937. He studied musicology at the Univ. of Berlin with Philipp Spitta. From 1896 to 1923 he lectured on music history at the Berlin Hochschule für Musik; in 1911 was elected secretary of the Academy. He wrote music criticism for several Berlin newspapers; publ. various historical essays in the scholarly musical journals; in 1898 he edited Beethoven's sonatas in their original form. He also publ. a valuable monograph on Dittersdorf, entitled *Dittersdorfiana* (Berlin, 1900); other publications were *Schaffen und Nachschaffen in der Musik* (Berlin, 1902); *Haydn, Mozart, Beethoven* (Leipzig, 1906; 3rd ed., 1920); *Meister des Taktstocks* (Berlin, 1919); and an interesting treatise, *Die Frauen in der Musik,* publ. in 1895 under the auspices of the feminist group Der Existenzkampf der Frau.

Krebs (real name, **Miedcke**), **Carl August,** German composer; b. Nuremberg, Jan. 16, 1804; d. Dresden, May 16, 1880. He studied music with the opera singer **Johann Baptist Krebs,** who legally adopted him. A precocious child, he is said to have composed the opera *Feodore* at the age of 7. He became a conductor at the Vienna Opera in 1826; in 1850 he was appointed principal conductor of the Dresden Opera, succeeding Wagner, who had been involved in revolutionary activities in Saxony; Krebs continued at his Dresden post until 1872. He produced 2 operas: *Silva* (Hamburg, 1830) and *Agnes* (Hamburg, Oct. 8, 1833; revised under the title *Agnes Bernauer* and produced in Dresden in 1858); but he was successful mainly as a song composer; his religious hymn *Vater unser* was popular for many years; he also wrote several masses and some brilliant piano pieces. He was married to the opera singer **Aloysia Michalesi** (1826–1904). Their daughter **Mary Krebs** (1851–1900) was a talented pianist.

Krebs, Helmut, German tenor; b. Dortmund, Oct. 8, 1913. He studied at the Berlin Hochschule für Musik; made his debut at the Berlin Volksoper in 1937; served in World War II; then sang with the Düsseldorf Opera. In 1948 he became a member of the Städtische Oper in Berlin; also made guest appearances in Hamburg, Munich, Milan, and London. In 1963 he was made a Kammersänger by the city of Berlin; from 1963–75 he taught at the Hochschule für Musik in Frankfurt. In addition to opera, he appeared widely as an oratorio singer.

Krebs, Johann Ludwig, German organist and composer; b. Buttelstädt, Oct. 10, 1713; d. Altenburg, Jan. 2, 1780. He received methodical training in musical subjects from his father, an organist, and was sent to study at the Thomasschule in Leipzig, where he became a pupil of Bach for 9 years (1726–35); was Bach's assistant at the harpsichord in Bach's Collegium Musicum there. Later he was organist at Zeitz, Zwickau, and Altenburg. He publ.: *Klavierübungen* in 4 parts (Nuremberg, 1743–49); sonatas for clavier and flute; suites and preludes for clavier; string trios; organ pieces (including an organ fugue on the name B-A-C-H); these were reprinted in the series Masterpieces of Organ Music (N.Y., 1944–45); Partita No. 2 is found in Pauer's *Alte Meister;* a Trio with Continuo, in Riemann's *Collegium Musicum;* his organ works were edited by K. Tittel in *Johann Ludwig Krebs: Ausgewählte Orgelwerke,* in *Die Orgel* (Lippstadt, 1963–75).
BIBLIOGRAPHY: Hans Löffler, "J.L. Krebs," *Bach-Jahrbuch* (1930); J. Horstmann, *The Instrumental Music of Johann Ludwig Krebs* (Diss., Boston Univ., 1959; with thematic catalogue); D. Mulberry, "Bach's Favorite Pupil: Johann Ludwig Krebs," *Music/The A.G.O. Magazine,* ii (1968).

Kreger, James, American violoncellist; b. Nashville, March 30, 1947. He received his early musical training taking piano lessons with local teachers. In 1965 the family moved to Beverly Hills, where he studied cello with Gabor Rejto; in 1966 he went to N.Y. and enrolled at the Juilliard School of Music as a student of Leonard Rose and Harvey Shapiro. He also took courses at Michigan State Univ., and played the cello in a student orch. in Tanglewood. On March 16, 1971, he gave an auspicious recital in N.Y., eliciting high praise from hardened music critics.

Krehbiel, Henry Edward, noted American music critic; b. Ann Arbor, Mich., March 10, 1854; d. New York, March 20, 1923. He was music critic of the *Cincinnati Gazette* (1874–80); then editor of the *N.Y. Musical Review* and critic for the *N.Y. Tribune;* the latter post he held for some 40 years, until his death; in 1909, he received the honorary degree of M.A. from Yale Univ. He publ. *Notes on the Cultivation of Choral Music, and the Oratorio Society of New York* (1884); *Review of the N.Y. Musical Seasons 1885–90* (5 vols.); *Studies in the Wagnerian Drama* (1891); *The Philharmonic Society of New York: A Memorial* (1892); *How to Listen to Music* (1896); *Annotated Biography of Fine Art* (with R. Sturgis; 1897); *Music and Manners in the Classical Period* (1898); *Chapters of Opera* (2nd ed., 1911); *A Book of Operas* (1909); *The Pianoforte, and Its Music* (1911); *Afro-American Folksongs* (1914); *A Second Book of Operas* (1917); *More Chapters of Opera* (1919); translations of Courvoisier's *Technic of Violin Playing* (N.Y., 1880; 2nd ed., 1896), Kerst's *Beethoven* (1905), and Kerst's *Mozart* (1905); also publ. and edited the Eng. version of Thayer's *Beethoven* (3 vols., 1921); he was consulting editor of *The Music of the Modern World* (1895–97) and American editor of the 2nd edition of *Grove's Dictionary of Music and Musicians* (1904–10); was also author, for many years, of the program notes of the N.Y. Phil. Society. He was a brilliant writer of music criticism, and was able to project his opinions (and his prejudices) in vivid prose in his newspaper reviews. He was an ardent champion of Wagner, and he also wrote with warm admiration for the late Romantic composers; but he deprecated the modern school of composition, hurling invectives on Stravinsky, Prokofiev, and Schoenberg (whose music he described as excrement).

Krehl, Stephan, German theorist and composer; b. Leipzig, July 5, 1864; d. there, April 7, 1924. He studied at the conservatories in Leipzig and Dresden. In 1889 he was appointed teacher of piano and theory at the Karlsruhe Cons.; from 1902, at the Leipzig Cons.; in 1911, became director there. He publ. the manuals *Praktische Formenlehre* (1902); *Allgemeine Musiklehre* (1904; 2nd ed., 1912; in Spanish, 1930); *Fuge: Erläuterung und Anleitung zur Komposition derselben* (1908); *Kompositionsunterricht und moderne Musik* (1909); *Musikerelend* (1912); *M. Hauptmann: Ein Dank- und Gedenkwort* (1918); *Theorie der Tonkunst und Kompositionslehre* (vol. I: *Elementarmusiklehre,* 1921; vol. II: *Harmonielehre,* 1923; 2nd ed., 1928). He also composed a Quintet for Clarinet, 2 Violins, Viola, and Cello; Cello Sonata; *Slovenische Tänze* for Piano, 4-hands; cantata, *Trostung;* prelude to Hauptmann's play *Hannelle.*
BIBLIOGRAPHY: F. Reuter, *Stephan Krehl* (1921).

Krein, Alexander, Russian composer; b. Nizhny-Novgorod, Oct. 20, 1883; d. Staraya Ruza, near Moscow, April 21, 1951. At the age of 13 he entered the Moscow Cons. and studied cello; also studied composition privately with Nikolayev and Yavorsky. Later he became an instructor at the People's Cons. of Moscow (1912–17); after the Revolution he worked in the music division of the Commissariat of Education and in the Ethnographic Dept. From 1923 he was associated with the productions of the Jewish Drama Theater in Moscow, and wrote music for many Jewish plays. Together with Gnessin, he was a leader of the National Jewish movement in Russia. In general, his style was influenced by Scriabin and Debussy, but he made considerable use of authentic Hebrew material.
WORKS: Operas: *Zagmuk,* on a revolutionary subject based on an ancient Babylonian tale (Moscow, May 29, 1930), and *Daughter of the People* (1946); ballet after Lope de Vega, *Laurencie* (1938); incidental music to the Jewish plays *The Eternal One* (1923), *Sabbati Zewi* (1924), *Ghetto* (1924), *The People* (1925), *The Doctor* (1925); *Salome* for Orch. (1923); *Elegy* for String Orch. (1914); *The Rose and the Cross,* symph. fragments (1917–21); *Kaddisch,* symph. cantata for Tenor Solo, Mixed Choir, and Orch. (1921); Symph. (1922–25); *U.S.S.R., Shock Brigade of the World Proletariat,* symph. dithyramb for Narrator, Chorus, and Orch. (1925); *Threnody in Memory of Lenin* for Chorus and Orch. (1925); various symph. suites on Hebrew themes; String Quartet; *Jewish Sketches* for Clarinet and String Quartet, *Elegiac Trio* for Violin, Cello, and Piano; *Jewish Capriccio* for Violin and Piano; Piano Sonata; *3 Poems* for Piano; *Jewish Songs* (to Russian words); vocalises.
BIBLIOGRAPHY: L. Sabaneyev, *Alexander Krein* (Moscow, 1928; in Russian and German).

Krein, Grigori, Russian composer, brother of **Alexander Krein;** b. Nizhny-Novgorod, March 18, 1879; d. Komarovo, near Leningrad, Jan. 6, 1955. He studied with Juon and Glière. His music underwent the influence of Jewish culture, and he wrote many works on Jewish themes; however, he also cultivated strict classical forms, adapting them to his needs. He wrote a descriptive symph. cycle on Lenin's life (1937); other works are a Violin Concerto; String Quartet; *Hebrew Rhapsody* for Clarinet and Orch.; piano pieces.

Krein, Julian, Russian composer, son of **Grigori Krein;** b. Moscow, March 5, 1913. He studied with his father; wrote his first compositions at the age of 13. In 1927 he went to Paris; took some lessons with Paul Dukas. In 1933 he went back to Moscow and remained there. Besides composing, he also wrote music criticism. His music is marked by a lyric quality; in his harmonic procedures he adopts advanced methods bordering on polytonality. Among his works are *5 Preludes* for Orch. (1927); symph. prelude, *Destruction* (1929); Cello Concerto (Barcelona, Oct. 18, 1931, Eisenberg, soloist); *Spring Symphony* (1938); piano pieces; songs.

Kreisler, Fritz, celebrated violinist; b. Vienna, Feb. 2, 1875; d. New York, Jan. 29, 1962. His talent manifested itself at an early age and was carefully fostered by his father, under whose instruction the boy made such progress that at the age of 6 he was sent to study with Jacob Dont; then was admitted to the Vienna Cons., where he studied with Jacques Auber and Hellmesberger (1882–85); in 1885, he carried off the gold medal. He then entered the Paris Cons., where he was a pupil of Massart (violin) and Delibes (composition); graduated in 1887 as winner of the Grand Prix (gold medal) over 40 competitors. He made his American debut at Steinway Hall in N.Y. on Nov. 10, 1888. In the following year, he made a very successful tour of the U.S. with Moriz Rosenthal. On his return to Europe, he abandoned music for some years; studied medicine in Vienna, and art in Rome and Paris; then entered the Austrian army, serving as an officer in an Uhlan regiment. At his reappearance in Berlin (March 1899) his playing created a sensation. Not only had he regained his outstanding virtuosity, but he had also developed into a great interpreter. On his 2nd visit to the U.S., in 1900–1, when he appeared as a soloist and in ensemble with Hofmann and Gerardy, he carried his audiences by storm; on his tour of England in the spring of 1901, he scored similar triumphs. In 1904 the London Phil. Society honored him by awarding him the Beethoven gold medal. At the outbreak of World War I in 1914, he joined his former regiment;

was wounded at Lemberg (Sept. 6, 1914) and excused from further service. Fortunately his wound was slight (his hip and shoulder were injured in a Russian cavalry attack), so that at the end of 1914 he resumed his artistic career in the U.S. He remained in the U.S. throughout the rest of World War I despite the embarrassment of his status as an enemy alien; after the Armistice, went back to Europe, but continued to make frequent visits to America. He was made Commander of the Legion of Honor by the French government, and received many other honors from foreign governments. In 1938 he became a French citizen; in 1940 he returned to N.Y.; in 1943, became an American citizen.

Kreisler's repertoire contained almost everything of value written for the violin since the 17th century. He was the owner of a Guarneri violin and of instruments by other masters; gathered a rich collection of invaluable MSS; in 1949 donated to the Library of Congress the original scores of Brahms's Violin Concerto and Chausson's *Poème* for Violin and Orch. He wrote some of the most popular violin pieces in the world, among them *Caprice viennois, Tambourin chinois, Schön Rosmarin, Liebesfreud,* etc. He also publ. a number of pieces in the classical vein, which he ascribed to various old composers (Vivaldi, Pugnani, Couperin, Padre Martini, Dittersdorf, Francœur, Stamitz, and others). In 1935 he reluctantly admitted that these pieces were his own, with the exception of the first 8 bars from the "Couperin" *Chanson Louis XIII,* taken from a traditional melody; he explained his motive in doing so by the necessity of building up well-rounded programs for his concerts that would contain virtuoso pieces by old composers, rather than a series of compositions under his own, as yet unknown, name. He also wrote the operettas *Apple Blossoms* (N.Y., Oct. 7, 1919) and *Sissy* (Vienna, Dec. 23, 1932); publ. numerous arrangements of early and modern music (Corelli's *La Folia,* Tartini's *The Devil's Trill,* Dvořák's *Slavonic Dances, Spanish Dance* by Granados, *Tango* by Albéniz, etc.). He publ. a book of reminiscences of World War I, *Four Weeks in the Trenches: The War Story of a Violinist* (Boston, 1915).

BIBLIOGRAPHY: L.P. Lochner, *Fritz Kreisler* (N.Y., 1950; not fully reliable as to factual details); Olin Downes, "Kreisler's Delectable Musical Hoax," *N.Y. Times* (March 3, 1935), reprinted in *Olin Downes on Music,* ed. by Irene Downes (N.Y., 1957).

Kreissle von Hellborn, Heinrich, Austrian writer; b. Vienna, Jan. 19, 1822; d. there, April 6, 1869. He studied law; was a Dr.Juris, and secretary in the Ministry of Finance in Vienna. A passionate admirer of Schubert, he publ. *Franz Schubert, Eine biographische Skizze* (1861), followed in 1865 by the exhaustive biography *Franz Schubert* (condensed Eng. trans. by Wilberforce, 1866; full trans. by A.D. Coleridge, 1869, in 2 vols., with an appendix by Sir George Grove).

Krejčí, Iša, important Czech composer and conductor; b. Prague, July 10, 1904; d. there, March 6, 1968. He studied composition with Jirák and Novák and conducting with Talich at the Prague Cons., graduating in 1929; was active as a conductor in Bratislava (1928–32), then at the Prague National Theater (1933–34) and at the Prague Radio (1934–45). From 1945 till 1958 he headed the opera in Olomouc; from 1958 to his death, he was music director of the National Theater in Prague. His music, in a neo-Classical idiom, is distinguished by vivacious rhythms and freely flowing melody; the national Czech element is not ostentatious, but its presence is well marked.

WORKS: 2 operas: *Antigone,* after Sophocles (1934), and *Pozdviženi v Efesu (The Revolt at Ephesus),* after Shakespeare's *Comedy of Errors* (1939–43; Prague, Sept. 8, 1946); Sinfonietta (1929); *Maly balet (Small Ballet)* for Chamber Orch. (1927–30); Concertino for Piano and Wind Instruments (1935); Concertino for Violin and Wind Instruments (1936); *Antické motivy (Antique Motifs)* for Low Male Voice, and Orch. or Piano (1936); Suite for Orch. (1939); *Sinfonietta-Divertimento* for Orch. (1939); Cello Concertino (1939–40); *20 Variations on an Original Theme* for Orch. (1946–47); Serenade for Orch. (1947–50); *14 Variations* on the folk song *Goodnight, My Beloved* for Orch. (1951–52); 4 symphs. (1954–55, 1956–57, 1961–63, 1961–66); *Vivat Rossini,* overture (1967); *Divertimento-Cassation* for Flute, Clarinet, Bassoon, and Trumpet (1925); 5 string quartets (1928, revised 1935; 1953; 1960; 1962; 1965); Viola Sonatina (1928–29); Clarinet Sonatina (1929–30); Trio for Oboe, Clarinet, and Bassoon (1935); Trio for Clarinet, Double Bass, and Piano (1936); Nonet (1937); *Sonatina concertante* for Cello and Piano (1939); Wind Quintet (1964); *4 Pieces* for Violin and Piano (1967); *A Little Mourning Music* for Alto, Violin, Cello, Double Bass, and Piano (1936); *Ohlasy (Night Sounds)* for Voice and Wind Quintet (1936); Piano Trio, with Female Voice, to words of a psalm (1967); Piano Sonatina (1934); *3 Scherzinos* for Piano (1945); songs.

Krejčí, Josef, Bohemian organist and composer; b. Milostin, Dec. 17, 1821; d. Prague, Oct. 19, 1881. He studied with Josef Proksch in Prague; was active as a church organist; in 1858 he became director of the Organ School in Prague, and in 1865 was appointed director of the Prague Cons. He wrote mainly for the organ and also composed many sacred choruses.

Krejčí, Miroslav, Czech composer; b. Rychnov nad Kněžnou, Nov. 4, 1891; d. Prague, Dec. 29, 1964. He studied science at Charles Univ. in Prague (1910–14); then became a schoolmaster there, remaining in that employment for nearly 30 years (1914–43). He was a prof. at Prague Univ. until his retirement (1943–53). His own music education was desultory; he studied 2 years with Vítězslav Novák as a youth (1911–13) and acquired a mastery of technique through actual composition.

WORKS: 2 operas: *Léto (Summer;* 1937; Prague, Dec. 4, 1940) and *Posledni Hejtman (The Last Captain;* 1944; Prague, March 18, 1948); cantatas: *The*

Wedding Song (1926); *Smrt Kristova* (*The Death of Christ;* 1937–40); *Better Love* (1954); *Rodné Zemi* (*Homeland;* 1958); *Mír* (*Peace;* 1959); Vocal Symph. (1930); 3 numbered symphs.: No. 1 (1944–46); No. 2 (1952–54); No. 3 (1955); *King Lávra,* symph. poem (1917); *Life and Time* for String Orch. and Horn (1927); Viola Concerto (1947); Clarinet Concerto (1949); *Capriccio* for Viola, Winds, and Percussion (1950); *Dance Suite* for Orch. (1950); Violin Concerto (1953); *Funeral Music* for Wind Orch. (1960); 7 string quartets (1913, 1918, 1926, 1941, 1943, 1953, 1955); Clarinet Quintet (1920); 3 string quintets (1926, 1952, 1957); Divertimento for Flute, Clarinet, Horn, and Bassoon (1926); 2 violin sonatas (1926, 1952); Viola Sonata (1942); Cello Sonata (1943); Sonatina for Bassoon or Oboe or Horn, and Piano (1950); Septet (1950); Nonet (1953); Quartet for Oboe, Clarinet, Bassoon, and Piano (1955); Wind Octet (1956); Suite for Solo Horn (1956); *3 Pieces* for 3 Violas and Piano (1957); Flute Sonata (1958); Divertimento for 10 Winds (1958); Horn Sonata (1959); Organ Sonata (1954); choruses; songs.

Krek, Uroš, Slovenian composer; b. Ljubljana, May 21, 1922. He studied composition with Škerjanc at the Music Academy in Ljubljana, graduating in 1947; in 1967 joined its staff as a lecturer in music. His style of composition is classical in form, but contains some elements of folk modalities.

WORKS: Violin Concerto (1949); Bassoon Concerto (1954); *Mouvements concertants* for String Orch. (1956); Horn Concerto (1960); *Inventiones ferales* for Violin and Orch. (1962); Concerto for Piccolo and Orch. (1966); *Capriccio* for Viola and 10 Instruments (1971); Sinfonia for Strings (1973); *Old Egyptian Stanzas* for Tenor and Orch. (1967); Violin Sonata (1946); Sonata for 2 Violins (1971).

Kremenliev, Boris, Bulgarian-American composer and musicologist; b. Razlog, May 23, 1911. In 1929 he came to the U.S.; studied composition with La Violette in Chicago and with Howard Hanson in Rochester, N.Y. He was a member of the Psychological Warfare Branch of the U.S. Army in Europe during World War II. In 1947 he was appointed to the staff of the Univ. of Calif. in Los Angeles. Several of his works are imbued with Bulgarian melorhythms; of these the most interesting are *Pravo Horo* for Orch. (Rochester, April 18, 1940) and *Bulgarian Rhapsody* for Orch. (1952); he also composed several pieces of chamber music and publ. a valuable treatise, *Bulgarian-Macedonian Folk Music* (Los Angeles, 1952).

Kremer, Gidon, violinist; b. Riga, Latvia, Feb. 27, 1947. He won the first prize of the Latvian Republic at the age of 16; then went to the Moscow Cons. to study with David Oistrakh. In 1970 he won first prize in the prestigious International Tchaikovsky Competition in Moscow, which catapulted him to a worldwide career. His vast repertoire includes several works by composers of the avant-garde.

Kremer, Isa, Jewish folksinger; b. Beltzi, Bessa-

rabia, 1885; d. Cordoba, Argentina, July 7, 1956. She acquired early fame as a singer of Russian, Yiddish, Polish, and German ballads; made many tours in Russia and Eastern Europe before coming to the U.S. in 1923; in N.Y. she appeared in vaudeville; gave her final concert in America at Carnegie Hall on Dec. 3, 1950. She married Dr. Gregorio Bermann, an Argentine psychiatrist, in 1940.

Kremlev, Yuli, Russian musicologist and composer; b. Essentuki, June 19, 1908; d. Leningrad, Feb. 19, 1971. He studied at the Leningrad Cons.; devoted himself mainly to musical biography; publ. monographs on Chopin (Moscow, 1949; revised ed., 1960), Grieg (Moscow, 1958), and Debussy (Moscow, 1964) and essays on esthetics. He also wrote a Symph., several piano sonatas, and songs.

Krempelsetzer, Georg, Bavarian composer; b. Vilsbiburg, April 20, 1827; d. there, June 9, 1871. He was by trade a cloth weaver; studied music in Munich with Franz Lachner; became chorus master at theaters in Munich (1865), Görlitz (1868), and Königsberg (1870). He wrote the opera *Der Onkel aus der Lombardei* (1861) and operettas: *Die Franzosen in Gotha; Der Vetter auf Besuch* (1863); *Die Kreuzfahrer* (1865); *Das Orakel in Delphi* (1867); *Die Geister des Weins* (1867); *Aschenbrödel; Rotmantel* (1868).

Kremser, Eduard, Austrian composer; b. Vienna, April 10, 1838; d. there, Nov. 27, 1914. He studied in Vienna; in 1869, became chorus master of the Männergesangverein there; also conducted various other choral societies. He wrote light operas: *Der Botschafter* (Vienna, Feb. 25, 1886); *Der kritische Tag* (Vienna, Dec. 6, 1891); etc.; several symph. sketches with Voices: *Balkanbilder; Prinz Eugen; Das Leben ein Tanz;* etc.; many part-songs (his settings of *6 altniederländische Volkslieder* are especially fine; of these the most celebrated is the Dutch *Prayer of Thanksgiving*); *Das Herzklopfen, Erinnerungen,* and *Fröhliche Armuth,* for Men's Chorus and Orch.; songs (*Jagdlied,* with accompaniment of 4 Horns; 2 songs from *Der Trompeter von Säkkingen,* with Solo Cornet); piano music; also edited *Wiener Lieder und Tänze* (2 vols., 1912, 1913).

BIBLIOGRAPHY: H. von Paumgarten, *Eduard Kremser* (Vienna, 1915).

Krenek, Ernst, noted modern composer; b. Vienna, Aug. 23, 1900. (Being of Czech origin, he used to spell his name Křenek [pronounced Krshenek] with a diacritical sign on the *r,* but dropped it after coming to America.) He studied in Vienna, and in Berlin with Franz Schreker; lived in Zürich (1923–25); then was an opera coach in Kassel under Paul Bekker (1925–27); in 1928 he returned to Vienna and became a correspondent of the *Frankfurter Zeitung;* also traveled widely in Europe as a lecturer and an accompanist in programs of his own songs. In 1937 he came to the U.S.; was a prof. of music at Vassar College (1939–42); then head of the music dept. at Hamline Univ. in St. Paul, Minn. (1942–47); lived in

Hollywood in 1947–50. In the summer of 1950 and in following years he made successful tours of Germany as a lecturer and a conductor of his own works. He became an American citizen on Jan. 24, 1945. He was married to Anna Mahler (daughter of Gustav Mahler) in 1923; they were divorced in 1925, and he married Berta Hermann, an actress. His evolution as a composer mirrors the development of modern music in general. The tradition of Mahler, strengthened by the domestic ties of Krenek's first marriage, was the dominant influence of his early life in music; he then became associated with the modern groups in Vienna, particularly Schoenberg, Berg, and Anton von Webern. In Germany he was associated with Hindemith as a creator of modern opera in a satiric manner. He achieved a masterly technique of composition in his earliest works, and developed his melodic and harmonic idiom in the direction of atonality and polytonality. His first international success came to him at the age of 26, with the production of his opera *Jonny spielt auf,* generally described as a "jazz opera" (although no such title appears in the score). It deals with a jazz fiddler whose fame sweeps the world; in the apotheosis, Jonny sits atop a gigantic globe. The opera was first performed in Leipzig (Feb. 10, 1927), producing a sensation; it was subsequently translated into 18 languages and performed all over the world; a brand of Austrian cigarettes was named after it; it was staged at the Metropolitan Opera House in N.Y. (Jan. 19, 1929) with the hero as a black-faced musician rather than a Negro as in the original. However, the opera fell into desuetude a few years later. Krenek produced several short operas, to which he wrote his own librettos, with transitory success. He also composed symphonic, choral, and chamber music; wrote books and articles on music history and modern methods of composition. In 1933 he adopted the 12-tone method of composition; his opera *Karl V* was written in this idiom; subsequent works use various ingenious applications of Schoenberg's basic method. In 1950 he completed a voluminous autobiography, the MS of which he deposited at the Library of Congress, not to be opened until 15 years after his death. Excerpts were publ. under the title *Self-Analysis.* He made his home in Palm Springs, Calif., but traveled widely as a conductor and pianist in his own works in Europe. In 1963 he was awarded the Grand State Prize of Austria.

WORKS: OPERAS AND DRAMAS WITH MUSIC: *Zwingburg* (Berlin, Oct. 16, 1924); *Der Sprung über den Schatten* (Frankfurt, June 9, 1924); *Orpheus und Eurydike* (Kassel, Nov. 27, 1926); *Jonny spielt auf* (Leipzig, Feb. 10, 1927); *Leben des Orest* (Leipzig, Jan. 19, 1930); *Cefalo e Procri* (Venice, Sept. 15, 1934); *Karl V* (Prague, June 15, 1938); *Tarquin* (Vassar College, May 13, 1941; first professional perf., Cologne, July 16, 1950); *What Price Confidence?* (1946); *Dark Waters* (1951); *Pallas Athene weint* (Hamburg, Oct. 17, 1955); *The Bell Tower* (Urbana, Ill., March 17, 1957); 3 short operas: *Der Diktator; Das geheime Königreich; Schwergewicht oder Die Ehre der Nation* (Wiesbaden, May 6, 1928); *Ausgerechnet und verspielt,* comic opera (Vienna, June 27, 1962); *Der goldene Bock,* fantastic chamber opera (Hamburg, June 16, 1964, composer conducting); *Das kommt davon, oder Wenn Sardakai auf Reisen geht (That's What Happened or, If Sardakai Goes Traveling),* to his own libretto (Hamburg State Opera, June 27, 1970).

BALLETS: *Der vertauschte Cupido,* after Rameau (Kassel, Oct. 25, 1925); *Mammon* (Munich, Oct. 1, 1927); *8-column Line* (Hartford, Conn., 1939).

FOR ORCH.: 5 symphs.: No. 1 (1921); No. 2 (1922); No. 3 (1922); No. 4 (N.Y., Nov. 27, 1947); No. 5 (Albuquerque, March 16, 1950); 2 *concerti grossi* (1921); *Symphonische Musik* for 9 Solo Instruments (Donaueschingen, July 30, 1922); Piano Concerto No. 1 (1923); Concertino for Flute, Violin, Harpsichord, and String Orch. (1924); Violin Concerto (Dessau, Jan. 5, 1925); *Symphonie* for Brass and Percussion (1924–25); *3 Military Marches* (Donaueschingen, 1926); *Potpourri* (Cologne, Nov. 15, 1927); *Kleine Symphonie* (Berlin, Nov. 1, 1928); *Theme and Variations* (1931); *Music for Wind Orchestra* (1931); Piano Concerto No. 2 (Amsterdam, March 17, 1938); *Symphonic Piece* for String Orch. (Ann Arbor, Mich., Aug. 1, 1939); *Little Concerto* for Piano and Organ, with Chamber Orch. (1940); *I Wonder as I Wander,* variations on a North Carolina folk song (1942); *Tricks and Trifles,* orch. version of the *Hurricane Variations* (1945); *Symphonic Elegy* for Strings, on the death of Anton von Webern (1946); Piano Concerto No. 3 (Minneapolis, Nov. 22, 1946, Mitropoulos, pianist-conductor; the 12-tone system consistently used by Krenek after 1936 is not applied in this concerto); Piano Concerto No. 4 (1950); Double Concerto for Violin, Piano, and Chamber Orch. (Donaueschingen Festival, Oct. 6, 1951); Concerto for Harp and Chamber Orch. (Philadelphia, Dec. 12, 1952); Concerto for 2 Pianos and Orch. (N.Y., Oct. 24, 1953); *Medea* for Contralto and Orch. (Philadelphia, March 13, 1953); *11 Transparencies* (Louisville, Feb. 12, 1955); *Spass mit Karten,* ballet (1957); *Kette, Kreis und Spiegel,* symph. poem (1957); *Spiritus Intelligentiae, Sanctus* for Voices and Electronic Sounds (1957); *Hexaeder,* 6 pieces for Chamber Ensemble (1958); *Missa duodecim tonorum* for Mixed Chorus and Organ (1958); *Sestina* for Soprano and Small Ensemble (1958); *Quaestio temporis* for Chamber Orch. (Hamburg, Sept. 30, 1960); *La Corona,* cantata (1959); *From 3 Make 7* for Chamber Orch. (1961); *5 + 1 (Alpbach Quintet;* 1962).

CHAMBER MUSIC: Violin Sonata (1919); Serenade for Quartet (1919); 8 string quartets: No. 1 (1921); No. 2 (1921); No. 3 (1923); No. 4 (1923–24); No. 5 (1930); No. 6 (1937); No. 7 (1943); No. 8 (1952); Suite for Clarinet and Piano (1924); Solo Violin Sonata (1924–25); Suite for Cello Solo (1939); Sonatina for Flute and Viola (1942); Sonata for Violin Solo (1942); Sonata for Viola and Piano (1948); String Trio (1948); *Parvula Corona Musicalis ad honorem J.S. Bach* for String Trio (1950); *Fibonacci-Mobile* for String Quartet, 2 Pianos, and Coordinator (Hanover, N.H., July 7, 1965).

FOR PIANO: *Double Fugue* for Piano, 2-hands (1918); *Dance Studies,* in *Grotesken-Album* (ed. by K. Seeling, 1922); 6 sonatas: No. 1 (1919); No. 2 (1928);

No. 3 (1943); No. 4 (1948); No. 5 (1950); No. 6 (1951); 5 sonatinas (1920); *Toccata and Chaconne* on the chorale *Ja, ich glaub' an Jesum Christum* (1922; also a suite of pieces on the chorale); 2 suites (1924); 5 pieces (1925); *12 Short Piano Pieces* (1938); *Hurricane Variations* (1944); *8 Piano Pieces* (1946); *George Washington Variations* (1950).

FOR CHORUS: *Concert Aria*, to text from Goethe's *Stella* (1928); *Von der Vergänglichkeit des Irdischen*, cantata (1932); *Reisebuch aus den Österreichischen Alpen* (1935); 2 a cappella choruses for Women's Voices, on Elizabethan poems (1939); *Proprium Missae in Festo SS. Innocentium* for Women's Voices (1940); *Lamentatio Jeremiae Prophetae, Secundum Brevarium Sacrosanctae Ecclesiae Romanae* (1941); *Cantata for Wartime* (1943); *5 Prayers* for Women's Voices, from the *Litanie* by John Donne (1944); *The Santa Fe Time Table* for Chorus a cappella, to the text of names of railroad stops between Albuquerque and Los Angeles (1945); *In Paradisum*, motet for Women's Voices a cappella (1946). Krenek also composed an Organ Sonata (1941) and revised and orchestrated Monteverdi's *L'incoronazione di Poppea* (1937); he is the author of the books *Über neue Musik* (collected lectures; Vienna, 1937; in Eng. as *Music Here and Now*, N.Y., 1939); *Studies in Counterpoint* (N.Y., 1940; in German as *Zwölfton-Kontrapunkt Studien*, Mainz, 1952); *Selbstdarstellung*, autobiography (Zürich, 1948; in Eng. as *Self-Analysis*, Albuquerque, 1953); *Musik im goldenen Westen: Das Tonschaffen des U.S.A.* (Vienna, 1949); *Johannes Ockeghem* (N.Y., 1953); *De rebus prius factis* (Frankfurt, 1956); *Gedanken Unterwegs* (Munich, 1959).

BIBLIOGRAPHY: A. Weissmann, "Ernst Krenek," *Modern Music* (Dec. 1928); F. Evans, "Ernst Krenek," *Cobbett's Cyclopedic Survey of Chamber Music* (London, 1930; vol. 2, pp. 76–79); J.M. Schneider, "Ernst Krenek," *Revue Musicale* (Aug. 1930); F. Saathen, *Ernst Krenek, Ein Essay* (Munich, 1959); Lothar Knessl, *Ernst Krenek* (Vienna, 1967); W. Rogge, *Ernst Kreneks Opern—Spiegel der zwanziger Jahre* (Wolfenbüttel, 1970); O. Kolleritsch, ed., *Ernst Krenek* (Vienna, 1982); *Ernst Krenek: Katalog zur Ausstellung* (Vienna, 1982).

Krenn, Franz, Austrian composer and pedagogue; b. Dross, Feb. 26, 1816; d. St. Andrä, June 18, 1897. He studied music with his father; occupied posts as church organist in Vienna; in 1869–93 was a prof. of harmony and counterpoint at the Vienna Cons. Gustav Mahler was his pupil. Krenn left a large number of works, among them 29 masses, a Symph., chamber music, and a manual, *Musik- und Harmonielehre* (1890).

Krenn, Fritz, Austrian bass; b. Vienna, Dec. 11, 1897; d. there, July 17, 1964. He studied at the Vienna Academy of Music; made his debut as the Herald in *Lohengrin* in Trieste in 1917; then sang in Vienna at the Volksoper (1917–18) and in Bratislava (1918–19); subsequently joined the Vienna State Opera (1919–25, 1934–42, 1946–59); also sang with the Berlin State Opera (1927–43), and with Covent Garden in London (1935). He made his Metropolitan Opera debut in N.Y. on Jan. 5, 1951, as Baron Ochs in *Der Rosenkavalier;* then continued his career in Europe. He was highly successful in buffo roles.

Krenn, Werner, Austrian tenor; b. Vienna, Sept. 21, 1943. He sang in the Vienna Boys' Choir; then studied bassoon; later took voice lessons with Elisabeth Rado in Vienna. In 1966 he made his debut at the Deutsche Oper in West Berlin; then sang regularly at the Vienna State Opera. In addition to opera, he made a career as a concert and oratorio singer.

Krentzlin, Richard, German piano pedagogue and composer; b. Magdeburg, Nov. 27, 1864; d. Oldendorf (Hesse), Nov. 27, 1956, on the morning of his 92nd birthday. He studied at the Kullak Academy; became a successful piano teacher; publ. numerous character pieces (*Bunte Bilder, Aus meiner Jugendzeit,* etc.) and 8 books of piano studies, *Der gute Pädagoge.*

Krenz, Jan, Polish conductor and composer; b. Wloclawek, July 14, 1926. He managed to take music lessons as a boy in Warsaw during the German occupation; after the war, he studied composition with Sikorski, conducting with Wilkomirski and Górzyński, and piano with Drzewiecki at the State Academy of Music in Lodz. In 1948 he became conductor of the Poznan Phil. and the Poznan Opera; in 1950 he was named to the post of second conductor of the Polish Radio National Symph. Orch. in Katowice; in 1953 he became its conductor; led it on tours in Europe, in Russia, China, Japan, and Australia, and directed it intermittently until 1967. From 1967 until 1973 he served as artistic director of the Warsaw Opera; then went to Germany; in 1979 settled in Bonn as Generalmusikdirektor, resigning in 1983. His music is audaciously modernistic in its orientation, while preserving a classical form.

WORKS: *Toccata* for Piano and Orch. (1943); Symph. No. 1 (1947-49); *Nocturnes* for Orch. (1950); *Classical Serenade* for Orch. (1950); *Rozmowa dwóch miast (Conversation of Two Towns)* for 2 Choruses and Orch. (1950); *Rustic Serenade* for Orch. (1951); Piano Concertino (1952); *Rhapsody* for Xylophone, Tam-tam, Timpani, Celesta, and Strings (1952); *Capriccio* for 24 Instruments (1962); *Antisymphony* (1962).

Kresának, Jozef, Slovak musicologist and composer; b. Čičmany, Dec. 20, 1913. He studied composition with Karel at the Prague Cons. (1932–37) and with Novák at the Master School there (1937–39); taught in Prešov and in 1944 was appointed a lecturer at the Bratislava Univ., becoming a full prof. of musical science in 1963. As a music scholar, he dedicated himself mainly to the stylistic analysis and codification of Slovak folk songs, and publ. numerous treatises on the subject. He also publ. a monograph on Eugen Suchoň (Bratislava, 1961), *Considerations on Music* (Prague, 1965), and *Foundations of Musical Thought* (Bratislava, 1976). His compositions include a String Quartet (1935), Piano Trio (1939), 2 suites for Violin and Piano (1947, 1951), 2 suites for Orch. (1951; revised 1961; 1953), *Prelude and Toccata* for Orch. (1957), and a Piano Quintet (1975).

Kretschmer, Edmund, German composer; b. Ostritz, Aug. 31, 1830; d. Dresden, Sept. 13, 1908. He studied with Julius Otto (composition) and Johann Schneider (organ) in Dresden. In 1863 he became organist of the court, retiring in 1901. He was a successful composer; his choral work *Geisterschlacht* won a prize at the Dresden singing festival (1865); his 3-part Mass for Men's Chorus won the Brussels Academy's prize in 1868. He wrote several operas to his own librettos in a Wagnerian manner; at least 2 of them were successful: *Die Folkunger* (Dresden, March 21, 1874) and *Heinrich der Löwe* (Leipzig, Dec. 8, 1877); he also produced 2 light operas: *Der Flüchtling* (Ulm, 1881) and *Schön Rotraut* (Dresden, 1887); several choral works for festive occasions; church music; etc.
BIBLIOGRAPHY: O. Schmid, *Edmund Kretschmer* (Dresden, 1890).

Kretzschmar, August Ferdinand Hermann, eminent German music scholar; b. Olbernhau, Jan. 19, 1848; d. Nikolassee, near Berlin, May 10, 1924. He was a chorister and a pupil of Julius Otto in Dresden; then studied with Richter, Reinecke, Oskar Paul, and Papperitz at the Leipzig Cons., where he took his degree of Dr.Phil. with a thesis on ancient notation prior to Guido d'Arezzo, *De signis musicis* (1871). He then became a teacher of organ and harmony at the Leipzig Cons.; also conducted choral societies there. In 1876 he was a theater conductor at Metz; in 1877, music director at Rostock Univ.; in 1880, municipal music director there. In 1887 he joined the faculty of Leipzig Univ.; in 1888–97, was Riedel's successor as conductor of the Riedelverein; conducted the Akademische Orchesterkonzerte initiated by himself (1890–95). In 1904 he went to Berlin as a prof. at the Univ. there; in 1909–20, was also the director of the Berlin Hochschule für Musik. He was a thoroughly educated musician, a good organist as well as choral conductor, and composer of some secular and sacred vocal music. But his importance in musicology lies in his establishment of certain musical and esthetic concepts that elucidate the historical process. He introduced a convenient term (taken from theology), "Hermeneutik," applying it to the explanation of musical melodies and intervallic progressions as expressive of human emotions.
WRITINGS: *Peter Cornelius* (1880); *Führer durch den Konzertsaal*, in 3 vols.: I (1887; 6th ed., 1921), II (1888; 2nd ed., 1932, supplemented by Noack and Botstiber), III (1890; 4th ed., 1920; enlarged by Schnoor, 1932); *Geschichte des neuen deutschen Liedes* (1912; vol. 1 only, up to the songs of Zelter); *Geschichte der Oper* (1919); *Einführung in die Musikgeschichte* (1920); *Bach-Kolleg* (1922). His articles in various periodicals were publ. as *Gesammelte Aufsätze* (2 vols., 1911). He ed. vols. 8, 9, and

42 of Denkmäler Deutscher Tonkunst, of which he was general editor from 1911 to 1919; brought out a new ed. of Lobe's *Lehrbuch der musikalischen Komposition* (4 vols., 1884–87).
BIBLIOGRAPHY: *Festschrift zu Kretzschmars 70. Geburtstag* (Leipzig, 1918); H. Abert, "Kretzschmar," *Jahrbuch der Musikbibliothek Peters* (1924).

Kreubé, Charles Frédéric, French conductor and composer; b. Luneville, Nov. 5, 1777; d. near St.-Denis, 1846. He studied violin in Paris with R. Kreutzer (1800); joined the orch. of the Paris Opéra-Comique as violinist; from 1816–28, was first conductor. He wrote 16 operas; also violin pieces.

Kreuder, Peter Paul, German composer of light opera; b. Aachen, Aug. 18, 1905; d. Salzburg, June 28, 1981. He studied in Munich and in Hamburg; then became active as music director of the Reinhardt theaters in Berlin (1928–30) and at the drama theater in Munich (1930–33). In 1936 he was appointed state music director in Munich. In 1945 he went to Argentina, where he occupied educational posts under the regime of Juan Perón. He wrote an opera, *Der Zerrissene*, which was performed in Stockholm in 1940, and several operettas. His song *Schön war die Zeit* became extremely popular in Germany. It also served as the title of his autobiography (Munich, 1955).

Kreutz, Arthur, American composer; b. La Crosse, Wis., July 25, 1906. He studied music at the Univ. of Wisconsin and at Columbia Univ. in N.Y.; then was lecturer at the latter (1946–52); in 1952 he was appointed to the staff of the music dept. of the Univ. of Mississippi, where he remained until 1964. His works include a "ballad opera," *Acres of Sky* (Fayetteville, Ark., Nov. 16, 1951; symph. poem, *Winter of the Blue Snow* (1942); 2 symphs. (1945, 1946); opera, *The University Greys* (Clinton, Miss., March 15, 1954); folk opera, *Sourwood Mountain* (Clinton, Jan. 8, 1959); also *Dance Concerto* for Clarinet and Orch. (1958); Violin Concerto (1965); 2 "jazz sonatas" for Violin and Piano, and other pieces in a jazz vein; also *New England Folksing* for Chorus and Orch. (Brooklyn, Feb. 17, 1948) and *Mosquito Serenade* for Orch. (N.Y. Phil., Feb. 21, 1948).

Kreutzer, Auguste, French violinist, brother of **Rodolphe Kreutzer;** b. Versailles, Sept. 3, 1778; d. Paris, Aug. 31, 1832. He studied with his brother at the Paris Cons.; played in the orch. of the Paris Opéra-Comique and Opéra; also in the court orchs.; taught at the Paris Cons. He wrote 2 violin concertos, 3 sonatas, etc.

Kreutzer, Konradin (later known as **Conrad**), important German composer; b. Messkirch, Baden, Nov. 22, 1780; d. Riga, Dec. 14, 1849. He was a pupil of J.B. Rieger at Zwiefalten Abbey and of Ernst Weihrauch (1792–96). He then studied law at Freiburg for one year (1799–1800) before devoting himself to music. In 1800 he brought out his first operetta, *Die lächerliche Werbung*, in Freiburg. He lived for 5 years in Constance, and then in Vienna until 1811, studying counterpoint under Albrechtsberger. He produced, with considerable success, *Jerry und Bätely*, after Goethe (May 19, 1810); not being able to bring out 2 operas, *Konradin von Schwaben* and *Der Taucher*, in Vienna, he went, after a pianistic tour of a year, to Stuttgart, where, after the production of *Konradin von Schwaben* (March 30, 1812), he was appointed court conductor. In Stuttgart he produced 8 dramatic works, and then went to Donaueschingen in 1818 as conductor to Prince von Fürstenberg. There he produced, in 1819, *Adele von Budoy*, which was later successful in a revision entitled *Cordelia*. Returning to Vienna, he brought out *Libussa* (Dec. 4, 1822); was conductor at the Kärnthnertor Theater (1822–27, 1829–32, and 1835–40) and at the Josephstadt Theater (1833–35); his most successful work, *Das Nachtlager von Granada* (Jan. 14, 1834), appeared, and was followed a month later by *Der Verschwender* (Feb. 20, 1834), incidental music for Ferdinand Raimund's play of that name. Together with *Jerry und Bätely*, these 2 works held the stage until the end of the century. In 1840–42 he was conductor at the Municipal Theater in Cologne; after 2 years in Vienna (1847–49), he accompanied his daughter Cäcilie, a singer, to Riga, where he died. Besides his many operas, he wrote an oratorio, *Die Sendung Mosis*, and a cantata, *Die Friedensfeier;* also church music, chamber music, and piano pieces; songs, and some noteworthy men's choruses (*Die Capelle, Sonntagsmorgen, Der Tag des Herrn*, etc.).

BIBLIOGRAPHY: W.H. Riehl, *Musikalische Charakterköpfe* (vol. I, Stuttgart, 1879); R. Rossmayer, "Kreutzers Klaviermusik," *Zeitschrift für Musikwissenschaft* (vol. XIII, pp. 80ff.); H. Burkard, *Konradin Kreutzers Ausgang* (Tübingen, 1920); A. Landau, *Das einstimmige Kunstlied Konradin Kreutzers* (Leipzig, 1930).

Kreutzer, Léon, French composer and music critic, son of **Auguste Kreutzer;** b. Paris, Sept. 23, 1817; d. Vichy, Oct. 6, 1868. He studied piano with Fleche and composition with Benoist. He wrote for the *Revue et Gazette Musicale, Revue Contemporaine, La Quotidienne, L'Union,* etc.; publ. *Essai sur l'art lyrique au théâtre* (1845) and a treatise on modulation; also wrote an orch. prelude to Shakespeare's *The Tempest;* string quartets, piano sonatas, etc.

Kreutzer, Leonid, Russian pianist and pedagogue; b. St. Petersburg, March 13, 1884; d. Tokyo, Oct. 30, 1953. He studied piano with Anna Essipova and composition with Glazunov at the St. Petersburg Cons. In 1906 he went to Germany; from 1921 to 1932 taught at the Hochschule für Musik in Berlin. After the advent of the Nazi regime in 1933 he went to the U.S., and in 1938 traveled to Japan, where he became a prof. of piano at the Cons. of Tokyo; earned a fine reputation as a teacher there; many Japanese concert pianists were his pupils. He publ. *Das Wesen der Klaviertechnik* (Berlin, 1923).

Kreutzer, Rodolphe, famous violinist; b. Versailles, Nov. 16, 1766; d. Geneva, Jan. 6, 1831. His father, a German violinist and teacher in Versailles, and Anton Stamitz were his teachers. At the age of 13 he played a violin concerto by Stamitz at a Concert Spirituel; performed his own First Concerto there in May 1784; in 1785 he was appointed first violin in the Chapelle du Roi, and in 1790 solo violin in the Théâtre-Italien, bringing out his first opera, *Jeanne d'Arc à Orleans* (May 10, 1790). It was followed by over 40 others, given at the Opéra, the Opéra-Comique, or the Théâtre-Italien; *Lodoiska* (Aug. 1, 1791) was perhaps his best. A year after his appointment as a teacher of violin at the Cons., he made a triumphant concert tour through Italy, Germany, and The Netherlands (1796); was in Vienna in 1798. In 1801 he succeeded Rode as solo violin at the Opéra, of which he became 2nd conductor in 1816 and was first conductor in 1817–24. From 1802 he was also chamber musician to Napoleon; from 1815, to Louis XVIII; retired in 1826, and so far lost influence that his last opera, *Mathilde,* was contemptuously rejected by the direction of the Opéra. Although his own music could not withstand the test of time, his name became immortal because it was to him that Beethoven dedicated the celebrated *Kreutzer Sonata.*

WORKS: 43 operas; 19 violin concertos; 2 double concertos; *Symphonie concertante* for Violin and Cello, with Orch.; 15 string quartets; 15 string trios; also duets, sonatas, variations, etc., for violin; but his masterwork, wherein his worthiness to rank with the great masters of the classic Parisian school of violin playing is convincingly proved, is the *40 Etudes ou Caprices* for Violin Solo, republ. in countless eds., revised by Vieuxtemps and others. Kreutzer was joint author, with Rode and Baillot, of the great violin method used in the Paris Cons.

BIBLIOGRAPHY: H. Kling, *R. Kreutzer* (Brussels, 1898); B. Cutter, *How to Study Kreutzer* (1907); J. Hardy, *R. Kreutzer: Sa jeunesse à Versailles* (Paris, 1910); A. Moser, *Geschichte des Violinspiels* (pp. 394ff.); (Berlin, 1923, pp. 394ff.; 2nd ed., revised, 1966–67); M. Williams, *The Violin Concertos of Rodolphe Kreutzer* (Diss., Indiana Univ., 1973).

Křička, Jaroslav, eminent Czech composer and pedagogue; b. Kelč, Moravia, Aug. 27, 1882; d. Prague, Jan. 23, 1969. He first studied law in Prague (1900–2); then studied music at the Cons. there (1902–5) and in Berlin (1905–6); in 1906, taught music in Ekaterinoslav, Russia; in 1909, returned to Prague and conducted (1911–20) the famous choral society Hlahol; in 1919, became a prof. at the Cons., remaining on its staff until 1945; then devoted his time to composition.

WORKS: Operas: *Hypolita* (1910–16; Prague, Oct. 10, 1917); *Bílý pán (The White Gentleman),* after Oscar Wilde's *The Canterville Ghost* (1927–29; Brno, 1929; revised in 1930 as *Today Ghosts Have a Difficult Time;* Breslau, Nov. 14, 1931); *Kral Lavra (King Lawrence;* 1936–37; revised 1938–39; Prague, June 7, 1940); *České jesličky (The Czech Christmas Manger;* 1936–37; revised 1948; Prague, Jan. 15, 1949); *Jáchym* a *Juliána* (*Joachim and Julia;* 1945–48; Opava, 1951); *Serenáda,* opera buffa (Pilsen, 1950); *Kolébka (The Cradle),* musical comedy (1950; Opava, 1951); *Zahořanský hon* (*The Zahořany Hunt;* Opava, 1955); children's operas: *Ogaři* (*Country Lads;* 1918; Nové Město in Moravia, Sept. 7, 1919); *Dobře to dopadlo* or *Tlustý pradědeček* (*It Turned Out Well* or *The Fat Great-Grandfather;* 1932) and *Lupici a detekotyvove* (*Robbers and Detectives;* 1932; both operas, Prague, Dec. 29, 1932); several small operas for children's theater; television opera, *Kalhoty* (*A Pair of Trousers;* Czech television, 1962). For Orch.: symph., *Jarní* (*Spring;* 1905–6; revised 1942); *Nostalgie* for String Orch. and Harp (1905); *Faith,* symph. poem (1907); *A Children's Suite* (1907); *Scherzo Idyllic* (1908; Prague, Nov. 13, 1910; 3rd movement of an uncompleted Symph. No. 2); *Modrý pták* (*A Blue Bird),* overture after a Maeterlinck fairy tale (1911; Prague, March 3, 1912; composer conducting); *Adventus,* symph. poem (1920–21; Prague, Nov. 6, 1921); *Matěj Kopecký,* overture (1928); *Horácká suita* (*Suite montagnarde;* 1935; Prague, Sept. 8, 1935); Sinfonietta for String Orch. and Timpani (1940–41); *Majales,* overture (1942); Violin Concerto (1944); Concertino for Horn, and String Quartet or String Orch. (1951); *Variations on a Theme of Boccherini* for Bassoon, and String Quartet or String Orch. (1952); *Sinfonietta semplice* (1962). Cantatas: *Pokušeni na poušti* (*Temptation in the Desert;* 1921–22; *Jenny, the Thief* (1927–28); *Tyrolese Elegies* (1930–31); *A Eulogy to a Woman* (1933); *Recollections of Student Years* (1934); *Moravian Cantata* (1935–36); *The Golden Spinning Wheel* (1943); *To Prague* (1960); *Small Suite in Old Style* for 2 Violins and Piano (1907); 3 string quartets (1907; 1938–39; *Wallachian,* 1949); *Doma* (*At Home),* piano trio (1924–25); Violin Sonata (1925); Sonatina for 2 Violins (1926–27; revised for Violin and Viola); Concertino (septet) for Violin, Wind Quintet, and Piano (1940); *Partita* for Solo Violin (1941); Divertimento for Wind Quintet (1950); Flute Sonatina (1951); Variations for Solo Violin (1956); Violin Sonatina (1962); several albums of piano pieces; a number of songs; also, arrangements of folk songs.

Krieger, Adam, German composer; b. Driesen, Neumark, Jan. 7, 1634; d. Dresden, June 30, 1666. He studied organ with Samuel Scheidt in Halle; in 1655–57 he was organist at the Nikolaikirche in Leipzig; then went to Dresden in 1657 as keyboard teacher to the Elector's daughter; in 1658 was made chamber and court organist there. He was one of the most important of the early composers of German lieder; he called his "Arien," and for most of them wrote the words as well as the music; they contain instrumental ritornels, for 2 violins and continuo in the early songs, for 5 strings and continuo in the later ones. Many of these "Arien" have been preserved, although most of his original collection (1657) is lost; it was reconstructed by H. Osthoff (1929); the 2nd collection (1667) is reproduced in vol. 19 of Denkmäler Deutscher Tonkunst.
BIBLIOGRAPHY: H. Osthoff, *Adam Krieger*

(Leipzig, 1929).

Krieger, Armando, Argentine composer; b. Buenos Aires, May 7, 1940. He studied composition with Alberto Ginastera; gave piano concerts in programs of advanced modern music. In his compositions he adopts a serial technique in which rhythmic, melodic, and harmonic elements follow a predetermined formula of contrasts. Among his works the most significant are *Métamorfosis d'après une lecture de Kafka* for Piano and 15 Instruments (1968); he also wrote 2 chamber cantatas (1959, 1963), 2 string quartets (1960, 1963), and other chamber music.

Krieger, Edino, Brazilian composer; b. Brusque (Santa Catarina), March 17, 1928. He studied music with his father, Aldo Krieger, director of the local Cons., and H.J. Koellreutter. In 1948 he studied with Aaron Copland at the Berkshire Music Center in Tanglewood; then at the Juilliard School of Music in N.Y. with Peter Mennin; also with Ernst Krenek in Brazil in 1952 and with Lennox Berkeley in London. He adopted the dodecaphonic method of composition, but in 1953 turned toward neo-Classicism with national allusions. To the first period belong his *Epigramas* for Piano; Sonatina for Flute and Piano; *Música de câmara* for Flute, Trumpet, Violin, and Timpani; and *Melopeia* for Voice, Viola, Oboe, Saxophone, and Trombone; to the 2nd, *Abertura sinfonica;* String Quartet; 2 piano sonatas; *Concertante* for Piano and Orch.; *Fantasia* for Orch.; *Divertimento* for String Orch.; *Brasiliana* for Viola and Orch.; and 4-hand Piano Sonata. However, he applies dodecaphonic techniques in his Brazilian work *Chôro* for Flute and String Orch. and in *Variações elementares* for Chamber Orch. (1965).

Krieger (or **Krüger**), **Johann,** famous German contrapuntist and organist, brother of **Johann Philipp Krieger;** b. Nuremberg, Dec. 28, 1651; d. Zittau, July 18, 1735. He studied with his brother, and became his successor as chamber organist at Bayreuth in 1672. He was subsequently a court musician at Greiz (1678–81); then went to Zittau, where he was active as municipal organist; he remained there for 53 years, appearing for the last time on the day before he died. His music was appreciated by Handel; some of his organ compositions are regarded as presaging the grand style of Bach.
WORKS: *Neue musikalische Ergetzligkeit,* arias for 5–9 Voices (Frankfurt, 1684); *6 musikalische Partien,* dance music for Clavichord (Nuremberg, 1697); *Anmuthige Clavier-Übung,* containing preludes, fugues, etc. (Nuremberg, 1699); also sacred music. Max Seiffert edited (in Denkmäler Deutscher Tonkunst) 2 sacred choral works by Krieger (vol. 6, part 1) and complete keyboard works, with critical notes, lists of sacred and secular vocal music, dates of perf., notes on extant MSS, biographical details, etc. (vol. 18); an aria from the *Neue musikalische Ergetzligkeit* is reprinted in Schering's *Geschichte der Musik in Beispielen,* no. 235. F. Riedel ed. *Johann Krieger: Präludien und Fugen,* in *Die*

Orgel, ii/3 (Leipzig, 1957).

Krieger, Johann Philipp, German composer, brother of **Johann Krieger;** b. Nuremberg, Feb. 25, 1649; d. Weissenfels, Feb. 7, 1725. He was a pupil of Johann Drechsel and Gabriel Schütz in Nuremberg; went to Copenhagen, where he became a pupil and later assistant of court organist Johann Schröder (1663–69). In 1670 he was appointed court organist and chamber composer at Bayreuth, with an interval of study in Italy (1673). He was subsequently court musician at Kassel, and at Halle (from 1677); on Dec. 23, 1680, he was appointed court conductor at Weissenfels and Halle, remaining in this capacity until his death. He received the rank of nobility from Emperor Leopold I during a visit to Vienna (1677). He produced some 20 stage works in Halle, Weissenfels, Hamburg, and other German towns; publ. 12 trio sonatas for 2 Violins, with Continuo (op. 1, 1688); 12 sonatas for Violin, with Viola da Gamba (op. 2, 1693); *Musikalischer Seelenfriede,* 20 sacred arias for Violin, with Bass (1697); *Lustige Feldmusik,* 6 overtures for Wind or other Instruments (1704); etc. Modern reprints, edited by Seiffert, are in vols. 53/54 of Denkmäler Deutscher Tonkunst (contains a selection of 21 sacred compositions by Krieger with critical commentary, as well as a complete list of his sacred works performed at Weissenfels, notes of extant MSS, biographical details, etc.), vol. 6 (2 sacred choral works, one with a practical transcription), and the appendix to vol. 18 (3 keyboard pieces). Other reprints are: instrumental suite from *Lustige Feldmusik,* in *Perlen alter Kammermusik* (ed. by Schering, for Strings; 1912); in *Organum,* edited by Seiffert (vol. 3, containing no. 3 of the *Feldmusik,* for Chamber Orch.); selected organ pieces are in vol. 4 of *Organum,* etc.; 24 arias, in *Haus- und Kammermusik aus dem XVI.–XVIII. Jahrhundert,* edited by H.J. Moser (1930); 2 arias in Schering's *Geschichte der Musik in Beispielen;* Eitner edited 2 partitas, 2 sonatas, and various vocal works in *Monatshefte für Musikgeschichte* (supplement to vol. 30).

Kriens, Christian, Dutch-American pianist, violinist, and composer; b. Brussels, April 29, 1881; d. Hartford, Conn., Dec. 17, 1934. He was taken to the Netherlands as a child; studied with his father, a clarinetist, and later at The Hague Cons. At 14 he made his debut at Amsterdam, playing the *Emperor Concerto* and conducting his own 2nd Symph. From 1896 to 1899 he toured Europe as a violinist; then taught at The Hague Cons. He came to America as conductor of the French Opera Co. (1906); settled in N.Y. in 1907; was a violinist in the N.Y. Symph. and N.Y. Phil., and at the Metropolitan Opera. He then became director of the Traveller's Broadcasting Co., Station WTIC, Hartford, Conn. Despondent over his inability to find further work, he committed suicide.

Krigar, Hermann, German pianist; b. Berlin, April 3, 1819; d. there, Sept. 5, 1880. He studied at Leipzig with Schumann, Mendelssohn, and Hauptmann (1843–45); organized a singing society in Berlin; taught there. He wrote incidental music, motets, Psalms, piano pieces, and songs.

Krips, Henry, Austrian-born Australian conductor; b. Vienna, Feb. 10, 1912. He studied at the Vienna Cons. and the Univ. of Vienna; then made his conducting debut at Vienna's Burgtheater in 1932; subsequently was conductor in Innsbruck (1933–34), Salzburg (1934–35), and Vienna (1935–38). In 1938 he emigrated to Australia and became a citizen in 1944. He conducted ballet; from 1947 was a conductor with the Australian Broadcasting Commission; also conducted the Perth Symph. Orch. From 1949–72 he was conductor of the South Australia Symph. Orch. in Adelaide. He combined this activity with guest appearances as conductor at the Sadler's Wells Opera in London, which he joined in 1967; also had engagements in Vienna. He was best known for his performances of light Viennese music, especially that of the Strauss family. He was the brother of the noted conductor **Josef Krips.**

Krips, Josef, noted Austrian conductor; b. Vienna, April 8, 1902; d. Geneva, Oct. 13, 1974. He studied with Mandyczewski and Weingartner in Vienna; was violinist at the Volksoper there (1918–21); then became operatic coach and choirmaster of the Volksoper (1921); made his operatic conducting debut there in 1921. In 1924 he conducted opera in Aussig; in 1925, at the Municipal Theater in Dortmund; in 1926–33 was Generalmusikdirektor at Karlsruhe. In 1933 he was appointed conductor at the Vienna State Opera; in 1935, became a prof. at the Vienna Academy of Music. In 1938 he lost these positions, after the annexation of Austria to Germany; conducted a season of opera in Belgrade (1938–39). In 1945 he rejoined the staff of the Vienna State Opera; conducted in England, France, and Russia in 1947, producing an excellent impression; also conducted the Vienna Phil. and at the Salzburg Festival. In 1950 he was appointed conductor of the London Symph. Orch.; from 1954 to 1963 he was conductor of the Buffalo Phil. Orch., then conductor of the San Francisco Symph. Orch. (1963–70); also was a guest conductor of the N.Y. Phil. and other American and European orchs.

Kristofferson, Kris, American country-and-western singer, actor and songwriter; b. Brownsville, Texas, June 22, 1936. Of an intellectual bent, he took a writing course at Pomona College, winning such high grades that he was given a Rhodes scholarship to Oxford Univ., where he obtained his B.A. degree in 1960. Upon returning to the U.S., he served in the U.S. Army as a helicopter pilot stationed in Germany. He found his true vocation when he moved to Nashville in 1965 and produced a song *Me and Bobby McGee,* which had the right countrified twang to it; his subsequent songs *For the Good Times* and *Sunday Mornin' Comin' Down* made the top of the charts. He then recorded *Full Moon* with his fiancée, Rita Coolidge. The song was successful, the marriage was not. Overflowing with quaquaversal talents, Kristofferson turned to movies, and made a hit in the screen epic *A Star Is Born* with Barbra Streisand as the leading lady.

Kriukov, Nicolai, Russian composer, brother of **Vladimir Kriukov;** b. Moscow, Feb. 14, 1908; d. there (suicide), April 5, 1961. He studied with Vassilenko; devoted himself chiefly to folk-song arrangements and film music. He wrote orch. suites on folk themes gathered in various republics of the Soviet Union, sometimes including native instruments. He received 2 Stalin prizes for his film scores.

Kriukov, Vladimir, Soviet composer, brother of **Nicolai Kriukov;** b. Moscow, July 22, 1902; d. Staraya Rusa, near Moscow, June 14, 1960. He studied composition with Miaskovsky at the Moscow Cons., graduating in 1925. In 1949–50 he was director of the Moscow Phil. Inst.; in 1957–59 taught composition at the Gniessin Inst. in Moscow. His music is harmoniously and melodiously eclectic, while adhering to an effective Russian style.
WORKS: Operas: *Railroad Stationmaster,* after Pushkin's tale (Moscow, Oct. 30, 1940), and *Dmitri Donskoy* (1947); *October Cantata* (1947); *Russian Rhapsody* for Orch. (1944); symph. poems: *January 9,* commemorating the march on the Winter Palace in St. Petersburg in 1905 (1931), and *Dreadnought Potemkin* (1955); Piano Concerto (1959); chamber music; piano pieces; songs.

Křivinka, Gustav, Czech composer; b. Doubravice, April 24, 1928. He studied violin and composition in Brno, graduating in 1954 from the Brno Cons. He wrote 2 symphs.; 2 violin concertos; 2 piano concertos; several song cycles; chamber music.

Křížkovský, Karel (Pavel), Bohemian choral composer; b. Holasovice, Jan. 9, 1820; d. Brno, May 8, 1885. He was a chorister at Opava; then attended the Gymnasium there; became a schoolteacher; in 1845, joined the order of the Austin Friars, and assumed the name Pavel; was ordained priest in 1848. He was greatly interested in Moravian folk songs and collected many of them in the field. At the same time, he began to compose choruses in the national manner; one of his earliest works, *Utonulá (The Girl Who Drowned),* became popular; other favorites are *Žaloba (The Plaint)* and particularly *Odvedeného prosba (The Recruit's Prayer).* He also wrote much sacred music (Roman Catholic) for the Olomouc Cathedral, where he was music director from 1873. Among his pupils was Janáček. Publication of his collected works was begun at Prague in 1949.
BIBLIOGRAPHY: J. Geissler, *Křížkovský* (Prague, 1885); K. Eichler, *Křížkovský* (Brno, 1904); J. Racek, *Křížkovský* (Olomouc, 1946).

Kroeger, Ernest Richard, American organist and composer; b. St. Louis, Aug. 10, 1862; d. there, April 7, 1934. He studied piano in St. Louis; then was organist at various churches there; taught and lectured at a number of schools in the U.S. He composed orch. works, including the overtures *Thanatopsis, Endymion, Sardanapalus, Hiawatha,* and *Atala* and the symph. suites *Lalla Rookh* and *The Mississippi; A Masque of Dead Florentines* for declamation or action with music; Piano Trio; Piano Quartet; Piano Quintet; 4 string quartets; Violin Sonata; pieces for organ; songs.

Kroeger, Karl, American composer; b. Louisville, Ky., April 4, 1932. He studied music at the Univ. of Louisville and the Univ. of Illinois; then moved to N.Y., where he became head of the Americana Collection of the N.Y. Public Library's Music Division. In 1964 he was appointed composer-in-residence at the Univ. of Oregon; in 1972 became director of the Moravian Music Foundation in Salem, N.C., where he remained until 1980; in 1982 he became an associate prof. at the Univ. of Colorado at Boulder. He has written numerous articles on Moravian music and has edited MSS from the Foundation archives. He has written symph. and chamber music in a neo-Classical manner.

Krohn, Ernst C., American musicologist; b. New York, Dec. 23, 1888; d. Santa Fe, N.Mex., March 21, 1975. He settled in St. Louis in 1898; studied piano with his father and with Ottmar Moll, attaining a modicum of virtuosity; gave recitals and taught piano in various schools in St. Louis from 1909 to 1963; also composed songs and piano pieces. He was co-founder of the Bach Society of St. Louis in 1942.
WRITINGS: *A Century of Missouri Music* (St. Louis, 1924); *The History of Music: An Index to the Literature Available in a Selected Group of Musicological Publications* (St. Louis, 1952); *Music Publishing in the Middle Western States before the Civil War* (Detroit, 1972).

Krohn, Felix (Julius Theofil), Finnish conductor and composer; b. Tampere, May 20, 1898; d. Lahti, Nov. 11, 1963. He studied with his father; later at the Helsinki School of Music and the Hochschule für Musik in Berlin. Returning to Finland in 1922, he was active as a conductor and teacher.
WORKS: *Sotarukous (War Prayer)* for Orch. (1918); sinfonia brevis, *Vuodenajat (The Seasons;* 1921); *Kyllikki,* cantata (1923); *Odalisque* for Orch. (1924); 4 suites for Orch.: *Sysmäläinen (The Man from Sysma;* 1938); *Vihreä kulta (Green Gold;* 1939); *Anu and Mikko* (1940); *Linnaisten kartanon vihreä kamari (The Green Room at Linnainen Manor;* 1944); *Uskollinen sisar (The Faithful Sister),* opera for children (1945); chamber music.

Krohn, Ilmari (Henrik Reinhold), eminent Finnish music scholar; b. Helsinki, Nov. 8, 1867; d. there, April 25, 1960. After studying with Richard Faltin in Helsinki, he went to Germany, where he took courses at the Leipzig Cons. with Papperitz and Reinecke (1886–90); obtained his Dr.Phil. in 1900 with the thesis *Über die Art und Enstehung der geistlichen Volksmelodien in Finnland* (Helsinki, 1899). Returning to Finland, he joined the staff of the

Univ. of Helsinki (1900); also taught at the Cons. there; lectured at musical congresses in London, Paris, Basel, Vienna, and Rome (1891–1914). In 1906 he founded the musical journal *Säveletär;* was a member of the Songbook Commission (1918–23); proposed the construction of an "Acoustic Harmonium" of his own invention, and publ. a paper on it, *System Krohn* (Vienna, 1906). In 1918 he was promoted to prof. of musicology at the Univ. of Helsinki, the first person to hold that post there; he retired in 1935.

WRITINGS: *Guide for Acoustic Intonation* (Helsinki, 1911; in Swedish, 1912); a course of music theory, in 5 parts: I. *Rhythm* (1911–14); II. *Melody* (1917); III. *Harmony* (1923); IV. *Polyphony* (1929); V. *Form* (1937); *Der Formenbau in den Symphonien von Jean Sibelius* (Helsinki, 1942); *Der Stimmungsgehalt in den Symphonien von Jean Sibelius* (2 vols., Helsinki, 1945–46); *Sävelmuistoja elämäni varrelta,* memoirs (Helsinki, 1951). His most significant accomplishment is the compilation of some 7,000 Finnish folk songs, *Suomen kansan sävelmiä,* which he began in 1886 and methodically arranged in 4 categories: I. sacred melodies; II. secular melodies; III. dance melodies; IV. runic melodies. The publication of these important materials stretched from 1898 till 1933. He also ed. Psalms (1903), introits (1908), antiphons (1915), Easter matins, New Year vigils, vespers, and the Order of the Mass for the church year (1925); *Iltakellot, Completorium I–IV* (1928); began a complete ed. of the Finnish Psalter in 1952. He contributed valuable articles on Finnish music to various journals. Krohn was also a composer; wrote an opera, *Tuhotulva* (*Deluge;* Helsinki, Oct. 25, 1928); 2 oratorios: *Ikiaartehet* (*Eternal Treasures;* 1914) and *Viottajat* (*Victors;* 1937); many sacred choral works; a number of songs. On the occasion of his 60th birthday, his students publ. a collection of musical essays in his honor (Helsinki, 1927).

BIBLIOGRAPHY: Sulho Ranta, *Ilmari Krohn,* in *Suomen säveltäjiä* (Helsinki, 1945; pp. 273–84).

Kroll, Erwin, German musicologist; b. Deutsch-Eylau, Feb. 3, 1886; d. Berlin, March 7, 1976. He studied in Königsberg; later took lessons in music theory with Pfitzner and Sandberger in Munich. From 1919 to 1924 he served as répétiteur at the State Opera in Munich; from 1925 to 1933 was active in Königsberg as a music journalist; after a hiatus during the Nazi regime and war, he was employed as director of the Berlin studios of the Northwest Radio (1946–53); he composed songs and chamber music, but devoted himself mainly to musical biography.

PUBLICATIONS: *E.T.A. Hoffmann* (Leipzig, 1923); *Hans Pfitzner* (Munich, 1924); *Aus den Werdejahren der neudeutschen Musik* (Königsberg, 1933); *C.M. von Weber* (Potsdam, 1934); *C.M. von Weber, Sein Leben in Bildern* (Leipzig, 1936); *Musikstadt Königsberg* (Freiburg im Breisgau, 1966).

Kroll, Franz, German pianist and music editor; b. Bromberg, June 22, 1820; d. Berlin, May 28, 1877. He was first a student of medicine; then took lessons from Liszt; settled in Berlin as a music teacher. He was the editor of Bach's *Well-Tempered Clavier* for the Bach Gesellschaft, to which he contributed an introduction, summarizing bibliographical data; also edited Mozart's piano works.

Kroll, William, American violinist; b. New York, Jan. 30, 1901; d. Boston, March 10, 1980. He studied in Berlin and at the Inst. of Musical Art in N.Y. (graduated in 1922); then became first violinist of the Coolidge String Quartet, and appeared with it at numerous chamber music festivals in the U.S. and in Europe; subsequently organized a string quartet of his own, the Kroll Quartet.

Krombholc, Jaroslav, Czech conductor; b. Prague, Jan. 30, 1918; d. there, July 16, 1983. He was educated at the Prague Cons. and at the Charles Univ. in Prague. In 1940 he made his conducting debut at the Prague National Theater; from 1968–75 he was its chief conductor; from 1973–78 served as chief conductor of the Prague Radio Symph. Orch. He was especially renowned for his authentic performances of the works by Smetana, Dvořák, Janáček, and other Czech composers.

Krombholc, Karlo, Hungarian-Serbian composer; b. Budapest, Dec. 20, 1905. He studied at the Vienna Academy of Music; was active as a concert pianist from 1927 to 1939; in 1945 he went to Yugoslavia and settled in Novi Sad as a piano teacher. His works are influenced mainly by Béla Bartók, with ethnic modalities gadrooned by atonal extrapolations. Typical of these is his extensive piano work *Sazvezda* (*Constellation;* 1969). He also wrote orch. works based on Hungarian and Balkan folk tunes.

Krommer, Franz, violinist and composer; b. Kamenitz, Moravia, Nov. 27, 1759; d. Vienna, Jan. 8, 1831. He first studied with his uncle, an organist; went to Vienna; joined the orch. of Count Styrum-Limburg at Simontornya as violinist, then conductor; became choirmaster at Fünfkirchen, Pecs; then bandmaster of the Károlyi regiment; went to Gödöllö as Kapellmeister of Count Grassalkovic's orch. He returned to Vienna, and in 1818 became Imperial Kapellmeister. He wrote a Mass; 5 symphs.; 5 violin concertos; a quantity of chamber music; quintets and quartets for wind instruments; etc.

BIBLIOGRAPHY: W.H. Riehl, *Musikalische Charakterköpfe* (vol. 3, Stuttgart, 1879).

Kromolicki, Joseph, eminent musicologist; b. Posen, Jan. 16, 1882; d. Berlin, Oct. 11, 1961. He received a thorough education in music, studying with Haberl and Haller in Regensburg and with Pfitzner, Kretzschmar, and Johannes Wolf in Berlin; received his Dr.Phil. in 1909 with the thesis *Die Practica artis musicae des Amerus.* He was active as a choral conductor in Berlin churches; edited *Musica Sacra* from 1908 and vols. 45, 48, and 57 of Denkmäler Deutscher Tonkunst; composed 5 masses, a Te

Deum, organ preludes, sacred songs, etc.

Kronke, Emil, German pianist and composer; b. Danzig, Nov. 29, 1865; d. Dresden, Dec. 16, 1938. He was a pupil of Reinecke in Leipzig and of Nicodé and Kirchner in Dresden; won first prize for piano playing at the Dresden Cons. (1886). He was an ardent admirer of Liszt, and wrote several virtuoso pieces for piano; also publ. several manuals: *Das virtuose Arpeggiospiel; Chopin-Etüden; Die moderne Technik; Die hohe Schule des 4. und 5. Fingers;* edited more than 200 of Chopin's works.

Kronold, Hans, cellist, brother of **Selma Kronold;** b. Cracow, July 3, 1872; d. New York, Jan. 10, 1922. He studied in Leipzig and Berlin; came to America at the age of 14; joined the orch. of the Metropolitan Opera; then played in the N.Y. Symph. Orch.; taught at the N.Y. College of Music. He publ. cello pieces and songs.

Kronold, Selma, soprano, sister of **Hans Kronold;** b. Cracow, Aug. 18, 1861; d. New York, Oct. 9, 1920. She made her debut as Agatha in *Der Freischütz,* at Leipzig, when she was 16; then was engaged to sing Wagnerian roles in various European cities. In 1888 she came to America; sang the leading roles in the American premieres of *Cavalleria Rusticana* (Philadelphia, Sept. 9, 1891) and *Pagliacci* (N.Y., June 15, 1893); in 1896, joined the Metropolitan Opera; retired in 1904 and founded the Catholic Oratorio Society. Her repertoire included some 45 parts.

Kroó, György, Hungarian musicologist; b. Budapest, Aug. 26, 1926. He studied violin at the National Cons. and at the Academy of Music in Budapest; also attended classes in musicology there with Szabolcsi and Bartha. In 1957 he was named head of music education of the Hungarian Radio; in 1960 became a guest lecturer at the Academy of Music, joining its permanent faculty in 1967; was chairman of its musicology dept. from 1973. His writings include *Robert Schumann* (Budapest, 1958); *Hector Berlioz* (Budapest, 1960); *Bartók Béla szinpadi müvei* (*Bartók's Stage Works;* Budapest, 1962); *Wenn Schumann ein Tagebuch geführt hätte* (Budapest, 1962); *A "szabadito" opera* (*The "Rescue" Opera;* Budapest, 1966); *Richard Wagner* (Budapest, 1968); *Bartók kalauz* (*A Guide to Bartók;* Budapest, 1971; in Eng., 1974).

Krow, Josef Theodor, Czech singer and composer; b. Nové Strašeci, Dec. 19, 1797; d. Draguignan, near Nice, March 1, 1859. He studied cello, theory, and voice; appeared as an opera singer in minor roles in Hungary, Poland, and the Netherlands. From 1835 to 1840 he lived in London as a singing teacher; in 1858 he went to Nice, where he died a year later. His claim to a small niche in music history is that in 1825 he publ. a song to the Czech words "Těšme se blahou nadeji," claiming it to be an authentic melody of the time of the Bohemian religious reformer, martyr, and saint Ján Hus. This claim was widely believed; Liszt wrote a piano paraphrase of Krow's song under the title *Hussittenlied aus dem 15. Jahrhundert* ("a Hussite song from the 15th century"). Under the same misapprehension Balfe made use of it in his opera *The Bohemian Girl,* and the Italian composer Angelo Tessaro in the opera *Giovanni Huss.* Even more spectacular was Krow's success in setting the same tune to his own German words, "Polen wird für ewig Polen," publ. under the pseudo-Polish pseudonym **Workinski** ("Work" is the crab form of "Krow") in 1831; caught in the wave of universal sympathy for Poland after the unsuccessful Polish rebellion, the song achieved tremendous popularity all over Europe.

Kroyer, Theodor, eminent German musicologist; b. Munich, Sept. 9, 1873; d. Wiesbaden, Jan. 12, 1945. He studied piano with Lang, counterpoint with Rheinberger, and musicology with Sandberger; took the degree of Dr.Phil. in 1897 from the Univ. of Munich with the dissertation *Die Anfang der Chromatik im italienischen Madrigal des XVI. Jahrhunderts* (publ. Leipzig, 1902); completed his Habilitation there in 1902 with his *Ludwig Senfl und sein Motettenstil* (Munich, 1902); then became music critic of the *Münchener Allgemeine Zeitung;* was on the staff of the univs. of Munich (1902–20), Heidelberg (1920–23), and Leipzig (1923–33). In 1925 he purchased for the Univ. of Leipzig the rich collection of instruments, MSS, and portraits from the famous Heyer Museum in Cologne; also in 1925 he began issuing the valuable series Publikationen Älterer Musik (Deutsche Gesellschaft für Musikwissenschaft). In 1932 be became a prof. at the Univ. of Cologne; retired in 1938. He edited a vol. (motets and Magnificat) of the complete works of Senfl in Denkmäler der Tonkunst in Bayern, 5 (1903); also edited a selection from the works of G. Aichinger for the same series (vol. 8, 1909).

BIBLIOGRAPHY: *Kroyer-Festschrift* (Regensburg, 1933); O. Ursprung, "Theodor Kroyer," *Zeitschrift für Musikwissenschaft* (Nov. 1933).

Krstič, Petar, Serbian composer; b. Belgrade, March 2, 1877; d. there, Jan. 21, 1957. He studied at the Vienna Cons. with R. Fuchs. Returning to Belgrade, he conducted opera at the National Theater; in 1930, became inspector of several music schools. His works, based on Serbian national tunes, included the opera *Zulumćar* (Belgrade, Nov. 23, 1927); cantata, *Jutro Slobode* (1919); several orch. suites of national dances; choruses and songs. He edited a Serbian music dictionary.

Krückl, Franz, Moravian baritone; b. Edlspitz, Nov. 10, 1841; d. Strasbourg, Jan. 13, 1899. He studied with Dessoff; made his debut in 1868 in Brünn; then sang in Kassel, Augsburg, Hamburg, and Cologne (1874–86); taught at the Hoch Cons. in Frankfurt; in 1892, became director of the Municipal Theater in Strasbourg. He publ. *Der Vertrag zwischen Direktor und Mitglied der deutschen Bühne* (1899).

Krueger, Felix Emil, German music psychologist;

b. Posen, Aug. 10, 1874; d. Basel, Feb. 24, 1948. He studied at the univs. of Strasbourg, Berlin, and Munich (Dr.Phil., 1897); also at the Psychological Inst. of Leipzig Univ. and the Kiel Psychological and Physiological Inst. After lecturing at the Univ. of Leipzig (1903–6), he went to Argentina and was a prof. at the Univ. of Buenos Aires (1906–8); was a prof. at Halle Univ. (1910–12); an exchange prof. at Columbia Univ., in N.Y. (1912–13); in 1918, was appointed prof. and director of the Psychological Inst. of Leipzig Univ., succeeding Wilhelm Wundt; held an honorary LL.D. degree from Columbia Univ.; also honorary degrees from European institutions of learning. He retired in 1938; lived in Potsdam; then went to Switzerland, where he remained until his death.
WRITINGS: *Beziehungen der experimentellen Phonetik zur Psychologie* (1907); *Mitbewegungen beim Singen, Sprechen und Hören* (Leipzig, 1910); *Über Entwicklungspsychologie* (1915); *Über psychische Ganzheit* (1926). In 1934 his students and admirers publ. a Festschrift on his 60th birthday.

Krueger, Karl (Adalbert), American conductor; b. Atchison, Kans., Jan. 19, 1894; d. Elgin, Ill., July 21, 1979. He learned to play the cello and organ in his early youth; then began his formal study at Midland College in his hometown (B.A. 1913) and at the Univ. of Kansas (M.A., 1916); also took an intermediate course in Boston at the New England Cons. of Music (1914–15), where his instructors were Chadwick in composition and Wallace Goodrich in organ playing. Subsequently Krueger played organ at St. Ann's Episcopal Church in N.Y. (1916–20). In 1920 he made a concert tour of Brazil as an organist; then went to Vienna, where he studied music theory with Robert Fuchs and conducting with Franz Schalk. He also attended classes in economics at the Univ. of Vienna and the Univ. of Heidelberg. Returning to the U.S. in 1922, he married the heiress Emma McCormick Jewett, of Chicago. He held the posts of conductor of the Seattle Symph. Orch. (1926–32), the Kansas City Phil. (1933–43), and the Detroit Symph. Orch. (1943–49); he was thus the first American-born musician to serve as permanent conductor of a major American symph. orch. In 1958 he founded the Society for the Preservation of the American Musical Heritage and made numerous recordings of American works. He wrote *The Way of the Conductor: His Origins, Purpose and Procedures* (N.Y., 1958).

Krug, Dietrich, German music teacher; b. Hamburg, May 25, 1821; d. there, April 7, 1880. He studied with Melchert and J. Schmitt. He wrote studies for the piano; also publ. a method.

Krug, Friedrich, German composer; b. Kassel, July 5, 1812; d. Karlsruhe, Nov. 3, 1892. He was a baritone singer; was court music director at Karlsruhe. He wrote the operas *Die Marquise* (Kassel, 1843); *Meister Martin der Kufer und seine Gesellen* (Karlsruhe, 1845); *Der Nachtwächter* (Mannheim, 1846).

Krug, (Wenzel) Joseph (called **Krug-Waldsee**), German composer and conductor; b. Waldsee, Nov. 8, 1858; d. Magdeburg, Oct. 8, 1915. He developed precociously; entered the Stuttgart Cons. at 14, studying violin, piano, singing, and theory; graduated in 1880, and went to Switzerland, where he was active as a teacher in Hofwyl; then conducted a choral society in Stuttgart (1882–89); was subsequently chorus master in Hamburg (1889–92), and in Nuremberg and Augsburg (from 1894); then lived in Magdeburg. He wrote several cantatas in a grand manner; 4 operas; chamber music; songs.

Krüger, Eduard, German writer on music; b. Lüneburg, Dec. 9, 1807; d. Göttingen, Nov. 9, 1885. He studied philology in Berlin and Göttingen; also studied music; in 1861 became a prof. of music at Göttingen Univ. He publ. *De musicis Graecorum organis circa Pindari tempora* (1830); *Grundriss der Metrik* (1838); *Beiträge für Leben und Wissenschaft der Tonkunst* (1847); *System der Tonkunst* (1866); also contributed articles to various periodicals.

Krüger, Wilhelm, German pianist and composer; b. Stuttgart, Aug. 5, 1820; d. there, June 16, 1883. He studied piano with Ziegele and composition with Lindpaintner. In 1845 he settled in Paris, where he enjoyed an excellent reputation as a pianist and teacher; in 1870, the outbreak of the Franco-Prussian War compelled him to return to Germany; he was then active as a pedagogue. He publ. a number of brilliant salon pieces for piano (168 opus numbers in all), which included caprices, nocturnes, genre pieces (*Harpe éolienne, Guitare*), a *Polonaise-Boléro*, études (*Les Six Jours de la semaine,* etc.), and transcriptions, fantasias, etc., of and on operatic airs. He edited a 2-vol. edition of Handel's clavier works.

Kruis, M.H. van 't, Dutch organist and composer; b. Oudewater, March 8, 1861; d. Lausanne, Feb. 14, 1919. He studied in The Hague; then filled various posts as organist and teacher; in 1886 he founded the musical monthly *Het Orgel*. He publ. *Beknopt overzicht der muziekgeschiedenis* (1892); also wrote an opera, *De bloem van Island;* 3 symphs.; 8 overtures; organ music; piano pieces; etc.

Krul, Eli, Polish-American composer; b. Pabianice, Jan. 1, 1926. He studied at the Hochschule für Musik in Munich (1945–49); in 1950 he settled in N.Y. His works include String Quartet (1958); *O Come, Let Us Sing* for Chorus and Organ (1960); *Alleluia* for Chorus a cappella (1962); etc.

Krumpholtz, Johann Baptist, Bohemian harpist and composer; b. Budenice, near Zlonice, May 8, 1742; d. Paris, Feb. 19, 1790. He received his first instruction from his father, a bandmaster in a Paris regiment; gave concerts in Vienna in 1772; studied composition with Haydn; in 1773–76, was a member of Prince Esterházy's orch. Following a long concert tour in Germany, he returned to France, and in

Metz he married **Fräulein Meyer,** a 16-year-old harpist, with whom he subsequently gave concerts in Paris and London. Krumpholtz added to his fame as a harpist by inventing a harp with 2 pedals, loud and soft; he also stimulated Erard to make experiments that led to the invention of the modern pedal mechanism. His life ended tragically; he drowned himself in the Seine when his young wife eloped to England with another man. He wrote 6 concertos for Harp and Orch.; Duo for 2 Harps; 52 sonatas and other works entitled *Sonates pathétiques;* Symph. for Harp, with Small Orch.; many short pieces.

Krumpholtz, Wenzel, Austrian violinist, brother of **Johann Baptist Krumpholtz;** b. Budenice, near Zlonice, 1750; d. Vienna, May 2, 1817. He was a member of the orch. at the Vienna Opera in 1796, and was friendly with Beethoven; when Krumpholtz died, Beethoven was moved to write a *Gesang der Mönche,* dedicated to his memory. Wenzel Krumpholtz wrote several pieces for unaccompanied violin, among them *Abendunterhaltung* and *Eine Viertelstunde für eine Violine.*

Krupa, Gene, American jazz drummer; b. Chicago, Jan. 15, 1909; d. Yonkers, N.Y., Oct. 16, 1973. He joined a jazz band when still in his adolescence; made his first recording at 18. In 1935 he became Benny Goodman's drummer and scaled the heights of the swing world; having a phenomenal technique and being a natural showman, he "popularized" the drums with extended, virtuosic solos. He left Goodman in 1938, forming his own band; he toured Europe and the Orient and became internationally famous. A largely fictional film, *The Gene Krupa Story,* was produced in 1959.

Kruse, Georg Richard, German conductor and writer on music; b. Greiffenberg, Jan. 17, 1856; d. Berlin, Feb. 23, 1944. He studied at the Univ. of Bern and in Leipzig; then was an opera director and conductor in Germany. In 1894–96 he toured the U.S. as conductor of a troupe presenting Humperdinck's *Hansel und Gretel;* returned to Europe and was municipal theater director in Bern, St. Gall, and Ulm (1896–1900); from 1900 to 1909 he edited the *Deutsche Bühnengenossenschaft.* In 1906 he founded and was director of the Lessing Museum in Berlin; in 1908, founded the Lessing Society and the *Musik-Volksbibliothek des Tonkünstlerverein;* also was editor of dramatic and musical works for *Reclams Universalbibliothek* and contributed articles to various journals. He publ. a comprehensive biography of A. Lortzing (1899); *Lortzings Briefe* (1901; enlarged 2nd ed., Regensburg, 1913); biographies of Otto Nicolai and Hermann Götz; essays; etc.

Kruseman, Jacob Philip, Dutch music publisher; b. Amsterdam, Nov. 17, 1887; d. The Hague, Jan. 31, 1955. He studied singing, and appeared in recitals and light opera in the Netherlands until 1909, when he founded a publishing firm in The Hague, specializing in books on music and art; issued about 25 vols.

of biographies of famous composers, and himself wrote a booklet, *Beethoven's Eigen Woorden* (The Hague, 1947). His most important publication is *Geïllustreerd muzieklexicon,* edited by himself with G. Keller (The Hague, 1932; supplemented, ed. by Kruseman and Zagwijn, 1949); it is modeled after Riemann's *Musiklexikon,* but contains a great deal of information on Dutch musicians not available in other reference books. After his death, the management of his publishing firm was assumed by his widow.

Krushelnytska, Solomea, Ukrainian soprano; b. Belavyntsy, near Tarnopol, Sept. 23, 1872; d. Lwow, Nov. 16, 1952. As a child she sang in a village choir; entered the Lwow Cons. as a voice student; made her debut there in 1892; then went to Milan, where she took voice lessons with Crespi. From 1898 to 1902 she appeared in opera in Warsaw and St. Petersburg; subsequently made an extensive European tour; sang at La Scala in Milan under Toscanini. Her repertoire included some 60 works; she sang Aïda, Desdemona, Madama Butterfly, Elisabeth in *Tannhäuser,* and Elsa in *Lohengrin;* also appeared in the title role of *Elektra* by Richard Strauss. In 1925 she abandoned the opera stage and devoted herself to concert singing; particularly notable was her promotion of Ukrainian composers in her programs of songs. In 1939 she returned to Lwow, where she taught at the Cons. She was one of the few Russian and Ukrainian singers to win praise for idiomatic renditions of Italian operas. Her voice was of a wide range, spanning fully 3 octaves; she attained excellence in both lyric and dramatic roles. A collection of articles about her career was publ., in the Ukrainian language, in Lwow in 1956.

Kruyf, Ton de, Dutch composer; b. Leerdam, Oct. 3, 1937. He studied violin; attended seminars in new music in Darmstadt led by Maderna, Boulez, Stockhausen, and Ligeti; then took a course in composition with Wolfgang Fortner in Heidelberg. In his music he pursues the goal of maximum effect with a minimum of means; he makes use of serialism when it is structurally justified.
  WORKS: Opera, *Spinoza* (Amsterdam, June 15, 1971); short radio opera, *Quauhquauhtinchan in den vreemde (Quauhquauhtinchan in Foreign Parts;* Hilversum, June 3, 1972); ballet, *Chronologie II* (The Hague, 1968); *Mouvements symphoniques* for Orch. (1955; revised 1966); *Sinfonietta,* 3 dances for Strings (1956; revised 1965); *5 Impromptus* for Small Orch. (1958); *Einst dem Grau der Nacht enttäuscht,* after poems by the modern painter Paul Klee, for Mezzo-soprano and Chamber Ensemble (Hilversum, Sept. 15, 1964); *Pour faire le portrait d'un oiseau,* after Jacques Prévert, for Mezzo-soprano and Chamber Ensemble (Hilversum, Sept. 17, 1965); *De blinde zwemmers,* 3 fragments for Youth Chorus and 2 Instrumental Groups (1966); *Töne aus der Ferne,* after a poem by Paul Klee, for Alto and Chamber Orch. (Amsterdam, Sept. 11, 1968); *Sinfonia II* (Hilversum, May 14, 1969; developed from

an orch. interlude in the opera *Spinoza*); *4 pas de deux* for Flute and Orch. (1972); *Echoi* for Oboe and String Orch. (1973); *Twee uur (2 Hours)* for Speaker and Orch. (1973); Quartet for Flute, Violin, Trumpet, and Bassoon (1959); Flute Sonatina (1960); *Music* for String Quartet (1962); *Partita* for String Quartet (1962); Solo Cello Sonata (1964); *Aubade* for Horn, 2 Trumpets, Trombone, and Tuba (1965); *Fragments IV from Shakespeare Sonnets* for Mezzo-soprano, Flute, and Cello (1965); *Pas de deux* for Flute and Piano (1968); *Serenata per complesso da camera* for Flute, Clarinet, Harp, and String Quintet (1968); *Mosaico* for Oboe and String Trio (1969); *Séance* for Percussion, Piano, and Harp (1969); *Echoi* for Solo Oboe (1973); *Sgrafitti* for Piano (1960); *Arioso* for Piano, 4-hands (1975). BIBLIOGRAPHY: E. Vermeulen, "Ton de Kruyf: Spinoza," *Sonorum Speculum,* 47 (1971).

Krygell, Johan Adam, Danish organist; b. Næstved, Sept. 18, 1835; d. Copenhagen, July 27, 1915. He began his career as a painter, but turned his attention to music; entered the Copenhagen Cons. in 1867, studying organ under G. Matthison-Hansen; won the Ancker stipend, and spent 1874–75 studying in Germany; returning to Copenhagen in 1880, he became organist at St. Matthew's Church; also taught. He wrote an opera, *Saul* (not produced); an oratorio; a Mass; 24 string quartets; a Septet; symphs.; overtures; organ works.

Krylov, Pavel, Russian composer; b. Tver, March 3, 1885; d. Moscow, April 21, 1935. He studied at the Phil. Inst. in Moscow; graduated in 1910 with honors. In 1920 he joined the staff of the Moscow Cons. Among his works are an opera, *The Fountain of Bakhtchissaray;* Symph.; symph. poem, *The Spring;* symph. suite, *Volga;* Concerto for Clarinet and Orch.; 3 piano sonatas; songs.

Kryzhanovsky, Ivan, Russian theorist and composer; b. Kiev, March 8, 1867; d. Leningrad, Dec. 9, 1924. He studied medicine and music; took lessons with Rimsky-Korsakov at the St. Petersburg Cons.; worked in Pavlov's laboratory of conditioned reflexes; served in the medical corps in the Russian army during World War I, and was taken prisoner. After his release, he lectured on the physiology of piano technique. He wrote several symph. works, chamber music, and a Piano Concerto. His paper, *Biological Bases of the Evolution of Music,* was publ. in an Eng. trans. (London, 1928).

Kubelík, Jan, famous Czech violinist; b. Michle, near Prague, July 5, 1880; d. Prague, Dec. 5, 1940. He was taught by his father, who was a gardener; since he showed extraordinary talent, he was accepted by Ševčik as a student at the Prague Cons.; later he studied in Vienna, where he made his professional debut on Nov. 26, 1898. In 1900 he began a series of triumphant concerts in Europe and America. He was regarded as a counterpart to Paderewski in virtuosity, dramatic appeal, and ability to communicate his art to audiences everywhere. In 1903 he

married a Hungarian countess and became a naturalized Hungarian citizen. His career as a great virtuoso was stopped short with World War I; he appeared less frequently than before; lived mostly in Prague. He gave a series of farewell concerts in 1939–40; his last concert was in Prague on May 8, 1940, after his beloved homeland had been dismembered by the Nazis. He composed 6 violin concertos in a brilliant style; also a Symph.; and some chamber music. BIBLIOGRAPHY: J. Čeleda, *Jan Kubelík* (Prague, 1930); K. Hoffmeister, *Jan Kubelík* (Prague, 1941); a symposium in his memory, ed. by J. Dostál, was publ. at Prague in 1942.

Kubelík, Rafael, eminent Czech conductor, son of Jan Kubelík; b. Býchory, near Kolín, June 29, 1914. He studied at the Prague Cons.; made his conducting debut with the Czech Phil. in Prague on Jan. 24, 1934; he was subsequently conductor at the National Theater in Brno (1939–41); from 1942 to 1948 he was music director of the Czech Phil.; between 1948 and 1950 he conducted in England and elsewhere in Europe. In 1950 he was appointed principal conductor of the Chicago Symph. Orch.; he made it a rule to feature modern works (about 60 pieces in all) in his programs; this and his insistence on painstaking work on details in rehearsals antagonized some critics in the Chicago press, so that he was compelled to resign (1953). From 1955 to 1958 he was director of the Covent Garden Opera in London; during his tenure there he presented the complete performance of *Boris Godunov* in Mussorgsky's original version. In 1961 he became chief conductor of the orch. of the Bavarian Radio, and toured with it in Japan (1965) and the U.S. (1968); retired from the post in 1979; for a brief time he was music director of the Metropolitan Opera in N.Y. (1973–74), where he also became the epicenter of controversy; these contretemps, however, did not undermine his artistic integrity. In 1978 he was engaged to conduct 6 weeks of guest appearances with the N.Y. Phil. In 1967 he became a Swiss citizen. Kubelík is also a composer; he wrote 2 operas: *Veronika* (Brno, April 19, 1947) and *Cornelia Faroli* (1966); 3 symphs.; Violin Concerto; Cello Concerto; Requiem; other choral works; *4 Forms* for String Orch. (1965); *Orphikon: Music in 3 Movements* for Orch. (N.Y., April 2, 1981, composer conducting).

Kubiak, Teresa, Polish soprano; b. Ldzan, Dec. 26, 1937. She was educated at the Academy of Music in Lodz; made her debut with the Lodz Opera in 1967; also appeared with the Warsaw Opera; then began an international career, singing in Vienna, Leipzig, London, and Chicago. On Jan. 18, 1973, she made her debut at the Metropolitan Opera as Liza in *The Queen of Spades.*

Kubik, Gail (Thompson), American composer; b. South Coffeyville, Okla., Sept. 5, 1914; d. Covina, Calif., July 20, 1984, of the side effects of kala-azar, a visceral protozoan infection he had contracted on a trip to Africa. His father was of Bohemian extraction; his mother, of Irish origin, was trained as a concert singer. Kubik studied the rudiments of music with her; then enrolled at the Eastman School of Music, where he studied violin with Samuel Belov, and composition with Bernard Rogers, Edward Royce, and Irving McHose; in 1934 he received his B.M. degree. In the same year he wrote a Piano Trio, and a Violin Concerto in which he was soloist in its premiere with the Chicago Symph. (Jan. 2, 1938). He continued his study in composition with Leo Sowerby at the American Cons. of Music in Chicago (M.M., 1936). In the meantime, he organized a family ensemble with his mother and his 2 brothers, and played concerts with them. In 1936–37 he taught violin at the Dakota Wesleyan Univ. in Mitchell, S.Dak.; in 1937–38 he took a composition course with Walter Piston at Harvard Univ. In 1938–40 Kubik was on the faculty of Teachers College at Columbia Univ. Concurrently he was employed as staff composer for NBC, and wrote incidental music for several radio productions. During World War II he served in the U.S. Air Force with the rank of sergeant. In 1943 he received a Guggenheim fellowship. After the war he traveled in Europe as a conductor and lecturer. He was awarded the American Prix de Rome in 1950 and 1951 and spent 3 years at the American Academy in Rome. In 1952 he was a guest lecturer at the Santa Cecilia Academy there. One of the most important works of this period was his *Symphonie concertante* for piano, viola, trumpet, and orch., for which he received the Pulitzer Prize in Music. In 1970 he was appointed composer-in-residence at Scripps College in Claremont, Calif.; when he was asked to retire at the age of 65 in 1980, he brought an unsuccessful suit against the school, claiming that productivity and not age should determine the time of retirement for a creative person. Besides his symph. works, Kubik developed great skill in writing for documentary films. His gift of musical humor was expressed at its best in the music he wrote for the animated film cartoon *Gerald McBoing-Boing* (1950), which received both a Motion Picture Academy Award and the British Film Inst. Award, and which incidentally launched a vogue of twangy rhinogenic tunes in popular music. In his symphonic and other scores he cultivated a manner that was expressively modern, without abandoning the basic tenets of tonality; the rhythmic patterns of his music were apt to be stimulatingly asymmetric. WORKS: FOR THE STAGE: *A Mirror for the Sky,* folk opera on the life of Audubon (Eugene, Oreg., May 23, 1939); *Boston Baked Beans,* "opera piccola" (N.Y., March 9, 1952); *Frankie and Johnnie,* ballet for Dance Band and Folk Singer (1946). FOR ORCH.: *American Caprice* for Piano and Orch. (1936); *Scherzo* (1940); 2 violin concertos: No. 1 (1934; revised 1936; Chicago, Jan. 12, 1938); No. 2 (1940; revised 1941; won first prize in the Jascha Heifetz competition); *Spring Valley Overture* (1947); 3 symphs.: No. 1 (1949); No. 2 (Louisville, Ky., April 7, 1956); No. 3 (N.Y., Feb. 28, 1957); *Symphonie concertante* for Piano, Viola, Trumpet, and Orch. (N.Y., Jan. 27, 1952; received the Pulitzer Prize in 1952); *Thunderbolt Overture* (1953); *Scenario* (1957).

CHAMBER MUSIC: *Trivialities* for Flute, Horn, and String Quartet (1934); Piano Trio (1934); Wind Quintet (1937); *Suite* for 3 Recorders (1941); Sonatina for Violin and Piano (1944); *Toccata* for Organ and Strings (1946); *Little Suite* for Flute and 2 Clarinets (1947); *Soliloquy and Dance* for Violin and Piano (1948); Divertimento No. 1 for 13 Players (1959); Divertimento No. 2 for 8 Players (1959); *Prayer and Toccata* for Organ and Chamber Orch. (1968); Divertimento No. 3 for Piano Trio (1970–71); *5 Birthday Pieces* for 2 Recorders (1974). FOR VOICE: *In Praise of Johnny Appleseed* for Bass-baritone, Chorus, and Orch. (1938; revised 1961); *Choral Profiles, Folk Song Sketches* for Chorus (1938); *Puck: A Legend of Bethlehem,* radio music (NBC Network, Dec. 29, 1940); *Litany and Prayer* for Men's Chorus, Brass, and Percussion (1943–45); *Fables and Song* for Voice and Piano (1950–59); *A Christmas Set* for Chorus and Chamber Orch. (1968); *A Record of Our Time,* "protest piece" for Chorus, Narrator, Soloist, and Orch. (Manhattan, Kans., Nov. 11, 1970); *Scholastics* for a cappella Chorus (1972); *Magic, Magic, Magic* for Chorus and Chamber Orch. (San Antonio, Texas, April 25, 1976). FILM SCORES: *The World at War* (1942); *Memphis Belle* (1943); *Gerald McBoing-Boing* (1950); *The Miner's Daughter* (1950); *Two Gals and a Guy* (1951); *Translantic* (1952); *The Desperate Hours* (1955); *Down to Earth* (1959); also piano pieces.
BIBLIOGRAPHY: David Ewen, *American Composers* (N.Y., 1982).

Kubín, Rudolf, Czech composer; b. Moravská, Ostrava, Jan. 10, 1909; d. there, Jan. 11, 1973. He studied cello and music theory at the Prague Cons.; took a course in quarter-tone and sixth-tone composition from Alois Hába (1925–27). After World War II, he was a co-founder of the Ostrava Cons. and was its first director. He wrote music in disparate styles, some extremely modern, others designed for utilitarian purposes (Mass songs, military marches, patriotic cantatas, etc.).
WORKS: 3 operas: *Letní noc* (A Summer Night; 1930–31; Czech Radio, 1931; first Czech radio opera); *Naši furianti* (*Our Wild Ones;* 1942–45; Ostrava, Sept. 18, 1949); *Koleje mládí* (*The Rails of Youth;* 1948–49; radio opera); numerous operettas, including *Heva* (1955–57); *Prolog* for Orch. (1929); *Czech Overture* (1932); Sinfonietta for Orch. and Organ (1935–36); Overture to the unfinished opera *Zpěv uhlí* (*Song of Coal;* 1936); Trombone Concerto (1936); *Symphony concertante* for 4 Horns and String Orch. (1937); Clarinet Concerto (1939); 2 violin concertos (1940, 1960); *Moravian Rhapsody* for Orch. (1942); overture, *Květen* (*May;* 1945); Accordion Concerto (1950); symph. cycle, *Ostrava* (1950–51), consisting of 5 separate works: *Vítězství* (*Victory),* *Maryčka Magdónova, Ostrava, V Beskydách* (*In the Beskid Mountains),* and *Ocelové srdce* (*Heart of Steel);* symph. poem, *Geroj, In Memoriam K. Gottwalda* (1953); dramatic overture, *Julius Fučík* (1954); Cello Concerto (1960); *Salutation to Frenštát,* melodrama for Orch. (Ostrava, Jan. 9, 1969); *Reminiscence,* symph. (Ostrava, Jan. 9, 1969);

String Quartet (1925–26); *Scherzo* for 2 Clarinets and Piano (1933); *Jazzety* for Piano (1940); *Scherzo* for Violin and Piano (1942); Ballade for 4 Cellos (1942); Nonet (1946); Suite for Solo Cello (1970); songs; choruses; numerous quarter-tone pieces written during his studies with Alois Hába: 2 suites for Piano (1926, 1927); 2 fantasies for Piano (1926, 1927); Fantasy for Clarinet and Piano (1926); *5 Pieces* for Cello and Piano (1926); *Piano Piece* (1927).

Kučera, Václav, Czech composer; b. Prague, April 29, 1929. He studied music at Charles Univ. in Prague (1948–51); then went to Russia, where he took a course in composition with Shebalin at the Moscow Cons. (1951–56). Upon returning to Prague, he served as head of foreign music at Czech Radio (1956–59); in 1972 was appointed to the music dept. of the Academy of Arts in Prague. In his own music he follows the precepts of socialist realism, often using historical subjects in his radio productions, with the application of electronic sounds; but he is also a prolific composer of chamber music in purely structural techniques. He also publ. monographs on Czech and Russian composers. WORKS: BALLETS: *The Brigands' Fire* (1958); *Festival Fairy Tale* (1959); *Kinetic Ballet* (1968); *Heart and Dream* (1973); *Life without Fault* (1979); 2 dramatic radio sketches: *Lidice* for Narrator, 2 Reporters, Announcer, Solo Soprano, Chorus, Instrumental Ensemble, and Electronic sounds, commemorating the destruction of the Czech village by the Nazis (1972); *Spartacus* for Chorus and Electronic Sound (1976). FOR ORCH.: Symph. (1962); *Krysař (The Pied Piper),* stereophonic concertino for Flute and 2 Chamber Orchs. (1964); *Obraz (Picture)* for Piano and Orch. (1966–70); *Salut,* symph. mosaic (1975); *Operand* for Chamber Orch. (1979); *Fortunata (Omaggio a Vivaldi)* for Chamber Orch. (1979); *Avanti,* symph. movement (1981). CHAMBER MUSIC: *Dramas* for 9 Instruments (1961); *Protests,* chamber cycle for Violin, Piano, and Kettledrums (1963); *Genesis* for Flute and Harp (1965); *Hic sunt homines* for Piano Quartet (1965); *Spectra* for Dulcimer (1965); *Diptychon* for Flute, Bass Clarinet, Piano, and Percussion (1966); *Duodrama* for Bass Clarinet and Piano (1967); *To Be,* an affirmative optimistic reply to Hamlet's question, for Percussion Quartet (1968); *Panta Rhei (All Flows),* according to the Greek philosopher Heraclitus) for Flute, Vibraphone, and Percussion (1969); *Invariant* for Bass Clarinet, Piano, and Electronic Tape (1969); *Scenario* for Flute, Violin, Viola, and Cello (1970); *Argot* for Brass Quintet (1970); *Diario (Homage to Ché Guevara),* concert cycle for Solo Guitar (1971); *Taboo a due boemi* for Bass Clarinet, Piano, and Percussion (1972); *Manifesto of Spring (In Memory of Prague, May, 1945)* for 4 Players (1974); *Imaginable Connections* for String Quartet (1976); *Horizons* for 5 Players (1978); *Aphorisms* for Violin and Piano (1978); *Epigrams* for Violin and Cello (1978); *Science Fiction* for Jazz Ensemble (1980); *Furiant* for Clarinet, Trombone, Cello, and Piano (1980); *Aquarelles* for Flute and Guitar (1981); *Stenograms*

for Flute, Cello, and Piano (1981); *Boiling Point* for 4 Brass Instruments (1981); *Wagnerian Improvisations* for Solo Flute (1982); *Capriccios (Hommage à Paganini)* for Violin and Guitar (1982). FOR VOICE: *Orbis Pictus* for Mixed Chorus and Old Instruments (1975); *Amoroso* for Mezzo-soprano, Flute, and Harp (1975); *Gallant Songs* for Mezzo-soprano, Flute, Clarinet, and Viola (1978); *Catharsis,* concert monologue for Soprano and Chamber Ensemble (1979); *Ecco Homo,* 5 Greek and Latin sentences for Bass, Violin, Viola, Cello, Harp, and Percussion (1980); *Listening Time,* concert monodrama for Solo Voice and Percussion (1981).

Kucharz, Johann Baptist, Bohemian organist; b. Chotecz, March 5, 1751; d. Prague, Feb. 18, 1829. He studied at the Jesuit College in Königsgratz, at the Jesuit Seminary in Gitschin, then with Seegert in Prague; was organist at the Heinrichskirche, then at the Strahow Monastery; was conductor of the Prague Opera (1791–1800). He made the first piano scores of Mozart's operas.

Kücken, Friedrich Wilhelm, German conductor and composer; b. Bleckede, Nov. 16, 1810; d. Schwerin, April 3, 1882. He studied with his brother-in-law, Lührss, an organist, and with Aron at Schwerin; in 1832, went to Berlin, where he studied counterpoint with Birnbach; in 1841, studied with Sechter in Vienna; conducted festivals of male choruses in Switzerland; was Kapellmeister in Stuttgart (1851–61). He wrote the operas *Die Flucht nach der Schweiz* (Berlin, Feb. 26, 1839) and *Der Prätendent* (Stuttgart, April 21, 1847); also sonatas for violin and for cello; etc. He is most noted for his songs (*Ach wie wär's möglich dann; Das Sternelein; O weine nicht; Trab, trab; The Maid of Judah; The Swallows;* etc.).

Kuczinski, Paul, composer; b. Berlin, Nov. 10, 1846; d. there, Oct. 21, 1897. He was a banker by profession; also an excellent musician (studied with Bülow and Kiel). He was a friend of Adolf Jensen, whose letters he publ. in part as *Aus Briefen Adolf Jensens* (1879); also publ. *Erlebnisse und Gedanken, Dichtungen zu Musikwerken* (1898), showing his admiration for Wagner. He wrote the poems for his own numerous vocal scores. WORKS: *Die Bergpredigt* for Baritone Solo, Chorus, and Orch.; *Gesang des Turmwächters* for Tenor Solo and Orch.; *Geschenke der Genien* for Female Chorus and Orch.; *Neujahrgesang* for Tenor Solo, Chorus, and Orch.; also piano pieces (*Humoreske, Intermezzo, Karnevalswalzer, Phantasiestücke*).

Kudelski, Karl Matthias, German violinist; b. Berlin, Nov. 17, 1805; d. Baden-Baden, Oct. 3, 1877. He studied with Lafont; played first violin in the orch. of the City Theater in Berlin; played in a quartet in Dorpat (1830); was Kapellmeister to a Russian Prince (1839); in 1841–51, was leader and director in the Imperial Theater in Moscow. He publ. *Kurzgefasste Harmonielehre* (1865); also violin concertos;

cello concertos; violin sonatas; piano trios; fantasies for violin and piano; etc.

Kuerti, Anton, pianist; b. Vienna, July 21, 1938. He studied piano with Arthur Loesser at the Cleveland Inst. of Music; then with Rudolf Serkin at the Curtis Inst. of Music in Philadelphia; made his debut with the Boston Pops Orch. in 1948; in subsequent seasons appeared with other American orchs.; also toured in Europe. In 1965 he became a prof. and pianist-in-residence at the Univ. of Toronto.

Kufferath, Hubert Ferdinand, German pianist and organist, brother of **Johann Hermann** and **Louis Kufferath;** b. Mülheim an der Ruhr, June 11, 1818; d. Brussels, June 23, 1896. He studied first with his brothers; then with Hartmann (violin) in Cologne; with Ferdinand David and Mendelssohn in Leipzig. In 1841–44 he was conductor of the Männergesangverein of Cologne; then settled in Brussels, where he taught members of the royal family; in 1872, became a prof. at the Brussels Cons. He wrote symphs., piano concertos, piano pieces (*Capriccio, Etudes de concert, Charakterstücke,* etc.); also wrote *Praktische Chorschule für 4 Vocal- oder Instrumentalstimmen zum Studium der Harmonie, des Kontrapunktes und der Orgel* (1896).

Kufferath, Johann Hermann, German violinist and composer, brother of **Hubert Ferdinand** and **Louis Kufferath;** b. Mülheim an der Ruhr, May 12, 1797; d. Wiesbaden, July 28, 1864. He studied violin with Spohr and composition with Hauptmann; in 1823, became music director at Bielefeld; in 1830, at Utrecht, where he also taught singing at the School of Music and conducted various societies; retired to Wiesbaden in 1862. He wrote cantatas (*Jubelkantate,* etc.), overtures, and motets; also a *Manuel de chant.*

Kufferath, Louis, pianist and teacher, brother of **Hubert Ferdinand** and **Johann Hermann Kufferath;** b. Mülheim an der Ruhr, Nov. 10, 1811; d. near Brussels, March 2, 1882. He studied with his brother Johann Hermann, and with Schneider at Dessau. In 1836–50 he was director of the Cons. at Leeuwarden in the Netherlands; then in Ghent and Brussels. He publ. a Mass; 250 canons; a cantata, *Artevelde;* songs; etc.

Kufferath, Maurice, Belgian cellist and writer on music, son of **Hubert Ferdinand Kufferath;** b. Brussels, Jan. 8, 1852; d. there, Dec. 8, 1919. He studied cello with the Servais (*père* and *fils*), then at Brussels Univ.; from 1873 to 1900, wrote for *L'Indépendence Belge,* was editor of the *Guide Musical,* then proprietor; in 1900, became director of the Théâtre de la Monnaie, together with Guillaume Guidé; was co-founder of the Ysaÿe concerts, with Ysaÿe and Guidé. He publ. essays on Wagner's operas, and a comprehensive work, *Le Théâtre de Wagner de Tannhäuser à Parsifal* (Brussels, 1891–98; 6 vols.; of these, *Parsifal* was publ. in Eng. trans., N.Y., 1904);

also a brochure, *L'Art de diriger l'orchestre* (Brussels, 1891; an account of Hans Richter's conducting in Brussels); a sketch of Henri Vieuxtemps (Brussels, 1883). He wrote the report on the musical instruments at the Brussels Exposition of 1880. Under the pen name **Maurice Reymont** he trans. Wagner's librettos and texts of songs by Brahms into French. He was an ardent propagandist for Wagner's ideas in Belgium.

BIBLIOGRAPHY: L. Solvay, *Notice sur Maurice Kufferath* (Brussels, 1923).

Küffner, Joseph, German composer; b. Würzburg, March 31, 1776; d. there, Sept. 8, 1856. He wrote 2 operas: *Sporn und Schärpe* and *Der Cornett;* 7 symphs.; 10 overtures; music for military band and wind instruments; Fantasy for Violin, with Orch.; Quintet for Flute and Strings; string quartets; trios and duets for flutes; duets for clarinet; guitar music; violin sonatas; etc.

Kuhač, Franz Xaver, Croatian music theorist; b. Escheck, Croatia, Nov. 20, 1834; d. Agram, June 18, 1911. He studied at the Budapest Cons. and at the Leipzig Cons.; also with Hanslick in Vienna and Liszt in Weimar. He publ. several valuable studies on the music system, instruments, and notation of the South Slavic nations, and 4 vols. of Slavic folk songs. He claimed Haydn and Tartini as Croatian composers; publ. *Josip Haydn i hrvatske narodne popievke* (*Joseph Haydn and Croatian Folk Melodies;* Agram, 1880); *Das türkische Element in der Musik der Kroaten, Serben und Bulgaren* (1900); numerous minor essays.

Kuhe, Wilhelm, Bohemian pianist; b. Prague, Dec. 10, 1823; d. London, Oct. 9, 1912. He studied with Proksch, Tomaschek, and Thalberg. He went to London with the singer Pischek in 1845 and settled there; from 1886 to 1904, was a prof. at the Royal Academy of Music. He wrote salon music (*Feu follet, Gondola, Rosée du soir, Etude de concert,* etc.); operatic fantasias for piano; also publ. *My Musical Recollections* (London, 1897).

Kuhlau, Friedrich, prolific German composer; b. Ülzen, Sept. 11, 1786; d. Copenhagen, March 12, 1832. He lost an eye in a childhood accident; during his recovery studied piano; became a private tutor in Hamburg and studied composition there with E.F.G. Schwenke. He went to Copenhagen in 1810 in order to avoid conscription into Napoleon's army; there he prospered, and in 1813 was appointed court musician.

WORKS: He produced several stage works in Copenhagen: *Røverborgen* (*The Robber's Castle;* May 26, 1814); *Trylleharpen* (*The Magic Harp;* Jan. 30, 1817); *Elisa* (April 17, 1820); *Lulu* (Oct. 29, 1824); *William Shakespeare* (March 28, 1826); *Elverhøj* (*The Fairies' Mound;* Nov. 6, 1828; his most celebrated dramatic work); wrote 3 flute quartets; trios concertants, duets, etc., for flute; 8 violin sonatas; 2 piano concertos; instructive piano sonatas and perennially popular sonatinas, much used for teaching purposes; also various pieces for 4 hands; songs and male quartets, once in great vogue.

BIBLIOGRAPHY: C. Thrane, *Danske komponist-er* (Copenhagen, 1875; with a list of works); idem, *Friedrich Kuhlau. Zur 100-jährigen Wiederkehr seines Geburtstages* (Leipzig, 1886). D. Fog ed. a thematic and bibliographic catalogue (Copenhagen, 1977).

Kuhlmann, Kathleen, American mezzo-soprano; b. San Francisco, Dec. 7, 1950. She studied in San Francisco and at the Chicago Lyric Opera School, making her debut with that company in 1979; subsequently appeared there in *Andrea Chenier* and *The Love of 3 Oranges.* She made her European debut in 1980 with the Cologne Opera, and in 1982 sang Charlotte in *Werther* and Rosina in *Il Barbiere di Siviglia.* On her 30th birthday (Dec. 7, 1980) she made her debut at Milan's La Scala as Meg Page in *Falstaff.* She made her London debut in 1982 at the Royal Opera, Covent Garden, as Ino and Juno in a new production of Handel's *Semele.* In 1983 she sang the leading role in *La Cenerentola* with the Glyndebourne Opera. Her other appearances included performances in the Promenade Concerts in London and with the Vienna State Opera.

Kühmstedt, Friedrich, notable German theorist; b. Oldisleben, Dec. 20, 1809; d. Eisenach, Jan. 10, 1858. He studied with Rinck at Darmstadt; then taught music there (1831–36); settled in Eisenach, where he taught at the seminary. He publ. a *Gradus ad Parnassum; Kunst des Vorspiels für Orgel; Theoretisch-praktische Harmonie- und Ausweichungslehre* (1838); composed organ music (a Double Fugue, a *Fantasia eroica,* fugues, preludes, and postludes); also oratorios, a Mass, motets, piano concertos, etc.

Kuhn, Gustav, Austrian conductor; b. Turrach, Aug. 28, 1947. He studied conducting at the Mozarteum in Salzburg and with Hans Swarowsky at the Hochschule für Musik in Vienna; later had instruction from Bruno Maderna and Herbert von Karajan. He received his Ph.D. from the Univ. in Salzburg in 1970. He then served as conductor at the Istanbul Opera (1970–73) and first conductor at the Stadttheater in Dortmund (1975–77). In 1978 he was named conductor at the Vienna State Opera; in 1979–81 he was chief conductor of the Bern Symph. Orch. and music director of the Bern Opera. In 1980 he conducted at the Glyndebourne and Salzburg festivals; in 1981 he made his American debut with the Chicago Lyric Opera. In 1983 he became generalmusikdirektor in Bonn, heading both the Stadttheater orch. and the Orch. der Beethovenhalle.

Kuhnau, Johann (real family surname, **Kuhn**), erudite German musician, organist, and theorist; b. Geising, April 6, 1660; d. Leipzig, June 5, 1722. He studied at the Kreuzschule in Dresden with Salomon Krügner and Christoph Kittel; took lessons with Heringk and Albrici, then with Edelmann at Zittau, where he was acting cantor in 1681–82. He

attended the Univ. of Leipzig in 1682–88, studying law; meanwhile, in 1684 succeeded Kühnel as organist at the Thomaskirche; in 1688 he organized a Collegium Musicum and also began to practice law. He became music director of the Univ. of Leipzig in 1701, when he was also appointed cantor at the Thomaskirche; was Bach's predecessor in the post. He publ. *Jura circa musicos ecclesiasticos* (Leipzig, 1688); *Der musickalische Quacksalber . . . in einer kurtzweiligen und angenehmen Historie . . . beschrieben* (Dresden, 1700; a satire on Italian music); 3 treatises are in MS. Kuhnau was the first to publish a harpsichord sonata imitated from the instrumental sonata (properly a suite) in several movements. It is found in Part II of his *Neue Clavier-Übung* (1692) and contains 3 movements, Allegro, Adagio, and Allegro (Rondo); there followed 7 sonatas in his *Frische Clavier-Früchte* (1696), which show a marked advance in treatment and melodic invention; 6 more harpsichord sonatas appeared under the title *Biblische Historien nebst Auslegung in sechs Sonaten,* in the highly original form of illustrations to biblical stories, thus presaging the development of program music; they set forth the fight between David and Goliath, David's cure of Saul, Jacob's Wedding, etc. (1700; new ed. of the first 2 by J.S. Shedlock, 1895; new ed. of the first by H. Bauer, 1927). Kuhnau's complete clavier works were publ. by Päsler in vol. 2 of Denkmäler Deutscher Tonkunst; Schering publ. 4 church cantatas and a list of Kuhnau's sacred works in vols. 58/59.

BIBLIOGRAPHY: H. Bischoff, *Über J. Kuhnaus Vorstellung einiger biblischen Historien* (1877); J.S. Shedlock, *The Pianoforte Sonata* (London, 1895; pp. 38ff.); R. Münnich, "Kuhnaus Leben," *Sammelbände der Internationalen Musik-Gesellschaft* (1902; pp. 473ff.); J.C. Martin, *Die Kirchenkantaten J. Kuhnaus* (Leipzig, 1928); H.F. Menck, "J. Kuhnaus 'Musickalische Quacksalber,' " in *Der Musiker im Roman* (Heidelberg, 1931; pp. 61ff.); E. Rimbach, *The Church Cantatas of Johann Kuhnau* (Diss., Univ. of Rochester, 1966).

Kühner, Basil, German composer; b. Stuttgart, April 1, 1840; d. Vilna, Aug. 1911. He studied at the Stuttgart Cons. with Faiszt and Lebert; then studied violin with Massart in Paris, and piano with Henselt in St. Petersburg; was director of the Tiflis Cons. (1870–76). In 1878 he settled in St. Petersburg, where he established his own music school (1892). He wrote the opera *Taras Bulba* (after Gogol; St. Petersburg, Dec. 24, 1880; had only 3 perfs.); a symph. subtitled *Liberation of the Serfs in Russia* (St. Petersburg, 1866); String Quintet; 2 string quartets; Suite for Cello and Piano; *Snowflakes,* suite for Piano; other piano pieces.

Kühner, Konrad, German pianist and teacher; b. Markt-Streufdorf, Meiningen, March 2, 1851; d. Schmalkalden, Feb. 5, 1909. He studied at the Stuttgart Cons.; in 1889–99 he lived in Dresden as a piano teacher, then in Braunschweig. He wrote the symph. poem *Maria Stuart;* piano music; *Technik* *des Klavierspiels; Schule des 4-händigen Spiels* (12 vols.); *Vortragsalbum* (5 vols.); *Etüdenschule des Klavierspielers* (12 vols.); also edited many works for the *Edition Litolff.*

Kuhse, Hanne-Lore, German soprano; b. Schwaan, March 28, 1925. She was educated at the Rostock Cons. and the Stern Cons. in Berlin; later studied in Potsdam. She made her debut in Gera in 1951 as Leonore in *Fidelio;* from 1952 to 1959 she was a member of the Schwerin Opera; then sang at the Leipzig Opera (1959–64). In 1964 she joined the East Berlin State Opera. In 1974 she was appointed prof. at the Hochschule für Musik in East Berlin. In 1954 she was named a Kammersängerin. A versatile artist, she was as stylistically faithful to her roles in Mozart's operas as to the heroic and lyric Wagnerian parts.

Kulenkampff, Georg, German virtuoso violinist; b. Bremen, Jan. 23, 1898; d. Schaffhausen, Oct. 4, 1948. He studied violin with Willy Hess in Berlin; in 1916 became concertmaster of the Bremen Phil. From 1923–26 he taught violin at the Hochschule für Musik in Berlin; in 1943 went to Switzerland and taught at the Lucerne Cons. He is regarded as one of the most brilliant German violinists of his generation; his book *Geigerische Betrachtungen,* partly didactic, partly autobiographical in content, was publ. posthumously, ed. by G. Meyer-Stichtung (Regensburg, 1952).

Kulenkampff, Gustav, German composer; b. Bremen, Aug. 11, 1849; d. Berlin, Feb. 10, 1921. He studied music with Barth (piano) and Bargiel (composition). He organized in Berlin his own women's choir; taught musical subjects at various music schools; appeared as a pianist. He wrote operas: *Der Page* (Bremen, 1890); *Der Mohrenfürst* (Magdeburg, 1892); *Die Braut von Cypern* (Schwerin, 1897); *König Drosselbart* (Berlin, 1899); *Ammarei* (1903); *Anneliese* (Kassel, 1904); women's choruses; Piano Sonata; songs; etc.

Kulka, János, conductor; b. Budapest, Dec. 11, 1929. He studied conducting with Ferencsik and Somogyi; also composition with Kodály. He conducted at the Hungarian State Opera in 1950; in 1957 conducted in Vienna; in 1959 was appointed first conductor at the State Opera in Stuttgart; from 1964 to 1976 he was Generalmusikdirektor of Wuppertal.

Kullak, Adolf, German music theorist and critic, brother of **Theodor Kullak;** b. Meseritz, Feb. 23, 1823; d. Berlin, Dec. 25, 1862. He studied general subjects at the Univ. of Berlin, and music with Bernhard Marx; then taught at his brother's Academy; contributed music criticism to various periodicals; publ. some piano pieces and songs. He wrote *Das Musikalisch-Schöne* (Leipzig, 1858) and *Ästhetik des Klavierspiels* (Berlin, 1861; 4th ed. by W. Niemann, 1906; 5th ed., 1916; in Eng., N.Y., 1892), a valuable and instructive summary of piano methods.

Kullak, Franz, German pianist and composer, son of **Theodor Kullak;** b. Berlin, April 12, 1844; d. there, Dec. 9, 1913. He studied with his father; also with Liszt for a brief while. In 1867 he became a piano teacher at his father's Academy; assumed its directorship at his father's death in 1882, dissolving the institution in 1890. He wrote an opera, *Ines de Castro* (Berlin, 1877); piano pieces; songs; also an essay, *Der Vortrag in der Musik am Ende des 19. Jahrhunderts* (Leipzig, 1898).

Kullak, Theodor, famous German pianist and pedagogue; b. Krotoschin, Sept. 12, 1818; d. Berlin, March 1, 1882. He studied piano with local teachers; in 1837 he went to Berlin at his father's behest to study medicine; also studied music there with Dehn (theory); then in 1842 went to Vienna, where he took lessons with Czerny. Returning to Berlin in 1846, he became court pianist to the King of Prussia. In 1850 he founded a cons. in Berlin in partnership with Julius Stern and Bernhard Marx; however, dissension soon arose among them, and in 1855 Kullak established his own school, the Neue Akademie der Tonkunst, which greatly prospered and became famous as Kullak's Academy. He publ. valuable pedagogic works: *Materialien für den Elementar-Unterricht* (3 vols.); *Schule des Oktavenspiel;* various characteristic pieces for piano in a salon manner (*Ondine, Les Etincellese, Les Danaides, La Gazelle,* etc.); also *Kinderleben* (2 albums of piano pieces).
   BIBLIOGRAPHY: O. Reinsdorf, *Theodor Kullak und seine Neue Akademie der Tonkunst in Berlin* (1870); H. Bischoff, *Zur Erinnerung an Theodor Kullak* (1883).

Kullman, Charles, American operatic tenor; b. New Haven, Conn., Jan. 13, 1903; d. there, Feb. 8, 1983. He was of German parentage; his family name was originally spelled with two *n*'s. He entered Yale Univ., and sang at the Yale Glee Club at college; graduated in 1924; then took courses at the Juilliard School of Music in N.Y., graduating in 1927. His first experience in opera was as a member of the American Opera Co., established in Rochester, N.Y., by Vladimir Rosing. Seeking wider opportunities, he went to Berlin, where he made his debut on Feb. 24, 1931, as Pinkerton in *Madama Butterfly,* at the Kroll Opera, a subsidiary of the Berlin State Opera, conducted by Otto Klemperer. He sang in the Berlin State Opera in 1932–35; then appeared at the Vienna State Opera, at Salzburg summer festivals, and at Covent Garden in London (1934–36). On Dec. 19, 1935, he made his debut at the Metropolitan Opera in N.Y. as Faust in Gounod's opera, vociferously greeted by loyal supporters who came specially from New Haven to join in the deserved applause. He remained on the roster of the Metropolitan until 1960; sang for the last time there on Dec. 3, 1960. His repertoire comprised 33 roles, including tenor parts in most standard German and Italian operas. He scored a signal success in the role of Eisenstein in *Die Fledermaus,* which he sang 30 times. After relinquishing his active stage career, he accepted a teaching position at Indiana Univ., where he was prof. of music until his retirement in 1971.

Kummer, Friedrich August, German cellist, oboist, and composer; b. Meiningen, Aug. 5, 1797; d. Dresden, Aug. 22, 1879. His family moved to Dresden, where Kummer studied cello with Dotzauer; then he studied oboe in order to enter the court orch., which he did in Nov. 1814; in 1817 he again studied the cello and became a virtuoso of the first rank. He also taught at the Dresden Cons. He was a prolific composer; 163 of his compositions were printed; he wrote concertos, a Concertino, divertissements, etc., for the cello; also concert pieces for oboe, clarinet, horn, trumpet; and a method for cello.

Kummer, Kaspar, German flutist and composer; b. Erlau, Dec. 10, 1795; d. Coburg, May 21, 1870. He was a member of the court orch. at Coburg; then music director there. He wrote quintets and quartets for flute and strings; flute concertos, trios, duos, etc.; and a method for flute.

Kümmerle, Salomon, German collector of vocal music; b. Malmsheim, near Stuttgart, Feb. 8, 1838; d. Samaden, Aug. 28, 1896. He taught at a school in Samaden (1875–90); publ. several collections of vocal music, among them *Musica sacra; Grabgesänge; Zionsharfe; Choralbuch für evangelische Kirchenchöre; Encyklopädie der evangelischen Kirchenmusik* (3 vols., 1888–96).

Kunad, Rainer, German composer; b. Chemnitz, Oct. 24, 1936. He studied in Leipzig with Finke, Gerster, and Schenk; became active as a teacher. He excels particularly in light opera and ballet. WORKS: Pantomime with singing, *Das Schloss* (1962); one-act opera, *Bill Brook* (1965); *Ich: Orpheus* for Actors, Dancers, and Singers (1965); also orch. works, among them *Aphorismen* (1956); *Sinfonia variatione* (1959); *Sinfonie* (1964); *Sinfonietta* (1969); *Concerto per archi* (1967); Piano Concerto (1969); Wind Quintet (1965); *Die Ehe* for Oboe, Bassoon, and Piano (1970); Piano Sonata; Overture for 2 Pianos; organ pieces; several cantatas and various choral works.

Kunc, Božidar, Croatian-American pianist and composer; b. Zagreb, July 18, 1903; d. Detroit, April 1, 1964. He received his academic training at the Music Academy in Zagreb, graduating in 1927; taught there from 1929 to 1950, when he emigrated to the U.S. He was a brother of the singer **Zinka Milanov.** His music is impressionistic in its harmonic palette. WORKS: 2 violin concertos (1928, 1955); *Dramatic Prologue* for Orch. (1929); *Symphonic Intermezzo* (1934); 2 piano concertos: No. 1 (Zagreb, April 27, 1934, composer soloist) and No. 2 (1962); *Marcia funebre* for Orch. (1936); *Triptihon* for Cello and Orch. (1940); *3 Episodes* for Piano and String Orch. (1955); symphs.; several chamber works, including Cello Sonata (1927); *Cycle* for Piano and Percussion

(1956); *Pieces* for Solo Double Bass (1959); 4 piano sonatas (1930–43); several cycles and pieces; songs.
BIBLIOGRAPHY: K. Kovačević, *Hrvatski kompozitori i njihova djela* (Zagreb, 1960). •

Kunc, Jan, Czech composer; b. Doubravice, Moravia, March 27, 1883; d. Brno, Sept. 11, 1976. He studied with Janáček in Brno and with Novák in Prague; was a music critic in Brno (1909–18); in 1918–19 he toured as accompanist with his wife, a concert singer. In 1919 he became an instructor at the Brno Cons.; from 1923 till 1945 was its director; lectured at the Masaryk Univ. in Brno (1947–52). WORKS: Unfinished opera, *The Lady from the Seashore* (begun 1919); *Song of Youth,* symph. poem (1915–16); *Stála Kačenka u Dunaja (Catherine Stood by the Danube),* ballad for Alto and Orch. (1918–19); Piano Sonata (1903); Piano Trio (1905); String Quartet (1909); *4 Compositions* for Piano (1917); *Chronicle,* 20 variations on a Slovak folk song, for Piano (1926); Violin Sonata (1931); Serenade for Violin and Piano (1952); *Miniatures* for Piano (1954–57; also for Wind Quintet, 1958); *Sedmdesát tisíc (70,000)* for Chorus (1907); *Ostrava* for Male Chorus (1912); *35 Folk Songs of Moravian Slovakia* for Female Chorus (1960); many folk-song arrangements.

Kunits, Luigi von, Austrian violinist and conductor; b. Vienna, July 20, 1870; d. Toronto, Oct. 8, 1931. He studied composition with Anton Bruckner, history of music with Hanslick, and violin with Ševčik. In 1893 he came to America; in 1897–1910 was concertmaster of the Pittsburgh Symph.; taught at the Pittsburgh Cons.; later founded his own music school. After 2 years in Europe (1910–12), he went to Canada and settled in Toronto; taught at the Canadian Academy of Music; founded the *Canadian Journal of Music* (1915–19); from 1923 till 1931 was conductor of the New Symph. Orch. of Toronto (renamed Toronto Symph. Orch. in 1927). He publ. a book, *The Hero as Musician: Beethoven* (1913); also contributed articles to various periodicals. His compositions include 2 violin concertos; String Quartet; Viola Sonata; *3 Etudes* for Violin and Piano; *Romanza* for Violin and Piano; songs.

Kunkel, Charles, German-American pianist and publisher; b. Sipperfeld, Rheinpfalz, July 22, 1840; d. St. Louis, Dec. 3, 1923. He was taken to America in 1848 by his father, who gave him elementary musical training. In 1868 he and his brother, **Jacob,** also a musician, went to St. Louis, where he established a music publishing business and started a music periodical, *Kunkel's Musical Review,* which included sheet music and articles; with his brother he also opened a music store selling pianos and other instruments; in 1872 he founded the St. Louis Cons. of Music, which continued in business for several years; furthermore, he presented an annual series of concerts in St. Louis known as Kunkel's Popular Concerts (1884–1900). He taught piano to the last years of his life; also publ. a method of piano playing, which was commended favorably by Liszt; Anton Rubinstein praised him as a pianist during his visit to St. Louis in 1873. Kunkel was reputed to be quite formidable as a sight reader. Altogether, he was certainly a shining light in the German musical colony in middle America in the 2nd half of the 19th century. With his brother he gave, to tumultuous applause, a series of concerts playing piano duets. His publishing business put out a cornucopia of his own piano solos with such titles as *Nonpareil, Galop Brilliant, Philomel Polka, Snowdrops Waltz,* and *Southern Jollification,* most of these highly perishable; however, one piece, *Alpine Storm,* deserves retrieval, if for no other reason than its dedication: "To my son, Ludwig van Beethoven Kunkel." (This piece also contains "tone clusters" played with the palm of the hand in the bass to imitate thunder.)

Kunkel, Franz Joseph, German theorist and composer; b. Dieburg, Aug. 20, 1808; d. Frankfurt, Dec. 31, 1880. From 1828 to 1954 he was rector and music teacher in the Bensheim Teachers' Seminary. He wrote *Kleine Musiklehre; Die Verurteilung der Konservatorien zu Pflanzschulen des musikalischen Proletariats* (1855); *Kritische Beleuchtung des C.F. Weitzmannischen Harmonie-Systems; Die neue Harmonielehre im Streit mit der alten* (1863); etc.; also a cantata, Psalms, motets, etc.

Kunkel, Jacob, German-American pianist; b. Kleiniedesheim, Oct. 22, 1846; d. St. Louis, Oct. 16, 1882. He studied with his elder brother, **Charles Kunkel,** who was also a nominal pupil of Tausig, who, according to the Kunkel family report, refused to teach him because he thought that the younger man was equal to the master. He was taken to America with his brother, and participated in most of the latter's enterprises, in the music publishing business and in a general music store. The brothers also gave a series of concerts playing piano duets. Jacob Kunkel composed piano pieces in a salon manner.

Künneke, Eduard, German operetta composer; b. Emmerich, Jan. 27, 1885; d. Berlin, Oct. 27, 1953. He studied with Max Bruch in Berlin; was subsequently engaged as a choirmaster in various theaters in Germany; produced 2 operas, *Robins Ende* (Mannheim, 1909) and *Coeur As* (Dresden, 1913), with little success; he then turned to light opera, and his first work in this genre, a singspiel, *Das Dorf ohne Glocke* (Berlin, April 5, 1919), was received with great acclaim. His next light opera, *Der Vetter aus Dingsda* (Berlin, April 15, 1921), was no less successful; there followed *Lady Hamilton* (1926); *Glückliche Reise* (Berlin, Nov. 23, 1932); *Lockende Flamme* (1933); *Herz über Bord* (1935); *Der grosse Name* (1938); etc. His last operetta was *Hochzeit mit Erika* (1949). Besides his stage works, he wrote many film scores, an Overture, a Piano Concerto, and other instrumental compositions.

Kunsemüller, Ernst, German conductor; b. Rehme, June 24, 1885; d. (as a result of war wounds) Düssel-

dorf, April 25, 1918. He studied at the univs. of Berlin and Bonn (Dr.Phil., 1909), then at the Cologne Cons. with Friedberg, Wölsche, and Steinbach; in 1910–12, conducted an a cappella chorus at Neuss; in 1912, became conductor of the Verein der Musikfreunde and Gesangverein in Kiel; in 1914, was appointed music director at the Univ. of Kiel. He wrote Serenade for Small Orch.; 2 piano sonatas; choruses; songs; etc.

Kunst, Jaap (Jakob), Dutch ethnomusicologist; b. Groningen, Aug. 12, 1891; d. Amsterdam, Dec. 7, 1960. He started playing the violin at an early age; soon became interested in the folk songs of the Netherlands. He received a degree in law at the Univ. of Groningen (1917); then toured with a string trio in the Dutch East Indies, and decided to remain in Java, where he worked in a government post. He became interested in indigenous Javanese music, and founded an archive for folk instruments and recordings in Jakarta. He returned to the Netherlands in 1934; in 1936 became curator of the Royal Tropical Inst. in Amsterdam; in 1953 became a lecturer at the Univ. of Amsterdam. Kunst is credited with having coined the word "ethnomusicology" as a more accurate term than "comparative musicology."

WRITINGS: *A Study of Papuan Music* (Weltevreden, 1931); *Musicologisch onderzoek 1930* (Batavia, 1931); *De Toonkunst van Java* (The Hague, 1934; Eng. trans., 1949; enlarged as *Music in Java,* 1973); *Music in Flores: A Study of the Vocal and Instrumental Music among the Tribes Living in Flores* (Leiden, 1942); *The Cultural Background of Indonesian Music* (Amsterdam, 1949); *Metre, Rhythm and Multipart* (Leiden, 1950); *Musicologica: A Study of the Nature of Ethnomusicology, Its Problems, Methods and Representative Personalities* (Amsterdam, 1950; enlarged as *Ethnomusicology,* 1955); *Sociologische bindingen in de muziek* (The Hague, 1953); ed. collections of folk songs of the Netherlands and Northern New Guinea.

Kunst, Jos, Dutch composer; b. Roermond, Jan. 3, 1936. He studied composition with Ton de Leeuw at the Amsterdam Cons. (1965–70); upon graduation joined its staff. In his music he utilizes a great variety of modernistic techniques, especially metamorphoses of given thematic material.

WORKS: *Stenen eten (The Stone Eaters)* for 2 Pianos (1965); *Ijzer (Iron)* for Violin and Piano (1965); *Insecten* for 13 Strings (1966); *Glass Music* for Piano (1966); *Extérieur* for 2-track Tape (1967); *Arboreal* for Orch. (Rotterdam, Sept. 11, 1969); *Expulsion* for 2-track Tape (1969); *Trajectoire* for 16 Voices and 11 Instruments (1970); *XVII One Way* for Small Orch. (Amsterdam, March 13, 1971); *XVIII Outward Bound* for Solo Harp (1971); *Solo Identity I* for Solo Bass Clarinet (1972); *Solo Identity II* for Piano (1973); *Elements of Logic* for Wind Orch. (in collaboration with Jan Vriend; 1972; Scheveningen, Feb. 25, 1973); *No Time at All* for Bass Clarinet and Piano (1973; a fusion of *Solo Identity I* and *II*); *No Time* for 3 Clarinets, Bass Clarinet, Piano, and 3

Percussionists (1974; an amplified version of *No Time at All*); *XXII: Any 2* for Woodwinds (1975).

Kuntze, Karl, German composer; b. Trier, May 17, 1817; d. Delitzsch, Sept. 7, 1883. He studied in Berlin with A.W. Bach, Marx, and Rungenhagen; was cantor and organist at Pritzwalk, then organist at Aschersleben (1858); in 1873 settled in Delitzsch, where he taught at the seminary. He is best known for his humorous male choruses (*Adam und Eva, Der Hecht im Karpfenteich, Weingalopp, Der neue Bürgermeister, Die Schweigermutter*); also wrote an operetta, *Im Gebirge* (Dessau, 1875); motets and songs for mixed chorus; organ pieces; etc. He edited the 3rd edition of Seidel's *Die Orgel und ihr Bau* (1875).

Kunwald, Ernst, Austrian conductor; b. Vienna, April 14, 1868; d. there, Dec. 12, 1939. He studied law at Vienna Univ. (Dr.Juris., 1891); at the same time studied piano with Leschetizky and J. Epstein, and composition with H. Grädener; then studied at the Leipzig Cons. with Jadassohn. His first engagement as an opera conductor was in Rostock (1895–97); then he conducted opera in Sondershausen (1897–98), Essen (1898–1900), Halle (1900–1), Madrid (1901–2), and Frankfurt (1902–5), and at Kroll's Theater in Berlin (1905–6); served as 2nd conductor of the Berlin Phil. Orch. (1907–12). In 1906 he was guest conductor of the N.Y. Phil. Society; in 1912, became regular conductor of the Cincinnati Symph. Orch., and from 1914, also of the May Festival. He was arrested as an enemy alien on Dec. 8, 1917, but was released on bail and allowed to continue to conduct until his internment. In 1919 he went to Germany and conducted symph. concerts in Königsberg (1920–27); in 1928–31, conducted the Berlin Symph. Orch.; then returned to Vienna, where he remained until his death.

Kunz, Alfred, Canadian composer; b. Neudorf, Saskatchewan, May 26, 1929. He studied with Delamont and Weinzweig in Toronto (1949–55); then went to Europe; attended Stockhausen's classes of new music in Darmstadt and Cologne; returning to Canada, he held various teaching posts in Ontario.
WORKS: Operetta for High School, *The Watchful Gods* (1962); 7 ballets, including *Moses* (1965); 2 sinfoniettas (1957, 1961); Violin Sonata (1959); *The Song of the Clarinet* for Narrator, Flute, Oboe, Clarinet, Bassoon, and String Quintet (1961); *Behold the Beauty of the Sky* for High School Chorus and Orch. (1961); *Excursion* for Orch. (1964); *Emanation No. 1* for Violin, Horn, and Piano (1962); *Emanation No. 2* for Flute, Clarinet, Horn, and Bassoon (1964); *Fun for 2* for 2 Bassoons or 2 Bass Clarinets (1964); *Love, Death, and Full Moonnights* for Baritone and Instrumental Ensemble (1964); Wind Quintet (1964); *The Big Land*, oratorio (1967); *In the Park of October Colour*, a "song of love" for Solo Piano, Chorus, and Orch. (1969); *5 Night Scenes* for Orch. (1971); *The Creation* for Narrator, 3 Sopranos, Alto, Chorus, and Orch. (1972); Concerto for 8 Percussion Players and Orch. (1973); Piano Concerto

(1975).

Kunz, Erich, Austrian bass-baritone; b. Vienna, May 20, 1909. He was educated at the Vienna Academy of Music. He first sang in several provincial opera houses; then was on the roster of the Vienna State Opera; later sang in London and in Tokyo. He made his Metropolitan Opera debut in N.Y. on Nov. 26, 1952, as Leporello in *Don Giovanni*. He was chiefly known for his buffo roles, and also acquired popularity as an operetta singer.

Kunz, Ernst, Swiss composer and conductor; b. Bern, June 2, 1891. He studied in Munich; from 1916 to 1918 he was a conductor of the Munich Opera; returning to Switzerland, he was active mainly as a theater conductor. His music is neo-Romantic in essence; the influences of Richard Strauss and Pfitzner are especially pronounced. He wrote operas: *Der Fächer* (1924; Zürich, 1929); *Vreneli ab em Guggisberg* (in Swiss dialect; 1935); *Die Bremer Stadtmusikanten* (1937); *Der Traum ein Leben* (1968); singspiel, *Die Hochzeitsreise* (1960); oratorios: *Vom irdischen Leben* (1931–49); *Christmas Oratorio* (1936); *Weisheit des Herzens* (1946); *Einkehr* (1951); *Psalter und Harfe* (1956); 5 symphs. (1917, 1921, 1942, 1965, 1966); symph. triptych, *Drei Lebensalter* (1964); *Serenata strana* for Orch. (1971); Viola Concerto (1952); Chamber Concerto for Strings, Solo Flute, and Piano (1971); 3 string quartets; Piano Quartet; piano pieces; about 500 choruses; several song cycles.

Kunz, Konrad Max, German composer; b. Schwandorf, Dec. 30, 1812; d. Munich, Aug. 3, 1875. He studied in Munich with Hartmann Stuntz; was co-founder and conductor of the Munich Liedertafel. He wrote many popular male songs (*Elstein; Odin, der Schlachtengott;* etc.); also *200 Canons for Piano;* publ. the satirical pamphlet *Die Gründung der Moosgau-Brüderschaft Moosgrillia* (1866).

Kunzel, Erich, American conductor; b. New York, March 21, 1935. He was educated at Dartmouth College (A.B.), Harvard Univ., Brown Univ. (A.M.), and North Kentucky State Univ. (Litt.D.). He was a member of the faculty at Brown Univ. (1958–65); was also assistant conductor of the Rhode Island Phil. (1963–65); then joined the conducting staff of the Cincinnati Symph., developing a highly successful series of popular concerts. He then taught at the Cincinnati Cons. (1965–71); later served as music director of the New Haven Symph. Orch. (1974–77).

Kunzen, Adolf Carl, German pianist and organist; b. Wittenberg, Sept. 22, 1720; d. Lübeck, July 1781. At the age of 8 he toured in the Netherlands and England; finally settled in Wittenberg as organist at the Marienkirche. He wrote an oratorio, a Passion, symphs., 21 violin concertos, piano sonatas, etc. (Many MSS are in the library of the Brussels Cons.)

Kunzen, Friedrich Ludwig Aemilius, composer,

son of **Adolf Carl Kunzen;** b. Lubeck, Sept. 24, 1761; d. Copenhagen, Jan. 28, 1817. He studied music with his father, and jurisprudence at Kiel Univ. (1784–87); then settled in Copenhagen, where he taught music. He spent a few years in Berlin, and was Kapellmeister at Frankfurt and Prague; then became court conductor in Copenhagen (1795).

WORKS: Operas: *Holger Danske* (Copenhagen, March 31, 1789); *Die Weinlese* (Frankfurt, May 3, 1793); *Hemmeligheden* (*The Secret;* Copenhagen, Nov. 22, 1796); *Dragedukken* (*The Good Fairy;* Copenhagen, March 14, 1797); *Erik Ejegod* (Copenhagen, Jan. 30, 1798); *Min bedstemoder* (*My Grandmother;* Copenhagen, May 15, 1800); *Kœrlighed paa Landet* (*Love in the Country;* Copenhagen, March 23, 1810); also wrote oratorios; overtures; sonatas. His musical style paralleled the models of Mozart and Haydn.

Kuosmanen, Kari, Finnish composer; b. Helsinki, March 11, 1946. He studied piano with Flodin; composition with Allis Sallinen at the Sibelius Academy in Helsinki. After graduation, he obtained a teaching post at the Oulu (Uleaborg) School of Music.

WORKS: *Abacus* for Violin, Viola, Cello, and Orch. (1968); *Sinfonia da chiesa* for 4 String Quartets (Helsinki, Feb. 28, 1973).

Kupferberg, Herbert, American journalist and music critic; b. New York, Jan. 20, 1918. He was educated at Cornell Univ. (B.A., 1939) and at Columbia Univ. (M.A., 1940; M.S., 1941). From 1942–66 he was on the staff of the *N.Y. Herald Tribune;* was also music critic of the *Atlantic Monthly* from 1962–69 and of the *National Observer* from 1967–77. He served as rapporteur for the Twentieth Century Fund's N.Y. task force on cultural exchange with the Soviet Union, which led to the publication of the report *The Raised Curtain* in 1977.

WRITINGS: *Those Fabulous Philadelphians: The Life and Times of a Great Orchestra* (N.Y., 1969); *The Mendelssohns: Three Generations of Genius* (N.Y., 1972); *Opera* (N.Y., 1975); *Tanglewood* (N.Y., 1976); also 2 books for young readers, *Felix Mendelssohn: His Life, His Family, His Music* (N.Y., 1972) and *A Rainbow of Sound: The Instruments of the Orchestra and Their Music* (N.Y., 1973).

Kupferman, Meyer, American composer; b. New York, July 13, 1926. He came from a Jewish family; his father, an immigrant from Rumania, taught him to sing Rumanian folk songs; his mother, who was Russian-Jewish, taught him old Yiddish songs. He studied clarinet with Louis Levy and piano with Joel Newman. He acquired his knack for composition from imitating modern French music, and his early works bear a distinct impressionistic flavor; following the trends of the times, he adopted the 12-tone method, but soon abandoned its strictures in favor of a more general style of composition. Among his most original works is a series of some 50 pieces for various instruments, titled *Infinities.* In 1975 he received a Guggenheim fellowship. In

1981 he was given an award of $5,000 by the American Academy and Inst. of Arts and Letters. About 1970 he turned to the "gestalt" form, which effectuates a creative synthesis of incompatible elements. He was also engaged in teaching; in 1951 he joined the music faculty of Sarah Lawrence College.

WORKS: Operas: *In a Garden* (N.Y., Dec. 29, 1949); *The Curious Fern* and *Voices for a Mirror* (both produced in N.Y. on June 5, 1957); *Draagenfut Girl* (Bronx, N.Y., May 8, 1958); *Dr. Faustus Lights the Lights* (1952); *The Judgement* (*Infinities* No. 18; 1966–67); *Prometheus* (1975–77); 11 symphs. (1950–83); Piano Concerto No. 1 (1948); Concerto for Cello and Jazz Band (1962); Concerto for Cello, Tape, and Orch. (1974); Concerto for 6 Instruments and Orch. (1976); Violin Concerto (1976); Piano Concerto No. 2 (1977); Tuba Concerto (1982); Clarinet Concerto (1984); 7 string quartets; some 35 pieces for various ensembles, entitled *Cycle of Infinities;* Concertino for 11 Brass Instruments; *Sonata on Jazz Elements* for Piano; *Tunnel of Love* for Jazz Combo (N.Y., May 22, 1971); *Abracadabra Quartet* for Piano and String Trio (N.Y., Dec. 5, 1976); *The Red King's Throw* for Clarinet, Piano, Cello, and Percussion (1978); *Richter 7,* "musical earthquake" (1979); a number of works titled *Sound Objects* representing dream images.

BIBLIOGRAPHY: David Ewen, *American Composers* (N.Y., 1982).

Kupkovič, Ladislav, Slovak composer of the avant-garde; b. Bratislava, March 17, 1936. He studied violin in Bratislava at the High School of Music (1950–55) and at the Cons. (1955–61); played violin in the Slovak Phil. In 1963 he organized the chamber ensemble Hudba Dneška ("Music of Today"). He left Czechoslovakia after the Soviet incursion in 1968 and went to Germany; lived in Berlin and Cologne until 1973, when he was appointed instructor at the Hochschule für Musik in Hannover. His music utilizes the cosmopolitan resources of ultramodern music.

WORKS: *Dialogues* for Flute and Bassoon (1961); *Maso kríza* (*Flesh of the Cross*), an impression of a surrealist painting of the crucifix, for Trombone and 10 Percussion Players (1961–62); *Psalm* for 4 Horns (1962); *Skica* (*Sketch*) for 6 Players (1962); *Otázky a odpovedi* (*Questions and Answers*) for 3 Flutes and Tam-tam (1962); *Décolleté* for 4 Oboes, 4 Trumpets, and 12 Percussion Players (1964); *Výkřiky* (*Exclamations*) for Flute, Bass Clarinet, Piano, and Percussion (1964); *Rozhovor času s hmotou* (*A Conversation between Time and Matter)* for Bassoon and 3 Percussion Players (1965); *Ozveny* (*Echoes*) for 31 Players (1966); *Písmená* (*Letters*) for 4 Female and 4 Male Voices (1967); *Menej i viac* (*More and Less*) for Bass Clarinet and Piano (1967); *Pred s za* (*Before and After*) for Chamber Ensemble (1967); *Cluster—Dynamika—Glissando* for String Quartet (1967); *Dioe* for Orch., with Conductor (1968); *Oktoedr* (*Octohedron*) for Chamber Ensemble (1968); *Präparierte Texte* Nos. 1–7 for various combinations of Instruments (1968); *Les Adieux* for Piano (1968); *Etude* for Ensemble (1968); *Ad libi-*

tum, a "happening" for a random group of Performers (1969); *Klanginvasion auf Bonn,* a spectacle of indeterminate duration, representing the invasion of noise on the population of Bonn (1970); *Treffpunkt* for 4 groups of Wind Instruments (1970); *Notausgang* for Orch. and Microphones (1970); *Musikalische Ausstellung* for Chamber Ensemble (1970); *Erinnerungen* for Orch. and Tape (1970); *Souvenir* for Violin, and Piano or String Orch. (1971); *Monolith* for 48 Strings (1971); *Ein Gespräch mit Gott (A Conversation with God)* for Orch. (1972); *Das Gebet (The Prayer)* for String Orch. and Percussion (1972–73); *Concours* for the "orchestra of the future" (1973). Kupkovič also initiated "walking concerts," in which a group of musicians walk in the streets playing segments of familiar pieces ad nauseam.

BIBLIOGRAPHY: Monika Lichtenfeld, "Porträt des Komponisten und Dirigenten Ladislav Kupkovič," *Musica* (March–April 1975).

Kupper, Annelies, German soprano; b. Glatz, July 21, 1906. She studied in Breslau; made her debut there in 1935; then sang in Schwerin (1937–38) and Weimar (1938–39); was a principal member of the Hamburg State Opera (1940–46) and the Bavarian State Opera in Munich (1946–61); also sang at Bayreuth and Salzburg; from 1956 she taught voice at the Munich Academy of Music.

Kuri-Aldana, Mario, Mexican composer; b. Tampico, Aug. 15, 1931. He studied piano with Carlos del Castillo at the Academia Juan Sebastián Bach in Mexico City (1948–51) and theory with Juan Tercero at the National School of Music of the Autonomous Univ. of Mexico (1952–60); took conducting courses from Igor Markevitch and Jean Giardino at the National Inst. of Fine Arts in Mexico City (1957–58); privately studied advanced techniques of composition with Rodolfo Halffter and Luis Herrera de la Fuente (1961–62); took lessons in Buenos Aires with Ginastera. Returning to Mexico, he gave himself to teaching. WORKS: 3 symphs.: No. 1, *Sacrificio* (1959); No. 2 for String Orch. (1966); No. 3, *Ce Actal-1521* (1976); *Los cuatro Bacabs,* suite for Double Wind Orch. and optional Narrator (1960); *Máscaras,* concerto for Marimba and Wind Orch. (1962); *Pasos* for Piano and Orch. (1963); *Bacab de las plegarias* for 2 Flutes, 2 Clarinets, Trumpet, Harp, and Strings (1966); *Formas de otros tiempos* for String Orch. and Harp (1971); *Concierto de Santiago* for Flute, String Orch., and 2 Percussion Players (1973); *Concertino mexicano* for Violin and String Orch. (1974); numerous songs accompanied by various instrumental combinations, among them *Cantares para una niña muerta* for Mezzo-soprano, Flute, and Guitar (1961); *Este, ese y aquel (This, That and the Other)* for Mezzo-soprano, Flute, Violin, Viola, Cello, and Vibraphone (1964); *Amarillo era el color de la Esperanza (Yellow Was the Color of Hope),* secular cantata for Narrator, Mezzo-soprano, and Jazz Band (1966); *Noche de verano* for Narrator, Soprano, and Small Orch (1975); *A mi hermano* for Baritone,

Chorus, and Orch. (1977); *Canto de 5-Flor* for Cello and Piano (1957); *Sonatina mexicana* for Violin and Piano (1959); *Xilofonías* for Piccolo, Oboe, Bass Clarinet, Double Bassoon, and Percussion (1963); *Puentes* for String Quartet (1965; revised 1977); *Candelaria,* suite for Wind Quintet (1965); *3-Silvestre,* concerto for 9 Instruments (1966); *Fuga para metales* (1968). For piano: *Suite ingenua* (1953); *Villancico, Canción y Jarabe* (1965); Sonata (1972).

Kurka, Robert, American composer of Czech descent; b. Cicero, Ill., Dec. 22, 1921; d. New York, Dec. 12, 1957. He studied violin with Kathleen Parlow and Hans Letz; composition with Otto Luening and Darius Milhaud; received a Guggenheim fellowship in 1951 and 1952. His opera *The Good Soldier Schweik,* completed shortly before his untimely death from leukemia, was produced with extraordinary success at the N.Y. City Center on April 23, 1958, and has since been widely performed in America and in Europe. His other works include 2 symphs.; Serenade for Chamber Orch.; Violin Concerto; Concerto for 2 Pianos, String Orch., and Trumpet; Concerto for Marimba and Orch.; *Ballad* for French Horn and Strings; 5 string quartets; Piano Trio; 4 violin sonatas; piano pieces; choruses.

Kurpiński, Karol, Polish composer; b. Wloszakowice (Luschwitz), March 6, 1785; d. Warsaw, Sept. 18, 1857. He studied with his father, Marcian Kurpiński, an organist; in 1810 became a violinist at a Warsaw theater; then 2nd conductor at the Warsaw Opera; also taught at the Warsaw Cons. He wrote the operas *Jadwiga* (Warsaw, Dec. 23, 1814), *The New Cracovians, The Castle of Czorsztyn* (Warsaw, May 11, 1819), and others; also many Polish dances. Wagner used one of his themes in his symph. overture *Polonia.* Kurpiński publ. a collection, *Historical Songs* (Warsaw, 1816).

Kürsteiner, Jean Paul, American pianist and pedagogue; b. (of a French-Swiss father and American mother) Catskill, N.Y., July 8, 1864; d. Los Angeles, March 19, 1943. He studied in Leipzig with Jadassohn and R. Hofmann; piano with Weidenbach and Teichmüller. Returning to America in 1893, he was appointed an instructor of piano and theory at the Ogontz School in Philadelphia, holding this position until 1930. In 1938 he moved to Los Angeles. He wrote a number of piano pieces, of which *Invocation to Eros* became fairly well known. His works comprise 33 opus numbers. He publ. *Essays on Expert Aid to Artistic Piano Playing.*

Kurt, Melanie, Austrian soprano; b. Vienna, Jan. 8, 1880; d. New York, March 11, 1941. She studied piano at the Vienna Cons. (1887–94), winning the gold medal and Liszt prize; then took singing lessons from Fannie Mütter in Vienna, and made a successful operatic debut as Elisabeth in *Tannhäuser* (Lübeck, 1902). From 1905 to 1908 she sang in Braunschweig; then (1908–12) at the Berlin Opera. She became an outstanding Wagner interpreter and appeared in London, Brussels, Milan, Budapest, etc.

When the Deutsches Opernhaus in Charlottenburg was opened in 1912, she was engaged as chief soprano for heroic roles. On Feb. 1, 1915, she made her debut at the Metropolitan Opera House as Isolde. In 1917 she returned to Europe, living in Berlin and Vienna as a singing teacher. In 1939 she settled in N.Y., where she remained until her death.

Kurtág, György, Hungarian composer; b. Lugoj, Feb. 19, 1926. He learned to play piano as a child; then studied composition with Kadosa, Leo Weiner, Veress, and Farkas at the Budapest Academy of Music (1946–53); went to Paris and took lessons with Milhaud and Messiaen (1957–58); upon returning to Budapest, he taught at the Academy of Music. In his music he sometimes applies serial principles to classical melodic configurations and forms. WORKS: *Suite* for Piano Duet (1950); Piano Suite (1951); *Cantata* (1953); Viola Concerto (1954); String Quartet (1959); Wind Quintet (1959); *8 Piano Pieces* (1960); *8 Duets* for Violin and Cimbalom (1960–61); *Jelek (Signs)* for Solo Viola (1961); *5 Merrycate* for Guitar (1962); *Bornemissza Péter mondásai (The Sayings of Péter Bornemissza),* concerto for Soprano and Piano (1963–68); *In Memory of a Winter Sunset,* 4 fragments for Soprano, Violin, and Cimbalom (1969); *4 Capriccios* for Soprano and Chamber Ensemble (1971–72); *Game* for Piano (1974–75); *4 Songs* (1975); *Szálkák (Splinters)* for Solo Cimbalom (1975); *Messages of the Late Miss R. V. Troussova* for Soprano and Chamber Ensemble (Paris, Jan. 14, 1981); *Omaggio a Luigi Nono* (London, Feb. 3, 1981). BIBLIOGRAPHY: "György Kurtág," *Tempo* (March and Sept. 1982).

Kurth, Ernst, eminent Austrian musicologist; b. Vienna, June 1, 1886; d. Bern, Aug. 2, 1946. He studied at the Vienna Cons. with Guido Adler; received his Dr.Phil. with the thesis *Der Stil der Opera seria von Chr. W. Gluck bis zum Orfeo* (1908), which was publ. in Adler's *Studien zur Musikwissenschaft* (vol. 1); held various posts as a teacher and a conductor in Germany; then went to Bern in 1912, where he founded a Collegium Musicum; became a prof. in 1927. His principal work, *Grundlagen des linearen Kontrapunkts: Bachs melodische Polyphonie* (Bern, 1917), exercised a profound influence on musicology, and on practical composition as well; the term "linear counterpoint," which he introduced in it, became part of scientific nomenclature in music; a companion vol., *Romantische Harmonik und ihre Krise in Wagners Tristan* (Bern, 1920), is a psychological analysis of Romantic music. His vol. *Musikpsychologie* (Berlin, 1931) represents a synthesis of his theoretical ideas on musical perception. He also publ. a comprehensive biography of Bruckner (2 vols., Berlin, 1925) and several valuable studies: "Zur Ars cantus mensurabilis des Franko von Köln," in *Kirchenmusikalisches Jahrbuch* (1908); *Die Voraussetzungen der theoretischen Harmonik und der tonalen Darstellungssysteme* (Bern, 1913); "Zur Motivbildung Bachs," *Bach Jahrbuch* (1917). BIBLIOGRAPHY: E. Bücken, "Kurth als Musik-theoretiker," *Melos,* IV/7–8; K. von Fischer, "In memoriam Ernst Kurth," in *Musikalmanach* (Munich, 1948).

Kurtz, Edward Frampton, American violinist and composer; b. New Castle, Pa., July 31, 1881; d. Cedar Falls, Iowa, June 8, 1965. He studied at the Univ. of Iowa, the Detroit Cons., and the Cincinnati Cons.; took violin lessons with Eugène Ysaÿe while Ysaÿe was conductor of the Cincinnati Symph. Orch.; studied composition with Clapp, Goetschius, and E.S. Kelley. After teaching at various Midwestern colleges, he became head of the music dept. of Iowa State Teachers College, in 1940, and lived mostly in Iowa. He wrote 5 symphs. (1932, 1939, 1940, 1943, 1944); several symph. poems; a Suite for String Quartet, subtitled *From the West;* violin pieces.

Kurtz, Efrem, Russian-American conductor; b. St. Petersburg, Nov. 7, 1900. He studied academic subjects in Riga; then went to Germany and took music courses at the Stern Cons. in Berlin, graduating in 1922. Subsequently he devoted himself to ballet conducting. He came to the U.S. in 1943; was conductor of the Kansas City Phil. (1943–48) and of the Houston Symph. Orch. (1948–54). In 1966 he conducted some concerts in Moscow and Leningrad; then was active as a guest conductor in Europe and America; in 1977 he conducted in Tokyo; also filled in engagements with the Kansas City Phil. and with the Zürich Tonhalle Orch.; in 1979 conducted guest appearances in Houston, Texas. He makes his permanent home in Switzerland. He married the flutist **Elaine Shaffer.**

Kurz, Selma, coloratura soprano; b. Bielitz, Silesia, Nov. 15, 1874; d. Vienna, May 10, 1933. She studied with Ress; made her first appearances in Hamburg in 1895. In 1899 she was engaged by Mahler at the Vienna Court Opera, and remained on the roster until 1926. She made her London debut at Covent Garden as Gilda (June 7, 1904), creating a profound impression; subsequently appeared in America as a concert singer, also with success. She was married to the famous Viennese gynecologist Josef Halban; they were the parents of the soprano **Desi Halban.** BIBLIOGRAPHY: H. Goldmann, *Selma Kurz* (Bielitz, 1933).

Kurz, Siegfried, German conductor and composer; b. Dresden, July 18, 1930. He studied conducting with Ernst Hintze, composition with Fidelio Finke, and trumpet with Gerd Seifert at the Staatlichen Akademie für Musik und Theater in Dresden (1945–50); from 1949–60 he was a conductor of music for dramatic productions at the Dresden State Theater. In 1960 he became a conductor at the Dresden State Opera; in 1975 he was named its music director; in 1979 he also became a prof. of composition at the Dresden Hochschule für Musik. He toured with the Dresden State Orch. to Austria, Japan, and the U.S. As a conductor, he was honored with the titles of Staatskapellmeister (1965) and Generalmusikdirektor (1971) ;as a composer, he received the

Kunstpreis and the Nationalpreis of the German Democratic Republic. His compositions combine the principles of Classical lucidity with the dissonant counterpoint of the modern era.

WORKS: 2 symphs. (1958, 1959); *Sinfonia piccola* (1953); Trumpet Concerto (1953); Piano Concerto (1964); Wind Quintet (1950); Sonatina for 7 Brass Instruments (1952); Chamber Concerto for Wind Quintet and String Orch. (1962); Piano Concerto (Dresden, Oct. 2, 1964); Variations for Orch. (1968); *Sonatine* for Orch. (1969); Music for Winds, Percussion, and Strings (1969); Horn Concerto (Dresden, Dec. 20, 1973).

Kusche, Benno, German bass-baritone; b. Freiburg im Breisgau, Jan. 30, 1916. He studied in Karlsruhe; made his operatic debut in Koblenz in 1938; then sang in Augsburg (1939–44); was subsequently a leading member of the Bavarian State Opera in Munich (1946–57). On Dec. 27, 1971, he made his debut at the Metropolitan Opera in N.Y. as Bechmesser in *Die Meistersinger.*

Kusevitsky, Moshe, Jewish cantor; b. Smorgon, Poland, June 9, 1899; d. Kings Point, Long Island, N.Y., Aug. 23, 1966. He studied in Vilna; became a cantor at Warsaw in 1926, and also pursued a concert career; made his Paris debut as a concert singer in 1930; then appeared several times in England; in 1934, gave concerts in Palestine; in 1938, sang in the U.S. He returned to Warsaw before the outbreak of World War II; escaped to Russia, where he remained from 1939 until 1946, and gave concerts in Leningrad, Moscow, Odessa, etc.; in 1946–47, toured in England; then settled in N.Y. Although his last name is identical (in Russian characters) with that of Serge Koussevitzky, the two are not related.

Kusser (or **Cousser**), **Johann Sigismund,** composer; b. Pressburg, Feb. 13, 1660; d. Dublin, Nov. 1727. He received his early musical training from his father, Johann Kusser (1626–75), a minister and organist. He lived in Stuttgart as a boy; then spent 8 years in Paris (1674–82), where he became a pupil of Lully. He subsequently was in Ansbach (1682–83); then in Braunschweig (1690). In 1694 he became co-director of the Hamburg Opera, but left 2 years later, and was active in Nuremberg and Augsburg as an opera composer. He was again in Stuttgart from 1700 to 1704. In 1705 he appeared in London, and after a year proceeded to Dublin, where he was a chapelmaster and teacher. He revisited Stuttgart briefly, but returned to Dublin, and remained there until his death. He was greatly esteemed as an operatic conductor; Mattheson, in his *Volkommener Capellmeister,* holds him up as a model of efficiency. Kusser is historically significant for being the mediator between the French and the German styles of composition, and the first to use Lully's methods and forms in German instrumental music. Lully's influence is shown in Kusser's set of 6 suites for strings, *Composition de musique suivant la méthode française* (Stuttgart, 1682).

WORKS: Operas: produced in Braunschweig:

Julia (1690); *Kleopatra* (1691); *Ariadne* (Feb. 15, 1692); *Andromeda* (Feb. 20, 1692); *Jason* (Sept. 1, 1692); *Narcissus* (Oct. 14, 1692); *Porus* (1693); in Hamburg: *Erindo* (1694) and *Der grossmüthige Scipio Africanus* (1694); in Stuttgart: *Der verliebte Wald* (1698) and *Erminia* (Oct. 11, 1698); 18 suites from the lost operas *Le Festin des Muses, La Cicala delle cetra d'Eunomio,* and *Apollen enjoué,* 6 operatic overtures, and several arias are extant; an aria from *Erindo* is publ. in Schering's *Geschichte der Musik in Beispielen* (No. 250); an overture was ed. by H. Osthoff (1933).

BIBLIOGRAPHY: F. Chrysander, "Die Hamburger Oper unter der Direktion von J.S. Kusser," *Allgemeine musikalische Zeitung* (1879); Hans Scholz, *J.S. Kusser* (Munich, 1911).

Kussevitsky, Serge. See **Koussevitzky, Serge.**

Küster, Hermann, German writer on music; b. Templin, July 14, 1817; d. Herford, March 17, 1878. He studied in Berlin with A.W. Bach, Ludwig Berger, Marx, and Rungenhagen; in 1845–52, was music director at Saarbrücken; then settled in Berlin as a music teacher; in 1857, became court and Cathedral organist. He publ. *Über Händels Israel in Ägypten* (1854); *Populäre Vorträge über Bildung und Begründung eines musikalischen Urteils* (4 vols., 1870–77); *Methode für den Unterricht im Gesang auf höheren Schulanstalten* (1872); *Über die Formen in der Musik* (1872); etc.; also wrote 7 oratorios; orch. music; church music; songs; etc.

Kutavičius, Bronislovas, Lithuanian composer; b. Molainiai, near Panevežys, Sept. 13, 1932. He studied composition with Antanas Račiunas at the State Cons. in Vilnius, graduating in 1964. In 1975 he was appointed to the music faculty at the Arts School in Vilnius. In his music he evolves a complex system of varied techniques, impressionistic pointillism, intervallic serialism, and aleatory sonorism, all this intertwined with Lithuanian melorhythms.

WORKS: FOR THE STAGE: Opera-ballet for children, *Doddering Old Man on Iron Mountain* (1976); opera-poem, *The Green Bird* (1981). FOR ORCH.: *Sinfonietta* (1964); *Divertimento* for Piano and String Orch. (1967); Symph. with Male Chorus (1973); *Dzukija Variations* for String Orch. and Tape (1975). FOR VOICE: *Pantheistic Oratorio* for Soprano, Narrator, 4 Male Voices, and 12 Instruments (1970); *On the Shore* for High Voice and 4 Violas (1972); *Little Performance* for Actress, 2 Pianos, and 2 Violins (1975); *Two Birds in the Thick of the Woods,* cantata for Soprano, Oboe, Prepared Piano, and Electronic Tape (1978); *The Last Pagan Rites,* oratorio for Soprano, Girls' Chorus, Horns, and Organ (1978). CHAMBER MUSIC: Violin Sonata (1962); *Prelude and Fugue* for 4 Violins (1966); *Poem* for Cello, Piano, and Wind Quintet (1967); Viola Sonata (1968); *From Madrigal to Aleatory,* suite for children, for Violin and Piano (1972); 2 string quartets: No. 1 (1972); No. 2, *Anno cum tettigonia (Year with a Cicada;* 1980); *Prutiena (Buried Village)* for Violin, Organ, and Chimes (1977); String Quintet (1978);

Clocks of the Past for String Quartet and Guitar (1978); *Perpetuum Mobile* for Cello and Piano (1978). FOR PIANO: *3 Metamorphoses* (1966); *Collages* for 2 Pianos (1970); Piano Sonata (1975); *A Disputation with a Stranger,* concerto for 2 Pianos and Tape (1982).

Kutev, Filip, Bulgarian choral leader and composer; b. Aytos, June 13, 1903. After completing his education in Sofia, he became a military band leader. In 1951 he organized an ensemble of largely untutored folksingers, musicians, and dancers; he brought it to a high point of virtuosity and toured in Europe (1958) and in the U.S. (1963), eliciting great praise. Virtually all of his compositions are derived from Bulgarian melorhythms; among these are *Bulgarian Rhapsody* for Orch. (1937); cantata, *September the 9th,* in honor of the entry of the Soviet Army into Bulgaria in 1944; *Stalin Cantata* (1949); Symph. (1950).
BIBLIOGRAPHY: S. Stoyanov, *Filip Kutev* (Sofia, 1962).

Kutschera, Elsa, Austrian operatic soprano; b. Vienna, June 1, 1867; d. there, Dec. 29, 1945. She studied with Pauline Viardot-García and Padilla; sang in Berlin in 1892; made U.S. tours in 1895 and 1915.

Kutzschbach, Hermann Ludwig, German conductor; b. Meissen, Aug. 30, 1875; d. Dresden, Feb. 9, 1938. He studied at the Dresden Cons. with Draeseke and others; was opera coach at various German theaters; in 1906–9, conductor of the court opera at Mannheim; then returned to Dresden, where he became conductor of the court opera (1914).

Kuula, Toivo, Finnish composer; b. Vasa, July 7, 1883; d. Viipuri (Vyborg), May 18, 1918. He studied at the Helsinki Cons. with Wegelius, Järnefelt, and Sibelius (1900–8); then went to Italy, where he took courses with Bossi in Bologna; also studied in Paris with Marcel Labey; in 1910 he was appointed conductor of the orch. at Oulu; from 1911 to 1916 was assistant conductor of the Helsinki Phil.; then conductor of the orch. in Viipuri. He was shot to death during a street fight in the aftermath of the Finnish Civil War. His music, rooted in Finnish folk song, is occasionally touched with Impressionism. To commemorate his achievement, 2 societies were formed in Helsinki and Stockholm, in 1948 and 1949. WORKS: At his death he left unfinished a *Jupiter Symphony;* his *Stabat Mater* for Chorus, Organ, and Orch. (1914–18) was completed by Madetoja and first perf. in 1919 in Helsinki. Completed works: 2 *South Ostrobothnian Suites* for Orch. (1906, 1912); *Prelude and Fugue* for Orch. (1909); *Prelude and Intermezzo* for Strings and Organ (1909); *Orjanpoika (The Son of a Slave),* symph. legend (1910); *Kuolemattomuuden toivo (Hope of Immortality)* for Baritone, Chorus, and Orch. (1910); *Merenkylpijäneidot (Maids on the Seashore)* for Soprano and Orch. (1910); *Impi ja pajarinpoika (The Maid and the Boyar's Son)* for Soprano and Orch. (1911); *Both-*

nic Poem for Orch. (Petrograd, Oct. 26, 1918, composer conducting); Violin Sonata; music for plays; piano pieces; songs.
BIBLIOGRAPHY: T. Elmgreen-Heinonen and E. Roiha, *Toivo Kuula* (Helsinki, 1952).

Kuusisto, Ilkka Taneli, Finnish composer, son of **Taneli Kuusisto;** b. Helsinki, April 26, 1933. He studied organ at the Sibelius Academy in Helsinki; also composition with Arre Merikanto and Nils-Eric Fougstedt. In 1958 he went to N.Y. to study organ with Seth Bingham; later continued his studies in Germany and in Vienna. WORKS: 3 *Introductions* for Brass, Percussion, and Organ (1956); 3 *Chinese Songs* for Soprano, Flute, and Piano (1956); Duo for Flute and Cello (1957); *Valkeneva päivä (Daybreak),* cantata for Solo Voices, Youth Chorus, and Organ (1957); *Coelestis aulae nuntius* for Trombone and Organ (1959); *Crucifixus* for Baritone and String Quartet (1959); *Cassazione* for 2 Clarinets and 2 Horns (1961); *Jazzationes,* suite for Jazz Quartet and String Quartet (1965); *Ritornells* for Viola and Marimba (1970); *The Pain* and *Alfhid,* 2 songs for Baritone, 2 Clarinets, and Strings (1972); music for Brecht's play *Saint Joan of the Stockyards* (1972); *Sota valosta (The War Over Light),* opera (Helsinki, April 2, 1981); music for films; anthems; songs.

Kuusisto, Taneli, Finnish composer, father of **Ilkka Taneli Kuusisto;** b. Helsinki, June 19, 1905. He studied at the Univ. of Helsinki, in Paris, and in Leipzig with J.N. David; in 1936–42, was assistant conductor at the Helsinki Radio; in 1942–46, chorus director at the Opera there. In 1948 he began teaching at the Sibelius Academy; was director there in 1959–71; was vice-chairman of the board of directors of the Finnish National Opera in 1960–70; was a member of the Swedish Royal Academy of Music. WORKS: Sonatina for String Quartet (1927); *Pastorale* for Orch. (1934); Nocturne for Cello and Orch. (1936); *Sonatina di Natale* for Flute, Cello, and Piano (1936); *Psalm 40* for Baritone, Chorus, Organ, and Strings (1939); *Jouluyö (Christmas Night)* for Chorus, Organ, and Orch. (1941); *Laatokka (Lake Ladoga),* symph. legend (1944); *Kangastuksia (Mirages)* for Mezzo-soprano and Orch. (1945); Trio for Flute, Viola, and Piano (1945); *Saimoon helmi (The Pearl of Saimaa),* cantata (1949); *Toccata* for Orch. (1953); piano pieces; organ pieces; sacred music.
BIBLIOGRAPHY: Sulho Ranta, "Taneli Kuusisto," in *Suomen saveltajia* (Helsinki, 1945; pp. 655–64).

Kuyper, Elisabeth, Dutch conductor and composer; b. Amsterdam, Sept. 13, 1877; d. Lugano, Feb. 26, 1953. She studied with Max Bruch in Berlin. In 1908–20 she taught theory at the Hochschule für Musik there; was founder (1908) and conductor of the Berlin Tonkünstlerinnen Orch.; in 1922 she led a few concerts of the London Women's Symph. Orch., and in 1923 conducted the N.Y. Women's Symph. Orch.; later returned to Europe and lived at Lago Maggiore in Brissago. She composed a Symph.; Violin Concerto; several violin sonatas; Ballade for Cello and Piano; Piano Trio; songs.

Küzdö, Victor, Hungarian violinist and teacher; b. Budapest, Sept. 18, 1859; d. Glendale, Calif., Feb. 24, 1966, at the age of 106. He studied at the Budapest Cons. with Karl Huber; made his debut there in 1882; toured in Europe, and visited the U.S. in 1884 and 1887. In 1894 he settled in N.Y.; in 1918–31, taught at the summer school of the Chicago Musical College; in 1932, settled in Glendale. He became totally blind in 1950. He publ. several violin pieces, among them a Serenade and *Witches' Dance.*

Kuznetsova, Maria, Russian soprano; b. Odessa, 1880; d. Paris, April 26, 1966. She studied voice in St. Petersburg with Tartakov; then sang at the Maryinsky Theater (1905–13, 1916–17); in the interim, appeared in Paris, London (1909), and Chicago (1916). She left Russia in 1918; had engagements in Stockholm and Copenhagen, and again in London (1920). Among her roles, apart from the Russian repertoire, were Violetta, Elsa, and Carmen.

Kuznetzov, Konstantin, Russian musicologist; b. Novocherkassk, Sept. 21, 1883; d. Moscow, May 25, 1953. He studied at the Univ. of Heidelberg (Dr.Phil., 1906); was an instructor at the Univ. of Moscow (1912–14); a prof. at the Univ. of Odessa (1914–20); in 1921, returned to Moscow, where he remained until his death. An erudite musician, he wrote on music history from a broad sociological standpoint; publ. *Introduction to the History of Music* (Moscow, 1923); *Glinka and His Epoch* (Moscow, 1927); edited several publications for the Musicological Inst. of Moscow.

Kvandal, Johan, Norwegian composer, son of **David Monrad Johansen;** b. Oslo, Sept. 8, 1919. He studied piano and composition at the Oslo Cons.; later with Joseph Marx in Vienna and Nadia Boulanger in Paris. He was a church organist in Oslo (1959–74) and a member of the governing board of the Society of Norwegian Composers (1960–75); wrote music criticism in the Oslo newspapers *Morgenposten* (1959–74) and *Aftenposten* (after 1974).
WORKS: Piano Sonatina (1942); Divertimento for Strings (1945); String Trio (1951); *Song of Stella* for Soprano and String Orch. (1952); 3 solo cantatas: No. 1 for Soprano or Tenor, and Orch. (1953); No. 2, *O Domine Deus,* for Soprano and Organ (1966); No. 3 for Baritone and Organ (1970); 3 string quartets (1954, 1966, 1983); *Variations and Fugue* for Orch. (1954); *Norwegian Overture* (1959); Symph. No. 1 (1959); Duo for Violin and Cello (1959); *Symphonic Epos* for Orch. (1961–62); Concerto for Flute and Strings (1963); *Aria, Cadenza and Finale* for Violin and Piano (1964); orch. suite from incidental music to the play *Skipper Worse* (1967); *Sinfonia concertante* (1968); *Introduction and Allegro* for Horn and Piano (1969); *3 Fantasy Country Dances* for Piano (1969); *Da lontano* for Flute and Piano (1970); Wind Quintet (1971); *Nature,* chamber cantata for

Baritone, Violin, and Piano (1972); *Antagonia,* concerto for 2 String Orchs. and Percussion (1972); *Duo concertante* for 2 Pianos (1974); Quartet for Flute, Violin, Viola, and Cello (1975); Concerto for Oboe and String Orch. (1977); Violin Concerto (1979); *Triptychon* for Orch. (1979); Concerto for Chamber Orch. (1980); *Night Music,* nonet (1981); *Overture Fantasy* for 8 Winds and Double Bass (1982); songs.

Kvapil, Jaroslav, significant Czech composer; b. Fryšták, April 21, 1892; d. Brno, Feb. 18, 1958. He studied with Janáček in Brno (1906–9) and at the Leipzig Cons. (1911–13) with Leichmüller (piano) and Max Reger (composition). He was in the Austrian army during World War I; then was music director of the Phil. Society in Brno (1919–47); taught at the Janáček Academy of Music in Brno (1947–57). His works show the double influence of Janáček's national and rhapsodic style and Max Reger's strong polyphonic idiom.
WORKS: Opera, *Pohádka máje (A Romance in May;* 1940–43; Prague, May 12, 1950; revised 1955; Brno, 1955); oratorio, *Lví srdce (The Lion's Heart;* 1928–31; Brno, Dec. 7, 1931); 2 cantatas: *A Song on Time That Is Passing* (1924) and *Small Italian Cantata* (1950); 4 symphs.: No. 1 (1913–14); No. 2 (1921); No. 3 (1936–37); No. 4, *Vítězná (Victory;* 1943); *Thema con variazioni e fuga* for Orch. (1912); 2 violin concertos (1927–28, 1952); *Z těžkých dob (From Anxious Times),* symph. variations (1939); *Slavonic (Jubilee) Overture* (1944); *Burlesque* for Flute and Orch. (1945); *Svítání (Daybreak),* symph. poem (1948–49); Oboe Concerto (1951); Piano Concerto (1954); 3 violin sonatas, with Piano (1910, 1914, 1931); Sonata for Violin and Organ (1931); Piano Trio (1912); Cello Sonata (1913); 6 string quartets (1914, 1926, 1931, 1935, 1949, 1951); Piano Quintet (1914–15); Brass Quintet (1925); Variations for Trumpet and Piano (1929); Suite for Trombone and Piano (1930); *Intimate Pictures* for Violin and Piano (1934); Wind Quintet (1935); Violin Sonatina (1941); *Fantasy* for Cello and Piano (1942); Nonet (1944); Quartet for Flute, Violin, Viola, and Cello (1948); Duo for Violin and Viola (1949); Suite for Viola and Piano (1955). He also wrote 3 piano sonatas (1912, 1925, 1946); Variations for Piano (1914); *Fantasy in the Form of Variations* for Piano (1952); Piano Sonatina (1956); *10 Pieces* for Piano (1957); Fantasy for Organ (1935); several song cycles; many transcriptions of folk songs; a piano album of 100 folk songs from Moravian Slovakia (1914).
BIBLIOGRAPHY: L. Kundera, *Jaroslav Kvapil* (Prague, 1944).

Kvernadze, Alexander, Soviet Georgian composer; b. Signahi, Georgia, June 29, 1928. He studied with Andrey Balanchivadze at the Cons. of Tiflis, graduating in 1953. Among his works are 2 piano concertos (1950, 1965); Violin Concerto (1956); *Dance-Fantasy* for Orch. (1959); Symph. (1961); violin pieces; film music.

Kwalwasser, Helen, American violinist, daughter of **Jacob Kwalwasser;** b. Syracuse, N.Y., Oct. 11,

1927. She showed a gift for violin playing at an early age; studied with Louis Persinger (1936–39), with Zimbalist at the Curtis Inst. of Music in Philadelphia (1939–41), then with Galamian (1941–48); made her debut in N.Y. on March 25, 1947; then toured Europe (1949); returning to N.Y., was active as a violinist and teacher.

Kwalwasser, Jacob, music psychologist and educator, father of **Helen Kwalwasser;** b. New York, Feb. 27, 1894; d. Pittsburgh, Aug. 7, 1977. He received his education at the Univ. of Pittsburgh and the Univ. of Iowa, obtaining his Ph.D. in 1926; taught in the public schools in Pittsburgh (1918–23); was head of public school music at the Univ. of Iowa (1923–26); in 1926, was appointed prof. and head of the dept. of music education at Syracuse Univ. He is the co-author of the Kwalwasser-Dykema Music Tests; publ. a manual on the subject in 1913; also collaborated in establishing the Kwalwasser-Ruch Musical Accomplishment Test, and various other melodic, harmonic, and instrumental tests; publ. numerous magazine articles on music education.
    WRITINGS: *Tests and Measurements in Music* (1927; an influential code of rules, adopted in many educational institutions); *Problems in Public School Music* (1932; revised ed., 1941; treats objectives of music education); *Exploring the Musical Mind* (N.Y., 1955).

Kwast, James, famous German pianist and teacher; b. Nijkerk, the Netherlands, Nov. 23, 1852; d. Berlin, Oct. 31, 1927. He studied with his father and Ferdinand Böhme; later with Reinecke and Richter at the Leipzig Cons.; also with Theodor Kullak and Wüerst at Berlin, and with Brassin and Gevaert at Brussels. In 1874 he became an instructor at the Cons. of Cologne; from 1883 till 1903 he taught at the Hoch Cons. in Frankfurt; from 1903 to 1906, was a prof. of piano at the Klindworth-Scharwenka Cons. in Berlin; then at the Stern Cons. there. He was greatly esteemed by his colleagues and students as a piano pedagogue; many well-known pianists were his pupils at Frankfurt and Berlin. His first wife,

Antonia (d. Stuttgart, Feb. 10, 1931), was a daughter of Ferdinand Hiller; his 2nd wife, **Frieda Hodapp-Kwast** (b. Bargen, Aug. 13, 1880; d. Bad Wiessee, Sept. 14, 1949), was a concert pianist. He wrote a Piano Concerto and other piano music; edited works of Handel and Clementi for the *Tonmeister* edition.

Kwiatkowski, Ryszard, Polish composer; b. Jaranowo Kujawy, June 27, 1931. He studied composition with T. Szeligowski and W. Rudziński at the State College of Music in Warsaw (1958–63); then took private lessons with Petrassi in Rome. His style of composition is free from repressive modernism, but is imbued with impressionistic metaphors, even when he wanders into the forbidding fields of dodecaphony.
    WORKS: *Serenade* for Trombone and Orch. (1957); 4 symphs.: No. 1 (1958); No. 2 (1964); No. 3 (1969); No. 4 (1970); *Pictures* for Chamber Orch. (1963); *Colors* for Orch. (1963); *Shapes* for Orch. (1963); 3 string quartets (1963, 1966, 1970); *Lights* for Orch. (1964); *Polyphonic Music* for Orch. (1967); Piano Quintet, with Metronome (1968); *Music* for Winds, Percussion, and Piano (1968); 2 percussion quartets (1968, 1971); *Pulsations* for Orch. (1969; Szczecin, Sept. 10, 1976); *Lyrical Music* for Violin and Double Bass (1969); *7 Photographs from the Moon* for Piano (1970); *Apotheosis of October* for Orch. (1972); *Marine Impressions* for String Quartet (1973); *Legend* for Viola and Piano (1975); *Seascapes* for Piano Trio (1975); Piano Sonata (1975); *Baltic Pictures* for Mezzo-soprano, 2 Violins, Cello, and Piano (1975); Violin Sonata (1976).

Kyriakou, Rena, Greek pianist; b. Iraklion, Feb. 25, 1918. She was a proverbial child prodigy who made her public debut in Athens at 6; later studied in Vienna with Paul Weingarten and Richard Stohr; then went to Paris and joined the piano class of Isidor Philipp at the Paris Cons.; she also studied composition there with Henri Busser; received its Premier Prix at the age of 15. She then embarked on a concert career in programs of neglected piano pieces by obscure Baroque composers.

L

La Rosa Parodi, Armando, Italian conductor and composer; b. Genoa, March 14, 1904; d. Rome, Jan. 21, 1977. He studied in Genoa and Milan; began his career as a conductor in 1929. He was active as a guest conductor in Genoa, Milan, Turin, and Rome; in 1963 he was named chief conductor of the RAI Orch. of Rome, a post he held until his death. He composed the operas *Il Mercante e l'avvocato* (1934) and *Cleopatra* (1938), and several symph. works.

La Barbara, Joan, American composer and experimental vocalist; b. Philadelphia, June 8, 1947. Her grandfather taught her to play nursery songs on the piano; later she sang in church and school choirs; joined a folk music group in Philadelphia; then went to N.Y., where she sang in radio commercials and at the same time made contacts with the most uninhibited representatives of the American avant-garde. In her compositions she usually makes use of graphic notation. Among her works are *Ides of March* for Strings and Voices (1974); *An Exaltation of Larks* for Voice and Electronics (1975); *Cyclone,* a sound sculpture for White Noise and Voices (1975; first perf. in Bonn, Germany, May 14, 1977; *Thunder* for Voice Electronics and Timpani (1976); *Circular Song* for Voice employing circular breathing (1975). She introduced many other vocal improvements, including vocalizing while breathing in and out.

Labarre, Théodore, eminent French harpist; b. Paris, March 5, 1805; d. there, March 9, 1870. He studied privately with Cousineau, Boscha, and Naderman; then at the Paris Cons. with Dourlen, Eler, Fétis, and Boieldieu. In 1824–47 he lived alternately in London and Paris; became conductor of the Opéra-Comique; in 1851, was appointed conductor of Louis Napoleon's private orch.; in 1867, became prof. of harp at the Paris Cons. He wrote 4 operas, 5 ballets, numerous pieces for harp, songs, etc.; also a *Méthode complète* for the harp.

La Bassée, Adam de, medieval poet; b. La Bassée; d. Lille, Feb. 25, 1286. He was an ecclesiastic at Lille; created religious songs by adapting his own words to sacred and secular melodies; some of these were publ. by Abbé D. Charnel in the *Messager des sciences historiques* (Ghent, 1858).

Labatt, Leonard, Swedish tenor; b. Stockholm, Dec. 4, 1838; d. there, March 7, 1897. He studied with J. Günther; then with Masset in Paris; made his debut in Stockholm as Tamino in *Die Zauberflöte* (1866); in 1868–69 was at the Dresden Opera; from 1869 till 1883 at the Vienna Opera; he sang in London in 1881; made an American tour in 1888–89. He was especially fine in Wagnerian roles.

BIBLIOGRAPHY: F. Hedberg, *Svenska opera-sängare* (Stockholm, 1885).

L'Abbé, Joseph Barnabé Saint-Sevin (real name, **Saint-Sevin**), French violinist and composer; b. Agen, June 11, 1727; d. Paris, July 20, 1803. A precocious musician, he began his study with his father and became a member of the orch. of the Comédie-Française at the age of 12; then studied with Leclair; was a violinist at the Opéra (1742–62); also played at the Concert Spirituel (1741–55); devoted his later years to teaching and composition. He had an excellent violin technique, and was an innovator in that he wrote out cadenzas in full.

WORKS: 2 books of violin sonatas, with Continuo (1748–64); symphs. for 3 Violins and Continuo (c.1754); 5 collections of airs arranged for one and 2 violins; a manual, *Les Principes du violon* (1761).

BIBLIOGRAPHY: L. de La Laurencie, *L'Ecole française de violon de Lully à Viotti* (vol. 2, Paris, 1923).

Labey, Marcel, French conductor and composer; b. Le Vésinet, Seine-et-Oise, Aug. 6, 1875; d. Nancy, Nov. 25, 1968. He studied law in Paris, receiving his degree in 1898; then turned his attention to music, studying piano with Delaborde, harmony with Lenormand, and composition with Vincent d'Indy at the Schola Cantorum; taught piano there, and at d'Indy's death in 1931, became vice-principal of the school.

WORKS: Opera, *Bérengère* (1912; Le Havre, April 12, 1929); 3 symphs. (1903, 1908, 1934); *Suite champêtre* for Orch. (1923); *Ouverture pour un drame* (Paris, Jan. 22, 1921); Piano Sonata; Viola Sonata; 2 violin sonatas; String Quartet; Piano Trio; Piano Quartet; Piano Quintet; songs; etc. He publ. piano arrangements of several orch. works of d'Indy (Symph. in B-flat, *Jour d'été à la montagne,* etc.).

Labia, Fausta, Italian opera singer, sister of **Maria Labia;** b. Verona, April 3, 1870; d. Rome, Oct. 6, 1935. She became a great favorite in Sweden, but retired in 1908 after her marriage. She then lived many years in Rome and taught at the Santa Cecilia Academy. Her method, *L'arte del respiro nello recitazione e nel canto,* was publ. posthumously in 1936.

Labia, Maria, Italian soprano, sister of **Fausta Labia;** b. Verona, Feb. 14, 1880; d. Malcesine del Garda, Feb. 10, 1953. She received her musical education from her mother, an excellent amateur singer; made her operatic debut in Stockholm on May 19, 1905, as Mimi. From 1906 to 1908 she was on the roster of the Komische Oper in Berlin. She was then engaged by the Manhattan Opera, where she first appeared on Nov. 9, 1908, as Tosca. After the demise of that company she joined the Vienna Opera; then

taught voice at the Music Academy of Siena. She was an actress of great emotional power, and was particularly successful in such dramatic roles as Carmen, Santuzza, Nedda, and Violetta.

Labitzky, August, German violinist and conductor, son of **Joseph Labitzky;** b. Bečov (Petschau), Oct. 22, 1832; d. Reichenhall, Aug. 28, 1903. He studied at the Prague Cons., and with Ferdinand David and Hauptmann in Leipzig. He became conductor of the Karlsbad resort orch. in 1853; composed piano pieces, etc.

Labitzky, Joseph, German dance composer and violinist, father of **August Labitzky;** b. Schönfeld, Eger, July 5, 1802; d. Karlsbad, Aug. 19, 1881. He studied with Veit in Bečov (Petschau); in 1820, joined the orch. in Marienbad as first violinist; then occupied a similar post in Karlsbad; organized his own orch. and toured southern Germany. He studied with Winter in Munich, where he publ. his first dances (1827); returning to Karlsbad in 1835, he organized an orch. and toured Europe. Many of his waltzes, galops, quadrilles, etc. (about 300 opus numbers) enjoyed a great vogue.

Lablache, Luigi, famous Italian bass of French and Irish descent; b. Naples, Dec. 6, 1794; d. there, Jan. 23, 1858. He studied voice with Valesi at the Naples Cons. della Pietà dei Turchini; at 18 he commenced his career there as a *basso buffo.* In 1812 he married Teresa Pinotti, the daughter of an actor. In 1813 he went to Palermo as *primo basso cantante;* then appeared at La Scala in Milan; made his debut in London as Geronimo in *Il matrimonio segreto* (March 30, 1830), with instantaneous success; appeared in Paris in the same role on Nov. 4, 1830. In 1836–37 Lablache lived in England as singing master to Queen Victoria. He also sang in Naples, Vienna, and St. Petersburg, always winning acclaim. He was greatly esteemed by his contemporaries; Schubert dedicated to him his 3 Italian songs (1827).

BIBLIOGRAPHY: F.H.J. Castil-Blaze, *Biographie de Lablache* (Paris, 1850); G. Widén, *Luigi Lablache* (Göteborg, 1897).

Labor, Josef, Austrian pianist, organist, and composer; b. Horowitz, June 29, 1842; d. Vienna, April 26, 1924. He lost his sight as a youth; studied with Sechter at the Vienna Cons.; in 1863 was tutor to the princesses of Hannover, who were then living in exile with their family in Vienna. He played in London (1865), Paris, and in Russia; in 1868 returned to Vienna, where he settled as a teacher; among his students were Julius Bittner and Arnold Schoenberg. Labor wrote several sonatas; a Piano Quartet; pieces for organ and for piano; church music; songs; etc.; also edited Biber's violin sonatas for Denkmäler der Tonkunst in Österreich.

BIBLIOGRAPHY: P. Kundi, *Josef Labor, Sein Leben und Wirken* (Vienna, 1963; contains a thematic catalogue).

Laborde, Jean Benjamin de, French violinist and

composer; b. Paris, Sept. 5, 1734; d. there (on the guillotine), July 22, 1794. He studied violin with Dauvergne and composition with Rameau; was chamberlain to Louis XV, and a member of the Compagnie des Fermiers-Généraux; then withdrew from the court and devoted himself to composition. He wrote 32 operas, and songs; also an *Essai sur la musique ancienne et moderne,* containing an early study of folk songs (1780); *Recueils de chansons avec un accompagnement de violon et la basse continue; Choix de chansons mises en musique* (4 vols., 1773); *Mémoires historiques sur Raoul de Coucy* (1781).

BIBLIOGRAPHY: Jacques Devisme, *J.B. de La Borde, Un favori des dieux* (Paris, 1936).

Labroca, Mario, Italian composer; b. Rome, Nov. 22, 1896; d. there, July 1, 1973. He studied composition with Malipiero and Respighi and graduated from the Parma Cons. in 1921. He held numerous administrative and teaching posts; was music director of the Teatro La Fenice in Venice (from 1959); lectured at the Univ. of Perugia (from 1960). He was closely connected with the theater and the cinema in Italy and composed many scores for plays and films.

WORKS: 2 operas: *La Principessa di Perepepè* (Rome, Dec. 11, 1927) and *Le tre figliuole di Pinco Pallino* (Rome, Jan. 27, 1928); Stabat Mater for Soprano, Mixed Chorus, and Orch. (Rome, Dec. 15, 1935); Symph. (1934); *Sinfonia* for String Orch. (1927); 2 string quartets (1925, 1934); Piano Trio (1925); Suite for Viola and Piano (1926); *3 cantate dalla Passione secondo San Giovanni* (1950).

Labunski, Felix, Polish-American composer and teacher, brother of **Wiktor Labunski** (1895–1974); b. Ksawerynów, Dec. 27, 1892; d. Cincinnati, April 28, 1979. Brought up in a musical environment (his father, a civil engineer, was an amateur singer; his mother played the piano), he began studying piano as a child; then entered the Warsaw Cons., where he was a student of Marczewski and Maliszewski. He met Paderewski, who arranged for him a stipend at the Ecole Normale de Musique in Paris, where he studied with Nadia Boulanger and Paul Dukas. In 1927 he formed, with Czapski, Perkowski, and Wiechowicz, the Association of Young Polish Musicians in Paris. Returning to Poland, Labunski held the post of director of the dept. of classical music of the Polish Radio in Warsaw (1934–36). In 1936 he emigrated to America; became a naturalized citizen in 1941. He lived in N.Y. until 1945, when he joined the staff of the Cincinnati College of Music, continuing in this position when it merged with the Cincinnati Cons. of Music in 1955; he retired in 1964 as prof. emeritus in composition. In his music, Felix Labunski remains faithful to the legacy of Romanticism as cultivated in Poland and Russia.

WORKS: Between 1923 and 1931, Labunski wrote mainly for piano; his first orch. work of importance was *Triptyque champêtre* (1931). Other works were *Polish Cantata* (1932); *Ptaki (The Birds)* for Soprano and Orch. (1934); String Quartet No. 1 (1935);

Divertimento for Flute and Piano (1936); Symph. No. 1 in G minor (1937); *In Memoriam,* symph. poem in memory of Paderewski (1941); *Suite* for String Orch. (1941; perf. at the Festival of the International Society for Contemporary Music, Berkeley, Calif., Aug. 2, 1942); *Song without Words* for Soprano and Strings (1946); *There Is No Death,* cantata (1950); Variations for Orch. (1951); Symph. No. 2 in D (1954); *Elegy* for Orch. (Cincinnati, Dec. 11, 1955); *Images of Youth,* cantata (Cincinnati May Festival, May 11, 1956); *Xaveriana,* fantasy for 2 Pianos and Orch., commissioned for the 125th anniversary of Xavier Univ. (1956); *Divertimento* for Flute, Oboe, Clarinet, and Bassoon (1956); *Diptych* for Oboe and Piano (1958); *Symphonic Dialogues* (Cincinnati, Feb. 9, 1961); String Quartet No. 2 (1962); *Canto di aspirazione* for Orch. (a revision of the slow movement of Symph., No. 2, 1963); *Polish Renaissance Suite* for Orch. (1967); *Intrada festiva* for Brass Choir (1968); *Salut à Paris,* ballet suite for Orch. (1968); *Music* for Piano and Orch. (1968); *Primavera* for Orch. (Cincinnati, April 19, 1974).

Labunski, Wiktor, pianist and composer, brother of **Felix Labunski**; b. St. Petersburg, April 14, 1895; d. Kansas City, Jan. 26, 1974. He studied at the St. Petersburg Cons. with Nikolayev (piano), Kalafati and Vitols (composition); later, piano with Felix Blumenfeld and Safonov, and conducting with Emil Mlynarski. From 1919 till 1928 he was head of the piano dept. at the Cons. of Cracow; then came to the U.S.; made his debut in 1928 as a pianist at Carnegie Hall in N.Y.; was an instructor at the Nashville Cons. (1928–31); prof. and director of the Memphis (Tenn.) College of Music (1931–37); in 1937, was appointed prof. and director of the Cons. of Music of Kansas City. In 1920 he married Wanda Mlynarska, daughter of his teacher Emil Mlynarski.

WORKS: Symph. in G minor (1936); Piano Concerto (Kansas City, Feb. 16, 1939, composer soloist); Concerto for 2 Pianos and Orch. (Kansas City, May 31, 1957); many piano pieces (*Impromptu, Minuet, 4 Variations on a Theme by Paganini, Reminiscence,* etc.).

Laccetti, Guido, Italian singer and composer; b. Naples, Oct. 1, 1879; d. Cava dei Tirreni, Oct. 8, 1943. He studied at the Cons. of Naples; from 1925 taught at the Palermo Cons. His works include the operas *La Contessa di San Remo* (1904); *Hoffmann* (Naples, 1912); *Il miracolo* (Naples, 1915); *Carnasciali* (Rome, 1925); and *La favola dei gobbi* (1935).

Lacerda, Francisco de, Portuguese conductor and musicologist; b. Ribeira Seca, S. Jorge, Azores, May 11, 1869; d. Lisbon, July 18, 1934. He studied at the Lisbon Cons.; received a government stipend for study in Paris, where he took a course with Vincent d'Indy at the Schola Cantorum. In Paris he associated himself with Bourgault-Ducoudray and worked with him in the International Folklore Assoc.; also conducted concerts. At the outbreak of World War I he returned to Portugal; in 1913 he organized the Orquestra Filarmonica in Lisbon. He compiled the important *Cancioneiro musical portugues,* containing some 500 folk songs; wrote a number of original compositions, among them the symph. works *Adamastor, Almorol, Rapsodia insular,* etc.

BIBLIOGRAPHY: A. Pinot, *Musica moderna portuguesa* (Lisbon, 1930; pp. 70–73); F. de Sousa, *Exposição commemorativa do primeiro centenario do nascimento, Francisco de Lacerda,* a centennial memoir (Lisbon, 1969).

Lach, Robert, Austrian musicologist and composer; b. Vienna, Jan. 29, 1874; d. Salzburg, Sept. 11, 1958. He was a pupil of R. Fuchs at the Cons. of the Gesellschaft der Musikfreunde in Vienna (1893–99); also studied philosophy and musicology there, with Wallaschek, Rietsch, and Adler; received a Dr.Phil. from the Univ. of Prague in 1902, with the dissertation *Studien zur Entwicklungsgeschichte der ornamentalen Melopöie* (publ. in Leipzig, 1913), viewing the entire field of musical history in the light of new discoveries of ethnographic investigation. From 1911 to 1920 he was chief of the music division of the Vienna State Library; in 1915, joined the faculty of the Univ. of Vienna. He recorded for the Phonogram Archives of Vienna the songs of Russian prisoners of World War I (with particular emphasis on Asian and Caucasian nationalities), and publ. numerous papers on these melodies. He was pensioned in 1939, and lived in Vienna in retirement, devoting his time to the compilation of oriental glossaries (Babylonian, Sumerian, Egyptian, etc.). In 1954 he became general editor of the new Denkmäler der Tonkunst in Österreich. The dedicatory brochure, *Robert Lach, Persönlichkeit und Werk, zum 80. Geburtstag* (Vienna, 1954), contains a complete list of his works and scholarly writings. His list of musical works attains 150 opus numbers, among them 10 symphs.; 25 string quartets; 14 string quintets; 7 string sextets; a Septet, Octet, Nonet, and Decet; trios; sonatas; cantatas; 8 masses; etc. He also wrote philosophical poems and mystical plays; contributed dozens of articles on various subjects to music periodicals.

Lachenmann, Helmut, German composer; b. Stuttgart, Nov. 27, 1935. He studied piano with Jürgen Uhde and composition with Johann Nepomuk David at Stuttgart and later took lessons with Nono in Venice. He subsequently worked in electronic music at the Univ. of Ghent, Belgium. In 1966–70 he was instructor in music theory at the Hochschule für Musik in Stuttgart; from 1970 to 1976 taught at the Ludwigsburg Pädagogische Hochschule; from 1976 at the Hochschule für Musik in Hannover; also conducted a master class in composition at the Basel Music Academy. Among his works are *Souvenir* for 41 Instruments (1959); *Introversion I* and *II* for 6 Instrumentalists (1964, 1966); String Trio (1966); *Trio fluido* for Clarinet, Marimba, and Viola (1968); *Pression* for Cello Solo (1969); *Kontrakadenz* for Orch. (1970); *Gran Torso* for String Quartet (1971); *Fassade* for Orch. (1973).

Lachmann, Robert, noted German musicologist; b. Berlin, Nov. 28, 1892; d. Jerusalem, May 8, 1939. He studied languages in Berlin and London; served in the German army during World War I, when he began to collect folk melodies from African and Indian war prisoners; later studied musicology with Stumpf and Johannes Wolf, and Arabic with Mittwoch at the Univ. of Berlin; received his Ph.D. (1922) with the thesis *Die Musik in den tunesischen Städten,* publ. in the *Archiv für Musikwissenschaft* (1923). He was librarian of the music division of the Prussian State Library from 1927 until 1933, when he was ousted by the Nazi authorities as a Jew. In 1935 he went to Jerusalem, where he worked at the Hebrew Univ.

WRITINGS: *Musik des Orients* (Breslau, 1929); *Die Musik der aussereuropäischen Natur- und Kulturvölker,* in Bücken's Handbuch series (1929); *Jewish Cantillation and Song in the Isle of Djerba* (Jerusalem, 1940; contains a list of Lachmann's publications).

Lachmund, Carl Valentine, American pianist and teacher; b. Booneville, Mo., March 27, 1857; d. Yonkers, N.Y., Feb. 20, 1928. He studied at the Cologne Cons. with Hiller, and later with Liszt, of whom he was one of the last pupils (1881–84); taught at the Scharwenka Cons. in Berlin, and appeared as a pianist, touring America with August Wilhelmj in 1880. Settling in N.Y. in 1891, he established his own cons. He also founded the Women's String Orch., which he directed for 12 seasons.

Lachner, Franz, German composer and conductor, brother of **Ignaz** and **Vincenz Lachner;** b. Rain-am-Lech, April 2, 1803; d. Munich, Jan. 20, 1890. He studied with Sechter and Stadler in Vienna; became an intimate friend of Schubert; from 1827 to 1834 was conductor of the Kärntnertor Theater in Vienna; in 1834, became conductor of the Mannheim Opera; in 1836, court conductor in Munich, then Generalmusikdirektor (1852–65).

WORKS: 2 oratorios: *Moses* (1833) and *Die vier Menschenalter* (1829); 4 operas: *Die Bürgschaft* (Pest, Oct. 30, 1828); *Alidia* (Munich, April 12, 1839); *Catarina Cornaro* (Munich, Dec. 3, 1841); *Benvenuto Cellini* (Munich, Oct. 7, 1849); 8 symphs.; a Requiem; masses; choral works; much chamber music; piano pieces; songs.

BIBLIOGRAPHY: O. Kronseder, "Franz Lachner," *Altbayrische Monatsschrift,* 4 (contains a complete catalogue of works); M. von Schwind, *Die Lachner-Rolle* (Munich, 1904); A. Würz, *Franz Lachner als dramatischer Komponist* (Munich, 1927); G. Wagner, *Franz Lachner als Liederkomponist* (Giebing, 1970).

Lachner, Ignaz, German organist, conductor, and composer, brother of **Franz** and **Vincenz Lachner;** b. Rain-am-Lech, Sept. 11, 1807; d. Hannover, Feb. 24, 1895. He studied music with his father; in 1824 joined Franz in Vienna, where he became an assistant conductor at the Kärntnertor Theater (1825); in 1828 became assistant Kapellmeister at the Vienna Court Opera. In 1831 he went to Stuttgart as court music director; in 1842, occupied a similar post in Munich; became conductor at the theater in Hamburg (1853); in 1858, became court conductor in Stockholm; in 1861, settled in Frankfurt as a music director.

WORKS: 3 operas: *Der Geisterturm* (Stuttgart, 1837); *Die Regenbrüder* (Stuttgart, May 20, 1839); *Loreley* (Munich, 1846); several singspiels, among them the popular *Letzte Fensterle;* ballets; melodramas; symphs.; chamber music; masses; piano compositions; violin pieces; etc.

BIBLIOGRAPHY: H. Müller, *Ignaz Lachner: Versuch einer Würdigung, mit Werkverzeichnis* (Celle, 1974).

Lachner, Vincenz, German organist, conductor, and composer, brother of **Franz** and **Ignaz Lachner;** b. Rain-am-Lech, July 19, 1811; d. Karlsruhe, Jan. 22, 1893. He first studied with his father, and later in Vienna with his brothers, succeeding Ignaz as organist and Franz as conductor at the Kärnthnertor Theater there in 1834, and Franz as court Kapellmeister at Mannheim in 1836. He conducted the German opera in London in 1842, and the municipal opera in Frankfurt in 1848. In 1873 he received a pension and settled in Karlsruhe, joining the faculty of the Cons. there in 1884. His 4-part male choruses are celebrated, particularly his settings of nearly all of Scheffel's songs, among the best being *Alt Heidelberg, du feine; Im schwarzen Wallfisch; Nun grüss' dich Gott;* he also wrote symphs., overtures, string quartets, a Piano Quartet, and numerous songs.

Lachnith, Ludwig Wenzel, Bohemian composer; b. Prague, July 7, 1746; d. Paris, Oct. 3, 1820. He was a member of the court orch. in Pfalz-Zweibrücken; in 1773 went to Paris and studied with Rudolph (horn) and Philidor (composition). He is known chiefly for his pasticcios, works in which he combined the music of several different composers; an instance is his oratorio *Saul,* with music taken from scores by Mozart, Haydn, Cimarosa, Paisiello, Gossec, and Philidor. He also arranged the music of Mozart's *Zauberflöte,* to a libretto reworked by Etienne Morel de Chefdeville, and produced it under the title *Les Mystères d'Isis,* justly parodied as *Les Misères d'ici.* In several of his ventures he had the older Kalkbrenner as his collaborator. Original compositions by Lachnith include the operas *L'Heureuse Réconciliation* (1785), *L'Antiquaire* (1789), and *Eugénie et Linval* (1798); 3 piano concertos; chamber music.

Lack, Théodore, French pianist and composer; b. Quimper, Finistère, Sept. 3, 1846; d. Paris, Nov. 25, 1921. A precocious musician, Lack was appointed organist of his village church when he was only 10 years old. At 14 he entered the Paris Cons., where he studied piano with Marmontel, harmony with Bazin, and theory with Lefébure-Wély. Graduating from the Cons. at 18, he became a piano instructor there, and held this position for 57 years (1864–1921) until his death, without ever leaving Paris. He wrote a great many salon pieces for piano (*Taren-*

telle, Boléro, Etudes élégantes, Valse espagnole, Scènes enfantines, Souvenir d'Alsace, Polonaise de concert, etc.).

Lacombe, Louis (Trouillon), French pianist and composer; b. Bourges, Nov. 26, 1818; d. Saint-Vaast-la-Hougue, Sept. 30, 1884. He studied at the Paris Cons. with Zimmermann, winning the first piano prize at the age of 13. After touring through France, Belgium, and Germany, he took courses with Czerny, Sechter, and Seyfried in Vienna. Following another concert tour, he settled in Paris (1839), concentrating on composition.

WORKS: Melodrama, *L'Amour* (Paris, Dec. 2, 1859); one-act opera, *La Madone* (Paris, Jan. 16, 1861); 2-act comic opera, *Le Tonnelier* (produced as *Meister Martin und seine Gesellen* at Coblenz, March 7, 1897); 4-act grand opera, *Winkelried* (Geneva, Feb. 17, 1892); cantata, *Sapho* (1878; won a prize at the Paris Exhibition); grand *Epopée lyrique* for Orch.; 2 dramatic symphs. with Soli and Chorus: *Manfred* (1847) and *Arva ou Les Hongrois* (1850); *Lassan et Friss,* Hungarian fantasy for Orch.; *Au tombeau d'un héros,* elegy for Violin and Orch.; Quintet for Piano, Violin, Cello, Oboe, and Bassoon; 2 piano trios; numerous piano pieces (*Etudes en octaves; 6 romances sans paroles;* etc.); also choruses. His essay *Philosophie et musique* was publ. posthumously (Paris, 1895).

BIBLIOGRAPHY: E. Bourdin, *Louis Lacombe* (Paris, 1882); H. Boyer, *Louis Lacombe et son œuvre* (Paris, 1888); L. Gallet, *Conférence sur Louis Lacombe et son œuvre* (Paris, 1891); E. Jongleux, *Un Grand Musicien méconnu: Louis Lacombe* (Bourges, 1935).

Lacombe, Paul, French composer; b. Carcassonne, Aude, July 11, 1837; d. there, June 5, 1927. He studied in Carcassonne with François Teysserre, an organist. He was a prolific composer; his works total more than 150, including *Ouverture symphonique* (1876); 3 symphs. (No. 3 won the prize of the Société des Compositeurs de Musique, 1886); *Suite pastorale* for Orch.; *Marche dernière* for Orch.; *Scène au camp* for Orch.; *Dialogue sentimental* for Flute, Bassoon, and Piano (1917); 3 violin sonatas; Cello Sonata; 3 trios; String Quartet; Mass; Requiem; songs; characteristic piano pieces (*Aubade aux mariés, Arabesques,* etc.).

BIBLIOGRAPHY: Léon Moulin, *Paul Lacombe et son œuvre* (Paris, 1924).

Lacome, Paul (Paul-Jean-Jacques Lacome de l'Estalenx), French composer; b. Houga, Gers, March 4, 1838; d. there, Dec. 12, 1920. In 1860 he went to Paris; became known as a composer of operettas, including *Jeanne, Jeannette et Jeannot* (1876); *Le Beau Nicolas* (1880); *Madame Boniface* (1883); *Myrtille* (1885); *Ma mie Rosette* (1890); *Le Cadeau de noces* (1893); *La Bain de Monsieur* (1895); *Le Maréchal Chaudron* (1898); and *Les Quatre Filles Aymon* (1898); also the orch. suites *Clair de lune, Suite ancienne, La Verbena;* quartets; trios; Psalms; piano pieces (*Les Succès de fa-*

mille, etc.); over 200 songs (*L'Estudiantina,* etc.). He publ. *Introduction à la vie musicale* (1911).

Laderman, Ezra, American composer; b. New York, June 29, 1924. He studied at Brooklyn College and at Columbia Univ. with Otto Luening and Douglas Moore (composition) and Paul Henry Lang (musicology); received 3 Guggenheim grants. He taught at Sarah Lawrence College in 1960–61 and again in 1965–66; from 1971 taught at the State Univ. of N.Y. at Binghamton; in 1978 was appointed director of the music program of the National Endowment for the Arts. WORKS: Operas: *Jacob and the Indians* (Woodstock, N.Y., July 26, 1957); *Sarah,* television opera (N.Y., Nov. 30, 1958); *Goodbye to the Clown* (N.Y., May 22, 1960); *The Hunting of the Snark,* children's opera after Lewis Carroll (N.Y., March 25, 1961); *Galileo Galilei,* opera oratorio for television (N.Y., May 14, 1967); reworked into a stage opera, Binghamton, Feb. 4, 1979); *Magic Prison* for 2 Narrators and Orch. (N.Y., June 12, 1967); 4 symphs.: No. 1 (1945); No. 2 (1963–64); No. 3 (1968); No. 4 (1973); Concerto for Orch.; Violin Concerto; *Sonore* for Orch. (Denver, Nov. 10, 1983); *Celestial Bodies* for Flute and Strings; *Double Helix* for Flute, Oboe, and Strings; Nonet for Wind Instruments; Octet for Wind Instruments; 2 piano sonatas. He also wrote the score for the film *The Eleanor Roosevelt Story,* which won an Oscar. His cantata *And David Wept* was produced by CBS Television in N.Y. on April 10, 1971.

Ladmirault, Paul-Emile, French composer; b. Nantes, Dec. 8, 1877; d. Kerbili, near Penestin (Morbihan), Oct. 30, 1944. As a child, he studied piano, organ, and violin; entered the Nantes Cons. in 1892, winning first prize in 1893; he was only 15 when his 3-act opera *Gilles de Retz* was staged in Nantes (May 18, 1893); he entered the Paris Cons. in 1895, studying with Gédalge and Fauré; subsequently returned to Nantes, where he taught at the Cons. His *Suite bretonne* (1902–3) and symph. prelude *Brocéliande au matin* (Colonne concert, Nov. 28, 1909) were extracts from a 2nd opera, *Myrdhin* (1902–9), which was never performed; the ballet *La Prêtresse de Koridwen* was produced at the Paris Opéra (Dec. 17, 1926). Other works include the operetta *Glycère* (Paris, 1928); Symph. (1910); *La Brière* for Orch. (Paris, Nov. 20, 1926); *En forêt,* symph. poem (1932); incidental music to *Tristan et Iseult* (1929); *Valse triste* for Piano and Orch.; *Airs anciens* for Tenor, String Quartet, and Piano (1897); *Ballet bohémien* for Flute, Oboe, Double String Quartet, and Piano (1898); *Fantaisie* for Violin and Piano (1899); *Chanson grecque* for Flute and Piano (1900); Violin Sonata (1901); *De l'ombre à la clarté* for Violin and Piano (1936); piano pieces; songs; many arrangements of Breton folk songs. He contributed articles on music to various periodicals. BIBLIOGRAPHY: Claude Debussy, "Paul-Emile Ladmirault," in *Gil Blas* (March 9, 1903); Octave Séré, *Musiciens français d'aujourd'hui* (Paris, 1922).

Ladnier, Tommy (Thomas), black American jazz trumpeter; b. Mandeville, La., May 28, 1900; d. New York, June 4, 1939. He studied trumpet with "Bunk" Johnson; after working in Chicago with King Oliver, he played in Europe with Sam Wooding's band (1925–26), with Fletcher Henderson (1926–27), and again with Wooding in Europe (1928–29). He continued to make appearances in Europe until his return to the U.S. in 1931; then played with Sidney Bechet, and later led his own quintet.

Ladunka, Naum, Russian composer; b. Dec. 13, 1730; d. St. Petersburg, Aug. 2, 1782. One of the few secular Russian composers of the 18th century, he is chiefly known for his arrangements of many Russian folk songs.

Ladurner, Ignaz Anton Franz Xaver, Austrian composer; b. Aldein, Tyrol, Aug. 1, 1766; d. Massy, Seine-et-Oise, March 4, 1839. He studied at the monastery of Benediktbeuren, succeeding his father as organist there (1782–84); studied in Munich under the patronage of Countess Heimhausen. In 1788 he settled in Paris, teaching at the Cons. there; Auber was one of his students. He wrote 2 operas: *Wenzel, ou Le Magistrat du peuple* (Paris, 1794) and *Les Vieux Fous* (Paris, 1796); 12 piano sonatas; 6 violin sonatas; Sonata for Piano, 4-hands; variations; divertissements; etc.

La Fage, Juste-Adrien-Lenoir de, eminent French writer on music; b. Paris, March 28, 1801; d. Charenton, March 8, 1862. He studied in Paris with Perne and Choron, and in Rome with Baini. Returning to Paris, he devoted himself to scholarly analysis of music theory. He ended his life at the Charenton Insane Asylum. WRITINGS: *Manuel complet de musique vocale et instrumentale* (6 vols., 1836–38; elaborated from Choron's sketches and notes); *Séméiologie musicale,* elements of music after Choron's principles (1837; an epitome was also publ. in 1837 as *Principes élémentaires de musique*); *De la chanson considérée sous le rapport musical* (1840); *Histoire générale de la musique et de la danse* (2 vols., 1844; incomplete); *De l'unité tonique et de la fixation d'un diapason universel* (1859); *Essais de diphthérographie musicale,* a valuable collection of source material); many works on plainsong: *De la reproduction des livres de plain-chant romain* (1853); *Cours complet de plain-chant* (2 vols., 1855–56; an important manual); *Nouveau traité de plain-chant* (1859; a supplement to the former); *Routine pour accompagner le plain-chant;* etc. BIBLIOGRAPHY: R.D. Denne-Baron, *La Fage* (Paris, 1863).

L'Affilard, Michel, French composer; b. c.1656; d. 1708. He was a singer at the Sainte-Chapelle in 1679, and at the royal chapel (1696–1709). His major work is a book on sight singing, *Principes très faciles, pour bien apprendre la musique* (Paris, 1691; Amsterdam, 1717), which is notable because the tempo of the airs is indicated according to a pendulum,

thus anticipating the use of a metronome. Some of L'Affilard's MSS are in the Versailles Library.
BIBLIOGRAPHY: M. Brenet, *Les Musiciens de la Sainte-Chapelle du Palais* (Paris, 1910).

Lafont, Charles-Philippe, French violinist and composer; b. Paris, Dec. 1, 1781; d. Tarbes, Aug. 14, 1839. He received his first violin instruction from his mother; then studied in Paris with Kreutzer and Rode. In 1801–8 he toured Europe; then became Rode's successor at the Russian court in St. Petersburg (1808); returned to Paris in 1815 as solo violinist to Louis XVIII. He engaged in a violin-playing debate with Paganini in Milan (1816). During an extended tour with the pianist Henri Herz beginning in 1831, Lafont was killed in a carriage accident in southern France. He wrote 7 violin concertos; fantasias, variations, etc., for violin with various instrumental groups; about 200 *romances* for voice; and 2 comic operas.

La Forge, Frank, American pianist, vocal teacher, and composer; b. Rockford, Ill., Oct. 22, 1879; d. New York, May 5, 1953. He studied piano with Leschetizky in Vienna; toured Germany, France, Russia, and the U.S. as accompanist to Marcella Sembrich (1908–18) and to Schumann-Heink (1919). In 1920 he settled in N.Y. as a voice teacher; among his students were Lawrence Tibbett, Marian Anderson, Lucrezia Bori, and Richard Crooks. He died while playing the piano at a dinner given by the Musicians Club in N.Y. He wrote many effective songs (*To a Violet, Retreat, Come unto these yellow sands, My love and I, To a Messenger, I came with a song, Before the crucifix,* etc.) and piano pieces (*Gavotte and Musette, Valse de concert, Improvisations,* etc.).

Lagger, Peter, Swiss bass; b. Buchs, Sept. 7, 1930; d. Berlin, Sept. 17, 1979. He studied at the Zürich Cons. and at the Academy of Music in Vienna; made his debut in Graz in 1953; then sang at the Zürich Opera in 1955, in Wiesbaden (1957–59), and in Frankfurt (1959–63); from 1963 he was a leading member of the Berlin City Opera. He made appearances in Hamburg, Vienna, Paris, and Geneva, and also at the Salzburg, Aix-en-Provence, and Glyndebourne festivals. He won acclaim in lieder recitals as well.

Lagoanère, Oscar de, French composer; b. Bordeaux, Aug. 25, 1853; d. Paris, May 23, 1918. He studied at the Paris Cons. with Marmontel, Duprato, and Savard. In 1876–1908 he conducted operettas at various theaters in Paris; in 1908–14, was administrator and director of music at the Théâtre de la Gaîté. He was a prolific composer of operettas, the most successful of which were *Le Cadeau d'Alain* (Paris, Sept. 14, 1902); *L'Habit de César* (Paris, May 14, 1906); *Amour et sport* (Paris, July 28, 1907); *Un Ménage au violon;* also piano pieces and songs.

La Guerre, Elisabeth Jacquet de, French composer, organist, and clavecinist; b. Paris, 1659; d. there,

June 27, 1729. A member of a family of professional musicians, she evinced talent at an exceptionally early age; was favored by the court of Louis XIV, completing her education under the patronage of Mme. de Montespan. She married Marin de La Guerre, organist of several Paris churches. Her works include an opera, *Céphale et Procris* (Paris, March 15, 1694); a ballet (1691); keyboard suites; a Violin Sonata; cantatas, mostly sacred; etc.

La Guerre, Michel, French organist and composer; b. Paris, c.1605; d. there, Nov. 13, 1679. He was organist at Sainte-Chapelle from 1633 until his death. His historical importance rests upon his being the author of the first French opera, a "comédie de chansons," *Le Triomphe de l'amour sur bergers et bergères* (Paris, Louvre, Jan. 22, 1655), to a libretto by Charles de Beys, court poet. At least, this is the claim made for La Guerre by H. Quittard, in his article "La Première Comédie Française en musique" (*Bulletin Français de la Société Internationale de Musique,* April–May, 1908). The claim is disputed by Romain Rolland and others.

Lahee, Henry, English pianist and composer, father of **Henry Charles Lahee;** b. Chelsea, April 11, 1826; d. London, April 29, 1912. He studied with Sterndale Bennett, C. Potter (piano), and J. Goss (composition). He was organist at Holy Trinity Church, Brompton (1847–74); also a concert pianist; was a member of the Phil. Society. He wrote madrigals and glees: *Hark, how the birds* (1869); *Hence, loathed melancholy* (1878); *Away to the hunt* (1879); *Love in my Bosom* (1880); etc.

Lahee, Henry Charles, American writer on music, son of **Henry Lahee;** b. England, July 2, 1856; d. Hingham, Mass., April 11, 1953, as a result of injuries sustained in an automobile accident. He served in the British mercantile marine (1871–79); in 1880, settled in Boston; was secretary of the New England Cons. (1891–99); then established a musical agency (1899); retired in 1951.
WRITINGS: (all publ. in Boston): *Famous Singers of Today and Yesterday* (1898; new ed., 1936); *Famous Violinists of Today and Yesterday* (1899; 2nd ed., 1912); *Famous Pianists of Today and Yesterday* (1901); *Grand Opera in America* (1902); *The Organ and Its Masters* (1903; new revised ed., 1927); *The Grand Opera Singers of Today* (1922); *Annals of Music in America* (1922; very valuable; contains a chronology of performances of major works); *The Orchestra: A Brief Outline of Its Development in Europe and America* (1925).

La Hèle, George de, composer; b. Antwerp, 1547; d. Madrid, Aug. 27, 1586. After early training as a chorister, he was sent to Madrid to join the royal chapel of Philip II in 1560, remaining in Spain for 10 years. In 1571, he entered the Univ. of Louvain; in 1572, became choirmaster at the church of Saint-Rombaud in Malines, remaining there until 1574, when he accepted a similar post at the Tournai Cathedral; he returned to Madrid in 1582 to take charge of music in the royal chapel. In 1576 he won prizes in the competition at Evreux for his motet *Nonne Deo subjecta* and his chanson *Mais voyez mon cher esmoy.* His 8 masses (1577; printed by Plantin, Antwerp, 1578), are dedicated to Philip II, are all parody masses and are modeled on works by Josquin, Lassus, Rore, and Crecquillon; he also wrote other sacred works. A modern edition of his works was compiled by L. Wagner: *Collected Works of George de la Hèle,* in Corpus Mensurabilis Musicae, LVI (1972).

BIBLIOGRAPHY: G. van Doorslaer, *George de la Hèle, Maître de chapelle–compositeur* (Antwerp, 1924).

Lahire, Philippe de, French writer; b. Paris, March 18, 1640; d. there, April 21, 1719. He was a prof. of mathematics at the Univ. of Paris; wrote *Explications des différences des sons de la corde tendue sur la trompette marine* and *Expériences sur le son.*

Lahoussaye, Pierre, French violinist and composer; b. Paris, April 12, 1735; d. there, 1818. He studied with Pagin; later in Padua with Tartini. He played in the court orch. of Parma; in 1768 went to London with Guglielmi; returning to Paris, was appointed chef d'orchestre of the Concert Spirituel (1777–81); was conductor of the Comédie-Italienne (1781–90); then at the Théâtre de Monsieur (1790–1801); he also taught at the Paris Cons. He wrote a comic opera, *Les Amours de Courcy* (Paris, Aug. 22, 1790); of his compositions, 6 violin sonatas were publ.

Laidlaw, Anna Robena, English pianist; b. Bretton, Yorkshire, April 30, 1819; d. London, May 29, 1901. She studied in Edinburgh with Robert Müller, in Königsberg, and in London with Henry Herz. In 1837 she played with the Gewandhaus Orch. in Leipzig; continued her successful career as a concert pianist until her marriage in 1855. She was an acquaintance of Schumann, whose *Fantasiestücke* are inscribed to her.

Laine, Cleo, remarkably versatile English singer; b. Southall, Middlesex, Oct. 28, 1927. After local appearances as a singer, she joined the jazz orch. of **John Dankworth** as a vocalist in 1953; they were married in 1958. She made her first tour of the U.S. in 1972 with Dankworth; they later gave many concerts together in programs of extraordinary scope and interest. In 1979 she received the Order of the British Empire.

Laistner, Max, German musician; b. Stuttgart, Feb. 16, 1853; d. London, July 3, 1917. He settled in London, where he founded the first German Glee Club; wrote a number of choral works. His arrangement of Chopin's "Minute Waltz" is included in the anthology *13 Transcriptions of Chopin's Waltz in D-flat, Op. 64,* ed. by D.M. Garvelmann (N.Y., 1969).

Lajarte, Théodore-Edouard Dufaure de, French writer on music and composer; b. Bordeaux, July 10, 1826; d. Paris, June 20, 1890. He studied at the Paris Cons. with Leborne; was archivist of the Grand Opéra (1873–90). He is best known for his writings on music: *Bibliothèque musicale du Théâtre l'Opéra* (2 vols., 1876–78; reprint, Geneva, 1969); *Instruments Sax et fanfares civiles* (1867); *Traité de composition musicale* (with Bisson; 1880); *Grammaire de la musique* (1880); *Petite encyclopédie musicale* (1881–84); *Curiosités de l'Opéra* (1883); also publ. a collection of *Airs à danser de Lulli à Méhul;* and the series Chefs-d'œuvre Classiques de l'Opéra Français. Early in his career Lajarte wrote the operettas *Monsieur de Floridor* (Paris, Oct. 11, 1880); *Mamzelle Pénélope; Duel du Commandeur; Portrait; Roi de Carreau;* the ballet *Les Deux Jumeaux de Bergame* (Paris, Jan. 26, 1886); also marches and dances for military band.

Lajeunesse, Marie Louise Cecilia Emma. See **Albani, Emma.**

Lajtha, László, significant Hungarian composer; b. Budapest, June 30, 1892; d. there, Feb. 16, 1963. He studied piano with Arpád Szendy and theory with Victor von Herzfeld at the Budapest Academy of Music; traveled to Leipzig, Geneva, and Paris; returned to Budapest in 1913 to become an associate of the Ethnographical Dept. of the Hungarian National Museum. From 1919 to 1949 he was a prof. at the National Cons., and after 1952 was prof. of musical folklore at the Academy of Music in Budapest. In 1951 he was awarded the Kossuth Prize for his work on Hungarian folk music. He was a brilliant symphonist; his instrumental music is distinguished by consummate mastery of contrapuntal writing.

WORKS: 3 ballets: *Lysistrata* (1933; Budapest, Feb. 25, 1937); *Le Bosquet des quatre dieux* (1943); *Capriccio* (1944); 10 symphs.: No. 1 (1936); No. 2 (1938); *Les Soli,* symph. for String Orch., Harp, and Percussion (1941); No. 3 (1947–48); No. 4, *Le Printemps (The Spring;* 1951); No. 5 (1952; Paris, Oct. 23, 1954); No. 6 (1955; Brussels, Dec. 12, 1960); No. 7 (1957; Paris, April 26, 1958); No. 8 (1959; Budapest, May 21, 1960); No. 9 (1961; posthumous, Paris, May 2, 1963); *Hortobágy Suite* for Orch. (1935); 2 divertissements for Orch. (1936, 1939); *3 Nocturnes* for Chorus and Orch. (1941); *In Memoriam* for Orch. (1941); 2 sinfoniettas for String Orch. (1946, 1956); *11 Variations* for Orch. (1947); *Missa in tono phrygio* for Chorus and Orch. (1949–50); *Dramma per musica,* piano quintet (1922); 10 string quartets (1923; 1926; 1929; 1930; 1937; 1950; 1951; 1953; *Suite Transylvaine,* 1953); Piano Quartet (1925); 3 string trios (1927, 1932, 1945); Piano Trio (1928); Violin Sonatina (1930); Cello Sonata (1932); 2 trios for Harp, Flute, and Cello (1935, 1949); 2 quintets for Flute, Violin, Viola, Cello, and Harp (*Marionettes,* 1937; 1948); *Sonata en concert* for Cello and Piano (1940); *Sonata en concert* for Flute and Piano (1958); *Sonata en concert* for Violin and Piano (1962); *Des esquisses d'un musicien* for Piano (1913); *Contes I* for Piano (1913); Piano Sonata (1914); *Scherzo and Toccata* for Piano (1930); Mass for Chorus and Organ (1951–52).

Lake, George Ernest, English organist and composer; b. London, May 29, 1854; d. there, March 15, 1893. He served as a church organist in London and Edinburgh; wrote anthems and hymns; also a musical comedy, *Sweepstakes* (London, May 21, 1891).

Lakner, Yehoshua, Czech-born Israeli composer; b. Bratislava, April 24, 1924. He went to Palestine in 1941; studied there with Partos, Boscovich, and Pelleg in Haifa, Jerusalem, and Tel Aviv; in 1952 attended Copland's classes in composition at the Berkshire Music Center in Tanglewood; in 1959–60 was in West Germany, where he worked with Stockhausen and Kagel in the electronic studio of the West German Radio and with Bernd-Aloys Zimmermann in Cologne. He then moved to Zürich, where he wrote music for the municipal theater; in 1974 joined the faculty of the Zürich Cons. His music follows the tenets of the modern Central European school of Abstract Expressionism and its concomitant atonality, with an application of serial techniques.
WORKS: Flute Sonata (1948); Sextet for Piano and Woodwinds (1951); *Toccata* for Orch. (1953); *Improvisations* for Solo Viola (1958); *Hexachords* for Orch. (1960); *Kaninchen* for Speaker, Percussion, and Tape (1973); *Umläufe* for Flute, Bass Clarinet, Piano, and 2 Tapes (1976).

Laks, Simon, Polish composer; b. Warsaw, Nov. 1, 1901. He studied at the Warsaw Cons. with Melcer (conducting) and Statkowski (composition); went to Paris in 1925, continuing his musical studies under Rabaud and Vidal at the Paris Cons. In 1941 he was interned by the Nazis at the Auschwitz concentration camp, but he survived and returned to Paris in May 1945.
WORKS: Symph. poem, *Farys* (1924); *Symphonic Blues,* jazz fantasy (1928); *Suite polonaise* (1936); Sinfonietta for Strings (1936); *Suite on Silesian Tunes* for Small Orch. (1945); *Songs of the Polish Earth* for Orch. (1946); *3 Warsaw Polonaises* for Chamber Orch. (1947); 5 string quartets; Quintet for Flute, Oboe, Clarinet, Bassoon, and Horn; Piano Trio, etc. He publ. his reminiscences, *La Musique d'un autre monde* (Paris, 1948).

Lalande, Michel-Richard de. See **Delalande.**

La Laurencie, Lionel de, important French musicologist; b. Nantes, July 24, 1861; d. Paris, Nov. 21, 1933. After studying law and science, he became a pupil of Léon Reynier (violin) and Alphonse Weingartner (harmony), and of Bourgault-Ducoudray at the Paris Cons. In 1898 he became a lecturer at the Ecole des Hautes Etudes Sociales; he contributed regularly to several musical journals.
WRITINGS: *La Légende de Parsifal et le drame musical de R. Wagner* (1888–94); *España* (1890); *Le Goût musical en France* (1905); *L'Académie de musique et le concert de Nantes* (1906); "Rameau,"
in *Musiciens célèbres* (1908); "Lully," in *Les Maîtres de la Musique* (1911); "Contribution à l'histoire de la symphonie française vers 1750," *L'Année Musicale* (with G. de Saint-Foix; 1911); *Les Créateurs de l'opéra français* (1920; 2nd ed., 1930); *L'Ecole française de violon, de Lully à Viotti* (3 vols., 1922–24); *Les Luthistes,* in *Musiciens célèbres* (1928); *La Chanson royale en France* (1928); *Inventaire critique du fonds Blancheton à la Bibliothèque du Conservatoire* (2 vols., 1930–31); *Chansons au luth et airs du XVIe siècle* (with Thibault and Mairy; 1931); *Orfée de Gluck* (1934). In 1916 La Laurencie became editor of Lavignac's *Encyclopédie de la musique et dictionnaire du Conservatoire,* to which he contributed articles on French music of the 17th and 18th centuries. The *Catalogue des livres de musiciens de la bibliothèque de l'Arsénal à Paris,* ed. by La Laurencie and A. Gastoué, was publ. in 1936.
BIBLIOGRAPHY: *Mélanges de musicologie offerts à M. Lionel de la Laurencie* (Paris, 1933); B. Brook, "Lionel de la Laurencie's *L'Ecole francaise de violon,*" *Notes* (Sept. 1969).

Lalewicz, Georg, Russian pianist; b. Suwalki, Poland, Aug. 21, 1875; d. Buenos Aires, Dec. 1, 1951. He studied piano with Annette Essipov and composition with Liadov and Rimsky-Korsakov at the St. Petersburg Cons. Upon graduation, he taught piano at the Odessa Cons. (1902–5), the Cracow Cons. (1905–12), and the Vienna Imperial Academy (1912–19). In 1921 he went to Argentina, settling in Buenos Aires as a prof. at the Cons. Nacional; changed his name to **Jorge Lalewicz.** An international prize for piano performance was established in his memory in 1952.

Laliberté, Alfred (full Christian name, **Joseph François Alfred**), Canadian pianist and composer; b. St. Jean, Quebec, Feb. 10, 1882; d. Montreal, May 7, 1952. He studied in Berlin (1900–1905) with Lutzenko (piano) and Klatte (theory); later took lessons with Teresa Carreño. In 1906 he formed a friendship with Scriabin and became an ardent propagandist of his music. Laliberté wrote an opera, *Sœur Béatrice* (after Maeterlinck), 2 string quartets, several piano pieces (some on Canadian themes); also made arrangements of some 800 Canadian songs. Most of his music remains in MS; a few original songs have been publ.

Lalo, Charles, French writer on musical matters; b. Périgueux, Feb. 24, 1877; d. Paris, April 1, 1953. He studied philosophy in Bayonne and Paris.
WRITINGS: *L'Esthétique expérimentelle contemporaine* (1908); *Esquisse d'une esthétique musicale scientifique* (1908; 2nd ed., 1939, as *Eléments d'une esthétique*); *Les Sentiments esthétiques* (1909); *Introduction à l'esthétique* (1912); *L'Art et la vie sociale* (1921).

Lalo, Edouard (-Victoire-Antoine), distinguished French composer (of Spanish descent); b. Lille, Jan. 27, 1823; d. Paris, April 22, 1892. He studied with Baumann at the Lille branch of the Paris

Cons.; then at the Paris Cons. with Habeneck (violin) and Schulhoff and Crèvecœur (composition); he played with equal skill on the violin and viola, and was violist of the Armingaud-Jacquard Quartet, a group organized in Paris for the purpose of spreading the works of the German masters. In 1848–49 he publ. his first songs (*L'Adieu au désert, L'Ombre de Dieu, Le Novice, 6 Romances populaires de Béranger*) and subsequently some chamber music. All of this music met with indifference, and Lalo was discouraged to the point of abandoning composition for several years; his ambition, however, was stimulated again by his marriage (in 1865) to **Mlle. Bernier de Maligny,** a fine contralto singer, who performed many of his songs. He wrote a 3-act opera, *Fiesque,* and sent the score to the competition established in 1867 by the Théâtre-Lyrique; it was ranked 3rd, and failed to reach production; the ballet music from it was performed under the title *Divertissement* at the Concert Populaire (Dec. 8, 1872), with excellent success. His next signal success was the performance of his Violin Concerto, played by Sarasate (Jan. 18, 1874) at a Châtelet concert; then came his most famous work, *Symphonie espagnole,* also performed by Sarasate (Feb. 7, 1875). This work, a true virtuoso piece with vibrant Spanish rhythms, became one of the greatest favorites in the violin repertoire, and secured for Lalo international fame. His *Fantaisie norvégienne* for Violin and Orch. followed; it was subsequently rearranged for orch. alone, and performed as *Rapsodie norvégienne* (Colonne Concerts, Oct. 26, 1879). He had not, however, abandoned his efforts at writing for the stage. As early as 1875 he began work on the opera *Le Roi d'Ys;* after several revisions, the work was produced at the Opéra-Comique (May 7, 1888), obtaining enormous success; repeated performances followed, in France and elsewhere in Europe; the American premiere took place at New Orleans, Jan. 23, 1890. In 1888 Lalo was made an officer of the Legion of Honor; also was awarded the Prix Monbinne by the Académie des Beaux-Arts. Besides the works already mentioned, there were the following: one act from an unfinished opera, *La Jacquerie* (completed by Artur Coquard; posthumously produced in Monte Carlo, March 9, 1895); ballets: *Namouna* (Paris, March 6, 1882) and *Néron* (Paris, March 28, 1891); 3 symphs., 2 of them unpubl.; Cello Concerto (Paris, Dec. 9, 1877); Piano Concerto (1889); 3 piano trios; String Quartet; Violin Sonata; 4 impromptus for Violin and Piano; *Soirées parisiennes* for Violin and Piano; *Guitare* for Violin and Piano; Cello Sonata; songs.

BIBLIOGRAPHY: M. Dufour, *Edouard Lalo* (Lille, 1908); centennial issue of the *Revue Musicale,* with articles by Paul Dukas, Adolphe Jullien, and Pierre Lalo (May 1923); J. Tiersot, "Edouard Lalo," *Musical Quarterly* (Jan. 1925); G. Servières, *Lalo* (Paris, 1925).

Lalo, Pierre, French critic, son of **Edouard Lalo;** b. Puteaux, Seine, Sept. 6, 1866; d. Paris, June 9, 1943. He became music critic of *Le Temps* in Oct. 1898; publ. *La Musique,* a selection of his articles (Paris,

1898–99); *De Rameau à Ravel: Portraits et souvenirs* (Paris, 1947; posthumous).

Laloy, Louis, French musicologist and critic; b. Grey, Haute-Saône, Feb. 18, 1874; d. Dôle, March 3, 1944. He studied philosophy in Paris, receiving the degree of docteur ès lettres in 1904; in 1899–1905, was also a pupil of Breéille and d'Indy at the Schola Cantorum. He was co-founder (1901) of the *Revue d'Histoire et de Critique Musicale;* in 1905 he founded, with J. Marnold, the *Mercure Musical;* contributed articles to *Revue de Paris, Grande Revue, Mercure de France,* and *Gazette des Beaux-Arts.* He publ. *Aristoxène de Tarente et la musique de l'antiquité* (1904); *Rameau* (1908); *Debussy* (1909; new ed., 1944); *Notes sur la musique cambodgienne* (in the *Bericht über den zweiten Kongress* of the Internationale Musik-Gesellschaft at Basel, 1906; publ. in Leipzig, 1907); *La Musique chinoise* (1910); *The Future of Music* (London, 1910); "L'Opéra," in *Cinquante ans de musique française, 1874–1923* (1924); *La Musique retrouvée, 1902–27* (1928); *Une Heure de musique avec Beethoven* (1930). He also provided the poem for Roussel's opera-ballet *Padmâvati* and for Debussy's *Ode à la France;* publ. a vol. of transcriptions of Chinese compositions; and supplied the French versions of a number of Russian opera librettos.

La Mara. See **Lipsius, Marie.**

LaMarchina, Robert, American cellist and conductor; b. New York, Sept. 3, 1928. He studied cello with his father; appeared as a *wunderkind* in public; continued his studies with Gregor Piatigorsky and Emanuel Feuermann; in 1944 played in the NBC Symph. under Toscanini; later joined the Los Angeles Phil.; sporadically conducted orchs. near and around Los Angeles; ultimately became primarily a conductor. From 1967 to 1979 he conducted the Honolulu Symph. Orch.

La Marre (Lamare), Jacques-Michel-Hurel de, French cellist; b. Paris, May 1, 1772; d. Caen, March 27, 1823. He toured Europe, including Russia, with great success; Clementi called him "the Rode of the violoncello." Four cello concertos and an *air varié* publ. under La Marre's name are actually by Auber.

Lambardi, Camillo, Italian tenor and composer; b. Naples, c.1560; d. there, Nov. 1634. He sang at the Santa Casa dell'Annunziata at Naples; studied there with Gian Domenico da Nola, whom he succeeded as a maestro di cappella in 1592; retired in 1631. He publ. music for Holy Week for 2 choirs (1592); 2 books of madrigals; etc.

Lambardi (Lombarodo), Francesco, Italian tenor, organist, and composer, son of **Camillo Lambardi;** b. Naples, 1587; d. there, July 25, 1642. As a youth he was a "sopranello" in the Santa Casa dell'Annunziata at Naples; later was tenor there; then organist of the royal chapel; was first organist there (1615–

36). He publ. 3 sets of *villanelle* for 3–5 Voices (Naples, 1607, 1614, 1616).

Lambelet, George, Greek composer and musicologist; b. Corfu, Dec. 24, 1875; d. Athens, Oct. 30, 1945. Both his father and his older brother were musicians. He studied in Naples; returned to Greece in 1901; co-edited *Critique* with Axiotis, and *Musical Chronicles* with J. Papadopoulos; publ. a number of studies on Greek folk music, including *Nationalism in Art and Greek Folk Music* (Athens, 1928). He is noted for *La Musique populaire grecque* (Athens, 1934), a collection of 60 Greek folk songs and dances, together with harmonizations and a critical study. Lambelet's musical compositions have a strong national flavor. He wrote choral works: *The Hymn to Peace; Balkan Hymn; Hymn to Greece;* etc.; *The Feast,* symph. poem; *Elegy* for Orch.; *Dirge* for Orch.; songs.

Lambert, Alexander, Polish-American pianist, composer, and teacher; b. Warsaw, Nov. 1, 1862; d. New York, Dec. 31, 1929. He studied piano with his father and with Julius Epstein at the Vienna Cons.; also worked with Liszt at Weimar for a brief period. He went to N.Y. in 1880; was director of the N.Y. College of Music (1887–1905); taught piano privately. He publ. a number of effective piano pieces (*Etude and Bourrée, Tarantella, Mazurka, Valse-Impromptu, Canzonetta,* etc.), and a valuable piano method, *A Systematic Course of Studies* (3 vols., 1907); also a brief *Piano Method for Beginners.*

Lambert, Constant, English composer, conductor, and writer on music; b. London, Aug. 23, 1905; d. there, Aug. 21, 1951. He was a member of an artistic family; studied at the Royal College of Music with R.O. Morris and Vaughan Williams. While he was still a student, Diaghilev commissioned a ballet from him (*Romeo and Juliet;* Monte Carlo, May 4, 1926). This early association with the dance proved decisive, for Lambert spent most of his life as a composer and conductor of ballets. His compositions are notable for the assimilation of a jazz idiom: in his *Elegiac Blues* (1927), in his very successful *Rio Grande* (on a poem of Sacheverell Sitwell) for Solo Piano, Chorus, and Orch. (Manchester, Dec. 12, 1929), and in his Piano Sonata (1928–29) and Piano Concerto with Small Orch. (1931). He wrote the ballets *Pomona* (Buenos Aires, Sept. 9, 1927) and *Horoscope* (London, Jan. 27, 1938); *The Bird Actors,* overture for Orch. (1925); *Summer's Last Will and Testament,* masque for Chorus and Orch. (after Thomas Nashe; London, Jan. 29, 1936); *King Pest* for Orch. (London, 1937); *Aubade héroïque* for Orch. (1942); *Prizefight* for Band (1923); *8 Chinese Songs* (on poems by Li-Po). Lambert also transcribed and edited works by Boyce, Handel, Roseingrave, etc.; rescored Vaughan Williams's *Job* for theater orch. (1931). He was music critic of the *Sunday Referee,* and publ. a provocative book, *Music Ho! A Study of Music in Decline* (London, 1934).
BIBLIOGRAPHY: R.J. McGrady, "The Music of

Constant Lambert," *Music & Letters* (July 1970); C. Palmer, "Constant Lambert—A Postscript," ibid. (April 1971).

Lambert, Herbert, English clavichord and harpsichord maker; b. Bath, Dec. 22, 1881; d. there, March 7, 1936. Originally a professional photographer, he turned his craftsmanship and research activity to the building of old keyboard instruments, especially clavichords. His name is perpetuated in *Lambert's Clavichord* (1928), a small book of compositions for this instrument by Herbert Howells.

Lambert, Johann Heinrich, German music theorist; b. Mühlhausen, Aug. 29, 1728; d. Berlin, Sept. 25, 1777. A member of the Berlin Academy, he wrote *Sur quelques instruments acoustiques* (1763; German ed., 1796); *Sur la vitesse du son* (1768); *Remarques sur le tempérament en musique* (1774; German trans. in Marpurg's *Historisch-kritische Beiträge,* vol. 5); and *Observations sur les sons des flûtes* (1775); all of the above are printed in the reports of the Berlin Academy.

Lambert, Juan Bautista, Catalan composer; b. Barcelona, 1884; d. there, May 4, 1945. He studied with Morera; was active in Barcelona as an organist and a conductor. He composed a successful light opera, *La alborada;* a symph. poem, *Vallencis;* also wrote numerous choral works, marches, and songs.

Lambert, Lucien, French composer and pianist; b. Paris, Jan. 5, 1858; d. Oporto, Portugal, Jan. 21, 1945. He studied first with his father; after a tour of America and Europe, returned to Paris to study at the Cons. with Dubois and Massenet, taking the Prix Rossini in 1885 with his cantata *Prométhée enchaîné.* He settled in Portugal in 1914; was a prof. of composition at the Oporto Cons. (1922–37).
WORKS: Operas: *Brocéliande* (Rouen, Feb. 25, 1893); *Le Spahi* (Paris, Oct. 18, 1897); *La Marseillaise* (Paris, July 14, 1900); *La Flamenca* (Paris, Oct. 31, 1903); *Harald* (1937); *Penticosa; La Sorcière;* ballets: *La Roussalka* (Paris, Dec. 8, 1911) and *Les Cloches de Porto* (1937); *Florette,* lyric comedy (1921); *Légende roumaine,* symph. poem; *Fantaisie monothématique* for Orch., on an oriental theme (Paris, March 19, 1933); *Tanger le soir,* Moorish rhapsody for Orch.; *Esquisses créoles,* orch. suite, on themes by Gottschalk; *Andante et fantaisie tzigane* for Piano and Orch.; String Quartet; String Sextet; Mass; piano pieces; songs.

Lambert, Michel, French lutenist and singer; b. Champigny-sur-Veude, near Chinon (Indre-et-Loire), 1610; d. Paris, June 29, 1696. He was master of chamber music at the court of Louis XIV; also a celebrated singing teacher. His daughter married Lully. He publ. *Airs et brunettes* (1666; 2nd ed., 1689) and *Airs et dialogues* (1698; posthumous).

Lambeth, Henry Albert, British organist, conductor, and composer; b. Hardway, near Gosport, Jan.

16, 1822; d. Glasgow, June 27, 1895. He studied with Thomas Adams; went to Glasgow about 1853 as city organist; was conductor of the Glasgow Choral Union (1859–80); harmonized Scottish melodies; wrote several songs and piano pieces; with D. Baptie, edited the *Scottish Book of Praise* (1876).

Lambillotte, Louis, French writer and church composer; b. Charleroi, Hainault, March 27, 1796; d. Vaugirard, Feb. 27, 1855. He was an organist at Charleroi, then at Dinant; in 1822, became maître de chapelle at the Jesuit Seminary at St.-Acheul, joining the order in 1825; subsequently settled in Vaugirard.
WORKS: 4 masses, one in the Lydian mode; other sacred music; organ pieces; fugues; etc.
WRITINGS: *Antiphonaire de Saint-Grégoire, Facsimile du manuscrit de Saint-Gall* (1851); *Clef des mélodies grégoriennes* (1851); *Quelques mots sur la restauration du chant liturgique* (1855); *Esthétique, théorie et pratique du chant grégorien* (1855); other essays.
BIBLIOGRAPHY: J. Dufour, *Mémoire sur les chants liturgiques restaurés par Lambillotte* (Paris, 1857); T. Nisard, *Le Père Lambillotte et Dom A. Schubiger* (Paris, 1857); M. de Monter, *Lambillotte et ses frères* (Paris, 1871).

Lambord, Benjamin, American organist and composer; b. Portland, Maine, June 10, 1879; d. Lake Hopatcong, N.J., June 6, 1915. He studied in Boston with A. Whiting, at Columbia Univ. with MacDowell, and in Paris with Vidal. He was organist and choirmaster in various churches in N.Y.; organized the Lambord Choral Society and the Modern Music Society. He wrote *Introduction and Variations on an English Dance Theme* for Orch.; *Clytie* for Soprano and Orch.; *Verses from Omar Khayyam* for Mixed Chorus and Orch.; *10 Lyric Studies for Piano;* piano pieces; part songs; songs.

Lamm, Pavel, Russian musicologist; b. Moscow, July 27, 1882; d. Nicolina Gora, near Moscow, May 5, 1951. He studied piano at the Moscow Cons.; toured Europe as accompanist of the singer Olenine d'Alheim; then was on the editorial board of the Russian State Publishing Dept. He edited the vocal score of Mussorgsky's original version of *Boris Godunov* (Moscow, 1928); was editor in chief for Mussorgsky's complete works in the aborted edition begun in 1928.

Lammers, Gerda, German soprano; b. Berlin, Sept. 25, 1915. She studied at the Hochschule für Musik in Berlin; then began her career as a concert singer. In 1955 she sang at Bayreuth; in 1957 appeared at Covent Garden in London. On March 16, 1962, she made her American debut at the Metropolitan Opera in N.Y. as Elektra in the opera of Richard Strauss.

Lammers, Julius, German composer; b. Leipzig, April 20, 1829; d. there, Sept. 20, 1888. He taught at the Leipzig Cons.; composed numerous songs and

some piano pieces.

Lamond, Frederic Archibald, Scottish pianist; b. Glasgow, Jan. 28, 1868; d. Stirling, Feb. 21, 1948. He played organ as a boy in a local church; also studied oboe and violin; in 1882, entered the Raff Cons. in Frankfurt, studying with Heermann (violin), Max Schwarz (piano), and Urspruch (composition); then piano with Hans von Bülow, Clara Schumann, and Liszt. A brilliant concert pianist, Lamond appeared in Berlin, Vienna, London, N.Y., and in Russia. He became renowned for his skillful interpretation of Beethoven; publ. an edition of Beethoven's sonatas (1923). He married Irene Triesch, a German actress, in 1904 and settled in Berlin, until the outbreak of World War II, when he moved to London. He was also a composer; wrote a Symph. (Glasgow, Dec. 23, 1889), some chamber music, and numerous piano pieces. He publ. an interesting vol. of reminiscences about Liszt and others, entitled *Memoirs* (Glasgow, 1949).

La Montaine, John, American composer; b. Oak Park, Ill., March 17, 1920. He studied piano in Chicago with Rudolph Ganz, and in Rochester at the Eastman School of Music, with Howard Hanson and Bernard Rogers; at the Juilliard School in N.Y. with Bernard Wagenaar; and with Nadia Boulanger. He received 2 Guggenheim fellowships in composition (1959, 1960); in 1962 served as composer-in-residence at the American Academy in Rome; was a visiting prof. at the Eastman School of Music in 1964–65. He received the Pulitzer Prize for his Piano Concerto in 1959. In 1977 he became holder of the Nixon Chair as a Nixon Distinguished Scholar at Nixon's alma mater, Whittier College, in California.
WORKS: Piano Concerto (Washington, D.C., Nov. 25, 1958); *Jubilant Overture; Colloquy* for String Orch.; Symph. No. 1; *From Sea to Shining Sea* for Orch.; *Novellis, Novellis,* Christmas pageant opera (Washington Cathedral, Dec. 24, 1961); *The Shepherdes Playe,* opera television production (Washington, Dec. 24, 1967); *Erode the Great,* cantata (Washington, Dec. 30, 1969); *Be Glad, Then, America,* Bicentennial opera (Univ. Park, Pa., Feb. 6, 1976); *Birds of Paradise* for Piano and Orch.; Te Deum; *Songs of the Rose of Sharon* for Soprano and Orch.; Cello Sonata; String Quartet; Flute Concerto (1981); organ pieces; songs.

Lamote de Grignon, Juan, Catalan conductor and composer; b. Barcelona, July 7, 1872; d. there, March 11, 1949. He studied at the Cons. of Barcelona, and upon graduation, taught piano there; made his debut as a conductor in Barcelona (April 26, 1902). In 1910 he founded the Orquesta Sinfónica de Barcelona, which carried on its activity until 1924; also led the municipal band (from 1914).
WORKS: One-act opera, *Hesperia* (Barcelona, Jan. 25, 1907); for Orch.: *Andalucía; Hispanicas; Scherzo; Cantos populares españoles; Poema romántico;* oratorio, *La Nit de Nadal;* numerous songs: *12 chansons catalanes; Violetas; 3 motetes; 3*

cantos espirituales; Passioneras; etc. He publ. *Musique et musiciens français à Barcelona, catalans à Paris* (Barcelona, 1935).

Lamote de Grignon, Ricard, Catalan cellist, conductor, and composer, son of **Juan Lamote de Grignon;** b. Barcelona, Sept. 23, 1899; d. there, Feb. 5, 1962. He studied cello and composition at the Barcelona Cons.; played cello in the Orquesta Sinfónica, conducted by his father; then conducted provincial orchs.; became assistant conductor of the municipal band of Barcelona.
WORKS: Opera, *La caperucita verde;* children's opera, *La flor;* symph. poem, *Boires; Tríptico de Rabindranath Tagore* for Soprano and Orch.; Piano Trio; songs. On April 19, 1936, he conducted, at the Barcelona Festival of the International Society for Contemporary Music, his symph. legend *Joan de Os;* his *Enigmas* for Orch. received the municipal prize of Barcelona in 1951. He publ. a manual, *Síntesis de técnica musical* (Barcelona, 1948).

Lamothe, Georges, French composer; b. 1837; d. Courbevoie, Oct. 15, 1894. He was a very prolific composer of dance music; wrote more than 1,000 opus numbers.

Lamoureux, Charles, noted French conductor and violinist; b. Bordeaux, Sept. 28, 1834; d. Paris, Dec. 21, 1899. He studied at the Paris Cons. with Girard (violin), taking first prize in 1854; also studied with Tolbecque (harmony), Leborne (counterpoint), and Alexis Chauvet (theory). In 1850 he became solo violinist in the Théâtre du Gymnase orch.; then became a member of the Paris Opéra orch. In 1860 he and Colonne, Adam, and A. Pilet founded a society for chamber music; in 1873, he organized the Société de l'Harmonie Sacrée; he became known as conductor of the Cons. Concerts (1872–73); was conductor of the Paris Opéra (1877–79). He founded the celebrated Concerts Lamoureux (Nouveaux Concerts) on Oct. 23, 1881; retired as its conductor in 1897, and was succeeded by his son-in-law, Chevillard. More than any other French musician, Lamoureux educated Parisians to appreciate Wagner; he was responsible not only for highly competent performances of classical masterpieces, but also for presentation of compositions of his contemporaries.
BIBLIOGRAPHY: Romain Rolland, *Musiciens d'aujourd'hui* (Paris, 1914; pp. 234ff.).

Lampe, Walther, German pianist, composer and pedagogue; b. Leipzig, April 28, 1872; d. Munich, Jan. 23, 1964. He studied piano with Clara Schumann; composition with Knorr in Frankfurt and with Humperdinck in Berlin; was a prof. of piano at the Munich Academy of Music from 1920 to 1937. His edition of Mozart piano sonatas (2 vols., Munich, 1954), based on the original MSS, is valuable. Among his works are piano pieces and songs.

Lamperti, Francesco, Italian singing teacher; b. Savona, March 11, 1811; d. Cernobbio, May 1, 1892. He studied at the Milan Cons.; was director at the Teatro Filodrammatico in Lodi; tutored many distinguished singers, including Albani, Mme. Artôt, both Cruvelis, Campanini, Collini, and Mme. Lagrange; taught at the Milan Cons. (1850–75). He publ. *Guida teorico-pratico-elementare per lo studi del canto; Studi di bravura per soprano; Esercizi giornalieri per soprano o mezzo-soprano; L'arte del canto; Osservazioni e consigli sul trillo; Solfeggi;* etc. His methods and studies in voice production have also appeared in Eng. trans.: *Studies in Bravura Singing for the Soprano Voice* (N.Y., 1875); *A Treatise on the Art of Singing* (London, 1877; revised ed., N.Y., 1890).

Lamperti, Giovanni Battista, Italian singing teacher, son of **Francesco Lamperti;** b. Milan, June 24, 1839; d. Berlin, March 18, 1910. At the age of 9 he was a choirboy at the Milan Cathedral; studied piano and voice at the Milan Cons.; served as accompanist in his father's class there. He taught first in Milan; subsequently in Dresden for 20 years; then in Berlin. Among his pupils were Sembrich, Schumann-Heink, Bulss, Stagno, etc. He publ. *Die Technik des Bel Canto* (1905; Eng. trans. by T. Baker; N.Y., 1905); *Scuola di canto* (8 vols. of solfeggi and vocalises); other technical exercises. His pupil W.E. Brown publ. *Vocal Wisdom; Maxims of G.B. Lamperti* (N.Y., 1931; new ed., 1957).

Lampugnani, Giovanni Battista, Italian teacher and composer; b. Milan, 1706; d. after 1784. In 1743 he became conductor of the Italian Opera in London; later was maestro al cembalo at La Scala in Milan. Over the period of 1732–69, he wrote 32 operas in the style of Hasse, which were presented in London, Venice, and Milan; publ. some trio sonatas; also wrote symphs. and concertos.

Lancen, Serge Jean Mathieu, French composer and pianist; b. Paris, Nov. 5, 1922. He studied at the Paris Cons. with Aubin, Büsser, and Noël Gallon. During World War II he went to Switzerland; returning to Paris, he continued his studies; obtained the Premier Prix de Rome for composition in 1949.
WORKS: *La Mauvaise Conscience,* chamber opera (Paris, Jan. 4, 1964); *Les Prix,* ballet (Bordeaux, March 13, 1954); Piano Concerto (1947); Concerto for Mouth Harmonica, written for Larry Adler (1955); Concerto for Double Bass and Orch. (1960); *Manhattan Symphony* (1962); *Concert à 6* for 6 Clarinets (1962); light pieces for radio: *Cadence, Promenade, Bahamas, Brazilia, En route for Monte-Carlo, Suite Gastronomique, Futilités;* also *Marche triomphale,* commissioned by the convention of the League against Rheumatism (Amsterdam, June 15, 1955).

Lanchbery, John, English conductor; b. London, May 15, 1923. He studied at the Royal Academy of Music in London; was then music director of the Metropolitan Ballet (1948–50) and the Sadler's Wells Theatre Ballet (1951–60); subsequently occupied a similar post with the Royal Ballet at Covent Garden (1960–72). In 1972 he was named music director of the Australian Ballet.

de Lancie, John, American oboist; b. Berkeley, Calif., July 26, 1921. He was educated at the Curtis Inst. of Music, Philadelphia (1936–40), where he studied oboe with Marcel Tabuteau; played oboe in the Pittsburgh Symph. (1940–42); then served in the U.S. Army. He persuaded Richard Strauss to write an oboe concerto. In 1946 de Lancie joined the Philadelphia Orch. as oboist; in 1954 he succeeded Tabuteau as principal oboist, a post he held until 1974; also taught at the Curtis Inst. (1954–74). In 1977 he became its director. He commissioned and gave the first performances of Jean Françaix's *L'Horloge de Flore* and of the Oboe Concerto by Benjamin Lees.

Land, Jan Pieter Nicholaas, Dutch orientalist and musicologist; b. Delft, April 23, 1834; d. Arnhem, April 30, 1897. In 1864 he was prof. of classical and oriental languages and of philosophy at the Amsterdam Academy; then was prof. of philosophy at Leyden Univ. (1872–94). He was an accomplished linguist, specializing in Semitic philology; was deeply interested in musico-historical research, to which he made most valuable contributions.
WRITINGS: *Noord Nederlands muziekgeschiedenis* (1874–81); *Over de toonladders der arabische muziek* (1880); *Musique et musiciens au XVIIe siècle. Correspondance et œuvres musicales de Constantijn Huygens* (with Jonckbloet; Leyden, 1882); *Recherches sur l'histoire de la gamme arabe* (Leyden, 1884); *Essai de notation musicale chez les arabes et les persans* (1885); *Over onze kennis der javaansche muziek* (Amsterdam, 1891).

Landau, Siegfried, German-American conductor and composer; b. Berlin, Sept. 4, 1921. He studied at the Stern Cons. in Berlin and also at the Klindworth-Scharwenka Cons. Early in 1939 he went to England, where he continued his studies at Trinity College; in November 1940 he arrived in the U.S., where he studied conducting with Pierre Monteux. In 1955 he organized the Brooklyn Philharmonia, which he conducted until 1971; concurrently conducted performances of the Chattanooga Opera Co. (1960–73).
WORKS: *Chassidic Suite* for Viola and Piano (1941); *Longing for Jerusalem* for Soprano and Orch. (1941); ballet, *The Golem* (1946); *The Sons of Aaron,* opera (Scarsdale, N.Y., Feb. 28, 1959); etc.

Landi, Stefano, Italian singer and composer; b. Rome, c.1586; d. there, Oct. 28, 1639. He studied at the Collegio Germanico in Rome; attended the Seminario Romano from 1602 to 1607. In 1618–20 he was maestro di cappella to Bishop Cornaro of Padua; returned to Rome in 1620, and was appointed to a similar post at Santa Maria dei Monti (1624); in 1629, became contralto singer at the Cappella Giulia, St. Peter's. He was one of the most eminent contrapuntists of the Roman school; was a pupil of the 2 Naninis; was one of the creators of the can-

tata, and one of the earliest operatic composers in Rome.
WORKS: *La morte d'Orfeo,* pastoral opera (Venice, 1619); *Il Sant' Alessio,* sacred opera (Rome, Feb. 23, 1632); also *Missa in benedictione nuptiarum* for 6 Voices (1628); a book of masses a cappella for 4–5 Voices; madrigals for 4–5 Voices (1619 and 1624); arias for one to 2 Voices (5 vols., 1620–38); etc.

Landini, Benedetto, Italian organist and composer; b. Calenzano, Jan. 31, 1858; d. Florence, July 11, 1938. He studied at the Florence Cons., graduating in 1886; became a teacher of organ there in 1888; also, for many years, was organist of the Church of Santissima Annunziata in Florence, and choirmaster at San Lorenzo and Santa Trinità; from 1891, was active in church music reforms in Tuscany. He wrote a Mass, a Requiem, *De profundis, Hymnus,* Psalms, and other sacred works; also a children's opera, *L'Arancia di Codino* (1913); edited works of Frescobaldi, Marco da Gagliano, and Corteccia, and numerous old Tuscan folk songs.

Landini (Landino), Francesco, Italian instrumentalist and composer; b. Fiesole, 1325; d. Florence, Sept. 2, 1397. Blinded by smallpox as a youth, he turned early to music, becoming proficient in the art of playing the lute, guitar, flute, and organ. He was one of the most celebrated organ virtuosos of his time; was known as "Francesco degli organi." He studied with Giovanni da Cascia and Jacopo da Bologna; was organist at the monastery of Santa Trinità in 1361; from 1365 until his death was "cappellanus" at the church of San Lorenzo in Florence. Although not the first, he was probably the most famous master of the Florentine "Ars nova" of the 14th century; his works, of which more than 150 are preserved in the libraries of Italy and southern Germany, represent about a quarter of extant Italian 14th-century music; he wrote madrigals, *cacce, ballate,* etc. Modern reprints: *The Works of Francesco Landini,* ed. by L. Ellinwood (Medieval Academy of America Publication 36; Cambridge, Mass., 1939); *The Works of Francesco Landini,* ed. by L. Schrade (Polyphonic Music of the 14th Century, vol. 4; Monaco, 1958).
BIBLIOGRAPHY: F. Villani, *Liber de civitatis Florentiae famosis civibus* (written c.1400; ed. by C. Galletti, 1874); F. Ludwig, "Die mehrstimmige Musik des 14. Jahrhunderts," *Sammelbände der Internationalen Musik-Gesellschaft* (1902); J. Wolf, *Geschichte der Mensuralnotation* (3 vols., 1904); idem, *Florenz in der Musikgeschichte des 14. Jahrhunderts, Sammelbände der Internationalen Musik-Gesellschaft,* 3; F. Ludwig in Adler's *Handbuch* (vol. 1); idem in *Zeitschrift für Musikwissenschaft,* 5; G. Carducci in *Opere,* 8; H. Riemann in *Handbuch der Musikgeschichte* (vol. 2); idem, "Das Kunstlied im 14.–15. Jahrhundert," *Sammelbände der Internationalen Musik-Gesellschaft,* 7; A. Schering, "Das Kolorierte Orgelmadrigal des Trecento," *Sammelbände der Internationalen Musik-Gesellschaft,* 13; A. Schering, *Studien zur Musikgeschichte der Frührenaissance* (1914); M. Schneider,

Die Ars nova des 14. Jahrhunderts in Frankreich und Italien (Wolfenbüttel, 1930); H. Besseler, *Die Musik des Mittelalters und der Renaissance* (1931); E. Li Gotti and N. Pirrotta, *Il Sacchetti e la tecnica del trecento italiano* (Florence, 1935); L. Ellinwood, "Francesco Landini and His Music," *Musical Quarterly* (April 1936); Hélène Nolthenius, *Renaissance in Mei; Florentijns leven rond Francesco Landino* (Utrecht, 1956); C. Schachter, "Landini's Treatment of Consonance and Dissonance," *Music Forum,* 2 (1970); D. Baumann, *Die dreistimmige Satztechnik bei Francesco Landini* (Baden-Baden, 1978).

Landon, H(arold) C(handler) Robbins, eminent American musicologist; b. Boston, March 6, 1926. He studied music history and theory with Alfred J. Swan at Swarthmore College, and composition there with Harl McDonald; he also took a course in English literature with W.H. Auden (1943–45); then went to Boston, where he enrolled in the musicology class of Karl Geiringer at Boston Univ. (B.Mus., 1947). In 1948 he traveled to Europe and settled in Vienna; in 1949 he founded the Haydn Society, with a view to preparing a complete edition of Haydn's works. He also instituted an energetic campaign to locate music MSS which had disappeared or been removed; thus, he succeeded in finding the MS of Haydn's Mass No. 13; he also found the MS of the so-called Jena Symph., erroneously ascribed to Beethoven, and proved that it had actually been composed by Friedrich Witt. In 1983 Landon discovered and edited for performance Handel's *Roman Vespers.* In *The Symphonies of Joseph Haydn* (London, 1955; supplement, 1961), he analyzes each symph. and suggests solutions for numerous problems of authenticity; in his new edition of the symphs. (Vienna, 1965–68), he carefully establishes the version nearest to the original authentic text. He subsequently publ. his massive study *Haydn: Chronicle and Works* in 5 vols. (Bloomington, Ind., and London): Vol. I, *Haydn: The Early Years, 1732–1765* (1980); Vol. II, *Haydn at Esterháza, 1766–1790* (1978); Vol. III, *Haydn in England, 1791–1795* (1976); Vol. IV, *Haydn: The Years of "The Creation," 1796–1800* (1977); Vol. V, *Haydn: The Late Years, 1801–1809* (1977). His other publications include *The Mozart Companion* (ed. with Donald Mitchell; London, 1956; 2nd ed., revised, 1965); *The Collected Correspondence and London Notebooks of Joseph Haydn* (London, 1959); a foreword with many emendations to C.S. Terry's *John Christian Bach* (London, 1929; 2nd ed., revised, 1967); *Beethoven: A Documentary Study* (London, 1970); *Essays on the Viennese Classical Style: Gluck, Haydn, Mozart, Beethoven* (London and N.Y., 1970); *Haydn: A Documentary Study* (London, 1981); *Mozart and the Masons* (London, 1983). During Landon's early years in Europe, his wife, Christa Landon (1922–77), joined him as a research partner in the search for rare MSS in libraries, churches, and monasteries. She publ. editions of works by Haydn, Mozart, and Bach; her edition of Haydn's piano sonatas (Vienna, 1963) supersedes the one by Hoboken. In 1983 Landon was named Distinguished Prof. of the Humanities at Middlebury College in Vermont.

Landormy, Paul (Charles-René), French musicologist and critic; b. Issy, Jan. 3, 1869; d. Paris, Nov. 17, 1943. For a number of years he taught philosophy in the provinces; going to Paris in 1892, he studied singing with Sbriglia and Pol Plançon. With Romain Rolland he organized a series of lectures on music history at the Ecole des Hautes Etudes Sociales; established an acoustic laboratory there; was music critic of *La Victoire* (1918); also contributed articles to *Le Temps* and various other journals. He publ. *Histoire de la musique* (Paris, 1910; augmented ed., 1923; Eng. trans., N.Y., 1923); *Brahms* (1920) and *Bizet* (1924) in the series Les Maîtres de la Musique; *La Vie de Schubert* (Paris, 1928); *Gluck* (Paris, 1941); *Gounod* (Paris, 1942); *La Musique française de Franck à Debussy* (Paris, 1943).

Landowska, Wanda (Alexandra), celebrated harpsichordist and authority on old music; b. Warsaw, July 5, 1879; d. Lakeville, Conn., Aug. 16, 1959. She studied piano at the Warsaw Cons. with Michalowski and in Berlin with Moszkowski. In 1900 she went to Paris, where she married Henry Lew, a writer. She traveled widely in Europe as a pianist; in 1909 made a tour of Russia, and played for Tolstoy, who showed great interest in her ideas on classical music. Subsequently, she devoted her efforts principally to reviving the art of playing upon the harpsichord. In 1912 she commissioned the Pleyel firm of Paris to construct a harpsichord for her; this was the first of the many keyboard instruments built for her in subsequent years. In 1913 she was invited by Kretzschmar to give a special course in harpsichord playing at the Berlin Hochschule für Musik. The outbreak of World War I found her in Germany, and she was interned there until the Armistice; in 1918 her husband was killed in an automobile accident in Berlin. In 1919 she gave master classes of harpsichord playing at the Basel Cons.; then returned to Paris. In 1925 she bought a villa in St.-Leu-la-Forêt, near Paris, and established there a school for the study of early music. A concert hall was built there in 1927; she presented regular concerts of early music, and gave lessons on the subject; also assembled a large collection of harpsichords. Her school attracted students from all over the world; she also taught at the Cons. of Fontainebleau, and frequently appeared at concerts in Paris, both as a pianist and as a harpsichordist. She commissioned Manuel de Falla to compose a Chamber Concerto for Harpsichord, and played the solo part in its first performance in Barcelona (Nov. 5, 1926); another commission was Poulenc's *Concert champêtre* for Harpsichord and Small Orch. (Paris, May 3, 1929). She appeared for the first time in America on Nov. 20, 1923, as soloist with the Philadelphia Orch., under Stokowski; then returned to France. When the Germans invaded France in 1940, Landowska fled to Switzerland, abandoning her villa, her library, and her instruments. In 1941 she reached N.Y.; presented a concert of harpsichord music there on Feb. 21, 1942; then devoted herself mainly to teaching; also made recordings; settled in her new home at Lakeville, Conn. She is acknowledged as one of the greatest performers on the modern harpsichord; her interpretations of Baroque music are notable in their balance between Classical precision and freedom from rigidity, particularly in the treatment of ornamentation. She wrote *Bach et ses interprètes* (Paris, 1906); *Musique ancienne* (Paris, 1909; 7th ed., 1921; Eng. trans., N.Y., 1924); many articles in various French and German magazines (on Bach, Chopin, harpsichord playing, etc.). A collection of her articles was publ. posthumously under the title *Landowska on Music*, edited and trans. by Denise Restout and Robert Hawkins (N.Y., 1964). She also wrote cadenzas for Mozart's concertos.

BIBLIOGRAPHY: A. Schaeffner, "Wanda Landowska et le retour aux 'humanités' de la musique," *Revue Musicale* (June 1927); R. Gelatt, *Music Makers* (N.Y., 1953; pp. 254–86); B. Gavoty, *Wanda Landowska* (Geneva, 1957); D. Restout, ed., *Landowska on Music* (Briarcliff Manor, N.Y., 1969).

Landowski, Marcel, French composer; b. Prêt L'Abbé (Finistère), Feb. 18, 1915. He studied with Büsser, Gaubert, and Munch; has been active as a conductor as well as a composer. His works include the opera *Le Rire de Nils Halerius* (Mulhouse, Jan. 19, 1951); oratorio, *Rythmes du monde* (1941); *Clairs-Obscurs,* suite for Orch. (Paris, 1938); *Edina,* symph. poem (1946); *Le Petit Poucet,* symph. suite (Paris, 1947); Symph. (Paris, 1949); Piano Concerto (Paris, March 1, 1942); Cello Concerto (Paris, 1946); *Le Ventriloque,* lyric comedy (Paris, Feb. 8, 1957); *Les Adieux,* one-act lyric drama (Paris, Oct. 8, 1960); *L'Orage,* symph. poem (1961); *L'Opéra de poussière,* opera in 2 acts (Avignon, Oct. 25, 1962); *Les Notes de nuit* for Narrator and Orch. (Boulogne, Dec. 16, 1962); Piano Concerto No. 2 (Paris, Feb. 28, 1964); Symph. No. 2 (Strasbourg, June 24, 1965); Symph. No. 3 (1965); Concerto for Flute and String Orch. (1968); also music for films.

BIBLIOGRAPHY: A. Goléa, *Marcel Landowski: L'Homme et son œuvre* (Paris, 1969).

Landowski, Mme. W.-L. (Alice-Wanda), French writer on music; b. Paris, Nov. 28, 1899; d. there, April 18, 1959. She studied piano in Paris at the Marguerite Long School; theory with Gustave Bret. She taught music history at the Cons. of Clermont; in 1945, became a prof. at the Rouen Cons., a branch of the Paris Cons.; also was engaged as music critic of *Le Parisien.* She adopted the initials W.-L. (L. for Ladislas, her father's name) to avoid confusion with Wanda Landowska, who was not a relation.

WRITINGS: *L'Année Musicale* (Paris, 1936–39; annual reports of musical events); *La Musique à travers les âges* (1937); *Maurice Ravel* (1938); *Les Grands Musiciens* (1938); *Histoire universelle de la musique moderne* (1941); *Histoire générale de la musique* (1945); *L'Œuvre de Claude Delvincourt* (1947); *Chopin et Fauré* (1946); *Le Travail en musique* (1949); *La Musique américaine* (1952);

Paul Paray (1956).

Landré, Guillaume (Louis Frédéric), important Dutch composer, son of **Willem Landré;** b. The Hague, Feb. 24, 1905; d. Amsterdam, Nov. 6, 1968. He took music lessons from Zagwijn and Pijper (1924–29); studied jurisprudence at Utrecht Univ., receiving a master's degree in 1929; then was a teacher of economics in Amsterdam (1930–47). He was general secretary of the Netherlands Arts Council (1947–58) and president of the Society of Netherlands Composers (1950–62). As a composer, he endeavored to revive the spirit and the polyphonic technique of the national Flemish School of the Renaissance in a 20th-century guise, with euphonious dissonances and impressionistic dynamics creating the modern aura. In his later works he experimented with serial devices.

WORKS: 3 operas: *De Snoek (The Pike),* comic opera (1934; Amsterdam, March 24, 1938); *Jean Lévecq,* after Maupassant (1962–63; Holland Festival, Amsterdam, June 16, 1965); *La Symphonie pastorale,* after André Gide (1965–67; Rouen, March 31, 1968); 4 symphs.: No. 1 (1932; Amsterdam ISCM Festival, June 9, 1933); No. 2 (1942; The Hague, March 6, 1946); No. 3 (Amsterdam, June 16, 1951); No. 4, *Symphonie concertante* (1954–55; Stockholm ISCM Festival, June 5, 1956); Suite for String Orch. and Piano (1936); *4 Pieces* for Orch. (1937); *Concert Piece* for Orch. (1938); Cello Concerto (1940); *Sinfonietta* for Violin and Orch. (1941); *Piae memoriae pro patria mortuorum* for Chorus and Orch. (1942); *Groet der martelaren (Salute to the Martyrs)* for Baritone and Orch. (1943–44); *Symphonic Music* for Flute and Orch. (1947–48); *Sinfonia sacra in memoriam patris* (1948; Rotterdam, Nov. 7, 1948; uses motifs from his father's *Requiem*); *4 mouvements symphoniques* (1948–49; The Hague, Jan. 17, 1950); *Berceuse voor moede mensen* for Soloists, Chorus, and Orch. (1952); Chamber Symph. for 13 Instruments (1952; Amsterdam, Feb. 24, 1953); *Sonata festiva* for Chamber Orch. (1953); *Kaleidoscope,* symph. variations (1956); *Symphonic Permutations* (1957); Clarinet Concerto (Amsterdam, June 25, 1959); *Concertante* for Contrabass Clarinet and Orch. (1959); *Anagrams* for Orch. (1960); *Variazioni senza tema* for Orch. (Amsterdam, Dec. 11, 1968); Violin Sonata (1927); 4 string quartets (1927, 1942–43, 1949, 1965); Piano Trio (1929); 2 wind quintets (1930, 1960); *4 Miniatures* for Clarinet, and String Quartet or String Orch. (1950); Sextet for Flute, Clarinet, and String Quartet (1959); *Quartetto piccolo* for 2 Trumpets, Horn, and Trombone (1961); incidental music to the play *Cortez.*

Landré, Willem, Dutch writer on music and composer, father of **Guillaume Landré;** b. Amsterdam, June 12, 1874; d. Eindhoven, Jan. 1, 1948. He was a pupil of Bernard Zweers. In 1901 he became music critic of the *Oprechte Haarlemsche Courant* in Haarlem; was music editor of the *Nieuwe Courant* in The Hague (1901–5), then of the *Nieuwe Rotterdamsche Courant* in Rotterdam (1905–37); taught theory, composition, and the history of music at the

Rotterdam Cons.; was editor of *Caecilia, Het Muziekcollege.*

WORKS: Operas: *De Roos van Dekama* (Haarlem, 1897) and *Beatrix* (The Hague, 1925); for Orch.: *In memoriam matris; 3 Mood Pictures; Le Jardin de Marguerite; Requiem in memoriam uxoris; Fragments from the Book of Baruch* for Chorus; Piano Concerto; Piano Trio; numerous part-songs and songs.

Landshoff, Ludwig, German musicologist and conductor; b. Stettin, June 3, 1874; d. New York, Sept. 20, 1941. He studied music with Thuille, Urban, and Max Reger in Munich and Berlin; musicology with Sandberger, Max Friedlaender, and O. Fleischer; received a Dr.Phil. (1901) from the Univ. of Munich with his treatise *Johann Rudolph Zumsteeg: Ein Beitrag zur Geschichte des Liedes und der Ballade.* He established concerts at which old music was played on instruments of its time; was director of the Munich Bach Society (1919–28). He went to Paris in 1933, and to N.Y. in 1939. He edited *Alte Meister des Belcanto* (5 vols., 1912–27; contains numerous 17th- and 18th-century unpubl. arias); Bach's *15 zweistimmige Inventionen und 15 dreistimmige Sinfonien, Trio-Sonaten; Musikalisches Opfer; 6 suites avec leurs préludes.*
BIBLIOGRAPHY: A. Einstein, "In Memoriam, Ludwig Landshoff," *Musical Quarterly* (April 1942).

Lane, Burton, American song composer; b. New York, Feb. 2, 1912. He studied with Simon Bucharoff; began to compose for musicals on Broadway; contributed songs for the musical *On a Clear Day You Can See Forever;* wrote for the films *St. Louis Blues* and *Ship Ahoy.* Among others, Ira Gershwin, Frank Loesser, and E.Y. Harburg wrote lyrics for his songs.

Lane, Eastwood, American composer; b. Brewerton, N.Y., May 22, 1879; d. Central Square, Oswego County, N.Y., Jan. 22, 1951. He attended Syracuse Univ.; then devoted himself to composition. His works are mostly in a light, descriptive vein, for piano; 2 of his piano sketches, *Sea Burial* and *Persimmon Pucker,* were orchestrated by Ferde Grofé for performance by Paul Whiteman; other works are piano suites: *Sleepy Hollow, Adirondack Sketches,* and *5 American Dances;* he also wrote 2 ballets: *Abelard and Heloise* and *A Caravan from China Comes.*
BIBLIOGRAPHY: J.T. Howard, *Eastwood Lane* (N.Y., 1925); N.P. Gentieu, "Eastwood Lane," *Journal of Jazz Studies* (Spring 1976).

Lane, Louis, American conductor; b. Eagle Pass, Texas, Dec. 25, 1923. He studied at the Univ. of Texas, at the Eastman School of Music in Rochester, N.Y., and at the Berkshire at Music Center in Tanglewood. In 1947 he won a competition to become apprentice conductor to George Szell, the music director of the Cleveland Orch.; in 1956 he was appointed assistant conductor to Szell. In 1959 he was appointed regular conductor of the Akron (Ohio) Symph. Orch. In addition, he appeared as guest conductor with the Chicago Symph. Orch. and with the Detroit Symph. Orch. He conducted several Cleveland Orch. concerts during its 1965 European (and Russian) tour. From 1970 to 1973 he was resident conductor of the Cleveland Orch.; in 1968–73 was associate director of the Blossom Festival School; in 1973 was named principal guest conductor, and in 1974–77 co-principal conductor, of the Dallas Symph. In 1971 he was awarded the prestigious Mahler Medal. In 1983 he became principal conductor of the National Symph. Orch. of the South African Broadcasting Corp. and also principal guest conductor of the Atlanta Symph. Orch.

Lang, Benjamin Johnson, American pianist and conductor; b. Salem, Mass., Dec. 28, 1837; d. Boston, April 3, 1909. He studied with his father and with Alfred Jaëll. In 1855 he went to Berlin for advanced studies; for a time took piano lessons with Liszt. Returning to America, he was engaged as a church organist; was also organist of the Handel and Haydn Society in Boston for many years (1859–95); then was its conductor (1895–97); directed the Apollo Club and the Cecilia Society from their foundation (1868 and 1874, respectively); gave numerous concerts of orchestral, choral, and chamber music on his own account. As a pianist, teacher, conductor, and organizer, he was in the first rank of Boston musicians for a third of a century, and brought out a long list of important works by European and American composers. Among his pupils were Arthur Foote and Ethelbert Nevin. He was also a composer; wrote an oratorio, *David,* and a great many sacred works; also songs and piano pieces.

Lang, Eddie (real name, **Salvatore Massaro**), American jazz guitarist; b. Philadelphia, Oct. 25, 1902; d. New York, March 26, 1933. He studied the violin; then took up the banjo and the guitar. He made solo appearances throughout the U.S., playing with Joe Venuti, Red Nichols, Paul Whiteman, and Bing Crosby. He was a pioneer among jazz guitarists; his early death was widely lamented in jazz circles.

Lang, Hans, Austrian operetta composer; b. Vienna, July 15, 1908. He studied at the Vienna Cons.; wrote popular songs; composed the operettas *Lisa, Benimm dich!* (Vienna, March 21, 1939; his most successful work); *Der Hofrat Geiger; Der alte Sünder; Mädel im Frack; X für ein U; Höchste Eisenbahn;* etc.

Lang, Henry Albert, American pianist, teacher, and composer; b. (of German parents) New Orleans, Oct. 9, 1854; d. Philadelphia, May 27, 1930. He studied at the Stuttgart Cons. Following a concert tour of Germany, he taught piano at the Karlsruhe Cons.; then at Riga and Königsberg. He came to the U.S. in 1890; settled in Philadelphia, where he was an instructor at several music schools. He wrote 2 symphs., *Fantastic Dances* for Orch.; Violin Concerto; Cello Sonata; Piano Quintet; 2 piano trios; 2 string quartets; songs.

Láng, István, Hungarian composer; b. Budapest, March 1, 1933. He studied with Viski (1951–56) and Ferenc Szabó (1956–58) at the Budapest Academy of Music; in 1966 he was appointed director of the Hungarian Marionette Theater. His music is rooted in euphonious dissonance, without venturing into fashionable ugliness.

WORKS: 2 operas: *Pathelin mester (Master Pathelin;* Budapest, 1958) and *A gyáva (The Coward;* Budapest, 1968); 4 ballets: *Mario és a varázsló (Mario and the Magician,* after Thomas Mann's novel; 1962); *Hiperbola* (1963; suite, 1968); *Lebukott (Nabbed;* 1968); ballet-cantata, *Csillagra-török (Star Fighters;* 1971); Viola Concerto (1957); Concerto for String Orch. (1960); Concertino for Xylophone and Orch. (1961; revised 1967); *Variazioni ed Allegro* for Orch. (1965; revision of a discarded symph.); *Gyászzene (Funeral Music)* for Orch. (1969); *Impulsioni* for Oboe and Instrumental Groups (1969); *3 Sentences from Romeo and Juliet* for Strings (1969–70); *Concerto bucolico* for Horn and Orch. (1970–71); *Tüzoszlop (Firepillar)* for Orch. (1972); Symph. No. 2 (1972–74); *Chamber Cantata* for Soprano, Clarinet, Cello, Piano, and Percussion (1962); Solo Cello Sonata (1960); 2 string quartets (1961, 1966); Duo for 2 Flutes (1963); 3 wind quintets (1964; *Transfigurazioni,* 1965; 1975); *Pezzi* for Soprano, Flute, Clarinet, Viola, and 2 Percussionists (1964); *Monodia* for Solo Clarinet (1965); *Dramma breve* for Solo Flute (1970); *Cassazione* for Brass Septet (1971); *Töredékek (Fragments)* for Female Voice, Oboe, Bassoon, and Harp (1971–72); *Rhymes* for Flute, Clarinet, Viola, Cello, and Piano (1972); *Villanások (Flashes)* for Solo Violin (1973); *Improvisazioni* for Solo Cimbalom (1973); *Constellations* for Oboe, Violin, Viola, and Clarinet (1974–75); *Surface Metamorphosis* for Tape (1975); *Solo* for Bass Flute (1975); *Monologue* for Horn (1975); *Waves* for Soprano and Vibraphone (1975); *Constellations* for Oboe and String Trio (1975–76).

Lang, Josephine, German composer of art songs, daughter of the German singer **Sabina Hitzelberger;** b. Munich, March 14, 1815; d. Tübingen, Dec. 2, 1880. She studied music with her mother and also took lessons with Mendelssohn; composed and publ. a considerable number of surprisingly competent lieder in an amiably songful, Germanically Romantic vein, in addition to some very playable piano pieces. She was married to a poet who wrote under the nom de plume Christian Reinhold.

Lang, Margaret Ruthven, American composer, daughter of **Benjamin J. Lang;** b. Boston, Nov. 27, 1867; d. Boston, May 29, 1972, at the age of 104(!). She studied in Boston with her father and later in Munich; also with Chadwick and MacDowell. Her works include the overture *Witichis* (1893); *Dramatic Overture* (1893); the overture to *Totila; Ballade* for Orch. (1901); *Sappho's Prayer to Aphrodite,* aria for Contralto, with Orch. (1895); *Phoebus,* aria for Baritone and Orch.; *In the Manger* for Mixed Choir; *The Heavenly Noël* for Solo, Women's Chorus, Piano, and String Orch.; *Christmas Cycle* for Vocal Quartet; piano pieces; some 200 songs. She stopped composing about 1930. She attended Boston Symph. concerts from their foundation; was present at a concert 3 days before her 100th birthday, at which Erich Leinsdorf included in the program the psalm tune *Old Hundredth* in her honor.

Lang, Paul Henry, eminent American musicologist and teacher; b. Budapest, Aug. 28, 1901. He studied bassoon and took courses in composition at the Budapest Music Academy with Kodály and Leo Weiner; played bassoon in various orch. groups in Budapest; also appeared as a pianist in chamber music recitals; was chorus répétiteur at the Royal Opera in Budapest (1923–24); then attended the Univ. of Heidelberg, and the Sorbonne in Paris, where he studied musicology with André Pirro (1924–28); in 1928 he went to the U.S., where he enrolled in Cornell Univ., in the class of Otto Kinkeldey; obtained his Ph.D. in 1934 with the dissertation *A Literary History of French Opera.* He was an assistant prof. at Vassar College (1930–31); associate prof., Wells College (1931–33); visiting lecturer, Wellesley College (1934–35); associate prof. of musicology, Columbia Univ. (1933–39); full prof., 1939; emeritus, 1970. He was vice-president of the American Musicological Society (1947–49) and president of the International Musicological Society (1955–58). From 1945 to 1972 he was editor of the *Musical Quarterly;* from 1954 to 1963, music editor of the *N.Y. Herald Tribune.* He publ. a valuable and very popular vol., *Music in Western Civilization* (N.Y., 1941; many subsequent reprints); an important biography, *George Frideric Handel* (N.Y., 1966); *Critic at the Opera* (N.Y., 1971); further brought out *A Pictorial History of Music* (with O. Bettman, N.Y., 1963); edited *One Hundred Years of Music,* a collection of articles marking the centennial of the G. Schirmer, Inc., music publishing house (N.Y., 1961); *Problems of Modern Music* (N.Y., 1962; separate publication of articles from the *Musical Quarterly,* 1960); *Stravinsky. A New Appraisal of His Work* (N.Y., 1963); *The Creative World of Mozart* (N.Y., 1963); *Contemporary Music in Europe. A Comprehensive Survey* (with Nathan Broder; N.Y., 1965; a reprint of the semicentennial issue of the *Musical Quarterly).*

Lang, Walter, Swiss pianist and composer; b. Basel, Aug. 19, 1896; d. Baden, Switzerland, March 17, 1966. He was a pupil of Jaques-Dalcroze; taught at the Dalcroze School in Geneva; then studied in Munich with Klose, and in Zürich with Andreae and W. Frey; appeared as a concert pianist and as an accompanist; then taught theory in Basel (1920–22); was a prof. of piano at the Zürich Cons. (1922–41); music director of Monte Ceneri Radio (1942–48); in 1948, he became an instructor at the Basel Cons. He was married to the coloratura soprano **Mimi Lang-Seiber.**

WORKS: Symph. (1946); overture, *Jour de Fête* (1947); *Scherzo fugato* for String Orch. (1939); Piano Concerto (1940); Cello Concerto (1951); String Quartet (1919); 2 violin sonatas (1920, 1939); Piano Trio

(1925); Flute Sonata (1956); numerous piano pieces.

Langbecker, Emanuel Christian Gottlieb, German authority on Protestant chorales; b. Berlin, Aug. 31, 1792; d. there, Oct. 24, 1843. He was secretary to Prince Waldemar of Prussia; his research on the origin of the Protestant chorale is embodied in *Das deutsch-evangelische Kirchenlied* (1830); *Johann Crügers Choral-Melodien* (1835); *Gesangblätter aus dem 16. Jahrhundert* (1838); and *Paul Gerhardts Leben und Lieder* (1841).

Langdon, Michael, English bass; b. Wolverhampton, Nov. 12, 1920. He studied at the Guildhall School of Music in London; subsequently took voice lessons with Alfred Jerger in Vienna, Maria Carpi in Geneva, and Otakar Kraus in London. In 1948 he joined the chorus at the Royal Opera House, Covent Garden; made his operatic debut there in 1950. He created several bass roles in operas by Benjamin Britten; was also noted for his command of the standard operatic repertoire. In 1978 he became director of the National Opera Studio. He was made a Commander of the Order of the British Empire in 1973.

Langdon, Richard, English composer and organist; b. Exeter, c.1729; d. there, Sept. 8, 1803. He studied at Oxford (Mus.Bac., 1761); was organist of Exeter Cathedral (1753–77); Bristol Cathedral (1778–82), and Armagh Cathedral (1782–94); publ. *Divine Harmony,* a collection of Psalms and anthems (1774); also *12 Glees* for 3–4 Voices (1770); 2 cantatas; 12 songs.

Lange, Daniel de, Dutch cellist and composer, brother of **Samuel de Lange;** b. Rotterdam, July 11, 1841; d. Point Loma, Calif., Jan. 31, 1918. He studied cello with Servais and composition with Verhulst. As a young man he taught at the Lwow Cons. (1860–63); returning to Amsterdam, he occupied various teaching posts; in 1895 became director of the Amsterdam Cons., remaining in that post until 1913; gave numerous choral concerts of old Dutch music; also wrote music criticism. In 1913 he went to California, where he lived at the headquarters of the Universal Brotherhood and Theosophical Society at Point Loma. He wrote an opera, *De val van Kuilenburg;* 2 symphs.; Cello Concerto; chamber music; sacred works; also publ. *Exposé d'une théorie de la musique.*
BIBLIOGRAPHY: Henry Viotta, *Onze hedendaagsche toonkunstenaars* (Amsterdam, 1894); A. Averkamp, *Levensbericht van Daniel de Lange* (Leyden, 1918); *Theosophical Field* (March 1918).

Lange, Francisco Curt, German musicologist; b. Eilenburg, Dec. 12, 1903. He studied music with Abert, Bekker, Bücken, and Sandberger. He received his Ph.D. in 1929 from the Univ. of Bonn with the dissertation *Über die Mehrstimmigkeit der Niederländischen Motetten.* In 1930 he went to Uruguay; established the Instituto Interamericano de Música, and Editorial Cooperativo In-

teramericano de Compositores, which publ. a long series of works by Latin American composers. Beginning in 1935, he edited the *Boletín Latino-Americano de Música,* a series of bulky vols. containing documentary data on Latin American music and composers; separate vols. appeared in Montevideo, Lima, Bogota, Caracas, Rio de Janeiro, etc. He also publ. numerous essays and pamphlets dealing with literature, philosophy, pedagogy, and sociology (all in Spanish); brought out an anthology, *Latin-American Art Music for the Piano* (G. Schirmer, Inc., N.Y., 1942), with biographical sketches of 12 composers; also publ. a collection of Brazilian church music of the 18th century. In 1948 he founded the musicology dept. of the National Univ. of Cuzo in Mendoza, Argentina.

Lange, Gustav, German pianist and composer; b. Schwerstedt, near Erfurt, Aug. 13, 1830; d. Wernigerode, July 19, 1889. He studied with A.W. Bach, Grell, and Löschhorn. For many years he lived in Berlin; wrote more than 400 piano pieces, generally facile, elegant, and effective, many of which gained great vogue.

Lange, Hans, German-American violinist and conductor; b. Constantinople, Feb. 17, 1884 (of German parents); d. Albuquerque, N.Mex., Aug. 13, 1960. He studied the violin as a child, then at the Prague Cons. with Ševčík, graduating in 1902 with highest honors. In 1903 he joined the Berlin Phil.; later played in the orch. of the Frankfurt Opera; settled in the U.S. in 1923; was assistant conductor of the N.Y. Phil. (1923–33) and later an associate conductor (1933–36); then associate conductor of the Chicago Symph. Orch. (1936–46). He was conductor of the Albuquerque Symph. Orch. from 1951 to 1958.

Lange, Konrad von, German esthetician; b. Göttingen, March 15, 1855; d. Tübingen, July 28, 1921. In his theories he introduced the basic concept of "illusion" in the creation and appreciation of art and music. He publ. *Die Bewusste Selbsttäuschung* (1895); *Das Wesen der Kunst* (2 vols., 1907); *Das Wesen der künstlerischen Erziehung* (1902); *Der Zweck der Kunst* (1912).

Lange, Samuel de, Dutch organist and composer, brother of **Daniel de Lange;** b. Rotterdam, Feb. 22, 1840; d. Stuttgart, July 7, 1911. He studied with Verhulst in the Netherlands and with Winterberger in Vienna. He was with his brother in Lwow (1859–63); then taught successively at the Rotterdam Music School (1863–74), the Basel Music School (1874–76), and the Cologne Cons. (1876–85); then was conductor of the Oratorio Society at The Hague (1885–93); finally was a prof. of organ and composition at the Stuttgart Cons. (1894); became its director in 1900. He wrote a Piano Concerto; 3 symphs.; 4 string quartets; 2 piano trios; 4 violin sonatas; 2 cello sonatas; 8 sonatas for organ; an oratorio, *Moses;* 3 cantatas: *De Opstanding, Die Totenklage,* and *Eines Königs Tränen;* male choruses; songs.

Lange-Müller, Peter Erasmus, Danish composer; b. Frederiksborg, near Copenhagen, Dec. 1, 1850; d. Copenhagen, Feb. 26, 1926. He studied at the Copenhagen Cons. His early compositions show the influence of J.P.E. Hartmann; those of his later period exhibit distinct individuality.
WORKS: Operas (all produced in Copenhagen): *Tove* (Jan. 19, 1878); *Spanske studenter* (Oct. 21, 1883); *Fru Jeanna* (Feb. 4, 1891); *Vikingeblod* (April 29, 1900); incidental music for *Fulvia* and *Det var en gang; Niels Ebbeson* for Baritone, Men's Chorus, and Orch.; 2 symphs.; orch. suites: *Alhambra* and *Weyerburg;* Trio for Violin, Cello, and Piano; piano pieces; etc.; some 200 songs, many of which gained great popularity.

Langendorff, Frieda, German contralto; b. Breslau, March 24, 1868; d. New York, June 11, 1947. She studied with Mme. Leffler-Burckard; made her debut in Strasbourg (1901); sang at the Metropolitan Opera in N.Y. (debut, Dec. 7, 1907, as Ortrud in *Lohengrin)* in 1907–8 and 1911. She then made an extensive concert tour throughout the U.S. (1912–13). In 1914 she was engaged by the Dresden Royal Opera; also sang at Bayreuth, Berlin, Helsinki, Brussels, and Amsterdam. She returned to N.Y. after World War II. Among the 76 operatic roles (which included mezzo-soprano parts) in her repertoire were Ortrud, Fricka, Amneris, Azucena, and Dalila.

Langenus, Gustave, Belgian clarinetist; b. Malines, Aug. 6, 1883; d. New York, Jan. 30, 1957. He studied at the Brussels Cons. As a youth of 18, he traveled with Sousa's band in Europe; then lived in England; in 1910, came to the U.S.; was a clarinetist with the N.Y. Symph. (1910–20); was one of the founders of the Chamber Music Society in N.Y. (1914); a member of the N.Y. Phil. from 1920–23; taught at the Juilliard School of Music and the Dalcroze School of Music. He publ. *Fingered Scale Studies for the Boehm Clarinet* (N.Y., 1911); *Modern Clarinet Playing* (N.Y., 1913); *Virtuoso Studies and Duos for Clarinet* (N.Y., 1915); *Complete Method for the Boehm Clarinet* (8 vols., N.Y., 1916).

Langer, Eduard, Russian pianist and composer; b. Moscow, May 3, 1835; d. there, June 5, 1905. He was a pupil at the Leipzig Cons. of Moscheles, Richter, and Hauptmann; upon returning to Moscow, he taught at the Cons. there; publ. numerous arrangements for 2 pianos (4- and 8-hands) of operas and orch. works by Russian composers; his own compositions include: String Quartet; String Trio; 2 violin sonatas; many piano pieces.

Langer, Ferdinand, German composer and cellist; b. Leimen, near Heidelberg, Jan. 21, 1839; d. Kirneck (Black Forest), Aug. 5, 1905. An excellent cellist, he joined the orch. of the Mannheim Court Theater; later became 2nd Kapellmeister there. With Emil Heckel, he founded the first Wagnerverein in Germany (1883). He produced several locally successful operas in Mannheim: *Die gefährliche Nachbarschaft* (1868); *Dornröschen* (1873); *Aschenbrödel*

(1878); *Murillo* (1887); and the "romantische Volksoper" *Der Pfeiffer von Haardt* (1894). He revised Weber's *Silvana* for its revival in 1885.

Langer, Hermann, German organist and theorist; b. Höckendorf, near Tharandt, July 6, 1819; d. Dresden, Sept. 8, 1889. He studied in Leipzig with K.F. Becker; in 1843, became organist of the Leipzig Univ. church; in 1845, teacher of liturgical song at Leipzig Univ.; in 1857, music director there; went to Dresden in 1887 as Inspector of Organ Building. He publ. *Repertorium für Männergesang; Der erste Unterricht im Gesang* (3 courses; 1876–77); also edited the *Musikalische Gartenlaube.*

Langer, Victor, Hungarian composer; b. Budapest, Oct. 14, 1842; d. there, March 19, 1902. He studied in Budapest with R. Volkmann, and later at the Leipzig Cons. Returning to Budapest, he was active as a teacher, theater conductor, and editor of a Hungarian music journal. His songs *Ógyek dalai,* Hungarian dances, arrangements, etc., publ. under the pen name of **Aladar Tisza,** are in the genuine national vein; they enjoyed great popularity.

Langert, Johann August Adolf, German composer; b. Coburg, Nov. 26, 1836; d. there, Dec. 27, 1920. He was a theater conductor in Coburg, Mannheim, and Basel; in 1873, became court conductor at Gotha, retiring in 1897 to his native town. He composed several operas: *Die Jungfrau von Orleans* (Coburg, 1861); *Des Sängers Fluch* (Coburg, 1863); *Dona Maria* (Darmstadt, 1866); *Die Fabier* (Coburg, 1866); *Dornröschen* (Leipzig, 1871); and *Jean Cavallier* (Coburg, 1880; rewritten and produced as *Die Camisarden,* 1887).

Langey, Otto, German-American cellist and composer; b. Leichholz, near Frankfurt an der Oder, Oct. 20, 1851; d. New York, March 16, 1922. He studied cello with Specht in Sorau, Ullrich in Halle, and Cabisius in Bremen; theory and composition with W. Fritze in Liegnitz. In 1877 he went to London, playing in the Hallé and Richter concerts; came to the U.S. in 1889, and made a tour as soloist with the Boston Symph. Club; settled in N.Y. as a teacher; in 1909, became arranger of orch. music for G. Schirmer, Inc. He publ. the *Langey Tutors* (methods for 28 different instruments) and numerous compositions for orch. (*Arabian Serenade, Liberty Overture, 3 Oriental Sketches,* etc.).

Langgaard, Rued, Danish composer and organist; b. Copenhagen, July 28, 1893; d. Ribe, July 10, 1952. His father, **Siegfried Langgaard** (1852–1914), was a pupil of Liszt and an accomplished pianist. Rued Langgaard studied organ with Gustav Helsted; from his early youth he was occupied mainly as a church organist. As a composer, he followed neo-Romantic trends, in the manner of Bruckner and Mahler, scaling heights and plumbing depths of grandiose designs.
WORKS: Biblical opera, *Antichrist* (1921–30); 16

symphs.: No. 1, *Klippepastoraler* (1908–11; Berlin, 1913); No. 2, *Vaarbrud (Spring Song)*, with Solo Soprano (1912–13; Copenhagen, 1914; revised and perf. on Danish Radio, 1948); No. 3, *Ungdomsbrus (The Sound of Youth)*, with Piano, Chorus, and Ad Libitum (1915; Copenhagen, 1918; revised 1926); No. 4, *Løvfald (The Fall of the Leaf;* 1916; Copenhagen, 1917); No. 5, *Steppenatur* (1918; Copenhagen, 1926; revised, Danish Radio, 1938); No. 6, *Det Himmelrivende (The Heaven Rending;* 1919); No. 7, *Ved Tordenskjold i Holmens Kirke* (1925–26; Copenhagen, 1926; revised, Danish Radio, 1935); No. 8, *Minder om Amalienborg* (1928); No. 9, *Dronning Dagmar* (1942; Danish Radio, 1943); No. 10, *Hin Tordenbolig* (1944); No. 11, *Ixion* (1945; Danish Radio, July 29, 1968); No. 12, *Helsingeborg* (1946); No. 13, *Undertro (Belief in Miracles;* 1947); No. 14, *Morgenen (Morning)*, suite for Chorus and Orch. (1948); No. 15, *Søstormen (The Storm at Sea;* 1948); No. 16, *Syndflod af Sol (Flood of Sun;* 1951; Copenhagen, March 17, 1966); for Voices, with Orch.: *Musae triumphantes* (1906); *Angelus (The Gold Legend;* 1915–37); *Sfaerernes Musik (Music of the Spheres;* 1916–18; his most interesting work; perf. in Karlsruhe, 1921); *Endens Tid (The End of Time;* 1921–39); 2 church cantatas: *Krematio* (1928–36) and *Jephta* (1948); *Højsangen (Song of Solomon;* 1949; Danish Radio, Feb. 24, 1969); *Heltedød (Death of a Hero)* for Orch. (1907); *Drapa* for Orch. (1907); *Sfinx,* overture (1909); *Saga blot* for Orch. (1917); Violin Concerto (1943–44; Danish Radio, July 29, 1968); dedicatory overture, *Carl Nielsen vor store Komponist (Carl Nielsen Our Great Composer)*, for Orch. (1948); 6 string quartets (1914–31); 5 violin sonatas (1915–49); *Dies irae* for Tuba and Piano (1948); many minor organ pieces, motets, and songs.

Langhans, Friedrich Wilhelm, German composer and violinist; b. Hamburg, Sept. 21, 1832; d. Berlin, June 9, 1892. He studied at the Leipzig Cons. with David (violin) and Richter (composition); then in Paris with Alard (violin). In 1852–56 he played violin in the Gewandhaus Orch. at Leipzig; in 1857–60 he was concertmaster at Düsseldorf; then a teacher and violinist in Hamburg, Paris, and Heidelberg; received his Dr.Phil. at Heidelberg (1871). He taught music history at Kullak's Neue Akademie der Tonkunst in Berlin (1874–81); in 1881, joined the faculty of the Scharwenka Cons. In 1858 he married the concert pianist **Louise Japha** (divorced in 1874). He publ. *Das musikalische Urteil* (1872; 2nd ed., 1886); *Die königliche Hochschule für Musik in Berlin* (1873); *Musikgeschichte in 12 Vorträgen* (1878); *Die Geschichte der Musik des 17., 18. und 19. Jahrhunderts* (2 vols., 1882–86; a well-written continuation of Ambros's great work). He composed a Symph.; String Quartet; Violin Sonata; and studies for violin.

Langlais, Jean, French organist and composer; b. La Fontenelle, Feb. 15, 1907. He was blind from infancy; studied organ with Dupré at the Paris Cons., winning first prize in 1930; studied composition with Paul Dukas. He became organist at Montrouge; from 1945, was organist at Ste.-Clotilde in

Paris; also taught organ at the School for the Blind. His works are mainly for organ (*2 offertoires pour tous les temps, 3 paraphrases grégoriennes,* etc.); he also wrote a symph. poem, *Cloches;* Suite for Cello and Orch.; numerous choral works; Trio for Flute, Violin, and Viola.

BIBLIOGRAPHY: A. Machabey, *Portraits de trente musiciens français* (Paris, 1949; pp. 109–13).

Langlé, Honoré François Marie, French music theorist and composer; b. Monaco, 1741; d. Villiers-le-Bel, near Paris, Sept. 20, 1807. He studied in Naples at the Cons. della Pietà dei Turchini, with Cafaro. In 1768 he went to Paris, becoming a singing teacher at the Ecole Royale de Chant in 1784; then was a prof. of harmony and librarian at the Paris Cons. He wrote an important *Traité d'harmonie et de modulation* (1793; 2nd ed., 1797; chord building by thirds); *Traité de la basse sous le chant* (1798); *Nouvelle méthode pour chiffrer les accords* (1801); *Traité de la fugue* (1805); also collaborated with Cherubini on the latter's *Méthode de chant;* edited Mengozzi's *Méthode de chant du Conservatoire* after Mengozzi's death. Langlé composed a number of operas, only one of which was presented: *Corisandre, ou Les Fous par enchantement* (Paris, March 8, 1791).

Langley, Allan Lincoln, American violinist; b. Newport, R.I., June 11, 1892; d. (of a heart attack) in a Hudson tube train between Jersey City and New York City, Nov. 12, 1949. He studied at Brown Univ. in Providence (B.A., 1914), and at the New England Cons. with Shepherd, Chadwick, Winternitz, and Mason; played violin and viola in the Boston Symph. (1918), National Symph. (1920–21), N.Y. Phil. (1921–27), and Richmond Symph. Orch. (1932–33).

Langlotz, Karl A., German-American composer; b. Saxe-Meiningen, June 20, 1834; d. Trenton, N.J., Nov. 25, 1915. He was a member of the Liszt circle in Weimar; in 1853, came to America; lived in Philadelphia as a music teacher; in 1857–68 was an instructor of German at Princeton; in 1868, entered the Theological Seminary there, graduating in 1871; in 1874, moved to Trenton, where he taught music. He is known for composing the famous Princeton song *Old Nassau* (1859), at the suggestion of Princeton students and teachers who gathered regularly to sing college songs; the song was first publ. in the earliest Princeton songbook, *Songs of Old Nassau* (N.Y., 1859).

BIBLIOGRAPHY: W.S. Conrow, "Old Nassau" (N.Y., 1905).

Langstroth, Ivan Shed, American pianist, teacher, and composer; b. Alameda, Calif., Oct. 16, 1887; d. New York, April 18, 1971. He studied in San Francisco with T. Vogt, then in Berlin with Juon, Humperdinck, and Lhevinne. In 1915 he was coach at the Kiel Opera; in 1916, organist at the American Church in Berlin; in 1917–20, toured Scandinavia as a concert pianist; in 1921–28, was a teacher at the New Cons. in Vienna; then returned to America; in

1943–45 he was a lecturer on music at Brooklyn College; then taught privately in N.Y. He wrote orch. and choral works, chamber music, piano pieces, and songs.

Lanier (Laniere), Nicholas, English composer, lutenist, and painter; b. Greenwich (baptized, Sept. 10), 1588; d. London, Feb. 24, 1666. He is important as having been probably the first to introduce the Italian recitative style into England, in his music to masques, of which the first was Ben Jonson's *Lovers Made Men* (London, Feb. 22, 1617). He was Master of the King's Musick under Charles I and Charles II. He wrote a pastoral on the birth of Prince Charles; a funeral hymn for Charles I; a cantata, *Hero and Leander;* and some New Year's songs; his songs are found in MS in the British Museum, Bodleian Music School, Christ Church, and Fitzwilliam Museum; also in the publ. collections *Select Musicall Ayres and Dialogues* (1653, 1659); *The Musical Companion* (1667); *The Treasury of Musick* (1669); *Choice Ayres and Songs* (1685); and J.S. Smith's *Musica Antiqua* (1812).
BIBLIOGRAPHY: J. Pulver, *A Biographical Dictionary of Old English Music* (1927); *Dictionary of National Biography* (vol. II; reprinted, Oxford, 1921–22); V. Duckles, "English Song and the Challenge of Italian Monody," in *Words to Music* (includes a complete transcription of *Hero and Leander;* Los Angeles, 1967).

Lanier, Sidney, American poet and musician; b. Macon, Ga., Feb. 3, 1842; d. Lynn, N.C., Sept. 7, 1881. Best known for his poetry, Lanier learned as a child to play the piano, flute, guitar, violin, and organ. After serving in the Civil War, he was organist and choirmaster for a short period at a church in Montgomery, Ala. In 1873 he became first flutist of the Peabody Symph. Orch. in Baltimore. He wrote a number of articles on music (collected in *Music and Poetry: Essays upon Some Aspects and Interpretations of the Two Arts,* 1898; reprinted, N.Y., 1969) and composed songs and flute pieces.
BIBLIOGRAPHY: H.C. Thorpe, "Sidney Lanier: A Poet for Musicians," *Musical Quarterly* (July 1925); A. H. Starke, "Sidney Lanier as a Musician," ibid. (Oct. 1934).

Lankow, Anna, noted German singing teacher; b. Bonn, Jan. 13, 1850; d. there, March 19, 1908. She studied singing in Cologne, Leipzig, and Dresden; began her career as a concert singer; then was engaged as a contralto in the Weimar Opera; however, because she had been lame since childhood, she was forced to abandon the stage. In 1883 she married the sculptor Paul Pietsch of Berlin; after his death in 1885, she came to America, settling in N.Y. as a singing teacher; subsequently returned to Germany. She publ. a valuable treatise, *Die Wissenschaft des Kunstgesangs* (1899, in German and Eng.).

Lanner, August (Joseph), Austrian violinist and composer, son of **Joseph (Franz Karl) Lanner;** b. Vienna, Jan. 23, 1834; d. there, Sept. 27, 1855. A talented violinist, dance composer, and conductor, he died in his 22nd year.

Lanner, Joseph (Franz Karl), historically significant Austrian violinist and dance composer; b. Vienna, April 12, 1801; d. Oberdöbling, near Vienna, April 14, 1843. A self-taught violinist and composer, he joined Pamer's dance orch. when he was 12. In 1818 he formed a trio; Johann Strauss, Sr., joined it, making it a quartet. The group grew in size, and by 1824 it was a full-sized classical orch. which became famous and performed in coffeehouses, taverns, at balls, etc. The orch. was subsequently divided into 2 ensembles, with Lanner leading one, and Strauss the other. Lanner and Strauss are credited with the creation of the mid-19th-century Viennese waltz. Lanner's output totals 207 popular pieces, including 112 waltzes, 25 Ländler, 10 quadrilles, 3 polkas, 28 galops, and 6 marches; overture to *Der Preis einer Lebensstunde; Banquet-Polonaise; Tarantella;* and *Bolero.* His complete works in 8 vols., ed. by E. Kremser, were publ. by Breitkopf & Härtel in 1889 (reprinted N.Y., 1971); selections were brought out by Oskar Bie (Munich, 1920) and Alfred Orel, in Denkmäler der Tonkunst in Österreich, 65 (33.ii).
BIBLIOGRAPHY: H. Sachs, *J. Lanner* (Vienna, 1889); F. Rebay and O. Keller, *J. Lanner* (Vienna, 1901); F. Lange, *J. Lanner und Johann Strauss, Ihre Zeit, ihr Leben und ihre Werke* (Vienna, 1904; 2nd ed., 1919); A.Weinmann, *Verzeichnis der im Druck erschienen Werke von Joseph Lanner* (Vienna, 1948).

Lannoy, Eduard, Austrian composer; b. Brussels, Dec. 4, 1787; d. Vienna, March 28, 1853. His family moved to Graz when he was a child; he studied there and in Paris. In 1813 he went to Vienna, where he became an active promoter of the Gesellschaft der Musikfreunde; in 1830–35 he was a member of the executive board of the Vienna Cons. He wrote several operas and singspiels, a Symph., overtures, chamber music, piano pieces, and songs.

Lans, Michael J.A., Dutch composer and authority on Gregorian chant; b. Haarlem, July 18, 1845; d. Amsterdam, Feb. 3, 1908. A Roman Catholic priest, he started publication of an ecclesiastical periodical, *Gregoriusblad* (1876); composed several masses; publ. *Palestrina* (1882) and a manual of strict counterpoint (1889).

Lantins, Arnold de, Netherlandish composer; b. probably at Lantin, near Liège, c.1400; date of death unknown. He traveled in Italy about 1427; was a singer in the Papal Chapel in Rome between Nov. 1431 and July 1432. His employment of carefully connected chords suggesting purely harmonic procedures is of historical interest. Two motets, *Tota pulchra es* and *O pulcherrima mulierum* (from the Song of Solomon), are reproduced in Charles Van den Borren's *Polyphonia Sacra: A Continental Miscellany of the 15th Century* (1932). Other works are found in J. Stainer, *Dufay and His Contemporaries* (London, 1898); in J. Wolf, *Ge-*

schichte der Mensural-Notation; and in vol. 61 (31) of Denkmäler der Tonkunst in Österreich.
BIBLIOGRAPHY: Charles Van den Borren, *Hugo et Arnold de Lantins* (Liège, 1935); G. Reese, *Music in the Renaissance* (N.Y., 1954; 2nd ed., revised, 1959).

Lantins, Hugo de, Netherlandish singer and composer, possibly related to **Arnold de Lantins;** b. probably at Lantin, near Liège, shortly before 1400; death date unknown. As a young man, he was in Italy, where he wrote an ode, *Tra quante regione,* for the marriage of Theodore Palaiologos (1421); several motets and other ecclesiastical pieces are extant.
BIBLIOGRAPHY: Charles Van den Borren, *Arnold et Hugo de Lantins* (Liège, 1935); G. Reese, *Music in the Renaissance* (N.Y., 1954; 2nd ed., revised, 1959).

Lanza, Mario (real name, **Alfredo Arnold Cocozza**), American singer of Italian descent; b. Philadelphia, Jan. 31, 1921; d. Rome, Oct. 7, 1959. He studied singing with Enrico Rosati; appeared in recitals and opera. In 1951 he starred in the title role of a highly successful film, *The Great Caruso.*

Lanzetti, Salvatore, Italian cellist; b. Naples, c.1710; d. Turin, c.1780. He was one of the earliest virtuosos on the cello; during his residence in London (c.1739–56) he succeeded in establishing the cello there as a favorite solo instrument; returned to Italy as a member of the royal chapel at Turin. He publ. 2 books of cello sonatas (1736); 6 cello solos; 6 sonatas for 2 Cellos, with Continuo; also a method, *Principes de doigter pour le violoncelle dans tous les tons.*

Lanzky-Otto, Ib, Danish-born Swedish horn player; b. Gentoste, July 8, 1940. He studied with his father, a horn player in the Stockholm Phil.; then played horn in the Stockholm Royal Opera Orch. (1958–61); subsequently was a member of the Stockholm Phil. (1961–67); succeeded his father as first horn player in 1967. In 1970 he organized workshops of the International Horn Society.

Laparra, Raoul, French composer; b. Bordeaux, May 13, 1876; killed during an air raid near Paris, April 4, 1943. He studied at the Paris Cons. with Gédalge, Massenet, and Fauré; won the Grand Prix de Rome with his cantata *Ulysse* (June 27, 1903). He was music critic of *Le Matin,* resigning in 1937 to dedicate himself entirely to composition. He was at his best in music inspired by Spanish subjects.
WORKS: Operas: *Peau d'âne* (Bordeaux, 1899); *La Habanera* (Paris, Feb. 26, 1908; his best-known work); *La Jota* (Paris, April 26, 1911); *Le Joueur de viole* (Paris, Dec. 24, 1925); *Las toreras* (Lille, Feb. 1929); *L'Illustre Fregona* (Paris, Feb. 16, 1931); incidental music to *El Conquistador; Un Dimanche basque,* suite for Orch. and Piano; etc.

Laporte, André, Belgian composer; b. Oplinter, July 12, 1931. He studied musicology and philosophy at the Catholic Univ. of Louvain, graduating in 1956; studied organ with Flor Peeters and counterpoint with Marinus De Jong (1956–58). In 1963 he was engaged as a producer for Belgian Radio; in 1968 he was appointed to the faculty of the Brussels Cons.
WORKS: Piano Sonata (1954); *Psalm* for 6 Voices and Brass (1956); *Introduction and Fughetta* for Guitar (1956); *Sequenza I* for Solo Clarinet (1964); *Sequenza II* for Bass Clarinet and 3 Clarinets (1965); *Jubilius* for 12 Brasses and 3 Percussionists (1966); *Ludus fragilis* for Solo Oboe (1967); *Story* for 3 Viole de Gamba and Harpsichord (1967); *Ascension* for Piano (1967); *Inclinations* for Flute (1968); *Alliances* for Cello and Piano (1968); *De profundis* for Mixed Choir (1968); *Le morte chitarre* for Tenor, Flute, and 14 String Soloists (1969); *Reflection* for Clarinet (1970); *Night Music* for Orch. (1970; Brussels, March 15, 1971); *La vita non è sogno* for Narrator, Tenor, Baritone, Chorus, and Orch. (Ghent, Sept. 13, 1972); *Péripétie* for Brass Sextet (1973); *Arboreal,* film music for Piano and Tape (1974); *Chamber Music* for Soprano, Flute, Clarinet, Violin, and Piano (1975).

Laporte, Joseph de, French writer on theater and music; b. Belfort, 1713; d. Paris, Dec. 19, 1779. He was a Jesuit abbé; wrote *Anecdotes dramatiques* (3 vols., 1775; contains all varieties of theatrical works); *Dictionnaire dramatique* (3 vols., 1776); *Almanach des spectacles de Paris, ou Calendrier historique des théâtres de l'Opéra, des Comédies française et italienne et des foires* (48 vols. in all; those from 1750–79 by Laporte; the rest by Duchesne and others).

La Pouplinière, Alexandre-Jean-Joseph Le Riche de, French musical amateur; b. Chinon, July 26, 1693; d. there, Dec. 5, 1762. A wealthy member of the nobility and a statesman, he was a patron of music and a pupil of Rameau. The musical soirées he gave in his private theater were famous; he engaged Gossec as music director (1751); introduced Johann Stamitz to the Parisian public; upon Stamitz's advice, he added horns, clarinets, and a harp to his orch., instruments seldom heard in a concert orch. before that time. La Pouplinière wrote a number of arias, some of which Rameau incorporated into his own works.
BIBLIOGRAPHY: Ancelet, *Observations sur la musique et les instruments* (Amsterdam, 1757); P. Hédouin, *Gossec* (Paris, 1852); idem, *Mosaïque* (Paris, 1856); G. Cucuel, *La Pouplinière et la musique de chambre au XVIIIᵉ siècle* (Paris, 1913).

La Prade, Ernest, American composer; b. Memphis, Tenn., Dec. 20, 1889; d. Sherman, Conn., April 20, 1969. He studied violin at the Cincinnati College of Music, at the Royal Cons. in Brussels with César Thomson, and in London with J. Jongen (composition). He subsequently taught at the Cincinnati College of Music; was a member of the Cincinnati

Symph. Orch. (1909–12), the Belgian and Holbrook Quartets in London (1914–17), and the N.Y. Symph. Orch. (1919–28); in 1929, he joined the staff of NBC; in 1950, became supervisor of music research there. He wrote a comic opera, *Xantha* (London, 1917), and songs; publ. *Alice in Orchestralia* (1925); *Marching Notes* (1929); *Broadcasting Music* (1947).

La Presle, Jacques de, French composer; b. Versailles, July 5, 1888; d. Paris, May 6, 1969. He studied at the Paris Cons.; received the Grand Prix de Rome in 1921; in 1937, was appointed prof. of harmony at the Paris Cons. His works include *Apocalypse de St.-Jean* (1928); *Album d'images,* suite for Orch. (1935); Piano Concerto (1949); chamber music; songs.

Laquai, Reinhold, Swiss composer; b. Zürich, May 1, 1894; d. Oberrieden, Oct. 3, 1957. He studied at the Zürich Cons.; later with Busoni in Berlin. In 1920 he became a teacher at the Zürich Cons.
WORKS: Operas: *Der Schleier der Tanit* and *Die Revisionsreise;* many orch. works (3 symphs., 5 overtures, 2 serenades, a concert piece for piano and orch., etc.); chamber music (trios; sonatas for violin, flute, cello, bassoon, and horn, clarinet, etc.; Piano Quintet); piano pieces; and more than 200 songs.

Lara, Agustín, Mexican composer of popular songs; b. Tlacotalpán, Oct. 14, 1900; d. Mexico City, Nov. 5, 1970. He learned to play piano by ear; earned his living as an entertainer in a Mexican house of tolerance, where he wrote his first successful song, *Rosa;* an encounter with a woman who impulsively slashed his face during an altercation inspired him to write a paean to womanhood, *Morucha,* which acquired great popularity. His other songs that became famous are *Tus pupilas, Gotas de amor,* and the most famous, *Mujer.*

Lara, Isidore de. See **De Lara, Isidore.**

Lara-Bareiro, Carlos, Paraguayan composer; b. Capiatá, March 6, 1914. He played in the boy scout band conducted by his father; then studied violin in Asunción and in Rio de Janeiro; during his stay in Brazil he also took lessons in composition and conducting. Returning to Paraguay in 1951, he organized in Asunción the Symph. Orch. of the Assoc. of Musicians of Paraguay. Eventually he moved to Buenos Aires. His works reflect the modes and moods of Paraguayan folk music. He wrote several symph. suites on Paraguayan themes and a Piano Concerto.

Laredo, Jaime, Bolivian violinist; b. Cochabamba, June 7, 1941. He was brought to the U.S. as a child; studied violin with Antonio de Grassi and Frank Houser in San Francisco, Josef Gingold in Cleveland, and Ivan Galamian at the Curtis Inst. of Music in Philadelphia. In 1959, a week before his 18th birthday, he won the Queen Elisabeth of Belgium

Competition in Brussels, and subsequently appeared with great success in America and Europe as a soloist with leading orchs. The proud Bolivian government issued a series of airmail stamps with Laredo's picture and a musical example with the notes A, D, C in the treble clef, spelling his name in Latin notation (La-Re-Do). In 1960 he married the pianist **Ruth Meckler** (divorced in 1974); his second wife, **Sharon Robinson,** was a cellist. With her and the pianist Joseph Kalichstein, he formed a trio which gave successful concerts.

Laredo, Ruth (née **Meckler**), American pianist; b. Detroit, Nov. 20, 1937. She studied with Rudolf Serkin at the Curtis Inst. of Music in Philadelphia; in 1962 made her debut with Leopold Stokowski and the American Symph. in N.Y. In 1965 she played in Europe with Rudolf Serkin and his son Peter Serkin; in 1977 she toured Japan. In 1960 she married the Bolivian violinist **Jaime Laredo,** with whom she played numerous recitals; but they were divorced in 1974. She is particularly fond of Russian music, and plays piano works of Rachmaninoff and Scriabin with passionate devotion.

La Rocca, Nick (Dominick James), American jazz cornetist; b. New Orleans, April 11, 1889; d. there, Feb. 22, 1961. After graduating from high school he became a cornetist and local bandleader. He formed the Original Dixieland Jazz Band, which gained wide popularity and brought attention to the New Orleans style of jazz; it played at Reisenweber's in N.Y. during World War I and toured throughout the U.S. and Europe; the group is most noted for having made, in 1917, the first jazz recordings, these becoming a major influence on the next generation (the "Chicago School") of white jazz musicians.
BIBLIOGRAPHY: H.O. Brunn, *The Story of the Original Dixieland Jazz Band* (Baton Rouge, 1960). La Rocca's memorabilia are on deposit at Tulane Univ.

Laroche, Hermann, Russian music critic; b. St. Petersburg, May 25, 1845; d. there, Oct. 18, 1904. He studied with Rubinstein and Zaremba at the St. Petersburg Cons., and with Tchaikovsky in Moscow. He became a prof. at the Moscow Cons. (1867–70); then at the St. Petersburg Cons. (1872–79); contributed numerous articles to Russian journals; collected his essays and criticisms and publ. them in 1894. His most important work is *M.I. Glinka and His Place in Russian Music* (1868; new ed., 1953); with N. Kashkin he wrote *Reminiscences of Tchaikovsky* (1894).

La Rotella, Pasquale, Italian composer and conductor; b. Bitonto, Feb. 26, 1880; d. Bari, March 20, 1963. He studied in Naples; was choral conductor at the Bari Cathedral (1902–13); in 1934–49, taught at the Liceo Musicale there; toured Italy as an opera conductor. His works include the operas *Ivan* (Bari, Jan. 20, 1900); *Dea* (Bari, April 11, 1903); *Fasma* (Milan, Nov. 28, 1908); *Corsaresca* (Rome, Nov. 13, 1933); *Manuela* (Nice, March 4, 1948); much sacred music.

Larrivée, Henri, French bass-baritone; b. Lyons, Jan. 9, 1737; d. Vincennes, Aug. 7, 1802. He sang in the chorus of the Paris Opéra; made his debut there in Rameau's *Castor et Pollux* in 1755; he subsequently distinguished himself in the operas of Gluck, creating the roles of Agamemnon in *Iphigénie en Aulide* (1774) and Orestes in *Iphigénie en Tauride* (1779). His wife, **Marie Jeanne Larrivée** (née **Le Mière;** b. Sedan, Nov. 29, 1733; d. Paris, Oct. 1786), was a soprano who sang minor roles at the Paris Opéra (1750–77); she created the title role of Ernelinde in Philidor's opera of 1767, and also the role of Eponine in *Sabinus* (1773) by Gossec.

Larrocha, Alicia de, brilliant Spanish pianist; b. Barcelona, May 23, 1923. She studied piano with Frank Marshall and theory with Ricardo Lamote de Grignon. She made her first public appearance at the age of 5; was soloist with the Orquesta Sinfónica of Madrid at the age of 11. In 1940 she launched her career in earnest; from 1947 made extensive concert tours in Europe and America. Her interpretations of Spanish music have evoked universal admiration for their authentic quality, but she has also been exuberantly praised by sober-minded critics for her impeccable taste and exquisitely polished technique in classical works.

L'Arronge, Adolf, composer and conductor; b. Hamburg, March 8, 1838; d. Berlin, May 25, 1908. He studied at the Leipzig Cons. with R. Genée; was a theater conductor in Cologne, Danzig, Königsberg, Würzburg, Stuttgart, Budapest, etc.; in 1866, became director of the Kroll Opera in Berlin; then of the Lobetheater in Breslau (1874–78). Returning to Berlin, he bought the Friedrich-Wilhelmstädtisches Theater in 1881, and managed it until 1894 as the Deutsches Theater. He brought out many musical farces, singspiels, etc. at the Wallnertheater, including his comic operas *Das Gespenst* and *Der zweite Jakob,* the "Volksstücke" *Das grosse Los* (1868) and *Mein Leopold,* etc.; also wrote many songs.

Larsen, Jens Peter, distinguished Danish musicologist; b. Copenhagen, June 14, 1902. He studied mathematics and musicology at the Univ. of Copenhagen; also took private organ lessons with Wöldike. He received his M.A. in 1928 from the Univ. of Copenhagen; then joined its staff; obtained his Ph.D. there in 1939 with the dissertation *Die Haydn-Überlieferung* (publ. in Copenhagen, 1939); he retired in 1970. A leading authority on the music of Haydn, he served as general editor of the critical edition sponsored by the Joseph Haydn Inst. of Cologne from 1955 to 1960; his studies on the music of Handel are also of value. WRITINGS: *Drei Haydn-Kataloge in Faksimile: Mit Einleitung und ergänzenden Themenverzeichnissen* (Copenhagen, 1941; 2nd ed., revised, 1979); *Weyses sange: Deres betydning for sangen i hjem, skole og kirke* (Copenhagen, 1942); *Handel's "Messiah": Origins, Composition, Sources* (Copenhagen, 1957; 2nd ed., revised, 1972).

BIBLIOGRAPHY: N. Schiørring, H. Glahn, and C. Hatting, eds., *Festskrift Jens Peter Larsen: Studier udgivet af Musikvidenskabeligt institut ved Københavns universitet* (Copenhagen, 1972).

Larsen, Nils, Norwegian pianist; b. Oslo, June 7, 1888; d. there, Nov. 7, 1937. He studied in Oslo with M. Knutzen and in Berlin with Ganz and da Motta. He wrote a number of piano pieces; edited the works of Christoph Graupner.

Larsén-Todsen, Nanny, Swedish soprano; b. Hagby, Kalmar county, Aug. 2, 1884; d. Stockholm, May 26, 1982. She studied at the Stockholm Cons. and in Germany and Italy. In 1906 she made her debut at the Royal Theater in Stockholm as Agathe in *Der Freischütz;* was a member of the Royal Theater (1907–22), specializing in Wagnerian roles; sang at La Scala in Milan (1923–24), at the Metropolitan Opera House in N.Y. (1925–27; debut there Jan. 31, 1925, as Brünnhilde in *Götterdämmerung*), and at Bayreuth (1927–31); made guest appearances at most of the European opera houses. Her principal roles were the 3 Brünnhildes, Isolde, Fricka, and Leonore. She married H. Todsen in 1916; following her retirement from the stage, she became a teacher in Stockholm.

Larsson, Lars-Erik, important Swedish composer; b. Åkarp, near Lund, May 15, 1908. He studied composition (with Ellberg) and conducting (with Olallo Morales) at the Royal Academy of Music in Stockholm (1925–29); then went to Vienna, where he took lessons with Alban Berg (1929–30); upon returning to Sweden, he was choirmaster of the Royal Opera in Stockholm (1930–31) and conducted the Swedish Radio orch. (1937–54); taught at the Royal Academy (1947–59) and was music director of Uppsala Univ. (1961–65). His early compositions were in a classical spirit, but with time his idiom became increasingly complex; there are also some instances of the application of dodecaphonic procedures in his later compositions. WORKS: FOR THE STAGE: Opera, *Prinsessan av Cypern* (*The Princess of Cyprus;* 1930–36; Stockholm, April 29, 1937); opera-buffa, *Arresten på Bohus* (*The Arrest at Bohus;* 1938–39); ballet, *Linden* (1958). FOR ORCH.: 3 symphs. (1927–28, 1936–37, 1945); 3 concert overtures (1929, 1934, 1945); *Symphonic Sketch* (1930); *Sinfonietta* for Strings (1932); *Little Serenade* for Strings (1934); Saxophone Concerto (1934); *Divertimento* for Chamber Orch. (1935); *Little March* (1936); *Ostinato* (Stockholm, Nov. 24, 1937); *En vintersaga* (*A Winter Tale*), suite (1937); *Pastoral Suite* (1938); *The Earth Sings,* symph. poem (1940); *The Land of Sweden,* suite (1941); *Gustavian Suite* for Flute, Harpsichord, and Strings (1943); Cello Concerto (1947); *Music for Orchestra* (1948-49); Violin Concerto (1952); 12 concertinos, with String Orch., for solo instruments: Flute, Oboe, Clarinet, Bassoon, Horn, Trumpet, Trombone, Violin, Viola, Cello, Double Bass, and Piano (1953-57); *Adagio* for Strings (1960); *3 Pieces* (1960); *Orchestral Variations* (1962); *Lyric Fantasy* for Small

Orch. (1967); *2 auguri* (1971); *Barococo*, suite (1973). VOCAL MUSIC: *Förklädd gud (The Disguised God)*, lyric suite for Narrator, Soprano, Baritone, Chorus, and Orch. (1940); *Väktarsånger (Watchman's Songs)* for Narrator, Baritone, Male Chorus, and Orch. (1940); *Missa brevis* for a cappella Chorus (1954); *Intrada Solemnis* for 2 Choruses, Boys' Chorus, Winds, and Organ (1964); *Soluret och urnan (The Sundial and the Urn)*, cantata (1965–66). CHAMBER MUSIC: Violin Sonatina (1928); *Duo* for Violin and Viola (1931); *Intimate Miniatures* for String Quartet (1938); 3 string quartets (1944, 1955, 1975); *4 tempi*, divertimento for Wind Quintet (1968); Cello Sonatina (1969); *3 Pieces* for Clarinet and Piano (1970); *Aubade* for Oboe, Violin, and Cello (1972). PIANO MUSIC: 3 sonatinas (1936, 1947, 1950); *Croquiser* (1947); *7 Little Preludes and Fugues* (1969).

La Rue, Jan (full Christian name, **Adrian Jan Pieters**), eminent American musicologist; b. Kisaran, Sumatra, July 31, 1918, of American parents (his ancestor who was a French Huguenot who fled first to the Palatinate and then came to America, landing in Massachusetts in 1670; LaRue's parents spent 3 years in Indonesia, where his father served as a botanist and developed a basic budding process used on rubber trees). He studied at Harvard Univ. (Ph.D., 1952) and at Princeton Univ.; taught at Wellesley College; in 1957 became a prof. at N.Y. Univ. His dual specialties are 18th-century music and style analysis. He prepared a thematic catalogue of about 10,000 entries on symphs. and instrumental concertos of the Classical period; contributed to various publications a number of original articles bringing informing light on obscure subjects. His most important papers include: "Native Music in Okinawa," *Musical Quarterly* (April 1946); "The Okinawan Notation System," *Journal of the American Musicological Society* (1951); "Die Datierung von Wasserzeichen im 18. Jahrhundert," *Kongress-Bericht*, Mozart-Jahr, 1956 (also in Eng., "Watermarks and Musicology," *Acta Musicologica*, 1961). He publ. *Guidelines for Style Analysis* (N.Y., 1970); was editor of the *Report of the Eighth Congress of the International Musicological Society, New York 1961* (Kassel, 1961); co-editor of the Festschrift for Otto Erich Deutsch (Kassel, 1963) and of the Festschrift for Gustave Reese (N.Y., 1965). In 1966–68 he was president of the American Musicological Society.

La Rue, Pierre de (Petrus Platensis, Pierchon, Pierson, Pierzon, Perisone, Pierazon de la Ruellien), eminent Netherlandish contrapuntist and composer; b. in all probability between 1455 and 1460, in Tournai, where his family is known to have resided; d. Courtrai, Nov. 20, 1518. He was at the court of Burgundy (1477); a singer at the Cathedral of Siena intermittently from 1482 to 1485; was attached to the chapel of Archduke Maximilian of Austria (April 1485) and the chapel of Notre-Dame in Bois-le-Duc (1490–91); was a chapel singer at the court of Burgundy (1492–1510); canon at the court of Philippe le Beau in Malines (1501); prebend at Courtrai, Namur, and Termonde (from 1501); *cantor principis* at Courtrai (1502). He returned to the Netherlands about 1508; was a singer at the court of Margaret of Austria at Mechelen; then served Archduke Karl (1514–16). He wrote about 50 masses, of which many were publ.; others are in MS in libraries in Brussels, Malines, Rome, Vienna, Berlin, etc. One of Petrucci's early publications using movable type was 7 "Misse Petri de La Rue," issued at Venice in 1503. Motets and chansons were printed in collections of the time. A motet was scored by Dreher in his *Cantiones sacrae* (1872); the mass *Ave Maria* was publ. by H. Expert in *Les Maîtres-Musiciens de la renaissance française* (1890); a Kyrie in A. Schering, *Geschichte der Musik in Beispielen* (no. 65); some motets in R.J. van Maldeghem, *Trésor musical* (1865–93); motets and a Requiem in F. Blume, *Das Chorwerk* (vols. 11 and 91); 3 masses in *Monumenta musicae belgicae*, 8.

BIBLIOGRAPHY: A.W. Ambros, *Geschichte der Musik* (vol. 3, pp. 234ff.); P. Wagner, *Geschichte der Messe* (pp. 166ff.); K.E. Roediger, *Die geistlichen Musikhandschriften der Universitäts-Bibliothek Jena* (1935); H. Riemann, *Handbuch der Musikgeschichte* (vol. 2, pp. 286ff.); Josef Robyns, *Pierre de la Rue* (Brussels, 1954; in Flemish); G. Reese, *Music in the Renaissance* (N.Y., 1954; 2nd ed., revised, 1959); M. Staehelin, "Pierre de la Rue in Italien," *Archiv für Musikwissenschaft* (April–June 1970).

La Salette, Joubert de, French music theorist; b. Grenoble, Sept. 4, 1743; d. there, Feb. 4, 1833. He wrote *Sténographie musicale* (1805; an unsuccessful invention on the lines of German tablature); *Considérations sur les divers systèmes de la musique ancienne et moderne* (1810; his best work); *De la notation musicale en général, et en particulier de celle du système grec* (1817); *De la fixité et de l'invariabilité des sons musicaux* (1824); and other essays.

Lasalle, Jean-Louis. See **Lassalle, Jean-Louis.**

Laserna, Blas de, Spanish composer; b. Corella, Navarre, Feb. 4, 1751; d. Madrid, Aug. 8, 1816. He was official composer for several theaters; composed the music for Ramón de la Cruz's comedy *El café de Barcelona* (Barcelona, Nov. 4, 1788); also the operas *La gitanilla por amor* (Madrid, 1791; successful) and *Idomeneo* (Madrid, Dec. 9, 1792); incidental music to plays of Calderón, Lope de Vega, Moreto, etc.; composed many *tonadillas, sainetes,* etc.

Las Infantas, Fernando de. See **Infantas, Fernando de las.**

Láska, Gustav, Bohemian composer and double-bass player; b. Prague, Aug. 23, 1847; d. Schwerin, Oct. 16, 1928. He studied at the Prague Cons. with Hrabe, Kittl, and Krejči. Following a year of giving double-bass concerts, he joined the court orch. in Kassel (1868–72); then in Sondershausen (1872–75); was a theater conductor in Göttingen, Eisleben, and

Halberstadt; played double bass in Berlin; in 1878, became double-bass player in the court orch. in Schwerin. WORKS: Opera, *Der Kaisersoldat;* cantata, *Deutsches Aufgebot;* 2 symphs.; 2 overtures; Double-bass Concerto; 3 masses; several works for double bass and piano *(3 Romanzen, Rhapsodie, Erotik, Ballade und Polonaise, Schlummerlied, Karneval von Venedig,* etc.); piano pieces; songs.

Laskine, Lily, French harpist; b. Paris, Aug. 31, 1893. She studied at the Paris Cons. with Alphonse Hasselmans and Georges Marty; won a Premier Prix there in 1905; was then a member of the orch. of the Paris Opéra (1909–26); from 1934 made numerous tours as a soloist; was a prof. of harp at the Paris Cons. (1948–58).

Lasner, Ignaz, cellist; b. Drosau, Bohemia, Aug. 8, 1815; d. Vienna, Aug. 18, 1883. He studied with Goltermann in Prague, and Merk and Servais in Vienna. He was an orch. player in Vienna; composed cello pieces.

Lassalle, Jean-Louis, French baritone; b. Lyons, Dec. 14, 1847; d. Paris, Sept. 7, 1909. After training in industrial design and painting, he entered the Paris Cons. to study voice; also studied privately with Novelli. In 1869 he sang in Liège, Lille, Toulouse, and Brussels; had his debut at the Paris Opéra, on June 7, 1872; remained there for more than 20 years, with extended leaves of absence, during which he toured throughout Europe, Russia, and the U.S. (debut, Metropolitan Opera House, N.Y., Jan. 15, 1892, as Nelusko in *L'Africaine);* remained at the Metropolitan until 1897. He returned to Paris in 1901 and settled there as a singing teacher; in 1903, became a prof. at the Paris Cons. His repertoire comprised about 60 operas, ranging from Donizetti to Wagner.

Lassen, Eduard, eminent Danish conductor and composer; b. Copenhagen, April 13, 1830; d. Weimar, Jan. 15, 1904. His family moved to Brussels when he was a child; he entered the Brussels Cons., taking the Belgian Prix de Rome (1851). Following a tour through Germany and Italy, he went to Weimar, where Liszt fostered the presentation of his 5-act opera *Landgraf Ludwigs Brautfahrt* (1857). He became court music director in Weimar (1858); then was conductor of the Weimar Opera (1860–95); led the world premiere of Saint-Saëns's opera *Samson et Dalila* (Weimar, Dec. 2, 1877). He also wrote the operas *Frauenlob* (Weimar, 1860) and *Le Captif* (Brussels, April 24, 1865); a ballet, *Diana;* 2 symphs.; *Fest-Cantate;* 2 overtures; Te Deum; a set of *Biblische Bilder* for Chorus and Orch.; songs; etc.; also incidental music to *Oedipus* (1874); Hebbel's *Nibelungen;* Goethe's *Faust* (parts 1 and 2; 1876); Scheffel's *Die Linde am Ettersberg* (1878); *Circe* (1881); Goethe's *Pandora* (1886).

Lassus, Ferdinand de, eldest son of **Roland de Lassus;** b. Munich, c.1560; d. Aug. 27, 1609. He was a musician at the Munich court (1584–85); court conductor at Sigmaringen (1585–90); a tenor singer in Munich (1590); went with the court to Landshut (1595) and later became court conductor there (1602). He brought out a book of *Cantiones sacrae suavissimae* (1587; motets); edited, with his brother **Rudolph,** his father's *Magnum opus musicum.*
   BIBLIOGRAPHY: H. Delmotte, *Notice biographique sur Roland Delattre* (Valenciennes, 1836; includes biography and list of works by Ferdinand de Lassus).

Lassus, Ferdinand de, son of **Ferdinand** and grandson of **Roland de Lassus;** d. c.1635. He studied in Rome (1609); was court conductor (1616) and official (1629) under the Duke of Bavaria. Of his works, written for 8- to 16-voiced double choruses in the style made popular by the Venetian school, few remain. He publ. *Apparatus musicus* (motets, Mass, Magnificat, Litany, etc.; 8 voices; 1622).

Lassus, Roland de (Latin, **Orlandus Lassus;** Italian, **Orlando di Lasso;** French, **Roland Delattre**), one of the greatest of the Netherlandish composers and one of the foremost contrapuntists of the Renaissance; b. Mons, 1532; d. Munich, June 14, 1594. At the age of 18, he was placed in the service of Constantino Castrioto of Naples (1550). From April 1553 to Dec. 1554 he was chorus master at St. John Lateran in Rome. His parents died in 1554; Lassus subsequently joined J. Cesare Brancaccio, a music lover from Naples; with him he supposedly visited England and France; this visit was of brief duration, if it took place at all. In 1555 he settled in Antwerp. Both socially and artistically, he enjoyed a fine reputation in Antwerp, despite his youth; he had his first works printed in Venice (1555), containing 22 madrigals to poems of Petrarch; in the same year he publ. in Antwerp a collection of madrigals and motets to words in Italian, French, and Latin. In 1556 he was offered a highly desirable post at the court of Duke Albrecht V of Bavaria, and settled in Munich; in 1558 he married an aristocratic lady, Regina Wechinger (Wäckinger). He remained in Munich for most of the next 38 years, until his death. He did make occasional trips, including to Flanders to recruit singers (1560); to Frankfurt for the coronation of Emperor Maximilian II in 1562; to Northern Italy in 1567; and to the French court in 1571, 1573, and 1574. He brought Giovanni Gabrieli to Munich in 1575. On Dec. 7, 1570, he received from the Emperor Maximilian a hereditary rank of nobility. His last journey was to Regensburg, a year before his death. Lassus represents the culmination of the great era of Franco-Flemish polyphony; his superlative mastery in sacred as well as secular music renders him one of the most versatile composers of his time; he was equally capable of writing in the most elevated style and in the popular idiom; his art was supranational; he wrote Italian madrigals, German lieder, French chansons, and Latin motets. Musicians of his time described him variously as the "Belgian Orpheus" and the "Prince of Music." The sheer scope of his production is amazing; he left more than 2,000 works in various genres. The Patrocinium Musices (1573–98), a 12-vol. series publ. in Munich by Adam Berg, under ducal patronage, contains 7 vols. of Lassus's works: vol. I, 21 motets; vol. II, 5 masses; vol. III, Offices; vol. IV, a Passion, vigils, etc.; vol. V, 10 Magnificats; vol. VI, 13 Magnificats; vol. VII, 6 masses. Lassus's sons publ. 516 of his motets under the title *Magnum opus musicum* (1604). Eitner publ. *Chronologisches Verzeichnis der Druckwerke des Orlando di Lassus* (Berlin, 1874). His collected works (21 vols., 1894–1926), were issued by Breitkopf & Härtel of Leipzig under the editorship of Haberl and Sandberger; a new series was begun in 1956 (12 vols. completed as of 1977) by the Bärenreiter Verlag under the editorship of W. Boetticher, who also publ. a complete catalogue of works (Berlin, 1956). Various works are contained in vols. 13, 34, 37, 41, and 48 of *Das Chorwerk,* and there are a considerable number in the catalogues of leading publishers.

BIBLIOGRAPHY: H. Delmotte, *Notice biographique sur Roland Delattre connu sous le nom d'Orland de Lassus* (Valenciennes, 1836); A. Mathieu, *Biographie de Roland de Lattre* (Mons, 1851); *Register für die Geschichte der Musik in Bayern,* ed. by D. Mettenleiter (Brixen, 1868); W. Bäumker, *Orlandus de Lassus, der letzte grosse Meister der niederländischen Tonschule* (Freiburg, 1878); J. Declève, *Roland de Lassus: Sa vie et ses œuvres* (Mons, 1894); F.X. Haberl, "Synchronistische Tabelle über den Lebensgang von Giovanni Pierluigi da Palestrina und Orlando di Lasso," *Kirchenmusikalisches Jahrbuch,* 9 (1894); A. Sandberger, *Beiträge zur Geschichte der bayrischen Hofkapelle* (vols. I and III; Leipzig, 1894); E. Destouches, *Orlando di Lasso: Ein Lebensbild* (Munich, 1894); E. Schmitz, *Orlando di Lasso* (Leipzig, 1915); E. Closson, *Roland de Lassus* (1919); R. Casimiri, *Orlando di Lasso, maestro di cappella al Laterano nel 1553* (Rome, 1920); Charles Van den Borren, *Orlande de Lassus* (Paris, 1920); A. Sandberger, *Ausgewählte Aufsätze* (Munich, 1921); idem, *Orlando di Lasso und die geistigen Strömungen seiner Zeit* (Munich, 1926); Charles Van den Borren, *En quelle année Roland de Lassus est-il né?* (The Hague, 1926); E. Lowinsky, *Der Motettenstil Orlando di Lassos* (Heidelberg, 1933); L. Behr, *Die deutschen Gesänge Orlando di Lassos* (Erlangen, 1935); E. Lowinsky, *Das Antwerpener Motettenbuch Orlando di Lassos und seine Beziehungen zum Motettenschaffen der niederländischen Zeitgenossen* (The Hague, 1937); Lucie Balmer, *Orlando di Lassos Motetten* (Berne, 1938); J. Huschke, *Orlando di Lassos Messen* (Leipzig, 1941); F. Blume, "Lasso und Palestrina," *Deutsche Musikkultur,* 9 (1944); C. Van den Borren, *Roland de Lassus* (1944); A. Einstein, *The Italian Madrigal* (Princeton, 1949); G. Reese, *Music in the Renaissance* (N.Y., 1954); W. Boetticher, *Orlando di Lasso* (2 vols., Berlin, 1956; contains complete list of works); Horst Leuchtmann, *Die musikalischen Wortausdeutungen in den Motetten des Magnum Opus Musicum von Orlando di Lasso* (Strasbourg, 1959); idem, *Orlando di Lasso, Sein Leben; Briefe* (2 vols., Wiesbaden, 1977).

Lassus, Rudolph de, organist and composer, son of **Roland de Lassus;** b. Munich, c.1563; d. there, 1625. He was a musician in the court orch. at Munich from 1585 until his death; was an organist and composer of merit and repute; from 1609 was court composer to the Duke; various works by him were publ.; 3 masses and 3 Magnificats are in MS in Munich; 2 motets are included in Proske's *Musica divina* (vol. I). With his brother Ferdinand he edited his father's *Magnum opus musicum.*

BIBLIOGRAPHY: H. Delmotte, *Notice biographique sur Roland Delattre connu sous le nom d'Orland de Lassus* (Valenciennes, 1836; includes biography and list of works).

László, Alexander, Hungarian composer; b. Budapest, Nov. 22, 1895. He studied at the Budapest Academy with A. Szendy (piano) and Herzfeld (composition); in 1915 he went to Berlin; was active as a pianist; also worked on the radio and in film enterprises. In 1938 he emigrated to the U.S.; in 1945, settled in Hollywood. He cultivated the idea of music expressed through colors; introduced a specially constructed "color pianoforte" (*Farblichtklavier*) at the Kiel music festival (June 14, 1925); for the projection of the colors corresponding to music in proportional wavelengths he invented the Sonchromatoscope and a new system of notation called Sonchromography. His book *Die Farblichtmusik* (1925) discusses this new technique. His works include, besides special compositions for color lights, the pantomimes *Marionetten* (Budapest, 1916); *Die schöne O-sang* (Hamburg, 1919); *Panoptikum;* etc.; for Piano: *News of the Day, Hungarian Dance Suite,* and *Fantasy of Colors; Mechanized Forces* for Orch.; *Hollywood Concerto* and *The Ghost Train of Marshall Pass* for Piano and Orch.; arrangements for piano of various works by classical composers; film music. His sophisticated ideas about music and color found a fertile ground in Hollywood, where he supplied many musical scores to television; also wrote a musical, *Wanted: Sexperts and Serpents for Our Garden of Maidens* (1968); *Pacific Triptych* for Orch. (1962); symph. fantasy, *Roulette hématologique* (1969).

Lateiner, Jacob, American pianist; b. Havana, May 31, 1928. He studied piano with Jascha Fischermann in Havana, and with Isabelle Vengerova at the Curtis Inst. of Music in Philadelphia; also attended the chamber music classes given by Piatigorsky and Primrose. He made his debut with the Philadelphia Orch. in 1945; subsequently performed throughout America and in Europe. He appeared regularly in chamber music recitals with Heifetz and Piatigorsky. From 1963–70 he taught at the Mannes College of Music in N.Y.; in 1966 was appointed to the faculty of the Juilliard School of Music in N.Y.

Latham, William P(eters), American composer and educator; b. Shreveport, La., Jan. 4, 1917. He studied trumpet at the Cincinnati Cons. of Music (1936–38); received his B.S. degree in music education from the Univ. of Cincinnati (1938) and continued his studies at the College of Music in Cincinnati (B.M., 1940; M.M., 1941); subsequently he studied composition with Howard Hanson and Herbert Elwell at the Eastman School of Music in Rochester, N.Y. (Ph.D., 1951). During World War II, he served in the U.S. Army as a cavalry bandsman and later as an infantry platoon leader in active combat in Germany in 1945. After the war, he taught at Iowa State Teacher's College in Ames (1946–65); became a prof. at North Texas State Univ. in Denton in 1965, director of graduate studies in music in 1969, and Distinguished Prof. in 1978; he retired in 1984. He excelled as a composer of sacred choruses and band music; in the latter, he boldly experimented with modern techniques, as exemplified by his *Dodecaphonic Set* and, most spectacularly, in *Fusion*, in which he endeavored to translate the process of atomic fusion into musical terms through an ingenious application of asymmetrical rhythms.

WORKS: Opera, *Orpheus in Pecan Springs* (1979–80; Denton, Dec. 4, 1980); ballet, *A Modern Trilogy* (Cincinnati, April 2, 1941). For Orch.: *The Lady of Shalott* (1939; Cincinnati, March 7, 1941); *Fantasy Concerto* for Flute, String Orch., and Harp (NBC radio broadcast, Cincinnati, May 5, 1941); *River to the Sea* for Baritone and Orch. (Cincinnati, Dec. 11, 1942); *Fantasy* for Violin and Orch. (1946; Minneapolis, May 23, 1948); *And Thou America* (1947; Rochester, Oct. 18, 1948); Symph. No. 1 (Rochester, April 25, 1950); Suite for Trumpet and String Orch. (Rochester, May 4, 1951); Symph. No. 2, *Sinfonietta* (1953; Fish Creek, Wis., Aug. 20, 1955); Concerto Grosso for 2 Saxophones and Symph. Wind Ensemble (Chicago, Dec. 16, 1960; revised, 1962, for 2 Saxophones and Chamber Orch.); Concertino for Saxophone and Symph. Wind Ensemble (1968; revised, 1969, for Saxophone and Orch.); *American Youth Performs* (Fort Worth, Aug. 1, 1969); *A Lenten Letter* for Soprano, String Orch., and Percussion, to a text by Alexander Solzhenitsyn (Denton, Oct. 9, 1974); *Jubilee 13/50* (Sherman, Texas, Nov. 4, 1978); *Supernovae* (1983). For Band: *Brighton Beach*, march (1954); *Proud Heritage*, march (1955); *3 Chorale Preludes* (1956); *Court Festival* (1957); *Passacaglia and Fugue* (1959); *Plymouth Variations* (1962); *Escapades* (1965); *Dionysian Festival* (1965); *Dodecaphonic Set* (Colorado Springs, Colo., March 11, 1966); *Prayers in Space* (1971); *The Music Makers*, with Chorus, Rock Group, Tape, and Guru (1972); *Dilemmae* (1973); *Prolegomena* (1974); *Revolution!* (1975); *Fusion* (1975; New Orleans, April 12, 1976); *March 6* (Dallas, Feb. 23, 1979); *Drones, Airs, and Games* (1983). Chamber music: 3 string quartets (1938–40); 3 string trios (1938–39); Sonatina for Flute and Piano (1937); *5 Pieces for Solo Clarinet* (1941; later renamed *5 Atonal Studies*); Sonata for Oboe and Piano (1947); Sonatina for Piano (1949); Sonata for Violin and Piano (1949); *Suite in Baroque Style* for Flute and Piano (1954); Sonata for Recorder and Harpsichord (1959); *Sisyphus 1971* for Alto Saxophone and Piano (1971); *Preludes before Silence*, 9 pieces for Solo Flute and Piccolo (1974); *Bravoure* for Piano (1976); *Eidólons* for Euphonium and Piano (1977); *Ex Tempore* for Alto Saxophone (1978). Choral music: *Peace* for Chorus and Orch., to a text by Rupert Brook (1943); *Prayer after World War* for Chorus a cappella (1945); *Prophecy of Peace*, with Organ, Piano, and Cymbals (1951; also versions with Orch., 1952, and Small Wind Ensemble, 1961); *Music for 7 Poems*, to texts by James Hearst, for Chorus and Orch. (1958); *Blind with Rainbows*, cantata (1962); *Te Deum*, with Wind Ensemble and Organ (1964); *Epigrammata* for Chorus a cappella (1978). Songs: *Te Deum Tejas*, 8 songs for Soprano, Flute, and Percussion, to texts by the composer (1981).

Latilla, Gaetano, Italian composer; b. Bari, Jan. 21, 1711; d. Naples, Jan. 15, 1788. As a child, he sang in the choir of the Cathedral in Bari; then studied at the Cons. di Sant' Onofrio in Naples. He was 2nd maestro di cappella at Santa Maria Maggiore in Rome from 1738 to 1741, when illness forced him to return to Naples; in 1756 he became chorus master at the Cons. della Pietà in Venice; in 1762, 2nd maestro di cappella at St. Mark's in Venice. In 1772 Latilla again returned to Naples, where he remained until his death. He wrote about 50 operas, including *Li Mariti a forza* (Naples, 1732); *Angelica ed Orlando* (Naples, 1735); *Gismòndo* (Naples, 1737; also known as *La finta giardiniera;* perf. as *Don Colascione* in London, 1749); *Madama Ciana* (Rome, 1738; perf. as *Gli Artigiani arrichiti* in London, 1750, and in Paris, 1753); *I Sposi incogniti* (Naples, 1779); also the oratorio *L'onnipotenza e la misericordia divina;* 6 string quartets; church music; etc.

La Tombelle, Fernand de, French organist and composer; b. Paris, Aug. 3, 1854; d. Château de Fayrac, Dordogne, Aug. 13, 1928. He first studied with his mother; then at the Paris Cons. with Guilmant (organ) and Dubois (composition); also with Saint-Saëns. In 1885–98 he was assistant organist at the Madeleine; in 1896–1904, prof. of theory at the Schola Cantorum.

WORKS: Oratorios: *Crux, L'Abbaye,* and *Jeanne d'Arc;* operettas: *Un Bon Numéro* and *Un Rêve au pays du bleu* (1892); ballets: *La Muse fleurie* and *La Roche aux fées;* orch. suites: *Impressions matinales, Livres d'images, Tableaux musicaux, Suite féodale;* symph. poem, *Antar;* cantatas: *Ste.-Cécile* and *Ste.-Anne;* incidental music to *La Magdaléenne, Yannic, Conte bleu;* chamber music (quartets, trios, sonatas for violin and piano); Mass; numerous sacred choruses; works for organ; songs. He also wrote a method for the harmonium.

Lattuada, Felice, Italian composer; b. Caselle di Morimondo, Milan, Feb. 5, 1882; d. Milan, Nov. 2, 1962. He studied at the Milan Cons. with Ferroni, graduating in 1911.

WORKS: Operas: *La tempestà* (Milan, Nov. 23, 1922); *Sandha* (Genoa, Feb. 21, 1924); *Le Preziose ridicole* (Milan, Feb. 9, 1929); *Don Giovanni* (Naples, May 18, 1929); *La caverna di Salamanca* (Genoa, March 1, 1938); *Caino* (Milan, Jan. 10, 1957); *Canto augurale per la Nazione Eletta* for Tenor, Chorus, and Orch.; orch. works: *Sinfonia roman-*

tica (1911); *Cimitero di guerra; Il mistero della Passione di Cristo; Incanti della notte; Divertimento rustico; Prelude and Fugue;* other choral, orch., and chamber works; also music for films.

Laub, Ferdinand, Austrian violinist and composer; b. Prague, Jan. 19, 1832; d. Gries, near Bozen, Tyrol, March 18, 1875. A precocious violinist, he entered the Prague Cons. as a child; under the patronage of the Grand Duke Stephen, he went to Vienna for further study (1847); then made a German tour, visited Paris, and played in London; in 1853, became concertmaster at Weimar; in 1855, leader of the court orch. in Berlin; in 1855–57, taught at the Stern Cons. there. After spending some time in Vienna (1862–65), he went on a Russian tour, after which he became a prof. of violin at the Moscow Cons. (1866). He spent his last years in Karlsbad and Tyrol. He wrote an opera, *Die Griesbäcker;* brought out 2 collections of Czech melodies; publ. violin pieces.
BIBLIOGRAPHY: B. Šich, *Ferdinand Laub* (Prague, 1951).

Laubenthal, Horst (original name, **Horst Neumann**), German tenor; b. Duderstadt, March 8, 1939. He was legally adopted by the German tenor **Rudolf Laubenthal,** with whom he studied. He made his debut in Würzburg in 1967; in 1968 joined the Württemberg State Theater in Stuttgart; he also sang in Vienna, Munich, Hamburg, and Berlin.

Laubenthal, Rudolf, German tenor; b. Düsseldorf, March 18, 1886; d. Pöcking, near Starnberg, Oct. 2, 1971. At first he studied medicine in Munich and Berlin; simultaneously took vocal lessons with Lilli Lehmann; in 1913 he made his debut in Berlin at the Deutsches Opernhaus; in 1919 he was engaged by the Bavarian State Opera in Munich. He made his Metropolitan Opera debut in N.Y. as Walther in *Die Meistersinger von Nürnberg* on Nov. 9, 1923; continued on the company's roster until 1933; he also sang with the Covent Garden Opera in London (1926–30) and made guest appearances in Chicago and San Francisco. He was primarily noted as a Wagnerian singer.

Lauber, Joseph, Swiss composer; b. Ruswil, Lucerne canton, Dec. 27, 1864; d. Geneva, May 28, 1952. He studied in Zürich with Hegar, in Munich with Rheinberger, and in Paris with Massenet and Diémer. Returning to Switzerland, he taught at the Zürich Cons.; then conducted a theater orch. in Geneva (1905–7). He wrote more than 200 compositions, including the opera *Die Hexe;* an oratorio, *Ad gloriam Dei;* 6 symphs. and other orch. works; 5 concertos (including one for Double Bass, with Orch.); chamber works; choral music; piano pieces; songs; etc.

Laufer, Beatrice, American composer; b. New York, April 27, 1923. She studied at the Juilliard School of Music with Roger Sessions, Marion Bauer, and Vittorio Giannini. Her works include 2 symphs.

(1944, 1961), a Violin Concerto (1966), and a number of choruses. Her opera *'Ile* was produced in N.Y. on the radio on Feb. 14, 1954; the stage premiere took place at the Brooklyn Museum, on April 28, 1957.

Launis, Armas Emanuel (real name, **Lindberg**), Finnish musicologist and composer; b. Hämeenlinna (Tavastehus), April 22, 1884; d. Nice, Aug. 7, 1959. He studied composition with Sibelius in Helsinki; took courses at the Univ. of Helsinki with Ilmari Krohn; earned his doctorate with the valuable thesis *Über Art, Entstehung und Verbreitung der Estnisch-Finnischen Runenmelodien* (Helsinki, 1913). In 1930 he settled in Nice.
WORKS: Operas: *Seitsemän veljestäf (The 7 Brothers;* Helsinki, April 11, 1913); *Kullervo* (Helsinki, Feb. 28, 1917); *Aslak Hetta* (Helsinki, 1922); *Noidan laulu (The Sorcerer's Song;* 1932); *Lumottu silkkihuivi (The Magic Silk Kerchief;* 1937); *Jehudith* (1940); 2 cantatas (1906, 1910); *Andante religioso* for Violin and Orch. (1932); *Northern Suite* for Violin and Orch. (1950); *Karelian Suite* for Orch. (1952); Piano Quintet and other chamber music; piano pieces; songs.

Laurence, Frederick, English composer; b. London, May 25, 1884. After beginning his career in business, he studied music privately with Josef Holbrooke; also in Germany, France, and Austria. Returning to London, he was for a while active in music publishing.
WORKS: For Orch.: *The Spirit's Wayfaring* (London, Oct. 2, 1918); *The Dance of the Witch Girl* (London, Oct. 12, 1920); *A Miracle; Enchantment; Fire Earth; Milandor; Night; The Dream of Harlequin; The Passionate Quest; The Gate of Vision;* chamber music; piano pieces.

Laurencie, Lionel de la. See **La Laurencie, Lionel de.**

Laurencin, Ferdinand Peter, Bohemian writer on music; b. Kremsier, Moravia, Oct. 15, 1819; d. Vienna, Feb. 5, 1890. He studied in Prague with Tomaschek and Pitsch; subsequently settled in Vienna as a writer; publ. the essays *Zur Geschichte der Kirchenmusik bei den Italienern und Deutschen* (1856), *Das Paradies und die Peri von R. Schumann* (1859), *Dr. Hanslicks Lehre vom Musikalisch Schönen: Eine Abwehr* (1859), and *Die Harmonik der Neuzeit* (1861); also contributed articles to the *Neue Zeitschrift für Musik,* which printed a biographical sketch of him by J. Schucht after his death (1890).

Laurens, Edmond, French composer and pedagogue; b. Bergerac, Nov. 10, 1852; d. Paris, Nov. 27, 1925. He studied with Guiraud at the Paris Cons.; later became a teacher of harmony and composition there.
WORKS: *La Harpe et le glaive,* grand opera; *Les Amours d'un soldat de plomb,* pantomime; *La Neuvaine,* lyric play; other works for the stage: *Irlande,*

Conte d'amour, Roses d'automne; Suite japonaise for Orch.; *Silhouettes* for Piano and Orch.; piano pieces; numerous songs. He also was the author of the manuals *Cours d'enseignement musical pianistique* and *L'Art du correcteur.*

Laurenti, Bartolomeo Girolamo, Italian violinist and composer; b. Bologna, c.1644; d. there, Jan. 18, 1726. He played violin at the Basilica San Petronio; was one of the earliest members of the Accademia Filarmonica in Bologna. He wrote *Sonate per camera a violino e violoncello* (1691); *Sei concerti a 3, cioè violino, violoncello ed organo* (1720); Sonata for Violin and Continuo; etc.

Lauri-Volpi, Giacomo, Italian tenor; b. Lanuvio, near Rome, Dec. 11, 1892; d. Valencia, Spain, March 17, 1979. He studied law; then went to Rome, where he took singing lessons with Enrico Rosati. He made his debut in Viterbo in 1919; then sang in the opera houses in Florence and at La Scala in Milan. He made his first American appearance at the Metropolitan Opera House in N.Y., on Jan. 26, 1923, as the Duke in *Rigoletto;* remained a member of the Metropolitan until 1933, while filling guest engagements at Covent Garden in London, at the Paris Opéra, and at the Teatro Colón in Buenos Aires. In 1934 he returned to Europe, and lived mostly in Burjasot, near Valencia. During World War II he continued to sing in Spain in concert and in opera, and in a remarkable demonstration of his tenorial vim and vigor, he sang an aria of Calaf from Puccini's opera *Turandot* at the Teatro Liceo in Barcelona in 1972, at the age of 80. He publ. several books of reminiscences, among them *L'equivoco* (Milan, 1939); *Cristalli viventi* (Rome, 1948); *A visa aperto* (Milan, 1953); 2 books on voices of the present and past, *Voci paralele* (Milan, 1955) and *Misteri della voce umana* (Milan, 1957).
BIBLIOGRAPHY: A. Gustarelli, *Chi è Giacomo Lauri-Volpi?* (Milan, 1932).

Laurischkus, Max, German composer; b. Insterburg, Feb. 18, 1876; d. Berlin, Nov. 17, 1929. He studied with Bargiel and Herzogenberg at the Hochschule für Musik in Berlin. He wrote *Zug des Todes* for Chorus and Orch.; Cello Concerto; *Konzertstück* for Violin and Orch.; *Pastorale* for "Mustel" Harmonium and Celesta; choruses for women's voices; etc.

Lauro, Antonio, Venezuelan guitarist and composer; b. Ciudad Bolívar, Aug. 3, 1917. He studied in Caracas; became a proficient guitar player; was soloist in the first performance of his Guitar Concerto (Caracas, July 25, 1956). He wrote many pieces for guitar; a choral symph. poem, *Cantacharo;* several symph. suites; choruses; songs.

Lauska, Franz (Seraphinus Ignatius), Bohemian pianist and composer; b. Brünn, Jan. 13, 1764; d. Berlin, April 18, 1825. He studied in Vienna with Albrechtsberger; was a chamber musician in Munich;

in 1794–98, taught in Copenhagen; settled in Berlin in 1798; became a teacher at the court; among his pupils was Meyerbeer. He wrote 24 sonatas (*Grande sonate, Sonate pathétique,* etc.); Cello Sonata; pieces for Piano, 4-hands (*6 Easy and Agreeable Pieces, Polonaise,* etc.); and variations for 2-hands; rondos; etc.

Lautenbacher, Susanne, German violinist; b. Augsburg, April 19, 1932. She studied at the Hochschule für Musik in Munich; took private lessons with Henryk Szeryng; then appeared in Europe as a soloist and chamber music player; also taught violin. She was praised for her sensitive performances of the classical violin repertoire.

Lauterbach, Johann Christoph, German violinist and composer; b. Culmbach, July 24, 1832; d. Dresden, March 28, 1918. He studied in Würzburg with Bratsch and Fröhlich; then at the Brussels Cons. with Bériot and Fétis, receiving a gold medal in 1851; taught violin there; in 1853, became a prof. of violin and concertmaster at the Munich Cons.; in 1861, at the court orch. in Dresden; also head of the violin dept. of the Dresden Cons. (1861–77). He wrote *Cavatine* for Violin and Orch.; *Capriccio* for Violin and Orch.; works for violin and piano (*2 Konzertetüden, Legende, Allegro scherzoso, Polonaise, Tarentelle,* etc.).

Laux, Karl, German writer on music; b. Ludwigshafen, Aug. 26, 1896; d. Dresden, June 27, 1978. He studied at the Univ. of Heidelberg; later taught at the Hochschule für Musik in Dresden, retiring in 1963; was active as a music critic. He publ. a biography of Anton Bruckner (Leipzig, 1940; revised ed., 1947); *Musik und Musiker der Gegenwart* (Essen, 1949); *Die Musik in Russland und in der Sowjetunion* (Berlin, 1958), and a number of valuable monographs and special articles on music in the German Democratic Republic.

Lavagne, André, French composer; b. Paris, July 12, 1913. He studied at the Paris Cons.; won first prize in piano (1933) and Premier 2nd Grand Prix de Rome (1938); in 1941, was appointed inspector of music in Paris schools.
WORKS: Operas: *Comme ils s'aiment* (Paris, 1941) and *Corinne* (Enghiens-les-Bains, 1956); *Concert dans un parc* for Piano and Orch., inspired by Watteau's painting (1941); *Concerto romantique* for Cello and Orch. (1941); *Nox,* symph. poem for Voice and Orch.; *Spectacle rassurant* for Voice and Orch.; several ballets (*Le Pauvre Jongleur, Kermesse,* etc.).
BIBLIOGRAPHY: A. Machabey, *Portraits de trente musiciens français* (Paris, 1949; pp. 115–19).

Lavagnino, Angelo Francesco, Italian composer; b. Genoa, Feb. 22, 1909. He studied with Renzo Rossi and Vito Frazzi at the Milan Cons., graduating in 1933; from 1948 to 1962 he was a prof. of film music at the Accademia Musicale in Siena.

WORKS: Opera, *Malafonte* (Antwerp, 1952); for Orch.: *Volo d'api* (1932) and *Tempo alto* (1938); Violin Concerto (1941); Piano Quintet (1942); Violin Sonata (1943); *Pocket Symphony* (title in Eng.; 1949).

Lavalle-García, Armando, Mexican composer; b. Ocotlán, Jalisco, Nov. 23, 1924. He studied violin at the National Cons. of Music in Mexico City and took courses in composition with Bernal Jiménez, Revueltas, and Rodolfo Halffter; subsequently played the viola with the National Symph. Orch. of Mexico City and conducted the Xalapa Symph. Orch. His music is permeated with the essence of Mexican folklore, even in pieces of ostensibly abstract connotations.
WORKS: 3 ballets: *La canción de los Buenos Principios* (1957); *3 tiempos de amor* (1958); *Corrido* (1959); *Mi viaje,* symph. poem (1950); *Estructuras geométricas* for String Orch. and Percussion (1960); Concerto for Viola and String Orch., (1965); Concerto for Violin, String Orch., and Percussion (1966); *Divertimento* for Wind Quintet (1953); Violin Sonata (1966); Oboe Sonata (1967); *Potencial* for Spanish Guitar, Psaltery, Harp, and Percussion (1967); *Trígonos* for Flute, Clarinet, and Bassoon (1968); Trio for Oboe, Bassoon, and Cello, with Percussion accompaniment (1969).

Lavallée, Calixa, Canadian pianist and composer; b. Verchères, Quebec, Dec. 28, 1842; d. Boston, Jan. 21, 1891. He first studied with his father; then at the Paris Cons. with Marmontel (piano), and Bazin and Boieldieu *fils* (composition). Returning to Canada, he made tours of his native country and the U.S.; took part in the Civil War; in 1881, became soloist in the company of Mme. Gerster, the German singer. He wrote the music to the Canadian national song *O Canada* (first perf. in Montreal, June 24, 1880; poem by Judge Routhier). He subsequently settled in Boston, where he became an instructor at the Petersilea Academy; wrote a comic opera, *The Widow* (Springfield, Ill., March 25, 1882).
BIBLIOGRAPHY: S. Salter, "Early Encouragement to American Composers," *Musical Quarterly* (Jan. 1932); E. Lapierre, *C. Lavallée, Musicien national du Canada* (Montreal, 1937).

Lavigna, Vincenzo, Italian composer and eminent music teacher; b. Altamura, Feb. 21, 1776; d. Milan, Sept. 14, 1836. He studied at the Cons. di Santa Maria di Loreto in Naples; subsequently went to Milan, where he was "maestro al cembalo" at La Scala until 1832; also was prof. of solfeggio at the Milan Cons.; he was a teacher of Verdi. He wrote 10 operas, of which his first, *La muta per amore, ossia Il Medico per forza* (Milan, 1803), was his best; also 2 ballets.
BIBLIOGRAPHY: G. De Napoli, *La triade melodrammatica altamurana: G. Tritto, V. Lavigna, S. Mercadante* (Milan, 1931; pp. 47–66).

Lavignac, (Alexandre Jean) Albert, eminent French musicologist and pedagogue; b. Paris, Jan. 21, 1846; d. there, May 28, 1916. He studied at the Paris Cons. with Marmontel (piano), Bazin and Benoist (harmony), and A. Thomas (composition), winning first prize for *solfège* in 1857, for piano in 1861, for harmony and accompaniment in 1863, and for counterpoint and fugue in 1864; he won 2nd prize for organ in 1865; was appointed assistant prof. of *solfège* (1871), prof. of *solfège* (1875), and then prof. of harmony (1891) there.
WRITINGS: His *Cours complet théorique de dictée musicale* (6 vols., 1882) attracted considerable attention and led to the introduction of musical dictation as a regular subject in all the important European conservatories; it was followed by *Dictées musicales* (additional exercises) in 1900. His magnum opus was the famous *Encyclopédie de la musique et Dictionnaire du Conservatoire,* which he edited from 1913 until his death. Other works: *Solfèges manuscrits* (6 vols.); *50 leçons d'harmonie; Ecole de la pédale du piano* (1889); *La Musique et les musiciens* (1895; 8th ed., 1910; entirely revised, 1950; Eng. trans. with additions on American music by H.E. Krehbiel, 1899; *Le Voyage artistique à Bayreuth* (1897; Eng. trans. as *The Music Dramas of Richard Wagner,* 1898); *Les Gaîtés du Conservatoire* (1900); *L'Education musicale* (1902; Eng. trans., 1903); *Notions scolaires de musique* (1905; Spanish trans., 1906); *Théorie complète des principes fondamentaux de la musique moderne* (1909). Lavignac's compositions (chiefly for the piano) are of little importance; together with T. Lack, he publ. arrangements for 2 pianos of Beethoven's First and 2nd Symphs.

Lavigne, Antoine-Joseph, French oboist; b. Besançon, March 23, 1816; d. Manchester, Aug. 1, 1886. He studied at the Paris Cons.; settled in England in 1841; played in the Drury Lane Promenade Concerts; then in Hallé's Manchester orch. He applied Böhm's ring-key system to the oboe. In his later years he became destitute, and died in the poorhouse.

La Violette, Wesley, American composer; b. St. James, Minn., Jan. 4, 1894; d. Escondido, Calif., July 29, 1978. He studied at Northwestern Univ. and at Chicago Musical College (M.M.; Mus.Doc., 1925); taught at Chicago Musical College (1923–33); in 1940 he went to California and lived in La Jolla.
WORKS: Opera, *Shylock* (1927; awarded the David Bispham Memorial Medal, 1930; excerpts perf., Chicago, Feb. 9, 1930); opera on the life of Buddha, *The Enlightened One* (1955); Symph. No. 1 (Rochester, N.Y., Oct. 19, 1938); Symph. No. 2, subtitled *Miniature,* or *Tom Thumb Symphony* (Chicago, May 25, 1942); *The Song of the Angels,* choral symph. (1952); cantata, *The Road to Calvary* (1952); 2 violin concertos (1929, 1938); *Penetrella* for Divided Strings, 18 parts (Chicago, Nov. 30, 1928); *Osiris,* Egyptian tone poem (1929); *Chorale* for Large Orch. (Chicago, July 31, 1936); *Music from the High Sierras* (San Francisco, March 4, 1941); Symph. No. 4 for Band (1942); Concertino for Flute and Orch. (1943); 3 string quartets; Piano Quintet (1927); Octet (1937);

Sextet for Piano, Flute, Oboe, Clarinet, Bassoon, and Horn (1940); Flute Quintet (1943); Flute Sonata; 2 violin sonatas; Viola Sonata; Piano Sonata; etc. He is the author of several publications on philosophy and religion: *The Creative Light* (N.Y., 1947); *The Wayfarer* (Los Angeles, 1956); etc. He publ. a book, *The Crown of Wisdom* (Bombay, 1960).

Lavista, Mario, Mexican composer of the extreme avant-garde; b. Mexico City, April 3, 1943. He studied harmony with Rodolfo Halffter and composition with Héctor Quintanar; then attended classes and seminars of Stockhausen, Pousseur, Xenakis, and Ligeti in Darmstadt and Cologne. Returning to Mexico in 1970, he founded Quanta, an improvisational music group. In his music he explores all resources of sound, and all idiomatic textures, from deliberate homophony to horrendous explosions of ear-splitting dissonance.
WORKS: *Monologue,* after Gogol's *Diary of a Madman,* for Baritone, Flute, Vibraphone, and Double Bass (1966); *5 Pieces* for String Quartet (1967); *Divertimento* for Wind Quintet, 5 Woodblocks, and 3 Shortwave Radios (1968); *Homage to Samuel Beckett* for 3 Amplified Choruses (1968); *Diacronia* for String Quartet (1969); *Kronos* for a minimum of 15 Alarm Clocks, and Loudspeakers and Tapes, with an indeterminate chronometric duration of 5 to 1,440 minutes (1969); *Piece for One Pianist and One Piano* (1970; also a version called *Piece for 2 Pianists and 2 Pianos,* in which a 2nd pianist maintains an absolute silence that must be "communicated" to the listeners); *Game* for Solo Flute (1970); *Continuo* for Brass, Percussion, 2 Prepared Pianos, and Strings (1970); Trio for 2 String Instruments and Ring Modulator (1972); *Diafonia* for One Performer on 2 Pianos and Percussion (1973); *Cluster* for Piano (1973); *Antinomia* for Tape (1973); *Antifonia* for Flute, 2 Bassoons, and Percussion (1974); *Dialogos* for Violin and Piano (1974); *Espejos (Mirrors)* for Piano, 4-hands (1975); *Quotations* for Cello and Piano (1975); *Lyhannh* for Orch. (1976; the title is Swift's word for the "swallow" in Part 4 of *Gulliver's Travels*); Piano Trio (1976); *Jaula* for any number of Prepared Pianos and Pianists (1976).

Lavoix, Henri-Marie-François, French writer on music; b. Paris, April 26, 1846; d. there, Dec. 27, 1897. He was graduated from the Sorbonne; then studied harmony and counterpoint with H. Cohen; in 1865, became librarian of the Bibliothèque Nationale; contributed articles to the *Revue et Gazette Musicale.*
WRITINGS: *Les Traducteurs de Shakespeare en musique* (1869); *La Musique dans l'ymagerie du moyen-âge* (1875); *La Musique dans la nature* (1873); *Histoire de l'instrumentation* (1878); *Le Chant, ses principes et son histoire,* in collaboration with T. Lemaire (1881); *La Musique du siècle de Saint-Louis* (1884); *La Musique française* (1891). His chief work was *Histoire de la musique* (Paris, 1884; reprinted 1891; trans. into Spanish and publ. in Buenos Aires in 1943).

Lavrangas, Denis, Greek conductor and composer; b. Argostoli, Cephalonia, Oct. 17, 1864; d. Razata, Cephalonia, July 30, 1941. He studied first in Argostoli with N. Serao (violin) and N. Tzanis (theory); then at the Cons. of San Pietro a Majella in Naples; and at the Paris Cons. with Delibes, Massenet, and Dubois; conducted an opera company touring through France; went to Italy and conducted theater orchs. in Turin, Venice, etc. Returning to Greece in 1894, he became artistic director of the Phil. Society of Athens.
WORKS: Operas: *Elda di Vorn* (Naples, 1890); *The 2 Brothers* (Athens, July 22, 1900); *The Sorceress* (Athens, 1901); *Dido* (Athens, April 19, 1909; his best work); *Black Butterfly* (Athens, 1928); *Redeemer* (Corfu, 1935); *Facanapas* (1935; perf. posthumously, Athens, Dec. 2, 1950); operettas: *White Hair* (Athens, 1915) and *Sporting Club* (Athens, 1919); *Ouverture grecque, Suites grecque,* and other works for Orch.; 2 masses; choruses; piano pieces; songs. He also publ. teaching manuals.

Lavry, Marc, significant Israeli composer; b. Riga, Dec. 22, 1903; d. Haifa, March 20, 1967. He studied with Teichmüller at the Leipzig Cons.; then was active as a conductor in Germany and in Sweden. In 1935 he went to Palestine; in 1951 he was appointed head of the music section of the Jerusalem Broadcasting Service. In 1952 he visited the U.S. His music is imbued with intense feeling for Jewish folk motifs. Among his works prior to his going to Palestine, the most notable is *Fantastische Suite* for Orch. (1932). He was the composer of the first Palestinian opera in Hebrew to receive a stage performance, *Dan Hashomer (Dan the Guard),* which he conducted in Tel Aviv on Feb. 17, 1945; another opera, *Tamar and Judah,* in the form of a series of cantillations with homophonic instrumental accompaniment, composed in 1958, was first performed in concert form, at the Jewish Arts Festival of Congregation Rodeph Sholom in N.Y., posthumously, March 22, 1970; he further composed *Israeliana I* for Orch. (1966); symph. poems: *Stalingrad* and *Emek (The Valley);* 2 piano concertos; many songs *(The Song of Emek* appearing in numerous eds.) and smaller works.

Law, Andrew, American singing teacher and composer; b. Milford, Conn., March 21, 1749; d. Cheshire, Conn., July 13, 1821. He graduated from Rhode Island College, receiving his M.A. in 1778; then studied theology and was ordained in Hartford (1787); subsequently he was active as a preacher in Philadelphia and Baltimore; later as a pioneer singing teacher in New England. He invented a new system of notation, patented in 1802, which employed 4 (later increased to 7) different shapes of notes without the staff; it was not successful and was used in only a few of his own books. A 2nd innovation (at least as far as American usages were concerned) was his setting of the melody in the soprano instead of in the tenor. In 1786 he received an honorary M.A. degree from Yale; in 1821, an LL.D. from Allegheny College in Meadville, Pa. He compiled *A Select*

Number of Plain Tunes Adapted to Congregational Worship (1775); *Select Harmony* (Cheshire, 1778); *A Collection of Hymns for Social Worship* (Cheshire, 1782); *The Rudiments of Music* (Cheshire, 1783); *The Art of Singing,* in 3 parts, each separately paged: I. *The Musical Primer;* II. *The Christian Harmony;* III. *The Musical Magazine* (Cheshire, 1792–93; 4th ed., Windsor, Vt., 1803; part III contains 6 books of tunes); *Harmonic Companion, and Guide to Social Worship: Being a Choice Selection of Tunes Adapted to the Various Psalms and Hymns* (Philadelphia, 1807); *The Art of Playing the Organ and Pianoforte* (Philadelphia, 1809); *Essays on Music* (Philadelphia, 1814). Only one of his hymn tunes, *Archdale,* acquired some popularity; but his teaching books, quaintly but clearly written, contributed considerably to early music education in America.

BIBLIOGRAPHY: F.J. Metcalf, *American Psalmody* (N.Y., 1917); idem, *American Writers and Compilers of Sacred Music* (N.Y., 1925); *Dictionary of American Biography* (vol. 11); Richard Crawford, *Andrew Law, American Psalmodist* (Evanston, Ill., 1968).

Lawes, Henry, English composer, brother of **William Lawes;** b. Dinton, Wiltshire, Jan. 5, 1596; d. London, Oct. 21, 1662. He studied in London with Coperario; in 1626, became Epistler and Gentleman of the Chapel Royal, then clerk; was a member of the King's private band; also music master to the Earl of Bridgewater; lost these appointments during the Protectorate, but was reinstated in 1660. He is interred in the cloisters of Westminster Abbey. Lawes is historically important because his infinite care in setting texts with proper note and accent marked a step in the development of vocal composition which culminated in Purcell.

WORKS: *Coelum Britannicum,* masque (London, Feb. 17, 1634); *Comus,* masque (Sept. 29, 1634); *The Triumphs of Peace,* masque; *A Paraphrase upon the Psalmes of David* (1637); *Choice Psalmes put into Musick for 3 Voices* (1648; includes many compositions by his brother **William Lawes**); *Ayres and Dialogues for 1, 2, and 3 Voices* (3 vols., 1653, 1655, 1658); music to poems by Milton, Herrick, W. Cartwright, Davenant, etc.; songs and anthems in contemporary collections: *The Treasury of Musick* (1669); Clifford's *Divine Services and Anthems* (1664); MSS are in the libraries of the British Museum and Christ Church, Oxford.

BIBLIOGRAPHY: *Dictionary of National Biography,* vol. 11 (Oxford, 1921–22); Willa McClung Evans, *Henry Lawes, Musician and Friend of Poets* (N.Y., 1941); E.F. Hart, "Introduction to Henry Lawes," *Music & Letters* (1951); J.G. Demaray, *Milton and the Masque Tradition* (Cambridge, Mass., 1968); A. Davidson, "Milton on the Music of Henry Lawes," *Milton Newsletter* (May 1968); R.J. McGrady, "Henry Lawes and the Concept of Just Note and Accent," *Music & Letters* (Jan. 1969); Pamela J. Willett, *The Henry Lawes Manuscript* (London, 1969); N.C. Carpenter, "Milton and Music: Henry Lawes, Dante, and Casella," *English Literary Renaissance* (1972).

Lawes, William, English composer, brother of **Henry Lawes;** b. Salisbury (baptized, May 1), 1602; d. Chester, Sept. 24, 1645. He studied with Coperario in London; was "musician in ordinary" to Charles I. He was killed in the service of the Royalist army during the Civil War. He is best known for his part-song *Gather ye rosebuds while ye may;* other works include music to Shirley's *The Triumph of Peace* (with Simon Ives; 1633); *The Triumph of Prince d'Amour* (1635); one of his anthems appears in Boyce's *Cathedral Music;* songs and vocal works in *Select Musicall Ayres and Dialogues* (1653 and 1659); *Catch that catch can* (1652), *The Treasury of Musick* (1669), *Choice Psalms* (1648); instrumental music in *Courtly Masquing Ayres* (1662); *The Royal Consort* (66 short pieces for viols, lutes, etc.) and some *Airs* for violin and bass can be found in the British Museum; his *Great Consort* (6 suites for 2 Treble Viols, 2 Theorbos, and 2 Bass Viols) is in the library of Christ Church, Oxford; other MSS of his anthems and canons are in the British Museum and the library of Christ Church, Oxford; *Select Consort Music of William Lawes* is publ. in *Musica Britannica,* 21.

BIBLIOGRAPHY: *Dictionary of National Biography,* vol. 11; J. Pulver, *A Biographical Dictionary of Old English Music* (1927); M. Lefkowitz, *William Lawes* (London, 1960).

Lawrence, Marjorie, Australian soprano; b. Dean's Marsh, Victoria, Feb. 17, 1907; d. Little Rock, Ark., Jan. 13, 1979. She studied in Melbourne with Ivor Boustead; then in Paris with Cécile Gilly. She made her American debut at the Metropolitan Opera House on Dec. 18, 1935, as Brünnhilde in *Die Walküre;* remained on its roster until 1941; made guest appearances with the Chicago, San Francisco, St. Louis, and Cincinnati operas. An attack of poliomyelitis while she was in Mexico (1941) interrupted her career. However, she staged a remarkable return at a concert in N.Y. on Nov. 9, 1942, when she sang reclining upon a couch. Her last appearance as an opera singer took place on Dec. 18, 1943, as Venus in *Tannhäuser.* She subsequently devoted herself to teaching. She publ. an autobiography, *Interrupted Melody, The Story of My Life* (N.Y., 1949), which was made into a motion picture in 1955.

Lawrence, Steve (real name, **Sidney Leibowitz**), American singer of popular music and actor; b. Brooklyn, July 8, 1935. He dropped out of high school to pursue a career as a singer; in 1953 he joined the "Steve Allen Show" on NBC-TV in N.Y., which became the nationally televised "Tonight" show in 1954; there he met the singer **Eydie Gorme,** whom he married in 1957; they subsequently appeared successfully in numerous nightclub engagements; he also acted in Broadway musicals, among them *What Makes Sammy Run?* in 1964, and co-starred with his wife in *Golden Rainbow* (1967).

Lawrence, Vera Brodsky, American pianist and

music editor; b. Norfolk, Va., July 1, 1909. She studied with Josef and Rosina Lhévinne at the Juilliard School of Music in N.Y. (1929–32); gave duo-piano concerts with Harold Triggs, and appeared as a soloist with American orchs. In a radical change of direction, she abandoned her concert career in 1965 to become a historian of American music. In 1967 she was appointed administrator of publications for the Contemporary Music Project, and supervised publication of numerous works by American composers. In 1969 she brought out the collected piano works of Louis Moreau Gottschalk, in 5 vols.; in 1970 she compiled, edited, and produced the collected works of Scott Joplin, in 2 vols., and in 1975 publ. the valuable vol. *Music for Patriots, Politicians, and Presidents,* tracing American history as reflected in popular music, profusely illustrated with title pages and musical excerpts from publ. songs and dances celebrating historical events, and campaign ballads written during presidential elections; this work received the ASCAP–Deems Taylor award in 1976.

Lawton, Dorothy, English music librarian; b. Sheffield, July 31, 1874; d. Bournemouth, Feb. 19, 1960. She came to the U.S. as a child; studied in N.Y. with Stojowski (piano), lectured on and taught piano, and theory and history of music until 1920, when she organized and became director of the music branch (circulation dept.) of the N.Y. Public Library; she established a similar dept. in the American Library in Paris in 1930. She returned to England in 1946, and settled in London.

Layton, Billy Jim, American composer and musicologist; b. Corsicana, Texas, Nov. 14, 1924. He studied at the New England Cons. with Carl McKinley, graduating in 1948; at Yale Univ. with Quincy Porter; and at Harvard Univ. with Walter Piston (composition) and Gombosi and Pirrotta (musicology); obtained his Ph.D. with the dissertation *Italian Music for the Ordinary of the Mass* (1960); was on the faculty of Harvard Univ. (1960–66); in 1966 was appointed a prof. of music at the State Univ. of N.Y. at Stony Brook.
WORKS: *An American Portrait,* symph. overture (1957); *Dante Fantasy* for Orch. (1964); *3 Dylan Thomas Poems* for Chorus and Brass Sextet (1955); chamber music of various descriptions.

Layton, Robert, English musicologist; b. London, May 2, 1930. He was educated at Worcester College, Oxford (B.A., 1953); then went to Sweden, learned the language, and took courses at the univs. of Uppsala and Stockholm; in 1959 he joined the staff of the BBC in London, where he prepared music seminars. He became an authority on Scandinavian music; his books include *Franz Berwald* (in Swedish, Stockholm, 1956; in Eng., London, 1959); *Sibelius and His World* (London, 1970; 3rd revised ed., 1983). He also contributed the majority of the articles on Scandinavian composers to *The New Grove,* and in a spirit of mischievous fun also inserted a biography of a nonexistent Danish composer, making up

his name from the stations of the Copenhagen subway. The editor was not amused, and the phony entry had to be painfully gouged in the galleys for the new printing.

Lazar, Filip, Rumanian composer; b. Craiova, May 18, 1894; d. Paris, Nov. 3, 1936. He studied with Kiriac and Castaldi at the Bucharest Cons. (1907–12) and with Teichmüller and Krehl at the Leipzig Cons. (1913–14). In 1915 he went to Paris; was a founding member of the modern musical society Triton (1928). His music is brilliantly hedonistic, with the ethnic Rumanian element furnishing an exotic element *à la moderne.*
WORKS: *Prelude* for Orch. (1919); *Suita română* for Orch. (1921); *Divertissement* for Orch. (1924); *Suite valaque* for Small Orch. (1925); *Tziganes,* scherzo for Orch. (Boston, Oct. 29, 1926); *Music for an Orchestra* (Boston, March 23, 1928); *Le Ring: Un Round de 4 minutes* (Paris, Jan. 10, 1930); 4 concertos: No. 1, *Concerto Grosso in the Old Style* (Boston, Feb. 21, 1930); No. 2 for Piano and Small Orch. (1931); No. 3 for Piano and Orch. (Paris, Nov. 4, 1934); No. 4, *Concerto da camera,* for Percussion and 12 Instruments (Paris, Dec. 11, 1935); *Musică pentru radio (Music for Radio),* overture for Small Orch. (Paris, Triton concerts, Feb. 26, 1931); 2 piano sonatas (1913, 1929); Violin Sonata (1919); 2 suites for Piano (1924, 1925); *Bagatelles* for Cello and Piano (1925); *3 Dances* for Violin and Piano (1927); *Bagatelles* for Piano (1927); Trio for Oboe, Clarinet, and Bassoon (1934); String Trio (1935); *Petite suite* for Oboe, Clarinet, and Bassoon (1936); choruses; songs.

Lazare, Martin, Belgian pianist and composer; b. Brussels, Oct. 27, 1829; d. there, Aug. 6, 1897. He studied in The Hague with van der Does, and at the Paris Cons. with Zimmerman; traveled to London, Germany, the U.S., and Canada.
WORKS: Opera, *Le Roi de Bohème* (The Hague, 1852); operetta, *Les Deux Mandarins* (Brussels, 1878); chamber music; piano works *(Sicilienne, Valses de salon, 6 études de concert, 6 études de genre).*

Lazaro, Hippolito, Spanish tenor; b. Barcelona, Aug. 13, 1887; d. Madrid, May 14, 1974. He studied in Milan; then sang operetta in Barcelona; went to London in 1912, singing at the Coliseum under the name of **Antonio Manuele;** in 1913 returned to Italy, where Mascagni chose him to create the role of Ugo in *Parisina* at La Scala in Milan. He made his Metropolitan Opera debut in N.Y. on Jan. 31, 1918, as the Duke of Mantua in *Rigoletto;* remained on its roster until 1920. In 1921 he created the role of Piccolo Marat in Mascagni's opera in Rome; also the role of Giannetto in *La cena delle beffe* by Giordano at La Scala in 1924. He made guest appearances with the Vienna State Opera, the Budapest Opera, and the Teatro Colón in Buenos Aires. He retired in 1950.

Lazarof, Henri, brilliant Bulgarian-American composer; b. Sofia, April 12, 1932. He left Bulgaria in

1948 for Palestine, and studied composition with Paul Ben-Haim in Jerusalem; then took courses with Goffredo Petrassi at the Santa Cecilia Academy in Rome (1955–57). He received a study fellowship from Brandeis Univ., where he studied with Harold Shapero (1957–59); in 1962 he joined the music faculty at the Univ. of Calif., Los Angeles; in 1970–71 he was named artist-in-residence at the Univ. in West Berlin; then returned to U.C.L.A. His music is marked by inventive originality in its thematic structure and subtle "sonorism" in instrumentation, without imperiling the pragmatic quality of the basic design; instances of serial procedures are unobtrusive.

WORKS: Piano Concerto (1957); *Piccola serenata* for Orch. (Boston, June 14, 1959); Viola Concerto (Monaco, Feb. 20, 1962; first prize at the International Competition of Monaco); Concerto for Piano and 20 Instruments (Milan Radio, May 28, 1963); *Odes* for Orch. (1963); *Concertino da camera* for Woodwind Quintet (1959); *Tempi concertati,* double concerto for Violin, Viola, and Chamber Orch. (1964); 2 string quartets (1956, 1962); String Trio (1957); Sonata for Violin Solo (1958); *Inventions* for Viola and Piano (1962); *Asymptotes* for Flute and Vibraphone (1963); *Quantetti* (a telescoped title for "Quattro canti per quartetto di pianoforte"), scored for 4 Pianos (1964); *Structures sonores* for Orch. (1966; received first International Prize of the City of Milan, La Scala Award); *Rhapsody* for Violin and Piano (1966); *Espaces* for 10 Instruments (1966); Octet for Wind Instruments (1967); *Mutazione* for Orch. (1967); Concerto for Cello and Orch. (1968; Oslo, Sept. 12, 1969); *Omaggio,* chamber concerto for 19 Players (1968); *Divertimenti* for 5 Players (1969); *Textures* for Piano and 5 Ensembles (1970); *Continuum* for Strings (1970); *Events,* ballet (1973); *Partita* for Brass Quintet (1973); *Concertazioni* for Orch. (1973); Chamber Concerto No. 3 (1974); *Duo-1973* for Piano and Cello (1974)); *Spectrum* for Trumpet, Orch., and Tape (Salt Lake City, Jan. 17, 1975); *Volo* for Solo Viola and 2 String Ensembles (1976); *Chamber Symphony* (1977); Concerto for Orch. (1977); *Canti,* ballet (1980); *Mirrors, Mirrors,* ballet (1981).

Lazarus, Daniel, French composer; b. Paris, Dec. 13, 1898; d. there, June 27, 1964. He studied at the Paris Cons., taking first prize in composition (1915). His works include the ballet *Le Roseau* (Paris, Nov. 15, 1924); *Symphonie avec Hymne,* a large work in 5 parts for Chorus and Orch. portraying the destiny of the Jewish people; an "épopée lyrique," *Trumpeldor* (Paris, April 30, 1946; perf. in concert form); *Fantaisie* for Cello and Orch.; Violin Sonata; piano pieces; etc.

Lazarus, Gustav, German pianist and composer; b. Cologne, July 19, 1861; d. Berlin, May 24, 1920. He studied with I. Seiss, G. Jensen, and F. Wüllner; was a prof. of piano at the Scharwenka Cons. in Berlin (1887–99); in 1899, became director of the Breslaur Cons. and Seminary in Berlin; appeared with success as a pianist in Germany, France, and England.

He wrote 170 opus numbers, including the operas *Mandanika* (Elberfeld, 1899) and *Das Nest der Zaunkönige;* choral works, with Orch.; an Orch. Suite; chamber music; choruses; piano works; songs.

Lazzari, Sylvio, French composer; b. Bozen, Dec. 30, 1857; d. Paris, June 18, 1944. He entered the Paris Cons. in 1883, studying with César Franck and Guiraud; became a naturalized French citizen, settling in Paris. Up to 1894 he was an active propagandist for the works of Wagner, contributing essays to various journals; then he devoted himself entirely to composition, adopting the principles of Impressionism. He visited the U.S. to conduct the world premiere of his opera *Le Sautériot* (Chicago, Jan. 19, 1918). He also wrote the operas *Armor* (Prague, Nov. 7, 1898); *La Lépreuse* (Paris, Feb. 7, 1912); *Melaenis* (Mulhouse, 1927); *La Tour de feu* (Paris, Jan. 16, 1928); a pantomime, *Lulu* (1887); orch. works: Symph.; *Rapsodie espagnole; Ophélie,* symph. poem; *Impressions d'Adriatique; Effet de nuit,* symph. poem (1904); *Marche pour une fête joyeuse; Tableau symphonique d'après Verlaine; Chanson de Moulin; Au bois de Misène; Cortège nocturne; Fête bretonne; Et la jeune fille parla; Perdu en mer; Rapsodie* for Violin and Orch.; *Le Nouveau Christ* for Baritone and Orch.; *Des choses des choses* for Soprano and Orch.; *Apparitions* for Soprano and Orch.; incidental music to *Faust;* Piano Trio; String Quartet; Octet for Wind Instruments; Violin Sonata; piano works; songs; etc.

Lazzari, Virgilio, Italian bass; b. Assisi, April 20, 1887; d. Castel Gandolfo, Oct. 4, 1953. He studied in Rome with Antonio Cogni; made his debut in 1908 with the Virale Light Opera Co.; then sang in South America. From 1918 to 1932 he was a member of the Chicago Opera. On Dec. 28, 1933, he made his Metropolitan Opera debut in N.Y. as Pedro in *L'Africaine;* remained on the roster until 1940; then returned for the 1943–51 seasons.

Lear, Evelyn, outstanding American soprano; b. Brooklyn, Jan. 8, 1926. Her maiden name was **Evelyn Shulman.** Her grandfather, Zavel Kwartin, was a synagogue cantor; her mother was a professional singer; her father, a lawyer, was an amateur musician. She studied piano and also practiced on the French horn, and played in a student orch. at the Berkshire Music Center in Tanglewood. She married Dr. Walter Lear at 17, and assumed his name in her professional career, keeping it after her divorce. She began to take voice lessons in Washington, D.C., with the baritone John Yard and sang in musicals. Realizing her inadequacies in vocal technique, she enrolled in the class of Sergius Kagen at the Juilliard School of Music in N.Y. There she met the baritone **Thomas Stewart,** who in 1955 became her second husband. They obtained Fulbright grants and went to Berlin for further study; she took voice with Maria Ivogün at the Berlin Hochschule für Musik. Soon both she and Stewart received a contract to sing at the Städtische Oper in Berlin. She made her debut there in 1959. An extraordinary

opportunity to show her expertise was presented to her when she was asked to sing the challenging title role in a concert performance of Alban Berg's opera *Lulu* in Vienna on May 24, 1960. She acquitted herself brilliantly, and was engaged to sing Lulu in the stage performance in Vienna in 1962. She was then invited to sing parts in other modern operas; she also gave fine performances of Baroque operas. She made her debut at the Metropolitan Opera in N.Y. on March 17, 1967, as Lavinia in David Levy's opera *Mourning Becomes Electra*. Later she sang at the Metropolitan the parts of the Countess in *Le nozze di Figaro*, Donna Elvira in *Don Giovanni*, and the Marschallin in *Der Rosenkavalier*. On April 2, 1969, she scored a signal success at the Metropolitan in the role of Marie in *Wozzeck*. She often appeared with her husband in the same opera, for instance as Count Almaviva and Cherubino in *Le nozze di Figaro*, as Donna Elvira and Don Giovanni, as Desdemona and Iago in *Otello*, and as Tosca and Scarpia.
BIBLIOGRAPHY: David Ewen, *Musicians since 1900* (N.Y., 1978).

Le Bé, Guillaume, early French type-founder; b. Troyes, 1525; d. Paris, 1598. He was trained in Rome and Venice; in 1550 he settled in Paris. He followed the method of Petrucci, printing notes and staff lines separately, thus necessitating 2 impressions. He also made tablature type. His punches and other equipment were acquired by Ballard, and were in use for another couple of centuries.

Lebègue, Nicolas-Antoine, French organist; b. Laon, 1631; d. Paris, July 6, 1702. From 1664 until his death he was organist at St. Merry in Paris; from 1678 was also one of the court organists. He publ. 3 books of organ music (I, 1676; II and III, after 1678); a vol. of *Pièces de clavessin* (1677); and *Airs* for 2–3 Voices, with Continuo. His complete organ works are to be found in Guilmant's *Archives des maîtres de l'orgue,* 9 (1909); a new ed. of his complete keyboard works is N. Dufourcq's *Œuvres de clavecin* (Monaco, 1956); selections from his clavecin music are printed in Farrenc's *Trésor Musical.*
BIBLIOGRAPHY: N. Dufourcq, *Nicolas-Antoine Lebègue* (Paris, 1954).

Lebert, Siegmund (real name, **Sigmund Levi**), German pianist and pedagogue; b. Ludwigsburg, near Stuttgart, Dec. 12, 1821; d. Stuttgart, Dec. 8, 1884. He was a pupil of Tomaschek in Prague. In 1856 he founded, with Faiszt, Stark, Brachmann, and Speidel, the Stuttgart Cons. His *Grosse Klavierschule* (which included numerous studies of his own composition), publ. in cooperation with Stark, ran through many editions (revised by Max Pauer, 1904), and appeared also in Eng., French, Italian, and Russian translations. He also publ. an *Instructive Edition* of classical piano works and edited Clementi's *Gradus ad Parnassum.*

Lebeuf, Abbé Jean, French music scholar; b. Auxerre, March 6, 1687; d. Paris, April 10, 1760. In 1740 he succeeded to Lancelot's chair in the Académie. He wrote about 180 essays on all manner of subjects, including a series publ. in the *Mercure de France* (1725–28) dealing with plainchant, in strong opposition to Motz's newly invented style of notation; other musical essays by him are: "Lettre sur les orgues," in the *Mercure de France* (1737); *Traité historique et pratique sur le chant ecclésiastique précédé d'une nouvelle méthode pour l'enseigner et l'apprendre facilement* (1741).

Leborne, Aimé-Ambroise-Simon, French composer; b. Brussels, Dec. 29, 1797; d. Paris, April 2, 1866. He went to France as a child; studied at the Paris Cons. with Berton and Cherubini; won the 2nd Prix de Rome (1818) and then the First Prix de Rome (1820); joined the faculty of the Paris Cons., as a prof. first of counterpoint, then of fugue, and finally of composition; retained this post until his death; was also librarian of the Paris Opéra and of the Royal Chapel. He wrote the operas *Le Camp du drap d'or* (Paris, Feb. 28, 1828); *Cinq ans d'entr'acte,* and *Lequel* (Paris, March 21, 1838); adapted Carafa's *Les Deux Figaros;* also edited a new edition of Catel's *Traité d'harmonie,* making numerous additions to the practical part (1848).

Leborne, Fernand, French music critic and composer; b. Charleroi, March 10, 1862; d. Paris, Jan. 15, 1929. He was a pupil at the Paris Cons. of Massenet, Saint-Saëns, and César Franck. He lived mostly in Paris; was music critic for *Le Monde Artiste,* later for the *Petit Parisien;* as a composer, he won the Prix Chartier in 1901.
WORKS: Operas: *Daphnis et Chloé* (Brussels, May 10, 1885); *Hedda* (Milan, 1898); *Mudarra* (Berlin, April 19, 1899); *Les Girondins* (Lyons, March 25, 1905); *La Catalane* (Paris, May 24, 1907); *Cléopâtre* (Rouen, 1914); *Néréa* (Marseilles, Jan. 12, 1926); for Orch.: *Suite intime, Symphonie dramatique, Aquarelles, Temps de guerre, Fête bretonne, Marche solennelle, Ouverture guerrière, Ouverture symphonique; Symphonie-Concerto* for Violin and Piano, with Orch.; incidental music to *L'Absent* (Paris, 1903); String Quartet; Piano Trio; Violin Sonata; Mass; motets; piano pieces; songs.

Lebouc, Charles-Joseph, French cellist and composer; b. Besançon, Dec. 22, 1822; d. Hyères, March 6, 1893. He studied at the Paris Cons. with Franchomme, Halévy, and Colet (composition), winning first prize for cello (1842) and for harmony (1844). He played in the Paris Opéra orch. (1844–48); was a member of the Société des Concerts from 1842; was founder of the Soirées de Musique Classique. He wrote *Trio de concert* for Piano, Violin, and Cello; *Ave verum* for Voice, with Piano and Cello; duos for cello, with piano; cello pieces; also a method for cello.

Lebrun, Franziska (née **Danzi**), renowned German soprano, wife of **Ludwig August Lebrun;** b. Mannheim, March 24, 1756; d. Berlin, May 14, 1791. She made her debut in Schwetzingen on Aug. 9, 1772, as

Sandrina in Sacchini's *La Contadina in corte;* her London debut was on Nov. 8, 1777, as Ariene in Sacchini's *Creso.* She sang in Paris at the Concert Spirituel, and in Milan during the first season of the Teatro alla Scala; also appeared in Naples and Berlin. She was also a composer; publ. 36 sonatas for violin and piano.

Lebrun, Jean, French horn player; b. Lyons, April 6, 1759; d. Paris, c.1809. He studied in Paris with Punto. His playing was remarkable for its purity of tone and for the ease with which he took the high notes. He played first horn in the Paris Opéra orch. (1786–92); after a visit to England, he entered the court orch. at Berlin; following extended tours, returned to Paris in 1806, but found no employment, and in despair, committed suicide. The mute for the horn is his innovation.

Lebrun, Louis-Sébastien, French tenor and composer; b. Paris, Dec. 10, 1764; d. there, June 27, 1829. Unsuccessful as a singer in the Paris Opéra and Opéra-Comique, he became one of the 4 "maîtres de chant" at the Opéra; in 1807, became a tenor in Napoleon's chapelle, and in 1810, "chef du chant" there. He wrote 16 operas, the most successful being *Marcelin* (Paris, March 22, 1800) and *Le Rossignol* (Paris, April 23, 1816); also a Te Deum (1809); *Missa solemnis* (1815); and a collection of *romances.*

Lebrun, Ludwig August, German oboe player, one of the greatest of his time; b. Mannheim (baptized, May 2), 1752; d. Berlin, Dec. 16, 1790. He studied with his father; was a member of the court orch. at Mannheim (1764–78); then toured with his wife, the singer **Franziska Lebrun,** in Germany, Italy, Austria, France, and England; his concerts in London (1781) and Paris (1784), both solo and with his wife, created a sensational success. He composed the ballets *Armida* and *Agus;* also 7 oboe concertos; 12 trios for Oboe, Violin, and Cello; duos for flutes.

Lebrun, Paul Henri Joseph, Belgian conductor and composer; b. Ghent, April 21, 1863; d. Louvain, Nov. 4, 1920. He was a pupil at the Cons. in Ghent; won the Belgian Prix de Rome in 1891 with his cantata *Andromeda,* and first prize of the Belgian Académie for a symph.; in 1890 became prof. of theory at the Ghent Cons. and conductor of the Orpheon at Cambrai; in 1895 became conductor of the Cercle Artistique at Ghent; from 1913 until his death, was director of the music school in Louvain. He wrote an opera, *La Fiancée d'Abydos* (Ghent, 1897); orch. and choral works; chamber music; etc.

Leça, Armando Lopes, Portuguese composer and folk-song specialist; b. Leça da Palmeira, Aug. 9, 1893; d. Vila Nova de Gaia, Sept. 7, 1977. He studied with Oscar da Silva; was active as a choral conductor and a collector of native folk songs; publ. an authoritative edition of popular Portuguese music (1922; expanded ed. in 2 vols., 1947). He wrote several dance suites for orch., of which the *Dansa de Don Pedro* attained considerable popularity; 2 operettas: *Maio florido* (1918) and *Bruxa* (1919); many piano pieces of pictorial character; songs.

Le Caine, Hugh, Canadian acoustician; b. Port Arthur, Ontario, May 27, 1914. He received a B.S. degree from Queen's Univ. in Kingston, Ontario, in 1938 and an M.S. in 1939; obtained his Ph.D. in nuclear physics from the Univ. of Birmingham, England, in 1952; cooperated with the first Canadian Electronic Music Studio at the Univ. of Toronto in 1959, and at McGill Univ. in Montreal in 1964; exhibited electronic-music instruments at Expo '67 in Montreal. He has contributed papers on electronic music to various scholarly journals; realized a number of electronic compositions for the radio and television studios in Toronto and Montreal, among them *Dripsody* (1959), *Alchemy* (1964), and *Perpetual Motion* for Data Systems Computer (1970).

Le Carpentier, Adolphe-Clair, French pianist and composer; b. Paris, Feb. 17, 1809; d. there, July 14, 1869. He was a pupil of Lesueur and Fétis at the Paris Cons. (1818), winning several prizes. He publ. an excellent *Méthode de piano pour les enfants;* also 25 *Etudes élémentaires* (op. 59), and a collection of 24 études, *Le Progrès;* also nearly 300 fantasias on operatic and national airs, well arranged and of moderate difficulty.

Lechner, Leonhard (Leonardus Lechner Athesinus), composer; b. in the valley of Adige (Athesinus; hence his surname) in the Austrian Tyrol, c.1550; d. Stuttgart, Sept. 9, 1606. He was a boy chorister under Roland de Lassus in Munich and Ivo de Vento in Landshut; then a teacher in Nuremberg (1570); was Kapellmeister in Hechingen (1584); from 1585 lived in Tübingen; became a tenor at the Hofkapelle in Stuttgart in 1585, and in 1595 was made Kapellmeister there. His later works, as illustrated by his *Johannispassion, Hohelied Salomonis,* and *Deutsche Sprüche vom Leben und Tod,* show him to be one of the most gifted of the German composers in the period immediately preceding Heinrich Schütz. He publ. *Motectaesacrae* (in 4–6 voices; 2 vols., 1575, 1581, the latter vol. bearing the title *Sacrae cantiones,* partly reprinted by Commer); *Newe teutsche Lieder* (3-voiced villanelles; 2 vols., 1576, 1577; collected ed., 1586, 1590); *Newe teutsche Lieder* (in 4–5 voices; 1577); *Newe teutsche Lieder* (in 4–5 voices; 1582; reprinted by E. Fritz Schmid, 1926); 8 Magnificats (in 4 voices; 1578); 3 masses (in 5–6 voices; 1584); 10 introits (in 5–6 voices; 1584); *Newe lustige teutsche Lieder, nach Art der welschen Canzonen* (in 4 voices; 1586, 1588); 7 *Psalmi Poenitentiales* (in 6 voices; 1587); *Harmoniae miscellae,* collection (1583); *Johannispassion* (1594; reprinted by Ameln, 1926); *Hohelied Salomonis* (in 4 voices; 1606; ed. by Ameln and Lipphardt, 1927); *Deutsche Sprüche vom Leben und Tod* (in 4 voices; 1606; ed. by Ameln and Lipphardt, 1927); other Psalms and motets for 4–18 voices (1575 –1604). He also made arrangements for 5 voices of 3-part villanelles by Regnart (1579; partly reprinted in *Monatshefte für Musikgeschichte,* vol. 19, ed. by Eitner); publ. works of Lassus. A complete ed. of Lechner's works was begun in 1954 under the general editorship of Konrad Ameln; by 1977, vols. 1–5, 7–9, 12, and 13 were issued.

BIBLIOGRAPHY: O. Kade, "Leonhard Lechner und sein Streit mit dem Grafen Eitel Friedrich von Hohenzollern im Jahre 1585," *Monatshefte für Musikgeschichte* (vol. 1, 1869, with musical supplement); J. Sittard, in *Zur Geschichte der Musik und des Theaters am Württembergischen Hofe* (1890; p. 27 et seq.); O. Koller, "Leonhard Lechner," *Musikbuch aus Österreich* (1904); M. Schreiber, *Leonhard Lechner* (Munich, 1932); idem, *Die Kirchenmusik des Kapellmeisters Leonhard Lechner Athesinus* (Regensburg, 1935); K. Ameln, *Gedenkrede auf Leonhard Lechner* (Lüdenscheid, 1961); idem, "Leonhard Lechner in His Time," in J. Riedel, ed., *Cantors at the Crossroads* (Buszin Festschrift; St. Louis, 1967).

Lechthaler, Josef, Austrian church composer and musicologist; b. Rattenberg, Dec. 31, 1891; d. Vienna, Aug. 21, 1948. He studied philology in Innsbruck, and musicology with Guido Adler in Vienna; obtained his degree of Dr.Phil. in 1919; from 1925, taught theory at the Vienna Academy of Music; was director of the church music school there from 1933 until 1938, and again from 1945 to his death. He wrote "Der katholische Organist als Baumeister des Gesamtkunstwerks," in *Kongress-Bericht für Kirchenmusik* (Berlin, 1927); composed cantatas: *Der lichte Tag* and *Lieder der Wanderschaft;* a cappella choruses; 2 string quartets; Trio for Violin, Viola da Gamba, and Harpsichord; song cycle, *Conjunx conjugi;* Piano Sonata; choruses, much guitar music; various songs and pieces for children.

BIBLIOGRAPHY: E. Tittel, *Josef Lechthaler* (Vienna, 1966).

Leclair, Jean Marie (l'aîné), celebrated French violinist; b. Lyons, May 10, 1697; d. Paris, Oct. 22, 1764. At first he was a dancer; was a ballet master at Turin, where the violinist Somis was attracted by dance music he wrote, and gave him further instruction. In 1729–31, he played the violin in the orch. of the Paris Opéra; was a frequent performer at the Concert Spirituel (1728–34). Thenceforth he lived in Paris as a composer and teacher; made brief visits to the Netherlands and Spain in 1743–44. He was assassinated in his own house; the circumstances that no robbery was attempted and that he was stabbed 3 times, in the front part of his body, suggest that the murderer was known to him; it may have been his estranged wife, who was also his publisher and engraver of his music. (See "The Murder of Leclair" in N. Slonimsky's *A Thing or Two about Music;* N.Y., 1948; pp. 86–90.) Leclair was one of the best composers for the violin in the 18th century; although he followed the Italian school in his early works, he developed a distinct style in his later music; he used technical devices in the virtuoso category.

WORKS: Opera, *Glaucus et Scylla* (Paris, Oct. 4, 1746); opera ballet, *Apollon et Climène* (1750); *Concerti grossi* for 3 Violins, Viola, Cello, and Organ; 6 trios, and 2 easy trios, for 2 Violins, with Bass; duos for violins; and (his finest compositions) 48 sonatas for Violin, with Continuo. New eds. have been publ. by F. David (in his *Hohe Schule des Violinspiels* and *Vorschule*), Eitner (in *Publikationen der Gesellschaft für Musikforschung,* vol. 31), D. Alard, M. Herwegh, Bouillard, Moffat, L. Lichtenberg, etc. The violin sonatas opp. 5, 9, and 15 are issued in the series Recent Researches in the Music of the Baroque Era (Madison, Wis., 1968–69). A complete ed. of his works in 16 vols. was begun in Paris in 1953, under the direction of M. Pincherle.

BIBLIOGRAPHY: L. de La Laurencie, "Le Rôle de Leclair dans la musique instrumentale," *Revue Musicale* (April 1923); A. Moser, *Geschichte des Violinspiels* (1923; p. 372 et seq.); H. Engel, *Das Instrumentalkonzert* (Part I, vol. 3, of Kretzschmar's *Führer,* p. 172 et seq.); M. Pincherle, *Jean-Marie Leclair l'aîné* (Paris, 1952); G. Nutting, "J.-M. Leclair," *Musical Quarterly* (Oct. 1964); N. Zaslaw, "Handel and Leclair," *Current Musicology,* 9 (1969).

Leclair, Jean Marie (le cadet), younger brother of the preceding; b. Lyons, Sept. 23, 1703; d. there, Nov. 30, 1777. Like his brother, he was a violinist; he spent most of his life in his native town; publ. a book of violin sonatas; wrote several divertissements.

BIBLIOGRAPHY: Léon Vallas, "Une Famille de violinistes lyonnais, les Leclair," *Bulletin de la Société Française de Musicologie* (July 1921).

Lecocq, Charles, French composer of light opera; b. Paris, June 3, 1832; d. there, Oct. 24, 1918. He studied at the Paris Cons. under Bazin (harmony), Halévy (composition), and Benoist (organ); obtained first prize for harmony (1850) and 2nd prize for fugue (1852). In 1857 he shared with Bizet a prize offered by Offenbach for the best opera buffa, with his *Le Docteur Miracle* (Paris, April 8, 1857). From that time on, he composed industriously for the stage; after several transient successes he produced an operetta, *Fleur de thé* (1868), which had a run of a hundred nights in Paris, and was also well received in England and Germany. He produced 9 more operettas before *La Fille de Mme. Angot* (Brussels, Dec. 4, 1872; Paris, Feb. 21, 1873), which brought him fame. In Paris alone it enjoyed an uninterrupted series of performances for over a year. It was closely followed by its rival in popularity, *Giroflé-Girofla* (Brussels, March 21, 1874). Altogether, he produced some 40 operettas and comic operas, distinguished by melodic grace, instrumental finish, and dramatic acumen, not inferior to the productions of Offenbach and Hervé. His serious opera *Plutus* (Opéra-Comique, March 31, 1886) was unsuccessful. He publ. a ballet pantomime for Piano, *Les Fantoccini;* 24 "morceaux de genre," *Les Miettes;* and a gavotte; also an aubade; melodies and chansons for voice with piano; sacred songs for women's voices (*La Chapelle au couvent*); etc.

BIBLIOGRAPHY: L. Schneider, *Les Maîtres de l'operette, Hervé et Charles Lecocq* (Paris, 1924).

Le Couppey, Félix, French pianist; b. Paris, April 14, 1811; d. there, July 5, 1887. He was a pupil at the Paris Cons.; from 1843, taught piano and harmony there. He publ. several successful piano methods: *Ecole du mécanisme du piano, 24 études primaires; Cours de piano élémentaire et progressif; L'Art du piano* (50 études with annotations); and a pamphlet, *De l'enseignement du piano: Conseils aux femmes professeurs* (1865); also piano character pieces and songs.

Lecuna, Juan Vicente, Venezuelan composer; b. Valencia, Nov. 20, 1891; d. Rome, Italy, April 15, 1954. He studied at the Escuela Normal, graduating in 1906; then went to Caracas and studied music theory with Juan Vicente at the Caracas Cons.; also took piano lessons with Salvador Llamozas. In 1918 he went to N.Y., where he earned a living by playing at hotels and restaurants. He then returned to Caracas and entered the diplomatic service. In 1936 he was appointed a civil employee at the Venezuelan embassy in Washington, D.C. Concurrently, he took courses in orchestration with Gustav Strube in Baltimore. In 1943 he was sent by the Venezuelan dept. of education to study musical education in Brazil, Uruguay, Argentina, and Chile. In 1947 he was named Secretary of the Legation of Venezuela in Rome, and later was appointed a member of the Venezuelan legation at the Vatican. He composed a Piano Concerto; *Suite venezolana* for 4 Guitars; a String Quartet; and a suite of 4 Venezuelan dances for Piano. BIBLIOGRAPHY: Walter Guido, "Ficha biográfica y catálogo de la obra musical de Juan Vicente Lecuna," *Revista Musical de Venezuela* (Jan.–April 1981).

Lecuona, Ernesto, Cuban composer of popular music; b. Havana, Aug. 7, 1896; d. Santa Cruz de Tenerife, Canary Islands, Nov. 29, 1963. He played piano as a child, and wrote his first song when he was 11 years old. He graduated from the National Cons. of Havana (1911); toured South America and Europe as leader of a Cuban dance band. Among his melodies, the most successful are *Malagueña, Andalucía,* and *Siboney.*

Ledbetter, Huddie (Leadbelly), black American folksinger and guitarist; b. Mooringsport, La., Jan. 21, 1885; d. New York, Dec. 6, 1949. He never had an education but possessed a genuine talent for folksong singing. He was jailed for murder in 1918; released in 1925; served another term for attempted homicide (1930–34) and another for assault (1939–40). It was during this last incarceration that he was discovered by folk researchers John and Alan Lomax, and they were instrumental in obtaining his early release and starting him on a career as a professional and renowned performer. The recordings of prison songs he made for the Lomaxes are now on deposit at the Library of Congress. After his release, he played and sang in nightclubs. The authenticity of his performance gives him a historic niche in folk-song history. A cult arose around his name after his death; the "hootenanny" movement was much influenced by his style. He is the composer of the song *Good Night, Irene,* but it did not become popular until after his death.

Ledebur, Carl, German writer on music; b. Schildesche, near Bielefeld, April 20, 1806; d. Stolp, Oct. 25, 1872. He was a Prussian cavalry officer; publ. *Tonkünstlerlexikon Berlins von den ältesten Zeiten bis auf die Gegenwart* (1861; reprint, Tutzing, 1965) and essays on Berlin court music.

Ledenev, Roman, Soviet composer; b. Moscow, Dec. 4, 1930. He studied composition at the Moscow Cons. with Rakov and Anatoly Alexandrov; later was an instructor there. His music is marked by a typically Russian lyric quality touched with permissible dissonances in harmonic treatment. WORKS: Oratorio, *The Chronicle of the Campaign of Igor* (1954); *The Song of Freedom* for Chorus, to words by Asian and African poets (1961); Violin Concerto (1964); Viola Concerto (1964); Sonata in memory of Prokofiev (1956); numerous songs.

Ledent, Félix-Etienne, Belgian pianist and composer; b. Liège, Nov. 20, 1816; d. there, Aug. 23, 1886. He studied at the Liège Cons. with J. Jalheau, and in Paris with Daussoigne-Méhul, taking the 2nd Prix de Rome (1843); in 1844, became prof. of piano at the Liège Cons. He publ. *Adagio et Rondo* for Piano and Orch.; piano pieces and songs.

Lederer, Felix, Bohemian conductor; b. Prague, Feb. 25, 1877; d. Berlin, March 26, 1957. He studied at the Prague Cons.; then at the Vienna Cons.; was conductor at the Municipal Theater in Nuremberg (1899–1903), at Augsburg (1903–5), Barmen (1905–8), Bremen (1908–10), and Mannheim (1910–22); in 1922, was appointed opera conductor at Saarbrücken; from 1945 until his death, he was in Berlin as a prof. at the Hochschule für Musik.

Ledger, Philip, English conductor, organist, harpsichordist, pianist, editor, and arranger; b. Bexhill-on-Sea, Sussex, Dec. 12, 1937. He was educated at King's College, Cambridge, and at the Royal College of Music, London. He served as Master of the Music at Chelmsford Cathedral (1962–65), as director of music at the Univ. of East Anglia (1965–73), and as dean of the School of Fine Arts and Music (1968–71). In 1968 he was named an artistic director of the Aldeburgh Festival; subsequently was engaged as conductor of the Cambridge Univ. Musical Society (1973) and director of music and organist at King's (1974). In 1982 he was appointed principal of the Royal Scottish Academy of Music and Drama in Glasgow. He edited *The Oxford Book of English Madrigals* (1978) and works of Byrd, Purcell, and Handel. A versatile musician, he is renowned as an elegant performer of early English music.

Leduc, Alphonse, French music publisher; b. Nantes, March 9, 1804; d. Paris, June 17, 1868. He

studied with Reicha at the Paris Cons.; played piano and bassoon. In 1841 he founded a music business in Paris; after his death, his son **Alphonse II** (1844–92) inherited the business; at the death of the latter, his widow directed the firm until 1904, when their son **Emile Alphonse III** (b. Nov. 14, 1878; d. Paris, May 24, 1951) became the next owner; his sons **Claude** and **Gilbert Leduc** (partners with their father from 1938) continued the business. From 1860 to 1895 the firm publ. *L'Art Musical,* which was then assimilated with the *Guide Musical.*
BIBLIOGRAPHY: Cecil Hopkinson, *Parisian Music Publishers, 1700–1950* (London, 1954).

Leduc, Jacques, Belgian composer; b. Jette, near Brussels, March 1, 1932. He studied music at the Royal Cons. in Brussels and privately with Jean Absil. In 1962 he was appointed to the faculty of the Music Academy in Uccle; in 1968 became a prof. of harmony at Brussels Cons., and in 1972 a prof. of counterpoint there.
WORKS: Lyric comedy, *Nous attendons Sémiramis* (Belgian Television, Feb. 6, 1973); cantata, *L'Aventure* (1961); *Antigone,* symph. poem (1960); Concertino for Oboe and String Orch. (1962); *Divertissement* for Flute and String Orch. (1962); *Fantaisie sur le thème de "La Folia"* for Clarinet, and Chamber Orch. or Piano (1964); *4 Etudes* for Chamber Orch. (1966); *Le Printemps,* symph. sketch (1967); *Ouverture d'été* (1968); Symph. (1969); Piano Concerto (1970); *5 croquis* for Orch. (1971); *Dialogue* for Clarinet, and Chamber Orch. or Piano (1972); *Instantanés,* 5 pieces for String Ensemble (1972); Wind Quintet (1960); *3 petites pièces en quatuor* for 4 Flutes or Clarinets (1963); String Trio (1963); *Suite en quatuor* for 4 Saxophones (1964); *3 Impromptus* for Harp (1964); *Sortilèges africains,* sequence for Voice, Saxophone, Percussion, and Piano (1966); Flute Sonata (1966); *Ballade* for Clarinet and Piano (1967); Violin Sonata (1967); *Capriccio* for Wind Quartet (1969); *3 pièces* for Solo Cello (1973); *4 pièces brèves* for Piano (1965); *Prelude, Variations, and Fugato* for Piano (1965); *Contrastes* for Piano (1967); *Apostrophes* for Piano (1971); choruses; songs.

Le Duc, Simon, French composer; b. Jan. 15, 1742; d. Paris, Jan. 20, 1777. He studied violin with Gaviniès; made his debut as a soloist on Sept. 8, 1763, at the Concert Spirituel in Paris. He subsequently became active as a composer of instrumental music and a publisher. His works comprise 3 symphs., *Symphonie concertante,* and concertante string trios, with orch.
BIBLIOGRAPHY: Barry S. Brook, "Simon Le Duc l'aîné, a French Symphonist at the Time of Mozart," *Musical Quarterly* (Oct. 1962).

Lee, Brenda, American vocalist; b. Atlanta, Ga., Dec. 11, 1944. She was baptized as **Brenda Mae Tarpley,** but she abbreviated her last name to a monosyllable evocative of her southern heritage. She won a local television prize as a babbling babe, and at the age of 12 made a hit with a recording of *One Step*

at a Time. She never joined a band, and thus owed all her successes to herself. Among her successful singles were *Dum Dum* and *Rockin' around the Christmas Tree;* in 1962 she produced the smash hit *All Alone Am I.* She also recorded several autobiographical discs, such as *The Brenda Lee Story, Sincerely, Brenda Lee,* and *Let It Be Me.*

Lee, Dai-Keong, Hawaiian composer of Chinese parentage; b. Honolulu, Sept. 2, 1915. He studied in the U.S. with Roger Sessions, Frederick Jacobi, and Aaron Copland.
WORKS: Operas: *The Poet's Dilemma* (N.Y., April 12, 1940); *Speakeasy* (N.Y., Feb. 8, 1957); *Hawaiian Festival Overture* (1940); Symph. No. 1 (1942); Violin Concerto (1946); 2nd Symph. (San Francisco, March 14, 1952); *Polynesian Suite* for Orch. (1958); *Canticle of the Pacific* for Chorus and Orch. (1968).

Lee, Ernest Markham, English organist and writer on music; b. Cambridge, June 8, 1874; d. Eastbourne, Nov. 13, 1956. While a student at Emanuel College, he acted as organist at All Saints', Woodford Green; in 1917 he was appointed prof. of organ at the Guildhall School of Music and examiner at the univs. of London, Oxford, and Cambridge; visited Canada and New Zealand (1929–30), Jamaica and Canada (1933), and India (1934); then lived in London.
WORKS: Services, anthems, sacred and secular songs, piano pieces *(Hesperis, Serapis, Modern Suite).*
WRITINGS: *Edvard Grieg* (1908); *The Story of Opera* (1909); *Brahms: The Man and His Music* (1915); *The Story of Symphony* (1916); *On Listening to Music* (1918); *Musical Theory and Knowledge* (1923); *Brahms' Orchestral Works* (1931).

Lee, Louis, German cellist and composer, brother of **Maurice** and **Sebastian Lee;** b. Hamburg, Oct. 19, 1819; d. Lübeck, Aug. 26, 1896. He studied cello with J.N. Prell; gave concerts at the age of 12 in German cities and in Copenhagen. He organized chamber music soirées (with Hafner, then with Boie) in Hamburg; taught at the Hamburg Cons. until 1884; also was first cellist of the Phil. Society. He publ. a Piano Quartet; Piano Trio; Cello Sonata; Cello Sonatina; pieces for piano and cello; piano pieces; music to Schiller's *Jungfrau von Orleans* and *Wilhelm Tell;* etc.

Lee, Maurice, German piano teacher, brother of **Louis** and **Sebastian Lee;** b. Hamburg, Feb. 1821; d. London, June 23, 1895. For many years before his death, he lived in London as a piano teacher and composer of popular salon music.

Lee, Peggy (née **Norma Dolores Egstrom**), American singer of popular music; b. Jamestown, N.Dak., May 26, 1920. After graduating from high school, she sang on a radio station in Fargo; in 1941 Benny Goodman chose her as vocalist with his band; she gained her first success with *Why Don't You Do Right?* She soon launched a solo career; with her first husband, Dave Barbour, she collaborated on writing such hits as *Mañana, Golden Earrings,* and *I Don't Know Enough about You,* which she interpreted with great acumen; she was equally successful with her sophisticated renditions of *Lover, Fever,* and particularly *Is That All There Is?* which became her theme song. With the composer Paul Horner and the playwright William Luce, she wrote the autobiographical musical *Peg* (1983).

Lee, Sebastian, German cellist and composer, brother of **Louis** and **Maurice Lee;** b. Hamburg, Dec. 24, 1805; d. there, Jan. 4, 1887. He studied with J.N. Prell; in 1837–68, was solo cellist at the Opéra in Paris; returned to Hamburg in 1868, remaining there until his death. He publ. an excellent method for cello; also variations, divertissements, and fantasies for cello, with orch.; variations for cello with string quartet; cello duos.

Leedy, Douglas, American composer, pianist, and conductor; b. Portland, Oreg., March 3, 1938. He studied at Pomona College (B.A., 1959) and at the Univ. of Calif. at Berkeley (M.A., 1962). He played the French horn in the Oakland (Calif.) Symph. Orch. and in the San Francisco Opera and Ballet orchs. (1960–65); in 1965–66 he held a joint U.S.-Polish government grant for study in Poland; from 1967 to 1970 was on the faculty of the Univ. of Calif., Los Angeles; from 1973 to 1978 he taught at Reed College in Portland, Oreg. His early works cultivated avant-garde methods of electronic application to mixed media, but later he sought to overcome the restrictions of Western music and its equal temperament; for this purpose, he began in 1979 to work with the Carnatic vocalist K.V. Narayanaswámy in Madras, India. Parallel to that, he evinced an interest in early Western music; edited *Chansons from Petrucci in Original Notation . . .* in the Musica Sacra et Profana series (1983), and also led the Oregon Telemann Ensemble (later known as the Harmonie Universelle).
WORKS: *Exhibition Music* (1965; continued indefinitely); *Decay,* theater piece for Piano, Wagner Tuba, and Tape (1965); *Antifonia* for Brass Quartet (1965); *Usable Music I for Very Small Instruments with Holes* (1966); *Usable Music II* for Brass Instruments (1966); *Teddy Bear's Picnic,* audio-tactile electronic theater piece (1968); *Ave Maris Stella* for Soprano, Instrumental Trio, Organ, and Electronic Sound (1968); *88 is Great,* theater piece for many-handed Piano (1968); *The Electric Zodiac,* electronic music (1969); *Entropical Paradise: 6 Sonic Environments* for Electronic Recordings (1970); *Gloria* for Soprano, Chorus, and Instruments (1970); *The 24th Psalm* for 6 Solo Soprano Voices, Chorus, and Orch. (1972); *Sebastian,* chamber opera based on documents of J.S. Bach, for Soprano, Baritone, Chamber Ensemble, and Tape (1971–74); chorale fantasia, *Wie schön leuchtet der Morgenstern,* for Organ and unseen Soprano (1972); String Quartet, in just tuning (1965–75); *Canti: Music for Con-*

trabass and Chamber Ensemble (1975); *Symphoniae sacrae* for Soprano, Bass, Viola da Gamba, and Harpsichord (1976); *Sur la couche de miettes* for Flute, Oboe, Violin, Viola, Cello, Guitar, Piano, equal-temperament Harpsichord, and just-intonation Harpsichord (1981); *Harpsichord Book, Parts I–II,* in traditional meantone temperament (1974, 1982); *Harpsichord Book, Part III,* in just tuning (1982); *4 Hymns from the Rigveda* for Chorus and Javanese or American Gamelan (1982–83); *5 Organ Chorales* (1983); *Music for Meantone Organ* (1983–84).

Lees, Benjamin, outstanding American composer; b. Harbin, Manchuria, Jan. 8, 1924, of Russian parents (his family name was **Lysniansky**). He was brought to the U.S. in infancy; studied piano in San Francisco and Los Angeles; served in the U.S. Army (1942–45); then enrolled at the Univ. of Southern Calif., Los Angeles, as a student in theory of composition with Halsey Stevens, Ingolf Dahl, and Ernst Kanitz; also took private lessons with George Antheil. He held a Guggenheim fellowship in 1955. In 1956 he went to Finland on a Fulbright fellowship, returning to America in 1962, after several years in Europe; in 1967 he visited Russia under the auspices of the State Dept. He taught composition at the Peabody Cons. in Baltimore, and at Queens College and the Manhattan School of Music in N.Y. Eventually he made his home in Great Neck, Long Island, N.Y., and devoted himself mainly to composition. He writes mostly for instruments; his music possesses an ingratiating quality, modern but not arrogantly so; his harmonies are lucid and are couched in euphonious dissonances; he favors rhythmic asymmetry; the formal design of his works is classical in its clarity. An interesting idiosyncrasy is the use of introductory instrumental solos in most of his symphs. and concertos. The accessibility of his musical expression makes his music attractive to conductors and soloists.
WORKS: 4 piano sonatas (1949, 1950, 1951, 1963); Sonata for 2 Pianos (1951); *Profile* for Orch. (1952; NBC Symph. Orch., N.Y., Milton Katims conducting, April 18, 1954); String Quartet No. 1 (1952); Sonata for Horn and Piano (1952); *Declamations* for String Orch. and Piano (1953; Oklahoma City, Feb. 15, 1956); Toccata for Piano (1953); Symph. No. 1 (1953); *Fantasia* for Piano (1953); Violin Sonata No. 1 (1954); *10 Kaleidoscopes* for Piano (1954); *3 Variables* for Wind Quartet and Piano (1955); *The Oracle,* music drama, libretto by the composer (1955); String Quartet No. 2 (1955); Piano Concerto No. 1 (Vienna, April 26, 1956); *Divertimento burlesca* for Orch. (1957); Symph. No. 2 (Louisville, Dec. 3, 1958); Violin Concerto (1958; Boston, Feb. 8, 1963); *Concertante breve* for Oboe, 2 Horns, Piano, and Strings (1959); *Prologue, Capriccio, and Epilogue* (Portland, April 9, 1959); *Concerto for Orchestra* No. 1 (1959; Rochester, N.Y., Feb. 22, 1962); *Epigrams* for Piano (1960); *Visions of Poets,* dramatic cantata to texts of Walt Whitman's words (Seattle, May 15, 1962); Concerto for Oboe and Orch. (1963); *Spectrum* for Orch. (1964); *The Gilded Cage,* opera (N.Y.,

1964); Concerto for String Quartet and Orch. (Kansas City, Jan. 19, 1965); *Invenzione* for Solo Violin (1965); Concerto for Chamber Orch. (1966); Piano Concerto No. 2 (Boston, March 15, 1968); *Silhouettes* for Wind Instruments and Percussion (1967); *Medea of Corinth* for Vocal Soloists, Wind Quintet, and Timpani (London, Jan. 10, 1971); *Odyssey* for Piano (1970); *Study No. 1* for Cello Solo (1970); *The Trumpet of the Swan* for Narrator and Orch. (Philadelphia, May 13, 1972); *Collage* for String Quartet, Woodwind Quintet, and Percussion (Milwaukee, May 8, 1973); Violin Sonata No. 2 (1972); *Etudes* for Piano and Orch. (Houston, Oct. 28, 1974); *Labyrinths* for Wind Ensemble (Bloomington, Ind., Nov. 18, 1975); Variations for Piano and Orch. (Dallas, March 31, 1976); *Passacaglia* for Orch. (Washington, D.C., April 13, 1976); Concerto for Woodwind Quintet and Orch. (Detroit, Oct. 7, 1976); *Dialogue* for Cello and Piano (N.Y., March 2, 1977); *Scarlatti Portfolio,* ballet (San Francisco, March 15, 1979); *Mobiles* for Orch. (N.Y., April 13, 1979); String Quartet No. 3 (1980); Double Concerto for Piano, Cello, and Orch. (N.Y., Nov. 7, 1982); Concerto for Brass and Orch. (Dallas, March 18, 1983).

BIBLIOGRAPHY: Deryck Cooke, "The Music of Benjamin Lees," *Tempo* (Summer 1959); Deryck Cooke, "The Recent Music of Benjamin Lees," ibid. (Spring 1963); N. Slonimsky, "Benjamin Lees in Excelsis," ibid. (June 1975).

Leeuw, Reinbert de, Dutch composer and pianist; b. Amsterdam, Sept. 8, 1938. He studied at the Amsterdam Cons.; in 1963 was appointed to the faculty of the Cons. of The Hague. Apart from his professional occupations, he became a political activist; collaborated with Louis Andriessen, Mischa Mengelberg, Peter Schat, and Jan van Vijmen on the anti-American multimedia spectacle *Reconstructie,* produced during the Holland Festival in Amsterdam on June 29, 1969. He further wrote an opera, *Axel* (with Vlijmen; 1975–76); *Solo I* for Solo Cello (1961); *3 Positions* for Solo Violin (1963); String Quartet (1963); *Interplay* for Orch. (1965); *Hymns and Chorals* for 15 Winds, 2 Electric Guitars, and Electric Organ (Amsterdam, July 5, 1970); *Duets* for Solo Recorder (1971); *Abschied (Farewell),* symph. poem, a stylistically historical recapitulation of the late Romantic period of German music between 1890 and 1910, culminating in the emergence of Schoenberg (1971–73; Rotterdam, May 11, 1974). Leeuw publ. a book about Ives (in collaboration with J. Bemlef; Amsterdam, 1969) and a collection of 17 articles, *Muzikale anarchie* (Amsterdam, 1973).

BIBLIOGRAPHY: E. Schonberger, "Reinbert de Leeuw," *Key Notes,* 1 (Amsterdam, 1975; pp. 3–18).

Leeuw, Ton de, Dutch composer; b. Rotterdam, Nov. 16, 1926. He studied piano and theory with Louis Toebosch in Breda (1947–49), composition with Badings in Amsterdam (1947–49) and with Messiaen and Thomas de Hartmann in Paris (1949–50); also took courses in ethnomusicology with Jaap Kunst in Amsterdam (1950–54). He was director of

sound for the Netherlands Radio Union in Hilversum (1954–59); then was engaged as a teacher of music in Utrecht and Amsterdam. In his works he explores all thinkable, and some unthinkable but conceptually plausible, ways, pathways, and byways of musical techniques. A government grant enabled him to make a tour of Iran and India in 1961, to study non-European systems of composition.

WORKS: Television opera, *Alceste* (Dutch Television, March 13, 1963); opera, *De droom (The Dream),* based on 14 haiku (Holland Festival, June 16, 1965); radio oratorio, *Hiob (Job),* for Soloists, Chorus, Orch., and Tape (1956); television play, *Litany of Our Time,* for Soprano, Chorus, Instruments, and Electronic Sound (1969; Dutch Television, Jan. 1, 1971); 2 ballets: *De bijen (The Bees;* Arnhem, Sept. 15, 1965) and *Krishna and Radha* for Flute, Harp, and Percussion (1964); Concerto Grosso for String Orch. (1946); *Treurmuziek in memoriam Willem Pijper* for Chamber Orch. (1948); Symph. for Strings and Percussion (1950); Symph. for String Orch. (1951); *Plutos-Suite* for Chamber Orch. (1952); 2 violin concertos (1953, 1961); *Suite* for Youth Orch. (1954); *10 mouvements rétrogrades* for Orch. (1957); *Brabant,* symph. song for Middle Voice and Orch. (1959); *Nritta,* orch. dance (1961); *Ombres* for Orch. (1961); *Symphonies for Winds,* an homage to Stravinsky, for 29 Winds (1962–63); *Haiku I* for Voice and Piano (1963); *Haiku II* for Soprano and Orch. (Rotterdam, July 5, 1968); *Spatial Music I* for 32–48 Players (1965–66); *Spatial Music II* for Percussion (1971); *Spatial Music III* for Orch. in 4 groups (1967); *Spatial Music IV (Homage to Stravinsky)* for 12 Players (1968); *Syntaxis I* for Tape (1966) and *II* for Orch. (1966; Utrecht, May 16, 1966); *Lamento pacis* for Chorus and 16 Instruments (1969); *Music for 12 Strings* (1970); *Music* for Organ and 12 Players (Zwolle, June 29, 1972); *Gending* for Javanese Gamelan Orch. (Hilversum, Oct. 11, 1975); String Trio (1948); Flute Sonata (1949); Violin Sonata (1951); Trio for Flute, Clarinet, and Piano (1952); *5 Sketches* for Oboe, Clarinet, Bassoon, Violin, Viola, and Cello (1952); 2 string quartets (1958; with Tape, 1964); *Antiphony* for Wind Quintet and 4 Electronic Tracks (1960); *Schelp* for Flute, Viola, and Guitar (1964); *The 4 Seasons* for Harp (1964); *Night Music* for one Performer on 3 different Flutes (1966); *Music* for one or 2 Violins (1967); *Music* for Solo Oboe (1969); *Reversed Night* for Solo Flute (1971); *Midare* for Solo Marimba (1972); *Music* for Solo Trombone (1973–74); *Canzone* for 4 Horns, 3 Trumpets, and 3 Trombones (1973–74); *Rime* for Flute and Harp (1974); *Mo-Do* for Amplified Harpsichord (1974); *Modal Music* for Accordion (1978–79); Piano Sonatina (1949); *Introduzione e Passacaglia* for Organ (1949); 2-piano Sonata (1950); *5 Etudes* for Piano (1951); *4 Rhythmic Etudes* for Piano (1952); *Lydische Suite* for Piano (1954); *3 African Studies* for Piano (1954); *Men Go Their Ways* for Piano (1964); *Sweelinck Variations* for Organ (1972–73); *De Toverfluit,* 4 songs for Soprano, Flute, Cello, and Piano (1954); *Car nos vignes sont en fleur* for 12 Mixed Voices (1981); *And They Shall Reign Forever* for Mezzo-soprano, Clarinet, Horn, Piano, and Percussion (1981); *Electronic Suite* for Tape (1958); *Clair-Obscur* for Electronic Sounds (1982); solo songs; choruses. He publ. a book, *Muziek van de twintigate eeuw (Music of the Twentieth Century;* Utrecht, 1964). See *Key Notes,* 3 (1976; pp. 67–74).

LeFanu, Nicola, British composer, daughter of **Elizabeth Maconchy;** b. Wickham Bishops, Essex, April 28, 1947. She studied music at St. Hilda's College, Oxford (B.A., 1968); also took private lessons with Goffredo Petrassi in Italy and with Thea Musgrave and Peter Maxwell Davies in England. Although she scrutinized her mother's works with great care and interest, she never engaged in a course of formal instruction with her. Brought up in an extremely cultured and sophisticated environment (her father, William LeFanu, made a mark in the British literary world), she absorbed the seemingly conflicting musical influences in the modern world with elegance and ease; her own style of composition represents a median line of modernism which she developed *sine ira et studio,* without discrimination even against such obsolescent resources as major triads. As a result, her music pleased the public and appealed to unprejudiced judges of musical competitions. Thus, in 1970, she won first prize at the BBC National Competition for her Variations for Oboe Quartet (1968). Most of her compositions are set for distinctive chamber music groups.

WORKS: *Soliloquy* for Oboe Solo (1965); *Preludio* for Chamber Orch. (1967); *Chiaroscuro* for Piano (1969); *Quartettsatz* for String Quartet (1970); Quintet for Clarinet and Strings (1970); *The Hidden Landscape* for Orch. (London, Aug. 7, 1973); *Columbia Falls* for Percussion, Harp, and Strings (Birmingham, Nov. 20, 1975); *Farne* for Orch. (Bradford, March 28, 1980); *Collana* for Solo Percussion and Ensemble (Boston, April 25, 1976); *Deva* for Solo Cello and 7 Players (London, March 23, 1979) *Christ Calls Man Home,* music for church service (1971); *The Valleys Shall Sing* for Chorus and Winds (1973); *The Same Day Dawns* for Soprano and 5 Players (1974; Boston, Nov. 1974); *For We Are the Stars* for 16 Solo Voices, to a text based on an American Indian poem (1978); *Like a Wave of the Sea* for Mixed Choir and Ensemble of Early Instruments (1981); *The Old Woman of Beare* for Soprano and 13 Players (1981); *Anti-World* for Dancer, Soprano, Baritone, and Ensemble (1972); *The Last Laugh* for Soprano, Tape, and Instrumental Ensemble (1972); *Dawnpath,* chamber opera (London, Sept. 29, 1977).

Lefébure, Louis-François Henri, French musician; b. Paris, Feb. 18, 1754; d. there, Nov. 1840. He was a government official until 1814; publ. several instructive books on singing: *Nouveau Solfège,* a 23-page pamphlet (1780), containing ideas put into practice by Gossec in the *Ecole royale de chant;* a polemical brochure, *Bévues, erreurs et méprises de différents auteurs célèbres en matières musicales* (1789); etc. He also composed 2 oratorios and other choral works.

Lefebure, Yvonne, French pianist; b. Ermont, Seine-et-Oise, June 29, 1904. She began piano studies as a child; at 9 won the "prix de petits prodiges" of the Paris Cons.; then studied there with Maurice Emanuel, Georges Caussade, and Charles Widor, winning 6 premiers prix; also took private lessons with Cortot. She married the music critic **Frédérick Goldbeck.**

Lefébure-Wély, Louis James Alfred, French organist and composer; b. Paris, Nov. 13, 1817; d. there, Dec. 31, 1869. A pupil of his father, he took, at the age of 8, the latter's place as organist of the church of Saint-Roch, becoming its regular organist at 14. Entering the Paris Cons. in 1832, he was taught by Benoist (organ) and Laurent and Zimmerman (piano); studied composition with Berton and Halévy. In 1847–58 he was organist at the Madeleine; then at St. Sulpice.

WORKS: Opera, *Les Recruteurs* (1861); cantata, *Après la victoire* (1863); 3 masses; 3 symphs.; String Quintet; String Quartet; much elegant salon music for piano (his most celebrated piece is *The Monastery Bells*); 50 piano études; harmonium music.

Lefebvre, Charles Edouard, French composer; b. Paris, June 19, 1843; d. Aix-les-Bains, Sept. 8, 1917. He studied at the Paris Cons.; won the Premier Grand Prix de Rome in 1870 for his cantata *Le Jugement de Dieu;* following his study in Rome, joined the faculty of the Paris Cons. in 1895.

WORKS: Operas: *Le trésor* (Angers, 1883); *Zaïre* (Lille, 1887); *Djelma* (Paris, May 25, 1894); *Singoalla; Judith,* biblical drama (Paris, 1879); *Ouverture dramatique; Dalila,* symph. poem; *Eloa,* "poème lyrique"; legend, *Melka; Sainte Cécile* for Solo Voice, Chorus, and Orch. (Paris, 1896); Serenade for Orch.; *Toggenburg,* overture (Paris, 1904); *La Messe du fantôme* for Voice and Orch.; chamber music (sonatas, trios, quartets, suites for both strings and woodwinds, etc.).

Lefeld, Jerzy Albert, Polish pianist, composer, and pedagogue; b. Warsaw, Jan. 17, 1898; d. there, Feb. 22, 1980. He studied piano with Michalowski and composition with Statkowski at the Warsaw Cons.; in 1918 he joined its faculty. He became known principally as a fine piano accompanist. His own compositions include 2 symphs., a string sextet, piano pieces, and songs.

Lefèvre, Jean Xavier, French clarinetist; b. Lausanne, March 6, 1763; d. Paris, Nov. 9, 1829. He studied with Michel Yost in Paris; from 1787, played in concerts; in 1791–1817, was at the Paris Opéra; in 1795–1825, a prof. at the Cons. He wrote a clarinet method (1802); also 6 concertos for clarinet, and trios, duos, sonatas, etc., for his instrument. He popularized the sixth key of the clarinet, but did not invent it, as is often stated.

BIBLIOGRAPHY: F.G. Rendall, *The Clarinet* (London, 1954; p. 74).

Leffler-Burckard, Martha, German soprano; b.

Berlin, June 16, 1865; d. Wiesbaden, May 14, 1954. She made her debut as a coloratura soprano in Strasbourg (1890); then sang at Breslau, Cologne, and Bremen; in 1898–1900, was at the court theater in Weimar; in 1900–1902, was at Wiesbaden; after that, at the principal German opera houses; in 1906, at Bayreuth; in 1908, at the Metropolitan Opera House in Wagner roles; in 1912–19, was a member of the Berlin Opera. Her best roles were Fidelio, Isolde, and the 3 Brünnhildes.

Le Flem, Paul, French composer and music critic; b. Lézardrieux, Côtes-du-Nord, March 18, 1881; still verifiably alive, albeit nearly blind, in Paris in October 1983, in his 103rd year of an active long life. He studied philosophy at the Sorbonne in Paris; in 1901 traveled to Russia; then studied music with Lavignac at the Paris Cons. and later with Vincent d'Indy and Albert Roussel at the Schola Cantorum. He subsequently taught a course in counterpoint at the Schola Cantorum; was engaged as a chorus conductor at the Opéra-Comique in 1924; then devoted himself mainly to music criticism; was for 17 years principal music critic of *Comœdia;* was one of the founders of the modern concert series *La Spirale* in Paris in 1935. He received the Grand Prix Musical of the City of Paris in 1951 in appreciation of his work as a writer, scholar, and composer. In his writings he energetically promoted the cause of modern music. His own compositions followed the musical methods of the French neo-Classical school; in several of his works he employed the melodic patterns of his native Brittany. WORKS: For the stage: *Aucassin et Nicolette,* fairy tale (Paris, July 20, 1923); *Le Rossignol de St. Malo* (Paris, Opéra-Comique, May 5, 1942); *La Clairière des fées,* lyric fantasy (1943; Paris Radio, Nov. 29, 1968); *La Magicienne de la mer,* lyric opera (Paris, Oct. 29, 1954). For Orch.: 4 symphs. (1908, 1958, 1967, 1977–78); *Konzertstück* for Violin and Orch. (1965); *La Maudite,* dramatic legend for Voices and Orch. (1967; new version, 1971); chamber music; piano pieces; choruses; songs.

Le Fleming, Christopher (Kaye), English composer; b. Wimborne, Feb. 26, 1908. He studied piano, and has been active in teaching at primary schools. He has written *The Singing Friar* for Tenor Solo, Chorus, and Orch.; 5 Psalms; *Peter Rabbit Music Books* for Piano; orch. suite, *London River* (1956); incidental music for plays.

Le Gallienne, Dorian, Australian composer; b. Melbourne, April 19, 1915; d. there, July 27, 1963. He graduated from Melbourne Univ. in 1938; then went to England, and studied with Arthur Benjamin and Howells at the Royal College of Music in London; during World War II he worked with the Dept. of Information and the Australian Broadcasting Commission. On another trip to England he took private lessons in composition with Gordon Jacob; in 1953 returned to Melbourne. His music is marked by clear linear procedures, often in dissonant counterpoint.

WORKS: 2 ballets: *Contes heraldiques* (1947) and *Voyageur* (1954); *3 Psalms* for Chorus and Orch. (1948); *Overture* (1952); Symph. in E (1952–53); Sinfonietta (1951–56); *Symphonic Study* for Orch. (1962–63; a posthumous work derived from material intended as a 2nd Symph.); Flute Sonata (1943); Violin Sonata (1945); Duo for Violin and Viola (1956); Trio for Oboe, Violin, and Viola (1957); 2 *Pieces:* No. 1 for Violin, Cello, Clarinet, Percussion, and Harp, and No. 2 for 2 Clarinets and String Quartet (both 1959); piano pieces; numerous songs, including *3 Sonnets of Shakespeare* (1946) and *4 Divine Poems of John Donne* (1947–50); incidental and film music.

Legge, Walter, British record producer; b. London, June 1, 1906; d. St. Jean-Cap Ferrat, France, March 22, 1979. Although not a professional musician by education or training, he became an ardent promoter of high-grade recordings of classical music; artists who appeared in recording sessions with him described him as a rigorous taskmaster who was willing to work endless hours until satisfactory results were achieved. Among the singers who performed for him was **Elisabeth Schwarzkopf,** whom he married in 1953. He also supervised records by Artur Schnabel and Wanda Landowska. In 1945 he sponsored the Philharmonia of London, conducted by Sir Thomas Beecham and later by Otto Klemperer. An important contribution to the auditory preservation of great performances was Legge's recordings of the piano performances by Dinu Lipatti, the brilliant Rumanian musician who died at an early age. Elisabeth Schwarzkopf edited a memorial publication, *On and Off the Record: A Memoir of Walter Legge* (N.Y., 1982). Incidentally, Legge pronounced his name "leg," as in a leg of lamb.

Leginska, Ethel (real name, **Liggins**), English pianist, teacher, and composer; b. Hull, April 13, 1886; d. Los Angeles, Feb. 26, 1970. She showed a natural talent for music at an early age; the pseudonym Leginska was given to her by Lady Maud Warrender, under the illusion that a Polish-looking name might help her artistic career. She studied piano at the Hoch Cons. in Frankfurt, and later in Vienna with Leschetizky. She made her debut as a pianist in London; also toured Europe; on Jan. 20, 1913, she appeared for the first time in America, at a recital in N.Y. Her playing was described as having masculine vigor, dashing brilliance, and great variety of tonal color; however, criticism was also voiced against an individualistic treatment of classical works. In the midst of her career as a pianist, she developed a great interest in conducting; she organized the Boston Phil. Orch. (100 players), later the Women's Symph. Orch. of Boston; appeared as a guest conductor with various orchs. in America and in Europe. In this field of activity she also elicited interest, leading to a discussion in the press of a woman's capability of conducting an orch. While in the U.S., she took courses in composition with Rubin Goldmark and Ernest Bloch; wrote music in various genres, distinguished by rhythmic display and a certain measure of modernism. She married the composer **Emerson Whithorne** in 1907 (divorced in 1916). In 1939 she settled in Los Angeles as a piano teacher.

WORKS: Operas: *Gale* (Chicago Civic Opera Co., Nov. 23, 1935, composer conducting) and *The Rose and the Ring* (1932; perf. for the first time, Los Angeles, Feb. 23, 1957, composer conducting); *From a Life* for 13 Instruments (N.Y., Jan. 9, 1922); *Beyond the Fields We Know,* symph. poem (N.Y., Feb. 12, 1922); *2 Short Pieces* for Orch. (Boston Symph., Feb. 29, 1924, Monteux conducting); *Quatre sujets barbares,* inspired by Gauguin, suite for Orch. (Munich, Dec. 13, 1924, composer conducting); *Fantasy* for Orch. and Piano (N.Y., Jan. 3, 1926); *Triptych* for 11 Instruments (Chicago, April 29, 1928); String Quartet, after 4 poems by Tagore (Boston, April 25, 1921); *6 Nursery Rhymes* for Soprano and Chamber Orch.; piano pieces; songs.

Legley, Victor, outstanding Belgian composer; b. Hazebrouck, French Flanders, June 18, 1915. He studied viola and music theory at the Brussels Cons. (1933–35); also took private lessons in composition with Jean Absil (1941), who was mainly influential in shaping Legley's style; in 1947 he became a programmer for the Flemish broadcasts of Belgian Radio; from 1949 taught at the Brussels Cons. In his works he adheres to the pragmatic tenets of modern music, structurally diversified and unconstricted by inhibitions against dissonance.

WORKS: Opera, *La Farce des deux nus* (Antwerp, Dec. 10, 1966); ballet, *Le Bal des halles* (1954); *Symphonic Variations on an Old Flemish Folk Song* (1941); 5 symphs. (1942, 1947, 1953, 1964, 1965); *Concert à 13,* chamber symph. (1944); *Suite* for Orch. (1944); *Music for a Greek Tragedy* for Orch. (1946); *Symphonie miniature* for Chamber Orch. (1946); 2 violin concertos: No. 1 (1947) and No. 2 (1966; Brussels, May 22, 1967; mandatory work of the 1967 Queen Elisabeth violin competition finals); *The Golden River,* symph. sketch (1948); Piano Concerto (1952); *Divertimento* for Orch. (1952); *Little Carnaval Overture* (1954); Concertino for Timpani and Orch. (1956); *Serenade* for String Orch. (1957); *La Cathédrale d'acier (The Steel Cathedral),* symph. sketch after a painting by Fernand Steven (1958); *Overture to a Comedy by Goldoni* (1958); *3 Pieces* for Chamber Orch. (1960); *Dyptiek* for Orch. (1964); *Harp Concerto* (1966); *Paradise Regained* for Orch. (1967); *Prélude for a Ballet* (1969); *3 Movements* for Brass and Percussion (1969); *Espaces* for String Orch. (1970); Viola Concerto (1971); 5 string quartets (1941; 1947; 1956; 1963; *Esquisses,* 1970); Trio for Oboe, Clarinet, and Bassoon (1942); Quartet for 4 Flutes (1943); Violin Sonata (1943); Viola Sonata (1943); Sextet for Piano and Wind Quintet (1945); Cello Sonata (1945); *Musique de midi,* nonet (1948); Clarinet Sonata (1952); Trumpet Sonata (1953); *Serenade* for 2 Violins and Piano (1954); *Burlesque* for Violin and Piano (1956); *Poème d'été* for Violin and Piano (1957); *Serenade* for Flute, Violin, and Cello (1957); *5 Miniatures* for 4 Saxophones (1958); Trio for Flute, Viola, and Guitar (1959); Wind Quintet (1961); *4 Pieces* for Guitar (1964); *Rhapsodie* for

Trumpet and Piano (1967); Piano Quartet (1973); Piano Trio (1973); String Trio (1973); 4 *Ballades* for either Violin, Viola, Cello, or Double Bass, each with Piano (1975); 2 piano sonatas (1946, 1974); *4 Portraits* for Piano (1954–55); *Music* for 2 Pianos (1966); *3 Marches* for Piano (1968); *Brindilles* for Piano (1974); *Brieven uit Portugal* for Voice and Piano (1955); *Zeng* for Soprano, and String Quartet or String Orch. (1965); other works for voice.

Legrand, Michel, French composer of popular music; b. Paris, Feb. 24, 1932. He entered the Paris Cons. at the age of 11; while still a student, he began making professional jazz arrangements; wrote for radio, television, and the cinema. His inventive score for the motion picture *Les Parapluies de Cherbourg* (1965), written throughout in singsong fashion, received merited praise.

Legrenzi, Giovanni, celebrated Italian composer; b. Clusone, near Bergamo (baptized, Aug. 12), 1626; d. Venice, May 27, 1690. He was the son of a violinist and composer named **Giovanni Maria Legrenzi.** In 1645 he became organist at S. Maria Maggiore in Bergamo; in 1651 he was ordained and made resident chaplain there; in 1653 became first organist. In 1656 he was named maestro di cappella of the Accademia dello Spirito Santo in Ferrara; his first opera, *Nino il giusto,* was given in Ferrara in 1662. He left Ferrara in 1665; in 1671 he settled in Venice, where he served as an instructor at the Conservatorio dei Mendicanti; in 1683 was its maestro di coro. In 1677 he was maestro of the Oratorio at S. Maria della Fava. In 1681 he became vice-maestro of San Marco; in 1685 was elected maestro there; under his regimen the orch. was increased to 34 instrumental parts (8 violins, 11 violettas, 2 viole da braccio, 3 violones, 4 theorbos, 2 cornets, one bassoon, and 3 trombones). Legrenzi was a noted teacher; among his pupils were Gasparini, Lotti, and Caldara, as well as his own nephew, **Giovanni Varischino.** Legrenzi's sonatas are noteworthy, since they served as models of Baroque forms as later practiced by Vivaldi and Bach. His operas and oratorios were marked by a development of the *da capo* form in arias, and his carefully wrought orch. support of the vocal parts was of historic significance as presaging the development of opera.

WORKS: OPERAS: *Nino il giusto* (Ferrara, 1662; not extant); *L'Achille in Sciro* (Ferrara, 1663; not extant); *Zenobia e Radamisto* (Ferrara, 1665); *Tiridate* (based upon the preceding; Venice, 1668; not extant); *Eteocle e Polinice* (Venice, 1675); *La divisione del mondo* (Venice, 1675); *Adone in Cipro* (Venice, 1676; not extant); *Germanico sul Reno* (Venice, 1676); *Totila* (Venice, 1677); *Il Creso* (Venice, 1681); *Antioco il grande* (Venice, 1681); *Il Pausania* (Venice, 1682); *Lisimaco riamato* (Venice, 1682); *L'Ottaviano Cesare Augusto* (Mantua, 1682; not extant); *Giustino* (Venice, 1683); *I due Cesari* (Venice, 1683); *L'anarchia dell'imperio* (Venice, 1684; not extant); *Publio Elio Pertinace* (Venice, 1684; not extant); *Ifianassa e Melampo* (Pratolino, 1685; not extant). ORATORIOS: *Oratorio del giuditio*

(Vienna, 1665; not extant); *Gli sponsali d'Ester* (Modena, 1676; not extant); *Il Sedicia* (Ferrara, 1676); *La vendita del core humano* (Ferrara, 1676); *Il Sisara* (Ferrara, 1678; not extant); *Decollatione di S. Giovanni* (Ferrara, 1678; not extant); *La morte del cor penitente* (Vienna, 1705); also the following published sacred works: *Concerti musicali per uso di chiesa* (Venice, 1654); *Harmonia d'affeti devoti* for 2–4 Voices (Venice, 1655); 13 *Salmi a 5* (Venice, 1657); *Sentimenti devoti* for 2–3 Voices (Venice, 1660); *Compiete con le lettanie & antifone della BV a 5* (Venice, 1662); *Sacri e festivi concenti, messa e psalmi a due chori* (Venice, 1667); *Acclamationi divoti* for one Voice (Bologna, 1670); *Sacri musicali concerti* for 2–3 Voices (Venice, 1689); *Motetti sacri* for one Voice (G. Varischino, ed.; Venice, 1692); additional sacred works include psalms, motets, etc. His secular vocal works include *Cantate e canzonette* for one Voice (Bologna, 1676; modern ed. in *Recent Researches in the Music of the Baroque Era,* XIV–XV, 1972); *Idee armonische* for 2–3 Voices (Venice, 1678); *Echi di riverenza di cantate e canzoni* (Bologna, 1678); cantatas; etc. INSTRUMENTAL MUSIC: 18 *Sonate a 2–3* (Venice, 1655); 30 *Sonate da chiesa e da camera . . . a 3* (Venice, 1656); 16 *Sonate a 2, 3, 5, & 6* (Venice, 1663); *La cetra, sonate a 2–4* (Venice, 1673); *Balletti e correnti a 5* (G. Varischino, ed.; Venice, 1691); *Sonate, 2–7 insts. con trombe e senza, overo flauti* (Venice, c.1695; not extant); several of the sonatas have been published in *Hortus musicus,* XXXI (1949) and LXXXIII and LXXXIV (1951), and in Le Pupitre, IV (Paris, 1968).

BIBLIOGRAPHY: H. Nüssle, *Giovanni Legrenzi als Instrumentalkomponist* (Diss., Univ. of Munich, 1917); G. Tebaldini, "Giovanni Legrenzi," *Musica d'Oggi* (April 1937); P. Fogaccia, *Giovanni Legrenzi* (Bergamo, 1954); S. Bonta, *The Church Sonatas of Giovanni Legrenzi* (Diss., Harvard Univ., 1964); J. MacDonald, *The Sacred Vocal Music of Giovanni Legrenzi* (Diss., Univ. of Michigan, 1964); A. Meli, "L'esordio di Giovanni Legrenzi da Clusone in Santa Maria Maggiore dal 1645 al 1655," *L'Eco di Bergamo* (Aug. 23, 1970); C. Sartori, "Due Legrenzi ricuperati," *Acta Musicologica,* XLVI (1974).

Legros, Joseph, French tenor; b. Monampteuil, Sept. 7, 1739; d. La Rochelle, Dec. 20, 1793. He was a choirboy in Laon; made his debut at the Paris Opéra in 1764 as Titon in Mondonville's *Titon et l'Aurore;* subsequently created several roles in operas by Gluck, including Achilles in *Iphigénie en Aulide* (1774) and Pylades in *Iphigénie en Tauride* (1779); he also sang in operas by Piccinni, Grétry, and others; he retired from the stage in 1783. He served as director of the Concert Spirituel (1777–90). He also was a composer; he wrote several operas and a number of songs.

Lehár, Franz, celebrated Austrian operetta composer; b. Komorn, Hungary, April 30, 1870; d. Bad Ischl, Oct. 24, 1948. He was first instructed in music by his father, Franz Lehár (1838–98), a military bandmaster; entered the Prague Cons. at 12 and studied violin with A. Bennewitz and theory with J. Foerster. In 1885 he was brought to the attention of Fibich, who gave him lessons in composition independently from his studies at the Cons. In 1887 Lehár submitted 2 piano sonatas to Dvořák, who encouraged him in his musical career. In 1888 he became a violinist in a theater orch. in Elberfeld; in 1889, entered his father's band (50th Infantry) in Vienna, and assisted him as conductor; after 1890 he led various military bands in Pola, Trieste, Budapest, and Vienna. His first success as a stage composer came with the production of his opera *Kukuschka* (Leipzig, Nov. 28, 1896); most of his subsequent productions took place in Vienna. His most celebrated operetta is *Die lustige Witwe (The Merry Widow);* the first production, in Vienna in 1905, was followed by innumerable performances throughout the world; in Buenos Aires it was played simultaneously in 5 languages (1907); other operettas that achieved tremendous success were *Der Graf von Luxemburg* (1909) and *Zigeunerliebe* (1910). Lehár's music exemplifies the spirit of gaiety and frivolity that was the mark of Vienna early in the century; his superlative gift of facile melody and infectious rhythms is combined with genuine wit and irony; a blend of nostalgia and sophisticated humor made a lasting appeal to audiences, undiminished by the upheavals of wars and revolutions.

WORKS: Opera, *Kukuschka* (Leipzig, Nov. 28, 1896; rewritten as *Tatjana,* Brünn, Feb. 24, 1905); operettas: *Wiener Frauen* (Vienna, Nov. 25, 1902; in Berlin as *Der Klavierstimmer;* rewritten as *Der Schlüssel zum Paradiese,* Leipzig, 1906); *Der Rastelbinder* (Vienna, Dec. 20, 1902); *Der Göttergatte* (Vienna, Jan. 20, 1904); *Die Juxheirat* (Vienna, Dec. 22, 1904); *Die lustige Witwe* (Vienna, Dec. 28, 1905); *Mitislaw der Moderne* (Vienna, Jan. 5, 1907); *Der Mann mit den drei Frauen* (Vienna, Jan. 21, 1908); *Das Fürstenkind* (Vienna, Oct. 7, 1909); *Der Graf von Luxemburg* (Vienna, Nov. 12, 1909); *Zigeunerliebe (Gypsy Love;* Vienna, Jan. 8, 1910); *Eva* (Vienna, Nov. 24, 1911); *Endlich allein* (Vienna, Feb. 10, 1914; revised and produced as *Schön ist die Welt,* Vienna, Dec. 21, 1934); *Der Sterngucker* (Vienna, Jan. 14, 1916; revised and produced in Milan as *La danza delle libellule,* Sept. 27, 1922); *Wo die Lerche singt* (Budapest, Feb. 1, 1918); *Die blaue Mazur* (Vienna, May 28, 1920); *Die Tangokönigin* (Vienna, Sept. 9, 1921); *Frasquita* (Vienna, May 12, 1922); *Die gelbe Jacke* (Vienna, Feb. 9, 1923; revised and produced as *Das Land des Lächelns,* Berlin, Oct. 10, 1929); *Clo-Clo* (Vienna, March 8, 1924); *Paganini* (Vienna, Oct. 30, 1925); *Der Zarewitsch* (Vienna, Feb. 21, 1927); *Friederike* (Berlin, Oct. 4, 1928); *Giuditta* (Vienna, Jan. 20, 1934). Besides his operettas, Lehár wrote an *Ungarische Fantasie* for Violin and Small Orch.; *Huldigungsouvertüre; Ein Märchen aus 1001 Nacht; Il guado,* symph. poem for Orch. and Piano; *Eine Vision,* overture; symph. poem, *Fieber;* song cycle, *Musikalischer Roman* (1936); numerous marches and dances for orch.

BIBLIOGRAPHY: E. Decsey, *Franz Lehár* (Vienna, 1924; 2nd ed., Munich, 1930); A. von Lehár, *Unsere Mutter* (1930); A. Rivoire, *Une Heure de musique avec Franz Lehár* (Paris, 1930); S. Czech,

Franz Lehár, Weg und Werk (Berlin, 1942); M. von Pereani, *Franz Lehár* (Vienna, 1949); W. Macqueen-Pope and D.L. Murray, *Fortune's Favorite: The Life and Times of Franz Lehár* (London, 1953); W. Zentner and A. Würz, eds., *Reclams Opern- und Operettaführer* (contains the plots of Lehár's most famous operettas; Stuttgart, 1955); *Katalog der Bühnenwerke von Franz Lehár* (Vienna, 1955); B. Grun, *Gold and Silver: The Life and Times of Franz Lehár* (London, 1970); M. Schönherr, *Franz Lehár, Bibliographie zu Leben und Werk* (Baden-bei-Wien, 1970).

Lehel, György, Hungarian conductor; b. Budapest, Feb. 10, 1926. He was educated at the Budapest Academy of Music; made his conducting debut in 1946. In 1950 he began his long and successful association with the Hungarian Radio; was named chief conductor of the Radio-Television Symph. Orch. in 1962. In addition to performing traditional Hungarian music, Lehel was also a determined champion of contemporary music.

Lehmann, Friedrich J., American music pedagogue; b. Cleveland, Sept. 17, 1866; d. Oberlin, Ohio, April 23, 1950. He studied piano and voice at the Oberlin Cons.; then went to Germany, and took lessons with Fritz von Bose and Gustav Schreck in Leipzig. He taught at the Oberlin Cons. for 30 years (1902–32). He publ. *A Treatise on Simple Counterpoint in 40 Lessons* (N.Y., 1907); *Harmonic Analysis* (Oberlin, 1910); *The Analysis of Form in Music* (Oberlin, 1919).

Lehmann, Fritz, German conductor; b. Mannheim, May 17, 1904; d. Munich, March 30, 1956. He studied at the univs. of Heidelberg and Göttingen; was a conductor in Göttingen (1923–27) and taught conducting at the Folkwangschule in Essen (1927–29); also conducted in Hildesheim and Hannover. In 1934 he became conductor of the Handel Festival in Göttingen; also Generalmusikdirektor in Bad Pyrmont (1935–38), in Wuppertal (1938–47), and at the Göttingen Opera (1946–50); subsequently was a teacher at the Hochschule für Musik in Munich. He was particularly distinguished as an interpreter of Handel, Bach, and other Baroque composers.
BIBLIOGRAPHY: J. Herrmann and F. Hamel, "Abschied von Fritz Lehmann," *Musica,* X (1956).

Lehmann, George, American violinist; b. New York, July 31, 1865; d. Yonkers, N.Y., Oct. 14, 1941. He was a pupil at the Leipzig Cons., studying with Schradieck (violin), Lammers (harmony), and Jadassohn (counterpoint and fugue); then took some violin lessons with Joachim in Berlin. In 1886 he returned to the U.S.; was concertmaster of the Cleveland Symph. Orch. (1886–89); then was in Europe (1889–92). In 1893 he settled in N.Y.; in 1907–14, lived in Berlin; after 1914, was again in N.Y. He publ. *True Principles of the Art of Violin Playing* (N.Y., 1899) and *The Violinist's Lexicon* (N.Y., 1918), also *4 Melodious Sketches* for Violin and Piano; etc.

Lehmann, Hans Ulrich, Swiss composer; b. Biel, May 4, 1937. He studied cello in Biel and music theory in Zürich; took courses in advanced composition at seminars of Pierre Boulez and Karlheinz Stockhausen in Basel (1960–63). In 1964 he was appointed to the faculty of the Musik-Akademie in Basel; from 1969, taught music theory at the Univ. of Zürich; from 1972 was a prof. of composition and theory at the Zürich Hochschule für Musik and Cons. As a composer, he adheres to progressive neo-Classicism with serial connotations.
WORKS: *Structures transparentes* for Piano, Viola, and Clarinet (1961); *Quanti I* for Flute and Chamber Ensemble (1962); *Régions pour un flûtiste* (1963); *Episoden* for Wind Quintet (1964); *Mosaik* for Clarinet (1964); *Komposition für 19* for Chamber Group 1965); *Spiele* for Oboe and Harp (1965); *Rondo* for Voice and Orch. (1967); *Instants* for Piano (1968); *Konzert* for 2 Wind Instruments and Strings (1969); *Régions III* for Clarinet, Trombone, and Cello (1970); *Monodie* for a Wind Instrument (1970).

Lehmann, Lilli, celebrated German soprano; b. Würzburg, Nov. 24, 1848; d. Berlin, May 16, 1929. Her mother, **Marie Loew** (1807–83), who had sung leading soprano roles and had also appeared as a harpist at the Kassel Opera under Spohr, became harpist at the National Theater in Prague in 1853, and there Lilli Lehmann spent her girlhood. At the age of 6 she began to study piano with Cölestin Müller, and at 12 progressed so far that she was able to act as accompanist to her mother, who was the only singing teacher she ever had. She made her professional debut in Prague on Oct. 20, 1865, as the First Page in *Die Zauberflöte;* then sang in Danzig (1868) and Leipzig (1869–70). In 1870 she became a member of the Berlin Opera, and soon established a reputation as a brilliant coloratura singer. During the summer of 1875 she was in Bayreuth, and was coached by Wagner himself in the parts of Wöglinde (*Rheingold* and *Götterdämmerung*), Helmwige, and the Forest Bird; these roles she created at the Bayreuth Festival the following summer. She then returned to Berlin under a life contract with the Berlin Opera; she was given limited leaves of absence, which enabled her to appear in the principal German cities, in Stockholm (1878), and in London (debut as Violetta, June 3, 1880; as Isolde, July 2, 1884; as Fidelio in 1887). She made her American debut at the Metropolitan Opera in N.Y. on Nov. 25, 1885, as Carmen; 5 days later she sang Brünnhilde in *Die Walküre;* then sang virtually all the Wagner roles through subsequent seasons until 1890; her last season there was 1898–99; also appeared as Norma, Aida, Donna Anna, Fidelio, etc. She sang Isolde at the American premiere of *Tristan* (Dec. 1, 1886), and appeared in Italian opera with the De Reszkes and Lassalle during the season of 1891–92. In the meantime her contract with the Berlin Opera was canceled (1889), owing to her protracted absence, and it required the intervention of Wilhelm II to reinstate her (1891). In 1896 she sang the 3 Brünnhildes at the Bayreuth Festival. Her great admiration for Mozart caused her to take an active part in the annual Mozart Festivals held at Salzburg, and from 1905 she was practically the chief organizer of these festivals. In 1909 she still sang Isolde in Vienna. Her operatic repertoire comprised 170 roles in 114 operas (German, Italian, and French). She possessed in the highest degree all the requisite qualities of a great interpreter; she had a boundless capacity for work, a glorious voice, and impeccable technique; she knew how to subordinate her fiery temperament to artistic taste; on the stage she had plasticity of pose, grace of movement, and regal presence; her ability to project her interpretation with conviction to audiences in different countries was not the least factor in her universal success. Although she was celebrated chiefly as an opera singer, she was equally fine as an interpreter of German lieder; she gave recitals concurrently with her operatic appearances, and continued them long after she had abandoned the stage; her repertoire of songs exceeded 600. She was also a successful teacher; among her pupils were Geraldine Farrar and Olive Fremstad. On Feb. 24, 1888, she married the tenor **Paul Kalisch** in N.Y.; they appeared together as Tristan and Isolde; some years later, they were legally separated (but not actually divorced). After Lilli Lehmann's death, Paul Kalisch inherited her manor at Salzkammergut, and remained there until his death in 1946, at the age of 90.

Lilli Lehmann was the author of the books *Meine Gesangskunst* (1902; Eng. trans. by Richard Aldrich, under the title *How to Sing*, N.Y., 1902; 3rd revised and supplemented ed., trans. by Clara Willenbücher, N.Y., 1924; reprint, 1949); *Studie zu Fidelio* (1904); *Mein Weg*, an autobiography (1913; 2nd ed., 1920; in Eng. as *My Path through Life*, 1914). She also edited arias of Mozart and many classical songs for the Peters Edition.

BIBLIOGRAPHY: J.H. Wagenmann, *Lilli Lehmanns Geheimnis der Stimmbänder* (Berlin, 1905; 2nd ed., 1926); L. Andro, *Lilli Lehmann* (Berlin, 1907).

Lehmann, Liza (Elizabetha Nina Mary Frederica), English soprano and composer; b. London, July 11, 1862; d. Pinner, Middlesex, Sept. 19, 1918. She was of German-Scotch parentage; grew up in an intellectual and artistic atmosphere: her grandfather was a publisher, her father a painter, her mother a singer. From her childhood she lived in Germany, France, and Italy; among the guests at her house in Rome was Liszt. She studied voice with Alberto Randegger in London, and composition with Wilhelm Freudenberg in Wiesbaden. She made her professional debut as a singer at a Monday Popular Concert in London (Nov. 23, 1885), and subsequently appeared at various festivals in England. On Oct. 10, 1894, she married the English painter and composer **Herbert Bedford,** and retired from the stage; she then applied herself with great earnestness to composition, for she was able to produce a number of works (mostly vocal) of undeniable merit, and was the first English woman composer to enjoy success

with a large public, in England and in America. Her best-known work, which has become a perennial favorite, is *In a Persian Garden,* to words from Omar Khayyám's *Rubaiyát,* in Fitzgerald's version; it is a song cycle, with recitatives, scored for 4 voices, with piano accompaniment; while the music itself is entirely conventional, the vocal parts are eminently effective, both in dramatic and in lyrical passages. In 1910 Liza Lehmann made a tour in the U.S., presenting concerts of her songs, with herself at the piano.

WORKS: *Sergeant Brue,* musical farce (London, June 14, 1904); *The Vicar of Wakefield,* "romantic light opera" (Manchester, Nov. 12, 1906); *Everyman,* one-act opera (London, Dec. 28, 1915); *Once upon a Time,* "fairy cantata" (London, Feb. 22, 1903); *Young Lochinvar* for Baritone Solo, Chorus, and Orch.; *Endymion* for Soprano and Orch.; *Romantic Suite* for Violin and Piano; *In a Persian Garden* for Vocal Quartet and Piano (London, Jan. 10, 1897, first American perf., Boston, Jan. 5, 1910); song cycles (several of a humorous nature): *The Daisy Chain* (12 songs of childhood); *More Daisies; Prairie Pictures; In Memoriam* (after Tennyson); *Nonsense Songs* (from *Alice in Wonderland*); *The Cautionary Tales and a Moral* (after Hilaire Belloc); also piano pieces (*Cobweb Castles,* etc.). Her memoirs, *The Life of Liza Lehmann, by Herself,* were publ. shortly after her death (London, 1919).

Lehmann, Lotte, celebrated German soprano; b. Perleberg, Feb. 27, 1888; d. Santa Barbara, Calif., Aug. 26, 1976. She studied in Berlin with Erna Tiedke, Eva Reinhold, and Mathilde Mallinger. She made her debut on Sept. 2, 1910, as the 2nd Boy in *Die Zauberflöte* at the Hamburg Opera, but soon was given important parts in Wagner's operas, establishing herself as one of the finest Wagnerian singers. In 1916 she was engaged at the Vienna Opera. Richard Strauss selected her to sing the Young Composer in *Ariadne auf Naxos* when it was first performed in Vienna; then she appeared as Octavian in *Der Rosenkavalier,* and later as the Marschallin, which became one of her most famous roles. In 1922 she toured in South America. On Oct. 28, 1930, she made her U.S. debut as Sieglinde with the Chicago Opera, and on Jan. 11, 1934, sang Sieglinde at the Metropolitan Opera in N.Y. She continued to appear at the Metropolitan, with mounting success, in the roles of Elisabeth in *Tannhäuser,* Tosca, and the Marschallin in *Der Rosenkavalier.* In 1939 she toured Australia. In 1945 she became an American citizen; she eventually settled in Santa Barbara, Calif. She publ. a novel, *Orplid mein Land* (1937; in Eng. as *Eternal Flight,* 1938), and an autobiography, *Anfang und Aufstieg* (Vienna, 1937; London, as *Wings of Song,* and N.Y., as *Midway in My Song,* 1938); *More Than Singing* (N.Y., 1945); *My Many Lives* (N.Y., 1948; a sequel to the previous vol.); she also publ. a book of reminiscences, *Five Operas and Richard Strauss* (N.Y., 1964).

BIBLIOGRAPHY: B.W. Wessling, *Lotte Lehmann, Mehr als eine Sängerin* (Salzburg, 1969).

Lehmann, Marie, dramatic soprano, sister of **Lilli Lehmann;** b. Hamburg, May 15, 1851; d. Berlin, Dec. 9, 1931. She was a pupil of her mother, and later of her sister; made her debut in Leipzig (May 1, 1867); in 1876 she created the parts of Wellgunde (*Rheingold* and *Götterdämmerung*) and Ortlinde (*Walküre*) at Bayreuth; from 1881 until her retirement in 1902 she was a member of the Vienna Court Opera; then lived in Berlin as a teacher.

Lehmann, Robert, German cellist; b. Schweidnitz, Silesia, Nov. 26, 1841; d. Stettin, June 12, 1912. He studied organ and cello; settled in Stettin in 1875 as a church organist and conductor. He publ. a series of waltzes for orch. under the title *Briefe aus Wien;* melodious pieces for cello; some church music; also wrote an autobiography, *Erinnerungen eines Künstlers* (1895).

Leibowitz, René, Polish-French composer and theorist; b. Warsaw, Feb. 17, 1913; d. Paris, Aug. 28, 1972. His family settled in Paris in 1926; from 1930 till 1933 he studied in Berlin with Schoenberg and in Vienna with Anton von Webern; under their influence he adopted the 12-tone method of composition; upon his return to France he became the foremost exponent of the 12-tone method in France; he had numerous private students, among them Boulez. He publ. *Schoenberg et son école* (Paris, 1947; in Eng., N.Y., 1949); *Introduction à la musique de douze sons* (Paris, 1949); a manual of orchestration, *Thinking for Orchestra* (with Jan Maguire; N.Y., 1958); *Histoire de l'Opéra* (Paris, 1957); *Erich Itor Kahn, Un Grand Représentant de la musique contemporaine* (with Konrad Wolff; Paris, 1958; in Eng., N.Y. 1958).
WORKS: Operas: *La Nuit close* (1949); *La Rumeur de l'espace* (1950); *Ricardo Gonfolano* (1953); *Les Espagnols à Venise,* opera buffa (1963; Grenoble, Jan. 27, 1970); *Labyrinthe,* after Baudelaire (1969); *Todos caerán,* to Leibowitz's own libretto (1970–72); for Orch.: *Fantaisie symphonique* (1956); Violin Concerto (1959); *3 Bagatelles* for String Orch. (1959); Concertino for Trombone (1960); Cello Concerto (1962); *Rapsodie symphonique* (1964–65); chamber music: *Marijuana* for Violin, Trombone, Vibraphone, and Piano (1960); *Sinfonietta da camera* (1961); *Capriccio* for Flute and Strings (1967); *Suite* for 9 Instruments (1967); Saxophone Quartet (1969); *Petite suite* for Clarinet Sextet (1970); 8 string quartets (1940, 1950, 1952, 1958, 1963, 1965, 1966, 1968); vocal works: *Tourist Death* for Soprano and Chamber Orch. (1943); *L'Explication des métaphores* for Speaker, 2 Pianos, Harp, and Percussion (1947); *Chanson Dada* for Children's Chorus and Instruments (1968); *Laboratoire central* for Speaker and Chorus (1970); numerous solo songs.
BIBLIOGRAPHY: Jan Maquire, "René Leibowitz," *Tempo* (Feb. and March, 1980).

Leibrock, Joseph Adolf, German cellist and harpist; b. Braunschweig Jan. 8, 1808; d. Berlin, Aug. 8, 1886. He studied in Berlin; received his Dr.Phil.; was cellist and harpist in the court orch. at Braun-

schweig. He wrote music to Schiller's *Räuber;* partsongs; arrangements for piano and cello; *Musikalische Akkordenlehre;* etc.

Leichtentritt, Hugo, eminent German-American music scholar; b. Pleschen, Posen, Jan. 1, 1874; d. Cambridge, Mass., Nov. 13, 1951. He was educated at Harvard Univ. (1891–94) and took a music course with Prof. Paine; went to Berlin in 1895 to complete his musical studies; obtained the degree of Dr.Phil. at Berlin Univ. with the dissertation *Reinhard Keiser in seinen Opern* (1901); he subsequently taught at the Klindworth–Scharwenka Cons. and wrote music criticism for German and American publications. In 1933 he left Germany and became a lecturer on music at Harvard Univ.; retired from Harvard in 1940. Although known chiefly as a scholar, Leichtentritt was also a composer; he wrote a Symph.; Violin Concerto; Cello Concerto; Piano Concerto; much chamber music; several song cycles; numerous piano pieces. He also wrote a comic opera, *Der Sizilianer,* which was produced in Freiburg on May 28, 1920. All his music MSS were donated after his death to the Library of Congress in Washington, D.C.
WRITINGS: *Chopin* (1905); *Geschichte der Motette* (Leipzig, 1908; a fundamental source on the subject); *Musikalische Formenlehre* (Leipzig, 1911; 5th ed., 1952; in Eng. as *Musical Form,* Cambridge, Mass., 1951); *Erwin Lendvai* (Berlin, 1912); *Ferruccio Busoni* (Leipzig, 1916); *Analyse der Chopinschen Klavierwerke* (2 vols., Berlin, 1920, 1922); *Händel* (Berlin, 1924; very valuable); *The Complete Piano Sonatas of Beethoven* (analytical notes; N.Y., 1936); *Everybody's Little History of Music* (N.Y., 1938); *Music, History, and Ideas* (Cambridge, Mass., 1938; very successful; 14 printings); *The Boston Symphony Orchestra and the New American Music* (Cambridge, Mass., 1946); *Music of the Western Nations* (posthumous; ed. and amplified by N. Slonimsky; Cambridge, Mass., 1956).

Leider, Frida, German opera soprano; b. Berlin, April 18, 1888; d. there, June 3, 1975. She was employed as a bank clerk in Berlin, and studied voice with Otto Schwarz on the side. She made her debut in Halle in 1915 as Venus in *Tannhäuser;* then sang at Rostock, Königsberg, and Hamburg. She was engaged by the Berlin State Opera in 1923, and remained on its roster until 1940; she also made guest appearances at La Scala in Milan, at the Paris Opéra, and in Vienna, Munich, Stockholm, Amsterdam, and Brussels. In 1928 she made her American debut at the Chicago Opera Co. as Brünnhilde in *Die Walküre;* appeared at the Metropolitan Opera in N.Y. on Jan. 16, 1933, as Isolde. In 1934 she returned to Germany; she encountered difficulties because her husband, a violinist named **Rudolf Deman,** was Jewish. She was confronted by the Nazis with the demand to divorce him, but refused; then she succeeded in going to Switzerland. After the war and the collapse of the Nazi regime, she maintained a vocal studio at the Berlin State Opera until 1952; then taught at the Hochschule für Musik in Berlin until 1958. She publ.

a memoir, *Das war mein Teil, Erinnerungen einer Opernsängerin* (Berlin, 1959; publ. in Eng. as *Playing My Part,* N.Y., 1966).

Leifs, Jón, foremost Icelandic composer and writer; b. Sólheimar, May 1, 1899; d. Reykjavik, July 30, 1968. After completing his primary education at Reykjavik, he went to Germany, where he studied at the Leipzig Cons. with Teichmüller, Szendrei, Scherchen, Lohse, and Graener; then conducted concerts in various German towns; in 1926 led the Hamburg Phil. when it visited Iceland; in 1934–37, was music director of Icelandic Radio; also president of the Council of Northern Composers (1951) and other musical societies in Iceland and Scandinavia. His music is technically derived from the German Romantic tradition; but in several of his works he makes use of Icelandic melodies and rhythms; often he abandons opulent harmonic accoutrements to portray Arctic nature in bleak, organum-like diaphony.
WORKS: Wordless music dramas: *Loftr* (Copenhagen, Sept. 3, 1938) and *Baldr* (1950); *Hljomkvida,* symph. trilogy (Karlsbad, 1925); *Icelandic Overture* (Oslo, 1926; his most successful work); *Kyrie on Icelandic Themes* for a cappella Chorus; *Island-Kantate* (Greifswald, 1930); *Saga–symfoni* (Helsinki, Sept. 18, 1950); 2 string quartets; several piano cycles based on Icelandic dance tunes; songs. He publ. (in Icelandic) a manual on musical forms; in German, *Islands künstlerische Anregung* (Reykjavik, 1951); contributed articles on Icelandic music to *Die Musik* (Oct. 1923), *Volk und Rasse* (Munich, 1932), and other publications.

Leigh, Mitch, American composer and arranger; b. Brooklyn, Jan. 30, 1928. He studied at Yale Univ.; upon graduation, entered the field of commercial music productions; founded Music Makers, Inc. His most successful production was *Man of La Mancha* (1965), for which he wrote the score, and which included the hit song *The Impossible Dream.*

Leigh, Walter, English composer; b. London, June 22, 1905; killed in action near Tobruk, Libya, June 12, 1942. He was a student of Edward Dent at Cambridge; also took lessons with Harold Darke and later with Paul Hindemith at the Hochschule für Musik in Berlin (1927–29). He was particularly adept in his writing for the theater.
WORKS: 2 light operas: *The Pride of the Regiment, or Cashiered for His Country* (Midhurst, England, Sept. 19, 1931) and *The Jolly Roger, or The Admiral's Daughter* (Manchester, Feb. 13, 1933); musical revue, *9 Sharp* (London, 1938); several pieces designated for amateur orch.; Sonatina for Viola and Piano (perf. at the Festival of the International Society for Contemporary Music, Vienna, June 17, 1932); Trio for 3 Pianos (1934); Trio for Flute, Oboe, and Piano (1935); several scores of incidental music for the theater; piano pieces and songs.

Leighton, Kenneth, English composer; b. Wakefield, Yorkshire, Oct. 2, 1929. He enrolled at Queen's College, Oxford, to study classics and music (B.Mus., 1951); later took courses with Goffredo Petrassi in Rome. In 1956–68 he was a lecturer in composition at the Univ. of Edinburgh; then a lecturer in music at Worcester College, Oxford (1968–70), and from 1970 again at the Univ. of Edinburgh.
WORKS: FOR ORCH.: Symph. for Strings (1948); *Primavera romana,* overture (1951); Piano Concerto No. 1 (1951); Concerto for Viola, Harp, Timpani, and Strings (1952); Violin Concerto (1952); Concerto for Oboe and Strings (1953); Concerto for 2 Pianos, Timpani, and Strings (1953); Cello Concerto (1956); Piano Concerto No. 2 (1960); Concerto for String Orch. (1961); Symph. No. 1 (1964); *Dance Suite* No. 1 (1968); *Dance Suite* No. 2 (1970); Piano Concerto No. 3 (1969); Organ Concerto (1970); Symph. No. 2, *Sinfonia Mistica,* for Soprano, Chorus, and Orch. (1977); *The Birds,* choral suite for Soprano, Tenor, Chorus, and Orch. (1954); *Laudes Montium,* psalm with orch. (1975); *Columba,* opera (Glasgow, June 16, 1981). CHAMBER MUSIC: Piano Quintet (1959); 2 violin sonatas (1951, 1956); 2 string quartets (1956, 1957); *Fantasy on a Chorale* for Violin and Organ (Washington, D.C., May 4, 1980); *Animal Heaven* for Soprano and Instruments, to texts by Walt Whitman and James Dickey (1980); Fantasy-Octet, "Homage to Percy Grainger" (1982). FOR CHORUS: *Sinfonia sacra, The Light Invisible* for Tenor, Chorus, and Orch., to texts from the Bible and poems by T.S. Eliot (1958). FOR KEYBOARD: *Fantasia contrapuntistica* for Piano (1956); organ pieces.

Leighton, Sir William, English musician, "gentleman pensioner"; b. Plash, Shropshire(?), c.1565; d. (buried, London, July 31) 1622. He publ. *The Teares or Lamentacions of a Sorrowfull Soule Composed with Musicall Ayres and Songs both for Voyces and Divers Instruments* (1614), containing 54 metrical Psalms and hymns, 17 being for 4 voices with accompaniments in tablature for the lute, bandora, and cittern, and 13 for 4 voices and 24 for 5 voices without accompaniment. The first 8 are by Leighton himself; the others are by Bull, Byrd, Dowland, Gibbons, Coperario, Weelkes, Wilbye, etc. A complete modern edition of his works was edited by C. Hill in *Early English Church Music,* XI (London, 1970).
BIBLIOGRAPHY: M. Seiffert, in the *Bulletin de la Société Musicologique* (1922); J. Pulver, *A Biographical Dictionary of Old English Music* (1927).

Leimer, Kurt, German pianist and composer; b. Wiesbaden, Sept. 7, 1920; d. Vaduz, Liechtenstein, Nov. 20, 1974. He studied piano with his great-uncle Karl Leimer (1858–1944), who was the teacher of Gieseking. After a brief concert career, Leimer took lessons in composition with Kurt von Wolfurt; made rapid progress as a composer, and produced 4 piano concertos (one for left hand), all very effective in their high-flown Romantic style; he was soloist in his 4th Piano Concerto in N.Y., on Oct. 14, 1956, with Stokowski conducting; Karajan also conducted some of his works. Leimer became an Austrian citizen in 1956, but lived in Vaduz.

Leinsdorf, Erich, eminent Austrian-born American conductor; b. Vienna, Feb. 4, 1912. He was a scion of a cultural Jewish family; his real last name was **Landauer.** His mother gave him his first music lessons; later he studied piano with Paul Emerich and Hedwig Kammer-Rosenthal; at 13 he began to study cello with Lilly Kosz. He also had private lessons in composition with Paul Pisk. In 1930 he took a master class in conducting at the Mozarteum in Salzburg, and then studied for a short time in the music dept. of the Univ. of Vienna; from 1931 to 1933 he took courses at the State Academy of Music, making his debut as a conductor at the Musikvereinsaal upon his graduation. In 1933 he served as assistant conductor of the Workers' Chorus in Vienna; in 1934 he went to Salzburg, where he had a successful audition with Bruno Walter and Toscanini at the Salzburg Festivals, and was appointed their assistant. In 1937 he was engaged as a conductor of the Metropolitan Opera in N.Y.; he made his American debut there conducting *Die Walküre* on Jan. 21, 1938, with notable success; he then conducted other Wagnerian operas, ultimately succeeding Bodanzky as head of the German repertoire there in 1939. In 1942 he became an American citizen. In 1943 he was appointed music director of the Cleveland Orch.; however, his induction into the U.S. Army in Dec. 1943 interrupted his term there. After his discharge in 1944, he once again conducted at the Metropolitan in 1944–45; also conducted several concerts with the Cleveland Orch. in 1945 and 1946, and made appearances in Europe. From 1947 to 1955 he was music director of the Rochester (N.Y.) Phil. Orch. In the fall of 1956 he was briefly music director of the N.Y. City Opera; then returned to the Metropolitan as a conductor and musical consultant in 1957. He also appeared as a guest conductor in the U.S. and Europe. In 1962 he received the prestigious appointment of music director of the Boston Symph. Orch., a post he retained until 1969; then he conducted opera and symph. concerts in many of the major music centers of America and in Europe; from 1977 to 1980 he held the post of principal conductor of the (West) Berlin Radio Symph. Orch. He publ. a semi-autobiographical and rather candid book of sharp comments, *Cadenza: A Musical Career* (Boston, 1976); also *The Composer's Advocate: A Radical Orthodoxy for Musicians* (New Haven, 1981).

BIBLIOGRAPHY: David Ewen, *Musicians since 1900* (N.Y., 1978).

Leisinger, Elisabeth, German coloratura soprano; b. Stuttgart, May 17, 1864; d. there, Dec. 15, 1933. She was a daughter of the singer **Bertha Leisinger** (1825–1913), from whom she received her training; subsequently studied with Pauline Viardot-García in Paris. In 1884 she was engaged at the Berlin Opera; sang there for 10 seasons; she married in 1894, and retired from the stage.

Leitch, Donovan ("Donovan"), Scottish folksinger; b. Glasgow, May 10, 1946. He played the guitar and improvised psychedelic and mystical tunes. He belonged to the generation of "flower children" who hid their troubled psyches behind the curtain of strewn petals in an atmosphere filled with clouds of incense. His song *Season of the Witch* was typical of the hallucinatory aspect of his personality, and *Mellow Yellow* reflected his tender nature. His album *A Gift from a Flower to a Garden* was a terrific hit. Other hits were *Hurdy Gurdy Man* and *Lalena.*

Leite, Antonio da Silva, Portuguese composer; b. Oporto, May 23, 1759; d. there, Jan. 10, 1833. He was conductor at the Oporto Cathedral from 1787 to 1826. He wrote 2 operas; publ. *Rezumo de todas as regras e preceitos de cantoria assim da musica metrica como da cantochão* (Oporto, 1787) and a guitar method, *Estudo de guitarra* (Oporto, 1796).

Leitert, Johann Georg, German pianist and composer; b. Dresden, Sept. 29, 1852; d. Hubertusburg, near Dresden, Sept. 6, 1901. He studied with Kragen and Reichel (piano) and Rischbieter (harmony). In 1865 he made his concert debut in Dresden; then played in Leipzig, Berlin, Prague, etc.; toured successfully in England in 1867; also gave concerts in Austria and Russia. From 1879–81 he taught at the Horák Music School in Vienna; wrote many characteristic pieces for piano: *Esquisses, Chants du crépuscule, Herbstblätter, Strahlen und Schatten, Aus schönern Stunden, Feuilles d'amour, Lose Blätter, Valse Caprice,* etc.; also transcriptions for piano (chiefly from Wagner's works).

Leitner, Ferdinand, eminent German conductor, b. Berlin, March 4, 1912. He studied at the State Academy of Music in Berlin; then served as Generalmusikdirektor of the Hamburg State Opera (1945–46) and of the Bavarian State Opera in Munich (1946–47). In 1947 he became Generalmusikdirektor of the Württemberg State Theater in Stuttgart. He left Stuttgart in 1969 to become chief conductor of the Zürich Opera, retiring from this post in 1984. He also was named chief conductor of the Residentie Orch. at The Hague (1976–80).

Leitzmann, Albert, German theorist and musicologist; b. Magdeburg, Aug. 3, 1867; d. Jena, April 16, 1950. He studied chiefly literature and esthetics; established himself as Privatdozent for German language and literature at the Univ. of Jena. Besides numerous books dealing with literature and philology, he publ. *Beethovens Briefe* (1909; 3rd ed., 1933); *Mozarts Briefe* (1910); *Mozarts Persönlichkeit* (1914); *Beethovens Persönlichkeit* (2 vols., 1914); *Beethovens persönliche Aufzeichnungen* (1918); *Ludwig van Beethoven. Berichte der Zeitgenossen* (2 vols., 1921); *W.A. Mozart. Berichte der Zeitgenossen* (1926).

Leiviskä, Helvi, Finnish composer; b. Helsinki, May 25, 1902. She studied under Erkki Melartin at the Helsinki School of Music, and with Arthur Willner in Vienna; subsequently served as a librarian of the Sibelius Academy in Helsinki. She is one of the very few women composers of symph. music in Finland.

WORKS: *Folk Dance Suite* for Orch. (1929; revised 1971); Piano Concerto (1935); 2 orch. suites (1934, 1938); *Triple Fugue* for Orch. (1935); *Pimeän peikko (Goblin of Darkness)* for Chorus and Orch. (1942); 3 symphs. (1947, 1954, 1971); *Mennyt manner (The Lost Continent)* for Solo Voices, Chorus, and Orch. (1957); *Sinfonia brevis* (1962; revised 1972); Piano Quartet (1926); String Quartet (1926); Violin Sonata (1945).

Le Jeune, Claude (or **Claudin**), French composer; b. Valenciennes, 1528; d. Paris, Sept. 25, 1600. He was active chiefly in Paris, where he appears to have been for some time associated with the poet Antoine de Baïf in the Académie de Musique, founded to encourage the growth of a new style of musical composition known as "musique mesurée," in which the music is made to follow the metrical rhythm of the text in conformity with the rules of classical prosody. The type of poetry set to music in this manner was called "vers mesurez," and 33 examples of such settings by Le Jeune are to be found in the work entitled *Le Printemps*, publ. posthumously at Paris in 1603 by his sister Cécile Le Jeune. The metrical scanning is given at the head of each song. In the preface to this work Le Jeune is given credit for having been the first to achieve the "mating of ancient rhythm and modern harmony"; if not the first, he was at least, together with his contemporary and friend Jacques Mauduit, one of the earliest and most notable cultivators of this new and significant style. Le Jeune also cultivated every other variety of vocal music known in his time, such as French chansons in "vers rimez," Italian madrigals, Latin motets, etc. Special mention must be made of his settings of the Psalms, of which several collections appeared in 1564–1606. So great was his renown even during his lifetime that a wood engraving dated 1598 bore the legend: "Le Phénix des Musiciens." His best-known work is his setting of the Genevan Psalter *a* 4 and 5, publ. by Cécile Le Jeune in 1613. This simple contrapuntal setting of the Psalms was widely used in the Reformed churches of France and the Netherlands, and it was also publ. in a German trans. Some of these harmonizations even found their way into early New England psalmbooks, such as *The Ainsworth Psalter* (cf. *Early Psalmody in America*, ed. by C.S. Smith for the N.Y. Public Library, 1939). A more elaborate setting of some Psalms, *12 psaumes de David*, in motet style for 2 to 7 voices, was contained in the work entitled *Dodecacorde*, publ. at La Rochelle in 1598. On the title page of this work, Le Jeune is described as "compositeur de la musique de la chambre du roy," showing that he was then attached to the court of Henri IV. It is known that he had espoused the Huguenot cause during the wars of the Catholic League, and it is said that his MSS narrowly escaped destruction during the siege of Paris in 1588, having been saved only by the intervention of his Catholic colleague Mauduit. In 1612 a nephew of Le Jeune publ. a *Second livre de meslanges à 4–10*, containing miscellaneous vocal pieces and 2 instrumental fantasias. The most important works of Le Jeune have been reprinted by H. Expert in his *Maîtres musiciens de la renaissance française*, as follows: *Dodecacorde* (vol. 11); *Le Printemps* (vols. 12–14); one part of the *Livre de meslanges* (vol. 16); *Psaumes en vers mesurez* (vols. 20–22); also, in *Monuments de la musique française* (vols. 1 and 8) are *Octonaires de la vanité et inconstance du monde* and other works; *Missa ad placitum* is in Le Pupitre, 2; chansons in *Florilège du concert vocal de la renaissance*, 6; the *Airs* (1608) are publ. in 4 vols. by D.P. Walker in the Miscellenea series of the American Inst. of Musicology.

BIBLIOGRAPHY: E. Bouton, *Esquisse biographique et bibliographique sur Claude Le Jeune* (Valenciennes, 1845); M. Cauchie, "La Mort de Claude Le Jeune," *Revue de Musicologie* (Aug. 1927); D.P. Walker and F. Lesure, "Claude Le Jeune and *Musique mesurée*," *Musica Disciplina* (1949).

Lekeu, Guillaume, talented Belgian composer; b. Heusy, near Verviers, Jan. 20, 1870; d. Angers, Jan. 21, 1894. He went to school in Poitiers; after graduation, followed his family to Paris, where he studied with Gaston Vallin; he also received some advice from César Franck and took a course with Vincent d'Indy. He subsequently went to Brussels to compete for the Belgian Prix de Rome; won 2nd prize with his cantata *Andromède* (1891). Returning to Paris, he wrote several works of excellent quality, but death (of typhoid fever) intervened when he was barely 24 years old. His style of composition was influenced mainly by César Franck; his most durable work, a Violin Sonata with modal inflections and chromatic progressions, closely follows the procedures of Franck's Violin Sonata.

WORKS: The list of his works is necessarily small: Cello Sonata (1888); *Adagio* for Strings (1888); *Chant de triomphale délivrance* for Orch. (1889); *Hamlet* for Orch. (1890); *Fantaisie sur un cramignon liégois* for Orch. (1890); *Chant lyrique* for Chorus and Orch. (1891); *Introduction et Adagio* for Tuba and Wind Orch. (1891); Piano Trio (1891); Violin Sonata (1891; his most frequently perf. work); Piano Sonata (1891); *Fantaisie sur 2 airs angevins* for Orch. (1892); *Suite* for Voice and Orch (1892); *Barberine* (fragments for an opera); *Chanson de mai* for Chorus and Orch.; *Adagio* for String Quartet; *Epithalame* for Strings, Trombones, and Organ; String Quartet; *Meditation* and *Minuet* for String Quartet; *Noël* for Soprano, String Quartet, and Piano; Piano Quartet (unfinished; completed by Vincent d'Indy); Piano Sonata; *Tempo di mazurka* for Piano; a group of songs.

BIBLIOGRAPHY: A. Tissier, *Guillaume Lekeu* (Verviers, 1906); R. Vandelle, "Guillaume Lekeu," *Revue Musicale* (1921); M. Lorrain, *Guillaume Lekeu, Sa correspondance, sa vie et son œuvre* (Liège, 1923); R. Stengel, *Lekeu* (Brussels, 1944); P. Prist, *Guillaume Lekeu* (Brussels, 1946).

Lemacher, Heinrich, German composer; b. Solingen, June 26, 1891; d. Cologne, March 16, 1966. He studied at the Cons. of Cologne; in 1928, he became

a teacher at the Cologne Hochschule für Musik. A disciple of the German Romantic school, he elaborated its principles in a number of choral and instrumental works; the chief influences are Bruckner and Reger; he wrote several symph. suites; chamber music; piano pieces. More important than these are his compositions for the Catholic service: several masses, offertories, motets, cantatas with organ accompaniment, etc., in which he succeeded in establishing a practical style of modern polyphony. Written shortly before his death, his last work, Sextet for 3 Trumpets, 2 Trombones, and Tuba, bears the opus number 208. He publ. several books on music theory: *Lehrbuch des Kontrapunktes* (Mainz, 1950; 4th ed., 1962); *Harmonielehre* (Cologne, 1958; 5th ed., 1967); *Formenlehre der Musik* (with H. Schroeder, Cologne, 1962; in Eng. as *Musical Form,* 1967).
BIBLIOGRAPHY: Karl Laux, "Heinrich Lemacher," in *Musik und Musiker der Gegenwart* (Essen, 1949; pp. 153–62).

Lemaire (or **Le Maire**), **Jean,** French musician; b. Chaumont en Bassigny, 1581; d. c.1650. He is said to have proposed the adoption of a 7th solmisation syllable *si* (so asserted by Rousseau in his *Dictionnaire de musique; za,* according to Mersenne's *Harmonie universalle).* However, the designation *si* seems to have been proposed even earlier, so the question of priority remains moot. Lemaire constructed a lute which he called the "Almérie" (anagram of Lemaire).
BIBLIOGRAPHY: J.R. Knowlson, "Jean Le Maire, the Almérie, and the 'Musique Almerique': A Set of Unpublished Documents," *Acta Musicologica* (1968).

Lemaire, Jean Eugène Gaston, French composer; b. Château d'Amblainvilliers, Seine-et-Oise, Sept. 9, 1854; d. (suicide; body found in the Seine) Paris, Jan. 9, 1928. He studied at the Ecole Niedermeyer; was a prolific composer of light music (operettas, piano pieces, and characteristic pieces for orch.).
WORKS: *Pierrette et le pot au lait,* pantomime (Paris, Feb. 11, 1891); *Conte de printemps,* pantomime (Paris, May 18, 1892); *La Belle Tunisienne,* opera in one act (Paris, Aug. 26, 1892); operettas: *Les Maris de Juanita, Le Supplice de Jeannot, Le Rêve de Manette; Rose,* lyric fairy tale (Paris, March 14, 1895); ballets: *Feminissima* (1902) and *Pierrot venge son rival* (1917). He also wrote a number of fox-trots, one of which, *La Grenouille,* became popular; and songs, of which *Vous dansez, marquise,* was a great favorite.

Le Maistre (or **Le Maître**), **Mattheus,** Flemish composer; b. near Liège, c.1505; d. Dresden, 1577. In 1554 he succeeded J. Walter as Kapellmeister at the court in Dresden; retired on a pension, Feb. 12, 1568. Fétis and Otto Kade wrongly identified him with Hermann Matthias Werrekoren, choirmaster in Milan.
WORKS: *Magnificat octo tonorum* (1577); *Catechesis numeris musicis inclusa* (1563; for the choirboys of the Dresden Chapel); *Geistliche und weltliche teutsche Gesänge* for 4–5 Voices (1566); motets for 5 Voices (1570); *Officia de nativitate et Ascensione Christi* for 5 Voices (1574); *Schöne und auserlesene teutsche und lateinische geistliche Lieder* (1577). A motet for 4 Voices, *Estote prudentes,* is in Commer's *Collectio* (vol. 8); 2 lieder for 4 Voices are in Ambros's *Geschichte der Musik* (vol. 5, *Beispielband,* ed. by O. Kade, 1882).
BIBLIOGRAPHY: O. Kade, monograph on Le Maistre (Mainz, 1862); René Vannes, *Dictionnaire des musiciens* (Brussels, 1947; pp. 242–44).

Lemare, Edwin Henry, British-American organist; b. Ventnor, Isle of Wight, Sept. 9, 1865; d. Los Angeles, Sept. 24, 1934. He received his early training from his father, an organist; then studied at the Royal Academy of Music in London; at the age of 19 he played at the Inventions Exhibition in London; in 1892 he began a series of weekly organ recitals at Holy Trinity Church in London; from 1897 to 1902 he was organist at St. Margaret's, Westminster. In 1901 he made a concert tour through the U.S. and Canada; from 1902 to 1905 he was organist at the Carnegie Inst. in Pittsburgh; then held the post of municipal organist in San Francisco (1917–21), Portland, Maine (1921–23), and Chattanooga, Tenn. (1924–29). He publ. about 200 organ works and made many arrangements. His *Andantino in D-flat* acquired wide popularity when it was used for the American ballad *Moonlight and Roses.* His booklet of reminiscences, *Organs I Have Met,* was publ. posthumously in 1957.

Lemeshev, Sergei, Russian tenor; b. Knyazevo, near Tver, July 10, 1902; d. Moscow, June 26, 1977. In his youth he worked as a cobbler's shop in Petrograd; then went to Moscow, where he studied at the Moscow Cons. with Raysky, graduating in 1925. He made his operatic debut at Sverdlovsk in 1926; then was a member of the Kharbin Opera in Manchuria (1927–29) and at the Tiflis Opera (1929–31). In 1931 he joined the Bolshoi Theater in Moscow, and gradually created an enthusiastic following; he was particularly admired for his performance of the role of Lensky in *Eugene Onegin;* in 1972, on his 70th birthday, he sang it again at the Bolshoi Theater. Other roles in which he shone, apart from the Russian repertoire, included Faust, Romeo, and Werther. He also made numerous appearances in solo recitals; was the first to present an entire cycle of Tchaikovsky's songs in 5 concerts.
BIBLIOGRAPHY: M. Lvov, *Sergei Lemeshev* (Moscow, 1947); E. Grosheva, *Sergei Lemeshev* (Moscow, 1960); S. Lemeshev, *My Life* (Moscow, 1968).

Lemit, William, French ethnomusicologist; b. Paris, Dec. 15, 1908; d. there (suicide), Aug. 21, 1966. He was entirely autodidact in music; traveled through the French countryside collecting popular songs. He publ. several song anthologies of French children's rhymes, among them *La Vie du garçon* (1950) and *Les Jeux chantés enfantins du folklore fran-*

çais (1957).

Lemmens, Nicolas Jacques, Belgian organist; b. Zoerle-Parwys, Jan. 3, 1823; d. Castle Linterport, near Malines, Jan. 30, 1881. He was trained in music by his father; then attended the Brussels Cons., where he was appointed prof. of organ in 1849. He composed principally for organ and publ. the useful *Ecole d'orgue.* His book *Du chant grégorien, sa mélodie, son rhythme, son harmonisation* was publ. posthumously in 1886; 4 vols. of his sacred choral works and organ pieces were publ. by Breitkopf & Härtel.

Lemmens-Sherrington, Helen, noted English soprano; b. Preston, Oct. 4, 1834; d. Brussels, May 9, 1906. She studied in Rotterdam and Brussels; gave concerts in London; then joined the Royal English Opera at Covent Garden (1864–65); sang with the Royal Italian Opera there (1866–68); in later years she taught voice at the Brussels Cons. She married the Belgian organist and composer **Nicolas Lemmens.**

Lemnitz, Tiana, noted German soprano; b. Metz, Oct. 26, 1897. She received her musical education in Metz and Frankfurt; then sang at Heilbronn and Aachen. She was subsequently a principal member of the Opera in Hannover (1929–34); from 1934 until her retirement in 1957 she sang at the State Opera in Berlin. She also made guest appearances at Covent Garden in London and at the Teatro Colón in Buenos Aires. Her repertoire was most extensive, including leading roles in German, Italian, French, and Russian operas.

Lemoine, Antoine-Marcel, French music publisher, violinist, and guitar player, father of **Henry Lemoine;** b. Paris, Nov. 3, 1753; d. there, April 10, 1816. A self-taught musician, he played viola at the Théâtre de Monsieur, conducted at minor Parisian theaters, and finally founded a music publishing firm.

Lemoine, Henry, French music publisher, son of **Antoine-Marcel Lemoine;** b. Paris, Oct. 21, 1786; d. there, May 18, 1854. He studied at the Paris Cons. (1798–1809); in 1821 he also had harmony lessons from Reicha; taught piano; at his father's death, succeeded to the latter's music publishing business. He publ. methods for harmony, piano, and solfeggio; *Tablettes du pianiste: Memento du professeur de piano;* sonatas, variations, dances, etc., for piano.

Lemont, Cedric Wilmont, organist; b. Fredericton, New Brunswick, Canada, Dec. 15, 1879; d. New York, April 27, 1954. He studied with Carl Faelten (piano) and Dunham (organ) in Boston; filled various positions as organist and choirmaster in Canada; in 1907, settled in the U.S.; taught in Chicago and Brooklyn. He publ. over 600 compositions, including piano pieces, anthems, etc.; also publ. 3 vols. of the *American History and Encyclopedia of Music.*

Lemoyne, Jean Baptiste, French conductor and composer; b. Eymet, Périgord, April 3, 1751; d. Paris, Dec. 30, 1796. He studied with Graun and Kirnberger at Berlin, where he became 2nd Kapellmeister to Frederick the Great. Returning to Paris, he brought out an opera, *Electre* (July 2, 1782), pretending to be a pupil of Gluck, an imposture that Gluck did not see fit to expose until the failure of Lemoyne's piece. In his next operas, Lemoyne abandoned Gluck's ideas, copied the style of Piccinni and Sacchini, and produced several successful works, including *Phèdre* (Fountainebleau, Oct. 26, 1786) and *Nephté* (Paris, Dec. 15, 1789).

Lenaerts, Constant, Belgian conductor and composer; b. Antwerp, March 9, 1852; d. there, March 20, 1931. He studied with Peter Benoît; began to conduct at the Flemish National Theater at the age of 18; in 1914, was appointed a teacher at the Antwerp Cons. He wrote a cantata, *De triomf van 't licht* (1890), songs, and some instrumental music.

Lendvai, Erwin, Hungarian conductor and composer; b. Budapest, June 4, 1882; d. Epsom, Surrey, March 31, 1949. He studied with Koessler; later went to Milan, where he had some lessons with Puccini; taught at Jaques Dalcroze's School of Eurhythmics for a season (1913–14); then was an instructor of dramatic composition at the Hoch Cons. in Frankfurt; later at the Klindworth-Scharwenka Cons. in Berlin (1919–22); was a teacher at the Hamburg Volksmusikschule (1923–25); a choral conductor in Coblenz (1926–27), then in Munich and in Erfurt; in 1938 he went to Switzerland, and later to London, where he remained until his death. He composed a Symph. (1909); *Archaische Tänze* for Small Orch.; *Masken,* orch. scherzo; *Nippon,* choral suite for Women's Voices; String Quartet; several piano trios and other chamber music; an opera, *Elga* (Mannheim, Dec. 6, 1916). He publ. a valuable method, *Chorschule.*

BIBLIOGRAPHY: Hugo Leichtentritt, *Erwin Lendvai* (Berlin, 1912).

Lendvay, Kamilló, Hungarian composer; b. Budapest, Dec. 28, 1928. He studied composition with Viski at the Budapest Academy of Music; devoted himself mainly to the musical theater, as a composer and a conductor; in 1973 was appointed conductor of the Capitol Operetta Theater; also taught at the Budapest Academy.

WORKS: Television opera buffa, *Abüvös szék* (*The Magic Chair;* 1972); 4 musicals: *The 3 Musketeers* (1962); *10 Days That Shook the World* (1967); *Ex* (1968); *Knock Out* (1968); 2 ballets: *Eszmélés* (*Awakening;* 1964) and *Musica leggiera* (jazz ballet; 1965); oratorio, *Orogenesis* (1969); *Tragic Overture* (1958); *Mauthausen* for Orch. (1958); Concertino for Piano, Wind Instruments, Percussion, and Harp (1959); *The Indomitable Tin Soldier,* orch. suite, with Narrator (1961); Violin Concerto (1961–62); *4 Invocations* for Orch. (1966); *Chamber Concerto* for 13 Instruments (1969); *Kifejezések* (*Expressions)* for 11 Strings or String Orch. (1974); *Pez-*

zo concertato for Cello and Orch. (Trieste, Oct. 18, 1975); *Fantasy* for Violin and Piano (1951); *Rhapsody* for Violin and Piano (1955); String Quartet (1962); *4 Duos* for Flute and Piano (1965); *Disposizioni* for Solo Cimbalom (1975); choruses; songs.

Lenepveu, Charles (Ferdinand), French composer and pedogogue; b. Rouen, Oct. 4, 1840; d. Paris, Aug. 16, 1910. While a law student, he took music lessons from Servais; won first prize at Caen in 1861 for a cantata; entered Ambroise Thomas's class at the Paris Cons. in 1863, and in 1865 took the Grand Prix de Rome with the cantata *Renaud dans les jardins d'Armide* (Paris, Jan. 3, 1866). His comic opera *Le Florentin* also won a prize, offered by the Ministry of Fine Arts (1867), and was performed at the Opéra-Comique (Feb. 26, 1874). The grand opera *Velléda* was produced at Covent Garden in London (July 4, 1882), with Adelina Patti in the title role. In 1891 Lenepveu succeeded Guiraud as prof. of harmony at the Cons., and in 1893 again succeeded him as prof. of composition, taking an advanced class in 1894. In 1896 he was elected to Ambroise Thomas's chair in the Académie des Beaux-Arts; was a Chevalier of the Legion of Honor, and an Officer of Public Instruction.
BIBLIOGRAPHY: R. de Saint-Arroman, *Charles Lenepveu* (Paris, 1898).

Léner, Jenö, Hungarian violinist; b. Szabadka, April 7, 1894; d. New York, Nov. 4, 1948. He studied at the Hungarian Music Academy in Budapest; worked as a violinist in theater orchs.; in 1918 organized the Léner String Quartet (with Joseph Smilovits, Sándor Roth, and Imre Hartmann), which became one of the most renowned string quartets of modern times; it was particularly noted for its interpretation of Beethoven's quartets. In 1925 Léner took his quartet to London, and in 1929 to the U.S.; it was disbanded in 1942, but reorganized, with a partly new membership, in 1945. The fame enjoyed by the Léner quartet can be judged by Aldous Huxley's discussion of its performance of Beethoven's last quartets in his novel *Point Counterpoint* (1928).
BIBLIOGRAPHY: Antal Molnár, *The Léner Quartet* (Budapest, 1968; also in Eng., in the series Great Hungarian Performers, 1969).

Leng, Alfonso, Chilean composer; b. Santiago, Feb. 11, 1884; d. there, Nov. 7, 1974. He was of mixed German and English descent; studied dentistry, and became a professional dentist in Santiago; also took music lessons with Enrique Soro. In his leisure time, he composed short symph. sketches in a Romantic vein, songs, and evocative piano pieces.
WORKS: *5 dolores* for Orch. (1920); *La muerte de Alsino,* symph. poem (1920; Santiago, May 30, 1931); *Canto de Invierno* for Orch. (1932); *Fantasia* for Piano and Orch. (Santiago, August. 28, 1936); *Psalm 77* for Soloists, Chorus, and Orch. (1941); *Fantasia quasi Sonata* for Piano (1909); *10 Preludes* for Piano (1919–32); *Andante* for Piano and String Quartet (1922); *2 Otoñales* for Piano (1932); 2 piano sonatas (1927, 1950); many songs. A special issue of the *Revista Musical Chilena* (Aug./Sept. 1957) was publ. in his honor, with articles by Domingo Santa Cruz, Alfonso Letelier, and others.

Lennon, John (Winston), English rock-'n'-roll singer, guitarist, poet, and instinctive composer, member of the celebrated rock group The Beatles; b. Liverpool, Oct. 9, 1940, during a German air raid on the city; d. Dec. 8, 1980, gunned down by a wacko in front of his apartment in New York. He was educated by an aunt after his parents separated; played the mouth organ as a child; later learned the guitar; was encouraged to become a musician by the conductor of a Liverpool-Edinburgh bus. Emotionally rocked over by Elvis Presley's animal magnetism, he became infatuated with American popular music. With 3 other rock-crazed Liverpudlians, Paul McCartney, George Harrison, and Stuart Sutcliffe, he formed a pop combo. Inspired by the success of a local group, The Crickets, Lennon hit upon the name The Beatles, which possessed the acoustical ring of the coleopterous insect *beetle* and the rock-associated *beat*. The Beatles opened at the pseudo-exotic Casbah Club in Liverpool in 1959; soon moved to the more prestigious Cavern Club, where they co-opted Pete Best as a drummer. In 1960 they played in Hamburg, scoring a gratifyingly vulgar success with the beer-sodden customers by their loud, electrically amplified sound. Back in England, The Beatles crept on to fame. In 1961 they were taken up by the perspicacious promoter Brian Epstein, who launched an extensive publicity campaign to put them over the footlights. Sutcliffe died of a brain hemorrhage in 1962. Pete Best left the group and was replaced by Richard Starkey, whose "nom-de-beatle" became Ringo Starr. The quartet opened at the London Palladium in 1963 and drove the youthful audience to a frenzy, a scene that was to be repeated elsewhere in Europe, in America, in Japan, and in Australia. After a period of shocked recoil, the British establishment acknowledged the beneficial contribution of The Beatles to British art and the Exchequer. In 1965 each beatle was made a Member of the Order of the British Empire. Although American in origin, the type of popular music plied by John Lennon and The Beatles as a group has an indefinably British lilt. The meter is square; the main beat is accentuated; syncopation is at a minimum; the harmony is modal, with a lowered submediant in major keys as a constantly present feature; a propensity for plagal cadences and a proclivity for consecutive triadic progressions create at times a curiously hymnal mood. But professional arrangers employed by The Beatles invested their bland melodies in raucous dissonance; electronic amplification made the music of The Beatles the loudest in the world for their time. The lyrics, most of them written by John Lennon and Paul McCartney, are distinguished by suggestive allusions, sensuous but not flagrantly erotic, anarchistic but not destructive, cynical but also humane. There are covert references to psychedelic drugs. The Beatles produced the highly original films *A Hard Day's*

Night, Help!, Yellow Submarine, and *Let It Be.* The most successful individual songs in the Beatles' repertoire were *Love Me Do, I Want to Hold Your Hand, Can't Buy Me Love, Ticket to Ride, Day Tripper, All My Loving, I Wanna Be Your Man, And I Love Her, Eight Days a Week, Yesterday, Michelle, Eleanor Rigby, With a Little Help from My Friends, Sergeant Pepper's Lonely Hearts Club Band, Magical Mystery Tour, Lady Madonna, You're Gonna Lose That Girl, Norwegian Wood, Good Day Sunshine, Hey Jude;* also title songs of the films. Lennon's 2nd wife, the Japanese-American artist Yoko Ono, greatly influenced the development of his social consciousness; they collaborated on his last album, *Double Fantasy,* which achieved great popularity. The shock waves produced by Lennon's murder reverberated throughout the world; crowds in deep mourning marched in N.Y., Liverpool, and Tokyo; Yoko Ono issued a number of declarations urging Lennon's fans not to give way to despair. Not even the death of Elvis Presley generated such outbursts of grief. A photograph taken on the afternoon before his murder, of John in the nude, embracing a fully dressed Yoko Ono, was featured on the cover of a special issue of *Rolling Stone* magazine (Jan. 22, 1981).

BIBLIOGRAPHY: Hunter Davies, *The Beatles,* "the authorized biography" (N.Y., 1968); Ned Rorem, "The Beatles," *N.Y. Review of Books* (Jan. 18, 1968); G. Geppert, *Songs der Beatles. Texte und Interpretationen* (2nd ed., Munich, 1968); E. Davies, "The Psychological Characteristics of Beatle Mania," *Journal of the History of Ideas* (April–June 1969); P. McCabe and R.D. Schonfeld, *Apple to the Core; The Unmaking of the Beatles* (N.Y., 1972); F. Seloron, *Les Beatles* (Paris, 1972); W. Mellers, *Twilight of the Gods: The Music of the Beatles* (N.Y., 1973).

Lenormand, René, French composer; b. Elbeuf, Aug. 5, 1846; d. Paris, Dec. 3, 1932. He received his musical training from his mother, who was an excellent pianist; in 1868 he went to Paris, where he studied with Damcke. Lenormand's main interest was in the creation of an international type of the German lied, and for that purpose he organized in Paris a society which he called Le Lied en Tous Pays. Besides his songs, Lenormand wrote an opera, *Le Cachet rouge* (Le Havre, 1925); Piano Concerto; *Le Lahn de Mabed* (on an old Arabian theme) for Violin and Orch.; *Le Voyage imaginaire,* symph. tableaux after Loti; *2 esquisses sur des thèmes malais* for Orch.; piano pieces (*Une Journée à la campagne, Le Nuage vivant, Valses sérieuses, Pièces exotiques,* etc.; for 4-hands: *Divertissement américain, La Nouba Medjenneba,* etc.); also publ. a valuable manual on harmony, *Etude sur l'harmonie moderne* (Paris, 1912; Eng. trans. as *A Study of Modern Harmony,* London, 1915).

BIBLIOGRAPHY: H. Woollett, *Un Mélodiste français: René Lenormand* (Paris, 1930).

Lent, Ernest, German cellist and composer; b. Brandenburg, Sept. 18, 1856; d. Washington, D.C., Dec. 22, 1922. He studied at the Leipzig Cons. (1878–81); toured in Europe as a concert cellist; in 1884, settled in Washington as a teacher. He publ. numerous pieces for cello and piano, and some songs; also a manual, *Elementary Technics for the Violin* (4 books).

Lentz, Daniel, American composer of the avant-garde; b. Latrobe, Pa., March 10, 1942. He began his career as a follower of the medieval troubadours and goliards; like them, he traveled far and wide; like them, he was the recipient of bounties from foundations and individuals in power. He received 2 grants from the National Endowment for the Arts, a Fulbright grant, and a Tanglewood Composition fellowship. He traveled in the Netherlands in 1970 and in Germany in 1973, and presented concerts and multimedia exhibitions in California and other receptive regions of the U.S. The titles of some of his works are inscrutable, as *Fermentation Notebooks, North American Eclipse;* or alliterative, as *The Iridescence of Eurydice.* Perhaps his most startling composition is *Love and Conception,* in sonata form, in which 2 naked young people, one of each gender, are told to crawl under the lid of a grand piano and simulate sexual intercourse; the piece was actually performed at the Univ. of Calif., Santa Barbara, on Feb. 26, 1969, but as a result, the composer was fired from his teaching job there. A similarly audacious work was his *Kissing Song* for 24 amplified Unisex Voices, performing vocalized osculations, with each kissing pair sliding their respective tongues into his (or her) mouth (1971); it was scheduled for public performance at the Metamusik Festival in Berlin in 1978 but was canceled because of the reluctance of the kissers to sing between someone else's lips.

Lenya, Lotte, Austrian actress and singer; b. Vienna, Oct. 18, 1898; d. New York, Nov. 27, 1981. She began her stage career as a dancer in Zürich, where she went at the outbreak of World War I in 1914; after the end of the war she went to Berlin. There she met **Kurt Weill,** whom she married in 1926; in 1927 she made her debut as a singer in the Brecht-Weill scenic cantata *Mahagonny;* in 1928 she sang in the production of the Brecht-Weill *Die Dreigroschenoper* in Berlin; from then on she identified herself with practically all of Weill's musicals. She and Weill fled Nazified Berlin in 1933, and after a couple of years in Paris and London, went to America. Although not a singer of a professional caliber, Lotte Lenya adapted herself to the peculiar type of half-spoken, half-sung roles in Weill's works with total dedication.

BIBLIOGRAPHY: H. Marx, ed., *Weill-Lenya* (N.Y., 1976).

Lenz, Wilhelm von, Russian writer on music; b. Riga, June 1, 1809; d. St. Petersburg, Jan. 31, 1883. He traveled in Europe; studied piano in Paris with Liszt and Chopin (1842); returning to Russia, he became a government councillor in St. Petersburg. His writings are historically valuable because of the intimate personal experience that they reflect. His most notable book is *Beethoven et ses trois styles* (2 vols., St. Petersburg, 1852; new ed., by Calvocoressi, Paris, 1909), in which he proposed for the first time the division of Beethoven's works into 3 chronological periods: the first (opp. 1–21) entirely Classical; the 2nd (opp. 22–95), and to Lenz the best, truly Beethovenian in its nobility and individuality; and the 3rd (from op. 96) marking partly a decline, partly an attempt to scale unattainable heights. Lenz further publ. *Beethoven: Eine Kunststudie* (6 vols., 1855–60); vols. 4–6 were separately publ. as *Kritischer Katalog der sämmtlichen Werke nebst Analysen derselben* (Hamburg, 1860), and vol. 1 as *Beethoven: Eine Biographie* (2nd ed., 1879; reprinted, with additions by A. Kalischer, 1908); *Die grossen Pianoforte-Virtuosen unserer Zeit* (brief character sketches of Liszt, Chopin, Tausig, and Henselt; 1872; Eng. trans., N.Y., 1899).

Leo, Leonardo (Lionardo Ortensio Salvatore de Leo), important Italian composer; b. San Vito degli Schiavi, near Brindisi, Aug. 5, 1694; d. Naples, Oct. 31, 1744. In 1709 he went to Naples, where he studied with Fago at the Conservatorio S. Maria della Pietà dei Turchini; his sacred drama *S. Chiara, o L'infedeltà abbattuta* was given there in 1712. In 1713 he was made supernumerary organist in the Viceroy's Chapel; also served as maestro di cappella to the Marchese Stella. His first opera, *Il Pisistrato,* was performed in Naples on May 13, 1714. His first comic opera, *La 'mpeca scoperta* in the Neapolitan dialect, was given in Naples on Dec. 13, 1723. In all, he wrote some 50 operas, most of them for Naples. Following Alessandro Scarlatti's death in 1725, he was elevated to the position of first organist at the viceregal chapel. In 1730 he became provicemaestro of the Royal Chapel; in 1737 vicemaestro. He taught as vicemaestro at the Conservatorio S. Maria della Pietà dei Turchini from 1734 to 1737; from 1741 was primo maestro in succession to his teacher, Fago; also was primo maestro at the Conservatorio S. Onofrio from 1739. In Jan. 1744 he became maestro di cappella of the Royal Chapel, but died that same year. Among his famous pupils were Piccinni and Jommelli. Leo's music for the theater (especially his comic operas) is noteworthy; of no less significance were his theoretical works, *Istituzioni o regole del contrappunto* and *Lezione di canto fermo.*

WORKS: OPERAS: All premiered in Naples unless otherwise given: *Il Pisistrato* (May 13, 1714); *Sofonisba* (Jan. 22, 1718); *Caio Gracco* (April 19, 1720); *Arianna e Teseo* (Nov. 26, 1721); *Baiazete, imperator dei Turchi* (Aug. 28, 1722); *Timocrate* (Venice, 1723); *La' mpeca scoperta* (comic opera; Dec. 13, 1723); *Il Turno Aricino* (with L. Vinci; 1724); *L'ammore fedele* (comic opera; April 25, 1724); *Lo pazzo apposta* (comic opera; Aug. 26, 1724); *Zenobia in Palmira* (May 13, 1725); *Il trionfo di Camilla, regina dei Volsci* (Rome, Jan. 8, 1726); *Orismene, ovvero Dalli sdegni l'amore* (comic opera; Jan. 19, 1726); *La semmeglianza de chi l'ha fatta* (comic opera; Fall 1726); *Lo matrimonio annascuso* (comic opera;

1727); *Il Cid* (Rome, Feb. 10, 1927); *La pastorella commattuta* (comic opera; Fall 1727); *Argene* (Venice, Jan. 17, 1728); *Catone in Utica* (Venice, 1729); *La schiava per amore* (comic opera; 1729); *Semiramide* (Feb. 2, 1730); *Rosmene* (comic opera; Summer 1730); *Evergete* (Rome, 1731); *Demetrio* (Oct. 1, 1732); *Amor da' senno* (comic opera; 1733); *Nitocri, regina d'Egitto* (Nov. 4, 1733); *Il castello d'Atlante* (July 4, 1734); *Demofoonte* (Jan. 20, 1735; Act 1 by D. Sarro, Act 2 by F. Mancini, Act 3 by Leo, and intermezzos by G. Sellitti); *La clemenza di Tito* (Venice, 1735); *Emira* (July 12, 1735; intermezzos by I Prota); *Demetrio* (Dec. 10, 1735; different setting from earlier opera of 1732); *Onore vince amore* (comic opera; 1736); *Farnace* (Dec. 19, 1736); *L'amico traditore* (comic opera; 1737); *Siface* (Bologna, May 11, 1737; revised version as *Viriate,* Pistoia, 1740); *La simpatia del sangue* (comic opera; Fall 1737); *Olimpiade* (Dec. 19, 1737); *Il conte* (comic opera; 1738); *Il Ciro riconosciuto* (Turin, 1739); *Amor vuol sofferenze* (comic opera; Fall 1739; revised version as *La finta frascatana,* Nov. 1744); *Achille in Sciro* (Turin, 1740); *Scipione nelle Spagne* (Milan, 1740); *L'Alidoro* (comic opera; Summer 1740); *Demetrio* (Dec. 19, 1741; different setting from the earlier operas of 1732 and 1735); *L'ambizione delusa* (comic opera; 1742); *Andromaca* (Nov. 4, 1742); *Il fantastico, od Il nuovo Chisciotte* (comic opera; 1743; revised version, Fall 1748); *Vologeso, re dei Parti* (Turin, 1744); *La fedeltà odiata* (comic opera; 1744); he also contributed to a pasticcio setting of Demetrio (June 30, 1738); he likewise composed prologues, arias, etc., to operas by other composers. A number of operas long attributed to Leo are now considered doubtful.

Leo also composed serenatas, feste teatrali, chamber cantatas, etc. He wrote the following sacred dramas and oratorios: *S. Chiara, o L'infedeltà abbattuta* (Naples, 1712); *Il trionfo della castità di S. Alessio* (Naples, Jan. 4, 1713); *Dalla morte alla vita di S. Maria Maddalena* (Atrani, July 22, 1722); *Oratorio per la Ss. vergine del rosario* (Naples, Oct. 1, 1730); *S. Elena al Calvario* (Bologna, 1734); *La morte di Abele* (Bologna, 1738); *S. Francesco di Paola nel deserto* (Lecce, 1738); *Il verbo eterno e la religione* (Florence, 1741); he also composed 6 Neapolitan masses, various mass movements, 2 Magnificats, offertories, antiphons, motets, etc.; most notable is his *Miserere* for Double Choir and Organ (1739), publ. in a modern ed. by H. Wiley Hitchcock (St. Louis, 1961). His instrumental works include 6 concerti for Cello, String Orch., and Basso Continuo (1737–38); of these, one in D major has been ed. by F. Cilea (Milan, 1934), one in A major by E. Rapp (Mainz, 1938), and 3 in the Series of Early Music, VII (1973); Concerto in D major for 4 Violins and Basso Continuo (publ. in *Musikschätze der Vergangenheit,* XXIV, Berlin, 1952); works for harpsichord; etc.

BIBLIOGRAPHY: C.V. Leo, *Leonardo Leo e sua epoca musicale* (Brindisi, 1894); G. Leo, *Leonardo Leo, musicista del secola XVIII e le sue opere musicali* (Naples, 1905); E. Dent, "Leonardo Leo," *Sammelbände der Internationalen Musik-Gesellschaft,* VIII (1906–7); F. Piovano, "A propos d'une récente biographie de Leonard Leo," *Sammelbäned der Internationalen Musik-Gesellschaft,* VIII (1906–7); K. Geiringer, "Eine Geburtstagskantate von P. Metastasio und Leonardo Leo," *Zeitschrift für Musikwissenschaft* (1927); E. Faustini-Fasini, "Leonardo Leo e la sua famiglia," *Note d'Archivio per la Storia Musicale,* XIV (1937); F. Walker, "Cav. Giacomo Leo and His Famous 'Ancestor,' " *Music Review* (Nov. 1948); F. Schlitzer, ed., *Tommaso Traetta, Leonardo Leo, Vincenzo Bellini: Noti e documenti raccolti da F. Schlitzer* (Siena, 1952); G.A. Pastore, *Leonardo Leo* (Galatina, 1957).

Léonard, Hubert, Belgian violinist and pedagogue; b. Bellaire, near Liège, April 7, 1819; d. Paris, May 6, 1890. His first violin teacher was Rouma, at Liège; he then became a pupil of Habeneck at the Paris Cons.; in 1844 he embarked on an extended European tour; then succeeded Bériot as prof. of violin at the Brussels Cons. In 1867 he went to Paris, where he remained until his death. He publ. *Petite gymnastique du jeune violiniste; 24 études classiques; Etudes harmoniques;* a method for violin, *Ecole Léonard; L'Ancienne Ecole italienne,* a collection of special studies in double stopping, including examples from Corelli, Tartini, Geminiani, and Nardini; *Le Violon au point de vue de l'orchestration;* also 5 violin concertos; 6 concert pieces, with Piano; Serenade for 3 Violins; Concert Duo for 2 Violins; fantasias and character pieces.

Leoncavallo, Ruggero, Italian dramatic composer; b. Naples, April 23, 1857; d. Montecatini, Aug. 9, 1919. He attended the Naples Cons., where his teachers were B. Cesi (piano) and M. Ruta and L. Rossi (composition), and at 16 made a pianistic tour. His first opera, *Tommaso Chatterton,* was about to be produced in Bologna (1878) when the manager disappeared, and the production was called off. Leoncavallo earned his living as a young man by playing piano in cafés; this life he continued for many years, traveling through Egypt, Greece, Turkey, Germany, Belgium, and the Netherlands before settling in Paris. There he found congenial company; composed chansonettes and other popular songs; wrote an opera, *Songe d'une nuit d'été (Midsummer Night's Dream,* after Shakespeare), which was privately sung in a salon. He began to study Wagner's scores, and became an ardent Wagnerian; he resolved to emulate the master by producing a trilogy, *Crepusculum,* depicting in epical traits the Italian Renaissance; the separate parts were to be *I Medici, Girolamo Savonarola,* and *Cesare Borgia.* He spent 6 years on the basic historical research; having completed the first part, and with the scenario of the entire trilogy sketched, he returned to Italy in 1887. There, the publisher Ricordi became interested in the project, but kept delaying the publication and production of the work. Annoyed, Leoncavallo turned to Sonzogno, the publisher of Mascagni, whose opera *Cavalleria rusticana* had just obtained a tremendous vogue. Leoncavallo submitted a short opera in a similarly realistic vein; he wrote his own libretto based on a factual story of passion and murder in a Calabrian village, and named it *Pagliacci.* The opera was given with sensational success at the Teatro dal Verme in Milan under the direction of Toscanini (May 21, 1892), and rapidly took possession of operatic stages throughout the world; it is often played on the same evening with Mascagni's opera, both works being of brief duration. Historically, these 2 operas signalized the important development of Italian operatic *verismo,* which influenced composers of other countries also. The holograph score of *Pagliacci* is in the Library of Congress.

The enormous success of *Pagliacci* did not deter Leoncavallo from carrying on his more ambitious projects. The first part of his unfinished trilogy, *I Medici,* was finally brought out at La Scala in Milan on Nov. 9, 1893, but the reception was so indifferent that Leoncavallo turned to other subjects; the same fate befell his youthful *Tommaso Chatterton* at its production in Rome (March 10, 1896). His next opera, *La Bohème* (Venice, May 6, 1897), won considerable success, but had the ill fortune of coming a year after Puccini's masterpiece on the same story, and was dwarfed by comparison. There followed a light opera, *Zazà* (Milan, Nov. 10, 1900), which was fairly successful, and was produced repeatedly on world stages. In 1904 Leoncavallo was commissioned by the German Emperor Wilhelm II to write an opera for Berlin; this was *Der Roland von Berlin,* on a German historic theme; it was produced in Berlin on Dec. 13, 1904, but despite the high patronage it proved a fiasco. In 1906 Leoncavallo made a tour of the U.S. and Canada, conducting his *Pagliacci* and a new opera, *La Jeunesse de Figaro,* specially written for his American tour; it was so unsuccessful that Leoncavallo never attempted to stage it in Europe. Back in Italy he resumed his industrious production; 2 new operas, *Maia* (Rome, Jan. 15, 1910) and *Malbruk* (Rome, Jan. 19, 1910), were produced within the same week; another opera, *La Reginetta delle rose,* was staged simultaneously in Rome and in Naples (June 24, 1912). In the autumn of that year, Leoncavallo visited London, where he presented the premiere of his *Gli Zingari* (Sept. 16, 1912); a year later, he revisited the U.S., conducting in San Francisco. He wrote several more operas, but they made no impression; 3 of them were produced during his lifetime: *La Candidata* (Rome, Feb. 6, 1915), *Goffredo Mameli* (Genoa, April 27, 1916), and *Prestami tua moglie* (Montecatini, Sept. 2, 1916); the following were produced posthumously: *A chi la giarettiera?* (Rome, Oct. 16, 1919), *Edipo re* (Chicago, Dec. 13, 1920), and *Il primo bacio* (Montecatini, April 29, 1923); yet another opera, *Tormenta,* remained unfinished. Salvatore Allegra collected various sketches by Leoncavallo and arranged from them a 3-act operetta, *La maschera nuda,* which was produced in Naples on June 26, 1925.

Leonhard, Julius Emil, German composer; b. Lauban, June 13, 1810; d. Dresden, June 23, 1883. He became a prof. of piano at the Munich Cons. in 1852, and at the Dresden Cons. in 1859. He wrote an oratorio, *Johannes der Täufer;* 3 cantatas for Soli,

Chorus, and Orch.; Symph.; overture to Oehlenschläger's *Axel und Walpurg;* Piano Sonata; 2 violin sonatas; 3 string trios; Piano Quartet; etc.

Leonhardt, Gustav, eminent Dutch organist and harpsichord player; b. 's Graveland, May 30, 1928. He studied in the Netherlands and Switzerland; toured widely in Europe; made 6 tours in America as a performer and lecturer. He edited collections of keyboard music; publ. *The Art of Fugue, Bach's Last Harpsichord Work* (The Hague, 1952).

Leoni, Franco, Italian composer; b. Milan, Oct. 24, 1864; d. London, Feb. 8, 1949. He studied at the Milan Cons. with Dominiceti and Ponchielli; in 1892 went to London, where he remained for 25 years, until 1917; then lived in France and Italy, eventually returning to England.
WORKS: Operas: *Raggio di luna* (Milan, June 5, 1890); *Rip van Winkle* (London, Sept. 4, 1897); *Ib and Little Christina,* "a picture in 3 panels" (London, Nov. 14, 1901); *The Oracle* (London, June 28, 1905; Metropolitan Opera, N.Y., Feb. 4, 1915; his most successful opera); *Tzigana* (Genoa, Feb. 3, 1910); *Le baruffe chiozzotte* (Milan, Jan. 2, 1920); *La terra del sogno* (Milan, Jan. 10, 1920); cantatas: *Sardanapalus* (1896) and *Golgotha* (1911); oratorio, *The Gate of Life* (London, March 16, 1898); songs.

Leoni, Leone, Italian composer; b. Verona, c.1560; d. Vicenza, June 24, 1627. He studied at the "academy" maintained by Count Mario Bevilacqua in Verona; was maestro di cappella in Vicenza from Oct. 4, 1588, until his death. He was a disciple of the Venetian school; his works are characteristic for their application of chromatic devices in harmony, and antiphonal choral usages. He publ. 5 books of madrigals for 5 Voices (Venice, 1588–1602); 4 books of motets, with Organ, under the title *Sacri fiori* (1606–22); *Aurea corona* for 4 Voices accompanied by 6 Instruments (1618). His motets are particularly fine.
BIBLIOGRAPHY: H. Wing, *The Polychoral Motets of Leone Leoni* (Diss., Boston Univ., 1966).

Leonin (Leoninus), great master of the Notre Dame School and of the Ars Antiqua; flourished probably before the cornerstone of Notre Dame de Paris was laid in 1163; was theretofore active at the earlier church, Beatae Mariae Virginis. According to the treatise of Anonymus IV (Coussemaker, *Scriptores,* I, 342), he complied the *Magnus Liber organi de graduali et antiphonario pro servitio divino multiplicando,* a cycle of 2-part liturgical settings for the whole church year, a work later revised by Leonin's successor, Perotin. The original of this collection has not been preserved, but there are 4 extant MSS containing music from it; of these, MS Wolfenbüttel 677 (formerly Helmstedt 628), dating from the 14th century (facsimile reprint in J.H. Baxter, *An Old St. Andrews Music Book,* 1931), though not the oldest, appears to preserve music from the *Magnus Liber* in purest form; the other 3 MSS are Pluteus 29.1 in the Biblioteca Medicea-Lau-

renziana of Florence, Wolfenbüttel 1206, and Madrid Biblioteca Nacional 20486. Leonin was the chief figure of his period, standing midway between the St. Martial school and Perotin; his technique is characterized by the juxtaposition in individual pieces of the note-against-note style, and the style in which, over a lower part characterized by long sustained notes, an upper part moves in freely flowing rhythm. (Both styles had already been used at St. Martial.)
BIBLIOGRAPHY: Fr. Ludwig, "Die liturgische Organa Leonins und Perotins," *Reimann–Festschrift* (1909); idem, *Repertotium organorum recentioris et motetorum vetustustissimi stili:* vol. I, *Catalogue raisonné der Quellen* (1910); J. Handschin, "Zur Notre Dame Rhythmik," *Zeitschrift für Musikwissenschaft* (1925); H. Schmidt, "Zur Melodiebildung Leonins und Perotins," ibid., (1931); M. Schneider, "Zur Satztechnik der Notre Dame-Schule," ibid., (1932); G. Reese, *Music in the Middle Ages,* chap. 11 (N.Y., 1940); W.G. Waite, *The Rhythm of Twelfth Century Polyphony* (New Haven, 1954); H. Husmann, "The Origin and Destination of the Magnus liber organi," *Musical Quarterly,* XLIX (1963); F. Salzer, "Tonality in Early Medieval Polyphony," *Music Forum,* I (1967).

Leonova, Darya, Russian contralto; b. Vyshny-Volochok, March 9, 1829; d. St. Petersburg, Feb. 6, 1896. She studied singing in St. Petersburg; in 1852 sang the part of Vanya in Glinka's *A Life for the Tsar,* and was greatly praised by Glinka himself. In 1875 she went on a concert tour around the world, through Siberia, China, Japan, and America. In 1879 she traveled in southern Russia and the Crimea with Mussorgsky as accompanist; sang arias from Mussorgsky's operas and his songs; in 1880 opened a singing school in St. Petersburg, with Mussorgsky acting as coach.
BIBLIOGRAPHY: V. Yakovlev, *D. Leonova* (Moscow, 1950).

Leopold I, Austrian emperor who reigned from 1658 till 1705; b. Vienna, June 9, 1640; d. there, May 5, 1705. During his reign Vienna became the center of the world's operatic activity, no fewer than 400 new operas having been produced in that time; he was not only an enthusiastic patron but also a practically trained musician and diligent composer. His complete works are in MS in the State Library at Vienna: 15 oratorios, 7 operas, 17 ballet suites, 155 arias, 79 sacred compositions (2 masses, 5 Offices for the Dead, 4-part Miserere with Instruments, etc.).

Leplin, Emanuel, American composer; b. San Francisco, Oct. 3, 1917; d. Martinez, Calif., Dec. 1, 1972. He studied violin with Georges Enesco; conducting with Pierre Monteux; composition with Roger Sessions.
WORKS: *Galaxy* for 2 Cellos and Orch. (1942); *Cosmos* for Violin and Orch. (1949); 2 symph. poems: *Landscapes* and *Skyscrapers* (San Francisco, May 5, 1960); Symph. (San Francisco, Jan. 3, 1962); 3 string

quartets; chamber music for various instrumental combinations; piano pieces.

Leppard, Raymond, English conductor and harpsichordist; b. London, Aug. 2, 1927. He studied at Trinity College, Cambridge; was a lecturer in music at Cambridge Univ. (1958–68). In 1963 he organized the English Chamber Orch. and traveled with it to Japan in 1970. In 1973 he became principal conductor of the Northern Symph. Orch. in England, resigning in 1980; then lived in N.Y. In 1978 he was guest conductor of the N.Y. Phil.; in 1983 he was made a Commander of the Order of the British Empire; in 1984 he became principal guest conductor of the St. Louis Symph. Orch. He took particular interest in early Baroque music; gave harpsichord recitals.

Leps, Wassili, Russian conductor and composer; b. St. Petersburg, May 12, 1870; d. Toronto, Dec. 22, 1943. He went to Germany, where he studied at the Dresden Cons. with Draeseke, Wüllner, and Theodor Kirchner. In 1894 he settled in America; taught at the Philadelphia Music Academy; then became conductor of the Philadelphia Operatic Society, which he led until 1923, producing 47 operas. In 1932 he organized the Providence Symph. Orch.; was its conductor until 1941, when he retired and went to Toronto to reside with a daughter. He wrote an opera on a Japanese subject, *Hoshi-San,* which he conducted with the Philadelphia Operatic Society on May 21, 1909; a cantata, *Yo-Nennen,* and some symph. music.
BIBLIOGRAPHY: E.E. Hipsher, *American Opera and Its Composers* (Philadelphia, 1934; pp. 290–94).

Le Roux, Maurice, French composer and conductor; b. Paris, Feb. 6, 1923. He studied with Messiaen at the Paris Cons.; then worked at the electronic studios of Radiodiffusion Française. In his music he adopts serial procedures. In 1952 he embarked on a conductor's career.
WORKS: *Le Petit Prince,* ballet (1950); *Sables,* ballet (1956); *Le Cercle des métamorphoses* for Orch. (1953); *Trois visages* for Trumpet and Piano; *Pièces dodécaphoniques* for Piano; songs. He publ. *Introduction à la musique contemporaine* (Paris, 1947); *Claudio Monteverdi* (Paris, 1951).

Leroux, Xavier, French composer; b. Velletri, Papal States, Oct. 11, 1863; d. Paris, Feb. 2, 1919. He was a pupil of Dubois and Massenet at the Paris Cons.; won first Grand Prix de Rome in 1885; was appointed a prof. at the Cons. in 1896.
WORKS: Operas: *Cléopâtre* (Paris, Oct. 23, 1890); *Evangeline* (Brussels, 1895); *Astarté* (Paris, Feb. 15, 1901); *La Reine Fiammette* (Paris, Dec. 23, 1903; Metropolitan Opera, N.Y., Jan. 24, 1919); *Vénus et Adonis* (Nîmes, 1905); *William Ratcliff* (Nice, Jan. 26, 1906); *Théodora* (Monte Carlo, March 19, 1907); *Le Chemineau* (Paris, Nov. 6, 1907; Metropolitan Opera, Jan. 31, 1919); *Le Carillonneur* (Paris, March 20, 1913); *La Fille de Figaro* (Paris, March 11, 1914); *Les Cadeaux de Noël* (Paris, Dec. 25, 1915); *1814*

(Monte Carlo, April 6, 1918); *Nausithoé* (posthumous; Nice, April 9, 1920); *La Plus Forte* (posthumous; Paris, Jan. 11, 1924); *L'Ingénu* (Bordeaux, Feb. 13, 1931); songs; piano pieces.

Le Roy, René, French flutist; b. Maisons-Laffitte, near Paris, March 4, 1898. He studied at the Paris Cons. with Hennebains, Lafleurance, and Gaubert. In 1918 he won first prize for flute playing; in 1919 succeeded his teacher Gaubert as director of the Société des Instruments à Vent; in 1922 he founded the Quintette Instrumental de Paris, with which he gave numerous concerts in Europe and America. He subsequently occupied various teaching positions; was prof. of chamber music for wind instruments at the Paris Cons. (1955–64). He compiled (with Cl. Dorgeuille) the manual *Traité de la flûte, historique, technique et pédagogique* (Paris, 1966).

Lert, Ernst Josef Maria, Austrian opera Intendant and writer; b. Vienna, May 12, 1883; d. Baltimore, Jan. 30, 1955. He studied at the Univ. of Vienna with G. Adler; in 1908 received his Dr.Phil.; was dramatic coach at the Municipal Theater in Breslau and in Leipzig; in 1920–23, opera director of the Municipal Theater and teacher at the Hoch Cons. in Frankfurt; in 1923–29, stage director at La Scala in Milan (with Toscanini); in 1929–31, stage director at the Metropolitan Opera House in N.Y.; in 1936–38, head of the opera dept. of the Curtis Inst. of Music in Philadelphia; after 1938, head of the opera dept. of the Peabody Cons., in Baltimore. He publ. *Mozart auf dem Theater* (Berlin, 1918; 4th ed., 1922); *Otto Lohse,* a biography (Leipzig, 1918).

Lert, Richard Johanes, Austrian conductor, brother of **Ernst Lert;** b. Vienna, Sept. 19, 1885; d. Los Angeles, April 25, 1980. He studied with Heuberger; then served as a conductor in Düsseldorf, Darmstadt, Frankfurt, Hannover, and Mannheim; later was guest conductor with the Staatsoper in Berlin. He emigrated to the U.S. in 1934 and settled in Pasadena, Calif., as a conductor and teacher. In 1916 he married the novelist Vicki Baum. He celebrated his 90th birthday in 1975, but continued to be active, conducting summer concerts at Orkney Springs, Va.; also gave courses in conducting.

Leschetizky, Theodor, great Austrain pianist and famous pedagogue; b. Lancut, Austrian Poland, June 22, 1830; d. Dresden, Nov. 14, 1915. He first studied with his father, who took him to Vienna, where he became a pupil of Czerny. He acquired a mastery of the piano in an amazingly short time, and was only 15 when he himself began to teach. He also attended the Univ. of Vienna as a student of philosophy, until its closure in the wake of the 1848 revolution. In 1852 he went to Russia; his initial concerts in St. Petersburg were extremely successful, and gradually he attracted many pupils. He was also active as music director to the Grand Duchess Helen. In 1862 Anton Rubinstein, director of the newly opened St. Petersburg Cons., engaged him as a teacher. After 16 years in Russia, Leschetizky returned to Vienna; there he married his former pupil Anna Essipova (she was his 2nd wife); they were divorced in 1892; Leschetizky contracted 2 more marriages after that. He continued to make occasional concert tours, but concentrated mainly on teaching; his fame grew, and pupils flocked from all over the world to his studio in Vienna. His most celebrated pupil was Paderewski; other pupils were Gabrilowitsch, Schnabel, Isabelle Vengerova, etc., as well as his 3rd and 4th wives, Dominirska Benislavska and Marie Rozborska. His method of playing with the "Kugelhand" (arched hand) was to secure fullness of tone and finger dexterity, with the flexible wrist reserved for octave playing and chord passages. A Leschetizky Society, composed of his pupils, was organized after his death; a branch was established in the U.S.

Leschetizky was also a composer; he wrote an opera, *Die erste Falte* (Prague, Oct. 9, 1867), and some chamber music; but it is his piano pieces that still remain of interest and value; of these, the following are the most effective: *Les 2 Alouettes; Grand polka de caprice; La Cascade; Perpetuum mobile; Valse chromatique; Souvenirs d'Italie; A la campagne,* and *3 études caractéristiques.*

BIBLIOGRAPHY: Malwine Brée, *Die Grundlage der Methode Leschetizky* (Vienna, 1902; also in Eng. and French translations); Countess Angèle Potocka, *Theodor Leschetizky* (London, 1903); Annette Hullah, *Theodor Leschetizky* (London, 1906); Ethel Newcomb, *Leschetizky as I Knew Him* (London, 1921).

Leslie, Henry David, English conductor and composer; b. London, June 18, 1822; d. Llansaintfraid, near Oswestry, Feb. 4, 1896. He was a pupil of Charles Lucas; cellist in the Sacred Harmonic Society, and its conductor from 1853–61. In 1855 he organized (with Heming) an a cappella singing society, which won first prize at Paris in 1878. He composed the operas *Romance, or Bold Dick Turpin* (1857) and *Ida* (1864); oratorios: *Immanuel* (1853) and *Judith* (1858); cantatas: *Holyrood* (1860); *Daughter of the Isles* (1861); and a "biblical pastoral," *The First Christian Morn* (1880); Symph.; overture, *The Templar.*

Lessel, Franz, Polish pianist and composer; b. Pulawy, c.1780; d. Petrikow, Dec. 26, 1838. He went to Vienna in 1797 to study medicine, but became a pupil of Haydn and one of his few intimate friends; returned to Poland upon Haydn's death, continuing to compose. He left in MS a great number of instrumental works; his publ. compositions show a fine talent; he wrote a Piano Concerto; 2 fantasias for Piano; 3 piano sonatas; a Piano Trio; several symphs.; his songs (to Polish words) were often performed.

Lessmann, Otto, German pianist and critic; b. Rüdersdorf, near Berlin, Jan. 30, 1844; d. Jena, April 27, 1918. He studied with Hans von Bülow (piano), Kiel (theory), and Teschner (voice); taught piano at the Stern Cons. in Berlin; was owner and editor of the

Allgemeine Musik-Zeitung (1882–1907).

Lester, Thomas William, English organist and composer; b. Leicester, Sept. 17, 1889; d. Berrien Springs, Mich., Dec. 4, 1956. He came to the U.S. in 1902; studied with Wilhelm Middelschulte in Chicago; wrote music criticism for the *Chicago Record-Herald;* also served as organist in various Chicago churches. He wrote 8 cantatas (sacred and secular); several suites for piano; organ pieces; numerous choruses; songs.

Le Sueur (or **Lesueur**), **Jean François,** French composer; b. Drucat–Plessiel, near Abbeville, Feb. 15, 1760; d. Paris, Oct. 6, 1837. At 7 he was a choirboy at Abbeville; at 14, in Amiens, where he took a course of studies; interrupting his academic education, he became maître de musique at the Cathedral of Séez; then an assistant at the Church of the Innocents in Paris. Abbé Roze gave him some instruction in harmony; this constituted practically all of his musical training; he developed his musical talent without teachers. His subsequent positions were as maître de musique at the Cathedral of Dijon (1781), at Le Mans (1783), and at Tours (1784). He then returned to Paris, now serving (upon the recommendation of Grétry) as maître de chapelle at the Innocents. When the competition for the post of maître de chapelle at Notre Dame was announced in 1786, Le Sueur entered it, and won. He organized an orch. for the chief festive days, and brought out masses, motets, services, etc., using a full orch., thus completely transforming the character of the services; he was greatly successful with the congregation, but the conservative clergy strongly objected to his innovations; other critics called his type of musical productions "opéra des gueux" (beggars' opera). He expounded his ideas of effective and descriptive music in a pamphlet, *Essai de musique sacrée ou musique motivée et méthodique, pour la fête de Noël, à la messe du jour* (1787); this evoked an anonymous attack, to which he replied with another publication, *Exposé d'une musique unie, imitative, et particulière à chaque solennité* (1787), reasserting his aim of making church music dramatic and descriptive. He retired temporarily in 1788, and spent 4 years in the country. Upon his return to Paris, he brought out at the Théâtre Feydeau 3 operas: *La Caverne* (Feb. 16, 1793), which had a popular success, *Paul et Virginie* (Jan. 13, 1794), and *Télémaque* (May 11, 1796). When the Paris Cons. was organized in 1795, Le Sueur was appointed inspector, and a member of the Committee on Instruction; with Méhul, Langlé, Gossec, and Catel, he wrote the *Principes élémentaires de la musique* and the *Solfèges du Conservatoire*. Le Sueur was dismissed in 1802 because of an altercation that occurred following the rejection, by the Opéra, of 2 of his operas in favor of *Sémiramis*, written by Catel. For 2 years he lived in poverty and suffering, until Napoleon, in 1804, raised him to the highest position attainable by a musician in Paris by appointing him as maître de chapelle, succeeding Paisiello. His rejected opera, *Les Bardes,* was then produced (Paris,

July 10, 1804) with great applause, and *La Mort d'Adam,* the other rejected work, was also staged (Paris, March 21, 1809). After the restoration of the monarchy, and despite Le Sueur's avowed veneration of Napoleon, the government of Louis XVIII appointed him superintendent and composer to the Chapelle du Roi; from 1818 he was also prof. of composition at the Paris Cons.; he had several celebrated pupils, among them Berlioz, Gounod, and Ambroise Thomas. He taught at the Cons. until his death; was a member of the Institut (1813), and held several other honorary positions. His last 3 operas were accepted for performance, but were not produced; these were *Tyrtée* (1794), *Artaxerse* (1797), and *Alexandre à Babylone;* other works were 2 secular cantatas: *L'Inauguration du temple de la Victoire* (Paris, Jan. 2, 1807) and *Le Triomphe de Trajan* (Paris, Oct. 23, 1807); several sacred oratorios (*Debora, Rachel, Ruth et Noémi, Ruth et Booz*); Solemn Mass for 4 Voices, Chorus, and Orch.; cantata, *L'Ombre de Sacchini;* 3 Te Deums; 2 Passions; *Stabat Mater;* these, and some other works, were publ.; he left many more (over 30 masses, etc.) in MS. He publ. *Notice sur la mélopée, la rythmopée, et les grands caractères de la musique ancienne* (Paris, 1793); a sketch of Paisiello (1816); and some pamphlets. In 1980 J. Mongredien publ. *Jean-François Le Sueur: A Thematic Catalogue of his Complete Works* (N.Y.).

BIBLIOGRAPHY: C.P. Ducanel, *Mémoire pour J.F. Lesueur* (Paris, 1802); Raoul-Rochette, *Notice historique sur la vie et les œuvres de Jean-François Le Sueur* (Paris, 1837); Stéphen de la Madeleine, *Biographie de Jean-François Le Sueur* (Paris, 1841); P.O. Fouque, "Le Sueur comme prédecesseur de Berlioz," in *Les Révolutionnaires de la musique* (Paris, 1882); H. Berlioz, *Les Musiciens et la musique* (Paris, 1903; on Le Sueur's oratorios); C. Pierre, *Hymnes et chants de la Révolution* (Paris, 1904); W. Buschkötter, *Jean François Le Sueur* (Halle, 1912); F. Lamy, *Jean François Le Sueur* (Paris, 1912); G. Servières, "Les Oratoires de Jean-François Le Sueur," in *Episodes d'histoire musicale* (Paris, 1912); J. Mongrédien, "La Musique du sacre de Napoléon Ier," *Revue de Musicologie* (1967); W. Dean, "Opera under the French Revolution," *Proceedings of the Royal Music Association* (1967–68); M.M. Herman, "The Turbulent Career of Jean-François Le Sueur," *Recherches sur la musique française classique* (1969).

Lesur, Daniel, French composer, pianist, and organist; b. Paris, Nov. 19, 1908. He studied at the Paris Cons. with Tournemire, Caussade, and Ferté; was assistant organist at Ste.-Clothilde (1927–37) and prof. of counterpoint at the Schola Cantorum (1935–39). In 1936 he and Yves Baudrier, O. Messiaen, and Jolivet organized "La Jeune France." His works include the ballet *L'Infante et le monstre* (with A. Jolivet; 1938); *Ave Maria sur un Noël* for Soprano, Contralto, Women's Chorus, and Organ (1938); *Andrea del Sarto,* symph. poem (Paris, June 21, 1949); *Andrea del Sarto,* opera (Marseille, Jan. 24, 1969); *Suite française* for Orch. (1935); *Pastorale* for

Chamber Orch. (1938); *Ricercare* for Orch. (1939); *Passacaille* for Piano and Orch. (1937); *L'Etoile de Séville,* suite for Chamber Orch. (1941); *Chansons cambodgiennes* for Voice and Chamber Orch. (1947); Suite for Piano and String Trio (1943); *Suite médiévale* for Flute, Violin, Viola, Cello, and Harp (1946); *Le Village imaginaire* for 2 Pianos (1947); piano pieces (*Soirs, Les Carillons, Bagatelle, Pavane, 2 Noëls, Pastorale variée, Ballade,* etc.); organ music; songs (*Les Harmonies intimes, La Mort des voiles, 3 poèmes de Cécile Sauvage, L'Enfance de l'art, Clair comme le jour,* etc.).

Lesure, François, French music librarian, musicologist, and writer; b. Paris, May 23, 1923. He studied at the Ecole des Chartres, then at the Ecole Pratique des Hautes Etudes and the Sorbonne, and musicology at the Paris Cons. A member of the music dept. at the Bibliotheque Nationale since 1950, he was made its chief curator in 1970. From 1953 to 1967 he headed the Paris office (responsible for Series B) of the Répertoire International des Sources Musicales (RISM), for which he himself edited 3 vols.: *Recueils imprimés: XVIe–XVIIe siècles* (Munich, 1960); *Recueils imprimés: XVIIIe siècle* (Munich, 1964; supplement in *Notes,* March 1972, vol. XXVIII, pp. 397–418, and the 2 vols. of *Ecrits imprimés concernant la musique* (Munich, 1971). His other posts have included a professorship at the Free Univ. of Brussels and editorship, since 1967, of the series reprinting early music known as Le Pupitre. He has also edited such non-serial works as the report of the 1954 Arras Conference, *La Renaissance dans les provinces du Nord* (Paris, 1956); *Anthologie de la chanson parisienne au XVIe siècle* (Monaco, 1953); 6 vols. of *Chansons polyphoniques* (Monaco, 1967–72; with A.T. Merritt; the first 5 vols. constitute the collected works of C. Janequin); P. Trichet's *Traité des instruments de musique (vers 1640)* (Neuilly, 1957); and a collected edition of Debussy's writings on music, *Monsieur Croche et autres écrits* (Paris, 1971; in Eng., N.Y., 1977). In 1971 he became president of the Société Française de Musicologie and in 1973 director of the published *Archives* of the Ecole Pratique des Hautes Etudes. His own publications include a *Bibliographie des éditions d'Adrian Le Roy et Robert Ballard, 1551–1598* (with G. Thibault, Paris, 1955; supplement in *Revue de Musicologie,* 1957); *Musicians and Poets of the French Renaissance* (N.Y., 1955); *Mozart en France* (Paris, 1956); *Collection musicale A. Meyer* (with N. Bridgman, Abbeville, 1961); *Musica e società* (Milan, 1966; German version as *Musik und Gesellschaft im Bild: Zeugnisse der Malerei aus sechs Jahrhunderten,* Kassel, 1966; in Eng. as *Music and Art in Society,* Univ. Park, Pa., 1968); *Bibliographie des éditions musicales publiées par Estienne Roger et Michel-Charles Le Cene, Amsterdam, 1696–1743* (Paris, 1969); and *Musique et musiciens français du XVIe siècle* (Geneva, 1976, a reprinting in book form of 24 vols. of Lesure's many articles originally publ. 1950–69). He contributed *L'Opéra classique français: 17e et 18e siècles* (Geneva, 1972) and *Claude Debussy* (Geneva, 1975) to the series Iconographie

Musicale. For the Bibliothèque Nationale he prepared a series of exhibition catalogs, most notably one on Berlioz (Paris, 1969). The culmination of his Debussy studies is a *Catalogue de l'œuvre de Claude Debussy* (Geneva, 1977).

Letelier, Alfonso, Chilean composer and teacher; b. Santiago, Oct. 4, 1912. He studied with Allende at the Cons. Nacional in Santiago, where he became a prof. of harmony (1947); aided in establishing the Escuela Moderna de Música. His compositions include a symph. poem, *La vida del campo,* for Piano and Orch.; *Aculeo,* suite for Orch. (Louisville, Ky., Jan. 30, 1957); *Los sonetos de la muerte* for Female Voice and Orch.; String Quartet; Variations for Piano; Mass for Chorus, String Orch., and Organ; songs. From 1952 to 1962 he was dean of the Faculty of Fine Arts of the Univ. of Chile.

Letorey, Omer, French composer; b. Châlon-sur-Saône, May 4, 1873; d. Paris, March 21, 1938. He studied at the Ecole Niedermeyer, and with Pessard at the Paris Cons.; in 1895 won the Prix de Rome with his scena *Clarisse Harlowe.* Other works include the operas *Cléopâtre* (1918); *L'Œillet blanc* (1930); *Le Sicilien ou L'Amour peintre* (Paris, Opéra-Comique, March 19, 1930).

Lettvin, Theodore, American pianist; b. Chicago, Oct. 29, 1926. He studied at the Curtis Inst. of Music in Philadelphia with Rudolf Serkin and Mieczyslaw Horszowski. In 1955–56 he became artist-in-residence at the Univ. of Colorado; then was head of the piano dept. of the Cleveland Music School Settlement (1956–68). In 1968 he was appointed to the piano faculty at the New England Cons. of Music.

Letz, Hans, German violinist; b. Ittenheim, Alsace, March 18, 1887; d. Hackensack, N.J., Nov. 14, 1969. He studied violin with H. Schuster at the Strasbourg Cons., and later with Joachim at the Hochschule für Musik in Berlin. In 1908 he emigrated to the U.S.; made his debut in N.Y. on Nov. 3, 1908; subsequently was concertmaster of the Chicago Sym. Orch. (1909–12), and 2nd violinist of the Kneisel Quartet (1912–17). In 1917 he settled in N.Y. as a teacher at the Inst. of Musical Art; also formed his own string quartet. He publ. a guide, *Music for the Violin and Viola* (N.Y., 1949).

Leuckart, F. Ernst Christoph, German music publisher; b. Halberstadt, March 21, 1748; d. Breslau, Feb. 2, 1817. He established a music business at Breslau in 1782; it was acquired in 1856 by Constantin Sander, who removed it to Leipzig in 1870, and added to it by buying out the firms of Weinhold & Förster (Breslau), Damköhler (Berlin), and Witzendorf (Vienna). The new firm, Constantin Sander, vormals F.E.C. Leuckart, publ. many learned works (e.g., by Ambros, Lussy, Westphal, Niecks, Molitor, etc.) and compositions of R. Franz, Rheinberger, Draeseke, Bossi, Hausegger, Huber, Klose, Duparc, Richard Strauss, Max Reger, Atterberg, Bantock,

Ernest Bloch, Johan Wagenaar, Schjelderup, and others. Constantin Sander's son Martin (b. Breslau, Nov. 11, 1859; d. Leipzig, March 14, 1930) was head of the firm until his death.

Lev, Ray, Russian pianist; b. Rostov, May 8, 1912; d. New York, May 20, 1968. Her father was a synagogue cantor, and her mother a singer. The family came to the U.S. in 1913; she sang in her father's synagogue choirs in N.Y.; studied piano with Walter Ruel Cowles in New Haven and with Gaston Déthier. She also took lessons with Tobias Matthay in London (1930–33); then returned to N.Y. and appeared in recitals.

Leva, Enrico de, Italian composer of popular music; b. Naples, Jan. 19, 1867; d. there, July 28, 1955. He studied with d'Arienzo; early in life, began writing popular ballads that proved of wide appeal *(Non mi guarda, E spingole frangese, Triste aprile, Ultima serenata,* etc.) and earned him great financial returns. He also wrote an opera, *La Camargo* (Turin, March 2, 1898).

Levadé, Charles (Gaston), French composer; b. Paris, Jan. 3, 1869; d. there, Oct. 27, 1948. He was a pupil of Massenet at the Paris Cons.; won the Grand Prix de Rome in 1899.
  WORKS: Opera, *Les Hérétiques* (Béziers, Aug. 27, 1905); lyric comedies: *La Rôtisserie de la reine Pédauque,* after Anatole France (Paris, Jan. 12, 1920) and *La Peau de chagrin,* after Balzac (Paris, April 24, 1929); orch. suites; chamber music; piano pieces; songs.

Levant, Oscar, American pianist and composer; b. Pittsburgh, Dec. 27, 1906; d. Beverly Hills, Aug. 14, 1972. He studied piano with Stojowski; also took a few composition lessons with Schoenberg and Schillinger. As a pianist, he established himself by his authentic performances of Gershwin's music *(Rhapsody in Blue, Concerto in F);* also emerged as a professional wit on the radio; publ. a brilliant book, *A Smattering of Ignorance* (N.Y., 1940). He wrote music of considerable complexity, in the modern vein; was soloist in his Piano Concerto (NBC Symph. Orch., Feb. 17, 1942); other works are *Nocturne* for Orch. (Los Angeles, April 14, 1937); String Quartet (1937); piano pieces; film scores.

Levarie, Siegmund, Austrian-American musicologist and conductor; b. Lemberg, Galicia, July 24, 1914. He studied conducting with Joseph Mertin at the Vienna Cons., musicology with Robert Haas at the Univ. of Vienna (Ph.D., 1938); concurrently, took private lessons in composition with Hugo Kauder. He emigrated to the U.S. in 1938; became a U.S. citizen in 1943. He was director of concerts at the Univ. of Chicago (1938–52); conducted the Collegium Musicum there, mostly in programs of medieval and Renaissance music; in 1954 was appointed a prof. of music at Brooklyn College.
  WRITINGS: *Fugue and Form* (Chicago, 1941);

Mozart's "Le Nozze di Figaro" (Chicago, 1952; reprint, N.Y., 1977); *Fundamentals of Harmony* (N.Y., 1954; reprint, N.Y., 1962); *Guillaume de Machaut* (N.Y., 1954; reprint, N.Y., 1970); *Musical Italy Revisited* (N.Y., 1963; reprinted 1973); *Tone: A Study in Musical Acoustics* (with Ernst Lévy; Kent, Ohio, 1968); edited music of Salomone Rossi: *Sinfonie a 3* (Vienna, 1937) and *Canzoni a 4* (N.Y., 1942); contributed articles on early music, opera, and acoustics to various journals.

Levasseur, Jean-Henri, French cellist and composer; b. Beaumont-sur-Oise, May 29, 1764; d. Paris, c.1826. He studied with Cupis and Duport; was a member of the Paris Opéra orch. (1789–1820); a prof. of cello at the Paris Cons. (1795–1826); belonged to the Imperial Chapel. He publ. sonatas, études, and duets for cello; was co-editor of the cello method used at the Paris Cons.

Levasseur, Nicolas-Prosper, French bass; b. Bresles, March 9, 1791; d. Paris, Dec 7, 1871. He was admitted to the Paris Cons. in 1807, and he entered Garat's singing class in 1811; made his debut at the Paris Opéra (Oct. 14, 1813); sang subordinate roles until 1820, when his success at Milan in Meyerbeer's *Marguerite d'Anjou* (Nov. 14, 1820) attracted attention, and he was engaged for 5 years at the Théâtre Italien in Paris; later took leading bass roles at the Opéra. He was also a prof. at the Paris Cons. (1841–69).

Levasseur, Rosalie (real Christian names, **Marie Claude Josèphe**), French soprano; b. Valenciennes, Oct. 8, 1749; d. Neuwied-on-Rhine, May 6, 1826. She was born out of wedlock to Jean-Baptiste Levasseur and Marie-Catherine Tournay; the parents were married when she was 11. She was described by contemporaries as being not at all attractive; still, she must have possessed a fine voice and musical ability, for she was a formidable rival of Sophie Arnould. She first appeared on the stage under the name of **Mlle. Rosalie;** in 1775 she assumed the name Levasseur. The Austrian ambassador in Paris used his influence to promote her career; they lived as husband and wife.

BIBLIOGRAPHY: J.-G. Prod'homme, "Rosalie Levasseur: Ambassadress of Opera," *Musical Quarterly* (April 1916).

Levens, Charles, French music theorist and organist; b. Marseilles, 1689; d. Bordeaux, March 11, 1764. He received his musical training at the St.-Sauveur Cathedral in Aix-en-Provence; subsequently was maître de chapelle at the Cathredral St.-Pierre in Vannes; then went to Bordeaux, where he was maître de musique at the St.-André church. He publ. in 1743 an elaborate book on harmony, *Abrégé des règles de l'Harmonie, pour apprendre la composition, avec un nouveau projet sur un système de musique sans tempérament ni cordes mobiles,* in which he attempted to correlate the ascending harmonic progression, in natural overtones, with the descending arithmetical progression in undertones,

thereby obtaining a dual harmonic basis; his elucubrations proved futile in practice.

Levenson, Boris, Russian composer and conductor; b. Ackerman, Bessarabia, March 10, 1884; d. New York, March 11, 1947. He studied at the St. Petersburg Cons. with Glazunov and Rimsky-Korsakov, graduating in 1907; in 1920, emigrated to America; lived mostly in N.Y. He wrote a Symph., an orch. suite, *Palestine* (N.Y., 1927); *Night in Bagdad,* oriental tone poem (N.Y. Phil., Aug. 17, 1938); *Volga,* tone poem; *Hebrew Suite* for 8 Instruments; 2 string quartets; songs.

Leveridge, Richard, English singer and composer; b. London, c.1670; d. there, March 22, 1758. According to contemporary reports, he possessed a powerful bass voice, and was a successful singer in Italian operas; sang at Covent Garden and Drury Lane. He publ. a collection of songs (1727) in a popular style; of these, *The Roast Beef of Old England* became a favorite. He wrote incidental music for *Macbeth,* a number of masques, etc. He was also the owner of a coffeehouse in London.

Levey, Richard Michael, Irish composer and conductor; b. Dublin, Oct. 25, 1811; d. there, June 28, 1899. He received a practical musical education playing in various orchs. in Dublin and writing incidental music for production of plays. About 1835 he became a theater conductor; wrote some 50 overtures and a number of ballad scores. He publ. a collection of old Irish airs.

Levey, William Charles, Irish conductor and composer, son of **Richard Michael Levey;** b. Dublin, April 25, 1837; d. London, Aug. 18, 1894. He studied with Auber, Thalberg, and Prudent in Paris; then became a conductor at Drury Lane in London (1868–74), Covent Garden, and other theaters. He wrote the operettas *Fanchette* (London, Jan. 4, 1864); *Punchinello* (London, Dec. 28, 1864); *The Girls of the Period* (London, Feb. 25, 1869); incidental music to *Anthony and Cleopatra, King o' Scots, Amy Robsart, Lady of the Lake, Rebecca, Esmeralda;* various pantomimes; 3 cantatas; many songs; piano pieces; etc.

Levi, Hermann, eminent German conductor; b. Giessen, Nov. 7, 1839; d. Munich, May 13, 1900. He was a pupil of Vincenz Lachner in Mannheim (1852–55) and at the Leipzig Cons. (1855–58). He conducted at Saarbrücken (1859–61) and at the German Opera in Rotterdam (1861–64). He became court conductor at Karlsruhe in 1864, and in 1872 he received his most important appointment, at the court theater in Munich; became its Generalmusikdirektor in 1894; retired in 1896. He enjoyed great respect among German musicians, and was influential in spreading the Wagnerian gospel. He conducted the first performance of *Parsifal* at Bayreuth (July 26, 1882), and his interpretation received complete approval from Wagner himself, who, for the nonce, repressed his opposition to Jews. Levi conducted the musical program at Wagner's funeral. He was also a friend of Brahms; his correspondence with Brahms was publ. in vol. 7 of *Brahms Briefwechsel* (Berlin, 1912). He wrote *Gedanken aus Goethes Werken* (1901; 3rd ed., 1911).

BIBLIOGRAPHY: E. Possart, *Erinnerungen an Hermann Levi* (Munich, 1901); A. Ettlinger, "Hermann Levi," necrology in Bettelheim's *Biographisches Jahrbuch* (1903).

Levidis, Dimitri, Greek composer; b. Athens, April 8, 1886; d. there, May 30, 1951. He studied at the Athens Cons., then with A. Denéréaz in Switzerland; in 1910, settled in Paris; from 1939 till his death, was again in Greece. He was the first to write works for the Martenot "Ondes Musicales," including *Poème symphonique pour solo d'Ondes Musicales et Orchestre* (Paris, Dec. 23, 1928) and *De profundis* for Voice and 2 Soli of Ondes Musicales (Paris, Jan. 5, 1930). Other works include a ballet, *Le Pâtre et la nymphe* (Paris, April 24, 1924); *Divertissement* for English Horn, Harps, Strings, Celesta, and Percussion (Paris, April 9, 1927); oratorio, *The Iliad; Poem* for Violin and Orch. (1927); *Chant payen* for Oboe and Strings; compositions for the "Dixtuor æolien d'orchestre"; pieces for chamber ensembles; song cycles; piano pieces.

Levina, Zara, Soviet composer; b. Simferopol, Crimea, Feb. 5, 1906; d. Moscow, June 27, 1976. She studied piano at the Cons. of Odessa, graduating in 1923; then entered the Moscow Cons., where she was a student of Felix Blumenfeld in piano and of Miaskovsky in composition, graduating in 1931. She subsequently gave piano recitals. She distinguished herself primarily as a composer of children's songs, which achieved great popularity; also set to music some 100 texts by Russian poets. She wrote 2 piano concertos (1945, 1975); 2 violin sonatas (1928, 1948); piano pieces.

BIBLIOGRAPHY: N. Mikhailovskaya, *Zara Levina* (Moscow, 1960).

Levine, James (Lawrence), brilliant American pianist and conductor; b. Cincinnati, June 23, 1943. His maternal grandfather was a cantor in a synagogue; his father was a violinist who led a dance band; his mother was an actress. He absorbed music by osmosis and began playing the piano as a small child. At the age of 10 he was soloist in Mendelssohn's 2nd Piano Concerto at a youth concert of the Cincinnati Symph. Orch.; he then studied music theory with Walter Levin, first violinist in the La Salle Quartet; in 1956 he took piano lessons with Rudolf Serkin at the Marlboro School of Music; in 1957 he began piano studies with Rosina Lhévinne at the Aspen Music School. In 1961 he entered the Juilliard School of Music in N.Y., and took courses in conducting with Jean Morel; he also had conducting sessions with Wolfgang Vacano in Aspen. In 1964 he graduated from the Juilliard School and joined the American Conductors Project connected with the Baltimore Symph. Orch., where he had occasion to practice conducting with Alfred Wallen-

stein, Max Rudolf, and Fausto Cleva. In 1964–65 he served as an apprentice to George Szell with the Cleveland Orch.; then became a regular assistant conductor with it (1965–70). In 1966 he organized the Univ. Circle Orch. of the Cleveland Inst. of Music; also led the student orch. of the summer music institute of Oakland Univ. in Meadow Brook, Mich. (1967–69). In 1970 he made a successful appearance as guest conductor with the Philadelphia Orch. at its summer home at Robin Hood Dell; subsequently appeared with other American orchs. In 1970 he also conducted the Welsh National Opera and the San Francisco Opera. He made his Metropolitan Opera debut in N.Y. on June 5, 1971, in a festival performance of *Tosca;* his success led to further appearances and appointment as principal conductor in 1973; he was named music director in 1975. In 1973 he also became music director of the Ravinia Festival, the summer home of the Chicago Symph. Orch.; in addition, he was music director of the Cincinnati May Festival from 1974 to 1978. In 1975 he began to conduct at the Salzburg Festivals; in 1982 he conducted at the Bayreuth Festival for the first time. He continued to make appearances as a pianist, playing chamber music with impeccable technical precision. But it is as a conductor and an indefatigable planner of the seasons at the Metropolitan Opera that he inspired respect. Unconcerned with egotistical projections of his own personality, he presided over the singers and the orch. with concentrated efficiency.

BIBLIOGRAPHY: David Ewen, *Musicians since 1900* (N.Y., 1978); P. Hart, *Conductors: A New Generation* (N.Y., 1979; pp. 221–66).

Levitzki, Mischa, Russian pianist; b. Kremenchug, May 25, 1898; d. Avon-by-the-Sea, N.J., Jan. 2, 1941. When he was 8 years old, his parents, who were naturalized American citizens, returned to the U.S. He studied at the Inst. of Musical Art in N.Y. with Stojowski (1906–11). In 1911 he went to Germany, where he studied with Dohnányi at the Hochschule für Musik in Berlin; won the Mendelssohn Prize. In 1915 he returned to America; appeared in a N.Y. recital on Oct. 17, 1916; subsequently made numerous tours in the U.S. and in the Orient. He publ. a number of attractive piano pieces (*Valse in A, Arabesque valsante, Valse tzigane, Gavotte, The Enchanted Nymph,* etc.).

Lévy, Alexandre, Brazilian composer; b. São Paulo, Nov. 10, 1864; d. there, Jan. 17, 1892. He studied with Emile Durand in Paris. His compositions include a Symph., which received a Columbus Celebration prize in 1892; *Comala,* symph. poem; *Suite brasileira* for Orch.; chamber music and piano works (*Schumanniana,* suite; *Allegro appassionato;* etc.). Although his music is steeped in the European Romantic tradition and his technique is limited, he appears an important figure in Brazilian music because of his contribution to the nationalist movement in music; he was one of the earliest Brazilian composers to use native folk material in instrumental works.

BIBLIOGRAPHY: Renato Almeida, *Compendio de historia da musica brasileira* (Rio de Janeiro, 1947).

Levy, Burt, American composer; b. Brooklyn, Aug. 5, 1936. He studied composition with George Rochberg, Salvatore Martirano, and others; received degrees from the Univ. of Oregon and Temple Univ. in Philadelphia. He joined the faculty at the Univ. of Illinois in Urbana. His works are of an experimental variety. In *Orbs with Flute* he applies such effects as slapping keys, pitchless clacks, tongue blocking the embouchure hole, etc.

Lévy, Ernst, distinguished Swiss pianist and composer; b. Basel, Nov. 18, 1895; d. Morges, Switzerland, April 19, 1981. He studied in Basel with Huber and Petri, and in Paris with Pugno. In 1941 he came to the U.S.; taught at the New England Cons. in Boston (1941–45), Bennington College in Vermont (1946–51), the Univ. of Chicago (1951–54), the Mass. Inst. of Technology in Boston (1954–59), and Brooklyn College of the City Univ. of N.Y. (1959–66). In 1966 he went to Switzerland and lived in Morges. A man of profound culture, he was also a virtuoso pianist. Besides his musical accomplishments, he was an alpinist and a master carpenter; his writings on philosophical subjects remain unpubl. He composed 15 symphs. between 1920 and 1967; much chamber music and many choral works; pieces for solo cello, solo viola, solo violin; *Soliloquy* for Solo Clarinet; 55 pieces for clavichord; a study on wholetone scales for piano; organ pieces; etc. He publ. a theoretical study (with S. Levarie), *Tone: A Study in Musical Acoustics* (Kent, Ohio, 1968).

Levy, Frank, American cellist and composer, son of **Ernst Lévy;** b. Paris, Oct. 15, 1930. He went to America with his father; studied at the Juilliard School of Music in N.Y. (B.S., 1951) and at the Univ. of Chicago (M.A., 1954); studied cello with Leonard Rose and Janos Starker in N.Y.; was a cellist in various orchs. WORKS: *Ricercar* for 4 Cellos (1958); Sonata for Unaccompanied Cello (1959); Quintet for Flute and Strings (1959); Bassoon Concerto (1961); Trio for Clarinet, Horn, and Bassoon (1961); Sonata for Bassoon and Piano (1963); *Fantasy* for Tuba, Harp, Timpani, and Strings (1965); choruses and solo songs.

Lévy, Heniot, Polish-American pianist and composer; b. Warsaw, July 19, 1879; d. Chicago, June 16, 1946. He was a pupil at the Hochschule für Musik in Berlin, and of Max Bruch (composition); made his debut as a pianist with the Berlin Phil. Orch. (1899); in 1900 he emigrated to America, and became a piano teacher at the American Cons. in Chicago. Among his works are *24 Variations on an Original Theme* for Orch. (Chicago, April 9, 1942); Piano Concerto; String Sextet; String Quintet; 2 piano quintets; 4 string quartets; 2 piano trios; Cello Sonata; numerous piano pieces; songs.

Levy, Jules, Bulgarian composer; b. Salonika, June 19, 1930. He studied in Sofia with Stoyanov at the Bulgarian State Cons., graduating in 1957; was subsequently engaged as conductor of the Stefan Makedonsky Theater of Music in Sofia. WORKS: 3 musicals: *The Girl I Was in Love With* (1963); *The World Is Small* (1970); *The Phone Which...* (1975); ballet, *Fair in Sofia* (1968); choreographic oratorio, *Onward to the Rising World* (1973); *Youth Concerto* for Violin and Orch. (1953); 3 symphs.: No. 1, *Life and Death* (1958); No. 2 (1970); No. 3 (1976); *Divertimento-Concertante No. 1* for Trumpet and Pop Orch. (1961) and *No. 2* for Flute and Orch. (1971); *Overture-Poem* (1962); *The Blacksmith,* symph. fantasy (1964); *Pirin Mountain Rhapsody* for Jazz and Symph. Orchs. (1972); string quartet, *Masks* (1974); chamber pieces; choral songs; popular music.

Lévy, Lazare, distinguished French pianist and pedagogue; b. (of French parents) Brussels, Jan. 18, 1882; d. Paris, Sept. 20, 1964. He studied with Diémer at the Paris Cons. (1894–98), where he was awarded first prize for piano; also studied harmony with Lavignac and composition with Gédalge; gave concerts with the principal orchs. of Europe; in 1920, succeeded Alfred Cortot as a prof. at the Paris Cons. He publ. numerous piano pieces.

Levy, Marvin David, American composer; b. Passaic, N.J., Aug. 2, 1932. He studied composition with Philip James at N.Y. Univ., and with Otto Luening at Columbia Univ.; was awarded an American Prix de Rome and a Guggenheim fellowship. He showed a particular disposition toward the musical theater. In his vocal and instrumental writing Levy adopts an expressionistic mode along atonal lines, in an ambience of cautiously dissonant harmonies vivified by a nervously asymmetric rhythmic pulse. WORKS: One-act operas: *Sotoba Komachi* (N.Y., April 7, 1957); *The Tower* (Sante Fe, Aug. 2, 1957); *Escorial* (N.Y., May 4, 1958). In 1961 he was commissioned to write an opera for the Metropolitan Opera at Lincoln Center, N.Y., to a libretto from O'Neill's play *Mourning Becomes Electra.* It was produced at the Metropolitan on March 17, 1967; although critical reception was indecisive, the opera was retained in the repertoire for several seasons, a signal honor to an American composer; he also wrote the opera *The Balcony* (1978). His other works include String Quartet (1955); *Rhapsody* for Violin, Clarinet, and Harp (1956); *Chassidic Suite* for French Horn and Piano (1956); Christmas oratorio, *For the Time Being* (1959); *Caramoor Festival Overture* (1959); Symph. (1960); *Sacred Service* for the Park Avenue Synagogue in N.Y. (1964); Piano Concerto (Chicago, Dec. 3, 1970).

Lévy, Michel-Maurice, French composer; b. Ville-d'Avray, June 28, 1883; d. Paris, Jan. 24, 1965. He studied at the Paris Cons. with Lavignac and Leroux. In 1920–32 he was popular as a musical parodist in vaudeville under the name of **Bétove** (i.e., Beethoven); wrote operettas under that name: *Pom-Pom* (1928); *Les Exploits galants du Baron de Crac*

(1932); *D'Artagnan* (1945). Under his own name he wrote the operas *Le Cloître* (Lyons, 1932) and *Dolorés* (Paris, 1952); operettas: *Lydia* (Brussels, 1936) and *La Demoiselle de Carentan* (Paris, 1951); *Les Trois Pantins de bois,* ballet suite for Orch.; *Le Chant de la terre,* symph. poem (1945); *Moïse,* "fresque lyrique" (Mulhouse, 1955); film music; choral works; songs.

Lewandowski, Louis, eminent Jewish scholar; b. Wreschen, near Posen, April 3, 1821; d. Berlin, Feb. 3, 1894. He studied at the Academy of Music in Berlin; became music director of the Berlin Synagogue from 1840; established himself as a voice teacher. His greatest accomplishment is the compilation of the Jewish service music for use by Berlin's Jewish community; in his arrangements of the traditional tunes, Lewandowski applied the technique of German Romantic music, and often reduced the exotic and asymmetrical pattern of the Jewish cantilena to simple song meters; his compositions for organ also employed ordinary 19th-century harmonies. This treatment contributed to the popularity of Lewandowski's service music, but at the same time traduced the true spirit of Jewish cantillation, so that the more nationalistic Jewish scholars refused to accept it.

Lewenthal, Raymond, American pianist; b. San Antonio, Texas, Aug. 29, 1926. He was taken to Hollywood as a child; studied piano with local teachers. He then enrolled at the Juilliard School of Music in N.Y., as a student of Olga Samaroff; continued his studies in Europe with Alfred Cortot; spent a year in Rio de Janeiro as a piano teacher. Returning to the U.S., he devoted himself to promoting the piano music of neglected Romantic composers, among them Thalberg, Hummel, and Henselt, whose works he performed at his recitals. Particularly meritorious is his redemption from undeserved oblivion of the voluminous output of Charles-Valentin Alkan. He edited a collection of Alkan's piano works for G. Schirmer, Inc.

Lewinger, Max, Polish violinist and composer; b. Sulkow, near Cracow, March 17, 1870; d. Dresden, Aug. 31, 1908; He studied at the conservatories of Cracow, Lwow, and Vienna; in 1893 became a teacher of violin at the Bucharest Cons.; then played in the Gewandhaus Orch. in Leipzig (1897) and in Dresden (from 1898). He publ. *Legende* for Violin and Orch., and a number of pieces for violin and piano (*Tarantella, Polonaise, Capriccio, Dumka, Serenade,* etc.).

Lewis, Sir Anthony, renowned English musicologist, conductor, and composer; b. Bermuda, March 2, 1915; d. Haslemere, England, June 5, 1983. He was educated at Wellington College and Cambridge Univ.; also took courses with Nadia Boulanger in Paris. From 1947–68 he was a prof. of music at the Univ. of Birmingham; then was dean of the faculty of fine arts there (1961–64). From 1968–82 he served as principal of the Royal Academy of Music in Lon-

don. He was knighted in 1972. His specialty was the music of the Baroque period; he edited, conducted, and recorded works by Purcell, Rameau, and Handel. His own works reveal his devotion to Baroque formulas. He wrote *Elegy and Capriccio* for Trumpet and Orch. (1947); *A Tribute of Praise* for Voices a cappella (1951); Concerto for Horn and Orch. (1956). He was one of the founders of the prestigious collection *Musica Britannica* (1951; 42 vols. to date).

Lewis, Daniel, American conductor; b. Flagstaff, Ariz., May 10, 1925. He studied composition with Nino Marcelli in San Diego, Calif. (1939–41); also took violin lessons in Boston; graduated from San Diego State College (B.M., 1949); attended the Claremont (Calif.) Graduate School (M.A., 1950). In 1959 he went to Germany, where he attended the Munich Hochschule für Musik and studied conducting with Eugen Jochum; also participated in a conducting seminar with Herbert von Karajan in Salzburg (1959–60). Returning to the U.S., he served as associate conductor with the San Diego Symph.; was also a conductor at the Alaska Music Festival in Anchorage. His other conducting engagements were at La Jolla, Calif. (1961–69), and with the Orange County (Calif.) Symph. (1966–70). In 1972 he was appointed music director and conductor of the Pasadena Symph., which he brought to a high degree of excellence, presenting programs of Classical, Romantic, and modern music. He also served as guest conductor with the Phoenix Symph. and Atlanta Symph. (1975–76), with the Philharmonia in the Aspen Music Festival (1975–77), with the Los Angeles Phil. (1974–76), with the Oakland Symph. (1978), and with the Minnesota Orch. (1979). He gave summer classes in Anchorage, Alaska (1958–65); he also taught at Calif. State Univ. at Fullerton (1963–70) and the Univ. of Southern Calif. (from 1970).

Lewis, Henry, black American conductor; b. Los Angeles, Oct. 16, 1932. He learned to play piano and string instruments as a child; at the age of 16 was engaged as a double-bass player in the Los Angeles Phil.; in 1955–59 played double bass in the 7th Army Symph. Orch. overseas, and also conducted it in Germany and the Netherlands. Returning to the U.S., he founded the Los Angeles Chamber Orch.; in 1963 traveled with it in Europe under the auspices of the State Dept. From 1968 to 1976 he was conductor and musical director of the New Jersey Symph. Orch. in Newark; subsequently conducted opera and orch. guest engagements. He married **Marilyn Horne** on July 2, 1960, but they were eventually separated.

Lewis, Jerry Lee, American rock pianist and vocal stylist; b. Ferriday, La., Sept. 29, 1935. He assaulted the piano keys with unusual ferocity as if seeking the rock bottom of the sound, and whenever he had a chance also vocalized in a frenetic seizure of the larynx. He tried every style, including rock, folk, western, and rhythm-and-blues, always hitting hard on mental torment. He never wrote his own songs, but he sure could metamorphosize and transmogrify ready-made tunes such as *Great Balls of Fire*. His rendition of *Whole Lotta Shakin' Going On* became a rock-'n'-roll classic. His career came to a halt in 1958 during his English tour after it was revealed in lurid headlines that he was traveling with a 13-year-old girl, who he said was his first cousin and child wife. Even his records were put on the shelf at radio stations, and he was reduced to playing at village fairs and roadhouses. It was not until 1963 that he was able to return to public favor, with records such as *Another Place, Another Time* and *What's Made Milwaukee Famous (Has Made a Loser Out of Me)*. In 1977 he recorded an autobiographical single, *Middle-Age Crazy*.

Lewis, John Aaron, American jazz pianist and composer; b. La Grange, Ill., May 3, 1920. He served in the U.S. Army during World War II; enrolled in the Manhattan School of Music (M.A., 1953); became an arranger. From 1952 to 1977 he led the Modern Jazz Quartet (piano, vibraphone, drums, double bass), a group that for 25 years was one of the focal points of both "cool" jazz and "classical" jazz, a merger known as Third Stream. To this end Lewis composed and arranged works that, while leaving room for jazz improvisation, also include such formal devices as fugal counterpoint; he also has composed extended compositions requiring the additional forces of string quartet or orch., and has written several movie scores (*Odds against Tomorrow, No Sun in Venice, A Milanese Story*) and a ballet, *Original Sin* (San Francisco Ballet, March 1961). Significantly, the Modern Jazz Quartet (known as MJQ) abandoned the usual nightclub habitat of jazz in favor of formal, tuxedoed performances in concert halls. Lewis has taught at several colleges, and in 1966 became a member of the Board of Trustees of the Manhattan School of Music.

Lewis, Leo Rich, American music educator; b. South Woodstock, Vt., Feb. 11, 1865; d. Cambridge, Mass., Sept. 8, 1945. He graduated from Tufts College (A.B., 1887); attended Harvard Univ. (M.A., 1889); then studied composition with Rheinberger at the Akademie der Tonkunst in Munich. From 1895 until his death he headed the music dept. and taught theory and music history at Tufts. He originated a card system of thematic cataloguing of music.
BIBLIOGRAPHY: H.A. Hersey, *A History of Music in Tufts College* (Manchester, N.H., 1947; pp. 302–16).

Lewis, Meade ("Lux"), black American jazz pianist; b. Chicago, Sept. 4, 1905; d. (in an automobile accident) Minneapolis, June 7, 1964. He was nicknamed "The Duke of Luxembourg" as a child, hence the contraction "Lux." He studied violin and piano; played in nightclubs and bars in Chicago; then went to N.Y., where he played with Pete Johnson and Albert Ammons. He was a leading exponent of the boogie-woogie style; his recording of *Honky Tonk Train Blues* was a landmark of the era.

Lewis, Ramsey, black American jazz pianist; b. Chicago, May 27, 1935. He studied at the Chicago Musical College (1947–54), the Univ. of Illinois at Urbana (1953–54), and DePaul Univ. (1954–55). He began his career as a member of a local jazz group; in 1956 he formed his own Ramsey Lewis Trio, and filled engagements at nightclubs, college campuses, and jazz festivals; he also wrote music for his group.

Lewis, Richard, noted English tenor; b. Manchester, May 10, 1914. He studied at the Royal Manchester College of Music; then took courses with Norman Allin at the Royal Academy of Music in London; made his operatic debut with the Carl Rosa Opera Co. in 1939; in 1947 he sang at the Glyndebourne Festival and at Covent Garden. In 1955 he appeared with the San Francisco Opera; also sang with it as a guest artist between 1962 and 1968. In 1963 he was named a Commander of the Order of the British Empire. His repertoire was extensive, including roles in operas ranging from Monteverdi and Mozart to Schoenberg, Britten, and Tippett.

Lewisohn, Adolph, German-American musical philanthropist; b. Hamburg, May 27, 1849; d. Saranac Lake, N.Y., Aug. 17, 1938. The principal services to music and education performed by this prominent industrialist were the erection in 1914 of the Lewisohn Stadium, which he donated to the College of the City of N.Y., and the inauguration of summer concerts by the N.Y. Phil. there. He also founded the Lewisohn chamber music education courses at Hunter College in N.Y.

Lewkowitch, Bernhard, Danish organist and composer; b. Copenhagen, May 28, 1927 (of Russian parents). He studied organ and composition at the Copenhagen Cons. (1946–50) with Schierbeck and Jersild. From 1947 to 1963 he served as organist and choirmaster at the Catholic Church of St. Ansgar, in Copenhagen. In 1953 he founded in Copenhagen a choral society, Schola Cantorum, with which he performed medieval and Renaissance music. In 1963 he was awarded the prestigious Carl Nielsen Prize; in 1966 he was given a lifetime Danish government pension. His own music is primarily choral, to Latin texts, and is derived essentially from the Renaissance paradigms of modal counterpoint; it has an affinity with sacred works of Stravinsky, but is otherwise sui generis in its stylized archaisms; several of these works have become repertoire pieces in Denmark, and were also performed at the international festivals of contemporary music in Haifa (1954), Cologne (1960), Amsterdam (1963), and Copenhagen (1964).
WORKS: *Mariavise* for Chorus (1947); *Tres orationes* for Tenor, Oboe, and Bassoon (1958); *Il cantico delle creature* for 8 Voices, after St. Francis of Assisi (1963); *Laudi a nostra Signora* for Chorus, to medieval texts (1969); 4 piano sonatas; madrigals; lieder.

Ley, Henry George, English organist and composer; b. Chagford, Dec. 30, 1887; d. Ottery-Saint-Mary, Devonshire, Aug. 24, 1962. He studied with Parratt at the Royal College of Music in London; was active mainly as a church organist in Oxford and London; was music director at Eton College (1926–45); also taught organ at the Royal College of Music in London. He wrote *Variations on a Theme by Handel* for Orch.; some chamber music; many organ pieces.

Ley, Salvador, Guatemalan pianist and composer; b. Guatemala City, Jan. 2, 1907. At the age of 15 he went to Berlin, where he studied piano with Georg Bertram and theory with Hugo Leichtentritt. He appeared as a pianist in Berlin in 1927; returned to Guatemala in 1934; in 1938 he gave a recital in N.Y.; then became a teacher of piano at the Cons. of Guatemala.
WORKS: *Lera,* opera in 2 acts (1959); *Danza exotica* for Piano (1959); Suite for Flute and Piano (1962); *Concertante* for Viola and String Orch. (1962); *Toccatina* for Piano (1965); *Introduction and Movement* for Unaccompanied Cello (1965); piano pieces; songs.

Leybach, Ignace, Alsatian pianist and composer; b. Gambsheim, July 17, 1817; d. Toulouse, May 23, 1891. He studied in Paris with Pixis, Kalkbrenner, and Chopin; in 1844, became organist at the Cathedral of Toulouse. He publ. some 225 piano pieces, in a facile and pleasing manner. His 5th Nocturne, op. 52, became famous, and its popularity continued among succeeding generations of piano students; it was reprinted in countless anthologies of piano music. Other piano compositions are: *Boléro brillant; Ballade; Valse poétique; Les Batelières de Naples;* etc.; he also publ. an extensive organ method (3 vols.; 350 pieces).

Leyden, Norman, American conductor; b. Springfield, Mass., Oct. 17, 1917. He studied at Yale Univ. (B.A., 1938; Mus.B., 1939) and at Teachers College of Columbia Univ. (M.A., 1965; Ed.D., 1968). He organized the Westchester Youth Symph. Orch. in White Plains, N.Y., in 1957; led it until 1968. In 1974 he became associate conductor of the Oregon Symph. Orch. in Portland; also pursued a successful career as a guest conductor with leading U.S. orchs. in concerts of popular fare.

Leygraf, Hans, Swedish pianist; b. Stockholm, Sept. 7, 1920. He appeared as a soloist with the Stockholm Orch. at the age of 10; then studied at the Stockholm Cons., in Munich, and in Vienna; acquired a fine reputation as a concert pianist; was particularly noted as a Mozart interpreter. In 1944 he married the Viennese pianist **Margarete Stehle** (b. Vienna, April 26, 1921). In 1956 he joined the faculty of the Salzburg Mozarteum.

Lhévinne, Josef, celebrated Russian pianist; b. Orel, Dec. 13, 1874; d. New York, Dec. 2, 1944. After some preliminary study in his native town, he was taken to Moscow, and entered Safonov's piano class at the Moscow Cons.; at the age of 15 he played the *Emperor Concerto,* with Anton Rubinstein conducting; he graduated in 1891; won the Rubinstein Prize in 1895. In 1900 he traveled to the Caucasus; taught piano at the Cons. of Tiflis; in 1902–6, taught at the Moscow Cons. In 1906 he went to the U.S.; made his American debut in N.Y. with the Russian Symph. Orch., conducted by Safonov (Jan. 27, 1906); afterward he made numerous concert tours in America. He lived mostly in Berlin from 1907 till 1919; was interned during World War I, but was able to continue his professional activities. In 1919 he returned to the U.S.; appeared in recitals, and with major American orchs.; also in duo recitals with his wife, **Rosina.** They established a music studio, where they taught numerous pupils; also taught at the Juilliard Graduate School. Lhévinne's playing was distinguished not only by its virtuoso quality, but by an intimate understanding of the music, impeccable phrasing, and fine gradations of singing tone. He was at his best in the works of the Romantic school; his performances of the concertos of Chopin and Tchaikovsky were particularly notable.
BIBLIOGRAPHY: Robert E. Wallace, *A Century of Music-Making: The Lives of Josef and Rosina Lhévinne* (Bloomington, Ind., 1976).

Lhévinne, Rosina, Russian pianist and teacher, wife of **Josef Lhévinne;** b. Kiev, March 28, 1880; d. (at the age of 96) Glendale, Calif., Nov. 9, 1976. She graduated from the Kiev Cons. in 1898, winning the gold medal; in 1899 she married Josef Lhévinne in Moscow; appeared as a soloist in Vienna (1910), St. Petersburg (1911), and Berlin (1912); remained in Berlin with her husband through World War I; in 1919, came to the U.S.; taught in the Juilliard Graduate School; also privately in N.Y., establishing a reputation as a fine pedagogue. Among her many pupils was Van Cliburn.

Lhotka, Fran, Czech-Yugoslav composer and teacher; b. Wožice, Dec. 25, 1883; d. Zagreb, Jan. 26, 1962. He took lessons with Dvořák in Prague, and with Janáček and Klička (1899–1905). After a season of teaching in Ekaterinoslav, Russia (1908–9), he settled in Zagreb; in 1919, was appointed an instructor at the Cons. of Zagreb, and conductor of the Lisinski Chorus, with which he toured Central Europe; from 1923 to 1940 and again from 1948 to 1952 he was rector of the State Music Academy in Zagreb.
WORKS: Operas: *Minka* (Zagreb, 1918) and *The Sea* (Zagreb, 1920); ballets: *The Devil of the Village* (Zürich, 1935; also perf. in Vienna, Prague, etc.); *Ballad of Medieval Love* (Zürich, 1937; also at the Edinburgh Festival, 1951); *Luk* (Munich, 1938); Symph.; *Yugoslav Capriccio* for Orch.; Violin Concerto; Suite for 4 Flutes; choral works; songs; a manual of harmony (Zagreb, 1948).

Lhotka-Kalinski, Ivo, Croatian composer, son of **Fran Lhotka;** b. Zagreb, July 30, 1913. He studied with Pizzetti in Rome; after the end of World War II he taught singing at the Music Academy of Zagreb; in 1967 became its regional director. He has a natural flair for stage composition in the folk style; he wrote several brilliant musical burlesques, among them *Analfabeta (The Illiterate;* Belgrade, Oct. 19, 1954); *Putovanje (The Journey),* first television opera in Yugoslavia (Zagreb, June 10, 1957); *Dugme (The Button;* Zagreb, April 21, 1958); *Vlast (Authority;* Zagreb Television, Oct. 18, 1959); *Svjetleći grad (The Town of Light;* Zagreb, Dec. 26, 1967); also a children's opera, *Velika coprarija (The Great Sorcerer;* 1952); *Misli (Thoughts)* for Clarinet and Strings (1965); a number of choral works, songs, and piano pieces.

Liadov, Anatoli, significant Russian composer, son of **Konstantin Liadov;** b. St. Petersburg, May 10, 1855; d. on his estate of Polynovka, in the district of Novgorod, Aug. 28, 1914. He was a member of an exceptionally gifted musical family. His father was an outstanding opera conductor; his grandfather was conductor of the St. Petersburg Phil. Society; Liadov's uncles were also professional musicians. After his primary education at home, Liadov entered the St. Petersburg Cons. (1870); studied piano with G.G. Kross, theory with J. Johannsen, composition with Rimsky-Korsakov; he was expelled from the school for failing to attend classes (1876), but was allowed to compete for a diploma in 1878, and passed the final examination brilliantly. He was immediately engaged as an instructor of theory and harmony at the Cons., and held this post until his death. Among his students were Prokofiev, Miaskovsky, Asafiev, and other notable Russian composers. From his first attempts at composition, Liadov was fascinated by Russian folklore, and most of his works possess the imaginative quality of Russian fairy tales. He was not a prolific composer; he was at his best in miniatures, which he worked out with a fine artistic sense; of these, the piano cycle *Birulki* (1876) and *Tabatière à musique (Music Box;* 1893) are particularly popular; for orch. he wrote the symph. tableaux *Baba Yaga, Enchanted Lake,* and *Kikimora,* which are still in the permanent repertoire of Russian orchs.; his arrangements of Russian songs are valuable for their authentic harmonization.
WORKS: For Orch.: *Scherzo* (1887); *Mazurka* (1888); *Polonaise* (1900); *Baba Yaga* (St. Petersburg, March 18, 1904); *8 Russian Folk Songs* (1906); *Enchanted Lake* (St. Petersburg, Feb. 21, 1909); *Kikimora* (St. Petersburg, Dec. 12, 1909); *Fragments from Apocalypse* (St. Petersburg, Dec. 8, 1912); *Nenie,* threnody (1914). For Piano: *Birulki* (1876); *4 Arabesques* (1879); *4 Intermezzos* (1882–83); *2 Mazurkas* (1887); *Novelette* (1889); *Ballade* (1890); *Marionnettes* (1892); *Bagatelle* (1892); *Tabatière à musique* (1893; also for Small Orch.); *Variations on a Polish Theme* (1901); 4 pieces: *Grimaces, Twilight, Temptation, Recollection* (1910); several sets of preludes and études; etc. Vocal works: 120 Russian folk songs for Voice and Piano (1903); other Russian song arrangements and harmonizations. Liadov contributed a movement to a string quartet

on the theme B-La-F, in honor of the publisher Belaiev (1895), and a polka for string orch. to the collection *Fridays* (1899).
BIBLIOGRAPHY: M.D. Calvocoressi and Gerald Abraham, *Masters of Russian Music* (London, 1936; pp. 424–30); N. Zaporozhets, *A.K. Liadov, Life and Work* (Moscow, 1954).

Liadov, Konstantin, Russian conductor, father of **Anatoli Liadov;** b. St. Petersburg, May 10, 1820; d. there, Dec. 19, 1868. He studied at the Theatrical School; in 1850 became conductor of the Imperial Opera; resigned shortly before his death, and was succeeded by Napravnik. He was an efficient drillmaster, and did much to raise the standard of performance; produced several Russian operas for the first time, and was instrumental in encouraging Russian music; he was greatly appreciated by his co-workers; Glinka often sought his advice on details of production of his operas.

Liapunov, Sergei, important Russian pianist and composer; b. Yaroslavl, Nov. 30, 1859; d. Paris, Nov. 8, 1924. He studied piano at the Moscow Cons. with Pabst and Klindworth, and composition with Hubert and Taneyev. From 1894 to 1902 he was subdirector of the Imperial Choir at St. Petersburg; from 1902 to 1910, inspector of music at St. Helen's Inst.; in 1910 became a prof. at the St. Petersburg Cons.; following the Russian Revolution, he lived in Paris. He was a member of the Imperial Geographic Society, which commissioned him to collect the folk songs of the regions of Vologda, Viatka, and Kostroma (publ. with piano accompaniments in 1897). As a composer, he followed the tradition of the Russian national school, but was also willing to experiment with harmonic innovations; his writing for piano possesses excellent expertise; his First Piano Concerto is still in the repertoire of Russian pianists.
WORKS: Symph. No. 1 (1887; St. Petersburg, April 23, 1888; also perf. in Berlin, Jan. 15, 1907); *Ouverture solennelle,* on Russian themes (St. Petersburg, May 6, 1896); *Zelazova Vola,* named after Chopin's birthplace and composed for Chopin's centennial (1910); *Hashish,* oriental symph. poem (1914); Symph. No. 2 (1910–17; Leningrad, Dec. 28, 1950); Violin Concerto; 2 piano concertos (1890, 1909); *Ukrainian Rhapsody* for Piano and Orch. (Berlin, March 23, 1908; Busoni, soloist); numerous piano compositions, of which *12 études d'exécution transcendante,* all in sharp keys, were written in emulation of Liszt's similarly titled piano studies in flat keys.
BIBLIOGRAPHY: M. Shifman, *S. Liapunov* (Moscow, 1960).

Liatoshinsky, Boris, Ukrainian composer; b. Zhitomir, Jan. 3, 1895; d. Kiev, April 15, 1968. He studied jurisprudence at the Univ. of Kiev, simultaneously taking lessons in composition at the Kiev Cons. with Glière, graduating in 1919. In 1920 he was appointed a prof. at the Kiev Cons.; also taught at the Moscow Cons. (1935–38 and 1941–43). His style of composition follows the broad outlines of national music, with numerous thematic allusions to folk songs.

WORKS: Operas: *The Golden Hoop* (Odessa, March 26, 1930); *Shchors* (Kiev, Sept. 1, 1938; glorifying the exploits of the Soviet partisan leader Nicolai Shchors); *Grazina,* symph. ballad (Kiev, Nov. 26, 1955); 5 symphs. (1918–67); *Reunion,* symph. poem (1949); *Slavonic Concerto* for Piano and Orch. (1953); 4 string quartets (1915–43); 2 piano trios (1925, 1942); Ukrainian Quintet for Piano (1946); numerous arrangements for chorus of Ukrainian folk songs; piano pieces; etc.

BIBLIOGRAPHY: Igor Boelza, *Boris Liatoshinsky* (Moscow, 1947).

Liberace, Walter (Wladziu Valentino), popular American pianist of Italian-Polish parentage; b. West Allis, Wis., May 16, 1919. He received rudimentary musical training from his father, a French-horn player. Encouraged by Paderewski, he began to study piano; played in nightclubs, billed as **Walter Busterkeys.** In 1940 he moved to N.Y.; evolved a facile repertoire of semiclassical arrangements; made a synthesis of the first movement of Beethoven's *Sonata quasi una fantasia* and Rachmaninoff's Prelude in C-sharp minor, taking advantage of the fact that both works are in the same key. He prospered; made lucrative inroads on television; built a home in California with a piano-shaped swimming pool. Inspired by a movie on Chopin, he placed a candelabrum on the piano at his concerts; this decorative object identified him as a Romantic pianist, an impression enhanced by the dress suit of white silk mohair he habitually wears. In 1959 he won a suit for defamation of character against the London *Daily Mirror* and its columnist W. Connor (Cassandra), who suggested in print that Liberace was a deviate. In 1982 his chauffeur-bodyguard-companion brought a lawsuit against Liberace for $380 million for services rendered in "an exclusive non-marital relationship," but lost.

BIBLIOGRAPHY: "Liberace Bombshell—Boyfriend Tells All," *National Enquirer* (Nov. 2, 1982).

Libert, Henri, French organist; b. Paris, Dec. 15, 1869; d. there, Jan. 14, 1937. He studied at the Paris Cons. with Marmontel and Diémer (piano), César Franck and Widor (organ), and Massenet and Godard (composition); took first organ prize (1894); was titular organist at the Basilica of St. Denis in Paris, and a prof. of organ at the American Cons. in Fontainebleau. He wrote many organ works, including *Variations symphoniques, Chorals, Préludes et fugues;* piano pieces; motets; songs; also publ. didactic works.

Libon, Philippe, French violinist and composer; b. (of French parents) Cadiz, Aug. 17, 1775; d. Paris, Feb. 5, 1838. He studied in London with Viotti; in 1796, became a chamber violinist in Lisbon; in 1798, was a member of the court orch. in Madrid. In 1800 he settled in Paris as a member of the court orch. He publ. 6 violin concertos; 6 string trios; duets; 2 vols. of *Airs variés; 30 caprices* for Violin Solo.

Licad, Cecile, pianist; b. Manila, Philippines, May 11, 1961. She studied piano with Rosario Picazo; made her public concert debut at the age of 7; then went to the U.S.; enrolled at the Curtis Inst. of Music in Philadelphia in the classes of Rudolf Serkin, Seymour Lipkin, and Mieczyslaw Horszowski. In 1979 she was soloist with the Boston Symph. Orch. at the Berkshire Music Center in Tanglewood; in 1981 she won the Leventritt Gold Medal, which launched her on a fine career; she was a soloist with the N.Y. Phil., Chicago Symph., London Symph., Pittsburgh Symph., Cleveland Orch., and Philadelphia Orch.; also gave recitals.

Lichard, Milan, Slovak authority on folk songs; b. Uhorská Skalica, Feb. 24, 1853; d. Užhorod, April 21, 1935. He studied music in Budapest; also worked for the railway administration. He devoted his entire life to collecting and editing Slovak songs; contributed numerous articles on the subject to various scholarly magazines. From 1921 he lived in Užhorod, where he was also active as a choral conductor.

Lichey, Reinhold, German organist and composer; b. Pohlsdorf, near Liegnitz, March 26, 1879; d. Plaue, Dec. 5, 1957. He studied music in Breslau; then went to Berlin, where he took lessons with Max Bruch. He subsequently held numerous positions as a church organist and a chorus leader in Aachen, Königsberg, Naumburg, Pforta, and finally Plaue, near Arnstadt, where he remained until his death. He was a voluminous composer; wrote mostly for organ and chorus; also composed the *Goethe-Symphonie* (1948) and *Deutsches Friedens-Quartett.*

Lichnowsky, Prince Carl, nobleman of Polish origin, friend of Mozart and Beethoven; b. Vienna, June 21, 1761; d. there, April 15, 1814. He received the title of nobility from the Russian government in 1773, but spent most of his life in Vienna. He was a pupil of Mozart, who accompanied him on a visit to the Prussian court in 1789. Beethoven's opp. 1, 13, 26, and 36 are dedicated to Lichnowsky. In his home, Lichnowsky presented regular chamber music concerts with a quartet composed of Schuppanzigh, Sina, Weiss, and Kraft. Lichnowsky's younger brother, Count Moritz (1771–1837), was also a friend of Beethoven, who dedicated his opp. 35, 51, and 90 to the Count and his wife.

Lichtenberg, Leopold, American violinist; b. San Francisco, Nov. 22, 1861; d. Brooklyn, May 16, 1935. As a child, he began to study with Wieniawski; traveled as a concert violinist in Belgium and the Netherlands; then returned to America; was a member of Theodore Thomas's orch. in N.Y., and also of the Boston Symph.; in 1899, was appointed head of the violin dept. of the National Cons. in N.Y.; gave chamber music concerts.

Lichtenberger, Henri, French writer on music; b. Mulhouse, March 12, 1864; d. Biarritz, Nov. 4, 1941. In 1887 he became a prof. of literature at the Univ.

of Nancy; from 1905, was a prof. of German language and literature at the Univ. of Paris. He made a special study of Wagner's art and ideas, and publ. *Richard Wagner, poète et penseur* (1890) and *Wagner,* a biography (1909; revised ed., 1925).

Lichtenstein, Karl August von, German theater manager and composer; b. Lahm, Franconia, Sept. 8, 1767; d. Berlin, Sept. 10, 1845. He studied music in Göttingen with Forkel; then was Intendant of court theaters at Dessau (1798), Vienna (1800), Bamberg (1811), and Berlin (1823); in 1825, became director of the Berlin Opera; composed 11 operas and vaudevilles.

Lichtenthal, Peter, Austrian composer and writer on music; b. Pressburg, May 10, 1780; d. Milan, Aug. 18, 1853. He was a doctor by profession, and composed music as an avocation; settled in Milan in 1810; produced 3 operas and 5 ballets at La Scala; publ. a String Quartet, 2 piano trios, and piano pieces. His chief writings are: *Cenni biografici intorno al celebre maestro Wolfgang Amadeus Mozart* (1814); *Dizionario e bibliografia della musica* (4 vols., 1826); *Estetica, ossia Dottrina del bello e delle belle arti* (1831); *Mozart e le sue creazioni* (1842).

Lichtenwanger, William, learned American librarian; b. Asheville, N.C., Feb. 28, 1915. He studied at the Univ. of Michigan at Ann Arbor (B.Mus., 1937; M.Mus., 1940); played double bass, oboe, and other instruments in the band and orch.; wrote pieces with whimsical titles, e.g., *Phrygidair* (in Phrygian mode, naturally). He served as assistant reference librarian of the Music Division at the Library of Congress in Washington, D.C. (1940–53, except for service in the U.S. Army, 1941–45); assistant head (1953–60) and head (1960–74) of the music reference section there; was associate editor of *Notes* of the Music Library Assoc. (1946–60), then its editor (1960–63); in 1975 he was made a member emeritus of the Music Library Assoc. In addition, he was music editor of Collier's Encyclopedia (1947–50) and consultant for the biographical dictionary *Notable American Women* (1971); also was a contributor to supplements II and III of the *Dictionary of American Biography;* was chairman and compiler of *A Survey of Musical Instrument Collections in the U.S. and Canada,* publ. by the Music Library Assoc. (1974). A polyglot and a polymath, he is fluent in German, French, and Turkish; nearly fluent in Japanese, and fairly fluent in personalized Russian. With his excellent wife, Carolyn, he edited an analytic index to *Modern Music* (N.Y., 1976). Among his scholarly achievements, perhaps the highest is his incandescent essay "The Music of *The Star-Spangled Banner*—From Ludgate Hill to Capitol Hill," in the *Quarterly Journal of the Library of Congress* (July 1977), in which he furnishes documentary proof that the tune of the American national anthem was indeed composed by John Stafford Smith, all demurrings by various estimable historians to the contrary notwithstanding. To the 6th edition of

Baker's Biographical Dictionary of Musicians he contributed incalculably precious verifications, clarifications, rectifications, and refutations of previous inadvertent and/or ignorant fabrications and unintentional prevarications; he also edited *Oscar Sonneck and American Music* (Urbana, Ill., 1984).

Lichtveld, Lou (Lodewijk Alphonsus Maria), Dutch composer; b. Paramaribo, Surinam, Nov. 7, 1903. He went to Amsterdam in 1922 and was active as an organist and music critic. In 1936 he joined the International Brigade on the Loyalist side in the Spanish Civil War. During the Nazi occupation of the Netherlands he served in the resistance movement, and became its representative in the emergency parliament of 1945. He returned to Surinam in 1949, and served as Minister of Education and Public Health and later President of the Exchequer; organized the facilities for musical education. From 1961 to 1969 he was in the diplomatic service of the Netherlands, stationed in Washington, D.C., and at the United Nations; then retired and lived mostly on the island of Tobago in the West Indies. He wrote about 2 dozen novels and essays under the pen name of **Albert Helman.** His musical works include an oratorio, *Canciones* (1934; MS lost in the Spanish Civil War); Piano Concertino (1932); Flute Sonata (1930); Violin Sonata (1931); *Triptych* for Piano (1925); Piano Sonata (1927); also experimental pieces employing oriental scales. He used a 24-tone scale for 2 Dutch documentary films produced by Joris Ivens: *Regen* (1929; musical score added in 1932) and *Philips-Radio* (1930; also known as *Industrial Symphony*). He also composed several choruses a cappella.

Lickl, Johann Georg, Austrian composer and conductor; b. Korneuburg, April 11, 1769; d. Pécs, May 12, 1843. He was associated with Schikaneder in Vienna, where he wrote the music for various light operas. His large opera *Slawina von Pommern* was produced in Vienna in 1812. He settled in Pécs as a church choir leader. Among his publ. works are several string quartets. He also publ. a periodic edition, *Wiener Salon-Musik* (arrangements for piano and harmonium from popular classics).

Lidholm, Ingvar, Swedish composer; b. Jönköping, Feb. 24, 1921. He studied violin and music theory at the Royal College of Music in Stockholm (1940–45) with Charles Barkel, Hilding Rosenberg, and Tor Mann; was a stipendiary of the Jenny Lind Foundation for studies in France, Switzerland, and Italy; then had private lessons with Mátyás Seiber in England. He played viola; then was engaged as conductor of the municipal orch. in Örebro (1947–56) and director of chamber music at the Swedish Broadcasting Corp. (1956–65); from 1965 to 1971 he taught at the Royal College of Music in Stockholm, and in 1974 became head of planning at the music dept. of the Swedish Radio. He became associated with the cosmopolitan avant-garde active in Sweden; contributed greatly to the formulation of methods and aims of modern music; with Ligeti and Lutoslawski he compiled the brochure *Three Aspects of New Music. From the Composition Seminar in Stockholm,* publ. in Eng. (Stockholm, 1968). In his own works he applies constructivist methods with various serial algorithms.

WORKS: *Toccata e canto* for Chamber Orch. (1944); Concerto for String Orch. (1945); Solo Flute Sonata (1945); *Laudi* for a cappella Chorus (1947); Piano Sonata (1947); *Music* for String Orch. (1952); Concertino for Flute, Oboe, English Horn, and Cello (1954); *Ritornell* for Orch. (Stockholm, Feb. 17, 1956); *4 Pieces* for Cello and Piano (1955); *Canto LXXXI* for a cappella Chorus, after Ezra Pound (1956); *Skaldens Natt (The Night of the Poet)* for Soprano, Chorus, and Orch. (Hamburg, April 6, 1959); *Mutanza* for Orch. (Örebro, Nov. 15, 1959); ballet, *Riter (Rites;* Stockholm, March 26, 1960); *Motus Colores* for Orch. (Cologne Festival, June 13, 1960); *Poesis* for Orch. (Stockholm, Jan. 14, 1964); *Nausikaa ensam (Nausikaa Alone),* lyrical scene, based on a section of Eyvind Johnson's novel *Return to Ithaca,* for Soprano, Chorus, and Orch. (Ingesund, June 2, 1963); *Holländarn (The Dutchman),* opera, after Strindberg (Swedish Television, Dec. 10, 1967); *Stamp Music,* an improvisatory piece in graphic notation for Variable Performers (1970; composed for a Swedish postage stamp; version for Soprano and Tam-tam, 1971).

Lídl, Václav, Czech composer; b. Brno, Nov. 5, 1922. He studied at the Brno Cons., graduating in 1948; devoted himself principally to composing for films. However, he took time off to write *Romantic Sonata* for Violin and Piano; 2 string quartets; Divertimento for Flute, Clarinet, and Bassoon; children's choruses.

Lidón, José, Spanish organist and composer; b. Béjar, June 2, 1748; d. Madrid, Feb. 11, 1827. He first served as an organist in Málaga; in 1787 obtained the post of organist at the Chapel Royal in Madrid. He wrote an opera, *Glauca y Coriolano,* which was performed in Madrid (1792); also music for organ and keyboard pieces. A keyboard sonata is printed in S. Kastner's collection *Silva iberica* (Mainz, 1954). Lidón also publ. *Reglas muy útiles para los organistas y aficionados al piano.*

Lie (Lie-Nissen), Erika, Norwegian pianist; b. Kongsvinger, Jan. 17, 1845; d. Christiania, Oct. 27, 1903. She studied with Kjerulf in Christiania and with Theodor Kullak in Berlin; later taught at Kullak's Academy there. She made concert tours throughout Europe; was particularly noted for her interpretation of Chopin. In 1870 she joined the faculty of the Copenhagen Cons. Returning to Norway, she married Dr. Oscar Nissen in 1874, and settled in Christiania.

Lie, Harald, Norwegian composer; b. Oslo, Nov. 21, 1902; d. there, May 23, 1942. At the age of 21 he went to America, where he earned his living as a piano tuner; then studied piano manufacturing in Leipzig. Returning to Norway in 1929, he took lessons in composition with Fartein Valen. During 12 years of composing he produced 2 symphs. (1934, 1937); *Symphonic Dance* (1942); some choral works; only 12 opus numbers in all. He died of tuberculosis.

Lie, Sigurd, Norwegian composer; b. Drammen, May 23, 1871; d. there, Sept. 29, 1904. He was a pupil of Lindeman and Holter; then studied at the Leipzig Cons. (1891–93); spent several years in Berlin; then returned to Norway, where he was appointed conductor of the Handelsstand Sangforening in Christiania (1902).

WORKS: Symph. in A minor (Christiania, Feb. 28, 1903); *Oriental Suite* for Orch. (Christiania, Oct. 28, 1899); Violin Concerto (Bergen, Feb. 13, 1896); *Erling Skjalgson* for Baritone Solo, Men's Chorus, and Orch. (Christiania, Oct. 28, 1899); *Norske dans* for Violin and Piano; men's choruses; a song cycle, *Wartburg;* many separate songs, of which *Schnee* became famous.

Liebe, Eduard Ludwig, German composer; b. Magdeburg, Nov. 19, 1819; d. Chur, Feb. 4, 1900. He studied in Kassel with Spohr and Baldewein; then was a music director at Coblenz, Mainz, and Worms; went to Strasbourg as a teacher; later taught in London. He wrote an opera, *Die Braut von Azola* (Karlsruhe, 1868); also publ. popular songs and piano pieces.

Liebermann, Rolf, Swiss composer and opera director; b. Zürich, Sept. 14, 1910. He studied composition with Wladimir Vogel, then resident in Switzerland; most of his works were in an experimental idiom, sharing the influence of hedonistic eclecticism, French neo-Classicism, and Viennese dodecaphony; he became particularly attracted to theatrical applications of modernistic procedures. He soon veered away from composition and made an extremely successful career as an opera administrator. In 1959 he became Intendant of the Hamburg State Opera, and in 1962 its artistic director; in this post he instituted an audacious program of commissioned works from avant-garde composers (among them Krenek, Schuller, and Penderecki). Concurrently he was program director of the North German Radio and the West Berlin Radio. In 1973 he was named director of the Paris Opéra.

WORKS: Operas: *Leonore 40/45* (Basel, March 25, 1952); *Penelope* (Salzburg, Aug. 17, 1954); *The School for Wives* (Louisville, Dec. 3, 1955; revised as a 3-act opera, *Die Schule der Frauen,* and produced in Salzburg in 1957); *Volkslieder Suite* (BBC broadcast, Jan. 10, 1947); *Furioso* for Orch. (1947; Dallas, Dec. 9, 1950); *Concerto for Jazzband and Orchestra* (Donaueschingen Festival, Oct. 17, 1954); cantatas: *Streitlied zwischen Leben und Tod* and *Une des fins du monde; Les Echanges* for 52 Industrial Machines recorded on tape (composed for an exhibition in Lausanne, where it was perf. on April 24, 1964); several piano pieces and songs. A Festschrift in his honor was presented to him on his 60th birthday (Hamburg, 1970).

Lieberson, Goddard, American composer and music executive; b. Hanley, Staffordshire, England, April 5, 1911; d. New York, May 29, 1977. He was brought to the U.S. as a child; studied at the Eastman School of Music in Rochester, N.Y.; settled in N.Y. in 1936. In 1939 he became a member of the staff of Columbia Records, Inc., and rapidly progressed in business; was president of Columbia Records (1955–66, 1973–75); in 1964 he was named president of the Record Industry Assoc. of America while continuing as head of Columbia Records. In this latter position he was the chief catalyst in promoting long-playing records since their introduction in 1948, and was also responsible for Columbia Records' liberal policy in recording modern works. He composed the orch. suites *5 Modern Painters* (1929); *Piano Pieces for Advanced Children or Retarded Adults;* edited *Columbia Book of Musical Masterpieces* (N.Y., 1950).

Liebeskind, Joseph, German music editor; b. Leipzig, April 22, 1866; d. there, Aug. 10, 1916. He studied at the Leipzig Cons. with Sitt, Reinecke, and Jadassohn; lived most of his life in Leipzig; edited and arranged a number of works by Gluck, Mozart, and Dittersdorf. He was a notable music collector; owned a large library rich in Gluck items, including some MSS.

Liebich, Ernst (Johann Gottlob), eminent German violin maker; b. Breslau, April 13, 1830; d. there, Sept. 23, 1884. His father and grandfather were violin makers, and he was trained in their workshop; also worked with Vuillaume in Paris, Hart in London, and Bausch in Leipzig. His instruments were awarded several prizes at international exhibitions.

Liebig, Karl, German conductor; b. Schwedt, July 25, 1808; d. Berlin, Oct. 6, 1872. He was engaged as an oboist in the Alexander Grenadier Regiment in Berlin; in 1843 he organized the Berlin Symphoniekapelle, which under his leadership attained a very high standard of performance; in 1867 the orch. elected another conductor; Liebig's attempts to form a rival organization proved futile.

Liebling, Emil, German-American pianist, brother of **Georg Liebling;** b. Pless, Silesia, April 12, 1851; d. Chicago, Jan. 20, 1914. He studied piano with Theodor Kullak in Berlin, Dachs in Vienna, and Liszt in Weimar; composition with Dorn in Berlin. In 1867 he came to America and lived in Chicago from 1872, actively engaged as a concert pianist and teacher. He wrote a number of effective piano pieces in a light vein (*Florence Valse, Feu follet, Albumblatt, 2 Romances, Cradle Song, Canzonetta, Menuetto scherzoso, Mazurka de concert, Spring Song.*) He edited *The American History and Encyclopedia of Music* and co-edited a *Dictionary of Musical Terms.*

Liebling, Estelle, American singer and vocal pedagogue, sister of **Leonard Liebling,** niece of **Emil** and **Georg Liebling;** b. New York, April 21, 1880; d. New York, Sept. 25, 1970. She studied with Mathilde Marchesi in Paris and S. Nicklass-Kempner in Berlin; made her debut as Lucia at the Dresden Royal Opera; also appeared at the Stuttgart Opera, the Opéra-Comique in Paris, and the Metropolitan Opera House in N.Y. (1902–3); was a soloist with leading symph. orchs. in the U.S., France, and Germany; also with Sousa; in 1936–38 was a prof. at the Curtis Inst. of Music in Philadelphia; then settled in N.Y. as a vocal teacher. She publ. *The Estelle Liebling Coloratura Digest* (N.Y., 1943).

Liebling, Georg, German-American pianist and composer, brother of **Emil Liebling;** b. Berlin, Jan. 22, 1865; d. New York, Feb. 7, 1946. He studied piano with Theodor and Franz Kullak, and Liszt; composition with Urban and Dorn; toured Europe (1885–89); was court pianist to the Duke of Coburg (1890). In 1894–97 he directed his own music school in Berlin; in 1898–1908, was a prof. at the Guildhall School of Music in London. He came to the U.S. in 1924; made his N.Y. concert debut on Nov. 19, 1924. He used the pseudonym **André Myrot.**

WORKS: *Great Mass* for Soli, Chorus, Orch., and Organ (Los Angeles, 1931); *Concerto eroico* for Piano and Orch. (1925); 2 violin concertos; 2 violin sonatas; 3 Preludes for Violin and Piano; *Aria e Tarantella* for Cello and Piano; *Légende* for Violin and Piano; etc.; piano pieces; songs.

BIBLIOGRAPHY: G. Braun, *Hofpianist Georg Liebling* (Berlin, 1896).

Liebling, Leonard, American music critic and editor, nephew of **Georg** and **Emil Liebling** and brother of **Estelle Liebling;** b. New York, Feb. 7, 1874; d. there, Oct. 28, 1945. He studied at City College in N.Y., and privately with Leopold Godowsky (piano); then in Berlin with Kullak and Barth (piano) and Urban (composition); toured Europe and America as a pianist. In 1902 he joined the staff of the *Musical Courier* in N.Y., and in 1911 became its editor in chief; his weekly columns on topical subjects were both entertaining and instructive. He also served as music critic of the *N.Y. American* (1923–34, 1936–37). He wrote some chamber music, piano pieces, and songs, as well as librettos of several light operas, including Sousa's *The American Maid.*

Lienau, Robert, German music publisher; b. Neustadt, Holstein, Dec. 28, 1838; d. there, July 22, 1920. In 1864 he purchased Schlesinger's business in Berlin, and in 1875, Haslinger's in Vienna; with the latter, he acquired the most important works of Weber, Meyerbeer, Liszt, Spohr, and others. In 1910 the management of the business was taken over by his sons **Robert** and **Wilhelm Lienau.**

Liepe, Emil, German singer and composer; b. Potsdam, Jan. 16, 1860; d. Berlin, Feb. 18, 1940. He studied in Leipzig and Vienna; in 1884–90, sang in various German opera theaters; in 1891–92 he appeared at the Bayreuth Festival; then retired from the stage, and taught voice at the Cons. of Sondershausen (1903–7) and, after 1907, in Berlin. He wrote an opera, *Colomba* (Danzig, 1894); symph. poems: *Fatum* and *Rückblick;* Symph.; a number of songs.

Lier, Bertus van. See **Van Lier, Bertus.**

Lier, Jacques van. See **Van Lier, Jacques.**

Lierhammer, Theodor, Austrian baritone and teacher; b. Lwow, Nov. 18, 1866; d. Vienna, Jan. 6, 1937. He was a practicing physician when he began to study singing with Ress in Vienna, Carafa in Milan, and Stockhausen in Frankfurt; made his debut at Vienna in 1894 in a concert with Fritz Kreisler; toured Austria and Hungary (1896), Germany (1898), Russia (1899), France and England (1900), and the U.S. (1904). In 1904–14 he was a prof. of singing at the Royal Academy of Music in London; served as an army physician during World War I; in 1922–24 he was in London as a singer and teacher; in 1924, was named prof. of singing at the State Academy of Music in Vienna; in 1932–35, taught at the Austro-American Summer Cons., in Mondsee (Salzburg). One of his American pupils was Roland Hayes.

Lieurance, Thurlow, American composer; b. Oskaloosa, Iowa, March 21, 1878; d. Boulder, Colo., Oct. 9, 1963. He studied at the Cincinnati College of Music; served as an army bandmaster during the Spanish-American War. He became interested in American Indian music, and lived on various reservations, studying the culture of Indian tribes; this research resulted in the composition of music showing the influence of Indian melodies; one of the songs, *By the Waters of Minnetonka,* achieved tremendous popularity; he further publ. *9 Indian Songs* (1919); *Songs of the North American Indian* (1921); *8 Songs from the Green Timber* (1922); *Forgotten Trails* (1923); wrote several symph. pieces: *Medicine Dance, Colonial Exposition Sketches, Scenes Southwest, Prairie Sketches, Water Moon Maiden,* etc. In 1940 he was appointed dean of the music dept. of Municipal Univ. of Wichita, Kans.; in 1957, was named dean emeritus.

Ligendza, Catarina, Swedish soprano; b. Stockholm, Oct. 18, 1937. She studied in Würzburg and Saarbrücken; then sang opera in Linz (1963) and at the Deutsche Oper in West Berlin (1969); her subsequent engagements were at Salzburg (1970) and Bayreuth (1971). She made her American debut at the Metropolitan Opera in N.Y. as Leonore in *Fidelio* on Feb. 25, 1971.

Ligeti, György, innovative Hungarian composer of the avant-garde; b. Dicsöszentmartin, Transylvania, May 28, 1923. He studied composition with Sándor Veress and Ferenc Farkas at the Budapest Music Academy (1945–49) and became an instructor there (1950–56). In 1956 he left Budapest; worked in the Studio for Electronic Music in Cologne (1957–

59); then lived mostly in Vienna (1959–69) and in Berlin (1969–73); in summers he lectured at the International Courses for New Music in Darmstadt; from 1961 was a guest prof. of composition at the Musical High School in Stockholm; in addition, he gave lectures in Spain, the Netherlands, Germany, and Finland, and at Tanglewood in the U.S.; in 1972 was composer-in-residence at Stanford Univ.; in 1973 was appointed prof. of composition at the Hochschule für Musik in Hamburg. In his bold and imaginative experimentation with musical materials and parameters, Ligeti endeavors to bring together all aural and visual elements in a synthetic entity, making use of all conceivable effects, employing homely kitchen utensils and plebeian noisemakers or grandiose electronic blasts, alternating tremendous sonorous upheavals with static chordal masses and shifting dynamic colors.

WORKS: *Rumanian Concerto* for Orch. (1951); *Glissandi* for Electronic Sound (1957); *Articulation* for Electronics (1958); *Apparitions* for Orch. (1959); *Atmospheres* for Orch. (1961); *Volumina* for Organ (1962); *Aventures* for 3 Singers and 7 Instruments (1962); *Nouvelles aventures* for Soprano and 7 Instruments (1962–65); *Requiem* for Soprano, Mezzosoprano, 2 Choruses, and Orch. (1963–65; Stockholm, March 14, 1965; the *Kyrie* from it was used in the film score for *2001: A Space Odyssey*); Cello Concerto (Berlin, April 19, 1967); *Lontano* for Orch. (Donaueschingen, Oct. 22, 1967); *10 Pieces* for Wind Quintet (Malmö, Jan. 19, 1969); *Ramifications* for String Orch. (1969); *Chamber Concerto* for 13 Instruments (Ottawa, April 2, 1970); Double Concerto for Flute, Oboe, and Orch. (1972); *Clocks and Clouds* for Female Chorus and Orch. (1973); *San Francisco Polyphony* for Orch. (1974); *Monument-Selbstporträt-Bewegung* for 2 Pianos (1976); opera, *Le Grand Macabre,* after Ghelderode's play (Stockholm, April 12, 1978); Trio for Violin, Horn, and Piano (1981); also 2 string quartets (1954, 1968). Ligeti's *Poème symphonique* for 100 Metronomes, all running at different speeds, was performed at the Buffalo Festival of the Arts Today (March 4, 1965), causing a sensation.

BIBLIOGRAPHY: Ove Nordwall, *Från Mahler till Ligeti* (Stockholm, 1965); Erkki Salmenhaara, *Das musikalische Material und seine Behandlung in den Werken von György Ligeti* (Helsinki-Regensburg, 1969); U. Dibelius, ed., *György Ligeti,* catalogue of works (Mainz, 1970).

Lightfoot, Gordon, Canadian singer and composer in the popular-music genres; b. Orillia, Ontario, Nov. 17, 1938. He learned to play folk guitar; then enrolled in Westlake College of Music in Los Angeles to acquire the rudiments of music theory. After working in Canada and England, he met Bob Dylan, who impressed him with the importance of social concerns in songs. In 1966 he brought out an album, *Lightfoot,* in which he demonstrated his facile talents as singer, composer, and guitarist.

Lilburn, Douglas, New Zealand composer; b. Wanganui, Nov. 2, 1915. He studied with Vaughan Williams at the Royal College of Music in London; then returned to New Zealand, where he became a prof. of music at Victoria Univ. in Wellington. Among his works are *Forest*, symph. poem (1937); *Aoteroa*, overture (London, April 16, 19⁓0); *Song of the Antipodes* for Orch. (Wellington, Aug. 20, 1947); *Diversions* for String Orch. (London, June 28, 1947); 3 symphs.: No. 1 (first full-fledged symph. by a New Zealand composer; Wellington, May 12, 1951); No. 2 (1955); No. 3 (1961); 2 string quartets; 3 violin sonatas; String Trio; Clarinet Sonata; Piano Sonata; other piano pieces; songs.

Liliencron, Rochus von, eminent German music scholar; b. Plön, Dec. 8, 1820; d. Coblenz, March 5, 1912. He studied law and theology in Kiel and Berlin; took a course in Nordic philology in Copenhagen; in 1850 became prof. of Norse literature at Kiel Univ.; in 1852, prof. of German literature at Jena Univ.; then privy-councillor at Saxe-Meiningen (1855–68); in 1869, went to Munich; there he edited the *Allgemeine deutsche Biographie* (1875–1900); collected and annotated German folk songs of the Middle Ages, publ. as *Historische Volkslieder der Deutschen vom 13.–16. Jahrhundert* (4 vols. and an appendix, Leipzig, 1865–69); from 1876 he lived in Schleswig as provost of St. John's Monastery; in 1894 was appointed editor of Denkmäler Deutscher Tonkunst.
WRITINGS: *Lieder und Sprüche aus der letzten Zeit des Minnesangs* (1854; contains 20 melodies with texts from the Jena Minnesänger Codex, c.1320); *Über den Chorgesang in der evangelischen Kirche* (1881); *Deutsches Leben im Volkslied um 1530*, containing 147 polyphonic German folk songs of the 16th century (1885; 2nd ed., 1925); *Chorordnung für die Sonn- und Festtage des evangelischen Kirchenjahres* (1900; 2nd ed., by H.J. Moser, 1929). He wrote an autobiography, *Frohe Jugendtage* (1902). In 1910, in honor of his 90th birthday, a Festschrift was publ., to which many of the foremost German musicologists contributed (Riemann, Adler, Friedlaender, Kretzschmar, Sandberger, Seiffert, and others).
BIBLIOGRAPHY: A. Bettelheim, *Leben und Wirken des Freiherrn Rochus von Liliencron* (1917).

Lilienthal, Abraham W., American composer and teacher; b. New York, Feb. 13, 1859; d. there, March 15, 1928. He received his entire musical training in N.Y.; for many years, played the viola in the N.Y. String Quartet; then lived in N.Y. as a teacher and composer. He wrote a String Quartet; String Quintet; String Sextet; Piano Trio; Cello Sonata; a series of orch. dances.

Liljeblad, Ingeborg, Finnish soprano; b. Helsinki, Oct. 17, 1887; d. there, Feb. 28, 1942. She studied in Berlin with Etelka Gerster, and in Paris with Félia Litvinne; was engaged at the Mannheim Opera (1911–13) and in Hamburg for the season of 1913–14. Returning to Helsinki in 1927, she taught at the Sibelius Academy. She was married to the conduc-

tor **Leo Funtek.**

Liljefors, Ingemar, Swedish composer, son of **Ruben Liljefors;** b. Göteborg, Dec. 13, 1906; d. Stockholm, Oct. 14, 1981. He studied at the Royal Academy of Music in Stockholm (1923–27 and 1929–31); in 1938 was appointed to its staff. From 1947 to 1963 he was chairman of the Assoc. of Swedish Composers. He publ. a manual on harmony from the functional point of view (1937) and one on harmonic analysis along similar lines (1951). His compositions frequently employ elements of Swedish folk music.
WORKS: Opera, *Hyrkusken* (*The Coachman*, 1951); *Rhapsody* for Piano and Orch. (1936); *3 Studies* for Piano (1939); Piano Concerto (1940); 2 piano trios (1940, 1961); Symph. (1943); Piano Concertino (1949); Violin Sonatina (1954); 3 piano sonatinas (1954, 1964, 1965); Violin Concerto (1956); Cello Sonatina (1958); *En Tijdh-Spegel* (*A Mirror of the Times*) for Soli, Chorus, and Orch. (1959; Swedish Radio, April 16, 1961); Sinfonietta (1961); String Quartet (1963); *2 Intermezzi* for Strings (1966); Sonatina for Solo Violin (1968); *Divertimento* for Strings (1968).

Liljefors, Ruben, Swedish composer and conductor; b. Uppsala, Sept. 30, 1871; d. there, March 4, 1936. He studied in Uppsala; then with Jadassohn at the Leipzig Cons.; later in Dresden with Draeseke; and with Max Reger in Leipzig. Returning to Sweden, he was active as a choral conductor in Uppsala (1902) and in Göteborg (1903–11); in 1912 he went to Gävle as conductor of the Orchestral Society.
WORKS: Cantata, *Blomsterfursten* (*The Flower-Prince*); Symph. (1906); *Sommer-Suite* (1920); *3 Bagatelles* for String Orch.; *Romance* for Violin and Orch.; Piano Concerto (1899; rewritten 1922); incidental music to *Fritjof och Ingeborg;* Violin Sonata; men's choruses; piano pieces; songs; etc.

Lill, John, English pianist; b. London, March 17, 1944. He studied at the Royal College of Music in London; made his debut at a concert in the Royal Festival Hall in 1963. In 1970 he won first prize in the International Tchaikovsky Competition in Moscow, which was the beginning of his successful international career. In 1978 he received the Order of the British Empire.

Lillo, Giuseppe, Italian composer; b. Galatina, Lecce, Feb. 26, 1814; d. Naples, Feb. 4, 1863. He studied at the Naples Cons. with Furno, Lanza, and Zingarelli; in 1846, became a teacher of harmony at the Naples Cons.; later (1859), a teacher of counterpoint and composition there. He had to retire from active life in 1861 because of mental illness.
WORKS: Operas: *Una moglie per 24 ore* (Naples, 1834); *L'osteria d'Andujar* (Naples, 1840; his most successful work); etc.; symphs.; Piano Quartet; much good piano music; also church music.

Limantour, José Yves, Mexican conductor; b. Paris (of Mexican parents), Aug. 9, 1919. He was educated at Trinity College, Cambridge; settled in Mexico in 1939; studied there at the Cons. Nacional; in 1940–41 he was in the U.S., where he took courses with Hindemith; in 1942–43 he was conductor of the orch. of the Ballets Russes de Monte Carlo in Mexico; in 1944–51, conductor of the Jalapa Symph. Orch.

Limbert, Frank, conductor and composer; b. New York (of German parents), Nov. 15, 1866; d. Hanau, Nov. 19, 1938. He was taken to Germany at the age of 8, and remained there; studied at the Hoch Cons. in Frankfurt; received his Dr.Phil. at the Univ. of Strasbourg (1894) with the dissertation *Beitrag zur Kenntnis der volkstümlichen Musik, insbesondere der Balladen-Komposition in England;* from 1895 lived mostly in Hanau, where he conducted an oratorio society. He publ. a *Konzertstück* for Piano and Orch.; Violin Sonata; Viola Sonata; *Ein Zyklus von Sonetten* for Chorus a cappella; other choruses; songs; piano pieces.

Limnander de Nieuwenhove, Armand Marie Ghislain, Belgian composer; b. Ghent, May 22, 1814; d. Moignanville, near Paris, Aug. 15, 1892. He studied in Freiburg with Lambillotte and in Brussels with Fétis; in 1835, became a choral director in Malines; in 1845, settled in Paris.
WORKS: Grand opera, *Le Maître-chanteur* (Paris, 1853); comic operas: *Les Monténégrins* (Paris, 1849); *Le Château de la Barbe-Bleue* (1851); *Yvonne* (1859); symph., *La Fin des Moisson; Scènes druidiques* for Orch.; String Quartet; Cello Sonata; church music; songs; etc.

Lin, Cho-Liang, Chinese violinist; b. Taiwan, Jan. 29, 1960. He began to study the violin as a child; when he was 10 he won the Taiwan National Youth Competition. He then studied with Robert Pikler at the New South Wales State Conservatorium of Music in Sydney; at 15 he came to the U.S., where he enrolled at the Juilliard School of Music in N.Y. as a scholarship student of Dorothy DeLay. In 1977 he won first prize in the Queen Sofia International Competition in Madrid, and subsequently appeared as a soloist with the N.Y. Phil., Philadelphia Orch., Chicago Symph., Pittsburgh Symph., Cleveland Orch., Los Angeles Phil., London Symph., Royal Phil. of London, London Phil., Bavarian Radio Symph., and Royal Danish Orch. In 1981 he toured the People's Republic of China; he also played in Hong Kong, New Zealand, and Japan.

Lincke, Joseph, Austrian cellist; b. Trachenberg, Silesia, June 8, 1783; d. Vienna, March 26, 1837. He was cellist in Schuppanzigh's famous quartet (1808–16) in Vienna; was first cellist at the Theater an der Wien (1818); finally at the Vienna Court Opera (1831). He composed some cello pieces.

Lincke, Paul, German composer of light music; b. Berlin, Nov. 7, 1866; d. Klausthal-Zellerfeld, near Göttingen, Sept. 3, 1946. He was active in many fields; played violin and bassoon; conducted theater orchs.; engaged in music publishing; after World War I he conducted revues at the Folies-Bergère in Paris (1918–20). His chief fame comes from his operettas; he is generally credited as being the progenitor of a special type of "Berlin operetta," as distinguished from the Vienna genre. The best known of these are *Venus auf Erden* (1897); *Im Reiche des Indra* (Berlin, Dec. 17, 1899); *Frau Luna* (Berlin, Dec. 31, 1899); *Fräulein Loreley* (Berlin, 1900); *Lysistrata* (Berlin, 1902), which contains the famous tune *Glühwürmchen-Idyll (Glowworm); Prinzessin Rosine* (1905); *Grigri* (1911); *Casanova* (1913). His last operetta was *Ein Liebestraum,* which was produced in Hamburg in 1940; a postage stamp in Lincke's honor, with a musical example showing the melody *Berliner Luft* from *Frau Luna,* was issued by the West German government in 1957.
BIBLIOGRAPHY: Edmund Nick, *Paul Lincke* (Hamburg, 1953).

Lincoln, Robert Dix, American pianist and composer; b. Woodstock, Ohio, Dec. 3, 1924. He studied with Nadia Boulanger in Paris. Upon his return to the U.S. he taught at various colleges. He wrote numerous teaching pieces for piano of a descriptive nature, among them *Lions and Tigers, Bouncing Clowns, Marching Musicians,* etc.

Lind, Jenny, famous soprano, called "the Swedish Nightingale"; b. Stockholm, Oct. 6, 1820; d. at her villa, Wynd's Point, Malvern Wells, England, Nov. 2, 1887. At the age of 10 she entered the Royal Opera School in Stockholm; her early teachers there were C.M. Craelius and I. Berg; she later studied with A.F. Lindblad and J.A. Josephson. She made her professional debut as Agathe in *Der Freischütz* at the Stockholm Opera on March 7, 1838; she then sang Euryanthe in Weber's opera, and several parts in French operas. In 1840 she was appointed a regular member of the Royal Swedish Academy of Music, and was also given the rank of court singer. However, she felt the necessity of improving her voice, and in 1841 went to Paris, where she studied for about a year with Manuel García, who gave her a thorough training according to his well-known "scientific" method. In Paris Meyerbeer heard her, and was so impressed that he wrote for her the part of Vielka in his opera *Ein Feldlager in Schlesien.* Jenny Lind returned to Stockholm in 1842; in 1844 she went to Berlin; sang there, and also in Hannover, Hamburg, Cologne, and Coblenz; then appeared in Frankfurt, Darmstadt, Copenhagen, and again in Berlin; her other important engagements were at the Gewandhaus in Leipzig (Dec. 6, 1845), and at the Vienna Opera (April 18, 1846). By this time, her fame became legendary in Europe; she was engaged to sing in London, and her appearance there was preceded by an extraordinary publicity campaign. She made her London debut as Alice in *Robert le Diable* on May 4, 1847, with sensational success; as Chorley reported, the town "went mad about the Swedish Nightingale." If her success in England was great, her American tour exceeded all expectations in public agitation and monetary reward. She arrived in America in 1850, under the sponsorship of P.T. Barnum, the circus manager, who presented Jenny Lind as a natural phenomenon rather than as an artist; nonetheless, she made a fine impression on the musical public as well; she sang recitals in N.Y., Boston, St. Louis, and other cities; a 4-page broadside in folio format with golden type was issued in anticipation of her Boston appearance by the F. Gleason Publishing Co. (1850); poems were written in her honor, and accounts of her concerts were publ. in hundreds of newspapers. She earned fantastic fees, and made generous donations to various charitable institutions in Sweden. On Feb. 5, 1852, she married, in Boston, her accompanist, **Otto Goldschmidt;** with him she returned to Europe; remained for some time in Dresden; in 1856 she went to London, and remained in England for the rest of her life, with the exception of a few appearances in Europe. She had left the operatic stage in 1849, before her American tour; in England she sang with her husband's Bach Choir; her final public appearance was at the Rhenish Music Festival in 1870, when she sang the principal part in her husband's oratorio *Ruth*; in 1883 she joined the faculty of the Royal College of Music in London. Unlike many other celebrated singers of her era, Jenny Lind was a paragon of domestic virtue, and was distinguished by her lack of vanity; even her most ardent worshipers did not claim that she was beautiful, but there was no disagreement as to the quality of her voice and her musicianship. She possessed a fine coloratura, with a compass reaching high G; never striving for dramatic effect, she was able to maintain a perfect phrase. Among her best operatic parts were La Sonnambula and Lucia. A bust of Jenny Lind was unveiled in Westminster Abbey on April 20, 1894. A Jenny Lind Association was formed in N.Y. in 1922, and a Jenny Lind Society was organized in Stockholm in 1943.

BIBLIOGRAPHY: J.B. Lyser, *G. Meyerbeer und Jenny Lind* (Vienna, 1847); C.G. Rosenberg, *Jenny Lind in America* (N.Y., 1851); H.S. Holland and W.S. Rockstro, *Memoir of Mme. Jenny Lind-Goldschmidt* (2 vols., London, 1891; condensed ed., one vol., 1893); W.S. Rockstro and O. Goldschmidt, *Jenny Lind-Goldschmidt: A Record and Analysis of the Method of the Late Jenny Lind-Goldschmidt* (London, 1894); C.A. Wilkens, *Jenny Lind: Ein Cäcilienbild aus der evangelischen Kirche* (Gütersloh, 1854; 5th ed., 1926); "Jenny Lind's Singing Method" (a letter written by her), *Musical Quarterly* (July 1917); T. Norlind, *Jenny Lind* (Stockholm, 1919); M.R. Werner, *Barnum* (N.Y., 1923); Mrs. Raymond Maude, *The Life of Jenny Lind* (London, 1926); Grace Humphrey, *Jenny Lind* (Philadelphia, 1928); E.C. Wagenknecht, *Jenny Lind-Goldschmidt* (Boston, 1931); Laura Benet, *Enchanting Jenny Lind* (N.Y., 1939); H. Headland, *The Swedish Nightingale: A Biography of Jenny Lind* (Rock Island, Ill., 1940); M. Pergament, *Jenny Lind* (Stockholm, 1945); K. Rotzen and T. Meyer, *Jenny Lind* (Stockholm, 1945); Joan Bulman, *Jenny Lind* (London, 1956); G.D. Schultz, *Jenny Lind, the Swedish Nightingale* (Philadelphia, 1962); W.P. Ware and T.C. Lockard,

Jr., translators and eds., *The Lost Letters of Jenny Lind* (London, 1966); A.M. Dunlop, *The Swedish Nightingale* (N.Y., 1965); E.P. Myers, *Jenny Lind, Songbird from Sweden* (Champaign, Ill., 1968).

Lindberg, Oskar Fredrik, Swedish composer and organist; b. Gagnef, Feb. 23, 1887; d. Stockholm, April 10, 1955. He studied at the Stockholm Cons. with Andreas Hallén and Ernst Ellberg; was organist at Trinity Church, Stockholm (1906–14); in 1919, was appointed a teacher of harmony at the Stockholm Cons.

WORKS: Opera, *Fredlös* (after Selma Lagerlöf's story *The Outlaw;* Stockholm, Nov. 25, 1943); *Det ljusa Landet* for Chorus and Orch. (1935); *Skansen Cantata; Bergslags Cantata* (1947); Symph. (1912); *Dalmålningar (Pictures from Dalarna;* 1908); symph. poems: *Florez och Blanzeflor, Från de stora skogarna, Hemifrån, Vildmark, Gesunda;* overtures; orch. suites; Piano Quartet; Piano Quintet; Requiem; piano pieces; songs.

Lindblad, Adolf Fredrik, Swedish composer; b. Skänninge, near Stockholm, Feb. 1, 1801; d. Linköping, Aug. 23, 1878. He studied in Berlin with Zelter. His numerous songs, tinged with national color, won deserved popularity, especially after Jenny Lind, his pupil, sang them in public; he was called the "Schubert of the North."

WORKS: Opera, *Frondörerna (The Frondists;* Stockholm, May 11, 1835); 2 symphs.; 7 string quartets; Piano Trio; Duo for Piano and Violin; songs (*The Song of the Dalecarlian Maiden, Lament, The Wood by the Aren Lake, A Day in Spring, A Summer's Day, Autumn Evening,* etc.).

BIBLIOGRAPHY: M. Grandinson, *Brev till A.F. Lindblad från Mendelssohn* (Stockholm, 1913).

Lindblad, Otto (Jonas), Swedish composer; b. Karlstorp, March 31, 1809; d. Mellby, Jan. 26, 1864. He is chiefly known for his vocal ensemble music; formed a vocal and instrumental trio; also was an opera and choral conductor. He wrote 66 vocal quartets; 5 choruses with solos; 14 vocal trios; 3 duets; 36 solo songs.

BIBLIOGRAPHY: Ture Nerman, *Otto Lindblad* (Uppsala, 1930).

Linde, Bo, Swedish composer; b. Gävle, Jan. 1, 1933; d. there, Oct. 2, 1970. He studied composition with Lars-Erik Larsson at the Royal Academy of Music in Stockholm; then took courses in conducting in Vienna (1953–54). In 1960 he returned to Gävle. In his music he follows a healthy Scandinavian style of composition, liberally diversified with cosmopolitan neo-Classical techniques, bordering on polytonality.

WORKS: *Sinfonia fantasia* (1951); *6 Character Studies* for Piano (1952); *Ballet blanc* (1953; Gävle, May 11, 1969); 2 piano trios (1953, 1969); String Quartet (1953); Violin Sonata (1953); 2 piano concertos (1954, 1956); *Suite in an Old Style* for Orch. (1954); 2 piano sonatinas (1955, 1962); *Preludium and Final* for Strings (1955); Violin Concerto (1957); Suite for

Orch. (1959); *Slotts-skoj (Fun in the Castle)*, children's opera for radio (1959); *Sinfonia* (1960); Concerto for Orch. (1961–62); *6 Pieces* for Piano (1962); *Concert Music* for Small Orch. (1963); *Vårbilder (Spring Scenes)* for Soli, Chorus, and Orch. (1963); Cello Concerto (1964); *Serenata nostalgica* for 11 Strings (1965); *Quartet in Miniature* for Clarinets (1965); *Suite Boulogne* for Orch. (1966); *Little Concerto* for Wind Quintet and Strings (1966); *Pensieri sopra un cantico vecchio* for Orch. (Gävle, Jan. 1, 1968); String Trio (1968); *Pezzo concertante*, concertino for Bass Clarinet and Strings (Gävle, Sept. 9, 1970); *6 Italian Songs* for Baritone, Violin, Cello, and Piano (1970).

Linde, Hans-Martin, German flutist; b. Werne, May 24, 1930. He studied at the Freiburg Hochschule für Musik; gave recitals throughout Europe; made his first American tour in 1967. In 1957 he became a lecturer at the Basel Music Academy; also taught at the Schola Cantorum Basiliensis; was a regular soloist with the Cappella Coloniensis of the Cologne Radio. He was particularly noted for his performances of Baroque music.

Lindegren, Johan, Swedish teacher and authority on church music; b. Ullared, Jan. 7, 1842; d. Stockholm, June 8, 1908. He studied at the Stockholm Cons., where he became a teacher of counterpoint in 1881; in 1884, was organist and cantor of St. Nicholas's Church. Among his pupils were Alfvén, Melchers, Bäck, Håkanson, and Wiklund. He edited *Tidning för kyrkomusik* (1881–82); also publ. a *Koralbok* (1905). Of his numerous compositions, only a few were publ.: *Hösttankar (Autumn Thoughts),* elegy; *Till Vegas jhältar (For Vega's Heroes),* festival march; String Quartet; Piano Sonata, and Fugue.

Lindeman, Ludvig Mathias, Norwegian organist and folk-song collector; b. Trondheim, Nov. 28, 1812; d. Christiania, May 23, 1887. He turned from theology to the study of music; in 1839, became organist at Our Saviour's Church in Christiania; in 1849, a teacher of church singing at the Theological Seminary of Christiania Univ.; in 1883 he and his son Peter Lindeman (1858–1930) founded a music school, which later developed into the Christiania Cons. He was one of the earliest and most active collectors of Norwegian folk songs; publ. nearly 600 folk melodies in the collection *Older and Newer Norwegian Mountain Melodies* (3 vols., 1853–67); also *68 Norwegian Mountain Melodies* (1841); *50 Norwegian Melodies* (1862); and *30 Norwegian Ballads* (1863). His *Chorale Book for the Norwegian Church* (1877) remains a standard work; it contains some melodies by Lindeman, including *Kirken den er et gammelt hus,* one of the best-known Norwegian hymn tunes; he also composed *Draumkvoedet (Dream Chant)* for Chorus; organ fugues; etc.
BIBLIOGRAPHY: O.M. Sandvik, *Ludvig Mathias Lindeman og folkemelodien* (Oslo, 1950).

Lindeman, Osmo, Finnish composer; b. Helsinki, May 16, 1929. He studied with Eino Linnala and Nils-Eric Fougstedt at the Sibelius Academy in Helsinki. In 1959 he was awarded a UNESCO grant to the Munich Music Academy, where he studied for a year with Carl Orff; upon returning to Finland, he taught at the Sibelius Academy. In his works he at first adopted a traditional Romantic manner, but after 1968 devoted himself to electronic music.
WORKS: Symph. No. 1, surnamed *Sinfonia inornata* (1959); Piano Concerto No. 1 (1963); Symph. No. 2 (1964); Piano Concerto No. 2 (1965); *Music* for Chamber Orch. (1966); Concerto for Chamber Orch. (1966); *Huutokauppa (Auction),* ballet with 6 Reciters, Chorus, 2 Pianos, and Orch. (1967); *Variabile* for Orch. (1967); String Trio (1958); *Partita* for Percussion (1962); *2 Expressions* for Vibraphone and Marimba (1965); String Quartet (1966). For Tape: *Kinetic Forms* (1969); *Mechanical Music* (1969); *Tropicana* (1970); *Midas* (1970); *Ritual* (1972; won first prize in the electronic and computer music category of the Sixth International Composition Contest, in Italy).

Lindholm, Berit, Swedish soprano, b. Stockholm, Oct. 18, 1934. She studied music in Stockholm and made her professional debut at the Royal Opera there in 1963. In 1966 she sang at Covent Garden in London; later also appeared at Bayreuth. In 1972 she sang at the San Francisco Opera; on Feb. 20, 1975, she made her debut at the Metropolitan Opera in N.Y. as Brünnhilde in *Die Walküre.* Her effective performances of Wagnerian roles established her reputation as an opera singer.

Lindley, Robert, English cellist; b. Rotherham, Yorkshire, March 4, 1776; d. London, June 13, 1855. He studied cello with Cervetto; from 1794 to 1851 was first cellist at the Royal Opera in London; in 1822 became prof. of cello at the Royal Academy of Music. He wrote pieces for the cello.

Lindner, August, German cellist; b. Dessau, Oct. 29, 1820; d. Hannover, June 15, 1878. He studied with Drechsler; in 1837 he became first cellist in the court orch. at Hannover. He composed a Cello Concerto and numerous vocal pieces.

Lindner, Ernst Otto Timotheus, German music scholar; b. Breslau, Nov. 28, 1820; d. Berlin, Aug. 7, 1867. He was editor of the *Vossische Zeitung;* also conducted the Berlin Bach-Verein. He wrote *Meyerbeers "Prophet" als Kunstwerk beurteilt* (1850); *Die erste stehende deutsche Oper* (1855); *Geschichte des deutschen Liedes im 18. Jahrhundert* (1871; ed. by Erk).

Lindpaintner, Peter Joseph von, German conductor and composer; b. Coblenz, Dec. 9, 1791; d. Nonnenhorn, Lake Constance, Aug. 21, 1856. He studied violin and piano in Augsburg; theory in Munich with Winter and Joseph Grätz; in 1812, became music director of the Isarthor Theater in Munich; from 1819 until his death, was conductor of the court orch. at Stuttgart, where his ability made the orch. famous.

WORKS: 28 operas, including *Der Bergkönig* (Stuttgart, Jan. 30, 1825); *Der Vampyr* (Stuttgart, Nov. 21, 1828); *Die Genueserin* (Vienna, Feb. 8, 1839); *Lichtenstein* (Stuttgart, Aug. 26, 1846); 3 ballets (*Joko,* etc.); 5 melodramas; 5 oratorios; symphs.; overture to *Faust;* incidental music to *Lied von der Glocke;* 6 masses; *Stabat Mater;* songs (*Die Fahnenwacht, Roland,* etc.).

BIBLIOGRAPHY: R. Hänsler, *Lindpaintner als Opernkomponist* (Munich, 1928).

Lineva, Evgenia (née **Papritz**), Russian folk-song collector; b. Brest-Litovsk, Jan. 9, 1854; d. Moscow, Jan. 24, 1919. She studied voice with her mother, who was a pupil of Glinka; then took lessons with Mathilde Marchesi in Vienna; later sang opera in Paris, London, and Moscow. In 1889 she married the engineer A.L. Linev (1840–1916); because of his revolutionary activities, he served a prison term, and was then forced to emigrate. Lineva was with him in London (1890–92) and in America; she gave concerts with a Russian choir (which she organized) at Carnegie Hall in N.Y. (Dec. 10, 1892) and at the Chicago Exposition (1893). In America they experimented with phonograph recording. Upon their return to Russia (1894), Lineva undertook a series of trips in the Volga region, using a phonograph constructed by her husband to record folk songs. She publ. her findings in 2 vols. (with photographs and musical examples) in Russian, and in Eng. under the title *The Peasant Songs of Great Russia* (St. Petersburg, 1904); she further publ. *Songs of the Novgorod Region* (1909).

BIBLIOGRAPHY: E. Kann-Novikova, *Evgenia Lineva* (Moscow, 1952).

Linjama, Jouko, Finnish composer; b. Kirvu, Feb. 4, 1934. He studied with Aarre Merikanto and Joonas Kokkonen at the Sibelius Academy in Helsinki; then at the Staatliche Hochschule für Musik in Cologne with Bernd Alois Zimmermann and G.M. Koenig (1962–64); later taught at the Sibelius Academy (1964–68). His production is marked with serial canonic techniques following the paradigm of Anton von Webern.

WORKS: *5 Metamorphoses on 5 Canons from op. 16 of Anton Webern* for Piano, Harpsichord, Guitar, Celesta, and Vibraphone (1963); *Orationes St. Thomae Aqvinatis* for Chorus, Flute, Oboe, Clarinet, Bassoon, Trumpet, and Trombone (1964; revised 1973); *Millaista on (How It Is),* chamber oratorio, to fragments of S. Beckett's text, for Baritone, 6 Male Voices, 3 Tapes, and Orch. (1964–68); *Kiittäkäät Herraa (Thank the Lord),* cantata for Soprano, Chorus, and Organ (1967); organ sonata, *Veni Creator Spiritus* (1968); *Missa de angelis* for Chorus, English Horn, Clarinet, Bassoon, Horn, and Trombone (1969); Concerto for Organ (1971); *Triptychon* for 2 Organs (1971); *Partita* for Organ (1973); incidental music; numerous choral pieces a cappella; songs.

Linko, Ernst, Finnish composer and pianist; b. Hel-

sinki, July 14, 1889; d. there, Jan. 28, 1960. He studied piano at the Helsinki School of Music (1909–11); then in Berlin, St. Petersburg, and Paris. He was director of the Sibelius Academy (1939–59); for many years was active as a concert pianist. He wrote 4 piano concertos (1916, 1920, 1931, 1957); *Symphonie chevaleresque* (1949); *Ariette* for Wind Ensemble; *Rigaudon* for Strings; Piano Trio; String Quartet; numerous piano pieces.

Linley, George, English composer and author; b. Leeds, 1798; d. London, Sept. 10, 1865. He settled in London, where he wrote words and music of songs, many of which acquired great vogue (*Ever of thee; I cannot mind my wheel, mother; Thou art gone from my gaze;* etc.); he also wrote the cantata *The Jolly Beggars;* the operas *Francesca Doria* (1849); *La Poupée de Nuremberg* (London, 1861); *The Toy Makers* (1861); *Law versus Love* (1862); part-songs, trios, duets, hymns; edited the collections *Scottish Melodies, Songs of the Camp, Original Hymn Tunes,* etc.; publ. *The Musical Cynics of London* (1862), a satirical poem aimed at the critic Chorley, and *Modern Hudibras* (1864).

Linley, Thomas, Jr., English violinist and composer, eldest son of **Thomas Linley, Sr.;** b. Bath, May 7, 1756; d. Grimsthorpe, Aug. 5, 1778. He was extremely gifted as a child, and played a violin concerto in public at the age of 8. He studied music in London with his father and with Boyce; was then sent to Florence, where he studied violin with Nardini, and while there, met Mozart, with whom he subsequently formed a close friendship. Returning to England, he played at his father's concerts at Bath and in London. He wrote incidental music for various plays in London. He lost his life by drowning at the early age of 22. Some of his vocal pieces were included in the posthumous collection of his father's music.

BIBLIOGRAPHY: G. Beechey, "Thomas Linley, Junior," *Musical Quarterly* (Jan. 1968; includes a list of surviving works).

Linley, Thomas, Sr., English composer; b. Badminton, Jan. 17, 1733; d. London, Nov. 19, 1795. He first studied with a church organist in Bath; then with Paradisi. He organized performances of oratorios in Bath; in 1774 he went to London, where he produced several oratorios, and various stage works, to which he contributed an occasional song; also arranged and orchestrated ballets, comic operas, etc., by other composers. He publ. *6 Elegies* for 3 Voices (his finest work) and *12 Ballads;* 2 vols. of miscellaneous vocal pieces by him were publ. posthumously. The writer Sheridan was his son-in-law; Linley wrote 7 numbers for the production of Sheridan's *The Duenna,* and arranged the other musical works for the opera; it was produced at Covent Garden in London on Nov. 21, 1775, and became one of the most successful comic operas in England of the 18th century (about 75 perfs. during the season). Linley's 3 sons and 3 daughters were also professional musicians.

BIBLIOGRAPHY: C. Black, *The Linleys of Bath* (London, 1926).

Linnala, Eino, Finnish composer; b. Helsinki, Aug. 19, 1896; d. there, June 8, 1973. He studied composition with Melartin at the Univ. of Helsinki and with Arthur Willner in Vienna. Upon his return to Finland he acted as chairman of the Finnish Composers' Copyright Bureau, TEOSTO (1960–68); publ. music textbooks. He composed 2 symphs. (1927, 1935); *Finnish Rhapsody* (1932); *Overture* (1934); 3 cantatas; numerous choral works and songs.

Linstead, George Frederick, Scottish pianist and composer; b. Melrose, Jan. 24, 1908. He wrote an oratorio at the age of 13, and an opera, *Agamemnon,* at 16; was church organist at Sheffield; in 1947, was appointed a prof. at Sheffield Univ. Besides his youthful compositions, he has written an opera, *Eastward of Eden* (1937); *Moto perpetuo* for Orch. (1947); Violin Sonata (1934); String Quartet (1941); piano pieces.

Lintermans, François-Joseph, Belgian composer and conductor; b. Brussels, Aug. 18, 1808; d. Ixelles, May 14, 1895. He was director of the Brussels choral society Les Artisans Réunis; composed choruses (*Cri de guerre, Réveil, Chœur des buveurs,* etc.).

Lioncourt, Guy de, French composer; b. Caen, Dec. 1, 1885; d. Paris, Dec. 24, 1961. He studied at the Schola Cantorum with Vincent d'Indy, who was his uncle by marriage; in 1918 he won the Grand Prix Lasserre with his fairy-tale opera *La Belle au bois dormant* (1912). In 1935 he was co-founder, with L. de Serres, of the Ecole César Franck in Paris.
WORKS: Dramatic: *Le Petit Faune aux yeux bleus* (1911); *Les Dix Lépreux* (1920); *Jean de la lune* (1921); *Le Mystère de l'Emmanuel* (Liège, 1924); *Le Mystère de l'Alléluia* (1927); *Le Réniement de St.-Pierre* (1928); *Le Dict de Mme. Sante-Barbe* (1937); *Le Navrement de Notre Dame* (1944); *Le Mystère de l'Esprit* (1946); String Quartet; Piano Quartet; 3 *Mélodies grégoriennes* for Organ; *Elevations liturgiques* for Organ; 3 masses; motets. He publ. *Un Témoignage sur la musique et sur la vie au XXᵉ siècle* (Reims, 1956).

Lipatti, Dinu, outstanding Rumanian pianist and composer; b. Bucharest, April 1, 1917; d. Chêne-Bourg, near Geneva, Dec. 2, 1950. His father was a violinist who had studied with Sarasate, and his mother, a pianist. He received his early training from his parents; then studied with Florica Musicescu at the Bucharest Cons. (1928–32). He received a 2nd prize at the International Competition at Vienna in 1934; then studied piano with Cortot, conducting with Munch, and composition with Paul Dukas and Nadia Boulanger in Paris (1934–39). He gave concerts in Germany and Italy, returning to Rumania at the outbreak of World War II. In 1943 he made his way to Stockholm, and then to Geneva, where he taught piano at the Geneva Cons. He visit-

ed England 4 times between 1946 and 1950; projected tours in America and Australia had to be canceled owing to his illness (lymphogranulomatosis), which led to his early death. He was generally regarded as one of the most sensitive interpreters of Chopin, and was also praised for his deep understanding of the Baroque masters. Lipatti was married to **Madeleine Cantacuzene,** herself a concert pianist. He was also a fine composer.
WORKS: Piano Sonata (1932); Violin Sonatina (1933); *Sätrarii,* symph. poem (1933); *Concertino in the Classic Style* for Piano and String Orch. (1936; Bucharest, Oct. 5, 1939); *Fantasy* for Piano Trio (1936); *Nocturne* for Piano (1937); *Suite* for 2 Pianos (1938); *Symphonie concertante* for 2 Pianos and Orch. (1938); *Improvisation* for Piano Trio (1939); 3 *Nocturnes* for Piano (1939); *Fantasy* for Piano (1940); Piano Sonatina for the Left Hand (1941); 3 *Rumanian Dances* for 2 Pianos (1943); or Piano and Orch. (1945; Geneva, Oct. 11, 1945); *Aubade* for Wind Quartet (1949); songs.
BIBLIOGRAPHY: *Hommage à Dinu Lipatti* (Geneva, 1952); A. Lipatti, *La Vie du pianiste Dinu Lipatti, écrite par sa mère* (1954).

Lipawsky, Josef, Austrian composer; b. Hohenmauth, Bohemia, Feb. 22, 1769; d. Vienna, Jan. 7, 1810. He studied philosophy in Prague; then settled in Vienna, where he enjoyed the friendship of Mozart, who gave him some instruction; was house musician for Count Adam Teleky; also gave public piano concerts. He wrote a Symph.; *Grande sonate pathétique* for Piano; songs. His music was highly regarded by his contemporaries.

Lipinsky, Carl, Polish violinist and composer; b. Radzyn, Oct. 30, 1790; d. near Lwow, Dec. 16, 1861. His father was a professional musician and gave him his primary education. He met Paganini, who agreed to teach him the violin; in 1835 he visited Leipzig; Schumann was greatly impressed by his playing and dedicated *Carnaval* to him. Lipinsky appeared in London on April 25, 1836, as soloist in his *Military Concerto* for Violin and Orch.; in 1839 he settled in Dresden as concertmaster of the Dresden Orch.; Liszt once played at the same concert with him. Lipinsky wrote a comic opera, *Klótnia przez zaklad* (Lwow, May 27, 1814), and other stage pieces; polonaises and *Rondos alla polacca* for violin and piano; numerous technical violin studies.

Lipkin, Malcolm Leyland, English composer; b. Liverpool, May 2, 1932. He studied at Liverpool College (1944–48) and at the Royal College of Music in London (1949–53); also took private lessons with Mátyás Seiber in London. In 1967 he was appointed tutor in the dept. of external studies at Oxford Univ. He wrote *Sinfonia di Roma* (1965); *Mosaics* for Chamber Orch. (1966); 2 violin concertos (1952, 1962); Piano Concerto (1957); Violin Sonata (1957); *Pastorale* for Horn and Strings (1963); *Suite* for Flute and Cello (1961); String Trio (1964); *Capriccio* for Piano and String Quartet (1966); *Psalm 96* (1969); Symph. No. 2, *The Pursuit* (1975–79; Manchester, Feb. 9, 1983); *Clifford's Tower* for Flute, Oboe, Clarinet, Bassoon, Horn, Violin, Viola, and Cello (1977); 4 piano sonatas; some choruses and lieder.

Lipkin, Seymour, American pianist and conductor; b. Detroit, May 14, 1927. He studied piano at the Curtis Inst. of Music in Philadelphia with Rudolf Serkin and Mieczyslaw Horszowski; later took courses in conducting with Serge Koussevitzky at Tanglewood. In 1959–60 he was assistant conductor of the N.Y. Phil.; then music adviser and conductor with the Joffrey Ballet in N.Y. He also taught piano at the Curtis Inst.

Lipkovska, Lydia, Russian soprano; b. Babino, Khotin district, Bessarabia, May 10, 1884; d. Beirut, Jan. 22, 1955. She studied voice with Madame Iretzkaya in St. Petersburg, and made her professional debut there in the spring of 1909. She sang in Paris with great success, and received a contract for an American tour. Her American debut took place with the Boston Opera on Nov. 12, 1909, when she sang *Lakmé;* on Nov. 18, 1909, she appeared at the Metropolitan Opera House in *La Traviata* with Caruso. She was reengaged for the following season in the U.S.; also appeared in London (July 11, 1911). During World War I she was in Russia; after the Revolution she went to France; in 1919 she married Pierre Bodin, a lieutenant in the French army; toured the U.S. again in 1920. She then lived in France and her native Bessarabia; during the Rumanian occupation of Odessa (1941–44) she appeared at the Odessa Opera in her favorite role of Violetta; also acted in drama. In 1944 she went to Paris; then accepted a teaching position in Beirut; during her last years of life she was supported by the Tolstoy Foundation of America.

Lipowsky, Felix Joseph, German music lexicographer and composer, son of **Thaddäus Ferdinand Lipowsky;** b. Wiesensteig, Jan. 25, 1764; d. Munich, March 21, 1842. He was engaged in many scholarly pursuits, as a legal scientist, politician, art historian, etc. He was active as a church organist and choir leader; in 1787 he obtained his Dr.Jur. degree; then served as a municipal officer in Bavaria. He publ. *Bairische Musiklexikon* (Munich, 1811), which contains valuable material despite many faults of commission and omission. He wrote several sacred choral works and some instrumental music.

Lipowsky, Thaddäus Ferdinand, German composer; b. St. Martin, Bavaria, Dec. 28, 1738; d. Wiesensteig, March 18, 1767. He studied with Leopold Mozart in Salzburg; obtained a law degree in Wiesensteig (1763); composed many violin pieces. A lengthy account of his career is found in the *Baierisches Musik-Lexikon* compiled by his son, **Felix Joseph Lipowsky.**

Lipp, Wilma, Austrian soprano; b. Vienna, April 26, 1925. She studied at the Vienna Cons. and with Toti Dal Monte in Milan. In 1945 she joined the Vienna State Opera; then sang in Milan (La Scala), London (Covent Garden), Hamburg, Paris, Munich, and Berlin; took part at the music festivals in Salzburg, Bayreuth, and Edinburgh. She was equally distinguished as a coloratura and as a lyric soprano.

Lipphardt, Walther, German musicologist; b. Wiescherhöfen bei Hamm, Oct. 14, 1906; d. Frankfurt, Jan. 17, 1981. He studied musicology with Moser at the Univ. of Heidelberg and with Gurlitt at the Univ. of Freiburg im Breisgau; then took additional courses at the Univ. of Heidelberg with Besseler, graduating with a dissertation on medieval German Marian litanies. He subsequently was appointed to the faculty of the Hochschule für Musik in Frankfurt as a docent in Catholic church music; retired in 1970. He publ. numerous valuable papers dealing with liturgical music, and edited works of Renaissance composers.

Lipps, Theodor, German writer on music; b. Wallhalben, July 28, 1851; d. Munich, Oct. 17, 1914. He occupied the chair of philosophy at the univs. of Bonn (1889), Breslau (1890–94), and Munich (from 1894). Besides the musical sections of his *Ästhetik* (2 vols., 1903–6), his writings on music comprise *Zur Theorie der Melodie* (1901); *Psychologische Studien* (vol. 2: *Das Wesen der musikalischen Harmonie und Disharmonie;* 1885; 2nd ed., 1905); "Tonverwandtschaft und Tonverschmelzung," *Zeitschrift für Psychologie und Physiologie* (1899).

BIBLIOGRAPHY: P. Moos, *Theodor Lipps als Musikästhetiker* (1907); F. Liuzzi, *Essenza dell'arte e valore estetico nel pensiero di Theodor Lipps* (Bologna, 1924).

Lipsius, Marie (pen name, **La Mara**), German writer on music; b. Leipzig, Dec. 30, 1837; d. Schmölen, near Wurzen, March 2, 1927. She received her entire education from her father, Dr. Adalbert Lipsius, rector of the Thomasschule in Leipzig; through R. Pohl, she was introduced to Liszt; in Liszt's circle at Weimar she had the happy fortune of meeting the foremost musicians of the time. Her writings on Liszt and Wagner, and on other German composers of the Romantic school, possess a stamp of authority and intimate understanding.

WRITINGS: *Beethoven* (1870; 2nd ed., 1873); *Musikalische Studienköpfe* (5 vols., 1868–82; often republ.); *Musikalische Gedanken-Polyphonie: Eine Sammlung von Aussprüchen berühmter Musiker über ihre Kunst* (1873); *Das Bühnenfestspiel in Bayreuth* (1877); *Musikerbriefe aus fünf Jahrhunderten* (2 vols., 1886); *Klassisches und Romantisches aus der Tonwelt* (1892); *Briefe an August Roeckel, von Richard Wagner* (Leipzig, 1895); *Briefe von H. Berlioz an die Fürstin Carolyne zu Sayn-Wittgenstein* (1903); *Aus der Glanzzeit der Weimarer Altenburg, Bilder und Briefe aus dem Leben der Fürstin C. Sayn-Wittgenstein* (1906); *Marie von Muchanov-Kalergis in Briefen an ihre Tochter* (1907; 2nd ed., 1911); *Beethovens "Unsterbliche Geliebte." Das Geheimnis der Gräfin Bruns-*

wik und ihre Memoiren (1909); *Liszt und die Frauen* (1911); *Durch Musik und Leben im Dienste des Ideals,* autobiography (2 vols., 1917; 2nd ed., 1926); *Beethoven und die Brunsviks* (1920); *An der Schwelle des Jenseits: Letzte Erinnerungen an die Fürstin Carolyne Sayn-Wittgenstein* (1925). She also publ. popular biographies of many composers (Wagner, Berlioz, Rubinstein, Schumann, etc.).

Lipton, Martha, American mezzo-soprano; b. New York, April 6, 1913. She was educated at the Juilliard School of Music in N.Y.; made her debut in recital. In 1944 she appeared with the Metropolitan Opera and remained on its roster until 1960; she sang with the N.Y. City Opera. In Europe she sang in Amsterdam and The Hague, and at the Holland and Edinburgh festivals, the Vienna State Opera, and the Paris Opéra; also made appearances in South America. In 1960 she became a prof. of voice at the Indiana Univ. School of Music.

Lirou, Jean François Espic, Chevalier de, French composer and theorist; b. Paris, 1740; d. there, 1806. He was an officer in the "Mousquetaires du roi," for whom he wrote *Marche des Mousquetaires*, which was performed until the Revolution. He publ. *Explication du système de l'harmonie* (1785); this was the first French theory of harmony that opposed Rameau's system and sought to establish the laws of chord progressions from the inherent affinities of tonality.

Lishin, Grigori, Russian composer; b. St. Petersburg, May 5, 1854; d. there, June 27, 1888. He studied piano with his mother; became a proficient accompanist; also wrote music criticism. He composed 2 operas, *Don Caesar* (Kiev, 1888) and *Count Nulin* (after Pushkin), to his own librettos. His sentimental ballad *She Laughed* was extremely popular with Russian singers.

Lisinski, Vatroslav, important Croatian composer; b. Zagreb, July 8, 1819; d. there, May 31, 1854. He was a student of Sojka and Wiesner von Morgenstern in Zagreb; as late as 1847, he went to Prague to study with Pitsch and Kittl. Although he never acquired a solid technique of composition, he was notable in that he tried to establish a national style in dramatic writing. He was the composer of the first Croatian opera, *Ljubav i zloba (Love and Malice),* for which he wrote only the vocal score; it was orchestrated by his teacher Wiesner von Morgenstern, and performed in Zagreb on March 28, 1846. His 2nd opera, *Porin,* also in Croatian, was given many years after his death, in Zagreb, on Oct. 2, 1897. He further wrote 7 overtures and a number of choruses and songs.
   BIBLIOGRAPHY: F. Kuhač, *Vatroslav Lisinski* (Zagreb, 1887); L. Zupanović, *Vatroslav Lisinski* (Zagreb, 1969).

Lisitsyan, Pavel, Armenian baritone; b. Vladikavkaz, Nov. 6, 1911. He studied in Leningrad; sang at the Maly Theater there (1935–37); then was a member of the Armenian Opera Theater in Erevan (1937–40); in 1940 he joined the Bolshoi Theater in Moscow, remaining on its roster until 1966, but in the interim filled engagements all over Europe, in India, and in Japan. From 1967–73 he was on the faculty of the Erevan Cons. On March 3, 1960, he made his Metropolitan Opera debut in N.Y. as Amonasro in *Aida.* He was best known for his roles in Russian operas.

Liška, Zděnek, Czech composer; b. Smecno, March 16, 1922; d. Prague, July 13, 1983. He studied at the Prague Cons.; beginning in 1945 he was active as a composer for the State Studios of Documentary Films. For the Czech spectacle *Laterna Magica,* he wrote a modernistic violin concerto in which actors and musicians alternate with their screen images without loss of continuity. This work, first performed in Leningrad on Dec. 5, 1960, was featured in the presentation of *Laterna Magica* in N.Y. in the summer of 1964.

Lissa, Zofia, outstanding Polish musicologist; b. Lwow, Oct. 19, 1908; d. Warsaw, March 26, 1980. She studied with Chybinski. The outbreak of the war interrupted her further studies; in 1947–54 she was vice-president of the Union of Polish Composers; in 1957 was appointed a prof. of musicology at Warsaw Univ.; she also served as a member-correspondent with the Berlin Academy of Fine Arts (from 1957) and of the Academy of Sciences and Literature of Mainz (1972). She wrote voluminously on a variety of subjects connected with music history, education, broadcasting, film music, psychology of music, and social implications of music; publ. *The Outlines of Musical Science* (Lwow, 1934; new ed., 1948); *Some Problems of Musical Esthetics* (Cracow, 1952; in Japanese, 1956; in Chinese, 1962); *Essays on Musical Esthetics* (Cracow, 1964; in German, Berlin, 1969; in Hungarian, Budapest, 1973; in Serbian, Belgrade, 1973); of peculiar interest is her publication *The Marxist Method in Musicology* (Cracow, 1951) in which she propounds the interpretation of socialist realism and other doctrines of Marxist science as applied to both musical composition and musical evaluation. She contributed numerous articles on Polish music to *Die Musik in Geschichte und Gegenwart.*

Lissenko, Nicolai, significant Ukrainian composer; b. Grinki, near Kremenchug, March 22, 1842; d. Kiev, Nov. 6, 1912. He was the son of a landowner; grew up in a musical atmosphere; the singing of Ukrainian songs by local peasants produced a lasting impression on him, and determined his future as a national composer. He studied natural sciences at the Univ. of Kiev, graduating in 1864; was a justice of the peace in the Kiev district (1864–66); then abandoned his nonmusical pursuits and went to Leipzig, where he entered the Cons., and took courses with Richter (theory), Reinecke (piano), and Papperitz (organ). Returning to Russia in 1868, he taught piano at the Kiev Inst. of the Daughters of Nobility; in 1874–76 he studied orchestration with Rimsky-Korsakov in St. Petersburg. As early as 1868 he publ. his first collection of Ukrainian songs (printed in Leipzig); subsequent issues comprised 240 songs in 5 books, arranged according to their categories (Spring Songs, Midsummer Night Songs, Christmas Songs, etc.); he set to music a great number of poems from *Kobzar* by the Ukrainian poet Shevchenko (5 albums for 2, 3, and 4 voices; publ. in Kiev, 1870–97). In 1903, on the occasion of the 35th anniversary of the publication of his first collection of Ukrainian songs, Lissenko received a gift of 5,000 rubles from his admirers.

In his pamphlet *The Characteristics of the Ukrainian Dumki* (1874), Lissenko presents a theory that Ukrainian modes are derived from Greek music, and that antiphonal construction is one of the main features of Ukrainian songs, while the persistence of symmetrical rhythms distinguishes them from Russian songs. In his original compositions, Lissenko asserted himself as an ardent Ukrainian nationalist; he wrote several operas to Ukrainian librettos: *Chernomortsy* (1870); *Rizdviana Nitch,* after Gogol's *Christmas Eve Night* (1870); *Winter and Spring* (1880); *Utoplena,* after Gogol's *May Night* (1885); *Taras Bulba,* after Gogol's novel of the same name (1890; Kiev, Dec. 20, 1903; revised by Liatoshinsky and produced in Kiev in 1937); and his most popular stage work, after Kotlarevsky's play, *Natalka-Poltavka* (*Natalie from Poltava*), originally in the form of incidental music, then expanded into a 3-act opera (1890). He further wrote the opera *Sappho,* with a Ukrainian text, which was unsuccessful; and 2 children's operas, *Pan Kotsky* (*Puss-in-Boots;* 1891) and *Koza-Dereza* (Kiev, April 20, 1901). Other works include 2 cantatas: *The Torrents Roar* (1877) and *Rejoice, Field Unplowed* (1883); also *Cossack Scherzo* for Orch. (1872); *Capriccio elegiaco* for Violin and Orch. (1894); 2 rhapsodies on Ukrainian themes for Piano; vocal pieces.

List, Emanuel, Austrian bass; b. Vienna, March 22, 1888; d. there, June 21, 1967. He was a chorister at the Theater-an-der-Wien; studied voice in Vienna, and made his debut at the Volksoper there in 1922 as Méphistophélès in *Faust;* in 1923, was engaged at the Berlin State Opera, remaining there until 1933; specialized in Wagnerian roles. On Dec. 27, 1933, he made his first American appearance at the Metropolitan Opera in N.Y., as the Landgraf in *Tannhäuser;* in subsequent seasons, sang almost all Wagnerian bass roles; remained with the company until 1948; sang at Bayreuth and Salzburg; also appeared as a singer of German lieder.

List, Eugene, American pianist; b. Philadelphia, July 6, 1918. He was taken to Los Angeles when a year old; studied there at the Sutro-Seyler Studios and made his debut with the Los Angeles Phil. at the age of 12; later studied in Philadelphia with Olga Samaroff, and at the Juilliard Graduate School in N.Y.; made his N.Y. debut playing the solo part in the American premiere of Shostakovich's Piano

Concerto No. 2 with the Philadelphia Orch. (Dec. 12, 1934). As a sergeant in the U.S. Army, he was called upon to play the piano at the Potsdam Conference in July 1945, in the presence of Truman, Churchill, and Stalin. In 1964 he was appointed a prof. of piano at the Eastman School of Music in Rochester, N.Y.; left there in 1975; then joined the faculty of N.Y. Univ.

List, Kurt, Austrian-American musician; b. Vienna, June 21, 1913; d. Milan, Nov. 16, 1970. He studied music at the Vienna Academy of Music (M.A., 1936) and at the Univ. of Vienna (Ph.D., 1938); also took private lessons with Alban Berg (1932–35) and Anton von Webern (1935–38). He went to the U.S. in 1938; became active in the field of recording; wrote music criticism. After World War II he returned to Europe and lived mostly in Italy. His String Quartet and a Wind Quintet were performed in N.Y.; he also wrote 2 unperformed operas, *Der Triumph des Todes* and *Mayerling,* stylistically influenced by Richard Strauss.

Listemann, Bernhard, German-American violinist and conductor; b. Schlotheim, Aug. 28, 1841; d. Chicago, Feb. 11, 1917. He studied with Ferdinand David in Leipzig, with Vieuxtemps in Brussels, and with Joachim in Hannover; became concertmaster of the court orch. in Rudolstadt (1859–67); then went with his brother **Fritz Listemann** to America; in 1871–74, was concertmaster of the Thomas Orch. in N.Y.; in 1874 he went to Boston, where he founded the Phil. Club, and later the Phil. Orch., which he conducted until 1881, when he became concertmaster of the newly established Boston Symph. Orch.; meanwhile, he started the Listemann Quartet; also was director of the Listemann Concert Co. (1885–93). In 1893 he went to Chicago, where he taught violin at the Chicago College of Music.

Listemann, Franz, American cellist, son of **Bernhard Listemann;** b. New York, Dec. 17, 1873; d. Chicago, March 11, 1930. He studied with Fries in Boston, with Julius Klengel in Leipzig, and with Haussmann in Berlin. After a year as first cellist in the Pittsburgh Orch., he settled in N.Y.; he was soloist at the American premiere of Dvořák's Cello Concerto (1896).

Listemann, Fritz, German violinist, brother of **Bernhard Listemann;** b. Schlotheim, March 25, 1839; d. Boston, Dec. 28, 1909. Like his brother, he studied with Ferdinand David at the Leipzig Cons.; was a member of the court orch. at Rudolstadt (1858–67); he went with his brother to America; played violin in the Thomas Orch. in N.Y. (1871–74); then was in Boston, where he played in various chamber music organizations, and (from 1878) in his brother's Phil. Orch.; in 1881–85, was a violinist in the Boston Symph. Orch.; then played in the Listemann Concert Co. directed by his brother. He wrote 2 violin concertos; violin pieces.

Listemann, Paul, American violinist, son of **Bern-**

hard **Listemann;** b. Boston, Oct. 24, 1871; d. Chicago, Sept. 20, 1950. He was taught by his uncle **Fritz Listemann,** and also by his father; as a boy, participated in the various organizations directed by his father; then went to Germany, where he studied in Leipzig with Brodsky and in Berlin with Joachim; he was subsequently engaged as an orch. violinist in Pittsburgh, N.Y., etc.; was a member of the Metropolitan Opera Orch. from 1903 to 1920. In 1930 he moved to Chicago.

Listov, Konstantin, Soviet composer; b. Odessa, Sept. 19, 1900; d. Moscow, Sept. 6, 1983. He learned music by ear; then studied piano in Tsaritsin (Stalingrad) and in Saratov. In 1923 he went to Moscow and began to write music for the theater. His Red Army song *Tachanka* became immensely popular. He also wrote a Symph. in commemoration of the centennial of Lenin (1970).
   BIBLIOGRAPHY: A. Tishchenko, *Konstantin Listov* (Moscow, 1962).

Liszt, Franz (Ferencz), greatly celebrated Hungarian pianist and composer, creator of the symphonic poem and a reformer of modern piano technique; b. Raiding, near Ödenburg, Oct. 22, 1811; d. Bayreuth, July 31, 1886. His father was an excellent amateur musician and trained him in music from earliest childhood; at the age of 9 young Liszt played the difficult Piano Concerto in E-flat major by Ries. A group of Hungarian aristocrats provided sufficient funds (600 florins annually) to finance his musical education for 6 years. In 1822 the family moved to Vienna, where Liszt became a pupil of Czerny in piano and studied music theory with Salieri. Liszt's ambitious father was eager to introduce him to Beethoven, and as a legend (supported by Liszt himself in his later years) had it, Beethoven kissed him on the brow after Liszt played an arrangement of Beethoven's Trio, op. 97, for him entirely from memory. Beethoven's factotum, Schindler, made an earnest effort to persuade Beethoven to come to Liszt's concert in Vienna on April 13, 1823, but Beethoven did not acquiesce. After concerts in Munich and Stuttgart, young Liszt proceeded to Paris, where he applied for admission to the Cons.; but Cherubini, then director of the Paris Cons., who was opposed to infant prodigies, refused to accept him as a student, using as an excuse a rule forbidding the entrance of foreigners. As a consequence, Liszt took no more piano lessons; he studied composition for a short time with Paër and then with Reicha. At the age of 13 Liszt composed an operetta, *Don Sanche, ou Le Château d'Amour,* which was performed 4 times at the Académie Royale de Musique in 1825. Liszt's father died in 1827, and he settled in Paris. He was already well-known as a virtuoso pianist, and in Paris he moved in the highest circles of letters and arts; he was fascinated by the new Romantic spirit of the age; the socialistic ideas of St.-Simon, the revolutionary rumblings of 1830, greatly affected him. Paganini's spectacular performances on the violin inspired Liszt to emulate him in creating a new pianistic

technique that exploited all possible sonorities of the instrument; the corresponding ideas of Berlioz in enlarging orch. sonorities found in Liszt an enthusiastic supporter. At the same time Liszt never abandoned the basic Romantic feeling for music as an expressive art, the voice of the human soul translated into musical tones; in this he was an ardent companion of Chopin, his close contemporary. He formed a liaison with the Countess d'Agoult, who wrote literary works under the nom de plume of Daniel Stern, and went to live with her in Geneva (1835–36). Three children were born to them: Cosima, the younger of 2 daughters, eventually became the wife of Richard Wagner. After his Geneva sojourn Liszt set out on a concert tour through Europe, which proved to be a series of triumphs. To underline the narrative Romantic quality of his playing and his compositions, he accepted the suggestion of his London friend Frederick Beale to use the word "recital," and the term became universally accepted. Since Liszt himself acknowledged that in his piano works he set Paganini as a model, it was only natural that he was often described as the "Paganini of the piano." But he maintained that his virtuosity was but a means of re-creating great music, and held that the interpreter's duty was to reveal the composer's innermost intentions. His spiritual affinity with Beethoven moved him to superlative renditions of the master's piano sonatas; but he was also able to give intimate interpretations of Chopin. Withal, Liszt was a man of the world, a practical musician who was willing to give to his public what was expected of him. On stage he was often an actor; he wore white gloves, as was the custom of the day, and took them off ceremoniously in front of the audience; at some concerts he had 2 pianos on the stage, and played a group of pieces on each in alternation so that his hands could be seen from every area of the audience. He included in some of his programs free improvisations on themes proffered to him by musical amateurs. His private life underwent another upheaval when he formed a new liaison with the Polish Princess Carolyne Sayn-Wittgenstein, who took up residence with Liszt; she was very influential in turning him toward established religion. Liszt became a Freemason in 1841; a tertiary of St. Francis in 1857. In 1865 Pope Pius IX conferred on him the dignity of Abbé. In 1879 he received the tonsure and the 4 minor orders (ostuary, lector, exorcist, and acolyte) and an honorary canonry; however, he was never ordained a priest, and could not say Mass, or hear confession. But he could discard his cassock and even marry if he so wished. He practically abandoned his concert career in 1842, when he accepted the position of court Kapellmeister at Weimar. When Wagner was exiled from Saxony, Liszt arranged the production of his opera *Lohengrin* in Weimar on Aug. 28, 1850; he also was instrumental in supervising performances of Wagner's *Der fliegende Holländer* and *Tannhäuser* and the music of Berlioz. In 1861 he left Weimar and lived for the most part in Rome. In 1870 he returned to Weimar to conduct a centennial Beethoven festival there. In 1875 he was made president of the New Hungarian Academy of Music in Budapest; the last years of his life were spent in Weimar, Budapest, and Rome. In Weimar he formed a faithful retinue of loyal and admiring students, and he displayed great interest in new movements in musical composition. He was an eager correspondent; his letters, many of them still unpubl., number in the thousands, written in French and German, in longhand; he did not employ a secretary. According to a will he made in 1860, Liszt's MSS passed into the possession of the Princess Carolyne Sayn-Wittgenstein; after her death in 1887, they were inherited by her daughter Marie Hohenlohe-Schillingsfürst. She in turn left these materials to the Weimar court; eventually they became part of the Liszt Museum.

Liszt's achievement as a composer is of revolutionary significance. He created the transcendental style of piano playing and introduced a new concept of the spiritual relationship between music and literature; he was allied with Wagner in the movement that was called, both in derision and admiration, *Zukunftsmusik,* the music of the future. The term applied to a mystical synthesis of the arts, which for Liszt implied the adoption of a programmatic design in a musical composition and a liberation from the classical rules of musical form. Such a synthesis was accomplished by Liszt in the creation of the symph. poem, explicitly descriptive and connected with a literary work or a philosophical idea. "Music of the future" also embraced the field of harmony, modulation, and melody. Both Liszt and Wagner greatly enhanced the type of chromatic harmony resulting from instant modulation into unrelated keys. In the last years of his life, Liszt experimented with melodic patterns, such as those derived from the whole-tone scale, which tend to obscure tonality, and with harmonic combinations rich in dissonance produced by long-delayed resolutions. Liszt defied tradition when he boldly outlined the main subject of his *Faust Symphony,* formed of 4 arpeggiated, chromatically descending, augmented triads, the whole aggregating into 12 different notes. In his orchestration he summoned large sonorities following the precedent of Berlioz. It was this unremitting flow of sound that outraged the music critics of Liszt's day and moved them to denounce Liszt as a purveyor of noise in the guise of music. But Liszt was also capable of writing music of intimate lyric quality; his songs to German or French words possess the deepest lyrical expressiveness; his piano pieces distill the poetry and the drama of the literary program to the finest gradation of sentiment. His B-minor Piano Sonata introduces a new dimension into this classical form: in place of an orderly succession and development of basic themes, Liszt cultivates here an association of motifs, thus transforming the work into a musical narrative. His 3 albums of *Années de pèlerinage* for piano are tone paintings, evoking the scene with pictorial vividness. His 2 piano concertos, his brilliant *Hungarian Rhapsodies,* his *Mephisto-Waltz,* and particularly his *Études d'exécution transcendante,* are unsurpassed in their sonorous grandeur and authentic virtuosity. In his transcriptions of Schubert's and Schumann's songs, he transmutes their vocal lines and accompanying harmonies into new tonal creations. Finally, his flamboyant arrangements of operatic arias by Auber, Donizetti, Gounod, Meyerbeer, Mozart, Rossini, Verdi, and Wagner are exhibitions of the highest art of transmutation from one medium into another. Liszt never wrote a full-fledged opera, but he composed oratorios that are operatic in substance and presentation. His many sacred works enhance the originality of his secular harmonies without losing their devotional character. Liszt was deeply conscious of his Hungarian heritage, but he spent most of his life in France, Germany, and Italy. Contrary to the natural assumption that Liszt, being the greatest Hungarian composer, spoke the language, it appears that his mother tongue was German, and that he could not converse in Hungarian at all; in later years he took lessons in Hungarian with Father Zsigmond Vadász, but abandoned the attempt after a few sessions. He never went into the countryside in quest of the folk origins of Hungarian music, as the 2 modern Hungarians Kodály and Bartók did; rather, he gathered the ethnic materials that he so brilliantly used in his *Hungarian Rhapsodies* and other works of Hungarian inspiration from Gypsy bands he frequently heard in public places in Budapest; in one extraordinary instance, he borrowed the theme for the most famous of these, No. 2, from an unpubl. work by an obscure Austrian musician named Heinrich Ehrlich, who had sent him his MS on approval; Ehrlich recounted this episode in his *30 Jahre Künstlerleben* (1893).

WORKS: FOR THE STAGE: *Don Sanche, ou Le Château d'Amour,* one-act operetta, a juvenile work (1825; the score, believed to have been lost, was discovered in 1903; the overture and an aria from it were publ. in the May 1904 issue of *Die Musik*).

FOR ORCH.: Symph. poems (all conducted for the first time by Liszt himself, except where otherwise noted): *Ce qu'on entend sur la montagne,* after Victor Hugo (Weimar, Jan. 7, 1857); *Tasso, Lamento e Trionfo* (Weimar, Aug. 28, 1849; revised version, Weimar, April 19, 1854); *Les Préludes,* after Lamartine's "Méditations poétiques" (Weimar, Feb. 23, 1854); *Orpheus* (Weimar, Feb. 16, 1854); *Prometheus* (Weimar, Aug. 24, 1850); *Mazeppa,* after Victor Hugo (Weimar, April 16, 1854); *Festklänge* (Weimar, Nov. 9, 1854); *Héroïde funèbre* (sketched in 1830 as *Symphonie révolutionnaire;* revised and orchestrated in 1850; Breslau, Nov. 10, 1857, Moritz Schön conducting); *Hungaria* (sketched in 1848; revised in 1856; first perf., Budapest, Sept. 8, 1856); *Hamlet* (1858; Sondershausen, July 2, 1876, Max Erdmannsdörfer conducting); *Hunnenschlacht,* after Kaulbach's painting (Weimar, Dec. 29, 1857); *Die Ideale,* after Schiller (Weimar, Sept. 5, 1857); *Eine Faust-Symphonie,* in 3 characteristic pictures, after Goethe, with a choral finale (Weimar, Sept. 5, 1857); a *Symphony* to Dante's *Divina commedia,* with a Female Chorus (Dresden, Nov. 7, 1867); *2 Episodes* from Lenau's "Faust" (1860–61); *2 Mephisto Waltzes* (1860, 1880); *3 odes funèbres,* with Male Chorus (1860–66); *Salve Polonia* (1863); *Festival March* for Goethe's jubilee (1849); for Piano and Orch.: Concerto No. 1, in E-flat, nicknamed the "Triangle Concerto" because of the prominent use of a triangle solo (1849; revised 1853; Weimar, Feb. 16, 1855; Berlioz conducting, composer at the piano); Concerto No. 2, in A major (1848; revised 1856–61; Weimar, Jan. 7, 1857; Hans von Bronsart, soloist, composer conducting); *Fantasie* on motifs from Beethoven's *Ruins of Athens* (Budapest, June 1, 1853); *Totentanz*, paraphrase on *Dies irae* (1849; revised 1853–59; The Hague, April 15, 1865, Hans von Bülow, soloist).

FOR PIANO SOLO: *Album d'un voyageur* (3 books); *3 apparitions; Rondo sur un thème espagnol (El Contrabandista); Napolitana; Rhapsodie espagnole* (arranged for Piano and Orch. by Busoni); *3 études de concert; 2 études de concert (Waldesrauschen, Gnomenreigen); Harmonies poétiques et religeuses* (10 pieces); *Liebesträume,* 3 nocturnes (originally they were songs); *3 sonetti del Petrarca; Valse impromptu; Mazurka brillante;* 2 *Polonaises; Scherzo and March; Grand solo de concert* (also for 2 Pianos); *Grand galop chromatique; 12 grandes études* (originally publ. as *Etudes en forme de 12 exercices pour piano); Ab irato, étude de perfectionnement;* Sonata in B minor (1854); *Berceuse; 2 ballades; 3 valses-caprices; 6 consolations; 20 Hungarian Rhapsodies* (No. 3 is the *Héroïde funèbre;* No. 9, the *Carnaval de Pest;* No. 15, the *Rákoczy March;* No. 20 is unpubl.; the MS is in the Liszt Museum at Weimar); *3 airs suisses; Années de pèlerinage* (3 series; contains such famous pieces as *Au bord d'une source, Venezia e Napoli,* and *Les Jeux d'eau à la Villa d'Este;* Book I is a revised version of Book I of the *Album d'un voyageur); Ave Maria; 3 élégies; 12 études d'exécution transcendante; Mephisto-Waltz* (originally for Orch.; 3 versions for Piano Solo; No. 4, unpubl., subtitled "Bagatelle sans tonalité"); *Via Crucis; Epithalamium; Bülow March; 3 valses oubliées; valse élégiaque; Weihnachtsbaum* (12 pieces); *Mosonyi's Grabgeleit; Mephisto-Polka; Impromptu* in F-sharp; 2 *légendes: St. François d'Assise prédicant aux oiseaux* and *St. François de Paule marchant sur les flots; La Lugubre Gondole; Heroischer Marsch im ungarischen Stil; 2 arabesques; Czardas obstiné; Czardas macabre; Hymne du Pape; 7 Ungarische Bildnisse; Rhapsody, nach Siebenbürgischen und Walachischen Motiven; Phantasy and Fugue on B-A-C-H;* Variations on a theme from Bach's B-minor Mass; Variations on Bach's prelude *Weinen, Klagen; Technische Studien* (12 books); transcriptions of Beethoven's symphs., of Berlioz's *Symphonie fantastique, Harold en Italie,* and overtures to *Les Francs-juges* and *King Lear,* of Wagner's overture to *Tannhäuser,* of 6 of Chopin's *Chants polonais,* of 10 songs by Robert Franz, 7 songs by Mendelssohn, songs from several cycles by Schubert (*Schwanengesang, Winterreise, Geistliche Lieder, Müllerlieder,* also *Die Forelle,* etc.), Schumann's *Liebeslied,* and other songs, etc.

VOCAL WORKS: *Missa solemnis* (the *Gran* festival Mass); *Hungarian Coronation Mass;* Mass in C minor, with Organ; *Missa choralis* in A minor, with Organ; Requiem; 3 oratorios: *Die Legende von der Heiligen Elisabeth; Christus; Stanislaus* (unfinished); 9 choruses, with Organ; *Die Seligkeiten* for Baritone Solo, Chorus, and Organ; *Pater noster* for Mixed Chorus and Organ; *Pater noster* and *Ave Maria* for Men's Voices and Organ; *Psalm 13* for Tenor Solo, Chorus, and Orch.; *Psalm 18* for Men's Chorus, Orch., and Organ; *Psalm 23* for Tenor (or Soprano) Solo, with Harp (or Piano) and Organ (or Harmonium); *Psalm 116* for Soli, Men's (or Mixed) Chorus, Organ, and Orch.; *Psalm 137* for Solo, Women's Chorus, Violin, Harp, Piano, and Organ; *Christus ist geboren* for Chorus, with Organ; *An den heiligen Franziskus* for Men's Voices, Organ, Trombones, and Drums; *Les Morts* for Men's Chorus and Orch.; numerous minor sacred compositions; cantatas: *Die Glocken des Strassburger Münsters, Die heilige Cäcile, An die Künstler* (for Soli, Men's Chorus, and Orch.), *Hungaria* (for Soli, Mixed Chorus, and Orch.; has nothing in common with the symph. poem bearing the same title; score lost for many years, discovered by P. Raabe in 1912); *Zur Säcular-Feier Beethovens; Festalbum* (for Goethe's 100th birthday); *Festchor* (for the unveiling of the Herder monument, Weimar, 1850); numerous 4-part men's choruses (*Das Lied der Begeisterung; Weimars Volkslied; Was ist das Deutsche Vaterland?,* with Piano; *Festgesang,* with Organ; about 60 songs with Piano, many strikingly beautiful (*Du bist wie eine Blume, Es muss ein wunderbares sein, Die Macht der Musik, Jeanne d'Arc au bûcher*). Vol. 2 of Peter Raabe's biography (1931) includes a complete catalogue of works. Thematic catalogues of Liszt's works were publ. by Breitkopf & Härtel in 1855 and 1876; a complete catalogue of the publ. works, by A. Göllerich, appeared in the *Neue Zeitschrift für Musik* (1887–88); a *Chronologisch-systematisches Verzeichnis* by L. Friwitzer was publ. in the *Wiener Musikalische Chronik* (Nov. 1887–March 1888).

In 1905 plans were made to publ. Liszt's complete works, to be issued periodically by Breitkopf & Härtel of Leipzig. Vol. I appeared in 1907; by 1936 Breitkopf & Härtel had issued 34 vols., but world conditions put an end to the project. In 1950 the Liszt Society of London, with E.J. Dent as president, began to issue a new series, but by 1968 only 56 vols. had appeared, 5 of them devoted to Liszt's lesser-known piano works, one to selected songs. A Neue Liszt-Ausgabe was begun in 1970 under the editorial direction of Zoltán Gárdonyi and István Szelényi, and by 1977, 8 vols. had been issued jointly by the Bärenreiter Verlag of Kassel and Editio Musica of Budapest.

WRITINGS: *De la fondation Goethe* (Goethestiftung) *à Weimar* (1851); *Lohengrin et Tannhäuser de Richard Wagner* (1851; also in German); *Frédéric Chopin* (1852; 2nd ed., in French, Leipzig, 1879; in Eng., 1901); *Über Fields Notturnos* (1859); *Des Bohémiens et de leur musique en Hongrie* (in French, 1859; also in Hungarian, German; in Eng. as *The Gypsy in Music); Robert Franz* (1872); *Keine Zwischenaktmusik mehr* (1879). His *Gesammelte Schriften* were ed. by Lina Ramann and publ. in 6 vols. (Leipzig, 1800–83); also a selection as *Volksausgabe* (4 vols., Leipzig, 1910); J. Kapp publ. an *Allgemeine Inhaltsübersicht* with full indices (1910).

BIBLIOGRAPHY: BIOGRAPHY: J.W. Christern, *Franz Liszt* (Hamburg, 1841); Lina Ramann, *Franz*

Liszt als Künstler und Mensch (3 vols., Leipzig, 1880–94; Eng. trans. of vol. 1, London, 1882); R. Pohl, *Franz Liszt: Studien und Erinnerungen* (Leipzig, 1883); L. Nohl, *Liszt* (Leipzig, 1884; Part 2 by A. Göllerich, 1887; Eng. trans., Chicago, 1887); T.C. Martin, *Franz Liszt* (London, 1886); E. Reuss, *Franz Liszt* (Dresden, 1898); R. Louis, *Franz Liszt* (Berlin, 1900); A.O. von Pozsony, *Liszt und Hans von Bülow* (Munich, 1900); M.-D. Calvocoressi, *Franz Liszt* (Paris, 1905; Eng. trans., in *Musical Observer*, N.Y., 1910–11); A. Göllerich, *Franz Liszt* (Berlin, 1908); J. Kapp, *Richard Wagner und Franz Liszt: Eine Freundschaft* (Berlin, 1908); idem, *Franz Liszt. Eine Biographie* (Berlin, 1909; 20th ed., 1924; a standard biography); A.W. Gottschalg, *Franz Liszt in Weimar und seine letzten Lebensjahre* (publ. posthumously, 1910); J. Chantavoine, *Liszt* (Paris, 1910; 5th ed., 1928); R. Ledos de Beaufort, *Franz Liszt: The Story of His Life* (Boston, 1910; with a list of works and pupils); A. Hervey, *Franz Liszt and His Music* (London, 1911); J. Kapp, *Franz Liszt und die Frauen* (Berlin, 1911); La Mara, *Liszt und die Frauen* (Leipzig, 1911); Cosima Wagner, *Franz Liszt: Ein Gedenkblatt von seiner Tochter* (Munich, 1911); J.G. Huneker, *Franz Liszt* (N.Y., 1911; in German, Munich, 1922); F. Barberio, *Liszt e la principessa de Sayn-Wittgenstein* (Rome, 1912); A. von Schorn, *Zwei Menschenalter, Erinnerungen und Briefe aus Weimar und Rom* (Stuttgart, 1913); Sir A. Mackenzie, *Liszt* (London, 1913); B. Schrader, *Franz Liszt* (Leipzig, 1914); K. Grunsky, *Franz Liszt* (Leipzig, 1924); R. Wetz, *Franz Liszt* (Leipzig, 1925); F. Corder, *Liszt* (London, 1925; new ed., 1933); Guy de Pourtalès, *La Vie de Franz Liszt* (Paris, 1926; also in Eng., N.Y., 1926); C. van Wessem, *Franz Liszt* (The Hague, 1927); Marie d'Agoult, *Erinnerungen an Franz Liszt* (ed. by Siegfried Wagner; 2 vols., 1928); A. Stradal, *Erinnerungen an Franz Liszt* (Bern, 1929); M. Herwegh, *Au banquet des dieux: Franz Liszt, Richard Wagner et leurs amis* (Paris, 1931); P. Raabe, *Franz Liszt* (2 vols., Stuttgart and Berlin, 1931); B. Kellermann, *Erinnerungen an Franz Liszt* (1932); Sacheverell Sitwell, *Liszt* (London, 1934; revised 1955); R. Bory, *Liszt et ses enfants: Blandine, Cosima et Daniel* (Paris, 1936); A. de Hevésy, *Liszt, ou Le Roi Lear de la musique* (Paris, 1936); R. Hill, *Liszt* (London, 1936); H. Engel, *Liszt* (Potsdam, 1936); Blandine Ollivier, *Liszt, le musicien passionné* (Paris, 1936); Z. Harsányi, *Magyar Rapszódia: Franz Liszt* (Budapest, 1936; in Eng., London, 1936, as *Hungarian Melody*, and N.Y., 1937, as *Immortal Franz*); E. von Liszt, *Franz Liszt* (Vienna, 1937; family documents, etc.); M. Tibaldi Chiesa, *Vita romantica di Liszt* (Milan, 1937); C. Aragonnès, *Marie d'Agoult: Une Destinée romantique* (Paris, 1938); P. Raabe, *Wege zu Liszt* (Regensburg, 1943); Jacques Vier, *La Comtesse d'Agoult et son temps* (6 vols., Paris, 1955–63); Y. Milstein, *Liszt* (Moscow, 1956); J. Rousselot, *Franz Liszt* (London, 1960); C. Rostand, *Liszt* (Paris, 1960); W.G. Armando, *Franz Liszt: Eine Biographie* (Hamburg, 1961); J. Hankiss, *Wenn Liszt ein Tagebuch geführt hätte* (Budapest, 1961); M. Bagby, *Liszt's Weimar* (N.Y., 1961); A. Leroy, *Franz Liszt* (Lausanne, 1967); C.V. Lachmund, *Mein Leben mit Franz Liszt* (Esch-

wege, 1970); E. Perényi, *Liszt: The Artist as Romantic Hero* (Boston, 1974); D. Legány, *Liszt and His Country 1869–1873* (Budapest, 1983); A. Walker, *Franz Liszt: Vol. I, The Virtuoso Years, 1811–1847* (London, 1983). Pictorial biographies: R. Bory, *La Vie de Franz Liszt par l'image* (Geneva, 1936); W. Füssmann and Béla Mátéka, *Franz Liszt. Ein Künstlerleben in Wort und Bild* (Berlin, 1936); Z. László and B. Mátéka, *Franz Liszt: Sein Leben in Bildern* (Budapest, 1967).

APPRECIATION, CRITICISM: W. Lenz, *Die grossen Pianoforte Virtuosen unserer Zeit* (Berlin, 1872; Eng. trans., N.Y., 1899); L. Nohl, *Beethoven, Liszt, Wagner* (Vienna, 1874); R. Wagner, *Über Franz Liszts Symphonische Dichtungen,* in *Gesammelte Schriften und Dichtungen* (vol. 5; Leipzig, 1883); Otto Lessmann, *Franz Liszt: Eine Huldigung* (in German and Eng.; N.Y., 1883); B. Vogel, *Franz Liszt als Lyriker* (Leipzig, 1887); A. Habets, *A. Borodin et Franz Liszt* (Paris, 1893; Eng. trans., London, 1895); O. Bie, *Das Klavier und seine Meister* (Munich, 1898); E. Segnitz, *Franz Liszt und Rom* (Leipzig, 1901); H. Gerstenberg, *Aus Weimars nachklassischer Zeit* (Hamburg, 1901); E.O. Nodnagel, *Jenseits von Wagner und Liszt* (Königsberg, 1902); La Mara, *Aus der Glanzzeit der Weimarer Altenburg* (Leipzig, 1906); F.H. Clark, *Liszts Offenbarung: Schlüssel zur Freiheit des Individuums* (Berlin, 1907); A. de Angelis, *Franz Liszt a Roma* (Turin, 1911); A. Kohut, *Franz Liszt in seinen Wirken als Mensch und als Tonkünstler* (Leipzig, 1911); A. von Schorn, *Das nachklassische Weimar unter der Regierungszeit Karl Friedrichs und Maria Paulownas* (Weimar, 1911; also *Zweiter Teil: Unter der Regierungszeit von Karl Alexander und Sophia,* Weimar, 1912); E. Segnitz, *Liszts Kirchenmusik* (Langensalza, 1911); E. Hughes, "Liszt as a Lieder Composer," *Musical Quarterly* (April 1917); O.G. Sonneck, "Liszt's Huldigungsmarsch and Weimar's Volkslied," *Musical Quarterly* (Jan. 1918); C. Boissier, *Liszt pédagogue* (Paris, 1928); J. Heinrichs, *Über den Sinn der Lisztschen Programmusik* (Kempen, 1929); H. Arminski, *Die ungarischen Fantasien von Franz Liszt* (Vienna, 1929); T. Weber, *Die symphonischen Dichtungen Liszts* (Vienna, 1929); E. Major, *Liszt's Hungarian Rhapsodies* (in Hungarian; Budapest, 1929); J. Bergfeld, *Die formale Struktur der symphonischen Dichtungen Franz Liszts* (Eisenach, 1931); Z. Gárdonyi, *Die ungarischen Stileigentümlichkeiten in den musikalischen Werken Franz Liszts* (Berlin, 1931); K. Isóz, *Liszt and Budapest* (in Hungarian; Budapest, 1931); H. Dobiey, *Die Klaviertechnik des jungen Liszt* (Berlin, 1931); I. Philipp, *La Technique de Liszt* (2 vols.; Paris, 1932); R. Kokai, *Franz Liszt in seinen frühen Klavierwerken* (Leipzig, 1933); E. Newman, *The Man Liszt: A Study of the Tragi-Comedy of a Soul Divided against Itself* (London, 1934); H. Westerby, *Liszt the Composer and His Piano Works* (London, 1936); Liszt issue of the *Musical Quarterly* (July 1936); G. Falk, *Liszt Breviarium* (in Hungarian; Budapest, 1936); E. Haraszti, "Franz Liszt—Author Despite Himself," *Musical Quarterly* (Oct. 1947); H. Searle, *The Music of Liszt* (London, 1954); E.N. Waters, "Liszt and Longfellow," *Musical Quarterly* (Jan. 1955); P. Rehberg, *Franz Liszt: Die Geschichte seines Leben, Scheffens und Wirkens* (Zürich, 1961); Alan Walker, ed., *Franz Liszt: The Man and His Music* (N.Y., 1970). Separate analyses of all the larger works, including the oratorios, masses, and Psalms, are found in H. Kretzschmar's *Führer durch den Konzertsaal* (3 vols., Leipzig, 1887; 4th ed., 1913); in Breitkopf & Härtel's *Kleiner Konzertführer* (Leipzig) and Schlesinger's *Der Musikführer* and *Meisterführer* (Berlin).

CORRESPONDENCE: *Briefwechsel zwischen Wagner und Liszt* (2 vols., Leipzig, 1887; 2nd ed., 1900; Eng. trans., London, 1888; 2nd ed., 1897, with index; the first 2 eds. contain only the letters from 1841–61, and many passages referring to persons still living at the time of publication were omitted; in the 3rd ed., prepared by Erich Kloss in 1910, all letters up to Wagner's death are included, and the omitted portions restored); La Mara, *Franz Liszts Briefe* (8 vols., Leipzig, 1893–1905; about 2,500 letters in the original French or German; those to Carolyne Sayn-Wittgenstein, in vols. 4–7, all in French); C. Bache, *Letters of Franz Liszt* (2 vols., London, 1894; in Eng. trans.); La Mara, *Briefwechsel zwischen Franz Liszt und Hans von Bülow* (Leipzig, 1898); R. von Seydlitz, *Ungedruckte Originalbriefe des Meisters an G. Freiherrn von Seydlitz* (Dresden, 1902); A. Stern, *Franz Liszts Briefe an Karl Gille* (Leipzig, 1903); La Mara, *Franz Liszt et Charles-Alexandre, grand-duc de Saxe: Correspondance* (Leipzig, 1909); C.A. René, 48 letters to A.W. Gottschalg, in *Franz Liszt in Weimar und seine letzten Lebensjahre* (1910); E. Reuss, *Franz Liszt in seinen Briefen* (Stuttgart, 1911); W. von Csapó, *Franz Liszts Briefe an Baron Anton Augusz, 1846–1878* (Budapest, 1911); N. de Gutmannsthal, *Souvenirs de Franz Liszt: Lettres inédites* (Leipzig, 1913); K. von Schlözer, *Römische Briefe, 1864–69* (Stuttgart, 1913); P. Raabe, *Briefwechsel zwischen Franz Liszt und dem Grossherzog Karl Alexander von Sachsen* (1918); A. Orel, *Briefe Liszts* (Vienna, 1930); correspondence with Mme. d'Agoult (in French), publ. by Daniel Ollivier, first series, 1833–40 (1933), 2nd series, 1840–64 (1934); correspondence with Liszt's daughter, Blandine, publ. by Ollivier, in *Revue des Deux Mondes* (Dec. 15, 1935; Jan. 1, 1936); *The Letters of Franz Liszt to Marie Sayn-Wittgenstein*, ed. by H.E. Hugo (N.Y., 1953). Liszt's letters to Olga von Meyendorff (1871–86), trans. by William B. Tyler, were publ., with an introduction and notes by Edward N. Waters (Washington, D.C., 1978). See also La Mara, *Briefe hervorragender Zeitgenossen an Franz Liszt* (3 vols., Leipzig, 1895–1904). For a comprehensive bibliography, see Charles Suttoni, "Franz Liszt's Published Correspondence: An Annotated Bibliography," *Fontes Artis Musicae*, XXVI (1979).

Litaize, Gaston, French composer and organist; b. Ménil-sur-Belvitte, Aug. 11, 1909. He was blind from infancy; studied at the National Inst. of the Blind; also at the Paris Cons.; won the 2nd Prix de Rome (unprecedented for a blind person); was appointed organist at the church of St.-François Xavier in Paris; also was on the staff of the National Inst. of the Blind. In the autumn of 1957 he made his first American tour as a concert organist. He holds the post of organ teacher at the Inst. Nationale des Jeunes Aveugles in Paris. He composed a number of organ pieces and several sacred choruses, among them *Messe solennelle en français* (1966).

Literes Carrión, Antonio, Spanish composer; b. Arta, Majorca(?), June 18, 1673; d. Madrid, Jan. 18, 1747. He was a composer and bass-viol player at the Royal Choir School in Madrid under Charles II, Philip V, and Ferdinand VI. In 1693 he was appointed to the royal chapel as bassist. After the fire at the old Alcazar in Madrid on Christmas Eve of 1734, Literes and Nebra were charged with the reconstruction of musical MSS that were damaged or completely burned. They also wrote new music for church services to replace the material destroyed. Literes composed excellent church music (14 Psalms, 8 Magnificats, etc.); some of his sacred works are reprinted in Eslava's *Lira Sacro-Hispana;* he also wrote an opera, *Los elementos*, and a zarzuela, *Accis y Galatea* (1709). His son **Antonio Literes Montalbo** (d. Madrid, Dec. 2, 1768) was a composer and organist under Ferdinand VI.

BIBLIOGRAPHY: N.A. Solar Quintes, "Antonio Literes Carrión y sus hijos," *Anuario Musical*, vol. 5 (Barcelona, 1950); F. Pedrell, *Teatro lírico español* (vols. 2 and 4); J. Nin, *Classiques espagnols du chant* (Paris, 1926).

Litinsky, Genrik (Heinrich), distinguished Russian composer; b. Lipovetz, March 17, 1901. He studied composition with Glière at the Moscow Cons., graduating in 1928; subsequently taught there (1928–43); among his students were Khrennikov, Zhiganov, Arutiunian, and other Soviet composers. In 1945 he went to Yakutsk as an ethnomusicologist; in collaboration with native Siberian composers he produced the first national Yakut operas, based on authentic folk melorhythms and arranged in contemporary harmonies according to the precepts of socialist realism: *Nurgun Botur* (Yakutsk, June 29, 1947); *Sygy Kyrynastyr* (Yakutsk, July 4, 1947); *Red Shaman* (Yakutsk, Dec. 9, 1967). He wrote 3 Yakut ballets: *Altan's Joy* (Yakutsk, June 19, 1963); *Field Flower* (Yakutsk, July 2, 1947); *Crimson Kerchief* (Yakutsk, Jan. 9, 1968). Other works include: Symph. (1928); *Dagestan Suite* for Orch. (1931); Trumpet Concerto (1934); *Festive Rhapsody* for Orch. (1966); 12 string quartets (1923–61); String Octet (1944); 12 concert studies for Cello (1967); 12 concert studies for Trumpet and Piano (1968); 15 concert studies for Oboe and Piano (1969). He publ. the valuable manuals *Problems of Polyphony* (3 vols., 1965, 1966, 1967), ranging from pentatonic to dodecaphonic patterns and from elementary harmonization to polytonality; also *Formation of Imitation in the Strict Style* (1970). In 1964 he was named a People's Artist of the Yakut Soviet Socialist Republic and of the Tatar Autonomous Soviet Socialist Republic.

Litolff, Henry Charles, pianist, composer, and publisher; b. London (of an Alsatian father and English mother), Feb. 6, 1818; d. Colombes, near Paris, Aug. 6, 1891. A precocious pianist, he studied with Moscheles; made his professional debut in London on July 24, 1832, at the age of 14. An early marriage (at 17) forced him to seek a livelihood in Paris, where he attracted attention by his brilliant concerts; then he became an itinerant musician, traveling in Poland, Germany, and the Netherlands; was in Vienna during the Revolution of 1848, and became involved, so that he was compelled to flee. He then settled in Braunschweig; after the termination of his first marriage, he married the widow of the music publisher Meyer, acquiring the business. Litolff was one of the pioneers in the publication of cheap editions of classical music (Collections Litolff). In 1860 he turned over the firm to his adopted son, **Theodor Litolff** (1839–1912). Then he went to Paris, marrying for a 3rd time (the Comtesse de Larochefoucauld); after her death (1870) he married a 15-year-old girl.

WORKS: Besides his business pursuits, he was a prolific composer; 115 of his works were publ.; of these, the most famous is the overture *Robespierre* (Paris, Feb. 2, 1870), which carries the idea of programmatic music to its utmost limit, with a vivid description of Robespierre's execution (drumbeats, etc.); operas: *Die Braut von Kynast* (Braunschweig, 1847); *Les Templiers* (Brussels, Jan. 25, 1886); *Héloïse et Abélard* (Paris, Oct. 17, 1872); oratorio, *Ruth et Booz* (1869); *Szenen aus Goethes Faust* for Soli, Chorus, and Orch.; 5 *Concertos-Symphonies* for piano and Orch., of which the 4th contains a brilliant scherzo which became a perennial favorite; *Eroica*, violin concerto; a funeral march for Meyerbeer; 3 piano trios; 6 *études de concert* for Piano; many character pieces for piano, of which *Chant de la fileuse* became popular.

BIBLIOGRAPHY: H. Berlioz, *Les Musiciens et la Musique* (Paris, 1878); P. Magnette, *Litolff* (Paris, 1914); T. Blair, *Henry Charles Litolff (1818–1891): His Life and Piano Music* (Diss., Univ. of Iowa, 1968).

Litta, Giulio, Italian composer; b. Milan, 1822; d. Vedano, near Monza, May 29, 1891. A composer of precocious talent and excellent training, he produced an opera at 20, *Bianca di Santafiora* (Milan, Jan. 2, 1843), followed by 6 more operas: *Sardanapalo* (Milan, Sept. 2, 1844); *Maria Giovanna* (Turin, Oct. 28, 1851); *Edita di Lorno* (Genoa, June 1, 1853); *Il Viandante* (Milan, April 17, 1873); *Raggio d'amore* (Milan, April 6, 1879); *Il violino di Cremona* (Milan, April 18, 1882). He also wrote an oratorio, *La Passione;* church music; songs.

Litvinne, Félia (real name, **Françoise-Jeanne Schütz**), Russian soprano; b. St. Petersburg, 1861; d. Paris, Oct. 12, 1936. She studied in Paris with Mme. Barth-Banderoli and Victor Maurel; made her debut there in 1885 at the Théâtre des Italiens; then sang at the Academy of Music in N.Y. with Mapleson's company; made successful appearances in St. Petersburg, Moscow, and Italy; returned to Paris, where she sang at the Opéra-Comique and the Thé-

âtre Lyrique de la Gaîté; also sang at Monte Carlo, La Scala, Covent Garden, and the Metropolitan Opera House; made a tour of South America. In 1927 she was appointed prof. of singing at the American Cons. of Fontainebleau. She publ. her memoirs, *Ma vie et mon art* (Paris, 1933).

Litzau, Johannes Barend, Dutch organist and composer; b. Rotterdam, Sept. 9, 1822; d. there, July 18, 1893. He studied with J.B. Bremer and B. Tours; in 1855, succeeded Bremer as organist of the Lutheran church in Rotterdam. He founded an organ school and wrote a number of organ works in the Classical style: 3 organ sonatas; *Konzertsatz im strengen Stil mit 4 Subjekten,* etc.; also a cantata, *Sneeuw-vermaak.*

Litzmann, Berthold, German writer on music; b. Kiel, April 18, 1857; d. Munich, Oct. 13, 1926. He wrote an exhaustive biography, *Clara Schumann, Ein Künstlerleben, nach Tagebüchern und Briefen* (3 vols., Leipzig, 1902–10; Eng. trans., 1913); also prepared for publication the correspondence between Brahms and Clara Schumann (2 vols., Leipzig, 1927; Eng. trans., N.Y., 1927).

Liuzzi, Fernando, Italian composer and musicologist; b. Senigallia, Dec. 19, 1884; d. Florence, Oct. 6, 1940. He studied in Bologna with Fano, and at the Liceo di Santa Cecilia in Rome; then went to Munich, where he studied with Mottl and Reger. He taught at the Cons. of Parma (1910–17), the Cons. "Luigi Cherubini" in Florence (1917–23), the Univ. of Florence (1923–27), and the Royal Univ. in Rome (1927–38). In 1939 he went to Belgium; returned to Italy in 1940.

WORKS: Operetta, *L'Augellin bel verde* (Rome, 1917); *Le Vergini savie e le vergini folli (The Wise and the Foolish Virgins),* a liturgical drama transcribed and rearranged for Soli, Chorus, and Orch. from a French MS of the 12th century (Florence, 1930); *La Passione* for Soli, Chorus, and Orch., based on religious melodies of the 13th century (1930); *Hyla,* symph. poem; *Gaiola e Marechiaro,* Neapolitan rhapsody for Orch.; Violin Sonata; *Sonata-fantasia* for Violin and Organ; songs; etc.

WRITINGS: *Estetica della musica* (Florence, 1924); *Essenza dell'arte e valore estetico nel pensiero di T. Lipps* (Bologna, 1924); *La Lauda e i primordi della melodia italiana* (2 vols. of facsimiles and transcriptions of medieval Italian music; Rome, 1935).

BIBLIOGRAPHY: E.T. Ferand, "In Memoriam: Fernando Liuzzi," *Musical Quarterly* (Oct. 1942).

Liverati, Giovanni, Italian composer; b. Bologna, March 27, 1772; d. Florence, Feb. 18, 1846. He studied voice, and was engaged as a tenor in Spain; in 1796 he traveled with an Italian opera company in Germany; then turned to composition, and wrote various operas for traveling troupes. He was in Stockholm in 1803, Paris in 1808, Vienna in 1811, and London in 1815; remained in London until about 1840; then went back to Italy.

WORKS: Operas: *La prova mancàta* (1801); *Enea in Cartagine* (1809); *I Selvaggi* (London, June 27, 1815); *Gastone e Bajardo* (London, Feb. 26, 1820); oratorio, *David* (1811). He contributed a setting of *In questa tomba oscura* to Mollo's collection (1808), which includes also the famous Beethoven setting of these words.

Liviabella, Lino, Italian composer; b. Macerata, April 7, 1902; d. Bologna, Oct. 21, 1964. He studied with Respighi at the Santa Cecilia Academy in Rome; was director of the Cons. of Pesaro from 1953 to 1959; then taught at Parma.

WORKS: *L'usignola e la Rosa* for Chamber Orch. (1926); *I canti dell'amore*, triptych for String Orch. (1929); *Suite per una fiaba* for Orch. (1933); *Il Vincitore,* written for the Berlin Olympiad (1936); *Il Poeta e sua moglia* for Orch. (1938); *La mia terra* for Orch. (1942); oratorios: *Sorella Chiara* (1947); *Caterina da Siena* (1949); *O Crux Ave* (1953); *Conchiglia,* dramatic musical play (1955); 3 violin sonatas; String Quartet; songs.

Ljungberg, Göta (Albertina), Swedish soprano; b. Sundsval, Oct. 4, 1893; d. Lidingö, near Stockholm, June 28, 1955. She studied at the Royal Academy of Music and the Royal Opera School in Stockholm; also privately in Berlin; in 1918, made her debut (as Elsa) at the Royal Stockholm Opera; appeared in London, in the title role of *Judith* by Goossens (1929); then sang at the Strauss Festival in Mannheim, etc.; her American debut was at the Metropolitan Opera in N.Y., on Jan. 20, 1932; she remained on the roster until 1935; created the role of Lady Marigold Sandys in Hanson's *Merry Mount.* After World War II, she lived in N.Y. as a voice teacher; then returned to Sweden.

Llobet, Miguel, Catalan guitar virtuoso; b. Barcelona, Oct. 18, 1875; d. there, Feb. 22, 1938. He began his career as a painter; then turned to music and studied with Tarrega; lived in Paris (1904–14); toured in Argentina (1910), Chile (1912), the U.S. (1915–17), and throughout Europe. Manuel de Falla composed his *Homenaje* (for the *Tombeau de Debussy*) for him, and Llobet himself made many arrangements for the guitar.

Llongueras y Badía, Juan, Catalan composer; b. Barcelona, June 6, 1880; d. there, Oct. 13, 1953. He studied in Barcelona with Morera, Millet, and Granados, and with Jaques-Dalcroze in Dresden and Geneva; founded the Inst. Catala de Rítmica i Plástica in Barcelona for the exposition in Spain of the Dalcroze methods; was also a music critic, writer, and prof. of music education in Barcelona. His compositions include piano pieces (*La vida sencilla, L'estiu efimer,* etc.), a quantity of *Canciones y juegos infantiles,* and other songs; he also wrote *Les cançuons de Nadal* (Catalan Christmas songs); publ. the essays *Couperin o la gracia, Bach o el fervor, Beethoven o la Passió,* etc.; also a book of reminiscences, *Evocaciones y recuerdos de mi primera vida musical en Barcelona* (Barcelona,

1944).

Lloyd, Albert Lancaster, noted English ethnomusicologist and folk singer; b. London, Feb. 29, 1908; d. Greenwich, Sept. 29, 1982. His early commitment to the Socialist cause contributed to his interest in folk-song research; he collected folk songs in Australia, and in later years in Eastern Europe; he lectured widely in England and the U.S., and also produced radio programs and documentary films. He publ. the valuable books *Come All Ye Bold Miners: Songs and Ballads of the Coalfields* (1952), *The Penguin Book of English Folk Song* (with Vaughan Williams; 1959), and the standard text *Folk Song in England* (1967).

Lloyd, Charles Harford, English organist and composer; b. Thornbury, Gloucestershire, Oct. 16, 1849; d. Slough, Oct. 16, 1919. He attended Magdalen Hall, Oxford (Mus.Bac., 1871; B.A., 1872; M.A., 1875; Mus.Doc., 1892); in 1887–92 was a teacher of organ and composition at the Royal College of Music; in 1892, an instructor at Eton College; from 1914 until his death, organist at the Chapel Royal, St. James'.

WORKS: Cantatas: *Hero and Leander* (Worcester, 1884); *The Song of Balder* (Hereford, 1885); *Andromeda* (Gloucester, 1886); *A Song of Judgment* (Hereford, 1891); *Sir Ogie and Lady Elsie* (Hereford, 1894); church music, including the anthems *Art thou weary?, Blessed is he, Fear not, O land, Give the Lord the honor,* and *A Hymn of Thanksgiving;* organ works.

Lloyd, David, American tenor; b. Minneapolis, Feb. 29, 1920. He studied in Minneapolis, and later at the Curtis Inst. of Music in Philadelphia and the Berkshire Music Center in Tanglewood. After singing with the N.Y. City Opera and the New England Opera Co., he made appearances at the Festival of Athens and the Glyndebourne Festival. He later served as director of the opera program at Hunter College in N.Y., while continuing his career as a concert singer.

Lloyd, George, English composer; b. St. Ives, June 28, 1913. He learned to play piano and violin at home; then studied composition with Harry Farjeon. He was in the Royal Marines during World War II; served in the Arctic on convoys to Russia, and nearly lost his life when his ship was sunk. He composed mainly for the theater; among his works are the operas *Iernin* (Penzance, Nov. 6, 1934); *The Serf* (London, Oct. 20, 1938); *John Socman* (Bristol, May 15, 1951); he also wrote 9 symphs.; 4 piano concertos; Violin Concerto; pieces of chamber music. In 1970 he was made an Officer of the Order of the British Empire.

Lloyd, Norman, American composer and music theorist; b. Pottsville, Pa., Nov. 8, 1909; d. Greenwich, Conn., July 31, 1980. He studied at N.Y. Univ.; received a D.Mus. from the Philadelphia Cons. in 1963, and was engaged as a teacher there and at other music schools. He served as director of the Juilliard School of Music in N.Y. (1946–49) and remained on its faculty until 1963. He became greatly interested in rural and urban folk music, including ragtime; also worked with choreographers on musical arrangements for modern dances. In 1952 he publ. *The Fireside Book of Favorite American Songs;* also edited *The Fireside Book of Folk Songs* and *The Golden Encyclopedia of Music.* With his wife, the pianist **Ruth Dorothy Lloyd,** he compiled *The Complete Sight Singer.*

Lloyd Webber, Andrew, highly successful British composer of musicals; b. London, March 22, 1948. His father, **William Southcombe Lloyd Webber,** was the director of the London College of Music; his mother was a piano teacher; his brother was a cellist. Conditioned by such an environment, Lloyd Webber learned to play piano, violin, and French horn, and soon began to improvise music, mostly in the form of American musicals. He attended Westminster School in London, then went to Magdalen College, Oxford, and to the Royal College of Music. In college he wrote his first musical, *The Likes of Us,* dealing with a philanthropist. At the age of 19, in 1967, he composed the theatrical show *Joseph and the Amazing Technicolor Dreamcoat,* which was performed at St. Paul's Junior School in London in 1968; it was later expanded to a full-scale production, and achieved considerable success for its amalgam of a biblical subject with rock music, French chansonnettes, and country-western songs. In 1970 it was produced in America and in 1972 was shown on television. Lloyd Webber achieved his first commercial success with *Jesus Christ Superstar,* an audacious treatment of the religious theme in terms of jazz and rock. It was produced in London on Aug. 9, 1972, and ran for 3,357 performances; it was as successful in America. Interestingly enough, the "rock opera," as it was called, was first released as a record album, which eventually sold 3 million copies. *Jesus Christ Superstar* opened on Broadway on Oct. 12, 1971, even before the London production. There were protests by religious groups against the irreverent treatment of a sacred subject; particularly offensive was the suggestion in the play of a carnal relationship between Jesus and Mary Magdalen; Jewish organizations, on the other hand, protested against the implied portrayal of the Jews as guilty of the death of Christ. The musical closed on Broadway on June 30, 1973, after 720 performances; it received 7 Tony awards. In 1981 the recording of *Jesus Christ Superstar* was given the Grammy award for best cast show album of the year. The great hullabaloo about the musical made a certainty of Lloyd Webber's further successes. His early musical *Joseph and the Amazing Technicolor Dreamcoat* was revived at the off-Broadway Entermedia Theatre in N.Y.'s East Village on Nov. 18, 1981, and from there moved to the Royale Theater on Broadway. In the meantime Lloyd Webber produced a musical with a totally different chief character, *Evita,* a semi-fictional account of the career of Mrs. Perón of Argentina; it was staged in London

on June 21, 1978; a N.Y. performance soon followed, with splendid success. But perhaps the most spectacular production of Lloyd Webber's was *Cats,* inspired by T.S. Eliot's *Old Possum's Book of Practical Cats;* it was produced in London on May 11, 1981, and was brought out in N.Y. in Oct. 1982 with fantastic success; *Evita* and *Joseph and the Amazing Technicolor Dreamcoat* were still playing on Broadway, so that Lloyd Webber had the satisfaction of having 3 of his shows running at the same time. Apart from his popular shows, Lloyd Webber wrote a mini-opera, *Tell Me on a Sunday,* about an English girl living in N.Y., which was produced by BBC Television in 1980; he also composed *Variations* for Cello for his cellist brother **Julian Lloyd Webber;** the work is derived from Paganini.

BIBLIOGRAPHY: *Current Biography* (June 1982).

Lloyd-Jones, David, English conductor; b. London, Nov. 19, 1934. He studied at Magdalen College; became a regular conductor at Covent Garden; also conducted at the English National Opera. In 1978 he was named music director of the English National Opera North in Leeds.

Lloyd-Webber, Julian, English cellist; b. London, April 14, 1951. He studied at the Royal College of Music; his principal teacher was Douglas Cameron; he also studied with Pierre Fournier in Geneva. He made his concert debut at London's Queen Elizabeth Hall in 1972; subsequently played many engagements as a soloist with English orchs. He made his American debut in N.Y. in 1980. In 1978 he became prof. of cello at the Guildhall School of Music in London. He is the brother of the composer **Andrew Lloyd Webber.**

Lobe, Johann Christian, German flutist, writer on music, and composer; b. Weimar, May 30, 1797; d. Leipzig, July 27, 1881. He studied with A.E. Müller; played a flute solo with the Gewandhaus Orch. in Leipzig (1811); then was a flutist, later a viola player, in the Weimar Court Orch. until 1842; founded a music school; in 1846–48 was in Leipzig as editor of the *Allgemeine Musikzeitung;* in 1853 publ. the periodical *Fliegende Blätter für Musik;* was music editor of *Illustrierte Zeitung;* also contributed articles to various journals.

WORKS: Operas (all produced in Weimar): *Wittekind, Die Flibustier, Die Fürstin von Granada* (Sept. 28, 1833), *Der rote Domino,* and *König und Pächter;* 2 symphs.; overtures; concertos; piano quartets; variations and solos for flute.

WRITINGS: *Die Lehre von der thematischen Arbeit* (1846); *Lehrbuch der musikalischen Komposition* (vol. I, *Harmony,* 1850; revised by Kretzschmar, 5th ed., 1884; vol. II, *Instrumentation,* 3rd ed., 1879; vol. III, *Canon, Fugue, etc.,* 1860; vol. IV, *Opera,* 1867; revised by Kretzschmar, 1884–87); *Katechismus der Musik* (1851; 28th ed., 1904; revised by Leichtentritt, 1926; Eng. trans., N.Y., 1896); *Musikalische Briefe eines Wohlbekannten* (1852; 2nd ed., 1860); *Fliegende Blätter für Musik* (3 vols., 1853–57);

Aus dem Leben eines Musikers (1859); *Vereinfachte Harmonielehre* (1861); *Katechismus der Kompositionslehre* (1872; 7th ed., 1902; Eng. trans., N.Y., 1891); *Consonanzen und Dissonanzen* (1869).

BIBLIOGRAPHY: W. Bode, ed., *Goethes Schauspieler und Musiker, Erinnerungen von Eberwein und Lobe* (1912); O. Coon, ed., *A New Catechism of Music on the Plan of Johann Christian Lobe* (N.Y., 1905).

Lobkowitz, Prince Franz Joseph (Maximilian Ferdinand) von, Austrian art patron; b. Vienna, Dec. 7, 1772; d. Raudnitz an der Elbe, Dec. 16, 1816. Beethoven dedicated to him the quartet op. 18; the 3rd, 5th, and 6th symphs.; the Triple Concerto; the quartet op. 74; and the song cycle *An die ferne Geliebte.*

Lobo, Duarte (also Latinized as **Eduardus Lupus**), Portuguese composer; b. Alcáçovas, c.1565 (he was not identical with the person of the same name baptized on Sept. 19, 1565; his date of birth must therefore remain uncertain); d. Lisbon, Sept. 24, 1646. He was a pupil of Manuel Mendes at Evora; served as choirmaster there before moving to Lisbon; in 1594, became master of the chapel at the Cathedral. As a composer of church music, he enjoyed considerable renown; his mastery of polyphony inspired respect, but comparisons with Victoria Benevoli and other great composers of his time are exaggerations. The following works were printed in his lifetime: *Natalitiae noctis responsoria, a* 4–8; *Antiphonae, a* 8; *Salve, a* 3–11 (Antwerp, 1602); *Officium defunctorum* (Lisbon, 1603); Magnificat, *a* 4 (Antwerp, 1605); 2 books of masses, *a* 4–8 (Antwerp, 1621, 1639); MSS are in the British Museum, in the Fitzwilliam Collection in Cambridge, and at the cathedrals of Granada and Toledo. An antiphon and 2 masses are reprinted in J.E. dos Santos, *A polifonia clássica portuguêsa* (Lisbon, 1937); 16 Magnificats for 4 Voices, transcribed by M. Joaquim (Lisbon, 1945).

BIBLIOGRAPHY: Manuel Joaquim, *20 libros de música polifónica* (Lisbon, 1953; pp. 58–59).

Locatelli, Pietro, Italian violinist and composer; b. Bergamo, Sept. 3, 1695; d. Amsterdam, March 30, 1764. As a youth he was appointed violinist at S. Maria Maggiore in Rome; played violin at the basilica of S. Lorenzo in Damaso (1717–23); subsequently made long professional tours, including appearances outside Italy; in 1729 he settled in Amsterdam, establishing regular public concerts, and enjoying fame there. His technical feats, particularly in double stops, were considered marvelous at the time; by changing the tuning of his violin, he produced apparently impossible effects; Paganini is said to have profited by Locatelli's innovations. A modern edition of his works was publ. by A. Koole, *Pietro Antonio Locatelli: Gesamtausgabe,* in Monumenta Musicae Neerlandicae, IV (1961).

WORKS: 12 *Concerti grossi* (Amsterdam, 1721); Flute Sonatas with Bass (Amsterdam, 1732); *L'arte del violino,* containing 12 concertos and 24 caprices for 2 Violins, Viola, Cello, and Continuo (1733); 6 *introduzioni teatrali* and 6 concertos (1735); 6 *Sonates en trio* (1737); 6 Sonatas for Solo Violin (1737); 6 *Concerti a 4* (1741); Trios for 2 Violins and Bass (1741); *L'arte di nuova modulazione: Caprices énigmatiques; Contrasto armonico: Concerto a 4.* Some of Locatelli's works appear in modern eds.: 6 Sonatas for Solo Violin; a few pieces in Alard's and David's methods; a theme with variations in Schering's *Alt-Meister des Violinspiels;* "Tragic Symphony," publ. by Schering; 2 trio sonatas, publ. by Moffat; etc.

BIBLIOGRAPHY: J.W. von Wasielewski, *Die Violine und ihre Meister* (1920); C. Vanbianchi, "Un celebre violinista bergamasco percursore di Nicolo Paganini," *Bolletino della Civica Biblioteca di Bergamo* (May 1920); A. Schering, *Geschichte des Instrumental-Konzerts* (1927); A. Moser, *Geschichte des Violinspiels* (1923; pp. 224ff.); M. Pincherle, *Les Violinistes* (Paris, 1924); A. Koole, *Leven en werken van Pietro Locatelli* (Amsterdam, 1949); A. Koole, *Pietro Antonio Locatelli. Conferenza* (Bergamo, 1970).

Locke, Matthew, English composer; b. Exeter, c.1620; d. London, Aug. 1677. He was a chorister at Exeter Cathedral, studying under Edward Gibbons and William Wake; then was composer to Charles II (1660); became a Roman Catholic, and was appointed organist to Queen Catherine. Prominent among English composers of his era, he wrote music to *The Tempest* and *Macbeth,* and to Shadwell's *Psyche* (London, March 9, 1675; the music for *The Tempest* and *Psyche* were publ. in 1675 as *The English Opera),* to Shirley's masque *Cupid and Death,* and to Stapleton's comedy *The Stepmother;* also 6 suites, anthems, etc. He also wrote the first English work on thoroughbass, *Melothesia, or Certain General Rules for Playing upon a Continued Bass* (1673); and pamphlets versus Salmon's attempt at reducing music notation to one universal character. P. Warlock and A. Mangeot publ. 6 *Consorts a 4* (London, 1932). Chamber music is reprinted in vols. 31–32 of *Musica Brittanica,* anthems and motets in vol. 38. R.E.M. Harding compiled *A Thematic Catalogue of the Works of Matthew Locke* (1971).

BIBLIOGRAPHY: J. Pulver, *A Biographical Dictionary of Old English Music* (1927); R. Covell, "17th-Century Music for *The Tempest," Studies in Music,* 2 (1968); C.D.S. Field, "Matthew Locke and the Consort Suite," *Music & Letters* (Jan. 1970); M. Tilmouth, "Revisions in the Chamber Music of Matthew Locke," *Proceedings of the Royal Music Association,* 98 (1971–72).

Lockhart, James, Scottish conductor; b. Edinburgh, Oct. 16, 1930. He studied at Edinburgh Univ. and at the Royal College of Music in London. He served as assistant conductor of the Yorkshire Symph. Orch. (1954–55); assistant conductor and coach at Münster (1955–56), Munich (1956–57), Glyndebourne (1957–59), and Covent Garden in London (1959–68). Intercalatorily, he was music director of the Opera Workshop of the Univ. of Texas in Austin (1957–59), and conductor of the BBC Scottish Symph. Orch.

(1960–61). From 1968–72 he was music director of the Welsh National Opera; from 1972–80 he served as Generalmusikdirektor of the State Theater in Kassel. In addition, he appeared as a guest conductor with several orchs. in England; in 1981 he became Generalmusikdirektor of the Rheinische Phil. in Koblenz and at the Koblenz Opera.

Lockspeiser, Edward, English writer on music; b. London, May 21, 1905; d. there, Feb. 3, 1973. He studied in Paris with Alexandre Tansman and Nadia Boulanger; then attended the classes of C.H. Kitson and Malcolm Sargent at the Royal College of Music in London. He dedicated himself to musical journalism, particularly to the cause of French music; publ. valuable monographs on Debussy (London, 1936; revised ed., 1951), Berlioz (1940), and Bizet (1947), and an exhaustive biography, *Debussy: His Life and Mind* (2 vols., London, 1962, 1965). He also edited *Claude Debussy: Lettres inédites à André Caplet, 1908–1914* (Monaco, 1957).

Lockwood, Anna, composeress of the militant avant-garde; b. Christchurch, New Zealand, July 29, 1939. She studied at Canterbury Univ. in New Zealand; then went to London, where she took courses with Peter Racine Fricker at the Royal College of Music; subsequently attended classes at the Hochschule für Musik in Cologne and at the Electronic Music Center in Bilthoven, the Netherlands. In 1968 she gave non-lectures at the Anti-University of London. With her husband, Harvey Matusow, she undertook a series of experiments in total art, including aural, oral, visual, tactile, gustatory, and olfactory demonstrations and sporadic transcendental manifestations; of these, the most remarkable was the summoning (in German) of Beethoven's ghost at a séance held in London on Oct. 3, 1968, with sound recorded on magnetic tape, which in playback revealed some surprisingly dissonant music of apparently metapsychic origin, tending to indicate that Beethoven was a posthumous avant-garde composer (the tape was not released in order to avoid unanswerable controversy); the séance was preceded by the burning of a combustible piano and of an inflammable microphone. Not content with setting the piano afire, she also demonstrated the drowning of an upright piano in a lake in Amarillo, Texas (Dec. 27, 1972). Anna Lockwood also experimented with surgical piano transplants. Her other works, some of them consisting of controlled glossolalia and notated optically on graphic paper, are *A Abélard, Héloïse* for Mezzo-soprano and 10 Instruments (1962); *Aspects of a Parable* for Baritone and 12 Instruments (1963); *Love Field* for Tape, a lament for John F. Kennedy, with reference to the name of the Dallas Airport (1964); *Glass Concert I* (1967); *Glass Concert II,* scored for Sheets of Armor-plate Glass, Spotlight Bulbs, Wineglasses, Milk Bottles, Glass Curtains, Fluorescent Tubes, Glass Mobiles, and other vitreous objects (1969; blueprint and directions publ. in *Source, 5*); *Dark Touch* for Tactile-Aural Equipment (1970); *Gentle Grass,* a ritual for 6 Players (1970); *Humm* for 70 or more Hummers (1971); *Bus Trip,* a moving event with Food, Free Love, and Realistic Sound Effects (1971); *River Archives,* an anthology of Sounds from world rivers (1971); *World Rhythms,* incorporating Ambient Recorded Sounds, inspired by long sessions of transcendental meditation (1975).

Lockwood, Lewis (Henry), distinguished American musicologist; b. New York, Dec. 16, 1930. He studied musicology with Lowinsky at Queens College in N.Y. (B.A., 1952) and with Strunk and Mendel at Princeton Univ. (M.F.A., 1955; Ph.D., 1960, with the dissertation *The Counter-Reformation and the Sacred Music of Vincenzo Ruffo,* publ. in Venice, 1970). In 1958 he joined the faculty of Princeton Univ. In 1980 he was appointed prof. at Harvard Univ. He is regarded as a prime authority on Renaissance music; his studies on music in Italy in the 15th and 16th centuries are especially thorough; he publ. a valuable book, *Music in Renaissance Ferrara, 1400–1505* (London, 1984). He was a senior consulting editor of *The New Grove Dictionary of Music and Musicians* (London, 1980).

Lockwood, Normand, American composer; b. New York, March 19, 1906. He studied at the Univ. of Michigan; in 1925 went to Europe and took lessons with Respighi in Rome and Nadia Boulanger in Paris; he was a Fellow at the American Academy in Rome (1929–31); upon his return to America he was an instructor in music at the Oberlin (Ohio) Cons. (1932–43); from 1945 to 1953, was a lecturer at Columbia Univ.; then at Trinity Univ. in San Antonio, Texas (1953–55); also taught at the Univ. of Hawaii and at the Univ. of Oregon. In 1961 he was appointed a member of the faculty of the Univ. of Denver; became prof. emeritus in 1974.

WORKS: Operas: *Scarecrow* (Columbia Univ., N.Y., May 19, 1945); *Early Dawn* (Denver, Aug. 7, 1961); *The Wizards of Balizar* (Denver, Aug. 1, 1962); *The Hanging Judge* (Denver, March 1964); *Requiem for a Rich Young Man* (Denver, Nov. 24, 1964); *Moby Dick* for Chamber Orch. (1946); Oboe Concerto (1966); *Symphonic Sequences* (1966); *From an Opening to a Close* for Wind Instruments and Percussion (1967); 2 concertos for Organ and Brass (1950, 1970); Clarinet Quintet (1960); Mass for Children and Orch.; 8 duets for 2 Trumpets; Flute Sonata; *Sonata-Fantasia* for Accordion; *Valley Suite* for Violin and Piano; *4 Excursions* for 4 String Basses; *4 Songs from James Joyce's "Chamber Music"* for Medium Voice and String Quartet (N.Y., March 28, 1948); oratorios: *Light out of Darkness* (1956) and *Children of God* (Cincinnati, Feb. 1, 1957); numerous other sacred works.

Loeb, John Jacob, American composer of popular songs; b. Chicago, Feb. 18, 1910; d. Valley Stream, Long Island, N.Y., March 2, 1970. He began writing songs for Broadway shows and jazz bands at the age of 18. Among his best-known songs are *Sweetie Pie, Masquerade,* and *Reflections in the Water.* In collaboration with Carmen Lombardo, he wrote the tune of *Boo Hoo.*

Loeffler, Charles Martin (Tornow), outstanding American composer; b. Mulhouse, Alsace, Jan. 30, 1861; d. Medfield, Mass., May 19, 1935. His father was a writer who sometimes used the nom de plume Tornow, which Loeffler later added to his name. When he was a child, the family moved to Russia, where his father was engaged in government work in the Kiev district; later they lived in Debrecen in Hungary, and in Switzerland. In 1875 Loeffler began taking violin lessons in Berlin with Rappoldi, who prepared him for study with Joachim; he studied harmony with Kiel; also took lessons with Bargiel. He then went to Paris, where he continued his musical education with Massart (violin) and Guiraud (composition). He was engaged briefly as a violinist in the Pasdeloup Orch.; then was a member of the private orch. of the Russian Baron Paul von Derwies at his sumptuous residences near Lugano and in Nice (1879–81). When Derwies died in 1881, Loeffler went to America, with letters of recommendation from Joachim. He played in the orch. of Leopold Damrosch in N.Y. In 1882 he became 2nd concertmaster of the newly organized Boston Symph. Orch., but was able to accept other engagements during late spring and summer months; in the spring of 1883, he traveled with the Thomas Orch. on a transcontinental tour; the summers of 1883 and 1884 he spent in Paris, where he took violin lessons with Hubert Léonard. He resigned from the Boston Symph. in 1903, and devoted himself to teaching and composition, living in Boston and suburban Medfield. He was married to Elise Burnett Fay (1910). After his death, she donated to the Library of Congress all of his MSS, correspondence, etc.; by his will, he left the material assets of his not inconsiderable estate to the French Academy and the Paris Cons. He was an officer of the French Academy (1906); a Chevalier in the French Legion of Honor (1919); a member of the American Academy of Arts and Letters; Mus.Doc. (*honoris causa*), Yale Univ. (1926).

Loeffler's position in American music is unique, brought up as he was under many different national influences, Alsatian, French, German, Russian, and Ukrainian. One of his most vivid scores, *Memories of My Childhood,* written as late as 1924, reflects the modal feeling of Russian and Ukrainian folk songs. But his esthetic code was entirely French, with definite leanings toward Impressionism; the archaic constructions that he sometimes affected, and the stylized evocations of "ars antiqua," are also in keeping with the French manner. His most enduring work, *A Pagan Poem,* is cast in such a neo-archaic vein. He was a master of colorful orchestration; his harmonies are opulent without saturation; his rhapsodic forms are peculiarly suited to the evocative moods of his music. His only excursion into the American idiom was the employment of jazz rhythms in a few of his lesser pieces.

WORKS: *The Nights in the Ukraine,* after Gogol, suite for Violin and Orch. (Boston, Nov. 20, 1891); *Fantastic Concerto* for Cello and Orch. (Boston, Feb. 2, 1894); *Divertimento* for Violin and Orch. (Boston, Jan. 4, 1895); *La Mort de Tintagiles,* after Maeterlinck, dramatic poem for 2 Viole d'Amore

and Orch. (revised for Orch. and Viola d'Amore, 1900; first perf., Boston, Feb. 16, 1901); *Divertissement espagnol* for Orch. and Saxophone (1901); *La Villanelle du Diable,* symph. fantasy for Orch. and Organ (Boston, April 11, 1902); *Poem* for Orch., inspired by Verlaine's *La Bonne Chanson* (Boston, April 11, 1902; reorchestrated, and perf. by the Boston Symph., Nov. 1, 1918); *A Pagan Poem,* after Virgil, for Orch., with Piano, English Horn, and 3 Trumpets obbligati (originally as chamber music, 1901; revised for Orch. and Piano, 1906; first perf., Boston Symph., Nov. 22, 1907, Karl Muck conducting); *Hora mystica* for Orch. and Men's Chorus (Boston Symph., March 2, 1917, Karl Muck conducting); *5 Irish Fantasies* for Voice and Orch. (3 numbers perf., Boston, March 10, 1922); *Memories of My Childhood (Life in a Russian Village)* for Orch. (awarded the Chicago North Shore Festival Assoc. prize, 1924; Chicago Symph., Evanston, Ill., May 30, 1924); *Canticum fratris solis (The Canticle of the Sun)* for Solo Voice and Chamber Orch. (commissioned by the E.S. Coolidge Foundation; first perf. at the Library of Congress Festival of Chamber Music, Oct. 28, 1925); *Evocation* for Women's Voices and Orch. (on lines from the *Select Epigrams of Greek Anthology* by J.W. Machail; commissioned for the opening of Severance Hall, Cleveland; perf. there, Feb. 5, 1931); Psalm 137, *By the Rivers of Babylon,* for 4-part Women's Chorus, with Organ, Harp, 2 Flutes, and Cello obbligato (1907); *For one who fell in battle* for 8-part Mixed Chorus a cappella (1911); *Beat! Beat! Drums!,* after Whitman, for Men's Chorus in unison, 6 Piccolos, 3 Saxophones, Brass, Drums, and 2 Pianos (1917; Cleveland, Nov. 17, 1932); 2 rhapsodies for Oboe, Viola, and Piano (*L'Etang* and *La Cornemuse,* after poems by Maurice Rollinat; 1905); Octet for 2 Clarinets, 2 Violins, Viola, Cello, Double Bass, and Harp; String Sextet; *Music for 4 Stringed Instruments* (in memory of the American aviator Victor Chapman; 1917); Quintet for 3 Violins, Viola, and Cello; *4 Melodies* for Voice and Piano, to poems by G. Kahn (1903); *4 Poems* for Voice, Viola, and Piano (1904); *4 Poems* for Voice and Piano (1906); *The wind among the reeds* for Voice and Piano to poems by Yeats (1908); *The Reveller* for Solo Voice, Violin, and Piano (1925); *Partita* for Violin and Piano (1930). In MS, a 4-act Chinese opera, *Life Is but a Dream;* and an opera based on a short play by Cecil Sharp. He also wrote *Violin Studies for the Development of the Left Hand* (publ. 1936).

BIBLIOGRAPHY: Carl Engel contributed an extensive essay on Loeffler to the *International Cyclopedia of Music and Musicians,* ed. by Oscar Thompson (N.Y., 1938). Engel also wrote articles on Loeffler in the *Chesterian* (March 1920), in *Musical Quarterly* (July 1925), and in *Cobbett's Cyclopedic Survey of Chamber Music* (1929). See also L. Gilman, *Nature in Music and Studies in Tone Poetry of Today* (1914); Paul Rosenfeld, *Musical Portraits* (1923); idem, *An Hour with American Music* (N.Y., 1929; pp. 52–59).

Loeillet, Jacques, oboe player, brother of **Jean-**

Baptiste Loeillet; b. Ghent, July 7, 1685; d. there, Nov. 28, 1748. He played in court orchs. in Brussels and Munich. In 1727 he went to France; demonstrated his virtuosity, performing on several wind instruments and on the violin, at the Versailles court, and was appointed chamber musician to Louis XV. He publ. 6 sonatas for 2 flutes; 6 sonatas for solo flute, with continuo.

Loeillet, Jean-Baptiste (known in England as **John Loeillet**), notable harpsichordist and flutist, brother of **Jacques Loeillet;** b. Ghent, Nov. 18, 1680; d. London, July 19, 1730. The family name has been variously spelled **L'Oeillet, Luly, Lulli, Lullie,** and even **Lully,** which form led to a great deal of confusion, so that Loeillet's Minuet in A has been misattributed in some editions to the great Lully. Loeillet studied in Ghent and in Paris. In 1705 he went to London, where he played the oboe and the flute at the Queen's Theatre (until 1710). He became extremely successful as a teacher, harpsichord player, and collector of musical instruments. He popularized the German transverse flute in England. In his music he followed the Italian tradition; his writing for the flute shows a thorough understanding of the virtuoso possibilities of the instrument.
WORKS: He publ. in London, under the name of John Loeillet, the following works: 6 suites of lessons for the harpsichord; 6 sonatas for various instruments; 12 sonatas for violins, German flutes, and common flutes; 12 solos for a German flute, common flute, and violin; the following were publ. under the name of **Jean-Baptiste Loeillet de Gand:** 4 books of solos for a flute and a bass; 6 sonatas for 2 flutes; and 6 sonatas for 2 German flutes. There are 2 different sets of opus numbers, which suggests that there was another Loeillet, possibly identifiable with John Loeillet's cousin, also named Jean-Baptiste, and active in Lyons. Reprints of authentic and putative works by John Loeillet include a set of sonatas ed. by Béon (Paris, 1911); a sonata ed. by Moffat; harpsichord pieces ed. by J. Watelet (Antwerp, 1932); 2 sonatas for flute and piano ed. by J. van Etsen (Antwerp, 1938); etc.
BIBLIOGRAPHY: Paul Bergmans, *Une Famille de musiciens belges du XVIIIe siécle: Les Loeillet* (Brussels, 1927); prime source book, providing documentary information on members of the family; but see B. Priestman, "Catalogue thématique des œuvres de Jean-Baptiste, John et Jacques Loeillet," *Revue Belge de Musicologie* (Oct.–Dec. 1952; pp. 219–74), separating John Loeillet's works from those purported to be by his cousin; see also Priestman's article, "The Keyboard Works of John Loeillet," *Music Review* (May 1955).

Loeillet, John. See **Loeillet, Jean-Baptiste.**

Loeschhorn, Albert. See **Löschhorn, Albert.**

Loesser, Arthur, brilliant American pianist and imaginative writer on music, brother of **Frank Loesser;** b. New York, Aug. 26, 1894; d. Cleveland, Jan. 4, 1969. He studied with Stojowski and Goet-schius at the Inst. of Musical Art in N.Y.; began an auspicious concert career in 1913; toured Australia and the Orient in 1920–21. In 1926 he was appointed a prof. of piano at the Cleveland Inst. of Music. In 1943 he was commissioned in the U.S. Army as an officer in the Japanese intelligence dept.; mastered the language and, after the war, gave lectures in Japanese in Tokyo; was the first American musician in uniform to play for a Japanese audience (1946). He publ. *Humor in American Song* (N.Y., 1943) and an entertaining vol., *Men, Women and Pianos: A Social History* (N.Y., 1954).

Loesser, Frank, American composer of popular music, brother of **Arthur Loesser;** b. New York, June 29, 1910; d. there, July 28, 1969. He was educated at City College in N.Y., where he began writing songs for college activities; he subsequently was active as a reporter, singer, and vaudeville performer. In 1931 he settled in Hollywood and devoted himself mainly to writing musical comedies. During World War II he was in the U.S. Army, and wrote several Army songs (*What Do You Do in the Infantry?; Salute to the Army Service Forces; Praise the Lord and Pass the Ammunition; They're Either Too Young or Too Old;* etc.); continued to produce popular songs after the war (*On a Slow Boat to China; Small Fry; The Moon of Manakoora; Dolores; How Sweet You Are; Now That I Need You; Roger Young; Just Another Polka; Two Sleepy People; Spring Will Be a Little Late This Year; A Touch of Texas; Jingle Jangle Jingle; I Wish I Didn't Love You So; My Darling, My Darling, Baby, It's Cold Outside;* etc.); also wrote music for several highly successful Broadway plays: *Where's Charley?, Guys and Dolls, The Most Happy Fella,* etc.
BIBLIOGRAPHY: Arthur Loesser, "My Brother Frank," *Notes* (March 1950).

Loevendie, Theo, Dutch composer and saxophone player; b. Amsterdam, Sept. 17, 1930. He studied composition and clarinet at the Amsterdam Cons. (1956–61); taught clarinet at the Toonkunst Music School in Haarlem and at the Amsterdam Cons. (1960–65); in 1968 was appointed instructor in improvisation at the Rotterdam Cons. In 1973 he organized STAMP concerts with the purpose of presenting contemporary music of various styles (jazz, folk music, avant-garde, etc.).
WORKS: Opera for young people, *Esperanza* (Holland Festival, Amsterdam, July 1971); *Conflux-us* for Jazz and Symph. Orchs. (1966); *3 Pieces* for 3 different Clarinets (1968); *Scaramuccia* for Clarinet and Orch. (Utrecht, April 14, 1971); *Music for Bass Clarinet and Piano* (1971); *Music for Double Bass and Piano* (1971); *Aulos* for Winds and/or Strings (1972); *2 Trios* for 3 Percussionists (1973); *Timbo* for 6 Percussionists (1974); *Prelude* for 6 Percussionists (1974); *De nachtegaal,* musical theater piece (1974); *Incantations* for Bass Clarinet and Orch. (The Hague, Oct. 25, 1975); *Orbits* for Solo Horn, 4 Obbligato Horns, and Orch. (Rotterdam, Feb. 28, 1976); *Strides* for Piano (1976); *6 Turkish Folk Poems* for Female Voice and 7 Instruments

Loevensohn – Loewe

(Holland Festival, The Hague, June 21, 1977); *Flexio* for Orch. (1979).

Loevensohn, Marix, Belgian cellist; b. Courtrai, March 31, 1880; d. Montauban, France, April 24, 1943. He studied at the Brussels Cons.; made his public debut in London at the age of 14; then toured England as a joint artist with celebrated musicians, among them Paderewski and Adelina Patti; was, successively, a member of the string quartets of Wilhelmj, Ysaÿe, and Thomson. In the interim, he taught in Berlin, Amsterdam, and Brussels.

Loewe, (Johann) Carl (Gottfried), outstanding German composer of lieder; b. Löbejün, near Halle, Nov. 30, 1796; d. Kiel, April 20, 1869. His father, a schoolmaster and cantor, taught him the rudiments of music; when he was 12 he was sent to the Francke Inst. in Halle, where his attractive manner, excellent high voice, and early ability to improvise brought him to the attention of Jerome Bonaparte, who granted him a stipend of 300 thalers annually until 1813. His teacher was Türk, the head of the Francke Inst.; after Türk's death in 1813, Loewe joined the Singakademie founded by Naue. He also studied theology at the Univ. of Halle, but soon devoted himself entirely to music. He had begun to compose as a boy; under the influence of Zelter, he wrote German ballades, and developed an individual style of great dramatic force and lyrical inspiration; he perfected the genre, and was regarded by many musicians as the greatest song composer after Schubert and before Brahms. His setting of Goethe's poem *Erlkönig* (1818), which came before the publication of Schubert's great song to the same poem, is one of Loewe's finest creations; other songs that rank among his best are *Edward, Der Wirthin Töchterlein, Der Nöck, Archibald Douglas, Tom der Reimer, Heinrich der Vogler, Oluf, Die verfallene Mühle,* etc. Loewe was personally acquainted with Goethe, and also met Weber. In 1820 he became a schoolmaster at Stettin, and organist at St. Jacobus there. He lived in Stettin, except for frequent travels, until 1866, when he settled in Kiel. He visited Vienna (1844), London (1847), Sweden and Norway (1851), and Paris (1857), among other places. Loewe was an excellent vocalist, and was able to perform his ballades in public.

WORKS: 5 operas, only one of which, *Die drei Wünsche,* was performed (Berlin, Feb. 18, 1834); 17 oratorios; cantata, *Die Hochzeit der Thetis; Die erste Walpurgisnacht,* after Goethe, ballade for Soli, Chorus, and Orch.; 368 ballades for voice and piano, publ. in his collected ed. and in numerous anthologies (Peters and Schlesinger publ. "Loewe-Albums" containing 20 and 16 numbers, respectively). Loewe's instrumental works (symphs., overtures, 3 string quartets, Piano Trio, several piano sonatas, etc.) are mostly in MS. He publ. several pedagogic works: *Gesanglehre für Gymnasien, Seminarien und Bürgerschulen* (Stettin, 1826; 5th ed., 1854); *Musikalischer Gottesdienst; Methodische Anweisung zum Kirchengesang und Orgelspiel* (1851, and subsequent eds.); *Klavier- und Gene-*ralbass-Schule (2nd ed., 1851). A *Gesamtausgabe der Balladen, Legenden, Lieder und Gesänge,* in 17 vols., ed. by Max Runze, was publ. by Breitkopf & Härtel (1899–1905). A Loewe-Verein was founded in Berlin in 1882.

BIBLIOGRAPHY: *Selbstbiographie,* ed. by K.H. Bitter (Berlin, 1870); A. Wellmer, *Carl Loewe: Ein deutscher Tonmeister* (Leipzig, 1886); M. Runze, *Loewe redivivus* (Berlin, 1888); A.B. Bach, *The Art-Ballad: Loewe and Schubert* (London, 1890; 3rd ed., 1891); M. Runze, *Ludwig Giesebrecht und Carl Loewe* (Berlin, 1894); W. Wossidlo, *Carl Loewe als Balladenkomponist* (Berlin, 1894); A. Niggli, *Carl Loewe* (Zürich, 1897); H. Bulthaupt, *Carl Loewe, Deutschlands Balladenkomponist* (Berlin, 1898); M. Runze, *Goethe und Loewe* (as introduction to vols. 11 and 12 of the *Gesamtausgabe* of Loewe's works; Leipzig, 1901); idem, *Die musikalische Legende* (introduction to vols. 13 and 14 of the same; Leipzig, 1902); H. Draheim, *Goethes Balladen in Loewes Komposition* (Langensalza, 1905); K. Anton, *Beiträge zur Biographie Carl Loewes* (Halle, 1912); idem, "Carl Loewe als Lehrer Walter von Goethes," *Goethe Jahrbuch* 23 (1913); H. Kleemann, *Beiträge zur Ästhetik und Geschichte der Loeweschen Ballade* (Halle, 1913); L. Hirschberg, *Loewe als Instrumentalkomponist* (Langensalza, 1919); O. Altenburg, *Carl Loewe* (Stettin, 1924); Hans Engel, *Carl Loewe: Überblick und Würdigung* (Greiswald, 1934); W. Serauky, "Zu Carl Loewes Biographie und musikalischen Schaffen," in *Festschrift A. Schering* (Berlin, 1937); R. Sietz, *Carl Loewe: Ein Gedenkbuch zum 150. Geburtstag* (Cologne, 1948).

Loewe, Ferdinand. See **Löwe, Ferdinand.**

Loewe, Frederick, Austrian-American composer of popular music; b. Vienna, June 10, 1904. He studied piano in Berlin with Busoni and Eugène d'Albert; composition with Reznicek. In 1924 he emigrated to the U.S.; was active as a concert pianist; then devoted himself chiefly to production of popular music. Adapting himself adroitly to the American idiom, he became one of the most successful writers of musical comedies; among them are *Salute to Spring; Great Lady; The Life of the Party; What's Up?; The Day before Spring; Brigadoon; Paint Your Wagon;* and (the most spectacularly successful of them all) *My Fair Lady,* after Shaw's *Pygmalion* (1956; 2,717 perfs.); this was followed by another hit, *Camelot* (1960); in all these his lyricist was Alan Jay Lerner.

BIBLIOGRAPHY: David Ewen, *Great Men of American Popular Song* (Englewood Cliffs, N.J., 1970).

Loewe, Sophie, German soprano; b. Oldenburg, March 24, 1815; d. Budapest, Nov. 28, 1866. She studied in Vienna with Ciccimarra and in Milan with Lamperti; made her debut in Vienna in 1832; sang in London in 1841; also in 1841, appeared at La Scala in Milan, where she created Donizetti's Maria Padilla; also created Verdi's Elvira in *Ernani* and Odabella in *Attila* at the Teatro La Fenice in Venice. She retired from the stage in 1848.

Loewenberg, Alfred, German musicologist; b. Berlin, May 14, 1902; d. London, Dec. 29, 1949. He studied at Jena Univ. (Ph.D., 1925); settled in London in 1935. His unique achievement is the compilation of *Annals of Opera: 1597–1940* (Cambridge, 1943; new ed., Geneva, 1955; revised and corrected, 1978), tabulating in chronological order the exact dates of first performances and important revivals of some 4,000 operas, with illuminating comments of a bibliographical nature. He also publ. *Early Dutch Librettos and Plays with Music in the British Museum* (London, 1947), and a number of articles.

Loewengard, Max Julius, German writer on music and pedagogue; b. Frankfurt, Oct. 2, 1860; d. Hamburg, Nov. 19, 1915. He was a pupil of Raff in Frankfurt; from 1891 to 1904 he was on the faculty of the Scharwenka Cons. in Berlin, and wrote music criticism for the *Börsen-Zeitung;* in 1904–8, taught at the Hamburg Cons.; founded the Inst. für Musikwissenschaft there. His compositions include an opera, *Die vierzehn Nothelfer* (Berlin, 1896); Serenade for Orch.; many songs.
WRITINGS: Several highly successful manuals: *Lehrbuch der Harmonie* (1892; 6th ed., 1906; Eng. trans. by H.M. Peacock, 1905; F. Liebing, 1907; T. Baker, 1910); *Lehrbuch des Kontrapunkts* (1902; Eng. trans. by F. Liebing, 1907); *Aufgabenbuch zur Harmonielehre* (1903); *Lehrbuch des Kanons und der Fuge* (1903); *Lehrbuch der musikalischen Formen* (1904); *Praktische Anleitung zum Generalbasspiel, Harmonisieren, Transponieren und Modulieren* (1913).

Logan, Frederick Knight, American composer of popular songs; b. Oskaloosa, Iowa, Oct. 15, 1871; d. June 11, 1928. He wrote a number of sentimental ballads in collaboration with his mother, **Virginia Logan.** He was the composer of the celebrated *Missouri Waltz,* which he publ. as a piano solo in 1914 with his name on the cover of the sheet music as an "arranger," for he was reluctant to admit the authorship of the tune that seemed beneath his estimate of himself as a composer. But when the words were added in 1916, the thing became a sensational hit. The state of Missouri accepted it as its official song. Harry Truman loved to play it on the piano and, for better or for worse, the *Missouri Waltz* became associated with his (Truman's) political deeds and misdeeds.

Logar, Mihovil, Croatian composer; b. Fiume, Oct. 6, 1902. He studied in Prague with K.B. Jirák and J. Suk. In 1927 he returned to Belgrade and became a prof. of composition at the Belgrade Musical Academy. A highly prolific composer, he writes in all genres, employing a restrained modern idiom.
WORKS: Operas: *Pokondirena tikva (Middleclass Noblewoman;* Belgrade, Oct. 20, 1956); *Četrdesetprva (The Year of 1941;* Sarajevo, Feb. 10, 1961); ballet, *Zlatna ribica (The Golden Fish,* after

Pushkin's tale; Belgrade, Nov. 11, 1953); *4 Scenes from Shakespeare,* incidental music for Orch. (1954); *Rondo rustico* for Orch. (1945); Violin Concerto (1954); Clarinet Concerto (1956); *Vatra (Fire),* cantata (Belgrade, Sept. 27, 1960); *Kosmonauti,* concert overture in honor of the Soviet cosmonauts (Belgrade, June 8, 1962); *Sinfonia italiana* (Belgrade, Nov. 24, 1964); *Doppio Concerto* for Clarinet and French Horn (Belgrade, April 5, 1968).

Logier, Johann Bernhard, German pianist, teacher, and composer; b. Kassel, Feb. 9, 1777; d. Dublin, July 27, 1846. He received his early musical training at home; as a youth he went to England and played the flute in a regimental band; he was employed as an organist in Westport, Ireland, where he perfected his invention of the "chiroplast," for holding the hands in the most convenient positions during piano practice; he patented it in 1814 and promoted it with fanatic persistence. Amazingly enough, it obtained great vogue in England, and was equally successful in Germany; in 1821 he was invited to Berlin, where he taught his method from 1822 to 1826; then returned to Ireland, and settled in Dublin in 1829. In reply to numerous polemical attacks on his invention Logier publ. equally bitter assaults on his detractors, among them the pamphlets *An Explanation and Description of the Royal Patent Chiroplast, or Hand-Director for Pianoforte* (London, 1816) and *An Authentic Account of the Examination of Pupils Instructed on the New System of Musical Education, by J.B. Logier* (London, 1818). He further publ. *The First Companion to the Royal Patent Chiroplast* (London, 1818; it went through numerous eds.) and *Logier's Practical Thorough-Bass,* and in German, *System der Musikwissenschaft und der musikalischen Komposition* (Berlin, 1827). He also introduced a method of simultaneous practice on different pianos, which for a time was adopted even in such a bastion of traditional music instruction as the Paris Cons. In the end, Logier's "chiroplast" joined a number of other equally futile pseudo-scientific inventions in the repository of musical curiosities.
BIBLIOGRAPHY: G. Pügner, *Johann Bernhard Logier, Ein Musikerzieher des 19. Jahrhunderts* (Diss., Univ. of Leipzig, 1959).

Logothetis, Anestis, Bulgarian-born avant-garde composer of Greek extraction; b. Burgas, Oct. 27, 1921. He was trained in mechanical engineering in Vienna (1942–45); then took lessons in composition there with Ratz and Uhl (1945–51); exhibited in Vienna galleries a series of polymorphic graphs capable of being performed as music by optional instrumental groups. He employs a highly personalized "integrating" musical notation, making use of symbols, signs, and suggestive images, playing on a performer's psychological associations.
WORKS: *Integration* for Violin, Cello, and Piano (1953); *Peritonon* for Horn and Piano (1954); *Polynom* for Orch. in 5 groups (1958); *2 Textures* for 2 Piano Groups (1959); *Kompression* for Any Instrument (1959); *Textur–Struktur–Spiegel–Spiel*

(1959); *Fantasmata and Meditation*, tape ballet music (1959); *Agglomeration* for Solo Violin (1960); *5 Portraits of Love*, ballet (1960); *Koordination* for 5 Orch. Groups (1960); *Himmelsmechanik*, ballet (1960); *Katalysator* for Horns (1960). The following "polymorphic" pieces are for variable Chamber Instrumental Groups: *Kulmination I + II + III* (1961); *Meditation* for Any Instruments or Voices (1961); *Impulse* (1961); *Vibration* (1962); *Määndros* (1963); *Odyssee* (1963); *Dynapolis* (1963); *Dispersion* (1963); *Kentra* (1964); *Seismographie I* and *II* (1964); *Osculations* (1964); *Ichnologia* (1964); *Labyrinthos* (1965); *Reversible Bijunktion* (1965); *1.65AL* (1965); *Orbitals* (1965); *Enòsis* (1965); *Diffusion* (1965); *Integration* (1966); *Enclaves* (1966); *Diptychon* for Piano (1966); *Desmotropie* for Orch. (1967); *Karmadharmadrama*, musical theater (1967; Graz, Oct. 12, 1972); *Polychron* (1967); *Syrroi* (1967); *Konvektionsströme* for Orch. (1968); *Styx* for Orch. of Plucked Strings (1968); *Evektion* (1968); *Anastasis*, stage piece for Voices, Tape Film, Television, and Instruments (1969); *Kollisionen* (1970); *Komplementäres* (1970); *Pyrifleghethon—Acheron—Kokkytos* for 3 Choirs and Optional Instruments (Athens, Sept. 26, 1971; refers to the 3 rivers of the Greek netherworld); *Klangraum I* and *II* for Orch. (1972); *Musik-Fontäne für Robert Moran* (1972); *Emanationen* for Clarinet and Tape (1973).

Logroscino, Nicola, Italian composer; b. Bitonto (baptized, Oct. 22), 1698; d. Palermo, after 1765. He was a pupil of Veneziano and Perugino (1714–27) at the Cons. di Santa Maria di Loreto in Naples; in 1728–31, was organist at Conza (Avellino); in 1731, was again in Naples. In 1747 he became first prof. of counterpoint at the Cons. dei Figliuoli Dispersi in Palermo; then went to Naples, where he produced his most successful operas; he is regarded as the creator of Neapolitan opera buffa in the local dialect, among them *Il Governatore*, *Il vecchio marito*, and *Tanto bene che male*. Of his serious operas, *Giunio Bruto* (1748) and *Olimpiade* (1753) were the most notable.

BIBLIOGRAPHY: H. Kretzchmar, "Zwei Opern Nicola Logroscinos," *Jahrbuch Peters* (1908); U. Prota-Giurleo, *Nicola Logroscino, Il Dio dell'opera buffa* (Naples, 1927); E.P. Morello, *A Scarlatti e Nicolo Logroscino* (1927); A. della Corte, *L'opera comica italiana nel 1700* (Bari, 1923; vol. 1, p. 172 et seq.).

Löhlein, Georg Simon, German composer; b. Neustadt, near Coburg, July (baptized, July 16) 1725; d. Danzig, Dec. 16, 1781. On account of his tall stature (6 feet 2 inches), he was seized on a journey and forced into the Prussian Guard; he was stationed at Potsdam and served at the palace of Frederick the Great. He was severely wounded at the battle of Collin during the Seven Years' War, but recovered and went to Jena, where he completed his interrupted musical education; at the age of 38 he enrolled at the Univ. of Leipzig; there he was active as both a violinist and a pianist. In 1781 he received a post as organist at the St. Mary Church in Danzig,

but suffered from the rigors of the climate, and died a few months after arrival there. Löhlein wrote a singspiel, *Zemire und Azor* (Leipzig, 1775);·several instrumental concertos; chamber music; etc.; but he became known mainly through his pedagogical work, *Clavier-Schule* (2 vols., 1765 and 1781), which passed through many editions and was revised by Czerny; he also publ. *Violinschule* (1774).

BIBLIOGRAPHY: F. von Glasenapp, *G.S. Löhlein* (Halle, 1937).

Lohmann, Peter, German poet and writer on music; b. Schwelm, April 24, 1833; d. Leipzig, Jan. 10, 1907. From 1856 he lived in Leipzig, and wrote (1858–61) for the *Neue Zeitschrift für Musik*. He publ. *Über R. Schumanns Faustmusik* (1860) and *Über die dramatische Dichtung mit Musik* (1861; 2nd ed., 1864; 3rd ed. as *Das Ideal der Oper*, 1886).

Lohse, Otto, German conductor and composer; b. Dresden, Sept. 21, 1858; d. Baden-Baden, May 5, 1925. He was a pupil at the Dresden Cons. of Richter (piano), Grützmacher (cello), Draeseke and Wüllner (composition). In 1880 he went to Russia and conducted theater music in Riga; in 1893 he was in Hamburg; there he married the famous singer **Katharina Klafsky,** and in the spring of 1896 both artists were members of the Damrosch Opera Co. in N.Y., with Lohse as conductor. From 1897 to 1904, Lohse conducted opera in Strasbourg; in 1904–11, in Cologne; in 1911–12, at the Théâtre de la Monnaie in Brussels; in 1912–23, at the Leipzig Stadttheater. He composed an opera, *Der Prinz wider Willen* (Riga, 1890), and songs.

BIBLIOGRAPHY: Ernst Lert, *Otto Lohse* (Leipzig, 1918).

Lolli, Antonio, Italian violinist and composer; b. Bergamo, c.1730; d. Palermo, Aug. 10, 1802. Little is known of his early life; he was in Stuttgart at the court of the Duke of Württemberg from 1758 till 1772; asked for a leave of absence, but did not return to Stuttgart; however, he drew his salary until 1774. He gave violin concerts in Hamburg, Lübeck, and Stettin in 1773–74; then proceeded to St. Petersburg, where he became a special favorite of Catherine II, and also ingratiated himself with Potemkin. He received 4,000 rubles annually as violinist to the Empress and chapel master of the court. In Dec. 1777 he visited Stockholm, and then went to Germany. An incorrigible gambler, he dissipated the fortune of 10,000 florins he had accumulated from the Russian emoluments, and in 1780, after protracted journeys through Europe, went back to St. Petersburg; there he was able to regain his social and artistic position; gave concerts at Potemkin's palace in St. Petersburg, and also played in Moscow. Despite his frequent derelictions of duty, he was retained at the court until 1783, when his contract was canceled and he was succeeded as chapel master by Paisiello. However, he continued to give some public concerts, and also lessons, before leaving Russia in 1784. In 1785 he appeared in London; then was in Paris and in Naples, finally settling in Palermo.

Contemporary accounts indicate that Lolli was a violinist of great ability, but also addicted to eccentricities in playing technical passages. He composed and publ. several sets of violin works, among them *5 Sonates et Divertissement* for Violin, with Continuo (1776; dedicated to Potemkin); other violin pieces (concertos, sonatas, etc.); also an *Ecole du violon en Quatuor* (Berlin, 1776; many reprints by various German and French publishers).
BIBLIOGRAPHY: A. Moser, "Arcangelo Corelli und Antonio Lolli; Zwei künstlerische Ehrenrettungen," *Zeitschrift für Musikwissenschaft* (April 1921); R.-Aloys Mooser, *Annales de la Musique et des Musiciens en Russie* (Geneva, 1950; vol. II, pp. 161–68).

Lomakin, Gavriil, Russian singer and composer; b. St. Petersburg, April 6, 1812; d. Gatchina, May 21, 1885. He studied theory with Sapienza; in 1830, became choirmaster and singing master at several institutions in St. Petersburg, and later conductor of the court chapel (1848–59). Together with Balakirev, he established in 1862 the Free School for Music, and had charge of the singing classes until 1870. He wrote 10 *Cherubim Songs;* 14 *Penitential Songs;* a Liturgy; etc.; publ. a *Treatise on Choral Singing;* arrangements for chorus of old Russian hymns.

Lomax, Alan, American ethnomusicologist; b. Austin, Texas, Jan. 31, 1915. He acquired his métier from his father, **John Avery Lomax;** studied at the Univ. of Texas in Austin (B.A., 1936) and at Columbia Univ. During the years 1933–42 he undertook the task of collecting folk songs of the Southwestern and Midwestern regions of the U.S.; in 1963 was appointed head of the Bureau of Applied Social Research. With his father he brought out several collections of unknown American folk songs, among them *The Folk Songs of North America in the English Language* (N.Y., 1960); *Hard-Hitting Songs for Hard-Hit People* (N.Y., 1967); *Folk Song Style and Culture* (Washington, D.C., 1968). They also supervised field recordings of rural and prison work songs, and it was on one such occasion that they discovered Leadbelly. Another "discovery" was "Jelly Roll" Morton, and their recorded interviews, made at the Library of Congress in 1938, resulted in the book *Mr. Jelly Roll* (N.Y., 1950; 2nd ed., Berkeley, 1973).

Lomax, John Avery, American ethnomusicologist; b. Goodman, Miss., Sept. 23, 1867; d. Greenville, Miss., Jan. 26, 1948. He began collecting and notating American folk songs in his early youth; studied music at the Univ. of Texas in Austin; founded the Texas Folklore Society. In 1933 his son **Alan Lomax** joined him in his research.
WRITINGS: *American Ballads and Folk Songs* (N.Y., 1934); *Cowboy Songs and Other Frontier Ballads* (with Alan Lomax; N.Y., 1938; enlarged ed., 1945); *Our Singing Country* (with Alan Lomax; N.Y., 1941); *Best Songs from the Lomax Collections for Pickers and Singers* (posthumous, ed. by Alan Lomax; N.Y., 1966). He also publ. an autobiography,

Adventures of a Ballad Hunter (N.Y., 1947).

Lombard, Alain, French conductor; b. Paris, Oct. 4, 1940. He studied with Gaston Poulet and Suzanne Desmarques in Paris. In 1961 he became a conductor at the Lyons Opera. From 1966–74 he was conductor and music director of the Miami Phil. Orch. In 1971 he was named chief conductor of the Strasbourg Phil. Orch., resigning this post in 1983.

Lombardo, Carmen, Canadian-born American songwriter and saxophone player; b. London, Ontario, July 16, 1903; d. North Miami, Fla., April 17, 1971. He was a brother of **Guy Lombardo** and played the saxophone in his band from 1929 until the year of his death. Carmen Lombardo's lush saxophone tone contributed greatly to the emotional euphony of the Lombardo sound, and his vibrato was most ingratiating. He was also a composer; among his popular hits are such tunes as *Sailboat in the Moonlight, Powder Your Face with Sunshine,* and the lachrymose classic *Boo Hoo,* which he composed in collaboration with John Jacob Loeb.

Lombardo, Guy, Canadian-born American bandleader; b. London, Ontario, June 19, 1902 (of Italian parents); d. Houston, Nov. 5, 1977. With his brother **Carmen Lombardo,** the saxophone player, he organized a dance band, The Royal Canadians, and took it to the U.S. in 1924; 2 other brothers, **Lebert** and **Victor,** were also members of the band. The band rapidly rose to success on the commercial wave of pervasive sentimentality; in 1928 it was publicized as the purveyor of "the sweetest music this side of Heaven." The rendition of *Auld Lang Syne* by the Guy Lombardo Band at the Waldorf-Astoria Hotel in N.Y. at New Year's Eve celebrations every winter from 1929 to 1977 (with the exception of 1959) became a nostalgic feature. In his arrangements, Guy Lombardo cultivated unabashed emotionalism; in his orchestrations, all intervallic interstices are well filled and saxophones are tremulous with vibrato. The result is a velvety, creamy, but not necessarily oleaginous harmoniousness, which possesses an irresistible appeal to the obsolescent members of the superannuated generation of the 1920s. His preferred dynamics was *mezzo-forte,* and his favorite tempo, *andante moderato;* he never allowed the sound of his band to rise to a disturbing *forte* or to descend to a squeaking *pianissimo.* He was a wizard of the golden mean, and his public loved it.

London, George, American bass-baritone; b. Montreal, May 5, 1919, of Russian-Jewish parents. His real name was **Burnstein.** The family moved to Los Angeles in 1935; there he took lessons in operatic interpretations with Richard Lert; also studied voice with Hugo Strelitzer and Nathan Stewart; made his public debut in the opera *Gainsborough's Duchess* by Albert Coates in a concert performance in Los Angeles on April 20, 1941. He appeared as Dr. Grenvil in Verdi's *La Traviata* on Aug. 5, 1941, at the Hollywood Bowl; also sang with the San Francisco Opera on Oct. 24, 1943, in the role of Monterone in

Rigoletto. He took further vocal lessons with Enrico Rosati and Paola Novikova in N.Y.; then, anticipating a serious professional career, he changed his name from the supposedly plebeian and ethnically confining Burnstein to a resounding and patrician London. In 1947 he toured the U.S. and Europe as a member of the Bel Canto Trio, with Frances Yeend, soprano, and Mario Lanza, tenor. His European operatic debut took place, as Amonasro, at the Vienna State Opera on Sept. 3, 1949; he made his Metropolitan Opera debut in N.Y. in the same role on Nov. 13, 1951; this was also the role he sang at his last Metropolitan appearance on March 10, 1966. Altogether he sang with the Metropolitan 249 times in N.Y. and 54 times on tour. On Sept. 16, 1960, he became the first American to sing Boris Godunov (in Russian) at the Bolshoi Theater in Moscow. In 1967 he was stricken with a partial paralysis of the larynx, but recovered sufficiently to be able to perform administrative duties. From 1968–71 he was artistic administrator of the John F. Kennedy Center for the Performing Arts in Washington, D.C.; was also executive director of the National Opera Inst. from 1971–77. He was general director of the Opera Society of Washington, D.C., from 1975–77, when he suffered a cardiac arrest that precluded any further public activities. Among his best roles were Wotan, Don Giovanni, Scarpia, Escamillo, and Boris Godunov.

BIBLIOGRAPHY: J. Wechsberg, "The Vocal Mission," a "profile" of George London, in the *New Yorker* (Oct. 26 and Nov. 2, 1957).

Long, Marguerite, notable French pianist and pedagogue; b. Nîmes, Nov. 13, 1874; d. Paris, Feb. 13, 1966. She studied piano with Marmontel at the Paris Cons.; was appointed an instructor there in 1906, her tenure running until 1940; in 1920 she founded her own music school; in 1940 Jacques Thibaud, the violinist, joined her; with him she gave numerous recitals and established the Long-Thibaud Competitions. She played an important role in promoting French music; in 1931 gave the first performance of the Piano Concerto by Ravel, dedicated to her. She was married to Joseph de Marliave. She publ. *Au piano avec Claude Debussy* (Paris, 1960); *Au piano avec Gabriel Fauré* (Paris, 1963).

BIBLIOGRAPHY: Janine Weill, *Marguerite Long: Une Vie fascinante* (Paris, 1969).

Longas, Federico, Spanish pianist and composer; b. Barcelona, July 18, 1893; d. Santiago, Chile, June 17, 1968. He was a pupil of Granados and Malats; toured widely in the U.S., South America, and Europe as accompanist to Tito Schipa and as a soloist. He founded a piano school, the Longas Academy, in Barcelona; later he went to Paris; then to the U.S., settling in N.Y. His works include effective piano pieces (*Jota, Aragon,* etc.) and over 100 songs (*Castilian Moonlight, La guinda, Muñequita,* etc.).

Longhurst, William Henry, English organist and composer; b. London, Oct. 6, 1819; d. Canterbury, June 17, 1904. He was a chorister at Canterbury Cathedral (1828–36); then assistant organist (1836–73); in 1873, became first organist, retiring in 1898 after 70 years of uninterrupted service in the Cathedral. He received the degree of Mus.Doc. in 1875; was a music lecturer at St. Augustine's College, Canterbury. He wrote an oratorio, *David and Absalom* (1872); a cathedral service; other church music; etc.

Longo, Achille, Italian composer, son of **Alessandro Longo;** b. Naples, March 28, 1900; d. there, May 28, 1954. He studied at the Naples Cons.; taught harmony there (1926–30); then at the Cons. of Parma (1930–34); in 1934 returned to Naples and taught composition at the Cons. until his death.

WORKS: Suite for Flute, Oboe, Clarinet, Bassoon, and Piano (1926; won the Bellini Prize); Piano Concerto (Venice, 1932); Piano Quintet (1934); Violin Concerto (1937); *Notturno* and *Corteo* for Orch. (1942); Requiem (1947); *Serenata in do* for Orch. (1950).

Longo, Alessandro, Italian pianist and music editor; b. Amantea, Dec. 30, 1864; d. Naples, Nov. 3, 1945. He studied with Cesi (piano) and Serrao (composition); in 1887, was appointed prof. of piano at the Naples Cons. In 1892 he founded the Circolo Scarlatti to promote the works of Domenico Scarlatti; from 1914, edited the periodical *L'Arte Pianistica.* His most important achievement is the complete edition of Domenico Scarlatti's harpsichord works (10 vols. and a supplement; the order of sonatas was partly superseded by Kirkpatrick's catalogue). He was also a prolific composer; publ. numerous pieces for piano solo and piano, 4-hands; Piano Quintet; *Tema con variazioni* for Harp; Suite for Clarinet and Piano; songs.

Longy, Georges, French oboe virtuoso; b. Abbeville, Aug. 29, 1868; d. Mareuil (Dordogne), March 29, 1930. He studied at the Paris Cons. (first prize, 1886); was a member of the Lamoureux Orch. (1886–88) and of the Colonne Orch. (1888–98). In 1898 he was engaged as first oboe player of the Boston Symph. Orch., and remained there until 1925. From 1899 to 1913 he conducted the Boston Orchestral Club. In 1900 he founded the Longy Club for chamber music; in 1916 he established his own music school in Boston (later the Longy School of Music in Cambridge, Mass.).

Lonque, Georges, Belgian composer; b. Ghent, Nov. 8, 1900; d. Brussels, March 3, 1967. He studied with Moeremans, Mathieu, and Lunssens at the Ghent Cons.; was awarded the 2nd Prix de Rome for his cantatas *Le Rossignol* in 1927 and for *Antigone* in 1929. He was a prof. of harmony at his alma mater after 1932, and was director of the music academy in Renaix (1938–64). His music was influenced mainly by Debussy, Fauré, and Ravel.

WORKS: *Impressions d'Hemelrijk* for Orch. (1925); *Vieux quai* for Violin or Cello, and Orch. (1928); *Aura,* symph. poem and ballet (1930); *Wiener Walzer* for Small Orch. (1933); *Poème de la mer* for Cello and Orch. (1935); *Images d'Orient* for Saxophone or Viola, and Orch. (1935); *Porcelaines de Saxe* for Small Orch. (1939); *Prélude et Aria* for Cello and Orch. (1943); *Estrelle* for Violin and Orch. (1944); Violin Concerto (1948); *Afgoden (Idoles)* for Clarinet and Orch. (1950); Violin Sonata (1925); *Caprice* for Violin and Piano (1930); String Quartet (1937); piano pieces, including *Nuit d'automne* (1929), 2 sonatinas (1939, 1944), *Voilier* (1952), *Tableaux d'une chambre bleue* (1952), and *Nocturne* (1955); *Missa pro pace* for Male Chorus and Organ (1941); numerous songs, including *Faune* (1933), *Why Don't You Come?* (1944), *La Question* (1957), and *Portrait* (1957).

Loomis, Clarence, American pianist and composer; b. Sioux Falls, S.Dak., Dec. 13, 1889; d. Aptos, Calif., July 3, 1965. He studied at the American Cons. of Chicago with Heniot Levy (piano) and Adolph Weidig (composition); subsequently took lessons with Leopold Godowsky in Vienna. Returning to the U.S., he held various positions as a music teacher; taught piano and organ at Highland Univ. in New Mexico (1945–55); in 1960 he settled in Aptos, Calif..
WORKS: As a composer, he was mainly successful in writing light operas in a Romantic vein; among them are *Yolanda of Cyprus* (London, Ontario, Sept. 25, 1929; also given in Chicago, Washington, D.C., and N.Y.); *A Night in Avignon* (Indianapolis, July 1932); *The White Cloud* (1935); *The Fall of the House of Usher* (Indianapolis, Jan. 11, 1941); *Revival* (1943); *The Captive Woman* (1953); he further wrote a comic ballet, *The Flapper and the Quarterback,* which was first performed in Kyoto, Japan, at the coronation of Emperor Hirohito, Nov. 10, 1928; for Orch.: *Gargoyles,* symph. prelude (1936); *Gaelic Suite* for Strings (1953); *Fantasy* for Piano and Orch. (1954); *Macbeth* (1954); *The Passion Play* for Chorus and Orch.; 2 string quartets (1953, 1963); cantata, *Song of the White Earth* (1956); numerous sacred choruses; *Susanna Don't You Cry,* a stage extravaganza (1939); piano suites; songs; organ pieces.
BIBLIOGRAPHY: E.E. Hipsher, *American Opera and Its Composers* (Philadelphia, 1934; pp. 298–301).

Loomis, Harvey Worthington, American composer; b. Brooklyn, Feb. 5, 1865; d. Boston, Dec. 25, 1930. He was a pupil in composition of Dvořák at the National Cons. in N.Y. (1891–93) when Dvořák was director there; later lived mostly in Boston; became interested in Indian music, and publ. many arrangements of Indian melodies; also original works in that style (*Lyrics of the Red Man,* etc.).
WORKS: Grand opera, *The Traitor Mandolin;* 2 melodramas: *The Song of the Pear* and *The Story of a Faithful Soul;* 4 comic operas: *The Maid of Athens, The Burglar's Bride, Going Up?, The Bey of Baba;* musical pantomimes: *Put to the Test, Her Revenge, In Old New Amsterdam, The Enchanted Fountain, Love and Witchcraft, Blanc et Noir;* incidental music to *The Tragedy of Death* and *The Coming of the Prince; Fairy Hill; Song Flowers for Children to Gather* (2 books); *Toy Tunes;* etc. Many of his MSS are in the Music Division of the Library of Congress.
BIBLIOGRAPHY: Rupert Hughes, *Contemporary American Composers* (Boston, 1900; pp. 77–92).

Loose, Emmy, Austrian soprano; b. Karbitz, Bohemia, Jan. 22, 1914. She was educated at the Prague Cons.; then made her debut at the Hannover Opera (1940). After 1941 she sang with the Vienna State Opera; also appeared in South America. In 1970 she was appointed to the faculty of the Vienna Academy of Music.

Looser, Rolf, Swiss cellist and composer; b. Niederscherli, near Bern, May 3, 1920. He studied cello with Richard Sturzenegger at the Cons. of Bern and theory with Moeschinger; he received his concert diploma in 1944 and subsequently took additional cello lessons with Pierre Fournier in Paris; he also continued his composition study with Willy Burkhardt in Zürich and with Frank Martin in Geneva. In 1953 he joined the staff of the Bern Cons. as a cello instructor; in 1963 he took up residence in Biel. Among his works are a *Fantasie* for Cello and Orch. (1958); *Rhapsodie* for Cello and Chamber Orch. (1961); *Fantasia a quattro* (1966); *Alyssos,* 5 pieces for String Orch. and Percussion (1968).

Lopatnikoff, Nicolai, outstanding Russian-American composer; b. Reval, Estonia, March 16, 1903; d. Pittsburgh, Oct. 7, 1976. He studied at the St. Petersburg Cons. (1914–17); after the Revolution, continued his musical training at the Helsinki Cons. with Furuhjelm (1918–20); then went to Germany, where he studied with Hermann Grabner in Heidelberg (1920) and Ernst Toch and Willy Rehberg in Mannheim (1921); concurrently took civil engineering at the Technological College in Karlsruhe (1921–27). He lived in Berlin (1929–33) and London (1933–39); came to the U.S. in 1939; became a naturalized citizen in 1944. He taught in N.Y. and Connecticut; in 1945 became a prof. of composition at the Carnegie Inst. of Technology (now Carnegie-Mellon Univ.) in Pittsburgh, retiring in 1969. In 1951 he married the poet Sara Henderson Hay. He was elected to the National Inst. of Arts and Letters in 1963. His music is cast in a neo-Classical manner, distinguished by a vigorous rhythmic pulse, a clear melodic line, and a wholesome harmonic investment. A prolific composer, he wrote music in all genres; being a professional pianist, he often performed his own piano concertos with orchs.
WORKS: FOR THE STAGE: Opera, *Danton* (1930–32), unperf.; a *Danton Suite* for Orch., excerpted from the opera, was first perf. in Pittsburgh, March 25, 1967; a ballet in 6 scenes, *Melting Pot* (1975; Indianapolis, March 26, 1976).
FOR ORCH.: *Prelude to a Drama* (1920; lost); 2 piano concertos: No. 1 (1921; Cologne, Nov. 3, 1925) and No. 2 (1930; Düsseldorf, Oct. 16, 1930); *Introduction and Scherzo* (1927–29; first complete perf., N.Y., Oct. 23, 1930); 4 symphs.: No. 1 (1928; Karlsruhe, Jan. 9, 1929); No. 2 (1938–39; 4-movement version, Boston,

Dec. 22, 1939; withdrawn and revised in 3 movements); No. 3 (1953–54; Pittsburgh, Dec. 10, 1954); No. 4 (1970–71; Pittsburgh, Jan. 21, 1972); *Short Overture* (1932; lost); *Opus Sinfonicum* (1933; revised 1942; first prize of the Cleveland Orch.; Cleveland, Dec. 9, 1943); *2 Russian Nocturnes* (1939; originally the 2 middle movements of the 2nd Symph.); Violin Concerto (1941; Boston, April 17, 1942); Sinfonietta (1942; first public perf., Festival of International Society for Contemporary Music, Berkeley, Calif., Aug. 2, 1942); Concertino for Orch. (1944; Boston, March 2, 1945); Concerto for 2 Pianos and Orch. (1950–51; Pittsburgh, Dec. 7, 1951); Divertimento (1951; La Jolla, Calif., Aug. 19, 1951); *Variazioni concertanti* (1958; Pittsburgh, Nov. 7, 1958); *Music for Orchestra* (1958; Louisville, Ky., Jan. 14, 1959); *Festival Overture* (1960; Detroit, Oct. 12, 1960); Concerto for Orch. (1964; Pittsburgh, April 3, 1964; orch. version of Concerto for Wind Orch.); *Partita concertante* for Chamber Orch. (1966); *Variations and Epilogue* for Cello and Orch. (1973; Pittsburgh, Dec. 14, 1973; orchestration of 1946 chamber piece). FOR WIND ORCH.: Concerto for Wind Orch. (1963; Pittsburgh, June 23, 1963); *Music for Band* (1963; transcribed by William Schaefer from *Music for Orchestra*). CHAMBER MUSIC: 2 piano trios (1918, lost; 1935); 3 string quartets (1920; 1924, revised 1928; 1955); Duo for Violin and Cello (1927); Sonata for Violin, Piano, and Snare Drum (1927; revised in 1967 as Sonata for Violin, Piano, and Percussion); Cello Sonata (1929); *Arabesque* for Cello or Bassoon, and Piano (1931); 3 Pieces for Violin and Piano (1931); *Variations and Epilogue* for Cello and Piano (1946; orchestrated 1973); Violin Sonata No. 2 (1948); *Fantasia concertante* for Violin and Piano (1962); *Divertimento da camera* for 10 Instruments (1965). FOR PIANO: *4 Small Piano Pieces* (1920); Prelude and Fugue (1920); Sonatina (1926; revised 1967); *2 Pieces* for Mechanical Piano (1927; lost); *2 danses ironiques* (1928; revised 1967); *5 Contrasts* (1930); *Dialogues* (1932); *Variations* (1933); Sonata (1943); *Intervals,* 7 studies (1957). FOR VOICE: Songs. BIBLIOGRAPHY: *Composers of the Americas,* vol. 12 (Washington, D.C., 1966); a privately publ. monograph, *The Compositions of Nikolai Lopatnikoff: A Catalogue,* compiled by William Critser (Pittsburgh, 1979).

Lopes-Graça, Fernando, eminent Portuguese pianist, composer, and musicologist; b. Tomar, Dec. 17, 1906. He took piano lessons at home; studied composition with Tomás Borba and musicology with Luís de Freitas Branco at the Lisbon Cons. (1923–31); subsequently was an instructor at the Instituto de Música in Coimbra (1932–36); was compelled to leave Portugal in 1937 for political reasons, and went to Paris, where he studied composition with Charles Koechlin. After the outbreak of World War II he returned to Lisbon and became active in the modern musical movement; taught at the Academia de Amadores de Música there (1940–54); in 1958 went to Brazil as a pianist; in 1959 made a concert tour in Angola, a Portuguese colony at the time; and in 1977 toured the Soviet Union with the Portuguese tenor Fernando Serafim. His music is inspired by nationalistic themes, and is inherently lyrical.

WORKS: FOR THE STAGE: Cantata-melodrama in 2 parts, *D. Duardos e Flérida,* for Narrator, 3 Soloists, Chorus, and Orch. (1964–69; Lisbon, Nov. 28, 1970); revue-ballet, *La Fièvre du temps,* for 2 Pianos (1938). FOR ORCH.: *Poemeto* for Strings (1928); *Prelúdio, Pastoral e Dança* (1929); 2 piano concertos (1940, 1942); *3 Portuguese Dances* (1941); Sinfonia (1944); *5 estelas funerárias* (1948); *Scherzo heróico* (1949); *Suite rústica No. 1* (1950–51); *Marcha festiva* (1954); Concertino for Piano, Strings, Brass, and Percussion (1954); *5 Old Portuguese Romances* (1951–55); *Divertimento* for Winds, Kettledrums, Percussion, Cellos, and Double Basses (1957); *Poema de Dezembro* (1961); Viola Concertino (1962); *4 bosquejos (4 Sketches)* for Strings (1965); *Concerto da camera,* with Cello obbligato (Moscow, Oct. 6, 1967, Rostropovich, soloist); *Viagens na minha terra* (*Travels in My Country;* 1969–70); *Fantasia* for Piano and Orch., on a religious song from Beira-Baixa (1974). FOR VOICE: *Pequeno cancioneiro do Menino Jesus* (*Little Songbook of the Child Jesus*) for Women's Chorus, 3 Flutes, String Quartet, Celesta, and Harp (1936–59); *História trágico-marítima* for Baritone, Contralto, Chorus, and Orch. (1942–59); *9 Portuguese Folk Songs* for Voice and Orch. (1948–49); *4 Songs of Federico García Lorca* for Baritone, 2 Clarinets, Violin, Viola, Cello, Harp, and Percussion (1953–54); *Cantos do Natal (Christmas Carols)* for Female Voices and Instrumental Ensemble (1958); *9 cantigas de amigo* for Voice and Chamber Ensemble (1964); *6 cantos sefardins (Sephardite Songs)* for Voice and Orch. (1971); choruses; songs. CHAMBER MUSIC: *Estudo-Humoresca* for Flute, Oboe, Clarinet, 2 Violins, Viola, and Cello (1930); 2 violin sonatinas (1931, revised 1951; 1931, revised 1970); Piano Quartet (1939; revised 1963); *Prelúdio, Capricho e Galope* for Violin and Piano (1941; revised 1951); *Página esquecida (Forgotten Leaf)* for Cello and Piano (1955); *Pequeno tríptico* for Violin and Piano (1960); *Prelúdio e Fuga* for Solo Violin (1961); *Canto de Amor e de Morte* for Piano Quintet (1961); *4 invençoes* for Solo Cello (1961); String Quartet (1964); *Suite rústica No. 2* for String Quartet (1965); *14 anotaçoes (14 Annotations)* for String Quartet (1966); *7 souvenirs* for Vieira da Silva for Wind Quintet (1966); *The Tomb of Villa-Lobos* for Wind Quintet (1970); *3 inflorescências* for Solo Cello (1973); *3 capriccetti* for Flute and Guitar (1975); *2 Airs* for Solo Flute (1976); *2 Movements* for Solo Flute (1977). FOR PIANO: 5 sonatas (1934; 1939, revised 1956; 1952; 1961; 1977); *8 Bagatelles* (1939–48; No. 4, 1950); *Glosas; (Glosses;* 1950); *24 Preludes* (1950–55); *Album do jovem pianista (Album for a Young Pianist;* 1953–63); *2 sonatinas recuperadas (2 Restored Sonatinas;* 194?; rewritten 1960); *In Memoriam Béla Bartók,* 8 progressive suites (1960–75); *4 Impromptus* (1961); *Piano Music for Children* (1968–76); *4 Pieces* for Harpsichord (1970–71).

FOR GUITAR: *Prelúdio e Baileto* (1968); *Partita* (1970–71); *Sonatina* (1974).

WRITINGS: About 25 books, including *Música e músicos modernos* (Oporto, 1943); *Dicionário de música* (with Borba, Lisbon: vol. 1, 1956; vol. 2, 1958); *Escritos musicológicos* (Lisbon, 1977); biographies of Mozart, Chopin, Bartók; essay on Portuguese music. In 1960 he ed., with Michel Giacometti, the first vol. of the *Antologia da Música Regional Portuguesa,* the first attempt to collect, in a systematic way, the regional songs of Portugal.

BIBLIOGRAPHY: M.V. Henriques, *Fernando Lopes Graça na música portuguesa contemporanea* (Sacavém, 1956).

Lopez, Vincent, American jazz pianist, composer, and bandleader; b. Brooklyn, Dec. 30, 1894; d. North Miami Beach, Fla., Sept. 20, 1975. His father, of Portuguese ancestry, a bandmaster in the U.S. Navy, taught Lopez the rudiments of music. However, he sent him to St. Mary's Passionist Monastery in the hope that he would become a Roman Catholic priest. But Lopez turned to music, and as a teenager played in the beer halls of Brooklyn. Later he led restaurant orchs. in N.Y. On Nov. 27, 1921, he inaugurated a regular broadcasting hour of dance band music over the radio station WJX in Newark, on which he popularized the song *Nola,* using it as a signature, opening with a greeting, "Hello, everybody ... Lopez speaking." He had the first sustaining television show, "Dinner Date with Lopez," which featured show-business personalities. Among his song hits were *Rockin' Chair Swing, Knock, Knock, Who's There?,* and *The World Stands Still.* He also gave lectures on numerology and related pseudo-sciences.

López-Buchardo, Carlos, Argentine composer; b. Buenos Aires, Oct. 12, 1881; d. there, April 21, 1948. He studied piano and harmony in Buenos Aires; composition with Albert Roussel in Paris; became director of the National Cons. in Buenos Aires. His music is set in a vivid style, rooted in national folk song; particularly successful in this respect is his symph. suite *Escenas argentinas* (Buenos Aires, Aug. 12, 1922, under Felix Weingartner). Other works are the opera *El sueño de alma* (Buenos Aires, Aug. 4, 1914; won the Municipal Prize); lyric comedies: *Madame Lynch* (1932); *La perichona* (1933); *Amalia* (1935); several piano pieces in an Argentine folk manner; songs.

Lopez-Cobos, Jesús, Spanish conductor; b. Toro, Feb. 25, 1940. He studied philosophy at Madrid Univ.; at the same time he took courses in music; then went to Vienna to study conducting with Hans Swarowsky. In 1969 he won first prize in the International Conductors' Competition in Besançon. He then conducted in Italy and West Germany. In 1972 he made his American debut with the San Francisco Opera. In 1980 he was named Generalmusik-direktor of the Deutsche Oper in West Berlin.

Lo Presti, Ronald, American composer; b. Williamstown, Mass., Oct. 28, 1933. He studied composition with Louis Mennini and Bernard Rogers at the Eastman School of Music in Rochester, N.Y. (M.M., 1956); subsequently was engaged as a clarinet teacher in public schools; in 1964 was appointed an instructor in music theory at Arizona State Univ. at Tempe. He obtained popular success with his score *The Masks,* which was commissioned for the space exhibit at the aerospace building at the Smithsonian Inst.

WORKS: One-act opera, *The Birthday* (1962; Winfield, May 1962); children's opera, *Playback* (Tucson, Ariz., Dec. 18, 1970); *The Masks* for Orch. (Rochester, May 8, 1955); *Nocturne* for Small Orch. (1955–56); *Nocturne* for Viola and String Orch. (1959); *Kansas Overture* (1960); *Kanza Suite* for Orch. (1961); *Llano estacado (The Staked Plain)* for Orch. (1961); *Port Triumphant* for Orch. (1962); 2 symphs. (1966, 1968); *From the Southwest* for Orch. (1967); *Rhapsody* for Marimba, Vibraphone, and Orch. (1975). For Voice: *Alleluia* for Chorus, Brass, and Timpani (1960); *Kanza* for 4 Narrators, Chorus, and Orch. (1961); *Tribute* for Chorus, and Orch. and/or Band (1962); *Scarecrow* for Children's Ballet Co., Mixed Voices, and Cello Orch. (1973); *Ode to Independence* for Baritone, Chorus, and Band (1974); *Requiem* for Chorus and Orch. (1975); *Memorials* for Chorus and Orch. (1975); choruses; songs. For Symph. Band: *Pageant* (1956); *Prelude* (1959); *Introduction, Chorale and Jubilee* (1961); *Tundra* (1967); *A Festive Music* (1968). Chamber music: *Suite* for 8 Horns (1952); *Sketch* for Percussion (1956); *Suite* for 4 Horns (1958); *5 Pieces* for Violin and Piano (1960); *Scherzo* for Violin Quartet (1960); *Chorale* for 3 Tubas (1960); *Fanfare* for 38 Brasses (1960); *Requiescat* for Brass Ensemble (1961); *Suite* for 5 Trumpets (1961); *Miniature* for Brass Quartet (1962); *Rondo* for Timpani and Piano (1969); Trio for 3 Percussionists (1971); String Quartet (1970); *Suite* for 6 Bassoons (1971); Fantasy for 5 Horns (1972); *Cantalena* for Cello Orch. (1972); Wind Quintet (1975).

Lorengar, Pilar, Spanish soprano; b. Saragossa, Oct. 12, 1921. She studied at the Cons. in Barcelona; also in Madrid. She made her debut in Barcelona in 1949; then sang in Paris and London. She came to America in 1955; appeared with the San Francisco and Chicago operas; made her Metropolitan Opera debut in N.Y. on Feb. 11, 1966, as Donna Elvira.

Lorentz, Alfred, German composer and conductor; b. Strasbourg, March 7, 1872; d. Karlsruhe, April 23, 1931. He studied with Rheinberger in Munich (composition), and with Mottl at Karlsruhe (conducting). He was chorus master, and later conductor, at the Municipal Theater in Strasbourg; from 1899 to 1925, was court conductor in Karlsruhe. He wrote the operas *Der Mönch von Sendomir* (Karlsruhe, 1907); *Die beiden Automaten* (Karlsruhe, 1913); *Liebesmacht* (Karlsruhe, 1922); *Schneider Fips* (Coburg, 1928); an operetta, *Die Mondscheindame* (Karlsruhe, 1919); some orch. works.

Lorentzen – Lorenzani

Lorentzen, Bent, Danish composer; b. Stenvad, Feb. 11, 1935. He studied with Jeppesen at the Aarhus Cons., and with Hjelmborg, Halmboe, Jersild, and Hoffding at the Royal Cons. in Copenhagen; had training in electronic music in Stockholm (1967–68). He subsequently taught at the Jutland Cons. in Aarhus. In his music he employs a variety of quaquaversal techniques, often utilizing purely sonoristic effects.
WORKS: 6 operas: *Stalten Mettelil (Haughty Little Mette;* 1963; Aarhus, Nov. 20, 1963; revised 1972); *Dissonances* (1964); *Eurydice,* radio opera (1965; Danish Radio, Dec. 16, 1969; first stage production, Aarhus, Sept. 1973; Prix Italia, 1970); *Tårnet (The Tower),* a film opera (1966); *Tristan Variations* for 3 Voices and Tape (1969); *This Music Seems Very Familiar,* comic skit based on Mozart's operas, for 4 Singers and Tape (1973–74; Kiel, Germany, May 3, 1974); 2 ballets: *Jomfru i fugleham (Young Maiden as a Bird)* for Orch. and Tape (1967) and *Afgrundens Brønd (The Bottomless Pit)* for Tape (1972); *The Night* for Soprano, Chorus, and Orch. (1965; Aarhus, April 4, 1979); *Shiftings* for Orch. (1966–67); *Cyclus 4* for String Orch. and Percussion (1966); *Music for Mozart Orchestra* (1966–67); *The Unconscious* for Orch. (1967); *Tide* for Orch. (1971; revised 1977); *My Bride Is an Enclosed Garden* for Solo Voice, Tape, and Orch. (1972); *Quadrata* for String Quartet (1963); *Cyclus 1* for Violin, Cello, and Double Bass (1966); *Cyclus 2* for 3 Percussionists (1966); *Cyclus 3* for Cello and Triple Playback (1966); *Studie für 2* for Cello and Percussion (1967); *Music Theater for 3* for Soprano, Cello, and Percussion (1968); *The End* for Solo Cello (1969); *Danish Wind* for Wind Quintet (1970); *Intersection* for Organ (1970); *Syncretism* for Clarinet, Trombone, Cello, and Piano (1970); *3 Mobiles* for Accordion, Guitar, and Percussion (1971); *Quartetto Rustico* for String Quartet (1971); *Quartz* for Solo Violin (1971); *Granite* for Solo Cello (1971); *Puncta* for Organ (1973); *Triplex* for Organ (1973); *Groppe* for Organ (1974); *Carnaval* for 3 Voices and Tape (1976); choruses.

Lorenz, Alfred Ottokar, Austrian musicologist, composer, and conductor; b. Vienna, July 11, 1868; d. Munich, Nov. 20, 1939. He studied at the Univ. of Vienna with Spitta; conducted opera at Königsberg and Elberfeld (1894–97), and at Coburg-Gotha (1898–1916); from 1920, lived in Munich; lectured at Munich Univ. from 1923. He made a specialty of Wagnerian research; publ. the comprehensive work *Das Geheimnis der Form bei Richard Wagner,* in 4 vols.: *Die musikalische Formgebung in Richard Wagners Ring des Nibelungen* (1924), *Der musikalische Aufbau von Tristan und Isolde* (1926), *Die Meistersinger* (1930), and *Parsifal* (1933); the musical architecture and form of the operas are here analyzed in minute detail. He further publ. *Alessandro Scarlattis Jugendoper* (1927); *Abendländische Musikgeschichte im Rhythmus der Generationen* (1928); and numerous smaller essays in various music magazines, on Bach, Mozart, Beethoven, Weber, Wagner, Richard Strauss, etc. He composed an opera, *Helges Erwachen* (Schwerin, 1896); incidental

music to various plays; the symph. poems *Bergfahrt* and *Columbus;* some chamber music; and songs.

Lorenz, Franz, Austrian writer on music; b. Stein, April 4, 1805; d. Vienna, April 8, 1883. He was a physician by profession; took great interest in music, and publ. valuable pamphlets on Mozart: *In Sachen Mozarts* (Vienna, 1851); *Mozart als Klavier-Komponist* (Breslau, 1866); numerous articles in Vienna newspapers and magazines.

Lorenz, Julius, German composer; b. Hannover, Oct. 1, 1862; d. Glogau, Oct. 1, 1924. He was a pupil of Reinecke and Jadassohn at the Leipzig Cons.; in 1884–95, he conducted the singing academy at Glogau; in 1895 he settled in N.Y. as a choral conductor; led the singing society Arion; in 1911, returned to Glogau. He wrote an opera, *Die Rekruten;* many choral works, both sacred and secular; some chamber music.

Lorenz, Karl Adolf, German composer; b. Köslin, Aug. 13, 1837; d. Stettin, March 3, 1923. He studied music in Berlin with Dehn, Kiel, and Gehrig; also at Berlin Univ. (Dr.Phil., 1861). He settled in Stettin, becoming conductor of the symph. concerts of the Lehrer-Gesangverein; succeeded Loewe as municipal director of music; founded the Stettiner Musikverein (for oratorio).
WORKS: Secular oratorios: *Otto der Grosse, Winfried, Krösus, Die Jungfrau von Orleans, Das Licht;* Passion cantata, *Golgotha;* 2 operas: *Die Komödie der Irrungen* and *Harald und Theano;* Symph.; Piano Trio; etc.
BIBLIOGRAPHY: K. König, *Karl Adolph Lorenz* (Stettin, 1937).

Lorenz, Max, German tenor; b. Düsseldorf, May 17, 1901; d. Salzburg, Jan. 11, 1975. He studied with Grenzebach; sang with the Dresden Opera; made his American debut with the Metropolitan Opera Co. in N.Y. as Walther in *Die Meistersinger* (N.Y., Nov. 12, 1931); appeared there again in 1933–34. From 1934 to 1939 he sang in Berlin and in Vienna; joined the Chicago Opera for one season; also made appearances in London, at La Scala in Milan, and at the Paris Opéra. He sang the roles of Tristan and Siegfried at the Bayreuth Festival (1933, 1942, 1952).
BIBLIOGRAPHY: W. Hermann, *Max Lorenz* (1976).

Lorenzani, Paolo, Italian composer; b. Rome, 1640; d. there, Oct. 28, 1713. He was a pupil of Orazio Benevoli at the Vatican; having failed to obtain Benevoli's position after the latter's death in 1672, he was given the post of maestro di cappella at the Jesuit College and at the Seminario Romano in Rome in 1675; in 1675–76 held a similar position at the Cathedral of Messina; when Sicily was captured by the French, the Duc de Vivonne, who was the French viceroy, induced Lorenzani to go to Paris (1678); he found favor with Louis XIV, and became court musician; in 1679 he was sent to Italy to recruit singers for the French court; he produced his Italian pastoral, *Nicandro e Fileno,* at Fontainebleau (1681); in 1679–83 he was "surintendant" of music to the Queen; after the Queen died he became choirmaster at the Italian religious order of Théatins in Paris (1685). For several years Lorenzani was supported by the Paris faction opposed to Lully; after Lully's death, Lorenzani produced an opera with a French libretto, *Orontée* (Paris, Aug. 23, 1687). This having failed, Lorenzani turned to the composition of motets, which proved his best works; the famous Paris publisher Ballard brought them out in an impressively printed edition; Ballard also publ. a book of Italian airs by Lorenzani. In 1694 Lorenzani returned to Italy, and was appointed maestro of the Cappella Giulia at St. Peter's, the post he had tried unsuccessfully to secure in 1672; there he remained until his death. His printed works include 25 motets for one to 5 voices (Paris, 1693); 6 Italian airs (Paris, 1690); and several separate vocal numbers; Henry Prunières reproduced a scene from Lorenzani's opera *Nicandro e Fileno* in the *Revue Musicale* (Aug. 1922).

BIBLIOGRAPHY: M. Brenet, *Les Concerts en France sous l'ancien régime* (Paris, 1900); Henry Prunières, *L'Opéra italien en France avant Lulli* (Paris, 1913); idem, "Paolo Lorenzani à la cour de France," *Revue Musicale* (Aug. 1922).

Lorenzi-Fabris, Ausonio de, Italian composer; b. Montebelluna, Jan. 18, 1861; d. Venice, July 30, 1935. He studied at the Liceo Benedetto Marcello in Venice. He composed the operas *Gli Adorati del fuoco* (Venice, Jan. 27, 1891); *Maometto II* (Venice, July 9, 1892; revised, Florence, May 9, 1903); *Il Re si annoia* (Trieste, Dec. 19, 1904); a religious play, *Refugium peccatorum* (Venice, March 24, 1897).

Lorenzo, Leonardo de, Italian flutist; b. Viggiano, Aug. 29, 1875; d. Santa Barbara, Calif., July 27, 1962. He studied at the Naples Cons.; from 1897 to 1907, was a flutist in various traveling orchs. In 1910 he emigrated to the U.S.; was first flutist of the N.Y. Phil. (1910–12); later, with the Minneapolis Symph. Orch., the Los Angeles Phil., and the Rochester Phil.; taught flute at the Eastman School of Music in Rochester, N.Y.; in 1935, settled in California. He publ. several books of flute studies and some solo pieces, and an informative book on flute playing and flute players, *My Complete Story of the Flute* (N.Y., 1951).

Loriod, Yvonne, French pianist; b. Houilles, Jan. 20, 1924. She studied at the Paris Cons. with Lazar Lévy and composition with Messiaen and Milhaud. She toured as a concert pianist in Germany and Austria; made her American debut in 1949 as piano soloist in Messiaen's work *Turangalila;* subsequently joined the faculty of the Paris Cons. She was the 2nd wife of **Olivier Messiaen.**

Lortzing, (Gustav) Albert, celebrated German opera composer; b. Berlin, Oct. 23, 1801; d. there, Jan. 21, 1851. His parents were actors, and the wandering life led by the family did not allow him to pursue a methodical course of study. He learned acting from his father, and music from his mother at an early age. After some lessons in piano with Griebel and in theory with Rungenhagen in Berlin, he continued his own studies, and soon began to compose. On Jan. 30, 1823, he married the actress Rosina Regina Ahles in Cologne; they had 11 children. In 1824 he wrote his first opera (to his own libretto), *Ali Pascha von Janina,* which, however, was not produced until 4 years later (Münster, Feb. 1, 1828). In 1832 he brought out the liederspiel *Der Pole und sein Kind* and the singspiel *Scenen aus Mozarts Leben,* which were well received on several German stages. From 1833 to 1844 he was engaged at the Municipal Theater of Leipzig as a tenor; there he launched a light opera, *Die beiden Schützen* (Feb. 20, 1837), which became instantly popular; on the same stage he produced, on Dec. 22, 1837, his undoubted masterpiece, *Czaar und Zimmermann* (later spelling, *Zar und Zimmermann*), to his own libretto derived from various French plays, and based on the true history of Peter the Great of Russia, who worked as a carpenter in the Netherlands. The opera was produced in Berlin in 1839, and from then on its success was assured; after a few years it became a favorite on most European stages. Lortzing's next opera, *Caramo, oder Das Fischerstechen* (Leipzig, Sept. 20, 1839), was a failure; there followed *Hans Sachs* (Leipzig, June 23, 1840) and *Casanova* (Leipzig, Dec. 31, 1841), which passed without much notice; subsequent comparisons showed some similarities between *Hans Sachs* and *Die Meistersinger,* not only in subject matter, which was derived from the same source, but also in some melodic patterns; however, no one seriously suggested that Wagner was influenced by Lortzing's inferior work. There followed a Romantic opera, *Der Wildschütz* (Leipzig, Dec. 31, 1842), which was in many respects the best that Lortzing wrote, but its success, although impressive, never equaled that of *Zar und Zimmermann.* At about the same time, Lortzing attempted still another career, that of opera impresario, but it was short-lived; his brief conductorship at the Leipzig Opera was similarly ephemeral. Composing remained his chief occupation; he produced *Undine* in Magdeburg (April 21, 1845) and *Der Waffenschmied* in Vienna (May 31, 1846). In Vienna he also acted as a conductor; after a season or two at the Theater an der Wien, he returned to Leipzig, where he produced the light opera *Zum Grossadmiral* (Dec. 13, 1847), which was only moderately successful. The revolutionary events of 1848 seriously affected his position in both Leipzig and Vienna; after the political situation became settled, he produced in Leipzig an opera of a Romantic nature, *Rolands Knappen* (May 25, 1849). Although at least 4 of his operas were played at various German theaters, Lortzing received no honorarium, owing to a flaw in the regulations protecting the rights of composers. He was compelled to travel again as an actor, but could not earn enough money to support his large family, left behind in Vienna. In the spring of 1850 he was engaged as music director at a small theater in Berlin; on Jan. 20, 1851, his last opera, *Die Opernprobe,* was produced in Frankfurt while he was on his deathbed in Berlin; he died the next day. His opera *Regina, oder Die Marodeure,* written in 1848, was edited by Richard Kleinmichel, with the composer's libretto revised by Adolf L'Arronge, and performed in Berlin on March 21, 1899; another opera, *Der Weihnachtsabend,* was not produced. Lortzing also wrote an oratorio, *Die Himmelfahrt Christi;* some incidental music to various plays; and songs. But it is as a composer of characteristically German Romantic operas that Lortzing holds a distinguished, if minor, place in the history of dramatic music. He was a follower of Weber, without Weber's imaginative projection; in his lighter works, he approached the type of French operetta; in his best creations he exhibited a fine sense of facile melody, and infectious rhythm; his harmonies, though unassuming, were always proper and pleasing; his orchestration, competent and effective.

BIBLIOGRAPHY: P.J. Düringer, *Albert Lortzing, Sein Leben und Wirken* (Leipzig, 1851); G.R. Kruse, *Albert Lortzing* (Berlin, 1899; standard biography); R. Bürner, *Albert Lortzing in Detmold* (Detmold, 1900); G.R. Kruse, *Lortzings Briefe* (Leipzig, 1902; augmented ed., 1913; 3rd ed., 1947); H. Wittmann, *Lortzing* (Leipzig, 1902); H. Laue, *Die Operndichtung Lortzings* (Bonn, 1932; a valuable analysis); H. Killer, *Albert Lortzing* (Potsdam, 1938); O. Schumann, *Albert Lortzing, Sein Leben in Bildern* (Berlin, 1941); E.W. Böhme, *Albert Lortzing in Lüneburg* (1951); J. Knodt, *Albert Lortzing* (1955).

Löschhorn, (Carl) Albert, German pianist, composer, and pedagogue; b. Berlin, June 27, 1819; d. there, June 4, 1905. He studied at the Royal Inst. for Church Music with L. Berger, Killitschgy, Grell, and A.W. Bach; became a piano teacher there in 1851. He publ. a series of excellent piano studies, including *Melodious Studies, La Vélocité, Universal Studies, Le Trille,* and *School of Octaves,* which became standard pedagogical works; also wrote attractive piano solos: *La Belle Amazone, 4 pièces élégantes, Tarentelle; 2 valses,* the barcarolle *A Venise,* and *3 mazurkas;* suites, sonatas, sonatinas, etc. With J. Weiss he publ. a *Wegweiser in die Pianoforte-Literatur* (1862; 2nd ed., 1885, as *Führer durch die Klavierliteratur).*

Lott, Felicity, English soprano; b. Cheltenham, May 8, 1947. She studied at the Royal Academy of Music in London; in 1976 she sang at Covent Garden in the world premiere of Henze's *We Come to the River;* she also appeared there as Anne Trulove in Stravinsky's *The Rake's Progress,* as Octavian in *Der Rosenkavalier,* and in various other roles. She appeared in Paris for the first time in 1976; made her Vienna debut in 1982 singing the *4 Letze Lieder* of Strauss; in 1984 was engaged as soloist with the Chicago Symph. Orch.

Lotti, Antonio, Italian organist and composer; b. Venice, c.1667; d. there, Jan. 5, 1740. He was a pupil of Legrenzi in Venice; in 1687 he became chorister at San Marco; in 1690, assistant organist there, and in 1692, 2nd organist. On Aug. 17, 1704, he was appointed first organist; in 1736 he was elected primo maestro di cappella. While at San Marco, he industriously composed church music, masses, anthems, etc.; he also wrote dramatic music. As a teacher, he was highly renowned; among his pupils were Alberti, Gasparini, Galuppi, and Marcello. He absented himself from Venice but once (1717–19), when he went to Dresden at the Crown Prince's invitation.

WORKS: 21 operas, including *Alessandro Severo* (Venice, Dec. 26, 1716); *Giove in Argo* (Dresden, Oct. 25, 1717); *Teofane* (Dresden, Nov. 13, 1719); *Costantino* (Vienna, Nov. 19, 1716; in collaboration with Fux and Caldara); 7 oratorios, including *Il voto crudele, L'umiltà coronata, Gioa re di Giuda,* and *Giuditta;* many masses, motets, etc., none of which were publ. by him. Lück's *Sammlung ausgezeichneter Compositionen* contains 4 masses and other numbers; Rochlitz, Proske, Trautwein, Commer, Schlesinger, and others have printed Misereres and other sacred music by Lotti; 8 masses were ed. by H. Müller in Denkmäler Deutscher Tonkunst, 60. During Lotti's lifetime his only work publ. was *Duetti, Terzetti e Madrigali a più voci* (Venice, 1705, dedicated to Joseph I; includes the madrigal *In una siepe ombrosa,* the appropriation of which caused Bononcini's downfall).

BIBLIOGRAPHY: Charlotte Spitz, *Antonio Lotti in seiner Bedeutung als Opernkomponist* (Leipzig, 1918); idem, "Ottone von Händel und *Teofane* von Lotti," in *Sandberger-Festschrift;* A. Moser, "Arcangelo Corelli und Antonio Lotti: Zwei künstlerische Ehrenrettungen," *Zeitschrift für Musik* (April 1921); A. Schering, *Geschichte des Oratoriums* (pp. 202ff.); R. Holden, *Six Extant Operas of Antonio Lotti (1667–1740)* (Diss., Univ. of Conn., 1967); K. O'Donnell, *The Secular Solo Cantatas of Antonio Lotti* (Diss., Iowa State Univ., 1975). The correspondence regarding the controversy with Bononcini was reproduced in *Letters from the Academy of Ancient Music at London to Signor Antonio Lotti of Venice with His Answers and Testimonials* (London, 1732); the case was described in the article "The Fall of Bononcini," *Musical Times* (Jan. 1892).

Lotze, Rudolf Hermann, German writer on music; b. Bautzen, May 21, 1817; d. Berlin, July 1, 1881. He became a prof. of philosophy at Leipzig Univ. in 1842; in 1844, prof. in ordinary, and court councillor at Göttingen; he settled in Berlin shortly before his death. He publ. *Geschichte der Ästhetik in Deutschland* (1868), which contains criticism of Helmholtz, Hauptmann, and others; also interesting ideas on musical esthetics.

Loucheur, Raymond, French composer; b. Tourcoing, Jan. 1, 1899; d. Nogent-sur-Marne, Sept. 14, 1979. He studied music with Henry Woollett at Le Havre (1915–18) and with Nadia Boulanger, Gédalge, d'Indy, Fauchet, and Paul Vidal at the Paris Cons. (1920–23). In 1928 he won the Premier Grand Prix de Rome for his cantata *Héracles à Delphe.* From 1925 to 1940 he was a teacher in Paris; in 1941, became the principal inspector of musical education in the Paris city schools and later was director of the Paris Cons. (1956–62). His music is chromatically lyrical and displays rhythmic spontaneity.

WORKS: Ballet, *Hop-Frog,* after Poe (1935–48; Paris, June 17, 1953; for Orch.: 2 symph. suites, Paris, June 30, 1949); cantata, *Héracles à Delphe* (Le Havre, June 12, 1929); 3 symphs.: No. 1 (1929–33; first complete perf., Concerts Colonne, Dec. 15, 1936; revised 1969); No. 2 (1944; Paris, Feb. 15, 1945); No. 3 (1971; Paris, Oct. 17, 1972); *En famille* for Chamber Orch. or Clarinet Sextet (1932; orchestrated 1940); *3 Duos* for Soprano, Chorus, and Orch. (1934); *Défilé* for Orch. (1936); *L'Apothéose de la Seine* for Narrator, Mezzo-soprano, Chorus, Ondes Martenot, and Orch. (1937; Paris, July 7, 1937); *Pastorale* for Orch. (1939); *Rapsodie malgache* for Orch. (1945; Paris, Oct. 10, 1945); *Divertissement* for Orch. (1951); Concertino for Trumpet, and Orch. or Clarinet Sextet (1954; orchestrated 1956); Violin Concerto (1960–63; Paris, Feb. 28, 1965); Percussion Concertino (1963; Paris, Jan. 9, 1966); *Cortège, Interlude, et Danse* for Winds, Harp, and Percussion (1964–65); Cello Concerto (1967–68; Radio Luxembourg, July 11, 1968); *Thrène* for String Orch. and Flute (1971); *Hommage à Raoul Dufy* for Orch. (1973; Paris, Oct. 27, 1964); *Evocations* for Wind Orch. (1974; Paris, March 7, 1976); chamber music: String Quartet (1930); *En famille* for Clarinet Sextet (1932; orchestrated 1940); *La Ballade des petites filles qui n'ont pas de poupée* for 4 Soli, Chorus, and Piano (1936); *Portraits* for Clarinet, Oboe, and Bassoon (1947); *4 pièces en quintette* for Harp, Flute, Violin, Viola, and Cello (1953); Concertino for Trumpet and Clarinet Sextet (1954; orchestrated 1956); *5 poèmes de R.-M. Rilke* for Mezzo-Soprano and String Quartet (1952–57); Solo Violin Sonata (1959); *Dialogues* for Flute and Harp; *Rencontres* for Oboe and Cello (1972); *Divertissement sur les flûtes* for 4 Flutes (1975); *Reflets* for Brass Quintet (1976); songs.

BIBLIOGRAPHY: *Courrier Musical de France,* no. 68 (1979).

Loudová, Ivana, Czech composer; b. Chlumec nad Cidlinou, March 8, 1941. She studied composition with Kabeláč at the Prague Cons. (1958–61) and with Hlobil at the Prague Academy of Arts (1961–66); in 1971 she went to Paris, where she took lessons with Messiaen and André Jolivet. Her music is richly dissonant and impressionistically colorful.

WORKS: *Fantasy* for Orch. (1961); Concerto for Chamber Orch. (1962); Symph. No. 1 (1964); Symph. No. 2 for Contralto, Chorus, and Orch. (1965); *Spleen (Hommage à Charles Baudelaire)* for Orch. (1971); *Chorale* for Wind Orch., Percussion, and Organ (1971); *Hymnos* for Wind Orch. and Percussion (1972); Concerto for Orch. (1974); Violin Sonata (1960–61); Clarinet Sonata (1963); String Quartet (1964); *Per tromba,* 5 studies for Solo Trumpet (1969); *Agamemnon* for Solo Percussionist (1973); *Romeo and Juliet,* suite for Flute, 2 Violins, Cello, and Harp (1973); children's cantata, *Le Petit Prince,* after Saint-Exupéry (1967); *Gnomai* for Soprano, Flute, and Harp (1970).

Louel, Jean, Belgian composer and conductor; b. Ostend, Jan. 3, 1914. He studied at the Ghent Cons. with Joseph Ryelandt (composition) and at the Brussels Cons. with Joseph Jongen (theory) and Désiré Defauw (conducting); then went to Paris to study conducting with Eugene Bigot and Paul Paray. He was director of music academies in Alost (1945–49) and Anderlecht (1949–56); in 1956 became inspector of music schools in Flemish Belgium. He obtained the Belgian Prix de Rome in 1943 for his cantata *La Navigation d'Ulysse.*

WORKS: *Fantaisie sur 2 chansons de trouvères* for Orch. (1942); *Suite* for Chamber Orch. or Piano (1942); *Burlesque* for Bassoon and Orch. (1943); *March funèbre* and *Triomfmarch* for Orch. (both in 1945); 2 piano concertos (1945, 1949); *Concerto da camera* for Flute and Orch. (1946–47); 2 violin concertos (1950, 1971); Symph. No. 2 for String Orch. (1968; his youthful Symph. No. 1 had been withdrawn); *Toccata and Fugue* for Winds (1974); Clarinet Sonata (1935); Brass Trio (1951); *Theme and Variations* for Violin and Piano (1953); Sonatina for 2 Violins and Piano (1955); Wind Quintet (1958); Violin Sonata (1960); *Suite* for Flute, Cello, Vibraphone, and Harp (1967); *Invention* for Solo Horn (1973).

Loughran, James, Scottish conductor; b. Glasgow, June 30, 1931. He began his conducting career as an assistant conductor at the Bonn Opera; also held similar posts in Amsterdam and Milan. In 1962 he became associate conductor of the Bournemouth Symph. In 1965 he was named principal conductor of the BBC Scottish Symph. in Glasgow. In 1971 he was appointed principal conductor of the Hallé Orch. of Manchester, succeeding the late Sir John Barbirolli. In 1979 he became principal conductor of the Bamberg Symph. in West Germany.

Louis Ferdinand, Prince of Prussia, nephew of **Frederick the Great;** b. Friedrichsfelde, near Berlin, Nov. 18, 1772; fell at Saalfeld, Oct. 10, 1806. He was an excellent amateur musician. While traveling in 1804, he met Beethoven, and showed great interest in the master's music. Beethoven's 3rd Piano Concerto in C minor is dedicated to Louis Ferdinand, which testifies to their mutual esteem. However, the statement sometimes made that Louis Ferdinand imitated Beethoven in his own works is untenable inasmuch as the Prince fell in battle 2 years after his first acquaintance with Beethoven's music. The following compositions by Louis Ferdinand are publ.: 2 piano quintets; 2 piano quartets; 4 piano trios; Octet for Clarinet, 2 Horns, 2 Violins, 2 Cellos, and Piano; *Notturno* for Flute, Violin, Cello, and Piano; *Andante and Variations* for Viola, Cello, and Piano; *Rondo* for Piano and Orch.; *Rondo* for Piano Solo. H. Kretzschmar edited his collected works (Leipzig, 1915–17).

BIBLIOGRAPHY: Elisabeth Wintzer, *Louis Ferdinand, als Mensch und Musiker* (1916); H. Wahl, *Prinz Louis Ferdinand von Preussen* (1917); F. Lewald, *Prinz Louis Ferdinand* (1929); A. Semrau, *Prinz Louis Ferdinand* (1930); R. Hahn, *Louis Fer-*

dinand (Breslau, 1934); E. Poseck, *Prinz Louis Ferdinand* (Berlin, 1938; 2nd ed., 1943).

Louis, Rudolf, German writer on music; b. Schwetzingen, Jan. 30, 1870; d. Munich, Nov. 15, 1914. He studied philosophy at the univs. of Geneva and Vienna (Dr.Phil., 1894); music with Klose and Mottl; was conductor at the State Theater in Landshut (1895–96), and in Lübeck (1896–97); in 1897, settled in Munich, where he became critic for the influential periodical *Neueste Nachrichten* (from 1900). WRITINGS: *Der Widerspruch in der Musik* (1893); *Richard Wagner als Musikästhetiker* (1897); *Die Weltanschauung Richard Wagners* (1898); *Franz Liszt* (1900); *Hector Berlioz* (1904); *Anton Bruckner* (1905); *Die deutsche Musik der Gegenwart* (1909; 3rd ed., 1912); *Aufgaben für den Unterricht in der Harmonielehre* (1911); with L. Thuille he wrote *Harmonielehre* (1907; 8th ed., 1924; abridged as *Grundriss der Harmonielehre*, 1908). He was also a composer; publ. a symph. fantasy, *Proteus* (1903); *Zum Hochzeitstage* and *Albumblatt* for Piano, 4-hands; songs.

Louis XIII, King of France from 1610 to 1643; b. Paris, Sept. 27, 1601; d. there, May 14, 1643. He was an amateur musician, and wrote madrigals. The well-known *Amaryllis,* arranged by Henri Ghis and widely publ. as "Air of Louis XIII," is a misattribution; the melody first appears in print as "La Clochette" in the *Ballet-Comique de la Reine* by Balthazar de Beaujoyeux, produced in 1582, long before Louis XIII was born. A gavotte, also entitled *Amaryllis,* with a melody totally different from the apocryphal "Air of Louis XIII" and dated 1620, may be an authentic composition of Louis XIII.

Loulié, Etienne, 17th-century French writer on music and inventor of the "chronomètre," the precursor of the metronome; b. Paris c.1655; d. there, c.1707. He studied with Gehenault and Ouvrard under the patronage of Mlle. de Guise; was at the Saint-Chapelle in Paris in 1663–73. He publ. *Eléments ou principes de musique dans un nouvel ordre . . . avec l'estampe et l'usage du chronomètre* (Paris, 1696; Eng. trans., 1965), which describes and illustrates his invention, an unwieldy device 6 feet tall; and a *Nouveau système de musique* (1698), describing the "sonomètre" (a monochord to aid in tuning), which he also invented.

Lourié, Arthur (Vincent), Russian composer; b. St. Petersburg, May 14, 1892; d. Princeton, N.J., Oct. 13, 1966. He studied at the St. Petersburg Cons.; participated in various modernistic groups, and wrote piano music, much influenced by Scriabin (*Préludes fragiles, Synthèses,* etc.); experimented in futuristic composition (e.g., *Formes en l'air,* dedicated to Picasso, and graphically imitating a cubist design by omitting the staves instead of using rests); also composed religious music (*Lamentations de la Vierge,* etc.). After the Soviet Revolution, he was appointed chief of the music dept. of the Commissariat for Public Instruction; in 1921 he left Russia,

and lived in Paris; in 1941, emigrated to the U.S., and became an American citizen. In his music written after 1920 he followed mainly Stravinsky's practice of stylizing old forms, secular and sacred. WORKS: *Nash marsh (Our March),* to a poem by Mayakovsky, for Declamation with Piano (1918); *La Naissance de la beauté,* cantata for a Chorus of 6 Sopranos, Soprano Solo, and Piano (1922); *Dithyrambes* for Flute Solo (1923); *Liturgical Sonata* for Orch., Piano, and Chorus (1928); *Concerto spirituale* for Piano, Chorus, and Double Basses (N.Y., March 26, 1930); *Sinfonia dialectica,* Symph. No. 1 (Philadelphia, April 17, 1931); *Kormtschaya,* Symph. No. 2 (Boston, Nov. 7, 1941); *The Feast during the Plague,* opera-ballet after Pushkin (1935; arranged for Soprano Solo, Mixed Chorus, and Orch.; Boston, Jan. 5, 1945); *De ordinatione angelorum* for Chorus (1948); *Piano Gosse* (1917; republ. in N.Y., 1944, under the title *8 Scenes of Russian Childhood*); 2 pieces for Piano: *Berceuse de la chevrette* (1936) and *A Phoenix Park Nocturne* (1938); *The Mime* for Solo Clarinet (1956); *Concerto da camera* for Violin Solo and String Orch. (1957); *The Blackamoor of Peter the Great,* opera (1961). He publ. a biography of Koussevitzky (N.Y., 1931). BIBLIOGRAPHY: "The Music of Arthur Lourié," *Ramparts* (Menlo Park, Calif., Jan. 1965); D. Gojowy, "Zwölftontechnik in Russland," *Melos* (May–June 1972).

Love, Shirley, American mezzo-soprano; b. Detroit, Jan. 6, 1940. She studied voice in Detroit with Avery Crew and in N.Y. with Marinka Gurewich and Margaret Harshaw; then sang with the Baltimore Opera (1962). She first appeared in a minor role at the Metropolitan Opera in N.Y. on Nov. 30, 1963; subsequently gained experience as a singer with other American opera companies; returned to the Metropolitan in 1970.

Løveberg, Aase (née **Nordmo**), Norwegian soprano; b. Målselv, June 10, 1923. She was born into a peasant family; spent her childhood on a farm near the Arctic Circle. When she was 19 she went to Oslo, where she studied voice with Haldis Ingebjart; made her opera debut in Oslo on Dec. 3, 1948; then sang in Stockholm, Vienna, Paris, and London. She made her first American appearance as a soloist with the Philadelphia Orch. (Dec. 6, 1957).

Løvenskjold, Herman Severin, Norwegian organist and composer; b. Holdensjärnbruk, July 30, 1815; d. Copenhagen, Dec. 5, 1870. At the age of 13 his parents took him to Copenhagen, where he studied music; in 1836 he brought out his ballet *Sylphiden* there with much success. After the production of his 2nd ballet, *Sara,* in 1839, he went to Vienna, where he took some lessons with Seyfried; returned to Denmark in 1851; was appointed organist at the Slottskyrka in Christiansborg. He wrote an opera, *Turandot* (Copenhagen, Dec. 3, 1854); *Festouvertüre* (for the coronation of Christian VIII); *Ouverture de concert idyllique;* the overture *Fra Skoven ved Furesø;* Piano Trio; Piano Quartet; piano pieces for 2- and 4-hands.

Lover, Samuel, Irish novelist, poet, painter, and composer; b. Dublin, Feb. 24, 1797; d. St. Heliers, Jersey, July 6, 1868. He wrote music to several Irish plays, and to many songs; publ. *Songs and Ballads* (London, 1859). Among his most popular songs (some of which are set to old Irish tunes) are *The Angel's Whisper, Molly Bawn,* and *the Low-Backed Car.* He wrote an opera, *Grana Uile, or The Island Queen* (Dublin, Feb. 9, 1832). He devised a very successful musical entertainment, *Irish Evenings* (1844), with which he toured the British Isles and the U.S. (1846). He was **Victor Herbert**'s grandfather.

Löw, Joseph, Bohemian pianist and composer; b. Prague, Jan. 23, 1834; d. there, Oct. 5, 1886. In 1854 he toured through Moravia, Silesia, Galicia, and the Bukovina; returning to Prague in 1856, he was active as a concert pianist and composer. He publ. over 450 numbers of light piano music, including *Jugend-Album; 2 impromptus romantiques; Allegro brillant* for 2 Pianos; *Soir de printemps; Maiengruss;* etc.

Löwe, Ferdinand, Austrian conductor; b. Vienna, Feb. 19, 1865; d. there, Jan. 6, 1925. He studied with Dachs, Krenn, and Bruckner at the Vienna Cons.; then taught piano and choral singing there (1883–96). In 1897 he became conductor of the Kaim Orch. in Munich; then of the court opera in Vienna (1898–1900); of the Gesellschaftskonzerte (1900–1904); in 1904 he became conductor of the newly organized Vienna Konzertverein Orch., which he made one of the finest instrumental bodies in Europe; he returned to Munich as conductor of the Konzertverein (1908–14), which comprised members of the former Kaim Orch.; also conducted in Budapest and Berlin; from 1918 to 1922 was head of the Vienna Staatsakademie für Musik. He was a friend and trusted disciple of Bruckner; edited (somewhat liberally) several of Bruckner's works even during the master's lifetime; conducted the 3 finished movements of Bruckner's posthumous 9th Symph. (Vienna, Feb. 11, 1903), with considerable cuts and alterations, adding Bruckner's Te Deum in lieu of the unfinished finale.

Löwe, Karl. See **Loewe, Carl.**

Lowens, Irving, eminent American musicologist, music critic, and librarian; b. New York, Aug. 19, 1916; d. Baltimore, Nov. 14, 1983. He studied at Teachers College, Columbia Univ. (B.S. in Music, 1939). During World War II he served as an air-traffic controller for the Civil Aeronautics Administration; he continued in this capacity at the National Airport in Washington, D.C.; then took special courses in American civilization at the Univ. of Maryland (M.A., 1957; Ph.D., 1965). In 1953 he began to write music criticism for the *Washington Star;* from 1960–78 he was its chief music critic; received the ASCAP Deems Taylor Award for the best arti-

cles on music in 1972 and 1977. From 1960–66 he was a librarian in the Music Division of the Library of Congress in Washington, D.C. From 1978–81 he was dean of the Peabody Inst. of the Johns Hopkins Univ. in Baltimore; also wrote music criticism for the *Baltimore News American.* A linguist, he traveled widely on numerous research grants in Europe; in 1970 he was the sole American representative at the Enesco Festival in Bucharest. He was a founding member of the Music Critics' Assoc., and from 1971–75 served as its president.

PUBLICATIONS: *The Hartford Harmony: A Selection of American Hymns from the Late 18th and Early 19th Centuries* (Hartford, 1953); *Music and Musicians of Early America* (N.Y., 1964); *Source Readings in American Music History* (N.Y., 1966); *Lectures on the History and Art of Music at the Library of Congress, 1946–63* (N.Y., 1968); *A Bibliography of American Songsters Published before 1821* (Worcester, Mass., 1976); *Haydn in America* (Smithsonian Institution, Washington, 1977). He ed. *An Introduction to the Singing of Psalm-Tunes, 1726* (Philadelphia, 1954).

Lowenthal, Jerome, American pianist; b. Philadelphia, Feb. 11, 1932. He studied piano at an early age; made his debut in Philadelphia at the age of 13; then took lessons with William Kapell and with Eduard Steuermann at the Juilliard School of Music in N.Y.; received a Fulbright grant and went to Paris to study with Alfred Cortot at the Ecole Normale de Musique. He then traveled to Israel, where he gave concerts and taught at the Jerusalem Academy of Music; returned to the U.S. in 1961. His repertoire embraced the standard piano literature as well as contemporary works; among composers who wrote special works for him were George Rochberg and Ned Rorem.

Lowinsky, Edward, eminent German-born American musicologist; b. Stuttgart, Jan. 12, 1908. He studied at the Hochschule für Musik in Stuttgart (1923–28); took his Ph.D. at the Univ. of Heidelberg in 1933 with the dissertation *Das Antwerpener Motettenbuch Orlando di Lassos und seine Beziehungen zum Motettenschaffen der niederländischen Zeitgenössen* (publ. in The Hague, 1937). When the Nazis came to power, he went to the Netherlands; in 1940 he emigrated to the U.S.; became an American citizen in 1947. He held the positions of assistant prof. of music at Black Mountain College (1942–47), associate prof. of music at Queens College, N.Y. (1948–56); prof. of music at the Univ. of Calif., Berkeley (1956–61); and prof. of music at the Univ. of Chicago (1961–76), where he also held a post-retirement professorship until 1978. He held Guggenheim fellowships in 1947–48 and 1976–77; was a Fellow at the Inst. for Advanced Study at Princeton Univ. from 1952 to 1954; was made a Fellow of the American Academy of Arts and Sciences in 1973; was named Albert A. Bauman Distinguished Research Fellow of the Newberry Library in 1982. He was general editor of the Monuments of Renaissance Music series; publ. the valuable studies *Secret*

Chromatic Art in the Netherlands Motet (N.Y., 1946) and *Tonality and Atonality in Sixteenth-Century Music* (Berkeley and Los Angeles, 1961; 2nd revised printing, 1962). He also prepared the vol. *Josquin des Prez. Proceedings of the International Josquin Festival-Conference* (London, 1976). He was married to the musicologist **Bonnie Blackburn.**

Löwlein, Hans, German conductor; b. Ingolstadt, June 24, 1909. He was educated at the Munich Academy of Music; then was répétiteur at the Bavarian State Opera. He conducted at the City Theater in Stettin; in 1946 was appointed first conductor of the Dresden State Opera. In 1949–50 he conducted at the Komische Oper in East Berlin; was then conductor of the East Berlin State Opera (1950–61) and later deputy Generalmusikdirektor of the Frankfurt State Opera (1961–64); subsequently held the post of chief conductor of the City Theater in Basel (1964–72); also made appearances as a conductor of opera and symph. in Japan.

Lowry, Robert, American hymn writer; b. Philadelphia, March 12, 1826; d. Plainfield, N.J., Nov. 25, 1899. He was a Baptist preacher and studied music in his middle age. His most popular hymn tune is *Something for Jesus.*
BIBLIOGRAPHY: R.G. McCutchan, *Our Hymnody* (N.Y., 1937).

Lowtzky, Hermann, Russian composer; b. Kamenetz-Podolsk, June 20, 1871; d. Zürich, Dec. 8, 1957. He studied law, philosophy, and music; went to St. Petersburg in 1899 and enrolled in Rimsky-Korsakov's class at the Cons. there. He moved to Switzerland in 1910. His music preserves the Russian elements of style and idiom. Among his publ. works are the opera *Lucretia,* to his own libretto (Kiev, Dec. 18, 1912); Piano Trio (1905); cantata, *Paradies und Peri.* In MS are an opera, *Mozart,* and *Kol Nidre* for Cello and Orch.

Loy, Max, German comductor and composer; b. Nuremberg, June 18, 1913; d. there, Feb. 15, 1977. He studied piano and music theory; in 1938 he became conductor of the Nuremberg Opera, and in 1971 was appointed its deputy Generalmusikdirektor. He also traveled as pianist-accompanist to celebrated singers, among them Erna Sack and Sigrid Onegin. He composed a Piano Concerto, 5 string quartets, a Piano Quintet, and songs.

Lualdi, Adriano, Italian composer, conductor, and critic; b. Larino, Campobasso, March 22, 1885; d. Milan, Jan. 8, 1971. He studied composition with Falchi in Rome and Wolf-Ferrari in Venice; began his musical career as an opera conductor; in 1918 went to Milan, where he was active as a music critic and government administrator on musical affairs; from 1936 to 1943 he was director of the Cons. of San Pietro a Majella in Naples; then was appointed director of the Florence Cons. (1947–56). He was a voluminous composer, excelling particularly in op-

era. His opera *Le nozze di Haura,* written in 1908, had a concert performance by the Radio Italiano on Oct. 15, 1939, and its first stage production in Rome on April 17, 1943. His subsequent operas were *La Figlia del re,* after the *Antigone* of Sophocles (Turin, March 18, 1922); *Le furie d'Arlecchino* (Milan, May 10, 1915); *Il Diavolo nel campanile* (La Scala, Milan, April 22, 1925); *La granceola* (Venice, Sept. 10, 1932); *La luna dei Caraibi,* one-act opera after O'Neill (Rome, Jan. 29, 1953); mimodrama, *Lumawig e la saetta* (Rome, Jan. 23, 1937); *Il testamento di Euridice,* lyric tragedy (1939–52); satiric radio comedy, *Tre alla radarstratotropojonosferaphonotheca del Luna Park* (1953–58); cantata, *La rosa di Saron* (1915; also titled *Il cantico;* Milan, May 10, 1915); symph. poems: *La leggenda del vecchio marinaio* (1910) and *L'interludio del sogno* (1917); *Suite adriatica* for Orch. (1932); *Africa,* rhapsody for Orch. (1936); *Divertimento* for Orch. (1941); numerous choruses and minor pieces for various instruments. Lualdi was also an industrious writer on musical subjects. He publ. several vols. of reminiscences of his "musical voyages": *Viaggio musicale italiano* (1931); *Viaggio musicale in Europa* (1928); *Viaggio musicale nel Sud-America* (Milan, 1934); *Viaggio musicale nel l'U.R.S.S.* (1941); also *L'arte di dirigere l'orchestra* (1940) and *Tutti vivi,* a collection of miscellaneous articles (Milan, 1955).

Lübeck, Ernst, Dutch pianist and composer, son of **Johann Heinrich Lübeck;** b. The Hague, Aug. 24, 1829; d. Paris, Sept. 17, 1876. He was trained as a pianist by his father; as a youth, he made a voyage to America, playing concerts in the U.S., Mexico, and Peru (1849–54); then returned to Europe and settled in Paris, where he acquired the reputation of a virtuoso; Berlioz wrote enthusiastically about his playing. He became mentally unbalanced following the events of the Paris Commune of 1871; there his career ended. He wrote some pleasing salon pieces for piano, among them *Berceuse; Tarentelle; Polonaise; Trilby the Sprite; Rêverie caractéristique.*

Lübeck, Johann Heinrich, Dutch violinist and composer; b. Alphen, Feb. 11, 1799; d. The Hague, Feb. 7, 1865. He was a Prussian regimental musician (1813–15); studied music in Potsdam; then was a player in theater orchs. in Riga and Stettin; in 1823, settled in the Netherlands, giving violin concerts. From 1827 until his death he was director of the Cons. of The Hague; was also conductor of the "Diligentia" concerts there, and in 1829, became court conductor.

Lübeck, Louis, Dutch cellist, son of **Johann Heinrich Lübeck;** b. The Hague, Feb. 14, 1838; d. Berlin, March 8, 1904. He studied with Jacquard in Paris; in 1863–68, taught cello at the Leipzig Cons.; toured Germany, the Netherlands, England, and the U.S. (1875–81); in 1881 he settled in Berlin as a cellist in the court orch. He wrote 2 concertos for cello, and solo pieces.

Lübeck, Vincentius (Vincenz), German organist

and composer; b. Padingbüttel, Sept. 1654; d. Hamburg, Feb. 9, 1740. He studied with his father; from 1675 to 1702 was an organist at Stade; in 1702, became organist at the Nicolaikirche in Hamburg, remaining in that post until his death. Lübeck's works, including 3 cantatas, chorale preludes for organ, etc., were publ. by Gottlieb Harms (Klecken, 1921). An edition of the complete organ works was publ. by K. Beckmann (Wiesbaden, 1973).

Lubin, Germaine, French soprano; b. Paris, Feb. 1, 1890; d. there, Oct. 27, 1979. She studied at the Paris Cons.; made her debut at the Opéra-Comique in 1912; in 1914 she joined the Paris Opéra, remaining on its roster until 1944. In 1931 she sang at Salzburg, in 1937 at Covent Garden in London; in 1938 she became the first French singer to appear at Bayreuth, gaining considerable acclaim for her Wagnerian roles. She continued her career in Paris during the German occupation and was briefly under arrest after the liberation of Paris, charged with collaboration with the enemy. She was later absolved of this charge, and upon retirement from the stage gave private voice lessons, dying in her 90th year.

Luboshutz (real name, **Luboshits**), **Léa,** Russian violinist; b. Odessa, Feb. 22, 1885; d. Philadelphia, March 18, 1965. She studied violin with her father; played in public at the age of 7; after study at the Odessa Music School, she went to the Moscow Cons., graduating with a gold medal (1903); gave concerts in Germany and France, and also took additional lessons from Eugène Ysaÿe in Belgium; returned to Russia, and organized a trio with her brother **Pierre** (piano) and sister **Anna** (cello); left Russia after the Revolution and lived in Berlin and Paris (1921–25). In 1925 she settled in N.Y.; played the American premiere of Prokofiev's First Violin Concerto (Nov. 14, 1925); made several appearances in joint recitals with her son, **Boris Goldovsky,** a pianist. From 1927, she was on the faculty of the Curtis Inst. of Music.

Luboshutz, Pierre, Russian pianist, brother of **Léa Luboshutz;** b. Odessa, June 17, 1891; d. Rockport, Maine, April 17, 1971. He studied violin with his father; then turned to the piano, and entered the Moscow Cons. as a pupil of Igumnov, graduating in 1912; also studied in Paris with Edouard Risler; returning to Russia, he played in a trio with his 2 sisters, **Léa** (violin) and **Anna** (cello); in 1926 went to America as accompanist to Zimbalist, Piatigorsky, and others. In 1931 he married **Genia Nemenoff** (b. Paris, Oct. 23, 1905); with her he formed a piano duo (N.Y. debut, Jan. 18, 1937); as Luboshutz-Nemenoff, they gave annual concerts with considerable success. From 1962 to 1968, they headed the piano dept. at Michigan State Univ.; then returned to N.Y.

Lubrich, Fritz, Jr., German organist, son of **Fritz Lubrich, Sr.;** b. Neustädtel, Jan. 26, 1888; d. Hamburg, April 15, 1971. He received his early training from his father; then was a student of Straube in organ

playing in Leipzig and of Max Reger in composition. From 1948 to 1952 he was the choir leader of the Hamburg Singakademie. He publ. several valuable articles on the history of choral organizations in Germany.

Lubrich, Fritz, Sr., German organist and writer on music; b. Bärsdorf, July 29, 1862; d. Eberswalde, March 29, 1952. He studied music in Breslau; was active as a church organist in various cities in Silesia. He edited several periodicals of Protestant church music and publ. a number of valuable articles on Lutheran liturgy.

Luca, Sergiu, Rumanian-born Israeli violinist; b. Bucharest, April 4, 1943. He began to study violin as a child; his parents took him to Israel in 1950; later he continued his studies in London, and at the Bern Cons. (1956–59); eventually he came to the U.S., as a student of Ivan Galamian at the Curtis Inst. of Music in Philadelphia. He began his professional American career as a soloist with the Philadelphia Orch. in 1965; subsequently appeared with many American and European orchs. with considerable success.

Lucantoni, Giovanni, Italian composer and singing teacher; b. Rieti, Jan. 18, 1825; d. Paris, May 30, 1902. He studied with his parents, who were both good amateur musicians; then with Giovanni Pacini in Lucca and Nicola Vaccaj in Milan. In 1857 he settled in Paris as a singing teacher; also lived in London. His vocal compositions were very popular for a time; particularly well known was the vocal duet *Una notte a Venezia;* he also wrote an opera, *Elisa* (Milan, June 20, 1850); a 4-part Mass; a cantata; a Symph.; and various "ballabili" for piano.

Lucas, Leighton, English conductor and composer; b. London, Jan. 5, 1903; d. there, Nov. 1, 1982. He was trained to be a dancer, and for several years (1918–21) was a member of Diaghilev's Ballets Russes in Paris and in London. Then he learned conducting and traveled with various ballet companies. He made arrangements of classical pieces for ballet and composed his own ballet scores, among them *The Wolf's Ride* (1935) and *The Horses* (1946). He also wrote some chamber music, including *Divertissement* for Harp and 8 Instruments (1955); Clarinet Concerto (1956); *Disquisition* for 2 Cellos and Piano, 4-hands (1967); String Trio (1969); etc. He publ. a pamphlet, *Mini-Music* (London, 1967).

Lucas, Mary Anderson, English composer; b. London, May 24, 1882; d. there, Jan. 14, 1952. She studied piano at the Dresden Cons.; later took lessons in composition with R.O. Morris and Herbert Howells. She adopted an advanced harmonic style of composition; her works include a ballet, *Sawdust* (1941), which had considerable success; 6 string quartets; Trio for Clarinet, Viola, and Piano; *Rhapsody* for Flute, Cello, and Piano; many songs.

Lucca, Pauline, Austrian soprano; b. Vienna, April 25, 1841; d. there, Feb. 28, 1908. She was a daughter of an Italian father and a German mother; she studied singing in Vienna and sang in the chorus of the Vienna Opera. Her professional debut took place in Olmütz as Elvira in *Ernani* on Sept. 4, 1859. Her appearance in Prague as Norma attracted the attention of Meyerbeer, who arranged her engagements in Berlin. In 1863 she sang in London with excellent success; in 1872 she made her first appearance in the U.S. Returning to Europe, she joined the staff of the Vienna Opera (1874–89); then retired from the stage. In her prime she was regarded as "prima donna assoluta," and her private life and recurring marriages and divorces were favorite subjects of sensational press stories; a curious promotional pamphlet, entitled *Bellicose Adventures of a Peaceable Prima Donna,* was publ. in N.Y. in 1872, presumably to whip up interest in her public appearances, but it concerned itself mainly with a melodramatic account of her supposed experiences during the Franco-Prussian War.

BIBLIOGRAPHY: Anna Mara-Jansen and D. Weisse-Zehrer, *Die Wiener Nachtigall: Der Lebensweg der Pauline Lucca* (Berlin, 1935).

Luciani, Sebastiano Arturo, Italian musicologist; b. Acquaviva delle Fonti, June 9, 1884; d. there, Dec. 7, 1950. He studied in Naples and Rome; devoted his energies mainly to documentation of biographies of Italian composers. He publ. a monograph on Domenico Scarlatti (Turin, 1942); edited *Antonio Vivaldi: Note e documenti sulla vita e sulla opere* (1939) and *La scuola veneziana* (1940).

Lucier, Alvin, American composer; b. Nashua, N.H., May 14, 1931. He studied theory with Quincy Porter at Yale Univ. and with Arthur Berger, Irving Fine, and Harold Shapero at Brandeis Univ.; also took a course with Lukas Foss at Tanglewood. He spent 2 years in Rome on a Fulbright scholarship. Returning to America in 1962, he was appointed to the faculty at Brandeis Univ.

WORKS: In his works he exploits serial and electronic techniques. Among them are *Music for Solo Performer* (1965), derived from amplified electroencephalographic waves, which activate percussion instruments; *Whistlers,* depicting magnetic disturbances in the ionosphere; *Shelter 999,* amplifications of mini-sounds in the immediate environment with parietal filters; *Music for High Structures; Chambers,* derived from the noises of displaced objects; *Vespers,* produced by acoustic orientation by means of echolocation; *The Only Talking Machine of Its Kind in the World* for Mixed Media, featuring electronic ventriloquy (1969); *Reflections of Sounds from the Wall.* He wrote a computer-controlled environmental work for the Pepsi-Cola pavilion at Expo '70 in Osaka, Japan, a sound mosaic with hundreds of tape recorders; also a biographical composition for oboe, accompanied by the Atlantic Ocean, a chest of drawers, and the Federal Bureau of Investigation (1970); also produced an experimental composition,

Still and Moving Lines of Silence in Families of Hyperbolas (N.Y., Feb. 21, 1975); and 4 pieces for multimedia (1975–77), involving electronic sound and a modified birdcall. In 1970 he resigned from Brandeis Univ. and joined the staff of Wesleyan Univ. In 1977 he was teaching at Wesleyan Univ.; was music director of the Viola Farber Dance Co. and a member of the Sonic Arts Union.

Luciuk, Juliusz, Polish composer; b. Brzeźnica, Jan. 1, 1927. He studied musicology with Jachimecki at the Jagiellonian Univ. in Cracow (1947–52), concurrently taking courses in composition with Wiechowicz at the State College of Music in Cracow (1947–56); then had lessons with Nadia Boulanger and Max Deutsch in Paris (1948–49). He evolved a sui generis technique according to the pragmatic purposes of each specific composition.

WORKS: Ballets: *Niobe* (1962); *Battleship Potemkin* (1967); *Orpheus* (1973); *Medea* (1975); *So Pass 5 Years* for Prepared Piano and Chamber Ensemble (Amsterdam, Oct. 9, 1972); oratorio, *Francis of Assisi* (Cracow, Oct. 3, 1976); cantata, *Dzikie wino* (*Virginia Creeper;* 1955); *Pour un ensemble* for Narrator and 24 Strings (1961); *Melorythmes* for Orch. (1962); *Lirica di timbri,* 5 pieces for Prepared Piano (1963); *Metamorphoses* for Orch. (1963); *Pacem in terris* for Vocalizing Soprano and Prepared Piano (1964); *Variété* for Trumpet and Orch. (1965); *Poème de Loire,* 5 songs for Soprano and Orch. (1968); *Speranza sinfonica* (1969); *Lamentazioni in memoriam Grazyna Bacewicz* for Orch. (1970); *Mini-Opus* for Piano, 4-hands (1971); Concertino for Piano and Chamber Orch. (1973); *Portraits lyriques* for Mezzo-soprano, 2 Violins, Cello, and Piano (1974).

Lucký, Štěpán, Czech composer; b. Žilina, Jan. 20, 1919. He studied quarter-tone composition with Alois Hába at the Prague Cons. (1936–39). During the occupation of Czechoslovakia he was interned in concentration camps at Bucharest, Auschwitz, and Buchenwald, but survived; after the war he enrolled in the Prague Cons., where he studied with Řídký, graduating in 1947. His music is couched in a pragmatic modernistic manner without circumscription by any particular doctrine or technique.

WORKS: Opera, *Půlnoční překvapení* (*Midnight Surprise;* 1958; Prague, 1959); *Divertimento* for 3 Trombones and String Ensemble (1946); Cello Concerto (1946); Piano Concerto (1947); Violin Concerto (1963–65); Octet for Strings (1970); *Double Concerto* for Violin, Piano, and Orch. (1971); Wind Quintet (1946); *Sonata brevis* for Violin and Piano (1947); *Elegy* for Cello and Piano (1948); Brass Quartet (1949); *Elegy* for Horn and Piano (1965); Sonata for Solo Violin (1967–69); *3 Pieces for Due Boemi* for Bass Clarinet and Piano (1969–70; Due Boemi is a Czech duo); *Sonata doppia* for 2 Violins (1971); Flute Sonata (1973); *Divertimento* for Wind Quintet (1974); Piano Sonata (1940); Piano Sonatina (1945); *3 Etudes* for Quarter-tone Piano (1946); *Little Suite* for Piano (1971); songs.

Ludford, Nicholas, English composer; b. c.1485; d. c.1557. He was one of the musicians at the Royal Free Chapel of St. Stephen's, Westminster, until it was dissolved in 1547; in 1521 he was admitted to the Fraternity of St. Nicholas, a guild of musicians. His surviving works (all in MS) include masses, motets, and a Magnificat. His *Collected Works,* ed. by J.D. Bergsagel, are being issued by the American Inst. of Musicology (1965—).

BIBLIOGRAPHY: H. Baillie, "Nicholas Ludford (c.1485–c.1557)," *Musical Quarterly* (April 1958).

Ludgin, Chester, American baritone; b. New York, May 20, 1925. After service in the U.S. Army (1943–46), he was a student of the American Theatre Wing Professional Training Program (1948–50); studied voice with Armen Boyajian. He began his career by singing in nightclubs; made his operatic debut in 1956 as Scarpia with the New Orleans Experimental Opera Theatre of America; in 1957 became a member of the N.Y. City Opera; sang leading roles with the San Francisco Opera from 1964; made his European debut with the Netherlands Opera in 1977. He created major roles in Ward's *The Crucible* (N.Y., 1961), Imbrie's *Angle of Repose* (San Francisco, 1967), and Bernstein's *A Quiet Place* (Houston, 1983); also made successful appearances in productions of Broadway musicals.

Ludikar, Pavel, Austrian bass; b. Prague, March 3, 1882; d. Vienna, Feb. 19, 1970. He studied law in Prague; then took piano lessons, acquiring sufficient proficiency to be able to play accompaniment to singers; then finally devoted himself to his real profession, that of opera singing. He appeared in Vienna, Dresden, Milan, and Buenos Aires; was a member of the Boston Civic Opera (1913–14); from 1926 to 1932 he was on the staff of the Metropolitan Opera Co.; his most successful role was that of Figaro in *Il Barbiere di Siviglia,* which he sang more than 100 times in the U.S.; he was also renowned for bass parts in Russian operas, and sang the title role of Krenek's opera *Karl V* in Prague on June 22, 1938. His repertoire included about 18 operatic roles in 4 languages.

Ludkewycz, Stanislaus, significant Polish composer; b. Jaroslav, Austrian Galicia, Jan. 24, 1879; d. Lwow, Sept. 10, 1979, at the age of 100. He studied philosophy in Lemberg (Lwow), graduating in 1901; then went to Vienna, where he studied musical composition with Grädener and Zemlinsky at the Vienna Cons.; received his Dr.Phil. in 1908. He then settled in Lemberg. From 1910 to 1914 he served as director of the Inst. of Music there; then was recruited in the Austrian army, and was taken prisoner by the Russians (1915). After the Russian Revolution he was evacuated to Tashkent; liberated in 1918, he returned to Lwow; from 1939 to 1972, until the age of 93, he was a prof. of composition at the Cons. there. When the city was incorporated into the Ukrainian Soviet Republic after World War II, Ludkewycz was awarded the Order of the Red Banner by the Soviet government (1949). On the occasion of his 100th birthday in 1979 he received the Order of Hero of Socialist Labor. His music followed the precepts of European Romanticism, with the representational, geographic, and folkloric aspects in evidence. Stylistically, the influence of Tchaikovsky was paramount in his vocal and instrumental compositions.

WORKS: Opera, *Dovbush,* to his own libretto (1955); *Caucasus,* symph. ode for Chorus and Orch. (1905–13); *The Testament,* cantata (1934; revised 1955). For Orch.: *Carpathian Symphony* (1952); symph. poems: *Stone Carvers* (1926); *Valse mélancolique* (1920); *Dnieper* (1947); *Moses* (1956); 2 piano concertos (1920, 1957); Violin Concerto (1945); Piano Trio (1919); *Variations on a Ukrainian Theme* for Violin and Piano (1949). Choral works, with Orch.: *Eternal Revolutionary* (1898); *Conquistadores* (1941); *A Testament for the Pioneers* (1967)· numerous piano pieces, songs, and arrangements of popular melodies.

BIBLIOGRAPHY: M. Zagaikevycz, *S. Ludkewycz* (Kiev, 1957); S. Pavlishin, *S. Ludkewycz* (Kiev, 1974).

Ludwig, August, German composer and musical journalist; b. Waldheim, Jan. 15, 1865; d. Dresden, April 9, 1946. He studied at the Cons. of Cologne, and later in Munich; brought out a number of orch. compositions, notably the overtures *Ad astra* and *Luther-Ouvertüre;* also a comic opera, *Kunst und Schein* (1906). From 1894 till 1903 he was editor of the *Neue Berliner Musikzeitung.* He publ. *Geharnischte Aufsätze über Musik* (a collection of essays); *Der Konzertagent* (1894); *Stachel und Lorbeer* (1897); *Zur Wertschätzung der Musik* (1898); *Tannhäuser redivivus* (1908). He attracted unfavorable attention by his abortive attempt to "complete" Schubert's "Unfinished" Symph., adding 2 movements, a *Philosophen-Scherzo,* and a *Schicksalsmarsch.*

Ludwig, Christa, remarkable German soprano; b. Berlin, March 16, 1928. She stemmed from a musical family; her father managed an opera; her mother sang. Christa Ludwig studied at the Hochschule für Musik in Frankfurt; in 1946 she made her opera debut in Frankfurt, in the role of Orlofsky in *Die Fledermaus.* In 1954 she sang the roles of Cherubino and Octavian at the Salzburg Festival; in 1955 was engaged by the Vienna State Opera. She made her artistic impact as a Wagnerian singer, and was equally successful in such disparate roles as Kundry in *Parsifal,* Fricka in *Das Rheingold,* Venus in *Tannhäuser,* and Magdalene in *Die Meistersinger.* She obtained brilliant success as the Marschallin in *Der Rosenkavalier,* and in other operas by Richard Strauss. In the Italian repertoire she gave fine interpretations of the roles of Amneris in *Aida,* Rosina in *The Barber of Seville,* and Lady Macbeth in Verdi's opera. Her career took her to opera theaters all over the world; she sang at La Scala in Milan, Covent Garden in London, the Teatro Colón in Buenos Aires, and the Nissei Theater in Tokyo. Sober-minded, skeptical music critics in Europe and America exerted their vocabularies to extol Christa Ludwig

Ludwig – Luening

as a superb singer not only in opera but also in the art of German lieder; some even praised her physical attributes. In 1962 she was named Kammersängerin of Austria, and in 1969 she received the Cross of Merit, First Class, of the Republic of Austria. On Sept. 29, 1957 she married **Walter Berry,** the Austrian baritone; they frequently appeared in the same opera together; when she sang Carmen, Walter Berry was her conquering torero, Escamillo; they separated and in 1970 were divorced; in 1972 she married the French actor Paul-Emile Deiber, and became a French citizen.

BIBLIOGRAPHY: P. Lorenz, *Christa Ludwig; Walter Berry* (Vienna, 1968); David Ewen, *Musicians since 1900* (N.Y., 1978).

Ludwig, Franz, Bohemian composer and musicologist; b. Graslitz, July 7, 1889; d. Münster, June 15, 1955. He studied first with his father, director of the Graslitz Music School; then with Pembaur, Reger, and Krehl at the Leipzig Cons., and with Riemann (musicology) at Leipzig Univ. He publ. a *Kurzgefasste Musikgeschichte des Erzgebirges* (1924); biographies of Franz Wüllner, etc. He composed an opera, *Schlag zwölf* (Münster, 1928); a scenic oratorio, *Das Lambertusspiel* (Bremerhaven, 1933); *Lustspielouvertüre* for Orch.; Piano Concerto; Horn Concerto; *Serenade* for 8 Wind Instruments; sonatas and other pieces for piano; men's choruses; songs.

Ludwig, Friedrich, German musicologist; b. Potsdam, May 8, 1872; d. Göttingen, Oct. 3, 1930. He studied music history at the Univ. of Marburg, and later at Strasbourg; in 1911 became a member of the faculty at the Univ. of Strasbourg; then went over to the Univ. of Göttingen. He was an authority on medieval music and publ. numerous valuable articles on the subject, covering all aspects of the period. He also edited the musical works of Guillaume de Machaut (1926–34).

BIBLIOGRAPHY: J. Müller-Blattau, *Dem Andenken Friedrich Ludwigs* (Kassel, 1931).

Ludwig, Leopold, Austrian conductor; b. Witkowitz (Ostrava), Jan. 12, 1908; d. Lüneburg, April 25, 1979. He studied piano in Vienna; then conducted provincial theater orchs. in Austria and Germany, in Oldenburg (1936–39), at the Vienna Staatsoper (1939–43), and at the Städtische Oper in Berlin (1943–50). In 1951 he was appointed Generalmusikdirektor of the Hamburg Staatsoper, and remained at this post until 1970; during his tenure there he introduced a number of new German operas, among them Krenek's *Pallas Athene weint* (1955) and Henze's *Der Prinz von Homburg* (1960). As guest conductor, Ludwig made special appearances in Edinburgh (1956) and San Francisco (1959). From 1968 until his death he taught at the Univ. of Hamburg.

BIBLIOGRAPHY: B.W. Wessling, *Leopold Ludwig* (Bremen, 1968).

Ludwig, Walther, German tenor; b. Bad Oeynhausen, March 17, 1902; d. Lahr, May 15, 1981. He studied

jurisprudence and also medicine before deciding on a singing career. In 1932 he joined the staff of the Municipal Opera in Berlin, remaining on its roster until 1945. From 1952–69 he was a prof. at the Berlin Hochschule für Musik. He also resumed his medical studies, and obtained the degree of Dr.Med. in Berlin in 1971.

Ludwig II, Bavarian king, royal patron of Wagner; b. in the Nymphenburg castle in Munich, Aug. 25, 1845; d. insane, by suicide, in the Starnberg Lake, June 13, 1886. As a crown prince he conceived an extreme adulation for Wagner, and when he became King, at 19, he declared his intention to sponsor all of Wagner's productions, an event that came at the most difficult time of Wagner's life, beset as he was by personal and financial problems. In sincere gratitude, Wagner spoke of his future plans of composition as "a program for the King." In his total devotion to Wagner, Ludwig converted his castle Neuschwanstein into a "worthy temple for my divine friend," installing in it architectural representations of scenes from Wagner's operas. His bizarre behavior caused the government of Bavaria to order a psychiatric examination of Ludwig, and he was eventually committed to an asylum near the Starnberg Lake. During a walk, he overpowered the psychiatrist escorting him, and apparently dragged him to his death in the lake, and drowned himself, too. Much material on Ludwig II is found in Wagner's bibliography; for a detailed account of his life see Wilfrid Blunt, *The Dream King, Ludwig II of Bavaria* (London, 1970).

Luening, Otto (Clarence), multifaceted American musician, composer, conductor, flutist, educator, and pioneer of electronic music; b. Milwaukee, June 15, 1900, of deeply rooted German ancestry, traceable to one Manfried von Lüninck, who flourished in 1350; one of Luening's maternal ancestors was said to be a descendant of Martin Luther's sister. Luening's great-grandfather emigrated to the U.S. in 1839 and settled in Wisconsin; he made the first barley beer in Milwaukee. Luening's paternal grandfather was American-born; he became active in bilingual culture in Wisconsin and was an organizer of the German-English Academy. Luening's father was an educated musician who received his training at the Leipzig Cons.; he had met Wagner and sung in performances of Beethoven's 9th Symph., with Wagner conducting; returning to Milwaukee, he became active in German-American music; he kept his cultural associations with Germany, and in 1912 took his family to Munich. There Otto Luening enrolled in the Akademie der Tonkunst; he studied flute with Alois Schellhorn, piano with Josif Becht, and composition with Beer-Walbrunn. He gave his first concert as a flutist in Munich on March 27, 1916. When America entered the war in 1917, Luening went to Switzerland, where he continued his musical education, studying with Philip Jarnach and Volkmar Andreae at the Zürich Cons.; he also had an opportunity to take private lessons with Busoni; pursuing his scientific interests, he attended a seminar in abnormal psychology at the Univ. of Zürich, and also appeared as an actor in the English Players Co. in Switzerland. He began to compose; his violin sonata and a sextet were performed at the Zürich Cons. Luening returned to the U.S. in 1920; he earned a living playing the flute in theater orchs. In 1925 he moved to Rochester, N.Y., where he served as coach and executive director of the opera dept. at the Eastman School of Music; in 1928 he went to Cologne; in 1930–31 he held a Guggenheim fellowship; in 1932–34 he was on the faculty of the Univ. of Arizona in Tucson. In 1934 he became chairman of the music dept. at Bennington College in Vermont, keeping this position until 1964; concurrently he also taught at Barnard College in N.Y.; in 1949 he joined the philosophy faculty at Columbia Univ., holding seminars in composition; retired in 1968 as prof. emeritus. While thus occupied, he continued to compose. His opera *Evangeline*, to his own libretto after Longfellow, which he completed in 1932 but revised numerous times, finally achieved production at Columbia Univ. on May 5, 1948, with Luening conducting; the opera received what is usually described as mixed reviews. As an inveterate flute blower, Luening used flutes in a number of his works; of these, the most self-indulgent was *Sonority Canon*, projecting a murmuration of innumerable flutes, written in 1962. He also was active as a conductor; he led the premiere of Menotti's opera *The Medium* in N.Y. on May 8, 1946, and of Virgil Thomson's *The Mother of Us All* in N.Y. on May 12, 1947.

An important development in Luening's career as a composer took place in 1952, when he began to experiment with the resources of the magnetic tape; he composed a strikingly novel piece, *Fantasy in Space*, in which he played the flute with its accompaniment electronically transmuted on tape; Stokowski conducted it in N.Y. on Oct. 28, 1952, along with Luening's 2 other electronic pieces, *Low Speed* and *Invention*. He found a partner in Vladimir Ussachevsky, who was also interested in musical electronics. Together, they produced the first work that combined real sounds superinduced on an electronic background, *Rhapsodic Variations* for tape recorder and orch., performed by the Louisville Orch. on March 30, 1954; its performance anticipated by a few months the production of Varèse's similarly constructed work, *Déserts*. Another electronic work by Luening and Ussachevsky, *A Poem in Cycles and Bells* for tape recorder and orch., was played by the Los Angeles Phil. on Nov. 18, 1954; on March 31, 1960, Leonard Bernstein gave the first performance with the N.Y. Phil. of still another collaborative composition by Luening and Ussachevsky, *Concerted Piece* for tape recorder and orch. Thenceforth, Luening devoted a major part of his creative effort to an integration of electronic sound into the fabric of a traditional orch., without abondoning the fundamental scales and intervals; most, but not all, of these works were in collaboration with Ussachevsky. Unaided, he produced *Synthesis* for electronic tape and orch. (1960) and *Sonority Canon* (1962). He also wrote straightforward pieces without electronics; of these the most

important is *A Wisconsin Symphony*, a sort of musical memoir of a Wisconsin-born composer; it was performed in Milwaukee, Luening's birthplace, on Jan. 4, 1976. His native state reciprocated proudly, awarding Luening an hononary doctorate from the Univ. of Wisconsin in Madison, a medal from the Wisconsin Academy of Sciences, Arts and Letters, and a citation from the Wisconsin State Assembly. Luening described his career, with its triumphs and disappointments, in an autobiography, *The Odyssey of an American Composer*, publ. in 1980.

WORKS: OPERA: *Evangeline*, to Luening's libretto after Longfellow's peom (1928–33; revised 1947; produced at Columbia Univ., N.Y., May 5, 1948, composer conducting). FOR ORCH.: Concertino for Flute and Chamber Orch. (1923; Philadelphia, Jan. 30, 1935); *First Symphonic Fantasia* (Rochester, N.Y., Nov. 25, 1925); *2 Symphonic Interludes* (1935; N.Y., April 11, 1936); *Preludes to a Hymn Tune*, after William Billings (N.Y., Feb. 1, 1937); *Kentucky Concerto* (1951); *Pilgrim's Hymn* (N.Y., Oct. 12, 1952); *Wisconsin Suite: Of Childhood Tunes Remembered* (1955); *2nd Symphonic Fantasia* (N.Y., Oct. 18, 1957); *Fantasia* for String Quartet and Orch. (1961); *Sonority Forms* (1973); *A Wisconsin Symphony* (Milwaukee, Jan. 4, 1976). CHAMBER MUSIC: Violin Sonata No. 1 (1917); Sextet for Flute, Clarinet, Horn, Violin, Viola, and Cello (1918); String Quartet No. 1 (1919–20); Sonatina for Flute and Piano (1919); Piano Trio (1921); Violin Sonata No. 2 (1922); String Quartet No. 2 (1923); Sonata No. 1 for Cello Solo (1924); *Serenade* for 3 Horns and Strings (1927); String Quartet No. 3 (1928); *Fantasia brevis* for Flute and Piano (1929); *Short Fantasy* for Violin and Horn (1930); *Mañana* for Violin and Piano (1933); *Fantasia brevis* for Violin, Viola, and Cello (1936); *Fantasia brevis* for Clarinet and Piano (1936); *Short Sonata* for Flute and Piano No. 1 (1937); *Short Fantasy* for Violin and Piano (1938); *Fuguing Tune* for Woodwind Quintet (1938); *The Bass with the Delicate Air* for Flute, Oboe, Clarinet, and Bassoon (1940); Violin Sonata No. 2 (1943); Suite for Cello and Piano (1946); Suite for Flute Solo No. 1 (1947); *3 Nocturnes* for Oboe and Piano (1951); *Legend* for Oboe and Strings (1952); Trio for Flute, Violin, and Piano (1952); Sonata for Bassoon and Piano (1952); Suite for Flute Solo No. 2 (1953); Sonata for Trombone and Piano (1953); *Song, Poem and Dance* for Flute and Strings (1957); Sonata for Viola Solo (1958); Sonata No. 2 for Solo Cello (1958); Sonata No. 1 for Violin Solo (1958); *Lyric Scene* for Flute and Strings (1958); *3 Fantasias* for Guitar Solo (1960); Suite for Flute Solo No. 3 (1961); Trio for Flute, Cello, and Piano (1962); *Sonority Canon* for 2 to 37 Flutes (1962); 3 Duets for 2 Flutes (1962); Suite for Flute Solo No. 4 (1963); Duo for Violin and Viola (1963); *Short Sonata* for Flute and Piano No. 2 (1966); *Fantasia* for Cello Solo (1966); Trio for 3 Flutes (1966); Violin Sonata No. 3 (1966); *14 Easy Duets* for Recorders (1967); Sonata No. 2 for Violin Solo (1968); Suite for Flute Solo No. 5 (1969); Trio for Trumpet, Horn, and Trombone (1969); Sonata No. 3 for Violin Solo (1970); *8 Tone Poems* for 2 Violas (1971); *Short Sonata* No. 2 for Flute and Piano

(1971); *Elegy for the Lonesome Ones* for 2 Clarinets and Strings (1974); *Prelude* for Flute, Clarinet, and Bassoon (1974); *Mexican Serenades* for Wind Instruments, Double Bass, and Percussion (1974); Suite for 2 Flutes and Piano (1976); *Canons* for 2 Violins and Flute (1976); *Fantasias on Indian Motives* for Flute Solo. FOR PIANO: *6 Short and Easy Piano Pieces* (1928); Dance Sonata (1929); *5 Intermezzi* (1932); 6 Piano Preludes (1935); 8 Preludes (1936); 8 Inventions (1938); *Short Sonata* No. 1 (1940); 10 Pieces for 5 Fingers (1946); *Gay Picture* (1957); *Short Sonata* No. 2 (1958); *Short Sonata* No. 3 (1958); *Short Sonata* No. 4 (1967); *Short Sonatas* Nos. 5, 6, 7 (1979). VOCAL MUSIC: *The Soundless Song* for Soprano, Instruments, Dancers, Light Projections (1923); *Alleluia* for Chorus (1944). ELECTRONIC MUSIC: *Fantasy in Space* for Flute and Electronic Tape (1952; N.Y., Oct. 28, 1952, Stokowski conducting); *Low Speed* for Flute and Tape (1952); *Invention in 12 Tones* for Flute and Tape (1952); electronic background music for *King Lear*, produced by Orson Welles (N.Y., Jan. 12, 1956); *Theatre Piece No. 2* for Electronic Tape, Voice, Brass, Percussion, and Narrator (choreographed by Doris Humphrey and José Limon; N.Y., April 20, 1956, composer conducting); also incidental music in electronics for a production of G.B. Shaw's *Back to Methuselah* (N.Y., March 5, 1958); *Gargoyles* for Violin Solo and Synthesized Sound (1960); *Synthesis* for Electronic Sound and Orch. (1960; Erie, Pa., Oct. 22, 1963); *Electronic Doubles of Choral Fantasy and Fugue* (1973). The following were produced in collaboration with Vladimir Ussachevsky: *Rhapsodic Variations* for Orch. and Electronic Tape, the first score ever composed which combined electronic sound with human musicians (Louisville, Ky., March 30, 1954; numerous subsequent perfs. in the U.S. and in Europe); *A Poem in Cycles and Bells* for Tape and Orch. (Los Angeles, Nov. 18, 1954); *Concerted Piece* for Tape Recorder and Orch. (N.Y., March 31, 1960).
BIBLIOGRAPHY: David Ewen, *American Composers* (N.Y., 1980).

Lugert, Josef, Bohemian music educator and composer; b. Frohnau, Oct. 30, 1841; d. Prague, July 24, 1936. He studied organ in Prague; in 1868 was appointed to the faculty of the Prague Cons.; later organized schools for instrumentalists in the provinces. He wrote a Symph. and several pieces of chamber music; publ. the manual *Musikalische Formenlehre* and various school manuals.

Luigini, Alexandre (-Clément-Léon-Joseph), French composer; b. Lyons, March 9, 1850; d. Paris, July 29, 1906. He was the son of the Italian musician Giuseppe Luigini (1820–98), who conducted at the Théâtre-Italien in Paris; studied at the Paris Cons. with Massart (violin) and Massenet (composition); then entered his father's orch. at Lyons (1869) as a violinist, and began his very successful career as a ballet composer with the production of his first stage work, *Le Rêve de Nicette* (Lyons, 1870); in 1877 he became conductor at the Grand Théâtre at Lyons and a prof. of harmony at the Lyons Cons.; after 20

years there, went to Paris as conductor at the Opéra-Comique, where he remained till his death, except during 1903, when he conducted the orch. at the Théâtre-Lyrique. His greatest success as a composer came with the production of *Ballet égyptien* (Lyons, Jan. 13, 1875), still one of the most popular ballet scores; it was inserted, with Verdi's permission, in the 2nd act of *Aida* at its performance in Lyons in 1886. Other works: comic operas: *Les Caprices de Margot* (Lyons, 1877); *La Reine des fleurs* (Lyons, 1878); *Faublas* (Paris, 1881); ballets: *Ballet égyptien* (Lyons, 1875); *Anges et démons* (1876); *Les Noces d'Ivanovna* (1883); *Le Bivouac* (1889); *Les Echarpes* (1891); *Rayon d'or* (1891); *Rose et Papillon* (1891); *Le Meunier* (1892); *Arlequin écolier* (1894); *Dauritha* (1894); also *Romance symphonique* for Orch.; 3 string quartets (all won prizes); marches for orch.; numerous piano pieces.

Lukačić, Ivan, Croatian organist and composer; b. Šibenik (baptized, April 17), 1587; d. Split, Sept. 20, 1648. He studied music in Italy, and in 1597 entered the Franciscan order. In 1620 he became prior of the Franciscan monastery and music master at the Cathedral of Split. His book of *Sacrae cantiones* (Venice, 1620; destroyed in World War II) includes 27 motets; they reflect the influence of the early Baroque style and employ instrumental accompaniment. Modern editions of his works appear in D. Plamenac, ed., *Odabarani moteti* (Zagreb, 1935) and J. Andreis, ed., *Sesnaesi moteta* (Zagreb, 1970).
BIBLIOGRAPHY: N. O'Loughlin, "A Note on Lukačić," *Musical Times*, CXIV (1973).

Lukács, Miklós, Hungarian conductor; b. Gyula, Feb. 4, 1905. He was educated at the Berlin Hochschule für Musik; from 1930 he conducted in Germany. In 1943 he returned to Hungary; served as a regular conductor at the Hungarian State Opera in Budapest; also conducted symph. concerts there.

Lukáš, Zdeněk, Czech composer; b. Prague, Aug, 21, 1928. He studied music theory with Kabeláč in Prague; then lived mostly in Pilsen as a choral conductor (1955–65). In his music he avails himself of several advanced techniques of composition, including serialism.
WORKS: Radio opera, *At žije mrtvý* (*Long Live the Dead Man;* 1967; Prague, Dec. 11, 1968); one-act opera, *Domácí karneval* (*Home Carnival;* 1968; Prague, March 29, 1969); Piano Concerto (1955); Violin Concerto (1956); Cello Concerto (1957); 4 symphs. (1960, 1961, 1965, 1966); Concerto for Soprano Saxophone and Orch. (1962); *Concerto grosso* for String Quartet and String Orch. (1964); *Symphonietta solemnis* (1965); *Sonata concertata* for Piano, Winds, and Percussion (1966); *Musica ritmica* for Percussion and Winds (1966); Concerto for Violin, Viola, and Orch. (Prague, March 7, 1969); Variations for Piano and Orch. (1970); 3 string quartets (1960, 1965, 1973); Trio for Violin, Piano, and Side Drum (1962); *Partita semplice* for 4 Violins and Piano (1964); Wind Quintet (1969); *Amoroso* for Clarinet, Bagpipes, and Double Bass (1970); *Thou Shalt Not Kill,*

electronic oratorio for Chorus, Instruments, and Tape (1971); *Verba laudata,* 4 songs for Soprano, String Quartet, and Piano (1967); *Modlitba (Prayer)* for Chorus, Organ, and Percussion (1968).

Luke, Ray, American composer and conductor; b. Fort Worth, Texas, May 30, 1926. He studied at the Texas Christian Univ. (B.M., 1949; M.M., 1950) and at the Eastman School of Music in Rochester, N.Y., with Bernard Rogers (Ph.D., 1960). In 1969 he received the gold medal at the Queen Elizabeth of Belgium International Competition for his Piano Concerto. He taught at the East Texas State College from 1951–62; in 1962 was appointed to the faculty of Oklahoma City Univ. He served as associate conductor of the Oklahoma City Symph. (1968–73), then as principal guest conductor (1974–78).
WORKS: For the stage: Opera, *Medea* (New England Cons., Boston, May 3, 1979); ballet, *Tapestry* (Oklahoma City, May 8, 1975). For Orch.: 4 symphs.: No. 1 (Rochester, March 26, 1959); No. 2 (Oklahoma City, Feb. 3, 1963); No. 3 (Oklahoma City, Feb. 21, 1964); No. 4 (Oklahoma City, March 30, 1970); Piano Concerto (Brussels, Nov. 26, 1970); Bassoon Concerto (1965); Suite No. 1 (Rochester, April 15, 1958); Suite No. 2 (1967); *Incantation* for Cello, Harp, and Strings (1968); *Compressions* No. 1 (Oklahoma City, Jan. 9, 1973); *Compressions* No. 2 (Fort Worth, Nov. 9, 1973); *Miniatures* (1957); *Epilogue* (1958); *Symphonic Dialogues* for Violin, Oboe, and Orch. (1965). Chamber music: Trio for Flute, Clarinet, and Piano (1974); *2 Odes* for Mezzo-soprano, Flute, and Piano (1965); String Quartet (1966); Septet (1979).
BIBLIOGRAPHY: David Ewen, *American Composers* (N.Y., 1982).

Lully (or **Lulli**), **Jean-Baptiste,** celebrated Italian-born French composer; b. Florence, Nov. 28, 1632; d. Paris, March 22, 1687. The son of a poor Florentine miller, he was taught the elements of music by a Franciscan monk, and also learned to play the guitar, and later the violin. Attracted by his vivacious temperament and a talent for singing, the Chevalier de Guise took him to Paris in 1646 as a page to Mademoiselle d'Orléans, a young cousin of Louis XIV. He soon adapted himself to the ways and manners of the French court, and quickly mastered the language, although he could never rid himself of a pronounced Italian accent. The story that he was once a scullery boy is apocryphal, but he kept company with the domestic servants, and his talent as a violin player was first revealed by his improvisations in the royal kitchen; the Count de Nogent heard him, and secured for him a position in the private band of Mademoiselle d'Orléans. When he set to music a satirical poem reflecting on his patroness, he lost favor with her, but entered the service of young Louis XIV (1652), winning his first success as a ballet dancer. He contrived to obtain instruction on the harpsichord and in composition from Nicolas Métru, organist of St. Nicolas-des-Champs, and François Roberday, organist at the Eglise des Petits-Pères. He attended opera and concerts at the court, led by his compatriot Luigi Rossi,

and conceived a passion for the theater, which became the determining factor of his entire career. After a brief association with the King's private orch., "les 24 violons du roi," he organized his own band of 17 instruments (later 21), "les petits violons," which he developed into a fine ensemble. He rose fast in royal favor; became a favorite composer of court ballets for various occasions; in several of these productions Louis XIV himself took part next to Lully, who danced and acted as "M. Baptiste." In 1661 he received the lucrative post of composer to the king, and in 1662, a further appointment as maître de musique of the royal family. In 1662 he married Madeleine Lambert, daughter of the court musician Michel Lambert. From 1663 to 1671 he wrote music for several comic ballets by Molière, including *Le Mariage forcé, L'Amour médecin,* and *Le Bourgeois Gentilhomme,* which foreshadowed the development of opéra-comique. In 1672 he obtained letters patent for the establishment of the Académie Royale de Musique (which eventually became the Grand Opéra), taking the privilege from Perrin and Cambert, who originally launched the enterprise in 1668. With the formation of a national opera house, Lully found his true calling, that of creating French operatic art, setting French texts to music with sensitivity to the genius of the language, and abandoning the conventional Italian type of opera, with its repetitive extensions of arias, endless fioned rituras, etc. In the theater, Lully did not confine himself to the composer's functions, but also acted as director, stage manager, conductor, and even, upon occasion, machinist. From 1672 he worked in close cooperation with a congenial librettist, Quinault, who followed Lully's ideas with rare understanding. Lully developed a type of overture which became known as the "Lully overture" or "French overture" and of which the earliest example occurs in his ballet *Alcidiane* (1658); this type of overture opens with a slow, solemn, homophonic section with sharply dotted rhythms, followed by a fast section with some elements of imitation; frequently the overture ends with a return to the tempo and rhythm of the opening. In vocal writing, Lully demonstrated his mastery of both dramatic recitative and songful arias; he imparted dramatic interest to his choral ensembles; the instrumental parts were also given more prominence than in early Italian opera. That an Italian-born musician should have become the founder of French opera is one of the many paradoxes of music history. As a man, Lully was haughty, arrogant, and irascible, tolerating no opposition; his ambition was his prime counsellor; considerations of morality played a small part in his actions. With those in power, he knew how to be submissive; a shrewd courtier, he often gained his aims by flattery and obsequiousness; the manner in which he secured for himself the directorship of the Académie Royale de Musique, through the royal favorite Mme. de Montespan, moved some of his critics to berate him savagely. Yet, thanks to his volcanic energy and his disregard of all obstacles, he was able to accomplish an epoch-making task. His death resulted from a symbolic accident: while conducting, he vehemently struck his foot with a sharp-pointed cane used to pound out the beat; gangrene set in, and he died of blood poisoning.

WORKS: BALLETS (produced at court in Paris, Versailles, Saint-Germain, and Fontainebleau): *La Nuit* (Feb. 23, 1653); *Alcidiane* (Feb. 14, 1658); *La Raillerie* (Feb. 19, 1659); *L'Impatience* (Feb. 19, 1661); *Les Saisons* (July 30, 1661); *Hercule amoureux* (ballet music for Cavalli's opera *Ercole amante;* Feb. 7, 1662); *Les Arts* (Jan. 8, 1663); *Les Noces de village* (Oct. 3, 1663); *Le Mariage forcé* (Jan. 29, 1664); *Les Amours déguisés* (Feb. 15, 1664); *Les Plaisirs de l'isle enchantée* (May 8, 1664); *La Naissance de Vénus* (Jan. 26, 1665); *L'Amour médecin* (Sept. 15, 1665); *Les Muses* (Dec. 2, 1666); *Le Sicilien, ou L'Amour peintre* (Feb. 10, 1667); *Le Carnaval* (Jan. 18, 1668); *Georges Dandin* (July 18, 1668); *Flore* (Feb. 13, 1669); *Monsieur de Pourceaugnac* (Oct. 6, 1669); *Les Amants magnifiques* (Feb. 4, 1670); *Le Bourgeois Gentilhomme* (Oct. 14, 1670); *Psyché* (Jan. 17, 1671); *Le Triomphe de l'Amour* (Jan. 21, 1681).

OPERAS: *Les Fêtes de l'Amour et de Bacchus* (1672); *Cadmus et Hermione* (April 27, 1673); *Alceste, ou Le Triomphe d'Alcide* (Jan. 19, 1674); *Thésée* (Jan. 12, 1675); *Atys* (Jan. 10, 1676); *Isis* (Jan. 5, 1677); *Psyché* (a different work from the similarly named ballet; April 19, 1678); *Bellérophon* (Jan. 31, 1679); *Proserpine* (Feb. 3, 1680); *Persée* (April 18, 1682); *Phaéton* (Jan. 9, 1683); *Amadis de Gaule* (Jan. 18, 1684); *Roland* (Jan. 8, 1685); *Idylle sur la paix* (July 16, 1685); *Le Temple de la paix* (Oct. 20, 1685); *Armide et Renaud* (Feb. 15, 1686); *Acis et Galatée* (Sept. 17, 1686); *Achille et Polyxène* (Nov. 7, 1687). For further details about productions and revivals of Lully's operas, see A. Loewenberg, *Annals of Opera* (1943; new ed., 1955). Ten stage works produced at the French court between 1653 and 1657 had several numbers contributed by Lully. Most of Lully's operas have been publ. by Breitkopf & Härtel, in *Chefs-d'œuvre classiques de l'opéra français; Armide et Renaud* in Eitner's *Publikationen älterer Musikwerke* (vol. 14; full score, and a piano score). Besides his stage works, Lully wrote a Te Deum, a Miserere, a 4-part Mass a cappella, many motets; instrumental works (string trios, airs for violin, etc.). Henry Prunières undertook a complete ed. of Lully's works (9 vols., publ. 1930–39).

BIBLIOGRAPHY: Le Prevost d'Exmes, *Lully Musicien* (Paris, 1779); Th. Lajarte, *Lully* (Paris, 1878); E. Radet, *Lully, Homme d'affaires, propriétaire et musicien* (Paris, 1891); R. Gandolfi, *Accademia dedicata a G.B. Lulli e Luigi Cherubini* (Florence, 1902); Romain Rolland, *Musiciens d'autrefois* (Paris, 1908; in Eng., 1915); Henry Prunières, *Lully* (Paris, 1909); L. de La Laurencie, *Lully* (Paris, 1911); idem, *L'Opéra italien en France avant Lully* (Paris, 1913); idem, *Le Ballet de cour en France avant Lully* (Paris, 1914); special issue of the *Revue Musicale* (Jan. 1925); Henry Prunières, "Lully and the Académie de Musique et de Danse," *Musical Quarterly* (Oct. 1925); idem, *La Vie illustre et libertine de J.B. Lully* (Paris, 1929; a somewhat romanticized biography, based on factual data); F. Böttger, *Die Comédie-Ballets von Molière und Lully* (Berlin, 1931); E. Borrel, *J.-B. Lully: Le Cadre, la vie, la personnalité, le rayonnement, les œuvres* (Paris, 1949); Th. Valensi, *Louis XIV et Lully* (Nice, 1951); N. Slonimsky's article in the *Guide du Concert* (Feb. 1, 1952), which reproduces the text of Lully's birth certificate, establishing his birth date as Nov. 28, 1632; J. Eppelsheim, *Das Orchester in den Werken J.B. Lullys* (Tutzing, 1961); M. Ellis, "Inventory of the Dances of Jean-Baptiste Lully," *Recherches sur la Musique Française Classique,* 9 (1969); A. Ducrot, "Les Représentations de l'Académie royale de musique à Paris au temps de Louis XIV (1671–1715)," *Recherches sur la Musique Française Classique,* 10 (1970).

Lumbye, Hans Christian, Danish composer of light music; b. Copenhagen, May 2, 1810; d. there, March 20, 1874. He played in military bands as a youth; in 1839 formed his own orch., soon achieving fame as a conductor and composer of dance music, especially with his concerts in the Tivoli amusement park in Copenhagen. He composed about 400 pieces of dance music (waltzes, galops, polkas, marches, etc.), which earned him the sobriquet of "the Johann Strauss of the North." His 2 sons were also musicians; the elder, **Carl Lumbye** (b. Copenhagen, July 9, 1841; d. there, Aug. 10, 1911), was a violinist, conductor, and composer of dance music; the younger son, **Georg Lumbye** (b. Copenhagen, Aug. 26, 1843; d. there, Oct. 30, 1922), studied at the Paris Cons., conducted dance music in Copenhagen, wrote the operetta *Heksefløtjen* (*The Witch's Flute;* 1869) and numerous vaudevilles.

BIBLIOGRAPHY: G. Skjerne, *H.C. Lumbye og hans Samtid* (Copenhagen, 1912; 2nd ed., 1946).

Lumsdaine, David, Australian composer; b. Sydney, Oct. 31, 1931. He studied piano, viola, and composition at the Sydney Cons. and at the Univ. of Sydney (B.A., 1953). After graduation in 1954 he moved to England, taking private lessons in composition with Mátyás Seiber in London. A precocious composer, he wrote his first pieces at the age of 12. In his mature works he developed a highly complex idiom of composition. In 1961 he was engaged by the Royal Academy of Music in London to organize a series of seminars on contemporary composition; in 1970 he obtained a lectureship in music at Durham Univ., where he established an electronic music studio.

WORKS: *Variations for Orchestra* (1957); *Short Symphony* (1959); *Annotations from Auschwitz,* chamber cantata (1964; his most powerful work); Cantata No. 2 (1964); *Missa brevis* (1964); *Bach Music* for Large Orch., based on material from Bach's *The Art of the Fugue,* transformed into a complex continuum of metric elements; Cantata No. 3, *Story from a Time of Disturbance,* for Baritone and Chamber Ensemble (1965); *Easter Frescoes* for Soprano and Chamber Orch., after the *New Testament* (1966); *Flights* for 2 Pianos (1967); *Mandala I* for Wind Quintet (1968); *Bourbon* for Computer and Tape (1968); *Babel* for Magnetic Tape (1968); *Episodes* for Orch. (1969); *Mandala II* for Flute, Clari-

net, Viola, Cello, and Percussion (1969); *Looking Glass Music* for Brass Quintet and Magnetic Tape (1971); *Kangaroo Hunt* for Piano and Percussion (1971); *Caliban Impromptu* for Piano Trio and Electronic Instruments, after Shakespeare's play *The Tempest* (1972); *Salvation Creek with Eagle* for Chamber Orch. (1974); *Sunflower* for Chamber Orch. (1975); *Evensong* for Brass Ensemble (1975); *Hagoromo* for Orch. (1975).
BIBLIOGRAPHY: James Murdoch, *Australia's Contemporary Composers* (Melbourne, 1972); R. Cooke, "David Lumsdaine," *Music and Musicians* 21 (1972–73); N. LeFanu, "David Lumsdaine," *Musical Times*, CXVII (1976).

Lunceford, James Melvin ("Jimmie"), black American jazz instrumentalist and bandleader; b. Fulton, Mo., June 6, 1902; d. Seaside, Oreg., July 12, 1947. He studied music with Wilberforce Whiteman, the father of Paul Whiteman; he mastered the saxophone and the guitar, trombone, and flute; then went to Fisk Univ. in Nashville, Tenn. (B.M., 1926). In 1929 he formed his own band, with which he made numerous tours of the U.S., becoming one of the most popular figures of the big-band period.

Lund, Signe, Norwegian composer; b. Oslo, April 15, 1868; d. there, April 6, 1950. She studied in Berlin, Copenhagen, and Paris; spent several years in America. As a composer, she was completely under the lyrical domination of Grieg's music, and her works are eminently perishable. She wrote a ceremonial overture, *The Road to France*, on the occasion of America's entry into World War I in 1917; also various instrumental pieces and songs. She publ. an autobiography, *Sol gjennem skyer* (Oslo, 1944).

Lundquist, Torbjörn, Swedish composer; b. Stockholm, Sept. 30, 1920. He studied composition with Dag Wirén; acquired proficiency on the accordion, and wrote many works for this popular instrument. In his music he followed the Romantic "Scandinavian" tradition; during his travels in the North he collected songs of Lapland, which he used in heterophonic counterpoint in some of his works. He also experimented with ultramodern techniques of "organized spontaneity."
WORKS: *Divertimento* for Chamber Orch. (1951); 3 symphs.: No. 1, *Kammarsymfoni* (1952–56; revised 1971); No. 2, *For Freedom* (1956–70); No. 3, *Sinfonia dolorosa* (1971–75); *Elegies from Bergen* for Tenor, Male Chorus, and Orch. (1958); *Via tomheten (Via the Emptiness),* "visions" for Soli, Chorus, and Chamber Orch. (1959); *Anrop (Call)* for Soprano and Orch. (1963–64); works for Solo Concert Accordion: *Partita piccola* (1964); *Metamorphoses* (1965); *9 2-part Inventions* (1966); *Plasticity* (1966); *Sonatina piccola* (1967); *Botany Play* (1968); *Microscope* (1971); *Concerto da camera* for Accordion and Orch. (1965; Gävle, Feb. 20, 1966); *Movements* for Accordion and String Quartet (1966); *Duell* for Accordion and Percussion (1966); *Combinazione* for Violin and Percussion (1966); 2 string quartets (1966, 1969); *Férvor* for Violino Grande and Orch. (1967); *Hangarmusik,* "concerto sinfonico" for Piano and Orch. (1967); *Teamwork* for Wind Quintet (1967); *Confrontation* for Orch. (Stockholm, Oct. 5, 1968); *Evoluzione* for Strings (1968); *Intarzia* for Accordion and Strings (1968); *Sogno* for Oboe and Strings (1968); *Sound on Sound* for Audience, Speaker, Composer, and Stereo Orch. (Stockholm, Jan. 25, 1969); *Stereogram III* for Xylorimba, Electric Guitar, and Accordion (1969); *4 rondeaux* for Wind Quartet and Piano (1969); *Tempera* for 6 Brass Instruments (1969); *Galax* for Orch. (1971); Marimba Concerto (1972); opera, *Sekund av evighet* (Stockholm, May 27, 1974); *Concerto grosso* for Violin, Cello, and String Orch. (1974); *Trio fiorente* for Piano Trio (1975).

Lundsten, Ralph, Swedish composer and film director; b. Neder-Luleå, Oct. 6, 1936. He is a pioneer in Swedish electronic composition.
WORKS: His electronic works include many ballets (often in collaboration with choreographer Ivo Cramér): *Ristningar (Carvings;* 1969); *Erik XIV* (1969); *Nattmara (Nightmare;* 1970); *Gustav III* (1971); *Fader vår (Our Father;* 1971); *Ringbunden* (1971); *Midnattstimmen* (1972); *Stretch* (1972); *Nordisk natursymfoni Nr 1, Strömkarlen (The Water Sprite;* 1972); *Gunnar på Lidarände* (1973); *Isländska dansbilder* (1974); *Johannes og anima* (ballet version of the *Nordic Nature Symphony No. 2,* 1975). Other electronic scores include *Främmande planet (Unknown Planet;* 1959–60); *Composition in 3 Movements* (1964); *Atomskymning (Atom Nightfall;* 1964); *EMS Nr 1* (1966); *Vintermusik* (1968); *Suite for Electronic Accordion* (1968); *Burmusik (Cage Music;* 1968); *Cosmic Love* (1970); *Through a Landscape of Mirrors* (1970); *Cosmic Love—Trial and Discussion* (1970); *Landskapsmusik* (1972); *På vingliga tår* (1973); *Shangri-La* (1973); *Terje möter Monstret och Mobben* (1973); *Heaven by Night* (1975); *Nordisk natursymfoni Nr 2, Johannes och huldran* (1975); *Spöken dansar* (1975); *Vattensymfoni (Water Symphony;* 1975). Electronic works in collaboration with Leo Nilson: *Kalejdoskop* (1965); *Aloha Arita* (1965–66); *3 Electronic Pop Pieces* (1966); *Visioner av flygande tefat (Visions of Flying Saucers;* 1966); *Music for the Ether Hypothesis* (1967); *Lyckomusik (Bliss Music;* 1968); *Feel* (1968); *It* (1968); *Sveagris* (1968); *Tellus* (1968); *Mizar* (1968); *Holmia* (1969); *Fågel blå (Bluebird,* 1969).

Lunetta, Stanley G., American avant-garde composer; b. Sacramento, Calif., June 5, 1937. He received his B.A. at Sacramento State College and completed graduate work at the Univ. of Calif., Davis, where he studied composition with Larry Austin, Jerome Rosen, and Richard Swift; also took a course with Karlheinz Stockhausen when the latter lectured at Davis. In 1963 Lunetta formed the New Music Ensemble, devoted to contemporary music. His works explore the potentialities of electronic media; a major project is to build a computer capable of independent creative composition, both in ultramodern and infra-classical fields.

WORKS: His pieces, most of them for mixed media characterized by disestablishmentarian latitudinarianism, include *A Piece for Bandoneon and Strings* (1966); *Funkart* for Mixers, Lights, and Audiovisual Input Material (1967); *TA-TA* for Chorus, with Mailing Tubes (Santa Barbara, May 15, 1969); *I Am Definitely Not Running for Vice President* for Photocells, Modulators, and 4 Governors (1967); *TWOMANSHOW,* an evening of environmental theater (1968); *Spider-Song,* a comic book and a situation (in collaboration with Larry Austin, first demonstrated in N.Y., Dec. 17, 1968); *Mr. Machine* for Flute and Electronics (1969); an epithalamium for a married percussionist couple (1970). He was one of the editors of the fantastically screwed-up hyper-modern music magazine *Source,* publ. (where else?) in California.

Lunn, Charles, English tenor; b. Birmingham, Jan. 5, 1838; d. London, Feb. 28, 1906. He studied in Italy with Sangiovanni, Cattaneo, and Vizione; then sang in concert and oratorio (1864–67); settled as a teacher in Birmingham, where his pupils' concerts, given in the Town Hall, became important local events; in 1895 he moved to London. He wrote *The Philosophy of Voice,* a valuable work (1874; 10th ed., 1906), followed by a sequel, *Vox Populi* (1880); also *Vocal Expression, Empirical or Scientific* (1878).

Lunssens, Martin, Belgian conductor and composer; b. Molenbeek-Saint-Jean, April 16, 1871; d. Etterbeek, Feb. 1, 1944. He studied with Gevaert, Jehin, and Kufferath at the Brussels Cons., gaining the First Belgian Prix de Rome in 1895 with the cantata *Callirhoé;* then became a prof. at the Brussels Cons.; subsequently was director of the Music Academy at Courtrai (1905–16); at Charleroi (1916–21); at the Cons. of Louvain (1921–24); and finally at Ghent (from 1924). He was also known as an excellent conductor; was in charge of the Flemish Opera in Antwerp, where he conducted many Wagner operas.

WORKS: 4 symphs., the first 3 with the programmatic titles *Symphonie romaine, Symphonie florentine,* and *Symphonie française;* several symph. poems (*Roméo et Juliette; Phèdre; Le Cid; Timon d'Athènes*); 3 violin concertos; Viola Concerto; Cello Concerto; much chamber music; songs.

Lupi, Roberto, Italian composer and music scholar; b. Milan, Nov. 28, 1908; d. Dornach, Switzerland, April 17, 1971. He studied at the Milan Cons.; then became a prof. of harmony and counterpoint at the Cherubini Cons. in Florence. Among his works are the cantata *Orfeo; Sacra sinfonia;* Cello Sonata; songs. He publ. a treatise, *Armonia di gravitazione* (Rome, 1946), emphasizing the importance of the focal tone in composition rather than key. He edited several works by Galuppi, Caldara, Stradella, and other Italian composers.

Luporini, Gaetano, Italian opera composer; b. Lucca, Dec. 12, 1865; d. there, May 12, 1948. He was a pupil of Primo Quilici, and a protégé of Ricordi, the publisher. After graduating from the Pacini Music Inst. in Lucca, he studied at the Milan Cons. with Carlo Angeloni and Catalani; returning to Lucca in 1902, he became director of the Pacini Music Inst.; also choirmaster of the Lucca Cathedral.

WORKS: OPERAS: *I dispetti amorosi* (Turin, Feb. 27, 1894); *La collana di Pasqua* (Naples, Nov. 1, 1896; renamed *Nora,* and perf. under that title in Lucca, Sept. 7, 1908); *L'aquila e le colombe* (Rome, Feb. 17, 1914); *Chiaro di luna* (Bologna, Nov. 20, 1925); also orch. pieces and songs.

Lupu, Radu, Rumanian pianist; b. Galati, Nov. 30, 1945. After studies in his native country he was awarded a scholarship to continue his education at the Moscow Cons.; his teachers there included Heinrich Neuhaus and his son Sviatoslav. In quick succession he won first prize in the Van Cliburn (1966), Enesco (1967), and Leeds (1969) competitions. In 1972 he made his American debut as soloist with the Cleveland Orch., and subsequently played with the Chicago, Los Angeles, N.Y., and Boston orchs. In Europe he made successful appearances in Berlin, Paris, and Amsterdam in varied programs ranging from classical to modern works.

Lupus, Eduardus. See **Lobo, Duarte.**

Lupus (Latinized name of **De Wolf**), **Michael,** Flemish composer; b. c.1500; d. Lierre, July 15, 1567. Biographical data are scant, and identity uncertain. He had a prebend at Soignies in 1535; in the same year was named chaplain to the court of Charles V at Naples. Upon his return to the Netherlands, he received a new prebend at Lierre. He traveled with Charles V in Germany (1547–48); when the Emperor abdicated in 1555, Lupus lost his positions. Four motets by Lupus are found in Fuenllana's collection of 1554, and in Petrucci's *Motetti de la Corona* (1526).

BIBLIOGRAPHY: René Vannes, *Dictionnaire des Musiciens* (Brussels, 1947); B. Blackburn, *The Lupus Problem* (Diss., Univ. of Chicago, 1970); idem, "Johannes Lupi and Lupus Hellinck: A Double Portrait," *Musical Quarterly,* LIX (1973).

Lussan, Zélie de, American soprano; b. Brooklyn, Dec. 21, 1862; d. London, Dec. 18, 1949. She was trained in singing by her mother, and made her first public appearance at the age of 16 at the Academy of Music in Brooklyn; in 1885 joined the Boston Ideal Opera Co., and in 1888 went to London, where she sang with the Carl Rosa Co.; in 1894–95 she appeared with the Metropolitan Opera in N.Y., and sang with it again in 1898 and 1899–1900. She sang off and on at Covent Garden from 1890 to 1910. On Sept. 11, 1907, she married the pianist **Angelo Fronani** in London; after his death in 1918 she remained in London until her own death.

Lussy, Mathis, Swiss writer on music and piano teacher; b. Stans, April 8, 1828; d. Montreux, Jan. 21, 1910. He studied with Businger and Nägeli; went to

Paris in 1847 as a piano teacher. He wrote *Exercices de mécanisme* (1863); *Traité de l'expression musicale* (1873; partial reprint as *Le Rythme musical,* 1883); *Histoire de la notation musicale* (1882; written with E. David); *L'Anacrouse dans la musique moderne* (1903); "De la diction musicale et grammaticale," in *Riemann-Festschrift* (1909); *La "Sonate pathétique" de Beethoven* (publ. posthumously, 1912; ed. by A. Dechevrens).
BIBLIOGRAPHY: E. Monod, *Mathis Lussy et le Rythme Musical* (Neuchâtel, 1912).

Lütgendorff, Willibald Leo, German art historian; b. Augsburg, July 8, 1856; d. Weimar, Dec. 31, 1937. He studied at the Kunstakademie in Munich; in 1889, became director of the Kunstschule and curator of the Art Gallery in Lübeck. Besides writings on the plastic arts, he publ. *Die Geigen- und Lautenmacher vom Mittelalter bis zur Gegenwart* (1904; enlarged ed., 1913; in 2 vols., 1922), which is regarded as a standard authority.

Luther, Martin, great religious reformer; b. Eisleben, Nov. 10, 1483; d. there, Feb. 18, 1546. His reform of the church extended to the musical services, in which he took the deepest interest. After leaving the Wartburg, near Eisenach (March 22, 1522), he gave his ideas practical shape; his *Formula missae* (1523) and *Deutsche Messe* ("German Mass"; 1526; facsimile ed. by J. Wolf, Kassel, 1934) established the new service. He changed the order of the Mass; a German psalm took the place of the introit; the German Creed was substituted for the Latin Credo. The German Mass was sung for the first time in the Parish Church at Wittenberg on Christmas Day, 1524. Kapellmeister Conrad Rupsch and cantor Johann Walter aided Luther in organizing the musical part of the Mass. Walter states that Luther invented chorale melodies on the flute (he was an excellent flutist), and that these were noted down by Walter and Rupsch. It is impossible to establish with certainty which hymn tunes ascribed to Luther are really his; *Jesaia dem Propheten das geschah* is definitely Luther's; and the celebrated hymn tune *Ein' feste Burg ist unser Gott* is most probably authentic. Most important, the words of many chorales were written, arranged, or translated from Latin by Luther. In *Geschichte des Kirchenlieds* Koch gives a list of 36.
BIBLIOGRAPHY: A.J. Rambach, *Über Luthers Verdienst um den Kirchengesang* (Hamburg, 1813); K. von Winterfeld, *Luthers deutsche geistliche Lieder* (Leipzig, 1840); Karl Loewe, *Lutherstudien* (1846; publ. Wittenberg, 1918); H. von Stephen, *Luther als Musiker* (Bielefeld, 1899); M. Rade, *Martin Luthers Leben, Taten und Meinungen* (3 vols., Tübingen, 1883; 2nd ed., 1901); F. Zelle, *Das älteste lutherische Haus-Gesangbuch* (Göttingen, 1903; with commentary); J.W. Lyra, *Luthers Deutsche Messe* (1904); idem, *Die Lieder Luthers in ihrer Bedeutung für das evangelische Kirchenlied* (Göttingen, 1905); idem, *Studien zu Luthers Liedern* (Göttingen, 1907); H. Lehmann, *Luther im deutschen Lied* (Halle, 1910); H. Kretzschmar, "Luther und die

Musik," in *Jahrbuch Peters* (1917); K. Anton, *Luther und die Musik* (1918); H. Preuss, *Luther der Künstler* (1931); H.J. Moser, *Die Melodien der Lutherlieder* (Leipzig, 1935); G. Wolfram, "Ein' feste Burg ist unser Gott" (Berlin, 1936); C. Mahrenholz, *Luther und die Kirchenmusik* (Kassel, 1937); Charles Schneider, *Luther poète et musicien et les Enchiridiens de 1524* (Geneva, 1942); Walter E. Buszin, "Luther on Music," *Musical Quarterly* (Jan. 1946); F. Smend, *Luther und Bach* (Berlin, 1947); Paul Nettl, *Luther and Music* (Philadelphia, 1948); W. Stapel, *Luthers Lieder und Gedichte* (Stuttgart, 1950).

Lutkin, Peter Christian, American organist and hymnologist; b. Thompsonville, Wis., March 27, 1858; d. Evanston, Ill., Dec. 27, 1931. He studied music in Chicago; then went to Europe, and took lessons with A. Haupt (organ) and W. Bargiel (composition) in Berlin; had further instruction in piano from Moszkowski in Paris and Leschetizky in Vienna. Returning to America, he filled various posts as an organist in Chicago; taught theory at the American Cons. of Music in Chicago. In 1883 he became an instructor in piano and organ at Northwestern Univ. in Evanston, Ill.; from 1895 to 1928 was dean of the School of Music there; also taught church music at the Garrett Biblical Inst. at Evanston (1915–28); for 20 seasons conducted the Chicago North Shore Festival Assoc. (1909–30); publ. church music and pedagogical works for piano; edited the *Methodist Sunday School Hymnal;* was co-editor of the *Episcopal Church Hymnal.*

Lutoslawski, Witold, outstanding Polish composer; b. Warsaw, Jan. 25, 1913. He played piano and violin as a child; then took formal piano lessons with Lefeld (1932–36) and composition with Maliszewski (1932–37) at the Warsaw Cons. At the beginning of World War II he was in the Polish army; became a German prisoner of war, but got back to Warsaw; earned a living by playing piano in cafés and cabarets. After the war he dedicated himself to composition and teaching. His *renommée* soon reached the outside world; he received invitations to give seminars and to lecture in England, West Germany, Denmark, and Sweden; he gave a seminar at the Berkshire Music Center in Tanglewood in 1962; was composer-in-residence at Dartmouth College in Hanover, N.H., in 1966. He received numerous awards: 3 first mentions in the International Rostrum of Composers, UNESCO (1958, 1964, 1968); Grand Prix du Disque, Paris (1965); Ravel Prize, Paris (1971); Sibelius Prize, Helsinki (1973); was made an honorary member of the Free Academy of Arts in Hamburg (1966); extraordinary member of the Academy of Arts in West Berlin (1968); honorary member of the International Society for Contemporary Music (1969); associate member of the German Academy of Arts in East Germany (1970); corresponding member of the American Academy of Arts and Letters (1975) and Royal Academy of Music in London (1976). He received honorary D.Mus. degrees from the Cleveland Inst. of Music (1971) and the Univ. of Warsaw (1973), and an honorary degree of D.F.A. from Northwestern Univ. (1974). His early works are marked by a neo-Classical tendency, with an influx of national Polish motifs; gradually he turned to a more structural type of composition in which the melodic and rhythmic elements are organized into a strong unifying network, with occasional incursions of dodecaphonic and aleatory practices; the influence of Béla Bartók is felt in the constantly changing colors, angular intervallic progressions, and asymmetrical rhythms. In this respect, Lutoslawski's *Musique funèbre* for String Orch., dedicated to the memory of Béla Bartók, thematically built on a concatenation of upward tritones and downward semitones, is stylistically significant.

WORKS: FOR ORCH.: *Symphonic Variations* (1936–38; Cracow, June 17, 1939); 3 symphs.: No. 1 (1941–47; Katowice, April 6, 1948); No. 2 (1966–67; Katowice, June 9, 1967); No. 3 (1972–73; Chicago, Sept. 29, 1983); *Overture* for Strings (1949; Prague, Nov. 9, 1949); *Little Suite* for Chamber Orch. (1950; Warsaw, April 20, 1951); Concerto for Orch. (1950–54; Warsaw, Nov. 26, 1954); *5 Dance Preludes* for Clarinet, Harp, Piano, Percussion, and Strings (1955; a version for Nonet, 1959); *Musique funèbre* for String Orch., in memory of Béla Bartók (1958; Katowice, March 26, 1958); *3 Postludes:* No. 1 for the centennial of the International Red Cross (1958); No. 2 (1960); No. 3 (1960); *Jeux vénitiens* (1961; Venice, April 24, 1961); *Livre* (The Hague, Nov. 18, 1968; individual movements are called Chapters); Cello Concerto (1970; London, Oct. 14, 1970; Rostropovich, soloist); *Mi-parti* (Rotterdam, Oct. 22, 1976); *Novelette* for Orch. (1979; Washington, D.C., Jan. 29, 1980); Double Concerto for Oboe, Harp, and Chamber Orch. (Lucerne Festival, Aug. 24, 1980). CHAMBER MUSIC: Trio for Oboe, Clarinet, and Bassoon (1945); *Recitativo e Arioso* for Violin and Piano (1951); *5 Folk Melodies* for Strings (1952); *Bucoliche,* 5 pieces for Viola and Piano (1952); *Preludia taneczne* for Clarinet and Piano (1954); String Quartet (1964); *Preludes and Fugue* for 13 Solo Strings (1971; Festival of the International Society for Contemporary Music, Graz, Oct. 22, 1972). VOCAL WORKS: *Belated Nightingale* and *Mr. Tralala,* 2 songs for Voice and Orch. (1947); *A Straw Chain* for Soprano, Mezzo-soprano, Flute, Oboe, 2 Clarinets, and Bassoon (1951); *Silesian Triptych* for Soprano and Orch. (Warsaw, Dec. 2, 1951); *5 Songs* for Female Voice and 30 Solo Instruments (1958); *3 poèmes d'Henri Michaux* for Choir, Wind Instruments, Percussion, 2 Pianos, and Harp (Zagreb, May 9, 1963; perf. requires 2 conductors reading from separate scores); *Paroles tissées* for Tenor, String Ensemble, Harp, Piano, and Percussion (Aldeburgh [England] Festival, June 20, 1965); *Les Espaces du sommeil* for Baritone and Orch. (1975; Berlin, March 12, 1978); piano pieces.

BIBLIOGRAPHY: S. Jarociński, "Witold Lutoslawski," in *Polish Music* (Warsaw, 1965; in Eng.; pp. 191–99); Ove Nordwall, *Lutoslawski* (Stockholm, 1968). B.A. Varga, *Lutoslawski Profile: Witold Lutoslawski in Conversation with Baliant Andras Varga* (London, 1976); Steven Stucky, *Luto-*

slawski and His Music (Cambridge, 1981).

Lütschg, Karl, renowned piano pedagogue; b. St. Petersburg, Oct. 15, 1839; d. Blankenburg, Germany, June 6, 1899. He studied piano with Henselt in Russia, and with Moscheles in Germany; composition with Richter and Kiel. Returning to St. Petersburg, he became a prof. at the Cons. there; publ. a number of valuable piano studies and instructive editions of classical works: *Ecole d'études* (12 books), *Bibliothèque des œuvres classiques et modernes* (420 nos.); etc. His son, **Waldemar Lütschg** (b. St. Petersburg, May 16, 1877; d. Berlin, Aug. 29, 1948), was also a pianist; after his father's death in 1899 he settled in Berlin; taught piano at the Chicago Musical College in 1905–6.

Lutyens, Elisabeth, important and remarkably prolific English composer; b. London, July 9, 1906; d. Hampstead, April 14, 1983. She was a daughter of the noted architect Sir Edwin Lutyens, and was brought up in an atmosphere of cultural enlightenment. She studied composition with Harold Darke and viola with Ernest Tomlinson at the Royal College of Music in London (1926–30); then went to Paris and took lessons with Caussade. In her vivid autobiography, *A Goldfish Bowl* (London, 1972), she recounted her search for a congenial idiom of musical expression, beginning with the erstwhile fashionable Romantic manner and progressing toward a more individual, psychologically tense writing in an atonal technique using a sui generis dodecaphonic method of composition. In 1969 she received the honorary title of Commander of the Order of the British Empire.

WORKS: FOR THE STAGE: *The Pit,* dramatic scene for Tenor, Bass, Women's Chorus, and Orch. (Palermo, April 24, 1949); *Penelope,* radio opera (1950); *Infidelio,* chamber opera (1956; London, April 17, 1973); *The Numbered,* an opera (1965–67); "a charade in 4 acts and 3 interruptions," *Time Off? Not a Ghost of a Chance* (1967–68; Sadler's Wells, London, March 1, 1972); *Isis and Osiris,* lyric drama for 8 Voices and Chamber Orch. (1969); *The Linnet from the Leaf,* musical theater for 5 Singers and 2 Instrumental Groups (1972); *The Waiting Game,* 5 scenes for Mezzo-soprano, Baritone, and Chamber Orch. (1973); *One and the Same,* scena for Soprano, Speaker, and Mimes (1973); *The Goldfish Bowl,* ballad opera (1975); *Like a Window,* extracts from letters of Van Gogh (1976); ballet, *The Birthday of the Infanta* (London, 1932).

FOR ORCH.: *3 Pieces* (1939); 6 chamber concertos, some with Solo Instruments (1939–48); *3 Symphonic Preludes* (1942); Viola Concerto (1947); *Music I* (1954); *Music II* (1962); *Music III* (1964); *Quincunx* (1960); *En voyage,* symph. suite (London, July 2, 1960); *Symphonies* for Piano, Wind Instruments, Harps, and Percussion (London, July 28, 1961); *Music* for Piano and Orch. (1964); *Novenaria* (1967); *Plenum II* for Oboe and Chamber Orch. (London, June 14, 1974); *The Winter of the World* for Cello and Chamber Ensemble (London, May 5, 1974); *Eos* for Chamber Orch. (1975); *Rondel* (1976); *6 Baga-*

telles for Chamber Orch. (1976); *Nox* for Piano and 2 Chamber Orchs. (1977); *Wild Decembers* (1980); *Music for Orchestra IV* (1981).

CHAMBER MUSIC: Solo Viola Sonata (1938); 13 string quartets (1938–82); String Trio (1939); *9 Bagatelles* for Cello and Piano (1942); *Aptote* for Solo Violin (1948); *Valediction* for Clarinet and Piano (1954); *Nocturnes* for Violin, Cello, and Guitar (1956); *Capricci* for 2 Harps and Percussion (1956); *6 Tempi* for 10 Instruments (1957); Wind Quintet (1960); String Quintet (1963); Trio for Flute, Clarinet, and Bassoon (1963); *Scena* for Violin, Cello, and Percussion (1964); *Music for Wind* for Double Wind Quintet (1964); *Music for 3* for Flute, Oboe, and Piano (1964); *The Fall of the Leafe* for Oboe and String Quartet (1967); *Horai* for Violin, Horn, and Piano (1968); *The Tides of Time* for Double Bass and Piano (1969); *Driving Out the Death* for Oboe and String Trio (1971); *Rape of the Moone* for Wind Octet (1973); *Plenum II* for Oboe and 13 Instruments (1973); *Plenum III* for String Quartet (1974); *Kareniana* for Viola and Instrumental Group (1974); *Go, Said the Bird* for Electric Guitar and String Quartet (1975); *Mare et Minutiae* for String Quartet (1976); *Fantasia* for Alto Saxophone and 3 Instrumental Groups (1977); *O Absalom* for Oboe and String Trio (1977); *Constants* for Cello and Piano (1977); *Doubles* for String Quartet (1978); *Footfalls* for Flute and Piano (1978); *Prelude* for Solo Violin (1979); Trio for Clarinet, Cello, and Piano (1979); *Morning Sea* for Oboe and Piano (1979); *Rapprochement* for Solo Horn, Solo Harp, Wind Quartet, String Quartet, Piano, and Percussion (1980); *Six* for an ensemble of 6 Instruments and Percussion (1980); *Soli* for Clarinet, interchangeable with Bass Clarinet, and Double Bass (1980); *Branches of the Night and of the Day* for Horn and String Quartet (1981); *The Living Night* for Percussion (1981); *Echo of the Wind* for Solo Viola (1981); *Triolet I* for Clarinet, Mandolin, and Cello (1982); *Triolet II* for Cello, Marimba, and Harp (1982).

FOR PIANO: *5 Intermezzi* (1942); *Piano e Forte* (1958); *Plenum I* (1973); *The Ring of Bone* (1975); 5 impromptus (1977); *3 Books of Bagatelles* (1979); *La natura dell'acqua* (1981).

FOR ORGAN: *Sinfonia* (1956); *Plenum IV* (1975).

VOCAL: *O Saisons, O Châteaux,* cantata for Soprano, Mandolin, Guitar, Harp, and Strings (1946); *Requiem for the Living* for Soloists, Chorus, and Orch. (1948); *Bienfaits de la lune* for Soprano, Tenor, Chorus, Strings, and Percussion (1952); *De Amore,* cantata (1957; London, Sept. 7, 1973); *Catena* for Soprano, Tenor, and 21 Instruments (1961–62); *Encomion* for Chorus, Brass, and Percussion (1963); *The Valley of Haisu-Se* for Soprano and Instrumental Ensemble (1965); *Akapotik Rose* for Soprano and Instrumental Ensemble (1966); *And Suddenly It's Evening* for Tenor and 11 Instruments (1967); *Essence of Our Happiness,* cantata (1968; London, Sept. 8, 1970); *Phoenix* for Soprano, Violin, Clarinet, and Piano (1968); *Anerca* for Women's Speaking Chorus, 10 Guitars, and Percussion (1970); *Vision of Youth* for Soprano, 3 Clarinets, Piano, and Percussion (1970); *Islands* for Soprano, Tenor, Narrator, and Instrumental Ensemble (London, June 7, 1971); *The Tears of Night* for Countertenor, 6 Sopranos, and 3 Instrumental Ensembles (1971); *Requiescat,* in memoriam Igor Stravinsky, for Soprano and String Trio (1971); *Dirge for the Proud World* for Soprano, Countertenor, Harpsichord, and Cello (1971); *Counting Your Steps* for Chorus, 4 Flutes, and 4 Percussion Players (1972); *Chimes and Cantos* for Baritone and Instrumental Ensemble (1972); *Voice of Quiet Waters* for Chorus and Orch. (1972; Huddersfield, April 14, 1973); *Laudi* for Soprano, 3 Clarinets, Piano, and Percussion (1973); *Chorale Prelude and Paraphrase,* to text from a letter of Keats, for Tenor, String Quintet, and Percussion (1977); *Cascando* for Contralto, Violin, and Strings (1977); *Elegy of the Flowers* for Tenor and 3 Instrumental Groups (1978); *Echoi* for Mezzo-soprano and Orch. (1979); Cantata for Dramatic Soprano and Instruments (1979); Cantata, to text by Baudelaire, for 3 Soloists and Instrumental Ensemble (1979); *The Roots of the World,* to text by Yeats, for Chorus and Cello Obbligato (1979); *Echoes* for Contralto, Alto Flute, English Horn, and String Quartet (1979); *Mine Eyes, My Bread, My Spade* for Baritone and String Quartet (1980); *Fleur du silence,* to words by Rémi de Gourmont, for Tenor, Flute, Oboe, Horn, Harp, Violin, Viola, and Percussion (1980); *The Singing Birds* for Actress and Solo Viola (1980).

Lutz, Wilhelm Meyer, operetta composer and conductor; b. Männerstadt, near Kissingen, 1822; d. London, Jan. 31, 1903. He studied music with his father, an organist, and later at Würzburg. In 1848 he settled in England; played organ in various churches in Birmingham, Leeds, and London; conducted theater music in London from 1851; in 1869 was appointed music director at the Gaiety Theatre, for which he wrote numerous light operas; the following were successful: *Faust and Marguerite* (1855); *Blonde and Brunette* (1862); *Zaida* (1868); *Miller of Milburg* (1872); *Legend of the Lys* (1873). He also wrote the popular dance *Pas de quatre.*

Luvisi, Lee, American pianist; b. Louisville, Ky., Dec. 12, 1937. He first studied at the Curtis Inst. of Music in Philadelphia with Rudolf Serkin and Mieczyslaw Horszowski; upon graduation in 1957, he joined its faculty. In 1962 he was named artist-in-residence at the Univ. of Louisville School of Music; later became chairman of its piano dept. He appeared as soloist with many of the major American and European orchs.; gave numerous solo recitals.

Lux, Friedrich, German composer; b. Ruhla, Nov. 24, 1820; d. Mainz, July 9, 1895. He studied with his father, a cantor at Ruhla; at 12 he gave an organ concert at Gotha; then studied with F. Schneider at Dessau, where he remained for 10 years as music director at the court theater. From 1851 to 1877 he was conductor at the City Theater in Mainz; from 1867 also conducted the Oratorio Society there.

WORKS: Operas: *Das Käthchen von Heilbronn* (Dessau, March 23, 1846); *Der Schmied von Ruhla* (Mainz, March 28, 1882); *Die Fürstin von Athen*

(Frankfurt, 1890); 4 symphs. (No. 3 subtitled *Die vier Menschenalter;* No. 4, *Durch Nacht zum Licht,* with Chorus); 3 string quartets; Piano Trio; many choral works and songs. He publ. transcriptions of Beethoven's symphs. (except the 9th) for piano, 4-hands.

BIBLIOGRAPHY: A. Reissmann, *F. Lux: Sein Leben und seine Werke* (Leipzig, 1888).

Luxon, Benjamin, English baritone; b. Redruth, March 24, 1937. He was educated at the Guildhall School of Music in London; made his debut with the English Opera Group in 1963. He gained wide recognition for his performance of the title role in Britten's television opera *Owen Wingrave,* produced in London by the BBC on May 16, 1971. From 1972 he sang at Covent Garden; also appeared at the Glyndebourne and Edinburgh festivals. On Feb. 2, 1980, he sang the title role in Tchaikovsky's *Eugene Onegin* at his Metropolitan Opera debut in N.Y.

Luython, Charles, Flemish composer; b. Antwerp, c.1556; d. Prague, 1620. After receiving elementary training as a chorister in his native land, he was sent, at the age of 10, to the Imperial Chapel in Vienna, where he remained until he was 15. He wrote 2 masses for Emperor Maximilian II; in 1582 was appointed court organist by Rudolph II, for whom he wrote a book of madrigals (publ. by Gardano in Venice). He remained with Rudolph II at his residence in Prague; in 1603 became successor to Philippe de Monte as court composer while continuing to hold his post as court organist. He retired from the service in 1611. Apart from his book of madrigals (Venice, 1582), he publ. *Sacrae cantiones* for 6 Voices (Prague, 1603); *Lamentationes* for 6 Voices (Prague, 1604); 9 masses for 3–7 Voices (Prague, 1609). Among his extant works for instruments, there is a *Fuga suavissima* (publ. in Woltz's *Tabulatur-Buch,* 1617). Luython was a composer of considerable ingenuity; Michael Praetorius recounts in his *Syntagma musicum* that Luython owned a keyboard instrument with 3 manuals, representing the diatonic, chromatic, and enharmonic intervals (18 notes to the octave), thus securing theoretically correct modulations through sharps or flats.

BIBLIOGRAPHY: L. de Burbure, *Charles Luython* (Brussels, 1880); A.A. Smijers, *Luython als Motettenkomponist* (Vienna, 1917); A.G. Ritter, *Zur Geschichte des Orgelspiels* (1884; pp. 51–52).

Luzzaschi, Luzzasco, Italian composer; b. Ferrara, 1545; d. there, Sept. 11, 1607. He studied with Cypriano de Rore as a child (until 1558); became a singer at the Este court in 1561; was first organist there from 1564; also directed one of the orchs., composed, and taught there; was also organist at the Ferrara Cathedral and at the Accademia della Morte; later was director of Duke Alfonso's private musica da camera. He attained great renown as a teacher; Frescobaldi was one of his many pupils.

WORKS: 7 books of madrigals for 5 Voices, of which 5 are extant (1571–1604); *Sacrae cantiones* for 5 Voices (1598); madrigals for one to 3 sopranos, with keyboard accompaniment (1601). Diruta's collection *Il Transilvano* contains an organ toccata and 2 ricercari by Luzzaschi; the toccata is reprinted in Ritter's *Zur Geschichte des Orgelspiels;* a 4-part *Canzon da sonar* is given in Rauerij's collection (1608); the accompanied madrigal *Ch'io non t'ami,* in Otto Kinkeldey's *Orgel und Klavier in der Musik des 16. Jahrhunderts* (Leipzig, 1910; p. 291). Other reprints are found in L. Torchi's *L'arte musicale in Italia* (vol. 4), in Riemann's *Musikgeschichte in Beispielen* (no. 73), and in Schering's *Geschichte der Musik in Beispielen* (no. 166).

BIBLIOGRAPHY: Otto Kinkeldey, "Luzzasco Luzzaschis Solo Madrigale mit Klavierbegleitung," *Sammelbände der Internationalen Musik-Gesellschaft* (1908); A. Einstein, *The Italian Madrigal* (Princeton, 1949); G. Reese, *Music in the Renaissance* (N.Y., 1954, pp. 411–13; 2nd ed., revised, 1959); E. Stainchamps, *Luzzasco Luzzaschi and His Five-part Madrigals* (Diss., Columbia Univ., 1960); A. Spiro, *The Five-part Madrigals of Luzzascho Luzzaschi* (Diss., Boston Univ., 1961).

Luzzi, Luigi, Italian composer; b. Olevano di Lomellina, March 28, 1828; d. Stradella, Feb. 23, 1876. He studied medicine at Turin, but later entered the musical profession; wrote successful songs (*Mia madre,* etc.); an opera, *Tripilla* (Novara, Feb. 7, 1874); Symph.; hymns for chorus and orch.; piano pieces.

Lvov, Alexei, Russian violinist and composer, author of the Russian national anthem under the Czars; b. Reval, June 5, 1798; d. Romano, near Kovno, Dec. 28, 1870. He was the son of the director of the Imperial Court Chapel in St. Petersburg; received his primary education at home; attended the Inst. of Road Engineering (graduated in 1818); at the same time studied violin. In 1827 he was sent to the Turkish front in Bulgaria; then was attached to the court. He wrote the national anthem *God Save the Czar* in 1833, and it was first performed in Moscow on the name day of Czar Nicholas I, on Dec. 6 (18), 1833; it remained the official anthem until the Revolution of 1917. In 1837 he succeeded his father as director of the Imperial Chapel (until 1861); in 1839 he organized instrumental classes there; edited a collection of services for the entire ecclesiastical year of the Greek Orthodox Church. In 1840 he traveled in Europe; played his Violin Concerto with the Gewandhaus Orch. in Leipzig (Nov. 8, 1840); Schumann greatly praised his playing. Returning to Russia, he established a series of orch. concerts in St. Petersburg, presenting classical programs. Growing deafness forced him to abandon his activities in 1867. As a composer, he slavishly followed the Italian school.

WORKS: 3 operas: *Bianca* (Dresden, Oct. 13, 1844); *Ondine* (in Russian; St. Petersburg, Sept. 20, 1847); *Starosta Boris, or The Russian Muzhik and the French Marauders* (on the 1812 war; St. Petersburg, May 1, 1854); several violin works, including a concerto; he publ. an essay, *On Free or Non-sym-*

metrical Rhythm (St. Petersburg, 1858).
BIBLIOGRAPHY: I. Yampolsky, *Russian Violin Art* (Moscow, 1951; vol. 1, pp. 205–27).

Lybbert, Donald, American composer; b. Cresco, Iowa, Feb. 19, 1923; d. Norwalk, Conn., July 26, 1981. He studied at the Univ. of Iowa (B.M., 1946), at the Juilliard School of Music with Robert Ward and Bernard Wagenaar (1946–48), at Columbia Univ. with Elliott Carter and Otto Luening (M.A., 1950), and with Nadia Boulanger at Fontainebleau, France (1961). He engaged in teaching; was on the music faculty at Hunter College (1967–80) while continuing to compose. His music was evolved from classical foundations, but he refrained from using key signatures and often applied quasi-serial procedures in his melodic patterns; in his rhythmic textures he often resorted to asymmetrical beat formations.
WORKS: Opera, *The Scarlet Letter* (1964–67); operetta, *Monica* (Amsterdam, Nov. 2, 1952); 2 piano sonatas (1947, 1954); Octet for Wind Instruments (1947); *Concert Overture* (1952); *From Harmonium,* song cycle (1954); *Introduction and Toccata* for Brass Instruments and Piano (1955); Trio for Clarinet, Horn, and Bassoon (1956); *Chamber Sonata* for Viola, Horn, and Piano (1957); *Leopardi Canti,* song cycle for Soprano, Flute, Viola, and Bass Clarinet to poems by Giacomo Leopardi (1959); *Movement* for Piano, 4-hands (1960); *Sonorities* for 11 Instruments (1960); *Sonata brevis* for Piano (1962); *Praeludium* for Brass and Percussion (1962); *Lines for the Fallen* for Soprano and 2 Pianos tuned a quarter-tone apart (1967); *Zap,* after a text from Ecclesiastes, for Multiantiphonal Chorus, Instruments, and Rock Group, composed for the centennial of Hunter College (1970); *Variants* for 5 Wind Instruments (1971); *Octagon* for Soprano and 7 Chamber Players, to text of Molly Bloom's erotic monologue in the conclusion of James Joyce's *Ulysses* (1975); choral pieces; songs.

Lyford, Ralph, American composer; b. Worcester, Mass., Feb. 22, 1882; d. Cincinnati, Sept. 3, 1927. He began to study piano and violin as a child; entered the New England Cons. in Boston at 12, studying piano with Helen Hopekirk, organ with Goodrich, and composition with Chadwick; then went to Leipzig to study conducting with Artur Nikisch (1906). Returning to America, he became assistant conductor of the San Carlo Opera Co. (1907–8); then was with the Boston Opera Co. (1908–14). In 1916 he settled in Cincinnati, where he taught at the Cons., and also conducted the summer seasons of opera at the Zoölogical Gardens there; in 1925 he became associate conductor of the Cincinnati Symph. Orch.
WORKS: Opera, *Castle Agrazant* (Cincinnati, April 29, 1926; won the David Bispham Medal); Piano Concerto (1917); chamber music; songs.
BIBLIOGRAPHY: E.E. Hipsher, *American Opera and Its Composers* Philadelphia, 1934; pp. 304–8).

Lyman, Howard Wilder, American voice teacher; b. Lancaster, Mass., Feb. 2, 1879; d. Herkimer, N.Y.,

Feb. 27, 1980, at the age of 101. He studied at the New England Cons., graduating in 1909; was for many years on the music faculty at the Univ. of Syracuse (1912–45) and concurrently director of music at the Methodist church there (1926–53). In his extreme old age he took shelter at the Folts Home in Herkimer.

Lympany, Moura, English pianist; b. Saltash, Aug. 18, 1916. She was educated at the Royal Academy of Music in London; also studied in Vienna with Paul Weingarten; then returned to England for further training with Mathilda Verne and Tobias Matthay. In 1938 she won second prize in the Ysaÿe Competition in Brussels; subsequently she developed an international career; made her American debut in 1948. In her programs she championed works by British composers; in 1969 she performed the Piano Concerto by Cyril Scott on the occasion of his 90th birthday, with the composer himself present and joining in appreciative applause. In 1979 she was made a Commander of the Order of the British Empire.

Lyne, Felice, American soprano; b. Slater, Mo., March 28, 1887; d. Allentown, Pa., Sept. 1, 1935. Her family moved to Allentown when she was a child; she studied there with F.S. Hardman; then in Paris with Mme. Marchesi, J. de Reszke, and L. d'Aubigne. She made a successful debut as Gilda in *Rigoletto* at Hammerstein's London Opera (Nov. 25, 1911), and appeared there 36 times that season, creating the principal soprano parts in the English premieres of Massenet's *Don Quichotte* and *Jongleur de Notre-Dame,* and Holbrooke's *Children of Don;* toured with the Quinlan Opera Co. Returning to the U.S., she became a member of the Boston Opera Co.; also appeared in concerts.

Lynes, Frank, American composer and organist; b. Cambridge, Mass., May 16, 1858; d. Bristol, N.H., June 24, 1913. He was a student at the New England Cons.; later studied piano and organ with B.J. Lang and harmony with J.K. Paine. He then went to Germany and enrolled in the Leipzig Cons. (1883–85), where his teachers were Reinecke (piano) and Jadassohn (theory). Returning to America, he settled in Boston. He held various positions as a church organist; for some years conducted the Cantabrigia Ladies' Chorus. He wrote mainly for piano.
WORKS: *Analytical Sonatinas* (a set of 4, so named to emphasize the formal element); *10 Bagatelles; 12 Recreations; 8 Fairy Tales for Musical Children; Woodland Notes* (6 pieces); *Scenes from Alice in Wonderland* (10 pieces); *Independence* (16 studies); also pedagogical works: *Key Circle Exercises; 10 Special Studies;* pieces for piano, 4-hands and 6-hands; pieces for 2 pianos, 8-hands; many songs; anthems.
BIBLIOGRAPHY: Olin Downes, *Frank Lynes* (Boston, 1914; contains a complete list of works).

Lynn, George, American choral conductor and composer; b. Edwardsville, Pa., Oct. 5, 1915. He studied composition with Roy Harris at Westminster Choir College, organ with Carl Weinrich, and conducting with John Finley Williamson. In 1964 he succeeded Williamson as director of Westminster Choir College and conductor of the Westminster Choir.

WORKS: Symph.; Piano Concerto; *Gettysburg Address* for Baritone Solo, Chorus, and Orch.; *Greek Folksong Rhapsody* for Contralto, Chorus, and Orch.; 3 sacred symphs. for Chorus; 3 string quartets; 30 organ pieces; 40 songs; about 130 choruses. He is editor of the Westminster Choir Series, publ. by G. Schirmer, Inc.

Lynn, Loretta, American country-music singer and songwriter; b. Butcher Hollow, Ky., April 14, 1932. A coal miner's daughter, she taught herself the rudiments of guitar playing; making her way to Nashville, Tenn., she joined the Grand Ole Opry; later organized her own group, The Blue Kentuckians, with which she toured widely. Unable to read music, she nevertheless scored enormous success with such compositions as *Don't Come Home A-Drinkin' (with Lovin' on Your Mind), You Ain't Woman Enough (to Take My Man),* and *Coal Miner's Daughter.* She publ. an autobiography in 1976, aptly named *Coal Miner's Daughter;* it was later made into a motion picture.

Lyon, David, English composer; b. Walsall, Staffordshire, Dec. 29, 1938. He was educated in London. His compositions include a String Quartet (1962); *Divertimento* for Small Orch. (1963); Piano Concerto (1964); *Partita* for Solo Horn (1964); *Dance Prelude* for Small Orch. (1964).

Lyon & Healy, American manufacturers of musical instruments. The firm was founded in Chicago in 1864 by **George Washburn Lyon** (b. 1820) and **Patrick Joseph Healy** (b. March 17, 1840; d. Chicago, April 3, 1905). They began originally as dealers in sheet music, books, and the smaller musical instruments; in 1871 they took over the piano business of Smith & Dixon, and gradually began also to manufacture other instruments. After the retirement of Lyon in 1889, Healy became the sole head and general manager; he expanded the manufacturing dept. and erected larger factories. Among the firm's instruments, the Lyon & Healy harp, put on the market in 1899, has become universally known; its collection of old violins once rivaled those of the world's most famous dealers. Besides the parent store in Chicago, there are several branches in other cities.

Lyon, James, early American composer; b. Newark, N.J., July 1, 1735; d. Machias, Maine, Oct. 12, 1794. He graduated from the College of New Jersey at Princeton in 1759; in 1764, accepted a pastorate in Nova Scotia; then in Machias, Maine (1772 until his death). The *N.Y. Mercury* of Oct. 1, 1759, speaks of an ode composed by Lyon, a member of the graduating class of Princeton, and mentions its performance at the graduation exercises on Sept. 26; but the music of this work, written in the same year that Hopkinson wrote his first songs, is lost. The first known compositions of Lyon are 6 psalm tunes publ. by him in the collection *Urania* (Philadelphia, 1761; facsimile reproduction, with introduction by R. Crawford, N.Y., 1973); he also wrote settings of 2 poems by Watts, *A Marriage Hymn* and *Friendship,* and of Psalms 8, 17, 19, 23, 95, 104, and 150.

BIBLIOGRAPHY: O.G. Sonneck, *Francis Hopkinson and James Lyon: Two Studies in Early American Music* (Washington, D.C., 1905; reprint, with new introduction by R. Crawford, N.Y., 1969); G.T. Edwards, *Music and Musicians of Maine* (Portland, 1928); *Dictionary of American Biography,* vol. VI (N.Y., 1933).

Lyons, James, American music critic and editor; b. Peabody, Mass., Nov. 24, 1925; d. New York, Nov. 13, 1973. He studied musicology with Karl Geiringer at Boston Univ. and music history with Warren Storey Smith at the New England Cons. of Music. He subsequently dedicated himself to musical journalism; settled in N.Y. in 1952; was a music critic for the *N.Y. Herald Tribune* (1953–62); in 1957 became editor and publisher of the *American Record Guide.* He was co-author (with John Tasker Howard) of *Modern Music* (N.Y. 1957); contributed articles to various music journals on a variety of subjects, ranging from oriental music to musical psychology.

Lyra, Justus Wilhelm, German cleric and song composer; b. Osnabrück, March 23, 1822; d. Gehrden, Dec. 30, 1882. He studied philosophy and theology in Berlin; filled various church offices in Germany; eventually became "pastor primarius" at Gehrden and Hannover. As a student, he wrote many scholastic songs, which became very popular in German univs. (e.g., *Der Mai ist gekommen, Durch Feld und Buchenhallen, Zwischen Frankreich und dem Böhmerwald, Meine Mus' ist gegangen*); he also wrote church music (Christmas cantata, 1872); publ. 5 books of songs, ranging from one voice to mixed chorus; *Die liturgischen Altarweisen des lutherischen Hauptgottesdienstes* (1873); *Andreas Ornithoparchus und dessen Lehre von den Kirchenakzenten* (Gütersloh, 1877); *Luthers Deutsche Messe* (posthumously publ., 1904).

BIBLIOGRAPHY: Bär and Ziller, *J.W. Lyra* (Leipzig, 1901).

Lysberg, Charles-Samuel. See **Bovy-Lysberg, Charles-Samuel.**

M

Ma, Yo-Yo, remarkable Chinese cellist; b. Paris, Oct. 7, 1955. He first studied with his father; then came to America to study with Leonard Rose at the Juilliard School of Music in N.Y. His rise on the violoncellistic firmament was spectacular; he was unreservedly praised for his unostentatious musicianship, for the freedom of his technical resources, and for the unforced tone of his melodious lyricism. He appeared with equal success as a soloist with American and European orchs. and as a chamber music player, commending himself as a foremost cello virtuoso.

Maag, Peter, distinguished Swiss conductor; b. St. Gallen, May 10, 1919. His father was the Lutheran minister and educated musician Otto Maag; his mother played violin in the Capet Quartet. After studying music at home, he went to the univs. of Zürich, Basel, and Geneva; among his teachers were Karl Barth in theology and Karl Jaspers in philosophy. He studied piano and music theory with Czeslaw Marek in Zürich; then went to Paris, where he had private lessons with Cortot; he studied conducting with Franz von Hoesslin and Ernest Ansermet in Geneva. He began his professional career as répétiteur and chorus master at the town theater in Biel-Solothurn. In 1952 he was appointed first con-

ductor of the Düsseldorf Opera under the directorship of Eugen Szenkar; from 1955–59 he was Generalmusikdirektor of the Bonn Opera; from 1964–68, chief conductor of the Vienna Volksoper; in 1972–74, artistic director of the Teatro Regio in Parma; held a similar post with the Teatro Regio in Turin from 1974–76. He conducted at Covent Garden in London in 1958. He made his U.S. debut in 1959 as a guest conductor of the Cincinnati Symph. Orch.; in 1961 conducted at the Chicago Lyric Opera. On Sept. 23, 1972, he made his Metropolitan Opera debut in N.Y. conducting *Don Giovanni;* was guest conductor with the Boston Symph., Detroit Symph., and National Symph. of Washington, D.C. He also toured South America and Japan.

BIBLIOGRAPHY: Dennis McIntire, "Peter Maag: Switzerland's Musical Ambassador," *Northern Light* (Jan. 1979).

Maas, Louis (Philipp Otto), composer and pianist; b. Wiesbaden, Germany, June 21, 1852; d. Boston, Sept. 17, 1889. He studied with Reinecke and Papperitz at the Leipzig Cons. (1867–71), and for 3 summers with Liszt. From 1875–80 he taught at the Leipzig Cons.; in 1880 he emigrated to the U.S., settling in Boston; conducted the Boston Phil. Concerts (1881–82). As a token of gratitude to his adoptive country, he wrote an "American Symphony," *On the Prairies,* dedicated to President Chester A. Arthur, which he conducted in Boston, Dec. 14, 1882. This symph., Germanic in form and harmonic language, contained some Indian themes. Maas further wrote overtures, suites, marches, fantasias, etc., for orch.; a String Quartet; a Piano Concerto; 3 sonatas, 3 impromptus, and 12 *Phantasiestücke* for Piano; violin sonatas; and songs.

Maasalo, Armas, Finnish composer; b. Rautavaara, Aug. 28, 1885; d. Helsinki, Sept. 9, 1960. He studied at the Helsinki School of Music; for 34 years directed the National Chorus (1915–49) and later headed the music dept. of the Sibelius Academy in Helsinki (1951–55). As a composer, he excelled particularly in Finnish church music.

WORKS: *Ricordanza* for Cello, Piano, and Orch. (1919); Piano Concerto (1919); *Karelian Scenes* for Orch. (1920); *The Path of Man,* cantata (1926); *2 Stars* for Alto, Chorus, and Orch. (1929); *Partita seria* for Strings (1934); *Christmas Oratorio* (1945); organ pieces; religious songs for chorus and solo voice.

Ma'ayani, Ami, Israeli composer; b. Ramat-Gan, Jan. 13, 1936. He studied composition privately with Ben-Haim (1956–60); concurrently attended courses in architecture at the Technion School in Haifa, receiving a diploma in 1960; then worked on electronic music with Ussachevsky at Columbia Univ. in N.Y. (1964–65). In 1971 he was appointed conductor of the Israeli National Youth Orch.

WORKS: Opera-oratorio, *The War of the Sons of Light,* for 4 Soloists, Chorus, Ballet, and Orch. (1970–72); *Divertimento concertante* for Chamber Orch. (1957); 2 harp concertos (1960, 1966); *Mizorim (Psalms)* for Soprano, Flute, Bass Clarinet, Harp, Percussion, and Strings (1965); Concerto for 8 Wind Instruments and Percussion (1966); *Regalim (Festivals)* for Soprano or Tenor, and Orch. (1966); Violin Concerto (1967); Cello Concerto (1967); 2-piano Concerto (1969); *Qumran,* symph. metaphor (1970); *Symphony Concertante* for Wind Quintet and Orch. (1972); Symph. No. 2 (1975); Viola Concerto (1975); Guitar Concerto (1976); *Poème* for Flute and String Trio (1965); *Improvisation variée* for Flute, Viola or Violin, and Harp (1966); *4 Preludes* for 4 Percussionists and Piano (1968); *2 Madrigals* for Harp and Wind Quintet (1969); 2 pieces for Harp Solo: *Magamat* (1960) and *Toccata* (1962); piano pieces.

Maazel, Lorin, brilliant American conductor; b. Neuilly, France, March 6, 1930, of American parents. They took him to Los Angeles when he was an infant. At a very early age he showed innate musical ability; he had perfect pitch and could assimilate music osmotically; he began to study violin at age 5 with Karl Moldrem, and then piano at age 7 with Fanchon Armitage. Fascinated by the mysterious art of conducting, he went to symph. concerts and soon began to take lessons in conducting with Vladimir Bakaleinikov, who was an associate con-

ductor of the Los Angeles Phil.; on July 13, 1938, at the age of 8, he was given a chance to conduct a performance of Schubert's *Unfinished Symphony* with the visiting Univ. of Idaho orch. In 1938 Bakaleinikov was appointed assistant conductor of the Pittsburgh Symph. Orch., and the Maazel family followed him to Pittsburgh. From Bakaleinikov, Lorin Maazel quickly learned to speak Russian. On Aug. 18, 1939, he made a sensational appearance in N.Y. conducting the National Music Camp Orch. of Interlochen at the World's Fair, eliciting the inevitable jocular comments (he was compared to a trained seal). Maazel was 11 when he conducted the NBC Symph. Orch. (1941) and 12 when he led an entire program with the N.Y. Phil. (1942). He survived these traumatic exhibitions, and took academic courses at the Univ. of Pittsburgh; in 1948 he joined the Pittsburgh Symph. Orch. as a violinist, and at the same time was appointed its apprentice conductor. In 1952 he received a Fulbright fellowship for travel in Italy, where he undertook a serious study of Baroque music; he also made his adult debut as a conductor in Catania on Dec. 24, 1953. On Feb. 20, 1955, he conducted at the Florence Music Festival; in 1956 he was guest conductor in Argentina; in 1957 he led the Vienna Festival; in 1958 he conducted at the Edinburgh Festival. In 1960 he became the first American to conduct at the Bayreuth Festival, where he led 8 performances of *Lohengrin.* In 1962 he toured the U.S. with the Orchestre National de France; on Nov. 1, 1962, he made his Metropolitan Opera debut in N.Y. in *Don Giovanni,* conducting it from memory. In the summer of 1963 he made a tour of Russia, conducting concerts in Moscow and Leningrad. From 1965 to 1971 he was artistic director of the Deutsche Oper in West Berlin; from 1965 to 1975 also served as chief conductor of the West Berlin Radio Symph. Orch. He was associate principal conductor of the New Philharmonia Orch. of London from 1970 to 1972, and its principal guest conductor from 1976 to 1980. In 1972 he became music director of the Cleveland Orch., a position he held with great distinction until 1982; was then made conductor emeritus. He led the Cleveland Orch. on 10 major tours abroad, including Australia and New Zealand (1973), Japan (1974), twice in Latin America, and twice in Europe, and maintained its stature as one of the world's foremost orchs. He was also chief conductor of the Orchestre National de France from 1977 to 1982; then became its principal guest conductor. In 1980 he became conductor of the famous Vienna Phil. New Year's Day Concerts. In 1982 he assumed the positions of artistic director and general manager of the Vienna State Opera, the first American to be so honored.

Maazel is equally adept as an interpreter of operatic and symph. scores; he is blessed with a phenomenal memory, and possesses an extraordinary baton technique. He also maintains an avid interest in nonmusical pursuits; a polyglot, he is fluent in French, German, Italian, Spanish, Portuguese, and Russian. He was married twice; first in 1952, to the Brazilian-American pianist Miriam Sandbank, and, after their divorce in 1969, to the Israeli pianist Isra-

ela Margit. Maazel was the recipient of many awards; he received an honorary doctorate from the Univ. of Pittsburgh in 1965, the Sibelius Prize in Finland, the Commander's Cross of the Order of Merit from West Germany, and, for his numerous recordings, the Grand Prix de Disque in Paris and the Edison Prize in the Netherlands.
BIBLIOGRAPHY: David Ewen, *Musicians since 1900* (N.Y., 1978).

Mabellini, Teodulo, Italian composer; b. Pistoia, April 2, 1817; d. Florence, March 10, 1897. He studied with Pillotti in his native town, and then at the Istituto Reale Musicale at Florence; at the age of 19, he produced there an opera, *Matilda a Toledo* (Aug. 27, 1836), which made so favorable an impression that Grand Duke Leopold II gave him a stipend to study with Mercadante at Novara. His 2nd opera, *Rolla* (Turin, Nov. 12, 1840), was no less successful; thereupon he wrote many more operas, among them *Ginevra degli Almieri* (Turin, Nov. 13, 1841), *Il Conte di Lavagna* (Florence, June 4, 1843), *I Veneziani a Costantinopoli* (Rome, 1844), *Maria di Francia* (Florence, March 14, 1846), and *Fiammetta* (Florence, Feb. 12, 1857). He also wrote several effective oratorios and cantatas: *Eudossia e Paolo* (Florence, 1845), *Etruria* (Florence, August 5, 1849), *Lo spirito di Dante* (Florence, May 15, 1865), and a patriotic hymn, *Italia risorta* (Florence, Sept. 12, 1847); *Grande fantasia* for Flute, Clarinet, Horn, Trumpet, and Trombone; sacred works for chorus and orch. He lived in Florence from 1843 until his death; conducted the concerts of the Società Filarmonica (1843–59); taught composition at the Istituto Reale Musicale (1859–87).
BIBLIOGRAPHY: M. Giannini, *Mabellini e la musica* (Pistoia, 1899); A. Simonatti, *Teodulo Mabellini* (Pistoia, 1923).

Macal, Zdenek, Czech conductor; b. Brno, Jan. 8, 1936. He was educated at the Brno Cons. and the Janáček Academy of Music. He made his conducting debut in Olmütz in 1963. In 1966 he won the first Mitropoulos prize in N.Y.; in 1970–74 served as chief conductor of the Cologne Radio Orch.; in 1980 he was appointed chief conductor of the Orch. of Hannover Radio.

MacArdle, Donald Wales, American musicologist; b. Quincy, Mass., July 3, 1897; d. Littleton, Colo., Dec. 23, 1964. He studied science at the Mass. Inst. of Technology, obtaining an M.S. in chemical engineering; he also took courses at the Juilliard School of Music in N.Y., and studied musicology at N.Y. Univ. Although he earned his living as an engineer, he devoted much time to scholarly research, mainly to the minutiae of Beethoven's biography; he contributed a number of valuable articles on the subject to the *Musical Quarterly* and other journals. He edited, with L. Misch, *New Beethoven Letters* (Norman, Okla., 1957); edited and translated Schindler's *Biographie von Ludwig van Beethoven,* 3rd ed., 1860, as *Beethoven as I Knew Him* (London and Chapel Hill, 1966); he further prepared *An Index to*

Beethoven's Conversation Books (Detroit, 1962) and, with S. Pogodda, *Beethoven Abstracts* (Detroit, 1973).

Macbeth, Allan, Scottish organist and composer; b. Greenock, March 13, 1856; d. Glasgow, Aug. 25, 1910. He studied at the Leipzig Cons. with Richter, Reinecke, and Jadassohn (1875–76). His subsequent musical activities were largely confined to playing the organ in Glasgow churches and directing choral groups; from 1890 he was principal of the School of Music at the Glasgow Athenaeum. He wrote an operetta, *The Duke's Doctor;* 2 cantatas: *The Land of Glory* (1890) and *Silver Bells; Jubilee Chorus* (1896); *Intermezzo* for Strings; *Danze pizzicate* for Orch.; also chamber music and songs.

Macbeth, Florence, American coloratura soprano; b. Mankato, Minn., Jan. 12, 1891; d. Hyattsville, Md., May 5, 1966. She studied in Europe; in 1913 made her operatic debut as Rosina in *Il Barbiere di Siviglia* in Braunschweig, Germany. On Jan. 14, 1914, she made her American debut with the Chicago Opera Co. and remained on its staff as prima coloratura soprano until 1930; for a season she undertook an American tour with the Commonwealth Opera Co., singing in Gilbert and Sullivan operettas. So melodious and mellifluous were her fiorituras that she was dubbed the "Minnesota Nightingale." In 1947 she married the novelist James M. Cain and settled in Maryland.

MacCunn, Hamish, Scottish composer and conductor; b. Greenock, March 22, 1868; d. London, Aug. 2, 1916. He studied at the Royal College of Music (1883–86) with Parry; then taught at the Royal Academy of Music (1888–94); in 1898, became conductor of the Carl Rosa Opera Co.; from 1900 to 1905 conducted at the Savoy Theatre; later he toured with various troupes, conducting light opera.
WORKS: Operas: *Jeanie Deans,* after Scott's *The Heart of Midlothian* (Edinburgh, Nov. 15, 1894); *Diarmid* (London, Oct. 23, 1897); *The Masque of War and Peace* (London, Feb. 13, 1900); *The Golden Girl,* musical comedy (Birmingham, Aug. 5, 1905); cantatas: *Lord Ullin's Daughter,* after Walter Scott (London, Feb. 18, 1888); *Bonny Kilmeny* (Edinburgh, Dec. 15, 1888); *The Lay of the Last Minstrel* (Glasgow, Dec. 18, 1888); *The Cameronian's Dream* (Edinburgh, Jan. 27, 1890); *Queen Hynde of Caledon* (Glasgow, Jan. 28, 1892); *The Wreck of the Hesperus,* after Longfellow (London, Aug. 28, 1905); overtures: *Cior Mhor* (London, Oct. 27, 1885); *The Land of the Mountain and the Flood,* after Scott (London, Nov. 5, 1887); *The Ship o' the Fiend* (London, Feb. 21, 1888); *The Dowie Dens o' Yarrow* (London, Oct. 13, 1888); *Highland Memories,* orch. sketch (London, March 13, 1897); *Scotch Dances* for Piano; songs; etc.

MacDermid, James G., American pianist, vocalist, and composer; b. Utica, Ontario, June 10, 1875; d. Brooklyn, Aug. 16, 1960. He studied in London, Ontario; in 1893 went to Chicago for further studies, and remained in the U.S.; became an American citizen in 1906; for several seasons toured as accompanist to his wife, **Sibyl Sammis MacDermid,** soprano (b. Foreston, Ill., May 15, 1876; d. New York, Nov. 2, 1940). He publ. about 75 sacred and secular songs.

MacDonald, Hugh, English musicologist; b. Newbury, Berkshire, Jan. 31, 1940. He was educated at Pembroke College, Cambridge (B.A., 1961; M.A., 1965; Ph.D., 1969); in 1966 he became a lecturer at Cambridge Univ., then at Oxford Univ. in 1971; in 1979 he was a visiting prof. at Indiana Univ. in Bloomington; in 1980 he was named Gardiner Prof. of Music at Glasgow Univ. His special field of interest is 19th-century music; he is particularly noted for his studies in French music, and is a leading authority on the life and works of Berlioz; in 1965 he became general editor of the *New Berlioz Edition.* He publ. *Berlioz: Orchestral Music* (London, 1969) and *Skryabin* (London, 1978).

MacDowell, Edward Alexander, greatly significant national American composer; b. New York, Dec. 18, 1860; d. (insane) there, Jan. 23, 1908. His father was a Scotch-Irish tradesman; his mother, an artistically inclined woman who encouraged MacDowell's musical studies. He took piano lessons with one Juan Buitrago and later with Paul Desvernine. In 1876, after traveling in Europe with his mother, MacDowell enrolled as an auditor in Augustin Savard's elementary class at the Paris Cons.; on Feb. 8, 1877, he was admitted as a regular student; also studied piano with Antoine-François Marmontel, and solfège with Marmontel's son. Somewhat disappointed with his progress, he withdrew from the Cons. on Sept. 30, 1878, and went to Germany for further study; there he took private lessons with Louis Ehlert, a pupil of Mendelssohn, in Wiesbaden; in 1879 he enrolled at the newly founded but already prestigious Hoch Cons. in Frankfurt as a student of Carl Heymann in piano, and in composition with the director of the school, the illustrious teacher and composer Joachim Raff. During MacDowell's stay there, Raff's class had a visit from Liszt, and MacDowell performed the piano part in Schumann's Quintet, op. 44, in Liszt's presence. At another visit, MacDowell played Liszt's *Hungarian Rhapsody* No. 14 for him; 2 years later MacDowell visited Liszt in Weimar, and played his own First Piano Concerto for him, accompanied by Eugène d'Albert at the 2nd piano. Encouraged by Liszt's interest, MacDowell sent him the MS of his *Modern Suite,* op. 10, for piano solo; Liszt recommended the piece for performance at the meeting of the Allgemeiner Deutscher Musikverein held in Zürich on July 11, 1882; Liszt also recommended MacDowell to the publishers Breitkopf & Härtel, and the firm brought out the first works of MacDowell to appear in print, the *Modern Suites* for piano, opp. 10 and 14. Despite his youth, MacDowell was given a teaching position at the Darmstadt Cons.; he also accepted private pupils; among them was Marian Nevins of Connecticut; they were married on July 9, 1884. During the early

years of their marriage, the MacDowells made their 2nd home in Wiesbaden, where MacDowell composed industriously; his works were performed in neighboring communities; the famous pianist Teresa Carreño put several of his piano pieces on her concert programs. There were also performances in America. However, the MacDowells were beset by financial difficulties; his mother offered him help, but he declined her proposed plan for him and his wife to live on the family property. MacDowell also declined an offer to teach at the National Cons. in N.Y. at a munificent fee of $5 an hour. Similarly, he rejected an offer to take a clerical position at the American Consulate in Crefeld, Germany. In 1888 he finally returned to the U.S. for good, and was welcomed in artistic circles as a famous composer and pianist; musical America at the time was virtually a German colony, and MacDowell's German training was a certificate of his worth. The Boston Symph. conductors Gericke, Nikisch, and Paur, all Germans, played his orch. works. On Nov. 19, 1888, MacDowell made his American debut as a composer and pianist at a N.Y. concert of the Kneisel String Quartet, featuring his *Modern Suite,* op. 10. On March 5, 1889, he was the soloist with the N.Y. Phil. in his 2nd Piano Concerto, under the direction of the famous German musician Theodore Thomas, in its world premiere. Then Frank van den Stucken invited MacDowell to play his concerto at the spectacular Paris Exposition on July 12, 1889. MacDowell had no difficulty having his works publ., although for some reason he preferred to have his early piano pieces printed under the pseudonym **Edgar Thorn.** When Columbia Univ. established its music dept. in 1896, MacDowell was offered a position as the first incumbent, being cited as "the greatest musical genius America has produced." Unfortunately, mutual disenchantment soon developed between MacDowell and the univ. authorities, and in 1904 he resigned his post. It is idle to speculate as to whether this event was a contributing cause of MacDowell's mental deterioration; he was already showing signs of depression: extreme irritability and gradual loss of vital functions; he eventually lapsed into total insanity. He spent the last years of his life in a childlike state, unaware of his surroundings. In 1906 a public appeal was launched to raise funds for MacDowell's care; among the signers were Horatio Parker, Victor Herbert, Arthur Foote, George Chadwick, Frederick Converse, Andrew Carnegie, J. Pierpont Morgan, and former President Grover Cleveland. MacDowell was only 47 years old when he died. The sum of $50,000 was raised for the organization of the MacDowell Memorial Assoc. Mrs. MacDowell, who outlived her husband by nearly half a century (she died at the age of 99, in 1956), deeded to the association her husband's summer residence at Peterborough, N.H. This property became a pastoral retreat, under the name of the MacDowell Colony, for American composers and writers, who could spend summers working undisturbed in separate cottages, paying a minimum rent for lodgings and food. During the summer of 1910, Mrs. MacDowell arranged an elaborate pageant with music from

MacDowell's works; the success of this project led to the establishment of a series of MacDowell Festivals at Peterborough.

Among American composers, MacDowell occupies a historically important place as the first American whose works were accepted as comparable in quality and technique with those of the average German composers of his time. His music adhered to the prevalent representative Romantic art. Virtually all of his works bear titles borrowed from mythical history, literature, or painting; even his piano sonatas, set in Classical forms, carry descriptive titles—Tragica, Eroica, Norse, Keltic—indicative of the mood of melodic resources, or as an ethnic reference. MacDowell lived in Germany during his formative years, and German musical culture was decisive in shaping his musical development; even the American rhythms and melodies in his music seem to be European reflections of an exotic art. A parallel with Grieg is plausible, for Grieg was also a regional composer trained in Germany. But Grieg possessed a much more vigorous personality, and he succeeded in communicating the true spirit of Norwegian song modalities in his works. Lack of musical strength and originality accounts for MacDowell's gradual decline in the estimation of succeeding generations; MacDowell's romanticism was apt to lapse into salon sentimentality. The frequency of performance of his works in concert (he never wrote for the stage) declined in the decades following his death, and his influence on succeeding generations of American composers receded to a faint recognition of an evanescent artistic period.

WORKS (opp. 1–7 were publ. under the pseudonym Edgar Thorn): FOR ORCH.: *Hamlet and Ophelia,* symph. poem, op. 22 (1885; Boston Symph., Jan. 27, 1893); *Lancelot and Elaine,* symph. poem, op. 25 (1888; Boston Symph., Jan. 10, 1890); *Lamia,* symph. poem, op. 29 (1889; Boston Symph., Oct. 23, 1908); *The Saracens* and *The Lovely Alda,* 2 symph. poems, op. 30 (Boston Phil., Nov. 5, 1891); Suite No. 1 for Orch., op. 42 (Worcester Festival, Sept. 24, 1891); Suite No. 2, *Indian Suite* (N.Y., Jan. 23, 1895; Boston Symph. Orch., Jan. 31, 1895); Piano Concerto No. 1, in A minor, op. 15 (1882; Vienna, April 17, 1898); Piano Concerto No. 2, in D minor, op. 23 (N.Y., March 5, 1889, composer soloist); *Romance* for Cello and Orch., op. 35 (1888).

FOR CHORUS: 2 choruses for Men's Voices, op. 3: *Love and Time* and *The Rose and the Gardener* (1897); *The Witch* for Men's Chorus, op. 5 (1898); *War Song* for Men's Chorus, op. 6 (1898); 3 songs for Men's Chorus, op. 27 (1887); 2 songs for Men's Chorus, op. 41 (1890); *2 Northern Songs* for Mixed Voices, op. 43 (1891); 3 choruses for Men's Voices, op. 52 (1897); *2 Songs from the 13th Century* for Men's Chorus (1897); 2 choruses for Men's Voices, op. 53 (1898); 2 choruses for Men's Voices, op. 54 (1898); *College Songs* for Men's Voices (1901); *Summer Wind* for Women's Chorus (1902).

FOR VOICE AND PIANO: *2 Old Songs,* op. 9 (1894); 3 songs, op. 11 (1883); 2 songs, op. 12 (1883); *From an Old Garden* (6 songs), op. 26 (1887); 3 songs, op. 33 (1888; revised 1894); 2 songs, op. 34 (1888); *6 Love Songs,* op. 40 (1890); 8 songs, op. 47 (1893); 4 songs, op.

56 (1898); 3 songs, op. 58 (1899); 3 songs, op. 60 (1902).

FOR PIANO: *Amourette,* op. 1 (1896); *In Lilting Rhythm,* op. 2 (1897); *Forgotten Fairy Tales (Sung outside the Prince's Door, Of a Tailor and a Bear, Beauty in the Rose Garden, From Dwarfland),* op. 4 (1898); *6 Fancies (A Tin Soldier's Love, To a Humming Bird, Summer Song, Across Fields, Bluette, An Elfin Round),* op. 7 (1898); *Waltz,* op. 8 (1895); *First Modern Suite,* op. 10 (1880); *Prelude and Fugue,* op. 13 (1883); *2nd Modern Suite,* op. 14 (1881); *Serenata,* op. 16 (1883); *2 Fantastic Pieces (Legend, Witches' Dance),* op. 17 (1884); *2 Pieces (Barcarolle, Humoresque),* op. 18 (1884); *Forest Idyls (Forest Stillness, Play of the Nymphs, Reverie, Dance of the Dryads),* op. 19 (1884); *4 Pieces (Humoresque, March, Cradle Song, Czardas),* op. 24 (1887); *6 Idyls after Goethe (In the Woods, Siesta, To the Moonlight, Silver Clouds, Flute Idyl, The Bluebell),* op. 28 (1887); *6 Poems after Heine (From a Fisherman's Hut, Scotch Poem, From Long Ago, The Post Wagon, The Shepherd Boy, Monologue),* op. 31 (1887); *4 Little Poems (The Eagle, The Brook, Moonshine, Winter),* op. 32 (1888); *Etude de concert* in F-sharp, op. 36 (1889); *Les Orientales,* after Victor Hugo *(Clair de lune, Danse le Hamac, Danse Andalouse),* op. 37 (1889); *Marionnettes,* 8 Little Pieces *(Prologue, Soubrette, Lover, Witch, Clown, Villain, Sweetheart, Epilogue),* op. 38 (1888; originally only 6 pieces; *Prologue* and *Epilogue* were added in 1901); 12 Studies, Book I *(Hunting Song, Alla Tarantella, Romance, Arabesque, In the Forest, Dance of the Gnomes);* Book II *(Idyl, Shadow Dance, Intermezzo, Melody, Scherzino, Hungarian),* op. 39 (1890); Sonata No. 1, *Tragica,* op. 45 (1893); 12 Virtuoso Studies *(Novelette, Moto perpetuo, Wild Chase, Improvisation, Elfin Dance, Valse triste, Burleske, Bluette, Träumerei, March Wind, Impromptu, Polonaise),* op. 46 (1894); *Air and Rigaudon,* op. 49 (1894); Sonata No. 2, *Eroica,* op. 50 (1895); *Woodland Sketches,* 10 pieces *(To a Wild Rose, Will o' the Wisp, At an Old Trysting Place, In Autumn, From an Indian Lodge, To a Water Lily, From Uncle Remus, A Desert Farm, By a Meadow Brook, Told at Sunset),* op. 51 (1896); *Sea Pieces (To the Sea, From a Wandering Iceberg, A.D. 1620, Star-light, Song, From the Depths, Nautilus, In Mid-Ocean),* op. 55 (1898); Sonata No. 3, *Norse,* op. 57 (1900); Sonata No. 4, *Keltic,* op. 59 (1901); *Fireside Tales (An Old Love Story, Of Br'er Rabbit, From a German Forest, Of Salamanders, A Haunted House, By Smouldering Embers),* op. 61 (1902); *New England Idyls,* 10 pieces *(An Old Garden, Midsummer, Midwinter, With Sweet Lavender, In Deep Woods, Indian Idyl, To an Old White Pine, From Puritan Days, From a Log Cabin, The Joy of Autumn),* op. 62 (1902); 6 Little Pieces on Sketches by J.S. Bach (1890); Technical Exercises, 2 Books (1893, 1895). MacDowell's writings were collected by W.J. Baltzell and publ. as *Critical and Historical Essays* (1912; reprinted, with new introduction by I. Lowens, N.Y., 1969).

BIBLIOGRAPHY: L. Gilman, *Edward MacDowell: A Study* (N.Y., 1908; corrected reprint, N.Y., 1969); E.F. Page, *Edward MacDowell: His Works and Ideals* (N.Y., 1910); J. Adams, *What the Piano Writings of MacDowell Mean to the Piano Student*

(Chicago, 1913); T.P. Currier, "MacDowell as I Knew Him," *Musical Quarterly* (Jan. 1915); O.G. Sonneck, *Suum cuique: Essays in Music* (N.Y., 1916); idem, *Catalogue of First Editions of Edward MacDowell* (Washington, D.C., 1917; reprint, N.Y., 1973); W.H. Humiston, *MacDowell* (N.Y., 1921); J.F. Porte, *A Great American Tone Poet: Edward MacDowell* (London, 1922); J.B. Matthews, *Commemorative Tributes to MacDowell* (N.Y., 1922); Abbie F. Brown, *The Boyhood of Edward MacDowell* (N.Y., 1924); Upton Sinclair, "MacDowell," *American Mercury* (1926); J.F. Cooke, *Edward MacDowell, A Short Biography* (Philadelphia, 1928); R.W. Brown, "A Listener to the Winds, Edward MacDowell," in *Lonely Americans* (N.Y., 1929); Paul Rosenfeld, *An Hour with American Music* (Philadelphia, 1929; pp. 31-51); Anita Brown, *A Mosaic of Muses of the MacDowell Club of New York* (N.Y., 1930); *Catalogue of an Exhibition Illustrating the Life and Work of Edward MacDowell* (N.Y., 1938); J.T. Howard, *Our American Music* (N.Y., 1939; 4th ed., 1965); Marian MacDowell, "MacDowell's Peterborough Idea," *Musical Quarterly* (Jan. 1932); idem, *Random Notes on Edward MacDowell and His Music* (Boston, 1950); Irving Lowens, "Edward MacDowell," *Hi-Fi Stereo Review* (Nov. 1967); Arnold T. Schwab, "Edward MacDowell's Birthdate: A Correction," *Musical Quarterly* (April 1975).

Macfarlane, William Charles, English-born American organist and composer; b. London, Oct. 2, 1870; d. North Conway, N.H., May 12, 1945. In 1874 he was taken to N.Y.; was taught by his father, Duncan Macfarlane (1836–1916), and by S.P. Warren. He made his debut as an organist in N.Y. on March 22, 1886; from 1898 to 1919 held various positions as an organist and a choral conductor; in 1941, retired to North Conway. He wrote *America First, A Boy Scout Operetta* (1917); light operas: *Little Almond Eyes* (Portland, 1916) and *Sword and Scissors* (1918); cantata, *The Message from the Cross* (1907); *The Church Service Book* (N.Y., 1912); numerous anthems and other sacred music; organ pieces (*Lullaby, Serenade, Scherzo, Romanza,* etc.).

Macfarren, Sir George Alexander, eminent English composer and pedagogue; b. London, March 2, 1813; d. there, Oct. 31, 1887. He received general education from his father, George Macfarren, the dramatist, and studied at the Royal Academy of Music; after graduation, he joined its faculty as a tutor in 1834. After many years as a prof. there, in 1875 he was appointed a prof. of music at Cambridge Univ., as successor to Sterndale Bennett. He was knighted in 1883. He had the great satisfaction of having his early overture *Chevy Chace* performed by Mendelssohn in Leipzig (1843) and by Wagner in London (1855). Macfarren's greatest ambition was to write an opera that would reflect the spirit of England, as the operas of Weber were redolent of the mythical lyricism of German folklore, but he signally failed in this endeavor. His 9 symphs. enjoyed some transient favor, but attempts at their revival foundered in future years. His wife, **Natalie Macfarren** (née Clarina Thalia Andrae; b. Lübeck, Dec. 14, 1826; d. Bakewell, April 9, 1916), a singer, studied music with Macfarren, whom she married in 1844; she dutifully sang her husband's operas in England. She publ. a *Vocal Method* and an *Elementary Course of Vocalising and Pronouncing the English Language.*

WORKS: OPERAS: *An Adventure of Don Quixote* (London, Feb. 3, 1846); *King Charles II* (London, Oct. 27, 1849); *Robin Hood* (London, Oct. 11, 1860); *Helvellyn* (London, Nov. 3, 1864). FOR ORCH.: 9 symphs. (1828, 1831, 1832, 1833, 1833, 1836, 1840, 1845, 1874); Piano Concerto (1835); Flute Concerto (1863); Violin Concerto (1871–74); overtures: *The Merchant of Venice* (1834); *Romeo and Juliet* (1836); *Chevy Chace* (1836); *Don Carlos* (1842); *Hamlet* (1856); *Festival Overture* (1874). FOR VOICE: Oratorios and cantatas: *The Sleeper Awakened* (London, Nov. 15, 1850); *Lenora* (London, April 25, 1853); *Christmas* (London, May 9, 1860); *St. John the Baptist* (Bristol, Oct. 23, 1873); *The Resurrection* (Birmingham, 1876); *Joseph* (Leeds, 1877); *King David* (Leeds, 1883); numerous sacred and secular vocal works; part-songs; trios; duets; and some 160 solo songs. CHAMBER MUSIC: 5 string quartets (1834, 1842, 1846, 1849, 1878); Quintet for Violin, Viola, Cello, Double Bass, and Piano (1844); Violin Sonata (1887); 3 piano sonatas; various piano and organ pieces. ARRANGEMENTS: *Popular Music of the Olden Time* (1859); *Popular Songs of Scotland* (1874). EDUCATIONAL WORKS: *Rudiments of Harmony* (1860; 14 eds.); *Six Lectures on Harmony* (London, 1867).

BIBLIOGRAPHY: H.C. Banister, *George Alexander Macfarren: His Life, Works and Influence* (London, 1892).

Macfarren, Walter Cecil, English pianist and composer, brother of **George Alexander Macfarren;** b. London, Aug. 28, 1826; d. there, Sept. 2, 1905. He was a chorister at Westminster Abbey; then studied at the Royal Academy of Music, with Holmes (piano) and with his brother (composition). From 1846 until 1903 he was a prof. of piano at the Royal Academy of Music; conducted its concerts from 1873 till 1880. He composed a number of overtures on Shakespearean subjects; a Piano Concerto; many piano pieces; edited Beethoven's sonatas, and several albums of piano pieces under the title *Popular Classics.* He publ. *Memories; An Autobiography* (London, 1905).

Mach, Ernst, eminent German acoustician; b. Turas, Moravia, Feb. 18, 1838; d. Vaterstetten, near Munich, Feb. 19, 1916. He was a prof. of physics in Prague (1864) and in Vienna (1895). Besides his scientific works of far-reaching importance, he publ. a number of books and studies dealing with musical acoustics: *Zwei populäre Vortraäge uüber musikalische Akustik* (1865); *Einleitung in die Helmholtz'sche Musiktheorie* (1866); *Zur Theorie des Gehöörorgans* (1872); *Beitrag zur Geschichte der Musik* (1892); *Die Analyse der Empfindungen und das Verhaältnis des Physischen zum Psychischen* (5th ed., 1906); "Zur Geschichte der Theorie der Konsonanz," in *Populärwissenschaftliche Vorträge* (3rd ed., 1903). The unit of velocity of sound "Mach" is named after him.

Mácha, Otmar, Czech composer; b. Ostrava, Oct. 2, 1922. He studied with Jaroslav Řídký at the Prague Cons. (1942–46); was chief dramaturgist for musical programs at Czech Radio in Prague (1945–62); from 1969 worked at Czech Radio.
  WORKS: 3 operas: *Polapenaá nevěra* (*Entrapped Faithlessness;* 1956–57; Prague, Nov. 21, 1958); *Jezero Ukereve* (*Lake Ukereve;* 1960–63; Prague, May 27, 1966); opera buffa, *Svatba na oko* (*Feigned Wedding;* 1974–76); musical comedy, *Cradle for Sinful Maidens* (1975–76); oratorio, *The Heritage of Jan Amos Comenius* (1952–55); *Symphonic Intermezzo* (1958); *Noc a naděje* (*Night and Hope),* symph. poem (Prague Spring Festival, May 26, 1960); *Azur Tarantella* for Orch. (1962); *Variations on a Theme by Jan Rychlík* for Orch. (Prague, March 15, 1966); *4 Monologues* for Soprano, Baritone, and Orch. (1966); *Variants,* short studies for Orch. (Czech Radio, April 21, 1969); *Janinka zpívá* (*Janinka Sings),* suite for Soprano and Orch. (1969); Sinfonietta (1970–71); *Double Concerto* for Violin, Piano, and Orch. (1975–76); String Quartet (1943); Violin Sonata (1948); Cello Sonata (1949); Bassoon Sonata (1963); *Funeral Toccata* for Organ (1964); *The Weeping of the Saxophone* for Saxophone and Piano (1968); *Folklore* for Piano (1969); *Psalm No. 2* for Baritone and Organ (1969); *Small Triptych,* 3 songs for Soprano, Flute, and Tam-tam (1971); *Wedding Toccata* for Organ (1974); *Eyes and Hands,* chamber cantata for Mezzo-soprano, Clarinet, Viola, and Piano (1975–76); choruses; songs.

Machabey, Armand, French musicologist; b. Pont-de-Roide, Doubs, May 7, 1886; d. Paris, Aug. 31, 1966. He studied with Vincent d'Indy and André Pirro; received his doctorat ès lettres from the Univ. of Paris in 1928 with the dissertation *Essai sur les formules usuelles de la musique occidentale des origines à la fin du XVᵉ siècle* (publ. in Paris, in a revised ed. in 1955, as *Genèse de la tonalité musicale classique);* subsequently was active as a music historian and essayist; also was one of the editors of *Larousse de la musique* (Paris, 1957). His writings include *Sommaire de la méthode en musicologie* (Paris, 1930); *Précis-manuel d'histoire de la musique* (Paris, 1942; 2nd ed., 1947); *La Vie et Maurice Ravel* (Paris, 1947); *Traité de la critique musicale* (Paris, 1947); *L'Œuvre d'Anton Bruckner* (Paris, 1947); *Le "bel canto"* (Paris, 1948); *Portraits de trente compositeurs français* (Paris, 1950); *Gerolamo Frescobaldi Ferrarensis* (Paris, 1952); *La Musique et la médicine* (Paris, 1952); *La Notation musicale* (Paris, 1952; 3rd ed., revised, 1971); *Guillaume de Machaut: La vie et l'œuvre musicale* (Paris, 1955); *Problèmes de notation musicale* (Paris, 1958); *La Musicologie* (Paris, 1962; 2nd ed., 1969); *Embryologie de la musique occidentale* (Paris, 1963); *La Musique de danse* (Paris, 1966).

Machado, Augusto, Portuguese composer; b. Lisbon, Dec. 27, 1845; d. there, March 26, 1924. He was a pupil of Junior, Lami, and D'Almeide in Lisbon, and of Lavignac and Danhauser in Paris; in 1892–1908, was director of the San Carlos Theater in Lisbon; in 1894–1910, director of the Cons. there. Besides numerous operettas, he wrote the operas *A Cruz de oiro* (Lisbon, 1873); *A Maria da Fonte* (Lisbon, 1879); *Lauriane* (Marseilles, Jan. 9, 1883; his most successful work); *Os Dorias* (Lisbon, 1887); *Mario Wetter* (Lisbon, 1898); *Venere* (Lisbon, 1905); *La Borghesina* (Lisbon, 1909). For the 3rd centenary of the death of Camoëns he wrote the symph. ode *Camões es os Luziadas* (1880); also wrote organ and piano pieces.

Machaut (or **Machault, Machaud**), **Guillaume de (Guillelmus de Mascaudio),** important French composer and poet, probably a native of Machaut in the Champagne; b. c.1300; d. Rheims, 1377. He studied theology; took Holy Orders; in 1323–40 was in the service of King John of Bohemia (Duke of Luxembourg) as almoner (1330), notary (1332), and secretary (1335), traveling widely with that prince (their visits extended to Russia). Later he was at the court of Charles V of France. He held various ecclesiastical benefices (Houdain, Arras, Verdun), and from 1337 was canon of Rheims, where he resided from 1340 until his death (he visited Paris in 1363). His works include ballades, rondeaux, virelais, and motets. He wrote the earliest polyphonic (4 voices) setting of the complete Mass by a single composer. A complete ed. of Machaut's musical works was prepared by Friedrich Ludwig for the *Publikationen älterer Musik* (vols. I, 1; III, 1; IV, 2; 1926–34, containing about two-thirds of his *opera omnia* and a commentary); the Mass, lais, and hocket, not included in Ludwig's collection, were brought out for the *Publikationen* by H. Besseler in 1943, but the printed copies were destroyed in an air raid. After the war, several editions of the Mass were publ. (by Chailley, Paris, 1948; by Machabey, Liège, 1948; by de Van, Rome, 1949; by Hübsch, Heidelberg, 1953; and Besseler's again, Leipzig, 1954). The complete works are publ. in L. Schrade, ed., *Polyphonic Music of the 14th Century* (vols. 2 and 3, Monaco, 1956); 14 works (including parts of the Mass) are found in J. Wolf's *Geschichte der Mensuralnotation von 1250–1450* (Leipzig, 1904); 2 pieces in Schering's *Geschichte der Musik in Beispielen;* other pieces in Davison and Apel, *Historical Anthology of Music* (Cambridge, Mass., 1946). *La Louange des dames,* lyric poems, was ed. by N. Wilkins (Edinburgh, 1972).
  BIBLIOGRAPHY: Machaut's poems were publ. by V. Chichmaref, as *Poésies lyriques de Guillaume Machaut* (2 vols., Paris, 1909). H. Quittard, "Notes sur Guillaume de Machaut et son œuvre," *Bulletin de la Société Française de Musicologie* (1918); H. Besseler, in the *Freiburger-Orgelbericht* (1926; pp. 146ff.); A. Machabey, "Guillaume de Machaut, La Vie et l'homme," *Revue Musicale* (May 1930; April–May 1931); G. Reese, *Music in the Middle Ages,* chapter 12 (N.Y., 1940); A. Douce, *Guillaume de Machaut, Musicien et poète rémois* (Rheims, 1948); George Perle, "Integrative Devices in the Music of

Machaut," *Musical Quarterly* (April 1948); Otto Gombosi, "Machaut's Messe Notre-Dame," *Musical Quarterly* (April 1950); S. Levarie, *Guillaume de Machaut* (N.Y., 1954); A. Machabey, *Guillaume de Machaut: La Vie et l'œuvre musicale* (2 vols., Paris, 1955); G. Reaney, "Notes on the Harmonic Technique of Guillaume de Machaut," in H. Tischler, *Essays in Musicology* (Apel Festschrift; Bloomington, Ind., 1968); H.H. Eggebrecht, "Machauts Motette Nr. 9," *Archiv für Musikwissenschaft* (Aug. 1968); S.J. Williams, "Vocal Scoring in the Chansons of Machaut," *Journal of the American Musicological Society* (Fall 1968); W. Dömling, *Die mehrstimmigen Balladen, Rondeaux und Virelais von Guillaume de Machaut* (Tutzing, 1970); M. Hasselman and T. Walker, "More Hidden Polyphony in a Machaut Manuscript," *Musica Disciplina* (1970); G. Reaney, *Guillaume de Machaut* (London, 1971).

Machavariani, Alexei, Georgian composer; b. Gory, Sept. 23, 1913. He studied at the Cons. of Tiflis, graduating in 1936; in 1940 became an instructor in music theory there. His music is profoundly infused with Caucasian melorhythms. He wrote the operas *Deda da shvili* (*Mother and Son;* Tiflis, May 1, 1945), on a patriotic subject connected with the struggle for independence in the Caucasus, and *Hamlet* (1964); ballet, *Knight in a Tiger's Skin* (1965); symph. poems: *Mumly Muhasa* (1939); *Satchidao* (1940); *On the Death of a Hero* (1948); overture, *The People's Choice* (1950); cantata, *For Peace, for Fatherland* (1951); Piano Concerto (1944); Violin Concerto (1950); oratorio, *The Day of My Fatherland* (1954); many songs, of which *Blue Light* (1949) achieved great popularity in Russia; *Khorumy,* a Georgian military dance, for Piano (1941; very popular); 2 symphs. (1947, 1973).

Mâche, François-Bernard, remarkable French composer and classical scholar; b. Clermont-Ferrand, April 4, 1935. Of a musical family, he studied piano locally; in 1955 entered L'Ecole Normale Supérieure in Paris, studying classical languages and literature; received his diploma in 1958; then enrolled at the Paris Cons., in the composition class of Olivier Messiaen; continued his classical studies, and in 1962 was given a professorship in classical literature. He also learned modern Greek, and translated contemporary Greek poetry and prose into English; several of his works are inspired by Greek mythology. In musical composition, Mâche became an adherent of experimental methods; in 1980 he received a national doctorate for his thesis on models of new music. He adopted the ideal of "organized sound" as enunciated by Varèse; but he also annexed sounds of nature; for resources he studied ornithology, but rather than translate the intonations of bird songs into human melorhythms performable on instruments, as his teacher Messiaen professed to do, Mâche transmutes the natural material into suggestive images of sound; in one of his works, *Amorgos,* named after an island in the Aegean Sea, he uses as a background the actual sound of the sea waves recorded on magnetic tape.

In one score, *Naluan,* he used recorded animal sounds. He also publ. an essay, *Musique, mythe, nature ou Les Dauphins d'Arion* (1982).
WORKS: *La Peau du silence* for Orch. (1962); *Rituel d'Oubli* for Orch. and Concert Band (1969); *Danae* for 12 Solo Voices and Percussion (1970); *Naluan* for 8 Instruments and Animal Sounds (1974); *Marae* for 6 Percussionists and Sounds of Nature (1974); *Kassandra* for 14 Instruments and Band (1977; Paris Radio, Oct. 16, 1977); *Andromède* for Orch., Double Chorus, and 3 Pianos (1979); *Amorgos* for 12 Instruments and Recorded Sea Waves (1979; Metz Festival, Nov. 16, 1979); *Sopiana* for Flute, Piano, and Magnetic Tape (1980; Pecs, Hungary, July 12, 1980); *Temboctou,* musical spectacle (1982).

Machl, Tadeusz, Polish organist, composer, and pedagogue; b. Lwow, Oct. 22, 1922. He studied composition with Malawski and organ with Rutkowski at the State College of Music in Cracow (1949–52); subsequently occupied various teaching and administrative positions in Cracow.
WORKS: *3 miniatury symfoniczne* (1946); 5 symphs.: No. 1, with Chorus (1947); No. 2 (1948); No. 3, *Tatry* (1949); No. 4 (1954); No. 5 for Soprano, Female Chorus, and Orch. (1963); many concertos, including 4 for Organ (1950, 1952, 1953, 1958) and one each for Soprano (1958), Violin (1960), Harpsichord (1962), Piano (1965), and Harp (1967); *Double Concerto* for Piano, Harpsichord, and Orch. (1967); 2 triple concertos: No. 1 for 3 Organs (1969) and No. 2 for 2 Pianos, Organ, and Orch. (1971); *Lyrical Suite* for Orch. (1956); *Jubilee Overture* (1971); *Dzień pracy (Labor Day)* for Chorus and Small Orch. (1948); 3 string quartets (1952, 1957, 1962); Piano Sonata (1940); pieces for organ solo and for piano; choruses; songs.

Machlis, Joseph, American music historian and pedagogue; b. Riga, Latvia, Aug. 11, 1906. He was brought to the U.S. as an infant. He studied at the College of the City of N.Y. (B.A., 1927), and at the Inst. of Musical Art of the Juilliard School (Teachers Diploma, 1927); also took an M.A. in English literature from Columbia Univ. (1938). In 1938 he was appointed to the music faculty at Queens College of the City Univ. of N.Y. He publ. several well-written texts: the immensely popular *The Enjoyment of Music* (N.Y., 1955; 3rd ed., 1970); *Introduction to Contemporary Music* (N.Y., 1961); *American Composers of Our Time* for young people (N.Y., 1963); *Getting to Know Music* for high school students (N.Y., 1966). He trans. a number of operatic librettos for the NBC Opera Co. (*Rigoletto, La Traviata, Fidelio, La Bohème, Cavalleria rusticana,* Prokofiev's *War and Peace,* etc.); *Boris Godunov, Tosca,* and Manuel de Falla's *Atlántida* for other opera companies. He is the author of 2 novels: *57th Street,* about the "concert industry" (N.Y., 1970), and *Lisa's Boy* (N.Y., 1982), publ. under the phonetically palindromic pseudonym **George Selcamm.**

Maciejewski, Roman, Polish composer, pianist, and choral conductor; b. Berlin, to Polish parents, Feb. 28, 1910. His mother taught him to play piano at an early age; he then took regular piano lessons with Goldenweiser (1916–19). His family returned to Poland in 1920, and Maciejewski studied piano there with Zalewski and in 1926 became a composition student of Wiechowicz; later studied with Sikorski in Warsaw and finally with Nadia Boulanger in Paris (1934–35). He lived in Sweden after 1938; in 1952 emigrated to the U.S., settling in Redondo Beach, Calif., as a church organist and director of the Roman Choir. He excels in writing lush, resonant, protracted choruses in self-confident tonal harmonies.

WORKS: Requiem for Soloists, Chorus, and Orch. (part I, 1944–60, premiered at the Warsaw Autumn Festival, Sept. 1960, composer conducting); *Allegro concertante* for Piano and Orch. (1944; Göteborg, Jan. 11, 1945; composer soloist); *Song of Bilitis* for Soprano and Orch. (1932); Brass Quartet (1937); String Quartet (1938); Violin Sonata (1940); String Trio (1948); *Nocturne* for Flute, Celesta, and Guitar (1951); *Variations* for Wind Quintet (1971); *Bajka (Fairy Tale)*, ballet for children for 2 Pianos (1931); Concerto for 2 Solo Pianos (1935); 2 piano sonatas (1926, 1932); *25 Mazurkas* for Piano (1928–38); several masses with organ; a cappella songs.

Mackenzie, Sir Alexander Campbell, distinguished British composer and educator; b. Edinburgh, Aug. 22, 1847; d. London, April 28, 1935. A scion of a musical family (there were 4 generations of musicians in his paternal line), he showed musical aptitude as a child; was sent to Germany, where he studied violin with K.W. Ulrich and theory with Eduard Stein, at the Sondershausen Cons. (1857–62); returning to England, he studied violin with Sainton, piano with Jewson, and music theory with Charles Lucas at the Royal Academy of Music; subsequently was active in Edinburgh as a violinist and teacher (1865–79). Between 1879 and 1888 he spent part of each year in Florence. In 1888 he was elected principal of the Royal Academy of Music in London, holding this post until 1924. From 1892 to 1899 he conducted the concerts of the Phil. Society of London. His reputation as an educator and composer was very high among musicians. He was knighted in 1895. As a composer, he was a staunch believer in programmatic music; he introduced national Scottish elements in many of his works; his *Pibroch Suite* for Violin and Orch., first introduced by Sarasate at the Leeds Festival (1889), acquired considerable popularity; Paderewski gave the first performance of his *Scottish Concerto* with the Phil. Society of London (1897). In 1922 he was made a Knight Commander of the Royal Victorian Order.

WORKS: OPERAS (all first perf. in London): *Colomba* (April 9, 1883); *The Troubadour* (June 8, 1886); *His Majesty* (Feb. 20, 1897); *The Cricket on the Hearth* (composed 1900; perf. June 6, 1914); *The Knights of the Road* (Feb. 27, 1905). CANTATAS: *Jason* (1882); *The Rose of Sharon* (Norwich Festival, Oct. 16, 1884); *The Story of Sayid* (1886); *The Witches' Daughter* (1904); *The Sun-God's Return* (1910). FOR ORCH.: *Cervantes,* overture (1877); *Scottish Rhapsody* No. 1 (1880); *Burns (Scottish Rhapsody* No. 2; 1881); *La Belle Dame sans merci,* after Keats (1883); *Twelfth Night,* after Shakespeare (1888); *Coriolanus,* suite (1901); *London Day by Day,* suite (1902); *Canadian Rhapsody* (1905); *Tam o' Shanter (Scottish Rhapsody* No. 3; 1911); *Youth, Sport and Loyalty,* overture (1922); Violin Concerto (1885); *Pibroch Suite* for Violin and Orch. (Leeds, Oct. 10, 1889); Suite No. 2 for Violin and Orch. (London, Feb. 18, 1897); *Scottish Concerto* for Piano and Orch. (London, March 24, 1897). CHAMBER MUSIC: Piano Trio (1874); String Quartet (1875); Piano Quartet (1875); *From the North,* 9 pieces for Violin and Piano (1895); *4 Dance Measures* for Violin and Piano (1915); several characteristic piano suites (*Rustic Suite, In the Scottish Highlands, Odds and Ends, Jottings, In Varying Moods*); a number of songs; arrangements of Scottish songs; etc. He publ. an autobiography, *A Musician's Narrative* (London, 1927).

Mackerras, Sir Charles, eminent Australian conductor; b. Schenectady, N.Y., of Australian parents, Nov. 17, 1925. He was taken to Sydney, Australia, as an infant; studied oboe, piano, and composition at the New South Wales Conservatorium there; then played oboe in the Sydney Symph. Orch. He won a British Council scholarship in 1947, and went to Prague to study conducting with Vaclav Talich at the Prague Academy of Music. Returning to London in 1948, he joined the conducting staff at the Sadler's Wells Opera; then was engaged as principal conductor of the BBC Concert Orch. (1954–56); subsequently appeared as a guest conductor with British orchs.; also had engagements on the Continent. From 1966 to 1970 he held the post of first conductor at the Hamburg State Opera. In 1970 he became music director at the Sadler's Wells Opera (it was renamed the English National Opera in 1974), a position he held until 1977. He further served as chief guest conductor of the BBC Symph. (1978–79). In 1978 he was named principal guest conductor of the English National Opera. In 1979 he visited the U.S.; was a guest conductor with the Metropolitan Opera and the N.Y. Phil. Returning to Europe, he made an appearance with the Vienna Phil. on Nov. 24, 1979. He was made a Commander of the Order of the British Empire in 1974, and was knighted in 1979. In 1982 he was named chief conductor of the Sydney (Australia) Symph. Orch. His conducting method is marked by carefully delineated instrumental and vocal parts, with a scrupulously high regard for the stylistic characteristics of each work.

Mackinlay, Malcolm Sterling, English bass and singing teacher, son of the famous contralto **Antoinette Sterling;** b. London, Aug. 7, 1876; d. there, Jan. 10, 1952. He studied at Trinity College, Oxford (M.A., 1901); studied singing with Manuel García; then traveled as joint artist with his mother; in 1904 he gave up his concert career and established himself in London as a singing teacher; organized the Sterling Mackinlay Operatic Society. He publ. the following books: *Antoinette Sterling and Other Celebrities* (1906); *Garcia, the Centenarian, and His Times* (1908); *The Singing Voice and Its Training* (1910); *Light Opera* (technique and theater craft; 1926); *Origin and Development of Light Opera* (1927); also 2 novels.

Maclean, Alexander Morvaren (Alick), English composer and conductor, son of **Charles Donald Maclean;** b. Eton, near Windsor, July 20, 1872; d. London, May 18, 1936. He studied with Sir Joseph Barnby; later conducted the Spa Orch. at Scarborough (from 1911) and the New Queen's Hall Light Orch. (1915–23). He wrote several operas; of these, 2 were produced in German, in Mainz: *Die Liebesgeige* (April 15, 1906) and *Waldidyll* (March 23, 1913); and 3 in London: *Petruccio* (June 29, 1895), *The King's Price* (April 29, 1904), and *Maître Seiler* (Aug. 20, 1909). His most successful opera, *Quentin Durward* (after Walter Scott), written in 1892, was not produced until many years later, at Newcastle upon Tyne (Jan. 13, 1920). He also wrote an oratorio, *The Annunciation* (London, 1910); *Rapsodie monégasque* for Orch. (1935); choral works.

Maclean, Charles Donald, English organist; b. Cambridge, March 27, 1843; d. London, June 23, 1916. He studied theory with Ferdinand Hiller in Cologne; later at Oxford Univ. (D.Mus., 1865). He was music director at Eton College (1871–75); then entered the Indian Civil Service, returning to London in 1898. He was the English editor of the International Musical Society.

Maclean, Quentin Stuart Morvaren, English-Canadian organist and composer; b. London, May 14, 1896; d. Toronto, July 9, 1962. He studied organ with Karl Straube and composition with Max Reger in Leipzig (1912–14); was interned as an enemy alien in Germany during World War I. Upon his return to London, he was active as an organist; in 1939 he emigrated to Canada.
WORKS: *Concert Piece* for Organ and Orch. (1932); *Rhapsody on 2 English Folk Tunes* for Harp and Small Orch. (1938); *Stabat Mater* for Tenor, Chorus, Organ, and Strings (1941); *Concerto Grosso in Popular Style* for 4 Electric Instruments (Solovox, Electric Organ, Electric Guitar, Theremin) and Small Orch. (1942); *Concerto* for Electric Organ and Dance Orch. (1945); *The Well-tempered Orchestra,* prelude and fugue on a tuning formula, for Orch. (1950); *Concerto Romantico* for Piano and Orch. (1953); *Rustic Rhapsody* for Orch. (1954); *Theme and Variatons* for Harpsichord and Orch. (1954); *Concerto Rococo* for Violin and Orch. (1957); String Quartet (1937); Piano Trio (1937); Trio for Flute, Viola, and Guitar (1937); organ pieces; choruses; songs.

Maclennan, Francis, American tenor; b. Bay City, Mich., Jan. 7, 1879; d. Port Westminster, Long Island, N.Y., July 17, 1935. He studied voice in N.Y., and later with Henschel in London and Franz Emerich

in Berlin; made his debut as Faust at Covent Garden (1902); in 1904 he sang Parsifal in Savage's Opera Co. on a tour of the U.S.; from 1907 till 1913 he sang at the Berlin Opera, where he had the distinction of being the first foreigner to sing Tristan in Germany; also performed Wagnerian roles in England; from 1915–17 he was a member of the Chicago Opera Co., appearing chiefly as a Wagnerian singer. In 1904 he married **Florence Easton,** with whom he appeared in duo recitals.

MacMillan, Sir Ernest (Alexander Campbell), eminent Canadian conductor and composer; b. Mimico, Ontario, Aug. 18, 1893; d. Toronto, May 6, 1973. He studied organ in Toronto and then at Edinburgh Univ. with Alfred Hollins and Frederick Niecks; in the summer of 1914 he went to Bayreuth to attend the Wagner Festival and was interned as an enemy alien at the outbreak of World War I; after the Armistice he returned to Canada and settled in Toronto; was director of the Toronto Cons. (1926–42) and dean of the faculty of music at the Univ. of Toronto (1927–52); was also conductor of the Toronto Symph. Orch. (1931–56) and the Mendelssohn Choir in Toronto (1942–57); filled in engagements as guest conductor in the U.S., England, Australia, and South America. He held several important administrative posts, including the presidency of the Canadian Music Council (1947–66), and of the Canadian Music Centre (1959–70). He was knighted by King George V in 1935 and received 9 honorary doctorates from Canadian and American univs.
WORKS: *England,* an ode, after Swinburne, for Soprano, Baritone, Chorus, and Orch. (composed in the prisoner-of-war camp in Germany, 1914–18; first perf. Sheffield, England, March 17, 1921); *Overture* (1924); *2 Sketches* on French-Canadian airs, for String Orch. (1927); *A Song of Deliverance* for Chorus and Orch. (1944); *Fantasy on Scottish Melodies* for Orch. (1946); *6 Bergerettes du Bas Canada* for Soprano, Alto, Tenor, Oboe, Viola, Cello, and Harp; *3 Indian Songs of the West Coast* for Voice and Piano; many other songs and choruses; etc. He publ. several educational works: *On the Preparation of Ear Tests; Graded Piano Sight Reading Exercises* (with Healey Willan); *The Modern Piano Student* (with Boris Berlin); ed. *Music in Canada* (Toronto, 1955).

Macmillen, Francis, American violinist; b. Marietta, Ohio, Oct. 14, 1885; d. Lausanne, Switzerland, July 14, 1973. A precocious child, he was sent to Germany at the age of 10 and was accepted by Joachim as a pupil; later he studied with César Thomson at the Brussels Cons., winning the first prize in 1901; continued his studies with Carl Flesch in Berlin and Leopold Auer in St. Petersburg. He made his professional debut as a concert violinist at the age of 17 in Brussels (March 30, 1903); appeared with the N.Y. Symph. Orch. on Dec. 7, 1906; then embarked on a concert tour of Europe; after the outbreak of World War I in 1914 he returned to the U.S. and taught violin at Ithaca, N.Y.; resumed his European tours in 1929; then lived in N.Y., Florence, Italy, and lastly, Switzerland.

MacNeil, Cornell, American opera baritone; b. Minneapolis, Sept. 24, 1922. He began to earn his living as a machinist, and simultaneously made appearances as a radio actor and operetta singer. His professional singing debut was in the baritone role in Menotti's opera *The Consul* in N.Y. on March 1, 1950. He joined the N.Y. City Opera in 1953; also made guest appearances in San Francisco, Chicago, and Mexico City. On March 5, 1959, he sang the role of Charles V in Verdi's opera *Ernani* at La Scala in Milan. On March 21, 1959, he sang Rigoletto at the Metropolitan Opera in N.Y. and became a regular member of the company; also sang in Europe. He attracted unexpected notoriety when he walked off the stage during the 3rd act of Verdi's opera *Un ballo in maschera* on Dec. 27, 1964, in Parma, Italy, in protest against the offensive attitude of the audience, and engaged in a fistfight with the opera manager. Pacified, he resumed his career in America, but also became active in labor union affairs; in 1969 he was elected president of the American Guild of Musical Artists.

Maconchy, Elizabeth, significant English composer of Irish extraction; b. Broxbourne, Hertfordshire, March 19, 1907. She studied with Vaughan Williams and Charles Wood at the Royal College of Music in London (1923–29); in 1930 went to Prague, where she absorbed the styles and techniques of Expressionism; upon returning to England, she composed prolifically in all genres; developed a style peculiarly her own: tonally tense, contrapuntally dissonant, and coloristically sharp in instrumentation. In 1977 she was made a Dame Commander of the Order of the British Empire. WORKS: FOR THE STAGE: 3 one-act operas: *The Sofa,* to a libretto by Ursula Vaughan Williams (London, Dec. 13, 1959); *The Departure* (London, Dec. 16, 1962); *The 3 Strangers,* after Thomas Hardy (London, June 5, 1968); *The Birds,* operatic extravaganza, after Aristophanes (London, June 5, 1968, on the same day with *The 3 Strangers*); church masque, *The Jesse Tree* (Dorchester Abbey, Oct. 7, 1970); ballets: *Great Agrippa* (1933); *The Little Red Shoes* (1935); *Puck Fair* (1940). FOR ORCH.: *The Land,* symph. suite (1929); Piano Concerto (1930); *Theme and Variations* for Strings (1942); Symph. (1945–48); Viola Concerto (1937); *Dialogue* for Piano and Orch. (1940); Concertino for Clarinet and Strings (Copenhagen Festival of the International Society for Contemporary Music, June 2, 1947); Symph. for Double String Orch. (1953); *Proud Thames,* overture (1953); *Serenata concertante* for Violin and Orch. (1962); *An Essex Overture* (1966); *3 Cloudscapes* for Orch. (1968); *Sinfonietta* (1975–76); *Epyllion* for Cello and 14 Strings (1975); *Romanza* for Viola and Chamber Orch. (London, March 12, 1979); Little Symph. (1980; Norwich, July 28, 1981); *Music for Strings* (Proms concert, London, July 26, 1983). CHAMBER MUSIC: 12 string quartets (1933, 1936, 1938, 1943, 1948, 1951, 1956, 1966, 1967, 1970, 1978, 1979);

Quintet for Oboe and Strings (1932); *Prelude, Interlude and Fugue* for 2 Violins (Prague Festival of the International Society for Contemporary Music, Sept. 4, 1935); Viola Sonata (1938); Violin Sonata (1944); Concertino for Piano and Strings (1951); Concertino for Bassoon and Strings (1954); String Trio (1957); Double Concerto for Oboe, Clarinet, Viola, and Harp (1960); Clarinet Quintet (1963); *Music* for Double Bass and Piano (1970); *3 Bagatelles* for Oboe and Harp (1972); *Contemplation* for Cello and Piano (1978); *Colloquy* for Flute and Piano (1979); *Fantasia* for Clarinet and Piano (1979); *Piccola musica* for String Trio (Cheltenham, July 13, 1981); *Trittico* for 2 Oboes, Bassoon, and Harpsichord (1981); Wind Quintet (1982); *Tribute* for Violin and 8 Wind Instruments (1983). VOCAL WORKS: *Samson at the Gates of Gaza* for Chorus and Orch. (1963); *The Starlight Night and Peace* for Soprano and Chamber Orch. (1964); *Witnesses* for 2 Sopranos, Flute, Oboe, Clarinet, Horn, Cello, Percussion, and Ukelele (1966); *3 Donne Songs* for Tenor and Piano (1966); *The Leaden Echo and the Golden Echo* for Chorus, Flute, Viola, and Harp (1978); *Creatures* for Chorus (1979); 3 settings of poems by Gerard Manley Hopkins for Soprano and Orch. (1964–70); *Ariadne* for Soprano and Orch. (1970); *Heloise and Abelard,* cantata for Soloists, Chorus, and Orch. (1978); *My Dark Heart,* after Petrarch, for Soprano and Instrumental Ensemble (1982); *L'Horloge* for Soprano, Clarinet, and Piano (1983); piano pieces. BIBLIOGRAPHY: F. Howes, "Elizabeth Maconchy," *Monthly Musical Record* (July–Aug. 1938); Elizabeth Maconchy, "A Composer Speaks," *Composer* (1971–72).

Macpherson, Charles, Scottish organist and composer; b. Edinburgh, May 10, 1870; d. London, May 28, 1927. He was a chorister at St. Paul's Cathedral; studied organ with George Martin; then took courses at the Royal Academy of Music; held various positions as an organist; succeeded his teacher George Martin as organist of St. Paul's in 1916; conducted the London Church Choirs Assoc. from 1914 until his death. He wrote several overtures on Scottish themes; a number of choral works; edited 144 Scottish songs in 8 vols.; publ. *A Short History of Harmony* (London, 1917).

Macpherson, Stewart, English organist and educator; b. Liverpool, March 29, 1865; d. London, March 27, 1941. He studied with W.C. Macfarren at the Royal Academy of Music (piano) and with G.A. Macfarren (composition); then taught harmony there; conducted the Westminster Orch. Society (1885–1902); in 1898 was appointed examiner to the Associated Board, in which capacity he visited Canada, Australia, and New Zealand (1900). He wrote a symph., several overtures, and a Mass; edited the *Music Student's Library* and the Joseph Williams Handbooks on Music series; publ. *Practical Harmony* (1894); *Practical Counterpoint* (1900); *Rudiments of Music* (1907); *350 Exercises in Harmony* (1907); *Evolution of Musical Design; Form in Music* (1908); *Music and Its Appreciation* (1910);

Aural Culture Based upon Musical Appreciation (with Ernest Read; in 3 parts: 1912, 1914, 1918); *Studies in Phrasing and Form* (1911); *Musical Education of the Child* (1915); *Studies in the Art of Counterpoint* (1928); *A Simple Introduction to the Principles of Tonality* (1929); *Cameos of Musical History* (1937).

Macque, Giovanni (Jean) de, Flemish composer; b. Valenciennes, c.1550; d. Naples, Sept. 1614. On his marriage certificate (1592) he is named "Fiammingo della città de Valencena"; a book of motets (Rome, 1596) describes him as a Belgian from Valenciennes. He studied with Philippe de Monte; then went to Rome (c.1570), where he became a member of the Compagnia dei Musici di Roma (organized in 1584); other members were Palestrina and Marenzio. In 1586 Macque went to Naples and entered the service of Don Fabrizio Gesualdo da Venosa, father of the composer Carlo Gesualdo. On May 20, 1590, Macque was appointed 2nd organist of the Church of the Annunciation in Naples. In 1594 he was appointed organist of the viceregal chapel, and in Dec. 1599 became its choir director. Among his pupils in Naples were Ascanio Mayone, Giovanni Maria Trabaci, Luigi Rossi, and Falconieri. Several of Macque's madrigals are found in Younge's *Musica transalpina* (1588) and in Morley's collection of Italian works (1598); extant keyboard pieces are reproduced in the *Monumenta musicae belgicae* (Antwerp, 1938; with a list of sources and a biographical sketch). Macque was one of the first to employ rhythmic transformations of a single theme (in canzonas), which were later used extensively by Frescobaldi; Macque also applied the keyboard technique of Cabezón's "diferencias" (variations).
BIBLIOGRAPHY: U. Prota-Giurleo, "Notizie storico-biografiche sul musicista belga Jean Macque," *Report of the First Congress of the International Society for Musical Research* (1930); A. Davison and W. Apel, *Historical Anthology of Music* (Cambridge, Mass., 1946); G. Reese, *Music in the Renaissance* (N.Y., 1954; 2nd ed., revised, 1959); L. Anderson, *Giovanni de Macque of Valencienes and the Evolution of Polyphonic Music in Naples at the End of the Sixteenth Century* (Diss., Univ. of Liège, 1970); W. Shindle, *The Madrigals of Giovanni de Macque* (Diss., Indiana Univ., 1970); F. Lippman, "Giovanni de Macque tra Roma e Napoli: Nuovi documenti," *Rivista Musicale Italiana,* XIII (1978).

MacRae, Gordon, American singer of popular music and actor; b. East Orange, N.J., March 12, 1921. He began making stage appearances as a child; then went to Hollywood, where he entered the movies; he sang in the screen versions of the Rodgers and Hammerstein musicals *Oklahoma* and *Carousel;* also performed as a vocalist in nightclubs and on television. In later years he was joined by his wife, **Sheila MacRae** (b. London, Sept. 24, 1924), who was also successful as a singer of popular music.

Macurdy, John, American bass; b. Detroit, March 18, 1929. He was educated at Wayne State Univ.; then began vocal studies with Avery Crew and studied dramatic interpretation with Boris Goldovsky. He joined the N.Y. City Opera in 1959; on Dec. 8, 1962, he made his Metropolitan Opera debut in a minor role; he remained on its roster for several seasons. In addition, he sang opera in Baltimore, Houston, San Francisco, Philadelphia, Glasgow, Milan, and Salzburg.

Madatov, Grigori, Russian flutist and composer; b. Baku, April 2, 1898; d. Moscow, March 14, 1968. He studied at the Moscow Cons. Upon graduation, he taught flute playing in Baku (1920–37) and at the Cons. of Tiflis (1938–44). In 1947 he joined the staff of the Musical Pedagogical Inst. in Moscow. He wrote many pieces for flute suitable as teaching material.

Maddy, Joseph Edgar, American educator and conductor; b. Wellington, Kans., Oct. 14, 1891; d. Traverse City, Mich., April 18, 1966. He studied at Bethany College, Wichita College, and the Columbia School of Music in Chicago; played the viola and clarinet; was a member of the Minneapolis Symph. Orch. (1909–14) and St. Paul Symph. (1914–18); supervisor of instrumental music in the public schools of Rochester, N.Y. (1918–20), and Richmond, Ind. (1920–24); instructor of public school methods at Earlham College (1922–24); in 1924, was appointed to the faculty of the Univ. of Michigan as a prof. of music education; in 1926 founded and conducted the National High School Orch., for which he established, with T.P. Giddings, the National Music Camp at Interlochen, Mich., in 1928.
BIBLIOGRAPHY: N. Browning, *Joe Maddy of Interlochen* (Chicago, 1963).

Madeira, Francis, American conductor; b. Jenkintown, Pa., Feb. 21, 1917. He studied piano and conducting at the Juilliard School of Music in N.Y. (1937–43). He was appointed to the faculty of Brown Univ. in 1943. In 1945 he organized the Rhode Island Phil. Orch. in Providence; resigned in 1980. He was also active as a concert pianist in the U.S. and in Europe; composed a number of symph. and other works.

Madeira, Jean (née **Browning**), American contralto; b. Centralia, Ill., Nov. 14, 1918; d. Providence, July 10, 1972. She studied piano with her mother, and was regarded as a child prodigy; at the age of 12, she was piano soloist with the St. Louis Symph. Orch.; took vocal lessons in St. Louis; then studied both piano and voice at the Juilliard School in N.Y. Subsequently she became a member of the Chautauqua Opera Co., and the San Carlo Opera Co. In 1948 she sang minor roles at the Metropolitan Opera; went to Europe; sang Carmen with the Vienna State Opera on Sept. 18, 1955, obtaining extraordinary success; on March 17, 1956, she appeared as Carmen with the Metropolitan Opera in N.Y., and this role became one of her best; she remained on the Metropolitan's roster until 1971. Her European tours included appearances at Covent Garden, La Scala, Paris Opéra, and Bayreuth. She was married to **Francis Madeira** on June 17, 1947.

Maderna, Bruno, remarkable Italian conductor and composer of modern propensities; b. Venice, April 21, 1920; d. Darmstadt, Germany, Nov. 13, 1973. He played violin as a child, instructed by his grandfather; his father was also a musician. He entered the Cons. of Milan, but his musical education was interrupted when he was drafted into the Alpine Regiment and was sent to fight on the Russian front. After the war, he studied in Milan and in Rome; then attended master classes in composition in Venice with Malipiero. In 1949 he went to Darmstadt, where he took conducting lessons with Scherchen. In his own conducting career Maderna promoted the most advanced works of the modern avant-garde. In 1955 he founded, with Luciano Berio, the electronic music studio at Milan Radio; from 1954 to 1967 he lectured at the summer courses in new music at Darmstadt, and after 1961 led the International Chamber Ensemble there; later taught at the Cons. of Rotterdam; in 1971 and 1972 he gave summer courses at the Berkshire Music Center in Tanglewood. He lived mostly in West Germany; became a naturalized German citizen in 1963. Stricken with cancer, he continued to conduct concerts as long as it was physically possible. Maderna was held in great esteem by composers of the international avant-garde, several of whom wrote special works for him. He was also a significant composer in his own right. WORKS: FOR THE STAGE: *Don Perlimplin,* radio opera after Lorca (1961; RAI Radio, Aug. 12, 1962); *Hyperion,* a "Lirica in forma di spettacolo" (1964; Venice Festival, Sept. 6, 1964; a composite of *Dimensioni III, Aria de Hyperion,* and tape); *Von A bis Z,* opera (1969; Darmstadt, Feb. 22, 1970); *Oedipe-Roi,* electronic ballet (Monte Carlo, Dec. 31, 1970); *Satyrikon,* opera after Petronius (1972; Scheveningen, the Netherlands, March 16, 1973; U.S. premiere, Tanglewood, Aug. 6, 1973). FOR ORCH.: *Introduzione e passacaglia* (1947); Concerto for 2 Pianos, Percussion, and 2 Harps (1948; Venice, Sept. 17, 1948); *Composizioni No. 1* (1949); *Composizioni No. 2* for Chamber Orch. (1950); *Improvvisazione I* and *II* (1951, 1952); *Composizioni in 3 tempi* (1954; Hamburg Radio, Dec. 8, 1954); Flute Concerto (1954); *Dark Rapture Crawl* (1957); Piano Concerto (1959; Darmstadt, Sept. 2, 1959); 3 oboe concertos: No. 1, with 23 Instruments (1962; revised 1965); No. 2 (1967; Cologne Radio, Nov. 10, 1967); No. 3 (1973; Amsterdam, July 6, 1973); *Dimensioni III* for Flute and Orch. (1963; Paris Radio, Dec. 12, 1963); *Stele per Diotima* for Orch., with cadenzas for Violin, Clarinet, Bass Clarinet, and Horn (1965; Cologne Radio, Jan. 19, 1966); *Dimensioni IV* (combination of *Dimensioni III* and *Stele per Diotima*); *Amanda* for Chamber Orch. (1966; Naples, Nov. 22, 1966); *Quadrivium* for 4 Percussionists and 4 Orch. Groups (1969); Violin Concerto (1969; Venice, Sept. 12, 1969); *Grande aulodia* for

Flute, Oboe, and Orch. (1969; Rome, Feb. 7, 1970); *Juilliard Serenade (Free Time I)* for Chamber Orch. and Tape Sounds (1970; N.Y., Jan. 31, 1971); *Music of Gaiety* for Solo Violin, Oboe, and Chamber Orch., based on pieces in the "Fitzwilliam Virginal Book" (1970); *Aura* (1971; Chicago Symph., March 23, 1972); *Biogramma* (1972); *Giardino religioso* for Chamber Ensemble (1972; Tanglewood, Aug. 8, 1972). FOR VOICE: *3 Greek Lyrics* for Soprano, Chorus, and Instruments (1948); *Studi per "Il Processo" di Kafka* for Narrator, Soprano, and Small Orch. (1949); *4 Briefe* for Soprano, Bass, and Chamber Orch. (1953); *Aria de "Hyperion"* for Soprano, Flute, and Orch. (1964); *Hyperion II* (combination of *Dimensioni III, Cadenza* for Flute, and *Aria da "Hyperion"*); *Hyperion III* (combination of *Hyperion* and *Stele per Diotima*); *Ausstrahlung* for Soprano, Chorus, and Orch. (1971); *Boswell's Journal* for Tenor and Chamber Orch. (N.Y., March 12, 1972). CHAMBER MUSIC: *Serenata* for 11 Instruments (1946; revised 1954); *Musica su 2 dimensioni* for Flute and Tape (1952; revised 1958); String Quartet (1955); *Serenata No. 2* for 11 Instruments (1957); *Serenata No. 4* for 20 Instruments and Tape (1961); *Honey rêves* for Flute and Piano (1961); *Aulodia per Lothar* for Oboe d'Amore and Guitar ad lib. (1965); *Widmung* for Solo Violin (1967); *Serenata per un satellite* for 7 Instruments (1969). ELECTRONIC MUSIC: *Notturno* (1955); *Syntaxis* for 4 different but unspecified timbres produced electronically (1956); *Continuo* (1958); *Dimensioni II, "Invenzioni sue una voce"* (1960); *Serenata No. 3* (1962); *Le Rire* (1964); *Ages* (with G. Pressburger, 1972). FOR PIANO: *B-A-C-H Variations* for 2 Pianos (1949). BIBLIOGRAPHY: K. Jansen, *"Bruno Maderna and Dutch Concert Life,"* containing an intimate account of Maderna's private life, *Keynote* (Amsterdam, 1980).

Madetoja, Leevi, outstanding Finnish composer; b. Oulu (Uleaborg), Feb. 17, 1887; d. Helsinki, Oct. 6, 1947. He studied in Helsinki with Järnefelt and Sibelius (1906–10); took lessons in Paris with Vincent d'Indy (1910–11) and in Vienna with Robert Fuchs (1911–12). Returning to Finland, he conducted the Helsinki Phil. (1912–14) and the Viipuri (Vyborg) Orch. (1914–16); taught at the Helsinki Cons. (1916–39); was also active as a music critic. Madetoja's music is inspired by Finnish melos; he is held in great esteem in Finland as a worthy continuator of the national Finnish school of composition, according to precepts established by Sibelius. WORKS: 2 operas: *Pohjalaisia* (*The Ostrobothnians;* Helsinki, Oct. 25, 1924) and *Juha* (Helsinki, Feb. 17, 1935); *Symphonic Suite* (1910); *Concert Overture* (1911); *Tanssinäky* for Orch. (*Dance Vision;* 1911–12); *Kullervo,* symph. poem (1913); 3 symphs. (1916, 1918, 1926); *Comedy Overture* (1923); ballet-pantomime, *Okon Fuoko* (Helsinki, Dec. 2, 1930); Piano Trio (1909); Violin Sonatina (1914); *Lyr-*

Madey – Maelzel

ic Suite for Cello and Piano (1922); many cantatas and solo songs; 40 a cappella works for male chorus; incidental music for plays; film music.

BIBLIOGRAPHY: K. Tuukkanen, *Leevi Madetoja* (Helsinki, 1947).

Madey, Boguslaw, Polish conductor and composer; b. Sosnowiec, May 31, 1932. He received diplomas in composition, piano, and conducting from the Academy of Music in Poznan; then went to England, where he took a course in conducting with Norman del Mar at the Guildhall School of Music in London (1959–60). Returning to Poland, he became conductor at the Warsaw Opera (1960–72); later was music director at the Grand Theater of Opera and Ballet in Lodz. He composed a Piano Concerto (1957); Flute Concerto (1960); a concerto for Voice and Instruments entitled *Transfiguration* (1965); some short piano pieces.

Madge, Geoffrey Douglas, extraordinary Australian pianist; b. Adelaide, Oct. 3, 1941. He studied piano with Clemens Leski at the Elder Cons. of the Univ. of Adelaide, graduating in 1959; toured Australia as a pianist in a piano trio (1959–63). In 1963 he went to Europe; studied piano with Géza Anda in Switzerland (1964) and with Peter Solymos in Hungary (1967). In 1971 he was appointed senior lecturer of classical and contemporary piano repertoire at the Royal Cons. of The Hague. As a pianist, he became known chiefly by his propaganda of ultra-modern music; his repertoire includes works by Ives, Sorabji, Xenakis, Boulez, Cage, Stockhausen, Wolpe, Barraqué, and Bussotti; a specialty is rarely played music of the Russian modernists, Mossolov, Obouhov, Roslavetz, Lourié, Alexandrov, and Wyschnegradsky. On June 11, 1982, at Utrecht, during the annual Holland Festival, he gave the 2nd complete performance (after 50 years) of Kaikhosru Sorabji's mammoth *Opus Clavicembalisticum;* he began it at 8:16 P.M. and finished it at 12:47 the next morning. On April 24, 1983, he gave another performance of the work at the Univ. of Chicago; then repeated the feat at Bonn, Germany, on May 10, 1983. On Sept. 19, 1979, as part of that year's International Society for Contemporary Music Festival in Athens, he gave the first complete performance of Nikos Skalkottas's 2-hour set of *32 Piano Pieces,* as well as his *4 Etudes.* His technical powers as a pianist are astonishing, and possibly without equal; certainly no other pianist has assembled such a repertoire of formidable modern works. Madge is a self-taught composer; he wrote a Viola Sonata (1963); a String Quartet (1965); a Violin Sonatina (1966); *Monkeys in a Cage,* a ballet for 12 Instruments (1976; Sydney Opera House, 1977); *Tendrils of the Rock,* 3 movements for Piano (1979); and a Piano Concerto (1979; Amsterdam, 1980).

Madriguera, Enric, Catalan-American composer; b. Barcelona, Feb. 17, 1904; d. Danbury, Conn., Sept. 7, 1973. He studied violin at the Barcelona Liceo Musical; in 1916 emigrated to the U.S., where he took a master course with Leopold Auer. Abandon-

ing a concert career, he devoted himself to the composition of tunes in the Latin American vein; of these the most popular were *Take It Away* and *Adios.* He organized a Latin American orch., and was named "Music Ambassador of the Americas" by the U.S. Congress.

Maegaard, Jan, Danish composer; b. Copenhagen, April 14, 1926. He studied music theory with Poul Schierbeck and B. Hjelbmborg; counterpoint with Knud Jeppesen and orchestration with J. Jersild at the Royal Cons. in Copenhagen (1945–50), and at the Univ. of Copenhagen, where he took a course in musicology with Jens Peter Larsen (*magister artis,* 1957). He then went to the U.S., where he studied musicography with Robert Nelson at the Univ. of Calif., Los Angeles (1958–59). Returning to Denmark, he taught at the Copenhagen Cons.; was appointed prof. at the Musicological Inst. of the Univ. of Copenhagen in 1971; received his D.Phil. for a 3-vol. dissertation, *Studies of the Evolution of Schoenberg's Dodecaphonic Method* (Copenhagen, 1972). Once more in America, he was guest lecturer at the State Univ. of N.Y. at Stony Brook (1974) and at the Univ. of Calif., Los Angeles (1978). He served on the board of the Society for Publishing Danish Music (1958–78).

WORKS: *Chamber Concerto No. 1* (1949); *Chamber Concerto No. 2* (1961–62); *Gaa udenom sletterne (Avoid the Plains)* for Chorus and Orch. (1953; Copenhagen, March 21, 1957); *Due tempi* for Orch. (Copenhagen, Aug. 31, 1961); music for a television production of *Antigone* for Chorus, Orch., and Tape (1966); *Suite* for Violin and Piano (1949); Trio for Oboe, Clarinet, and Bassoon (1950); Wind Quintet (1951); *Suite* for 2 Violins (1951); *Den gyldne harpe (The Golden Harp)* for Mezzo-soprano, Oboe, Cello, and Piano (1951); *Quasi una sonata* for Viola and Piano (1952); Bassoon Sonata (1952); *Variations impromptus* for Violin, Viola, Cello, and Piano (1953); *Jaevndøgnselegi (Equinox Elegy)* for Soprano, Cello, and Organ (1955); *Alter Duft aus Märchenzeit* for Piano Trio (1960); *Movimento* for Clarinet, Horn, Hammond Organ, String Quartet, and Percussion (1967); *Musica riservata No. 1* for String Quartet (1970); *Musica riservata No. 2* for Oboe, Clarinet, Saxophone, and Bassoon (1976); *Pastorale* for 2 Clarinets (1976); Piano Sonata (1955); choruses; songs; cadenzas; transcriptions of Bach, Mozart, and Schoenberg. He publ. a textbook on new music, *Musikalsk modernisme 1945–62* (Copenhagen, 1964; 2nd ed., 1971).

Maelzel, Johannes Nepomuk, German inventor of the metronome; b. Regensburg, Aug. 15, 1772; d. on board the brig *Otis* in the harbor of La Guaira, Venezuela, en route to Philadelphia, July 21, 1838. He studied music with his father, an organ manufacturer. In 1972 he went to Vienna, where he began constructing mechanical instruments, which attracted great attention in Vienna and subsequently in other European cities; of these the Panharmonicon was particularly effective; in 1812 he inaugurated an Art Cabinet, where he exhibited his inventions, including an automatic trumpeter. In 1816 he constructed the metronome, the idea for which he obtained from Winkel of Amsterdam (who had exhibited similar instruments, but without the scale divisions indicating the number of beats per minute). Maelzel put the metronome on the market, despite a lawsuit brought by Winkel, and the initial of his last name was thenceforth added to the indication of tempo in musical compositions (M.M., Maelzel's metronome). Beethoven wrote a piece for Maelzel's Panharmonicon, which he subsequently orchestrated and publ. as *Wellington's Victory.* Maelzel also exhibited an "automatic chess player." Though he claimed it as his invention, it was really designed and built by Wolfgang von Kempelen. He was able to impress the public by his "scientific" miracle, but it was soon exposed by skeptical observers, among them Edgar Allan Poe, as an ingenious mechanical contrivance concealing a diminutive chess master behind its gears. (In this connection, see C.M. Carroll, *The Great Chess Automaton,* N.Y., 1975.)

Maes, Jef, Belgian composer and violist; b. Antwerp, April 5, 1905. He enrolled at the Royal Flemish Cons. in Antwerp in 1922 and studied viola and chamber music; took private lessons in composition with Karel Candael. He played viola in several orchs. in Antwerp; from 1932 he taught violin at the music academy in Boom (near Antwerp), becoming its director in 1943; from 1942 to 1970 was on the faculty of the Flemish Cons. in Antwerp. In his compositions he continues the traditions of the Belgian national school.

WORKS: Opera buffa, *Marise* (1946); television opera, *De antikwaar* (*The Antique Dealer;* 1959; Antwerp Television, March 1963); ballet, *Tu auras nom . . . Tristan* (1960; Geneva, June 1963); orch. suite, 1963–64); *3 rythmen in dansvorm* for Orch. (1931); *Légende* for Violin and Orch. (1933); Viola Concerto (1937); *Concertstück* for Orch. (1938); *Ouvertura buffa* (1939); *Concertstück* for Trombone and Orch. (1944); Piano Concerto (1948); Violin Concerto (1951); 3 symphs. (1953, 1965, 1975); Concerto for Harpsichord and String Orch. (1955); *Burlesque* for Bassoon and Orch. (1957); *Rosa mystica* for Soprano, and Orch. or Piano (1959); *Kempische Suite* for Orch. or Wind Orch. (1960); *Concertante ouverture* (1961); *Arabesque en scherzo* for Flute and Orch. (1963); *Praeludium, Pantomime, Scherzo,* suite for Orch. (1966); *Partita* for String Orch. (1966); *Ouverture op een Belcanto Thema van Verdi* for Orch. or Wind Orch. (1967); *De verloofden* for Orch. (1969); *Mei 1871* for Narrator and Orch. (1971); *Music pour le podium* for Wind Orch. (1971); *Dialogue* for Violin and Orch. (1972); Sonatina for Flute and Viola (1934); Violin Sonata (1934); *Concertstück* for Trumpet and Piano (1957); *Prelude and Allegro* for 2 Trumpets, Horn, Trombone, and Tuba (1959); *Fantasia* for 2 Pianos (1960); Duo for Violin and Piano (1962); Trio for Violin, Viola, and Percussion (1964); *4 contrastes* for 4 Clarinets (1965); *Suite* for Percussion and Piano (1968); Piano Quartet (1970); songs.

Mága, Otmar, conductor; b. Brno, Czechoslovakia, to German-Hungarian parents, June 30, 1929. His family moved to Germany when he was 16, and he was educated at the Stuttgart Hochschule für Musik and the Univ. of Tübingen. He studied conducting with Paul van Kempen and Sergiu Celibidache in Siena; also with Ferdinand Leitner in Stuttgart. In 1963 he was named chief conductor of the Göttingen Symph.; in 1967, of the Nuremberg Symph. In 1970 he was appointed Generalmusikdirektor of the Bochum Symph (resigned this post in 1982); also served as permanent guest conductor of the NHK Symph. in Tokyo. He appeared as guest conductor also in Italy and France.

Magaloff, Nikita, Russian-Swiss pianist; b. St. Petersburg, Feb. 21, 1912. His family left Russia after the Revolution; he enrolled in the Paris Cons. as a student of Isidor Philipp; graduated with the Premier Prix at the age of 17. In 1939 he settled in Switzerland; in 1947 made his first American tour; also toured South America, South Africa, etc. From 1949 to 1960 he conducted a school of piano virtuosity at the Geneva Cons.; then gave summer courses at Taormina, Sicily, and at the Accademia Musicale Chigiana in Siena. In 1956 he became a Swiss citizen, living mostly in Coppet (Vaud). He is renowned for his lyrico-dramatic interpretations of Chopin, with lapidary attention to detail. He is also a composer; he wrote a Piano Toccata; Sonatina for Violin and Piano; songs; cadenzas for Mozart's piano concertos.

Maganini, Quinto, American flutist, conductor, arranger, and composer; b. Fairfield, Calif., Nov. 30, 1897; d. Greenwich, Conn., March 10, 1974. He played the flute in the San Francisco Symph. Orch. (1917) and in the N.Y. Symph. (1919–28); studied flute playing with Barrère in N.Y. and composition with Nadia Boulanger in France, at the American Cons. in Fontainebleau; in 1927, won a Pulitzer scholarship; in 1928–29, was awarded a Guggenheim fellowship; in 1930, became conductor of the N.Y. Sinfonietta; in 1932 he organized his own orch., the Maganini Chamber Symph., with which he toured widely. From 1939 till 1970 he was conductor of the Norwalk (Conn.) Symph.

WORKS: *Toulumne,* "a Californian Rhapsody," for Orch., with Trumpet obbligato (N.Y., Aug. 9, 1924); *South Wind,* orch. fantasy (N.Y., April 7, 1931); *Sylvan Symphony* (N.Y., Nov. 30, 1932); *Napoleon,* an orch. portrait (N.Y., Nov. 10, 1935); *The Royal Ladies,* orch. suite on airs ascribed to Marie Antoinette (Greenwich, Conn., Feb. 3, 1940); opera, *Tennessee's Partner* (American Opera Festival, Radio Station WOR, N.Y., May 28, 1942); numerous arrangements for small orch. of classical and modern works.

Mager, Jörg, German music theorist and pioneer in electronic music; b. Eichstätt, Nov. 6, 1880; d. Aschaffenburg, April 5, 1939. After completing his univ. studies, he became interested in electronic reproduction of sounds; constructed several instruments capable of producing microtonal intervals by electronic means, which he named Sphärophon, Elektrophon, and Partiturophon; he was also active in visual music for film. He publ. *Vierteltonmusik* (Aschaffenburg, 1916) and *Eine neue Epoche der Musik durch Radio* (Berlin, 1924).

Maggini, Giovanni Paolo, Italian violin maker; b. Brescia, Nov. (baptized, Nov. 29) 1579; d. there, c.1630. He worked in the shop of Gasparo da Salò; after his marriage in 1615, he set up his own workshop and became prosperous, thanks to the excellence of his manufacture; about 50 violins and 20 violas and cellos are extant; his instruments are prized particularly because of the softness of their tone in deep registers. His label reads: Gio. Paolo Maggini, Brescia.
BIBLIOGRAPHY: M.L. Huggins, *Giovanni Paolo Maggini, His Life and Work* (London, 1892); A. Berenzi, *Gli artefici liutai bresciani* (Brescia, 1890); A. Berenzi, *Di Giovanni Paolo Maggini* (Cremona, 1907).

Maggioni, Aurelio Antonio, Italian composer; b. Milan, April 8, 1908. He studied at the Milan Cons.; graduated as a pianist (1926) and composer (1933). He subsequently taught music theory in Parma (1938), in Florence (1939–51), in Milan (1952–54), in Lima, Peru (1954–59), and again in Milan from 1959. He wrote the opera *Il gioco di Soleima* (Bergamo, 1955); during his stay in Peru he composed a *Suite incaici* for Orch., making use of indigenous themes; also a mandatory amount of chamber music and minor pieces, all set in a competent Italianate style.

Magnard, (Lucien-Denis-Gabriel-) Albéric, French composer; b. Paris, June 9, 1865; d. Baron, Oise, Sept. 3, 1914 (killed by German soldiers in his house). He was brought up in an intellectual family; his father was editor of *Le Figaro.* He studied at the Paris Cons. with Dubois and Massenet, and later with Vincent d'Indy. He fell under the influence of Wagner, but succeeded in generating an element of national French music in his works; his mastery of instrumentation is incontestable, and the rhapsodic sweep of his symphs. is impressive. Despite these qualities, Magnard's symph. music never gained a stable place in the orch. repertoire; his operas were even less successful.
WORKS: Operas: *Yolande* (Brussels, Dec. 27, 1892); *Guercœur* (1900; revised by Guy-Ropartz, and produced at the Paris Opéra, April 24, 1931); *Bérénice* (Opéra-Comique, Paris, Dec. 15, 1911); 4 symphs. (1894, 1899, 1902, 1913); *Suite dans le style ancien* for Orch. (1892); *Hymne à la Justice* (1903); *Hymne à Vénus* (1906); Quintet for Wind Instruments and Piano (1904); String Quartet (1904); Piano Trio (1906); Violin Sonata; Cello Sonata; songs.
BIBLIOGRAPHY: M. Boucher, *Albéric Magnard* (Lyons, 1919); C. Laforêt, "L'Esthétique d'Albéric Magnard," *Revue Musicale* (1920); G. Carraud, *La Vie, l'œuvre et la mort d'Albéric Magnard* (Paris, 1921); B. Bardet, *Albéric Magnard, 1865–1914* (Paris, 1966).

Magne, Michel, French composer; b. Lisieux, March 20, 1930. He began to compose as a very young man, adopting at once an ultramodern method; his film score *Le Pain vivant* (1955) received critical acclaim; he has also experimented with electronic music; on May 26, 1955, he conducted in Paris his *Symphonie humaine* for 150 Performers, making use of inaudible "infrasounds" to produce a physiological reaction by powerful low frequencies. He wrote the musical score for Françoise Sagan's ballet *Le Rendez-vous manqué* (1957).

Magomayev, Muslim, Azerbaijani composer; b. Shusha, Sept. 18, 1885; d. Baku, July 28, 1937. He began his musical career as an improviser, and his first opera, *Shah Ismail* (1916), was a series of songs and interludes on native themes. His 2nd opera, *Nergiz* (Baku, Jan. 1, 1936), is based on the events of the Russian Revolution.
BIBLIOGRAPHY: G. Ismailova, *Muslim Magomayev* (Baku, 1975).

Mahaim, Ivan, Swiss physician, amateur violinist, and writer on music; b. Liège, June 25, 1897; d. Lausanne, Dec. 3, 1965. He studied violin with Alfred Pochon in Lausanne; held the post of associate prof. in cardiology at the Univ. of Lausanne. He publ. a highly valuable 2-vol. edition, *Beethoven, Naissance et renaissance des derniers quatuors* (Paris, 1964); contributed many articles on Beethoven to various publications.

Mahillon, Victor, Belgian manufacturer of musical instruments and writer on acoustics; b. Brussels, March 10, 1841; d. Saint-Jean, Cap-Ferrat, June 17, 1924. He was the son of **Charles Mahillon** (1813–87), founder of the manufacturing firm of that name; he worked in his father's shop as a youth; applied himself to a study of acoustics; in 1869 he began publishing a periodical, *L'Echo Musical,* which he abandoned shortly before his father's death; then assumed the management of the factory; made excellent reproductions of rare instruments, among them a complete collection of all the wind instruments in use during the 16th and 17th centuries. In 1876 he became custodian of the instrumental museum of the Cons. of Brussels (founded by Fétis) and greatly enlarged the collection (more than 3,500 specimens).
WRITINGS: *Tableau synoptique des voix et de tous les instruments de musique; Tableau synoptique de la science de l'harmonie; Elements d'acoustique musicale et instrumentale* (1874); *Catalogue descriptif et analytique du Musée instrumental du Conservatoire Royal de Musique de Bruxelles* (1880; 2nd ed., 5 vols., 1893–1922); *Le Matériel sonore des orchestres de symphonie, d'harmonie, et de fanfares* (1897); *Les Instruments à vent: I. Le Trombone, Son histoire, sa théorie, sa construction;* II. *Le Cor;* III. *La Trompette* (1907).

Mahler, Fritz, Austrian-American conductor, nephew of **Gustav Mahler;** b. Vienna, July 16, 1901; d. Winston-Salem, N.C., June 18, 1973. He studied composition in Vienna with Schoenberg, Anton von Webern, and Alban Berg; musicology with Guido Adler at the Univ. of Vienna (1920–24); conducting with Leopold Reichwein. He conducted summer orchs. in Bad Hall (1924–26); light opera at the Volksoper in Vienna; in 1930–35, was conductor of the radio orch. in Copenhagen; in 1936 emigrated to America, where he taught at the Juilliard Summer School; was conductor of the Erie (Pa.) Phil. Orch. (1947–53); in 1953–64, conductor of the Hartford (Conn.) Symph. Orch.

Mahler, Gustav, great Austrian composer and conductor; b. Kalischt, Bohemia, July 7, 1860; d. Vienna, May 18, 1911. He attended school in Iglau; in 1875 entered the Vienna Cons. where he studied piano with Julius Epstein, harmony with Robert Fuchs, and composition with Franz Krenn. He also took academic courses in history and philosophy at the Univ. of Vienna (1877–80). In the summer of 1880 he received his first engagement as a conductor, at the operetta theater in the town of Hall in Upper Austria; subsequently he held posts as theater conductor at Ljubljana (1881), Olmütz (1882), Vienna (1883), and Kassel (1883-85). In 1885 he served as 2nd Kapellmeister to Anton Seidl at the Prague Opera, where he gave several performances of Wagner's operas. From 1886 to 1888 he was assistant to Arthur Nikisch in Leipzig; in 1888 he received the important appointment of music director of the Royal Opera in Budapest. In 1891 he was engaged as conductor at the Hamburg Opera; during his tenure there he developed a consummate technique for conducting. In 1897 he received a tentative offer as music director of the Vienna court opera, but there was an obstacle to overcome. Mahler was Jewish, and although there was no overt anti-Semitism in the Austrian government, an Imperial appointment could not be given to a Jew. Mahler was never orthodox in his religion, and had no difficulty in converting to Catholicism, which was the prevailing faith in Austria. He held this position at the Vienna court opera for 10 years; under his guidance it reached the highest standards of artistic excellence. Mahler became an undisputed dictator of music in Vienna. Even the imperial Cosima Wagner adopted a deferential tone in her requests for Mahler's favors, especially when it concerned Siegfried Wagner's operas, which Mahler reluctantly accepted for performances. In 1898 Mahler was engaged to succeed Hans Richter as director of the Vienna Phil. Concerts. Here, as in his direction of opera, he proved a great interpreter, but he also allowed himself considerable freedom in rearranging the orchestration of classical scores when he felt it would redound to greater effect. He also aroused antagonism among the players by his autocratic behavior toward them. He resigned from the Vienna Phil. in 1901; in 1907 he also resigned from the Vienna court opera. In the meantime, he became immersed in strenuous work as a composer; he confined himself exclusively to composition of symph. music, sometimes with vocal parts; because of his busy schedule as conductor, he could compose

only in the summer months, in a villa on the Wörthersee in Carinthia. In 1902 he married Alma Schindler; they had 2 daughters. The younger daughter, Anna Mahler, was briefly married to Ernst Krenek; the elder daughter died in infancy. Alma Mahler studied music with Zemlinsky, who was the brother-in-law of Arnold Schoenberg.

Having exhausted his opportunities in Vienna, Mahler accepted the post of principal conductor of the Metropolitan Opera in N.Y. in 1907. He made his American debut there on Jan. 1, 1908, conducting *Tristan und Isolde.* In 1909 he was appointed conductor of the N.Y. Phil. Society. His performances both at the Metropolitan and with the N.Y. Phil. were enormously successful with the audiences and the N.Y. music critics, but inevitably he had conflicts with the board of trustees in both organizations, which were mostly commanded by rich women. He resigned from the Metropolitan Opera; on Feb. 21, 1911, he conducted his last concert with the N.Y. Phil. and then returned to Vienna; he died there of pneumonia on May 18, 1911, at the age of 50. The N.Y. newspapers published lurid accounts of his struggle for artistic command with the regimen of the women of the governing committee. Alma Mahler was quoted as saying that although in Vienna even the Emperor himself did not dare to order Mahler about, in N.Y. he had to submit to the whims of 10 ignorant women. The newspaper editorials mourned Mahler's death, but sadly noted that his N.Y. tenure was a failure. As to Mahler's own compositions, the *N.Y. Tribune* said bluntly, "We cannot see how any of his music can long survive him." His symphs. were sharply condemned in the press as being too long, too loud, and too discordant. It was not until the 2nd half of the 20th century that Mahler became fully recognized as a composer, the last great Romantic symphonist. Mahler's symphs. were drawn on the grandest scale, and the technical means employed for the realization of his ideas was correspondingly elaborate. The sources of his inspiration were twofold: the lofty concepts of universal art, akin to those of Bruckner, and ultimately stemming from Wagner; and the simple folk melos of the Austrian countryside, in pastoral moods recalling the intimate episodes in Beethoven's symphs. True to his Romantic nature, Mahler attached descriptive titles to his symphs.; the first was surnamed *Titan;* the 2nd, *Resurrection;* the 3rd, *Ein Sommermorgentraum;* and the 5th, *The Giant.* The great 8th became known as "symph. of a thousand," because it required about 1,000 instrumentalists, vocalists, and soloists for performance; however, this sobriquet was the inspiration of Mahler's agent, not of Mahler himself. Later in life Mahler tried to disassociate his music from their programmatic titles; he even claimed that he never used them in the first place, contradicting the evidence of the MSS, in which the titles appear in Mahler's own handwriting. Mahler was not an innovator in his harmonic writing; rather, he brought the Romantic era to a culmination by virtue of the expansiveness of his emotional expression and the grandiose design of his musical structures. Morbid by nature, Mahler brooded upon the inevitability of death; one of his

Mahler

most poignant compositions was the cycle for voice and orch. *Kindertotenlieder (Songs of the Death of Children);* he wrote it shortly before the death of his little daughter, and somehow he blamed himself for this seeming anticipation of his personal tragedy. In 1910 he consulted Sigmund Freud in Vienna, but the treatment was brief and apparently did not help Mahler to resolve his psychological problems. Unquestionably, Mahler suffered from an irrational feeling of guilt. In the 2nd movement of his unfinished 10th Symph., significantly titled *Purgatorio,* he wrote on the margin, "Madness seizes me, annihilates me," and appealed to the Devil to take possession of his soul. But he never was clinically insane.

Mahler's importance to the evolution of modern music is very great; the early works of Schoenberg and Alban Berg show the influence of Mahler's concepts. A society was formed in the U.S. in 1941 "to develop in the public an appreciation of the music of Bruckner, Mahler and other moderns." An International Gustav Mahler Society was formed in Vienna in 1955, with Bruno Walter as honorary president. On Mahler's centennial, July 7, 1960, the government of Austria issued a memorial postage stamp of one-and-a-half shillings, with Mahler's portrait.

WORKS: SYMPHS.: No. 1, in D, *Titan* (1883–88; Budapest, Nov. 20, 1889, composer conducting; U.S. premiere, N.Y., Dec. 16, 1909, composer conducting; a rejected movement, entitled *Blumine,* was reincorporated and perf. separately by Benjamin Britten at the Adleburgh Music Festival on June 18, 1967); No. 2, in C minor, *Resurrection,* with Soprano, Contralto, and Chorus (1887–94; Berlin, Dec. 13, 1895, composer conducting; American premiere, N.Y., Dec. 8, 1908, composer conducting; No. 3, in D minor, *Ein Sommermorgentraum* (1893–96; Krefeld, June 9, 1902, composer conducting; American premiere, N.Y., Feb. 8, 1922, Mengelberg conducting); No. 4, in G (1899–1901; Munich, Nov. 25, 1901, composer conducting; American premiere, N.Y., Nov. 6, 1904); No. 5, in C-sharp minor, *The Giant* (1901–2; Cologne, Oct. 18, 1904, composer conducting; American premiere, Cincinnati, March 24, 1905); No. 6, in A minor (1903–5; Essen, May 27, 1906, composer conducting; American premiere, N.Y., Dec. 11, 1946, Mitropoulos conducting); No. 7, in E minor (1904–6; Prague, Sept. 19, 1908, composer conducting; American premiere, Chicago, April 15, 1921); No. 8, in E-flat, "Symphony of a Thousand," with 8 Solo Voices, Adult and Children's Choruses (1906–7; Munich, Sept. 12, 1910, composer conducting; American premiere, Philadelphia, March 2, 1916, Stokowski conducting); No. 9, in D (1909–10; posthumous premiere, Vienna, June 26, 1912, Bruno Walter conducting; American premiere, Boston, Oct. 16, 1931, Koussevitzky conducting); No. 10, in F-sharp minor (sketched 1909–10, unfinished; 2 movements, *Adagio* and *Purgatorio,* perf. in Vienna, Oct. 12, 1924, Franz Schalk conducting; publ. in facsimile, 1924, by Alma Mahler; a performing version of the 10th Symph., using the sketches then available and leaving the 2 scherzo movements in fragmentary form, was made by Deryck Cooke; it

was broadcast by the BBC from London for the first time on Dec. 19, 1960; Alma Mahler approved of Cooke's realization; further sketches were made available, and a full performing version was premiered in London, Aug. 13, 1964; the U.S. premiere followed in Philadelphia on Nov. 5, 1965; a final revision of the score was made in 1972).

FOR VOICE: *Das klagende Lied* for Soprano, Contralto, Tenor, Chorus, and Orch. (1878–80; revised 1896–98; Vienna, Feb. 17, 1901, composer conducting); *Lieder und Gesänge aus der Jugendzeit,* 14 songs for Voice and Piano (1880–91); *Lieder eines fahrenden Gesellen,* 4 songs with Orch. (1883–85; Berlin, March 16, 1896, Mahler conducting); 14 Lieder from *Das Knaben Wunderhorn* for Voice and Orch. (1892–1901); 5 songs, to poems by Rückert (1901–3); *Kindertotenlieder,* 5 songs, with Piano or Orch., to poems by Rückert (1901–4; Vienna, Jan. 29, 1905, composer conducting); *Das Lied von der Erde,* symph. for Contralto or Baritone, Tenor, and Orch. (1907–9; Munich, Nov. 20, 1911, Bruno Walter conducting; Philadelphia, Dec. 14, 1916, Stokowski conducting).

Mahler destroyed the MSS of several of his early works, among them a piano quintet, performed in Vienna on July 11, 1878, with the composer at the piano, and 3 unfinished operas: *Herzog Ernst von Schwaben,* to a drama by Uhland; *Die Argonauten,* from a trilogy by Grillparzer, and *Rübezahl,* after Grimm's fairy tales. He further made an arrangement of Weber's *Die drei Pintos* (Leipzig, Jan. 20, 1888, composer conducting) and *Oberon* (c.1907); also arranged Bruckner's 3rd Symph. for 2 Pianos (1878). Mahler made controversial reorchestrations of symphs. by Beethoven, Schumann, and Bruckner, and a version for String Orch. of Beethoven's String Quartet in C-sharp minor, op. 131.

BIBLIOGRAPHY: L. Schiedermair, *Gustav Mahler* (Leipzig, 1901); Paul Stefan, *Gustav Mahlers Erbe* (Munich, 1908; a polemic against Felix Weingartner, Mahler's successor in Vienna); *Gustav Mahler. Ein Bild seiner Persönlichkeit in Widmungen* (Munich, 1910); Paul Stefan, *Gustav Mahler. Eine Studie über Persönlichkeit und Werk* (Munich, 1910; 4th augmented ed., 1921; Eng. trans., N.Y., 1913); R. Specht, *Gustav Mahler* (Berlin, 1913); Guido Adler, *Gustav Mahler* (Vienna, 1916); A. Neisser, "Gustav Mahler," *Reclams Universal-Bibliothek* (Berlin, 1918); H.F. Redlich, *Gustav Mahler: Eine Erkenntnis* (Nuremberg, 1919); Paul Bekker, *Mahlers Sinfonien* (Berlin, 1921); A. Roller, *Die Bildnisse Gustav Mahlers* (Leipzig, 1922); R. Mengleberg, *Gustav Mahler* (1923); Natalie Bauer-Lechner, *Erinnerungen an Gustav Mahler* (Vienna, 1923); Alma Maria Mahler, *Briefe Gustav Mahlers* (Berlin, 1924); W. Hutschenruyter, *Gustav Mahler* (The Hague, 1927); H. Holländer, "Gustav Mahler," *Musical Quarterly* (Oct. 1931); G. Engel, *Gustav Mahler* (Vienna, 1936; also in Eng. trans., N.Y., 1957); Alma Maria Mahler, *Gustav Mahler: Erinnerungen und Briefe* (Amsterdam, 1940; in Eng. as *Memories and Letters,* London, 1946); Egon Wellesz, "The Symphonies of Gustav Mahler," *Music Review* (Jan.–April 1940); Bruno Walter (with Ernst Krenek), *Gustav Mahler* (N.Y., 1941); Dika Newlin,

Bruckner—Mahler—Schoenberg (N.Y., 1947; 2nd ed., revised, 1978); Arnold Schoenberg, "Gustav Mahler," *Style and Idea* (N.Y., 1950); N. Loeser, *Gustav Mahler* (Haarlem, 1950); Hans Tischler, "Mahler's Impact on the Crisis of Tonality," *Music Review* (April 1951); Theodore Reik, *The Haunting Melody* (N.Y., 1953); Erwin Stein, *Orpheus in New Guises* (London, 1953); H.F. Redlich, *Bruckner and Mahler*, The Master Musicians Series (London, 1955; 2nd ed., revised, 1963); Donald Mitchell, "Some Notes on Mahler's Tenth Symphony," *Musical Times* (Dec. 1955); idem, *Gustav Mahler: The Early Years* (London, 1958; revised ed., 1980); Willi Reich, ed., *Gustav Mahler: Im eigenen Wort, im Wort der Freunde* (Zürich, 1958); T. Adorno, *Mahler: Eine musikalische Physiognomik* (Frankfurt, 1960); S. Vestdijk, *Gustav Mahler* (The Hague, 1960); N. Cardus, *Gustav Mahler: His Mind and His Music*, vol. I (London, 1965); Heinrich Kralik, *Gustav Mahler* (Vienna, 1968); Jack Diether, "Notes on Some Mahler Juvenilia," *Chord and Discord*, III/I (1969); Kurt Blaukopf, *Gustav Mahler, oder Zeitgenosse der Zukunft* (Vienna, 1969); Henry-Louis de La Grange, *Mahler*, vol. I (N.Y., 1973); David Holbrook, *Gustav Mahler and the Courgage to Be* (N.Y., 1975); Donald Mitchell, *Gustav Mahler: The Wunderhorn Years* (Boulder, Colo., 1976); Anne Shelley, ed., *Gustav Mahler in Vienna* (N.Y., 1976); Kurt Blaukopf, ed., *Mahler. A Documentary Study* (N.Y., 1976); P. Ruzicka, *Mahler: Eine Herausforderung* (Wiesbaden, 1977); C. Floros, *Gustav Mahler* (2 vols.; Wiesbaden, 1977); Egon Gartenberg, *Mahler: The Man and His Music* (N.Y., 1978); Edward R. Reilly, *Gustav Mahler und Guido Adler: Zur Geschichte einer Freundschaft* (Vienna, 1978; in Eng., Cambridge, 1982); Bruno and Eleanore Vondenhoff, *Gustav Mahler Dokumentation* (Tutzing, 1978); D. Cooke, *Gustav Mahler: An Introduction to His Music* (London, 1980); H.H. Eggebrecht, *Die Musik Gustav Mahlers* (Munich, 1982); E. Seckerson, *Mahler: His Life and Times* (N.Y., 1982); D. Greene, *Mahler: Consciousness and Temporality* (N.Y., 1984).

Mahrenholz, Christhard, German musicologist and writer on ecclesiastical subjects; b. Adelebsen, near Göttingen, Aug. 11, 1900. He studied organ as a youth; took courses at the Leipzig Cons. with Schering; received his Ph.D. in 1923 from the Univ. of Göttingen with the dissertation *Samuel Scheidt: Sein Leben und Werk* (Leipzig, 1924; reprinted 1968); upon graduation, devoted himself mainly to the cause of Lutheran music. In 1933 he was elected president of the Association of Evangelical German Church Choirs; was co-editor of the magazine *Musik und Kirche*. In 1960 he became abbott of the Amelungsborn Cloister; in 1967 he retired from active work. Among his publications are *Luther und die Kirchenmusik* (Kassel, 1937); *Die Orgelregister* (Kassel, 1930; 2nd ed., 1944; reprinted 1968); *Die Berechnung der Orgelpfeifenmensuren vom Mittelalter bis zur Mitte des 19.Jh.* (Kassel, 1938). He edited works by Scheidt and other German composers; was co-editor of *Handbuch der deutschen evangelischen Kirchenmusik* (Göttingen, several vols., beginning 1932). A collection of his articles, *Musicologica et liturgica: Gesammelte Aufsätze von Christhard Mahrenholz*, edited by K.F. Müller, was publ. in Kassel in 1960, as an homage on his 60th birthday; a Festschrift, *Kerygma und Melos*, containing a bibliography of his writings from 1960 to 1970, was publ. for his 70th birthday in 1970 in Kassel and Berlin.

Maiboroda, Georgi, Ukrainian composer; b. in a farmhouse in Pelekhovshchina, near Poltava, Dec. 1, 1913. He studied at the Kiev Cons. with Revutsky, graduating in 1941; from 1952 he taught there. His music tends toward heroically patriotic themes according to the precepts of socialist realism.
WORKS: Operas: *Milana* (1957); *The Arsenal* (1960); *Taras Shevchenko* (1964); *Yaroslav the Wise* (1975); cantata, *Friendship of Peoples* (1948); 3 symphs. (1940, 1952, 1976); Concerto for Voice and Orch. (1969); numerous vocal pieces.
BIBLIOGRAPHY: O.S. Zinkevich, *Georgi Maiboroda* (Kiev, 1973; in Ukrainian).

Maichelbeck, Franz Anton, German composer of keyboard music; b. Reichenau, July 6, 1702; d. Freiburg im Breisgau, June 14, 1750. He studied theology in Freiburg, then went to Rome to study music; returned to Freiburg and became organist at the Cathedral and a prof. of Italian at the Univ. He publ. *Die auf dem Clavier spielende Caecilia* (1736; contains 8 sonatas) and *Die auf dem Clavier lehrende Caecilia* (1738; a book of studies).

Maier, Guy, American pianist; b. Buffalo, Aug. 15, 1891; d. Santa Monica, Calif., Sept. 24, 1956. He studied at the New England Cons. in Boston, and privately with Schnabel. After a series of solo appearances in the U.S., he formed, with Lee Pattison, a partnership as duo-pianists, and gave numerous concerts with him (until 1931). From 1933 till 1946 he taught at the Juilliard School of Music in N.Y.; in 1946 he went to California. He made numerous transcriptions of various classical works for piano.

Maier, Julius Joseph, German music scholar; b. Freiburg im Breisgau, Dec. 29, 1821; d. Munich, Nov. 21, 1889. He studied for a government career, but in 1849 took up music under Haussmann in Leipzig; taught for a time at the Munich School of Music; in 1857 was appointed custodian of the music dept. of the Munich Library. He publ.: *Klassische Kirchenwerke alter Meister* (1845; arranged for Men's Chorus); *Auswahl englischer Madrigale* (1863); the valuable catalogue *Die musikalischen Handschriften der Königlichen Hof- und Staatsbibliothek in München* (1879; only Part I, *Die Handschriften bis zum Ende des 17. Jahrhunderts*).

Maillart, Louis (called **Aimé**), French composer; b. Montpellier, March 24, 1817; d. Moulins, May 26, 1871. He studied at the Paris Cons. with Halévy and Leborne (composition) and with Guérin (violin); won the Grand Prix de Rome in 1841.

WORKS: 6 operas, all first perf. at Paris: *Gastibelza* (Nov. 15, 1847); *Le Moulin des tilleuls* (1849); *La Croix de Marie* (1852); *Les Dragons de Villars* (Sept. 19, 1856; his most successful opera, perf. also in Germany under the title *Das Glöckchen des Eremiten*); *Les Pêcheurs de Catane* (Dec. 19, 1860); *Lara* (March 21, 1864); also several cantatas and other sacred works.

Maillart, Pierre, Belgian theorist; b. Valenciennes, 1551; d. Tournai, July 16, 1622. He was chorister at the Flemish chapel in Madrid (1563–70); returning to his native land, he entered the Univ. of Louvain; was later in Antwerp (1574) and Tournai (1581), where he became cantor in 1589. He publ. *Les Tons, ou Discours sur les modes de musique* (Tournai, 1610; reprinted 1972).

Mailly, Alphonse-Jean-Ernest, Belgian organist and composer; b. Brussels, Nov. 27, 1833; d. there, Jan. 10, 1918. He studied at the Cons. of Brussels; taught piano and organ there; gave numerous and successful organ concerts in France and England; wrote various pieces for piano and organ.

Mailman, Martin, American composer; b. New York, June 30, 1932. He studied composition with Louis Mennini, Wayne Barlow, Bernard Rogers, and Howard Hanson at the Eastman School of Music in Rochester, N.Y., graduating in 1954 (M.M., 1955; Ph.D., 1960); taught at the U.S. Navy School of Music (1955–57), Eastman School of Music (1958–59), Ford Foundation Young Composers Project (1959–61), and East Carolina College (1961–66); in 1966 he was appointed to the faculty of North Texas State Univ. in Denton. In 1982 he received a grant from the National Endowment for the Arts.
WORKS: OPERA: *The Hunted* (Rochester, April 27, 1959). FOR ORCH.: 2 symphs. (1969, 1979); *Dance in 2 Moods* (1952); *Autumn Landscape* (1954); *Jubilate* (1955); *Elegy* (1955); *Cantiones* (1957); Prelude and Fugue No. 1 (1959); *Partita* for String Orch. (1960); *Gateway City Overture* (1960); *Suite in 3 Movements* (1961); Prelude and Fugue No. 2 (1963); Sinfonietta (1964); *Generations 2* for 3 String Orchs. and Percussion (1969); Violin Concerto (1982). FOR BAND: *Partita* (1958); *Commencement March* (1960); *4 Miniatures* (1960); *Geometrics* No. 1 (1961); *Geometrics in Sound* No. 2 (1962); *Alarums* (1962); Concertino for Trumpet and Band (1963); *Liturgical Music* (1964); *Geometrics* No. 3 (1965); *Geometrics* No. 4 (1968); *Associations No. 1* (1968–69); *In Memoriam Frankie Newton* (1970); *Shouts, Hymns and Praises* (1972); *Geometrics* No. 5 (1976); *Night Vigil* (1980); *Exaltations* (1981). VOCAL MUSIC: *Alleluia* for Chorus and Band (1960); *Leaves of Grass* for Narrator, Chorus, and Band (1963); *Shakespearean Serenade* for Chorus and 9 Instruments (1968); *Requiem, Requiem* for Chorus, Soloists, and Orch. (1970); *Let Us Now Praise Famous Men* for Solo Voice, Narrators, and Band (1975); *Generations 3: Messengers* for Children's Choirs, Solo Voice, and Stage Band (1977). CHAMBER MUSIC: *Promenade* for Brass and Percussion (1953); *Brevard Fanfare* for Brass (1961); String Quartet (1962); *4 Divisions* for Percussion Ensemble (1966); *Partita* No. 4 for 9 Players (1967); *2 Fanfares* for Brass (1970); *Clastics: Formations* for Solo Cello (1977); *Clastics 2* for Euphonium and Percussion (1979). FOR PIANO: *Petite Partita* (1961); *Variations on a Short Theme* (1966); *Martha's Vineyard* (1969); *In Memoriam Sylvia Scionti* (1974); *Clastics 3* for 2 Pianos (1980).

Mainardi, Enrico, Italian cellist and composer; b. Milan, May 19, 1897; d. Munich, April 10, 1976. He studied cello and composition at the Milan Cons., graduating in 1920; then went to Berlin, where he was a student of Hugo Becker. He played chamber music; appeared in concerts with Dohnányi; then formed a trio with the flutist Gazzelloni and the pianist Agosti; taught cello at the Santa Cecilia Academy in Rome, beginning in 1933; later went to live in Germany.
WORKS: 3 cello concertos: No. 1 (1943; Rome, May 13, 1947; composer soloist) No. 2 (1960); No. 3, with String Orch. (1966); *Musica per archi; Elegie* for Cello and String Orch. (1957); Concerto for 2 Cellos and Orch. (1969; Freiburg, West Germany, Oct. 12, 1970); *Divertimento* for Cello and String Orch. (1972); 2 unnumbered string trios (1939, 1954); *Suite* for Cello and Piano (1940); Cello Sonatina (1943); *Notturno* for Piano Trio (1947); String Quartet (1951); Cello Sonata (1955); Sonata and *Sonata breve* for Solo Cello; *7 studi brevi* for Solo Cello (1961); *Sonata quasi fantasia* for Cello and Piano (1962); Violin Sonata; Piano Quartet (1968); Viola Sonata (1968); *Burattini,* suite of 12 pieces for Cello and Piano (1968); Trio for Clarinet, Cello, and Piano (1969); String Quintet (1970); Piano Sonatina (1941); other piano pieces.

Maine, Basil Stephen, English writer on music; b. Norwich, March 4, 1894; d. Sheringham, Norfolk, Oct. 13, 1972. He studied with Stanford, Rootham, and Dent at Queen's College in Cambridge; was active after graduation as a schoolteacher and occasionally an actor; in 1921 he became a music director in London; was music critic there in 1925–37; was ordained a priest in 1939. He publ. a number of monographs about music, among them biographies of *Elgar* (2 vols., London, 1933); *Chopin* (London 1933; 2nd ed., 1948); also collections of essays: *The Glory of English Music* (1937); *The Best of Me; A Study in Autobiography* (London, 1937); *Basil Maine on Music* (1945); *Twang with Our Music, Being a Set of Variants to Mark the Completion of Thirty Years' Practice in the Uncertain Science of Music Criticism* (London, 1957). He also composed some choral works and organ pieces.

Mainwaring, John, English churchman and first biographer of Handel; b. Drayton Manor, Staffordshire, c.1724; d. Church Stetton, April 15, 1807. He was educated at St. John's College, Cambridge; was ordained in 1748; in 1749 became rector of Church Stetton, Shropshire; was a Fellow of St. John's College, 1748–88; then became Lady Margaret Prof. of Divinity at Cambridge Univ. His biography of Handel, which utilized material provided by John Christopher Smith, appeared under the title *Memoirs of the Life of the Late George Frederic Handel* (London, 1760); a portion of the biography was written by Robert Price; it was trans. into German by J. Mattheson (Hamburg, 1761).

Mainzer, Joseph, German singing teacher and musical journalist; b. Trier, Oct. 21, 1801; d. Salford, Lancashire, Nov. 10, 1851. He was a chorister at the Trier Cathedral; then studied music in Darmstadt, Munich, and Vienna; returning to his native town, he was ordained a priest; taught at the seminary there, and publ. a sight-singing method, *Singschule* (1831). He then abandoned the priesthood; moved to Brussels (1833), and then to Paris (1834), where he started the short-lived *Chronique Musicale de Paris* (1838). In 1841 he went to England; lived for a time in London, and finally established himself in Manchester as a singing teacher. In 1844 he began publication of the monthly *Mainzer's Musical Times and Singing Circular,* which in 1846 became the *Musical Times* (publ. without interruption through nearly one and a half centuries). Mainzer mastered the English language to such an extent that he was able to engage in aggressive musical journalism. His methods of self-advertising were quite uninhibited; he arranged singing courses in open-air gatherings, and had pamphlets printed with flamboyant accounts of receptions tendered him. WRITINGS: *Singschule* (Trier, 1831); *Méthode de chant pour les enfants* (Paris, 1835); *Méthode de chant pour voix d'hommes* (Paris, 1836); *Bibliothèque élémentaire de chant* (Paris, 1836); *Méthode pratique de piano pour enfants* (Paris, 1837); *Abécédaire de chant* (Paris, 1837); *École chorale* (Paris, 1838); *Esquisses musicales, ou Souvenirs de voyage* (Paris, 1838–39); *Cent mélodies enfantines* (Paris, 1840); *Singing for the Million* (London, 1841).

BIBLIOGRAPHY: Percy A. Scholes, "The Mainzer Movement," in *The Mirror of Music* (London, 1947; vol. 1, pp. 3–10).

Mair, Franz, Austrian composer; b. Weikersdorf, in the Marchfeld, March 15, 1821; d. Vienna, Nov. 14, 1893. He was founder (1883) and conductor of the Vienna Schubertbund; composed music to *Die Jungfrau von Orleans* and other theatrical productions; wrote a number of male choruses and a cycle of 15 folk songs of various nations, arranged for Men's Chorus and Orch., as *Die Völker und ihre Lieder.* His reminiscences were publ. by the Schubertbund under the title *Aus meinem Leben* (Vienna, 1897).

Maison, René, Belgian tenor; b. Frameries, Nov. 24, 1895; d. Mont-Dore, France, July 15, 1962. He studied at the Cons. of Brussels, and later went to the Paris Cons.; was on the roster of the Monte Carlo Opera (1922), then of the Opéra-Comique in Paris, and at Covent Garden in London. He was a member of the Chicago Civic Opera Co. (1927–32) and the Teatro Colón in Buenos Aires (1934–37); then joined

the Metropolitan Opera in N.Y. (debut as Walther in *Die Meistersinger,* Feb. 3, 1936), remaining there until 1943.

Maitland, John Alexander Fuller. See **Fuller-Maitland, John Alexander.**

Maitland, Rollo F., American organist; b. Williamsport, Pa., Dec. 10, 1884; d. Philadelphia, April 7, 1953. He was taught the rudiments of music by his father; then studied violin, piano, and organ with various teachers in Philadelphia; was active as a church organist there; taught theory and other subjects at the Zeckwer-Hahn Music Academy in Philadelphia; he publ. a number of compositions for organ; also contributed articles to the *Diapason* and other publications.

Maizel, Boris, significant Russian composer; b. St. Petersburg, July 17, 1907. He graduated from the Leningrad Cons. in 1936, in the composition class of Riazanov; during the siege of Leningrad by the Germans in 1942 he was evacuated to Sverdlovsk; in 1944 he settled in Moscow. WORKS: For Orch.: 9 symphs.: No. 1 (1940); No. 2, subtitled *Ural Symphony* (1944); No. 3, *Victoriously Triumphant,* written in celebration of the victory over Germany (1945); No. 4 (1947); No. 5 (1962); No. 6 (1967); No. 7 (1970); No. 8 (1973); No. 9 (1976); Double Concerto for Violin, Piano, and Orch. (1949); Double Concerto for Flute, Horn, Strings, and Percussion (1971); Concerto for 10 Instruments (1977); Concerto for 2 Pianos and String Orch. (1978); 3 symph. poems: *Distant Planet* (1961; also as a ballet, 1962); *Leningrad Novella* (1969); *Along Old Russian Towns* (1975). For the stage: *The Shadow of the Past,* opera (1964); *Snow Queen,* ballet (1940; also a symph. suite, 1944); *Sombrero,* children's ballet (1959). Chamber music: Cello Sonata (1936); Piano Trio (1951); 2 string quartets (1937, 1974). Also, song cycles; piano pieces; various theatrical compositions based on the themes of the Buryat Soviet Republic; film music.

Majeske, Daniel, American violinist; b. Detroit, Sept. 17, 1932. He began studying violin at the age of 4, and at 16 appeared as a soloist with the Detroit Symph. Orch.; continued his studies at the Curtis Inst. in Philadelphia with Ivan Galamian. In 1955 he joined the violin section of the Cleveland Orch.; in 1969 he was named its concertmaster. He appeared as a soloist with major American orchs.; in 1965 he was appointed to the faculty of the Cleveland Music School Settlement. He owns the "Marquis de Riviera" Stradivarius violin of 1718.

Majo, Gian Francesco (called **Ciccio di Majo**), Italian composer, son of **Giuseppe Majo;** b. Naples, March 24, 1732; d. there, Nov. 17, 1770. He received his primary education from his father; also studied with his uncle Gennaro Manno and his great-uncle Francesco Feo; was a church organist; then began to compose for the stage; wrote some 20 operas, of which the first was *Ricimero, re dei Goti* (Rome, Feb. 7, 1759); also wrote separate arias for various pasticcios.

BIBLIOGRAPHY: D. Di Chiera, *The Life and Operas of Gian Francesco de Majo* (Diss., Univ. of Calif., Los Angeles, 1962).

Majo, Giuseppe, Italian composer, father of the preceding; b. Naples, Dec. 5, 1697; d. there, Nov. 18, 1771. He studied with Nicola Fago at the Cons. della Pietà dei Turchini in Naples; in 1744 became master of the royal chapel in Naples, retaining this post until his death. He wrote a considerable amount of church music; also several comic operas and 2 serious operas.

Majone (Mayone), Ascanio, Neapolitan organist and composer; lived in the late 16th to early 17th centuries. He was a pupil of Giovanni Macque, and his assistant at the viceregal chapel at Naples, c.1600. Existing musical publications by Majone are: *Primo libro di diversi capricci per sonare* (Naples, 1603); *Il primo libro di madrigali a 5 voci* (Naples, 1604); *Secondo libro di diversi capricci per sonare* (Naples, 1609; reprinted in *Orgue et Liturgie,* 63 and 65; Paris, 1964). Two of his madrigals are included in the collection *Teatro di madrigali a 5 v. de div. excell. musici Napolitani, posti in luce da Scipione Ricci, Libraro* (Naples, 1609). Majone is mentioned in Scipione Cerreto's *Della prattica musica vocale e strumentale* (Naples, 1601) as an outstanding performer on the organ and harp. Majone's keyboard toccatas are among the earliest examples of the affective Baroque style found later in Frescobaldi.

BIBLIOGRAPHY: W. Apel, "Neapolitan Links between Cabezón and Frescobaldi," *Musical Quarterly* (Oct. 1938); M. Bukofzer, *Music in the Baroque Era* (N.Y., 1947).

Major, Ervin, Hungarian music scholar and composer; b. Budapest, Jan. 26, 1901; d. there, Oct. 10, 1967. He studied with his father, **Jakab Gyula Major;** then took lessons with Kodály (1917–21). He made a profound study of Hungarian folk music as it relates to the works of classical composers, and publ. numerous essays on the subject. He composed mostly in small forms; among his works are a Bassoon Sonata (1938); Sonata for Double Bass and Piano (1943); piano pieces and choruses.

Major (real name, **Mayer**), **Jakab Gyula,** Hungarian pianist, conductor, and composer; b. Kosice, Dec. 13, 1858; b. Budapest, Jan. 30, 1925. He studied with Robert Volkmann; graduating from the Budapest Cons. in 1882, he became a teacher in Hungarian schools. He toured in Europe as a pianist; then returned to Budapest. His music follows the Romantic tradition of the German school. He wrote the operas *Erzsike* (Budapest, Sept. 24, 1901), *Széchy Mária* (1906), and *Mila* (1913); 5 symphs.; Piano Concerto; Violin Concerto; Cello Concerto; 4 string quartets; Piano Quintet; 2 violin sonatas; much piano music.

Makarov, Nicolai, Russian guitarist; b. Chukhloma, Feb. 16, 1810; d. Funtikovo-Rozhestvino, near Tula, Dec. 17, 1890. He appeared as a soloist in Tula in 1841; in 1852 went abroad; in 1856 he organized in Brussels an international competition for the best works for the guitar. In his leisure time he wrote unsuccessful novels and compiled a French dictionary. He publ. an autobiography, *My Septuagenarian Reminiscences* (1881).

Makarova, Nina, Russian composer; b. Yurino, Aug. 12, 1908; d. Moscow, Jan. 15, 1976. She studied with Miaskovsky at the Moscow Cons., graduating in 1936. Her early works show a Romantic flair, not without some coloristic touches of French Impressionism. She wrote an opera, *Zoya* (1955); a Symph. (1938), which she conducted herself in Moscow on June 12, 1947; a number of violin pieces; a Sonatina and 6 études for piano; several song cycles; a cantata, *The Saga of Lenin* (1970). She was married to **Aram Khachaturian.**

BIBLIOGRAPHY: Ivan Martinov, *Nina Makarova* (Moscow, 1973).

Makeba, Miriam, black South African singer; b. Prospect, near Johannesburg, March 4, 1932. She sang in a mission choir in Pretoria; then joined an itinerant minstrel show. She first attracted attention when she sang the leading part in the African opera *King Kong* (Johannesburg, Feb. 2, 1959). In 1959 she went to the U.S.; appeared in N.Y. nightclubs and on television; testified at the United Nations on racist policies of South Africa; made a successful tour of Europe; also traveled to Ethiopia and Kenya as a representative of Negro art.

BIBLIOGRAPHY: *Current Biography* (June 1965).

Makedonski, Kiril, Macedonian composer; b. Bitol, Jan. 19, 1925. After completing his academic schooling in Skoplje, he studied with Krso Odak at the Music Academy in Zagreb; later continued his composition studies with Brkanović in Sarajevo, and in Ljubljana with Škerjanc. He is the composer of the first national Macedonian opera, *Goce* (Skoplje, May 24, 1954); his 2nd opera was *Tsar Samuil* (Skoplje, Nov. 5, 1968). He also wrote 4 symphs., chamber music, and a number of choruses. His idiom follows the fundamental vocal and harmonic usages of the Russian national school.

BIBLIOGRAPHY: Branko Karakaš, *Muzicki Stvaraoci u Makedoniji* (Belgrade, 1970; pp. 68–70).

Maklakiewicz, Jan Adam, Polish composer; b. Chojnaty, near Warsaw, Nov. 24, 1899; d. Warsaw, Feb. 7, 1954. He studied with Statkowski at the Warsaw Cons. and with Paul Dukas in Paris. Returning to Poland, he became an instructor in harmony at the Warsaw Cons.; from 1932 he was organist at the Church of the Holy Cross; in 1934 he established the musical periodical *Chor* and was also active as a music critic. From 1947 to his death Maklakiewicz was director of the Cons. of Cracow.

WORKS: Under the influence of French modernism, Maklakiewicz wrote a number of works in an advanced style; his *4 Japanese Songs* were perf. at the Oxford Festival of the International Society for Contemporary Music (July 23, 1931). Other works include a ballet, *Cagliostro in Warsaw* (Poznan, Oct. 1, 1946); symph. poem, *Grünewald* (Cracow, Sept. 1, 1945); *Uwertura praska (The Prague Overture;* Prague, May 8, 1947); Cello Concerto (1932); Violin Concerto (1933); some chamber music; many arrangements of Polish folk songs.

Maksimović, Rajko, Serbian composer; b. Belgrade, July 27, 1935. He studied at the Academy of Music in Belgrade; later joined its faculty; also took a postgraduate course at Princeton Univ. His style of composition combines formal neo-Classicism with serial procedures and ethnic Balkan thematics.

WORKS: *Muzika posta-janja,* based on an atonally treated motif, B-A-C-H (Belgrade, July 20, 1965); *Partita concertante* for Violin and Strings (1965); *Kad su živi zavideli mrtvima (When the Living Envied the Dead),* cantata to texts from medieval Serbian chronicles (Belgrade, April 21, 1964); *3 Haiku* for Female Choir and Chamber Orch., with the application of aleatory devices (Zagreb, May 16, 1967).

BIBLIOGRAPHY: Vlastimir Peričić, *Muzički Stvaraoci u Srbiji* (Belgrade, 1969; pp. 238–43).

Maksymiuk, Jerzy, Polish conductor; b. Grodno, April 9, 1936. He studied composition and conducting at the Warsaw Cons.; won several prizes for composition. He began his conducting career with the Polish National Radio Symph. Orch. in Katowice; in 1972 he founded the Polish Chamber Orch. of Warsaw, and subsequently toured with it. In 1983 he became engaged as principal conductor of the BBC Scottish Symph. Orch. of Glasgow, dividing his time between Poland and the U.K.

Malanotte, Adelaide, Italian contralto; b. Verona, 1785; d. Salò, Dec. 31, 1832. She made her debut in 1806 in Verona; created the title role in the first production of Rossini's opera *Tancredi* in Venice at the Teatro La Fenice in 1813. She retired from the stage in 1821.

Malashkin, Leonid, Russian composer; b. 1842; d. Moscow, Feb. 11, 1902. He was an ardent song collector; his anthology *50 Ukrainian Folksongs* is valuable. His original compositions were not successful; he wrote an opera, *Ilya Murometz* (Kiev, 1879), a *Russian Symphony on Folk Themes* (Moscow, March 27, 1873), and a great deal of church music.

Malawski, Artur, Polish violinist and composer; b. Przemyśl, July 4, 1904; d. Cracow, Dec. 26, 1957. He graduated as a violinist from the Cracow Cons. in 1928; then studied composition with Kazimierz Sikorski, and conducting at the Warsaw Cons. (1936–39). In his music he utilized Polish folk songs as thematic material; the treatment is in a general modern idiom.

WORKS: *Allegro capriccioso* for Small Orch. (1929); *Sinfonietta* (1936); *Symphonic Variations* (1937); cantata, *Wyspa Gorgon (Gorgons' Island;* 1939); 2 symphs. (1938–43, 1955); ballet-pantomime, *Wierchy (The Peaks;* 1944; revised 1950); *6 Symphonic Etudes* for Piano and Orch. (Sopot, April 30, 1948); *Tryptyk góralski (Highland Triptych)* for Small Orch. or Piano (1949); *Toccata and Fugue* for Piano and Orch. (1949); cantata, *Stara baśń (The Old Tale;* 1950); *Suite popularna* for Orch. (1952); *Hungaria 1956* for Orch. (1957; Warsaw, Feb. 14, 1958; descriptive of the Hungarian insurrection of 1956); 2 string quartets (1926, 1943); String Sextet (1935); *Ziabia Ballad (Ballad of the Frogs),* 2 recitations for Voice and Wind Ensemble (1934); *Burlesque* for Violin and Piano (1940); *Miniatures* for Piano (1947); Violin Sonata (1951); Piano Trio (1953).

BIBLIOGRAPHY: B. Schäffer, ed., *Artur Malawski: Zycie i twórczość* (Cracow, 1969).

Malcolm, George, English harpsichordist, pianist, and conductor; b. London, Feb. 28, 1917. He studied at Balliol College, Oxford, and at the Royal College of Music, London. He was Master of Music at Westminster Cathedral (1947–59) and artistic director of the Philomusica of London (1962–66), which gave performances of Baroque music. In 1965 he was made a Commander of the Order of the British Empire.

Malcuzynski, Witold, outstanding Polish pianist; b. Warsaw, Aug. 10, 1914; d. Palma, Majorca, July 17, 1977. He studied with Turczynski at the Warsaw Cons.; graduated in 1936; then took lessons with Paderewski in Switzerland. After his marriage to the French pianist **Colette Gaveau,** he went to Paris (1939); then toured in South America (1940–42); made his American debut in 1942; gave concerts in Australia in 1950. He made in all 14 U.S. tours, 9 South American tours, and 2 world tours (1949; 1956). He was particularly distinguished as an interpreter of Chopin.

BIBLIOGRAPHY: B. Gavoty, *Witold Malcuzynski* (London, 1957).

Maldeghem, Robert Julien van, Belgian music editor; b. Denterghem, Oct. 9, 1806; d. Brussels, Nov. 13, 1893. He studied with Fétis at the Brussels Cons., winning the Belgian Prix de Rome; obtained a post as church organist; undertook a thorough research of old Flemish music, and eventually publ. an anthology of choral works in 29 vols., *Trésor musical,* an edition of great documentary and historic importance, despite many errors of transcription; comments and rectifications were made by Charles Van den Borren in *Acta Musicologica,* 5/6, and by G. Reese, "Maldeghem and His Buried Treasure: A Bibliographical Study," in *Notes* (Dec. 1948).

Maldere (Malderre), Pierre van, Belgian violinist and composer; b. Brussels, Oct. 16, 1729; d. there, Nov. 1, 1768. In 1746 he became a member of the ensemble of the Royal Chapel of Brussels. From

1751 to 1753 he was in Dublin as a violinist, conductor, and composer. He then traveled to Paris (1754) and Austria (1757–58); returning to Brussels, he became conductor of the Opera, and also wrote stage works for production there; in 1762–67 was director of the Grand Théâtre in Brussels. Three of his brothers were also violinists.

WORKS: Operas: *Le Déguisement pastoral* (Vienna, July 12, 1756); *Les Amours champêtres* (Vienna, Nov. 5, 1758; not extant); *Les Précautions inutiles* (1760); *Les Sœurs rivals* (1762); *La Bagarre* (Paris, Feb. 10, 1763; not extant); *Le Médecin de l'amour* (Brussels, 1766; not extant); *Le Soldat par amour* (Brussels, Nov. 4, 1766; not extant); a number of instrumental works, of which many were publ. during his lifetime: 6 symphs. (Brussels, 1759); *6 sinfonie a più stromenti* (Paris, 1760), and a similar set, publ. in Paris (1768); also violin sonatas.

BIBLIOGRAPHY: S. Clercx, *Pierre van Maldere* (Brussels, 1948).

Maleingreau (or **Malengreau**), **Paul de,** Belgian composer and organist; b. Trélon-en-Thiérache, Nov. 23, 1887; d. Brussels, Jan. 9, 1956. He studied with Edgar Tinel at the Brussels Cons.; in 1913, became a prof. of harmony there; in 1919, was appointed instructor of organ; in 1946 he was elected president of the Froissart Academy. His performances of Bach organ works were highly regarded in Belgium. Among his compositions are 2 symphs.; *Légende de St. Augustin* for Solo Voices, Chorus, and Orch. (1934); Easter Mass (1925); 2 diptychs for Orch. (1947); organ works; piano pieces.

Maler, Wilhelm, German composer and music educator; b. Heidelberg, June 21, 1902; d. Hamburg, April 29, 1976. He studied music history with Kroyer and composition with Grabner in Heidelberg; then took courses with Haas in Munich and Jarnach in Berlin. He subsequently occupied several teaching positions in Cologne, Bonn, Detmold, and Hamburg; also was active in theatrical organizations. His music is marked by a strong polyphonic strain; in his works as well as in his theoretical writings he developed structural ideas promulgated by Hindemith.

WORKS: Concerto for Cembalo and Chamber Orch. (1927); *Orchesterspiel* (1930); Violin Concerto (1932); *Flämisches Rondo* for Orch. (1937); 2 string quartets; String Trio; 6 piano sonatas; various minor pieces. He publ. a manual of harmony, *Beitrag zur Harmonielehre* (Leipzig, 1931; revised as *Beitrag zur durmolltonalen Harmonielehre,* 1950; 3rd revised ed., 1957).

Malfitano, Catherine, American soprano; b. New York, April 18, 1948. She had her early training at home with her father, a violinist in the Metropolitan Opera orch.; later took regular voice lessons at the Manhattan School of Music. She made her formal debut in 1972; then sang with opera companies in Minneapolis, Santa Fe, N.Y., Houston, and also London.

Malgoire, Jean-Claude, French oboist, conductor, and musicologist; b. Avignon, Nov. 25, 1940. He studied from 1957–60 at the Paris Cons., where he won first prizes in the categories of oboe and chamber music; in 1968 he won the International Prize of Geneva for his performances as an oboist. In 1974 he founded La Grande Ecurie et La Chambre du Roy, with the avowed purpose of presenting old French music in historically authentic instrumentation; he toured with this ensemble in Europe, South America, Australia, and the U.S. He also appeared as a guest conductor, leading performances of rarely heard operas in Copenhagen, Stockholm, and London.

Malherbe, Charles-Théodore, French writer on music and conductor; b. Paris, April 21, 1853; d. Cormeilles, Eure, Oct. 5, 1911. First he studied law, and was admitted to the bar; but then took up music under A. Danhauser, A. Wormser, and J. Massenet. After a tour (as Danhauser's secretary) through Belgium, the Netherlands, and Switzerland in 1880–81, to inspect the music in the public schools, he settled in Paris; in 1896, was appointed assistant archivist to the Grand Opéra, succeeding Nuitter as archivist in 1899. He edited *Le Ménestrel,* and contributed to many leading reviews and musical journals. His collection of musical autographs, which he left to the Paris Cons., was probably one of the finest private collections in the world.

WRITINGS: *L'Œuvre dramatique de Richard Wagner* (1886); *Précis d'histoire de l'Opéra-Comique* (1887); *Notice sur Ascanio* (1890); *Mélanges sur R. Wagner* (1891); *Histoire de la seconde Salle Favart* [Opéra-Comique] (2 vols., 1893–93, "couronnée par l'Institut"); *Catalogue des œuvres de Donizetti* (1897); *Programmes et concerts* (1898); *Auber* (1911). Malherbe was secretary of the edition of Rameau's complete works publ. by Durand, editing the historical and biographical notices therein; also editor, with Weingartner, of the complete edition of Berlioz's works (Breitkopf & Härtel).

Malherbe, Edmond Paul Henri, French composer; b. Paris, Aug. 21, 1870; d. Corbeil-Essonnes (Seine-et-Oise), March 7, 1963. He studied at the Paris Cons. with Massenet and Fauré; in 1898, won the Premier Second Prix de Rome, and in 1899, the Deuxième Premier Grand Prix; 3 times winner of the Prix Trémont of the Académie des Beaux-Arts (1907, 1913, 1921); in 1950 received the Grand Prix Musical of the City of Paris for the total of his works. A productive composer, he continued to write music in his 80s, but very few of his larger compositions were performed, and virtually none publ.

WORKS: Operas: *Madame Pierre* (1903; Paris, 1912); *L'Avare,* after Molière (1907); *L'Emeute* (1911; Paris, 1912); *Cléanthis* (1912); *Anna Karénine* (1914); *Le Mariage forcé,* after Molière (1924); *Néron* (1945); *L'Amour et Psyché,* lyric tragedy with ballet (1948; State Prize, 1950); *Monsieur de Pourceaugnac,* pantomime with chorus, after Molière (1930); a series of "tableaux symphoniques" after great paintings; 3 symphs. (1948, 1956, 1957); Violin Concerto; Nonet; Sextet; many choruses, songs, piano pieces. He publ. *L'Harmonie du système musical actuel à demi-tons* (1920) and *Le Tiers-de-ton: Deux Systèmes: Tempéré et non-tempéré* (1900, 1950).

Malibran, María Felicità (née **García**), famous contralto, daughter of **Manuel García;** b. Paris, March 24, 1808; d. Manchester, Sept. 23, 1836. Taken to Naples, she played a child's part in Paër's opera *Agnese;* later she studied solfeggio with Panseron; from the age of 15, however, she was her father's pupil in singing. Her debut in London (June 7, 1825), as Rosina in the *Barbiere,* procured her engagement for the season. The family then voyaged to N.Y., where for 2 years she was the popular favorite, singing in *Otello, Romeo, Don Giovanni, Tancredi, Cenerentola,* and the 2 operas which her father wrote for her, *L'Amante astuto* and *La Figlia dell'aria.* In N.Y. she married the French merchant Malibran; he soon became bankrupt, and they separated. Returning to Paris, her immense success led to an engagement at a salary of 50,000 francs; after 1829 she sang every season at London; also appeared at Rome, Naples, Bologna, and Milan. She married the violinist **Bériot** in 1836, only a few months before her death, which was caused by overexertion after a severe fall from her horse. As a singer and actress, she exercised over her audiences the fascination of a highly endowed personality. Her voice was of extraordinary compass, but the medium register had several "dead" tones. She was also a good pianist, and composed numerous nocturnes, romances, and chansonnettes, publ. in album form as *Dernières pensées.*
BIBLIOGRAPHY: *Cenni biografici* (Venice, 1835); G. Barbieri, *Notizie biografiche di Maria Malibran* (Milan, 1836); I. Nathan, *The Life of Mme. Maria Malibran de Bériot* (London, 1836); A. von Treskow, *Mme. Malibran* (Leipzig, 1837); Comtesse Merlin, *Loisirs d'une femme de monde* (Paris, 1838; German trans. by G. Lotz as *Maria Malibran als Weib und Künstlerin,* Leipzig, 1839; Eng. trans., London, 1844; more romantic than trustworthy); E. Legouvé, "Maria Malibran," in *Etudes et souvenirs de théâtre* (Paris, 1880); E. Heron-Allen, "A Contribution towards an Accurate Biography of Ch. de Bériot and Maria Malibran," *De fidiculis opuscula* 6 (1894); A. Pougin, *Maria Malibran: Histoire d'une cantatrice* (Paris, 1911; Eng. trans., London, 1911); Clément Lanquine, *La Malibran* (Paris, 1911); J.-G. Prod'homme, "La Fayette and Maria Malibran," *Chesterian* (Sept. 1919); Louise Héritte-Viardot, *Une Famille de grands musiciens* (1923); Carl Engel, "Again La Fayette and Maria Malibran," *Chesterian* (Jan.–Feb. 1925); "6 Unpublished Letters from La Fayette to Maria Malibran," *Chesterian* (March–April 1925); A. Flament, *Une Etoile en 1830: La Malibran* (Paris, 1928); Phyllis Crump, *Musset and Malibran* (Cambridge, England, 1932); P. Larionoff, *Maria Malibran e i suoi tempi* (Florence, 1935); D. Bielli, *Maria Malibran* (1936); M. Lorenzi de Bradi, *La Brève et Merveilleuse Vie de la Malibran* (Paris, 1936); G.G. Bernardi, "La Malibran a Venezia," *Musica d'Oggi* (Aug.–Sept. 1936); H. Malherbe, *La Passion de la Malibran* (Paris, 1937); A. Flament, *L'Enchanteresse errante, la Malibran* (Paris, 1937); S. Desternes and H. Chandet, *La Malibran et Pauline Viardot* (Paris, 1969); Carmen de Reparaz, *María Malibran* (Madrid, 1976).

Malipiero, Francesco, Italian composer, grandfather of **Gian Francesco Malipiero;** b. Rovigio, Jan. 9, 1824; d. Venice, May 12, 1887. He studied with Melchiore Balbi at the Liceo Musicale in Venice. At the age of 18 he wrote an opera, *Giovanna di Napoli,* which was produced with signal success; Rossini praised it. Other operas by Malipiero were *Attila* (Venice, Nov. 15, 1845; renamed later *Ildegonda di Borgogna*); *Alberigo da Romano* (Venice, Dec. 26, 1846; his best); *Fernando Cortez* (Venice, Feb. 18, 1851).

Malipiero, Gian Francesco, greatly distinguished Italian composer; b. Venice, March 18, 1882; d. Treviso, near Venice, Aug. 1, 1973. He was reared in a musical environment: his grandfather, Francesco Malipiero, wrote operas; his father, Luigi Malipiero, was also a musician. In 1898 Malipiero enrolled at the Vienna Cons. as a violin student; in 1899 he returned to Venice, where he studied at the Liceo Musicale Benedetto Marcello with Marco Bossi, whom he followed to Bologna in 1902; he took a diploma in composition at the Liceo Musicale G.B. Martini in Bologna in 1904. In 1913 he went to Paris, where he absorbed the techniques of musical Impressionism, cultivating parallel chord formations and amplified tonal harmonies with characteristic added sixths, ninths, and elevenths. However, his own style of composition was determined by the polyphonic practices of the Italian Baroque. In 1921 Malipiero returned to Italy; taught composition at the Univ. of Parma (1921–23); afterwards lived mostly in Asolo, near Venice. He became director of the Liceo Musicale Benedetto Marcello in Venice in 1939; was named a member of the National Inst. of Arts and Letters in N.Y. in 1949, of the Royal Flemish Academy in Brussels in 1952, of the Institut de France in 1954, and of the Akademie der Künste in West Berlin in 1967. Apart from his activities as composer and educator, Malipiero was the erudite and devoted editor of collected works of Monteverdi and Vivaldi.
WORKS: OPERAS: *Canossa* (1911; Rome, Jan. 24, 1914; destroyed); *Sogno d'un tramonto d'autunno* (1914; not perf. until nearly half a century later, when it was brought out in concert production on the Milan Radio, Oct. 4, 1963); *L'Orfeide,* in 3 parts: *La morte della maschere, 7 canzoni,* and *Orfeo* (1919–22; first complete perf., Düsseldorf, Nov. 5, 1925), the 2nd part, *7 canzoni* (Paris, July 10, 1920), often being perf. separately; the trilogy *3 commedie goldoniane* (1920–22; consisting of *La bottega da caffè, Sior Todaro Brontolon,* and *Le baruffe chiozzotte,* first perf. in its entirety, Darmstadt, March 24, 1926); *Filomela e l'Infatuato* (1924–25; Prague, March 31, 1928); *Merlino, Maestro d'organi* (1927;

Rome Radio, Aug. 4, 1934); *Il mistero di Venezia,* in 3 parts: *Le aquile di aquileia, Il finto Arlecchino,* and *I corvi di San Marco* (1925–28; first perf. in its entirety, Coburg, Germany, Dec. 15, 1932); *Torneo notturno* (1929; Munich, May 15, 1931); *Il festino* (1930; Turin Radio, Nov. 6, 1937); *La favola del figlio cambiato* (1933; Braunschweig, Germany, in a German version, Jan. 13, 1934); *Giulio Cesare* (1935; Genoa, Feb. 8, 1936); *Antonio e Cleopatra* (1937; Florence, May 4, 1938); *Ecuba* (1939; Rome, Jan. 11, 1941); *La vita è sogno* (1940; Breslau, Poland, June 30, 1943); *I capricci di Callot* (1941–42; Rome, Oct. 24, 1942); *L'allegra brigata* (1943; Milan, May 4, 1950); *Mondi celesti e infernali* (1948–49; concert version, Turin Radio, Jan. 12, 1950); *Il Figliuol prodigo* (1952; first stage perf., Florence May Festival, May 14, 1957); *Donna Urraca* (1953; Bergamo, Oct. 2, 1954); *Venere prigioniera* (1955; Florence May Festival, May 14, 1957); *Il Capitan Spavento* (1955; Naples, March 16, 1963); *Il Marescalco* (1960; Treviso, Oct. 1969); *Rappresentazione e festa del Carnasciale e della Quaresima* (1961; Venice, Jan. 20, 1970); *Don Giovanni,* after Pushkin (1962; Naples, Sept. 22, 1963); *Le metamorfosi di Bonaventura* (1963–65; Venice, Sept. 5, 1966); *Don Tartufo bacchettone* (1966; Venice, Jan. 20, 1970); *Gli Eroi di Bonaventura* (1968; Milan, Feb. 5, 1969); *L'Iscariota* (1970; Siena, Aug. 28, 1971); *Uno dei dieci* (1970; Siena, Aug. 28, 1971).
BALLETS: *Pantea* (1918–19; Venice, Sept. 6, 1932); *La mascherata delle principesse prigioniere* (1919; Brussels, Oct. 19, 1924); *Stradivario* (1947–48; Florence, June 20, 1949); *Il mondo novo* (1951; Rome, Dec. 16, 1951; revised as *La lanterna magica,* 1955).
DIALOGHI: No. 1, *con M. de Falla,* for Orch.; No. 2 for 2 Pianos; No. 3, *con Jacopone da Todi,* for Voice and 2 Pianos; No. 4 for Wind Quintet; No. 5 for Viola and Orch.; No. 6 for Harpsichord and Orch.; No. 7 for 2 Pianos and Orch.; No. 8, *La morte di Socrate,* for Baritone and Small Orch. (all 1956–57).
OTHER WORKS FOR ORCH.: *Sinfonia degli eroi* (1905; lost); *Sinfonia del mare* (1906); *Sinfonie del silenzio e della morte* (1908); *Impressioni dal vero* in 3 parts (first part, Milan, May 15, 1913; 2nd part, Rome, March 11, 1917; 3rd part, Amsterdam, Oct. 25, 1923); *Armenia,* on Armenian folk songs (1917); *Ditirambo tragico* (1917; London, Oct. 11, 1919); *Pause del silenzio* in 2 parts (first part, his most famous orch. work, Rome, Jan. 27, 1918; 2nd part, Philadelphia, April 1, 1927); *Per una favola cavalleresca* (1920; Rome, Feb. 13, 1921); *Oriente immaginario* for Chamber Orch. (Paris, Dec. 23, 1920); *Variazioni senza tema* for Piano and Orch. (1923; Prague, May 19, 1925); *L'esilio dell'eroe,* symph. suite (1930); *Concerti per orchestra* (1931; Philadelphia, Jan. 29, 1932); *Inni* (Rome, April 6, 1933); 2 violin concertos: No. 1 (1932; Amsterdam, March 5, 1933) and No. 2 (1963; Venice, Sept. 14, 1965); *7 invenzioni* (1932; Rome, Dec. 24, 1933); *4 invenzioni* (1932; Dresden, Nov. 11, 1936); 11 numbered symphs.: No. 1 (1933; Florence, April 2, 1934); No. 2, *Elegiaca* (1936; Seattle, Jan. 25, 1937); No. 3, *Delle campane* (1944; Florence, Nov. 4, 1945); No. 4, *In Memoriam* (1946; Boston, Feb. 27, 1948; dedicated to the memory of Natalie Koussevitzky); No. 5, *Concertante, in eco,*

for 2 Pianos and Orch. (London, Nov. 3, 1947); No. 6, *Degli archi,* for Strings (1947; Basel, Feb. 11, 1949); No. 7, *Delle canzoni* (1948; Milan, Nov. 3, 1949); No. 8, *Symphonia brevis* (1964); No. 9, *Dell'ahimè* (1966; Warsaw, Sept. 21, 1966); No. 10, *Atropo* (1967); No. 11, *Delle cornamuse* (1969); 6 piano concertos: No. 1 (1934; Rome, April 3, 1935); No. 2 (1937; Duisburg, Germany, March 6, 1939); No. 3 (1948; Louisville, Ky., March 8, 1949); No. 4 (1950; Turin Radio, Jan. 28, 1951); No. 5 (1958); No. 6, *Delle macchine* (1964; Rome, Feb. 5, 1966); Cello Concerto (1937; Belgrade, Jan. 31, 1939); *Concerto a 3* for Violin, Cello, Piano, and Orch. (1938; Florence, April 9, 1939); *Sinfonia in un tempo* (1950; Rome, March 21, 1951); *Sinfonia dello zodiaco* (1951; Lausanne, Jan. 23, 1952); *Passacaglie* (1952); *Fantasie di ogni giorni* (*Fantasies of Every Day;* 1953; Louisville, Nov. 17, 1954); *Elegy-Capriccio* (1953); 4 *Fantasie concertanti* (all 1954): No. 1 for String Orch.; No. 2 for Violin and Orch.; No. 3 for Cello and Orch.; No. 4 for Piano and Orch.; Concerto for 2 Pianos and Orch. (Besançon Festival, Sept. 11, 1957); *Notturno di canti e ballo* (1957); *Serenissima* for Saxophone and Orch. (1961); *Sinfonia per Antigenida* (1962); Flute Concerto (1968).
OTHER VOCAL WORKS: *San Francesco d'Assisi,* mystery for Soli, Chorus, and Orch. (1920; N.Y., March 29, 1922); *La Principessa Ulalia,* cantata (1924; N.Y., Feb. 19, 1927); *La cena* for Soli, Chorus, and Orch. (1927; Rochester, N.Y., April 25, 1929); *Il commiato* for Baritone and Orch. (1934); *La Passione* for Soli, Chorus, and Orch. (Rome, Dec. 15, 1935); *De Profundis* for Solo Voice, Viola, Bass Drum, and Piano (1937); *Missa pro mortuis* for Solo Baritone, Chorus, and Orch. (Rome, Dec. 18, 1938); *4 vecchie canzoni* for Solo Voice and 7 Instruments (1940; Washington, D.C., April 12, 1941); *Santa Eufrosina,* mystery for Soli, Chorus, and Orch. (Rome, Dec. 6, 1942); *Universa Universis* for Male Chorus and Chamber Orch. (1942; Liviano, April 11, 1943); *Vergilii Aeneis,* heroic symph. for 7 Soli, Chorus, and Orch. (1943–44; Turin, June 21, 1946; scenic version, Venice, Jan. 6, 1958); *Le 7 allegrezze d'amore* for Solo Voice and 14 Instruments (Milan, Dec. 4, 1945); *La Terra* for Chorus and Orch. (1946; Cambridge, Mass., May 2, 1947, with Organ); *I 7 peccati mòrtali* for Chorus and Orch. (1946; Monteceneri, Nov. 20, 1949); *Mondi celesti* for Solo Voice and 10 Instruments (1948; Capri, Feb. 3, 1949); *La festa de la Sensa* for Baritone, Chorus, and Orch. (1948; Brussels Radio, July 2, 1954); *5 favole* for Solo Voice and Small Orch. (Washington, Oct. 30, 1950); *Passer mortuus est* for a cappella Chorus (Pittsburgh, Nov. 24, 1952); *Magister Josephus* for 4 Voices and Small Orch. (1957); *Preludio e Morte di Macbeth* for Baritone and Orch. (1958); *L'asino d'oro* for Baritone and Orch., after Apuleius (1959); *Concerto di concerti ovvero Dell'uom malcontento* for Baritone, Concertante Violin, and Orch. (1960); *Abracadabra* for Baritone and Orch. (1962); *Ave Phoebe, dum queror* for Chorus and 20 Instruments (1964); *L'Aredodese* for Reciter, Chorus, and Orch. (1967).
OTHER CHAMBER MUSIC: 8 string quartets: No. 1, *Rispetti e Strombotti* (1920); No. 2, *Stornelli e Ballate* (1923); No. 3, *Cantari alla madrigalesca* (1930; also for String Orch.); No. 4 (1934); No. 5, *Dei capricci*

(1940); No. 6, *L'arca di Noè* (1947); No. 7 (1950); No. 8, *Per Elisabetta* (1964); *Ricercari* for 11 Instruments (Washington, Oct. 7, 1926); *Ritrovari* for 11 Instruments (1926; Gardone, Italy, Oct. 26, 1929); *Sonata a 3* for Piano Trio (1927); *Epodi e giambi* for Violin, Viola, Oboe, and Bassoon (1932); *Sonata a 5* for Flute, Violin, Viola, Cello, and Harp (1934); Cello Sonatina (1942); *Sonata a 4* for 4 Winds (1954); *Serenata mattutini* for 10 Instruments (1959); *Serenata* for Bassoon and 10 Instruments (1961); *Macchine* for 14 Instruments (1963); *Endecatode,* chamber symph. for 14 Instruments and Percussion (1966; Dartmouth College, Hanover, N.H., July 2, 1967).

OTHER WORKS FOR PIANO: *6 morceaux* (1905); *Bizzarrie luminose dell' alba, del meriggio e della notte* (1908); *Poemetti lunari* (1910); *Preludi autunnali* (1914); *Poemi asolani* (1916); *Barlumi* (1917); *Risonanze* (1918); *Maschere che passano* (1918); *3 omaggi* (1920); *Omaggio a Claude Debussy* (1920); *Cavalcate* (1921); *La siesta* (1921); *Il tarlo* (1922); *Pasqua di Risurrezione* (1924); *Preludi a una fuga* (1926); *Epitaffio* (1931); *Omaggio a Bach* (1932); *Preludi, ritmi e canti gregoriani* (1937); *Preludio e fuga* (1941); *Hortus conclusus* (1946); *5 studi per domani* (1959).

Malipiero, Riccardo, Italian composer, nephew of **Gian Francesco Malipiero;** b. Milan, July 24, 1914. He studied piano and composition at the Milan and Turin conservatories (1930–37); completed studies with his uncle at the Benedetto Marcello Cons. in Venice (1937–39); traveled as a lecturer and pianist in Europe, South America, and the U.S. As a composer, he followed the Italian neo-Baroque, but about 1950 he adopted a fairly consistent method of 12-tone composition. WORKS: FOR THE STAGE: 3 operas: *Minnie la Candida* (Parma, Nov. 19, 1942); *La Donna è mobile,* opera buffa (1954; Milan, Feb. 22, 1957); television opera, *Battono alla Porta* (Italian Television, Feb. 12, 1962; stage version, Genoa, May 24, 1963). FOR ORCH.: Piano Concerto (1937); *3 Dances* for Orch. (1937); 2 cello concertos (1938, 1957); *Balleto* for Orch. (1939); *Piccolo concerto* for Piano and Orch. (1945); *Antico sole* for Soprano and Orch. (1947); *Cantata sacra* for Soprano, Chorus, and Orch. (1947); 3 symphs.: No. 1 (1949); No. 2, *Sinfonia Cantata,* for Baritone and Orch. (1956; N.Y., March 19, 1957); No. 3 (1959; Univ. of Florida, Miami, April 10, 1960); Violin Concerto (1952; Milan, Jan. 31, 1953); *Studi* for Orch. (1953; Venice Festival, Sept. 11, 1953); *Ouverture-Divertimento "del Ritorno"* (1953); Concerto for Piano and Chamber Orch. (1955); *Concerto breve* for Ballerina and Chamber Orch. (1956; Venice Festival, Sept. 11, 1956); *Cantata di natale* for Soprano, Chorus, and Orch. (1959; Milan, Dec. 21, 1959); Sonata for Oboe and Strings (1960); *Concerto per Dimitri* for Piano and Orch. (1961; Venice Festival, April 27, 1961); *Nykteghersia* for Orch. (1962); *Cadencias* for Orch. (1964; Geneva Radio, Jan. 13, 1965); *Muttermusik* for Orch. (1965–66; Milan, Feb. 28, 1966); *Mirages* for Orch. (1966; Milan, Feb. 6, 1970); *Carnet de notes* for Chamber Orch. (1967); *Rapsodia* for Violin and Orch. (1967); *Serenata per Alice Tully* for Chamber Orch. (1969; N.Y., March 10, 1970); *Monologo* for Female Voice and Strings (1969); Concerto for Piano Trio and Orch. (1971; Milan, Jan. 16, 1976); *Requiem 1975* for Orch. (Florence, Nov. 6, 1976); *Go Placidly* for Baritone and Chamber Orch. (1976; N.Y., Nov. 10, 1976). CHAMBER MUSIC: *Musik I* for Cello and 9 Instruments (1938); 3 string quartets (1941, 1954, 1960); Violin Sonata (1956); Piano Quintet (1957); *Musica da camera* for Wind Quintet (1959); Oboe Sonata (1959); *6 poesie di Dylan Thomas* for Soprano and 10 Instruments (1959); *Mosaico* for Wind and String Quintets (1961); *Preludio Adagio e Finale* for Soprano, 5 Percussionists, and Piano (1963); *In Time of Daffodils,* to poems by e.e. cummings, for Soprano, Baritone, and 7 Instrumentalists (Washington, D.C., Oct. 30, 1964); *Nuclei* for 2 Pianos and Percussion (1966); *Cassazione* for String Sextet (1967); Piano Trio (1968); *Ciaccona di Davide* for Viola and Piano (1970); *Memoria* for Flute and Piano (1973); *Giber Folia* for Clarinet and Piano (1973). FOR PIANO: *14 Inventions* (1938); *Musik* for 2 Pianos (1939); *Piccolo musica* (1941); *Invenzioni* (1949); *Costellazioni* (1965); *Le Rondini de Alessandro* (1971). He publ. several monographs: *J.S. Bach* (Brescia, 1948); *Debussy* (Brescia, 1948); *Guida alla dodecafonia* (Milan, 1961); *Musica ieri e oggi* (with E. Radius and G. Severi; 6 vols., Rome, 1970). BIBLIOGRAPHY: Claudio Sartori, *Riccardo Malipiero* (in Eng.; Milan, 1957); C. Sartori and P. Santi, *Due tempi di Riccardo Malipiero* (Milan, 1964).

Maliponte, Adriana, Italian soprano; b. Brescia, Dec. 26, 1938. Her family moved to Mulhouse, and she studied at the Cons. there. She made her operatic debut as Mimi in *La Bohème* at the Teatro Nuovo, Milan, in 1958; also sang minor roles at La Scala; subsequently had engagements at the Paris Opéra and the Opéra-Comique. She made her American debut in Philadelphia in 1963; then sang in Chicago and Cincinnati. On March 19, 1971, she made her Metropolitan Opera debut in N.Y. as Mimi.

Maliszewski, Witold, Polish composer; b. Mohylev-Podolsk, July 20, 1873; d. Zalesie, July 18, 1939. He studied piano in Warsaw and violin in Tiflis; then enrolled in the St. Petersburg Cons., in the class of Rimsky-Korsakov. He became director of the Odessa Cons. in 1908; went to Poland in 1921, and was active there mainly as a teacher; in 1932 he joined the staff of the Warsaw Cons. As a composer, he followed the Russian Romantic tradition; some of his symph. works had a modicum of success. He wrote the operas *The Mermaid* (Warsaw, 1928) and *Boruta* (1930); 4 symphs.; Piano Concerto (1932); 4 string quartets; Violin Sonata; Cello Sonata; many piano pieces; songs. BIBLIOGRAPHY: E. Wrocki, *Witold Maliszewski* (Warsaw, 1932).

Malkin, Jacques, Russian-American violinist; b. Slobodka, near Odessa, Dec. 16, 1875; d. New York, Dec. 8, 1964. He studied in Odessa, and later enrolled at the Paris Cons.; in 1893 he played the viola d'amore in the Société des Instruments Anciens in Paris. In 1918 he went to America and settled in N.Y. as a violin teacher; with his brothers **Joseph** and **Manfred**, he formed a trio.

Malkin, Joseph, Russian-American cellist; b. Propoisk, near Odessa, Sept. 24, 1879; d. New York, Sept. 1, 1969. After studying in Odessa, he went to Paris and studied cello at the Paris Cons., graduating in 1902; then went to Germany and became the first cellist at the Berlin Phil. (1902–8); toured America as a member of the Brussels Quartet. He remained in the U.S.; was first cellist of the Boston Symph. Orch. (1914–19) and of the Chicago Symph. (1919–22); with his brothers **Jacques** and **Manfred** he organized the Malkin Trio, which presented concerts in N.Y. and Boston. In 1933 he organized the Malkin Cons. in Boston, and was instrumental in inviting Arnold Schoenberg to teach there during Schoenberg's first American season (1934–35); the Cons. closed in 1943; from 1944 to 1949, Malkin played cello in the N.Y. Phil., before retiring. He died in a nursing home. He publ. a number of arrangements and studies for the cello.

Malkin, Manfred, Russian-American pianist; b. Odessa, Aug. 11, 1884; d. New York, Jan. 8, 1966. He studied at the Paris Cons.; in 1905 went to the U.S.; established his own music school in N.Y. (1914–31); with his brothers **Jacques** and **Joseph,** formed a trio.

Malko, Nicolai, eminent Russian conductor; b. Brailov, May 4, 1883; d. Sydney, Australia, June 23, 1961. He studied philology at the Univ. of St. Petersburg, graduating in 1906; also studied composition and orchestration with Rimsky-Korsakov, Liadov, and Glazunov; conducting with Tcherepnin. After graduation he went to Munich, where he took a conducting course with Mottl. Returning to Russia, he conducted opera in St. Petersburg; was conductor of the Leningrad Phil. (1926–28), with which he performed many new works by Soviet composers, including the premiere of Shostakovich's First Symph. In 1928 he left Russia; conducted orchs. in Vienna, Buenos Aires, Prague, etc.; was particularly successful in Denmark, where he made frequent appearances, and established a conducting class; many Danish musicians became his pupils, including the King of Denmark, who was a talented amateur. In 1938 he visited the U.S. as a lecturer; also appeared as guest conductor with several American orchs.; became an American citizen on May 7, 1946. He subsequently conducted the Yorkshire Symph. Orch. in England (1954–56). In 1956 he was appointed resident conductor of the Sydney Symph. Orch. in Australia, where he established a fine tradition of orch. performance, striving above all for clarity and balance of sonorities. He publ. a manual, *The Conductor and His Baton* (Copenhagen, 1950), and his memoir, *A Certain Age* (N.Y., 1966); also composed various works, among them a Clarinet Concerto (Copenhagen, Sept. 27, 1952). The Danish Radio inaugurated in his honor a triennial Malko International Contest for conductors.

BIBLIOGRAPHY: N. Malko, *Reminiscences* (Leningrad, 1972).

Malling, Jørgen, Danish composer; b. Copenhagen, Oct. 31, 1836; d. there, July 12, 1905. He studied with Gade; was first winner of the Ancher stipend in 1861; went to Paris and there became enthusiastic over Chevé's system of vocal notation, which he tried (unsuccessfully) to introduce in various cities in Scandinavia and Russia; was an organist in Svendborg (1869–72); lived in Vienna from 1879 to 1882, and in Munich from 1882 to 1895; returned to Copenhagen in 1901; was active there as a teacher and composer. He wrote the operas *Lisenka* and *Frithjof;* a cantata, *Küvala;* String Quartet; Piano Trio; numerous piano pieces and songs.

Malling, Otto (Valdemar), Danish composer; b. Copenhagen, June 1, 1848; d. there, Oct. 5, 1915. He studied with Gade and J.P.E. Hartmann at the Copenhagen Cons.; conducted the Student's Choral Society (1872–84); was an organist at various churches in Copenhagen (1878–1910); became conductor of the Concert Society there (1874–93); in 1885 was appointed instructor of music theory at the Copenhagen Cons.; in 1899 became its director. WORKS: His publ. works, comprising about 100 opus numbers, include a Symph.; Fantasia for Violin and Orch.; *Oriental Suite, Musique de ballet;* Piano Concerto; several cantatas; works for organ; numerous songs; characteristic pieces for piano; ballet, *Askepot (Cinderella;* Copenhagen, Sept. 25, 1910); and a treatise on instrumentation.

Mallinger, Mathilde (née **Lichtenegger**), soprano; b. Agram, Croatia, Feb. 17, 1847; d. Berlin, April 19, 1920. She studied in Prague and Vienna; made her debut in Munich as Norma (Oct. 4, 1866), and created the role of Eva in *Die Meistersinger* (Munich, June 21, 1868). In 1873 she appeared in the U.S.; also sang in Russia. Subsequently she was active mainly as a singing teacher, in Prague (1890–95) and, after 1895, in Berlin. She was married to Baron von Schimmelpfennig of Berlin.

Mallinson, Albert, English composer and organist; b. Leeds, Nov. 13, 1870; d. Elsinore, Denmark, April 5, 1946. He was a pupil of W. Creser; then a church organist in Leeds; in 1903, married the Danish singer **Anna Steinhauer,** and with her made successful tours of Denmark and Germany, introducing his own songs; from 1904 until 1914 he was organist of the English Church in Dresden; at the outbreak of World War I he went to Denmark, where he remained most of his life. He wrote about 300 songs to German, Eng., and Danish texts.

Malm, William, American ethnomusicologist; b. La Grange, Ill., March 6, 1928. He studied composition at Northwestern Univ. (B.M., 1949; M.M., 1950); then joined the faculty at the Univ. of Illinois (1950) and at the U.S. Naval School of Music (1951–53). He continued his music studies at the Univ. of Calif., Los Angeles, receiving his Ph.D. in 1959 with the dissertation *Japanese Nagauta Music;* also taught there (1958–60). In 1960 he was engaged at the Univ. of Michigan; became a prof. there in 1966. As an ethnomusicologist, he specializes in Asian music; he publ. *Japanese Music and Musical Instruments,* the first scholarly and comprehensive survey of the subject in English.

WRITINGS: *Nagauta: The Heart of Kabuki Music* (Tokyo, 1963); *Music Cultures of the Pacific, the Near East and Asia* (Englewood Cliffs, N.J., 1967; 2nd ed., 1977); *The Special Characteristics of Gagaku* (Tokyo, 1971); ed., with J. Crump, *Chinese and Japanese Music-dramas* (Ann Arbor, Mich., 1975); ed., with J. Brandon and D. Shively, *Studies in Kabuki* (Honolulu, 1977).

Malotte, Albert Hay, American organist and song composer; b. Philadelphia, May 19, 1895; d. Los Angeles, Nov. 16, 1964. He was a chorister at St. James Episcopal Church; studied with W.S. Stansfield, and later in Paris with Georges Jacob; then moved to Hollywood, where he became a member of the music staff of the Walt Disney Studios; composed the scores for some of Disney's "Silly Symphonies" and "Ferdinand, the Bull." He was the composer of the enormously popular setting *The Lord's Prayer* (1935); he also set to music the 23rd Psalm and other religious texts.

Malovec, Jozef, Slovak composer; b. Hurbanovo, March 24, 1933. He studied with A. Moyzes at the High School of Musical Arts in Bratislava (1951–53) and with Sommer and Řídký at the Prague Academy (1953–57); subsequently was active in program making on the Bratislava Radio.

WORKS: *Scherzo* for Orch. (1956); *3 Studies* for String Quartet (1962); *Little Chamber Music* for Flute, Clarinet, Trumpet, Vibraphone, Viola, Cello, and Percussion (1964); *Kryptogram* for Piano, Bass Clarinet, and Percussion (1965); *Suite* for Strings and Harpsichord (1974); *5 National Songs* for Alto and Orch. (1975); *Prelude and Burlesque* for Wind Quintet (1976); electronic pieces: *Orthogenesis* (1967); *Punctum Alpha* (1968); *Theorem* (1971).

Malten (real name, **Müller**), **Therese,** German soprano; b. Insterburg, June 21, 1855; d. Neuzchieren, near Dresden, Jan. 2, 1930. She studied with Gustav Engel in Berlin; made her operatic debut in Dresden in 1873, and remained for some 30 years the principal singer on the roster of the Dresden Opera; also sang in Berlin, Vienna, and London. Wagner heard her and suggested her engagement as Kundry at the premiere of *Parsifal* at Bayeuth in 1882. She was particularly renowned as a Wagnerian singer; was also a fine dramatic actress.

Mamangakis, Nikos, Greek composer; b. Rethymnon, Crete, March 3, 1929. He studied music at the Hellikon Cons. in Athens (1947–53); then composition with Carl Orff and Harald Genzmer at the Hochschule für Musik in Munich (1957–61) and electronic music at the Siemens Studio in Munich (1961–62); subsequently divided his time between Athens and Berlin. His works reflect modern quasimathematical procedures, with numerical transformations determining pitch, rhythm, and form.

WORKS: *Music for 4 Protagonists* for 4 Voices and 10 Instrumentalists, on a text by Kazantzakis (1959–60); *Constructions* for Flute and Percussion (1959–60); *Combinations* for Solo Percussionist and Orch. (1961); *Speech Symbols* for Soprano, Bass, and Orch. (1961–62); "Cycle of Numbers": No. 1, *Monologue,* for Solo Cello (1962); No. 2, *Antagonisms,* for Cello and One Percussionist moving in an arc along the stage (1963); No. 3, *Trittys (Triad),* for Guitar, 2 Double Basses, Santouri, and Percussion (1966); and No. 4, *Tetraktys,* for String Quartet (1963–66); *Kassandra* for Soprano and 6 Performers (1963); *Erotokritos,* ballad for 3 Voices and 5 Instruments in an old style (1964); *Ploutos,* popular opera after Aristophanes (1966); *Theama-Akroama,* visual-auditive event (happening) for Actor, Dancer, Painter, Singer, and 8 Instruments (Athens, April 3, 1967); *Scenario for 2 Improvised Art Critics* for Voice, Instruments, and Tape (1968); *Antinomies* for Solo Voice, Flute, Electric Double Bass, 2 Harps, 4 Cellos, 2 Percussionists, Hammond Organ, 4 Basses, and 4 Sopranos (Athens, Dec. 18, 1968); *Bolivar,* folk cantata in pop-art style (1968); *The Bacchants,* electronic ballet (1969); *Parastasis* for various Flutes, Voice, and Tape (1969); *Askesis* for Solo Cello (1969-70); *Perilepsis* for Solo Flute (1970); *Erophili,* popular opera (1970); *Anarchia* for Solo Percussion and Orch. (Donaueschingen, Oct. 16, 1971); *Penthima,* in memory of Jani Christou, for Solo Guitar (1970–71); *Monologue II* for Violin and Tape (1971); *Kykeon* for several Solo Instruments (1972); *Olophyrmos* for Magnetic Tape (1973).

Mamiya, Michio, brilliant Japanese composer; b. Asahikawa, Hokkaido, June 29, 1929. He studied with Ikenouchi at the State Music School in Tokyo; upon graduation he devoted himself mainly to the cultivation of national Japanese music in modern forms, with inventive uses of dissonant counterpoint and coloristic instrumentation.

WORKS: Opera, *Mukashi banashi hitokai Tarobê (A Fable from Olden Times about Tarobê, the Slavedealer;* 1959); oratorio, *15 June 1960,* an homage to an activist Japanese student killed during the demonstration against the renewal of the Japanese-American defense treaty (1961); a musical, *Elmer's Adventure* (Tokyo Radio, Aug. 28, 1967); 2 piano concertos (1954, 1970); Sonata for Violin, Piano, Percussion, and Double Bass (1966); Violin Concerto (Tokyo, June 24, 1959); Quartet for Japanese Instruments (1962); Sonata for Violin Solo (1971); Nonet (1972); a number of choral works.

Mana-Zucca (real name, **Augusta Zuckermann**), American pianist and composer; b. New York, Dec. 25, 1887; d. Miami Beach, March 8, 1981. She studied piano with Alexander Lambert in N.Y.; then went to Europe, where she took some lessons with Leopold Godowsky and Busoni in Berlin. Upon her return to the U.S., she was exhibited as a piano prodigy. In 1916 she changed her name by juggling around the syllables of her real last name and dropping her first name altogether. She was soloist in her own Piano Concerto in N.Y. on Aug. 20, 1919; her Violin Concerto, op. 224, was performed in N.Y. on Dec. 9, 1955. She further wrote 2 operas, *Hypatia* and *The Queue of Ki-Lu;* a ballet, *The Wedding of the Butterflies;* and a number of unpretentious orch. pieces, such as *Frolic for Strings, Fugato Humoresque, Bickerings,* and *Havana Nights.* She publ., under the title *My Musical Calendar,* a collection of 366 piano pieces, one to be played every day, with the supernumerary opus to account for leap years. But she attained real success with her lyrically soaring songs, most of them to her own words, with such appealing titles as *I Love Life* and *There's Joy in My Heart.* In 1940 she settled in Florida.

Manchester, Melissa, American songwriter and singer of popular music; b. New York, Feb. 15, 1951. She studied at the High School of Performing Arts in N.Y.; then launched a career as a pop vocalist; made numerous appearances on television. Her recording albums brought her a number of awards and citations.

Mancinelli, Luigi, distinguished Italian conductor and composer; b. Orvieto, Feb. 5, 1848; d. Rome, Feb. 2, 1921. He studied organ and cello with his brother, Marino; then was a cellist in the Orvieto cappella and the orch. of the Teatro della Pergola in Florence; he also studied cello with Sbolà and composition with Mabellini in Florence; then was first cellist and maestro concertatore at the Teatro Morlacchi in Perugia; in 1874 he made his conducting debut there in *Aida* after the regular conductor was unable to lead the performance owing to a temporarily inebriated condition. He then was called to Rome, where he was conductor of the Teatro Apollo from 1874 to 1881; subsequently he served as director of the Cons. in Bologna. On June 18, 1886, he made his London debut conducting a concert performance; in 1887 he conducted at Drury Lane; from 1888 to 1905 he was chief conductor at Covent Garden; from 1887 to 1893 conducted opera in Madrid. He joined the roster of the Metropolitan Opera in N.Y. in 1893, and continued to conduct there until 1903. On May 25, 1908, he led the first performance at the newly opened Teatro Colón in Buenos Aires; he returned there in 1909, 1910, and 1913. He enjoyed a fine reputation as a competent, dependable, and resourceful opera conductor; naturally, he excelled in the Italian repertoire, but he also conducted Wagner's operas, albeit in dubious Italian translation. From his experience as an opera conductor, he learned the art of composing for the theater; his operas are indeed most effective; of these, *Ero e Leandro* became a favorite.

WORKS: OPERAS: *Isora de Provenza* (Bologna, Oct. 2, 1884); *Tizianello* (Rome, June 20, 1895); *Ero e Leandro* (Norwich Festival, Oct. 8, 1896; his most famous opera, produced all over Europe, and also at the Metropolitan Opera, N.Y.); *Paolo e Francesca* (Bologna, Nov. 11, 1907); a posthumous opera, *Sogno di una notte d'estate,* after Shakespeare's *Midsummer Night's Dream* (not produced). ORATORIOS: *Isaia* (Norwich, England, Oct. 13, 1887) and *Santa Agnese* (Norwich, Oct. 27, 1905); cinematic cantata *Giuliano l'Apostata* (Rome, 1920); *Intermezzi sinfonici* for *Cleopatra* by Cossa, a symph. suite that became popular.

BIBLIOGRAPHY: L. Arnedo, *Luigi Mancinelli y su opera Hero y Leandro* (Madrid, 1898); G. Orefice, *Luigi Mancinelli* (Rome, 1921); L. Silvestri, *Luigi Mancinelli; Direttore e compositore* (Milan, 1966).

Mancini, Francesco, Italian composer; b. Naples, Jan. 16, 1672; d. there, Sept. 22, 1737. He studied at the Cons. di S. Maria della Pietà dei Turchini in Naples; in 1704 held the post of first organist in the Royal Chapel; was its director in 1707–8, and again from 1725 until his death; from 1720 until he suffered a stroke in 1735, was maestro di cappella at the Cons. S. Maria di Loreto in Naples. He wrote some 20 operas for Naples, which established his reputation as a notable composer. His opera *Idaspe fedele* was sung in Italian at the Haymarket Theatre in London on April 3, 1710, with considerable success.

BIBLIOGRAPHY: J. Wright, *The Secular Cantatas of Francesco Mancini (1672–1737)* (Diss., N.Y. Univ., 1975).

Mancini, Henry, American composer of film and television music; b. Cleveland, April 16, 1924, of Italian parents. He took piccolo lessons from his father, a member of the Sons of Italy band in Aliquippa, Pa. After playing in dance bands, he studied at Carnegie Inst. in Pittsburgh and at the Juilliard School of Music in N.Y. He further studied composition in Los Angeles with Castelnuovo-Tedesco, Ernst Krenek, and Alfred Sendrey. In 1952 he became a composer for Universal-International film studios and in 1958 began writing background music for television. His jazzy theme for the Peter Gunn series placed him at once as one of the most adroit composers of melodramatic music; he won 5 television awards and several Academy Awards for film scores.

Mandac, Evelyn, soprano; b. Malaybalay, Mindanao, Aug. 16, 1945. She studied voice at the Univ. of the Philippines; then went to the U.S. and enrolled at Oberlin College and later at the Juilliard School of Music. She began her career in 1968 with a concert debut in Mobile, Alabama; then sang with opera companies in Washington, D.C., and San Francisco. On Dec. 19, 1975, she made her debut as Lauretta in *Gianni Schicchi* at the Metropolitan Opera in N.Y.

Mandel, Alan, brilliant American pianist; b. New York, July 17, 1935. He began taking piano lessons with Hedy Spielter at the incredible underage of 3½, and continued under her pianistic care until he was 17. In 1953 he entered the class of Rosina Lhévinne at the Juilliard School of Music in N.Y. (B.S., 1956; M.S., 1957); later took private lessons with

Leonard Sure (1957–60). In 1961 he obtained a Fulbright fellowship; went to Salzburg, where he studied advanced composition with Hans Werner Henze (1961–63). Returning to the U.S., he taught piano at Pa. State College (1963–66). In 1966 he was appointed head of the piano division at the American Univ. in Washington, D.C. In 1980 he founded the Washington Music Ensemble with the aim of presenting modern music of different nations. As a pianist, he made 24 tours in 45 countries, not counting islands, north and south; toured Australia twice. One of Mandel's chief accomplishments was the recording of the complete piano works of Charles Ives; he also recorded 40 piano works of Gottschalk and all the piano sonatas of **Elie Siegmeister** (his father-in-law). Mandel's own compositions include a Piano Concerto (1950), a Symph. (1961), and a number of pieces for piano solo.

Mandić, Josip, Croatian composer; b. Trieste, April 4, 1883; d. Prague, Oct. 5, 1959. He studied music in Trieste, Zagreb, and Vienna; composed 4 symphs. (1929, 1930, 1953, 1954); a Croatian Mass; several cantatas and other vocal music; a Nonet and String Quartet; also the operas *Mirjana* (Olomouc, Feb. 20, 1937) and *Kapetan Niko* (1944).

Mandl, Richard, Austrian composer; b. Prossnitz, May 9, 1859; d. Vienna, April 1, 1918. He studied at the Vienna Cons.; then went to Paris, where he attended the classes of Delibes at the Cons.; returned to Vienna in 1900. He wrote a one-act comic opera, *Nächtliche Werbung* (Prague, 1888); cantata, *Griselidis;* symph. poem, *Stimme des Orients;* symph. rhapsody, *Algier;* dance suite, *Viennensia;* several violin pieces; String Quintet; songs. He was married to **Camilla Barda** (1872–1922), who publ. a valuable pedagogical work, *Kompendium der gesamten Klaviertechnik* (3 vols.).

Mandrell, Barbara (Ann), American country-music singer and instrumentalist; b. Houston, Dec. 25, 1948. She learned to play the accordion; then took up the steel guitar and performed at local entertainment places; later went to Nashville, where she joined the "Grand Ole Opry." She quickly gained a wide following with her performances of such songs as *I've Been Loving You Too Long, Standing Room Only, Woman to Woman, Midnight Angel, Midnight Oil,* and *Best of Strangers.* In 1980 she starred in her own television show, which proved to be quite successful.

Mandyczewski, Eusebius, eminent Austrian musicologist; b. Czernowitz, Aug. 17, 1857; d. Vienna, July 13, 1929. He studied with Robert Fuchs and Nottebohm in Vienna; in 1880 he became choirmaster of the Vienna Singakademie, and archivist to the Gesellschaft der Musikfreunde; in 1896 he joined the faculty of the Vienna Cons., where he taught music history and composition. He was subsequently engaged as one of the editors of the great edition of Haydn's works undertaken by Breitkopf & Härtel; collaborated in many other scholarly editions, including the complete works of Brahms, who was a friend of his; his correspondence with Brahms was publ. by Karl Geiringer in the *Zeitschrift für Musikwissenschaft* (May 1933).

Manelli, Francesco, Italian composer; b. Tivoli, Sept. 1594; d. Parma, July 1667. He served as a chorister at the Cathedral of Tivoli in 1605, and continued his service there as chapel singer (1609–24); he then was maestro di cappella there (1627–28). He produced an opera, *Gelia,* in Bologna (1630); in 1636 he went to Venice, where he was chapel singer at San Marco; from 1645 to his death he was in the service of the Duke of Parma. In 1637, the Teatro San Cassiano in Venice, the first public opera house in Europe, was opened with Manelli's opera *L'Andromeda;* he wrote several other operas, which enjoyed considerable popularity. All the musical scores of Manelli are lost, but some librettos are preserved. His op. 4, *Musiche varie* (Venice, 1626), a collection of cantatas, arias, *canzonette,* and *ciacone,* shows that he had adopted the "parlando" recitative.
  BIBLIOGRAPHY: G. Radicotti, *L'arte musicale in Tivoli nei secoli XVI, XVII e XVIII* (Tivoli, 1907; 2nd ed., 1921).

Manén, Juan, Catalan composer; b. Barcelona, March 14, 1883; d. there, June 26, 1971. He studied both piano and violin, and was exhibited as a piano prodigy in public; then decided to switch to the violin, and went on a European tour; was particularly welcome in Germany, where he resided most of the time from 1908 on. His music is redolent of Spanish, and more specifically Catalan, melorhythms. He wrote an autobiography in 2 vols., titled, with a wistful retrospection, *El niño prodigioso* and *El jóven artista* (Barcelona, 1944, 1964).
  WORKS: FOR THE STAGE: Operas: *Juana de Nápoles* (Barcelona, 1902); *Acté* (Barcelona, 1903; revised and performed with a German libretto as *Nero und Akté,* Karlsruhe, Jan. 28, 1928); *Der Fakkeltanz* (Frankfurt, 1909); *Soledad* (Barcelona, 1952); "theater symph.," *Camino del sol* (Braunschweig, May 2, 1926); theater triptych, *Don Juan* (unperformed); ballet, *Triana* (1952). FOR ORCH.: Concertino for Violin and Orch. (1965); *Sinfónia ibérica* (1966); *Festividad,* overture (1966); *Rapsodia catalana* for Piano and Orch. (1968); *Nova Catalonia, Romanza mistica,* and *Romanza amorosa* for Violin and String Orch.; Fantasia-Sonata for Guitar; pieces for violin.

Manfredini, Francesco, Italian violinist and composer; b. Pistoia (baptized, June 22), 1684; d. there, Oct. 6, 1762. He was engaged as a violinist in Ferrara and Bologna (1704–11); was maestro di cappella at the Cathedral of Pistoia from 1727. He publ. *Concertini per camera* (1704); *12 sinfonie da chiesa* (1709); *12 concerti grossi* (1718). His *Concerto grosso per il santissimo natale* (which includes a fine *Pastorale*) was publ. for 2 Violins, String Quartet, and Piano (Leipzig, 1906); his 6 sonatas for 2 Violins and Cello appeared in London (c.1764); his Sinfonia No.

10, in Vienna (1935); the Concerto Grosso No. 9 was edited for string orch. by E. Bonelli (Padua, 1948); the Sinfonia No. 12, was edited by R. Nielsen (Rome, 1949).

BIBLIOGRAPHY: *U. Bolletino Storico Pistoiese,* III (1968).

Manfredini, Vincenzo, Italian composer, son of **Francesco Manfredini;** b. Pistoia, Oct. 22, 1737; d. St. Petersburg, Aug. 16, 1799. He was a pupil of his father; later studied with Perti in Bologna and with Fioroni in Milan. In 1758 he went to Russia, where he was attached to the court (until 1769); then returned to Italy; lived in Bologna and Venice; in 1798 was engaged by Paul I (who was his former pupil) to come to Russia again; he died there the following year. During his first visit to Russia he produced the following works: *Amour et Psyché,* ballet (Moscow, Oct. 20, 1762); *L'Olimpiade,* opera (Moscow, Nov. 24, 1762); *Pygmalion,* ballet (St. Petersburg, Sept. 26, 1763); *Carlo Magno,* opera (St. Petersburg, Nov. 24, 1763); wrote 6 clavecin sonatas for Catherine the Great (1765).

BIBLIOGRAPHY: "Les Dernières Œuvres de Vincenzo Manfredini," in R.-Aloys Mooser, *Annales de la musique et des musiciens en Russie au XVIIIᵉ siècle* (Geneva, 1950; vol. II, pp. 28–43).

Mangione, "Chuck" (Charles Frank Mangione), American jazz musician and composer; b. Rochester, N.Y., Nov. 29, 1940. He studied at the Eastman School of Music, where he earned his bachelor's degree; gained practical experience as a member of a jazz combo with his brothers. He also began to compose, producing *Friends and Love* for his appearance as guest conductor with the Rochester Phil. in 1970; subsequently made numerous tours with his own band. His record album *Bellavia* was a major success; it was followed by *Feels So Good,* an instrumental number of his own composition which found acclaim among jazz and pop-music lovers.

Mangold, Karl (Ludwig Amand), German composer, brother of **Wilhelm Mangold;** b. Darmstadt, Oct. 8, 1813; d. Oberstdorf, Aug. 5, 1889. He studied at the Paris Cons. with Berton and Bordogni; returning to Darmstadt, became a violinist in the court orch.; from 1848–69, was court music director; also conducted various choral societies there. He wrote an opera, *Tannhäuser,* which was produced in Darmstadt on May 17, 1846, only a few months after the premiere of Wagner's great work; in order to escape disastrous comparisons, the title was changed to *Der getreue Eckart,* and the libretto revised; the new version was produced posthumously in Darmstadt on Jan. 17, 1892. Mangold wrote 2 more operas, *Gudrun* and *Dornröschen;* several "concert dramas" (*Frithjof, Hermanns Tod, Ein Morgen am Rhein, Barbarossas Erwachen*); also oratorios (*Abraham, Wittekind, Israel in der Wüste*); chamber music; and a number of male quartets, which attained great popularity in Germany.

Mangold, (Johann) Wilhelm, German composer and violinist, brother of **Karl Mangold;** b. Darmstadt, Nov. 19, 1796; d. there, May 23, 1875. He studied with Rinck and Abbé Vogler; then went to Paris for lessons with Cherubini at the Paris Cons.; in 1825, became court conductor at Darmstadt; was pensioned in 1858. He wrote 3 operas, chamber music, and melodies for clarinet with piano, which were popular for a time.

Manilow, Barry, American singer, arranger, and composer of popular music; b. Brooklyn, N.Y., June 17, 1946. He played the accordion and piano in his youth; then worked as a successful arranger and composer of radio and television commercials; scored enormous success with his pop hits *Mandy; It's a Miracle; Could It Be Magic?; I Write the Songs; Looks Like We Made It; Can't Smile without You;* and others.

Mankell, Henning, Swedish composer; b. Härnösand, June 3, 1868; d. Stockholm, May 8, 1930. He studied piano and composition in Stockholm; composed a number of works, mostly for piano; in his style he followed some models of French impressionist music. Among his works are a Piano Concerto (1917); 3 piano sonatas; 8 ballads for Piano; 3 string quartets; Piano Quintet; Piano Trio; songs.

Mann, Alfred, German-born American musicologist; b. Hamburg, April 28, 1917. He studied at the Milan Cons. and the Berlin Hochschule für Musik; emigrated to America and enrolled at the Curtis Inst. of Music in Philadelphia, receiving his diploma in 1942; later took courses in musicology at Columbia Univ. (Ph.D., 1955, with the dissertation *The Theory of Fugue*). In 1947 he was appointed a prof. of music at Rutgers Univ. in Newark, N.J.

WRITINGS: *Die Lehre vom Kontrapunkt* (Celle, 1938; 2nd ed., 1951); *Steps to Parnassus* (partial Eng. trans. of J.J. Fux's *Gradus ad Parnassum,* N.Y., 1943; new ed., under the title *The Study of Counterpoint,* N.Y., 1965); *The Study of Fugue* (New Brunswick, N.J., 1958; 2nd ed., 1965); ed. the series Documents of the Musical Past (New Brunswick, N.J., 1953–65) and Fux's *Gradus ad Parnassum* in the *Sämtliche Werke* (Kassel, 1967); contributed articles to *The Musical Quarterly* and other scholarly journals.

Mann, Arthur Henry, English organist and editor; b. Norwich, May 16, 1850; d. Cambridge, Nov. 19, 1929. He studied at Oxford (B.Mus., 1882); from 1876 to his death was organist at King's College, Cambridge. He was a noted student of Handel's music; with Ebenezer Prout, he discovered at the Foundling Hospital the original wind-instrument parts of Handel's *Messiah,* and reconstructed the score in accordance with these parts; the work was performed in London in this version on June 13, 1894. Mann was co-editor (with Fuller-Maitland) of the Fitzwilliam Catalogue (publ. 1893); edited Tallis's motet for 40 voices, *Spem in alium* (1888); was music editor of *The Church of England Hymnal* (1895). He composed an oratorio, *Ecce Homo* (1882), and several sacred works.

Mann, Herbie, American jazz flutist; b. New York, April 16, 1930. He studied at the Manhattan School of Music, and became a successful jazz flutist. He made extensive solo tours and played in pop concerts with the leading American orchs.

Mann, Leslie, Canadian composer and clarinetist; b. Edmonton, Alberta, Aug. 13, 1923; d. Balmoral, Manitoba, Dec. 7, 1977. He studied music in Toronto; in 1957 went to Winnipeg and became first clarinetist of the CBC Winnipeg Orch. there. His music follows tradition, and contributes to listening pleasure without straining.
WORKS: Chamber opera, *The Donkey's Tale* (1971); *Concertino in the Old Style* for String Orch. (1955); Flute Concerto (1964); Clarinet Concerto (1970); *Sinfonia Concertante* for Bassoon and Chamber Orch. (1971); *Concerto Grosso No. 1* for Chamber Orch. (1972); 3 symphs. (No. 1, 1973; No. 2, 1974; No. 3, *Typhoon,* 1976); *Weep You No More Sad Fountains,* 7 songs to Elizabethan poems, for Voice and Chamber Orch. (1974); *5 Bagatelles* for Clarinet or Viola, and Piano (1951); Trio for Flute, Clarinet, and Cello (1952); Cello Sonata (1953); *5 Improvisations* for Flute and Piano (1954); *Toccata alla Barocco* for Flute, Clarinet, and Cello (1956); Wind Quintet (1961); Clarinet Sonata (1962); *Suite* for Clarinet Solo (1963); *Suite* for Flute Solo (1963); Trio for Clarinet, Cello, and Piano (1967); *4 Studies in the Blues Idiom* for Wind Quintet (1969); *Music* for Clarinet, Viola, and Piano (1971); *Partita* for Violin and Bassoon (1972); Sonata for Solo Violin (1974); *Vocalise* for Oboe or Clarinet, and Piano (1974); String Quartet (1975); Suite for Solo Saxophone (1976); Flute Sonata (1977); songs.

Mann, Paul, Austrian-American song composer; b. Vienna, Sept. 3, 1910; d. Queens, N.Y., May 27, 1983. He was educated at the Vienna Music Academy, where he studied composition with Joseph Marx. He came to the U.S. after the Nazi Anschluss in 1938 and wrote music for Broadway productions and for films. His song, *Put Your Dreams Away* was popularized by Frank Sinatra. Other successful songs were *The Finger of Suspicion* and *Angel in Disguise.*

Mann, Robert, American violinist, composer, and conductor; b. Portland, Oreg., July 19, 1920. He studied violin with Edouard Déthier at the Juilliard Graduate School in N.Y., and had instruction in chamber music with Adolfo Betti, Felix Salmond, and Hans Letz; also took courses with Edgar Schenkman in conducting, and Bernard Wagenaar and Stefan Wolpe in composition. In 1941 he won the Naumburg Competition, and made his N.Y. debut as a violinist. From 1943 to 1946 he was in the U.S. Army; then joined the faculty of the Juilliard School and in 1948 founded the Juilliard String Quartet, in which he plays first violin, and which was to become one of the most highly regarded chamber music groups; in 1962 it was established as the quartet in residence under the Whittall Founda-

tion at the Library of Congress, without suspending its concert tours in America and abroad. As a conductor, Robert Mann specializes in contemporary music; was associated as a performer and lecturer with the Music Festival and Inst. at Aspen, Colo., and also served with the National Endowment for the Arts; in 1971 he was appointed president of the Walter W. Naumburg Foundation, with his wife, Lucy Rowan, as secretary and executive administrator. He has composed a String Quartet (1952); *Suite* for String Orch. (1965); several "lyric trios" for violin, piano, and narrator.

Mann, William, English music critic and writer on music; b. Madras, Feb. 14, 1924. He studied piano with Ilona Kabos and composition with Mátyás Seiber; also studied at Magdalene College, Cambridge, with Patrick Hadley, Hubert Middleton, and Robin Orr. He became a member of the music staff of the *Times* of London in 1948; in 1960 he became its chief music critic. In addition, he appeared in radio broadcasts for the BBC; also made serviceable English translations of opera libretti and texts of German lieder. He publ. *Introduction to the Music of Johann Sebastian Bach* (London, 1950); *Richard Strauss: A Critical Study of the Operas* (London, 1964); and *The Operas of Mozart* (London, 1977).

Manneke, Daan, Dutch composer; b. Kruiningen, Nov. 7, 1939. He studied organ at the Brabant Cons. (1960–66) and compostion with Ton de Leeuw in Amsterdam (1967–73); in 1973 was appointed lecturer on modern music at the Amsterdam Cons.
WORKS: Opera, *De passie van Johannes Lanckohr* (1977); *Walking in Fog Patches* for Wind Quintet (1971); *Jeu* for Solo Flute (1971); *Plein jeu* for Brass Quintet (1972); *4 Sonatas* for Youth Orch. (1972); *Stages* for Variable Ensemble (1972); *Music about Poor and Bad People* for a cappella Chorus (1972); *3 Times* for Chorus and Small Orch. (1974; winner of the 1976 Fontein Tuynhout Prize for best perf. by amateurs); *Ordre* for 4 Recorders (1975); *Sinfonia* for 13 String Instruments (1975); *Job* for Male Chorus, 4 Brasses, and 3 Percussionists (1976); *En passant (Touching in Passing)* for Small Orch. (1977).

Manners, Charles (real name, **Southcote Mansergh**), Irish bass singer and impresario; b. London, Dec. 27, 1857; d. Dublin, May 3, 1935. He studied in Dublin; then at the Royal Academy of Music in London and in Florence. In 1882 he made his stage debut with the D'Oyly Carte company, creating the role of Private Willis in Sullivan's *Iolanthe.* In 1890 he married the soprano **Fanny Moody;** in 1897 organized the Moody-Manners Opera Co., with her as a partner, for the production of grand opera in the English language; in 1902, after several successful seasons in the provincial theaters, he took his enterprise to London; retired in 1913.

Mannes, Clara Damrosch, pianist, daughter of **Leopold Damrosch;** b. Breslau, Dec. 12, 1869; d. New York, March 16, 1948. At the age of 6 she began to study piano in N.Y.; then went to Dresden, where she took lessons with H. Scholtz; later also was a pupil of Busoni in Berlin (1897). On June 4, 1898, she married the violinist **David Mannes,** with whom she toured the U.S. and England for 20 years in joint recitals; was co-director of the Mannes School in N.Y.

BIBLIOGRAPHY: *Notable American Women* (N.Y., 1971, vol. II).

Mannes, David, American violinist and conductor; b. New York, Feb. 16, 1866; d. there, April 25, 1959. He studied violin in Berlin, and was briefly a student of Ysaÿe in Brussels (1903). He was a member of the N.Y. Symph. Orch. conducted by Walter Damrosch, beginning in 1891, and was its concertmaster from 1898 to 1912; married **Clara Damrosch,** June 4, 1898. In 1912 he founded in N.Y. the Music School Settlement for Colored People; conducted a series of free symph. concerts at the Metropolitan Museum in N.Y. (1919–47). In 1916 he opened his own music school in N.Y., known as the David Mannes School of Music; continued to be active until a very advanced age; on his 90th birthday, in 1956, a special concert was organized in his honor at the Metropolitan Museum. He publ. an autobiography, *Music Is My Faith* (N.Y., 1938).

Mannes, Leopold Damrosch, American pianist, son of **David Mannes** and **Clara Damrosch Mannes;** b. New York, Dec. 26, 1899; d. Martha's Vineyard, Cape Cod, Mass., Aug. 11, 1964. He graduated from Harvard Univ. (B.A., 1920); studied at the David Mannes School and at the Inst. of Musical Art in N.Y.; was a pupil of Elizabeth Quaile, Guy Maier, and Alfred Cortot (piano), and Schreyer, Scalero, and Goetschius (theory); won a Pulitzer scholarship (1925) and a Guggenheim fellowship (1926); subsequently taught composition and piano at the Inst. of Musical Art and at the Mannes School; succeeded his father as director of the latter. He temporarily abandoned music as a profession to enter the research laboratory of the Eastman Kodak Co. at Rochester, N.Y., and was a co-inventor, with Leopold Godowsky (son of the pianist), of the Kodachrome process of color photography. Among his works are: Suite for 2 Pianos (1924); String Quartet (1928; perf. many times by the Kneisel Quartet); *3 Short Pieces* for Orch. (1926); incidental music to Shakespeare's *Tempest* (1930).

Manney, Charles Fonteyn, American music editor and composer; b. Brooklyn, Feb. 8, 1872; d. New York, Oct. 31, 1951. He was first a church singer; then studied theory with W.A. Fisher in N.Y., and with Goodrich and Goetschius in Boston. In 1898 he was engaged as music editor for the Oliver Ditson Co., and held this position until 1930; also conducted the Footlight Orch. and various choral groups; after retirement, he moved to N.Y. He wrote an opera, 3 cantatas, songs, and piano pieces.

Manning, Jane, English soprano; b. Norwich, Sept. 20, 1938. She studied at the Royal Academy of Music in London; in 1964 she made her debut in London in a program of contemporary music, and subsequently established herself as a leading interpreter of modern music in England. She is married to the composer **Anthony Payne.**

Manning, Kathleen Lockhart, American composer; b. Hollywood, Oct. 24, 1890; d. Los Angeles, March 20, 1951. She played as a child pianist in public concerts; took lessons with Moszkowski in Paris; also appeared as an opera singer with the Hammerstein Opera Co. in London (1911–12). She wrote 2 operas (*Mr. Wu* and *For the Soul of Rafael*) and several song cycles: *Sketches of Paris* (which includes *In the Luxemburg Gardens*), *Sketches of London, Songs of Egypt, Sketches of New York,* etc.; also piano pieces (*3 Dance Impressions, In the Summer,* etc.).

Mannino, Franco, Italian pianist, conductor, and composer; b. Palermo, April 25, 1924. He studied piano with R. Silvestri and composition with V. Mortari at the Santa Cecilia Academy in Rome; made his debut as a pianist at the age of 16; subsequently toured as a pianist in Europe and America. In 1957 he conducted the orch. of the Maggio Musicale of Florence on a tour of the U.S. He subsequently conducted in Europe, South America, and the Far East; was a frequent guest conductor in the Soviet Union, where he regularly appeared with the Leningrad Phil. In 1969 he became artistic director of the Teatro San Carlo in Naples; from 1974 its artistic adviser. In 1982 he was appointed principal conductor and artistic adviser of the National Arts Centre Orch. in Ottawa. He was a prolific composer; his operas and other works are written in traditional melodramatic Italian style, diversified by occasional modernistic procedures.

WORKS: OPERAS: *Mario e il mago* (1952; Milan, Feb. 23, 1956); *Vivi* (1955; Naples, March 28, 1957; many subsequent perfs.); *La speranza* (1956; Trieste, Feb. 14, 1970); *La stirpe di davide* (1958; Rome, April 19, 1962); *Le notti della paura* (1960; RAI, Rome, May 24, 1963); *Il Diavolo in giardino* (1962; Palermo, Feb. 28, 1963); *Luisella* (1969; Palermo, Feb. 28, 1963); *Il quadro delle meraviglie* (1963; Rome, April 24, 1963); *Il ritratto di Dorian Gray* (1973; Catania, Jan. 12, 1982); *Il Principe Felice* (1981). FOR ORCH.: Piano Concerto (1954; Remschied, Dec. 1, 1954); *Sinfonia Americana* (1954; Florence, Nov. 11, 1956); *Sinfonia* (1958); *Demoniaca,* overture (1963); Concerto for 3 Violins (1965; Moscow, March 21, 1966); *Laocoonte* for Orch. (1966; Trieste, May 8, 1968); Concerto for Piano, 3 Violins, and Orch. (1969); *Notturno Napoletano* (1969; Naples, March 13, 1970); *Concerto grosso* (1970); Violin Concerto (1970; Milan, May 14, 1971); Concerto No. 2 for Piano (1974; Cagliari, April 22, 1980); Cello Concerto (1974; Naples, July 14, 1975); *Supreme Love,* cantata for Solo Voices, Chorus, and Orch. (1977; Naples, Sept. 30, 1978); *Settecento* for Orch. (1979); *Olympic Concert* for 6 Violins, 2 Pianos, and Orch. (1979); *Nirvana,* poem for Orch. (1980; Cagliari, April 22, 1980); Concerto for 6 Violins, 2

Pianos, and Orch. (1980); Symph. No. 4, *Leningrad* (1981; Lecce, May 11, 1982).

Manns, Sir August, German-English conductor; b. Stolzenberg, near Stettin, March 12, 1825; d. London, March 1, 1907. He learned to play the violin, clarinet, and flute; was a member of various bands in Danzig and Berlin; then conducted bands in Königsberg and Cologne. In 1854 he went to London, where he became a conductor at the Crystal Palace; in 1855 he inaugurated the famous Saturday Concerts at the Crystal Palace, which he conducted for 45 seasons, until 1901, presenting about 14,000 concerts in all, in programs of a regular symph. repertoire. He became a celebrated musical and social figure in London, and was knighted in 1903. Besides the Saturday Concerts, he conducted 6 Triennial Handel Festivals (1883–1900) and the orch. concerts of the Glasgow Choral Union (1879–92).

BIBLIOGRAPHY: H.S. Wyndham, *August Manns and the Saturday Concerts* (London, 1909); *Dictionary of National Biography* (Supplement; Oxford, 1920).

Mannstädt, Franz, German conductor; b. Hagen, July 8, 1852; d. Wiesbaden, Jan. 18, 1932. He studied at the Stern Cons. in Berlin; was Hans von Bülow's assistant conductor at Meiningen, and also conducted some concerts of the Berlin Phil., which he took on a major tour in 1885; then went to Wiesbaden as court conductor, retiring in 1924.

Manojlović, Kosta, Serbian composer; b. Krnjevo, Dec. 3, 1890; d. Belgrade, Oct. 2, 1949. He studied in Munich and at Oxford Univ., receiving a bachelor's degree in 1919. He wrote a Serbian liturgy, and a cantata, *By the Waters of Babylon;* characteristic piano pieces (*Danse fantastique,* etc.) and songs. He publ. several studies on Serbian folk music; his collection of 337 songs of east Serbia was publ. posthumously (Belgrade, 1953).

Manowarda, Josef von, Austrian bass; b. Cracow, July 3, 1890; d. Berlin, Dec. 24, 1942. He studied in Graz; made his debut there in 1911; then sang at the Vienna Volksoper (1915–18) and in Wiesbaden (1918–19); in 1919 he joined the Vienna State Opera, where he had a distinguished career; also sang at Salzburg, Bayreuth, La Scala in Milan, Rome, and the Berlin State Opera; taught at the Vienna Academy of Music (1932–35). He was also a fine concert singer.

Manrique de Lara, Manuel, Spanish composer and student of folklore; b. Cartagena, Oct. 24, 1863; d. St. Blasien, Germany, Feb. 27, 1929. He entered the Spanish army and rose to the rank of brigadier general; studied music with Chapí; became a leading authority on old Spanish ballads, including those sung by Jewish communities in the Near East. He wrote *La Orestiada,* symph. trilogy (1900); chamber music; etc.

Manschinger, Kurt, Austrian composer; b. Zeil-Wieselburg, in a castle of which his father was an administrator, July 25, 1902; d. New York, Feb. 23, 1968. He studied musicology at the Univ. of Vienna, and at the same time took private lessons with Anton von Webern (1919–26). After graduation he was mainly active as a theatrical conductor in Austria and Germany. His practical acquaintance with operatic production led to his decision to write operas, for which his wife, the singer **Greta Hartwig,** wrote librettos. Of these, his first opera, *Madame Dorette,* was to be performed by the Vienna State Opera, but the invasion of Austria by the Nazi troops in 1938 made this impossible. Manschinger and his wife fled to London, where they organized an émigré theater, The Lantern. In 1940 they emigrated to America; Manschinger changed his name to **Ashley Vernon** and continued to compose; earned his living as a musical autographer by producing calligraphic copies of music scores for publishers.

WORKS: Operas: *The Barber of New York* (N.Y., May 26, 1953); *Grand Slam* (Stamford, Conn., June 25, 1955); *Cupid and Psyche* (Woodstock, N.Y., July 27, 1956); *The Triumph of Punch* (Brooklyn, Jan. 25, 1969); *Der Talisman* for Voices, Violin, Viola, Cello, and Piano (London, Feb. 24, 1940); Sinfonietta (1964); Symph. (1967); chamber music.

Mansfield, Orlando Augustine, English organist and composer; b. Warminster, Nov. 28, 1863; d. Cheltenham, July 6, 1936. He studied with E.H. Turpin in London and later at Trinity Univ. in Toronto; held various positions as organist in England; from 1892 to 1912 was examiner for London College of Music. He publ. about 600 works for piano and for organ; and some 100 arrangements of choral and other works; publ. his original compositions under the pen names **Oscar Liemann** and **Sofie N. Adlam.** He contributed numerous articles to Eng. and American journals; publ. *Student's Harmony* (1896), which passed through several editions.

Mansfield, Purcell James, English organist, son of **Orlando Augustine Mansfield;** b. Torquay, May 24, 1889; d. Glasgow, Sept. 24, 1968. He received his entire education from his father. In 1905 he won the gold and silver medals at the Bristol Eisteddfod (Welsh Festival); then was organist at various churches in London and Glasgow. He publ. miscellaneous pieces for organ and arrangements of Scottish airs for mixed choir.

Manski, Dorothée, American soprano; b. New York, March 11, 1895; d. Atlanta, Feb. 24, 1967. She went to Germany as a child; appeared at Berlin in Max Reinhardt's productions; made her first American appearance with the Metropolitan Opera in N.Y., on Nov. 5, 1927, as the Witch in *Hänsel und Gretel;* remained with the Metropolitan Opera until 1941; then joined the faculty of the School of Music at Indiana Univ. as a vocal teacher.

Manskopf, (Jakob Friedrich) Nicholas, German collector of musical materials; b. Frankfurt, April

25, 1869; d. there, July 2, 1928. After extensive travels in France and England, he founded in his native city the Musikhistorisches Museum, containing MSS, books, documents, rare scores, theater programs, medals, caricatures, autographs, etc., of musicians from the 14th to the 20th century— about 30,000 items in all.

Mansurian, Tigran, Lebanese-born Armenian composer; b. Beirut, Jan. 27, 1939. His family moved to Soviet Armenia when Mansurian was 8 years old. He studied with Sarian at the Erevan Cons. (1960–65). In 1968 he was appointed to the faculty of his alma mater. His music is substantially neo-Classical in form and ethnic Armenian in its thematic and rhythmic material.
WORKS: FOR ORCH.: Concerto for String Orch. (1962); Concerto for Organ and Chamber Orch. (1964); *Partita* (1965); *Preludes* (1975); Cello Concerto, to the memory of Shostakovich (1976); Concerto for Violin, Cello, and Orch. (1979); *Praeludium* (1980). CHAMBER MUSIC: Solo Cello Sonata (1960); 2 string quartets (1960, 1963); Viola Sonata (1961); *Suite* for Wind Instruments and Piano (1961); Flute Sonata (1962); *Scherzo* for Violin and Piano (1962); *Allegro Barbaro* for Cello and Piano (1963); Violin Sonatina (1964); 2 violin sonatas (1964, 1965); Piano Trio (1965); *Psalm* for 2 Flutes and Violin (1966); *Music* for 12 Instruments (1966); *Arabesques I* and *II* for Chamber Ensemble (1969, 1970); *Bird's Silhouette I, II,* and *III* for Harpsichord and Percussion (1971, 1972, 1973); *2 Elegies* for Violin and Piano (1972); *Interior* for String Quartet (1972); 2 cello sonatas (1973, 1974). FOR VOICE: *Ariens,* after the 15th-century Armenian poet Naapet Kuchack, for Soprano and Chamber Orch. (1967); *Intermezzo* for Vocal and Instrumental Ensemble (1972); *2 Maidens,* madrigal after Kostan Sarian, for Soprano and Chamber Ensemble (1981); choruses; songs. FOR PIANO: Sonatina (1963); *3 Preludes* (1965); Sonata (1965); *4 Miniatures* (1969); *3 Pieces* (1971).

Mantelli, Eugenia, Italian mezzo-soprano; b. c.1860; d. Lisbon, March 3, 1926. She made her debut in Treviso in 1883 as Kalad in *Le Roi de Lahore;* subsequently sang in Germany, South America, England, and Russia. On Nov. 23, 1894, she made her Metropolitan Opera debut in N.Y. as Amneris; she continued to make appearances there until the 1902–3 season. She retired in 1910.

Mantovani, Annunzio Paolo, Italian conductor of popular music; b. Venice, Nov. 15, 1905; d. Tunbridge Wells, England, March 29, 1980. He went to London as a youth; studied at the Trinity College of Music there; became a British subject in 1933. He formed an orch. of his own in Birmingham at the age of 18; then led bands in hotels and in theaters. His ingratiatingly harmonious orch. arrangements made his name famous; the "Mantovani sound" became a byword with sedentary music-lovers seeking relaxation and listening pleasure as an antidote to the dramatic enervation of hazardous modern living and raucous popular music.

Mantovani, Tancredi, Italian writer on music; b. Ferrara, Sept. 27, 1863; d. Rome, Feb. 24, 1932. He was a pupil of A. Busi in Bologna; in 1894 he became a prof. of music history and librarian at the Liceo Rossini in Pesaro; was editor of the *Cronaca Musicale* (1896–1904); in 1919 was appointed prof. of literature at the Santa Cecilia Academy in Rome.
WRITINGS: *Estetica musicale* (1892); *Orlando di Lasso* (1895); *Rossini a Lugo* (1902); *Cristoforo Gluck* (1914); *Angelo Mariani* (1921); a guide to Berlioz's *Damnation de Faust* (1923); etc.

Mantuani, Josef, Austrian music scholar; b. Laibach (Ljubljana), March 28, 1860; d. there, March 18, 1933. He studied composition with Bruckner and others in Vienna; musicology at the Univ. of Vienna, obtaining the degree of Dr.Phil.; became librarian in the Vienna Library in 1893, and later chief of the music division; from 1909 taught in his native town of Laibach. He edited several vols. of Denkmäler der Tonkunst in Österreich; publ. *Tabulae codicum manuscriptorum ... asservatorum* (2 vols., 1897 and 1899; a complete catalogue of the MSS in the Vienna Library); *Katalog der Ausstellung anlässlich der Centenafeier D. Cimarosas* (1901); *Über den Beginn des Notendrucks* (1901); *Ein unbekanntes Druckwerk* (1902); *Geschichte der Musik in Wien. I. Teil: Von den Römerzeiten bis zum Tode des Kaisers Max I.* (1904); "Die Musikpflege Laibachs zur Zeit Schuberts," in the *Adler Festschrift* (1930).

Manuel, Roland. See **Roland-Manuel, Alexis.**

Manzoni, Giacomo, Italian composer; b. Milan, Sept. 26, 1932. He studied music in Messina and Milan; taught composition at the Milan Cons. (1962–64) and at the Bologna Cons. (1965–75). His opera *Atomtod (Atom Death),* descriptive in apocalyptic sounds of the ultimate atomic war, attracted a great deal of attention at its production (Milan, March 17, 1965). Other works: opera, *La sentenza* (Bergamo, Oct. 13, 1960); *5 Vicariote* for Chorus and Orch. (Radio Turin, Nov. 29, 1968); *Don Chisciotte* for Soprano, Small Chorus, and Chamber Orch. (1961; Venice Festival, Sept. 14, 1964); *4 poesie spagnole* for Baritone, Clarinet, Viola, and Guitar (1961); *Studio per 24* for Chamber Orch. (1962); *Studio No. 2* for Orch. (Milan, April 20, 1963); *Studio No. 3* for Tape (1964); *Musica notturna* for 5 Wind Instruments, Piano, and Percussion (1966); *Insiemi* for Orch. (Milan, Oct. 30, 1969); *Spiel* for 11 Strings (1969); *Parafrasi con finale* for 10 Instruments (1969); *Variabili* for Orch. (1973); *Percorso C* for Bassoon and String Orch. (1976).

Mapleson, Col. James Henry, English impresario; b. London, May 4, 1830; d. there, Nov. 14, 1901. He studied at the Royal Academy of Music in London; subsequently was engaged as a singer and a viola player; sang in Italy under the name of **Enrico Mariani.** In 1861 he became the manager of the Italian Opera at the Lyceum Theatre in London; then of Her Majesty's Theatre (1862–67); at Drury Lane

(1868–69); in partnership with Gye at Covent Garden (1869–70); again at Drury Lane (1871–76); at the reconstructed (after the fire of 1868) Her Majesty's Theatre (from 1877). He gave several seasons of opera in the U.S. (during intervals of his London enterprises); his American ventures fluctuated between success and disaster; his last season was 1896–97 at the N.Y. Academy of Music. On March 17, 1890, he married the American singer **Laura Schirmer.** An exuberant personality, he dominated the operatic news in both England and America by his recurrent professional troubles and his conflicts with, and attachments to, prima donnas. He was known as "Colonel" Mapleson by his intimates, but held no such rank. He publ. *The Mapleson Memoirs* (2 vols., London, 1888). His nephew, **Lionel S. Mapleson** (b. London, Oct. 23, 1865; d. New York, Dec. 21, 1937), came to the U.S. as a violinist; in 1889 joined the orch. of the Metropolitan Opera in N.Y.; then, for a half century, was librarian there; left his own valuable library to the Metropolitan Opera, including the first recordings, made by himself, ever taken of actual performances, with the voices of de Reszke, Calvé, and others.

Mara, Gertrud Elisabeth (née **Schmeling**), German soprano; b. Kassel, Feb. 23, 1749; d. Reval, Russia, Jan. 20, 1833. She learned to play the violin as a child; gave concerts in Vienna and London; returning to Germany, she studied voice and developed an extraordinary range, reaching high E; she sang in Hiller's concerts in Leipzig in 1766; then sang with the Dresden Opera (1767–71) and was engaged by the Berlin Opera (1771–79). She married the cello player Mara, and appeared under her married name. From 1784 to 1802 she lived mostly in London; in 1799 she separated from her husband; then went to Russia, where she supported herself as a singing teacher; she lived in Moscow until 1812, when Napoleon's invasion forced her to seek refuge elsewhere; from 1813 she was a singing teacher in Reval, where she remained until the end of her life. She was a famous prima donna in her time, and there was much literature written about her.
BIBLIOGRAPHY: G.C. Grosheim, *Das Leben der Künstlerin Mara* (Kassel, 1823; reprinted 1972); G. Bürkli, *Gertrud Elisabeth Mara* (Zürich, 1835); "Autobiographie" (ed. by Riesemann), *Allgemeine musikalische Zeitung* (1875); A. Niggli, "Gertrud Elisabeth Mara," in Waldersee's *Sammlung musikalischer Vorträge* (Leipzig, 1881; after the autobiography); E. Wolff, *Mignon* (Munich, 1909); Rosa Kaulitz-Niedeck, *Die Mara: Das Leben einer berühmten Sängerin* (Heilbronn, 1929); O. Anwand, *Die Prima Donna Friedrichs des Grossen* (Berlin, 1930); also V. Huber, *Flirt und Flitter; Lebensbilder aus der Bühnenwelt* (Düsseldorf, 1970).

Maragno, Virtú, Argentine composer; b. Santa Fé, March 18, 1928. He studied in Buenos Aires and later in Rome with Goffredo Petrassi. Returning to Argentina, he became active as a choral conductor and teacher. He writes in a distinctly modernistic vein, leaning toward serial techniques.

WORKS: *Triste y Danza* for Small Orch. (1947); *Divertimento* for Wind Quintet (1952); *Scherzo sinfónico* (Buenos Aires, June 16, 1953); Concertino for Piano and 14 Instruments (1954); 2 string quartets (1958, 1961); *Expresión* for Double Orch. and Percussion (Rome, June 23, 1961); *Intensidad y Espacio* for Orch. (1962); *Composición I* for Voices, Instruments, and Magnetic Tape (Buenos Aires, Oct. 5, 1962); music for the theater; film scores; choruses; songs.

Marais, Josef, American folksinger and composer; b. Sir Lowry Pass, South Africa, Nov. 17, 1905; d. Los Angeles, April 27, 1978. He studied at the South African College of Music and at the Royal Academy of Music in London; then took violin lessons with Otakar Sevčik in Prague. He emigrated to the U.S. in 1939; worked at the Office of War Information in N.Y. and broadcast songs from the South African *veld;* in 1947 married Roosje Baruch de la Bardo, a Dutch immigrant *chanteuse,* who took on the professional name Miranda. Together they publ. a number of song collections; Marais wrote the music for several stage productions, including Alan Paton's *Too Late the Phalarope;* he composed the orch. work *Paul Gauguin Suite* and other descriptive pieces.

Marais, Marin, great French player of the viola da gamba and composer; b. Paris, May 31, 1656; d. there, Aug. 15, 1728. He was apprenticed as a choirboy at the Sainte-Chapelle; studied bass viol with Sainte-Colombe and composition with Lully (whom he addresses as teacher in a letter publ. in his first book of pieces for his instrument). He then became "joueur de viole du roi" (Aug. 1, 1679). In 1686 he presented at Versailles an *Idylle dramatique;* in 1701 he was called upon to write a Te Deum for the convalescence of the Dauphin. He retired in 1725. Marais possessed matchless skill as a virtuoso on the viola da gamba, and set a new standard of excellence by enhancing the sonority of the instrument. He also established a new method of fingering, which had a decisive influence on the technique of performance. As a composer, he followed Lully's French manner; his recitatives comport with the rhythm of French verse and the inflection of the rhyme. The purely instrumental parts in his operas were quite extensive; in *Alcione* (Paris, Feb. 18, 1706) he introduced a "tempeste," which is one of the earliest attempts at stage realism in operatic music. His other operas are *Alcide* (1693), *Ariane et Bacchus* (1696), and *Sémélé* (1709). He publ. 5 books of pieces for gamba (1686–1725); trios (or "symphonies") for violin, flute, and viola da gamba (1692); a book of trios for violin, viola da gamba, and harpsichord under the title *La Gamme* (1723). An edition of his instrumental works, edited by J. Hsu, began publication in N.Y. in 1980. He was married on Sept. 21, 1676, and had 19 children; in 1709 he played a concert with 3 of them for Louis XIV. His son **Roland** was also a talented gambist; he publ. 2 books of pieces for the instrument with a basso continuo and a *Nouvelle méthode de musique pour servir d'in-*

troduction aux acteurs modernes (1711).

BIBLIOGRAPHY: L. de La Laurencie, *L'Ecole Française de violon* (Paris, 1924); F. Lesure, "Marin Marais," and M. Barthélemy, "Les Opéras de Marin Marais" (both *Revue Belge de Musicologie,* 1953); C. Thompson, *Marin Marais, 1656–1728* (Diss., Univ. of Michigan, 1956); M. Urquhart, *Style and Technique in the "Pièces de violes" of Marin Marais* (Diss., Univ. of Edinburgh, 1970); B. McDowell, *Marais and Forqueray: A Historical and Analytical Study of their Music for Solo Basse de Viole* (Diss., Columbia Univ., 1974); J. Vertrees Sadie, "Marin Marais and His Contemporaries," *Musical Times,* CXIX (1978).

Mařák, Otakar, Czech tenor; b. Ostrihom, Hungary, Jan. 5, 1872; d. Prague, July 2, 1939. He studied with Paršova-Zikešová at the Prague Cons.; made his debut as Faust in 1899 in Brno; then sang with the Prague National Theater Opera (1900–7, 1914–34), in Vienna, Berlin, London, Paris, and Chicago. He died in poverty after the failure of a business venture.

Marazzoli, Marco, significant Italian composer; b. Parma, between 1602 and 1608; d. Rome, Jan. 26, 1662. In 1631 he gained the patronage of Cardinal Antonio Barberini in Rome; in 1637 he settled in Rome in the cardinal's service and became a tenor in the Papal Chapel, a position he held until his death; he also was engaged by Cardinal Mazarin in Paris in 1643; returned to Rome in 1645; in 1656 he became virtuoso di camera to Queen Christina of Sweden, who held her court in Rome at the time. Marazzoli was a prolific composer of choral music; about 375 of his cantatas and oratorios are extant. His name is also associated with that of Virgilio Mazzocchi; they collaborated on the first comic opera, *Chi soffre, speri* (Rome, Feb. 27, 1639), which was a revision of *Il facone* (Rome, Feb. 1637). His other operas include *L'amore trionfante dello sdegno* (also known as *L'Armida;* Ferrara, Feb. 1641); *Gli amori di Giasone e d' Issifile* (Venice, 1642; not extant); *Le pretensioni del Tebro e del Po* (Ferrara, March 4, 1642); *Il capriccio* or *Il giudizio della ragione fra la Beltà e l'Affetto* (Rome, 1643); *Dal male il bene* (with A.M. Abbatini; Rome, 1653); *Le armi e gli amori* (Rome, 1654); *La vita humana, ovvero Il trionfo della pietà* (Rome, Jan. 31, 1656).

BIBLIOGRAPHY: A. Loewenberg, *Annals of Opera* (Cambridge, 1943; revised 1955); M. Grace, *Marco Marazzoli and the Development of the Latin Oratorio* (Diss., Yale Univ., 1974).

Marbé, Myriam, Rumanian composer; b. Bucharest, April 9, 1931. She began her musical studies at home with her mother, a professional pianist; then entered the Bucharest Cons., where she studied with Negrea (1944–54). In 1954 she joined the staff of the Bucharest Cons. Her compositions are permeated with Rumanian melorhythms, but her harmonic investiture is quite modern. In later works she experiments with "sonorism," serialism, and "spatial" music.

WORKS: *The World of Children* for Piano (1952); Viola Sonata (1955); Piano Sonata (1956); cantata, *Noapte țărănească* (*Night of the Land;* 1958); *Lyrical Piece* for Oboe, String Orch., 2 Horns, Piano, Celesta, and Percussion (1959); Clarinet Sonata (1961); *Musica festiva,* divertissement for Strings, Brass, and Percussion (1961); *Incantation,* sonata for Solo Clarinet (1964); Sonata for 2 Violas (1965); *Clime* for Mezzo-soprano and Chamber Orch. (1966); *Ritual pentru setea pămîntului* (*Ritual for the Thirst of the Earth)* for 7 Singers scattered and staggered through the hall, and optional Percussion (1968); *Le Temps inévitable* for Piano (1968); ditto for Piano and Orch. (1971); *Jocus secundus* for Small Vocal Group, Tape, Violin, Viola, Cello, Clarinet, Piano, and Percussion (1969); *Cluster Studies* for Piano (1970); *Accents* for Piano (1971); *Temps et espace* for Orch. (1972); *Cycle* for Flute, Guitar, and Percussion (1974); *Petite musique du soleil* for Orch. (1974); *Vocabulaire I—Chanson* for Soprano, Clarinet, Piano, and Bells (1974); choruses; songs.

Marbeck (Merbecke), John, English composer and theologian; b. Windsor, c.1510; d. there, c.1585. He was a chorister in St. George's Chapel, Windsor (1531); narrowly escaped burning as a heretic in 1544; was imprisoned, but pardoned by Henry VIII; Mus.Bac., Oxford, 1550; lay clerk and organist of St. George's Chapel. His chief work is *The Booke of Common Praier noted* (1550), an adaptation of the plainchant of earlier rituals to the first ritual of Edward VI; reprinted in facsimile, 1939: republ. in Jebb's *Choral Responses and Litanies* (1857; vol. II). One of his hymns appears in Hawkins's *General History of the Science and Practice of Music.* Marbeck was also the compiler of a concordance of the English Bible (1550).

BIBLIOGRAPHY: J. Pulver, *A Biographical Dictionary of Old English Music* (London, 1927); J. Eric Hunt, *Cranmer's First Litany, 1544, and Merbecke's Book of Common Prayer noted, 1550* (London, 1939); R. Stevenson, "John Marbeck's *Noted Booke* of 1550," *Musical Quarterly* (April 1951).

Marcel (real name, **Wasself**), **Lucille,** American soprano; b. New York, 1885; d. Vienna, June 22, 1921. She studied in Paris with Jean de Reszke, who recommended her for the role of Elektra at the Vienna premiere of Strauss's opera; she made her debut in this very difficult part on March 24, 1908, under the direction of **Felix Weingartner,** whom she married in 1907; she was the principal soprano when Weingartner became conductor of the Hamburg Opera (1912–14). She sang with the Boston Opera Co., making her American debut as Tosca on Feb. 14, 1912; later she returned to Vienna, where she remained until her death.

Marcelli, Nino, Chilean composer and conductor; b. Santiago, Jan. 21, 1890; d. San Diego, Calif., Aug. 16, 1967. He studied at the National Cons. of Santiago. In 1920 he went to the U.S.; played cello in the San Francisco Symph.; in 1927 organized the San Diego Symph. Orch., which he conducted until 1937.

He composed several orch. marches and overtures, and also a *Suite Araucana* based on motifs of Chilean Indians.

Marcello, Alessandro, Italian scholar and composer, brother of **Benedetto Marcello;** b. Venice, Aug. 24, 1669; d. Padua, June 19, 1747. He publ. his works under the name of **Eterico Stinfalico;** extant are *Concerti a cinque con violino solo e violoncello obbligato* (op. 1); various pieces for flutes and oboes with strings, etc. Alessandro Marcello seems to have been the composer of the Oboe Concerto transcribed by Bach, which is usually attributed to Benedetto Marcello.
BIBLIOGRAPHY: F.C. Walker, "A Little Bach Discovery," *Music & Letters* (April 1950).

Marcello, Benedetto, famous Italian composer and poet; b. Venice, Aug. 9, 1686; d. Brescia, July 24, 1739. He received an excellent education; studied jurisprudence as well as music; studied violin with his father; then singing and counterpoint with Gasparini and Lotti; had a political career: was a member of the Council of Forty for 14 years, "Provveditore" at Pola for 8 years, and finally papal chamberlain at Brescia, a position he retained from 1738 until his death. His masterwork is the settings of Giustiniani's paraphrases of the first 50 Psalms (*Estro poetico-armonico; Parafrasi sopra i cinquanta primi Salmi;* Venice, publ. by D. Lovisa, 1724–26, in 8 vols. folio); they are for one, 2, 3, and 4 voices, with basso continuo for organ or clavicembalo; a few with cello obbligato or 2 violas; they have been often republ. (by Carli in Paris, etc.). He also publ. *Concerti grossi* for 5 parts (1701); *Sonate per cembalo, Sonate a cinque, e flauto solo con basso continuo* (1712), *Canzoni madrigaleschi ed Arie per camera a 2–4* (1717); a satire on operatic manners, *Il teatro alla moda, o sia Metodo sicuro e facile per ben comporre ed eseguire opere italiane in musica* (1720; 2nd ed., 1722; modern ed. by E. Fondi, Lanciano, 1913; Eng. trans. by R.G. Pauly in the *Musical Quarterly,* July 1948, and January 1949; German trans. by A. Einstein in *Perlen älterer romanischer Prosa,* 24); the pamphlet *Lettera famigliare* (1705), a rather captious critique of Lotti, was printed incomplete, with a statement that it no longer corresponded to the views of the author. Both *Il teatro alla moda* and *Lettera famigliare* were publ. anonymously, but Marcello's authorship was never in dispute. Besides the works named above, Marcello composed oratorios and over 400 secular cantatas, preserved in MS in the libraries of Dresden and Vienna, and sacred works.
BIBLIOGRAPHY: G. Sacchi, *Vita di Benedetto Marcello* (Venice, 1788; trans., with supplementary material, of F.L. Fontana's Latin biography of Marcello in vol. 9 of *Vitae Italorum Doctrinae Excellentium,* Pisa, 1787); O. Chilesotti, *I nostri maestri del passato* (Milan, 1882; pp. 83–91); Leonida Busi, *Benedetto Marcello* (Bologna, 1884); O. Chilesotti, *Sulla lettera critica di Benedetto Marcello contro A. Lotti* (Bassano, 1885; contains polemics with Busi; appends a list of Marcello's publications and bibliography); E. Fondi, *La vita e l'opera letteraria del musicista Benedetto Marcello* (Rome, 1909); A. Della Corte, "La Morale d'una satira," *Il pianoforte* (1921); U. Rolandi, "I 50 salmi," *Musica d'Oggi* (XI/1); A. d'Angeli, *Benedetto Marcello* (Milan, 1940); R.G. Pauly, "Benedetto Marcello's Satire on Early 18th-Century Opera," *Musical Quarterly* (April 1948); W.S. Newman, "The Keyboard Sonatas of Benedetto Marcello," *Acta Musicologica* (1957); C. Sites, *Benedetto Marcello's Chamber Cantatas* (Diss., Univ. of North Carolina, 1959).

Marchal, André, distinguished French organist and pedagogue; b. Paris, Feb. 6, 1894. He was blind from birth; studied at the Institution Nationale des Jeunes Aveugles; later entered the Paris Cons. in the class of Gigout. In 1915 he became organist at St. Germain-des-Prés in Paris; then served at St. Eustache from 1945–63. He began a concert career in 1923; also gave master classes for organists.

Marchand, Louis, French organist, harpsichordist, and composer; b. Lyons, Feb. 2, 1669; d. Paris, Feb. 17, 1732. He went to Paris as a youth; in 1691 he received the post of organist of the Jesuit church in the rue St. Jacques there; he was also organist at other Parisian churches; in 1708 he was named an organiste du roi, in which capacity he earned a considerable reputation; in 1713 he made a major tour of Germany. Marchand's name is historically connected with that of Bach because both were scheduled to meet in open competition in Dresden in 1717; however, Marchand failed to appear and Bach was deemed the superior virtuoso by default. Marchand composed 3 books for clavecin (1–2, Paris, 1702; 3, Paris, 1707). A number of his organ works are included in Guilmant's *Archives de maîtres de l'orgue;* his *Plein jeu* (in 6 parts) is reproduced in J. Bonnet's *Historical Organ Recitals* (vol. 1). See also T. Dart, ed., *Louis Marchand: Pièces de clavecin* (Paris, 1960).
BIBLIOGRAPHY: G. Sharp, "Louis Marchand, 1669–1732: A Forgotten Virtuoso," *Musical Times,* CX (1969).

Marchant, Sir Stanley (Robert), English organist and composer; b. London, May 15, 1883; d. there, Feb. 28, 1949. He studied organ at the Royal Academy of Music in London; occupied various posts as organist in London churches; was on the staff of the Royal Academy of Music from 1913, in executive as well as teaching capacities; was knighted in 1943. As a composer, he confined himself to organ music, vocal works for church services, and school manuals.

Marchesi, Blanche (Baroness André Caccamisi), famous dramatic soprano, daughter of **Salvatore** and **Mathilde Marchesi;** b. Paris, April 4, 1863; d. London, Dec. 15, 1940. She was first trained as a violinist; took lessons with Nikisch in Germany and with Colonne in Paris. In 1881 she began to study singing with her mother, and, until her marriage to Baron Caccamisi, acted as her mother's assistant. She made her concert debut in Berlin (1895);

when she sang in London (1896), the reception was so enthusiastic that she made England her home; her operatic debut followed in Prague in 1900 as Brünnhilde in *Die Walküre;* then she sang with the Moody-Manners company in London; from 1902 sang the Wagner roles at Covent Garden; made tours of Russia and Central Europe; also made 2 concert tours of the U.S. (1899, 1909); gave her farewell concert in 1938. In her last years, she established herself as a highly esteemed teacher in London. She publ. her memoirs under the title *A Singer's Pilgrimage* (London, 1923).

Marchesi, Luigi, celebrated male soprano, known as **"Marchesini,"** b. Milan, Aug. 8, 1754; d. Inzago, Dec. 14, 1829. He was a chorister in Milan; made his debut at Rome at age 17, scoring an immediate success. His fame as a sopranist grew rapidly after his visits to other Italian cities. In 1785 he was engaged as a singer at the court of Catherine the Great; on his way to St. Petersburg, he stopped over in Vienna, where he sang at the Imperial court of Joseph II. He made his Russian debut in St. Petersburg, early in 1786, as Rinaldo in Sarti's opera *Armida e Rinaldo;* the Italian female soprano Luiza-Rosa Todi intrigued against him, and despite his successes, he left Russia before the expiration of his contract. On March 9, 1787, he sang in Berlin, winning great acclaim; then toured through Switzerland and Italy. He sang for the last time at the age of 66 in Naples; then returned to Milan.

BIBLIOGRAPHY: R.-Aloys Mooser, *Annales de la musique et des musiciens en Russie au XVIIIᵉ siècle* (Geneva, 1950; vol. II, pp. 497–98).

Marchesi de Castrone, Mathilde (née **Graumann**), famous German vocal teacher; b. Frankfurt, March 24, 1821; d. London, Nov. 17, 1913. She studied singing in Frankfurt with Felice Ronconi, in Vienna with Nicolai, and in Paris with Manuel García; made her concert debut in Frankfurt on Aug. 31, 1844. In 1849 she went to London; in 1852 she married the Italian baritone **Salvatore Marchesi de Castrone.** Later in life she devoted herself mainly to teaching; had classes at the Vienna Cons. (1854–61 and 1869–78); also taught privately in Paris. Among her famous pupils were Murska, Gerster, Melba, Eames, Calvé, and Sanderson. She wrote an autobiography, *Erinnerungen aus meinem Leben* (Vienna, 1877), which was publ. in a revised and amplified edition under the title *Marchesi and Music: Passages from the Life of a Famous Singing Teacher* (N.Y., 1897). She further publ. a vocal manual, *10 Singing Lessons* (N.Y., 1910), which was reprinted under a new title, *Theoretical and Practical Vocal Method* (N.Y., 1970, with an introduction by Philip L. Miller).

Marchesi de Castrone, Salvatore (complete name and title, **Cavaliere Salvatore de Castrone, Marchese della Rajata**), baritone and famous teacher; b. Palermo, Jan. 15, 1822; d. Paris, Feb. 20, 1908. Of a noble family, he was destined for a government career and studied law in Palermo; however,

he turned to music, and took lessons in singing and theory with Raimondi in Palermo, and with Lamperti in Milan. He was involved in the revolutionary events of 1848, and was compelled to leave Italy; went to N.Y., where he made his operatic debut in Verdi's *Ernani.* He then studied with García in London; married **Mathilde Graumann (Mathilde Marchesi de Castrone)** in 1852, and sang with her in opera on the Continent. From 1854 till 1861, they both taught at the Vienna Cons.; later at the Cologne Cons. (1865–68), and again in Vienna (1869–78); after that they resided in Paris.

Marchetti, Filippo, Italian opera composer; b. Bolognola, near Camerino, Feb. 26, 1831; d. Rome, Jan. 18, 1902. He was a pupil of Lillo and Conti at the Royal Cons. in Naples. His first opera, *Gentile da Varano* (Turin, Feb. 1856), was extremely well received, and he repeated his success with another opera, *La Demente,* for Turin (Nov. 27, 1856); however, his next opera, *Il Paria,* never reached the stage. He was not discouraged by this and wrote his *Romeo e Giulietta* (Trieste, Oct. 25, 1865), which had a pronounced success in performances at La Scala in Milan and other Italian theaters. He achieved his greatest success with *Ruy-Blas* (La Scala, April 3, 1869), which was produced also in Germany and England; the remaining operas were *Gustavo Wasa* (La Scala, Feb. 7, 1875) and *Don Giovanni d'Austria* (Turin, March 11, 1880). In 1881 he was appointed president of the Santa Cecilia Academy in Rome; then was director of the Liceo Musicale (1886–1901).

Marchetto da Padua, an early proponent of *Ars Nova* who flourished in the 14th century and worked in Florence; author of the important treatises *Lucidarium in arte musicae planae* (on plainsong, early 14th century) and *Pomerium artis musicae mensurabilis* (on mensural music, 1318); the latter is included (in part) in Strunk's *Source Readings in Music History* (N.Y., 1950); a modern edition is found in *Corpus scriptorum de musica,* VI (1961). He also wrote *Brevis compilatio in arte musicae mensuratae,* which has been edited by G. Vecchi, "Su la composizione del *Pomerium* di Marchetto de Padova e la *Brevis compilatio,*" in *Quadrivium,* i (1956).

BIBLIOGRAPHY: O. Strunk, "Intorno a Marchetto da Padua," *Rassegna Musicale* (Oct. 1950); N. Pirotta, "Marchettus de Padua and the Italian Ars Nova," *Musica Disciplina,* IX (1955); M. Martinez-Göllner, "Marchettus of Padua and Chromaticism," *L'ars nova italiana del tracento II: Certaldo 1969;* F. Gallo, "Marchettus in Padua und die 'Franco-venetische' Musik des frühen Trecentos," *Archiv für Musikwissenschaft,* XXXI (1974).

Marchisio, Barbara, Italian contralto; b. Turin, Dec. 6, 1833; d. Mira, April 19, 1919. She studied in Turin with L. Fabbrica; made her debut as Rosina in Madrid in 1856; then sang with the major opera houses in Europe; was very successful in her appearances in Paris (1860) and London (1862); following her retirement from the stage, she was active as a voice teacher.

Marco, Tomás, Spanish composer; b. Madrid, Sept. 12, 1942. He studied violin and composition at the Univ. of Madrid (1959–64). An ardent modernist, he founded in 1967 the magazine *Sonda,* dedicated to new music. His own compositions are of an experimental, almost exhibitionistic, theatrical nature.

WORKS: *Los caprichos* for Orch. (1959–67); *Trivium* for Piano, Tuba, and Percussion (1963); *Roulis-Tangage* for Trumpet, Cello, Guitar, Piano, Vibraphone, and 2 Percussionists (1962–63); *Glasperlenspiel* for Chamber Orch. (1963–64); *Car en effet* for 3 Clarinets and 3 Saxophones (1965); *Piraña* for Piano (1965); *Jabberwocky* for Actors, Tenor, Saxophone, Piano, 4 Percussionists, Tape, 6 Radios, Lights, and Slides (1966); *Schwan* for Trumpet, Trombone, Viola, Cello, and 2 Percussionists (1966); *Cantos del pozo artesiano* for Actress, 3 Chamber Ensembles, and Lights (1967); *Vitral (Música celestial No. 1)* for Organ and String Orch. (1968); *Maya* for Cello and Piano (1968–69); *Anábasis* for Orch. (1968–70); *Rosa-Rosae,* quartet for Flute, Clarinet, Violin, and Cello (1969); *Tea Party* for 4 Vocal Soloists, Clarinet, Trombone, Cello, and Vibraphone (1969); *Floreal* for a Percussionist (1969); *Kukulcan* for Wind Quintet (1969–72); *Mysteria* for Chamber Orch. (1970–71); *Albor* for Flute, Clarinet, Violin, Cello, and Piano (1970); *Evos* for Piano (1970); *Necronomicon,* choreography for 6 Percussionists (1971); *L'Invitation au voyage* for Soprano, optional Narrator, 3 Clarinets, Piano, and Percussion (1971); *Angelus novus (Hommage à Mahler)* for Orch. (1971); *Jetzzeit* for Clarinet and Piano (1971); Violin Concerto, subtitled *Les Mécanismes de la mémoire* (1971–72; Royan Festival, April 19, 1973); *Nuba* for Flute, Oboe, Clarinet, Violin, Cello, and Percussion (1973); *Ultramarina* for Soprano, Clarinet, Piano, and Percussion (1975).

BIBLIOGRAPHY: G. Gomez Amat, *Tomás Marco* (Madrid, 1971).

Marcoux, Vanni (full name, **Jean Emile Diogène Marcoux**), dramatic baritone; b. (of French parents) Turin, June 12, 1877; d. Paris, Oct. 21, 1962. He was a law student at the Univ. of Turin; then went to France, where he enrolled at the Paris Cons. He made his debut in Turin in 1894 as Sparafucile in *Rigoletto;* subsequently obtained considerable success at his debut at the Paris Opéra as Colonna in the premiere of Février's *Monna Vanna* (Jan. 13, 1909). Massenet entrusted to him the part of Don Quichotte in the premiere of his opera of that name (Monte Carlo, Feb. 19, 1910). In 1912 he sang with the Boston Opera Co., and later with the Chicago Opera Co. His repertoire included more than 200 roles in several languages. He eventually returned to Paris and was instructor in lyric declamation at the Paris Cons.; sang at the Paris Opéra for nearly 40 years; was also director of the Grand Theater in Bordeaux (1948–51). In professional appearances, he used the hyphenated name **Vanni-Marcoux.**

Marcovici, Silvia, Rumanian violinist; b. Bacau, Jan. 30, 1952. She studied at the Bucharest High School for Music; made her professional debut in The Hague in 1968; in 1970 she won first prize in the Georges Enescu Competition. In 1972 she played in London, and subsequently appeared with several English orchs. She made a successful American debut in N.Y. in 1977.

Maréchal, Adolphe, Belgian tenor; b. Liège, Sept. 26, 1867; d. Brussels, Feb. 1, 1935. He studied at the Liège Cons.; made his debut in Tournai in 1891; then sang in Rheims, Bordeaux, and Nice; in 1895 he became a member of the Opéra-Comique in Paris, where he remained until 1907; during that time, he created the roles of Julien in *Louise,* Alain in *Grisélidis,* and Danielo in *La Reine fiammette;* also Jean in *Le Jongleur de Notre-Dame* at Monte Carlo. He retired in 1907 after the loss of his singing voice.

Maréchal, Henri-Charles, French composer; b. Paris, Jan. 22, 1842; d. there, May 12, 1924. He studied piano and theory at the Paris Cons.; composition with Victor Massé; won the Grand Prix de Rome (1870) with the cantata *Le Jugement de Dieu.* After his return from Rome he produced an oratorio, *La Nativité* (1875), and several operas: *Les Amoureux de Catherine* (Paris, May 8, 1876), *La Taverne des Trabans* (1881), *Calendal* (Rouen, Dec. 21, 1894), *Ping-Sin* (Paris, Jan. 25, 1918), etc.; also wrote several orch. suites, choral works, etc. He publ. 2 vols. of reminiscences: *Rome: Souvenirs d'un musicien* (Paris, 1904; 2nd ed., 1913) and *Paris: Souvenirs* (Paris, 1907); also *Monographie universelle de l'Orphéon* (Paris, 1910; on singing societies) and *Lettres et Souvenirs, 1871–1874* (Paris, 1920).

Maréchal, Maurice, French cellist; b. Dijon, Oct. 3, 1892; d. Paris, April 19, 1964. He won first prize at the Paris Cons. in 1911; then gave concerts as a cello soloist in Boston, Chicago, N.Y., Paris, London, and other European cities; also toured in Russia, China, and Japan. Returning to Paris, he taught cello at the Paris Cons. (1942–63).

Marek, Czeslaw, Polish composer and pianist; b. Przemysl, Sept. 16, 1891. He studied piano with Leschetizky in Vienna and composition with Pfitzner in Strasbourg. In 1915 he went to Zürich, and in 1932 became a Swiss citizen. In his later years he devoted himself mainly to pedagogy; publ. a manual, *Lehre des Klavierspiels* (Zürich, 1972). He composed a Symph. (1927); *Echos de la jeunesse* for Piano (1914); and several minor piano pieces, as well as songs.

Marenco, Romualdo, Italian composer; b. Novi Ligure, March 1, 1841; d. Milan, Oct. 9, 1907. He played the violin, then the bassoon at the Doria Theater in Genoa, for which he wrote his first ballet, *Lo sbarco di Garibaldi a Marsala.* He studied counterpoint under Fenaroli and Mattei; traveled; and became in 1873 director of ballet at La Scala in Milan. He composed over 20 ballets (*Sieba, Excelsior,*

Sport, etc.); operas: *Lorenzio de' Medici* (Lodi, 1874); *I Moncada* (Milan, 1880); *Le Diable au corps* (Paris, 1884); and the "idilio giocoso" *Strategia d'amore* (Milan, 1896). A posthumous opera, *Federico Struensea,* was produced in Milan in 1908.

Marenzio, Luca, important Italian composer; b. Coccaglio, near Brescia, 1553 or 1554; d. Rome, Aug. 22, 1599. Little is known of his early life; he may have studied with Giovanni Contino in Brescia; about 1574 he entered the service of Cardinal Cristoforo Madruzzo in Rome; following Madruzzo's death in 1578, he entered the service of Cardinal Luigi d'Este; he made an extended visit with the cardinal to the court of Duke Alfonso II d'Este in Ferrara, where he spent the months of Nov. 1580 to May 1581; he dedicated 2 volumes of madrigals to the duke and his sister Lucrezia. After the death of the cardinal in 1586, he entered the service of Ferdinando de' Medici, the grand duke of Florence (1588); in 1589 he returned to Rome, where he apparently received the patronage of several cardinals; about 1593 he entered the service of Cardinal Cinzio Aldobrandini; he subsequently served at the court of Sigismund III of Poland (1596–98); he then returned to Rome, where he died the following year. Marenzio was one of the foremost madrigalists of his time; his later works in the genre are historically significant for their advanced harmonic procedures. He also composed about 75 motets. He was called by his contemporaries "il più dolce cigno d'Italia" and "divino compositore."

WORKS: His secular works were publ. as follows: *Il primo libro de madrigali* for 5 Voices (Venice, 1580); *Il primo libro de madrigali* for 6 Voices (Venice, 1581); *Il secondo libro de madrigali* for 5 Voices (Venice, 1581); *Il terzo libro de madrigali* for 5 Voices (Venice, 1582); *Il secondo libro de madrigali* for 6 Voices (Venice, 1584); *Madrigali spirituali* for 5 Voices (Rome, 1584; enlarged ed., 1610); *Il quarto libro de madrigali* for 5 Voices (Venice, 1584); *Il primo libro delle villanelle* for 3 Voices (Venice, 1584); *Il quinto libro de madrigali* for 5 Voices (Venice, 1585); *Il terzo libro de madrigali* for 6 Voices (Venice, 1585); *Il secondo libro delle canzonette alla napolitana* for 3 Voices (Venice, 1585); *Madrigali . . . libro primo* for 4 Voices (Rome, 1585); *Il terzo libro delle villanelle* for 3 Voices (Venice, 1585; 4th ed., enlarged, 1600); *Il quarto libro de madrigali* for 6 Voices (Venice, 1587; 3rd ed., revised, 1593); *Il quarto libro delle villanelle* for 3 Voices (Venice, 1587; 4th ed., revised, 1600); *Il quinto libro delle villanelle* for 3 Voices (Venice, 1587); *Madrigali . . . libro primo* for 4, 5, and 6 Voices (Venice, 1588); *Il quinto libro de madrigali* for 6 Voices (Venice, 1591); *Il sesto libro de madrigali* for 5 Voices (Venice, 1594); *Il sesto libro de madrigali* for 6 Voices (Venice, 1595); *Il settimo libro de madrigali* for 5 Voices (Venice, 1595); *L'ottavo libro de madrigali* for 5 Voices (Venice, 1598); *Il nono libro de madrigali* for 5 Voices (Venice, 1599); also *Il secondo libro de madrigali* for 4 Voices, which is not extant. His sacred works were publ. as follows: *Motectorum pro festis totius anni cum Communi*

Sanctorum for 4 Voices (Venice, 1585); *Completorium et antiphonae* for 6 Voices (Venice, 1595; not extant); *Motetti* for 12 Voices (Venice, 1614); *Sacrae cantiones* for 5, 6, and 7 Voices (Venice, 1616). B. Meier and R. Jackson are editing the *Opera omnia* in Corpus Mensurabilis Musicae (1976—); S. Ledbetter and P. Myers are also editing *The Secular Works* (N.Y., 1977—).

BIBLIOGRAPHY: F. Haberl, "Luca Marenzio: Eine bio-bibliographische Skizze," *Kirchenmusikalisches Jahrbuch,* XV (1900); J. Orbaan, "Notizie inedite su Luca Marenzio," *Bolletino Bibliographico Musicale,* III/3 (1928); A. Einstein, *The Italian Madrigal* (Princeton, 1949; pp. 614–618 and 628–637); P. Guerrini, *Luca Marenzio, il più dolce cigno d'Italia nel centenario della nascita* (Brescia, 1953); G. Reese, *Music in the Renaissance* (N.Y., 1954; 2nd ed., revised, 1959); H. Engel, *Luca Marenzio* (Florence, 1956); D. Arnold, *Marenzio* (London, 1965); J. Steele, "The Later Madrigals of Luca Marenzio," *Studies in Music* (1969); R. Jackson, "Two Newly-Found Motets by Marenzio (?)," *Journal of the American Musicological Society,* XXIV (1971); S. Ledbetter, *Luca Marenzio: New Biographical Findings* (Diss., N.Y. Univ., 1971); W. Kirkendale, "Franceschina, Girometta, and Their Companions in a Madrigal 'A diversi linguaggi' by Luca Marenzio and Orazio Vecchi," *Acta Musicologica,* XLIV (1972); N. Pirrotta, "Note su Marenzio e il Tasso," *Scritti in onore di Luigi Ronga* (Milan and Naples, 1973); J. Chater, "Fonti poetichi dei madrigali di Luca Marenzio," *Rivista Italiana di Musicologia,* XIII (1978); S. Ledbetter, "Marenzio's Early Career," *Journal of the American Musicological Society,* XXXII (1979); J. Chater, *Luca Marenzio and the Italian Madrigal* (London, 1981).

Maresch, Johann Anton, inventor of the Russian "hunting-horn music," in which each player has a horn producing a single tone; b. Chotěboř, Bohemia, 1719; d. St. Petersburg, June 10, 1794. He studied horn with Hampel in Dresden, and cello in Berlin. In 1748 he was engaged by the Russian Chancellor Bestuzhev as horn player in his private orch. in St. Petersburg, and later became chamber musician to the Russian court. In 1751 he was commissioned to organize an ensemble of hunting horns for the court; he formed a group comprising 2 complete octaves tuned chromatically, adding large drums with church bells suspended within them; also constructed wooden horns for soft accompaniment to operas. The vogue of horn orchs. in Russia continued for about 50 years after Maresch's death; the players were recruited usually from among serfs. After the emancipation of serfs in Russia in 1861, the horn orchs. gradually disappeared.

BIBLIOGRAPHY: J.C. Hinrichs, *Entstehung, Fortgang und jetzige Beschaffenheit der russischen Jagdmusik* (St. Petersburg, 1796); K. Vertkov, *Russian Horn Music* (Moscow, 1948); "Les Orchestres de cors russes," in R.-Aloys Mooser, *Annales de la musique et des musiciens en Russie au XVIIIe siècle* (Geneva, 1951; vol. III, pp. 859–76).

Mareschall, Samuel, Flemish composer; b. Tournai, May 22, 1554; d. Basel, 1640. He studied at the Univ. of Basel. In 1577 became a prof. of music there and organist at the Basel Cathedral; in 1576 was appointed prof. at the Univ. there. His collection of 4-part vocal settings of the Psalms (1606) became a traditional Lutheran hymnbook; another book of Psalms (including hymns by Luther) appeared in 1616. He also compiled *Melodiae suaves* (1622); much earlier he publ. a disquisition, *Porta Musica, mit einem kurtzen Bericht und Anleitung zu den Violen* (Basel, 1589).
BIBLIOGRAPHY: R. Kendall, "The Life and Works of Samuel Mareschall," *Musical Quarterly* (Jan. 1944).

Marescotti, André-François, Swiss composer; b. Carouge, near Geneva, April 30, 1902. He studied at the Geneva Cons., and in Paris with Roger-Ducasse; from 1924 he was chorus master at Sacre-Cœur; from 1940, at the St. Joseph Church in Geneva; from 1931, a prof. at the Geneva Cons.
WORKS: *Aubade* for Orch. (Geneva, Jan. 27, 1938); *Concert carougeois* for Orch. (1942); *Les Anges du Greco,* ballet (Zürich, June 1, 1947); *Giboulées* for Bassoon and Orch. (1949); *La Lampe d'argile,* dramatic legend (Strasbourg, April, 1951); overture, *Festa* (1961); *Concert carougeois* for Orch. (1966); numerous piano pieces. He publ. a valuable vol. (in folio), *Les Instruments d'orchestre, Leurs caractères, leurs possibilités et leur utilisation dans l'orchestre moderne,* with 900 musical examples (Paris, 1950).

Maretzek, Max, operatic impresario; b. Brünn, Moravia, June 28, 1821; d. Staten Island, N.Y., May 14, 1897. He studied medicine and law at the Univ. of Vienna; music with Ignaz von Seyfried (a pupil of Mozart and Haydn). He progressed rapidly, and at the age of 22 conducted his first opera, *Hamlet* (Brünn, 1843). He then traveled in France and England as a theater conductor and composer of ballet music. In 1848 he arrived in N.Y. as conductor and manager of the Italian Opera Co. He presented Adelina Patti for the first time in opera (as Lucia, 1859); in 1876 he staged his own play with music, *Baba;* conducted his pastoral opera *Sleepy Hollow; or, The Headless Horseman,* after Washington Irving (N.Y., Sept. 25, 1879). As a worldly impresario, he was extremely successful; traveled to Mexico and Cuba, but lived mostly in N.Y., and became an American citizen. He publ. a book of reminiscences, *Crotchets and Quavers, or Revelations of an Opera Manager in America* (N.Y., 1855); and a sequel, *Sharps and Flats* (N.Y., 1870).
BIBLIOGRAPHY: E. Hipsher, *American Opera and Its Composers* (Philadelphia, 1934; pp. 310–12).

Marez Oyens, Tera de, Dutch composer; b. Velzen, Aug. 5, 1932. She studied piano, violin, composition, and conducting at the Amsterdam Cons., graduating in 1953; attended a course in electronic music given by Koenig; was subsequently associated with the Inst. of Sonology in Utrecht.

WORKS: 2-Piano Sonatina (1961); *Der Chinesche Spiegel,* 3 songs for Tenor and Orch. (1962); *2 Sketches* for Wind Quintet (1963); *Deducties* for Oboe and Harpsichord (1964); *Photophonie I* for Tape (1969); *Introduzione* for Orch. (1969); *Communication* for Chorus and Dancers (1970); *Ryoanji Temple* for Contralto, Oboe, Violin, Viola, and Cello (1972); *Transformation* for Orch. (1972); Wind Octet (1972); *Canzone per Sonar* for variable instrumentation (1972); *Delta Ballet* for Tape (1973); *Mixed Feelings* for 4-track Tape and Percussion (1973); *3 Modi* for 3 Violins, Cello, and Recorder Quartet (1973); *From Death to Birth* for Chorus (1974); *Starmobile* for variable instrumentation (1974); Trio for Cello, Percussion, and Tape (1974); *Human* for Orch. and Tape (1975); *Ode to Kelesh* for Chorus and Instruments (1975); *Shoshadre,* in 2 parts, for Strings (1976); *Episodes* for Orch. and variable Ensemble (1976); *Inter-Times* for Oboe, Bassoon, Piano, and Harpsichord (1977); music for radio broadcasts of poetry, plays, and various "verbosonic" compositions.

Margaritis, Loris, Greek pianist; b. Aigion, Aug. 15, 1895; d. Athens, Sept. 27, 1953. He began his career as an infant prodigy; studied in Berlin and Munich. When his early promise failed to materialize, he returned to Greece in 1915, and became an instructor at the Cons. of Salonika.

Margola, Franco, Italian composer; b. Orzinuovi, near Brescia, Oct. 30, 1908. He studied violin and composition at the Cons. of Parma; then took a course in advanced music theory with Casella at the Santa Cecilia Academy in Rome. He then taught at the Cons. of Cagliari and at the Cons. of Parma. He wrote an opera, *Il mito di Caino* (Bergamo, 1940); 2 symphs.; a children's Concerto for Piano, with Small Orch., and a similar Concerto for Violin; Piano Concerto (Florence, Feb. 12, 1944); Cello Concerto (1955); Horn Concerto (1960); Double Concerto for Violin, Piano, and String Orch. (1960); Oboe Concerto, with String Orch. (1962); *4 Episodi* for Flute and Guitar (1970); 10 string quartets; 4 violin sonatas; 3 cello sonatas; etc. He publ. a manual, *Guida pratica per lo studio della composizione* (Milan, 1954).

Marguste, Aiti, Estonian composer; b. Are, Aug. 5, 1931. He studied composition at the Cons. of Tallinn; then devoted himself to teaching there. He applies modernistic techniques to classical forms of composition. Among his works are 5 symphs. (1960, 1964, 1966, 1967, 1970); *Estonian Rhapsody* for Orch. (1974); Concertino for Piano and Orch. (1958); numerous pieces for various instrumental combinations.

Maria Antonia Walpurgis, Electress of Saxony, daughter of the Elector of Bavaria (Emperor Charles VII); b. Munich, July 18, 1724; d. Dresden, April 23, 1780. She was not only a generous patroness of the fine arts, but a trained musician, pupil of Hasse and Porpora (1747–52); under the pseudonym

E.T.P.A. (Ermelinda Talea Pastorella Arcada, her name as member of the Academy of Arcadians) she produced and publ. 2 Italian operas to her own librettos, *Il trionfo della Fedeltà* (Dresden, 1754) and *Talestri* (Nymphenburg, near Munich, Feb. 6, 1760; Dresden, Aug. 24, 1763); the former was one of the earliest publications of Breitkopf & Härtel printed from their new types (1765); she also wrote texts of oratorios and cantatas for Hasse and Ristori.
BIBLIOGRAPHY: K. von Weber, *Maria Antonia Walpurgis* (2 vols., Dresden, 1857); H. Drewes, *Maria Antonia Walpurgis als Komponistin* (Leipzig, 1934); A. Yorke-Long, *Music at Court: 4 Eighteenth-Century Studies* (London, 1954).

Mariani, Angelo, Italian conductor and composer; b. Ravenna, Oct. 11, 1821; d. Genoa, June 13, 1873. He studied violin and composition; had some lessons with Rossini in Bologna; made his principal career as an opera conductor, first in Italy (1844–47), then in Denmark (1847–48). He took part in the Italian war of independence of 1848; then was compelled to leave Italy, and spent 4 years in Istanbul. In 1852 he returned to Italy as opera conductor and director of the Teatro Carlo Felice in Genoa, a post he held until his death; introduced Wagner's *Lohengrin* in Bologna, where he was also music director of the Teatro Comunale from 1860 until his death. He was also favorably known as a composer; wrote several attractive songs (*Liete e tristi rimembranze, Il Trovatore nella Liguria, Rimembranze del Bosforo,* etc.); also some orch. music. He arranged 3 operas by Verdi (in their entirety) for string quartet: *Macbeth, I vespri Siciliani,* and *Un ballo in maschera.*
BIBLIOGRAPHY: T. Mantovani, *Angelo Mariani* (Rome, 1921); U. Zoppi, *Angelo Mariani, Giuseppe Verdi e Teresa Stolz in un carteggio inedito* (Milan, 1947); S. Martinotti, "Angelo Mariani, direttore e musicista, nel suo tempo," *Studi Musicali,* ii (1973).

Marić, Ljubica, remarkable Serbian composer; b. Kragujevac, March 18, 1909. She studied with Josip Slavenski in Belgrade; then went to Prague, where she took composition courses with J. Suk and Alois Hába; also studied conducting with Malko in Prague (1929–32) and with Scherchen in Strasbourg (1933); she returned to Prague for more study with Hába in his special quarter-tone classes (1936–37). She subsequently taught at a music school in Belgrade. During the period of Nazi occupation of Serbia she was an active participant in the resistance. After the war she was a member of the teaching staff of the Belgrade Music Academy (1945–67). In her music she adopted a global type of modern technique, utilizing variable tonal configurations, atonal melodic progressions, and microtonal structures while adhering to traditional forms of composition.
WORKS: String Quartet (1931); Wind Quintet (1932); Trio for Clarinet, Trombone, and Double Bass in quarter-tones (1937); Violin Sonata (1948); *Passacaglia* for Orch. (Belgrade, April 21, 1958); cantatas: *Pesme prostora (Songs of Space),* based on inscriptions on the graves of Bogomils, a heretical

religious sect of the Middle Ages (Belgrade, Dec. 8, 1956; her most acclaimed work); *Slovo svetlosti (Sound of Light),* oratorio to texts from medieval Serbian poetry (1966); *Prag sna (Threshold of Dream),* chamber cantata for Narrator, Soprano, Alto, and Instrumental Ensemble (1961; Opatija, Oct. 30, 1965); numerous piano pieces and songs. Apart from her experimental works, Ljubica Marić became deeply immersed in the study of ancient Byzantine chants, and wrote several modern realizations of the Serbian Octoichos; to this category belong her *Muzika Oktoiha No. 1* for Orch. (Belgrade, Feb. 28, 1959); *Vizantijski koncert (Byzantine Concerto)* for Piano and Orch. (Belgrade, June 4, 1963); *Ostinato super thema octoicha* for String Quintet, Harp, and Piano (Warsaw, Sept. 27, 1963); and *Simfonija oktoiha,* begun in 1964.
BIBLIOGRAPHY: V. Peričić, *Muzički Stvaraoci u Srbiji* (Belgrade, 1969; pp. 251–62).

Marie, Gabriel, French composer of light music; b. Paris, Jan. 8, 1852; d. Puigcerda, Catalonia, Aug. 29, 1928. He studied at the Paris Cons.; was chorus master of the Lamoureux Concerts (1881–87); conductor of the orch. concerts of the Société Nationale de Musique (1887–94); of Ste.-Cécile in Bordeaux; at Marseilles and (during the summer months) at the Casino in Vichy. He wrote a number of melodious pieces for orch., of which *La Cinquantaine* (in arrangements for violin or cello, with piano) became immensely popular. He also wrote music criticism, collected in *Pour la musique* (Paris, 1930).

Marini, Biagio, Italian violinist and composer; b. Brescia, c.1587; d. Venice, March 20, 1665. He was a violinist under Monteverdi at San Marco in Venice (1615–18); then was music director of the Accademia degli Erranti in Brescia (1620); subsequently was a violinist in the Farnese court in Parma (1621); then went to Germany and served at the courts in Neuberg and Düsseldorf (1623–49). In 1649 he was appointed maestro di cappella at S. Maria della Scala in Milan; in 1652 he was director of the Accademia della Morte in Ferrara. He publ. about 25 opus numbers of vocal and instrumental music. His op. 1, *Affetti musicali* (1617), contains the earliest specimen of the Italian solo violin sonata, entitled *La Gardana* (reprinted in Schering's "Zur Geschichte der Solosonate in Der ersten Hälfte des 17. Jahrhunderts," in *Riemann-Festschrift* (Leipzig, 1909); other reprints are in J. von Wasielewski, *Die Violine im 17. Jahrhundert* and in L. Torchi, *L'arte musicale in Italia* (vol. 8).
BIBLIOGRAPHY: A. Einstein, *Italienische Musiker am Hofe der Neuberger-Wittelsbacher, Sammelbände der Internationalen Musik-Gesellschaft,* IX/3; A. Schering, in *Riemann-Festschrift* (1909); A. Moser, *Geschichte des Violinspiels* (Berlin, 1923; 2nd ed., revised, 1966–67); Dora J. Iselin, *Biagio Marini, Sein Leben und seine Instrumentalwerke* (Diss., Univ. of Basel, 1930); W. Clark, *The Vocal Music of Biagio Marini* (Diss., Yale Univ., 1966); T. Durm, "The Sonata of Biagio Marini: Structure and Style," *The Music Review,* XXXVI (1975).

Marini, Ignazio, noted Italian bass; b. Tagliuno, Nov. 28, 1811; d. Milan, April 29, 1873. In 1833 he joined La Scala in Milan, where he sang until 1847; then appeared at London (1847–49) and N.Y. (1850–52); in 1856 he went to St. Petersburg, where he remained until 1863. He was one of the leading bass singers of his day; created the title roles in Verdi's *Oberto* and *Attila;* was a distinguished interpreter of bass parts in Rossini's operas.

Marino, Amerigo, American conductor; b. Chicago, Feb. 5, 1925. He studied violin at the Chicago Cons. and conducting with Nicolai Malko, George Szell, Max Rudolf, and Alfred Wallenstein. He conducted the Glendale (Calif.) Orch.; in 1964 was appointed music director of the Birmingham (Ala.) Symph. Orch., which he successfully led for a number of years.

Marinov, Ivan, Bulgarian composer and conductor; b. Sofia, Oct. 17, 1928. He studied conducting with Goleminov and composition with V. Stoyanov and Khadjiev at the Bulgarian State Cons. in Sofia, graduating in 1955. In 1956 he became a conductor of the People's Opera in Plovdiv; then was appointed conductor of the Sofia State Opera House (1966). He wrote *Dvuboj (Duel),* poem for Tenor and Orch. (1953); *Suite on 4 Folk Songs* for Orch. (1955); *Ilinden,* symph. poem (1956); *Paraphrases* for Orch. (1957); *Fantastic Scenes* for Orch. (1959); *Divertimento* for Orch. (1961); *Pentagram* for Bass, String Orch., Piano, and Timpani (1965–66); Symph. No. 1 for Bass and Orch. (1967); *Festive Suite* for Orch. (1968); *Ode on Liberty* for Orch. (1969); chamber music; songs.

Marinuzzi, Gino, Italian conductor and composer, son of **Giuseppe Marinuzzi;** b. New York, April 7, 1920. He studied at the Milan Cons. with Renzo Bossi, graduating as a pianist and composer in 1941. He began his career as conductor at the Rome Opera in 1946. He was one of the first Italian composers to explore the potentialities of electronic music; in collaboration with Ketoff he developed an electronic synthesizer, the "Fonosynth," and made a founder of an electronic studio in Rome. His compositions include a Violin Concerto, a Piano Concerto, and several other works for various instrumental combinations; also a radio opera, *La Signora Paulatim* (Naples, 1966), as well as a number of pieces specially adapted for electronic tape.

Marinuzzi, Giuseppe (Gino), Italian conductor and composer; b. Palermo, March 24, 1882; d. Milan, Aug. 17, 1945. He studied with Zuelli at the Palermo Cons.; began his career as a conductor in Catania; conducted in Italy and Spain; went to South America on tour with the Teatral Opera Co.; then was director of the Liceo Musicale in Bologna (1915–18); in 1919 conducted in Rome; in 1920 came to the U.S. as artistic director of the Chicago Opera Association; returned to Italy in 1921; was chief conductor of the Rome Opera in 1928–34, and of La Scala from 1934 to his death. False dispatches about his assassi-nation at the hands of the Italian anti-Fascists found their way into periodicals and eventually into reputable reference works, but upon verification, it appears that he died peacefully in a hospital, a victim not of a bullet but of hepatic anemia. He wrote 3 operas: *Barberina* (Palermo, 1903); *Jacquerie* (Buenos Aires, Aug. 11, 1918); *Palla de' Mozzi* (La Scala, Milan, April 5, 1932); and several works for orch., on Italian themes.

BIBLIOGRAPHY: A. Garbelotto, *Gino Marinuzzi* (Ancona, 1965).

Mario, Giovanni, celebrated tenor; b. Cagliari, Sardinia, Oct. 17, 1810; d. Rome, Dec. 11, 1883. He was of noble birth (his real name was **Mario Cavaliere di Candia**), and was destined for a military career; after a period of training at the Turin Military Academy, he joined the regiment of which his father was the colonel, but eloped to Paris with a ballerina in 1836; there he studied with Bordogni and Poncharde at the Cons., and made his debut at the Opéra in *Robert le Diable* (Nov. 30, 1838); in 1840 he joined the roster of the Italian Opera in Paris, and won triumphs by the freshness and power of his voice and his exquisite vocal style; this was combined with a handsome figure, which made him the idol of the pleasure-loving women of Paris. In order not to embarrass his aristocratic relatives, he appeared under his Christian name, Mario, without a surname, achieving fame not only in opera, but also in concerts; he was as successful in London and St. Petersburg as in France. For some years, he, Tamburini, Lablache, and **Giulia Grisi** formed a celebrated vocal quartet; he married Grisi; retired in 1867, and lived in Paris and Rome.

BIBLIOGRAPHY: L. Engel, *From Mozart to Mario* (London, 1886); Mrs. Godfrey Pearce (Cecilia Maria de Candia, Mario's daughter) and F. Hird, *The Romance of a Great Singer* (London, 1910).

Mario, Queena (real name, **Tillotson**), American soprano; b. Akron, Ohio, Aug. 21, 1896; d. New York, May 28, 1951. She was a practicing journalist in N.Y. before she began to study music; took voice lessons with Oscar Saenger and Marcella Sembrich; made her debut with the San Carlo Opera in N.Y. (Sept. 4, 1918); then joined the staff of the Metropolitan Opera; her first appearance there was as Micaela in *Carmen* (Nov. 30, 1922); retired from the opera stage in 1938, but continued to give concerts; taught at the Curtis Inst. of Music in Philadelphia from 1931 as successor to Marcella Sembrich. She married the conductor **Wilfred Pelletier** in 1925; they divorced in 1936. She was the author of several mystery novels (*Murder in the Opera House,* etc.).

Mariotte, Antoine, French opera composer; b. Avignon, Dec. 22, 1875; d. Izieux (Loire), Nov. 30, 1944. He was trained at the Naval Academy; in 1897 he became a pupil of Vincent d'Indy at the Schola Cantorum; in 1899 was appointed conductor of the symph. concerts at St.-Etienne, Loire; from 1902 until 1919 he taught at the Cons. of Orléans; in 1920 was appointed its director; from 1936 to 1938 he was director of the Paris Opéra-Comique.

WORKS: Operas: *Salomé* (Lyons, Oct. 30, 1908); *Le Vieux Roi* (Lyons, 1911); *Léontine Sœurs* (Paris, May 21, 1924); *Esther, Princesse d'Israël* (Paris, May 5, 1925); *Gargantua* (Paris, Feb. 13, 1935); also a symph. suite, *Impressions urbaines;* numerous teaching pieces for piano; and songs.

Mariz, Vasco, Brazilian musicologist, diplomat, and bass; b. Rio de Janeiro, Jan. 22, 1921. He studied composition with Oscar Lorenzo Fernandez and voice with Vera Janacopoulos; also took courses in law at the Univ. of Rio de Janeiro, obtaining his D.J. degree in 1943. He sang minor roles in opera at Rio de Janiero, São Paulo, and Porto Alegre, and gave solo recitals as a lieder singer; also recorded Brazilian songs. In 1945 he entered the diplomatic service; was vice-consul at Oporto, Portugal (1948–49); attaché in Belgrade (1950–51); consul in Rosario, Argentina (1952–53); consul in Naples (1956–58); counselor of the Brazilian embassy in Washington, D.C. (1959–60); counselor of the Brazilian mission to the U.N. (1961–62); Brazilian envoy to the Organization of American States in Washington, D.C. (1967–69); head of the Cultural Dept. of the Brazilian Ministry of Foreign Affairs (1970); Brazilian ambassador to Ecuador (1971–74); assistant secretary of state for legislative affairs in Brasilia (1975–76); Brazilian ambassador to Israel (1977–82); Brazilian ambassador to Peru (1983–84).

PUBLICATIONS: *Figuras da musica brasileira contemporánea* (Oporto, 1948; 2nd ed., Brasilia, 1970); *Dicionário biográfico musical* (Rio de Janeiro, 1948; 2nd ed., 1984); *Hector Villa-Lobos, Compositor brasileiro* (Rio de Janeiro, 1949; 6th ed., 1983); *Canção brasileira* (Oporto, 1948; 4th ed., Rio de Janeiro, 1980); *Alberto Ginastera* (Rosario, 1954); *Vida musical I* (Oporto, 1950); *Vida musical II* (Rio de Janeiro, 1970); *Historia de musica no Brasil* (Rio de Janeiro, 1981; 2nd ed., 1983); *Tres musicologos brasileiros* (Rio de Janeiro, 1983).

Markevitch, Igor, greatly talented Russian-born composer and conductor; b. Kiev, July 27, 1912; d. Antibes, France, March 7, 1983. He was taken to Paris in his infancy; in 1916 the family settled in Vevey, Switzerland, which remained Markevitch's home for the next decade. He began to study piano with his father, subsequently took piano lessons with Paul Loyonnet; he also took academic courses at Vevey College. In 1925 he joined the piano class of Alfred Cortot in Paris at the Ecole Normale de Musique, and studied harmony, counterpoint, and composition with Nadia Boulanger. He attracted the attention of Serge Diaghilev, who commissioned him to write a piano concerto and also to collaborate with Boris Kochno on a ballet. Markevitch was soloist in his Piano Concerto at Covent Garden in London on July 15, 1929. Diaghilev died on Aug 19, 1929, and Markevitch interrupted his work on the ballet for him; he used the musical materials from it in his cantata to a text by Jean Cocteau; it was produced in Paris on June 4, 1930, achieving extraordinary success. On December 8, 1930, Markevitch's Concerto Grosso was performed for the first time in Paris with even a greater acclaim. Finally, his ballet, *Rebus,* was produced in Paris on Dec. 15, 1932, to enthusiastic press reviews. Markevitch was hailed, only half-facetiously, as "Igor II" (the first Igor being, of course, Igor Stravinsky). In 1933 Markevitch also began his career as a conductor, with a concert in Amsterdam. On June 26, 1933, his new ballet, *L'Envol d'Icare,* was given for the first time in Paris; Darius Milhaud opined that the occasion would probably "mark a date in the evolution of music." But swift as was Markevitch's Icarus-like ascent as a composer, even more precipitous was his decline. He began to be sharply criticized for his penchant toward unrelieved dissonance. When he conducted the world premiere of his oratorio, *Le Paradis perdu,* in London on Dec. 20, 1935, it was roundly condemned for sins of dissonance. Although Markevitch continued to compose, his main activities turned toward conducting. In 1934–36 he took conducting lessons in Switzerland with Hermann Scherchen. On Jan. 31, 1938, Markevitch conducted in Warsaw his new symph. work, *Le Nouvel Age,* for the first time anywhere. In 1940, with the war already raging in Europe, Markevitch stayed in Florence, where he composed his sinfonia concertante *Lorenzo il magnifico.* In 1941 he completed his last original work, the *Variations, Fugue and Envoi on a Theme of Handel,* and devoted himself almost exclusively to conducting; he held permanent conducting posts in Stockholm, Montreal, Madrid, Monte Carlo, and Rome; was principal guest conductor of the Lamoureux Orch. in Paris; also made successful tours of Russia. For several years he led seminars in conducting in Salzburg. He settled in southern France.

WORKS: *Noces,* suite for Piano (1925); *A la foire* (1926); *Sinfonietta in F* (Brussels, Nov. 30, 1929); Piano Concerto (London, July 15, 1929, composer soloist); *Cantate,* to a text by Jean Cocteau (Paris, June 4, 1930); Concerto Grosso (Paris, Dec. 8, 1930); Partita (Paris, May 13, 1932); *Serenade* for Violin, Clarinet, and Bassoon (Wiesbaden, Aug. 5, 1931); *Ouverture Symphonique* (1931); *Rébus,* ballet, dedicated to the memory of Serge Diaghilev (Paris, Dec. 15, 1931); *Galop* for 8 Players (1932); *L'Envol d'Icare,* ballet (Paris, June 26, 1933; also arranged for Piano Solo under the title *La Mort d'Icare);* *Hymnes* for Orch. (Paris, June 26, 1933, composer conducting); *Petite suite d'après Schumann* for Orch. (1933); *Psaume* for Soprano and Chamber Orch. (Amsterdam, Dec. 3, 1933, composer conducting); *Le Paradis perdu,* oratorio after Milton (London, Dec. 20, 1935, composer conducting); *3 poèmes* for Voice and Piano (1935); *Hymne à la mort* for Chamber Orch. (1936); *Cantique d'amour* for Chamber Orch. (Rome, May 14, 1937); *Le Nouvel Age,* sinfonia concertante for Orch. (Warsaw, Jan. 21, 1938, composer conducting); *La Taille de l'homme* for Soprano and 12 Instruments; unfinished; first perf. as *Oraison musicale* (1939; Maastricht, Feb. 7, 1982); *Duo* for Flute and Bassoon (1939); *Stefan le poète* for Piano (1939–40); *Lorenzo il magnifico,* sinfonia concertante for Soprano and Orch. (Florence, Jan. 12, 1941); *Variations, Fugue and Envoi on a Theme of Handel* for Piano (Rome, Dec. 14, 1941); *Inno della liberazione nazionale,* songs for the Italian underground resistance (1943–44); *Le Bleu Danube* for Chamber Orch. (Florence, May 24, 1946, composer conducting).

BIBLIOGRAPHY: Bernard Gavoty, *Igor Markevitch* (Geneva, 1954); special issue of *Tempo* (September 1980); Josef Heinzelmann, *Igor Markevitch* (Bonn, 1982).

Markova, Juliana, Bulgarian pianist; b. Sofia, July 8, 1945. She studied piano at the Sofia Cons.; then went to Italy and worked with Ilonka Deckers at the Verdi Cons. in Milan, graduating with the highest honors; she subsequently won prizes in the Enesco Competition in Bucharest and the Marguerite Long Competition in Paris. This opened for her an opportunity to give concerts; she appeared as soloist with leading orchs. of Europe and the U.S., including the London Symph., Philharmonia Orch., Royal Phil., Los Angeles Phil., Chicago Symph., Cleveland Orch., and Philadelphia Orch.; also toured in solo recitals. She settled in London; married the English pianist **Michael Roll.** A technically brilliant pianist, she excels in the Romantic and the early modern repertoire.

Marks, Alan, talented American pianist; b. Chicago, May 14, 1949. His family moved to St. Louis when he was a child; he studied piano with Shirley Parnas Adams. In 1965 he won a prize in Interlochen; gave his first piano recital in St. Louis in 1966. In 1967 he went to N.Y., where he studied at the Juilliard School of Music with Irwin Freundlich until 1971; then with Leon Fleisher at the Peabody Cons. in Baltimore (1971–72). Subsequently he gave successful recitals in Boston, Washington, Philadelphia, Los Angeles, San Francisco, and other cities. In 1976 played the first performance of *Caprichos* for Piano by Carlos Chávez; also participated in numerous concerts of chamber music. He possesses an innate virtuoso technique, and seems to be able to interpret with perfect stylistic fidelity piano works by classical as well as modern composers.

Markull, Friedrich Wilhelm, German composer; b. Reichenbach, near Elbing, Prussia, Feb. 17, 1816; d. Danzig, April 30, 1887. He studied organ playing and in 1836 was appointed organist at a Danzig church. He also gave concerts as a pianist. His 3 operas were performed in Danzig: *Maja und Alpino* (Dec. 23, 1843); *Der König von Zion* (March 22, 1850); and *Das Walpurgisfest* (Jan. 14, 1855). He also wrote 2 oratorios, symphs., and organ pieces.

BIBLIOGRAPHY: W. Neumann, *F. W. Markull* (Kassel, 1857).

Markwort, Johann Christian, German singer and voice teacher; b. Reisling, near Braunschweig, Dec. 13, 1778; d. Bessungen, near Darmstadt, Jan. 13, 1866. He took courses in theology in Leipzig; then went to Vienna to study voice; sang tenor in opera in Munich and in Liechtenstein; in 1810 was engaged as choirmaster in Darmstadt. In 1830 he dedicated himself entirely to teaching; he publ. several pedagogical books: *Umriss einer Gesammt- Tonwissenschaft überhaupt wie auch einer Sprach- und Tonsatzlehre* (Darmstadt, 1826); *Gesang-, Ton- und Rede-Vortraglehre* (Mainz, 1827); *Über Klangveredelung der Stimme* (Mainz, 1847); also a pianoforte method.

Marley, Bob, Jamaican reggae singer; b. in the village of Rhoden Hall, Feb. 6, 1945, of a white father, a British army captain, and a native black mother; d. Miami, May 11, 1981. He was taken to Kingston as a child and worked as an electrical welder. He picked up popular tunes in the streets and from the radio, opened a small recording shop of his own, and then began making records of some of his own tunes, a mixture of calypso and "soul" music. He joined the Rastafarian religious group, followers of Haile Selassie of Ethiopia (whose original name was Ras Tafari). In 1976 he became embroiled in politics, supporting the People's National Party; as he was preparing to sing at a band concert on Dec. 3, 1976, he was shot and wounded. After that episode, he went to Europe, scoring an unusual popular success, particularly in England, Sweden, the Netherlands, and West Germany. In 1977 he made a tour of the U.S., where his fame had preceded him via his record albums. His songs, in black Jamaican dialect, preach revolution; typical of them are *Rebel Music, Everywhere Be War,* and *Death to the Downpressors.*

Marliani, Marco Aurelio, Italian composer; b. Milan, Aug. 1805; d. Bologna, May 8, 1849. He studied philosophy; took some lessons with Rossini in Paris, where he went in 1830; under Rossini's influence, he wrote several operas, which reached the stage in Paris: *Il Bravo* (Feb. 1, 1834); *Ildegonda* (March 7, 1837); *Xacarilla* (Oct. 28, 1839); a ballet, *La Gypsy* (with A. Thomas; Jan. 28, 1839). He returned to Italy in 1847; produced another opera in Bologna, *Gusmano il Buono* (Nov. 7, 1847). He was involved in the revolutionary struggle of 1848; was wounded in a skirmish near Bologna, and died as a result of his injuries.

Marliave, Joseph de, French writer on music; b. Toulouse, Nov. 16, 1873; d. (killed in battle at Verdun) Aug. 24, 1914. He wrote a valuable monograph, *Les Quatuors de Beethoven,* which was publ. posthumously in Paris in 1917 and reprinted, with preface by Gabriel Fauré, in 1925. He was the husband of the pianist **Marguerite Long**.

Marlowe, Sylvia (original name, **Sylvia Sapira**), American harpsichordist; b. New York, Sept. 26, 1908; d. there, Dec. 11, 1981. She studied piano; went to Paris to take courses with Nadia Boulanger at the Ecole Normale de Musique; later became a student of Wanda Landowska in harpsichord playing. In 1953 she joined the faculty of the Mannes School of Music in N.Y. In 1957 she founded the Harpsichord Music Society, which commissioned works by Elliott Carter, Ned Rorem, Vittorio Rieti, Henri Sauguet, and others. Although her primary devotion was to the Baroque style of composition, she adventurously espoused the cause of popular American music; she was a member of the pop group called Chamber Music Society of Lower Basin Street and even performed in nightclubs, ostentatiously proclaiming her belief in music as an art in flux. She was married to a landscape painter named Leonid Berman, who died in 1976.

Marmier, Jules, German composer; b. Freiburg, March 15, 1874; d. Estavayer, July 28, 1975, at the age of 101. He composed several operatic works and organized religious spectacles for amateurs.

Marmontel, Antoine-François, celebrated French pedagogue and pianist; b. Clermont-Ferrand, July 16, 1816; d. Paris, Jan. 17, 1898. He studied at the Paris Cons. with Zimmermann (piano), Dourlen (harmony), Halévy (fugue), and Lesueur (composition); won first prize for piano playing in 1832. In 1837 he became instructor in solfeggio at the Cons.; in 1848 he succeeded Zimmermann as head of a piano class, and won enduring fame as an imaginative and efficient teacher; among his pupils were Bizet, Vincent d'Indy, Th. Dubois, E. Guiraud, Paladilhe, Diémer, Planté, and Debussy. He continued to teach until 1887. He publ. numerous didactic works: *L'Art de déchiffrer* (100 easy studies); *Ecole élémentaire de mécanisme et de style* (24 studies); *Ecole de mécanisme;* 5 *Etudes de salon; L'Art de déchiffrer à 4 mains;* also sonatas, serenades, characteristic pieces, salon music, dances, etc.

WRITINGS: *Les Pianistes célèbres* (1878); *Symphonistes et virtuoses* (1880); *Virtuoses contemporains* (1882); *Elements d'esthétique musicale, et considérations sur le beau dans les arts* (1884); *Histoire du piano et de ses origines* (1885).

Marmontel, Antonin Emile Louis, French pianist, son of **Antoine-François Marmontel;** b. Paris, Nov. 22, 1850; d. there, July 23, 1907. He studied at the Paris Cons., and in 1901 was appointed to its faculty as an instructor and piano player.

Maros, Miklós, Hungarian-born Swedish composer, son of **Rudolf Maros;** b. Pécs, Nov. 14, 1943. He studied with Rezso Sugár and Ferenc Szabó in Budapest; in 1968 settled in Stockholm, where he took composition lessons with Lidholm. In 1971 he became a member of the Electronic Music Studio Foundation in Stockholm.

WORKS: One-act opera, *Jag önskar jag vore . . . (If Only . . . ;* 1971); *Inversioni* for Soprano and Chamber Ensemble (1968); *Turba* for Chorus (1968); *Coalottino* for Baritone Saxophone, 3 Pianos, Harpsicord, Hammond Organ, 2 Violins, Viola, and 2 Cellos (1969); *Spel* for Clarinet, Trombone, Percussion, and Cello (1969); *Dénique* for Soprano and Orch. (Norrköping, Jan. 14, 1972); *Anenaika* for Soprano, Clarinet, Trombone, Viola, and Cello (1970); *Cartello* for Piano, Flute, Harp, and Strings (1970); *Pantomim* for Piano, Celeste, Harpsichord, Hammond

Organ, and Tape (1970); Viola Sonata for Tape (1970); *Izé,* musical theater for Flute and Percussion (1970); *In H* for Tape (1970); *Mutazioni* for Winds (1971); Concertino for Double Bass or Tuba, and 6–24 Winds (1971); *Descort* for Soprano, Flute, and Double Bass (1971); *Diversion* for Soprano, Alto, Alto Flute, Guitar, Viola, and 3 Percussionists (1971); *HCAB-BACH* for Piano (1971); *Sorg,* musical theater for Clarinet, Trombone, Piano, and ad libitum Instruments (1971); *Orömhir* for Trumpet, Violin, and Viola (1971); *Aspectus* for 10 Instruments (1972); *Laus Pannoniae (Praise for Hungary)* for Soprano, Chorus, Recorder, Oboe, Harp, Harpsicord, and Organ (1972); *Causerie* for Flute and Piano (1972); *Confluentia* for Small String Orch. (1972); *Sirens* for 4 Harps (1972); *Oratio* for Male Chorus and Tape (1973); *Proportio* for Wind Orch. (1973); *Etyder* for Tuba (1973); *Air* for Bassoon (1973); Symph. No. 1 (1974); *Oolit* for 11 Instruments (1974); *3 Epigrams* for Horn, Cello, and Piano (1975).

Maros, Rudolf, Hungarian composer; b. Stachy, Jan. 19, 1917; d. Budapest, Aug. 2, 1982. He studied composition with Kodály and Siklós and viola at the Budapest Academy of Music (1938–42); played viola in the Budapest Concert Orch. (1942–49); from 1949–78 he was on the faculty of the Budapest Academy of Music. The early period of his music is marked by nationalistic tendencies; later he adopted serial techniques and began to explore the field of "sonorism," or sound for sound's sake, making use of all available sonorous resources, such as tone clusters and microtones.

WORKS: BALLETS: *The Wedding at Ecser* (1950); *Bányászballada (Miner's Ballad;* 1961); *Cinque studi* (1967; after the orch. set of the same title); *Quadros soltos (Musica da ballo)* (1968); *Reflexionen* (1970); *Dance Pictures* (1971); *Metropolis* (1972); *The Poltroon* (1972). FOR ORCH.: *Puppet Show Overture* (1944); 2 sinfoniettas (1944, 1948); Bassoon Concertino (1954); *Symphony for Strings* (1956); *Ricercare* (1959); *Musica da ballo,* suite (1962; based on the ballet *Miner's Ballad*); *Cinque studi* (1960; as a ballet, 1967); *3 Eufonias: I* for Strings, 2 Harps, and Percussion (1963); *II* for 24 Winds, 2 Harps, and Percussion (1964); *III* for Orch. (1965); *Gemma (In Memoriam Kodály)* (1968); *Monumentum* (1969); *Notices* for Strings (1972); *Landscapes* for Strings (1974); *Fragment* (1977). CHAMBER MUSIC: String Quartet (1948); *Serenade* for Oboe, Clarinet, and Bassoon (1952); *Musica leggiera* for Wind Quintet (1956); String Trio (1957); *Musica da camera per 11* (1966; Dartmouth College, Hanover, N.H., July 12, 1967); Trio for Violin, Viola, and Harp (1967); *Consort* for Wind Quintet (1970); *Albumblätter* for Double-bass Solo (1973); *Kaleidoscope* for 15 Instruments (1976); *4 Studies* for 4 Percussionists (1977); *Contrasts* for Chamber Ensemble (1979); FOR VOICE: *2 Laments* for Soprano, Alto Flute, Harp, Piano, and Percussion (1962); *Lament* for Soprano and Chamber Ensemble (1967); *Messzeségek (Remoteness)* for Chorus a cappella (1975); *Strophen* for Soprano, Harp, and Percussion (1975); *Nyúlfarkkantáta (Tiny Cantata)* for Voices, Strings, and Piano (1976);

Cheremiss Folksongs for Chorus a cappella (1977).

Marpurg, Friedrich, German opera composer, great-grandson of **Friedrich Wilhelm Marpurg;** b. Paderborn, April 4, 1825; d. Wiesbaden, Dec. 2, 1884. He played the violin and piano as a child; studied composition later with Mendelssohn and Hauptmann at Leipzig. He became conductor at the Königsberg Theater, then at Sondershausen (1864); succeeded Mangold as court music director at Darmstadt (1868); then was at Freiburg (1873), Laibach (1875), and Wiesbaden, where he became conductor of the Cäcilienverein.
WORKS: Operas: *Musa, der letzte Maurenkönig* (Königsberg, 1855); *Agnes von Hohenstaufen* (Freiburg, 1874); *Die Lichtensteiner* (not perf.).

Marpurg, Friedrich Wilhelm, German theorist; b. Seehof bei Seehausen, Brandenburg, Nov. 21, 1718; d. Berlin, May 22, 1795. While secretary to General von Rothenburg at Paris (1746–49), he became acquainted with Rameau and his theories; after a short stay in Berlin, and a prolonged sojourn in Hamburg, he joined the Prussian lottery at Berlin (1763), and was its director from 1766 until his death.
WRITINGS: *Die Kunst das Clavier zu spielen* (2 vols.: Vol. I, 1750; Vol. II, 1761); *Anleitung zum Clavier-spielen, der schönern Ausübung der heutigen Zeit gemäss entworfen* (1755; 2nd ed., 1765; also in French and Dutch); *Abhandlung von der Fuge* (his *magnum opus;* 1753–54, in 2 parts; French ed. by Marpurg himself, 1756; revised by Sechter, Vienna, 1843, and Dehn, Leipzig, 1858); *Historisch-kritische Beyträge zur Aufnahme der Musik* (5 vols., 1754–78); *Handbuch bey dem General basse und der Composition* (1755–58: 3 parts; supplement 1760; 2nd ed., 1762; French by Choron and Lafage, 1836–38); a German trans. of d'Alembert's *Elements de la musique* (*Systematische Einleitung in die musikalische Setzkunst,* according to Rameau; 1757); *Kritische Einleitung in die Geschichte und Lehrsätze der alten und neuen Musik* (1759; only on ancient music); *Kritische Briefe über die Tonkunst* (a weekly publication appearing 1759–63); *Anleitung zur Musik überhaupt und zur Singkunst besonders* (1763); *Neue Methode, allerley Arten von Temperaturen dem Claviere aufs bequemste mitzutheilen* (1790); etc. He composed 6 keyboard pieces, organ music, songs (sacred and secular), and an unfinished 4-part Mass.
BIBLIOGRAPHY: H. Riemann, *Geschichte der Musiktheorie* (2nd ed., 1921, pp. 496ff.); E. Bieder, *Über Friedrich Wilhelm Marpurgs System der Harmonie des Kontrapunkt und der Temperatur* (Diss., Univ. of Berlin, 1923); H. Serwer, *Friedrich Wilhelm Marpurg (1718–1795): Music Critic in a Galant Age* (Diss., Yale Univ., 1969).

Marqués y García, Pedro Miguel, Spanish composer of light opera; b. Palma de Mallorca, May 20, 1843; d. there, Feb. 25, 1918. He studied in Paris with Alard and Armingaud, then at the Paris Cons. with Massart (violin) and Bazin (composition); also stud-

ied privately with Berlioz, and in 1867 at Madrid with Monasterio. From 1870–96 he was one of the most successful of the "zarzuela" composers, his most popular works being *El anillo de hierro* (1878), *El reloj de Lucerna, La monja alférez, El plato de dia,* etc. He wrote orch. variations, and was the author of a number of books (mostly on philosophy).

Marriner, Neville, outstanding English violinist and conductor; b. Lincoln, April 15, 1924. He studied at the Royal College of Music in London and at the Paris Cons.; was a member of the Martin String Quartet (1946–53); then was assistant concertmaster with the London Symph. Orch. (1956–68); Monteux, who conducted same, encouraged Marriner to become a symph. conductor. Following this advice, Marriner joined a summer class in conducting which Monteux had maintained at Hancock, Maine. In 1959 Marriner organized the Academy of St.-Martin-in-the-Fields in a London church of that name, this being an "academy" in the old German nomenclature descriptive of concert activity. In 1968 he was invited to Los Angeles to organize a local chamber orch.; as at his London "academy," so with the Los Angeles Chamber Orch., Marriner presented programs of Baroque music; he made a European tour with it in 1974. He founded, concurrently, a similar organization in Australia. In 1977 he was named artistic director of the Meadow Brook Music Festival in Rochester, Mich. In 1978 he accepted the prestigious appointment of conductor and music director of the Minnesota Orch. in Minneapolis; in 1981 he became principal guest conductor of the Stuttgart Radio Symph. Orch. In 1979 he was made a Commander of the Order of the British Empire.

Marrocco, William Thomas, American violinist and musicologist; b. West New York, N.J., Dec. 5, 1909. After initial music studies in the U.S. he went to Italy and entered the Cons. di Musica S. Pietro a Majella in Naples, receiving his diploma di Magistero in 1930; then studied violin and musicology at the Eastman School of Music in Rochester, N.Y. (M.A., 1940); earned his Ph.D. at the Univ. of Calif. in Los Angeles with the dissertation *Jacopo da Bologna and His Works* (1952; publ. as *The Music of Jacopo da Bologna,* Berkeley, 1954); was on the music faculty of the Univ. of Kansas in Lawrence (1946–49); in 1950 was appointed a prof. of music at the Univ. of Calif. in Los Angeles. He publ. numerous informative essays dealing with old Italian and American music; edited *14th-Century Italian Cacce* (Cambridge, Mass., 1940; revised 1961) and an anthology, *Music in America* (in collaboration with Harold Gleason; N.Y., 1964).

Marsalis, Wynton, outstanding black American trumpet virtuoso; b. New Orleans, Oct. 18, 1961. He attended the Berkshire Music Center at Tanglewood, where, at the age of 17, he was singled out as the most gifted trumpet player; continued his studies at the Juilliard School of Music in N.Y. He subsequently joined Art Blakey's big band, and played with it at the Jazz Festival at Montreux, Switzer-

Marschalk – Marschner

land, in 1980; then toured with his own quintet, which included his brother, Branford, a fine saxophonist; he also worked with Miles Davis. Concurrently he showed interest in the classical repertoire, and proceeded to perform trumpet concertos of the Baroque period with great aplomb. In 1983 he achieved unprecedented success when he won Grammy Awards in both the jazz and classical categories for his recordings.

Marschalk, Max, German music critic; b. Berlin, April 7, 1863; d. Poberow-on-the-Ostsee, Aug. 24, 1940. He was a pupil of H. Urban; from 1894 until its dissolution in 1933, was music critic of the *Vossische Zeitung;* from 1934, music director of the Dreililien publishing company in Berlin. He composed a short opera, *In Flammen* (Gotha, 1896); a "Liederspiel," *Aucassin und Nicolette* (Stuttgart, 1907); incidental music to Hauptmann's *Hanneles Himmelfahrt* (1894), *Die versunkene Glocke* (1898), and *Und Pippa tanzt* (1906); also to Maeterlinck's *Sœur Béatrice*, etc.

Marschner, Franz, Bohemian pianist, pedagogue, and writer on music; b. Leitmeritz, March 1855; d. Weissphyra, Aug. 22, 1932. He studied with Skuhershý at the Prague Cons. and with Bruckner in Vienna. He publ. some valuable essays on the techniques of piano playing, among them *Entwurf einer Neugestaltung der Theorie und Praxis des kunstgemässen Anschlags* (on piano touch; Vienna, 1888); also wrote essays on musical esthetics; composed choral pieces, some chamber music, and songs.

Marschner, Heinrich (August), important German opera composer; b. Zittau, Saxony, Aug. 16, 1795; d. Hannover, Dec. 14, 1861. He sang in the school choir at the Zittau Gymnasium, and also studied music with Karl Hering. In 1813 he went to Leipzig, where he studied jurisprudence at the Univ.; encouraged by the cantor of the Thomasschule, J.C. Schicht, he turned to music as his main vocation. In 1816 he became a music tutor in Count Zichy's household in Pressburg, and also served as Kapellmeister to Prince Krasatkowitz. In his leisure hours he began to compose light operas; his first opera, *Titus* (1816), did not achieve a performance, but soon he had 2 more operas and a singspiel produced in Dresden. His first signal success was the historical opera *Heinrich IV und d'Aubigné*, which was accepted by Weber, who was then music director at the Dresden Opera, and was produced there on July 19, 1820. In 1817 he was in Vienna, where he was fortunate enough to meet Beethoven. In 1821 Marschner moved to Dresden and had his singspiel *Der Holzdieb* staged at the Dresden Opera (Feb. 22, 1825). He expected to succeed Weber as music director at the Dresden Opera after Weber died suddenly in London, but failed to obtain the post. He went to Leipzig, where he became Kapellmeister of the Stadttheater, and wrote for it 2 Romantic operas, in the manner of Weber: *Der Vampyr,* performed there on March 29, 1828, and *Der Templer und die*

Jüdin, after the famous novel *Ivanhoe* by Sir Walter Scott (Dec. 22, 1829). In 1830 he was offered the position of Kapellmeister of the Hannover Hoftheater, and there he produced his most successful opera, *Hans Heiling,* which exhibited the most attractive Romantic traits of his music: a flowing melody, sonorous harmony, and nervous rhythmic pulse; the opera formed a natural transition to the exotic melodrama of Meyerbeer's great stage epics and to Wagner's early lyrical music dramas. Historically important was Marschner's bold projection of a continuous dramatic development, without the conventional type of distinct arias separated by recitative. In this respect Marschner was the heir of Weber and a precursor of Wagner.

WORKS: For the stage: *Titus,* opera (1816; not perf.); *Der Kyffhäuserberg,* singspiel (1816; Zittau, Jan. 2, 1822); *Heinrich IV und d'Aubigné,* opera (1817–18; Dresden, July 19, 1820); *Saidar und Zulima,* romantic opera (Pressburg, Nov. 26, 1818); *Der Holzdieb,* singspiel (1823; Dresden, Feb. 22, 1825; revised in 1853 as *Geborgt*); *Lukretia,* opera (1820–26; Danzig, Jan 17, 1827); *Der Vampyr,* romantic opera (1827; Leipzig, March 29, 1828); *Der Templer und die Jüdin,* romantic opera (Leipzig, Dec. 22, 1829); *Des Falkners Braut,* comic opera (1830; Leipzig, March 10, 1832); *Hans Heiling,* romantic opera (1831–32; Berlin, May 24, 1833); *Das Schloss am Atna,* romantic opera (1830–35; Leipzig, Jan. 29, 1836); *Der Bäbu,* comic opera (1836–37; Hannover, Feb. 19, 1838); *Kaiser Adolf von Nassau,* romantic opera (Dresden, Jan 5, 1845); *Austin,* romantic opera (1850–51; Hannover, Jan. 25, 1852); *Sangeskönig Hiarne, oder Das Tyringsschwert,* romantic opera (1857–58; Frankfurt, Sept. 13, 1863); ballet, *Die stolze Bäuerin* (Zittau, 1810); incidental music. Apart from his stage productions, he wrote a number of choral works, but his attempts to compose instrumental music were not successful; his 2 symphs. remained unfinished.

BIBLIOGRAPHY: W. Neumann, *Heinrich Marschner* (Kassel, 1854); H. Borges, "Heinrich Marschners Oper 'Hiarne,'" *Neue Zeitschrift für Musik,* LXXIX (1883); E. Danzig, *Heinrich Marschner in seinen minderbekannten Opern und Liedern* (Leipzig, 1890); M. Wittmann, *Heinrich Marschner* (Leipzig, 1897); G. Münzer, *Heinrich Marschner* (Berlin, 1901); L. Hirschberg, "Marschner als Balladenkomponist," *Musikwelt,* XXXVII (1905); C. Preiss, *Templer und Jüdin* (Graz, 1911); L. Hirschberg, "Heinrich Marschners Balladen," *Die Musik,* XI (1911–12); H. Gaartz, *Die Opern Heinrich Marschners* (Leipzig, 1912); L. Hirschberg, "Heinrich Marschners Chöre," *Neue Musik-Zeitung,* XXXIII (1912); H. Wetzel, "Heinrich Marschners Balladen," *Musikpädagogische Blätter* (1914); G. Fischer, *Marschner Erinnerungen* (Hannover, 1918); H. Pfitzner, "Marschners Vampyr," *Neue Musik-Zeitung,* XLV (1924); A. Bickel, *Heinrich Marschner in seinen Opern* (Diss., Univ. of Erlangen, 1929); A. Gnirs, *Hans Heiling* (Karlsbad, 1931); G. Hausswald, *Heinrich Marschner* (Dresden, 1938); V. Köhler, *Heinrich Marschners Bühnenwerke* (Diss., Univ. of Göttingen, 1956); idem, "Heinrich Marschner," *Hannoversche Geschichtsblätter,* new series, XVI (1962); idem, "Rezitativ, Szene und Melodram in Heinrich Marschners Opern," *Gesellschaft für Musikforschung Kongressbericht* (Bonn, 1970); A. Dean Palmer, *H.A. Marschner, 1795–1861: His Life and Stage Works* (1980).

Marsh, Robert Charles, American music critic; b. Columbus, Ohio, Aug. 5, 1924. At Northwestern Univ. he studied journalism (B.S., 1945) and philosophy (A.M., 1946); earned a doctorate in education at Harvard (1951); synchronously he took courses in music theory with Robert Palmer at Cornell Univ. (1946–47) and attended lectures of Hindemith at Harvard (1949–50); studied musicology with Thurston Dart and theory of criticism with H.S. Middleton at Cambridge, England (1955–56). He held teaching positions at the Univ. of Illinois (1947–49); Chicago City Junior College (1950–51); Univ. of Kansas City (1951–52); State Univ. of N.Y. (1953–54); and Univ. of Chicago (1956–58). He became music critic with the *Chicago Sun Times* in 1956; contributed articles on music to various literary publications and philosophical journals; edited *Logic and Knowledge of Bertrand Russell* (1956); publ. *Toscanini and the Art of Orchestral Performance* (Philadelphia, 1956; revised as *Toscanini and the Art of Conducting*, 1962); also a book on the Cleveland Orch. (1967).

Marshall, John Patton, American music educator; b. Rockport, Mass., Jan. 9, 1877; d. Boston, Jan. 17, 1941. He studied music with MacDowell, Chadwick, B.J. Lang, and others; was organist at various churches; lectured on music at the Harvard Summer School. In 1903 he was appointed a prof. at Boston Univ., and in 1928 became dean of the College of Music there. He publ. the teaching manuals *Syllabus of History of Music* (1906), *Syllabus of Music Appreciation* (1911), etc.

Marshall, Margaret, Scottish soprano; b. Stirling, Jan. 4, 1949. She studied at the Royal Scottish Academy of Music in Glasgow; also took voice lessons with Hans Hotter. In 1974 she won first prize at the International Competition in Munich; made her London debut in 1975; in 1978 she made her operatic debut in Florence as Euridice in *Orfeo;* she then sang the role of the Countess in the 1979 Florence production of *Le nozze di Figaro,* and made her Covent Garden debut in the same role in 1980. In 1982 she appeared in Milan and at the Salzburg Festival. She made her first appearances in the U.S. in 1980 as a soloist with the Boston Symph. and N.Y. Phil.; subsequently made several American tours as a concert artist.

Marsick, Armand, eminent Belgian composer, nephew of **Martin-Pierre-Joseph Marsick;** b. Liège, Sept. 20, 1877; d. Haine-Saint-Paul, April 30, 1959. He studied with his father, Louis Marsick; then took a course in composition with Sylvain Dupuis at the Liège Cons.; became first violinist in the Théâtre Municipal in Nancy; completed composition studies with Guy Ropartz at the Cons. there. In 1898 he

became concertmaster at the Concerts Colonne in Paris. In 1908 he obtained the position of instructor at the Cons. of Athens; he remained in Greece until 1921; was appointed conductor at the Music Academy of Bilbao, Spain, in 1922. He returned to Belgium in 1927; was a prof. at the Liège Cons. (1927–42) and conductor of the Société des Concerts Symphoniques (1927–39).
WORKS: 3 operas: *La Jane* (1903; first produced as *Vendetta corsa* in Rome, 1913; then at Liège, March 29, 1921); *Lara* (1913; Antwerp, Dec. 3, 1929); *L'Anneau nuptial* (1920; Brussels, March 3, 1928); radio play, *Le Visage de la Wallonie* (1937); symph. poems: *Stèle funéraire* (1902) and *La Source* (1908); *Improvisation et Final* for Cello and Orch. (1904); 2 suites: *Scènes de montagnes* (1910) and *Tableaux grecs* (1912); *Tableaux de voyage* for Small Orch. (1939); *Loustics en fête* for Small Orch. (1939); *3 morceaux symphoniques* (1950); Violin Sonata (1900); Quartet for 4 Horns (1950); *4 pièces* for Piano (1912); several sets of songs; choruses. A catalogue of his works was publ. by the Centre Belge de Documentation Musicale (Brussels, 1955).

Marsick, Martin-Pierre-Joseph, distinguished violinist; b. Jupille, near Liège, Belgium, March 9, 1848; d. Paris, Oct. 21, 1924. He studied at the Liège Cons.; at the age of 12, played the organ at the Cathedral; then studied violin with Léonard at the Brussels Cons. and with Massart at the Paris Cons., taking first prize there. In 1870 he became a pupil of Joachim in Berlin. After a brilliant debut at Paris in the Concerts Populaires (1873), he undertook long tours in Europe; also played in the U.S. (1895–96). In 1892 he was appointed prof. of violin at the Paris Cons. Among his pupils were Carl Flesch and Jacques Thibaud. He wrote 3 violin concertos and numerous solo pieces for the violin (*Adagio scherzando; 2 Reveries; Songe; Romance; Tarentelle; Agitato; Intermezzo; Berceuse;* etc.).

Marsop, Paul, German librarian and writer on music; b. Berlin, Oct. 6, 1856; d. Florence, Italy, May 31, 1925. He studied with Hans von Bülow; from 1881 lived in Munich and (during the winter) in Italy. He founded in Munich the Musikalische Volksbibliothek, which he turned over to the city in 1907; also aided in the establishment of similar libraries in other cities.
WRITINGS: *Musikalische Essays* (1899); *Studienblätter eines Musikers* (1903); *Neue Kämpfe* (1913); *Musikalische Satiren und Grotesken* (1924); and various pamphlets dealing mostly with Wagner (*Die Aussichten der Wagnerschen Kunst in Frankreich, Der Kern der Wagnerfrage,* etc.).

Marston, George W., American organist, choral conductor, and composer; b. Sandwich, Mass., May 23, 1840; d. there, Feb. 2, 1901. He studied organ; moved to Portland, Maine, as a youth and established himself there as a church organist and music teacher. He composed some choral music suitable for performances by amateur groups.

Marteau – Martenot

Marteau, Henri, famous French violinist; b. Reims, March 31, 1874; d. Lichtenberg, Bavaria, Oct. 3, 1934. He studied violin with Léonard at the Paris Cons. and began his concert career as a youth; was soloist with the Vienna Phil. at the age of 10, and played a concert in London at 14. In 1892, 1893, 1894, 1898, and 1906 he also toured the U.S.; gave concerts in Scandinavia, Russia, France, and Germany. In 1900 he was appointed prof. of violin at the Geneva Cons., and in 1908 succeeded Joachim as violin teacher at the Hochschule für Musik in Berlin. In 1915 he left Germany and went to Sweden, becoming a Swedish citizen in 1920; then taught at the German Music Academy in Prague (1921–24), at the Leipzig Cons. (1926–27), and (from 1928) at the Dresden Cons. He was greatly appreciated by musicians of Europe; Max Reger, who was a personal friend, wrote a violin concerto for him, as did Massenet; his teacher Léonard bequeathed to him his magnificent Maggini violin, formerly owned by the Empress Maria Theresa. Marteau was also a competent composer; he wrote an opera, *Meister Schwable* (Plauen, 1921); a symph. work, *Gloria naturae* (Stockholm, 1918); 2 violin concertos; Cello Concerto; *Sonata fantastica* for Violin alone; 3 string quartets; String Quintet; Clarinet Quintet; numerous violin pieces and arrangements of classical works.

BIBLIOGRAPHY: B. Marteau, *Henri Marteau, Siegeszug einer Geige* (Tutzing, 1971).

Martelli, Henri, French composer; b. Santa Fe, Argentina, Feb. 25, 1895; d. Paris, July 15, 1980. He studied law at the Univ. of Paris; simultaneously took courses in composition with Widor and Caussade. He was secretary of the Société Nationale de Musique (1945–67) and director of programs there from 1968; from 1953 to 1973 was president of the French section of the International Society for Contemporary Music. In his compositions he attempted to re-create the spirit of old French music in modern techniques.

WORKS: Opera, *La Chanson de Roland* (1921–23; revised 1962–64; Paris, April 13, 1967); opera buffa, *Le Major Cravachon* (1958; French Radio, June 14, 1959); 2 ballets: *La Bouteille de Panurge* (Paris, Feb. 24, 1937) and *Les Hommes de sable* (1951); *Rondo* for Orch. (1921); *Sarabande, Scherzo et Final* for Orch. (1922); *Divertissement sarrasin* for Orch. (1922); *Sur la vie de Jeanne d'Arc* for Orch. (1923); *Scherzo* for Violin and Orch. (1925); *Mors et Juventas* for Orch. (1927); *Bas-reliefs assyriens* for Orch. (1928; Boston, March 14, 1930); *Passacaille sur un thème russe* for Orch. (1928); Concerto for Orch. (1931; Boston, April 22, 1932); 3 suites for Orch.: No. 1, *Suite sur un thème corse* (1936); No. 2 (1950); No. 3 (1971); Concerto No. 1 for Violin and Chamber Orch. (1938); *Ouverture pour un conte de Boccace* (1942); *Suite concertante* for Wind Quintet and Orch. (1943); *Divertimento* for Wind Orch. (1945); *Fantaisie* for Piano and Orch. (1945); Sinfonietta (1948); 3 symphs.: No. 1 for Strings (1953; French Radio, March 13, 1955); No. 2 for Strings (1956; Paris, July 17, 1958); No. 3 (1957; Paris, March 8, 1960); Concertino No. 2 for Violin and Chamber Orch.

(1954); Concertino for Oboe, Clarinet, Horn, Bassoon, and String Orch. (1955); Double Concerto for Clarinet, Bassoon, and Orch. (1956); *Le Radeau de la Méduse,* symph. poem (1957); *Variations* for String Orch. (1959); *Scènes à danser* for Orch. (1963); *Rapsodie* for Cello and Orch. (1966); Oboe Concerto (1971); *Le Temps,* cantata for Voice and 8 Instruments (1945); *Chrestomathie* for a cappella Chorus (1949); *Invention* for Cello and Piano (1925); Duo for Oboe and English Horn (1925); 2 string quartets (1932–33, 1944); Piano Trio (1935); Violin Sonata (1936); *Suite* for 4 Clarinets (1936); *Introduction et Final* for Violin and Piano (1937); Wind Octet (1941); *Scherzetto, Berceuse et Final* for Cello and Piano (1941); Bassoon Sonata (1941); Cello Sonatina (1941); Flute Sonata (1941); *3 esquisses* for Saxophone and Piano (1943); *Préambule et Scherzo* for Clarinet and Piano (1944); *7 Duos* for Violin and Harp (1946); *Fantaisiestück* for Flute and Piano (1946); Wind Quintet (1974); Cornet Sonatina (1948); *Adagio, Cadence et Final* for Oboe and Piano (1949); 2 quintets for Flute, Harp, and String Trio (1950, 1952); Trio for Flute, Cello, and Piano (1951); *Cadence, Interlude et Rondo* for Saxophone and Piano (1952); *15 études* for Solo Bassoon (1953); Bass Trombone Sonata (1956); Viola Sonata (1959); *Suite* for Solo Guitar (1960); *Concertstück* for Viola and Piano (1962); Concertino for Cornet and Piano (1964); *Dialogue* for Trombone, Tuba or Bass Saxophone, and Piano (1966); Oboe Sonata (1972); String Trio (1973–74); Trio for Flute, Cello, and Harp (1976); *Suite galante* for Piano (1924); *Guitare* for Piano (1931); 3 *Petites suites* for Piano (1935, 1943, 1950); *Suite* for Piano (1939); 2-piano Sonata (1946); *Sonorités* for Piano, left-hand (1974); 17 radiophonic works (1940–62); songs.

Martenot, Maurice, French inventor of the electronic instrument "Ondes musicales," a.k.a. "Ondes Martenot"; b. Paris, Oct. 14, 1898; d. there, Oct. 10, 1980, as a result of a velocipede accident. He studied composition at the Paris Cons. with Gédalge; began to work on the construction of an electronic musical instrument with a keyboard, which he called Ondes musicales. He gave its first demonstration in Paris on April 20, 1928, and on Dec. 23, 1928, the first musical work for the instrument, *Poème symphonique pour solo d'Ondes musicales et orchestre,* by Dimitri Levidis, was presented in Paris. Martenot publ. *Méthode pour l'enseignement des Ondes musicales* (Paris, 1931). The instrument became popular, especially among French composers: it is included in the score of Honegger's *Jeanne d'Arc au bûcher* (1935); Koechlin's *Le Buisson ardent,* part 1 (1938); Martinot's 2nd Symph., subtitled *Hymne à la vie* (1944); and Messiaen's *Turangalîla-Symphonie* (1946–48). It was used as a solo instrument in Koechlin's *Hymne* (1929), Jolivet's *Concerto* (1947), Landowski's *Concerto* (1954), Bondon's *Kaleidoscope* (1957), and Charpentier's *Concertino "alla francese"* (1961); Milhaud, Jolivet, Rivier, Koechlin, Chaynes, Eloy, Tessier, Louvier, Bussotti, Goeyvaerts, Schibler, Mestres-Quadreny, and Calvin Hampton contributed to the growing literature of symph. and chamber music works that include the Ondes Martenot. Of all the early electronic instruments—Ondes Martenot, Trautonium, and Theremin—only Martenot's has proved a viable musical instrument. When Varèse's *Ecuatorial,* written in 1934 for a brass ensemble and including a Theremin, was publ. in 1961, the publ. score substituted an Ondes Martenot for the obsolescent Theremin. Martenot's sister, **Ginette Martenot** (b. Paris, Jan. 27, 1902), became the chief exponent of the Ondes Martenot in concert performances in Europe and America.

Martens, Frederick Herman, American writer on musical subjects; b. New York, July 6, 1874; d. Mountain Lakes, N.J., Dec. 18, 1932. He studied in N.Y. with local teachers; from 1907, was active mainly as a writer; publ. *Leo Ornstein: The Man, His Ideas, His Work* (1918); *Violin Mastery* (1919); *Art of the Prima Donna and Concert Singer* (1923); *String Mastery* (1919; revised ed., 1923); *A Thousand and One Nights of Opera* (1926); *Book of the Opera and the Ballet* (1925); contributed articles to the *Musical Quarterly* and other publications.

Martienssen, Carl Adolf, German musicologist and pedagogue; b. Güstrow, Dec. 6, 1881; d. Berlin, March 1, 1955. He studied with Klindworth and Wilhelm Berger in Berlin; musicology with Kretzschmar. In 1914 he was appointed instructor of piano at the Leipzig Cons.; in 1932 became prof. at the Musical Inst. for Foreigners in Berlin. He taught at the Hochschule für Musik in Berlin from 1934 to 1945; then at the Hochschule für Musik in Rostock (1945–50); subsequently at the Hochschule für Musik in East Berlin (1950–52). WRITINGS (all publ. in Leipzig): *Die individuelle Klaviertechnik auf der Grundlage des schöpferischen Klangwillens* (1930); *Die Methodik des individuellen Klavierunterrichts* (1934); *Grundlage einer deutschen Klavierlehre* (1942); *Das Klavierkunstwerk* (1950); and shorter studies.

Martín, Edgardo, Cuban composer and writer on music; b. Cienfuegos, Oct. 6, 1915. He studied with his maternal grandmother, the pianist **Aurea Suárez;** later took piano lessons in Havana with Jascha Fischermann and studied composition with José Ardévol. He taught music history at the Cons. Municipal (1945–68) and music analysis in the Escuela Nacional de Arte (1969–73) in Havana. From 1962 to 1971 he served as executive secretary of the National Committee of Music for UNESCO. As a composer, he pursues the plausible genre of pleasurable modern music. He publ. *Catálogo biográfico de compositores de Cuba* (Havana, 1970) and *Panorama histórico de la música en Cuba* (Havana, 1971). WORKS: Ballet, *El Caballo de coral* (Havana, 1960); 2 symphs. (1947, 1948); Concerto for 9 Wind Instruments (1944); Trio for Oboe, Clarinet, and Bassoon (1963); 2 string quartets (1967, 1968); *Recitativo y aria* for Viola and Piano (1979); *Los 2 abuelos* for Chorus and Instrumental Ensemble

(1949); *Canto de héroes* for Voices, with Orch. (1967); *La carta del soldado* for Narrator, Tenor, Chorus, Speaking Chorus, and Orch. (1970); *Granma* for Chorus and Instruments (1976); songs: *4 cantos de la Revolución* (1962); *7 cantos del Amor Imposible* (1964); *Antiquas comuniones* (1972); *Cantos de Martí* (1976); for Piano: Sonata (1943); *2 Preludios* (1950); *Soneras:* No. 1 (1950); No. 2 (1971); No. 3 (1975); also pieces for guitar.

Martin, Frank, greatly renowned Swiss composer; b. Geneva, Sept. 15, 1890; d. Naarden, the Netherlands, Nov. 21, 1974. He studied with Joseph Lauber in Geneva (1906–14); then took courses in Zürich (1918–20), Rome (1921–23), and Paris (1923–25). He returned to Geneva in 1926 as a pianist and harpsichordist; taught at the Inst. Jaques-Dalcroze (1927–38); was founder and director of the Technicum Moderne de Musique (1933–39); president of the Assoc. of Swiss Musicians (1942–46). He moved to the Netherlands in 1946 and while living there taught classes in composition at the Cologne Hochschule für Musik (1950–57). His early music showed the influence of César Franck and French impressionists, but soon he succeeded in creating a distinctive style supported by a consummate mastery of contrapuntal and harmonic writing, and a profound feeling for emotional consistency and continuity. Still later he became fascinated by the logic and self-consistency of Schoenberg's method of composition with 12 tones, and adopted it in a modified form in several of his works. He also demonstrated an ability to stylize folk-song materials in modern techniques. In 1944, the director of Radio Geneva asked Martin to compose an oratorio to be broadcast immediately upon the conclusion of World War II. He responded with *In terra pax* for 5 Soli, Double Chorus, and Orch., which was given its broadcast premiere from Geneva at the end of the war in Europe, May 7, 1945; a public performance followed in Geneva 24 days later. WORKS: FOR THE STAGE: Operas: *Der Sturm (The Tempest),* after Shakespeare (1952–54; Vienna, June 17, 1956), and *Monsieur de Pourceaugnac,* after Molière (1960–62; Geneva, April 23, 1963). Ballets: *Das Märchen vom Aschenbrödel,* after the Cinderella legend (1941; Basel, March 12, 1942), and *Ein Totentanz zu Basel im Jahre 1943* (Basel, May 27, 1943); play with music, *La Nique à Satan,* for Baritone, Male and Female and Children's Choruses, Winds, Percussion, 2 Pianos, and Double Bass (1930–31; Geneva, Feb. 25, 1933); incidental music to *Oedipus Rex* (1923), *Oedipus Coloneus* (1924), *Le Divorce* (1928), *Romeo and Juliet* (1929), and *Athalic* (1946). VOCAL WORKS: In addition to *In terra pax, 3 poèmes païens* for Baritone and Orch. (1910); *Les Dithyrambes* for 4 Soli, Mixed Chorus, Children's Chorus, and Orch. (1918); *4 sonnets à Cassandre* for Mezzo-soprano, Flute, Viola, and Cello (1921); *Messe* for Double Chorus a cappella (1922); *Musique pour les Fêtes du Rhône* for Chorus and Winds (1929); *Cantate sur la Nativité* for Soli, Chorus, String Orch., and Piano (1929; unfinished); *Chanson en canon* for Chorus a cappella (1930); *Le Vin herbé,* oratorio after the Tristan legend, for 12 Solo Voices, 7 Strings, and Piano (1938–41; first complete production, Zürich, March 26, 1942); *Cantate pour le 1er août* for Chorus, and Organ or Piano (1941); *Der Cornet* or *Die Weise von Liebe und Tod des Cornets Christoph Rilke*, after Rilke, cycle for Alto and Orch. (1942–43; Basel, Feb. 9, 1945); *Sechs Monologe aus "Jedermann" (6 Monologues from "Everyman")*, after Hofmannsthal, for Baritone or Alto, and Piano (1943; orchestrated 1949); *Dédicace* for Tenor and Piano (1945); *3 Chants de Noël* for Soprano, Flute and Piano (1974); *Golgotha*, oratorio for 5 Soli, Chorus, Orch., and Organ (1945–48; Geneva, April 29, 1949); *5 chansons d'Ariel* for Small Chorus a cappella (1950); *Psaumes de Genève*, psalm cantata for Chorus, Children's Chorus, Orch., and Organ (1958); *Le Mystère de la Nativité*, oratorio (1957–59; Geneva, Dec. 24, 1959); *3 Minnelieder* for Soprano and Piano (1960); *Ode à la musique* for Chorus, Trumpet, 2 Horns, 3 Trombones, Double Bass, and Piano (1961); *Verse à boire* for Chorus a cappella (1961); *Pilate*, short oratorio (Rome, Nov. 14, 1964); *Maria Triptychon* for Soprano, Violin, and Orch. (consists of the separate works *Ave Maria, Magnificat*, and *Stabat Mater*, 1967–69; Rotterdam, Nov. 13, 1969); *Poèmes de la Mort* for 3 Male Voices and 3 Electric Guitars (1969–71); *Requiem* (1971–72; Lausanne, May 4, 1973); *Et la vie l'emporta*, chamber cantata for Small Vocal and Instrumental Ensembles (1974; his last work; orchestration completed by Bernard Reichel in 1975).

INSTRUMENTAL WORKS: Suite for Orch. (1913); 2 violin sonatas (1913, 1931–32); *Symphonie pour orchestre burlesque sur des thèmes savoyards*, with Children's Instruments (1915); Piano Quintet (1919); *Esquisses* for Small Orch. (1920); *Pavane couleur de temps* for String Quintet or String Orch. or Small Orch. (1920); *Foxtrot*, overture for 2 Pianos (1924; also for Orch.); Piano Trio on popular Irish themes (1924); *Rythmes*, 3 symph. movements (1926; International Society for Contemporary Music Festival, Geneva, April 6, 1929); *Guitare*, 4 small pieces for Guitar (1933; versions for Piano and Orch.); 2 piano concertos: No. 1 (1933–34; Geneva, Jan. 22, 1936) and No. 2 (1968–69; The Hague, June 27, 1970); *Rhapsodie* for String Quintet (1935); *Danse de la peur* for 2 Pianos and Small Orch. (1936; music from an uncompleted ballet, *Die blaue Blume*); String Trio (1936); Symph., with Jazz Instruments (1937; Geneva, March 10, 1938); *Ballade* for Saxophone, Strings, Piano, and Percussion (1938); *Sonata da chiesa* for Viola d'Amore or Flute, and Organ or Orch. or String Orch. (1938); *Ballade* for Flute, and Orch. or String Orch. (1939); *Ballade* for Piano and Orch. (1939); *Ballade* for Trombone or Saxophone, and Piano or Orch. (1940); *Passacaille* for Organ (1944; versions for String Orch., 1952, and for Full Orch., 1962); *Petite symphonie concertante* for Harp, Harpsichord, Piano, and Double String Orch. (1944–45; Zürich, May 17, 1946; an alternate version, retitled *Symphonie concertante*, was created in 1946 for Full Orch., eliminating the solo instruments); *8 Preludes* for Piano (1947–48); Concerto for 7 Winds, Strings, and Percussion (1949; Bern, Oct. 25, 1949); *Ballade* for Cello, and Piano or Small Orch. (1949);

Violin Concerto (1950–51; Basel, Jan. 24, 1952); Concerto for Harpsichord and Small Orch. (Venice, Sept. 14, 1952); *Clair de lune* for Piano (1953); *Etudes* for String Orch. or 2 Pianos (1955–56); *Ouverture en hommage à Mozart* (1956); *Pièce brève* for Flute, Oboe, and Harp (1957); *Ouverture en rondeau* (1958); *Inter arma caritas* for Orch. (1963); *Les Quatre Eléments* for Orch. (1963–64; Geneva, Oct. 7, 1964); *Etude rythmique* and *Etude de déchiffrage* for Piano (both 1965); Cello Concerto (1965–66; Basel, Jan. 26, 1967); String Quartet (1966–67); *Erasmi monumentum* for Orch. and Organ (Rotterdam, Sept. 24, 1969); *3 danses* for Oboe, Harp, and String Orch. (Zürich, Oct. 9, 1970); *Ballade* for Viola, Winds, Harp, and Harpsichord (1972); *Polyptyque*, 6 images of the Passion of Christ, for Violin and 2 String Orchs. (1972–73; Lausanne, Sept. 9, 1973); *Fantaisie sur des rythmes flamenco* for Piano (1973).

BIBLIOGRAPHY: R.-Aloys Mooser, *Regards sur la musique contemporaine, 1921–1946* (Lausanne, 1947); B. Billeter, *Frank Martin, Ein Aussenseiter der neuen Musik* (Basel, 1970). The Sept./Oct. 1976 issue of *Schweizerische Musikzeitung*, devoted to Frank Martin, includes an extensive bibliography.

Martin, Freddy, American bandleader; b. Cleveland, Dec. 9, 1906; d. Newport Beach, Calif., Sept. 30, 1983. He played the tenor saxophone in his youth; he formed his own band while still in high school; in time he became one of the most popular bandleaders of the "Swing" era of the 1930s and 1940s. He also gained popular success with his arrangements of themes from classical scores; these included Tchaikovsky's First Piano Concerto as *Tonight We Love* and Grieg's Piano Concerto as *I Look at Heaven*. He was instrumental in launching the careers of Dinah Shore and other prominent vocalists.

Martin, Sir George (Clement), English organist and composer; b. Lambourne, Berkshire, Sept. 11, 1844; d. London, Feb. 23, 1916. He was a pupil of J. Pearson and Dr. Stainer; received the degree of B.Mus. at Oxford in 1868. He was knighted in 1897. In 1888 he succeeded Stainer as organist of St. Paul's Cathedral, which post he held until his death. He publ. the primer *The Art of Training Choir Boys*.

Martin, (Nicolas-) Jean-Blaise, famous French baritone; b. Paris, Feb. 24, 1768; d. Ronzières, Rhône, Oct. 28, 1837. He made his debut at the Théâtre de Monsieur in 1789 in *Le Marquis de Tulipano;* sang at the Théâtre Feydeau and the Théâtre Favart from 1794 until they were united as the Opéra-Comique in 1801, and there until 1823. In 1816–18 and again in 1832–37, he was a prof. at the Paris Cons. His voice, while essentially baritone in quality, had the extraordinary range of 3 full octaves, reaching high C.

Martin, Mihaela, Rumanian violinist; b. Bucharest, Sept. 10, 1958. She studied violin first with her father, and later with Elena Schmitzer and Stefan

Gheorghiu. In 1978 she won 2nd prize at the International Tchaikovsky Competition in Moscow and first prize at the Tibor Varga Competition in Sion, Switzerland; in 1982 she won first prize at the first International Violin Competition of Indianapolis, and was awarded its Gold Medal and $10,000; these awards stimulated her further successes; she played with orchs. in Indianapolis, Detroit, St. Louis, Salt Lake City (Utah Symph.), N.Y. (American Symph.), Manchester (Hallé Orch.), and London (BBC Symph.).

Martin, Riccardo (real name, **Hugh Whitfield Martin**), American tenor; b. Hopkinsville, Ky., Nov. 18, 1874; d. New York, Aug. 11, 1952. He studied violin in Nashville and singing in N.Y.; was a pupil in composition of MacDowell at Columbia Univ.; in 1901 went to Paris, where he took singing lessons with Sbriglia; made his debut as Faust in Nantes (1904) and his American debut as Canio (in *Pagliacci*) with the San Carlo Opera Co. in New Orleans (1906); was a member of the Metropolitan Opera Co. from 1907 to 1915; then was with the Boston Grand Opera Co. (1916–17); again with the Metropolitan (1917–18); then with the Chicago Opera Co. (1920–22); subsequently settled in N.Y. and taught singing.

Martin, Thomas, Austrian-born American opera conductor and translator of opera librettos; b. Vienna, May 28, 1909; d. New York, May 14, 1984. He studied at the Vienna Cons.; conducted at the Volksoper; in 1937–38 toured the U.S. with the Salzburg International Opera Guild. In 1939 he married Ruth Kelley of Jersey City, who became his collaborator in numerous translations of opera librettos. In 1941 their translation of Mozart's opera *Die Zauberflöte* was accepted by the Metropolitan Opera. From 1944 to 1956 he was conductor at the N.Y. City Opera, and from 1966 to 1981 conducted school performances there. From 1958 to 1965 he served as associate chorus master at the Metropolitan Opera. The translations (from German and Italian) of opera librettos made by Thomas Martin and his wife include: Mozart's *Die Zauberflöte, Die Entführung von dem Seraglio, Le nozze di Figaro, Don Giovanni,* and *Così fan tutte;* Rossini's *Il Barbiere di Siviglia* and *L'Italiana in Algeri;* Verdi's *La Traviata* and *Rigoletto;* Lortzing's *Der Wildschütz* and *Der Waffenschmied;* Puccini's *La Bohème* and *Madama Butterfly;* Johann Strauss's *Die Fledermaus.* Martin also publ. a collection, *Treasury of Grand Opera Librettos.* In 1981 he and his wife were awarded a Medal of Honor First Class by the government of Austria.

Martinček, Dušan, Slovak composer; b. Prešov, June 19, 1936. He studied piano at the Bratislava Cons. and composition with Cikker and Zimmer; upon graduation, devoted himself to teaching.

WORKS: *Dialogues in the Form of Variations* for Piano and Orch. (1961); *Simple Overture* (1963); *Rhapsody* for Piano and Orch. (1965–66); 3 piano sonatas; *Elegy* for String Orch. (1973); Sonata for Solo Viola (1974).

Martinelli, Giovanni, famous Italian tenor; b. Montagnana, near Padua, Oct. 22, 1885; d. New York, Feb. 2, 1969. One of the 14 children of a fertile Italian family, he played clarinet in the town band; then went to Milan and studied voice there with Mandolini. On Dec. 3, 1910, he made his debut in Milan singing in Rossini's *Stabat Mater;* he made his operatic debut at the Teatro del Varme in Milan as Ernani; Puccini heard him and invited him to sing in the European premiere of *La Fanciulla del West* (Rome, June 12, 1911); he sang for the first time at London's Covent Garden on April 22, 1912. He made his American debut on Nov. 3, 1913, in Philadelphia as Cavaradossi in *Tosca.* On Nov. 20, 1913, he appeared at the Metropolitan Opera in N.Y. as Rodolfo in *La Bohème,* scoring an immediate success with the public and the press; he remained with the Metropolitan for 30 years, until 1943; he returned in 1944, giving his farewell on March 8, 1945; during his final season there (1945–46), he appeared as a concert artist. He then taught voice in N.Y. while making occasional appearances as a singer; he made his last appearance in a production of *Turandot* in Seattle in 1967 in his 82nd year. At the Metropolitan, he sang Radames in *Aida* 126 times, Don José in *Carmen* 75 times, Canio in *Pagliacci* 68 times, and Manrico in *Il Trovatore* 70 times; other parts in his rich repertoire were the title roles in *Faust, Samson and Delilah, Andrea Chénier,* and *Otello.* However, he shunned the Wagnerian characters in opera.

BIBLIOGRAPHY: David Ewen, *Musicians since 1900* (N.Y., 1978).

Martinet, Jean-Louis, French composer; b. Ste.-Bazeille, Nov. 8, 1912. He studied music theory with Charles Koechlin, Roger-Ducasse, and Messiaen; also took lessons in conducting with Charles Munch and Roger Desormière. He naturally absorbed the harmonic essence of French Impressionism and the contrapuntal rigor of the neo-Classical style as practiced by Stravinsky and Béla Bartók; in later works he succumbed to the fashionable temptation of dodecaphony *à la française.* Among his works are a symph. poem, *Orphée* (1945); 6 pieces, each entitled *Mouvement symphonique* (1953–59); *Variations* for String Quartet (1946, in dodecaphonic technique); cantatas: *Episodes* (1950); *Elsa* (1959); *Les Amours* for Chorus a cappella (1960); *Les Douze* for Narrator, Chorus, and Orch., after a revolutionary poem by Alexander Blok (1961); symph., *In memoriam* (1963); *Divertissement pastoral* for Piano and Orch. (1966); *2 images* for Orch. (1966).

Martínez, Marianne di, Austrian singer, pianist, and composer; b. Vienna, May 4, 1744; d. there, Dec. 13, 1812. She was the daughter of Nicoló Martínez, who went to Vienna as "gentiluomo" to the papal nuncio. Thanks to his privileged social position in the diplomatic circles in Vienna, her father was able to engage the best instructors for her; Metastasio arranged for her to study singing with Porpora, piano and theory with Haydn, and advanced composition with Giuseppe Bonno. She appeared as a singer and pianist in aristocratic salons. After Metastasio's death, the family inherited his estate, and continued to play an important role in Viennese artistic life by holding regular soirées. Marianne di Martínez learned enough from her exalted tutors to write her own music; she composed several oratorios and cantatas, a Symph., 2 piano concertos, and a group of minor instrumental pieces. None of these was in any way remarkable, but her works are of historical interest as examples of musical composition by a woman of high society who contributed to the artistic life of the Austrian capital during its greatest ascendance on the international scene. Manuscripts of some of her works are preserved in the archives of the Gesellschaft der Musikfreunde in Vienna.

Martini, Giovanni Battista, known as **Padre Martini;** illustrious Italian pedagogue, writer on music, and composer; b. Bologna, April 24, 1706; d. there, Aug. 3, 1784. He received the rudiments of musical knowledge from his father, a violinist; then took courses with Angelo Predieri, Giovanni Antonio Ricieri, and Francesco Antonio Pistocchi. A man of unquenchable intellectual curiosity, he studied mathematics with Zanotti, and took a seminar in ecclesiastical music with Giacomo Perti. In 1721 he entered the Franciscan conventual monastery in Lugo di Romagna, but abandoned monastic aspirations and returned to Bologna in 1722; there he became organist, and later maestro di cappella, at S. Francesco in 1725, and was ordained a priest in 1729. He was a prolific composer and a learned scholar; his *Storia della musica* (3 vols., Bologna, 1757, 1770, and 1781; reprinted 1967) gives an extensive survey of music in ancient Greece. But it is as a pedagogue that Padre Martini achieved lasting fame. His magnum opus in music theory was *Esemplare ossia Saggio fondamentale practico di contrappunto* (2 vols., Bologna, 1774 and 1775). J.C. Bach, Jommelli, Grétry, and Mozart were his students. A by-product of his various activities was the accumulation of a magnificent library, which Burney estimated at nearly 17,000 vols.; after Martini's death, it became the foundation of the collection in the library of the Liceo Musicale (later the Civico Museo Bibliografico Musicale). He received many honors during his long life; in 1758 he became a member of the Accademia dell' Istituto delle Scienze di Bologna and of the Accademia dei Filarmonici di Bologna. In 1776 he was elected to membership in the Arcadi di Roma, where his Arcadian title was "Aristosseno Anfioneo" ("Aristoxenos Amphion"). He conducted a voluminous correspondence; about 6,000 letters are extant; it included communications with scholars, kings, and popes.

WORKS: Oratorio, *L'assunzione di Salomone al tronto d'Israello* (1734); masses, introits, graduals, offertories, vespers, hymns; *Litaniae atque antiphonae finales B. Virginis Mariae* for 4 Voices, Organ, and Instruments, publ. in Bologna in 1734; secular vocal works: 24 sinfonias, numerous concertos for various instruments, about 100 keyboard sonatas.

WRITINGS: *Regola agli organisti per accompagnare il canto fermo* (Bologna, 1756); *Compendio della teoria de' numeri per uso del musico* (Bologna, 1769).

CORRESPONDENCE: A selection of his letters was ed. by F. Parisini as *Carteggio inedito del G. Martini, coi più celebri musicisti del suo tempo* (Bologna, 1888). An annotated index was prepared by A. Schnoebelen as *Padre Martini's Collection of Letters* (N.Y., 1979).

BIBLIOGRAPHY: A. Eximeno, *Dubbio sopra il saggio fondamentale pratico di contrappunto del Padre Giovanni Battista Martini,* (Rome, 1775); G. Della Valle, *Memorie storiche del p. m. Giambattista Martini* (Naples, 1785); G. Gandolfi, *Elogio di Giovanni Battista Martini* (Bologna, 1813); F. Parisini, *Della vita e delle opere del Padre G.B. Martini* (Bologna, 1887); L. Busi, *Il Padre G.B. Martini* (Bologna, 1891); F. Haberl, "Padre Giovanni Battista Martini als Musiker und Componist," *Kirchenmusikalisches Jahrbuch,* VII (1892); W. Reich, *Padre Martini als Theoretiker und Lehrer* (Diss., Univ. of Vienna, 1934); G. Tebaldini, "La scolastica del P. Martini," *Rivista Musicale Italiana,* XLIII (1939) and XLIV (1940); P. Pauchard, *Ein italienischer Musiktheoretiker: Pater Giambattista Martini* (Lugano, 1941); N. Gallini, "Le dimissioni di Padre Martini," *La Scala* (Sept. 1953); P. Zaccaria, *P. Martini compositore* (Diss., Pontificio Istituto di Musica Sacra, Rome 1959); H. Brofsky, *The Instrumental Music of Padre Martini* (Diss., N.Y. Univ., 1963); idem, "The Symphonies of Padre Martini," *Musical Quarterly,* LI (1965); idem, "The Keyboard Sonatas of Padre Martini," *Quadrivium,* VIII (1967); P. Wiechens, *Die Kompositionstheorie und das kirchenmusikalische Schaffen Padre Martinis* (Regensburg, 1968); P. Zaccaria, *Padre Giambattista Martini: Compositore musicologo e maestro* (Padua, 1969); H. Brofsky, "J.C. Bach, G.B. Sammartini, and Padre Martini: A *Concorso* in Milan in 1762," in *A Musical Offering: Essays in Honor of Martin Bernstein* (N.Y., 1977).

Martini (real name, **Schwarzendorf**), **Jean Paul Egide** (properly, **Johann Paul Ágid**), German organist and composer; b. Freystadt in the Palatinate (baptized, Aug. 31), 1741; d. Paris, Feb. 10, 1816. At the age of 10 he enrolled in the Jesuit Seminary in Neuburg an der Donau, becoming organist there. In 1760, having studied organ, he settled in Nancy, and Italianized his name; then was attached to the retinue of King Stanislas at Lunéville (1761–66). In 1766 he went to Paris, where he won a prize for a military march for the Swiss Guard; this introduced him into army circles in France; he enlisted as an officer of a Hussar regiment, and wrote more band music; also composed an opera, *L'Amoureux de quinze ans,* which was produced with extraordinary success at the Italian Opera in Paris (April 18, 1771). Leaving the army, he became music director to the Prince of Condé, and later to the Comte d'Artois. He purchased the reversion of the office of First Intendant of the King's Music, a speculation brought to naught by the Revolution, which caused him to resign in haste his position as conductor at the Théâtre Feydeau, and flee to Lyons in 1792. He returned to Paris in 1794, and was appointed Inspector of the Paris Cons. in 1798; also taught composition there until 1802. In appreciation of his royalist record, he was given the post of Royal Intendant at the Restoration in 1814, but died 2 years later. He wrote 13 operas, a Requiem for Louis XVI, Psalms, and other church music, but he is chiefly remembered as the composer of the popular air *Plaisir d'amour,* which was arranged by Berlioz for voice and orch.

BIBLIOGRAPHY: A Pougin, *J.P.E. Martini* (Paris, 1864).

Martini, Nino, Italian tenor; b. Verona, Aug. 7, 1902; d. there, Dec. 9, 1976. He studied voice in Italy and in the U.S.; took lessons with Giovanni Zenatello in N.Y. In 1931 he made his American debut as an opera singer with the Philadelphia Opera Co.; sang at the Metropolitan Opera House in N.Y. for the first time as the Duke in *Rigoletto* on Dec. 28, 1933, and remained on its roster until 1946.

Martino, Donald, American composer; b. Plainfield, N.J., May 16, 1931. He learned to play the clarinet, oboe, and saxophone in his youth; then studied composition with Ernst Bacon at Syracuse Univ. (B.M., 1952) and with Milton Babbitt and Roger Sessions at Princeton Univ. (M.F.A., 1954); continued his studies with Luigi Dallapiccola in Florence, Italy, on a Fulbright scholarship (1954–56). In 1958–59 he was an instructor at Princeton Univ.; from 1959 to 1969 taught theory and composition at Yale Univ.; then was a prof. of composition at the New England Cons. of Music (1970–80), where he served as chairman of the composition dept. He was Irving Fine Prof. of Music at Brandeis Univ. (1980–83); in 1983 became a prof. of music at Harvard Univ. He received 3 Guggenheim fellowships (1967, 1973, 1982); was awarded the Pulitzer Prize in Music in 1974 for his chamber music piece *Notturno;* in 1981 was made a member of the American Academy and Inst. of Arts and Letters. In his music he adopts a quasi-mathematical method of composition based on arithmetical permutations of tonal and rhythmic ingredients.

WORKS: *Quodlibets* for Flute (1954); *A Set for Clarinet,* (1954); *Portraits,* secular cantata for Mezzo-soprano, Bass-baritone, Mixed Chorus, and Orch., to texts by Walt Whitman, Edna St. Vincent Millay, and e.e. cummings (1955); *7 canoni enigmatici* for String Quartet or other instrumental combinations (1955); *Composition* for Orch. (retitled *Contemplations;* 1957); Quartet for Clarinet, Violin, Viola, and Cello (1957); *Piano Fantasy* (1958); Trio for Violin, Cello, and Piano (1959); *5 frammenti* for Oboe and Double Bass (1961); *Fantasy-Variations* for Violin (1962); Concerto for Wind Quintet (1964); *Parisonatina al'dodecafonia* for Cello (1964); Piano Concerto (1965); *B,A,B,B,IT,T* for Clarinet (1966); *Strata* for Bass Clarinet (1966); *Mosaic for Grand Orchestra* (1967); *Pianississimo,* piano sonata (1970); *7 Pious Pieces* for Chorus, to a text by Robert Herrick (1971); Cello Concerto (1972); *Augenmusik: A Mixed Mediacritique* for "actress, danseuse or uninhibited female percussionist and electronic tape" (1972); *Notturno* for Flute, Clarinet, Violin, Cello, Percussion, and Piano (1973); *Paradiso Choruses,* oratorio for 12 Soloists, Mixed Chorus, Children's Chorus ad libitum, Orch., and Tape, after Dante's *Divine Comedy* (1974); *Ritorno* for Orch. (1975); Triple Concerto for Clarinet, Bass Clarinet, Contrabass Clarinet, and Chamber Orch. (1977); *Fantasies and Impromptus* for Piano (1980); *Parody Suite* for Piano (1982); String Quartet (1983).

Martinon, Jean, significant French conductor and composer; b. Lyons, Jan. 10, 1910; d. Paris, March 1, 1976. He studied violin at the Paris Cons. (1926–29), winning a premier prix; then took lessons in composition with Albert Roussel and Vincent d'Indy and in conducting with Charles Munch. He was in the French army during World War II; was taken prisoner in 1940 and spent 2 years in a German prison camp (Stalag IX); during imprisonment he wrote several works of a religious nature, among them *Psalm 136, Musique d'exil ou Stalag IX,* and *Absolve Domine,* in memory of French musicians killed in the war. After the war he conducted the Concerts du Conservatoire de Paris; in 1946 he was appointed conductor of the Bordeaux Symph. Orch.; later had guest engagements as a conductor in England and South America. From 1947 to 1950 he served as associate conductor of the London Phil.; made his American debut with the Boston Symph. Orch., March 29, 1957, conducting the American premiere of his 2nd Symph. His other engagements were as principal conductor of the Lamoureux Orch. in Paris (1950–57), the Israel Phil. (1958–60), and the Düsseldorf Symph. (1960–66). In 1963 he was appointed conductor of the Chicago Symph. Orch.; during the 5 years of his tenure he conducted about 60 works by modern American and European composers of the modern school; this progressive policy met opposition from some influential people in Chicago society and in the press, and he resigned in 1968. He returned to France and led the Orch. National of Paris Radio; also conducted the Residente Orch. in The Hague. His own compositions follow the spirit of French neo-Classicism, euphonious in their modernity and expansive in their Romantic élan.

WORKS: FOR THE STAGE: Opera, *Hécube,* after Euripides (1949–54; first scenic perf., Strasbourg, Nov. 10, 1956); ballet, *Ambohimanga ou La Cité bleue,* with Soloists and Chorus (1946; Paris, 1947). FOR ORCH.: 4 symphs.: No. 1 (1934–36; Paris, March 1940); No. 2, *Hymne à la vie* (1942–44; Paris, Feb. 13, 1944); No. 3, *Irlandaise* (Radio Eirean, Dublin, 1949); No. 4, *Altitudes* (1964–65; Chicago, Dec. 30, 1965); *Symphoniette* for Strings, Piano, Harp, and Percussion (1935; Paris, May 30, 1938); 2 violin concertos: No. 1, *Concerto giocoso* (1937–42); No. 2 (1958; Selle, Bavaria, May 28, 1961); *Musique d'exil ou Stalag IX,* a musical reminiscence of imprisonment (1941; Paris, Jan. 11, 1942); *Divertissement* (1941); *Obsession* for Chamber Orch. (1942); *Romance bleue,* rhapsody for Violin and Orch. (1942); *Concerto Lyrique* for String Quartet and Chamber Orch. (1944; transcribed as Concerto for 4 Saxophones and Chamber Orch. in 1974); *Overture for a Greek Tragedy* (1949; prelude to the 2nd act of *Hécube*); *Symphonies de voyages* (1957); *Introduction and Toccata* (1959; orchestration of piano piece *Prelude and Toccata*); Cello Concerto (1963; Hamburg, Jan. 25, 1965); *Le Cène (The Last Supper*, 1962–63); *Hymne, Variations et Rondo* (1967; Paris, Feb. 15, 1969); Flute Concerto (1970–71); *Sonata Movimento Perpetuo* (1973). CHAMBER MUSIC: 7 sonatinas: No. 1 for Violin and Piano (1935); No. 2 for Violin and Piano (1936); No. 3 for Piano (1940); No. 4 for Wind Trio (1959); No. 5 for Violin and Piano (1942); No. 6 for Solo Violin (1958); No. 7 for Flute and Piano (1958); *Domenon* for Wind Quintet (1939); String Trio (1943) *Suite nocturne* for Violin and Piano (1944); Piano Trio (1945); *Scherzo* for Violin and Piano (1945); 2 string quartets (1946, 1963–66); *Prelude and Toccata* for Piano (1947); *Duo* for Violin and Piano (1953); *Introduzione, Adagio et Passacaille* for 13 Instruments (1967); *Vigentuor* for 20 Instruments (1969); Octet (1969). FOR VOICE: *Absolve Domine* for Male Chorus and Orch. (1940; perf. at Stalag IX prison camp, Nov. 2, 1940); *Appel de parfums* for Narrator, Male Chorus or Mixed Chorus, and Orch. (1940); *Psalm 136 (Chant de captifs)* for Narrator, Soloists, Chorus, and Orch. (1942); *Ode au Soleil né de la Mort* for Narrator, Chorus, and Orch. (1945); *Le Lis de Sharon*, oratorio (1951; Tel Aviv, 1952); songs.

BIBLIOGRAPHY: A. Machabey, *Portraits de trente musiciens français* (Paris, 1950; pp. 121–125); *Le Courrier Musical de France*, no. 26 (1969) and no. 40 (1973).

Martins, João Carlos, Brazilian pianist; b. São Paulo, June 25, 1940. He studied piano with José Kliass; made his professional debut at Teresopolis in 1954; other concerts followed in Brazilian cities; in 1960 he made his American debut at Carnegie Hall in N.Y., evoking superlatives for his "passionate subjectivity" from the critics; later he made a specialty of performing all of Bach's 48 preludes and fugues in 2 consecutive concerts; he also appeared as a soloist with orchs. in N.Y., Philadelphia, and Boston. But at the height of his successes, in 1969, he was knocked down during a soccer match, and hurt his arm to the point of a painful neuralgia, so that he had to stop playing piano. But in a surprising change of direction, he went into banking, managed a champion prizefighter, started a construction company, and became a multimillionaire in devalued Brazilian currency. An even more surprising development followed when, in 1981, he was appointed to the post of the Brazilian State Secretary of Culture; in this capacity he exhibited an extraordinary knack for urban recovery in the direction of futuristic Americanization. In the meantime, his neurological ailment subsided, and he returned to his career as a virtuoso pianist.

Martinů, Bohuslav, remarkable Czech composer; b. Polička, Dec. 8, 1890; d. Liestal, near Basel, Swit-

zerland, Aug. 28, 1959. He studied violin at home; in 1907–9 he was enrolled at the Prague Cons.; then entered the Prague Organ School, where he studied organ and theory, but was expelled in 1910 for lack of application; played in the 2nd violin section in the Czech Phil. in Prague (1913–14), returning to Polička (1914–18) to avoid service in the Austrian army; after World War I he reentered the Prague Cons. as a pupil of Suk, but again failed to graduate. In 1923 he went to Paris and participated in the progressive musical circles there; took private lessons with Albert Roussel. In a relatively short time his name became known in Europe through increasingly frequent performances of his chamber works, ballets, and symph. pieces; several of his works were performed at the festivals of the International Society for Contemporary Music. In 1932 his String Sextet won the Elizabeth Sprague Coolidge Award. He remained in Paris until June 1940, when he fled the German invasion and went to Portugal and finally to America in 1941; settled in N.Y.; was a visiting prof. of music at Princeton (1948–51); spent the last 2 years of his life in Switzerland. On Aug. 27, 1979, his remains were taken from Schönenberg, Switzerland, to Polička, Czechoslovakia, where they were placed in the family mausoleum. His music is characterized by a strong feeling for Bohemian melorhythms; his stylizations of Czech dances are set in a modern idiom without losing their simplicity. In his large works he followed the neo-Classical trend, with some impressionistic undertones; his mastery of modern counterpoint was extraordinary. In his music for the stage, his predilections were for chamber forms; his sense of operatic comedy was very strong, but he was also capable of poignant lyricism.

WORKS: OPERAS: *Voják a tanečnice (The Soldier and the Dancer)*, in 3 acts (1926–27; Brno, May 5, 1928); *Les Larmes du couteau (The Knife's Tears)*, in one act (1928); *Trois souhaits, ou Les Vicissitudes de la vie (3 Wishes, or The Fickleness of Life)*, "opera-film in 3 acts" (1929; perf. posthumously, Brno, June 16, 1971; the normal orch. is augmented by a Jazz Flute, Saxophones, Flexatone, Banjo, and Accordion); *La Semaine de bonté*, in 3 acts (1929; unfinished); *Hry o Marii (The Miracle of Our Lady)*, in 4 parts (1933–34; Brno, Feb. 23, 1935); *Hlas lesa (The Voice of the Forest)*, radio opera in one act (1935; Czech Radio, Oct. 6, 1935); *Divadlo za bránou (The Suburban Theater)*, opera buffa in 3 acts (1935–36; Brno, Sept. 20, 1936); *Veselohra na mostě (Comedy on a Bridge)*, radio opera in one act (1935; revised 1950; Czech Radio, March 18, 1937); *Julietta, or The Key to Dreams*, lyric opera in 3 acts (1936–37; Prague, March 16, 1938); *Alexandre bis*, opera buffa in one act (1937; Mannheim, Feb. 18, 1964); *What Men Live By (Čím člověk žije)*, pastoral opera after Tolstoy, in one act (1951–52; N.Y., May 20, 1955); *The Marriage (Ženitba)*, television opera after Gogol, in 2 acts (1952; NBC television, N.Y., Feb. 7, 1953); *La Plainte contre inconnu*, in 3 acts (1953; unfinished); *Mirandolina*, comic opera in 3 acts (1954; Prague, May 17, 1959); *Ariadne*, lyric opera in one act (1958; Gelsenkirchen, West Germany, March 2, 1961); *Greek Passion (Řecké pašije)*, musical drama after

Kazantzakis, in 4 acts (1955–59; Zürich, June 9, 1961).

BALLETS: *Noc (Night)*, a "meloplastic scene" in one act (1913–14); *Stín (The Shadow)*, in one act (1916); *Istar*, in 3 acts (1918–22; Prague, Sept. 11, 1924); *Who Is the Most Powerful in the World? (Kdo je na světě nejmocnější)*, ballet comedy, after an English fairy tale (1922; Brno, Jan. 31, 1925); *The Revolt (Vzpoura)*, ballet sketch in one act (1922–23; Brno, Feb. 11, 1928); *The Butterfly That Stamped (Motýl, ktery dupal)*, after Kipling, in one act (1926); *La Revue de cuisine (The Kitchen Revue;* Prague, 1927); *On tourne (Natáčí se)*, for a cartoon and puppet film (1927); *Le Raid merveilleux (Báječný let)*, "ballet mechanique" for 2 Clarinets, Trumpet, and Strings (1927); *Échec au roi (Checkmating the King)*, jazz ballet in one act (1930); *Špalíček (The Chap Book)*, with Vocal Soloists and Chorus (1931; revised 1940; Prague, Sept. 19, 1933; revision, Prague, April 2, 1949); *Le Jugement de Paris* (1935); *The Strangler (Uškreovač)*, for 3 Dancers (1948; New London, Conn., Aug. 15, 1948).

FOR ORCH.: 6 symphs.: No. 1 (1942; Boston, Nov. 13, 1942); No. 2 (1943; Cleveland, Oct. 28, 1943); No. 3 (1944; Boston, Oct. 12, 1945); No. 4 (1945; Philadelphia, Nov. 30, 1945); No. 5 (1946; Prague, May 27, 1947); and No. 6, *Fantaisies symphoniques* (1951–53; Boston, Jan. 7, 1955); Concertino for Cello, Wind Instruments, and Piano (1924); 5 piano concertos: No. 1 (1925; Prague, Nov. 21, 1926); No. 2 (1934; rescored 1944; Prague, 1935); No. 3 (1947–48; Dallas, Nov. 20, 1949); No. 4, *Incantation* (1955–56; N.Y., Oct. 4, 1956); No. 5 *Fantasia concertante* (1957; Berlin, Jan. 31, 1959); Concertino for Piano, left hand, and Chamber Orch. (1926; Prague, Feb. 26, 1947; originally titled *Divertimento*); 2 cello concertos: No. 1 for Cello and Chamber Orch. (1930; revised for Full Orch., 1939, and rescored in 1955) and No. 2 (1944–45); Concerto for String Quartet and Orch. (1931; also known as String Quartet with Orch.); 2 violin concertos: No. 1 (1931–32; Chicago, Oct. 25, 1973) and No. 2 (1943; Boston, Dec. 31, 1943); *Divertimento (Serenade No. 4)* for Violin, Viola, Oboe, Piano, and String Orch. (1932); Concertino for Piano Trio and Orch. (1933; Basel, Oct. 16, 1936); Concerto for Harpsichord and Chamber Orch. (1935); Concerto for Flute, Violin, and Chamber Orch. (1936); *Duo concertante* for 2 Violins and Orch. (1937); *Suite concertante* for Violin and Orch. (1937; revised 1945); Piano Concertino (1938; London, Aug. 5, 1948); *Sonata da camera* for Cello and Chamber Orch. (1940); *Sinfonietta giocosa* for Piano and Chamber Orch. (1940; revised 1941; N.Y., March 16, 1942); *Concerto da camera* for Violin, String Orch., Piano, and Timpani (1941; Basel, Jan. 23, 1942); 2-Piano Concerto (1943; Philadelphia, Nov. 5, 1943); *Sinfonia concertante* for Oboe, Bassoon, Violin, Cello, and Small Orch. (1949; Basel, Dec. 8, 1950); 2-Violin Concerto (1950; Dallas, Jan. 8, 1951); *Rhapsody-Concerto* for Viola and Orch. (1952; Cleveland, Feb. 19, 1953); Concerto for Violin, Piano, and Orch. (1953); Oboe Concerto (1955); *Smrt Tintagilova (The Death of Tintagile)*, music for the Maeterlinck drama (1910); *Anděl smrti (Angel of Death)*, symph. poem (1910; also for Piano); *Nocturno No. 1* (1914); *Ballada*

(1915); *Míjející půlnoc (Vanishing Midnight;* 1921–22); *Half-Time*, rondo (1924; Prague, Dec. 7, 1924); *La Bagarre (The Tumult)*, rondo (1926; Boston, Nov. 18, 1927); *Jazz Suite* (1928); *La Rhapsodie* (1928; Boston, Dec. 14, 1928); *Praeludium*, in the form of a scherzo (1930); *Serenade* for Chamber Orch. (1930); *Sinfonia concertante* for 2 Orchs. (1932); *Partita* (Suite No. 1) (1932); *Invence (Inventions;* 1934); Concerto Grosso for Small Orch. (1938; Boston, Nov. 14, 1941); *3 ricercari* for Chamber Orch. (1938; Venice, 1938); Double Concerto for 2 String Orchs., Piano, and Timpani (1938; Basel, Feb. 9, 1940); *Memorial to Lidice* (1943; N.Y., Oct. 28, 1943); *Thunderbolt P-47*, scherzo (1945; Washington, D.C., Dec. 19, 1945); *Toccata e due canzone* for Small Orch. (1946; Basel, Jan. 21, 1947); *Sinfonietta La Jolla* for Chamber Orch. and Piano (1950); *Intermezzo* for Orch. (1950; Louisville Orch., Carnegie Hall, N.Y., Dec. 29, 1950); *Les Fresques de Piero della Francesca*, impressions of 3 frescoes (1955; Salzburg Festival, Aug. 28, 1956); *The Rock*, symph. prelude (1957; Cleveland, April 17, 1958); *Parables* (1957–58; Boston, Feb. 13, 1959); *Estampes*, symph. suite (1958; Louisville, Feb. 4, 1959).

FOR VOICE: *Nipponari*, 7 songs for Female Voice and Chamber Ensemble (1912); cantata, *Česká rapsódie* (1918; Prague, Jan. 12, 1919); *Kouzelné noci (Magic Nights)*, 3 songs for Soprano and Orch. (1918); *Le Jazz*, movement for Voice and Orch. (1928); a cantata on Czech folk poetry, *Kytice (Bouquet of Flowers;* 1937; Czech Radio, May 1938); *Polní mše (Field Mass)* for Male Chorus, Baritone, and Orch. (1939; Prague, Feb. 28, 1946); *Hora tři světel (The Hill of 3 Lights)*, small oratorio for Soloists, Chorus, and Organ (1954; Bern, Oct. 3, 1955); *Hymnus k sv. Jakubu (Hymn to St. James)* for Narrator, Soloists, Chorus, Organ, and Orch. (1954; Polička, July 31, 1955); *Gilgameš (The Epic of Gilgamesh)* for Narrator, Soloists, Chorus, and Orch. (1954–55; Basel, Jan. 24, 1958); *Otvírání studánek (The Opening of the Wells)* for Narrator, Soloists, Female Chorus, 2 Violins, Viola, and Piano (1955); *Legend from the Smoke of Potato Fires* for Soloists, Chorus, and Chamber Ensemble (1957); *Mikeš z hor (Mikesh from the Mountains)* for Soloists, Chorus, 2 Violins, Viola, and Piano (1959); *The Prophesy of Isaiah (Proroctví Izaiášovo)* for Male Chorus, Soloists, Viola, Trumpet, Piano, and Timpani (1959; Jerusalem, April 2, 1963; his last work; posthumous perf.); numerous part-songs and a cappella choruses.

CHAMBER MUSIC: 7 string quartets: No. 1 (1918; reconstructed, with the addition of a newly discovered 4th movement, by Jan Hanuš in 1972); No. 2 (1925); No. 3 (1929); No. 4 (1937); No. 5 (1938); No. 6 (1946); No. 7, *Concerto da camera* (1947); 5 violin sonatas: in C major (1919); in D minor (1926); No. 1 (1929); No. 2 (1931); No. 3 (1944); 2 string trios (1923, 1934); Quartet for Clarinet, Horn, Cello, and Drum (1924); 2 unnumbered nonets: for Violin, Viola, Cello, Flute, Clarinet, Oboe, Horn, Bassoon, and Piano (1924–25), and for Violin, Viola, Cello, Double Bass, Flute, Clarinet, Oboe, Horn, and Bassoon (1959); 2 duos for Violin and Cello (1927, 1957); *Impromptu* for Violin and Piano (1927); String Quintet (1927); Sextet for Winds and Piano (1929); *5 Short Pieces* for

Violin and Piano (1929); Wind Quintet (1930); *Les Rondes,* 6 pieces for 7 Instruments (1930); 3 piano trios (*5 Brief Pieces,* 1930; 1950; 1951); Sonatina for 2 Violins and Piano (1930); *Etudes rythmiques* for Violin and Piano (1931); *Pastorales* and *Nocturnes* for Cello and Piano (both 1931); *Arabesques* for Violin or Cello, and Piano (1931); String Sextet (1932); Sonata for 2 Violins and Piano (1932); *Serenade* No. 1 for 6 Instruments; No. 2 for 2 Violins and Viola; No. 3 for 7 Instruments (all 1932; No. 4 is the *Divertimento* for Violin, Viola, Oboe, Piano, and String Orch.); 2 piano quintets (1933, 1944); Sonata for Flute, Violin, and Piano (1936); *4 Madrigals* for Oboe, Clarinet, and Bassoon (1937); Violin Sonatina (1937); *Intermezzo,* 4 pieces for Violin and Piano (1937); Trio for Flute, Violin, and Bassoon (1937); 3 cello sonatas (1939, 1944, 1952); *Bergerettes* for Piano Trio (1940); *Promenades* for Flute, Violin, and Harpsichord (1940); Piano Quartet (1942); *Madrigal Sonata* for Flute, Violin, and Piano (1942); *Variations on a Theme of Rossini* for Cello and Piano (1942); *Madrigal Stanzas,* 5 pieces for Violin and Piano (1943); Trio for Flute, Cello, and Piano (1944); Flute Sonata (1945); *Czech Rhapsody* for Violin and Piano (1945); *Fantasia* for Theremin, Oboe, String Quartet, and Piano (1945); 2 duos for Violin and Viola (*3 Madrigals,* 1947; 1950); Quartet for Oboe, Violin, Cello, and Piano (1947); *Mazurka-Nocturne* for Oboe, 2 Violins, and Cello (1949); *Serenade* for Violin, Viola, Cello, and 2 Clarinets (1951); Viola Sonata (1955); Clarinet Sonatina (1956); Trumpet Sonatina (1956); *Divertimento* for 2 Flutes-à-bec (1957); *Les Fêtes nocturnes* for Violin, Viola, Cello, Clarinet, Harp, and Piano (1959); *Variations on a Slovak Theme* for Cello and Piano (1959). FOR PIANO: *Puppets,* small pieces for children (in 3 sets, 1914–24); *Scherzo* (1924; discovered 1971); *Fables* (1924); *Film en miniature* (1925); *3 Czech Dances* (1926); *Le Noël* (1927); *4 Movements* (1928); *Borová,* 7 Czech dances (1929; also for Orch.); *Préludes (en forme de . . .)* (1929); *Fantaisie* for 2 Pianos (1929); *A trois mains* (1930); *Esquisses de danse,* 5 pieces (1932); *Les Ritournelles* (1932); *Dumka* (1936); *Fenêtre sur le jardin (Window in the Garden),* 4 pieces (1938); *Fantasia and Toccata* (1940); *Mazurka* (1941); *Etudes and Polkas* (in 3 books, 1945); *The 5th Day of the 5th Moon* (1948); *3 Czech Dances* for 2 Pianos (1949); Sonata (1954); *Reminiscences* (1957). FOR HARPSICHORD: *2 Pieces* (1935); Sonata (1958); *Impromptus* (1959). FOR ORGAN: *Vigilie* (1959).

BIBLIOGRAPHY: M. Šafránek, "Bohuslav Martinů," *Musical Quarterly* (July 1943); idem, *Bohuslav Martinů: The Man and His Music* (N.Y., 1944); Jan Löwenbach, *Martinů pozdravuje domov* (Prague, 1947); M. Šafránek, *Bohuslav Martinů: His Life and Works* (London, 1962); H. Halbreich, *Bohuslav Martinů* (Zürich, 1968); C. Martinů, *Můj život s Bohuslav Martinů (My Life with Bohuslav Martinů*; Prague, 1971), reminiscences by his wife, Charlotte; B. Large, *Martinů* (N.Y., 1975). See also *"Modern Music" . . . Analytic Index,* compiled by Wayne Shirley, ed. by Wm. and C. Lichtenwanger (N.Y., 1976; pp. 132–33).

Martín y Soler, Vicente, Spanish opera composer; b. Valencia, June 18, 1754; d. St. Petersburg, Jan. 30, 1806. He was church organist at Alicante as a youth, before going to Madrid, where he produced his first opera, *I due avari* (1776). He then went to Italy, where he was known as Martini lo Spagnuolo (the Spaniard); wrote operas for Naples, Turin, and Lucca. He secured the services of Da Ponte as librettist, and produced with him the operas *Il Burbero di buon cuore* (*The Grumbler with a Good Heart;* Vienna, Jan. 4, 1786; much acclaimed; revived there, Nov. 9, 1789, with 2 additional airs written expressly for it by Mozart); *Una cosa rara* (his undoubted masterpiece; Vienna, Nov. 17, 1786; numerous productions in other European capitals; Mozart borrowed a theme from this opera for his *Don Giovanni*); *L'arbore di Diana* (Vienna, Oct. 1, 1787). Having achieved fame in Italy, where he was favorably compared with Cimarosa and Paisiello, Martín y Soler was engaged as court composer by Catherine the Great (1788). In St. Petersburg, he produced the operas *Gorye Bogatyr Kosometovitch* (libretto by Catherine II; Feb. 9, 1789); *La melomania* (Jan. 7, 1790); *Fedul and His Children* (Jan. 16, 1791); *La Festa del villaggio* (Jan. 26, 1798); ballets: *Didon abandonnée* (1792); *L'Oracle* (1793); *Amour et Psyché* (1793); *Tancrède* (1799). In 1795 he went to London; his operas *La scola de' maritati* (Jan. 27, 1795) and *L'isola del piacere* (May 26, 1795), both to librettos by Da Ponte, were presented there with excellent success. In 1796 he returned to Russia, and remained there until his death.

BIBLIOGRAPHY: J.R. de Lihory, *La música en Valencia* (Valencia, 1903); R.-Aloys Mooser, "Un Musicien espagnol en Russie," *Rivista Musicale Italiana* (1936); R.-Aloys Mooser, *Annales de la musique et musiciens en Russie au XVIIIᵉ siècle,* vol. II (Geneva, 1951; pp. 455–61).

Martirano, Salvatore, American composer; b. Yonkers, N.Y., Jan. 12, 1927. He studied piano and composition at the Oberlin Cons. of Music (B.M., 1951); then at the Eastman School of Music in Rochester, N.Y., with Bernard Rogers (M.M., 1952); later went to Italy, where he took courses with Luigi Dallapiccola at the Cherubini Cons. of Music in Florence (1952–54). He served in the U.S. Marine Corps; played clarinet and cornet with the Parris Island Marine Band; in 1956–59 he held a fellowship to the American Academy in Rome, and in 1960 received a Guggenheim fellowship and the American Academy of Arts and Letters Award. In 1963 he joined the faculty of the Univ. of Illinois at Urbana. He writes in a progressive avant-garde idiom, applying the quaquaversal techniques of unmitigated radical modernism, free from any inhibitions.

WORKS: Sextet for Wind Instruments (1949); Prelude for Orch. (1950); Variations for Flute and Piano (1950); String Quartet No. 1 (1951); *The Magic Stones,* chamber opera after the *Decameron* (Oberlin Cons., April 24, 1952); *Piece for Orchestra* (1952); Violin Sonata (1952); *Contrasto* for Orch. (1954); *Chansons innocentes* for Soprano and Piano (1957); *O, O, O, O, That Shakespeherian Rag* for Mixed

Chorus and Instrumental Ensemble (1958); *Cocktail Music* for Piano (1962); *Octet* (1963); *Underworld* for 4 Actors, 4 Percussion Instruments, 2 Double Basses, Tenor Saxophone, and Tape (1965); *Ballad* for amplified nightclub Singer and Instrumental Ensemble (1966); *L's.G.A.* for a gas-masked Politico, Helium Bomb, 3 16mm Movie Projectors, and Tape (1968); *The Proposal* for Tapes and Slides (1968); *Action Analysis* for 12 People, Bunny, and Controller (1968); *Selections* for Alto Flute, Bass Clarinet, Viola, and Cello (1970).

Marton, Eva, Hungarian soprano; b. Budapest, June 18, 1948. She studied at the Franz Liszt Academy of Music in Budapest with Endre Rösler and Jenö Sipos, graduating in 1968; was on the roster of the Budapest State Opera from 1968–72; sang with the Frankfurt Opera from 1972–77; then joined the Hamburg State Opera. She also made appearances at the Florence May Festival, the Bayreuth Festival, the Salzburg Festival, the San Francisco Opera, and the Metropolitan Opera. Among her finest roles are Tosca, Desdemona, Elsa in *Lohengrin*, Leonore in *Fidelio*, and Elisabeth in *Tannhäuser*. She is also noted for her performances as an oratorio and lieder singer.
BIBLIOGRAPHY: C. Wilkens, *Eva Marton* (Hamburg, 1982).

Marttinen, Tauno, Finnish composer; b. Helsinki, Sept. 27, 1912. He studied piano, composition, and conducting at the Viipuri (Vyborg) Inst. of Music and the Sibelius Academy in Helsinki; conducted the Hameenlinna (Tavastehus) City Orch.: was director of the Hameenlinna Music Inst. from 1950 to 1975. A remarkably prolific composer, he began writing music in a traditional "Scandinavian" manner; about 1955 he adopted a serial technique. His adventurous style, marked by a sense of enlightened eclecticism and drawing its inspiration from national sources, caused some enthusiastic Finnish commentators to compare him to Charles Ives.
WORKS: FOR THE STAGE: *Neiti Gamardin talo (The House of Lady Gamard),* opera after Balzac (1960–71); *Päällysviitta (The Cloak),* opera after Gogol's story (1962–63); *Kihlaus (The Engagement),* opera after Aleksis Kivi (1964); *Apotti ja ikäneito (The Abbot and the Old Maid),* opera based on Balzac (1965); *Hymy tikkaiden juurella (The Smile at the Foot of the Ladder),* ballet after Henry Miller (1965); *Tulitik uja lainaamassa (Borrowing Matches),* opera after Maiju Lassila (1965); *Lea,* opera after Aleksis Kivi (1967); *Poltettu oranssi (Burnt Orange),* TV opera after Eva-Liisa Manner (1968); *Dorian Grayn muotokuva (The Portrait of Dorian Gray),* ballet after Oscar Wilde (1969); *Lumikuningatar (The Snow Queen),* children's ballet after H.C. Andersen (1970); *Beatrice,* ballet from the play after Dante's *Divine Comedy* (1970; Helsinki, Feb. 24, 1972); *Mestari Patelin (Master Patelin),* chamber opera (1969–72); *Laestadiuksen saarna (Laestadius's Sermon),* opera (1974–76); *Psykiatri (The Psychiatrist),* opera (1974); *Meedio (The Medium),* a cappella opera (1975–76); *Jaarlin sisar (The Earl's*

Sister), ballad opera (1977); *Faaraon kirje (The Pharaoh's Letter),* opera (1978–80); *The Sun out of the Moon,* ballet (1975–77).
FOR ORCH.: 7 symphs.: No. 1 (1957–58); No. 2 (1959); No. 3 (1963); No. 4 (1965; co-winner of first prize in the orch. section of the 1967 Camden Festival of Finnish music held in London); No. 5, *The Shaman* (1967; revised 1972); No. 6 (1974–75); No. 7 (1977); *Suite* (1960); *Linnunrata (The Milky Way),* variations (1960–61); *Rembrandt* for Cello and Orch. (1962); Violin Concerto (1958–62); *Panu, tulen jumala (Panu, God of Fire;* 1963); *Manalan linnut (Birds of the Underworld;* 1964); 2 piano concertos (1964, 1973); *Fauni,* fantasy (1965); cello concerto, *Dalai Lama* (1964–66); *Maailman luominen (The Creation of the World),* symph. poem (1966); *Intrada* for Wind Ensemble (1967); Bassoon Concerto (1966–68); *Mont Saint Michel* (1969); *Vanha linna (An Old Castle;* 1969); *Pentalia* (1969); *Harmonia* (1970); *Hämeenlinna,* Sept. 27, 1972); *Concert Piece* for Trumpet and Chamber Orch. (1971); *Pohjola (The North)* for Wind Orch. (1972; Helsinki, Nov. 22, 1972); Flute Concerto (1974); *Hirvenhiihto (On the Tracks of the Winter Moose),* concerto for Clarinet and Orch. (1974).
VOCAL WORKS: *Kokko, ilman lintu (Eagle, Bird of the Air)* for Mezzo-soprano and Orch. (1956; the first work in his new style); *Tumma maa (Dark Land)* for Alto and Orch. (1960); *Pidot (Feast)* for Soprano, Tenor, and Orch. (1962); *Gabbata,* cantata for Reciter, Tenor, Baritone, 2 Choruses, and Strings (1965); 3 cantatas based on Kalevala themes (1964–65); *Kuoleman unia (Dreams of Death)* for Alto, and Orch. or Piano (1967); *Ohikulkija (Passer-by)* for Soprano and Chamber Ensemble (1969); *Raahab* for Soloists, Male Chorus, and Wind Orch. (1971); *Ääniä Nooan arkista (Voices in Noah's Ark)* for Male Chorus and Instrumental Ensemble (1971).
CHAMBER MUSIC: *Delta* for Clarinet and Piano (1962); *Hahmoja (Silhouettes)* for Piano and Percussion (1962); *Loitsu (Incantation)* for Percussion Trio (1963); *Alfa* for Flute and 7 Cymbals (1963); *Nonetto* (1963); *Vipusessa käynti (Visiting Vipunen)* for 7 Double Basses (1969); 2 string quartets (1969, 1970); *Kupoli (Cupola)* for Organ and Tamtam (1971); Duo for Clarinet and Percussion (1971).
FOR PIANO: 4 *Preludes* (1965); *Titisee* (1965); *Taara* (1967); Sonatina (1970); *Easter* (1971); also *Himalaja* for Solo Percussionist (1969); numerous songs and a cappella choral works; music for films and plays.

Martucci, Giuseppe, eminent Italian composer and conductor; b. Capua, Jan. 6, 1856; d. Naples, June 1, 1909. A pupil of his father (a trumpet player), he made his debut as a child pianist at the age of 7; at 11 he was admitted to the Cons. di San Pietro a Majella in Naples; there he studied piano with B. Cesi, and composition with P. Serrao, but left in 1871. Subsequently he traveled as a pianist in Italy, France, Germany, and England; in 1880 he became a prof. of piano at the Naples Cons.; conducted symph. concerts established by Prince d'Ardore, and was the director of the Neapolitan Società del Quartetto. From 1886 until 1902 he was director of the Bologna Cons.; in 1902 he returned to Naples, and became director of the Cons. there, a post he held until his death. His activities as a fine symph. conductor contributed much to Italian musical culture, and he was greatly esteemed by his colleagues and the public; an ardent admirer of Wagner, he conducted the Italian premiere of *Tristan und Isolde* (Bologna, June 2, 1888); also led performances of other operas by Wagner. In his own works, he followed the ideals of the German school; the influences of Wagner and Liszt are particularly pronounced. As a composer, he was greatly admired by Toscanini, who repeatedly performed his orch. music.

WORKS: 2 symphs. (1895, 1904); *4 piccoli pezzi* for Orch.; 2 piano concertos; Piano Quintet; 2 piano trios; *Momento musicale e minuetto* for String Quartet; Cello Sonata; several sets of piano pieces; numerous songs; piano arrangements of classical works.

BIBLIOGRAPHY: R. Prati, *Giuseppe Martucci* (Turin, 1914); a commemorative vol., *Capua a Giuseppe Martucci* (Capua, 1915); Perrachio, "L'opera pianistica di Martucci," *Il Pianoforte* (March 1922); M. Limoncelli, *Giuseppe Martucci* (Naples, 1939); F. Fano, *Giuseppe Martucci* (Milan, 1950; contains complete chronology of Martucci's life, and exact dates of first perfs. of works).

Martucci, Paolo, Italian pianist, son of **Giuseppe Martucci;** b. Naples, Oct. 8, 1883. He studied with his father; made his concert debut in Bologna with Tchaikovsky's First Piano Concerto, on June 27, 1902; from 1904 to 1911 he lived in England; then went to the U.S.; taught at the Cincinnati Cons. (1911–13); in 1913 moved to N.Y. and taught piano.

Marty, Georges-Eugène, French composer and conductor; b. Paris, May 16, 1860; d. there, Oct. 11, 1908. He attended the Paris Cons. (1872–82), winning the Grand Prix de Rome with the cantata *Edith;* in 1894 was appointed instructor at the Paris Cons.; in 1903 succeeded Taffanel as conductor of the famous Société des Concerts du Conservatoire. He wrote 3 operas (*Le Duc de Ferrare, Daria,* and *La Grande Mademoiselle);* a symph. poem, *Merlin enchanté; Suite romantique* for Orch.; choruses, songs, much piano music.

Martzy, Johanna, Hungarian violinist; b. Timişoara, Rumania, Oct. 26, 1924; d. Glarus, Switzerland, Aug. 13, 1979. She studied at the Academy of Music in Budapest (1932–42); after the war she went to England; also made appearances in America. She gained a reputation as a fine chamber music player.

Marvin, Frederick, American pianist; b. Los Angeles, June 11, 1923. He studied voice with his mother and appeared as a boy soprano on the radio; then took piano lessons with Rudolf Serkin at the Curtis Inst. of Music in Philadelphia. During World War II he worked as a musical therapist in U.S. Army hospitals; resuming his performing career after 1945, he gave concerts in the U.S.; made his first Euro-

pean tour in 1954. He did research in Spain on the works of Antonio Soler; edited 6 vols. of Soler's music, including an interesting *Fandango.*

Marx, Adolf Bernhard, eminent German music theorist and writer; b. Halle, May 15, 1795; d. Berlin, May 17, 1866. Intended for the law, he matriculated at the Univ. of Halle, but also studied music with Türk, and gave up a subsequent legal appointment at Naumburg to gratify his love for art. He continued the study of composition in Berlin with Zelter; in 1824 he founded the *Berliner Allgemeine Musikalische Zeitung* (with the publisher Schlesinger); he edited this publication with ability, and proved himself a conspicuous advocate of German music; however, the publication ceased in 1830. After taking the degree of Dr.Phil at Marburg (1827), Marx lectured on music at the Berlin Univ.; was appointed a prof. in 1830; became music director of the scholastic choir there in 1832. He was co-founder (with Kullak and Stern) of the Berlin Cons. (1850), retiring in 1856 to devote himself to literary and univ. work. He was an intimate friend of the Mendelssohn family, and advised young Mendelssohn in musical matters.

WRITINGS: His writings on musical theory and esthetics include: *Die Lehre von der musikalischen Komposition* (4 vols., 1837–47; several times reprinted; new eds. by Hugo Riemann, 1887–90); *Allgemeine Musiklehre* (1839; 10th ed., 1884; trans. into Eng.); *Über Malerei in der Tonkunst* (1828); *Über die Geltung Händelscher Sologesänge für unsere Zeit* (1829); *Die alte Musiklehre im Streit mit unserer Zeit* (1841); *Die Musik des 19. Jahrhunderts und ihre Pflege* (1855); *Ludwig van Beethoven, Leben und Schaffen* (1859; 6th ed., by G. Behnke, 1911); *Gluck und die Oper* (2 vols., 1863); *Anleitung zum Vortrag Beethoven'scher Klavierwerke* (1863; new ed. by E. Schmitz, 1912; Eng. trans., 1895); *Erinnerungen aus meinem Leben* (2 vols., 1865); *Das Ideal und die Gegenwart* (1867). A collection of his essays was publ. by L. Hirschberg as *Über Tondichter und Tonkunst* (3 vols., 1912–22). While Marx was greatly esteemed as a music theorist, his own compositions were unsuccessful; he wrote a singspiel, *Jery und Bätely,* after Goethe (1824); the oratorio *Mose* (1841); etc.

BIBLIOGRAPHY: G.F. Selle, *Aus Adolf Bernhard Marx's literarischem Nachlass* (Berlin, 1898); L. Hirschberg, "Der Tondichter Adolf Bernhard Marx," *Sammelbände der Internationalen Musik-Gesellschaft* (1908).

Marx, (Walter) Burle, Brazilian conductor; b. São Paulo, July 23, 1902. He studied piano with his mother; then went to Germany, where he took lessons with Barth and Kwast; also studied composition with Reznicek. In 1930 he returned to Brazil, where he became active primarily as a conductor. He conducted a concert of Brazilian music at the N.Y. World's Fair in 1939; after 1953 taught at the Settlement Music School in Philadelphia. He wrote several effective orch. pieces; contributed articles on Brazilian music to various publications.

Marx, Josef, German-American oboist, musicologist, and publisher; b. Berlin, Sept. 9, 1913; d. New York, Dec. 21, 1978. He emigrated to America in his early youth; studied oboe with Marcel Dandois at the Cincinnati Cons. and later with Leon Goossens in London. He then took lessons in music theory with Stefan Wolpe. As an orch. oboe player, he was a member of the Palestine Orch. (1936–37) and the Pittsburgh Symph. Orch. (1942–43); also played English horn in the orch. of the Metropolitan Opera in N.Y. (1943–51); in addition, he appeared as an oboe soloist; several contemporary composers wrote special works for him. In 1945 he founded the McGinnis-Marx Edition in N.Y., which publ. works by Wolpe, Wuorinen, Sydeman, Schuller, and other contemporary composers. In 1956–60 he taught oboe playing at the Hartt College of Music in Hartford.

Marx, Joseph, Austrian composer and pedagogue; b. Graz, May 11, 1882; d. there, Sept. 3, 1964. He studied musicology with Degner at the Univ. of Graz, taking the degree of Dr.Phil. with the dissertation *Über die Funktionen von Intervallen, Harmonie und Melodie beim Erfassen von Tonkomplexen.* In 1914 he went to Vienna, where he taught at the State Academy; was its director (1922–24); then rector of the Hochschule für Musik in Vienna (1924–27); for 3 years was adviser to the Turkish government on music education, traveling to Ankara in that capacity; later resumed his teaching in Vienna until 1952; taught at the Univ. of Graz (1947–57). As a composer, he styled himself a "Romantic realist." WORKS: *Herbstchor an Pan* for Chorus, Children's Chorus, Orch., and Organ (1911); a *Ballade,* a *Scherzo,* and a *Quartett in Form einer Rhapsodie,* all for Piano Quartet (1911); *Frühlingssonate* for Violin and Piano (1913); *Trio Phantasie* for Piano Trio (1913); *Romantische Klavierkonzert* (1919–20); *Eine Herbstsymphonie* (1920–21; Vienna, Feb. 5, 1922; its final movement, *Ein Herbstpoem,* is often played as a separate piece); *Naturtrilogie* for Orch., consisting of the separate pieces *Eine symphonische Nachtmusik, Idylle,* and *Eine Frühlingsmusik* (1922–25); *Nordlands-Rhapsodie* for Orch. (1928–29); *Castelli Romani,* 3 pieces for Piano and Orch. (1930); *Verklärtes Jahr,* 5 songs for Middle Voice and Orch. (1930–32); 3 string quartets: No. 1, *Quartetto chromatico* (1937); No. 2, *in modo antico* (1938); No. 3, *in modo classico* (1941); *Alt-Wiener Serenaden* for Orch. (1941–42; Vienna, April 14, 1942); *Sinfonische Rhapsodie* (1943); *Sinfonietta in modo classico* for Strings (1944; arrangement of the 3rd string quartet); *Sinfonia in modo antico* for Strings (1947; arrangement of the 2nd string quartet).

Marx, Karl, German composer and pedagogue; b. Munich, Nov. 12, 1897. He served in the German army during World War I and was a prisoner of war in England; after the Armistice, studied with Carl Orff, Hausegger, Beer-Walbrunn, and Schwickerath. In 1924 he was appointed to the faculty of the Akademie der Tonkunst in Munich; in 1928 became the conductor of the Bach Society in Munich; from 1939 to 1946 was instructor at the Hochschule für Musikerzeihung in Graz; subsequently taught at the Hochschule für Musik in Stuttgart (1946–66). A master of German polyphony, Marx excels in choral composition, both sacred and secular; he is greatly esteemed as a pedagogue. WORKS: FOR ORCH.: Concerto for 2 Violins and Orch. (1926); Piano Concerto (1929; revised 1959); Viola Concerto (1929); *Passacaglia* (1932); Violin Concerto (1935); Concerto for Flute and Strings (1937); *15 Variations on a German Folk Song* (1938); *Musik nach alpenländischen Volksliedern* for Strings (1940); *Festival Prelude* (1956); Concerto for String Orch. (1964; a reworking of his 1932 *Passacaglia*); *Fantasia sinfonica* (1967; revised 1969); *Fantasia concertante* for Violin, Cello, and Orch. (1972). VOCAL MUSIC: Several large cantatas, including *Die heiligen drei Könige* (1936); *Rilke-Kantate* (1942); *Und endet doch alles mit Frieden* (1952); *Raube das Licht aus dem Rachen der Schlange* (1957); *Auftrag und Besinnung* (1961); chamber cantatas; including *Die unendliche Woge* (1930); also cantatas for special seasons, children's cantatas, and the like; a cappella pieces; songs, many with Orch., including *Rilke-Kreis* for Voice and Piano (1927; version for Mezzo-soprano and Chamber Orch., 1952) and *3 Songs,* to texts by Stefan George, for Baritone and Chamber Orch. (1934). Also, *Fantasy and Fugue* for String Quartet (1927); *Variations* for Organ (1933); *Divertimento* for 16 Winds (1934); *Turmmusik* for 3 Trumpets and 3 Trombones (1938); *Divertimento* for Flute, Violin, Viola, Cello, and Piano (1942); 6 sonatinas for various instrumental combinations (1948–51); *Kammermusik* for 7 Instruments (1955); Trio for Piano, Flute, and Cello (1962); Cello Sonata (1964); *Fantasy* for Solo Violin (1966); *Partita über "Ein' feste Burg"* for String Quartet or String Orch. (1967); Wind Quintet (1973). BIBLIOGRAPHY: R. von Saalfeld, "Karl Marx," *Zeitschrift für Musik* (May 1931); F. Oberborbeck, "Karl Marx," *Hausmusik,* XXI (1957); E. Karkoschka, "Über späte Instrumentalwerke von Karl Marx," *Musica,* XXVI (1972).

Marxsen, Eduard, German organist and teacher; b. Nienstädten, near Altona, July 23, 1806; d. Altona, Nov. 18, 1887. He was a pupil of his father, an organist; later studied with Seyfried and Bocklet in Vienna; then returned to Hamburg, where he studied with J.H. Clasing; became known there as a pedagogue. He was a teacher of Brahms; composed about 70 works in various genres.

Maryon, Edward (full name, **John Edward Maryon-d'Aulby**), English composer; b. London, April 3, 1867; d. there, Jan. 31, 1954. He began to compose early in life; went to Paris, where his first opera, *L'Odalisque,* won the Gold Medal at the Exposition of 1889; however, he regarded the work as immature and destroyed the score. In 1891 he studied with Max Pauer in Dresden; later took lessons with F. Wüllner in Cologne; then lived in France; in 1914–19 he was in Montclair, N.J., where he established a cons. with a fund for exchange of music students between England and America; in 1933 he returned to London. Besides *L'Odalisque,* Maryon wrote the following operas: *Paolo and Francesca; La Robe de plume; The Smelting Pot; The Prodigal Son; Werewolf; Rembrandt; Greater Love;* and *Abelard and Heloise.* In his opera *Werewolf* he applied a curious system of musical symbolism, in which the human part was characterized by the diatonic scale and the lupine self by the whole-tone scale; Maryon made a claim of priority in using the whole-tone scale consistently as a leading motive in an opera. His magnum opus was a grandiose operatic heptalogy under the title *The Cycle of Life,* comprising 7 mystical dramas: *Lucifer, Cain, Krishna, Magdalen, Sangraal, Psyche,* and *Nirvana.* He further wrote a symph. poem, *The Feather Robe,* subtitled *A Legend of Fujiyama* (1905), which he dedicated to the Emperor of Japan; and *Armageddon Requiem* (1916), dedicated to the dead of World War I. Of his works, only the following were publ.: *Beatitudes* for Baritone, Double Chorus, and Orch. (1907); *6 Melodies* for Voice and Piano (1907); *The Paean of Asaph,* a festival cantata (1931). After Maryon's death, his complete MSS were donated by his heirs to the Boston Public Library. Maryon developed a theory of universal art, in which colors were associated with sounds; an outline of this theory was publ. in his pamphlet *Marcotone* (N.Y., 1919).

BIBLIOGRAPHY: E.E. Hipsher, *American Opera and Its Composers* (Philadelphia, 1934; pp. 313–16).

Märzendorfer, Ernst, Austrian conductor; b. Oberndorf, May 26, 1921. He studied in Graz; then conducted at the Opera there. In 1953 he became a conductor of the Salzburg Mozarteum Orch.; in 1958 he went to the Berlin City Opera. He became a conductor at the Vienna State Opera in 1966; also appeared as a regular conductor at the Vienna Volksoper, beginning in 1971. He conducted in the U.S. as well, making his American debut with the N.Y. City Opera in 1965.

Marzo, Eduardo, Italian pianist, organist, and composer; b. Naples, Nov. 29, 1852; d. New York, June 7, 1929. As a boy of 15, he settled in N.Y., and appeared in concerts as a pianist; was accompanist to many celebrated artists, among them Carlotta Patti, Mario, and Sarasate on their American tours. From 1878 he played the organ in various N.Y. churches. He held numerous honorary orders, conferred on him by the King of Italy; was co-founder of the American Guild of Organists. He wrote many masses and other sacred choral works; cantatas; operettas; songs; piano pieces.

BIBLIOGRAPHY: F.H. Martens, in *Dictionary of American Biography,* vol. VI.

Mascagni, Pietro, famous Italian opera composer; b. Livorno, Dec. 7, 1863; d. Rome, Aug. 2, 1945. His father was a baker who wished him to continue in that trade, but yielded to his son's determination to study music. He took lessons with Alfredo Soffredi-ni in his native town until he was enabled, by the aid of an interested patron, to enter the Cons. of Milan, where he studied with Ponchielli and Saladino (1882). However, he became impatient with school discipline, and was dismissed from the Cons. in 1884. The following year he obtained a post as conductor of the municipal band in the small town of Cerignola. He composed industriously; in 1888 he sent the MS of his one-act opera *Cavalleria rusticana* to the music publisher Sonzogno for a competition, and won first prize. The opera was performed at the Costanzi Theater in Rome on May 17, 1890, with sensational success; the dramatic story of village passion, and Mascagni's emotional score, laden with luscious music, combined to produce an extraordinary appeal to opera lovers. The short opera made the tour of the world stages with amazing rapidity, productions being staged all over Europe and America with never-failing success; the opera was usually presented in 2 parts, separated by an "intermezzo sinfonico" (which became a popular orch. number performed separately). *Cavalleria rusticana* marked the advent of the operatic style known as *verismo,* in which stark realism was the chief aim and the dramatic development was condensed to enhance the impressions. When, 2 years later, another "veristic" opera, Leoncavallo's *Pagliacci,* was taken by Sonzogno, the 2 operas became twin attractions on a single bill. Ironically, Mascagni could never duplicate or even remotely approach the success of his first production, although he continued to compose industriously and opera houses all over the world were only too eager to stage his successive operas. Thus, his opera *Le Maschere* was produced on Jan. 17, 1901, at 6 of the most important Italian opera houses simultaneously (Rome, Milan, Turin, Genoa, Venice, Verona); it was produced 2 days later in Naples. Mascagni himself conducted the premiere in Rome, but the opera failed to fire the imagination of the public; it was produced in a revised form in Turin 15 years later (June 7, 1916), but was not established in the repertoire even in Italy. In 1902 Mascagni made a tour of the U.S., conducting his *Cavalleria rusticana* and other operas, but owing to mismanagement, the visit proved a fiasco; a South American tour in 1911 was more successful. Mascagni also appeared frequently as a conductor of symph. concerts. In 1890 he was made a Knight of the Crown of Italy; in 1929 he was elected a member of the Academy. At various times he also was engaged in teaching; from 1895 until 1902 he was director of the Rossini Cons. in Pesaro. His last years were darkened by the inglorious role that Mascagni assumed in his ardent support of the Fascist regime, so that he was rejected by many of his old friends. It was only after his death that his errors of moral judgment were forgiven; his centennial was widely celebrated in Italy in 1963.

WORKS: Operas: *Pinotta* (written in 1880; score recovered after 50 years, and first produced in San Remo, March 23, 1932); *Guglielmo Ratcliff* (c.1885; Milan, Feb. 16, 1895); *Cavalleria rusticana* (Rome, May 17, 1890); *L'Amico Fritz* (Rome, Oct. 31, 1891; the only fairly successful opera by Mascagni after *Cavalleria rusticana;* still perf. in Italy); *I Rantzau*

(Florence, Nov. 10, 1892); *Silvano* (Milan, March 25, 1895); *Zanetto* (Pesaro, March 2, 1896); *Iris* (Rome, Nov. 22, 1898); *Le Maschere* (premiere in 6 cities, Jan. 17, 1901); *Amica* (Monte Carlo, March 16, 1905); *Isabeau* (Buenos Aires, June 2, 1911); *Parisina* (Milan, Dec. 15, 1913); *Lodoletta* (Rome, April 30, 1917); *Scampolo* (1921); *Il piccolo Marat* (Rome, May 2, 1921); *Nerone* (Milan, Jan. 16, 1935); *I Bianchi ed i Neri* (1940). Other works include 2 symphs.: No. 1 (1879) and No. 2 (1881); *Poema Leopardiano* (for the centenary of G. Leopardi, 1898); Hymn in honor of Admiral Dewey (July 1899); *Rapsodia satanica* for Orch. (music for a film, Rome, July 2, 1917); *Davanti Santa Teresa* (Rome, Aug. 1923); chamber music.

BIBLIOGRAPHY: G. Monaldi, *Pietro Mascagni: L'Uomo e l'artista* (Rome, 1899); G. Marvin, *Pietro Mascagni: Biografia aneddotica* (Palermo, 1904); G. Bastianelli, *Pietro Mascagni, con nota delle opere* (Naples, 1910); E. Pompei, *Pietro Mascagni, nella vita e nell'arte* (Rome, 1912); G. Orsini, *L'arte di Pietro Mascagni* (Milan, 1912); G. Scuderi, *Iris* (1923); T. Mantovani, *Iris* (1930); A. Donno, *Modernità di Pietro Mascagni* (1931); G. Cogo, *Il nostro Mascagni* (1931); "Bibliografia delle opere di Pietro Mascagni," *Bolletino Bibliografico Musicale* (Milan, 1932); A. de Donno, *Mascagni nel 900 musicale* (Rome, 1935); A. Jeri, *Mascagni, 15 Opere, 1000 Episodi* (Milan, 1940); D. Cellamare, *Mascagni e la "Cavalleria" visti da Cerignola* (Rome, 1941); *Mascagni parla* (Rome, 1945). Numerous publications were issued on Mascagni's centennial in 1963: *Comitato nazionale delle onoranze a Pietro Mascagni nel primo centenario della nascità* (Livorno, 1963); M. Morini, ed., *Pietro Mascagni* (2 vols., Milan, 1964); G. Gavazzeni, *Discorso per Mascagni nel centenario della nascità* (Rome, 1964); D. Cellamare, *Pietro Mascagni* (Rome, 1965); D. Stivender, ed. and translator, *The Autobiography of Pietro Mascagni* (N.Y., 1975).

Maschera, Fiorenzo or **Florentio,** Italian organist and composer; b. probably in Brescia, c.1540; d. there, c.1584. He first studied with his father; then was a pupil of Merulo; served as organist at Santo Spirito in Venice; on Aug. 22, 1557, he succeded Merulo as organist at the Cathedral in Brescia. Of his compositions, 23 are extant; all are 4-part instrumental canzonas. He published *Libro primo de canzoni da sonare a quattro voci* (Brescia, 1584), which has been edited by W. McKee in *The Music of Florentio Maschera (1540–1584)* (Diss., North Texas State Univ., 1958).

Mascheroni, Edoardo, Italian conductor and composer; b. Milan, Sept. 4, 1852; d. Ghirla, near Varese, March 4, 1941. As a boy, he showed special interest in mathematics and literature; wrote literary essays for the journal *La Vita Nuova* before he decided to study music seriously; took lessons with Boucheron in Milan, and composed various pieces. In 1880 he began a career in Brescia as a conductor, and it was in that capacity that he distinguished himself. He was first a theater conductor in Livorno; then went to Rome, where he established his

reputation as an opera conductor (1884). Upon Verdi's explicit request, he was selected to conduct the premiere of *Falstaff* at La Scala in Milan (1893); he remained on the staff of La Scala until 1897; then conducted in Germany, Spain, and South America; also was successful as a symph. conductor. He wrote 2 operas: *Lorenza* (Rome, April 13, 1901) and *La Perugina* (Naples, April 24, 1909).

Mašek, Vincenz, Bohemian pianist; b. Zwikovecz, April 5, 1755; d. Prague, Nov. 15, 1831. He was a pupil of Seeger and F.X. Dussek; became an accomplished player of the piano and harmonica; after long tours, he settled in Prague as an organist and music dealer. His brother **Paul Mašek** (1761–1826) was a good pianist and a teacher in Vienna.

Masetti, Enzo, Italian composer; b. Bologna, Aug. 19, 1893; d. Rome, Feb. 11, 1961. He studied with Franco Alfano at the Liceo Musicale in Bologna; devoted his life mainly to film music; from 1942 until his death he was connected with the Centro Sperimentale di Cinematografia in Rome; publ. *La musica nel film* (Rome, 1950) and composed about 60 film scores. He wrote several dramatic fables, among them *La fola delle tre ochette* (Bologna, 1928), *La mosca mora* (Bologna, 1930), and *La bella non può dormire* (Bologna, 1957). His other works include *Contrasti* for Orch. (1921); *Il gioco del cucù* for Piano and Orch. (1928); a number of piano pieces and songs.

Masini, Angelo, Italian tenor; b. Terra del Sole, near Forli, Nov. 28, 1844; d. Forli, Sept. 28, 1926. He studied with Gilda Minguzzi; made his debut as Pollione in 1867 in *Finale Emilia;* then sang throughout Italy, Spain, and Russia; was chosen by Verdi to sing in the Requiem, appearing under Verdi's direction in London, Paris, and Vienna. He retired from the stage in 1907.

Mason, Colin, English music critic; b. Northampton, Jan. 26, 1924; d. London, Feb. 6, 1971. He studied at the Trinity College of Music in London; after the war he received a Hungarian state scholarship for the purpose of writing a book on Béla Bartók and entered as a student at the Budapest Academy of Music (1947–49). Returning to England, he was the music critic of the *Manchester Guardian* (1951–64) and of the *Daily Telegraph* (from 1964); also edited the music magazine *Tempo* (from 1962); was editor of the revised printing of Cobbett's *Cyclopedic Survey of Chamber Music* (London, 1963; with a supplementary 3rd vol.); publ. *Music in Britain, 1951–61* (London, 1963).

Mason, Daniel Gregory, eminent American composer and educator; b. Brookline, Mass., Nov. 20, 1873; d. Greenwich, Conn., Dec. 4, 1953. He was a scion of a famous family of American musicians; grandson of **Lowell Mason** and nephew of **William Mason**; his father, **Henry Mason,** was a co-founder of the piano manufacturing firm Mason & Hamlin.

He entered Harvard Univ., where he studied with John K. Paine (B.A., 1895); after graduation he continued his studies with Arthur Whiting (piano), P. Goetschius (theory), and Chadwick (orchestration). Still feeling the necessity for improvement of his technique as a composer, he went to Paris, where he took courses with Vincent d'Indy. Returning to America, he became active as a teacher and composer. In 1905 he became a member of the faculty of Columbia Univ.; in 1929, was appointed MacDowell Professor of Music; he was chairman of the music dept. until 1940, and continued to teach there until 1942, when he retired. As a teacher, he developed a high degree of technical ability in his students; as a composer, he represented a conservative trend in American music; while an adherent to the idea of an American national style, his conception was racially and regionally narrow, accepting only the music of Anglo-Saxon New England and "the old South"; he was an outspoken opponent of the "corrupting" and "foreign" influences of 20th-century Afro-American and Jewish-American music. His ideals were the German masters of the Romantic school; but there is an admixture of impressionistic colors in his orchestration; his harmonies are full and opulent, his melodic writing expressive and songful. The lack of strong individuality, however, has resulted in the virtual disappearance of his music from the active repertoire, with the exception of the overture *Chanticleer* and the Clarinet Sonata.

WORKS: FOR ORCH.: Symph. No. 1, in C minor (Philadelphia, Feb. 18, 1916; revised radically, and perf. in a new version, N.Y., Dec. 1, 1922); *Chanticleer,* a festival overture (Cincinnati, Nov. 23, 1928); Symph. No. 2, in A (Cincinnati, Nov. 7, 1930); Symph. No. 3, *Lincoln* (N.Y., Nov. 17, 1937); *Prelude and Fugue* for Piano and Orch. (Chicago, March 4, 1921); *Scherzo-Caprice* for Chamber Orch. (N.Y., Jan. 2, 1917); *Suite after English Folksongs* (1918); *Russians* for Baritone and Orch. (1918). CHAMBER MUSIC: Quartet for Piano and Strings (1912); *Pastorale* for Violin, Clarinet, and Piano (1913); Sonata for Clarinet and Piano (1915); *String Quartet on Negro Themes* (1919); 3 pieces for Flute, Harp, and String Quartet (1922); *Variations on a Theme of John Powell* for String Quartet (1926); *Divertimento* for Flute, Oboe, Clarinet, Horn, and Bassoon (1927); *Fanny Blair,* folk-song fantasy for String Quartet (1929); *Serenade* for String Quartet (1932); *Sentimental Sketches,* 4 short pieces for Violin, Cello, and Piano (1935); *Variations on a Quiet Theme* (1939); a choral work, *Songs of the Countryside* (1926).

WRITINGS: *From Grieg to Brahms* (1902; revised ed., 1930); *Beethoven and His Forerunners* (1904); *The Romantic Composers* (1906; reprint, Westport, Conn., 1970); *The Appreciation of Music* (1907; with T.W. Surette); *The Orchestral Instruments and What They Do* (1909; reprint, Westport, 1971); *A Guide to Music* (1909); *A Neglected Sense in Piano Playing* (1912); *Great Modern Composers* (1916); *Short Studies of Great Masterpieces* (1917); *Contemporary Composers* (1918); *Music as a Humanity: And Other Essays* (1921); *From Song to Symphony* (1924); *Artistic Ideals* (1925); *The Dilemma of American Music* (1928; reprint, Westport, 1970); *Tune In, America!* (1931; reprint, 1969); *The Chamber Music of Brahms* (1933); *Music in My Time and Other Reminiscences* (1938; reprint, Westport, 1970); *The Quartets of Beethoven* (1947); contributed articles to the *Musical Quarterly* and other periodicals; was editor in chief of *The Art of Music.*

BIBLIOGRAPHY: B.C. Tuthill, "Daniel Gregory Mason," *Musical Quarterly* (Jan. 1948); Sister Mary Justina Klein, *The Contribution of Daniel Gregory Mason to American Music* (Washington, D.C., 1957); H. Earle Johnson, in *Dictionary of American Biography,* Supplement V (N.Y., 1977).

Mason, Lowell, American composer, organist, and conductor; b. Medfield, Mass., Jan. 8, 1792; d. Orange, N.J., Aug. 11, 1872. As a youth he studied singing with Amos Albee and Oliver Shaw; at 16 he directed the church choir at Medfield; from 1812–19 worked in a dry-goods store, then as a bank clerk in Savannah, Ga., also teaching and conducting; in 1827 went to Boston, becoming a church organist; was president of the Handel and Haydn Society (1827–32); established classes on Pestalozzi's system, teaching it privately from 1829 and in the public schools from 1838. He founded the Boston Academy of Music in 1833, with George J. Webb; in 1855, was made honorary Mus.Doc. by N.Y. Univ. (one of the first instances of the conferring of that degree in America); studied pedagogic methods in Zürich in 1837; publ. his experiences in *Musical Letters from Abroad* (N.Y., 1853); in 1851, went to N.Y.; after 1854, resided in Orange, N.J. He became wealthy through the sale of his many collections of music: *Handel and Haydn Society's Collection of Church Music* (1822; 16 later eds.); *Juvenile Psalmist* (1829); *Juvenile Lyre* (1830); *Lyra Sacra* (1832); *Sabbath School Songs* (1836); *Boston Academy Collection of Church Music* (1836); *Boston Anthem Book* (1839); *The Psaltery* (1845); *Cantica Laudis* (1850); *New Carmina Sacra* (1852); *Normal Singer* (1856); *Song Garden* (3 parts; 1864–65); etc. Many of his own hymn tunes, including *Missionary Hymn (From Greenland's Icy Mountains), Olivet, Boylston, Bethany, Hebron,* and *Olmutz,* are still found in hymnals. His valuable library, including 830 MSS and 700 vols. of hymnology, was given to Yale College after his death.

BIBLIOGRAPHY: T.F. Seward, *The Educational Work of Dr. Lowell Mason* (Boston, 1885); F.J. Metcalf, *American Writers and Compilers of Sacred Music* (1925); E.B. Birge, *History of Public School Music in the U.S.* (1928); H.L. Mason, *Hymn Tunes of Lowell Mason, A Bibliography* (Cambridge, Mass., 1944); idem, *Lowell Mason: An Appreciation of His Life and Work* (N.Y., 1944); A.L. Rich, *Lowell Mason; The Father of Singing among the Children* (Chapel Hill, N.C., 1946); J.V. Higginson, "Notes on Lowell Mason's Hymn Tunes," *Hymn* (April 1967); E.J. O'Meara, "The Lowell Mason Library," *Notes* (Dec. 1971); C. Pemberton, *Lowell Mason: His Life and Work* (Diss., Univ. of Minnesota, 1971).

Mason, Luther Whiting, American music educator; b. Turner, Maine, April 3, 1828; d. Buckfield, Maine, July 4, 1896. He was chiefly self-taught; in 1853 became superintendent of music in Louisville schools, later in Cincinnati, where he invented the "National System" of music charts and books, which had instant success, and made him famous. He settled in Boston in 1865, and reformed music instruction in the primary schools; in 1879 he was invited by the Japanese government to supervise music in the schools of Japan, where he labored 3 years with notable results (school music in Japan is termed "Mason-song"). He spent some time in Germany perfecting his principal work, *The National Music-Course.*

Mason, William, American pianist and pedagogue; b. Boston, Jan. 24, 1829; d. New York, July 14, 1908. The son of **Lowell Mason,** he had excellent opportunities for study; after piano lessons from Henry Schmidt in Boston, and frequent public appearances (first in Boston, March 7, 1846, at an Academy of Music concert), he studied in Leipzig (1849) under Moscheles, Hauptmann, and Richter; in Prague under Dreyschock; and under Liszt at Weimar. He played in Weimar, Prague, and Frankfurt; in 1853, in London; in 1854–55, in various American towns, settling in 1855 in N.Y. With Theodore Thomas, Bergmann, and Matzka, he founded the Mason and Thomas Soirées of Chamber Music, a series of classic concerts continued until 1868; thereafter he won wide celebrity as a composer and teacher. In 1872 Yale College conferred on him the degree of Mus.Doc. His principal textbook for piano playing is *Touch and Technic* (op. 44); others are *A Method for the Piano,* with E.S. Hoadley (1867); *System for Beginners* (1871); and *Mason's Pianoforte-Technics* (1878). His compositions, classical in form and refined in style and treatment, include a *Serenata* for Cello and Piano; some 40 numbers for piano solo, including *Amitié pour moi, Silver Spring, Monody, Rêverie poétique,* etc.; publ. *Memories of a Musical Life* (1901).

BIBLIOGRAPHY: F.H. Martens, in *Dictionary of American Biography,* vol. VI.

Mason & Hamlin Co., celebrated firm of piano manufacturers. The house was founded as the M. & H. Organ Co. in Boston in 1854 by **Henry Mason,** a son of **Dr. Lowell Mason,** and **Emmons Hamlin.** The latter, a brilliant mechanic, turned his attention to improving the quality of the reeds and obtaining great variety of tonal color, with the result that in 1861 the firm introduced the American Cabinet Organ. The firm became internationally famous, when at the Paris Exposition of 1867 its organs were awarded first prize over numerous European competitors; since then the firm has exhibited at every important exposition in Europe and America. In 1882 it began the construction of pianofortes, introducing a new system of stringing which found immediate favor; of several improvements patented by Mason & Hamlin, the most important is the Tension-Resonator (1902; described in *Scientific American,* Oct. 11, 1902), a device for preserving the tension of the sounding board. The firm subsequently became a subsidiary of the Aeolian American Corp. and eventually of the American Piano Corp. **Henry Lowell Mason,** son of the founder, was president of the firm until 1929. He died in Boston on Oct. 18, 1957, at the age of 93.

Massa, Juan Bautista, Argentine composer; b. Buenos Aires, Oct. 29, 1885; d. Rosario, March 7, 1938. He studied violin and composition; became a choral conductor; moved to Rosario, where he was active as a teacher.

WORKS: Operas: *Zoraide* (Buenos Aires, May 15, 1909); *L'Evaso* (Rosario, June 23, 1922); *La Magdalena* (Buenos Aires, Nov. 9, 1929); 3 operettas: *Esmeralda* (1903); *Triunfo del corazón* (1910); *La eterna historia* (1911); ballet, *El cometa* (Buenos Aires, Nov. 8, 1932); symph. poem, *La muerte del Inca* (Buenos Aires, Oct. 15, 1932); 2 Argentine Suites for Orch.; other pieces on native themes.

BIBLIOGRAPHY: F.C. Lange, "Juan Bautista Massa," *Boletín Latino-Americano de Música* (Dec. 1938).

Massa, Nicolò, Italian composer; b. Calice Ligure, Oct. 26, 1854; d. Genoa, Jan. 24, 1894. He studied at the Milan Cons. with Bazzini; wrote the operas *Aldo e Clarenza* (Milan, April 11, 1878); *Il Conte di Chatillon* (Reggio Emilia, Feb. 11, 1882); *Salammbò* (Milan, April 15, 1886; his most successful opera); *Eros* (posthumous; Florence, May 21, 1895); also composed *Inno al lavoro* (1892).

Massarani, Renzo, Italian composer; b. Mantua, March 26, 1898; d. Rio de Janeiro, March 28, 1975. He studied in Rome with Respighi; in 1935 went to Rio de Janeiro, where he was active as a music critic and teacher. He wrote mainly for the stage; among his works are the ballets *Guerin meschino* (Darmstadt, 1928) and *Boè* (Bergamo, 1937); violin pieces and songs.

BIBLIOGRAPHY: "Renzo Massarani," *Il Pianoforte* (Dec. 1924).

Massart, Lambert-Joseph, eminent violinist; b. Liège, July 19, 1811; d. Paris, Feb. 13, 1892. He was a pupil of R. Kreutzer at Paris, where, as a foreigner, he was refused admission to the Cons. by Cherubini; but he became so celebrated as a teacher that he was appointed prof. of violin there (1843–90). Wieniawski, Marsick, and Teresina Tua were his pupils. His wife, **Louise-Aglaë Massart** (b. Paris, June 10, 1827; d. there, July 26, 1887), was a pianist and teacher. In 1875 she succeeded Farrenc as teacher at the Paris Cons.

Massart, Nestor-Henri-Joseph, Belgian tenor; b. Ciney, Oct. 20, 1849; d. Ostend, Dec. 19, 1899. He was an officer in the Belgian army when his remarkable voice attracted the attention of the royal family, through whose influence he was granted a leave of absence for study. He sang with success in Brussels, Lyons, Cairo, New Orleans, San Francisco, and

Mexico.

Massé, Victor (real name, **Félix-Marie**), French opera composer; b. Lorient, Morbihan, March 7, 1822; d. Paris, July 5, 1884. He was a child prodigy; was accepted at the Paris Cons. at the age of 12, and studied with Zimmerman (piano) and Halévy (composition); in 1844 he won the Grand Prix de Rome with the cantata *Le Renégat de Tanger*. While in Rome he sent home an Italian opera, *La Favorita e la schiava*. After his return, his *romances* had great vogue, and his first French opera, *La Chambre gothique* (Paris, 1849), was fairly successful. In 1866 he succeeded Leborne as prof. of counterpoint at the Paris Cons.; and in 1872 he was elected member of the Institut de France, as successor to Auber. His most successful light opera was *Les Noces de Jeannette* (Paris, Feb. 4, 1853); the list of his other operas, performed in Paris, includes: *La Chanteuse voilée* (Nov. 26, 1850); *Galathée* (April 14, 1852); *La Fiancée du Diable* (June 3, 1854); *Miss Fauvette* (Feb. 13, 1855); *Les Saisons* (Dec. 22, 1855); *La Reine Topaze* (Dec. 27, 1856); *Fior d'Aliza* (Feb. 5, 1866); and *Le Fils du Brigadier* (Feb. 25, 1867); his last opera, *Une Nuit de Cléopatre,* was performed posthumously (April 25, 1885).
BIBLIOGRAPHY: L. Delibes, *Notice sur Victor Massé* (Paris, 1885); J.G.M. Ropartz, *Victor Massé* (Paris, 1887); C. Delaborde, *Notice sur la vie et les ouvrages de Victor Massé* (Paris, 1888).

Masselos, William, American pianist; b. Niagara Falls, N.Y., Aug. 11, 1920. He studied piano with Carl Friedberg at the Juilliard School of Music in N.Y. (1932–42) and ensemble playing with Felix Salmond and Louis Persinger; music theory with Bernard Wagenaar. He made his professional debut in N.Y. in 1939; was a soloist with the N.Y. Phil. in 1952 under Mitropoulos; then played with Monteux in 1959 and with Bernstein in 1973. He served as pianist-in-residence at Indiana Univ. (1955–57); at Catholic Univ. of America in Washington, D.C. (1965–71); and at Georgia State Univ. in Atlanta (1972–75); in 1976 he was appointed to the piano faculty at Juilliard.

Massenet, Jules (-Emile-Frédéric), illustrious French composer; b. Montaud, near St.-Etienne, Loire, May 12, 1842; d. Paris, Aug. 13, 1912. At the age of 9 he was admitted to the Paris Cons.; studied with Laurent (piano), Reber (harmony), Savard and Ambroise Thomas (composition); after taking first prizes for piano playing and fugue (1859), he carried off the Grand Prix de Rome with the cantata *David Rizzio* (1863). In 1878 he was appointed prof. of composition at the Paris Cons., and at the same time was elected a member of the Académie des Beaux-Arts; he continued to teach at the Paris Cons. until his death; among his students were Alfred Bruneau, Gabriel Pierné, and Gustave Charpentier. As a pedagogue, he exercised a profound influence on French opera. After Gounod, Massenet was the most popular French opera composer; he possessed a natural sense of graceful melody in a distinctive French style; his best operas, *Manon, Werther,* and *Thaïs,* enjoy tremendous popularity in France; the celebrated *Meditation* for Violin and Orch. from *Thaïs* is a regular repertoire number among violinists.
WORKS: OPERAS: *La Grand'-Tante* (Paris, April 3, 1867); *Don César de Bazan* (Paris, Nov. 30, 1872); *Le Roi de Lahore* (Paris, April 27, 1877); *Hérodiade* (Brussels, Dec. 19, 1881); *Manon* (Paris, Jan. 19, 1884); *Le Cid* (Paris, Nov. 30, 1885); *Esclarmonde* (Paris, May 14, 1889); *Le Mage* (Paris, March 16, 1891); *Werther* (Vienna, Feb. 16, 1892); *Thaïs* (Paris, March 16, 1894); *Le Portrait de Manon* (Paris, May 8, 1894); *La Navarraise* (London, June 20, 1894); *Sapho* (Paris, Nov. 27, 1897); *Cendrillon* (Paris, May 24, 1899); *Grisélidis* (Paris, Nov. 20, 1901); *Le Jongleur de Notre Dame* (Monte Carlo, Feb. 18, 1902); *Chérubin* (Monte Carlo, Feb. 14, 1905); *Ariane* (Paris, Oct. 31, 1906); *Thérèse* (Monte Carlo, Feb. 7, 1907); *Bacchus* (Paris, May 5, 1909); *Don Quichotte* (Monte Carlo, Feb. 19, 1910); *Roma* (Monte Carlo, Feb. 7, 1912); posthumous: *Panurge* (Paris, April 25, 1913); *Cléopatre* (Monte Carlo, Feb. 23, 1914); *Amadis* (Monte Carlo, April 1, 1922). INCIDENTAL MUSIC: *Les Erynnies* (1873); *Un Drame sous Philippe II* (1875); *Nana-Sahib* (1883); *Théodora* (1884); *Le Crocodile* (1886); *Phèdre* (1900); *Le Grillon du foyer* (1904); *Le Manteau du Roi* (1907); *Perce-Neige et les sept gnomes* (1909). BALLETS: *Le Carillon* (1892); *La Cigale* (1904); *Espada* (1908). ORATORIOS: *Marie-Magdeleine* (1873); *Eve* (1875); *La Terre promise* (1900). OTHER CHORAL WORKS: *Narcisse; La Vierge; Biblis.* FOR ORCH.: 7 suites: No. 1 (1865); No. 2, *Scènes hongroises* (1871); No. 3, *Scènes dramatiques* (1873); No. 4, *Scènes pittoresques* (1874); No. 5, *Scènes napolitaines* (1876); No. 6, *Scènes de féerie* (1879); No. 7, *Scènes alsaciennes* (1881); 3 overtures: *Ouverture de concert* (1863); *Phèdre* (1873); *Brumaire* (1899); symph. poem, *Visions* (1890); *Parade militaire* (1887); *Devant la Madone* (1897); *Marche solennelle* (1897); *Les Rosati* (1902); *Fantasie* for Cello and Orch. (1897); Concerto for Piano and Orch. (1903); about 200 songs; 12 vocal duets; piano pieces for 2- and 4-hands. Massenet completed and orchestrated Delibes's opera *Kassya* (1893).
BIBLIOGRAPHY: E. de Solenière, *Massenet: Etude critique et documentaire* (Paris, 1897); A. Bruneau, *La Musique française* (Paris, 1901); C. Fournier, *Etude sur le style de Massenet* (Amiens, 1905); L. Aubin, *Le Drame lyrique* (Tours, 1908); L. Schneider, *Massenet: L'Homme et le musicien* (Paris, 1908; the most comprehensive biography; new ed., 1926); H.T. Finck, *Massenet and His Operas* (N.Y., 1910); O. Séré, *Musiciens français d'aujourd'hui* (revised ed. Paris, 1921); A. Soubies, *Massenet historien* (Paris, 1913); A. Pougin, *Massenet* (Paris, 1914); G. Jean-Aubry, "Un Mot sur Massenet," in *La Musique française d'aujourd'hui* (Paris, 1916); René Brancour, *Massenet* (1922; 2nd ed., 1930); J. Loisel, *Manon de Massenet* (1922); C. Bouvet, *Massenet* (Paris, 1929); J. d'Udine, *L'Art du lied et les mélodies de Massenet* (1931); A. Bruneau, *Massenet* (Paris, 1935); A. Morin, *Jules Massenet et ses opéras* (Montreal, 1944). Massenet's autobiography (completed by X. Leroux) appeared shortly after his

death as *Mes souvenirs* (Paris, 1912; Eng. trans., as *My Recollections,* Boston, 1919); James Harding, *Massenet* (London, 1970).

Masséus, Jan, Dutch composer; b. Rotterdam, Jan. 28, 1913. He studied at the Cons. in Rotterdam; was a music critic in Rotterdam from 1956 to 1960; then moved to Leeuwarden, where he was director of the Music School from 1961 to 1972.

WORKS: Sinfonietta for Chamber Orch. (1952); Concerto for Violin and Chamber Orch. (1953); Concerto for 2 Flutes and Orch. (1956); *Cassazione,* 4 dances for Small Orch. (1960); Piano Concerto (1966); *Schermutselingen (Skirmishes)* for Chorus and Orch. (Leeuwarden, Dec. 17, 1975); *Gezelle liederen* for Soprano, Alto, Piano, 4-hands, and Percussion (1955); *Camphuysen-liederen* for Chorus, 3 Trumpets, 3 Trombones, and Tuba (1967); *4 Songs* for Chorus, 9 Brasses, Double Bass, and Percussion (1970); *The 7 Tile Tableaux* for Baritone, Brass Instruments, Double Bass, and Percussion (1973); 2 violin sonatas (1946, 1950); Trio for Flute, Violin, and Piano (1948); *Quintetto* for Piano and String Quartet (1952); *Introduction and Allegro* for Oboe, Clarinet, and Piano (1952); *Partita* for Violin and Piano (1956); Flute Sonata (1957); *Serenade* for Oboe, Bassoon, Violin, and Viola (1958); *7 Minutes of Organized Sound* for 3 Winds, Guitar, and Percussion (1968); *Symphonic Fantasy* for 2 Pianos (1947); *Helicon Suite* for Piano, 4-hands (1952); *Zoological Impressions* for Piano, 4-hands (1954), *Balletto piccola* for 2 Pianos (1955); *Confetti* for Piano, 4-hands (1969); *Pentatude,* 5 studies for Piano (1974).

Masson, Gérard, French composer; b. Paris, Aug. 12, 1936. He took courses in advanced techniques with Stockhausen, Pousseur, and Earle Brown, working along the lines of serial methods and acoustical coordination of sonorous blocs; experienced profound influence of the theory and practice of Varèse's "organized sound." His music is marked by strict constructivism, enlivened by lyric exoticism.

WORKS: *Pièce* for 14 Instruments and Percussion (1964); *Dans le deuil des vagues I* for 14 Instruments (Royan Festival, April 1, 1967); *Ouest I* for 10 Instruments (Vienna, April 25, 1968); *Dans le deuil des vagues II* for Orch. (London, Nov. 20, 1968); *Ouest II* for Voice and Instruments (Paris, April 26, 1971). Stravinsky, who had an opportunity to examine some of Masson's scores, commended him in one of his last publ. interviews.

Masson, Paul-Marie, eminent French musicologist; b. Sète, Hérault, Sept. 19, 1882; d. Paris, Jan. 27, 1954. He studied music history with Romain Rolland at the Sorbonne; received his degree with the dissertation *La Musique mesurée à l'Antique au XVIe siècle* (1907); subsequently enrolled in the Schola Cantorum as a pupil of Vincent d'Indy; also took lessons with Koechlin. In 1910 he was appointed prof. of the history of music at the Univ. of Grenoble, and entrusted with the organization of the Institut Français de Florence, with the aim of publishing complete editions of works of the early Italian masters. He taught music history at the Sorbonne (1931–52); in 1937 he was elected vice-president of the Société Française de Musicologie, and in 1949, its president. He publ. valuable books: *Lullistes et Ramistes* (1912); *Musique italienne et musique française* (1912); *Berlioz* (1923); *L'Opéra de Rameau* (1930); ed. *Chants de carnaval florentins* (vol. I) and 5-part madrigals by Gesualdo; contributed numerous articles to European music magazines, etc. He was also a competent composer; his works include a cantata to his own words, *Chant des peuples unis; Suite pastorale* for Wind Quintet; songs and piano pieces. A 2-vol. offering, *Mélanges d'histoire et d'esthétique musicale offertes à Paul-Marie Masson* (containing a brief biographical sketch and bibliography), was presented to him by his colleagues, friends, and pupils on his retirement from the Sorbonne in 1952; it was publ. posthumously (Paris, 1955).

Masterson, Valerie, English coloratura soprano; b. Birkenhead, June 3, 1937. She studied at the Matthay School of Music in Liverpool and the Royal College of Music in London; also in Milan. She made her debut with the Salzburg Landestheater in 1964; then sang with the D'Oyly Carte Opera in London; became a member of the Sadler's Wells Opera in London in 1971; from 1974 sang at Covent Garden.

Masurok, Yuri, Russian baritone of Polish birth; b. Krasnik, Poland, July 18, 1931. He studied at the Lwow Inst. and the Moscow Cons.; won prizes in singing competitions in Prague (1960), Bucharest (1961), and Montreal (1967); in 1964 made his debut as Eugene Onegin at the Bolshoi Theater in Moscow, where he later sang Prince Andrei in Prokofiev's *War and Peace.* He made his London debut at Covent Garden in 1975 as Anckarström, the same role he chose for his U.S. debut with the San Francisco Opera in 1977. In 1979 he sang Escamillo in Zeffirelli's production of *Carmen* at the Vienna State Opera, and has also appeared there as Scarpia and Luna. His other roles include Rossini's Figaro, Giorgio Germont, and Rodrigo in *Don Carlos.*

Maszynski, Piotr, Polish choral composer; b. Warsaw, July 3, 1855; d. there, Aug. 1, 1934. He studied piano and composition at the Warsaw Cons.; taught there from 1892 till his death; also conducted a choral society. He wrote several attractive choruses, 2 cantatas, a Violin Sonata, and some 100 songs; publ. textbooks for music schools; edited instructive anthologies of vocal music.

Mata, Eduardo, noted Mexican conductor and composer; b. Mexico City, Sept. 5, 1942. He studied composition with Rodolfo Halffter at the National Cons. of Mexico (1954–60); then took lessons in composition and conducting with Carlos Chávez (1960–65) and Julian Orbón (1960–63); in 1964 went to the Berkshire Center in Tanglewood, Mass., where he attended conducting seminars led by Max Rudolf,

Gunther Schuller, and Erich Leinsdorf. He was conductor of the Symph. Orch. of Guadalajara (1964–66); in 1970–78 he was principal conductor of the Phoenix (Ariz.) Symph. Orch.; in 1977 was appointed conductor and music director of the Dallas Symph. Orch. He proved his excellence as an interpreter of Classical and Romantic music to the satisfaction and even delectation of audiences that expect to be pleased by beautiful music, and his success with the public made it possible for him to introduce into his programs some decidedly unpleasing pieces by such un-Romantic composers as Boulez and Berio and by such forbidding representatives of the uncompromising avant-garde as Stockhausen and Cage. Eduardo Mata's own music finds the golden mean between neo-Classicism and ultramodernism; however, during the most hectic period of his activities as a conductor, beginning with 1970, he practically abandoned composition.

WORKS: *Trio a Vaughan Williams* for Clarinet, Snare Drum, and Cello (1957); Piano Sonata (1960); incidental music for Shakespeare's *Twelfth Night* for Soprano Recorder, Viola, and Guitar (1961); *Improvisaciones* for Clarinet and Piano (1961); 3 symphs.: No. 1, *Clásica* (Mexico City, March 24, 1962); No. 2, *Romántica* (Mexico City, Nov. 29, 1963); No. 3 for Horn obbligato and Wind Orch. (1966–67); *Débora*, ballet music (1963); *La venganza del pescador*, suite for 2 Flutes, Trombone, Violin, Guitar, and Percussion (1964); *Improvisaciones No. 1* for String Quartet and Piano, 4-hands (1964), *No. 2* for Strings and 2 Pianos (1965), and *No. 3* for Violin and Piano (1965); *Aires sobre un tema del siglo XVI* for Mezzo-soprano, 2 Flutes, Oboe, Bassoon, 2 Violas, Cello, and Double Bass (1964); Cello Sonata (1966).

Matačić, Lovro von, noted Yugoslav conductor; b. Sušak, Feb. 14, 1899. He was educated at the Vienna Academy of Music; served as an assistant at the Salzburg Festival, eventually settling in Ljubljana as conductor at the Opera. In 1938 he became chief conductor of the Belgrade Phil. Orch. and Opera. He then was Generalmusikdirektor of the German Opera in West Berlin and chief conductor of the Dresden Phil. In 1961 he became Generalmusikdirektor of the Frankfurt State Opera. In 1970 he was named chief conductor of the Zagreb Phil.

Matěj, Josef, Czech composer; b. Brušperk, Feb. 19, 1922. He learned to play the trombone from his father; studied composition with Emil Hlobil at the Prague Cons. (1942–47) and Jaroslav Řídký at the Academy of Musical Arts (1947–51). His early works are characterized by folk-song inflections of the Lachian region of his birth; after 1960 he introduced into his works some coloristic oriental elements; also made discreet use of dodecaphonic techniques.

WORKS: 2 string quartets (1948–49, 1966); Quartet for Trombones (1950); 2 trombone concertos (1951, 1952); Symph. No. 1 for Soloists, Chorus, and Orch. (1953–55); *Sonata da camera* for Oboe and Chamber Orch. (1955); Wind Quintet (1955–56); Symph. No. 2 (1959–60); *Rhapsody* for Viola and

Orch. (1961–63); Violin Concerto (1961–63); Trumpet Concerto (1961–63; Prague, April 15, 1965); *Informatorium* for Trombone and Piano (1964); *Jewish Folk Poetry* for Chorus (1964); Sonata for Trombone, 12 Strings, and Piano (1966); Concerto for Flute, Strings, and Harpsichord (1968); 10 2-part and 10 3-part *Inventions* for 2 and 3 Trombones (1967); *Initials,* vocal fantasy on the text of a letter of St. Paul to the Corinthians, for Tenor, Speaker, Chorus, and Orch. (1968); Concertino for Trumpet, French Horn, and Trombone (1969); Symph. No. 3, *Sinfonia dramatica* (1969); Concerto for Clarinet, Strings, and Piano (1970); Violin Sonata (1971); Cello Concerto (Prague, March 7, 1973); *Triple Concerto* for Trumpet, French Horn, Trombone, and Chamber Orch. (1973); songs.

Materna, Amalie, Austrian soprano; b. St. Georgen, Styria, July 10, 1844; d. Vienna, Jan. 18, 1918. She was a church singer; married the actor Karl Friedrich; together they sang in light opera. She made her debut in Graz in 1865; in 1869 she first sang at the Vienna Court Opera, and remained on its staff until 1894. Her dramatic talent, powerful voice, and beauteous features attracted the notice of Wagner, who selected her for the role of Brünnhilde in the first Bayreuth Festival of 1876; the following year she sang at Wagner festival in London, under the composer's own direction, and also sang in Wagner festivals in N.Y., Chicago, and Cincinnati. Her American opera debut took place on Jan. 5, 1885, as Elisabeth in *Tannhäuser* during the first season of German opera at the Metropolitan Opera House; in 1894 she became a member of Walter Damrosch's German company in N.Y. In 1902 she returned to Vienna and opened a singing studio there.

Mather, Bruce, Canadian composer and pianist; b. Toronto, May 9, 1939. He studied composition with Ridout, Morawetz, and Weinzweig at the Toronto Cons. (1952–59); took summer courses in piano with Alexandre Uninsky at the Aspen School of Music in Colorado (1957–58); then went to Paris and studied with Simone Plé-Caussade, Messiaen, and Milhaud (1959–61); returning to America, he continued his musical education with Leland Smith at Stanford Univ. (M.A., 1964) and studied for his doctorate at the Univ. of Toronto (Ph.D., 1967). In 1966 he joined the faculty of McGill Univ. in Montreal; in 1970 became a prof. at the Univ. of Montreal. Mather's own music follows the path of unprejudiced modernism, extending from neo-Classicism to Expressionism and comprising elements of serialism and microtonality.

WORKS: Violin Sonata (1956); *2 Songs,* after Thomas Hardy, for Bass-baritone and Small Orch. (1956); *Venice,* after Byron, for Soprano, Clarinet, Cello, and Piano (1957); *3 Songs,* to poems of Robert Graves, for Soprano and String Orch. (1957–58); Concerto for Piano and Chamber Orch. of Wind Quintet and String Quartet (Aspen, Aug. 20, 1958; composer, soloist); *Elegy* for Saxophone and Strings (1959); *Cycle Rilke* for Voice and Guitar (1959–60);

Etude for Solo Clarinet (1962); *Orphée* for Soprano, Piano, and Percussion (1963); *Symphonic Ode* for Orch. (Toronto, March 28, 1965); *Orchestra Piece 1967* (Toronto, Jan. 11, 1967); *Ombres* for Orch. (Montreal, May 1, 1968); 5 *Madrigals: I* for Soprano, Alto, Flute, Mandolin, Harp, Violin, and Cello (1967); *II* for Soprano, Alto, Flute, Harp, Violin, Viola, and Cello (1968); *III* for Alto, Marimba, Harp, and Piano (1971); *IV* for Soprano, Flute, Piano, and Tape (1972); *V* for Soprano, Alto, and 17 Instrumentalists (1972–73); *Music for Vancouver* for Small Orch. (1969); 2-Piano Sonata (1970); *Musique pour Rouen* for String Orch. (1970–71); *Mandola* for Mandolin and Piano (1971); *Music for Organ, Horn and Gongs* (1973); *In memoriam Alexandre Uninsky* for Piano (1974); *Eine kleine Bläsermusik* for Wind Quintet 1975); *Au Château de Pompairain* for Mezzo-soprano and Orch. (Ottawa, May 4, 1977); *Clos de Vougeot* for 4 Percussionists (1977).

Mathews, William Smythe Babcock, American organist and writer on music; b. London, N.H., May 8, 1837; d. Denver, April 1, 1912. He studied music in Boston; occupied various teaching posts in Georgia, North Carolina, Alabama, Chicago, and Denver; was organist in Chicago churches; edited the *Musical Independent* (1868–72); was music critic of the *Chicago Tribune* (1878–86); in 1891, founded and edited the monthly magazine *Music.* He publ. *Outlines of Musical Form* (1867); *Emerson Organ-Method,* with L.O. Emerson (1870); *Mason's Piano Techniques,* with William Mason (1876); *How to Understand Music* (2 vols., 1880 and 1888); *100 Years of Music in America* (1889); *Popular History of Music* (1889; 2nd ed., 1906); *Pronouncing and Defining Dictionary of Music* (1896); *Music, Its Ideals and Methods* (1897); *The Masters and Their Music* (1898); *The Great in Music* (3 vols., 1900–1903).

Mathias, Franz Xaver, Alsatian church musician; b. Dinsheim, July 16, 1871; d. Strasbourg, Feb. 2, 1939. He studied in Germany with Hugo Riemann; was organist at the Strasbourg Cathedral (1898–1908); then a prof. of sacred music at the Univ. of Strasbourg. Among his works the best known is the oratorio *Mystère de Joseph,* containing an instrumental *Ballet égyptien.* He also wrote an oratorio of gigantic dimensions, *Urbem Virgo tuam serva* for 2 choruses (with the assistance of a "crowd" of many voices); 28 cantatas; several masses; Psalms; motets; many organ pieces; publ. a manual of accompaniment of Gregorian chant.

Mathias, Georges (-Amédée-Saint-Clair), French composer; b. Paris, Oct. 14, 1826; d. there, Oct. 14, 1910. As a youth he had the privilege of taking piano lessons with Chopin; studied composition with Halévy and others at the Paris Cons.; in 1862 was appointed prof. of piano there, and taught until 1893. He composed 2 piano concertos; 6 piano trios; *5 morceaux symphoniques* for Piano and Strings; and a number of studies, under the promising titles *Etudes de style et de mécanisme* and

Etudes de genre. He also publ. a collection of attractive piano pieces for 2- and 4-hands; his overtures and other symph. works are less interesting.

Mathias, William, Welsh composer; b. Whitland, Dyfed, Nov. 1, 1934. He studied at the Univ. College of Wales, Aberystwyth (B.Mus., 1956); then at the Royal Academy of Music with Lennox Berkeley (composition) and Peter Katin (piano). In 1965 he was elected a Fellow of the Royal Academy of Music; was awarded the D.Mus. degree by the Univ. of Wales in 1966; in 1968 he received the Bax Society Prize for composition. In 1969 he became a lecturer in music at the Univ. College of North Wales; in 1970 was appointed prof. and head of the dept. of music at the Univ. College of North Wales, Bangor. He was commissioned by Prince Charles to write a choral work for the royal bride at Westminster in July 1981. His style of composition may be described as civilized modernism, sophisticated but free of exhibitionistic affectation, optimistically tonal but occasionally somber, brilliantly idiomatic in instrumentation, and unequivocally populist in its euphonious appeal. WORKS: FOR ORCH.: *Divertimento* for String Orch. (1958); *Dance Overture* (London, Aug. 10, 1962); *Invocation and Dance* (Cardiff Festival, March 1, 1962); *Serenade* for Chamber Orch. (1962); Concerto for Orch. (Liverpool, March 29, 1966); Symph. No. 1 (Birmingham, June 23, 1966); Sinfonietta (1967); *Litanies* (1968); *Festival Overture* (1970); *Holiday Overture* (BBC radio broadcast, Sept. 30, 1971); *Vistas* (Swansea Festival, Oct. 25, 1975); Piano Concerto No. 1 (1955); Piano Concerto No. 2 (1960); Piano Concerto No. 3 (Swansea, Oct. 15, 1968); Harp Concerto (Bournemouth, June 1, 1970); Concerto for Harpsichord, Strings, and Percussion (1971); Clarinet Concerto (North Wales Music Festival, Sept. 22, 1975); Symph. No. 2, *Summer Music* (Liverpool, May 14, 1983). CHAMBER MUSIC: Violin Sonata (1961); Quintet for Flute, Oboe, Clarinet, Horn, and Bassoon (1963); *Divertimento* for Flute, Oboe, and Piano (1963); Concertino for Flute, Oboe, Bassoon, and Harpsichord (1964); String Quartet (1967); several organ pieces; choruses; songs; anthems; carols and Psalms, with organ or a cappella; piano pieces.

Mathieu, Emile (-Louis-Victor), Belgian composer and pedagogue; b. Lille, France (of Belgian parentage), Oct. 18, 1844; d. Ghent, Aug. 20, 1932. He studied at the Brussels Cons. with Fétis and Auguste Dupont; taught at Louvain (1867–73); then was in Paris as a theater conductor; returning to Louvain, he became director of the music school there (1881–98); in 1898 was appointed director of the Ghent Cons. In 1869, in 1871, and for a 3rd time in 1873, he won the 2nd Grand Prix de Rome in Brussels; retired in 1924. WORKS: Cantatas: *La Dernière Nuit de Faust; Le Songe de Colomb; Debout; Peuple; Les Bois;* comic operas: *L'Echange* (Liège, 1863); *Georges Dandin* (Brussels, 1877); *La Bernoise* (Brussels, 1880); grand operas: *Richilde* (Brussels, 1888) and *L'Enfance de*

Roland (1895); Violin Concerto; other instrumental works; symph. poems: *Noces féodales; Le Lac;* etc.

Mathieu, Rodolphe, Canadian composer; b. Grondines, Portneuf, Quebec, July 10, 1890; d. Montreal, June 29, 1962. He moved to Montreal at the age of 16; had composition lessons from Alexis Contant; then went to Paris, where he took courses with Vincent d'Indy and Louis Aubert at the Schola Cantorum (1920–27); in 1927 returned to Montreal. His music is cast in a modern French manner.

WORKS: *Les Yeux noirs* for Tenor and Piano (1911); *Chevauchée* for Piano (1911); *3 Preludes* for Piano (1912–15); *Un Peu d'ombre* for Tenor and Chamber Orch. (1913); String Quartet (1920); Piano Trio (1921); *12 études modernes* for Solo Violin (1920–23); *Harmonie du soir* for High Voice, Violin, and Orch. (1924); Piano Sonata (1927); Violin Sonata (1928); *2 poèmes* for Voice and String Quartet (1928); *Lève-toi, Canadien* for Chorus and Orch. (Montreal, Oct. 25, 1934); Piano Quintet (1942).

Mathis, Edith, Swiss soprano; b. Lucerne, Feb. 11, 1938. She studied in Zürich and Lucerne, where she made her operatic debut at the age of 18; was subsequently engaged at the Cologne Opera (1959), at the Salzburg Festival (1960), and in Glyndebourne (1962). In 1963 she joined the staff of the Deutsche Oper in Berlin; in 1960–75 was a member of the Hamburg State Opera. She made her debut at the Metropolitan Opera House in N.Y. on Jan. 19, 1970, as Pamina in *The Magic Flute.*

Mathis, Johnny (John Royce Mathis), black American singer of popular music; b. San Francisco, Sept. 30, 1935. He received classical vocal training before deciding upon a singing career as a popular vocalist; appeared as a nightclub singer; subsequently made tours of the U.S., Europe, Africa, and the Far East. He was particularly adept in renditions of pseudo-romantic ballads such as *Misty, Chances Are, The Twelfth of Never,* and *Wonderful, Wonderful.*

Matičič, Janez, Slovenian composer; b. Ljubljana, June 3, 1926. He studied in Paris and worked in the electronic studios of Radiodiffusion Française; wrote numerous works using the resources of *musique concrète.* He also composed music in a traditional manner: a Symph. (1953); songs; piano pieces.

Mátray, Gábor, Hungarian music scholar; b. Nágykáta, Nov. 23, 1797; d. Budapest, July 17, 1875. He studied law and at the same time learned to compose. In 1812, at the age of 15, he wrote the earliest surviving Hungarian piece of stage music, *Cserni György;* also publ. a general history of music (1828–32), the first such history in the Hungarian language; wrote treatises on folk music and Gypsy music, and made arrangements of Hungarian folk songs. His own works (for piano, guitar, and chorus) are mostly salon music, but some of them are historically important because of the use of native rhythms.

BIBLIOGRAPHY: P. Varnai, "Gábor Mátray," *Zenetudományi Tanulmányok,* vol. II (Budapest, 1954).

Matsudaira, Yori-aki, Japanese composer of the avant-garde, son of **Yoritsuné Matsudaira;** b. Tokyo, March 27, 1931. He studied biology in Tokyo (1948–57); then formed a composing collective, "Group 20.5," with which he produced *Variation on the Theme of Noh* for Flute, Clarinet, 3 Percussionists, Piano, Violin, Viola, and Cello (1960). His own works include: *Variations* for Piano Trio (1957); *Speed Coefficient* for Flute, Piano, and Keyboard Percussion (1958); *Orbits I–III* for Flute, Clarinet, and Piano (1960); *Instruction* for Piano (1961); *Configuration* for Chamber Orch. (1961–63; Tokyo, March 29, 1967); *Co-Action I & II* for Cello and Piano (1962); *Parallax* for Flute, Oboe, Clarinet, Bassoon, and Saxophone (1963); *Tangent '64* for Tape (1964); *Rhymes for Gazelloni* for Solo Flute (1965–66); *Distribution* for String Quartet and Ring Modular (1966–67); *What's Next!* for Soprano and 2 Noisemakers (1967; revised 1971); *Alternation for Combo* for Trumpet, Percussion, Piano, Double Bass, and Ring Modulator (1967); *Assemblage* for Tape (1968); *Assemblage* for Female Voice and Ring Modulator (1968); *Wand Waves* for Narrator and Tape (1970); *Allotropy* for Piano (1970); *Why Not?* for 4–5 Operators with Live Electronics (1970); *"The Symphony"* for 14 Players (1971); *Gradation* for Violin, Viola, and Oscillator (1971); *Substitution* for Soprano and Piano (1972); *Messages* for Wind Orch. and Tape (1972).

Matsudaira, Yoritsuné, Japanese composer; b. Tokyo, May 5, 1907. He studied composition with Alexander Tcherepnin when the latter was in Japan; won the Weingartner Prize in 1937 and the International Composition Competition Prize in Rome in 1962. His music amalgamates old Japanese modalities with modern harmonies.

WORKS: *Theme and Variations* on popular Japanese songs, for Orch. (Tokyo, Dec. 17, 1939); *Ancient Japanese Dance* for Orch. (Berlin, Oct. 9, 1953); *Negative and Positive Figures* for Orch. (Tokyo, May 28, 1954); *Metamorphoses on "Saibara"* (an old Japanese melody) for Soprano and 18 Instruments (Haifa Festival, June 3, 1954); *Koromogae (Love Song)* for Soprano and 19 Instruments (1954; Venice, Dec. 11, 1968); *Figures sonores* for Orch. (1956; Zürich Festival, June 1, 1957); *U-Mai,* ancient dance for Orch. (Darmstadt, Sept. 11, 1958); *Samai* for Chamber Orch. (Rome Festival, June 15, 1959); *Dance Suite* for 3 Orchs. (Donaueschingen, Oct. 18, 1959); *Bugaku* for Chamber Orch. (Palermo, Oct. 6, 1962); *3 Movements* for Piano and Orch. (Stockholm, March 20, 1964); *Ritual Dance and Finale* for Orch. (1963); *Serenata* for Flute and 10 Instruments (1963); Piano Concerto (Madrid Festival, May 20, 1965); *Concerto da camera* for Harpsichord, Harp, and Instrumental Ensemble (1964); *Dialogo coreografico* for 2 Pianos and Chamber Ensemble (1966; Royan, France, April 3, 1967); *Roei*

"Jisei" (2 Stars in Vega) for Voice and Instrumental Ensemble (1967); *Music* for 17 Instruments (1967); *Mouvements circulatoires* for 2 Chamber Orchs. (Graz Festival, Oct. 10, 1972); *Prelude, Interlude and Aprèslude* for Orch. (1973); Sonatina for Flute and Clarinet (1940); Cello Sonata (1942); Concerto for 2 Solo Pianos (1946); Piano Trio (1948); 2 string quartets (1948, 1951); 2 violin sonatas (1948, 1952); *Suite* for Flute, Bassoon, and Piano (1950); Piano Sonata (1953); *Katsura* for Soprano, Harp, Harpsichord, Guitar, and Percussion (1957; revised 1967); *Somaksah* for Solo Flute (1961); *Portrait B* for 2 Pianos and 2 Percussionists (1967–68); *12 pezzi facili* for Piano (1968–69).

Matsumura, Teizo, Japanese composer; b. Kyoto, Jan. 15, 1929. He studied composition with Akira Ifukube, Tomojiro Ikenouchi, and Yosuji Kiyose; subsequently lectured at the Tokyo Inst. Geijutsu Daigaku. Among his works are *Introduction et Allegro concertant* for Orch. (1955); *Achimè* for Soprano, Percussion, and 11 Instruments (1957); *Cryptogram* for Chamber Orch. (1958); Symph. (1965); *Flute of Evil Passions,* poetic drama for Baritone, Male Chorus, 2 Japanese Instruments, and Orch. (1965); *Prélude* for Orch. (Tokyo, Feb. 28, 1969); *Poem I* for Shakuhachi (Japanese vertical flute) and Koto (1969); *Totem Ritual* for Chorus and Orch. (1970); *Poem II* for Shakuhachi (1972); Piano Concerto (1973).

Matsushita, Shin-ichi, Japanese composer; b. Osaka, Oct. 1, 1922. He graduated in mathematics from the Kyushu Univ. in Fukuoka in 1947; concurrently studied music. In 1958 he went to work in an electronic-music studio in Osaka; taught both mathematics and music at the Univ. of Osaka City. In his music he follows cosmopolitan modernistic techniques, mostly of a functional, pragmatic nature. WORKS: *Ouvrage symphonique* for Piano and Orch. (1957); *Correlazioni per 3 gruppi* for 12 Players (1958); *Composizione da camera per 8* (1958); *Isomorfismi* for Orch. (1958); *5 tempi per undici* for 11 Instruments (1958–59); *Le Croître noir* for Chorus, Electronic, and Musique Concrète Sounds, Piano, Harp, and Percussion (1959; Osaka, Nov. 14, 1959); *Faisceaux* for Flute, Cello, and Piano (1959); *Jet Pilot* for Narrator, Orch., String Quartet, and Female Chorus (1960); 2 radio operas: *Comparing Notes on a Rainy Night* and *Amayo* (both 1960); *Sinfonia "Le Dimensioni"* (1961); *Cube for 3 Players* for Flute, Celesta, and Viola (1961); *Successioni* for Chamber Orch. (Radio Palermo, Oct. 1, 1962); *Meta-Musique* No. 1 for Piano, Horn, and Percussion (1962); *Uro* for Chamber Ensemble (1962); *Sinfonia "Vita"* (1963); *Musique* for Soprano and Chamber Ensemble (Osaka, Sept. 14, 1964); *Fresque sonore* for 7 Instruments (1964); *Hexahedra A, B* and *C* for Piano and Percussion (1964–65); *Spectra 1–4* for Piano (1964; 1967; for 2 Players, 1971; 1971); *Kristalle* for Piano Quartet (1966); *Alleluja in der Einsamkeit* for Guitar, Piccolo, and 2 Percussionists (1967); *Serenade* for Flute and Orch. (1967); *Sub-*

ject 17 for Piano, Percussion, Horn, Trumpet, and Trombone (San Francisco, Oct. 31, 1967); *Sinfonie Pol* for Orch., Harp, and Piano (1968); *Haleines astrales* for Chamber Ensemble (1968); *Astrate Atem* for Orch., Harp, and Piano (1969–70); *Requiem on the Place of Execution* for 4 Soloists, Chorus, Orch., and Tape (1970); *Musik von der Liebe* for Flute, Vibraphone, Harp, Piano, Electone, and Tape (1970); *Musik der Steinzeit* for Violin, Ondes Martenot, Tape, and the sound of Cracking Stone (1970); *Ostinato obbligato* for Piano (1972).

Mattei, Tito, Italian pianist and composer; b. Campobasso, near Naples, May 24, 1841; d. London, March 30, 1914. He studied with Parisi, Conti, and Thalberg; made rapid progress, so that at the age of 11 he obtained a nominal appointment as "professore" of the Santa Cecilia Academy in Rome; received a gold medal for playing before Pope Pius XI, and was appointed pianist to the King of Italy. About 1865 he settled in London, where he was active principally as an opera conductor. He himself composed several operas: *Maria di Gand* (London, 1880); *The Grand Duke* (London, 1889); *La Prima Donna* (London, 1889); a ballet, *The Spider and the Fly* (London, 1893); also songs and piano pieces.

Matteis, Nicola, Italian violinist, who settled in London in 1672, and publ. there 4 books of violin pieces (airs, preludes, fugues, allemandes, sarabands, etc.) under varying Italian and English titles; also *The False Consonances of Musick, or, Instructions for playing a true Base upon the Guitarre, with Choice Examples and Clear Directions to enable any man in a short time to play all Musicall Ayres,* etc. In addition, he wrote *A Collection of New Songs* (2 vols., London, 1696). His son, also named **Nicola** (d. 1749), lived in Vienna, and in Shrewsbury, England. He was Burney's teacher.
BIBLIOGRAPHY: Paul Nettl, "An English Musician at the Court of Charles VI in Vienna," *Musical Quarterly* (April 1942).

Matteo da Perugia, Italian church composer; b. Perugia in the 2nd half of the 14th century; date of death unknown. He was principal maestro di cappella of the Milan Cathedral; occupied this post from 1402 to 1416. He wrote 4 Glorias in 3 parts; one Gloria in 4 parts; a number of motets and other sacred works for services at the Milan Cathedral. The first vol. of the new series of the Istituzioni e Monumenti dell'Arte Musicale Italiana (1957) is devoted to music by Matteo, ed. by F. Fano; 22 pieces are transcribed in modern notation by Willi Apel in his anthology *French Secular Music of the Late 14th Century* (Cambridge, Mass., 1950).
BIBLIOGRAPHY: F. Fano in the *Rivista Musicale Italiana* (Jan.–March 1953); C. Sartori, "Matteo da Perugia e Bertrand Feragut," *Acta Musicologica* (1956).

Mattfeld, Julius, American librarian and musicographer; b. New York, Aug. 8, 1893; d. there, July 31, 1968. He studied at the N.Y. German Cons. In 1910 he joined the staff of the N.Y. Public Library; resigned in 1926 to become music librarian of the National Broadcasting Co. (until 1929); then was librarian of the Columbia Broadcasting System; was also organist of the Fordham Lutheran Church in N.Y. (1915–32). He publ. *The Folk Music of the Western Hemisphere* (1925); *A Hundred Years of Grand Opera in New York, 1825–1925* (1927); *Variety Music Cavalcade*, 1620–1950 (N.Y., 1952; revised ed., 1962); *A Handbook of American Operatic Premieres, 1731–1962* (Detroit, 1963).

Mattfeld, Victor Henry, American organist and music editor; b. Bunceton, Mo., Sept. 1, 1917. He studied at Concordia College, River Forest, Ill.; then at the Univ. of Chicago (B.A., 1942) and at the American Cons. of Music in Chicago (M.Mus., 1946); took a course in conducting with Malko; was organist and choirmaster at Zion Lutheran Church in Chicago (1938–47); instructor at the American Cons. of Music (1945–47); from 1947 till 1956 was organist and choirmaster at various churches in N.Y. and New Haven; was an instructor in music history at the Yale School of Music (1952–55).

Matthaei, Karl, Swiss organist; b. Olten, April 23, 1897; d. Winterthur, Feb. 8, 1960. He studied piano and organ at the Basel Cons.; also took courses in musicology there with Karl Nef; then went to Leipzig, where he pursued his organ studies with Straube (1920–23); subsequently was organist in Wadenswil; from 1925 was organist and director of the Winterthur music school; from 1938 served also as organist of the city church. He edited *J. Pachelbel: Ausgewählte Orgelwerke* (4 vols., Kassel, 1928–36), *M. Praetorius: Sämtliche Orgelwerke* (Wolfenbüttel, 1930), and *J.J. Froberger: Ausgewählte Orgelwerke* (Kassel, 1932). He further edited a *Bach-Gedenkschrift* (Zürich, 1950); publ. the books *Vom Orgelspiel* (Leipzig, 1936) and *Die Baugeschichte der Stadtkirchenorgel in Winterthur* (Winterthur, 1941).
BIBLIOGRAPHY: *Karl Matthaei: Gedenkschrift* (Winterthur, 1960).

Matthay, Tobias (Augustus), eminent English pianist and pedagogue; b. London, Feb. 19, 1858; d. High Marley, near Haslemere, Surrey, Dec. 14, 1945. He began to play the piano at the age of 6; was taught by private teachers; in 1871 he entered the Royal Academy of Music as a pupil of Dorrell (piano); won the Sterndale Bennett scholarship, and continued to study piano (with Macfarren); took courses with Sterndale Bennett, and after the latter's death (1875) completed his studies with Ebenezer Prout and Arthur Sullivan; was appointed sub-prof. of piano at the Royal Academy of Music in 1876; sub-prof. of harmony in 1878, and full prof. of piano in 1880. In that year he gave his first public recital, and for the next 15 years he appeared frequently on the concert platform; but his interest in teaching gradually engrossed his attention, so that in 1895 he gave up his career as a concert pianist, and in 1900 established his own piano school in London. The Matthay System, as his teaching method was known, became famous not only in England but on the Continent and in America. Students flocked to him and carried his method abroad. Matthay wrote about 100 piano pieces, a *Konzertstück* for Piano and Orch., a Piano Quartet, and some other works. His didactic publications include: *The Art of Touch* (1903); *The First Principles of Pianoforte Playing* (1905); *Relaxation Studies* (1908); *Commentaries on the Teaching of Pianoforte Technique* (1911); *The Rotation Principle* (1912); *The Child's First Steps in Piano Playing* (1912); *Musical Interpretation* (1913); *Pianist's First Music Making* (3 books); *The Nine Steps towards Finger-individualization; On Memorizing;* etc.
BIBLIOGRAPHY: : Jessie Henderson Matthay, *The Life and Works of Tobias Matthay* (London, 1945); A Coviello, *What Matthay Meant* (London, 1948); R. Hoare, "What Did Matthay Mean?" *Piano Teacher,* IV (1962).

Mattheson, Johann, famous German composer, theorist, and lexicographer; b. Hamburg, Sept. 28, 1681; d. there, April 17, 1764. He received a thorough education in the liberal arts at the Johanneum; acquired proficiency in English, Italian, and French; studied music there with the Kantor, Joachim Gerstenbüttel. He received private musical instruction studying keyboard music and composition with J.N. Hanff; also took singing lessons and learned to play the violin, gamba, oboe, flute, and lute. At a very early age he began to perform as an organist in the churches of Hamburg; also sang in the chorus at the Hamburg Opera. He graduated from the Johanneum in 1693; concurrently took courses in jurisprudence. He then served as a page at the Hamburg court of Graf von Güldenlöw, who held the title of Vice-König of Norway. He made his debut as a singer in a female role with the Hamburg Opera during its visit to Kiel in 1696; from 1697 to 1705 he was a tenor with the Hamburg Opera, conducted rehearsals, and also composed works for it. He befriended Handel in 1703; together they journeyed to Lübeck to visit Buxtehude, who was about to retire as organist, and to apply for his post. The unwritten requirement for the job was marriage to one of Buxtehude's five daughters, whose attractions seemed dubious; both Mattheson and Handel declined the opportunity. In 1704 a violent quarrel broke out between Mattheson and Handel during a performance of Mattheson's opera *Cleopatra* at the Hamburg Opera. Mattheson sang the principal male role of Antonius while Handel acted as conductor from the keyboard in the capcity of maestro al cembalo. Upon the conclusion of his role on stage, Mattheson asked Handel to let him assume the position at the keyboard, since he was the composer. Handel refused and an altercation ensued. The dispute was finally decided by a duel, during which Mattheson broke his sword on a metal button of Handel's coat, or so at least the most credible report of the episode went. They were, however, soon reconciled and remained friends. In 1704 Mattheson became the tutor of Cyrill Wich, the son of Sir John Wich, British envoy at Hamburg. In 1706 he became secretary to Sir John; when the younger Wich became ambassador in 1715, he retained Mattheson as secretary, a position he held for most of his life. During this period Mattheson diligently studied English politics, law, and economics, thereby adding to his many other accomplishments. In 1715 he assumed the post of music director of the Hamburg Cathedral. He composed much sacred music for performance there, including many oratorios. In 1719 he also became Kapellmeister to the court of the Duke of Holstein. Growing deafness compelled him to resign his post at the Cathedral in 1728. In 1741 he was given the title of Legation Secretary to the Duke of Holstein, and was made counsel in 1744. Mattheson's output as a composer was substantial, but little of his music has survived. Of his major compositions, only the MSS of one of his operas, *Cleopatra* (modern ed., by G. Buelow in *Das Erbe deutscher Musik*, LXIX, 1975), and one of his oratorios, *Das Lied des Lammes* (modern ed. by B. Cannon, Madison, Wis.), are extant; the bulk of his MSS kept in the Hamburg Stadtbibliothek were destroyed during the hideous "fire-storm" bombing of Hamburg during World War II. However, most of his numerous literary writings are preserved. Outstanding among his books is *Der vollkommene Capellmeister* (1739), an original theoretical treatise on the state of music in his era. Also valuable is his *Grosse General-Bass-Schule* (1731; based on his earlier work *Exemplarische Organisten-Probe*, 1719) and the *Kleine General-Bass-Schule* (1735). Of great historical value is his biographical dictionary, *Grundlage einer Ehren-Pforte . . .* (1740), which contains 149 entries. Many of the entries on musicians of his own time were compiled from information provided by the subjects themselves, and several prepared complete autobiographical accounts for his lexicon.

WRITINGS: All of the following were publ. in Hamburg: *Das neu-eröffnete Orchester, oder gründliche Anleitung, wie ein "galant homme" einen vollkommenen Begriff von der Hoheit und Würde der edlen Musik erlangen möge* (1713); *Das beschützte Orchester* (1717); *Exemplarische Organisten-Probe im Artikel vom General-Bass* (1719; publ. in an enlarged ed. as *Grosse-General-Bass-Schule, oder: Der exemplarischen Organisten-Probe zweite, verbesserte und vermehrte Auflage,* 1731; reprint, 1968); *Réflexions sur l'éclaircissement d'un problème de musique pratique* (1720); *Das forschende Orchester* (1721; reprint, 1976); *Melotheta, das ist der grundrichtige, nach jetziger neuesten Manier angeführte Componiste* (1721–22); *Critica musica* (1722–25; reprint, 1964); *Der neue gottingische, aber viel schlechter, als die alten lacedämonischen urtheilende Ephorus* (1727); *Der musicalische Patriot* (1728; reprint, 1975); *De eruditione musica, ad virum plurimum reverendum, amplissimum atque doctissimum, Joannes Christophorum Krüsike* (1732); *Kleine General-Bass-Schule* (1735); *Kern melodischer Wissenschaft* (1737; reprint, 1976); *Gültige Zeugnisse über die jüngste Matthesonisch-Musicalische Kern-Schrift* (1738); *Der vollkommene Capellmeister, das ist gründliche Anzeige aller derjenigen Sachen, die*

einer wissen, können und vollkommen inne haben muss, der eine Capelle mit Ehren und Nützen verstehen will, Mattheson's fundamental publication, which served a generation of musicians of the time (1739; facsimile reprint, Kassel, 1954; revised Eng. trans. by E.C. Harriss, 1980); this was followed by the biographical compilation, the "Honor gate" of composers and performing artists, *Grundlage einer Ehren-Pforte, woran die tüchtigsten Capellmeister, Componisten, Musikgelehrten, Tonkünstler, etc. Leben, Werke, Verdienste, etc., erscheinen sollen* (1740; new ed., with addenda, by M. Schneider, Berlin, 1910; reprint, 1969); *Die neuste Untersuchung der Singspiele, nebst beygefügter musicalischen Geschmacksprobe* (1744; reprint, 1975); *Das erläuterte Selah, nebst einigen andern nützlichen Anmerkungen und erbaulichen Gedanken über Lob und Liebe* (1745); *Behauptung der himmlischen Musik aus den Gründen der Vernunft, Kirchen-Lehre und heiligen Schrift* (1747); *Matthesons Mithridat wider den Gift einer welschen Satyre, genannt: La Musica* (by S. Rosa; 1749); *Matthesons bewährte Panacea, als eine Zugabe zu seinem musicalischen Mithridat, erste Dosis* (1750); *Wahrer Begriff der harmonischen Lebens. Der Panacea zwote Dosis* (1750); *Sieben Gespräche der Weisheit und Musik samt zwo Beylagen: als die dritte Dosis der Panacea* (1751); *Philologisches Tresespiel, als ein kleiner Beytrag zur kritischen Geschichte der deutschen Sprache* (1752; reprint, 1975); *Plus ultra, ein Stückwerk von neuer und mancherley Art* (4 vols., 1754, 1755, 1755, 1756); *Georg Friederich Händels Lebensbeschreibung* (German trans. of J. Mainwaring's biography; 1761; reprint, 1976); etc.

WORKS: All of the following were first perf. in Hamburg unless otherwise stated: OPERAS: *Die Plejades oder Das Sieben-Gestirne* (1699); *Der edelmüthige Porsenna* (1702); *Victor, Hertzog der Normannen* (pasticcio; Act 1 by Schiefferdecker; Act 2 by Mattheson; Act 3 by Bronner; 1702); *Die unglückselige Cleopatra* (1704); *Le Retour du siècle d'or* (Holstein, 1705); *Boris Goudenow* (1710); *Die geheimen Begebenheiten Henrico IV* (1711); he also prepared a German version of Orlandini's *Nero* (1723), with additions.

ORATORIOS: *heylsame Geburth und Menschwerdung unsers Herrn und Heylandes Jesu Christi* (1715); *Die gnädige Sendung Gottes des Heiligen Geistes* (1716); *Chera, oder Die Leidtragende und getröstete Wittwe zu Nain* (1716); *Der verlangte und erlangte Heiland* (1716); *Der Altonaische Hirten-Segen, nebst einer Passions-Andacht über den verlassenen Jesum* (1717); *Der reformirende Johannes* (1717); *Der für die Sünde der Welt gemartete und sterbende Jesus* (1718); *Der aller-erfreulichste Triumph oder Der überwindende Immanuel* (1718); *Die glücklich-streitende Kirche* (1718); *Die göttliche Vorsorge über alle Creaturen* (1718); *Die Frucht des Geistes* (1719); *Christi Wunder-Wercke bey den Schwachgläubigen* (1719); *Die durch Christi Auferstehung bestägte Auferstehung aller Todten* (1720); *Das gröste Kind* (1720); *Der Blut-rünstige Kelter-Treter und von der Erden erhöhete Menschen-Sohn* (1721); *Das irrende und*

wieder zu recht gebrachte Sünde-Schaaf (1721); *Die Freuden-reiche Geburt und Menschwerdung unsers Herrn und Heilandes Jesu Christi* (1721); *Der unter den Todten gesuchte, und unter den lebendigen gefundene Sieges-Fürst* (1722); *Das Grosse in dem Kleinen, oder Gott in den Herzen eines gläubigen Christen* (1722); *Das Lied des Lammes* (1723); *Der liebreiche und gedultige David* (1723); *Der aus dem Löwen-Graben befreyte, himmlische Daniel* (1725); *Das gottseelige Geheimnis* (1725); *Der undanckbare Jerobeam* (1726); *Der gegen seine Brüder barmherzige Joseph* (1727); *Das durch die Fleischwerdung des ewigen Wortes erfüllte Wort der Verheissung* (1727). Additional vocal works include many secular wedding cantatas, 18 Italian secular cantatas, serenades, etc. He also composed his own funeral oratorio, *Das fröhliche Sterbelied.*
INSTRUMENTAL MUSIC: *Sonate à due cembali per il Signore Cyrillo Wich gran virtuoso* (1705; ed. by B. Cannon, London, 1960); *Suite für 2 Cembali* (1705; ed. by B. Cannon, London, 1960); *XII sonates à deux et trois flûtes sans basse* (publ. in Amsterdam, 1708); Sonate for Harpsichord (1713); *Pièces de clavecin en deux volumes* (publ. in London, 1714; German ed. as *Matthesons Harmonisches Denkmahl, aus zwölff erwählten Clavier-Suiten,* publ. in London, 1714; reprint, 1965); *Der brauchbare Virtuoso, welcher sich ... mit zwölff neuen Kammer-Sonaten* for Flute, Violin, and Harpsichord (1720); *Die wol-klingende Finger-Sprache, in zwölff Fugen, mit zwey bis drey Subjecten* (first part, 1735; 2nd part, 1737; ed. by L. Hoffmann-Erbrecht, Leipzig, 1954).
BIBLIOGRAPHY: L. Meinardus, *Mattheson und seine Verdienste um die deutsche Tonkunst,* in Waldersee's *Sammlung musikalischer Vorträge* (Leipzig, 1879); H. Schmidt, *Johann Mattheson, ein Förderer der deutschen Tonkunst, im Lichte seiner Werke* (Diss., Univ. of Munich, 1897); F. Stege, "Johann Mattheson und die Musikkritik des 18. Jahrhunderts," *Zeitschrift für Musik,* CVI (1939); B. Cannon, *Johann Mattheson, Spectator in Music* (New Haven, 1947); H. Becker, "Johann Mattheson handschriftliche Einzeichnungen im 'Musikalischen Lexicon' Johann Gottfried Walthers," *Die Musikforschung,* V (1952); W. Braun, *Johann Mattheson und die Aufklärung* (Diss., Univ. of Halle, 1952); F. Feldmann, "Mattheson und die Rhetorik," *Gesellschaft für Musikforschung Kongressbericht* (Hamburg, 1956); H. Reddick, *Johann Mattheson's Forty-eight Thorough-bass Test-Pieces: Translation and Commentary* (Diss., Univ. of Michigan, 1956); H. Lenneberg, "Johann Mattheson on Affect and Rhetoric in Music," *Journal of Music Theory,* II (1958); F. Feldmann, "Der Hamburger Johann Mattheson und die Musik Mittel-und Ostdeutschlands," *Hamburger Mittel- und Ostdeutsche Forschungen,* V (1966); G. Buelow, "Johann Mattheson, the Composer, An Evaluation of His Opera *Cleopatra* (Hamburg, 1704)," in *Studies in Eighteenth Century Music: A Tribute to Karl Geiringer* (London and N.Y., 1970); J. Wenzel, *Geschichte der Hamburger Oper, 1678–1978* (Hamburg, 1978); H. Marx, *Johann Mattheson* (Hamburg, 1982).

Matthews, (Harry) Alexander, American organist and composer; b. Cheltenham, England, March 26, 1879; d. Middletown, Conn., April 12, 1973. He studied with his father, John A. Matthews; then went to America; taught at the Univ. of Pa. He retired in 1954, and lived in Middletown; he died at the age of 94. He publ. *The Introits and Graduals of the Church Year* (Philadelphia, 1924) and wrote a cantata, *The Story of Christmas.* His brother, **John Sebastian Matthews** (b. Cheltenham, Dec. 11, 1870; d. Pawtucket, R.I., July 23, 1934), was also an organist who went to America. He publ. several anthems, organ pieces, and songs.

Matthews, Denis, English pianist; b. Coventry, Feb. 27, 1919. He studied at the Royal Academy of Music in London; made his debut in 1939; then played with British orchs.; also gave solo recitals. In 1972 he became a prof. at the Univ. of Newcastle upon Tyne. His autobiography, *In Pursuit of Music,* was publ. in 1966. In 1975 he was made a Commander of the Order of the British Empire.

Matthison-Hansen, (Johan) Gottfred, Danish organist and composer, son of **Hans Matthison-Hansen;** b. Roskilde, Nov. 1, 1832; d. Copenhagen, Oct. 14, 1909. He studied piano with his father; later took lessons in piano and theory with W.H. Barth; then enrolled at the Univ. of Copenhagen as a law student. Although mainly self-taught, he trained himself so as to hold several church positions as an organist, at the Fredericks Church (1859), St. John's (1871), and the Trinity Church (1881) in Copenhagen; also made tours in organ recitals in Denmark and Germany. In 1867 he began teaching organ at the Copenhagen Cons.; in 1884 he also assumed the position of piano teacher there. He composed a number of works for organ which he included in his recitals; in addition to the Classical repertoire, he championed the Romantic works of the time.

Matthison-Hansen (originally **Matthias Hansen**), **Hans,** Danish organist, father of **(Johan) Gottfred Matthison-Hansen;** b. Adelby, near Flensburg, Feb. 6, 1807; d. Roskilde, Jan. 7, 1890. He learned to play the violin, viola, and cello at the Copenhagen Academy of Art; then took general music courses with C.E.F. Weyse. In 1832 he was appointed organist of the Cathedral in Roskilde, a position he retained until his death. He gave solo recitals in Denmark, Norway, Sweden, and Germany (1861–62); visited London in 1864. He also composed some works for organ.

Matthus, Siegfried, German composer; b. Mallenuppen, East Prussia, April 13, 1934. He studied composition with Wagner-Régeny at the Deutsche Hochschule für Musik in East Berlin (1952–58) and with Eisler at the Deutsche Akademie der Künste (1958–60); in 1964 he was appointed a composer and dramatist at the East Berlin Komische Oper; in 1972 became a member of the presidium of the Deutsche Akademie der Künste.
WORKS: FOR THE STAGE: 4 operas: *Lazarillo vom Tormes* (1960–63); *Der letzte Schuss* (1966–67); *Noch*

ein Löffel Gift, Liebling (1971–72); *Omphale* (1972–73). FOR ORCH.: *Concerto for Orchestra* for 2 Flutes, 3 Trombones, Harp, Piano, Percussion, and Strings (1963); *Inventions* (1964); *Tua res agitur* for 15 Instruments and Percussion (1965); Violin Concerto (1968; East Berlin, Feb. 24, 1969); 2 symphs.: No. 1, *Dresdener Sinfonie* (1969), and No. 2 (1976); Piano Concerto (1970; East Berlin, Feb. 18, 1971); *Orchesterserenade* (1974); Cello Concerto (1975); *Werther,* "musical metaphor" (1976); *Responso,* concerto for Orch. (1977); *Visions* for Strings (1978); Flute Concerto (1978); *Kammerkonzert* for Solo Flute, Harpsichord, and Strings (1980–81). FOR VOICE: *Es wird ein grosser Stern in meinen Schoss fallen,* 5 love songs for Soprano and Orch. (1961–62; East Berlin, Oct. 5, 1962); *Das Manifest,* cantata (1965); *Kammermusik* for Alto, 3 Female Voices, and 10 Instruments (1965); *Galileo* for Voice, 5 Instruments, and Tape (1966); *Vokalsinfonie* for Soprano, Baritone, 2 Choruses, and Orch. (1967; from the opera *Der letzte Schuss*); *Kantate von den Beiden* for Narrator, Soprano, Baritone, and Orch. (1968); *Vokalisen* for Soprano, Flute, Double Bass, and Percussion (1969); *Laudate pacem,* oratorio (1974); *Unter dem Holunderstrauch,* scene after Kleist for Soprano, Tenor, and Orch. (1976); *Holofernes-Portrait* for Baritone and Orch. (1981); choruses; songs. CHAMBER MUSIC: Sonatina for Piano and Percussion (1960); Sonata for Brasses, Piano, and Kettledrums (1968); Music for 4 Oboes and Piano (1968); Octet (1970); String Quartet (1971); Harp Trio for Flute, Viola, and Harp (1971). FOR PIANO: *Variations* (1958); *Konzertstück* (1958).

BIBLIOGRAPHY: Ursula Stürzbecher, *Komponisten in der DDR: 17 Gespräche* (Hildesheim, 1979).

Matton, Roger, Canadian composer; b. Granby, Quebec, May 18, 1929. He studied piano at the Cons. of Montreal; later was a composition student of Claude Champagne there (1946–49). He then went to Paris and studied with Nadia Boulanger and others. In 1956–76 he was a researcher and ethnomusicologist at the Archives de folklore at the Laval Univ. in Quebec City. His music is marked by dramatic lyricism enlivened by propulsive rhythms. WORKS: *Danse brésilienne* for 2 Pianos (1946); *Etude* for Clarinet and Piano (1946); *Danse lente (Gymnopédie)* for Small Orch. (1947); Concerto for Saxophone and Strings (1948); *3 Préludes* for Piano (1947–49); *Esquisse* for String Quartet (1949); *Pax,* symph. suite (1950); *Suite on Gregorian Themes* for Organ (1952); Concerto for 2 Pianos and Percussion (1954–55); *L'Escaouette,* suite of folk songs for 4 Soloists, Chorus, and Orch. (1957); *L'Horoscope,* choreographic suite (Toronto, Oct. 12, 1958); 4 *Mouvements symphoniques:* No. 1 (Quebec City, Nov. 14, 1960); No. 2, *Music for a Drama* (Montreal, April 17, 1962); No. 3 (Quebec City, May 7, 1974); No. 4 (1977); Concerto for 2 Pianos and Orch. (1964; Quebec City, Nov. 30, 1964); *Te Deum* for Baritone, Chorus, and Orch., with Electronic Sound (Quebec City, Nov. 27, 1967).

Matys, Jiří, Czech composer; b. Bakov, Oct. 27, 1927. He studied organ with František Michálek at the Brno Cons., graduating in 1947; then took a course in composition with Kvapil at the Janáček Academy of Music in Brno; joined its faculty after graduation (1953–57); was then headmaster of the School of Music at Králové Pole in Brno (1957–60). In 1960 he moved to Ostrava, where he was active as a music administrator.

WORKS: Horn Sonata (1948); *Fantasy* for String Orch. (1949); *Partita* for Piano Trio (1949); *To Those Fallen in May 1945,* symph. poem (1949); Piano Sonata (1950); Wind Quartet (1951); Symph. (1951); Viola Sonata (1954); *The Bells of Velice,* chamber cantata (1954); *Impromptus* for Violin and Piano (1955); 4 string quartets (1957, 1961, 1962–63, 1973); *Lyrical Melodramas* for Narrator and Piano 1957; *Children's Ballets* for Wind Quintet (1959); *Variace na smrt (Variations on Death)* for Narrator, Horn, and String Quartet (1959); Quartet for 4 Violins (1960); *Inventions* for 3 Violins (1960); *Jitřní hudba (Mourning Music)* for String Orch., 2 Trumpets, and Percussion (1961–62); *Pictures of Winter* for Piano (1962); Solo Viola Sonata (1963); Duet for Violin and Viola (1963); Violin Sonata (1964–65); *Sonata balladica* for Piano (1966); *5 Bagatelles* for Accordion (1966); *Inventions* for Flute and Cello (1969); *3 Movements* for Wind Quintet (1969); *Suite* for Trumpet and Piano (1969); *Music* for Wind Quintet (1970); *Pictures,* 3 pieces for Cello and Piano (1970); *Allusions,* 3 compositions for 4 Flutes (1971); *Music for String Quartet and Orch.* (1971); *Written by Grief into Silence* for Medium Voice and Orch. (1972); *Suite* for Viola and Bass Clarinet (1972–73); *Symphonic Overture* (1973–74); *Partita* for Solo Oboe (1974); *Poetic Movements,* 3 compositions for Flute, Violin, and Piano (1975).

Matz, Rudolf, Croatian cellist and composer; b. Zagreb, Sept. 19, 1901. He studied cello and composition at the Music Academy of Zagreb; in 1950 was appointed instructor in cello there; then taught chamber music at the Music Academy of Ljubljana. He publ. a manual for cello playing (Zagreb, 1951).

WORKS: *Classical Concert* for Cello and Orch. (1949); *Lyric Sketches* for Cello Solo and String Orch. (1959); Flute Concerto (1963); 4 string quartets (1924, 1932, 1935, 1944); *Baroque Concerto* for 3 Cellos and Piano (1952); *12 Pieces* for 3 Cellos and Piano (1960); Violin Sonata (1941); 2 cello sonatas (1941, 1942); *11 Caprices* in 12-tone technique for Cello Solo (1964); *24 Songs on Croatian Folk Poems* and other pieces based on native themes.

Matzenauer, Margarete, celebrated Hungarian-born singer; b. Temesvar, June 1, 1881; d. Van Nuys, Calif., May 19, 1963. Her father was a symph. conductor, and her mother a dramatic soprano; she grew up in favorable musical surroundings, and began to study singing at an early age, first in Graz, then in Berlin, and finally in Munich. In 1901 she joined the staff of the Strasbourg Opera; then sang contralto roles at the Munich Court Opera (1904–11); also sang at Bayreuth in 1911. She made her

Matzka – Maurel

American debut as Amneris in *Aida* at the Metropolitan Opera House in N.Y. (Nov. 13, 1911) and remained one of its leading members until 1930; in the interim she sang in opera in Germany and South America. She began her operatic career as a contralto, but also sang soprano parts; from 1914 on she called herself a soprano singer. After a farewell concert recital in Carnegie Hall, N.Y., in 1938, she retired from the stage and lived in California.

Matzka, George, German-American violinist and composer; b. Coburg, Oct. 31, 1825; d. New York, June 15, 1883. He was a member of the N.Y. Phil., and its conductor in 1876. He wrote overtures, choruses, and some chamber music.

Matzke, Hermann, German musicologist; b. Breslau, March 28, 1890; d. Constance, Switzerland, May 22, 1976. He studied musical sciences in Breslau with Kretzschmar, J. Wolf, and Kinkeldey; then in Berlin, where at the Univ. he received his Ph.D. in 1920; in 1924 he returned to Breslau and developed a concept of musical technology, dealing mainly with instrumental construction; edited *Zeitschrift für Instrumentenbau* (1934–43); in 1946 settled in Constance. He publ. *Musikökonomik und Musikpolitik* (Breslau, 1927); *Grundzüge einer musikalischen Technologie* (Breslau, 1931); *Musikgeschichte der Welt im Überblick* (Bonn, 1949; new amplified ed., 1961).

Mauceri, John, American conductor; b. New York, Sept. 12, 1945. He studied at Yale Univ. (B.A., 1967); served as conductor of the Yale Symph. Orch. (1968–74), with which he toured France and Austria. In 1976–77 he conducted the Israel Phil. on its tour of Germany and Austria, as well as in Tel Aviv and Jerusalem. He also was guest conductor of the Los Angeles Phil. (1974), San Francisco Symph. (1974), National Symph. Orch. in Wolf Trap Farm Park (1975), L'Orchestre National de France in Paris (1975), Scottish National Orch. (Edinburgh, 1976) and Philadelphia Orch. at Robin Hood Dell (1976).

Mauduit, Jacques, French composer; b. Paris, Sept. 16, 1557; d. there, Aug. 21, 1627. He served as registrar in a Paris court, and studied music by himself, progressing so well that at the age of 24 he won the first prize for a motet at a competition. When the poet Antoine Baïf established in Paris the Académie Française de Musique et de Poésie (1570), Mauduit became associated with him, and made several settings of Baïf's poems (Paris, 1586; reprinted by Henry Expert in *Les Maîtres-Musiciens de la Renaissance française*). He is reputed to have saved the musical MSS of Le Jeune when the latter was arrested for his Huguenot sympathies. Mauduit's 5-part Requiem, included in Mersenne's *Harmonie Universelle*, is reprinted in R.E. Chapman's Eng. trans. of Mersenne's books on instruments (The Hague, 1957).
BIBLIOGRAPHY: G. Reese, *Music in the Renaissance* (N.Y., 1954; 2nd ed., revised, 1959).

Mauersberger, Rudolf, German choral conductor; b. Mauersberg, Erzgebirge, Jan. 29, 1889; d. Dresden, Feb. 22, 1971. He studied piano and organ at the Leipzig Cons.; won the Nikisch Prize for composition in 1914; served as organist and choirmaster in Aachen (1919–25); then was in charge of church music in Thuringia (1925–30), directing the choir at Eisenach's Georgenkirche. In 1930 he became choirmaster of the Kreuzkirche in Dresden; directed its famous boys' choir, taking it on numerous tours in Europe and abroad. He composed a number of choral works, including the *Dresdner Requiem* (1948), written in memory of those who lost their lives during the barbarous bombing of the beautiful porcelaneous city just a few weeks before the end of the war.

Mauke, Wilhelm, German composer; b. Hamburg, Feb. 25, 1867; d. Wiesbaden, Aug. 24, 1930. He first studied medicine; then turned to music; was a pupil of Huber in Basel. He then established himself as a music critic in Munich; wrote the operas *Der Taugenichts* (1905), *Fanfreluche* (1912), *Die letzte Maske* (1917), *Das Fest des Lebens* (1926); other stage works: *Romantische Sinfonie*; an oratorio, *Die Vertreibung aus dem Paradies*; a symph. poem, *Einsamkeit*, after Nietzsche; a Piano Concerto; 160 songs. A list of his works was publ. by F.X. Osterrieder (Munich, 1927).
BIBLIOGRAPHY: W. Nagel, *Wilhelm Mauke* (1919).

Maunder, John Henry, British composer of hymns; b. London, Feb. 21, 1858; d. there, Jan 25, 1920. He studied at the Royal Academy of Music in London; served as organist in several London churches. He began his career as a theater composer; wrote an operetta, *Daisy Dingle* (1885); later devoted himself exclusively to sacred music; his oratorio *The Martyrs* (Oxford, May 25, 1894) became a perennial favorite; even more successful was his oratorio *From Olivet to Calvary;* he further wrote sacred works for chorus a cappella *(Praise the Lord, Blessed be Thy Name, Christ Awake, Conquering Kings, This Is the Day, Worship the King, Sing of Heaven);* other choral works are *Bethlehem, Song of Thanksgiving,* and *Christ Is Risen* for Voice, with Orch. Accompaniment.

Maurel, Victor, famous French baritone; b. Marseilles, June 17, 1848; d. New York, Oct. 22, 1923. He studied singing at the Paris Cons.; made his debut at the Paris Opéra in 1868; then sang in Italy, Spain, England, and Russia; in 1873 he made an American tour. Returning to Paris, he was on the staff of the Opéra (1879–94). He made his debut at the Metropolitan Opera House in N.Y. on Dec. 3, 1894, as Iago in *Otello;* sang there until 1896; then was a member of the Opéra-Comique in Paris until 1904. In 1909 he emigrated to the U.S., where he remained until his death; in his last years he was active as stage designer in N.Y. He created the role of Iago in Verdi's *Otello* (Milan, Feb. 5, 1887) and the title role in *Falstaff* (Milan, Feb. 9, 1893); also distinguished himself in Wagnerian roles. He publ. several monographs on the esthetics of singing and also autobiographical reminiscences, among them *Le Chant renové par la science* (1892); *Un Problème d'art* (1893); *L'Art du chant* (1897); *Dix ans de carrière* (1898).

BIBLIOGRAPHY: F. Rogers, "Victor Maurel: His Career and His Art," *Musical Quarterly* (Oct. 1926).

Maurer, Ludwig (Wilhelm), German violinist and composer; b. Potsdam, Feb. 8, 1789; d. St. Petersburg, Oct. 25, 1878. A precocious child musician, he appeared in concerts at the age of 13; at 17 he went to Russia, remaining there for 10 years, giving concerts and serving as house musician to Russian aristocrats. From 1817 until 1832 he traveled in Europe, and was successful as a violinist in Berlin and in Paris. He was in Russia again (1832–45), then lived in Dresden, eventually returning to St. Petersburg. He produced 2 operas in Hannover, *Der neue Paris* (Jan. 27, 1826) and *Aloise* (Jan. 16, 1828); also wrote many stage pieces in Russia; with Aliabiev and Verstovsky, he contributed the music to Chmelnitsky's comedy *A Novel Prank, or Theatrical Combat* (1822). In addition, he wrote a curious quadruple concerto, *Symphonie concertante,* for 4 Violins with Orch. (1838); 3 violin concertos; string quartets, and other chamber music. His 2 sons **Vsevolod** (1819–92), a violinist, and **Alexis,** a cellist, remained in Russia.

Maurice, Alphons, German composer; b. Hamburg, April 14, 1862; d. Dresden, Jan. 27, 1905. He studied with Dessoff, Krenn, and Grädener at the Vienna Cons.; wrote the operas *Josepha, Schatz,* and *Der Wundersteg; Waldestraum* for Orch.; *Spanische Serenade* for Violin and Orch.; choruses; piano pieces; songs.

Maurice, Pierre, Baron de, Swiss composer; b. Geneva, Nov. 13, 1868; d. there, Dec. 25, 1936. He attended the Cons. at Geneva, then for a short time studied at Stuttgart, finishing his musical education with Lavignac and Massenet at the Paris Cons. He lived many years in Munich; composed the operas *Die weisse Flagge* (Kassel, 1903), *Misé brun* (Stuttgart, 1908), *Lanval* (Weimar, 1912), and *Kalif Storch* (not perf.); a biblical drama, *La Fille de Jephthé* (Geneva, 1899); a symph. suite, *Die Islandfischer* (after Loti); *Chanson des quatre saisons* for Piano, and other piano pieces; songs.

Mauricio, José, Portuguese composer and music theorist; b. Coimbra, March 19, 1752; d. Figueira, Sept. 12, 1815. He studied theology at Coimbra Univ.; was mestre de capela there from about 1784 to 1786; then served as organist at the Santa Cruz monastery in Coimbra. In 1791 he became director of the music school in the bishop's palace and mestre de capela of Coimbra Cathedral; in 1802 he was appointed prof. of music at Coimbra Univ. He wrote a great deal of church music and some instrumental works revealing the influence of Haydn. He also publ. a *Metodo de musica* (Coimbra, 1806).

BIBLIOGRAPHY: J. Vasconcellos, *Os musicos portugueses* (Oporto, 1870; pp. 229–48).

Maurin, Jean-Pierre, French violinist; b. Avignon, Feb. 14, 1822; d. Paris, March 16, 1894. He studied violin with Abillot and Habeneck at the Paris Cons., where he succeeded Alard as a teacher in 1875. He was co-founder of the Société des Derniers Quatuors de Beethoven, in Paris.

Maury, Lowndes, American composer; b. Butte, Mont., July 7, 1911; d. Encino, Calif., Dec. 11, 1975. He earned his B.A. degree in music at the Univ. of Montana in 1931; went to Los Angeles, where he studied composition with Wesley La Violette and Schoenberg; became active in Hollywood as a pianist, arranger, and teacher.

WORKS: *In Memory of the Korean War Dead* for Violin and Piano (1952); *Proud Music of the Storm,* cantata to words by Walt Whitman (1953); *Passacaglia* for String Orch. (1959); *Springtime Digressions* for Piano, Flute, and String Quintet (1961); *Speculations* for Piano and 3 String Instruments (1964); *Summer of Green,* rhapsody for Alto Flute and String Orch. (1964); *Scène de ballet* for Piccolo and String Quartet (1965); 11 *Sketches* for Piano Trio (1968); *The Imprisoned Cellist,* suite for Solo Cello (1973)

PUBLICATIONS: *Magic Lines and Spaces,* a series of piano instruction books in correlated notation, a system employing a 3-line staff (1974).

Maus, Octave, Belgian journalist and musician; b. Brussels, June 12, 1856; d. Lausanne, Nov. 26, 1919. He studied music with Louis Brassin. An ardent admirer of Wagner, he went to Bayreuth to attend the first Wagner Festival in 1876; in 1881 he was co-founder of the weekly magazine *L'Art Moderne,* in Brussels, which promoted Wagnerian ideas; then participated in the musical society "XX," the title of which symbolized the future 20th century; it was active from 1884 to 1893. From 1894 to the outbreak of World War I in 1914 he led in Brussels a concert group, Libre Esthétique. He spent the last years of his life in Switzerland.

BIBLIOGRAPHY: Madeleine Maus, *Trente années de lutte pour art* (a memoir by his wife, describing his activities on behalf of new music); Albert Van Der Linden, *Octave Maus et la vie musicale belge* (Brussels, 1950; contains 55 letters from Vincent d'Indy to Maus).

Maw, Nicholas, remarkable English composer; b. Grantham, Lincolnshire, Nov. 5, 1935. He played clarinet and piano; studied composition with Lennox Berkeley and Paul Steinitz at the Royal Academy of Music in London (1955–58) and with Nadia Boulanger and Max Deutsch in Paris (1958–59). From 1966 to 1970 he was composer-in-residence at Trinity College, Cambridge. In his music he makes use of serial methods of composition without abandoning the principle of tonality.

WORKS: FOR THE STAGE: *One Man Show,* comic opera (London, Nov. 12, 1964); *The Rising of the*

Moon, opera (1967–70; Glyndebourne, July 19, 1970). FOR ORCH.: *Scenes and Arias* for Solo Voices and Orch. (London, Aug. 31, 1962); *Sinfonia* for Chamber Orch. (Newcastle upon Tyne, May 30, 1966); *Severn Bridge Variations* (1967); Sonata for String Orch. and 2 Horns (Bath, June 7, 1967); *Serenade* (Singapore, March 31, 1973); *Summer Dances* for Youth Orch. (Aldeburgh, July 27, 1981); *Toccata* (Norwich, Oct. 15, 1982). VOCAL MUSIC: *Nocturne* for Mezzo-soprano and Chamber Orch. (1957–58); *5 Epigrams* for Mixed Voices a cappella (1960); *Our Lady's Song* for Mixed Voices a cappella (1961); *The Angel Gabriel* for Mixed Chorus (1963); *Round* for Children's Chorus, Mixed Chorus, and Piano (1963); *6 Interiors* for High Voice and Guitar (1966); *The Voice of Love* for Mezzo-soprano and Piano (1966); *5 Irish Songs* for Mixed Chorus (Cork, May 4, 1973); *Reverdie,* 5 songs for Male Voices (Glasgow, Oct. 29, 1975); Te Deum for Soprano, Tenor, Mixed Chorus, and Organ (Bruton, May 29, 1975); *20 Nonsense Rhymes* for Voices and Piano (1976); *Annes!* for Mixed Chorus (1976); *La vita nuova* for Soprano and Chamber Ensemble (London, Sept. 2, 1979); *The Ruin* for Double Chorus and Solo Horn (Edinburgh, Aug. 27, 1980). CHAMBER MUSIC: Sonatina for Flute and Piano (1957); *Essays* for Organ (1961); *Chamber Music* for Oboe, Clarinet, Horn, Bassoon, and Piano (1962); 2 string quartets (1965, 1982); *Personae* for Piano (1973); *Life Studies* for 15 Solo Strings (1973); Quartet for Flute and Strings (1981); *Night Thoughts* for Solo Flute (1982).

BIBLIOGRAPHY: Susan Bradshaw, "Nicholas Maw," *Musical Times* (Sept. 1962).

Maxfield, Richard (Vance), American avant-garde composer; b. Seattle, Wash., Feb. 2, 1927; d. (by self-defenestration from a hotel room) Los Angeles, June 27, 1969. He studied at the Univ. of Calif., Berkeley, with Roger Sessions, and at Princeton Univ. with Milton Babbitt; also took courses with Ernst Krenek and Luigi Dallapiccola. He became deeply engaged in acoustical electronics; taught experimental music at the New School for Social Research in N.Y. and at San Francisco State College; contributed essays to avant-garde publications; 2 of them, in free verse, were publ. in *Contemporary Composers on Contemporary Music,* edited by Elliot Schwartz and Barney Childs (N.Y., 1967). He acquired an excellent technique of composition in the traditional idiom before adopting an extreme avant-garde style. WORKS: *Classical Overture* (1942); Trio for Clarinet, Cello, and Piano (1943); Septet for 2 Flutes, 3 Clarinets, French Horn, and Bassoon (1947); Sonata for Unaccompanied Violin (1949); Violin Sonata (1950); String Trio (1951); Sonata for Unaccompanied Flute (1951); *Structures* for 10 Wind Instruments (1951); *11 Variations* for String Quartet (1952); *5 Movements* for Orch. (1956); Chamber Concerto for 7 Instruments (1957); *Structures* for Orch. (1958); *Sine Music* (1959); *Stacked Deck,* opera for Tape, Actors, and Lighting (1959); *Perspectives* for Violin and Tape (1960); *Peripeteia* for Violin, Saxophone, Piano, and Tape (1960); *Clarinet Music* for 5 Clarinets and Tape (1961); *Cough Music,* with sonic materials obtained from coughs and other bronchial sound effects recorded during a modern dance recital and electronically arranged in a piece of tussive polyphony (perf. for the first time as the opening number in an audiovisual spectacle, "Musical Essays in Time, Space and Sound," by the Division of Adult Education of the Cooper Union for the Advancement of Science and Art in N.Y. on Jan. 13, 1961); *Toy Symphony* for Flute, Violin, Wooden Boxes, Ceramic Vase, and Tape (1962); *African Symphony* (1964); *Venus Impulses* for Electronic Sound (1967).

Maxson, Frederick, American organist and composer; b. Beverly, N.J., June 13, 1862; d. Philadelphia, Jan. 21, 1934. He studied with Guilmant in Paris; for many years played organ in Philadelphia churches; was a successful teacher; publ. organ pieces, anthems, and songs.

May, Edward Collet, English organist and singing teacher; b. Greenwich, Oct. 29, 1806; d. London, Jan. 2, 1887. He studied with C. Potter and Crivelli; was organist of Greenwich Hospital (1837–69); prof. of vocal music at Queen's College, London. A disciple of Hullah, he taught in numerous schools and private classes, doing much to popularize singing among the masses; publ. *Progressive Vocal Exercises for Daily Practice* (1853); songs.

May, Florence, English pianist and writer, daughter of **Edward Collett May;** b. London, Feb. 6, 1845; d. there, June 29, 1923. She studied music with her father and with an uncle, Oliver May; began a promising career as a pianist in London; in 1871 went to Germany; took lessons with Clara Schumann in Baden-Baden; there she made the acquaintance of Brahms, who gave her some lessons. She became his enthusiastic admirer; upon her return to England, she started a vigorous campaign for performances of the music of Brahms; she herself gave many first performances of his works in London. The important result of her dedication to Brahms was her comprehensive work *The Life of Johannes Brahms* (2 vols., London, 1905; revised ed., publ. posthumously, 1948); she also publ. *The Girlhood of Clara Schumann* (London, 1912).

Mayall, John, English rhythm-and-blues singer; b. Manchester, Nov. 29, 1933. An ardent promoter of black American blues, he formed a group called The Bluesbreakers, serving as a laboratory for instrumentalists, which included Eric Clapton, Peter Green, John McVie, Mick Taylor, Aynsley Dunbar, and Mick Fleetwood. The Bluesbreakers released a number of successful albums, among them *A Hard Road* and *The Turning Point,* and the first classic of British blues, under the title *Bluesbreakers with Eric Clapton.* Another album, *U.S.A. Union,* produced a workable amalgam of jazz and blues. Eventually Mayall emigrated to America.

Maybrick, Michael (pseudonym, **Stephen Adams**),

English baritone and composer; b. Liverpool, Jan. 31, 1844; d. Buxton, Aug. 25, 1913. He studied at the Leipzig Cons. with Plaidy, Moscheles, and Richter (1866–68), and was a vocal pupil of Nava at Milan. He sang at the principal concerts in London and the provinces, and toured the U.S. and Canada in 1884. Many of his songs (sung by himself) had great vogue (e.g., *Nancy Lee*). His sacred solo *The Holy City* is still sung in churches in England and America.

Mayer, Charles, German pianist and composer; b. Königsberg, March 21, 1799; d. Dresden, July 2, 1862. He was taken to Russia as a child; was taught by John Field, who was in Russia at the time; lived in Moscow until Napleon's invasion in 1812; then went to St. Petersburg, and in 1814 to Paris. He returned to Russia in 1819 and formed a large class of pupils in St. Petersburg; in 1845 he made a tour of Scandinavia and Germany; in 1850 he settled in Dresden. He publ. an enormous number of piano pieces, in salon style; one of his mazurkas was once misattributed to Chopin.

Mayer, Frederick Christian, American organist; b. Columbus, Ohio, March 4, 1882; d. Amarillo, Texas, Oct. 20, 1973, in consequence of an automobile accident, while driving alone, at the age of 91, across the continent from a visit in California to his retirement home in Florida. He studied at the Cincinnati Cons., graduating in 1905; then went to Europe for further study of organ playing, at the Stern Cons. in Berlin and at the Cons. of Fountainebleau. Returning to the U.S., he taught at the Cincinnati Cons.; in 1911 was appointed organist of Cadet Chapel, West Point Military Academy; although he reached the mandatory retirement age of threescore and ten in 1952, he was allowed to carry on for another couple of years. He was reputed as a fine carillon builder; inspected and supervised dozens of carillons in the U.S., Canada and Belgium.

Mayer, Joseph Anton, German composer and pedagogue; b. Pfullendorf, Baden, Dec. 5, 1855; d. Stuttgart, Dec. 3, 1936. He studied at the Stuttgart Cons., and later in Berlin with Bargiel; then taught at the Stuttgart Cons. He wrote the operas *Der Stern von Bethlehem* and *Magdelenenbrunnen;* the choral works with Orch. *Der Geiger von Gmünd, Jephtha, Würde der Frauen,* etc.; also piano pieces and songs.

Mayer, Max, pianist and pedagogue; b. Hamburg, May 31, 1859; d. Manchester, England, Oct. 26, 1931. He studied with local teachers; then with Seyfriz in Stuttgart, and finally with Liszt in Weimar. In 1883 he settled in Manchester; appeared frequently in chamber music concerts, and as accompanist in his own songs, which were first introduced by Muriel Foster. From 1908 he taught at the Royal College of Music in Manchester.

Mayer, Wilhelm (pseudonym, **W.A. Rémy**), Aus-trian pianist and pedagogue; b. Prague, June 10, 1831; d. Graz, Jan. 22, 1898. He studied with C.F. Pietsch; also took a course in law; received a Dr.Jur. (1856). In 1862 he became conductor of the Graz Musical Society, resigning in 1870 to apply himself to pedagogy; he taught both piano and composition, and achieved great renown; among his pupils were Busoni, Kienzl, Rezniček, and Weingartner.

Mayer, William, American composer; b. New York, Nov. 18, 1925. He studied at Yale Univ. and the Mannes College of Music; then had theory sessions with Sessions. His most successful compositions are for the theater and the radio.
WORKS: *The Greatest Sound Around,* short children's opera (1954); *Hello World!* ("a musical trip around the world"), children's opera for Narrator, Orch., and Audience Participation (N.Y., Nov. 10, 1956); *One Christmas Long Ago,* one-act opera (Philadelphia, Dec. 12, 1964); *Brief Candle,* "micro-opera" (1964); *A Death in the Family,* opera based on James Agee's eponymous novel and Tad Mosel's play *All the Way Home* (Minneapolis, March 11, 1983); *The Snow Queen,* ballet (1963); *Andante for Strings* (1955); *Hebraic Portrait* for Orch. (1957); *Overture for an American* (1958); *Two Pastels* for Orch. (1960); *Country Fair* for Brass Trio (1962); *Elegy* for Brass Quintet (1964); *Octagon* for Piano and Orch. (N.Y., American Symph., William Masselos, soloist; Leopold Stokowski conducting, March 21, 1971); many choruses (*The Passionate Shepherd to His Love, The Nymph's Reply to the Passionate Shepherd, Corinna's Going A-Maying,* etc.); a String Quartet and other chamber music; a Piano Sonata; children's pieces for piano; songs.

Mayer-Mahr, Moritz, German pianist and teacher; b. Mannheim, Jan. 17, 1869; d. Göteborg, Sweden, July 30, 1947. After a course of study in Mannheim, he went to Berlin; in 1892, was appointed prof. of piano at the Klindworth-Scharwenka Cons. In 1933 he left Germany and settled in Sweden, remaining there until his death. He publ. *Die Technik des Klavierspiels* (3 vols.) and *Der musikalische Klavier-Unterricht;* edited the studies of Czerny and Heller.

Mayer-Reinach, Albert, German musicologist; b. Mannheim, April 2, 1876; d. Örebro, Sweden, Feb. 25, 1954. He studied in Munich and Berlin; received his Dr.Phil. with the dissertation *K.H. Graun als Opernkomponist* (Berlin, 1899); was lecturer on music at the Univ. of Kiel (1904–30); conducted various choral societies; edited 2 vols. of works by early Königsberg composers; publ. valuable papers on German operas, etc. In 1933 he went to Sweden; in 1936 he became director of a music school in Örebro.

Mayer-Serra, Otto, eminent Spanish musicologist; b. Barcelona, July 12, 1904, of German-Catalan parentage; d. Mexico City, March 19, 1968. He studied in Germany with H. Abert, Curt Sachs, J. Wolf, and E. von Hornbostel; received his Ph.D. in 1929 with the dissertation *Die romantische Klavier-*

sonaten, from the Univ. of Greifswald. He returned to Spain in 1933, and was music critic of the Catalan weekly *Mirador*. In 1936, at the outbreak of the Spanish Civil War, he was appointed head of the music division of the propaganda ministry of the Catalan government; served in the Loyalist Army in 1938–39; after its defeat, he fled to France. In 1940 he reached Mexico, where he became active as a writer, editor, lecturer, and manager.

WRITINGS: *El romanticismo musical* (Mexico, 1940); *Panorama de la música mexicana* (Mexico, 1941); *Panorama de la música hispano-americana* (Mexico, 1944); *Música y músicios de Latino-América* (of fundamental importance; contains detailed biographies of Latin American musicians and descriptions of folk songs; 2 vols.; Mexico City, 1947).

Mayfield, Curtis, black American songwriter; b. Chicago, June 3, 1942. Extremely precocious, he produced a song, *For Your Precious Love,* at 16; then joined Jerry Butler's band The Impressions, as a guitarist, and co-authored with him the hit solo *He Will Break Your Heart.* In 1961 he practically took over Butler's band, and led it until 1970, scoring hits with *Hey Little Girl, Gypsy Woman,* and *This Is My Country.* Self-confident to the point of arrogance, he put out a solo album egotistically named *Curtis,* and followed it up with *Curtis Live!* They were successful. But a greater success came with his soundtrack to the film *Superfly.*

Maykapar, Samuil, Russian pianist, composer, and teacher; b. Kherson, Dec. 18, 1867; d. Leningrad, May 8, 1938. He studied at the St. Petersburg Cons. with B. Cesi (piano) and Soloviev (theory); then in Vienna with Leschetizky; gave concerts in Germany (1903–10). From 1910 to 1930 he was a prof. at the St. Petersburg Cons. He composed almost exclusively for piano; was particularly successful in miniature forms. His piano works include: *Biriulki* (a suite of 26 pieces); *24 Miniatures; The Marionette Theater* (an album of 7 pieces); 2 sonatinas; etc.; also piano studies and special exercises (for pedaling, for wrist actions, etc.). He publ. the books *The Musical Ear* (Moscow, 1900) and *The Years of Study and of Musical Activity* (partly autobiographical; Moscow, 1938).

Maylath, Heinrich, pianist and pedagogue; b. Vienna, Dec. 4, 1827; d. New York, Dec. 31, 1883. He was a pupil of his father; traveled as a concert pianist in Europe, including Russia. In 1867 he settled in America, and became a teacher in N.Y. He publ. some excellent, instructive piano music, as well as concert pieces; made numerous transcriptions of various works for piano.

Maynor, Dorothy, American soprano; b. Norfolk, Va., Sept. 3, 1910. Her father was a Methodist minister; she entered Hampton Inst. as a young woman and later toured Europe with the Institute's famous Negro chorus. She made her N.Y. debut on Nov. 19, 1939, creating an excellent impression. In 1963 she

founded the Harlem School of the Arts, dedicated to the music education of underprivileged children; retired as its executive director in 1979.

Mayr, Richard, Austrian bass; b. Henndorf, near Salzburg, Nov. 18, 1877; d. Vienna, Dec. 1, 1935. He was a student of medicine in Vienna. At the age of 21, he enrolled in the Vienna Cons.; studied voice; and in 1902 made his operatic debut at Bayreuth as Hagen. He was then engaged by Gustav Mahler at the Vienna Opera, of which he remained a member until his death. He made his American debut on Nov. 2, 1927, with the Metropolitan Opera Co. as Pogner; sang there until 1930. He possessed a rich and powerful voice, equally suited for tragic and comic parts; was particularly distinguished as Wotan; his performance of Baron Ochs in *Der Rosenkavalier* was also notable.

BIBLIOGRAPHY: H.J. Holz, *Richard Mayr* (Vienna, 1923); Otto Kunz, *Richard Mayr* (Vienna, 1933).

Mayr (Mayer), (Johannes) Simon (Giovanni Simone), outstanding German opera composer; b. Mendorf, Bavaria, of Italian parentage, June 14, 1763; d. Bergamo, Dec. 2, 1845. He first studied music with his father, a schoolteacher and organist; he sang in a church choir, and played organ. In 1774 he entered the Jesuit college in Ingolstadt; in 1781 he began a study of theology at the Univ. of Ingolstadt. In 1787 a Swiss Freiherr, Thomas von Bassus, took him to Italy to further his musical education; in 1789 he commenced studies with Carlo Lenzi in Bergamo; he then was sent to Ferdinando Bertoni in Venice. He began his career as a composer of sacred music; his oratorios were performed in Venice. After the death of his patron, Count Presenti, in 1793, he was encouraged by Piccinni and Peter von Winter to compose operas. His first opera, *Saffo o sia I riti d'Apollo Leucadio,* was performed in Venice in 1794. He gained renown with his opera *Ginevra di Scozia* (Trieste, April 21, 1801), and it remained a favorite with audiences; also successful were his operas *La rosa bianca e la rosa rossa* (Genoa, Feb. 21, 1813) and *Medea in Corinto* (Naples, Nov. 28, 1813). In 1802 he became maestro di cappella at S. Maria Maggiore in Bergamo; in 1805 he reorganized the choir school of the Cathedral as the Lezioni Caritatevoli di Musica and assumed its directorship; intractable cataracts, which led to total blindness in 1826, forced him to limit his activities to organ playing. In 1822 he founded the Società Filarmonica of Bergamo. Mayr's operas, while reflecting the late Neapolitan school, are noteworthy for their harmonization and orchestration, which are derived from the German tradition. After 1815 he devoted most of his time to composing sacred music, which totals some 600 works in all. He was also an eminent pedagogue. Donizetti was his pupil.

WORKS: OPERAS: *Saffo o sia I riti d'Apollo Leucadio,* dramma per musica (Venice, Feb. 17, 1794); *La Lodoiska,* dramma per musica (Venice, Jan. 26, 1796; revised for Milan, Dec. 26, 1799); *Un pazzo ne fa cento [I Rivali delusi; La Contessa immaginaria],* dramma giocoso (Venice, Oct. 8, 1796);

Telemaco nell'isola di Calipso, dramma per musica (Venice, Jan. 16, 1797); *Il segreto,* farsa (Venice, Sept. 24, 1797); *L'intrigo della lettera [Il pittore astratto],* farsa (Venice, Fall 1797); *Avviso ai maritati,* dramma giocoso (Venice, Jan. 15, 1798); *Lauso e Lidia,* dramma per musica (Venice, Feb. 14, 1798); *Adriano in Siria,* dramma per musica (Venice, April 23, 1798); *Che originali [Il trionfo della musica; Il fanatico per la musica: La musicomania],* farsa (Venice, Oct. 18, 1798); *Amor ingegnoso,* farsa (Venice, Dec. 27, 1798); *L'ubbidienza per astuzia,* farsa (Venice, Dec. 27, 1798); *Adelaide di Gueselino,* dramma per musica (Venice, May 1, 1799); *Labino e Carlotta,* farsa (Venice, Oct. 9, 1799); *L'Avaro,* farsa (Venice, Nov. 1799); *L'accademia di musica,* farsa (Venice, Fall 1799); *Gli sciti,* dramma per musica (Venice, Feb. 1800); *La Locandiera,* farsa (Vicenza, Spring 1800); *Il carretto del venditore d'aceto,* farsa (Venice, June 28, 1800); *L'Imbroglione e il castigamatti,* farsa (Venice, Fall 1800); *L'equivoco, ovvero Le bizzarie dell'amore,* dramma giocoso (Milan, Nov. 5, 1800); *Ginevra di Scozia [Ariodante],* dramma serio eroico per musica (Trieste, April 21, 1801; inaugural perf. at the Teatro Nuovo there); *Le due giornate [Il Portatore d'acqua],* dramma eroicomico per musica (Milan, Aug. 18, 1801); *I Virtuosi [I Virtuosi a teatro],* farsa (Venice, Dec. 26, 1801); *Argene,* dramma eroico per musica (Venice, Dec. 28, 1801); *Elisa, ossia Il monte S. Bernardo,* dramma sentimentale per musica (Malta, 1801); *I misteri eleusini,* dramma per musica (Milan, Jan. 6, 1802); *I castelli in aria, ossia Gli Amanti per accidente,* farsa (Venice, May 1802); *Ercole in Lidia,* dramma per musica (Vienna, Jan. 29, 1803); *Gl'intrighi amorosi,* dramma giocoso (Parma, Carnival 1803); *Le finte rivali,* melodramma giocoso (Aug. 20, 1803); *Alonso e Cora,* dramma per musica (Milan, Dec. 26, 1803; revised as *Cora* for Naples, 1815); *Amor non ha ritegno [La fedeltà delle vedove],* melodramma eroicomico (Milan, May 18, 1804); *I due viaggiatori,* dramma giocoso (Florence, Summer 1804); *Zamori, ossia L'Eroe dell'Indie,* dramma per musica (Piacenza, Aug. 10, 1804; inaugural perf. at the Nuovo Teatro Communale); *Eraldo ed Emma,* dramma eroico per musica (Milan, Jan. 8, 1805); *Di locanda in locanda e sempre in sala,* farsa (June 5, 1805); *L'amor coniugale [Il custode di buon cuore],* dramma giocoso (Padua, July 26, 1805); *La rocca di Frauenstein,* melodramma eroicomico (Venice, Oct. 26, 1805); *Gli Americani [Idalide],* melodramma eroico (Venice, Carnival 1806; *Palmira, o sia Il trionfo della virtù e dell'amore,* dramma per musica (Florence, Fall 1806); *Il piccolo compositore di musica,* farsa (Venice, 1806); *Nè l'un, nè l'altro,* dramma giocoso (Milan, Aug. 17, 1807); *Belle ciarle e tristi fatti [L'imbroglio contro l'imbroglio],* dramma giocoso (Venice, Nov. 1807); *Adelasia e Aleramo,* melodramma serio (Milan, Dec. 25, 1807; *I cherusci,* dramma per musica (Rome, Carnival 1808); *Il vero originale,* burletta per musica (Rome, Carnival 1808); *La finta sposa, ossia Il Barone burlato,* dramma giocoso (Rome, Spring 1808); *Il matrimonio per concorso,* dramma giocoso (Bologna, Carnival 1809); *Il ritorno di Ulisse,* azione eroica per musica (Venice, Carnival 1809); *Amor non soffre opposizione,* dramma giocoso (Venice, Carnival 1810); *Raùl di Créqui,* melodramma serio (Milan, Dec. 26, 1810); *Il sacrifizio d'Ifigenia [Ifigenia in Aulide],* azione seria drammatica per musica (Brescia, Carnival 1811); *L'amor figliale [Il Disertore],* farsa sentimentale (Venice, Carnival 1811); *La rosa bianca e la rosa rossa [Il trionfo dell'amicizia],* melodramma eroica (Genoa, Feb. 21, 1813); *Medea in Corinto,* melodramma tragico (Naples, Nov. 28, 1813); *Tamerlano,* melodramma serio (Milan, Carnival 1813); *Elena [Elena e Costantino],* dramma eroicomico per musica (Naples, Carnival 1814); *Atar, o sia Il serraglio d'Ormus,* melodramma serio (Genoa, June 1814); *Le due duchesse, ossia La caccia dei lupi [Le due amiche],* dramma semiserio per musica (Milan, Nov. 7, 1814); *La Figlia dell'aria, ossia La vendetta di Giunone,* dramma per musica (Naples, Lent 1817); *Nennone e Zemira,* dramma per musica (Naples, March 22, 1817); *Amor avvocato,* commedia per musica (Naples, Spring 1817); *Lanassa,* melodramma eroico (Venice, Carnival 1818); *Alfredo il grande,* melodramma serio (Rome, Feb. 1818); *Le Danaide [Danao],* melodramma serio (Rome, Carnival 1819); *Fedra,* melodramma serio (Milan, Dec. 26, 1820); *Demetrio,* dramma per musica (Turin, Carnival 1824).

ORATORIOS: *Iacob a Labano fugiens* (Venice, 1791); *Sisara* (Venice, 1793); *Tobia, o Tobiae matrimonium* (Venice, 1794); *La Passione* (Forli, 1794); *David in spelunca Engaddi* (Venice, 1795); *Il sacrifizio di Iefte* (Forli; year unknown); *Samuele* (Bergamo, 1821); *S. Luigi Gonzaga* (Bergamo, 1822); also the sacred dramas *Ifigenia in Tauride* (Florence, Spring 1817) and *Atalia* (Naples, Lent 1822). He also composed about 50 cantatas, 18 masses, over 200 mass movements, 2 Requiems, 20 Requiem movements, 43 hymns, 14 antiphons, 13 motets, etc. His secular vocal works include over 40 canzonettas, arias, songs, lieder, etc. His instrumental works include 2 symphs., 2 piano concertos, chamber music, and keyboard pieces.

WRITINGS: In addition to his *Breve notizie storiche della vita e delle opere di Giuseppe Haydn* (Bergamo, 1809) and *Regolamento delle Lezioni Caritatevoli di musica* (Bergamo, 1822), many other writings remain in MS.

BIBLIOGRAPHY: G. Calvi, *Musica sacra di S. Mayr* (Milan, 1848); G. Finazzi, *Per la solenne inaugurazione del monumento eretto alla memoria del celebre maestro G.S. Mayr nella basilica di S. Maria Maggiore in Bergamo* (Bergamo, 1853); F. Alborghetti and M. Galli, *Gaetano Donizetti e G. Simone Mayr: Notizie e documenti* (Bergamo, 1875); C. Schmidl, *Cenni biografici su G.S. Mayr* (Trieste, 1901); C. Scotti, *Giovanni Simone Mayr: Discorso* (Bergamo, 1903); H. Kretzschmar, "Die musik geschichtliche Bedeutung S. Mayrs," *Jahrbuch der Musikbibliothek Peters 1904;* L. Schiedermair, *Beiträge zur Geschichte der Oper um die Wende des 18. und 19. Jahrhunderts: Simon Mayr* (2 vols., Leipzig, 1907 and 1910); A. Gazzaniga, *Il Fondo musicale Mayr della biblioteca civica di Bergamo* (Bergamo, 1963); M. Carner, "Simone Mayr and His *L'amor coniugale,*" *Music & letters* (July 1971); J. Freeman, "Johann Simon Mayr and

His *Ifigenia in Aulide,*" *Musical Quarterly* (April 1971); A. Gazzaniga, "Su *L'amor coniugale* di Giovanni Simone Mayr," *Nuova Rivista Musicale Italiana* (Sept.–Oct. 1971).

Mayseder, Joseph, Austrian violinist and composer; b. Vienna, Oct. 26, 1789; d. there, Nov. 21, 1863. He was a pupil of Suche and Wranitzky (violin); and of E. Förster (piano and composition). He joined the famous Schuppanzigh Quartet as 2nd violin; became concertmaster of the court theater in 1810; entered the court orch. in 1816; became solo violinist at the court opera in 1820 and chamber violinist to the Emperor in 1835; music director of the court chapel in 1836; retired in 1837. He never went on tours, and rarely gave concerts; yet he was a finished virtuoso, admired even by Paganini. In Vienna he was very successful as a teacher. His works include several violin concertos, 5 string quintets, 8 string quartets, trios, and solo violin pieces, all effectively written.
BIBLIOGRAPHY: E. Hellsberg, *Joseph Mayseder* (Diss., Univ. of Vienna, 1955).

Mayuzumi, Toshirō, eminent Japanese composer; b. Yokohama, Feb. 20, 1929. He studied at the National Music Academy in Tokyo (1945–51); then took courses at the Paris Cons. with Aubin. Returning to Japan, he organized the modern group Ars Nova Japonica and also worked at the electronic studio in Tokyo. He became known in Europe with the production of his *Sphenogramme,* a modernistic piece for Voice and Instruments (Frankfurt Festival of the International Society for Contemporary Music, June 25, 1951), and *Ectoplasme* for Electronic Instruments, Percussion, and Strings (Stockholm Festival of the International Society for Contemporary Music, June 5, 1956). His style of composition embodies sonorous elements from old Japanese music, serial techniques, and electronic sound, all amalgamated in a remarkably effective manner; he was quite successful in writing film scores, and spent several years in Hollywood.
WORKS: Violin Sonata (1946); *Divertimento* for 10 Instruments (1948); *Symphonic Mood* (1950); *Mikrokosmos* for 7 Instruments (Modern Music Festival, Karuizawa, Japan, Aug. 12, 1957); *Phonologie symphonique* (Tokyo, May 28, 1957); *Nirvana Symphony* (Tokyo, April 2, 1958); *U-So-Ri,* oratorio (Tokyo, June 12, 1959); *Mandala-Symphonie* (Tokyo, March 27, 1960); *Bunraku* for Cello Solo (1960); *Music with Sculpture* for Winds (Pittsburgh, June 29, 1961); *Prelude* for String Quartet (1961); *Bugaku,* ballet (N.Y., March 20, 1963); *Samsara,* symph. poem (Tokyo, June 12, 1962); *Texture* for Band (Pittsburgh, June 10, 1962); *Essay in Sonorities* (Osaka, Jan. 21, 1963); *Fireworks* for Band (Pittsburgh, June 13, 1963); *Pratidesana,* Buddhist cantata (Kyoto, Sept. 5, 1963); *The Ritual Overture* for Band (Pittsburgh, July 2, 1964); *The Birth of Music,* symph. poem (Tokyo, Oct. 10, 1964); symph. poem, *Showa Tempyo Raku* (*Old and Present Music;* Tokyo, Oct. 31, 1970); opera, *Kinkakuji* (*The Temple of the Golden Pavilion;* Berlin, June 23, 1976).

Mazas, Jacques-Féréol, French violinist; b. Lavaur (Tarn), Sept. 23, 1782; d. Bordeaux, Aug. 25, 1849. He was a pupil of Baillot at the Paris Con., winning first prize as violinist (1805); then played in the orch. of the Italian Opera in Paris; toured Europe (1811–29); then was a teacher in Orléans, and director of a music school in Cambrai (1837–41). He spent the last years of his life in Bordeaux. He wrote a method for violin (new ed. by J. Hrímalý) and numerous valuable studies; also a method for viola; concertos, string quartets, trios, violin duets, fantasias, variations, romances, etc.; also 3 operas, one of which, *Le Kiosque,* was performed at Paris in 1842. A set of 6 études was publ. in a new ed. by Hubay.

Mazura, Franz, Austrian bass-baritone; b. Salzburg, April 21, 1924. Following vocal studies, he began his career in Germany; in 1949 he sang in Kassel, and subsequently appeared at the opera houses of Mainz, Braunschweig, and Mannheim. In 1963 he became a member of the Städtische Oper in West Berlin. He sang at the Bayreuth Festival in 1974. In addition to the Wagnerian repertoire, he sang Pizzaro in *Fidelio,* Jochanaan in *Salomé,* and Moses in Schoenberg's *Moses und Aron.*

Mazzinghi, Joseph, English pianist and composer; b. London, Dec. 25, 1765; d. Downside, near Bath, Jan. 15, 1844. He was the son of Thomas Mazzinghi, of Corsican extraction, who made his home in England. Joseph Mazzinghi studied with John Christian Bach in London; he was a mere child when his father died, and succeeded him as organist of the Portuguese Chapel. He subsequently took lessons with Anfossi and Sacchini. He wrote 2 Italian operas for the King's Theatre: *La bella Arsena* (Dec. 12, 1795) and *Il tesoro* (June 14, 1796), and a number of light stage works to Eng. texts: *A Day in Turkey* (Covent Garden, Dec. 3, 1791), *The Turnpike Gate* (Covent Garden, Nov. 14, 1799), *The Wife of 2 Husbands* (Drury Lane, Nov. 1, 1803). He also wrote a large number of arias, glees, and songs; one of them, *Tell Me Shepherds,* attained great popularity.

Mazzocchi, Domenico, Italian composer; b. Veja, near Città Castellana (baptized, Nov. 8), 1592; d. Rome, Jan. 21, 1665. A learned Roman lawyer, he studied music with Nanini; in 1621 entered the service of Cardinal Ippolito Aldobrandini; publ. a book, *Madrigali a 5 voci in partitura* (1638), in which appear, for the first time, the conventional symbols for *crescendo* (◁) and *decrescendo* (>), *piano* (*p*), *forte* (*f*), and *trillo* (*tr*), which he explains in a preface. He also composed the operas *La catena d'Adone* (Rome, 1626) and *L'innocenza difesa,* several oratorios, and various pieces of church music.
BIBLIOGRAPHY: A. Cardinali, *Cenni biografici su Domenico e Virgilio Mazzocchi* (Subiaco, 1926); W. Witzenmann, *Domenico Mazzocchi, 1592–1665: Dokumente und Interpretationen,* in *Analecta Musicologica,* no. 8 (1970).

Mazzocchi, Virgilio, Italian composer, brother of **Domenico Mazzocchi;** b. Veja (baptized, July 22), 1597; d. there, Oct. 3, 1646. He studied music with his brother in Rome; served as maestro di cappella at the Chiesa del Gesù; then was at St. John Lateran (1628–29). In 1629 he was engaged at Cappella Giulia, at St. Peter's, and served there until his death. His opera, *Chi soffre, speri,* was produced in Rome on Feb. 27, 1639; excerpts from it were publ. by H. Goldschmidt; an *Argomento et allegoria* relating to it was publ. at the time of its first performance; a copy is in the Library of Congress in Washington, D.C.

BIBLIOGRAPHY: A. Salza, "Mazzocchi," *Rivista Musicale Italiana* (1917); A. Cardinali, *Cenni biografici su Domenico e Virgilio Mazzocchi* (Subiaco, 1926).

Mazzolani, Antonio, Italian composer; b. Ruina, near Ferrara, Dec. 26, 1819; d. Ferrara, Jan. 25, 1900. He studied with Zagagnoni (composition) and Lodi (piano); wrote the operas *Gismonda* (Ferrara, May 17, 1854) and *Enrico Charlis* (Ferrara, Nov. 25, 1876); his choruses, with extensive soli, were very popular in Italy during his time.

Mazzoleni, Ettore, conductor and composer, of Italian and Swiss extraction; b. Brusio, Switzerland, June 18, 1905; d. Toronto, as a result of an automobile accident, June 1, 1968. He studied music in Oxford and London; in 1929 was appointed teacher at Upper Canada College, Toronto, remaining until 1945; from 1932 taught at the Toronto Cons., and conducted concerts there; became its principal in 1945; also appeared as a guest conductor in other Canadian cities. He made several transcriptions of folk songs for various instrumental and vocal groups.

Mazzucato, Alberto, Italian violinist, composer, and writer on music; b. Udine, July 28, 1813; d. Milan, Dec. 31, 1877. He first studied mathematics; then turned to music, his teacher being Bresciano in Padua, where his first opera, *La Fidanzata di Lammermoor,* was given (Feb. 24, 1834); he wrote 8 more operas: *Don Chisciotte* (Milan, April 26, 1836), *Esmeralda* (Mantua, Feb. 10, 1838; his most successful stage work), *I Corsari* (Milan, Feb. 15, 1840), *I due sergenti* (Milan, Feb. 27, 1841), *Luigi V* (Milan, Feb. 25, 1843), *Hernani* (Genoa, Dec. 26, 1843); *Alberico da Romano* (Padua, 1847) and *Fede* (not perf.). Verdi's ascendance soon put him into the shade. He joined the faculty of the Milan Cons. in 1839, and from 1872 until his death was its director. From 1859 till 1869 he was concertmaster in the orch. of La Scala, Milan; for several years was editor of the influential *Gazzetta Musicale*; publ. *Trattato d'estetica musicale.*

McBride, Robert Guyn, American composer; b. Tucson, Ariz., Feb. 20, 1911. He learned to play the clarinet and saxophone and played in dance bands as a youth. He studied music theory at the Univ. of Arizona (1928–35); was a member of the Tucson Symph. Orch. (1928–35). From 1935 to 1946 he taught wind instrument playing at Bennington College; was then arranger for Triumph Films, N.Y. (1946–57); from 1957 to 1978 he was on the music faculty of the Univ. of Arizona. An exceptionally prolific composer, he wrote over 1000 pieces in various genres, many of them on American or Mexican themes with an infusion of jazz elements.

WORKS: *Mexican Rhapsody* for Orch. (1934); *Workout* for Oboe and Piano (1936); *Swing Stuff* for Clarinet and Piano (1938); *Jam Session* for Woodwind Quintet (1941); *Side Show* for Orch. (1944); Violin Concerto (1954); *Swing Foursome* for String Quartet (1957); *Five Winds Blowing* for Wind Quintet (1957); *Hill Country Symphony* (1964); *Lament for the Parking Problem* for Trumpet, Horn, and Trombone (1968).

McCabe, John, English pianist and composer of considerable attainments; b. Liverpool, April 21, 1939, of mixed Scottish-Irish stock on his father's side and of German-Scandinavian-Spanish ancestry on his mother's. He played piano, violin, and cello as a child and, according to family lore, composed 13 symphs. and an opera before the advent of puberty. He studied composition with Thomas Pitfield at Manchester Univ. (Mus.B., 1960), at the Royal Manchester College of Music, and in Munich with Harald Genzmer; was pianist-in-residence at Univ. College in Cardiff (1965–68); then settled in London. In 1978 he made a tour of the U.S. as a pianist-composer.

WORKS: FOR THE STAGE: *This Town's a Corporation Full of Crooked Streets,* an entertainment for Speaker, Tenor, Children's Chorus, Mixed Chorus, and Instrumental Ensemble (1969); *The Lion, the Witch, and the Wardrobe,* children's opera (1969); *The Teachings of Don Juan,* ballet (1973); *The Play of Mother Courage,* chamber opera (1974); *Mary Queen of Scots,* ballet (Glasgow, March 3, 1976). FOR ORCH.: 3 piano concertos: No. 1 (1966); No. 2 (1970); No. 3 (1977); 2 violin concertos: No. 1 (1959) and No. 2 (1980); 3 Symphs.: No. 1 (1965); No. 2 (1970); No. 3 (1978); *Concertante Music* (1968); *Metamorphoses* for Harpsichord and Orch. (1968); *Concerto funèbre* for Viola and Chamber Orch. (1962); Chamber Concerto for Viola, Cello, and Orch. (1965); Concerto for Chamber Orch. (1962; revised 1968); *Notturni ed Alba* for Soprano and Orch. (1970); *Concertante Variations* on a theme of Nicholas Maw, for Strings (1970); Concerto for Oboe d'Amore and Orch. (1972); *The Chagall Windows* (1974); Clarinet Concerto (1977); *The Shadow of Light* (1979); Concerto for Orch. (London, Feb. 10, 1983). VOCAL WORKS: *Aspects of Whiteness,* cantata for Mixed Chorus and Piano (1967); *Voyage Cantata* for Soloists, Chorus, and Orch. (1972); *Stabat Mater* for Soprano, Chorus, and Orch. (1976); *Reflections on a Summer Night,* cantata for Mixed Chorus and Orch. (1977); many choruses. CHAMBER MUSIC: *Movements* for Clarinet, Violin, and Cello (1964); *Concertante* for Harpsichord and Chamber Ensemble (1965); String Trio (1966); *Nocturnal* for Piano Quintet (1966); *Miniconcerto* for Organ, Percussion, and 485 Penny-whistles

(1966); *Dance Movements* for Horn, Violin, and Piano (1967); *Rounds* for Brass Quintet (1967); Sonata for Clarinet, Cello, and Piano (1969); 3 string quartets: No. 1 (1960); No. 2 (1972); No. 3 (1979); many piano pieces and organ works.

McCartney, John Paul, English rock-'n'-roll singer and composer; member of the famous Liverpudlian quartet The Beatles; b. Liverpool, June 18, 1942. He picked out chords on a family piano (his father was an amateur ragtime player), and at puberty began playing a left-handed guitar. He is the only Beatle who attended college, and studied English literature. Fascinated by Elvis Presley, he tried to emulate the spirit of American rock 'n' roll *à l'anglaise*. He joined John Lennon and George Harrison in the Casbah Club in Liverpool in 1959; this fruitful and fantastically lucrative association with them, and later with Ringo Starr, continued until the breakup of the group in 1970, when McCartney went to High Court to end the partnership and asked for an accounting of assets and income. Endowed with an authentic poetic gift, McCartney infused a literary quality into the lyrics used by The Beatles, fashioning them in archaic English prosody, which in combination with the modal harmony of the arrangements imparted a somewhat distant quality to their products. Like his co-Beatles, McCartney went through a period of transcendental meditation when he sat at the feet of a hirsute Indian guru, but his British common sense soon overrode this metaphysical infatuation.
BIBLIOGRAPHY: Hunter Davies, *The Beatles* (N.Y., 1968); Ned Rorem, "The Beatles," *N.Y. Review of Books* (Jan. 18, 1968); G. Geppert, *Songs der Beatles. Texte und Interpretationen* (2nd ed.; Munich, 1968); E. Davies, "The Psychological Characteristics of Beatle Mania," *Journal of the History of Ideas* (April–June 1969); P. McCabe and R.D. Schonfeld, *Apple to the Core: The Unmaking of the Beatles* (N.Y., 1972); F. Seloron, *Les Beatles* (Paris, 1972); W. Mellers, *Twilight of the Gods: The Music of the Beatles* (N.Y., 1973).

McCauley, William, Canadian composer; b. Tofield, Alberta, Feb. 14, 1917. He studied piano with Margaret Parsons and music theory with Healy Willan at the Royal Cons. of Toronto (1945–47); later took courses in composition with Bernard Rogers and Howard Hanson at the Eastman School of Music in Rochester, N.Y. (1957–60; M.Mus., 1959; D.Mus., 1961). He was a music director at Crawley Films (1949–57), where he composed and conducted music for over 100 television films and documentaries; then was director of music at York Univ. (1961–69); in 1970 was appointed head of the music dept. of Seneca College in Toronto. His music is pleasing, lyrical, and inoffensive, with some officious modernities.
WORKS: *Newfoundland Scene* for Orch. (1952); *Saskatchewan Suite* for Orch. (1956); *5 Miniatures* for Flute and Strings (1958); *Contrasts* for Orch. (1958); Horn Concerto (1959); *5 Miniatures* for Bass Trombone, Harp, and Strings (1959); *Theme and

Deviations for Orch. (1960); *Wilderness* for Orch., music from the film (1963); *Canadian Folk Song Fantasy* for Symph. Band (1966); *Metropolis*, concert suite for Symph. Band (1967); *2 Nocturnes* for Strings (1968); *Sunday Morning at Wahanowin* for String Orch. (1968); *Concerto grosso* for Solo Brass Quintet and Orch. (1973); *Christmas Carol Fantasies* for Orch. (1975); *5 Miniatures* for 6 Percussionists (1962); *5 Miniatures* for 10 Winds (1968); *5 Miniatures* for 4 Saxophones (1972); *Miniature Overture* for Brass Quintet (1973); *Kaleidoscope Québécois* for Flute, Clarinet, Violin, Cello, and 2 Pianos (1974); *5 Miniatures* for Brass Quintet (1974); *Space Trip* for Piano (1968); choruses; songs, many with instrumental accompaniment.

McClellan, John Jasper, American organist and conductor; b. Payson, Utah, April 20, 1874; d. Salt Lake City, Aug. 2, 1925. He studied piano with A. Jonás, organ with A.A. Stanley, and composition with J.E. Schmaal. In 1900 he became organist at the Mormon Tabernacle at Salt Lake City; made a transcontinental tour with its choir. In 1905 he founded the Salt Lake City Symph. Orch., and conducted it until 1910; was a Bachelor of Didactics of the Mormon Church; composed an *Ode to Irrigation;* organ pieces; numerous anthems.

McCorkle, Donald Macomber, American musicologist; b. Cleveland, Feb. 20, 1929; d. Vancouver, Feb. 6, 1978. He studied clarinet, and took courses in musicology at Indiana Univ. with Willi Apel and Paul Nettl; was granted a Ph.D. degree there (1958). In 1954 he was appointed assistant prof. of musicology at Salem College, Winston-Salem, N.C.; served as music editor of the Moravian Church in America; was executive director of the Moravian Music Foundation; then went to Vancouver, where he was active as a teacher. He wrote a valuable dissertation, *Moravian Music in Salem: A German-American Heritage.*

McCormack, John, famous Irish tenor; b. Athlone, June 14, 1884; d. Glena, Booterstown, Sept. 16, 1945. Without previous training, he took part in the National Irish Festival at Dublin in 1903, and carried off the gold medal; in 1903 he became a member of the Dublin Cathedral Choir and began to study seriously with the organist and choirmaster, Vincent O'Brien; he made his operatic debut at Savona on Jan. 13, 1906, and his debut as a concert singer at a concert of the Sunday League in London (Feb. 17, 1907); in 1909 he sang at the San Carlo Opera in Naples, and was engaged by Hammerstein for the Manhattan Opera House in N.Y., where he made his American debut on Nov. 10, 1909, as Alfredo Germont in *La Traviata;* he made his debut at the Metropolitan Opera House in N.Y. on Nov. 29, 1910; also appeared there in 1912–14 and in 1917–19; during the 1910–11 season he was with the Chicago Opera Co.; after that, he appeared seldom in opera, but became tremendously successful as a concert tenor. He was naturalized as an American citizen in 1919; was given the title of Count by Pope Pius XI in 1928 and named Papal Chamberlain. Postage stamps in his honor were issued in June 1984 to mark his centennial of birth: a 22-pence Irish stamp, and a 20-cent denomination in the U.S.

BIBLIOGRAPHY: L.A.G. Strong, *John McCormack* (London, 1941; reprint, 1949); Lily McCormack (his widow), *I Hear You Calling Me* (Milwaukee, 1949); L.F.X. McDermott Roe, *John McCormack, The Complete Discography* (London, 1956); R. Foxall, *John McCormack* (N.Y., 1964); *Dictionary of American Biography*, Supplement III (N.Y., 1973).

McCoy, Seth, black American tenor; b. Sanford, N.C., Dec. 17, 1928. He studied voice in Cleveland and N.Y.; began his career as a tenor soloist with the Robert Shaw Chorale on its tours of the U.S. and South America; subsequently established himself as one of the leading concert and oratorio singers in the U.S. through his numerous appearances with the Boston Symph., Chicago Symph., Cleveland Orch., Philadelphia Orch., and Pittsburgh Symph. On Feb. 17, 1979, he made his Metropolitan Opera debut in N.Y. as Tamino in *Die Zauberflöte*.

McCoy, William J., American composer; b. Crestline, Ohio, March 15, 1848; d. Oakland, Calif., Oct. 15, 1926. His family moved to California when he was a child; he began to compose at the age of 12; then was sent to N.Y. to study with William Mason; he later studied at the Leipzig Cons. with Reinecke and Hauptmann. His Symph. in F was conducted in Leipzig by Reinecke in 1872. He returned to California and wrote some theater music for the Bohemian Club there (*Harmadryads, The Cave Man,* etc.); also wrote an opera, *Egypt* (2 acts presented at the Berkeley Music Festival, Sept. 17, 1921), for which he received the Bispham Medal of the American Opera Society of Chicago; *Yosemite,* overture; Violin Concerto; a suite from *A Masque of Apollo* (*Prelude, Dance,* and *The Naiad's Idyl*); numerous songs, and a textbook, *Cumulative Harmony.*

BIBLIOGRAPHY: E.E. Hipsher, *American Opera and Its Composers* (Philadelphia, 1934; pp. 317–20).

McCracken, James, remarkable American tenor; b. Gary, Ind., Dec. 16, 1926. His father was a singing fireman; his mother played the piano, although she could not read music. This created a musical environment, and McCracken began to play the clarinet. When he graduated from Horace Mann High School he was voted the most likely to succeed in music among his classmates, who matriculated mostly in baseball. He also married a school sweetheart, but then came the war and he joined the navy. After the war he enrolled at Columbia Univ. and began to study singing in earnest. He obtained engagements to sing secondary and tertiary roles in Broadway musicals, and held a regular job as a vocalist at the Roxy Theater in N.Y. In 1952 he made his opera debut as Rodolfo in *La Bohème* with the Central City Opera Co. in Colorado. He successfully auditioned for the Metropolitan Opera and was giv-

en a chance to sing minor roles there. In the meantime he was divorced and remarried. With his new wife, he went to Europe, and succeeded in making a number of respectable appearances with various European opera houses. He took an intensive course in Italian singing with Marcello Conati in Milan. Upon his return to the U.S., he was engaged to sing the title role in Verdi's *Otello* with the Opera Society in Washington, D.C., on Jan. 22, 1960. He sang Otello at the Zürich Festival on June 15, 1961, and with the San Francisco Opera on Oct. 2, 1962, with excellent success. On March 10, 1963, he sang this role at the Metropolitan Opera in N.Y. His career was now assured. In 1964 he sang Otello at Covent Garden in London. Other roles in which he excelled were Canio in *Pagliacci,* Manrico in *Il Trovatore,* Don José in *Carmen,* Radames in *Aida,* Don Alvaro in *La forza del destino,* and Tannhäuser in Wagner's opera.

BIBLIOGRAPHY: David Ewen, *Musicians since 1900* (N.Y., 1978).

McCutchan, Robert Guy, American choral conductor and hymnologist; b. Mount Ayr, Iowa, Sept. 13, 1877; d. Claremont, Calif., May 15, 1958. He was active as a music educator and choral conductor in the schools and churches of Iowa, Kansas, and Indiana; made a thorough study of American hymnals and publ. a valuable compilation, *Our Hymnody* (Nashville, 1937; 2nd ed., 1942; contains detailed biographical information on American hymn composers); also *Hymn Tune Names: Their Sources and Significance* (Nashville, 1957).

McDaniel, Barry, American baritone; b. Lyndon, Kans., Oct. 18, 1930. He studied at the Juilliard School of Music in N.Y.; then was awarded a Fulbright scholarship in Germany; he took voice lessons in Stuttgart; made his operatic debut with the Württemberg State Theater there in 1959; subsequently sang with the Karlsruhe Opera, the Städtische Oper in Berlin, the Bavarian State Opera in Munich, and the Vienna State Opera; also made guest appearances at the Salzburg and Bayreuth festivals. On Jan. 19, 1972, he sang the role of Pelléas in Debussy's *Pelléas et Mélisande* in his debut with the Metropolitan Opera in N.Y. His operatic repertoire is quite extensive; he is equally adept in Baroque operas and in modern roles.

McDonald, Harl, American composer and music administrator; b. near Boulder, Colo., July 27, 1899; d. Princeton, N.J., March 30, 1955. He studied at the Univ. of Southern Calif.; became a professional pianist; also did research in the measurement of instrumental and vocal tones; publ. its results in *New Methods of Measuring Sound* (Philadelphia, 1935). In 1939 he was appointed business manager of the Philadelphia Orch., but continued to compose. His music gained performance almost exclusively by courtesy of the Philadelphia Orch., conducted by Stokowski and Ormandy.

WORKS (all perf. in Philadelphia): 4 symphs.: No. 1, *The Santa Fé Trail* (Nov. 16, 1934); No. 2, *The*

Rhumba Symphony (Oct. 4, 1935); No. 3, *Lamentations of Fu Hsuan*, for Orch., Chorus, and Soprano Solo (Jan. 3, 1936); No. 4 (April 8, 1938); *Festival of the Workers* (April 26, 1934); *3 Poems on Traditional Aramaic Themes* (Dec. 18, 1936); Concerto for 2 Pianos and Orch. (April 2, 1937); Violin Concerto (March 16, 1945); *Saga of the Mississippi* (April 9, 1948); *From Childhood,* suite for Harp and Orch. (Jan. 17, 1941); 2 nocturnes for Orch., *San Juan Capistrano* (Boston Symph., Oct. 30, 1939); *Arkansas Traveler,* humoresque (Detroit, March 3, 1940); *Bataan,* tone poem (Washington, July 3, 1942); chamber music: 2 piano trios (1931, 1932); *Fantasy for String Quartet* (1932); *Quartet on Negro Themes* (1933); many choral works.
BIBLIOGRAPHY: Madeleine Goss, *Modern Music-Makers* (N.Y., 1952; pp. 303–13).

McDonald, Susann, American harpist; b. Rock Island, Ill., May 26, 1935. She studied with Lily Laskine in Paris; received the premier prix de harpe at the Paris Cons. (1955); her principal harp teacher was Henriette Renié, whose method she adopted in her own playing and teaching; she also had some lessons with Marcel Grandjany. She made her American debut in Los Angeles in 1956; then gave concerts in N.Y. (1959) and toured Europe and South America; in 1967 she was appointed prof. of harp at the Univ. of Southern Calif., Los Angeles; also taught at the Univ. of Arizona; in 1975 she joined the faculty of the Juilliard School in N.Y. She is noted for her excellent interpretations of contemporary music, for which she has developed a perfect technique.

McDowell, John Herbert, American composer; b. Washington, D.C., Dec. 21, 1926. He studied at Colgate Univ. (B.A., 1948) and at Columbia Univ. with Otto Luening, Jack Beeson, and Roger Goeb (M.A., 1957); held a Guggenheim fellowship in 1962. He devoted his energies chiefly to music for the theater and dance.
WORKS: Cantata, *Good News from Heaven* (1957); *Four Sixes and a Nine* for Orch. (1959); *Accumulation* for 35 Flutes, Strings, and Percussion (1964); 100-odd pieces for dance, among them *Insects and Heroes* (1961); *From Sea to Shining Sea,* an homage to Ives (1965); *Dark Psalters* (1968).

McEwen, Sir John Blackwood, Scottish composer and pedagogue; b. Hawick, April 13, 1868; d. London, June 14, 1948. He studied at Glasgow Univ. (M.A., 1888) and at the Royal Academy of Music in London, with Corder, Matthay, and Prout; taught piano in Glasgow (1895–98) and composition at the Royal Academy of Music in London (1898–1936); in 1924 he succeeded Alexander Mackenzie as principal, retiring in 1936. He was knighted in 1931. He continued to compose until his last years.
WORKS: 2 symphs., of which the one subtitled *Solway* (1911) was the best known; 4 orch. suites (1893–1941); *7 Bagatelles* for Strings; Viola Concerto (1901); 17 string quartets (1893–1947); 6 violin sonatas (1913–29); Viola Sonata (1930); *Scottish Rhapso-*

dy for Violin and Piano (1915); piano pieces; songs. He publ. *Text Book of Harmony and Counterpoint* (1908); *The Elements of Music* (1910); *A Primer of Harmony* (1911); *The Thought in Music* (1912); *Tempo Rubato* (1928); *Introduction to the Piano Sonatas of Beethoven* (1931).
BIBLIOGRAPHY: S. Dyke's article on McEwen's string quartets in Cobbett's *Cyclopedic Survey of Chamber Music* (London, 1930; 2nd ed., 1963).

McGill, Josephine, American composer and collector of American folk songs; b. Louisville, Ky., Oct. 20, 1877; d. there, Feb. 24, 1919. She studied with Alexander Lambert at the New York College of Music; collected material for the publication *Folk Songs of the Kentucky Mountains* (1917, 1922, 1926, and 1937).

McHose, Allen Irvine, American music theorist and educator; b. Lancaster, Pa., May 14, 1902. He studied at Franklin and Marshall College (B.S., 1923; D.F.A., 1948), at the Eastman School of Music in Rochester, N.Y. (B.M., 1928; M.M., 1929), and at Oklahoma City Univ. (D.Mus., 1945). From 1930–67 he was on the faculty at the Eastman School; from 1931–62 was chairman of the theory dept. there. He developed a theory of musical analysis based upon a statistical survey of works of J.S. Bach, and propounded it persuasively in his books *Contrapuntal Harmonic Technique of the 18th Century* (1947) and *Basic Principles of the Technique of 18th and 19th Century Composition* (1951). He also publ. *Sight Singing Manual* (1944, with Ruth N. Tibbs); *Keyboard and Dictation Manual* (1949, with Donald White); *Teachers' Dictation Manual* (1948); and *Musical Style 1850–1920* (1950). He wrote a Violin Sonata (1929) and a Concerto for Oboe and Orch. (1932).

McHugh, Jimmy, American composer of popular songs; b. Boston, July 10, 1894; d. Beverly Hills, May 22, 1969. He was a rehearsal accompanist for the Boston Opera Co. before embarking on composition. He moved to N.Y. in 1921. His first Broadway show was *Blackbirds of 1928,* which included his greatest hit song, *I Can't Give You Anything but Love, Baby.* In 1930 he went to Hollywood and began to write for films; one of his most famous songs of the period was *South American Way.* During the war he wrote the inspirational song *Comin' in on a Wing and a Prayer.* He was awarded a Presidential Certificate of Merit for his work on war bonds. He also received honorary doctor's degrees from Harvard Univ., Georgetown Univ. and Holy Cross College.

McIntyre, Donald, New Zealand bass-baritone; b. Auckland, Oct. 22, 1934. He went to London and studied at the Guildhall School of Music; in 1959 he made his debut with the Welsh National Opera; from 1960 was a member of the Sadler's Wells Opera; in 1967 he made his debut at Covent Garden; beginning in 1967, he sang at the Bayreuth Festivals. On Feb. 15, 1975, he made his Metropolitan Opera debut as Wotan in *Das Rheingold;* also sang in Hamburg, Paris, and Milan. He was particularly distinguished in Wagnerian roles.

McKay, George Frederick, American composer; b. Harrington, Wash., June 11, 1899; d. Stateline, Nev., Oct. 4, 1970. He studied at the Univ. of Washington, Seattle, and subsequently at the Eastman School of Music in Rochester, with Palmgren and Sinding; graduated in 1923. In 1941 he was appointed to the faculty of the Univ. of Washington, where he retired in 1968.

WORKS: 4 sinfoniettas (1925–42); *Fantasy on a Western Folk Song* (Rochester, May 3, 1933); *Bravura Prelude* for Brass Ensemble (Rochester, April 30, 1939); *To a Liberator,* symph. poem (Indianapolis, March 15, 1940); *Introspective Poem* for Strings (Philadelphia, April 3, 1941); *A Prairie Portrait* (San Francisco, Sept. 4, 1941); *Pioneer Epic* (Oakland, Feb. 17, 1942); Wind Quintet (1930); Piano Trio (1931); a quintet subtitled *American Street Scenes,* for Clarinet, Trumpet, Saxophone, Bassoon, and Piano (1935); 2 organ sonatas; Violin Concerto (1940); Cello Concerto (1942); a suite on Negro folk songs for Strings, entitled *Port Royal, 1861* (1939).

McKellar, Kenneth, Scottish tenor; b. Paisley, June 23, 1927. He took a course in philology at the Univ. of Aberdeen and received a B.S. degree; then studied voice at the Royal College of Music in London. He subsequently sang with the Carl Rosa Opera Co. in London; later toured the U.S. as a concert singer. He was also a fine interpreter of traditional Scottish ballads, which he included in his concert programs.

McKinley, Carl, American composer and organist; b. Yarmouth, Maine, Oct. 9, 1895; d. Boston, July 24, 1966. He studied with Edward Burlingame Hill at Harvard Univ.; in 1929 was appointed instructor of organ and composition at the New England Cons. in Boston. Many of his works are inspired by American subjects. He wrote *The Blue Flower,* symph. poem (N.Y., Jan. 18, 1924); *Masquerade,* American rhapsody for Orch. (his most popular work; Chicago North Shore Festival, May 29, 1926); *Caribbean Holiday* (Boston, Nov. 18, 1948); String Quartet, Cello Sonata, and other pieces of chamber music, as well as organ pieces and songs.

McKinney, Mathilde, American pianist and composer; b. South Bend, Ind., Jan. 31, 1904. She studied piano and composition at the Juilliard School of Music in N.Y.; was a member of the faculty of Westminster State College, Princeton, N.J. (1960–70). Among her piano pieces are *Rain Drops* and *Sad Waltz.*

McKuen, Rod, American minstrel and lyricist; b. Oakland, Calif., April 29, 1933. He ran away from a previously broken home at the age of 11; bummed as a logger and roadman; roped calves and dogged bulls in and out of rodeo shows; became a disc jockey and scriptwriter in a psychological warfare unit during the Korean War. Returning to the U.S., he appeared as a folksy balladeer in San Francisco nightclubs; obtained a music theory book and learned to write tunes; supported himself by playing supporting roles in otherwise unsupportable bit parts in the movies; eked out a posh living by crashing parties and gorging himself on choice comestibles. He became a roving poet, dispensing a plethora of facile country-style songs with monosyllabic assonances for rhymes and a simple appeal of scenes of non-obscene free love against an artificially flavored pastoral landscape. His first anthology of verse, *An Autumn Came,* was a failure, but he stumbled into a poetic bonanza with the commercially issued vols. *Stanyan Street* and *Listen to the Warm.* He never indentured himself to an agent, and so was able to reap a lucrative harvest of success, blandly chanting, "I have no special bed, I give myself to those who offer love." He publ. a memoir, *Finding My Father* (N.Y., 1976) in which he stated, "I was born a bastard; some people spend their entire lives becoming one." His putative natural father was a lumberjack who died about 1965.

McLaughlin, John, British guitarist; b. Yorkshire, Jan. 4, 1942. He played piano and guitar as a child, and formed a band as a schoolboy. In 1969 he issued his first solo album, *Extrapolation,* which displayed his virtuosity on the guitar. He subsequently got together with Miles Davis, with whom he made *Bitches Brew* and *In a Silent Way.* In 1970 he sought spiritual expansion through a worshipful association with a Bengal mystic, and recorded *My Goal's Beyond,* an album of transcendental meditation containing group improvisation; a further development was his starting a Mahavishnu orchestra, mixing Hindu religiosity with pseudo-Baroque classicism; in a new album, *Birds of Fire,* he made use of a synthesizer. Still immersed in a misty mysticism, he produced, in company with other turbaned converts, an album called *Love, Devotion, Surrender* and, even closer to Nirvana, a set recorded in Central Park called *Between Nothingness and Eternity.* He sobered up about 1976, and tried to combine Hindu instrumentation with jazz; then reverted to the primordial mentality with an album *Friday Night in San Francisco,* issued in 1981.

McNair, Barbara, black American singer of popular music and actress; b. Racine, Wis., March 4, 1939. She studied music at the Univ. of Southern Calif. in Los Angeles; then went to N.Y., where she sang in Broadway musicals, including *Body Beautiful* (1958); and *The Merry World of Nat King Cole* (1961); she also appeared as a television actress.

McNair, Sylvia, American soprano; b. Mansfield, Ohio, June 23, 1956. She played violin; then began to take vocal lessons with Virginia Zeani at the Indiana Univ. School of Music in Bloomington. In 1982 she won a National Metropolitan Opera Audition and made an impressive appearance as Sandrina in Haydn's *L'Infedeltà delusa* in N.Y. She also sang with the Atlanta Symph., the San Francisco

Symph., and the National Symph. in Washington, D.C. Her repertoire includes most of the standard operas; she also is able to acquit herself laudably in difficult parts in contemporary operas.

McNaught, William (Gray), English music journalist and editor; b. London, March 30, 1849; d. there, Oct. 13, 1918. He studied at the Royal Academy of Music; was active as a choral conductor; in 1892 until his death he was editor of the *School Music Review,* publ. by Novello; in 1909 he became editor of the *Musical Times.* His son, also named **William McNaught** (b. London, Sept. 1, 1883; d. there, June 9, 1953), was assistant editor of the *Musical Times* when his father was editor; wrote program notes and reviews for many years; in 1944 he became its editor, succeeding Harvey Grace. He publ. *A Short Account of Modern Music and Musicians* (London, 1937); *Beethoven* (London, 1940) and *Elgar* (London, 1947).

McPartland, Jimmy (James), American jazz trumpeter; b. Chicago, March 15, 1907. He studied violin, then took up the cornet; at the age of 16, he organized a band with his brother; subsequently played with Bix Beiderbecke, Ben Pollack, and Jack Teagarden. After military service in World War II, he resumed his career by organizing his own quartet in Chicago; later led his own band on tours.

McPartland, Marian, English jazz pianist; b. Windsor, March 20, 1920. She first played violin; then won a scholarship to the Guildhall School of Music, where she studied piano. She began her career as a jazz pianist in joint appearances with the jazz pianist Billy Mayerl; in 1945 she married the jazz trumpeter **Jimmy McPartland;** in 1946 went to America and played in a combo with her husband; in 1951 she organized her own trio. She was also active as a composer of songs in the popular vein.

McPhatter, Clyde, black American vocalist; b. Durham, N.C., Nov. 15, 1933; d. New York, June 13, 1972. His father was a preacher in a Baptist church, and McPhatter began singing gospel songs under his tutelage. Still in school, he formed a gospel group called Mt. Lebanon Singers; then sang with a choral ensemble, The Dominoes, making a hit with *Have Mercy, Baby.* In 1953 he organized his own group called The Drifters, which established the mix of gospel and pop that came to be known as "soul" music. His best renditions were the rhythm-and-blues *Money Honey,* and pop favorites *There Goes My Baby, Dance with Me, A Lover's Question,* and *Lover Please.*

McPhee, Colin, outstanding American composer; b. Montreal, Canada, March 15, 1901; d. Los Angeles, Jan. 7, 1964. He studied at the Peabody Cons. with Gustav Strube, graduating in 1921; then took piano lessons with Arthur Friedheim in Toronto and with Isidor Philipp in Paris. Returning to America in 1926, he joined the modern movement in N.Y.; wrote a Concerto for Piano and Wind Octet (1928; Boston, March 11, 1929) and also scores for the experimental films *H₂O* and *Mechanical Principles.* In 1934 he went to live on the island of Bali in Indonesia; in 1936 he was in Mexico, where he wrote his major work, *Tabuh-Tabuhan,* for 2 Pianos and Orch.; then was again in Bali, until 1939. From 1958 until his death he was at the Inst. of Ethnomusicology at the Univ. of Calif. in Los Angeles. He wrote *Balinese Ceremonial Music* for Flute and 2 Pianos (1942); *Transitions* for Orch. (1951); 3 symphs. (1955, 1957, 1962); *4 Iroquois Dances* for Orch.; *Invention and Kinesis* for Piano; publ. *A House in Bali* (N.Y., 1946) and *Music in Bali* (posthumous, New Haven, Conn., 1966).
BIBLIOGRAPHY: *"Modern Music" ... Analytic Index,* compiled by Wayne Shirley and ed. by W. and C. Lichtenwanger (N.Y., 1976; pp. 129–130).

McRae, Carmen, black American jazz vocalist; b. New York, April 8, 1922. She joined Benny Carter's band in 1944; subsequently sang with the bands of Count Basie, Mercer Ellington, and others; made tours in Europe and Japan. She was married to Kenny Clarke, and recorded several songs as **Carmen Clarke.**

McShann, Jay ("Hootie"), black American jazz pianist, blues singer, and bandleader; b. Muskogee, Okla., Jan. 12, 1909. He took up the piano at an early age; led his own group during the big-band era in Kansas City. Among his hits were *Hootie Blues* (a title from which he got his nickname), *Confessin' the Blues,* and *Swingmatism.* The legendary jazz figure Charlie Parker was a member of McShann's band. After a stint in the U.S. Army (1943–45), he resumed his career, working mainly in California. He continued to be active well into old age; in 1974 he toured Europe with the show *The Musical Life of Charlie Parker;* in 1975 he took part in the Montreux Jazz Festival; in 1979 he played at the Alexandra Palace Jazz Festival in London. He publ. *Boogie Woogie and Blues Piano Solos.* He also appeared in the film *The Last of the Blue Devils.*

Meader, George, American tenor; b. Minneapolis, July 6, 1888; d. Hollywood, Dec. 19, 1963. He studied law at the Univ. of Minnesota; after graduation in 1908 he went to Germany, where he took voice lessons with Anna Schoen-René; he remained in Germany and sang at the Stuttgart Opera (1911–19). Returning to America in 1919, he gave recitals before making his operatic debut with the Metropolitan Opera in N.Y., as Victorin in Korngold's opera *Die tote Stadt* (Nov. 19, 1921); he resigned from the Metropolitan in 1931 and sang in operetta; was particularly successful in Jerome Kern's *Cat and the Fiddle.*

Meale, Richard, Australian composer; b. Sydney, Aug. 24, 1932. He studied piano, harp, and clarinet at the New South Wales Cons. of Music (1947–55); in 1960 he took a course in Asian music at the Ethnomusicological Inst. at the Univ. of Calif. in Los

Angeles; traveled to France and Spain before returning to Australia in 1961; was program planning officer of the Australian Broadcasting Commission (1962–69); then was on the faculty of the Univ. of Adelaide (1969–73). In his music he followed the precepts of ethnomusicology, seeking to create a synthesis of primitive natural melorhythms with modernistic counterpoints.

WORKS: *Stonehenge* for Piano (1945); *Rhapsody* for Violin and Piano (1952); Quintet for Oboe and Strings (1952); *Rhapsody* for Cello and Piano (1953); Horn Sonata (1954); ballet, *The Hypnotist* (1956); Solo Flute Sonata (1957); *Divertimento* for Piano Trio (1959); Flute Concerto (1959); *Sinfonia* for Piano, 4-hands and Strings (1959); *Orenda* for Piano (1959, revised 1968); Flute Sonata (1960); ballet, *At Five in the Afternoon* (1961); *Las Alboradas* for Flute, Violin, Horn, and Piano (1963); *Homage to García Lorca* for Double String Orch. (1964); *Intersections* and *Cyphers* for Flute, Viola, Vibraphone, and Piano (both 1965); graphic scores; *Images (Nagauta)* for Orch. (1966); *Nocturnes* for Solo Vibraphone, Harp, Celesta, and Orch. (1965–67); *Very High Kings* for Orch., Organ, 2 Amplified Pianos, and 6 Spatially Positioned Trumpets (1968); *Clouds Now and Then* for Orch. (1969); *Soon It Will Die* for Orch. (1969); *Interiors/Exteriors* for 2 Pianos and 3 Percussionists (1970); *Variations* for Orch. (1970); Wind Quintet (1970); *Coruscations* for Piano (1971); *Incredible Floridas,* an homage to Rimbaud, for Flute, Guitar, Violin, Cello, Piano, and Percussion (1971); *Plateau* for Wind Quintet (1971); *Evocations* for Oboe, Chamber Orch., and Obbligato Violin (1972); String Quartet (1974).

Mechem, Kirke Lewis, American composer; b. Wichita, Kans., Aug. 16, 1925. After finishing high school in Topeka, Kans., he enrolled at Stanford Univ., where his teachers were Harold Schmidt, Leonard Ratner, and Sandor Salgo. He later took courses in composition at Harvard Univ. with A. Tillman Merritt and Randall Thompson (M.A., 1953). In his works he adopted a candidly euphonious method of composition, not shirking resolvable dissonances and circumtonal melodic patterns, but faithfully observing basic tonality; as a result, his music gives unadulterated aural satisfaction to unprejudiced ears.

WORKS: *Tartuffe,* opera, after Molière (San Francisco, May 27, 1980); Symph. No. 1 (1958–59; San Francisco Symph., Josef Krips conducting, Jan. 6, 1965); Symph. No. 2 (San Francisco Symph., March 29, 1967, Krips conducting; radically revised version, San Francisco Symph., Jan. 15, 1969, Krips conducting); *Divertimento* for Flute and String Trio; String Quartet; numerous sacred choruses.

Meck, Nadezhda von, friend and benefactress of Tchaikovsky; b. Znamenskoye, near Smolensk, Feb. 10, 1831; d. Wiesbaden, Jan. 13, 1894. She became interested in Tchaikovsky's music through Nicholas Rubinstein, director of the Moscow Cons., of which she was a patroness. At first offering Tchaikovsky commissions, she later granted him a yearly

allowance of 6,000 rubles in order that he might compose undisturbed by finanical considerations. He lived for long periods in close proximity to her, at Brailov (near Kiev) and in Florence, Italy, but although they carried on an extensive and intimate correspondence (publ. in 3 vols., Moscow, 1934–36), they never met face to face. Tchaikovsky's allowance was abruptly cut off in 1890 on the pretext of financial difficulties, leading to a complete break between him and Mme. von Meck in 1891. She employed the youthful Debussy as a pianist in her household.

BIBLIOGRAPHY: Barbara von Meck and Catherine Drinker Bowen, *Beloved Friend* (biographical romance; N.Y., 1937); Olga Bennigson, "More Tchaikovsky–von Meck Correspondence," *Musical Quarterly* (April 1938).

Medek, Tilo, German composer; b. Jena, Jan. 22, 1940. He studied composition with Wagner-Régeny at the Deutsche Hochschule für Musik in East Berlin; attended classes in musicology with Vetter and E.H. Meyer at Humboldt Univ. in East Berlin (1959–64), and later with Wagner-Régeny at the Deutsche Akademie der Künste (1964–67). In 1977 he moved to West Germany.

WORKS: FOR THE STAGE: Short opera after Isaac Babel, *Einzug* (1969); 2 singspiels: *Iche und die Hexe Yu* (1970–71) and *Appetit auf Frühkirschen* (1971); ballet, *David und Goliath* (1972). FOR ORCH.: *Triade* (1964); *Rezitativ und Arie* (1965); *Porträt eines Tangos* (1968); *Das zögernde Lied* (1970); Flute Concerto (1973); *Grosser Marsch* (1974); Concerto for Piccolo and Orch. (1975; East Berlin, Feb. 2, 1976); *König Johann,* concert overture (1976); Marimba Concerto (1975–76); Cello Concerto (1978; East Berlin, Oct. 8, 1978); Organ Concerto (1977–79; Baden-Baden, March 7, 1981); Violin Concerto (1979–80; Cologne, Nov. 14, 1980); *König Johann oder Der Ausstieg* for Organ and Orch. (1980). CHAMBER MUSIC: *Tanzstudie* for Horn, Harpsichord, and Piano (1963); Flute Sonata (1963); 3 wind quintets (1965, 1974–76, 1979); String Trio (1965); *Terzinen,* duo for Flute and Piano (1966); *Divertissement* for Wind Quintet and Harpsichord (1967); *Stadtpfeifer,* "Schwanengesang" for Clarinet, Trombone, Cello, and Piano (1973); *Schattenspiele* for Solo Cello (1973); *Sensible Variationen um ein Schubertthema* for Flute, Violin, and Cello (1973); Nonet (1974); *3 Tagzeiten* for Marimba, Piano, and Percussion (1976); *Tagtraum* for 7 Instruments (1976); *Giebichenstein* for 8 Instruments (1976); *Eine Stele für B.A. Zimmermann* for Solo Cello (1976); *Zur Unzeit Erblühtes,* 5 pieces for Marimba (1977); *Erdrauch* for Guitar (1979). FOR VOICE: *Altägyptische Liebeslieder* for 2 Voices and Orch. (1963); *Johann Wallbergens natürliche Zauberkünste 1768* for Narrator, Soprano, and Salon Orch. (1965; Gelsenkirchen, Jan. 18, 1979); *Sintflutbestanden,* triptych for Tenor, Piano, and Horn (1967); *Gethsemane,* cantata (1980). FOR PIANO: *Miszellen I–III* (1965–75); *Kaminstücke,* 12 pieces (1968–70); *Adventskalender,* 24 pieces (1972–73); *Tag- und Nachtstücke* (Book I, Nos. 1–8, 1976–78). FOR ORGAN:

Verschüttete Bauernflöte (1969); *Praeludium—Choralspiel—Postludium* (1971–78); *Ranken* (1978); *Rückläufige Passacaglia* (1979); *Schnurrpfeifereien* (1979).

BIBLIOGRAPHY: Ursula Stürzbecher, *Komponisten in der DDR: 17 Gespräche* (Hildesheim, 1979).

Medinš, Jānis, foremost Latvian composer; b. Riga, Oct. 9, 1890; d. Stockholm, March 4, 1966. He graduated from the First Riga Musical Inst. in 1909; was violist and conductor of the Latvian Opera in 1913–15; In 1914–16 he was head of the piano dept. of the firm of A. Diederichs in St. Petersburg; in 1916–20, was military bandmaster there. In 1920 he returned to Riga; conducted opera at the Latvian National Theater (1920–28); was chief conductor of the Latvian Radio Symph. Orch. (1928–44); in 1929–44 was also a prof. at the Riga Cons. In 1944, as the Soviet armies approached Latvia, Medinš went to Germany, and in 1948 went to Stockholm. He wrote the operas *Uguns un nakts* (*Fire and Night;* Riga, May 26, 1921) and *Deevi un cilveki* (Riga, May 23, 1922); symph. and chamber music; choruses.

Medtner, Nicolai, notable Russian composer; b. (of German parents) Moscow, Jan. 5, 1880; d. London, Nov. 13, 1951. He first studied with his uncle, Theodore Goedicke; in 1892 entered Moscow Cons., where he took courses with Sapelnikov and Safonov (piano), and with Taneyev (composition); he graduated in 1900, winning the gold medal; in the same year he won the Rubinstein prize in Vienna; for the next 2 years he appeared with much success as a pianist in the European capitals; returning to Russia, he taught at the Moscow Cons. for one academic year (1902–3); was again prof. there from 1918 till 1921, when he left Russia; he lived in Berlin and Paris; eventually settled in London; made U.S. tours in 1924–25 and in 1929–30. In Russian music he was a solitary figure; he never followed the nationalist trend, but endeavored to create a new type of composition, rooted both in the Classical and the Romantic tradition; his sets of fairy tales in sonata form are unique examples of his favorite genre. He wrote his best compositions before he left Russia; although he continued to compose during his residence abroad, his late music lacks the verve and Romantic sincerity that distinguish his earlier works. He wrote almost exclusively for the piano and for the voice. A revival of his music was begun in Russia after his death.

WORKS: 3 piano concertos: No. 1 (1916–18); No. 2 (Moscow, March 13, 1927); No. 3 (London, Feb. 19, 1944, composer soloist); Piano Quintet (1950). For Piano: *3 Mood Pictures* (1902); *3 Improvisations* (1902); *3 Arabesques* (1905); 34 *Fairy Tales* (1905–29); *3 Dithyrambs* (1906); *Sonata-Triad* (1907); *3 Novels* (1909); *4 Sonatas* (1909–14); *Fairy-tale Sonata* (1912); *Sonata-Ballade* (1913); *Sonata romantica* (1930); *Sonata minacciosa* (1931); *Sonata idillica* (1935); *4 Lyric Fragments* (1912); 3 sets of *Forgotten Melodies* (1919–20); 4 sets of *Romantic Sketches* (1933); *2 Elegies* (1945). Vocal works: 104 songs;

Sonata-Vocalise, for Voice and Piano, without words (1921); *Suite-Vocalise* (1923). Chamber music: 2 violin sonatas; various pieces for Violin and Piano. A collection of Medtner's literary essays was publ. in an Eng. trans. by Alfred Swan, as *The Muse and the Fashion* (Haverford, Pa., 1951).

BIBLIOGRAPHY: E. Newman, "N. Medtner," *Musical Times* (Jan. 1915); V. Yakovlev, *N. Medtner,* in Russian and German (Moscow, 1927); A. Swan, "Medtner and the Music of Our Time," *Music & Letters* (Jan. 1927); R. Holt, *Medtner and His Music* (London, 1948); idem, ed., *N. Medtner,* a symposium (London, 1956); B. Dolinskaya, *Nicolai Medtner* (Moscow, 1966). His collected works were publ. in 12 vols. in Moscow (1959–63).

Meerens, Charles, Belgian acoustician; b. Bruges, Dec. 26, 1831; d. Schaerbeek, near Brussels, Jan. 14, 1909. He studied cello under Bessems, Dumont, and Servais; then became a tuner in his father's piano factory, and devoted himself to acoustical research.

WRITINGS: *Le Métromètre, ou Moyen simple de connaître le degré de vitesse d'un mouvement indiqué* (1859); *Instruction élémentaire de calcul musical* (1864); *Phénomènes musico-physiologiques* (1868); *Hommage à la mémoire de M. Delezenne* (1869); *Examen analytique des expériences d'acoustique musicale de M.A. Cornu et E. Mercadier* (1869); *Le Diapason et la notation musicale simplifiées* (1873); *Mémoire sur le diapason* (1877); *Petite méthode pour apprendre la musique et le piano* (1878); *La Gamme musicale majeure et mineure* (1890); *Acoustique musicale* (1892); *L'Avenir de la science musicale* (1894); *La Science musicale à la portée de tous les artistes et amateurs* (1902).

Meerts, Lambert (-Joseph), Belgian violinist and pedagogue; b. Brussels, Jan. 6, 1800; d. there, May 12, 1863. He studied with Lafont and Habeneck at Paris; from 1835, was prof. at the Brussels Cons. Among his important instructive works for violin are *Etudes pour violon avec accompagnement d'un second violon; Mécanisme du violon* (advanced studies); 12 books of studies on rhythm, on motifs by Beethoven; etc.

Mees, Arthur, American conductor; b. Columbus, Ohio, Feb. 13, 1850; d. New York, April 26, 1923. He was a pupil, in Berlin, of Kullak (piano), Weitzmann (theory), and Dorn (conducting); from 1880 to 1886, he conducted the Cincinnati May Festival Chorus; from 1888 to 1911, was conductor of the Orange Mendelssohn Union; in 1891–1913, was conductor of the Albany Musical Assoc.; from 1913, was also conductor of the Bridgeport Oratorio Society; from 1896, was assistant conductor of the Chicago Symph. Orch.; wrote analytical program notes for it, and also for the N.Y. Phil. Society (1887–96). He publ. *Choirs and Choral Music* (1901); also composed piano studies.

Meester, Louis de, Belgian composer; b. Roeselare, Oct. 28, 1904. He traveled widely in his youth as a popular musician; lived in Algeria (1928–30);

was a teacher at the Cons. in Meknes, French Morocco (1932–37); returned to Belgium in 1938 and studied briefly with Jean Absil; served as acoustical director at the Belgian Radio (1945–61). From 1961 to 1969 he was director of the Inst. for Psychoacoustics and Electronic Music at Ghent Univ.

WORKS: 3 operas: *La Grande Tentation de Saint Antoine*, opera buffa (1957; Antwerp, Nov. 11, 1961); *2 is te weinig, 3 is te veel* (*2 Is Too Little, 3 Is Too Much*, 1966; Palermo, June 13, 1969); *Paradijsgeuzen* (*Beggars in Heaven*, 1966; Ghent, March 26, 1967); *Van een trotse vogel*, musical comedy for Narrator and Small Orch. (1948); *Magreb* for Viola and Orch. (1946); *Capriccio* for Orch. (1948); *Sprookjesmuziek* for Orch. (1949); 2 works serving as introductions for children to instruments of the orch.: *Betje Trompet* for Narrator and Small Orch. (1949) and *Betje Trompet en de Reus* (*Betje Trumpet and the Giant*) for 2 Narrators and Orch. (1965); *Sinfonietta Buffa* (1950); 2 piano concertos (1952, 1956); *La Voix du silence*, cantata for Baritone, Narrators, Female Chorus, and Chamber Orch. (1951–54); *Musica per archi* (1955); *Amalgames* for Orch. (1956); *Marine* for Orch. (1957); Concertino for 2 String Orchs. (1965); *Serenade* for Flute, Oboe, and Strings (1967); Cello Sonatina (1945); *Divertimento* for Wind Quintet (1946); 3 string quartets (1947, 1949, 1954); String Trio (1951); *Tafelmuziek* for Flute, Oboe, Violin, Viola, and Cello (1953); Sonata for Solo Guitar (1954); Violin Sonata (1957); *Serenade* for Harpsichord and 11 Strings (1958–59); *Postludium* for Organ and Brass (1959); *Divertimento* for Piano Quartet (1970); Piano Sonata (1946); *3 Nocturnes* for Piano (1947); *Variations* for 2 Pianos (1947); *Petite Suite* for Piano (1953); *Petites Variations* for Piano (1954); *Mimes* for Piano (1958); Piano Sonatina (1964); 9 electronic pieces; choruses; film music.

Meeuwisse, Willy, Dutch pianist and composer; b. Arnhem, Dec. 18, 1914; d. Amsterdam, Aug. 6, 1952. He was a student of Sem Dresden in Amsterdam; his *Suite of Old Dutch Dances* for Piano Solo enjoyed a certain popularity. He also was active as a concert pianist.

Méfano, Paul, French composer; b. Basra, Iraq, March 6, 1937. He studied at the Paris Cons. with Dandelot, Messiaen, Martenot, and Milhaud; attended seminars of Boulez, Stockhausen and Pousseur in Basel. He received a grant from the Harkness Foundation for residence in the U.S. (1966–68) and in Berlin (1968–69). In his music he pursues a constructivist style, with an emphasis on rhythmic percussion and electronic sound; the influences of Stravinsky and Varèse are particularly in evidence. WORKS: *Incidences* for Orch. and Piano (1960); *Paraboles* for Soprano and Chamber Ensemble (Paris, Jan. 20, 1965); *Interférences* for a Chamber Group (1966); *Lignes* for Bass Voice, Brass, Percussion, Bassoon, and Amplified Double Bass (1968); *Aurélia* for 3 Choruses, 3 Orchs., and 3 Conductors (1968); *La Cérémonie* for Voices, Instrumental Groups, and Speaking Choruses (1970); *Intersec-*

tion, electronic piece for 2 Generators and Ring Modulator (1971).

Mehegan, John, American jazz pianist and theorist; b. Hartford, Conn., June 6, 1916; d. New Canaan, Conn., April 3, 1984. He was self-taught as a pianist; took some courses at the Julius Hartt School of Music in Hartford. In 1941 he went to N.Y., where he became a nightclub pianist. Taking up jazz as a legitimate musical form, he taught jazz at the Juilliard School of Music from 1947 until 1964; also was a lecturer in jazz improvisation at the Yale School of Music. He wrote a number of articles on the technique of jazz-piano playing. His magnum opus was a 4-vol. edition, *Jazz Improvisation.* He appeared with Billie Holiday, Charles Mingus, and Lionel Hampton as pianist. He died of a brain tumor; when it became clear his condition was terminal, his colleagues and admirers arranged for him a pre-memorial concert on March 23, 1984, at Symphony Space, a jazz emporium in Westport, Conn., with Dave Brubeck and other jazz notables lending their talents to the occasion.

Mehrkens, Friedrich Adolf, German conductor and teacher; b. Neuenkirchen, near Ottendorf-on-Elbe, April 22, 1840; d. Hamburg, May 31, 1899. He studied at the Leipzig Cons. (1861–62), then settled in Hamburg as a pianist, teacher, and conductor of singing societies. He was conductor of the Bach-Gesellschaft from 1871. He wrote a Symph., a Te Deum, and chamber music.

Mehta, Mehli, Indian violinist and conductor, father of **Zubin Mehta;** b. Bombay, Sept. 25, 1908. He studied violin in Bombay and at Trinity College in London, obtaining his licentiate there in 1929. In 1935 he founded the Bombay Symph. Orch.; in 1942 organized the Bombay String Quartet. He was assistant concertmaster of the Hallé Orch. in Manchester from 1955 to 1959; then settled in the U.S. In 1964 he became conductor of the orch. of the Univ. of Calif., Los Angeles, which he brought up to a high degree of excellence.

Mehta, Zubin, exuberant, effulgent, and eloquent Indian conductor; b. Bombay, April 29, 1936. The family belonged to the historic tribe of Parsi nobles, the fire-worshiping followers of Zarathustra who fled en masse from the turbulence of Persia 13 centuries before Zubin Mehta's birth. He was tutored in music by his father, Mehli Mehta, who played violin in a hotel and also conducted a local orch.; he learned to play violin and piano; when he was 16 he successfully conducted a rehearsal of the Bombay Symph. Orch. Before deciding on a musical career, he took a course in medicine at St. Xavier College in Bombay; but he turned away from the unesthetic training in dissection, and instead went to Vienna, where he practiced to play the double bass at the Vienna Academy of Music and took conducting lessons with Hans Swarowsky. During the summers of 1956 and 1957 he attended conducting classes at the Accademia Chigiana in Siena with Carlo Zecchi and Alceo Galliera. In 1957 he graduated from the Vienna Academy of Music, and made his professional debut conducting the Tonkünstler Orch. in the Musikverein. In 1958 he married the Canadian singer **Carmen Lasky;** they had 2 children, but were divorced in 1964; she married Zubin Mehta's brother Zarin in 1966, thus making Zubin an uncle by marriage of his own children. On July 20, 1969, he married the actress Nancy Kovack in a dual ceremony, Methodist and Zoroastrian. In the meantime his career progressed by great strides; he won the competition of the Royal Liverpool Phil. in 1958, and conducted it for a season as an assistant; later he obtained guest engagements in Austria and Yugoslavia. When Eugene Ormandy needed a surrogate conductor on a date with the Vienna Phil. he was unable to fill in, Mehta became a successful substitute. In 1959 he competed in a conducting test in Tanglewood, and won 2nd prize. In 1960 he received a bona fide engagement to conduct the Vienna Symph. Orch. In July 1960 he made his formal American conducting debut at Lewisohn Stadium; later in 1960 he conducted 2 concerts of the Montreal Symph. and produced such a fine impression that he was appointed its music director. In 1962 Mehta took the Montreal Symph. to Russia, where he gave 8 concerts; then conducted 2 concerts with it in Paris and one in Vienna, where he took 14 bows in response to a vociferous ovation. In the meantime he received a contract to conduct the Los Angeles Phil., thus becoming the holder of 2 major conducting jobs, in Montreal and Los Angeles, a feat he was able to accomplish by commuting on newfangled jet airplanes; he was also the youngest conductor to function in this dual capacity. His career was now assuming the allure of a gallop, aided by his ability, rare among conductors, to maintain his self-control under trying circumstances. He has the reputation of a bon vivant; his joy of life is limitless. Professionally, he maintains an almost infallible reliability; he conducts all of his scores, even the most mindboggling modern productions, and operas as well, from memory. He is also a polyglot; not only is he eloquent in English and Hindi, but he is fluent in German, French, and Spanish; he even speaks understandable Russian. He made his debut at the Metropolitan Opera in N.Y. on Dec. 29, 1965, conducting *Aida.* His performances of *Carmen* and *Turandot* were highly praised. In 1967 he resigned his post in Montreal; in 1968 he was named music adviser of the Israel Phil.; in 1977 he became its music director. In 1978 he left the Los Angeles Phil. after he received an offer he could not refuse, the musical directorship of the N.Y. Phil.; in 1980 he toured with it in Europe. His association with the Israel Phil. was particularly affectionate; he conducted it during the Six-Day War and at the 25th anniversary of Israel's independence; in 1974 he was given an honorary Ph.D. by Tel Aviv Univ. No Jew could be more Israeli than the Parsi Mehta. *Time* glorified him with a cover story in its issue of Jan. 19, 1968.

BIBLIOGRAPHY: David Ewen, *Musicians since 1900* (N.Y., 1978); M. Bookspan and R. Yockey, *Zubin: The Zubin Mehta Story* (N.Y., 1978); P. Hart, *Conductors: A New Generation* (N.Y., 1979; pp. 127–

63).

Méhul, Etienne-Nicholas, famous French composer; b. Givet, Ardennes, June 22, 1763; d. Paris, Oct. 18, 1817. His father apprenticed him to the old blind organist of the Couvent des Récollets in Givet; he then went to Lavaldieu, where he studied with the German organist Wilhelm Hansen, director of music at the monastery there. In 1778 he went to Paris, where he continued his musical studies with the composer Jean-Frédéric Edelmann. His first opera to receive a performance was *Euphrosine, ou Le Tyran corrigé* (Théâtre Favart, Paris, Sept. 4, 1790); another opera, *Alonso et Cora* (later known as *Cora*), was staged at the Paris Opéra on Feb. 15, 1791. His next opera, *Adrien,* was in rehearsal by the end of 1791, but the revolutionary turmoil prevented a performance; it finally received its premiere at the Paris Opéra on June 4, 1799. His opera *Stratonice* was given at the Théâtre Favart in Paris on May 3, 1792, and was highly successful. Then followed his opera *Le Jeune Sage et le vieux fou,* which was performed at the same theater on March 28, 1793. In 1793 Méhul became a member of the Institut National de Musique, which had been organized by the National Convention under the revolutionary regime. He composed a number of patriotic works during these turbulent years of French history, including the popular *Chant du départ* (first perf. publicly on July 4, 1794). He also continued to compose for the theater, shrewdly selecting subjects for his operas allegorically suitable to the times. In 1794 he was awarded an annual pension of 1,000 francs by the Comédie-Italienne. In 1795 he became one of the 5 inspectors of the newly established Cons., and was also elected to the Institut. He became a member of the Légion d'Honneur in 1804. Between 1795 and 1807 Méhul composed 18 operas, some of which were written in collaboration with other composers. His greatest opera from this period is the biblical *Joseph* (Opéra-Comique, Feb. 17, 1807); its success in Paris led to performances in Germany, Austria, Hungary, Russia, the Netherlands, Belgium, Switzerland, England, Italy, and America. Also noteworthy is his *Chant national du 14 juillet 1800,* an extensive work calling for 2 choirs with an additional group of high voices and orchestral forces. Apart from operas, he composed several symphs. In spite of his poor health, he nevertheless continued to teach classes at the Paris Cons.; among his students was the opera composer Hérold. Méhul's last opera was *La Journée aux aventures,* which was given at the Opéra-Comique on Nov. 16, 1816. Although Méhul's operas practically disappeared from the active repertoire, his contribution to the operatic art remains of considerable historical importance. Beethoven, Weber, and Mendelssohn were cognizant of some of his symph. works.

WORKS: OPERAS: *Euphrosine, ou Le Tyran corrigé* (Théâtre Favart, Paris, Sept. 4, 1790; revised as *Euphrosine et Coradin*); *Alonso et Cora* (Paris Opéra, Feb. 15, 1791; later known as *Cora*); *Stratonice* (Théâtre Favart, Paris, May 3, 1792); *Le Jeune*

Sage et le vieux fou (Théâtre Favart, Paris, March 28, 1793); *Horatius Coclès* (Paris Opéra, Feb. 18, 1794); *Le Congrès des rois* (Théâtre Favart, Paris, Feb. 26, 1794; in collaboration with 11 other composers); *Mélidore et Phrosine* (Théâtre Favart, Paris, May 6, 1794); *Doria, ou La Tyrannie détruite* (Théâtre Favart, Paris, March 12, 1795); *La Caverne* (Théâtre Favart, Paris, Dec. 5, 1795); *La Jeunesse d'Henri IV* (Théâtre Favart, Paris, May 1, 1797; later known as *Le Jeune Henri*); *La Prise du pont de Lodi* (Feydeau, Paris, Dec. 15, 1797); *Adrien, empéreur de Rome* (Paris Opéra, June 4, 1799, later known as *Adrien*); *Ariodant* (Théâtre Favart, Paris, Oct. 11, 1799); *Épicure* (Théâtre Favart, Paris, March 14, 1800; in collaboration with Cherubini); *Bion* (Théâtre Favart, Paris, Dec. 27, 1800); *L'Irato, ou L'Emporté* (Opéra-Comique, Paris, Feb. 17, 1801); *Une folie* (Opéra-Comique, Paris, April 5, 1802); *Le Trésor supposé, ou Le Danger d'écouter aux portes* (Opéra-Comique, Paris, July 29, 1802); *Joanna* (Opéra-Comique, Paris, Nov. 23, 1802); *Héléna* (Opéra-Comique, Paris, March 1, 1803); *Le Baiser et la quittance, ou Une Aventure de garnison* (Opéra-Comique, Paris, June 18, 1803; in collaboration with Boieldieu, R. Kreutzer, and Nicolo); *L'Heureux malgré lui* (Opéra-Comique, Paris, Dec. 29, 1803); *Les 2 Aveugles de Tolède* (Opéra-Comique, Paris, Jan. 28, 1806); *Uthal* (Opéra-Comique, Paris, May 17, 1806); *Gabrielle d'Estrées, ou Les Amours d'Henri IV* (Opéra-Comique, Paris, June 25, 1806); *Joseph* (Opéra-Comique, Paris, Feb. 17, 1807); *Amphion, ou Les Amazones* (Paris Opéra, Dec. 17, 1811; later known as *Les Amazones, ou La Fondation de Thèbes*); *Le Prince troubadour* (Opéra-Comique, Paris, May 24, 1813); *L'Oriflamme* (Paris Opéra, Feb. 1, 1814; overture by Méhul; remainder in collaboration with H.-M. Berton, R. Kreutzer, and Paer); *La Journée aux aventures* (Opéra-Comique, Paris, Nov. 16, 1816); *Valentine de Milan* (Opéra-Comique, Paris, Nov. 28, 1822); the opera *Lausus* and the opera-ballet *L'Amour et Psyché* are considered doubtful works in the Méhul canon. BALLETS: *Le Jugement de Paris* (Paris Opéra, March 5, 1793; with music by Gluck, Haydn, and others); *La Dansomanie* (Paris Opéra, June 14, 1800; with music by Mozart and others); *Daphnis et Pandrose* (Paris Opéra, Jan. 14, 1803; with music by Gluck, Haydn, and others); *Persée et Andromède* (Paris Opéra, June 8, 1810; with music by Haydn, Paer, and Steibelt). He also composed several pieces of incidental music, many choral works (including the *Chant national du 14 juillet 1800*), numerous songs and patriotic works, etc. FOR ORCH.: Several symphs. including those numbered by Méhul as No. 1 in G minor (1809), No. 2 in D major (1809), No. 3 in C major (1809), and No. 4 in E major (1810). He also composed 2 books of keyboard sonatas: *3 sonates,* book 1 (1783), and *3 sonates,* book 2 (1788); in addition, a chamber music work entitled *Ouverture burlesque,* for Piano, Violin, 3 Mirlitons, Trumpet, and Percussion. BIBLIOGRAPHY: A. Quatremère de Quincy, *Funérailles de M. Méhul, Institut Royal de France* (Paris, 1817); idem, "Notice historique sur la vie et les œuvres de M. Méhul," *Institut Royal de France: Séance publique de l'Académie Royale des Beaux-*Arts du 2 octobre 1819 (Paris, 1819); F.-J. Fétis, "Biographie: Méhul (Etienne Henri)," *Revue Musicale,* VII (1830); P. Vieillard, *Méhul, Sa vie et ses œuvres* (Paris, 1859); J.-B. Weckerlin, "Les Quatre Versions de la romance de Joseph, opéra de Méhul," *Revue et Gazette Musicale de Paris,* XLII (1875); A. Pougin, *Méhul: Sa vie, son génie, son caractère* (Paris, 1889; 2nd ed., 1893); H. Parent de Curzon, "Méhul, Sa vie et son œuvre," *Musiciens du temps passé* (Paris, 1893); C. Pierre, *Musique des fêtes et cérémonies de la Révolution française* (Paris, 1899); C. Jourday, "A propos du Chant national du 14 juillet," *Revue d'Histoire et de Critique Musicales,* I (1901); C. Pierre, *Les Hymnes et chansons de la Révolution* (Paris, 1904); R. Brancour, *Méhul* (Paris, 1912); H. Strobel, "Die Opern von E.N. Méhul," *Zeitschrift für Musikwissenschaft,* VI (1923–24); C. Barzel, "Notes et documents de musique: La Jeunesse et le roman de Méhul," *Mercure de France* (Sept. 15, 1932); P.-M. Masson, "L'Œuvre dramatique de Méhul," *Annales de l'Université de Paris,* XII (Paris, 1937); H. Gougelot, *La Romance française sous la Révolution et l'Empire* (Melun, 1937–43; includes many songs of Méhul); B. Schwartz, *French Instrumental Music between the Revolutions (1789 to 1830)* (Diss., Columbia Univ., 1950); A. Ringer, "A French Symphonist at the Time of Beethoven: Etienne Nicolas Méhul," *Musical Quarterly* (Oct. 1951); W. Dean, "Opera under the French Revolution," *Proceedings of the Royal Musical Association,* XCIV (1967–68); W. Dudley, *Orchestration in the Musique d'harmonie of the French Revolution* (Diss., Univ. of Calif., Berkeley, 1968); D. Charlton, *Orchestration and Orchestral Practice in Paris, 1789–1810* (Diss., Cambridge Univ., 1973); idem, "Motive and Motif: Méhul before 1791," *Music & Letters,* LVII (1976).

Meibom (or **Meibomius, Meiboom, Meybom**), **Marcus,** erudite scholar; b. Tönning, Schleswig, c.1620; d. Utrecht, Feb. 15, 1710. He was for some years prof. at the Univ. of Uppsala; in 1674 visited England; lived thereafter principally in Utrecht. His chief work is *Antiquae musicae auctores septem, graece et latine, Marcus Meibomius restituit ac notis explicavit* (Amsterdam, 1652; 2 vols.); it contains treatises on music by Aristoxenos, Euclid (*Introductio harmonica*), Nicomachos, Gaudentius Philosophos, Bacchius Senior, Aristides Quintilianus, and M. Capella (Book IX of the *Satyricon*); until the publication of the new ed. of those authors by Karl Jan, Meibom's work was the only accessible source of information.

Meier, Johanna, American soprano; b. Chicago, Feb. 13, 1938. She was a scholarship student at the Manhattan School of Music in N.Y. She made her debut with the N.Y. City Opera in 1969 as the Countess in Strauss's *Capriccio;* during the next 10 years she sang the roles of the Marschallin, Tosca, Senta, Rosalinda, etc., with the N.Y. City Opera. In 1979 she made her Metropolitan Opera debut in N.Y. as Ariadne, and subsequently appeared there as the Marschallin, Senta, and Marguerite; also sang with the opera companies of Chicago, Cincinnati, Pittsburgh, Seattle, and Baltimore. In Europe, she had guest engagements in opera in Zürich, Vienna, Hamburg, and Berlin; made her Bayreuth debut as Isolde in 1981.

Meiland, Jakob, German composer; b. Senftenberg, Lausitz, 1542; d. Hechingen, Dec. 31, 1577. He was a choirboy in the Dresden Hofkapelle; in 1558 he enrolled at the Univ. of Leipzig; in 1563 joined the Kantorei of the Protestant Margrave Georg Friedrich of Brandenburg-Ansbach; in 1564 became its director; in 1565 founded its Hofkapelle and served as its first director. He moved to Frankfurt in 1572 and to Celle in 1576. In 1577 he became Kapellmeister to Count Eitel Friedrich von Hohenzollern of Hechingen, but died that same year.
WORKS: *Cantiones sacrae cum harmonicis numeris, a* 5, 6 (Nuremberg, 1564; 4th ed., 1573); *Selectae cantiones, a* 5, 6 (1572); *Cantiones aliquot novae . . . quibus adiuncta sunt officia due, a* 5 (Frankfurt, 1575); *Sacrae aliquot cantiones latinae et germanicae . . . sequentes duas cantiones in honorem domini Sigismundi Feyerabend et Hieronymi eius filii, a* 4, 5 (Frankfurt, 1575); *Harmoniae sacrae selectae ac compositiones divinae, a* 5 (Erfurt, 1588); *Cygneae cantiones latinae et germanicae, a* 4, 5 (Wittenberg, 1590); 3 Passions; Mass; secular songs; etc.
BIBLIOGRAPHY: R. Oppel, *Jakob Meiland (1542–1577)* (Diss., Munich, 1911).

Meinardus, Ludwig (Siegfried), German composer and writer; b. Hooksiel, Oldenburg, Sept. 17, 1827; d. Bielefeld, July 10, 1896. He was a pupil at the Leipzig Cons.; also studied in Berlin, in Weimar (with Liszt), and with Marx in Berlin. In 1853–65 he was conductor of the Singakademie at Glogau; then was a teacher at the Dresden Cons.; from 1874 till 1887 he lived in Hamburg as a composer and critic, then going to Bielefeld.
WRITINGS: *Kulturgeschichtliche Briefe über deutsche Tonkunst* (2nd ed., 1872); *Ein Jugendleben* (1874, 2 vols.; a sort of autobiography); *Rückblick auf die Anfänge der deutschen Oper* (1878); *Mattheson und seine Verdienste um die deutsche Tonkunst* (1879); *Mozart: Ein Künstlerleben* (1882); *Die deutsche Tonkunst im 18.–19. Jahrhundert* (1887); *Klassizität und Romantik in der deutschen Tonkunst* (1893); *Eigene Wege* (1895).

Meitus, Yuli, Ukrainian composer; b. Elizavetgrad, Jan. 28, 1903. He studied in Kharkov; from 1942 to 1946 he worked in Turkestan; then lived mostly in Kiev. Meitus is one of the most prolific opera composers in the Soviet Union; virtually all of his operas deal with subjects of the Russian Revolution and Civil War. They are: *Perekop* (Kiev, Jan. 20, 1939); *Gaidmaki* (Ashkhabad, Oct. 15, 1943); *Leili and Medzhun* (Ashkhabad, Nov. 2, 1946); *The Young Guard* (Kiev, Nov. 7, 1947; revised, Leningrad, Feb. 22, 1950); *Dawn over the Dvina* (Kiev, July 5, 1955); *Stolen Happiness* (Lwow, Sept. 10, 1960); *Makhtumkuli* (Ashkhabad, Dec. 29, 1962);

The Daughter of the Wind (Odessa, Oct. 24, 1965); *The Brothers Ulyanov* (Ufa, Nov. 25, 1967; revised and produced in Alma-Ata, 1970); *Yaroslav the Wise* (Donetsk, March 3, 1973); he also wrote a *Turkmenian Symphony* (1946) and 5 symph. suites on Ukrainian and other ethnic motifs.
BIBLIOGRAPHY: Y. Malyshev, *Yuli Meitus, Essays on His Work* (Moscow, 1962).

Melachrino, George Miltiades, English bandleader; b. London, May 1, 1909; d. there, June 18, 1965. He studied at the Trinity College of Music; formed his own band; then launched a new group, the Melachrino Strings, which he imbued with a sort of black-velvet coloration that made the "Melachrino sound" a byword among music lovers. He could play every instrument except harp and piano. His recording albums bore titles of irresistible sentimentality, e.g. *Music for Two People Alone, Music for a Nostalgic Traveler* (known in Europe under the name of *Reverie*), and *Music for Relaxation.*

Melani, Jacopo, Italian opera composer; b. Pistoia, July 6, 1623; d. there, Aug. 19, 1676. He was a member of an exceptionally gifted family of Italian musicians; his 7 brothers were singers and composers. He became organist of the Pistoia Cathedral in 1645, and maestro di cappella there in 1657. He specialized in comic operas, of which the following, performed in Florence, are the most important: *Il Podestà di Colognole* (Dec. 1656), *Ercole in Tebe* (July 8, 1661), and *Il Girello* (Jan. 20, 1670); regarding the last, see the discussion by R. Weaver, "*Il Girello,* a 17th-century Burlesque Opera," in *Quadrivium,* XII/2 (1971).

Melartin, Erkki Gustaf, Finnish composer; b. Käkisälmi (Kexholm), Feb. 7, 1875; d. Pukinmäki (near Helsinki), Feb. 14, 1937. He was a pupil of Wegelius at the Cons. in Helsinki and of Robert Fuchs in Vienna; taught theory at the Helsinki Cons. (1898; 1901–7); succeeded Wegelius as director in 1911, and remained at this post until 1936. His compositions are marked by a lyrical strain, with thematic materials often drawn from Finnish folk songs.
WORKS: Opera, *Aino* (1907; Helsinki, Dec. 10, 1909); 6 symphs. (1902; 1904; 1906–7; 1912; *Sinfonia brevis,* 1916; 1924–25); Violin Concerto (Helsinki, 1913); ballet, *Sininen helmi* (*The Blue Pearl*, 1930); numerous symph. suites and poems; incidental music for 10 plays; 2 commemorative cantatas; 4 string quartets; Piano Sonata; Violin Sonata; piano pieces; choruses; about 300 songs.
BIBLIOGRAPHY: K. Flodin, *Finska musiker* (Stockholm, 1900); E. Marvia, "Erkki Melartin," in *Suomen Säveltäjiä,* ed. by Sulho Ranta (Helsinki, 1945; pp. 342–59).

Melba, Dame Nellie (stage name of **Mrs. Helen Porter Armstrong,** née **Mitchell**), famous Australian coloratura soprano; b. Burnley, near Richmond, May 19, 1861; d. Sydney, Feb. 23, 1931. Her father, who had decided objections to anything connected with the stage, was nevertheless fond of music and proud of his daughter's talent. When she was only 6 years old he allowed her to sing at a concert in the Melbourne Town Hall, but would not consent to her having singing lessons; instead, she was taught piano, violin, and harp, and even had instruction in harmony and composition. As she grew older she frequently played the organ in a local church, and was known among her friends as an excellent pianist, while all the time her chief desire was to study singing. Not until after her marriage in 1882 to Captain Charles Armstrong was she able to gratify her ambition, when she began to study with a local teacher, Cecchi; her first public appearance as a singer was on May 17, 1884, in a benefit concert in Melbourne. The next year her father received a government appointment in London, and she accompanied him, determined to begin an operatic career. Her first concert in London (June 1, 1886) convinced her of the necessity of further study, and she went to Mme. Marchesi in Paris. Her debut as Gilda at the Théâtre de La Monnaie in Brussels (Oct. 13, 1887) created a veritable sensation; the famous impresario Sir Augustus Harris immediately engaged her for the spring season at Covent Garden, where she appeared on May 24, 1888, as Lucia, arousing great enthusiasim; a similar success attended her appearance in Paris, where she sang Ophelia in Ambroise Thomas's *Hamlet* (May 8, 1889); St. Petersburg (1891); Milan (La Scala, 1893; immense triumph over a carefully planned opposition); Stockholm and Copenhagen (Oct. 1893); N.Y. (Metropolitan Opera, as Lucia, Dec. 4, 1893); Melbourne (Sept. 27, 1902). From her first appearance at Covent Garden she sang there off and on until 1914; besides being one of the most brilliant stars of several seasons at the Metropolitan Opera, she also sang with Walter Damrosch's Opera Co. (1898) and at Hammerstein's Manhattan Opera (1906–7 and 1908–9), and made several transcontinental concert tours of the U.S. Bemberg wrote for her *Elaine,* (1892), and Saint-Saëns, *Hélène* (1904), in both of which she created the title roles. In 1915 she began teaching at the Albert Street Conservatorium in Melbourne; returned to Covent Garden for appearances in 1919, 1923, and a farewell performance on June 8, 1926. Then she returned to Australia and retired from the stage. Melba was by nature gifted with a voice of extraordinary beauty and bell-like purity; through her art she made this fine instrument perfectly even throughout its entire compass (*b*-flat–*f³*) and wonderfully flexible, so that she executed the most difficult *fioriture* without the least effort. As an actress she did not rise above the conventional, and for this reason she was at her best in parts demanding brilliant coloratura (Gilda, Lucia, Violetta, Rosina, Lakmé, etc.). On a single occasion she attempted the dramatic role of Brünnhilde in *Siegfried* (Metropolitan Opera, N.Y., Dec. 30, 1896), and met with disaster. In 1918 she was created a Dame of the British Empire. She was a typical representative of the golden era of opera; a prima donna *assoluta,* she exercised her powers over the public with perfect self-assurance and a fine command of her singing voice. As a measure of Melba's uni-

versal popularity, it may be mentioned that her name was attached to a delicious dessert (Peach Melba) consisting of half a cooked peach served with vanilla ice cream and a clear raspberry sauce (Melba sauce); and also to Melba toast, a crisp, thinly sliced toasted bread, patented in 1929 by Bert Weil (1890–1965), president of the Devonsheer Melba Corp. A motion picture based on her life was produced in 1953, with Patrice Munsel as Melba. She wrote an autobiography, *Melodies and Memories* (London, 1925).

BIBLIOGRAPHY: Agnes Murphy, *Melba, A Biography* (London, 1909; contains a chapter on singing written by Melba); P. Colson, *Melba, An Unconventional Biography* (London, 1931); J. Wechsberg, *Red Plush and Black Velvet: The Story of Melba and Her Times* (Boston, 1961); G.W. Hutton, *Melba* (Melbourne, 1962); J. Hetherington, *Melba* (London, 1967).

Melcer, Henryk, Polish pianist and composer; b. Kalisch, Sept. 21, 1869; d. Warsaw, April 18, 1928. He was a pupil of Moszkowski at the Warsaw Cons. and of Leschetizky in Vienna (1892–94). After successful concert tours of Russia, Germany, and France, he taught piano for a short time at the Cons. of Helsinki; then taught in Lwow and at the Vienna Cons. (1903–6); in 1908, became conductor of the Warsaw Phil. Society; from 1922 to 1927 was director of the Warsaw Cons.

WORKS: Operas: *Marja* (Warsaw, Nov. 16, 1904) and *Protasilas and Laodamia;* a choral ballad, *Pani Twardowska;* 2 piano concertos: No. 1 in E minor (won the Rubinstein prize, 1895) and No. 2 in C minor (won the Paderewski prize, 1898); Piano Trio; Violin Sonata; piano pieces; songs.

Melchers, Henrik Melcher, Swedish violinist and composer; b. Stockholm, May 30, 1882; d. there, April 9, 1961. He studied there at the Cons. and with J. Lindegren; later at the Paris Cons. He lived in Paris (1905–19), then in Brussels, and in Sondershausen. In 1925 he became a prof. at the Stockholm Cons.

WORKS: *Swedish Rhapsody* for Orch. (Stockholm, 1914), the symph. poems *Näcken* (1916), *La Kermesse* (1919), and others; *Poem* for Violin and Orch. (1922); songs.

Melchior, Lauritz, celebrated tenor; b. Copenhagen, March 20, 1890; d. Santa Monica, Calif., March 18, 1973. He studied with Paul Bang at the Royal Opera School, Copenhagen; in 1913, made his operatic debut in *Pagliacci* (as a baritone) at the Royal Opera, where he was engaged from 1914–21; studied at the same time with Wilhelm Herold, and in 1918 appeared as a tenor; in 1921–23, he studied with Beigel in London, then with Grenzebach in Berlin and Anna Bahr-Mildenburg in Munich; made his London debut at Covent Garden on May 14, 1924; he studied the Bayreuth traditions under Kittel, at the invitation of Cosima and Siegfried Wagner, and made his first appearance at the Festspielhaus there on July 23, 1924, as Siegfried; he sang at Bayreuth regularly till 1931, and acquired the reputation of being one of the finest Wagnerian tenors. He sang Tannhäuser at his first appearance with the Metropolitan Opera, N.Y. (Feb. 17, 1926); remained on its roster until 1950, the 1927–28 season excepted; then settled in California. He became an American citizen on June 13, 1947.

Melichar, Alois, Austrian music critic; b. Vienna, April 18, 1896; d. Munich, April 9, 1976. He studied theory at the Vienna Academy of Music with Joseph Marx (1917–20) and at the Hochschule für Musik in Berlin with Schreker (1920–23). In 1923–26 he was in the Caucasus, where he collected materials on Caucasian folk songs; then lived in Berlin and Vienna. In his compositions he follows the safe footpath of Reger, Pfitzner, and Graener; he wrote a symph. poem *Der Dom* (1934); *Rhapsodie über ein schwedisches Volkslied* (1939); *Lustspiel-Ouvertüre* (1942); lieder; film music. As a music critic, he acquired notoriety by his intemperate attacks on better composers than himself. His publications, written in his virulent, polemical manner, include *Die unteilbare Musik* (Vienna, 1952); *Musik in der Zwangsjacke* (Vienna, 1958), and (particularly vicious) *Schönberg und die Folgen* (Vienna, 1960).

Melik-Pashayev, Alexander, Soviet conductor; b. Tiflis Georgia, Oct. 23, 1905; d. Moscow, June 18, 1964. He received his primary music education at home; learned to play the piano; served as rehearsal pianist at the opera house in Tiflis; made his debut as conductor there in 1923. He then went to Leningrad, where he took a course in conducting with Gauck at the Leningrad Cons., graduating in 1930. In 1931 he was engaged as a member of the conducting staff of the Bolshoi Theater in Moscow, and served as its principal conductor from 1953 to 1962. For the excellence of his productions of Russian operas he received 2 consecutive Stalin Prizes (1942, 1943). He also conducted performances of the Bolshoi Theater abroad (London, 1961; Budapest, 1963).

Melikov, Arif, Soviet composer; b. Baku, Sept. 13, 1933. He studied with Kara Karayev at the Cons. of Baku; in 1965 he joined its faculty. His music hews to the tenets of socialist realism, representational and stylistically inoffensive to untutored ears.
WORKS: Ballet, *Legend of Love* (1961); *Ali-Baba and the 40 Thieves* (1973); cantata, *The Voice of the Earth* (1972); 3 symphs. (1958, 1959, 1973); symph. poem, *Fatherland* (1963); 3 suites for Native Instruments; choruses; songs; music for the theater.

Melis, Carmen, Italian dramatic soprano; b. Cagliari, Sardinia, Aug. 14, 1885; d. Longone al Segrino, Dec. 19, 1967. She studied with Teresina Singer and Carlo Carignani in Milan, and later with Jean de Reszke in Paris; made a successful debut at Naples in 1906; then sang in Rome, Milan, Venice, Cairo, Warsaw, and Odessa. She was engaged by Hammerstein for the Manhattan Opera, and made her American debut there as Tosca (N.Y., Nov. 26, 1909); subsequently was a member of the Boston Opera

Co. (1911–13). Later she became a teacher; Renata Tebaldi studied with her for 3 years.

Melkikh, Dmitri, Russian composer; b. Moscow, Feb. 11, 1885; d. there, Feb. 22, 1943. He studied at the People's Cons. in Moscow with Yavorsky, under whose influence he wrote music in archaic Russian modes; his few symph. works reveal traits of French Impressionism. Among his works are 3 symphs. (1925, 1933, 1938); 4 string quartets; a symph. poem, *Alladine et Palomides* (after Maeterlinck), and several song cycles.

Melkus, Eduard, Austrian violinist; b. Baden-bei-Wien, Sept. 1, 1928. He was educated at the Vienna Academy of Music and the Univ. of Vienna; also studied in Paris, Zürich, and Winterthur. He then played in several Swiss orchs. In 1965 he founded the Cappella Academica of Vienna, an ensemble devoted to performances of Baroque music on original instruments.

Mell, Gertrud Maria, Swedish organist and composer; b. Ed, Aug. 15, 1947. She studied at the Lund Cons.; subsequently was active as a radio lecturer. At the same time she studied navigation and received a certificate as a seawoman in 1971. During her sea travels she became convinced that music must be free from all restraints and follow only the dictates of one's creative spirit. She wrote 5 symphs. (1964, 1965, 1966, 1967, 1978); a String Quartet (1969); and some piano pieces.

Mellers, Wilfrid (Howard), English musicologist and composer; b. Leamington, April 26, 1914. He enrolled in Leamington College and at Cambridge Univ. (1933–38); studied composition with Wellesz and Rubbra; then taught at Dartington Hall (1938–40) and Downing College, Cambridge (1945–48); subsequently was on the faculty of the Univ. of Birmingham (1948–59) and served as Andrew W. Mellon Professor of Music at the Univ. of Pittsburgh (1960–63). In 1964 he was appointed to the music faculty of York Univ.
WRITINGS: *Music and Society: England and the European Tradition* (London, 1946); *Studies in Contemporary Music* (London, 1947); *François Couperin and the French Classical Tradition* (London, 1950); *Music in the Making* (London, 1952); *Romanticism and the 20th Century* (London, 1957); *The Sonata Principle* (London, 1957); *Music in a New Found Land: Themes and Developments in the History of American Music* (London, 1964); *Harmonious Meeting: A Study of the Relationship between English Music, Poetry and Theatre, c.1600–1900* (London, 1965); *Caliban Reborn: Renewal in Twentieth-Century Music* (N.Y., 1967); *Twilight of the Gods: The Music of the Beatles* (N.Y., 1973) *Bach and the Dance of God* (N.Y., 1980); *Beethoven and the Voice of God* (London, 1983).
WORKS: Operas: *The Tragical History of Christopher Marlowe* (1952); *The Ancient Wound* (Univ. of Victoria, British Columbia, July 27, 1970). Instrumental and vocal music: *Sinfonia ricercata* (1947);

Alba, in 9 Metamorphoses for Flute and Orch. (1961); *Noctambule and Sun-Dance* for Wind Instruments (1962); *Voices and Creatures* for Speaker, Flute, and Percussion (1962); *De Vegetalibus et Animalibus* for Soprano, Clarinet, Violin, Cello, and Harp (1971); *Venery for 6 Plus* for Dancing Singers and Instruments (1972); *The Gates of the Dream* for Soloists, Chorus, and Orch. (York, May 8, 1974).

Melles, Carl, Hungarian conductor; b. Budapest, July 15, 1926. He received his musical training in Budapest; in 1951 was appointed conductor of the Hungarian State Orch. and the Symph. Orch. of Hungarian Radio and Television; was also a prof. at the Budapest Academy of Music (1954–56). After the abortive rebellion in 1956, he led the Radio Orch. of Luxembourg (1958–60); also conducted at Bayreuth and Salzburg. He eventually made his home in Vienna and became a regular conductor of the Vienna Symph. and on the Austrian Radio.

Mellnäs, Arne, Swedish composer; b. Stockholm, Aug. 30, 1933. He studied with Larsson and Blomdahl at the Royal Academy of Music in Stockholm (1953–63), in Berlin with Blacher (1959), in Vienna with Ligeti (1961–62), and in Bilthoven with Koenig (1962–63), where Mellnäs specialized in electronic music. In 1964 he traveled to America and worked at the San Francisco Tape Music Center. From 1963 to 1972 he taught at the Stockholm Musikhögskolan.
WORKS: Oboe Sonata (1957); Concerto for Clarinet and Strings (1957); *Music* for Orch. (1959); *Chiasmos* for Orch. (1961); *Växlingar* for Flute, or Piccolo, and Clarinet (1961); *Collage* for Orch. (1962); *Per caso* for Saxophone, Trombone, Violin, Double Bass, and 2 Percussionists (1963); *Tombola* for Horn, Trombone, Electric Guitar, and Piano (1963); electronic pieces: *Cem/63* (1963), *Nite Music* (1964), *Intensity 6.5* (1966; dedicated to the memory of Edgar Varèse, containing electronically modified quotations from Varèse's works, particularly from *Density 21.5*), Conglomérat (1968), *Eufoni* (1969), *Monotrem* (1969), *Kaleidovision,* ballet for television (1969), *Appassionato* (1970), *Far Out* (1970), *Splinters* (1970), *Aura* for Orch. (Malmö, June 5, 1964); *Gestes sonores* for any ensemble (1964); *Sic transit* for Instruments and Tape (1964); *Succsim* for Chorus (1964); *Siamfoni* for Trumpet, Horn, and Trombone (1964); *Minibuff,* opera for 2 Singers and Tape (1966); *Drones* for Jazz Combo (1967); *Fixations* for Organ (1967); *Quasi niente* for one to 4 String Trios (1968); *Spots and Spaces,* after e.e. cummings, for Male Chorus, 11 Strings, and Winds (1968); *Aglepta* for Chorus (1969); *Capricorn Flakes* for Piano, Harpsichord, and Vibraphone (1970); *Cabrillo* for Clarinet, Trombone, Cello, and Percussion (1970); *Schizofoni* for One, 2, or 3 Pianos (1971); *Noël,* after e.e. cummings, for 2 Sopranos, Children's Chorus, and Instrumental Ensemble (1971); *Transparence* for Orch. (1972); *Vae* for Chorus and Organ (1972); *Ceremus* for Flute, Clarinet, Trumpet, Trombone, Double Bass, and Percussion (1973); *Sub luna* for Soprano, Flute, Violin, and Harp (1973);

Mara Mara Minne for Chorus and Tape (1973); *Fragile* for any kind and number of Instruments (1973); *Blow* for Wind Orch. (1974); a church opera, *Erik den helige (Erik the Holy;* Stockholm, May 18, 1976).

Melnikov, Ivan, Russian baritone; b. St. Petersburg, March 4, 1832; d. there, July 8, 1906. He was a choirboy in school; was engaged in trade, and for a time served as inspector of Volga boats; he began to study seriously late in life; took lessons with Lomakin (1862); then went to Italy, where he studied with Repetto. He made his debut in Bellini's *Puritani* (St. Petersburg, Oct. 6, 1867); created the title role in Mussorgsky's *Boris Godunov* (St. Petersburg, Feb. 8, 1874).

Melton, James, American tenor; b. Moultrie, Ga., Jan. 2, 1904; d. New York, April 21, 1961. He attended high school and college in Florida; later entered the Univ. of Georgia, where he played the saxophone in the college band. Subsequently, he went to Vanderbilt College, Nashville, Tenn., where he took lessons in singing with Gaetano de Luca. He obtained several lucrative engagements on the radio; made his concert debut in N.Y. on April 22, 1932; made his first opera appearance in Cincinnati on June 28, 1938. On Dec. 7, 1942, he appeared for the first time with the Metropolitan Opera in N.Y., remaining on its roster until 1950; also toured the U.S. as a concert singer.

Meltzer, Charles Henry, English journalist and translator; b. London, 1852; d. New York, Jan. 14, 1936. He studied music in London and Paris; was foreign correspondent for the *N.Y. Herald* and the *Chicago Tribune;* settled in N.Y. in 1888. He was an ardent proponent of opera in Eng., and trans. the librettos of *Die Walküre* and *Das Rheingold, Les Contes d'Hoffmann,* Monteverdi's *Orfeo,* etc.

Meluzzi, Salvatore, Italian composer of church music; b. Rome, July 22, 1813; d. there, April 17, 1897. He was maestro di cappella at the basilica of St. Peter's in the Vatican, and for 45 years was director of the Cappella Giulia. Thoroughly versed in the art of the old Italian masters, he emulated them in writing masses, Requiems, antiphons, motets, hymns, and Psalms; among his best pieces are a *Stabat Mater* and a *Miserere.*

Membrée, Edmond, French composer; b. Valenciennes, Nov. 14, 1820; d. Château Damont, near Paris, Sept. 10, 1882. He studied at the Paris Cons. with Alkan and Zimmerman (piano) and Carafa (composition).
WORKS: Operas: *François Villon* (Paris, April 20, 1857); *L'Esclave* (Paris, July 17, 1874); *Les Parias* (Paris, Nov. 13, 1876); *La Courte Echelle* (Paris, 1879); cantata, *Fingal* (Paris, May 14, 1861); ballads; songs; etc.
BIBLIOGRAPHY: L. Mention, *Un Compositeur valenciennois: Edmond Membrée* (Paris, 1908).

Menager, Laurent, Luxembourg composer; b. Luxembourg, Jan. 10, 1835; d. there, Feb. 7, 1902. He was a song composer and a respected pedagogue. A postage stamp was issued in his honor by the government of Luxembourg in 1951.

Menasce, Jacques de, Austrian pianist and composer; b. Bad Ischl, Austria, Aug. 19, 1905, of a French-Egyptian father and a German mother; d. Gstaad, Switzerland, Jan. 28, 1960. He studied in Vienna with Sauer (piano) and with J. Marx, Paul Pisk, and Alban Berg (composition). From 1932 until 1940 he gave concerts in Europe as a pianist; in 1941 he came to America, living mostly in N.Y., but continued his concert career in Europe.
WORKS: 2 piano concertos (1935, 1939); *5 Fingerprints* for Piano (1943); *Romantic Suite* for Piano (1950); *Divertimento* for Piano and String Orch. (1940); *Le Chemin d'écume* for Soprano and Orch. (Geneva, 1942); ballet, *Status Quo* (1947); Violin Sonata (1940); Viola Sonata (1955); songs, choruses.

Menchaca, Angel, Paraguayan music theorist; b. Asunción, March 1, 1855; d. Buenos Aires, May 8, 1924. He was trained as a jurist; also taught history and literature at the National College in Buenos Aires. In 1914 he publ. a provocative book, *Sistema teórico-gráfico de la música,* in which he proposed a new system of notation, employing a basic alphabet of 12 notes and dispensing with the established signatures, staff, etc. He toured Europe for the purpose of lecturing on this device; invented a special keyboard to facilitate its application. He was also a composer; his compositions include songs and school choruses.

Mendel, Arthur, eminent American music scholar; b. Boston, June 6, 1905; d. Newark, N.J., Oct. 14, 1979. He studied at Harvard Univ. (A.B., 1925); also took courses in theory with Nadia Boulanger in Paris (1925–27); returning to America, he was literary editor of G. Schirmer, Inc. (1930–38); also wrote music criticism in the *Nation* (1930–33); from 1936 to 1953 he conducted in N.Y. a chorus, The Cantata Singers, specializing in Baroque music; taught at the Dalcroze School of Music from 1938; was its president in 1947–50; also lectured at Columbia Univ. (1949) and the Univ. of Calif., Berkeley (1951); he was then prof. of music and chairman of the music dept. at Princeton Univ. (1952–67); held the Henry Putnam Univ. Professorship there from 1969 to 1973. He edited (with H.T. David) the valuable "documentary biography" *The Bach Reader* (N.Y., 1945; revised N.Y., 1966); edited Bach's *St. John Passion* (1951), Schütz's *Christmas Story* (1949) and *Musicalische Exequien* (1957), and other works of the Baroque period. He publ. numerous important articles on the history of pitch, reprinted in *Studies in the History of Musical Pitch* (Amsterdam, 1969) and also promoted the possibility of music analysis with the aid of a computer, publ. in *Computers and the Humanities* (1969–70). A Festschrift, *Studies in Renaissance and Baroque Music in Honor of Arthur Mendel,* ed. by R. Marshall, was publ. in Kassel in 1974.

Mendel, Hermann, German music lexicographer; b. Halle, Aug. 6, 1834; d. Berlin, Oct. 26, 1876. He was a pupil of Mendelssohn and Moscheles in Leipzig, and of Wieprecht in Berlin. In 1870 he founded and edited the *Deutsche Musiker-Zeitung,* also edited *Mode's Opernbibliothek* (about 90 librettos, with commentaries and biographies of composers) and a *Volksliederbuch.* He publ. 2 small books on Meyerbeer (1868, 1869). His great work was the *Musikalisches Conversations-Lexikon,* which he began to publ. in 1870, but was able to continue only to the letter M; the rest was completed by August Reissmann; the entire edition was in 11 vols.; a supplementary vol. was publ. in 1883.

Mendelsohn, Alfred, Rumanian composer; b. Bucharest, Feb. 17, 1910; d. there, May 9, 1966. He studied in Vienna with Joseph Marx, Franz Schmidt, Egon Wellesz and others (1927–31), and at the Bucharest Cons. with Jora (1931–32). From 1946 to 1954 he was conductor of the Rumanian Opera in Bucharest; in 1949 was prof. at the Bucharest Cons., remaining there until his death. An exceptionally prolific composer, he produced a great amount of highly competent, technically accomplished music. Influenced primarily by the programmatic Romanticism of the Vienna School, he also probed the potentialities of motivic structures, suggesting the serial concepts of modern constructivists while remaining faithful to basic tonalitarianism.
WORKS: Dramatic symph., with libretto, in 7 tableaus, *Imnul iubirii (The Love Hymn,* 1946); operas: *Meșterul Manole* (1949); *Michelangelo* (1964; Timisoara, Sept. 29, 1964); *Spinoza,* a lyrical scene (1966); operetta, *Anton Pann* (Bucharest, 1963); ballets: *Harap Alb (The White Moor,* 1948) and *Călin* (1956); oratorios and cantatas: *1917* (1956; on the Russian Revolution); *Inimă vitează* (1952); *Canata Bucureștiului* (1953); *Horia* (1955); *1907* (1957; deals with the 1907 peasant uprising in Rumania); *Glasul lui Lenin (The Voice of Lenin,* 1957); *Sub cerul de vară* (1959); *Pentru Marele Octombrie* (1960); *Cei puternici* (1965); *Suite Concertante* for Flute and String Orch. (1957); *Suite* for Chamber Orch. (1940); *Suită comemorativă* for String Orch. (1943); 9 symphs.: No. 1 (1944); No. 2, *Veritas* (1947); No. 3, *Reconstrucția* (1949); No. 4, *Apelul păcii* (1951); No. 5 (1953); No. 6 (1955); No. 7 (1960); No. 8 (1963); No. 9, *Concertante,* for Organ and Orch. (1964); symph. poems: *Prăbușirea Doftanei (Doftana's Assault,* 1949); *Eliberarea (Liberation,* 1954); *Va înflori acel Arminden (The May Tree Will Blossom,* 1959); *Schite dobrogene (Dobrudjan Sketches,* 1961); Chamber Symph. (1961); 2 piano concertos (1946, 1949); Cello Concerto (1949); 3 violin concertos (1953, 1957, 1964); Concertino for Harp and Strings (1955); *Divertimento* for Horn and Strings (1957); Concerto Grosso for String Quartet and Strings (1958); Concerto for Organ and Chamber Orch. (1960); Viola Concerto (1965); *Epitaph* for Orch. (1965); Concerto for Orch. (1965); Concerto for String Orch. (1965); 10 string quartets (1930–64);

Piano Quintet (1953); Harp Quintet (1955); String Sextet (1957); Piano Trio (1959); *Theme and Variations* for 7 Cellos (1963); Octet for 8 Cellos (1963); numerous sonatas for violin, viola, and cello; Piano Sonata (1947) and smaller pieces; song cycles.

Mendelssohn, Arnold, German composer; son of a cousin of **Felix Mendelssohn;** b. Ratibor, Dec. 26, 1855; d. Darmstadt, Feb. 19, 1933. He studied law at the Univ. of Tübingen; then entered the Hochschule für Musik in Berlin, where he studied with Löschhorn (piano), Haupt (organ), Grell, Kiel, and Taubert (composition). He was subsequently an instructor in Bielefeld (1883–85); a prof. at the Cologne Cons. (1885–90); then director of church music in Darmstadt. In 1912 he was appointed a prof. at the Hoch Cons. in Frankfurt; among his pupils there was Hindemith. He wrote 3 operas: *Elsi, die seltsame Magd* (Cologne, 1896), *Der Bärenhäuter* (Berlin, Feb. 9, 1900), and *Die Minneburg* (Mannheim, 1909); 2 cantatas: *Aus tiefer Not* and *Auf meinen lieben Gott;* a German Mass for 8-part Chorus a cappella; 3 symphs.; a Violin Concerto; 2 string quartets; a Cello Sonata; 2 piano sonatas; several sets of songs. He edited Schütz's oratorios and some of Monteverdi's madrigals. His book on esthetics, *Gott, Welt und Kunst,* was brought out by W. Ewald (Wiesbaden, 1949).

BIBLIOGRAPHY: E.O. Nodnagel, *Jenseits von Wagner und Liszt* (Königsberg, 1902); W. Nagel, *Arnold Mendelssohn* (Leipzig, 1906); H. Hering, *Arnold Mendelssohn: Die Grundlagen seines Schaffens und seiner Werke* (Regensburg, 1930).

Mendelssohn, Fanny. See **Hensel, Fanny Cäcilia.**

Mendelssohn, Felix (full name, **Jacob Ludwig Felix Mendelssohn-Bartholdy**), illustrious German composer; b. Hamburg, Feb. 3, 1809; d. Leipzig, Nov. 4, 1847. He was a grandson of the philosopher Moses Mendelssohn and the son of the banker Abraham Mendelssohn; his mother was Lea Salomon; the family was Jewish, but upon its settlement in Berlin the father decided to become a Protestant and added Bartholdy to his surname. Mendelssohn received his first piano lessons from his mother; subsequently studied piano with Ludwig Berger and violin with Carl Wilhelm Henning and Eduard Rietz; he also had regular lessons in foreign languages and in painting (he showed considerable talent in drawing with pastels); he also had piano lessons with Marie Bigot in Paris, where he went with his father for a brief stay in 1816. His most important teacher in his early youth was Carl Friedrich Zelter, who understood the magnitude of Mendelssohn's talent; in 1821 Zelter took him to Weimar and introduced him to Goethe, who took considerable interest in the boy Mendelssohn after hearing him play. Zelter arranged for Mendelssohn to become a member of the Singakademie in Berlin in 1819 as an alto singer; on Sept. 18, 1819, Mendelssohn's *19th Psalm* was performed by the Akademie. In 1825 Mendelssohn's father took him again to Paris to consult Cherubini on Mendelssohn's prospects in music; however, he re-

turned to Berlin, where he had better opportunities for development. Mendelssohn was not only a precocious musician, both in performing and in composition; what is perhaps without a parallel in music history is the extraordinary perfection of his works written during adolescence. He played in public for the first time at the age of 9, on Oct. 28, 1818, in Berlin, performing the piano part of a trio by Wölffl. He wrote a remarkable octet at the age of 16; at 17 he composed the overture for the incidental music to Shakespeare's *A Midsummer Night's Dream,* an extraordinary manifestation of his artistic maturity, showing a mastery of form equal to that of the remaining numbers of the work, which were composed 15 years later. Mendelssohn proved his great musicianship when he conducted Bach's *St. Matthew Passion* in the Berlin Singakademie on March 11, 1829, an event that gave an impulse to the revival of Bach's vocal music. In the spring of 1829 Mendelssohn made his first journey to England, where he conducted his Symph. in C minor (seated, after the fashion of the time, at the keyboard); later he performed in London the solo part in Beethoven's "Emperor" Concerto; he then traveled through Scotland, where he found inspiration for the composition of his overture *Fingal's Cave (Hebrides),* which he conducted for the first time during his 2nd visit to London, on May 14, 1832; 10 days later he played in London the solo part of his G minor Concerto and his *Capriccio brillante.* He became a favorite of the English public; Queen Victoria was one of his most fervent admirers; altogether he made 10 trips to England as a pianist, conductor, and composer. In 1830–32 he traveled in Germany, Austria, Italy, and Switzerland, and also went to Paris. In May 1833 he led the Lower-Rhine Music Festival in Düsseldorf; then conducted at Cologne in June 1835. He was still a very young man when, in 1835, he was offered the conductorship of the celebrated Gewandhaus Orch. in Leipzig; the Univ. of Leipzig bestowed upon him an honorary degree of Dr.Phil. Mendelssohn's leadership of the Gewandhaus Orch. was of the greatest significance for the development of German musical culture; he engaged the violin virtuoso Ferdinand David as concertmaster of the orch., which soon became the most prestigious symph. organization in Germany. On March 28, 1837, Mendelssohn married Cécile Charlotte Sophie Jeanrenaud of Frankfurt, the daughter of a French Protestant clergyman. Five children (Carl, Marie, Paul, Felix, and Elisabeth) were born to them, and their marriage was exceptionally happy. At the invitation of King Friedrich Wilhelm IV, Mendelssohn went in 1841 to Berlin to take charge of the music of the court and in the Cathedral; Mendelssohn received the title of Royal Generalmusikdirektor, but residence in Berlin was not required. Returning to Leipzig in 1842, Mendelssohn organized the famous "Conservatorium." Its splendid faculty comprised—besides Mendelssohn himself, who taught piano, ensemble playing, and later composition—Schumann, who taught classes in piano and composition; Hauptmann, in music theory; David, in violin; Becker, in organ; and Plaidy and Wenzel, in piano. The Conservatorium was officially opened on April 3, 1843. The financial nucleus of the foundation was a bequest from Blümner of 20,000 thaler, left at the disposal of the King of Saxony for the promotion of the fine arts, and Mendelssohn made a special journey to Dresden to petition the King on behalf of the Leipzig Cons. During Mendelssohn's frequent absences, the Gewandhaus Concerts were conducted by Hiller (1843–44) and Gade (1844–45). In the summer of 1844 Mendelssohn conducted the Phil. Concerts in London; this was his 8th visit to England; during his 9th visit he conducted the first performance of his oratorio *Elijah* in Birmingham, on Aug. 26, 1846. It was in England that the "Wedding March" from Mendelssohn's music to *A Midsummer Night's Dream* began to be used to accompany the bridal procession; it became particularly fashionable when it was played at the wedding of the Princess Royal in 1858. Mendelssohn made his 10th and last visit to England in the spring of 1847; this was a sad period of his life, for his favorite sister, Fanny, died on May 14, 1847. Mendelssohn's own health began to deteriorate, and he died in Leipzig at the age of 38. The exact cause of his early death is not determined; he suffered from severe migraines and chills before he died, but no evidence could be produced by the resident physicians for either a stroke or heart failure. A detailed account of Mendelssohn's illness and death is found in Dieter Kerner's *Krankheiten grosser Musiker* (Stuttgart, 1969; vol. 2, pp. 23–44). The news of Mendelssohn's death produced a profound shock in the world of music; not only in Germany and England, where he was personally known and beloved, but in distant America and Russia as well, there was genuine sorrow among musicians. Mendelssohn societies were formed all over the world; in America the Mendelssohn Quintette Club was founded in 1849. A Mendelssohn Scholarship was established in England in 1856; its first recipient was Arthur Sullivan.

Mendelssohn's influence on German, English, American, and Russian music was great and undiminishing through the years; his symphs., concertos, chamber music, piano pieces, and songs became perennial favorites in concerts and at home, the most popular works being the overture *Hebrides,* the ubiquitously played Violin Concerto, the *Songs without Words* for Piano, and the "Wedding March" from incidental music to *A Midsummer Night's Dream.* Professional music historians are apt to place Mendelssohn below the ranks of his great contemporaries, Schumann, Chopin, and Liszt; in this exalted company Mendelssohn is often regarded as a phenomenon of Biedermeier culture. A barbaric ruling was made by the Nazi regime to forbid performances of Mendelssohn's music as that of a Jew; his very name was removed from music history books and encyclopedias publ. in Germany during that time. This shameful episode was of but a transitory nature, however; if anything, it served to create a greater appreciation of Mendelssohn's genius.

WORKS: FOR THE STAGE: *Ich, J. Mendelssohn . . . ,* Lustspiel (1820); *Die Soldatenliebschaft,* comic opera (1820; Wittenberg, April 28, 1962); *Die beiden Pädagogen,* singspiel (1821; Berlin, May 27, 1962); *Die wandernden Komödianten,* comic opera (1822; dialogue not extant); *Der Onkel aus Boston oder Die beiden Neffen,* comic opera (1823; Berlin, Feb. 3, 1824; dialogue not extant); *Die Hochzeit des Camacho,* op. 10, opera (1825; Berlin, April 29, 1827; dialogue not extant); *Die Heimkehr aus der Fremde,* op. 89, Liederspiel (1829, written for the silver wedding anniversary of Mendelssohn's parents, perf. at their home, Berlin, Dec. 26, 1829); *Der standhafte,* incidental music to Calderón's play (1833); *Trala. A frischer Bua bin i* (1833); *Ruy Blas,* incidental music to Hugo's play (1839); *Antigone,* op. 55, incidental music to Sophocles' play (Potsdam, Oct. 28, 1841); *A Midsummer Night's Dream,* op. 61, incidental music to Shakespeare's play (1842; Potsdam, Oct. 14, 1843); *Oedipus at Colonos,* op. 93, incidental music to Sophocles' play (Potsdam, Nov. 1, 1845); *Athalie,* op. 74, incidental music to Racine's play (Berlin-Charlottenburg, Dec. 1, 1845); *Lorelei,* op. 98, opera (begun in childhood but unfinished; *Ave Maria,* a vintage chorus, and finale to Act I only; Birmingham, Sept. 8, 1852).

ORATORIOS: *St. Paul,* op. 36 (1834–36; Düsseldorf, May 22, 1836, composer conducting); *Elijah,* op. 70 (1846; Birmingham, Aug. 26, 1846, composer conducting); *Christus,* op. 97 (unfinished).

OTHER SACRED MUSIC: *Die Himmel erzählen* for 5 Voices (1820); *Gott, du bist unsre Zuversicht* for 5 Voices (1820); *Ich will den Herrn nach seiner Gerechtigkeit preisen* for 4 Voices (1820); *Tag für Tag sei Gott gepriesen* for 5 Voices (1820); *Das Gesetz des Herrn ist ohne Wandel* for 5 Voices (1821–22); *Er hat der Sonne eine Hütte gemacht* for 5 Voices (1821–22); *Jube Domine* for Solo Voices and Double Chorus (1822); *Psalm LXVI* for Double Female Chorus and Basso Continuo (1822); Magnificat in D major for Chorus and Orch. (1822); Kyrie in C minor for Solo Voices and Chorus (1823); *Jesus, meine Zuversicht* for Solo Voices and Chorus (1824); *Salve Regina* in E-flat major for Soprano and Strings (1824); 2 sacred pieces for Chorus: *Wie gross ist des Allmächt'gen Güte* (1824) and *Allein Gott in der Höh' sey Ehr* (1824); Te Deum in D major for Double Chorus and Basso Continuo (1826); *Jesu, meine Freude,* chorale cantata for Double Chorus and Strings; *Tu es Petrus* for Chorus and Orch., op. 111 (1827); *Ave Maria Stella* for Soprano and Orch. (1828); *Hora est* for 16 Voices and Organ (1828); 3 sacred pieces for Tenor, Chorus, and Organ, op. 23: *Aus tiefer Not, Ave Maria,* and *Mitten; Psalm CXV* for Solo Voices, Chorus, and Orch., op. 31 (1830); *Zum Feste der Dreieinigkeit (O beata et benedicta)* for 3 Sopranos and Organ (1830); 3 motets for Female Chorus and Organ, op. 39 (1830): *Hear my prayer, O Lord (Veni, Domine), O praise the Lord (Laudate pueri),* and *O Lord, thou hast searched me out (Surrexit Pastor); Verleih uns Frieden* for Chorus and Orch. (1831); Te Deum in A major for Solo Voices, Chorus, and Organ (1832); *Lord have mercy upon us* for Chorus (1833); 2 sacred choruses for Male Chorus, op. 115 (1833); *Responsorium et hymnus* for Male Voices, Cello, and Organ, op. 121 (1833); *Psalm XLII* for Solo Voices, Chorus, and Orch., op. 42 (1837); *Psalm XCV* for Tenor, Chorus, and Orch., op. 46 (1838); *Psalm V, Lord hear the voice* for Chorus (1839); *Psalm XXXI, Defend me, Lord* for Chorus (1839); *Hymn* in A major for Solo Voice, Chorus, and Orch., op. 96 (1840); *Psalm CXIV* for Double Chorus and Orch., op. 51 (1839); *Geistliches Lied* in E-flat major for Solo Voice, Chorus, and Organ (1840); *Psalm C, Jauchzet den Herrn* for Chorus (1842); *Herr Gott, dich loben wir* for Solo Voices, Chorus, Organ, and Orch. (1843); *Psalm XCVIII* for Double Chorus and Orch., op. 91 (1843); *Ehre sei dem Vater* for 8 Voices (1844); *Hear my prayer*, hymn for Soprano, Chorus, and Organ (1844); *Ehre sei dem Vater* in C major for 4 Voices (1845); *Er kommt aus dem kindlichen Alter der Welt* for 6 Voices (1846); *Lauda Sion* for Chorus and Orch., op. 73 (1846; Liège, June 11, 1846); *Die deutsche Liturgie* for 8 Voices (1846); *3 English Church Pieces* for Solo Voices and Chorus, op. 69 (1847): *Nunc dimittis, Jubilate,* and *Magnificat;* 3 Psalms for Solo Voices and Double Chorus, op. 78: *Psalm II* (1843), *Psalm XLIII* (1844), and *Psalm XXII* (1844); 6 *Anthems* for Double Chorus, op. 79: *Rejoice, O ye people; Thou, Lord, our refuge hast been* (1843); *Above all praises* (1846); *Lord, on our offences* (1844); *Let our hearts be joyful* (1846); *For our offences* (1844). Other works include: *Ach Gott vom Himmel sieh darein,* chorale cantata for Solo Voices, Chorus, and Orch.; *Cantique pour l'Eglise wallonne de Francfort (Venez chantez)* for 4 Voices; *Christe, du Lamm Gottes,* chorale cantata for Chorus and Orch.; *Gloria patri (Ehre sei dem Vater)* for 4 Voices; *Glory be to the Father* for 4 Voices; *Gloria* in E-flat major for Solo Voices, Chorus, and Orch. (unfinished); Kyrie for Chorus and Orch.; Kyrie in A major for 8 Voices; *Vom Himmel hoch,* chorale cantata for Solo Voices, Chorus, and Orch.; etc.

SECULAR CANTATAS: *In feierlichen Tönen,* wedding cantata for Soprano, Alto, Tenor, Chorus, and Piano (1820); *Grosse Festmusik zum Dürerfest* for Solo Voices, Chorus, and Orch. (Berlin, April 18, 1828); *Begrüssung (Humboldt Cantata),* festival music for Solo Male Voices, Male Chorus, and Wind (Berlin, Sept. 18, 1828); *Die erste Walpurgisnacht* for Chorus and Orch., op. 60 (1832; Berlin, Jan. 1833; revised 1843; Leipzig, Feb. 2, 1843); *Gott segne Sachsenland* for Male Voices and Wind (Dresden, June 7, 1843); *An die Künstler,* festival song for Male Voices and Brass, op. 68 (Cologne, June 1846).

CHORAL SONGS: *Einst ins Schlaraffenland zogen* for 4 Male Voices (1820); *Lieb und Hoffnung* for Male Voices (1820); *Jägerlied (Kein bess're Lust in dieser Zeit)* for 4 Male Voices (1822); *Lob des Weines (Seht, Freunde, die Gläser)* for Solo Male Voices and Male Chorus (1822); *Lass es heut am edlen Ort* for 4 Male Voices (1828); *Worauf kommt es überall an* for 4 Male Voices (1837); *Im Freien zu singen* for Mixed Voices, op. 41: 1, *Im Walde* (1838); 2, *Entflieh mit mir* (1838); 3, *Es fiel ein Reif* (1838); 4, *Auf ihrem Grab* (1834); 5, *Mailied* (1838); 6, *Auf dem See* (1838); *Der erste Frühlingstag* for Mixed Voices, op. 48 (1839): 1, *Frühlingsahnung;* 2, *Die Primel;* 3, *Frühlingsfeier;* 4, *Lerchengesang;* 5, *Morgengebet;* 6, *Herbstlied; Ersatz für Unbestand* for 4 Male Voices (1839); *Festgesang* for Male Voices (Leipzig,

June 25, 1840; No. 2 adapted by W.H. Cummings for *Hark! the Herald Angels Sing*); 6 male choruses, op. 50: 1, *Türkisches Schenkenlied* (1839–40); 2, *Der Jäger Abschied* (1840); 3, *Sommerlied* (1839–40); 4, *Wasserfahrt* (1839–40); 5, *Liebe und Wein* (1839); 6, *Wanderlied* (1842); *Nachtgesang* for 4 Male Voices (1842); *Die Stiftungsfeier* for 4 Male Voices (1842); *Im Grünen* for Mixed Voices, op. 59: 1, *Im Grünen* (1837); 2, *Frühzeitiger Frühling* (1843); 3, *Abschied vom Wald* (1843); 4, *Die Nachtigall* (1843); 5, *Ruhetal* (1843); 6, *Jagdlied* (1843); *Sahst du ihn herniederschweben,* funeral song for Mixed Voices, op. 116 (1845); *Der Sänger* (1845; Leipzig, Nov. 10, 1846); *Wandersmann* for Male Voices, op. 75: 1, *Der frohe Wandersmann* (1844); 2, *Abendständchen* (1839); 3, *Trinklied;* 4, *Abschiedstafel* (1844); 4 male choruses, op. 76: 1, *Das Lied vom braven Mann;* 2, *Rheinweinlied* (1844); 3, *Lied für die Deutschen in Lyon* (1846); 4, *Comitat;* 6 choruses for Mixed Voices, op. 88: 1, *Neujahrslied* (1844); 2, *Der Glückliche* (1843); 3, *Hirtenlied* (1839); 4, *Die Waldvögelein* (1843); 5, *Deutschland* (1839–43); 6, *Der wandernde Musikant* (1840); 4 choruses for Mixed Voices, op. 100: 1, *Andenken* (1844); 2, *Lob des Frühlings* (1843); 3, *Frühlingslied* (1843–44); 4, *Im Wald* (1839); 4 male choruses, op. 120: 1, *Jagdlied* (1837); 2, *Morgengruss des Thüringischen Sängerbundes* (1847); 3, *Im Süden;* 4, *Zigeunerlied; Lob der Trunkenheit (Trunken müssen wir alle sein)* for 4 Male Voices; *Musikantenprügelei (Seht doch diese Fiedlerbanden)* for 2 Male Voices.—Also concert arias: *Che vuoi mio cor?* for Mezzo-soprano and Strings, and *Infelice* for Soprano and Orch., op. 94 (1834; revised 1843).

SONGS: *Ave Maria* (1820); *Raste Krieger, Krieg ist aus* (1820); *Die Nachtigall (Da ging ich hin)* (1821–22); *Der Verlassene (Nacht ist um mich her)* (1821–22); *Von allen deinen zarten Gaben* (1822); *Wiegenlied (Schlummre sanft)* (1822); *Sanft weh'n im Hauch der Abendluft* (1822); *Der Wasserfall (Rieselt hernieder)* (1823); 12 songs, op. 8 (1828): 1, *Minnelied;* 2, *Das Heimweh* (by Fanny Mendelssohn); 3, *Italien* (by Fanny Mendelssohn); 4, *Erntelied;* 5, *Pilgerspruch;* 6, *Frühlingslied;* 7, *Maienlied;* 8, *Andres Maienlied (Hexenlied);* 9, *Abendlied;* 10, *Romanze;* 11, *Im Grünen;* 12, *Suleika und Hatem* (by Fanny Mendelssohn); *The Garland (Der Blumenkranz)* (1829); 12 songs, op. 9 (1829–30): 1, *Frage;* 2, *Geständnis;* 3, *Wartend;* 4, *Im Frühling;* 5, *Im Herbst;* 6, *Scheidend;* 7, *Sehnsucht* (by Fanny Mendelssohn); 8, *Frühlingsglaube;* 9, *Ferne;* 10, *Verlust* (by Fanny Mendelssohn); 11, *Entsagung;* 12, *Die Nonne* (by Fanny Mendelssohn); 4 songs (1830): 1, *Der Tag (Sanft entschwanden mir);* 2, *Reiterlied (Immer fort);* 3, *Abschied (Leb wohl mein Lieb);* 4, *Der Bettler (Ich danke Gott dir); Seemanns Scheidelied* (1831); *Weihnachtslied (Auf schicke dich recht feierlich)* (1832); 6 songs, op. 19a (1830–34): 1, *Frühlingslied;* 2, *Das erste Veilchen;* 3, *Winterlied;* 4, *Neue Liebe;* 5, *Gruss;* 6, *Reiselied; Mailied (Ich weiss mir'n Mädchen)* (1834); 2 romances: *There be none of beauty's daughters* (1833) and *Sun of the Sleepless* (1834); 2 songs: *Das Waldschloss* (1835) and *Pagenlied* (1835); 6 songs, op. 34 (1834–36): 1, *Minnelied;* 2, *Auf Flügeln des Gesanges;* 3, *Früh-*

lingslied; 4, *Suleika;* 5, *Sonntagslied;* 6, *Reiselied;*
Lied einer Freundin (Zarter Blumen leicht Ge-
winde) (1837); *Im Kahn* (1837); *O könnt ich zu dir*
fliegen (1838); 6 songs, op. 47 (1832–39): 1, *Min-*
nelied; 2, *Morgengruss;* 3, *Frühlingslied;* 4, *Volks-*
lied; 5, *Der Blumenstrauss;* 6, *Bei der Wiege;* 2
songs: *Todeslied der Bojaren* (1840) and *Ich hör ein*
Vöglein (1841); 6 songs, op. 57 (1839–43): 1, *Altdeut-*
sches Lied; 2, *Hirtenlied;* 3, *Suleika;* 4, *O Jugend;* 5,
Venetianisches Gondellied; 6, *Wanderlied;* 6 songs,
op. 71 (1842–47): 1, *Tröstung;* 2, *Frühlingslied;* 3, *An*
die Entfernte; 4, *Schilflied;* 5, *Auf der Wander-*
schaft; 6, *Nachtlied;* 3 songs, op. 84 (1831–39): 1, *Da*
lieg' ich unter den Bäumen; 2, *Herbstlied;* 3, *Jagd-*
lied; 6 songs, op. 86 (1831–51): 1, *Es lauschte des*
Laub; 2, *Morgenlied;* 3, *Die Liebende schreibt;* 4,
Allnächtlich im Traume; 5, *Der Mond;* 6, *Altdeut-*
sches Frühlingslied; 6 songs, op. 99: 1, *Erster Ver-*
lust; 2, *Die Sterne schau'n;* 3, *Lieblingsplätzchen;* 4,
Das Schifflein; 5, *Wenn sich zwei Herzen scheiden;*
6, *Es weiss und rät es doch keiner;* 2 sacred songs,
op. 112: *Doch der Herr, er leitet die Irrenden recht*
and *Der du die Menschen lässest sterben;* also *Des*
Mädchens Klage; Warnung vor dem Rhein; Der
Abendsegen (The Evening Service); Gretchen
(Meine Ruh ist hin); Lieben und Schweigen (Ich
flocht ein Kränzlein schöner Lieder); Es rauscht
der Wald; Vier trübe Monden sind entfloh'n; Wein-
end seh' ich in die Nacht; Weiter, rastlos atemlos
vorüber.—Vocal duets: *Ein Tag sagt es dem andern*
for Soprano and Alto (1821); 6 duets, op. 63 (1836–45):
1, *Ich wollt' meine Lieb';* 2, *Abschiedslied der Zug-*
vögel; 3, *Gruss;* 4, *Herbstlied;* 5, *Volkslied;* 6, *Mai-*
glöckchen und die Blümelein; 3 duets, op. 77 (1836–
47): 1, *Sonntagsmorgen;* 2, *Das Aehrenfeld;* 3, *Lied*
aus "Ruy Blas"; 3 folk songs: 1, *Wie kann ich froh*
und lustig sein; 2, *Abendlied;* 3, *Wasserfahrt;* also
various canons.

FOR ORCH.: 13 youthful sinfonias for Strings: No. 1,
in C major (1821); No. 2, in D major (1821); No. 3, in
E minor (1821); No. 4, in C minor (1821); No. 5, in
B-flat major (1821); No. 6, in E-flat major (1821); No.
7, in D minor (1821–22); No. 8, in D major (1822); No.
9, in C major (1823); No. 10, in B minor (1823); No.
11, in F major (1823); No. 12, in G minor (1823); No.
13, in C minor (1823; one movement only); symphs.:
No. 1, in C minor, op. 11 (1824); No. 2, in B-flat major,
a symph.-cantata for Solo Voices, Chorus, and
Orch., *Lobgesang* or *Hymn of Praise,* op. 52 (Leipzig,
June 25, 1840, composer conducting); No. 3, in A minor, *Scottish,* op. 56 (1830–42; Leipzig, March 3, 1842,
composer conducting); No. 4, in A major, *Italian,*
op. 90 (London, May 13, 1833, composer conducting);
No. 5, in D major, *Reformation,* op. 107 (1830–32;
Berlin, Nov. 15, 1832, composer conducting); Violin
Concerto in D minor for Strings (1822; Yehudi
Menuhin gave its first perf. from the MS, N.Y., Feb.
4, 1952); Piano Concerto in A minor for Strings
(1822); Concerto in D minor for Violin, Piano, and
Strings (1823); Concerto in E major for 2 Pianos and
Orch. (1823; Berlin, Nov. 14, 1824); Concerto in A-flat
major for 2 Pianos and Orch. (1824; Stettin, Feb. 20,
1827); Overture in C major for Wind Instruments,
op. 24 (1824); *Capriccio brillant* in B minor for
Piano and Orch., op. 22 (1825–26; London, May 25,

1832); Overture (*Trumpet* Overture) in C major, op.
101 (1826; revised 1833); *Ein Sommernachtstraum,*
overture for Shakespeare's *A Midsummer Night's*
Dream, op. 21 (1826; Stettin, April 29, 1827); *Meeres-*
stille und glückliche Fahrt (Calm Sea and Prosper-
ous Voyage), overture after Goethe, op. 27 (Berlin,
April 18, 1828); *Die Hebriden* or *Fingals Höhle (The*
Hebrides or *Fingal's Cave),* overture, op. 26 (1830;
London, May 14, 1832); Piano Concerto No. 1, in G
minor, op. 25 (Munich, Oct. 17, 1831, composer soloist); *Die schöne Melusine (The Fair Melusina),*
overture after Grillparzer, op. 32 (1833; London,
April 7, 1834); *Rondo brillant* in E-flat major for
Piano and Orch., op. 29 (1834); *Trauermarsch* in A
minor for Wind, op. 103 (1836); Piano Concerto No.
2, in D minor, op. 40 (Birmingham, Sept. 1837, composer soloist); *Serenade* and *Allegro giocoso,* in B
minor, for Piano and Orch., op. 43 (1838); *Ruy Blas,*
overture after Hugo, op. 95 (Leipzig, March 1839);
March in D major, op. 108 (1841); Violin Concerto in
E minor, op. 64 (1844; Leipzig, March 13, 1845; Ferdinand David, soloist; composer conducting).

CHAMBER MUSIC: Trio in C minor for Violin, Viola,
and Piano (1820); Presto in F major for Violin and
Piano (1820); Violin Sonata in F major (1820); 15
fugues for String Quartet (1821); Piano Quartet in D
minor (1822); Piano Quartet No. 1, in C minor, op. 1
(1822); String Quartet in E-flat major (1823); Piano
Quartet No. 2, in F minor, op. 2 (1823); Viola Sonata
in C minor (1824); Sextet in D major for Violin, 2
Violas, Cello, Double Bass, and Piano, op. 110 (1824);
Clarinet Sonata in E-flat major (1824); Piano Quar-
tet No. 3, in B minor, op. 3 (1825); Violin Sonata in
F minor, op. 4 (1825); Octet in E-flat major for 4
Violins, 2 Violas, and 2 Cellos, op. 20 (1825); Quintet
No. 1, in A major, for 2 Violins, 2 Violas, and Cello,
op. 18 (1826; revised 1832); String Quartet No. 2, in
A major, op. 13 (1827); Fugue in E-flat major for
String Quartet (1827); Fugue in E-flat major for
String Quartet, op. 81/4 (1827); *Variations concer-*
tantes for Cello and Piano, op. 17 (1829); String
Quartet No. 1, in E-flat major, op. 12 (1829); *The*
Evening Bell for Harp and Piano (1829); Concert
Piece in F major for Clarinet, Basset Horn, and
Piano or Orch., op. 113 (1833); Concert Piece in D
minor for Clarinet and Basset Horn, op. 114 (1833);
string quartets: Nos. 3–5, op. 44 (1837–38); Violin
Sonata in F major (1838); Cello Sonata No. 1, in
B-flat major, op. 45 (1838); Piano Trio No. 1, in D
minor, op. 49 (1839); *Capriccio* in E minor for String
Quartet, op. 81/3 (1843); Cello Sonata No. 2, in D
major, op. 58 (1843); Quintet No. 2, in B-flat major,
op. 87 (1845); Piano Trio No. 2, in C minor, op. 66
(1845); *Lied ohne Worte* in D major for Cello and
Piano, op. 109 (1845); String Quartet No. 6, in F minor, op. 80 (1847); *Andante* in E major for String
Quartet, op. 81/1 (1847); *Scherzo* in A minor for
String Quartet, op. 8½ (1847).

FOR PIANO: *Andante* in F major (1820); piano
piece in E minor (1820); 2 little pieces (1820); 2 little
pieces (1820); 5 little pieces (1820); *Largo-Allegro* in
C minor (1820); *Recitativo (Largo)* in D minor
(1820); Sonata in F minor (1820); Sonata in A minor
(1820); *Presto* in C minor (1820); Sonata in E minor
(1820); 2 studies (1820); *Allegro* in A minor (1821);

Study in C major (1821); Sonata in G minor, op. 105 (1821); *Largo-Allegro molto* in C minor/major (1821–22); 3 fugues: D minor, D minor, and B minor (1822); *Allegro* in D minor (1823); *Fantasia (Adagio)* in C minor (1823); *Rondo capriccioso* in E major, op. 14 (1824); *Capriccio* in F-sharp minor, op. 5 (1825); Fugue in C-sharp minor (1826); Sonata in E major, op. 6 (1826); *7 charakteristische Stücke*, op. 7 (1827); *Fantasia* in E major, on "The Last Rose of Summer," op. 15 (1827); Sonata in B-flat major, op. 106 (1827); Fugue in E minor (1827); *Scherzo* in B minor (1829); *3 fantaisies ou caprices*, op. 16 (1829); *Andante* in A major (1830); *Lieder ohne Worte (Songs without Words)*: 8 books, opp. 19 (1829–30), 30 (1833–34), 38 (1836–37), 53 (1839–41), 62 (1842–44), 67 (1843–45), 85 (1834–45), 102 (1842–45); *Fantasia (Sonate écossaise)* in F-sharp minor, op. 28 (1833); *3 Caprices*, op. 33 (1833–35); *Scherzo a capriccio* in F-sharp minor (1835–36); Study in F minor (1836); *Andante* in A-flat major (1836); *Lied* in F-sharp minor (1836); *Prelude* in F minor (1836); *3 Preludes*, op. 104a (1836); *6 Preludes* and *Fugues*, op. 35 (1832–37); *Gondellied (Barcarole)* in A major (1837); *Capriccio* in E major, op. 118 (1837); *Albumblatt (Lied ohne Worte)* in E minor, op. 117 (1837); *Andante cantabile* and *Presto agitato*, in B major (1838); 3 Studies, op. 104b (1834–38); *Prelude* and *Fugue* in E minor (1827–41); *Variations sérieuses* in D minor, op. 54 (1841); *Variations* in E-flat major, op. 82 (1841); *Variations* in B-flat major, op. 83 (1841); *Kinderstücke (Christmas Pieces)*, op. 72 (1842–47); *Perpetuum mobile* in C major, op. 119; etc.—For Piano Duet: *Lento-Vivace* in G minor (1820); *Fantasia* in D minor (1824); *Allegro brillant* in A major, op. 92 (1841); *Variations* in B-flat major, op. 83a (1841).—For 2 Pianos: *Duo concertant:* Variations on the march from Weber's *Preciosa* (1833; with Moscheles).—Also several works for organ, including 3 *Preludes* and *Fugues*, op. 37 (1837), and 6 sonatas, op. 65 (1844–45).

BIBLIOGRAPHY: COLLECTED EDITIONS, SOURCE MATERIAL: The first collected ed. of his works, *Felix Mendelssohn-Bartholdy: Werke: Kritisch durchgesehene Ausgabe,* was ed. by Julius Rietz and publ. by Breitkopf & Härtel (Leipzig, 1874–77); this ed. omits a number of works, however. A new ed. of the complete works, the *Leipziger Ausgabe der Werke Felix Mendelssohn-Bartholdys,* began publication in Leipzig in 1960 by the Internationale Felix-Mendelssohn-Gesellschaft. Breitkopf & Härtel publ. a *Thematisches Verzeichnis im Druck erschienener Compositionen von Felix Mendelssohn-Bartholody* (Leipzig, 1846; 2nd ed., 1853; 3rd ed., 1882). Other sources include the following: Y. Rokseth, "Manuscrits de M. à la Bibliothèque du Conservatoire," *Revue de Musicologie,* XV (1934); E. Walker, "An Oxford Collection of Mendelssohniana," *Music & Letters,* XIX (1938); M. Schneider, "Eine M.-Sammlung in Basel," *Der Amerbach Bote: Almanach* (Basel, 1947); E. Werner, "M. Sources," *Notes,* II (1954–55); *M.-Festwoche aus Anlass der 150. Wiederkehr des Geburtstages am 3. Februar 1959* (Leipzig, 1959); M. Schneider, *M.-Archiv der Staatsbibliothek Stiftung Preussischer Kulturbestiz* (Berlin, 1965); R. Elvers, *F. M.-B.: Dokumente seines Lebens: Ausstellung zum 125. Todestag* (Berlin, 1972); P. Krause, *Autographen, Erstausgaben und Frühdrucke der Werke von F. M.-B. in Leipziger Bibliotheken und Archiven* (Leipzig, 1972). BIOGRAPHICAL: W. Lampadius, *F. M.-B.: Ein Denkmal für seine Freunde* (Leipzig, 1848; Eng. trans., with additional articles by others, N.Y., 1865; 2nd greatly augmented German ed., as *F. M.-B.: Ein Gesammtbild seines Lebens und Wirkens,* Leipzig, 1886); L. Stierlin, *Biographie von F. M.-B.* (Zürich, 1849); J. Benedict, *A Sketch of the Life and Works of the Late F. M.-B.* (London, 1850; 2nd ed., 1853); W. Neumann, *F. M.-B.: Eine Biographie* (Kassel, 1854); A. Reissmann, *F. M.-B.: Sein Leben und seine Werke* (Berlin, 1867; 3rd ed., revised, 1893); H. Barbedette, *F. M.-B.: Sa vie et ses œuvres* (Paris, 1868); C. Mendelssohn-Bartholdy, *Goethe und F. M.-B.* (Leipzig, 1871; Eng. trans., London, 1872; 2nd ed., 1874); S. Hensel, *Die Familie M. 1729–1847, nach Briefen und Tagebüchern* (3 vols., Berlin, 1879; 18th ed., 1924; Eng. trans., 2 vols., London, 1881); J. Sittard, *F. M.-B.* (Leipzig, 1881); W. Rockstro, *M.* (London, 1884; revised ed., 1911); E. David, *Les M.-B. et Robert Schumann* (Paris, 1886); J. Eckardt, *Ferdinand David und die Familie M.-B.* (Leipzig, 1888); J. Hadden, *M.* (London, 1888; 2nd ed., 1904); S. Stratton, *M.* (London, 1901; 6th ed., 1934); V. Blackburn, *M.* (London, 1904); E. Wolff, *F. M.-B.* (Berlin, 1906; 2nd ed., revised, 1909); C. Bellaigue, *M.* (Paris, 1907; 4th ed., 1920); J. Hartog, *F. M.-B. en zijne werken* (Leyden, 1908); P. de Stoecklin, *M.* (Paris, 1908; 2nd ed., 1927); M. Jacobi, *F. M.-B.* (Bielefeld, 1915); W. Dahms, *M.* (Berlin, 1919; 9th ed., 1922); J. Esser, *F. M.-B. und die Rheinlande* (Diss., Univ. of Bonn, 1923); C. Winn, *M.* (London, 1927); J. Cooke, *F. M.-B.* (Philadelphia, 1929); E. Vuillermoz, *Une Heure de musique avec M.* (Paris, 1930); S. Kaufmann, *M.: A Second Elijah* (N.Y., 1934; 2nd ed., 1936); J. Petitpierre, *Le Mariage de M. 1837–1847* (Lausanne, 1937; Eng. trans. as *The Romance of the M.s,* London, 1947); B. Bartels, *M.-B.: Mensch und Werk* (Bremen, 1947); K. Wörner, *F. M.-B.: Leben und Werk* (Leipzig, 1947); M. Schneider, *M. im Bildnis* (Basel, 1953); P. Radcliffe, *M.* (London, 1954; 2nd ed., revised, 1967); R. Sterndale Bennett, "The Death of M.," *Music & Letters,* XXXVI (1955); E. Werner, "New Light on the Family of F. M.," *Hebrew Union College Annual,* XXVI (1955); H. Worbs, *F. M.-B.* (Leipzig, 1956; 2nd ed., 1957); idem, *F. M.-B.: Wesen und Wirken im Spiegel von Selbstzeugnissen und Berichten der Zeitgenossen* (Leipzig, 1958); H. Jacob, *F. M. und seine Zeit: Bildnis und Schicksal eines Meisters* (Frankfurt, 1959–60; Eng. trans., 1963); E. Werner, *M.: A New Image of the Composer and His Age* (N.Y., 1963); E. Rudolph, *Der junge F. M.: Ein Beitrag zur Musikgeschichte des Stadt Berlin* (Diss., Humboldt Univ., Berlin, 1964); K.-H. Köhler, *F. M.-B.* (Leipzig, 1966; 2nd ed., revised, 1972); H. Schonberg, *The Great Conductors* (N.Y., 1967; pp. 117–24); S. Grossmann-Vendrey, *F. M.-B. und die Musik der Vergangenheit* (Regensburg, 1969); M. Hurd, *M.* (London, 1970); W. Reich, *F. M. im Spiegel eigener Aussagen und zeitgenössischer Dokumente* (Zürich, 1970); H. Kupferberg, *The M.s: Three Generations of Genius* (N.Y., 1972); G. Marek, *Gentle Genius: The Story of F. M.* (N.Y.,

1972); P. Ranft, *F. M.-B.: Eine Lebens chronik* (Leipzig, 1972); Y. Tiénot, *M.: Musicien complet* (Paris, 1972); D. and M. Jenkins, *M. in Scotland* (London, 1978); M. Moshansky, *M.* (Tunbridge Wells, 1982).

CRITICAL, ANALYTICAL: F. Zander, *Über M.s Walpurgisnacht* (Königsberg, 1862); C. Seldon, *La Musique en Allemagne: M.* (Paris, 1867); F. Edwards, *The History of M.'s Oratorio "Elijah"* (London, 1896; 2nd ed., 1900); J. Hathaway, *An Analysis of M.'s Organ Works: A Study of Their Structural Features* (London, 1898); O. Mansfield, *Organ Parts of M.'s Oratorios and Other Choral Works Analytically Considered* (London, 1907); idem, "Some Characteristics and Peculiarities of M.'s Organ Sonatas," *Musical Quarterly* (July 1917); H. Waltershausen, *M.s Lieder ohne Worte* (Munich, 1920); J. Koffler, *Die orchestrale Koloristik in den symphonischen Werken von M.* (Diss., Univ. of Vienna, 1923); H. Mandt, *Die Entwicklung des Romantischen in der Instrumentalmusik F. M.-B.s* (Diss., Univ., of Cologne, 1927); G. Schünemann, "Die Bachpflege der Berliner Singakademie," *Bach-Jahrbuch 1928;* R. Werner, *F. M.-B. als Kirchenmusiker* (Frankfurt, 1930); C. Wilkinson, *How to Interpret M.'s "Songs without Words"* (London, 1930); T. Armstrong, *M.'s R 'Elijah'* (London, 1931); G. Kinsky, "Was M. Indebted to Weber?," *Musical Quarterly* (April 1933); G. Wilcke, *Tonalität und Modulation im Streichquartett M.s und Schumanns* (Leipzig, 1933); L. Hochdorf, *M.s "Lieder ohne Worte" und der "Lieder ohne Worte"-Stil in seinen übrigen Instrumentalwerken* (Diss., Univ. of Vienna, 1938); J. Horton, *The Chamber Music of M.* (London, 1946); L. and H. Tischler, "M.'s Songs without Words," *Musical Quarterly* (Jan. 1948); P. Young, *Introduction to the Music of M.* (London, 1949); D. Mintz, "Melusine: A M. Draft," *Musical Quarterly* (Oct. 1957); idem, *The Sketches and Drafts of Three of M.'s Major Works (Elijah,* Symph. No. 4, and D minor Trio; Diss., Cornell Univ., 1960); S. Vendrey, *Die Orgelwerke von F. M.-B.* (Diss., Univ. of Vienna, 1964); J. Werner, *M.'s "Elijah": A Historical and Analytical Guide to the Oratorio* (London, 1965); G. Friedrich, *Die Fugenkomposition in M.s Instrumentalwerk* (Bonn, 1969); F. Krummacher, *M. der Komponist; Studien zur Kompositionsweise am Beispiel der Kammermusik für Streicher* (Habilitationschrift, Univ. of Erlangen, 1972); M. Thomas, *Das Instrumentalwerk F. M.-B.s: Eine systematisch-theoretische Untersuchung unter besonderer Berücksichtigung der zeitgenössischen Musiktheorie* (Kassel, 1972); C. Dahlhaus, ed., *Das Problem M.* (Rengensburg, 1974); R. Larry Todd, *M.'s Musical Education* (Cambridge, 1982).

CORRESPONDENCE: P. Mendelssohn-Bartholdy, *Reisebriefe ... aus den Jahren 1830–32* (Leipzig, 1861; 5th ed., 1882; Eng. trans. by Lady Wallace, as *Letters from Italy and Switzerland,* London, 1862); idem, *Briefe aus den Jahren 1833–47* (Leipzig, 1863; 8th ed., 1915; Eng. trans. by Lady Wallace, London, 1863); L. Nohl, *Musiker-briefe* (Leipzig, 1867); E. Polko, *Erinnerungen an F. M.-B.* (Leipzig, 1868; Eng. trans. by Lady Wallace, London, 1869); E. Devrient, *Meine Erinnerungen an F. M.-B. und seine Briefe an mich* (Leipzig, 1869; Eng. trans. by Lady Macfarren, London, 1869); *Acht Briefe und ein Faksimile* (Leipzig, 1871; Eng. trans. in *Macmillan's Magazine,* June 1871); F. Hiller, *F. M., Briefe und Erinnerungen* (Cologne, 1874; Eng. trans. by M.E. von Glehn, London, 1874); S. Hensel, *The M. Family, 1729–1847, from Letters and Journals* (2 vols., 1882; reprint, N.Y., 1969); F. Moscheles, *Brief von F. M. an Ignaz und Charlotte Moscheles* (Leipzig, 1888; Eng. trans. as *Letters of F. M.,* London, 1888); M. Friedlaender, "Briefe an Goethe," *Goethe-Jahrbuch* (1891); E. Wolff, *F. M.-B., Meisterbriefe* (Berlin, 1907; 2nd augmented ed., 1909); K. Klingemann, *F. M.-B.s Briefwechsel mit Legationsrat Karl Klingemann* (Essen, 1909); G. Selden-Goth, *M.'s Letters* (selections from the letters, trans. by Lady Wallace, with additional correspondence; N.Y., 1945); R. Sietz, ed., *F. M.-B.: Sein Leben in Briefen* (Cologne, 1948). A new collection of letters is being publ. by the Veröffentlichungen der Historischen Kommission zu Berlin: vol. 1, *Briefe an deutsche Verleger,* ed. by R. Elvers (Berlin, 1968); H.-J. Rothe and R. Szeskus, eds., *Briefe aus Leipziger Archiven* (Leipzig, 1972).

Mendelssohn, Felix Robert, German cellist, great-grandnephew of the famous composer; b. Berlin, Sept. 27, 1896; d. Baltimore, May 15, 1951. He studied at the Stern Cons.; later taught cello there. In 1936 he settled in the U.S.; taught in N.Y.; in 1941 joined the Baltimore Symph. Orch. He died in Cadoa Hall, Baltimore, while playing Dohnányi's *Konzertstück.*

Mendizábel, Rosendo Cayetano, Argentinian composer of popular music; b. Buenos Aires, April 21, 1868; d. there, June 30, 1913. He was a pianist at Laura Montserrat's fancy dancing bordello, improvising his music. His most popular tune was *El entrerriano* (1897).

Mendoza, Emilio, Venezuelan composer; b. Caracas, Aug. 8, 1953. He played guitar as a child; in his compositions he first followed conventional forms, but expanded his musical resources to include a lot of creative noise. His *Alborada* for Viola and Piano (1975) represents a dialogue between traditional and raucous sounds.

Mengal, Jean-Baptiste, Belgian horn virtuoso and composer; b. Ghent, Feb. 21, 1792; d. Paris, Dec. 19, 1878. He learned the rudiments of music from his father, who was an experienced horn player, and from his brother **Martin-Joseph Mengal,** whom he succeeded as first horn player at the Ghent municipal theater. In 1812 he entered the Paris Cons., graduating with first prize; then played in the orch. of the Grand Opéra. He wrote a number of works for his instrument: fantasies, duets, solos; also publ. a method of horn playing.

Mengal, Martin-Joseph, Belgian horn player and conductor; brother of **Jean-Baptiste Mengal;** b. Ghent, Jan. 27, 1784; d. there, July 4, 1851. He studied with his father; played in Paris orchs.; in 1825 was appointed director of the Ghent municipal theater; then was conductor at Antwerp; in 1835 became director of the Ghent Cons. He wrote a great number of sacred works; his MSS are preserved at the Ghent Cons.

Mengelberg, Karel, Dutch composer and conductor; nephew of **Willem Mengelberg;** b. Utrecht, July 18, 1902. He studied with Pijper and later took a course at the Hochschule für Musik in Berlin. He conducted theater orchs. in provincial German towns and was a musician with Berlin Radio (1930–33); subsequently was conductor of the municipal band in Barcelona (1933); then went to Kiev, Russia, where he was in charge of the music dept. in the Ukrainian film studio. He returned to Amsterdam in 1938.

WORKS: 2 ballets: *Bataille* (1922) and *Parfait Amour* (1945); *3 songs from Tagore's "The Gardener"* for Soprano and Orch. (1925); String Quartet (1938); Sonata for Solo Oboe (1939); Trio for Flute, Oboe, and Bassoon (1940); a short *Requiem* for Orch. (1946); *Divertimento* for Small Orch. (1948); Horn Concerto (1950); *Toccata* for Piano (1950); *Jan Hinnerik* for a cappella Chorus (1950); *Anion,* symph. sketch (1950); *Soliloquio* for Solo Flute (1951); *Ballade* for Flute, Clarinet, Harp, and String Quartet (1952); *Serenade* for String Orch. (1952); *Recitatief* for Baritone, Viola da Gamba, and Harpsichord (1953); *Suite* for Small Orch. (1954); *Roland Holst,* cantata for Chorus and Small Orch. (1955); *Soneria, Romanza e Mazurca* for Harp (1958). In 1961 he completed the revision, with a simplified orchestration, of Willem Pijper's 2nd Symph. (Pijper's own revised score was destroyed during a Nazi air raid on Rotterdam in May 1940).

Mengelberg, Kurt Rudolf, German-born musicologist and composer of Dutch descent, nephew of the conductor **Willem Mengelberg;** b. Krefeld, Feb. 1, 1892; d. Beausoleil, near Monte Carlo, Oct. 13, 1959. He studied piano with Neitzel in Cologne and musicology with Hugo Riemann at the Univ. of Leipzig, receiving his doctorate in 1915. He then went to Amsterdam, where he studied music theory with his uncle; in 1917, through his uncle's intervention, he became artistic assistant of the Concertgebouw Orch. in Amsterdam; then was artistic manager there in 1925–35, and finally director in 1935–54. Among his publications are the valuable program book *Das Mahler-Fest, Amsterdam Mai 1920* (Vienna, 1920); a biography of Mahler (Leipzig, 1923); *Nederland, spiegeleener beschaving (The Netherlands, Mirror of a Culture;* Amsterdam, 1929); a commemorative publication on the semi-centennial of the Concertgebouw (Amsterdam, 1938); *Muziek, spiegel des tijds (Music, Mirror of Time,* Amsterdam, 1948); and a biography of Willem Mengelberg. His own compositions are mainly liturgical; among them are *Missa pro pace* (1932); *Stabat Mater* (1940), and *Victimae Paschali laudes* (1946); he also wrote *Symphonic Variations* for Cello and Orch. (1927); Violin Concerto (1930); *Ca-*

priccio for Piano and Orch. (1936); Concertino for Flute and Chamber Orch. (1943); solo songs and piano pieces.

Mengelberg, Misha, Dutch composer, son of **Karel Mengelberg;** b. Kiev, June 5, 1935. He was born in Kiev while his father was working in the U.S.S.R.; came in 1938 to the Netherlands, where he studied with Kees van Baaren at the Royal Cons. in The Hague, graduating in 1964. He was a co-founder of the Instant Composers Pool in 1967; in 1972 became president of the Guild of Improvising Musicians, a jazz organization.

WORKS: *Musica* for 17 Instruments (1959); *Medusa* for String Quartet (1962); *Commentary* for Orch. (1965); *Exercise* for Solo Flute (1966); *Omtrent een componistenactie (Concerning a Composer's Action)* for Wind Quintet (1966); *3 Piano Pieces + Piano Piece 4* (1966); *Amaga* for 3 Different Guitars and Electronic Equipment (1968); *Anatoloose* for Orch. and Tape (1968; Holland Festival, July 8, 1971); *Hello Windy Boys* for Double Wind Quintet (1968); *Met welbeleefde groet van de kameel (With the Very Polite Greetings of the Camel)* for Orch. with Electronic Sawing and Excavating Drills (1971–73); *Onderweg (On the Way)* for Orch. (1973; Bergen, Norway, Jan. 13, 1974). He participated in creating an anti-imperialistic collective opera, *Reconstructie* (1968–69; Holland Festival, June 29, 1969; in collaboration with Louis Andriessen, Reinbert de Leeuw, Peter Schat, and Jan van Vlijmen).

Mengelberg, Willem, celebrated Dutch conductor; b. Utrecht, March 28, 1871; d. Chur, Switzerland, March 21, 1951. He studied at the Cons. of Utrecht, and later at the Cologne Cons. with Seiss, Jensen, and Wüllner. He was appointed municipal music director in Lucerne in 1891, and his work there attracted so much attention that in 1895 he was placed at the head of the famous Concertgebouw Orch. in Amsterdam, holding this post for 50 years (resigning in 1945), a record tenure for any conductor; during his directorship, he elevated that orch. to a lofty position in the world of music. In addition, he became conductor of the Toonkunst choral society in Amsterdam (1898); appeared frequently as guest conductor in all the European countries; in England was an annual visitor from 1913 until World War II; appeared with the N.Y. Phil. in 1905; in 1908 was appointed conductor in Frankfurt; left in 1921 and accepted an invitation to conduct the National Symph. Orch. in N.Y., which was absorbed at his suggestion by the Phil. Society Orch.; he led the N.Y. Phil. at various intervals from 1922 till 1930; in 1928 he received the degree of Mus.Doc. at Columbia Univ. (*honoris causa*); in 1933 was appointed prof. of music at Utrecht Univ. During the occupation of the Netherlands by the Germans, Mengelberg openly expressed his sympathies with the Nazi cause, and lost the high respect and admiration that his compatriots had felt for him; after the country's liberation he was barred from professional activities there, the ban to be continued until 1951, but he died in that year in exile in Switzerland. Mengelberg was one of the finest representatives of the Romantic tradition in symph. conducting; his interpretations extracted the full emotional power from the music, and yet he never transgressed the limits imposed by the structural forms of classical music; his renditions of Beethoven's symphs. were inspiring. He was a great admirer of Mahler and conducted a festival of Mahler's music in Amsterdam in May 1920; he was also a champion of works by Richard Strauss (who dedicated the score of *Ein Heldenleben* to him), Max Reger, and Debussy.

BIBLIOGRAPHY: Hugo Nolthenius, *Willem Mengelberg* (Amsterdam, 1920); Rudolf Mengelberg, *Das Mahlerfest in Amsterdam* (Amsterdam, 1920); A. Van den Boer, *De psychologische beteekenis van Willem Mengelberg als dirigent* (Amsterdam, 1925); Edna R. Sollitt, *Mengelberg and the Symphonic Epoch* (N.Y., 1930); Edna R. Sollitt, *Mengelberg spreckt* (speeches of Mengelberg; The Hague, 1935); W. Paap, *Willem Mengelberg* (Amsterdam, 1960).

Menges, Herbert, English conductor, brother of **Isolde Menges;** b. Hove, Aug. 27, 1902; d. London, Feb. 20, 1972. He played violin as a child; then took piano lessons with Mathilda Verne and attended courses in composition with Vaughan Williams at the Royal College of Music in London. He began his conducting career in Brighton, and conducted the Brighton Phil. Society (which was founded by his mother) from 1925 until his death. He was also a music director of the Old Vic Theatre (1931–50); in 1945 he became conductor of the Southern Phil. Orch. at Southsea. In 1963 he was made an Officer of the Order of the British Empire.

BIBLIOGRAPHY: Donald Brook, *International Gallery of Conductors* (Bristol, 1951; pp. 113–16).

Menges, Isolde, English violinist, sister of **Herbert Menges;** b. Hove, May 16, 1893; d. Richmond, Surrey, Jan. 13, 1976. Both her parents were violinists, and she studied at home; then went to St. Petersburg for lessons with Leopold Auer. She made her London debut on Feb. 4, 1913, and her N.Y. debut on Oct. 21, 1916. In 1931 she was appointed to the faculty of the Royal College of Music in London; also organized the Menges Quartet there.

Mengewein, Karl, German composer and teacher; b. Zaunroda, Thuringia, Sept. 9, 1852; d. Berlin, April 7, 1908. From 1876 until 1886 he was a teacher at Freudenberg's Cons., Wiesbaden, and with the latter founded a Cons. at Berlin in 1886, of which he was co-director till 1896. He founded the Oratorienverein (1895) and the next year the "Madrigal" for the production of a cappella music. He wrote an oratorio, *Johannes der Täufer* (1892); festival cantata, *Martin Luther;* operetta, *Schulmeisters Brautfahrt* (Wiesbaden, 1884); overture, *Dornröschen;* several singspiels; a Requiem; female choruses; etc. He also publ. *Die Ausbildung des musikalischen Gehörs* (1908).

Ménil, Félicien de, French musicologist; b. Boulogne-sur-Mer, July 16, 1860; d. Neuilly, near Paris, March 28, 1930. He studied with Henri Maréchal and Lenepveu at the Paris Cons.; undertook extensive travels in America, India, and Africa; returning to Paris, he was appointed prof. of history of music at the Ecole Niedermeyer (1899). His publications include: *Monsigny* (1893); *Josquin des Près* (1897); *L'Ecole flamande du XVᵉ siècle* (Paris, 1895; considerably augmented and publ. as *L'Ecole contrapuntique flamande au XVᵉ et au XVIᵉ siècle,* 1905); *Histoire de la danse à travers les âges* (1904). He was an ardent adherent of Esperanto, and wrote the hymn of the Esperantists (1928).

Mennicke, Karl, German writer on music; b. Reichenbach, May 12, 1880; killed in action during World War I in Galicia, late June 1917. He studied music with Hugo Riemann; received his Dr.Phil. in 1905 with the dissertation *Hasse und die Brüder Graun als Symphoniker* (with thematic catalogue).

Mennin, Peter, eminent American composer and educator; b. Erie, Pa., May 17, 1923; d. New York, June 17, 1983. His family stemmed from Italy; Mennin's real name was **Mennini;** his brother, **Louis Mennini,** also a composer, did not cut off the last letter of his name as Peter did. His early environment was infused with music, mostly from phonograph recordings; he studied piano with Tito Spampani. In 1940 he enrolled in the Oberlin Cons. in Ohio, where he took courses in harmony with Normand Lockwood. He quickly learned the basics of composition, and at the age of 18 wrote a symph. and a string quartet. In 1942 he enlisted in the U.S. Army Air Force; was discharged in 1943, and resumed his musical studies at the Eastman School of Music in Rochester, N.Y., where his teachers were Howard Hanson and Bernard Rogers. He worked productively; wrote another symph. in 1944; a movement from it, entitled *Symphonic Allegro,* was performed by the N.Y. Phil., Leonard Bernstein conducting, on March 27, 1945. His 3rd Symph. was performed by Walter Hendl with the N.Y. Phil. on Feb. 27, 1947. Mennin progressed academically as well; he obtained his Ph.D. from the Eastman School of Music in 1947. He received a Guggenheim fellowship grant in 1948; a 2nd Guggenheim grant followed in 1956. From 1947 to 1958 he taught composition at the Juilliard School of Music; in 1958 he assumed the post of director of the Peabody Cons. in Baltimore. In 1962 he received his most prestigious appointment, that of president of the Juilliard School of Music, serving in that capacity until his death. Despite his academic preoccupations, he never slackened the tempo of his activities as a composer; he diversified his symphs. by adding descriptive titles; thus his 4th Symph. was subtitled *The Cycle* and was scored for chorus and orch.; his 7th Symph. was called *Variations Symphony;* the 4 movements of his 8th Symph. bore biblical titles. Increasingly also, he began attaching descriptive titles to his other works; his Concertato for Orch. was surnamed *Moby Dick;* there followed a *Canto* *for Orchestra,* a *Sinfonia capricciosa,* a *Cantata de Virtute, Voices,* and *Reflections of Emily,* to texts by Emily Dickinson. It is remarkable that Mennin never wrote operas, ballets, or any other works for the stage; his musical mind was directed toward pure structural forms; his music is characterized by an integrity of purpose and teleological development of thematic materials, all this despite the bold infusion of dissonant sonorities in contrapuntal passages. Mennin held honorary doctorates from the Univ. of Chicago, the Univ. of Wisconsin, Temple Univ., and the Univ. of Heidelberg in Germany.

WORKS: 9 symphs.: No. 1 (1942); No. 2 (Rochester, March 27, 1945); No. 3 (N.Y., Feb. 27, 1947); No. 4, *The Cycle,* for Chorus and Orch. (N.Y., March 18, 1949); No. 5 (Dallas, April 2, 1950); No. 6 (Louisville, Ky., Nov. 18, 1953); No. 7, *Variations Symphony* (Cleveland, Jan. 23, 1964); No. 8, in 4 movements, titled *In Principio, Dies Irae, De Profundis, Laudate Dominum* (N.Y., Nov. 21, 1974); No. 9 (Washington, D.C., March 10, 1981); *Sinfonia* for Chamber Orch. (Rochester, May 24, 1947); *Fantasia* for String Orch. (N.Y., Jan. 11, 1948); *Folk Overture* (Washington, D.C., Dec. 19, 1945); Violin Concerto (1950); Concertato, *Moby Dick,* for Orch. (Erie, Pa., Oct. 20, 1952); Cello Concerto (Juilliard School, Leonard Rose, soloist, Feb. 19, 1956); Piano Concerto (Cleveland, Feb. 27, 1958); Concertino for Flute, Strings, and Percussion (1945); *Canto for Orchestra* (San Antonio, Texas, March 4, 1963); *Sinfonia capricciosa* (Washington, D.C., March 10, 1981); *Cantata de Virtute* for Tenor, Baritone, Narrator, Chorus, Children's Chorus, and Orch., originally planned as a setting of Robert Browning's poem *The Pied Piper of Hamelin* (Cincinnati, May 2, 1969); *Symphonic Movements* (Minneapolis, Jan. 21, 1971; later perf. under the title *Sinfonia*); *Voices* for Mezzo-soprano, Percussion, Piano, Harp, and Harpsichord, to texts from Thoreau, Melville, Whitman, and Emily Dickinson (N.Y., March 28, 1976); *Reflections of Emily* for Treble Voices, Piano, Harp, and Percussion, to texts from poems by Emily Dickinson (N.Y., Jan. 18, 1979); Flute Concerto (N.Y., May 5, 1983); 2 string quartets (1941, 1951); *Sonata concertante* for Violin and Piano (Washington, D.C., Oct. 19, 1956); Piano Sonata (1963).

BIBLIOGRAPHY: David Ewen, *American Composers* (N.Y., 1982).

Mennini, Louis, American composer; brother of **Peter Mennin** (whose real name was **Mennini**); b. Erie, Pa., Nov. 18, 1920. He studied at the Oberlin Cons. (1939–42); then served in the U.S. Army Air Force (1942–45); subsequently studied composition with Bernard Rogers and Howard Hanson at the Eastman School of Music, Rochester, N.Y. (B.M., 1947; M.M., 1948); was on its faculty from 1949 to 1965; then served as dean of the School of Music, North Carolina School of the Arts at Winston-Salem (1965–71); in 1973 was appointed chairman of the dept. of music of Mercyhurst College in Erie, Pa. His music is pragmatic and functional, with occasional modernistic touches.

WORKS: 2 chamber operas: *The Well* (Rochester, May 8, 1951) and *The Rope,* after Eugene O'Neill (Berkshire Music Festival, Aug. 8, 1955); *Overtura breve* (1949); 2 symphs.: No. 1, *Da chiesa* (1960); No. 2, *Da festa* (1963); String Quartet (1961); *Tenebrae* for Orch. (1963); Concerto Grosso for Orch. (1975); numerous pieces for violin and for piano.

Menotti, Gian Carlo, remarkable composer; b. Cadegliano, Italy, July 7, 1911; was the 6th of 10 children. He learned the rudiments of music from his mother, and began to compose as a child, making his first attempt at an opera, entitled *The Death of Pierrot,* at the age of 10. He studied for several years (1923–27) at the Milan Cons.; then came to the U.S., and entered the Curtis Inst. in Philadelphia (1927–33), where he studied with Rosario Scalero; subsequently taught composition at the Curtis Inst.; traveled often to Europe; made his home at Mt. Kisco, N.Y. Although Menotti has associated himself with the cause of American music, and spends most of his time in the U.S., he has retained his Italian citizenship. As a composer, he is unique on the American scene, being the first to create American opera possessing such an appeal to audiences as to become established in the permanent repertoire. Inheriting the natural Italian gift for operatic drama and an expressive singing line, he has adapted these qualities to the peculiar requirements of the American stage and to the changing fashions of the period; his serious operas have a strong dramatic content in the realistic style stemming from the Italian *verismo.* He writes his own librettos, marked by an extraordinary flair for drama and for the communicative power of the English language; with this is combined a fine, though subdued, sense of musical humor. Menotti makes no pretensions at extreme modernism, and does not fear to approximate the successful formulas developed by Verdi and Puccini; the influence of Mussorgsky's realistic prosody is also in evidence, particularly in recitative. When dramatic tension requires a greater impact, Menotti resorts to atonal and polytonal writing, leading to climaxes accompanied by massive dissonances. His first successful stage work was *Amelia Goes to the Ball,* an opera buffa in one act (originally to an Italian libretto by the composer, as *Amelia al ballo*), staged at the Academy of Music, Philadelphia, on April 1, 1937. This was followed by another comic opera, *The Old Maid and the Thief,* commissioned by the National Broadcasting Co., first performed on the radio, April 22, 1939, and on the stage, by the Philadelphia Opera Co., on Feb. 11, 1941. Menotti's next operatic work was *The Island God,* produced by the Metropolitan Opera, N.Y., on Feb. 20, 1942, with indifferent success; but with the production of *The Medium* (N.Y., May 8, 1946), Menotti established himself as the foremost composer-librettist of modern opera. The imaginative libretto, dealing with a fraudulent spiritualist who falls victim to her own practices when she imagines that ghostly voices are real, suited Menotti's musical talent to perfection; the opera had a long and successful run in N.Y., an unprecedented occurrence in the history of the American lyric theater.

A short humorous opera, *The Telephone*, was first produced by the N.Y. Ballet Society, Feb. 18, 1947, on the same bill with *The Medium;* these 2 contrasting works were subsequently staged all over the U.S. and in Europe, often on the same evening. Menotti then produced *The Consul* (N.Y., March 1, 1950), his best tragic work, describing the plight of political fugitives vainly trying to escape from an unnamed country but failing to obtain the necessary visa from the consul of an anonymous power; very ingeniously, the author does not include the title character in the cast, since the consul never appears on the stage but remains a shadowy presence. *The Consul* exceeded Menotti's previous operas in popular success; it had a long run in N.Y., and received the Pulitzer Prize. On Christmas Eve, 1951, the National Broadcasting Co. presented Menotti's television opera *Amahl and the Night Visitors,* a Christmas story of undeniable poetry and appeal; it became an annual television production every Christmas in subsequent years. His next opera was *The Saint of Bleecker Street,* set in a N.Y. locale (N.Y., Dec. 27, 1954); it won the Drama Critics' Circle Award for the best musical play of 1954, and the Pulitzer Prize for 1955. A madrigal ballet, *The Unicorn, the Gorgon and the Manticore,* commissioned by the Elizabeth Sprague Coolidge Foundation, was first presented at the Library of Congress, Washington, Oct. 21, 1956. His opera *Maria Golovin,* written expressly for the International Exposition at Brussels, was staged there on Aug. 20, 1958. In 1958 he organized the Festival of 2 Worlds in Spoleto, Italy, staging old and new works; in 1977 he inaugurated an American counterpart of the festival in Charleston, S.C. In many of the festival productions Menotti acted also as stage director. In the meantime he continued to compose; he produced in quick succession *Labyrinth,* a television opera to his own libretto (N.Y., March 3, 1963); *Death of the Bishop of Brindisi,* dramatic cantata with the text by the composer (Cincinnati, May 18, 1963); *Le Dernier Sauvage,* opera buffa, originally with an Italian libretto by Menotti, produced at the Opéra-Comique in Paris in a French trans. (Oct. 21, 1963; produced in Eng. at the Metropolitan Opera, N.Y., Jan. 23, 1964); *Martin's Lie,* chamber opera to Menotti's text (Bath, England, June 3, 1964); *Help, Help, the Globolinks!,* "an opera in one act for children and those who like children" to words by Menotti, with electronic effects (Hamburg, Dec. 19, 1968); *The Most Important Man,* opera to his own libretto (N.Y., March 12, 1971); *The Hero,* comic opera (Philadelphia, June 1, 1976); *The Egg,* a church opera to Menotti's own libretto (Washington Cathedral, June 17, 1976); *The Trial of the Gypsy* for Treble Voices and Piano (N.Y., May 24, 1978); *Miracles* for Boys' Choir (Fort Worth, Texas, April 22, 1979); *La loca,* opera to Menotti's own libretto dealing with a mad daughter of Ferdinand and Isabella (San Diego, June 3, 1979); *A Bride from Pluto,* opera (Washington, D.C., April 14, 1982). Among Menotti's non-operatic works are the ballets *Sebastian* (1944) and *Errand into the Maze* (N.Y., Feb. 2, 1947); Piano Concerto No. 1 (Boston, Nov. 2, 1945); *Apocalypse,* symph. poem (Pittsburgh, Oct. 19, 1951); Violin Con-

certo (Philadelphia, Dec. 5, 1952, Zimbalist soloist); *Triplo Concerto a Tre,* triple concerto in 3 movements (N.Y., Oct. 6, 1970); *Landscapes and Remembrances,* cantata to his own autobiographical words (Milwaukee, May 14, 1976); *First Symphony,* subtitled *The Halcyon* (Philadelphia, Aug. 4, 1976); Piano Concerto No. 2 (Miami, Fla., June 23, 1982); *Nocturne* for Soprano, String Quartet, and Harp (N.Y., Oct. 24, 1982); Double-bass Concerto (N.Y. Phil., Oct. 20, 1983, James VanDemark, soloist; Zubin Mehta conducting). He also wrote a number of *pièces d'occasion* such as *Trio for a House-Warming Party* for Piano, Cello, and Flute (1936); *Variations on a Theme by Schumann; Pastorale* for Piano and String Orch.; *Poemetti per Maria Rosa* (piano pieces for children); etc. Menotti is the author of the librettos for Samuel Barber's operas *Vanessa* (Metropolitan Opera, N.Y., Jan. 15, 1958) and *A Hand of Bridge* (1959), and wrote a play without music, *The Leper* (Tallahassee, Fla., April 22, 1970).

After many years in America, he bought an estate, Yester House, in Scotland, and made it his permanent abode in 1974 with his legally adopted son, Francis Phelan, who thenceforth bore his name.

BIBLIOGRAPHY: Robert Tricoire, *Gian Carlo Menotti, L'Homme et son œuvre* (Paris, 1966); John Gruen, *Menotti: A Biography* (N.Y., 1978).

Menter, Joseph, German cellist; b. Teisbach, Bavaria, Jan. 23, 1808; d. Munich, April 18, 1856. He began his career as a violinist; then studied cello with Moralt in Munich, and became a member of the orch. of the Bavarian Royal Opera (1833). His daughter, **Sophie Menter,** was a celebrated pianist.

Menter, Sophie, German pianist and teacher; daughter of **Joseph Menter;** b. Munich, July 29, 1846; d. there, Feb. 23, 1918. She studied piano with Niest in Munich and with Lebert in Stuttgart; made her professional debut in 1867 at the Gewandhaus Concerts in Leipzig, and later took lessons with Tausig and Liszt. In 1872 she married the cellist **David Popper** (divorced, 1886). From 1883 to 1887 she taught piano at the St. Petersburg Cons.; then lived mostly in the Tyrol. She composed a number of attractive pieces. Tchaikovsky orchestrated her work *Ungarische Zigeunerweisen* for piano and orch., and she played it under his direction in Odessa, on Feb. 4, 1893.

Menuhin, Hephzibah, American pianist; b. San Francisco, May 20, 1920; d. London, Jan. 1, 1981. Like her brother, **Yehudi Menuhin,** she appeared in public at a very early age. In her concert career she devoted herself exclusively to chamber music; played numerous sonata recitals with her brother.

Menuhin, Yehudi, celebrated American violinist; b. New York, April 22, 1916, of Russian-Jewish parents (the family surname was originally Mnuhin). As a child, he was taken to San Francisco, where he began to study violin with Sigmund Anker; in 1923 he began taking lessons with Louis Persinger, who was then concertmaster of the San Francisco

Symph. Orch. On Feb. 29, 1924, he made his public debut in Oakland playing Bériot's *Scène de ballet* with Persinger as accompanist; Menuhin was only 7 at the time. On Jan. 17, 1926, when he was 9 years old, he played a recital in N.Y. He made his European debut in Paris on Feb. 6, 1927, with Paul Paray and the Lamoureux Orch. In Paris he began to study with Georges Enesco, who became his most influential teacher, and who guided his future career. Returning to America, Menuhin played the Beethoven Concerto with Fritz Busch and the N.Y. Symph. Orch. on Nov. 25, 1927, winning unanimous acclaim from the public and the press. He subsequently made tours throughout America and Europe; on April 12, 1929, he appeared with Bruno Walter and the Berlin Phil., playing concertos by Bach, Beethoven, and Brahms on the same program; on Nov. 4, 1929, he made his London debut. He continued to pursue his studies with Enesco, and also received additional instruction from Adolf Busch. On the sesquicentennial of the first concert given at the Gewandhaus in Leipzig, he appeared as soloist with the Gewandhaus Orch. in the Mendelssohn Concerto (Nov. 12, 1931). In 1935 he completed his first world tour, giving concerts in 73 cities in 13 countries, including Australia. He also became active in organizing music festivals; in 1956 he established the Gstaad Festival in Switzerland. In 1959 he made his home in London, and founded the Bath Festival, which he directed until 1968; he also founded the Windsor Festival and directed it from 1969 to 1972. He toured as soloist with his own chamber orch.; later he devoted much time to conducting and musical education. He toured Japan in 1951 and Russia in 1956. In 1963 he founded his own boarding school for musically gifted children at Stoke d'Abernon, Surrey. In 1965 he received an honorary knighthood from Queen Elizabeth II. In 1970 he received honorary citizenship from the community of Saanen, Switzerland, and assumed Swiss national allegiance while preserving his American citizenship. In 1971 he succeeded Barbirolli as president of Trinity College of Music in London. In 1976 he was awarded an honorary doctorate by the Sorbonne of Paris, the first musician to be so honored during its entire history. On Sept. 10, 1981, he celebrated the 50th anniversary of his first appearance in Leipzig by performing the Brahms Concerto with Kurt Masur and the Gewandhaus Orch.

Apart from his musical activities, he became deeply interested in art, politics, and above all, psychology and philosophy. He embraced the cause of oriental religions, practiced yoga exercises, and even lectured on these abstruse subjects. In 1963 he appeared over BBC in London in a discussion entitled "Yehudi Menuhin and His Guru." He also adopted a health diet eschewing carbohydrates and some other foods. In his political utterances he antagonized many factions in many lands. He was enthusiastically received in Israel during his tours in 1950, 1951, 1952, and 1953, but aroused Israeli animosity when he gave benefit concerts for Palestinian refugees. He embarrassed the Russians at a music congress in Moscow in 1971 when in his speech, which he read in understandable Russian, he appealed to them on behalf of human rights; he was never invited to Russia again. In the meantime, his artistry suffered somewhat; critics began to notice a certain unsteadiness in his intonation and technique; as a conductor he performed not more than satisfactorily. Still, he never slackened his energetic activities; on July 3, 1976, at a concert at Wolf Trap near Washington, D.C., he introduced a new violin concerto by Alan Hovhaness. He publ. a collection of essays under the title *Theme and Variations* (London, 1972); an autobiography, *Unfinished Journey* (N.Y., 1977); and, with Curtis W. Davis, *The Music of Man* (London, 1980), based on the television series of the same title.

BIBLIOGRAPHY: B. Gavoty, *Yehudi Menuhin et Georges Enesco* (Geneva, 1955); R. Magidoff, *Yehudi Menuhin: The Story of the Man and the Musician* (Garden City, N.Y., 1955; 2nd ed., 1973); N. Wymer, *Yehudi Menuhin* (London, 1961); E. Fenby, *Menuhin's House of Music* (London, 1969); David Ewen, *Musicians since 1900* (N.Y., 1978); R. Daniels, *Conversations with Menuhin* (London, 1979).

Mercadante, (Giuseppe) Saverio (Raffaele), important Italian opera composer and teacher; b. Altamura, near Bari (baptized, Sept. 17), 1795; d. Naples, Dec. 17, 1870. He was born out of wedlock; was taken to Naples when he was about 11. In 1808 he was enrolled in the Collegio di San Sebastiano; he had no means to pay for his tuition; besides, he was over the age limit for entrance, and was not a Neapolitan; to gain admission he had to change his first Christian name and adjust his place and date of birth. He studied solfeggio, violin, and flute; also took classes in figured bass and harmony with Furno and counterpoint with Tritto; subsequently studied composition with the Collegio's director, Zingarelli (1816–20). He began to compose while still a student, writing marches, concertos, sinfonias, trios, quartets, and other works. In 1818 he composed 3 ballets; the success of the 3rd, *Il flauto incantato,* encouraged him to try his hand at an opera. His first opera, *L'apoteosi d'Ercole,* had a successful premiere at Naples on Jan. 4, 1819. He wrote 5 more operas before *Elisa e Claudio,* produced at La Scala in Milan on Oct. 30, 1821, which established his reputation. Other important operas were *Caritea, regina di Spagna* (Venice, Feb. 21, 1826); *Gabriella di Vergy* (Lisbon, Aug. 8, 1828); *I Normanni a Parigi* (Turin, Feb. 7, 1832); *I Briganti* (Paris, March 22, 1836); *Il giuramento* (Milan, March 10, 1837; considered his masterpiece); *Le due illustri rivali* (Venice, March 10, 1838); *Elena da Feltre* (Naples, Dec. 26, 1838); *Il Bravo* (Milan, March 9, 1839); *La Vestale* (Naples, March 10, 1840; one of his finest operas); *Il Reggente* (Turin, Feb. 2, 1843); *Leonora* (Naples, Dec. 5, 1844); *Orazi e Curiazi* (Naples, Nov. 10, 1846; a major success in Italy); and *Virginia* (Naples, April 7, 1866; his last opera to be perf. although composed as early as 1845; its premiere was delayed for political reasons). Mercadante wrote about 60 operas in all, for different opera houses, often residing in the city where they were produced; thus he lived in Rome, Bologna, and

Milan; he also spent some time in Vienna (where he composed 3 operas in 1824) and in Spain and Portugal (1826–31). From 1833 to 1840 he was maestro di cappella at the Cathedral of Novara; about that time he suffered the loss of sight in one eye, and in 1862 he became totally blind. In 1839 Rossini offered him the directorate of the Liceo Musicale in Bologna, but he served in that post only a short time; in 1840 he was named director of the Naples Cons. in succession to his teacher Zingarelli. Mercadante's operas are no longer in the active repertoire, but they are historically important, and objectively can stand comparison with those of his great compatriots Rossini, Bellini, and Donizetti.

WORKS: OPERAS: *L'apoteosi d'Ercole*, dramma per musica (Teatro San Carlo, Naples, Jan. 4, 1819); *Violenza e costanza, ossia I falsi monetari*, dramma giocoso (Teatro Nuovo, Naples, Jan. 19, 1820; also known as *Il castello dei spiriti*); *Anacreonte in Samo*, dramma per musica (Teatro San Carlo, Naples, Aug. 1, 1820); *Il geloso ravveduto*, melodramma buffo (Teatro Valle, Rome, Oct. 1820); *Scipione in Cartagine*, melodramma serio (Teatro Argentina, Rome, Dec. 26, 1820); *Maria Stuarda regina di Scozia [Maria Stuart]*, dramma serio (Teatro Comunale, Bologna, May 29, 1821); *Elisa e Claudio, ossia L'amore protetto dall'amicizia*, melodramma semiserio (Teatro alla Scala, Milan, Oct. 30, 1821); *Andronico*, melodramma tragico (Teatro La Fenice, Venice, Dec. 26, 1821); *Il posto abbandonato, ossia Adele ed Emerico*, melodramma semiserio (Teatro alla Scala, Milan, Sept. 21, 1822); *Amleto*, melodramma tragico (Teatro alla Scala, Milan, Dec. 26, 1822); *Alfonso ed Elisa*, melodramma serio (Teatro Nuovo, Mantua, Dec. 26, 1822); *Didone abbandonata*, dramma per musica (Teatro Regio, Turin, Jan. 18, 1823); *Gli sciti*, dramma per musica (Teatro San Carlo, Naples, March 18, 1823); *Costanzo ed Almeriska*, dramma per musica (Teatro San Carlo, Naples, Nov. 22, 1823); *Gli Amici di Siracusa*, melodramma eroico (Teatro Argentina, Rome, Feb. 7, 1824); *Doralice*, dramma semiserio (Kärnthnertortheater, Vienna, Sept. 18, 1824); *Le nozze di Telemaco ed Antiope*, azione lirica (Kärnthnertortheater, Vienna, Nov. 5, 1824; in collaboration with others); *Il Podestà di Burgos, ossia Il Signore del villaggio*, melodramma semiserio (Kärnthnertortheater, Vienna, Nov. 20, 1824; 2nd version as *Il Signore del villaggio*, in Neapolitan dialect, Teatro Fondo, Naples, May 28, 1825); *Nitocri*, melodramma serio (Teatro Regio, Turin, Dec. 26, 1824); *Impermestra*, dramma tragico (Teatro San Carlo, Naples, c.1824); *Erode, ossia Marianna*, dramma tragico (Teatro La Fenice, Venice, Dec. 27, 1825); *Caritea, regina di Spagna [Donna Caritea], ossia La morte di Don Alfonso re di Portogallo*, melodramma serio (Teatro La Fenice, Feb. 21, 1826); *Ezio*, dramma per musica (Teatro Regio, Turin, Feb. 2, 1827); *Il montanaro*, melodramma comico (Teatro alla Scala, Milan, April 16, 1827); *La testa di bronzo, ossia La capanna solitaria*, melodramma eroico comico (private theater of Barone di Quintella, Lisbon, Dec. 3, 1827); *Andriano in Siria*, dramma serio (Sao Carlos, Lisbon, Feb. 24, 1828); *Gabriella di Vergy*, melodramma serio (Sao Carlos, Lisbon, Aug. 8, 1828); *La rap-*

presaglia, opera buffa (Cadiz, Nov. 20?, 1829); *Don Chisciotte [alle nozze di Gamaccio]*, opera buffa (Cadiz, c.1829); *Francesca da Rimini*, melodramma (Madrid, c.1830); *Zaira*, melodramma tragico (Teatro San Carlo, Naples, Aug. 31, 1831); *I Normanni a Parigi*, tragedia lirica (Teatro Regio, Turin, Feb. 7, 1832); *Ismalia, ossia Amore e morte*, melodramma serio fantastico (Teatro alla Scala, Milan, Oct. 27, 1832); *Il Conte d'Essex*, melodramma (Teatro alla Scala, Milan, March 10, 1833); *Emma d'Antiochia*, tragedia lirica (Teatro La Fenice, Venice, March 8, 1834); *Uggero il danese*, melodramma (Teatro Riccardi, Bergamo, Aug. 11, 1834); *La gioventù di Enrico V*, melodramma (Teatro alla Scala, Milan, Nov. 25, 1834); *I due Figaro*, melodramma buffo (first confirmed perf., Madrid, Jan. 26, 1835); *Francesca Donato, ossia Corinto distrutta*, melodramma semiserio (Teatro Regio, Turin, Feb. 14, 1835); *I Briganti*, melodramma (Théâtre-Italien, Paris, March 22, 1836); *Il giuramento*, melodramma (Teatro alla Scala, Milan, March 10, 1837; also known as *Amore e dovere*); *Le due illustri rivali*, melodramma (Teatro La Fenice, Venice, March 10, 1838); *Elena da Feltre*, dramma tragico (Teatro San Carlo, Naples, Dec. 26, 1838); *Il Bravo [La Veneziana]*, melodramma (Teatro alla Scala, Milan, March 9, 1839); *La Vestale*, tragedia lirica (Teatro San Carlo, Naples, March 10, 1840); *La Solitaria delle Asturie, ossia La Spagna ricuperata*, melodramma (Teatro La Fenice, Venice, March 12, 1840); *Il proscritto*, melodramma (Teatro San Carlo, Naples, Jan. 4, 1842); *Il Reggente*, dramma lirico (Teatro Regio, Turin, Feb. 2, 1843); *Leonora*, melodramma semiserio (Teatro Nuovo, Naples, Dec. 5, 1844); *Il Vascello de Gama*, melodramma romantico (Teatro San Carlo, Naples, March 6, 1845); *Orazi e Curiazi*, tragedia lirica (Teatro San Carlo, Naples, Nov. 10, 1846); *La Schiava saracena, ovvero Il campo di Gerosolima*, melodramma tragico (Teatro alla Scala, Milan, Dec. 26, 1848); *Medea*, tragedia lirica (Teatro San Carlo, Naples, March 1, 1851); *Statira*, tragedia (Teatro San Carlo, Naples, Jan. 8, 1853); *Violetta*, melodramma (Teatro Nuovo, Naples, Jan. 10, 1853); *Pelagio*, tragedia lirica (Teatro San Carlo, Naples, Feb. 12, 1857); *Virginia*, tragedia lirica (Teatro San Carlo, Naples, April 7, 1866).

BALLETS: *Il Servo balordo o La disperazione di Gilotto* (Teatro San Carlo, Naples, Feb. 1, 1818); *Il Califfo generoso* (Teatro Fondo, Naples, 1818); *Il flauto incantato o Le convulsioni musicali* (Teatro San Carlo, Naples, Nov. 19, 1818; revised version for Teatro alla Scala, Milan, Jan. 12, 1828); *I Portoghesi nelle Indie o La conquista di Malacca* (Teatro San Carlo, Naples, May 30, 1819; in collaboration with Gallenberg).

In addition to his music for the theater, he composed much sacred music, including masses, motets, 8 Magnificats, several Salve Reginas, 2 Tantum ergos, etc.; of particular interest is his *Le sette [ultime] parole di Nostro Signore* for 2 Sopranos, Tenor, Baritone, Mixed Voices, 2 Violas, Cello, and Double Bass (1838); also his *Christus e Miserere* for Alto, Tenor, Bass, Chorus a cappella, English Horn, Horn, Bassoon, and Harp (Cons., Naples, March 19, 1856). He furthermore composed a number of cantatas and hymns with orch., including a hymn for Garibaldi (Naples, 1861) and another designed for the inauguration of a statue to Rossini (Pesaro, Aug. 21, 1864). His orch. music includes sinfonias (actually free variations in the form of an overture), fantasias on themes by other composers, marches, etc. He also wrote a number of chamber music pieces and songs.

BIBLIOGRAPHY: W. Neumann, *Saverio Mercadante* (Kassel, 1855); R. Colucci, *Biografia di Saverio Mercadante* (Venice, 1867); F. Florimo, "Saverio Mercadante," in *Cenno storico sulla scuolo musicale di Napoli* (2 vols., Naples, 1869–71; 2nd ed., revised and enlarged in 4 vols., 1880–83, as *La scuola musicale di Napoli e i suoi conservatorii*); O. Serena, *I musicisti altamurani . . . in occasione del centenario di S. Mercadante* (Altamura, 1895); G. Bustico, "Saverio Mercadante a Novara," *Rivista Musicale Italiana*, XXVIII (1921); A. Pomè, *Saggio critico sull'opera musicale di S. Mercadante* (Turin, 1925); G. Pannain, "Saggio su la musica a Napoli nel secolo XIX, da Mercadante a Martucci," *Rivista Musicale Italiana*, XXXV (1928); G. de Napoli, *La triade melodrammatica altamurana: Giacomo Tritto, Vincenzo Lavigna, Saverio Mercadante* (Milan, 1931); G. Solimene, *La patria e i genitori di Mercadante* (Naples, 1940); B. Notarnicola, *Saverio Mercadante: Biografia critica* (Rome, 1945; 3rd ed., much revised, 1951, as *Saverio Mercadante nella gloria e nella luce; Verdi non ha vinto Mercadante*); F. Schlitzer, *Mercadante e Cammarano* (Bari, 1945); a sesquicentennial publication prepared by the committee "Pro Mercadante," *Saverio Mercadante: Note e documenti* (Bari, 1945); F. Walker, "Mercadante and Verdi," *Music & Letters* (Oct. 1952 and Jan. 1953); A. Sardone, *Mercadante, le due patrie e "La gran madre Italia"* (Naples, 1954); E. Brizio, "Saverio Mercadante: Cause e rimedi di una ingiustizia," *Altamura: Bolletino dell'Archivio* (Jan. 1967); G. Carli Ballola, "Incontro con Mercadante," *Chigiana*, XXVI–XXVII (Florence, 1969–70); M. Rinaldi, "Significato di Mercadante," *Ritratti e fantasie musicale* (Rome, 1970); G. Carli Ballola, "Mercadante e *Il Bravo*," *Il melodramma italiano dell'ottocento: Studi e ricerche per Massimo Mila* (Turin, 1977).

Mercadier, Jean Baptiste, French music theorist; b. Belesta, Ariège, April 18, 1750; d. Foix, Jan. 14, 1815. He wrote *Nouveau système de musique théorique et pratique* (1776), a critique of Tartini's and Rameau's systems, favoring Rameau.

Mercer, Johnny, American lyricist and composer of popular songs; b. Savannah, Ga., Nov. 18, 1909; d. Los Angeles, June 25, 1976. He went to N.Y. as a youth, and attracted the attention of Paul Whiteman; subsequently wrote songs for him, Benny Goodman, and Bob Crosby. In 1940 he went to Hollywood, where he founded Capitol Records. His first success as a lyric writer was *Lazybones*, with music by Hoagy Carmichael; another great success was *Accentuate the Positive*, which he wrote for his psychoanalyst. He wrote both words and music for *Something's Gotta Give*, and other hits. He received 4 Academy Awards ("Oscars") for his lyrics.

Mercer, Mabel, English-born American songstress; b. Burton-on-Trent, Staffordshire, Feb. 3, 1900; d. Pittsfield, Mass., April 20, 1984. Her father, a black American, died before she was born; her mother was a white British vaudeville singer; Mabel Mercer became a stage performer in her early adolescence; was a dancer in a music hall in London; after World War I she went to Paris, where she made a success as a nightclub singer; she became a vedette at Bricktop's in Paris, managed by Ada Smith. In 1938 she went to America and settled in N.Y. She continued her career as a nightclub singer, but also gave regular recitals of popular songs. In 1982 she sang at the Kool Jazz Festival. In 1983 she received the Presidential Medal of Freedom from President Reagan. She was briefly married to jazz musician **Kelsey Pharr.**

Mercure, Pierre, Canadian composer; b. Montreal, Feb. 21, 1927; d. in an ambulance between Avallon and Auxerres, France, on Jan. 29, 1966, after an automobile crash while driving from Paris to Lyons. He studied composition with Claude Champagne at the Montreal Cons. (1944–49) and in Paris with Nadia Boulanger (1949–50); also took courses with Dallapiccola at the Berkshire Music Center in Tanglewood, and at Darmstadt and Dartington with Pousseur, Nono, and Berio. He played bassoon with the Montreal Symph. (1947–52); then became producer of musical broadcasts on the French radio network in Montreal. In his music he explored electronic sonorities in combinations with traditional instrumentation.

WORKS: *Kaléidoscope* for Orch. (1947–48); *Pantomime* for Winds and Percussion (1948); 3 short choreographed pieces: *Dualité*, with Trumpet and Piano; *La Femme archaïque*, with Viola, Piano, and Timpani; and *Lucrèce Borgia*, with Trumpet, Piano, and Percussion (all composed in 1949); *Emprise* for Clarinet, Bassoon, Cello, and Piano (1950); *Cantate pour une joie* for Soprano, Chorus, and Orch. (1955); *Divertissement* for Solo String Quartet and String Orch. (1957); *Triptyque* for Orch. (1959); 6 tape pieces with optional choreography: *Improvisation, Incandescense, Structures Métalliques I* and *II* (all 1961), *Manipulations* (1963), and *Surimpressions* (1964); *Répercussions,* for Japanese Wind Chimes on Tape (1961); *Jeu de Hockey* on Tape (1961); *Structures Métalliques III* for Tape (1962); *Tétrachromie*, ballet for 3 Winds, 4 Percussionists, and Tape (1963); *Psaume pour abri*, radiophonic cantata for Narrator, 2 Choirs, Chamber Ensemble, and Tape (Montreal, May 15, 1963); *Lignes et Points* for Orch. (1964; Montreal, Feb. 16, 1965); *H₂O per Severino* for 4–10 Flutes and/or Clarinets (1965); film scores.

Merian, Hans, Swiss musicologist; b. Basel, 1857; d. Leipzig, May 28, 1905. He publ. *Mozarts Meisteropern* (1900); *Geschichte der Musik im 19. Jahrhundert* (1902; 3rd ed. as *Illustrierte Geschichte der Musik*, 1914) and wrote a number of analytical notes to instrumental and operatic masterpieces.

Merian, Wilhelm, Swiss musicologist; b. Basel, Sept. 18, 1889; d. there, Nov. 15, 1952. He studied with Nef in Basel and with Rezniček in Berlin; also studied musicology at the Univ. of Berlin; received a Dr.Phil. in 1915, with the dissertation *Die Tabulatur des Organisten H. Kotter: Ein Beitrag zur Musikgeschichte des beginnenden 16. Jahrhunderts* (publ. in Leipzig, 1916). From 1920 to 1951 he was music editor of the *Basler Nachrichten;* was docent (1921), then (1930) prof. of musicology, at the Univ. of Basel. With Paul Sacher he helped to found the Schola Cantorum Basiliensis.

WRITINGS: *Gedenkschrift zum 50-jährigen Bestehen der Allgemeinen Musikschule in Basel* (1917); *Basels Musikleben im 19. Jahrhundert* (1920); *Die Klaviermusik der deutschen Koloristen* (1921); *Der Tanz in den deutschen Tabulaturbüchern* (1927); *Formuntersuchung zu Mozarts Klaviersonaten,* in the Nef-Festschrift (1932); *Hermann Suter: Der Dirigent und der Komponist* (Basel, 1936); *Hermann Suter: Ein Lebensbild als Beitrag zur schweizerischen Musikgeschichte* (Basel, 1936). He was the ed. of the *Basel Kongress-Bericht* (1924), *Geistliche Werke des 16. Jahrhunderts,* and other publications.

Méric-Lilande, Henriette, French soprano; b. Dunkirk, 1798; d. Chantilly, Sept. 7, 1867. She studied with her father, who was the director of a provincial opera company; she made her debut in Nantes in 1814; her first appearance in Paris came in 1823 in a pasticcio. On March 7, 1824, she took part in the Venice premiere of Meyerbeer's *Il Crociatto in Egitto;* after further study in Italy, she created Bianca in Bellini's *Bianca e Gernando* (Naples, May 30, 1826), Imogene in *Il Pirata* (Milan, Oct. 27, 1827), and Alaide in *La Straniera* (Milan, Feb. 14, 1829), even though Bellini himself declared that she was "incapable of delicate sentiment." She appeared in London at the King's Theatre in 1830 as Imogene and sang in 1831 as Rossini's *Semiramis;* she retired shortly after creating the title role in Donizetti's *Lucrezia Borgia* (Milan, Dec. 26, 1833).

Mériel, Paul, French composer; b. Mondonbleau, Loire-et-Cher, Jan. 4, 1818; d. Toulouse, Feb. 24, 1897. As a boy, he earned his living playing the violin in theater orchs.; later studied with Napoleão in Lisbon; produced a comic opera, *Cornelius l'argentier,* in Amiens; then settled in Toulouse, where he brought out a symph. poem, *Le Tasse (Tasso),* a grand opera, *L'Armorique* (1854); and the comic opera *Les Précieuses ridicules* (1877).

Merikanto, Aarre, Finnish composer, son of **Oskar Merikanto;** b. Helsinki, June 29, 1893; d. there, Sept. 29, 1958. He studied in Leipzig with Max Reger (1912–14) and with Vasilenko in Moscow (1916–17). In 1936 he joined the faculty at the Sibelius Academy in Helsinki, and in 1951 he succeeded Palmgren as head of the dept. of composition there; he held this post until his death. Like his father, he wrote on

themes of Finnish folklore, but he also produced a few pieces that had elements of French Impressionism.

WORKS: Opera, *Juha* (1920–22; first perf. on the Finnish Radio in Helsinki, Dec. 3, 1958, as a memorial to him; first stage perf. took place in Lahti, Oct. 28, 1963); 3 piano concertos (1913, 1937, 1955); 3 symphs. (1916, 1918, 1953); 4 violin concertos (1916, 1925, 1931, 1954); symph. suite, *Lemminkainen* (1916); 2 cello concertos (1919, 1941–44); *Pan,* symph. poem (1924); Concerto for Violin, Clarinet, French Horn, and String Sextet (1925); *Concert Piece* for Cello and Chamber Orch. (1926); *Notturno,* symph. poem (1929); *Kyllikin ryöstö (The Abduction of Kyllikki),* symph. poem (1935); *Scherzo* for Orch. (1937); *3 Impressions* for Orch. (1940); *Soitelma kesäyölle (Music to the Summer Night)* for Orch. (1942); *Genesis* for Soprano, Chorus, and Orch. (1956); *Tuhma (Simpleton)* for Male Chorus and Orch. (1956); 2 string quartets (1913, 1939); String Trio (1912); Piano Trio (1917); Nonet (1926); String Sextet (1932); *Partita* for Harp and Woodwinds (1936); songs.

Merikanto, Oskar, Finnish composer; b. Helsinki, Aug. 5, 1868; d. Hausjärvi-Oiti, Feb. 17, 1924. After preliminary study in his native city, he went to Leipzig and Berlin to continue his musical education (1887). Returning to Finland, he became organist of St. John's Church, and from 1911 till 1922 was conductor of the National Opera in Helsinki. He wrote a great number of songs, which became very popular in Finland; organ works and manuals for organ playing; various instrumental pieces; and 3 operas: *Pohjan Neiti (The Maid of Bothnia;* Viborg, June 18, 1908), *Elinan surma (Elina's Death;* Helsinki, Nov. 17, 1910), and *Regina von Emmeritz* (Helsinki, Jan. 30, 1920).

BIBLIOGRAPHY: Yrjö Suomalainen, *Oskar Merikanto* (Helsinki, 1950).

Meriläinen, Usko, Finnish composer; b. Tampere, Jan. 27, 1930. He studied with Aarre Merikanto and Leo Funtek at the Sibelius Academy in Helsinki (1951–55); then took private lessons with Ernst Krenek at Darmstadt and with Wladimir Vogel in Switzerland. In 1956–57 he was a conductor and teacher in Kuopio; subsequently was theater conductor in Tampere (1957–60); then taught at the music inst. there (1961–66) and from 1965 at the Univ. In his music he adopted a pragmatic modern idiom, with structural foundations of tonal and/or dodecaphonic procedures, depending on the basic concept.

WORKS: 3 ballets: *Arius* (1958–60; 2 suites, 1960 and 1962, and an *Introduction and Variations,* 1964, from the ballet), *Psyche* for Tape (1973), and *Alasin (The Anvil,* 1975); *Sumu (The Mist),* symph. fantasy (1952); 5 symphs.: No. 1 (1952–55); No. 2 (1964); No. 3 (1971); No. 4, *The Anvil,* dance pantomime for Tape (1975); No. 5 (1976); 2 piano concertos (1955, 1969); Concerto for Orch. (1956); Chamber Concerto for Solo Violin, Double String Orch., and Percussion (1962); *Epyllion 1* for Orch. (1963); *Musique du Printemps* for Orch. (1969); Cello Concerto (1975); *Dialogues* for Piano and Orch. (1977; Tampere, Sept. 29, 1978); *Mobile,* game for Orch. (1978); *Kinetic Poem* for Piano and Orch. (Helsinki, Oct. 14, 1982); *4 Bagatelles* for String Quartet (1962); *Arabesques* for Solo Cello (1963); *Hommage à Jean Sibelius* for Violin and Piano (1965); *Impression* for Wind Quintet, Piano, Viola, Cello, Double Bass, and Percussion (1965); String Quartet (1965); *Divertimento* for Wind Quintet, Harp, Viola, and Cello (1968); *Metamorfora for 7* for Clarinet, Bassoon, Trumpet, Trombone, Percussion, Violin, and Double Bass (1969); *Concerto for 13* for 7 Violins, 3 Violas, 2 Cellos, and Double Bass (1971); *Concerto* for Double Bass and Percussion (1973); *Aspects of the Ballet "Psyche"* for Tape Instrumental Ensemble (1973); *Simultus* for Flute, Saxophone, Guitar, and Percussion (1979); *Kyma* for String Quartet (1979); *Suite* for Piano (1955); Piano Sonatina (1958); 4 piano sonatas (1960, 1966, 1972, 1974); *Riviravi,* small piano pieces for children (1962); *3 Notturni* for Piano (1967); *Papillons* for 2 Pianos (1969); *4 Love Songs* for Soprano and Piano (1961).

Merk, Joseph, Austrian cellist; b. Vienna, March 18, 1795; d. Ober-Döbling, June 16, 1852. He was trained in Vienna; in 1818 became first cellist at the Vienna Opera; in 1823, a teacher at the Cons. He wrote 2 cello concertos, fantasias, polonaises, etc.; his cello études are of value to students.

Merkel, Gustav (Adolf), German organist and composer; b. Oberoderwitz, Nov. 12, 1827; d. Dresden, Oct. 30, 1885. He studied organ with J. Schneider and theory with J. Otto. He was organist in several churches in Dresden; wrote many organ works: 9 sonatas (for 4-hands, with double pedal); 5 fantasias; 30 pedal studies; an organ method; also motets and songs.

Merklin, Joseph, German organ builder; b. Oberhausen, Baden, Jan. 17, 1819; d. Nancy, France, June 10, 1905. He worked in his father's workshop in Freiburg; in 1843 went to Brussels; in 1853 took his brother-in-law, **F. Schütze,** into partnership, changing the name of his firm to Merklin, Schütze & Cie. In 1855 he bought out the Ducroquet firm in Paris; in 1858 he reorganized his partnership as the Société Anonyme pour la Fabrication des Orgues, Etablissement Merklin-Schütze. The firm supplied organs to several cathedrals in Europe. Merklin publ. an interesting technical paper, *Notice sur l'électricité appliquée aux grandes orgues* (Paris, 1887), containing some surprising insights on the possible manufacture of electric organs. His nephew **Albert Merklin** (1892–1925) went to Madrid at the outbreak of World War I in 1914 and established a Spanish branch of the firm. Merklin's Paris factory was acquired by Guttschenritter in 1899, and his branch in Lyons was bought in 1906 by the Swiss organ builder Theodor Kuhn; it was incorporated in 1926 as Société Anonyme des Anciens Établissements Michel, Merklin & Kuhn. After several further changes of ownership, the firm was taken over in 1967 by Fredrich Jakob in Zürich.

Merli, Francesco, Italian tenor; b. Milan, Jan. 27, 1887; d. there, Dec. 11, 1976. He studied with Borghi and Negrini in Milan; had a successful career singing in provincial opera houses in Italy, culminating in his appearance at La Scala in Milan in 1922, in the role of Walther in *Die Meistersinger;* he continued to be on its roster until 1946; also made frequent guest appearances at the Teatro Colón in Buenos Aires; between 1926 and 1930 he sang at Covent Garden in London. He made his debut at the Metropolitan Opera in N.Y. as Radames in *Aida* on March 2, 1932; then returned to Italy. He retired from the stage in 1950 and was active mainly as a voice teacher.

Merman, Ethel (real name, **Ethel Agnes Zimmerman**), famous American singer of popular music; b. Queens, N.Y., Jan. 16, 1908; d. New York, Feb. 14, 1984. She was of German-Scottish extraction. She took a commercial course in high school and held several jobs as a secretary while trying to satisfy her desire to be a singing actress. She never took vocal lessons but developed her booming powerful voice naturally. She obtained some bookings at Long Island night spots, and soon attracted the attention of Broadway managers. She auditioned for George Gershwin, who hired her to sing in his musical *Girl Crazy,* and she made a hit with the feature song *I Got Rhythm;* she held a high C for 16 bars in the coda against the orch. playing the melodic line. She had unbounded confidence in her stardom; she could also act in an uninhibited manner, which suited most of the roles she sang on Broadway. She was arrogant and foul-mouthed in her dealings with agents, managers, directors, and even composers, but she knew how to put the music across; her ability to make the most of each song, and her sense of perfect intonation, made her the darling of Broadway. "Broadway has been very good for me," she once said, "but I've been very good for Broadway." Among the musicals in which she starred were Cole Porter's *Anything Goes* (1934); Irving Berlin's *Annie Get Your Gun* (1946) and *Call Me Madam* (1950); Styne's *Gypsy;* and many others. She also made 14 movie musicals, among them *There's No Business Like Show Business* and *It's a Mad, Mad, Mad, Mad World.* Her last public appearance was in 1982, when she took part in a Carnegie Hall benefit concert. Her private life was tempestuous; she married and divorced 4 times; her daughter from the 2nd marriage committed suicide. In April 1983 she underwent surgery to remove a brain tumor. When the news of her death arrived on the radio, all the Broadway theaters observed a minute of silence during the performance to honor her memory.

Merö, Yolanda, Hungarian-American pianist; b. Budapest, Aug. 30, 1887; d. New York, Oct. 17, 1963. She studied piano with her father; made her American debut with the Russian Symph. Orch. in N.Y. on Nov. 3, 1909; married Hermon Irion of Steinway & Sons, and remained in the U.S.

Merola, Gaetano, conductor and impresario; b. Naples, Jan. 4, 1881; d. San Francisco, Aug. 30, 1953. He studied at the Naples Cons.; came to the U.S. in 1899, and was appointed assistant conductor at the Metropolitan Opera House; also conducted with the Henry Savage English Opera in N.Y. (1903), the Manhattan Opera Co. in N.Y. (1906), etc.; in 1923 he became general director of the San Francisco and Los Angeles operas. He collapsed and died while conducting a concert at the Sigmund Stern Grove in San Francisco.

Merriam, Alan P(arkhurst), American anthropologist and ethnomusicologist; b. Missoula, Mont., Nov. 1, 1923; d. near Warsaw in a plane crash, March 14, 1980. He studied at the Univ. of Montana (B.A., 1947); took courses in anthropology from Melville Herskovits and Richard Waterman at Northwestern Univ. (M.M., 1948; Ph.D., 1951); taught anthropology there in 1953–54 and again from 1956–62, and at the Univ. of Wisconsin (1954–56); in 1962 became a prof. of anthropology at Indiana Univ. in Bloomington; was chairman of the dept. there in 1966–69. In 1976 he was engaged as a senior scholar in anthropology at the Univ. of Sydney. He was involved in field research among the Flathead Indians and the tribes in Zaïre.
WRITINGS: *The Anthropology of Music* (Evanston, Ill., 1964); with F. Gillis, *Ethnomusicology and Folk Music: An International Bibliography of Dissertations and Theses* (Middletown, Conn., 1966); *Ethnomusicology of the Flathead Indians* (Chicago, 1967); *African Music on LP: An Annotated Discography* (Evanston, 1970); *The Arts and Humanities in African Studies* (Bloomington, Ind., 1972).

Merrick, Frank, English pianist and composer; b. Clifton, Bristol, April 30, 1886; d. London, Feb. 19, 1981. He studied piano and composition with his father, a professional pedagogue; in 1905 went to Vienna to take piano lessons with Leschetizky. Returning to England, he taught at the Royal Manchester College of Music (1910–29); then became a prof. at the Royal College of Music in London; in 1956 he joined the piano faculty of the Trinity College of Music in London. In 1928 he entered a rather ill-conceived contest launched by the Columbia Phonograph Co. to nail down the centenary of Schubert's death by finishing his Unfinished Symph. Merrick did finish it, and won a prize. He was married to the pianist **Hope Squire** and gave duo-piano concerts with her. Somewhat off-center in his propensities, proclivities, and predilections, he learned Esperanto and wrote songs to his own texts in that artificial language invented by a Polish oculist in 1887. But Merrick also wrote 2 playable piano concertos and some pleasurable instrumental pieces, such as *Celtic Suite* and *Dream Pageant.* He publ. a didactic volume, *Practising the Piano* (London, 1958), and edited John Field's piano concertos.

Merrill, Robert, noted American baritone; b. Brooklyn, June 4, 1917. He first studied voice with his mother, Lillian Miller Merrill, a concert singer;

subsequently took lessons with Samuel Margolis. He began his career as a popular singer on the radio; then made his operatic debut as Amonasro in *Aida* in Trenton, N.J., in 1944. After winning the Metropolitan Opera Auditions of the Air in N.Y., he made his debut with the Metropolitan on Dec. 15, 1945, as Germont in *La Traviata.* He remained on the roster of the Metropolitan Opera for 30 years; also gave solo recitals. He was briefly married to the American soprano **Roberta Peters.** He publ. 2 autobiographical books, *Once More from the Beginning* (N.Y., 1965) and *Between Acts* (N.Y., 1977).

Merriman, Nan (Katherine-Ann), American mezzo-soprano; b. Pittsburgh, April 28, 1920. She studied with Alexia Bassian in Hollywood; made her operatic debut as La Cieca in *La Gioconda* with the Cincinnati Summer Opera in 1942; from 1943 she sang with Toscanini and the NBC Symph. Orch.; also appeared in opera at Aix-en-Provence, Edinburgh, and Glyndebourne. Her best operatic roles included Magdalena in *Rigoletto* and Emilia in *Otello.* She also sang the part of Baba the Turk in Stravinsky's *The Rake's Progress.* She retired in 1965.

Merritt, A(rthur) Tillman, American musicologist and pedagogue; b. Calhoun, Mo., Feb. 15, 1902. He studied at the Univ. of Missouri (B.A., 1924; B.F.A., 1926) and Harvard Univ. (M.A., 1927); then went to Europe on a J.K. Paine traveling scholarship from Harvard, and studied in Paris with Nadia Boulanger and Paul Dukas; upon his return to America, he taught at Trinity College in Hartford, Conn. (1930–32). In 1932 he joined the faculty of the music dept. of Harvard Univ.; was its chairman from 1942–52 and from 1968 to 1972, when he retired. He publ. the valuable treatise *Sixteenth-century Polyphony: A Basis for the Study of Counterpoint* (Cambridge, Mass., 1939); also edited works by Janequin. On his retirement he was honored with a Festschrift, *Words and Music: The Scholar's View* (Cambridge, Mass., 1972).

Merseburger, Carl Wilhelm, founder of the music publishing firm in Leipzig bearing his name; b. 1816; d. 1885. In 1849 he purchased the publishing business of Carl Fredrich Meusel; specializing in school music, he brought out a great number of useful manuals and songbooks; also was the publisher of *Euterpe,* a periodical on education. His successor was his brother **Otto Merseburger** (1822–1898); the latter was succeeded by his son, **Max Merseburger** (1852–1935). The entire stock was destroyed during the air raids on Leipzig in 1944; after the war, the business was resumed, with headquarters in Berlin, and temporary subsidies in Darmstadt and Heidelberg. A centennial Festschrift was publ. in Leipzig, 1949, by the grandson of the founder. The firm was acquired by Adolf Strube in 1956, and became a limited company in 1964.

Mersenne, Marin, important French theorist; b. La Soultière (Maine), Sept. 8, 1588; d. Paris, Sept. 1,

1648. He studied at the college of Le Mans; then at the Jesuit School at La Flèche (from 1604); then at the Collège Royal and the Sorbonne in Paris from 1609; in 1611 he joined the Order of Minims; between 1640 and 1645 made 3 trips to Italy; maintained a correspondence with the leading philosophers and scientists of his time. His writings provide souce material of fundamental importance for the history of 17th-century music.

WRITINGS: *Traité de l'harmonie universelle* (1627), later expanded to *Harmonie universelle* (1636–37; 2 large folio vols. with illustrations and musical examples; includes a *Traité des instruments,* depicting and describing all instruments of the 17th century; his most important work); *Quaestiones celeberrimae in Genesim* (1623; chiefly on Hebrew music); *Questions harmoniques* (1634); *Les Préludes de l'harmonie universelle* (1634); *Harmonicorum libri XII* (1635; enlarged ed., 1648); etc.

BIBLIOGRAPHY: C. Adam, *Le Père Mersenne et ses correspondants en France* (Paris, 1897); A. Pirro, "Les Correspondants du Père Mersenne," *Bulletin de la Société Internationale de Musique* (1909); P. Tannery, *Correspondance du Père Marin Mersenne* (Paris, 1933); H. Ludwig, *Marin Mersenne und seine Musiklehre* (Halle, 1934); R. Lenoble, *Mersenne ou La Naissance du mécanisme* (Paris, 1943). The 7 books of the *Traité des instruments* were trans. into Eng. for the first time by Roger E. Chapman and publ. under the title *Harmonie Universelle: The Books on Instruments* (The Hague, 1957); *Marin Mersenne: Correspondance,* ed. by C. de Waard (Paris, 1959).

Mersmann, Hans, German musicologist; b. Potsdam, Oct. 6, 1891; d. Cologne, June 24, 1971. He studied in Munich with Sandberger and Kroyer, in Leipzig with Riemann and Schering, and at the Univ. of Berlin with Wolf and Kretzschmar; received a Dr.Phil. with the dissertation *Christian Ludwig Boxberg und seine Oper "Sardanapalus" (Ansbach 1698), mit Beiträgen zur Ansbacher Musikgeschichte* (1914). He subsequently occupied various teaching positions: at the Stern Cons. in Berlin, and at the Technische Hochschule there, until 1933; was in charge of the folk-song archives of the Prussian Volksliederkommission (1917–33); also organized numerous seminars on musicology and modern music; from 1924 edited the periodical *Melos;* wrote music criticism. In 1946–47 he taught at the Hochschule für Musik in Munich; from 1947 to 1958 was director of the Hochschule für Musik in Cologne. As a historian and analyst of modern music, Mersmann occupies an important position in contemporary research.

WRITINGS: Apart from numerous papers in German periodicals, he publ. *Angewandte Musikästhetik* (collected papers on esthetics; Berlin, 1926); *Kulturgeschichte der Musik in Einzeldarstellungen* (Berlin, 1921–25; 4 vols.: *Das deutsche Volkslied; Beethoven; Musik der Gegenwart; Mozart);* *Angewandte Musikästhetik* (Berlin, 1926); *Die moderne Musik seit der Romantik,* in Bücken's *Handbuch der Musikwissenschaft* (1928); "Die Ton-

sprache der neuen Musik," in *Melosbücherei* (ed. by Mersmann, 1928; 2nd ed., 1930); *Das Musikseminar* (Leipzig, 1931); *Kammermusik* (Leipzig, 1930–34; in 4 vols.: *Die Kammermusik des 17. und 18. Jahrhunderts; Beethoven; Deutsche Romantik; Europäische Kammermusik des 19. und 20. Jahrhunderts);* *Eine deutsche Musikgeschichte* (Potsdam, 1934; enlarged to include music history of other Western nations, publ. as *Musikgeschichte in der abendländischen Kultur,* 1955; 3rd ed., 1973); *Volkslied und Gegenwart* (Potsdam, 1936); *Musikhören* (Berlin, 1938; enlarged ed., 1952); *Neue Musik in den Strömungen unserer Zeit* (Bayreuth, 1949); *Die Kirchenmusik im XX. Jahrhundert* (Nuremberg, 1958); *Stilprobleme der Werkanalyse* (Mainz, 1963); *Die moderne Oper und die Neue Musik unserer Zeit* (Kassel, 1967).

BIBLIOGRAPHY: W. Wiora, ed., *Musikerkenntnis und Musikziehung. Dankesgaben für H. Mersmann zu seinem 65. Geburtstag* (1957).

Mertens, Joseph, Belgian composer; b. Antwerp, Feb. 17, 1834; d. Brussels, June 30, 1901. He was the first violinist at the Opéra in Brussels; was a violin teacher at the Cons.; was conductor of the Flemish Opera there (1878–89); then inspector of the Belgian music schools, and finally director of the Royal Theater at The Hague. He composed a number of Flemish and French operettas and operas which had local success: *De zwaarte Kapitein* (The Hague, 1877); *De Vrijer in de strop* (1866); *La Méprise* (1869); *L'Egoïsa* (1873); *Thécla* (1874); *Liederik l'intendent* (1875); *Les Trois Etudiants; Le Vin, le jeu et le tabac; Le Capitaine Robert; Les Evincés;* etc.

Mertke, Eduard, pianist and composer; b. Riga, June 17, 1833; d. Cologne, Sept. 25, 1895. He studied with S. von Lützau (piano) and Agthe (theory); appeared in public as a child pianist; toured Russia and Germany; in 1869 was appointed to the faculty of the Cologne Cons., where he continued to teach until his death. He wrote 3 operas: *Lisa, oder Die Sprache des Herzens* (Mannheim, Feb. 24, 1872), *Resi vom Hemsensteig,* and *Kyrill von Thessalonica;* many piano pieces; technical exercises for piano; he also publ. a collection, *Melodies of the Ukraine.*

Mertz, Joseph Kasper, Austrian guitar virtuoso; b. Pressburg (Bratislava), Aug. 17, 1806; d. Vienna, Oct. 14, 1856. He moved to Vienna in 1840; gave concerts there and in Germany, using a 10-string guitar. His works for the guitar enjoyed a modicum of popularity; his *Concertino* received first prize at the International Competition in Brussels, in 1856. He was married to the pianist **Josephine Plantin.**

BIBLIOGRAPHY: F. Buck, *Die Gitarre und ihre Meister* (Vienna, 1926; 2nd ed., Berlin, 1952).

Merula, Tarquinio, significant Italian organist and composer; b. Cremona, c.1594; d. there, Dec. 10, 1665. In 1616 he received an appointment as organist of S. Maria Incoronata in Lodi. In 1621 he went to Poland, where he served as court organist. Returning to Italy, he became maestro di cappella at the Cathedral in Cremona in 1627; in 1631 he was engaged as maestro di cappella of S. Maria Maggiore in Bergamo; these positions he held until his death; from 1633 to 1635 he was also maestro di cappella for the Laudi della Madonna. He was a versatile composer and wrote both secular and sacred music; remarkably enough for a church organist, he also wrote instrumental music in a concertante style; his ensemble canzonas are especially fine.

WORKS: VOCAL MUSIC: SACRED: *Il primo libro de motetti e sonate concertati,* op. 6, for 2–5 Voices (Venice, 1624); *Libro secondo de concerti spirituali con alcune sonate,* op. 8, for 2–5 Voices (Venice, 1628); *Pegaso . . . salmi, motetti, suonate . . .* for 2–5 Voices, *libro terzo,* op. 11 (c.1633–37); *Concerto . . . messi, salmi . . . concertati,* op. 15, for 2–8 and 12 Voices, with Instruments (Venice, 1639); *Arpa Davidica . . . salmi, et messe,* op. 16, *a 4* (Venice, 1640); *Il terzo libro delle salmi et messa concertati,* op. 18, *a 3–4* (Venice, 1652. VOCAL MUSIC: SECULAR: *La finta savia,* opera in collaboration with others (Venice, 1643); *Il primo libro de madrigaletti,* op. 4, for 3 Voices and Basso Continuo (Venice, 1624); *Il primo libro de madrigali concertate,* op. 5, for 4–8 Voices and Basso Continuo (Venice, 1624); *Satiro e Corisca dialogo musicale,* op. 7, for 2 Voices and Basso Continuo (Venice, 1626); *Madrigali et altre musiche concertate a 1–5, libro secondo,* op. 10 (Venice, 1633); *Curtio precipitato et altri capricii, libro secondo,* op. 13, for One Voice (Venice, 1638); *Canzonetta a 3 et 4,* op. 14? (date unknown; not extant). INSTRUMENTAL MUSIC: *Il primo libro delle canzoni, a 4,* op. 1 (Venice, 1615); *Il secondo libro delle canzoni da suonare,* op. 9, for 3 Instruments and Basso Continuo (c.1631–33); *Canzoni overo sonate concertate per chiesa e camera, a 2–3, libro terzo,* op. 12 (Venice, 1637); *Il quarto libro delle canzoni da suonare, a 2–3,* op. 17 (Venice, 1651). See A. Sutkowski, ed., *Tarquinio Merula: Opere complete,* I/i (Brooklyn, 1974).

BIBLIOGRAPHY: J.W. von Wasielewski, *Die Violine im 17. Jahrhundert* (Bonn, 1874); E. Schmitz, *Geschichte der weltlichen Solokantate* (Leipzig, 1914; 2nd ed., revised, 1955); E. van der Straeten, *The History of the Violin* (London, 1933); E. Crocker, *An Introductory Study of the Italian Canzona for Instrumental Ensembles* (Diss., Radcliffe College, 1943); N. Fortune, *Italian Secular Song from 1600 to 1635: The Origins and Development of Accompanied Monody* (Diss., Cambridge Univ., 1954); W. Newman, *The Sonata in the Baroque Era* (Chapel Hill, 1959; 2nd ed., 1966); A. Curtis, "L'opera cembalo-organistica di Tarquinio Merula," *L'Organo,* I (1960); J. Roche, "Music at S. Maria Maggiore, Bergamo, 1614–1643," *Music & Letters,* XLVII (1966); C. Palisca, *Baroque Music* (Englewood Cliffs, N.J., 1968); J.L.A. Roche, *North Italian Liturgical Music in the Early 17th Century* (Diss., Cambridge Univ., 1968); A. Colzani, "La cappella della Laudi a Cremona fino al servizio di Tarquinio Merula," *Contributi e studi di liturgia e musica nella regione padana* (Bologna, 1972); M. Padoan, "Tarquinio Merula nelle fonte documentarie," *Contributi e studi di*

liturgia e musica nella regione padana (Bologna, 1972); E. Ferrari Barassi, "Tarquinio Merula i jego dialog 'Satiro e Corsica,'" *Pagine* (1974).

Merulo (real name, **Merlotti**), **Claudio** (called **da Correggio**), Italian composer, organist, and music publisher; b. Correggio, April 8, 1533; d. Parma, May 4, 1604. He studied with Tuttovale Menon and Girolamo Donato. On Oct. 21, 1556, he became organist at the Cathedral in Brescia, succeeding Vincenzo Parabosco; on July 2, 1557, was chosen as 2nd organist at San Marco in Venice; in 1566 he succeeded Padovano as first organist, a position he held until 1584. He composed a number of works for state occasions, including intermedi to Frangipane's *Tragedia* for the visit of Henry III of France in 1574. Active as a music publisher between 1566 and 1570, he brought out several first editions of his own works, as well as works by Primavera, Porta, and Wert. In 1586 he was appointed organist at the court of the Duke of Parma; in 1591 became organist to the company of the Steccata, a position he retained until his death. Merulo was reputed to be one of the greatest organists of his item; as a composer, he was an important representative of the Venetian school. His organ music is of especial merit; he also composed church music and madrigals.

WORKS: INSTRUMENTAL MUSIC: *Ricercari d'intabolatura d'organo . . . libro primo* (Venice, 1567); *Messe d'intavolatura d'organo* (Venice, 1568); *Il primo libro de ricercari da cantare a 4* (Venice, 1574); *Canzoni d'intavolatura d'organo a 4 fatte alla francese* (Venice, 1592); *Toccate d'intavolatura d'organo, libro primo* (Rome, 1598); *Toccate d'intavolatura d'organo, libro secondo* (Rome, 1604); *Libro secondo di canzoni d'intavolatura d'organo a fatte alla francese* (Venice, 1606); *Ricercari d'organo . . . libro secondo* (Venice, 1607); *Ricercari da cantare a 4 . . . libro terzo* (Venice, 1608); *Terzo libro de canzoni d'intavolatura d'organo a 5 fatte alla francese* (Venice, 1611); see S. Dalla Libera, *Claudio Merulo: Toccate per organo,* I–III (Milan, 1959). VOCAL MUSIC: SACRED: *Missarum liber primus* for 5 Voices (Venice, 1573); *Liber primus sacrarum cantionum* for 5 Voices (Venice, 1578); *Liber secundus sacrarum cantionum* for 5 Voices (Venice, 1578); *Il primo libro de mottetti* for 6 Voices (Venice, 1583); *Il primo libro de mottetti* for 4 Voices (Venice, 1584); *Il secondo libro de mottetti* for 6 Voices (Venice, 1593); *Sacrorum concentuum* for 5, 8, 10, 12, and 16 Voices (Venice, 1594); *Il terzo libro de mottetti* for 6 Voices (Venice, 1605); *Misse due* for 8 and 12 Voices, with Organ (Venice, 1609); an edition of his sacred music, ed. by J. Bastian in Corpus Mensurabilis Musicae, began publication in 1970. VOCAL MUSIC: SECULAR: *Il primo libro de madrigali* for 5 Voices (Venice, 1566); *Il primo libro de madrigali* for 4 Voices (Venice, 1579); *Il primo libro de madrigali* for 3 Voices (Venice, 1580); *Il secondo libro de madrigali* for 5 Voices (Venice, 1580); also intermedi to L. Dolce's drama *Le Troiane* (1566) and Frangipane's *Tragedia* (Venice, July 21, 1574).

BIBLIOGRAPHY: A. Catelani, "Memorie della

vita e delle opere di Claudio Merulo," *Gazzetta Musicale di Milano,* XVIII (1860); Q. Bigi, *Di Claudio Merulo da Correggio* (Parma, 1861); *Claudio Merulo da Correggio* (Parma, 1905; essays by 8 Italian scholars); A. Einstein, "Claudio Merulo's Ausgabe der Madrigale," *Sammelbände der Internationalen Musik-Gesellschaft,* VIII/2 (1906–7); O. Kinkeldey, *Orgel und Klavier in der Musik des 16. Jahrhunderts* (Leipzig, 1910); A. Einstein, *The Italian Madrigal* (Princeton, 1949); G. Reese, *Music in the Renaissance* (N.Y., 1954; 2nd ed., revised, 1959); L. Debes, *Die musikalischen Werke von Claudio Merulo (1533–1604)* (Diss., Julius-Maximilians Univ., Würzburg, 1964); J. Bastian, *The Sacred Music of Claudio Merulo* (Diss., Univ. of Michigan, 1967).

Merz, Karl, German-American musician; b. Bensheim, near Frankfurt, Sept. 19, 1836; d. Wooster, Ohio, Jan. 30, 1890. He was a pupil of his father and of F.J. Kunkel; went to the U.S. in 1854, and lived in Philadelphia as a teacher. He was a contributor to various periodicals; his collected essays, *Music and Culture,* edited by his son, Dr. Charles H. Merz, were publ. in Philadelphia (1890).

Messager, André (-Charles-Prosper), celebrated French composer and conductor; b. Montluçon, Allier, Dec. 30, 1853; d. Paris, Feb. 24, 1929. He studied at the Ecole Niedermeyer in Paris with Gigout (composition), A. Laussel (piano), and C. Loret (organ); then took lessons with Saint-Saëns. In 1874 he became organist at St.-Sulpice; subsequently was choir director at Sainte-Marie des Batignoles (1882–84). He began his career as a conductor at the Folies-Bergère; then conducted at the Eden-Theatre in Brussels in 1880; was music director at the Opéra-Comique (1898–1908); also directed the opera at Covent Garden, London (1901–7). From 1907 till 1915 he was the regular conductor of the Paris Opéra; was in charge of the Société des Concerts du Conservatoire from 1908 until his death; under the auspices of the French government he visited the U.S. with that orch., giving concerts in 50 American cities (1918). Returning to Paris, he again conducted at the Opéra-Comique; led a season of Diaghilev's Ballets Russes in 1924. As a conductor, he played an important role in Paris concert life; he directed the première of *Pelléas et Mélisande* (1902, with 21 rehearsals), the score of which Debussy dedicated to him. His initial steps as a composer were auspicious; his symph. (1875) was awarded the gold medal of the Société des Compositeurs and performed at the Concerts Colonne (Jan. 20, 1878); his dramatic scene *Don Juan et Haydée* (1876) was awarded a gold medal by the Academy of St. Quentin. He wrote several other works for orch. (*Impressions orientals, Suite funambulesque,* etc.) and some chamber music, but he was primarily a man of the theater. His style may be described as enlightened eclecticism; his music is characteristically French, and more specifically, Parisian, in its elegance and gaiety. He was honored in France; in 1926 he was elected to the Académie des Beaux Arts. He was married to

Hope Temple (real name, **Dotie Davis,** 1858–1938), who was the author of numerous songs. His operas (first perf. in Paris except where otherwise indicated) include *François les-bas-bleus* (Jan. 20, 1878; score begun by F. Bernicat and completed after his death by Messager); *La Fauvette du temple* (Nov. 17, 1885); *La Béarnaise* (Dec. 12, 1885); *Le Bourgeois de Calais* (April 6, 1887); fairy tale, *Isoline* (Dec. 26, 1888; the ballet suite from it is popular); *La Basoche* (May 30, 1890; greatly acclaimed); *Madame Chrysanthème* (after Loti; Jan. 26, 1893; to a story similar to Puccini's *Madame Butterfly,* produced 11 years later; but Puccini's dramatic treatment eclipsed Messager's lyric setting); *Le Chevalier d'Harmental* (May 5, 1896); *Véronique* (Dec. 10, 1898; successful); *Les Dragons de l'Impératrice* (Feb. 13, 1905); *Fortunio* (June 5, 1907); *Béatrice* (Monte Carlo, March 21, 1914); *Monsieur Beaucaire* (Birmingham, April 7, 1919). Among his successful operettas were *Le Mari de la Reine* (Dec. 18, 1889); *Miss Dollar* (Jan. 22, 1893); *La Fiancée en loterie* (Feb. 15, 1896); *Les P'tites Michu* (Paris, Nov. 16, 1897; many subsequent perfs.); *La Petite Fonctionnaire,* dance-hall operetta (Paris, May 14, 1921); *Passionnément* (Paris, Jan. 15, 1926). His ballets include *Fleur d'oranger* (1878); *Les Vins de France* (1879); *Mignons et vilains* (1879); *Les Deux Pigeons* (1886); *Scaramouche* (1891); *Amants éternels* (1893); *Le Chevalier aux fleurs,* in collaboration with Pugno (1897); *Le Procès des roses* (1897); *Une Aventure de la Guimard* (1900); *Passconnement* (Jan. 19, 1926). He also wrote incidental music to Delair's *Hélène* (1891) and Moreau and Carré's *La Montagne enchantée,* in collaboration with Leroux (1897).

BIBLIOGRAPHY: Autobiographical sketch and articles on Messager in *Musica* (Paris, Sept. 1908); O. Séré, *Musiciens français d'aujourd'hui* (1911; revised ed., 1921); H. Février, *André Messager; Mon maître, mon ami* (Paris, 1948); M. Augé-Laribé, *André Messager, Musicien de théâtre* (Paris, 1951).

Messchaert, Johannes Martinus, Dutch baritone; b. Hoorn, Aug. 22, 1857; d. Zürich, Sept. 9, 1922. He studied violin, then changed to singing; was a pupil of Stockhausen in Frankfurt and Wüllner in Munich; began his career as a choral conductor in Amsterdam; then appeared as a singer of the German repertoire; lived for many years in Berlin; in 1920 went to teach at the Cons. of Zürich.

BIBLIOGRAPHY: F. Martienssen, *Johannes Messchaert. Ein Beitrag zum Verständnis echter Gesangskunst* (Berlin, 1914; 2nd ed., 1920); idem, *Johannes Messchaert, Eine Gesangsstunde;* F. Martienssen also ed. 2 vols. of Schubert's songs with Messchaert's dynamic marks (Mainz, 1928). A collection of reminiscences about Messchaert was ed. by M.C. Canneman in 1968.

Messiaen, Olivier, outstanding French composer; b. Avignon, Dec. 10, 1908. A scion of an intellectual family (his father was a translator of English literature; his mother, Cécile Sauvage, a poet), he absorbed the atmosphere of culture and art as a child. A mystical quality was imparted by his mother's

Messiaen

book of verses *L'Ame en bourgeon (The Burgeoning Soul),* dedicated to her as yet unborn child. He learned to play piano; at the age of 8 composed a song, *La Dame de Shalott,* to a poem by Tennyson. At the age of 11 he entered the Paris Cons., where he attended the classes of Jean and Noël Gallon, Marcel Dupré, Maurice Emmanuel, and Paul Dukas, specializing in organ, improvisation, and composition; he carried first prizes in all these departments. After graduation in 1930 he became organist at the Trinity Church in Paris. That same year he began teaching at the Ecole Normale de Musique and at the Schola Cantorum. That same year he organized, with André Jolivet, Ives Baudrier, and Daniel-Lesur, the group La Jeune France, with the aim of promoting modern French music. He was in the French army at the outbreak of World War II in 1939; was taken prisoner; spent 2 years in a German prison camp in Görlitz, Silesia; he composed there his *Quatuor pour la fin du temps;* was repatriated in 1942 and resumed his post as organist at the Trinity Church in Paris; was also appointed to the faculty of the Paris Cons., where he taught harmony and musical analysis. After the war he gave courses at the Berkshire Music Center in Tanglewood (1948) and at Darmstadt (1950–53). Young composers seeking instruction in new music became his eager pupils; among them were Pierre Boulez, Jean-Louis Martinet, Stockhausen, Xenakis, and others who were to become important composers in their own right. He received numerous honors; was made a Grand Officier de la Légion d'Honneur; was elected a member of the Inst. de France, of the Bavarian Academy of the Fine Arts, of the Santa Cecilia Academy in Rome, of the American Academy of Arts and Letters, and of other organizations. He is married to the pianist **Yvonne Loriod.** Messiaen is one of the most original of modern composers; in his music he makes use of a wide range of resources, from Gregorian chant to oriental rhythms. A mystic by nature and Catholic by religion, he strives to find a relationship between progressions of musical sounds and religious concepts; in his theoretical writing he strives to postulate an interdependence of modes, rhythms, and harmonic structures. Ever in quest of new musical resources, he employs in his scores the "Ondes Martenot" and exotic percussion instruments; a synthesis of these disparate tonal elements finds its culmination in his grandiose orch. work *Turangalîla-Symphonie.* One of the most fascinating aspects of Messiaen's innovative musical vocabulary is the phonetic emulation of bird song in several of his works; in order to attain ornithological fidelity, he made a detailed study notating the rhythms and pitches of singing birds in many regions of several countries. The municipal council of Parowan, Utah, where Messiaen wrote his work *Des canyons aux étoiles,* glorifying the natural beauties of the state of Utah, resolved to name a local mountain Mt. Messiaen on Aug. 5, 1978. On Nov. 28, 1983, his first opera, *St. François d'Assise,* was produced, with international acclaim, at the Paris Opéra.

WORKS: Opera, *St. François d'Assise* (Paris Opéra, Nov. 28, 1983). For Orch.: Fugue in D minor (1928); *Le Banquet eucharistique* (1928); *Simple chant d'une âme* (1930); *Les Offrandes oubliées* (1930; Paris, Feb. 19, 1931); *Le Tombeau resplendissant* (1931; Paris, Feb. 12, 1933); *Hymne au Saint Sacrement* (1932; Paris, March 23, 1933; N.Y., March 13, 1947, Stokowski conducting); *L'Ascension* (1933; Paris, Feb. 1935); *3 Talas* for Piano and Orch. (Paris, Feb. 14, 1948); *Turangalîla-Symphonie* (1946–48; Boston, Dec. 2, 1949); *Réveil des oiseaux* for Piano and Orch. (Donaueschingen, Oct. 11, 1953); *Oiseaux exotiques* for Piano, 2 Wind Instruments, Xylophone, Glockenspiel, and Percussion (Paris, March 10, 1956); *Chronochromie* (Donaueschingen, Oct. 16, 1960); *7 Haï-kaï* for Piano, 13 Wind Instruments, Xylophone, Marimba, 4 Percussion Instruments, and 8 Violins (1962; Paris, Oct. 30, 1963); *Couleurs de la cité céleste* for Large Orch., with imitations of 2 New Zealand birds and one from Brazil (Donaueschingen, Oct. 17, 1964, Boulez conducting); *Et expecto resurrectionem mortuorum* for 18 Woodwinds, 16 Brass Instruments, and 3 Percussion Instruments (1964; Paris, May 7, 1965); *Des canyons aux étoiles* (1970–74; N.Y., Nov. 20, 1974). Chamber music: *Thème et variations* for Violin and Piano (1932); *Quatuor pour la fin du temps* for Violin, Clarinet, Cello, and Piano (perf. in Stalag 8A, Görlitz, Silesia, with the composer at the piano, Jan. 15, 1941); *Le Merle noir* for Flute and Piano (1951); *Le Tombeau de Jean-Pierre Guézec* for Horn (1971). Vocal works: *2 ballades de Villon* (1921); *3 mélodies* (1930); *La Mort du nombre* for Soprano, Tenor, Violin, and Piano (1930; Paris, March 25, 1931); Mass for 8 Sopranos and 4 Violins (1933); *Poèmes pour Mi* for Soprano and Piano (1936; Paris, April 28, 1937; orch. version, 1937; Paris, 1946); *O sacrum convivium!* for Chorus and Organ (1937); *Chants de terre et de ciel,* song cycle for Soprano and Piano to texts by the composer (1938); *Chœurs pour une Jeanne d'Arc* for Chorus a cappella (1941); *3 petites liturgies de la Présence Divine* for 18 Sopranos, Piano, Ondes Martenot, and Orch. (1944; Paris, April 21, 1945); *Harawi,* "chant d'amour et de mort," for Dramatic Soprano and Piano (1945); *5 rechants* for 12-voice Chorus (1949); *La Transfiguration de Notre Seigneur Jésus-Christ,* in 14 sections, for Chorus and Orch. (Lisbon, June 7, 1969). For Piano: *8 Preludes* (1929); *Pièce pour le tombeau de Paul Dukas* (1935); *Visions de l'Amen* for 2 Pianos (1942); *20 regards sur l'enfant Jésus* (1944); *Cantéyodjayâ* (1948); *4 études de rythme* (1949); *Catalogue d'oiseaux* (1956–58). For Organ: *Variations écossaises* (1928); *Le Banquet céleste* (1928); *Diptyque* (1929); *Apparition de l'église éternelle* (1932); *L'Ascension,* version of orch. work of 1933 with new 3rd movement (1934); *La Nativité du Seigneur* (1935); *Les Corps glorieux* (1939); *Messe de la Pentecôte* (1950); *Livre d'orgue* (1951); *Verset pour la fête de la dédicace* (1960); *Méditations sur le mystère de la Sainte Trinité* (1969).

WRITINGS: *20 leçons de solfèges modernes* (Paris, 1933); *20 leçons d'harmonie* (Paris, 1939); *Technique de mon langage musical* (2 vols., Paris, 1944; Eng. trans. as *The Technique of My Musical Language,* in 2 vols., 1957); individual articles on musical ornithology and other subjects.

BIBLIOGRAPHY: B. Gavoty, *Musique et mystique: Le "cas" Messiaen* (Paris, 1945); Virginie Zinke-Bianchini, *Olivier Messiaen. Notice biographique; catalogue détaillé des œuvres éditées* (Paris, 1946); Claude Rostand, *Olivier Messiaen* (Paris, 1958; contains a list of works and a discography); A. Goléa, *Rencontres avec Olivier Messiaen* (Paris, 1961); Claude Samuel, *Entretiens avec Olivier Messiaen* (Paris, 1967); Stuart Waumsley, *The Organ Music of Olivier Messiaen* (Paris, 1969; revised ed., 1975); Robert Sherlaw Johnson, *Messiaen* (Berkeley, Calif., 1975); Roger Nicols, *Messiaen* (London, 1975).

Messiter, Arthur Henry, organist; b. Frome, Somersetshire, England, April 12, 1834; d. New York, July 2, 1916. He was for 31 years (1866–97) organist and choirmaster at Trinity Church, N.Y.; publ. *A History of the Choir and Music of Trinity Church* (1906).

Messner, Joseph, Austrian organist; b. Schwaz (Tyrol), Feb. 27, 1893; d. St. Jakob Thurn, near Salzburg, Feb. 23, 1969. He studied in Innsbruck; then went to Munich, where he took courses in organ playing and composition with Friedrich Klose; in 1922 he was appointed cathedral organist in Salzburg; from 1926 to 1967 he led the concerts at the Salzburg Cathedral. At the same time he gave a seminar in church music at the Mozarteum there. He wrote 4 operas: *Hadassa* (Aachen, March 27, 1925); *Das letzte Recht* (1932); *Ines* (1933); *Agnes Bernauer* (1935); 3 symphs.; Violin Concerto; Cello Concerto; String Quartet; several sacred works, including 11 masses. He edited a collection of old Salzburg masters (Bernardi, Caldara, M. Haydn, Leopold Mozart, W.A. Mozart); also transcribed Bruckner's Mass in C and Choral Mass.

Mester, Jorge, talented American conductor; b. Mexico City, April 10, 1935, of Hungarian parents. He began to play the violin and viola as a youth. He attended an American school in Mexico City and later a military academy in Hollywood. In 1952 he enrolled at the Juilliard School of Music in N.Y., where he studied conducting with Jean Morel; he received a master's degree there in 1957; also attended conducting classes with Leonard Bernstein in Tanglewood (1955). He made his orch. debut as a conductor in Mexico City in 1955. From 1957 to 1967 he taught conducting at the Juilliard School of Music. In 1964 he led a few exhibitionistic concerts of the parodistic P.D.Q. Bach series in N.Y. inaugurated with a great thud by Peter Schickele. In 1967 he was appointed conductor and music director of the Louisville (Ky.) Orch., holding this post until 1979. Following the Louisville Orch.'s unique policy of commissioning new works and then giving their premieres, Mester conducted, during his tenure, something like 200 first performances, and made about 70 recordings of some of them. Concurrently, he served as principal conductor of the Kansas City Phil. (1971–74). In 1970 he assumed the post of music director of the Aspen Music Festival; in 1980 he was charged with the task of reorganizing the Casals Festival in Puerto Rico. In 1982 he resumed his teaching duties at the Juilliard School of Music in N.Y. Equally at home in the classical and modern repertoire, in symph. music and in opera, Mester knows how to impart a sense of color with a precision of technical detail.

Mestres-Quadreny, Josep Maria, Spanish composer; b. Manresa, March 4, 1929. He studied composition with Cristòfor Taltabull at the Univ. of Barcelona (1950–56); in 1960 collaborated in the founding of Música Abierta, an organization of avant-garde musical activity; later he joined composers Xavier Benguerel, Joaquim Homs, and Josep Soler in founding the Conjunt Català de Música Contemporània, for the propagation of Catalan music. In 1968 he went to work in an electronic music studio. In his music he consciously attempts to find a counterpart to Abstract Expressionism in art, as exemplified by the paintings of Miró; for this purpose he applies serial techniques and aleatory procedures.

WORKS: Piano Sonata (1957); *Epitafios,* cantata for Soprano, Strings, Harp, and Celesta (1958); opera, *El Ganxo* (1959); *Triade per a Joan Miró,* composed of *Música da cámara I* for Flute, Piano, Percussion, Violin, and Double Bass; *Música da cámara II* for 3 Clarinets, English Horn, Trumpet, Trombone, Percussion, and String Trio; and *3 Moviments per a orquesta de cámara* for 15 Instruments, formed by superimposing the previous 2 works (all 1961); *3 invenció mòvils: I* for Flute, Clarinet, and Piano; *II* for Voice, Trumpet, and Electric Guitar; and *III* for String Quartet (all 1961); *Tramesa a Tàpies* for Violin, Viola, and Percussion (1961); 3 ballets: *Roba i ossos (Things and Bones,* 1961); *Petit diumenge (Little Sunday,* 1962); *Vegetació submergida (Submerged Vegetation,* 1962); *Quartet de Catroc* for String Quartet (1962); *Digodal* for String Orch. (1963); *Concert per a representar,* musical theater for 6 Voices, 6 Instrumentalists, and Tape (1964); *3 cànons en homenatge a Galile,* in 3 versions: for Piano, for Percussion, and for Ondes Martenot, each with Tape (1965, 1968, 1969); *Conversa* for Chamber Orch. (1965); *Suite bufa,* musical theater for Ballerina, Mezzo-soprano, Piano, and Electronic Sound (1966); *Tríptic carnavalesc,* cantata for Soprano, Flute, Clarinet, Trumpet, Trombone, 2 Percussionists, and Piano (1966); *Música per a Anna* for Soprano and String Quartet (1967); String Trio (1968); *Ibemia* for 13 Instrumentalists (1969); *Quadre* for Chamber Orch. (1969); *Micos i Papellones* for Guitar and Metal Percussion (1970); *Double Concerto* for Ondes Martenot, Percussion, and Orch. (1970); *Variacions essencials* for String Trio and Percussion (1970); *Homenatge a Joan Prats* for 6 Actors, Electroacoustical Installation, String Quartet, 4 Percussionists, Flute, Clarinet, Trumpet, 2 Trombones, and Tuba (1972); *Frigoli-Frigola* and *Aronada* for any number or type of Instruments (1969, 1972).

Metallov, Vasili, Russian musicologist; b. Saratov,

March 13, 1862; d. Moscow, June 1, 1926. He studied theology and Russian church music; in 1901, was appointed prof. of the history of Russian church singing at the Moscow Cons. His works on Russian church music possess great authority; they include *Alphabet of the Neume Songs* (Moscow, 1899); *The Synodal Singers* (1898); *Outline of the History of the Orthodox Church Song in Russia* (1893); *The Strict Style* (1897); etc. Metallov twice received awards from the Russian Academy of Sciences.

Metastasio, Pietro Antonio Domenico Bonaventura, famous Italian poet and opera librettist; b. Rome, Jan. 3, 1698; d. Vienna, April 12, 1782. He was the son of a papal soldier named Trapassi, but in his professional career assumed the Greek trans. of the name, both Trapassi (or Trapassamento) and Metastasio, meaning transition. He was a learned classicist; began to write plays as a young boy; studied music with Porpora; he achieved great fame in Italy as a playwright; in 1730 was appointed court poet at Vienna by Emperor Charles VI. He wrote about 35 opera texts, which were set to music by Handel, Gluck, Mozart, Hasse, Porpora, Jommelli, and many other celebrated composers; some of them were set to music 60 or more times. His librettos were remarkable for their melodious verse, which naturally suggested musical associations; the libretto to the opera by Niccolo Conforto, *La Nitteti* (1754; first perf. in Madrid, Sept. 23, 1756), was on the same subject as *Aida*, anticipating the latter by more than a century. Metastasio's complete works were publ. in Paris (1780–82; 12 vols.), Mantua (1816–20; 20 vols.); ed. by F. Gazzani (Torino, 1968); ed. by M. Fubino (Milano, 1968); see also A. Wotquenne, *Verzeichnis der Stücke in Versen ... von Zeno, Metastasio und Goldoni* (Leipzig, 1905).
    BIBLIOGRAPHY: S. Mattei, *Memorie per servire alla vita del Metastasio* (Colle, 1785); C. Burney, *Life and Letters of Metastasio* (3 vols., 1796; reprinted N.Y., 1973); M. Zito, *Studio su Pietro Metastasio* (Naples, 1904). E.M. Leonardi, *Il melodramma del Metastasio* (Naples, 1909); L. Russo, *Metastasio* (1921); A. Gustarelli, *Metastasio* (1930); M. Apollonio, *Metastasio* (1931); A. Bonaventura, "Pietro Metastasio musicista," *Musica d'Oggi* (1932); A. Vullo, *Confronto fra i melodrammi di Zeno e Metastasio* (Agrigento, 1935); A. Salazar, "Un antecedente de Aida en España," *Nuestra Música* (Mexico, 1950); H.C. Wolff, "Das Märchen von der Neapolitanischen Oper und Metastasio," *Analecta Musicologica,* 9 (1970).

Metcalf, Frank J., American hymnologist; b. Ashland, Mass., April 4, 1865; d. Washington, D.C., Feb. 25, 1945. He studied at Boston Univ. (B.A., 1886); was for 42 years a clerk in the War Department. He owned a private collection of more than 2,000 hymn books, including Lyon's *Urania* (1761) and other rare editions; also a MS bibliography containing about 10,000 entries. He publ. *American Psalmondy* (N.Y, 1917); *American Writers and Compilers of Sacred Music* (N.Y., 1925); *Stories of Hymn Tunes* (N.Y., 1928); also numerous articles.

Methfessel, Albert Gottlieb, German composer; b. Stadtilm, Thuringia, Oct. 6, 1785; d. Heckenbeck, near Gandersheim, March 23, 1869. From 1832 until 1842 he was court composer at Braunschweig, then retired on a pension.
    WORKS: Opera, *Der Prinz von Basra;* oratorio, *Das befreite Jerusalem;* sonatas and sonatinas for Piano; part-songs, publ. in his *Liederbuch, Liederkranz,* and other collections.
    BIBLIOGRAPHY: W.H. Riehl, *Musikalische Charakterköpfe,* vol. 3 (Stuttgart, 1879). His brother, **Friedrich Methfessel** (b. Stadtilm, Aug. 27, 1771; d. there, May 14, 1807), publ. songs with guitar accompaniment.

Metianu, Lucian, Rumanian composer; b. Cluj, June 3, 1937. He studied with Olah, Vancea, Paul Constantinescu, and Chirescu at the Bucharest Cons. (1957–63).
    WORKS: *Cantata de camera* for Chorus and Chamber Orch. (1953); Concerto for String Orch. (1959); *2 Choreographic Tableaux* for Orch. (1964); *Echo* for Orch. (1966); *Ergodica* for Orch. (1967); *Conexe* for Speaking Chorus and Orch. (1969); *Elogiu* for Orch. (1969); Piano Quintet (1960); 2 string quartets (1961, 1968); Piano Sonata (1962); *Pithagoreis* for Tape (1970–71).

Metner, Nicolai. See **Medtner, Nicolai.**

Métra, (Jules-Louis-) Olivier, French composer of light music; b. Le Mans, June 2, 1830; d. Paris, Oct. 22, 1889. An actor's son, he became an actor himself as a boy; was first taught music by E. Roche; then was a pupil of Elwart at the Paris Cons. (1849–54). He played violin, cello, and double bass at Paris theaters; then conducted at various dance halls; the masked balls at the Opéra-Comique (1871); the orch. at the Folies-Bergère (1872–77); the balls at the Théâtre de la Monnaie, Brussels (1874–76); finally, the balls at the Paris Opéra. His waltzes, mazurkas, polkas, quadrilles, etc. were extremely popular; at the Folies-Bergère he produced 19 operettas and ballet divertissements; and at the Opéra, the ballet *Yedda* (1879).

Métru, Nicolas, French organist and composer; b. Bar-sur-Aube, c.1600; d. Paris, c.1670. He was organist at St.-Nicholas-des-Champs in Paris (1642); was Lully's teacher. Ballard publ. his *Fantaisies* in 2 parts for String Instruments (1642), 2 books of airs (1646), and an *Air sur la paix et le mariage du roy* (1662).

Mettenleiter, Dominicus, German music historian, brother of **Johann Georg Mettenleiter;** b. Tannhausen, near Ellwangen, May 20, 1822; d. Regensburg, May 2, 1868. He collaborated with his brother in the publication of his *Enchiridion chorale* and publ. on his own several valuable works dealing with music in Bavaria: *Aus der musikalischen Vergangenheit bayrischer Städte: Musikgeschichte der Stadt Regensburg* (Regensburg, 1866); *Musik-*

geschichte der Oberpfalz (Amberg, 1867); etc. He also wrote a biography of his brother (Brixen, 1866) and of Karl Proske (Regensburg, 1868; 2nd ed., 1895). His valuable music collection was incorporated with Proske's library in Regensburg.

Mettenleiter, Johann Georg, German church composer, brother of **Dominicus Mettenleiter;** b. St. Ulrich, near Ulm, April 6, 1812; d. Regensburg, Oct. 6, 1858, as choirmaster and organist at the Cathedral. An erudite church composer, he publ. *Manuale breve cantionum ac precum* (1852) and *Enchiridion chorale . . .* (1855), both with added organ accompaniments; also Psalm 95, for 6 Male Voices (1854); other works in MS (masses; a *Stabat Mater; 2 Miserere; Ave Maria* for Double Chorus, etc.). His brother wrote his biography, *Johann Georg Mettenleiter, Ein Künstlerbild* (1866).

Metzler, Valentin, music publisher and instrument dealer in London; b. Bingen, Germany; d. London, 1833. He settled in London about 1788 and opened a shop for the sale of musical instruments; after his death, his son **George Richard Metzler** (1797–1867) became the owner, and the name of the firm was changed to G. Metzler & Co. In 1816 the firm began to publ. music; in 1867 G. Metzler entered into partnership with Frank Chappell; the firm continued to carry on its business in London until 1930.

Meulemans, Arthur, Belgian composer; b. Aarschot, May 19, 1884; d. Brussels, June 29, 1966. He studied with Edgar Tinel in Mechelen; in 1916 founded the Limburg School for organ at Hasselt; he then moved to Brussels; conducted the radio orch. there (1930–42); in 1954 was elected president of the Royal Flemish Academy of Fine Arts. He produced a prodigious amount of highly competent works in all genres.
  WORKS: 3 operas: *Vikings* (1919), *Adriaen Brouwer* (1926), and *Egmont* (1944; Antwerp, 1960); 15 symphs.: No. 1 (1931); No. 2 (1933); No. 3, *Dennensymphonie* (1933); No. 4, for Winds and Percussion (1934); No. 5, *Danssymphonie,* with Female Chorus (1939); No. 6, *Zeesymphonie,* with Contralto and Mixed Chorus (1940); No. 7, *Zwaneven* (1942); No. 8, *Herfstsymphonie,* with Soli and Chorus (1942); No. 9 (1943); No. 10, *Psalmen-Symphonie,* with 2 Narrators, Soli, and Chorus (1943); No. 11 (1946); No. 12 (1948); No. 13, *Rembrandt-Symphonie* (1950); No. 14 (1954); No. 15 (1960); 3 sinfoniettas (1952, 1959–60, 1960); 2 ballet suites: *Josaphatpark* (1933) and *De Vogels* (1947); 3 oratorios: *Sacrum mysterium* (1917), *De zeven weeën* (1920), and *De dochtor van Jairus* (1922); various symph. poems, suites, and pieces that include: *Meinacht* (1912); *Plinius Fontein* (1913); *Karnaval-Suite* (1926); *Stadspark,* prelude and scherzo (1928); *Vlaamse rapsodie* (1932); *Verworvenheden* (1939); *Adagio* for Strings (1939); *4 Symphonic Sketches* (1940); *Fusillé à l'aube* (1948); *De Witte,* with Chorus (1949); *Symphonic Triptych* (1951); *Meterologisch Instituut* (1951); *Tableaux* (1952); *Peter Breugel* (1952); *Hertog Jan*

van Brabant, with Baritone (1953); *Social Security,* masquerade (1954); *Ionisatie,* choreographic movements (1956); *Relais* (1957), *Symphonic Dances* (1957); *Esquisses symphoniques* (1958); *Divertimento,* with Chorus (1958); *Aforismen* (1961); *Middelheim* (1961); *Partita* (1961); *Cirkus* (1961); *Torenhof* (1963); 2 *Concertos for Orchestra* (1953, 1956); many works for soloist and orch.: 3 piano concertos (1941, 1956, 1960), 2–Piano Concerto (1959); 3 violin concertos (1942, 1946, 1950); Viola Concerto (1942); 2 cello concertos (1920, 1944); Flute Concerto (1942); Oboe Concerto (1942); *Sonata concertante* for Clarinet and String Orch. (1948); 4–Clarinet Concertino (1963); 4–Clarinet Suite (1964); 4–Saxophone Concerto Grosso (1958); 4–Saxophone Concertino (1962); 2 horn concertos (1940, 1961); Trumpet Concerto (1943); Trombone Concertino (1953); Timpani Concerto (1954); Harp Concerto (1953); Harpsichord Concerto (1958); 2 organ concertos (1942, 1958); Concerto Grosso for 6 Winds, Strings, Harp, and Percussion (1962). Chamber music: 5 string quartets (1915, 1932, 1933, 1944, 1952); 2 violin sonatas (1915, 1953); Viola Sonata (1953); Cello Sonata (1953); Trumpet Sonata (1959); Piano Trio (1941); String Trio (1941); 2 woodwind trios (1933, 1960); 2 brass trios (1933, 1960); Piano Quartet (1915); Woodwind Quartet (1962); Saxophone Quartet (1953); *Suite* for 4 Trombones (1942); 3 wind quintets (1931, 1932, 1958); Concerto for Organ, Trumpet, Horn, and Trombone (1962); many other works and solo pieces. For piano: 3 sonatas (1916, 1917, 1951); 3 sonatinas (1927, 1928, 1941); *Refleksen* (1923); *Préludes* (1951); *Atmosferiliën* (1962). For organ: Sonata (1915); 2 symphs. (1949); *7 Pieces* (1959); *Pièce heroïque* (1959). He also wrote many pieces for carillon, a cappella choruses, and songs.

Mey, Kurt Johannes, German musicologist; b. Dresden, June 24, 1864; d. there, Sept. 21, 1912. He studied with K.A. Fischer in Dresden and with Spitta at the Univ. of Berlin; after filling various positions as répétiteur in provincial opera houses, he returned to Dresden. He publ. *Der Meistergesang in Geschichte und Kunst* (1892; revised ed., 1901); *Die Musik als tönende Weltidee* (part I, *Die metaphysischen Urgesetze der Melodik,* 1901); etc.

Meybom, Marcus. See **Meibom, Marcus.**

Meyer, Ernst Hermann, German musicologist and composer; b. Berlin, Dec. 8, 1905. His father was a medical doctor of artistic interests who encouraged him to study music; he took piano lessons with Walter Hirschberg and played in chamber music groups. During the economic disarray in Germany in the 1920s Meyer was obliged to do manual labor in order to earn a living. In 1926 he was able to enroll in the Univ. of Berlin, where he studied musicology with Johannes Wolf, Arnold Schering, Friedrich Blume, Erich Hornbostel, and Curt Sachs; in 1928 he had additional studies with Heinrich Besseler at the Univ. of Heidelberg, obtaining his Ph.D. with the dissertation *Die mehrstimmige Spielmusik des 17. Jahrhunderts in Nord- und Mittel-*

europa (publ. in 1934 in Kassel). In 1929 he met Hanns Eisler, who influenced him in the political aspect of music. In 1930 he joined the German Communist Party. He conducted workers' choruses in Berlin and composed music for the proletarian revue *Der rote Stern (The Red Star).* He also attended classes on film music given by Paul Hindemith. In 1931 he took a course in Marxism-Leninism with Hermann Duncker at the Marxist Workers' School in Berlin. He also began a detailed study of works by modern composers; in his own works, mostly for voices, he developed a style characteristic of the proletarian music of the time, full of affirmative action in march time adorned by corrosive discords, and yet eminently singable. When the Nazis bore down on his world with a different march, he fled to London, where, with the help of the English progressive musician Alan Bush, he conducted the Labour Choral Union. During the war he participated in the Chorus of the Free German Cultural Union in London and wrote propaganda songs; of these, *Radio Moskau ruft Frau Krämer* was widely broadcast to Germany. He returned to Germany in 1948 and became engaged in pedagogical activities; taught music history at Humboldt Univ. in East Berlin, retiring in 1970. He was acknowledged as one of the most persuasive theoreticians of socialist realism in music; he founded the periodical *Music und Gesellschaft,* which pursued the orthodox Marxist line. He publ. *English Chamber Music: The History of a Great Art from the Middle Ages to Purcell* (London, 1946; in German as *Die Kammermusik Alt-Englands,* East Berlin, 1958); *Das Werk Beethovens und seine Bedeutung für das sozialistisch-realistische Gegenwartsschaffen* (East Berlin, 1970). A Festschrift was publ. in his honor in Leipzig in 1973.

WORKS: OPERA: *Reiter der Nacht* (1969–72). FOR ORCH.: Symph. for Strings (1946–47; revised 1958); *Symphonischer Prolog,* dedicated to the memory of freedom fighters (1949); Symph. for Piano and Orch. (1961); *Poem* for Viola and Orch. (1962); Violin Concerto (1964); *Serenata pensierosa* (1965); Concerto Grosso (1966); Symph. in B-flat (1967); Harp Concerto (1969); Toccata (1971); *Divertimento* (1973). CHAMBER MUSIC: Trio for Flute, Oboe, and Harp (1935); Clarinet Quintet (1944); Piano Trio, subtitled *Reflections and Resolution* (1948); 3 string quartets (1956, 1959, 1967); *Sonatina Fantasia* for Violin Solo (1966). CHORAL WORKS: *Mansfelder Oratorium* (1950); cantata, *Nun, Steuermann,* after Walt Whitman's *Now Voyager* (1946; revised 1955); *Gesang von der Jugend* for Soloists, Mixed Chorus, Children's Chorus, and Orch. (1957); *Das Tor von Buchenwald* (1959); *Der Staat* for Chorus and Orch. (1967); *Lenin hat gesprochen* (1970); more than 200 mass songs; piano pieces; film music.

BIBLIOGRAPHY: K. Niemann, *E.H. Meyer* (Leipzig, 1975); H.A. Brockhaus and K. Neimann, eds., *Musikgeschichte der deutschen demokratischen Republik, 1945–1976* (East Berlin, 1979; pp. 46–54).

Meyer, Kerstin, Swedish mezzo-soprano; b. Stockholm, April 3, 1928. She studied at the Royal Academy of Music in Stockholm; made her debut at the Royal Theater in Stockholm in 1952; also sang in Rome, Hamburg, Milan, Vienna, Salzburg, and other European music centers. On Oct. 29, 1960, she made her Metropolitan Opera debut as Carmen. She subsequently sang in South America and Japan. In 1963 she was named Swedish court soloist.

Meyer, Krzysztof, remarkable Polish composer; b. Cracow, Aug. 11, 1943. He played piano as a child; then took lessons in composition with Stanislaw Wiechowicz; subsequently undertook formal studies at the State College of Music in Cracow, where he obtained 2 diplomas: in 1965 in composition with Krzysztof Penderecki, and in 1966 in general music theory with Aleksander Frączkiewicz. In 1964, 1966, and 1968 he went to Paris, where he took courses with Nadia Boulanger; won several prizes at various competitions in France and in Poland. In 1970 he won the Grand Prix of the Prince Rainier III Competition in Monaco for his opera *Cyberiada.* In 1965–67 he appeared as a pianist with the contemporary music group MW-2; in 1966 he was appointed to the faculty of the State College of Music in Cracow. In 1981 he lived in Hamburg; then returned to Poland. Among his honors was the Award of the Minister of Culture and Arts in Poland (1975) and the Medal of the Government of Brazil (1975). Apart from his activities as a pianist and a composer, he has also contributed to Polish music journals, and publ. the first Polish-language monograph on Shostakovich, which was also trans. into German. His musical intelligence and acoustical acuity are of the rarest quality. As a composer, he adopts an advanced idiom without ever transcending the practical limits of instrumental and vocal techniques or of aural perception. As a demonstration of his talent for sophisticated mimicry, he composed a Mozartean symph. that is apt to confuse and seduce the most solemn Mozartologist. (It was, perhaps coincidentally, first performed on April Fools' Day in 1977.) Nadia Boulanger wrote of Meyer: "Il est un musicien tout à fait exceptionnel" (*Le Figaro,* Paris, May 7, 1970).

WORKS: Fantastic comic opera, *Cyberiada,* libretto by composer after the novel by Stanislaw Lem (Grand Prix at the Prince Rainier III Competition, Monaco, 1970); 5 symphs.: No. 1 (Cracow, June 12, 1964); No. 2, with Mixed Chorus, *Epitaphium Stanislaw Wiechowicz in memoriam* (1967; Katowice, Feb. 15, 1969); No. 3, *Symphonie d'Orphée,* with Mixed Choir, to words by Paul Valéry (1968; Warsaw, Sept. 1972); No. 4 (1973; Zagreb, May 14, 1975); No. 5 for String Orch. (Bialystok, Sept. 17, 1979); Symph. in D major, in the style of Mozart (1976; Poznan, April 1, 1977); Chamber Concerto for Oboe, Percussion, and String Orch. (1964; Cracow, June 25, 1965); Violin Concerto (1965; Poznan, March 22, 1969); Cello Concerto (Poznan, April 1975); Chamber Concerto for Oboe, Percussion, and String Orch. (Katowice, April 1975); Trumpet Concerto (1975; Poznan, April 2, 1976); *Fireballs* for Orch. (1976; Warsaw, April 20, 1978); *Polish Chants* for Soprano and Orch. (1977; Bydgoszcz, Sept. 9, 1979); *Lyric Triptych* for Tenor and Chamber Orch., to words by W.H. Auden (1976; Aldeburgh, June 22, 1978).

CHAMBER MUSIC: *Introspection* for 5 Cellos (1960); *Music for 3 Cellos, Timpani and Piano* (1962); 5 string quartets (1963, 1969, 1971, 1974, 1977); *Songs of Resignation and Denial* for Soprano, Violin, and Piano (1963); *Quartettino* for Soprano, Flute, Cello, and Piano (1966); *5 Chamber Pieces* for Soprano, Clarinet, Violin, and Viola (1967); *Quattro colori* for Clarinet, Trombone, Cello, and Piano (1971); Concerto da Camera for Oboe, Percusson, and Strings (1972); Solo Violin Sonata (1975); *3 Pieces* for Percussion Solo (1976); *Concerto retro* for Flute, Violin, Cello, and Harpsichord (1976).

FOR PIANO: 5 sonatas (1962, 1963, 1967, 1969, 1975); *Aphorism* (1961); *Magic Pictures* (1975); *Children's Suite* (1978); *24 Preludes* (1978); Harpsichord Sonata (1973).

Meyer, Leonard B., American musicologist and writer on esthetics; b. New York, Jan. 12, 1918. He studied philosophy and composition at Columbia Univ. (M.A. in music, 1948) and humanities at the Univ. of Chicago (Ph.D., 1954); also took private lessons in composition with Stefan Wolpe and Aaron Copland. In 1946 he was appointed to the staff of the Univ. of Chicago; in 1961, became chairman of the music dept.; was prof. there until 1975; was prof. of music and humanities at the Univ. of Pa. from 1975. He publ. an important book dealing with the problems of communication and cultural contexts in the human response to music, *Emotion and Meaning in Music* (Chicago, 1956); *The Rhythmic Structure of Music* (with Grosvenor Cooper; Chicago, 1960); *Music, the Arts, and Ideas: Patterns and Predictions in Twentieth Century Culture* (Chicago, 1967); *Explaining Music: Essays and Explorations* (Berkeley, 1973); with E. Zonis, *Improvisation in Music: East and West* (Chicago, 1973). He also contributed valuable articles to various scholarly journals.

Meyer, Leopold von (called **Leopold de Meyer**), celebrated piano virtuoso; b. Baden, near Vienna, Dec. 20, 1816; d. Dresden, March 5, 1883. He studied with Czerny and Fischhof; at the age of 19, embarked on a series of pianistic tours in Europe; also toured in America (1845–47). At his concerts he invariably included his own compositions, written in a characteristic salon style; his agents spread sensational publicity about him in order to arouse interest. A *Biography of Leopold de Meyer* was publ. in London in 1845.

Meyer-Baer, Kathi, musicologist; b. Berlin, July 27, 1892. She studied piano in Berlin with Frieda Kwast-Hodapp and G. Bertram; then musicology at the Univ. of Berlin with Kretzschmar, Riemann, and Johannes Wolf, receiving her Ph.D. in 1916 with the dissertation *Der chorische Gesang der Frauen* (publ. in Leipzig, 1917). In 1922 she became librarian of the Paul Hirsch Music Library in Frankfurt (transferred in 1936 to Cambridge, England); was music critic for the *Frankfurter Zeitung* (1923–33).

In 1936 she went to Paris; in 1939 settled in N.Y., where she was active as a librarian, teacher, and writer. She publ. *Das Konzert* (Stuttgart, 1925), *Bedeutung und Wesen der Musik* (Strasbourg, 1932), and a great number of valuable publications, among them *Liturgical Music Incunabula. A Descriptive Catalogue* (London, 1962); *Music of the Spheres and the Dance of Death. Studies in Musical Iconography* (Princeton, 1970).

Meyer-Eppler, Werner, Dutch-German physicist and pioneer in electronic music; b. Antwerp, April 30, 1913; d. Bonn, July 8, 1960. He studied physics and mathematics in Cologne and Bonn. In 1949 he joined the faculty of the Univ. of Bonn, working on communication theory. He publ. a valuable treatise, *Musik, Raumgestaltung und Elektroakustik* (Mainz, 1955).

Meyer-Helmund, Erik, composer; b. St. Petersburg, April 25, 1861; d. Berlin, April 4, 1932. He studied music with his father; then in Berlin with Kiel; was first a singer, and traveled extensively in Europe, introducing his own songs; from 1911 he lived in Berlin. He is best known as a song composer; more than 200 of his light vocal numbers were publ.; he also composed 5 operas: *Margitta* (Magdeburg, 1889), *Der Liebeskampf* (Dresden, 1892), *Taglioni* (Berlin, 1912), *Traumbilder* (Berlin, 1912), and *Die schöne Frau Marlies* (Altenburg, 1916); also the operettas *Trischka* (Riga, 1894) and *Lucullus* (Riga, 1905); the ballet *Rübezahl* (Leipzig, 1893); male choruses; and piano pieces in a Romantic vein (*Wonnetraum, Sérénade rococo,* etc.); *Fantasie* for Violin and Orch.; etc.

Meyer-Olbersleben, Max, German pianist and composer; b. Olbersleben, near Weimar, April 5, 1850; d. Würzburg, Dec. 31, 1927. He first studied with his father; then with Liszt at Weimar. On Liszt's recommendation, he received a liberal allowance from the government for further study; took lessons in Munich with Cornelius and Rheinberger. In 1876 he became a teacher of piano and theory at Wüllner-Hartung's orch. school in Weimar; in 1877, was appointed to the staff of the Würzburg Cons., of which he became director in 1907; also conducted the famous Liedertafel from 1879. He was a composer of talent and ability; his chamber music is effectively and competently written; he also publ. songs and piano pieces. His "romantic opera" *Clare Dettin* was produced in Würzburg (1896); the comic opera *Der Haubenkrieg,* in Munich (1902).

Meyer-Siat, Pie, French musicologist; b. Ribeauvillé, Haut-Rhin, Oct. 15, 1913. He was educated at the Univ. of Strasbourg; received a degree in philosophy in 1937; took the agrégation in German in 1948; was awarded his Ph.D. in musicology in 1962 with the dissertation *Les Callinet, facteurs d'orgues à Rouffach, et leur œuvre en Alsace,* publ. in Strasbourg, 1965. He was an authority on organs in Alsace; contributed important articles for *Les*

Meyerbeer

Cahiers de la Société d'Histoire de Saverne; also publ. the books *L'Orgue Callinet de Masevaux* (Mulhouse, 1962); *L'Orgue Joseph Callinet de Mollau (Haut-Rhin)* (Strasbourg, 1963); *Les Orgues de Niedernai et d'Obernai* (Colmar, 1972); *Stiehr-Mockers, facteurs d'orgues* (Hagenau, 1972).

Meyerbeer, Giacomo, famous German opera composer; b. Vogelsdorf, near Berlin, Sept. 5, 1791; d. Paris, May 2, 1864. He was a scion of a prosperous Jewish family; his real name was **Jakob Liebmann Beer;** he added the name Meyer to his surname, forming the plausible compound Meyerbeer, and, following the Italian fashion in musical affairs, changed his German first name, Jakob, to Giacomo. He studied piano with Lauska, and also had a chance to have some instruction in piano from Clementi, who was for a while a guest at Meyerbeer's house in Berlin. He began to study music theory with Zelter, and later took additional courses with Anselm Weber. From 1810 to 1812 he studied with the renowned musician Abbé Vogler at Darmstadt; Carl Maria von Weber was one of his fellow pupils. In Darmstadt he wrote the oratorio *Gott und die Natur,* which was performed in Berlin on May 8, 1811, when Meyerbeer was only 19 years old; there followed the composition of 2 operas, *Jephthas Gelübde,* produced in Munich on Dec. 23, 1812, and *Wirth und Gast, oder Aus Scherz Ernst,* staged at Stuttgart on Jan. 6, 1813; the 2nd of these operas was accepted for production in Vienna under the alternative title *Alimelik.* Meyerbeer knew Salieri, who advised him to enliven the heavily contrapuntal and somewhat Germanic style of his music by the infusion of a free-flowing Italian melos; Meyerbeer followed Salieri's advice, to his great profit. In 1815 he went to Venice, where he wrote several operas in the Italian vein: *Romilda e Costanza,* produced in Padua on July 19, 1817; *Semiramide riconosciuta,* staged in Turin early in 1819; and *Emma di Resburgo,* presented in Venice on June 26, 1819, in an Italian version, and later in German as *Emma von Leicester.* There followed *Margherita d'Angiù* (Milan, Nov. 14, 1820), which attained moderate success. In his next opera, *Il Crociato in Egitto,* produced in Venice on March 7, 1824, Meyerbeer displayed his great talent for dramatic action and Italianate melodic invention. It had a successful production in London on July 23, 1825, followed by a Paris performance on Sept. 25, 1825. He also arranged his opera *Margherita d'Angiù* for the French stage under the title *Margherita d'Anjou;* it was produced in Paris on March 11, 1826. In 1827 Meyerbeer began his long and fruitful association with the famous French writer and librettist Eugène Scribe, with whom he wrote his opera to the French text *Robert le diable,* produced at the Paris Opéra on Nov. 21, 1831, with extraordinary success.

Personal events, both tragic and happy, intervened. His father died on Oct. 27, 1825. On May 25, 1826, he married his cousin Minna Mosson; 2 children, Eugénie and Alfred, were born to them but died in their infancy. He received the order of Chevalier of the Légion d'Honneur, and in 1834 was elected a member of the French Institut. From then on Meyerbeer took permanent residence in Paris. In 1832 he began work on his greatest opera, *Les Huguenots,* to a libretto mainly by Scribe; it was staged with enormous success at the Paris Opéra on Feb. 29, 1836, and eventually entered the repertoire of all major European opera houses. In 1836 Meyerbeer and Scribe began their collaboration on a new opera, *Le Prophète,* and in 1837 they completed the text and score of *L'Africaine;* both operas confirmed Meyerbeer's fame as a composer of tremendous power, capable of moving large audiences by their melodramatic effects, and at the same time impressing critics by the purely musical quality of the work. Meyerbeer became an undisputed king of the French opera establishment; indeed, it is said that Rossini, disgusted by the Meyerbeer cult in Paris, decided not to write anymore for the Paris Opéra. It was only in the early years of the 20th century that music historians began to question the gaudy brilliance of Meyerbeer's stellar flamboyance. After the production of *Les Huguenots* in Berlin in 1842, Meyerbeer was asked by King Friedrich Wilhelm IV to accept the position of Generalmusikdirektor at the capital. Meyerbeer accepted the flattering invitation and produced in Berlin his opera *Ein Feldlager Schlesien;* Jenny Lind lent her illustrious presence in a later performance of the opera, in the role of Vielka. A curious chapter in Meyerbeer's life was his association with Wagner, whom Meyerbeer, many years his senior, helped financially; Meyerbeer also conducted Wagner's opera *Rienzi* in Berlin. Wagner repaid Meyerbeer with ingratitude, attacking his operas as a harmful artistic influence and denigrating him as a Jew. The composition of *Le Prophète* proceeded slowly, but the work eventually received a brilliant stage performance at the Paris Opéra on April 16, 1849, with the celebrated prima donna Pauline Viardot-García in the role of Fidès. Meyerbeer's next opera was *L'Etoile du nord,* which utilized some musical material from *Ein Feldlager in Schlesien;* it was produced at the Opéra-Comique on Feb. 16, 1854; this was followed by the premiere, also at the Opéra-Comique, of Meyerbeer's next opera, *Le Pardon de Ploërmel,* on April 4, 1859. In 1862 Meyerbeer visited England to attend the first performance of a work he wrote for the World Exhibition in London, the *Fest-Ouverture im Marschstyl (Festive Overture in a March Style).* In the meantime, he continued work on a revision of his opera *L'Africaine;* this was greatly handicapped by Scribe's death in 1861. Meyerbeer supervised the rehearsals of the opera, but death supervened with dramatic suddenness on the night of May 2, 1864. Meyerbeer's body was taken to Berlin, where it was laid to earth in official ceremonies attended by the Prussian court and prominent dignitaries in the arts. Fétis was subsequently charged with making the final preparations for the first performance of *L'Africaine,* which was given at the Paris Opéra on April 28, 1865, with great acclaim. This opera, too, entered the general repertoire.

WORKS: OPERAS: *Jephthas Gelübde* (Munich, Dec. 23, 1812); *Wirth und Gast, oder Aus Scherz*

Ernst, Lustspiel (Stuttgart, Jan. 6, 1813; revised as *Die beyden Kalifen*, Vienna, Oct. 20, 1814; later known as *Alimelek*); *Das Brandenburger Tor*, singspiel (composed 1814 but not perf.); *Romilda e Costanza*, melodramma semiserio (Padua, July 19, 1817); *Semiramide riconosciuta*, dramma per musica (Turin, March 1819); *Emma di Resburgo*, melodramma eroico (Venice, June 26, 1819); *Margherita d'Angiù*, melodramma semiserio (Teatro alla Scala, Milan, Nov. 14, 1820; revised as *Margherita d'Anjou*, Odéon, Paris, March 11, 1826); *L'Almanzore* (composed 1821 but not perf.); *L'Esule di Granata*, melodramma serio (Teatro alla Scala, Milan, March 12, 1821); *Il Crociato in Egitto*, melodramma eroico (Venice, March 7, 1824); *Robert le diable*, grand opéra (Opéra, Paris, Nov. 21, 1831); *Les Huguenots*, grand opéra (Opéra, Paris, Feb. 29, 1836); *Ein Feldlager in Schlesien*, singspiel (Berlin, Dec. 7, 1844; later known as *Vielka*); *Le Prophète*, grand opéra (Opéra, Paris, April 16, 1849); *L'Etoile du nord*, opéra comique (Opéra-Comique, Paris, Feb. 16, 1854; much of the music based on *Ein Feldlager in Schlesien*); *Le Pardon de Ploërmel*, opéra comique (Opéra-Comique, Paris, April 4, 1859; also known as *Le Chercheur du trésor* and as *Dinorah, oder Die Wallfahrt nach Ploërmel*); *L'Africaine*, grand opéra (Opéra, Paris, April 28, 1865; originally known as *Vasco da Gama*); Meyerbeer also left a number of unfinished operas in various stages of development. Other stage works include *Der Fischer und das Milchmädchen, oder Viel Lärm um einen Kuss (Le Passage de la rivière, ou La Femme jalouse; Le Pêcheur et la laitière)*, ballet-pantomime (Berlin, March 26, 1810); *Gli amori di Teolinda (Thecelindens Liebschaften)*, monodrama (Genoa, 1816); *Das Hoffest von Ferrara*, masque (Berlin, Feb. 28, 1843); *Struensee*, incidental music for a drama by Michael Beer, Meyerbeer's brother (Berlin, Sept. 19, 1846); etc.

SACRED MUSIC: *Gott und die Natur*, oratorio (Berlin, May 8, 1811); *Geistliche Gesänge*, 7 odes after Klopstock, for Soprano, Alto, Tenor, and Bass (Leipzig, 1817 or 1818); *An Gott*, hymn for Soprano, Alto, Tenor, Bass, and Piano (Leipzig, 1817); Psalm XCI for Soprano, Alto, Tenor, Bass, and Double Mixed Chorus a cappella (Berlin, 1853); *Prière du matin* for 2 Choirs and Piano ad libitum (Paris, 1864); etc.

OCCASIONAL AND SECULAR CHORAL WORKS: *Festgesang zur Errichtung des Guttenbergischen Denkmals in Mainz* for 2 Tenors, 2 Basses, Men's Voices, and Piano ad libitum (Mainz, 1835); *Dem Vaterland* for Men's Voices (Berlin, 1842); *Le Voyageur au tombeau de Beethoven* for Bass Solo and Women's Voices a cappella (composed 1845); *Festhymne* for Solo Voices, Chorus, and Piano ad libitum (for the silver wedding anniversary of the King and Queen of Prussia, 1848); *Ode an Rauch* for Solo Voices, Chorus, and Orch. (in honor of the sculptor Christian Rauch; Berlin, 1851); *Maria und ihr Genius*, cantata for Soprano, Tenor, Chorus, and Piano (for the silver wedding anniversary of Prince and Princess Carl, 1852); *Brautgeleite aus der Heimat*, serenade for Chorus a cappella (for the wedding of Princess Luise, 1856); *Festgesang zur Feier des 100 jährigen Geburtsfestes von Friedrich Schiller* for

Soprano, Alto, Tenor, Bass, Chorus, and Orch. (composed 1859); *Festhymnus* for Solo Voices, Chorus, and Piano ad libitum (for the coronation of Wilhelm I, 1861); etc.

FOR ORCH.: Symph. in E-flat major (1811); Piano Concerto (1811); Concerto for Piano and Violin (1812); 4 *Fackeltänze* for Military Band or Orch. (1844, 1850, 1856, 1858); *Festmarsch* for the centenary of Schiller's birth (1859); *Krönungsmarsch* for 2 Orchs. (for the coronation of Wilhelm I, 1861); *Fest-Ouverture im Marschstyl* (for the opening of the World Exhibition in London, 1862); etc. He also composed many fine songs, as well as pieces for piano.

BIBLIOGRAPHY: A. Morel, *Le Prophète: Analyse critique de la nouvelle partition de Giacomo Meyerbeer* (Paris, 1849); E. Lindner, *Meyerbeers "Prophet" als Kunstwerk beurtheilt* (Berlin, 1850); E. de Mirecourt, *Meyerbeer* (Paris, 1854); A. de Lasalle, *Meyerbeer, Sa vie et le catalogue de ses œuvres* (Paris, 1864); A. Pougin, *Meyerbeer: Notes biographiques* (Paris, 1864); H. Blaze de Bury, *Meyerbeer et son temps* (Paris, 1865); H. Mendel, *Giacomo Meyerbeer* (Berlin, 1868); J. Schucht, *Meyerbeers Leben und Bildungsgang* (Leipzig, 1869); A. Body, *Meyerbeer aux eaux de Spa* (Brussels, 1885); A. Kohut, *Meyerbeer* (Leipzig, 1890); E. Destranges, *L'Œuvre théâtral de Meyerbeer* (Paris, 1893); J. Weber, *Meyerbeer: Notes et souvenirs d'un de ses secrétaires* (Paris, 1898); J.G. Prod'homme, "Die Hugenotten-Premiere," *Die Musik*, III/1 (1903–4); H. de Curzon, *Meyerbeer: Biographie critique* (Paris, 1910); H. Eymieu, *L'Œuvre de Meyerbeer* (Paris, 1910); L. Dauriac, *Meyerbeer* (Paris, 1913; 2nd ed., 1930); L. Hirschberg, "Meyerbeers religiöse Tonwerke," *Die Musik*, XIII/3 (1914); G. Kruse, "Meyerbeers Jugendopern," *Zeitschrift für Musikwissenschaft*, I (1918–19); J. Kapp, *Giacomo Meyerbeer* (Berlin, 1920; 8th ed., revised, 1932); J. Strelitzer, *Meyerbeers deutsche Jugendopern* (Diss., Univ. of Münster, 1920); A. Brent Smith, "The Tragedy of Meyerbeer," *Music & Letters*, VI (1925); E. Istel, "Meyerbeer's Way to Mastership," *Musical Quarterly* (Jan. 1926); G. Servières, "Les Transformations et tribulations de *L'Africaine*," *Rivista Musicale Italiana*, XXXIV (1927); R. Haudek, *Scribes Operntexte für Meyerbeer: Eine Quellenuntersuchung* (Diss., Univ. of Vienna, 1928); H. Abert, "Giacomo Meyerbeer," *Gesammelte Schriften und Vorträge* (Halle, 1929); J. Cooke, *Meyerbeer* (Philadelphia, 1929); J.-G. Prod'homme, "Meyerbeer à Paris avant 'Robert le diable,' d'après son journal inédit," *Mercure de France* (April 14, 1936); H. Becker, "Meyerbeers Ergänzungsarbeit an Webers nachgelassener Oper 'Die drei Pintos,'" *Die Musikforschung*, VII (1954); idem, *Der Fall Heine-Meyerbeer: Neue Dokumente revidieren ein Geschichtsurteil* (Berlin, 1958); idem, ed., *Giacomo Meyerbeer: Briefwechsel und Tagebücher* (Berlin, 1960—); idem, "Giacomo Meyerbeer," *Leo Baeck Institute: Yearbook*, IX (London, 1964); M. Brod, "Some Comments on the Relationship between Wagner and Meyerbeer," ibid.; H. Kirchmeyer, "Psychologie des Meyerbeer-Erfolges," *Neue Zeitschrift für Musik*, 125 Jg. (1964); J. Klein, "Giacomo Meyerbeer (1791–

1864)," *Music Review,* XXV (1964); J. Meyerowitz, "Giacomo Meyerbeer," *Musica,* XIX (1965); C. Frese, *Dramaturgie der grossen Opern Giacomo Meyerbeers* (Berlin, 1970); S. Döhring, "Les Œuvres tardives de Meyerbeer," *Schweizerische Musikzeitung/Revue Musicale Suisse,* XCV (1975); M. Loppert, "An Introduction to 'L'Etoile du nord,'" *Musical Times,* CXVI (1975); J. Thomson, "Giacomo Meyerbeer: The Jew and His Relationship with Richard Wagner," *Musica Judaica,* I (1975–76); H. Becker, *Meyerbeer: Bild-Monographie* (Reinbek, near Hamburg, 1980); J. Fulcher, "Meyerbeer and the Music of Society," *Musical Quarterly* (April 1981).

Meyerowitz, Jan, German-American composer; b. Breslau, April 23, 1913. In 1927 he went to Berlin, where he studied with Gmeindl and Zemlinsky at the Hochschule für Musik. Compelled to leave Germany in 1933, he went to Rome, where he took lessons in advanced composition with Respighi and Casella, and in conducting with Molinari. In 1938 he moved to Belgium and later to southern France, where he remained until 1946; he then emigrated to the U.S., becoming a naturalized citizen in 1951. He married the French singer **Marguerite Fricker** in 1946. He held a Guggenheim fellowship twice (1956, 1958). In the U.S. he taught at the Berkshire Music Center in Tanglewood and at Brooklyn College; in 1962 was appointed to the faculty of the City College of N.Y. In 1977 he received a grant from the National Endowment for the Arts. His music is imbued with expansive emotionalism akin to that of Mahler; in his works for the theater there is a marked influence of the tradition of 19th-century grand opera. His technical idiom is modern, enlivened by a liberal infusion of euphonious dissonance, and he often applies the rigorous and vigorous devices of linear counterpoint.
WORKS: OPERAS: *The Barrier,* to a libretto by Langston Hughes (N.Y., Jan. 10, 1950); *Eastward in Eden* (title changed later to *Emily Dickinson;* Detroit, Nov. 16, 1951); *Simoon* (Tanglewood, Aug. 2, 1950); *Bad Boys in School* (Tanglewood, Aug. 17, 1953); *Esther,* libretto by Langston Hughes (Univ. of Illinois, Urbana, May 17, 1957); *Port Town,* libretto by Langston Hughes (Tanglewood, Aug. 4, 1960); *Godfather Death* (Brooklyn, June 2, 1961); *Die Doppelgängerin,* after Gerhart Hauptmann (title changed later to conform with the original title of Hauptmann's play, *Winterballade;* Hannover, Germany, Jan. 29, 1967). FOR ORCH.: *Silesian Symphony* (1957); *Symphony Midrash Esther* (N.Y. Phil., Jan. 31, 1957); *Flemish Overture* (Cleveland, 1959); Flute Concerto (1962); Oboe Concerto (1963); *Sinfonia brevissima* (Corpus Christi, Texas, 1965); *6 Pieces for Orchestra* (Pittsburgh, May 27, 1967); *7 Pieces for Orchestra* (Turin, 1972). CANTATAS: *Music for Christmas* (N.Y., 1954); *The Glory around His Head* (N.Y. Phil., April 14, 1955); *Missa Rachel Plorans* (N.Y., Nov. 5, 1955); *The Rabbis* (text from the Talmud; Turin, 1965); several solo cantatas, among them *Emily Dickinson Cantata; 6 Songs* to poems by August von Platen for Soprano and Orch. (Co-

logne, Feb. 12, 1977). CHAMBER MUSIC: Woodwind Quintet (1954); String Quartet (1955); Cello Sonata (1946); Trio for Flute, Cello, and Piano (1946); Violin Sonata (1960); Flute Sonata (1961); Piano Sonata (1958); *Homage to Hieronymus Bosch* for 2 Pianos, 4-hands (1945); songs to German, French and Eng. texts. Meyerowitz publ. a monograph on Schoenberg (Berlin, 1967); also a booklet, *Der echte jüdische Witz* (Berlin, 1971).

Meylan, Jean, Swiss conductor; b. Geneva, Dec. 22, 1915. He studied at the Univ. of Geneva; also at the Geneva and Lausanne conservatories; his teachers in conducting were Weingartner, Kletzki, and Schuricht. He was chief conductor of the Cologne Radio Symph. Orch. (1947–49); then conducted at the Cologne Opera and with the Gurzenich Orch.; was permanent guest conductor of the City Orch. in St. Gallen (1953–56). From 1957 to 1962 he was chief conductor of the Geneva Opera; later was mainly active as a guest conductor.

Meylan, Pierre, Swiss musicologist and editor; b. Lucens (Vaud), Oct. 22, 1908; d. Morges, May 7, 1974. He studied philology at the univs. of Lausanne, Halle, and Leipzig, and piano in Lausanne. He publ. *Les Ecrivains et la musique* (2 vols.; Lausanne, 1944, 1952); edited the collections *Richard Strauss: Anecdotes et souvenirs* (Lausanne, 1951); *Les Plus Belles Lettres de Mozart* (Lausanne, 1956), etc. He was the editor of *Revue Musicale de Suisse Romande.*

Meyrowitz, Selmar, German conductor; b. Bartenstein, East Prussia, April 18, 1875; d. Toulouse, March 24, 1941. He studied at the Cons. of Leipzig, and later with Max Bruch in Berlin; in 1897, became assistant conductor at the Karlsruhe Opera under Mottl, with whom he went to America as conductor at the Metropolitan Opera House (1903); subsequently conducted in Prague (1905–6), Berlin (1907–10), and Hamburg (1913–16), where he was also director of the Cons. In 1917 he returned to Berlin; was conductor at the State Opera (1924–27); toured with the German Grand Opera Co. in the U.S. (1929–31); after a brief sojourn in Germany, he went to France in 1933, and remained there until his death.

Mézeray, Louis-Charles-Lazare-Costard de, conductor and composer; b. Braunschweig, Nov. 25, 1810; d. Asnières, near Paris, April 1887. As a young man he conducted theater orchs. in Strasbourg and elsewhere; at 17, he obtained the post of conductor at the Liège Theater; at 20, he became conductor at the Court Theater in The Hague, where he brought out his heroic opera *Guillaume de Nassau;* subsequently he studied with Reicha in Paris; again traveled as theater conductor in France, and also appeared as a baritone singer; finally, in 1843, he became chief conductor at the Grand Théâtre in Bordeaux, and brought the standard of performance there to a very high level, establishing a fine reputation for himself.

Miaskovsky, Nicolai, eminent Russian composer;

b. Novogeorgievsk, near Warsaw, April 20, 1881; d. Moscow, Aug. 8, 1950. His father was an officer of the dept. of military fortification; the family lived in Orenburg (1888) and in Kazan (1889–93). In 1893 he was sent to a military school in Nizhny-Novgorod; in 1895 he went to a military school in St. Petersburg, graduating in 1899. At that time he developed an interest in music, and tried to compose; took lessons with the composer Kazanli; his first influences were Chopin and Tchaikovsky. In 1902–3 he was in Moscow, where he studied harmony with Glière. Returning to St. Petersburg in 1903, he took lessons with Kryzhanovsky, from whom he acquired a taste for modernistic composition in the impressionist style. In 1906, at the age of 25, he entered the St. Petersburg Cons. as a pupil of Liadov and Rimsky-Korsakov, graduating in 1911. At the outbreak of World War I in 1914, Miaskovsky was called into active service in the Russian army; in 1916 he was removed to Reval to work on military fortifications; he remained in the army after the Bolshevik Revolution of 1917; in 1918 he became a functionary in the Maritime Headquarters in Moscow; was finally demobilized in 1921. In that year he became prof. of composition at the Moscow Cons., remaining at that post to the end of his life. A composer of extraordinary ability, a master of his craft, Miaskovsky wrote 27 symphs., a much chamber music, piano pieces, and songs; his music is marked by structural strength and emotional élan; he never embraced extreme forms of modernism, but adopted workable devices of tonal expansion short of polytonality, and freely modulating melody short of atonality. His style was cosmopolitan; only in a few works did he inject his style folkloric elements.

WORKS: Symphs. (all first perf. in Moscow, unless otherwise indicated): No. 1, C minor (1908; Pavlovsk, June 2, 1914); No. 2, C-sharp minor (July 24, 1912); No. 3, A minor (Feb. 27, 1915); No. 4, E minor (Feb. 8, 1925); No. 5, D major (July 18, 1920); No. 6, E-flat minor (May 4, 1924); No. 7, B minor (Feb. 8, 1925); No. 8, A major (May 23, 1926); No. 9, E minor (April 29, 1928); No. 10, F minor (April 7, 1928); No. 11, B-flat minor (Jan. 16, 1933); No. 12, G minor (June 1, 1932); No. 13, B minor (world premiere, Winterthur, Switzerland, Oct. 16, 1934); No. 14, C major (Feb. 24, 1935); No. 15, D minor (Oct. 28, 1935); No. 16, F major (Oct. 24, 1936); No. 17, G-sharp minor (Dec. 17, 1937); No. 18, C major (Oct. 1, 1937); No. 19, E-flat (Feb. 15, 1939); No. 20, E major (Nov. 28, 1940); No. 21, F-sharp minor (Nov. 16, 1940; perf. by the Chicago Orch. as a commissioned work on Dec. 26, 1940, under the title *Symphonie Fantaisie*); No. 22, subtitled *Symphonie Ballade* (Tiflis, Jan. 12, 1942); No. 23, A minor, *Symphony-Suite* (July 20, 1942); No. 24, F minor (Dec. 8, 1943); No. 25, D-flat (March 6, 1947); No. 26, C major (1948; on old Russian themes; Dec. 28, 1948); No. 27, C minor (perf. posthumously, Dec. 9, 1950). Other orch. works: *Silence*, symph. poem after Edgar Allan Poe (Moscow, June 13, 1911); *Alastor,* symph. poem after Shelley (Moscow, Nov. 18, 1914); Serenade for Small Orch. (Moscow, Oct. 7, 1929); *Lyric Concertino* for Small Orch. (Moscow, Oct. 7, 1929); Sinfonietta for String Orch. (Moscow, May 1930); Violin Concerto (Leningrad,

Nov. 14, 1938); *Salutatory Overture,* on Stalin's 60th birthday (Moscow, Dec. 21, 1939); Cello Concerto (Moscow, March 17, 1945). Also a cantata, *Kirov Is With Us* (1942); marches for military band; choruses; 13 string quartets; 2 cello sonatas; Violin Sonata; 9 piano sonatas; several sets of piano pieces; song cycles; etc. His collected works were issued in 12 vols. in Moscow in 1953–56.

BIBLIOGRAPHY: Miaskovsky's "Autobiographical Notes," *Sovietskaya Muzyka* (June 1936); L. Sabaneyev, *Modern Russian Composers* (N.Y., 1927); A. Ikonnikov, *Miaskovsky, His Life and Works* (Moscow, 1944; Eng. trans., N.Y., 1946); T. Livanova, *Miaskovsky* (Moscow, 1953); V. Vinogradov, *Guide to the Symphonies of N. Miaskovsky* (Moscow, 1954); S. Shlifstein, ed., *Miaskovsky, Articles, Letters, Reminiscences,* 2 vols. (Moscow, 1959).

Michael, David Moritz, German wind instrument player, violinist, and composer; b. Künhausen, near Erfurt, Oct. 27, 1751; d. Neuwied, on the Rhine, 1825. He spent some years as a Hessian army musician; in 1781 joined the Moravian church; from 1795 till 1815 he lived in the Moravian settlements at Nazareth and Bethlehem, Pa., and was the leading spirit in the musical performances in both towns; he played violin and most winds, and as a novelty, would amuse his audience by performing simultaneously on 2 French horns. A list of programs of the Collegium Musicum at Nazareth, beginning with 1796, is preserved in the Moravian Historical Society at Nazareth. Michael's compositions are listed in *A Catalogue of Music by American Moravians,* compiled by A.G. Rau and H.T. David (Bethlehem, 1938). They include a dozen choral works and 16 *Partien,* or suites, for 5, 6, and 7 Wind Instruments, among them one, a programmatic work, written for a boat ride on the Lehigh River.

BIBLIOGRAPHY: H.T. David, "Background for Bethlehem: Moravian Music in Pennsylvania," *American Magazine of Art* (April 1939); idem, "Musical Life in the Pennsylvania Settlements of the *Unitas Fratrum,*" *Transactions of the Moravian Historical Society* (1942; reprinted as Moravian Music Foundation Publication No. 6, Winston-Salem, N.C., 1959); K. Kroeger, "David Moritz Michael's Psalm 103," *Moravian Music Foundation Bulletin* (Fall–Winter 1976).

Michaelides, Solon, Greek musicologist, conductor, and composer; b. Nicosia, Cyprus, Nov. 25, 1905; d. Athens, Sept. 9, 1979. He studied first at the Trinity College of Music in London; then took courses in composition at the Ecole Normale de Musique in Paris with Nadia Boulanger, and later in conducting with Marcel Labey at the Schola Cantorum. Upon his return to Cyprus, he founded ahe Schola cons. at Limassol in 1934 and was its director until 1956; subsequently was director of the Salonika State Cons. (1957–70) and permanent conductor of the Symph. Orch. of Northern Greece (1959–70). In 1970 he was pensioned and he moved to Athens. He publ. *Modern British Music* (Nicosia, 1939), *Cyprus Folk Music* (ibid., 1944; 2nd ed., 1956), *Modern Greek*

Music (ibid., 1945; 2nd ed., 1952), the 2-vol. *Harmony of Contemporary Music* (Limassol, 1945), *The Neo-Hellenic Folk Music* (ibid., 1948) and *A Dictionary of Ancient Greek Music* (London, 1977). Among his compositions are an opera to his own libretto, *Ulysses* (1951); a ballet, *Nausicaa* (1961); *At the Cypriot Marriage,* symph. sketch for Flute and Strings (1934); *2 Byzantine Sketches* for Strings (1936); *2 Greek Symphonic Pictures* (1936); 2 cantatas: *The Tomb* (1936) and *Free Besieged* (1955); *Byzantine Offering* for Strings (1944); *Archaic Suite* for Flute, Oboe, Harp, and Strings (1962); Piano Concerto (1966); String Quartet (1934); Piano Trio (1946); *Suite* for Cello and Piano (1966); *Suite* for Piano (1966); *Hymn and Lament for Cyprus* for a cappella Chorus (1975).

Michalak, Thomas, Polish conductor; b. Cracow, Dec. 21, 1940. He studied violin in Warsaw; made his debut as a soloist with the Warsaw Phil. Orch. at the age of 16. His conducting debut was with the Ballets Russes de Monte Carlo during its tour of the U.S. in 1964. In 1967 he became a member of the faculty at Ithaca College. In 1972 he won first prize in the Koussevitzky awards at the Berkshire Music Center. He subsequently served on the conducting staff of the Pittsburgh Symph. Orch. (1974); later became music director of the Canton (Ohio) Symph. Orch. (1976–77). In 1977 he was appointed music director of the N.J. Symph. Orch. of Newark, retaining this post until 1983; in 1981–82 he served as music adviser of the Kansas City Phil.

Michalsky, Donal, American composer; b. Pasadena, Calif., July 13, 1928; d. (asphyxiated in a fire and burned to death with his wife, 2 small children, a house guest, and her daughter), Newport Beach, Calif., Jan. 1, 1976. He studied clarinet as a youth; then attended the Univ. of Southern Calif. at Los Angeles as a student in theory with Halsey Stevens and in orchestration with Ingolf Dahl, obtaining his doctorate in 1965. In 1958 he went to Germany, where he took a course with Wolfgang Fortner in Freiburg im Breisgau. In 1960 he was appointed prof. of composition at the Calif. State College at Fullerton, holding this position until his tragic death. In his music he adopted a powerful modern idiom in robust dissonant counterpoint, often written in dodecaphonic technique, and yet permeated with a lyric and almost Romantic sentiment. WORKS: 3 symphs.: No. 1, choral symph., *Wheel of Time* (1967); No. 2, *Sinfonia concertante* (1969); No. 3 (1975); Concertino for 19 Wind Instruments and Percussion (1964); Quintet for 2 Trumpets, 2 Trombones, and Piano (1951); *Divertimento* for 2 Clarinets and Bass Clarinet (1952); *Partita* for Oboe d'Amore, String Trio, and String Orch. (1956); Cello Sonata (1958); *Sonata concertante* for Piano Solo (1961); *Trio Concertino* for Flute, Oboe, and Horn (1961); *Cantata da Requiem* (1962); *Variations* for Clarinet and Piano (1962); *Partita piccola* for Flute and Piano (1964); *3 × 4* for Saxophone Quartet (1972); a number of pieces for band; songs. The MS of his projected opera *Der arme Heinrich* was

burned in the fire that took his life.

Micheelsen, Hans Friedrich, German composer of sacred music; b. Hennstedt, Dithmarschen, June 9, 1902; d. Glüsing, Holstein, Nov. 23, 1973. He studied in Hamburg and Berlin; was active as a church organist until 1938, when he was drafted into the German army; after demobilization he settled in Hamburg, where he taught at the Hochschule für Musik. He retired in 1962 and lived mostly in Schwarzwald. He wrote primarily choral music and pieces for organ; among his works are a *Luther Mass* (1933); a German Requiem, *Tod und Leben* (1938); an oratorio, *Wachstum und Reife* (1953); *Passion According to St. Mark* (1954); cantata, *Land der Väter* (1955); evangelical mass, *Unser Wandel ist im Himmel* (1957); *St. John's Passion* for chorus a cappella (1961); also a singspiel, *Münchhausen;* Organ Concerto (1952); Suite for Flute and Piano (1970); some songs in the Hamburg dialect.

Michel, Paul-Baudouin, Belgian composer; b. Haine-St.-Pierre, Sept. 7, 1930. He studied humanities at the Cons. in Mons; then took composition with Absil at the Queen Elisabeth Music Chapel in Brussels (1959–62) and conducting at the Royal Cons. in Brussels; attended summer courses in Darmstadt with Ligeti, Boulez, Maderna, and Messiaen. He was later appointed director of the Academy of Music in Woluwé-St.-Lambert. His music adheres to the doctrine of precisely planned structural formations in a highly modern idiom. WORKS: *Rex Pacificus,* radiophonic motet for Bass, Chorus, Orch., and Tape (1968); *La Boîte de Pandore,* ballet (1961); *Equateur,* cantata (1962); *Le Feu et le monde* for Narrator, Soli, Chorus, Organ, 12 Trumpets, and Percussion (1970); *Variations symphoniques* (1960); *5 inframorphoses* for String Orch. (1963); *Symphonium* for Orch. (1966); *Concaténation* for Chamber Orch. (1967); *Hors-Temps* for Orch. (1970); *Confluences* for 2 Chamber Groups (1974); String Trio (1956); Violin Sonata (1960); *Hommage à François Rabelais,* Wind Quintet (1960); Clarinet Sonatina (1960); String Quartet (1961); *Sérénade concertante* for Violin and Piano (1962); *Motet aléatoire sur le "Veni creator"* for Chorus, 19 Instruments, and Percussion (1962); *Quadrance* for String Quartet (1965); *Conduit et Danse hiératique* for Solo Harp (1964); *Monologue double* for Flute and Tape (1965); *Ultramorphoses* for Flute, Clarinet, Saxophone, Percussion, Piano, Violin, Viola, and Cello (1965); *Clarbassonance* for Bass Clarinet and Tape (1966); *Bassonance* for Bassoon and Tape (1966); *Oscillonance* for 2 Violins and Piano (1967); *Colloque* for Piano, Trumpet, and Percussion (1967); *Gravures* for 2 Trumpets and Horn (1972); *Intonations* for Brass (1972); *Systoles—Diastoles* for Soprano and Instruments (1973); *Parelléloide* for Clavichord and Tape (1974); several piano works, including *Partita No. 1* (1955); *Transsonance* (1965); *Libration I* (1971, revised 1973); *Lithophanie* (1971, for Prepared Piano); *Points cardinaux* (1968); *Variations concentriques* (1971); *Musicoïde* (1971, for 2 Prepared Pianos); and *Orbe*

(1972); *Transphonies pour plusieurs nefs* for Organ (1969); *Puzzlephonie* for Organ (1972); choruses.

Michelangeli, Arturo Benedetti, celebrated Italian pianist; b. Brescia, Jan. 5, 1920. He received his formal music training at the Venturi Inst. in Brescia, where he took violin lessons with Paolo Chiuieri; at the age of 10 he entered the Milan Cons. as a piano pupil of Giuseppe Anfossi, obtaining his diploma at the age of 13. In 1939 he won the Concours International de Piano in Geneva; later joined the piano faculty at the Martini Cons. in Bologna. He was a lieutenant in the Italian air force; after the formal surrender of Italy to the Allies and the German occupation, he was active in the country's anti-Fascist underground; he was taken prisoner by the Germans, but escaped after a few months. Despite these peripeteias he somehow managed to practice, acquiring a formidable virtuoso technique. However, he also developed idiosyncrasies, often canceling scheduled performances, and engaged in such distracting (and dangerous) activities as automobile racing, skiing, and mountain climbing. Both his virtuosity and his eccentricities contributed to his legend, and his rare concerts were invariably public successes. He toured the U.S. in 1950 and in 1966; played in the Soviet Union in 1964; also gave concerts in South America. Eventually he returned to Italy and dedicated himself to teaching; organized an International Academy for pianists in a rented palazzo in Brescia with a multitude of pianos in soundproof studios; among his pupils was Maurizio Pollini, who in time became himself a pianistic celebrity.
BIBLIOGRAPHY: David Ewen, *Musicians since 1900* (N.Y., 1978).

Michelet, Michel (real name, **Levin**), Russo-American composer; b. Kiev, June 26, 1894. He studied cello in Kiev and at the Vienna Cons. with Julius Klengel; then went to Leipzig, where he took lessons with Max Reger. Returning to Kiev in 1914, he studied composition with Reinhold Glière. He left Russia in 1921; went to Vienna and subsequently to Paris, where he became a composer of film music. In 1941 he made his way from France to the U.S. under difficult wartime conditions, and settled in Hollywood. His music has a certain lyric quality, in a Russian vein, with an infusion of characteristic devices of early French Impressionism.
WORKS: Opera, *Hannele,* after Hauptmann (1972); Violin Concerto (1943); *Lisztiana,* "romantic trio" for Violin, Cello, and Piano (1943); Cello Sonata No. 1 (1937); Cello Sonata No. 2 (1977); 3 violin sonatas; Sonata for Balalaika and Piano (1972); piano pieces; songs; nearly 200 film scores.

Michi, Orazio, called **della Arpa** (because of his virtuosity on the harp), Italian composer; b. Alifa Caserta, c.1595; d. Rome, Oct. 26, 1641. From 1614 till 1623 he was in Rome; after that, with Cardinal Maurizio of Savoy. Until 1914 his works were unknown except for 5 arias publ. in Bianchi's *Raccolta d'arie* (Rome, 1640) and a 6th one publ. by Torchi in vol. 5 of *L'arte musicale in Italia.* Then, A. Cametti publ., in the *Rivista Musicale Italiana* (April 1914), a full description and complete thematic catalogue of 43 pieces for one to 3 voices with continuo (chiefly arias) by Michi which he had discovered in various Italian libraries, and which prove that Michi was one of the earliest and most important Roman masters of the monodic style.

Middelschulte, Wilhelm, eminent German organist; b. Werne, near Dortmund, April 3, 1863; d. there, May 4, 1943. He studied at the Inst. für Kirchenmusik in Berlin with Löschhorn (piano), Haupt (organ), and Commer and Schröder (composition). After serving as organist at the Church of St. Luke in Berlin (1888–91), he went to America and settled in Chicago; was organist there at the Cathedral of the Holy Name (1891–95); also prof. of organ at the Wisconsin Cons. of Music in Milwaukee. He was greatly distinguished as a Bach player and pedagogue; in 1935 he became instructor of theory and organ at the Detroit Foundation Music School; in 1939 he returned to Germany.
BIBLIOGRAPHY: J.J. Becker, "Wilhelm Middelschulte," *Musical Quarterly* (April 1928).

Middleton, Hubert Stanley, British organist and music educator; b. Windsor, May 11, 1890; d. London, Aug. 13, 1959. He studied at the Royal Academy of Music in London and at Cambridge Univ. (M.A., 1920). He was appointed organist and director of music at Trinity College, Cambridge, in 1931; also taught at the Royal Academy of Music in London. His specialty was cathedral music. He himself composed a certain number of anthems and organ pieces. He was greatly esteemed as an educator, and his teaching methods exercised profound influence on his students, many of whom became educators in their own right.

Miedél, Rainer, German-American conductor; b. Regensburg, June 1, 1937; d. Seattle, March 25, 1983. He studied cello with André Navarra in Paris, and conducting with Istvan Kertesz and Carl Mellisz; also took conducting lessons with Franco Ferrara. In 1965 he was engaged as a cellist with the Stockholm Phil. Orch.; made his conducting debut with it in 1967. From 1969 to 1976 he was music director of the Gavleborgs Orch. in Sweden; concurrently served as assistant conductor of the Baltimore Symph. Orch. (1969–72) and then associate conductor (1972–73). In 1976 he was appointed music director and conductor of the Seattle Symph. Orch.; in 1980 he traveled with it on its first European tour. From 1980 to 1982 he served as interim music director of the Florida Phil.; he also had numerous guest conducting engagements in Berlin, Vienna, Leningrad, Bucharest, Hong Kong, Guadalajara, Copenhagen, Hamburg, Alaska, Chicago, Dallas, Toronto, Vancouver, Quebec, Indianapolis, Honolulu, etc. His career was ended when he was stricken with a peculiarly deadly form of cancer. He conducted his last concert in Seattle on Jan. 13, 1983.

Mieg, Peter, Swiss composer; b. Lenzburg, Sept. 5, 1906. He studied piano and theory in Basel; took courses in literature and archeology in Paris; received his Ph.D. in Zürich for a dissertation on art. He subsequently studied composition with Frank Martin; simultaneously was active as a professional painter. His works comprise a String Trio (1937); 2 string quartets (1938, 1945); Concerto for 2 Pianos and Orch. (1941); ballet, *Daphne* (1945); 2 piano concertos (1947, 1961); Violin Concerto (1949); *Concerto veneziano* for String Orch. (1955); Concerto for Oboe and Orch. (1957); *Sinfonie* (1958); Concerto for Flute and String Orch. (1962); several piano sonatas and other piano pieces; songs.

Mielck, Ernst, Finnish composer; b. Viipuri (Vyborg), Oct. 24, 1877; d. Locarno, Italy, Oct. 22, 1899 (2 days before his 22nd birthday). He studied piano in St. Petersburg, and composition with Max Bruch in Berlin. His early death deprived Finland of a major musical talent. He left several works showing considerable technical skill and inventive power; among these are String Quartet (1895); *Macbeth Overture* (1895); String Quintet (1896–97); *Finnish Symphony* (1897); *Dramatic Overture* (1898); two piano concertos (1895, 1898); *Finnish Suite* for Orch. (1899). A monograph on Mielck was publ. by W. Mauke (Leipzig, 1901).

Mielke, Antonia, German dramatic soprano; b. Berlin, c.1852; d. there, Nov. 15, 1907. At first she sang chiefly coloratura roles, but gradually assumed the great dramatic parts, for which she was particularly gifted. She sang the Wagner heroines at the Metropolitan Opera during the season of 1890–91 (succeeding Lilli Lehmann); also toured the U.S. in concert recitals; returning to Germany, she continued her operatic career until 1902, when she settled in Berlin as a teacher.

Miereanu, Costin, Rumanian-French composer; b. Bucharest, Feb. 27, 1943. He studied with Alfred Mendelsohn, Varga, and Dan Constantinescu at the Bucharest Cons. (1960–66); attended seminars with Günther Becker and Ligeti at the summer courses in new music held in Darmstadt (1967, 1968) and also had sessions with Pierre Schaeffer at the Cons. of Paris (1968–69) and with the Groupe de Recherches Musicales there; in 1968 settled in France, acquiring French citizenship in 1977. His music presents a totality of the cosmopolitan avant-garde: serialism, electronic sound, aleatory production, and musical-verbal theater. Some of his compositions have optional parts for magnetic tape and film.
WORKS: *Donum sacrum Brancusi* for Voice and Orch. (1963); *Espace dernier,* aleatory music for Chorus, 6 Instrumental Groups, and Tape (1965; Royan, April 14, 1973); *Variante* for Solo Clarinet (1966); *Finis coronat opus* for Pianist and 6 Instrumental Groups (1966); *Cadenza* for One or More Pianists (1966); *Monostructures I* for 2 Orchs. of Strings and Brass (1967) and *II* for Strings, Brass, and Tape (1967); *Sur-sum corda* for Piano, Violin, Viola, Cello, and Clarinet (1967–68); *Nuit* for Soprano and a cappella Chorus (1968); *Dans la nuit des temps,* aleatory music for Variable Ensemble and Tape (1968–69); *Couleurs du temps (Colors of Time)* in 3 versions: for String Orch. (1968), for String Quartet and Tape (1968), and for Double String Quartet and Double Bass (1969); *Espaces au-delà du dernier,* aleatory music for Chamber Ensemble (1969); *Espaces II* for 20 Strings, Piano, and Tape (1967–69); *Polymorphies 5 × 7,* in concert version, for ad libitum Chorus, Variable Ensemble, and Tape, or in stage version, for Actors, Chorus, Variable Ensemble, and Tape (1968–70); *Night Music* for Tape (1968–70); *Alba* for 12 Voices and 4 Percussionists (1972; version for 2 Voices and Objects, 1973); *Source de juin* for Flute, Clarinet, Trombone, Trumpet, Electric Guitar, and Percussion (1972); *Altar* in 3 versions that mix Voices, Instruments, Film, and Tape in various combinations (1973); 5 separate works (*Amnar, Rod, Amurg, Zbor,* and *Apo*) all subtitled "réécriture spatio-temporelle," for varying combinations of Instrumental and Vocal Soloists, Chamber Ensembles, Film, and Tape (1973; all 5 works, Paris, Feb. 5, 1974); *Silence Tisse* for Variable Vocal and Instrumental Ensembles (1973–74); *Domingo* for Variable Quintet of Voices and Instruments (1974); *Quintafeira* for 2 Trumpets, Horn, Trombone, and Tuba (1974); *Segundafeira* for 5 Different Flutes (1974); *Luna cinese* for Narrator, One Performer and One or More Electrophones (1975); *Planetarium I* for Piano, 2 Flutes, Trombone, and Vibraphone (1975); *Rêve sans (T) rêve,* a "kinéaquarium vidéophonique" (1975); *Sempre azzuro* for Variable Ensemble (1975); *Rosario* for Orch. and Optional Tenor (1973–76); *Musiques élémentaires pour la Messe,* cycle of 6 pieces for Variable Instruments (1976).

Miersch, Paul Friedrich Theodor, cellist and composer; b. Dresden, Jan. 18, 1868; d. New York, March 1, 1956. He studied at the Munich Academy with Werner (cello) and Rheinberger (composition); came to the U.S. in 1886, and lived in Washington, D.C.; during Tchaikovsky's American tour in 1891 he played the cello part in Tchaikovsky's trio in Washington, in the composer's presence. In 1892 he moved to N.Y.; was first cellist of the N.Y. Symph. Orch. (1893–98); then held a similar post at the Metropolitan Opera (1898–1912). After retirement from concert life, he remained in N.Y. as a teacher. He wrote a number of compositions, 46 of which have been publ.

Mies, Paul, noted German musicologist and pedagogue; b. Cologne, Oct. 22, 1889; d. there, May 15, 1976. He studied musicology, mathematics, and physics at the Univ. of Bonn, receiving his Ph.D. there in 1912 with the dissertation *Über die Tonmalerei;* then was active as a teacher of mathematics in Cologne (1919–39) while continuing his musicological work; in 1946 he became director of the Institut für Schulmusik at the Cologne Staatliche Hochschule für Musik, retaining this post until 1954.

WRITINGS: *Die Bedeutung der Skizzen Beethovens zur Erkenntnis seines Stiles* (Leipzig, 1925; in Eng., London, 1929); *Musik im Unterricht der höheren Lehranstalten* (2 vols., Cologne, 1926); *Skizzen aus Geschichte und Ästhetik der Musik* (Cologne, 1926); *Das romantische Lied und Gesänge aus Wilhelm Meister; Musik und Musiker in Poesie und Prosa* (2 vols., Berlin, 1926); *Schubert, der Meister des Liedes: Die Entwicklung von Form und Inhalt im Schubertschen Lied* (Berlin, 1928); *Johannes Brahms: Werke, Zeit, Mensch* (Leipzig, 1930); *Der Charakter der Tonarten: Eine Untersuchung* (Cologne, 1948); *Von Sinn und Praxis der musikalischen Kritik* (Krefeld, 1950); *Franz Schubert* (Leipzig, 1954); *Textkritische Untersuchungen bei Beethoven* (Munich and Duisburg, 1957); *Die geistlichen Kantaten Johann Sebastian Bachs und der Hörer von heute* (3 vols., Wiesbaden, 1958, 1959, and 1964); *Bilder und Buchstaben werden Musik* (Rodenkirchen, 1964); with H. Grundmann, *Studien zum Klavierspiel Beethovens und seiner Zeitgenossen* (Bonn, 1966; 2nd ed., 1970); *Die weltlichen Kantaten Johann Sebastian Bachs und der Hörer von heute* (Wiesbaden, 1967); *Das instrumentale Rezitativ: Von seiner Geschichte und seinen Formen* (Bonn, 1968); *Die Krise der Konzertkadenz bei Beethoven* (Bonn, 1970); *Das Konzert im 19. Jahrhundert: Studien zu Kadenzen und Formen* (Bonn, 1972); ed., *Reihenfolge,* a collection for school orchs.

Miessner, Benjamin Franklin, American inventor of electronic instruments; b. Huntingburg, Ind., July 27, 1890; d. Miami, Fla., March 25, 1976. He studied electrical engineering at Purdue Univ. (1913–16). About 1925 he organized his own company, Miessner Inventions, Inc. He perfected the Wurlitzer organ and electronic pianos before his retirement in 1959.

Mignan, Edouard-Charles-Octave, French organist and composer; b. Paris, March 17, 1884; d. there, Sept. 17, 1969. He studied at the Paris Cons. with Widor (organ) and Paul Vidal (compostion); was church organist at Orléans and later on at the Madeleine in Paris. He wrote a number of melodious orch. suites, a Symph., sacred choruses, numerous motets, and organ pieces.

Mignone, Francisco, eminent Brazilian composer; b. São Paulo, Sept. 3, 1897. He studied music with his father; then took courses in piano, flute, and composition at the São Paulo Cons.; then studied with Ferroni at the Milan Cons. (1920); returning to Brazil, he was appointed to the faculty of the Escola Nacional de Música in Rio de Janeiro (1933), and taught there until 1967. His music shows the influence of the modern Italian school of composition; his piano pieces are of virtuoso character; his orchestration shows consummate skill. In many of his works he employs indigenous Brazilian motifs, investing them in sonorous modernistic harmonies not without a liberal application of euphonious dissonances.

WORKS: OPERAS: *O Contractador dos diamantes* (Rio de Janeiro, Sept. 20, 1924); *O inocente* (Rio de Janeiro, Sept. 5, 1928); *O Chalaça* (1972); operetta, *Mizú* (1937). BALLETS: *Maracatú de Chico-Rei* (Rio de Janeiro, Oct. 29, 1934), *Quadros amazónicos* (Rio de Janeiro, July 15, 1949), *O guarda chuva* (São Paulo, 1954). FOR ORCH.: *Suite campestre* (Rio de Janeiro, Dec. 16, 1918); *Congada,* from the opera *O Contractador dos diamantes* (São Paulo, Sept. 10, 1922; his most popular piece); *Scenas da Roda,* symph. dance (São Paulo, Aug. 15, 1923); *Festa dionisiaca* (Rome, Oct. 24, 1923); *Intermezzo lirico* (São Paulo, May 13, 1925); *Momus,* symph. poem (Rio de Janeiro, April 24, 1933); *Suite brasileira* (Rio de Janeiro, Dec. 9, 1933); *Sonho de um Menino Travesso* (São Paulo, Oct. 30, 1937); *4 fantasias brasileiras* for Piano and Orch. (1931–37); *Seresta* for Cello and Orch. (Rio de Janeiro, March 31, 1939); *Miudinho,* symph. dance (São Paulo, June 28, 1941); *Festa das Igrejas* (N.Y., April 22, 1942); *Sinfonia tropical* (1958); Piano Concerto (1958); Violin Concerto (1961); Concerto for Violin, Piano, and Orch. (1966); Concertino for Clarinet and Small Orch. (1957); Bassoon Concertino (1957); Concerto for Violin and Chamber Orch. (1975). CHAMBER MUSIC: 2 Sextets (1935, 1968); String Octet (1956); 2 wind quintets (1960, 1962); 2 string quartets (1956, 1957); Sonata for 4 Bassoons (1966); 2 wind trios (1967, 1968); 3 violin sonatas (1964, 1965, 1966); Cello Sonata (1967); 2 sonatas for 2 Bassoons (1960, 1965); 2 sonatas for Flute and Oboe (1969, 1970); *Trifonia* for Oboe, Flute, and Bassoon (1963); *Tetrafonia* for Flute, Oboe, Clarinet, and Trumpet (1963); *Sonata a tre* for Flute, Oboe, and Clarinet (1970); Sonata for Trumpet Solo (1970); Clarinet Sonata (1971). FOR PIANO: 4 sonatas (1941, 1962, 1964, 1967); *Rondo* (1969); several waltzes in Brazilian popular style; *Samba rítmico* for 2 Pianos (1953); *Sonata humorística* for 2 Pianos (1968). VOCAL MUSIC: oratorio, *Alegrias de Nossa Senhora* (Rio de Janeiro, July 15, 1949); oratorio, *Santa Clara* (1962); many songs.

BIBLIOGRAPHY: N. Slonimsky, *Music of Latin America* (N.Y., 1945; pp. 134–36); Luiz Heitor Correa de Azevedo, "Francisco Mignone," *Música Brasileña Contemporánea* (Rosario, Argentina, 1952; pp. 125–57). An autobiographical brochure, *A parte do anjo,* was publ. for his 50th birthday, containing articles by Correa de Azevedo, Mario de Andrade, and L. Chiaffarelli (São Paulo, 1947); special issue of *Inter-American Music Bulletin* (1970–71).

Migot, Georges, significant French composer; b. Paris, Feb. 27, 1891; d. Levallois, near Paris, Jan. 5, 1976. He began taking piano lessons at the age of 6; entered the Paris Cons. in 1909; after preliminary courses in harmony, he studied composition with Widor, counterpoint with André Gedalge, and music history with Maurice Emmanuel; orchestration with Vincent d'Indy, and organ with Gigout and Guilmant. Before completing his studies at the Paris Cons., he was mobilized into the French army, was wounded at Longuyon in 1914, and was released from military service. In 1917 he presented in Paris a concert of his own works; received the Lily Boulanger Prize in 1918. He competed twice for the Prix de Rome in 1919 and 1920, but failed to win and abandoned further in 1919 and attempts. In the meantime he engaged in a serious study of painting; in fact, he was more successful as a painter than as a composer in the early years of his career; he exhibited his paintings in Paris art galleries in 1917, 1919, 1923, and in subsequent years. He also wrote poetry; virtually all of his vocal works are written to his own words. In his musical compositions he endeavored to recapture the spirit of old French polyphony, thus emphasizing the continuity of national art in history. His melodic writing is modal, often with archaic inflections, while his harmonic idiom is diatonically translucid; he obtains subtle coloristic effects through unusual instrumental registration. Profoundly interested in the preservation and classification of old musical instruments, Migot served as curator of the Instrumental Museum of the Paris Cons. (1949–61).

WORKS: *Hagoromo*, "symphonie lyrique et chorégraphique" for Baritone, Chorus, and Orch., to a text by Migot and Laloy (Monte Carlo, May 9, 1922); *Le Rossignol en amour*, chamber opera to a text by Migot (1926–28; Geneva, March 2, 1937); *La Sulamite*, concert opera to a libretto by Migot (1969–70); *L'Arche*, "polyphonie spatiale" for Soprano, Female Chorus, and Orch., to a poem by Migot (1971; Marseilles, May 3, 1974); 13 symphs. (some of their material was derived from earlier pieces of chamber music, and their numeration does not follow chronological order): No. 1, *Les Agrestides* (1919–20; Paris, April 29, 1922); No. 2 (1927; Festival of Besançon, Sept. 7, 1961); No. 3 (1943–49); No. 4 (1946–47); No. 5, *Sinfonia da chiesa,* for Wind Instruments (1955; Roubaix, Dec. 4, 1955); No. 6 for Strings (1944–51; Strasbourg, June 22, 1960); No. 7 for Chamber Orch. (1948–52); No. 8 for 15 Wind Instruments and 2 Double Basses (1953); No. 9 for Strings (incomplete); No. 10 (1962); No. 11 for Wind Instruments (1963); No. 12 (1954–64; Lille, May 29, 1972); No. 13 (1967); also *Petite Symphonie en trois mouvements enchaînés* for String Orch. (1970; Béziers, July 23, 1971). OTHER ORCH. WORKS: *Le Paravent de laque aux cinq images* (1920; Paris, Jan. 21, 1923); *Trois ciné-ambiances* (1922); *La Fête de la bergère* (1921; Paris, Nov. 21, 1925); *Prélude pour un poète* (Paris, June 7, 1929); *Le Livre des danceries,* orch. suite (Paris, Dec. 12, 1931); *Le Zodiaque* (1931–39); *Phonie sous-marine* (1962); *Dialogue* for Piano and Orch. (1922–26; Paris, March 25, 1926); *Dialogue* for Cello and Orch. (1922–26; Paris, Feb. 7, 1927); *Suite* for Violin and Orch. (1924; Paris, Nov. 14, 1925); *Suite* for Piano and Orch. (Paris, March 12, 1927); *Suite en concert* for Harp and Orch. (Paris, Jan. 15, 1928); *La Jungle*, "polyphonie" for Organ and Orch. (1928; Paris, Jan. 9, 1932); Piano Concerto (1962; Paris, June 26, 1964); Concerto for Harpsichord and Chamber Orch. (Paris, Dec. 12, 1967). CHAMBER MUSIC: *Les Parques* for 2 Violins, Viola, and Piano (1909); 3 string quartets (1921, 1957, 1966); Quartet for Flute, Violin, Cello, and Piano (1960); Quartet for Violin, Viola, Cello, and Piano (1961); Quartet for 2 Clarinets, Corno di Bassetto, and Bass Clarinet (1925); Quartet for Saxophones (1955); Quartet for 2 Violins and 2 Cellos (1955); Quintet for Flute, Oboe, Clarinet, Horn, and Bassoon (1954); *Introduction pour un concert de chambre* for 5 Strings and 5 Wind Instruments (1964); Trio for Oboe, Violin, and Piano (1906); Trio for Violin, Viola, and Piano (1918); Piano Trio (1935); Trio for Oboe, Clarinet, and Bassoon (1944); String Trio (1944–45); Trio for Flute, Cello, and Harp (1965); Guitar Sonata (1960); *Sonate luthée* for Harp Solo (1949); 2 sonatas for Violin Solo (1951, 1959); Violin Sonata (1911); *Dialogue No. 1* for Violin and Piano (1923); *Dialogue No. 2* for Violin and Piano (1925); Sonata for Viola Solo (1958); Sonata for Cello Solo (1954); *Dialogue No. 1* for Cello and Piano (1922); *Dialogue No. 2* for Cello and Piano (1929); Sonata for Cello and Piano (1958); *Suite* for 2 Cellos (1962); *Suite* for Flute Solo (1931); Flute Sonata (1945); *Pastorale* for 2 Flutes (1950); *Suite* for English Horn and Piano (1963); Sonata for Clarinet Solo (1953); Sonata for Bassoon Solo (1953). VOCAL WORKS: *6 tétraphonies* for Baritone, Flute, Violin, and Cello, to words by Migot (1945); *7 petites images du Japon* for Voice and Piano (1917); *Vini vinoque amor* for 2 Voices, Flute, Cello, and Piano (1937); numerous unaccompanied vocal trios and quartets; sacred choruses a cappella; double and triple choruses a cappella; *Liturgie œcuménique* for 3 Voices and Organ (1958); oratorio, *La Mise au tombeau* to Migot's text (1948–49); "lyric mystery," *La Nativité de Notre Seigneur* for Soloists, Chorus, and Instruments, to text by Migot (1954); *La Passion*, oratorio (1939–46; Paris, July 25, 1957); *L'Annonciation*, oratorio (1943–46); *Mystère orphique* for Voice and Orch. (1951; Strasbourg, March 18, 1964); *Cantate d'amour*, concert opera, to texts by Migot (1949–50); *La Résurrection*, oratorio (1953; Strasbourg, March 28, 1969); *Du ciel et de la terre*, "space symphony" for a film (1957); *Le Zodiaque*, "chorégraphie lyrique" with libretto by Migot (1958–60); *La plate, vaste savane* for Soprano and Instruments (1967); *3 chansons de joie et de souci* for Voice and Guitar (1969); *3 Dialogues* for Voice and Cello (1972); *5 Chants initiatiques* for Voice and Piano (1973); also much liturgical music; a group of albums of character pieces for piano; numerous works for organ. Migot publ. an autobiography, *Kaléidoscope et Miroirs* (Toulouse, 1970); *Essais pour une esthétique générale* (Paris, 1920); *Jean-Philippe Rameau et le génie de la musique française* (Paris, 1930); *Lexique de quelques termes utilisés en musique* (Paris, 1947); 2 vols. of poems (Paris, 1950, 1951).

BIBLIOGRAPHY: Léon Vallas, *Georges Migot* (Paris, 1923); Pierre Wolff, *La Route d'un musicien: Georges Migot* (Paris, 1933); Maurice Henrion, "La Musique vocale de Georges Migot," *Revue Musicale* (Nov. 1946); Marc Honegger, "Georges Migot," *Revue Musicale Suisse* (1954); Max Pinchard, *Connaissance de Georges Migot, musicien français* (Paris, 1959); Marc Honegger, ed., *Catalogue des œuvres musicales de Georges Migot* (Strasbourg, 1977). A collection of Migot's articles was publ. under the title *Les Ecrits de Georges Migot* (4 vols., Paris, 1932); C. Latham, ed. and trans., *Georges Migot: The Man and His Work* (Strasbourg, 1982).

Miguez, Leopoldo, Brazilian composer; b. Rio de

Janeiro, Sept. 9, 1850; d. there, July 6, 1902. He was a conductor, and was associated with various theatrical enterprises; began to compose marches and waltzes; won a prize for his *Hymn of the Republic* (1889). In 1890 he was appointed director of the Instituto Nacional de Musica in Rio de Janeiro, retaining this post until his death. In his theater works he pursued Wagnerian ideas, but his technique was insufficient for adequate orchestration.

WORKS: Operas: *Pelo Amor* (Rio de Janeiro, 1897) and *Os Saldunes* (Rio de Janeiro, Sept. 20, 1901); overtures; songs; marches.

BIBLIOGRAPHY: "Leopoldo Miguez e o Instituto Nacional de Musica," *Revista Brasileira de Musica* (1940).

Mihalovich, Edmund (Ödön) von, Hungarian composer; b. Fericsancze, Sept. 13, 1842; d. Budapest, April 22, 1929. He studied with Mosonyi in Budapest, and with Hauptmann in Leipzig; also took lessons with Peter Cornelius in Munich. From 1887 to 1919 he taught at the Hungarian Academy of Music in Budapest. He was an ardent Wagnerite and opposed Hungarian musical nationalism; the melodic materials of his own works are entirely Germanic.

WORKS: Operas: *Hagbart und Signe* (Dresden, March 12, 1882); *Eliane* (Budapest, Feb. 16, 1908); *Toldi szerelme* (*Toldi's Love*; Budapest, March 18, 1893); 4 symphs. (1879, 1892, 1900, 1902); *Hero and Leander*, symph. poem (1875); *Faust*, fantasy for Orch. (1880); Violin Sonata; piano pieces; songs.

Mihalovici, Marcel, significant Rumanian-French composer; b. Bucharest, Oct. 22, 1898. He studied composition privately with Cuclin in Bucharest; in 1919 went to Paris, where he settled; became a French citizen in 1955. He studied violin with Nestor Lejeune, Gregorian chant with Amédée Gastoué, and composition with Vincent d'Indy at the Schola Cantorum (1919–25). With Martinu, Conrad Beck, and Tibor Harsányi, he formed a freely associated "Ecole de Paris," consisting of emigrants, which later attracted several other Parisian composers, among them Alexandre Tcherepnin of Russia, Alexandre Tansman of Poland, and Alexander Spitzmueller of Austria. Mihalovici was a founding member of the modern music society "Triton" (1932); was elected a member of the Inst. de France in 1964. He married the noted pianist **Monique Haas**. Mihalovici's music presents a felicitous synthesis of French and Eastern European elements, tinted with a roseate impressionistic patina and couched in euphoniously dissonant harmonies.

WORKS: OPERAS: *L'Intransigeant Pluton* (1928; Paris, April 3, 1939); *Phèdre* (1949; Stuttgart, June 9, 1951); *Die Heimkehr* (Frankfurt, June 17, 1954); *Krapp ou La Dernière Bande*, libretto by Samuel Beckett (1959–60; Bielefeld, Germany, Feb. 25, 1961); opera-buffa, *Les Jumeaux* (1962; Braunschweig, Germany, Jan. 23, 1963). BALLETS: *Une Vie de Polichinelle* (Paris, 1923); *Le Postillon du Roy* (Paris, 1924); *Divertimento* (Paris, 1925); *Karagueuz*, ballet for marionettes (Paris, 1926; Chicago, 1926); *Thésée au labyrinthe* (1956; Braunschweig, April 4,

1957; revised version as *Scènes de Thésée*, Cologne, Oct. 15, 1958); *Alternamenti* (1957; Braunschweig, Feb. 28, 1958); *Variations* (Bielefeld, March 28, 1960). FOR ORCH.: *Notturno* (1923); *Introduction au mouvement symphonique* (1923; Bucharest, Oct. 17, 1926); *Fantaisie* (1927; Liège Festival, Sept. 6, 1930); *Cortège des divinites infernales* (1928; Bucharest, Dec. 7, 1930); *Chindia* for 13 Wind Instruments and Piano (1929); *Concerto quasi una Fantasia* for Violin and Orch. (1930; Barcelona Festival, April 22, 1936); *Divertissement* (1934); *Capriccio roumain* (1936); *Prélude et Invention* for String Orch. (1937; Warsaw Festival, April 21, 1939); *Toccata* for Piano and Orch. (1938, revised 1940); *Symphonies pour le temps présent* (1944); *Variations* for Brass and Strings (1946); *Séquences* (1947); *Ritournelles* (1951); 5 symphs.: *Sinfonia giocosa* (Basel, Dec. 14, 1951); *Sinfonia partita* for Strings (1952); *Sinfonia variata* (1960); *Sinfonia cantata* for Baritone, Chorus, and Orch. (1953–63); and No. 5 for Dramatic Soprano and Orch. (in memory of Hans Rosbaud, 1966–69; Paris, Dec. 14, 1971); *Etude en 2 parties* for Piano Concertante, 7 Wind Instruments, Celesta, and Percussion (Donaueschingen, Oct. 6, 1951); *Elegie* (1955); *Ouverture tragique* (1957); *Esercizio* for Strings (1959); *Musique nocturne* for Clarinet, String Orch., Harpsichord, and Celesta (1963); *Aubade* for Strings (1964); *Périples* for Orch. with Piano Concertante (1967; Paris, March 22, 1970); *Prétextes* for Oboe, Bass Clarinet, and Chamber Orch. (1968); *Variantes* for Horn, and Orch. or Piano (1969); *Borne* (1970); *Rondo* (1970); *Chant Premier* for Saxophone and Orch. (1973–74); *Follia*, paraphrases for Orch. (1976–77). VOCAL MUSIC: Cantata, *La Genèse* (1935–40); *Cantilène* for Mezzo-soprano and Chamber Orch. (1972); *Cascando*, invention for Music and Voice (1962); *Mémorial*, 5 a cappella motets, each dedicated to a different deceased composer (1952); songs, *Abendgesang* (1957), *Stances* (1967), and *Textes* (1974). CHAMBER MUSIC: 2 violin sonatas (1920, 1941); Piano Quartet (1922); 3 String quartets (1923, 1931, 1943–46); Oboe Sonatina (1924); *Serenade* for String Trio (1929); Sonata for 3 Clarinets (1933); Viola Sonata (1942); Sonata for Violin and Cello (1944); *Egloge* for Flute, Oboe, Clarinet, Bassoon, and Piano (1945); Sonata for Violin Solo (1949); Sonata for Cello Solo (1949); Wind Trio (1955); *Pastorale triste* for Flute and Piano (1958); Bassoon Sonata (1958); Clarinet Sonata (1958); *Improvisation* for Percussion (1961); *Dialogues* for Clarinet and Piano (1965); *Serioso* for Bass Saxophone and Piano (1971); *Récit* for Solo Clarinet (1973); *Melopeia* for Solo Oboe (1973). FOR PIANO: *3 Nocturnes* (1928); *4 Caprices* (1929); *Ricercari* (1941); *3 pièces nocturnes* (1948); Sonata (1964), *Cantus Firmus* for 2 Pianos (1970); *Passacaglia* for the Left Hand (1975); incidental music for productions of *Sappho* (1946), *Le Paradis perdu* (1951), *Meurtre dans la cathédrale* (1952), *Orphée* (1954), *Mélusine* (1957), and *Herakles* (1975).

BIBLIOGRAPHY: Georges Beck, *Marcel Mihalovici* (Paris, 1954); Viorel Cosma, *Muzicieni români* (contains a list of works with dates of perf.; Bucharest, 1970).

Mihály, András, Hungarian composer and conductor; b. Budapest, Nov. 7, 1917. He studied cello with Adolf Schiffer and chamber music with Leo Weiner and Imre Waldbauer at the Budapest Academy of Music (1934–38); took private composition lessons from Paul Kadosa and István Strasser. He played cello in the orch. of the Budapest Opera House (1948–50); in 1950 was appointed prof. of the Budapest Academy of Music. In 1968 he organized the Budapest Chamber Ensemble and conducted it in a series of concerts with programs of new music. As a composer, he writes in a compact contrapuntal style oxygenated by a breath of lyricism. He won the Kossuth Prize in 1955 and the Erkel Prize 3 times (1952, 1954, 1964).

WORKS: Opera, *Együtt és egyedül* (*Together and Alone,* 1964–65; Budapest, Nov. 5, 1966; 3 symphs.: (*Sinfonia da Requiem,* 1946, 1950, 1962); cantatas: *My Beloved Hungarian Fatherland* (1952); *The Red Cart* (1957); *Memory and Warning* (1959); *1871* (1960); *Fly, Poem!* (1967); Cello Concerto (1953); Piano Concerto (1954); *Fantasy* for Wind Quintet, String Orch., Harp, Celesta, and Percussion (1955); *Festive Overture* (1959); Violin Concerto, with Piano obbligato (1959); *3 Movements* for Chamber Ensemble (1969); *Monodia* for Orch. (1971); *Musica per 15* (1975); Piano Trio (1940); 2 string quartets (1942, 1960); *Rhapsody* for Viola and Piano (1947); *Serenade* for Wind Trio (1956); *Suite* for Cello and Piano (1957); Piano Sonata (1958); *3 Apocrypha* for Female Vocal Trio or Chorus, and Clarinet and Percussion (1962); *Movement* for Cello and Piano (1962); song cycles, *Chamber Music,* after Joyce (1958); *Attila József Songs* (1961); and *Psalms of Rapture,* after Radnóti (1969); incidental music to plays and films.

BIBLIOGRAPHY: J. Kárpáti, *Mihály András* (Budapest, 1965).

Mikhailova, Maria, Russian soprano; b. Kharkov, June 3, 1866; d. Perm, Jan. 18, 1943. She studied in St. Petersburg, and then in Paris and Milan; in 1892 she made her debut at the Imperial Opera in St. Petersburg as Marguerite de Valois in *Les Huguenots;* she remained a member there until 1912. On Oct. 29, 1895, she created the role of Electra in Taneyev's *Oresteia.* She visited Tokyo in 1907. She made over 300 recordings, achieving a considerable reputation through the gramophone alone.

Mikhashoff, Ivar, American pianist; b. Albany, N.Y., March 8, 1944. He studied at the Eastman School of Music; then enrolled at the Juilliard School of Music in N.Y. as a student of Beveridge Webster; subsequently traveled to Paris to take a course with Nadia Boulanger (1968–69). In 1973 he received a D.M.A. in composition from the Univ. of Texas; taught at the State Univ. of New York in Buffalo; in 1981 joined the faculty of the Boston Univ. Tanglewood Inst. He included in his repertoire a variety of works by modern composers, among them Aaron Copland, Lukas Foss, Charles Ives, and Dane Rudhyar. He also appeared as a multimedia performer. In 1980 he played the principal acting role in the La Scala premiere of Bussotti's opera *La Racine.* In 1982 he organized the Holland Festival's 2-week-long celebration of 200 years of Dutch-American friendship through a series of 9 thematic concerts covering 250 years of American music. He also composed some chamber music and a Piano Concerto.

Miki, Minoru, Japanese composer; b. Tokushima, Shikoku, March 16, 1930. He studied composition with Akira Ifukube and Ikenouchi at the Tokyo Univ. of Arts, graduating in 1955; organized the Ensemble Nipponia with 15 other members (1964); then was appointed a lecturer at the Tokyo College of Music.

WORKS: Opera, *Ada—An Actor's Revenge* (London, 1979); operetta, *Husband the Hen* (1963); musical drama for children, *Kikimimi* (Tokyo, Feb. 27, 1968); *Trinita Sinfonia* (1953); *Osabai* for 12 Winds and Percussion (1955); *Sinfonia Gamula* (1957); *Poema estiva* for Piano (1958); Symphony *"Joya"* (1960); *Requiem* for Baritone, Male Chorus, and Orch. (1963); Sextet for Piano and Wind Quintet (1965); *Time* for Solo Marimba (1968); Marimba Concerto (Tokyo, Oct. 11, 1969); *Jo-No-Kyoku,* prelude for Shakuhachi, Koto, Sangen, and Strings (1969); *Convexity,* concerto for 3 groups of "Sankyoku" and a Japanese Drum (1970); *Hakuyoh* for Violin and Koto (1973); *Ha-No-Kyoku,* koto concerto (1974); many pieces for Japanese instruments solo.

Mikorey, Franz, German composer and conductor; b. Munich, June 3, 1873; d. there, May 11, 1947. He studied in Munich with Thuille and H. Levi; later in Berlin with H. von Herzogenberg; conducted in Bayreuth (1894); then in Prague, Regensburg, Elberfeld, and Vienna; in 1902 was engaged as court conductor in Dessau; was appointed music director there in 1912. He conducted opera at Helsinki from 1919 to 1924; then returned to Germany.

WORKS: Opera, *Der König von Samarkand* (Dessau, 1910); 2 symphs. (*Tragische; An der Adria*); *Sinfonia Engadiana* for Soli, Chorus, and Orch.; Piano Concerto; Piano Quintet; Piano Trio; male choruses; songs. He publ. *Grundlagen des Dirigierens* (1929).

BIBLIOGRAPHY: E. Hamann, *Franz Mikorey* (Leipzig, 1907).

Miksch, Johann Aloys, famous baritone and singing teacher; b. Georgental, Bohemia, July 19, 1765; d. Dresden, Sept. 24, 1845. He was a choirboy in Dresden; then singer at the Court Church (1786); was a baritone in the Italian Opera of Dresden (1797); chorusmaster of the German Opera (1820); was pensioned in 1831. He was greatly renowned as a teacher; among his pupils was Schröder-Devrient.

BIBLIOGRAPHY: A. Kohut, *J. Miksch* (Leipzig, 1890).

Mikuli, Karl, Polish pianist and composer; b. Czernowitz, Oct. 20, 1819; d. Lwow, May 21, 1897. He first studied medicine in Vienna, but his pronounced talent for music made him decide to go to Paris for serious study; there he became a pupil of Chopin (1844); he also studied composition with Reicha. After the outbreak of the Revolution of 1848, he left Paris and made several tours in Russia and Austria; was appointed director of the Lwow Cons. (1858); 30 years later he established a music school of his own there. His edition of Chopin's works contains numerous emendations made by Chopin himself as marginal remarks in Mikuli's student copies. He publ. a number of piano pieces of his own, greatly influenced by Chopin's style; also *43 airs nationaux roumains* for Piano.

Mila, Massimo, Italian writer on music; b. Turin, Aug. 14, 1910. He studied literature at the Univ. of Turin; after graduation, he became a regular contributor to many Italian musical publications; was music critic of *L'Espresso* (1955–68) and of *La Stampa* (1968–74). He taught music history at the Turin Cons. (1953–73); also at the Univ. of Turin from 1960.
WRITINGS: *Il melodramma di Verdi* (Bari, 1933); *Cent' anni di musica moderna* (Milan, 1944); *W.A. Mozart* (Turin, 1945); *Breve storia della musica* (Milan, 1946; 2nd ed., 1963); *L'esperienza musicale e l'estetica* (Turin, 1950; 3rd ed., 1965); *"La carriera d'un libertino" di Strawinsky* (Milan, 1952); *Cronache musicale, 1955–1959* (Turin, 1959); *La musica pianistica di Mozart* (Turin, 1963); *Le sinfonie di Mozart* (Turin, 1967); *"I vespri siciliani" di Verdi* (Turin, 1973).
BIBLIOGRAPHY: G. Pestelli, ed., *Il melodramma italiano dell'ottocento: Studi e ricerche per Massimo Mila* (Turin, 1977).

Milán, Luis, Spanish musician, courtier, and poet; b. Valencia, c.1500; d. after 1561. He was a favorite at the viceregal court of Valencia under Germaine de Foix and her 3rd husband, Don Fernando of Aragón. In 1535–36 he brought out his most important work, *Libro de música de vihuela de mano intitulado El Maestro* (Valencia), intended as an instruction book for learning to play the vihuela (a large 6-stringed guitar). This was the first book of its kind to be publ. in Spain, and it is valuable for its many musical examples (*tientos,* fantasias, pavanes, and solo songs with guitar accompaniment: *villancicos,* romances, and *sonetos*), which reveal Milán's high qualities as a composer. Milán also publ. *El cortesano* (1561), giving a description of courtly life at Valencia in his day. *El Maestro,* with the original tablature and transcription into modern notation, was edited by Leo Schrade in *Publikationen älterer Musik, 2* (Leipzig, 1927); modern eds. have been publ. by R. Chiesa (Milan, 1965) and C. Jacobs (University Park, Pa., 1971).
BIBLIOGRAPHY: J.B. Trend, *L. Milán and the Vihuelistas* (London, 1925); J. Ward, *The Vihuela de Mano and Its Music (1536–1576)* (Diss., N.Y. Univ., 1953).

Milanov, Zinka (née **Kunc**), famous soprano; b. Zagreb, Yugoslavia, May 17, 1906. She studied with Milka Ternina in Zagreb, and made her professional debut with the Ljubljana Opera (1927); then sang opera in Hamburg and Vienna; in 1937 was soloist in Verdi's Requiem, under the direction of Toscanini in Salzburg. She made her American debut at the Metropolitan Opera House, N.Y., on Dec. 17, 1937, in *Il Trovatore*, remained on its staff, off and on, until 1966; then taught at the Indiana Univ. School of Music in Bloomington (1966–67). In 1937 she married Predrag Milanov; they were divorced in 1946; she married Ljubomir Ilic in 1947.

Milburn, Ellsworth, American composer; b. Greensburg, Pa., Feb. 6, 1938. He studied with Scott Huston at the College-Cons. of Music in Cincinnati (1956–58); later with Roy Travis and Henri Lazarof at the Univ. of Calif. at Los Angeles (1959–62) and at Mills College with Milhaud (1966–68). He was a teacher at the Cincinnati Cons. (1970–75); in 1975, was appointed to the faculty of Rice Univ. in Houston.
WORKS: *5 Inventions* for 2 Flutes (1965); *Massacre of the Innocents* for Chorus (1965); Concerto for Piano and Chamber Orch. (1967); String Trio (1968); *Soli* for 5 Players on 10 Instruments (1968); String Quintet (1969); *Soli II* for 2 players on Flutes and Double Bass (1970); *Voussoirs* for Orch. (1970); *Soli III* for Clarinet, Cello, and Piano (1971); *Soli IV* for Flute, Oboe, Double Bass, and Harpsichord (1972); Violin Sonata (1972); *Lament* for Harp (1972).

Milde, Hans Feodor von, opera baritone; b. Petronell, near Vienna, April 13, 1821; d. Weimar, Dec. 10, 1899. He studied singing with Manuel García; was a life member of the Weimar Court Opera, and created the role of Telramund in *Lohengrin* (1850). His wife, **Rosa Agthé** (b. Weimar, June 25, 1827; d. there, Jan. 26, 1906), created the role of Elsa, and sang at Weimar until 1876.
BIBLIOGRAPHY: Natalie von Milde, *P. Cornelius. Briefe . . . an Feodor und Rosa von Milde* (Weimar, 1901).

Mildenberg, Albert, American composer; b. Brooklyn, N.Y., Jan. 13, 1878; d. there, July 3, 1918. He was a member of a musical family; studied piano with his mother; then took lessons with Rafael Joseffy (piano) and Bruno Oscar Klein (composition). In 1905 he went to Rome, where he studied with Sgambati; later studied in Paris with Massenet; in 1907 he made a public appearance in Paris as a conductor. Returning to America, he became dean of the music dept. of Meredith College at Raleigh, N.C. He wrote a number of songs, many of them to his own texts; also wrote his own opera librettos. His style was in the Italian tradition; Massenet commended his gift of melody. His light opera *The Wood Witch* was produced in N.Y. on May 25, 1903; another comic opera, *Love's Locksmith,* was given in N.Y. in 1912.
BIBLIOGRAPHY: E.E. Hipsher, *American Opera and Its Composers* (Philadelphia, 1934, pp. 320–22).

Mildenburg, Anna von, famous dramatic soprano; b. Vienna, Nov. 29, 1872; d. there, Jan. 27,

1947. She studied at the Vienna Cons. with Rosa Papier and Pollini; made her opera debut in Hamburg, where her fine voice and acting ability attracted a great deal of attention; in 1897 she was engaged to sing in Bayreuth; in 1898 she became a member of the Vienna Opera; retired from the stage in 1917; went to Munich, where she taught singing at the State Academy; later taught in Berlin; eventually returned to Vienna. Her repertoire included all the great Wagnerian roles. In 1909 she married the playwright Hermann Bahr, with whom she wrote *Bayreuth und das Wagner Theater* (Leipzig, 1910; Eng. trans., London, 1912); she also publ. *Erinnerungen* (1921) and *Darstellung der Werke Richard Wagner aus dem Geiste ser Dichtung und Musik* (vol. 1, *Tristan und Isolde*; Leipzig, 1936). Bahr alone wrote *Parsifalschutz ohne Ausnahmegesetz* (Berlin, 1912).

BIBLIOGRAPHY: P. Stefan, *Anna Bahr-Mildenburg* (Vienna, 1922).

Milder-Hauptmann, Pauline Anna, soprano; b. Constantinople, Dec. 13, 1785; d. Berlin, May 29, 1838. She was the daughter of an Austrian diplomatic official; in Vienna she attracted the notice of Schikaneder. He recommended her to Tomaselli and Salieri, who taught her opera singing. She made her debut at the Vienna Opera on April 9, 1803, and soon became so well regarded as an artist and singer that Beethoven wrote the role of Fidelio for her. Her voice was so powerful that Haydn reportedly said to her: "Dear child, you have a voice like a house." In 1810 she married a Vienna merchant, Hauptmann. In 1812 she went to Berlin, where she created a sensation, particularly as Gluck's heroines (in *Iphigenia, Alcestis,* and *Armida*); she left Berlin in 1829; then sang in Russia, Sweden, and Austria; retired in 1836.

Miles, Maurice, English conductor; b. Epsom, Feb. 25, 1908. He studied piano and violin at home; then at the Royal Academy of Music, with Clifford Curzon (piano) and Sir Henry J. Wood (conducting). Later he took lessons with Clemens Krauss in Salzburg. Returning to England, he conducted the summer orch. at Buxton, and the regular season at Bath. He was in the British army from 1940 till 1943, when he was placed in charge of overseas music broadcasts at the BBC. In 1947 he was appointed conductor of the newly formed Yorkshire Symph. Orch.

BIBLIOGRAPHY: Donald Brook, *International Gallery of Conductors* (Bristol, 1951; pp. 117–20).

Miles, Philip Napier, English composer; b. Shirehampton, Jan. 21, 1865; d. Kingsweston, Bristol, July 19, 1935. He studied in London with Parry and Dannreuther; organized the Shirehampton Choral Society on his own estate and conducted festivals in various localities in England. He wrote several operas: *Westward Ho!* (London, Dec 4, 1914); *Fire Flies* (Clifton, England, Oct. 13, 1924; on the same program with his opera *Markheim*); *Good Friday; Demeter;* and *Queen Rosamond;* also some chamber music and many songs.

BIBLIOGRAPHY: H.C. Colles, "Philip Napier Miles," *Music & Letters* (1936).

Miletić, Miroslav, Croatian violinist and composer; b. Sisak, Aug. 22, 1925. He studied in Zagreb; organized there the renowned Pro Arte String Quartet, specializing in performances of modern music.

WORKS: Operas: *Hasanaginica* and *Der Fall Ruženka*; radio opera, *Auvergnanski Senatori* (1957); *Vision,* television ballet (1958); Suite for String Orch. (1955); Violin Concerto (1958); Viola Concerto (1959); Symph. (1959); *Rhapsodic Variations* for Violin and Piano (1962); 4 string quartets; Violin Sonata; *Proportions* for 6 Instruments; *Lamentation* for Viola and Magnetic Tape; piano pieces; Croatian songs arranged for recorder.

Milford, Robin, English composer; b. Oxford, Jan. 22, 1903; d. Lyme Regis, Dec. 29, 1959. He studied with Holst, Vaughan Williams, and R.O. Morris, at the Royal College of Music in London. While still a student, he composed a number of works, mostly in small forms, in a clear rhythmic manner, with thematic materials suggesting English folk music.

WORKS: Ballet, *The Snow Queen,* after Hans Christian Andersen (1946); oratorio, *The Pilgrim's Progress,* after John Bunyan (1932); *The Forsaken Merman,* after Matthew Arnold, for Tenor, Women's Chorus, Strings, and Piano (1938–50); *A Litany to the Holy Spirit,* after Robert Herrick (1947); Suite for Chamber Orch. (1924); *Miniature Concerto* for Strings (1933); *Ariel* for Small Orch. (1940); *Miniature Concerto* for Harpsichord and Chamber Orch. (1927); Violin Concerto (1937); *Elegiac Meditation* for Viola and Strings (1947); *Fantasia* for String Quartet (1945); Trio for Clarinet, Cello, and Piano (1948); Trio for 2 Violins and Piano (1949); Flute Sonata (1944); Violin Sonata (1945); *A Festival* for Strings (1951); *Fishing by Moonlight* for Piano and Strings (1952); opera, *The Scarlet Letter* (1959); piano pieces; songs; other works in various forms.

Milhaud, Darius, eminent French composer; b. Aix-en-Provence, Sept. 4, 1892; d. Geneva, June 22, 1974. He was the descendant of an old Jewish family, settled in Provence for many centuries. His father was a merchant of almonds; there was a piano in the house, and Milhaud improvised melodies as a child; then began to take violin lessons. He entered the Paris Cons. in 1909, almost at the age limit for enrollment; studied with Berthelier (violin), Lefèvre (ensemble), Leroux (harmony), Gédalge (counterpoint), Widor (composition and fugue), and Vincent d'Indy (conducting); he played violin in the student orch. of the Cons. under the direction of Paul Dukas. He received first "accessit" in violin and counterpoint, and 2nd in fugue; won the Prix Lepaulle for composition. While still a student, he wrote music in a bold modernistic manner; became associated with Erik Satie, Jean Cocteau, and Paul Claudel. When Claudel was appointed French minister to Brazil, he engaged Milhaud as his secretary; they sailed for Rio de Janeiro early in 1917; returned to Paris (via the West Indies and N.Y.) shortly after the Armistice of Nov. 1918. Milhaud's name became known to a larger public as a result of a newspaper article by Henri Collet in *Comœdia* (Jan. 16, 1920), grouping him with 5 other French composers of modern tendencies (Auric, Durey, Honegger, Poulenc, and Germaine Tailleferre) under the sobriquet Les Six, even though the association was stylistically fortuitous. In 1922 Milhaud visited the U.S.; he lectured at Harvard Univ., Princeton, and Columbia; appeared as pianist and composer in his own works; in 1925, he traveled in Italy, Germany, Austria, and Russia; returning to France, he devoted himself mainly to composition and teaching. At the outbreak of World War II, he was in Aix-en-Provence; in July 1940 he came to the U.S.; taught for several years at Mills College in Oakland, Calif. In 1947 he returned to France; was appointed prof. at the Paris Cons., but continued to visit the U.S. as conductor and teacher almost annually, despite his illness (arthritis), which compelled him to conduct while seated; he retained his post at Mills College until 1971; then settled in Geneva. Exceptionally prolific since his student days, he wrote a great number of works in every genre; introduced a modernistic type of music drama, "opéra à la minute," and also the "miniature symphony." He experimented with new stage techniques, incorporating cinematic interludes; has also successfully revived the Greek type of tragedy with vocal accompaniment. He has composed works for electronic instruments, and has demonstrated his contrapuntal skill in such compositions as his 2 string quartets (No. 14 and No. 15), which can be played together as a string octet. He was the first to exploit polytonality in a consistent and deliberate manner; has applied the exotic rhythms of Latin America and the West Indies in many of his lighter works; of these, his *Saudades do Brasil* are particularly popular; Brazilian movements are also found in his *Scaramouche* and *Le Bœuf sur le toit;* in some of his works he has drawn upon the resources of jazz. His ballet *La Création du monde,* produced in 1923, portraying the Creation in terms of Negro cosmology, constitutes the earliest example of the use of the blues and jazz in a symph. score, anticipating Gershwin in this respect. Despite this variety of means and versatility of forms, Milhaud has succeeded in establishing a style that is distinctly and identifiably his own; his melodies are nostalgically lyrical or vivaciously rhythmical, according to mood; his instrumental writing is of great complexity and difficulty, and yet entirely within the capacities of modern virtuoso technique; he has arranged many of his works in several versions each.

WORKS: OPERAS: *La Brebis égarée,* "roman musical" (1910–15; Paris, Dec. 10, 1923); *Agamemnon* (1913; Paris, April 16, 1927); *Le Pauvre Matelot,* "complainte en trois actes" (1926; Paris, Dec. 12, 1927); *Les Choéphores* (Paris, June 15, 1919, in concert form; stage perf., Brussels, March 27, 1935); *Les Euménides* (1922; Antwerp, Nov. 27, 1927); *Les Malheurs d'Orphée* (Brussels, May 7, 1926); *Esther de Carpentras,* opéra-bouffe (1925; Paris, Feb. 1, 1938); 3 "minute operas": *L'Enlèvement d'Europe* (Baden-Baden, July 17, 1927), *L'Abandon d'Ariane,* and *La*

Délivrance de Thésée (Wiesbaden, April 20, 1928); *Christophe Colomb,* grand opera in 26 scenes, to a book by Paul Claudel (Berlin, May 5, 1930); *Maximilien* (Paris, Jan. 4, 1932); *Médée* (Antwerp, Oct. 7, 1939); *Bolivar* (1943; Paris, May 12, 1950); *Le Jeu de Robin et Marion,* mystery play after Adam de la Halle (Wiesbaden, Oct. 28, 1951); *David,* opera in 5 acts and 12 scenes (Jerusalem, June 1, 1954, to celebrate the establishment of Jerusalem as the capital of Judea); *La Mère coupable,* to a libretto by Madeleine Milhaud, after Beaumarchais (Geneva, June 13, 1966); *Saint Louis, Roi de France,* opéra-oratorio to the poem by Paul Claudel (1970–71; Rio de Janeiro, April 14, 1972); *Jeux d'enfants* (short plays for children for voice and instruments); *A propos de bottes* (1932), *Un Petit Peu de musique* (1933), *Un Petit Peu d'exercice* (1937).

BALLETS: *L'Homme et son désir* (Paris, June 6, 1921); *Le Bœuf sur le toit* (Paris, Feb. 21, 1920); *Les Mariés de la Tour Eiffel* (Paris, June 19, 1921; with Honegger, Auric, Poulenc, and Tailleferre); *La Création du monde* (Paris, Oct. 25, 1923); *Salade,* "ballet chanté" (Paris, May 17, 1924); *Le Train bleu,* "danced operetta" (Paris, June 20, 1924); *Polka* for a ballet, *L'Éventail de Jeanne,* homage to Jeanne Dubost, patroness of music (other numbers contributed by Ravel, Ibert, Roussel, and others; Paris, June 16, 1927); *'adame Miroir* (Paris, May 31, 1948); *Jeux de printemps* (Washington, D.C., Martha Graham, choreographer, Oct. 30, 1944); *The Bells,* after Poe (Chicago, April 26, 1946); *Vendange* (1952; produced 20 years later, Nice, April 17, 1972); *La Rose des vents* (Paris, 1958); *La Branche des oiseaux* (Nice, 1965).

FOR ORCH: *Suite symphonique* No. 1 (Paris, May 26, 1914); *Suite symphonique* No. 2 (from incidental music to Paul Claudel's *Protée;* Paris, Oct. 24, 1920); 5 symphs. for Small Orch.: No. 1, *Le Printemps* (1917), No. 2, *Pastorale* (1918), No. 3, *Sérénade* (1921), No. 4, *Dixtuor à cordes* (1921), No. 5, *Dixtuor d'instruments à vent* (1922); 12 symphs. for Large Orch.: No. 1 (Chicago, Oct. 17, 1940, composer conducting); No. 2 (Boston, Dec. 20, 1946, composer conducting); No. 3, *Hymnus ambrosianus,* with Chorus (Paris, Oct. 30, 1947); No. 4 (Paris, May 20, 1948, composer conducting); No. 5 (Turin, Oct. 16, 1953); No. 6 (Boston, Oct. 7, 1955; composer conducting); No. 7 (Chicago, March 3, 1956); No. 8, subtitled *Rhodanienne* (Univ. of Calif., Berkeley, Festival, April 22, 1958); No. 9, (Fort Lauderdale, Fla., March 29, 1960); No. 10 (Portland, Oreg., April 4, 1961); No. 11, *Romantique* (1960; Dallas, Texas, Dec. 12, 1960); No. 12, *Rural* (Davis, Calif., Feb. 16, 1962); *Cinéma-Fantaisie sur Le Bœuf sur le toit* for Violin and Orch. (Paris, Dec. 4, 1920); *Caramel mou,* a shimmy, for Jazz Band (1920); *5 études* for Piano and Orch. (Paris, Jan. 20, 1921); *Saudades do Brasil,* suite of dances (also for Piano; 12 numbers; 1920–21); *Ballade* for Piano and Orch. (1921); *3 Rag Caprices* (Paris, Nov. 23, 1923); *Le Carnaval d'Aix,* for Piano and Orch. (N.Y., Dec. 9, 1926, composer soloist); *2 hymnes* (1927); Violin Concerto No. 1 (1927); Viola Concerto (Amsterdam, Dec. 15, 1929); Concerto for Percussion and Small Orch. (Paris, Dec. 5, 1930); Piano Concerto No. 1 (Paris, Nov. 23, 1934); *Concertino de printemps,* for Violin and Orch. (Paris, March 21, 1935); Cello Concerto No. 1 (Paris, June 28, 1935); *Suite provençale* (Venice Festival, Sept. 12, 1937); *L'Oiseau* (Paris, Jan. 30, 1938); *Cortège funèbre* (N.Y., Aug. 4, 1940); Piano Concerto No. 2 (Chicago, Dec. 18, 1941, composer soloist); Concerto for 2 Pianos and Orch. (Pittsburgh, Nov. 13, 1942); *Opus Americanum* (San Francisco, Dec. 6, 1943); Clarinet Concerto (1941; Washington, Jan. 30, 1946); *Suite française* (Goldman Band, N.Y., June 13, 1945; for Orch., N.Y. Phil., July 29, 1945); *Cain and Abel* for Narrator and Orch. (Hollywood, Oct. 21, 1945); *Le Bal martiniquais* (N.Y., Dec. 6, 1945, composer conducting); *2 Marches* (CBS, N.Y., Dec. 12, 1945); *Fête de la Victoire* (1945); Cello Concerto No. 2 (N.Y., Nov. 28, 1946); *Suite* for Harmonica and Orch. (1942; Paris, May 28, 1947, Larry Adler, soloist; also for Violin and Orch., Philadelphia, Zino Francescatti, soloist); Concerto No. 3 for Piano and Orch. (Prague, May 26, 1946); Violin Concerto No. 2 (Paris, Nov. 7, 1948); *L'Apothéose de Molière* for Harpsichord and Strings (Capri, Sept. 15, 1948); *Kentuckiana* (Louisville, Jan. 4, 1949); Concerto for Marimba, Vibraphone, and Orch. (St. Louis, Feb. 12, 1949); Piano Concerto No. 4 (Boston, March 3, 1950); Piano Concerto No. 5 (N.Y., June 25, 1956); *West Point Suite* for Band (West Point, May 30, 1952); *Concertino d'hiver* for Trombone and String Orch. (1953); *Ouverture méditerranéenne* (Louisville, May 22, 1954); Harp Concerto (Venice, Sept. 17, 1954); Oboe Concerto (1957); Concerto No. 3 for Violin and Orch. (*Concerto royal,* 1958); *Aubade* (Oakland; Calif., March 14, 1961); *Ouverture philharmonique* (N.Y., Nov. 30, 1962); *A Frenchman in New York* (Boston, June 25, 1963); *Odes pour les morts des guerres* (1963); *Murder of a Great Chief of State,* in memory of John F. Kennedy (Oakland, Calif., Dec. 3, 1963); *Pacem in terris,* choral symph. (Paris, Dec. 20, 1963); *Music for Boston* for Violin and Orch. (1965); *Musique pour Prague* (Prague, May 20, 1966); *Musique pour l'Indiana* (Indianapolis, Oct. 29, 1966); *Musique pour Lisbonne* (1966); *Musique pour Nouvelle Orléans* (commissioned by the New Orleans Symph. Orch., but unaccountably canceled, and perf. for the first time instead in Aspen, Colo., Aug. 11, 1968, with Milhaud conducting); *Musique pour l'Univers Claudelien* (Aix-en-Provence, July 30, 1968); *Musique pour Graz* (Graz, Nov. 24, 1970); *Musique pour San Francisco,* "with the participation of the audience"(1971); *Suite in G* (San Rafael, Calif., Sept. 25, 1971); *Ode pour Jerusalem* (1972).

CHAMBER MUSIC: 18 string quartets (1912–51), of which No. 14 and No. 15 are playable together, forming an octet; first perf. in this form at Mills College, Oakland, Calif., Aug. 10, 1949); 2 violin sonatas (1911, 1917); Sonata for Piano and 2 Violins (1914); *Le Printemps* for Piano and Violin (1914); Sonata for Piano, Flute, Clarinet, and Oboe (1918); Sonatina for Flute and Piano (1922); *Impromptu* for Violin and Piano (1926); *3 Caprices de Paganini* for Violin and Piano (1927); Sonatina for Clarinet and Piano (1927); *Pastorale* for Oboe, Clarinet, and Bassoon (1935); *Suite* for Oboe, Clarinet, and Bassoon (1937); *La Cheminée du Roi René,* suite for Flute, Oboe, Clarinet, Horn, and Bassoon (1939); Sonatina for 2 Violins (1940); *Sonatine à trois* for Violin, Viola, and Cello (1940); Sonatina for Violin and Viola (1941); *Quatre visages* for Viola and Piano (1943); 2 viola sonatas (1944); *Elegie* for Cello and Piano (1945); *Danses de Jacarémirim* for Violin and Piano (1945); Sonata for Violin and Harpsichord (1945); Duo for 2 Violins (1945); String Trio (1947); *Aspen Serenade* for 9 Instruments (1957); String Sextet (1958); Chamber Concerto for Piano, Wind Instruments, and String Quintet (1961); String Septet (1964); Piano Quartet (1966); Piano Trio (1968); *Stanford Serenade* for Oboe and 11 Instruments (Stanford, Calif., May 24, 1970); *Musique pour Ars nova* for 13 Instruments, with aleatory episodes (1969); Wind Quintet (1973).

VOCAL WORKS: 3 albums of songs to words of Francis Jammes (1910–12); *7 Poèmes de la Connaissance de l'Est,* to words by Paul Claudel (1913); *3 Poèmes romantiques* for Voice and Piano (1914); *Le Château,* song cycle (1914); *4 Poèmes* for Baritone, to words by Paul Claudel (1915–17); *8 Poèmes juifs* (1916); *Child poems,* to Tagore's words (1916); *3 poèmes,* to words by Christina Rossetti (1916); *Le Retour de l'enfant prodigue,* cantata for 5 Voices and Orch. (1917; Paris, Nov. 23, 1922, composer conducting); *Chansons bas,* to Mallarmé's words, for Voice and Piano (1917); *2 Poèmes de Rimbaud* for Voice and Piano (1917); *Psalm 136* for Baritone, Chorus, and Orch. (1918); *Psalm 129* for Baritone and Orch. (1919); *Les Soirées de Pétrograd,* in 2 albums: *L'Ancien Régime* and *La Révolution* (1919); *Machines agricoles* for Voice and 7 Instruments, to words from a commercial catalogue (1919); *3 Poèmes de Jean Cocteau* for Voice and Piano (1920); *Catalogue de fleurs* for Voice with Piano or 7 Instruments (1920); *Feuilles de température* for Voice and Piano (1920); *Cocktail* for Voice and 3 Clarinets (1921); *Psalm 126* for Chorus a cappella (1921); *4 Poèmes de Catulle* for Voice and Violin (1923); *6 Chants populaires hébraïques* for Voice and Piano (1925); *Hymne de Sion* for Voice and Piano (1925); *Pièce de circonstance,* to words by Jean Cocteau, for Voice and Piano (1926); *Cantate pour louer le Seigneur* for Soli, Choruses, and Orch. (1928); *Pan et Syrinx,* cantata (1934); *Les Amours de Ronsard* for Chorus and Small Orch. (1934); *Le Cygne* for Voice and Piano, to words by Paul Claudel (1935); *La Sagesse,* for Voices and Small Orch., to words by Paul Claudel (1935; Paris Radio, Nov. 8, 1945); *Cantate de la Paix,* to words by Paul Claudel (1937); *Cantate nuptiale,* after *Song of Songs* (Marseilles, Aug. 31, 1937); *Les Deux Cités,* cantata a cappella (1937); *Chanson du capitaine* for Voice and Piano (1937); *Les Quatre Eléments* for Soprano, Tenor, and Orch. (1938); *Récréation,* children's songs (1938); *3 élégies* for Soprano, Tenor, and Strings (1939); *Incantations* for Male Chorus (1939); *Quatrains valaisans* for Chorus a cappella, to Rilke's words (1939); *Cantate de la guerre* for Chorus a cappella, to Paul Claudel's words (1940); *Le Voyage d'été,* suite for Voice and Piano (1940); *4 chansons de Ronsard* for Voice and Orch. (1941); *Rêves,* song cycle (1942); *La Libération des Antilles* for Voice and Piano (1944); *Kaddisch* for Voice, Chorus, and Organ (1945); *Sabbath Morn-*

ing Service for Baritone, Chorus, and Organ (1947); *Naissance de Vénus,* cantata for Mixed Chorus a cappella (Paris Radio, Nov. 30, 1949); *Ballade-Nocturne* for Voice and Piano (1949); *Barba Garibo,* 10 French folk songs, with Orch. (for the celebration of the wine harvest in Menton, 1953); *Cantate de l'initiation* for Chorus and Orch. (1960); *Cantate de la croix de charité* (1960); *Invocation à l'ange Raphael* for 2 Women's Choruses and Orch. (1962); *Adam* for Vocal Quintet (1964); *Cantate de Psaumes* (Paris, May 2, 1968); choral comedy, *Les Momies d'Egypte* (1972).

FOR PIANO: *Le Printemps,* suite (1915–19); 2 sonatas (1916 and 1949); *Saudades do Brasil,* 12 numbers in 2 books (1921); *3 Rag Caprices* (1922; also for Small Orch.); *L'Automne,* suite of 3 pieces (1932); *4 romances sans paroles* (1933); 2 sets of children's pieces: *Touches noires; Touches blanches* (1941); *La Muse ménagère,* suite of 15 pieces (1944; also for Orch.); *Une Journée,* suite of 5 pieces (1946); *L'Enfant aimé,* suite of 5 pieces (also for Orch.; 1948); *Le Candélabre à sept branches,* piano suite (Ein Gev Festival, Israel, April 10, 1952); *Scaramouche,* version for 2 Pianos (1939); *Le Bal martiniquais,* version for 2 Pianos (1944); etc. *Paris,* suite of 6 pieces for 4 Pianos (1948); *6 Danses en 3 mouvements* for 2 Pianos (Paris, Dec. 17, 1970). Also film music; incidental music for plays by Claudel, Romain Rolland, etc. Milhaud publ. a collection of essays, *Etudes* (Paris, 1926), and an autobiography, *Notes sans musique* (Paris, 1949; in Eng. as *Notes without Music,* London, 1952); also *Entretiens avec Claude Rostand* (Paris, 1952), *Ma vie heureuse* (Paris, 1973).

BIBLIOGRAPHY: Paul Landormy, "Darius Milhaud," *Le Ménestrel* (Aug. 14, 21, 28, 1925); Géa Augsbourg, *La Vie de Darius Milhaud en images* (Paris, 1935); Ernst Krenek, "Darius Milhaud," in *The Book of Modern Composers,* ed. David Ewen (N.Y., 1942); Marion Bauer, "Darius Milhaud," *Musical Quarterly* (April 1942); Paul Collaer, *Darius Milhaud* (Antwerp, 1947); Georges Beck, *Darius Milhaud: Etude suivie du catalogue chronologique complet* (Paris, 1949; a detailed list of works, with dates of composition and perfomance; with a supplement, 1957); Colin Mason, "The Chamber Music of Milhaud," *Musical Quarterly* (July 1957); J. Roy, *Darius Milhaud* (Paris, 1968); Antonio Braga, *Darius Milhaud* (Naples, 1969). See also *"Modern Music"... Analytic Index,* compiled by Wayne Shirley, ed. by W. and C. Lichtenwanger (N.Y., 1976; pp. 137–39); C. Palmer, *Milhaud* (London, 1976).

Millard, Harrison, American composer; b. Boston, Nov. 27, 1829; d. there, Sept. 10, 1895. He sang in the chorus of the Handel and Haydn Society as a child; then went to Italy to study voice; was a concert tenor for several years, and made tours in England with the Irish soprano Catherine Hayes. Returning to America in 1854, he became a vocal instructor, first in Boston, then (from 1856) in N.Y. He publ. about 350 songs; wrote also many church works, and an opera, *Deborah,* to an Italian libretto (not performed). He also set to music *Uncle Tom's Cabin* by Harriet Beecher Stowe.

Miller, Dayton Clarence, American physicist and flutist; b. Strongsville, Ohio, March 13, 1866; d. Cleveland, Feb. 22, 1941. After graduation from Baldwin Univ. and Princeton (D.Sc., 1890), he became prof. of physics at the Case School of Applied Science (from 1893). An early interest in the flute led to his experimentation with various versions of the instrument (including a double-bass flute); he accumulated an extensive collection of flutes and various materials relating to the flute, which he left to the Library of Congress Washington, D.C. A leading authority in the field of acoustics and light, he was president of the American Physical Society (1925–26) and of the Acoustical Society of America (1931–32), and vice-president of the American Musicological Society (1939). He publ. *The Science of Musical Sounds* (1916; revised 1926; reprinted 1934); *Catalogue of Books and Literary Material Relating to the Flute and Other Musical Instruments* (1935); *Anecdotal History of the Science of Sound to the Beginning of the 20th Century* (1935); *Sound Waves, Their Shape and Speed* (1937); etc. He also trans. and annotated Böhm's *The Flute and Flute Playing* (Cleveland, 1908; revised ed., 1922).

BIBLIOGRAPHY: H. Fletcher, *Biographical Memoir of Dayton Clarence Miller* (Washington, 1944; contains an extensive list of writings); L.E. Gilliam and W. Lichtenwanger, *The Dayton C. Miller Flute Collection: A Checklist of the Instruments* (Washington, 1961); see also *Dictionary of American Biography,* Supplement III.

Miller, Glenn, American trombonist and band leader; b. Clarinda, Iowa, March 1, 1904; perished in a plane during World War II on a flight from England to France, Dec. 16, 1944. He studied at the Univ. of Colorado; went to N.Y. in 1930; in 1935 joined Ray Noble's band. He then went to Joseph Schillinger to study orchestration; began experimenting with special effects, combining clarinets with saxophones in the same register; the resultant sound became the Glenn Miller hallmark. At the outbreak of World War II, he assembled a large band and flew to England, where he played for the U.S. Air Force. A motion picture, *The Glenn Miller Story,* was produced in 1953.

BIBLIOGRAPHY: John Flower, *Moonlight Serenade: A Bio-Discography of the Glenn Miller Civilian Band* (New Rochelle, N.Y., 1972); C. Simon, *Glenn Miller and His Orchestra* (N.Y., 1974); see also G.T. Simon, in *Dictionary of American Biography,* Supplement III.

Miller, Mildred, American soprano; b. Cleveland, Dec. 16, 1924. Her parents came from Germany; the original family name was Müller. She studied at the Cleveland Inst. of Music (B.M., 1946), then with Sundelius at the New England Cons. in Boston (diploma, 1948). In 1949 she went to Germany; sang with the Stuttgart Opera and with the Munich Opera. In 1950 she married the American pilot Wesley W. Posvar. Returning to the U.S., she made her debut with the Metropolitan Opera Co. in N.Y., as

Cherubino in *Le nozze di Figaro* (Nov. 17, 1951); remained there until 1975.

Miller, Mitch(ell William), American oboist, recording executive, and conductor; b. Rochester, N.Y., July 4, 1911. He studied at the Eastman School of Music (B.Mus., 1932); played oboe in the Rochester Phil. Orch. (1930–33) and in the CBS Symph. Orch. (1935–47); was director of artists and repertoire for the classical division of Mercury Records (1947–50); then was in charge of the popular division of Columbia Records (1950–61); ultimately starred in his own television program, "Sing-Along with Mitch" (1960–65), which became extremely popular.

Miller, Philip Lieson, American librarian and musicologist; b. Woodland, N.Y., April 23, 1906. He studied at the Manhattan Music School and the Juilliard School of Music in N.Y.; from 1927, he worked in the Music Division of the N.Y. Public Library; was assistant chief (1946–59); chief (1959–1966). He was one of the principal founders and first president (1966–68) of the Assoc. for Recorded Sound Collections; in 1963–64, was president of the Music Library Assoc. He publ. many articles and reviews, dealing especially with singers and singing, and the books *Vocal Music* (N.Y., 1955) and *The Ring of Words. An Anthology of Song Texts* (very valuable; N.Y., 1963).

Miller, Robert, American pianist and lawyer; b. New York, Dec. 5, 1930; d. Bronxville, N.Y. Nov. 30, 1981. He studied piano with Mathilde McKinney and Abbey Simon; then enrolled at Princeton Univ., where he took classes in composition with Milton Babbitt and Edward T. Cone, graduating in 1952; also studied jurisprudence at Columbia Law School, graduating in 1957. He was admitted to the bar in 1958 and became a practicing Wall Street lawyer; among his clients were several composers. As a pianist, he made his debut in Carnegie Hall in N.Y. in 1957; had a fairly active, though unhappily brief, career as a recitalist, excelling particularly in ultramodern music. He gave the first performance in N.Y. in 1980 of a piano concerto by John Harbison; George Crumb wrote his *Makrokosmos* (vol. II) for him.

Miller, Roger, American country-music singer and songwriter; b. Fort Worth, Texas, Jan. 2, 1936. He abandoned his formal education before completing the 8th grade; he then set out on his own, took up the guitar and other instruments, and served a stint in the U.S. Army in Korea. After his discharge, he made his way to Nashville; although he never learned to read music, he became a successful composer of songs. He made his first song hit with his autobiographical *King of the Road* in 1965.

Millet, Luis, Catalan composer and conductor; b. Masnou, near Barcelona, April 18, 1867; d. Barcelona, Dec. 7, 1941. He studied with Vidiella and Pedrell; then became a choral conductor. In 1891 he founded the famous choral society Orfeó Català, which he continued to lead until the last years of his life; was also director of the municipal music school in Barcelona; composed several orch. fantasies on Catalan folk songs and many choral works; publ. 2 books on folk music: *De la canción popular catalana* and *Pel nostre ideal* (1917).

BIBLIOGRAPHY: Baltasar Sampler, *Luis Millet* (Barcelona, 1926).

Milligan, Harold Vincent, American organist and composer; b. Astoria, Oreg. Oct. 31, 1888; d. New York, April 12, 1951. He studied with Carl and Noble; was a church organist in Portland, Oreg., before coming to N.Y., in 1907; then taught organ at various schools and colleges; was church organist in Brooklyn and N.Y.; also lectured on American music. He publ. 4 collections of early American songs: *Pioneer American Composers* (2 vols.); *Washington Garland; The First American Composer; Colonial Love Lyrics;* also a biography of Stephen Foster (N.Y., 1920); *Stories of the Famous Operas* (N.Y., 1950); and with G. Souvaine, ed. *The Opera Quiz Book* (N.Y., 1948).

Millöcker, Karl, Austrian operetta composer; b. Vienna, April 29, 1842; d. Baden, near Vienna, Dec. 31, 1899. His father was a jeweler, and Millöcker was destined for that trade, but showed irrepressible musical inclinations and learned music as a child; played the flute in a theater orch. at 16; later took courses at the Cons. of the Gesellschaft der Musikfreunde in Vienna. Upon the recommendation of Franz von Suppé, he received a post as theater conductor in Graz (1864); produced his operettas *Der tote Gast* and *Die beiden Binder* there (both on Dec. 21, 1865). In 1866 he returned to Vienna; from 1869 to 1883 was conductor of the Theater an der Wien; there he presented a number of his operettas, among them *Drei Paar Schuhe* (Jan. 5, 1871); *Wechselbrief und Briefwechsel,* or *Ein nagender Wurm* (Aug. 10, 1872); *Ein Abenteuer in Wien* (Jan. 20, 1873); *Gräfin Dubarry* (Oct. 31, 1879); *Apajune der Wassermann* (Dec. 18, 1880); *Die Jungfrau von Belleville* (Oct. 29, 1881); *Der Bettelstudent* (Dec. 6, 1882; his most successful work; popular also in England and America as *Student Beggar;* N.Y., Oct. 29, 1883); *Gasparone* (Jan. 26, 1884); *Der Vice-Admiral* (Oct. 9, 1886); *Die sieben Schwaben* (Oct. 29, 1887); *Der arme Jonathan* (Jan. 4, 1890; new version by Hentschke and Rixner, 1939; quite successful); *Das Sonntagskind* (Jan. 16, 1892); *Der Probekuss* (Dec. 22, 1894); *Das Nordlicht* (Dec. 22, 1896). Millöcker possessed a natural gift for melodious music; although his popularity was never as great as that of Johann Strauss or Lehár, his operettas captured the spirit of Viennese life.

BIBLIOGRAPHY: C. Preiss, *Karl Millöcker* (Vienna, 1905).

Mills, Charles, American composer; b. Asheville, N.C., Jan. 8, 1914; d. New York, March 7, 1982. A scion of a long line of English settlers in the Carolinas, Mills spent his formative period of life in a rural environment; was active in sports, but at the same time played in dance bands. In 1933 he went to N.Y. and engaged in serious study of composition, first with Max Garfield and then with Aaron Copland (1935–37), Roger Sessions (1937–39), and Roy Harris (1939–41). He enjoyed composing; wrote mostly in a severe but eloquent contrapuntal style; in virtually his entire career as a composer he pursued the ideal of formal cohesion; his style of composition may be described as *Baroque à l'Américaine*. His quest for artistic self-discipline led him to the decision to become a Catholic, a faith in which no uncertainty exists. He was baptized according to the Roman Catholic rite on May 14, 1944. In 1952 he was awarded a Guggenheim fellowship; he also engaged in teaching. In his last works Mills gradually adopted the serial method of composition, which seemed to respond to his need of strong discipline.

WORKS: For Orch.: 5 symphs.: No. 1 (1940); No. 2 (1942); No. 3 (1955); *Crazy Horse Symphony*, a tribute to the legendary Sioux Indian chief known as Chief Crazy Horse (Cincinnati, Nov. 28, 1958); Symph. No. 5 (1980); Piano Concerto (1948); *Theme and Variations* (N.Y., Nov. 8, 1951); *In a Mule-Drawn Wagon* for String Orch. (1968); *Symphonic Ode* for String Orch. (1976); Chamber music: 5 string quartets (1939–59); 6 violin sonatas (1940–77); 2 suites for Solo Violin (1942, 1944); 2 cello sonatas (1940, 1942); Piano Trio (1941); Chamber Concerto for 10 Instruments (1946); Sonata for English Horn and Piano (1946); *Concerto sereno* for Woodwind Octet (1948); *Prologue and Dithyramb* for String Quartet (1951); Concertino for Oboe and Strings (1956); *Serenade* for Wind and String Instruments (1961); Brass Quintet (1962); Brass Sextet (1964); *Sonata da chiesa* for Recorder and Harpsichord (1972); *The 5 Moons of Uranus* for Recorder and Piano (1972); *Duo Dialogue* for Recorder and Organ. For Voice: *Canticles of the Sun* for Voice and Piano (1945); *The Ascension Cantata* for Tenor Solo and Chorus a cappella (1954); *The First Thanksgiving*, cantata for Chorus and Organ (1956). For Piano: 11 sonatinas (1942–45); 2 sonatas (1941–42); *30 Penitential Preludes* (1945). For Jazz Ensemble: *The Centaur and the Phoenix* (1960); *Summer Song* (1960); *Paul Bunyan Jump* (1964).

BIBLIOGRAPHY: David Ewen, *American Composers* (N.Y., 1982).

Mills, Frederick Allen ("Kerry"), American composer and music publisher (composed as Kerry Mills; his publishing house was called F.A. Mills); b. Philadelphia, Feb. 1, 1869; d. Hawthorne, Calif., Dec. 5, 1948. In 1892–93 he taught violin at the Univ. of Michigan; in 1895 he publ. in Detroit his own cakewalk march, *Rastus on Parade;* encouraged by favorable sales, he moved to N.Y., where he became one of the most important publishers of minstrel songs, cakewalks, early ragtime, and other popular music. His own compositions were particularly successful; *At a Georgia Campmeeting* (1897) became the standard against which all other cakewalks were measured; performed in Europe by John Philip Sousa, it became popular there as well; it was roundly denounced in the Leipzig *Illustrierte Zeitung* (Feb. 5, 1903), and could well have been the inspiration for Debussy's *Golliwog's Cakewalk.* Some of his other hits also reached Europe; his *Whistling Rufus* (1899) was publ. in Berlin as *Rufus das Pfeifergigerl.*

Mills-Cockell, John, Canadian composer; b. Toronto, May 19, 1943. He studied composition and electronic music at the Univ. of Toronto and at the Royal Cons. of Music there. In 1966 he developed, in collaboration with the writer Blake Parker, artist Michael Hayden, and designer Dick Zander, a method of composition and performance called Intersystems; he joined the rock bands Kensington Market in Toronto and Hydroelectric Streetcar in Vancouver, utilizing the Moog Synthesizer; in 1970 he organized his own band, Syrinx, a trio including electric hand drums, electric saxophone, and Moog Synthesizer. He also wrote electronic music for films. His works include *Canonic Variations* for Prepared Piano, Bassoon, and Stereo Tape; Wind Quartet; *Reverberations* for Solo Trombone and 2 Stereo Tape Loops; numerous pieces for mixed media, among them *Journey Tree, Father of Light, Apaloosa-Pegasus, Hollywood Dream Trip,* and *Gold Rush.*

Milner, Anthony, English composer; b. Bristol, May 13, 1925. He studied with Herbert Fryer and R.O. Morris at the Royal College of Music in London and privately with Mátyás Seiber. He taught at Morley College in London (1947–62); was appointed to the staff of the Royal College of Music in London in 1962. In 1965 he was named lecturer at the Univ. of London, King's College. He publ. *Harmony for Class Teaching* (2 vols.; 1950).

WORKS: FOR ORCH.: *Variations* for Orch. (1958); *Divertimento* for String Orch. (1961); *April Prologue* (1961); *Sinfonia pasquale* for String Orch. (1963); Chamber Symph. (1968); Symph. No. 1 (1972); Symph. No. 2 with Vocal Soloists and Chorus (Liverpool, July 13, 1978); Concerto for Strings (1982); Concerto for Symphonic Wind Band (Ithaca, N.Y., Oct. 12, 1979); Cantatas: *Salutatio Angelica* (1948); *The City of Desolation* (1955); *St. Francis* (1956); *The Water and the Fire* (1961); *Midway* for Mezzo-soprano and Chamber Orch. (London, July 10, 1974); *Motet for Peace* for Men's Chorus and Orch. (1974); *Emmanuel* for Counter-tenor, Chorus, and Orch. (1975); *The Leaden Echo and the Golden Echo* for Chamber Choir (1974). CHAMBER MUSIC: Quartet for Oboe and Strings (1953); Quintet for Wind Instruments (1964); String Quartet (1975). OTHER VOCAL MUSIC: Sacred choruses a cappella; song cycles.

Milnes, Sherrill, American baritone; b. Hinsdale, Ill., Jan. 10, 1935. His father managed a spacious farm at Downers Grove, some distance from Chicago; his mother sang and directed the Congregational church choir at Downers Grove. Sherrill Milnes helped his parents with daily chores, milking cows and removing fecal matter; after cleaning up, he would play piano and violin, which he had learned at home. He honked the tuba in a school band; then enrolled as a medical student in North Central College in Naperville. He finally turned to music, studied voice at Drake Univ. in Des Moines, and also played in jazz groups to earn a living. He transferred to Northwestern Univ. for further musical education, then joined the chorus of the Chicago Symph.; in 1960 he was induced by Boris Goldovsky to join his New England Opera Co., and Milnes traveled with it far and wide in the U.S., performing such prestigious roles as Figaro, Rigoletto, and Escamillo. In 1961 he met Rosa Ponselle in Baltimore, where she resided at the time, and she coached him in some of his roles. He won an award in the competition of the American Opera Auditions in 1964; subsequently made his European debut as Figaro in *The Barber of Seville* at the Teatro Nuovo in Milan on Sept. 23, 1964. Returning to the U.S., he sang, on Oct. 18, 1964, the part of Valentin in *Faust* with the N.Y. City Opera. On Dec. 22, 1965, he made his debut with the Metropolitan Opera in N.Y. as Valentin; he gradually rose to a stellar position with the Metropolitan, scoring acclaim in virtually all the baritone parts of the standard repertoire: Escamillo, Figaro, the Count di Luna, Tonio, Iago, Don Carlo, Rigoletto, and Scarpia; his greatest role was Don Giovanni. He also took time off for guest appearances in Europe. Among his avocations was conducting; he actually led the Milwaukee Symph. Orch. at two weekend concerts in 1975, acquitting himself with surprising allure.

BIBLIOGRAPHY: David Ewen, *Musicians since 1900* (N.Y., 1978).

Milojević, Miloje, Serbian composer and writer on music; b. Belgrade, Oct. 27, 1884; d. there, June 16, 1946. He was taught piano by his mother; then entered the Serbian school at Novi Sad. Returning to Belgrade after graduation (1904), he became a student of literature at Belgrade Univ. and a pupil at the Serbian School of Music. In 1907 he married the singer **Ivanka Milutinović;** they settled in Munich until 1910; Milojević served at the headquarters of the Serbian army in 1914. In 1917–19 he was in France; from 1919, was again in Belgrade. He publ. a school manual, *Elements of the Art of Music* (1922). As a composer, he wrote mostly in small forms; was influenced successively by Grieg, Strauss, Debussy, and Russian modernists; his music contains an original treatment of Balkan folk songs. His piano suite, *Grimaces rythmiques* (in a modern vein), was performed at the Paris Festival on June 26, 1937. His list of works contains 89 opus numbers.

BIBLIOGRAPHY: P. Konjović, *Miloje Milojević,* in Serbian, with a summary in French (Belgrade, 1954).

Milsap, Ronnie, blind American country-music singer; b. Robbinsville, N.C., Jan. 16, 1944. He entered the North Carolina State School for the Blind as a child and learned to play the violin, piano, and guitar; while in high school he formed his own rock band, but then turned to country music and went to Nashville to live. Very soon he reached the heights of country music, garnering numerous awards and honors. In 1976 he became a regular member of the Grand Ole Opry in Nashville.

Milstein, Nathan, celebrated Russian-born American violinist; b. Odessa, Dec. 31, 1904. His father was a well-to-do merchant in woolen goods; his mother was an amateur violinist who gave him his first lessons. He then began to study with the well-known Odessa violinist Pyotr Stolyarsky, remaining under his tutelage until 1914; then went to St. Petersburg, where he entered the class of the great teacher Leopold Auer at the St. Petersburg Cons. He began his concert career in 1919, with his sister as piano accompanist. In Kiev he met Vladimir Horowitz, and they began giving duo recitals; later they were joined by Gregor Piatigorsky, and organized a trio. Russia was just emerging from a devastating civil war, and communications with Western Europe were not established until much later. In 1925 Milstein was able to leave Russia; he went to Berlin and then to Brussels, where he met Eugène Ysaÿe, who encouraged him in his career. He gave several recitals in Paris, then proceeded to South America. On Oct. 28, 1929, he made his American debut with the Philadelphia Orch. conducted by Stokowski. In 1942 he became an American citizen. He celebrated the 50th anniversary of his American debut in 1979 by giving a number of solo recitals and appearing as soloist with American orchs. As an avocation, he began painting and drawing, arts in which he achieved a certain degree of self-satisfaction. He also engaged in teaching; held master classes at the Juilliard School of Music in N.Y., and also in Zürich. He composed a number of violin pieces, and wrote cadenzas for the violin concertos of Beethoven, Brahms, and Paganini.

BIBLIOGRAPHY: B. Gavoty, *Nathan Milstein* (Geneva, 1956); David Ewen, *Musicians since 1900* (N.Y., 1978).

Milstein, Yakov, Russian pianist, pedagogue, and writer on music; b. Voronezh, Feb. 4, 1911; d. Moscow, Dec. 4, 1981. He studied piano with Igumnov at the Moscow Cons., graduating in 1932; subsequently was a member of its faculty (1935–59, and after 1963). His main interest was an analysis of works of masters of Romantic music; particularly important is his biography of Liszt (Moscow, 1956; Hungarian ed., Budapest, 1965). He contributed an essay on the piano technique of Chopin and Liszt to *The Book of the First International Musicological Congress Devoted to the Works of Chopin* (Warsaw, 1963). He also publ. a monograph on his teacher, Igumnov (Moscow, 1975).

Milton, John, father of the poet; b. Stanton St. John, near Oxford, c.1563; d. London (buried, March 15), 1647. He was a chorister at Christ Church, Oxford (1572–77); apparently remained at Oxford for several years, and in 1585 went to London, where he was admitted to the Scriveners' Co. in 1600; in that year he married Sarah Jeffrey. His fine 6–part madrigal *Fayre Oriana in the Morn* was publ. in Morley's *Triumphes of Oriana* (1601); 4 anthems were publ. in Leighton's *Teares or Lamentacions* (1614); a motet and 5 anthems in Myriell's *Tristitiae remedium* (1616); and 3 Psalm settings in Ravenscroft's *Whole Booke of Psalms* (1621); 3 fantasias for 5 viols, and other works, are in MS.

BIBLIOGRAPHY: E. Brennecke, Jr., *John Milton the Elder and His Music* (N.Y., 1938; with bibliography and 16 musical examples).

Milveden, (Jan) Ingmar (Georg), Swedish composer, organist, and musicologist; b. Göteborg, Feb. 15, 1920. He studied cello and organ; then took a course in composition with Sven Svensson and in musicology with C.A. Moberg in Uppsala; earned his doctorate there in 1972 with the dissertation *Zu den liturgischen "Hystorie" in Schweden. Liturgie- und choralgeschichtliche Untersuchungen.* Milveden is one of the most important Swedish composers of modern church music. In 1967 he became organist at St. Per's Church in Uppsala; lectured at the Univ. of Stockholm in 1970–73 and at the Univ. of Uppsala from 1972.

WORKS: *Serenade* for String Orch. (1942); Piano Sonatina (1943); Duo for Flute and Piano (1953, revised 1975); Trio for Flute, Clarinet, and Viola (1955, revised 1973); *Canticula Linnaeana* for Chorus a cappella (1965); *Mässa i skördetid (Mass of the Harvest Time)* for Congregation, Liturgist, 2 Choruses, 2 Organs, and Orch. (1965); *Pezzo Concertante* for Orch. (1969; Uppsala, Feb. 5, 1970); *Concerto al Fresco* for Clarinet and Orch. (1970; Uppsala, Nov. 25, 1971); *Threnodia* for 3 Cellos (1970); church opera, *Vid en Korsväg* (1971; Lund, Nov. 30, 1974); *Nu . . . ,* 4 Linne quotations for Solo Voices, Chorus, and Instrumental Groups (1972; Ingesund, March 17, 1974); *Magnificat* for 2 Choral Groups, Organ, Winds, and Percussion (1973); *Toccata* for Organ (1973); *3 assaggi* for Solo Cello (1975); choruses; songs.

Mimaroglu, Ilhan Kemaleddin, Turkish-American composer and writer on music; b. Istanbul, March 11, 1926. He studied law at the Univ. of Ankara; in 1955 traveled to the U.S. on a Rockefeller fellowship, and settled in N.Y., where he studied theory with Jack Beeson and Chou Wen-chung, musicology with Paul Henry Lang, and electronic music with Vladimir Ussachevsky at Columbia Univ.; he took lessons in modern composition with Stefan Wolpe, and also received inspiring advice from Edgar Varèse. He was subsequently a recipient of a Guggenheim fellowship (1971–72). He publ. several books in Turkish (*Sounds of America, Jazz as an Art, 11 Contemporary Composers, A History of Music, Little Encyclopedia of Western Music,* etc.). In 1963 he began his association with the Columbia-Princeton Electronic Music Center, where he composed most of his electronic works, among them *Le Tombeau d'Edgar Poe* (1964), *Anacolutha* (1965), *Wings of the Delirious Demon* (1969), and music for Jean Dubuffet's *Coucou Bazar* (1973). He developed compositional methods viewing electronic music in a parallel to cinema, resulting in works for tape in which recorded performance dominates individual rendition. Concurrently, he displayed a growing political awareness in his choice of texts, conveying messages of New Left persuasion in such works as *Sing Me a Song of Songmy,* a protest chant against the war in Vietnam (1971) and *To Kill a Sunrise* (1974). Other works include *Parodie sérieuse* for String Quartet (1947); Clarinet Concerto (1950); *Metropolis* for Orch. (1955); *Pièces futiles* for Clarinet and Cello (1958); *Epicedium* for Voice and Chamber Ensemble (1961); *2 × e.e.* for Vocal Quartet, on poems of e.e. cummings (1963); *September Moon* for Orch. (1967); *Music Plus One* for Violin and Tape (1970); *Cristal de Bohème* for Percussion Ensemble (1971); various piano pieces and songs.

Minchev, Georgi, Bulgarian composer; b. Sofia, Jan. 29, 1939. He studied composition with Goleminov at the Bulgarian State Cons. in Sofia, graduating in 1963; went to Moscow and studied there with Shchedrin (1968–70); in 1972 he traveled to France, Great Britain, and the U.S. on a UNESCO scholarship. Returning to Bulgaria, he became chief of productions at the Committee for Television and Radio in Sofia.

WORKS: Oratorio, *Starobulgarski hroniky (Old Bulgarian Chronicles)* for Narrator, Soloists, Mixed Chorus, Folk Music Chorus, and Orch. (Sofia, Dec. 22, 1971); Symph. (1967); *Music for 3 Orch. Groups* (1968); *Intermezzo and Aquarelle* for Strings, 2 Flutes, and Harpsichord (1972); *3 Poems* for Mezzo-soprano and Orch. (1973); *Concert Music* for Orch. (1975); Piano Concerto (1976); *Symphonic Prologue* (1980); choruses; solo songs; folk-song arrangements.

Mingus, Charles, black American jazz musician; b. Nogales, Ariz., April 22, 1922; d. Cuernavaca, Mexico, Jan. 5, 1979. His signal achievement was to elevate the role of the double bass in the rhythm section of the jazz band to that of a melody carrier; by so doing, he created a peculiar type of black instrumentation. He worked in California before moving to N.Y., where he played with Duke Ellington and other famous jazz bandleaders. A highly explosive individual, he became known as the "angry man of jazz." He even expressed his disgust with the very term "jazz": "The word means nigger, second-class citizen." In his own groups he insisted on including white players. He toured Europe in 1972 and 1975, but later sank into depression and retired to Mexico, where he hoped to find a cure for his illness, an amyotrophic lateral sclerosis. A convert to Hinduism, he instructed his last wife to scatter his ashes over the Ganges River. He improvised a number of jazz pieces with sophisticated titles such as *Pithecanthropus Erectus,* which were eventually notated and publ. He also left an autobiography, dictated to a collaborator under the title *Beneath the Underdog: His World as Composed by Mingus* (N.Y., 1971).

Minkus, Alois (Louis), Austrian composer of ballet music; b. Vienna, March 23, 1826; d. there, Dec. 7, 1917. (The exact date of his death was established in 1976 from documentation available in the parish register and the burial records of the city of Vienna.) He was a violinist by profession; as a young man went to Russia, where he was engaged by Prince Yusupov as leader of his serf orch. in St. Petersburg (1853–55). From 1862 to 1872 he was concertmaster of the Bolshoi Theater in Moscow. In 1869 the Bolshoi Theater produced his ballet *Don Quixote* to the choreography of the famous Russian ballet master Petipa; its success was extraordinary, and its appeal to the Russian audiences so durable that the work retained its place in the repertoire of Russian ballet companies for more than a century, showing no signs of diminishing popularity. Equally popular was his ballet *La Bayadère,* produced by Petipa in St. Petersburg in 1877; another successful ballet by Minkus was *La Fiametta or The Triumph of Love,* originally produced in Paris in 1864. From 1872 to 1885 Minkus held the post of court composer of ballet music for the Imperial theaters in St. Petersburg; he remained in Russia until 1891 when returned to Vienna, where he lived in semi-retirement until his death at the age of 91. The ballets of Minkus never took root outside Russia, but their cursive melodies and bland rhythmic formulas suit old-fashioned Russian choreography to the airiest *entrechat.*

Minoja, Ambrogio, Italian composer and singing teacher; b. Ospitaletto Lodigiano, near Piacenza, Oct. 22, 1752; d. Milan, Aug. 3, 1825. He studied music in Lodi and Naples; served as maestro al cembalo at La Scala in Milan and at the Teatro Canobbiano there from 1780 to 1802. In 1814 he became censor of the Milan Cons., and held that position until his death. As an instructor of high repute, he publ. books of solfeggi and *Lettere sopra il canto* (Milan, 1812); composed a Symph. and wrote much choral music, as well as 2 operas: *Tito nelle Gallie* (La Scala, Milan, Dec. 26, 1786) and *Olimpiade* (Rome, Dec. 26, 1787).

Minton, Yvonne, Australian mezzo-soprano; b. Sydney, Dec. 4, 1938. She studied at the Sydney Cons. and in London. In 1961 she won the Kathleen Ferrier Prize; then made appearances with several opera groups in London. In 1965 she made a successful Covent Garden debut. On March 16, 1973, she made her first American appearance at the Metropolitan Opera in N.Y. as Octavian in *Der Rosenkavalier;* also sang at Bayreuth and Salzburg. In 1980 she was made a Commander of the Order of the British Empire.

Mintz, Shlomo, Russian-born Israeli violinist; b. Moscow, Oct. 30, 1957. He went to Isreal while very young, and came to the attention of Isaac Stern, who arranged for him to study at the Juilliard School of Music in N.Y. on a scholarship. Within a few years he began to concertize with increasing success in Israel and America.

Mirecki, Franz (Franciszek Wincenty), Polish composer, pianist, and singing teacher; b. Cracow (baptized, March 31), 1791; d. there, May 29, 1862. He studied with his father; made his debut as a pianist at the age of 9; later was a student of Hummel in Vienna (1814) and of Cherubini in Paris (1817). He lived in Milan in 1822–26 and in Genoa in 1831–38 before returning to Cracow, where he established himself as a singing teacher; also served as director of the Cracow Opera (1844–47).
  WORKS: Operas: *Cyganie (The Gypsies;* in Polish; Warsaw, May 23, 1822); *Evandro in Pergamo* (in Italian; Genoa, Dec. 26, 1824); *I due forzati* (Lisbon, March 7, 1826); *Cornelio Bentivoglio* (Milan, March 18, 1844); *Nocleg w Apeninach (A Night in the Apennines;* in Polish; Cracow, April 11, 1845); numerous piano pieces; eds., in 12 vols., of 50 Psalms of Benedetto Marcello, with added instrumental parts.

Mirouze, Marcel, French composer and conductor; b. Toulouse, Sept. 24, 1906; d. Aude (in an automobile accident), Aug. 1, 1957. He studied with Busser at the Paris Cons.; conducted the Paris Radio Orch. (1935–40) and in Monte Carlo (1940–43). He wrote an opera, *Geneviève de Paris,* for the 2,000th anniversary of the founding of the city of Paris; it was produced first as a radio play with music in 1952, and then on stage in Toulouse in the same year; he also composed 2 ballets, *Paul et Virginie* (1942) and *Les Bains de mer* (1946); 2 symph. tableaux, *Afrique* (1936) and *Asie* (1938); Piano Concerto (1948); film music; piano pieces; songs.

Mirovitch, Alfred, Russian-American pianist; b. St. Petersburg, May 4, 1884; d. Whitefield, N.Mex., Aug. 3, 1959. He graduated from the St. Petersburg Cons. with the first prize in piano as a student of Anna Essipova in 1909; began his concert career in 1911; made 7 world tours; made his American debut in 1921. He conducted master classes in piano at the Juilliard School of Music in N.Y. (1944–52); then joined the faculty of Boston Univ. He edited, for G. Schirmer, Inc., a number of collections of classical piano music for students: *Early Classics for the Piano; Introduction to Piano Classics* (3 vols. for different grades); *Introduction to the Romantics; Introduction to the Study of Bach* (2 vols.); *Introduction to Chopin* (2 vols.); he also edited piano pieces by Russian composers; wrote original piano compositions (*Spring Song, Toccata,* etc.).

Miry, Karel, Belgian composer; b. Ghent, Aug. 14, 1823; d. there, Oct. 3, 1889. He studied violin with Jean Andries and composition with Martin Joseph Mergal at the Ghent Cons.; in 1857 he was engaged as a prof. of harmony and counterpoint there; in 1871 was appointed assistant director; from 1875 he became inspector of music in the municipal schools of Ghent, and from 1881, inspector of state-supported music schools. As a composer, he cultivated the national Flemish style; wrote several symphs. and 18 operas and operettas to French and Flemish librettos. His opera *Boucherd d'Avesnes* was first staged in Ghent on Feb. 5, 1864, obtaining considerable success. But he owes his fame to the patriotic song *De Vlaamse Leeuw,* which he wrote at the age of 22, and which became the Flemish anthem of Belgium.

BIBLIOGRAPHY: J. Maertens, *De structuurontleding van de symfonieen van Karel Miry* (Diss., Univ. of Ghent, 1968).

Mirzoyan, Edvard, Armenian composer; b. Gori, Georgia, May 12, 1921. He studied at the Erevan Cons., graduating in 1941; then went to Moscow and entered the composition class of Litinsky at the Moscow Cons. In 1948 he was appointed instructor at the Erevan Cons.; in 1965 became a prof. there. In his music he follows a lucid neo-Classical style, while his thematic materials are of native Armenian provenance. He wrote a String Quartet (1947); the cantatas *Soviet Armenia* (1948) and *Lenin* (in collaboration with Arutyunian, 1950); a Symph. for Strings (1962, his strongest composition); songs.

BIBLIOGRAPHY: M. Ter-Simonyan, *Edvard Mirzoyan* (Moscow, 1969).

Misch, Ludwig, German-American musicologist; b. Berlin, June 13, 1887; d. New York, April 22, 1967. He studied music theory with Max Friedlaender at the Univ. of Berlin; simultaneously took courses in law, obtaining his doctor's degree in Heidelberg in 1911. He was music critic for the *Allgemeine Musikzeitung* (1909–13); conducted theater orchs. in Berlin, Essen, and Bremen. From 1921 to 1933 he was music critic of the *Berliner Lokalanzeiger.* Under the Nazi regime he conducted a Jewish madrigal choir in Berlin until he was sent to a concentration camp. In 1947 he emigrated to N.Y., where he became active as an organist and musicologist. He publ. the valuable books *Johannes Brahms* (Bielefeld, 1913; 2nd ed., Berlin, 1922); *Beethoven-Studien* (Berlin, 1950; also in Eng., Norman, Okla., 1953); trans. and annotated (with Donald W. MacArdle) *New Beethoven Letters* (Norman, 1957); also wrote *Die Faktoren der Einheit in der Mehrsätzigkeit der Werke Beethovens: Versuch einer Theorie der Einheit des Werkstils* (Bonn, 1958); *Neue Beethoven-Studien und andere Themen* (Bonn, 1967).

Mischakoff, Mischa, Russian-American violinist; b. Proskurov, April 3, 1895; d. Petoskey, Mich., Feb. 1, 1981. His original name was **Mischa Fischberg;** owing to a plethora of Russian-Jewish violinists named Fischberg, he decided to change his name to Mischakoff, formed by adding the Russian ending *-koff* to his first name, which itself is a Russian diminutive for Michael. He studied with Leopold Auer at the St. Petersburg Cons., graduating in 1912 with a gold medal for excellence; then taught at the Cons. of Nizhny-Novgorod (1918–20); emigrated to the U.S. in 1921 and became a naturalized citizen in 1927. He was concertmaster of the N.Y. Symph. Orch. (1924–27), the Philadelphia Orch. (1927–29), the Chicago Symph. Orch. (1930–36), the NBC Symph. Orch. under Toscanini (1937–51), and the Detroit Symph. Orch. (1951–68). He was a member

of the faculty of the Juilliard School of Music in N.Y. (1940–52); then taught at Oakland Univ. (1965–68) and the Peabody Cons. (1969–70), and was a guest prof. at the Aspen (Colo.) Music Festival (1970–73). At the time of his death, he was teaching at Wayne State Univ. in Detroit.

Misón, Luis, Spanish musician; b. Barcelona; d. Madrid, Feb. 13, 1776. He was a flutist in the Royal Chapel and the Royal Opera, Madrid (from 1748); became conductor there in 1756; composed stage music; was the first to introduce the "tonadilla escénica," a sort of miniature comic opera that developed from the musical interludes in early Spanish plays; also wrote "sainetes" (dramatic dialogues) and zarzuelas (operettas); his sonatas for flute and bass are in MS.

BIBLIOGRAPHY: J. Subirá, *La música er: la Casa de Alba* (Madrid, 1927); idem, *Tonadillas teatrales ineditas* (Madrid, 1932; with musical examples); idem, *Los maestros de la tonadilla esénica* (Barcelona, 1933; with musical examples).

Misra, Mahapurush, Indian virtuoso on the tabla; b. Calcutta, Jan. 1, 1933. He studied with eminent swamis and gurus; toured in Europe in 1959 and in the U.S. in 1961.

Missa, Edmond Jean Louis, French opera composer; b. Rheims, June 12, 1861; d. Paris, Jan. 29, 1910. He studied with Massenet at the Paris Cons.; received an honorable mention for the Prix de Rome in 1881; then served as organist at St. Thomas d'Aquin.

WORKS: Operas *Babette* (London, Oct. 22, 1900); *Muguette,* based on Ouida's *2 Little Wooden Shoes* (Paris, March 18, 1903; his most successful work; also perf. in Germany and England); *Maguelone* (London, July 20, 1903); several other operas were produced in Paris and Rheims.

Mitchell, Donald, eminent English music scholar and publishing executive; b. London, Feb. 6, 1925. He studied at Dulwich College in London (1939–42); after noncombatant wartime service (1942–45), he founded (1947) and then became co-editor (with Hans Keller) of *Music Survey* (1949–52); in 1953–57 he was London music critic of the *Musical Times.* In 1958 he was appointed music editor and adviser of Faber & Faber Ltd., book publishers; in 1965 he became business manager, and in 1973 director, of the firm. He edited *Tempo* (1958–62); was on the music staff of the *Daily Telegraph* (1959–64); in 1963–64 served as music adviser to Boosey & Hawkes Ltd.; in 1967 was a member of the BBC Central Music Advisory Council; in 1971–76 was prof. of music, and from 1976 visiting prof. of music, at the Univ. of Sussex; in 1973 was awarded by it an honorary M.A. degree; received his doctorate in 1977 from Southampton Univ., with a dissertation on Mahler. He lectured widely on musical subjects in the United Kingdom, U.S., and Australia; contributed articles to the *Encyclopædia Britannica* and other reference publications; was active in broadcasting plans for BBC dealing with musical subjects. As a music scholar, Mitchell made a profound study, in Vienna and elsewhere, of the life and works of Gustav Mahler; was awarded in 1961 the Mahler Medal of Honor by the Bruckner Society of America. His major work is a Mahler biography: vol. 1, *Gustav Mahler: The Early Years* (London, 1958; revised ed., 1980); vol. 2, *The Wunderhorn Years* (London, 1976); other publications are *The Language of Modern Music* (London, 1963; 3rd ed., 1970), *The Faber Book of Nursery Songs* (London, 1968) and *The Faber Book of Children's Songs* (London, 1970). He ed. and annotated Alma Mahler's *Gustav Mahler: Memories and Letters* (1968; 3rd revised ed., 1973); also publ. *W.A. Mozart: A Short Biography* (London, 1956). With Hans Keller he compiled the symposium *Benjamin Britten: A Commentary of All His Works from a Group of Specialists* (London, 1952); with H.C. Robbins Landon, *The Mozart Companion* (N.Y., 1956); with J. Evans, he ed. *Benjamin Britten, 1913–1976: Pictures from a Life* (London, 1978).

Mitchell, Dwike, American jazz pianist; b. Jacksonville, Fla., Feb. 14, 1930. He studied at the Philadelphia Music Academy; formed a duo with the French horn player and bassist Willie Ruff, a Yale graduate, and together they played in nightclubs with complete popular acceptance despite their academic education and ability to read music. In 1959 they gave impromptu sessions of jazz in Russia, arousing unrestrained enthusiasm among young Soviet audiences.

Mitchell, Howard, American cellist and conductor; b. Lyons, Nebr., March 11, 1911. His family moved to Sioux City, Iowa, when he was a child, and he studied piano and trumpet before taking up the cello at the Peabody Cons. in Baltimore; he then enrolled in the Curtis Inst., Philadelphia, as a cello student of Felix Salmond, graduating in 1935. He was first cellist at the National Symph. Orch. in Washington (1933–46); then served as its associate conductor (1946–49) and principal conductor (1949–70). In 1970 he was appointed conductor of the National Orch. of Uruguay.
BIBLIOGRAPHY: Hope Stoddard, *Symphony Conductors of the U.S.A.* (N.Y., 1957; pp. 119–25).

Mitchell, Joni, Canadian pop singer and songwriter; b. McLeod, Alberta, Nov. 7, 1943. Her maiden name was Roberta Joan Anderson. She sang to her own guitar accompaniment in clubs in Toronto, and met the folksinger Chuck Mitchell, whom she temporarily married. She kept his last name after their divorce. In her interpretations, she closely followed the folk-song style, with an admixture of jazzy syncopation. For a while she worked as a lyrics writer for the legendary jazz artist Charles Mingus, and after his death in 1979 wrote a moving song in his memory, somewhat sacrilegiously entitled *God Must Be a Boogie Man.* Among her hit records were *Clouds, Ladies of the Canyon, Help Me,* and *Raised on Robbery.*

Mitchell, Leona, talented black American soprano; b. Enid, Okla., Oct. 13, 1948. She was one of 15 children; her father, a Pentecostal minister, played several instruments by ear; her mother was a good amateur pianist. Leona Mitchell sang in local church choirs; then received a scholarship to Oklahoma City Univ., where she obtained her B.Mus. degree in 1971. She made her operatic debut in 1973 as Micaëla in *Carmen* with the San Francisco Spring Opera Theater. She then received the $10,000 Opera America grant, which enabled her to take voice lessons with Ernest St. John Metz in Los Angeles. On Dec. 15, 1975, she made her Metropolitan Opera debut in N.Y. as Micaëla; subsequently sang there the roles of Pamina in *Die Zauberflöte* and Musetta in *La Bohème;* she won critical acclaim for her portrayal of Leonora in *La forza del destino* in 1982.

Mitchell, William John, American musicologist; b. New York, Nov. 21, 1906; d. Binghamton, N.Y., Aug. 17, 1971. He studied at the Inst. of Musical Arts in N.Y. (1925–29); then at Columbia Univ. (B.A., 1930); went to Vienna for further studies (1930–32). Upon his return to N.Y. he was on the staff at Columbia Univ.; received his M.A. there in 1938; became a full prof. in 1952, then served as chairman of the music dept. from 1962 to 1967; concurrently he taught at the Mannes College of Music in N.Y. (1957–68); he subsequently joined the faculty of the State Univ. of N.Y. in Binghamton. Among his publications are *Elementary Harmony* (N.Y., 1939; 3rd ed., revised, 1965); he trans. C.P.E. Bach's *Versuch über die wahre Art das Clavier zu spielen,* publ. in N.Y., 1949, as *Essay on the True Art of Playing Keyboard Instruments;* with F. Salzer, he ed. the *Music Forum* (a hard-cover, unperiodical periodical emphasizing Schenkerian analysis; 1967—); contributed articles on the *Tristan Prelude* and a work of Orlando di Lasso. He also wrote valuable articles dealing with the evolution of chromaticism and chord symbolism.

Mitjana y Gordón, Rafael, eminent Spanish music historian; b. Málaga, Dec. 6, 1869; d. Stockholm, Aug. 15, 1921. He studied music with Eduardo Ocón in Málaga, Felipe Pedrell in Madrid, and Saint-Saëns in Paris; was employed in the Spanish diplomatic service in Russia, Turkey, Morocco, and Sweden.
WRITINGS: His most important work is the extensive contribution on the history of Spanish music in Lavignac's *Encyclopédie de la musique* (Paris, 1920; Part I, vol. IV). He also wrote numerous valuable works of a critical or historical nature, including: *L'Orientalisme musical et la musique arabe; El Cancionero de Uppsala; Catalogue critique et descriptif des imprimés de musique des XVIᵉ et XVIIᵉ siècles conservés à la Bibliothèque de l'Université Royale d'Uppsala* (vol. 1 only; Uppsala, 1911; vols. 2 and 3 completed by A. Davidsson); *Don Fernando de Las Infantas teólogo y músico* (Madrid, 1918); *Estudios sobre algunos músicos españoles del siglo XVI* (Madrid, 1918); *Francisco Guerrero* (Ma-

drid, 1922); *Cristóbal Morales* (Madrid, 1922); etc.

Mitrea-Celarianu, Mihai, Rumanian composer; b. Bucharest, Jan. 20, 1935. He studied with Rogalski, Alfred Mendelsohn, Vancea, and Negrea at the Bucharest Cons. (1948–53); also took private lessons with Jora (1949–51); was a prof. of harmony and music history in Bucharest (1954–60, 1962–68); then attended summer courses in new music given by Aloys Kontarsky, Caskel, and Karkoschka in Darmstadt (1968), and further studied with the Groupe de Recherches Musicales in Paris (1968–69) and with Pierre Schaeffer and Pousseur at the Paris Cons. (1968–69). His trademarks in composition are aleatory, electronic, and variable scoring.

WORKS: Violin Sonata (1957); Piano Sonata (1958); *Variations* for Orch. (1958); Piano Sonatina (1960); *Le Chant des étoiles,* cantata for Mezzo-soprano and 33 Instruments (1964); *Glosă (Comment)* for Solo Viola (1965); *Petite histoire d'avant-monde* for Small Chamber Ensemble (1967); *Convergences II (Colinda)* for Electronic Instruments and Percussion (1967), *III (Idéophonie M),* aleatory music for Narrator, Children's Choir, and 19 Instruments (1968), *IV* for One Performer on Optional Instrument or Variable Ensemble (1968) and *V (Jeux dans le blanc)* for Chorus, Percussion, and Tape (1969); *Trei pentru cinci* for Aleatorily Structured Orch. (in collaboration with Miereanu and Bosseur, 1969); *Seth* for 7 Instruments (1969); *ZN* "idéogramme photographique" for 3, 4, or 5 Performers (1971); *Signaux (Sur l'Océan U)* for 13 Players (1971); *Inaugural 71,* "action" for a Flutist, with Electro-acoustical Devices and a Projector (1971); *Piano de matin (Ecoute pour Anne Frank),* "action" for 5 Instruments, 5 Persons manipulating Divergent Sound Sources, Electro-acoustical Devices, and Projectors (1972); *Prérêve* for Voice, Harpsichord, Flute, and Percussion (1975); songs.

Mitropoulos, Dimitri, celebrated Greek conductor and composer; b. Athens, March 1, 1896; d. while on the podium conducting a La Scala rehearsal of Mahler's 3rd Symph., Milan, Nov. 2, 1960. He studied composition with Armand Marsick, the Belgian musician who spent many years in Greece, at the Odeon in Athens; wrote an opera after Maeterlinck, *Sœur Béatrice* (1918), performed at the Odeon (May 20, 1919); in 1920, after graduation from the Odeon, he went to Brussels, where he studied composition with Paul Gilson; in 1921 he went to Berlin, where he took piano lessons with Busoni; served as an assistant conductor at the Berlin Opera (1921–24); then returned to Greece, where he became conductor of the municipal orch. in Athens. In 1930 he was invited to conduct a concert of the Berlin Phil.; when the soloist Egon Petri became suddenly indisposed, Mitropoulos substituted for him as soloist in Prokofiev's Piano Concerto No. 3, conducting from the keyboard (Feb. 27, 1930). He played the same concerto in Paris in 1932, as a pianist-conductor, and later in the U.S. His Paris debut as a conductor (1932) obtained a spontaneous success; he conducted the most difficult works from memory, which

was a novelty at the time; also led rehearsals without a score. He made his American debut with the Boston Symph. on Jan. 24, 1937, with immediate acclaim; that same year he was engaged as permanent conductor of the Minneapolis Symph. Orch.; there he frequently performed modern music, including works by Schoenberg, Alban Berg, and other representatives of the atonal school; the opposition that naturally arose was not sufficient to offset his hold on the public as a conductor of great emotional power. He resigned from the Minneapolis Symph. in 1949 to accept the post of conductor of the N.Y. Phil.; shared the podium with Stokowski for a few weeks, and in 1950 became music director. In 1956 Leonard Bernstein was engaged as associate conductor with Mitropoulos, and in 1958 succeeded him as music director. With the N.Y. Phil., Mitropoulos continued his policy of bringing out important works by European and American modernists; he also introduced the innovation of programming modern operas (*Elektra, Wozzeck*) in concert form. A musician of astounding technical ability, Mitropoulos became very successful with the general public as well as with the musical vanguard whose cause he so boldly espoused. While his time was engaged mainly in the U.S., Mitropoulos continued to appear as guest conductor in Europe; he also appeared on numerous occasions as conductor at the Metropolitan Opera House and at various European opera theaters. He became an American citizen in 1946. Mitropoulos was one of the earliest among Greek composers to write in a distinctly modern idiom.

WORKS: Violin Sonata, entitled *Ostinata,* in a nearly precise Schoebergian idiom (1925–26); *Burial* for Orch. (1925); Concerto Grosso for Orch. (1928); *Concert Piece* for Violin and Piano (1913); Piano Sonata (1915); *Fauns* for String Quartet (1915); *Piano Piece* (1925); *Passacaglia, Preludio e Fuga* for Piano (c. 1925); *10 Inventions* for Soprano and Piano (1926); *4 Dances from Cythera* for Piano (1926); incidental music for *Electra* and *Hippolytus* (1936, 1937).

BIBLIOGRAPHY: Harold Schonberg, *The Great Conductors* (N.Y., 1967).

Mitsukuri, Shukichi, Japanese composer; b. Tokyo, Oct. 21, 1895; d. Chigasaki, Kanagawa Prefecture, May 10, 1971. He graduated in applied chemistry from the engineering dept. of the Imperial Univ. in Tokyo in 1921; then went to Berlin and studied composition with Georg Schumann; returned to Japan in 1925 and became an Imperial Navy engineering officer. In 1930 he founded a contemporary Japanese composers' society, Shinko Sakkyokuka; in 1954, was appointed a prof. at the Music Academy in Tokyo.

WORKS: *Sinfonietta classica* (Paris, March 6, 1936); *10 Haikai de Basho* for Orch. (Paris, Dec. 10, 1937); *Elegy* for Chorus and Orch. (1949); Symph. No. 1 (Tokyo, Aug. 22, 1951); Symph. No. 2 (1963); Piano Concertino (Tokyo, Aug. 22, 1953); Piano Concerto (Tokyo, April 23, 1955); Violin Sonata (1935); Piano Quintet (1955); *Night Rhapsody* for Piano

(1935); other piano pieces; 3 albums of Japanese folk songs (1950, 1954, 1955).

Mittelmann, Norman, Canadian baritone; b. Winnipeg, May 25, 1932. He studied with Martial Singher at the Curtis Inst. in Philadelphia, and with Lotte Lehmann in Santa Barbara, Calif. He was a member of the staff of the Toronto Opera. On Oct. 28, 1961, he made his debut in a minor role at the Metropolitan Opera; sang there until 1965; again in 1973–75.

Mitterer, Ignaz Martin, Austrian composer of church music; b. St. Justina, Feb. 2, 1850; d. Brixen, Aug. 18, 1924. He studied singing with his uncle, Anton Mitterer; piano and organ with B. Huber; was ordained a priest in 1874; studied again (1876–77) at the Kirchenmusikschule in Regensburg with F.X. Haberl; was Kapellmeister at the Cathedral there (1882–84); then at the Cathedral in Brixen. He won for himself a distinguished place among modern masters of the Palestrina style; wrote more than 200 opus numbers for the church; publ. *Praktischer Leitfaden für den römischen Choralgesang* (1896), *Die wichtigsten kirchlichen Vorschriften für Kirchenmusik* (4th ed., 1905), *Praktische Chor-Singschule* (4th ed., 1908), *Vademecum für Harmoniumspieler,* etc.

Mitterwurzer, Anton, famous Austrian baritone; b. Sterzing, April 12, 1818; d. Döbling, near Vienna, April 2, 1876. He was a nephew of Gänsbacher, and studied with him; after serving as chorister at St. Stephen's, Vienna, he sang in Austrian provincial theaters. In 1839 he was engaged by the Dresden Court Opera, and remained there for 30 years, until he was pensioned in 1870. He was particularly notable in Wagnerian roles.

Mittler, Franz, Austrian composer and pianist; b. Vienna, April 14, 1893; d. Munich, Dec. 28, 1970. He studied in Vienna with Heuberger and Prohaska; later in Cologne with Fritz Steinbach and Carl Friedberg. From 1921 to 1938 he lived in Vienna as a pianist and accompanist; in 1939 went to America, and settled in N.Y.
WORKS: Opera, *Rafaella* (Duisburg, 1930); Piano Trio; a number of piano pieces. In America he wrote numerous popular songs (*In Flaming Beauty, From Dreams of Thee, Soft through My Heart, Over the Mountains)*; also light piano suites: *Manhattan Suite, Suite in 3/4 Time, Newsreel Suite, Boogie-Woogie, Waltz in Blue, One-Finger Polka.*
BIBLIOGRAPHY: Diana Mittler Battipaglia, *Franz Mittler: Composer, Pedagogue and Practical Musician* (Diss., Univ. of Rochester, 1974).

Mittmann, Paul, German composer of choral music; b. Habelschwerdt, June 18, 1868; d. Breslau, Jan. 11, 1920. He studied with G. Kothe at the seminary in Habelschwerdt, and later with Riemenschneider; served as church organist in Breslau; also was music critic for the *Breslauer Zeitung.* He wrote a number of fine male and mixed choruses (several in Silesian dialect), and some 150 opus numbers for the church.

Miyagi, Michio, Japanese virtuoso on the koto and composer; b. Kobe, April 7, 1894; d. near Tokyo (in a railroad accident), June 25, 1956. He lost his eyesight at the age of 7; was instructed in koto playing by a blind musician named Nakajima; in 1908 he went to Korea; in 1917 moved to Tokyo, where he remained most of his life. In 1918 he introduced a koto with 17 strings. He was named a member of the Academy of Fine Arts in Tokyo in 1948; was the Japanese delegate at the Folk Music and Dance Festival in Europe in 1953. He composed more than 1,000 works for the koto and for other Japanese instruments; all of these are descriptive of poetic moods, or suggest a landscape. His Concerto for Koto, Flute, and Orch. entitled *Haru no Umi (Sea at Springtime)* was presented by André Kostelanetz with the N.Y. Phil. on Dec. 31, 1955, with Shinichi Yuize, a member of the Kabuki Dance Group, as soloist on the koto. Other works are *Variations on Etenkagu* for Koto and Orch. (1925); *Ochiba no Odori (Dance of Falling Leaves)* for Koto Solo; etc. He also publ. a book, *Ame no Nembutsu (Prayers for Rain).*

Miyoshi, Akira, Japanese composer; b. Tokyo, Jan. 10, 1933. He joined the Jiyû-Gakuen children's piano group at the age of 3, graduating at the age of 6. He studied French literature; in 1951 began to study music with Hirai, Ikenouchi, and the French musician Raymond Gallois-Montbrun, who was in Tokyo at that time. He obtained a stipend to travel to France and took lessons in composition with Henri Challan and again with Gallois-Montbrun (1955–57); upon his return to Japan, he resumed his studies in French literature at the Univ. of Tokyo, obtaining a degree in 1961. In 1965 he was appointed instructor at the Toho Gakuen School of Music in Tokyo.
WORKS: 2 poetical dramas: *Happy Prince* (1959) and *Ondine* (1959); *Symphonie concertante* for Piano and Orch. (1954); *Mutation symphonique* (1958); *3 mouvements symphoniques* (1960); Piano Concerto (1962); *Duel* for Soprano and Orch. (1964); Concerto for Orch. (Tokyo, Oct. 22, 1964); Violin Concerto (1965); *Odes metamorphosées* for Orch. (1969); Concerto for Marimba and String Ensemble (1969); 2 works of musical poesy: *The Red Mask of Death I* for Narrator, Orch., and Electronic Sound (1969) and *II* for Voice, Chorus, Orch., and Electronic Sound (1970); *Ouverture de fête* (1973); Sonata for Clarinet, Bassoon, and Piano (1953); Violin Sonata (1954–55); Sonata for Flute, Cello, and Piano (1955); *Torse I* for Chamber Orch. (1959), *II* for Chorus, Piano, Electone, and Percussion (1962), *III* for Solo Marimba (1968), *IV* for String Quartet and 4 Japanese Instruments (1972), and *V* for 3 Marimbas (1973); 2 string quartets (1962, 1967); *Conversation,* suite for Solo Marimba (1962); *8 poèmes* for Flute Ensemble (1969); *Transit* for Electronic and Concrete Sounds, Percussion, and Keyboard Instru-

ments (1969); *Hommage à musique de chambre, I, II, III,* and *IV* for Flute, Violin and Piano (1970, 1971, 1972, 1974); *Nocturne* for Marimba, Percussion, Flute, Clarinet, and Double Bass (1973); *Protase de loin à rien* for 2 Guitars (1974); Piano Sonata (1958); *In Such Time,* suite for Piano (1960); *Etudes en forme de Sonate* for Piano (1967); choruses; songs.

Mizelle, John, American avant-garde composer; b. Stillwater, Okla., June 14, 1940. He studied at Sacramento State College (B.A., 1965) and at the Univ. of Calif. at Davis (M.A., 1967), where he took courses with Larry Austin, Jerome Rosen, Karlheinz Stockhausen, Richard Swift, and David Tudor. He later joined the staff at Davis as associate prof. in music. He is a professional trombone player and a member of the New Music Ensemble. In his music he affects technological associations; uses graphic notation.

WORKS: *Piano Opus* (1966); *Light Sculpture* (1967); *Radial Energy I* (1967); *Mass for Voices and Electronics* (1967); *Tangential Energy II* (1968); *Wave Forms* (1968).

Mizler, Lorenz Christoph, learned German music scholar; b. Heidenheim, Franconia, July 25, 1711; d. Warsaw, March 1778. He entered the Ansbach Gymnasium when he was 13; also took music lessons from Ehrmann in Ansbach, and learned to play the violin and flute. In 1731 he enrolled as a theology student at the Univ. of Leipzig; he received his bachelor's degree in 1733, and his master's degree in 1734 with his *Dissertatio, Quod musica ars sit pars eruditionis philosophicae* (2nd ed., 1736; 3rd ed., 1740). He was a friend of J.S. Bach. In 1735 he went to Wittenberg, where he studied law and medicine. Returning to Leipzig in 1736, he gave his disputation *De usu atque praestantia philosophiae in theologia, jurisprudentia, medicina* (Leipzig, 1736; 2nd ed., 1740). In May 1737 he joined the faculty of the Univ. of Leipzig, where he lectured on Mattheson's *Neu-eröffnete Orchester* and music history. In 1738 he also established the Korrespondierende Sozietät der Musicalischen Wissenschaften. He likewise publ. the valuable music periodical *Neu eröffnete musikalische Bibliothek* (1739–54). In 1743 he entered the service of the Polish Count Malachowski of Konshie, working as a secretary, teacher, librarian, and mathematician; he learned the Polish language and devoted much time to the study of Polish culture. In 1747 he took his doctorate in medicine at the Univ. of Erfurt; that same year he went to Warsaw, where he was made physician to the court in 1752. He was ennobled by the Polish court as Mizler von Kolof in 1768. His vast erudition in many branches of knowledge impelled him to publish polemical works in which he, much in the prevalent manner of 18th-century philosophers, professed omniscience. Thus he publ. the pamphlet *Lusus ingenii de praesenti bello* (Wittenberg, 1735), in which he proposed, by means of a musical game, to advise the German emperor Karl VII on the proper conduct of the war waged at the time. Pugnacious by nature, he derided "the stupidities of con-

ceited self-grown so-called composers making themselves ridiculous" in a lampoon entitled "Musical Stabber" (*Musikalischer Starstecher, in welchem rechtschaffener musikverständigen Fehler bescheiden angemerket, eingebildeter und selbst gewachsener sogenannter Componisten Thorheiten aber lächerlich gemachet werden,* Leipzig, 1739–40). His theoretical writings include *Anfangs-Gründe des General-Basses nach mathematischer Lehr-Art abgehandelt* (an attempt to instruct figured bass by mathematical rules), publ. in Leipzig in 1739. He also translated into German Fux's *Gradus ad Parnassum,* with annotations (Leipzig, 1742). He prepared an autobiography for Mattheson's basic biographical music dictionary, *Grundlage einer Ehren-Pforte* (Hamburg, 1749; new ed. by M. Schneider, Berlin, 1910; reprint, 1969).

BIBLIOGRAPHY: F. Wöhlke, *Lorenz Christoph Mizler: Ein Beitrag zur musikalischen Gelehrtengeschichte des 18. Jahrhunderts* (Würzburg, 1940); J. Birke, *Christian Wolffs Metaphysik und die zeitgenössische Literatur- und Musiktheorie: Gottsched, Scheibe, Mizler* (Berlin, 1966).

Mlynarski, Emil, Polish conductor and composer; b. Kibarty, July 18, 1870; d. Warsaw, April 5, 1935. He studied at the St. Petersburg Cons. (1880–89), taking up both the violin, with Leopold Auer, and piano, with Anton Rubinstein; also took a course in composition with Liadov. He embarked on a career as a conductor; in 1897 he was appointed principal conductor of the Warsaw Opera, and concurrently conducted the concerts of the Warsaw Phil. (1901–5); from 1904 to 1907 he was director of the Warsaw Cons. He achieved considerable success as a conductor in Scotland, where he appeared with Scottish Orch. in Glasgow and Edinburgh (1910–16). He was director of the Warsaw Cons. in 1919–22, and of the Warsaw Opera in 1918–29. From 1929 to 1931 he taught conducting at the Curtis Inst. of Music in Philadelphia; in 1931 returned to Warsaw. He composed some effective violin music, including 2 concertos, of which the first won the Paderewski prize (1898). He also composed a comic opera, *Noc letnia* (*Summer Night*; Warsaw, March 29, 1924).

BIBLIOGRAPHY: A. Wach, *Zycie i twórczość Emila Mlynarskiego* (*Life and Works of Emil Mlynarski;* diss., Univ. of Cracow, 1953).

Moberg, Carl Allan, Swedish musicologist; b. Östersund, June 5, 1896; d. Uppsala, June 19, 1978. He studied with Norlind at the Univ. of Uppsala (1917–24); then took some lessons with Alban Berg in Vienna, and took a course in musicology with Peter Wagner in Freiburg, Switzerland (1924–27). Returning to Sweden, he was a reader (1928), then prof. at the Univ. of Uppsala (1947–61). Among his signal achievements was a journey to Lapland in the north to collect native songs. He was honored with a Festschrift on his 65th birthday in 1961. Most of his writings deal with Swedish music history; among them are *Über die schwedischen Sequenzen* (2 vols.; diss., Univ. of Uppsala, 1927); *Kyrkomusikens historia* (Stockholm, 1932); *Tonkonstens historia i*

Västerlandet (2 vols., Stockholm, 1933); *Dietrich Buxtehude* (Hälsingborg, 1946); *Die liturgische Hymnen in Schweden* (Uppsala, 1947); *Musikens historia i Västerlander intill 1600* (Oslo, 1973).

Mocquereau, Dom André, distinguished French scholar; authority on Gregorian chant; b. La Tessoualle, near Cholet (Maine-et-Loire), June 6, 1849; d. Solesmes, Jan. 18, 1930. In 1875 he joined the Order of Benedictines at the Abbey of Solesmes, devoted himself to the study of Gregorian chant under the direction of Dom Pothier, and became teacher of choral singing in the abbey. After the expulsion, in 1903, of the Order from France, they found a refuge of the Isle of Wight (Quarr Abbey, Ryde), where Mocquereau then became prior; later he returned to Solesmes. He was the founder and editor of the capital work *Paléographie musicale*, of which 17 vols. appeared between 1889 and 1958. Works by Mocquereau include *Le Nombre musical grégorien ou Rythmique grégorienne* (very valuable; 1908–27); *L'Art grégorien, Son but, ses procédés, ses caractères; Petit traité de psalmodie; La Psalmodie romaine et l'accent tonique latin* (1895); *Notes sur l'influence de l'accent et du cursus tonique latins dans le chant ambrosien* (1897); *Méthode de chant grégorien* (1899).
BIBLIOGRAPHY: F. Kosch, in the *Zeitschrift für Musikwissenschaft*, 12; J. Ward, *De greg. Zangen naar Dom Mocquereau* (Doornik, 1929); J.A. de Donostia, *A propos du nombre musical grégorien de Dom Mocquereau* (Paris, 1930); Maurice Blanc, *L'Enseignement musical de Solesmes* (Paris, 1953; chap. 3); see also special issues of the *Gregorian Review* (Jan.–Feb. 1955) and *Revue Grégorienne* (Jan.–April 1955).

Mödl, Martha, German soprano; b. Nuremberg, March 22, 1912. She studied at the Nuremberg Cons. and in Milan; made her debut as a mezzo-soprano in Remscheid in 1942; later sang in Düsseldorf; in 1948 she joined the Hamburg State Opera. After 1950 she sang dramatic soprano roles with notable success; made appearances at Bayreuth from 1951 to 1967; in 1955 she took part in the reopening celebrations at the Vienna State Opera. On March 2, 1957, she made her Metropolitan Opera debut as Brünnhilde in *Die Gotterdämmerung;* remained on its roster until 1960. She was made both an Austrian and German Kammersängerin. She was particularly distinguished in Wagnerian parts.
BIBLIOGRAPHY: W. Schäfer, *Martha Mödl* (Hannover, 1967).

Moeck, Hermann, German music publisher and instrument maker; b. Elbing, July 9, 1896; d. Celle, Oct. 9, 1982. He established his publishing business in Celle in 1930; in 1960 he handed it over to his son **Hermann Moeck, Jr.** (b. Lüneburg, Aug. 16, 1922). The firm was influential in the revival of the manufacture of the vertical flute (recorder) and other Renaissance and early Baroque instruments; Moeck also publ. arrangements and authentic pieces for recorders and the theretofore obsolete fidels. Hermann Moeck, Jr. wrote a valuable monograph, *Ursprung und Tradition der Kernspaltflöten* (2 vols., 1951), also publ. in an abridged form as *Typen europäischer Blockflöten* (Celle, 1967).

Moeller, Mathias, Danish organ builder; b. Bornholm, Denmark, Sept. 29, 1855; d. Hagerstown, Md., April 13, 1937. He came to the U.S. in 1872 and established a factory in Hagerstown which became the largest organ factory in the world; in it were built the organs for West Point, the N.Y. Hippodrome, etc. Moeller contributed a number of important improvements to the construction of the organ.

Moeran, E(rnest) J(ohn), English composer of Irish descent; b. Heston, Middlesex, Dec. 31, 1894; d. Kenmare, County Kerry, Ireland, Dec. 1, 1950. His father was a clergyman, and he learned music from hymnbooks; then studied at the Royal College of Music; was an officer in the British army in World War I, and was wounded. Returning to London, he took lessons in composition with John Ireland (1920–23); also became interested in folk music; he collected numerous folk songs in Norfolk, some of which were publ. by the Folksong Society (1922). Most of his compositions were inspired by simple folk patterns; his folk-song arrangements are aptly made and are authentic in feeling.
WORKS: 2 Rhapsodies for Orch. (first, Manchester, 1924; 2nd, Norwich Festival, 1924); Symph. in G minor (London, Jan. 13, 1938); Violin Concerto (London, July 8, 1942); *Rhapsody* for Piano and Orch. (London, Aug. 19, 1943); Cello Concerto (Dublin, Nov. 25, 1945; with Moeran's wife, **Peers Coetmore,** as soloist); *Serenade* in G major for Orch. (London, Sept. 2, 1948); Quartet for Oboe and Strings (1946); Cello Sonata (1947); piano and organ works; many songs.
BIBLIOGRAPHY: S. Wild, *E.J. Moeran* (London, 1973).

Moeschinger, Albert, Swiss composer; b. Basel, Jan. 10, 1897. He studied in Bern, Leipzig, and Munich. In his works he shows influences of German neo-Romanticism and French Impressionism. A prolific composer, he has written some 100 opus numbers; his works include 3 symphs.; 3 piano concertos; Violin Concerto; 6 string quartets; 2 piano trios; Quintet for Clarinet and Strings; 2 trios for Flute, Clarinet, and Bassoon; 2 cello sonatas; Sonata for Violin and Organ; *Variations mystérieuses* for Chamber Orch. (1977); *Blocs sonores* for Orch. (1977); many pieces for piano, organ, etc.; cantatas and other choral works.

Moevs, Robert W., American composer; b. La Crosse, Wis., Dec. 2, 1921. He studied at Harvard Univ. (A.B., 1942); after service as a pilot in the U.S. Air Force, he took courses in Paris with Nadia Boulanger (1946–51); was a Fellow at the American Academy in Rome (1952–55); returning to the U.S., he was on the music faculty at Harvard Univ. (1955–63); from 1963, was prof. of music at Rutgers Univ.

in New Brunswick, N.J. His music is marked by sonorous exuberance and rhythmic impulsiveness; his use of percussion is plangent. He favors ornamental variation forms.

WORKS: *14 Variations for Orchestra* (Boston, April 6, 1956); *Symphony in 3 Movements* (Cleveland, April 10, 1958); *Attis* for Orch. with Chorus and Tenor Solo (Boston, Feb. 24, 1960); *Et Occidentem Illustra* (Boston, Feb. 24, 1967); Piano Concerto (1960); *Cantata sacra* for Baritone, Male Chorus, Flute, 4 Trombones, and Timpani, to a Latin text from the Easter liturgy (1952); *Musica da camera* for Chamber Orch. (1968); *Pan* for Unaccompanied Flute (1951); *Fanfara canonica* for 6 Trumpets (1966); numerous choral works and solo songs.

Moffat, Alfred Edward, Scottish music editor and arranger; b. Edinburgh, Dec. 4, 1863; d. London, June 9, 1950. He studied with L. Bussler in Berlin (1882–88); then went to London, where he became active as an editor of violin music by old English composers; he publ. the series Old English Violin Music (London) and Meisterschule der Alten Zeit (Berlin); also publ. numerous arrangements: *The Minstrelsy of Scotland* (200 Scottish songs); *The Minstrelsy of Ireland*; *40 Highland Reels and Strathspeys*; *Songs and Dances of All Nations* (with J.D. Brown); various other eds. of string and vocal music; etc.

Moffo, Anna, American soprano; b. Wayne, Pa., June 27, 1932, of Italian parentage. She studied voice at the Curtis Inst. of Music in Philadelphia; later went to Italy on a Fulbright fellowship and studied at the Santa Cecilia Academy in Rome. She made her debut in Spoleto in 1955, and, progressing rapidly in her career, she was engaged at La Scala in Milan, at the Vienna State Opera, and in Paris. Returning to America, she sang with the Chicago Lyric Opera; on Nov. 14, 1959, she made her debut at the Metropolitan Opera in N.Y. as Violetta, obtaining a gratifying success; she continued to sing regularly at the Metropolitan, earning a stellar reputation for both her singing and acting ability.

Mohaupt, Richard, German composer; b. Breslau, Sept. 14, 1904; d. Reichenau, Austria, July 3, 1957. He studied with J. Prüwer and R. Bilke; began his musical career as an opera conductor; also gave concerts as pianist. After the advent of the Nazi regime in 1933, he was compelled to leave Germany because his wife was Jewish; he settled in N.Y. in 1939, and continued to compose; was also active as a teacher. In 1955 he returned to Europe.

WORKS: Operas: *Die Wirtin von Pinsk* (Dresden, Feb. 10, 1938); *Die Bremer Stadtmusikanten* (Bremen, June 15, 1949); *Double Trouble* (Louisville, Dec. 4, 1954); *Der grüne Kakadu* (Hamburg, Sept. 16, 1958). Ballets: *Die Gaunerstreiche der Courasche* (Berlin, Aug. 5, 1936); *Lysistrata* (1946); *The Legend of the Charlatan*, pantomime (1949); *Max und Moritz*, dance-burlesque, after Wilhelm Busch (Karlsruhe, Dec. 18, 1950). For Orch.: Symph. (N.Y. Phil., March 5, 1942); *Stadtpfeifermusik* (London Festival of the International Society for Contemporary Music, July 7, 1946); *Bucolica* for Double Chorus and Orch. (1948); *Trilogy* for Contralto Solo and Orch. (1951); Violin Concerto (N.Y. Phil., April 29, 1954); chamber music; songs; piano pieces.

Moiseiwitsch, Benno, pianist; b. Odessa, Feb. 22, 1890; d. London, April 9, 1963. He studied in Odessa, and won the Anton Rubinstein prize at the age of 9; then went to Vienna, where he studied with Leschetizky. He made his debut in Reading, England, on Oct. 1, 1908, and subsequently made London his home; made his American debut in N.Y. on Nov. 29, 1919, and toured many times in Australia, India, Japan, etc. He represented the traditional school of piano playing, excelling mostly in Romantic music.
BIBLIOGRAPHY: M. Moiseiwitsch, *Benno Moiseiwitsch* (London, 1965).

Mojsisovics, Roderich von, Austrian composer; b. Graz, May 10, 1877; d. there, March 30, 1953. He studied with Degner in Graz, with Wüllner and Klauwell at the Cologne Cons., and with Thuille in Munich. He conducted a choral group in Brno (1903–7); then taught in various Austrian towns. He became director of the Steiermärkische Musikverein in 1912; it became the Graz Cons. in 1920, and he remained as director until 1931; in 1932–35 he taught music history at the Univ. of Graz; then lectured in Munich and Mannheim; he returned to teach at the Graz Cons. from 1945 to 1948. In his music he was a decided follower of Wagnerian precepts. He wrote 8 operas; 5 symphs.; a symph. poem, *Stella;* 2 overtures; a Violin Concerto; numerous chamber works; songs; publ. the biographies *Max Reger* (1911) and *E.W. Degner* (1919); also *Bachprobleme* (1930); etc.
BIBLIOGRAPHY: M. Morold, *Roderich Mojsisovics* (1924); K. Haidmayer, *Roderich von Mojsisovics: Leben und Werk* (Diss., Univ. of Graz, 1951).

Mokranjac, Stevan, Serbian composer; b. Negotin, Jan. 9, 1856; d. Skoplje, Sept. 28, 1914. He studied in Munich with Rheinberger, and in Leipzig with Jadassohn and Reinecke; in 1887 he became director of the Serbian Choral Society in Belgrade, with which he also toured. In 1899 he founded the Serbian Music School in Belgrade, and remained its director until his death. He wrote 15 choral rhapsodies on Serbian and Macedonian melodies; a Liturgy of St. John Chrysostomos (publ. in Leipzig, 1901; also with an Eng. trans. as *Serbian Liturgy,* London, 1919); a Funeral Service ("Opelo"); he compiled a large collection of church anthems according to the Serbian usage and derived from old Byzantine modes; wrote a collection of songs for Mixed Chorus, *Rukoveti (Bouquets).*

Mokranjac, Vasilije, Serbian composer; b. Belgrade, Sept. 11, 1923. He was brought up in a musical enviroment (his father was a cellist, a nephew of the famous Serbian composer **Stevan Mokranjac**). He studied piano and composition at the Belgrade Academy of Music. His early works are Romantic in style, but he gradually began experimenting with serial techniques, while safeguarding the basic tonal connotations.

WORKS: Symph. No. 1 (Belgrade, Feb. 2, 1962); Symph. No. 2 (Belgrade, April 1, 1966); Symph. No. 3 (Belgrade, Oct. 25, 1968); *Dramatic Overture* (1950); *Concertino* for Piano, String Orch., and 2 Harps (Belgrade, March 15, 1960); chamber music; piano pieces; incidental music for dramatic plays.

BIBLIOGRAPHY: Vlastimir Peričić, *Muzički Stvaraoci u Srbiji* (Belgrade, 1969).

Mokrejs, John, American pianist, composer, and teacher of Czech descent; b. Cedar Rapids, Iowa, Feb. 10, 1875; d. there, Nov. 22, 1968. He studied piano with Leopold Godowsky and theory with Adolph Weidig at the American Cons. of Music in Chicago; was active as a piano teacher in N.Y.; from 1945 to 1966 lived in Los Angeles; then returned to Cedar Rapids.

WORKS: Opera, *Sohrab and Rustum*; operetta, *The Mayflower*; *American Cantata* (on the life of Abraham Lincoln); Piano Trio; String Quartet; songs. He is best known, however, for his teaching pieces for piano: *Valcik (Little Waltz), Boutade, Bird Rondo, Day in Summer, Indian Dance, Harvest Moon, Military Nocturne, Moravian Lullaby, Carillon,* and *Rainbow Pieces.* He also publ. instruction books: *Lessons in Sight Reading* (Chicago, 1909); *Lessons in Harmony* (N.Y., 1913); *Natural Counterpoint* (Chicago, 1941).

Mokrousov, Boris, Russian composer; b. Nizhny-Novgorod, Feb. 27, 1909; d. Moscow, March 27, 1968. He studied at the Moscow Cons. with Miaskovsky, graduating in 1936. While still a student, he wrote an orch. suite, *The Pioneers* (1933); a Quartet for 2 Trumpets and 2 Trombones (1934); and a Trombone Concerto (1935). His graduation piece was a politically inspired work, *Anti-Fascist Symphony,* for Orch., Chorus, and Military Band (Moscow, Aug. 1, 1937). He also wrote an opera, *Chapayev,* depicting the life of a Soviet hero.

Molchanov, Kirill, Soviet composer; b. Moscow, Sept. 7, 1922; d. there, March 14, 1982. He was attached to the Red Army Ensemble of Song and Dance during World War II; after demobilization, he studied composition with Anatoly Alexandrov at the Moscow Cons., graduating in 1949. From 1973 to 1975 he served as director of the Bolshoi Theater and accompanied it on its American tour in 1975. He was primarily an opera composer; his music style faithfully follows the precepts of socialist realism.

WORKS: Operas: *The Stone Flower* (Moscow, Dec. 2, 1950); *Dawn* (1956); *Romeo, Juliet and Darkness* (1963); *The Unknown Soldier* (1967); *A Woman of Russia* (1969); *The Dawns Are Quiet Here* (his most successful work, to his own libretto depicting the Russian struggle against the Nazis; its Moscow production at the Bolshoi Theater, on April 11, 1975, became a melodramatic event of the year, accompanied by an unabashed display of tearful emotion; however, its American perf. during the visit of the Bolshoi Theater to N.Y. in June 1975 met with a

disdainful dismissal on the part of the critics). Other works: 3 piano concertos (1945, 1947, 1953); cantata, *Song of Friendship* (1955); *Black Box,* suite for Voice, Recitation, and Piano (1968).

BIBLIOGRAPHY: Y. Korev, *Kirill Molchanov* (Moscow, 1971).

Moldavan, Nicolas, Russian-American viola player; b. Kremenetz, Jan. 23, 1891; d. New York, Sept. 21, 1974. He studied at the St. Petersburg Cons., graduating in 1912. In 1918 he left Russia and went on a tour of the Far East; he settled in the U.S.; was a member of the Flonzaley Quartet (1925–29); then played in the Coolidge Quartet.

Moldenhauer, Hans, German-American musicologist; b. Mainz, Dec. 13, 1906. He studied music with Dressel, Zuckmayer, and Rosbaud in Mainz; was active as a pianist and choral conductor there. In 1938 he went to the U.S., and settled in Spokane, Wash.; as an expert alpinist, he served in the U.S. Mountain Troops during World War II. After the war he organized the Spokane Cons. (founded by him in 1942), incorporated as an educational inst. in 1946. With his wife, the pianist **Rosaleen Moldenhauer** (1926–82), he inaugurated a series of radio broadcasts of 2-piano music; the outgrowth of this was the publ. of his valuable book *Duo-Pianism* (Chicago, 1950). As a music reseacher, he became profoundly interested in the life and works of Anton von Webern; he organized 6 international Webern festivals, in Seattle (1962), Salzburg (1965), Buffalo (1966), at Dartmouth College, Hanover, N.H. (1968), in Vienna (1972), and at Louisiana State Univ., Baton Rouge (1976). His major achievement in research was the formation of the Moldenhauer Archives ("Music History from Primary Sources") embodying a collection of some 10,000 musical autographs, original MSS, correspondence, etc., of unique importance to musical biography. Particularly rich is the MS collection of works of Webern, including some newly discovered works; for this accomplishment, Moldenhauer was awarded in 1970 the Austrian Cross of Honor for Science and Art. Moldenhauer's publications concerning Anton von Webern include *The Death of Anton Webern. A Drama in Documents* (N.Y., 1961; establishes for the first time the circumstances of Webern's tragic death in 1945); *Anton von Webern: Perspectives* (Seattle, 1966): *Anton von Webern, Sketches 1926–1945* (N.Y., 1968) and *Anton von Webern: Chronicle of His Life and Work* (in collaboration with Rosaleen Moldenhauer, N.Y., 1978). Moldenhauer suffered from a hereditary eye disease, Retinitis pigmentosa, and became totally blind in 1980. He remarried in 1982, a few months after his first wife's death.

Moldovan, Mihai, Rumanian composer; b. Dej, Nov. 5, 1937. He studied with Toduța and Comes at the Cluj Cons. (1956–59); then with Vancea, Vieru, and Jora at the Bucharest Cons. (1959–62); was active in various branches of Rumanian radio and television. His music fuses a Rumanian ethos with modern harmonic textures.

WORKS: Cantatas: *Soare al păcii* (*Sun of Peace*, 1962); *Prefigurarea primăverii*, chamber cantata, (1962); *Bocet* (1963); *6 stări de nuanță* (1966); and *Cintare omului* (1967); *Rituale*, suite for Soprano and Orch. (1963); Oboe Concerto (1964); *Texturi*, piece for Orch. (1967); *Poem* for Chamber Orch., with Ondes Martenot (1967); *Vitralii (Stained Glass Windows)*, 6 pieces for Orch. (1968); *Scoarțe (Tapestry)* for Orch. (1969); *Tulnice* for 4 Flutes, 8 Horns, Harp, 4 Cellos, 4 Double Basses, and Percussion (1971); *Sinfonia* for Strings (1972); Violin Sonatina (1967); String Quartet (1968); *Incantations* for Clarinet and Piano (1968); *Cadenza I* for Trombone and Percussion, *II* for Solo Double Bass, and *III* for Flute and Percussion (all 1971); *Cîntece străbune* (*Ancient Songs*) for Soprano, Flute, Clarinet, Horn, Trumpet, Trombone, Piano, Vibraphone, Xylophone, and String Quintet (1972).

Molina, Antonio J., Philippine composer and conductor; b. Quiapo, Manila, Dec. 26, 1894; received his primary education at the Boy's Catholic School in his native town; then studied with Bibiano Morales in Manila; founded and directed a string group, Rondalla Ideal; also was engaged as conductor of various theater and cinema orchs. in Manila; wrote popular waltzes; then began to compose more ambitious theater music; conducted at Manila the premiere of his lyric drama *Ritorna Vincitor* (March 10, 1918) and his zarzuelas *Panibuglo* (*Jealousy*, April 16, 1918) and *Ang Ilaw* (Nov. 23, 1918). In 1925 he became a teacher of harmony at the Univ. of the Philippines; in 1934 he joined the staff of the President's Committee on Filipino Folksongs and Dances. He wrote a Christmas carol for Mixed Chorus and Orch., *The Living Word* (Manila, Dec. 18, 1936); a Quintet for Piano and Strings, based on native folk songs (Manila, Jan 21, 1950); also numerous piano pieces and songs.

Molinari, Bernardino, eminent Italian conductor; b. Rome, April 11, 1880; d. there, Dec. 25, 1952. He studied with Falchi and Renzi at the Santa Cecilia Academy in Rome; in 1912, became conductor of the Augusteo orch. in Rome; also conducted throughout Europe and South America. In 1928 he made his American debut with the N.Y. Phil., which he conducted again during the 1929–30 and 1930–31 seasons; he also appeared with other American orchs. He was a champion of the modern Italian school, and brought out many works by Respighi, Malipiero, and other outstanding Italian composers; publ. a new ed. of Monteverdi's *Sonata sopra Sonata Maria* (1919) and concert transcriptions of Carissimi's oratorio *Giona*, Vivaldi's *Le quattro stagioni*, etc.; also orchestrated Debussy's *L'Isle joyeuse.*

BIBLIOGRAPHY: E. Mucci, *Bernardino Molinari* (Lanciano, 1941).

Molinari-Pradelli, Francesco, Italian conductor; b. Bologna, July 4, 1911. He studied in Bologna and in Rome. In 1946 he conducted at La Scala in Milan; in 1951 he was guest conductor in London; also conducted opera at San Carlo, Naples; from 1957 he led successful opera performances in San Francisco and Los Angeles. He is particularly renowned for his interpretations of Wagner and Puccini.

Molique, Wilhelm Bernhard, German violinist and composer; b. Nuremburg, Oct. 7, 1802; d. Cannstadt, near Stuttgart, May 10, 1869. He first studied with his father; King Maximilian I, hearing of his uncommon gifts, sent him to Munich (1816) to study with Rovelli, concertmaster of the Munich Court Orch.; he succeeded Rovelli in that post in 1820; in 1826 he became concertmaster of the Stuttgart orch., with the title of Musikdirektor. He won fame abroad with extended tours in the Netherlands, Russia, England, and France. The political crisis of 1849 caused him to settle in London, where he remained until 1866; he then returned to Germany. His works include 6 violin concertos; 8 string quartets; pieces for violin and piano, and for violin and flute; fantasias, rondos, and other works for solo violin; etc.

BIBLIOGRAPHY: Fritz Schröder, *Bernhard Molique und seine Instrumentalkompositionen* (Stuttgart, 1923).

Molitor, Raphael, German musicologist; b. Sigmaringen, Feb. 2, 1873; d. Beuron, Oct. 14, 1948. He was the son of Johann Baptist Molitor, a cathedral organist; he studied philosophy and theology in the Benedictine Monastery of Beuron; was ordained a priest in 1897; lectured there on canon law (1898–1904); in 1904, was appointed a member of the advisory board of the *Editio Vaticana*. He was one of the foremost authorities on Gregorian chant.

WORKS: *Reformchoral* (1901); *Die nach-tridentinische Choralreform zu Rom* (2 vols., 1901, 1902); *Choralweigendrucke; Der gregorianische Choral als Liturgie und Kunst; Josef Rheinberger;* etc.; contributed important articles to the *Gregoriusblatt; Kirchenmusikalisches Jahrbuch; Sammelbände der Internationalen Musik-Gesellschaft;* etc.

Moll, Kurt, German bass; b. Buir, April 11, 1938. He studied in Cologne; then sang opera there and in Aachen, Mainz, Wuppertal, and Hamburg. In 1968 he sang at Bayreuth; then made appearances at Salzburg (1970), La Scala in Milan (1972), and Covent Garden in London (1975). He made his Metropolitan Opera debut on Sept. 18, 1978, as the Landgrave in *Tannhäuser*. He was particularly successful in Wagnerian roles.

Möllendorff, Willi von, German pianist and composer; b. Berlin, Feb. 28, 1872; d. Stettin, April 27, 1934. He studied with Bargiel at the Berlin Hochschule für Musik (1891–93); was subsequently active as a pianist and theater conductor in Giessen, Berlin, and finally Stettin. He was known especially for his experimentation with quarter-tones, for the exposition of which he invented a bichromatic harmonium with a new keyboard. For this instrument he composed an *Adagio religioso* (with Cello Solo);

Mollenhauer – Molnár

also *5 kleine Stücke*. In addition, he wrote operas, a ballet, 2 symphs., choral works, etc.

Mollenhauer, Eduard, German violinist; b. Erfurt, April 12, 1827; d. Owatoma, Minn., May 7, 1914. He was a violin pupil of Ernst (1841) and Spohr (1843); after a brief concert career in Germany, he went to London, where he joined Jullien's Orch., of which an older brother, **Friedrich Mollenhauer** (1818–85), also a violinist, was a member; after a tour with Jullien's Orch. in the U.S. (1853), the brothers settled in New York as teachers; Eduard Mollenhauer also appeared as a soloist with the N.Y. Phil. Society. He wrote the operas *The Corsican Bride* (N.Y., 1861) and *Breakers* (N.Y., 1881); 3 symphs.; a Violin Concerto; solo pieces for violin (*La Sylphide*, etc.); songs.

Mollenhauer, Emil, American violinist and conductor; son of **Friedrich Mollenhauer;** b. Brooklyn, Aug. 4, 1855; d. Boston, Dec. 10, 1927. He studied violin with his father; in 1872 entered Theodore Thomas's orch.; then joined the Damrosch Orch.; from 1885 to 1888 was a member of the Boston Symph. Orch.; then assumed the conductorship of the Boston Festival Orch., and toured the U.S. with it, featuring many celebrated soloists (Calvé, Nordica, Melba, Campanari, Joseffy, Ysaÿe, Marteau, etc.). In 1899 he was elected conductor of the Boston Handel and Haydn Society, which he led until 1927.
BIBLIOGRAPHY: *Dictionary of American Biography* (vol. 13).

Mollenhauer, Henry, German cellist; brother of **Friedrich** and **Eduard Mollenhauer;** b. Erfurt, Sept. 10, 1825; d. Brooklyn, N.Y., Dec. 28, 1889. In 1853 he was a member of the Royal Orch. in Stockholm; toured the U.S. (1856–58) with Thalberg, Gottschalk, and Carlotta Patti; then settled in Brooklyn as a teacher; founded the Henry Mollenhauer Cons., which later flourished under the direction of his sons **Louis, Henry,** and **Adolph.**

Mollenhauer, Louis, American violinist; son of **Henry Mollenhauer;** b. Brooklyn, Dec. 17, 1863; d. there, Feb. 9, 1926. He studied with his uncle, **Eduard Mollenhauer;** was a member of the Mollenhauer Quintet Club; after his father's death, was director of his cons. (1889–91); then founded his own cons. in Brooklyn.

Möller, Heinrich, German musicologist; b. Breslau, June 1, 1876; d. Naumburg, March 3, 1958. He studied musicology with Riemann, Kretzschmar, and Friedlaender; lived in N.Y. from 1914 to 1921; then returned to Germany. From 1937 till 1945 he was docent at the Univ. of Jena; in 1953 was appointed instructor at the Hochschule für Musik in Weimar. He was editor of the valuable collection *Das Lied der Völker* (14 vols.); also trans. the librettos of operas of Mussorgsky and Rimsky-Korsakov into German.

Moller (or **Möller**), **Joachim.** See **Burck, Joachim.**

Moller, John Christopher, German composer and organist; b. 1755; d. New York, Sept. 21, 1803. In 1790 he appeared in N.Y. as a harpsichordist, but left immediately after his concerts for Philadelphia, where he became organist and composer for the Zion German Lutheran Church (appointed, Oct. 11, 1790). From 1791–92 he took part in the City Concerts (with Reinagle, and later Henri Capron) both as manager and performer. Apparently he was also proficient as a pianist, violinist, and performer on the glass harmonica. In 1793 he was joint proprietor, with Capron, of a music store, which he also used as a music school. Because of the destruction of the Zion Church by fire on Dec. 26, 1794, Moller's income was severely reduced, and in Nov. 1795 he returned to N.Y. In 1796 he succeeded Hewitt in the management of the N.Y. City Concerts with the Van Hagens. His attempt to continue this subscription series by himself, when Van Hagen later left for Boston, was unsuccessful.
WORKS: *6 Quartettos* (publ. in London by J. Betz); *Progressive Lessons for the Harpsichord* (op. 6, London); *Compleat Book of Instruction for the Pianoforte* (op. 6, London); *6 Sonatas for the forte piano or harpsichord, with a violin or violoncello accompaniment* (London); *12 Variations pour le clavecin* (1798); *Sinfonia, Rondo, Overture, Quartetto* for "Harmonica" (Benjamin Franklin's *armonica,* a glass harmonica) 2 Violas, and Cello; *Duetti* for Clarinet and Piano in the first issue of Moller & Capron's *Monthly Numbers* (1793); cantata, *Dank und Gebet*... (1794).
BIBLIOGRAPHY: J.T. Howard, *Our American Music* (N.Y., 1939; 4th ed., 1965); E.C. Wolf, *Lutheran Church Music in America during the 18th and Early 19th Centuries* (Diss., Univ. of Illinois, 1960; contains a copy of Moller's only extant cantata); R.D. Stetzel, *John Christopher Moller and His Role in Early American Music* (Diss., Univ. of Iowa, 1965); E.C. Wolf, "Music in Old Zion, Philadephia, 1750–1850," *Musical Quarterly* (Oct. 1972).

Molloy, James Lyman, Irish composer of light music; b. Cornalaur, King's County, Aug. 19, 1837; d. Wooleys, Bucks, Feb. 4, 1909. His operettas (*Students' Frolic, My Aunt's Secret, Very Catching*), numerous songs (*Love's Old Sweet Song, London Bridge, The Kerry-dance, The Postilion, Punchinello,* etc.), and Irish melodies with new accompaniments enjoyed great popularity.
BIBLIOGRAPHY: *Dictionary of National Biography* (Supplement; Oxford, 1920).

Molnár, Antal, Hungarian musicologist and composer; b. Budapest, Jan. 7, 1890. He studied violin and composition with Viktor Herzfeld at the Budapest Academy; then played viola in the Waldbauer String Quartet (1910–13) and later in the Dohnányi-Hubay Piano Quartet (1917–19); subsequently was for 40 years on the faculty of the Budapest Academy of Music (1919–59). He publ. his autobiography in Budapest in 1974.

WORKS: (in Hungarian, publ. in Budapest): *The Spirit of Music History* (1914); *The Spiritual Basis of Bach and Handel* (1920); *History of European Music before 1750* (1920); *Sociology of Music History* (1923); *The New Hungarian Music* (1925); *Jazzband* (1931); a monograph on Kodály (1936); *Music and Life* (1946); *The Spirit of New Music* (1948); *The Art of Béla Bartók* (1948); *Johannes Brahms* (1959); *Index to the Historical Repertory of Baroque Music* (1959); *Papers on Music,* collection of essays (1961); *On Music* (1963); *The Léner String Quartet* (1968; also in Eng., Budapest, 1969); *The World of the Composer* (1969); *Practical Aesthetics of Music* (1971). He is also a prolific composer; among his works are *Savitri,* stage music (1912); *Grotesque March* for Orch. (1914); Cello Concerto (1916); *Hungarian Dances* for Orch. (1917); *Operetta Music* for Orch. (1920); *Oriental Tale* for Orch. (1921); *Budapest,* overture (1921); *Past and Present* for Violin and Orch. (1923); *Suite* for Orch. (1925); *Variations on a Hungarian Theme* for Orch. (1928); *Hungarian Comedy Overture* (1928; *Kuruc-Music* for 4 Tárogatós (Hungarian instrument) and Chamber Orch. (1936); *Overture to a Comedy* (1948); Harp Concerto (1952); 2 piano trios (1912, 1917); 3 string quartets (1912, 1926, 1928); Wind Quintet (1926); songs; choruses; folk-song arrangements.

Momigny, Jérôme Joseph de, French music theorist; b. Philippeville, Namur, Jan. 20, 1762; d. in an insane asylum in Charenton, near Paris, Aug. 25, 1842. He studied music early in life, and at the age of 12 was already engaged as a church organist in St. Omer; in 1785 he went to Lyons. He became involved in the political struggle against the Jacobins in 1793; after their ouster he was appointed provisional municipal officer, and took part in the resistance against the troops of the National Convention; when that enterprise failed, he fled to Switzerland. After the fall of Robespierre he returned to Lyons; then went to Paris, where he remained under Napoleon and the restoration of the monarchy. He opened there a successful music publishing business which flourished for 28 years (1800–28) and which publ. about 750 works by 153 composers, including a number of his own compositions and treatises on music, in which he claimed to have invented a new and unfailing system of theory and harmony; the titles alone, containing such immoderate asseverations as "théorie neuve et générale," "seul système musical qui soit vraiment fondé et complet," "la seule vraie théorie de la musique," etc., reveal his uncommon faith in himself. He bolstered his self-assurance by such declarations as: there can exist only one true art of music; there is one and only one code of morals; there must be a sharp distinction between good and bad combinations of sounds, as there is between right and wrong in morality. By false analogy with order in music, he extolled monarchical rule and publ. numerous pamphlets in support of his reactionary convictions. Not finding a ready response from the authorities, he gradually sank into pathetic solitude and ended his days in an asylum. His tracts, both on

music and on politics, are of interest only to investigators of material on depraved mental states, and his own compositions fell into utter desuetude during his lifetime. Riemann publ. a devastating review of Momigny's theories which drove a mortuary nail into his hopes for recognition.

WRITINGS: (all publ. in Paris): *Cours complet d'harmonie et de composition d'après une théorie neuve et générale de la musique* (1806; 3 vols., dedicated to Talleyrand); *Nouveau Solfège avec accompagnement de piano, dans lequel le phrasé est réduit en principes* (1808); *Exposé succint du seul système musical qui soit vraiment fondé et complet* (1809); *La Seule Vraie Théorie de la musique* (1821; also in Italian, Bologna, 1823); *Cours général de musique de piano, d'harmonie et de composition depuis A jusqu'à Z* (1834; unfinished); also *Méthode de piano* (1802); *La Première Année de leçon de pianoforte* (1803).

WORKS: 6 string quartets; 6 violin sonatas; 2 piano sonatas; 12 fantasias for Piano; *Grand Nocturne* for Flute and Piano; 5 cantatas; 137 songs.

BIBLIOGRAPHY: Albert Palm, *Jérôme-Joseph de Momigny* (Paris, 1957).

Mompou, Federico, significant Spanish composer; b. Barcelona, April 10, 1893. After preliminary studies at the Cons. of Barcelona he went to Paris, where he studied piano with Isidor Philipp and composition with S.S. Rousseau. He returned to Barcelona during World War I; then was again in Paris until 1941, when he once more went back to Spain. He visited N.Y. in 1970, 1973, and 1978. His music is inspired by Spanish and Catalan melos, but its harmonic and instrumental treatment is entirely modern. He wrote mostly for piano: *6 impressions intimes* (1911–14); *Scènes d'enfants* (1915); *Suburbis* (1916–17); *3 pessebres* (1918); *Cants magics* (1919); *Festes Llunyanes* (1920); *6 charmes* (1921); *3 variations* (1921); *Dialogues* (1923); a series, *Canción y danza* (1918–53); *10 preludes* (1927–51); *3 paisajes* (1942, 1947, 1960); *Música callada* (4 albums, 1959–67); *Suite compostelana* for guitar (1963); choral works and songs.

BIBLIOGRAPHY: Santiago Kastner, *Federico Mompou* (Madrid, 1946); A. Iglesias, *Federico Mompou* (Madrid, 1977).

Monaco, Mario del. See **Del Monaco, Mario.**

Monasterio, Jesús de, famous Spanish violinist and pedagogue; b. Potes, near Santander, March 21, 1836; d. Casar del Periedo, Sept. 28, 1903. He played for the Queen in 1843, and she became his patroness; he made his debut in 1845 in Madrid, as an infant prodigy; studied at the Brussels Cons. with Bériot (violin) and with Fétis (theory). In 1857 he returned to Madrid as honorary violinist of the Royal Chapel; was appointed prof. of violin at the Madrid Cons., and taught there for many years; was its director from 1894 to 1897; conducted the Sociedad de Conciertos (1869–76), and was influential in forming a taste for classical music in Spain. He publ. a number of violin pieces, some of which (e.g.,

Adíos a la Alhambra) were very popular.

BIBLIOGRAPHY: J.M. Alonso, *Jesús de Monasterio* (Santander, 1954; contains a list of works).

Moncada, Eduardo Hernández. See **Hernández Moncada, Eduardo.**

Moncayo García, José Pablo, Mexican composer; b. Guadalajara, June 29, 1912; d. Mexico City, June 16, 1958. He studied with Chávez; from 1932 was a member of the Mexican Symph. Orch.; was conductor of the National Symph. Orch. in 1949–52; in company with Ayala, Contreras, and Galindo (also pupils of Chávez), he formed the so-called Grupo de Los Cuatro for the purpose of furthering the cause of Mexican music.

WORKS: Opera, *La mulata de Córdoba* (Mexico City, Oct. 23, 1948); *Huapango* for Orch. (1941), *Homenaje a Cervantes* for 2 Oboes and Strings (Mexico City, Oct. 27, 1947), *Cumbres* for Orch. (Louisville, Ky., June 12, 1954); piano pieces, choruses.

Mondonville, Jean-Joseph Cassanea de (de Mondonville was his wife's maiden name), French violinist and composer; b. Narbonne (baptized, Dec. 25), 1711; d. Belleville, near Paris, Oct. 8, 1772. He appeared as a violinist in the Concert Spirituel in Paris (1734); wrote numerous motets for that organization; succeeded Gervais in 1744 as intendant of the "musique de la chapelle" at Versailles; music director of the Concert Spirituel from 1755 till 1762. He produced several operas and pastorales: *Isbé* (Paris, April 10, 1742); *Le Carnaval du Parnasse* (Sept. 23, 1749; included ballet scenes); *Titon et l'Aurore* (Paris, Jan. 9, 1753); *Daphnis et Alcimadure* (Fontainebleau, Oct. 29, 1754); also wrote some instrumental music: *Pièces de clavecin en sonates* (with Violin; 1734); *Les Sons harmoniques* for Violin and Continuo (1736); and various other works.

BIBLIOGRAPHY: L. Galibert, *Jean-Joseph Cassanea de Mondonville* (Narbonne, 1856); F. Hellouin, *Feuillets d'histoire* (Paris, 1903); L. de La Laurencie, *L'Ecole française de violon de Lulli à Viotti* (Paris, 1922–24); A. Moser, *Geschichte des Violinspiels* (Berlin, 1923; 2nd ed., revised and enlarged, 1966–67); A. Tessier, "Madame de Mondonville," *Revue Musicale* (July 1926); E. Borroff, *The Instrumental Works of Jean-Joseph Cassanéa de Mondonville* (Diss., Univ. of Michigan, 1958).

Monestel, Alejandro, Costa Rican composer; b. San José, April 26, 1865; d. there, Nov. 3, 1950. He studied music at the Brussels Cons.; returning to Costa Rica in 1884, he was organist at the San José Cathedral (1884–1902); then lived in N.Y. (1902–37), where he was active as a church organist and composer. He wrote 14 masses, 4 Requiems, 5 cantatas on the life of Jesus; also *Rapsodia costarricense* for Orch. (San José, Aug. 28, 1935); he publ. arrangements of Costa Rican songs.

Monfred, Avenir H. de, composer of Franco-Russian ancestry; b. St. Petersburg, Sept. 17, 1903; d. Paris, April 11, 1974. He studied piano, organ, and composition at the St. Petersburg Cons., graduating in 1922. In 1924 he went to Paris and studied with Vincent d'Indy at the Schola Cantorum (1925–27). He promulgated an interesting theory of composition, "Diatonic Polymodality," expounded in detail in his book *The New Diatonic Modal Principle of Relative Music* (N.Y., 1970).

WORKS: 2 symphs. (1955, 1957); symph. poem, *Vienna, 1850* (1941); ballet, *Suite New-yorkaise* (Monte Carlo, Nov. 19, 1956); symph. suite, *Manhattan Sketches* (1958); *Rapsodie Juive* for Orch. (1926); String Quartet (1939); 3 violin sonatas (1922, 1926, 1947); Cello Sonata (1938); many pieces for piano and for organ; choruses; film scores.

Moniuszko, Stanislaw, famous Polish composer; b. Ubiel, province of Minsk, Russia, May 5, 1819; d. Warsaw, June 4, 1872. He studied with August Freyer in Warsaw (1827–30) and with Rungenhagen in Berlin (1837–39); served as church organist in Vilna (1840–58), where he also produced a number of his operas. In 1858 he settled in Warsaw; was prof. at the Warsaw Cons. He wrote about 20 operas and operettas; his masterpiece was *Halka*, the first genuinely national Polish opera, which attained a lasting success in Poland, in Russia, and to some extent in Germany. It was first presented in 2 acts in Vilna, by an amateur group (Jan. 1, 1848); then was expanded to 4 acts, and produced 10 years later in Warsaw (Jan. 1, 1858). Other operas are: *Loterya* (Warsaw, Sept. 12, 1846), *Jawnuta* (Vilna, May 20, 1852), *Flis* (*The Raftsman;* Warsaw, Sept. 24, 1858), *Hrabina* (*The Countess;* Warsaw, Feb. 7, 1860), *Verbum nobile* (Warsaw, Jan. 1, 1861), *Straszny dwór* (The Haunted Castle; Warsaw, Sept. 28, 1865), *Paria* (Warsaw, Dec. 11, 1869), *Beata* (Warsaw, Feb. 2, 1872); he also wrote about 270 songs (some of which are very popular in Poland); choral works; a symph. poem, *Bajka (Fairy Tale);* etc. Several biographies of Moniuszko have been publ. in Polish: by A. Walicki (1873); J. Karlowicz (1885); B. Wilczynski (1900); A. Koehler (1919); Z. Jachimecki (1924; revised 1961); H. Opienski (1924); S. Niewiadomski (1928); E. Wrocki (1930); T. Joteyko (1932); W. Hulewicz (1933); K. Stromenger (1946). Witold Rudzinski publ. a comprehensive biography with a complete list of works (Warsaw, 1954; 4th ed., 1972) and also brought out an *Almanach moniuszkowski 1872–1952*, on the 50th anniversary of Moniuszko's death (Warsaw, 1952).

BIBLIOGRAPHY: Z. Jachimecki, "Stanislaw Moniuszko," *Musical Quarterly* (Jan. 1928); Jan Prosnak, *Stanislaw Moniuszko* (Cracow, 1968).

Monk, Edwin George, English organist and music editor; b. Frome, Somerset, Dec. 13, 1819; d. Radley, near Oxford, Jan. 3, 1900. He studied with G.A. Macfarren; received a Mus.Bac. from Oxford in 1848; a Mus.Doc. in 1856. From 1858 till 1883 he was organist of York Minster. He edited *The Anglican Chant Book, The Anglican Choral Service Book, The Anglican Hymn Book* (with Singleton), *The Psalter* *and Canticles pointed for chanting* (with Ouseley), and *Anglican Psalter Chants* (with Ouseley).

Monk, Thelonious ("Sphere"), black American jazz pianist; b. Rocky Mount, N.C., Oct. 10, 1918; d. Englewood, N.J., Feb. 17, 1982. He spent most of his life in Harlem, where he played in nightclubs; gradually surfaced as a practitioner of bebop, set in angular rhythms within asymmetrical bar sequences. His eccentric behavior was signalized by his external appearance; he wore skullcaps and dark sunglasses; time and again he would rise from the keyboard and perform a tap dance. Although not educated in the formal sense, he experimented with discordant harmonies, searching for new combinations of sounds. Paradoxically, he elevated his ostentatious ineptitude to a weirdly cogent modern idiom, so that even deep-thinking jazz critics could not decide whether he was simply inept or prophetically innovative. Monk's own tunes, on the other hand, seemed surprisingly sophisticated, and he gave them impressionistic titles, such as *Crepuscule with Nellie* (Nellie was the name of his wife) and *Epistrophy,* or else ethnically suggestive ones, as in *Rhythm-a-ning.* A profoundly introspective neurotic, he would drop out of the music scene for years, withdrawing into his inner self. During the period between 1973 and 1976 he stayed with an admirer, the Baroness Nica de Koenigswarter, in her mansion in Weehawken, N.J., but was visited daily by his wife, Nellie. He made his last public appearance at the Newport Jazz Festival in 1976, but seemed a faint shadow, a weak echo of his former exuberant personality. His song *Criss-Cross* was used by Gunther Schuller for his *Variations on a Theme of Thelonious Monk.*

Monk, William Henry, English music editor; b. London, March 16, 1823; d. there, March 1, 1889. He was a pupil of T. Adams, J.A. Hamilton, and G.A. Griesbach; served as organist in various London churches; taught music at King's College in London, at the School for the Indigent Blind, the National Training School, etc. He edited for the Church of Scotland *The Book of Psalms in Metre, Scottish Hymnal, The Psalter,* and *Book of Anthems;* was the music editor of *Hymns, Ancient and Modern;* composed many popular hymn tunes (*Eventide,* etc.); edited *The Parish Choir.*
  BIBLIOGRAPHY: *Dictionary of National Biography* (vol. 13).

Monleone, Domenico, Italian opera composer; b. Genoa, Jan. 4, 1875; d. there, Jan. 15, 1942. He studied at the Cons. of Milan; from 1895 to 1901 was active as a theater conductor in Amsterdam and in Vienna. He attracted attention by producing in Amsterdam (Feb. 5, 1907) an opera, *Cavalleria Rusticana,* to a libretto by his brother **Giovanni,** on the same subject as Mascagni's celebrated work; after its first Italian performance (Turin, July 10, 1907), Mascagni's publisher, Sonzogno, brought a lawsuit against Monleone for infringement of copyright. Monleone was forced to change the title; his brother rewrote

the libretto, and the opera was produced as *La Giostra dei falchi* (Florence, Feb. 18, 1914). Other operas were: *Una novella di Boccaccio* (Genoa, May 26, 1909); *Alba eroica* (Genoa, May 5, 1910); *Arabesca* (Rome, March 11, 1913; won first prize at the competition of the City of Rome); *Suona la ritrata* (Milan, May 23, 1916); *Il mistero* (Venice, May 7, 1921); *Fauvette* (Genoa, March 2, 1926); *La ronda di notte* (Genoa, March 6, 1933); also an opera in Genovese dialect, *Scheûggio Campann-a* (Genoa, March 12, 1928). For some of his works he used the pseudonym **W. di Stolzing.**

Monn, Georg Matthias, Austrian composer; b. Lower Austria, April 9, 1717; d. Vienna, Oct. 3, 1750. For many years he was organist of the Karlskirche there. He wrote instrumental works marking a transition from the Baroque to the new style perfected by Johann Stamitz. A selection of his extant works appears in Denkmäler der Tonkunst in Österreich, 31 (15.ii), ed. by Horwitz and Riedel: 3 symphs. of which one, in E-flat, may possibly be by a younger relative, **Johann Christoph Monn** or **Mann** (1726–1782), and a trio sonata; in vol. 39 (19.ii), ed. by W. Fischer and Arnold Schoenberg: 5 symphs., Cello Concerto in G minor, and Harpsichord Concerto in D (together with thematic catalogue of instrumental works of Georg Matthias Monn and Johann Christoph Monn). He wrote several symphs.; one, in E-flat major, formerly ascribed to him, has been proved to be a work by F.X. Pokorný (see *Notes,* Summer 1966, p. 1179). The Quartet Fugues reprinted by Albrechtsberger are by Johann Christoph Monn. G.M. Monn's Harpsichord Concerto was transcribed by Schoenberg for cello and orch. (1933).

Monnikendam, Marius, Dutch composer; b. Haarlem, May 28, 1896; d. Amsterdam, May 22, 1977. He studied composition with Sem Dresden, and organ and piano with de Pauw at the Amsterdam Cons.; in 1925 went to Paris, where he took courses with Louis Aubert and Vincent d'Indy at the Schola Cantorum. Returning to the Netherlands, he taught composition at the Rotterdam Cons. and in Amsterdam; also served as music critic of the newspaper combine *De Tijd* and *De Maasbode.* He wrote a number of church works, in which he revived the most ancient form of plainchant, but injected asymmetric rhythms in a modern style; in his larger works, he employed the resources of advanced harmony, including polytonality. He publ. monographs on César Franck (Amsterdam, 1949), Igor Stravinsky (Haarlem, 1951), *50 Masterpieces of Music* (The Hague, 1953), and *Nederlandse Componisten van heden en verleden* (Amsterdam, 1968).
  WORKS: FOR ORCH.: *Arbeid* (*Labour*), symph. movement (1931); *Sinfonia super "Merck toch hoe sterck"* for Chamber Orch. (1944); *Mouvement symphonique* (1950); Concerto for Trumpet, Horn, and Orch. (1952); *Variations symphoniques super "Merck toch hoe sterck"* (1954); Concerto for Organ and Strings (1958); *Ouverture* for Organ and Orch. (1960); *Vision* for Chamber Orch. (1963); Concerto for Organ, Wind Instruments, Harp, Double Bass,

and Percussion (1968); Piano Concertino (1974). FOR VOICE: 2 Te Deums for Chorus and Orch. (1919, 1946); *Missa Nova* for 3 Voices and Organ (1928); *7 Boetpsalmen (7 Penitential Psalms)* for Chorus and Orch. (1934); *Noah,* oratorio (1937); *Samson,* oratorio (1938); *Solomon,* oratorio (1939); *Missa antiphonale* (1939); *Sinfonia sacra I* for Male Chorus and Orch. (1947); *Sinfonia sacra II (Domine salvum fac)* for Chorus and Orch. (1952); *Passion* for Speaker, Chorus, and Orch. (1948); *Van Riebeeck-Taferelen* for 2 Speakers, Chorus, and Orch. (1952); *Noé ou La Destruction du Premier Monde,* oratorio (1955); *Magnificat* for Soprano, Male Chorus, and Orch. without Strings (1956; transcribed for Mixed Chorus and Full Orch., 1965); *Missa festiva* for Chorus and Orch. (1956); *Hymne* for Alto, Male Chorus, and Orch. (1957); *Lamentations of Jeremiah* for Chorus and Orch. (1956); *Missa solenissima* for Chorus, Organ, and 7 Wind Instruments (1959); *Missa pro defunctis* for 3 Soloists, Organ, and Percussion (1961); *Apocalypse* for Chorus and Organ (1966); *Madrigalesca* for Chorus, 9 Winds, and Percussion (1966); *De Kinderkruistocht (The Children's Crusade)* for Mixed or Female Chorus, 7 Woodwinds, and Percussion (1967); *Via sacra (Way of the Cross)* for Speaker, Chorus, Organ, Percussion, and Projection Slides (1969); *3 psaumes pour le temps présent* for Soloists, Chorus, and Chamber Orch. (1971); *Missa concertanta* for Soloists, Chorus, and Orch. (1971); *Elckerlyc (Everyman),* mystery play for Chorus, Organ, and Orch. (The Hague, May 28, 1976); *Heart Rhythm* for Speaker, Male Chorus, Organ, Double Bass, and Percussion (1975); *Gloria* for Chorus, Organ, and Orch. (1976). CHAMBER WORKS: Cello Sonata (1925); 2 *toccatas* for Organ (1931, 1970); Concerto for Organ, 2 Trumpets, and 2 Trombones (1956); *10 Inventions* for Organ (1959); *Suite* for Flute, Oboe, Clarinet, Bassoon, and Harp (1960); Piano Sonatina (1967); *Suite biblique* for Piano, 4-hands (1967); *The Bells,* prelude for Organ (1971); *Toccata batalla* for Organ, 2 Trumpets, and 2 Trombones (1972); numerous small organ pieces.

Mononen, Sakari, Finnish composer; b. Korpiselkä, July 27, 1928. He studied composition with Nils-Eric Fougstedt and Einar Englund at the Sibelius Academy in Helsinki, graduating in 1961. In 1967 he was appointed director of the dept. of sacred music of the Kuopio Music Inst. He composed a Symph. (1961); Concerto Grosso for Winds and Strings (1968); *Divertimento* for Orch. (1971); *Legenda con espressione* for Orch. (1971); *Perspectives* for Orch. (1972); 2 suites for Piano (1959, 1970); String Trio (1960); String Quartet (1961); 3 organ sonatas (1963, 1964, 1965); *Vuorela Suite* for a cappella Chorus (1972); Clarinet Sonata (1973).

Monrad Johansen, David, Norwegian composer and music critic; b. Vefsn, Nov. 8, 1888; d. Oslo, Feb. 20, 1974. He studied at the Oslo Cons. (1904–9); also took private lessons with Elling and Holter (1909–15). In 1915 he went to Berlin, where he took a course in composition with Humperdinck. Upon returning to Norway, he was engaged in musical jour-

nalism; was music critic of *Aftenposten* (1925–45); publ. a monograph on Grieg (1934; in Eng., Princeton, 1938; new printings, 1943 and 1956). In his music he followed the lyrico-dramatic tradition of Grieg, inspired by Scandinavian folk melos.
WORKS: *Suite* for Orch. (1915); incidental music to the play *Jo Gjende* (1924); *Voluspaa (The Wise Woman's Prophesy),* after Edda poetry, for Soloists, Chorus, and Orch. (1922–26); *Sigvat skald* for Voice and Orch. (1928); *Me vigjer vår sang,* cantata (1930); *Ignis ardens,* cantata (1930–32); *Symphonic Fantasy* (1936); *Pan,* symph. poem (1939); *Symphonic Variations* (1944–46); Piano Concerto (1954); *Epigrams on Norwegian Motifs* for Orch. (1960); *Lamento* for String Orch. (1964); Violin Sonata (1912–13); 3 suites for Piano: *Nordlandsbilleder (Scenes from Northern Norway,* 1918), *Fra Gudbrandsdalen (From the Gudbrandsdal Valley,* 1922), and *Prillar-Guri* (1924); *Nordslands trompet,* song cycle (1925); *Balladesk suite* for Cello and Piano (1942); Piano quartet (1947–48); *Nordlandske danser* for Piano (1958); Flute Quintet (1967); String Quartet (1969); songs; choruses.

Monroe, Bill, American country-music instrumentalist, singer, and composer, a pioneer of bluegrass music; b. near Rosine, Ky., Sept. 13, 1911. He studied with his uncle, a fiddler; then played fiddle in a band formed by his brothers Birch and Charlie. In 1938 he organized his own band, the Blue Grass Boys, which gained fame through appearances on the "Grand Ole Opry" radio program in Nashville. His innovations in string-band music led to the development of the bluegrass style, notable for its syncopated rhythm and complex but invariably tonal harmonies. In 1971 he was elected a member of the Country Music Hall of Fame in Nashville.
BIBLIOGRAPHY: J. Rooney, *Bossmen: Bill Monroe & Muddy Waters* (N.Y., 1971); N. Rosenberg, *Bill Monroe and His Blue Grass Boys: An Illustrated Discography* (Nashville, 1974).

Monsigny, Pierre-Alexandre, French opera composer; b. Fauquembergues, near St.-Omer, Oct. 17, 1729; d. Paris, Jan. 14, 1817. He was forced at an early age, by his father's death, to support his family; he abandoned his study of music and took a position as clerk in the Bureaux des Comptes du Clergé (1749); then became maître d'hôtel (majordomo) to the Duke of Orléans; in 1754, a performance of Pergolesi's *Serva padrona* so fired his imagination that he decided to try his own skill at comic opera. He took a rapid course of harmony with the double-bass player Gianotti, and soon completed his first stage work, *Les Aveux indiscrets,* produced at the Théâtre de la Foire Saint-Germain (Feb. 7, 1759). In quick succession, and with increasing success, the same theater brought out 3 more of Monsigny's operas: *Le Maître en droit* (Feb. 13, 1760), *Le Cadi dupé* (Feb. 4, 1761), and *On ne s'avise jamais de tout* (Sept. 14, 1761). The members of the Comédie-Italienne, alarmed at the rising prestige of the rival enterprise, succeeded in closing it, by exercise of vested privilege, and took over its best actors. Monsigny thereafter wrote exclusively for the Comédie-Italienne; a few of his operas, however, were first presented at the private theater of the Duke of Orléans, at Bagnolet. The operas produced at the Comédie-Italienne in Paris were *Le Roi et le fermier* (Nov. 22, 1762), *Rose et Colas* (March 8, 1764), *Aline, reine de Golconde* (April 15, 1766), *L'Ile sonnante* (Bagnolet, June 5, 1767), *Le Déserteur* (March 6, 1769), *Le Faucon* (Fontainebleau, Nov. 2, 1771), *La Belle Arsène* (Fountainebleau, Nov. 6, 1773), and *Félix, ou L'Enfant trouvé* (Fountainebleau, Nov. 10, 1777). Here Monsigny stopped abruptly, perhaps (as he himself modestly explained it) for lack of ideas. After the Revolution, he lost the stewardship of the estates of the Duke of Orléans, but the Opéra-Comique allowed him a pension of 2,400 francs; in 1800 he was made Inspector of Instruction at the Cons. (resigning in 1802). In 1813 he was elected to Grétry's chair in the Institut de France. Monsigny possessed an uncommon and natural melodic invention, and sensibility in dramatic expression, but his theoretical training was deficient; still, his works attained the foremost rank among the precursors of the French comic operas.

BIBLIOGRAPHY: Quatremère de Quincy, *Notice historique sur la vie et les ouvrages de Monsigny* (Paris, 1818); M. Alexandre, *Eloge historique de Pierre Alexandre Monsigny* (Arras, 1819); M. Hédouin, *Eloge de Monsigny* (Paris, 1820); F. de Ménil, *Les Grands Musiciens du Nord: Monsigny* (Paris, 1893); A. Pougin, *Monsigny et son temps* (Paris, 1908); P. Druilhe, *Monsigny, Sa vie et son œuvre* (Paris, 1955).

Montagu-Nathan, Montagu, English writer on music; b. Banbury, Sept. 17, 1877; d. London, Nov. 15, 1958. His original name was **Montagu Nathan;** he changed it legally to Montagu Montagu-Nathan on March 17, 1909. He studied in Birmingham; then took violin lessons with Ysaÿe in Brussels, with Heermann in Frankfurt, and with Wilhelmj in London. He appeared as a violinist in Belfast and Leeds, but soon abandoned concerts in favor of music journalism. He learned the Russian language and wrote several books on Russian music: *A History of Russian Music* (1914), *Handbook to the Piano Works of A. Scriabin* (1916; reprinted 1922); *Contemporary Russian Composers* (1917); and monographs on Glinka, Mussorgsky, and Rimsky-Korsakov.

Montani, Nicola Aloysius, American choral conductor and composer; b. Utica, N.Y., Nov. 6, 1880; d. Philadelphia, Jan. 11, 1948. He studied with Lorenzo Perosi and others in Rome; had training in Gregorian music under Dom Mocquereau and Dom Eudine on the Isle of Wight (1905–6); was organist and choirmaster of the Church of St. John the Evangelist, Philadelphia (1906–23). In 1914 he founded the Society of St. Gregory of America (officially recognized by Pope Benedict XV) for the restoration of Gregorian chant and the early polyphonic style recommended in the "Motu Proprio" of Pius X; he edited the *Catholic Choirmaster*. Montani was also, for a time, editor in chief of the liturgical music

dept. of G. Schirmer, Inc., and of the Boston Music Co. He wrote 8 masses; a *Stabat Mater;* motets, songs, etc.; publ. *Essentials of Sight Singing* and *The Art of A Cappella Singing; St. Gregory Hymnal; Catholic Choir Book* (1920; also in Braille type, for use by the blind). The *Caecilia* devoted its Aug. 1935 issue to Montani, listing biographical data and a catalogue of works.

Monte, Philippe de (Filippo di Monte or **Philippus de Monte**), great Belgian composer; b. Mechlin, 1521; d. Prague, July 4, 1603. He went to Italy in his youth and was active there as a singer and teacher. From 1542 to 1551 he was in Naples in the service of the Pinelli family; then went to Rome, where he publ. his first book of madrigals (1554); from Rome he proceeded to Antwerp in 1554, and then to England, where he served as chorus praefectus in the private chapel of Philip II of Spain, the husband of the Queen, Mary Tudor. In Sept. 1555 he left England and went to Italy again; in 1567 he was in Rome. On May 1, 1568, he became Imperial Court Kapellmeister to the Emperor Maximilian II in Vienna; he held this position until his death, which occurred while the court was at Prague during the summer of 1603. In 1572 he was appointed treasurer of Cambrai Cathedral, and in 1577, also a canon (residence was not required for either position there). He was greatly esteemed as a composer; he wrote some 1,000 madrigals, about 40 masses, and many other works of sacred music.

WORKS: MASSES: *Missa ad modulum "Benedicta es"* for 6 Voices (Antwerp, 1579); *Liber primus* (7) *missarum* for 5, 6, and 8 Voices (Antwerp, 1587); Mass for 5 Voices (Venice, 1590); none of his other masses were publ. in his lifetime, and most of these remain in MS. MOTETS: *Sacrarum cantionum . . . liber primus* for 5 Voices (Venice, 1572); *Sacrarum cantionum . . . liber secundus* for 5 Voices (Venice, 1573); *Sacrarum cantionum . . . liber tertius* for 5 Voices (Venice, 1574); *Libro quarto de motetti* for 5 Voices (Venice, 1575); *Sacrarum cantionum . . . liber quintus* for 5 Voices (Venice, 1579); *Sacrarum cantionum . . . liber sextus* for 5 Voices (Venice, 1584; not extant); *Sacrarum cantionum . . . liber primus* for 6 and 12 Voices (Venice, 1585); *Sacrarum cantionum . . . liber secundus* for 6 Voices (Venice, 1587); *Sacrarum cantionum . . . liber primus* for 4 Voices (Venice, 1596); *Sacrarum cantionum . . . liber septimus* for 5 Voices (Venice, 1600); etc.

MADRIGALI SPIRITUALI: *Il primo libro de madrigali spirituali* for 5 Voices (Venice, 1581); *Il primo libro de madrigali spirituali* for 6 Voices (Venice, 1583); *Il secondo libro de madrigali spirituali* for 6 and 7 Voices (Venice, 1589); *Il terzo libro de madrigali spirituali* for 6 Voices (Venice, 1590); *Eccellenze di Maria vergine* for 5 Voices (Venice, 1593).

MADRIGALS: *Madrigali . . . libro primo* for 5 Voices (Rome, 1554); *Il primo libro de madrigali* for 4 Voices (Venice, 1562); *Il secondo libro de madrigali* for 5 Voices (Venice, 1567); *Il primo libro de' madrigali* for 6 Voices (c.1568; not extant; 2nd ed., Venice, 1569); *Il secondo libro delli madrigali* for 6 Voices

(Venice, 1569); *Il secondo libro delli madrigali* for 4 Voices (Venice, 1569); *Il terzo libro delli madrigali* for 5 Voices (Venice, 1570); *Il quarto libro delli madrigali* for 5 Voices (Venice, 1571); *Madrigali... libro quinto* for 5 Voices (Venice, 1574); *Il sesto libro delli madrigali* for 5 Voices (Venice, 1575); *Il terzo libro de madrigali* for 6 Voices (Venice, 1576); *Il settimo libro delli madrigali* for 5 Voices (Venice, 1578); *Il quarto libro de madrigali* for 6 Voices (Venice, 1580); *L'ottavo libro delli madrigali* for 5 Voices (Venice, 1580); *Il nono libro de madrigali* for 5 Voices (Venice, 1580); *Il terzo libro de madrigali* for 4 Voices (c.1580; not extant; 2nd ed., Venice, 1585); *Il decimo libro delli madrigali* for 5 Voices (Venice, 1581); *Il quarto libro de madrigali* for 4 Voices (Venice, 1581); *Il primo libro de madrigali* for 3 Voices (Venice, 1582); *Il quinto libro de madrigali* for 6 Voices (Venice, 1584); *L'undecimo libro delli madrigali* for 5 Voices (Venice, 1586); *Il duodecimo libro delli madrigali* for 5 Voices (Venice, 1587); *Il terzodecimo libro delli madrigali* for 5 Voices (Venice, 1588); *Il quartodecimo libro delli madrigali* for 5 Voices (Venice, 1590); *Il sesto libro de madrigali* for 6 Voices (Venice, 1591); *Il settimo libro de madrigali* for 6 Voices (Venice, 1591); *Il quintodecimo libro de madrigali* for 5 Voices (Venice, 1592); *Il sestodecimo libro de madrigali* for 5 Voices (Venice, 1593); *L'ottavo libro de madrigali* for 6 Voices (Venice, 1594); *Il decimosettimo libro delli madrigali* for 5 Voices (Venice, 1595); *Il decimottavo libro di madrigali* for 5 Voices (Venice, 1597); *Il decimonono libro delli madrigali* for 5 Voices (Venice, 1598); *La fiammetta... libro primo* for 7 Voices (Venice, 1599); *Musica sopra Il pastor fido... libro secondo* for 7 Voices (Venice, 1600); etc. A complete ed. of his works was edited by C. van den Borren and G. van Doorslaer as *Philippe de Monte: Opera* (31 vols., Bruges, 1927–39; reprint, 1965). R. Lenaerts and others are editing *Philippe de Monte: New Complete Edition* (Louvain, 1975—).

BIBLIOGRAPHY: G. van Doorslaer, *Philippe de Monte* (Mechelen, 1895); V. Eberstein, *Die Messen Philippe de Montes, mit besonderer Berücksichtigung seiner Parodietechnik* (Diss., Univ. of Vienna, 1912); P. Bergmans, *Quatorze lettres inédites du compositeur Philippe de Monte* (Brussels, 1921); G. van Doorslaer, *La Vie et les œuvres de Philippe de Monte* (Brussels, 1921); idem, *Deux lettres nouvelles de Philippe de Monte* (Mechelen, 1927); A. Einstein, "Filippo di Monte als Madrigalkomponist," *International Musicological Society Congress Report*, I (Liège, 1930); J. van Nuffel, "Philippe de Monte," *Proceedings of the Music Association*, 57 (1931); P. Oberg, *The Sacred Music of Philippe de Monte* (Diss., Univ. of Rochester, 1944); A. Einstein, *The Italian Madrigal* (Princeton, 1949); G. Reese, *Music in the Renaissance* (N.Y., 1954; 2nd ed., revised, 1959); P. Nuten, *De madrigali spirituali van Filip de Monte* (Brussels, 1958); G. Michael, *The Parody Mass Technique of Philippe de Monte* (Diss., N.Y. Univ., 1959); R. Lindell, *Die sechs- und siebenstimmige Madrigale von Filippo di Monte* (Diss., Univ. of Vienna, 1977); I. Bossuyt, "Newly-discovered Part Books of Early Madrigal Collections of Philippus de Monte (1521–1603)," *Fontes*

Artis Musicae, XXVI (1979).

Monte, Toti dal. See **Dal Monte, Toti.**

Montéclair, Michel Pignolet de, French composer; b. Andelot (baptized, Dec. 4), 1667; d. near St.-Denis, Sept. 22, 1737. He was one of the early players of the modern double bass; from 1699 to his death he played in the orch. of the Académie Royale de Musique; there he produced his ballet-opera *Les Fêtes de l'été* (June 12, 1716) and a lyric tragedy, *Jephté,* in 5 acts (Feb. 28, 1732), the first stage work on a biblical subject to be presented at the Académie. He also wrote a Requiem, 6 trio sonatas, flute duets, and "brunettes" (French love songs); publ. a *Nouvelle méthode pour apprendre la musique* (Paris, 1700; revised eds., 1709, 1736), a *Méthode facile pour apprendre à jouer du violon* (Paris, 1712; a pioneer violin method); and *Principes de musique* (Paris, 1736).

BIBLIOGRAPHY: E. Voillard, *Essai sur Montéclair* (Chaumont, 1879); J. Carlez, *Un Opéra biblique au XVIIIᵉ siècle* (on *Jephté;* Paris, 1879); A. Moser, *Geschichte des Violinspiels* (Berlin, 1923; 2nd ed., revised and enlarged, 1966–67); M. Pincherle, "Elementary Musical Instruction in the 18th Century: An Unknown Treatise by Montéclair," *Musical Quarterly* (Jan. 1948); J. Sadie, "Montéclair, the Viol Player's Composer," *Journal of the Viola da Gamba Society of America,* XV (1978).

Montella, Giovanni Domenico, Italian lutenist and composer; b. Naples, c.1570; d. before July 2, 1607. He studied with Giovanni de Macque; was a lutenist in the academy of Dom Fabrizio Gesualdo; in 1591 he was engaged as lutenist in the Royal Chapel, Naples; was also an organist and harpist. He wrote Psalms and other church music; publ. 2 vols. of *villanelles,* a vol. of motets, and 10 vols. of madrigals. Some of his sacred music is included in *Istituzioni e monumenti dell'arte musicale italiano* (vol. V, 1934).

Montemezzi, Italo, eminent Italian opera composer; b. Vigasio, near Verona, Aug. 4, 1875; d. there, May 15, 1952. He was a pupil of Saladino and Ferroni at the Milan Cons., and graduated in 1900; his graduation piece, conducted by Toscanini, was *Cantico dei Cantici,* for chorus and orch. He then devoted himself almost exclusively to opera. In 1939 he went to the U.S.; lived mostly in California; in 1949 he returned to Italy. Montemezzi's chief accomplishment is the maintenance of the best traditions of Italian dramatic music, without striving for realism or overelaboration of technical means. His masterpiece in this genre is the opera *L'amore dei tre re* (Milan, La Scala, April 10, 1913), which has become a standard work in the repertoire of opera houses all over the world. Other operas are: *Giovanni Gallurese* (Turin, Jan. 28, 1905); *Hellera* (Turin, March 17, 1909); *La nave* (libretto by Gabriele d'Annunzio; Milan, Nov. 1, 1918); *La notte di Zoraima* (Milan, Jan. 31, 1931); *L'incantesimo* (radio premiere, NBC, Oct. 9, 1943, composer conducting); he also wrote the symph. poems *Paolo e Virginia* (Rome, 1930) and *Italia mia!* (1944), etc.

BIBLIOGRAPHY: L. Tretti and L. Fiumi, eds., *Omaggio a Italo Montemezzi* (Verona, 1952).

Monteux, Claude, American flutist and conductor, son of **Pierre Monteux;** b. Brookline, Mass., Oct. 15, 1920. He studied flute with Georges Laurent; then played in the Kansas City Phil. (1946–49); subsequently began a career as a conductor; was music director of the Columbus (Ohio) Symph. Orch. from 1951 to 1956. He then was music director of the Hudson Valley Phil. in Poughkeepsie, N.Y., from 1959 to 1975. He also appeared as a guest conductor in the U.S. and Europe.

Monteux, Pierre, celebrated French conductor; b. Paris, April 4, 1875; d. Hancock, Maine, July 1, 1964. He studied at the Paris Cons. with Berthelier (violin), Lavignac (harmony), and Lenepveu (composition); received first prize for violin (1896); then was a viola player in the Colonne Orch., and later chorus master there; also played viola in the orch. of the Opéra-Comique. He then organized his own series, the Concerts Berlioz, at the Casino de Paris. In 1911 he became conductor for Diaghilev's Ballets Russes; his performances of modern ballet scores established him as one of the finest technicians of the baton. He led the world premieres of Stravinsky's *Petrouchka, Le Sacre du printemps,* and *Le Rossignol;* Ravel's *Daphnis et Chloé;* and Debussy's *Jeux;* conducted at the Paris Opéra (1913–14); founded the Société des Concerts Populaires in Paris (1914); appeared as guest conductor in London, Berlin, Vienna, Budapest, etc. In 1916–17 he toured the U.S. with the Ballets Russes; in 1917, conducted the Civic Orch. Society, N.Y.; in 1917–19, at the Metropolitan Opera House. In 1919 he was engaged as conductor of the Boston Symph. Orch., and held this post until 1924 (succeeded by Koussevitzky); from 1924 to 1934 he was associate conductor of the Concertgebouw Orch. in Amsterdam; in 1929–38 was principal conductor of the newly founded Orch. Symphonique de Paris. From 1936 until 1952 he was conductor of the reorganized San Francisco Symph. Orch.; then continued to conduct in Europe and America; was a frequent guest conductor with the Boston Symph. (conducted it on his 80th birthday, April 4, 1955); also led its concerts at Tanglewood; shared the podium with Munch during the European tour of the Boston Symph. in 1956 (which included Russia). In 1961 (at the age of 86) he became principal conductor of the London Symph. Orch., retaining this post until his death. He was married in 1927 to **Doris Hodgkins,** an American singer (b. Salisbury, Maine, 1895; d. Hancock, Maine, March 13, 1984) who co-founded in 1941 the Domaine School for Conductors and Orchestral Players in Hancock, Maine, of which Monteux was director. She publ. 2 books of memoirs, *Everyone Is Someone* and *It's All in the Music* (N.Y., 1965). After Monteux's death she established the Pierre Monteux Memorial Foundation. As an interpreter, Monteux endeavored to bring out the inherent essence of the music, without imposing his own artistic personality; unemotional and restrained in his podium manner, he nonetheless succeeded in producing brilliant performances.

BIBLIOGRAPHY: Harold Schonberg, *The Great Conductors* (N.Y., 1967).

Monteverdi, Claudio (Giovanni Antonio), great Italian composer; b. Cremona, (baptized, May 15) 1567; d. Venice, Nov. 29, 1643. His surname is also rendered as **Monteverde.** He was the son of a chemist who practiced medicine as a barber-surgeon; studied singing and theory with Marc' Antonio Ingegneri, maestro di cappella at the Cathedral of Cremona; he also learned to play the organ. He acquired the mastery of composition at a very early age; he was only 15 when a collection of his 3-part motets was publ. in Venice; there followed several sacred madrigals (1583) and canzonettas (1584). In 1589 he visited Milan, and made an appearance at the court of the Duke of Mantua; by 1592 he had obtained a position at the court in the service of Vincenzo I as "suonatore" on the viol (viola da gamba) and violin (viola da braccio). He came into contact with the Flemish composer Giaches de Wert, maestro di cappella at the Mantuan court, whose contrapuntal art greatly influenced Monteverdi. In 1592 Monteverdi publ. his 3rd book of madrigals, a collection marked by a considerable extension of harmonic dissonance. In 1595 he accompanied the retinue of the Duke of Mantua on forays against the Turks in Austria and Hungary, and also went with him to Flanders in 1599. He married Claudia de Cattaneis, one of the Mantuan court singers, on May 20, 1599; they had 2 sons; a daughter died in infancy. In 1601 he was appointed maestro di cappella in Mantua following the death of Pallavicino. The publication of 2 books of madrigals in 1603 and 1605 further confirmed his mastery of the genre. Having already composed some music for the stage, he now turned to the new form of the opera. *L'Orfeo,* his first opera, was given before the Accademia degli Invaghiti in Mantua in Feb. 1607. In this pastoral, he effectively moved beyond the Florentine model of recitative-dominated drama by creating a more flexible means of expression; the score is an amalgam of monody, madrigal, and instrumental music of diverse kinds. In 1607 Monteverdi was made a member of the Accademia degli Animori of Cremona. He suffered a grievous loss in the death of his wife in Cremona on Sept. 10, 1607. Although greatly depressed, he accepted a commission to compose an opera to celebrate the marriage of the heir-apparent to the court of Mantua, Francesco Gonzaga, to Margaret of Savoy. The result was *L'Arianna,* to a text by Rinuccini, presented in Mantua on May 28, 1608. Although the complete MS has been lost, the extant versions of the Lamento d'Arianna from the score testify to Monteverdi's genius in expressing human emotion in moving melodies. In 1614 Monteverdi prepared a 5-part arrangement of his 6th book of madrigals, also publ. separately (Venice, 1623). He further wrote 2 more works for wedding celebrations, the prologue to the pastoral play

Monteverdi

L'Idropica (not extant), and the French-style ballet *Il ballo delle ingrate.* His patron, Duke Vincenzo of Mantua, died in 1612; and his successor, Francesco, did not retain Monteverdi's services. However, Monteverdi had the good fortune of being called to Venice in 1613 to occupy the vacant post of maestro di cappella at San Marco, at a salary of 300 ducats, which was raised to 400 ducats in 1616. His post at San Marco proved to be the most auspicious of his career, and he retained it for the rest of his life. He composed mostly church music, but did not neglect the secular madrigal forms. He accepted important commissions from Duke Ferdinando of Mantua. His ballet, *Tirsi e Clori,* was given in Mantua in 1616. In 1619 he publ. his 7th book of madrigals, significant in its bold harmonic innovations. In 1624 his dramatic cantata, *Il combattimento di Tancredi e Clorinda,* after Tasso's *Gerusalemme liberata,* was performed at the home of Girolamo Mocenigo, a Venetian nobleman. The score is noteworthy for the effective role played by the string orch. Other works comprised intermedi for the Farnese court in Parma. A great inconvenience was caused to Monteverdi in 1627 when his son Massimiliano, a medical student, was arrested by the Inquisition for consulting books on the Index Librorum Prohibitorum; he was acquitted. In 1630 Monteverdi composed the opera *Proserpina rapita* for Venice; of it only one trio has survived. Following the plague of 1630–31, he wrote a mass of thanksgiving for performance at San Marco (the *Gloria* is extant); in 1632 he took Holy Orders. His *Scherzi musicali* for One and 2 Voices was publ. in 1632. Then followed his *Madrigali guerrieri et amorosi,* an extensive retrospective collection covering some 30 years, which was publ. in 1638. In 1637 the first public opera houses were opened in Venice, and Monteverdi found a new outlet there for his productions. His operas *Il ritorno d'Ulisse in patria* (1640), *Le nozze d'Enea con Lavinia* (1641; not extant), and *L'incoronazione di Poppea* (1642) were all given in Venice. The 2 extant operas may be considered the first truly modern operas in terms of dramatic viability. Monteverdi died at the age of 76 and was accorded burial in the church of the Fratri in Venice. A commemorative plaque was erected in his honor, and a copy remains in the church to this day.

Monteverdi's place in the history of music is of great magnitude. He established the foundations of modern opera conceived as a drama in music. For greater dynamic expression, he enlarged the orch., in which he selected and skillfully combined the instruments accompanying the voices. He was one of the earliest, if not the first, to employ such coloristic effects as string tremolo and pizzicato; his recitative assumes dramatic power, at times approaching the dimensions of an arioso. In harmonic usage he introduced audacious innovations, such as the use of the dominant seventh-chord and other dissonant chords without preparation. He is widely regarded as having popularized the terms "prima prattica" and "secunda prattica" to demarcate the polyphonic style of the 16th century from the largely monodic style of the 17th century, corresponding also to the distinction between "stile antico" and "stile moderno." For this he was severely criticized by the Bologna theorist Giovanni Maria Artusi, who publ. in 1600 a vitriolic pamphlet against Monteverdi, attacking the "musica moderna" which allowed chromatic usages in order to achieve a more adequate expression.

WORKS: In addition to various eds. of his works in separate format, G.F. Malipiero edited a complete ed. as *Claudio Monteverdi: Tutte le opere* (16 vols., Asolo, 1926–42; 2nd ed., revised, 1954; vol. 17, supplement, 1966). All of these are now being superseded by 2 new complete eds.: one, by the Fondazione Claudio Monteverdi, began publication in 1970; the other, ed. by B.B. de Surcy, began issuing simultaneously critical and facsimile eds. in 1972. A list of his works follows:

DRAMATIC: *L'Orfeo,* opera, designated "favola in musica" (Mantua, Feb. 1607; publ. in Venice, 1609); *L'Arianna,* opera (Mantua, May 28, 1608; not extant except for various versions of the Lament); *In ballo delle ingrate,* ballet (Mantua, 1608; publ. in *Madrigali guerrieri et amorosi,* Venice, 1638); Prologue to *L'Idropica,* comedy with music (Mantua, June 2, 1608; not extant); *Tirsi e Clori,* ballet (Mantua, 1616; publ. in *Concerto: Settimo libro,* Venice, 1619); *Le nozze di Tetide,* favola marittima (begun 1616 but unfinished; not extant); *Andromeda,* opera (begun c.1618 but unfinished; not extant); *Apollo,* dramatic cantata (unfinished; not extant); *Il combattimento di Tancredi e Clorinda* (Venice, 1624; publ. in *Madrigali guerrieri et amorosi,* Venice, 1638); *La finta pazza Licori* (composed for Mantua, 1627; never perf.; not extant); *Gli amori di Diana e di Endimione* (Parma, 1628; not extant); *Mercurio e Marte,* torneo (Parma, 1628; not extant); *Proserpina rapita,* opera (Venice, 1630; only one trio extant); *Volgendo il ciel,* ballet (Vienna, c.1636; publ. in *Madrigali guerrieri et amorosi,* Venice, 1638); *Il ritorno d'Ulisse in patria,* opera (Venice, 1640); *Le nozze d'Enea con Lavinia,* opera (Venice, 1641; not extant); *La vittoria d'Amore,* ballet (Piacenza, 1641; not extant); *L'incoronazione di Poppea,* opera (Venice, 1642).

SECULAR VOCAL: Places and dates of publication are included: *Canzonette* for 3 Voices (Venice, 1584); *Il primo libro de madrigali* for 5 Voices (Venice, 1587); *Il secondo libro de madrigali* for 5 Voices (Venice, 1590); *Il terzo libro de madrigali* for 5 Voices (Venice, 1592); *Il quarto libro de madrigali* for 5 Voices (Venice, 1603); *Il quinto libro de madrigali* for 5 Voices (Venice, 1605); *Musica tolta da i madrigali di Claudio Monteverde d'altri autori, e fatta spirituale da Aquilino Coppini* for 5 and 6 Voices (Milan, 1607); *Scherzi musicali di Claudio Monteverde, raccolti da Giulio Cesare Monteverde suo fratello* for 3 Voices (Venice, 1607); *Il secondo libro della musica di Claudio Monteverde e d'altri autori, fatta spirituale da Aquilino Coppini* for 5 Voices (Milan, 1608); *Il terzo libro della musica di Claudio Monteverde e d'altri autori, fatta spirituale da Aquilino Coppini* for 5 Voices (Milan, 1609); *Il sesto libro de madrigali* for 5 Voices, "con uno dialogo," and 7 Voices, with Basso Continuo (Venice, 1614); *Concerto: Settimo libro de madri-*

gali, con altri generi de canti for One to 4 and 6 Voices, with Basso Continuo (Venice, 1619); *Scherzi musicali cioè arie, et madrigali in stil recitativo, con una ciaccona . . . raccolti da Bartholomeo Magni* for One and 2 Voices, with Basso Continuo (Venice, 1632); *Madrigali guerrieri et amorosi con alcuni opuscoli in genere rappresentativo, che saranno per brevi episodii frà i canti senza gesto: libro ottavo* for One to 8 Voices and Instruments, with Basso Continuo (Venice, 1638); *Madrigali e canzonette . . . libro nono* for 2 and 3 Voices, with Basso Continuo (Venice, 1651).

SACRED VOCAL: *Sacrae cantiunculae . . . liber primus* for 3 Voices (Venice, 1582); *Madrigali spirituali* for 4 Voices (Brescia, 1583); *Musica tolta da i madrigali di Claudio Monteverde e d'altri autori, e fatta spirituale da Aquilino Coppini* for 5 and 6 Voices (Milan, 1607); *Il secondo libro della musica di Claudio Monteverde e d'altri autori, fatta spirituale da Aquilino Coppini* for 5 Voices (Milan, 1608); *Il terzo libro della musica di Claudio Monteverdi e d'altri autori, fatta spirituale da Aquilino Coppini* for 5 Voices (Milan, 1609); *Sanctissimae virgini missa senis vocibus ad ecclesiarum choros ac Vespere pluribus decantandae —cum nonnullis sacris concentibus ad sacella sive principum cubicula accommodata* for One to 3, 6 to 8, and 10 Voices and Instruments, with Basso Continuo (Venice, 1610); *Selva morale e spirituale* for One to 8 Voices and Instruments (Venice, 1641); *Messa* for 4 Voices, *et salmi* for One to 8 Voices, and *concertati, e parte da cappella, et con le letanie della beata vergine* for 6 Voices (Venice, 1650).

BIBLIOGRAPHY: S. Davari, *Notizie biografiche del distinto maestro di musica Claudio Monteverdi* (Mantua, 1884); E. Vogel, "Claudio Monteverdi," *Vierteljahrsschrift für Musikwissenschaft,* III (1887); G. Sommi Picenardi, *Claudio Monteverdi a Cremona* (Milan, 1896); H. Goldschmidt, "Monteverdis Ritorno d'Ulisse," *Sammelbände der Internationalen Musik-Gesellschaft,* IV (1902–3); idem, "Claudio Monteverdis Oper: Il ritorno d'Ulisse in patria," ibid., IX (1907–8); G. Cesari, "Die Entwicklung der Monteverdischen Kammermusik," *International Musical Society Congress Report,* III (Vienna, 1909); H. Leichtentritt, "Claudio Monteverdi als Madrigalkomponist," *Sammelbände der Internationalen Musik-Gesellschaft,* XI (1909–10); L. Schneider, *Un Précurseur de la musique italienne aux XVIe et XVIIe siècles: Claudio Monteverdi: L'Homme et son temps* (Paris, 1921); A. Tessier, "Les Deux Styles de Monteverde," *Revue Musicale,* III/8 (1922); H. Prunières, *La Vie et l'œuvre de Claudio Monteverdi* (Paris, 1924; Eng. trans., 1926; 2nd French ed., 1931); C. van den Borren, " 'Il ritorno d'Ulisse in patria' de Claudio Monteverdi," *Revue de l'Université de Bruxelles,* III (1925); J. Westrup, "Monteverde's 'Il ritorno d'Ulisse in patria,' " *Monthly Musical Record,* LVIII (1928); G.F. Malipiero, *Claudio Monteverdi* (Milan, 1929); issue of the *Rassegna Musicale* devoted to Monteverdi (Oct. 1929); K. Müller, *Die Technik der Ausdrucksdarstellung in Monteverdis monodischen Frühwerken* (Berlin, 1931); H. Redlich, *Claudio Monteverdi: Ein formgeschichtlicher Versuch* (Berlin,

1932); J. Westrup, "The Originality of Monteverde," *Proceedings of the Musical Association,* LX (1933–34); W. Kreidler, *Heinrich Schütz und der Stile Concitato von Claudio Monteverdi* (Stuttgart, 1934); H. Redlich, "Notationsprobleme in Cl. Monteverdis 'Incoronazione di Poppea,' " *Acta Musicologica,* X (1938); J. Westrup, "Monteverdi and the Orchestra," *Music & Letters,* XXI (1940); idem, "Monteverdi's 'Lamento d'Arianna,' " *Music Review,* I (1940); O. Tiby, *Claudio Monteverdi* (Turin, 1944); D. de' Paoli, *Claudio Monteverdi* (Milan, 1945); H. Redlich, "Monteverdi's Religious Music," *Music & Letters,* XXVII (1946); M. Bukofzer, *Music in the Baroque Era—from Monteverdi to Bach* (London, 1948); A. Einstein, *The Italian Madrigal* (Princeton, 1949); H. Redlich, *Claudio Monteverdi: Leben und Werk* (Olten, 1949; Eng. trans. and revision, London, 1952); J. Westrup, "Monteverdi and the Madrigal," *Score,* I (1949); L. Schrade, *Monteverdi, Creator of Modern Music* (London, 1950); M. le Roux, *Claudio Monteverdi* (Paris, 1951); C. Sartori, "Monteverdiana," *Musical Quarterly* (July 1952); idem, *Monteverdi* (Brescia, 1953); A.A. Abert, *Claudio Monteverdi und das musikalische Drama* (Lippstadt, 1954); H. Redlich, "Claudio Monteverdi: Some Problems of Textual Interpretation," *Musical Quarterly* (Jan. 1955); W. Osthoff, "Zu den Quellen von Monteverdis Ritorno d'Ulisse in Patria," *Studien zur Musikwissenschaft,* XXIII (1956); D. Arnold, " 'Seconda practica': A Background to Monteverdi's Madrigals," *Music & Letters,* XXXVIII (1957); W. Osthoff, "Monteverdi-Funde," *Archiv für Musikwissenschaft* (1957); idem, "Neue Beobachtungen zu Quellen und Geschichte von Monteverdis 'Incoronazione di Poppea," *Die Musikforschung,* XI (1958); G. Pannain, "Studi monteverdiana," *La Rassegna Musicale,* XXVIII (1958), XIX (1959), XXX (1960), XXXI (1961), and *Quaderni della Rassegna Musicale,* III (1965); R. Roche, *Monteverdi* (Paris, 1959); W. Osthoff, *Das dramatische Spätwerk Claudio Monteverdis* (Tutzing, 1960); C. Gallico, "Newly Discovered Documents Concerning Monteverdi," *Musical Quarterly* (Jan. 1962); F. Ghisi, "L'orchestra in Monteverdi," in *Karl Gustav Fellerer zum 60. Geburtstag* (Cologne, 1962); D. Arnold, *Monteverdi* (London, 1963); R. Tellart, *Claudio Monteverdi: L'Homme et son œuvre* (Paris, 1964); D. Arnold, *Monteverdi Madrigals* (London, 1967); G. Barblan et al., *Claudio Monteverdi nel quarto centenario della nascita* (Turin, 1967); H. Redlich, "Claudio Monteverdi: Some Editorial Problems of 1967," *Consort,* 24 (1967); E. Santoro, *La famiglia e la formazione di Claudio Monteverdi: Note biografiche con documenti inediti* (Cremona, 1967); D. Arnold and N. Fortune, eds., *The Monteverdi Companion* (London, 1968); *Congresso internazionale sul tema Claudio Monteverdi e il suo tempo: Venezia, Mantova e Cremona 1968* (Verona, 1969); N. Anfuso and A. Gianuario, *Preparazione alla interpretazione della Poïesis Monteverdiana* (Florence, 1971); W. Frobenius, "Zur Notation eines Ritornells in Monteverdis 'L'Orfeo,' " *Archiv für Musikwissenschaft,* XXVIII (1971); K. Mays, *Harmonic Style in the Madrigals of Claudio Monteverdi* (Diss., Indiana Univ., 1971); D. Stevens, "Monteverdi's Necklace," *Musi-*

cal *Quarterly* (July 1973); idem, *Monteverdi: Sacred, Secular and Occasional Music* (Rutherford, N.J., 1978); D. de' Paoli, *Monteverdi* (Milan, 1979); J. Kurtzman, *Essays on the Monteverdi Mass and Vespers of 1610* (Houston, 1979); D. Stevens, ed. and translator, *The Letters of Claudio Monteverdi* (London, 1980); D. Arnold, *Monteverdi Church Music* (London, 1982).

Monteverdi, Giulio Cesare, Italian organist, composer, and writer on music, brother of **Claudio Monteverdi;** b. Cremona, (baptized, Jan. 31) 1573; d. Salò, Lake Garda, during the plague of 1630–31. In 1602 he entered the service of the Duke of Mantua, where his famous brother was maestro di cappella. He composed the music for the 4th intermedio in Guarini's play *L'Idropica,* which was performed for the wedding celebration of the Mantuan heir-apparent, Francesco Gonzaga, with Margaret of Savoy in 1608. His opera *Il rapimento di Proserpina* was given in Casale Monferrato in 1611. In 1620 he was named maestro di cappella of the Cathedral in Salò. He publ. a collection of 25 motets under the title *Affetti musici, ne quali si contengono motetti a 1–4 et 6 voci, per concertarli nel basso per l'organo* (Venice, 1620). A madrigal for 3 Voices and Continuo (1605) and 2 pieces in his brother's *Scherzi musicali* (Venice, 1607) are extant. He contributed to the collection *Scherzi musicali* an important *Dichiaratione,* in which he expounded at length the musical ideas of his brother and gave a vigorous reply to the attacks on Monteverdi by Artusi; an Eng. trans. is found in O. Strunk, *Source Readings in Music History* (N.Y., 1950).

BIBLIOGRAPHY: C. Sartori, "Giulio Cesare Monteverdi a Salò: Nuovi documenti inediti," *Nuova Rivista Italiana* (Nov.–Dec. 1967).

Montgomery, Kenneth, English conductor; b. Belfast, Northern Ireland, Oct. 28, 1943. He received his formal musical education at the Royal College of Music in London; studied conducting in Siena with Sergiu Celibidache, and in London with Sir Adrian Boult; also had instruction with John Pritchard and Hans Schmidt-Isserstedt. In 1964 he joined the conducting staff of the Glyndebourne Festival; in 1966 conducted at the Sadler's Wells Opera. In 1970 he became assistant conductor of the Western Orch. Society at Bournemouth; in 1972 its associate conductor; in 1973 was appointed music director of the Bournemouth Sinfonietta. He was music director of the Glyndebourne Touring Opera (1975–76). From 1976–80 he was principal conductor of the Netherlands Radio; in 1981 he became chief conductor of its Groot Omroep Koor.

Montgomery, Merle, American pianist and composer; b. Davidson, Okla., May 15, 1904. She studied at the Univ. of Oklahoma and at the Eastman School of Music; then went to Paris, where she took piano lessons with Isidor Philipp and composition with Nadia Boulanger at the American Cons. in Fontainebleau. Returning to the U.S., she became active as a music editor, compiler of educational textbooks, etc. Under the pen name of **Aline Campbell,** she publ. a number of characteristic piano pieces, often with exotic titles, such as *A Camel Ride.*

Montgomery, Wes, black American jazz guitarist; b. Indianapolis, March 6, 1925; d. there, June 15, 1968. He played in a local club before joining Lionel Hampton's band in 1948; returned to Indianapolis in 1950, and then established himself as a leading jazz artist in the Midwest; after 1959 he made many tours in the company of his brothers or other small jazz groups. He gained wide recognition with his first record album, *Movin' Wes* (1965), which was followed by *Bumpin'* (1965), *Goin' Out of My Head* (1966), and *A Day in the Life* (1967). He was regarded as one of the great jazz guitarists of his time; his unique style resulted from his use of the thumb as a plectrum.

Montoya, Carlos, popular flamenco guitarist; b. Madrid, Dec. 13, 1903. He began to play the guitar when he was 8; within a few years he performed professionally with various dance groups, and later gave solo recitals which attracted faithful aficionados; he traveled in the U.S., in South America, in Spain, in Japan, and in South Vietnam. He also improvised a number of attractive pieces, among them a *Suite flamenca* for Guitar and Orch. (1966); they were notated by helpers, since Montoya himself never learned to read music.

Montsalvatge, Bassols Xavier, Catalan composer; b. Gerona, March 11, 1911. He studied with Morera and Pahissa; in 1936 received the Pedrell prize for his *Pequeña suite burlesca* for Violin and Woodwinds. He wrote the musical fables *El gato con botas* (Barcelona, 1947) and *Viaje a la luna* (in Catalan; Barcelona, 1966); *Sinfonía mediterránea* (1949); a string quartet, *Cuarteto indiano* (1952); *Concerto breve* for Piano and Orch. (1956); *3 danzas inciertas* for 2 Violins (1956); *Cant espiritual* for Chorus and Orch. (1958); song cycle, *5 Invocaciones al crucificado* for Soprano and 12 Instruments (1969).

Moodie, Alma, Australian violinist; b. Brisbane, Sept. 12, 1900; d. Frankfurt, Germany, March 7, 1943. She studied with César Thomson in Brussels (1907–10); played at a concert as a child prodigy (with Max Reger); gave concerts in Germany, where she lived most of her life; taught at the State Academy of Music at Frankfurt. Her prestige as a musician was high in Germany; she performed many new works; Pfitzner wrote his Violin Concerto for her.

Moody (Manners), Fanny, English dramatic soprano; b. Redruth, Cornwall, Nov. 23, 1866; d. Dundrum, County Dublin, July 21, 1945. She studied singing with Mme. Sainton-Dolby; after several appearances in the provinces, she sang Micaela at Drury Lane in London (April 30, 1887). She married **Charles Manners,** the singer and impresario, on

July 5, 1890, and thereafter accompanied her husband on his tours. Together they founded the Moody-Manners Opera Co., in 1897. She was at her best in lyric roles; also appeared successfully in Wagnerian parts (Elsa, Elisabeth, etc.).

Moog (pronounced Mohg), **Robert A.,** American electric engineer, inventor of the Moog music synthesizer; b. Flushing, N.Y., May 23, 1934. He attended the Bronx High School of Science (1948–52), Queens College (1952–55), Columbia Univ. (1955–57) and Cornell Univ. (1957–65); received his B.S. in physics from Queens College (1957); B.S. in electrical engineering from Columbia Univ. (1957); Ph.D. in engineering physics from Cornell Univ. (1965). He established the R.A. Moog Co. in 1954 for the purpose of perfecting electronic musical instruments; introduced components of electronic music synthesizers in 1964; the company was incorporated in 1968, with its office at Trumansburg, N.Y. His synthesizer, which has colloquially been dubbed as "The Moog," rapidly acquired popularity. Although even pre-Moog electronic generators could synthesize tone colors, the Moog has achieved a high degree of vitality, which made it an artistic musical medium. The 1969 Moog has a manual of 5½ octaves, with the keys responding to the touch of the fingers, enabling the player to secure an extended spectrum of dynamic gradations. As the technology of the Moog continued to improve, there arose a whole generation of Moog virtuosos; among these, Walter Carlos earned enviable fame for his colorful renditions of Bach's keyboard music in a manner which was popularized as "switched-on Bach."

Moór, Emanuel, Hungarian pianist and inventor; b. Kecskemét, Feb. 19, 1863; d. Mont Pèlerin, near Montreux, Switzerland, Oct. 20, 1931. He studied in Budapest and Vienna; toured the U.S. from 1885 to 1887, as director of the Concerts Artistiques, for which he engaged Lilli Lehmann, Ovide Musin, and other celebrated artists, and also acted as their accompanist. He then lived in London, Lausanne, and Munich. He invented the Moór-Duplex piano, consisting of a double keyboard with a coupler between the two manuals (an octave apart). With the introduction of this piano a new technique was made possible, facilitating the playing of octaves, tenths, and even chromatic glissandos. Some piano manufacturers (Steinway, Bechstein, Bösendorfer) have put the Moór mechanism into their instruments. Moór's 2nd wife, **Winifred Christie** (b. Stirling, Feb. 26, 1882; d. London, Feb. 8, 1965), an English pianist, aided him in promoting the Moór keyboard, and gave many performances on it in Europe and America. She publ. (in collaboration with her husband) a manual of technical exercises for the Moór piano. Needless to say, Moór's invention sank into innocuous desuetude along with phonetic alphabets, Volapük, and similar elucubrations of earnest but impractical innovators. Moór was also a composer; his works include 5 operas: *La Pompadour* (Cologne, Feb. 22, 1902), *Andreas Hofer* (Cologne, Nov. 9, 1902), *Hochzeitsglocken* (Kassel, Aug. 2,

1908; in London, under the title *Wedding Bells,* Jan. 26, 1911), *Der Goldschmied von Paris,* and *Hertha;* 8 symphs. and other orch. works; 4 piano concertos; 3 violin concertos; 2 cello concertos; Triple Concerto for Violin, Cello, and Piano; Concerto for 2 Cellos and Orch.; 2 piano quintets; 2 string quartets; 2 piano trios; *Suite* for 4 Cellos; 12 violin sonatas; 7 cello sonatas; 3 piano sonatas; Hungarian Dances for Piano; Harp Sonata; Sonata for 4 Harps; a great number of songs.

BIBLIOGRAPHY: L. Deutsch, *Die Technik der Doppelklaviatur Moór* (Leipzig, 1932); W. Reich, "Das Moórsche Doppelklavier," *Die Musik,* XXIV/4; D. Tovey, "The Pianoforte of Emanuel Moór," *Music & Letters* (Jan. 1922); Max Pirani, *Emanuel Moór* (London, 1959; with a preface by Pablo Casals).

Moor, Karel, Czech composer; b. Bělohrad, Dec. 26, 1873; d. Prague, March 30, 1945. His real name was **Mohr.** He studied at the Cons. of Prague; then went for further study to Vienna. From 1900 to 1923 he was active as a theatrical director and conductor in Bohemia and Serbia; then lived mainly in Prague. He achieved his first success as a composer with the operetta *Pan profesor v pekle (Professor in Hell),* produced in Brno in 1908; his other operas, *Viy,* after Gogol's fantastic tale (Prague, July 14, 1903), and *Hjoerdis* (Prague, Oct. 22, 1905), were also successful. A facile writer, he publ. an autobiography in the form of a novel (Prague, 1906), a vol. of reminiscences (Pilsen, 1917) and a semi-fictional book, *V dlani osudu (In the Hand of Destiny;* publ. posthumously in 1947).

Moore, Carman, American composer; b. Lorain, Ohio, Oct. 8, 1936. He studied with Hall Overton and Vincent Persichetti in N.Y.; later took lessons with Stefan Wolpe and Luciano Berio, who inculcated in him the most advanced, though diverse, methods of ultramodern composition. In 1968 he organized, with a few colleagues, the Society of Black Composers. In 1976 he received a commission from the N.Y. Phil. to compose a piece derived from the music of his racial background; the piece, entitled *Wild Fires and Field Songs,* was performed on Jan. 24, 1973. Another piece by Moore that attracted attention was *Museum Piece,* performed in N.Y. on April 22, 1975.

Moore, Douglas Stuart, distinguished American composer and music educator; b. Cutchogue, N.Y., Aug. 10, 1893; d. Greenport, Long Island, N.Y., July 25, 1969. He studied at Yale Univ. with D.S. Smith and Horatio Parker; wrote several univ. songs, among them the football song *Good Night, Harvard,* which became popular among Yale students; after obtaining his B.A. (1915) and Mus.Bac. (1917), he joined the U.S. Navy; following the Armistice of 1918, he attended classes of Vincent d'Indy at the Schola Cantorum in Paris and also took lessons in organ playing with Tournemire and in composition with Nadia Boulanger, and with Ernest Bloch in Cleveland. Returning to the U.S., he served as organist at the Cleveland Museum of Art (1921–23) and at Adelbert College, Western Reserve Univ. (1923–25); in 1925 he received a Pulitzer traveling scholarship in music and spent a year in Europe. In 1926 he was appointed to the faculty of Columbia Univ.; in 1940 he succeeded Daniel Gregory Mason as the head of the music dept. there; many American composers were his students. He retired in 1962. A fine musical craftsman, Moore applied his technical mastery to American subjects in his operas and symph. works. He achieved popular success with his "folk opera" *Ballad of Baby Doe,* dealing with the true story of an actual historic figure during the era of intensive silver mining; the opera was staged on July 7, 1956, at Central City, Colo., where its action took place; the opera had numerous revivals in America, and also in Europe. His other operas were *The Headless Horseman* (1936); *The Devil and Daniel Webster* (N.Y., May 18, 1939); *White Wings,* chamber opera (Hartford, Feb. 2, 1949); *The Emperor's New Clothes* (N.Y., Feb. 19, 1949); *Giants in the Earth* (N.Y., March 28, 1951; awarded the Pulitzer Prize); *Gallantry, a "Soap Opera"* (N.Y., March 15, 1958); *The Wings of the Dove* (N.Y., Oct. 12, 1961); *The Greenfield Christmas Tree* (Baltimore, Dec. 8, 1962); and *Carrie Nation,* to the story of a notorious temperance fighter (Lawrence, Kans., April 28, 1966); he wrote for orch. *Pageant of P.T. Barnum* (Cleveland, April 15, 1926); *Moby Dick,* symph. poem (1927); *A Symphony of Autumn* (1930); *Overture on an American Tune* (N.Y., Dec. 11, 1932); *Village Music* (N.Y., Dec. 18, 1941); *In Memoriam* (Rochester, N.Y., April 27, 1944); Symph. in A (Paris, May 5, 1946; received honorable mention by the N.Y. Music Critics' Circle, 1947); *Farm Journal* for Chamber Orch. (N.Y., Jan. 19, 1948); Violin Sonata (1929); String Quartet (1933); Wind Quintet (1942); Quintet for Clarinet, 2 Violins, Viola, and Cello (1946); Piano Trio (1953). He publ. *Listening to Music* (N.Y., 1932; revised 1963) and *From Madrigal to Modern Music: A Guide to Musical Styles* (N.Y., 1942).

Moore, Earl Vincent, American music educator; b. Lansing, Mich., Sept. 27, 1890. He studied at the Univ. of Michigan (B.A., 1912; M.A., 1915) and later in Europe with Widor, Holst, Boult, Heger, and others. He was an organist and teacher of theory at the Univ. of Michigan (1914–23); then was director of its School of Music, while continuing to teach (he was a prof. there from 1923–46); from 1946 to 1960 he was dean of the School of Music. In 1939–40 he was national director of the WPA Music Project; in 1960–70 was chairman of the music dept. at the Univ. of Houston. He served at various times as a consultant to the War Dept. and to univs.; in 1959–72 was a member of the E.S. Coolidge Foundation Committee in the Library of Congress; was a founder-member of the National Assoc. of Schools of Music and its president in 1936–38. He composed parts of the Michigan Union Operas and other pieces, but is famous at Michigan Univ. as composer of the football song *Varsity.*

Moore, Gerald, English pianist and preeminent accompanist; b. Watford, July 30, 1899. He studied at the Univ. of Toronto. After a brief career as a concert pianist, he devoted himself almost exclusively to the art of accompaniment, in which he attained the foremost rank and a well-nigh legendary fame. As a witty account of his experiences at the piano he publ. a sort of autobiography, *The Unashamed Accompanist* (London, 1943; revised ed., 1957), followed by an even more unzipped opus, *Am I Too Loud?*(N.Y., 1962), and concluding with a somewhat nostalgic vol., *Farewell Recital: Further Memoirs* (London, 1978), and a rip-roaring sequel, *Furthermoore [sic]: Interludes in an Accompanist's Life* (London, 1983). Of a purely didactic nature are his books *Singer and Accompanist: The Performance of 50 Songs* (London, 1953), *The Schubert Song Cycles* (London, 1975), and *"Poet's Lore" and Other Schumann Cycles and Songs* (London, 1984).

Moore, Grace, American soprano; b. Slabtown, Tenn., Dec. 5, 1898; d. Copenhagen, Jan. 26, 1947. She studied at the Wilson Greene School of Music in Chevy Chase, Md., and with Marafioti; first appeared in musical comedy in N.Y. (1921–26); then studied in France. Upon returning to America, she made her operatic debut as Mimi at the Metropolitan Opera House (Feb. 7, 1928), and sang there off and on until 1946; made successful appearances also at the Paris Opéra-Comique (1928); at Covent Garden, London (1935); and at other European centers; also sang with the Chicago City Opera (1937); appeared in several motion pictures. She was killed in an airplane accident, on a flight from Copenhagen to Stockholm. She publ. an autobiography, *You're Only Human Once* (1944).

Moore, John Weeks, pioneer American musicologist and lexicographer; b. Andover, N.H., April 11, 1807; d. Manchester, N.H., March 23, 1889. He was a newspaper publisher and editor at Bellows Falls, Vt., where he publ. the *Bellows Falls Gazette* (1838–55); also was for a time editor of the musical journals *World of Music* and *Musical Library.* His magnum opus is the *Complete Encyclopedia of Music, Elementary, Technical, Historical, Biographical, Vocal, and Instrumental* (Boston, 1854; 1004 pages; Appendix, 1875; also the *Dictionary of Musical Information* (1876); he publ. the collections *Sacred Minstrel* (1842), *American Collection of Instrumental Music* (1856), and *The Star Collection of Instrumental Music* (1858); also *Puritanism of Music in America* (18 numbers), *Musical Record* (5 vols.; 1867–70), *Song and Song Writers of America* (200 numbers; 1859–80), etc.

BIBLIOGRAPHY: *Dictionary of American Biography.*

Moore, Mary Carr, American composer; b. Memphis, Tenn., Aug. 6, 1873; d. Inglewood, Calif., Jan. 9, 1957. Her father was a cavalry officer in the U.S. Army, who sang; her mother authored several theater dramas; her uncle, **John Harraden Pratt,** was an organist. The family moved to California in 1885. Mary Moore studied theory with her uncle, and singing with H.B. Pasmore. In 1894 she wrote, to her own libretto, an operetta, *The Oracle,* which was produced in San Francisco in 1894, and she sang the leading part in it. In 1926 she settled in Los Angeles, where she taught at a private piano school. She dedicated herself to the composition of operas. On March 27, 1922, she herself conducted a performance in San Francisco of her "Indian Intermezzo" in one act, *The Flaming Arrow,* to a libretto by her mother. There followed a one-act musical tragedy, *The Leper,* never produced. In 1912 she wrote a "grand opera," *Narcissa,* to a book by her mother, dealing with missionaries and Indians; it was produced in Seattle on April 22, 1912, and revived in San Francisco, when Mary Moore conducted 9 performances of it during the week of Sept. 7, 1925. The next opera was *Rizzio,* based on the tragic fate of Mary Stuart's Italian lute instructor; it was produced in Los Angeles, on May 26, 1932. Her last opera to enjoy a production was *Los Rubios,* depicting the early history of Los Angeles; it was produced in Los Angeles on Sept. 10, 1931. Mary Moore also wrote a Piano Concerto, 2 string quartets, a String Trio, 3 piano trios, 67 piano pieces, 54 choruses, and 220 songs. She made no pretense at musical sophistication in her productions. Her integrity was total.

BIBLIOGRAPHY: E.E. Hipsher, *American Opera and Its Composers* (Philadelphia, 1934; pp. 328–36).

Moore, Melba, black American singer of popular music and actress; b. New York, Oct. 29, 1945. She studied at Newark's Arts High School and at the Montclair, N.J., State Teachers College; subsequently taught school for several years before setting out on a professional singing career. She served as a vocalist with the orch. of Babs Gonzales (1964); then sang in Broadway musicals, including the highly successful *Hair* (1968–70). She also appeared on the stage as a dramatic actress. Among her recording albums, the eponymous *Peach Melba* attracted attention.

BIBLIOGRAPHY: *Current Biography* (Jan. 1973).

Moore, Thomas, famous Irish poet, ballad singer, and song composer; b. Dublin, May 28, 1779; d. near Devizes, Wilts, Feb. 25, 1852. He had no regular musical training, but learned to play the piano with the aid of the organist William Warren. He was in London from 1799 to 1803; then received a position as a government functionary in Bermuda; however, he stayed there only a few months; then returned to London by way of the U.S. and Canada. In London he became extremely popular as a ballad singer in the houses of the aristocracy; in 1807 he publ. a volume of poetry, *Irish Melodies,* set to music by Sir John Stevenson. In 1817 he issued his celebrated poem *Lalla Rookh.* An ardent Irish nationalist, he played an important role in the creation and revival of Irish poetry and music. Among his own melodies are *Love thee, dearest, When midst the gay, One dear smile,* and *The Canadian Boat-Song.* He freely borrowed his musical materials from popular Irish tunes and in some cases modified them sufficiently to produce apparently new songs. He also composed short concerted vocal pieces; the terzetto *O lady fair* and the 3-part glee *The Watchman* won wide popularity. In 1895 Sir Charles Stanford publ. *The Irish Melodies of Thomas Moore: The Original Airs Restored.*

BIBLIOGRAPHY: S. Gwynn, *Thomas Moore* (London, 1905); W. Trench, *Tom Moore* (Dublin, 1934); S. MacCall, *Thomas Moore* (Dublin, 1936); *Dictionary of National Biography.*

Moos, Paul, German writer on esthetics; b. Buchau, March 22, 1863; d. Raeren, Belgium, Feb. 27, 1952. He studied with Thuille, Rheinberger, and others in Munich; publ. *Moderne Musikästhetik in Deutschland* (1902; 2nd ed., 1922, entitled *Die Philosophie der Musik von Kant bis Eduard von Hartmann*); *Richard Wagner als Ästhetiker* (1906); *Die psychologische Ästhetik in Deutschland* (1919); *Die deutsche Ästhetik der Gegenwart* (vol. I, 1929; vol. II, 1931); also contributed many valuable essays to German music magazines.

Mooser, Aloys, Swiss organ manufacturer; b. Niederhelfenschwyl, June 27, 1770; d. Fribourg, Dec. 19, 1839. He studied with his father, an Alsatian organist; attained fame as one of the greatest masters in organ building; the quality of the "vox humana" in his organs was particularly admired.

Mooser, R(obert) Aloys, Swiss writer on music; great-grandson of the preceding; b. Geneva, Sept. 20, 1876; d. there, Aug. 24, 1969. His mother was a Russian, and he acquired the knowledge of the Russian language in childhood. He studied with his father and Otto Barblan in Geneva. In 1896 he went to St. Petersburg, where he served as organist at the French church, wrote music criticism for the *Journal de St. Petersbourg,* and made an extensive study of Russian music in the archives. He took courses with Balakirev and Rimsky-Korsakov. In 1909 he returned to Geneva and became active as a music critic there. His reviews were collected in the vols.: *Regards sur la musique contemporaine: 1921–46* (Lausanne, 1946); *Panorama de la musique contemporaine: 1947–1953* (Geneva, 1953); *Aspects de la musique contemporaine: 1953–1957* (Geneva, 1957) *Visage de la musique contemporaine, 1957–1961* (Paris, 1962). He wrote the following books on Russian music: *L'Opéra-comique français en Russie au XVIIIᵉ siècle* (Geneva, 1932; 2nd ed., 1954); *Violonistes-compositeurs italiens en Russie au XVIIIᵉ siècle* (Milan, 1938–50); *Opéras, intermezzos, ballets, cantates, oratorios joués en Russie durant le XVIIIᵉ siècle* (Geneva, 1945; 2nd ed., 1955); *Annales de la musique et des musiciens en Russie au XVIIIᵉ siècle* (of prime importance for new, detailed, and accurate documentation; 3 vols.; Geneva, 1948–51); also wrote *Deux violonistes genevois, G. Fritz et Chr. Haensel* (Geneva, 1968).

Morales, Cristóbal de, eminent Spanish composer; b. Seville, c.1500; d. Málaga, 1553 (between Sept. 4 and Oct. 7). He was a pupil of Fernández de Castilleja, who was chapel master at the Seville Cathedral. From 1526 to 1528, Morales was choirmaster of the Avila Cathedral; then was in Plasencia until 1531. In 1535 he entered the papal choir in Rome (until 1540, and again in 1541–45); he composed much sacred music during this period. After a brief journey to Spain, he returned to Rome and increased his productivity as a composer; he also traveled in the retinue of the Pope to various towns in Italy. From 1545 to 1547 he was choirmaster at the cathedral of Toledo; in 1551 he obtained a similar post at Málaga, where he remained until his death. Morales was one of the outstanding masters of the polyphonic style; he was greatly esteemed by contemporary musicians; Bermudo described him as "the light of Spain in music." 2 books of masses, many motets, Magnificats, and Lamentations were publ. during his lifetime. Modern reprints are in Eslava's *Lira sacro-hispana;* Pedrell's *Hispaniae Schola musica sacra;* Martini's *Esemplare;* Rochlitz's *Sammlung;* etc. The *Opera omnia* are appearing in Monumentos de la Música Española, vols. 11, 13, 15, 17, 20, 21, 24, 34 (Madrid, 1952–).

BIBLIOGRAPHY: H. Collet, *Le Mysticisme musical espagnol au XVIᵉ siècle* (Paris, 1913); R. Mitjana, *Cristóbal de Morales, Estudio critico-biográfico* (Madrid, 1920); F.R. Piqueras, *Música y músicos toledanos* (Toledo, 1922); J.B. Trend, "Cristóbal Morales," *Music & Letters* (Jan. 1925); Elústiza and Castrillo Hernández, *Antología musical* (Barcelona, 1933); R. Stevenson, "Cristóbal Morales, A Fourth-Centenary Biography," *Journal of the American Musicological Society* (Spring 1953); R. Stevenson, "The Earliest Polyphonic Imprint in South America," *Notes* (March 1967); H. Anglès, "Problemas que presenta la nueva edición de las obras de Morales y de Victoria," in J. Robijns et al., eds., *Renaissance-Muziek* (Leuven, 1969); S. Rubio, *Cristóbal de Morales: Estudio critico de su polifonia* (El Escorial, 1969).

Morales, Melesio, Mexican composer; b. Mexico City, Dec. 4, 1838; d. San Petro de los Pinos, May 12, 1908. He began to compose salon music for piano and soon acquired sufficient technique to write for the stage; produced 2 operas, *Romeo y Julieta* (Mexico City, Jan. 27, 1863) and *Ildegonda* (Mexico City, Jan. 27, 1866); then went to France and Italy for additional study. Returning to Mexico after 4 years abroad, he presented 2 more operas: *Gino Corsini* (Mexico City, July 14, 1877) and *Cleopatra* (Mexico City, Nov. 14, 1891). Despite his passionate advocacy of national music, he followed conventional Italian models in his own works.

Morales, Olallo Juan Magnus, writer and composer; b. (of a Spanish father and Swedish mother) Almería, Spain, Oct. 15, 1874; d. Tällberg, April 29, 1957. Taken to Sweden as a child, he received his education there, first at Göteborg, then at the Stockholm Cons. with W. Stenhammar and others (1891–99), and in Berlin with H. Urban (composition) and Teresa Carreño (piano). In 1901 he returned to Sweden; was conductor of the Göteborg Symph. Orch.

(1905–9). From 1909 he lived in Stockholm; was a prof. at the Stockholm Cons. (1917–39); was secretary of the Academy of Music (1918–40). With T. Norlind, he compiled a history of the Royal Academy of Music on its sesquicentennial (1921); also publ. a handbook of conducting (Stockholm, 1946). His works include a Symph.; several overtures; Violin Concerto (1943); String Quartet; Piano Sonata; *Balada andaluza* for Piano (1946); *Nostalgia* and other character pieces for Piano; choral works; songs.

Moralt, Joseph, eldest brother and first violin in a famous Munich string quartet of brothers; b. Schwetzingen, Aug. 5, 1775; d. Munich, Nov. 13, 1855. **Johann Baptist Moralt,** the 2nd violin (b. Mannheim, March 10, 1777; d. Munich, Oct. 7, 1825), wrote symphs. and string quartets; **Philipp Moralt,** the cellist (b. Munich, Dec. 29, 1780; d. there, Jan. 10, 1830), also played in the Munich municipal band; **Georg Moralt,** the viola player (b. Munich, 1781; d. there, 1818), was a member of the quartet until his death.

Moralt, Rudolf, German conductor; b. Munich, Feb. 26, 1902; d. Vienna, Dec. 16, 1958. He was educated at the Academy of Music in Munich. He then conducted opera in Kaiserslautern (1923–28, 1932–34), Braunschweig (1934–36), and Graz (1937–40). In 1940 he became one of the principal conductors of the Vienna State Opera, continuing there until his death.

Moran, Robert Leonard, American composer of the avant-garde; b. Denver, Jan. 8, 1937. He studied piano; went to Vienna in 1958, where he took lessons in 12-tone composition with Hans Erich Apostel. Returning to America, he enrolled at Mills College, where he attended seminars of Luciano Berio and Darius Milhaud (M.A., 1963). At the same time he painted in the manner of Abstract Expressionism. In 1959 he toured Sweden as a pianist in programs of hyper-modernistic compositions. His music is written in graphic notation, and is animated by surrealistic imagination.

WORKS: *Eclectic Boogies* for 13 Percussionists (N.Y., Jan. 14, 1965); *Interiors* for Any Instrumental Ensemble (San Francisco, April 12, 1965); *Within the Momentary Illumination* for 2 Harps, Electric Guitar, Timpani, and Brass (Tokyo, Dec. 1, 1965); *L'Après-midi du Dracoula* for Any Group of Instruments capable of producing Any Kind of Sound (1966); *Elegant Journey with Stopping Points of Interest* for Orch. (1967); *Smell Piece for Mills College* for Frying Pans and Foods (Mills College, Nov. 20, 1967; originally intended to produce a conflagration sufficiently thermal to burn down the college); *Scream Kiss No. 1* for Harpsichord and Stereophonic Tape (1968); *Let's Build a Nut House,* opera in memory of Paul Hindemith (San Jose, April 19, 1969); *Titus* for Amplified Automobile and Players (1969); *39 Minutes for 39 Autos,* environmental work for 30 Skyscrapers, 39 Auto Horns, Moog Synthesizer, and Players, employing 100,000 Persons, directed from atop Twin Peaks in San Francisco, and making use of Autos, Airplanes, Searchlights and local Radio and Television Stations (San Francisco, Aug. 20, 1969); *Silver and the Circle of Messages* for Chamber Orch. (San Francisco, April 24, 1970); *Hallelujah,* "a joyous phenomenon with fanfares" for Marching Bands, Drum and Bugle Corps, Church Choirs, Organs, Carillons, Rock-'n'-Roll Bands, Television Stations, Automobile Horns, and any other sounding implements, commissioned by Lehigh Univ. for the city of Bethlehem, Pa., with the participation of its entire population of 72,320 inhabitants (staged in Bethlehem, April 23, 1971); *Divertissement No. 3,* a "street opera" (BBC Television, London, 1971); *Evening Psalm of Dr. Dracula* for Prepared Piano and Tape (1973).

Moran-Olden, Fanny, German soprano; b. Oldenburg, Sept. 28, 1855; d. Berlin, Feb. 13, 1905. She took lessons with Götze in Dresden, where she made her debut as **Fanny Olden** (her real name was **Tappenhorn**) in the role of Norma (1877); she then was at the Frankfurt Opera (1878–83), at the Leipzig City Theater (1884–91), and at the Munich Opera (1892–93); she sang in N.Y. during the 1888–89 season. She was twice married: in 1879 to the tenor **Karl Moran,** and in 1897 to **Bertram,** court singer in Munich.

Moravec, Ivan, Czech pianist; b. Prague, Nov. 9, 1930. His father, a lawyer, played piano and sang, which created a musical atmosphere at his home. He entered the Prague Cons., graduating in 1948 with first prize in piano playing; but his promising career was impeded by a spinal ailment resulting from a fall while ice-skating in his childhood, and it was not until he had a long period of electrotherapy and application of hot compresses that he was able to resume piano playing; in the meantime, he whiled away his enforced leisure by painting impressionist canvasses. But when he recuperated, he struck back with a vengeance, practicing from dawn to dusk. He concertized in Italy, Poland, and Hungary. On Jan. 30, 1964, he made his American debut as soloist with the Cleveland Orch. He did not play again in the U.S. until Oct. 24, 1982, when he gave a solo recital at Carnegie Hall in N.Y.

Morawetz, Oskar, significant Czech-born Canadian composer; b. Svetla, Jan. 17, 1917. He studied with Jaroslav Křička at Prague Univ. (1933–36); after the invasion of Czechoslovakia by the Nazis in 1939 he went to Paris; then proceeded to Canada by way of Italy and the Dominican Republic; entered the Univ. of Toronto (B.M., 1944; D.Mus., 1953). He taught at the Royal Cons. of Music in Toronto (1946–51) and from 1951 at the Univ. of Toronto. His music is Classical in format, Romantic in spirit, impressionistic in coloring, and modernistic in harmonic usage.
WORKS: *Carnival Overture* (1946; Montreal, July 1, 1947); *Divertimento* for Strings (1948); 2 symphs.: No. 1 (1951–53; first complete perf. Toronto, March 5, 1956; each movement is titled for separate perf.— *Fantasy, Dirge,* and *Scherzo*) and No. 2 (1959; Toronto, Feb. 2, 1960); *Overture to a Fairy Tale* (1956; Halifax, Feb. 8, 1957); *Capriccio* for Orch. (1960); Piano concerto (1962; Montreal, April 23, 1963); Sinfonietta for Strings (1963, revised 1968); *Passacaglia on a Bach Chorale* for Orch. (1964; Toronto, Nov. 24, 1964); Sinfonietta for Winds and Percussion (1965; Montreal, Feb. 22, 1966); Concerto for Brass Quintet and Orch. (Toronto, March 28, 1968); *Memorial to Martin Luther King,* elegy for Cello and Orch. (1968; the last movement employs the popular spiritual *Free at Last*); *Reflections after a Tragedy* for Orch. (1969); *Symphonic Intermezzo* (1971); *Improvisation* for Cello and Orch. (1973); Harp Concerto (1976); *Keep Us Free* for Chorus and Orch. (1951); *From the Diary of Anne Frank* for Soprano or Mezzo-soprano, and Orch. (1970; Toronto, May 26, 1970); *A Child's Garden of Verses,* after R.L. Stevenson, for Mezzo-soprano or Alto or Baritone, and Orch. (Toronto, Feb. 10, 1973); 3 string quartets (1944, 1952–55, 1959); Duo for Violin and Piano (1947); Violin Sonata (1956); Trio for Flute, Oboe, and Harpsichord or Piano (1960); *2 Fantasies* for Cello and Piano (1962, revised 1970); *2 Preludes* for Violin and Piano (1965); piano works, including *Sonata tragica* (1945), *Scherzo* (1947), *Fantasy in D minor* (1948), *Tarantelle* (1949), *Ballade* (1950), *Fantasy on a Hebrew Theme* (1951), *Scherzino* (1953), *Fantasy, Elegy and Toccata* (1958), *10 Preludes* (1966), *Suite* (1968), and *Fantasy* (1973); many songs, some with orch., all listed in *Contemporary Canadian Composers* (Toronto, 1975; pp. 156–160).

Moreau, Jean-Baptiste, French composer; b. Angers, 1656; d. Paris, Aug. 24, 1733. He was a chorister at the Cathedral of Angers; then was choirmaster at the Cathedral of Langres. After a year in Dijon, he went to Paris in 1686; was introduced at the French court by the Dauphine, and was commissioned by Louis XIV to write several divertissements, among them *Les Bergers de Marly* (1687). He won great success with his musical interludes (recitatives and choruses) for Racine's *Esther* (1698) and *Athalie* (1691), performed at the royal school of St.-Cyr, where Moreau was maître de chapelle; he also wrote music for Racine's *Cantiques spirituels,* for performance at St.-Cyr. His success at court was marred by his dissolute habits; however, he was greatly esteemed as a teacher of singing and composition; among his pupils were Montéclair, J.F. Dandrieu, Clérambault, and the singers Louise Couperin and his own daughter Marie-Claude Moreau. The music to *Esther* and *Athalie,* and the *Cantiques spirituels,* were publ. in the music supplement to P. Mesnard's *Œuvres de J. Racine* (Paris, 1873).
BIBLIOGRAPHY: Th. Lavallée, *Historire de la maison royale de St.-Cyr* (Paris, 1856); A. Taphanel, *Le Théâtre de St.-Cyr* (Paris, 1876); J. Tiersot, "Les Chœurs d'Esther et d'Athalie de Moreau," *Revue Musicale* (Jan. 1903); Kathi Meyer, *Der chorische Gesang der Frauen* (Leipzig, 1917); N. Demuth, "A Musical Backwater," *Musical Quarterly* (Oct. 1954).

Moreau, Léon, French composer; b. Brest, July 13, 1870; d. Paris, April 11, 1946. He studied at the Paris

Cons.; won the Grand Prix de Rome in 1899. Among his works are the operas *Myriade* and *Pierrot décoré;* the symph. poems *Sur la mer lointaine* and *Dionysos;* a Piano Concerto; many songs.

Moreira, Antonio, Portuguese composer; b. Abrantes, 1758; d. Lisbon, Nov. 21, 1819. He studied with João de Sousa Carvalho at the Lisbon Seminario Patriarcal; became his assistant in 1775; in 1787 was appointed mestre de capela of the royal chapel; then served as music director of the Italian Opera Theater in Lisbon (1790), and later was director at the Teatro San Carlos there (1793–1800). His opera *Il Disertore* was given at Turin in 1800.

Morel, Auguste-François, French composer; b. Marseilles, Nov. 26, 1809; d. Paris, April 22, 1881. He lived in Paris from 1836 to 1850; then returned to Marseilles, and became director of the Cons. there; produced a grand opera, *Le Jugement de Dieu* (1860); wrote a great deal of chamber music of excellent quality, for which he won the Prix Chartier twice; also 2 symphs. and a number of overtures.

Morel, François d'Assise, Canadian composer; b. Montreal, March 14, 1926. He studied piano with Trudel and composition with Claude Champagne, Isabelle Delorme, and Germaine Malépart at the Quebec Provincial Cons. in Montreal (1944–53); in 1958 was a founding member (along with Joachim, Garant, and Geanne Landry) of Musique de Notre Temps, an organization specializing in performances of new music; then joined the faculty of the Institut Nazareth in Montreal. His music parallels the esthetic fashions of the modern times, from Debussyan coloristic imagism to motoric neo-Classicism to the organized sound of Varèse to the stern serialism of the cosmopolitan avant-garde.
WORKS: *Esquisse* for Orch. (1946–47; Montreal, Oct. 7, 1947); *Diptyque* for 23 Instruments (1948, revised 1956; originally titled *Suite pour petit orchestre*); *Rondo Enfantin* for Piano (1949); *4 chants japonais* for Soprano and Piano (1949); 2 string quartets (1952, 1962–63); *Antiphonie* for Orch. (1953; N.Y., Oct. 16, 1953; Stokowski conducting); *2 études de sonorité* for Piano (1952–54); *Cassation* for Woodwind Septet (1954); *Les Rivages perdus* for Soprano or Tenor, and Piano (1954); *Litanies* for Winds, Brass, Harp, Piano, Celesta, and Percussion (1956, revised 1970); *Spirale* for Winds, Brass, Harp, Celesta, and Percussion (1956); *Symphonie* for Brass and Percussion (1956); *Intrada* for Chorus and Orch. (1957); *Rythomologue* for 8 Percussionists (1957, revised 1970); *Rituel de l'espace,* symph. poem (1956–58; Montreal, April 6, 1960); *Beatnik* for Jazz Band (1959); *Boréal* for Orch. (1959; Montreal, April 26, 1960); *Le Mythe de la roche percée* for Double Woodwinds and Percussion (1960–61; Pittsburgh, June 10, 1961); Brass Quintet (1962); *L'Etoile noire* for Orch. (Montreal, March 13, 1962); *Requiem* for Winds (1963); Sinfonia for Jazz Band (1963); *Trajectoire* for Orch. (1967; Montreal, April 20, 1967); *Neumes d'espace et Reliefs* for Orch. (1967; Edmonton, Oct. 29, 1967); *Prismes-Anamorphoses* for Winds, Percussion, Harp, Piano, and Celesta (1967); *Départs* for 14 Solo Strings, Harp, Guitar, and 2 Percussionists (Montreal, March 17, 1969); *Iikkii (Froidure)* for 18 Solo Instruments (Montreal, Feb. 3, 1972); *Radiance* for Small Orch. (1970–72); *Me duele España,* variations for Solo Guitar (1975).

Morel, Jean, French conductor; b. Abbeville, Jan. 10, 1903; d. New York, April 14, 1975. He studied piano with Isidor Philipp, music theory with Noel Gallon, music theory with Maurice Emmanuel, opera conducting with Reynaldo Hahn, and composition with Pierné; subsequently taught at the American Cons. in Fontainebleau (1921–36). At the outbreak of war in 1939 he emigrated to the U.S.; taught at Brooklyn College (1940–43); then conducted opera in Brazil and Mexico. In 1949 he was appointed to the faculty of the Juilliard School of Music in N.Y., and became conductor of the Juilliard Orch. He also conducted at the Metropolitan Opera House in 1956–1962, 1967–68, and 1969–71. He gained wide recognition as a teacher of conducting; retired from Juilliard in 1971.

Morell, Barry, American tenor; b. New York, March 30, 1927. He studied voice in N.Y.; made his operatic debut with the N.Y. City Opera in 1956. On Nov. 1, 1958, he appeared at the Metropolitan Opera in the role of Pinkerton in *Madama Butterfly.* Subsequently he toured in Europe, as a guest artist with the Städtische Oper in Berlin, at the Vienna State Opera, and at Covent Garden in London.

Morelli, Carlo (real name, **Carlos Zanelli**), Chilean baritone; b. Valparaiso, Dec. 25, 1897; d. Mexico City, May 12, 1970. He studied voice in Bologna with Angelo Queize, and in Florence with Leopoldo Mugnone. He sang at La Scala, Milan; toured South America (1925–31); made his first U.S. appearence with the Chicago City Opera in 1932; made his debut at the Metropolitan Opera on Dec. 21, 1935, as Marcello in *La Bohème;* remained there until 1940; then sang with the San Carlo Opera at the City Center, N.Y. (1940–49). In 1949 he settled in Mexico.

Morelli, Giacomo, Italian librarian and music scholar; b. Venice, April 14, 1745; d. there, May 5, 1819. He was librarian at San Marco; discovered fragments of the *Art of Rhythm* by Aristoxenos, and publ. them in 1785.

Morelli, Giuseppe, Italian conductor; b. Rome, Aug. 2, 1907. He served as a choirboy in St. Peter's in Rome and studied at the Santa Cecilia Cons., obtaining his diploma in composition in 1930. He subsequently took a course in conducting with Bernardino Molinari; rapidly earned a reputation as a fine opera conductor; in Italy he has had engagements with the Rome Opera and in Naples, Palermo, Parma, Bologna, and Venice. He also appeared as an opera conductor in Paris, Madrid, Vienna, Brussels, Amsterdam, West Berlin, Scandinavia, and Japan. He made a successful American debut as conductor at the N.Y. City Opera in 1970.

Morelot, Stéphen, French scholar; authority on sacred music; b. Dijon, Jan. 12, 1820; d. Beaumont, Oct. 7, 1899. He was dean of the faculty of jurisprudence at Dijon Univ.; was co-editor (from 1845) of the *Revue de la musique religieuse, populaire et classique;* he went to Italy in 1847 to study church music. He publ. numerous essays on the subject, among them *De la musique au XVe siècle . . .* (1856), *Eléments de l'harmonie appliqués à l'accompagnement du plain-chant, d'après les traditions des anciennes écoles* (1861). His *Manuel de Psalmodie en fauxbourdons à 4 voix . . .* (1855) is an ingenious attempt to revive the ancient style of harmonization.

Morena (real name, **Meyer**), **Berta,** German soprano; b. Mannheim, Jan. 27, 1878; d. Rottach-Egern, Oct. 7, 1952. Her buxom beauty attracted the attention of the famous painter von Lenbach; at his behest, she was engaged (after brief training under Sophie Röhr-Brajnin in Munich) to sing Agathe in *Der Freischütz* at the Munich Opera (1898), and was immediately successful. She remained at the Munich Opera until 1923; made her American debut with the Metropolitan Opera, N.Y., as Sieglinde (March 4, 1908), and returned to sing in 1910–12 and 1924–25. Her talent as an actress greatly helped her in her career; she was regarded in Germany as one of the most intelligent and musicianly singers; she excelled particularly in the Wagnerian parts (Elisabeth, Elsa, Eva, Isolde, the three Brünnhildes, etc.).

BIBLIOGRAPHY: A. Vogl, *Berta Morena und ihre Kunst* (Munich,1919).

Moreno, Segundo Luis, Ecuadorian composer; b. Cotacachi, Aug. 3, 1882; d. Quito, Nov. 18, 1972. He played the clarinet in a civil band in Quito. He studied at the Quito Cons.; then was active as a military band leader in various localities in Ecuador; in 1937, took over the newly established Cons. Nacional de Música in Cuenca; later was director of the Cons. of Guayaquil. He composed mostly for military band; many of his pieces celebrate various patriotic events in Ecuador, as the cantata *La emancipación* (1920); the overture *9 de Julio* (1925), and various pieces on native motifs, among them *3 suites ecuatorianas* for Orch. (1921, 1944, 1945). He publ. the valuable ethnomusicological treatises *Música y danzas del Ecuador* (1949, in Spanish and Eng.) and *La música de los Incas* (1957).

Morera, Enrique, Spanish composer; b. Barcelona, May 22, 1865; d. there, March 11, 1942. As a child, he was taken to Argentina, and studied in Buenos Aires; then took courses at the Cons. of Brussels. Returning to Barcelona, he studied piano with Albéniz and harmony with Felipe Pedrell. In 1896 he founded the choral society Catalunya Nova, which he conducted for several years; taught at the Escuela Municipal de Música in Barcelona (1910–28). He was an ardent propagandist of Catalan music,

and wrote a number of songs to Catalan words; also collected 193 melodies of popular origin. His opera *Emporium,* originally to a Catalan text, was performed first in Italian (Barcelona, Jan. 20, 1906); he wrote more than 50 other stage works (lyric comedies, zarzuelas, operettas, intermezzos, etc.); several symph. poems (*Atlántida, Traidoría,* etc.); a Cello Concerto; some chamber music; a set of 5 sardanas (national dances of Catalonia) for Piano, etc.

BIBLIOGRAPHY: I. Iglesias, *E. Morera* (Barcelona, 1921; in Catalan).

Morère (real name, **Couladère**), **Jean,** French tenor; b. Toulouse, Oct. 6, 1836; d. Paris, Feb. 1887. He studied with Paul Laget in Toulouse; made his debut as Manrico at the Paris Opéra in 1861, where he sang until 1869; created the title role in Verdi's *Don Carlos* there in 1867; also appeared in Brussels at the Théâtre Royal de la Monnaie (1865–66, 1869–70). He suffered a mental derangement in the wake of the Franco-Prussian War in 1871.

Moreschi, Alessandro, the last of the artificial male sopranos; b. Montecompatri, near Rome, Nov. 11, 1858; d. Rome, April 21, 1922. He studied with Capocci in Rome; from 1883 to 1913 was sopranist at the Sistine Chapel in the Vatican. His voice was of such purity and beauty that he was nicknamed "l'angelo di Roma."

BIBLIOGRAPHY: Angus Heriot, *The Castrati in Opera* (London, 1956; appendix; pp. 225–27).

Morgan, Maud, American harpist; b. New York, Nov. 22, 1860; d. there, Dec. 2, 1941. She received her musical training from her father, George Washbourne Morgan (1823–1892); then studied in London; made her public debut in 1875 in a concert with Ole Bull.

Morgan, Russ, popular American trombonist and band leader; b. Scranton, Pa., April 29, 1904; d. Las Vegas, Aug. 7, 1969. A son of a coal-mine foreman, he worked the mines from the age of 9; learned piano from his mother; then studied the trombone. In 1923 he formed his first band, The Scranton Sirens. Later he went to N.Y. and became an arranger for John Philip Sousa. Subsequently, he played in nightclubs and theaters; in 1936 he formed a band to assist Rudy Vallee on his radio show. He ingratiated himself with audiences by the emotional use of the waah-waah mute on the trombone, obtaining effective contrasts in the mellow style of "sweet jazz."

Morganfield, Mckinley. See **Waters, Muddy.**

Mori, Frank, English musician; son of **Nicolas Mori;** b. London, March 21, 1820; d. Chaumont, France, Aug. 2, 1873. He was educated by his father; wrote light music; his operetta *The River-Sprite* (London, Feb. 9, 1865) was fairly successful.

Mori, Nicolas, English violinist and music publish-

er (of Italian extraction); b. London, Jan. 24, 1796; d. there, June 14, 1839. He studied violin with Barthélemon and Viotti; gave many concerts as a soloist at an early age; also was a member of the London Phil. Society. He brought out the Eng. editions of works by Mendelssohn, and other music. An eccentric, he wrote flamboyant advertisements about his career, and shortly before his death announced his own memorial concert, punning on his name ("Memento Mori").
BIBLIOGRAPHY: E.W. Duffin, *Particulars of the Illness and Death of the Late Mr. Mori* (London, 1839).

Moriani, Napoleone, outstanding Italian tenor; b. Florence, March 10, 1806; d. there, March 4, 1878. He studied with C. Ruga; made his operatic debut in Pacini's *Gli Arabi delle Gallie* in Pavia in 1833; then sang throughout Italy, garnering great praise for his interpretations of Bellini, Donizetti, and Verdi; he created the role of Enrico in Donizetti's *Maria di Rudenz* in Venice in 1838, and that of Carlo in *Linda di Chamounix* in Vienna in 1842; he also sang in London (1844–45). He was forced to retire from the stage in 1847 as a result of the deterioration of his vocal cords.

Morillo, Roberto García, Argentine composer and music critic; b. Buenos Aires, Jan. 22, 1911. He studied composition with Aguirre and Juan José Castro; later took courses with Gaito and Ugarte. From 1926 to 1930 he was in Paris. Returning to Argentina, he taught at the National Cons. in Buenos Aires and wrote music criticism for *La Nación.* His music is marked by propulsive rhythms and a strong sense of dissonant counterpoint. Among his works are a symph. poem, *Berseker* (Buenos Aires, Dec. 29, 1932); Piano Concerto (Buenos Aires, Nov. 7, 1940); *Las pinturas negras de Goya* for Piano, Violin, Cello, Flute, Clarinet, and Bassoon (Montevideo, May 27, 1940); *The Fall of the House of Usher,* after Poe (Buenos Aires, May 12, 1943); 3 symphs. (1948, 1955, 1961); *Variaciones olímpicas* for Orch. (1958); *3 pinturas de Piet Mondrian* for Orch. (1960); *Ciclo de Dante Alighieri* for Chamber Orch. (1970); *Dionysos* for Orch. (1971); Quartet for Violin, Cello, Clarinet, and Piano (1937); *Concerto a 9* for 3 Clarinets and Strings (1943); String Quartet (1951); 5 piano sonatas (1935–62); *Cantata de los caballeros* for Soprano and Orch., to words by García Lorca (1965); *Divertimento sobre temas de Paul Klee* for Wind Quintet (1967; orchestrated 1971); *Cantata féstiva* a cappella (1971); also film music. Morillo publ. monographs on Mussorgsky (1943), Rimsky-Korsakov (1945), and Carlos Chávez (1960); also publ. *Julian Bautista en la música española contemporánea* (1949). His biographical sketch and a list of works are found in *Compositores de América,* vol. VIII (Washington, D.C., 1962).

Morin, Gösta, Swedish musicographer; b. Ludvika, April 14, 1900. He studied with T. Norlind at Uppsala Univ., and later in Germany, Austria, and Italy; in 1937 visited the U.S. He held the position of librarian at Uppsala Univ.; then at the Royal Music Academy in Stockholm; was editor in chief of the valuable new edition of *Sohlmans Musik Lexikon* (4 vols., Stockholm, 1948–53).

Morini, Erica (originally **Erika**), violinist; b. Vienna, Jan. 5, 1904. Her father was Italian, her mother Viennese. She studied at her father's school of music in Vienna; then with Ševčik; made her professional debut as a child prodigy, at the age of 12; played with the Gewandhaus Orch. in Leipzig, under the direction of Nikisch (1918). She made her U.S. debut in N.Y. on Jan. 26, 1921; in subsequent years played with virtually all major American orchs.; also toured South America, Australia, and the Orient; eventually settled in N.Y.

Morison, Elsie, Australian soprano; b. Ballarat, Aug. 15, 1924. She studied with Olive Carey at the Melbourne Cons.; made her debut at the Royal Albert Hall in London in 1948; then sang with the Sadler's Wells Opera (1948–54) and at Covent Garden (1953–62). She married the Czech conductor **Rafael Kubelik.**

Morlacchi, Francesco, Italian composer; b. Perugia, June 14, 1784; d. Innsbruck, Oct. 28, 1841. He was a pupil of Caruso in Perugia, and of Zingarelli at Loreto; received the diploma of "maestro compositore" from the Liceo Filarmonico of Bologna (1805). At the time of graduation, he wrote a cantata for the coronation of Napoleon as King of Italy (1805); even earlier he wrote church music and an opera. His first stage work to be performed was an operetta, *Il Poeta spiantata, o Il Poeta in campagna* (Florence, 1807); he showed his contrapuntal skill in the composition of a Miserere in 16 parts; then produced a comic opera, *Il ritratto* (Verona, April 1807), and a melodrama, *Il Corradino* (Parma, Feb. 25, 1808). His first signal success as an opera composer was the production of *Le Danaide* in Rome (Feb. 11, 1810). He was engaged as music director of the Italian Opera in Dresden in 1811; wrote there several operas and, in 1814, a Mass in celebration of the return of the King of Saxony to Dresden; also wrote music for the Russian governor of Dresden during the occupation, and other occasional pieces. He continued to compose operas, for Naples, Milan, Venice, and Genoa, among them *Gianni di Parigi* (Milan, May 30, 1818), *Tebaldo ed Isolina* (Venice, Feb. 4, 1822; his most famous work; produced also in London, Paris, Leipzig, Prague, etc.), and *Colombo* (Genoa, June 21, 1828). When the King of Saxony died in 1827, Morlacchi wrote a Requiem, one of his finest works. He spent the last years of his life partly in Dresden and partly in Italy; he died on his way to Italy, at Innsbruck.
BIBLIOGRAPHY: G.B. Rossi-Scotti, *Della vita e delle opere del cav. Francesco Morlacchi... memorie istoriche* (Perugia, 1860); E. Magni-Dufflocq, "Francesco Morlacchi," *Bolletino Bibliografico Musicale* (1934); W. Fischer, ed., *In memoriam Francisci Morlacchi* (Innsbruck, 1952); G. Ricci des Ferres-Cancani, *Francesco Morlacchi, Un maestro*

italiano alla corte di Sassonia (1784–1841) (Florence, 1956).

Morley, Thomas, famous English composer; b. Norwich, 1557 or 1558; d. London, Oct. 1602. He studied with William Byrd. From 1583 to 1587 he was organist and master of the choristers at Norwich Cathedral. In 1588 he received his B.Mus. from Oxford. About this time he became organist at St. Paul's Cathedral. By 1591 he had turned spy for the government of Queen Elizabeth I. In 1592 he was sworn in as a Gentleman of the Chapel Royal and was made Epistler and then Gospeller. He was also active as a printer, holding a monopoly on all music publishing under a patent granted to him by the government in 1598. In addition to publishing his own works, he acted as editor, arranger, translator, and publisher of music by other composers. Notable among his editions was *The Triumphes of Oriana* (1601), a collection of madrigals by 23 composers. He gained distinction as a music theorist; his *A Plaine and Easie Introduction to Practicall Musicke* (1597) became famous as an exposition of British musical schooling of his time.

WORKS: MADRIGALS: *Canzonets, or Little Short Songs to Three Voyces* (London, 1593; 3rd ed., enlarged, 1602, as *Canzonets... with Some Songs added by the Author*); *Madrigalls to Foure Voyces: the First Booke* (London, 1594; 2nd ed., enlarged, 1600, as *Madrigalls... with Some Songs added by the Author*); *The First Booke of Balletts to Fiue Voyces* (London, 1595; 3rd ed., 1600); *The First Booke of Canzonets to Two Voyces* (London, 1595); *Canzonets or Little Short Aires to Fiue and Sixe Voyces* (London, 1597); he ed. the last 3 in Italian editions as well; he also ed. *Madrigales: The Triumphes of Oriana, to Fiue and Six Voyces Composed by Divers Seurall Aucthors* (London, 1601). SOLO SONGS: *The First Booke of Aires or Little Short Songs to Sing and Play to the Lute with the Base-Viol* (London, 1600; it contains the song *It was a lover and his lasse* from Shakespeare's *As You Like It*). Many of the preceding works were ed. by E.H. Fellowes in *The English Madrigal School* (4 vols., 1913 et seq.: I, *Canzonets to 2 Voices* [1595] and *Canzonets to 3 Voices* [1593], revised by T. Dart, 1956; II, *Madrigals to 4 Voices* [1594], revised by T. Dart, 1963; III, *Canzonets to 5 and 6 Voices* [1597], revised by T. Dart, 1966; IV *Ballets to 5 Voices* [1600], revised by T. Dart, 1966). *The Triumphes of Oriana* was ed. by E.H. Fellowes in *The English Madrigal School, A Guide to Its Practical Use* (London, 1926; revised by T. Dart, 1962, in *The English Madrigalists*). *The First Booke of Aires* was ed. by E.H. Fellowes in *The English School of Lutenist Song Writers* (London, 1920–32; revised by T. Dart, 1966, in *The English Lute-Songs*). Modern eds. of additional works by Morley include H. Andrews and T. Dart, *Collected Motets* (London, 1959), and T. Dart, ed., *Keyboard Works*, in *English Keyboard Music* (London, 1959). Morley ed. *The First Booke of Consort Lessons, made by divers exquisite Authors for sixe Instruments to play together, viz. the Treble Lute, the Pandora, the Citterne, the Base Violl, the Flute,* *and the Treble Violl* (London, 1599; 2nd ed., corrected and enlarged, 1611; modern ed. by S. Beck, N.Y., 1959). His treatise *A Plaine and Easie Introduction to Practicall Musicke* (London, 1597) was publ. in a facsimile ed. by E.H. Fellowes (London, 1937); a modernized ed. was publ. by R. Alec Harman (London, 1952; 2nd ed., 1963).

BIBLIOGRAPHY: O. Bekker, *Die englischen Madrigalisten William Byrd, Thomas Morley und John Dowland* (Leipzig, 1901); E.H. Fellowes, *English Madrigal Verse* (Oxford, 1920; 3rd ed., revised, 1967, by F. Sternfeld and D. Greer); idem, *The English Madrigal Composers* (Oxford, 1921; 2nd ed., 1948); idem, *The English Madrigal* (Oxford, 1925); J. Pulver, "The English Theorists: XIII—Thomas Morley," *Musical Times,* LXXVI (1935); T. Dart, "Morley's Consort Lessons of 1599," *Proceedings of the Royal Musical Association,* LXXIV (1947–48); J. King, *An Aesthetic and Musical Analysis of the Madrigals of Thomas Morley, with Special Reference between Text and Music and Some Comparison with the Madrigals of John Wilby, John Bennet, and the "Triumphs Of Oriana"* (Diss., Univ. of Toronto, 1950); R. Stevenson, "Thomas Morley's 'Plaine and Easie' Introduction to the Modes," *Musica Disciplina,* VI (1952); J. Kerman, "Morley and the 'Triumphs Of Oriana,'" *Music & Letters,* XXXIV (1953); J. Uhler, *Morley's Canzonets for Two Voices* (Diss., Univ. of Louisiana, 1954); idem, "Thomas Morley's Madrigals for Four Voices," *Music & Letters,* XXXVI (1955); idem, *Morley's Canzonets for Three Voices* (Baton Rouge, 1957); D. Brown, "Thomas Morley and the Catholics: Some Speculations," *Monthly Musical Record,* LXXXIX (1959); T. Dart, "Morley and the Catholics: Some Further Speculations," ibid.; F. Zimmerman, "Italian and English Traits in the Music of Thomas Morley," *Anuario Musical,* XIV (1959); D. Brown, "The Style and Chronology of Thomas Morley's Motets," *Music & Letters,* XLI (1960); C. Murphy, *Thomas Morley Editions of Italian Canzonets and Madrigals* (Tallahassee, 1964); W. Shaw, "Thomas Morley of Norwich," *Musical Times,* CVI (1965); D. Greer, "The Lute Songs of Thomas Morley," *Lute Society Journal,* VIII (1966); R. McGrady, "Thomas Morley's First Booke of Ayres," *Music Review,* XXXIII (1972); M. Chibbett, "Dedications in Morley's Printed Music," *Royal Musical Association Research Chronicle,* XIII (1977); G. Beechey, "Morley's Church Music," *Musical Times* (Sept. 1981).

Mornington, Garrett Colley Wellesley, Earl of, father of the Duke of Wellington; b. Dangan, Ireland, July 19, 1735; d. London, May 22, 1781. He was a glee composer. In 1776 and 1777 the Catch Club awarded him prizes for catches; and in 1779 he won a prize for the glee *Here in a cool grot.* Sir Henry Bishop edited a complete collection of his glees and madrigals (1846). Mornington received a Mus.Doc. from the Univ. of Dublin, and was a prof. there from 1764 to 1774.

Moroi, Makoto, Japanese composer, son of **Saburo Moroi;** b. Tokyo, March 12, 1930. He studied composition with his father and Tomojiro Ikenouchi at the Tokyo Academy of Music (1948–52); later taught at the Osaka Univ. of Arts and Science. His music partakes of three different sources which sometimes fuse into a unified modality: ancient Japanese elements, serialism, and sonorism, i.e., organized sound with electronic instruments.

WORKS: *Composition No. 1* for Orch. (1951–53), *No. 2* for Orch. (1958), *No. 3* for Narrator, Male Chorus, and Orch. (1958), *No. 4* for Narrator, 3 Speaking Sopranos, Chorus, and Orch. (1960), and *No. 5, Ode to Arnold Schoenberg,* for Chamber Orch. (Osaka, Aug. 26, 1961); *Suite classique* for Orch. (1953); *Suite concertante* for Violin and Orch. (Kyoto, Sept. 7, 1963); Piano Concerto (1966); Symph. (Tokyo, Nov. 7, 1968); Concerto for Shakuhachi (Japanese bamboo flute), String Orch., and Percussion (1970-71); *Pitagorasu no hoshi (Stars of Pythagoras)* for Narrator, Chorus, Tape, and Chamber Orch. (1959); *Cantata da camera No. 1* for Ondes Martenot, Harpsichord, 3 Percussionists, Male Chorus, and Narrator (1959); *Cantata da camera No. 2, Blue Cylinder,* for Narrator, Solo Soprano, Chorus, and Chamber Orch. (1959); *The Red Cocoon* for Narrator, Pantomime, 2 Choruses, Tape, and Orch. (1960); *Phaeton, the Coachman* for Narrator, Solo Voice, Chorus, and Tape (1965); *Vision of Cain,* symph. sketch for ballet (1966); *Izumo, My Home!* for Baritone, Soprano, Chorus, Orch., and Tape (1970); Symph. for Voice, Percussion, Japanese Instruments, and Tape (1972); *Musica da camera No. 3* for Viola and Wind Quintet (1951); *Musica da camera No. 4* for String Quartet (1954); *Partita* for Solo Flute (1953); *Albumblätter* for Solo Oboe (1953); *Développements rarefiants* for Soprano and Chamber Group (Karuizawa, July 12, 1957); *Ordre* for Cello and Piano (1958); *5 epigrammes* for Flute, Clarinet, Vibraphone, Celesta, Harp, Violin, and Cello (Tokyo, Feb. 29, 1964); *Kusabira (Mushrooms)* for 2 Voices and Electronic Sound (1964); *Toccata, Sarabande and Tarantella* for Strings and Piano (1964); *5 Dialogues* for 2 Shakuhachi (1965); *Les Farces* for Solo Violin (1970); piano pieces: *Alpha and Beta* (1953–54), Sonatina (1966), and *8 Parables* (1967); *Contradiction I* and *II* (1972) and several other works for Japanese instruments alone.

Moroi, Saburo, Japanese composer, father of **Makoto Moroi;** b. Tokyo, Aug. 7, 1903; d. there, March 24, 1977. He studied literature at Tokyo Univ. (1926–28), later took lessons in composition with Max Trapp, orchestration with Gmeindl, and piano with Robert Schmidt at the Hochschule für Musik in Berlin (1932–34). Upon returning to Japan, he was active as a music teacher; among his students who achieved a reputation as composers in their own right were Dan, Irino, and his son **Makoto Moroi.**

WORKS: 2 piano concertos (1933, 1977); 5 symphs.: No. 1 (Berlin, Oct. 2, 1934), No. 2 (Tokyo, Oct. 12, 1938), No. 3, with Organ (Tokyo, May 26, 1950), No. 4 (Tokyo, March 26, 1951), and No. 5 (Tokyo, 1971); Cello Concerto (1936); Bassoon Concerto (1937); Violin Concerto (1939); *2 Symphonic Movements* (1942); Sinfonietta (1943); *Allegro* for Piano and Orch. (1947); *2 Songs* for Soprano and Orch. (1935); fantasy-oratorio, *A Visit of the Sun* (Tokyo, June 30, 1969); Violin Sonata (1930); String Quartet (1933); Piano Quartet (1935); Viola Sonata (1935); Flute Sonata (1937); String Sextet (1939); String Trio (1940); 2 piano sonatas (1933, 1940); *Preludio ed Allegro giocoso* for Piano (1971). Among his numerous publications are a text, *Junsui talicho,* on strict counterpoint, and the 5-vol. *Historical Research of Musical Forms* (Tokyo, 1957–67).

Moross, Jerome, American composer; b. Brooklyn, Aug. 1, 1913; d. Miami, July 25, 1983. He studied music at the Juilliard School in N.Y.; became associated with various ballet groups and wrote a number of scores for the dance, most of them on American subjects, all of them in a vivid folklike manner. In 1940 he went to Hollywood as an arranger; collaborated with Aaron Copland on the score for *Our Town.* He held 2 Guggenheim fellowships, in 1947 and 1948. His first film score was *Close Up* (1948); his other film scores were for *The Cardinal, The Proud Rebel,* and *The Big Country.* For Broadway he wrote music for *Parade* (1935). His works for the dance included *Paul Bunyan* (1934); *American Patterns* (1937); *Frankie and Johnny* (1938); *Guns and Castanets* (1939); *The Eccentricities of Davy Crockett* (1946); *Robin Hood* (1946). He also wrote ballets-operas: *Susanna and the Elders* (1940); *Willie the Weeper* (1945); *The Golden Apple* (1952); *Gentleman, Be Seated!* (N.Y., Oct. 10, 1963); a ballet suite, *The Last Judgment* (1953); several orch. works, including a Symph. (conducted by Sir Thomas Beecham in Seattle on Oct. 18, 1943); *Beguine* (N.Y., Nov. 21, 1934); and *A Tall Story* (N.Y., Sept. 25, 1938); chamber music, including Sonatina for Clarinet Choir (1966); Sonatina for Strings, Double Bass, and Piano (1967); Sonatina for Brass Quintet (1968); Sonatina for Woodwind Quintet (1970); Sonatina for Divers Instruments (1972); Sonata for Piano Duet and String Quartet (1975); and Concerto for Flute and String Quartet (1978). Shortly before his death he completed a one-act opera, *Sorry, Wrong Number.*

Morphy, Guillermo, Conde de, Spanish courtier and musician; b. Madrid, Feb. 29, 1836; d. Baden, Switzerland, Aug. 28, 1899. He was taken to Germany as a child; there he studied music; took courses with Fétis in Brussels, where he wrote an orch. *Serenata española,* which had several performances. In 1864 he was named "chamber gentleman" to the Prince of Asturias, the future Alfonso XII, and then became his secretary; received his nobiliary title in 1885. He spent much time in Vienna and Paris, and took up the study of Spanish tablature music of the 16th century. His transcriptions (marred by inaccuracies) were publ. posthumously, with an introduction by Gevaert, as *Les Luthistes espagnols du XVIe siècle* (2 vols., Leipzig, 1902; German text by Riemann). In his influential position at the Spanish court, Morphy helped many talented musicians; he was instrumental in procuring a stipend for Albéniz to enable him to study in Brussels.

Morris, Harold, American composer and pianist; b. San Antonio, Texas, March 17, 1890; d. New York, May 6, 1964. He studied at the Univ. of Texas (B.A.) and the Cincinnati Cons.; lectured at the Rice Inst. of Houston, Texas (1933), at Duke Univ. (1939–40), etc.; was on the faculty of the Juilliard School of Music (1922–39); Teachers College, Columbia Univ. (1939–46); received many awards (National Federation of Music Clubs, Philadelphia Music Guild Award, etc.); was one of the principal founders of the American Music Guild in N.Y. (1921). In his music, he reveals himself as a Romanticist; in the main direction of his creative development, he was influenced by Scriabin. Many of his works are of programmatic content; some of them include American thematic material.

WORKS: For Orch: *Poem,* after Tagore's *Gitanjali* (Cincinnati, Nov. 29, 1918); *Dum-A-Lum,* variations on a Negro spiritual, for Chamber Orch. (1925); Piano Concerto (Boston, Oct. 23, 1931, composer soloist; very successful); Symph. No. 1, after Browning's *Prospice* (1934); *Passacaglia and Fugue* (1939); *Suite* for Chamber Orch. (N.Y., Nov. 1, 1941); Violin Concerto (N.Y., May 25, 1939); *American Epic* (1942); Symph. No. 2, subtitled *Victory* (Chicago, Dec. 23, 1952); *Heroic Overture* (1943); Symph. No. 3, subtitled *Amaranth,* after the poem by Edwin A. Robinson (Houston, March 13, 1948). Chamber music: 2 piano trios; 2 string quartets; 2 piano quintets; Violin Sonata; *Prologue and Scherzo* for Flute, Violin, Cello, and Piano; *Rhapsody* for Flute, Cello, and Piano; 4 piano sonatas; other piano pieces.

Morris, James, American bass-baritone; b. Baltimore, Jan. 10, 1947. He studied in Baltimore with Rosa Ponselle, and in N.Y. with Frank Valentino and Nicola Moscona. He made his operatic debut in Baltimore in 1967 as Crespel in *Les Contes d'Hoffmann.* On Jan. 7, 1971, he made his debut with the Metropolitan Opera in N.Y. as the King in *Aida,* and continued to appear there successfully in subsequent seasons; also sang with other American and European opera houses. He specialized in the Italian repertoire.

Morris, R(eginald) O(wen), English composer and eminent pedagogue; b. York, March 3, 1886; d. London, Dec. 14, 1948. He studied at the Royal College of Music, with Charles Wood; from 1920, taught at the Royal College of Music, with the exception of 2 years (1926–28), when he taught theory at the Curtis Inst. of Music in Philadelphia.

WORKS: Symph. in D; Violin Concerto; *Concerto piccolo* for 2 Violins and String Orch.; *Fantasy* for String Quartet; songs. It is mainly as an excellent teacher that Morris established himself; he gave considerable freedom to his students in expressing their individuality without adhering too closely to academic dogma. He publ. *Contrapuntal Technique in the XVIth Century* (1922); *Foundations of Practical Harmony and Counterpoint* (1925); *Preparatory Exercises in Score Reading* (with H. Ferguson; 1931); *Figured Harmony at the Keyboard* (1933); *The Structure of Music* (1935); *The Oxford

Harmony (vol. 1 only; 1946).

BIBLIOGRAPHY: E. Rubbra, "R.O. Morris: An Appreciation," *Music & Letters* (Jan. 1949).

Morris, Wyn, Welsh conductor; b. Triech, Feb. 14, 1929. He studied at the Royal Academy of Music in London and the Salzburg Mozarteum; then was apprentice conductor with the Yorkshire Symph. Orch. (1950–51) and conductor of an army band (1951–53). In 1954 he founded the Welsh Symph. Orch.; in 1957 he went to the U.S., where he led the Cleveland Chamber Orch. and other groups. In 1960 he returned to Great Britain; served as conductor of the choir of the Royal National Eisteddfod of Wales (1960–62), of the Royal Choral Society of London (1968–70), and of the Huddersfield Choral Society (1969–74); then organized the Symphonica of London, with which he gave regular concerts in ambitious programs, particularly of Mahler's music.

Morrison, Jim, psychedelic American rock star; b. Melbourne, Fla., Dec. 8, 1943; d. Paris, France, July 3, 1971, under mysterious circumstances. He studied cinema at the Univ. of Calif., Los Angeles, where he met Ray Manzarek, who was pinch-hitting with a rhythm-and-blues band, Rick and the Ravens, and a jazz drummer, John Densmore. They organized a group called The Doors, in allusion to the doors of perception opening into the surreal worlds as revealed by Aldous Huxley's search for hallucinogenic substances. The Doors had morbid propensities and mixed sex with death in their songs; because of that chimera of intellectuality, The Doors were solemnly discussed on the pages of highbrow magazines. For some years they served as a house band at The Whiskey A Go-Go, a sleazy watering hole for psychedelic hippies on the Sunset Strip in Los Angeles. Jim Morrison acted out his exhibitionistic expressionism on the stage for the benefit of the receptive throng. The products of this period were such songs of altered states as *Light My Fire, Break On Through, Love Me Two Times, People Are Strange, When the Music's Over, My Eyes Have Seen You,* and *The End.* Morrison's erotomania, stooping to such indecencies as dry-humping the microphone and explicit masturbatory gestures, finally led to a bust in Miami in 1969. He went into a decline and his attempt to return to straight rock with sporadic releases such as *Touch Me, Love Her Madly, Roadhouse Blues, You Make Me Real,* and *L.A. Woman* were but partially successful. In trouble with authorities and besotted with alcohol, Morrison relocated to Paris and died at 27 of an apparent heart attack.

Morrison, Van, Irish-American rock vocalist and songwriter; b. Belfast, Aug. 13, 1945. His real name was **George Ivan.** He sang, playing guitar, harmonica, and saxophone. In 1964 he formed a band named Them, but left it 2 years later and went to Boston. His first song, *Brown-Eyed Girl,* was a success in 1967. In 1968 he issued a solo recording album under the name *Astral Weeks.* This established his expanded consciousness and galactic dreams; typical of his further development were his songs *Moondance, Into the Mystic, Wild Night,* and *Wavelengths.*

Morse, Charles Henry, American organist; b. Bradford, Mass., Jan. 5, 1853; d. Boston, June 4, 1927. He studied at the New England Cons. and at the Boston Univ. College of Music, with J.K. Paine; then taught at various Boston schools, in Minneapolis, and in Brooklyn, before returning to Boston. He publ. a number of anthems, Christmas carols, etc.; also many arrangements for organ, and several valuable compilations (*The Contemporary Organist, The Church Organist, The Junior Church Organist,* etc.).

Mortari, Virgilio, Italian composer and pianist; b. Passirana di Lainate, near Milan, Dec. 6, 1902. He studied at the Milan Cons. with Bossi and Pizzetti; after a few years as a concert pianist he became an instructor at the Cons. Benedetto Marcello in Venice (1933–40); in 1940 he was appointed prof. of music at the Santa Cecilia Academy in Rome, remaining at this post until 1973; in 1963 he became vice-president there. His music combines the traits of the Italian Baroque and the modern French school of composition. He wrote the operas *Secchi e Sberlecchi* (1927), *La scuola delle moglie* (1930), *La Figlia del diavolo* (Milan, March 24, 1954), and *Il contratto* (1962); he also completed Mozart's unfinished work *L'Oca del Cairo,* which was performed in his version in Salzburg, on Aug. 22, 1936. He further wrote the ballets *L'allegra piazetta* (1945), *Specchio a tre luci* (1973), and numerous orch. works, among them Fantasia for Piano and Orch. (1933), *Notturno incantato* (1940), Piano Concerto (1952), the overture *Eleonora d'Arborea* (1968), *Tripartita* (1972); concertos for solo instruments with orch.: Piano Concerto (1960), Viola Concerto (1966), Double-bass Concerto (1966), Violin Concerto (1967), Double Concerto for Violin and Piano (1968), Cello Concerto (1969), Harp Concerto (1972); also Concerto for String Quartet and Orch. (1937); Sonatina for Harp (1938), *Piccola serenata* for Cello Solo (1946), *Piccola serenata* for Violin Solo (1947), *Duettini concertati* for Violin and Double Bass (1966), *Capriccio* for Violin Solo (1967); vocal works: *2 Funeral Psalms* in memory of Alfredo Casella for Voice and Instruments (1947); *Alfabeto a sorpresa* for 3 Voices and 2 Pianos (1959); songs with piano. He publ. *La tecnica dell'orchestra contemporanea* (in collaboration with Casella; Milan, 1947; 2nd ed., 1950); also arranged fragments from operas by Galuppi, Pergolesi, and Monteverdi.

Mortelmans, Ivo, Belgian composer; son of **Lodewijk Mortelmans;** b. Antwerp, May 19, 1901. He studied at the Antwerp Cons.; upon graduation taught academic subjects and theory in Berchem (1925–66), and concurrently at Deurne (1939–70) and Mortsel (1946–67). He was active as an opera conductor. He wrote an oratorio, *Eeuwig vlecht de bruid haar kroon* (1964) and numerous other choral works, both sacred and secular.

Mortelmans, Lodewijk, Belgian composer; b. Antwerp, Feb. 5, 1868; d. there, June 24, 1952. He was a chorister in the Dominican Church; then studied with Benoit in Antwerp. In 1889 he won the 2nd Belgian Prix de Rome; gained first prize with his cantata *Lady Macbeth* in 1893; then taught at the Antwerp Cons. In 1921 he made a tour in the U.S.; was director of the Antwerp Cons. from 1924 to 1933.

WORKS: Opera, *De kinderen der Zee* (Antwerp, 1920); symph. poems: *Helios* (1894), *Mythe du printemps* (1895), *Avonlied* (1928), *Weemoedig aandenken* (1942), *Eenvoud* (1950); church cantata, *Jong Vlaanderen* (1907); *Symphonie homérique* (1898); 4 elegies for Orch.: *In memoriam* (1917), *Elevation du cœur* (1917), *Solitude* (1919), *Treurdicht* (1925); 3 sets of *Miniatures* for Piano; 27 *Old Flemish Folksongs* for Piano; a number of songs to Flemish words, which are his finest creations. Paul Gilson called him "Prince of the Flemish song."

BIBLIOGRAPHY: The Belgian Center of Musical Documentation publ. a complete catalogue of his works, with a brief biography in Flemish, French, and Eng. (Brussels, 1954); see also J.L. Broeckx, *Lodewijk Mortelmans* (Antwerp, 1945).

Mortensen, Finn, Norwegian composer; b. Oslo, Jan. 6, 1922; d. there, May 21, 1983. He studied harmony with Thorlief Eken (1942), vocal polyphony with Egge (1943), and in the winter of 1956, composition with Niels Viggo Bentzon in Copenhagen. In 1970 he was appointed to the faculty of the Oslo Cons. (renamed the Norwegian State Academy of Music in 1973); succeeded Egge as chairman of the Norwegian Society of Composers (1972–74). In some compositions he adopted a modified 12-tone idiom, supplemented by the devices of permutation and thematic rotation.

WORKS: FOR ORCH.: Symph. (1953; first complete perf., Bergen, Jan. 21, 1963); *Pezzo orchestrale* (1957); *Evolution* (1961); *Tone Colors* (1961); Piano Concerto (1963; Oslo, Sept. 11, 1963); *Fantasia* for Piano and Orch. (1965–66; Oslo, May 6, 1966); *Per orchestra* (1967; Oslo, Nov. 27, 1967); *Hedda* (1974–75); *Fantasia* for Violin and Orch. (1977). CHAMBER MUSIC: String Trio (1950); Wind Quintet (1951); Solo Flute Sonata (1953); Duo for Soprano and Violin (1956); Sonatina for Clarinet Solo (1957); Sonatina for Balalaika and Piano (1957); *5 Studies* for Solo Flute (1957); Sonatina for Solo Viola (1959); Oboe Sonatina (1959); *Fantasia* for Solo Bassoon (1959); Violin Sonata (1959); Viola Sonatina (1959); Piano Quartet (1960); *3 Pieces* for Violin and Piano (1961–63); *Constellations* for Accordion, Guitar, and Percussion (1971); *Neoserialism I* for Flute and Clarinet (1971), *II* for Flute, Clarinet, and Bassoon (1972), and *III* for Violin, Viola, and Cello (1973); *Suite* for Wind Quintet (1972); *Serenade* for Cello and Piano (1972); *3 Pieces* for Solo Accordion (1973); *Construction* for Solo Horn (1974–75); *Adagio and Fugue* for 16 Horns (1976); Sonata for Oboe and Harpsichord (1976); *Fantasia* for Solo Trombone (1977); *Suite* for 5 Recorders and String Quintet (1978–79); String Quartet (1981). FOR PIANO: 2 sonatinas (1943, 1949); 2

sonatas (1956, 1977); *Fantasia and Fugue* (1957–58); 2-Piano Sonata (1964); *Drawing* (1966); *Impressions for 2 Pianos* (1971).

BIBLIOGRAPHY: N. Grinde, *Contemporary Norwegian Music 1920–1980* (Oslo, 1981; pp. 90–92).

Mortensen, Otto, Danish composer; b. Copenhagen, Aug. 18, 1907. He studied piano, organ, and composition at the Cons. of Copenhagen; in 1939 went to Paris, where he studied with Darius Milhaud. In 1942 he joined the staff of the Cons. of Copenhagen, remaining until 1966; then lectured at the Univ. of Arhus (1966–74). He composed mostly vocal music; among his instrumental works are: String Quartet (1937); Quartet for Flute, Violin, Cello, and Piano (1938); Wind Quintet (1944); Oboe Sonata (1947); Piano Concerto (1948); Symph. (1957).

Morthenson, Jan W., Swedish composer; b. Örnsköldsvik, April 1, 1940. He studied academic musical subjects with Lidholm in Stockholm; then went to Cologne, where he worked with G.M. Koenig in electronic techniques; also attended the summer courses on new music in Darmstadt; in 1970 he visited the U.S., and gave lectures at the Cons. of San Francisco. In his compositions he devised a "nonfigurative" method in which "individual changes in sound are imperceptible," and publ. a treatise, *Nonfigurative Musik* (Copenhagen, 1966). WORKS: 4 pieces entitled *Coloratura: I* for Strings and Tape (1960), *II* for Orch. (1962), *III* for Chamber Orch. (1962–63), and *IV* for Orch. (1963); 3 *Wechselspiel: I* for Cello (1960), *II* for Flute and 3 Loudspeakers (1961), and *III* for Piano and Percussion (1961); *Canzona* for 6 Choral Groups, Percussion, and Loudspeakers (1961); *Chains-Mirrors,* electro-acoustical work for Soprano (1961); *Some of these. . .,* graphic music for Organ (1961); *Courante I, II* and *III,* graphic music for Piano (1962); *Pour Madame Bovary* for Organ (1962); 3 *Antiphonia: I* for Orch. (1963), *II* for Chamber Orch. (1963), and *III* for Chamber Orch. (1970); *Eternes* for Organ (1964); computer pieces: *Neutron Star* (1967), *Spoon River* (1967), *Ultra* (1971), and *Sensory Project I* and *II* (1971); electronic pieces: *Interferences* (1967), *Epsilon Eridani* (1967), *Ionosphères* (1969), and *Zero* (1969); *Decadenza I* for Organ and Tape (1968); *Decadenza II* for Orch. with Tape and Film (1970; Uppsala, Jan. 18, 1972); *Colossus* for Orch. (1970; Berlin, Nov. 26, 1972); *Farewell* for Organ (1970); *Senza* for Strings (1970); *Labor* for Chamber Orch. (1971); *Life* for Tenor, Orch., and Instrumental Group (1972); *Video I* for 8 Solo Strings (1972); *Alla marcia* for Female Chorus, Orch., Tape, and 8 Stroboscopes (1972–73; Stockholm, March 31, 1974); *5 Pieces* for Orch. (1973). He wrote several experimental picture-sound productions for video projection, including *Supersonics* (1970), *Camera humana* (1972), and *Sensory Project III* (1972); also a film score, *Interferences I* (1967).

Morton, "Jelly Roll" (real Christian names, **Ferdinand Joseph La Menthe**), black American (actually, a "Creole-of-color," having mixed African and

French-American ancestry) ragtime-blues-jazz pianist and composer; b. New Orleans, Sept. 20, 1885; d. Los Angeles, July 10, 1941. Born into a French-speaking family that proudly recalled its former days of wealth and position, Morton grew up surrounded by musical instruments and frequently attended performances at the New Orleans French Opera House. He played several instruments, but settled on the piano, and (against the wishes of his family) was playing professionally by the time he was 15; he worked with Bunk Johnson in 1900, and was particularly successful as a pianist in the local bordellos of "Storyville" (the red-light district of New Orleans). He left New Orleans in 1907 and traveled through much of the U.S., both spreading his concept of ragtime and jazz and learning the various regional styles; he was in N.Y. in 1911, Tulsa in 1912, San Francisco and Chicago in 1915, etc.; also traveled in Mexico and Canada. He was a colorful and flamboyant figure, given to extravagant boasting and flashy living; in addition to his being a musician, he was a professional gambler (cards and billiards), nightclub owner, and producer; he made and lost several fortunes. His early compositions (*King Porter Stomp,* composed 1902, publ. 1924; *Jelly Roll Blues,* composed 1905, publ. 1915) are important samples of the styles of the period. Around 1922 he made his first piano rolls, and in 1923 began recording, both solo and with the New Orleans Rhythm Kings (unusual, for this was a white group); his own band, the Red Hot Peppers, recorded during the years 1926–30 and produced some of the finest samples ever made of the New Orleans Dixieland style. In 1938 he recorded for the Library of Congress, playing piano, singing, demonstrating styles, relating anecdotes and stories, and creating, in sound, his view of the history of jazz; a major outgrowth of these recordings is his biography, Alan Lomax's *Mister Jelly Roll. The Fortunes of Jelly Roll Morton, New Orleans Creole and "Inventor of Jazz"* (N.Y., 1950; 2nd ed., Berkeley, 1973).

Morton, Robert, English composer; b. c.1440; d. 1475. He was clerk and *chappellain* of the chapel of Philip the Good and Charles the Bold of Burgundy (1457–76); was possibly identical with **Robertus Anglicus** (d. 1485), a singer at St. Peter's, Rome. Some of his compositions are preserved in the *Kopenhagener chansonnier,* publ. by K. Jeppesen (1927); several MSS are in Belgian archives. A modern ed. of his works, edited by A. Atlas, is in progress.

BIBLIOGRAPHY: D. Fallows, *Robert Morton's Songs: A Study of Styles in the Mid-fifteenth Century* (Diss., Univ. of Calif., Berkeley, 1978).

Mosca, Giuseppe, Italian composer of operas; b. Naples, 1772; d. Messina, Sept. 14, 1839. He studied with Fenaroli; was engaged as répétiteur at the Théâtre-Italien, Paris (1803–9); then was maestro di cappella in Palermo (1817–21); later was director of music at the Messina Theater (1827). He was a prolific composer; wrote 42 operas, which were produced on leading Italian stages; also ballets and other theatrical pieces.

Mosca, Luigi, Italian composer; brother of **Giuseppe Mosca;** b. Naples, 1775; d. there, Nov. 30, 1824. He was a pupil of Fenaroli; served as maestro al cembalo at the San Carlo Theater in Naples; later taught singing. He produced 16 operas, of which *I Pretendenti delusi* (Milan, Sept. 7, 1811) was the most successful.

Moscheles, Ignaz, eminent pianist, pedagogue, and composer; b. Prague, May 23, 1794; d. Leipzig, March 10, 1870. Of a well-to-do family (his father was a Jewish merchant), he was trained in music as soon as his ability was discovered; his first piano teacher was Dionys Weber at the Prague Cons.; at the age of 14, Moscheles performed publicly a concerto of his own composition. Soon afterward, following his father's death, he went to Vienna to study under Albrechtsberger and Salieri, at the same time earning his living as a teacher. His conspicuous talents won him access to the best circles; he prepared the piano score of Beethoven's *Fidelio.* At concerts in Munich, Dresden, and Leipzig (1816), and in Paris (1820), his remarkable playing was much applauded; he was a pioneer in developing various modifications of tone by touch, afterward exploited by Liszt. In 1821 Moscheles settled in London; made frequent trips to the Continent, and gave Mendelssohn piano lessons at Berlin in 1824. The teacher and the pupil became close friends; on July 13, 1829, they gave the first performance in London of Mendelssohn's Concerto for 2 pianos and orch. After the foundation of the Leipzig Cons. in 1846, Mendelssohn invited Moscheles to join its staff. There, a host of pupils from all quarters of the globe were trained by him with sympathetic consideration, and yet with unflinching discipline in musical matters. He was noted for his energetic, brilliant, and strongly rhythmical playing; his virtuosity equaled his emotional absorption in the music; his romantic pieces for piano expressed clearly his ideas of the extent and the limitations of the instrument.
WORKS: 8 piano concertos, of which Nos. 3, 5, and 6 were favorites; he also wrote, for Piano and Orch., *Marche d'Alexandre, Souvenirs d'Irlande, Souvenirs de Danemark,* etc.; *Grand Septuor* for Piano, Violin, Viola, Clarinet, Horn, Cello, and Double Bass; *Grand Sextuor* for Piano, Violin, Flute, 2 Horns, and Cello; Piano Trio; piano duos with Violin, with Horn, and with Guitar; for 2 Pianos, *Hommage à Haendel;* for 2 Pianos, 8-hands, *Les Contrastes;* for Piano, 4-hands, *Sonate symphonique;* for Piano Solo, *Sonate mélancolique, Allegro di bravura, La Tenerezza, Les Charmes de Paris;* also wrote excellent studies (*Characteristic Studies,* in 2 books; 54 *Etudes de concert;* the études *L'Ambition* and *L'Enjouement,* etc.). His output totals 142 opus numbers. See his thematic index, *Thematisches Verzeichnis im Druck erschienener Compositionen* (1885; reprinted London, 1967). Moscheles trans. Schindler's biography of Beethoven into Eng. (with numerous additions), publ. as *The Life of Beethoven* (2 vols., London, 1841). His wife, **Charlotte Moscheles,** née **Embden** (d. Detmold, Dec. 13, 1889), wrote *Aus Moscheles' Leben* (Leipzig, 1872; 2 vols.; Eng. trans., London, 1873). His correspondence with Mendelssohn was publ. by his son, **F. Moscheles,** who also publ. his father's memoirs, as *Fragments of an Autobiography* (London, 1899).
BIBLIOGRAPHY: Excerpts of Moscheles's diaries and letters were publ. in trans. by A.O. Coleridge: *Recent Music and Musicians as Described in the Diaries and Correspondence of Ignaz Moscheles* (1873; reprinted N.Y., 1970); G. Servières, "Moscheles," *Revue Pleyel* (Paris, Dec. 1926); H. Engel, *Die Entwicklung des deutschen Klavierkonzertes von Mozart bis Liszt* (1927); I. Heussner, *Ignaz Moscheles in seinen Klaviersonaten, Kammermusikwerken, und Konzerten* (Marburg, 1963); J. Roche, "Ignaz Moscheles," *Musical Times* (March 1970).

Moscona, Nicola, Greek operatic bass; b. Athens, Sept. 23, 1907; d. Philadelphia, Sept. 17, 1975. He studied singing at the Athens Cons. with Elena Theodorini. He sang opera in Greece and Eygpt; then went to Milan; in 1937 he was engaged to sing at the Metropolitan Opera in N.Y., and made a successful American debut there as Ramfis in *Aida* (Dec. 13, 1937); remained on its staff until 1962; then went to Philadelphia, where he taught at the Academy of Vocal Arts.

Mosel, Ignaz Franz von, Austrian composer, conductor, and writer on music; b. Vienna, April 1, 1772; d. there, April 8, 1844. He began his career as an opera conductor, and was the first in Vienna to use a baton (1812). In 1816 he conducted the first concert of the Gesellschaft der Musikfreunde. In 1820 he was appointed vice-director of the court theaters in Vienna, and in 1829, custodian of the Imperial Library.
WORKS: Three of his operas were produced at the Vienna Court Opera: *Die Feuerprobe* (April 28, 1811), *Salem* (March 5, 1813), and *Cyrus und Astyages* (June 13, 1818); he also publ. 3 collections of songs.
WRITINGS: *Versuch einer Ästhetik des dramatischen Tonsatzes* (1813); *Die Tonkunst in Wien während der letzten fünf Dezennien* (1818, in the Vienna *Allgemeine Musikalische Zeitung;* separate reprint, 1840); *Über das Leben und die Werke des Anton Salieri* (1827); *Über die Originalpartitur des Requiems von W.A. Mozart* (1839); *Geschichte der kaiserl. königl. Hofbibliothek zu Wien* (1835).
BIBLIOGRAPHY: R. Batka, "Moseliana," *Musikbuch aus Österreich* (1911, 1912).

Mosenthal, Joseph, German violinist and composer; b. Kassel, Nov. 30, 1834; d. New York, Jan. 6, 1896. He was a pupil of his father and Spohr, and played in the court orch. of Kassel under Spohr's direction. He emigrated to America in 1853; was organist at Calvary Church, N.Y. (1860–87); from 1867, was conductor of the N.Y. Mendelssohn Glee Club; also was a violinist in the N.Y. Phil. (for 40 years). He publ. anthems, hymns, and other sacred works for the Episcopal Church, and part-songs for male chorus *(Thanatopsis, Blest Pair of Sirens, Music of the Sea,* etc.); *Sunday Lyrics* (6 songs); a Psalm, *The Earth Is the Lord's;* numerous songs.

Moser, Andreas, notable German violinist and music scholar; b. Semlin, Hungary, Nov. 29, 1859; d. Berlin, Oct. 7, 1925. He studied first in Zürich, with Hegar; also took courses in engineering and architecture in Stuttgart; in 1878 he became a violin pupil of Joachim in Berlin; in 1883 was concertmaster in Mannheim; in 1884 settled in Berlin. In 1888 he was appointed a teacher at the Hochschule für Musik, a post he held until his death. He publ. valuable studies on the history of the violin.
WRITINGS: *Joseph Joachim. Ein Lebensbild* (Berlin, 1898; revised and enlarged 4th ed., 1908; Eng. trans. 1900); *Methodik des Violinsoiels* (2 parts; Leipzig, 1920); *Geschichte des Violinspiels* (Berlin, 1923; 2nd ed., revised and enlarged, 1966–67); *Technik des Violinspiels* (2 vols.; Leipzig, 1925); collaborated with Joachim on a 3-vol. *Violinschule* (Berlin, 1902–5; 2nd. ed., revised by M. Jacobsen, 1959; French trans. by Marteau; Eng. trans. by Moffat); ed. *Johannes Brahms im Briefwechsel mit Joseph Joachim* (1908; vols. V and VI of the Brahms correspondence) and, with Johannes Joachim, *Briefe von und an Joseph Joachim* (3 vols., 1911–13); ed. (with Joachim) Beethoven's string quartets and Bach's partitas for violin; also various other violin works.
BIBLIOGRAPHY: H.J. Moser, *Andreas Moser,* in Ebel's *Berliner Musikjahrbuch* (1926, pp. 106ff.).

Moser, Edda, German soprano, daughter of **Hans Joachim Moser;** b. Berlin, Oct. 27, 1938. She took vocal lessons in Berlin; made her professional debut at the Würzburg Opera in 1963, and in 1967 sang at the Deutsche Oper in West Berlin; in 1968–71 she was a member of municipal opera houses in Frankfurt; in 1971 joined the Vienna State Opera. She also sang at Easter Festivals in Salzburg. She made her American debut at the Metropolitan Opera in N.Y. on Nov. 22, 1968. She maintains an extensive repertoire, both in coloratura soprano and lyrico-dramatic roles, being equally successful in traditional and modern works.

Moser, Hans Joachim, eminent German musicologist, son of **Andreas Moser** and father of **Edda Moser;** b. Berlin, May 25, 1889; d. there, Aug. 14, 1967. He studied violin with his father; then took courses in musicology with Kretzschmar and Wolf at the Univ. of Berlin, with Schiedermair at the Univ. of Marburg, and with Riemann and Schering at the Univ. of Leipzig; also studied voice with Oskar Noë and Felix Schmidt, and took courses in composition with H. van Eyken, Robert Kahn, and G. Jenner; he received his Ph.D. from the Univ. of Rostock in 1910 with the dissertation *Die Musikergenossenschaften im deutschen Mittelalter.* Returning to Berlin, he was active as a concert singer (bass-baritone); then served in the German army during World War I. He subsequently completed his Habilitation at the Univ. of Halle in 1919 with his *Das Streichin-strumentenspiel im Mittelalter* (publ. in A. Moser's *Geschichte des Violinspiels,* Berlin, 1923; 2nd ed., revised and enlarged, 1966–67). In 1919 he joined the faculty of the Univ. of Halle as a Privatdozent of musicology, and then became a reader there in 1922; he then was a reader at the Univ. of Heidelberg from 1925 to 1927; he was honorary prof. at the Univ. of Berlin from 1927 to 1934, and also served as director of the State Academy for Church and School Music in Berlin from 1927 to 1933; he received the degree of doctor of theology at Königsberg in 1931. He retired from his public positions in 1934 but continued his musicological pursuits in Berlin; he later served as head of the Reichsstelle für Musik-Bearbeitungen from 1940 to 1945. After World War II, he resumed teaching by accepting appointments as a prof. at the Univ. of Jena and the Hochschule für Musik in Weimar in 1947; he then served as director of the Berlin Cons. from 1950 until 1960. He was an outstanding music historian and lexicographer; his numerous writings are notable for their erudition. However, his unquestionable scholarship was marred by his ardent espousal of the Nazi racial philosophy; so ferocious was his anti-Semitism that he excluded Mendelssohn from his books publ. during the Third Reich. He also composed a number of songs and choruses, as well as the school opera *Der Reisekamerad,* after Andersen; in addition, he wrote novels, short stories, and a comedy. He arranged operas by Handel and Weber; wrote an entirely new libretto for Weber's *Euryanthe* and produced it under the title *Die sieben Raben* (Berlin, March 5, 1915). He served as editor of a projected complete edition of Weber's works (Augsburg and Leipzig, 1926–33), but it remains unfinished. Other works he edited include *Luthers Lieder, Werke,* XXXV (Weimar, 1923; with O. Albrecht and H. Lucke); *Minnesang und Volkslied* (Leipzig, 1925; 2nd ed., enlarged, 1933); *Das Liederbuch des Arnt von Aich* (Kassel, 1930; with E. Bernoulli); *Das deutsche Sololied und die Ballade, Das Musikwerk,* XIV (1957; Eng. trans., 1958); *Heinrich Schütz: Italienische Madrigale, Neue Ausgabe sämtlicher Werke,* XXII (Kassel, 1962); etc.
WRITINGS: In addition to countless articles for various German music journals, he also wrote the following: *Technik der deutschen Gesangskunst* (Berlin, 1911; 3rd ed., 1955; with Oskar Noë); *Geschichte der deutschen Musik* (3 vols., Stuttgart and Berlin, 1920, 1922, and 1924; 2nd ed., enlarged, 1968); *Musikalisches Wörterbuch* (Leipzig and Berlin, 1923); *Paul Hofhaimer: Ein Lied- und Orgelmeister des deutschen Humanismus* (Stuttgart and Berlin, 1929; 2nd ed., enlarged, 1966); *Die Ballade* (Berlin, 1930); *Die Epochen der Musikgeschichte im Überblick* (Stuttgart and Berlin, 1930; 2nd ed., 1956); *Die mehrstimmige Vertonung des Evangeliums* (2 vols., Leipzig, 1931 and 1934); *Corydon: das ist: Geschichte des mehrstimmigen Generalbass-Liedes und des Quodlibets im deutschen Barock* (2 vols., Braunschweig, 1933); *Die Melodien der Luther-Lieder* (Leipzig and Hamburg, 1935); *Johann Sebastian Bach* (Berlin, 1935; 2nd ed., 1943); *Tönende Volksaltertümer* (Berlin, 1935); *Heinrich Schütz: Sein Leben und Werk* (Kassel, 1936; 2nd ed.,

revised, 1954; Eng. trans., 1959); *Lehrbuch der Musikgeschichte* (Berlin, 1936; 13th ed., 1959); *Das deutsche Lied seit Mozart* (Berlin and Zürich, 1937; 2nd ed., revised, 1968); *Die Musikfibel* (Leipzig, 1937); *Kleine deutsche Musikgeschichte* (Stuttgart, 1938; 4th ed., 1955); *Allgemeine Musiklehr* (Berlin, 1940); *Christoph Willibald Gluck* (Stuttgart, 1940); *Kleines Heinrich-Schütz-Buch* (Kassel, 1940; Eng. trans., 1967); *Carl Maria von Weber* (Leipzig, 1941; 2nd ed., 1955); *George Friedrich Händel* (Kassel, 1941; 2nd ed., 1952); *Goethe und die Musik* (Leipzig, 1949); *Lebensvolle Musikerziehung* (Vienna, 1952); *Musikgeschichte in hundert Lebensbildern* (Stuttgart, 1952); *Die evangelische Kirchenmusik in Deutschland* (Berlin, 1953); *Musikästhetik* (Berlin, 1953); *Die Musikleistung der deutschen Stämme* (Vienna, 1954); *Die Tonsprachen des Abendlandes* (Berlin and Darmstadt, 1954); *Dietrich Buxtehude* (Berlin, 1957); *Musik in Zeit und Raum* (Berlin, 1960; collected essays); *Bachs Werke: Ein Führer für Musikfreunde* (Kassel, 1964); etc. His major work was the *Musiklexikon* (Berlin, 1932–35; 2nd ed., 1943, withdrawn; 3rd ed., 1951; 4th ed., 1955; supplement, 1963).
BIBLIOGRAPHY: *Festgabe für Hans Joachim Moser* (Kassel, 1954; with complete list of writings).

Moser, Rudolf, Swiss composer; b. Niederuzwyl, St. Gall, Jan. 7, 1892; d. in a fall, while mountain climbing in Silvaplana (Graubünden), Aug. 20, 1960. He studied theology at Basel Univ. and musicology with Nef; then studied at the Leipzig Cons. (1912–14) with Max Reger, Sitt, and Klengel; further with Huber in Basel and Lauber in Geneva. He became conductor of the cathedral choir in Basel; was also active as a pedagogue.
WORKS: *Der Rattenfänger,* dance play (1950); Concerto Grosso for String Orch. (Basel, June 26, 1927); several suites for orch.; 3 violin concertos; Organ Concerto; Concerto for Violin, Viola, and Cello; Piano Concerto; Viola Concerto; 4 string quartets; Piano Trio; String Sextet; *Das Lied von der Sonne* for Soli, Chorus, Orch., and Organ; *Odes of Horace* for Baritone, Chorus, and Orch.; other vocal music; organ pieces.
BIBLIOGRAPHY: H. Buchli, *Rudolf Moser* (Zürich, 1964).

Mosewius, Johann Theodor, German conductor and musicologist; b. Königsberg, Sept. 25, 1788; d. Schaffhausen, Sept. 15, 1858. He began his career as an opera singer in Königsberg, and later in Breslau; became music director of the Königsberg Theater in 1814; in 1827 joined the faculty at the Univ. of Breslau; in 1832 became music director there; in 1831, became director of the Inst. for Church Music in Breslau. By establishing the Singakademie (1825) and giving competent performances of works of Bach to Beethoven, he exercised a cultural influence on the musical life of Breslau. He also publ. articles on composers; of these, 2 were reprinted separately; *J.S. Bach in seinen Kirchencantaten und Choralgesängen* (1845) and *J.S. Bachs Matthäus Passion* (1852).

BIBLIOGRAPHY: A. Kempe, *Erinnerungen an J.T. Mosewius* (Breslau, 1859).

Moskowa, Prince de la, Joseph Napoléon, eldest son of Marshal Ney; French musician; b. Paris, May 8, 1803; d. St.-Germain-en-Laye, July 25, 1857. A senator, and brigadier general under Napoleon III, he was also a talented musician. In 1843 he established the Société de Musique Vocale, Religieuse et Classique (for the perf. of works of the 16th–17th centuries), himself conducting the concerts in his palace; the society publ. 11 vols. of these works as *Recueil des morceaux de musique ancienne,* which included works by Allegri, Arcadelt, Bach, Bononcini, Carissimi, the 2 Gabrielis, Gesualdo, Orlando Gibbons, Gluck, Handel, Haydn, Janequin, Josquin Des Prez, Lotti, Marcello, Orlando Lasso, Palestrina, Scarlatti, Stradella, Victoria, etc. He composed 2 comic operas, *Le Cent-Suisse* (Paris, June 7, 1840) and *Yvonne* (Paris, March 16, 1855); also a Mass with Orch. in 1831.

Mosolov, Alexander, Russian composer of avant-garde tendencies; b. Kiev, Aug. 11, 1900; d. Moscow, July 12, 1973. He fought in the Civil War in Russia (1918–20); was wounded and decorated twice with the Order of the Red Banner for heroism. After the war, he studied composition with Glière in Kiev; also privately with Miaskovsky in Moscow; took piano lessons with Igumnov at the Moscow Cons., graduating in 1925. He played his First Piano Concerto in Leningrad on Feb. 12, 1928. In his earliest works he adopted modernistic devices; wrote songs to texts of newspaper advertisements. His ballet *Zavod (Iron Foundry;* Moscow, Dec. 4, 1927) attracted attention because of the attempt to imitate the sound of a factory at work by shaking a large sheet of metal. However, Mosolov's attempt to produce "proletarian" music by such means elicited a sharp rebuke from the official arbiters of Soviet music. On Feb. 4, 1936, he was expelled from the Union of Soviet Composers for staging drunken brawls and behaving rudely to waiters in restaurants. He was sent to Turkestan to collect folk songs as a move toward his rehabilitation.
WORKS: 4 operas: *The Hero* (Baden-Baden, July 15, 1928); *The Dam* (Leningrad, 1929); *Masquerade* (1940); *The Signal* (1941); an anti-fascist musical comedy, *Friedrich Barbarossa;* 6 symphs. (1928, 1932, 1937, 1942, 1947, 1950); 2 piano concertos (1927, 1932); 5 suites for Orch.: No. 1, *Turkmenian* (1933); No. 2, *Uzbekian Dance* (1935); No. 3, *Native Lands,* with Folk Instruments (1951); No. 4 (1955); No. 5, *Festive* (1955); Harp Concerto (1939; Moscow, Nov. 18, 1939); Concerto for Orch. (1943); Cello Concerto (1946); *Elegiac Poem* for Orch. (1961); 4 oratorios, among them *M.I. Kalinin* (1940) and *Moscow* (1948); patriotic cantata, *Minin and Pozharsky; Kirghiz Rhapsody* for Mezzo-soprano, Chorus, and Orch. (1933); *Ukraine* for Soloist, Chorus, and Orch. (1942); 2 string quartets (1926, 1942); Trio for Clarinet, Cello, and Piano (1926); Piano Trio (1927); Cello Sonata (1927); Viola Sonata (1928); *Dance Suite* for Piano Trio (1928); 4 piano sonatas (1923, 1924, 1925,

1926); choruses; songs.

Mosonyi, Mihály (real name, **Michael Brandt**), Hungarian composer; b. Frauenkirchen, Sept. 2, 1814; d. Budapest, Oct. 31, 1870. He learned to play violin, double bass, and organ as a child; then took some lessons with Karl Turányi in Pressburg; subsequently earned his living as a private tutor in aristocratic families in Hungary and Vienna; he also played double bass in various orchs. Although he was a product of the Classical school of composition, he became enamored of Hungarian national music; began to write in the Hungarian idiom, while his harmonies remained Germanic. Liszt took great interest in his works, and proposed to bring out Mosonyi's German opera *Kaiser Max auf der Martinswand* (1857), but Mosonyi delayed the final revision of the work, and it never reached performance. His 2nd opera, *Szêp Llon (Pretty Helen)*, was produced at Budapest on Dec. 19, 1861; another opera, *Almos,* was not staged until Dec. 6, 1934, 64 years after Mosonyi's death. He further wrote 5 masses and other church music; 2 symphs.: No.1 (Pest, March 1844); No. 2 (Pest, March 30, 1856); 6 string quartets; several choruses for men's voices; songs. His *Funeral Music for Széchenyi* employs the so-called Hungarian mode, and its strong national character established Mosonyi as one of the founders of the Hungarian School.

BIBLIOGRAPHY: K. Ábrányi, *Mosonyi* (Budapest, 1872); J. Káldor, *Michael Mosonyi* (Dresden, 1936); Béla Bartók, "Three Unpublished Liszt Letters to Mosonyi," *Musical Quarterly* (Oct. 1921); F. Bónis, *Mosonyi Mihály* (Budapest, 1960).

Moss, Lawrence, American composer; b. Los Angeles, Nov. 18, 1927. He studied music at Pomona College, the Univ. of Calif. at Los Angeles (A.B., 1949), the Eastman School of Music in Rochester (A.M., 1951), and the Univ. of Southern Calif. (Ph.D., 1957). In 1956–59 he taught at Mills College in Oakland, Calif.; in 1959 received a Guggenheim fellowship for travel in Italy; in 1960 was appointed to the faculty of Yale Univ.; remained there until 1969; then was a prof. at the Univ. of Maryland. His stylistic usages tend to polycentric tonality, with sporadic application of serial techniques. He wrote the operas *The Brute,* after Chekhov (Norfolk, Conn., July 15, 1961) and *The Queen and the Rebels* (N.Y., Nov. 1, 1962); *Suite* for Orch. (1950); *Fantasia* for Piano (1952); Trio for Flute, Violin, and Cello (1953); *Song of Myself,* to Whitman's words, for Baritone and Chamber Ensemble (1957); 2 string quartets (1958, 1975); Violin Sonata (1959); *Music for 5* for Wind Quintet (1965); *Windows* for Flute, Clarinet, and Double Bass (1966); *Remembrances* for Chamber Ensemble (1968); *Patterns* for Flute, Clarinet, Viola, and Piano (1968); *Exchanges* for Chamber Ensemble (1968); *Ariel* for Soprano and Orch. (1969); *Paths* for Orch. (1971); *Unseen Leaves* for Soprano, Oboe, Tapes, Slides, and Lights (Washington, D.C., Oct. 20, 1975); symphs. for Brass Quintet and Chamber Orch. (1977).

Moss, Piotr, Polish composer; b. Bydgoszcz, May 13, 1949. He graduated from the State Academy of Music in Warsaw; became engaged mainly in composing music for radio, television, and films, in a mandatory semi-classical manner. However, he writes concert pieces in an adult and civilized style.

WORKS: Violin Concerto (1971); Wind Quintet (1971); *Per esempio,* music for 13 Performers (1972); String Quartet (1973); *Charon,* a symph. (1973); Piano Concertino (1973); *Vowels* for 12 Voices and Instrumental Ensemble (1974); Piano Trio (1974); *Giorno* for 10 Performers (1975); Cello Concerto (1975).

Moszkowski, Alexander, music critic; brother of **Moritz Moszkowski**; b. Pilica, Poland, Jan. 15, 1851; d. Berlin, Sept. 26, 1934. He lived most of his life in Berlin; wrote criticism for various publications there; was also editor of *Lustige Blätter* (a humorous magazine); publ. the entertaining booklets *Anton Notenquetschers Neue Humoresken* (1893; 9th ed., 1904); *Anton Notenquetschers heitere Dichtungen* (1894); etc. A serious work is *Die Kunst in 1000 Jahren* (1910).

Moszkowski, Moritz, famous pianist, teacher, and composer; b. Breslau, Aug. 23, 1854; d. Paris, March 4, 1925. He studied at the Dresden Cons.; later at the Stern Cons. and at the Kullak Academy in Berlin; then became a teacher at the latter institution. He gave his first public concert in Berlin in 1873; then played elsewhere in Germany, and in Paris, where he established his reputation as a pianist; in 1897, he made Paris his headquarters. As a composer, he is most widely known by his pieces in the Spanish vein, particularly the 2 books of *Spanish Dances* for Piano Solo or Piano Duo; also popular were his études, concert waltzes, gavottes, *Skizzen,* a tarantella, a humoresque, etc. In larger forms he essayed an opera, *Boabdil der Maurenkönig* (Berlin, April 21, 1892), which contains a ballet number that became popular; he also wrote a ballet, *Laurin* (1896); a symph. poem, *Jeanne d'Arc; Phantastischer Zug* for Orch.; *Aus aller Herren Länder* for Orch.; Violin Concerto; Piano Concerto.

Moszumańska-Nazar, Krystyna, Polish composer; b. Lwow, Sept. 5, 1924. She studied composition with Wiechowicz and piano with Jan Hoffman at the State College of Music in Cracow (1948–55); in 1964 was appointed to its faculty. Her music is classic in its formal organization, but densely dissonant in harmony.

WORKS: Piano Concertino (1954); 2 overtures (1954, 1956); *Allegro symphonique* (1957); *4 Symphonic Essays* (1957); *5 Duets* for Flute and Clarinet (1959); *Hexaèdre* for Orch. (1960); *Music for Strings* (1961); *Exodus* for Orch. and Tape (1964); *Variazioni concertanti* for Flute and Chamber Orch. (1965–66); *Interpretations* for Flute, Percussion, and Tape (1967); *Intonations* for 2 Choruses and Orch. (1968); *Implications* for 2 Pianos and Percussion (1968); *Pour orchestre* (1969; Poznan, March 29, 1973); *Bagatelles* for Piano (1971); *Bel canto* for Soprano, Celesta, and Percussion (1972); String Quartet (1973–74); *Polish Madonnas*, poem for Chorus and Orch. (1974).

Moten, Bennie, black American jazz pianist and bandleader; b. Kansas City, Nov. 13, 1894; d. there, April 2, 1935. He studied baritone horn and piano; worked in local bands; then organized his own 5-piece group, which evolved into one of the major big bands of the late 1920s and early 1930s; he made many recordings and toured extensively.

Motta, José Vianna da. See **Da Motta, José Vianna.**

Mottl, Felix, celebrated Austrian conductor; b. Unter-St. Veit, near Vienna, Aug. 24, 1856; d. Munich, July 2, 1911. After preliminary studies at a seminary, he entered the Vienna Cons., and studied there with Door (piano), Bruckner (theory), Dessoff (composition), and Hellmesberger (conducting), graduating with high honors. In 1876 he acted as one of the assistants at the first Wagner festival at Bayreuth. In 1881 he succeeded Dessoff as court conductor at Karlsruhe; in 1893 was appointed Generalmusikdirektor there. He conducted *Tristan und Isolde* at the Bayreuth Festival in 1886; led a Wagner concert in London in 1894; and gave the entire *Ring* tetralogy at Covent Garden in 1898. In 1903 he was engaged to conduct the projected performances of *Parsifal* at the Metropolitan Opera in N.Y., but withdrew owing to the protests of the Wagner family. Mottl secured recognition for Peter Cornelius's *Der Barbier von Bagdad* by re-orchestrating the score, and producing it first at Karlsruhe, on Feb. 1, 1884; additional changes were made by him with Hermann Levi, and in this form the work finally became established in the opera repertoire. In 1903 he became Generalmusikdirektor of the Munich Court Opera; was conductor of the Vienna Phil. from 1904 to 1907. In Dec. 1905 he conducted, also in Karlsruhe, the first complete performance of both parts of Berlioz's *Les Troyens* (in German); he orchestrated Wagner's *5 Gedichte,* and edited Wagner's early overtures. Mottl composed 3 operas: *Agnes Bernauer* (Weimar, 1880), *Rama,* and *Fürst und Sänger;* a String Quartet; numerous songs. Among his arrangements, that of Chabrier's *Bourrée fantasque* enjoys continued popularity in the concert hall.
BIBLIOGRAPHY: Harold Schonberg, *The Great Conductors* (N.Y., 1967).

Mottu, Alexandre, Swiss pianist, organist, and composer; b. Geneva, June 11, 1883; d. there, Nov. 24, 1943. He studied organ with Otto Barblan in Geneva; piano with Teresa Carreño in Berlin. He was appointed prof. of piano and organ at the Cons. of Geneva in 1907. His works include various pieces for piano, violin, and organ, and much choral music.

Moulaert, Pierre, Belgian composer, son of **Raymond Moulaert;** b. Brussels, Sept. 24, 1907; d. there,

Nov. 13, 1967. He studied at the Royal Cons. in Brussels with his father and Joseph Jongen, and taught there from 1927 until his death. He was not a prolific composer, and wrote mostly in small forms, but his music has a distinctive quality of fine craftsmanship.
WORKS: *Passepied en Rondo* for Wind Quintet (1940); Concertino for Flute, Oboe, and Strings (1954); String Quartet (1956); *Sérénade* for Orch. (1956); *Petite musique concertante* for Orch. (1961); *Introduction et Fugue* for Flute, Oboe, Clarinet, Bassoon, and Strings (Uccle, March 7, 1963); *Séquences* for Orch. (1964).

Moulaert, Raymond, Belgian composer, father of **Pierre Moulaert;** b. Brussels, Feb. 4, 1875; d. there, Jan. 18, 1962. He studied at the Brussels Cons. with Arthur de Greef (piano) and Edgar Tinel (theory); then was appointed to its staff and taught composition (1939); concurrently was director of his own music school in St.-Gilles for 25 years (1913–38); also lectured at the Queen Elizabeth Chapel of Music in Brussels.
WORKS: *Theme and Variations* for Trumpet and Orch. (1910); *Appels pour un tournoi de chevalerie (Invitation to a Tournament of Chivalry)* for Wind Orch. (1923); *Passacaglia* for Orch. (1931); *Symphonie de valses* (1936); Trumpet Concertino (1937); Piano Concerto (1938); *Rhapsodie écossaise* for Clarinet and Orch. (1940); *Tango-caprice* for Saxophone and Orch. (1942); *Etudes symphoniques* (1943); *Symphonie de fugues* (1942–44); *Eroica* for Horn and Chamber Orch. (1946); *Légende* for Flute and Orch. (1951); *Variations symphoniques* (1952); Sinfonietta for Strings (1955; lost); *Andante* for 4 Horns (1903); *Andante, Fugue et Final* for 4 Saxophones (1907); Sextet for Wind Quintet and Piano (1925); *Passacaglia* for Solo Double Bass (1928); *Etudes rythmiques* for Percussion (1929); *Divertimento* for String Trio (1936); *Choral varié* for 4 Cellos (1937); *Suite* for 3 Trombones (1939); *Sonata en forme de passacaille* for Cello and Piano (1942); *Concert* for Wind Quintet and Harp (1950); *Bagatelles* for 2 Violins (1960); organ works, including Sonata (1907), *2 Pieces* (1910), *3 poèmes bibliques* (1916–20), *2 Fugues* (1929) and *Prelude et Choral* (1948); piano works, including Sonata (1917), *Toccata* (1938), *Ciels* (1938), and *Etudes-paraphrases,* after Paganini (1948); 5 sets of *Poèmes de la Vieille France* for variable vocal groups (1917–43); *L'Eau passe,* song cycle for Solo Voice. A catalogue of his works was publ. by the Centre Belge de Documentation Musicale (Brussels, 1954).

Mount-Edgcumbe, Richard, British nobleman (2nd Earl of Mount-Edgcumbe) and music amateur; b. Plymouth, Sept. 13, 1764; d. Richmond, Surrey, Sept. 26, 1839. He was the author of the book *Musical Reminiscences, containing an Account of the Italian Opera in England from 1773,* which he publ. anonymously in 1825. He also wrote an opera, *Zenobia* (in Italian), which was produced at London on May 22, 1800.

Mouquet, Jules, French composer; b. Paris, July 10, 1867; d. there, Oct. 25, 1946. He studied at the Paris Cons. with Leroux (harmony) and Dubois (composition); won the first Prix de Rome in 1896 with his cantata *Mélusine,* the Prix Trémont in 1905, and the Prix Chartier (for chamber music) in 1907; in 1913 he became prof. of harmony at the Paris Cons.

WORKS: Oratorios: *Le Sacrifice d'Isaac* and *Le Jugement dernier;* symph. poems: *Diane et Endymion* and *Persée et Andromède; Danse grecque* for Orch.; *Divertissement grec* for Flute and Harp; Sonata for Flute and Piano; pieces for oboe and piano, bassoon and piano, saxophone and piano, etc.; Septet for Wind Instruments; *Etudes antiques* for Solo Piano. He also publ. *Cours complémentaire d'harmonie.*

Mouret, Jean Joseph, French composer; b. Avignon, April 11, 1682; d. Charenton, Dec. 20, 1738. He was attached to the court in Paris; produced an opera-ballet, *Les fêtes ou Le Triomphe de Thalie* (Paris, Aug. 14, 1714); an opera, *Ariane* (Paris, April 6, 1717); *Les Amours des dieux,* opera-ballet (Paris, Sept. 14, 1727). He was director of the Concert Spirituel (1728–34); wrote motets for performances there; also divertissements for the Comédie-Italienne; about 50 of his chamber pieces were publ. during his lifetime.

BIBLIOGRAPHY: R. Viollier, *J.J. Mouret, Le Musicien des grâces* (Paris, 1950).

Moussorgsky, Modest. See **Mussorgsky, Modest.**

Mouton, Jean, important French composer; b. Holluigue (now Haut-Wignes), near Samer, c.1459; d. St. Quentin, Oct. 30, 1522. In 1477 he became a singer and teacher of religion (écolâtre-chantre) at the collegiate church of Notre Dame in Nesle. He became maître de chapelle in Nesle in 1483, and also entered the priesthood. In 1500 he was in charge of the choirboys at the Cathedral of Amiens. In 1501 he was director of music at the collegiate church of St. André in Grenoble, but left his position without permission in 1502. He subsequently entered the service of Queen Anne; later served Louis XII and François I. He was made canon in absentia at St. André in Grenoble, which conferred a benefice on him in 1510, and later was elected a canon at St. Quentin. Pope Leo X made him an apostolic notary. He was the teacher of Adrian Willaert. In his music he followed the precepts of Josquin Des Prez; he particularly excelled in the art of the canon. He composed more than 100 motets, some 15 masses, and over 20 chansons. About 50 of his works were publ. in his lifetime; several collections were publ. posthumously. His *Opera omnia,* edited by A. Minor, began publication in 1967 in the Corpus Mensurabilis Musicae series of the American Inst. of Musicology.

BIBLIOGRAPHY: J. Delporte, "L'Ecole polyphonique franco-flamande: Jean Mouton," *Revue Liturgique et Musicale,* XVI/3 (1932), XVII/4 (1933), XVIII/6 (1934), and XIX/2 (1935); idem, "Nouveaux documents sur Jean Mouton," *Musique et Liturgie,* XXI (1937); F. Lesure, "Un Document sur la jeunesse de Jean Mouton," *Revue Belge de Musicologie,* V (1951); A. Minor, *The Masses of Jean Mouton* (Diss., Univ. of Michigan, 1951); R. Dammann, *Studien zu den Motetten von Jean Mouton* (Diss., Univ. of Freiburg, 1952); J. Shine, *The Motets of Jean Mouton* (Diss., N.Y. Univ., 1953); G. Reese, *Music in the Renaissance* (N.Y., 1954; 2nd ed., revised, 1959); P. Kast, *Studien zu den Messen des Jean Mouton* (Diss., Univ. of Frankfurt, 1955); idem, "Zu Biographie und Werk Jean Moutons," *Kongressbericht: Wien Mozartjahr 1956;* L. Lockwood, "Jean Mouton and Jean Michel: New Evidence on French Music and Musicians in Italy, 1505–1520," *Journal of the American Musicological Society,* XXXII (1979).

Moyse, Louis, French flutist, son of **Marcel Moyse;** b. Scheveningen, the Netherlands, July 14, 1912. He was taken to Paris as an infant; learned to play the piano and flute at home; later took private piano lessons with Isidore Philipp (1925–27); in 1930 he entered the Paris Cons., where he studied flute with Philippe Gaubert and composition with Eugène Bigot; he graduated in 1932, with the Premier Prix in flute; then was his father's teaching assistant at the Paris Cons., and filled in with various jobs playing at movie theaters and restaurants. He served in the French army during World War II; after the war he organized the Moyse Trio, with his father as flutist, his wife, **Blanche Honegger-Moyse,** as violinist, and himself as pianist. In 1948 he went with his wife to the U.S.; became an American citizen in 1959. He joined his father at Marlboro College in Vermont, where he taught until 1975; then was appointed prof. of flute and chamber music at the Univ. of Toronto. He publ. in N.Y. several educational collections of flute pieces, among them *Solos for Flute Players,* *40 Little Pieces for Beginner Flutists,* *Album of Flute Duets,* *30 Easy Duets for Flutes,* etc.

WORKS: *Suite* for 2 Flutes and Viola (1957); *4 Dances* for Flute and Violin (1958); Woodwind Quintet (1961); *Divertimento* for Double Woodwind Quintet, 2 Cellos, Double Bass, and Timpani (1961); *4 Pieces* for 3 Flutes and Piano (1965); *3 Pieces* for Flute and Guitar (1968); *Marlborian Concerto* for Flute, English Horn, and Orch. (1969); *A Ballad for Vermont* for Narrator, Soloists, Chorus, and Orch. (1971–72); Flute Sonata (1975); *Serenade* for Piccolo, 4 Flutes, Alto Flute, Bass Flute, and Piano (1977); he also arranged for flute and various instrumental groups works by Bach, Telemann, Handel, Mozart, Beethoven, and Weber.

Moyse, Marcel, celebrated French flutist; b. Saint-Amour (Jura), May 17, 1889. He studied flute with Taffanel at the Paris Cons.; upon graduation was first flutist in several Paris orchs. (Lamoureux, Cologne, Pasdeloup, etc.). In 1932 he succeeded Philippe Gaubert as prof. of flute at the Paris Cons. In 1949 he went to the U.S.; in 1950 organized, with his son **Louis Moyse,** Rudolf Serkin, Adolf Busch, and Hermann Busch, the Marlboro School and Festival of Music in Brattleboro, Vt.; also conducted master classes in flute and chamber music in Switzerland; gave similar courses in Japan in 1973. At the age of 92 he conducted an instrumental ensemble in the music of Mozart and Dvořák, on Aug. 11, 1981, in N.Y. He publ. a series of excellent flute studies, among them *20 exercises et études, 24 petites études mélodiques, 25 études mélodiques, 100 études faciles et progressives, 25 études de virtuosité* (after Czerny), *12 études de grande virtuosité* (after Chopin), etc.; also wrote 50 variations on the Allemande from Bach's Flute Sonata in A minor and compiled a manual for flute, *Tone Developement through Interpretation.*

Moyzes, Alexander, Slovak composer, son of **Mikuláš Moyzes;** b. Kláštor pod Znievom, Sept. 4, 1906. He studied conducting with Ostrčkil, composition with Karel and Šín, and organ with Wiedermann at the Prague Cons. (1925–28); continued studies at the master school there with Vítězslav Novák (1929–30). Upon graduation from the Cons. in 1928, he taught at the Prague Academy of Music, transferring to the High School of Musical Arts in Bratislava in 1949; was chief of the music section of Bratislava Radio (1937–48); in 1965–71 was rector of the Bratislava High School of Musical Arts. His music uses the melodic resources of Slovak folk songs; his Symph. No. 1 is the first national Slovak symph.
    WORKS: Opera, *Udatný král'* (*The Brave King*, 1966; Bratislava, 1967); 9 symphs.: No. 1 (Bratislava, Feb. 11, 1929); No. 2 (1932, revised 1941); No. 3 (1942; orch. version of the wind quintet); No. 4 (1939–47); No. 5 (1948); No. 6 (1951); No. 7 (Bratislava, Oct. 23, 1955); No. 8 (1968); No. 9 (1971); *Symphonic Overture* (1929); Concertino for Orch. (1933); *Jánošík's Rebels* for Orch. (1933); *Nikola Šuhaj,* overture (1933); *Down the River Váh,* symph. suite (1936, revised 1945); *Dances from the Hron Region* for Orch. (1950); *February Overture* (1952); *Dances from Gemer,* suite for Orch. (1955); Violin Concerto (1958); *Sonatina giocosa* for Violin, Chamber String Orch., and Harpsichord (1962); Flute Concerto (1966); *Keeper of the House,* overture (1972); *Bonfires on the Mountains,* symph. suite (1973); *Musica Istropolitana* for Chamber String Orch. (1974); *Music to Woman,* symph. study (1975; Bratislava, May 13, 1976); *The Tale about Jánošik,* rhapsodic suite for Orch. (1976); cantatas: *Svätopluk* (1935); *Znejú piesne na chotari* (*Songs Resound in the Meadows,* 1948); 2 song cycles: *Jeseň (In Autumn)* for Mezzo-soprano, and Orch. or Piano (1960), and *Morning Dew* for Mezzo-soprano, and Orch. or Piano (1963); 2 string quartets (1928, 1969); Wind Quintet (1933); *Poetic Suite* for Violin and Piano (1948); *Duetta* for Violin and Piano (1960); *Small Suite* for Violin and Piano (1968); Sonatina for Flute and Guitar (1975); *Divertimento* for Piano (1929); *Jazz Sonata* for 2 Pianos (1932); Piano Sonata (1942).
    BIBLIOGRAPHY: L. Burlas, *Alexander Moyzes* (Bratislava, 1956).

Moyzes, Mikuláš, Slovak composer; b. Velká Slatina, Dec. 6, 1872; d. Prešov, April 2, 1944. He studied at the Budapest Academy of Music; in 1907 became director of the Municipal School of Music in Prešov, where he remained. He wrote a *Missa solemnis;* many choruses; Wind Quintet; Wind Sextet; made arrangements of Slovak songs. His popular overture *Naše Slovensko (Our Slovakia)* was reorchestrated by his son **Alexander Moyzes.**

Mozart, (Johann Georg) Leopold, German-born Austrian composer, violinist, and theorist, father of **Wolfgang Amadeus Mozart;** b. Augsburg, Nov. 14, 1719; d. Salzburg, May 28, 1787. A bookbinder's son, he studied at the Augsburg Gymnasium (1727–35); continued his studies at the Lyceum attached to the Jesuit school of St. Salvator (1735–36). In 1737 he went to Salzburg, where he studied philosophy and law at the Benedictine Univ.; he received his bachelor of philosophy degree in 1738. Subsequently he entered the service of Johann Baptist, Count of Thurn-Valsassina and Taxis, the Salzburg canon and president of the consistory, as both valet and musician. In 1743 he became 4th violinist in the Prince-Archbishop's court orch.; also taught violin and keyboard to the choirboys of the Cathedral oratory. In 1757 he became composer to the court and chamber; in 1758 he was promoted to 2nd violinist in the court orch.; in 1762 he was appointed Vice-Kappellmeister. He married Anna Maria Pertl of Salzburg on Nov. 21, 1747; of their 7 children, only "Nannerl" and Wolfgang survived infancy. He dedicated himself to the musical education of his children, but his methods of presentation of their concerts at times approached frank exploitation, and his advertisements of their appearances were in poor taste. However, there is no denying his great role in fostering his son's career. Leopold Mozart was a thoroughly competent composer; the mutual influence between father and son was such that works long attributed to his son proved to be his. Leopold Mozart was also important as a theorist. He produced an influential violin method in his *Versuch einer gründlichen Violinschule* (Augsburg, 1756; 2nd ed., revised, 1769–70; 3rd ed., enlarged, 1787; facsimile of 1756 ed., Vienna, 1922; also various translations, including one in Eng., London, 1939; 2nd ed., 1951). His *Nannerl-Notenbuch* is a model of a child's music album; it was publ. in 1759; edited in part by E. Valentin (Munich, 1956; 2nd ed., 1969). M. Seiffert edited *Leopold Mozart: Ausgewählte Werke* in Denkmäler der Tonkunst in Bayern, XVII, Jg. IX/2 (Leipzig, 1908). Leopold Mozart's vocal works include sacred cantatas, masses, litanies, school dramas, and secular lieder. He also composed symphs.; the famous *Kindersinfonie (Toy Symphony),* long attributed to Haydn, was in all probability a work by Leopold Mozart. On this, see E.F. Schmid, "Leopold Mozart und die Kindersinfonie," *Mozart Jahrbuch 1951,* and R. Münster, "Wer ist der Komponist der 'Kindersinfonie'?," *Acta Mozartiana,* XVI (1969). A.A. Abert attributes Wolfgang's Symph. in G major, K. Anh. 221; 45a, "Old Lambach" (1768), to Leopold; see her "Methoden der Mozartforschung," *Mozart Jahrbuch 1964,* and

"Stilistischer Befund und Quellenlage: Zu Mozarts Lambacher Sinfonie KV Anh. 221–45a," in *Festschrift Hans Engel* (Kassel, 1964). Other orch. works include several concertos, among them *Die musikalische Schlittenfahrt* (1755); dances; etc. He also composed chamber music and works for the keyboard.

BIBLIOGRAPHY: CORRESPONDENCE AND NOTEBOOKS: H. Abert, "Leopold Mozarts Notenbuch von 1762," *Gluck-Jahrbuch*, III (1917); A. Schurig, *Leopold Mozarts Reiseaufzeichnungen, 1763–1771* (facsimile ed.; Dresden, 1920); O.E. Deutsch and B. Paumgartner, *Leopold Mozarts Briefe an seine Tochter* (Salzburg and Leipzig, 1936); E. Anderson, ed. and translator, *Letters of Mozart and His Family* (3 vols., London and N.Y., 1938; 2nd ed., revised by A. Hyatt King and M. Carolan, 1966); E. Müller von Asow, "Leopold Mozarts Münchener Reise 1786," *Musikerziehung*, VIII (1954–55); A. Kozár, *Wolfgang Amadeus Mozart (1756–1791) im Spiegel der Briefe seines Vaters Leopold Mozart: Ein Beitrag zur Kulturgeschichte des 18. Jahrhunderts* (Diss., Univ. of Graz, 1955); E. Müller von Asow, "Zu Leopold Mozarts Wiener Reise 1785," *Musikerziehung*, IX (1955–56); H. Klein, "Unbekannte Mozartiana von 1766/67," *Mozart Jahrbuch 1957;* D.-R. de Lerma, "The Nannerl Notebook," *Music Review,* XIX (1958); W. Bauer, O.E. Deutsch, and J. Eibl, eds., *Mozart: Briefe und Aufzeichnungen* (contains letters, notebooks, etc. relating to Leopold; 7 vols., Kassel, 1962–75); W. Plath, "Leopold Mozarts Notenbuch für Wolfgang (1762)—Eine Fälschung?," *Mozart Jahrbuch 1971–72* (concerning a spurious notebook).

BIOGRAPHICAL, CRITICAL, ANALYTICAL, ETC.: M. Friedlaender, "Leopold Mozarts Klaviersonaten," *Die Musik,* IV/1 (1904); W. Renz, "Leopold Mozarts als Komponist," ibid., IV/4 (1905); G. Schünemann, "Leopold Mozart als Komponist," *Allgemeine Musik-Zeitung,* XXVI (1909); A. Moser, *Geschichte des Violinspiels* (Berlin, 1923; 2nd ed., revised and enlarged, 1966–67); K. Gerhartz, "Die Violinschule von Leopold Mozart (1756)," *Mozart-Jahrbuch,* III (1929); O.E. Deutsch, "Vater Mozarts Ende," *National-Zeitung Basel: Sonderausgabe* (May 30, 1937); F. Posch, "Leopold Mozart als Mensch, Vater und Erzieher der Aufklärung," *Neues Mozart-Jahrbuch,* I (1941); E. Theiss, *Die Instrumentalwerke Leopold Mozarts nebst einer Biographie* (Diss., Univ. of Giessen, 1942); E.F. Schmid, "Leopold Mozart," *Lebensbilder aus dem Bayerischen Schwaben,* III (Munich, 1954); idem, "Leopold Mozart: Vater und Mentor," *Österreichische Musikzeitschrift,* XI (1956); idem, "Neues zu Leopold Mozarts Bildungsgang," *Acta Mozartiana,* III/1 (1956); W. Egk, "Anmerkungen zur Violinschule von Leopold Mozart," *Gestalt und Gedanke,* IV (1957); W. Plath, "Beiträge zu Mozart-Autographie, I: Die Handschrift Leopold Mozarts," *Mozart Jahrbuch 1960–61;* J. Kay, *Mein Sohn Wolfgang Amadeus: Glück und Tragik des Vaters Leopold Mozart* (Vienna, 1965); W. Lievense, *De familie Mozart in Nederland: Een reisverslag* (Hilversum, 1965); R. Münster, "Neues zu Leopold Mozarts Augsburger Gymnasialjahren," *Acta Mozartiana,* XII (1965); L. Staehelin, *Die Reise der Familie Mozart durch die Schweiz* (Bern, 1968); L.

Wegele, ed., *Leopold Mozart, 1719–1787: Bild einer Persönlichkeit* (Augsburg, 1969); W. Plath, "Zur Echtheitsfrage bei Mozart: 2. Leopold Mozart," *Mozart Jahrbuch 1971–72;* D. Carlson, *The Sacred Vocal Works of Leopold Mozart* (Diss., Univ. of Michigan, 1976); A. Layer, *Eine Jugend in Augsburg—Leopold Mozart 1719–1787* (Augsburg, 1976).

Mozart, Maria Anna (Walburga Ignatia), nicknamed **"Nannerl,"** daughter of **Leopold Mozart** and sister of **Wolfgang Amadeus Mozart**; b. Salzburg, July 30, 1751; d. there. Oct. 29, 1829. She was taught music by her father from her earliest childhood, and appeared in public as a pianist with her brother; together they traveled to Vienna in 1768; upon her return to Salzburg, she devoted herself mainly to teaching. In 1784 she married Baron von Berchtold zu Sonnenburg, who died in 1801. She went blind in 1825. Although nearly 5 years older than Wolfgang Mozart, she survived him by 38 years, and lived long enough to survive also Beethoven and Schubert.

BIBLIOGRAPHY: W. Hummel, ed. *Nannerl Mozarts Tagebuchblätter mit Eintragungen ihres Bruders Wolfgang Amadeus* (Stuttgart, 1958).

Mozart, Wolfgang Amadeus (baptismal names, **Johannes Chrysostomus Wolfgangus Theophilus**), supreme genius of music whose works in every genre are unsurpassed in lyric beauty, rhythmic variety, and effortless melodic invention; b. Salzburg, Jan. 27, 1756; d. Vienna, Dec. 5, 1791. He and his sister, tenderly nicknamed "Nannerl," were the only 2 among the 7 children of Anna Maria and **Leopold Mozart** to survive infancy. Mozart's sister was 4½ years older; she took harpsichord lessons from her father, and Mozart as a very young child eagerly absorbed the sounds of music. He soon began playing the harpsichord himself, and later studied the violin. Leopold Mozart was an excellent musician, but he also appreciated the theatrical validity of the performances that Wolfgang and Nannerl began giving in Salzburg. On Jan. 17, 1762, he took them to Munich, where they performed before the Elector of Bavaria. In Sept. 1762 they played for Emperor Francis I at his palace in Vienna. The family returned to Salzburg in Jan. 1763, and in June 1763 the children were taken to Frankfurt, where Wolfgang Mozart showed his skill in improvising at the keyboard. In Nov. 1763 they arrived in Paris, where they played before Louis XVI and Marie Antoinette; it was in Paris that Wolfgang's first compositions were printed (4 sonatas for harpsichord, with violin ad libitum). In April 1764 they proceeded to London; there Wolfgang played for King George III. In London he was befriended by Bach's son Johann Christian Bach, who gave exhibitions improvising 4-hands at the piano with the child Mozart. By that time Mozart had tried his ability in composing serious works; he wrote 2 symphs. for a London performance, and the MS of another very early symph., purportedly written by Mozart in London, was discovered in 1980. Leopold Mozart wrote home with undisguised pride: "Our great and mighty Wolfgang seems to know everything at the age of 7 that a man acquires at the age of 40." Knowing the power of publicity, he diminished Wolfgang's age, for at the time the child was fully 9 years old. In July 1765 they journeyed to the Netherlands, then set out for Salzburg, visiting Dijon, Lyons, Geneva, Bern, Zürich, Donaueschingen, and Munich on the way. Arriving in Salzburg in Nov. 1766, Wolfgang applied himself to serious study of counterpoint under the tutelage of his father. In Sept. 1767 the family proceeded to Vienna, where Wolfgang began work on an opera, *La finta semplice;* his 2nd theater work was a singspiel, *Bastien und Bastienne,* which was produced in Vienna at the home of Dr. Franz Mesmer, the protagonist of the famous method of therapy by "animal magnetism," which became known as Mesmerism. On Dec. 7, 1768, Mozart led a performance of his *Missa solemnis* in C minor before the royal family and court at the consecration of the Waisenhauskirche. Upon Mozart's return to Salzburg in Jan. 1769, Archbishop Sigismund von Schrattenbach named him his Konzertmeister; however, the position was without remuneration. Still determined to broaden Mozart's artistic contacts, his father took him on an Italian tour. The announcement for a concert in Mantua on Jan. 16, 1770, just a few days before Mozart's 14th birthday, was typical of the artistic mores of the time: "A Symphony of his own composition; a harpsichord concerto, which will be handed to him, and which he will immediately play *prima vista;* a Sonata handed him in like manner, which he will provide with variations, and afterwards repeat in another key; an Aria, the words for which will be handed to him and which he will immediately set to music and sing himself, accompanying himself on the harpsichord; a Sonata for harpsichord on a subject given him by the leader of the violins; a Strict Fugue on a theme to be selected, which he will improvise on the harpsichord; a Trio in which he will execute a violin part *all' improvviso;* and, finally, the latest Symphony by himself." Legends of Mozart's extraordinary musical ability grew; it was reported, for instance, that Mozart wrote out the entire score of *Miserere* by Allegri, which he had heard in the Sistine Chapel at the Vatican only twice. Young Mozart was subjected to numerous tests by famous Italian musicians, among them Giovanni Sammartini, Piccini, and Padre Martini; he was given a diploma as an elected member of the Accademia Filarmonica in Bologna after he had passed examinations in harmony and counterpoint. On Oct. 10, 1770, the Pope made him a Knight of the Golden Spur. He was commissioned to compose an opera; the result was *Mitradate, rè di Ponto,* which was performed in Milan on Dec. 26, 1770; Mozart himself conducted 22 performances of this opera from the harpsichord; also in Milan he composed a serenata for the wedding festivities of Archduke Ferdinand, which was produced there on Oct. 17, 1771. He returned to Salzburg late in 1771; his patron, Archbishop Schrattenbach, died about that time, and his successor seemed to be indifferent to Mozart as a musician. Once more Mozart went to Italy, where his newest opera, *Lucio Silla,*

was performed in Milan on Dec. 26, 1772. In July 1773 he traveled to Vienna, where he became acquainted with the music of Haydn, who greatly influenced his instrumental style. Returning to Salzburg once more, he supervised the production of his opera *Il Rè pastore,* which was performed on April 23, 1775.

In March 1778 he visited Paris again for a performance of his "Paris" Symph. at a Concert Spirituel. Returning to Salzburg in Jan. 1779, he resumed his duties as Konzertmeister and also obtained the position of court organist at a salary of 450 gulden. In 1780 the Elector of Bavaria commissioned from him an opera seria, *Idomeneo,* which was successfully produced in Munich on Jan. 29, 1781. In May 1781 Mozart lost his position with the Archbishop in Salzburg and decided to move to Vienna, which became his permanent home. There he produced his operatic masterpiece *Die Entführung aus dem Serail,* staged at the Burgtheater on July 16, 1782, with excellent success. On August 4, 1782, he married Constanze Weber, the sister of Aloysia Weber, with whom Mozart had previously been infatuated. Two of his finest symphs. —No. 35 in D major, "Haffner," written for the Haffner family of Salzburg; and No. 36 in C major, the "Linz"— dated from 1782 and 1783, respectively. From this point forward Mozart's productivity reached extraordinary dimensions, but despite the abundance of commissions and concert appearances, he was unable to earn enough to sustain his growing family. Still, melodramatic stories of Mozart's abject poverty are gross exaggerations. He apparently felt no scruples in asking prosperous friends for financial assistance. Periodically he wrote to Michael Puchberg, a banker and a brother Mason (Mozart joined the Masonic Order in 1784), with requests for loans (which he never repaid); invariably Puchberg obliged, but usually granting smaller amounts than Mozart requested. (The market price of Mozart autographs has grown exponentially; a begging letter to Puchberg would fetch, some 2 centuries after it was written, a hundred times the sum requested.) In 1785 Mozart completed a set of 5 string quartets which he dedicated to Haydn; unquestionably the structure of these quartets owed much to Haydn's contrapuntal art. Haydn himself paid a tribute to Mozart's genius; Mozart's father quoted him as saying, "Before God and as an honest man I tell you that your son is the greatest composer known to me either in person or by name." On May 11, 1786, Mozart's great opera buffa, *Le nozze di Figaro,* was produced in Vienna, obtaining a real triumph with the audience; it was performed in Prague early in 1787 with Mozart in attendance. It was during that visit that Mozart wrote his 38th Symph., in D major, known as the "Prague" Symph.; it was in Prague, also, that Mozart's operatic masterpiece *Don Giovanni* was produced, on Oct. 29, 1787. It is interesting to note that at its Vienna performance the opera was staged under the title *Die sprechende Statue,* unquestionably with the intention of sensationalizing the story; the dramatic appearance of the statue of the Commendatore, introduced by the ominous sound of trombones, was a shuddering climax to the work. In Nov. 1787 Mozart was appointed Kammer-musicus in Vienna as a successor to Gluck, albeit at a smaller salary: Mozart received 800 gulden per annum as against Gluck's salary of 2,000 gulden. The year 1788 was a glorious one for Mozart and for music history; it was the year when Mozart composed his last 3 symphs.: No. 39 in E-flat major; No. 40 in G minor; and No. 41 in C major, known under the name "Jupiter" (the Jovian designation was apparently attached to the work for the first time in British concert programs; its earliest use was in the program of the Edinburgh Festival in Oct. 1819). In the spring of 1789 Mozart went to Berlin; on the way he appeared as soloist in one of his piano concertos before the Elector of Saxony in Dresden, and also played the organ at the Thomaskirche in Leipzig. His visits in Potsdam and Berlin were marked by his private concerts at the court of Friedrich Wilhelm II; the King commissioned from him a set of 6 string quartets and a set of 6 piano sonatas, but Mozart died before completing these commissions. Returning to Vienna, Mozart began work on his opera buffa *Così fan tutte* (an untranslatable sentence because *tutte* is the feminine plural, so that the full title would be "Thus do all women"). The opera was first performed in Vienna on Jan. 26, 1790. In Oct. 1790 Mozart went to Frankfurt for the coronation of Emperor Leopold II. Returning to Vienna, he saw Haydn, who was about to depart for London. In 1791, during his last years of life, he completed the score of *Die Zauberflöte*, with a German libretto by Emanuel Schikaneder. It was performed for the first time on Sept. 30, 1791, in Vienna. There followed a mysterious episode in Mozart's life; a stranger called on him with a request to compose a Requiem; the caller was an employee of Count Franz von Walsegg, who intended to have the work performed as his own in memory of his wife. Mozart was unable to finish the score, which was completed by his pupil Franz Xavier Süssmayr, who dutifully handed it over to Walsegg.

The immediate cause of Mozart's death at the age of 35 years, 10 months, and 9 days seems to have been acute nephritis. A detailed discussion of the clinical aspects of Mozart's illness is found in Dieter Kerner's *Krankheiten grosser Musiker* (Stuttgart, 1973; vol. I, pp. 9–87). Almost immediately after the sad event, myths and fantasies appeared in the press; the most persistent of them all was that Mozart had been poisoned by Salieri out of professional jealousy; this particularly morbid piece of invention gained circulation in European journals; the story was further elaborated upon by a report that Salieri confessed his unspeakable crime on his deathbed in 1825. Pushkin used the tale in his drama *Mozart and Salieri,* which Rimsky-Korsakov set to music in his opera of the same title; a fanciful dramatization of the Mozart-Salieri rivalry was made into a successful play, *Amadeus,* by Peter Shaffer, which was produced in London in 1979 and in N.Y. in 1980. A cheap attempt to cash in on the Mozart tragedy was made in a book publ. in 1983, which alleged that Mozart was poisoned by the husband of Mozart's putative mistress, but such repellent publications do not deserve bibliographic notice. The notion of Mozart's murder also appealed to the Nazis; in the ingenious version propagated by some German writers of the Hitlerian persuasion, Mozart was a victim of a double conspiracy of Masons and Jews who were determined to suppress the flowering of racial Germanic greatness; the Masons, in this interpretation, were outraged by Mozart's revealing of their secret rites in *Die Zauberflöte*, and allied themselves with plutocratic Jews to prevent further spread of Mozart's dangerous revelations. Another myth related to Mozart's death that found its way into the majority of Mozart biographies and even into respectable reference works was that a blizzard raged during Mozart's funeral and that none of his friends could follow his body to the cemetery; this story is easily refuted by the records of the Vienna weather bureau for the day (see in this connection N. Slonimsky, "The Weather at Mozart's Funeral," *Musical Quarterly,* Jan. 1960). It is also untrue that Mozart was buried in a pauper's grave; his body was removed from its original individual location because the family neglected to pay the mandatory dues.

The universal recognition of Mozart's genius during the 2 centuries since his death has never wavered among professional musicians, amateurs, and the general public. In his music, smiling simplicity was combined with somber drama; lofty inspiration was contrasted with playful diversion; profound meditation alternated with capricious moodiness; religious concentration was permeated with human tenderness. Devoted as Mozart was to his art and respectful as he was of the rules of composition, he was also capable of mocking the professional establishment. A delightful example of this persiflage is his little piece *Ein musikalischer Spass,* subtitled "Dorf Musikanten," a "musical joke" at the expense of "village musicians," in which Mozart all but anticipated developments of modern music, 2 centuries in the future; he deliberately used the forbidden consecutive fifths, allowed the violin to escape upward in a whole-tone scale, and finished the entire work in a welter of polytonal triads.

The variety of technical development in Mozart's works is all the more remarkable considering the limitations of instrumental means in his time; the topmost note on his keyboard was F above the 3rd ledger line, so that in the recapitulation in the first movement of Mozart's famous C major Piano Sonata, the subject had to be dropped an octave lower to accommodate the modulation. The vocal technique displayed in Mozart's operas is amazing in its perfection; to be sure, the human voice has not changed since Mozart's time, but Mozart knew how to exploit vocal resources to the utmost. This adaptability of his genius to all available means of sound production is the secret of the eternal validity of his music, and the explanation of the present popularity of Mozart mini-festivals, such as the N.Y. concert series advertised as "Mostly Mozart."

In the list of Mozart's works given below, the K. numbers represent the system of identification established by L. von Köchel in his *Chronologisch-thematisches Verzeichnis sämtlicher Tonwerke*

Mozart

Wolfgang Amade Mozarts (Leipzig, 1862; 6th ed., revised by F. Giegling, A. Weinmann, and G. Sievers, Wiesbaden, 1964); the revised K. numbers of the 6th edition are also included.

WORKS: OPERAS AND OTHER COMPOSITIONS FOR THE STAGE: *Apollo et Hyacinthus,* K. 38, Latin intermezzo (Salzburg Univ., May 13, 1767); *La finta semplice,* K. 51; 46a, opera buffa (Archbishop's palace, Salzburg, May 1?, 1769); *Bastien und Bastienne,* K. 50; 46b, singspiel (Franz Mesmer's residence, Vienna, Sept.?–Oct.? 1768); *Mitridate, Rè di Ponto,* K. 87; 74a, opera seria (Regio Ducal Teatro, Milan, Dec. 26, 1770); *Ascanio in Alba,* K. 111, festa teatrale (Regio Ducal Teatro, Milan, Oct. 17, 1771); *Il sogno di Scipione,* K. 126, serenata (Archbishop's palace, Salzburg, May? 1772); *Lucio Silla,* K. 135, opera seria (Regio Ducal Teatro, Milan, Dec. 26, 1772); *La finta giardiniera,* K. 196, opera buffa (Munich, Jan. 13, 1775; also produced as a singspiel, *Die verstellte Gärtnerin,* Augsburg, May 1, 1780); *Il Rè pastore,* K. 208, dramma per musica (Archbishop's palace, Salzburg, April 23, 1775); *Semiramis,* K. Anh. 11; 315e, duodrama (not extant); *Thamos, König in Ägypten,* K. 345; 336a, music for Gebler's play; *Zaide,* K. 344; 336b, singspiel (unfinished; dialogue rewritten and finished by Gollmick, with overture and finale added by Anton André, Frankfurt, Jan. 27, 1866); *Idomeneo, Rè di Creta,* K. 366, opera seria (Hoftheater, Munich, Jan. 29, 1781); *Die Entführung aus dem Serail,* K. 384, singspiel (Burgtheater, Vienna, July 16, 1782); *L'oca del Cairo,* K. 422, opera buffa (unfinished); *Lo Sposo deluso,* K. 430; 424a, opera buffa (unfinished); *Der Schauspieldirektor,* K. 486, singspiel (Schönbrunn Palace, Heitzing [suburb of Vienna], Feb. 7, 1786); *Le nozze di Figaro,* K. 492, opera buffa (Burgtheater, Vienna, May 1, 1786); *Il dissoluto punito, ossia Il Don Giovanni,* K. 527, opera buffa (National Theater, Prague, Oct. 29, 1787); *Così fan tutte, ossia La scuola degli amanti,* K. 588, opera buffa (Burgtheater, Vienna, Jan. 26, 1790); *Die Zauberflöte,* K. 620, singspiel (Theater auf der Wieden, Vienna, Sept. 30, 1791); *La clemenza di Tito,* K. 621, opera seria (National Theater, Prague, Sept. 6, 1791). —Arias and scenes for Voice and Orch.: 39 for Soprano (4 not extant); one for Alto; 11 for Tenor (one with only 48 bars extant); 8 for Bass. —Duets for Solo Voices and Orch.: One for 2 Tenors; one for Soprano and Tenor; 2 for Soprano and Bass. —Ensembles for Solo Voices and Orch.: one for Soprano, Tenor, and Bass; one for Tenor and 2 Basses; one for Soprano, Tenor, and 2 Basses; one for Soprano, Alto, Tenor, and Bass (not extant).—Ensembles for Solo Voices, and Piano or other Instruments: One for 2 Sopranos; 5 for 2 Sopranos and Bass; 2 for Soprano, Tenor, and Bass; one for 2 Sopranos and Bass; one for Soprano, 2 Tenors, and Bass.—34 songs for Solo Voices, with Piano (2 with Mandolin; 2 Masonic songs, with Male Chorus). —Numerous canons.

MASSES, ORATORIOS, CANTATAS, ETC.: Kyrie in F major, K. 33 (1766); *Die Schuldigkeit des ersten Gebots,* K. 35, sacred drama (1767; part one by Mozart, part 2 by Michael Haydn, part 3 by Adlgasser; Salzburg, March 12, 1767); *Grabmusik,* K. 42; 35a, cantata (1767; Salzburg Cathedral, April 7, 1767); *Missa sol-*

emnis in C minor, K. 139; 47a, "Waisenhausmesse" (1768; Vienna, Dec. 7, 1768); *Missa brevis* in G major, K. 49; 47d (1768; only fragments extant); *Missa brevis* in D minor, K. 65; 61a (1769; Collegiate Church, Salzburg, Feb. 5, 1769); *Missa* in C major, K. 66, "Dominicus" (1769; St. Peter, Salzburg, Oct. 15, 1769); *La Betulia liberata,* K. 118; 74c, oratorio (1771); *Missa brevis* in G major, K. 140; C 1.12 (1773; may not be by Mozart); *Missa* in C major, K. 167, "In honorem Ssmae Trinitatis" (1773); *Missa brevis* in F major, K. 192; 186f (1774); *Missa brevis* in D major, K. 194; 186h (1774); *Missa brevis* in G major, K. 220; 196b, "Spatzenmesse" (1775–76); *Missa* in C major, K. 262; 246a (1775); *Missa* in C major, K. 257, "Credo" (1776); *Missa brevis* in C major, K. 258, "Spaur" (1776); *Missa brevis* in C major, K. 259, "Organ Solo" (1776); *Missa brevis* in B-flat major, K. 275; 272b (1777; St. Peter, Salzburg, Dec. 21, 1777); *Missa* in C major, K. 317, "Coronation" (1779); *Missa solemnis* in C major, K. 337 (1780); *Kyrie* in D minor, K. 341; 368a (1780–81); *Missa* in C minor, K. 427; 417a (1782–83; unfinished; Kyrie and Gloria, St. Peter, Salzburg, Oct. 25, 1783); *Dir, Seele des Weltalls,* K. 429; 468a, cantata (1785; unfinished); *Davidde penitente,* K. 469, oratorio (1785; music from the *Missa* in C minor, K. 427; 417a, 2 arias excepted); *Die Maurerfreunde,* K. 471, cantata (1785; "Zur gekronten Hoffnung" Lodge, Vienna, April 24, 1785); *Die ihr des unermesslichen Weltalls Schöpfer ehrt,* K. 619, cantata (1791); *Eine kleine Freimaurer-Kantate,* K. 623 (1791; "Zur neugekronten Hoffnung" Lodge, Vienna, Nov. 18, 1791); Requiem in D minor, K. 626 (1791; unfinished; completed by Franz Xavier Süssmayr). —Also the following: *God Is Our Refuge* in G minor, K. 20, motet (1765); *Stabat Mater,* K. 33c (1766; not extant); *Scande coeli limina* in C major, K. 34, offertory (1767); *Veni Sancte Spiritus* in C major, K. 47 (1768); *Benedictus sit Deus* in C major, K. 117; 66a, offertory (1769); *Te Deum* in C major, K. 141; 66b (1769); *Ergo interest* in G major, K. 143; 73a, motet (1773); Miserere in A minor, K. 85; 73s (1770); *Cibavit eos* in A minor, K. 44; 73u, antiphon (1770; may not be by Mozart); *Quaerite primum* in D minor, K. 86; 73v, antiphon (1770); *Regina coeli* in C major, K. 108; 74d (1771); *Inter natos mulierum* in G major, K. 72; 74f, offertory (1771); *Regina coeli* in B-flat major, K. 127 (1772); *Exultate, jubilate* in F major, K. 165; 158a, motet (1773; Milan, Jan. 17, 1773); *Tantum ergo* in D major, K. 197; C 3.05 (1774; may not be by Mozart); *Sub tuum praesidium* in F major, K. 198; C 3.08, offertory (1774; may not be by Mozart); *Misericordias Domini* in D minor, K. 222; 205a, offertory (1775); *Venite populi* in D major, K. 260; 248a (1776); *Alma Dei creatoris* in F major, K. 277; 272a, offertory (1777); *Sancta Maria, mater Dei* in F major, K. 273, gradual (1777); Miserere, K. Anh. 1; 297a (1778; not extant); *Kommet her, ihr frechen Sünder* in B-flat major, K. 146; 317b, aria (1779); *Regina coeli* in C major, K. 276; 321b (1779?); *O Gottes Lamm; Als aus Aegypten,* K. 343; 336c, 2 German sacred songs (1787?); *Ave verum corpus* in D major, K. 618, motet (1791).—Additional works: *Litaniae Lauretanae* in B-flat major, K. 109; 74e (1771); *Litaniae de venerabili altaris sacramento* in B-flat major, K. 125 (1772); *Litaniae Lauretanae* in D major, K. 195;

186d (1774); *Dixit Dominus, Magnificat* in C major, K. 193; 186g (1774); *Litaniae de venerabili altaris sacramento* in E-flat major, K. 243 (1776); *Vesperae de Dominica* in C major, K. 321 (1779); *Vesperae solennes de confessore* in C major, K. 339 (1780).

For orch.: symphs.: No. 1, in E-flat major, K. 16 (1764–65); A minor, K. Anh. 220; 16a (1765; not extant); No. 4, in D major, K. 19 (1765); F major, K. Anh. 223; 19a (1765; considered lost until discovered in 1980); C major, K. Anh. 222; 19b (1765; not extant); No. 5, in B-flat major, K. 22 (1765); No. 43, in F major, K. 76; 42a (1767); No. 6, in F major, K. 43 (1767); No. 7, in D major, K. 45 (1767); G major, K. Anh. 221; 45a, "Old Lambach" (1768; may be by Leopold Mozart); G major, "New Lambach" (1768); B-flat major, K. Anh. 214; 45b (1768); No. 8, in D major, K. 48 (1768); D major, K. Anh. 215; 66c (1769; not extant); B-flat major, K. Anh. 217; 66d (1769; not extant); B-flat major, K. Anh. 218; 66e (1769; not extant); No. 9, in C major, K. 73 (1772); No. 44, in D major, K. 81; 731 (1770; may be by Leopold Mozart); No. 47, in D major, K. 97; 73m (1770); No. 45, in D major, K. 95; 73n (1770); No. 11, in D major, K. 84; 73q (1770; may not be by Mozart); No. 10, in G major, K. 74 (1770); B-flat major, K. Anh. 216; C 11.03 (1770–71; may not be by Mozart; No. 42, in F major, K. 75 (1771); No. 12, in G major, K. 110; 75b (1771); D major, K. 120; 111a (1771; finale only; perf. with the overture to *Ascanio in Alba,* K. 111, forming a symph.); No. 46, in C major, K. 96; 111b (1771); No. 13, in F major, K. 112 (1771); No. 14, in A major, K. 114 (1771); No. 15, in G major, K. 124 (1772); No. 16, in C major, K. 128 (1772); No. 17, in G major, K. 129 (1772); No. 18, in F major, K. 130 (1772); No. 19, in E-flat major, K. 132 (1772; with alternative slow movements); No. 20, in D major, K. 133 (1772); No. 21, in A major, K. 134 (1772); No. 50, in D major, K. 161, 163; 141a (1773–74); No. 26, in E-flat major, K. 184; 161a (1773); No. 27, in G major, K. 199; 161b (1773); No. 22, in C major, K. 162 (1773); No. 23, in D major, K. 181; 162b (1773); No. 24, in B-flat major, K. 182; 173dA (1773); No. 25, in G minor, K. 183; 173dB (1773); No. 29, in A major, K. 201; 186a (1774); No. 30, in D major, K. 202; 186b (1774); No. 28, in C major, K. 200; 189k (1774); D major, K. 121; 207a (1774–75; finale only; perf. with the overture to *La finta giardiniera,* K. 196, forming a symph.); D major (4 movements from the Serenade in D major, K. 204; 213a); C major, K. 102; 213c (1775; finale only; perf. with versions of the overture and first aria from *Il Rè pastore,* K. 208); D major (4 movements from the Serenade in D major, K. 250; 248b); No. 31, in D major, K. 297; 300a, "Paris" (1778: with 2 slow movements); No. 32, in G major, K. 318 (1779; in one movement); No. 33, in B-flat major, K. 319 (1779); D major (3 movements from the Serenade in D major, K. 320, "Posthorn"); No. 34, in C major, K. 338 (1780); C major, K. 409; 383f (1782; minuet only; may have been intended for the Symph. No. 34 in C major, K. 338); No. 35, in D major, K. 385, "Haffner" (1782; based on the Serenade in D major, K. 250; 248b, "Haffner"); No. 36, in C major, K. 425, "Linz" (1783); No. 37, in G major, K. 444; 425a (1783?; only the introduction is by Mozart; remainder by Michael Haydn; No. 38, in D major, K. 504, "Prague" (1786); No. 39, in E-flat major, K. 543 (1788); No. 40, in G minor, K. 550 (1788);

No. 41, in C major, K. 551, "Jupiter" (1788). A symph. listed as K. Anh. 8; 311A was never composed.

Piano concertos: No. 5, in D major, K. 175 (1773); No. 6, in B-flat major, K. 238 (1776); No. 8, in C major, K. 246 (1776); No. 9, in E-flat major, K. 271 (1777); No. 12, in A major, K. 414; 385p (1782); No. 11, in F major, K. 413; 387a (1782–83); No. 13, in C major, K. 415; 387b (1782–83); No. 14, in E-flat major, K. 449 (1784); No. 15, in B-flat major, K. 450 (1784); No. 16, in D major, K. 451 (1784); No. 17, in G major, K. 453 (1784); No. 18, in B-flat major, K. 456 (1784); No. 19, in F major, K. 459 (1784); No. 20, in D minor, K. 466 (1785); No. 21, in C major, K. 467 (1785); No. 22, in E-flat major, K. 482 (1785); No. 23, in A major, K. 488 (1786); No. 24, in C minor, K. 491 (1786); No. 25, in C major, K. 503 (1786); No. 26, in D major, K. 537, "Coronation" (1788); No. 27, in B-flat major, K. 595 (1790–91).— Also No. 10, in E-flat major, for 2 Pianos, K. 365; 316a (1779); No. 7, in F major, for 3 Pianos, K. 242 (1776); Rondo in D major, K. 382; new finale for No. 5, in D major, K. 175; Rondo in A major, K. 386 (1782).

Violin concertos: No. 1, in B-flat major, K. 207 (1775); No. 2, in D major, K. 211 (1775); No. 3, in G major, K. 216 (1775); No. 4, in D major, K. 218 (1775); No. 5, in A major, K. 219 (1775).—Also the following: Concertone in C major for 2 Violins, K. 190; 186e (1774); Adagio in E major for Violin, K. 261 (1776; for Violin Concerto No. 5, in A major, K. 219); Rondo in B-flat major for Violin, K. 269; 261a (1776); Sinfonia concertante in E-flat major for Violin and Viola, K. 364; 320d (1779); Rondo in C major for Violin, K. 373 (1781); Andante in A major for Violin, K. 470 (1785; not extant).

For wind instruments: Concerto for Trumpet, K. 47c (1768; not extant); Concerto for Bassoon in B-flat major, K. 191; 186e (1774); Concerto for Oboe, K. 271k (1777; not extant; perhaps a version of K. 314; 285d below); Concerto for Flute in G major, K. 313; 285c (1778); Concerto for Oboe or Flute in C/D major, K. 314; 285d (1778; oboe version may be for K. 271k above); Andante for Flute in C major, K. 315; 285e (1779–80); Sinfonia concertante for Flute, Oboe, Bassoon, and Horn, K. Anh. 9; 297B (1778?; not extant; may not have been composed); Sinfonia concertante in E-flat major for Oboe, Clarinet, Bassoon, and Horn, K. Anh. 9; C 14.01 (doubtful); Concerto for Flute and Harp in C major, K. 299; 297c (1778); Sinfonia concertante in G major for 2 Flutes, 2 Oboes, and 2 Bassoons, K. 320 (movements 3 and 4 of the Serenade in D major, K. 320, "Posthorn"); Rondo for Horn in E-flat major, K. 371 (1781; unfinished); concertos for Horn: No. 1, in D major, K. 412; 386b (1782–87); No. 2, in E-flat major, K. 417 (1783); No. 3, in E-flat major, K. 447 (1783?); No. 4, in E-flat major, K. 495 (1786); Concerto for Clarinet in A major, K. 622 (1791).

Serenades, divertimentos, cassations, etc.: *Gallimathias musicum,* K. 32 (1766); 6 divertimentos, K. 41a (1767; not extant); Cassation in D major, K. 100; 62a (1769); Cassation in G major, K. 63 (1769); Cassation in C major (1769; not extant); Cassation in B-flat major, K. 99; 63a (1769); Divertimento in E-flat major, K. 113 (1771); Divertimento in D major, K. 131 (1772); Divertimento in D major, K. 205; 167a

Mozart

(1773?); Serenade in D major, K. 185; 167a (1773); Serenade in D major, K. 203; 189b (1774); Serenade in D major, K. 204; 213a (1775); *Serenata notturna* in D major, K. 239 (1776); Divertimento in F major, K. 247 (1776); Serenade in D major, K. 250; 248b, "Haffner" (1776); Divertimento in D major, K. 251 (1776); *Notturno* in D major, K. 286; 269a (1776–77); Divertimento in B-flat major, K. 287; 271h (1777); Serenade in D major, K. 320, "Posthorn" (1779); Divertimento in D major, K. 334; 320b (1779–80); *Maurerische Trauermusik* in C minor, K. 477; 479a (1785); *Ein musikalischer Spass* in F major, K. 522 (1787; satirical; employs deliberate discords, consecutive fifths, etc.); *Eine kleine Nachtmusik* in G major, K. 525 (1787).—Also 14 divertimentos for Wind Ensemble; 15 marches (2 not extant); 10 German dances, *ländler;* 17 contredanses (several not extant); ballet, *Les Petits Riens,* K. Anh. 10; 299b (1778; Opéra, Paris, June 11, 1778); etc.

CHAMBER MUSIC: STRING QUARTETS: G major, K. 80; 73f (1770); Divertimento in D major, K. 136; 125a (1772); Divertimento in B-flat major, K. 137; 125b (1772); Divertimento in F major, K. 138; 125c (1772); D major, K. 155; 134a (1772); G major, K. 156; 134b (1772); C major, K. 157 (1772–73); F major, K. 158 (1772–73); B-flat major, K. 159 (1773); E-flat major, K. 160; 159a (1773); F major, K. 168 (1773); A major, K. 169 (1773); C major, K. 170 (1773); E-flat major, K. 171 (1773); B-flat major, K. 172 (1773); D minor, K. 173 (1773); G major, K. 387 (1782); D minor, K. 421; 417b (1783); E-flat major, K. 428; 421b (1783); B-flat major, K. 458, "Hunt" (1784); A major, K. 464 (1785); C major, K. 465, "Dissonance" (1785); D major, K. 499, "Hoffmeister" (1786); Adagio and Fugue in C minor, K. 546 (1788); D major, K. 575, "Prussian" (1789); B-flat major, K. 589, "Prussian" (1790); F major, K. 590, "Prussian" (1790).

STRING QUINTETS (2 Violins, 2 Violas, and Cello): B-flat major, K. 174 (1773); C major, K. 515 (1787); G minor, K. 516 (1787); C minor, K. 406; 516b (1788); D major, K. 593 (1790); E-flat major, K. 614 (1791).

FOR STRINGS AND WIND INSTRUMENTS: Duo in B-flat major for Bassoon and Cello, K. 292; 196c (1775); Quartet in D major for Flute, Violin, Viola, and Cello, K. 285 (1777); Quartet in G major for Flute, Violin, Viola, and Cello, K. 285a (1778); Quartet in C major for Flute, Violin, Viola, and Cello, K. Anh. 171; 285b (1781–82); Quartet in A major for Flute, Violin, Viola, and Cello, K. 298 (1786–87); Quartet in F major for Oboe, Violin, Viola, and Cello, K. 370; 368b (1781); Quintet in E-flat major for Horn, Violin, 2 Violas, and Cello, K. 407; 386c (1782); Quintet in A major for Clarinet, 2 Violins, Viola, and Cello, K. 581 (1789).

STRING SONATAS, DUOS, AND TRIOS: Solos for Cello and Bassoon, K. 33b (1766; not extant); *Nachtmusik* for 2 Violins and Bassoon, K. 41g (1767; not extant); Sonata in C major for Violin and Bassoon, K. 46d (1768); Sonata in F major for Violin and Bassoon, K. 46e (1768); Trio in B-flat major for 2 Violins and Bassoon, K. 266; 271f (1777); 4 preludes for Violin, Viola, and Cello, K. 404a (1782; may not be by Mozart); Duo in G major for Violin and Viola, K. 423 (1783); Duo in B-flat major for Violin and Viola, K. 424 (1783); Trio in E-flat major for Violin, Viola, and

Cello, K. 563 (1788).

FOR KEYBOARD AND OTHER INSTRUMENTS: Divertimento in B-flat major for Piano, Violin, and Cello, K. 254 (1776); Trio in D minor for Piano, Violin, and Cello, K. 442 (1783?–90; unfinished; completed by M. Stadler); Quintet in E-flat major for Piano, Oboe, Clarinet, Bassoon, and Horn, K. 452 (1784); Quartet in G minor for Piano, Violin, Viola, and Cello, K. 478 (1785); Quartet in E-flat major for Piano, Violin, Viola, and Cello, K. 493 (1786); Trio in G major for Piano, Violin, and Cello, K. 496 (1786); Trio in E-flat major for Piano, Clarinet, and Viola, K. 498 (1786); Trio in B-flat major for Piano, Violin, and Cello, K. 502 (1786); Trio in E major for Piano, Violin, and Cello, K. 542 (1788); Trio in C major for Piano, Violin, and Cello, K. 548 (1788); Trio in G major for Piano, Violin, and Cello, K. 564 (1788); Adagio and Rondo in C minor for Glass Harmonica, Flute, Oboe, Viola, and Cello, K. 617 (1791).

FOR KEYBOARD AND VIOLIN: Sonata in C major, K. 6 (1762–64); Sonata in D major, K. 7 (1762–64); Sonata in B-flat major, K. 8 (1763–64); Sonata in G major, K. 9 (1763–64); Sonata in B-flat major, K. 10 (1764); Sonata in G major, K. 11 (1764); Sonata in A major, K. 12 (1764); Sonata in F major, K. 13 (1764); Sonata in C major, K. 14 (1764); Sonata in B-flat major, K. 15 (1764); Sonata in E-flat major, K. 26 (1766); Sonata in G major, K. 27 (1766); Sonata in C major, K. 28 (1766); Sonata in D major, K. 29 (1766); Sonata in F major, K. 30 (1766); Sonata in B-flat major, K. 31 (1766); Sonata in G major, K. 301; 293a (1778); Sonata in E-flat major, K. 302; 293b (1778); Sonata in C major, K. 303; 293c (1778); Sonata in A major, K. 305; 293d (1778); Sonata in C major, K. 296 (1778); Sonata in E minor, K. 304; 300c (1778); Sonata in D major, K. 306; 300l (1778); Sonata in B-flat major, K. 378; 317d (1779?); Sonata in B-flat major, K. 372 (1781; unfinished; completed by M. Stadler); Sonata in G major, K. 379; 373a (1781); Variations in G major, K. 359; 374a (1781); Variations in G minor, K. 360; 374b (1781); Sonata in F major, K. 376; 374d (1781); Sonata in F major, K. 377; 374e (1781); Sonata in E-flat major, K. 380; 374f (1781); Sonata in C major, K. 403; 385c (1782; unfinished; completed by M. Stadler); Sonata in C major, K. 404; 385d (1782?; unfinished); Sonata in A major, K. 402; 385e (1782; unfinished; completed by M. Stadler); Sonata in C minor, K. 396; 385f (1782; one movement only; completed by M. Stadler); Sonata in B-flat major, K. 454 (1784); Sonata in E-flat major, K. 481 (1785); Sonata in A major, K. 526 (1787); Sonata in F major, K. 547, "für Anfänger" (1788).

FOR KEYBOARD SOLO: Sonata in G major, K. Anh. 199; 33d (1766; not extant); Sonata in B-flat major, K. Anh. 200; 33e (1766; not extant); Sonata in C major, K. 201; 33f (1766; not extant); Sonata in F major, K. 202; 33g (1766; not extant); Sonata in C major, K. 279; 189d (1775); Sonata in F major, K. 280; 189e (1775); Sonata in B-flat major, K. 281; 189f (1775); Sonata in E-flat major, K. 282; 189g (1775); Sonata in G major, K. 283; 189h (1775); Sonata in D major, K. 284; 205b (1775); Sonata in C major, K. 309; 284b (1777); Sonata in D major, K. 311; 284c (1777); Sonata in A minor, K. 310; 300d (1778); Sonata in C major, K. 330; 300h (1781–83); Sonata in A major, K. 331; 300i (1781–83);

Sonata in F major, K. 332; 300k (1781–83); Sonata in B-flat major, K. 333; 315c (1783–84); Sonata in C minor, K. 457 (1784); Sonata in F major, K. 533 (1786); Sonata in C major, K. 545, "für Anfänger" (1788); Sonata in F major, K. Anh. 135; 547a (1788; may not be by Mozart); Sonata in B-flat major, K. 570 (1789); Sonata in D major, K. 576 (1789).

FOR KEYBOARD DUET: Sonata in C major, K. 19d (1765); Sonata in D major, K. 381; 123a (1772); Sonata in B-flat major, K. 358; 186c (1773–74); Sonata in F major, K. 497 (1786); Sonata in C major, K. 521 (1787).—Also: Sonata in D major for 2 Keyboards, K. 448; 375a (1781); 17 variations for Keyboard Solo (one not extant) and one for Piano Duet; many miscellaneous pieces; 17 sonatas for Organ, most with 2 Violins and Bassoon; etc.

Since the publication of the Breitkopf & Härtel edition of Mozart's works, the list of doubtful and spurious compositions has grown extensively. The pioneering research of Wyzewa and Saint-Foix has been followed by the important studies of Wolfgang Plath, Alan Tyson, and other scholars. For detailed information, see the bibliography below. A selected compilation of doubtful and spurious works follows (those noted in the list of works above are excluded);

Masses: F major, K. 116; 90a, by Leopold Mozart; E-flat major, K. Anh. 235f; C 1.02, by B. Schack; G major, K. Anh. 232; C 1.04, "Twelfth Mass"; G major, K. *deest;* C 1.18, "Missa solemnis pastorita"; D minor, K. Anh. 237; C 1.90, "Requiem brevis"; Kyrie in C major, K. 340; C 3.06; Kyrie in C major, K. 221; A1, by Eberlin.—Also: *Lacrimosa* in C minor, K. Anh. 21; A2, by Eberlin; *Justum deduxit Dominus,* hymn, K. 326; A4, by Eberlin; *Adoramus te,* hymn, K. 327; A10, by Q. Gasparini; *De profundis clamavi,* Psalm, K. 93; A22, by Reutter; *Salve Regina,* K. 92; C 3.01; *Tantum ergo* in B-flat major, K. 142; C 3.04; *Offertorium sub exposito venerabili,* K. 177 and 342; C 3.09, by Leopold Mozart.

Symphs.: No. 2, in B-flat major, K. 17; C 11.02; B-flat major, K. Anh. 216; C 11.03; No. 3, in E-flat major, K. 18; A51, by C.F. Abel; F major, K. 98; C 11.04; B-flat major, K. 311a; C 11.05, the so-called "2nd Paris" Symph.—Also: Fugue in D major, K. 291; A52, by M. Haydn, finished by S. Sechter.

Piano concertos: The first 4 piano concertos, K. 37, 39, 40, and 41, are arrangements of sonata movements by Raupach, Honauer, Schobert, Eckard, and C.P.E. Bach; the 5th Piano Concerto, K. 107, consists of arrangements of 3 sonatas by Johann Christian Bach.

Violin concertos: Two violin concertos, one in D major, K. 271a; 271i, the other in E-flat major, K. 268; C 14.04, may contain some music composed by Mozart. The Violin Concerto in D major, K. Anh. 294a; C 14.05, the so-called "Adelaide" Concerto, which was widely performed after its alleged discovery in 1931, was actually composed by the French violinist Marius Casadesus; it was supposedly dedicated to Princess Adelaide, the daughter of Louis XV, by the boy Mozart during his visit to Paris at the age of 10.—Also: *Sinfonia concertante* in A major for Violin, Viola, and Cello, K. Anh. 104; 320e.

Sonatas for Keyboard and Violin: K. 55–60;

C 23.01–6 and K. 61, by Raupach.

BIBLIOGRAPHY: COLLECTED EDITIONS, SOURCE MATERIAL: The first collected edition of Mozart's works was edited by L. von Köchel et al. as *W.A. Mozarts Werke;* it was publ. by Breitkopf & Härtel (74 vols. in 24 series, Leipzig, 1877–83; 11 supplementary vols., Leipzig, 1877–1910). A new critical edition, *W.A. Mozart: Neue Ausgabe Sämtlicher Werke,* ed. by E. Schmid et al., began publication in Kassel in 1955; it is sponsored by the Internationale Stiftung Mozarteum Salzburg.

The standard thematic catalogue is L. von Köchel, ed., *Chronologisch-thematisches Verzeichnis sämtlicher Tonwerke Wolfgang Amade Mozarts* (Leipzig, 1862; 3rd ed., extensively revised by A. Einstein, Leipzig, 1937; reprint, with supplement, Ann Arbor, Mich., 1947; 6th ed., a major revision, by F. Giegling, A. Weinmann, and G. Sievers, Wiesbaden, 1964; the 6th ed. contains a revised K. numbering system; further supplementary material is found in the *Mozart-Jahrbuch 1971–2,* pp. 342–401, as prepared by P. van Reijen).

See also the following: Mozart's own *Verzeichnüss aller meiner Werke* (facsimile ed. by O. Deutsch as *W.A. M.: Verzeichnis aller meiner Werke: Faksimile der Handschrift mit dem Beiheft "M.s Werkverzeichnis 1784–1791,"* Vienna, 1938; Eng. ed., 1956; also another ed. by E. Müller von Asow as *W.A. M.: Verzeichnis aller meiner Werke und Leopold Mozart: Verzeichnis der Jugendwerke W.A. M.s,* Vienna, 1943; 2nd ed., 1956); A. André, *Thematischer Katalog wie M. solchen von 1784–91 eigenhändig geschrieben hat* (Offenbach, 1805; 2nd ed., augmented, 1828); K. Moyses, *Systematischer Katalog der im Mozarteum befindlichen Autographe M.s* (Salzburg, 1862); C. von Wurzbach, *M.-Buch* (Vienna, 1869); J. Horner, *Katalog des M.s-Museums zu Salzburg* (Salzburg, 1882; 2nd ed. by J. Engl, 1898); H. de Curzon, *Essai de bibliographie mozartienne: Revue critique des ouvrages relatifs à W.A. M. et ses œuvres* (Paris, 1906); L. Schiedermair, *W.A. M.s Handschrift in zeitlich geordneten Nachbildungen* (Bückeburg and Leipzig, 1919); M. Blaschitz, *Die Salzburger M.-Fragmente* (Diss., Univ. of Bonn, 1924); O. Keller, *W.A. M.: Bibliographie und Ikonographie* (Berlin, 1927); O. Deutsch and C. Oldman, "M.-Drucke: Eine bibliographisches Ergänzung zu Köchels Werkverzeichnis," *Zeitschrift für Musikwissenschaft,* XIV (1931–32); C. Oldman, "M. and Modern Research," *Proceedings of the Royal Musical Association,* LVIII (1931–32); H. Farmer and H. Smith, *New Mozartiana: The M. Relics in the Zavertal Collection at the University of Glasgow* (Glasgow, 1935); O. Deutsch, "M.s Nachlass: Aus den Briefen Constanzes an den Verlag André," *M.-Jahrbuch 1953;* idem, "M.s Verleger," *M.-Jahrbuch 1955;* A. Hyatt King, *M. in the British Museum* (London, 1956); H. Moldenhauer, "Übersicht der Musikmanuskripte W.A. M.s in den Vereinigten Staaten von Amerika (1956)," *M.-Jahrbuch 1956;* L. Nowak, "Die Wiener M.-Autographen," *Österreichische Musikzeitschrift,* XI (1956); M. and C. Raeburn, "M.'s Manuscripts in Florence," *Music & Letters* (Oct. 1959); W. Plath, "Beiträge zur M.-Autographie I: Die Handschrift Leopold Mozarts," *M.-Jahrbuch 1960–61;* O. Schneider and A. Algatzy, *M.-Handbuch: Chronik, Werk, Bibliographie* (Vienna, 1962); A. Abert, "Methoden der Mozartforschung," *M.-Jahrbuch 1964;* H. Engel, "Probleme der Mozartforschung," *M.-Jahrbuch 1964;* G. Rech, "M.: Results of Present-Day Research on His Works," *Universitas,* VII (1965); G. Croll, "Zu den Verzeichnissen von M.s nachgelassenen Fragmenten und Entwurfen," *Österreichische Musikzeitschrift,* XXI (1966); K. Pfannhauser, "Epilegomena Mozartiana," *M.-Jahrbuch 1971–2;* W. Plath, "Leopold Mozarts Notenbuch für Wolfgang (1762): Eine Falschung?," *M.-Jahrbuch 1971–2;* W. Plath et al., "Zur Echtheitsfrage bei M.," *M.-Jahrbuch 1971–2;* N. Zaslaw, "A Rediscovered M. Autograph at Cornell University," *M.-Jahrbuch 1971–2;* D. Leeson and D. Whitwell, "M.'s Thematic Catalogue," *Musical Times* (Aug. 1973); A. Hyatt King, "Some Aspects of Recent M. Research," *Proceedings of the Royal Musical Association,* C (1973–74); R. Angermüller and O. Schneider, "M.-Bibliographie (bis 1970)," *M.-Jahrbuch 1975;* W. Senn, "Beiträge zur Mozartforschung," *Acta Musicologica,* XLVIII (1976); W. Plath, "Beiträge zur M.-Autographie II: Schriftchronologie 1770–1780," *M.-Jahrbuch 1976–7;* R. Angermüller and O. Schneider, *M.-Bibliographie 1971–1975 mit Nachträgen bis 1970* (Kassel, 1978); O. Wessely, "Ergänzerungen zur M.-Bibliographie," *Studien zur Musikwissenschaft,* XXIX (1978).

YEARBOOKS AND OTHER PUBLICATIONS: *Jahresbericht des Mozarteums* (Salzburg, 1880–1917); *Mitteilungen für die Mozartgemeinde in Berlin* (Berlin, 1895–1925); *Mozarteums-Mitteilungen* (Salzburg, 1918–21); *M.-Jahrbuch* (3 vols., Munich, 1923, 1924, and 1929); *Wiener Figaro* (issued by the Mozartgemeinde of Vienna, 1931—); *Neues M.-Jahrbuch* (3 vols., Regensburg, 1941–43); *M.-Jahrbuch* (Salzburg, 1950—); *Mitteilungen der Internationalen Stiftung Mozarteum* (Salzburg, 1952—); *Acta Mozartiana* (issued by the Deutschen Mozart-Gesellschaft of Augsburg, 1954—).

CORRESPONDENCE: L. Nohl, *M.s Briefe nach den Originalen herausgegeben* (Salzburg, 1865; Eng. trans. by Lady Wallace, London, 1866; 2nd German ed., augmented, Leipzig, 1877); H. de Curzon, *Nouvelles lettres des dernières années de la vie de M.* (Paris, 1898); K. Storck, *M.s Briefe in Auswahl* (Stuttgart, 1906); A. Leitzmann, *M.s Briefe ausgewählt* (Leipzig, 1910); M. Weigel, *M.s Briefe* (Berlin, 1910); H. Leichtentritt, *M.s Briefe* (Berlin, 1912); L. Schiedermair, *Die Briefe W.A. M.s und seiner Familie: Erste kritische Gesamtausgabe* (5 vols., of which the last is an iconography, Munich and Leipzig, 1914); E. Anderson, ed. and trans., *Letters of M. and His Family* (the most extensive collection in Eng.; 3 vols., London and N.Y., 1938; 2nd ed., revised, by A. Hyatt King and M. Carolan, 1966); E. Müller von Asow, ed., *Gesamtausgabe der Briefe und Aufzeichnungen der Familie M.* (5 vols., Berlin, 1942); W. Bauer, O. Deutsch, and J. Eibl, eds., *M.: Briefe und Aufzeichnungen* (the standard ed., with commentaries; 7 vols., Kassel, 1962–75).

BIOGRAPHY: F. von Schlichtegroll, "Johannes Chrysostomus Wolfgang Gottlieb M.," *Nekrolog auf*

das Jahr 1791 (Gotha, 1793; new ed. by L. Landshoff, Munich, 1924); F. Niemtschek, *Leben des k. k. Kapellmeisters Wolfgang Gottlieb M. nach Originalquellen beschrieben* (Prague, 1798; 2nd ed., augmented, 1808; facsimile reprint of the latter, 1905; Eng. trans., London, 1956); I. Arnold, *M.s Geist: Seine kurze Biographie und ästhetische Darstellung* (Erfurt, 1803); idem, *Galerie der berühmtesten Tonkünstler des 18. und 19. Jahrhunderts ... W.A. M. und Joseph Haydn: Versuch einer Parallele* (Erfurt, 1810; 2nd ed., 1816); Stendhal, *Lettres ... sur le célèbre compositeur Haydn: Suivies d'une vie de M. et considérations sur Métastase* (Paris, 1814; 2nd ed., revised, as *Vies de Haydn, de M. et de Métastase;* Eng. trans., 1972); P. Lichtenthal, *Cenni biografici intorno al celebre maestro W.A. M.* (Milan, 1816); G. von Nissen, *Biographie W.A. M.s nach Originalbriefen* (Leipzig, 1828); A. Oulibicheff, *Nouvelle biographie de M., suivie d'un aperçu sur l'histoire générale de la musique* (3 vols., Moscow, 1843; German trans. by L. Gantter, Stuttgart, 1859; Russian trans. by M. Tchaikovsky, Moscow, 1890); E. Holmes, *The Life of M.* (London, 1845; 2nd ed., 1878); O. Jahn, *W.A. M.* (4 vols., Leipzig, 1856–59; 2nd ed., 1867; Eng. trans. by P. Townsend, London, 1882; German revisions by H. Deiters, 3rd ed., 1891–93 and 4th ed., 1905–7; exhaustively rewritten and revised by H. Abert as *W.A. M.: Neu bearbeitete und erweiterte Ausgabe von Otto Jahns "M.,"* 2 vols., Leipzig, 1919–21, rendering it the standard biography; further revision by A.A. Abert, 2 vols., Leipzig, 1955–56); L. Nohl, *M.* (Leipzig, 1863; 2nd ed., augmented, as *M.s Leben,* 1877; Eng. trans. by Lady Wallace, London, 1877; 3rd German ed., revised, by P. Sakolowski, Berlin, 1906); C. Pohl, *M. und Haydn in London* (Vienna, 1867); L. Nohl, *M. nach den Schilderungen seiner Zeitgenossen* (Leipzig, 1880); G. Nottebohm, *Mozartiana* (Leipzig, 1880); V. Wilder, *M., L'Homme et l'artiste* (Paris, 1880; 4th ed., 1889; Eng. trans., London, 1908); L. Meinardus, *M.: Ein Künstlerleben* (Leipzig, 1882); F. Gehring, *M.* (London, 1883; 2nd ed., 1911); L. Klasen, *W.A. M.: Sein Leben und seine Werke* (Vienna, 1897); O. Fleischer, *M.* (Berlin, 1899); R. Procházka, *M. in Prag* (Prague, 1899; revised and augmented ed. by P. Nettl as *M. in Böhmen,* Prague, 1938); E. Breakspeare, *M.* (London, 1902); E. Prout, *M.* (London, 1903); L. Mirow, *M.s letzte Lebensjahre: Eine Künstlertragödie* (Leipzig, 1904); C. Belmonte, *Die Frauen im Leben M.s* (Augsburg, 1905); C. Bellaigue, *M.* (Paris, 1906); F. Lentner, *M.s Leben und Schaffen* (Innsbruck, 1906); H. von der Pfordten, *M.* (Leipzig, 1908); K. Storck, *M.: Sein Leben und Schaffen* (Stuttgart, 1908); W. Flower, *Stray Notes on M. and His Music* (Edinburgh, 1910); L. Schmidt, *W.A. M.* (Berlin, 1912); T. de Wyzewa and G. de Saint-Foix, *W.A. M.: Sa vie musicale et son œuvre de l'enfance à la pleine maturité* (a useful study, especially on the origin and development of Mozart's style; 5 vols., Paris, 1912–46; vols. 3–5 by Saint-Foix alone); A. Schurig, *W.A. M.: Sein Leben und sein Werk* (2 vols., Leipzig, 1913; 2nd ed., 1923; French trans., 1925); H. de Curzon, *M.* (Paris, 1914; 2nd ed., 1927); E. Engel, *W.A. M.* (Vienna, 1914); J. Kreitmeier, *W.A. M.: Eine Charakterzeichnung des grossen Meisters nach literarischen Quellen*

(Düsseldorf, 1919); L. Schiedermair, *M.: Sein Leben und seine Werke* (Munich, 1922; 2nd ed., revised, 1948); E. Blümml, *Aus M.s Freundes und Familien Kreis* (Vienna, 1923); O. Keller, *W.A. M.* (Berlin, 1926); B. Paumgartner, *M.* (Berlin, 1927; 6th ed., 1967); D. Hussey, *W.A. M.* (London, 1928; 2nd ed., 1933); M. Morold, *M.* (Vienna, 1931); R. Tenschert, *M.* (Leipzig, 1931); M. Davenport, *M.* (N.Y., 1932); H. Ghéon, *Promenades avec M.* (Paris, 1932; 7th ed., 1948; Eng. trans. as *In Search of M.,* London, 1934); S. Sitwell, *M.* (N.Y., 1932); R. Haas, *W.A. M.* (Potsdam, 1933; 2nd ed., 1950); E. Schmid, *W.A. M.* (Lübeck, 1934; 3rd ed., 1955); J. Talbot, *M.* (London, 1934); E. Blom, *M.* (London, 1935; 3rd ed., revised, by J. Westrup, 1975); A. Boschot, *M.* (Paris, 1935; 2nd ed., 1949); C. Perriolat, *M., Révélateur de la beauté artistique* (Paris, 1935); A. Kolb, *M.* (Vienna, 1937); W. Turner, *M.: The Man and His Works* (London and N.Y., 1938; 3rd ed., 1966); I. Gyomai, *Le Cœur de M.* (Paris, 1939); W. Goetz, *M.: Sein Leben in Selbstzeugnissen, Briefen und Berichten* (Berlin, 1941); E. Komorzynski, *M.* (Berlin, 1941; Vienna, 1955); G. Schaeffner, *W.A. M.* (Bern, 1941); A. Albertini, *M.: La vita, le opere* (Milan, 1942); E. Valentin, *Wege zu M.* (Regensburg, 1942); A. Einstein, *M.: His Character, His Work* (N.Y., 1945; German ed., 1947; 4th ed., 1960); P. Espil, *Les Voyages de Chérubin, ou L'Enfance de M.* (Bayonne, 1946); M. Mila, *W.A. M.* (Turin, 1946); E. Valentin, *M.* (Hameln, 1947); R. Tenschert, *W.A. M.* (Salzburg, 1951; Eng. trans., London, 1952); M. Kenyon, *M. in Salzburg* (London, 1952); M. Röttger, *W.A. M.* (Stuttgart, 1952); M. Brion, *M.* (Paris, 1955); J. Dalchow, *W.A. M.s Krankheiten, 1756–1763* (Bergisch Gladbach, 1955); N. Medici di Marignano and R. Hughes, *A M. Pilgrimage: Being the Travel Diaries of Vincent and Mary Novello in the Year 1829* (London, 1955); A. Ostoja, *M. e l'Italia* (Bologna, 1955); E. Schenk, *W.A. M.: Eine Biographie* (Vienna and Zürich, 1955; 2nd ed., revised 1975; Eng. trans. in an abridged ed. as *M. and His Times,* N.Y., 1959); G. Barblan and A. Della Corte, *M. in Italia* (Milan, 1956); C. Fusero, *M.* (Turin, 1956); F. Hadamowsky and L. Nowak, *M.: Werk und Zeit* (Vienna, 1956); D. Kerner, "W.A. M.s Krankheiten und sein Tod," *Neue Zeitschrift für Musik* (Dec. 1956); E. Blom, "M.'s Death," *Music & Letters* (Oct. 1957); J. Burk, *M. and His Music* (N.Y., 1959); J. and B. Massin, *W.A. M.: Biographie, histoire de l'œuvre* (Paris, 1959; 2nd ed., 1970); C. Haldane, *M.* (London, 1960); O. Deutsch, *M.: Die Dokumente seines Lebens, gesammelt und erläutert* (an invaluable study; Kassel, 1961; Eng. trans. as *M.: A Documented Biography,* Palo Alto, Calif., 1965; 2nd ed., 1966; supplement, 1978); idem, "Die Legende von M.s Vergütung," *M.-Jahrbuch 1964;* S. Sadie, *M.* (London, 1965); C. Bär, *M.: Krankheit, Tod, Begräbnis* (Kassel, 1966; revised ed., 1972); A. Hyatt King, *M.: A Biography with a Survey of Books, Editions and Recordings* (a useful study; London, 1970); M. Levey, *The Life and Death of M.* (London, 1971); H. Schuler, *Die Vorfahren W. M.s* (Essen, 1972); J. Eibl, "Die M.s und der Erzbischof," *Österreichische Musikzeitschrift,* XXX (1975); A. Hutchings, *M.: The Man, the Musician* (London and N.Y., 1976); W. Hildesheimer, *M.* (Frankfurt, 1977; Eng. trans., 1979); C.

Bär, "Er war . . . kein guter Wirth: Eine Studie über M.s Verhältnis zum Geld," *Acta Mozartiana,* XXV (1978); I. Keys, *M.: His Life in His Music* (St. Albans, 1980); A. Steptoe, "M. and Poverty: A Re-examination of the Evidence," *Musical Times* (April 1984).

ICONOGRAPHY: R. Tenschert, *W.A. M. 1756–1791: Sein Leben in Bildern* (Leipzig, 1935); R. Bory, *La Vie et l'œuvre de W.-A. M. par l'image* (Geneva, 1948; in Eng. as *The Life and Works of W.A. M. in Pictures,* Geneva, 1948); G. Rech, *W.A. M.: Ein Lebensweg in Bildern* (Munich and Berlin, 1955); R. Petzoldt, *W.A. M.: Sein Leben in Bildern* (Leipzig, 1956); E. Valentin, *M.: Eine Bildbiographie* (Munich, 1959; Eng. trans., 1959); O. Deutsch, *M. und seine Welt in zeitgenossischen Bildern* (Kassel, 1961; in German and Eng.).

MOZART AND FREEMASONRY: O. Deutsch, *M. und die Wiener Logen: Zur Geschichte seiner Freimaurer-Kompositionen* (Vienna, 1932); P. Nettl, *M. und die königliche Kunst: Die freimaurerische Grundlage der Zauberflöte* (Berlin, 1932; 2nd ed., 1956); P. Nettl, *M. and Masonry* (N.Y., 1957); J. Chailley, *"La Flûte enchantée," opéra maconnique: Essai d'explication du livret et de la musique* (Paris, 1968; Eng. trans. as *The Magic Flute, Masonic Opera,* N.Y., 1971; London, 1972); F. Smyth, "Brother M. of Vienna," *Ars Quatuor Coronatorum,* 87, Transactions of Quatuor Coronati Lodge No. 2076, London (Lodge of research; 1974); K. Thomson, "M. and Freemasonry," *Music & Letters* (Jan. 1976); idem, *The Masonic Thread in M.* (London, 1977); H.C. Robbins Landon, *Mozart and the Masons* (London, 1983).

CRITICISM, ANALYSIS: GENERAL: A. Hammerle, *M. und einige Zeitgenossen: Neue Beiträge für Salzburgische Geschichte, Literatur und Musik* (Salzburg, 1877); K. Prieger, *Urtheile bedeutender Dichter, Philosopher und Musiker über M.* (Wiesbaden, 1885–86); E. Komorzynski, *M.s Kunst der Instrumentation* (Stuttgart, 1906); A. Cametti, *M. a Roma* (Rome, 1907); G. Schünemann, ed., *M. als achtjähriger Komponist: Ein Notenbuch Wolfgangs* (Leipzig, 1909; Eng. trans., 1909); W. Nagel, *M. und die Gegenwart* (Langensalza, 1912); A. Leitzmann, *M.s Persönlichkeit* (Leipzig, 1914); R. Lach, *W.A. M. als Theoretiker* (Vienna, 1918); E. Lert, *M. auf dem Theater* (Berlin, 1918; 4th ed., 1922); H. Mersmann, *M.* (vol. 4 of *Kulturgeschichte der Musik in Einzeldarstellungen,* Berlin, 1925); V. Heinrich, *Komik und Humor bei M.* (Vienna, 1931); W. Lüthy, *M. und die Tonartencharakteristik* (Strasbourg, 1931); D. Tovey, *Essays in Musical Analysis* (7 vols., London, 1935–44); C. Thieme, *Der Klangstil des Mozartorchesters* (Leipzig, 1936); P. Hirsch, "Some Early M. Editions," *Music Review,* I (1940); H. Deininger, ed., *Augsburger Mozartbuch: Zeitschrift des historischen Vereins für Schwaben,* LV–LVI (Augsburg, 1942–43); H. Socnik, *Das Pedal bei M.* (Danzig, 1943); M. Mila, *Saggi Mozartiani* (Milan, 1945); J. Chantavoine, *M. dans M.* (Paris, 1948); E. Schmid, *Ein schwäbisches Mozartbuch* (Stuttgart, 1948); R. Elvers, *Untersuchungen zu den Tempi in M.s Instrumentalmusik* (Diss., Univ. of Berlin, 1952); A. Hyatt King, *M. in Retrospect: Studies in Criticism and Bibliography* (London, 1955; 3rd ed., 1970); I. Bruce, "A Note on M.'s Bar-rhythms," *Music Review,* XVII (1956); A. Einstein, *Essays on Music* (N.Y., 1956); H. Engel, "M.s Instrumentation," *M.-Jahrbuch 1956;* R. Giazotto, *Annali Mozartiani* (Milan, 1956); H.C. Robbins Landon and D. Mitchell, eds., *The M. Companion* (N.Y. and London, 1956; 2nd ed., 1965); P. Schaller and H. Kühner, eds., *M.-Aspekte* (Olten and Freiburg, 1956); E. Schmid, "M. and Haydn," *Musical Quarterly* (April 1956); H. Albrecht, ed., *Die Bedeutung der Zeichen Keil, Strich, und Punkt bei M.* (Kassel, 1957); A. Della Corte, *Tutto il teatro di M.* (Turin, 1957); W. Siegmund-Schultze, *M.s Melodik und Stil* (Leipzig, 1957); H. Engel, "Haydn, M. und die Klassik," *M.-Jahrbuch 1959;* G. Massenkeil, *Untersuchungen zum Problem der Symmetrie in der Instrumentalmusik W.A. M.s* (Wiesbaden, 1962); *Neues Augsburger Mozartbuch: Zeitschrift des historischen Vereins für Schwaben,* LXII–LXIII (Augsburg, 1962); I. Eisley, "M. and Counterpoint: Development and Synthesis," *Music Review,* XXIV (1963); P. Lang, ed., *The Creative World of M.* (N.Y., 1963); *Mozartgemeinde Wien 1913 bis 1963: Forschung und Interpretation* (Vienna, 1964); S. Davis, "Harmonic Rhythm in M.'s Sonata Form," *Music Review,* XXVII (1966); M. Flothuis, *M.s Bearbeitungen eigener und fremder Werke* (Salzburg, 1969); K. Marx, *Zur Einheit der zyklischen Form bei M.* (Stuttgart, 1971); M. Schmid, *M. und die Salzburger Tradition* (Tutzing, 1976); F. Holbock, *W.A. M.: Der Salzburger Domorganist und seine Beziehungen zur katholischen Kirche* (Stein am Rhein, 1978); R. Leavis, "M.'s Divertimentos for Mixed Consort," *Musical Times* (June 1980); B. Brophy, "Da Ponte and M.," *Musical Times* (July 1981); G. Pestelli, *The Age of M. and Beethoven* (Cambridge, 1984).

OPERA AND VOCAL MUSIC: A. Oulibicheff, *M.s Opern: Kritische Erläuterungen* (Leipzig, 1848); W. Pole, *The Story of M.'s Requiem* (London, 1879); C. Gounod, *Le Don Juan de M.* (Paris, 1890; Eng. trans., 1895); A. Farinelli, *Don Giovanni: Note critiche* (Turin, 1896); A. Weltner, *M.s Werke und die Wiener Hoftheater: Statistisches und Historisches* (Vienna, 1896); K. Söhle, *M. Dramatisches Zeitbild* (Leipzig, 1907); E. Dent, *M.'s Operas: A Critical Study* (London, 1913; 2nd ed., 1947); H. Cohen, *Die dramatische Idee in M.s Operntexten* (Berlin, 1916); H. von Waltershausen, *Die Zauberflöte* (Munich, 1920); A. Lorenz, "Das Finale in M.s Meisteropern," *Die Musik,* XIX (1926–27); E. Blom, "The Literary Ancestry of Figaro," *Musical Quarterly* (Oct. 1927); R. Dumesnil, *Le "Don Juan" de M.* (Paris, 1927; 2nd ed., 1955); O. Beer, *M. und das Wiener Singspiel* (Vienna, 1932); K. Rosenthal, "The Salzburg Church Music of M. and His Predecessors," *Musical Quarterly* (Oct. 1932); S. Anheisser, "Die Urfassung des Figaro," *Zeitschrift für Musikwissenschaft,* XV (1932–33); F. Brukner, *Die Zauberflöte: Unbekannte Handschriften und seltene Drucke aus der Frühzeit der Oper* (Vienna, 1934); P. Stefan, *Die Zauberflöte: Herkunft, Bedeutung, Geheimnis* (Vienna, 1937); E. Komorzynski, "Die Zauberflöte: Entstehung und Bedeutung des Kunstwerks," *Neues M.-Jahrbuch* (vol. I, Regensburg, 1941); K. Rosenthal, "M.'s Sacramental Litanies and Their Forerunners," *Musical Quarterly* (Oct. 1941);

P. Jouve, *Le Don Juan de M.* (Freiburg, 1942; 3rd ed., Paris, 1948; Eng. trans., London, 1957); L. Conrad, *M.s Dramaturgie der Oper* (Würzburg, 1943); E. Wellesz, "Don Giovanni and the Dramma Giocoso," *Music Review,* IV (1943); C. Benn, *M. on the Stage* (London, 1946; 2nd ed., 1947); S. Levarie, *M.'s "Le nozze di Figaro": A Critical Analysis* (Chicago, 1952); D. Lauener, *Die Frauengestalten in M.s Opern* (Zürich, 1954); K. Fellerer, *M.s Kirchenmusik* (Salzburg, 1955); M. Brown, "M.'s Songs for Voice and Piano," *Music Review,* XVII (1956); A. Greither, *Die sieben grossen Opern M.s: Versuche über das Verhältnis der Texte zur Musik* (Heidelberg, 1956; 2nd ed., enlarged, 1970); C. Raeburn, "Die textlichen Quellen des 'Schauspieldirektor,'" *Österreichische Musikzeitschrift,* XIII (1958); E. Hess, "Zur Ergänzung des Requiems von M. durch F.X. Süssmayr," *M.-Jahrbuch 1959;* T. Volek, "Über den Ursprung von M.s Oper 'La clemenza di Tito,'" *M.-Jahrbuch 1959;* I. Kecskeméti, "Beiträge zur Geschichte von M.s Requiem," *Studia Musicologica Academiae Scientiarum Hungaricae,* I (1961); S. Kunze, "M.s Schauspieldirektor," *M.-Jahrbuch 1962–3;* K. Marguerre, "M. und Süssmayr," *M.-Jahrbuch 1962–3;* A. Livermore, "The Origins of Don Juan," *Music & Letters* (July 1963); B. Brophy, *M. the Dramatist: A New View of M., His Operas and His Age* (a Freudian interpretation; London and N.Y., 1964); O. Deutsch, "Zur Geschichte von M.s Requiem," *Österreichische Musikzeitschrift,* XIX (1964); C. Floros, "Das 'Programm' in M.s Meisterouverturnen," *Studien zur Musikwissenschaft,* XXVI (1964); C. Raeburn, "Die Entführungsszene aus 'Die Entführung aus dem Serail,'" *M.-Jahrbuch 1964;* A. Rosenberg, *Die Zauberflöte: Geschichte und Deutung* (Munich, 1964); A. Livermore, "Così fan tutti: A Well-kept Secret," *Music & Letters* (Oct. 1965); R. Moberly and C. Raeburn, "M.'s 'Figaro'; the Plan of Act III," *Music & Letters* (April 1965); L. Nowak, "Das Requiem von W.A. M.," *Österreichische Musikzeitschrift,* XX (1965); P. Branscombe, "'Die Zauberflöte': Some Textual and Interpretative Problems," *Proceedings of the Royal Musical Association,* XCII (1965–66); M. Chusid, "The Significance of D minor in M.'s Dramatic Music," *M.-Jahrbuch 1965–6;* G. Gruber, "Das Autograph der 'Zauberflöte,'" *M.-Jahrbuch 1967* and *1968–70;* D. Heartz, "The Genesis of M.'s Idomeneo," *M.-Jahrbuch 1967;* K.-H. Köhler, "M.s Kompositionsweise: Beobachtungen am Figaro-Autograph," *M.-Jahrbuch 1967;* R. Moberly, *Three M. Operas: Figaro, Don Giovanni, The Magic Flute* (London, 1967; N.Y., 1968); S. Döhring, "Die Arienformen in M.s Opern," *M.-Jahrbuch 1968–70;* H. Federhofer, "Die Harmonik als dramatischer Ausdrucksfaktor in M.s Meisteropern," *M.-Jahrbuch 1968–70;* E. Batley, *A Preface to The Magic Flute* (London, 1969); C. Henning, "Thematic Metamorphoses in Don Giovanni," *Music Review,* XXX (1969); A. Abert, *Die Opern M.s* (Wolfenbüttel, 1970; in Eng. in *The New Oxford History of Music,* vol. VII, London, 1973); B. Brophy, "'Figaro' and the Limitations of Music," *Music & Letters* (Jan. 1970); F. Beyer, "M.s Komposition zum Requiem: Zur Frage der Ergänzung," *Acta Mozartiana,* XVIII (1971); A. Dunning, "M.s Kanons," *M.-Jahrbuch*

1971–2; C. Rosenthal, "Der Einfluss der Salzburger Kirchenmusik auf M.s kirchenmusikalische Kompositionen," *M.-Jahrbuch 1971–2;* H. Eggebrecht, *Versuch über die Wiener Klassik: Die Tanzszene in M.s "Don Giovanni"* (Wiesbaden, 1972); S. Kunze, *Don Giovanni vor M.: Die Tradition der Don Giovanni-Opern im italienischen Buffo-Theater des 18. Jahrhunderts* (Munich, 1972); R. Moberly, "M. and His Librettists," *Music & Letters* (April 1973); D. Heartz, "Tonality and Motif in Idomeneo," *Musical Times* (May 1974); R. Moberly, "The Influence of French Classical Drama on M.'s 'La clemenza di Tito,'" *Music & Letters* (July 1974); K. Fellerer, "Liturgische Grundlagen der Kirchenmusik M.s," in *Festschrift Walter Senn* (Munich and Salzburg, 1975); G. Gruber, "Bedeutung und Spontaneität in M.s 'Zauberflöte,'" ibid.; H. Scheel, "'Le Mariage de Figaro' von Beaumarchais und das Libretto der 'Nozze di Figaro' von Lorenzo da Ponte," *Die Musikforschung,* XXVIII (1975); A. Tyson, "'La clemenza di Tito' and Its Chronology," *Musical Times* (March 1975); W. Mann, *The Operas of M.* (London, 1977); F. Noske, *The Signifier and the Signified: Studies in the Operas of M. and Verdi* (The Hague, 1977); D. Heartz, "M., His Father and 'Idomeneo,'" *Musical Times* (March 1978); C. Osborne, *The Complete Operas of M.* (London, 1978); C. Ballantine, "Social and Philosophical Outlook of M.'s Operas," *Musical Quarterly* (Oct. 1981); P. Branscombe, "Cosi in Context," *Musical Times* (July 1981); R. Donington, "Don Giovanni Goes to Hell," *Musical Times* (July 1981); D. Heartz, "'Che mi sembra di morir'; Donna Elvira and the Sextet," *Musical Times* (July 1981); A. Tyson, "Le nozze di Figaro: Lessons from the Autograph Score," *Musical Times* (July 1981); B. Williams, "M.'s Comedies and the Sense of an Ending," *Musical Times* (July 1981); C. Gianturco, *M.'s Early Operas* (London, 1982); D. Heartz, "La clemenza di Sarastro: Masonic Benevolence in Mozart's Last Operas," *Musical Times* (March 1983). ORCHESTRAL: D. Schultz, *M.s Jugendsinfonien* (Leipzig, 1900); H. Schenker, "M.: Sinfonie g-Moll," *Das Meisterwerk in der Musik,* II (1926); A. Dickinson, *A Study of M.'s Last Three Symphonies* (London, 1927; 2nd ed., 1940); G. de Saint-Foix, *Les Sinfonies de M.* (Paris, 1932; Eng. trans., 1947); N. Broder, "The Wind Instruments in M.'s Symphonies," *Musical Quarterly* (July 1933); C. Girdlestone, *W.A. M. et ses concertos pour piano* (2 vols., Paris, 1939; 3rd ed., 1978; in Eng., one vol., London and Norman, Okla., 1948); A. Hutchings, *A Companion to M.'s Piano Concertos* (London, 1948; 2nd ed., 1950); H. Engel, "Über M.s Jugendsinfonien," *M.-Jahrbuch 1951;* G. Hausswald, *M.s Serenaden: Ein Beitrag zur Stilkritik des 18. Jahrhunderts* (Leipzig, 1951; 2nd ed., revised, 1975); H. Engel, "Der Tanz in M.s Kompositionen," *M.-Jahrbuch 1952;* J. David, *Die Jupiter-Sinfonie: Eine Studie über die thematisch-melodischen Zusammenhänge* (Göttingen, 1953); E. Simon, "Sonata into Concerto: A study of M.'s First Seven Concertos," *Acta Musicologica,* XXXI (1959); A. Abert, "Stilistischer Befund und Quellenlage: Zu M.s Lambacher Sinfonie KV Anh. 221–45a," *Festschrift Hans Engel* (Kassel, 1964); H. Tischler, *A Structural Analysis of M.'s Piano Concertos* (N.Y.,

1966); D. Forman, *M.'s Concerto Form: The First Movements of the Piano Concertos* (London, 1971); P. Benary, "Metrum bei M.: Zur metrischen Analyse seiner letzten drei Sinfonien," *Studien zur Musikwissenschaft,* CXIV (1974); S. Wollenberg, "The Jupiter Theme: New Light on Its Creation," *Musical Times* (Sept. 1975); A. Hyatt King, *M. Wind and String Concertos* (London, 1978); N. Zaslaw, "M.'s Paris Symphonies," *Musical Times* (Sept. 1978); C. Wolff, "Zur Chronologie der Klavierkonzert-Kadenzen M.s," *M.-Jahrbuch 1978–9;* A. Tyson, "The Two Slow Movements of M.'s Paris Symphony K297," *Musical Times* (Jan. 1981); R. Dearling, *The Music of W.A. M.: The Symphonies* (Rutherford, N.J., 1982); E. Smith and M. Serenades, *Divertimenti and Dances* (London, 1982). CHAMBER MUSIC: T. Dunhill, *M.'s String Quartets* (London, 1927; 2nd ed., 1948); A. Einstein, "M.'s Ten Celebrated String Quartets," *Music Review,* III (1942); W. Fischer, "M.s Weg von der begleiteten Klaviersonata zur Kammermusik mit Klavier," *M.-Jahrbuch 1956;* K. Marguerre, "M.s Klaviertrios," *M.-Jahrbuch 1960–61;* A. Hyatt King, *M. Chamber Music* (London, 1968); W. Hummeke, *Versuch einer strukturwissenschaftlichen Darstellung der ersten und vierten Sätze der zehn letzten Streichquartette von W.A. M.* (Münster, 1970); I. Hunkemöller, *W.A. M.s frühe Sonaten für Violine und Klavier* (Bern and Munich, 1970); D. Leeson and D. Whitwell, "M.'s 'Spurious' Wind Octets," *Music & Letters* (Oct. 1972); R. Hellyer, "M.'s Harmoniemusik," *Music Review,* XXXIV (1973); A. Tyson, "New Light on M.'s 'Prussian' Quartets," *Musical Times* (Feb. 1975); R. Hellyer, "M.'s Harmoniemusik and Its Publishers," *Musical Times* (July 1981); C. Wolff, ed., *The String Quartets of Haydn, M., and Beethoven: Studies of the Autograph Manuscripts* (a valuable investigation; Cambridge, Mass., 1981). KEYBOARD: F. Lorenz, *W.A. M. als Clavier-Componist* (Breslau, 1866); F. Marks, *Questions on M.'s Pianoforte-sonatas* (London, 1929); N. Broder, "M. and the 'Clavier,'" *Musical Quarterly* (Oct. 1941); H. Dennerlein, *Der unbekannte M.: Die Welt seiner Klavierwerke* (Leipzig, 1951); P. and E. Badura-Skoda, *M.-Interpretation, Anregungen zur Interpretation der Klavierwerke* (Vienna and Stuttgart, 1957; revised ed. in Eng. as *Interpreting M. on the Keyboard,* N.Y., 1962); R. Rosenberg, *Die Klaviersonaten M.s: Gestalt- und Stilanalyse* (Hofheim, Hesse, 1972).

Mozart, Wolfgang Amadeus (Franz Xaver), son of the great composer; b. Vienna, July 26, 1791; d. Karlsbad, July 29, 1844. He studied with Hummel and Salieri in Vienna; gave a concert as pianist at the age of 13; lived many years as a private tutor in Lwow, where he founded the Cecilia Society. He wrote 2 piano concertos; a String Quartet; Piano Trio; Violin Sonata; many pieces for piano. BIBLIOGRAPHY: J. Fischer, *W.A. Mozart* (Karlsbad, 1888); Karl Geiringer, "W.A. Mozart the Younger," *Musical Quarterly* (Oct. 1941); W. Hummel, *W.A. Mozarts Söhne* (Kassel, 1956); A. Vander Linden, "Le Dernier Fils de W.A. Mozart," *Bulletin des*

Mraczek – Muck

Beaux-Arts de l'Academie Royale de Belgique (1968).

Mraczek, Joseph Gustav, Czech composer; b. Brno, March 12, 1878; d. Dresden, Dec. 24, 1944. He received his first instruction from his father, the cellist **Franz Mraczek;** was a chorister in various churches in Brno before going to Vienna, where he studied with Hellmesberger, Stocker, and Löwe at the Cons.; from 1897 to 1902 was concertmaster at the Stadttheater in Brno; then taught violin in Brno (until 1918). In 1919, he went to Dresden to teach composition at the Cons. there; conducted the Dresden Phil. (1919–24); remained in Dresden to the end of his life. He wrote 6 operas: *The Glass Slipper* (Brno, 1902); *Der Traum* (Brno, Feb. 26, 1909); *Aebelö* (Breslau, 1915); *Ikdar* (Dresden, 1921); *Herrn Dürers Bild oder Madonna am Wiesenzaun* (Hannover, Jan. 29, 1927); *Der Liebesrat* (not produced); his most successful piece was a symph. burlesque, *Max und Moritz* (Brno, 1911; also widely played throughout Germany, and in the U.S.); other works include: *Oriental Sketches* for Small Orch. (1918); symph. poem, *Eva* (1922); *Oriental Dance Rhapsody* (1931); a Piano Quintet; a String Quartet; piano pieces; songs.

BIBLIOGRAPHY: E.H. Müller, *J.G. Mraczek* (Dresden, 1918).

Mravina (original name, **Mravinskaya**), **Evgeniya,** noted Russian soprano; b. St. Petersburg, Feb. 16, 1864; d. Yalta, Oct. 25, 1914. She studied in St. Petersburg with Pryanishnikov, and later with Désirée d'Artôt in Berlin; then sang in Italy. After returning to Russia, she joined the Maryinsky Theater in St. Petersburg in 1886, remaining on its roster until 1900. In 1891–92 she toured in England, France, Belgium, and Germany. She had the privilege of going over the part of Marguerite in *Faust* with Gounod, and the part of Mignon in the opera of that name by Ambroise Thomas with the composer himself. She gave brilliant renditions of Italian soprano roles; was greatly praised in Russia for her performances of the Russian operatic parts. She retired from the operatic stage in 1900 but continued to appear in recital.

BIBLIOGRAPHY: A.P. Grigorieva, *E. Mravina* (Moscow, 1970).

Mravinsky, Evgeni, eminent Russian conductor; b. St. Petersburg, June 4, 1903. He studied biology at St. Petersburg Univ.; then joined the Imperial Ballet as a pantomimist and rehearsal pianist; in 1924 he enrolled in the Leningrad Cons., where he studied conducting with Gauk, graduating in 1931; also took additional training with Malko; had courses in composition with Vladimir Shcherbachev; then was conductor of the Leningrad Theater of Opera and Ballet (1932–38). In 1938 he was appointed principal conductor of the Leningrad Phil. Mravinsky represents the best of the Soviet school of conducting, in which technical precision and fidelity to the music are combined with individual and even Romantic interpretations. He is especially noted for his fine performances of Tchaikovsky's operas, ballets, and symphs.; he gave first performances of several symphs. of Prokofiev and Shostakovich; also conducted works by Béla Bartók and Stravinsky. In 1973 he was awarded the order of Hero of Socialist Labor.

BIBLIOGRAPHY: V. Bogdanov-Berezovsky, *The Soviet Conductor Mravinsky* (Leningrad, 1956); V. Fomin, *Mravinsky Conducts* (Leningrad, 1976).

Mshvelidze, Shalva, Georgian composer; b. Tiflis, May 28, 1904. He studied at the Tiflis Cons., graduating in 1930; then was associated with various theatrical groups in the Caucasus, and also worked in Leningrad. He joined the faculty of the Tiflis Cons. in 1929. Virtually all of his works for the theater are dedicated to the exploration of the national music of Soviet Georgia. He wrote the operas *Legend of Tariel* (Tiflis, Feb. 25, 1946); *The Grandmaster's Right Hand* (Tiflis, June 3, 1961); the oratorios *Caucasiana* (1949) and *The Legacy of Posterity*, for the centennial of Lenin's birth (1970); 5 symphs. (1943, 1944, 1952, 1968, 1974); symph. poems: *Azar* (1933); *Zviadauri* (1940); *Mindia* (1949); *Youngling and Tiger* (1962); chamber music; songs; incidental music to about 25 plays; film scores. He publ. a manual on orchestration in the Georgian language (1965).

Muck, Karl, great German conductor; b. Darmstadt, Oct. 22, 1859; d. Stuttgart, March 3, 1940. He received his first musical instruction from his father; also studied piano with Kissner in Würzburg; later pursued academic studies (classical philology) at the Univ. of Heidelberg and at Leipzig; received his Dr.Phil. in 1880. He also attended the Leipzig Cons., and shortly before graduation made a successful debut as pianist with the Gewandhaus Orch. However, he did not choose to continue a pianistic career; he obtained a position as chorus master at the municipal opera in Zürich; his ability soon secured him the post of conductor there; in subsequent years he was theater conductor in Salzburg, Brünn, and Graz; there Angelo Neumann, impresario of a traveling opera company, heard him, and engaged him as conductor for the Landestheater in Prague (1886), and then as Seidl's successor for his traveling Wagner Co. It was during those years that Muck developed his extraordinary qualities as a masterful disciplinarian and faithful interpreter possessing impeccable taste. In 1889 he conducted the Wagner tetralogy in St. Petersburg, and in 1891, in Moscow. In 1892 he was engaged as first conductor at the Berlin Opera, and also frequently conducted symph. concerts of the Royal Chapel there. From 1894 to 1911 he led the Silesian Music Festivals; in 1899 he conducted the Wagner repertoire at Covent Garden; from 1904 to 1906, he conducted the concerts of the Vienna Phil. (alternating with Mottl); he also appeared, with outstanding success, in Paris, Rome, Brussels, Madrid, Copenhagen, and other European centers. In 1901 he was selected to conduct the performances of *Parsifal* at Bayreuth. In 1906 he was engaged as conductor of the Boston

Symph. Orch., and led it for 2 seasons, returning to Berlin in 1908, as Generalmusikdirektor. He returned to America in the autumn of 1912 and assumed the post of permanent conductor of the Boston Symph. His farewell appearance at the Berlin Opera, conducting *Tristan und Isolde,* was made the occasion of a tumultuous demonstration. During the 20 years of his activity in Berlin he conducted 1,071 performances of 103 operas, of which 35 were novelties. With the entry of the U.S. into the war in the spring of 1917, Muck's position in Boston became ambiguous; he was known as a friend of Wilhelm II, and did not temper his intense German nationalism. Protests were made against the retention of Muck as conductor in Boston, and despite the defense offered by Major Higginson, the founder of the Boston Symph., Muck was arrested at his home on March 25, 1918, and interned as an enemy alien until the end of the war. In 1919 he returned to Germany; conducted the Hamburg Phil. from 1922 until 1933; then went to Stuttgart.

BIBLIOGRAPHY: N. Stücker, *Karl Muck* (Graz, 1939); Irving Lowens, "L'Affaire-Muck," *Musicology* I/3 (1947); H. Schonberg, *The Great Conductors* (N.Y., 1967; pp. 216–22).

Muczynski, Robert, American composer; b. Chicago, March 19, 1929. He played piano at home; then enrolled in the class of Alexander Tcherepnin at De Paul Univ. For his graduation, he played his own *Divertimento* for Piano and Orch. His music is influenced by the Russian modern school; rhythmic vivacity within a neo-Baroque framework creates an attractive aural effect.

WORKS: FOR ORCH.: *Divertimento* for Piano and Orch. (1951–52); Symph. No. 1 (1953); Piano Concerto (1954); *Galena: A Town,* suite (1957–58); *Dovetail Overture* (1959–60); *Dance Movements* for Chamber Orch. (1962–63); *Symphonic Dialogues* (1965); *Charade* (1970–71); *A Serenade for Summer* for Chamber Orch. (1976); *Cavalcade,* suite (1978); Concerto for Alto Saxophone and Chamber Orch. (1981; Kalamazoo, Mich., Nov. 1, 1981); CHAMBER MUSIC: *Allegro Deciso* for Brass Sextet and Timpani (1952); Flute Sonata (1960–61); *Movements* for Wind Quintet (1962); 2 piano trios (1966–67, 1975); Cello Sonata (1968); *Fantasy Trio* for Clarinet, Cello, and Piano (1969); *Voyage,* 7 pieces for Brass Trio (1969); Sonata for Alto Saxophone (1970); String Trio (1971–72). FOR PIANO: Sonatina (1949–50); *6 Preludes* (1953–54); 3 sonatas (1955–57, 1965–66, 1973–74); *Suite* (1960); *Toccata* (1961–62); *A Summer Journal* (1964); *Seven* (1970–71); *Maverick Pieces,* 12 miniatures (1976); *Masks* (1979–80).

Mudarra, Alonso, Spanish lutenist; b. c.1508; d. Seville, April 1, 1580. He was appointed canon of the Seville Cathedral in 1566. His important work, *Tres libros de música en cifra para vihuela* (i.e., lute music in tablature), originally publ. in Seville in 1546, was printed in modern notation by Emilio Pujol (Barcelona, 1946); this edition contains 77 works by Mudarra and his contemporaries, a biographical sketch, and commentary.

Muddy Waters. See **Morganfield, McKinley.**

Mudge, Richard, English composer; b. Bideford, 1718; d. Great Packington, near Birmingham, April 3, 1763. He publ. 6 concertos for strings, and also an Adagio for String Orch. with a finale for voices singing the melody of Byrd's canon *Non nobis Domine.* He entered Pembroke College, Oxford, in 1735 (B.A., 1738; M.A., 1741); was ordained a curate at Great Packington.

BIBLIOGRAPHY: S.R. Flint, *Mudge Memoirs* (1883; privately printed).

Mudie, Thomas Mollison, English composer and organist; b. London, Nov. 30, 1809; d. there, July 24, 1876. He studied at the Royal Academy of Music with Crotch and Potter; then taught piano there (1832–44); was organist at Galton, Surrey (1834–44); then taught at Edinburgh (1844–63), eventually returning to London. He wrote 5 symphs.; a Piano Quintet; a Piano Trio; and some vocal works.

Muench, Gerhart, German-born Mexican pianist and composer; b. Dresden, March 23, 1907. He studied piano with his father, a prof. at the Dresden Cons.; gave a public piano recital in Dresden at the age of 9. His auspicious career was halted by the Nazi takeover in Germany; Muench was drafted into the German army, but was discharged in 1944 as physically unfit; he emigrated to America in 1947; settled in Mexico in 1953; taught at the Univ. Nacional in Mexico City. In his piano recitals he introduced the new music of Stockhausen, Boulez, Pousseur, and others to Mexican audiences.

WORKS: He began composing at an early age; his *Concerto da camera* for Piano and Chamber Orch. was performed at the 1926 Contempoary Music Festival in Donaueschingen. His other works include a Cello Sonata (1938); *Capriccio variato* for Piano and Orch. (1941); chamber opera, *Tumulus Veneris* (1950); *Tesauras Orphei* for Oboe, Clarinet, Viola, Double Bass, and Harp (1951); *Vocationes* for Piano and Chamber Orch. (1951); Bassoon Concerto (1956); *Muerte sin fin* for Orch. (1957); Concerto for Piano and Strings (1957); Violin Concerto (1959); *Evoluta,* in 3 parts, for 2 Pianos (1961); *Pièce de résistance* for Piano (1962); *Tessellata Tacambarensia,* cycle of 9 chamber pieces for various instrumental groups or soloists (1964–76); *Labyrinthus Orphei* for Orch. (1965); *Itinera duo* for Piano and Orch. (1965); *Oxymora* for Orch. (1967); *Auditur* for Orch. (1968); *Asociaciones* for Coloratura, Soprano and Instruments (1969); *Epitomae Tacambarensiae* for Orch. (1974); *Out of Chaos* for Cello and Piano (1975); *Signa Flexanima* for Piano Trio (1975); *Tetrálogo* for String Quartet (1977); *Mini-Dialogos* for Violin and Cello (1977); *Proenza* for Piano Trio (1977); *Yuriko* for Violin and Piano (1977); 5 masses; choruses; songs.

Muffat, Georg, important organist and composer; b. Megève, Savoy (baptized, June 1), 1653; d. Passau, Feb. 23, 1704. He studied with Lully in Paris (1663–69); was named organist at the Molsheim Cathedral on March 31, 1671; in 1674, went to Ingolstadt to study law; then went to Vienna; in 1678, entered the service of the Archbishop of Salzburg. In 1681 he was in Italy; studied with Corelli and Pasquini in Rome; also spent several years in Paris. In 1687 he was appointed organist to the Bishop of Passau; in 1690, became Kapellmeister there. He was a significant composer; developed the German type of concerto grosso; publ. organ works, sonatas for various instruments, orch. suites, etc.

WORKS: *Armonico tributo*, polyphonic sonatas (1682; partly reprinted in Denkmäler der Tonkunst in Österreich, 89); *Florilegium*, orch. suites in the style of Lully (2 vols., 1695–96; reprinted by Rietsch in Denkmäler der Tonkunst in Österreich, 2, 4 [1.ii, 2.ii]); *Apparatus musico-organisticus*, toccatas for Organ (1960; reprinted by Lange, 1888, and by Kaller-Valentin, 1933); 12 concerti grossi, publ. under the title *Auserlesener ... Instrumentalmusik erste Versamblung* (1701; reprinted in Denkmäler der Tonkunst in Österreich, 23 [11.ii]); a toccata is included in J. Bonnet's *Historical Organ Recitals* (vol. 1).

BIBLIOGRAPHY: L. Stollbrock, *Die Komponisten Georg und Gottlieb Muffat* (Rostock, 1888); F. Raugel, "Georg Muffat en Alsace," *Revue de Musicologie* (Dec. 1954); W. Kolneder, *Georg Muffat: Zur Aufführungspraxis* (1970).

Muffat, Gottlieb (Theophil), Austrian organist and composer; son of **Georg Muffat;** b. Passau (baptized, April 25), 1690; d. Vienna, Dec. 9, 1770. In 1711 he went to Vienna, where he studied with J.J. Fux; from 1714, was in charge of the accompaniment of operas, church festivals, and chamber music at the Vienna court; became 2nd court organist in 1717; first organist, in 1741; retired on a pension in 1763.

WORKS: *72 Versetl sammt 12 Toccaten* for Organ (1726; reprinted by Guido Adler in Denkmäler der Tonkunst in Österreich, 58 [29.ii]); *Componimenti musicali* for Harpsichord (ibid., 7 [3.iii]; includes an essay on ornaments; Handel used this material for ornamental phrases in his oratorios).

BIBLIOGRAPHY: L. Stollbrock, *Die Komponisten Georg und Gottlieb Muffat* (Rostock, 1888); H. Knöll, *Die Klavier- und Orgelwerke von Theophil Muffat* (Vienna, 1916); F. Chrysander in *Supplement, enthaltend Quellen zu Händels Werken* (vol. 5 of the complete ed. of Handel's works).

Mugellini, Bruno, Italian composer; b. Potenza, Dec. 24, 1871; d. Bologna, Jan. 15, 1912. He studied with Busi and Martucci in Bologna; appeared as a concert pianist in Italy; then was appointed prof. of piano at the Liceo Musicale in Bologna (1898), and succeeded Martucci as its director in 1911. He wrote an opera, *Catullo*; a symph. poem, *Alla Fonte del Clitumno*; Piano Quartet; Cello Sonata; several sonatas and other pieces for piano; church music.

Mugnone, Leopoldo, Italian conductor; b. Naples, Sept. 29, 1858; d. there, Dec. 22, 1941. He studied with Cesi and Serrao at the Naples Cons.; began to compose as a young student; when he was 16, he pro-

duced a comic opera, *Don Bizarro e le sue figlie* (Naples, April 20, 1875); other operas were *Il Biricchino* (Venice, Aug. 11, 1892; fairly successful) and *Vita Bretone* (Naples, March 14, 1905). He also composed an attractive Neapolitan song, *La Rosella*, and other light music. But it was as a fine opera conductor that Mugnone achieved fame; his performances of Italian stage works possessed the highest degree of authority and an intense musicianly ardor. He also brought out Wagner's music dramas in Italy; conducted the first performance of Mascagni's *Cavalleria rusticana* (Rome, in May 17, 1890).

Mühlfeld, Richard, famous German clarinetist; b. Salzungen, Feb. 28, 1856; d. Meiningen, June 1, 1907. He first studied the violin and played in the Meiningen Court Orch.; then practiced on the clarinet without a teacher, and in 1876, at the age of 20, became first clarinetist at Meiningen. From 1884 to 1896 he was first clarinetist at the Bayreuth Festivals. Brahms wrote for him the Trio, op. 114 (for Clarinet, Cello, and Piano), the Quintet, op. 115 (for Clarinet, 2 Violins, Viola, and Cello), and the 2 clarinet sonatas, op. 120.

Mühling, August, German organist and composer; b. Raguhne, Sept. 26, 1786; d. Magdeburg, Feb. 3, 1847. He was for many years organist at the Magdeburg Cathedral; wrote the oratorios *Abbadona, Bonifazius, David, Die Leidensfeier Jesu*; 2 symphs.; Concerto for Bassoon and Orch.; 3 string quartets; Quintet for Flute, 2 Violins, Viola, and Cello; sacred duets and songs.

Mul, Jan, Dutch composer; b. Haarlem, Sept. 20, 1911; d. Overveen, Dec. 30, 1971. He studied with H. Andriessen and with Sem Dresden at the Amsterdam Cons.; was an organist and choral conductor in Overveen (1931–60); served as music editor of the Amsterdam daily *De Volkskrant* and chairman of the Guild of Dutch Composers. He orchestrated Sem Dresden's opera *François Villon* from the vocal score for the production at the 1958 Holland Festival (Amsterdam, June 12, 1958) and Sweelinck's *Keyboard variations on an Old Song* (Amsterdam, June 12, 1963). He wrote some fine sacred choral music; his secular works show the influence of the French modern school.

WORKS: 2 short operas, *De Varkenshoeder (The Swineherd)*, after H.C. Andersen (Amsterdam, June 25, 1953) and *Bill Clifford* (Hengelo, Oct. 5, 1964); several masses; *Stabat Mater* for Chorus and Small Orch. (1934); *Te Deum laudamus* for Chorus and Orch. (1955); *4 Coplas* for Voice and Orch. (1936); *Egmont onthalsd (Egmont Beheaded)* for Chorus and Orch. (1938); Piano Concerto (1940); Sonata for Mezzo-soprano, Baritone, and Small Orch. (1940–53); *Galant Quartet* for Soprano, and Small Orch. or Flute, Cello, and Piano (1952); *Felicitatie* for Orch. (1952); Concerto for Orch. (1956); Sinfonietta (1957; an orchestration of his Piano Sonata); *Mein junges Leben* for Orch. (1961); *Lettre de M. l'Abbé d'Olivet à M. le President Bouhier* for Baritone and Orch. (1962); Concerto for Piano, 4-hands, and Small Orch.

(1962); *Confetti musicali* for Orch. (1965); *Ik, Jan Mul (I, Jan Mul)* for Orch. (1965); *Divertimento* for Piano and Orch. (1967); *Balladino* for Cello, and Orch. or Piano (1968); *Variazioni "I due orsini"* for Orch. (1968); *The Old Familiar Faces* for Bass and Chamber Orch. (1969); *L'Homme désarmé,* cantata (1970–71; posthumously, Leyden, Sept. 25, 1973); 2 Piano sonatinas (1928, 1942); Piano Sonata (1940); *Intervallen,* 6 inventions for Piano (1942; orchestrated in 1954); Organ Sonata (1942); 2-piano Sonata (1953); Quintet for Clarinet, Bassoon, Violin, Viola, and Cello (1957); *De kwink,* ballad for Male Chorus, Bassoon, and Percussion (1965); *Les Donemoiselles,* punning tribute to the Dutch Society Donemus, 6 small pieces for Piano (1968); Trio for 2 Violins and Double Bass (1969).

Mulder, Ernest Willem, Dutch composer; b. Amsterdam, July 21, 1898; d. there, April 12, 1959. He studied at the Toonkunst Cons. in Amsterdam, later taught there; was a lecturer at the Univ. of Utrecht (1938–47), director of the Bussum Music School, and conductor of the Toonkunst Musical Society. He specialized in sacred music.
WORKS: Opera, *Dafne* (1932–34); *3 chansons* for Soprano and Orch. (1921–28); *Sinfonia sacra I* for 6 Soloists, Chorus, and Orch. (1922–32), *II, Dialogue mystique,* for Baritone, Chorus, and Orch. (1936–40), *III, super psalmos,* for Orch. (1948) and *IV, super passionem,* for Orch. (1949–50); *Requiem (Missa pro defunctis)* for Soloists, Chorus, and Orch. (1927–32); Piano Concerto (1935); *Holland* for Chorus and Orch. (1942); *Stabat Mater dolorosa* for Soloists, Chorus, and Orch. (1948); *Te Deum laudamus* for Chorus and Orch. (1951); *Symphonietta* for Medium Voice and Orch. (1958); 2 violin sonatas (1920); *Ars contrapunctica,* a collection of 7 small works for various instrumental combinations (1938–40); *Sonata (in modo classico)* for Solo Violin (1941); Trio for 3 Bassoons, (1942); String Quartet (1942); Sextet for Wind Quintet and Piano (1946); Quartet for Oboe, Bassoon, Cello, and Harp (1946); songs.

Mulder, Herman, Dutch composer; b. Amsterdam, Dec. 12, 1894. He studied harmony and voice, had a brief career as a concert singer. A prolific composer, he wrote 12 symphs.: No. 1 (1940), No. 2 (1952), No. 3 (1954), No. 4 (1959–60), No. 5 (1961), No. 6 (1962), No. 7 (1964), No. 8 (1967), No. 9 (1968), No. 10 (1971), No. 11 (1972–73), and No. 12 (1974–75); *Suite* for Orch. (1941); Piano Concerto (1943); Concerto for Orch. (1956); Concertino for Piano, 9 Wind Instruments, and Percussion (1964); Violin Concerto (1964); Concertino for Violin and String Orch. (1964); Concertino for Oboe and Orch. (1966); *Music* for Violin and Chamber Orch. (1967); 2-piano Concerto (1968); *Ouverture* (1967–70); *Capriccio* for Orch. (1970); *Funerailles* for Orch. (1971); 13 string quartets (Nos. 7–13, 1951–70); 5 sonatas, one each for Oboe, Flute, Clarinet, Horn, and Bassoon, all with Piano (1943–45); Piano Quintet (1947); English Horn Sonata (1950); 3 cello sonatinas (1956, 1956, 1967); 2 string quintets, with 2 Violas (1956, 1972); 2 string sextets (1957, 1973); 5 violin sonatas (1958–75); Viola

Sonata (1960); Trio for Flute, Oboe, and Bassoon (1960); String Quintet, with 2 Cellos (1961); 2 wind quintets (1961, 1966); Piano Trio (1965); Piano Quartet (1965); Violin Sonatina (1972); 2 string trios (1972); *Droomland (Dreamland),* after Edgar Allan Poe, for Baritone (or Contralto) and Piano (1949; orchestrated 1971); piano pieces; songs.

Muldowney, Dominic, British composer; b. Southampton, July 19, 1952. He studied with Jonathan Harvey at Southampton Univ. and later with Birtwistle in London and with Bernard Rands and David Blake at York Univ.; in 1976 he was appointed composer-in-residence at the National Theatre in London. He belongs to a group of British composers who reject esoteric musical abstractions and doctrinaire methodology in favor of an art which is readily accessible to a wide range of listeners.
WORKS: *Driftwood to the Flow* for 18 Strings (1972); *Klavier-Hammer* for one or more Pianos (1973); *Music at Chartres* for 16 Instruments (1973); String Quartet No. 1 (1973); String Quartet No. 2 (1980); Cantata for Soloists, 2 Speakers, 2 Cellos, and Percussion (1974); *Lovemusic for Bathsheba Evergreen and Gabriel Oak* for Chamber Group (1974); Solo/Ensemble for Chamber Group (1974); *The Earl of Essex's Galliard* for 3 Actors, Dancer, and Instruments (1975–76); *Double Helix* for 8 Players (1977); *Garland of Chansons* for 6 Oboes and 3 Bassoons (1978); *3 Hymns to Agape* for Chamber Orch. (1978); *Macbeth,* ballet music, for Orch. (1979); 6 Psalms for Choir, Soprano, Tenor, and Instruments (1979; Horsham, Dec. 6, 1980); *5 Theatre Poems,* after Brecht, for Mezzo-soprano and Instruments (1980–81; London, April 26, 1982); Piano Trio (1980; Bath Festival, May 25, 1982); *In Dark Times* for 4 Soloists and Chamber Group, to 8 poems by Brecht (1981; London, Feb. 23, 1982); *Sports et Divertissements,* after Satie, for Reciter and Chamber Group (1981); *The Duration of Exile* and *A Second Show* for Mezzo-soprano and Chamber Group (1983; London, June 2, 1983); Piano Concerto (1983; London, July 27, 1983).

Mulè, Giuseppe, Italian composer; b. Termini, Sicily, June 28, 1885; d. Rome, Sept. 10, 1951. He studied at the Cons. of Palermo; graduated as a cellist as well as in composition. In 1922 he was engaged as director of the Cons. of Palermo (until 1925); in 1925 he succeeded Respighi as director of the Santa Cecilia Academy in Rome; remained there until 1943. He wrote mostly for the stage, and was particularly successful in providing suitable music for revivals of Greek plays. He composed numerous operas in the tradition of the Italian *verismo*: *La Baronessa di Carini* (Palermo, April 16, 1912), *La Monacella della fontana* (Trieste, Feb. 17, 1923), *Dafni* (Rome, March 14, 1928), *Liolà* (Naples, Feb. 2, 1935); the oratorio *Il Cieco di Gerico*; the symph. poems *Sicilia canora* (1924) and *Vendemmia* (1936); also *3 canti siciliani* for Voice and Orch. (1930); a String Quartet and other chamber music; songs.

Mule, Marcel, French saxophone player; b. Aube,

June 24, 1901. He studied clarinet and saxophone with his father; was a member of the Garde Républicaine (1923–36); in 1929 he formed the Quatuor de Saxophones de Paris; in 1942 was appointed instructor of the newly established saxophone class at the Paris Cons. In 1957–58 he made his first American tour, appearing as soloist with leading American orchs. in concertos by modern French composers.

Müller, Adolf, Sr., Hungarian opera composer; b. Tolna, Oct. 7, 1801; d. Vienna, July 29, 1886. He began his career as a singer; in 1828 became conductor at the Theater an der Wien, and brought out there a number of singspiels, musical farces, etc.; also 2 operas: *Domi, der amerikanische Affe* (Jan. 28, 1831; fairly successful) and the comic opera *Das Zauberrütchen* (Dec. 2, 1831).

Müller, Adolf, Jr., Austrian composer and conductor; son of the preceding; b. Vienna, Oct. 15, 1839; d. there, Dec. 14, 1901. After completing his education in Vienna, he was engaged as a theater conductor in the provinces; was conductor of the German Opera at Rotterdam (1875–83); after that at the Theater an der Wien, where his father had directed before him. He produced there a number of operas: *Der Pfarrer von Kirchfeld* (Nov. 5, 1870), *Heinrich der Goldschmidt, Waldmeisters Brautfahrt, Van Dyke,* etc.; and the operettas *Der Hofnarr* (Nov. 20, 1886; his greatest success), *Der Teufels Weib* (Nov. 22, 1890), *Der Millionen-Onkel* (Nov. 5, 1892), *General Gogo* (Feb. 1, 1896), and *Der Blondin von Namur* (Oct. 15, 1898).

Müller, August Eberhard, German organist and composer; b. Nordheim, Hannover, Dec. 13, 1767; d. Weimar, Dec. 3, 1817. He was an organist at various churches at Magdeburg and Leipzig; in 1800 became assistant to Johann Adam Hiller at the Thomasschule in Leipzig, and succeeded him as cantor there in 1804; also was music director of the Thomaskirche and Nikolaikirche. In 1810 he became court conductor in Weimar. He wrote 3 piano concertos and 18 piano sonatas; 11 flute concertos; 11 church cantatas; a practical piano method (1805; actually the 6th ed. of Löhlein's *Pianoforte-Schule,* revised by Müller; Kalkbrenner's method is based on it; Czerny publ. the 8th ed. in 1825); a method for the flute. He also publ. cadenzas for, and a guide to the interpretation of, Mozart's concertos; arranged piano scores of Mozart's operas (very popular in his time).
BIBLIOGRAPHY: G. Haupt, *A.E. Müller's Leben und Klavierwerke* (Leipzig, 1926).

Müller, Franz (Karl Friedrich), German writer on Wagner and other subjects; b. Weimar, Nov. 30, 1806; d. there, Sept. 2, 1876. He was a government councillor in Weimar; was closely connected with the growing Wagner movement, and publ. a number of pamphlets on Wagner's operas: *Tannhäuser* (1853), *Richard Wagner und das Musikdrama* (1861), *Der Ring des Nibelungen* (1862), *Tristan und Isolde* (1865), *Lohengrin* (1867), and *Die Mei-*

stersinger von Nürnberg (1869), the last 3 at the express command of King Ludwig II of Bavaria; also *Im Foyer* (1868; on theatrical affairs in Weimar).

Müller, Friedrich, German clarinetist, conductor, and composer; b. Orlamünde, Dec. 10, 1786; d. Rudolstadt, Dec. 12, 1871. In 1803 he entered the royal orch. at Rudolstadt as a clarinet player; in 1831 became its conductor; was pensioned in 1854. He wrote 2 symphs.; 2 clarinet concertos and other music for clarinet; also clarinet studies; a Quartet for Clarinet and Strings; etc.

Müller, Georg Gottfried (also known as **George Godfrey**), American Moravian minister, violinist, and composer; b. Gross Hennersdorf, Saxony, May 22, 1762; d. Lititz, Pa., March 19, 1821. He came to America in 1784, and spent the major part of his life at Lititz, as a member of the culturally important group of Moravians in America. His works are listed by A.G. Rau and H.T. David in *A Catalogue of Music by American Moravians* (Bethlehem, 1938), and his music is represented in vol. I of the series Music by the Moravians in America, publ. by the N.Y. Public Library (1938).

Müller, Gottfried, German composer; b. Dresden, June 8, 1914. He studied with Sir Donald Tovey in Edinburgh, Scotland, and with Straube in Leipzig; was an instructor at the Hochschule für Musik in Leipzig and, from 1952 to 1961, an organist in Berlin. In 1961 he was appointed prof. of composition at the Cons. of Nuremberg. Among his works are a set of orch. variations on a German folk song, which became popular; *Deutsches Heldenrequiem* (1934); *Capriccio* (1959); *Dürersymphonie* (1962); Concertino for 3 Pianos (1963); String Quartet (1966); Concerto for 2 Pianos and Orch. (1967); Piano Concerto (1969).

Müller, Hans, German musicologist; son of the poet Wolfgang Müller von Königswinter; b. Cologne, Sept. 18, 1854; d. Berlin, April 11, 1897. He was appointed prof. of the history of music at the Hochschule für Musik, Berlin, in 1889; publ. *Hucbalds echte und unechte Schriften über Musik* (1884); *Abhandlung über Mensuralmusik in der Karlsruher Handschrift St. Peter Pergamen, 29a* (Leipzig, 1886); etc.

Müller, Heinrich Fidelis, German composer and choral leader; b. Fulda, April 23, 1827; d. there, Aug. 30, 1905. He was for many years choirmaster at the Cologne Cathedral; composed the oratorios *Weihnachtsoratorium, Die heilige Elisabeth, Die Passion unseres Herrn*; several masses, motets, choruses, etc.

Müller, Hermann, German music editor and ecclesiastic; b. Dortmund, Oct. 1, 1868; d. Paderborn, Jan. 17, 1932. He studied theology; received the degree of Dr.Theol.; in 1891, became a priest; later studied church music with Haberl and Haller in Regensburg (1894); from 1894, was cathedral choirmaster in Paderborn; was a specialist in church music. He publ. *Der feierliche Gottesdienst der Karwoche* (9th ed., 1928); *Gänge durchs Kirchenlied* (1926); numerous articles on church music in specialized publications.

Müller, Iwan, clarinetist and instrument maker; b. Reval, Estonia, Dec. 14, 1786; d. Bückeburg, Feb. 4, 1854. He developed the clarinet with 13 keys plus the "Altclarinett" (superseding the basset horn). In 1809 he went to Paris, where he established a clarinet workshop; although he faced the opposition of conservative instrument makers, his improved clarinet eventually won general popularity. He spent the last years of his life at Bückeburg as court musician; publ. a method for his new instruments; 6 clarinet concertos and 2 clarinet quartets.
BIBLIOGRAPHY: F.G. Rendall, *The Clarinet* (London, 1954; 3rd. ed., 1971).

Müller, Joseph, collector of musicians' portraits; b. Frankfurt, April 23, 1877; d. Closter, N.J., May 9, 1939. He studied at the Cons. of Ostend, Belgium, graduating in 1893; settled in N.Y. in 1933, and in 1934 became curator of musical iconography at the N.Y. Public Library; publ. *The Star Spangled Banner: Words and Music Issued between 1814–64,* an annotated bibliographical list of the different versions, with many facsimiles (N.Y., 1935); contributed articles on musical iconography to the *Musical Quarterly* and other publications.

Müller, Karl Christian, organist and teacher; b. Saxe-Meiningen, July 3, 1831; d. New York, June 4, 1914. He studied piano and organ with Heinrich Pfeiffer, and composition with Andreas Zöllner. He went to N.Y. in 1854; worked in a piano factory, then played violin in the orch. of the Barnum Museum. From 1879 to 1895 he taught harmony at the N.Y. College of Music; trans. Sechter's *Grundsätze der musikalischen Composition* (entitled *Fundamental Harmony,* N.Y., 1871; 9 subsequent eds.); also supplemented it by 4 sets of tables on modulation, chord succession, and harmonization (1882–93).
WORKS: *Pleasant Recollections* and *Golden Hours* for Piano; 3 organ sonatas; Sonata for Violin and Piano; String Quartet; choruses; songs; *March of the Crusaders* and *Resignation* for Organ; several large works in MS.

Müller, Maria, lyric soprano; b. Leitmeritz, Austria, Jan. 29, 1898; d. Bayreuth, March 13, 1958. She studied in Prague and Vienna; later with Max Altglass in N.Y.; made her debut in Linz in 1919; was a member of the Prague Opera (1921–23), Munich Opera (1923–24), and Metropolitan Opera (1924–35; debut as Sieglinde, Jan. 21, 1925). In 1926 she joined the Berlin Städtische Oper and later the Berlin State Opera; also sang at the Wagner festivals in Bayreuth (1930–44) and in Salzburg.

Müller, Peter, German composer; b. Kesselstadt, near Hanau, June 9, 1791; d. Langen, Aug. 29, 1877. He taught music at various schools in Germany; wrote his renowned *Jugendlieder;* male choruses; organ pieces; etc. In 1839 he became pastor at Staden. His opera (after Bulwer-Lytton), *Die letzten Tage von Pompeii,* was produced at Darmstadt on Dec. 25, 1853; he also wrote 7 string quintets and other chamber music.

Müller Quartets. Two famous German string quartets, the first to undertake regular concert tours, their members being: (1) The brothers **Karl** (1797–1873), **Gustav** (1799–1855), **Theodor** (1802–75), and **Georg** (1808–1855); they were all born in Braunschweig and belonged to the orch. there, Karl as concertmaster, Theodor as cellist, Gustav as violinist, and Georg as conductor. Their artistic tours included not only all the large German cities, but also Vienna and Paris (1833), Copenhagen (1838), St. Petersburg (1845), and the Netherlands (1852).
BIBLIOGRAPHY: L. Köhler, *Die Gebrüder Müller und das Streichquartett* (Leipzig, 1858); E. Stier, "Das Streichquartett der Gebrüder Müller," *Braunschweigisches Archiv* (July 1913).
(2) The four sons of Karl, all b. in Braunschweig (this quartet was organized in 1855, after the death of 2 members of the first one); **Karl,** first violin, b. April 14, 1829; d. Stuttgart, Nov. 11, 1907; **Hugo,** 2nd violin, b. Sept. 21, 1832; d. Braunschweig, June 26, 1886; **Bernhard,** viola, b. Feb. 24, 1825; d. Rostock, Sept. 4, 1895; and **Wilhelm,** cello, b. June 1, 1834; d. New York, Sept. 1897. For 10 years they constituted the court quartet at Meiningen; then, after extended and successful travels, they settled in Rostock as members of the city orch., Karl being appointed music director. The quartet was broken up by the appointment of Wilhelm (1873) to succeed Sweerts as first cello in the Royal Orch. at Berlin, and prof. in the Hochschule für musik. Karl lived from then on at Stuttgart and Hamburg; was also a noted composer.

Müller, Sigfrid Walther, German composer; b. Plauen, Jan. 11, 1905; d. in a Russian prison camp in Baku, Nov. 2, 1946. He studied at the Leipzig Cons. with Karg-Elert and Martienssen; also church music and organ with Straube; taught at the Leipzig Cons. (1929–32) and at the Hochschule für Musik in Weimar (1940–41); then was in the German army on the eastern front. His output comprised 62 op. numbers, mostly chamber music and organ works; also an opera, *Schlaraffenhochzeit* (Leipzig, 1937); *Böhmische Musik* for Orch.; *Gohliser Schlossmusik* for Small Orch.; Concerto for Flute and Chamber Orch. (1941).

Müller, Wenzel, Austrian composer; b. Tyrnau, Moravia, Sept. 26, 1767; d. Baden, near Vienna, Aug. 3, 1835. He studied with Dittersdorf; conducted theater orchs. in provincial towns; was director of the German Opera in Prague from 1807 to 1813; then went to Vienna as conductor at the Leopoldstadt Theater, a post he held almost to the end of his life. He wrote an enormous amount of stage music, and his singspiels were very popular in their day; among them were the following, which he brought out at the Leopoldstadt Theater: *Das Sonnenfest der Braminen* (Sept. 9, 1790); *Kaspar der Fagottist, oder Die Zauberzither* (June 8, 1791); *Das Neusonntagskind* (Oct. 10, 1793); *Die Schwestern von Prag* (March 11, 1794); *Die Teufelsmühle am Weinerberg* (an Austrian fairy tale; Nov. 12, 1799; his most popular stage work). A full list of his operas is in the 2nd Supplement to Riemann's *Opernhandbuch* (Leipzig, 1887).

BIBLIOGRAPHY: W. Krone, *Wenzel Müller* (Berlin, 1906); L. Raab, *Wenzel Müller* (Vienna, 1928); R. Haas, "Wenzel Müller," *Mozart-Jahrbuch 1953* (1954).

Müller-Blattau, Joseph Maria, German musicologist; b. Colmar, Alsace, May 21, 1895; d. Saarbrücken, Oct. 21, 1976. He studied musicology with Friedrich Ludwig at the Univ. of Strasbourg; also studied composition and conducting with Pfitzner and organ with Ernst Münch at the Strasbourg Cons. He served in the German army during World War I; after the Armistice of 1918, he resumed his studies in musicology with Wilibald Gurlitt at the Univ. of Freiburg im Breisgau; received his Ph.D. there in 1920 with the dissertation *Grundzüge einer Geschichte der Fuge* (publ. in Königsberg, 1923; 3rd ed., revised, 1963). He then completed his Habilitation at the Univ. of Königsberg in 1922 with his *Die Kompositionslehre Heinrich Schützens in der Fassung seines Schülers Christoph Bernhard* (publ. in Leipzig, 1926; 2nd ed., 1963). He taught at the Univ. of Königsberg; was promoted to reader there in 1928; then taught at the univs. of Frankfurt (1935–37) and Freiburg im Breisgau (1937–39); subsequently served in military administration (1939–42); then lectured at the Univ. of Strasbourg during the last years of World War II. From 1952 to 1958 he was director of the Staatliche Hochschule für Musik in Saarbrücken; he also taught at the Univ. of Strasbourg from 1952 to 1964. He was the editor of the abortive 12th edition of Riemann's *Musiklexikon* (1937–39), of which only a few issues appeared before the outbreak of World War II made further publication impossible.

WRITINGS: *Das Elsass, ein Grenzland deutscher Musik* (Freiburg, 1922); *Geschichte der Musik in Ost- und Westpreussen von der Ordenszeit bis zur Gegenwart* (Königsberg, 1931; 2nd ed., enlarged, 1968); *Hamann und Herder in ihren Beziehungen zur Musik* (Königsberg, 1931); *Das deutsche Volkslied* (Berlin, 1932; 2nd ed., 1958); *Einführung in die Musikgeschichte* (Berlin, 1932; 2nd ed., 1941); *Johannes Brahms* (Potsdam, 1933); *Georg Friedrich Händel* (Potsdam, 1933; 2nd ed., 1959); *Zur Erforschung des ostpreussischen Volksliedes* (Halle, 1934); *Johann Sebastian Bach* (Leipzig, 1935; 2nd ed., Stuttgart, 1950); *Geschichte der deutschen Musik* (Berlin, 1938; 3rd ed., 1942); *Hans Pfitzner* (Potsdam, 1940; 2nd ed., revised, 1969); *Gestaltung—Umgestaltung: Studien zur Geschichte der musikalischen Variation* (Stuttgart, 1950); *Das Verhältnis von Wort und Ton in der Geschichte der Musik: Grundzüge und Probleme* (Stuttgart, 1952); *Die Volksliedsammlung des jungen Goethe* (Kassel, 1955); *Von der Vielfalt der Musik: Musikgeschichte—Musikerziehung—Musikpflege* (Freiburg, 1966); *Goethe und die Meister der Musik* (Stuttgart, 1969).

BIBLIOGRAPHY: W. Salmen, ed., *Festgabe für Joseph Müller-Blattau zum 65. Geburtstag* (Saarbrücken, 1960; 2nd ed., 1962); C.-H. Mahling, ed., *Zum 70. Geburtstag von Joseph Müller-Blattau* (Kassel, 1966).

Müller-Hartmann, Robert, German composer; b. Hamburg, Oct. 11, 1884; d. Dorking, Surrey, Dec. 15, 1950. He studied at the Stern Cons. in Berlin; was a lecturer on music at Hamburg Univ. (1923–33); in 1937 settled in England, where he worked mainly as an arranger and translator. He wrote a number of symph. works, some of which were first performed by Richard Strauss and Karl Muck: a Symph., a Symph. Ballad, several sets of variations, etc; a Trio for Flute, Violin, and Viola; 2 violin sonatas; many organ works; piano pieces.

Müller-Hermann, Johanna, Austrian composer and pedagogue; b. Vienna, Jan. 15, 1878; d. there. April 19, 1941. She studied with Karl Nawratil, Josef Labor, Guido Adler, Zemlinsky, and J.B. Foerster; began to compose at an early age, in a Romantic vein, influenced chiefly by Mahler and Max Reger; was regarded as one of the foremost European women composers of orch. and chamber music. She wrote an oratorio, *In Memoriam*, to Walt Whitman's words; a Symph. for Voices with Orch.; a Symph. Fantasy on Ibsen's play *Brand*; String Quartet; String Quintet; Piano Quintet; Violin Sonata; Cello Sonata; Piano Sonata; several song cycles.

Müller-Kray, Hans, German conductor; b. Essen, Oct. 13, 1908; d. Stuttgart, May 30, 1969. He studied piano, cello, and theory in Essen; then was a conductor at the Essen Theater. He conducted in Münster (1934–41), Frankfurt (1942–45), and Wiesbaden (1945–48). In 1948 he became chief conductor of the Stuttgart Radio Symph., a post he held until his death. He was also a composer; wrote several ballet scores and other works.

Müller-Reuter, Theodor, German conductor and composer; b. Dresden, Sept. 1, 1858; d. there, Aug. 11, 1919. He studied piano with Alwin Wieck in Dresden and Clara Schumann in Frankfurt; also took lessons in composition with E.J. Otto and Meinardus in Dresden. He taught piano at the Strasbourg Cons. (1879–87), and at Dresden; subsequently conducted the Concert Society in Krefeld (1893–1918), returning to Dresden shortly before his death. He wrote the operas *Ondolina* (Strasbourg, 1883) and *Der tolle Graf* (Nuremberg, 1887) and many choral works; publ. a valuable *Lexikon der deutschen Konzert-Literatur* (Leipzig, 1909; Supplement, 1921); also a vol. of reminiscences and essays, *Bilder und Klänge des Friedens; musikalische Erinnerungen und Aufsätze* (Leipzig, 1919).

Müller von Asow, Erich Hermann, German musicologist; b. Dresden, Aug. 31, 1892; d. Berlin, June 4, 1964. He studied at the Univ. of Leipzig with Hugo Riemann (1912–15); during World War I was engaged as a military band conductor in the German army; then was in charge of the Pädagogium der Tonkunst in Dresden (1926–32); in 1936 he went to Austria; was briefly under arrest by the Gestapo in 1943; in 1945 returned to Germany, and lived mostly in Berlin. His publications include several valuable biographical studies, among them *Angelo und Pietro Mingotti* (Leipzig, 1917); *J.G. Mraczek* (Dresden, 1917); *Heinrich Schütz* (Dresden, 1922); *An die unsterbliche Geliebte: Liebesbriefe berühmter Musiker* (Dresden, 1934; 2nd ed., Vienna, 1942); *The Letters and Writings of G.F. Handel* (in Eng., London, 1935; in German, 1949); *J.S. Bach, Gesammelte Briefe und Schriften* (Regensburg, 1940; 2nd ed., 1950); *Egon Kornauth* (Leipzig, 1941); *Johannes Brahms und seine Welt* (Vienna, 1943); *Max Reger und seine Welt* (Berlin, 1944); numerous publications on Mozart. He began in 1955 a thematic catalogue of the works of Richard Strauss, which was completed by A. Ott and F. Trenner (3 vols.; Vienna, 1959–74). Anticipating the ominous zeitgeist, he regrettably publ. a *Handbuch der Judenfrage, Das Judentum in der Musik* (Leipzig, 1932). A Festschrift on the occasion of his 50th birthday was publ. in Salzburg (1942); and a compendium, *Epistolae et musica,* on his 60th birthday (Hamburg, 1952). A complete list of his writings is in *Kürschners deutscher Musiker-Kalender* (1954).

Müller von Kulm, Walter, Swiss composer; b. Kulm, Aug. 31, 1899; d. Arlesheim, near Basel, Oct. 3, 1967. He studied in Basel and Zürich; in 1947 was appointed director of the Basel Cons. He has written a number of stage works, among them an opera, *Der Erfinder* (1944); a ballet, *Die blaue Blume* (1936); an oratorio, *Vater unser* (1945); Symph. (1928); and several works of chamber music. He also publ. a manual of harmony, *Grundriss der Harmonielehre* (Basel, 1948).

Müller-Zürich, Paul, Swiss conductor and composer; b. Zürich, June 19, 1898. He studied at the Zürich Cons. (1917–20); also in Paris and Berlin. From 1927 to 1969 he was on the faculty of the Zürich Cons. His early works show Romantic influences; later he turned to a modern contrapuntal style.
WORKS: Viola Concerto (1935); 2 violin concertos (1936, 1957); 2 *Sinfonias* for String Orch. (1945, 1953); Cello Concerto (1954); 2 *Sinfoniettas* (1964); Concerto for 2 Violins, String Orch., and Harpsichord (1969); chamber music.
BIBLIOGRAPHY: F. Jakob, *Paul Müller: Biographie und Werkverzeichnis* (Zürich, 1963).

Mulligan, "Gerry" (Gerald Joseph Mulligan), American jazz saxophonist; b. New York, June 4, 1927. His formative years were spent in Philadelphia; in 1946 he began working as an instrumentalist and arranger for Gene Krupa; later became associated with Claude Thornhill and Miles Davis;

in 1952 he formed his own "pianoless" quartet, with which he toured and made recordings. He was an important figure in the development of "cool" jazz, as both a baritone saxophonist and an arranger.

Mullings, Frank, distinguished English tenor; b. Walsall, March 10, 1881; d. Manchester, May 19, 1953. He studied voice in Birmingham; made his debut in Coventry in 1907 as Faust; then sang Tristan in London in 1913, and performed the role of Otello in Manchester in 1916. In 1919 he was the first to sing Parsifal in English, at Covent Garden in London. From 1922–29 he was the principal dramatic tenor of the British National Opera Co., and appeared with it as Apollo in the first performance, in 1924, of Rudland Boughton's *Alkestis.* His other roles include Siegfried, Tannhäuser, Canio, and Radames. From 1930–45 he appeared mainly in concerts.

Mumma, Gordon, American avant-garde composer; b. Framingham, Mass., March 30, 1935. He began experimenting with electronic music at the age of 19, composing music and sound effects for an experimental theater in Ann Arbor. In 1957 he joined Robert Ashley and the artist Milton Cohen in a revolutionary theatrical art based on projected images; this developed into an esthetic medium called "Manifestations: Light and Sound" and later "Space Theatre"; in 1964 Mumma, Cohen, and Ashley gave a memorable presentation of the Space Theatre at the Biennial Exhibition in Venice, becoming pioneers in the electronic light-show. With the development of transistor circuitry in electronics, Mumma began a serious study of its technology. In 1961 Mumma became a founder of the annual contemporary music festival in Ann Arbor called ONCE. Working at the Inst. of Science and Technology in Ann Arbor, he developed a skill in seismology; made a study of tape recordings of earthquakes and underground nuclear explosions. In 1966 he joined the Merce Cunningham Dance Co. and moved to N.Y.; formed an ensemble called the Sonic Arts Union, which made 2 European tours. He gave courses in electronic circuitry at Brandeis Univ. (1966–67) and at the Univ. of Illinois in Urbana (1969–70); designed the Sound Modifier Console for the Pepsi-Cola Pavilion at EXPO '70 in Osaka, Japan; developed a process of "cybersonic" control of acoustical and electronic media. He also applied computer techniques to composition.
WORKS: For Magnetic Tape: *Vectors* (1959); *Densities* (1959); *Sinfonia* for 12 Instruments with Tape (1960); *Mirrors* (1960); *Meanwhile, a Twopiece* for Percussion and Tape (1961); *Epoxy* (1962); *Megaton for William Burroughs* (1963); *Le Corbusier* for Orch., Organ, Tape, and Cybersonic Concertante (1965). Instrumental works: *A Quarter of Fourpiece* for 4 Instruments (1963); a group of pieces with the punning titles *Very Small Size Mograph, Medium Size Mograph, Large Size Mograph* (1962–64) for Piano and Instruments; *Mesa* for Cybersonic Bandoneon with Electronic Accompaniment (1966; his most significant work); *Diastasis, As in Beer* for 2

Munch – Münnich

Cybersonic Guitars with Electronic Accompaniment (1967); *Swarmer* for Violin, Concertina, Musical Saw, and Cybersonic Modifiers (1968); *Digital Process with Poem Field* for Tape and Film Projections (1969); *Communication in a Noisy Environment* (produced in Automation House, N.Y., by Intermedia Inst., Nov. 19, 1970); also a number of works with the generic title *Conspiracy* for Digital Computer and Several Performers, intended to illustrate a democratic society in which the living enjoy civil rights on a par with computers; *Telepos* for Dancers and Telemetry Belts and Accelerometers (1971); *Phenomenon Unarticulated* for Frequency Modulated Ultrasonic Oscillators (1972); *Ambivex* for "surrogate myoelectrical telemetering system with pairs of performing appendages" (1972).

Munch, Charles, eminent Alsatian conductor; b. Strasbourg, Sept. 26, 1891; d. Richmond, Va., Nov. 6, 1968. The original spelling of his name was **Münch;** he was a son of **Ernst Münch,** a choral conductor in Alsace. He studied violin at the Strasbourg Cons., then went to Paris, where he studied violin with Lucien Capet, and later took further violin lessons with Carl Flesch in Berlin and conducting with Furtwängler in Leipzig. He was sergeant of artillery in the German army during World War I; was gassed at Peronne, and wounded at Verdun. In 1918, as an Alsatian, he became a French citizen; was concertmaster of the municipal orch. of Strasbourg (1919–26); later joined the Gewandhaus Orch. in Leipzig as concertmaster. He made his professional debut as a symph. conductor in Paris with the Straram Orch. (Nov. 1, 1932); in order to perfect his conducting technique he took some instruction with Alfred Szendrei (Sendrey), a Hungarian conductor then living in Paris (1933–40). Although he began his career as a conductor at the age of 41, he quickly rose to eminence; organized his own orch. in Paris, the Orch. de la Société Philharmonique (1935–38), performing many French works. In 1938 he was engaged to conduct the Société des Concerts du Conservatoire de Paris, and remained with it during the difficult time of the German occupation. He was awarded the French Légion d'Honneur in 1945. He made his American debut with the Boston Symph. Orch. on Dec. 27, 1946; in 1948 he made a transcontinental tour of the U.S. with the French Radio Orch. In 1949 he was selected as permanent conductor of the Boston Symph., to succeed Koussevitzky. In 1952 he traveled with the Boston Symph. to Europe on its first European tour; in 1956 the Boston Symph., with Munch and Monteux as conductors, made another European tour, which included Russia. He retired as conductor of the Boston Symph. Orch. in 1962. Returning to Paris, he organized there the Orch. de Paris; it was during an American tour of this orch. that he collapsed and died in Richmond, Va. In his conducting Munch combined a distinct individuality with a fine sense of authentic color and stirring rhythms; in Classical works he continued the traditions of the German school, striving mainly for precision and fidelity to the music, while making allowances for appropriate Romantic effusions. Modern French music occupied a prominent place on his programs; he brought out new works by Albert Roussel, Milhaud, Honegger and others. He publ. a book, *Je suis chef d'orchestre* (Paris, 1954; in Eng., *I Am a Conductor,* N.Y., 1955).

BIBLIOGRAPHY: Hope Stoddard, *Symphony Conductors of the U.S.A.* (N.Y., 1957; pp. 136–46).

Münch, Ernst, Alsatian organist and choral conductor; b. Niederbronn, Dec. 31, 1859; d. Strasbourg, April 1, 1928. He was appointed organist at St. Wilhelm (St. Guillaume) Church in Strasbourg in 1882, where he founded a choir which attained a great renown for its performance of Bach's cantatas and passions; Albert Schweitzer served as organist at these performances. His son, **Fritz Münch** (b. Strasbourg, June 2, 1890), succeeded him as conductor of the St. Wilhelm Choir in 1924; his second son, **Charles Münch (Munch),** became a celebrated conductor; his third son was **Hans Münch.**

Münch, Hans, Alsatian conductor; b. Mulhouse, March 9, 1893. He was a nephew of **Ernst Münch** and son of the organist **Eugen Münch** of Mulhouse. He studied organ, composition, and conducting at the Basel Cons. He conducted the choral society of Basel (1925–65) and also the subscription concerts of the Allgemeine Musikgesellschaft, from 1935 until 1966; was director of the Basel Music School in 1935–47. He composed several cantatas, a Symph. (1951), and *Symphonische Improvisationen* (1971).

Münchinger, Karl, German conductor; b. Stuttgart, May 29, 1915. He studied at the Hochschule für Musik in Stuttgart; then with Abendroth at the Leipzig Cons.; in 1941–43 he conducted symph. orchs. in Hannover, and in 1945 founded the Stuttgart Chamber Orch. From then on he pursued his conducting career mainly outside of Germany; toured America, Japan and Russia; made his U.S. debut in San Francisco in 1953, and during the following season made a U.S. tour with his Stuttgart Chamber Orch.; he visited the U.S. again in 1977. In 1966 he organized the "Klassische Philharmonie" in Stuttgart, with which he gave regular performances.

Munclinger, Milan, Czech flutist and conductor; b. Košice, July 3, 1923. He began to study the flute in his youth; then enrolled at the Prague Cons.; also studied at the Academy of Musical Arts and the Univ. of Prague. He gained distinction as founder-conductor of the Ars Rediviva ensemble, with which he gave performances of Baroque and Classical repertoire with much success; also toured widely with his ensemble.

Münnich, Richard, German music educator and theorist; b. Berlin, June 7, 1877; d. Weimar, July 4, 1970. He studied piano with his father, and cello with Otto Hutschenreuter; then took courses at the Univ. of Berlin with Max Friedlaender and Carl

Stumpf (1897–1901). He subsequently devoted himself to music education; held various teaching posts in Berlin and Stettin; for 25 years taught music theory at the Klindworth-Scharwenka Cons. in Berlin (1910–35); in 1935 he was appointed prof. and director at the Hochschule für Musik in Weimar; he retired in 1964. He publ. a number of practice books for school, among them *Widerholungsbüchlein für den Musikunterricht an höheren Schulen* (4th ed., 1928); *Jale, Ein Beitrag zur Tonsilbenfrage und zur Schulmusik-Propädeutik* (Lahr, 1930; new ed., Wolfenbüttel, 1957). In his numerous writings on harmony he followed Riemann's analytical theories. A Festschrift was presented to him on his 70th birthday (1947).

Munrow, David, English recorder player; b. Birmingham, Aug. 12, 1942; d. Chesham Bois, Buckinghamshire, May 15, 1976. He read English at Pembroke College, Cambridge; during this period (1961–64) he founded an ensemble for the furtherance of early English music and organized a recorder consort. In 1967 he formed the Early Music Consort of London, which gave many successful concerts of medieval and Renaissance music. He wrote *Instruments of the Middle Ages and Renaissance* (London, 1976). He killed himself for obscure reasons in his early maturity.

Munsel, Patrice Beverly, American soprano; b. Spokane, Wash., May 14, 1925. She studied in N.Y. with William Herman and Renato Bellini; won an audition at the Metropolitan Opera and made a successful debut there on Dec. 4, 1943, in the minor role of Philine in *Mignon* (the youngest singer ever accepted by the Metropolitan); she remained on the staff until 1958, excepting the 1945–46 season. She subsequently made several European tours. Her best roles are Gilda, Lucia, Rosina, Violetta, and Lakmé. She portrayed Melba in a motion picture on Melba's life (1953); also made successful appearances in operetta and in Broadway musicals.

Munz, Mieczyslaw, Polish-American pianist and pedagogue; b. Cracow, Oct. 31, 1900; d. New York, Aug. 25, 1976. He studied piano and composition at the Vienna Academy of Music, and later at the Hochschule für Musik in Berlin; his principal teacher there was Ferruccio Busoni. He made a brilliant debut in Berlin in 1920 as soloist in 3 works on the same program: the Brahms Piano Concerto in D minor, Liszt's Piano Concerto in A, and *Variations symphoniques* by César Franck. His American debut took place in a solo recital in N.Y. on Oct. 20, 1922; he subsequently was soloist with a number of orchs. in the U.S.; also toured Europe, South America, Australia, and Japan. He was on the faculty of the Curtis Inst. of Music in Philadephia from 1941 to 1963, when he was engaged as a prof. of piano at the Juilliard School of Music in N.Y. In 1975 he gave courses in Tokyo. His piano playing was distinguished by a fine Romantic flair supported by an unobtrusive virtuoso technique. He was highly esteemed as a teacher.

Münzer, Georg, German writer on music and teacher; b. Breslau, Sept. 4, 1886; d. Berlin, April 24, 1908. He studied in Berlin with Klindworth (piano) and Helmholtz (acoustics); also studied musicology with Bellermann and Spitta; received his Dr.Phil. with the dissertation *Beiträge zur Konzertgeschichte Breslaus;* lived in Breslau and Berlin.
WORKS: *Zur Einführung in Richard Wagners "Ring des Nibelungen"* (1900); *Heinrich Marschner* (1901); numerous essays in music journals.

Muradeli, Vano, Russian composer; b. Gori, Georgia, April 6, 1908; d. Tomsk, Siberia, Aug. 14, 1970. As a child he improvised songs, accompanying himself on the mandolin (there was no piano in his home); he did not learn to read music until he was 18, when he entered the Tiflis Cons.; after graduation (1934) he went to the Moscow Cons., where he studied first with Shekhter and then with Miaskovsky. His early compositions were influenced by his native folk music; he wrote a *Georgian Suite* (1935) and incidental music to plays on Caucasian subjects. His first important work was a symph. in memory of the assassinated Soviet dignitary Kirov (Moscow, Nov. 28, 1938); his 2nd Symph. (1946) received a Stalin prize. The performance of his opera *Great Friendship* (Moscow, Nov. 7, 1947) gave rise to an official condemnation of modernistic trends in Soviet music, culminating in the resolution of the Central Committee of the Communist Party of Feb. 10, 1948, which described the opera as "chaotic, inharmonious and alien to the normal human ear." Muradeli's reputation was rehabilitated by his subsequent works: *The Path of Victory* for Orch., a series of choruses (*Stalin's Will Has Led Us; Song of the Fighters for Peace; Hymn to Moscow,* which received a Stalin prize in 1951), and an opera, *October* (Moscow, April 22, 1964).

Muratore, Lucien, French tenor; b. Marseilles, Aug. 29, 1876; d. Paris, July 16, 1954. He studied at the Cons. of Marseilles, graduating with honors in 1897, but began his career as an actor. Later he studied opera at the Paris Cons.; made his opera debut at the Opéra–Comique on Dec. 16, 1902, in Hahn's *La Carmélite,* with extraordinary success. Muratore also sang in the premières of several operas by Massenet: *Ariane* (1906), *Bacchus* (1909), and *Roma* (1912); Février's *Monna Vanna* (1909) and Giordano's *Siberia* (1911); etc. In 1913 he made his American debut with the Boston Opera Co.; on Dec. 15, 1913, he sang Faust with the Chicago Opera Co. In 1914 he joined the French army; in 1917 he sang at the Teatro Colón in Buenos Aires; then returned to the Chicago Opera Co. In 1922 he went back to France; for 7 years he served as mayor of the town of Biot. He was married 3 times; his first 2 marriages (to **Marguerite Bériza,** a soprano, and to the famous prima donna **Lina Cavalieri**) ended in divorce; his 3rd wife was Marie Louise Brivaud.

Muris, Johannes de (original French rendering may have been **Jehan des Murs, de Murs, de Meurs,** etc.), important French music theorist, astronomer, and mathematician; b. in the diocese of Lisieux, Normandy, c.1300; d. c.1351. He was long confused with Julian des Murs, a Master of the Children of the Sainte-Chapelle of Paris (c.1350), who later served as secretary to Charles V of France; it seems most likely, however, that the 2 were close relatives. Johannes de Muris is listed as a baccalaureate student in the Faculty of Arts in Paris in 1318. During the next few years he was active in Evreux and Paris; was associated with the Collège de Sorbonne in Paris, where he achieved the academic degree of Magister. In 1326–27 he was at the monastery of Fontevrault (Maine-et-Loire); it is known that Julian des Murs was his clerk at this time. In 1332–33 he was in Evreux; then returned to Paris, where he was again associated with the Sorbonne (1336–37). In 1338–42 he was in service at the court of the King of Navarra, Philippe d'Evreux. In 1342 he was one of the 6 canons of the collegiate church in Mezières-en-Brenne (Indre); in 1344 he went, at the invitation of Pope Clement VI, to Avignon, where he participated in the conference on the reform of the calendar. There is extant a letter in verse which he wrote to Philippe de Vitry.

The writings by Johannes de Muris pose problems; titles and versions of the various works attributed to him are questionable. Those that appear authentic are as follows: *Ars novae musicae* or *Notitia artis musicae* (1321; although he gave it the title *Summa musicae,* the work is always known by the 2 preceding titles in order to avoid confusion with a spurious work of the same name); *Questiones super partes musicae* or *Compendium musicae practicae* (c.1322; apparently a condensed version of the 2nd book of the *Ars novae musicae*); *Musica speculativa secundum Boetium* (June 1323). Some scholars also attribute to him *Libellus cantus mensurabilis (secundum Johannes de Muris)* (c.1340) and *Ars contrapuncti secundum Johannes de Muris* (after 1340). The *Speculum musicae* (c.1325), long attributed to Muris, has been proved to be a work by Jacques de Liège.
BIBLIOGRAPHY: R. Hirschfeld, *Johann de Muris: Seine Werke und seine Bedeutung als Verfechter des Classischen in der Tonkunst: Eine Studie* (Leipzig, 1884); H. Riemann, *Geschichte der Musiktheorie im IX.–XIX. Jahrhundert* (Leipzig, 1898; 2nd ed., revised, 1921; Eng. trans., 1967); W. Grossmann, *Die einleitenden Kapitel des Speculum Musicae von Johannes de Muris: Ein Beitrag zu Musikanschauung des Mittelalters* (Leipzig, 1924; erroneous in ascribing the authorship of *Speculum musicae* to Johannes de Muris); L. Gushee, "New Sources for the Biography of Johannes de Muris," *Journal of the American Musicological Society,* XXII (1969); U. Michels, *Die Musiktraktate des Johannes de Muris* (Wiesbaden, 1970); M. Haas, "Musik zwischen Mathematik und Physik: Zur Bedeutung der Notation in den 'Notitia artis musicae' des Johannes de Muris (1321)," in *Festschrift für Arno Volk* (Cologne, 1974).

Muro, Bernardo de, Italian operatic tenor; b. Tempio Pausanio, Sardinia, 1881; d. Rome, Oct. 27, 1955. He studied at the Santa Cecilia Academy in Rome. He sang Turiddu in *Cavalleria rusticana* in 1911; in 1912 appeared in the title role of *Don Carlos* at La Scala in Milan; then sang major tenor roles in practically all the standard Italian operas; toured in South America, and briefly in the U.S., with the San Carlo Opera Co. He never became a star on the operatic firmament, yet knowledgeable critics regarded him as worthy of comparison with Caruso, both in the carrying force of his natural voice and in emotional appeal.

Murphy, Lambert, American tenor; b. Springfield, Mass., April 15, 1885; d. Hancock, N.H., July 24, 1954. He studied at Harvard Univ. (A.B., 1908); took singing lessons with T. Cushman in Boston and Luckstone in N.Y.; was a soloist in various Boston churches (until 1910); made tours with the Boston Festival Orch.; appeared at many festivals; from 1911 to 1914 was a member of the Metropolitan Opera.

Murphy, "Turk" (Melvin), American jazz trombonist and bandleader; b. Palermo, Calif., Dec. 16, 1915. After studying music theory, he took up the cornet and trombone; subsequently led his own band. He achieved distinction by reviving ragtime and jazz numbers from the early period of popular music.

Murray, (Morna) Anne, Canadian singer of popular and country-western music; b. Springhill, Nova Scotia, June 20, 1945. She attended Mount St. Vincent Univ. in Halifax; graduated from the Univ. of New Brunswick in Fredericton with a bachelor's degree in physical education in 1966. She made appearances on Canadian television and made several recordings; in 1970 she gained international recognition with her album *Snowbird.* After several more successful albums, she received the 1974 Grammy award as best female country vocalist for her recording of *Love Song.* Other successful albums followed, including *New Kind of Feeling* (1979), which won her a platinum award. In 1981 she again won the Grammy award as best female country vocalist for her recording of *Could I Have This Dance?* from the movie *Urban Cowboy.*

Murray, Bain, American composer and musicologist; b. Evanston, Ill., Dec. 26, 1926. He studied at Harvard Univ. with Walter Piston (composition), Otto Gombosi (musicology), and A. Tillman Merritt (theory), obtaining his M.A. in 1952. From 1955 to 1970 he taught at the Oberlin Cons.; in 1970 was appointed a prof. of music at the Cleveland State Univ. He composed a ballet, *Peter Pan,* some chamber music, and a number of songs.

Murrill, Herbert Henry John, English composer; b. London, May 11, 1909; d. there, July 24, 1952. He studied at the Royal Academy of Music in London with York Bowen, Stanley Marchant, and Alan Bush; then took courses at Oxford Univ. with Ernest

Walker and Sir Hugh Allen. He occupied various posts as organist and choral director; in 1933 he was appointed to the staff of the Royal Academy of Music, remaining there until his death. His relatively small output is in a modern vein, exemplified by a "jazz opera," *Man in Cage* (London, 1930). He also wrote 2 cello concertos (1935, 1950) and some chamber music, as well as songs and piano pieces.

Murschhauser, Franz Xaver Anton, German music theorist; b. Zabern, near Strasbourg, June (baptized, July 1) 1663; d. Munich, Jan. 6, 1738. He studied with J.K. Kerll; from 1691 was music director of the Frauenkirche there. He wrote the theoretical treatise *Academia musico-poetica bipartita, oder Hohe Schule der musikalischen Composition,* the first part of which appeared in 1721, provocatively described as being intended "to give a little more light to the excellent Herr Mattheson." The latter retaliated with such devastating effect in his *Melopoetische Lichtscheere (Critica musica,* 1722; pp. 1–88) that Murschhauser refrained from publishing the 2nd part of his work. His compositions for organ are reprinted in Denkmäler der Tonkunst in Bayern, 30 (18), edited by M. Seiffert, with a biographical sketch.

BIBLIOGRAPHY: M. Vogeleis, "F.X.A. Murschhauser," *Kirchenmusikalisches Jahrbuch* (1901).

Murska, Ilma di, Croatian soprano; b. 1836; d. (suicide by poison) Munich, Jan. 14, 1889. She studied with Mathilde Marchesi in Vienna, and later in Paris; made her debut in Florence (1862). After a European tour, she was engaged at the Vienna Opera. She made her London appeerence for the first time as Lucia (May 11, 1865) and was favorably received there for several seasons (until 1873); toured America and Australia (1873–76); was again in London in 1879. She taught at the National Cons., N.Y., in 1880. She led a turbulent life; was married 3 times; killed herself in a fit of despondency.

Musard, Philippe, famous French dance composer; b. Tours, Nov. 8, 1792; d. Auteuil (Paris), March 30, 1859. He studied music privately with Reicha; first came into public view at the promenade concerts in Paris, begun in Nov. 1833, in a bazaar of the Rue St. Honoré; there he introduced Dufresne, a remarkable player on the cornet, and wrote special solo pieces for him which became a great attraction; he also conducted balls at the Paris Opéra (1835–36), at which his orch. of 70 musicians won great acclaim. His quadrilles and galops enjoyed immense popularity, and he earned the sobriquet "le roi des quadrilles." In London he conducted the promenade concerts at Drury Lane during the season of 1840–41; he appeared at other concerts in England. His son **Alfred Musard** (1828–81) was also a composer of quadrilles, and a bandleader.

Musgrave, Thea, remarkable Scottish composer; b. Barnton, Midlothian, May 27, 1928. She planned to study medicine and enrolled in the Univ. of Edinburgh for preliminary studies; concurrently she attended courses in musical analysis with Mary Grierson and advanced composition and counterpoint with a visiting Austrian composer, Hans Gál. She received her B.M. degree in 1950 and went to Paris to study with Nadia Boulanger. Her first compositions were in a cautiously impressionistic manner. She wrote a ballet, with a scenario based on Chaucer's subject from *The Pardoner's Tale,* and she received a prize for her work. In 1954 she wrote a cantata for the BBC of Scotland which was successfully performed. In 1955 she completed a chamber opera, *The Abbot of Drimock,* based on a Scottish story, and it was successfully performed, first as a concert work, and later as a stage production. From 1959–65 she served as a lecturer on music at London Univ. in Teddington. All these years she followed the acceptable modern style of composition, but soon the diatonic lyricism of the initial period of her creative evolution gave way to increasingly chromatic constructions, eventually systematized into serial organization. She herself described her theatrical works as "dramatic-abstracts" in form, because even in the absence of a programmatic design, they revealed some individual dramatic traits. From 1955–70 she was active mainly as a choral conductor and accompanist; from 1970–78 she was on the music faculty at the Univ. of Calif., Santa Barbara. There she met a congenial colleague, the American viola player **Peter Mark;** they were married in 1971. In 1974 she received a Guggenheim fellowship; this enabled her to compose music without concern for fiscal matters. During this period, her most important work was *Mary, Queen of Scots,* commissioned by the Scottish Opera for the Edinburgh Festival in 1977. Appreciated by critics and audiences alike, her compositions, in a variety of styles but invariably effective and technically accomplished, enjoyed numerous performances in Europe and America.

WORKS: *The Abbott of Drimock,* chamber opera (London, 1955); *The Decision* (1964; London, Nov. 30, 1967); *The Voice of Ariadne,* after *The Last of the Valerii* by Henry James (Aldeburgh [England] Festival, June 11, 1974); *Mary, Queen of Scots* (Edinburgh Festival, Sept. 6, 1977); *A Christmas Carol* (Norfolk, Va., Dec. 7, 1979); *An Occurrence at Owl Creek Bridge,* radio opera for Baritone, 3 Speakers, Tape, and Orch. (London, Dec. 20, 1981); *A Tale for Thieves,* ballet (1953); *Orfeo,* ballet for Dancer, Flute, and Tape (1975); *4 Madrigals* for Unaccompanied Chorus (1953); *A Suite o' Bairnsangs* for Voice and Piano (1953); *Cantata for a Summer's Day* for Vocal Quartet, Speaker, Flute, Clarinet, String Quartet, and Double Bass (1954); *Song of the Burn* for Unaccompanied Chorus (1954); *5 Love Songs* for Tenor and Guitar (1955); *Divertimento* for String Orch. (1957); String Quartet (1958); *Obliques* for Orch. (1958); *A Song for Christmas* for Voice and Piano (1958); *Scottish Dance Suite* for Orch. (1959); *Triptych* for Tenor and Orch. (1959); *Colloquy* for Violin and Piano (1960); Trio for Flute, Oboe, and Piano (1960); *Monologue* for Piano (1960); *Serenade* for Flute, Clarinet, Harp, Viola, and Cello (1961); *Perspectives* for Orch. (1961); Chamber Concerto No. 1 for 9 Instruments (1962); *Theme and*

Interludes for Orch. (1962); *The Phoenix and the Turtle* for Chorus and Orch. (1962); *Marko the Miser,* "a tale for children to mime, sing and play" (1962); *Sinfonia* (1963); *The 5 Ages of Man* for Chorus and Orch. (1964); *Excursions* for Piano Duet (1965); *Festival Overture* (1965); Chamber Concerto No. 2 for 5 Instruments (1966); Chamber Concerto No. 3 for 8 Instruments (1966); *Nocturnes and Arias* for Orch. (1966); *Variations* for Brass Band (1966); *Sonata for 3* for Flute, Violin, and Guitar (1966); *Impromptu No. 1* for Flute and Oboe (1967); *Concerto for Orchestra* (1967); *Memento Creatoris* for Unaccompanied Chorus (1967); *Music* for Horn and Piano (1967); Clarinet Concerto (London, Feb. 5, 1969; a deft, chic virtuoso piece, requiring the soloist to promenade among members of the orch.); *Beauty and the Beast,* ballet for Chamber Orch. and Electronic Tape (1968–69; London, Nov. 19, 1969); *Soliloquy No. 1* for Guitar and Electronic Tape (1969); *Night Music* for Chamber Orch. (1969); *Memento Vitae* for Orch. (1969–70); *Elegy* for Viola and Cello (1970); *Impromptu No. 2* for Flute, Oboe, and Clarinet (1970); *From One to Another* for Viola and Electronic Tape (1970); Horn Concerto (1971); Viola Concerto (1973); *Space Play,* concerto for 9 Instruments (1974); *Rorate Coeli* for Mixed Chorus (1974); *Orfeo II,* orch. version of the ballet (1975; Los Angeles, March 28, 1976); *From One to Another* for Viola and Strings (1979–80; Minneapolis, March 1982); *The Last Twilight* for Chorus, Brass, and Percussion (Santa Fe, July 20, 1980); *Peripeteia* for Orch. (1981).
BIBLIOGRAPHY: David Ewen, *Composers since 1900* (N.Y., 1981).

Musicescu, Gavriil, Rumanian composer of sacred music and folk-song arranger; b. Ismail, March 20, 1847; d. Jassy, Dec. 21, 1903. He studied at the Cons. of Jassy and later at the St. Petersburg Cons. In 1872 he was appointed a prof. at the Jassy Cons. and became its director in 1901. He composed mainly choral music for the Orthodox Church; publ. a manual for voice teachers (Jassy, 1877). His arrangements of Rumanian folk songs have an authentic flavor, thanks to his skill in finding suitable harmonizations of intervallically peculiar melodic patterns.
BIBLIOGRAPHY: G. Breazul, *G. Musicescu* (Bucharest, 1962).

Musin, Ovide, Belgian violinist; b. Nandrin, near Liège, Sept. 22. 1854; d. Brooklyn, N.Y., Nov. 24, 1929. He studied with Heynberg and Léonard at the Liège Cons., taking first violin prize at the age of 13; he won the gold medal at 15; toured Europe from 1874 to 1882 with remarkable success. In 1883 he went to America; between 1892 and 1897 he made 2 world tours. From 1897 to 1908 he taught at the Cons. of Liège; in 1908 he established himself in N.Y., and opened his own school of music. He publ. a number of brilliant violin pieces; also the instructive works *System of Daily Practice* (1899) and *The Belgian School of the Violin* (4 vols.; 1916; a combination of his own methods with those of his teacher Léo-

nard); also publ. a book, *My Memories* (1920). His wife, **Annie Louise Tanner-Musin** (b. Boston, Oct. 3, 1856; d. there, Feb. 28, 1921), was a well-known coloratura soprano.
BIBLIOGRAPHY: *Dictionary of American Biography.*

Musiol, Robert Paul Johann, German writer on music and pedagogue; b. Breslau, Jan. 14, 1846; d. Fraustadt, Posen, Oct. 19, 1903. He studied in Liebenthal, Silesia; devoted himself to teaching. He publ. a useful lexicon, *Musikalisches Fremdwörterbuch; Katechismus der Musikgeschichte* (2nd ed., 1888); edited Tonger's *Konversations-Lexikon der Tonkunst* (1881–85) and *Musikerlexikon* (1890).

Mussolini, Cesare, Italian composer and theorist; b. Romagna, 1735; d. probably in London, where he went in 1780; publ. (in Eng.) *A New and Complete Treatise on the Theory and Practice of Music, with Solfeggios* (London, 1795); also canzonets. He was an ancestor of Benito Mussolini.

Mussolini, Romano, Italian jazz pianist; son of Il Duce; b. Carpena, Forli, Sept. 26, 1927. With the rest of Mussolini's family, he lived in Ischia after the war; picked up the accordion and piano; became a professional jazz band leader in Rome.

Mussorgsky, Modest, great Russian composer; b. Karevo, Pskov district, March 21, 1839; d. St. Petersburg, March 28, 1881. He received his first instruction on the piano from his mother; at the age of 10 was taken to St. Petersburg, where he had piano lessons with Anton Herke. In 1852 he entered the cadet school of the Imperial Guard; composed a piano piece entitled *Porte enseigne Polka,* which was publ. (1852); after graduation, he joined the regiment of the Guard. In 1857, he met Dargomyzhsky, who introduced him to Cui and Balakirev; he also became friendly with the critic and chief champion of Russian national music, Vladimir Stasov. These associations prompted Mussorgsky's decision to become a professional composer. He played and analyzed piano arrangements of works by Beethoven and Schumann; Balakirev helped him to acquire a knowledge of form; he tried to write music in classical style, but without success; his inner drive was directed toward "new shores," as Mussorgsky himself expressed it. The liquidation of the family estate made it imperative for Mussorgsky to take a paying job; he became a clerk in the Ministry of Communications (1863), resigning 4 years later. During this time, he continued to compose, but his lack of technique compelled him time and again to leave his various pieces unfinished. He eagerly sought professional advice from his friends Stasov (for general esthetics) and Rimsky-Korsakov (for problems of harmony); to the very end of his life, he regarded himself as being only half-educated in music, and constantly acknowledged his inferiority as a craftsman. But he yielded to no one in his firm faith in the future of national Russian music. When a group of compos-

ers from Bohemia visited St. Petersburg in 1867, Stasov published an article in which he for the first time referred to the "mighty handful of Russian musicians" pursuing the ideal of national art. The expression was picked up derisively by some journalists, but it was accepted as a challenge by Mussorgsky and his comrades-in-arms, Balakirev, Borodin, Cui, and Rimsky-Korsakov, the "mighty five" of Russian music. In 1869, Mussorgsky once more entered government service, this time in the forestry dept. He became addicted to drink, and had epileptic fits; he died a week after his 42nd birthday. The significance of Mussorgsky's genius did not become apparent until some years after his death. Most of his works were prepared for publication by Rimsky-Korsakov, who corrected some of Mussorgsky's harmonic crudities, and reorchestrated the symph. works. Original versions of Mussorgsky's music were preserved in MS, and eventually publ. But despite the availability of the authentic scores, Mussorgsky's works continue to be performed in Rimsky-Korsakov's editions, made familiar to the whole musical world. In his dramatic works, and in his songs, Mussorgsky draws a boldly realistic vocal line, in which inflections of speech are translated into a natural melody. His first attempt in this genre was an unfinished opera, *The Marriage*, to Gogol's comedy; here Mussorgsky also demonstrated his penetrating sense of musical humor. His ability to depict tragic moods is revealed in his cycle *Songs and Dances of Death;* his understanding of intimate poetry is shown in the children's songs. His greatest work is the opera *Boris Godunov* (to Pushkin's tragedy), which has no equal in its stirring portrayal of personal destiny against a background of social upheaval. In it, Mussorgsky created a true national music drama, without a trace of the Italian conventions that had theretofore dominated the operatic works by Russian composers. Mussorgsky wrote no chamber music, perhaps because he lacked the requisite training in contrapuntal technique. Of his piano music, the set of pieces *Pictures at an Exhibition* (somewhat after the manner of Schumann's *Carnaval*) is remarkable for its vivid representation of varied scenes (it was written to commemorate his friend, the painter Victor Hartmann, whose pictures were the subjects of the music); the work became famous in the brilliant orchestration of Ravel. Although Mussorgsky was a Russian national composer, his music influenced many composers outside Russia, and he came to be regarded as the most potent talent of the Russian national school.
WORKS: OPERAS: *The Marriage* (1868; only the first act completed; produced, St. Petersburg, April 1, 1909; completed and orchestrated by Alexander Tcherepnin; perf. in this form for the first time, Essen, Sept. 14, 1937); *Boris Godunov* (1868–69, with 7 scenes; Leningrad, Feb. 16, 1928; 2nd version, with prologue and 4 acts, St. Petersburg, Feb. 8, 1874; revised and reorchestrated by Rimsky-Korsakov in 1896; produced in this new form, St. Petersburg, Dec. 10, 1896, and subsequently all over the world; Mussorgsky's original score, ed. by Paul Lamm, publ. in 1928); *Khovanshchina* (on a historical sub-

ject from the time of Peter the Great; completed and orchestrated by Rimsky-Korsakov; first perf., St. Petersburg, Feb. 21, 1886); *The Fair at Sorochinsk* (unfinished, completed by Cui; Moscow, Oct. 21, 1913; also arranged and orchestrated by Nicolas Tcherepnin, and produced at Monte Carlo, March 17, 1923). CHORAL WORKS: *The Destruction of Sennacherib*, after Byron, for Chorus and Orch. (St. Petersburg, March 18, 1867) and *Joshua* for Contralto, Bass, Chorus, and Piano (1874–77). FOR ORCH.: *Scherzo* (St. Petersburg, Jan. 23, 1860); *Intermezzo in modo classico* (1867); *A Night on Bald Mountain* (1860–66; reorchestrated by Rimsky-Korsakov and perf. posthumously, St. Petersburg, Oct. 27, 1886). FOR PIANO: *Scherzo* (1858); *Jeux d'enfants–les quatre coins* (German subtitle *Ein Kinderscherz;* 1859); *Impromptu passionné* (1859); Sonata for Piano, 4-hands (1860); *Souvenirs d'enfance* (1865); *Rêverie* (1865); *La Capricieuse* (1865); *Intermezzo in modo classico* (piano version of the orch. piece; 1867); *Pictures at an Exhibition* (1874; *Promenade; Gnomus; Il vecchio castello; Tuileries; Bydlo; Ballet des poussins dans leurs coques; Deux juifs, l'un riche et l'autre pauvre; Promenade; Limoges—Le Marché; Catacombae; Cum mortuis in lingua mortua; La Cabane sur des pattes de poule; La Grande Porte de Kiev;* French titles by Mussorgsky); *En Crimée* (1880); *Méditation* (1880); *Une Larme* (1880); piano transcriptions of dances from the opera *The Fair at Sorochinsk;* many incomplete fragments of youthful works, etc. SONGS: *King Saul* (1863); *Cradle Song* (1865); *Darling Savishna* (1866); *The Seminarist* (1866); *Hopak* (1866); *On the Dnieper* (1879); *Hebrew Song* (1879); *The Classicist* (satirical; 1867); *The Garden by the Don* (1867); *The Nursery,* children's song cycle (1868–72); *Rayok* (*The Peep-show;* musical lampoon at assorted contemporaries; 1870); *Sunless,* song cycle (1874); *Forgotten* (1874); *Songs an Dances of Death,* cycle of 4 songs (1875–77); *Mephistopheles' Song of the Flea* (1879); a number of other songs. In 1928–34 the Soviet State Publishing House undertook, under the direction of Paul Lamm, the publication of his complete works, including variants, fragments, notations of folk songs, etc.
BIBLIOGRAPHY: V. Stasov, *M.* (St. Petersburg, 1881); V. Baskin, *M.* (Moscow, 1887); Pierre d'Alheim, *M.* (Paris, 3rd ed., 1896); Marie Olénine-d'Alheim, *Le Legs de Mussorgsky* (Paris, 1908); M.-D. Calvocoressi, *M.* (Paris, 1907, 2nd French ed., 1911; Eng. trans., London, 1919); Rosa Newmarch, "M.'s Operas," *Musical Times* (July 1913); M. Montagu-Nathan, *M.* (London, 1916); Oskar von Riesemann, *M.* (Munich, 1925; in Eng., N.Y., 1935); Alfred Swan, "M. and Modern Music," *Musical Quarterly* (April 1925); Kurt von Wolfurt, *M.* (Stuttgart, 1927); R. Godet, *En marge de Boris Godunov* (Paris, 1927); Igor Glebov, *M.* (Leningrad, 1928); H. van Dalen, *M.* (The Hague, 1930); Y. Keldish, *Lyricism in M.'s Songs* (Moscow, 1933); M.D. Calvocoressi, "M.'s Musical Style," *Musical Quarterly* (Oct. 1932); idem, "M.'s Youth," *Musical Quarterly* (Jan. 1934); V. Fedorov, *M.* (Paris, 1935); Maria Tibaldi Chiesa, *M.* (Milan, 1935); Gerald Abraham and M.D. Calvocoressi, "M.," in *Masters of Russian Music* (London 1936; pp.

178–248); C. Barzel, *M.* (Paris, 1939); G. Orlov, *Chronicle of the Life and Works of Mussorgsky* (Moscow, 1940); G. Gavazzeni, *M. e la musica russa dell' 800* (Florence, 1943); R. Garcia Morillo, *M.* (Buenos Aires, 1943); M.D. Calvocoressi, *M.* (completed by Gerald Abraham, London, 1946; 2nd ed., revised, 1974); R. Hofmann, *M.* (Paris 1952); M.D. Calvocoressi, *M. M., His Life and Works* (London, 1956; ed. by Gerald Abraham; a completely different book from the earlier ones by Calvocoressi); V. Serov, *M. M.* (N.Y., 1968); numerous publications in Russian, pertaining to various aspects of Mussorgsky's life and works; special numbers of Russian magazines. A collection of letters and documents were publ. by A. Rimsky-Korsakov (Moscow, 1932); materials, largely taken from this vol., were trans. and ed. by J. Leyda and S. Bertensson, as *The M. Reader* (N.Y., 1947). The paintings of Victor Hartmann that inspired Mussorgsky's *Pictures at an Exhibition* were reproduced by Alfred Frankenstein in his article on the subject in the *Musical Quarterly* (July 1939); Frankenstein also brought out an illustrated ed. of the work (1951).

Mustel, Victor, celebrated French builder of harmoniums; inventor of the celesta; b. Le Havre, June 13, 1815; d. Paris, Jan. 26, 1890. He began as a carpenter; in 1844 went to Paris, where he worked in several shops, becoming foreman in Alexandre's harmonium factory; established himself in 1853; the following year invented "the double expression," which won the first prize at the Paris Exposition of 1855; from 1866 the firm became famous as V. Mustel et ses Fils. He also constructed an instrument consisting of graduated tuning forks in a resonance box, operated by a keyboard; this was patented in 1886 by his son **Auguste** (1842–1919) as the "Celesta." Tchaikovsky heard the celesta in Paris, and became so enchanted with it that he used it (for the first time in any score) in his ballet *The Nutcracker.*

Müthel, Johann Gottfried, German organist and composer; b. Mölln, Jan. 17, 1728; d. Bienenhof, near Riga, July 14, 1788. He studied at Lübeck and became court organist at Schwerin in 1747. In 1750 he traveled to Leipzig to see Bach, and remained with him for a few days before Bach's death. He then journeyed to Potsdam, where he met Carl Philipp Emanuel Bach. In 1753 he went to Riga, where he became an organist at the Lutheran church. He composed a number of organ pieces, and also several piano works, including a duet, the title of which includes for the first time the word "Fortepiano." BIBLIOGRAPHY: Robert G. Campbell, *Johann Gottfried Müthel* (Diss., 2 vols., Indiana Univ., 1966).

Muti, Lorenzo, Italian singer and conductor; b. Spoleto, Sept. 2, 1951. Menotti chose him for the boy's role in the premiere of his opera *Maria Golovin* in Brussels in 1958. He was also the boy singer in Britten's *Abraham and Isaac* in 1965; in 1966 he sang Yniold in *Pelléas et Mélisande* in Spoleto. But as his voice was about to break, he decided to study music seriously and academically; took courses at the Curtis Inst. in Philadelphia and at the Juilliard School in N.Y., graduating in 1973. He made a successful debut in Spoleto as conductor of Salieri's opera buffa *Prima la musica, poi le parole* in the summer of 1974.

Muti, Riccardo, greatly talented and multiply gifted Italian conductor; b. Naples, July 28, 1941. His father was a medical doctor who possessed a natural Neapolitan tenor voice; under his guidance Muti began to play the violin and piano; later enrolled at the Cons. of San Pietro a Maiella in Naples, where he studied composition with Jacopo Napoli and Nino Rota; there he also obtained a diploma in piano; then went to Milan to study conducting with Antonino Votto and composition with Bruno Bettinelli at the Verdi Cons.; in 1965 he attended a seminar in conducting with Franco Ferrara in Venice. In 1967 he won the prestigious Guido Cantelli competition for conductors and received several engagements as a symph. conductor, first at RAI (Radiotelevisione Italiana) in Milan and then at the Maggio Musicale Fiorentino in Florence. In 1968 he conducted opera at the Autunno Musicale Napoletano. In 1970 he was appointed principal conductor at the Teatro Comunale in Florence, where he produced a number of operas in the standard Italian repertoire; he also continued to conduct the orch. of the Maggio Musicale Fiorentino. Soon he expanded his activities beyond Italy. He conducted performances at the festivals of Salzburg, Lucerne, Montreux, and Prague; also had guest engagements with the Berlin Phil., the Vienna Phil., and orchs. in Amsterdam, Budapest, Milan, and Madrid. On Oct. 27, 1972, Muti made his first American appearance, conducting the Philadelphia Orch., and later had a guest engagement with it in N.Y.; the critics were impressed with his musicianship and also with his handsome Roman profile. A cornucopia of engagements followed. In 1973 he succeeded Klemperer as principal conductor of the New Phil. Orch. of London (it restored its original name of Philharmonia Orch. in 1977); he was named its music director in 1979 and continued in that capacity until 1982; he also retained his post with the Maggio Musicale in Florence until 1982, when his main activities definitely shifted to America. He was a frequent guest conductor with the Philadelphia Orch. and formed an enthusiastic following in that city; in 1977 he was named the orch.'s principal guest conductor. Finally, after much discussion and speculation as to the inevitable succession to the energetic but aging Eugene Ormandy, Muti was announced in 1980 as his heir. In 1982 he took the Philadelphia Orch. on a tour of festivals in Europe. Muti's career was now firmly established on both sides of the Atlantic; if he follows the musical longevity of his Philadelphia predecessors, Stokowski and Ormandy, he will keep his symphonic aureole (he has a magnificent head of black hair, with no sign of incursive alopecia) until 2020 A.D.

BIBLIOGRAPHY: David Ewen, *Musicians since*

1900 (N.Y., 1978); P. Hart, *Conductors: A New Generation* (N.Y., 1979; pp. 105–24); D. Webster, "Riccardo Muti," *Ovation* (Feb. 1983).

Mutter, Anne-Sophie, talented German violinist; b. Rheinfeldin, June 29, 1963. At the age of 6 she won "First Prize with Special Distinction" at the "Jungen Musiziert" National Competition, the youngest winner in its annals. In 1976 she came to the notice of Herbert von Karajan during her appearance at the Lucerne Festival; in 1977 he invited her to be a soloist with him and the Berlin Phil. at the Salzburg Easter Festival; this was the beginning of an auspicious career. She subsequently appeared regularly with Karajan and the Berlin Phil., and also recorded standard violin concertos with him.

Muzio, Claudia, Italian dramatic soprano; b. Pavia, Feb. 7, 1889; d. Rome, May 24, 1936. Her baptismal name was **Claudina Muzzio,** but she adopted the altered form Claudia Muzio early in her career. She studied in Milan; also took voice lessons with Mme. Casaloni in Turin; made her debut as Manon at Arezzo (Jan. 15, 1910); then sang in Italy, South America, France, and England; made her first American appearance at the Metropolitan Opera as Tosca (Dec. 4, 1916), remaining on its roster until 1922; then was a member of the Chicago Opera until 1932; after returning to the Metropolitan for a season, she went back to Italy in 1934.
BIBLIOGRAPHY: H.M. Barnes, *Claudia Muzio; A Biographical Sketch and Discography* (Austin, Texas, 1947).

Muzio, Emanuele, Italian composer; b. Zibello, Aug. 25, 1825; d. Paris, Nov. 27, 1890. He studied piano with Margherita Barezzi (Verdi's first wife), and composition with Verdi himself; was one of the very few pupils Verdi ever had. In 1852 he was engaged as conductor of the Italian Opera in Brussels; he later traveled to England and America; settled in Paris in 1875 as a singing teacher. Carlotta Patti and Clara Louise Kellogg were his pupils. He wrote several operas: *Giovanna la pazza* (Brussels, April 8, 1851); *Claudia* (Milan, Feb. 7, 1853); *Le due regine* (Milan, May 17, 1856); *La Sorrentina* (Bologna, Nov. 14, 1857); also many songs and piano pieces.
BIBLIOGRAPHY: A. Belforti, *Emanuele Muzio, l'unico alievo di G. Verdi* (Milan, 1896); L.A. Garibaldi, ed., *Giuseppe Verdi nelle lettere di Emanuele Muzio ed Antonio Barezzi* (Milan, 1931).

Myagi, Ester, Estonian composer; b. Tallinn, Jan. 10, 1922. She studied at the Tallinn Cons., and later took a course with Shebalin at the Moscow Cons. In 1954 she was appointed instructor in music theory at the Tallinn Cons. In her music she cultivates Romantic motifs. Her prinicipal work is a cantata, *Kalevipoja teckond Soome,* written under the influence of Sibelius (1954). She also wrote a Symph. (1969), several pieces of chamber music, and choruses.

Mycielski, Zygmunt, Polish composer and musicologist; b. Przeworsk, Aug. 17, 1907. He studied in Cracow, and later in Paris with Nadia Boulanger and Paul Dukas. In 1929–36 he was a member of the Society of Young Polish Composers in Paris. After the end of World War II, he became active as a journalist; edited the principal Polish music magazine *Ruch Muzyczny* (1945–48, 1960–68). His music, couched in a modern idiom, contains elements of Polish folk inflections; but dodecaphonic usages are also encountered.
WORKS: Piano Trio (1934); *Lamento di Tristano* for Small Orch., in memory of Szymanowski (1937); *5 Symphonic Essays* (1945); *Portrait of a Muse* for Narrator, Chorus, and 15 Instruments (1947); 6 symphs.: No. 1 (1947); No. 2 (1960); No. 3, *Sinfonia breve* (1967; Warsaw, Sept. 23, 1972); No. 4 (1972–73; Poznan, April 2, 1976); No. 5 (1977); *Polish Symphony* (1951); *Silesian Overture* (1948); *Brzezina* for Soprano and String Quartet (1952); *Zabawa w Lipinach* (*Merrymaking at Lipiny*), ballet in one scene (1953); Piano Concerto (1954); *Nowy lirnik mazowiecki* (*New Mazovian Bard*), 9 songs and finale for Soprano, Baritone, Chorus, and Orch. (1955); *5 préludes* for Piano Quintet (1967); songs; orchestration of 13 Bach chorale preludes (1964). He publ. 2 collections of musical essays: *Uzieczki z pieciolinii* (*Flight of the Staff-lines,* Warsaw, 1956) and *Notatki o muzyce i muzykach* (*Notes on Music and Musicians,* Cracow, 1961).

Myer, Edmund J., American teacher of singing; b. York Springs, Pa., Jan. 21, 1846; d. Los Angeles, Jan. 25, 1934. He studied in Philadelphia and N.Y.; founded the National Summer School of Music at Lake Chautauqua and Round Lake, N.Y.; publ. a number of books and pamphlets on the voice: *Truths of Importance to Vocalists* (1883); *The Voice from a Practical Standpoint* (1886); *Voice Training Exercises* (1888); *Vocal Reinforcement* (1891); *Position and Action in Singing* (1897); *The Renaissance of the Vocal Art* (1902); *The Vocal Instructor* (1913); *A Revelation to the Vocal World* (1917).

Myers, Rollo, English writer on music; b. Chislehurst, Kent, Jan. 23, 1892. He studied briefly at the Royal College of Music in London; then was music correspondent for English newspapers in Paris (1919–34); was a member of the staff of the BBC in London (1935–44); was active as music journalist and editor; publ. the books *Modern Music: Its Aims and Tendencies* (London, 1923); *Music in the Modern World* (London, 1939); *Erik Satie* (London, 1948); *Debussy* (London, 1949; 2nd ed., revised, 1948); *Introduction to the Music of Stravinsky* (London, 1950); *Ravel: Life and Works* (London, 1960); *Emmanuel Chabrier and His Circle* (London, 1969); *Modern French Music* (Oxford, 1971). He edited an anthology, *Twentieth Century Music* (London, 1960; 2nd ed., enlarged, 1968); wrote numerous articles on music.

Mysliveček (Mysliweczek; Mislivecek), Josef, famous Bohemian composer, called "Il divino Boemo" and "il Venatorini" in Italy; b. Ober-Sárka, near Prague, March 9, 1737; d. Rome, Feb. 4, 1781. His father was a miller. He was a pupil at the Normalschule of the Dominicans of St. Jilgi (1744–47) and the Jesuit Gymnasium (1748–53), where he received his first instruction in music; he also sang in the choir of St. Michal under Felix Benda. He then was apprenticed as a miller, being made a master miller in 1761. He also pursued his musical studies, taking courses in counterpoint with František Habermann and organ with Josef Seger. In 1760 he publ. anonymously a set of 6 sinfonias, named after the first 6 months of the year. Determined upon a career as a composer, he went to Venice in 1763 to study the art of operatic writing with Giovanni Pescetti. His first opera, *Medea*, was produced in Parma in 1764. While in Parma, he met the singer Lucrezia Aguiari, who became his mistress in the first of his many romantic liaisons. He was commissioned to write another opera, *Il Bellerofonte,* for the Teatro San Carlo in Naples, where it was performed with considerable success on Jan. 20, 1767. This led to other commissions from Italian theaters. His opera *Ezio* (Naples, June 5, 1775) and his oratorio *Isacco figura del Redentore* (Florence, March 10, 1776) were successfully performed in Munich in 1777; his career was blunted, however, by syphilis and disfiguring facial surgery. He returned to Italy but never regained his social standing. He succumbed at the age of 43. Mysliveček was one of the most significant Bohemian composers; his operas and oratorios were frequently performed and publ. in his lifetime. Mozart expressed admiration of his talent.

WORKS: OPERAS: *Medea* (Parma, 1764); *Il Bellerofonte* (Naples, Jan. 20, 1767); *Farnace* (Naples, Nov. 4, 1767); *Il trionfo di Clelia* (Turin, Dec. 26, 1767); *Il Demofoonte* (Venice, Jan. 1769); *L'Ipermestra* (Florence, March 28, 1769); *La Nitteti* (Bologna, Spring 1770); *Montezuma* (Florence, Jan. 3, 1771); *Il gran Tamerlano* (Milan, Dec. 26, 1771); *Il Demetrio* (Pavia, Jan. 25, 1773); *Erifile* (Munich, 1773); *Romolo ed Ersilia* (Naples, Aug. 13, 1773); *La clemenza di Tito* (Venice, Dec. 26, 1773); *Antigona* (Turin, Carnival 1774); *Atide* (Padua, June 1774); *Artaserse* (Naples, Aug. 13, 1774); *Ezio* (Naples, June 5, 1775); *Merope* (Naples, 1775); *Adriano in Siria* (Florence, Fall 1776); *Las Calliroe* (Naples, May 30, 1778); *L'Olimpiade* (Naples, Nov. 4, 1778); *La Circe* (Venice, May 1779); *Il Demetrio* (Naples, Aug. 13,

1779); *Armida* (Milan, Dec. 26, 1779); *Medonte* (Rome, Jan. 1780); *Antigono* (Rome, April 1780). ORATORIOS: *La famiglia di Tobia* (Padua, 1769); *Adamo ed Eva* (Florence, May 24, 1771); *Giuseppe riconosciuto* (Padua, 1771); *La Passione di Gesù Cristo* (Prague, 1773); *La liberazione d'Israele* (1775); *Isacco figura del Redentore* (Florence, March 10, 1776); also sinfonias, overtures, keyboard concertos, sonatas for keyboard, string quartets, trios.

BIBLIOGRAPHY: H. Wilkemann, *Joseph Mysliweczek als Opernkomponist* (Diss., Univ. of Vienna, 1915); M. Pincherle, "Un Oublié: Il divino Boemo," *Feuillets d'histoire de violon* (Paris, 1927); G. de Saint-Foix, "Un Ami de Mozart: Joseph Mysliweczek," *La Revue Musicale,* IX/4–6 (1928); P. Nettl, "Mozart und Mysliveček," *Prager Rundschau,* VII (1937); idem, *Mozart in Böhmen* (Prague, 1938); J. Čeleda, *Josef Mysliveček, tvůrce pražského nářeči hudebniho rokoka tereziánského (Josef Mysliveček: Creator of the Prague Dialect of Theresian Musical Rococo;* Prague, 1946); U. Prota-Giurleo, "L'Abate Galiani messo in imbarazzo da un musicista boemo," *Nostro tempo* (1957); S. Špatová-Ramešová, *Il divino Boemo* (Prague, 1957); R. Pečman, *Josef Mysliveček und sein Opernepilog* (Brno, 1970; includes bibliography and list of sources).

Mysz-Gmeiner, Lula, Hungarian contralto; b. Kronstadt, Transylvania, Aug. 16, 1876; d. Schwerin, Aug. 7, 1948. She studied violin in her native town, and singing in Berlin with Etelka Gerster and Lilli Lehmann; made her debut there in 1900; then traveled in Europe as a concert singer; was greatly praised for her interpretations of German lieder. She married an Austrian officer, Ernst Mysz (1900).

Myszuga, Aleksander, Polish tenor; b. Nowy Witkw, near Lwow, June 7, 1853; d. Schwarzwald, near Freiburg, March 9, 1922. He was of Ukrainian descent; studied voice in Lwow and Milan; later took lessons with Sbriglia in Paris, adopting the name **Filippi** for his stage appearances. He sang widely in Italy, Vienna, and Prague in both lyrical and dramatic roles in French and Italian operas; he was also noted for singing tenor parts in Polish operas. In later years he taught voice in Kiev and Stockholm.

N

Nabokov, Nicolas, distinguished Russian-American composer; b. near Lubcha, Novogrudok district, Minsk region, April 17, 1903; d. New York, April 6, 1978. He was a scion of a distinguished Russian family; his uncle was a liberal member of the short-lived Duma (Russian parliament); the famous writer Vladimir Nabokov was his first cousin. (The name is pronounced with stress on the 2nd syllable, Nabókov.) Nabokov received his early education in St. Petersburg; after the Revolution he went to Yalta in the Crimea, where he took composition lessons with Rebikov; then he proceeded to Berlin, where he became a student of Busoni; finally moved to Paris, where he was introduced to Diaghilev, who commissioned him to write a work for the Ballets Russes; this was an auspicious beginning to Nabokov's career. In 1933 he went to the U.S.; taught at Wells College (1936–41) and at the Peabody Cons. of Music, Baltimore (1947–52). From 1952 to 1963 he was secretary-general of the Congress for Cultural Freedom; then served as artistic director of the Berlin Music Festivals (1963–68); lectured on esthetics at the State Univ. of N.Y. at Buffalo (1970–71) and at N.Y. Univ. (1972–73). In his music he adopted a cosmopolitan style, with an astute infusion of fashionable bitonality; in works of Russian inspiration, he reverted to melorhythms of Russian folk songs.

WORKS: Operas: *The Holy Devil,* on the subject of Rasputin (Louisville, Ky., April 18, 1958; revised and expanded, produced in Cologne under the title *Der Tod des Grigori Rasputin,* Nov. 27, 1959); *Love's Labour's Lost,* to a libretto of W.H. Auden after Shakespeare (Brussels, 1973); ballets: *Union Pacific* (Philadelphia, April 6, 1934); *Vie de Polichinelle* (1934); *The Wanderer* (1966); *Don Quichotte* (N.Y., 1966); ballet-cantata, *Ode, or Meditation at Night on the Majesty of God, as Revealed by the Aurora Borealis* (Ballets Russes, Paris, June 6, 1928); Symph. No. 1, *Symphonie lyrique* (Paris, Feb. 16, 1930); Symph. No. 2, *Sinfonia biblica* (N.Y., Jan. 2, 1941); Symph. No. 3, *A Prayer* (N.Y., Jan. 4, 1968); incidental music to Milton's *Samson Agonistes* (Wells College, Aurora, N.Y., May 14, 1938); *The Return of Pushkin* for Voice and Orch. (Boston, Jan. 2, 1948); *Vita nuova* for Soprano, Tenor, and Orch. (Boston, March 2, 1951); Cello Concerto, subtitled *Les Hommages* (Philadelphia, Nov. 6, 1953); *America Was Promises,* cantata (N.Y., April 25, 1950); oratorio, *Job* (1933); *Collectionneur d'échos* for Soprano, Bass, and 9 Percussion Instruments (1933); *Symboli Chrestiani* for Baritone and Orch. (1953); *5 Poems by Anna Akhmatova* for Voice and Orch. (1964); *Studies in Solitude* (1961); String Quartet (1937); Sonata for Bassoon and Piano (1941); 2 piano sonatas (1926, 1940); Piano Concerto (1932); Flute Concerto (1948); piano pieces; songs.

Nachbaur, Franz, German tenor; b. Giessen, near Friedrichshafen, March 25, 1830; d. Munich, March 21, 1902. He studied in Stuttgart and was a pupil of Pischek there; sang as a chorister at Basel; made his debut in Meiningen in 1858; then sang in opera at Mannheim, Hannover, Prague, Vienna, and other musical centers. In 1866 he joined the roster of the Munich Opera, and remained there until his retirement in 1890. He was the first to sing the part of Walther in *Die Meistersinger* (1868); sang Lohengrin in Rome (1878); appeared in London with a German opera company (1882).

Nachez, Tivadar (Theodor Naschitz), Hungarian violinist; b. Budapest, May 1, 1859; d. Lausanne, May 29, 1930. He studied in Berlin with Joachim, and in Paris with Léonard. He lived mostly in London; went to California during World War I; then returned to Europe and presented his farewell concert in London in 1926. He wrote a number of violin pieces derived from Hungarian folk songs.

Nadel, Arno, German composer and writer; b. Vilna, Lithuania, Oct. 3, 1878; d. Auschwitz, March 1943. He studied in Königsberg with Birnbaum and Schwalm; then at the Jewish Seminary in Berlin with Loewengard and L. Mendelssohn; in 1916 he became conductor of the Jewish Community Choir in Berlin. He compiled several anthologies of Jewish songs, among them *Jontefflieder,* in 10 vols. (1919); *Jüdische Volkslieder,* in 2 vols. (Leipzig, 1921; new ed., 1926). In 1943 he was taken to Auschwitz and put to death in the Nazi concentration camp there.

Nadermann, François Joseph, French harp virtuoso and composer; b. Paris, 1781; d. there, April 2, 1835. He was a pupil of Krumpholtz; from 1816 served at the Royal Chapel; in 1825 was appointed a prof. at the Paris Cons. He joined his brother Henri in the management of the harp-making business founded by their father. He composed 2 harp concertos and various other pieces for the instrument.

Nagel, Wilibald, German pianist and musicologist; b. Mülheim-an-der-Ruhr, Jan. 12, 1863; d. Stuttgart, Oct. 17, 1929. He studied in Berlin with Ehrlich, Spitta, Bellermann, and others. In 1888 he was appointed a lecturer in music history at the Univ. of Zürich; then lived in London (1893–96), where he studied early English music. Returning to Germany, he completed his Habilitation at the Technische Hochschule in Darmstadt in 1898 with his *Die Entwicklung der Musik in Frankreich und England* (publ. in Berlin, 1898); then served on its faculty as a prof. from 1905 to 1913. He then settled in Stuttgart, where he edited the *Neue Musikzeitung* (1917–21); from 1921 was a prof. at the Hochschule für Musik; also made frequent appearances as a concert pianist.

WRITINGS: *Die dramatisch-musikalischen Bearbeitungen der Genovefa-Legende; Ein Beitrag zur Geschichte der Oper* (Leipzig, 1889); *Johannes Brahms als Nachfolger Beethoven's* (Leipzig and Zürich, 1892); *Geschichte der Musik in England* (2 vols., Strasbourg, 1894 and 1897; down to Purcell's death); *Annalen der englischen Hofmusik, 1509–1649* (1894); *Geschichte der Musik am Darmstädter Hof, 1570–1800* (1901); *Beethoven und seine Klaviersonaten* (2 vols., Langensalza, 1903 and 1905; 3rd ed., 1933); *Studien zur Geschichte der Meistersänger* (1909); *Die Klaviersonaten von Johannes Brahms: Technisch-ästhetische Analysen* (Stuttgart, 1915); *Wilhelm Mauke* (Vienna and Leipzig, 1919); *Johannes Brahms* (Stuttgart, 1923).

Nägeli, Johann (Hans) Georg, Swiss publisher, writer, and composer; b. Wetzikon, near Zürich, May 26, 1773; d. there, Dec. 26, 1836. He was a music publisher at Wetzikon (established 1792); was founder and president of the Swiss Assoc. for the Cultivation of Music; was a singing teacher at a primary school, applying the Pestalozzian system. As a song composer he is best known by *Freut euch des Lebens* ("Life let us cherish"). He wrote *Gesangsbildungslehre nach Pestalozzischen Grundsätzen* (with M. Pfeiffer; 1810; popular ed., 1811); *Christliches Gesangbuch* (1828); *Vorlesungen über Musik mit Berücksichtigung der Dilettanten* (1826); *Musikalisches Tabellwerk für Volksschulen zur Herausbildung für den Figuralgesang* (1828); a polemical pamphlet against Thibaut; *Der Streit zwischen der alten und der neuen Musik* (1826); etc. Nägeli publ. (from 1803) a periodical, *Répertoire des Clavecinistes,* in which he brought out piano pieces by contemporary composers, including the first publication of Beethoven's sonatas, op. 31. With Beethoven he was on intimate terms, despite disagreements.

BIBLIOGRAPHY: Biographical sketches of Nägeli were written by Ott (1838), Bierer (1844), Keller (1848), and Schneebeli (1873); H. Kling, *Beethoven et ses relations avec Nägeli* (1912); R. Hunziker, *H.G. Nägeli* (Zürich, 1938); A.E. Cherbuliez, *Der unbekannte Nägeli* (Chur, 1938); I.I. Hassan, *Die Welt- und Kunstanschauung Hans Georg Nägelis* (Zürich, 1947); H. Schattner, *Volksbildung durch Musikerziehung: Leben und Wirken Hans Georg Nägelis* (Diss., Univ. of Saarbrücken, 1960). Willi Reich edited a collection of Nägeli's articles under the title *Von Bach zu Beethoven* (Basel, 1945).

Naginski, Charles, composer; b. Cairo, Egypt, May 29, 1909; d. by drowning, Lenox, Mass., Aug. 4, 1940. He was brought to America at an early age; studied piano with his father and other teachers; in 1928–33, held a fellowship at the Juilliard Graduate School as a pupil in composition of Rubin Goldmark.

WORKS: For Orch.: *Suite* (1931); 2 symphs. (1935, 1937); *1936,* orch. poem (1936); *Sinfonietta* (1937); *3 Movements* for Chamber Orch. (1937); *The Minotaur,* ballet for Orch. (1938); *Nocturne and Pantomime* (1938); *5 Pieces from a Children's Suite* (Boston, 1940); *Movement* for Strings; 2 string quartets (1933); songs.

Nancarrow, Conlon, remarkable American composer, innovator in the technique of recording notes on a player-piano roll; b. Texarkana, Ark., Oct. 27, 1912. He played the trumpet in jazz orchs.; then took courses at the Cincinnati Cons.; subsequently traveled to Boston, where he became a private student of Nicolas Slonimsky, Walter Piston, and Roger Sessions. In 1937 he joined the Abraham Lincoln Brigade and went to Spain to fight in the ranks of the Republican Loyalists against the brutal assault of General Franco's armies. Classified as a premature anti-Fascist after the Republican defeat in Spain, Nancarrow was refused a U.S. passport and moved to Mexico City, where he remained for 40 years, eventually obtaining Mexican citizenship. In 1981, with political pressures defused in the U.S., Nancarrow was able to revisit his native land and to participate at the New American Music Festival in San Francisco. In 1982 he was a composer-in-residence at the Cabrillo Music Festival in Aptos, Calif.; also traveled to Europe, where he participated at festivals in Austria, Germany, and France. An extraordinary event occurred in his life in 1983, when he was awarded the "genius grant" of $300,000 by the MacArthur Foundation of Chicago, enabling him to continue his work without any concerns about finances. The unique quality of Nancarrow's compositions is that they can be notated only by perforating player-piano rolls to mark the notes and rhythms, and can be performed only by activating such piano rolls. This method of composition gives Nancarrow total freedom in conjuring up the most complex contrapuntal, harmonic, and rhythmic combinations that no human pianist or any number of human pianists could possibly perform. The method itself is extremely laborious; a bar containing a few dozen notes might require an hour to stamp out on the piano roll. Some of Nancarrow's studies were publ. in normal notation in Cowell's *New Music Quarterly.* Aaron Copland, Ligeti, and other contemporary composers expressed their appreciation of Nancarrow's originality in high terms of praise. On Jan. 30, 1984, Nancarrow gave a concert of his works in Los Angeles, in a program including his *Prelude and Blues for Acoustic Piano* and several of his studies. An audiovisual documentary on Nancarrow was presented on slides by Eva Soltes. A number of Nancarrow's *Studies for Player Piano* which could be adequately notated were publ. in *Soundings 4* (1977), accompanied with critical commentaries by Gordon Mumma, Charles Amirkhanian, John Cage, Roger Reynolds, and James Tenney.

Nanino (Nanini), Giovanni Bernardino, Italian composer and teacher, brother of **Giovanni Maria Nanino;** b. c.1550; d. Rome, 1623. He was a boy soprano at the Cathedral in Vallerano; studied music with his brother. From 1591 to 1608 he was maestro di cappella at S. Luigi dei Francesi in Rome. His brother lived with him in a home maintained by the church, and they boarded and taught the boy sopranos. He subsequently was maestro di cappella at S. Lorenzo in Damaso, the small church in the home of Cardinal Montalto. He was a significant composer and teacher in his day.

WORKS: SACRED: *Motecta* for 2 to 4 Voices (Rome, 1610); *Motecta, liber secundus* for One to 5 Voices, with Basso Continuo (Rome, 1611); *Motecta, liber tertius* for One to 5 Voices, with Basso Continuo (Rome, 1612); *Motecta, liber quartus* for One to 5 Voices, with Basso Continuo (Rome, 1618); *Salmi vespertini* for 4 to 8 Voices (Rome, 1620; ed. by K. Proske, *Musica divina,* I/3 and II/2, Regensburg, 1860–74); *Venite exultemus* for 3 Voices, with Basso Continuo (Assisi, 1620); etc. SECULAR: *Il primo libro de madrigali* for 5 Voices (Venice, 1588); *Il secondo libro de madrigali* for 5 Voices (Venice, 1599); *Il terzo libro de madrigali* for 5 Voices (Rome, 1612); etc.

BIBLIOGRAPHY: H.-W. Frey, "Die Kapellmeister an der französischen Nationalkirche San Luigi dei Francesi in Rom im 16. Jahrhundert," *Archiv für Musikwissenschaft,* XXIII (1966).

Nanino (Nanini), Giovanni Maria, important Italian composer and teacher, brother of **Giovanni Bernardino Nanino;** b. Tivoli, 1543; d. Rome, March 11, 1607. He was a boy soprano at the Cathedral in Vallerano, and was a pupil of Palestrina in Rome. Following Palestrina's resignation as maestro di cappella at S. Maria Maggiore in 1567, Nanino was named his successor. From 1575 to 1577 he was maestro di cappella at S. Luigi dei Francesi. In 1577 he became a tenor in the papal choir, remaining a member until his death; he also was elected to the position of maestro di cappella several times after 1586. He continued an association with S. Luigi dei Francesi; after his brother was made maestro di cappella there in 1591, he lived with his brother in a home maintained by the church, where they boarded and taught the boy sopranos. His pupils included Paolo Agostino, Felice Anerio, Antonio Brunelli, and other outstanding musicians. Nanino was one of the most significant composers and teachers of the Roman school. His sacred and secular works are of great merit.

WORKS: SACRED: *Motecta ... nova inventione elaborata* for 3 to 5 Voices (Venice, 1586; 4 are found in K. Proske, ed., *Musica divina,* ½, 4, Regensburg, 1854–62; 14 are in R. Schuler, *The Life and Liturgical Works of Giovanni Maria Nanino,* Diss., Univ. of Minnesota, 1963); 5 Lamentations in F. Haberl, "G.M. Nanino," *Kirchenmusikalisches Jahrbuch,* VI (1891); 2 canons ed. by A. Cametti in *Rivista Musicale Italiana,* XXXV (1928); 14 motets are in R. Schuler, *G.M. Nanino: Fourteen Liturgical Works* (Madison, Wis., 1969). SECULAR: *Il primo libro de' madrigali* for 5 Voices (Venice, c.1571; not extant; 2nd ed., 1579); *Madrigali* for 5 Voices (Venice, 1581; with 13 pieces by A. Stabile); *Il terzo libro de madrigali* for 5 Voices (Venice, 1586; with one piece by G.B. Nanino); *Il primo libro delle canzonette* for 3 Voices (Venice, 1593); also *157 Contrappunti e canoni a 2–11 voci* (in MS).

BIBLIOGRAPHY: F. Haberl, "G.M. Nanino," *Kir-*

chenmusikalisches Jahrbuch, VI (1891); G. Radiciotti, *Giovanni Maria Nanino, musicista tiburtino ... Vita ed opere* (Pesaro, 1909); G. Reese, *Music in the Renaissance* (N.Y., 1954; 2nd ed., revised, 1959); R. Schuler, *The Life and Liturgical Works of Giovanni Maria Nanino* (Diss., Univ. of Minnesota, 1963); H.-W. Frey, "Die Gesänge der Sixtinischen Kapelle an den Sonntagen und hohen Kirchenfesten des Jahres 1616," *Mélanges Eugène Tisserant* (Vatican City, 1964); idem, "Die Kapellmeister an der französischen Nationalkirche San Luigi dei Francesi in Rom im 16. Jahrhundert," *Archiv für Musikwissenschaft,* XXII (1965) and XXIII (1966).

Napier, William, British music publisher; b. 1740; d. London, 1812. He was a violinist in the Chapel Royal; established a music publishing business; Haydn arranged 2 books of Scottish songs for him, with accompaniment for piano, violin, and cello (1792).
BIBLIOGRAPHY: F. Kidson, *British Music-publishers* (1900).

Napoli, Gennaro, Italian composer; b. Naples, May 19, 1881; d. there, June 28, 1943. He was a pupil of d'Arienzo and de Nardis at the Royal Cons. in Naples; in 1906, won the Pensionato Nazionale per la Musica; in 1912, became a teacher of composition at the Liceo Musicale in Naples; in 1915, joined the staff of the Royal Cons.; in 1926, became its assistant director; was editor of *L'Arte Pianistica.*
WORKS: Opera, *Jacopo Ortis;* dramatic scene, *Armida abbandonata* (1906); *In montagna,* orch. suite (1906); Symph. in D minor; *Il sole risorto* for Soli, Chorus, and Orch. (1909); piano pieces; songs; etc. He was the author of *Bassi imitati e fugati* (1915).

Napoli, Jacopo, Italian composer, son of **Gennaro Napoli;** b. Naples, Aug. 26, 1911. He studied at the Cons. San Pietro a Majella in Naples, with his father and S. Cesi; was subsequently appointed to the faculty, and eventually became director. He specialized in opera, often with a Neapolitan background, which gave him the opportunity to use Neapolitan songs in his scores. From 1962 to 1972 he was director of the Cons. of Milan; then taught at the Cremona Cons. The list of his operas includes *Il Malato immaginario* (Naples, 1939); *Miseria e nobilità* (Naples, 1945); *Un curioso accidente* (Bergamo, 1950); *Masaniello* (1951; won a prize of La Scala, Milan); *I Peccatori* (1954); *Il tesoro* (Rome, 1958); *Il rosario* (Brescia, 1962); *Il povero diavolo* (Triest, 1963); *Il Barone avaro* (Naples, 1970).

Napravnik, Eduard, celebrated Russian conductor of Czech origin; b. Býšt, near Hradec Králové, Bohemia, Aug. 24, 1839; d. St. Petersburg (Petrograd), Nov. 23, 1916. He studied music at home and in Prague; also took lessons with J.B. Kittl. In 1861 he was engaged by the Russian nobleman Yussupov to lead his private orch. in St. Petersburg; in 1863 he became a répétiteur at the Imperial Opera; became

2nd conductor in 1867, and chief conductor in 1869. He held this post for 47 years, until his death, and became greatly renowned as a thorough musician, possessing a fabulous sense of pitch and rhythm, and exceptional ability as a disciplinarian. His reputation and influence were very great in Russian operatic affairs; Dostoyevsky in one of his novels uses Napravnik's name as a synonym for a guiding spirit. Napravnik conducted the premiere of *Boris Godunov* and of many other Russian operas; his interpretations of the Russian repertoire established a standard emulated by other Russian conductors; yet he was deficient in emotional inspiration; his performances of symph. works were regarded as competent but not profound. He was himself a composer of several operas in the Russian style, imitative of Tchaikovsky; one of them, *Dubrovsky* (St. Petersburg, Jan. 15, 1895), has become part of the active repertoire in Russia. Other operas were *Nizhegorotzy* (St. Petersburg, Jan. 8, 1869); *Harold* (St. Petersburg, Nov. 23, 1886); *Francesca da Rimini* (St. Petersburg, Dec. 9, 1902). He also wrote 4 symphs., some chamber music, piano pieces, etc.
BIBLIOGRAPHY: P. Weymarn, *E. Napravnik* (St. Petersburg, 1881); N. Findeisen, *E. Napravnik* (St. Petersburg, 1898).

Narayana Menon, Yatakke Kurupath, Indian virtuoso on the vina; b. New Delhi, June 27, 1911. He specialized in comparative musicology; was for many years director of All India Radio; made many European tours as a performer and lecturer.

Nardini, Pietro, Italian violinist; b. Livorno, April 12, 1722; d. Florence, May 7, 1793. He was a pupil of Tartini at Padua; in 1762–65 was solo violinist in the Stuttgart Court Orch.; lived with Tartini until the latter's death in 1770; then was maestro of the court music at Florence. Both Leopold Mozart and Schubart praised his playing. Among his works are 6 violin concertos; 6 sonatas for Violin and Bass; 6 violin solos; 6 violin duets; 6 string quartets; 6 flute trios. Some of his sonatas are in Alard's *Les Maîtres classiques* and David's *Hohe Schule des Violinspiels;* other works appear in Jensen's *Klassische Violinmusik;* also in numerous new eds.
BIBLIOGRAPHY: A. Moser, *Geschichte des Violinspiels* (Berlin, 1923; 2nd ed., revised and enlarged, 1966–67); C. Pfäfflin, *Pietro Nardini: Seine Werke und sein Leben* (Stuttgart, 1930; 2nd ed., 1936).

Nares, James, English composer and organist; b. Stanwell, Middlesex, 1715 (baptized, April 19); d. London, Feb. 10, 1783. He was a chorister in the Chapel Royal under Gates; also studied with Pepusch. Nares was deputy he became organist of St. George's Chapel, Windsor; he became organist of York Minster in 1735; in 1756 he succeeded Greene as one of the organists to the Chapel Royal; he received a Mus.Doc. from Cambridge Univ. in 1757; was Master of the Children at the Chapel Royal, 1757–80. He publ. a dramatic ode, *The Royal Pastoral;* a collection of catches, canons, and glees (1772);

methods for harpsichord, organ, and singing; etc. Detached pieces are in Arnold's *Cathedral Music,* Page's *Harmonia Sacra,* and Stevens's *Sacred Music.*

BIBLIOGRAPHY: *Dictionary of National Biography,* XL.

Narváez, Luis de, Spanish guitar virtuoso of the 16th century. He was a native of Granada; was chamber musician to Philip II. He publ. *Los seys libros del Delphin de música de cifra para tañer vihuela* (Vallodolid, 1538; in tablature), containing the earliest examples of variation form publ. in Spain; it was reprinted in modern notation by E Pujol in *Monumentos de la música española* (vol. 3, Barcelona, 1945); some selections are in Morphy's *Les Luthistes espagnols du XVIᵉ siècle* (Leipzig, 1902); one is in A.T. Davison and W. Apel, *Historical Anthology of Music* (vol. 1, Cambridge, Mass., 1946); modern ed. by G. Tarragó (Madrid, 1971).

BIBLIOGRAPHY: E.M. Torner, *Collección de Vihuelistas españoles del siglo XVI* (Madrid, 1924); J.B. Trend, *Luis Milán and the Vihuelistas* (1925).

Nash, Heddle, English tenor; b. London, June 14, 1896; d. there, Aug. 14, 1961. He was a chorister at Westminster Abbey; then studied in London and Milan with Giuseppe Borgatti; made his operatic debut in Milan in 1924 as Count Almaviva; then returned to London, where he sang at the Old Vic and at the Sadler's Wells Opera (1925) and with the British National Opera Co. (1926–29). He was a leading tenor at Covent Garden (1929–39 and 1947–48); also had engagements at the Glyndebourne Festivals (1934–38); was particularly noted for his fine performances in operas by Mozart and Rossini. His son, **John Heddle Nash** (b. London, March 30, 1928), was a baritone.

Nasidze, Sulkhan, Georgian composer; b. Tiflis, March 17, 1927. He studied piano and composition at the Tiflis Cons.; in 1963 joined its staff; in 1974 became artistic director of the State Phil. of Georgia in Tiflis. His music is imbued with Georgian melorhythms, and is set in a fairly advanced idiom. He wrote the oratorio *Fatherland Mine* (1967); cantata, *Spring, Spring!* (1975); 5 symphs. (1958, 1964, 1970, 1972, 1975); *Rhapsody* on themes of old Tiflis for Orch. (1964); 2 piano concertos (1954, 1961); Cello Concerto (1974); Piano Trio (1958); 2 string quartets (1968, 1971); *Polyphonic Sonata* for Piano; vocal cycles; choruses.

Nastasijević, Svetomir, Serbian composer; b. Gornje Milanovec, April 1, 1902. He studied engineering and architecture; at the same time he learned to play the violin; wrote music criticism and publ. 2 manuals on music theory. His works include the music drama *Medjuluško blago* (*The Treasure of the Medjuluzje;* Belgrade, March 4, 1937); *Durad Branković,* national opera from medieval Serbian history (Belgrade, June 12, 1940); several symph. poems and choruses. In his operas, he adopts the Wagnerian system of leitmotifs.

BIBLIOGRAPHY: V. Peričić, *Muzički Stvaraoci u Srbiji* (Belgrade, 1969; pp. 342–50).

Nat, Yves, French pianist; b. Béziers, Dec. 28, 1890; d. Paris, Aug. 31, 1956. He studied at the Paris Cons. with Diémer; was appointed a prof. of piano there in 1934. He gave numerous recitals in France, where his reputation was very high; made an American tour as accompanist in 1911 and in 1914 (with Luisa Tetrazzini).

Natanson, Tadeusz, Polish composer; b. Warsaw, Jan. 26, 1927. He studied composition with Wilkomirski, Perkowski, and Poradowski at the State College of Music in Wroclaw (1952–56); in 1965 he joined its faculty.

WORKS: Opera, *Tamango* (1972); ballet-pantomime, *Quo Vadis* (1970); *Toccata* for Orch. (1956); Piano Concerto (1956); *Rondo Concertante* for Violin and Orch. (1958); Double Concerto for 2 Saxophones and Orch. (1959); *3 Pictures* for 7 Instruments and Percussion (1960); *Satires* for Chorus and Instrumental Ensemble (1960); 5 symphs.: No. 1, *Symphonie concertante,* for Piano and Orch. (1961); No. 2 (1962); No. 3, *In Memory of John F. Kennedy* (1965); No. 4 (1969); No. 5, for Baritone, Chorus, and Orch. (1975); *Concerto breve* for Trombone and Orch. (1963); Concertino for Piano, Strings, and Percussion (1966); *Vers libre* for Orch. (1966); *6 Pieces* for 6 Performers (1967); Viola Concerto (1971); *Triptyque* for Orch. (1976); *3 Pieces* for Double Bass and Piano (1976). He publ. *Contemporary Composers' Techniques,* in 2 vols. (1970, 1972).

Nathan, Hans, German-American musicologist; b. Berlin, Aug. 5, 1910. He took courses in musicology at Berlin Univ. (Dr.Phil., 1934); studied piano with Rudolph Schmidt and Claudio Arrau, theory with Grete von Zieritz, and conducting with Michael Taube; was active as a music critic in Berlin (1932–36). In 1936 he went to the U.S.; became an American citizen in 1944; in 1936–38 he did postgraduate study at Harvard Univ. After a year of teaching at Tufts Univ. he joined the faculty of Michigan State Univ. in East Lansing, in 1946; held a Guggenheim fellowship in 1957; was a visiting prof. at the Inst. for Advanced Study in Princeton, N.J., in 1957–58 and again in the summer of 1979; he retired in 1981. He wrote *Das Rezitativ der Frühopern Richard Wagners* for his dissertation at the Univ. of Berlin (1934); in the U.S. he devoted himself chiefly to subjects of American music; publ. the valuable books *Dan Emmett and the Rise of Early Negro Minstrelsy* (Norman, Okla., 1962) and *William Billings: Data and Documents* (Detroit, 1975). He is the editor of vol. 2 (1977) of the complete, critical edition of works by William Billings, in 4 vols.; contributed articles on folk music, history, and modern biography to various publications; these include important accounts of Luigi Dallapiccola's works: "Luigi Dallapiccola: Fragments from Conversations," *Music Review* (Nov. 1966) and "Considérations sur la manière de travailler de Luigi Dallapiccola," *Schweizerische Musikzeitung* (Aug. 1975).

Nathan, Isaac, English composer; b. Canterbury, 1790; d. Sydney, Australia, Jan. 15, 1864. He studied singing and composition with D. Corri in London; collaborated with Byron on the *Hebrew Melodies* (1815–19), his most successful effort; served as music librarian to George IV; also maintained a music publishing business. In 1841 he moved to Australia, where he continued his enterprises. He publ. *An Essay on the History and Theory of Music, and on the Qualities, Capabilities and Management of the Human Voice* (1823; 2nd ed., as *Musurgia Vocalis,* 1836) and *Memoirs of Madame Malibran de Bériot* (3rd ed., 1836).

WORKS: Comic operas: *Sweethearts and Wives* (London, July 7, 1823) and *The Alcaid, or The Secrets of the Office* (London, July 14, 1824); operatic farce, *The Illustrious Stranger, or Married and Buried* (London, Oct. 1, 1827); opera, *Don John of Austria* (Sydney, May 3, 1847); *Hebrew Melodies,* with Byron (1822, 1861); songs.

BIBLIOGRAPHY: Catherine Mackerras, *The Hebrew Melodist; A Life of Isaac Nathan* (Sydney, 1963).

Nathan, Montagu. See **Montague-Nathan, Montagu.**

Natorp, Bernhard Christoph Ludwig, German vocal pedagogue; b. Werden-am-Ruhr, Nov. 12, 1774; d. Münster, Feb. 8, 1846. He studied theology and pedagogics at Halle Univ.; became a pastor at Essen in 1798; counselor of the Consistory at Potsdam in 1808; general superintendent at Münster in 1819.

WRITINGS: *Anleitung zur Unterweisung im Singen für Lehrer in Volksschulen* (2 courses, 1813, 1820; often republ.); *Lehrbüchlein der Singekunst* (2 courses, 1816, 1820); *Über den Gesang in den Kirchen der Protestanten* (1817); *Über den Zweck, die Einrichtung und den Gebrauch des Melodienbuchs für den Gemeindegesang in den evangelischen Kirchen* (1822), followed by the *Melodienbuch* (1822); *Choralbuch für evangelische Kirchen* (1829; harmonized in 4 parts with preludes and interludes by Rinck; 4th ed., 1885); and *Über Rincks Präludien* (1834).

BIBLIOGRAPHY: H. Knab, *B.C.L. Natorp* (Kassel, 1933).

Natra, Sergiu, Rumanian-born Israeli composer; b. Bucharest, April 12, 1924. He studied composition with Leon Klepper at the Bucharest Cons. (1945–52); emigrated to Israel in 1961, where he became active mainly as a teacher.

WORKS: *Divertimento in a Classical Style* for String Orch. (1943); *March and Chorale* for Orch. (1944); String Quartet (1947); *Suite* for Orch. (1948); Symph. No. 1 (1952); *4 Poems* for Baritone and Orch. (1958); *Music* for Violin and Harp (1959); Sinfonia for Strings (1960); *Toccata* for Orch. (1963); *Music for Solo Harpsichord and 6 Instruments* (1964); Sonatina for Solo Harp (1965); *Music* for Oboe and Strings (1965); *Variations* for Piano and Orch. (1966); *Song of Deborah* for Mezzo-soprano and Chamber Orch. (1967); *Commentary on Nehemia*

for Baritone, Chorus, and Orch. (1967); 3 solo sonatinas: for Trombone, for Trumpet, and for Oboe (all 1969); *Environment for an Exhibition,* sound collage on tape (1970); Piano Trio (1971).

Nau, Maria Dolores Benedicta Josefina, operatic soprano; b. New York (of Spanish parentage), March 18, 1818; d. Levallois, near Paris, Jan., 1891. She was a pupil of Cinti-Damoreau at the Paris Cons.; in 1836–42 sang minor parts at the Paris Opéra, then appeared in Brussels and London; from 1844 she sang again at the Opéra, in leading roles; in 1849–50 was in London; in 1850 and 1854–56, in the U.S.; she returned to Paris in 1856 and retired from the stage.

Naudin, Emilio, tenor; b. (of French parentage) Parma, Oct. 23, 1823; d. Boulogne-sur-Mer, May 5, 1890. He was a pupil of Panizza in Milan; made his debut at Cremona, c.1845; appeared in Vienna, St. Petersburg, London, Madrid, and Paris (from 1862, at the Théâtre Italien). He created the role of Vasco da Gama in *L'Africaine* (in accordance with a stipulation in Meyerbeer's will); retired in 1879.

Naujalis, Juozas, Lithuanian composer; b. Raudondvaris, near Kaunas, April 9, 1869; d. Kaunas, Sept. 9, 1934. He studied at the Warsaw Musical Inst.; served as an organist in various Lithuanian towns; in 1919, became director of the Music School in Kaunas, later the State Musical Inst. His compositions include masses, a Lithuanian church hymn; also piano and organ works; etc. He edited a collection of contemporary organ masters (6 vols).

Naumann, Emil, German music scholar and composer, grandson of **Johann Gottlieb Naumann;** b. Berlin, Sept. 8, 1827; d. Dresden, June 23, 1888. He was a pupil of Schnyder von Wartensee in Frankfurt, and then of Mendelssohn in Leipzig (1842); he studied at the Leipzig Cons. (1843–44); later took courses at the Univ. of Bonn; received his Ph.D. at the Univ. of Berlin in 1867 with the dissertation *Das Alter des Psalmengesänge.* In 1850 he became Hofkirchen-Musikdirektor in Berlin. In 1873 he was made a lecturer in music history at the Dresden Cons. In his own works he faithfully followed the methods of his revered teacher Mendelssohn, without ever attaining the melodic grace and harmonic lucidity that made Mendelssohn's music a perennial art. Naturally, he opposed Wagner's innovations and wrote critically about "the music of the future."

WORKS: For the stage: *Judith,* opera (Dresden, 1858); *Die Muhlenhexe,* singspiel (Berlin, 1861); *Loreley,* grand opera (Berlin, 1889). Vocal music: *Christus der Friedensbote,* oratorio (Dresden, 1848); *Missa solennis* (1851); *Die Zerstörung Jerusalem's durch Titue,* cantata (1855); 12 Psalms in *Psalmen auf alle Sonn- und Fest-Tage des evangelischen Kirchenjahres* for *Musica sacra,* vols. VIII–X (Berlin and Posen, 1855); *Dank- und Jubel-Cantate zur Feier der Siege Preussens im Jahre 1866.* Also, Sonata for Piano and Violin, and several overtures.

WRITINGS: *Ueber Einführung des Psalmen-*

gesanges in die evangelische Kirche (Berlin, 1856); Die Tonkunst in ihren Beziehungen zu den Formen und Entwickelungsgesetzen alles Geisteslebens (2 vols., Berlin, 1869–70); Ludwig van Beethoven: Zur hundertjährigen Geburtstagsfeier (Berlin, 1871); Deutsche Tondichter von Sebastian Bach bis auf die Gegenwart (Berlin, 1871; 6th ed., 1895); Nachklänge: Eine Sammlung von Vorträgen und Gedenkblättern (Berlin, 1872); Deutschlands musikalische Heroen in ihrer Rückwirkung auf die Nation (Berlin, 1873); Italienische Tondichter von Palestrina bis auf die Gegenwart (Berlin, 1874–75; 2nd ed., 1883); Das goldene Zeitalter der Tonkunst in Venedig (Berlin, 1876); Musikdrama oder Oper? Eine Beleuchtung der Bayreuther Bühnenfestspiele (Berlin, 1876); Zukunftsmusik und die Musik der Zukunft (Berlin, 1877); Darstellung eines bisher unbekannt gebliebenen Stylgesetzes im Aufbau des classischen Fugenthemas (Berlin, 1878); Illustrierte Musikgeschichte (2 vols., Berlin and Stuttgart, 1880–85; Eng. trans. by F. Ouseley, 1882–86; 10th German ed., 1934, by E. Schmitz); Der moderne musikalische Zopf (Berlin, 1880).

Naumann, (Karl) Ernst, German organist, conductor, and composer, grandson of **Johann Gottlieb Naumann;** b. Freiberg, Saxony, Aug. 15, 1832; d. Jena, Dec. 15, 1910. He studied in Leipzig with Hauptmann, Richter, Wenzel, and Langer; received his Ph.D. in 1858 from the Univ. of Leipzig with the dissertation Über die verschiedenen Bestimmungen der Tonverhältnisse und die Bedeutung des pythagoreischen oder reinen Quintensystems für unsere heutige Musik (pub. in Leipzig, 1858); also took organ lessons in Dresden with Johann Schneider. In 1860 he was appointed music director and director of academic concerts at the Univ. of Jena; also served as city organist; was made a prof. in 1877; retired in 1906. He edited 6 vols. of Bach's cantatas and works for keyboard for the collected edition of the Bach Gesellschaft, and later edited several organ works for the Neue Bach Gesellschaft. He further edited a practical edition of Bach's organ music in 9 vols. (1899–1904). His own compositions include chamber music, sacred works, and lieder.

Naumann, Johann Gottlieb, distinguished German composer and conductor; b. Blasewitz, near Dresden, April 17, 1741; d. Dresden, Oct. 23, 1801. He received his first instruction in music at the Dresden Kreuzschule. In 1757 the Swedish violinist Anders Wesström took him to Italy, where he received valuable instruction from Tartini in Padua, Padre Martini in Bologna, and Hasse in Venice. His intermezzo Il tesoro insidiato was premiered in Venice on Dec. 28, 1762. In 1764 he returned to Dresden, where he was appointed 2nd church composer to the court; in 1765 he was named chamber composer. He made return trips to Italy (1765–68; 1772–74), where he brought out several operas. In 1776 he was appointed Kapellmeister in Dresden. In 1777 he visited Stockholm at the invitation of Gustavus III, and was charged with reorganizing the Hofkapelle. His most popular opera, Cora och Alonzo, received

its first complete performance in Stockholm during the consecration of the New Opera House on Sept. 30, 1782. Another important opera, Gustaf Wasa, was premiered there on Jan. 19, 1786, and was considered the Swedish national opera for many years. In 1785–86 he visited Copenhagen, where he carried out some reforms at the Hofkapelle and court opera. He composed the opera Orpheus og Eurydike for the Danish king's birthday, and it was premiered in Copenhagen on Jan. 31, 1786. He was named Oberkapellmeister for life in Dresden in 1786. At the request of Friedrich Wilhelm II, he made several visits to Berlin, where his operas Medea in Colchide (Oct. 16, 1788) and Protesilao (Jan. 26, 1789) were premiered at the Royal Opera. He also wrote masses, cantatas, oratorios, and lieder.

WORKS: FOR THE STAGE: All first performed at the Kleines Kurfürstliches Theater in Dresden unless otherwise given: Il tesoro insidiato, intermezzo (Teatro San Samuele, Venice, Dec. 28, 1762); Li creduti spiriti, opera buffa (Teatro San Cassiano, Venice, Carnival 1764; in collaboration with 2 other composers); L'Achille in Sciro, opera seria (Teatro San Cecilia, Palermo, Sept. 5, 1767); Alessandro nelle Indie, opera seria (1768; unfinished); La clemenza di Tito, opera seria; (Feb. 1, 1769); Il villano geloso, opera buffa (1770); Solimano, opera seria (Teatro San Benedetto, Venice, Carnival 1773); L'isola disabitata, azione per musica (Venice, Feb. 1773); Armida, opera seria (Teatro Nuovo, Padua, June 13, 1773); Ipermestra, opera seria (Teatro San Benedetto, Venice, Feb. 1, 1774); La villanella incostante, opera buffa (Teatro San Benedetto, Venice, Fall 1773); L'Ipocondriaco, opera buffa (March 16, 1776); Amphion, prologue and opera-ballet (Royal Theater, Stockholm, Jan. 1, 1778); Elisa, opera seria (April 21, 1781); Cora och Alonzo, opera seria (New Opera House, Stockholm, Sept. 30, 1782); Osiride, opera seria (Oct. 27, 1781); Tutto per amore, opera buffa (March 5, 1785); Gustaf Wasa, lyric tragedy (New Opera House, Stockholm, Jan. 19, 1786); Orpheus og Eurydike, opera seria (Royal Theater, Copenhagen, Jan. 31, 1786); La reggia d'Imeneo, festa teatrale (Oct. 21, 1787); Medea in Colchide, opera seria with ballet (Royal Opera, Berlin, Oct. 16, 1788); Protesilao, opera seria with ballet and choruses (Royal Opera, Berlin, Jan. 26, 1789; in collaboration with J.F. Reichardt); La dama soldato, opera buffa (March 30, 1791); Amore giustificato, festa teatrale (May 12, 1792); Aci e Galatea ossia I ciclopi amanti, opera buffa (April 25, 1801). ORATORIOS: All performed in Dresden unless otherwise given: La passione di Gesù Christo (Padua, 1767); Isacco, figura del Redentore (1772); S. Elena al calvario (1775); Giuseppe riconosciuto (1777); Il ritorno del figliolo prodigo (1785); La morte d'Abel (1790); Davide in Terebinto, Figura del Salvatore (1794); I pellegrini al sepolcro (1798); Il ritorno del figliolo prodigo (1800); Betulia liberata (1805); also masses, including a Missa solenne in A-flat major (Vienna, 1804), and sacred cantatas. LIEDER: Freimaurerlieder … zum Besten der neuen Armenschule (publ. in Leipzig, 1775); 40 Freymäurerlieder zum Gebrauch der teutschen auch französischen Tafellogen (publ. in Berlin, 1782; 2nd ed., 1784); Sammlung von Liedern (publ. in Pförten, 1784); *6 neue Lieder* (publ. in Berlin, 1795); *25 neue Lieder verschieden Inhalts* (publ. in Dresden, 1799); etc. His instrumental works include sinfonias, a Keyboard Concerto, quartets, sonatas for Keyboard and Violin, sonatas for Glass Harmonica, etc.

BIBLIOGRAPHY: A.G. Meissner, *Bruckstücke zur Biographie J.G. Naumann's* (2 vols., Prague, 1803–4; 2nd ed., Vienna, 1814); F. Rochlitz, "Johann Gottlieb Naumann und sein Vater-Unser, nach Klopstock," *Für Freunde der Tonkunst,* III (Leipzig, 1830); F. Mannstein, *Vollständiges Verzeichnis aller Kompositionen des Kurfürstlich Sächsischen Kapellmeisters Naumann* (Dresden, 1841); G. Schweizer, *Biographie von Johann Gottlieb Naumann* (3 vols., Zürich, 1843–45); M. Nestler, *Der kursächsische Kapellmeister Naumann aus Blasewitz* (Dresden, 1901); R. Engländer, *Johann Gottlieb Naumann als Opernkomponist (1741–1801)* (Leipzig, 1922); R. Engländer, "Die Dresdner Instrumentalmusik in der Zeit der Wiener Klassik," *Uppsala Universitets årsskrift 1956,* no. 5.

Naumann, Siegfried, Swedish composer and conductor; b. Malmö, Nov. 27, 1919. He studied at the Musical College in Stockholm, and later at the Santa Cecilia Academy in Rome (with Pizzetti and Malipiero); also took courses at the Mozarteum in Salzburg. From 1950 he made appearances as a conductor; conducted the Gavle Symph. Orch. in 1954–55; in 1962 he founded the Musica Nova ensemble, and toured with it in Scandinavia, Germany, and England. He wrote 3 symphs. and some other works in a traditionally acceptable infra-modern idiom, but at the age of 40 decided to adopt an austere structural style governed by serial procedures and diversified by aleatory passages. To mark this decisive avatar, he designated his first serial work, *Ruoli (Roles)* for 4 Clarinets, as op. 1 (1959). His subsequent compositions in this modern style are: *7 Sonetti de Petrarca* for Tenor, Harp, Vibraphone, and 4 Cellos (1959); *Phaedri: 4 Fabulae* for Soli, Chorus, and 8 Instruments (1961); *Improvviso sopra 28 strutture* for Keyboard and Percussion Instruments (1961); *Transformations* for Orch. (1962; Gävleborg, April 29, 1962); *Risposte I* for Flute and Percussion (1963); *Risposte II* for Piano, Hammond Organ, Electric Guitar, Trombone, and Percussion (1963); *Il cantico del sole* for Soli, Chorus, 10 Solo Instruments, and Orch. (1963; perf. at the Festival of the International Society for Contemporary Music in Stockholm, Sept. 14, 1966); *Cadenza* for 9 Players (1964); *Missa in onore della Madonna de Loreto* for Chorus, Organ, and Percussion (1964); *Solitude* for Harp and Percussion (1966); *Spettacolo I* for Soprano and Orch. (1967); *Spettacolo II* for 3 Soli, Chorus, and Orch. (1969); *Estate* for Chamber Orch. (1968); *Massa vibrante* for Percussion (1969); *Ljudposter (Soundposts)* for Wind Orch. (1970); *Due cori su testi latini* for Chorus, Double Bass, Hammond Organ, and Percussion (1970); *Teatro strumentale* for Chamber Ensemble (1971); *Il cielo del ponte a Moriano,* dialogue for Tenor, Chorus, and Chamber Orch. (1972); *Bombarda* for Organ and Percussion

(1973); *3 canti da cabaret* for Soprano and Percussion (1973).

Nauwach, Johann, German composer; b. Brandenburg, c.1595; d. probably in Dresden, c.1630. By 1607 he was a choirboy in Dresden; in 1612 he was sent to Italy for further study by the Elector of Saxony; he studied in Turin and Florence, receiving instruction on the lute from Lorenzo Allegri; in 1618 he returned to Dresden, and was later made a chamber musician. His first collection of songs shows the major influence of Caccini and other Italian monodists, while the 2nd collection is historically important as the first German vol. of continuo lieder.

WORKS: *Libro primo di arie passeggiate a una voce per cantar e sonar nel chitarrone* (Dresden, 1623); *Erster Theil teutscher Villanellen mit 1, 2 und Stimmen auf der Tiorba Laute, Clavicymbel und andere Instrumenta gerichtet* (Dresden, 1627).

BIBLIOGRAPHY: A. Einstein, "Ein unbekannter Druck aus der Frühzeit der Monodie," *Sammelbände der Internationalen Musik-Gesellschaft,* XIII (1911–12); W. Vetter, *Das frühdeutsche Lied,* II (Münster, 1928); R. Thomas, *Poetry and Song in the German Baroque* (Oxford, 1963); J. Baron, *Foreign Influences on the German Secular Solo Continuo Lied in the Mid-seventeenth Century* (Diss., Brandeis Univ., 1967).

Nava, Gaetano, Italian singing master; b. Milan, May 16, 1802; d. there, March 31, 1875. He was taught by his father, **Antonio Maria Nava** (1775–1826) and Pollini; then at the Milan Cons. In 1817–24 by Orlandi, Ray, Piantanida, and Frederici. From 1837 he was a prof. of solfeggio at the Cons., and of choral singing, from 1848. He wrote a great number of excellent solfeggi and vocalises; also *Metodo pratico di vocalizzazione.*

Navarra, André, noted French cellist; b. Biarritz, Oct. 13, 1911. He studied at the Cons. of Toulouse; also at the Paris Cons.; in 1949 he was appointed to its faculty. In 1954 he began teaching master classes in Siena; in 1958 became a prof. at the North West German Music Academy in Detmold. Despite his activity as a pedagogue, he never abandoned his career as a solo cellist; he also commissioned cello concertos to several French composers, and gave first performances of these works, among them the concertos by André Jolivet (1962) and Henri Tomasi (1970).

Navarrini, Francesco, distinguished Italian bass; b. Citadella, 1853; d. Milan, Feb. 23, 1923. He studied with Giuseppe Felix and Carlo Boroni in Milan; made his debut as Alfonso in *Lucrezia Borgia* in Ferrara in 1876. From 1883 to 1900 he was a member of La Scala in Milan; created the role of Lodovico in Verdi's *Otello* there (Feb. 5, 1887); then toured in England, France, and Russia. He made his first American appearance in 1902 as a member of Mascagni's traveling opera company. A giant of a man (he measured 6 and a half feet), he imposed his presence in heroic and buffo bass roles, including roles in Wagner's operas.

Navarro, García, Spanish conductor; b. Chiva, April 30, 1941. He was educated at the Valencia Cons., where he studied oboe; also took courses at the Cons. of Madrid. He then went to Vienna to study conducting with Hans Swarowsky, Karl Oesterreicher, and Reinhold Schmid; also took composition lessons with Alfred Uhl. In 1967 he won first prize at the conducting competition in Besançon, France. He was music director of the Valencia Symph. Orch. (1970–74); then was associate conductor of the North Hollywood Phil. (1974–78). In 1979 he made his debut as an opera conductor at Covent Garden, London. In 1980 he became music director of the National Opera at the São Carlos Theater in Lisbon; remained there until 1982. In 1980, he made his first appearances in America as a guest conductor, of the orchs. of St. Louis and Chicago.

Navarro, Juan, Spanish composer; b. Seville or Marchena, c.1530; d. Palencia, Sept. 25, 1580. He was a pupil of Fernández de Castilleja in Seville; sang as a tenor in the choir of the Duke of Arcos at Marchena in 1549; then sang at the Cathedral in Jaén; joined the choir at Málaga Cathedral in 1553; in 1554 applied unsuccessfully for the post of *maestro de capilla* there (F. Guerrero was the successful candidate); was *maestro de capilla* at Ávila (1563–66); then at Salamanca (1566–74); director of the choir at Ciudad Rodrigo (1574–78); from 1578 was *maestro de capilla* at the Cathedral in Palencia. Navarro's *Psalmi, Hymni ac Magnificat totius anni ... 4, 5 ac 6 v.* were publ. at Rome in 1590 (modern ed. by S. Rubio, Madrid, 1978). The book *Liber in quo 4 Passiones Christi Domini continentur ... 8 Lamentationes: Oratioque Hieremiae Prophetae* is by another Juan Navarro, a Franciscan monk born in Cádiz and serving in Mexico. Extant MSS: *Antifona a San Sebastian* (in Málaga); part of a *Magnificat* (in Seville); 8 pieces (in Toledo); *Recuerde el alma dormida,* madrigal a 5 (in the Collección del Patriarca, Valencia); madrigals: 7 for 4 voices; one for 5 voices (Biblioteca Medinaceli and Biblioteca Nacional, Madrid). The madrigal *Ay de mí, sin ventura* was printed by Pedrell in *Cancionero Musical Popular Español,* III; Eslava printed 3 Magnificats and 2 Psalms; several motets are in the *Antología Musical,* ed. by Elústiza and Castrillo Hernández (Barcelona, 1933; with biography).
BIBLIOGRAPHY: G. Chase, "Juan Navarro Hispalensis and Juan Navarro Gaditanus," *Musical Quarterly* (April 1945); Robert Stevenson, *Spanish Cathedral Music in the Golden Age* (Berkeley, Calif., 1961).

Navarro, Theodore ("Fats"), American jazz trumpeter; b. Key West, Fla., Sept. 24, 1923; d. New York, July 7, 1950. He first took up the tenor saxophone, then mastered the trumpet; subsequently played with several groups, including those of Andy Kirk (1943–44) and Billy Eckstine (1945–46); he later worked in N.Y. as a leading exponent of the bop style.

Navas, Juan, important Spanish composer of the 2nd half of the 17th century. He wrote numerous secular works, including some interesting *Pasacalles* with guitar accompaniment; also some sacred music.
BIBLIOGRAPHY: F. Pedrell, *Teatro lírico español anterior al siglo XIX,* vols. III and IV (1897).

Navrátil, Karel, Czech composer; b. Prague, April 24, 1867; d. there, Dec. 23, 1936. He was a pupil of Ondříček (violin) and G. Adler (theory); lived in Prague.
WORKS: Lyric drama, *Hermann;* opera, *Salammbô;* symph. poems: *Der weisse Berg, Lipany, Jan Hus, Žižka,* and *Zalco;* 2 symphs.; Violin Concerto; 2 piano concertos; Sonata for Violin; Sonata for Viola; men's choruses; songs.

Naylor, Bernard, English-born Canadian conductor and composer; b. Cambridge, Nov. 22, 1907. He studied composition with Vaughan Williams, Holst, and Ireland at the Royal College of Music in London (1924–26); then served as conductor of the Oxford Univ. Opera Club (1927–31). In 1932 he went to Canada, and was engaged to conduct the Winnipeg Symph. Orch.; returned to England in 1936 and was organist and director of music at Queen's College, Oxford, until 1939; once more in Canada, he conducted the Little Symph. Orch. in Montreal (1942–47); returned again to England and taught at Oxford (1950–52) and at Reading Univ. (1953–59). He moved permanently to Canada in 1959. As a composer, he specializes in sacred choral music.
WORKS: *Variations* for Small Orch. (1960); String Trio (1960); *The Living Fountain,* cycle of 4 songs for Tenor and String Orch. (1947); *Missa da camera* for 4 Vocal Soloists, Chorus, and Chamber Orch. (1954–66); *The Resurrection According to Saint Matthew,* Easter cantata (1965); *The Nymph Complaining for the Death of Her Faun* for Mezzosoprano, Flute, Oboe, Clarinet, Bassoon, and String Quartet (1965); *Festal Te Deum* for Chorus and Orch. (1968); *Scenes and Prophecies* for Soprano, Chorus, Brass, and Percussion (1968–69); several a cappella choruses, including *9 Motets* (1952), *Magnificat & Nunc Dimittis* (1964), and *Missa sine Credo* (1969); songs.

Naylor, Edward Woodall, English organist and composer, son of **John Naylor;** b. Scarborough, Feb. 9, 1867; d. Cambridge, May 7, 1934. He was a pupil of his father, and from 1888–92, at the Royal College of Music; received a Mus.Doc. from Cambridge Univ. in 1897; was organist at St. Mary's, Kilburn, 1896–98; from 1908, was organist at Emanuel College, Cambridge.
WORKS: Opera, *The Angelus* (London, Jan. 27, 1909; won the Ricordi prize); men's choruses; sacred music; overture, *Tokugawa,* for Orch. (Tokyo, 1919); chamber music; etc. He was the author of *Shakespeare and Music* (London, 1896); *An Elizabethan Virginal Book* (London, 1905); *The Poets and Music* (London, 1928).

Naylor, John, English composer; b. Stanningley, near Leeds, June 8, 1838; d. at sea, May 14, 1897. He was a choirboy at Leeds Parish Church; received a Mus.Doc. from Cambridge Univ. in 1872; was organist at various churches in England; in 1883, became organist and choirmaster of York Minster, and also (from 1892) conductor of the York Musical Society.

WORKS: 4 cantatas: *Jeremiah, The Brazen Serpent, Meribah,* and *Manna;* church services, anthems, hymns, part-songs, organ pieces, and a well-known book of chants.

Naylor, Ruth, Australian soprano; b. Adelaide, Aug. 3, 1908; d. London, Oct. 16, 1976. She studied voice in London, Berlin, Munich, and Salzburg. Between 1932 and 1948 she sang regularly with several opera companies in London, eliciting favorable comments for the precision of her fioriture; she excelled particularly in lyric roles in Italian opera.

Nazareth, Ernesto, Brazilian pianist and composer of dance music and songs; b. Rio de Janeiro, March 20, 1863; d. there, Feb. 4, 1934. He was a pioneer in fostering a national Brazilian type of composition, writing pieces in European forms with Brazilian melorhythmic inflections, pointedly entitled *Fado brasileiro, Tango brasileiro, Valsa brasileira, Marcha brasileira,* etc.; he also composed original dances in the rhythms of the samba and chôro. In his declining years he became totally deaf. A detailed list of his works is found in *Composers of the Americas,* vol. X (Washington, D.C., 1964).

Neal, Heinrich, German pianist and composer, son of the American painter David Neal; b. Munich, Sept. 8, 1870; d. Heidelberg, June 9, 1940. He studied in Munich with Rheinberger and in Dresden with Draeseke. In 1894 he was co-founder of a music school in Heidelberg and taught there until 1920. In subsequent years he gave private music lessons and publ. his piano pieces at his own expense. He wrote mostly teaching pieces for the piano, among them 24 études in all major and minor keys; a *Kinderovertüre* for 2 Pianos; several *Deutsche Rhapsodien;* 3 string quartets; songs and choral pieces.

Neate, Charles, English pianist and cellist; b. London, March 28, 1784; d. Brighton, March 30, 1877. He studied music with James Windsor and later took piano lessons with John Field; he further studied cello with W. Sharp and composition with Wölff. He started his career as a concert pianist in London; in 1813 became one of the founders of the London Phil. Society, with which he appeared as performer and conductor; in 1815 he went to Vienna, where he succeeded in entering into a friendly relationship with Beethoven. He composed 2 piano sonatas; a Quintet for Piano, Woodwinds, and Double Bass; 2 piano trios; also publ. *An Essay on Fingering* (1855). Literature on Beethoven frequently mentions Neate's relationship with him.

BIBLIOGRAPHY: E. Anderson, "Charles Neate: A Beethoven Friendship," in the Festschrift for O.E.

Deutsch (Kassel, 1963).

Neblett, Carol, American soprano; b. Modesto, Calif., June 1, 1946. She studied voice with William Vermond, and later with Lotte Lehmann and Pierre Bernac. In 1969 she joined the N.Y. City Opera; also made successful appearances with the Chicago Opera, the Dallas Opera, the Metropolitan Opera, and several opera houses in Europe.

Nebra (Blasco), José (Melchor de), Spanish composer; b. Catalayud, Zaragoza, 1702 (baptized, Jan. 6); d. Madrid, July 11, 1768. He was organist at the Convent of the Descalzas Reales in Madrid; was appointed 2nd organist to the Royal Chapel in 1724, and music director there in 1751. Together with Literes, he was engaged to reconstruct and compose new music when the archives of the Royal Chapel were destroyed in the fire of 1734. He was a prolific composer; wrote about 20 operas, a great deal of sacred music. His Requiem for Queen Barbara (1758) is reproduced in Eslava's *Lira Sacro-Hispana.*

BIBLIOGRAPHY: M. Soriano-Fuertes, *Historia de la música española,* IV (Madrid, 1859); E. Cotarelo y Mori, *Historia de la Zarzuela,* chap. III (Madrid, 1934).

Nechayev, Vasily, Russian pianist and composer; b. Moscow, Sept. 28, 1895; d. there, June 5, 1956. He studied at the Moscow Cons. with Goldenweiser (piano), graduating in 1917; then took composition lessons with Vasilenko. In 1925 he joined the staff of the Moscow Cons. He made a systematic study of the folk songs of the Ural region and made arrangements of folk songs of other lands. He composed the operas *7 Princesses,* after Maeterlinck (1923), and *Ivan Bolotnikov* (1930); a Septet, Quartet, Violin Sonata, Cello Sonata, songs, and a number of piano pieces.

Nedbal, Karel, Czech conductor; nephew of **Oskar Nedbal;** b. Dvur Králové, near Prague, Oct. 28, 1888; d. Prague, March 20, 1964. He studied with Novák in Prague and Foerster in Vienna; was conductor at the theater of Moravska-Ostrava, then of the Vinohrady Choral Society in Prague, and in 1914, of the Vinohrady Theater (with Ostrčil); in 1921–28, was opera director at Olomouc; in 1928–38, at Bratislava; in 1938–40, at Brno; from 1940 he worked in Prague as a radio and opera conductor.

Nedbal, Oskar, Czech composer and conductor; b. Tábor, Bohemia, March 26, 1874; d. (suicide) Zagreb, Dec. 24, 1930. He was a pupil of Bennewitz (violin), Knittl and Stecker (theory), and Dvořák (composition) at the Prague Cons., where he graduated in 1892. From 1891 to 1906 he played viola in the famous Bohemian String Quartet (Karl Hoffmann, Josef Suk, Nedbal, Hans Wihan); in 1896–1906 he conducted the Czech Phil.; in 1906–19, was conductor of the Tonkünstler-Orch. in Vienna; also of the Volksoper there for a time; from 1919, was a guest conductor in Czechoslovakia, Austria, and Yugoslavia; conducted the Sak Phil. in 1920–21. He later was director of the Slovak National Theater in Bratislava and head of Bratislava Radio.

WORKS: Ballets: *Der faule Hans* (1902); *Grossmütterchens Märchenschätze* (1908); *Prinzessin Hyazintha* (1911); *Des Teufels Grossmutter* (1912); *Andersen* (1914); operettas: *Die keusche Barbara* (Prague, 1910); *Polenblut* (Vienna, Oct. 25, 1913; successfully revived, Oct. 10, 1954); *Die Winzerbraut* (Vienna, Feb. 11, 1916); *Die schöne Saskia* (Vienna, Nov. 16, 1917); *Eriwan* (Vienna, Nov. 29, 1918); opera, *Sedlák Jakub (Farmer James;* Brno, Oct. 13, 1922); also instrumental works.

BIBLIOGRAPHY: J. Květ, *In memoriam Oskara Nedbala* (Bratislava, 1931); idem, *Oskar Nedbal* (Prague, 1947); M. Šulc, *Oskar Nedbal* (Prague, 1959); A. Buchner, *Oskar Nedbal: Život a dílo* (Prague, 1976).

Neefe, Christian Gottlob, German composer and conductor; b. Chemnitz, Feb. 5, 1748; d. Dessau, Jan. 26, 1798. He studied music in Chemnitz with Wilhelmi, the city organist; also with C.G. Tag, the cantor of Hohenstein. He began to compose when he was 12, and he studied the textbooks of Marpurg and C.P.E. Bach. He studied law at the Univ. of Leipzig (1769–71); subsequently continued his studies in music with A. Hiller; then succeeded Hiller as conductor of Seyler's traveling opera troupe (1776). In 1779 he became conductor of the Grossmann-Hellmuth opera enterprise in Bonn. Neefe's name is especially honored in music history because about 1780 Beethoven was his pupil in piano, organ, figured-bass practice, and composition in Bonn; there is evidence that Neefe realized the greatness of Beethoven's gift even as a child. In 1782 Neefe was named court organist. After the Grossmann theater closed in 1784, Neefe devoted himself mainly to teaching as a means of support. The theater was reopened in 1789, and Neefe served as its stage director until 1794, when the French army occupied Bonn and the theater was closed again. He then moved to Dessau. In 1796 he became music director of the Dessau theater. Neefe's autobiography, *Lebenslauf von ihn selbst geschrieben,* dated 1782, was revised by F. Rochlitz for publication in the *Allgemeine musikalische Zeitung* (1798–99; Eng. trans. in Paul Nettl, *Forgotten Musicians,* N.Y., 1951).

WORKS: *Die Apotheke,* comic opera (Berlin, Dec. 13, 1771); *Amors Guckkasten,* operetta (Leipzig, May 10, 1772); *Die Einsprüche,* operetta (Leipzig, Oct. 16, 1772); *Zemire und Azor* (Leipzig, March 5, 1776; not extant); *Heinrich und Lyda,* singspiel (Berlin, March 26, 1776); *Die Zigeuner* (Frankfurt, Nov. 1777); *Sophonisbe,* monodrama (Mannheim, Nov. 3, 1778); *Adelheit von Veltheim,* opera (Frankfurt, Sept. 23, 1780); lieder; concertos; keyboard music.

BIBLIOGRAPHY: M. Stöpgeschoff, *Neefe als Liederkomponist* (Diss., Univ. of Bonn, 1924); I. Leux, *Christian Gottlob Neefe, 1748–98: Biographie und Instrumentalkompositionen* (Leipzig,

1925); A. Becker, *Christian Gottlob Neefe und die Bonner Illuminaten* (Bonn, 1969).

Neel, Boyd, English conductor; b. Blackheath, Kent, July 19, 1905; d. Toronto, Canada, Sept. 30, 1981. He studied medicine and was trained as a medical doctor before taking up music. In 1933 he organized the Boyd Neel String Orch., originally counting 18 members, with a repertoire of Baroque music, supplemented by modern works for chamber orch. After a successful debut in London, he toured widely with his orch. all over the world, including the U.S., Australia, and New Zealand; he also conducted ballet and opera. From 1953 to 1971 he served as dean of the Royal Cons. of Music in Toronto. He publ. a book, *The Story of an Orchestra* (London, 1950), in which he recounted his musical adventures.

BIBLIOGRAPHY: Donald Brook, *International Gallery of Conductors* (London, 1951; pp. 125–28).

Nef, Albert, Swiss conductor and composer; brother of **Karl Nef;** b. St. Gall, Oct. 30, 1882; d. Bern, Dec. 6, 1966. He studied at the Leipzig Cons. and with Kretzschmar in Berlin (Dr.Phil., 1906); from 1907, was an opera conductor in Lübeck, Neustrelitz, and Rostock; from 1912 was in Bern, also was conductor of the Orch. Society there from 1922; from 1920, was president of the Swiss Stage Artists' Alliance. He was the author of *Das Lied in der deutschen Schweiz im letzten Drittel des 18. und am Anfang des 19. Jahrhunderts* (1909); also of *50 Jahre Berner Theater* (Bern, 1956). He composed a singspiel, *Graf Strapinski* (Bern, 1928); *Appenzeller Tänze* for Orch. (1926); *Wanderschaft,* song cycle for Tenor, Mixed Chorus, and Orch. (Bern, 1924); choruses; piano pieces; songs.

Nef, Karl, Swiss musicologist; b. St. Gall, Aug. 22, 1873; d. Basel, Feb. 9, 1935. He entered the Leipzig Cons. in 1891, studying with Reckendorf (piano), Julius Klengel (cello), and Jadassohn (theory); attended Kretzschmar's lectures on musicology at the Univ., and in 1896 received a Dr.Phil. with his dissertation *Die Collegia musica in der deutschen reformierten Schweiz* (publ. in St. Gall, 1897). He settled in Basel in 1897; in 1898–1909 was editor of the *Schweizerische Musikzeitung;* in 1900, became Privatdozent for musicology at the Univ.; in 1909, became associate prof.; in 1923, prof.

WRITINGS: *Ferdinand Fürchtegott Huber* (1898); "Zur Geschichte der deutschen Instrumentalmusik in der zweiten Hälfte des 17. Jahrhunderts," *Beihefte der Internationalen Musik-Gesellschaft,* 5 (1902); *Die Musik im Kanton St. Gallen, 1803–1903* (1903); *Katalog der Musikinstrumente im historischen Museum zu Basel* (1906); *Schriften über Musik und Volksgesang* (1908; bibliography of books and essays by Swiss writers); *Einführung in die Musikgeschichte* (1920; 3rd ed., 1945; in French, 1925, Eng. ed. as *Outline of the History of Music,* N.Y., 1935); *Geschichte der Sinfonie und Suite* (1921); *Geschichte unserer Musikinstrumente* (1926; new ed., 1949); *Die 9 Sinfonien*

Beethovens (1928); *Aufsätze* (posthumous; Basel, 1936). A dedicatory vol., *Karl Nef zum 60. Geburtstag*, was publ. at Basel in 1933.

Neff, Fritz, German composer; b. Durlach, Baden, Nov. 20, 1873; d. Munich, Oct. 3, 1904. He was a pupil of Thuille and Mottl in Karlsruhe; was a composer of great promise unfulfilled. He publ. choral works: *Ein schön teutsch Reiterlied, Chor der Toten, Schmied Schmerz, Die Weihe der Nacht;* songs (*Die Polenschänke*, etc.).

Negrea, Marțian, Rumanian composer; b. Vorumloc, Transylvania, Feb. 10, 1893; d. Bucharest, July 13, 1973. He studied with Timotei Popovici at the Andréien Seminary in Sibiu (1910–14); then took courses with Franz Schmidt and Mandyczewski in Vienna (1918–21). Returning to Rumania, he became a prof. of composition at the Cons. in Cluj (1921–41) and of harmony at the Cons. in Bucharest (1941–63). His music is marked by a Romantic quality; almost all of his compositions are programmatic in intent and folkloric in content. Thematically, he applies elements of Transylvanian melorhythms.
WORKS: 2-act opera, *Marin Pescarul* (1933; Cluj, Oct. 3, 1934); *Fantezie simfonică* (1921); 2 *Rapsodia română* for Orch. (1938, 1950); *Povești din Grui (Fairytale from Grui),* symph. poem (1940); *Divertissement* for Orch. (1951); *Prin munții apuseni (Through the Western Mountains),* suite for Orch. from music to the film (1952); *Recrutul (The Recruit),* symph. suite (1953); *Simfonia primăverii (Spring Symphony,* 1956); *Sărbătoarea muncii (Celebration of Work),* symph. poem (1958); Concerto for Orch. (1963); *Requiem* for Soloists, Chorus, and Orch. (1957); *Oratoriul patriei* for Narrator, Soloists, Chorus, and Orch. (1959); *Prelude and Fugue* for String Quartet (1920); *4 Pieces* for Harp (1945); String Quartet (1949); *4 Rumanian Sketches* for Clarinet and Piano (1958); *Suite* for Clarinet and Piano (1960); Piano Sonata (1921); Piano Sonatina (1922); choruses; songs.

Negri, Gino, Italian composer; b. Milan, May 25, 1919. He studied at the Milan Cons. with Renzo Bossi, graduating in 1942. In 1959 he was appointed artistic director of the Teatro del Popolo in Milan. He wrote a number of light operas, all to his own librettos, among them *Vieni qui, Carla* (Milan, Feb. 28, 1956); *Massimo* (Milan, April 12, 1958); *Il tè delle tre* (Como, Sept. 12, 1958); *Il Circo Max* (Venice, Sept. 23, 1959); *Publicità, ninfa gentile* (Milan, 1970).

Negri, Vittorio, Italian conductor; b. Milan, Oct. 16, 1923. He was educated at the Milan Cons., graduating with a degree in composition and conducting in 1946; began his professional career at the Salzburg Mozarteum, working with Bernhard Paumgartner; then served as a guest conductor of the Orch. del Teatro alla Scala in Milan, the Orch. National de France in Paris, the Dresden Staatskapelle, and the Boston Symph. Orch.; also made festival appearances in Salzburg, Montreux, Monte

Carlo, and Versailles.

Neidhardt (Neidhart, Nithart) von Reuenthal, German Minnesänger; b. c.1180; d. c.1240. He was in all probability the earliest German musician whose songs are extant. These are found in MS collections of the late 14th century; a complete list of sources is in Hagen's *Minnesinger* (vol. 4; 1838). An edition of Neidhardt's songs, with facsimile reproductions and transcriptions in modern notation, was brought out by Wolfgang Schmieder in Denkmäler der Tonkunst in Österreich, 71 (1930; 37.i). Another collection, *Neidhardt-Lieder,* ed. by F. Gennrich, was publ. as no. 9 in the series Summa Musica Medii Aevi (Darmstadt, 1962).
BIBLIOGRAPHY: L. Erk and F.M. Böhme, *Deutscher Liederhort* (Leipzig, 1894); H. Rietsch, *Die deutsche Liedweise* (1904); S. Singer, *Neidhartstudien* (Tübingen, 1920); E. Wiessner, *Kommentar zu Neidharts Liedern* (Leipzig, 1954); idem, *Vollständiges Wörterbuch zu Neidharts Liedern* (Leipzig, 1954); A. Hatto and R. Taylor, *The Songs of Neidhart von Reuental* (Manchester, 1958); D. Boueke, *Materialien zur Neidhart-Überlieferung* (Munich, 1967); K.H. Kohrs, "Zum Verhältnis von Sprache und Musik in den Liedern Neidharts von Reuental," *Deutsche Vierteljahrsschrift für Literaturwissenschaft und Geistesgeschichte,* XLIII/4 (1969).

Neidlinger, Günter, German conductor; b. Heidelberg, Oct. 4, 1930. He studied piano in Heidelberg and Stuttgart; then took a course in composition with Fortner in Freiburg; also studied conducting with Müller-Kray in Stuttgart. In 1962 he became conductor at the City Theater in Saarbrücken; in 1966 he was named chief conductor of the Bodensee Symph. Orch. at Konstanz. In 1970 he was named chief conductor of the Nuremberg Symph. Orch.; in his programs he introduced a considerable number of works of the Baroque period rarely performed by modern ensembles.

Neidlinger, Gustav, German baritone; b. Mainz, March 21, 1910. He received his musical training in Frankfurt; then sang with the operas in Mainz (1931–34), Hamburg (1936–50), and Stuttgart (from 1950). In 1952 he made his first appearance at the Bayreuth Festival; in 1953 he sang at La Scala in Milan; in 1956 at the Vienna State Opera. He also sang at Covent Garden in London (1963) and the Teatro Colón in Buenos Aires (1968). He made his Metropolitan Opera debut in N.Y. on Nov. 17, 1972, as Alberich in Wagner's *Siegfried*. It was in Wagnerian roles that he gained his best successes.

Neidlinger, William Harold, American choral conductor and music pedagogue; b. Brooklyn, July 20, 1863; d. East Orange, N.J., Dec. 5, 1924. He studied with Dudley Buck in N.Y. and with Dannreuther in London; was active as a choral leader and a singing teacher. He publ. *Small Songs for Small Singers* (1896), which became a standard work for kindergartens; he himself composed attractive, if not musically distinguished, children's songs, among them *Earth, Sky and Air in Song, Little Folks' Song Book,* etc.

Neitzel, Otto, German composer and writer; b. Falkenburg, Pomerania, July 6, 1852; d. Cologne, March 10, 1920. He was a pupil at Kullak's Academy in Berlin; studied also at the Univ. (Dr.Phil., 1875); then made a concert tour, as pianist, with Pauline Lucca and Sarasate; in 1878 became conductor of the Musikverein at Strasbourg, where (1879–81) he also conducted at the City Theater. Until 1885 he taught at the Moscow Cons.; then at the Cologne Cons.; from 1887 was also critic for the *Kölnische Zeitung;* he visited the U.S. in 1906–7 as a lecturer, pianist, and conductor; in 1919, became a member of the Academy of Arts in Berlin.
WORKS: Operas: *Die Barbarina* (Wiesbaden, Nov. 15, 1905) and *Der Richter von Kaschau* (Darmstadt, March 31, 1916); Piano Concerto (1900); etc. He wrote *Führer durch die Oper des Theaters der Gegenwart* (3 vols., 1890–93; 4th ed., 1908); *Beethovens Symfonien nach ihrem Stimmungsgehalt erläutert* (1891; 6th ed., 1924); *Saint-Saëns* (1899); *Aus meiner Musikantenmappe* (1914).
BIBLIOGRAPHY: A. Dette, *Die Barbarina* (Fulda, 1913; guide to Neitzel's opera; contains biographical sketch).

Nejedlý, Vít, Czech composer, son of **Zdeněk Nejedlý;** b. Prague, June 22, 1912; d. Dukla, Slovakia, Jan. 1, 1945. He studied composition with Jeremiáš and conducting with Talich at the Charles Univ. in Prague, obtaining his Ph.D. in 1936; after the occupation of Czechoslovakia by the Nazis in 1939 he went to the Soviet Union, where he was an editor of Czech programs for Radio Moscow foreign broadcasts; in 1943 joined the Czechoslovak contingent of the Red Army, and moved with it to the borders of Czechoslovakia, when he died of typhoid fever.
WORKS: Opera, *Tkalci (The Weavers),* after Hauptmann (1938; completed by Jan Hanuš; Pilsen, May 7, 1961); melodrama, *The Dying* (1933); 3 symphs.: No. 1 (1931); No. 2, *Bídy a smrti (Poverty and Death,* 1934); No. 3, *Španělská (Spanish,* 1937–38; dedicated to the Spanish Loyalist Army fighting Franco); *Overture* to Verhaeren's *Dawn* (1932); *Commemoration* for Orch. (1933); Sinfonietta (1937); *Dramatic Overture* (1940); *Lidová suita (Popular Suite)* for Orch. (1940); 2 cantatas, *Den (The Day,* 1935) and *To You—the Red Army* (1943); *2 Compositions* for Wind Quintet (1934); *2 Compositions* for Nonet (1934); *Small Suite* for Violin and Piano (1935); String Quartet (1937); Concertino for Nonet (1940); *Fantasy* for Piano (1937); many songs, military marches and choruses.
BIBLIOGRAPHY: J. Jiránek, *Vít Nejedlý* (Prague, 1959).

Nejedlý, Zdeněk, Czech music scholar, historian, and socialist politician; b. Litomysl, Feb. 10, 1878; d. Prague, March 9, 1962. He studied music with Zdenko Fibich in Prague and musicology with Hostinský at Charles Univ. in Prague. From 1899 to 1909 he was employed as an archivist of the National Museum in Prague; in 1905 he joined the staff, and from 1919 to 1939 was a prof. at, Charles Univ., where he organized the dept. of musicology. Intensely involved in political activities, he joined the Communist Party of Czechoslovakia in 1929. After the Nazi invasion of 1939 he went to Russia, where he was a prof. in the history dept. at Moscow Univ. In 1945 he returned to Czechoslovakia; served as minister of education (1948–53) and deputy premier (1953). He publ. a number of books on the history of Czech music; of these the most original is a history of Bohemian music, in the form of a catechism, in 3 vols. (Prague, 1904, 1907, 1913); he further publ. several monographs on Czech composers and their works, among them *Smetana's Operas* (1908; 3rd ed., 1954), *The Modern Bohemian Opera since Smetana* (1911), and *Vitězslav Novák* (1921); also biographies of Mahler (1913; 2nd ed., 1958) and Wagner (1916; 2nd ed., 1961).
BIBLIOGRAPHY: J. Teichmann, *Zdeněk Nejedlý* (Prague, 1938); V. Pekárek, *Zdeněk Nejedlý* (Prague, 1948); J. Jiránek, *Zdeněk Nejedlý* (Prague, 1952); F. Cervinka, *Zdeněk Nejedlý* (Prague, 1959).

Nelhybel, Vaclav, Czech-American composer; b. Polanka, Sept. 24, 1919. He studied composition and conducting with Rídký at the Prague Cons. (1938–42) and musicology at the Univ. of Prague (also 1938–42); in 1942 went to Switzerland and took courses in medieval and Renaissance music at the Univ. of Fribourg; was affiliated with Swiss National Radio (1947–50); then was music director of Radio Free Europe in Munich (1950–57). In 1957 he settled in the U.S., becoming a citizen in 1962; subsequently evolved energetic activities as a lecturer and guest conductor at American colleges and high schools. As a composer, he is especially notable for his fine pieces for the symphonic band. His harmonic idiom is of a freely dissonant texture, with melorhythmic components gravitating toward tonal centers.
WORKS: In 1976 he accomplished the setting for organ, brass, and timpani of 52 hymns and 6 church pieces, publ. in a collection entitled *Festival Hymns and Processionals.* FOR THE STAGE: 3 operas: *A Legend* (1953–54); *Everyman,* medieval morality play (Memphis, Oct. 30, 1974); *The Station* (1978); 2 ballets: *In the Shadow of a Lime Tree* (1946) and *The Cock and the Hangman* (Prague, Jan. 17, 1947). FOR ORCH.: Symph. No. 1 (1942); *Ballade* (1946); *Etude symphonique* (1949); Concertino for Piano and Chamber Orch. (1949); *Sinfonietta Concertante* (1960); Viola Concerto (1962); *Houston Concerto* (1967); *Concertino da camera* for Cello, 15 Winds, and Piano (1971); *Polyphonies* (1972); *Toccata* for Solo Harpsichord, 13 Winds, and Percussion (1972); *Cantus and Ludus* for Piano, 17 Winds, and Percussion (1973); *Polyphonic Variations* for Strings and Trumpet (1975); *Slavonic Triptych* (1976). FOR SYMPH. BAND: *Caucasian Passacaglia* (1963); *Concerto Antiphonale* for 14 Brasses (1964); *Symphonic Requiem,* with Baritone in the last of its 4 movements (1965); *Estampie,* with Antiphonal Brass Sextet (1965); *Yamaha Concerto* (1971); *Introit,* with Solo Chimes (1972); *Dialogues,* with Piano Solo

(1976); *Ritual* for Band (1978). FOR VOICE: *Caroli antiqui varii,* 7 a cappella choruses for 7 Voices (1962); *Epitaph for a Soldier* for Soloists and a cappella Chorus (1964); *Peter Piper* for Chorus, and Clarinet Choir or Piano (1965); *Cantata pacis* for 6 Soloists, Chorus, Winds, Percussion, and Organ (1965); *Dies ultima* for 3 Soloists, Mixed Chorus, Speaking Chorus, Orch., and Jazz Band (1967); *Sine nomine* for 4 Soloists, Chorus, Orch., and Tape (1968); *America Sings* for Solo Baritone, Chorus, and Band (1974); *Estampie natalis* for Double Chorus, Piccolo, Viola, Cello, and Percussion (1976); *6 Fables for All Time* for Narrator, Chorus, and Orch. (Ridgefield, Conn., Oct. 25, 1980; Skitch Henderson, narrator). CHAMBER MUSIC: *3 Organa* for 4 Bassoons (1948); 2 string quartets (1949, 1962); 3 wind quintets (1948, 1958, 1960); Quartet for 4 Horns (1957); Quartet for Piano and 3 Brass Instruments (1959); *4 Miniatures* for String Trio (1959); *Numismata* for Brass Septet (1961); Brass Trio (1961); 2 brass quintets (1961, 1965); *Impromptus* for Wind Sextet (1963); 9 clarinet trios (1963); *Scherzo concertante* for Horn and Piano (1963); *3 Pieces* for Saxophone Quartet (1965); *Quintetto concertante* for Violin, Trombone, Trumpet, Xylophone, and Piano (1965); Concerto for Percussion (1972); *Concerto spirituoso No. 1* for 12 Flutes, Electric Harpsichord, and Solo Voice (1974); *No. 2* for 12 Saxophones, Electric Harpsichord, and Solo Voice (1974); *No. 3* for Electric Violin, English Horn, Horn, Tuba, Vibraphone, Winds, Percussion, and Solo Voice (1975); *No. 4* for Voice, String Quartet, and Chamber Orch. (1977); *Oratio No. 1* for Piccolo, Solo Trumpet, Chimes, and String Quartet or String Orch. (1974) and *No. 2* for Solo Oboe and String Trio (1976); *Music* for 6 Trumpets (1975); *Ludus* for 3 Tubas (1975); Bassoon Quartet (1976); *Variations* for Solo Harp (1977). FOR PIANO: *103 Short Pieces* (1965). FOR ORGAN: *3 danses liturgiques* (1964); *26 Short Preludes* (1972); *Preambulum,* with Timpani (1977).

Nelle, Wilhelm, German authority on church music; b. Schwöbber, near Hameln, May 9, 1849; d. Münster, Oct. 15, 1918. He studied theology in Halle and Tübingen, where he also studied music with Robert Franz and Otto Scherzer. From 1872 he was active as a priest in various German cities. In 1895 he founded the Evangelischer Kirchengesang-Verein für Westfalen. He was prominent in the reform and organization of Evangelical church music in Germany.
    WRITINGS: *Das Evangelische Gesangbuch von 1835* (1883); *Liederbüchlein, 25 geistliche und weltliche Lieder* (1891); *Choralbuch zum Rheinisch-Westfälischen Evangelischen Gesangbuch* (with Hollenberg, 1892; 3rd ed., 1908); *Die Festmelodien des Kirchenjahres charakterisiert* (1895; 2nd ed., 1904, as *Aus dem Evangelischen Melodienschatz,* I); *Geschichte des deutschen evangelischen Kirchenliedes* (1904; 3rd ed., 1928); *Chorbuch* (with J. Plath, 1917).

Nelson, John, American conductor; b. San José, Costa Rica (of American missionary parents), Dec. 6, 1941. He received his primary musical training with local teachers in Costa Rica; then went to N.Y., where he studied conducting with Jean Morel at the Juilliard School of Music (1963–67). He began making professional appearances while still a student; conducted the Pro Arte Chorale in N.Y., eliciting high praise for his performance of *Les Troyens* of Berlioz. He subsequently made guest appearances with major American and European orchs.; also led the Jerusalem Symph. Orch. He revisited Costa Rica to conduct the National Symph. Orch. in San José. In 1976 he was appointed conductor and music director of the Indianapolis Symph. Orch.; in 1979–80 was artistic consultant and principal guest conductor of the Louisville Orch.

Nelson, Judith, American soprano; b. Chicago, Sept. 10, 1939. She studied at St. Olaf College in Northfield, Minn.; then sang with music groups of the Univ. of Chicago and the Univ. of Calif. at Berkeley; made her operatic debut as Drusilla in Monteverdi's *L'incoronazione di Poppea* in Brussels in 1979. She is particularly noted for her performances of Baroque music.

Nelson, Oliver E., black American composer and arranger; b. St. Louis, June 4, 1932; d. Los Angeles, Oct. 27, 1975. He studied piano, saxophone, taxidermy, dermatology, and embalming. After serving in the Marines, he studied composition with Robert Wykes at Washington Univ. in St. Louis (1954–58); had private lessons with Elliott Carter in N.Y. and George Tremblay in Los Angeles; in the 1950s and early 1960s, he played saxophone in several jazz orchs., among them those led by Wild Bill Davis, Louis Bellison, Duke Ellington, and Count Basie; then moved to Hollywood.
    WORKS: Saxophone Sonata (1957); *Songs* for Contralto and Piano (1957); Divertimento for 10 Woodwinds and Double Bass (1957); *Afro-American Sketches* for Jazz Ensemble (1960); *Blues and the Abstract Truth* for Jazz Ensemble (1960); Woodwind Quintet (1960); *Dirge* for Chamber Orch. (1961); *Soundpiece* for Contralto, String Quartet, and Piano (1963); *Soundpiece* for Jazz Orch. (1964); *Patterns* for Jazz Ensemble (1965); *A Study in 5/4* for Wind Ensemble (1966); Concerto for Xylophone, Marimba, Vibes, and Wind Orch. (1967); *The Kennedy Dream Suite* for Jazz Ensemble (1967); *Jazzhattan Suite* for Jazz Orch. (1967; N.Y., Oct. 7, 1967); Septet for Wind Orch. (1968); *Piece* for Orch. and Jazz Soloists (1969); *A Black Suite* for Narrator, String Quartet, and Jazz Orch. (1970); *Berlin Dialogue* for Jazz Orch. (1970; Berlin, 1970); *Concert Piece* for Alto Saxophone and Studio Orch. (1972); *Fugue and Bossa* for Wind Orch. (1973). In 1966 he made a sterling jazz arrangement of Prokofiev's *Peter and the Wolf;* then wrote music for films (*Death of a Gunfighter, Skullduggery,* and *Zig Zag*) and television (*It Takes a Thief, Ironside, The Name of the Game, Longstreet, The Six Million Dollar Man,* etc.). He publ. a valuable improvisation saxophone book, *Patterns for Jazz* (Los Angeles, 1966; originally titled *Patterns for Saxophone*).

BIBLIOGRAPHY: David N. Baker and others, eds., *The Black Composer Speaks* (Metuchen, N.J., 1978; pp. 203–37, including a complete list of works).

Nelson, Robert U., American musicologist; b. Brush, Colo., Sept. 16, 1902. He studied at the Univ. of Calif., Berkeley (A.B., 1923); later worked with Gaston Déthier and Percy Goetschius at the Inst. of Musical Art, N.Y. (diplomas in piano and organ, 1925), and with Walter Piston and Willi Apel at Harvard Univ. (M.A., 1937; Ph.D., 1944). He also studied composition with Gustav Holst and Eugene Zador. From 1925 to 1937 he was a faculty member at Washington State Univ.; in 1938 became an instructor at the Univ. of Calif., Los Angeles; was a prof. from 1955; retired in 1970. He publ. a valuable study, *The Technique of Variation* (Berkeley, 1948); contributed numerous articles to music magazines.

Nelson, Ron(ald Jack), American composer; b. Joliet, Ill., Dec. 14, 1929. He studied composition with Howard Hanson, Bernard Rogers, Louis Mennini, and Wayne Barlow at the Eastman School of Music in Rochester, N.Y. (1947–56); in the interim, went to Paris, where he took courses with Tony Aubin at the Ecole Normale de Musique (1954–55). In 1956 he joined the music staff of Brown Univ. in Providence, R.I.; was chairman of the music dept. there in 1963–73.
WORKS: Operas: *The Birthday of the Infanta* (Rochester, May 14, 1956) and *Hamaguchi* (1980). Ballet: *Dance in Ruins* (1954). For Orch.: *Savannah River Holiday* (1955; also for Band, 1973); *This Is the Orchestra* for Narrator and Orch. (1960); *Jubilee* (1960); *Overture for Latecomers* (1961); *Toccata* (1963); *Rocky Point Holiday* (1969; also for Band, 1969); *Trilogy: JFK—MLK—RFK* for Orch. and Tape (in memory of President John F. Kennedy, Martin Luther King, and Robert F. Kennedy; 1969); *5 Pieces for Orchestra after Paintings by Andrew Wyeth* (1976); *Meditation and Dance* for Orch. (1977); *6 Pieces for Chamber Ensemble* (1977). For Band: *Fanfare for a Celebration* (1982; also for Orch., 1983); *Medieval Suite* (1982); *Rocky Mountain Jubilee* (1984). Vocal music: *The Christmas Story,* cantata (1958); *Triumphal Te Deum* (1963); *What Is Man?,* oratorio (1964); *Meditation of the Syllable OM,* with Narrator (1970); *Mass of St. La Salle* (1981); songs; piano pieces.

Nelson, Willie, American country-music singer and songwriter; b. Abbott, Texas, April 30, 1933. For a short time he attended Baylor Univ. in Waco, Texas; then made appearances in local honky-tonk bars; also began to write songs, which included *Hello Walls, Crazy,* and *Night Life,* made famous by leading singers of the day. He then went to Nashville, Tenn., where he played bass in the band of Ray Price and gained renown with such songs as *The Party's Over* and *Little Things* in his many appearances with the Grand Ole Opry. He eventually returned to Texas and became instrumental in the development of the "Austin sound," a.k.a. "outlaw country" or "redneck rock."

Nelsova, Zara, brilliant Canadian-born American cellist; b. Winnipeg, Dec. 23, 1918, of Russian extraction. Her father, a flutist, gave her music lessons; she later studied with Dezso Mahalek (1924–28). In 1929 she went to London, where she continued her studies with Herbert Walenn in London (1929–35). In 1931, at the age of 13, she appeared as soloist with the London Symph. Orch. With her 2 sisters, a pianist and a violinist, she organized a group billed as the Canadian Trio, and toured in England, Australia, and South Africa. Returning to Canada, she served as principal cellist of the Toronto Symph. Orch. (1940–43); she was also a member of another Canadian Trio, this time with Kathleen Parlow and Sir Ernest MacMillan (1941–44). In 1942 she made her U.S. debut at Town Hall in N.Y.; also continued her studies, receiving valuable instruction from Feuermann, Casals, and Piatigorsky. In 1962 she joined the faculty of the Juilliard School of Music in N.Y. In 1953 she became an American citizen. From 1963 to 1973 she was the wife of the American pianist **Grant Johannesen.** She received rather rapturous press reviews for her lyrical interpretations of classical and modern cello music in a purportedly "Russian" (i.e., wonderful) style.

Němeček, Franz Xaver. See **Niemtschek, Franz Xaver.**

Nemescu, Octavian, avant-garde Rumanian composer; b. Pascani, March 29, 1940. He studied with Jora, Alfred Mendelsohn, Vieru, Ciortea, Vancea, and Paul Constantinescu at the Bucharest Cons. (1956–63); attended the summer courses of new music held in Darmstadt (1972); taught asymptotic approximations from infinitude to infinitesimality.
WORKS: Clarinet Sonata (1961–62); *Poliritmii* for Clarinet, Piano, and Prepared Piano (1962–63); *Triunghi (Triangle)* for Orch. (1964; Bucharest, Dec. 3, 1967); *4 Patru dimensiuni în timp (4 Dimensions in Time): I* for Orch. (1965), *II* for Chorus and Orch. (1966), *III* for Orch. (1967), and *IV* for Orch. (1968); *Combinații în cercuri (Combinations of Circles)* for Cello, Tape, and Multimedia Action (1965); *Plurisens,* cycle for Variable Group and Multimedia Action (1965–68); *Memorial I–V* for various combinations of Instruments, Tape, and Multimedia Action (1968–70); *Concentric* and *Efemeride,* both for Variable Ensemble, Tape, and Multimedia Action (1968–69); *Ego,* multimedia spectacle (1970); *Le Roi va mourir* for an Instrumentalist, Clock, Tape, and Multimedia Action (1971–72); *Ulysse* for Variable Group, Tape, and Multimedia Action (1972–73); *Jeu des sens,* music for a pair of ears, eyes, hands, a nose, and a mouth (1973–74); *Pourras-tu seul?* and *Cromoson,* both "imaginary music" (1973–74); *Natural!!,* space music (1973–74); *Kalendrier,* permanent music for the atmosphere of a room (1974).

Németh, Mária, Hungarian soprano; b. Kormend, March 13, 1897; d. Vienna, Dec. 28, 1967. She studied with Georg Anthes and Géza Laszló in Budapest, Giannina Russ in Milan, Fernando De Lucia in Naples, and Felicie Kaschowska in Vienna; made her debut as Sulamith in *Königin von Saba* in Budapest in 1923. In 1925 she became a member of the Vienna State Opera, where she remained until 1946; also made appearances at Covent Garden in London, La Scala in Milan, Munich, Rome, Paris, and Salzburg. She sang both lyric and coloratura roles during her career, excelling as the Queen of the Night, Aida, Donna Anna, and Tosca, among others.

Nemiroff, Isaac, American composer; b. Cincinnati, Feb. 16, 1912; d. New York, March 5, 1977. He studied at the Cincinnati Cons., and with Stefan Wolpe at the N.Y. College of Music; taught at various music schools in N.Y. and Brooklyn.

WORKS: Duo for Violin and Cello (1939); Concerto for Oboe and String Orch. (1955); Concertino for Flute Solo, Violin, and String Orch. (1958); *Lorca,* solo cantata for Voice, Flute, and Strings (1963); Woodwind Quintet (1968); Quintet for Flute, Clarinet, Cello, Voice, and Piano (1969); *Atomyriades* for Solo Oboe (1972); Duo for Oboe and Bass Clarinet (1973); 2 string quartets; 2 violin sonatas; Saxophone Sonata.

Nemtin, Alexander, Soviet composer; b. Perm, July 13, 1936. He studied at the Moscow Cons., graduating in 1960. He writes music in different genres, but his most notable creation is an intimately plausible reification of Scriabin's *Acte préalable,* the "preliminary act" of the planned *Mysterium.* Nemtin put together the score from sketches left by Scriabin after his death, supplemented by materials from his late opus numbers, endeavoring to recreate Scriabin's symph. textures. The first part of this work was performed in Moscow on March 16, 1973.

Nenna, Pomponio, Italian madrigalist; b. Bari, near Naples, c.1613. d. Rome, c.1613. Held in high regard by his contemporaries, he was created a Knight of the Golden Spur in 1603. He publ. 6 books of madrigals for 5 voices from 1582 to 1618, and a book of madrigals *a* 4 (1613; 2nd ed., 1621). Several responds are printed in *Istituzione e monumenti dell'arte musicale italiana,* vol. 5 (pp. LIII–LX); his madrigals, ed. by E. Dagnino, in *Pubblicazioni dell'Istituto Italiano per la Storia della Musica* (Rome, 1942).

Nenov, Dimiter, Bulgarian composer and pianist; b. Razgrad, Jan. 1, 1902; d. Sofia, Aug. 30, 1953. He studied piano and composition at the Cons. in Dresden; returning to Bulgaria, he taught piano at the Sofia Music Academy from 1937 until his death.

WORKS: Symph. No. 1 (1922); *Ballad* for Orch. (1926); Piano Concerto (1932–36); 2 ballads for Piano and Orch. (1942, 1943); *Rhapsodic Fantasy* for Orch. (1943); Violin Sonata (1921); Piano Sonata (1922).

Nepomuceno, Alberto, important Brazilian composer; b. Fortaleza, July 6, 1864; d. Rio de Janeiro, Oct. 16, 1920. He studied in Rome, Berlin, and Paris,

returning to Brazil in 1895. In 1902 he was appointed director of the Instituto Nacional de Musica in Rio de Janeiro, remaining only for a few months; he returned to this post in 1906, holding it until 1916. In 1910 he conducted Brazilian music at the International Exposition in Brussels. In some of his music he introduced thematic material from Brazilian folk music.

WORKS: Operas: *Artemis* (Rio de Janeiro, June 14, 1898); *O Garatuja* (Rio de Janeiro, Oct. 26, 1904); *Abul* (Buenos Aires, June 30, 1913); Symph. (an early work; publ. posthumously, 1937); *Suite brasileira* for Orch. (contains a popular *Batuque*); songs; piano pieces.

Neri, Saint Donna Filippo, one of the greatest spiritual leaders of the Renaissance; b. Florence, July 21, 1515; d. Rome, May 26, 1595. He was educated in Florence; by 1534 was in Rome; in 1548 he founded the Confraternità della Ss. Trinità; in 1551 took Holy Orders. He began by giving lectures on religious subjects and holding spiritual exercises in the oratory of the church of San Girolamo della Carità, and soon attracted a large following. These meetings invariably ended with the singing of hymns, or *laudi spirituali,* for which the poet Ancina wrote many of the texts, while Giovanni Animuccia, maestro di cappella at the Vatican and music director of the Oratory, set them to music. In 1575 the Congregation of the Oratory, as a seminary for secular priests, was officially recognized by Pope Gregory XIII, and in 1578 the Congregation transferred its headquarters to the church of Santa Maria in Vallicella. But the founder himself remained at S. Girolamo until 1583; from 1578 the great Spanish polyphonist Victoria lived with him there, as chaplain at this church. Another Spanish musician who was prominently associated with the Oratorio was Francisco Soto de Langa. S. Filippo was friendly with Palestrina, whose spiritual adviser he was, but there is no evidence that the latter succeeded Animuccia as music director of the Oratory. From the musical practice of the Oratory there eventually developed the form that we know as "oratorio." Contrary to general belief, this form did not make its first appearance in Cavalieri's *Rappresentazione di anima e di corpo,* performed at S. Maria in Vallicella in 1600, but in Giovanni Francesco Anerio's *Teatro Armonico spirituale di madrigali a 5, 6, 7 e 8 voci,* dating from 1619 and consisting of musical settings of the Gospels and of stories from the Bible. It was not until about 1635–40 that this form actually began to receive the title of oratorio, from the place where the performances were given. S. Filippo was beatified on May 25, 1615, and canonized on March 12, 1622.

BIBLIOGRAPHY: P.G. Bacci, *Vita di San F. Neri* (Naples, 1855; Eng. trans., 2 vols., St. Louis, 1903); L. Ponnelle and L. Bourdet, *St. Ph. Neri et la société romaine de son temps* (Paris, 1918; Eng. trans., London, 1932); P. Pasquetti, *L'oratorio musicale in Italia* (Florence, 1906), chaps. 4–8; L. Pastor, *Geschichte des Päpste* (Freiburg, 1886–1930; in Eng., London, 1930, vol. 19, chap. 4); D. Alaleona, *Storia dell'oratorio musicale in Italia* (Milan, 1945); C. Gasbarri, *L'oratorio filippino* (Rome, 1957); H. Smither, *A History of the Oratorio*, vol. 1 (Chapel Hill, 1977).

Neri, Giulio, Italian bass; b. Turilla di Siena, May 21, 1909; d. Rome. April 21, 1958. He studied with Ferraresi in Florence; made his debut at the Teatro delle Quattro Fontane in Rome in 1935; then sang at the Teatro Reale dell'Opera in Rome, where he soon established himself as a principal bass; also made guest appearances at La Scala in Milan, Florence, Venice, London, and Munich. An outstanding Verdi interpreter, he was equally distinguished as a Wagnerian.

Nerini, Emile, French composer; b. Colombes, near Paris, Feb. 2, 1882; d. Paris, March 22, 1967. Son of a piano manufacturer, he studied with Decombes, Diémer, Lenepveu, and Caussade at the Paris Cons.
WORKS: Lyric dramas: *Manoël* (Paris, May 11, 1905); *Le Soir de Waterloo* (Paris, April 17, 1910); *L'Epreuve dernière* (Monte Carlo, March 16, 1912); *Mazeppa* (Bordeaux, 1925); operetta, *Mademoiselle Sans-Gêne* (1944; Bordeaux, 1966); *Bacchus* for Chorus and Orch.; programmatic pieces for orch. (*Parmi les roses, Solitude, Rêve oriental,* etc.); chamber music; instrumental sonatas; songs; etc. He also publ. a *Traité d'harmonie.*

Nero, Peter, popular American pianist and conductor; b. New York, May 22, 1934. He studied at the Juilliard School of Music; then toured as a pianist with Paul Whiteman; subsequently launched a highly successful career as a pianist in the popular music genres. He also appeared as a conductor in his own arrangements of popular music and in his original compositions; he wrote the score for the film *A Sunday in New York,* in which he also played a cameo part.

Neruda, Franz Xaver, Bohemian cellist, brother of **Wilma Maria Francisca Neruda;** b. Brünn, Dec. 3, 1843; d. Copenhagen, March 20, 1915. At an early age he appeared in concerts with his father and sister; in 1864–76 was a member of the Royal Orch. in Copenhagen, where in 1868 he founded the Society for Chamber Music; he succeeded Gade in 1892 as conductor of a similar organization in Stockholm. He composed 5 cello concertos; *Aus dem Böhmerwald* and *Slovakische Märsche* for Orch.; string quartets; pieces for cello, for piano, and for organ; songs.

Neruda (Lady Hallé), Wilma Maria Francisca, Czech violinist; b. Brünn, March 21, 1839; d. Berlin, April 15, 1911. Her father was an organist; her brother, **Franz Xaver Neruda,** a cellist. She first played in public in Vienna when she was 7 years old, with her sister **Amalie,** a pianist; then made a tour with her father, sister, and brother through Germany. On June 11, 1849, she played at a Phil. Society concert in London; after prolonged travels on the Continent, including Russia, she married the Swedish conductor **Ludvig Norman,** from whom she was divorced in 1869; she returned to London the same year. On July 26, 1888, she married **Sir Charles Hallé,** and with him made tours to Europe, Australia, and South Africa until her husband's death in 1895. When she announced her intention of retiring, a number of admirers, headed by the Prince of Wales (Edward VII), raised a subscription and presented to her a palace at Asolo, near Venice. In 1899 she made an American tour. In 1901 Queen Alexandra conferred upon her the title of "Violinist to the Queen." Her instrument, a Stradivarius dated 1709, considered one of the finest in existence, was presented to her in 1876 jointly by the Duke of Saxe-Coburg and Gotha, Earl Dudley, and Earl Hardwicke.
BIBLIOGRAPHY: *Dictionary of National Biography* (Supplement, 1901–11), II, p. 190.

Nessler, Victor E., Alsatian composer; b. Baldenheim, Jan. 28, 1841; d. Strasbourg, May 28, 1890. He studied in Strasbourg, where he produced his first opera, *Fleurette* (1864). In 1870 he became conductor of the Caroltheater in Leipzig and produced there his opera *Der Rattenfänger von Hameln* (Leipzig, March 19, 1879), which established his reputation as an opera composer. An even greater success was achieved by his opera *Der Trompeter von Säkkingen* (Leipzig, May 4, 1884), which entered the repertoire of many European opera houses. In both operas Nessler adroitly appealed to the Romantic tastes of the German audiences, even though from a purely musical standpoint these productions offered little originality. His other operas, none of which achieved a comparable success, included *Dornröschens Brautfahrt* (1867), *Irmingard* (1876), *Der wilde Jäger* (1881), *Otto der Schütz* (1886), and *Die Rose von Strassburg* (1890). He also wrote several operettas: *Die Hochzeitsreise* (1867), *Nachtwächter und Student* (1868), and *Am Alexandertag* (1869).
BIBLIOGRAPHY: C. Schneider, "Victor Nessler, compositeur alsacien du *Trompette de Säkkingen,*" *La Musique en Alsace hier et aujourd'hui* (Strasbourg, 1970).

Nesterenko, Evgeni, Russian bass; b. Moscow, Jan. 8, 1938. He first studied architectural engineering; graduated from the Leningrad Structural Inst. in 1961; then enrolled in the Leningrad Cons., where he studied voice with Lukanin. He began his opera career at the Maly Theater in Leningrad (1963–67); then was a member of the Kirov Opera and Ballet Theater there (1967–71). In 1970 he won first prize at the International Tchaikovsky Competition in Moscow; in 1971 he joined the Bolshoi Theater. He then engaged on a European concert tour; also sang in the U.S. In 1975 he was appointed chairman of the voice dept. at the Moscow Cons. He excelled in such roles as Boris Godunov and Méphistophélès. In 1982 he was awarded the Lenin Prize.

Nestyev, Izrail, Russian musicologist; b. Kerch, April 17, 1911. He studied at the Moscow Cons., graduating in 1937; during World War II served as a military correspondent; subsequently was in charge of the programs of Moscow Radio (1945–48); in 1956, he joined the staff of the Moscow Cons., conducting seminars on European music. He is the author of the standard biography of Prokofiev (Moscow, 1946; in Eng., N.Y., 1946; new revised ed., Moscow, 1957; in Eng., Stanford, Calif., 1960, with a foreword by N. Slonimsky); other books are *Popular Song as Foundation of Musical Creativity* (Moscow, 1961); *How to Understand Music* (Moscow, 1962); *Hanns Eisler and His Songs* (Moscow, 1962); *Puccini* (Moscow, 1963); *Béla Bartók, Life and Works* (Moscow, 1969). He was a co-editor of the symposium *Sergei Prokofiev; Articles and Materials* (Moscow, 1962); and of *European Music of the 20th Century; Materials and Documents* (Moscow, 1975).

Nettl, Bruno, American musicologist, son of **Paul Nettl;** b. Prague, March 14, 1930. He was brought to the U.S. in 1939; studied at Indiana Univ. (A.B., 1950; M.A., 1951; Ph.D., 1953, with the dissertation *American Indian Music North of Mexico: Its Styles and Areas,* publ. as *North American Indian Musical Styles,* Philadelphia, 1954); he also received an M.A. degree in library science from the Univ. of Michigan in 1960. He taught at Wayne State Univ. (1953–64); in 1964 he joined the faculty of the Univ. of Illinois at Urbana, becoming a prof. of music and anthropology in 1967. His books include *Music in Primitive Culture* (Cambridge, Mass., 1956); *Cheremis Musical Styles* (Bloomington, Ind., 1960); *An Introduction to Folk Music in the United States* (Detroit, 1960; 3rd ed., revised and enlarged, 1976); *Reference Materials in Ethnomusicology* (Detroit, 1961; 2nd ed., 1967); *Theory and Method in Ethnomusicology* (N.Y., 1964); *Folk and Traditional Music of the Western Continents* (Englewood Cliffs, N.J., 1965; 2nd ed., 1973); etc.

Nettl, Paul, eminent American musicologist; b. Hohenelbe, Bohemia, Jan. 10, 1889; d. Bloomington, Ind., Jan. 8, 1972. He studied jurisprudence (LL.D., 1913) and musicology (Ph.D., 1915) at the German Univ. of Prague; from 1920 to 1937 was on its faculty. In 1939 he emigrated to the U.S.; from 1946 to 1959 he taught at Indiana Univ. in Bloomington. His writings include *Über den Ursprung der Musik* (Prague, 1920); *Alte jüdische Spielleute und Musiker* (Prague, 1923); *Musik und Tanz bei Casanova* (Prague, 1924); *Musik-Barock in Böhmen und Mähren* (Brunn, 1927); *Der Prager Kaufruf* (Prague, 1930); *Das Wiener Lied im Zeitalter des Barock* (Vienna, 1934); *Mozart in Böhmen,* after Prochazka's *Mozart in Prag* (Prague, 1938); *The Story of Dance Music* (N.Y., 1947); *The Book of Musical Documents* (N.Y., 1948); *Luther and Music* (N.Y., 1948); *Casanova und seine Zeit* (Esslingen, 1949); *Goethe und Mozart: Eine Betrachtung* (Esslingen, 1949); *The Other Casanova* (N.Y., 1950); *Forgotten Musicians* (N.Y., 1951); *National Anthems* (N.Y., 1952; 2nd ed., enlarged, 1967); *Beethoven Encyclopedia* (N.Y., 1956; 2nd ed., revised, 1967, as *Beethoven Handbook*); *Mozart and Masonry* (N.Y.,

1957); *Beethoven und seine Zeit* (Frankfurt, 1958); *Georg Friedrich Händel* (Berlin, 1958); *Mozart und der Tanz* (1960); *The Dance in Classical Music* (N.Y., 1963); R. Daniel, ed., *Paul Nettl: Selected Essays* (Bloomington, 1975). A bio-bibliographical brochure, *Ein Musikwissenschaftler in zwei Welten: Die musikwissenschaftlen und literarischen Arbeiten von Paul Nettl,* compiled by Thomas Atcherson, was publ. as part of a Festschrift in Vienna in 1962.

Neubauer, Franz Christoph, Czech violinist and composer; b. Melník, March 21, 1750; d. Bückeburg, Oct. 11, 1795. He was taught violin by the village schoolmaster; led a wandering life; produced an operetta, *Ferdinand und Yariko,* in Munich (1784); then proceeded to Vienna, where he met Mozart and Haydn; from 1790 to 1794 he served as Kapellmeister to Prince Weilburg; in 1795 succeeded Johann Christoph Friedrich Bach as court Kapellmeister at Bückeburg. He was a prolific composer; wrote 12 symphs.; the 11th symph. was entitled *La Bataille,* and included in the score some sounds imitative of battle.

BIBLIOGRAPHY: F. von Schlichtegroll, *Musiker-Nekrologe* (ed. R. Schaal, Kassel, 1953).

Neuendorff, Adolf, German conductor; b. Hamburg, June 13, 1843; d. New York, Dec. 4, 1897. He went to America in 1854 and studied violin with Matzka and Weinlich, and piano with Schilling. He appeared both as a concert violinist and pianist; gave violin concerts in Brazil in 1861. In 1863 he went to Milwaukee, then a center of German music, and served as music director of the German theater there; subsequently moved to N.Y., where he conducted German opera, including the first American performances of *Lohengrin* (April 3, 1871) and *Die Walküre* (April 2, 1877); in 1884 he moved to Boston and became the first conductor of the Music Hall Promenade Concerts (later Boston Pops); he then followed his wife, the singer **Georgine von Januschowsky,** to Vienna, where she was prima donna at the Imperial Opera (1893–95); he finally returned to N.Y., and in 1897 became conductor of the Metropolitan Permanent Orch., succeeding Seidl.

BIBLIOGRAPHY: *Dictionary of American Biography,* XIII.

Neuhaus, Heinrich, eminent Russian pianist and pedagogue; b. Elizavetgrad, April 12, 1888; d. Moscow, Oct. 10, 1964. He studied piano with his father, **Gustav Neuhaus** (1847–1938); other musical members of the family were his uncle, the pianist and composer **Felix Blumenfeld,** and his first cousin, the Polish composer **Karol Szymanowski.** Neuhaus began giving concerts at the age of 9; he made a concert tour in Germany in 1904, then studied composition with Paul Juon in Berlin; in 1912–14 he took piano lessons with Leopold Godowsky in Vienna. Returning to Russia, he taught piano at the Kiev Cons. (1918–22); then was a prof. from 1922 to his death at the Moscow Cons. Among his students were Gilels and Sviatoslav Richter. Neuhaus publ.

The Art of Piano Playing (Moscow, 1958; in Eng., London, 1983).
BIBLIOGRAPHY: V. Delson, *Heinrich Neuhaus* (Moscow, 1966).

Neuhaus, Rudolf, German conductor; b. Cologne, Jan. 3, 1914. He first studied violin; then took conducting lessons with Hermann Abendroth; also studied music theory with Philipp Jarnach. He was music director of the Landestheater in Neustrelitz (1934–44); then was conductor of the Landestheater in Schwerin (1945–52). In 1953 he joined the Dresden State Opera, where he was deputy Generalmusikdirektor until 1975; was noted for his performances of operas of Wagner and Richard Strauss. From 1953 he was a member of the faculty of the Dresden Hochschule für Musik; in 1959 was named prof. there.

Neukomm, Sigismund Ritter von, Austrian composer and conductor; b. Salzburg, July 10, 1778; d. Paris, April 3, 1858. He was a pupil of the organist Weissauer, and of Michael Haydn for composition; from 1798 to 1805 he studied in Vienna under Joseph Haydn, who showed him fatherly care. In 1804 he passed through Stockholm, where he was elected a member of the Academy, to St. Petersburg, there becoming conductor of the German Opera. The year 1809 found him in Paris, an intimate of Grétry and Cherubini, and pianist to Talleyrand after Dussek. For his Requiem in memory of Louis XVI (Vienna, 1814), Louis XVII ennobled him in 1815, decorating him with the cross of the Legion of Honor. In 1816 Neukomm went to Rio de Janeiro, and was appointed court music director by Emperor Dom Pedro, whom he accompanied to Lisbon on the outbreak of the revolution in 1821. He was in Talleyrand's service until 1826; then traveled for many years; and finally resided alternately in London and Paris. Despite his almost continuous travels, he was a most industrious composer; besides much church music, he produced several German operas; 2 symphs., 5 overtures, and 6 fantasias for orch.; chamber music; a Piano Concerto and many piano pieces; 57 organ pieces; about 200 French, English, Italian, and German songs; etc. His autobiography was publ. as *Esquisses biographiques de Sigismond Neukomm* (Paris, 1859).
BIBLIOGRAPHY: Gisela Pellegrini, *Sigismund Ritter von Neukomm: Ein vergessener Salzburger Musiker* (Salzburg, 1936); L.H. Corrêa de Azevedo, "S. Neukomm, An Austrian Composer in the New World," *Musical Quarterly* (Oct. 1959); R. Angermüller, *Sigismund Neukomm: Werkverzeichnis, Autobiographie, Beziehung zu seinen Zeitgenossen* (Munich, 1977).

Neumann, Angelo, Austrian tenor and opera administrator; b. Vienna, Aug. 18, 1838; d. Prague, Dec. 20, 1910. He began a mercantile career, but deserted it after taking vocal lessons from Stilke-Sessi, and after his debut as a lyric tenor in 1859; he sang at theaters in Cracow, Odenburg, Pressburg, Danzig, and the Vienna Court Opera (1862–76); in 1876–82 he

was manager of the Leipzig opera under Förster; then gathered together a traveling company for producing Wagner operas, journeying as far as Italy; from 1882 to 1885 he was manager of the Bremen opera; then until his death, of the German opera in Prague (Landestheater). He publ. *Erinnerungen an Richard Wagner* (1907; Eng. trans. by E. Livermore, 1908).

Neumann, Franz (František), Czech conductor and composer; b. Přerov, Moravia, June 16, 1874; d. Brno, Feb. 24, 1929. He was a pupil at the Leipzig Cons.; was répétiteur in Karlsruhe and Hamburg; Kapellmeister in Regensburg, Linz, and Reichenberg; in 1904, became 2nd Kapellmeister in Frankfurt; in 1919, first conductor of the Czech National Opera in Brünn; in 1925, its director. He composed the operas *Die Brautwerbung* (Linz, 1901), *Liebelei* (Frankfurt, Sept. 18, 1910), *Herbststurm* (Berlin, April 9, 1919), *Beatrice Caracci* (Brno, April 29, 1922; in Czech), and *Leyer und Schwert* (publ. 1901; not produced); 2 ballets; men's choruses; etc.

Neumann, Václav, Czech conductor; b. Prague, Sept. 29, 1920. He studied violin and viola at the Cons. of Prague; was principal viola player in the Czech Phil.; conducted it from 1948 to 1950; then was engaged as conductor of orchs. in Karlsbad and Brno; also led the Leipzig Opera (1964–68); from 1970 to 1972 he was music director and conductor of the Württemberg Symph. Orch. In 1972 he was appointed chief conductor of the Czech Phil.

Neumann, Věroslav, Czech composer; b. Citoliby, near Louny, May 27, 1931. He studied theory with Jaroslav Řídký at the Prague Cons. After a few works in a traditional style, he adopted the 12-tone method of composition. He wrote *Panoráma Prahy (Panorama of Prague)* for Baritone and Orch. (1962); *Peace Symphony* (1964); *Ode* for Orch. (1966); *Pozvánka na koktejl (Invitation to Cocktails)* for Orch. (1969); *Omaggio a Prokofieff* for 2 Violins (1969); a children's choral cycle, *Intervals* (1971).

Neumark, Georg, German hymn writer; b. Langensalza, March 3, 1621; d. Weimar, July 8, 1681. He was the author of the words and music of the hymn *Wer nur den lieben Gott lässt walten,* used by Bach in several of his cantatas, and by Mendelssohn in the oratorio *St. Paul.* Neumark publ. several vols. of verse, some with his own tunes; the most important is *Poetisch-musikalisches Lustwäldchen* (Jena, 1652; enlarged ed., as *Fortgepflanztes Lustwäldchen,* 1657).
BIBLIOGRAPHY: Franz Knauth, *Georg Neumark, Leben und Dichten* (Langensalza, 1881).

Neupert, Edmund, Norwegian-American pianist and pedagogue; b. Christiania, April 1, 1842; d. New York, June 22, 1888. He studied at Kullak's Academy in Berlin; then taught there. In 1868 he went to Denmark, where he taught piano at the Copenhagen

Cons.; for 2 years he was a piano instructor at the Moscow Cons. (1881–83); then emigrated to the U.S. and settled in N.Y. as a piano teacher. His collections of piano studies were much in use by American teachers.

Neupert, Hanns, German historian and builder of keyboard instruments; b. Bamberg, Feb. 22, 1902; d. there, Nov. 9, 1980. He was the son of the piano manufacturer Fritz Neupert (1872–1952); studied science and musicology; devoted himself to the manufacture of keyboard instruments. He publ. the books *Vom Musikstab zum modernen Klavier* (Bamberg, 1925); *Das Cembalo* (Bamberg, 1933; new ed., 1956); *Das Klavichord* (Kassel, 1948; 2nd ed., 1956; in Eng. as *The Clavichord,* 1965); *Die Frau und das Cembalo* (Bamberg, 1953). His collection of some 250 keyboard instruments was acquired in 1968 by the German National Museum in Nuremberg.

Nevada, Emma, stage name of **Emma Wixom,** operatic soprano; b. Alpha, near Nevada City, Calif., Feb. 7, 1859; d. Liverpool, June 20, 1940. She studied from 1877 with Marchesi in Vienna; made her debut in London on May 17, 1880, in *La Sonnambula;* sang at Trieste in the autumn; then in Florence, Livorno, Naples, Rome, and Genoa, and at La Scala, Milan. Her first appearance in Paris was at the Opéra-Comique, May 17, 1883, as Zora in F. David's *Perle du Brésil.* During the season of 1884–85 she was a member of Col. Mapleson's company at the old Academy of Music in N.Y., singing on alternate nights with Patti. She sang in Chicago at the Opera Festival in 1885, and again in 1889. She then sang mostly in Europe; retired in 1910.
BIBLIOGRAPHY: T. Williams, *Notable American Women,* II (N.Y., 1971); G. Jellinek, *Dictionary of American Biography,* Supplement II.

Nevada, Mignon Mathilde Marie, daughter of **Emma Nevada;** operatic soprano; b. Paris, Aug. 14, 1886; d. Long Melford, England, June 25, 1971. She made her debut at the Costanzi Theater, Rome, as Rosina in *Il Barbiere di Siviglia* in 1907; then sang a season at the San Carlos in Lisbon; after a season at the Pergola Theater in Florence, she made her London debut at Covent Garden as Ophelia (Oct. 3, 1910), and sang there in subsequent seasons; also appeared at La Monnaie in Brussels, and (1923) at La Scala in Milan; during World War II she engaged in war work at Liverpool, England; from 1954, lived in London.

Neveu, Ginette, French violinist; b. Paris, Aug. 11, 1919; d. in an airplane disaster at the Azores Islands, Oct. 28, 1949. She was a grandniece of **Widor;** studied with her mother, and later with Carl Flesch; first played in public with the Colonne Orch. in Paris at the age of 7. After graduating from the Paris Cons. with a first prize, she won the Wieniawski Grand Prize at the International Contest in Warsaw in 1934. Her American debut took place with the Boston Symph., on Oct. 24, 1947; her success was immediate and unmistakable. She was at the height of her career when she perished on her way to the U.S. for her 3rd annual tour.
BIBLIOGRAPHY: M.J. Ronze-Neveu, *Ginette Neveu; La Fulgurante Carrière d'une grande artiste* (Paris, 1952; in Eng., London, 1956).

Nevin, Arthur Finley, American composer and pedagogue, brother of **Ethelbert Nevin;** b. Edgeworth, Pa., April 27, 1871; d. Sewickley, Pa., July 10, 1943. He received a musical training at home, mainly from his father; then studied at the New England Cons. in Boston; in 1893 went to Berlin, where he studied piano with Klindworth and composition with Boise. Returning to the U.S., he devoted himself to teaching and conducting; was a prof. of music at the Univ. of Kansas (1915–20) and director of the municipal music dept. of Memphis, Tenn. (1920–22); lived for a time on Montana Indian reservations studying Indian music. He was unable to secure a performance for his "Indian" opera *Poia,* but succeeded in making arrangements with the Berlin State Opera to produce it; it was staged on April 23, 1910, but only 4 performances were given; the composer attributed the failure to the hostile anti-American Berlin group; another opera, *A Daughter of the Forest,* was produced in Chicago, January 5, 1918; among his other works were 2 orch. suites, *Lorna Doone* and *Love Dreams;* some chamber music; and a number of piano pieces.
BIBLIOGRAPHY: E.E. Hipsher, *American Opera and Its Composers* (Philadelphia, 1934; pp. 334–43).

Nevin, Ethelbert Woodbridge, popular American composer; brother of **Arthur Finley Nevin;** b. Edgeworth, Pa., Nov. 25, 1862; d. New Haven, Conn., Feb. 17, 1901. After preliminary musical studies in America, he went to Germany, where he took lessons in singing and piano with Franz Böhme (1877–78); returning to the U.S., he studied piano with Benjamin J. Lang and harmony with Stephen A. Emery in Boston. In 1884 he went again to Germany to study piano with Karl Klindworth (1884–86); then lived in Berlin, Paris, and Florence, before finally settling in New Haven. He had a natural talent for melodious songs and piano pieces in a semi-Classical manner. His *Narcissus* for Piano became a perennial favorite with sentimental piano teachers; his songs *The Rosary* and *Mighty Lak' a Rose* achieved tremendous popularity in women's clubs. His pantomime *Lady Floriane's Dream* was produced in N.Y. in 1898.
BIBLIOGRAPHY: V. Thompson, *The Life of Ethelbert Nevin* (Boston, 1913); F. Rogers, "Some Memories of Ethelbert Nevin," *Musical Quarterly* (July 1917); J.T. Howard, *Ethelbert Nevin* (N.Y., 1935).

Nevin, Gordon Balch, American composer; b. Easton, Pa., May 19, 1892; d. New Wilmington, Pa., Nov. 15, 1943. He studied organ and theory in N.Y.; was organist at various churches in Pennsylvania; also in Cleveland; publ. numerous songs (*In Memoriam, Song of Sorrow, Moonlight Serenade,* etc.); contributed to music magazines.

Neway, Patricia, American soprano; b. Brooklyn, Sept. 30, 1919. She studied at the Mannes College of Music in N.Y. After several appearances in minor roles, she achieved her first significant success as Magda in Menotti's opera *The Consul* (Philadelphia, March 1, 1950); appeared in another Menotti opera, *Maria Golovin,* at the Brussels World's Fair on Aug. 20, 1958. Her repertoire includes parts in operas by Alban Berg, Benjamin Britten, and Menotti.

Newcomb, Ethel, American pianist; b. Whitney Point, N.Y., Oct. 30, 1875; d. there, July 3, 1959. She went to Vienna in 1895, and studied with Leschetizky until 1903; served as his assistant from 1904 to 1908; made her debut on Feb. 28, 1903, with the Vienna Symph.; returning to America, she appeared in recitals; then settled at her home in Whitney Point.

Newlin, Dika, American writer on music and composer; b. Portland, Oreg., Nov. 22, 1923. She studied piano and theory at Michigan State Univ., East Lansing (B.A., 1939) and at the Univ. of Calif., Los Angeles (M.A., 1941); later took courses at Columbia Univ. in N.Y. (Ph.D., 1945); in the interim she attended the classes of Schoenberg in Los Angeles, acquiring a thorough knowledge of the method of composition with 12 tones; also had some sessions with Sessions, and took additional instruction in piano playing with Serkin and Schnabel. She taught at Western Maryland College (1945–49); at Syracuse Univ. (1949–51); at Drew Univ. in Madison, N.J. (1952–65); and at North Texas State Univ. in Denton (1965–75). In 1977 she joined the faculty of The New School for Social Research in N.Y. She publ. a valuable study on comparative musical styles, *Bruckner-Mahler-Schoenberg* (Diss., Columbia Univ., 1945; publ. in N.Y., 1947; totally revised ed., N.Y., 1978); she trans. into Eng. Leibowitz's *Schoenberg et son école* (N.Y., 1949), Schoenberg's *Style and Idea* (N.Y., 1951), and Rufer's *Das Werk A. Schönbergs* (London, 1962). Her compositions follow the Schoenbergian idiom; she wrote a *Sinfonia* for Piano (1947); Piano Trio (1948); Chamber Symph. (1949); *Fantasy on a Row* for Piano (1958); *Study in 12 Tones* for Viola d'Amore and Piano (1959); *Atone* for Chamber Ensemble (1976); *Second-Hand Rows* for Voice and Piano (1977–78).

Newman, Alfred, American film composer; b. New Haven, Conn., March 17, 1900; d. Hollywood, Feb. 17, 1970. He studied piano with Sigismund Stojowski and composition with Rubin Goldmark; also had private lessons with Schoenberg in Los Angeles. He began his career in vaudeville shows billed as "The Marvelous Boy Pianist"; later, when he led theater orchs. on Broadway, he was hailed as "The Boy Conductor" and "The Youngest Conductor in the U.S." In 1930 he went to Hollywood and devoted himself entirely to writing film music; he wrote about 230 film scores; 45 of this number were nominated for awards of the Motion Picture Academy,

and 9 were winners. However, only his musical scores for *The Song of Bernadette* and *Love Is a Many-Splendored Thing* were complete scores; the rest were merely incidental to the action on the screen. Among his most successful scores were *All about Eve, The Egyptian* (partly written by the original assignee, Bernard Herrman), *The Prisoner of Zenda* (1937), *Wuthering Heights* (1939), *Captain from Castille* (1947), and *The Robe* (1953). Stylistically he followed an eclectic type of theatrical Romanticism, often mimicking, almost literally, the most popular works of Tchaikovsky, Rachmaninoff, Wagner, and Liszt, and amalgamating these elements in colorful free fantasia; in doing so, he created a category of composition that was to become known, with some disdain, as "movie music."

BIBLIOGRAPHY: Frederick Steiner, *The Making of an American Film Composer: A Study of Alfred Newman's Music in the First Decade of the Sound Era* (Diss., Univ. of Southern Calif., 1981).

Newman, Anthony, American harpsichordist, pianist, organist, conductor, and composer; b. Los Angeles, May 12, 1941. He studied piano and organ; in 1959 went to Paris, where he took courses at the Ecole Normale de Musique with Pierre Cochereau and Nadia Boulanger; returning to the U.S., he studied organ at the Mannes College of Music in N.Y. (B.S., 1962) and composition with Leon Kirchner and Luciano Berio at Harvard Univ. (M.A., 1963); received his D.M.A. from Boston Univ. in 1966. He made his professional debut at Carnegie Hall in 1967, in a recital featuring the pedal harpsichord; subsequently toured widely as a harpsichordist, organist, pianist, and fortepianist. He served on the faculty of the Juilliard School of Music in N.Y. (1968–73), at the State Univ. of N.Y. at Purchase (1968–75), and at the Indiana Univ. School of Music in Bloomington (1978–81); also gave master classes. His own compositions are in a neo-Baroque style.

WORKS: For Orch.: Orch. Cycle I (1975); Violin Concerto, composed for the 50th anniversary of the Indianapolis Symph. Orch. (Indianapolis, Oct. 26, 1979; Hidetaro Suzuki, soloist; John Nelson, conductor). Chamber music: Violin Sonata (1976); Cello Sonata (1977); Sonata for Double Bass and Piano (1981); Piano Trio (1980); Piano Quintet (1981). For Piano: Piano Cycle I (1976). For Organ: *Bhajeb* (1970); *Symphony in the French Manner* (1979); *Prelude and Contrapunctus* (1981). For Guitar: *Variations and Grand Contrapunctus* (1979); Suite for Guitar (1982).

BIBLIOGRAPHY: J. Braider, "Anthony Newman: Renaissance Man of the Classical Keyboard," *Contemporary Keyboard* (Dec. 1980).

Newman, Ernest, renowned English music critic; b. Liverpool, Nov. 30, 1868; d. Tadworth, Surrey, July 7, 1959. His real name was **William Roberts;** he assumed his *nom de plume* to symbolize an "earnest new man." He prepared himself for the Indian Civil Service, but entered business in Liverpool, pursuing his musical studies as a favorite avocation. In 1904 he accepted an instructorship in the Midland Inst.,

Birmingham, and took up music as a profession; in 1905, he was in Manchester as critic of the *Guardian;* in 1906–18, in Birmingham as critic for the *Daily Post;* in 1919–20, in London as critic for the *Observer;* from March 1920 to 1958, was on the staff of the *London Sunday Times;* from 1923, was also a contributor to the *Glasgow Herald;* in 1924–25, was guest critic of the *N.Y. Evening Post.* One of the best equipped and most influential of the English music critics, he continued to write his regular column in the *Sunday Times* in his 90th year.

WRITINGS: *Gluck and the Opera* (1895); *A Study of Wagner* (1899); *Wagner* (1904); *Musical Studies* (1905; 3rd ed., 1914); *Elgar* (1906); *Hugo Wolf* (1907; German trans., 1910); *Richard Strauss* (1908); *Wagner as Man and Artist* (1914; 2nd ed., 1924); *A Musical Motley* (1919); *The Piano-Player and Its Music* (1920); *A Musical Critic's Holiday* (1925); *The Unconscious Beethoven* (1927); *What to Read on the Evolution of Music* (1928); *Stories of the Great Operas* (3 vols., 1929–31); *Fact and Fiction about Wagner* (1931); *The Man Liszt* (1934); *The Life of Richard Wagner* in 4 vols. (1933; 1937; 1941; 1946); *Opera Nights* (1943; U.S. ed. as *More Stories of Famous Operas*); *Wagner Nights* (1949; U.S. ed. as *The Wagner Operas*); *More Opera Nights* (1955; U.S. ed. as *17 Famous Operas*); *From the World of Music: Essays from "The Sunday Times"* (selected by F. Aprahamian; London, 1956); *More Musical Essays* (2nd selection from the *Sunday Times,* London, 1958). Newman trans. Felix Weingartner's book *Über das Dirigieren* (Leipzig, 2nd ed., 1925), Schweitzer's *J.S. Bach* (Leipzig, 1911), and Rolland's *Beethoven the Creator* (London, 1929; N.Y., 1937); for Breitkopf & Härtel's ed. of Wagner's works he wrote entirely new and remarkably fine translations. He edited *Fifty Songs of Hugo Wolf* (with critical introduction); was editor of *The New Library of Music* (historical and bibliographical monographs); was editor of a new revised edition (in Eng.) of Berlioz's *Memoirs* (1932); a collection of his essays was publ. under the title *Testament of Music* (London, 1962); he was a contributor to numerous Eng. and American journals.

BIBLIOGRAPHY: H. van Thal, ed., *Fanfare for Ernest Newman* (London, 1955); Vera Newman, *Ernest Newman: A Memoir by His Wife* (London, 1963).

Newman, Randy, American societal country-music songwriter; b. New Orleans, Nov. 28, 1943. He spent his childhood in southern California, where he took regular music lessons. His songs often veered toward the unacceptable, unthinkable, and inconceivable, as while ostensibly attacking the rednecks he used the word "nigger." In 1977 he produced the album *Little Criminals,* which assailed the bigots, but in which one number, *Short People,* was misconstrued as an attack on people short of stature and picayune in mind. As a result, his songs were dropped at some radio stations. He recouped with the song *Born Again* in 1979. In 1981 he proved his ability by supplying a fine sound track to the film *Ragtime.*

Newman, William S., distinguished American music scholar; b. Cleveland, April 6, 1912. He studied piano with Riemenschneider and Arthur Loesser; composition with Elwell and Shepherd, in Cleveland; received his Ph.D. at Western Reserve Univ. in 1939 with the dissertation *The Present Trend of the Sonata Idea;* then took courses in musicology with Paul Henry Lang at Columbia Univ. in 1940; during World War II served in the U.S. Army Air Force Intelligence. In 1945 he joined the staff of the Univ. of North Carolina at Chapel Hill; became prof. emeritus, 1976. He focused most of his research on the evolution of the instrumental sonata. His chief project was *A History of the Sonata Idea* in 3 vols.: *The Sonata in the Baroque Era* (Chapel Hill, 1959; 2nd ed., revised, 1966); *The Sonata in the Classic Era* (Chapel Hill, 1963; 2nd ed., revised, 1972); *The Sonata since Beethoven* (Chapel Hill, 1969; 2nd ed., revised, 1972). His other publications include 3 critical editions of works in sonata forms *(13 Keyboard Sonatas of the 18th and 19th Centuries; 6 Keyboard Sonatas from the Classic Era; 3 Keyboard Sonatas by the Sons of Bach);* he further contributed articles on the sonata to the *Enciclopedia della musica, Die Musik in Geschichte und Gegenwart,* and *Grove's Dictionary of Music and Musicians.* He publ. *Performance Practices in Beethoven's Piano Sonatas* (N.Y., 1971), and contributed numerous articles to American and European music magazines on various aspects of Classical sonata form. He began his musical career as a pianist, appearing in solo recitals and also with orchs. (until 1970); publ. a useful manual, *The Pianist's Problems* (N.Y., 1950; 4th ed., 1984). He composed an operetta, *Freddy and His Fiddle* (1936); *An American Tragedy,* concert overture (1941); several pieces for band; and some chamber music.

Newmarch, Rosa Harriet (née **Jeaffreson**), English writer on musical subjects; b. Leamington, Dec. 18, 1857; d. Worthing, April 9, 1940. Growing up in an artistic atmosphere, she entered the Hetherley School of Art to study painting, but after a time abandoned that career for literary pursuits; settled in London in 1880 as a contributor to various journals. There she married Henry Charles Newmarch, in 1883. She visited Russia in 1897 and many times afterward; established contact with the foremost musicians there; her enthusiasm for Russian music, particularly that of the Russian national school of composition, was unlimited, and she publ. several books on the subject which were of importance to the appreciation of Russian music in England, though her high-pitched literary manner was sometimes maintained to the detriment of factual material.

WRITINGS: *Tchaikovsky* (1900); *Songs to a Singer* (1906); *Poetry and Progress in Russia* (1907); *The Russian Opera* (1914; in French, 1922); *The Russian Arts* (1916); *The Devout Russian* (1919); *The Concert-Goer's Library* (collection of program notes, 6 vols., London, 1928–48); she trans. *The Life and Letters of Tchaikovsky* (1908; abridged from Modest Tchaikovsky's biography).

Newmark, John, Canadian pianist; b. Bremen, Germany, June 12, 1904. He studied in Leipzig; made a career as an accompanist; traveled all over the world with celebrated singers, violinists, and cellists, among them Kathleen Ferrier, Elisabeth Schumann, Richard Tucker, George London, Szymon Goldberg, and Maurice Eisenberg. He settled in Montreal.

Newsom, Hugh Raymond, American concert manager and composer; b. Cawnpore, India, Dec. 20, 1891; d. Baltimore, May 19, 1978. He was brought to America as an infant, and studied music at the Oberlin Cons. in Ohio; later had some lessons with George Chadwick at the New England Cons. in Boston. He became a successful concert manager; in 1937 married the harpist **Marjorie Brunton.** In the meantime, he composed industriously; wrote an oratorio-drama, *The Divine Tragedy;* several other oratorios; and a number of character pieces for piano and song cycles; also wrote a Harp Concerto, which was first performed by his wife in N.Y. on Nov. 6, 1968. His style of composition is disarmingly euphonious in an attractive lyric vein.

Newton, Ivor, English pianist; b. London, Dec. 15, 1892; d. there, April 21, 1981. He studied piano with Arthur Barclay; then went to Berlin, where he studied lieder with Zur Mühlen and the art of accompaniment with Conrad van Bos. An earnest student of the history of song and the proper role of accompaniment, he became one of the most appreciated piano accompanists of the time, playing at recitals with celebrated singers and instrumentalists, among them Dame Nellie Melba, John McCormack, Chaliapin, Kirsten Flagstad, Pablo Casals, Yehudi Menuhin, and Maria Callas. His career, which spanned more than 60 years, is chronicled in his interesting autobiography, *At the Piano —Ivor Newton* (London, 1966). In 1973 he was made a Commander of the Order of the British Empire.

Newton, Wayne, American singer of popular music; b. Roanoke, Va., April 3, 1942. He began his career on television as a pop singer; was then propelled to commercial greatness at the neon-lighted casinos of Las Vegas and other artistically repugnant but monetarily attractive haunts; he also shrewdly invested his lucre in real-estate ventures; his recordings sold into the millions. An additional plus was his loud proclamation of the American virtues of legitimate motherhood, honest capitalism, and right-wing Republicanism.

Newton-John, Olivia, English country-music singer; b. Cambridge, Sept. 26, 1948. She was taken to Australia as a child; returning to England at the age of 16, she began making appearances as a folksinger; eventually turned to country music. She made her first tour of America in 1974, becoming a part of the "Nashville scene." Among her greatest hits were *Have You Never Been Mellow* and *I Honestly Love You;* she also appeared in the highly successful, if tawdry, film *Grease* (1978).

Ney, Elly, German pianist; b. Düsseldorf, Sept. 27, 1882; d. Tutzing, March 31, 1968. She was a piano student of Leschetizky and Sauer in Vienna; made her debut in Vienna in 1905; gave successful recitals in Europe and America; then devoted herself mainly to teaching; lived mostly in Munich. She was married to Willem van Hoogstraten (1911–27); in 1928 she married P.F. Allais of Chicago. She publ. an autobiography, *Ein Leben für die Musik* (Darmstadt, 1952; 2nd ed. as *Erinnerungen und Betrachtungen; Mein Leben aus der Musik,* 1957).

BIBLIOGRAPHY: C. von Pidoll, *Elly Ney* (Leipzig, 1942); Zenta Maurina, *Begegnung mit Elly Ney* (Memmingen, 1956); E. Valentin, *Elly Ney, Symbol einer Generation* (Munich, 1962).

Nezhdanova, Antonina, Russian soprano; b. Krivaya Balka, near Odessa, June 16, 1873; d. Moscow, June 26, 1950. She studied at the Moscow Cons.; in 1902 joined the staff of the Bolshoi Theater. She was equally successful as a lyric, dramatic, and coloratura soprano; her range extended to high G. In 1912 she made an appearance as Gilda in *Rigoletto* at the Grand Opéra in Paris. Her best roles were Tatiana in *Eugene Onegin,* Marguerite in *Faust,* and Elsa in *Lohengrin.* In 1943 she became a prof. of voice at the Moscow Cons.

BIBLIOGRAPHY: G. Polyanovsky, *A. Nezhdanova* (Moscow, 1970).

Nibelle, Adolphe-André, French composer of operettas; b. Gien, Loiret, Oct. 9, 1825; d. Paris, March 11, 1895. His numerous light operas had considerable vogue in Paris. Among the most successful were *Le Loup-Garou* (1858), *Les Filles du lac* (1858), *L'Arche-Marion* (1868), *La Fontaine de Berny* (1869), *Le 15 août* (1869), *Les Quatre Cents Femmes d'Ali-Baba* (1872), and *L'Alibi* (1873); he also publ. *Heures musicales* (24 songs).

Nicholl, Horace Wadham, English organist and composer; b. Tipton, near Birmingham, March 17, 1848; d. New York, March 10, 1922. He studied music with his father and with the local organist, Samuel Prince; then served as church organist in the vicinity; in 1871 received an offer to go to Pittsburgh as organist at St. Paul's Cathedral; in 1878 he went to N.Y., where he was engaged as a teacher. He wrote several biblical oratorios, 2 symphs., and *Hamlet,* a "psychic sketch" for Orch.; also numerous piano pieces.

Nicholl, Joseph Weston, English composer; b. Halifax, Yorkshire, May 7, 1875; d. there, May 1925. He studied in Berlin, Munich, and Paris; returning to England, he led the Yorkshire Military Band. He wrote the symph. poem *In English Seas* and a number of pieces for band.

Nicholls, Agnes, English soprano; b. Cheltenham, July 14, 1877; d. London, Sept. 21, 1959. She studied singing with Visetti at the Royal College of Music in London; made her operatic debut in Manchester on

Nov. 20, 1895, as Dido in a revival of Purcell's opera; on May 14, 1901, she sang the role of the Dewman in *Hänsel und Gretel* at Covent Garden, London. On July 15, 1904, she married the conductor **Hamilton Harty.** She was quite successful in Wagnerian roles; in 1908 she sang Sieglinde in *Die Walküre* at Covent Garden under the direction of Hans Richter.

Nichols, Ernest Loring ("Red"), American jazz cornetist and bandleader; b. Ogden, Utah, May 8, 1905; d. Las Vegas, June 28, 1965. His father taught him cornet, and he played in his father's brass band from the age of 12; began his professional career in 1920 playing with local bands; then led his own groups. One of his bands, The Five Pennies, provided the title for a 1959 film concerning his career.

Nichols, "Red" (Ernest Loring Nichols), American jazz cornetist and bandleader; b. Ogden, Utah, May 8, 1905; d. Las Vegas, June 28, 1965. His father taught him cornet, and he played in his father's brass band from the age of 12. He then cut a swath in the world of popular music with his own band, advertised as "Red Nichols and His Five Pennies" (actually, the number of "Pennies" was 10); among its members were such future celebrities as Jimmy Dorsey, Benny Goodman, and Glenn Miller. A maudlin motion picture, *The Five Pennies,* was manufactured in 1959, and catapulted "Red" Nichols into the stratosphere of jazzdom. Heuristic exegetes of European hermeneutics bemoaned the commercialization of his style, giving preference to his earlier, immaculate, jazzification.

BIBLIOGRAPHY: G. Johnson, *The 5 Pennies: The Biography of Jazz Band Leader Red Nichols* (N.Y., 1959).

Nicodé, Jean-Louis, German pianist and composer; b. Jerczik, near Posen, Aug. 12, 1853; d. Langebrück, near Dresden, Oct. 5, 1919. He was taught by his father and by the organist Hartkäs; in 1869 entered Kullak's Academy in Berlin, where he studied piano with Kullak, harmony with Wüerst, and counterpoint and composition with Kiel. He made a concert tour (1878) with Mme. Artôt through Galicia and Rumania; in 1878–85, was a piano teacher at the Dresden Cons.; till 1888, was conductor of the Phil. Concerts; established the Nicodé Concerts in 1893, and, in order to enlarge their scope by the production of larger choral works, formed the Nicodé Chorus in 1896. In 1900 he abandoned these concerts, retired to Langebrück, and devoted himself to composition. He wrote a Symph.; symph. poems; 2 sonatas for Cello and Piano; many piano pieces; songs.

BIBLIOGRAPHY: Th. Schäfer, *Jean-Louis Nicodé. Ein Versuch kritischer Würdigung und Erläuterung seines Schaffens* (Berlin, 1907); O. Taubmann, "Jean-Louis Nicodé," *Monographien moderner Musiker,* III (Leipzig, 1909).

Nicolai, (Carl) Otto (Ehrenfried), famous German opera composer and conductor; b. Königsberg, June 9, 1810; d. Berlin, May 11, 1849. He studied piano at home; in 1827 he went to Berlin, where he took lessons in theory with Zelter; he also took courses with Bernhard Klein at the Royal Inst. for Church Music. On April 13, 1833, he made a concert debut in Berlin as a pianist, singer, and composer. He then was engaged as organist to the embassy chapel in Rome by the Prussian ambassador, Bunsen. While in Italy he also studied counterpoint with Giuseppe Baini. In 1837 he proceeded to Vienna, where he became a singing teacher and Kapellmeister at the Kärnthnertortheater. In Oct. 1838 he returned to Italy; on Nov. 26, 1839, he presented in Trieste his first opera, *Rosmonda d'Inghilterra,* given under its new title as *Enrico II.* His 2nd opera, *Il Templario,* was staged in Turin on Feb. 11, 1840. In 1841 he moved to Vienna, where he was appointed court Kapellmeister in succession to Kreutzer. There Nicolai was instrumental in establishing symph. concerts utilizing the musicians of the orch. of the Imperial Court Opera Theater; on March 28, 1842, he conducted this ensemble featuring Beethoven's 7th Symph.; this became the inaugural concert of the celebrated Vienna Phil. Orch. In 1848 he was appointed Kapellmeister of the Royal Opera in Berlin. On March 9, 1849, his famous opera *Die lustigen Weiber von Windsor,* after Shakespeare, was given at the Berlin Royal Opera; it was to become his only enduring creation. Nicolai died suddenly 2 months after its production. In 1887 Hans Richter, then conductor of the Vienna Phil., inaugurated an annual "Nicolai-Konzert" in his memory, and it became a standard occasion. It was conducted by Gustav Mahler in 1899–1901; by Felix Weingartner in 1909–27; by Wilhelm Furtwängler in 1928–31, 1933–44, and 1948–54; by Karl Böhm in 1955–57 and 1964–80; and by Claudio Abbado in 1980 and 1983.

WORKS: OPERAS: *Enrico II* (original title, *Rosmonda d'Inghilterra;* Trieste, Nov. 26, 1839); *Il Templario* (Turin, Feb. 11, 1840; revised as *Der Tempelritter,* Vienna, Dec. 20, 1845); *Gildippe ed Odoardo* (Genoa, Dec. 26, 1840); *Il proscritto* (Milan, March 13, 1841; revised as *Die Heimkehr des Verbannten,* Vienna, Feb. 3, 1846); *Die lustigen Weiber von Windsor* (Berlin, March 9, 1849). SACRED MUSIC: *Pater noster* for 8 Voices, op. 33; *In assumptione Beatae Mariae Virginis,* offertory for 5 Voices, op. 38; *Salve regina* for Soprano and Orch., op. 39; *Te Deum* for Solo Voices, 4 Voices, and Orch.; Mass in D major for 4 Solo Voices, 4 Voices, and Orch.; Psalms, motets, etc. SECULAR CHORAL MUSIC: *Preussens Stimme* for 4 Voices and Orch., op. 4; 6 lieder for 4 Voices, op. 6; *Verschiedene Empfindungen an einem Platz* for Soprano, 2 Tenors, Bass, and Piano, op. 9; 3 *Königslieder der älteren Berliner Liedertafel* for 4 Male Voices, op. 10; *Gesänge* for 4 Male Voices, op. 17; etc. FOR ORCH.: *In morte di Vincenzo Bellini,* a funeral march; symphs.: No. 1, in C minor (1831), and No. 2, in D major (1835; revised 1845); *Kirchliche Festouvertüre über . . . Ein feste Burg* for 4 Voices, Organ, and Orch., op. 32 (1844); *Weihnachtsouvertüre über Vom Himmel hoch* for 4 Voices ad libitum and Orch.; chamber music; solo songs.

BIBLIOGRAPHY: H. Mendel, *Otto Nicolai: Eine Biographie* (Berlin, 1866; 2nd ed., 1868); B. Schröder, ed., *Otto Nicolai: Tagebücher nebst biographischen Ergänzungen* (Leipzig, 1892); "Otto Nicolais Briefe aus den Jahren 1832–48," *Deutsche Rundschau* (Jan. 1897); G. Kruse, "Falstaff und Die lustigen Weiber," *Die Musik*, VI/4 (1906–7); idem, "Otto Nicolai als Sinfoniker," *Allgemeine Musik-Zeitung*, XXXV (1908); idem, "Goethe, Zelter und Otto Nicolai," *Goethe-Jahrbuch*, XXXI (1910); idem, "Otto Nicolais italienische Opern," *Sammelbände der Internationalen Musik-Gesellschaft*, XII/2 (1910–11); idem, *Otto Nicolai: Ein Künstlerleben* (Berlin, 1911); idem, *Otto Nicolais musikalische Aufsätze* (Regensburg, 1913); W. Altmann, ed., *Otto Nicolai: Briefe an seinen Vater* (Regensburg, 1924); G. Kruse, "Otto Nicolais 'Lustigen Weiber' ... mit unbekannt gebliebenen Nummern," *Die Musik*, XXVIII (1936); W. Altmann, ed., *Otto Nicolais Tagebücher* (Regensburg, 1937); E. Schliepe, "Das wiederentdeckte 'Tedeum' von Otto Nicolai," *Die Musik*, XXXI (1939); W. Jerger, ed., *Otto Nicolai: Briefe an die Wiener Philharmoniker* (Vienna, 1942); H. Kraus and K. Schreinzer, eds., *Wiener Philharmoniker 1842–1942* (Vienna, 1942); A. Würz, "Otto Nicolai: Eine Betrachtung zu seinem Gedenken," *Neue Musikzeitschrift* (April 1949); J. Klein, "Verdi and Nicolai: A Strange Rivalry," *Music Review*, XXXII (1971).

Nicolau, Antonio, Catalan composer and conductor; b. Barcelona, June 8, 1858; d. there, Feb. 26, 1933. He studied in Barcelona with Balart and Pujol; also in Paris, where he lived for 8 years; then became conductor of the Sociedad de Conciertos de Barcelona, with which he gave many important first performances in Spain; was director of the Barcelona Municipal Music School from 1896 and teacher of many of the leading Catalan musicians, including Lamote de Grignon.
WORKS: Operas: *El rapto* (Madrid, 1887) and *Constanza* (Barcelona); dramatic scene, *La tempestad* (Barcelona); symph. poems: *El triunfo de Venus* (Paris, 1882) and *Spes;* choral works: *Captant* (1904), *La mort del Escolà, Entre flors, La mare de deu;* songs.
BIBLIOGRAPHY: R. Mitjana, *Para música vamos!* (Valencia, 1909).

Nicolet, Aurèle, Swiss flutist; b. Neuchâtel, Jan. 22, 1926. He was educated in Zürich and Paris; then played flute in Swiss orchs.; later joined the Berlin Phil. (1950–59). He was a prof. at the Berlin Hochschule für Musik (1953–65); then taught at the Hochschule für Musik in Freiburg; also gave summer classes at the Salzburg Mozarteum. Apart from his activities as a pedagogue, he developed a wide international career giving worldwide flute recitals which took him to the U.S., Israel, and Japan.

Nicolini, stage name of **Ernest Nicolas,** French dramatic tenor; b. Saint-Malo, Feb. 23, 1834; d. Pau, Jan. 19, 1898. He studied at the Paris Cons.; made his debut in July 1857, in Halévy's *Mousquetaires de la Reine,* at the Opéra-Comique, where he was engaged till 1859; then went to Italy, and sang as "Nicolini" with moderate success. In 1862–70 he sang at the Salle Ventadour in Paris; in 1866 he visited London, where he made his debut at Covent Garden on May 29, 1866. In 1871 he sang opera at Drury Lane; from 1872 to 1884, at Covent Garden. After touring with **Adelina Patti,** he married her, on Aug. 10, 1886.

Niculescu, Stefan, Rumanian composer and musicologist; b. Moreni (Ploesti), July 31, 1927. He studied at the Bucharest Cons. with Mihail Jora, Ion Dumitrescu, Tudor Ciortea, Theodor Rogalski, and others; attended the summer courses on advanced music in Darmstadt; also worked in an electronic studio in Munich (1966); from 1963 was on the staff of the Bucharest Cons. In his music he follows the median course of serialism, without excluding tonality.
WORKS: Children's opera, *Le Livre avec Apolodore* (1975); Clarinet Sonata (1954–55); Symph. No. 1 (1955–56); String Trio No. 1 (1957); *Inventions* for Clarinet and Piano (1964); *Inventions* for Viola and Piano (1965); *Hétéromorphie* for Orch. (1967; Bucharest, April 12, 1968); *Formants* for 17 String Soloists (1968); *Tastenspiel* for Piano (1968); *Aphorisms by Heraclitus* for a cappella Chorus (1968–69); Wind Sextet (1970); *Unisonos I* for Orch. (Mainz, Germany, Sept. 26, 1970; a revised version, *Unisonos II,* 1971–72, first perf. at the Graz Festival, Oct. 17, 1972); *Triplum I* for Flute, Cello, and Piano (1971); *Ison I,* variations for 14 Instrumental Soloists (1971); *Triplum II* for Clarinet, Cello, and Piano (1972); *Ison II,* concerto for Winds and Percussion (1975); opera, *Cartea cu "Apolodor"* (Cluj, April 13, 1975); String Trio No. 2 (1976); Symph. No. 2 (1979–80); *Omaggio a Enescu e Bartók* for Chamber Orch. (1982); *Le Prince né des larmes,* ballet (1982). He publ. a monograph on Georges Enesco (Bucharest, 1971) and several analytic articles on the music of Webern, Xenakis, Boulez, Ligeti, and Cage.

Niecks, Friedrich (Frederick), German pedagogue and writer on music; b. Düsseldorf, Feb. 3, 1845; d. Edinburgh, June 24, 1924. He studied the violin under Langhans, Grünewald, and Auer, and piano and composition with J. Tausch; made his debut (as a violinist) at Düsseldorf in 1857; until 1867 he was a member of the orch. there, the last years as concertmaster; in 1868, became organist at Dumfries, Scotland, and viola player in a quartet with A.C. Mackenzie. After 2 terms at Leipzig Univ. (1877) and travels in Italy, he won a position in London as critic for the *Monthly Musical Record* and *Musical Times;* in 1891, was appointed Reid Prof. of Music at Edinburgh Univ. In 1901 Niecks founded the Music Education Society. He was made a Mus.Doc. (*honoris causa*) by Dublin Univ. in 1898; LL.D. by Edinburgh Univ. After his retirement in 1914 he lived in Edinburgh.
WRITINGS: *A Concise Dictionary of Musical Terms* (2nd ed., 1884; 5th ed., revised and enlarged, 1900); *Frédéric Chopin as a Man and Musician* (1888; 3rd ed., 1902; German ed., 1890); *Programme Music in the Last Four Centuries* (1907); *R. Schu-*

mann (posthumous, 1925).

Niedermeyer, Louis, Swiss composer; b. Nyon, April 27, 1802; d. Paris, March 14, 1861. He was a pupil in Vienna of Moscheles (piano) and Förster (composition); in 1819, of Fioravanti in Rome and Zingarelli in Naples. He lived in Geneva as an admired song composer, and settled in Paris in 1823; there he brought out 4 unsuccessful operas (*La casa nel bosco,* May 28, 1828; *Stradella,* March 3, 1837; *Marie Stuart,* Dec. 6, 1844; *La Fronde,* May 2, 1853). He then bent his energies to sacred composition, and reorganized Choron's Inst. for Church Music as the Ecole Niedermeyer, which eventually became a flourishing inst. with government subvention; he also founded (with d'Ortigue) a journal for church music, *La Maîtrise;* and publ. with him *Méthode d'accompagnement du plain-chant* (1856; 2nd ed., 1876; Eng. trans. by W. Goodrich, N.Y., 1905). Niedermeyer's masses, motets, hymns, etc. were well received; his romances (*Le Lac; Le Soir; La Mer; L'Automne;* etc.) are widely known; he also publ. organ preludes, piano pieces, etc.
   BIBLIOGRAPHY: A. Niedermeyer, *Louis Niedermeyer, Son œuvre et son école* (Paris, n.d.); Anon., *Vie d'un compositeur moderne* (by Niedermeyer's son; Fontainebleau, 1892; reprinted in Paris, 1893, with preface by Saint-Saëns); M. Galerne, *L'Ecole Niedermeyer* (Paris, 1928)

Nielsen, Alice, American soprano; b. Nashville, Tenn., June 7, 1876; d. New York, March 8, 1943. She was of partly Danish, partly Irish extraction; sang in a church choir in Kansas City; then joined the Burton Stanley Opera Co., where she sang in operettas; she made her debut as a grand-opera singer in Naples as Marguerite in *Faust* (Dec. 6, 1903); made her first American appearance in N.Y. (Nov. 10, 1905). In 1908 she toured with the San Carlo Co. in the U.S.; then achieved the status of a prima donna with the Boston Opera Co. (1909–13) and also sang with the Metropolitan Opera. She eventually settled in N.Y. as a singing teacher.

Nielsen, Carl (August), greatly significant Danish composer; initiator of the modern Danish school of composition; b. Nørre-Lyndelse, near Odense, on the island of Fyn (Funen), June 9, 1865; d. Copenhagen, Oct. 3, 1931. As a boy, he received violin lessons from his father; then played 2nd violin in his village orch. and took trumpet lessons; at the age of 14 became a trumpeter in the Odense military band. While in Odense he made his first efforts at composing, producing a few chamber pieces; a string quartet he wrote qualified him for admission to the Royal Cons. in Copenhagen, where he studied composition with O. Rosenhoff, violin with V. Tofte, and music history with Gade (1884–86). He played violin in the Royal Chapel Orch. in Copenhagen (1889–1905); later conducted at the Royal Opera in Copenhagen (1908–14) and led the Musikföreningen (Music Society) in Copenhagen (1915–27); also conducted concerts in Germany, the Netherlands, Sweden, and Finland; a few months before his death he was appointed director of the Royal Cons. in Copenhagen. The early style of his music, Romantic in essence, was determined by the combined influences of Gade, Grieg, Brahms, and Liszt, but later on he experienced the powerful impact of modern music, particularly in harmony, which in his works grew more and more chromatic and dissonant; yet he reserved the simple diatonic progressions, often in a folk-song manner, for his major climaxes; in his orchestration he applied opulent sonorities and colorful instrumental counterpoint; there are instances of bold experimentation in some of his works, as, for example, the insertion of a snare-drum solo in his 5th Symph., playing independently of the rest of the orch.; he attached somewhat mysterious titles to his 3rd and 4th symphs. (*Expansive* and *Inextinguishable*). Nielsen is sometimes described as the Sibelius of Denmark, despite obvious dissimilarities in idiom and sources of inspiration; while the music of Sibelius is deeply rooted in national folklore, both in subject matter and melodic derivation, Nielsen seldom drew on Danish popular modalities; Sibelius remained true to the traditional style of composition, while Nielsen sought new ways of modern expression. It was only after his death that Nielsen's major works entered the world repertoire; festivals of his music were organized on his centennial in 1965, and his symphs. in particular were played and recorded in England and America, so that Nielsen finally emerged as one of the most important composers of his time.
   WORKS: (all premieres in Copenhagen, except where otherwise noted): FOR THE STAGE: 2 operas: *Saul og David,* after E. Christiansen (*Saul and David,* 1898–1901; Nov. 28, 1902) and *Maskarade,* after V. Andersen (1904–6; Nov. 11, 1906); incidental music to 14 plays, including *Aladdin* (1918–19; Feb. 15, 1919) and *Moderen* (*The Mother,* 1920; Jan. 30, 1921). FOR ORCH.: 6 symphs.: No. 1 (1891–92; March 14, 1894); No. 2, *De fire temperamenter* (*The 4 Temperaments,* 1901–2; Dec. 1, 1902); No. 3, *Sinfonia espansiva* (1910–11; Feb. 28, 1912); No. 4, *Det uudslukkelige* (*The Inextinguishable,* 1915–16; Feb. 1, 1916); No. 5 (1921–22; Jan. 24, 1922); No. 6, *Sinfonia semplice* (1924–25; Dec. 11, 1925); *Little Suite* for Strings (1888; Sept. 8, 1888); *Symphonic Rhapsody* (1888; Feb. 24, 1893; lost); *Helios,* overture (1903; Oct. 8, 1903); *Saga-Drøm* (*Dream of Saga,* 1908; April 6, 1908); *Ved en ung kunstners baare* (*At the Bier of a Young Artist); Andante lamentoso* for String Orch. (1910); Violin Concerto (1911; Feb. 28, 1912); paraphrase on *"Naermere Gud til dig"* (*"Nearer My God to Thee"*) for Wind Orch. (1912; Aug. 22, 1915); *Pan og Syrinx,* pastorale (*Pan and Syrinx,* 1917–18; Feb. 11, 1918); Flute Concerto (1926; Paris, Oct. 21, 1926); *Rhapsodic Overture, En fantasirejse til Faerøerne* (*A Fantasy-Journey to the Faroe Islands,* 1927; Nov. 27, 1927); Clarinet Concerto (1928; Humlebaek, Sept. 14, 1928); *Bøhmisk-Dansk folketone* (*Bohemian and Danish Folktunes*), paraphrase for String Orch. (1928; Nov. 1, 1928). FOR VOICE: 10 cantatas for various ceremonial occasions; *Hymnus amoris* for Soprano, Tenor, Baritone, Bass, Chorus, and Orch. (1896–97; April 27, 1897); *Søvnen (Sleep)* for Chorus and Orch. (1903–4; March 21, 1905); *Fynsk foraar*

(Springtime in Funen), lyrical humoresque for Soprano, Tenor, Bass-baritone, Chorus, and Orch. (1921; Odense, July 8, 1922); *3 Motets* for Chorus a cappella (1929; April 11, 1930); numerous original songs to Danish words; harmonizations of Danish folk songs. CHAMBER MUSIC: String Quintet (1888); 4 string quartets: No. 1 (op. 13, 1888; revised 1897), No. 2 (op. 5, 1890), No. 3 (op. 14, 1898), and No. 4 (op. 44, 1906; originally titled *Piacevolezza,* op. 19); *2 Fantasias* for Oboe and Piano (1889); 2 violin sonatas (1895, 1912); *Serenata in Vano* for Clarinet, Bassoon, Horn, Cello, and Bassoon (1914); from incidental music to *Moderen: Faith and Hope Are Playing* for Flute and Viola, *The Fog Is Lifting* for Flute and Harp, and *The Children Are Playing* for Solo Flute (all 1920); Wind Quintet (1922; Oct. 9, 1922); *Prelude and Theme with Variations* for Solo Violin (1923); *Praeludio e Presto* for Solo Violin (1928); *Canto serioso* for Horn or Cello, and Piano (1928); *Allegretto* for 2 Recorders (1931). FOR PIANO: *5 Pieces* (1890); *Symphonic Suite* (1894); *6 Humoreske-Bagateller* (1894–97); *Festpraeludium* (1900); *Chaconne* (1916); *Theme with Variations* (1916); *Suite (Den Luciferiske)* (*Lucifer Suite,* 1919–20); *3 Pieces* (1928); *Klavermusik for smaa og store* (*Piano Music for Young and Old*), 24 short 5-tone pieces in all keys in 2 vols. (1930). FOR ORGAN: *29 Short Preludes* (1929); *2 Posthumous Preludes* (1929); *Commotio* (1930–31). Nielsen publ. the books *Levende musik* (Copenhagen, 1925; in Eng. as *Living Music,* London, 1953) and *Min Fynske barndom* (reminiscences of his childhood, Copenhagen, 1927; in Eng. under the title *My Childhood,* London, 1953).

BIBLIOGRAPHY: Hugo Seligmann, *Carl Nielsen* (Copenhagen, 1931); Knud Jeppesen, "Carl Nielsen: A Danish Composer," *Music Review* (1946); T. Meyer and F.S. Petersen, *Carl Nielsen* (2 vols.; Copenhagen, 1947–48); L. Dolleris, *Carl Nielsen* (Odense, 1949); H. Madsen, *Carl Nielsens Fyn* (Odense, 1950); R. Simpson, *Carl Nielsen, Symphonist, 1865–1931* (London, 1952; revised ed., 1979); idem, *Sibelius and Nielsen* (London, 1965); D. Fog (with T. Schousboe), *Carl Nielsen, Kompositioner; En bibliografi* (Copenhagen, 1965); A.M. Telmanyi, *Mit Barndomschjem* (Copenhagen, 1965); *Carl Nielsen: Centenary Essays* (London, 1966); *Carl Nielsen: Dagbøger og brevvesling med Anna Marie Carl Nielsen* (2 vols.; Copenhagen, 1983).

Nielsen, Ludolf, Danish violinist and composer; b. Nørre-Tvede, Jan. 29, 1876; d. Copenhagen, May 11, 1939. He was a pupil at the Copenhagen Cons. of V. Tofte (violin), A. Orth (piano), Bondesen (harmony), O. Malling, and J.P.E. Hartmann (composition); as winner of the Ancker stipend he traveled in 1907 in Germany, Austria, and Italy; then lived in Copenhagen as a teacher and composer.

WORKS: Operas: *Isabella* (Copenhagen, Oct. 8, 1915); *Uhret (The Clock); Lola* (Copenhagen, 1920); ballet, *Reisekameraden;* 3 symphs.; other orch. works; chamber music; choruses; songs; piano pieces; etc.

Nielsen, Riccardo, Italian composer; b. Bologna, March 3, 1908. He studied with Alfredo Casella and Carlo Gatti; began composing in the Italian Baroque manner but eventually made a decisive turn toward the 12-tone technique of composition. He occupied various administrative and teaching positions; from 1946 to 1950 was director of the Teatro Comunale in Bologna; in 1952 became director of the Liceo Frescobaldi in Ferrara, where he also taught composition.

WORKS: *Sinfonia concertante* for Piano and Orch. (1932); Violin Concerto (1933); *Sinfonia in G* (1934); *Divertimento* for Clarinet, Bassoon, Trumpet, Violin, Viola, and Cello (1934); Concerto for Orch. (1935); *Musica per archi* (1946); monodrama, *L'Incubo* (Venice, 1948); radio opera, *La via di Colombo* (1953); *Variations* for Orch. (1956); *Requiem nella miniera* (1957); *Invenzioni e sinfonie* for Soprano and Orch. (1959); *Varianti* for Orch. (1965); *6 + 5 fasce sonore* for Strings (1968); Piano Quartet (1961); *7 aforismi* for Clarinet and Piano (1958); Cello Sonata (1958); *Cadenza a due* for Cello and Piano (1967); Chamber Cantata for Voice, Women's Chorus, and Instruments (1969); *Ganymed* for Soprano, Clarinet, Cello, and Piano (1958); *4 poesie di Apollinaire* for Voice and Piano (1961). He publ. a theoretical work, *Le forme musicali* (Bologna, 1961).

Nielsen, Svend, Danish composer; b. Copenhagen, April 20, 1937. He studied music theory with Vagn Holmboe at the Copenhagen Cons., graduating in 1967; then continued to take lessons in advanced composition with Per Norgaard; in 1969 he became a music instructor at the Copenhagen Cons. Among his works are *Duetter* for Soprano, Contralto, Flute, Cello, Vibraphone, and Percussion (1964); *Prisma-suite* for Contralto, Flute, Viola, and Strings (1965); *Metamorfoser* for 23 Solo Strings (1968); *Nuages* for Orch. (1972); a chamber opera, *Bulen* (1968).

Nielsen, Tage, Danish composer; b. Frederiksborg, Jan. 16, 1929. He studied musicology at the Univ. of Copenhagen (1948–55); then was program director of Danish Radio (1957–63); in 1963 he was appointed rector at the Cons. of Aarhus.

WORKS: String Quartet (1947); Sonatina for 2 Bassoons (1948); Piano Sonata (1950); *Intermezzo gaio* for Orch. (1952); *4 Miniatures* for String Orch. (1963); *Bariolage* for Orch. (Aarhus, Feb. 7, 1966); *Variants* for Solo Flute (1966); *Il giardino magico* (Aarhus, March 24, 1969); *Elegy* for Guitar Solo (1975); organ pieces; songs; music for schools.

Niemann, Albert, German opera tenor; b. Erxleben, near Magdeburg, Jan. 15, 1831; d. Berlin, Jan. 13, 1917. He began his career as an actor and dramatist; then sang in a chorus in Dessau; made his debut there in 1849; had lessons with F. Schneider and the baritone Nusch; sang in Halle in 1852–54; then in Hannover; then went to Paris, where he studied with Duprez. In 1866 he was engaged at the Royal Court Opera in Berlin, and remained on the staff until 1888. Wagner thought highly of him and asked him to create the role of Tannhäuser in Paris

(March 13, 1861) and of Siegmund at the Bayreuth Festival in 1876. From 1886 to 1888 he was a member of the Metropolitan Opera Co. in N.Y.; his debut there was in his star role as Siegmund (Nov. 10, 1886); then he sang Tristan at the American premiere of *Tristan und Isolde* (Dec. 1, 1886) and Siegmund in *Götterdämmerung* (Jan. 25, 1888).

BIBLIOGRAPHY: R. Sternfeld, *Albert Niemann* (Berlin, 1904); Niemann's correspondence with Wagner was publ. by W. Altmann (Berlin, 1924).

Niemann, Walter, German writer on music and composer; b. Hamburg, Oct. 10, 1876; d. Leipzig, June 17, 1953. He was a pupil of his father, Rudolph Niemann, and of Humperdinck (1897); in 1898–1901, studied at the Leipzig Cons. with Reinecke and von Bose, and at the Univ. with Riemann and Kretzschmar (musicology); received a Dr.Phil. in 1901, with the dissertation *Über die abweichende Bedeutung der Ligaturen in der Mensuraltheorie der Zeit vor Johannes de Garlandia* (publ. in Leipzig, 1902; reprint, Wiesbaden, 1971); in 1904–6, was editor of the *Neue Zeitschrift für Musik* in Leipzig; in 1906–7, was a teacher at the Hamburg Cons.; in 1907–17, was again in Leipzig as a writer and critic of the *Neueste Nachrichten,* then gave up this position to devote himself to composition. Besides a Violin Sonata and a few works for orch. and string orch., he wrote numerous piano pieces (over 150 opus numbers).

WRITINGS: *Musik und Musiker des 19. Jahrhunderts* (1905); *Die Musik Skandinaviens* (1906); *Das Klavierbuch* (1907; 5th ed., 1920); *Edvard Grieg* (1908; with G. Schjelderup); *Die musikalische Renaissance des 19. Jahrhunderts* (1911); *Taschenlexikon für Klavierspieler* (1912; 4th ed., 1918); *Die Musik seit Richard Wagner* (1913; later eds. as *Die Musik der Gegenwart*); *Jean Sibelius* (1917); *Klavier-Lexikon* (1917); *Die nordische Klaviermusik* (1918); *Die Virginalmusik* (1919); *Meister des Klaviers* (1919); *Brahms* (1920; Eng. trans., N.Y., 1929; reprint, N.Y., 1969).

Niemtschek (Niemetschek, Němeček), Franz Xaver, Czech writer on music; b. Sadská, near Poděbrady, July 24, 1766; d. Vienna, March 19, 1849. He studied at the Prague Gymnasium (1776–82); then studied philosophy at Prague Univ. (Ph.D., 1800); was a prof. of philosophy at the Univ. of Prague from 1802 to 1820; is known in musical annals for his biography of Mozart, whom he greatly admired and evidently knew personally: *Leben des k. k. Kapellmeisters Wolfgang Gottlieb Mozart* (Prague, 1798; 2nd ed., 1808; in Eng., London, 1956).

Niessen-Stone, Matja von, American soprano; b. Moscow, Dec. 28, 1870; d. New York, June 8, 1948. At the age of 6 she was taken to Germany, where she studied singing in Dresden with Adolf Jansen and in Berlin with Lilli Lehmann and others; after a successful debut in Dresden in 1890 she toured Europe; in 1906 she went to the U.S. and sang at the Metropolitan Opera House in N.Y., during the season 1908–9. From 1910 to 1917 she taught voice at the Inst. of Musical Art in N.Y. In 1922 she went back to Europe and taught singing in Berlin until 1938, when she returned to N.Y.

Nietzsche, Friedrich, celebrated philosopher; b. Röcken, near Lützen, Oct. 15, 1844; d. Weimar, Aug. 25, 1900, after 11 years of insanity. He was prof. of classical philology at the Univ. of Basel (1869–79); was at first a warm partisan of Wagner, whom he championed in *Die Geburt der Tragödie aus dem Geiste der Musik* (1872; 2nd ed., 1874) and *Richard Wagner in Bayreuth* (1876). In *Der Fall Wagner* and *Nietzsche contra Wagner* (both 1888) and in *Götzendämmerung* (1889), he turned against his former idol and became a partisan of Bizet. Nietzsche was also a trained musician; he publ. 17 songs (1864) and *An das Leben* for Chorus and Orch. (1887); in MS are piano pieces (2- and 4-hands) and songs. His lieder have been edited by G. Göhler (Leipzig, 1924), and his *Complete Works,* by Curt Paul Jang (Basel, 1976).

BIBLIOGRAPHY: E. Förster-Neitzsche, *Das Leben F. N.s* (2 vols., Leipzig, 1895–1904; Eng. trans. [condensed], N.Y., 1912–15); J. Zeitler, *N.s Ästhetik* (Leipzig, 1900); Th. Lessing, *Schopenhauer, Wagner, N.* (Munich, 1906); H. Bélart, *F. N. und Richard Wagner* (Berlin, 1907); P. Lasserre, *Les Idées de N. sur la musique. La Période Wagnérienne (1871–6)* (Paris, 1907; new ed., 1930); E. Eckertz, *N. als Künstler* (Munich, 1930); H. Bélart, *F. N.s Freundschaftstragödie mit R. Wagner* (Dresden, 1912); E. Förster-Neitzsche, *Wagner und N. zur Zeit ihrer Freundschaft* (Munich, 1915); "Wagner and N.: The Beginning and End of Their Friendship," *Musical Quarterly* (July 1918; selection from E. Förster-Neitzsche's book, trans. by C.V. Kerr); W. Dahms, *Die Offenbarung der Musik. Eine Apotheose F. N.s* (1922); L. Griesser, *N. und Wagner* (1923); K. Hildebrandt, *Wagner und N., Ihr Kampf gegen das 19. Jahrhundert* (Breslau, 1924); H. Baugh, "N. and His Music," *Musical Quarterly* (April 1926); J.M. Verweyen, *Wagner und N.* (Stuttgart, 1926); E. Gürster, *N. und die Musik* (1929); J.G. Huneker, *Essays* (N.Y., 1929); G.B. Foster, *F. N.* (N.Y., 1931); P.G. Dippel, *N. und Wagner* (1934); E. Ruprecht, *Der Mythos bei Wagner und N.* (Berlin, 1938). See also *F. N.s gesammelte Briefe* (Berlin, 1900–8; vol. III, 2, contains letters to Bülow, H. von Senger, and M. von Meysenbug; vol. IV, letters to P. Gast) and H. Daffner's ed. of *N.s Randglossen zu Bizets "Carmen"* (Regensburg, 1912). P. Gast's letters to N. were publ. in 1924 (vol. I).

Niewiadomski, Stanislaw, Polish composer and music critic; b. Soposzyn, Galicia, Nov. 4, 1859; d. Lwow, Aug. 15, 1936. He studied in Lwow (with Mikuli), Vienna (F. Krenn), and Leipzig (Jadassohn); in 1886–87 and 1918–19, was manager of the Lwow Opera; in 1885–1914, was music critic there; in 1887–1914, was a teacher at the Lwow Cons.; in 1918–21, was editor of the *Gazeta Muzyczna;* from 1919, was a music critic in Warsaw and a teacher at the Cons. there; in 1929, became director of the Warsaw Music Inst. He composed numerous songs and piano pieces (about 500 works), and publ. biographies of Chopin and Moniuszko.

Nigg, Serge, French composer; b. Paris, June 6, 1924. He studied composition with Messiaen and Simone Plé-Caussande at the Paris Cons. (1941–46) and privately with René Liebowitz (1946–48), mainly the Schoenbergian method of composition with 12 tones. Nigg became one of the earliest representatives of dodecaphony in France; however, under the influence of his political convictions, he later abandoned modern techniques and began writing in a manner accessible to a broad public. In 1959 he formed, with Durey and others, the Assoc. of Progressive Musicians, advocating socialist realism in music.

WORKS: FOR THE STAGE: 2 ballets: *Billard* (1951; Amsterdam, 1951) and *L'Etrange Aventure de Gulliver à Lilliput* (1958, for radio; concert version for 12 Instruments).

FOR ORCH.: *Timour,* symph. poem (1944); Concertino for Piano, Wind Instruments, and Percussion (1946); *3 mouvements symphoniques* (1947); *Pour un poète captif,* symph. poem appealing for the liberation of a radical poet imprisoned for political disturbances (1950); 2 piano concertos: No. 1 (1954; Paris, Jan. 10, 1955) and No. 2 (1970–71; Strasbourg, June 10, 1971); Violin Concerto (1957; Paris, May 27, 1960); *Musique funèbre* for Strings (1958); *Jérôme Bosch—Symphonie (Hieronymus Bosch Symphony;* 1960; Strasbourg, June 21, 1960); Concerto for Flute and Strings (1961); *Visages d'Axël,* suite in 2 parts (1967; Paris, Sept. 4, 1967); *Fulgar* for Band, Percussion, 2 Harps, Piano, Celesta, and Tubular Chimes (1969; Paris, Oct. 9, 1969); *Scènes concertantes* for Piano and Strings (1976; Paris Radio, March 26, 1976); *Millions d'oiseaux d'or* (1980–81; Toulouse Orch. on U.S. tour, Boston, March 20, 1981).

FOR VOICE: *Perséphone,* melodrama (1942); *Le Fusillé inconnu,* oratorio (1949); *Les Vendeurs d'indulgences,* cantata (1953); *Prière pour le premier jour d'été,* cantata for Speaker, Chorus, and Orch. (1955); *La Croisade des Enfants (The Children's Crusade),* oratorio for Narrator, Baritone, Children's Chorus, Mixed Chorus, and Small Orch. (1959); *Histoire d'œuf* for 2 Speakers, 6 Percussionists, and Piano (1961); *Le Chant du dépossédé (The Song of the Dispossessed),* after Mallarmé, for Narrator, Baritone, and Orch. (Strasbourg, June 25, 1964).

CHAMBER MUSIC: *Variations* for Piano and 10 Instruments (1946; Paris, Jan. 29, 1947); Quintet for Flute, String Trio, and Harp (1952); Solo Violin Sonata (1965); *Pièce* for Trumpet and Piano (1972); *Pièce* for Flute and Piano (1976).

FOR PIANO: *Fantaisie* (1942); *Le Tombeau de Jérôme Bosch* (1958); 2 sonatas (1943, 1965).

BIBLIOGRAPHY: J. Roy, *Présences contemporaines de la musique française* (Paris, 1962; pp. 425–38).

Niggli, Arnold, Swiss writer and editor; b. Aarburg, Dec. 20, 1843; d. Zürich, May 30, 1927. He studied law at Heidelberg, Zürich, and Berlin. In 1875–1909, he was secretary to the town council at Aarau; in 1890–98, was editor of the *Schweizerische Musikzeitung;* later, he lived in Zürich. He publ. a valuable work, *Die Schweizerische Musikgesellschaft; Eine musik- und kulturgeschichtliche Studie* (1886), *Geschichte des Eidgenössischen Sängervereins, 1842–92,* and short studies of a number of great composers and performers (some of them in Waldersee's *Sammlung musikalischer Vorträge*).

Nikisch, Arthur, celebrated Hungarian conductor; b. Szent-Miklós, Oct. 12, 1855; d. Leipzig, Jan. 23, 1922. His father was head bookkeeper to Prince Lichtenstein. Nikisch attended the Vienna Cons., studying with Dessoff (composition) and Hellmesberger (violin), graduating in 1874. While still a student he had the honor of playing among the first violins under Wagner's direction at the laying of the cornerstone of the Bayreuth Theater (1872). He was at first engaged as a violinist in the Vienna Court Orch. (1874); then as 2nd conductor at the Leipzig Theater (1878). From 1882 to 1889 he was first conductor there. In 1889 he was engaged as conductor of the Boston Symph. Orch., with excellent success, remaining at this post until 1893. Returning to Europe, he was music director of the Budapest Opera (1893–95); also conducted the Phil. Concerts there; from 1895, was conductor of the Gewandhaus Concerts in Leipzig, succeeding Reinecke, and of the Phil. Concerts in Berlin. From 1897 he was in constant demand as a visiting conductor, and made a number of extended tours with the Berlin Phil. Orch.; he directed many of the concerts of the London Phil. Society, and works of Wagner and Richard Strauss at Covent Garden; in 1912 he made a tour of the U.S. with the entire London Symph. Orch. (85 performers). In 1902–7, he was director of studies at the Leipzig Cons.; in 1905–6, general director of the Stadttheater. As a symph. conductor he possessed an extraordinary Romantic power of musical inspiration; he was the first of his profession to open the era of "the conductor as hero," exercising a peculiar magnetism on his audiences equal to that of virtuoso artists; his personal appearance, a poetic-looking beard and flowing hair, contributed to his success. His son **Mitja Nikisch** (b. Leipzig, May 21, 1899; d. Venice, Aug. 5, 1936) was an excellent pianist; he toured South America in 1921; made his U.S. debut in N.Y., Oct. 23, 1923.

BIBLIOGRAPHY: F. Pfohl, *Arthur Nikisch als Mensch und als Künstler* (Leipzig, 1900; new ed., 1925); I. Lipaiev, *Arthur Nikisch* (Moscow, 1904; in Russian); E. Segnitz, *Arthur Nikisch* (1920); A. Dette, *Arthur Nikisch* (1922); H. Chevalley, *Arthur Nikisch, Leben und Wirken* (1922; 2nd ed., 1925); Harold Schonberg, *The Great Conductors* (N.Y., 1967); W. Stresemann, *The Berlin Philharmonic from Bülow to Karajan* (in German and Eng.; Berlin, 1979).

Nikolaidi, Elena, contralto; b. Izmir, Turkey, of Greek parents, June 13, 1909. She studied voice with Thanos Mellos, whom she married on April 27, 1936;

made her operatic debut at the Vienna State Opera, Dec. 16, 1936; later sang in Salzburg, London, Prague, and Cairo; made her American debut (in a concert) in N.Y., on Jan. 20, 1949.

Nikolais, Alwin, American choreographer, stage director, and composer of electronic ballet scores; b. Southington, Conn., Nov. 25, 1912. He studied piano; played in movie houses for the silent films. In 1929 he began to study dance with a pupil of Mary Wigman; became director of the Hartford Parks Marionette Theater and later chairman of the dance dept. of the Hartt School of Music in Hartford. In 1942–46 he served in military counterintelligence in Europe; then studied with Hanya Holm in N.Y. In 1948 he joined the dance faculty of the Henry Street Settlement, and in 1949 became co-director of the Henry Street Playhouse in N.Y. His principal choreographic innovation is the technique of body extension by tubular projections and disks attached to the head and upper and nether limbs, so that a biped dancer becomes a stereogeometrical figure; often in his productions clusters of dancers form primitivistic ziggurats. His portrayal of extraterrestrial creatures in Menotti's children's opera *Help, Help, the Globolinks!* was acclaimed for its imaginative quality at its premiere at the Hamburg State Opera (Dec. 19, 1968).

Nikolayev, Leonid, Russian pianist and pedagogue; b. Kiev, Aug. 13, 1878; d. Tashkent, Oct. 11, 1942. He was a pupil of Sergei Taneyev and Ippolitov-Ivanov at the Moscow Cons.; then settled in St. Petersburg, where he became prof. of piano at the Cons. in 1906, achieving a fine reputation as a teacher; among his piano pupils was Shostakovitch. Nikolayev went to Tashkent in Central Asia after the German invasion of Russia in 1941, and died there shortly afterward. He composed several symph. works; a *Hymn to Beauty* for Soli, Chorus, and Orch.; Cello Sonata; Violin Sonata; a number of piano works (sonata, *Tarantella,* etc.); also a suite for 2 Pianos; made arrangements for piano of organ works by Buxtehude and Pachelbel.

BIBLIOGRAPHY: S. Savshinsky, *Leonid Nikolayev* (Moscow, 1950).

Nikolayeva, Tatiana, Russian pianist and composer; b. Bezhitz, May 4, 1924. She studied at the Moscow Cons. with Goldenweiser (piano) and Golubev (composition). After a highly successful series of concerts in Russia, she appeared in Prague (1948); at the bicentennial Bach festival in Leipzig (1950) she won first prize for her playing of Bach's clavier works. In 1953 she visited Iceland as a member of the Soviet delegation; in the same year also toured Siberia. Among her works are 2 piano concertos; Piano Sonata; *24 Concert Etudes* for Piano; Symph.; *Song of Happiness,* cantata (1949); vocal cycle, *Iceland* (1953); many piano pieces.

Nikolov, Lazar, Bulgarian composer; b. Burgas, Aug. 26, 1922. He studied composition with Vladigerov at the Bulgarian State Cons. in Sofia (1942–

46); in 1961 joined its faculty. An experimenter by nature, he was one of the few composers in Bulgaria who adopted modern procedures of composition, melodically verging on atonality and harmonically on polytonality.

WORKS: 2 operas: *Prometheus Bound,* chamber opera (1963–69; Ruse, March 24, 1974), and *Uncles* (1975); 2 piano concertos: No. 1 (1947–48; Ruse, Nov. 21, 1949) and No. 2 (1954–55; Sofia, Feb. 28, 1963); Concerto for String Orch. (1949; Ruse, Nov. 30, 1951); Violin Concerto (1951–52; Varna, March 25, 1955); 2 symphs.: No. 1 (1953; Varna, Feb. 16, 1956) and No. 2, with 2 Pianos (1960–61); Piano Concertino (1964); *Symphonies* for 13 Strings (1965); *Divertimento concertante* for Chamber Orch. (1968); Cello Concertino (1973); *Chants* for Soloists, Chorus, and Chamber Instrumental Group (1969); Violin Sonata (1953–54); Viola Sonata (1955); Piano Quintet (1958–59); Flute Sonata (1962); Cello Sonata (1962); Clarinet Sonata (1962); 2 string quartets (1965, 1970); Sonata for 2 Harps (1971); Double-bass Sonata (1972); Bassoon Sonata (1976); Oboe Sonata (1976); 4 piano sonatas (1950, 1952, 1955, 1964); 2-piano Sonata (1952).

Niles, John Jacob, American folksinger and authority on folk music; b. Louisville, Ky., April 28, 1892; d. at his Boot Hill farm, near Lexington, Ky., March 1, 1980. He studied at the Cincinnati Cons.; later devoted himself to collecting and arranging the songs of the Southern Appalachians; also composed choruses in a folk-song manner. Among his publications are *7 Kentucky Mountain Songs* (1929); *7 Negro Exultations* (1929); *Songs of the Hill Folk* (1934); *10 Christmas Carols* (1935); *More Songs of the Hill Folk* (1936); *Ballads and Tragic Legends* (1937); *The Anglo-American Ballad Study Book* (1945); *The Anglo-American Carol Study Book* (1948); and *The Shape-Note Study Book* (1950). He also publ. *Songs My Mother Never Taught Me* (with Douglas Moore, 1929).

Nilius, Rudolf, Austrian conductor; b. Vienna, March 23, 1883; d. Bad Ischl, Dec. 31, 1962. He studied cello; was a member of the Vienna Phil. (1906–13); conducted the Tonkünstlerorchester in Vienna (1912–21). In 1921 he founded in Vienna the Phil. Chamber Orch. Concerts.

Nilson, Leo, Swedish composer of electronic music; b. Malmö, Feb. 20, 1939. He studied organ and piano at the Music Academy in Stockholm; was briefly an organist of the Swedish church in Paris, where he was exposed to *musique concrète;* upon his return to Sweden began writing electronic music for films, television, and various avant-garde exhibitions. His works include *Skorpionen* (1965); *Skulpturmusik I, II,* and *III* (1966, 1967, 1968); *Satellitmusik* (1967); *That Experiment H₂S* (1968); *Sirrah* (1971); *Star-75,* multimedia work with Dancers and Sculptor (1975).

Nilsson, Birgit, celebrated Swedish dramatic soprano; b. near Karup, May 17, 1918. She studied singing in Stockholm. In 1947 she joined the Royal Opera; sang Elsa at the Bayreuth Festival in 1954, and Isolde in 1957 and 1959; she also appeared at La Scala in Milan. She made her U.S. debut at the Hollywood Bowl on Aug. 9, 1956; sang Wagnerian roles with the San Francisco Opera and the Chicago Lyric Opera. In London she sang Brünnhilde in a complete cycle of Wagner's tetralogy in 1957. She made her long-delayed debut with the Metropolitan Opera in N.Y. as Isolde, on Dec. 18, 1959. At the peak of her career she was acclaimed as one of the greatest Wagnerian singers of all time. After an absence of 5 years from the Metropolitan she gave a gala concert there on Nov. 4, 1979; on Feb. 1, 1980, she returned to the Met roster; on Feb. 16, 1980, at the age of 62, she sang the title role in *Elektra* by Richard Strauss; the performance was taped for television and broadcast on Jan. 28, 1981.

Nilsson, Bo, Swedish composer of ultramodern tendencies; b. Skellefteaa, May 1, 1937. Largely autodidact, he experimented with techniques of serial composition, the phonetic possibilities of vocal music, and electronic sonorities; attended seminars on modern techniques in Cologne and Darmstadt. His works are constructed on precise quasi-mathematical, serial principles, and are often given abstract titles in German.
WORKS: *Frequenzen* for Piccolo, Flute, Percussion, Guitar, Xylophone, Vibraphone, and Double Bass (1955–56); *Bewegungen (Movements)* for Piano (1956); *Schlagfiguren* for Piano (1956); *Buch der Veränderungen (Book of Changes)* for Orch. (1957); *Zeiten im Umlauf (Times in Transit)* for 8 Woodwinds (1957); *Kreuzungen (Crossings)* for Flute, Vibraphone, Guitar, and Xylophone (1957); *Audiogramme* for Tape (1957–58); *Ett blocks timme (Stunde eines Blocks),* chamber cantata for Soprano and 6 Instrumentalists (1957–58); *20 Gruppen* for Piccolo, Oboe, and Clarinet, or any 3 instruments (1958); *Quantitäten* for Piano (1958); *Plexus* for Orch. (1959); *Stenogramm* for Percussion or Organ (1959); *Reaktionen* for 1–4 Percussionists (1960); *Szenes I–IV: I* for 2 Flutes, 2 Trumpets, Piano, Harp, and 2 Percussionists (1960); *II* for 6 Trumpets, 4 Violins, 4 Percussionists, Piano, Harp, Celesta, and Vibraphone (1961); *III* for Chamber Orch. (1961); *IV* for Saxophone, Orch., and Chorus (1974–75); *Versuchungen (Temptations)* for 3 Orch. Groups (1961); *La Bran* for Chorus and Orch. (1961); *Entrée* for Tape and Orch. (1963); *Litanei über das verlorene Schlagzeug (Litany for the Lost Drum)* for Orch. without Percussion, to conform to the title (1965); *Déjà-vu* for Wind Quartet (1967); *Revue* for Orch. (1967); *Attraktionen* for String Quartet (1968); *Design* for Violin, Clarinet, and Piano (1968); *Rendezvous* for Piano (1968); *Quartets* for 36 Winds, Percussion, and Tape (1969); *Caprice* for Orch. (1970); *Exit* for Tape and Orch. (1970); *Eurythmical Voyage* for Piano, Tape, and Orch. (1970); *Déjà-connu (Already Known)* for Wind Quintet (1973); *Nazm* for Speakers, Vocal Soloists, Chorus, Orch., and Tape (1972–73). He publ. an autobiography under the title *Spaderboken* (Stockholm, 1966).

Nilsson, Kristina (Christine), Swedish soprano; b. Sjöabol, near Växjö, Aug. 20, 1843; d. Stockholm, Nov. 22, 1921. Her teachers were Baroness Leuhausen, and F. Berwald in Stockholm; with him she continued study in Paris, and on Oct. 27, 1864, made her debut, as Violetta in *La Traviata,* at the Théâtre Lyrique, where she was engaged for 3 years. After successful visits to London, she was engaged in 1868–70 at the Paris Opéra; then made long tours with Strakosch in America (1870–72), and sang in the principal continental cities. In 1872 she married Auguste Rouzaud (d. 1882); her 2nd husband (married 1887) was the Spanish count Angel Vallejo y Miranda. She revisited America in the winters of 1873, 1874, and 1883, making her debut on the opening night of the Metropolitan Opera House in N.Y. on Oct. 22, 1883, as Marguerite in *Faust.* Her voice was not powerful, but it was brilliant. She excelled as Marguerite and Mignon.
BIBLIOGRAPHY: B. Carlsson, *Kristina Nilsson* (Stockholm, 1922); T. Norlind, *Kristina Nilsson* (Stockholm, 1923); H. Headland, *Christine Nilsson, the Songbird of the North* (Rock Island, Ill., 1943).

Nilsson, Torsten, Swedish organist and composer; b. Höör, Jan. 21, 1920. He studied church music at the Royal College of Music in Stockholm (1938–42); served as church organist in Köping (1943–53), Hälsingborg (1953–62), and, from 1962, in the Oscar Church in Stockholm. He excels in liturgical works; in his organ music he introduces many innovations, such as static tone-clusters and specified periods of thematic improvisation.
WORKS: 5 church opera-oratorios: *Ur jordens natt (Out of the Night of the Earth)* for Improvising Soli and Vocal Groups, with Organ (Stockholm, April 12, 1968); *Dantesvit (Dante Suite)* for Soli, Vocal Group, Percussion, Organ, Harpsichord, and Tape (Stockholm, April 23, 1969); *Skapelse (The Creation)* for Narrator, Chorus, Organ, and Instruments (Stockholm, May 11, 1970); *Ur jordens natt. Del 2 (Out of the Night of the Earth, Part 2;* Stockholm, April 12, 1974); *Den sista natten (The Last Night)* for 2 Actors, Mixed and Children's Chorus, Flute, Harp, Organ, and Percussion (Stockholm, Nov. 25, 1973); Concerto for Organ and 7 Woodwinds (1963); *Caresser,* after Pablo Neruda, for Baritone, Chorus, and Instrumental Ensemble (1969); *Verwerfungen* for Organ and 13 Percussion Instruments (1970); *Non est Deus?,* chamber oratorio on a biblical text (1971–72); *Baltassan* for Soli, Chorus, and Organ (1972); *Steget over Troskelm (Over the Threshold),* concerto for Piano, Wind Instruments, and Percussion (1975); many songs.

Nimsgern, Siegmund, German bass-baritone; b. St. Wendel, Jan. 14, 1940. He took vocal lessons with Sibylle Fuchs and Jakob Stampfli in Saarbrücken; sang at the Saarbrücken Opera (1967–71) and then at the Deutsche Oper am Rhein in Düsseldorf (1971–74); later engaged on an international career, appearing in Milan, Paris, Montreal, San Francisco, and London.

Nin (y Castellanos), Joaquín, Spanish composer and pianist; b. Havana, Sept. 29, 1879; d. there, Oct. 24, 1949. He studied piano with Carlos Vidiella in Barcelona, and M. Moszkowski in Paris; composition with d'Indy at the Schola Cantorum; in 1906–8, was a prof. there; in 1908–10, was in Berlin; then briefly in Havana and Brussels; he lived for many years in Paris; was a member of the French Legion of Honor, the Spanish Academy, etc. He was especially noted as an interpreter of early piano music.

WORKS: "Mimodrama," *L'Autre;* for Piano: *Suite de valses lyriques, Danza ibérica, Message à Claude Debussy,* "1830," *Variations on a Frivolous Theme,* etc.; for Violin and Piano: *En el jardín de Lindaraja, Suite espagnole,* etc.; *Chants d'Espagne* for Cello; etc. He publ. several essays on general problems of esthetics, among them *Pour l'art* (Paris, 1909; Eng. trans., London, 1915, as *In the Service of Art*), *Idées et commentaires* (1912), *Clavecin ou piano* (1921), and *Las tres grandes escuelas.* He edited 2 valuable collections of Spanish keyboard music: *16 sonatas anciennes d'auteurs espagnols* (Paris, 1925) and *17 sonates et pièces anciennes d'auteurs espagnols* (Paris, 1929); also 10 violin pieces by Herrando, etc.

BIBLIOGRAPHY: R. Villar, *Músicos españoles* (vol. II); H. Collet, *L'Essor de la musique espagnole au XXᵉ siècle* (Paris, 1929).

Nin-Culmell, Joaquín, Cuban-Spanish pianist and composer, son of **Joaquín Nin;** b. Berlin, Sept. 5, 1908. He studied piano in Paris at the Schola Cantorum; later took private lessons with Alfred Cortot, and composition at the Paris Cons. with Paul Dukas; in 1930–34 he had lessons in Granada with Manuel de Falla. He emigrated to the U.S. in 1936; was prof. of music and chairman of the music dept. of Williams College, Williamstown, Mass. (1940–49); in 1950 he was appointed to the faculty of the Univ. of Calif. at Berkeley; became prof. emeritus in 1974. His music retains its national Spanish element, the main influence being that of de Falla, but he employs modern harmonies and characteristic asymmetrical rhythms of the cosmopolitan modern school. He was soloist in his own Piano Concerto at a concert of the Rochester (N.Y.) Phil. in Williamstown, Mass. (Dec 5, 1946); other works are the opera *La Celestina;* Cello Concerto (1963); Piano Quintet (1938); *Tonadas* for Piano (4 books); *Dedication Mass* for Mixed Chorus and Organ; *Jorge Manrique* for Soprano and String Quartet (1963); *A Celebration for Julia,* one-movement string quartet in memory of Julia Hanes Hurley, a music patroness (N.Y., March 3, 1982); also several song cycles.

Nisard, Théodore, pen name of **Abbé Théodule-Eléazar-Xavier Normand,** French authority on Gregorian chant; b. Quaregnon, near Mons, Jan. 27, 1812; d. Jacqueville, Seine-et-Marne, Feb. 29, 1888. He was a chorister at Cambrai, and also studied music at Douay; attended the priests' seminary at Tournai; in 1839 was appointed director of the Enghien Gymnasium, occupying his leisure with the study of church music. In 1842 he became 2nd chef

de chant and organist at St. Germain des Prés, Paris; but soon devoted himself wholly to literary work; he publ. the first transcription of the Antiphonary of Montpellier (neumes and Latin letter notation from A to P), discovered by Danjou in 1847. Of his numerous books on plainchant the most important are a revised edition of Jumilhac's *La Science et la pratique du plain-chant* (1847; with Le Clercq) and *Dictionnaire liturgique, historique et pratique du plain-chant et de musique d'église au moyen âge et dans les temps modernes* (1854; with d'Ortigue). He also publ. *De la notation proportionelle au moyen âge* (1847); *Etudes sur les anciennes notations musicales de l'Europe* (1847); *Etudes sur la restauration du chant grégorien au XIXᵉ siècle* (1856); *Du rythme dans le plain chant* (1856); *Les Vrais Principes de l'accompagnement du plain-chant sur l'orgue d'après les maîtres des XVᵉ et XVIᵉ siècles* (1860); *Des chansons populaires chez les anciens et chez les Français* (1867); *L'Archéologie musicale et le vrai chant grégorien* (1890; 2nd ed., 1897).

Nissen, Georg Nikolaus, Danish Councillor of State; b. Hadersleben, Jan. 22, 1761; d. Salzburg, March 24, 1826. He married Mozart's widow in 1809, and collected materials for a biography of Mozart, publ. by his widow in 1828 as *Biographie W.A. Mozarts nach Originalbriefen.*

Nissen, Hans Hermann, German baritone; b. Zippnow, near Marienwerder, West Prussia, May 20, 1893; d. Munich, March 28, 1980. He began his career as a concert singer; then devoted himself to opera; he sang at the Berlin Volksoper and the Munich Opera. In 1930 he went to the U.S., where he became a member of the Chicago Civic Opera (1930–32); on Nov. 23, 1938, he made his appearance with the Metropolitan Opera in N.Y., as Wotan, and remained with it for a season. After 1945 he returned to Germany, where he joined the Bavarian State Opera in Munich, retiring in 1967. He remained in Munich as a voice teacher.

Nixon, Roger, American composer; b. Tulare, Calif., Aug. 8, 1921. He studied clarinet with a local teacher; in 1940 attended a seminar in composition with Arthur Bliss at the Univ. of Calif. at Berkeley, and in 1941, with Ernest Bloch. In 1942–46 he was in the U.S. Army; he returned in 1947 to Berkeley, where he had fruitful sessions with Sessions (Ph.D., 1952); in the summer of 1948 he took private lessons with Schoenberg. In 1959 he joined the staff of San Francisco State College. A prolific composer, he writes in a consistent modern idiom anchored in fluctuating tonality and diversified by atonal protuberances. His music is marked by distinctly American melorhythms; his miniature opera, *The Bride Comes to Yellow Sky,* is an exemplar of adroit modernistic Westernism fashioned in a non-ethnomusicological manner.

WORKS: String Quartet No. 1 (1949); *Air for Strings* (1952); Violin Concerto (1956); *The Wine of Astonishment,* cantata for Baritone Solo and Mixed Chorus (1960); *Reflections* for Symphonic Band

(1962); *Elegiac Rhapsody* for Viola and Orch. (1962); *3 Dances* for Orch. (1963); *Nocturne* for Symphonic Band (1965); opera, *The Bride Comes to Yellow Sky* (Eastern Illinois Univ., Feb. 20, 1968; revised and perf. by the San Francisco State College Opera Workshop, March 22, 1969); Viola Concerto (San Francisco, April 29, 1970); *A Solemn Processional* for Symphonic Band (San Francisco, May 9, 1971); Violin Concerto (1976); various pieces of chamber music; choruses; songs; piano pieces.

Niyazi (real name, **Taghi-zade-Khadzhibekov**), Soviet Georgian conductor and composer; b. Tiflis, Aug. 20, 1912. His father was the well-known composer **Zulfugar Khadzhibekov.** He studied music in Moscow, Erevan, and Baku. From 1937–65 he served, off and on, as conductor of the Azerbaijani Ballet. In 1961 he was named principal conductor of the Leningrad Theater of Opera and Ballet. He conducted a number of first performances of works by Azerbaijani composers.
WORKS: Opera, *Hosrov and Shirin* (1942); ballet, *Chitra,* after Rabindranath Tagore (1961); *In Combat,* symph. poem (1944); popular concert pieces; songs.

Noack, Friedrich, German musicologist; b. Darmstadt, July 10, 1890; d. there, Jan. 21, 1958. He studied musicology in Berlin with Kretzschmar, Stumpf, and J. Wolf. After World War I he studied at the Inst. für Kirchenmusik in Berlin; then taught music subjects at the Univ. of Darmstadt; from 1947 until his death he taught at the Hochschule für Musik in Frankfurt. He was also on the staff of the Cons. of Mainz (1926–39), of the Hochschule für Musik in Mannheim (1939–45), and of the Landesmusikschule in Darmstadt (1945–54). His publications include *Chr. Graupners Kirchenmusiken* (Leipzig, 1926) and numerous bibliographical articles in various German publications. He edited vols. 51 and 52 of Denkmäler Deutscher Tonkunst and vol. 10 of the works of Telemann (Kassel, 1955); also revised vol. 1 (on the symph.) of Kretzschmar's *Führer durch den Konzertsaal* (1932).

Nobel, Felix de, Dutch pianist and choral conductor; b. Haarlem, May 27, 1907; d. Amsterdam, March 25, 1981. He studied piano with Martha Autengruber and composition with Sem Dresden at the Amsterdam Cons.; from 1939 to 1973 led the Netherlands Chamber Choir. He was chiefly known as an excellent accompanist for singers; made arrangements of Dutch, Irish, and Jewish folk songs for women's chorus. In 1965 he was awarded the Elizabeth Sprague Coolidge Memorial Medal.

Noble, (John) Jeremy, English music critic; b. London, March 27, 1930. He studied at Worcester College, Oxford; wrote on music in the *Times* of London (1960–63); then went to the U.S., where he was a research fellow at the State Univ. of N.Y. at Buffalo (1963–70). Upon his return to England, he assumed the position of music critic of the *Sunday Telegraph* (1972–76); in 1976 resumed his post in

Buffalo. Apart from his writing, he was active as a broadcaster for the BBC in London.

Noble, Ray, English bandleader, composer, and arranger, nephew of **Thomas Tertius Noble;** b. Brighton, Dec. 17, 1903; d. London, April 2, 1978. He received a thorough musical training at Cambridge; formed a band in London, assembled mostly from hotel orch. groups. Most of his arrangements were of English folk tunes; then he began to compose; among his most popular songs was *Goodnight, Sweetheart,* which subsequently became his theme song on American radio shows. In 1934 he went to the U.S.; Glenn Miller helped him to assemble musicians for his band, and he opened at the Rainbow Room in N.Y. on June 1, 1935, seated at a white grand piano on a rotating platform, making tours among the guests at the floorside, and returning to the bandstand at the end of each number. He became extremely successful on network radio shows, appearing not only as a bandleader and composer but also as an actor, usually in the role of a comical Englishman. Besides his theme song— *Goodnight, Sweetheart*—he composed *The Very Thought of You, By the Fireside, The Touch of Your Lips,* and several other hit songs. His *Cherokee,* originally a section of his *American Indian Suite,* became a perennial favorite. Ray Noble demonstrated, in a chorus he wrote for 5 saxophones, his expertise in purely contrapuntal writing with a jazz flavor.

Noble, Thomas Tertius, English organist and composer; b. Bath, May 5, 1867; d. Rockport, Mass., May 4, 1953. He studied organ with Parratt at the Royal College of Music in London, where he also took courses in music theory with Bridge and Stanford. He was subsequently employed as a church organist in Colchester and Cambridge. In 1898 he organized the York Symph. Orch., which he conducted until 1912; he then emigrated to America and served as organist at St. Thomas's Episcopal Church in N.Y., until 1947; he gave his final organ recital, playing his own works, in N.Y. on Feb. 26, 1947. He publ. *The Training of the Boy Chorister* (N.Y., 1943).

Nobre, Marlos, Brazilian composer; b. Recife, Feb. 18, 1939. He studied piano and theory at the Pernambuco Cons. (1946–54); in 1960 went to Rio de Janeiro, where he took composition lessons with H.J. Koellreutter; later studied with Camargo Guarnieri at the São Paulo Cons. (1963–64) and with Alberto Ginastera in Buenos Aires (1963–64); took a course in electronic music with Ussachevsky at Columbia Univ. (1969); was music director of the National Symph. Orch. of Brazil (1971–76). Despite a somewhat quaquaversal efflux of styles and idioms to which he was exposed during his student days, he succeeded in forming a strongly individual manner of musical self-expression, in which sonorous and structural elements are effectively combined with impressionistic, pointillistic, and serial techniques, supplemented by restrained aleatory procedures. He is one of the few contemporary Latin-American composers who does not disdain to make use of native melorhythmic inflections, resulting in ingratiating harmoniousness.

WORKS: Concertino for Piano and Strings (1959); *Variations* for Solo Oboe (1960); Piano Trio (1960); *Theme and Variations* for Piano (1961); *16 Variations* for Piano (1962); Solo Viola Sonata (1963); *Divertimento* for Piano and Orch. (Rio de Janeiro, Nov. 10, 1965); *Rhythmic Variations* for Piano and Percussion (1963); *Ukrínmakrinkrín* for Soprano, Wind Instruments, and Piano, to a text derived from primitive Brazilian Negro and Indian rituals (Buenos Aires, Nov. 20, 1964); *Modinha* for Voice, Flute, and Viola (1966); *Sonata breve* for Piano (1966); *Canticum instrumentale* for Flute, Harp, Piano, and Timpani (1967); String Quartet No. 1 (1967); *Rhythmetron* for 32 Percussion Instruments (1968; choreographed 1969); *Convergencias* for Orch. (Rio de Janeiro, June 11, 1968); Wind Quintet (1968); *Tropicale* for Flute, Clarinet, Piano, and Percussion (1968); *Desafio* for Viola and String Orch. (1968; Recife, Oct. 30, 1974); *Concerto breve* for Piano and Orch. (Rio de Janeiro, May 27, 1969); *Ludus instrumentalis* for Chamber Orch. (1969); *Mosaico* for Orch. (1970; Rio de Janeiro, May 12, 1970); *Biosfera* for String Orch. (1970; Lisbon, Jan. 27, 1971); *Sonancias* for Piano and Percussion (1972); *O canto multiplicado* for Voice and String Orch. (1972); *In memoriam* for Orch. (Rio de Janeiro, Sept. 18, 1976); Concerto for String Orch. (1975–76).

Nobutoki, Kiyoshi, Japanese composer and pedagogue; b. Kyoto, Dec. 29, 1887; d. Tokyo, Aug. 1, 1965. He studied music in Japan and in Germany; composed a cantata, *Kaido Tosei* (Tokyo, Nov. 26, 1940), and other choral works; was primarily engaged in educational work in Tokyo.

Noda, Ken, fantastically precocious Japanese-American pianist and composer; b. New York, Oct. 5, 1962. He studied piano with Adele Marcus in N.Y.; made his professional debut at 14 as soloist with the Minnesota Orch. in Beethoven's 3rd Piano Concerto (Minneapolis, May 14, 1977); later played with the New York Phil., the St. Louis Symph., and the Baltimore Symph.; in the meantime he took composition lessons with Sylvia Rabinof and Thomas Pasatieri in N.Y. He was only 10 years old when his one-act opera, *The Canary,* was performed (to piano accompaniment) at the Music Festival in Brevard, N.C., on Aug. 18, 1973; the following year, it received first prize in the National Young Composers' Contest sponsored by the National Federation of Music Clubs; he wrote another one-act opera, *The Swing,* in 1974. So impressive were his achievements that in 1976 he was awarded a National Endowment of the Arts grant to write an opera, titled *The Rivalry,* to his own libretto based on a story of Andrew Jackson. He also composed *A Zoo Suite* for Piano (1973); Piano Sonatina (1974); *Prelude and Canon* for Piano (1974); *An Emily Dickinson Song Cycle, A Christina Rossetti Song Cycle,* and *A Cycle of German Poems* (all in 1977). With commendable modesty he acknowledges influences of Mozart, Verdi, Puccini, Rachmaninoff, Menotti, Barber, and Pasatieri.

Noda, Teruyuki, Japanese pianist and composer; b. Mie Prefecture, June 15, 1940. He studied at the Tokyo Univ. of Arts with Tomojiro Ikenouchi and Akio Yashiro.

WORKS: *Symphony in One Movement* (1963); Trio for Violin, Horn, and Piano (1963); Quartet for Horn, Cello, Timpani, and Piano (1965); *Choral Symphony* (Tokyo, July 10, 1968); *Mattinata (Morning Song)* for Marimba, 3 Flutes, and Contrabass (1968; Tokyo, Oct. 4, 1968); *A Mirror or A Journey,* symph. radio piece with Monologue (1968); 2 quartets for Japanese Instruments (1969, 1973); *Dislocation* for Orch. (Tokyo, Feb. 10, 1971); *Mutation* for 4 Japanese Instruments and Orch. (1971); *Shi-sha-no-Sho (Livre de Mort)* for Mixed Chorus (1971); Quartet No. 2 for Japanese Instruments (1973).

Nodermann, Preben (Magnus Christian), Danish composer; b. Hjörring, Jan. 11, 1867; d. Lund, Nov. 14, 1930. He was a pupil of O. Malling in Copenhagen (1888–90); in 1899–1903, was organist in Malmö; then was Kapellmeister at the Cathedral in Lund.

WORKS: Operas: *King Magnus* (Hamburg, 1898); *Gunnlögs Saga* (publ. but not produced); *Rokoko* (Leipzig, 1923); operetta, *Prinz Inkognito* (Copenhagen, 1909; publ. as *Die Jungfernstadt*); motets; sacred and secular choruses; pieces for violin and piano; organ preludes; etc. He made a new vocal score of Gluck's *Orfeo* (1906); publ. *Tragedien om Orpheus och Eurydice af J. Celcius* (1901) and *Studier i svensk hymnologi* (1911).

Noehren, Robert, American organist and organ builder; b. Buffalo, N.Y., Dec. 16, 1910. He studied at the Inst. of Musical Art in N.Y. and at the Curtis Inst. of Music in Philadelphia; served in the U.S. Army in World War II. After demobilization he studied at the Univ. of Michigan, receiving his B.Mus. degree in 1948; then joined its faculty in 1949. He made numerous appearances as an organist in the U.S.; also built organs for churches in Buffalo, San Francisco, and other cities. He composed a number of pieces for organ solo.

Noelte, A. Albert, German-American music pedagogue and composer; b. Starnberg, March 10, 1885; d. Chicago, March 2, 1946. He went to the U.S. in 1901 and studied music and literature in Boston; in 1908 he returned to Germany but frequently visited the U.S.; in 1931 settled there and was appointed a prof. at Northwestern Univ. in Evanston, Ill. He earned a fine reputation as a teacher; many American scholars and composers were his pupils. He composed an orch. piece, *Prologue to a Romantic Drama,* which was performed in Chicago on Jan. 16, 1941, and a number of other pieces of little consequence. His opera *François Villon* was produced in Karlsruhe in 1920.

Nohl, (Karl Friedrich) Ludwig, German writer on music; b. Iserlohn, Westphalia, Dec. 5, 1831; d. Heidelberg, Dec. 15, 1885. He studied jurisprudence at Bonn (1850), Heidelberg, and Berlin; entered the legal profession against his own desire, to please his father. In music he was instructed by Dehn; later (1857) by Kiel, in Berlin. Having embraced music as his profession, he became a lecturer at Heidelberg in 1860; was an associate prof. at Munich in 1865–68; retired to Badenweiler till 1872, when he settled in Heidelberg as a private lecturer, becoming a prof. in 1880.

WRITINGS: (several also in Eng.): *Mozarts Briefe* (1865; 2nd ed., 1877); *Briefe Beethovens* (1865); *Musikalisches Skizzenbuch* (1866); *Musiker-Briefe* (1867); *Beethovens Leben* (3 vols., 1867–77); *Neues Skizzenbuch* (1869); *Gluck und Wagner* (1870); *Die Beethoven-Feier und die Kunst der Gegenwart* (1871); *Beethoven, Liszt, Wagner* (1874); *Beethoven nach den Schilderungen seiner Zeitgenossen* (Stuttgart, 1877; in Eng. as *Beethoven as Depicted by His Contemporaries,* London, 1880); *Mozart nach den Schilderungen seiner Zeitgenossen* (1880); *Richard Wagners Bedeutung für die nationale Kunst* (1883); *Das moderne Musikdrama* (1884); *Die geschichtliche Entwickelung der Kammermusik* (1885). For Reclam's *Universal-Bibliothek* he wrote *Allgemeine Musikgeschichte* and biographies of Beethoven, Mozart, Wagner, Haydn, Weber, Spohr, and Liszt.

Nolte, Ewald Valentin, American music educator; b. Utica, Nebr., Sept. 21, 1909. He studied music with Albert Noelte (not a relation) at Northwestern Univ. in Evanston, Ill. (M.Mus., 1945; Ph.D., 1954), and with Paul Hindemith and Leo Schrade (1950–51) at Yale Univ. His professional career was devoted mainly to education and to conducting church choruses. From 1944 to 1964 he was on the music faculty of Northwestern Univ.; then at Salem College; in 1964–72, he was director of the Moravian Music Foundation. He publ. a series of anthologies, *Music for Young Americans;* arranged American folk songs; supplied accompaniments to hymns; composed choral sacred music; edited numerous works from the Moravian Foundation Archives.

Noni, Alda, Italian soprano; b. Trieste, April 30, 1916. She studied in Trieste and in Vienna; made her debut in Ljubljana in 1937 as Rosina in Rossini's *The Barber of Seville;* then sang at the Vienna State Opera (1942–46). In 1946 she appeared in London as Norina in Donizetti's *Don Pasquale;* also sang at the Glyndebourne Festivals (1949–53). She was entrusted by Richard Strauss with the role of Zerbinetta in the Vienna production of *Ariadne* in 1943. She became best known for her soubrette roles in Italian operas.

Nono, Luigi, prominent Italian composer of the musical and political avant-garde; b. Venice, Jan. 29, 1924. He studied jurisprudence at the Univ. of Padua, graduating in 1946; then took lessons in composition with Malipiero at the Cons. of Venice; later studied advanced harmony and counterpoint with Bruno Maderna and Hermann Scherchen. During the final years of World War II he was a participant in the Italian Resistance movement against the Nazis. He became a member of the Italian Communist Party and in 1975 was elected to its Central Committee. In his compositions he adopted Schoenberg's 12-tone method; his devotion to Schoenberg's ideas was strengthened by his marriage to Schoenberg's daughter Nuria. As a resolutely "engaged" artist, Nono mitigates the antinomy between the modern idiom of his music and the conservative Soviet ideology of socialist realism by his militant political attitude and his emphasis on revolutionary subjects in his works, so that even extreme dissonances may be dialectically justified as representing the horrors of Fascism. Nono made 3 visits to the Soviet Union (1963, 1973, 1976), but his works are rarely, if ever, performed there. He makes use of a variety of techniques: serialism, "sonorism" (employment of sonorities for their own sake), aleatory and concrete music, electronics. Perhaps his most militant composition, both politically and musically, is *Intolleranza 1960,* to texts by Brecht, Eluard, Sartre, and Mayakovsky, a protest against imperialist policies and social inequities; at its production in Venice on April 13, 1961, a group of neo-Fascists showered the audience with leaflets denouncing Nono for his alleged contamination of Italian music by alien doctrines, and even making a facetious allusion to his name as representing a double negative.

WORKS: (besides *Intolleranza*): *Variazioni canoniche* for Orch., based on the 12-tone row of Schoenberg's *Ode to Napoleon Buonaparte* (Darmstadt, Aug. 27, 1950); *Polifonica, Monodia, Ritmica* for Flute, Clarinet, Bass Clarinet, Saxophone, Horn, Piano, and Percussion (Darmstadt, July 10, 1951); *España en el corazón* (to words by F.G. Lorca) for Voices and Instruments (Darmstadt, July 21, 1952); ballet, *Der rote Mantel* (Berlin, Sept. 20, 1954); *La Victoire de Guernica* for Voices and Orch. (1954); *Canti* for 13 Instruments (Paris, March 26, 1955); *Incontri* for 24 Instruments (Darmstadt, May 30, 1955); *Varianti* for Violin Solo, Strings, and Woodwinds (Donaueschingen, Oct. 20, 1957); *La terra e la compagna* for Soli, Chorus, and Instruments (Hamburg, Jan. 13, 1958); *Il canto sospeso* for Solo Voices, Chorus, and Orch., to texts from letters by young men and women condemned to death by the Fascists (Cologne, Oct. 24, 1956); *Sarà dolce tacere* for 8 Solo Voices, to texts from "La terra e la morte" by Cesare Pavese (Washington, D.C., Feb. 17, 1961); *La fabbrica illuminata* for Voice and Magnetic Tape (1964); music for the documentary play *Die Ermittlung* by Peter Weiss, dealing with the trial of Nazi guards (Frankfurt, Oct. 19, 1965); *Sul ponte di Hiroscima,* commemorating the victims of the atomic attack on Hiroshima, for Soloists and Orch. (1962); *A Floresta é jovem e cheja de vida,* oratorio to texts from declarations by the Vietnam guerrilla fighters (1966); *Per Bastiana* for Electronic Tape and 3 Orch. Groups (1967); *Non consumiano Marx* for Electronic Sound (1968); *Voci destroying Muros* for Women's Voices and Instruments in Mixed

Media, featuring a machine gun pointed toward the audience (1970); *Y entonces comprendió* for Voices and Magnetic Tape, dedicated to Ché Guevara (1970); *Ein Gespenst geht um in der Welt (A Spectre Rises over Europe)*, to words from the Communist Manifesto, for Voice and Orch. (Cologne, Feb. 11, 1971); *Como una ola de fuerza y luz* for Singer, Piano, Magnetic Tape, and Orch. (1972); 2 piano concertos (1972, 1975); an opera, *Al gran sole carico d'amore* (1974); *...sofferte onde serene...* for Piano and Tape (1976); *Con Luigi Dallapiccola* for 6 Percussionists and Live Electronics (1979); *Fragmente-Stille, an Diotima* for String Quartet (1979–80); *Das atmende Klarsein* for Bass Flute, Choir, and Live Electronics (1980–81); *Quando stanno morendo...* for 4 Female Voices, Bass Flute, Cello, and Live Electronics (1982); *Omaggio a György Kurtág* for Trombone and Live Electronics.

Noone, Jimmie, black American jazz clarinetist; b. Cut-Off, La., April 23, 1895; d. Los Angeles, April 19, 1944. He first took up the guitar; began to play the clarinet at age 15; then studied with Sidney Bechet in New Orleans; subsequently made appearances there with Bechet's orch.; later played in Chicago and N.Y., appearing with various bands and leading his own groups. His limpid style of playing was preserved on many fine recordings.

Norby, Erik, Danish composer; b. Copenhagen, Jan. 9, 1936. He studied with Per Nørgaard at the Conservatories in Copenhagen and Aarhus, graduating in 1966; since then he has taught at the Aalborg Cons. His music is fairly advanced in harmony.
WORKS: *Variations* for Orch. (1965); *Illustrations* for Percussion (1965); *Music for 8 Sextets* (1966; withdrawn); *Sinfonia da Requiem* (1968); *Nocturne* for Orch. (1969); *Corps céleste* for Orch. (1970); *Chromatikon* for Organ (1971); *Cortège (Passacaglia)* for Orch. (1973; Aalborg, March 12, 1974); *3 Songs* for Soprano and 11 Instruments (1973); *Schubert-Variations* for 4 Flutes (1974); *Regnbueslangen (The Rainbow Snake)*, after an American Indian fable, for Orch. (Copenhagen, Nov. 20, 1975); *4 Songs* for Mezzo-soprano and Piano (1976); Capriccio for Trumpet, Strings, and Piano (1978).

Nordal, Jón, Icelandic composer; b. Reykjavik, March 6, 1926. He studied with Jón Thórarinsson at the Reykjavik School of Music; then in Zürich with Willy Burkhard (1949–51); finally in Paris and Rome (1955–57). He taught at the Reykjavik School of Music before becoming its director in 1959, a post he still holds. He is a member of the modern group Musica Nova, and in 1968 became a member of the Royal Swedish Academy. His early works are in the neo-Classical mold; in the course of time he adopted colorism in the French impressionist vein.
WORKS: *Concerto Grosso* for Orch. (1950); *Sinfonietta seriosa* (1954); Piano Concerto (1957); Concerto for Orch.; *Brotaspil (A Play of Fragments)* for Orch. (1963); *Adagio* for Flute, Harp, Piano, and String Orch. (1965); *Stiklur* for Orch. (1969); *Canto*

elegiaco for Cello and Orch. (1971); *Epitafion* for Orch. (1974); *Langnaetti (The Long Night)* for Orch. (1976); *Tvisong (Twinsong)*, double concerto for Violin, Viola, and Orch. (1979); *Choralis* for Orch. (1981); Violin Sonata; *Rórill* for Flute, Oboe, Clarinet, and Bass Clarinet.

Norden, Norris Lindsay, American composer and theorist; b. Philadelphia, April 24, 1887; d. there, Nov. 3, 1956. He studied with C. Rybner at Columbia Univ. (Mus.Bac., 1910; M.A., 1911); held various positions as a church organist in Philadelphia, and conducted choral societies.
WORKS: He wrote several large works for chorus and orch.: *Thanatopsis* (1922); *Te Deum* (1923); *Charity* (1928); overtures; symph. poems: *Silver Plume* (1924); *The White Swan* (1936); etc.; publ. about 150 choral arrangements of sacred works by Russian and Scandinavian composers; also publ. articles on music theory.

Nordgren, Pehr Henrik, Finnish composer; b. Saltvik, Jan. 19, 1944. He studied music with Joonas Kokkonen; traveled to Japan and took courses in Japanese music at the Tokyo Univ. of Arts and Music (1970–73). In his compositions he makes use of both advanced and traditional harmonies.
WORKS: *Euphonie I* for Orch. (1966–67); *Epiphrase* for Orch. (1967); *Euphonie II* for Orch. (1967); *Nattlig vaka (Nightly Wake)*, suite from music to the radio play by Nelly Sachs, for Chamber Ensemble (1967); *Minore* for Orch. (1968); *Neljä kuolemankuvaa (4 Scenes of Death)* for Chamber Ensemble (1968); 2 violin concertos (1969, 1977); *The Turning Point* for Orch. (Helsinki, March 14, 1974); *Autumnal Concerto* for Japanese Instruments and Orch. (Helsinki, Aug. 27, 1974); Symph. (1974); Piano Concerto (1975); *Symphony for Strings* (1978); 3 string quartets (1967, 1968, 1976); *Sonatina per sestetto* for Flute, Clarinet, Violin, Cello, Piano, and Percussion (1969); *Kolme maanitusta (3 Enticements)* for Wind Quintet (1970); *Ritornello* for Violin and Piano (1970); *Hoichi the Earless* for Piano (1972).

Nordheim, Arne, significant Norwegian composer; b. Larvik, June 20, 1931. He studied at the Oslo Cons. (1948–52) with Karl Andersen and Bjarne Brustad; in 1955 took additional instruction with Holmboe in Copenhagen. Returning to Oslo, he joined the avant-garde circles; experimented in pointillistic tone color; adopted a motivic method of melorhythmic structures without formal development. He was a music critic for the Oslo daily *Dagbladet*; in 1968 he visited the U.S. as a lecturer and composer.
WORKS: *Epigram* for String Quartet (1954); String Quartet (1956); *Aftonland (Evening Land)*, song cycle for Soprano and Chamber Ensemble (1957); *Canzona per orchestra* (Bergen, June 11, 1961); *Katharsis*, ballet based on the legend of St. Anthony, for Orch. and Tape (1962); *Kimaere*, ballet (1963); *Partita* for Viola, Harpsichord, and Percussion (1963); *Epitaffio* for Orch. and Tape (1963);

Favola, musical play for Soloists, Chorus, Orch., and Tape (1965); electronic pieces: *Evolution* (1966), *Warsawa* (1967–68), *Solitaire* (1968), *Pace* (1970), and *Lux et tenebrae* (1971); *3 Responses* for Percussion Groups and Tape (1967); *Eco* for Soprano, Chorus, and Orch. (1967–68); *Colorazione* for Hammond Organ, 2 Percussionists, and Tape (1967–68); *Signaler* for Accordion, Percussion, and Electric Guitar (1967); incidental tape music for Ibsen's *Peer Gynt* (1969); *Floating* for Orch. (Graz, Oct. 20, 1970); *Dinosaurus* for Accordion and Tape (1971); *Listen* for Piano (1971); *Partita II* for Electric Guitar (1971); *Greening* for Orch. (Los Angeles, April 12, 1973); *Zimbel* for Orch. (1974); *Spur* for Accordion and Orch. (1974); *Doria* for Tenor and Orch. (1974–75); 3 ballets: *Strender* (1974), *Aridadne,* with Tape and 2 Sopranos (1977), and *The Tempest,* with Tape (1979); *Be Not Afeared,* after Shakespeare, for Soprano, Baritone, Ensemble, and Tape (1978); *Tempora noctis* for Soprano, Mezzo-soprano, Orch., and Tape (1979); 3-act ballet, *The End of Time* (1981); *Tenebrae,* concerto for Cello and Orch. (1981–82; Washington, D.C., Nov 23, 1982).

Nordica, Lillian (real name, **Lillian Norton**), distinguished American soprano; b. Farmington, Maine, Dec. 12, 1857; d. Batavia, Java, May 10, 1914. She studied with John O'Neill at the New England Cons. in Boston; made her concert debut in Boston in 1876, and toured with the Handel and Haydn Society. In 1878 she traveled to Europe as a soloist with Gilmore's band. She then studied operatic roles in Milan with Antonio Sangiovanni, who suggested the stage name Nordica, which she used for her operatic debut there on March 8, 1879, as Elvira in *Don Giovanni.* In St. Petersburg, she sang for Czar Alexander II a week before he was assassinated in March 1881. After making appearances in several German cities, she made her Paris debut on July 22, 1882, as Marguerite, at the Opéra; on Jan. 22, 1883, she married Frederick A. Gower. With him she returned to America and made her American debut with Colonel Mapleson's company in N.Y. on Nov. 23, 1883. In 1884 she began proceedings for divorce from her first husband, but he mysteriously disappeared while attempting to cross the English Channel in a balloon. She made her debut at Covent Garden in London on March 12, 1886. She first sang at the Metropolitan Opera House in N.Y. on Dec. 18, 1891, as Valentine in *Les Huguenots.* She was heard for the first time as Isolde at the Metropolitan on Nov. 27, 1895, scoring an overwhelming success. From then on she sang chiefly Wagnerian roles; she continued to appear off and on at the Metropolitan until 1909, when she began to make extended concert tours. Her farewell appearance was in Reno, Nev., on June 12, 1913. In 1896 she married the Hungarian tenor Zoltan Doeme, from whom she was divorced in 1904; in 1909 she married the banker George W. Young in London. She died while on a trip around the world.

BIBLIOGRAPHY: Ira Glackens, *Yankee Diva; Lillian Nordica and the Golden Days of Opera* (N.Y., 1963).

Nordoff, Paul, American composer; b. Philadelphia, June 4, 1909; d. Herdecke, West Germany, Jan. 18, 1977. He studied piano with Olga Samaroff and composition with Rubin Goldmark at the Juilliard School of Music in N.Y. (1928–33). He subsequently taught composition classes at the Philadelphia Cons. (1937–42), Michigan State College (1945–49), and Bard College (1949–59); afterward devoted himself mainly to music therapy and work with mentally retarded children, in Germany, Finland, and England. He held two Guggenheim fellowships (1933, 1935).

WORKS: *The Masterpiece,* opera in one act (Philadelphia, Jan. 24, 1941); secular Mass for Mixed Chorus and Orch. (1934); *The Sun,* cantata with Eurhythmic Ballet (1945); *Winter Symphony* (1955); *The Frog Prince* for Narrator and Orch., to his own text (1955); Violin Concerto; 2 piano concertos; Piano Quintet; string quartets and other chamber music; song cycles and piano pieces. He publ. *Music Therapy for Handicapped Children* (with C. Robbins; N.Y.; 2nd ed., London, 1971, with a preface by Benjamin Britten) and *Music Therapy in Special Education* (N.Y., 1971).

Nordquist, Johan Conrad, Swedish conductor; b. Vänersborg, April 11, 1840; d. Charlottenlund, April 16, 1920. He was a pupil of the Music Academy in Stockholm (1856); joined the court orch. in 1859 as a viola player; in 1864 became regimental bandmaster; in 1876 became chorus master at the Royal Opera; in 1885, became court conductor; in 1888–92, was general director. From 1870 to 1872 and again from 1880 to 1900 he taught at the Stockholm Cons.; then occupied various posts as organist and conductor. He wrote a funeral march for the obsequies of Charles XV (1872) and a festival march for the golden wedding anniversary of Oscar II (1897), besides piano pieces and songs.

Nordraak, Rikard, composer of the Norwegian national hymn, *Ja, vi elsker;* b. Christiania, June 12, 1842; d. Berlin, March 20, 1866. He was a pupil of Kiel and Kullak in Berlin; was a composer with a strong Norwegian nationalist tendency; was a close friend of Grieg, upon whom he exerted a considerable influence, and who wrote a funeral march in his memory. His death at the age of 23 was a grievous loss to Norway's music. Besides the Norwegian national anthem, he wrote music to Björnson's *Mary Stuart in Scotland;* also songs and piano pieces.

BIBLIOGRAPHY: L. Greni, *Rikard Nordraak* (Oslo, 1941); A. van E. Sein, *Rikard Nordraak* (Oslo, 1942); also articles by Ö. Anker in *Norsk Musikkgranskning* for 1940.

Noren, Heinrich Gottlieb (real name, **Heinrich Suso Johannes Gottlieb**—in 1916 he added his wife's name, Noren, to his own), Austrian composer; b. Graz, Jan. 5, 1861; d. Rottach, Bavaria, June 6, 1928. He studied violin with Vieuxtemps in Brussels (1878) and with Massart in Paris (1883); music theory with Bussler in Berlin; in 1895 he settled in Krefeld, where he founded his own music school. He then taught at the Stern Cons. in Berlin (1902–7); in 1915 he moved to Rottach. His name attracted attention with the performance of his orch. variations, *Kaleidoskop* (Dresden, July 1, 1907), in which the last movement, dedicated to "a famous contemporary," was a variation on a theme from *Ein Heldenleben* by Richard Strauss. The publishers of Strauss instituted a lawsuit against Noren, which created a ripple of excitement in musical circles. Noren also composed an opera, *Der Schleier der Beatrice;* a Symph.; a Violin Concerto; and some chamber music.

Norena, Eide (real name, **Kaja Hansen Eide**), Norwegian soprano; b. Horten, April 26, 1884; d. Lausanne, Nov. 19, 1968. She studied voice in Oslo, then in Weimar, London, and Paris; was a pupil of Raimund von Zur Mühlen; began her career as a concert singer in Scandinavia, later joining the Oslo Opera Co.; sang at La Scala in Milan, then at Covent Garden; in 1926–32, she was a member of the Chicago Civic Opera; from 1932 to 1938, of the Metropolitan Opera Co. (made her debut as Mimi, on Feb. 9, 1933); from 1935, of the Paris Opéra; toured the U.S. in concert.

Nørgaard, Per, prominent Danish composer; b. Gentofte, near Copenhagen, July 13, 1932. He studied music theory at the Royal Danish Music Cons. in Copenhagen with Holmboe, Høffding, and Hjelmborg (1952–56) and also took courses with Nadia Boulanger in Paris (1956–57). Returning to Denmark, he taught at the Funen Cons. (1958–60), the Royal Cons. (1960–65), and from 1965, at the Aarhus Cons. After a period of adolescent emulation of Sibelius, he plunged into the mainstream of cosmopolitan music-making, exploring the quasi-mathematical serial techniques based on short tonal motifs, rhythmic displacement, metrical modulation, pointillism, graphic notation, and a "horizontal" invariant fixing certain notes to specific registers; then shifted to a pointillistically impressionistic colorism evolving in a tonal bradykinesis. WORKS: 4 operas: *The Labyrinth* (1963; Copenhagen, Sept. 2, 1967); *Gilgamesh* (1971–72; Aarhus, May 4, 1973); *Siddharta* (1977–79; Stockholm, March 18, 1983); *The Divine Tivoli,* chamber opera (1982); 3 ballets: *Le Jeune Homme à marier* (*The Young Man Is to Marry,* after Ionesco, 1964; Danish Television, April 2, 1965; first stage perf., Copenhagen, Oct. 15, 1967), *Tango Chicane* (Copenhagen, Oct. 15, 1967), and *Trio* for 3 Dancers and Percussion (Paris, Dec., 1972); 3 oratorios: *It Happened in Those Days,* Christmas oratorio for youth (1960); *Dommen (The Judgement),* Easter oratorio for youth (1962); *Babel* (1964; Stockholm, Sept. 15, 1966); *Metamorphose* for Strings (1952); 4 symphs.: No. 1, *Sinfonia austera* (1954; Danish Radio, Aug. 19, 1958); No. 2 (1970; Aarhus, April 13, 1970); No. 3, with Chorus and Organ (1972–75; Copenhagen, Sept. 2, 1976); No. 4, *Indian Rose Garden and Chinese Witch Lake* (Hamburg, Oct. 30, 1981); *Triptychon* for Mixed Voices, and Wind Instruments or Organ (1957); *Constellations,*

concerto for 12 Solo Strings or 12 String Groups (Copenhagen, Nov. 3, 1958); *Lyse Danse* for Chamber Orch. (1959); *Fragment VI* for 6 Orch. Groups: Winds, Brass, Percussion, Harp, Pianos, Timpani (1959–61; Aarhus, Feb. 12, 1962); *Nocturnes,* suite for Soprano, and Piano or 19 Instruments (1961–62); *3 Love Songs* for Contralto and Orch. (1963); *Prism* for 3 Vocalists and Instrumental Ensemble (1964); *Composition* for Small Orch. (1966); *Iris* for Orch. (Copenhagen, May 19, 1967); *Luna, 4 Phases* for Orch. (Danish Radio, Sept. 5, 1968); *Recall* for Accordion and Orch. (1968); *Voyage into the Golden Screen* for Chamber Orch. (Copenhagen, March 24, 1969); *Mosaic* for 16 Winds (1969); *Doing* for Wind Orch. (1969); *Lilá* for 11 Instruments (1972); Quintet for Flute, Violin, Viola, Cello, and Piano (1951–52); *Suite* for Flute and Piano (1952); *Solo intimo* for Solo Cello (1953); *Diptychon* for Violin and Piano (1953); 2 trios for Clarinet, Cello, and Piano (1955, 1974); *Songs from Aftonland* for Contralto, Flute, Harp, Violin, Viola, and Cello (1956); 3 string quartets: No. 1, *Quartetto brioso* (1958); No. 2, *In 3 Spheres* (1965); No. 3, *Inscape* (1969); *Miniatures* for String Quartet (1959); 2 piano sonatas (1952, 1957); *Trifoglio* for Piano (1953); *4 Sketches* and *9 Studies* for Piano (1959); *Travels* for Piano (1969); electronic pieces; incidental music; songs.

Nørholm, Ib, Danish composer; b. Copenhagen, Jan. 24, 1931. He studied with Bjørn Hjelmborg and Vagn Holmboe at the Royal Danish Cons. in Copenhagen (1950–54); became a church organist in Elsinore (1957–63) and then in Copenhagen; taught at the Royal Cons. and later at the Funen Cons. in Odense; wrote music criticism. His musical idiom is permeated with Scandinavian lyricism, even when he introduces modernistic devices. WORKS: Opera, *Invitation to a Beheading,* after Vladimir Nabokov's novel (1965, Danish Television, Oct. 10, 1967); chamber opera, *Den unge Park* (*The Young Park;* Aarhus, Oct. 14, 1970); 7 symphs.: No. 1 (Danish Radio, Aug. 13, 1959); No. 2, *Isola Bella* (Copenhagen, April 27, 1972); No. 3, *Day's Nightmare* (Copenhagen, Oct. 9, 1973); No. 4, *Modskabelse,* for Soloists, Chorus, and Orch. (1979); No. 5 (1981); No. 6 (1982); No. 7, *Ecliptical Instincts* (Copenhagen, May 20, 1983); *Fluctuations* for 34 Solo Strings, 2 Harps, Harpsichord, Mandolin, and Guitar (1962); *Relief I* and *II* for Chamber Ensemble (both 1963) and *III* for Orch. (1964); *Serenade of Cincinnatus* for Chamber Orch. (1964); *Exile* for Orch. (Copenhagen, Sept. 8, 1966); *Efter Ikaros (After Icarus),* suite for Orch. (1967); *Heretic Hymn,* fresco for Orch. (1974); *Idylles d'Apocalypse* for Organ and 20 Instruments (1980); *Jongleurs–69* for Soloists, Chorus, Ensembles, Loudspeaker Voice, and Orch. (Odense, Nov. 25, 1969); *Tys og lovsang (Light and Hymn of Thanksgiving)* for Soloists, Chorus, Organ, and Instrumental Ensemble (Copenhagen Cathedral, Dec. 5, 1972); *Day's Nightmare II* for Soloists, Chorus, and Orch. (Copenhagen, Nov. 29, 1973); *Rhapsody* for Viola and Piano (1955); 4 string quartets: No. 1, *In Vere* (1955); No. 2, *5 Impromptus* (1965); No. 3, *From My Green Herbarium* (1966); No.

4, *September—October—November* (1966); *Tombeau* for Cello and Piano (1956); Violin Sonata (1956–57); Trio for Clarinet, Cello, and Piano (1957); *Mosaic Fragments* for Flute and String Trio (1958); Piano Trio (1959); *Signature from a Province* for Piano (1970); songs.

Norlind, (Johan Henrik) Tobias, Swedish musicologist; b. Hvellinge, May 6, 1879; d. Stockholm, Aug. 13, 1947. He studied piano and music in Lund; then went to Germany, where he took courses in composition with Jadassohn at the Leipzig Cons. (1897–98) and with Thuille in Munich (1898–99); he also studied musicology with Sandberger at the Univ. of Munich, and subsequently with Friedlaender at the Univ. of Berlin. Returning to Sweden in 1900, he attended the univs. of Uppsala and Lund, obtaining the degree of Dr.Phil. in 1909. He then held several positions as an instructor in colleges and univs.; taught music history at the Stockholm Cons. (1918–45); in 1921 was appointed a prof. of music history at the Royal Academy of Music in Stockholm.
WRITINGS: *Svensk musikhistoria* (Stockholm, 1901; German trans., abridged, 1904); *Musiken vid svenska skolor under 1600 talet* (1906); *Beethoven* (1907); *Allmänt Musiklexikon* (2 vols., 1916; new ed., 1927; exceedingly valuable for Scandinavian and Finnish music); *Jenny Lind* (1919); *Wagner* (1923); *Svensk folkmusik och folkdans* (1930); *Bilder ur svenska musikens historia,* in 4 vols. (1947); numerous articles on Swedish music in various European publications.

Norman, Jessye, black American soprano; b. Augusta, Ga., Sept. 15, 1945. She received a scholarship to study at Howard Univ. in Washington, D.C.; then continued her musical training at the Peabody Cons. of Music in Baltimore; also studied with Pierre Bernac at the Univ. of Michigan. She made her operatic debut at the Deutsche Oper in West Berlin in 1969; then sang in Rome and Florence. In 1972 she appeared at La Scala in Milan; she made her debut at the Metropolitan Opera in N.Y. on Sept. 26, 1983, in *Les Troyens.* In addition to opera, she became a successful as a solo performer in recital.

Norman, (Fredrick Vilhelm) Ludvig, Swedish conductor; b. Stockholm, Aug. 28, 1831; d. there, March 28, 1885. He studied piano and composition at the Leipzig Cons. with Moscheles, Hauptmann, and Rietz (1848–52); returning to Stockholm, he became in 1859 conductor of the newly formed Phil. Society. He married the violinist **Wilma Neruda** in 1864 (divorced, 1869). He composed 4 symphs.; a Piano Concerto; String Octet; Piano Sextet; 11 books of songs; piano pieces; also publ. *Musikaliska uppsatser och kritiker* (posthumous; Stockholm, 1888).

North, Alex, American composer and conductor; b. Chester, Pa., Dec. 4, 1910. He studied at the Curtis Inst. in Philadelphia and at the Juilliard School of Music in N.Y.; also took private lessons with Ernst Toch in Los Angeles. He began his career as a com-

poser for documentary films and gradually established himself as a composer of imaginative cinema music; wrote the scores for *Death of a Salesman, Viva Zapata!, A Streetcar Named Desire, The Bad Seed, The Sound and the Fury, Spartacus, The Misfits, Cleopatra, The Agony and the Ecstasy,* and *Who's Afraid of Virginia Woolf?* His song *Unchained Melody* acquired great popularity. Apart from these lucrative tasks, he composed grand symphs., modernistic concertos, and unorthodox cantatas.
WORKS: *Rhapsody* for Piano and Orch. (N.Y., Nov. 11, 1941); *Revue* for Clarinet and Orch. (N.Y., Nov. 20, 1946, Benny Goodman, soloist; Leonard Bernstein conducting); Symph. No. 1 (1947); *Morning Star Cantata* (N.Y., May 18, 1947); *Little Indian Drum* for Narrator and Orch. (N.Y., Oct. 19, 1947); *Negro Mother Cantata* (N.Y., May 17, 1948); *Holiday Set* for Orch. (Saratoga, N.Y., July 10, 1948); Symph. No. 2 (1968); Symph. No. 3 (1971; incorporating parerga & paralipomena from the score originally written for the film *2001, A Space Odyssey,* which was not used in the actual production).

North, Roger, English musician; b. Tostock, Suffolk, Sept. 3, 1653; d. Rougham, March 1, 1734. He was a solicitor; rose to be named Attorney-General to King James II; music was his avocation. He publ. *Memoires of Musick* and *Musicall Gramarian,* containing comments on the musical mores of his era.
BIBLIOGRAPHY: J. Wilson, ed., *Roger North on Music; Being a Selection from His Essays Written During the Years c.1695–1728* (London, 1959).

Norvo, Red (real name, **Kenneth Norville**), American jazz vibraphonist and bandleader; b. Beardstown, Ill., March 31, 1908. He played piano and xylophone while attending classes in mining engineering at the Univ. of Missouri (1926–27); later joined Paul Whiteman's orch. In 1935 he organized his own band in N.Y.; also worked with Benny Goodman (1944–45) and Woody Herman (1945–46). He was temporarily married to the blues singer **Mildred Bailey.**

Noskowski, Sigismund (Zygmunt von), significant Polish conductor and composer; b. Warsaw, May 2, 1846; d. there, July 23, 1909. He studied at the Warsaw Music Inst.; then became an instructor in a school for the blind, and devised a music notation for the blind. He subsequently went to Germany, where he studied composition with Kiel in Berlin. After a brief period of professional activities in Western Europe, he returned to Warsaw and was director of the Music Society there (1881–92); in 1888 he was appointed a prof. at the Warsaw Cons.; later conducted at the Warsaw Opera and led some concerts of the Warsaw Phil. Society. He wrote the operas *Livia Quintilla* (Lwow, Feb. 1, 1898), *Wyrok* (Warsaw, Nov. 15, 1906), and *Zemsta* (Warsaw, 1909); 3 symphs. (1875, 1880, 1903); and several symph. poems, of which *Step* (1897) became quite popular in Poland; also chamber music and songs. He publ. 2 collections of folk melodies and was co-author with M. Zawirski of a book on harmony and counterpoint (Warsaw, 1909).

Noté, Jean, Belgian baritone; b. Tournai, May 6, 1859; d. Brussels, April 1, 1922. He studied at the Ghent Cons.; made his debut in a concert in Ghent in 1883; then sang opera in Lille, Brussels, Lyons, Marseilles, etc. He made his N.Y. Metropolitan Opera debut on Dec. 3, 1908, as Escamillo. In 1913 he joined the Paris Opéra, and remained on its roster until his death. Among his finest roles were Hamlet, Beckmesser, Rigoletto, and Wolfram.

Notker (Balbulus), a monk at the Monastery of St. Gall; b. Elgg, near Zürich (or Jonschwyl, near St. Gall), c.840; d. April 6, 912. He was one of the earliest and most important writers of sequences; his *Liber hymnorum* (sequence texts of the year 884) is of particular interest. Several short musical treatises in Latin and German are traditionally ascribed to him; but these should be more correctly attributed to a certain **Notker Labeo,** who was also a monk at St. Gall but who flourished about a century later than Notker "Balbulus" (a nickname meaning "the stammerer"). It has also been established that Notker Balbulus was not the author of the *Media in vita in morte sumus* (cf. P. Wagner, "Das Media vita," in *Schweizerisches Jahrbuch für Musikwissenschaft*, I). Gerbert (*Scriptores*, I) publ. 4 of the above-mentioned treatises, together with a commentary on the so-called "Romanian" letters (probably spurious). Two of these treatises, also a 5th one (presumably also by N. Labeo), are included in Riemann's *Studien zur Geschichte der Notenschrift*. All 5 treatises were publ. by Piper in 2 vols. as part of the projected collected edition of Notker Labeo's works.
BIBLIOGRAPHY: A.K. Henschel, *Zehn Sequenzen des Notker Balbulus, aus den ältesten Quellen übertragen und mit der Überlieferung verglichen* (Diss., Univ. of Erlangen, 1924); R. van Doren, *Etude sur l'influence musicale de l'Abbaye de St. Gall* (1925); H. Husmann, "Die St. Galler Sequenztradition bei Notker und Ekkehard," *Acta Musicologica*, 26 (1954); R.Crocker, *The Early Medieval Sequence* (Berkeley, Calif., 1977).

Nottebohm, (Martin) Gustav, distinguished German musicologist; b. Lüdenscheid, Westphalia, Nov. 12, 1817; d. Graz, Oct. 29, 1882. He studied with Berger and Dehn in Berlin (1838–39); then with Mendelssohn and Schumann in Leipzig (1840–45); finally with Sechter in Vienna (1846), where he settled as a music teacher. He revised the Beethoven edition publ. by Breitkopf & Härtel, prepared thematic catalogues of the works of Beethoven and Schubert, and edited some of the works of Mozart. Of particular importance are his studies of Beethoven's sketchbooks.
WRITINGS: *Ein Skizzenbuch von Beethoven* (Leipzig, 1865; 2nd ed., 1924, by P. Mies, as *Zwei Skizzenbücher von Beethoven aus den Jahren 1801 bis 1803*); *Thematisches Verzeichniss der im Druck erschienenen Werke von Ludwig van Beethoven* (Leipzig, 2nd ed., 1868, reprint, 1969); *Beethoveniana* (Leipzig, 1872; 2nd ed., 1925); *Beethovens Studien* (Leipzig, 1873; includes Beethoven's exercise books under Haydn, Albrechtsberger, and Salieri); *Thematisches Verzeichniss der im Druck erschienenen Werke von Franz Schubert* (Vienna, 1874); *Mozartiana* (Leipzig, 1880); E. Mandyczewski, ed., *Zweite Beethoveniana* (Leipzig, 1887; 2nd ed., 1925).

Nouguès, Jean, French composer; b. Bordeaux, April 25, 1875; d. Auteuil, Aug. 28, 1932. He showed remarkable precocity as a composer, having completed an opera, *Le Roi du Papagey,* before he was 16. After regular study in Paris, he produced his opera *Yannha* at Bordeaux in 1897. The next 2 operas, *Thamyris* (Bordeaux, 1904) and *La Mort de Tintagiles* (Paris, 1905), were brought out without much success; but after the production of his spectacular *Quo Vadis* (text by H. Cain, after Sienkiewicz's famous novel; Nice, Feb. 9, 1909) he suddenly found himself famous. The work was given in Paris on Nov. 26, 1909, in N.Y on April 4, 1911; had numerous revivals in subsequent years. His later operas failed to measure up to *Quo Vadis;* they included *L'Auberge rouge* (Nice, Feb. 21, 1910), *La Vendetta* (Marseilles, 1911), *L'Aiglon* (Rouen, Feb. 2, 1912), and *Le Scarabée bleu* (1931).

Nourrit, Adolphe, celebrated French tenor; b. Montpellier, March 3, 1802; d. (suicide) Naples, March 8, 1839. His father, **Louis Nourrit** (1780–1831), was a leading opera tenor in France; Adolphe Nourrit studied voice with the famous teacher Manuel García; at the age of 19 he made his debut as Pylaides in Gluck's opera *Iphigénie en Tauride* at the Paris Opéra (Sept. 10, 1821), with excellent success. He soon became known in Paris as one of the finest tenors of his generation, and famous opera composers entrusted him with leading roles at the premieres of their works; thus, he appeared in the title role of Meyerbeer's *Robert le Diable* (Paris, Nov. 21, 1831) and as Raoul in *Les Huguenots* (Paris, Feb. 29, 1836); in the title role in Rossini's *Le Comte Ory* (Paris, Aug. 20, 1828) and as Arnold in his *Guillaume Tell* (Paris, Aug. 3, 1829); as Masaniello in Auber's *La Muette de Portici* (Paris, Feb. 29, 1828); as Eléazar in Halévy's *La Juive* (Paris, Feb. 23, 1835); and others. He then traveled in Italy in Dec. 1837, and was particularly successful in Naples. His career seemed to be assured, but despite all these successes, vocal problems and a liver ailment led to depression, and he killed himself by jumping from the roof of his lodging in Naples.
BIBLIOGRAPHY: L.M. Quicherat, *Adolphe Nourrit* (3 vols., Paris, 1867); E. Boutet de Monvel, *Un Artiste d'autrefois, Adolphe Nourrit* (2 vols., Paris, 1903); F. Rogers, "Adolphe Nourrit," *Musical Quarterly* (Jan. 1939).

Nováček, Ottokar, American violinist and composer of Czech descent; b. Weisskirchen, Hungary, May 13, 1866; d. New York, Feb. 3, 1900. He studied violin with his father, Martin Joseph Nováček, and with Brodsky at the Leipzig Cons., graduating in 1885. In 1891 he was engaged by Nikisch to join the Boston Symph. Orch., of which Nikisch was the music director. In America, Nováček began to compose; his name became known chiefly through his brilliant violin piece *Perpetuum mobile;* he also wrote a Piano Concerto; 3 string quartets; *8 Concert-Caprices* for Violin and Piano; *Bulgarian Dances* for Violin and Piano; and songs.

Nováček, Rudolf, Czech violinist and composer; b. Bela Crkva, April 7, 1860; d. Prague, Aug. 12, 1929. He lived mostly in Temesvár; also held occasional positions as violin teacher and conductor in Rumania, Bulgaria, and Russia. His *Sinfonietta* for Wind Instruments (first perf. in Prague, Nov. 11, 1888) became popular.

Novães, Guiomar, extraordinary Brazilian pianist; b. São João da Bõa Vista, Feb. 28, 1895; d. São Paulo, March 7, 1979. She was the 17th of 19 offspring in a highly fecund family; studied piano with a local Italian teacher, Luigi Chiafarelli; soon began performing in public recitals. The Brazilian government sent her to France to take part in a competition for entering the Paris Cons.; she won first place among 388 contestants from a jury that included Debussy and Fauré; Debussy praised her for "the power of total inner concentration, rare among artists." She enrolled in the class of Isidor Philipp, who later described her as a true "force of nature." She graduated from the Paris Cons. in 1911, and made a successful concert tour in France, England, and Italy. She made her American debut at a N.Y. recital on Nov. 11, 1915, and subsequently made numerous tours of the U.S. Reviewing one of her concerts, James Huneker described her as "the Paderewska of the Pampas." In 1922 she married the Brazilian composer **Octavio Pinto.** She made her home in São Paulo, with frequent sojourns in N.Y. In 1956 the Brazilian government awarded her the Order of Merit as a goodwill ambassador to the U.S. She made her last American appearance in 1972. She was especially praised for her interpretations of the music of Chopin, Schumann, and other composers of the Romantic era; she also played pieces by South American composers, including some works written for her by her husband. Her playing was notable for its dynamic colors; she exuded a personal charm, while often disregarding the more pedantic aspects of the music.

Novák, Jan, Czech composer; b. Nová Říše, April 8, 1921. He studied piano with local teachers, and composition with Petrželka at the Brno Cons. (1940–46) and with Bořkovec at the Prague Academy of Musical Arts (1946–47); during the summer of 1947 he attended the composition classes of Aaron Copland at the Berkshire Music Center at Tanglewood, Mass., and also took lessons with Martinu in N.Y. (1947–48). Returning to Czechoslovakia, he lived in Brno; but left the country in the wake of the political events of 1968; he moved to Denmark (1968–70) and in 1970 settled in Rovereto, Italy, where he

taught piano at the municipal music school.
WORKS: Oboe Concerto (1952); *Balletti* for Nonet (1955); Concerto for 2 Pianos and Orch. (1955); *Toccata chromatica* for Piano (1957); Concertino for Wind Quintet (1957); *Capriccio* for Cello and Orch. (1958); *Musica Caesariana* for Wind Orch. (1960); *Passer Catulli* for Bass Singer and 9 Instruments (1961); *Ioci vernalis* for Bass, 8 Instruments, and Bird Songs on Tape (1964); *Testamentum* for Chorus and 4 Horns (1956); *Dido,* oratorio (1967); *Ignis pro Ioanne Palach,* cantata (1968; Prague, April 15, 1969); *Mimus magicus* for Soprano, Clarinet, and Piano (1969); *Rondini,* 8 rondos for Piano (1970); *Concentus Eurydicae* for Guitar and String Orch. (1970); *Orpheus et Eurydice* for Soprano, Viola d'Amore, and Piano (1971); *Invitatio pastorum,* cantata (1971); *Panisci fistula,* 3 preludes for 3 Flutes (1972); *Rosarium,* exercise for 2 Guitars (1972); choruses; songs.

Novák, Johann Baptist, Slovenian composer; b. Ljubljana, 1756; d. there, Jan. 29, 1833. He served as a government clerk and at the same time studied music; in 1799–1800 was conductor, and in 1808–25 music director, of the Phil. Society in Ljubljana; he gave concerts as a singer and violinist. A close contemporary of Mozart, he composed in a Mozartean manner. His historical importance lies in his incidental music to *Figaro,* a play in the Slovenian language based on the same comedy by Beaumarchais that served for Mozart's great opera. Novák's music forms a striking parallel to Mozart's procedures and yet contains some original traits.
BIBLIOGRAPHY: Dragotin Cvetko, "J.B. Novák —Ein slowenischer Anhänger Mozarts," *Bericht über den Internationalen Musikwissenschaftlichen Kongress Wien, Mozartjahr, 1956.*

Novák, Milan, Slovak composer; b. Trahovice, Aug. 12, 1927. He studied piano with Kafenda, composition with Alexander Moyzes, and conducting with Talich at the Bratislava Cons. In 1955 he was appointed conductor of the Military Artistic Ensemble in Bratislava.
WORKS: 2 ballets: *Where the Play Ends* (1964) and *Ballad about a Tree* (1967); Concertino for Trumpet, Strings, Piano, 4-hands, and Percussion (1964); *Reminiscences* for Cello and Orch. (1969); Concerto for Harp and Chamber Orch. (1972); *Mountains and the Heart,* song cycle for Bass and Orch. (1973); *30 Happy Years,* cantata for Children's Chorus and Orch. (1975); *So that There Is Life on Earth,* cantata (1976); Clarinet Sonatina (1959); Cello Sonatina (1961); String Quartet (1975); *Music* for Flute and String Quartet (1975); music for theater and films.

Novák, Vítězslav, eminent Czech composer; b. Kamenitz, Dec. 5, 1870; d. Skuteč, July 18, 1949. He studied jurisprudence and philosophy at the Univ. of Prague, and music at the Cons. there, where his teachers were Jiránek, Stecker, and Dvořák. From 1909 to 1920 he taught at the Prague Cons., and from 1918 to 1939 was a prof. of composition at the Master

School of the Czech State Cons. Brahms was the first to discover the extraordinary talent of Novák, and recommended him to his own publisher, Simrock. Novák's early works follow the general line of German Romantic composition, but in his operas and symph. poems he showed a profound feeling for national elements in Czech music. In 1946 he received the title of National Artist of the Republic of Czechoslovakia.

WORKS: OPERAS: *Zvikovský rarášek* (*The Imp of Zvikov;* Prague, Oct. 10, 1915); *Karlštejn* (Prague, Nov. 18, 1916); *Lucerna* (Prague, May 13, 1923); *Děduv odkaz* (*Old Man's Bequest;* Brno, Jan. 16, 1926). BALLETS: *Signorina Gioventù* and *Nikotina* (both perf. in Prague, Feb. 10, 1929). FOR ORCH.: *Slovácka Suite* (Prague, Feb. 4, 1906); *Lady Godiva,* overture (Prague, Nov. 24, 1907); *V Tatrach* (*In the Tatra Mountains;* Prague, Dec. 7, 1907); *Toman a lesní panna* (Prague, April 5, 1908); *Podzimni sinfonie* (*Autumn Symphony;* Prague, Dec. 18, 1934); *De profundis* (Brno, Oct. 9, 1941); *Majova sinfonie* (*May Symphony,* in celebration of the liberation of Prague by the Soviet Army in May 1945; dedicated to Stalin; Prague, Dec. 5, 1945); cantata, *Boure* (Brno, April 14, 1910); *12 ukolébavek* (*12 Lullabies),* variations on a poem for Women's Voices (Prague, 1938. CHAMBER MUSIC: Piano Trio; Piano Quartet; Piano Quintet; 2 string quartets; *Trio quasi una ballata;* Sonata for Viola, Cello, and Piano. Also numerous piano pieces, among them *Ballade, Czech Dances, Sonata eroica, Pan, Suite exoticon,* 6 sonatinas, etc.; *St. Wenceslas Triptych* for Organ; songs.

BIBLIOGRAPHY: Z. Nejedlý, *Vítězslav Novák* (Prague, 1921); K. Hoffmeister, *Tvorba V. Nováka, z let 1941–1948* (Prague, 1949); Bohumir Štědroň, *Vítězslav Novák v obrazech* (Prague, 1967); Vladimir Lebl, *Vítězslav Novák* (in Eng.; Prague, 1968).

Novello, (Joseph) Alfred, English music publisher, son of **Vincent Novello;** b. London, Aug. 12, 1810; d. Genoa, July 16, 1896. He was also a bass singer, organist, and composer; was choirmaster at Lincoln's Inn Chapel. He entered his father's business at 19. He inaugurated an important innovation, the printing of separate vocal parts for choir use; did much to popularize classical music in England by publishing cheap oratorio scores. After his retirement he lived in Genoa.

Novello, Clara Anastasia, daughter of **Vincent Novello;** English soprano; b. London, June 10, 1818; d. Rome, March 12, 1908. Having studied piano and singing in London, she entered the Paris Cons. in 1829, but returned home the following year because of the revolution. After a successful debut on Oct. 22, 1832, at Windsor, she was engaged for the Phil. Society, the Antient Concerts, and the principal festivals. In 1837 Mendelssohn engaged her for the Gewandhaus concerts; she then sang in Berlin, Vienna, and St. Petersburg. She made her operatic debut in Padua (July 6, 1841); sang with great success in the principal Italian cities. On Nov. 22, 1843, she married Count Gigliucci, withdrawing to private life for several years; she reappeared in 1850, sing-

ing in concert and opera (chiefly in England and Italy). After her farewell appearance in London in 1860, she retired to Rome. Schumann greatly admired Clara Novello, and coined the term Novelette for some of his pieces as an affectionate homage to her.

BIBLIOGRAPHY: Valeria Gigliucci, *Clara Novello's Reminiscences, compiled by her daughter* (London, 1910; with memoir by A.D. Coleridge); Averil Mackenzie-Grieve, *Clara Novello* (London, 1955).

Novello, Vincent, English music publisher; b. London, Sept. 6, 1781; d. Nice, Aug. 9, 1861. He was a chorister in the Sardinian Chapel on Duke Street; later deputy organist to Webbe and Danby, and in 1797–1822, organist at the chapel of the Portuguese Embassy. He was pianist to the Italian Opera in 1812; was a founder of the Phil. Society in 1813, sometimes conducting its concerts; in 1840–43, was organist at the Roman Catholic Chapel in Moorfields. In 1811 he founded the great London music publishing firm of **Novello & Co.** Himself a composer of sacred music (masses, motets, anthems, Kyries, etc.), he gathered together and publ. excellent collections: *A Collection of Sacred Music* (1811; 2 vols.); *Purcell's Sacred Music* (1829; 5 vols.); *Croft's Anthems; Greene's Anthems; Boyce's Anthems;* masses by Haydn, Mozart, Beethoven; etc. He retired to Nice in 1849.

BIBLIOGRAPHY: Mary Cowden-Clarke, *Life and Labours of Vincent Novello* (London, 1862); W. Barclay Squire, "Some Novello Correspondence," *Musical Quarterly* (April 1917); *Dictionary of National Biography,* vol. XLI; also N. Medici and R. Hughes, *A Mozart Pilgrimage* (London, 1955; travel diaries of Vincent Novello and his wife); M. Hurd, "Vincent Novello, 6 September 1781–9 August 1861," *Musical Times* (Oct. 1981).

Novello & Co., prominent firm of music publishers, founded 1811 in London by **Vincent Novello.** Under the management of his eldest son, **(Joseph) Alfred Novello,** the business increased enormously, and after the latter's retirement in 1856, **Henry Littleton** (b. London, Jan. 2, 1823; d. there, May 11, 1888), who became a partner in 1861, assumed the general management, becoming sole proprietor in 1866. The following year he acquired the business of Ewer and Co., and in 1867 changed the name of the firm to **Novello, Ewer & Co.** On his retirement in 1887 he was succeeded by his sons, **Alfred H.** and **Augustus J. Littleton,** and his sons-in-law, **George T.S. Gill** and **Henry W. Brooke.** In 1898 the house was formed into a limited company, under the name of Novello & Co., Ltd. In 1846 they acquired *Mainzer's Musical Times* (established 1844), which they have publ. since then as the *Musical Times.* The N.Y. branch, established in 1850, was taken over in 1906 by H.W. Gray & Co.

BIBLIOGRAPHY: J. Bennett, *A Short History of Cheap Music as Exemplified in the Records of the House of Novello, Ewer & Co.* (1887); "The Novello Centenary," *Musical Times* (June 1911).

Novello-Davies, Clara, Welsh singing teacher and choral conductor; b. Cardiff, April 7, 1861; d. London, March 1, 1943. Her real surname was Davies; her father (who was also her first teacher) called her "Clara Novello" after the celebrated singer of that name, and she adopted the combined name professionally. She sang at concerts; in 1881 she turned to choral conducting; organized a Royal Welsh Ladies' Choir, with which she traveled with fine success in Great Britain, France, America, and South Africa; at the World's Fair in Chicago (1893) and at the Paris Exposition of 1900 the chorus was awarded first prize. She was commended by Queen Victoria (1894) and by King George and Queen Mary (1928). She publ. a number of successful songs (*A Voice from the Spirit Land, The Vigil, Comfort,* etc.); was also author of the book *You Can Sing* and an autobiography, *The Life I Have Loved* (London, 1940). Her son, **Ivor Novello** (b. Cardiff, Jan. 15, 1893; d. London, March 6, 1951), wrote (at her request) the song *Keep the Home Fires Burning,* immensely popular during World War I.

Noverre, Jean-Georges, French dancer who introduced dramatic action into the ballet (ballet-pantomime); b. Paris, April 29, 1727; d. St.-Germain-en-Laye, Oct. 19, 1810. He was a solo dancer at Berlin; was ballet master at the Opéra-Comique in Paris, 1749; at London, 1757–75; at Lyons, Stuttgart, Vienna, Milan, and (1775–80) at the Grand Opéra, Paris. He publ. *Lettres sur la danse, et sur les ballets* (1760; several eds.; Eng. trans., London, 1782, 1930, 1951).
BIBLIOGRAPHY: C.E. Noverre, *Life and Works of the Chevalier Noverre* (London, 1882); H. Abert, "Jean Georges Noverre und sein Einfluss auf die dramatische Ballet-Komposition," *Jahrbuch Peters* (1908); H. Niedecken, *J.G. Noverre; Sein Leben und seine Beziehungen zur Musik* (Halle, 1914); D. Lynham, *The Chevalier Noverre* (London, 1950).

Novikov, Anatoly, Russian composer; b. Skopin, Oct. 30, 1896. He studied at the Moscow Cons. with Glière, Vasilenko, and Catoire; devoted himself to organizing chorus groups in the Soviet Military Academy; composed a number of patriotic songs which entered the Soviet popular repertoire, among them *5 Bullets;* wrote the political cantata *We Need Peace* (1954); *Hymn of the Democratic Youth of the World; My Fatherland, Russia; March of Communist Brigades;* etc.; also some lively musical comedies. On the occasion of his 80th birthday in 1976 he was awarded the order of Hero of Socialist Labor, the Order of Lenin, and the Sickle and Hammer gold medal.

Novotná, Jarmila, Czech soprano; b. Prague, Sept. 23, 1907. She studied with Emmy Destinn; made her debut in *La Traviata* (Prague, June 27, 1926); in 1928 joined the roster of the Berlin State Opera. She made her American debut at San Francisco, in *Madama Butterfly* (Oct. 18, 1939); first sang at the Metropolitan Opera in N.Y. in *La Bohème,* on Jan. 5, 1940; remained on its staff until 1951; again from

1952–56; then retired to Vienna.

Novotný, Václav Juda, Bohemian composer; b. Wesetz, near Počatek, Sept. 17, 1849; d. Prague, Aug. 1, 1922. He studied at the Prague Organ School with Skuherský; for many years was editor of the Bohemian musical paper *Dalibor;* composed pieces for violin and songs; compiled a large collection of Bohemian folk songs; trans. into Czech about 100 opera texts, among them all the dramatic works of Wagner.

Nowak, Leopold, eminent Austrian musicologist; b. Vienna, Aug. 17, 1904. He studied piano and organ with Louis Dité and counterpoint with Franz Schmidt at the Vienna Academy of Music; then took courses in musicology with Guido Adler and Robert Lach at the Univ. of Vienna; received his Ph.D. there in 1927 with the dissertation *Das deutsche Gesellschaftslied bei Heinrich Finck, Paul Hofhaymer und Heinrich Isaac;* completed his Habilitation with his *Grundzüge einer Geschichte des Basso ostinato* (publ. in Vienna, 1932). He lectured at the Univ. of Vienna from 1932 until 1973; in 1945 he became editor of the critical edition of Bruckner's works; from 1946 to 1969 he was director of the music division of the Nationalbibliothek in Vienna, where he compiled valuable catalogues for special exhibitions on Bruckner, Bach, Mozart, Haydn, and others. His exhaustive studies on the life and music of Bruckner are of prime value.
WRITINGS: *Franz Liszt* (Innsbruck, 1936); *Te Deum laudamus: Gedanken zur Musik Anton Bruckners* (Vienna, 1947); *Joseph Haydn* (Vienna, 1951; 3rd ed., 1965); *Gegen den Strom: Leben und Werk von Emil Nikolaus von Rezniček* (with F. von Rezniček, the composer's daughter; Vienna, 1960); *Anton Bruckner: Musik und Leben* (a brief study; Vienna, 1964); *Reden und Ansprachen* (Vienna, 1964); *Anton Bruckner: Musik und Leben* (a voluminous pictorial biography; Linz, 1973); *Das Geburtshaus Anton Bruckners [Ansfelden]: Führer* (Linz, 1975).
BIBLIOGRAPHY: F. Grasberger, ed., *Bruckner-Studien: Leopold Nowak zum 60. Geburtstag* (Vienna, 1964).

Nowak, Lionel, American composer and pianist; b. Cleveland, Sept. 25, 1911. He studied piano with Beryl Rubinstein and Edwin Fischer; composition with Herbert Elwell and Quincy Porter; also had fruitful sessions with Sessions. Upon graduation from the Cleveland Inst. of Music in 1936 he was music director for the Humphrey-Weidman Dancers; then taught at Converse College in Spartanburg, S.C. (1942–46) and at Syracuse Univ. (1946–48); in 1948 he was appointed to the faculty of Bennington College, and was still a prof. of piano there in 1984.
WORKS: Concertino for Piano and Orch. (1944); Oboe Sonata (1949); 3 cello sonatas (1950, 1951, 1960); *Diptych* for String Quartet (1951); Trio for Clarinet, Violin, and Cello (1951); Quartet for Oboe and Strings (1952); Sonata for Solo Violin (1952);

Piano Trio (1954); *Concert Piece* for Kettledrums and String Orch. (1961).

Nowowiejski, Felix, Polish composer; b. Wartenburg, Feb. 7, 1877; d. Poznan, Jan. 18, 1946. He studied with Bussler at the Stern Cons. in Berlin; won the Paderewski Prize in 1903. He lived mostly in Berlin; after World War I taught organ and church music at the State Cons. in Poznan (1920–27). A competent composer, he followed the line of German Romanticism.
WORKS: Opera, *Legenda Baltyku (Baltic Legend),* produced in Poznan in 1924; 5 symphs.; 3 symph. poems; Piano Concerto (1941); Cello Concerto (1938); and a considerable amount of chamber music. His best-known work was the oratorio *Quo vadis* (1907), after Sienkiewicz's novel.
BIBLIOGRAPHY: Jan Boehm, *F. Nowowiejski* (Olsztyn, 1968).

Nozzari, Andrea, Italian tenor; b. Vertrova, near Bergamo, 1775; d. Naples, Dec. 12, 1832. He studied with Petrobelli in Bergamo; made his operatic debut in 1894; then made appearances in Rome, Milan, and Paris; was a principal tenor in Naples (1811–25); created tenor roles in several operas of Rossini; then retired and taught singing.

Nucius (Nucis, Nux), Johannes, German composer and theorist; b. Görlitz, c.1560; d. Himmelwitz, March 25, 1620. He studied music with Johannes Winckler, the cantor of the Görlitz Gymnasium; c.1586 he took Holy Orders at the monastery of Rauden; in 1591 was made abbot of the monastery of Himmelwitz in Silesia. He publ. 50 *Modulations sacrae modis musicis* for 5 and 6 Voices (Prague, 1591; 2nd ed., 1609, as *Cantionum sacrarum liber primus*); 52 *Cantionum sacrarum diversarum vocum, liber secundus,* some for 7, others for 8, Voices (Liegnitz, 1609); a theoretical work, *Musices poeticae sive De compositione cantum praeceptiones ultissimae* (Neisse, 1613).
BIBLIOGRAPHY: B. Widmann, *Johannes Nucius, Abt von Himmelwitz* (Bregenz, 1921); E. Kirsch, *Von der Persönlichkeit und dem Stil des schlesischen Zisterzienser-Komponisten Johannes Nucius* (Breslau, 1926).

Nuitter (real name, **Truinet**), **Charles Louis Etienne,** French writer on music; b. Paris, April 24, 1828; d. there, Feb. 23, 1899. He was a lawyer by profession; then became interested in the theater; was custodian of the archives of the Paris Opéra. He changed his real name, Truinet, to Nuitter by anagrammatic transposition of letters, and under that name wrote librettos for many operas and operettas, including some by Offenbach; also translated librettos of operas by Weber, Mozart, Wagner, and Verdi; wrote scenarios for Delibes (*Coppélia*) and others. He publ. *Le Nouvel Opéra* (1875); *Les Origines de l'opéra français* (1886; with Thoinan); many articles in music magazines.

Nummi, Seppo, Finnish composer, music critic, and festival administrator; b. Oulu, May 30, 1932; d. Tampere, Aug. 1, 1981. He studied at the Univ. of Helsinki and at the Sibelius Academy; his composition teacher was Yrjö Kilpinen. He began writing music criticism for the newspaper *Uusi Suomi* in 1953; in 1967 he founded the noted Helsinki Festival, serving as its director until 1977. As a composer, he is best known for his many songs in a fine lyrical mode, in the tradition of Hugo Wolf and his teacher Kilpinen; he also wrote some chamber music. He publ. *Musica fennica* (with T. Makinen; Helsinki, 1965; trans. into Eng. and several other languages) and *Modern Musik* (Stockholm, 1966; also in Finnish).

Nunn, Edward Cuthbert, English organist, conductor, and composer; b. Bristol, Feb. 23, 1868; d. London, Nov. 26, 1914. He studied at the Royal Academy of Music; then served as organist at various churches, and conducted opera. He composed the children's operas *Kamar-al-Zaman, The Fairy Slipper, The Shepherdess and the Sweep, The Garden of Paradise,* and *The Wooden Bowl;* also cantatas and other choral works.

Nunó, Jaime, Spanish bandmaster; composer of the Mexican national anthem; b. San Juan de las Abadesas, Sept. 8, 1824; d. Auburndale, N.Y., July 18, 1908. He studied with Mercadante in Italy; in 1851 went to Cuba, and in 1854 to Mexico, where he was appointed chief of military bands; was commissioned to write a national anthem for Mexico; it was sung for the first time on Sept. 15, 1854. Subsequently he was active as an impresario for Italian opera companies in Cuba, Mexico, and the U.S.

Nussio, Otmar, Italian composer; b. Grosseto, Oct. 23, 1902. He studied flute, piano, and composition at the Cons. in Milan and with Respighi in Rome. He conducted concerts of light music and wrote a number of overtures and orch. suites, among them *Escapades musicales* (1949); *Tzigana* (1954); *Portraits musicaux* (1955); *Episodio* (1958); *Monologhi di vita e di morte* (1958); and *Alborada* (1971); also a Flute Concerto (1936); Piano Concerto (1960); *Passatempo donchisciottesco* for Clarinet and Orch. (1971); *Cantata ticinese* for Voices and Orch. (1962). His suite for Harpsichord, Flute, Violin Solo, and Strings, *Rubensiana,* was performed for the first time in the Rubens House in Antwerp, on May 21, 1950.

Nyiregyházi, Erwin, remarkable Hungarian pianist; b. Budapest, Jan. 19, 1903. He absorbed music by a kind of domestic osmosis, from his father, a professional tenor, and his mother, an amateur pianist. An exceptionally gifted *wunderkind,* he had perfect pitch and a well-nigh phonographic memory as a very small child; played a Haydn sonata and pieces by Grieg, Chopin, and himself at a concert in Fiume at the age of 6. In 1910 he entered the Budapest Academy of Music, studying theory with Albert Siklós and Leo Weiner, and piano with István Tomán. In 1914 the family moved to Berlin, where he became a piano student of Ernst von Dohnányi. He made his debut in Germany playing Beethoven's 3rd Piano Concerto with the Berlin Phil. (Oct. 14, 1915). In 1916 he began studying with Frederic Lamond, a pupil of Liszt, who was instrumental in encouraging Nyiregyházi to study Liszt's music, which was to become the most important part of his concert repertoire. In 1920 he went to the U.S.; his American debut (Carnegie Hall, N.Y., Oct. 18, 1920) was sensationally successful; the word "genius" was freely applied to him by critics usually restrained in their verbal effusions. Inexplicably, his American career suffered a series of setbacks; he became involved in a lawsuit with his manager; he married his next manager, a Mrs. Mary Kelen, in 1926, but divorced her a year later. He then went to California, where he became gainfully employed as a studio pianist in Hollywood; in 1930 he made a European tour; then lived in N.Y. and in Los Angeles. Beset by personal problems, he fell into a state of abject poverty, but resolutely refused to resume his concert career; he did not even own a piano. He married frequently, and as frequently divorced his successive wives. In 1972 he married his 9th wife, a lady 10 years his senior; she died shortly afterward. Attempts were made in vain by friends and admirers in California to induce him to play in public; a semi-private recital was arranged for him in San Francisco in 1974; a recording of his playing of Liszt was issued in 1977; it was greeted with enthusiastic reviews, all expressing regret for his disappearance from the concert stage. Nyiregyházi composed several hundred works, mostly for piano; they remain in MS. As a child, Nyiregyházi was the object of a "scientific" study by Dr. Géza Révész, director of the Psychological Laboratory in Amsterdam, who made tests of his memory, sense of pitch, ability to transpose into different keys at sight, etc.; these findings were publ. in German as *Psychologische Analyse eines musikalisch hervorragenden Kindes* (Leipzig, 1916) and in Eng. as *The Psychology of a Musical Prodigy* (London, 1925), but the examples given and the tests detailed in the book proved to be no more unusual than the capacities of thousands of similarly gifted young musicians.

Nystedt, Knut, Norwegian composer, organist, and choral conductor; b. Christiania, Sept. 3, 1915. He studied organ with A. Sandvold, conducting with Fjeldstad, and composition with Per Steenberg and Bjarne Brustad at the Oslo Cons. (1931–43); then organ with E. White and composition with Aaron Copland in N.Y. (1947). Returning to Norway, he became organist at the Torshov Church in Oslo; in 1950 he organized the Norwegian Soloist Choir and took it on a series of successful tours in Europe and in the U.S. He gave lectures on Norwegian music in Long Beach, Calif., in 1962; conducted a musical seminar in Minneapolis in 1964; was composer-in-residence at Berea College in Kentucky in 1968, and at Augsburg College in Minnesota in 1969. As a composer, he continues the tradition of Scandinavian Romanticism.
WORKS: Christmas opera, *Med krone og stjerne*

(*With Crown and Star,* 1971); *Høgfjell (The Mountains),* suite for Orch. (1940–41); *Naadevegen,* oratorio (1943–46); *Norge, mitt land (Norway, My Country)* for Chorus and Orch. (1944); *Concerto Grosso* for 3 Trumpets and Strings (1946); *Spenningens land (Land of Suspense),* symph. fantasy (1947; Oslo, Sept. 29, 1948); *Festival Overture* (1950); *Symphony for Strings* (1950; 2 earlier symphs. were withdrawn); Concertino for Clarinet, English Horn, and Strings (1952); *De syv segl (The 7 Seals),* visions for Orch. (1958–60); *Collocations* for Orch. (1963); *Lucis Creator Optime* for Soloists, Chorus, Organ, and Orch. (1968); *Spes mundi,* mass for Chorus, Church Play Group, Orff School Instruments, Trumpet, Organ Liturgist, and Congregation (1970); *Mirage* for Orch. (1974); *Celebration* for Symphonic Band (1982); *Sinfonia del mare* for Orch. (1983); 4 string quartets (1938, 1948, 1956, 1966); Violin Sonata (1941); numerous organ pieces; *The Moment* for Soprano, Celesta, and Percussion (1962); *Suoni* for Flute, Marimba, and Female Chorus (1970); *Pia memoria,* Requiem for 9 Winds (1971); *Music for 6 Trombones* (1980); church motets; a hymn, *De profundis,* his most popular work (1964).

Nystroem, Gösta, Swedish composer; b. Silvberg, Oct. 13, 1890; d. Särö, near Göteborg, Aug. 9, 1966. He studied piano with his father and theory with Hallen. In 1919 he went to Paris, where he took courses with Vincent d'Indy, Chevillard, and the Russian musician Leonid Sabaneyev, at that time living in France. In 1932 Nystroem returned to Sweden. His music is marked with Romantic tendencies, tinged with Impressionism.
WORKS: Radio drama, *De Blinda (The Blind,* 1949); ballet, *Ungersvennen och de sex prinsessorna (The Young Lad and the 6 Princesses,* 1951); radio opera, *Herr Arnes penningar (Sir Arne's Hoard),* based on a novel by Selma Lagerlöf (Swedish Radio, Nov. 26, 1959). FOR ORCH.: *Rondo capriccioso* for Violin and Orch. (1917); symph. poem, *Is havet (The Arctic Ocean,* 1924); symph. poem, *Babels torn (The Tower of Babel,* 1928); 2 concertos for String Orch. (1930, 1955); 6 symphs. with subtitles: No. 1, *Sinfonia breve* (1931; Göteborg, Oct. 19, 1932); No. 2, *Sinfonia espressiva* (1932–35; Göteborg, Feb. 18, 1937); No. 3, *Sinfonia del mare,* with Soprano Solo (1947–48; Stockholm, March 24, 1949); No. 4, *Sinfonia Shakespeareana* (1952; Göteborg, Nov. 5, 1952); No. 5, *Sinfonia seria* (1963; Stockholm, Oct. 9, 1963); No. 6, *Sinfonia Tramontana* (1965; Stockholm, Oct. 30, 1966); 4 suites of incidental music: No. 1, *Konungen (The King,* 1933; after Lagerkvist); No. 2, *The Tempest* (1934; after Shakespeare); No. 3, *Bödeln (The Hangman,* 1935); No. 4, *The Merchant of Venice* (1936; after Shakespeare); *Suite* for Small Orch. (1950); *Partita* for Flute, Strings, and Harp (1953); Violin Concerto (1954); *Concerto ricercante* for Piano and Orch. (1959; Stockholm, May 15, 1960); *Summer Music* for Soprano and Orch. (1964); 2 string quartets (1956, 1961); 3 *Havsvisioner (Visions of the Sea)* for a cappella Chorus (1956); piano pieces, among them the sentimental *Regrets* (1923; also for Orch.); songs.

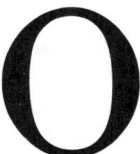

O

Oakeley, Sir Herbert Stanley, English composer; b. Ealing, Middlesex, July 22, 1830; d. London, Oct. 26, 1903. He studied at Oxford; later attended the Leipzig Cons.; also took organ lessons in Dresden and Bonn. In 1865 he was appointed a prof. of music at Edinburgh Univ., and held this post until 1891; was influential in the musical affairs of Scotland in general. He wrote a cantata, *Jubilee Lyric; Suite in the Olden Style* for Orch.; many pieces of church music; choruses; arrangements of Scottish national melodies; etc.

BIBLIOGRAPHY: E.M. Oakeley, *The Life of Sir H.S. Oakeley* (London, 1904).

Oberhoffer, Emil Johann, German conductor; b. near Munich, Aug. 10, 1867; d. San Diego, Calif., May 22, 1933. He received his musical training from his father, an organist; learned to play violin and organ; later studied piano in Paris with Isidor Philipp. He then came to the U.S.; in 1897 settled in St. Paul, Minn.; became conductor of the Phil. Choral Society in Minneapolis (1901); succeeded in securing an endowment for the establishment of a permanent orch.; gave his first concert with the newly organized Minneapolis Symph. Orch. on Nov. 5, 1903; led it until 1923; then retired, and lived in California.

BIBLIOGRAPHY: Article by J.T. Howard in *Dictionary of American Biography*, Supplement I.

Oberlin, Russell, American countertenor; b. Akron, Ohio, Oct. 11, 1928. He studied at the Juilliard School of Music in N.Y., graduating in 1951; in 1952 he joined the N.Y. Pro Musica Antiqua, appearing as a soloist in works from the medieval and Renaissance periods; in 1960 he sang the role of Oberon in Britten's *A Midsummer Night's Dream* at Covent Garden, London. In 1971 he joined the faculty at Hunter College in N.Y.

Oberthür, Karl, German harp player and composer; b. Munich, March 4, 1819; d. London, Nov. 8, 1895. He studied with Elise Brauchle and G.V. Röder in Munich; after playing at various theaters in Switzerland and Germany, he went to London in 1844; established himself as a teacher there. He wrote 2 operas; several cantatas; a symph. legend, *Lorelei,* for Harp and Orch.; a Nocturne for 3 Harps; many elegant soli for harp (*Elégie, Pensées musicales, Réveil des elfes, Miranda, Le Sylphe,* etc.).

Obin, Louis-Henri, French bass singer; b. Ascq, near Lille, Aug. 4, 1820; d. Paris, Nov. 11, 1895. From 1844 till 1869 he was a renowned singer at the Paris

Opéra; after his retirement from the stage, he taught at the Paris Cons. (1871–91).

Oborin, Lev, Russian pianist; b. Moscow, Sept. 11, 1907; d. Moscow, Jan. 5, 1974. He studied at the Moscow Cons. with Igumnov, graduating in 1926; in 1928, was appointed an instructor in piano there; in 1935 was named a prof. there; in 1964 was made a People's Artist of the U.S.S.R. He received various prizes as a pianist, but dedicated himself mainly to teaching.
BIBLIOGRAPHY: S. Khentova, *Lev Oborin* (Moscow, 1964).

Obouhov, Nicolas, remarkable Russian composer; b. Moscow, April 22, 1892; d. Paris, June 13, 1954. He studied at the St. Petersburg Cons. with Nicolas Tcherepnin and Maximilian Steinberg; after the Revolution he emigrated to France and lived in Paris, where he had some instruction from Ravel. As early as 1914 he began experimenting with harmonic combinations containing 12 different notes without duplication (he called his system "absolute harmony"). In 1915 he devised a special notation for this type of harmony, entirely enharmonic, with crosses indicating sharps or flats; several composers, among them Honegger, wrote pieces in Obouhov's notation. He gave a demonstration of his works written and notated in this system in Petrograd at a concert organized by the editors of the review *Muzykalnyi Sovremennik* on Feb. 3, 1916. He devoted his entire life to the composition of his magnum opus, *Le Livre de vie,* for Solo Voices, Chorus, 2 Pianos, and Orch. The MS score, some 2,000 pages long, was deposited after his death at the Bibliothèque Nationale in Paris. A mystic, Obouhov signed his name "Nicolas l'illuminé" and used his own blood to mark sections in the score; the finale represented the spiritual and religious apotheosis in which both the old and the new Russian societies and political factions become reunited. In this and some other scores Obouhov introduced shouting, screaming, sighing, and groaning sounds for the voice parts. A section of *Le Livre de vie* was performed by Koussevitzky in Paris on June 3, 1926. In quest of new sonorities, Obouhov devised an electronic instrument, the "croix sonore," in the form of a cross, and composed works for it, which were performed by Mme. Aussenac de Broglie. He publ. *Traité d'harmonie tonale, atonale et totale* (Paris, 1946), which presents an exposition of his system.
BIBLIOGRAPHY: Boris de Schloezer, "Nicolas Obouhov," *Revue Musicale* (1921); C. Laronde, *Le Livre de vie de Nicolas Obouhow* (Paris, 1932).

Oboussier, Robert, Swiss composer; b. Antwerp (of Swiss parents), July 9, 1900; d. (stabbed to death by his roommate), Zürich, June 9, 1957. He studied at the Cons. of Zürich, with Volkmar Andreae and Philipp Jarnach (composition); then with Siegfried Ochs in Berlin (conducting). He then lived in Florence (1922–28); was music editor of the *Deutsche Allgemeine Zeitung;* but in 1938 political conditions in Germany impelled him to leave for Switzerland; in 1942 he became director of the Central Archive of Swiss Music. Of cosmopolitan background, he combined in his music the elements of both Germanic and Latin cultures. His collection of critical reviews, *Berliner Musik-Chronik 1930–38,* was publ. posthumously in 1969.
WORKS: Opera, *Amphitryon* (Berlin, March 13, 1951); *Trilogia sacra* for Chorus and Orch. (1929); Piano Concerto (1933; revised 1944); Symph. (1936); *Antigone,* cantata (1939); Violin Concerto (1953); *3 Psalms* for Soli, Chorus, and Orch. (1947); *Vie et mort,* song cycle for Contralto; piano pieces.
BIBLIOGRAPHY: K.H. Wörner, "Robert Oboussier," *Musica* (Oct. 1954).

Obradović, Aleksandar, Serbian composer; b. Bled, Aug. 22, 1927. He studied composition with Logar at the Belgrade Academy of Music, graduating in 1952; had advanced studies with Lennox Berkeley in London (1959–60); traveled to Russia in 1963; spent a year in the U.S. studying at the Columbia Univ. electronic music center in N.Y. (1966–67); in 1969 he was appointed a prof. at the Belgrade Academy of Music. Formally, his music adheres to the architectonic Classical design with strongly discernible tonal centers, but he experiments with atonal thematics and polytonal harmonies; in some of his works he applies explicit dodecaphonic formulas.
WORKS: Ballet, *Prolećni uranak (Spring's Awakening,* 1949); 5 symphs.: No. 1 (1952; Belgrade, March 11, 1953); No. 2 (1959–61; Belgrade, Jan. 22, 1965); No. 3, *Mikrosimfonija,* for Tape and Orch. (1967; Opatija, Oct. 27, 1968); No. 4 (1972; Belgrade, May 24, 1972); No. 5 (1973); *Symphonic Kolo* (1949); *Symphonic Scherzo* (1955); *Plameni vjetar (Flaming Wind),* song cycle for Baritone and Orch. (1955; Belgrade, Jan. 13, 1959); Concertino for Piano and String Orch. (1956); Concerto for Clarinet and String Orch. (1958; Belgrade, May 26, 1959); *Symphonic Epitaph* for Narrator, Chorus, and Orch. (1959; Belgrade, May 21, 1959); *Scherzo-Overture* (1959); *Kroz svemir (Through the Universe),* suite for Orch. (1961); *Scherzo in modo dodecaphonico* for Orch. (1962; Belgrade, May 24, 1962); *Prelude and Fugue* for Voice and String Orch. (1963); *Epitaph H* for Orch. and Tape (1965; Berlin, Oct. 6, 1965); *Sutjeska* for Narrator, Chorus, and Orch. (1968); *Dramatična fuga* for Wind Orch. (1972; Belgrade, Nov. 17, 1972); Quintet for Flute, Clarinet, and String Trio (1950); *Platani* for Chamber Ensemble (1964); *Microsonata I* for Solo Clarinet (1969); *Microsonata II* for Solo Bassoon (1971); choruses; songs; electronic pieces.
BIBLIOGRAPHY: V. Peričić, *Muzički Stvaraoci u Srbiji* (Belgrade, 1969; pp. 351–63).

Obraztsova, Elena, outstanding Russian mezzo-soprano; b. Leningrad, July 7, 1937. Her father was an engineer who played the violin. She studied voice at the Leningrad Cons., graduating in 1964; made her operatic debut at the Bolshoi Theater in Moscow during the 1964–65 season as Marina in *Boris Godunov;* won first prize at the International

Tchaikovsky Competition in Moscow in 1970. She made her first tour of the U.S. with the Bolshoi troupe in June–July 1975; on Oct. 12, 1976, she made her Metropolitan Opera debut in N.Y. as Princess de Bouillon in Cilèa's *Adriana Lecouvreur.* She was awarded the Lenin prize in 1976. She possesses a remarkably even tessitura, brilliant in all registers; her roles include virtually the entire Russian operatic repertoire, and such parts of the standard operas as Norma, Amneris, and Carmen.

Obrecht (Hobrecht, Obreht, Obertus, Hobertus), Jacob, famous Netherlandish contrapuntist; b. Bergen-op-Zoom, Nov. 22, 1450 (or 1451); d. Ferrara, 1505 (of the pestilence). The son of a city trumpeter, he received his rudimentary musical training in his native town; he entered the Univ. of Louvain on Aug. 17, 1470; then returned to Bergen-op-Zoom; took Holy Orders, and said his first Mass as an ordained priest there on April 23, 1480. He was named *maître des enfants* at Cambrai on July 28, 1484; was in Bruges from 1485 to 1487; at the request of the Duke of Ferrara, he obtained a leave of absence for 6 months to travel to Italy; arrived in Ferrara in Dec. 1487; returned to Bruges in 1488, and remained there until 1491, when he became music director at Notre-Dame in Antwerp; he visited Bergen-op-Zoom in 1496–97, after which he went again to Bruges; at various times was also in Antwerp. In 1504 he once more entered the service of the ducal court at Ferrara, where he remained until his death. He was a prolific composer; his masses, motets, hymns, etc., are found in various collections of the period, and also in the Archives of the Papal Chapel. He was well known in Italy during his lifetime; Petrucci publ. the collection *Missae Obrecht* (1503), containing the masses *Je ne demande, Grecorum, Fortuna desperata, Malheur me bat,* and *Salve diva parens;* the collection *Missae diversorum* (vol. I) includes Obrecht's mass *Si dedero.* The extensive edition of Obrecht's works in 7 vols., edited by Johannes Wolf (1908–21, Amsterdam and Leipzig), contains 24 masses, 22 motets, chansons, and the famous 4-part Passion according to St. Matthew, the oldest known polyphonic setting of this text. Since the publication of this edition, additional works by Obrecht have been brought to light. On the other hand, some works formerly attributed to him have been proved to be spurious; thus another Passion, long thought to have been by Obrecht, was apparently by a chapel singer named Longueval, in the court of King Louis XII of France. A new *Opera omnia,* edited by A. Smijers, began publication in 1953 (Vereeniging voor Nederlandse Muziekgeschiedenis, Amsterdam).

BIBLIOGRAPHY: O.J. Gombosi, *Jakob Obrecht. Eine stilkritische Studie* (Leipzig, 1925); E.H. Juten, "Obrecht," *Annales de l'Académie Royale d'Archéologie de Belgique* (series 7, vol. 7, Antwerp, 1930); A.W. Ambros, *Geschichte der Musik* (vol. III, pp. 182ff.; vol. V contains 6 examples); Anny Piscaer, *Jacob Obrecht* (Bergen-op-Zoom, 1938); article on Obrecht in *Dictionnaire des musiciens,* ed. by René Vannes (Brussels, 1947); Gustave Reese, *Music in the Renaissance* (N.Y., 1954); Bain Murray, "New Light on Jacob Obrecht's Development," *Musical Quarterly* (Oct. 1957); C. Dahlhaus, "Zu Marcus van Crevels neuer Obrecht-Ausgabe," *Die Musikforschung* (Oct.–Dec. 1967); L.G. van Hoorn, *Jacob Obrecht* (The Hague, 1968).

Obretenov, Svetoslav, Bulgarian composer; b. Provadia, Nov. 25, 1909. He studied at the Sofia Cons.; was active as a choral conductor. He has written mostly for chorus; his oratorio *The Partisans* was performed for the first time in Sofia on June 25, 1949.

BIBLIOGRAPHY: V. Krstev, *Svetoslav Obretenov* (Sofia, 1959).

O'Brien, Charles, Scottish composer; b. Edinburgh, Sept. 6, 1882; d. there, June 27, 1968. He studied with H. MacCunn; later devoted himself to teaching. Among his compositions are a Symph., 3 overtures, 2 piano trios, a Clarinet Sonata, a number of piano pieces, and songs.

Obrist, Aloys, Italian conductor and music editor; b. San Remo, March 30, 1867; d. (by suicide, after having killed the singer Anna Sutter out of jealousy) Stuttgart, June 29, 1910. He studied at the Univ. of Berlin; received his Dr.Phil. (1892) with the dissertation *Melchior Franck.* He filled posts as conductor in Rostock, Augsburg, etc.; then became court conductor at Stuttgart; from 1900, was custodian of the Liszt Museum in Weimar, and chairman of the editorial board for the publication of Liszt's works. He was a connoisseur of old instruments, and owned a valuable collection, which passed to the Bach Museum in Eisenach.

Obukhova, Nadezhda, Russian mezzo-soprano; b. Moscow, March 6, 1886; d. Feodosiya, Aug. 14, 1961. She studied with Masetti at the Moscow Cons., graduating in 1912. She made her debut at the Bolshoi Theater there in 1916 as Pauline in *The Queen of Spades;* remained on its roster until 1943. In addition to the Russian repertoire, she was noted for her portrayals of Carmen, Dalila, Amneris, and others. She was greatly esteemed in Russia; in 1943 she was awarded the State Prize of the U.S.S.R.

BIBLIOGRAPHY: E. Grosheva, *Nadezhda Obukhova* (Moscow, 1953); G. Polyanovsky, *My Meetings with N. Obukhova* (Moscow, 1971).

Očenáš, Andrej, Slovak composer; b. Selce, near Banská Bystrica, Jan. 8, 1911. He studied composition with Alexander Moyzes at the Bratislava Academy, graduating in 1937; then took a course with Vitězslav Novák at the Prague Cons., graduating in 1939. He worked at Czech Radio in Bratislava (1939–50) and was director of musical programs there (1957–62); taught at the Bratislava Cons. (1943–73); was director there in 1950–54. His music is imbued with a Slovak ethos.

WORKS: Musical play, *Rok na dedine* (*Year in a Village;* Bratislava, Dec. 11, 1948); 3 ballets: *At the*

Ochman – Ockeghem

Brigand's Ball (1941), *Highlander's Songs* (1954–56), and *The Romance of the Rose,* a "stage symphony" with Narrator, Solo Singers, Chorus, and Orch. (1969–71); *Tales of My Native Land,* suite for Orch. (1943); *Resurrection,* symph. trilogy (1946); *To My Nation,* symph. poem (1947); Cello Concerto (1952); *Ruralia Slovaca* for String Orch., 2 Flutes, 2 Clarinets, 2 Trumpets, Horns, and Piano (1957); Piano Concerto (1959); *Concertino rustico* for Cimbalom, Strings, and Piano (1963); Sinfonietta (1967); *O zemi a človeku (About Earth and Man),* symph. for Chorus and Small Orch. (1970); *May Overture* (1972); Violin Concerto (1974); *Margarita and Besná,* cantata (1939); *Prophecies,* oratorio (1949–50); *Monuments of Glory,* symph. tetralogy for Tenor, Children's and Mixed Choruses, and Orch. (1963); *Pastorale of Orava* for Soloists, Chorus, and Orch. (1961); *I Loved You,* laudatorium for Soloists, Chorus, Organ, and Orch. (1974); 2 string quartets (*Pictures of the Soul,* 1942; *Etude,* 1970); Concertino for Flute and Piano (1961–62); Piano Trio (1967); *Frescoes* for Violin and Piano (1967); *Poem of the Heart* for Solo Violin (1968); *Don Quixote,* duo for Violin and Cello (1969); *Zvony (The Bells),* piano sonata (1972); piano pieces: *Rainstorm* (1946), *New Spring* (1954), *Youth* (1956), and *Pictures of Legends* (1957); *Pastels* for Organ (1961); choruses; songs.

Ochman, Wieslaw, Polish tenor; b. Warsaw, Feb. 6, 1937. He studied at the State Academy of Music in Cracow. In 1964 he appeared with the Cracow Opera; also sang in Warsaw. He was later engaged at the Deutsche Oper in West Berlin (1966–68). On March 12, 1975, he sang for the first time at the Metropolitan Opera in N.Y.

Ochs, Siegfried, German choral conductor and composer; b. Frankfurt, April 19, 1858; d. Berlin, Feb. 5, 1929. He studied medicine and chemistry before turning to music; took private lessons with Friedrich Kiel and Heinrich Urban. In 1882 he organized in Berlin a choral union under his own name, working in close collaboration with the Berlin Phil. under the direction of Hans von Bülow. In 1920 it was merged with the chorus of the Berlin Hochschule für Musik and earned a reputation as one of the best choral ensembles in Germany. Ochs was also a composer; he wrote a comic opera, *Im Namen des Gesetzes* (Hamburg, 1888), 2 operettas, and several song cycles; publ. an autobiography, *Geschehenes, Gesehenes* (Leipzig, 1922); compiled a valuable history of German choral singing, *Der deutsche Gesangverein* (4 vols., Berlin, 1923–28); publ. *Über die Art, Musik zu Hören* (Berlin, 1926); edited Bach's cantatas; and publ. choral arrangements of German folk songs. BIBLIOGRAPHY: M. Stappenbeck, *Chronik des Philharmonischen Chors in Berlin* (Berlin, 1932); K. Singer, *Siegfried Ochs, Der Bergründer des Philharmonischen Chors* (Berlin, 1933).

Ockeghem (or **Okeghem, Okenghem, Ockenheim,** etc.), **Johannes** (or **Jean de**), great Flemish contrapuntist and teacher; b. East Flanders, c.1410; d. Tours, Feb. 6, 1496 (old-style calendar), according to an entry in the Archives Nationales, Paris. He was probably a pupil of Binchois; was a boy chorister at Antwerp Cathedral (1443–44); a chorister in the chapel of Duke Charles of Bourbon (1446–48); a pupil of Dufay in Cambrai (1449); a chorister in the royal chapel (1452–53); from 1454, was composer and first chaplain to 3 successive kings of France: Charles VII, Louis XI, and Charles VIII; was treasurer of the Abbey of St.-Martin at Tours; in 1465 was "maître de la chapelle du roy"; in 1469 he traveled to Spain, and in 1484 to Flanders, at the King's expense. Upon Ockeghem's death, Guillaume Crétin wrote a poetic "Déploration," and Josquin Des Prez (his greatest pupil) and Lupi composed musical epitaphs. Important both as a teacher and composer, Ockeghem was the leader of the 2nd generation of the great Franco-Flemish school of the 15th century (which includes Busnois, Regis, and Caron). His art expresses the mysticism of the Netherlands in the late Middle Ages; his technical skill in the development of purely formal resources, while very important, is not the most prominent characteristic of his style, as most historians have asserted. At the same time, Ockeghem's achievements in the art of imitative counterpoint unquestionably make his music a milestone on the way to the a cappella style of the coming generations.

WORKS: 16 masses and individual sections of masses; 9 motets; a ninefold canon-motet, *Deo gratias,* in 36 parts (of doubtful authenticity); about 20 chansons and one canon (*Fuga a 3 in epidiatessaron* = the chanson *Prenez sur moi*). Burney, Forkel, Kiesewetter, Schlecht, Ambros-Kade, Wooldridge, and P. Wagner have printed fragments of the mass *Cujusvis toni (ad omnem tonum);* Bellermann *(Die Mensuralnoten und Taktzeichen),* a fragment of the *Missa Prolationum;* Riemann, in *Musikgeschichte in Beispielen* (1912; no. 16) and in *Handbuch der Musikgeschichte* (II, 1), fragments of the mass *Pour quelque peine* (probably not by Ockeghem); the masses *Caput* and *Le Serviteur* (the latter probably a work of V. Faugues, according to Tinctoris [Coussemaker, *Scriptores,* IV, 146a]) are publ. in their entirety in Denkmäler der Tonkunst in Österreich, 38 (19.i); the mass *Mi mi* (ed. for practical use by H. Besseler) is in F. Blume's *Das Chorwerk,* #4 (1928); 2 sections of the mass *L'Homme armé* are in A.T. Davison and W. Apel, *Historical Anthology of Music* (Cambridge, Mass., 1947); a motet, *Alma redemptoris mater,* is in *Altniederländische Motetten* (Kassel, 1929), ed. by H. Besseler; another motet, *Ut heremita solus,* in Schering's *Geschichte der Musik in Beispielen* (1931; no. 52); the "Déploration" on the death of Binchois, *Mort tu as navré,* in J. Marix's *Les Musiciens de la cour de Bourgogne au XVe siècle* (1937; no. 54); the motet *Intemerata Dei Mater,* in Smijers's *Muziekgeschiedenis in Voorbeelden,* I (1939); the canon-motet in 36 parts, in Riemann's *Handbuch der Musikgeschichte,* II, 1. Regarding the chansons, there are 4 in Ambros-Kade's *Geschichte,* V; 4 in O. Gombosi's *Jacob Obrecht* (1925); one in J. Wolf's *Sing- und Spielmusik aus älterer Zeit* (1926); 8 in *Trois chansonniers français du XVe siècle,* I (1927), ed. by Droz-Rokseth-Thibault; 2 in K. Jeppesen's *Der Kopenhagener Chansonnier* (1927); and 2 in Davison and Apel, *Historical Anthology of Music.* A 3-part chanson, *O rosa bella,* by Hert, with a new discantus added to it by Ockeghem, is in Denkmäler der Tonkunst in Österreich, 14/15 (7). The *Fuga in epidiatessaron* has been discussed, reprinted, and solved with more or less success by innumerable writers; reprints are to be found in Jeppesen, Droz-Rokseth-Thibault, and J.S. Levitan (see below). A complete ed. of Ockeghem's works, edited by D. Plamenac, was begun in 1927 in the *Publikationen älterer Musik* of the Deutsche Musikgesellschaft, with a vol. containing 8 masses (new ed. of this vol., N.Y., 1958; vol. 2, containing 8 masses and Mass sections, N.Y., 1947; revised 1966).

BIBLIOGRAPHY: L. de Burbure, *J. de Ockeghem* (1853; 2nd ed., 1868); E. Thoinan, *Déploration de Guillaume Crétin sur le trépas de J. Ockeghem* (Paris, 1864); M. Brenet, *J. de Ockeghem* (Paris, 1893; 2nd ed. in *Musique et musiciens de la vieille France,* 1911; with bibliography); A. Schering, "Ein Rätseltenor Ockeghems" (Kretzschmar-Festschrift, 1918); D. Plamenac, *J. Ockeghem als Motetten- und Chansonkomponist* (Vienna, 1924); M. Cauchie, "Les Véritables Noms et prénoms d'Ockeghem," *Revue de Musicologie* (1926); W. Stephan, *Die burgundisch-niederländische Motette zur Zeit Ockeghems* (Heidelberg, 1937); J.S. Levitan, "Ockeghem's Clefless Compositions," *Musical Quarterly* (Oct. 1937); Ernst Krenek, *J. Ockeghem* (N.Y., 1953); Gustave Reese, *Music in the Renaissance* (N.Y., 1954); several important essays in *Essays in Music in Honor of Dragan Plamenac,* ed. by G. Reese and R.J. Snow (Pittsburgh, 1969); *Johannes Ockeghem en zijn tijd* (Dendermonde, 1970).

O'Connell, Charles, American conductor and music executive; b. Chicopee, Mass., April 22, 1900; d. New York, Sept. 1, 1962. He studied at the Catholic School and College of the Holy Cross (B.A., 1922); also studied organ in Paris with Widor. From 1930 to 1944 he was head of the artist and repertoire dept. of the RCA Victor Co., then music director of Columbia Masterworks (1944–47). He publ. *The Victor Book of the Symphony* (1934; new ed., 1948); *The Victor Book of the Opera* (1937); *The Other Side of the Record* (relating personal experiences in dealing with musical celebrities; N.Y., 1947); *The Victor Book of Overtures, Tone Poems and Other Orchestral Works* (1950).

Odak, Krsto, Croatian composer; b. Siverić, Dalmatia, March 20, 1888; d. Zagreb, Nov. 4, 1965. He studied composition with P. Hartmann in Munich (1911–13) and with Novák in Prague. Upon his return to Yugoslavia, he was prof. of composition at the Music Academy of Zagreb, retiring in 1961. He wrote 4 symphs. (1940, 1953, 1961, 1965); the operetta *Dorica pleše* (*Dorrit Dances;* 1934); the radio opera *Majka Margarita* (*Mother Margaret;* Zagreb, 1955); Piano Concerto (1963); 4 string quartets (1925, 1927, 1934, 1957); 2 masses in the old Slavonic language; other sacred works; song cycles.

Odaka, Hisatada. See **Otaka, Hisatada.**

O'Day, Anita, American jazz singer; b. Chicago, Dec. 18, 1919. She began her career in Chicago as a vocalist with the Max Miller Combo in 1939, and became one of the leading jazz singers of the era; she sang with the big bands of Gene Krupa, Roy Eldridge, and Stan Kenton, and she also gave solo recitals.

Oddone Sulli-Rao, Elisabetta, Italian composer; b. Milan, Aug. 13, 1878; d. there, March 3, 1972. She studied at the Milan Cons.; composed a one-act opera, *A gara colle rondini* (Milan, 1920), and a children's opera, *Petruccio e il cavallo cappuccio* (Milan, 1916); also several oratorios; chamber music; and a number of songs. She did some valuable work on dissemination of Italian folk songs; publ. *Canzoniere popolare italiano, Canzoncine per bimbi, Cantilene popolari dei bimbi d'Italia,* etc.

Odetta (née **Odetta Holmes;** a.k.a. **Odetta Felious Gordon**), black American folk singer; b. Birmingham, Ala., Dec. 31, 1930. Her family moved to Los Angeles when she was a child; she studied voice at Los Angeles City College, and also learned to play the guitar. She sang in nightclubs in California; made her concert debut in N.Y. in 1959; then appeared on the radio, and took singing parts in several films, including *Sanctuary* (1960). In 1974 she made a tour in the Soviet Union which attracted much attention; the Russians were stunned by the spectacle of a black woman singing Negro spirituals and accompanying herself on the guitar. As the liberation movement spread in the South, she was awarded, in 1965, a Key to the City from the Birmingham municipality.

Odington, Walter (Walter of Evesham), a Benedictine monk at the monastery of Evesham; he was at Oxford in 1316, and at Merton College there in 1330. He is one of the chief medieval writers on mensural notation; his *De speculatione musices* (MS in Corpus Christi College, Cambridge) was printed by Coussemaker in 1864 (*Scriptores,* I; modern ed. by F. Hammond, *Walteri Odington Summa de speculatione musicae,* in Corpus Scriptorum de Musica, XIV, 1970). This work is particularly valuable for the light it throws on musical rhythm as practiced in the late 13th century; it also discusses intervals, notation, musical instruments, and musical forms (rondellus, motet, etc.). His views on consonance and dissonance are interesting for their acceptance of thirds and sixths as legitimate consonances. He was also noted as an astronomer.

BIBLIOGRAPHY: J. Wolf, "Early English Musical Theorists," *Musical Quarterly* (Oct. 1939); G. Reese, *Music in the Middle Ages* (N.Y., 1940).

Odnoposoff, Adolfo, Argentine cellist, brother of **Ricardo Odnoposoff;** b. Buenos Aires, Feb. 22, 1917.

He studied with Alberto Schiuma; then went to Berlin, where he took lessons with Feuermann, and to Paris, where he became a student of Diran Alexanian. He was subsequently active as a concert cellist in Palestine (1936–38), Peru (1938–40), Chile (1940–44), Havana (1944–58), and Mexico City, where he also taught at the Cons. Nacional de Música (1958–64); then was a prof. of cello and chamber music at the Cons. of Music in San Juan, Puerto Rico. In 1975 he became a prof. of cello at North Texas State Univ., in Denton. Several Latin American composers (Roque Cordero, Rodolfo Halffter, Eduardo Mata, Floro Ugarte, Antonio Tauriello, and others) wrote special works for him.

Odonoposoff, Ricardo, Argentine violinist, brother of **Adolfo Odonoposoff**; b. Buenos Aires, Feb. 24, 1914. He studied with Aaron Klasse in Buenos Aires (1919–26), Rudolph Deman in Berlin (1927–28), and Carl Flesch in Berlin (1928–32). A precocious musician, he played in public as an infant; was a soloist with the Berlin Phil. at 17; won first prize at the International Contest for Violinists in Vienna at 18. He evolved a brilliant career as a concert violinist, appearing in all parts of the world; eventually settled in Vienna as a prof. of the Music Academy.

Odo de Cluny (Saint), important musical theorist of the 10th century; b. near Le Mans, 879; d. Tours, Nov. 18, 942. A pupil of Rémy d'Auxerre in Paris, he took Holy Orders at 19, and in 899 was canon and choir singer at Tours; in 909 he entered the Benedictine monastery at Baume, near Besançon, and then was successively abbot at Aurillac, Fleuri, and (from 927) Cluny. The famous medieval treatise *Dialogus de musica* (also known as *Enchiridion musices*) is attributed to him without foundation (it is printed in Gerbert's *Scriptores* and, in Eng. trans., in Oliver Strunk's *Source Readings in Music History,* N.Y., 1950). In the development of pitch notation through letter-names, he was the first to give a complete series (2 octaves and a fifth) of letter-names (G, A, B, C, D, E, F, G, etc.) corresponding to our modern series; but whereas we change from capital to lower-case letters at *c* to designate the pitches of the 2nd octave, in Odo's system the change was made at *a*. He was also the first to add the sign *gamma* (Greek "G") to designate the note corresponding to G on the first line of our bass clef. He distinguished between b flat and b natural (b *rotundum* and b *quadratum*), but only at one point in the gamut, namely, the note lying one degree below middle C in our system.

BIBLIOGRAPHY: Th. Nisard, *St.-Odo de Cluny* (Paris, 1866); M. Huglo, "L'Auteur du *Dialogue sur la musique* attribué à Odo," *Revue de Musicologie* (1969).

O'Dwyer, Robert, English-Irish composer and conductor; b. Bristol, Jan. 27, 1862; d. Dublin, Jan. 6, 1949. He was a conductor of the Carl Rosa Opera Co. in London and on tour (1891); then with the Arthur Rousbey Opera Co. in England and Ireland (1892–96); in 1899 became music director at the Univ. of Ireland in Dublin; from 1914 to 1939, was prof. of Irish music there; was music director (from 1901) of the Gaelic League choir, for which he arranged many Irish songs. He wrote one of the earliest operas with a Gaelic text, *Eithne,* produced in Dublin on May 16, 1910; also composed songs with Gaelic words; organ pieces. He left a book in MS, *Irish Music and Its Traditions.*

Oehl, Kurt, eminent German musicologist; b. Mainz, Feb. 24, 1923. He was educated at the Johannes Gutenberg Univ. in Mainz; obtained his Ph.D. (1952) with the dissertation *Beitrage zur Geschichte der deutschen Mozart-Übersetzungen.* After working as a dramaturge, he became a member of the editorial staff of the *Riemann Musiklexikon* in 1960. In this capacity, he helped to prepare the vol. on musical terms and historical subjects (*Sachteil*) for the 12th edition (Mainz, 1967); also served as a biographical editor for the *Supplement* (2 vols.; Mainz, 1972, 1975). He then became an editor for the *Brockhaus-Riemann Musiklexikon* (2 vols.; Mainz, 1979). In 1973 he joined the faculty of the Johannes Gutenberg Univ.

Oesterlein, Nikolaus, Austrian music scholar; b. Vienna, May 4, 1842; d. there, Oct. 8, 1898. An ardent admirer of Wagner, he amassed an enormous collection of materials relating to Wagner's life and works. This collection, known as the "Wagner Museum," was subsequently given to the town of Eisenach; the catalogue, publ. by Breitkopf & Härtel (1882–95), fills 4 vols. Oesterlein also publ. a vol. entitled *Bayreuth,* on the inauguration of the festival plays in 1876, and *Über Schicksale des Wagner-Museums in Wien* (1892).

Oestvig, Karl, Norwegian tenor; b. Oslo, May 17, 1889; d. there, July 21, 1968. He studied in Cologne; made his debut at the Stuttgart Opera in 1914; remained on its roster until 1919; was then a member of the Vienna State Opera (1919–27), where he created the role of the Emperor in Strauss's *Die Frau ohne Schatten* in 1919; also sang at the Berlin State Opera and the Städtische Oper. He accepted the post of director of the Oslo Opera (1941) during the Nazi occupation of Norway, an action which brought him disgrace after the war. As an opera singer, he was at his best in the Wagnerian repertoire.

Oetting, William H., American organist and pedagogue; b. Pittsburgh, Oct. 14, 1875; d. there, Oct. 29, 1969. He studied in Berlin with Riemann, Egidi, Boise, and Hutcheson; while there, he taught at the Klindworth-Scharwenka Cons. In 1901 he returned to the U.S., and for half a century was organist at various churches in Pittsburgh. He publ. *Preparatory Exercises for Manuals and Pedals* (2nd ed., 1953).

Oettingen, Arthur Joachim von, German physicist and musical theorist; b. Dorpat, Russia, March 28, 1836; d. Leipzig, Sept. 6, 1920. He studied physics at the Univ. of Dorpat; then in Paris and Berlin; from 1863 to 1893, was a prof. of physics at the Univ. of Dorpat; from 1894 to 1919, at the Univ. of Leipzig. He publ. *Das Harmoniesystem in dualer Entwicklung* (1866; revised ed. as *Das duale Harmoniesystem*, 1913), reconciling and developing the systems of Helmholtz and Hauptmann; *Die Grundlage der Musikwissenschaft* (Leipzig, 1916); etc.

Offenbach, Jacques, the creator of French burlesque opera; b. Cologne, June 20, 1819; d. Paris, Oct. 5, 1880. He was the son of a Jewish cantor, whose original surname was Eberst; Offenbach was the town where his father lived. He went to Paris in Nov. 1833; studied cello with Vaslin at the Cons. (1833–34); then played the cello in the orch. of the Opéra-Comique; composed various pieces for his instrument. In 1850 he was engaged as conductor at the Théâtre Français; wrote *Chanson de Fortunio* for the production of Alfred de Musset's *Chandelier* (1850); the song proved tremendously popular; he then undertook the composition of operettas, a genre in which he became a master.

WORKS: He wrote a one-act operetta, *Pepito* (Théâtre des Variétés, Oct. 28, 1853); in 1855 he ventured to open a theater of his own, the old Théâtre Comte, in the Passage Choiseul, which under a new name, Bouffes-Parisiens, became celebrated; he carried on the enterprise until 1866, producing a number of his most popular pieces, among them *Les Deux Aveugles,* for the opening of the Bouffes-Parisiens (July 5, 1855), *Le Violoneux* (Aug. 31, 1855), *Madame Papillon* (Oct. 3, 1855), *Ba-ta-clan* (Dec. 29, 1855), *La Bonne d'enfants* (Oct. 14, 1856), *Les Trois Baisers au diable* (Jan. 15, 1857), *Le Mariage aux lanternes* (Oct. 10, 1857), *Mesdames de la Halle* (March 3, 1858), *Orphée aux enfers* (one of his most celebrated pieces; Oct. 21, 1858), *Geneviève de Brabant* (Nov. 19, 1859), *Daphnis et Chloé* (March 27, 1860), *Barkouf* (Dec. 24, 1860), *La Chanson de Fortunio* (a new operetta to Musset's *Chandelier*), *Le Pont des soupirs* (March 23, 1861), *Monsieur et Madame Denis* (Jan. 11, 1862), etc. Having abandoned the management of the Bouffes-Parisiens, he produced several operettas in Ems, Germany, and an opera-ballet, *Die Rheinnixen*, in Vienna (Feb. 8, 1864); then returned to Paris, where he staged, at the Variétés, one of his most spectacular successes, *La Belle Hélène* (Dec. 17, 1864), an operetta that was soon taken over by theater enterprises all over the world; another fabulously successful operetta was *La Vie parisienne* (Palais Royal, Oct. 31, 1866); subsequent productions were *La Grande Duchesse de Gérolstein* (Variétés, April 12, 1867), *La Périchole* (Variétés, Oct. 6, 1868; one of the most enduringly popular operas of Offenbach; recurring revivals in many countries), and *Les Brigands* (Variétés, Dec. 10, 1869). In 1870, the Franco-Prussian War interrupted his activities in Paris; he resumed the production of operettas with *Boule-de-neige* (Bouffes-Parisiens, Dec. 14, 1871); in 1873 he took over the management of the Théâtre de la Gaîté, and produced there a new enlarged version of *Orphée aux enfers,* as an "opéra-féerique" (Feb. 7,

1874). In 1877 he undertook a tour in America, which was not wholly successful; he described his impressions in *Notes d'un musicien en voyage* (Paris, 1877) and in *Offenbach en Amérique* (Paris, 1877; in Eng., 1877, as *Offenbach in America;* republ. as *Orpheus in America* by the Indiana Univ. Press in Bloomington, 1957). His last operetta produced in his lifetime was *La Fille du tambour-major* (Paris, Folies-Dramatiques, Dec. 13, 1879). A posthumous work, *La Belle Lurette,* was revised by Delibes, and staged in Paris on Oct. 30, 1880. Offenbach's only grand opera, and his true masterpiece, *Les Contes d'Hoffmann,* remained unfinished at his death; recitatives were added by Ernest Guiraud. The famous barcarolle was taken from Offenbach's opera-ballet *Die Rheinnixen* (1864), where the tune was used for a ghost song. *Les Contes d'Hoffmann* was produced at the Opéra-Comique on Feb. 10, 1881, with immediate and decisive success; it was presented in N.Y. on Oct. 16, 1882; also all over Europe. Offenbach's music is characterized by an abundance of flowing, rollicking melodies, seasoned with ironic humor, suitable to the extravagant burlesque of the situations. His irreverent treatment of mythological characters gave Paris society a salutary shock; his art mirrored the atmosphere of precarious gaiety during the 2nd Empire.

BIBLIOGRAPHY: E. de Mirecourt, *Offenbach* (Paris, 1867); A. Martinet, *Offenbach* (Paris, 1887); H. Berlioz, *Les Musiciens et la musique* (ed. by A. Hallays, Paris, 1903); P. Bekker, *Offenbach* (Berlin, 1909); E. Rieger, *Offenbach und seine Wiener Schule* (Vienna, 1920); L. Schneider, *Offenbach* (Paris, 1923); R. Brancour, *Offenbach* (Paris, 1929); A. Henseler, *Jakob Offenbach* (Berlin, 1930); H. Kristeller, *Der Aufstieg des Kölners Jacques Offenbach* (Berlin, 1931); S. Kracauer, *Jacques Offenbach* (Paris, 1937; 2nd ed., 1962; in Eng., London, as *Offenbach and the Paris of His Time;* N.Y., as *Orpheus in Paris,* 1938); S. Sitwell, *La Vie Parisienne: A Tribute to Offenbach* (London, 1937); J. Brindejont-Offenbach, *Offenbach, mon grand-père* (Paris, 1940). For details of productions see A. Loewenberg, *Annals of Opera* (Cambridge, 1943; 3rd ed., 1978); A. Decaux, *Offenbach, Roi du Second Empire* (Paris, 1958; 3rd ed., 1975); P. Jacob, *Jacques Offenbach in selbstzeugnissen und Bilddokumenten* (Hamburg, 1969); R. Pourvoyeur, *Jacques Offenbach: Essay in Toengepaste Muzieken Toneelsociologie* (Brussels, 1977); P. Gammond, *Offenbach: His Life and Times* (Tunbridge Wells, 1980); J. Harding et al., *Offenbach, 1819–1880: A Tribute* (London, 1980); R. Pourvoyeur, *Offenbach: Idillio e Parodia* (Turin, 1980); also the special issue "Jacques Offenbach, 1819–1880," *Musical Times* (Oct. 1980).

Ogdon, John (Andrew Howard), English pianist; b. Manchester, Jan. 27, 1937. He studied at the Royal Manchester College of Music; made appearances in recitals and as a soloist with orchs. In 1962 he won the world's most prestigious contest, the Tchaikovsky Competition in Moscow (another first prize was awarded that year to Vladimir Ashkenazy); from 1976 to 1980 was on the faculty of

Indiana Univ. in Bloomington. A man of massive physique, he handles the piano with masculine power, but is also capable of the finest quality of lyricism.

BIBLIOGRAPHY: B. Ogdon and M. Kerr, *Virtuoso: The Story of John Ogdon* (London, 1981).

Ogihara, Toshitsugu, Japanese composer; b. Osaka, June 6, 1910. He studied composition with Yoritsuné Matsudaira at Nihon Univ.; took private lessons with Alexander Tcherepnin during the latter's stay in Japan. His music follows the classical models.

WORKS: Ballet, *Springtime* (1973); *2 Movements* for Percussion and Orch. (1942); *Sôshun no Hiroba,* symph. poem (1955); Symph. No. 1 (1958); *Rhapsody* for Orch. (1960); 2 violin concertos (1962, 1963); Violin Concertino (1962); *Capriccio* for String Orch. (1964); *4 Pieces* for Horn and String Orch. (1972); 4 string quartets (1940, 1949, 1953, 1969); 2 string trios (1947, 1961); Violin Sonata (1959); Concerto for Clarinet and String Quartet (1955); *Capriccio* for Woodwinds and Strings (1958); Trio for Clarinet, Cello, and Piano (1962); English Horn Sonata (1962); Quartet for 4 Flutes (1963); Trio for Flute, Violin, and Piano (1965); Piano Quintet (1970); Trio for Clarinet, Violin, and Cello (1970); Trio for Oboe, Cello, and Piano (1970); Trio for Cello, Bassoon, and Piano (1970); *7 Poems* for Soprano, Violin, Cello, and Piano (1971); *Serenade* for Cello, Violin, and Clarinet (1972); *4 Pieces* for Tuba, 3 Tenor Trombones, and Bass Trombone (1972); *2 Suites* for Flute and Piano (1974); piano pieces; songs.

Oginski, Prince Michael Cleophas, Polish composer; b. Guzow, near Warsaw, Sept. 25, 1765; d. Florence, Oct. 15, 1833. He was a Polish nobleman of a musical family; his uncle, Michael Casimir Oginski (1731–1803), was an amateur composer of some talent. Oginski pursued the career of diplomacy; as a Polish patriot, he left Poland after its partition, and agitated in Turkey and France for the Polish cause. In 1799 he wrote an opera, *Zelis et Valcour ou Bonaparte au Caire,* to ingratiate himself with Napoleon; it was revived in a radio performance in Cracow on June 29, 1953. Of historical interest are his polonaises, many of which were publ.; the one in A minor, known as *Death Polonaise,* became extremely popular; he also wrote mazurkas and waltzes for piano, and a patriotic Polish march (1825).

Ogura, Roh, Japanese composer; b. Kitakyūshu, Jan. 19, 1916. He studied with Fukai, Sugawara, and Ikenouchi; then was engaged in teaching.

WORKS: Opera, *Neta* (1957); *Orly—A Bugbear at Sea* for Narrator and Orch. (1963); Symph. in A (1941); Piano Concerto (Tokyo, March 24, 1946); Symph. in F (Tokyo, April 25, 1951); *5 Movements on Japanese Folk Songs* for Orch. (1957); Symph. in G (1968); Violin Concerto (1971); 3 string quartets (1941, 1946, 1954); Violin Sonata (1950); Violin Sonatina (1960); *Divertimento* for 7 Winds (1964); *Divertimento* for 8 Winds (1972); *Dance Suite* for 2 Pianos (1953); choruses; songs.

Ohana, Maurice, French composer and pianist; b. Casablanca, June 12, 1914, of Spanish parentage. He studied piano with Lazare Lévy in Paris and composition with Daniel Lesur; subsequently took lessons with Alfredo Casella in Rome. He settled in Paris.

WORKS: Operas: *Syllabaire pour Phèdre* (Avignon, 1969) and *Autodafé,* for puppet theater (Lyons, 1972); ballet, *Etudes chorégraphiques* (1955); *Synaxis* for Percussion, 2 Pianos, and Orch. (1966); *Chiffres de clavecin* for Harpsichord and 21 Instruments (1968); *Silenciaire* for Percussion and 12 Strings (1969); *Signes* for Flute, Piano, Guitar, and Percussion (1965); *5 séquences* for String Quartet (1962–64); *Syrtes* for Cello and Piano (1972); 24 preludes for Piano (1973); oratorios: *Llanto por Ignacio Sanchez Mejias* (1950) and *Récit de l'an Zéro* (1959); numerous choral pieces; film scores.

BIBLIOGRAPHY: J. Roy, *Présences contemporaines, Musique française* (Paris, 1962); N. Quist, *Maurice Ohana* (Diss., Univ. of Heidelberg, 1973).

O'Hara, Geoffrey, American song composer; b. Chatham, Ontario, Canada, Feb. 2, 1882; d. St. Petersburg, Fla., Jan. 31, 1967. He settled in the U.S. in 1904; became an American citizen in 1922. He studied with Homer Norris and J. Vogler; played organ in the Chatham Episcopal church; then acted in vaudeville as a pianist, singer, and composer; wrote the song *Your eyes have told me* for Caruso. In 1913 he was appointed an instructor in American Indian music as part of a program of the Dept. of the Interior; in 1917, became an army song leader; was instructor in community singing at Teachers College, Columbia Univ. (1936–37); charter member of the American Society of Composers, Authors and Publishers (1914).

WORKS: He wrote several operettas, among them *Peggy and the Pirate, Riding Down the Sky, The Count and the Co-ed, The Smiling Sixpence;* about 300 songs, of which the following were extremely popular: *K-K-K-Katy, I Love a Little Cottage, Wreck of the Julie Plante, Leetle Bateese, The Living God, I Walked Today Where Jesus Walked, Give a Man a Horse He Can Ride, Where Heaven Is, Tomasso Rotundo, A Little Close Harmony, The Old Songs, Sing Awhile Longer, Forward to Christ, One World,* etc.; he also publ. a collection of Canadian folk songs.

Ohlsson, Garrick, American pianist; b. Bronxville, N.Y., April 3, 1948. He entered the preparatory division of the Juilliard School of Music in 1961 as a student of Sascha Gorodnitzki; in 1968 he enrolled in the master class of Rosina Lhévinne. He came to public notice in 1969, when he won the international Busoni competition in Bolzano and the Montreal contest for pianists. A giant leap in his career was made when he became the first American pianist to win the prestigious quinquennial Chopin International Piano Competition in Warsaw in 1970, contending against topnotch Polish and Russian performers. A Polish writer described Ohlsson as a "bear-butterfly" for his ability to traverse the entire spectrum of 18 dynamic degrees discernible on the modern pianoforte, from the thundering fortississimo to the finest pianississimo, with reference also to his height (6 foot, 4 inches), weight (225 lbs.), and stretch of hands (an octave and a fifth in the left hand and an octave and a fourth in the right hand). His interpretations are marked by a distinctive Americanism, technically flawless and free of Romantic mannerisms.

Ohms, Elisabeth, Dutch soprano; b. Arnhem, May 17, 1888; d. Marquardstein, Oct. 16, 1974. She studied in Amsterdam, Frankfurt, and Berlin; made her debut in Mainz in 1921; in 1922 she joined the Bavarian State Opera in Munich, of which she was a principal member until 1936; also sang at La Scala in Milan (1927–29) and at Covent Garden in London (1928–29, 1935). On Jan. 17, 1930, she made her debut with the Metropolitan Opera in N.Y. as Brünnhilde; remained on its roster until 1932. She made guest appearances with the Vienna State Opera and at the Bayreuth Festivals. She excelled in Wagner's operas; among her finest roles were Brünnhilde, Kundry, Venus, and Isolde.

Oistrakh, David, famous Russian violinist; b. Odessa, Sept. 30, 1908; d. Amsterdam, Oct. 24, 1974. He studied violin as a child with Stolarsky in Odessa; then entered the Odessa music school, graduating in 1926; appeared as soloist in Glazunov's Violin Concerto under the composer's direction in Kiev in 1927. In 1928 he went to Moscow; in 1934 was appointed to the faculty of the Moscow Cons. His name attracted universal attention in 1937 when he won first prize at the International Competition in Brussels, in which 68 violinists from 21 countries took part. He played in Paris and London in 1953 with extraordinary success; made his first American appearances in 1955, as soloist with major American orchs. and in recitals, winning enthusiastic acclaim; his playing was marked, apart from a phenomenal technique, by stylistic fidelity to works by different composers of different historical periods. Soviet composers profited by his advice as to technical problems of violin playing; he collaborated with Prokofiev in making an arrangement for violin and piano of his Flute Sonata. (He also played a chess match with Prokofiev.) A whole generation of Soviet violinists numbered among his pupils, first and foremost his son **Igor Oistrakh** (b. Odessa, April 27, 1931), who has had a spectacular career in his own right; he won first prize at the International Festival of Democratic Youth in Budapest (1949) and the Wieniawski Contest in Poznan (1952); some critics regarded him as equal to his father in virtuosity.
BIBLIOGRAPHY: V. Bronin, *David Oistrakh* (Moscow, 1954); I. Yampolsky, *David Oistrakh* (Moscow, 1964); D. Naberin, *David und Igor Oistrakh* (Berlin, 1968); V. Josefowitsch, *D. Oistrach* (Stuttgart, 1977); Y. Soroker, *David Oistrakh* (Jerusalem, 1982).

Okeghem, Johannes. See **Ockeghem, Johannes.**

Oki, Masao, Japanese composer; b. Iwata, Shizuoka, Oct. 3, 1901; d. Kamakura, April 18, 1971. He studied engineering and music; then devoted himself mainly to teaching and composition. He wrote 6 symphs., of which the 5th was subtitled *Atomic Bomb;* it was performed in Tokyo on Nov. 6, 1953; the 6th Symph. (1970) was entitled *Vietnam.* His other works included a cantata, *Take Back the Human* (1961–63); a String Quartet; and some choral works.

Olah, Tiberiu, Rumanian composer; b. Arpasel, Jan. 2, 1928. He studied at the Cons. in Cluj (1946–49); then went to Russia, where he studied at the Moscow Cons. (1949–54); in each of the years from 1966 to 1969, he attended the summer courses in new music at Darmstadt. In 1958 he was appointed to the staff of the Bucharest Cons. In his music Olah adopts a strong contrapuntal style, with some excursions into the atonal domain and dodecaphonic organization.
WORKS: Piano Sonatina (1950); String Quartet (1952); Trio for Violin, Clarinet, and Piano (1954); Symph. No. 1 (1955); Violin Sonatina (1955); 4 cantatas: *Cantata* for Female Chorus, 2 Flutes, Strings, and Percussion (1956); *Prind visele aripi (Dreams Become Reality,* 1959); *Lumina lui Lenin (The Light of Lenin,* 1959); *Constelaţia omului (The Galaxy of Man,* 1960); a cycle of 5 works inspired by the works of the Rumanian sculptor Constantin Brâncuşi: *Coloana fără sfîrşit (Endless Column),* symph. poem (1962); Sonata for Solo Clarinet (1963); *Spaţiu şi ritm (Space and Rhythm),* étude for 3 Percussion Groups (1964); *Poarta sărutului (Archway of the Kiss),* symph. poem (1966); *Masa tăcerii (The Table of Silence),* symph. poem (1967–68); *5 Pieces* for Orch. (1966); *Echinocţii (Equinoxes)* for Voice, Clarinet, and Piano (1967); *Translations* for 16 Strings (1968); *Perspectives* for 13 Instruments (1969); Sonata for Solo Cello (1971); *Invocation* for 5 Instruments (1971); *Crescendo* for Orch. (1972); *Evenimente 1907* for Orch. (1972); *The Time of Memory* for Chamber Ensemble (1973; N.Y., Dec. 6, 1974); songs.

Olczewska, Maria (real name, **Marie Berchtenbreitner**), German mezzo-soprano; b. Augsburg, Aug. 12, 1892; d. Klagenfurt, Austria, May 17, 1969. She sang in operetta in Hamburg; then was engaged at the Leipzig Opera (1920–23); subsequently was a member of the Vienna State Opera (1923–36) and of Covent Garden in London (1924–32), where she sang Wagnerian operas with excellent success. She was then engaged at the Chicago Opera and at the Metropolitan Opera in N.Y., making her debut as Brangäne (Jan. 16, 1933) and remaining on its staff until 1935. In 1947 she returned to Vienna, where she taught at the Cons. She had a powerful voice, which made it possible for her to master the Wagner roles; but she was also excellent in dramatic parts, such as Carmen. Furthermore, she had a genuine talent as a stage actress.

Oldberg, Arne, American composer; b. Youngstown, Ohio, July 12, 1874; d. Evanston, Ill., Feb. 17, 1962. He studied composition with Middelschulte; then went to Vienna, where he was a piano pupil of Leschetizky (1893–95); also took courses with Rheinberger in Munich. Returning to America in 1899, he became head of the piano dept. at Northwestern Univ.; retired in 1941. Most of his orch. works were performed by the Chicago Symph. Orch., among them *Paolo and Francesca* (Jan. 17, 1908), *At Night* (April 13, 1917), Symph. No. 4 (Dec. 31, 1942), Symph. No. 5 (Jan. 19, 1950), and *St. Francis of Assisi* for Baritone and Orch. (Ravinia Festival, July 16, 1954). Other works are: *Academic Overture* (1909); *The Sea,* symph. poem (1934); 2 piano concertos, of which the 2nd won the Hollywood Bowl prize and was performed there (Aug. 16, 1932); Violin Concerto (1933; Chicago, Nov. 7, 1946); 2 rhapsodies for Orch.; chamber music; piano pieces.

Oldham, Arthur, English composer; b. London, Sept. 6, 1926. He studied at the Royal College of Music with Herbert Howells, and privately with Benjamin Britten. From 1945 he was active as music director of various London theaters. He has written the ballets *Mr. Punch* (1946), *The Sailor's Return* (1947), *Circus Canteen* (1951), and *Bonne-Bouche* (1952); a symph. poem, *The Apotheosis of Lucius* (1952); a musical for children, *The Land of Green Ginger* (1964); *Hymns for the Amusement of Children* for Voices and Organ (1962); various sacred and secular works.

Oldman, Cecil Bernard, English music librarian; b. London, April 2, 1894; d. there, Oct. 7, 1969. He studied at Exeter College, Oxford; in 1920 received an appointment in the Dept. of Printed Books in the British Museum; from 1948 to 1959 was Principal Keeper. His specialty was documentation on Mozart; he publ. and annotated the letters of Constanze Mozart to J.A. André, in the 3rd vol. of Emily Anderson's *Letters of Mozart and His Family* (1938); he contributed numerous valuable papers to British, German, and Dutch publications. In 1951 he became chairman of the Council of the British Union Catalogue of Music.

Oldroyd, George, English organist and composer; b. Healey, Yorkshire, Dec. 1, 1886; d. London, Feb. 26, 1951. He studied organ and music theory with Eaglefield Hull; violin with Frank Arnold. After a year in Paris as organist of the English Church there (1915), he played at various London churches; taught at Trinity College; in 1949 succeeded Stanley Marchant as prof. at the Univ. of London. He wrote a number of sacred works, of which a *Stabat Mater* is notable; publ. *The Technique and Spirit of Fugue: An Historical Study* (London, 1948); *Polyphonic Writing for Voices, in 6 and 8 Parts* (London, 1953); and some essays on Gregorian chant.

Olds, Gerry, American composer; b. Cleveland, Feb. 26, 1933. He studied at the Cleveland Inst. and at the Chicago Cons. (M.A., 1957). His works include a *Short Symphony* (1956); Violin Concerto (1957); Toccata for String Orch. (1958); Wind Quintet (1958); 2nd Symph., in one movement (1958); String Trio (1959); and Piano Concerto (1960).

Olenin, Alexander, Russian composer, brother of the singer **Marie Olénine d'Alheim;** b. Istomino, Riazan district, June 13, 1865; d. Moscow, Feb. 15, 1944. He studied with P. Pabst and with Erdmannsdörfer; lived most of his life in Moscow. He wrote an opera in a folk style, *Kudeyar* (Moscow, Nov. 26, 1915); a symph. poem, *After the Battle; Préludes prairiales* for 2 Oboes, Violin, and Piano (1927); Piano Sonata; Violin Sonata; several song cycles (*The Street, The Peasant's Son, The Autumn, Home,* etc.); 52 songs to texts by Heine.
    BIBLIOGRAPHY: V. Belaiev, "Olenin's Reminiscences of Balakirev," *Musical Quarterly* (Jan. 1930).

Olénine d'Alheim, Marie, Russian soprano; b. Istomino, Riazan district, Oct. 2, 1869; d. Moscow, Aug. 27, 1970, at the age of 100. She studied in Russia and later in Paris; made her debut in Paris in 1896. Through her brother, the composer **Alexander Olenin,** she met Stasov, Balakirev, and Cui, and became interested in Russian vocal music. In 1893 she married the French writer Pierre d'Alheim (1862–1922), translator of the text of *Boris Godunov;* together they organized, in Moscow and in Paris, numerous concerts and lectures on Russian music, particularly on Mussorgsky; she was an outstanding interpreter of Russian songs; publ. a book, *Le Legs de Mussorgsky* (Paris, 1908). In 1935 she settled in Paris as a voice teacher; in 1949 joined the French Communist Party; in 1959 she returned to Russia.

Olevsky, Julian, violinist; b. Berlin, May 7, 1926. He studied violin in Germany; in 1947 he went to the U.S.; was naturalized in 1951. He developed a fine career as a solo violinist; was also active as a teacher; served on the faculty of the Univ. of Mass., Boston (1967–74).

Oliphant, Thomas, British composer; b. Condie, Perthshire, Dec. 25, 1799; d. London, March 9, 1873. Of Scottish birth, he settled in London in 1830 and became a member of the Madrigal Society of London; publ. *A Brief Account of the Madrigal Society* (1835), *A Short Account of Madrigals* (1836), and *La Musa Madrigalesca* (1837; the words of 400 madrigals, chiefly of the Elizabethan period); he also wrote English words for Italian madrigals; publ. several collections of glees, catches, and rounds.
    BIBLIOGRAPHY: *Dictionary of National Biography.*

Olitzka, Rosa, German contralto; b. Berlin, Sept. 6, 1873; d. Chicago, Sept. 29, 1949. She studied with Désirée Artôt and Julius Hey; sang at Berlin (1891); then was engaged at the Hannover Opera (1892–93), at Covent Garden in London (1894), and in N.Y. with the German Opera Co., conducted by Damrosch

(1895–97); was also with the Metropolitan Opera (1895–97, 1899–1901). After a season with the Chicago Opera Co. (1910–11), she left the stage and was active as a vocal teacher in Chicago.

Olitzki, Walter, German baritone; b. Hamburg, March 17, 1903; d. Los Angeles, Aug. 2, 1949. After a career in Germany, he appeared as Beckmesser at the Metropolitan Opera in N.Y. (Dec. 2, 1939); he specialized in Wagnerian roles; was with the Metropolitan Opera until 1947. He was a nephew of **Rosa Olitzka.**

Oliveira, Elmar, American violinist; b. Waterbury, Conn., June 8, 1950. He studied violin at the Hartt College of Music in Hartford, Conn., and later at the Manhattan School of Music. In 1975 he won the Walter W. Naumburg Competition in N.Y. In 1978 he won the Gold Medal of the International Tchaikovsky Competition in Moscow, which catapulted him onto an international career.

Oliveira, Jocy de, Brazilian pianist and avant-garde composer; b. Curitiba-Parana, Brazil, April 11, 1936, of French and Portuguese origin. She studied piano in São Paulo with J. Kliass and in Paris with Marguerite Long; then traveled to the U.S.; obtained her M.A. at Washington Univ. in St. Louis in 1968. She appeared as a piano soloist with major orchs. in Europe and America, specializing in the modern repertoire; in 1966 she played the piano part in Stravinsky's *Capriccio* in St. Louis, under Stravinsky's direction. As a composer, she occupies the aphelion of ultra-modernism, experimenting in electronic, environmental, theatrical, cinematic, and television media, as exemplified by *Probabilistic Theater* I, II, and III for Musicians, Actors, Dancers, Television and Traffic Conductor, and other environmental manifestations. Her *Polinteracões I, II, III* present the culmination of "total music" involving the visual, aural, tactile, gustatory, and olfactory senses, with an anatomic chart serving as a score for guidance of the participants, supplemented by a phonemic table indicating the proper verbalization of vocal parts. (Complete score and illustrations were reproduced in *Source,* no. 7, Sacramento, Calif., 1970.) A performance of *Polinteracões* was attempted on the occasion of the Catalytic Celebration of the 10th Anniversary Festival of the New Music Circle in St. Louis on April 7, 1970, but was stopped by the management as a noisy, noisome nuisance. Jocy de Oliveira is also active in belles-lettres; she wrote a sociological fantasy, *O 3° Mundo (The Third World;* a utopian, optimistic vision of the future); a controversial play, *Apague meu (Spotlight),* first produced in São Paulo in 1961; poetical works; etc. She also composed a number of advanced sambas, precipitating the vogue of the Brazilian bossa nova. She is the wife of the Brazilian conductor **Eleazar de Carvalho.**

Oliver, Henry Kemble, American composer of hymn tunes; b. Beverly, Mass., Nov. 24, 1800; d. Salem, Aug. 12, 1885. He was a chorister at Park Street Church in Boston; graduated from Dartmouth College in 1818; played the organ in various churches in Salem and Boston; in 1826, founded and managed the Salem Mozart Association; subsequently went to Lawrence, Mass., where he was mayor in 1859; later was also mayor of Salem; in 1861–65, was treasurer of the State of Massachusetts. He was given B.A. and M.A. degrees by Harvard Univ. (1862) and was made a Mus.Doc. by Dartmouth College (1883). He wrote many well-known hymn tunes (*Federal Street, Morning, Harmony Grove, Beacon Street, Hudson*), motets, chants, and a *Te Deum;* publ. *The National Lyre* (1848; with Tuckerman and Bancroft; contains many of his own compositions), *Oliver's Collection of Hymn and Psalm Tunes* (1860), and *Original Hymn Tunes* (1875).

BIBLIOGRAPHY: F.J. Metcalf, *American Writers and Compilers of Sacred Music* (1925; pp. 230–33); *Dictionary of American Biography* (vol. XIV).

Oliver, John, American conductor; b. Teaneck, N.J., June 4, 1939. He studied at the Univ. of Notre Dame (B.M., 1961) and the New England Cons. of Music (M.M. in choral conducting, 1967). After serving as an assistant to Erich Leinsdorf at the Berkshire Music Center at Tanglewood (1968–70), he was named head of vocal and choral activities there; founded his own John Oliver Chorale in 1977. He joined the staff of the Mass. Inst. of Technology in 1964; was a technical instructor there in the humanities dept. (1970–77), then lecturer (1977–81) and, from 1981, senior lecturer.

Oliver, Joseph ("King"), black American jazz cornetist and bandleader; b. on a plantation near Abend, La., May 11, 1885; d. Savannah, Ga., April 8, 1938. In 1907 he was working in Storyville (the brothel district of New Orleans) with the Melrose Brass Band; in subsequent years he was with a number of other brass bands there, and in 1915 he formed his own group, eventually known as the Creole Jazz Band; in 1917 he acquired the nickname "King," traditionally reserved for the leading jazz musicians. Also in 1917, the government closed the bordellos in Storyville, putting most of the musicians (among others) out of work; the following year Oliver moved his band to Chicago, leading a migration of jazz musicians to the city that was largely responsible for the dispersion of the black New Orleans jazz style throughout the country. In 1922 Louis Armstrong, whom he had known in New Orleans, joined the band, helping to make it the most polished exponent of New Orleans collectively improvised jazz; the group's 1923 recordings were the most influential early jazz recordings ever made; they have been reissued by the Smithsonian Inst. Subsequent bands formed by Oliver remained a potent force in jazz until around 1928. Oliver is the uncle of the composer **Ulysses Kay.**

BIBLIOGRAPHY: W.C. Allen, *King Joe Oliver* (London, 1958); M. Williams, ed., *Jazz Panorama* (contains essays on Oliver by Edmond Souchon and Larry Gushee; N.Y., 1964); F. Ramsey, Jr., in *Dictio-*

nary of American Biography, Supplement II.

Olivero, Magda, Italian soprano; b. Saluzzo, near Turin, March 25, 1912. She studied at the Turin Cons.; made her debut in Turin in 1933; then sang in the Italian provinces. She temporarily retired from the stage when she married in 1941, but resumed her career in 1951; made successful appearances at La Scala in Milan, and in Paris and London. In 1966 she made her American debut in Dallas in the title role of Cherubini's *Medea;* she was 63 years old when she made her first appearance with the Metropolitan Opera, N.Y., on April 3, 1975, as Tosca, an unprecedented occurrence in the annals of opera; on Dec. 5, 1977, she gave a highly successful recital in a program of Italian art songs at Carnegie Hall, N.Y. Among her operatic roles were Violetta, Mimi, and Tosca; she was praised mainly for her dramatic penetration of each character and her fine command of dynamic nuances.

Oliveros, Pauline, American composer; b. Houston, Texas, May 30, 1932. She was of a musical family; her mother and grandmother were piano teachers from whom she learned the rudiments of music; she also took violin lessons with William Sydler and studied accordion playing with Marjorie Harrigan. From her earliest days she became sensitive to pleasing animal sounds, and was able aurally to suppress the rude noise of motorcars in her environment. She added to her practical musical knowledge by studying the French horn with J.M. Brandsetter. From 1949 to 1952 she studied composition with Paul Koepke at the Univ. of Houston; in 1954 she enrolled at San Francisco State College (B.A., 1958); also studied privately with Robert Erickson (1954–60), who initiated her into modern harmony, the art of asymmetrical rhythms, group improvisation, and acoustical sonorism. Gradually, she expanded her receptivity into the range of subliminal sounds, derived from the overtone series, differential tones, and sonic abstractions. In 1960 she composed a piano sextet which explored a variety of such elusive tonal elements; it received the Pacifica Foundation National Prize. Advancing further into the domain of new sonorities, she wrote a choral work, *Sound Patterns,* to wordless voices (1962), which received a prize in the Netherlands. With Morton Subotnick and others she organized the San Francisco Tape Music Center, and experimented with the resources of magnetic tape. On July 22, 1967, she presented in San Francisco a 12-hour marathon of recorded electronic music of her own composition. In 1967 she joined the music faculty of the Univ. of Calif. at San Diego, where she remained until 1981. There she was able to develop her ideas further afield. Taking advantage of her skill as a gardener, she arrayed garden hoses and lawn sprinklers as part of a musical ensemble accompanied by the sounds of alarm clocks and various domestic utensils. Occasionally, a musician was instructed to bark. To this enriched artistic vocabulary was soon added a physical and psychosomatic element; performers had to act the parts of a magician, a juggler, and a fortune-teller. Page turners, piano movers, and floor sweepers were listed as performing artists. In her later works she reduced such kinetic activities and gradually began to compose ceremonial works of sonic meditation, sotto voce murmuration, lingual lallation, and joyful ululation, with the purpose of inducing an altered state of consciousness or unconsciousness; sometimes an exotic but usually digestible meal was served at leisurely intervals. Pauline Oliveros often presided over such sessions, singing and playing her faithful accordion; sometimes this music was left to be unheard by ordinary ears, but it could be perceived mystically. In 1979 she took part in the Berlin Festival of Metamusic, to audible acclaim. In 1977 she obtained first prize from the city of Bonn for a work commemorating the sesquicentennial of Beethoven's death; the piece was verbally notated with the intention to subvert perception of the entire city so that it would become a perceptual theater. As she moved higher into the realm of cosmic consciousness, Pauline Oliveros introduced the psychic element into her works; in 1970 she drew an equation for an indefinite integral of the differential *psi* (for psychic unit), to create the state of Oneness. Apart from her metamusical activities, she became a karate expert, the holder of the third Kyu black belt in Shotokan-style karate.

WORKS: *Variations for Sextet* for Flute, Clarinet, Trumpet, Horn, Cello, and Piano (1960); *Sound Patterns* for Chorus (1961); Trio for Trumpet, Piano, and Page Turner (1961); Trio for Trumpet, Accordion, and Double Bass (1961); *7 Passages* for 2-channel Tape, Mobile, and Dancer (1963); *Five* for Trumpet and Dancer (1964); *Duo* for Accordion and Bandoneon, with possible Mynah Bird Obbligato (1964); *Apple Box Orchestra* for 10 Performers, Amplified Apple Boxes, etc. (1964); *Pieces of Eight* for Wind Octet and a number of Props, including a Cash Register (1965); *7 Sets of Mnemonics,* multimedia piece (1965); *George Washington Slept Here* for Amplified Violin, Film Projections, and Tape (1965); *Bye Bye Butterfly* for Oscillators, Amplifiers, and Tapes (1965); *Winter Light* for Tape, Mobile, and Figure (1965); *Participle Dangling in Honor of Gertrude Stein* for Tape, Mobile, and Work Crew (1966); *Theater Piece for Trombone Player* for Garden Hose, Instruments, and Tape (1966); *Night Jar* for Viola d'Amore (1968); *Festival House* for Orch., Mimes, Light, and Film Projections (1968); *Double Basses at Twenty Paces* for 2 Double Basses, Tape, and Projections (1968); *The Dying Alchemist Preview* for Narrator, Violinist, Trumpet, Piccolo, Percussion, and Slides (1969); *The Wheel of Fortune,* suggested by the trump cards in the tarot deck, for Solo Clarinet (1969); *Aeolian Partitions* for Flute, Clarinet, Violin, Cello, and Piano (1969); *To Valerie Solanis and Marilyn Monroe, in Recognition of Their Desperation,* verbally notated score (1970; Solanis, the founder of SCUM, i.e. the Society to Cut Up Men, tried unsuccessfully to shoot the pop artist Andy Warhol; Marilyn Monroe destroyed her own beautiful and desirable body by feeding herself sleeping pills to mortal excess); *Meditation on the Points of the Compass* for

Chorus and Percussion (1970); *Bonn Feier,* intended to convert the city of Bonn into an imagined total theater (1971); *Post Card Theater,* multimedia event (1972); *Phantom Fathom,* mixed-media event with an Exotic Potluck Dinner (1972); *1000 Acres* for String Quartet (1972); *Sonic Images,* subliminal auditory fantasy (1972); *Crow Two,* ceremonial opera (1974); *Rose Mountain Slow Runner* for Voice and Accordion (1975; renamed *Horse Sings from Cloud,* inspired by a dream image of a horse lifted to a cloud by birds); *Willow Brook Generations and Reflections* for Wind Instruments and Vocalists (1976); *The Yellow River Map,* ceremonial meditation for a lot of people (1977); *King Kong Sings Along* for Chorus (1977); *Rose Moon,* ceremonial for Chorus and Percussion (1977); *The Witness* for Virtuoso Instrumentalists (1978); *El relicario de los animales* for Soprano and 20 Instruments (1979); *Carol Plantamura* for Voice and 20 Instruments (1979); *Gone with The Wind, 1980* for Assorted Ensembles (1980); *Wheel of Times,* for String Quartet and Electonics (1982); *The Mandala* for 4 Clarinets, 8 Crystal Glasses, Bass Drum, and Finger Cymbals (timeless date of composition).

BIBLIOGRAPHY: David Ewen, *American Composers* (N.Y., 1982); Heidi von Gunden, *The Music of Pauline Oliveros* (Metuchen, N.J., 1983).

d'Ollone, Max (full name, **Maximilien-Paul-Marie-Félix**), French composer and writer on music; b. Besançon, June 13, 1875; d. Paris, May 15, 1959. He studied with Lavignac, Massenet, and Lenepveu at the Paris Cons.; received the Grand Prix de Rome in 1897 with his cantata *Frédégonde;* was active as an opera conductor in Paris and the French provinces. A prolific composer, he wrote 5 operas: *Le Retour* (Angers, Feb. 13, 1913), *Les Uns et les autres* (Paris, Nov. 6, 1922), *L'Arlequin* (Paris, Dec. 24, 1924), *George Dandin,* after Molière (Paris, March 19, 1930), and *La Samaritaine* (Paris, June 25, 1937); also *Dans la cathédrale* for Orch. (1906); *Fantaisie* for Piano and Orch. (1899); chamber music; many songs; he contributed to French magazines on musical subjects; publ. a book, *Le Théâtre lyrique et le public* (Paris, 1955).

Olman, Abe, American songwriter; b. Cincinnati, Dec. 20, 1888; d. Rancho Mirage, Calif., Jan. 4, 1984. He worked as a song demonstrator in Cleveland in 1910; then moved to Chicago, where he established a music publishing firm, La Salle Music. From 1946–56 he was a director of ASCAP. Among his hits were *Oh, Johnny Oh* and *Down among the Sheltering Palms,* which was sung by Al Jolson. He supplied many songs to movie musicals in the early years of the talkies.

Olmeda de San José, Federico, Spanish musicologist and composer; b. Burgos de Osma, 1865; d. Madrid, Feb. 11, 1909. He studied violin and music theory at Burgos; was appointed organist at the Cathedral of Burgos in Dec. 1887; in 1907 went to Madrid as choirmaster of the Convent of Las Descalzas Reales; founded and edited the review *La Voz de la Música* (1907); publ. manuals of solfeggio, the essays *Folklore de Burgos* (Burgos, 1902), *Pío X y el canto romano* (Burgos, 1904), etc.; also an important study on the 12th-century Codex of Calixtus II, in *Viaje musical a Santiago de Galicia* (1895). He wrote 4 symphs.; a symph. poem, *Paraíso perdido;* an *Oda* for String Orch.; several church works: *32 rimas* for Piano (1890–91), organ pieces, etc. (altogether some 350 works).

BIBLIOGRAPHY: H. Collet, *L'Essor de la musique espagnole au XXᵉ siècle* (Paris, 1929).

Olsen, Ole, Norwegian composer; b. Hammerfest, July 4, 1850; d. Oslo, Nov. 10, 1927. He studied with J. Lindeman; was active as an organist and theater conductor in Trondheim and other provincial towns; in 1870 went to Leipzig, where he studied with Richter and Reinecke. Returning to Norway in 1874, he became a piano teacher in Oslo; was conductor of the Music Society there (1878–81), instructor of music at the Military Academy (1887–1903), and inspector of military music (1899–1919). He wrote the operas *Stig Hvide* (1876), *Stallo* (1902), and *Klippeøerne* (1905), which were not produced, and *Lajla* (Oslo, Oct. 8, 1908); also some incidental music; a Symph. (1878); the symph. poems *Aasgaardsreien* (1878) and *Alfedans* (*Elf Dance;* 1880); Concerto for Horn and Orch. (Oslo, April 1, 1905); numerous choruses; songs; piano music.

Olsen, Poul Rovsing, Danish composer and ethnomusicologist; b. Copenhagen, Nov. 4, 1922; d. there, July 2, 1982. He studied law at the Univ. of Aarhus (1940–42) and at the Univ. of Copenhagen (1942–48); concurrently, took lessons in composition with Knud Jeppesen at the Royal Cons. of Music in Copenhagen (1943–46); later studied with Nadia Boulanger in Paris (1948–49). Between 1958 and 1963 he took part in ethnomusicological expeditions to Arabia, India, Greece, and eastern Greenland and wrote numerous valuable papers on the folklore and musical cultures of the areas he visited. He worked until 1960 for the Danish Ministry of Education as a legal expert on music copyright; served as chairman of the Danish Society of Composers (1962–67); taught ethnomusicology at the Univ. of Lund, Sweden (1967–69), and subsequently at the Univ. of Copenhagen. He was president of the International Council of Traditional Music (formerly the International Folk Music Council) from 1977 until his death. He was a music critic for the newspapers *Morgenbladet* (1945–46), *Information* (1949–54), and *Berlingske Tidende* (1954–74). Much of his music embodies materials of non-European cultures, reflecting the influence of his travels. His *Elegy* for Organ (1953) is the first piece in the serial system by a Danish composer.

WORKS: FOR THE STAGE: 2 operas: *Belisa,* after García Lorca (1964; Copenhagen, Sept. 3, 1966) and *Usher,* after Poe (1980); 4 ballets: *Ragnarök (Twilight of the Gods;* 1948; Copenhagen, Sept. 12, 1960); *La Création* (1952; Copenhagen, March 10, 1961); *Bryllupet (The Wedding;* 1966; Copenhagen, Sept. 15, 1969); *Den Fremmede (The Stranger;* 1969;

Copenhagen, July 17, 1972). FOR ORCH.: *Symphonic Variations* (1953); Piano Concerto (1953–54); *Sinfonia I* (1957–58; Copenhagen, April 13, 1959); *Sinfonia II, Susudil,* based on Arab and Turkish modes (1966; Copenhagen, Oct. 31, 1966); *Capriccio* (1961–62); *Et russisk bal (The Russian Ball),* 3 dances (1965); *Au Fond de la nuit* for Chamber Orch. (1968); *Randrussermarchen* (1977); *Lux Coelestis* (1978). FOR VOICE: *Schicksalslieder,* after 4 Hölderlin poems, for Soprano or Tenor, and 7 Instruments (1953); *Evening Songs* for Mezzo-soprano and Flute (1954); *Alapa-Tarana,* vocalise for Mezzo-soprano and Percussion (1959); *A l'inconnu* for Soprano or Tenor, and 13 Instruments (1962); *Kejseren (The Emperor)* for Tenor, Male Chorus, and Orch. (1963; Copenhagen, Sept. 5, 1964); *A Song of Mira Bai* for Chorus, 3 Trumpets, and Percussion (1971); *Air* for Mezzo-soprano, Saxophone, and Piano (1976); *The Planets* for Mezzo-soprano, Flute, Viola, and Guitar (1978). CHAMBER MUSIC: *2 Pieces* for Clarinet and Piano (1943); *Romance* for Cello and Piano (1943); Violin Sonata (1946); 2 string quartets (1948, 1969); Serenade for Violin and Piano (1949); 2 piano trios (1950, 1976); *Prolana* for Clarinet, Violin, and Piano (1955); Cello Sonata (1956); *The Dream of Pan* for Solo Flute (1959); *Nouba,* 6 movements for Harp (1960); *Passacaglia* for Flute, Violin, Cello, and Piano (1960); *Patet* for 9 Musicians (1966); *How to Play in D major without Caring about It,* fantasy for 2 Accordions (1967); *Arabesk* for 7 Musicians (1968); *Shangri-La* for Flute, Viola d'Amore, and Piano (1969); *Pour une Viola d'Amour* (1969); *Rencontres* for Cello and Percussion (1970); *Poème* for Accordian, Guitar, and Percussion (1973); Concertino for Clarinet, Violin, Cello, and Piano (1973); *Partita* for Solo Cello (1974); *Nostalgie* for Guitar (1976); *Danse élégiaque* for Flute and Guitar (1978); *A Dream of Violet* for String Trio (1982). FOR PIANO: 3 sonatinas (1941, 1951, 1967); *Theme with Variations* (1947); 2 sonatas for Piano, 4-hands (1948, 1967); *12 Preludes* (1948); 2 sonatas (1950, 1952); *3 Nocturnes* (1951); *Medardus,* suite (1956); *5 Inventions* (1957); *Bagatelles* (1962); *Images* (1965); *4 Innocent Sonatas* (1969); *Many Happy Returns* (1971).

PUBLICATIONS: *Musiketnologi* (Copenhagen, 1974) and *Music and Musical Instruments in the World of Islam* (with Jean Jenkins, London, 1976).

Olsen, Sparre, Norwegian composer; b. Stavanger, April 25, 1903. He studied composition with Valen in Oslo (1925–30), then with Max Butting in Berlin, and with Percy Grainger in London; was a violinist with the Oslo Phil. Orch. (1923–33) and in Bergen (1933–40); in 1936 became a recipient of the State Salary of Art (a government life pension); in 1968 was awarded the Order of St. Olav. His music is in the national tradition.

WORKS: *Variations on a Norwegian Folk Song* for Orch. or Piano (1930); *Little Overture* (1931); *2 Edda Songs* for Voice, and Orch. or Piano (1931); *2 Modelle für Musik als Hörkulisse* for Orch. (1931); *Gneisten (The Spark)* for Male Chorus and Orch. (1933); *Cantata for Bergen* (1934); *Røystene (The*

Voices) for Soloists, Chorus, and Chamber Orch. (1935); *Prelude and Fugue* for Orch. (1935); *Draumkvedet (The Dream Ballad)* for Narrator, Soloists, Chorus, and Orch. (Bergen, April 19, 1937); 3 *Symphonic Fantasias:* No. 1 (1938–39; Oslo, Sept. 21, 1939); No. 2 (1957; Oslo, Oct. 6, 1957); No. 3 (1973; Bergen, Nov. 28, 1974); *Nidarosdomen (The Nidaros Cathedral),* fugue and chorale for Orch. (1940); *From Telemark,* suite for Small Orch. or Piano (1940–41); *Ver sanctum* for Chorus and Orch. (1941); *De profundis sursum corda,* peace cantata (1945; Bergen, May 1946); *Music for Orchestra* (Oslo, Nov. 3, 1948); *Pastoral and Dance* for Orch. (1949); *Leitom Suite* for Orch. or Piano (1951); *Serenade* for Flute and String Orch. (1954); *Intrada* for Orch. with Choral Finale (1956); *Canticum* for Orch. (1972); *Suite* for Flute, Oboe, and Clarinet (1933); Wind Quintet (1946); *3 Pieces* for Flute and Viola (1970); String Quartet (1972); songs; sacred choruses.

Olson, Lynn Freeman American composer and piano pedagogue; b. Minneapolis, June 5, 1938. He studied music at the Univ. of Minnesota; after graduation, he devoted himself mainly to musical education; ran a successful radio series under the inviting title "It's Time for Music." He publ. hundreds of semi-classical piano pieces suitable for teaching, songs, and choruses. He served as consultant to Carl Fischer, publishers, and as a contributing editor to *Clavier Magazine.*

Olsson, Otto Emanuel, eminent Swedish organist and composer; b. Stockholm, Dec. 19, 1879; d. there, Sept. 1, 1964. He studied with Lagergren and Dente at the Stockholm Cons. (1897–1901); from 1908 until 1945, taught there; was organist of the Gustav Vasa Church in Stockholm (1908–56); became a member of the Royal Academy of Music in 1915.

WORKS: *Requiem* for Soli, Chorus, and Orch. (1903); 3 string quartets (1903, 1906, 1947); 2 organ symphs. (1903, 1918); 3 sets of *Preludes and Fugues* for Organ (1910–11, 1918, 1935); *6 Latin Hymns* for a cappella Chorus (1911–13); solo songs.

Oncina, Juan, Spanish tenor; b. Barcelona, April 15, 1925. He studied in Barcelona; made his debut there in 1946. He then went to Italy and became a leading interpreter of Italian opera. From 1952 to 1961 he was a regular member of the Glyndebourne Festival Opera.

Ondříček, Emanuel, Czech violinist, son of **Jan Ondříček** and brother of **Franz Ondříček;** b. Pilsen, Dec. 6, 1882; d. Boston, Dec. 30, 1958. He studied with his father and with Ševčik at the Prague Cons.; after a series of concerts in Europe, he settled in the U.S. in 1912; became an eminent teacher in Boston and N.Y.; publ. a manual, *Mastery of Tone Production and Expression on the Violin.*

Ondříček, Franz, Czech violinist; b. Prague, April 29, 1857; d. Milan, April 12, 1922. He studied with his father, **Jan Ondříček,** and later with Bennewitz at the Prague Cons., winning first prize (1876–79); then with Massart at the Paris Cons., where he also won first prize (1879–81). He undertook extensive concert tours of Europe, America, Siberia, and the Far East before settling in Vienna (1907), where he founded the celebrated Ondříček Quartet (with Silbiger, Junck, and Jelinek); was a prof. at the New Vienna Cons. (1910–19); from 1919 taught at the Prague Cons. In 1885 he married **Anna Hlaváček,** a singer at the National Theater of Prague. As a concert player, he impressed his audiences with his fiery temperament, but in his later years developed a grand Classical style, marked by dignified repose. He publ. *Rapsodie bohème* for Violin and Orch.; a cadenza to the Violin Concerto of Brahms; numerous pieces for violin with piano. In collaboration with S. Mittelmann, he brought out *Neue Methode zur Erlangung der Meistertechnik des Violinspiels auf anatomisch-physiologischer Grundlage* (2 parts, 1909) with 15 of his own études.

Ondříček, Jan, Czech violinist; b. Běleč, near Bratronice, May 6, 1832; d. Prague, March 13, 1900. He was the son of a village violinist, and studied with him; played in various orchs., and also conducted; was a friend of Dvořák. He had 9 children, all of whom were musicians.

Onégin, Sigrid (neé **Hoffmann;** full name, **Elizabeth Elfriede Emilie Sigrid**), contralto; b. Stockholm (of a German father and a French mother), June 1, 1889; d. Magliaso, Switzerland, June 16, 1943. She studied in Frankfurt with Resz, in Munich with E.R. Weiss, and with di Ranieri in Milan. She made her first public appearance, using the name **Lilly Hoffmann,** in Wiesbaden, Sept. 16, 1911, in a recital, accompanied by the Russian pianist and composer **Eugene Onégin** (b. St. Petersburg, Oct. 10, 1883; d. Stuttgart, Nov. 12, 1919; real name, Lvov; he was a grandnephew of Alexis Lvov, author of the Russian Czarist hymn). She married him on May 25, 1913; after his death, she married a German doctor, Fritz Penzoldt (Nov. 20, 1920). She made her first appearance in opera as Carmen, in Stuttgart, on Oct. 10, 1912; made her American operatic debut at the Metropolitan Opera House, N.Y., as Amneris, on Nov. 22, 1922; revisited America several times, her last tour (in recitals) being in 1938. From 1931 she lived mostly in Switzerland.
BIBLIOGRAPHY: Fritz Penzoldt, *Alt-Rhapsodie; Sigrid Onegin, Leben und Werk* (Neustadt, 1953; includes several chapters written by Sigrid Onégin herself, originally publ. 1939, Magdeburg).

O'Neill, Norman, English conductor and composer; b. London, March 14, 1875; d. there, March 3, 1934. He was a direct descendant of the notable English musician **John Wall Callcott;** his father was a painter. He studied in London with Arthur Somervell, and later with Knorr in Frankfurt. Returning to London in 1899, he married the pianist **Adine Rückert** (1875–1947). He wrote incidental music for the Haymarket Theatre, of which he was music direc-

tor from 1908 to 1919; also produced the ballets *Before Dawn* (1917), *Punch and Judy* (1924), *Alice in Lumberland* (1926), etc.
BIBLIOGRAPHY: D. Hudson, *Norman O'Neill: A Life of Music* (London, 1945).

Onofri, Alessandro, Italian organist and composer; b. Spoleto, May 29, 1874; d. Varese, Aug. 27, 1932. He studied in Rome with Mascagni, Rossi, and others; in 1904 settled in Boston, where he was a church organist. He wrote the operas *Biancospino* (Venice, March 31, 1910) and *Assiuolo* (Rome, Sept. 25, 1912); the light operas *La famiglia modello* (Livorno, 1913) and *Il bocciuolo di rosa* (Rome, 1916). During his stay in the U.S., he wrote a set of American dances for piano.

Onslow, George (full name, **André Georges Louis Onslow**), noted French composer; b. Clermont-Ferrand, July 27, 1784; d. there, Oct. 3, 1853. He was the grandson of the first Lord Onslow; studied in London with Hüllmandel, Dussek, and Cramer (piano) and in Paris with Reicha (composition). He wrote 3 comic operas, produced in Paris: *L'Alcalde de la Vega* (Aug. 10, 1824), *Le Colporteur* (Nov. 22, 1827), and *Le Duc de Guise* (Sept. 8, 1837); 4 symphs.; and some other orch. music. However, these works failed to maintain interest; Onslow's real achievement was the composition of a great number of chamber works, in which he demonstrated an uncommon mastery of counterpoint; he wrote 34 string quintets; 36 string quartets; 6 piano trios; a Sextet for Flute, Clarinet, Horn, Bassoon, Double Bass, and Piano (the double-bass part was expressly written for the famous virtuoso Dragonetti); Nonet for Violin, Viola, Cello, Double Bass, Flute, Oboe, Clarinet, Bassoon, and Horn; Septet for Flute, Oboe, Clarinet, Horn, Bassoon, Double Bass, and Piano; violin sonatas; cello sonatas; piano sonatas, 4-hands; a number of piano pieces. As a result of a hunting accident in 1829, when a stray bullet injured him, he became deaf in one ear; his Quintet No. 15, subtitled *Le Quintette de la balle (Quintet of the Bullet),* was the musical rendering of this episode.
BIBLIOGRAPHY: L. Halévy, *Notice sur George Onslow* (Paris, 1855).

Oosterzee, Cornelie van, Dutch composer; b. Batavia, Java, Aug. 16, 1863; d. Berlin, Aug. 8, 1943. She studied in Berlin, and settled there in 1890; her opera *Das Gelöbnis* was produced in Weimar on May 1, 1910.

Opieński, Henryk, eminent Polish music scholar and composer; b. Cracow, Jan. 13, 1870; d. Morges, Switzerland, Jan. 21, 1942. He studied with Zelenski in Cracow, with Vincent d'Indy in Paris, and with H. Urban in Berlin; then went to Leipzig, where he studied musicology with Riemann and conducting with Nikisch. In 1907 he was appointed an instructor at the Warsaw Musical Society; from 1908 to 1912 he conducted the Warsaw Opera; in 1912 he went again to Germany, where he took his degree of

Dr.Phil. (Leipzig, 1914). He spent the years of World
War I at Morges, Switzerland; returning to Poland,
he was director of the Poznan Cons. (1919–26); then
settled again in Morges.

WORKS: Operas: *Maria* (1904; Poznan, April 27,
1923) and *Jakub lutnista* (*Jacob the Lutenist;* 1916–
18; Poznan, Dec. 21, 1927); oratorio, *The Prodigal
Son* (1930); symph. poems: *Lilla Weneda* (1908) and
Love and Destiny (1912); *Scènes lyriques en forme
de quatuor* for String Quartet; violin pieces; songs;
an album of 15 Polish songs (with French words;
1928); another album of 15 Polish songs (with Eng.
words; 1936). He publ. several books and essays on
Chopin (Lwow, 1910; 2nd ed., 1922; Warsaw, 1911;
Warsaw, 1912, etc.); also the collected letters of Chopin, in Polish, German, French, and Eng. (1931); oth-
er writings include a history of music in Polish
(Warsaw, 1912; 2nd ed., 1922); *La Musique polonaise*
(Paris, 1918; 2nd ed., 1929); a valuable monograph on
Moniuszko (Warsaw, 1924); a monograph on Pade-
rewski (Lwow, 1910; 2nd ed., Warsaw, 1928; in
French, Lausanne, 1928; 2nd ed., 1948).
BIBLIOGRAPHY: A. Fornerod, *H. Opieński* (Lau-
sanne, 1942).

Oppens, Ursula, talented American pianist; b.
New York, Feb. 2, 1944. She studied economics and
English literature at Radcliffe College (B.A., 1965);
then studied with Rosina Lhévinne and Leonard
Shure at the Juilliard School of Music. She won first
prize at the Busoni Competition in Italy in 1969;
co-founded Speculum Musicae in N.Y., a chamber
music ensemble devoted to performing contemporary music. In 1976 she was awarded the Avery
Fisher Prize.

Orbison, Roy, American rock singer; b. Wink, Texas, April 23, 1936. He possessed an excellent lyric
tenor voice, so unusual among the common breed of
rockers that he won a distinctive niche uncontested
by others in the field of popular music. He also was
an able songwriter of the pop type. In 1962 he made
a tour in England. Among his hits were *Crying,
Many Moods,* and *Regeneration.* His song *Pretty
Woman* became his identification number in signing off on the air. Among his self-centered anthologies were such albums as *Orbisongs* and *There Is
Only One Roy Orbison.*

Orbón (de Soto), Julián, Spanish-born composer;
b. Avilés, Aug. 7, 1925. He received the rudiments of
a musical education from his father, a professional
pianist. After the Spanish Civil War the family emigrated to Cuba; he studied music theory with José
Ardevol, with whom he also formed the Grupo de
Renovación Musical (1942–49); was director of his
father's Orbón Cons. in Havana in 1946–60. After
the revolution of 1959 in Cuba, Orbón went to Mexico; taught at the National Cons. in Mexico City in
1960–63; in 1964 he settled in N.Y. In his music he
follows a neo-Classical mode of composition;
among his works are: Symphony in C (1945); *Danzas
sinfónicas* (1955); Concerto Grosso (1958); *Oficios de
3 días* for Chorus and Orch. (1970); String Quartet

(1951); numerous piano pieces and choruses.

Orchard, William Arundel, Australian pianist,
conductor, and composer; b. London, April 13, 1867;
d. during a voyage in the South Atlantic, off the
coast of South Africa (23°49′S; 9°33′E), April 17, 1961.
He studied in London and Durham; in 1903 went to
Australia and lived in Sydney, where he was active
as a conductor and music educator; served as director of the New South Wales State Cons. (1923–34);
later taught at the Univ. of Tasmania. He wrote an
opera, *The Picture of Dorian Gray,* after Oscar
Wilde; a Violin Concerto; String Quartet; String
Quintet; choruses; songs. He publ. 2 books dealing
with Australian music: *The Distant View* (Sydney,
1943) and *Music in Australia* (Melbourne, 1952).

Ordoñez, Carlos, Austrian composer of Spanish
extraction; b. Vienna, April 19, 1734; d. there, Sept.
6, 1786. He was employed as a clerk, but studied
violin and performed successfully at chamber music concerts. He wrote numerous singspiels and
much instrumental music, some of which was publ.
during his lifetime. His singspiel *Diesmal hat der
Mann den Willen* was performed in Vienna on
April 22, 1778; his marionette opera *Alceste* was introduced by Haydn in Esterház on Aug. 30, 1775.
Ordoñez developed an excellent métier, and several
of his symphs. possessed enough merit to be misattributed to Haydn.
BIBLIOGRAPHY: A. Brown, *Carlo d'Ordoñez
(1734–1786): A Thematic Catalogue* (Detroit, 1978);
idem, "The Symphonies of Carlos d'Ordoñez,"
Haydn Yearbook, XII (Cardiff, 1981).

Orefice, Giacomo, Italian composer; b. Vicenza,
Aug. 27, 1865; d. Milan, Dec. 22, 1922. He studied with
Mancinelli and Busi in Bologna; in 1909 became a
prof. at the Verdi Cons. in Milan; also wrote music
criticism.
WORKS: Operas: *Mariska* (Turin, Nov. 19, 1889);
Consuelo (Bologna, Nov. 27, 1895); *Il Gladiatore*
(Madrid, March 20, 1898); *Chopin* (Milan, Nov. 25,
1901); *Cecilia* (Vicenza, Aug. 16, 1902); *Mosè* (Genoa,
Feb. 18, 1905); *Il pane d'altrui* (Venice, Jan. 19,
1907); *Radda* (Milan, Oct. 25, 1912); *Castello dei so-
gni* (unfinished); ballet, *La Soubrette* (Milan, 1907);
a Symph.; orch. suites: *Sinfonia del bosco* (1898),
Anacreontiche, and *Laudi francescane* (1920);
chamber music; piano pieces; etc. He arranged
Monteverdi's *Orfeo* (produced in Milan, Nov. 30,
1909); publ. a monograph on his teacher Mancinelli
(Rome, 1921).

Orel, Alfred, Austrian musicologist; b. Vienna,
July 3, 1889; d. there, April 11, 1967. He studied law
at the Univ. of Vienna, graduating in 1912; then was
employed in the Ministry of Finance until 1918;
subsequently studied musicology with Guido Adler
at the Univ. of Vienna, where he received his Ph.D.
in 1919 with the dissertation *Die Hauptstimme in
den "Salve regina" der Trienter Codices;* he completed his Habilitation there in 1922 with his *Über
rhythmische Qualität in mehrstimmigen Tonsät-*

zen des 15. Jahrhunderts. He was librarian of the Inst. of Musicology at the Univ. of Vienna from 1918 to 1922; later was a reader in music history there, from 1929 to 1945. He was particularly noted for his work on the life and music of Anton Bruckner.

WRITINGS: *Unbekannte Frühwerke Anton Bruckners* (Vienna, 1921; with an edition of the Overture in G minor); *Ein Wiener Beethoven-Buch* (Vienna, 1921); *Anton Bruckner: Das Werk—Der Künstler—Die Zeit* (Vienna and Leipzig, 1925); *Wiener Musikerbriefe aus zwei Jahrhunderten* (Vienna, 1925); *Beethoven* (Vienna, 1927); with R. Stöhr and H. Gál, *Formenlehre der Musik* (Leipzig, 1933; 2nd ed., 1954); *Anton Bruckner, 1824–1896: Sein Leben in Bildern* (Leipzig, 1936); *Kirchenmusikalische Liturgik* (Augsburg, 1936); *Franz Schubert, 1797–1828: Sein Leben in Bildern* (Leipzig, 1939); *Aufsätze und Vorträge* (Vienna and Berlin, 1939); *Ein Harmonielehrekolleg bei Anton Bruckner* (Vienna and Berlin, 1940); *Der junge Schubert* (Vienna, 1940); *Mozarts deutscher Weg: Eine Deutung aus Briefen* (Vienna, 1940; 2nd ed., 1943); *Grillparzer und Beethoven* (Vienna, 1941); *Mozart in Wien* (Vienna, 1944); *Hugo Wolf: Ein Künstlerbildnis* (Vienna, 1947); *Johannes Brahms: Ein Meister und sein Weg* (Olten, 1948); *Goethe als Operndirektor* (Bregenz, 1949); *Bruckner-Brevier: Briefe, Dokumente, Berichte* (Vienna, 1953); *Musikstadt Wien* (Vienna, 1953); *Mozart, Gloria Mundi* (Salzburg, 1956); ed. *Johannes Brahms und Julius Allgeyer: Eine Künstlerfreundschaft in Briefen* (Tutzing, 1964).

BIBLIOGRAPHY: H. Federhofer, ed., *Festschrift Alfred Orel zum 70. Geburtstag überreicht von Kollegen, Freunden und Schülern* (Vienna and Wiesbaden, 1960).

Orel, Dobroslav, Czech ecclesiastical music scholar; b. Ronov, near Prague, Dec. 15, 1870; d. Prague, Feb. 18, 1942. He studied music with Novák and Hostinský in Prague; later musicology with Guido Adler in Vienna. In 1914 he received a Dr.Phil. there with the dissertation *Der Mensuralkodex Speciálník, Ein Beitrag zur Geschichte der Mensuralmusik und der Notenschrift in Böhmen bis 1540.* He was ordained a priest; was a prof. at the Prague Cons. (1907–19); in 1909–18 he was editor of the Prague church music periodical *Cyrill;* in 1921–38, a prof. of musicology at the Komensky Univ., Bratislava; he was conductor of various choral societies in Bratislava. His writings, some in Czech, some in German, include: *Handbook of the Roman Plainchant* (1899); *The Franus Cantional of 1505* (1921); *Czech Hymnal* (1921); *Old Czech Rorate Songs* (1922); *J.L. Bella,* a biography (1924). He edited (with M. Springer) the liturgical works *Graduale parvum* (Regensburg, 1912) and *Proprium Provinciae Pragensis ad Grad. Rom.* (1913); (with Hejčl) *Marian Folk-Vespers* (1912).

Orem, Preston Ware, American composer, conductor, and teacher; b. Philadelphia, 1865; d. there (while conducting a school orch.), May 26, 1938. He studied at the Univ. of Pa.; taught at Combs Cons.,

Philadelphia (1896–1905); in 1900, became editor for the Theodore Presser Co. and conductor of the Presser Choral Society. He publ. a harmony book for beginners; composed *American Indian Rhapsody* for Piano; a symph. sketch, *Out of the West;* chamber music; piano pieces; songs.

Orff, Carl, outstanding German composer; b. Munich, July 10, 1895; d. there, March 29, 1982. He studied at the Academy of Music in Munich, and with Heinrich Kaminski; from 1950 to 1960, was a prof. at the Hochschule für Musik in Munich. In his music he sought to revive the old monodic forms and to adapt them to modern tastes by means of dissonant counterpoint, with lively rhythm in asymmetrical patterns. Apart from his compositions, Orff initiated a highly important method of musical education, which was adopted not only in Germany but in England, America, and Russia; it stemmed from the Günther School for gymnastics, dance, and music which Orff founded in 1924 with Dorothee Günther in Munich, with the aim of promoting instrumental playing and understanding of rhythm among children; he commissioned the piano manufacturer Karl Maendler to construct special percussion instruments that would be extremely easy to play; the "Orff instruments" became widely adopted in American schools. Orff's ideas of rhythmic training owe much to the eurhythmics of Jaques-Dalcroze, but he simplified them to reach the elementary level; as a manual, he compiled a set of musical exercises, *Schulwerk* (1930–35, revised 1950–54).

WORKS: His most famous work is the scenic oratorio, *Carmina Burana* (Frankfurt, June 8, 1937; numerous productions in Europe and America); the words (in Latin and German) are from 13th-century student poems found in the monastery of Benediktbeuren in Bavaria ("Burana" is the Latin adjective of the locality). Other works: *Der Mond,* opera, after a fairy tale by Grimm (Munich, Feb. 5, 1939; revised version, Munich, Nov. 26, 1950); *Die Kluge,* opera, also after a fairy tale by Grimm (Frankfurt, Feb. 20, 1943); *Catulli Carmina,* scenic cantata after Catullus (Leipzig, Nov. 6, 1943); *Die Bernauerin,* musical play (Stuttgart, June 15, 1947); *Antigonae,* musical play after Sophocles (Salzburg, Aug. 9, 1949); *Trionfo di Afrodite* (3rd part of a triology under the general title *Trionfi,* the first and 2nd parts being *Carmina Burana* and *Catulli Carmina;* Milan, Feb. 13, 1953); *Astutuli,* opera-ballet (Munich, Oct. 20, 1953); *Comoedia de Christi Resurrectione,* Easter cantata (Munich, March 31, 1956); *Oedipus der Tyrann,* musical play after Sophocles (Stuttgart, Dec. 11, 1959); *Ludus de nato infante mirificus,* Nativity play (Stuttgart, Dec. 11, 1960); *Prometheus,* opera (Stuttgart, March 24, 1968); *Rota* for Voices and Instruments, after the canon *Sumer is icumen in,* composed as a "salute to youth" for the opening ceremony of the Munich Olympics (1972); stage play *De temporum fine comoedia* (Salzburg, 1973). He further wrote a dance play, *Der Feuerfarbene* (1925); *Präludium* for Orch. (1925); Concertino for Wind Instruments and Harpsichord (1927); *Entrata* for Orch., based on melodies of William Byrd (1928;

revised 1940); Festival Music for Chamber Orch. (1928); *Bayerische Musik* for Small Ensemble (1934); *Olympischer Reigen* for Various Instruments (1936); revised versions of Monteverdi's *Orfeo* (Mannheim, April 17, 1925; 2nd version, Munich, Oct. 13, 1929; 3rd version, Dresden, Oct. 4, 1940) and Monteverdi's *Ballo delle ingrate, Lamento d'Arianna,* and *L'incoronazione di Poppea.*

BIBLIOGRAPHY: A. Liess, *Carl Orff* (Zürich, 1955; 2nd ed., 1977); E. Helm, "Carl Orff," *Musical Quarterly* (July 1955); I. Kiekert, *Die musikalische Form in den Werken Carl Orffs* (Regensburg, 1957); A. Liess, *Carl Orff: His Life and His Music* (N.Y., 1966); M. Devreese-Papgnies, *Sur les traces du Schulwerk de Carl Orff, Méthodologie pour l'usage des instruments d'orchestre scolaire* (Brussels, 1968); R.B. Glasgow and G.H. Dale, *Study to Determine the Feasibility of Adapting the Carl Orff Approach to Elementary Schools in America* (Washington, D.C., 1968); L. Barenboim, ed., *Carl Orff's System of Musical Education of Children* (Leningrad, 1971); Gertrud Orff, *The Orff Music Therapy* (Eng. trans., London, 1980); U. Klement, *Das Musiktheater Carl Orffs* (Leipzig, 1982).

Orgad, Ben-Zion, German-born Israeli composer; b. Gelsenkirchen, Aug. 21, 1926. He came to Palestine in 1933; studied composition with Ben-Haim (1940–46); made several trips to America and took courses in composition with Copland at Tanglewood (1949, 1952, 1961) and with Irving Fine and Harold Shapero at Brandeis Univ. (1960–61); lectured on Israeli music in the U.S. (1970). Returning to Israel, he worked in the Ministry of Culture in Jerusalem.

WORKS: *Toccata* for Piano (1946); *Ballade* for Solo Flute (1947); *Hatsvi Israel (The Beauty of Israel),* symph. for Baritone and Orch. (1949); biblical cantata, *Isaiah's Vision* (1952); *Min He'afar (Out of the Desert),* quintet for Mezzo-soprano or Contralto, Flute, Bassoon, Viola, and Cello (1956); *Building the King's Stage* for Orch. (1957); *Monolog* for Solo Viola (1957); Septet for Clarinet, Bassoon, Horn, Violin, Viola, Cello, and Double Bass (1959); *Music* for Orch., with Solo Horn (1960); String Trio (1961); *7 Variations on C* for Piano (1961); *Tak'sim* for Solo Harp (1962); *Movement on A* for Orch. (1965); *Kaleidoscope* for Orch. (1965); *Mizmorim,* cantata on Psalms (1966–67); *Songs of an Early Morning* for Mezzo-soprano, Baritone, and Chamber Orch. (1968); *Landscapes* for Wind Quintet (1969); *First Watch* for String Orch. (1969); *Melodic Dialogues on 3 Scrolls* for Violin, Oboe, Percussion, String Quartet, and String Orch. (1969); *Songs without Words,* sextet for Violin, Cello, Flute, Clarinet, Percussion, and Piano (1970); *Ballade* for Orch. (1971); *A Tale of a Pipe* for Soloists, Female Chorus, and 19 Instruments (1971); *The Second Watch* for Chamber Orch. (1973); Duo for Violin and Cello (1973).

Orgeni, Aglaja (real name, **Görger St. Jorgen**), Hungarian coloratura soprano; b. Roma Szombat, Dec. 17, 1841; d. Vienna, March 15, 1926. She was a pupil of Mme. Viardot-García at Baden-Baden; made her debut on Sept. 28, 1865, as Amina, at the Berlin Opera; made her first appearance in London on April 7, 1866, as Violetta, at Covent Garden; she sang later in Vienna, Dresden, Berlin, Copenhagen, etc.; from 1886, taught singing at the Dresden Cons.; was made a Royal Professor in 1908 (the first case of the title being conferred on a woman). In 1914 she settled in Vienna. Among her distinguished pupils were Erika Wedekind and Edyth Walker.

BIBLIOGRAPHY: Erna Brand, *Aglaja Orgeni* (Munich, 1931).

Orlov, Nicolai, Russian pianist; b. Elets, Feb. 26, 1892; d. Grantown-on-Spey, Scotland, May 31, 1964. He studied at the Moscow Cons. with Igumnov; also privately with Taneyev; in 1921, left Russia and gave concerts throughout Europe; also appeared in the U.S.; made his headquarters mainly in Paris.

Ormandy, Eugene (real name, **Blau**), outstanding conductor; b. Budapest, Nov. 18, 1899. He studied violin with his father; entered the Royal Academy of Music in Budapest at the age of 5; began studying with Hubay at 9; received an artist's diploma for violin in 1914; received a teacher's certificate at the Royal Academy in 1917; then was concertmaster of the Blüthner Orch. in Germany; also gave recitals and played with orchs. as soloist. In 1921, he came to the U.S.; obtained the position of concertmaster of the Capitol Theater Orch., N.Y., and remained there for 2½ years; made his debut as conductor with that orch. in Sept. 1924; in 1925, became its associate music director; in 1929, conducted the N.Y. Phil. at Lewisohn Stadium; in 1930, became guest conductor with the Robin Hood Dell Orch., Philadelphia; on Oct. 30, 1931, conducted the Philadelphia Orch. In 1931, he was appointed music director and permanent conductor of the Minneapolis Symph. Orch.; in 1936, was engaged as associate conductor of the Philadelphia Orch. (with Stokowski); on Sept. 28, 1938, became permanent conductor; traveled with it on transcontinental tours in 1937, 1946, 1948, 1957, 1962, 1964, 1971, 1974, and 1977; in 1949, made an extended tour in England; in the spring of 1955, presented concerts with the Philadelphia Orch. in 10 European countries; in the summer of 1958 he led it on another European tour (including Russia). He appeared on numerous occasions as guest conductor with European orchs.; in Australia (summer of 1944); South America (summer of 1946); Latin America (1966); the Far East (1967, 1978); and Japan (1972). In 1970 he received the Presidential Medal of Freedom. In 1973 he took the Philadelphia Orch. to China and led it in several cities there; this was the first appearance of an American symph. orch. in the People's Republic of China. Ormandy was made an officer of the French Legion of Honor (1952; was promoted to Commander in 1958); was made a Knight of the Order of the White Rose of Finland (1955); became a holder of the medal of the Bruckner Society (1936); received an honorary Mus.Doc. from the Univ. of Pa. in 1976 he was named an honorary Knight Commander of the British Empire by Queen Elizabeth in honor of the American Bicentennial; altogether, he has received 26 awards and 23 honorary doctorates. In his interpretations, Ormandy reveals himself as a Romanticist; he excels in the works of Beethoven, Schumann, and Richard Strauss; his renditions of music by Debussy and of the moderns are marked by color without extravagance; he conducts all his scores from memory. After 42 seasons as music director of the Philadelphia Orch., he retired at the close of the 1979–80 season, and was named Conductor Laureate.

BIBLIOGRAPHY: Hope Stoddard, *Symphony Conductors of the U.S.A.* (N.Y., 1957; pp. 147–59); H. Kupferberg, *Those Fabulous Philadelphians* (N.Y., 1969); idem, "Eugene Ormandy," *Ovation* (Feb. 1984).

Ornithoparchus (Greek form of his real name, **Vogelsang**), **Andreas**, German music scholar; b. Meiningen, c.1485; d. Münster, c.1535. He matriculated at the Univ. of Rostock (M.A., 1512) and at the Univ. of Tübingen (M.A., 1515); was rector of the parochial school in Münster in 1514; also matriculated at Wittenberg (1516), Leipzig (1516), and Greifswald (1518). He publ. a valuable theoretical treatise, *Musice active micrologus* (1517; 6th ed., 1540; Eng. trans. by Dowland, London, 1609; reprinted 1977).

BIBLIOGRAPHY: J.W. Lyra, *Andreas Ornithoparchus und dessen Lehre von den Kirchenakzenten* (Gütersolh, 1877).

Ornstein, Leo, remarkable Russian pianist and composer; b. Kremenchug, Dec. 11, 1892. The son of a synagogal cantor, he studied music at home; then with Vladimir Puchalski in Kiev; at the age of 10 he was accepted as a pupil at the St. Petersburg Cons. As a consequence of anti-Semitic disturbances in Russia, the family decided to emigrate to the U.S. in 1907. Ornstein studied piano with Mrs. Bertha Feiring Tapper at the New England Cons. in Boston, and with Percy Goetschius; also attended the Inst. of Musical Art in N.Y. He gave his first concert in N.Y., as a pianist, on March 5, 1911; then played in Philadelphia and other cities. About 1910 he began to compose; he experimented with percussive sonorities, in dissonant harmonies; made a European tour in 1913; played in Norway, Denmark, and in Paris; appeared in London on March 27, 1914, in a piano recital announced as "futuristic music" and featuring his Sonata and other works. Returning to the U.S. early in 1915, he gave a series of recitals at the Bandbox Theater in N.Y., comprising works by Debussy, Ravel, Schoenberg, Scriabin, and other modern composers; also his own music; his *Danse sauvage* excited his audiences by its declared wildness. Ornstein was hailed as the prophet of a new musical era, but soon ceased to attract attention. He continued to compose, although the titles of his works were no longer wild and provocative; in 1974 he completed his major work, *Biography in Sonata Form.* His 90th birthday was celebrated by a special concert of his works in N.Y. in 1982.

WORKS: For Orch.: *3 Moods: Anger, Peace, Joy* (1914); *The Fog,* symph. poem (1915); Piano Concerto (Philadelphia Orch., Feb. 13, 1925, composer soloist); *Lysistrata Suite* (1933); *Nocturne and Dance of Fates* (St. Louis, Feb. 12, 1937); *3 Russian Choruses* a cappella (1921); Piano Quintet; 3 String Quartets: No. 1; No. 2 (1975); No. 3 (1979); Violin Sonata; Cello Sonata; *Nocturne* for Clarinet and Piano; 4 piano sonatas; many pieces for piano: *A la chinoise; Suicide in an Airplane* (1913); *Danse sauvage* (1915); *Suite russe;* songs (*The Corpse,* etc.).

BIBLIOGRAPHY: Carl Van Vechten, *Music and Bad Manners* (N.Y., 1916; pp. 229–43); C.L. Buchanan, "Ornstein and Modern Music," *Musical Quarterly* (April 1918); F.H. Martens, *Leo Ornstein: The Man, His Ideas, His Work* (N.Y., 1918); Paul Rosenfeld, in *Musical Chronicle, 1917–1923* (N.Y., 1923); idem, in *An Hour with American Music* (N.Y., 1929); Vivian Perlis, "The Futurist Music of Leo Ornstein," *Notes* (June 1975).

Orozco, Rafael, Spanish pianist; b. Córdoba, Jan. 24, 1946. He studied at the Cons. in Córdoba, then at the Madrid Cons., where he graduated in 1964; also took piano lessons with Alexis Weissenberg at the Accademia Chigiana in Siena; in 1966 he won the Leeds International Piano Competition; subsequently toured extensively, receiving praise as a fine interpreter of the Romantic repertoire.

Orr, Charles Wilfred, English composer; b. Cheltenham, July 31, 1893; d. Stroud, Gloucestershire, Feb. 24, 1976. He studied at the Guildhall School of Music in London; wrote songs in the manner of German lieder, to words by English poets; his set of 7 songs to texts from Housman's *A Shropshire Lad* is notable.

BIBLIOGRAPHY: S. Northcote, "The Songs of C. W. Orr," *Music & Letters* (1937).

Orr, Robin, Scottish composer; b. Brechin, June 2, 1909. He studied organ, piano, and composition at the Royal College of Music in London (1926–29) and at Cambridge Univ. (1929–32); subsequently took courses with Edward J. Dent in London, Alfredo Casella in Siena, and Nadia Boulanger in Paris. From 1938 to 1950 he was active as an organist and music instructor at St. John's College, Cambridge; received his Mus.D. from Cambridge Univ. in 1951; taught there until 1956; then at the Univ. of Glasgow (1956–65); in 1965 was appointed a prof. of music at Cambridge Univ.; he retired in 1976. His works include *Symphony in One Movement* (London, Dec. 12, 1963); *Full Circle,* opera (Perth, Scotland, April 10, 1968); *Journeys and Places* for Mezzosoprano and String Quintet (1971); String Quartet; choral pieces. He edited *The Kelvin Series of Scots Songs.*

Orrego-Salas, Juan, Chilean composer and music educator; b. Santiago, Jan. 18, 1919. He studied at the School of Architecture of the Catholic Univ. of Santiago (1938–42); studied composition with Humberto Allende and Domingo Santa Cruz at the National Cons. of Music of the Univ. of Chile (1936–43); came to the U.S. and attended classes in musicology with Paul Henry Lang and George Herzog at Columbia Univ. in N.Y. (1944–45); subsequently studied composition with Randall Thompson at Princeton Univ. (1945–46) and with Aaron Copland at Tanglewood, Mass. (summer 1946); in 1953 received a diploma as Profesor Extraordinario de Composición (Ph.D.) from the Univ. of Chile; was awarded the honorary degree of Doctor Scientiae by the Catholic Univ. of Santiago (1971). From 1942 to 1961 he taught at the Univ. of Chile; in 1961 was engaged as prof. of composition and Latin-American music history at Indiana Univ. in Bloomington, and director of the Latin-American Music Center there.

WORKS: Opera-oratorio, *El retablo del rey pobre* for 3 Sopranos, Mezzo-soprano, Contralto, Tenor, Baritone, Chorus, and Small Orch. (1950–51); 3 ballets: *Juventud* (after Handel's *Solomon*, 1948); *Umbral del sueño* (1951); *The Tumbler's Prayer* (1960); oratorio, *The Days of God* (Washington, D.C., Nov. 2, 1976); 2 cantatas: *Cantata de Navidad* for Soprano and Orch. (1946) and *América, no en vano invocamos tu nombre* (1966); *Missa, in tempore discordiae* for Tenor, Chorus, and Orch. (1968–69); *Psalms* for Narrator and Wind Orch. (1962); *Songs,* in 3 movements, for Medium Voice and String Quartet (1945); *Canciones castellanas* for Soprano and 8 Instruments (1948); *Cantos de advenimiento* for Medium Voice, Cello, and Piano (1948); *Words of Don Quixote* for Baritone and Chamber Ensemble (Washington, Oct. 31, 1970); numerous songs and choruses. FOR ORCH.: *Escenas de Cortes y Pastores,* suite (1946); *Obertura festiva* (1948); 4 symphs.: No. 1 (1949; Santiago, July 1950); No. 2, *a la memoria de un vagabundo* (1954; Minneapolis, Feb. 17, 1956); No. 3 (1961; Washington, April 22, 1961); No. 4, *de la respuesta lejana* (Bloomington, Ind., 1967); Piano Concerto (1950); *Concerto da camera* for Woodwind Quartet, 2 Horns, Harp, and Strings (1952); *Serenata concertante* (1954–55; Louisville, May 3, 1955); *Jubileaus musicus* (1956); *Concerto a tre* for Violin, Cello, Piano, and Orch. (Washington, May 7, 1965); concerto for Wind Orch. (1963–64); *Volte* for Piano, 15 Winds, Harp, and Percussion (1971); *Variaciones serenas* for String Orch. (1971). CHAMBER MUSIC: Violin Sonata (1945); *Sonata a duo* for Violin and Viola (1945); *Suite* for Solo Bandoneon (1952); Sextet for Clarinet, String Quartet, and Piano (1954); *Duo concertante* for Cello and Piano (1955); *Pastorale and Scherzo* for Violin and Piano (1956); 2 *Divertimentos* for Flute, Oboe, and Bassoon (1956); String Quartet No. 1 (1957); Concertino for Brass Quartet (1963); *Sonata a quattro* for Flute, Oboe, Harpsichord, and Double Bass (1964); Piano Trio (1966); *Quattro liriche breve* for Saxophone and Piano (1967); *Mobili* for Viola and Piano (1967); *Esquinas* for Solo Guitar (1971); *Serenata* for Flute and Cello (1972); *Sonata de Estío* for Flute and Piano (1972); *Presencias* for Flute, Oboe, Clarinet, Violin, Viola, Cello, and Harpsichord (1972). FOR PIANO: 2 *Suites* (1946, 1951); *Variaciones y fuga sobre un pregón* (1946); *Diez prezas simples* (1951); *Canción y Danza* (1951); *Rústica* (1952); Sonata (1967).

Orsi, Romeo, Italian clarinetist and manufacturer of wind instruments; b. Como, Oct. 18, 1843; d. Milan, June 11, 1918. He studied at the Royal Cons. of Milan (1856–64); in 1873 became a prof. of clarinet there; for 40 years was first clarinetist of La Scala (1871–1911); gave concerts in Italy and in Paris. In 1881 he constructed a combination clarinet capable of performing both B-flat and A clarinet parts; it had a temporary acceptance among orch. players; he also manufactured a bass clarinet in A for use in Verdi's *Otello;* publ. a method for the saxophone.

Orth, John, American organist and composer; b. Annweiler, Bavaria, Dec. 2, 1850; d. Boston, May 3, 1932. His parents settled in Taunton, Mass., when he was a year old; he studied organ with his father; then went to Germany, where he took courses with Kullak and Deppe (piano); also had lessons with Liszt; studied composition with Faiszt, Weitzmann, Kiel, and P. Scharwenka. In 1875 he settled in Boston as a pianist and teacher; in lecture-recitals became a propagandist for Liszt's music in America. In 1883 he married his pupil Lizette E. Blood, known as **L.E. Orth** (d. Boston, Sept. 14, 1913), who was herself a composer of songs and piano pieces. Orth publ. a number of teaching pieces for piano.

Orthel, Léon, Dutch composer and pianist; b. Roosendaal, North Brabant, Oct. 4, 1905. He studied composition with Johan Wagenaar at the Royal Cons. of The Hague (1921–26); a government fellowship enabled him to study with Paul Juon at the Hochschule für Musik in Berlin (1928–29). From 1941 to 1971 he taught piano and theory at the Royal Cons. at The Hague; concurrently taught composition at the Amsterdam Cons. (1949–71); was chairman of the Composers' Section of the Royal Dutch Society of Musicians (1947–70). He gave concerts as a pianist in the Netherlands. As a composer, he followed the Romantic trends.

WORKS: Among his best lyric works are 13 separate song cycles to the poems of Rainer Maria Rilke (1934–72). Other works include a *Concertstuk* for Violin and Orch. (1924); *Scherzo* for Piano and Orch. (1927); Cello Concerto (1929); *Concertino alla burla* for Piano and Orch. (1930); 6 symphs.: No. 1 (1931–33); No. 2, *Piccola sinfonia* (1940; Rotterdam, Oct. 31, 1941; his finest work and one of the most frequently played); No. 3 (1943); No. 4, *Sinfonia concertante,* for Piano and Orch. (1949); No. 5, *Musica iniziale* (1959–60); No. 6 (1960–61); *Nonnen-Klage* for Soprano, and Orch. or Piano (1943); 2 *Scherzos* for Orch. (1954–55, 1956–57); *3 movimenti ostinati* for Orch. (1971–72; Amsterdam, Sept. 1, 1973); Trumpet Concerto (1973–74); *Une Martyre (Dessin d'un maître inconnu)* for High Voice and Orch. (1974–75); *Album di disegni* for Orch. (1976–77); *Music* for Double Bass and Orch. (1981). CHAMBER MUSIC: 2 violin sonatas (1924, 1933); 2 cello sonatas (1925, 1958); *Burleske* for Cello and Piano (1926); *Ballade* for Cello and Piano (1927); *5 pezzettini* for Clarinet and Piano (1963); String Quartet (1964); Viola Sonata (1964–65); *Ballade* for Flute and Piano (1970); *8 abbozzi* for Flute, Cello, and Piano (1971); *5 Bagatelles* for Solo Harp (1973); Organ Sonata (1973). FOR

PIANO: Sonata (1923); *4 Pieces* (1923–24); 8 sonatinas (1924; *Minatuure sonatine*, 1942; 1945; 1953; for the left hand, 1959; 1974; *Uit 1920 en 1922*, 1975; *Sonatina capricciosa*, 1975); *Preludes* (1925); *Epigrams* (1938); *5 études-caprices* (1957); *2 hommages en forme d'étude* (1958); *3 pezzettini* (1958); *3 exempelkens* (1963); pieces for children.

d'Ortigue, Joseph-Louis, French musicologist; b. Cavaillon, Vaucluse, May 22, 1802; d. Paris, Nov. 20, 1866. He studied law in Aix-en-Provence; in 1829 settled in Paris, where he wrote articles on music for various journals. In 1857 he founded *La Maîtrise* (with Niedermeyer) and in 1862, the *Journal des Maîtrises* (with F. Clément), both periodicals for church music; in 1863 he became editor of *Le Ménestrel;* succeeded Berlioz as critic for the *Journal des Débats*. In his various positions he exercised considerable influence on musical life in Paris. WRITINGS: *Le Balcon de l'opéra* (Paris, 1833; a book of essays); *De l'Ecole musicale italienne et de l'administration de l'Académie Royale de Musique* (1839; republ. 1840 as *Du Théâtre italien et de son influence* ...); *Abécédaire du plain chant* (1844); *Dictionnaire liturgique*, etc. (1854); *Introduction à l'étude comparée des tonalités, et principalement du chant grégorien et de la musique moderne* (1853); *La Musique à l'église* (1861); *Traité théorique et pratique de l'accompagnement du plainchant* (with Niedermeyer; 1856; Eng. trans. by W. Goodrich, N.Y., 1905). BIBLIOGRAPHY: M. Barber, *Joseph-Louis d'Ortigue* (Paris, 1919).

Ortiz, Cristina, Brazilian pianist; b. Bahia, April 17, 1950. She began piano studies in Brazil, then went to Paris, where she studied with Magda Tagliaferro; subsequently she traveled to the U.S. and enrolled at the Curtis Inst. of Music in Philadelphia as a student of Rudolf Serkin. She made her N.Y. recital debut in 1971; also appeared as a soloist with orchs. in America. She made her London debut in 1973 with the London Symph. Orch. and played with orchs. on the Continent.

Ortiz, Diego, Spanish composer; b. Toledo, c.1510; d. Naples, c.1570. He was in the service of the Duke of Alba as maestro de capilla at the vice-regal court in Naples from 1558 until 1565. He was one of the earliest masters of variations (divisions). His greatest work is *Trattado de glosas sobre clausulas y otros géneros de puntos en la música de violones* (Rome, 1553; modern ed. by M. Schneider, Berlin, 1913; 3rd ed., Kassel, 1967), containing early examples of instrumental variations and ornamental cadenzas (for viola da gamba alone with harpsichord). An Italian version of this work was also publ. at Rome in 1553 (*Il primo libro de Diego Ortiz Toletano*, etc.). In addition, Ortiz publ. a vol. of sacred music at Venice in 1565 (hymns, motets, Psalms, etc., for 4–7 voices). Some motets by him (in lute tablature) were included in Valderrábano's *Silva de Sirenas* (1547). Modern reprints of his sacred music are in the collections of Proske, Eslava, and Pedrell.
BIBLIOGRAPHY: J. Subirá, *La música en la Casa de Alba* (Barcelona, 1927); R. Borrowdale, *The "Musies Liber Primus" of Diego Ortiz, Spanish Musician* (Diss., Univ. of Southern Calif., 1952); P. Strassler, *Hymns for the Church Year, Magnificats, and other Sacred Choral Works of Diego Ortiz* (Diss., Univ. of North Carolina, 1966).

Ortmann, Otto Rudolph, American music educator, b. Baltimore, Jan. 25, 1889; d. there, Oct. 22, 1979. After studying at the Peabody Cons. of Music in Baltimore, he joined its faculty in 1913; from 1928 to 1942 served as its director. He then taught at Goucher College (1942–57); upon retirement he continued to give private instruction in piano, voice, and corrective speech despite advanced age and almost total blindness. Among his publications are *The Physical Basis of Piano Touch and Tone* (1925) and *The Psychological Mechanics of Piano Technique* (1929; 2nd ed., 1962).

Orto, Marbriano (Marbrianus) de, Netherlandish composer and singer; b. diocese of Tournai, c.1460; d. Nivelles, Feb. 1529. As a young man he was a singer in the papal choir at Rome (1484–99); was dean of the collegiate church of St. Gertrude in Nivelles (1489–96); in 1505 he was in the service of Philip the Fair of Burgundy; went to Spain with him in 1506, and was ennobled. In 1509–17 he was in the chapel of Archduke Charles (later Emperor Charles V). Petrucci publ. a book of 5 masses by him (1505), also 11 chansons for 4 voices in the *Odhecaton* (1500–1503), and a Lamentation in *Lamentationum Jeremias prophetae liber I* (1506); several MSS are in the Vienna Library and at the Univ. of Jena; Ambros reproduced an *Agnus* from the so-called "Mimi" Mass (based on the theme of 2 notes, E, A) in the supplement of his *Geschichte der Musik*.
BIBLIOGRAPHY: G. van Doorslaer, "La Chapelle musicale de Philippe le Beau," *Revue Belge d'Archéologie et d'Histoire de l'Art*, IV (1934); K.E. Roediger, *Die geistlichen Musikhandschriften der Universitäts-Bibliothek Jena* (2 vols.; 1935); G. Reese, *Music in the Renaissance* (N.Y., 1954; 2nd ed., revised, 1959).

Ory, Edward ("Kid"), black American jazz trombonist and bandleader; b. La Place, La., Dec. 25, 1886; d. Honolulu, Jan. 23, 1973. He played the banjo as a child; took up trombone; later joined bands led by Louis Armstrong and King Oliver. After a hiatus from performing (1933–42), he organized his own band and toured with it in Europe (1956–59). He was known for his "tailgate" style of trombone playing. He was the composer of the well-known *Muskrat Ramble*.

Osborn-Hannah, Jane, American soprano; b. Wilmington, Ohio, July 8, 1873; d. New York, Aug. 13, 1943. She received her first singing lessons from her mother; then went to Europe, where she studied with Marchesi and Sbriglia in Paris; was engaged at the Leipzig Opera (1904–7); then sang in Dresden,

Berlin, and Munich; appeared in London in 1908; made her American debut at the Metropolitan Opera House as Elisabeth (Jan. 5, 1910) and sang there until 1911; was a member of the Chicago Opera Co. (1910–14); was particularly notable in Wagnerian roles; after 1914 lived mostly in N.Y. She was married to Frank Hannah, American consul at Magdeburg.

Osborne (real name, **Eisbein**), **Adrienne,** American contralto; b. Buffalo, Dec. 2, 1873; d. Zell am Ziller, Austria, June 15, 1951. She studied with August Götze and Max Stägemann in Leipzig; later with **Felix von Kraus,** whom she married in 1899. She sang at the Municipal Opera in Leipzig; in 1908 settled in Munich, where she received the rank of Royal Chamber Singer. After the death of her husband in 1937, she went to live in Zell am Ziller, and remained there until her death.

Osborne, Bob (b. Hyden, Ky., Dec. 7, 1931) and **Sonny** (b. Hyden, Oct. 29, 1937), American country-music singers and instrumentalists. They learned to play the banjo and mandolin, and in 1953 began to make appearances on the radio, billed as the Osborne Brothers, and to take their bluegrass renditions to college campuses and other country-music haunts; their use of amplified electric guitars contributed to their success. Their hits included *Midnight Flyer, Rocky Top,* and *Georgia Pinewoods.*

Osborne, Conrad L(eon), American music critic; b. Lincoln, Nebr., July 22, 1934. He studied at Columbia Univ.; also took voice lessons with Cornelius Reid and acting instruction with Frank Corsaro; subsequently appeared as an actor in N.Y. theaters and on television; also sang in opera and concerts as a baritone. He was chief voice critic and a contributing editor to *High Fidelity* from 1959 to 1969; also served as the N.Y. music critic of the *Financial Times* of London from 1962 to 1969; the subject of his articles is mostly vocal music.

Osborne, Nigel, English composer; b. Manchester, June 23, 1948. He studied at Oxford Univ. with Egon Wellesz and Kenneth Leighton; then traveled to Poland and worked with Witold Rudziński and at the Polish Radio Experimental Studio in Warsaw (1970–71); in 1978 became a lecturer in music at the Univ. of Nottingham. In his compositions he strives to present the olden modalities of remote musical eras with the aid of modern techniques, including electronic sound.
WORKS: *Beautiful Thing I* and *Beautiful Thing II* for Chamber Ensemble (1969–70); *Byzantine Epigrams* for Chorus a cappella (1969); *7 Words,* cantata (1969–71); *Charivari* for Orch. (1973); *Chansonnier* for Chamber Ensemble (1975); *Passers By* for Bass Recorder, Cello, Electronic Synthesizer, and Diapositive (1976); *I am Goya* for Bass-baritone and 4 Instruments (1977); *Concert piece* for Cello and Orch. (1977); *Sinfonia* (London, Aug. 2, 1982).
BIBLIOGRAPHY: N. O'Loughlin, "The Music of Nigel Osborne," *Musical Times* (May 1980).

Osghian, Petar, Serbian composer; b. Dubrovnik, April 27, 1932. He studied in Belgrade; adopted a free neo-Romantic style of composition.
WORKS: *Poema eroico* for Orch. (Belgrade, Dec. 8, 1959); *Symphoniette* for Strings (Belgrade, Dec. 20, 1960); Concerto for Orch. (Belgrade, Feb. 25, 1964); *Sigogis* for Orch. (Zagreb, May 12, 1967); *Meditation* for 2 Pianos; numerous other piano pieces.

Osgood, George Laurie, American singer and vocal teacher; b. Chelsea, Mass., April 3, 1844; d. Godalming, England, Dec. 12, 1922. He studied at Harvard Univ.; led the Glee Club there; then went to Germany, where he studied singing and interpretation with Haupt and Robert Franz; gave concerts in Germany; in 1872 returned to the U.S., and settled in Boston as a successful vocal teacher. He subsequently lived in Switzerland and England. He publ. *Guide in the Art of Singing,* which went through 8 editions; also anthems, choruses, and some 50 songs.
BIBLIOGRAPHY: *Dictionary of American Biography* (vol. XIV).

Osgood, Henry Osborne, American music journalist; b. Peabody, Mass., March 12, 1879; d. New York, May 8, 1927. He was educated in Boston; also studied music in Germany, Italy, and France; was correspondent in Munich and Paris for the N.Y. *Musical Courier;* returning to the U.S. in 1914, he became its associate editor. He publ. *So This Is Jazz* (N.Y., 1926); composed *The Rouge Bouquet* (words by Joyce Kilmer) for Men's Chorus; also songs.

Osten, Eva von der, German soprano; b. Insel, Aug. 19, 1881; d. Dresden, May 10, 1936. She studied with August Iffert in Dresden; made her debut as Urbain in *Les Huguenots* in Dresden in 1902; was a principal member of the Dresden Court (later State) Opera until 1927; created the role of Octavian in *Der Rosenkavalier* there in 1911; also appeared at Covent Garden (1913–14) and in the U.S. with the German Opera Co. After her retirement, she became a producer of opera in Dresden. Her most famous roles were Kundry, Ariadne, and Tosca.

Osterc, Slavko, Yugoslav composer; b. Verzej, June 17, 1895; d. Ljubljana, May 23, 1941. He studied at the Prague Cons. with Jirák and Novák (1925–27); took a course in the quarter-tone system with Alois Hába; returning to Yugoslavia, he became a prof. at the Cons. of Ljubljana. He was associated with the modern movement in Europe; experimented with various techniques, including quarter-tone writing.
WORKS: Ballets: *The Masque of the Red Death* (after Edgar Allan Poe; 1930); *Illegitimate Mother* (1940); *Illusions* (1941); symph. poem, *Mermaid* (1924); *Nocturne* for Strings (1940); Sonata for 2 Clarinets (1929); Quintet for Wind Instruments (1932); Saxophone Sonata (1941); a number of piano pieces. The following works by him were performed at the festivals of the International Society for Contemporary Music: Concerto for Piano and Wind Instruments (Prague, Sept. 1, 1935), *Mouvement sym-*

phonique (London, June 24, 1938), and *Passa-caglia-Chorale* for Orch. (Warsaw, April 14, 1939).

Osthoff, Helmuth, distinguished German musicologist, father of **Wolfgang Osthoff;** b. Bielefeld, Aug. 13, 1896; d. Würzburg, Feb. 9, 1983. He studied music in Bielefeld and in Münster. He served in the German army during World War I; after the Armistice he resumed his studies at the Univ. of Münster (1919), and later (1920–22) took courses with Wolf, Kretzschmar, and Schünemann at the Univ. of Berlin, where he received his Ph.D. in 1922 with the dissertation *Der Lautenist Santino Garsi da Parma: Ein Beitrag zur Geschichte der oberitaliensischen Lautenmusik der Spätrenaissance* (publ. in Leipzig, 1926). He subsequently studied conducting with Brecher, composition with Klatte, and piano with Kwast at the Stern Cons. (1922–23). In 1923–26 he served as répétiteur at the Leipzig Opera; in 1926 he became assistant lecturer to Arnold Schering in the dept. of musicology at the Univ. of Halle; in 1928 he was appointed chief assistant to Schering in the dept. of music history at the Univ. of Berlin; completed his Habilitation there in 1932 with his treatise *Die Niederländer und das deutsche Lied 1400–1640* (publ. in Berlin, 1938). In 1938 he became a prof. and director of the inst. of musicology at the Univ. of Frankfurt, positions he held until his retirement in 1964. He was especially noted for his astute studies of Renaissance music. His other publications include *Adam Krieger; Neue Beiträge zur Geschichte des deutschen Liedes in 17. Jahrhundert* (Leipzig, 1929; 2nd ed., 1970); *Johannes Brahms und seine Sendung* (Bonn, 1942); *Josquin Desprez* (2 vols., Tutzing, 1962–65). A Festschrift was publ. in Tutzing in 1961 to honor his 65th birthday, a 2nd in 1969 for his 70th birthday (contains a bibliography of his writings), and a 3rd in 1977 for his 80th birthday.

Osthoff, Wolfgang, German musicologist, son of **Helmuth Osthoff;** b. Halle, March 17, 1927. He studied piano and theory at the Frankfurt Staatliche Hochschule für Musik (1939–43); then took lessons in conducting with Kurt Thomas (1946–47). He subsequently studied musicology with his father at the Univ. of Frankfurt (1947–49) and with Georgiades at the Univ. of Heidelberg (1949–54); received his Ph.D. there in 1954 with the dissertation *Das dramatische Spätwerk Claudio Monteverdis* (publ. in Tutzing, 1960). He taught at the Univ. of Munich (1957–64); completed his Habilitation there in 1965 with his *Theatergesang und darstellende Musik in der italienischen Renaissance* (publ. in Tutzing, 1969). He became a lecturer at the Univ. of Munich in 1966. In 1968 he was named a prof. of musicology at the Univ. of Würzburg. In addition to many scholarly articles dealing with music history from the 15th to the 19th century, he also contributed to many music reference works.

Ostrčil, Otakar, eminent Czech conductor and composer; b. Smichov, near Prague, Feb. 25, 1879; d. Prague, Aug. 20, 1935. He studied languages at the Univ. of Prague, and then taught at a school in Prague (until 1920); at the same time took courses in piano with Adolf Mikeš (1893–95) and studied composition privately with Fibich (1895–1900). From 1909 till 1922 he conducted an amateur orch. in Prague; also conducted opera there (1914–19); in 1920 he succeeded Karel Kovařovic as principal conductor at the Prague National Theater. In his compositions, Ostrčil continued the Romantic tradition of Czech music, with some modern elaborations revealing the influence of Mahler.
WORKS: Operas: *Vlasty skon* (*The Death of Vlasta;* Prague, Dec. 14, 1904); *Kunálovy oči* (*Kunala's Eyes;* Prague, Nov. 25, 1908); *Poupě* (*The Bud;* Prague, Jan. 25, 1911); *Legenda z Erinu* (*The Legend of Erin;* Brno, June 16, 1921); *Honzovo království* (*Johnny's Kingdom;* Brno, May 26, 1934); Symph. (1905); Sinfonietta (1921); *Summer,* 2 symph. movements (1926); *Calvary,* set of variations (1928); several cantatas; String Quartet; Trio for Violin, Viola, and Piano; several song cycles.
BIBLIOGRAPHY: J. Bartoš, *Otakar Ostrčil* (Prague, 1936).

O'Sullivan, Patrick, American pianist and pedagogue; b. Louisville, Ky., Aug. 23, 1871; d. Los Angeles, March 18, 1947. He studied piano with Harold Bauer in Paris and P. Scharwenka in Berlin; composition with Wilhelm Berger in Berlin. Returning to America, he occupied various posts as a choral conductor and teacher; was a prof. at the Louisville Cons. (1915–39) and at the Cons. of Memphis (Tenn.), run by Roman Catholic sisters. Among his works are *Heraklius* for Orch.; *Fantaisie irlandaise* for Piano and Orch.; *Epithalamium* for Chorus and String Quartet; he also publ. a collection of 65 Irish melodies for 2 voices.

Otaka, Hisatada, Japanese composer; b. Tokyo, Sept. 26, 1911; d. there, Feb. 16, 1951. He went to Europe in 1931 and studied music theory with Richard Stöhr and Joseph Marx in Vienna; also took lessons in conducting with Felix Weingartner at the Vienna Academy (1934–38); returned to Japan in 1940; conducted the Nippon Symph. Orch. (1942–51) in Tokyo.
WORKS: 2 *Japanese Suites* for Orch.: No. 1 (Budapest, Nov. 8, 1938) and No. 2 (Vienna, Nov. 3, 1939); Sinfonietta for Strings (1937); *Midare* for Orch. (Berlin, Dec. 10, 1939); Cello Concerto (Tokyo, May 23, 1943); *Rhapsody* for Piano and Orch. (Tokyo, Dec. 10, 1943); *Fatherland* for Orch. (Tokyo, Oct. 22, 1945); Symph. (1948); Flute Concerto (Tokyo, March 5, 1951); Violin Sonata (1932); 2 string quartets (1938, 1943); Piano Trio (1941); many piano pieces and songs.

Otaño, (José María) Nemesio, Spanish composer and musicologist; b. Azcoitia, Dec. 19, 1880; d. San Sebastián, April 29, 1956. He studied with V. Arregui and V. Goicoechea; became a Jesuit priest; founded the Schola Cantorum at Comillas and, in 1907, the journal *Música Sácro-Hispana,* of which he was editor until 1922. He energetically supported the study of Spanish folk music; made a study of the Spanish *villancico;* from 1940 till 1951 was director of the Madrid Cons. He publ. an important collection of old and new Spanish organ music, *Antología de organistas españoles;* an essay on folklore, *El canto popular montañés;* a collection of Spanish military music of the 18th century (Burgos, 1939); also composed a number of sacred works; wrote a book, *La música religiosa y la legislación eclesiástica* (Barcelona, 1912).

Otescu, Ion Nonna, Rumanian composer and conductor; b. Bucharest, Dec. 15, 1888; d. there, March 25, 1940. He studied at the Bucharest Cons. with Kiriac and Castaldi (1903–7); then with Widor at the Paris Cons. and with Vincent d'Indy at the Schola Cantorum (1908–11). He was a prof. of composition at the Bucharest Cons. (1913–40) and its director (1918–31). He also conducted opera at the National Theater (1921–39); from 1927 led the concerts of the Bucharest Phil.; was a founding member (1920) of the Society of Rumanian Composers.
WORKS: Musical comedy, *Bubi* (1903); 2 operas: *Ilderim* (libretto by Queen Marie of Rumania; Bucharest, 1920) and *De la Matei cetire* (1938; revised and completed by Aurel Stroe; posthumous premiere, Cluj, Dec. 27, 1966); 2 ballets: *Ileana Cosînzeana* (1918) and *Rubinul miraculos* (1919); *Idilă* for String Orch. (1908); symph. poems: *Templul din Gnid* (1908), *Legenda trandafirului roşu* (1910), *Narcis* (1911), and *Vrăjile Armidei* (1915); *Din bătrîni,* symph. sketch (1912); *Peisaj de iarnă,* symph. tableau (1913); *Scherzo* for Orch. (1923); songs.

Othegraven, August von, German composer; b. Cologne, June 2, 1864; d. Wermelskirchen, March 11, 1946. He studied at the Cons. of Cologne; from 1889 taught there; became a prof. in 1914. He composed chiefly for chorus; his oratorio *Marienleben* (Cologne, 1919) was fairly successful; he also wrote a musical fairy tale, *Die schlafende Prinzessin* (Cologne, 1907), and an operetta, *Poldis Hochzeit* (Cologne, 1912).
BIBLIOGRAPHY: B. Voss, *August von Othegraven, Leben und Werk* (Cologne, 1961).

Othmayr, Caspar, German composer; b. Amberg, March 12, 1515; d. Nuremberg, Feb. 4, 1553. He studied at the Univ. of Heidelberg; in 1536 became "magister," and in 1545 rector, of the monastery school at Heilsbronn, near Ansbach; in 1548 became provost in Ansbach. He was celebrated not only for his sacred works but also for his ingenious polyphonic settings of secular songs; of the latter, the most important are *Reuterische und jegerische Liedlein* for 4 and 5 Voices (1549). Sacred works include: *Cantilenae* (1546); *Epitaphium Lutheri* (1546); *Bicinia sacra* (1547); *Symbola principum* (1547; new ed. by H. Albrecht, 1941); *Trincina* (1549).
BIBLIOGRAPHY: H. Albrecht, *Caspar Othmayr, Leben und Werk* (Kassel, 1950).

Otis, Philo Adams, American writer and composer of sacred music; b. Berlin Heights, Ohio, Nov. 24, 1846; d. Chicago, Sept. 23, 1930. He studied music with Dudley Buck in N.Y., and with Clarence Eddy in Chicago. He served as chorusmaster at the First Presbyterian Church in Chicago (1905–12); publ. *The First Presbyterian Church, 1833–1913* (a history, 1913); *Impressions of Europe, 1873–1874: Music, Art and History* (1922); *The Chicago Symphony Orchestra* (a history, 2 vols., 1925); *The Hymns You Ought to Know* (1928); he also composed 2 sacred cantatas: *Wondrous Words of Love* and *The Risen Christ; Pastorale* for Violin, Cello, Double Bass, Harp, and Organ; many hymns and anthems.

Otterloo, Willem van, Dutch conductor and composer; b. Winterswijk, Dec. 27, 1907; d. as a result of an automobile accident, Melbourne, Australia, July 27, 1978. He studied cello with Orobio de Castro and composition with Sem Dresden at the Amsterdam Cons.; after graduation he was engaged as cellist in the Utrecht Orch.; in 1933 became its assistant conductor, and in 1937, associate conductor. From 1949 to 1972 he conducted the Residente Orch. at The Hague, bringing it to a state of excellence. In 1967 he went to Australia as conductor of the Melbourne Symph. Orch. until 1971. From 1973 until his death he was chief conductor of the Sydney Symph. Orch.; in the interim he served as Generalmusikdirektor of the Düsseldorf Symph. Orch. (1974–77).

Ottman, Robert W., American music theorist and pedagogue; b. Fulton, N.Y., May 3, 1914. He studied music theory with Bernard Rogers at the Eastman School of Music in Rochester, N.Y. (M.Mus., 1943). During and after World War II he served in the infantry in the U.S. Army (1943–46); then took lessons in composition with Alec Rowley at Trinity College of Music in London; in 1946 was engaged as a lecturer in music at North Texas State Univ., from which he also received his Ph.D. (1956). He publ. a number of excellent school manuals: *Music for Sight Singing* (N.Y., 1956); *Elementary Harmony, Theory and Practice* (N.Y., 1961; 3rd ed., 1983); *Advanced Harmony, Theory and Practice* (N.Y., 1961; new ed., 1972); *The 371 Chorales of J.S. Bach* (with Frank Mainous; very successful; N.Y., 1966); *Workbook for Elementary Harmony* (N.Y., 1974); *Programmed Rudiments of Music* (with Frank Mainous; N.Y., 1978).

Otto, (Ernst) Julius, German choral conductor and composer; b. Königstein, Sept. 1, 1804; d. Dresden, March 5, 1877. He studied with Weinlig in Dresden; then was a teacher there. In 1830 he was appointed cantor at the Kreuzkirche, and held this position for 45 years; his choir became one of the most celebrated in Germany; he also conducted several choral societies. His best works are the excellent male choruses in his collection *Ernst und Scherz,* which became extremely popular (*Burschenfahrten, Gesellenfahrten, Soldatenleben, Der Spinnabend, Der Sängersaal,* etc.); also 2 grand operas and 4 comic operas for amateur performance (*Die Mordgrundbruck bei Dresden* is the best); 3 oratorios; many songs for solo voice (*In die Ferne, Des deut-*

schen Rheines Braut, etc.); piano sonatas, rondos, etc.

BIBLIOGRAPHY: A.R. Scheumann, *Julius Otto* (Dresden, 1904).

Otto, Lisa, German soprano; b. Dresden, Nov. 14, 1919. She was educated at the Hochschule für Musik in Dresden; made her debut in 1941 at the Landestheater in Beuthen. She was a member of the Dresden State Opera (1945–50); then sang at the Deutsche Oper in West Berlin and at the Bayreuth Festival. She toured widely, visiting the U.S., South America, and Japan.

Ötvos, Gabor, Hungarian conductor; b. Budapest, Sept. 21, 1935. He was educated at the Franz Liszt Academy of Music in Budapest; left Hungary in 1956 and settled in Italy. He conducted in Venice and Trieste; then went to Germany. From 1967 to 1972 he was first conductor and deputy Generalmusikdirektor of the Frankfurt Opera. He also conducted in America; made his Metropolitan Opera debut on Oct. 27, 1971. In 1972 he became Generalmusikdirektor of Augsburg, a post he held until 1981, when he was appointed chief conductor of the Royal Danish Theater in Copenhagen.

Oudin, Eugène (Espérance), American baritone; b. New York, Feb. 24, 1858; d. London, Nov. 4, 1894. He was of French extraction; studied law at Yale Univ.; was an amateur singer, and made his debut in N.Y., on Aug. 30, 1886, in an operetta. On Jan. 31, 1891, he created the role of Ivanhoe in Arthur Sullivan's opera of that name, and won immediate acclaim. He remained in England most of his life, but also made several appearances in Europe, including Russia; scored notable successes in Wagnerian roles (Wolfram, Telramund, etc.).

Oudrid (y Segura), Cristóbal, Spanish composer; b. Badajoz, Feb. 7, 1825; d. Madrid, March 12, 1877. He studied music with his father; acquired his craft by arranging works of Haydn and Mozart for wind instruments; in 1844 went to Madrid, where he took lessons with Saldoni. He showed a decided talent for writing melodious zarzuelas, among them *Buenas noches, Señor Don Simon* (Madrid, April 16, 1852), *El postillon de la Rioja* (Madrid, June 7, 1856), *El último mono* (Madrid, May 30, 1859), and *El molinero de Subiza* (1870).

BIBLIOGRAPHY: A. Pena y Goni, *La opera española en el siglo XIX* (Madrid, 1881).

Oulibicheff, Alexander, Russian official and music amateur; b. Dresden, April 13, 1794; d. Nizhny-Novgorod, Feb. 5, 1858. He studied violin at home in Dresden, where his father was Russian ambassador; was educated in Germany. When the family returned to Russia after 1812, he was employed in the Ministry of Finance, and later in the Ministry of Foreign Affairs (1816–30). He was the editor of the French periodical *Journal de St. Petersbourg* (1812–30); retired to his estate in Nizhny-Novgorod in

1841. His greatest admiration was for Mozart; his magnum opus is *Nouvelle biographie de Mozart, suivie d'un aperçu sur l'histoire générale de la musique* (3 vols., Moscow, 1843; 2nd German ed., 1859; Russian trans. by Modest Tchaikovsky, Moscow, 1890). By way of praising Mozart, he inserted deprecating remarks on Beethoven's later style; when he was taken to task for this lack of appreciation (by Lenz and others), he publ. *Beethoven, ses critiques et ses glossateurs* (Leipzig and Paris, 1857), in which he emphatically reiterated his sharp criticism of Beethoven's harmonic and formal procedures.

Oury, Anna Caroline (née **Belleville**), German pianist; b. Landshut, June 24, 1808; d. Munich, July 22, 1880. Her father, a French nobleman named Belleville, was director of the Munich Opera. She studied with Czerny in Vienna; made her debut there; then gave concerts in Munich and in Paris; settled for many years in London, where she married the violinist **Antonio James Oury** (b. London, c.1880; d. Norwich, July 25, 1883) in 1831; toured with him in Russia, Germany, Austria, and France. She wrote a number of piano pieces in the salon style, of which nearly 200 were publ.

Ouseley, Sir Frederick Arthur Gore, English composer and theorist; b. London, Aug. 12, 1825; d. Hereford, April 6, 1889. He was the son of Sir Gore Ouseley, ambassador to Persia; studied at Oxford Univ. (B.A., 1846; M.A., 1849; D.Mus., 1854). He was ordained a priest in 1849; was curate at St. Barnabas, Pimlico (1849–51). In 1855 he succeeded Sir Henry Bishop as prof. of music at Oxford Univ. He was a fine organist, and excelled in fugal improvisation.

WORKS: 2 oratorios: *The Martyrdom of St. Polycarp* (1855) and *Hagar* (1873); 11 church services; 70 anthems; *The Psalter, Arranged for Chanting, with Appropriate English Chants; Anglican Psalter Chants; Cathedral Services by English Masters* (2 vols.). He also publ. *Treatise on Harmony* (1868); *Counterpoint, Canon and Fugue,* after Cherubini (1868); *Musical Form and General Composition* (1875). He left his fine music library to St. Michael's College, Tenbury.

BIBLIOGRAPHY: F.T. Havergal, *Memorials of F.A.G. Ouseley, Bart.* (London, 1889); F.W. Joyce, *Life of Rev. Sir F.A.G. Ouseley, Bart., etc.* (London, 1892; revised, 1896, with an appendix by J.S. Bumpus, containing a list of all of Ouseley's extant works); M.F. Alderson and H.C. Colles, *History of St. Michael's College, Tenbury* (London, 1943).

Ovchinnikov, Viacheslav, Soviet composer and conductor; b. Voronezh, May 29, 1936. He studied composition with Khrennikov at the Moscow Cons., graduating in 1962; also studied conducting with Lev Ginzburg; upon graduation he conducted various orchs. in Moscow and on Soviet radio, television, etc. He composed an opera, *On the Dawn of Misty Youth* (1974–78); ballet, *Sulamith* (1962); oratorio, *Hymn to the Fatherland* (1974); heroic poem, *Yuri*

Gagarin (1974); 3 symphs. (1956, 1973, 1978); 6 symph. suites (1955–72); *Elegy in Memory of Rachmaninoff* (1973); also made orch. arrangements of Rachmaninoff's piano works; wrote the background score for the film *War and Peace* (1961–67) and other film music; also choruses, songs, piano pieces.

Overton, Hall, American composer; b. Bangor, Mich., Feb. 23, 1920; d. New York, Nov. 24, 1972. He studied piano at the Chicago Musical College; served in the U.S. Army overseas (1942–45). After the war, he studied composition with Persichetti at the Juilliard School of Music, N.Y., graduating in 1951; also took private lessons with Wallingford Riegger and Darius Milhaud. At the same time, he filled professional engagements as a jazz pianist and contributed to the magazine *Jazz Today.* WORKS: Operas: *The Enchanted Pear Tree,* after Boccaccio's *Decameron* (Juilliard School of Music, N.Y., Feb. 7, 1950); *Pietro's Petard* (N.Y., June 1963); *Huckleberry Finn,* after Mark Twain (Juilliard American Opera Center, N.Y., May 20, 1971); 2 symphs. (1955, 1962); 2 string quartets; String Trio; Viola Sonata; Cello Sonata; *Pulsations* for Chamber Ensemble (his last work; 1972).

Owens, "Buck" (Alvis Edgar Owens, Jr.), American country-music entertainer; b. Sherman, Texas, Aug. 12, 1929. He took up the piano in his youth, and then the electric guitar; he began playing in honky-tonks when he was 16, and later established himself as one of the most successful country-music entertainers; made many appearances on radio, television, and on tours. In 1969 he became co-host (with Roy Clark) of the inane but highly successful "Hee Haw" television program.

Ozawa, Seiji, glamorous Japanese conductor of extraordinary accomplishments; b. Hoten, Manchuria, of Japanese parents, Sept. 1, 1935. His father was a Buddhist, his mother a Christian. The family went back to Japan in 1944, at the end of Japanese occupation of Manchuria. Ozawa began to study piano; at 16 he enrolled at the Toho School of Music in Tokyo, where he studied composition and conducting; one of his teachers, Hideo Saito, a professional cellist, profoundly influenced his development as a musician; he graduated in 1959 with first prizes in composition and conducting. By that time he had already conducted concerts with the NHK (Japan Broadcasting Corp.) Symph. Orch. and the Japan Phil.; upon Saito's advice, he went to Europe; to defray his expenses he became a motor-scooter salesman for a Japanese firm, and promoted the product in Italy and France. In 1959 he won first prize at the international competition for conductors in Besançon, and was befriended by Charles Munch and Eugène Bigot; he then studied conducting with Bigot in Paris. Munch arranged for Ozawa to come to the U.S. and to study conducting at the Berkshire Music Center in Tanglewood; in 1960 he won its Koussevitzky Prize, and was awarded a scholarship to work with Herbert von Karajan and the Berlin Phil. Leonard Bernstein heard him in

Berlin and engaged him as an assistant conductor of the N.Y. Phil. On April 14, 1961, he made his first appearance with the orch. at Carnegie Hall; later that year, he accompanied Bernstein and the orch. on its tour of Japan. In 1962 he was invited to return as a guest conductor of the NHK Symph. Orch., but difficulties arose between him and the players, who objected to being commanded in an imperious manner by one of their own countrymen; still, he succeeded in obtaining engagements with other Japanese orchs., which he conducted on his periodic visits to his homeland.

In the meantime, Ozawa advanced significantly in his American career; from 1964 to 1968 he was music director of the Ravinia Festival, the summer home of the Chicago Symph. Orch.; in 1969 he served as its principal guest conductor; from 1965 to 1969 he also was music director of the Toronto Symph. Orch., which he took to England in 1965. From 1970 to 1976 he was music director of the San Francisco Symph. Orch., and then its music adviser in 1976–77. In the spring of 1977 Ozawa took the San Francisco Symph. on a tour of Europe, visiting 15 cities, some in Russia, where he was received with exceptional acclaim. Even before completing his tenure in San Francisco, he had begun a close association with the Boston Symph. Orch.; with Gunther Schuller, he became co-artistic director of its Berkshire Music Center in 1970; in 1972 he assumed the post of music adviser of the Boston Symph., and in 1973 he became its conductor and music director, and sole artistic director of the Berkshire Music Center, an astonishing event in American music annals, marking the first time an oriental musician was chosen solely by his merit to head the Boston Symph. Orch., which was for years since its foundation the exclusive preserve of German, and later French and Russian, conductors. In 1976 Ozawa took the Boston Symph. on a tour of Europe; in 1978 he escorted it to Japan, where those among Japanese musicians who had been skeptical about his abilities greeted his spectacular ascendance with national pride. Another unprecedented event took place in the spring of 1979, when Ozawa traveled with the Boston Symph. to the People's Republic of China on an official cultural visit; in August 1979 Ozawa and the orch. went on a tour of European music festivals. The centennial of the Boston Symph. Orch. in 1981 was marked by a series of concerts, under Ozawa's direction, which included appearances in 14 American cities and a tour of Japan, France, Germany, Austria, and England.

With dormant racial prejudices finally abandoned in American society, Ozawa's reputation rose to universal recognition of his remarkable talent. He proved himself a consummate master of orchestral playing, equally penetrating in the classical repertoire as in the works of modern times; his performances of such demanding scores as Mahler's 8th Symph. and Schoenberg's *Gurrelieder* constituted proofs of his commanding technical skill, affirmed *a fortiori* by his assured presentation of the rhythmically and contrapuntally intricate 4th Symph. of Charles Ives. All these challenging scores Ozawa consuetudinarily conducted from memory, an astonishing feat in itself. He was married twice: first to the Japanese pianist **Kyoko Edo,** and 2nd, to a Eurasian, Vera Ilyan. He received an honorary doctorate in music from the Univ. of San Francisco in 1971, and one from the New England Cons. of Music in 1982.

BIBLIOGRAPHY: David Ewen, *Musicians since 1900* (N.Y., 1978); P. Hart, *Conductors: A New Generation* (N.Y., 1979; pp. 165–94).

P

Paap, Wouter, eminent Dutch musicologist and composer; b. Utrecht, May 7, 1908; d. Lage Vuursche (Baarn), Oct. 7, 1981. He studied piano and music theory; devoted himself mainly to musicology; served as editor in chief of the Dutch music periodical *Mens en Melodie;* was also co-editor of the valuable music encyclopedia in the Dutch-language *Algemene Muziekencyclopedie* (6 vols., Amsterdam, 1957–63).

PUBLICATIONS: Monographs on Bruckner (Bilthoven, 1963), Eduard van Beinum (Baarn, 1956), Willem Mengelberg (Amsterdam, 1958, as part of *Music in Holland*); *De Symphonieen van Beethoven* (Utrecht, 1947); *Moderne Kermuziek in Nederland* (Amsterdam, 1948); *Muziek, Moderne en klassiek* (Utrecht, 1961); *Mozart* (Utrecht, 1962).

COMPOSITIONS: *Sterre der zee* for Soprano, Chorus, and Orch. (1937); Sinfonietta for Chamber Orch. (1938); *Wals* for Chamber Orch. (1940); *Declamatorium* for Recitation with Orch. (1940); *Passacaglia* for Orch. (1943); *Muziek ter Bruiloft,* solo cantata for Tenor and Orch. (1945); *Studentenmuziek* for String Orch. (1948); *Guirlanden van Muziek* for String Orch. (1951); *Ballet suite* for Chamber Orch. (1953); *Luchtige suite* for Carillon (1955); *Overture Electora* for Orch. (1956); *5 Liederen* for Voice and Orch. (1956); Sonatina for Carillon (1963); various pieces for wind instruments.

Pablo, Luis de, Spanish composer; b. Bilbao, Jan. 28, 1930. He studied jurisprudence at Madrid Univ., receiving a law degree in 1952. He attended the Cons. of Madrid; traveled to Paris, where he received musical advice from Messiaen and Boulez; also took courses at the summer seminars for new music at Darmstadt. Returning to Spain, he organized the modern performance groups Tiempo y Música and Alea. Like most Spanish composers, he followed in his youth the precepts of the national school, with the music of Manuel de Falla as principal influence, but soon he adopted hyperserial techniques, in which whole tonal complexes, chords, or groups of chords become thematic units; similarly, dynamic processes assume the role of compositional determinants, eventually attaining the ultimate libertarianism in promiscuous cross-fertilization of all media, all styles, and all techniques of musical composition.

WORKS: *Coral* for Woodwinds (1953); *Comentarios* for Soprano, Piccolo, Vibraphone, and Double Bass (1956); Clarinet Quintet (1954); 2 string quartets (1955, 1957); *Elegía* for String Orch. (1956); Harpsichord Concerto (1956); Piano Sonata (1958); *Movil I* and *Movil II* for 2 Pianos (1958, 1968); *Radi-*

al for 24 Instruments (1960); *Polar* for Voice, Saxophone, Bass Clarinet, and Percussion (1961); *4 Inventions* for Orch. (1955–62); *Tombeau* for Orch. (1963); 6 *Modulos:* No. 1, for Chamber Ensemble (1965); No. 2, for Double Orch. (1966); No. 3, for 17 Instruments (1967); No. 4, *Ejercicio,* for String Quartet (1965); No. 5, for Organ (1967); No. 6, *Parafrasis,* for 24 Instruments (1968); *Sinfonías* for 17 Wind Instruments (1955–66); *Cesuras* for Double Trio of Woodwinds and Strings (Festival of American and Spanish Music, Madrid, Oct. 22, 1964); *Imaginario I* for Harpsichord and 3 Percussionists (1967); *Imaginario II* for Orch. (1967); *Heterogéneo* for 2 Narrators, Hammond Organ, and Orch. (1968; Donaueschingen, Oct. 18, 1970); *Protocolo,* opera (1968; Paris, Oct. 23, 1970); *Quasi una fantasia* for String Sextet and Orch. (1968; Paris, April 17, 1972); *Por diversos motivos* for Voice, Projected Images, and Chamber Orch. (1969); *Oroïtaldi* for Orch. (1971); *Eléphants ivres (Drunken Elephants),* in 4 parts, for differing orch. formations (1972–73); *Je mange, tu manges* for Small Orch. and Tape (1972; Royan, April 14, 1973); *Masque* for Flute, Clarinet, Piano, and Percussion (1973). He publ. *Aproximación a una estética de la música contemporánea* (Madrid, 1968).

Pabst, Louis, German pianist and composer; b. Königsberg, July 18, 1846; d. Moscow, 1903. He made his first appearance as a pianist in his native city in 1862; was in England from 1867 to 1869; then established a music school in Riga, Russia (1869–75); subsequently toured Australia; there he founded the Academy of Music of Melbourne (1887); revisited London in 1894; in 1897 went again to Russia; became an instructor at the music school of the Phil. Society in Moscow in 1899; in 1903 became court councillor of the Ministry of the Interior. He publ. a number of piano pieces.

Pabst, Paul, German pianist, brother of **Louis Pabst;** b. Königsberg, May 27, 1854; d. Moscow, June 9, 1897. He studied with Liszt; went to Russia, and taught at the Moscow Cons. He made a number of effective paraphrases for piano of operatic works; particularly well known is the one on *Eugene Onegin.*

Pacchiarotti, Gasparo, famous Italian male soprano; b. Fabriano, near Ancona, 1740 (baptized, May 21); d. Padua, Oct. 28, 1821. He studied under Bertoni at St. Mark's in Venice; was principal soloist in San Marco in 1765–68; from 1769, sang at the principal Italian theaters with brilliant success; in 1778, went to London with Bertoni, returning there in 1781–84 and 1791. In 1793 he retired and settled in Padua; sang for Napoleon when the latter passed through Padua in 1796. A. Calegari publ. *Modi generali del canto* (1836), based on Pacchiarotti's method.
BIBLIOGRAPHY: G.C. Pacchiarotti (his adopted son), *Cenni biografici intorno a Gaspare Pacchiarotti* (Padua, 1844); R. Sassi, *Un celebre musico fabrianese, Gaspare Pacchiarotti* (Fabriano, 1935); A.

Heriot, *The Castrati in Opera* (London, 1956; pp. 163–71).

Pacchierotti, Ubaldo, Italian composer and conductor; b. Cervarese-Croce (Padua), Oct. 30, 1875; d. Milan, April 18, 1916. He studied at the Cons. S. Pietro a Majella in Naples; conducted in Livorno and Buenos Aires.
WORKS: Operas: *La lampada* (Buenos Aires, 1899); *L'albatro* (Milan, 1905); *Eidelberga mia!* (Genoa, Feb. 27, 1908; in N.Y. as *Alt Heidelberg,* 1910); *Il Santo* (Turin, 1913); and other works.
BIBLIOGRAPHY: C.M. Rietmann, "Ubaldo Pacchierotti," *Pensiero Musicale* (Nov.–Dec. 1926).

Pache, Joseph, German pianist and conductor; b. Friedland, Silesia, June 1, 1861; d. Baltimore, Dec. 7, 1926. He studied piano with Klindworth in Berlin (1883–85); composition with Max Bruch in Breslau (1885–86); then studied voice with J. Hey in Berlin. He emigrated to the U.S. in 1891; from 1894, was conductor of the Oratorio Society in Baltimore.

Pachelbel, Carl Theodorus, son of **Johann Pachelbel;** b. Stuttgart, Nov. 24, 1690; d. Charleston, S.C., Sept. 14, 1750. He emigrated to Boston in the 1730s and in 1733 assisted in the erection of the organ of Trinity Church in Newport, R.I., of which he was organist for about a year. On Jan. 21, 1736, he advertised a concert in N.Y., the first there of which details have been recorded, and on March 8, a 2nd one. He then moved to Charleston, became organist of St. Philip's Church, and on Nov. 22, 1737, gave a public concert in his home. An 8-part Magnificat, the only known composition of Carl Pachelbel, is in the State Library in Berlin (publ. N.Y., 1937).
BIBLIOGRAPHY: O.G. Sonneck, *Early Concert-Life in America (1731–1800)* (in Eng., Leipzig, 1907); J.T. Howard, *Our American Music* (N.Y., 1939, and later eds.); V.L. Redway, "A New York Concert in 1736," *Musical Quarterly* (April 1936); idem, "C.T. Pachelbel, Musical Emigrant," *Journal of the American Musicological Society* (Spring 1952).

Pachelbel, Johann, great German composer and organist; b. Nuremberg (baptized, Sept. 1), 1653; d. there (buried, March 9), 1706. He studied music in Nuremberg with Heinrich Schwemmer; received instruction in composition and instrumental performance from G.C. Wecker; pursued his academic studies at the local St. Lorenz school; also attended the lectures at the Auditorium Aegidianum. He then took courses briefly at the Univ. of Altdorf (1669–70), and served as organist at the Lorenzkirche there. He subsequently was accepted as a scholarship student at the Gymnasium Poeticum in Regensburg, and took private music lessons with Kaspar Prentz. In 1673 he went to Vienna as deputy organist at St. Stephen's Cathedral. In 1677 he assumed the position of court organist in Eisenach. In 1678 he became organist at the Protestant Predigerkirche in Erfurt. It was in Erfurt that he established his reputation as a master organist, composer, and teacher. He was a friend of the Bach family, and was the teacher of Johann Christoph Bach, who in turn taught Johann Sebastian Bach. On Oct. 25, 1681, Pachelbel married Barbara Gabler; she and their infant son died during the plague of 1683. He then married Judith Drommer on Aug. 24, 1684; they had 5 sons and 2 daughters. Two of their sons, **Wilhelm Hieronymus** and **Carl Theodorus,** became musicians; another son, Johann Michael, became an instrument maker; a daughter, Amalie, became a painter. In 1690 he accepted an appointment as Württemberg court musician and organist in Stuttgart. However, with the French invasion in the fall of 1692 he fled to Nuremberg; in November of that year he became town organist in Gotha. In 1695 he succeeded his teacher Wecker as organist at St. Sebald in Nuremberg, a position he held until his death. Pachelbel was one of the most significant predecessors of Johann Sebastian Bach. His liturgical organ music was of the highest order, particularly his splendid organ chorales. His non-liturgical keyboard music was likewise noteworthy, especially his fugues and variations (of the latter, his *Hexachordum Apollinis* of 1699 is extraordinary). He was equally gifted as a composer of vocal music. His motets, sacred concertos, and concertato settings of the *Magnificat* are fine examples of German church music. Pachelbel was a pioneer in notational symbolism of intervals, scales, and pitch levels arranged to correspond to the meaning of the words. Thus, his setting of the motet *Durch Adams Fall* is accomplished by a falling figure in the bass; exaltation is expressed by a rising series of arpeggios in a major key; steadfast faith is conveyed by a repeated note; satanic evil is translated into an ominous figuration of a broken diminished-seventh-chord. Generally speaking, joyful moods are portrayed by major keys, mournful states of soul by minor keys, a practice which became a standard mode of expression through the centuries.

WORKS: In addition to various separate editions of his works, major publications include M. Seiffert and A. Sandberger, eds., *Johann Pachelbel: Klavierwerke,* in Denkmäler der Tonkunst in Bayern, II, Jg. II/1 (1901); M. Seiffert, ed., *Johann Pachelbel: Orgelkompositionen,* in Denkmäler der Tonkunst in Bayern, VI, Jg. IV/1 (1903); K. Matthaei and W. Stockmeier, eds., *Johann Pachelbel: Ausgewählte Orgelwerke* (vols. 1–4 by Matthaei, Kassel, 1928–36; vols. 5–6 by Stockmeier, Kassel, 1972–74).
CHORALES FOR ORGAN: *8 Choräle zum Praeambulieren* (Nuremberg, 1693). Fugues: *Ach Gott, vom Himmel sieh darein; Ach Herr, mich armen Sünder; Christe, der du bist Tag und Licht; Da Jesus an dem Kreuze stund* (may not be by Pachelbel); *Der Herr ist mein getreuer Hirt* (2 versions); *Dies sind die heil'gen zehn Gebot; Es woll uns Gott genädig sein* (2 versions); *In dich hab' ich gehoffet, Herr; Wo Gott zum Haus nicht gibt sein Gunst.* Three-part Cantus firmus: *Allein Gott in der Höh sei Ehr* (may not be by Pachelbel); *Christ unser Herr zum Jordan kam; Durch Adams Fall; Erbarm dich mein, o Herre Gott; Erhalt uns Herr, bei deinem Wort* (may not be by Pachelbel); *Gelobet seist du, Jesu Christ; Gott Vater, der du deine Sonn'; Herr*

Gott, dich loben alle wir; Ich hab' mein' Sach' Gott heimgestellt; Ich ruf zu dir; Jesus Christus, unser Heiland, der den Tod (2 versions); *Kommt her zu mir, spricht Gottes Sohn; Lob sei Gott in des Himmels Thron; Meine Seele erhebt den Herren [tonus peregrinus]* (2 versions); *Nun freut euch, lieben Christen g'mein'; O Mensch bewein dein Sünde gross; Vom Himmel hoch da komm ich her; Warum betrübst du dich, mein Herz; Was mein Gott will, das g'scheh allzeit; Wenn wir in höchsten Nöten sein; Wie schön leuchtet der Morgenstern; Wo Gott der Herr nicht bei uns hält* (2 versions); *Wo Gott zum Haus nicht gibt sein Gunst.* Four-part Cantus firmus: *Gott hat das Evangelium; Gott Vater, der du deine Sonn'; Komm, Gott Schöpfer, heiliger Geist; Mag ich Unglück nicht widerstahn; Nun lasst uns Gott dem Herren; Vater unser im Himmelreich.* Combination-form: *Ach Gott, vom Himmel sieh darein; Ach Herr, mich armen Sünder; Ach wie elend ist unsre Zeit; Allein Gott in der Höh sei Ehr* (may not be by Pachelbel); *An Wasserflüssen Babylon* (2 versions); *Auf meinen lieben Gott; Christ lag in Todesbanden; Der Tag der ist so freudenreich; Durch Adams Fall; Ein feste Burg; Es spricht der Unweisen Mund wohl; Herr Christ, der einig Gott's Sohn; Herr Jesu Christ, ich weiss gar wohl; Ich ruf zu dir; Nun komm der Heiden Heiland; O Lamm Gottes unschuldig; Vater unser im Himmelreich; Vom Himmel hoch da komm ich her; Warum betrübst du dich, mein Herz; Wenn mein Stündlein vorhanden ist; Wenn wir in höchsten Nöten sein; Wo Gott der Her nicht bei uns hält.* Bicinia: *Durch Adams Fall; Es spricht der Unweisen Mund wohl* (may not be by Pachelbel); *Jesus Christus, unser Heiland, der von uns; Was mein Gott will, das g'scheh allzeit.* Other kinds: *Allein zu dir, Herr Jesu Christ* (2 versions); *Nun lob, mein' Seel', den Herren; Wir glauben all' an einen Gott.* He also composed 95 *Magnificat* fugues. His non-liturgical music for organ includes 26 fugues, 16 toccatas, 7 preludes, 6 fantasias, 6 ciacconas, 3 ricercari, etc. Additional keyboard music includes his arias with variations known as *Hexachordum Apollinis, sex arias exhibens ... quam singulis suae sunt subjectae variationes* (Nuremberg, 1699), about 17 suites, and the following chorale variations: *Ach was soll ich Sünder machen; Alle Menschen müssen sterben; Christus, der ist mein Leben; Freu dich sehr, o meine Seele [Treuer Gott, ich muss dir klagen]; Herzlich tut mich verlangen; Was Gott tut, das ist wohlge-tan; Werde munter, mein Gemüte.*
CHAMBER MUSIC: *Canon and Gigue* in D major for 3 Violins and Basso Continuo (the *Canon* is one of his most famous works, being extremely popular with modern audiences; it has been publ. and republ. in numerous arrangements for various instruments); *Musicalische Ergötzung bestehend in 6 verstimten Partien* for 2 Violins and Basso Continuo (Nuremberg, 1695); *Partie* in G major for 2 Violins, 2 Violas, Cello, and Basso Continuo.
VOCAL MUSIC: Motets for 2 4-part choruses: *Der Herr ist König, darum toben die Völker; Der Herr ist König und herrlich geschmückt; Gott ist unser Zuversicht; Jauchzet dem Herrn; Jauchzet Gott,*

alle Lande; Nun danket alle Gott; Singet dem Herrn; Tröste uns Gott; also the unfinished *Der Herr ist König und herrlich geschmückt* for 5 Voices and Basso Continuo; in addition, 2 Latin motets: *Exsurgat Deus* and *Paratum cor meum.* Sacred concertos: *Christ lag in Todesbanden* for 4 Voices, 2 Violins, 3 Violas, and Basso Continuo; *Der Name des Herren sei gelobet* for 3 Voices, 2 Violins, and Basso Continuo; *Gott ist unser Zuversicht* for 4 Voices, 2 Violins, 2 Violas, Bassoon, and Basso Continuo; *Gott sei uns gnädig* for 5 Voices, 5 Trumpets, Timpani, 2 Violins, 4 Violas, Bassoon, Basso Continuo, and Organ; *Jauchzet dem Herrn, alle Welt* for 5 Voices, 2 Oboes, 2 Violins, 3 Violas, Viole, and Basso Continuo; *Jauchzet dem Herrn, alle Welt* for 5 Voices, 4 Trumpets, Timpani, 2 Violins, 3 Violas, Bassoon, and Basso Continuo; *Kommt her zu mir* for 4 Voices, 2 Violins, 2 Cornets, and Basso Continuo; *Lobet den Herrn in seinem Heiligtum* for 5 Voices, 2 Flutes, Bassoon, 5 Trumpets, Trombone, Timpani, Cymbal, Harp, 2 Violins, 3 Violas, Basso Continuo, and Organ; *Meine Sünde betrüben mich* for Voice, Chorus of 4 Voices, 4 Viole da Gamba, Bassoon/Viole, and Basso Continuo (fragment only extant); etc. Arias: *Auf, werte Gäst* for Voice, 2 Violins, and Basso Continuo; *Augen, streuet Perlen-Tränen* for 2 Voices, 4 Violas, Viola pro Basso, and Organ; *Das angenehmste Wetter* for Voice, 2 Violins, and Basso Continuo (unfinished); *Das Gewitter* for Voice, 2 Violins, and Basso Continuo; *Das Jahr fängt an* for Voice, 2 Violins, 2 Violas, and Basso Continuo; *Der Widder Abrahams* for 2 Voices, 2 Violins, and Basso Continuo; *Die freuderfüllten Abendstunden* for Voice, 2 Violins, 2 Violas, and Basso Continuo; *Es muss die Sinne ja erfreuen* for Voice, 2 Violins, and Basso Continuo; *Geliebtes Vaterherz* for Voice, 2 Violins, 2 Violas, and Basso Continuo/Viole; *Guter Walter unsers Rats* for Voice, 2 Violins, 2 Violas, and Basso Continuo; *Hör, grosser Mäcenat* for Voice, 2 Violins, 2 Violas, and Basso Continuo; *Mäcenas lebet noch* for Voice, 2 Violins, Trumpet, and Basso Continuo; *Mein Leben, dessen Kreuz* for Voice, 4 Violas, Viola pro Basso, and Organ; *O grosses Musenlicht* for Voice, 2 Violins, 2 Viole da Gamba, and Basso Continuo; *So ist denn dies der Tag* for Voice, Chorus of 4 Voices, 2 Violins, 3 Violas, 4 Trumpets, Timpani, and Basso Continuo; *So ist denn nur die Treu* for 2 Voices, Chorus of 5 Voices, 2 Flutes, 2 Violins, 3 Violas, and Basso Continuo; *Voller Wonder, voller Kunst* for 4 Voices and Basso Continuo (unfinished); *Wie nichtig, ach* for Voice, 3 Violas, and Basso Continuo; *Wohl euch, die ihr in Gott verliebt* for 4 Voices (unfinished). Music for Vespers: *Ingressus* in C major for 4 Voices, 2 Violins, Viola, and Basso Continuo; *Ingressus* in C major for 4 Voices, 2 Violins, 3 Violas, and Basso Continuo; *Ingressus* in C major for 5 Voices, 4 Trumpets, Timpani, 2 Violins, 3 Violas, Bassoon, Basso Continuo, and Organ; *Ingressus* in D major for 4 Voices, 2 Violins, Viola, and Basso Continuo; *Ingressus* in D major for 4 Voices, 2 Violins, 3 Violas, Bassoon, and Basso Continuo; *Ingressus* in D minor for 5 Voices, 2 Violins, 3 Violas, Bassoon, and Basso Continuo; *Ingressus* in F major for 5 Voices, 2 Violins, 4 Violas, Bassoon, and Basso Continuo; *Ingressus* in G major for 4 Voices, 2 Violins, 3 Violas ad libitum, Bassoon ad libitum, and Basso Continuo; *Ingressus* in G minor for 4 Voices, 2 Violins, Bassoon, and Basso Continuo; *Ingressus* in G minor for 5 Voices, 2 Violins, Viola, 2 Viole da Gamba, Bassoon, and Basso Continuo; *Ingressus* in A major for 5 Voices, 2 Violins, 3 Violas, Bassoon, and Basso Continuo; *Ingressus* in A minor for 5 Voices, 2 Violins, 3 Violas, Bassoon, and Basso Continuo; *Magnificat* in C major for 5 Voices, 2 Oboes, 2 Violins, 3 Violas, Bassoon, and Basso Continuo; *Magnificat* in C major for 5 Voices, 4 Trumpets, Timpani, 2 Violins, Viola, 2 Viole da Gamba, Bassoon, Basso Continuo, and Organ; *Magnificat* in C major for 4 Voices, 2 Trumpets, 2 Violins, 2 Violas, and Basso Continuo; *Magnificat* in C major for 5 Voices, 4 Trumpets, Timpani, 2 Violins, Viola, 2 Viole da Gamba, Bassoon, and Basso Continuo; *Magnificat* in D major for 5 Voices, 2 Violins, 2 Cornets/Oboes, 3 Violas, Bassoon, and Basso Continuo; *Magnificat* in D major for Double Chorus of 5 Voices and Double Orch., each with 2 Violins, 3 Violas, Bassoon, and Basso Continuo; *Magnificat* in D major for 4 Voices and 4 Violas ad libitum; *Magnificat* in E-flat major for 4 Voices, 2 Violins, 3 Violas, Bassoon, Basso Continuo, and Organ; *Magnificat* in F major for 4 Voices, 2 Violins, Bassoon, and Basso Continuo; *Magnificat* in F major for 5 Voices, 2 Violins, Bassoon, and Basso Continuo; *Magnificat* in G major for 4 Voices, 2 Violins, and Basso Continuo; *Magnificat* in G minor for 4 Voices; *Magnificat* in B-flat major for 5 Voices, 2 Oboes, 2 Violins, 3 Violas, Bassoon, Basso Continuo, and Organ. He also composed a *Missa* in C major for 4 Voices, 2 Violins, Clarino, and Basso Continuo, and a *Missa brevis* in D major for 4 Voices.

BIBLIOGRAPHY: J. Mattheson, *Grundlage einer Ehren-Pforte* (Hamburg, 1740; new ed. by M. Schneider, Berlin, 1910; reprint, 1969); P. Spitta, *Johann Sebastian Bach* (2 vols., Leipzig, 1873–80; Eng. trans. by C. Bell and J. Fuller Maitland, 3 vols., London, 1884–85; 2nd ed., 1899; reprint, 2 vols., N.Y., 1951); A. Ritter, "Tabulatur Buch ... von Johann Pachelbeln ... 1704," *Monatshefte für Musikgeschichte,* VI (1874); idem, *Zur Geschichte des Orgelspiels im 14. bis zum Anfange des 18. Jahrhunderts* (Leipzig, 1884); M. Seiffert, *Geschichte der Klaviermusik* (Leipzig, 1899); M. Seiffert, "Johann Pachelbels musikalische Sterbensgedanken," *Sammelbände der Internationalen Musik-Gesellschaft,* V (1903–4); G. Beckmann, "Johann Pachelbel als Kammerkomponist," *Archiv für Musikwissenschaft,* I (1918–19); F. Blume, *Die evangelische Kirchenmusik,* in Bücken's *Handbuch der Musikwissenschaft,* X (1931; 2nd ed., revised, as *Geschichte der evangelischen Kirchenmusik,* 1965; Eng. trans. as *Protestant Church Music: A History,* 1974); O. Kaul, "Zwei unbekannte Kompositionen von Johann Pachelbel," *Zeitschrift für Musikwissenschaft,* XVI (1933–34); G. Frotscher, *Geschichte des Orgelspiels und der Orgelkomposition,* I (Berlin, 1935; 3rd ed., enlarged, 1966); E. Doflein, "Pachelbels Kammermusik," *Zeitschrift für Hausmusik,* VII (1938); E. von Rumohr, *Der Nürnbergische Tasteninstrumentalstil im 17. Jahrhundert, dargestellt an Arie,*

Variation und Suite (Diss., Univ. of Münster, 1938); E. Born, *Die Variation als Grundlage handwerklicher Gestaltung im musikalischen Schaffen Johann Pachelbels* (Berlin and Frankfurt, 1941); H. Woodward, *A Study of the Tenbury Manuscripts of Johann Pachelbel* (Diss., Harvard Univ., 1952); K. Matthaei, "Johann Pachelbel: Zu seinem 300. Geburtstag," *Musik und Gottesdienst,* VII (1953); H.J. Moser, "Johann Pachelbel: Zur 300. Wiederkehr seines Geburtstages," *Musik und Kirche,* XXIII (1953); H.H. Eggebrecht, "Johann Pachelbel als Vokalkomponist," *Archiv für Musikwissenschaft,* XI (1954); E. Nolte, *The Instrumental Works of Johann Pachelbel* (Diss., Northwestern Univ., 1954); H.H. Eggebrecht, "Johann Pachelbel: Zu seinem 250. Todestag," *Musica,* X (1956); E. Nolte, "The Magnificat Fugues of Johann Pachelbel: Alternation or Intonation?," *Journal of the American Musicological Society,* IX (1956); idem, "Classic Contract between Pachelbel and Erfurt Church," *Diapason,* XLVIII (1957); S. Orth, "Johann Pachelbel: Sein Leben und Wirken in Erfurt," *Aus der Vergangenheit der Stadt Erfurt,* II/4 (1957); F. Riedel, *Quellenkündliche Beiträge zur Geschichte der Musik in der 2. Hälfte des 17. Jahrhunderts* (Kassel, 1960); H. Samuel, *The Cantata in Nuremberg during the Seventeenth Century* (Diss., Cornell Univ., 1963); H.H. Eggebrecht, "Das Weimarer Tabulaturbuch von 1704," *Archiv für Musikwissenschaft,* XXII (1965); F. Krummacher, "Kantate und Konzert im Werk Johann Pachelbels," *Die Musikforschung,* XX (1967).

Pachelbel, Wilhelm Hieronymus, German organist and composer, son of **Johann Pachelbel;** b. Erfurt (baptized, Aug. 29), 1686; d. Nuremberg, 1764. His only known teacher was his father, who gave him instruction in both keyboard instruments and composition. He is believed to have begun his career as an organist in Fürth; then was organist of the Predigerkirche in Erfurt. In 1706 he became organist of the Jakobikirche in Nuremberg; that same year was named organist at St. Egidien there. In 1719 he became organist at St. Sebald, a post he held until his death. Little of his music is extant, all of it being for keyboard instruments. He publ. *Musicalisches Vergnügen bestehend in einem Praeludio, Fuga und Fantasia, sowohl auf die Orgel als auch auf das Clavier... vorgestellt und componiert* in D major (Nuremberg, 1725?) and *Praeludium und Fuga* in C major (Nuremberg, 1725?). He also composed *Fantasia super "Meine Seele, lass es gehen"; Fantasia* in B-flat major; *O Lamm Gottes unschuldig* for Clavier; *Toccata* in G major. See H.J. Moser and T. Fedtke, *Wilhelm Hieronymus Pachelbel: Gesamtausgabe der erhaltenen Werke für Orgel und Clavier* (Kassel, 1957).

BIBLIOGRAPHY: J. Mattheson, *Grundlage einer Ehren-Pforte* (Hamburg, 1740; new ed. by M. Schneider, Berlin, 1910; reprint, 1969); A. Ritter, *Zur Geschichte des Orgelspiels im 14. bis zum Anfange des 18. Jahrhunderts* (Leipzig, 1884); M. Seiffert, *Geschichte der Klaviermusik* (Leipzig, 1899); G. Frotscher, *Geschichte des Orgelspiels und der Or-*

gelkomposition, I (Berlin, 1935; 3rd ed., enlarged, 1966); F. Riedel, *Quellenkündliche Beiträge zur Geschichte der Musik in der 2. Hälfte des 17. Jahrhunderts* (Kassel, 1960).

Pachler-Koschak, Marie Leopoldine, Austrian pianist; b. Graz, Oct. 2, 1792; d. there, April 10, 1855. She was an enthusiastic admirer of Beethoven, who wrote to her in 1817: "I have found no one, not excepting the great pianists, who interprets my compositions as well as you." In 1816 she married Dr. Karl Pachler, a lawyer in Graz. In their house Franz Schubert spent several weeks in the summer of 1827. Schubert wrote a little 4-hand march for their son, Faust Pachler, who publ. *Beethoven und M. Pachler-Koschak* (Berlin, 1866), which contains valuable details concerning Beethoven's last days.

Pachmann, Vladimir de, eccentric Russian pianist; b. Odessa, July 27, 1848; d. Rome, Jan. 6, 1933. He received his primary music education at home from his father, an Austrian violinist; then went to Vienna, where he enrolled in the piano class of Prof. Dachs at the Vienna Cons. He began his concert career with a tour of Russia in 1869; he was 40 years old before he made a decisive impact on the international scene; his first American tour, in 1891, was sensationally successful, and it was in America that he began exhibiting his curious eccentricities, some of them undoubtedly calculated to produce shock effect: he made grimaces when he did not like his own playing and shouted "Bravo!" when he played a number to his satisfaction; even more bizarre was his crawling under the grand piano after the concert, claiming that he was looking for the wrong notes he had accidentally hit; all this could be explained as idiosyncratic behavior; but he also allowed himself to mutilate the music itself, by inserting arpeggios between phrases and extra chords at the end of a piece. Most American critics were outraged by his shenanigans, but some, notably Philip Hale, found mitigation in the poetic quality of his interpretations. Pachmann was particularly emotional in playing Chopin, when his facial contortions became quite obnoxious; James Huneker dubbed him "Chopinzee." Pachmann did not lack official honors; in 1885, on his tour of Denmark, he was made a Knight of the Order of Danebrog; in 1916 the London Phil. Society awarded him the Beethoven Medal. His personal life was turbulent; he married frequently (the exact number of his wives is in dispute). His first wife was Maggie Oakey, whom he married in 1884; she edited several Chopin études, indicating Pachmann's own fingering; they were divorced in 1895.

BIBLIOGRAPHY: H.C. Schonberg, *The Great Pianists* (N.Y., 1963).

Pacini, Giovanni, Italian composer; b. Catania, Feb. 17, 1796; d. Pescia, Dec. 6, 1867. He was a pupil of Marchesi and Padre Mattei at Bologna, and of Furlanetto at Venice; his first opera was *Don Pomponio* (1813; not perf.); then came *Annetta e Lucinda* (Milan, Oct. 17, 1813); up to 1835 he had produced over 40 operas on various Italian stages, when the failure of *Carlo di Borgogna* (Feb. 21, 1835) at Venice temporarily checked the flow of dramatic composition; he went to Viareggio, near Lucca, and established a very successful school of music there, for which he wrote several short treatises—*Corso teoretico-pratico di lezioni di armonia* (1863), *Cenni storici sulla musica e trattato di contrappunto* (1864)—and built a private theater. Later he removed the school to Lucca. In 1840 Pacini, who prided himself on rapid work, wrote his dramatic masterpiece, *Saffo,* in 28 days (Naples, Nov. 29, 1840; enthusiastically received). Forty more operas followed up to 1867; the best were *Medea* (Palermo, Nov. 28, 1843), *La Regina di Cipro* (Turin, Feb. 7, 1846), and *Niccolò de' Lapi* (Florence, Oct. 29, 1873; posthumous production). Pacini also wrote numerous oratorios, cantatas, masses, etc.; a *Dante* symph.; an Octet; 6 string quartets; other chamber music, vocal duets, and arias. He was an active contributor to several musical papers; publ. memoirs, *Le mie memorie artistiche* (Florence, 1865; enlarged by Cicconetti, 1872; revised by F. Magnani, 1875). His brother, **Emilio Pacini** (b. 1810; d. Neuilly, near Paris, Dec. 2, 1898), was a distinguished librettist.

BIBLIOGRAPHY: *Giovanni Pacini* (Pescia, 1896); M. Davini, *Il Maestro Giovanni Pacini* (Palermo, 1927); A. Cametti, *Il Corsaro di Pacini* (1931); F. Lippmann, "Giovanni Pacini: Bemerkungen zum Stil seiner Opern," *Chigiana,* XXIV (1967).

Pacini, Leonardo, Italian composer; b. near Pistoia, May 26, 1885; d. Viareggio, April 13, 1937. He was a pupil of Pizzetti at Florence; in 1921, graduated from the Liceo Martini of Bologna. He was a Franciscan friar.

WORKS: Operas: *Alla Muda* (1924; Viareggio, 1925) and *Mirta;* operetta, *Il Pirata* (Viareggio, 1927); oratorios: *Transitus Divi Dominici* (Bologna, 1921) and *Frate Francesco* (Viareggio, 1929); cantatas: *La Sagra dei Caduti* (1922); *Portiuncola Pia; Clara Discipula* (Viareggio, 1924); *Sinfonia del giglio* for Chorus and Orch.; Psalms, motets, and other church music; chamber music; songs; etc.

Paciorkiewicz, Tadeusz, Polish composer and organist; b. Sierpc, Oct. 17, 1916. He studied organ with Rutkowski and composition with Sikorski at the Warsaw Cons. (1936–43). He taught in music schools in Plock (1945–49), Lodz (1949–54), and Warsaw (from 1954).

WORKS: Opera, *Romanza from Gdańsk* (1964); 2 radio operas: *Ushiko* (1962) and *Ligea* (1964); ballet, *Legenda Warszawy* (1959); oratorio, *De revolutionibus* (1972–73; Olsztyn, Feb. 19, 1973); 2 piano concertos (1952, 1954); 2 symphs. (1953, 1957); Violin Concerto (1955); *Duet koncertujacy* for Organ and Orch. (1962); Organ Concerto (1967); *Divertimento* for Clarinet and String Orch. (1968); Trombone Concerto (1971); Viola Concerto (1976); Wind Quintet (1951); Violin Sonata (1954); Bassoon Sonatina (1954); String Quartet (1960); *4 Capriccios (Quasi una sonata)* for Clarinet and Piano (1960); Trio for

Oboe, Clarinet, and Bassoon (1963); Trio for Flute, Viola, and Harp (1966); *6 Miniatures* for 4 Trombones (1972); Piano Quintet (1972); *Duet concertante* for Clarinet and Piano (1973); *Missa brevis* for Chorus and Organ (1973–74); Cello Sonata (1975); *3 Pieces* for Harp (1976); Organ Sonata (1946); 2 piano sonatinas (1952, 1953); songs.

Pacius, Fredrik (Friedrich), German-born Finnish composer; b. Hamburg, March 19, 1809; d. Helsinki, Jan. 8, 1891. He studied violin with Spohr and composition with Hauptmann. He served as a violinist in the Royal Chapel in Stockholm (1828–34); then went to Helsinki, where he organized a choral society (1835) and later (1845) established regular symph. concerts there. Pacius wrote the first Finnish opera, *Kung Karls jakt* (to a Swedish libretto); it was staged in Helsinki on March 24, 1852. He was the author of the Finnish national anthem, *Maamme laulu,* set to the words of the Swedish poem *Vartland,* later trans. into Finnish (1848); he also wrote many other songs of a Swedish-Finnish inspiration. Among his other works are the opera *Loreley* (Helsinki, April 28, 1887); Violin Concerto (1845); numerous choral works and songs.

BIBLIOGRAPHY: M. Collan-Beaurain, *F. Pacius* (Helsinki, 1921); Otto E. Andersson, *Den unge Pacius* (Helsinki, 1938); J. Rosas, *F. Pacius som tonsättare* (Åbo, 1949).

Paderewski, Ignacy (Ignace) Jan, celebrated Polish pianist and composer; b. Kurylowka, Podolia (Russian Poland), Nov. 18, 1860; d. New York, June 29, 1941. His father was an administrator of country estates; his mother died soon after his birth. From early childhood, Paderewski was attracted to piano music; he received some musical instruction from Peter Sowinski, who taught him 4-hands arrangements of operas. His first public appearance was in a charity concert at the age of 11, when he played piano with his sister. His playing aroused interest among wealthy patrons, who took him to Kiev. He was then sent to Warsaw, where he entered the Cons., learned to play trombone, and joined the school band. He also continued serious studies of piano playing; his teachers at the Warsaw Cons. were Schlözer, Strobl, and Janotha. In 1875 and 1877 he toured in provincial Russian towns with the Polish violinist Cielewicz; in the interim periods he took courses in composition at the Warsaw Cons., and upon graduation in 1878 he was engaged as a member of the piano faculty there. In 1880 he married a young music student named Antonina Korsak, but she died 9 days after giving birth to a child, on Oct. 10, 1880. In 1882 he went to Berlin to study composition with Kiel; there he met Anton Rubinstein, who gave him encouraging advice and urged him to compose piano music. He resigned from his teaching job at the Warsaw Cons. and began to study orchestration in Berlin with Heinrich Urban. While on a vacation in the Tatra Mountains (which inspired his *Tatra Album* for piano) he met the celebrated Polish actress Modjeska, who proposed to finance his further piano studies with Leschetiz-

Paderewski

ky in Vienna. Paderewski followed this advice and spent several years as a Leschetizky student. He continued his career as a concert pianist. On March 3, 1888, he gave his first Paris recital, and on Nov. 10, 1888, played a concert in Vienna, both with excellent success. He also began receiving recognition as a composer. Anna Essipoff (who was married to Leschetizky) played his piano concerto in Vienna under the direction of Hans Richter. Paderewski made his London debut on May 9, 1890. On Nov. 17, 1891, he played for the first time in N.Y., and was acclaimed with an adulation rare for pianists; by some counts he gave 107 concerts in 117 days in N.Y. and other American cities and attended 86 dinner parties; his wit, already fully developed, made him a social lion in wealthy American salons. At one party, it was reported, the hostess confused him with a famous polo player who was also expected to be a guest, and greeted him effusively. "No," Paderewski is supposed to have replied, "he is a rich soul who plays polo, and I am a poor Pole who plays solo." American spinsters beseeched him for a lock of his luxurious mane of hair; he invariably obliged, and when his valet observed that at this rate he would soon be bald, he said, "Not I, my dog." There is even a story related by a gullible biographer that Paderewski could charm beasts by his art and that a spider used to come down from the ceiling in Paderewski's lodgings in Vienna and sit at the piano every time Paderewski played a certain Chopin étude. Paderewski eclipsed even Caruso as an idol of the masses. In 1890 he made a concert tour in Germany; also toured South America, South Africa, and Australia. In 1898 he purchased a beautiful home, the Villa Riond-Bosson on Lake Geneva, Switzerland; in 1899 he married Helena Gorska, Baroness von Rosen. In 1900, by a deed of trust, Paderewski established a fund of $10,000 (the original trustees were William Steinway, Major H.L. Higginson, and Dr. William Mason), the interest from which was to be used for triennial prizes given "to composers of American birth without distinction as to age or religion" for works in the following categories: symphonies, concertos, and chamber music. In 1910, on the occasion of the centennial of Chopin's birth, Paderewski donated $60,000 for the construction of the Chopin Memorial Hall in Warsaw; in the same year he contributed $100,000 for the erection of the statue of King Jagiello in Warsaw, on the quinquecentennial of his victory over the Teutonic Knights in 1410. In 1913 he purchased a ranch in Paso Robles in California.

Although cosmopolitan in his culture, Paderewski remained a great Polish patriot. During the First World War he donated the entire proceeds from his concerts to a fund for the Polish people caught in the war between Russia and Germany. After the establishment of the independent Polish state, Paderewski served as its representative in Washington; in 1919 he was named prime minister of the Polish Republic, the first musician to occupy such a post in any country at any period. He took part in the Versailles Treaty conference; it was then that Prime Minister Clemenceau of France welcomed Paderewski with the famous, if possibly apocryphal, remark: "You, a famous pianist, a prime minister! What a comedown!" Paderewski resigned his post on Dec. 10, 1919. He reentered politics in 1920 in the wake of the Russian invasion of Poland that year, when he became a delegate to the League of Nations; he resigned on May 7, 1921, and resumed his musical career. On Nov. 22, 1922, he gave his first concert after a hiatus of many years at Carnegie Hall in N.Y. In 1939 he made his last American tour. Once more during his lifetime Poland was invaded, this time by both Germany and Russia. Once more Paderewski was driven to political action. He joined the Polish government-in-exile in France and was named president of its parliament on Jan. 23, 1940. He returned to the U.S. on Nov. 6, 1940, a few months before his death. At the order of President Roosevelt, his body was given state burial in Arlington National Cemetery, pending the return of his remains to Free Poland. Paderewski received many honors. He held the following degrees: Ph.D. from the Univ. of Lemberg (Lwow, 1912); D.Mus. from Yale Univ. (1917); Ph.D. from the Univ. of Cracow (1919); D.C.L. from Oxford Univ. (1920); LL.D. from Columbia Univ. (1922); Ph.D. from the Univ. of Southern Calif. (1923); Ph.D. from the Univ. of Poznan (1924); and Ph.D. from the Univ. of Glasgow (1925). He also held the Grand Cross of the French Legion of Honor (1922). A postage stamp with his picture was issued in Poland in 1919, and 2 postage stamps honoring him in the series "Men of Liberty" were issued in the U.S. in 1960.

As an artist, Paderewski was a faithful follower of the Romantic school, which allowed free, well-nigh improvisatory declensions from the written notes, tempi, and dynamics; judged by 20th-century standards of precise rendering of the text, Paderewski's interpretations appear surprisingly free, but this very personal freedom of performance moved contemporary audiences to ecstasies of admiration. Also, Paderewski's virtuoso technique, which astonished his listeners, has been easily matched by any number of pianists of succeeding generations. Yet his position in the world of the performing arts remains undiminished by the later achievements of younger men and women pianists. As a composer, Paderewski also belongs to the Romantic school. At least one of his piano pieces, the *Menuet in G* (which is a movement of his set of *6 Humoresques* for piano), achieved enormous popularity. His other compositions, however, never sustained a power of renewal and were eventually relegated to the archives of unperformed music. His opera *Manru*, composed in 1897–1900, dealing with folk life in the Tatra Mountains, was produced in Dresden on May 29, 1901, and was also performed by the Metropolitan Opera in N.Y. on Feb. 14, 1902. Another major work, a Symph. in B minor, was first performed by the Boston Symph. Orch. on Feb. 12, 1909. His other works included a Piano Concerto in A minor (1888); *Fantaisie polonaise* for Piano and Orch. (1893); Violin Sonata (1880); songs; and the following compositions for piano solo: *Prelude and Capriccio; 3 Pieces (Gavotte, Mélodie, Valse mélancholique); Krakowiak; Elégie; 3 Polish Dances; Introduction and*

Toccata; Chants du voyageur (5 pieces); *6 Polish Dances; Album de mai* (5 pieces), *Variations and Fugue; Tatra Album* (also arranged for Piano, 4-hands); *6 Humoresques de concert* (which includes the famous *Menuet in G*); *Dans le désert; Miscellanea* (7 pieces); *Légende;* Sonata in E-flat minor (1903). A complete list of Paderewski's works was publ. in the *Bolletino bibliografico musicale* (Milan, 1932).

BIBLIOGRAPHY: F. Buffen, *Ignacy Paderewski* (N.Y., 1891); C.F. Tretbar, *Paderewski: A Biographical Sketch* (N.Y., 1892); H.T. Fink, *Paderewski and His Art* (N.Y., 1895); A. Nossig, *Paderewski* (Leipzig, 1901); E.A. Baughan, *I. Paderewski* (London, 1908); A.E. Chybiński, *Paderewski* (Warsaw, 1910); S. Popielowna, *Ignacy Paderewski* (Tarnow, 1919); F.H. Martens, *Paderewski* (N.Y., 1923); J.F. Cooke, *Paderewski* (Philadelphia, 1928); *To J. Paderewski* (Kosciuszko Foundation, N.Y., 1928); H. Opieński, *Paderewski* (Warsaw, 1928); B. Sidorowicz, *Ignacy Paderewski* (Poznan, 1924); C. Philips, *Paderewski* (N.Y., 1933); R. Landau, *Paderewski* (N.Y., 1934); *Paderewski's Diamond Anniversary* (N.Y., 1936); Mary Lawton, *The Paderewski Memoirs* (to 1914 only; N.Y., 1938); E. Ligocki, *Homage to Paderewski* (Edinburgh, 1941); A. Gronowicz, *Paderewski: Pianist and Patriot* (Edinburgh, 1943); B. Sarrazin, *Imageries de Paderewski* (Annonay, 1945); S. Giron, *Le drame Paderewski* (Geneva, 1948); A. Baumgartner, *La Vérité sur le prétendu drame Paderewski* (polemical response to Giron's book; Geneva, 1948); A. Strakacz, *Paderewski as I Knew Him* (New Brunswick, N.J., 1949); C. Kellogg, *Paderewski* (N.Y., 1956); J. Cieplinski, *Ignacy Paderewski* (N.Y., 1960); R.F. and P. Hume, *The Lion of Poland: The Story of Paderewski* (N.Y., 1962); R. Halski, *Paderewski* (London, 1964); W. Dulaba, *Ignacy Paderewski* (Cracow, 1966); Adam Zamoyski, *Paderewski* (N.Y., 1982).

Padilla, Lola Artôt de, Spanish soprano, daughter of the baritone **Mariano Padilla y Ramos;** b. Sèvres, near Paris, Oct. 5, 1876; d. Berlin, April 12, 1933. She was trained solely by her mother, the singer **Désirée Artôt.** After singing in salons and concerts, she was engaged by Albert Carré for the Opéra-Comique in 1903. Later she toured as a concert singer through Europe; was engaged at the Komische Oper in Berlin in 1905–8 as prima donna; in 1909–27, was a member of the Royal (later State) Opera in Berlin; then retired.

Padilla y Ramos, Mariano, Spanish baritone; b. Murcia, 1842; d. Auteuil, near Paris, Nov. 23, 1906. He studied with Mabellini in Florence; made his debut in Messina; sang in opera with great success in Italy, Austria, Germany, and Russia. In 1869 he married the singer **Désirée Artôt.**

Paër, Ferdinando, significant composer; b. Parma, June 1, 1771; d. Paris, May 3, 1839. He was a pupil of Fortunati and Ghiretti. His career as an opera composer began in 1792, when he produced the operas *Circe* (Venice) and *Le astuzie amorose* (Parma). In

that year he was also appointed honorary maestro di cappella to the court of Parma. In Vienna, from 1797–1802, his style underwent a change, both harmony and orchestration showing increased variety and fullness; *Camilla, ossia Il sotterraneo* (Vienna, Feb. 23, 1799) is considered his best opera. Paër succeeded Naumann as court Kapellmeister at Dresden in 1802; *Leonara, ossia L'amore conjugale* (Dresden, Oct. 3, 1804) is identical in subject with Beethoven's *Fidelio.* In 1807 he went to Paris, becoming maître de chapelle to Napoleon and conductor of the Opéra-Comique; later (1812) he succeeded Spontini at the Italian Opera, where he remained, through the vicissitudes of Catalini's domination and the joint conductorship of Rossini (1824–26), his successful rival on the stage, until his forced resignation in 1827 (he was held to blame for the poor financial condition of the theater). In 1828 he received the cross of the Legion of Honor; was elected to the Institut in 1831; and in 1832 was appointed conductor of the royal chamber music. Although some of his 43 operas were successful—e.g., *Sargino* (Dresden, May 26, 1803) and *Agnese* (first perf. privately, near Parma, Oct. 1809)—they have all disappeared from the repertoire, except for *Le Maître de chapelle* (Paris, March 29, 1821), which is occasionally performed in France; he also wrote 2 oratorios and a Passion, 10 cantatas, and much other vocal music; a *Symphonie bacchante* and variations on *Vive Henri IV,* for Full Orch.; 4 grand military marches; many piano variations; etc.

BIBLIOGRAPHY: T. Massé and A. Deschamps, *Paër et Rossini* (Paris, 1820); C. de Colobrano, *Funérailles de F. Paër* (Paris, 1893).

Paganelli, Giuseppe Antonio, Italian composer; b. Padua, March 6, 1710; d. Madrid, c.1762. He was employed as a cembalo player in an Italian opera company; was in Venice (1732), then at Bayreuth (1737–38). In 1755 he went to Madrid. He wrote several operas; but his historical importance lies in his works for the harpsichord. His *Divertisement de le Beau Sexe* (6 sonatas) was publ. by Gino Tagliapietra (Milan, 1936).

BIBLIOGRAPHY: F. Torrefranca, "Poeti minori del clavicembalo," *Rivista Musicale Italiana* (1910); E. Schenk, *Giuseppe Antonio Paganelli* (Salzburg, 1928); W. Newman, *The Sonata in the Classic Era* (Chapel Hill, N.C., 1963).

Paganini, Niccolò, most famous of violin virtuosos; b. Genoa, Oct. 27, 1782; d. Nice, May 27, 1840. His father, a poor shopkeeper with little musical knowledge, but loving the art, taught him to play on the mandolin, and then procured abler teachers for his gifted son; under G. Servetto, and after him the maestro di cappella G. Costa, Niccolò's progress in violin playing was rapid; at 8 he composed a sonata for violin; in 1793 he appeared in public; from 1795 he studied with Ghiretti and began to compose seriously. His career as an independent virtuoso dates from 1798, when he ran away from his father after a concert at Lucca, and made a tour by himself to Pisa and other places. Though only 16, he was passionately fond of gambling, and addicted to all forms of dissipation; at Livorno he had to part with his violin to pay a gambling debt, but a French merchant named Levron lent him a fine Guarnerius violin, and was so charmed with his playing that he made him a present of it. In 1804 Paganini went home, and spent a year in assiduous practice; he set out again on his travels in 1805, arousing unbounded enthusiasm; was soon appointed court solo violinist at Lucca (where his novel performances on the G string began), and stayed there until 1808; then up to 1827 he traveled throughout Italy, his renown spreading from year to year and his vast technical resources maturing and augmenting so that victory over would-be rivals (Lafont at Milan, 1816, and Lipinski at Piacenza, 1817) was easy. When he left Italy for the first time in 1828, his opening concert, at Vienna, was a veritable triumph; from the municipality he received the great gold medal of St. Salvator; from the Emperor, the (honorary) title of court virtuoso. He reached Berlin in March 1829, Paris in March 1831; played for the first time in London on June 3, 1831. Within a year he accumulated a fortune in Britain. The winter of 1833–34 was passed in Paris; he then retired for a time to his villa at Parma, though often visiting Paris. He spent the winter of 1838 in Paris, where his chief disorder, laryngeal phthisis, was aggravated by the climate. In search of sun and fresh air he went to Nice, but soon died there.

Paganini's stupendous technique (in double stops, left-hand pizzicato, staccato, harmonics), great power, and perfect control of tone, the romantic passion and intense energy of his style, quite apart from mere tricks of virtuosity (such as tuning up the A string by a semitone or playing the *Witches' Dance* on one string after severing the other 3 on stage, in sight of the audience, with a pair of scissors), made him the marvel of his time. He was an artist quite sui generis, whose dazzling genius held his audiences spellbound, and impressed musicians and amateurs alike.

WORKS: 24 *Capricci per violino solo,* op. 1; (piano transcriptions by Schumann and Liszt); 6 *Sonate per violino e chitarra,* op. 2; same, op. 3; 6 *Gran quartetti a violino, viola, chitarra e violoncello,* opp. 4, 5; Concerto in B minor, *La Campanella,* with rondo "à la clochette," op. 7; *Le Streghe,* variations on a theme by Süssmayr, op. 8; Variations on *God Save the King,* op. 9; *Il Carnevale di Venezia,* 20 variations, op. 10; *Concert allegro moto perpetuo,* op. 11; Variations on *Non più mesta,* op. 12; Variations on *Di tanti palpiti,* op. 13; *Variazioni di bravura* on airs from *Mosè;* 60 studies in 60 progressive variations on the air *Barucabà* (of these only opp. 1–5 were publ. during his life, the others posthumously). A number of works are still in MS. A piece for violin and guitar, written by Paganini in 1815, was publ. in 1977 as his Concerto No. 6, ed. by Ruggiero Ricci. His collected works are being publ. in an Edizione Nazionale, ed. by L. Ronga et al. (1976–).

BIBLIOGRAPHY: J.M. Schottky, *Paganinis Leben und Treiben als Künstler und als Mensch* (Prague and Hamburg, 1830; reprinted 1909); L.F. L'Héritier, *Notice sur le célèbre violiniste N. Paganini* (Paris, 1830; Eng. trans., London, 1830); F.C.J. Schuetz, *Leben, Charakter und Kunst des Ritters N. Paganini* (Illmenau, 1830); K.F. Guhr, *Über Paganinis Kunst, die Violine zu spielen* (Mainz, 1831; Eng. trans. by S. Novello, London, 1831); F.J. Fétis, *Notice biographique sur N. Paganini* (Paris, 1851; Eng. trans., London, 1852); G. Conestabile, *Vita di N. Paganini* (Perugia, 1851; new ed., Milan, 1936); O. Bruni, *N. Paganini, Racconto storico* (Florence, 1873; new ed., 1903); A. Niggli, "N. Paganini," in Waldersee's *Sammlung musikalischer Vorträge* (Leipzig, 1882); S.S. Stratton, *N. Paganini: His Life and Work* (London, 1907); J.-G. Prod'homme, *Paganini* (Paris, 1907; Eng. trans., N.Y., 1911); A. Bonaventura, *N. Paganini* (Modena, 1911); J. Kapp, *N. Paganini* (Berlin, 1913; revised ed., 1928); E. Istel, *Paganini* (1919); J. Siber, *Paganini* (Berlin, 1920); G. Kinsky, "Paganinis musikalischer Nachlass," in the *Heyer Catalogue,* IV (pp. 402–47); L. Day, *Paganini* (N.Y., 1929); A. Günther, *Paganini in Lucca* (Munich, 1929); A. Montanelli, *Paganini a Forlì* (Forlì, 1930); E. Istel, "The Secret of Paganini's Technique," *Musical Quarterly* (Jan. 1930); A. Codingola, *Paganini intimo* (a very important documentary compilation; Genoa, 1935); J. Pulver, *Paganini, the Romantic Virtuoso* (London, 1936); R. de Saussine, *Paganini le magicien* (Paris, 1938; Eng. trans., N.Y., 1954); I. Pizzetti, *N. Paganini* (Turin, 1940); N. Podenzani, *Il romanzo di N. Paganini* (Milan, 1944); M. Tibaldi Chiesa, *Paganini, La vita e l'opera* (3rd ed., Milan, 1944); H. Spivacke, *Paganiniana* (Washington, D.C., 1945); T. Valensi, *Paganini* (Nice, 1950); A. Mell, "Paganiniana in the Muller Collection of the New York Public Library," *Musical Quarterly* (Jan. 1953); G.I.C. de Courcy, *Paganini: The Genoese* (Norman, Okla., 1957); R. de Saussine, *Paganini* (Milan, 1958); A. Codignola, *Arte e magia di Niccolò Paganini* (Milan, 1960); W.G. Armando, *Paganini: Eine Biographie* (Hamburg, 1960); D.F. Botti, *Paganini e Parma* (Parma, 1961); P. Berri, *Paganini: Documenti e testimonianze* (Genoa, 1962); L. Day, *Paganini of Genoa* (London, 1966).

Page, "Hot Lips" (Oran), black American jazz trumpeter; b. Dallas, Jan. 27, 1908; d. New York, Nov. 5, 1954. He took up the trumpet when he was 12 years of age; was a member of the Blue Devils (1927–30); then played in Bennie Moten's band in St. Louis (1931–35) and briefly with Count Basie (1935–36). He was a leading blues trumpeter of his day.

Page, Jimmy, British guitarist; b. Heston, Middlesex, Jan. 9, 1945. He studied art; then turned to guitar and became one of the most successful "ghost guitarists" on records for which others took credit. In 1966 he joined The Yardbirds as a lead guitarist; the group broke up, and Page went over to another band bearing the inexplicable name Led Zeppelin (some rockologists maintain the Led is a deliberate misspelling of Lead, and that Led Zeppelin is a heteronymous appellation for a "heavy metal" sound, like a dirigible that cannot fly). Led Zeppelin led a successful American tour in 1969, precipitating a "heavy metal" craze, and its albums, including songs such as *Communication Breakdown,* sold prodigiously. Another album, *Led Zeppelin II,* containing the hits *Whole Lotta Love* and *Ramble On,* was even more successful. During their fifth American tour in 1970, the group recorded the album *Led Zeppelin III,* which contained the provocative *Immigrant Song.* In 1976 Led Zeppelin issued its certified platinum award album, *Presence.* In America, the group became the greatest crowd-gathering magnet, but in 1980, one of their charter members was found dead, drowned in his own vomit. This was the signal for Led Zeppelin to disgorge.

Page, John, English tenor and anthologist; b. c.1760; d. London, Aug. 16, 1812. He was a lay clerk at St. George's, Windsor; Gentleman of the Chapel Royal; Vicar-choral at St. Paul's (1801). He compiled *Harmonica sacra* (3 vols., 1800; a collection of 74 anthems in score, by eminent English composers of the 16th–18th centuries; new ed. by Rimbault); *Festive Harmony* (4 vols., 1804; madrigals, glees, and elegies); *Collection of Hymns* (1804); *The Burial Service, Chant, Evening Service, Dirge and Anthems App. to be Perf. at the Funeral of Lord Nelson* (1806); anthems, Psalms, etc.

Page, Kate Stearns, American piano pedagogue; b. Brookline, Mass., Aug. 21, 1873; d. New York, Jan. 19, 1963. She taught at the Denison House Settlement in Boston for 10 years and at the Parke School in Brookline, Mass., for 5 years; from 1933 she was a piano teacher at the Diller-Quaile School of Music in N.Y. She publ. valuable pedagogical material, some of it in collaboration with Angela Diller.

Page, Nathaniel Clifford, American music editor; b. San Francisco, Oct. 26, 1866; d. Philadelphia, May 12, 1956. He was a pupil of E. Stillman Kelley; from 1905–9 was an editor for O. Ditson Co. in Boston; from 1909, for C.C. Birchard & Co., Carl Fischer, Theodore Presser, etc.; then again for O. Ditson Co.; from 1921–29, conducted summer classes in orchestration at Columbia Univ. He made a special study of oriental music.
WORKS: Light opera, *The First Lieutenant* (San Francisco, 1889); other stage works; many band and orch. pieces; cantatas; songs; etc. He publ. over 400 vocal and instrumental arrangements of popular pieces.

Page, Patti (born **Clara Ann Fowler**), American pop singer; b. Claremore, Okla., Nov. 8, 1927. She sang in a church choir in Tulsa; then appeared on a local radio program, adopting the name Patti Page. She subsequently went to Chicago. She gained fame with her recording of *Tennessee Waltz* in 1950; also made guest appearances in pop concerts with American orchs.

Page, Robert, American conductor; b. Abilene,

Texas, April 27, 1927. He studied at Abilene Christian College; then received an M.M. from Indiana Univ.; also did advanced study at N.Y. Univ. He was director of choral activities at Temple Univ. in Philadelphia (1956–75); then was chairman of the dept. of music at Carnegie-Mellon Univ. in Pittsburgh (1975–80). In 1971 he became director of choruses of the Cleveland Orch.; in 1979 he was named assistant conductor of the orch., and concurrently he became music director of the Mendelssohn Choir of Pittsburgh. As a guest conductor, he has appeared with the Philadelphia Orch., Pittsburgh Symph., Minnesota Orch., and the orch. of the Teatro Colón in Buenos Aires.

Page, Willis, American conductor; b. Rochester, N.Y., Sept. 18, 1918. He received his musical training at the Eastman School of Music; studied conducting with Pierre Monteux. He served as conductor of the New Orch. Society, Boston (1950–54); then was associate conductor of the Buffalo Phil. (1955–59). From 1959 to 1967 he was music director of the Nashville Symph.; also conducted the Yomiuri Nippon Symph. in Tokyo (1962–63). Later he taught conducting at the Eastman School of Music (1967–69). In 1969 he became music director of the Des Moines Symph.; in 1971 he was appointed music director of the Jacksonville (Fla.) Symph.; acted also as guest conductor with several other orchs.

Pagliughi, Lina, American-born Italian soprano; b. New York, May 27, 1907; d. Rubicone, Oct. 2, 1980. She was encouraged to pursue a career as a singer by Tetrazzini; studied voice in Milan with Manlio Bavagnoli; made her operatic debut at the Teatro Nazionale in Milan as Gilda in 1927; then made appearances throughout Italy; sang at La Scala in Milan in 1930, and continued to make appearances there until 1947; then sang with Italian Radio until her retirement in 1956. She was married to the tenor **Primo Montanari.** She was best known for her roles in operas by Rossini, Bellini, and Donizetti.

Pahissa, Jaime, Catalan composer; b. Barcelona, Oct. 7, 1880; d. Buenos Aires, Oct. 27, 1969. He was a practicing architect for 4 years before turning to music as a profession; studied composition with Morera in Barcelona. He associated himself with the Catalan nationalist movement in art, obtaining his first important success in 1906 with the Romantic opera *La presó de Lleida (The Prison of Lérida),* which had 100 consecutive performances in Barcelona; it was later rewritten and produced in Barcelona on Feb. 8, 1928, under the title *La Princesa Margarita,* again obtaining a notable success. Other operas produced in Barcelona were *Gala Plácida* (Jan. 15, 1913) and *Marinela* (March 31, 1923). Among his orch. works the most remarkable is *Monodia,* written in unisons, octaves, double octaves, etc., without using any other intervals, and depending for its effect only on instrumental variety (Barcelona, Oct. 12, 1925); in a different vein is his *Suite Intertonal* (Barcelona, Oct. 24, 1926), based on his own method of free tonal and polytonal composition. In 1935 Pahissa emigrated to Argentina, settling in Buenos Aires, where he continued to compose; he also established himself as a teacher and writer there. He publ. in Buenos Aires several books: *Espíritu y cuerpo de la música* (1945); *Los grandes problemas de la música* (1945; new ed., 1954); *Vida y obra de Manuel de Falla* (Buenos Aires, 1947; also in Eng., London, 1954); *Sendas y cumbres de la música española* (1955). A detailed account of Pahissa's career in Barcelona is found in the *Diccionario de la música ilustrado* (1930).

Pahlen, Kurt, Austrian writer on music; b. Vienna, May 26, 1907. He studied at the Vienna Cons., and also at the Univ. of Vienna (with Guido Adler, Lach, and Orel), graduating in 1929. In 1939 he settled in Buenos Aires, where he became a successful teacher and writer on musical subjects; he publ. a music history: *Historia gráfica universal de la música* (Buenos Aires, 1944; in Eng. as *Music of the World*, N.Y., 1949); also a general manual of musical knowledge, *Síntesis del saber musical* (Buenos Aires, 1948); *Ins Wunderland der Musik* (Zürich, 1948); *Manuel de Falla und die Musik in Spanien* (Olten, 1953); *Musiklexikon der Welt* (Zürich, 1956).

Paik, Nam June, Korean-American avant-garde composer and experimenter in the visual arts; b. Seoul, July 20, 1932. He studied first at the Univ. of Tokyo; then went to Germany, where he took courses in music theory with Thrasybulos Georgiades in Munich and with Wolfgang Fortner in Freiburg im Breisgau. Turning toward electronics, he did experimental work at the Electronic Music Studio in Cologne (1958–60); attended the summer seminars for new music at Darmstadt (1957–61). In his showings he pursues the objective of total art as the sum of integrated synesthetic experiences, involving all sorts of actions—walking, talking, dressing, undressing, drinking, smoking, moving furniture, engaging in quaquaversal commotion—intended to demonstrate that any human or inhuman action becomes an artistic event through the power of volitional concentration of an ontological imperative. Paik attracted attention at his duo recitals with the topless cellist Charlotte Moorman, at which he acted as a surrogate cello, with his denuded spinal column serving as the fingerboard for Ms. Moorman's cello bow, while his bare skin provided an area for intermittent pizzicati. About 1963 Paik began experimenting with videotape as a medium for sounds and images; his initial experiment in this field was *Global Groove,* a high-velocity collage of intermingled television bits, which included instantaneous commercials, fragments from news telecasts, and subliminal extracts from regular programs, subjected to topological alterations. His list of works (some of them consisting solely of categorical imperatives) includes *Ommaggio a Cage* for piano demolition, breakage of raw eggs, spray painting of hands in jet black, etc. (Düsseldorf, Nov. 13, 1959); *Symphony for 20 Rooms* (1961); *Variations on a Theme of Saint-Saëns* for Cello and Piano, with the pianist playing *Le Cygne* while the cellist dives into an oil drum filled with water (N.Y., Aug. 25, 1965, composer at the keyboard, cellist Charlotte Moorman in the oil drum); *Performable Music,* wherein the performer is ordered to make with a razor an incision of no less than 10 centimeters on his left forearm (Los Angeles, Dec. 2, 1965); *Opéra sextronique* (1967); *Opéra électronique* (1968); *Creep into the Vagina of a Whale* (c.1969); *Young Penis Symphony,* a protrusion of 10 erectile phalluses through a paper curtain (c.1970; produced for the first time at "La Mamelle" in San Francisco, Sept. 21, 1975, under the direction of Ken Friedman, who also acted as one of the 10 performers). Of uncertain attribution is a symph. designated as No. 3, which Paik delegated to Ken Friedman, who worked on it in Saugus, Calif., the epicenter of the earthquake of Feb. 9, 1971, and of which the earthquake itself constituted the finale.

BIBLIOGRAPHY: Calvin Tomkins, "Video Visionary," *New Yorker* (May 5, 1975); autobiographical note in *Source,* 11 (1973).

Pailliard, Jean-François, noted French conductor; b. Vitry-le-François, April 18, 1928. He received his musical training at the Paris Cons.; later took courses in conducting with Igor Markevitch at the Salzburg Mozarteum. In 1953 he founded the Jean-François Pailliard Chamber Orch., with which he toured widely. He also acted as a guest conductor in Europe and America. In 1970 he appeared with the Osaka Phil. in Japan. He was furthermore active as an editor of Baroque music, including works by Corelli, Torelli, and Delalande.

Paine, John Knowles, American composer and teacher; b. Portland, Maine, Jan. 9, 1839; d. Cambridge, Mass., April 25, 1906. His father kept a music store in Portland, and conducted the local band. Paine's first music teacher was H. Kotzschmar. He then went to Berlin and studied under Haupt (counterpoint), Fischer (singing), and Wieprecht (instrumentation) from 1858 to 1861. After organ concerts in Berlin and various American cities, he settled in Boston as organist of the West Church on Cambridge St. In 1862 he became a teacher of music at Harvard Univ., and organist at Appleton Chapel in Cambridge, Mass.; from 1875 until his death he occupied the newly created professorship of music at Harvard, the first in any American univ. In 1866–67 he toured Germany and conducted his Mass at Berlin. He was awarded the honorary degrees of M.A. (Harvard, 1869) and Mus.Doc. (Yale, 1890). He was one of the most notable pioneers in American musical development. Among his many pupils were J.A. Carpenter, A. Foote, E.B. Hill, F.S. Converse, H.T. Finck, and D.G. Mason.

WORKS: *Domine salvum fac* for Men's Chorus and Orch. (1863); Mass in D for Soli, Chorus, and Orch.; oratorio, *St. Peter; Centennial Hymn* for Chorus and Orch. (Philadelphia, 1876); music to *Œdipus tyrannus* (Sophocles) for Men's Voices and Orch.; *The Realm of Fancy,* cantata for Soprano Solo, Chorus, and Orch.; *Phœbus, arise; The Nativity,* cantata for Soli, Chorus, and Orch.; *Song of*

Promise, cantata for Soprano, Chorus, and Orch.; incidental music to *The Birds* of Aristophanes; *Columbus March and Hymn,* for the Chicago Exposition (1893); *Hymn of the West,* for the St. Louis Exposition (1904); 2 symphs.: in C minor and in A (*Spring Symphony;* Cambridge, Mass., March 10, 1880); 2 symph. poems: *The Tempest* and *An Island Fantasy;* overture to *As You Like It; Duo concertante* for Violin and Cello, with Orch.; String Quartet; Piano Trio; Larghetto and Scherzo for Piano, Violin, and Cello; Romanza and Scherzo for Piano and Cello; Sonata for Piano and Violin; characteristic pieces for piano; variations and fantasias for organ; motets, part-songs, and songs. An opera, *Azara* (text by himself), was publ. in 1901, and had a concert performance in Boston in 1907. He wrote *The History of Music to the Death of Schubert* (posthumous, 1907). His *Lecture Notes* was publ. in 1885.

BIBLIOGRAPHY: G.T. Edwards, *Music and Musicians of Maine* (1928); M.A.DeW. Howe, "J.K. Paine," *Musical Quarterly* (July 1939); K. Roberts, *John Knowles Paine* (Diss., Univ. of Michigan, 1962); John C. Schmidt, *The Life and Works of John Knowles Paine* (N.Y., 1980).

Paisible, Louis Henri, French violinist and composer; b. St. Cloud, near Paris, July 21, 1748; d. St. Petersburg, March 19, 1782 (suicide). He studied with Gaviniès; played in the orch. of the Concert Spirituel in Paris; then traveled through Europe; in 1778 was engaged at the Russian court in St. Petersburg. Although well received at first, he was unable to make headway with a series of concerts for which he solicited subscriptions; deprived of resources, he shot himself. Twelve of his string quartets and 2 violin concertos have been publ. in Paris and London.

BIBLIOGRAPHY: A. Mooser, *Annales de la musique et des musiciens en Russie au XVIIIᵉ siècle* (Geneva, 1950; vol. II, pp. 274–78).

Paisiello, Giovanni, famous Italian composer; b. Taranto, May 9, 1740; d. Naples, June 5, 1816. From the age of 5 he studied at the Jesuit school in Taranto, where he was taught by a priest, Resta, and where his singing so delighted Guaducci, maestro at the Capuchin church, that he advised the boy's father to place him in the Cons. di S. Onofrio at Naples. There he studied under Durante, Cotumacci, and Abos, from 1754 to 1759, remaining 4 years longer as a teacher, and occupying himself with sacred composition (masses, oratorios, etc.). But a comic intermezzo performed at the Cons. in 1763 disclosed such dramatic talent that he was commissioned to write an opera for the Marsigli Theater at Bologna; here his first comic opera was produced, *La pupilla, ossia Il mondo alla rovescia* (1764). For 12 years, during which he brought out some 50 operas, his successes were many and reverses few, even in rivalry with Piccinni and Cimarosa. Important works of this period are *Le finte Contesse* (Rome, Feb. 1766), *L'idolo cinese* (Naples, Spring 1767), and *La Frascatana* (Venice, Nov. 1774). Invit-

ed to St. Petersburg by Empress Catherine II in 1776, he lived there 8 years on a princely salary; he produced several operas, including *Il Barbiere di Siviglia* (St. Petersburg, Sept. 26, 1782), which became so popular in Italy that it still stood as a rival to Rossini's masterpiece in 1816. During the next 15 years he acted as maestro di cappella to Ferdinand IV of Naples (1784–99); of his productions of this period, especially noteworthy are *Il Re Teodoro in Venezia* (Vienna, Aug. 23, 1784; perhaps his best opera), *Le Gare generose* (Naples, Spring 1786), *L'amor contrastato* (later called *La Molinara;* Naples, Summer 1788), *Nina, o La Pazza per amore* (Caserta, June 25, 1789; a charming "opera semiseria," a genre in which Paisiello excelled), and *I Zingari in fiera* (Naples, Nov. 21, 1789). During the revolutionary period of 1799–1801 Paisiello stood well with the republican government, but lost the favor of the King, together with his place and salary. In 1802–3 he was Napoleon's maître de chapelle at Paris. From 1803 until the Bourbon restoration of 1815, he held his former position at Naples, and other posts of importance, all of which later he lost on Ferdinand's return in 1815, being retained solely as maestro di cappella. Paisiello was an extraordinarily productive composer, and one of the most popular of his time; yet of his 100 or more operas, only a few are ever revived nowadays. His vein of melody was original, fresh, and natural; although he introduced instrumental effects that were novel in Italy, he carefully avoided the overelaborate numbers common to the period, obtaining his effect by the grace, beauty, and dramatic truthfulness of his melody.

WORKS: Operas: *Il Marchese di Tulipano; La Serva padrona; Il Barbiere de Siviglia; Il Re Teodoro; La Molinara; Nina; Proserpine.* Church music: Passion oratorio (Warsaw, 1784); 3 solemn masses for Double Choir and 2 Orchs.; Te Deum for the same; Requiem for 4 Voices and Orch. (perf. at his own funeral); 30 masses for the same; 2 5-part masses; *Dixit,* Magnificat, *Miserere,* about 40 motets with Orch.; etc. Instrumental music: 12 symphs.; funeral march for Gen. Hoche; 6 piano concertos; 12 piano quartets; 6 string quartets; Sonata and Concerto for Harp; 2 vols. of sonatas, caprices, etc., for piano.

BIBLIOGRAPHY: I.F. Arnold, *G. Paisiello: Seine kurze Biographie* (Erfurt, 1810); J.F. Lesueur, *Notice sur Paisiello* (Paris, 1816); Gagliardo, *Onori funebri ... di Paisiello* (Naples, 1816); Quatremère de Quincy, *Notice historique de Paisiello* (Paris, 1817); F. Schizzi, *Della vita a degli studi di G. Paisiello* (Milan, 1833); C.G. Pupino, *Paisiello* (Naples, 1908); S. Panareo, *Paisiello in Russia* (Trani, 1910); H. Abert, "Paisiellos Buffokunst und ihre Beziehungen zu Mozart," *Archiv für Musikwissenschaft,* I/3 (1919); A. Della Corte, *Settecento italiano: Paisiello* (Turin, 1922); F. Barberio, "I primi dieci anni di vita artistica di Paisiello," *Rivista Musicale Italiana* (1922); A. Cametti, *Paisiello e la corte di Vienna* (Rome, 1929); G.C. Speciale, *G. Paisiello* (Naples, 1931); P. Petrosellini, *Il Barbiere di Siviglia di G. Paisiello* (1932); A. Loewenberg, "Paisiello's and Rossini's *Barbiere di Siviglia,*" *Music & Letters*

(April 1939); E. Faustini-Fasini, *Opere teatrali, oratori e cantate di G. Paisiello* (Bari, 1940); M.F. Robinson, *Naples and Neapolitan Opera* (London, 1972).

Paita, Carlos, Argentine conductor; b. Buenos Aires, March 10, 1932. He studied with Juan Neuchoff and with Jacobo Fischer. Impressed by Furtwängler's concerts in Argentina, he decided to study conducting. He became moderately successful in his ambitious plans; conducted concerts with the National Radio Orch. in Argentina and opera at the Teatro Colón. He then went to Europe to pursue his career. In 1966 he led the Stuttgart Radio Symph.; in 1979 he made his American debut with the Houston Symph. A musician of passionate Latin temperament, he often aroused wonderment among Anglo-Saxon audiences in the U.S., but he was invariably successful in Buenos Aires.

Pakhmutova, Alexandra, Soviet composer; b. Beketovka, near Stalingrad, Nov. 9, 1929. She studied at the Moscow Cons. with Shebalin, graduating in 1953. She was particularly successful in the genre of urban ballads, close to contemporary reality; of these, especially popular were her *Songs of Turbulent Youth* (1961); *Cuba, My Love,* (1962); *Keep Your Heart Young* (1963); *Young Eagles Learn to Fly* (1965); *A Coward Will Not Play Hockey* (1968); *Let Us Embrace the Sky* (1966); *Gagarin's Constellation* (1971); *Sport Heroes* (1972); *Hope* (1974). Her Trumpet Concerto acquired great popularity in Russia.
WORKS: For the stage: Ballet, *Lucid Vision* (1973). For Orch.: *Russian suite* (1952); Trumpet Concerto (Moscow, June 11, 1955); Concerto for Orch. (1971). For Voice: *Lenin Is in Our Hearts,* suite for Narrator, Children's Chorus, and Orch. (1957); *Young Pioneer Songs,* cantata (1972); choruses; songs. Chamber music: *4 Miniatures on Russian Folk Themes* for String Quartet (1950); *Nocturne* for Horn and Piano (1956).
BIBLIOGRAPHY: E. Dobrynina, *Alexandra Pakhmutova* (Moscow, 1973).

Paladilhe, Emile, French composer; b. Montpellier, June 3, 1844; d. Paris, Jan. 6, 1926. He entered the Paris Cons. in 1853; was a pupil of Marmontel (piano), Benoist (organ), and Halévy (counterpoint); won first prize for piano and organ in 1857; won the Grand Prix de Rome in 1860 with the cantata *Le Czar Ivan IV* (Paris Opéra, 1860). He brought out the one-act comic opera *Le Passant* at the Opéra-Comique (April 24, 1872), followed by *L'Amour africain* (May 8, 1875); *Suzanne* (Dec. 30, 1878); *Diana* (Feb. 23, 1885); the 5-act opera *Patrie* (Opéra, Dec. 20, 1886); and *Les Saintes Maries de la mer,* a sacred lyric drama (Montpellier, 1892). He also produced 2 masses; Symph. in E-flat; some sacred music; numerous songs (*Mandolinata, Premières pensées, Mélodies écossaises*). In 1892 he succeeded Guiraud as member of the Institut de France.

Palange, Louis Salvador. American conductor, composer, and arranger, of Italian descent; b. Oakland, Calif., Dec. 17, 1917; d. Burbank, June 8, 1979. He played the clarinet and bassoon in school bands; in 1936 went to Los Angeles, where he took lessons with Wesley La Violette. In 1955 he became conductor of the Beach Cities Symph. Orch.; in 1965, formed the Southeast Symph. Continuing to accumulate orch. groups, he assumed in 1967 the direction of 3 more orchs.: the Downey Symph. Orch., Hollywood-Wilshire Symph. Orch., and Metropolitan Symph. Orch. of Los Angeles.
WORKS: *Symphony in Steel* for Band (Los Angeles, March 8, 1941); Symph. No. 1, *Invasion Symphony,* (1946); Violin Concerto (1950); String Quartet (1950); *Hollywood Panorama,* tone poem (Burbank, Sept. 21, 1952); *A Romantic Piano Concert* (Cleveland, May 13, 1954); *Poker Deck Ballet Suite* for Orch. (Redondo Beach, Calif., Dec. 9, 1960); Symph. No. 2 (Los Angeles, March 22, 1968).

Palau, Manuel, Spanish composer and conductor; b. Valencia, Jan. 4, 1893; d. there, Feb. 18, 1967. He studied first at the Cons. of Valencia; later in Paris, where he took lessons from Koechlin and Ravel. Returning to Valencia, he established himself as a teacher, conductor, and composer. Most of his thematic material is inspired by Catalan folk songs; his instrumental music usually bears programmatic content; his technique of composition follows the French impressionist procedures.
WORKS: Zarzuelas: *Beniflors, Amor torna,* etc.; *Gongoriana,* orch. suite (1927); 2 symphs.; *Concierto levantino* for Guitar and Orch.; *Homenaje a Debussy* for Orch.; Sonata for Guitar Solo; numerous songs of a popular nature; piano pieces: *Valencia, Levantina, Sonatina Valenciana, 3 impresiones fugaces, Campanas y paisaje balear, Danza hispalense, Danza iberica, Evocación de Andalucía,* etc.
BIBLIOGRAPHY: A. Mingote, *Manuel Palau* (Valencia, 1946); F.J. León Tello, *La obra pianistica de Manuel Palau* (Valencia, 1956).

Palazzesi, Matilde, Italian soprano; b. Montecarotto, March 1, 1802; d. Barcelona, July 3, 1842. She studied with Giacomo Solarto in Pesaro; made her debut in 1824 in Dresden; sang with the Italian Opera there until 1833; then appeared at La Scala in Milan and other Italian opera houses; went to Barcelona, where she sang at the Opera from 1841. She was a leading interpreter of soprano roles in the operas of Rossini, Bellini, Donizetti, and Spontini.

Páleníček, Josef, Czech composer and pianist; b. Travnik, July 19, 1914. He studied with Otakar Šín and Vítězslav Novák at the Prague Cons.; then went to Paris and took lessons with Albert Roussel (1936–37). He traveled as pianist in the Czech Trio; in 1963 was appointed to the staff of the Prague Cons. In 1977 he received the State Prize for his interpretations of Janáček's piano works, his specialty.
WORKS: 3 piano concertos: No. 1, with String Orch. and Timpani (1939); No. 2 (1953); No. 3, for young pianists, with Small Orch. (1961); Saxophone

Concerto (1944); Concertino for Orch. (1937–45); Flute Concerto (1955); *Concertino da camera* for Clarinet and Orch. (1957); *Symphonic Variations on an Imaginary Portrait of Ilya Ehrenburg* for Orch. (1971); Cello Concerto (1973); oratorio, *Song of Man* (1952–58); Piano Quintet (1933); *Preludium a capriccio* for Violin and Piano (1935); Clarinet Sonatina (1936); *Choral Variations* for Cello and Piano (1942); *Little Suite* for Clarinet and Piano (1943); String Quartet No. 1 (1954); *Masks*, 2 pieces for Saxophone and Piano (1957); *Little Suite* for Violin and Piano (1958); *Trio Sonata* for Mezzo-soprano, Oboe, and Piano (1965); *Variations* for Cello and Piano (1972); *Rondo concertante* for Cello and Piano (1972); *In modo antico,* suite for Cello and Guitar (1973); Piano Sonata (1936); *Piano Sketchbook,* cycle of 5 pieces (1939); instructive works for children.

Palester, Roman, Polish composer; b. Śniatyñ, Dec. 28, 1907. He studied with Soltys at the Cons. of Lwow and with Sikorski at the Warsaw Cons.; he went to France in 1925, and after a brief visit in Poland, settled in Paris. In his music Palester adopted the modernistic devices of the French school, but preserved elements of Polish folk songs in the thematic structure of his works; harmonically he did not choose to transcend the limits of enhanced tonality. Several of his works were performed at festivals of the International Society for Contemporary Music: *Symphonic Music* (London, July 27, 1931); *Danse polonaise* for Orch. (Barcelona, April 22, 1936); Violin Concerto (London, July 14, 1946). Other works are: 5 symphs.: No. 1 (1935); No. 2 (1942); No. 3 for 2 Chamber Orchs. (1948); No. 4 (1951; revised 1971); No. 5 (1970–72); *Requiem* (1948); Sonatina for 3 Clarinets (1936); Concertino for Piano and Orch. (1942); *Serenade* for 2 Flutes and String Orch. (Cracow, Nov. 9, 1947); 2 string trios (1946, 1958); *Sonnets for Orpheus* for Voice and Chamber Orch. (1952); *Passacaglia* for Orch. (1953); *Variations* for Orch. (1955); Concertino for Harpsichord and Instrumental Ensemble (1955); one-act opera, *La Mort de Don Juan* (1959–60; Brussels, 1965); *Varianti* for 2 Pianos (1963); *Metamorphoses* for Orch. (1965–66); 2 piano sonatas (1968, 1975); Trio for Flute, Viola, and Harp (1969); Duo for 2 Violins (1972); *Suite à quatre* for Oboe and String Trio (1973); *Passacaglia and Variations* for Piano (1974); *Songs,* after Milosz, for Soprano and Chamber Orch. (1976); Viola Concerto (1977–78); *Te Deum* for 3 Choirs and Instruments (1978–79).

Palestrina (Giovanni Pierluigi, called da Palestrina), the greatest composer of the Catholic Church and of the Roman School; b. Palestrina, near Rome, c.1525; d. Rome, Feb. 2, 1594. He was a chorister at the Cathedral of his native town c.1532; in 1534, when Cardinal della Valle, Bishop of Palestrina, was made Archbishop of S. Maria Maggiore in Rome, he took Palestrina with him and entered him in the choir school of that church. In 1537 we find him listed as an elder choirboy; in 1539, his voice having broken, he left the choir and returned home. But by 1540, or soon after, he was back in Rome, studying music; his teacher may have been Firmin Le Bel, choirmaster of S. Maria Maggiore. In 1544 he was appointed organist and choirmaster at the Cathedral of St. Agapit in Palestrina; the bishop there was Cardinal del Monte, who in 1550 became Pope under the name of Julius III, and who in 1551 bestowed upon Palestrina the post of maestro of the Cappella Giulia. Meanwhile, Palestrina had married (June 12, 1547) and had become father of 2 sons. In 1554 he publ. his first book of masses, dedicated to Julius III, who rewarded him by making him a member of the Pontifical Choir (Jan. 1555); this aroused much resentment, for Palestrina was admitted without taking the entrance examination, and it is said that he had a poor voice. A few months later he was dismissed with a small pension by the new Pope, Paul V, on the ground that he was a married man. He then received the appointment of maestro of the church of St. John Lateran, for which he wrote his celebrated *Lamentations.* In 1560 he resigned this post, and in March of the following year he became maestro of S. Maria Maggiore. In 1563 his first book of motets was publ. About this time the Council of Trent concerned itself with the reform of church music, decreeing the exclusion of all profane and impure elements; contrapuntal music, which lent itself to many abuses, might also have been forbidden, had it not been for the determined opposition of the Emperor Ferdinand I. Palestrina's role in influencing the decisions of the Council, especially as regards the proposed exclusion of contrapuntal music, has been grossly exaggerated and misrepresented by most historians, beginning with Baini. Palestrina's famous *Missa Papae Marcelli* is undoubtedly a model of the purest religious style; but there is no evidence that it played much part in shaping the fate of church music at that time. From 1565 to 1571 Palestrina was music director at the new Roman Seminary, where his elder sons were students. In 1567 he resigned his post at S. Maria Maggiore and entered the service of Cardinal Ippolito d'Este (d. 1572). In 1568 the Emperor Maximilian offered him the post of maestro at the court of Vienna, but Palestrina demanded so high a salary that the matter was dropped. In 1571 he resumed his old post as maestro of the Cappella Giulia, retaining this office until his death. In 1576 Pope Gregory XIII issued a decree for the revision of the Gradual, which was to be carried out by Palestrina and Annibale Zoilo; but the revised version, known as the "Medicean Gradual," was not printed until 20 years after Palestrina's death (1614). In 1580, having suffered several family bereavements, including the death of his wife, Palestrina decided to enter the priesthood; but soon he changed his mind, and on March 28, 1581, he married the widow of a prosperous furrier. He then took a partner and successfully carried on the fur business. In 1583 he was invited to become maestro at the court of Mantua, but again his terms were rejected as too high. In 1584 he brought out his settings of the Song of Solomon, and in 1589 his harmonized version of the Latin Hymnal was publ. At his death he was buried in the Cappella Nuova of old St.

Peter's Church. In his music Palestrina aimed at technical smoothness and beauty of sound rather than at forceful expression and originality. In the "Motu Proprio" (1903) of Pope Pius X, on sacred music, Palestrina's works are recommended as "of excellent quality from a liturgical and musical standpoint."

WORKS: A monumental ed. of his complete compositions was publ. by Breitkopf & Härtel in 33 vols. (1862–1907), comprising 181 motets, 113 hymns and offertories, 93 masses, 9 Lamentations, 10 litanies, 4 Psalms, 35 Magnificats, 83 secular madrigals, 56 Italian sacred madrigals, miscellaneous compositions, and documents. After the completion of this great ed., the same firm began the separate publication of several of the most famous works. Breitkopf & Härtel also publ. a special catalogue. A new collected ed. was begun in 1939 under the editorship of R. Casimiri, reaching 32 vols. as of 1977.

BIBLIOGRAPHY: G. Baini, *Memorie storico-critiche della vita e delle opere di G.P. a Palestrina* (2 vols., Rome, 1828.; German trans., abridged, Leipzig, 1834); K. von Winterfeld, *Joh. P. von Palestrina* (Breslau, 1832); W. Bäumker, *Palestrina* (Freiburg, 1887); correspondence with the Duke of Mantua, in *Kirchenmusikalisches Jahrbuch* (1886); P. Wagner, *Palestrina als weltlicher Komponist* (Strasbourg, 1890); F.X. Haberl, "Die Kardinals-Kommission von 1564 und Palestrinas *Missa Papae Marcelli*," *Kirchenmusikalisches Jahrbuch* (1892); Ph. Spitta, "Palestrina im 16. und 19. Jahrhundert," *Deutsche Rundschau* (July 1894); F.X. Haberl, *G.P. da Palestrina e il Graduale romanum officiale dell'editio medicaea (1614)* (Regensburg, 1894); A. Cametti, *Cenni biografici di G.P. da Palestrina* (Milan, 1895); G. Félix, *Palestrina et la musique sacrée (1594–1894)* (Lille, 1896); C. Respighi, *Nuovo studio su G.P. da Palestrina e l'emendazione del Graduale romano* (Rome, 1899); A. Cametti, "Un nuovo documento sulle origini di G.P. da Palestrina," *Rivista Musicale Italiana* (1903); Michel Brenet, *Palestrina* (Paris, 1905); J. Gloger, *Die "Missa Prima." Eine Studie über den Palestrinastil* (Leobschütz, 1910); E. Schmitz, *G.P. Palestrina* (Leipzig, 1914); K. Weinmann, *Palestrinas Geburtsjahr* (Regensburg, 1915); R. Casimiri, *G.P. da Palestrina. Nuovi documenti biografici* (Rome, 1918); idem, *Il "Codice 59" dell'archivio musicale lateranense* (Rome, 1919); Zoë K. Pyne, *G.P. da Palestrina. His Life and Times* (London, 1922); A. Cametti, *G.P. da Palestrina e il suo commercio di pelliccerie* (Rome, 1922); idem, "G.P. da Palestrina e le sue alleanze matrimoniali," *Rivista Musicale Italiana* (1923); idem, *Le Case dei Pierluigi in Palestrina* (Rome, 1925); idem, *Palestrina* (Milan, 1925); idem, "Bibliografia palestriniana," *Bollettino Bibliografico Musicale* (Sept. 1926); K. Jeppesen, *The Style of Palestrina and the Dissonance* (Danish, 1923; German, 1925; Eng., 1927; 2nd Eng. ed., 1946); idem, in the P. Wagner-Festschrift (1926), Adler-Festschrift (1930), and Liège Kongress-Bericht (1931); L.P. Manzetti, "Palestrina," *Musical Quarterly* (July 1928); K.G. Fellerer, *Palestrina* (Regensburg, 1930; 2nd ed., Düsseldorf, 1960); F. Raugel, *Palestrina* (Paris, 1930); W. Widmann, "Die 6-stimmigen Messen Palestrinas," *Kir-*

chenmusikalisches Jahrbuch (1930–31); O. Ursprung, *Die katholische Kirchenmusik* (1933); H. Coates, *Palestrina* (London, 1938); O. Strunk, "Guglielmo Gonzaga and Palestrina's *Missa Dominicalis*," *Musical Quarterly* (April 1947); J. Samson, *Palestrina ou La Poésie de l'exactitude* (Geneva, 1950); K. Jeppesen, "The Recently Discovered Mantova Masses of Palestrina," *Acta Musicologica* (1950); A.I.M. Kat, *Palestrina* (Haarlem, 1951); G. Reese, *Music in the Renaissance* (N.Y., 1954); H.K. Andrews, *An Introduction to the Technique of Palestrina* (London, 1958); K. Jeppesen, "Palestrina," in *Die Musik in Geschichte und Gegenwart;* R.L. Marshall, "The Paraphrase Technique of Palestrina in His Masses Based on Hymns," *Journal of the American Musicological Society* (1963); T. Day, "Echoes of Palestrina's *Missa ad fugam* in the Eighteenth Century," ibid. (Fall 1971); L. Lockwood, Norton Critical Score ed. of *Pope Marcellus Mass,* containing score, backgrounds, and analyses (N.Y., 1975).

Palisca, Claude Victor, American musicologist; b. Fiume, Yugoslavia, Nov. 24, 1921. He came to the U.S. in 1930; attended public schools in N.Y. and Florida; studied at Queens College (B.A., 1943) with Karol Rathaus (composition) and at Harvard Univ. with Walter Piston and Randall Thompson (composition) and with Otto Kinkeldey, Gombosi, and Davison (musicology); obtained his M.A. in 1948, and his Ph.D. in 1954 with the dissertation *The Beginnings of Baroque Music: Its Roots in Sixteenth-century Theory and Polemics.* He was a member of the faculty at the Univ. of Illinois at Urbana (1953–59); in 1959 joined the staff of Yale Univ. He held a John Knowles Paine Traveling Fellowship (1949–50), a Fulbright grant for Italy (1950–52), and a Guggenheim fellowship (1960–61).

WRITINGS: *Girolamo Mei: Letters on Ancient and Modern Music to Vincenzo Galilei and Giovanni Bardi* (Rome, 1960); *17th-Century Science and the Arts* (with others; Princeton, 1961); *Musicology* (with others; Englewood Cliffs, N.J., 1963); *Baroque Music* (Englewood Cliffs, N.J., 1968); trans. (with G.A. Marco) Gioseffo Zarlino's *Le istitutioni harmoniche* (Part 3, 1558; New Haven, 1968); ed. *Norton Anthology of Western Music* (N.Y., 1980).

Palkovský, Oldřich, Czech composer; b. Brušperk, Feb. 24, 1907. He studied composition with Petrželka at the Brno Cons. (1926–31) and with Suk at the Prague Cons. (1931–33); was director of the State Testing Commission for Music (1939–54) and taught at the Kroměříž branch of the Brno Cons.

WORKS: 6 symphs. (1933–34, 1939, 1944, 1947, 1956–57, 1962); Concerto for Cimbalom and Small Orch. (1952–53); *Scherzo capriccio* for Orch. (1953); *Morvarian Dances* for Orch. (1956); *Variations and Fugue* for Cimbalom, String Orch., and Timpani (1959); Flute Concerto (1959); Oboe Concerto (1961); Accordion Concerto (1961); *3 Symphonic Movements* (1971); 6 string quartets (1931, 1933, 1937, 1957, 1962, 1970); 2 piano trios (1940, 1968); Violin Sonata (1942); Viola Sonata (1944); Concertino for

Winds (1945); Cello Sonata (1946); Clarinet Sonata (1947); 2 wind quintets (1949, 1958); Quartet for Flute, Violin, Viola, and Cello (1950); Horn Sonata (1963); *Chamber Music* for 8 Instruments (1964); *Balladic Sonata* for Bassoon and Piano (1969); *Sonnets* for Flute, Bass Clarinet, and Piano (1969); piano pieces; songs.

Palkovský, Pavel, Czech composer, son of **Oldřich Palkovský;** b. Zlín, Dec. 18, 1939. He studied composition with Schaefer at the Brno Cons., graduating in 1960, and with Kapr at the Janáček Academy of Music in Brno, graduating in 1964.
WORKS: Cello Sonata (1963); 2 symphs.: No. 1 (1964) and No. 2 for Piano and Orch. (1968–69); *Chamber Music I* for Strings, Piano, and Percussion (1964); *Chamber Music II* for Piano, Organ, Celesta, and Percussion (1968); Horn Sonata (1967); *3 Studies* for Accordion and 9 Winds (1969); Trio for 3 Accordions (1969).

Pallantios, Menelaos, Greek composer and pedagogue; b. Piraeus, Jan. 29, 1914. He studied with Mitropoulos in Greece and with Alfredo Casella in Rome; in 1936 became an instructor at the Cons. of Athens, and in 1962 was appointed its director. In 1969 he was elected to the Athens Academy. He wrote music to several ancient Greek tragedies, endeavoring to re-create the classical modes in modern investiture. Among his works are: Symph. (1948); *Divertimento* for Orch. (1952); Piano Concerto (1961); *5 Character Pieces* for Oboe, Clarinet, and Bassoon (1962).

Pallavicini, Carlo, Italian composer; b. Salò, near Brescia (date unknown); d. Dresden, Jan. 29, 1688. He served as an organist at S. Antonio in Padua in 1665–66, and in 1673–74 was maestro dei concerti there; then went to Venice; in 1687 he was appointed music director of the new Italian Opera at Dresden; wrote several operas for it. A scene from *Le Amazoni nell'isole fortunate* (Piazzola, near Padua, Nov. 11, 1679) was publ. in the *Sammelbände der Internationalen Musik-Gesellschaft* (vol. 2), and the complete score of *La Gerusalemme liberata* (Venice, Jan. 3, 1687) was edited by Abert in the Denkmäler Deutscher Tonkunst (vol. 55).

Pallavicino, Benedetto, Italian composer; b. Cremona, 1551; d. Mantua (date unknown). He was a court singer in Mantua from 1582 and maestro di cappella to the Duke from 1596. Monteverdi mentions Pallavicino's death in a letter applying for his post to the Duke of Mantua in Nov. 1601. Pallavicino publ. one book of madrigals *a* 4 (1579), 8 books *a* 5 (1581, ?, 1585, 1588, 1593, 1600, 1604, 1612), one book *a* 6 (1587), and other madrigals in collections; also a book of motets *a* 8, 12, and 16 (1595).
BIBLIOGRAPHY: D. de Paoli, *Monteverdi* (Milan, 1945); G. Sartori, "Monteverdiana," *Musical Quarterly* (July 1952); P. Flanders, *A Thematic Index to the Works of Benedetto Pallavicino* (N.Y., 1971).

Pallemaerts, Edmundo, Belgian composer; b. Malines, Dec. 21, 1867; d. Buenos Aires, April 20, 1945. He studied music with De Greef and Kufferath at the Brussels Cons.; settled in Buenos Aires in 1889, and founded there the Cons. Argentino, of which he was the first director (1894). He wrote a *Fantasia Argentina* for Orch.; many minor works for piano; also songs.

Pallo, Imre, Hungarian conductor; b. Budapest, May 15, 1941. He studied with Kodály at the Budapest Cons.; then took courses in conducting with Hans Swarowsky at the Vienna Academy of Music. He became music assistant to Herbert von Karajan and Karl Böhm at the Vienna and Salzburg festivals (1962–64); also conducted the orch. of the Vienna Academy. He made his American debut with the National Symph. Orch., Washington, D.C., in 1973. He then became a regular conductor at the N.Y. City Opera. In addition, he served as music director of the Hudson Valley Phil. Orch. at Poughkeepsie, N.Y., in 1976. He also conducted at the opera houses of Washington, Philadelphia, and Cincinnati.

Palm, Siegfried, German cellist and opera administrator; b. Barmen, April 25, 1927. He studied cello with his father, a member of the City Orch. in Wuppertal. After making his debut with the City Orch. in Lübeck, he joined the North German Radio Symph. in Hamburg (1947). He served as a member of the Cologne Radio Symph. (1962–68); in 1962 joined the faculty of the Cologne Hochschule für Musik; was appointed its director in 1972. From 1976 to 1981 he was general administrator of the Deutsche Oper in West Berlin, without abandoning his career as a cellist. He traveled widely in Africa and Asia with the purpose of studying native music. He commissioned several modern composers, among them Blacher, Kagel, Keleman, Ligeti, Penderecki, Xenakis, and Zimmermann, to write special works which he performed in world premieres. He also contributed scholarly treatises on the new techniques of string instruments.

Palma, Athos, Argentine composer; b. Buenos Aires, June 7, 1891; d. Miramar, Jan. 10, 1951. He studied with C. Troiani (piano) and other teachers in Buenos Aires; in 1904, went to Europe, returning to Buenos Aires in 1914. There he was busily engaged as a teacher. His music follows the Italian tradition, although the subject matter is derived from South American history and literature. He wrote the operas *Nazdah* (Buenos Aires, June 19, 1924) and *Los Hijos del Sol (The Sons of the Sun,* after an Inca legend; Buenos Aires, Nov. 10, 1928); *Cantares de mi tierra* for Strings (1914); symph. poems: *Jardines* and *Los Hijos del Sol;* Violin Sonata; Cello Sonata; Piano Sonata; many songs; pedagogical works: *Teoría razonada de la música* and *Tratado completo de armonía.*
BIBLIOGRAPHY: N. Lamuraglia, *Athos Palma: Vida, arte, educación* (Buenos Aires, 1954).

Palmer, Felicity, English soprano; b. Cheltenham,

April 6, 1944. She studied at the Guildhall School of Music in London; then went to Munich, where she studied voice with Marianne Schech at the Hochschule für Musik; was a member of the John Alldis Choir and the Purcell Consort; in 1970 won the Kathleen Ferrier Memorial Scholarship. She made her operatic debut at the Houston Opera in 1973.

Palmer, Horatio Richmond, American music pedagogue; b. Sherburne, N.Y., April 26, 1834; d. Yonkers, N.Y., Nov. 15, 1907. He was taught by his father and sister, later by various teachers in N.Y., Berlin, and Florence. He settled in Chicago after the Civil War; from 1873 he had charge of the New Church Choral Union there, giving concerts with as many as 4,000 singers; in 1877–91 he was dean of the Summer School of Music at Chautauqua. Of his collections, *The Song Queen, The Song King, The Song Herald,* and *Concert Choruses* had great success; he also publ. *Theory of Music, Class Method* (of elementary teaching), *Manual for Teachers* (in public schools), etc.

BIBLIOGRAPHY: *Dictionary of American Biography,* vol. XIV (1934).

Palmer, Robert, American composer; b. Syracuse, N.Y., June 2, 1915. He studied at the Eastman School of Music in Rochester with Howard Hanson and Bernard Rogers (1934–38); then had lessons with Roy Harris and Aaron Copland (1939–40). In 1940–43 he was on the faculty at the Univ. of Kansas; in 1943 was appointed to the staff of Cornell Univ. In his music he adheres to the neo-Classical mold; in his melodic progressions he frequently employs a scale of alternating whole-tones and semitones, known as the "Rimsky-Korsakov scale," so called because Rimsky-Korsakov liked to use it for exotic effects in his operas. WORKS: FOR ORCH.: *Poem* for Violin and Chamber Orch. (1938); Concerto for Chamber Orch. (1940); *K 19,* symph. elegy for Thomas Wolfe (1945); Chamber Concerto for Violin, Oboe, and Strings (1949); *Variations, Chorale and Fugue* (1947–54); 2 symphs.: No. 1 (1953–54, revised 1979); No. 2 (1966); *Memorial Music* for Chamber Orch. (1959–60); *A Centennial Overture* (1965); *Choric Songs and Toccata* for Wind Ensemble (1969); Concerto for Piano and String Orch. (1968–70); *Organon II* for String Orch. (1975). FOR VOICE: *Abraham Lincoln Walks at Midnight* for Chorus and Orch. (1948); *The Trojan Women* for Women's Chorus, Wind Instruments, and Percussion (1955); *Of Night and the Sea,* chamber canata (1956); *Nabuchodonosor,* dramatic oratorio (1960–64); *Portents of Aquarius (Visions and Prophecies)* for Narrator, Chorus, and Organ (1975); *Carmina Amoris,* cycle for Soprano, Violin, Clarinet, and Piano (1978). CHAMBER MUSIC: 4 string quartets (1939, 1947, 1954, 1959); 2 piano quartets (1945–47; 1973); Piano Quintet (1950); Viola Sonata (1951); Wind Quintet (1951); Quintet for Clarinet, Strings, and Piano (1952, revised 1964); Violin Sonata (1956); Piano Trio (1958); *Organon I* for Flute, Clarinet, Violin, and Cello (1961–77); Trumpet Sonata (1971–72); *Sinfonia Concertante* for 9 Instruments (1972);

Cello Sonata (1976–78). FOR PIANO: 3 sonatas (1938, 1942–48, 1978–79); Sonata for 2 Pianos (1944); *Evening Music* (1956); Sonata for Piano, 4-hands (1952–57); *11 Epigrams* (1958–67); *Transitions* (1977).

BIBLIOGRAPHY: W. Austin, "The Music of Robert Palmer," *Musical Quarterly* (Jan. 1956).

Palmgren, Selim, eminent Finnish composer; b. Pori (Björneborg), Feb. 16, 1878; d. Helsinki, Dec. 13, 1951. He studied piano and composition at the Cons. of Helsinki (1895–99); then went to Berlin, where he continued his piano studies with Ansorge, Berger, and Busoni. Returning to Finland, he became active as a choral conductor in Helsinki (1902–4); in 1909–12 he was director of the Music Society in Turku. In 1921 he made a tour of the U.S. as a pianist; from 1923 to 1926 taught piano and composition at the Eastman School of Music in Rochester, N.Y.; then returned to Helsinki; became a prof. of harmony and composition at the Sibelius Academy in 1936, remaining there until his death. He was married to the Finnish soprano **Maikki Pakarinen** in 1910, after her divorce from Armas Järnefelt; after her death Palmgren married Minna Talwik. He excelled in piano compositions, often tinged with authentic Finnish colors; some of his pieces are marked by effective impressionistic devices, such as whole-tone scales and consecutive mild dissonances. Among his piano miniatures, *May Night* enjoys considerable popularity with music students and their teachers.

WORKS: 5 piano concertos: No. 1 (1903); No. 2, *Virta (The Stream;* 1913); No. 3, *Metamorphoses* (1915); No. 4, *Huhtikuu (April;* 1924–26); No. 5 (1939–41); 2 operas: *Daniel Hjort* (April 15, 1910; revised version, Helsinki, 1938) and *Peter Schlemihl; Pastorale* for Orch. (1920); *Turun lilja (The Lily of Turku),* cantata (1929); *Ballet Music* for Orch. (1944); *Concert Fantasy* for Violin and Orch. (1945); for Piano: 2 sonatas; *Fantasia; 24 Preludes; Ballade* (in the form of a theme with variations); *Finnische Lyrik* (12 pieces); *Finnische Suite (The Seasons); Maskenball,* suite; 24 *Etudes* (1921–22); etc.; songs and men's choruses. He publ. a book, *Minusta Tuli Muusikko* (Helsinki, 1948).

BIBLIOGRAPHY: K. Maasalo, "Selim Palmgren," *Suomalaisia Sävellyksiä,* II (Borgå, 1969).

Palombo, Paul Martin, American composer; b. Pittsburgh, Sept. 10, 1937. He was trained in electronics; studied composition at the Peabody Cons. in Baltimore and at the Eastman School of Music in Rochester, N.Y., with Wayne Barlow and Bernard Rogers (1963–69); in 1969 he was appointed to the faculty of the Univ. of Cincinnati College-Cons. of Music; in 1973 assumed the direction of the electronic music studio there; remained until 1978; then taught at the Univ. of Washington in Seattle from 1978 to 1981; in 1981 he joined the faculty of the Univ. of Wisconsin. WORKS: *Serenade* for String Orch. (1964); Piano Sonata (1965); Sinfonietta for Chamber Orch. (1965); Cello Sonata (1966); String Quartet No. 1 (1966–67); *Movement* for Orch. (1967); *Variations* for Orch. (1967–68); *Proteus,* ballet for Tape and Orch. (1969); *Morphosis,* electronic ballet (1970); *Metatheses* for Flute, Oboe, Double Bass, and Harpsichord (1970); *Montage* for Violin and Piano (1971); *Crystals,* electronic multimedia score (1971); *Ritratti anticamente* for Viola and Piano (1972; revised 1974); 4 *Sonos: I* for Harpsichord and Tape (1972); *II* for Harp and Tape (1972); *III* for Double Bass and Tape (1973); *IV* for String Trio and Tape (1974); *Etcetera,* electronic ballet (1973); *Stegowagenvolkssaurus,* electronic music for a sculpture (1973–74).

Pálsson, Páll P., Austrian-born Icelandic composer and conductor; b. Graz, May 9, 1928. He studied with Michl, Mixa, and Brugger in Graz; settled in Iceland in 1949 and was first trumpet player in the Iceland Symph. Orch. In 1964 he was appointed director of the Reykjavik Male Choir and later became one of the conductors of the Icelandic Symph. Orch. and the Reykjavik Chamber Ensemble.
WORKS: Divertimento for 18 Winds (1963); *Hringspil I* for Violin, Viola, Clarinet, and Bassoon (1964) and *II* for 2 Trumpets, Horn, and Trombone; *Crystals* for String Quartet and Wind Quintet (1970); *Requiem* for a cappella Chorus (1970); *Dialog* for Orch. (1973); *Mixed Things* for Flute and Piano (1977); *Hugledhing um L (Meditation über L)* for Orch. (1977; the "L" is for Ludwig van Beethoven); Clarinet Concerto (Reykjavik, Jan. 6, 1983).

Pampanini, Rosetta, Italian soprano; b. Milan, Sept. 2, 1896; d. Corbola, Aug. 2, 1973. She studied with Emma Molajoli in Milan; made her debut in Rome in 1920; then continued her vocal studies; in 1925 she joined La Scala in Milan, remaining on its roster until 1937; also sang at Covent Garden in London (1928, 1929, 1933) and in Chicago (1931–32). After retiring in 1942 she taught voice. Her most distinguished roles were Mimi and Desdemona.

Panassié, Hugues, French music critic, expert on jazz; b. Paris, Feb. 27, 1912; d. Montauban, Dec. 8, 1974. He founded the Hot Club de France (1932); lectured on jazz at the Sorbonne in 1937, and in America in 1938; publ. *Le Jazz Hot* (basic treatise on the subject; Paris, 1934; in Eng. as *Hot Jazz,* N.Y., 1936); *The Real Jazz* (N.Y., 1942; in French, *La Véritable Musique de jazz,* Paris, 1946); *La Musique de jazz et le swing* (Paris, 1945); *Douze années de jazz (1927–1938)* (Paris, 1946); *Louis Armstrong* (Paris, 1947); *Jazz panorama* (Paris, 1950); *Discographie critique* (Paris, 1951); *Dictionnaire du jazz* (with Madeleine Gautier; Paris, 1954; in Eng. as *Dictionary of Jazz,* London, 1956; American ed., Boston, 1956, as *Guide to Jazz*).

Pandolfini, Angelica, Italian soprano; b. Spoleto, Aug. 21, 1871; d. Lenno, July 15, 1959. She was the daughter of the Italian baritone **Francesco Pandolfini.** She studied with Jules Massart in Paris; made her debut as Marguerite in 1894 in Modena; after singing in the Italian provinces, she appeared at La Scala in Milan (1897–99, 1906). She created the title

role in *Adriana Lecouvreur* at the Teatro Lirico in Milan in 1902; retired from the stage in 1908. She was best known for her convincing portrayals of *verismo* roles.

Pandolfini, Francesco, Italian baritone; b. Termini Imerese, Palermo, Nov. 22, 1836; d. Milan, Feb. 15, 1916. He studied with Ronconi and Vannuccini in Florence; made his debut in *Gemma di Vergy* in Pisa in 1859; then sang throughout Italy. In 1871 he appeared with notable success at La Scala in Milan; he created the role of Arnoldo in *I Lituani* by Ponchielli there in 1874; also sang at Covent Garden in London (1877, 1882); retired from the stage in 1890. His daughter, **Angelica Pandolfini,** was a soprano.

Panerai, Rolando, Italian baritone; b. Campi Bisenzio, near Florence, Oct. 17, 1924. He studied at the Florence Cons. with Frazzi; also with di Armani and G. Tess in Milan; after winning first prize in the voice competition in Spoleto, he made his operatic debut at the Teatro San Carlo in Naples in 1947; in 1951 he joined the La Scala Opera in Milan; also sang at Covent Garden in London, the Vienna State Opera, and the Salzburg Festivals. He specialized in the Italian repertoire.

Panizza, Ettore, Argentine conductor and composer of Italian extraction; b. Buenos Aires, Aug. 12, 1875; d. Milan, Nov. 27, 1967. He studied at the Cons. of Milan, graduating in 1898 with prizes for piano and composition; began his career as an operatic conductor in Italy in 1899, and continued successfully for more than half a century. From 1907 to 1914 he conducted Italian operas at Covent Garden in London; then at La Scala in Milan (1916–26) and at the Metropolitan Opera in N.Y. (1934–42). He publ. an autobiography, *Medio siglo de vida musical* (Buenos Aires, 1952).
WORKS: Operas: *Il Fidanzato del mare* (Buenos Aires, Aug. 15, 1897); *Medio evo latino* (Genoa, Nov. 17, 1900); *Aurora* (Buenos Aires, Sept. 5, 1908); *Bisanzio* (Buenos Aires, July 25, 1939); also *Il Re della foresta* for Soli, Chorus, and Orch.; *Tema con variaciones* for Orch.; Violin Sonata; Cello Sonata; String Quartet; piano pieces; songs.

Pankiewicz, Eugeniusz, Polish pianist and composer; b. Siedlce, Dec. 15, 1857; d. Tworki, near Warsaw, Dec. 24, 1898. He studied piano in Lublin; then went to Warsaw to study with J. Wieniawski; later took master classes with Leschetizky in St. Petersburg; he also studied composition with Noskowski in Warsaw. He subsequently taught piano at the Warsaw Inst. of Music; also composed attractive songs. His career was cut short by a mental illness; he had to be confined to a mental institution, and died at 41 years of age.
BIBLIOGRAPHY: W. Pozniak, *Eugeniusz Pankiewicz* (Cracow, 1958).

Pannain, Guido, distinguished Italian musicologist and composer; b. Naples, Nov. 17, 1891; d. there,

Sept. 6, 1977. He studied composition with C. de Nardis at Naples; upon graduation, devoted himself mainly to research, into both old and new aspects of music.

WRITINGS: *La teoria musicale di G. Tinctoris* (1913); *Le origini della scuola musicale napoletana* (1914); *Le origini e lo sviluppo dell' arte pianistica in Italia dal 1500 al 1700 circa* (1917); *Lineamenti di storia della musica* (1922; 9th ed., 1970); *Musica e musicisti in Napoli nel secolo XIX* (1922); *Storia del Conservatorio di Napoli* (1942); *La vita del linguaggio musicale* (1947); *Ottocento musicale italiano* (1952); collaborated with A. Della Corte in *Storia della musica,* in 3 vols. (1936; 3rd ed., 1952). Beginning in 1928, he was one of the chief contributors to the *Rassegna musicale* (essays on modern composers; publ. as *Musicisti dei tempi nuovi,* Turin, 1932; Eng. trans. by Bonavia, London, 1932, as *Modern Composers*); *Ottocento musicale italiano* (Milan, 1952); *L'opera e le opere ed altri scritti di letteratura musicale* (Milan, 1958); *Verdi* (Turin, 1964); *Wagner* (Milan, 1964).

WORKS: Operas: *L'Intrusa* (1926; Genoa, 1940); *Beatrice Cenci* (Naples, Feb. 21, 1942); *Madame Bovary* (Naples, April 16, 1955); 2 violin concertos (1930, 1960); Viola Concerto (1955); Harp Concerto (1968); Piano Concerto (1968); *Requiem* (1955).

Panofka, Heinrich, German singing teacher; b. Breslau, Oct. 3, 1807; d. Florence, Nov. 18, 1887. He began his career as a violinist; after playing some concerts in Germany, he went to Paris in 1832 and began taking singing lessons with Bordogni. With Bordogni he organized, in 1842, the Académie de Chant, which failed to prosper. In 1844 he went to London, where he became a fashionable singing teacher; eventually he went to Florence, spending his last days there. He publ. a manual, *L'Art de chanter* (Paris, 1853), which had a considerable vogue.

Panseron, Auguste-Mathieu, French singing teacher; b. Paris, April 26, 1795; d. there, July 29, 1859. His father, who orchestrated many operas for Grétry, taught him until he entered the Paris Cons. in 1804; he studied under Gossec, Levasseur, and Berton, winning the Prix de Rome in 1813. After study in Bologna, Rome, Naples, Vienna (with Salieri), and Munich, he returned to Paris in 1818, taught singing, was an accompanist at the Opéra-Comique, and wrote 3 one-act operas; became a prof. of solfeggio at the Cons. in 1826, of vocalization in 1831, and of singing in 1836. In 1825–40 he brought out some 200 *romances;* he also composed church music, but attained real eminence as a vocal teacher and as a writer of instructive works on singing.

Pantaleoni, Adriano, Italian baritone; b. Udine, Oct. 7, 1837; d. there, Dec. 18, 1908. He studied in Udine and Milan; was a principal member of La Scala in Milan (1871–77, 1896); also sang in London and the U.S.; after his retirement, he taught voice in Udine and Trieste. He was particularly noted for his roles in Verdi's operas. His sister, **Romilda Pan-**

taleoni, was well known as an operatic soprano.

Pantaleoni, Romilda, Italian soprano; b. Udine, 1847; d. Milan, May 20, 1917. She studied with Prati, Rossi, and Lamperti in Milan; made her debut at the Teatro Carcano in Milan in Foroni's *Margherita* in 1868; then sang in Turin and at La Scala in Milan, where she created the role of Desdemona in Verdi's *Otello* in 1887 and Tigrana in Puccini's *Edgar* in 1889. Her brother, **Adriano Pantaleoni,** was a noted baritone.

Panufnik, Andrzej, eminent Polish composer and conductor; b. Warsaw, Sept. 24, 1914. His mother was an Englishwoman who studied violin in Warsaw, his father a manufacturer of string instruments. Panufnik studied composition with Sikorski at the Warsaw Cons. (1932–36); then took lessons in conducting with Weingartner at the Vienna Academy (1937–38) and briefly with Philippe Gaubert in Paris. He returned to Warsaw in 1939, and remained there during the Nazi occupation of the city; had an underground performance in 1942 of his *Tragic Overture.* In 1945–46 he conducted the Cracow Phil., then conducted the Warsaw Orch. (1946–47). In 1954 he went to England, and in 1961 became a British subject. From 1957 to 1959 he was conductor and music director of the Birmingham Symph. Orch., and frequently a guest conductor in London. In his youth, before the war, he belonged to the vanguard group among Polish composers; he made use of advanced techniques, including quarter-tones, which he employed in the instrumental *Berceuse (Lullaby).* Even in the matter of notation he was an innovator; in several of the orch. scores he left blank spaces instead of rests in the inactive instrumental parts. In his music of the later period he adopted a more circumspect idiom—expressive, direct, and communicative. He constantly revised his old scores for better effect.

WORKS: Piano Trio (1934; recomposed 1945 and revised 1967); *5 Polish Peasant Songs* for Treble Chorus, 2 Flutes, 2 Clarinets, and Bass Clarinet (1940; recomposed 1945; London Festival of the International Society for Contemporary Music, July 12, 1946; revised 1959); *Tragic Overture* (1942; score lost in Warsaw fires; recomposed 1945; first public perf., N.Y., March 24, 1949; revised 1955); *Lullaby* for 29 String Instruments, and 2 Harps (1947; Paris, April 26, 1948; revised 1955); *Nocturne* for Orch. (1947; revised 1955); *12 Miniature Studies* for Piano (1947; revised 1955); *Sinfonia rustica* (1948; Warsaw, May 13, 1949; revised 1955); *Hommage à Chopin* in 2 versions: for Soprano and Piano (1949) and for Flute and String Orch. (1966); *Old Polish Suite* for String Orch. (1950; revised 1955); *Concerto in modo antico (Gothic Concerto)* for Orch. (1951; revised 1955); *Symfonia pokoju (Symphony of Peace)* for Chorus and Orch. (Warsaw, May 25, 1951); *Heroic Overture* (1952; Helsinki Olympiad, July 27, 1952; revised 1965); *Rhapsody* for Orch. (1956; first public perf., London, Aug. 26, 1957); *Sinfonia elegiaca* (1957; revised 1966; first and 3rd sections arranged as a ballet, *Elegy,* N.Y., 1957); *Polonia,* suite for Orch. (1959; London, Aug. 21, 1959); *Autumn Music* for Orch. (1962); Piano Concerto (1962; revised 1972); *Sinfonia sacra* (1963; Monaco, Aug. 12, 1964; as a ballet, *Cain and Abel*, West Berlin, Nov. 1968); *Landscape* for String Orch. (London, Nov. 13, 1965); *Divertimento* for String Orch. (London, Sept. 24, 1966); *Jagiellonian Triptych* for Strings (London, Sept. 24, 1966); *Epitaph for the Victims of Katyn* for Woodwinds, Strings, and Timpani (N.Y., Nov. 17, 1968, Stokowski conducting); *Reflections* for Piano (1968); *Universal Prayer*, a setting of Alexander Pope's poem, for 4 Soloists, Chorus, 3 Harps, and Organ (Cathedral Church of St. John the Divine, N.Y., May 24, 1970, Stokowski conducting); *Thames Pageant*, cantata for Young Players and Singers (1969); ballet, *Miss Julie* (Stuttgart, March 8, 1970); Concerto for Violin and String Orch. (London, July 18, 1972); *Invocation for Peace* for Youth Chorus and Youth Orch. (Southampton, Nov. 28, 1972); *Winter Solstice* for Soprano, Baritone, Chorus, and Instruments (London, Dec. 16, 1972); *Sinfonia concertante* for Flute, Harp, and String Orch. (1973; London, May 20, 1974); *Sinfonia di sfere (Symphony of Spheres;* 1975; London, April 13, 1976); 2 string quartets: No. 1 (1976) and No. 2, *Messages* (1980); *Sinfonia mystica* (1977); *Metasinfonia* for Organ, Strings, and Timpani (1978); *Concerto festivo* for Orch. (1979); Concertino for Percussion, and Piano, 4-hands, or String Orch. (1980); *Sinfonia votiva* (1980–81; Boston, Jan 28, 1982); *A Procession for Peace* for Orch. (1982).

BIBLIOGRAPHY: Scarlett Panufnik (his wife), *Out of the City of Fear* (recounting Panufnik's flight from Poland; London, 1956).

Panula, Jorma, Finnish conductor and composer; b. Kauhajoki, Aug. 10, 1930. He studied at the Helsinki School of Church Music, at the Sibelius Academy in Helsinki with Leo Funtek, and with Dean Dixon at Lund. As a conductor, he has appeared with the Helsinki Phil. Orch. and also with several European orchs. In his works he often explores modernistic ideas and idioms, as exemplified by his *Jazz capriccio* for Piano and Orch. (1965) and *Terässinfonia (Steel Symphony;* 1969). He also composed a Violin Concerto (1954).

Panum, Hortense, Danish musicologist; b. (of Danish parents) Kiel, Germany, March 14, 1856; d. Copenhagen, April 26, 1933. Her father, a prof. of physiology at Kiel Univ., returned to Copenhagen in 1864. She studied music history with W. Tappert in Berlin (1886–87). After her return to Denmark, she devoted herself to historical studies (especially concerning old instruments).

WRITINGS: *Illustreret musikhistorie* (1895–1905; Part II by W. Behrend); *Musiken og musiklivet i Danmark för anno 1880* (1904); *Musiken og musiklivet i Danmark efter anno 1800* (1906); *Haydn, Mozart, og Beethoven* (1908); *Middelalderens strengeinstrumenter og dares Forlöbere i Oldtiden* (profusely illustrated; I, 1915; II, 1928; III, 1931; Eng. ed. in one vol., by J. Pulver, as *The Stringed Instruments of the Middle Ages, Their Evolution,*

etc., London, 1939; reprinted N.Y., 1972); *Af musikhistoriens Billedbog* (1916; 2nd ed., 1930); *Langelegen som dansk folkeinstrument* (1918); *Illustreret musiklexikon* (Copenhagen, 1924–26; with W. Behrend and O.M. Sandvik; new ed., 1940).

Panzéra, Charles, French baritone; b. Hyères, Feb. 16, 1896; d. Paris, June 6, 1976. He studied at the Paris Cons.; made his debut at the Opéra-Comique in 1919; then gave concerts in Europe and America; also taught at the Juilliard School in N.Y. In 1949 he was appointed a prof. at the Paris Cons. He publ. a manual, *L'Art de chanter* (Paris, 1945).

Panzner, Karl, German conductor; b. Teplitz, Bohemia, March 2, 1866; d. Düsseldorf, Dec. 17, 1923. He studied piano and composition at the Dresden Cons.; then was a private pupil of Anton Rubinstein, who advised him to adopt the career of a concert pianist. Instead, he became a theater conductor; in 1893 he succeeded E. Paur as Kapellmeister at the Leipzig Stadttheater, where he remained 6 years. In 1899 he was called to Bremen to conduct the Phil. and (in 1904) also the Lehrer Gesangverein, with which he made several successful tours (notably to Paris in 1907); from 1907 to 1909 he filled numerous engagements as a visiting conductor in Barcelona, Paris, St. Petersburg, Moscow, Rome, and N.Y. From 1909 he was municipal music director in Düsseldorf; also conductor of the Phil. Society concerts at Hamburg.

BIBLIOGRAPHY: W. Gareiss, *Karl Panzner* (Leipzig, 1909).

Papaioannou, Yannis, Greek composer; b. Kavala, Jan. 6, 1911. He studied piano and music theory at the Hellenic Odeon in Athens (1929–34); then had some composition lessons with Honegger in Paris (1949). In 1953 he was appointed to the staff of his alma mater; introduced into his courses a study of modern techniques of composition. His own music traversed from a fairly conservative neo-Classical idiom to dodecaphony and eventually integral serialism.

WORKS: *Daphnis and Chloe* for Chorus and Orch. (1934); *Idyll* for Orch. (1938); *Choreographic Prelude* for Orch. (1939); symph. poems: *The Corsair* (1940); *Poem of the Forest* (1942); *Vassilis the Albanian* (1945); *Matins of Souls* (1947); *Pygmalion* (1951); *Hellas* (1956); *Symphonic Tableau* (1968); 5 symphs. (1946, 1951, 1953, 1963, 1964); *Triptych* for Strings (1947); Piano Concerto (1950); *Concerto for Orchestra* (1954); 3 suites for Orch. (Nos. 1 and 2, *Pictures from Asia;* No. 3, *Egypt,* 1961); Concertino for Piano and String Orch. (1962); *Sarpidon's Funeral,* cantata (1965); *3 Byzantine Odes* for Soprano and Chamber Ensemble (1966); *Electra Monologues* for Soprano and Instrumental Ensemble (1968); *Footsteps* for Mezzo-soprano, Narrator, Chorus, and Instrumental Ensemble (1969); *India,* suite for Orch. (1969); *4 Orphic Hymns* for Narrator and Instrumental Ensemble (1971); Concerto for Violin and Chamber Orch. (1971); Concerto for Violin, Piano, and Orch. (1972–73); Violin Sonata (1947);

Winter Fantasy, ballet for Flute, Clarinet, Violin, Cello, and Piano (1950); String Quartet (1959); *Suite for Guitar* (1960); Sonatina for Flute and Guitar (1962); Quartet for Flute, Clarinet, Guitar, and Cello (1962); Trio for Oboe, Clarinet, and Bassoon (1962); *Archaic* for 2 Guitars (1962); String Trio (1963); Trio for Flute, Viola, and Guitar (1967); Quartet for Oboe, Clarinet, Viola, and Piano (1968); *5 Characters*, brass quintet (1970); *Aphigissis (Narration)* for Solo Violin (1970); *The Harlequin's Prattling* for Solo Tuba (1971); *Portrait* for Solo Tuba (1972); *Syneirmoi (Associations)* for 9 Instruments (1973); *Echomorphes (Sound-figures)* for Solo Violin (1975); *Rhythms and Colors* for Solo Cello (1976); *Puck* for Solo Cello (1976); Piano Trio (1977); Piano Sonata (1958); other pieces for Piano: *Odalisque* (1937); *24 Preludes* (1938); 2 suites (1948, 1959); *Partita in modo antico* (1957); *12 Inventions* (1958); *Oraculum* (1965); *7 Piano Pieces* (1969); *Enigma* (1969); also, choruses, songs, theater music.

Papandopulo, Boris, Croatian conductor and composer; b. Bad Honneft am Rhein, Feb. 25, 1906. He studied in Zagreb and Vienna; in 1959 was appointed conductor of the National Theater in Zagreb; from 1964 to 1968 he conducted in Split and Rijeka; later filled engagements as a guest conductor in Yugoslavia. His operas and most of his instrumental works are written in a national Croatian idiom; but he also experimented with the 12-tone techniques, as exemplified by his pointedly titled *Dodekafonski concert* for 2 Pianos (1961).

WORKS: Operas: *Amphytrion* (1940); *Sunflower* (1942); *Rona* (Rijeka, May 25, 1956); *Marulova Pisan,* dedicated to the town of Split and dealing with the siege of a neighboring town by the Turks c.1500 and its liberation by Spalatines (Split, Aug. 14, 1970); a "fantastic opera," *Madame Buffault* (1972); ballets: *Zlato (Gold;* Zagreb, 1931); *Žetva (The Harvest;* Sarajevo, 1950); *Beatrice Cenci* (Gelsenkirchen, 1959); *Gitanella* (1965); *Dr. Atom,* subtitled $Qu + H^3 + H^2 = He^4 + n + 9$ (Rijeka, 1966); *Ljudi u hotelu* (perf. in Vienna as *Menschen im Hotel,* 1967); *Teuta* (1973); cantata, *Legend of Comrade Tito* (Zagreb, May 10, 1962); 2 symphs.: No. 1 (1930) and No. 2 (Zagreb, May 8, 1946, composer conducting); String Symphonietta (his most frequently perf. work); 4 piano concertos (1938, 1942, 1947, 1958); Concerto for 4 Timpani and Orch. (1969); Concerto for Harpsichord and String Orch. (1962); Double-bass Concerto (1968); 5 string quartets (1927, 1933, 1945, 1950, 1970); many choral works and piano pieces.

BIBLIOGRAPHY: Kovačević, *Hrvatski Kompozitori i Njihova Djela* (Zagreb, 1960).

Papi, Gennaro, Italian-American conductor; b. Naples, Dec. 21, 1886; d. New York, Nov. 29, 1941. He studied with de Nardis at the S. Pietro a Majella Cons. in Naples (graduated 1904); was an assistant conductor in Warsaw (1909–10), Turin (1911), London (Covent Garden, 1911–12), Milan, Odessa, and Buenos Aires; in 1913–16, was assistant to Toscanini at the Metropolitan Opera House; in 1916–26, con-

ductor of Russian and Italian opera there; in 1925–32, conductor of the Chicago Civic Opera; then made appearances in Milan, Mexico City, and Buenos Aires until 1935, when he was re-engaged at the Metropolitan; he remained with the company until his death.

Papier, Rosa, Austrian mezzo-soprano; b. Baden, near Vienna, Sept. 15, 1858; d. Vienna, Feb. 9, 1932. She sang at the Imperial Opera in Vienna; later taught at the Vienna Cons. In 1881 she married the pianist **Hans Paumgartner.**

Papineau-Couture, Jean, Canadian composer; b. Outremont (part of metropolitan Montreal), Nov. 12, 1916. He studied piano with Léo-Pol Morin (1939–40) and theory with Gabriel Cusson in Montreal (1937–40); then in the U.S. (1940–45) with Quincy Porter at the New England Cons. in Boston, with Nadia Boulanger at the Longy School in Cambridge, Mass., and in California. Upon returning to Montreal, he devoted himself to teaching and musical organization; was founding president of the Société de Musique Contemporaine du Québec (1966–73) and dean of the music faculty at the Univ. of Montreal (1968–73). His music underwent an evolution, common to many Canadian composers, from a neo-Baroque idiom to Expressionism, with judicious excursions into serial techniques.

WORKS: *Concerto grosso* for Small Orch. (1943; revised 1955); Symph. (1947–48; revised 1956); *Papotages (Tittle-Tattle),* ballet (1949; Montreal, Nov. 20, 1950); Concerto for Violin and Chamber Orch. (1951); *Poème* for Orch. (1952); *Prélude* for Orch. (1953); *Psaume CL* for Soprano, Tenor, Chorus, Wind Ensemble, and One or 2 Organs (1954); 5 *Pièces concertantes:* No. 1, *Repliement (Folding Back),* for Piano and String Orch. (1956); No. 2, *Eventails,* for Cello and Chamber Orch. (1959); No. 3, *Variations,* for Flute, Clarinet, Violin, Cello, Harp, and String Orch. (1959); No. 4, *Additions,* for Oboe and String Orch. (1959); No. 5, *Miroirs (Mirrors),* for Orch. (1963); *3 Pieces* for Orch. (1961); Piano Concerto (1965; Toronto, Feb. 6, 1966); *Paysage* for 8 Narrators, 8 Singers, Wind Quintet, String Quintet, Piano, Harp, and Percussion (1968; Zagreb, May 9, 1969); *Oscillations* for Orch. (1969); *Contraste* for Voice and Orch. (1970); *Obsession* for 16 Players (1973); *Eglogues* for Alto, Flute, and Piano (1942); *Suite* for Piano (1942); Violin Sonata (1944; revised 1953); *Suite* for Flute and Piano (1944–45); *Rondo* for Piano, 4-hands (1945); *Aria* for Solo Violin (1946); *Quatrains* for Soprano and Piano (1947); *Suite* for Flute, Clarinet, Bassoon, Horn, and Piano (1947); 2 string quartets (1953, 1967); *Suite* for Solo Violin (1956); *Eclosion,* stage music for a Mime, Violin, Piano, and Tape (1961); *3 Caprices* for Violin and Piano (1962); *Fantaisie* for Wind Quintet (1963); *Canons* for Brass Quintet (1964); *Dialogues* for Violin and Piano (1967); Sextet for Oboe, Clarinet, Bassoon, Violin, Viola, and Cello (1967); *Nocturnes* for Flute, Clarinet, Violin, Cello, Harpsichord, Guitar, and Percussion (1969); *Complémentarité* for Piano (1971); *Dyarchie* for Harpsichord (1971); *Chanson de Rahit* for Voice, Clarinet, and Piano (1972); Trio for Clarinet, Viola, and Piano (1974); *Départ* for Solo Alto Flute (1974); *Versegères* for Solo Bass Flute (1975); *Slano* for String Trio (1975); *J'aime les tierces mineures* for Solo Flute (1976); *Le Débat du cœur et du corps* for Narrator, Cello, and Percussion (1977).

Pâque, Désiré, remarkable Belgian composer; b. Liège, May 21, 1867; d. Bessancourt, France, Nov. 20, 1939. He began to compose as a child; wrote a Mass at the age of 12; studied at the Liège Cons.; lived in Sofia, Athens, Lisbon, and Geneva, settling in Paris in 1914. He wrote 144 opus numbers, among them the one-act opera *Vaima* (1903); 8 symphs. (1895, 1905, 1912, 1916, 1919, 1927, 1934, 1936); 2 piano concertos (1888, 1935); Cello Concerto (1893); *Ouverture sur 3 thèmes bulgares* (Ostende, Aug. 17, 1895); *Ouverture libre* (1899; Munich, Dec. 29, 1911); Requiem (1900); 10 string quartets (1892–1939); 3 piano quintets (1896, 1924, 1938); 2 sextets (1909, 1919); 5 suites for Piano, Violin, and Viola (1891–96); 3 piano trios (1903–30); 4 violin sonatas (1890–1934); 4 piano sonatas (1911); Viola Sonata (1915); 13 albums of piano pieces; choral works. His production falls into 3 periods: cosmopolitan and formal (1886–1908); freely episodic, in an *adjonction constante* of recurrent themes (1909–18); atonal and polytonal (1919–39). His last manner is exemplified by *10 pièces atonales pour la jeunesse* for Piano (1925). Only a few of his works are publ.; the bulk of his music remains in MS.

Paradies (originally **Paradisi**), **Pietro Domenico,** Italian composer and harpsichordist; b. Naples, 1707; d. Venice, Aug. 25, 1791. He was a pupil of Porpora; brought out several operas in Italy; in 1747 went to London, where he earned a living mainly as a teacher of harpsichord playing, but also produced an opera, *Fetonte* (Jan. 17, 1747); publ. *12 sonate di gravicembalo* (London, 1754). Toward the end of his life he returned to Italy. Some of his MS works are preserved in the Fitzwilliam Museum at Cambridge; his sonatas were brought out by G. Benvenuti and D. Cipollini in Milan (1920).

Paradis, Maria Theresia von, Austrian pianist and composer; b. Vienna, May 15, 1759; d. there, Feb. 1, 1824. Blind from her 5th year, she was taught by Richter and Koželuh (piano), Salieri and Righini (singing), and Friberth and Abbé Vogler (composition), becoming an excellent pianist and organist; she played in Paris in 1784, and made a tour to London, Brussels, and German capitals in 1786. By the aid of a system of notation invented by a friend, she became a skillful composer, her chief works being a melodrama, *Ariadne und Bacchus* (Laxenburg, June 20, 1791; not extant); an operetta, *Der Schulkandidat* (Vienna, Dec. 5, 1792); the fairy opera *Rinaldo und Alcina* (Prague, June 30, 1797; not extant); a funeral cantata on the death of Louis XVI (1794); a Piano Trio; sonatas and variations for piano; songs; etc. In her last years she taught singing and piano playing.

BIBLIOGRAPHY: F. Niecks, in the *Monthly Musical Record* (Jan. 1913); H. Ullrich, "M.T. Paradis and Mozart," *Music & Letters* (Oct. 1946); E. Komorzynski, "Mozart und M.T. Paradis," *Mozart-Jahrbuch* (Salzburg, 1952).

Paranov, Moshe, American pianist and conductor; b. Hartford, Conn., Oct. 28, 1895. He studied piano with Julius Hartt and Harold Bauer, composition with Ernest Bloch and Rubin Goldmark. He married Hartt's daughter, Pauline; was co-founder of the Julius Hartt School of Music in Hartford in 1920; in 1957, was named president of the Julius Hartt Musical Foundation of the Univ. of Hartford.

Paratore, Anthony (b. Boston, June 17, 1944) and his brother **Joseph** (b. Boston, March 19, 1948), outstanding American duo-pianists. They followed separate courses of study as pianists, graduating from the Boston Univ. School of Fine and Applied Arts; both entered the Juilliard School of Music in N.Y., in the class of Rosina Lhévinne, who suggested that they try a career as duo-pianists; they subsequently appeared as duo-pianists with Arthur Fiedler and the Boston Pops Orch., and then made their N.Y. recital debut in 1973. In 1974 they won first prize at the Munich International Competition, and scored successes as duo-soloists with the Chicago Symph., San Francisco Symph., National Symph. of Washington, D.C., Indianapolis Symph., Detroit Symph., and N.Y. Phil. In Europe they played with the Berlin Phil., Warsaw Phil., BBC Symph. of London, and Rotterdam Phil.

Paray, Paul, distinguished French conductor and composer; b. Le Tréport, Normandy, May 24, 1886; d. Monte Carlo, Oct. 10, 1979. He received his musical education from his father, a church organist; in 1904 he entered the Paris Cons. as a composition student; studied there with Leroux, Caussade, Lenepveu, and Vidal; received the Premier Grand Prix de Rome with his cantata *Yanitza* (1911). He was drafted into the French army during World War I and was taken prisoner by the Germans; composed a string quartet while interned at Darmstadt; after the Armistice, he became conductor of the orch. of the Casino de Cauterets. Substituting for an ailing André Caplet, Paray made his Paris debut on Feb. 20, 1920, and soon became assistant conductor of the Lamoureux Orch., succeeding Chevillard as first conductor in 1923; was appointed conductor of symph. concerts in Monte Carlo in 1928, and in 1932 he succeeded Pierné as conductor of the Concerts Colonne, remaining until the orch. was disbanded by the Nazi occupiers of Paris in 1940; conducted briefly in Marseilles and, following the liberation of Paris, resumed duties with the Colonne Orch. (1944–52). Paray made his American debut in N.Y. on July 24, 1939, in a program of French music. In 1952 he was engaged to conduct the reorganized Detroit Symph. Orch., and on Oct. 18, 1956, inaugurated the new Ford Auditorium in Detroit in a program that included his own *Mass for the 500th Anniversary of the Death of Joan of Arc,* a work first heard in the Cathedral in Rouen, France, in 1931; he resigned in 1963 and returned to France, though he continued to guest-conduct internationally. In July 1977, at the age of 91, he conducted an orch. concert in honor of Marc Chagall's 90th birthday celebration in Nice, and, at age 92, made his last conducting appearance in the U.S., leading the orch. of the Curtis Inst. of Music in Philadelphia; at the time of his death (in 1979), he had commitments through 1981. As a conductor, he concentrated on the Classics and Romantics, and French music. He was the composer of several highly competent works, including, besides *Yanitza* and his *Mass,* a ballet entitled *Artémis troublée* (Paris Opéra, April 28, 1922, perf. as a symph. poem, *Adonis troublé*); *Fantaisie* for Piano and Orch. (Paris, March 25, 1923); 2 full symphs., in C (1935) and in A (1940); Symph. for Strings; String Quartet (1918); Violin Sonata (1908); Cello Sonata (1919); piano pieces.

BIBLIOGRAPHY: W.L. Landowski, *Paul Paray* (Lyons, 1956); Hope Stoddard, *Symphony Conductors of the U.S.A.* (N.Y., 1957; pp. 160–70); Nancy Shear, "Paul Paray at 92: A Link with History," *High Fidelity/Musical America* (March 1979; pp. MA 32–33).

Parelli, Attilio (real last name, **Paparella**), Italian conductor and composer; b. Monteleone d'Orvieto, near Perugia, May 31, 1874; d. there, Dec. 26, 1944. He studied at the Santa Cecilia Academy in Rome; graduated in 1899; held various posts as a conductor in Italy and France; went to the U.S. as assistant conductor to Campanini at the Manhattan Opera in N.Y. (1906); also conducted for the Chicago Grand Opera Co. In 1925 he returned to Europe. He wrote the operas *Hermes* (Geneva, Nov. 8, 1906); *I dispettosi amanti* (Philadelphia, March 6, 1912); *Fanfulla* (Trieste, Feb. 11, 1921); Symph.; orch. suite, *Rapsodia umbra;* symph. poem, *La Chimera;* songs.

Parent, Armand, Belgian violinist; b. Liège, Feb. 5, 1863; d. Paris, Jan. 19, 1934. He was a pupil at the Liège Cons. of L. Massart (violin) and S. Dupuis (harmony). From 1883 to 1889, he was concertmaster with the Colonne Orch.; from 1900, a prof. of violin at the Schola Cantorum. In 1892 he founded (with Loiseau, Vieux, and Fournier) the Quatuor Parent, which for many years enjoyed an excellent reputation. Parent wrote 2 string quartets, a String Quintet, a Violin Sonata, and a number of minor pieces for violin and piano; also *Gymnastique du violon, 20 études de virtuosité, Etudes pour violon, Exercises pour le violon d'après les 17 quatuors de Beethoven,* and a 5-part *Méthode complète.*

Parepa-Rosa (née **Parepa de Boyescu**), **Euphrosyne,** English soprano; b. Edinburgh, May 7, 1836; d. London, Jan. 21, 1874. Her father was a native of Bucharest; her mother, **Elizabeth Seguin,** was a well-known singer. She made her operatic debut at the age of 16 in Malta; then sang in principal Italian music centers, in Madrid, and in Lisbon. She made her first London appearance as Elvira in *I Puritani* on May 21, 1857, and became a great favorite of the English public. She married the impresario Carlo Rosa in 1867 during an American tour. She returned to England in 1873 and remained there until her death.

BIBLIOGRAPHY: *Dictionary of National Biography,* vol. XLIII.

Pareto, Graziella, Spanish soprano; b. Barcelona, March 6, 1889; d. Rome, Sept. 1, 1973. She studied with Vidal in Milan; made her debut as Micaela in Barcelona in 1906; then sang at the Teatro Colón in Buenos Aires, in Turin, and in St. Petersburg. In 1914 she appeared at La Scala in Milan; subsequently sang at Covent Garden in London (1920), in N.Y., and in Salzburg (1931).

Paribeni, Giulio Cesare, Italian teacher and critic; b. Rome, May 27, 1881; d. Milan, June 13, 1960. He studied at the Univ. of Rome and at the Liceo di S. Cecilia; was first a conductor, then, from 1911–15, head of the publishing firm of Sonzogno; from 1914 was a teacher of composition and harmony at the Royal Cons. in Milan; from 1922, an opera critic of *L'Ámbrosiano* in Milan. He was the author of *Storia e teoria della antica musica greca* (Milan, 1912) and *Muzio Clementi,* a biography (Milan, 1921); also, a composer of orch. works, chamber music, and church music.

Parík, Ivan, Slovak composer; b. Bratislava, Aug. 17, 1936. He studied composition with Očenáš at the Bratislava Cons.; then with Cikker and Alexander Moyzes at the Bratislava Academy of Music, graduating in 1962; was then appointed to its faculty. In his music he utilizes a wide range of contemporary resources, from serialism to pointillistic minimalism and expressionistic abstractions.

WORKS: *Music* for 4 String Instruments (1958); *2 Songs,* to Japanese poetry, for Mezzo-soprano, Violin, Clarinet, Xylophone, and Gong (1960); Sonata for Flute Solo (1962); *Epitaph* for Flute, Viola, and Cello (1962); *Music for 3* for Flute, Oboe, and Clarinet (1964); *Koláže (Collage)* for a variable Chamber Ensemble (1968); *Exercises* for Solo Trumpet (1968); *Vežová hudba (Tower Music)* for 12 Brasses, 2 Tapes, and Bells (1969); *Sonata-Canon* for Flute and Tape (1971); *Meditation* for Viola and Piano (1975); *Epitaph* for Flute and Guitar (1975); electronic pieces.

Parish-Alvars, Elias, English harpist; b. Teignmouth, Feb. 28, 1808; d. Vienna, Jan. 25, 1849. He studied harp with Bochsa; from 1831–36 gave concerts in Germany. While in Leipzig he was associated with Mendelssohn. In 1847 he settled in Vienna. His compositions for harp enjoyed a certain popularity during his lifetime.

Parkening, Christopher, outstanding American guitarist; b. Los Angeles, Dec. 14, 1947. He began to play the guitar as a child; gave a public recital at the age of 12; subsequently engaged in a brilliant international career, touring throughout the U.S.,

Europe, and the Far East. He also publ. transcriptions of sacred music for the guitar and a valuable guitar method.

Parker, Charlie, nicknamed **"Yardbird"** or **"Bird"** (real Christian name, **Charles Christopher**), black American jazz saxophonist, the leading exponent of bebop; b. Kansas City, Aug. 29, 1920; d. New York, March 12, 1955. He was self-taught, on an alto saxophone given to him at age 11 by his mother; at 15 he left school and became a professional musician; in 1939 went to N.Y., and in 1941 was in the big band of Jay McShann, with which he made his first recordings. In 1943 he played tenor sax (his only extended period on that instrument) in Earl Hines's band; met Dizzy Gillespie and other young musicians dissatisfied with the prevailing big band swing style; after work they would meet in a club called Minton's, and there gradually evolved the new style of bebop. Parker became the acknowledged leader of this style as he developed an improvising technique characterized by virtuosic speed, intense tone, complex harmonies, and florid melodies having irregular rhythmic patterns and asymmetric phrase lengths. After the mid-1940s he usually worked in small combos led either by himself or by one of the other members of the small, close-knit circle of bopsters; occasionally he also worked with larger ensembles (including a string orch. for which he wrote the arrangements). As a composer, he usually worked with the 12-bar blues patterns (but always in an unstereotyped manner; he made 175 blues recordings, all markedly different) or with chord progressions of well-known "standard" tunes: his *Ornithology,* for instance, is based on the progressions of *How High the Moon.* He achieved a prominence that made him a living legend (a leading N.Y. club, Birdland, was named after him); his life, though, in addition to being tragically short, was plagued by the consequences of narcotics addiction (acquired when he was in his mid-teens) and alcoholism. He had a nervous breakdown in 1946 and was confined at Camarillo State Hospital in California for 6 months; because of suspected narcotics possession, the N.Y. City police rescinded his cabaret license in 1951, thereby denying him the right to work in N.Y. clubs; he attempted suicide twice in 1954, and subsequently entered Bellevue Hospital in N.Y. He died in the N.Y. apartment of a fervent admirer, Rothschild Baroness Pannonica de Konigswarter.

BIBLIOGRAPHY: M. Harrison, *Charlie Parker* (London, 1960); R.G. Reisner, *Bird: The Legend of Charlie Parker* (N.Y., 1962); J.G. Jepsen, *A Discography of Charlie Parker* (Copenhagen, 1968); T. Williams, "Charlie Parker Discography," *Discographical Forum* (1968–70; 13 installments); R. Russell, *Bird Lives!* (N.Y., 1973); P. Koster and D.M. Bakker, *Charlie Parker* (discography, 4 vols.; Alphen aan den Rijn, the Netherlands, 1974); L.O. Koch, "Ornithology: A Study of Charlie Parker's Music," *Journal of Jazz Studies* (Dec. 1974 and June 1975); J. Patrick, "Charlie Parker and Harmonic Sources of Bebop Composition," ibid. (June 1975).

Parker, Henry Taylor, American critic and writer on music; b. Boston, April 29, 1867; d. there, March 30, 1934. He attended Harvard Univ.; then served as N.Y. correspondent of the *Boston Evening Transcript* and later as its London correspondent; in 1905 he became the paper's principal drama and music critic, holding this position until his death. Although not trained as a musician (he could not read notes), Parker possessed an extraordinary sense of esthetic values and often gave unstinting praise to composers of the modern school who were disdained by the musical establishment; he was equally capable of appreciating fresh talents among performers. He wrote a curiously antiquated prose, employing archaic turns of phrase, but his articles, often very long, were uniquely artistic. He signed his name H.T.P., which was facetiously deciphered by some as an acronym for "Hard To Please," or "Hell To Pay." He publ. a collection of essays on music, *Eighth-Notes* (N.Y., 1922).

BIBLIOGRAPHY: D.T.W. McCord, *H.T.P.; Portrait of a Critic* (N.Y., 1935).

Parker, Horatio William, eminent American composer and pedagogue; b. Auburndale, Mass., Sept. 15, 1863; d. Cedarhurst, N.Y., Dec. 18, 1919. He studied piano with John Orth, theory with Emery, and composition with Chadwick in Boston; subsequently went to Germany, where he took courses in organ and composition with Rheinberger in Munich (1882–85); under his tutelage he wrote a cantata, *King Trojan* (1885). Returning to N.Y., he taught at the cathedral schools of St. Paul and St. Mary (1886–90), at the General Seminary (1892), and at the National Cons. of Music (1892–93); was organist and choirmaster at St. Luke's (1885–87), St. Andrew's (1887–88), and the Church of the Holy Trinity (1888–93); in 1893 went to Boston as organist and choirmaster at Trinity Church. He attracted attention with the first performance of his oratorio *Hora novissima* (N.Y., May 3, 1893), in which he demonstrated his mastery of choral writing, while his harmonic and contrapuntal style remained securely tied to German practices. In 1894 he was engaged as a prof. of theory at Yale Univ.; in 1904 became dean of its School of Music, and remained there until his death. Many American composers received the benefit of his excellent instruction; among them was Charles Ives, who kept his sincere appreciation of Parker's teaching long after he renounced Parker's conservative traditions. Parker conducted performances of his works in England in 1900 and 1902; received an honorary degree of Mus.Doc. at Cambridge Univ. in 1902. Returning to the U.S., he served as organist and choirmaster at the collegiate church of St. Nicholas in Boston in 1902–10. He continued to compose industriously, without making any concessions to the emerging modern schools of composition; his choral works are particularly notable. In 1911 his opera *Mona* won the $10,000 prize offered by the Metropolitan Opera Co. in N.Y., and was produced there on March 14, 1912; he also won a prize offered by the National Federation of Women's Clubs for his 2nd opera, *Fairyland,* which was produced in Los Angeles on July 1, 1915. Neither of the operas possessed enough power to survive in the repertoire. Besides the 2 operas and the oratorio *Hora novissima*, Parker wrote 2 symph. poems: *A Northern Ballad* and *Vatheil* (1903); a masque, *Cupid and Psyche*, for the 50th anniversary of the founding of the Yale Art School (New Haven, June 16, 1916); Concerto for Organ and Orch. (Boston, Dec. 26, 1902); 2 string quartets; Piano Trio and other pieces of chamber music; a great number of choral works, for which he is mainly distinguished: *The Lord Is My Shepherd; The Ballad of a Knight and His Daughter; King Trojan; Blow, Blow, Thou Winter Wind; The Norsemen's Raid; Morning and Evening Service; Harald Harfager; Dream-King and His Love; 6 Part-songs; The Holy Child; The Legend of St. Christopher; Adstant Angelorum Chori; A Wanderer's Psalm; Hymnos Andron; A Star Song; King Gorm the Grim; A Song of Times; Morven and the Grail; The Dream of Mary;* etc.; numerous songs, with orch. or piano accompaniments; patriotic odes, such as *Union and Liberty*, composed for the inauguration of Theodore Roosevelt in 1905, and the World War I song *The Red Cross Spirit Speaks;* he also wrote a Sonata for Organ and other organ pieces of various dimensions; publ. the educational vols. *The Progressive Music Series* (8 vols.) and *Music and Public Entertainment* (1911).

BIBLIOGRAPHY: G.W. Chadwick, *Horatio Parker* (N.Y., 1921); D.S. Smith, "A Study of Horatio Parker," *Musical Quarterly* (April 1930); Isabel Parker Semler, with Pierson Underwood, *Horatio Parker, A Memoir for His Grandchildren* (N.Y., 1942; with complete list of works).

Parker, James Cutler Dunn, American organist and composer; b. Boston, June 2, 1828; d. Brookline, Mass., Nov. 27, 1916. He studied law in Boston, and music in Leipzig (1851–54) under Moscheles (piano) and Hauptmann and Richter (composition); then lived in Boston; was organist and choir director of Trinity Church (1864–91) and a prof. at the Boston Univ. College of Music. His choral works include *Redemption Hymn* (1877); cantata, *The Blind King* (1886); *St. John: The Life of Man,* oratorio; several church services. He publ. a *Manual of Harmony* (1855) and *Theoretical and Practical Harmony* (1870).

BIBLIOGRAPHY: *Dictionary of American Biography,* vol. XIV.

Parkhurst, Howard Elmore, American organist; b. Ashland, Mass., Sept. 13, 1848; d. (accidentally drowned) Lavalette, N.J., Aug. 18, 1916. He publ. *A Complete System of Harmony* (1908), *A Complete Method for the Modern Organ* (1911), *The Church Organist* (1913), *The Beginnings of the World's Music* (1915), *Rambles in Music-Land* (1914); wrote an oratorio, an orch. overture, and church music.

Parlow, Kathleen, Canadian violinist; b. Calgary, Sept. 20, 1890; d. Oakville, Ontario, Aug. 19, 1963. Her family moved to San Francisco when she was a child, and she had her early instruction in violin

there; in 1906 she was sent to St. Petersburg, Russia, where she was accepted by Leopold Auer in his violin class at the St. Petersburg Cons. She subsequently developed an extensive concert career; played in England, Scandinavia, the U.S., and the Orient. In 1929–36 she was a violin instructor at Mills College in Oakland, Calif.; in 1941, joined the faculty of the Royal Cons. of Music in Toronto; there she organized in 1942 the Parlow String Quartet.

BIBLIOGRAPHY: M.P. French, *Kathleen Parlow, A Portrait* (Toronto, 1967).

Parnas, Leslie, American cellist; b. St. Louis, Nov. 11, 1931. He studied cello with Piatigorsky at the Curtis Inst. of Music in Philadelphia. In 1958 he won the Casals Prize in Prades. In 1959 he made his N.Y. debut; then appeared as soloist with a number of American orchs.; also toured in Europe, Israel, and Russia.

Parodi, Lorenzo, Italian pedagogue and composer; b. Genoa, Aug. 10, 1856; d. there, March 28, 1926. He studied in Genoa and with Guiraud and Massenet in Paris. He taught esthetics and history of music at the Liceo Amilcare Zanella in Genoa, of which he was also director.

WORKS: Oratorios: *Joannes Baptista* and *Calvario;* masses and hymns; cantatas; a *Stabat mater; Suite greca* and *Ouverture triomphale* for Orch.; pieces for violin, and for piano; songs. Also publ. *Musicologia, L'estetica del canone,* and a treatise on instrumentation.

Parratt, Sir Walter, English organist; b. Huddersfield, Feb. 10, 1841; d. Windsor, March 27, 1924. He was a pupil of his father; at 7 played his first church service; at 11, was organist at Armitage Bridge, and passed through successive similar positions to Magdalen College, Oxford (1872), and St. George's Chapel, Windsor (1882), succeeding Elvey. He received a Mus.Bac. from Oxford in 1873; became a prof. of organ at the Royal College of Music in 1883; was knighted in 1892; was made Master of Music in Ordinary to the Queen (1893), to King Edward VII (1901), and to King George V (1910); from 1908 he was a prof. of music at Oxford (resigned on Jan. 1, 1918); from 1916, dean of music at London Univ.; in 1894 he received from Oxford a Mus.Doc. *honoris causa;* was named Commander of the Victorian Order; etc.

WORKS: Music to Aeschylus's *Agamemnon* and *Orestes; Elegy to Patroclus* (1883); anthems, songs, music for organ and piano.

BIBLIOGRAPHY: *Musical Times* (July 1902); *Dictionary of National Biography* (Supplement, 1922–30; pp. 655–57); Sir Donald Tovey and G. Parratt, *Walter Parratt, Master of Music* (London, 1941).

Parris, Herman, American physician and a composer by avocation; b. Ekaterinoslav, Russia, Oct. 30, 1903; d. Philadelphia, Jan. 14, 1973. He was brought to America in his infancy; studied at the Jefferson Medical College in Philadelphia, obtaining his M.D.

in 1926. Concurrently he studied music at the Univ. of Pa. and graduated in 1921. He was a diligent and competent composer; wrote 4 symphs. (1946, 1947, 1949, 1952), 8 piano concertos (one a year between 1946 and 1953), 4 string quartets (1946, 1948, 1960, 1964), 22 piano sonatas (at least one a year between 1946 and 1965), 115 piano preludes (averaging 5 annually between 1946 and 1965), *Hebrew Rhapsody* for Orch. (1949), *Lament* for String Orch. (in memory of Olin Downes; 1956), and various pieces of chamber music. All these compositions remain largely in limbo, and are seldom if ever visibly, audibly, or plausibly performed, but once in his lifetime he gained a flickering moment of notoriety when he produced an orch. piece entitled *Hospital Suite,* realistically portraying bloody events in the sickroom; it was brought to light in a collegiate spirit by the Doctors' Orch. Society in N.Y. on May 13, 1948. Unfortunately, no further performances were given (all the patients in the suite died).

Parris, Robert, American composer and pianist; b. Philadelphia, May 21, 1924. He studied piano as a youth; enrolled at the Univ. of Pa. (B.S., 1945; M.S., 1946); then studied composition with Peter Mennin at the Juilliard School of Music in N.Y. (B.S., 1948) and with Ibert and Copland at the Berkshire Music Center in Tanglewood (1950–51); in 1952–53 he received a Fulbright fellowship to study with Honegger at the Ecole Normale de Musique in Paris. He taught at several univs. before settling in Washington, D.C., where he joined the faculty of The George Washington Univ. in 1963. His music is distinguished by strong formal structure and tonal cohesion; when pragmatically justifiable, he applies serialistic techniques with deliberate circumspection.
WORKS: FOR ORCH.: Symph. (1952); Piano Concerto (1954); Concerto for 5 Kettledrums and Orch. (1955; Washington, D.C., March 25, 1958); Viola Concerto (1956; Washington, May 20, 1971); Violin Concerto (1958); Flute Concerto (1964); Concerto for Trombone and Chamber Orch. (Washington, Sept. 19, 1964); Concerto for Percussion, Violin, Cello, and Piano (1967); *The Phoenix,* concerto for Timpani and Orch. (1969; Detroit, Jan. 2, 1970); *The Messengers* for Orch. (later retitled *Angels;* 1974; Albany, N.Y., March 14, 1975); *Rite of Passage* for Clarinet, Electric Guitar, and Chamber Orch. (1978); *Chamber Music for Orchestra* (1984). CHAMBER MUSIC: 2 string trios (1948, 1951); 2 string quartets (1951, 1952); Sonatina for Brass (1948); Sonatina for Winds (1954); Sonata for Viola and Piano (1956); Sonata for Violin and Piano (1956); Quintet for Violin, Cello, Flute, Oboe, and Bassoon (1957); Trio for Clarinet, Piano, and Cello (1959); Sinfonia for Brass (1963); Sonatina for Recorder Quartet (1964); Duo for Flute and Violin (1965); Sonata for Solo Violin (1965); *The Book of Imaginary Beings* for Flute, Violin, Viola, Cello, and Percussion (1972); *The Book of Imaginary Beings, Part II,* for Clarinet, Violin, Viola, Cello, and Percussion (1983). VOCAL MUSIC: *Night* for Baritone, String Quartet, and Clarinet (1951); *Alas, for the Day,* cantata (1954); *Mad Scene* for Soloists and Chamber Orch. (1960); *The Raids: 1940* for Soprano, Piano, and Violin (1960); *Hymn for the Nativity* for Chorus and Brass Ensemble (1962); *Dreams* for Soprano and Chamber Orch. (1976).

Parrish, Carl, American musicologist and composer; b. Plymouth, Pa., Oct. 9, 1904; d. (as a result of injuries incurred in an automobile accident) Valhalla, N.Y., Nov. 27, 1965. After receiving his Ph.D at Harvard with the dissertation *The Early Piano and Its Influences on Keyboard Technique and composition in the Eighteenth Century* (1939), he taught at Wells College (1939–43), Fisk Univ. (1943–46), Westminster Choir College (1946–49), and Pomona College (1943–46); from 1953 he was a prof. at Vassar College. He publ. *The Notation of Medieval Music* (N.Y., 1957; 2nd ed., 1959) and *A Treasury of Early Music* (N.Y., 1958). In collaboration with John F. Ohl, he publ. *Masterpieces of Music before 1750* (N.Y., 1951); wrote choral settings of folk songs; a String Quartet; a song cycle; piano pieces.

Parrott, Andrew, English conductor; b. Walsall, March 10, 1947. He studied at Oxford Univ., where he pursued research into the performing practices of 16th- and 17th-century music. In 1973 he founded the Taverner Choir, and subsequently the Taverner Consort and Players. He conducted Monteverdi's *Vespers* at London's Promenade Concerts in 1977; gave the first performance in London of Bach's *B-minor Mass* with period instruments; also presented in authentic style the *St. Matthew Passion* and the *Brandenburg Concertos.* He appeared as a guest conductor with the English Chamber Orch., the London Bach Orch., and the Concerto Amsterdam.

Parrott, Ian, British composer; b. London, March 5, 1916. He studied at the Royal College of Music and at Oxford Univ., where he received his degrees of B.Mus. and D.Mus. During World War II he served in the Royal Corps of Signals in the Middle East and North Africa; after the war was a lecturer in music at Birmingham Univ. (1947–50) and from 1950 to 1983 at the Univ. College of Wales in Aberystwyth. He wrote the opera *The Black Ram* (in the Welsh language, Aberystwyth, March 9, 1966); ballet, *Maid in Birmingham* (1951); 3 symphs. (1946, 1960, 1966); symph. prelude, *El Alamein* (1944); symph. impression, *Luxor* (1948); Piano Concerto (1948); Wind Quintet (1948); *Fantasy Trio* for Piano, Violin, and Cello (1950); *Solemn Overture* (1956); Concerto for English Horn and Orch. (1956); Concerto for Trombone and Wind Instruments (1967); 4 string quartets. He publ. a number of useful manuals: *Pathway to Modern Music* (London, 1947); *A Guide to Musical Thought* (London, 1955); *Method in Orchestration* (London, 1957); and a monograph, *Elgar* (London, 1971).

Parry, Sir (Charles) Hubert (Hastings), eminent English composer and pedagogue; b. Bournemouth, Feb. 27, 1848; d. Knight's Croft, Rustington, Oct. 7, 1918. While at Eton, from 1861, he studied composition with G. Elvey; took part in the concerts of the

Musical Society as pianist, organist, violinist, and composer. At 19, while still a student at Eton, he took the degree of Mus.Bac. at Oxford. He entered Exeter College, Oxford, in 1867. There he began to study music in earnest under Bennett and Macfarren, also taking piano lessons from Dannreuther (1872–79). His public career as a composer began with the production of an *Intermezzo religioso* for Strings at the Gloucester Festival of 1868. In 1883 Parry was appointed Choragus of Oxford Univ.; in that year Cambridge conferred on him the honorary degree of Mus.Doc., followed by Oxford (1884) and Dublin (1891) degrees. In 1894 he succeeded Sir George Grove as director of the Royal College of Music, which post he held until his death; in 1899–1908 he was a prof. of music at Oxford Univ.; in 1898 he was knighted.

WORKS: Opera, *Guinevere* (1885–86); 4 symphs. (1878–82, 1883, 1889, 1889); overture, *Guillem de Cabestanh* (1878–79); *Overture to an Unwritten Tragedy* (1893); Piano Concerto in F-sharp (1878–79); *Suite moderne* (1886); *Lady Radnor's Suite* for Strings (1894); *An English Suite* (publ. posthumously, 1921); symph. fantasy in B minor, *1912* (1912); symph. poem, *From Death to Life* (1914); other works for orch.; 3 oratorios: *Judith* (Birmingham, 1888); *Job* (Gloucester, 1892; his best work); *King Saul* (Birmingham, 1894); *Scenes from Shelley's Prometheus Unbound* (Gloucester, 1880); choral song, *Jerusalem* (publ. 1916); many anthems, hymns, motets, odes, part-songs, etc.; 3 string quartets (1867, 1868, 1878–80); 3 piano trios (1878, 1884, 1884–90); String Quintet (1884); Piano Quartet (1879); Nonet for Winds (1877); Fantasy-Sonata for Violin and Piano (1878); Cello Sonata (1883); etc.; songs; organ pieces; piano pieces.

WRITINGS: His publ. writings include numerous excellent articles in *Grove's Dictionary, Studies of Great Composers* (1886; 8th ed., 1904); *The Art of Music* (1893; enlarged as *The Evolution of the Art of Music,* 1896; new revised ed. by H.C. Colles, N.Y., 1930); *Summary of the History and Development of Medieval and Modern European Music* (1893); *The Music of the 17th Century* (vol. III of the *Oxford History of Music,* 1902; 2nd ed., 1938, ed. by E.J. Dent); *J.S. Bach* (1909; revised ed., 1934); *Style in Musical Art* (1911). His college addresses were publ. by H.C. Colles (1920).

BIBLIOGRAPHY: R.O. Morris, "H. Parry," *Music & Letters* (April 1920); C.L. Graves, *H. Parry, His Life and Works* (2 vols., London, 1926); G.M. Greene, *Two Witnesses* (N.Y., 1930); J.A. Fuller-Maitland, *The Music of Parry and Stanford* (Cambridge, 1934).

Parry, John (called **"Bardd Alaw,"** "master of song"), Welsh musician; b. Denbigh, Feb. 18, 1776; d. London, April 8, 1851. He played clarinet in a band; then was a bandmaster; was composer to Vauxhall in 1809; conductor of "Eisteddfodau" in Wales for years; was a critic for the *Morning Post* (1834–48), and treasurer of the Royal Society of Musicians (1831–49).

WORKS: *The Welsh Harper* (1839–48; collection of Welsh music, with a historical introduction); various other collections; also much original music (incidental music to several plays, harp sonatas, glees, songs, part-songs, etc.).

BIBLIOGRAPHY: *Dictionary of National Biography,* vol. XLIII (1895).

Parry, John, blind Welsh bard; b. Nevin, South Caernarvonshire, North Wales, 1710; d. Wynnstay, Denbighshire, Oct. 7, 1782. He served as harper to Sir W.W. Wynne. He collected several vols. of folk songs: *Antient British Music* (tunes of Cambro-Britons, 1742); *Collection of Welsh, English and Scotch Airs* (1760–65); *Cambrian Harmony: A Collection of Antient Welsh Airs* (1781).

Parry, Joseph, Welsh composer; b. Merthyr Tydfil, May 21, 1841; d. Penarth, near Cardiff, Feb. 17, 1903. His parents emigrated to America, but he returned to Britain, won Eisteddfod prizes for songs, and entered the Royal Academy of Music in 1868, studying under Bennett, Garcia, and Steggall; received his Mus.Bac. degree from Cambridge in 1871; then was appointed a prof. of music at the Univ. College in Aberystwyth.

WORKS: 5 operas: *Blodwen* (Aberdare, 1878); *Virginia* (Aberdare, 1883); *Arianwen* (Cardiff, 1890); *Sylvia* (Cardiff, 1895); *King Arthur* (finished 1897); oratorios: *Emmanuel* (1880) and *Saul of Tarsus* (1892); cantatas: *The Prodigal Son; Nebuchadnezzar; Cambria; The Maid of Cefu Idfa;* also, *Druids' Chorus;* an orch. ballade; overtures; String Quartet; piano music, anthems, songs.

BIBLIOGRAPHY: *Dictionary of National Biography* (Supplement, 1901–11; vol. III, pp. 73–74).

Parsch, Arnošt, avant-garde Czech composer; b. Bučovice, Moravia, Feb. 12, 1936. In 1967 he joined in Brno a modern group of composers, organized by Alois Piňos.

WORKS: Concerto for Instruments, Percussion, and Piano (1964); Trio for Clarinet, Violin, and Viola (1965); Sonata for Chamber Orch. and Tape (1966); *Didacticas 1; Didacticas 2* for Double Bass and Piano (1966–68); *Didacticas 3* for Violin, Piano, and Percussion (1969); *4 Poetics* for various instrumental combinations and Tape (1966–69); 2 symphs. (1967, 1970–72); *Structures* for Bass Clarinet and Piano (1967); *Transpositions* for Wind Quintet (1967); Concertino for Violin, Piano, Guitar, and Percussion (1968); 2 string quartets (1969, 1973); *Rota* for Violin and Double Bass (1971); *Esercizii per uno, due, tre e quattro* for 2 Flutes, Cello, and Guitar (1971); *Contraposizioni per Due Boemi* for Bass Clarinet and Piano (1972); *Znamení touhy (Sign of Desire),* melodramatic cantata (1972); *4 pezzi* for Clarinet, Violin, Double Bass, and Piano (1972); *Útěk (Escape),* symph. poem (1973; Prague, March 30, 1974); *Night of Fire* for Children's Chorus, Organ, and Piano (1975); *Les Fleurs* for Bass Clarinet and Piano (1976); Double Concerto for Flute, Trombone, and Orch. (1976); *Sitting Bull,* jazz cantata (1975).

Parsley (**Parseley, Persleye, Parcele,** etc.), **Osbert,** English church-music composer; b. 1511; d. Norwich, 1585. He was a lay clerk at Norwich Cathedral for about 50 years. *Tudor Church Music* (vol. 10) contains reprints of 5 of his works; MSS in the British Museum include several motets; *Perslis clocke for 5 Voices;* etc.

BIBLIOGRAPHY: *Dictionary of National Biography,* vol. XLIII (1895).

Parsons, Albert Ross, American piano pedagogue; b. Sandusky, Ohio, Sept. 16, 1847; d. Mount Kisco, N.Y., June 14, 1933. He studied with F.L. Ritter in N.Y.; then went to Germany, where he took piano lessons with Moscheles, Reinecke, Wenzel, and Papperitz at the Leipzig Cons. and music theory with Richter and Paul there; later he received additional instruction with Tausig, Kullak, Weitzmann, and Wüerst in Berlin. In 1871 he settled in N.Y., where he earned the reputation of a piano teacher according to the best German traditions of the art. He publ. the manuals *Science of Pianoforte Practice* (1886) and *The Virtuoso Handling of the Pianoforte* (1917), and wrote some choral and piano music.

BIBLIOGRAPHY: *Dictionary of American Biography,* vol. XIV.

Parsons, Geoffrey, Australian pianist; b. Sydney, June 15, 1929. He studied at the New South Wales State Conservatorium of Music; in 1950 he went to London; subsequently established himself as a fine accompanist, appearing with such leading musicians as Hans Hotter, Elisabeth Schwarzkopf, Nicolai Gedda, and Dame Janet Baker. He was made a Commander of the Order of the British Empire in 1977.

Parsons, Graham, short-lived American country-rock musician and songwriter; b. Winterhaven, Fla., Sept. 5, 1946; d. Joshua Tree, Calif., Sept. 19, 1973. He twanged the guitar in Georgia bands, and somehow managed to take time out to study theology at Harvard; it was in those patrician surroundings that he organized a country-rock group, which he called The International Submarine Band. He also contributed to the Byrds in their famous album *Sweetheart of the Rodeo.* On his own he put out *Hickory Wind* and *One Hundred Years from Now.* In 1968 he formed the Flying Burrito Brothers, which recorded his greatest success, *The Gilded Palace of Sin.* There followed *Burrito Deluxe* and *The Last of the Red Hot Burritos.* Just before dying of immoderate drug use, he composed his last song, ironically titled *Grievous Angel.*

Pärt, Arvo, remarkably inventive Estonian composer; b. Paide, Sept. 11, 1935. He studied composition with Heino Eller at the Tallinn Cons., graduating in 1963; from 1958 to 1967 was attached to the music division of Estonian Radio. In 1980 he emigrated; in 1982 he settled in West Berlin. He began to compose in a traditional manner, writing instrumental pieces in a neo-Baroque idiom, strict to form, freely dissonant in harmony; under the influence of Western musical modernism he gradually levitated toward the empyreal emporium of empiric sonorism, without renouncing, however, the historic foundation of tonality. The spectrum of his musical vocabulary extends from abecedarian minimalism to quaquaversal polytonality, from impressionistic pointillism to austere serialism. One of his original specialities is a technique he calls "tintinnabuli," in which he applies shifting phases of a given chord. Pärt was the first Estonian composer to use the authentic Schoenbergian method of composition with 12 different tones related only to one another to form melodic and harmonic dodecaphonic structures. He applied it in his arresting *Nekrolog,* dedicated to the victims of the Holocaust. Extending the concept of integral dodecaphony, he makes use of pandiatonic and panpentatonic tone-clusters, culminating in the formation of a Brobdingnagian blob of "white noise." When at a loss for new ideas, he resorts to aleatory proceedings. He also harks upon occasion back to historic antecedents in applying the austere precepts of *ars antiqua.* In this, Pärt commends himself as a true *Homo ludens,* a musician playing a diversified game.

WORKS: FOR ORCH.: *Nekrolog,* dedicated to the victims of fascism (1960); 3 symphs.: No. 1, *Polyphonic* (1963); No. 2 (1966); No. 3 (1971); *Perpetuum mobile* (1963); *Collage on the Theme B-A-C-H* for Strings, Oboe, and Harpsichord (1964); *Pro et contra* for Cello and Orch. (1964); *Wenn Bach Bienen gezüchtet hätte (If Bach Had Raised Bees),* on the theme B-A-C-H, concertino for Harpsichord, Electric Bass Guitar, Electronic Tape, and Ensemble (1978; Graz, Oct. 7, 1983; version B for Harpsichord and 20 Strings, 1980); *Cantus in Memory of Benjamin Britten* for String Orch. and Glockenspiel (1977); *Tabula Rasa* ("scraped tablet," alluding to the epistemological philosophy propagated by John Locke asserting that the human mind possesses no innate notions), concerto for Violin, String Orch., and Prepared Piano (1977); *Fratres I,* version B, for String Orch. and Percussion (1977–82; Göteborg, Sweden, May 19, 1983); Concerto for Violin, Cello, and Chamber Orch. (1978–79; London, April 23, 1981); *Spiegel im Spiegel (Mirror in Mirror),* version B, for Violin, Piano, and Strings (1980); Cello Concerto (1983).

FOR VOICE: *Meie Aed (Our Garden),* cantata for Children's Chorus and Orch. (1959); *Maailma samm (The World's Stride),* oratorio (1961); *Solfeggio* for Mixed Chorus and String Quartet (1964); *Credo* for Solo Piano, Mixed Chorus, and Orch. (1968); *Laul armastatule (Song for the Beloved),* cantata-symph. to poems by Rustaveli (1973); *Calix (Dies irae)* for Chorus, Organ, Trumpet, Trombone, Glockenspiel, Tam-tam, 2 Electric Guitars, and Kettledrum (1976); *Modus (Tintinnabulum 2)* for Soprano and Instrumental Ensemble (1976); *Missa sillabica* for 4 Voices or Chamber Choir, and 6 Instruments (1977); *Cantate Domino canticum novum (Psalm 95)* for 4 Voices and 4 Instruments (1977); *De profundis* for Male Chorus, Organ, and Percussion ad lib. (1970; *Summa* for Tenor, Baritone, and 6 Instruments (1978); *Passio Domini nos-*

tri Jesu Christi secundum Joannem for Chorus and Ensemble (1981–82; Munich, Nov. 28, 1982).

CHAMBER MUSIC: String Quartet (1959); Quintettino for 5 Wind Instruments (1964); *Musica syllabica* for 12 Instruments (1964); *Kriips ja punkt (Dash and Dot)* for Ensemble (1967); *Fratres I*, version A, for String Quintet and Wind Quintet (1977), and version C, for Nonet (1977); *Fratres II* for Solo Violin (1980); *Fratres III* for Solo Cello (1980); *Arbos* for 7 Instruments (1977); *Spiegel im Spiegel*, version A, for Violin and Piano (1978); *Pari Intervallo*, version A, for 4 Instruments (1980); *Die Brüder* for Violin and Piano (1980).

FOR PIANO: 2 sonatinas (1958, 1959); *Partita* (1959); *Diagrams,* aleatory work (1964); *Für Alina* (1976); *Variationen zur Gesundung von Arinuschka (Variations for Arinuschka's Recuperation)* (1977); *Pari Intervallo,* version C (1980).

FOR ORGAN: *Trivium* (1976); *Annum per annum* (1980); *Pari intervallo,* version B (1980).

Partch, Harry, remarkable American composer; b. Oakland, Calif., June 24, 1901; d. San Diego, Sept. 3, 1974. Largely autodidact, he began experimenting with instruments capable of producing fractional intervals, which led him to the formulation of a 43-tone scale; he expounded his findings in his book, *Genesis of a Music* (1949). Among new instruments constructed by him are elongated violas, a chromelodeon, kitharas with 72 strings, harmonic canons with 44 strings, boos (made of giant Philippine bamboo reeds), cloud-chamber bowls, blow-boys (a pair of bellows with an attached automobile horn), etc. Seeking intimate contact with American life, he wandered across the country, collecting indigenous expressions of folkways, inscriptions on public walls, etc., for texts in his productions. WORKS: *8 Hitchhiker Inscriptions from a California Highway Railing* and *U.S. Highball, A Musical Account of a Transcontinental Hobo Trip* for Chorus and Instruments (both perf. for the first time in Carnegie Chamber Hall, N.Y., April 22, 1944); *The Letter, A Depression Message from a Hobo Friend* for Voices and Instrumental Ensemble (1944); *Oedipus,* music drama (Mills College, Oakland, March 14, 1952); *The Bewitched,* dance satire (Univ. of Illinois, Urbana, March 26, 1957); *Revelation in the Courthouse Park,* musical tragedy (Univ. of Illinois, Urbana, April 11, 1961); *Water, Water,* an American ritual (Univ. of Illinois, March 9, 1962). BIBLIOGRAPHY: Peter Yates, "Genesis of a Music," *High Fidelity* (July 1963); P. Earls, "Harry Partch: *Verses* in Preparation for *Delusion of the Fury,*" *Inter-American Institute for Musical Research: Yearbook III* (1967).

Parton, Dolly (Rebecca), American singer and songwriter of country and pop-rock music; b. Locust Ridge, near Sevierville, Tenn., Jan. 19, 1946. Born into a poverty-stricken family, she began to sing as a child; after graduating from high school, she went to Nashville, Tenn., to seek her fortune; in 1967 she became a member of Porter Wagoner's band. She quickly assumed a leading place among country-music stars; in 1976 she moved into the pop-rock field, and toured widely with her own group, Gypsy Fever. She composed such popular songs as *Coat of Many Colors, Tennessee Mountain Home, Joshua, Jolene,* and *Love Is Like a Butterfly;* she was particularly successful with the country album *Here You Come Again* and the pop-rock album *Heartbreakers.* To top it all, she made herself famous by appearing as one of the 3 rather odd secretaries in the comedy film *Nine to Five.*

Partos, Oedoen, Hungarian-born Israeli composer and violist; b. Budapest, Oct. 1, 1907; d. Tel Aviv, July 6, 1977. He studied violin with Hubay and composition with Kodály at the Royal Academy of Music in Budapest (1918–24). In 1938 he went to Palestine; was first violist in the Palestine Symph. Orch. (later Israel Phil.) from 1938 to 1956. In 1951 he was appointed director of the Tel Aviv Academy of Music (later the Israel Rubin Academy of Tel Aviv Univ.); from 1961, he was a prof. there. He was the soloist for the premieres of his 3 viola concertos. His early works followed the rhythmical and melodic patterns of the oriental tradition, emphasized the chromatic melodic turns, and developed a free accumulation of variations on a theme that is never stated in its entirety. In 1971 Partos went to the Netherlands and experimented with the possibilities of 31-tone scales proposed by the 17th-century Dutch physicist and mathematician Christiaan Huygens. WORKS: 2 string quartets: No. 1, *Concertino* (1932; revised 1939; N.Y., May 24, 1941), and No. 2, *Tehilim* (*Psalms;* 1960; also for String Orch., without Double Basses, 1960); *4 Folk Songs* for Alto and String Quartet (1939); *Yizkor (In memoriam)* for Viola or Violin or Cello, and String Orch. (1947); *Rondo* for Violin and Piano (1947); *4 Israeli Tunes* for Violin or Viola or Cello, and Piano (1948); 3 viola concertos: No. 1, *Songs of Praise* (Tel Aviv, Jan. 22, 1949); No. 2 (1957); No. 3, *Sinfonia concertante* (Jerusalem, 1963); *Ein Gev,* symph. fantasy (1951–52; Ein Gev, Oct. 1, 1953; UNESCO Prize, 1952; Israel State Prize, 1954); *Oriental Ballad* for Viola and Cello, and Orch. or Piano (1956); Violin Concerto (1958); *Maqamat* for Flute and String Quartet (1959); *Agada (A Legend)* for Viola, Piano, and Percussion (1960; London Festival of the International Society for Contemporary Music, June 6, 1962); *Iltur (Improvisation)* for 12 Harps (1960); *Prelude* for Piano (1960); *Dmuyoth (Images)* for Orch. (1960); *Daughter of Israel,* cantata (1961); *5 Israeli Songs* for Tenor, Oboe, Piano, and Cello (1962); *Symphonic Movements* (1966); *Arpiliyot (Nebulae)* for Wind Quintet (1966); *Netivim (Paths),* symph. elegy (1969); *Shiluvim (Fuses)* for Viola and Chamber Orch. (Tel Aviv, June 21, 1970); Concertino for Flute and Piano (1969); *Metamorphoses* for Piano (1971); *Music* for Chamber Orch. (1971); *3 Fantasies* for 2 Violins (1972; composed in the 31-tone system); *Arabesque* for Oboe and Chamber Orch. (1975); *Ballad,* piano quartet (1977); *Fantasy,* piano trio (1977); *Invenzione a 3 (Homage à Debussy)* for Flute, Harp, and Viola (1977).

BIBLIOGRAPHY: W. Elias, *Oedoen Partos* (Tel Aviv, 1978).

Partridge, Ian, English tenor; b. London, June 12, 1938. He received his musical training at New College, Oxford; Clifton College; the Royal College of Music; and the Guildhall School of Music. He first sang in the Westminster Cathedral Choir; then began a solo career. He specialized in German lieder; often appeared in local duos with his sister **Jennifer Partridge.**

Pasatieri, Thomas, talented American opera composer; b. New York, Oct. 20, 1945. He began to play the piano by spontaneous generation, and picked up elements of composition, particularly vocal, by a similar subliminal process; between the ages of 14 and 18 he wrote some 400 songs. He persuaded Nadia Boulanger to take him as a student by correspondence between Paris and N.Y. when he was 15; at 16 he entered the Juilliard School of Music, where he became a student of Vittorio Giannini and Vincent Persichetti; he also took a course with Darius Milhaud in Aspen, Colo., where his first opera, *The Women,* to his own libretto, was performed when he was only 19. It became clear to him that opera was his natural medium, and that the way to achieve the best results was by following the evolutionary line of Italian operatic productions characterized by the felicity of *bel canto,* facility of harmonic writing, and euphonious fidelity to the lyric and dramatic content of the subject. In striving to attain these objectives, Pasatieri ran the tide of mandatory inharmoniousness; while his productions were applauded by hoi polloi, they shocked music critics and other composers; one of them described Pasatieri's music as "a stream of perfumed urine." This attitude is akin to that taken by some toward Vittorio Giannini and Gian Carlo Menotti (interestingly, all 3 are of Italian genetic stock). From 1967 to 1969 Pasatieri taught at the Juilliard School; then was engaged at the Manhattan School of Music (1969–71); from 1980 was Distinguished Visiting Prof. at the Univ. of Cincinnati College-Cons. of Music.

WORKS: The list of Pasatieri's operas grows with every passing year: *The Women* (Aspen, Aug. 20, 1965); *La Divina* (N.Y., March 16, 1966); *Padrevia* (Brooklyn, Nov. 18, 1967); *Calvary* (Seattle, April 7, 1971); *The Trial of Mary Lincoln,* television opera (Boston, Feb. 14, 1972); *Black Widow* (Seattle, March 2, 1972); *The Seagull,* after Chekhov's play (Houston, March 5, 1974); *Signor Deluso,* after Molière's comedy *Sganarelle* (Greenway, Va., July 27, 1974); *The Penitentes* (Aspen, Aug. 3, 1974); *Ines de Castro* (Baltimore, March 30, 1976); *Washington Square,* after Henry James (Detroit, Oct. 3, 1976); *Before Breakfast* (1980); *Maria Elena* (Tucson, April 8, 1983). He further wrote *Héloïse and Abelard* for Soprano, Baritone, and Piano (1971); *Rites de passage* for Voice and Strings (1974); *3 Poems of James Agee* for Voice and Piano (1974); 2 piano sonatas and other piano pieces.

BIBLIOGRAPHY: Peter G. Davis, "They Love Him in Seattle," *N.Y. Times Magazine* (March 21, 1976).

Pasdeloup, Jules-Etienne, famous French conductor; b. Paris, Sept. 15, 1819; d. Fontainebleau, Aug. 13, 1887. He studied piano at the Cons. with Laurent and Zimmerman; from 1841 he was répétiteur of a solfeggio class; in 1847–50, teacher of a piano class, which he gave up to organize the celebrated symph. concerts of the Société des Jeunes Elèves du Conservatoire (1853), developing (1861) into the Concerts Populaires de Musique Classique at the Cirque Napoléon, a pioneer series of good, inexpensive popular concerts which were a success from the start. Pasdeloup also taught a vocal ensemble class at the Cons. (1855–68). His popular concerts gradually lost ground in competition with Colonne and Lamoureux, ceasing in 1884; he revived them in 1886–87, just before his death. A grand popular music festival at the Trocadéro (1884), instituted for his benefit, netted him nearly 100,000 francs.

BIBLIOGRAPHY: A. Elwart, *Histoire des Concerts Populaires de Musique Classique* (Paris, 1864); E. Bernard, "Jules Pasdeloup et les Concerts Populaires," *Revue de Musicologie,* LVII (1971).

Pasero, Tancredi, Italian bass; b. Turin, Jan. 11, 1893; d. Milan, Feb. 17, 1983. He studied in Turin; made his debut in 1917 as Rodolfo in *La Sonnambula* in Vicenza; in 1926 he joined La Scala in Milan, remaining on its roster until 1952. He made his Metropolitan Opera debut in N.Y. on Nov. 1, 1929, as Alvise in *La Gioconda;* continued on its roster until 1933. He also had guest engagements in South America; his repertoire was extensive and included Italian, German, French, and Russian operas; he excelled in the bass roles in Verdi's operas, and made a distinctive appearance as Boris Godunov.

Pashchenko, Andrei, prolific Russian composer; b. Rostov, Aug. 15, 1883; d. Moscow, Nov. 16, 1972. He studied with Vitols and Steinberg at the St. Petersburg Cons., graduating in 1917; occupied various clerical positions; was librarian of the Leningrad Phil.; in 1961 he went to live in Moscow. An exceptionally fertile composer, he wrote some 14 operas and 15 symphs.; the style of his music is a natural continuation of the traditions of the Russian national school; in his later works he allowed a certain influx of impressionistic harmonies and unresolved dissonant combinations.

WORKS: Operas: *Eagles in Revolt* (Leningrad, Nov. 7, 1925); *King Maximilian* (1927); *The Black Cliff* (Leningrad, June 12, 1931); *The Pompadours* (1939); *Jester Balakirev* (1949); *The Capricious Bride* (1956); *Radda and Loyko* (1957); *Nila Snishko* (1961); *The Great Seducer* (1966); *Woman, This Is the Devil* (1966); *African Love* (1966); *The Horse in the Senate* (1967); *Portrait* (1968); *Master and Margarita* (1971); 15 symphs. (1915, 1929, 1933, 1938, 1952, 1954, 1956, 1957, 1958, 1963, 1964, 1966, 1969, 1969, 1970); 4 sinfoniettas (1943, 1945, 1953, 1964); *Volga Fantasy* for Orch. (1961); *Ukrainiada,* symph. poem (1963); *Icarus,* symph. poem (1964); *Dance Triptych* for Orch. (1965); *The Voice of Peace,* symph. poem (1971); *Poem of Stars,* symph. poem (1971); Cello Concerto (1964); 9 string quartets; numerous works for chorus. He publ. *Essays on the History and Theory of Music* (Leningrad, 1939).

BIBLIOGRAPHY: Y. Meylikh, *Andrei Pashchenko* (Leningrad, 1960).

Pashkalov, Viacheslav, Russian ethnomusicologist; b. Moscow, May 14, 1873; d. Leningrad, Dec. 26, 1951. He studied literature and music in Moscow; in 1919 was appointed head of the ethnographic division of the Moscow State Library. He publ. the valuable treatises *Survey of the Musical Structure of the Russian Songs of the Province of Voronezh* (1914); *The Musical Structure of the Songs of the Crimea* (1924); *Songs of the Orient* (1925). He was also a composer; wrote a number of songs in a national Russian style.

Pashkevich, Vasily, Russian violinist and composer; b. c.1740; d. March 20, 1797. In 1763 he was admitted as a violinist to the 2nd court orch. in St. Petersburg; in 1779 was engaged as a theater conductor there. His Russian opera *A Carriage Accident* was performed in St. Petersburg on Nov. 7, 1779; in 1782 he presented 2 comic operas in Russian: *The Miser* (Moscow) and *The Pasha of Tunis* (St. Petersburg). In 1783 he was transferred to the first court orch.; in 1786 was commissioned by Catherine the Great to write a comic Russian opera, *Fevey,* for which the Empress herself wrote the libretto. It was produced in St. Petersburg on April 19, 1786, and Pashkevich received an award of 1,000 rubles. In 1789 he was appointed chief of ball music at the Imperial Palace, and simultaneously was elevated to the rank of concertmaster of the first court orch. In 1790 he collaborated with Sarti and Canobbio on another Russian opera to a text of Catherine the Great, *The Early Reign of Oleg,* which was first produced at the palace, and publicly performed in St. Petersburg on Nov. 2, 1790. In collaboration with Martín y Soler, he wrote still another comic opera to a text by the Empress, *Fedul and His Children* (perf. at the palace, Jan. 27, 1791; publicly, St. Petersburg, March 2, 1791). He was given the honorary rank of colonel. His Mass according to the Russian Orthodox liturgy was publ. in Moscow in 1796.

BIBLIOGRAPHY: R.-Aloys Mooser, *Annales de la musique et des musiciens en Russie au XVIII*ᵉ *siècle* (Geneva, 1950; vol. II, pp. 55–57).

Pasini (-Vitale), Lina, Italian soprano; b. Rome, Nov. 8, 1872; d. there, Nov. 23, 1959. She studied in Rome; made her debut in 1893 as Cecilia in Cilea's *Tilda* at the Teatro dal Verme in Milan; then sang at La Scala in Milan, Turin, the Teatro Colón in Buenos Aires, Rome, and Naples; retired from the stage in 1928. She married the conductor **Edoardo Vitale.** At the height of her career, she was widely regarded as one of the finest Wagnerian sopranos on the Italian stage.

Paskalis, Kostas, Greek baritone; b. Livadia, Sept. 1, 1929. He studied at the Athens Cons.; made his debut as Rigoletto in Athens in 1951, singing at the Opera there until 1960. In 1958 he made his first appearance with the Vienna State Opera, and subsequently sang there regularly; also sang in Berlin, Moscow, Leningrad, and London. On Feb. 17, 1965, he made his Metropolitan Opera debut in N.Y. as Carlo in *La forza del destino.*

Pasmore, Henry Bickford, American singing teacher and composer; b. Jackson, Wis., June 27, 1857; d. San Francisco, Feb. 23, 1944. He studied in San Francisco; then went to Leipzig and London, where he took courses in singing with various teachers. Returning to America, he taught singing at the Univ. of the Pacific, San Jose, at Stanford Univ., and at Mills College. He wrote an exotic opera, *Lo-ko-rah;* another opera on a libretto based on Californian history, *Amor y oro;* an overture, *Miles Standish;* a symph. poem, *Gloria California;* a Mass; several cantatas; church music; songs.

Pasquali (Pascale, Paschali), Francesco, Italian composer, one of the earliest musicians to write instrumental pieces with figured bass; b. Cosenza, c.1590; d. after 1633. He studied in Rome, and remained there for most of his life. Between 1615 and 1633 he brought out 3 books of madrigals for 4 and 5 voices, and several vols. of secular and sacred songs for one, 2, 3, 4, and 5 voices.

Pasquali, Nicolò, Italian violinist and composer; b. c.1718; d. Edinburgh, Oct. 13, 1757. He settled in Edinburgh in 1740; was in Dublin between 1748 and 1752, then briefly in London, before returning to Edinburgh. He publ. sonatas for violin with accompaniments; 12 overtures; and an instructive book, *Thorough-bass Made Easy* (Edinburgh, 1757).

Pasquini, Bernardo, Italian organist and composer; b. Massa di Valdinievole, Tuscany, Dec. 7, 1637; d. Rome, Nov. 21, 1710. He came to Rome in 1650 and studied with Vittori and Cesti; was employed as a church organist at Chiesa Nuova (1661–63), at S. Maria Maggiore (1663), at Santa Maria in Aracoeli (1664 until his death), and at S. Luigi dei Francesi (1673–75); served as first organist at the Oratory of SS. Crocifisso (1664–85), and was at one time in the employ of Prince Giambattista Borghese as a chamber musician. He was renowned as a teacher; Durante, G. Muffat, and Della Ciaja were his pupils. He wrote about 17 oratorios, 14 operas (1672–92), and chamber cantatas, but was distinguished mainly for his keyboard composition; his toccatas and suites were publ. during his lifetime in the collection *Toccates et suites pour le clavecin de MM. Pasquini, Poglietti et Gaspard Kerle* (Paris, 1704). Other clavier works were brought out by L. Torchi in *L'arte musicale in Italia,* by Cesi, by Tagliapietra in *Antologia di musica antica e moderna per pianoforte,* and in other anthologies. His vocal pieces were publ. by F. Boghen (1923, 1930). His collected works for keyboard, edited by M.B. Haynes, were publ. in 7 vols. (Rome, 1964–68); a Sonata for 2 Claviers was brought out by W. Danckert (Kassel, 1971).

BIBLIOGRAPHY: V. Virgili, *Bernardo Pasquini* (Pescia, 1908); A. Bonaventura, *Bernardo Pasquini* (Ascoli Piceno, 1923); F. Boghen, *L'arte di Bernardo Pasquini* (1931); G. Roncaglia, "Il Tirinto di Bernardo Pasquini e i suoi intermezzi," *Rassegna Musicale* (Nov. 1931); G. Crain, *The Operas of Bernardo Pasquini* (Diss., Yale Univ., 1965); W.S. Newman, *The Sonata in the Baroque Era* (Chapel Hill, N.C., 1966).

Pasquini, Ercole, Italian organist and composer; b. Ferrara; d. Rome, between 1608 and 1620. He studied with Alessandro Milleville; was an organist in Ferrara and later at St. Peter's in Rome (1597–1608). His set of *Canzone francese per cembalo* is reprinted by Torchi in *L'arte musicale in Italia* (vol. III); W. Shindle edited *Ercole Pasquini: Collected Keyboard Works,* in *Corpus of Early Keyboard Music,* XII (1966).

BIBLIOGRAPHY: Fr. Superbi, *Apparato degli Huomini illustri della città di Ferrara* (1620); W. Shindle, *The Keyboard Works of Ercole Pasquini* (Diss., Indiana Univ., 1963).

Pasquotti, Corrado, Italian composer; b. Vittorio Veneto, March 11, 1954. He studied in Padua, Venice, and Milan. In 1977 he received the diploma of merit of the Teatro Angelicum in Milan. He subsequently taught at the Cons. Rossini of Pesaro. In his works he strives to achieve intimate synergy of visual images and auditory projections; his written scores literally follow the parameters of a given painting, with notes corresponding to the lines of the design and rests occupying the spaces of the object; depending on a chart for such correspondences, different musical versions are achieved in actual performances. A typical product of this method is *Forma Magistra Ludi* for Chamber Orch., to images by Yasmin Brandolini d'Adda (1980).

Passereau, Pierre, French composer of the first half of the 16th century. He was chapel singer to the Duke of Angoulême (Francis I); 23 of his chansons appear in various anthologies publ. between 1533 and 1547; 2 of them are reprinted in F. Lesure, ed., *Anthologie de la chanson parisienne au XVIe siècle* (Monaco, 1953); his *Opera omnia,* edited by G. Dottin, was issued by the American Inst. of Musicology (1967).

Passy, (Ludvig Anton) Edvard, Swedish pianist and pedagogue; b. Stockholm, Sept. 3, 1789; d. Drottningholm, Aug. 16, 1870. He received his first music instruction from his brother; then studied with L. Piccinni (who was Kapellmeister in Stockholm from 1796–1801), with John Field in St. Petersburg, and with Eggert in Stockholm. After several successful tours of Germany he settled in his native city as a highly esteemed teacher, and organist of the court chapel (1833–66).

WORKS: 2 piano concertos; Fantasy for Piano and Orch.; 3 string quartets; 2 piano trios; organ fugues; piano pieces; songs; etc.

Pasta (née **Negri**), **Giuditta,** famous Italian dramatic soprano; b. Saronno, near Milan, Oct. 28, 1797; d. at her villa on Lake Como, April 1, 1865. She studied with Asioli at the Milan Cons. and made her debut in 1815; after indifferent appearances in London and Paris, she returned to Italy for further vocal study with Scappa. At her appearances in Paris in 1822 she was acclaimed as a vocal phenomenon; the range of her voice was from A in the low register to D in the high treble; but what contributed chiefly to her success was her extraordinary dramatic power, so that she won out with the audiences and critics against all possible rivals. So great was her fame at the peak of her career that renowned composers wrote into their operas roles to suit her voice; Bellini did so in *La Sonnambula* and *Norma,* Donizetti in *Anna Bolena,* and Pacini produced his *Niobe* for her.

BIBLIOGRAPHY: Maria Ferranti Giulini, *Giuditta Pasta e i suoi tempi* (Milan, 1935).

Pasternack, Josef Alexander, Polish-American conductor; b. Czestochowa, Poland, July 1, 1881; d. Chicago, April 29, 1940. He studied at the Warsaw Cons. with Michalowski (piano) and Noskowski (composition); came to America in 1895; played the viola in the Metropolitan Opera orch. (1900–10); was assistant conductor there during the season of 1909–10; then was conductor of various opera companies in N.Y. and Chicago; composed popular orch. pieces and songs; made numerous arrangements.

Pasterwitz, Georg von, German church composer; b. Bierhütten, near Passau, June 7, 1730; d. Kremsmünster, Jan. 26, 1803. He studied music with Eberlin in Salzburg; after touring Europe, entered the order of the Benedictines in 1755; was choirmaster at the monastery in Kremsmünster (1767–83); lived in Vienna (1783–95); in 1795 resumed his post in Kremsmünster. He publ. 24 organ fugues and 300 *Themata und Versetten zum Präambulieren.* In MS there exists about 20 masses, numerous Psalms, offertories, vespers, motets, etc.; also several operas, intermezzi, and detached arias interpolated in various operas of other composers.

BIBLIOGRAPHY: G. Huemer, *Die Pflege der Musik im Stifte Kremsmünster* (Wels, 1877); A. Kellner, *Musikgeschichte des Stiftes Kremsmünster* (Kassel, 1956).

Pastou, Etienne-Jean Baptiste, French vocal educator; b. Vigan, Gard, May 26, 1784; d. Ternes, near Paris, Oct. 8, 1851. He founded a singing school in Paris in 1819; was made a prof. at the Paris Cons. in 1836; publ. a method for ensemble singing, *Ecole de la lyre harmonique* (Paris, 1822).

Patachich, Iván, Hungarian composer; b. Budapest, June 3, 1922. He studied composition with Szabó, Siklós, and Viski at the Budapest Academy;

was active mainly as a theater conductor; in 1953 became music director of the Budapest Film Studio; established the first electronic music studio in Budapest in 1972.

WORKS: 2 operas: *Theomachia* (1962) and *Fuente Ovejuna* (1969); 3 ballets: *Black and White* (1958); *Sunday Romance* (1963); *Mngongo and Mlaba* (1965); 2 cantatas: *Country of Cliffs* (1953) and *Music of the Bible* (1968); 2 harp concertos (1956, 1968); Double-bass Concertino (1957); Flute Concerto (1958); Viola Concerto (1959); Oboe Concerto (1959); *3 Pieces* for Clarinet and Orch. (1961); Guitar Concerto (1961); *Concerto breve* for Cello and Orch. (1962); 2 divertimentos for Orch. (1962, 1969); 2 piano concertos (1963, 1968); *Sinfonietta Savariensis* (1964); Violin Concerto (1964); *Quadri di Picasso* for Orch. (1965); Bassoon Concerto (1965); 2 symphs. (1965, 1966); Percussion Concerto (1966); *Colori 67* for Orch. (1967); *3 schizzi* for Orch. (1969); Concerto for Violin, Piano, and Orch. (1969); *2 pezzi* for Trumpet and Chamber Orch. (1969); *2 pezzi* for Trombone and Chamber Orch. (1969); Organ Concerto (1972); Concertino for Piano and Wind Orch. (1972); 2 violin sonatas (1948, 1964); Wind Quintet (1960); Double-bass Sonatina (1961); 2 piano trios (1962, 1967); Sonata for Harp and Horn (1964); *Canzone moro e caccia* for Horn and Piano (1971); *Ritmi pari e dispari* for 2 Horns (1971); *Proporzioni* for Percussion (1972); *Quartettino* for Saxophones (1972); *Aquarelli* for 2 Trombones (1972); Piano Sonata (1965); Piano Sonatina (1966); *4 pezzi piccoli* for Piano (1971).

Patanè, Giuseppe, talented Italian conductor; b. Naples, Jan. 1, 1932. He was a son of **Franco Patanè** (1908–68), a noted opera conductor; studied at the Cons. S. Pietro a Majella in Naples; made his debut as a conductor at the age of 19, when he led a performance of *La Traviata* at the Teatro Mercadante in Naples; he was subsequently 2nd conductor at the Teatro San Carlo in Naples (1951–56); became principal conductor of the Linz Opera in 1961, and in 1962 to 1968 was conductor of the Deutsche Oper in Berlin; he further filled engagements at La Scala in Milan, at the Vienna Opera, and in Copenhagen, with excellent acclaim; he also conducted the Radio Orch. of Berlin, the Orch. de la Suisse Romande in Switzerland, etc. In 1978 he conducted Italian opera at the Metropolitan Opera in N.Y.; in 1982 was appointed co-principal conductor of the American Symph. in N.Y., remaining at this post until 1984.

Patey, Janet Monach (née **Whytock**), English contralto; b. London, May 1, 1842; d. Sheffield, Feb. 28, 1894. She was married to the bass singer **John Patey** (1835–1901). After singing at various English festivals, she made an American tour in 1871; also sang in Australia (1890). In her prime she was regarded as the foremost English contralto.

Patiño, Carlos, Spanish cleric and composer; b. Santa Maria del Campo; d. Madrid, Sept. 5, 1675. In 1632 he received a grant from King John IV of Portugal; from 1633 to 1648 he was maestro de capilla at the Spanish court; in 1660 was appointed to a similar position at the Royal Cloister of the Incarnation. He was one of the most important composers of sacred music of his time; he particularly excelled in polyphonic works for 8–12 voices; most of his music is preserved in MS in the archives of El Escorial and in Salamanca. His *Missa in devotione* for Double Chorus is reproduced in Eslava's *Lira sacro-hispana;* Felipe Pedrell transcribed some of Patiño's *Tonos humanos* in vols. 3 and 4 of *Teatro lírico español anterior al siglo XIX.*

BIBLIOGRAPHY: Varela Silvari, *Galeria biográfica de músicos gallegos* (Coruña, 1874); V. Torres, *Galeria de gallegos ilustres* (Madrid, 1875; vol. 5).

Paton, Mary Ann, Scottish soprano; b. Edinburgh, Oct. 1802; d. Bulcliffe Hall, Chapelthorpe, July 21, 1864. Of a musical family, she sang in concerts as a child; made her first operatic appearance as Susanna in the *Marriage of Figaro* (London, Aug. 3, 1822). She sang the part of Rezia in the premiere of Weber's *Oberon* in London (April 12, 1826) and was praised by Weber himself. She had a very fine voice, and could sing lyric and coloratura parts with equal brilliance. She was married to **Joseph Wood,** the tenor.

BIBLIOGRAPHY: "Miss Paton," *Quarterly Music Magazine and Review* (London, 1823); *Memoir of Mr. and Mrs. Wood* (Philadelphia, 1840).

Patterson, Annie Wilson, Irish collector of folk songs and writer on music; b. Lurgan, Oct. 27, 1868; d. Cork, Jan. 16, 1934. She studied organ at the Royal Irish Academy of Music with Sir R. Stewart; was an organist at various churches in Dublin; in 1909, settled in Cork; was awarded the degree of Mus.Doc. by the National Univ. of Ireland. She organized the Feis Ceoil (Irish Music Festival), held annually from 1897.

WORKS: *6 Original Gaelic Songs; Rallying Song of the Gaelic League* (with Orch.); *The Bells of Shandon* for Chorus; *Invernia,* arrangement of Irish airs; 2 Irish operas: *The High-King's Daughter* and *Oisin;* cantatas; symph. poems; etc.

WRITINGS: *The Story of Oratorio* (1902); *Schumann* (1903; in Master Musician Series; new revised ed., 1934); *Chats with Music-Lovers* (1908); *How to Listen to an Orchestra* (1913; new ed., 1928); *Great Minds in Music; Beautiful Song and the Singer; The Music of Ireland; The Profession of Music* (1926).

Patterson, Franklin Peale, American composer; b. Philadelphia, Jan. 5, 1871; d. New Rochelle, N.Y., July 6, 1966. He studied at the Univ. of Pa., and later in Munich with Thuille and Rheinberger.

WORKS: His opera *The Echo,* produced in Portland, Oreg., on June 9, 1925, was awarded the David Bispham Memorial Medal and the medal award of the National Federation of Music Clubs. Other works: the short operas *Beggar's Love (A Little Girl at Play), Mountain Blood,* and *The Forest Dwellers;* the grand operas *Through the Narrow Gate* and *Caprice.* He also publ. various instructive pamphlets: *How to Write a Good Tune* (1924); *Practical Instrumentation* (1923); *Leit-Motives of the Nibelungen Ring* (1896); *The Perfect Modernist* (1921); etc.

BIBLIOGRAPHY: E. Hipsher, *American Opera and Its Composers* (Philadelphia, 1934; pp. 355–58).

Patti, Adelina (Adela Juana Maria), one of the greatest coloratura singers of the 19th century, in both opera and concert; b. Madrid, Feb. 10, 1843; d. Brecknock, Wales, Sept. 27, 1919. The daughter of 2 Italian singers, she was taken to N.Y. at an early age; from 1851–55 she sang in many concerts there. She was taught piano by her sister **Carlotta,** and singing by her half-brother, Ettore Barili; her formal debut was made in N.Y. on Nov. 24, 1859, as Lucia (under the stage name of "the little Florinda"). In London she first appeared in *La Sonnambula* on May 14, 1861, at Covent Garden, her success rivaling that of Grisi; her Paris debut was in the same role, at the Théâtre Italien, on Nov. 19, 1862. In Paris in 1868 she married the Marquis de Caux, from whom she separated in 1877; they were divorced in 1885. She sang for the first time in Italy at La Scala in Milan on Nov. 3, 1877, Violetta in *La Traviata* being the role selected. She sang in all the chief cities of Europe, and was everywhere received with enthusiasm; made guest appearances at the Metropolitan Opera House in N.Y. in April 1892. She commanded very large fees. She retired from the stage in 1895, but continued to appear in concerts, giving an official "farewell" concert at Albert Hall in London on Dec. 1, 1906. Her last public appearance was at a benefit concert for the Red Cross in the same hall, on Oct. 20, 1914. Her 2nd husband, the tenor **Nicolini,** whom she married in 1886, died in 1898; she married a Swedish nobleman, Baron Cederström, in 1899. Although her voice was not powerful, it possessed a wide range (c^1–f^3), wonderful flexibility, and perfect evenness throughout; it probably excelled that of any other singer in voluptuous sweetness and bell-like purity. Her vocalization and technical skill were above all criticism, and the ease with which she took the highest notes was astonishing. But she was a poor actress, she lacked temperament, and her musical intelligence was ordinary. Her operatic repertoire included about 30 roles in the operas of Rossini, Bellini, Donizetti, Meyerbeer, Gounod, Auber, and Verdi (earlier works).

BIBLIOGRAPHY: Th. de Grave, *Biographie d'A. Patti* (Paris, 1865); G. de Charnacé, *A. Patti* (Paris, (1868); G.M. Dalmazzo, *A. Patti's Life* (London, 1877); L. Lauw, *Fourteen Years with A. Patti* (London, 1884); E. Hanslick, "A. Patti," in *Musikalische Stationen* (Berlin, 1885; Eng. trans. in Hanslick, *Vienna's Golden Years of Music,* N.Y., 1950, pp. 187–208); A. Weismann, *Die Primadonna* (1919); H. Klein, *The Reign of Patti* (N.Y., 1920).

Patti, Carlotta, concert singer, sister of **Adelina Patti;** b. Florence, Oct. 30, 1835; d. Paris, June 27, 1889. Her father and mother were her first teachers in singing; she had piano lessons with Henri Herz in Paris. Her early youth was spent in N.Y. Lameness prevented success on the stage, but she was more fortunate as a concert singer, making her debut in N.Y. in 1861, followed by an American tour with the impresario Ullmann. Here, and in Europe, she became a favorite on the concert stage, more especially as a coloratura vocalist of exquisite technique united with great sentiment. In 1871 she married the cellist **De Munck.**

Pattiera, Tino, Yugoslav tenor; b. Cavtat, near Ragusa, June 27, 1890; d. there, April 24, 1966. He studied at the Vienna Academy of Music with Ranieri; in 1915 he joined the Dresden Court (later State) Opera, where he was a principal member of the company until 1941; also sang with the Berlin State Opera (1924–29); was a guest artist in Chicago, Vienna, Budapest, Paris, Prague, and other music centers. He gave a farewell concert in 1948; from 1950 he taught voice at the Vienna Academy of Music. He was most renowned for the lyric roles in Verdi's operas.

Pattison, John Nelson, American pianist and composer; b. Niagara Falls, Oct. 22, 1845; d. New York, July 27, 1905. He studied piano in Germany with celebrated teachers (Thalberg, Henselt, Hans von Bülow) and also had lessons from Liszt. He gave a series of concerts in the U.S., and toured as accompanist for Parepa-Rosa, Louise Kellogg, Albani, Pauline Lucca, and others. He wrote a symph. work, *Niagara;* marches and overtures for military band; a Concerto-Fantasia for Piano and Orch.; some 200 pieces for piano solo. He publ. *Memoir of J.N. Pattison* (N.Y., 1868).

Pattison, Lee, American pianist; b. Grand Rapids, Mich., July 22, 1890; d. Claremont, Calif., Dec. 22, 1966. He first studied at the New England Cons. of Music; later in Berlin with Schnabel. In 1917 he formed a duo-piano team with Guy Maier; they gave a number of successful concerts until 1931, when the partnership was dissolved. From 1932 till 1937 he was head of the piano dept. at Sarah Lawrence College; also taught at the Juilliard Summer School; lived mostly in N.Y. His compositions include *Florentine Sketches* for Piano and a piano suite of 7 pieces, *Told in the Hills.*

Patton, Willard, American singer and composer; b. Milford, Maine, May 26, 1853; d. Minneapolis, Dec. 12, 1924. He studied with Dudley Buck and others in N.Y.; was active as a tenor in oratorios; in 1883 settled in Minneapolis as a vocal teacher.

WORKS: Oratorio, *Isaiah* (1897); operettas: *The Gallant Garroter* (1882) and *La Fianza* (1889); grand opera, *Pocahontas* (Minneapolis, Jan. 4, 1911); 2 musical "epics": *The Star of Empire* (1900) and *Foot-Stones of a Nation* (1906); symph. fantasy, *The Spirit of 1861* (1915).

Patzak, Julius, Austrian tenor; b. Vienna, April 9, 1898; d. Rottach-Egern, Bavaria, Jan. 26, 1974. He studied at the Univ. of Vienna, where he attended the classes of Guido Adler and Mandyczewski; made his debut in 1926; sang at the State Opera in Munich from 1928 to 1945; then was on the staff of the Vienna Opera (1946–59); continued to fill guest engagements in Berlin. He was also distinguished as a singer in oratorio and in recitals. He retired from the stage in 1966 and lived in Rottach-Egern.

Pauer, Ernst, Austrian pianist; b. Vienna, Dec. 21, 1826; d. Jugenheim, near Darmstadt, May 9, 1905. He studied piano with Mozart's son, W.A. Mozart, Jr., and composition with Sechter. In 1851 he went to London; taught at the Royal Academy of Music (1859–64); in 1861 he began a series of historical performances of harpsichord and piano music in chronological order, which attracted considerable attention. After a number of concerts in Germany and Austria he was appointed pianist to the Austrian court (1866). He continued his activities until 1896, when he retired and lived in Jugenheim. He publ. in English a number of educational works of some value, among them *The Art of Pianoforte-playing* (1877); *Musical Forms* (1878); *The Elements of the Beautiful in Music* (1877); also, *The Birthday Book of Musicians and Composers* (London, 1881) and *A Dictionary of Pianists and Composers for the Pianoforte* (1895); he further brought out collections for piano students: *The New Gradus ad Parnassum; Classical Companion: Celebrated Concert-studies;* and *Cultures of the Left Hand.* He made excellent arrangements of symphs. by Beethoven and Schumann, for piano solo, piano, 4-hands, and piano, 8-hands; also arranged Mendelssohn's orch. works for piano, 4-hands and 8-hands; these arrangements were widely used in the 19th century and were extremely useful for young pianists until the advent of the phonograph administered a lethal blow to this type of musical activity.

Pauer, Jiří, Czech composer; b. Libušín, near Kladno, central Bohemia, Feb. 22, 1919. He studied composition with Otakar Šín; then with Alois Hába at the Prague Cons. (1943–46) and with Borkovec at the Prague Academy of Music (1946–50). He occupied various administrative posts with the Ministry of Education and Culture and with Czech Radio; was artistic director of the Opera of the National Theater in Prague (1953–55, 1965–67); then taught at the Prague Academy. In 1979 he was appointed general manager of the Prague Opera; was director of the Czech Phil. from 1958 to 1980. His music follows the pragmatic precepts of socialist realism in its modern application, broadly lyrical and tensely dramatic by turns.
  WORKS: For the stage: 5 operas: *Žvanivý Slimejš* (*The Talkative Snail;* 1949–50; Prague, April 5, 1958); *Zuzana Vojířová* (1954–57; Prague, May 11, 1958); *Červená Karkulka* (*Little Red Riding Hood;* 1958–59; Olomouc, 1960); *Manželské kontrapunkty* (*Marital Counterpoints;* 1961; 3 operatic satirical sketches, Ostrava, 1962; 2nd version as 5 satires, Liberec, 1967); *Zdravý nemocný* (*Le Malade imaginaire),* after Molière (1966–69; Prague, May 22,

1970); children's ballet, *Ferdy the Ant* (1974; Prague, 1976). For Orch.: *Comedy Suite* (1949); Bassoon Concerto (1949); *Youth Suite* (1951); *Scherzo* (1951); *Children's Suite* for Chamber Orch. (1953); *Rhapsody* (1953); Oboe Concerto (1954); Horn Concerto (1958); Symph. (1963); *Panychide,* symph. picture (1969); *Canto festivo* (1970–71); Trumpet Concerto (1972); *Initials* (1974). Vocal music: *Canto triste,* cycle for Medium Voice and Orch. (1971); *Swan Song,* monodrama for Male Voice and Orch. (1973); *Tragédie o vose a nose (Tragedy of Wasp and Nose)* for Bass and Orch. (1976). Chamber music: *Partita* for Solo Harp (1947); *Divertimento* for 3 Clarinets (1949); *Capriccio* for Flute or Oboe, Clarinet or Bassoon, and Piano (1952); Violin Sonatina (1953); Cello Sonata (1954); 3 string quartets (1960, 1969, 1970); *Divertimento* for Nonet (1961); Wind Quintet (1961); Piano Trio (1963); *Monologues* for Solo Clarinet (1964); *Interpolations* for Solo Flute (1969); *Rhapsody* for Solo Cello (1969); *Musica da concerto* for 13 Winds (1971); *Trompetina* for Trumpet and Piano (1972). For Piano: *My Notebook* (1942–43); *For a Happy Journey* (1950); *Bagatelles* (1968); also songs and choruses.

Pauer, Max, eminent English pianist and teacher, son of **Ernst Pauer;** b. London, Oct. 31, 1866; d. Jugenheim, May 12, 1945. He studied with his father; embarked on several successful concert tours in Germany; in 1887 was appointed prof. of piano at the Cologne Cons.; in 1897 became a prof. at the Stuttgart Cons.; was its director in 1908–20; in 1920 it became the Hochschule für Musik, which he directed until 1924; then he became director of the Leipzig Cons. (1924–32) and of the Mannheim Hochschule für Musik (1933–34); retired in 1934. He made an American tour in 1913–14. Following his father's excellent example in arranging Classical symphs. for piano, he made transcriptions of symphs. by Mozart and Haydn for piano solo and piano, 4-hands. He publ. an ironic autobiography, *Unser seltsames Ich* (Stuttgart, 1942).

Pauk, György, Hungarian violinist; b. Budapest, Oct. 26, 1936. He studied at the Franz Liszt Academy of Music in Budapest. After the unsuccessful Hungarian rebellion of 1956, he went to the Netherlands. He then won several violin competitions, including the prestigious Jacques Thibaud International Competition in 1959; eventually made his home in England. With the pianist Peter Frankl and the cellist Ralph Kirshbaum, he formed a successful concert trio.

Paul, Oscar, German music theorist; b. Freiwaldau, April 8, 1836; d. Leipzig, April 18, 1898. He studied theology; then took private lessons in piano with Plaidy and theory with Hauptmann and Richter. He adapted Hauptmann's *Lehre von der Harmonik* for practical usages and publ. the result under the title *Lehrbuch der Harmonik* (1880; in Eng., N.Y., 1885). He also publ. *Geschichte des Klaviers* (Leipzig, 1868); *Handlexikon der Tonkunst* (Leipzig, 1873); *Musikalische Instrumente* (Braunschweig, 1874).

Paul, Thomas, distinguished American bass; b. Chicago, Feb. 22, 1934. He studied with Howard Swan and Robert Gross at Occidental College in Los Angeles (B.A., 1956); then took courses in conducting with Jean Morel and Frederic Waldman at the Juilliard School of Music in N.Y.; also studied voice privately in N.Y. He made his vocal debut in Handel's *Belshazzar* at Carnegie Hall on April 10, 1961. He sang with the N.Y. City Opera (1963–70), and with the opera companies of Philadelphia, Houston, Washington, D.C., Cincinnati, and New Orleans; was also a soloist with orchs., including the N.Y. Phil., Chicago Symph., Boston Symph., Cleveland Orch., Philadelphia Orch., Pittsburgh Symph., and Los Angeles Phil. He made his European debut in Zürich on April 3, 1976, in a performance of Bach's *St. Matthew Passion.* In 1971 he became a prof. of voice at the Eastman School of Music in Rochester, N.Y., and was also appointed to the faculty of the Aspen Music School. His finest roles include Boris Godunov, Figaro, and Méphistophélès.

Paull, Barberi, American composer of the avant-garde; b. New York, July 25, 1946. She began to play piano as an infra-adolescent, in private and in public; with the awakening of consciousness, she opted for jazz and multimedia forms of self-expression, but went through the motions of academic training at the Juilliard School of Music in N.Y., where she studied composition with Hall Overton and Jacob Druckman (1970–71); later she took courses with Charles Wuorinen at the Manhattan School of Music (1972) and attended the Musical Theatre Workshop conducted by Lehman Engel (1973). Then, in a dash of feminist self-assertion, she founded the Barberi Paull Musical Theatre, Inc., and presented with it a series of mixed-media events. In her compositions she elevates eclecticism to an article of democratic faith, embracing jazz, pop tunes, and electronic sound in a context of ostentatious and unapologetic cosmic sentimentality.
WORKS: Electronic ballet, *Time* (1971); *Earth Pulse,* choreographic cantata, making use of musique concrète (1971); *The Mass* for Tape, Percussion, and Visual Projections (1974); *A Land Called The Infinity of Love* for Multimedia (1975); *Sheer Silver Sheen Flower Sky* for Chorus (1971–74); *O Wind* for Mezzo-soprano and String Quartet (1975); *Song for Orchestra* (1977); *A Christmas Carol,* after Dickens, for Chorus and Instrumental Trio (1977; also in a jazz version); many unabashed pop tunes.

Paulli, Holger Simon, Danish conductor; b. Copenhagen, Feb. 22, 1810; d. there, Dec. 23, 1891. He studied violin with Schall and Wexschall; at the age of 12, entered the court orch. in Copenhagen; then became its concertmaster (1849) and principal conductor (1863–83). In 1866 he was appointed co-director, with Gade and Hauptmann, of the newly founded Copenhagen Cons. He was an admirer of Wagner, and conducted the first performances in Denmark of *Lohengrin* (1870), *Die Meistersinger* (1872), and *Tannhäuser* (1875). He composed a sing-

spiel, *Lodsen (The Pilot),* which was produced in Copenhagen on Sept. 25, 1851; also wrote some ballet music, violin pieces, and songs.
BIBLIOGRAPHY: F. Bendix, *Af en Kapelmusikers Erindringer* (Copenhagen, 1913).

Paulmüller, Alexander, Austrian conductor; b. Innsbruck, March 4, 1912. He studied musicology with Lach and Orel, and also piano, composition, and conducting, at the Vienna Academy of Music; then worked as a coach under Bruno Walter at the Vienna State Opera. Later he conducted in several Austrian and German regional opera houses; served as first conductor of the Frankfurt State Opera. From 1964 to 1972 he was chief conductor of the Stuttgart Phil. Orch. In 1973 he became a guest conductor of the State Theater in Salzburg.

Paulson, Gustaf, Swedish composer and organist; b. Hälsingborg, Jan. 22, 1898; d. there, Dec. 17, 1966. He studied composition in Copenhagen with Peder Gram; from 1929 until his death, served as church organist in Hälsingborg. He was an extraordinarily prolific composer; wrote 13 symphs. and 19 concertos for every instrument of the orch. His music reflected the type of Scandinavian Romanticism associated with Sibelius and Nielsen, pervaded by streaks of coherent polyphony.
WORKS: 13 symphs.: No. 1 (1928); No. 2 (1933); No. 3, *Sinfonia da chiesa* (1945); No. 4, *Uppstandelse* (*The Resurrection;* 1947); No. 5, *Aron Bergenson in memoriam* (1948); No. 6 (1952); No. 7 (1953); No. 8 (1954); No. 9 (1956); No. 10 (1957); No. 11, *Stabat Mater* (1959; Hälsingborg, March 26, 1961); No. 12 (1963; Hälsingborg, Nov. 28, 1963); No. 13 (1966); 2 sinfonias for String Orch. (1953, 1954); 19 concertos: 2 for Piano (1940, 1961); 2 for Cello (1944, 1957); 2 for Oboe (1950, 1957); 2 for English Horn, with Strings (1958, 1959); 2 for Clarinet (1958, 1959); one each for Bassoon (1959); for Saxophone (1959); for Violin (1960); for Flute, with Female Choir, subtitled *Arets tider* (1962); for Horn (1964); for Trombone (1965); for Trumpet (1965); for Viola (1965); for Double Bass (1965–66); *Symphonic Variations* (1934); *Metamorphoses on a Theme by Clementi* for Orch. (1951); *Passion* for Cello and Orch. (1961); *Stabat Mater* for Soli, Female Chorus, Strings, and Percussion (1956; Hälsingborg, March 17, 1957); *Vid korset,* oratorio (1957); 5 string quartets; Violin Sonata (1958); Cello Sonata (1960); piano pieces; organ pieces; songs.

Paulus, Olaf, Norwegian composer; b. Christiania, Jan. 25, 1859; d. Stavanger, June 29, 1912. He was a pupil of C. Cappelen and J. Svendsen; also studied at the Leipzig Cons.; from 1889 he was organist at the Cathedral in Stavanger; made a trip to the U.S. in 1902, directing choral concerts in Minneapolis and St. Paul. In his native country he is highly esteemed as a national composer; his men's choruses are in the repertoire of all Norwegian societies; he also wrote songs and piano pieces, and edited a collection of songs, *De 1,000 hjems sange (Home Songs;* 1888).

Pauly – Pavarotti

Pauly, Rosa, Hungarian dramatic soprano; b. Eperjes, March 15, 1894; d. Herzlia, Israel, Dec. 14, 1975. She studied voice with Rosa Papier-Paumgartner in Vienna, and made her operatic debut at the Vienna Opera as Desdemona in Verdi's *Otello* in 1918. She subsequently sang in Hamburg, Cologne, and Mannheim. In 1927–31 she was a member of the staff at the Kroll Opera in Berlin; she was also on the staff of the Vienna State Opera (1929–35); in 1934 she sang the challenging role of Elektra in Strauss's opera in Salzburg, gathering encomiums; in 1935 she appeared at La Scala in Milan. She made her American debut as Elektra in a concert performance with the N.Y. Phil. on March 21, 1937; sang it again at her first appearance with the Metropolitan Opera on Jan. 7, 1938; appeared there until 1940; also sang at the Teatro Colón in Buenos Aires in 1939. In 1946 she went to Palestine, and devoted herself to teaching in Tel Aviv. She was reputed to be one of the best dramatic sopranos of her era.

Paumann, Conrad, historically significant German organist and composer; b. Nuremberg, between 1410 and 1415; d. Munich, Jan. 24, 1473. He was blind from birth; through the patronage of Ulrich Grundherr, and later his son Paul Grundherr, he was able to obtain instruction in music. By 1446 he was appointed organist at St. Sebald in Nuremberg; in 1447 he became town organist. In 1450 he was called to Munich to serve as court organist to Duke Albrecht III of Bavaria. He won great renown as an organist, and traveled to Austria and Italy. He also achieved mastery as a player on the harp, the lute, and the recorder; he was particularly noted for his improvisations. Some of his extant works have been publ. in *Das Erbe deutscher Musik,* first series (1958); see also the *Fundamentum organisandi magistri Conradi Paumanns ceci de Nürenberga anno 1452* as ed. by W. Apel in *Keyboard Music of the Fourteenth and Fifteenth Centuries, Corpus of Early Keyboard Music,* I (1963).
BIBLIOGRAPHY: F. Arnold and H. Bellerman, "Das Locheimer Liederbuch nebst der Ars organisandi von Conrad Paumann," *Jahrbuch für musikalische Wissenschaft,* II (1867); L. Schrade, *Die handschriftliche Überlieferung der ältesten Instrumental-Musik* (Lahr, 1931); B. Wallner, "Konrad Paumann," in *Münchner Characterköpfe der Gotik* (Munich, 1938); G. Reese, *Music in the Renaissance* (N.Y., 1954; 2nd ed., revised, 1959); T. Göllner, *Formen früher Mehrstimmigkeit in deutschen Handschriften des späten Mittelalters* (Tutzing, 1961); F. Krautwurst, "Konrad Paumann in Nördlingen," in *Festschrift für Heinrich Besseler* (Leipzig, 1961); F. Krautwurst, "Neues zur Biographie Konrad Paumanns," *Jahrbuch für fränkische Landesforschung,* XXII (1962); C. Wolff, "Conrad Paumanns Fundamentum organisandi und seine verschiedenen Fassungen," *Archiv für Musikwissenschaft,* XXV (1968).

Paumgartner, Bernhard, eminent Austrian musicologist and conductor; b. Vienna, Nov. 14, 1887; d. Salzburg, July 27, 1971. He was a son of **Hans Paum-**gartner (1843–96), who was for many years a chorus master of the Vienna Court Opera, and of **Rosa Papier,** a well-known singer. He studied with Bruno Walter; in 1917 was engaged as director of the Mozarteum in Salzburg, which he headed until 1938, and again from 1945 to 1959. Shortly before his death he was elected an honorary president of the Salzburg Festival. A versatile musician, he was active as a conductor, composer, and writer on musical subjects. He wrote an opera, *Rossini in Neapel* (Zürich, March 27, 1936), and some other stage music, including ballets: *Pagoden* (Munich, 1927); *Ballo medico* (Vienna, 1943); *Salzburger divertimento* (Salzburg, 1955, using Mozart's music); *Ouvertüre zu einem ritterlichen Spiel* for Orch.; various instrumental pieces in a Baroque manner. Among his publications were *Mozart* (Berlin, 1927; 6th ed., enlarged, 1967); *Franz Schubert: Eine Biographie* (Zürich, 1943; 3rd ed., 1960); *J.S. Bach* (Zürich, 1950); he also contributed numerous articles on Mozart and on music to various publications in Salzburg. He publ. an autobiographical memoir, *Erinnerungen* (Salzburg, 1969). A collection of his articles and essays was publ. posthumously (Kassel, 1973).

Paunović, Milenko, Serbian composer; b. Šajkaš, Nov. 28, 1889; d. Belgrade, Oct. 1, 1924. He studied in Leipzig with Max Reger and Hugo Riemann; became a choral conductor in Novi Sad. In his music he followed Wagnerian concepts, and wrote several music dramas to his own texts. He also composed a *Yugoslav Symphony* (Ljubljana, March 17, 1924).

Paur, Emil, Austrian conductor; b. Czernowitz, Bukovina, Aug. 29, 1855; d. Mistek, Bohemia, June 7, 1932. He was trained in the rudiments of music by his father, and played the violin and piano in public at the age of 8; at 11 he entered the Vienna Cons., where he studied violin with Hellmesberger and composition with Dessoff, graduating in 1870. He achieved an excellent reputation as a competent drillmaster, and in 1893 was engaged as conductor of the Boston Symph. Orch. to succeed Nikisch; he held this post for 5 seasons; from 1898 to 1902 he conducted the N.Y. Phil. Society; during the season of 1899–1900 he led the Wagner repertoire at the Metropolitan Opera in N.Y.; from 1899 to 1902 he served as director of the National Cons. in N.Y., succeeding Dvořák; from 1902 to 1904 he filled engagements in Europe; in 1904 he was again engaged in the U.S., as conductor of the Pittsburgh Symph. Orch. (until 1910). In 1912 he returned to Berlin, but failed to impress the fastidious concert audiences there; for the rest of his life he conducted occasional engagements. He was married to the pianist **Maria Bürger** (1862–99).

Pavarotti, Luciano, spectacularly popular silver-throated Italian tenor; b. Modena, Oct. 12, 1935. His father was a baker who liked to sing and wanted his son to sing, too; but his mother, who worked in a tobacco factory, hoped he would become a bank clerk. He followed the advice of neither, and earned his living by teaching school and selling insurance. He did not abandon his voice training, however, and took lessons with Arrigo Pola and Ettore Campogalliani. In 1961 he sang his first operatic role, that of Rodolfo in *La Bohème*, in Reggio Emilia; then received engagements in Venice and Palermo. There followed appearances in Amsterdam, Vienna, Dublin, and London. In 1963 he sang in Spain and in Poland. In 1965, he revisited London, and sang the role of Alfredo in *La Traviata* at Covent Garden. In 1966 he made his American debut in Miami; then went on a tour in Australia, with a troupe that included the famous soprano Joan Sutherland. Returning from this long tour, he made an important debut at La Scala in Milan. His repertoire now included most of the standard operas, and he received engagements all over Europe. In 1967 he sang with the San Francisco Opera. One of his major feats of sheer virtuosity was to perform the classical arias in Donizetti's operas in their original key, requiring repeated high C's, which he delivered with insouciant aplomb, fully conscious of the effect he was producing on the public and the critics. On Nov. 23, 1968, he made his debut with the Metropolitan Opera in N.Y., singing Rodolfo, with unqualified acclaim. His fame was established, and critics exhausted their vocabulary of superlatives to describe his renditions of the parts of the Duke in *Rigoletto*, Riccardo in *Un ballo in maschera*, Cavaradossi in *Tosca*, and other favorites of the Italian repertoire. (He carefully avoided singing Wagner.) Apart from opera, he appeared in recitals in the U.S., in Europe, and in Japan. Idolized by the public as no tenor had been since the days of Caruso, he plays the part of being Pavarotti with succulent delectation. Like Caruso, he is a gastronome. Unlike Caruso, he wears a substantial beard. Like Caruso, he is arrestingly corpulent (c.290 lbs.). Like Caruso, like Mario del Monaco, and like many other Italian tenors, he paints nicely. Like most tenors, he likes himself immensely. Unlike most tenors, he does not get involved in scandal, and ostentatiously projects himself in words and pictures as a family man. Like most successful artists, he plays tennis and swims for relaxation. In 1982 he agreed to appear in an American film with an idiotic title, *Yes, Giorgio!* It proved that he had no talent as a dramatic actor, outside of opera. He publ. an autobiography, *Pavarotti: My Own Story* (with W. Wright; Garden City, N.Y., 1981).

Pavlova, Anna, celebrated Russian dancer; b. St. Petersburg, Feb. 12, 1881; d. The Hague, Jan. 23, 1931. Of humble origin (her father was a soldier, her mother a domestic laundress), she joined the Imperial Ballet at a very early age, and in 1906 received the rank of prima ballerina. Her fame spread, and in 1914 she left Russia for a fabulously successful career abroad. In 1909 she took part in the season of the Ballets Russes in Paris; in 1910 she organized her own troupe, with which she toured in Europe, America, and Asia. She was celebrated for her performance of Giselle, but the greatest image she left for posterity was the solo dance *The Dying Swan*, to the music of Saint-Saëns, originally choreographed by Fokine. The correct pronunciation of her name is Pav-ló-va (not Páv-lo-va, as is commonly heard).

BIBLIOGRAPHY: Theodore Stier, *With Pavlova round the World* (1927); Valerian Svetlov, *Anna Pavlova* (1930); Walford Hyden, *Pavlova* (1931); Victor André (Pavlova's husband), *Anna Pavlova* (1932); Cyril W. Beaumont, *Anna Pavlova* (1932); Paul D. Magriel, ed., *Pavlova* (1947; profusely illustrated); A.H. Franks, ed., *Pavlova* (1956); Harcourt Algeranoff, *My Years with Pavlova* (1957).

Payne, Albert, German music publisher; b. Leipzig, June 3, 1842; d. there, April 1, 1921. From 1858–61, he was a pupil at the Leipzig Cons. of David (violin), Dreyshock (piano), and E.F. Richter and Hauptmann (theory); then, for a short time, of Massart in Paris. In 1862 he entered his father's publishing firm; under the title *Payne's kleine Kammermusik Partiturausgabe*, he began in 1886 the publication of a low-priced pocket edition of chamber music of the Classical masters, which immediately met with pronounced favor, so that he soon added the works of the Romanticists; in 1892 he sold the edition (212 numbers) to Ernst Eulenburg, who enlarged its scope still further.

Payne, Anthony, English composer; b. London, Aug. 2, 1936. He studied at Dulwich College and at Durham Univ. (1958–61); then wrote music criticism for the *Daily Telegraph*. He is married to soprano **Jane Manning.** His style of composition is structurally disciplined, but inwardly Romantic and inspired by northern moods and modes.

WORKS: *Phoenix Mass* for Chorus, 3 Trumpets, and 3 Trombones (1965–72); *Paraphrases and Cadenzas* for Clarinet, Viola, and Piano (1969); *2 Songs without Words* for 5 Male Voices a cappella (1970); *Sonatas and Ricercars* for Wind Quintet (1970–71); Concerto for Orch. (London, Jan. 8, 1975); *First Sight of Her and After,* song cycle to poems by Thomas Hardy, for 16 Voices (1975); *The World's Winter* for Soprano and 8 Players, to words by Tennyson (1976); *A Little Ascension Cantata* for Chorus a cappella (1978); *A Little Whitsuntide Cantata* for Chorus a cappella (1978); String Quartet (1978); *The Stones and Lonely Places Sing* for 7 Players (1979); *Song of the Clouds* for Oboe and Chamber Orch. (1979); *Footfalls Echo* for Violin and Piano (1980); *Spring's Shining Wake* for Chamber Orch. (1980–81); *A Day in the Life of a Mayfly* for 6 Players (1982).

Payne, John, American composer; b. New York, May 23, 1941. He studied psychology at Brown Univ. (B.A., 1962); played in jazz bands. Bypassing the traditional forms of conventional modernism, he devoted his energies to total environmental art. He collaborated with Carol Law and Charles Amirkhanian in producing a live-electronic theater event, *Ode to Gravity* (San Francisco, Sept. 21, 1968); staged the audience-participation happenings *Thursday Mix* (San Francisco, March 27, 1969, a

Thursday) and *Friday Mix* (San Francisco, May 2, 1969, a Friday). He also programmed a number of electronic scores, among them *Elevator Music* and *Toot le fromage*, making use of inchoate concrete noises.

Paz, Juan Carlos, significant Argentine composer; b. Buenos Aires, Aug. 5, 1901; d. there, Aug. 25, 1972. He studied composition with Constantino Gaito in Argentina and later with Vincent d'Indy in Paris; in 1929, with several young composers of radical tendencies, he organized in Buenos Aires the "Grupo Renovación," and in 1937 inaugurated a series of concerts of new music; became a music critic and author of several books. His early works, after 1921, are marked by strong polyphony, in a neo-Classical style; about 1927, he adopted atonal and polytonal procedures; in 1934 he began to compose almost exclusively in the 12-tone idiom; after 1950 he modified his musical language, adopting a less rigid and more personal style of composition.

WORKS: FOR ORCH.: *Canto de Navidad* (1927; instrumented 1930); *Movimiento sinfónico* (1930); Suite for Ibsen's *Juliano Emperador* (1931); *3 Pieces* (1931); *Passacaglia* (1936; Paris Festival of the International Society for Contemporary Music, June 25, 1937; revised 1952–53); *Música (Preludio y fuga)* (1940); *Passacaglia* for String Orch. (1944; revised 1949); *Rítmica constante* (1952); *6 superposiciones* (1954); *Transformaciones canónicas* (1955–56); *Música* for Bassoon, Strings, and Percussion (1955–56); *Continuidad 1960* (1960–61; 3rd Festival of Music, Caracas, May 11, 1966); *Estructuras 1962* for Chamber Orch. (1962); *Música* for Piano and Orch. (1964; 3rd Inter-American Music Festival, Washington, D.C., May 12, 1965).

CHAMBER MUSIC: *Tema y transformaciones* for 11 Winds (1929); Wind Octet (1930); 3 sonatinas: No. 1 for Clarinet and Piano (1930); No. 2 for Flute and Clarinet (1932); No. 3 for Oboe and Bassoon (1933; later transcribed for Piano); *Concierto No. 1* for Flute, Oboe, Clarinet, Bassoon, Trumpet, and Piano (1932) and *No. 2* for Oboe, Trumpet, 2 Trombones, Bassoon, and Piano (1935); *4 Composiciónes dodecafónica:* No. 1 for Flute, English Horn, and Cello (1934; lost); No. 2 for Flute and Piano (1935); No. 3 for Clarinet and Piano (1937); No. 4 for Solo Violin (1938); Overture for 12 Instruments (1936); 4 pieces for Solo Clarinet (1936); *3 Composiciónes en trío:* No. 1 for Flute, Clarinet, and Bassoon (1937); No. 2 for Clarinet, Trumpet, and Alto Saxophone (1938); No. 3 for Flute, Oboe, and Bass Clarinet or Bassoon (1940; revised 1945); 2 string quartets (1938, 1940–43); *Música* for Flute, Saxophone, and Piano (1943); *Dédalus 1950* for Flute, Clarinet, Violin, Cello, and Piano (1950–51); *Continuidad 1953* for Piano and Percussion (1953–54); *3 contrapuntos* for Clarinet, Electric Guitar, Celesta, Trumpet, Trombone, and Cello (1955); *Invención* for String Quartet (1961); *Concreción* for Flute, Clarinet, Bassoon, Horn, Trumpet, Trombone, and Tuba (1964).

FOR PIANO: 3 sonatas (1923, 1925, 1935); *Tema con transformaciones* (1928); *3 movimientos de jazz* (1932); Sonatina No. 3 (1933; originally for Oboe and

Bassoon); *10 piezas sobre una serie dodecafónica* (1936); *Música 1946; Núcleos,* first series (1962–64).

FOR ORGAN: *Galaxia 64* (1964).

BIBLIOGRAPHY: J.C. Beschinsky, *Juan Carlos Paz* (Buenos Aires, 1964); J. Romano, "Juan Carlos Paz," in *Boletín Latino-Americano de Música* (no. 54, 1966); "Juan Carlos Paz," *Sonda* (no. 1, 1967). A complete list of his works to 1956 is found in *Composers of the Americas,* vol. 2 (Washington, D.C., 1956).

Peace, Albert Lister, English organist and composer; b. Huddersfield, Jan. 26, 1844; d. Liverpool, March 14, 1912. He played organ in the parish church as a child; in 1865, he became an organist in Glasgow; then studied at Oxford Univ. (Mus.Bac., 1870; Mus.Doc., 1875). From 1879 to 1897 he was organist at Glasgow Cathedral; in 1897, became successor to W.T. Best as organist of St. George's Hall in Liverpool. He wrote a cantata, *St. John the Baptist; Psalm 138* for Soli, Chorus, and Orch.; many organ pieces; anthems; church services.

Pearce, Stephen Austen, English-American organist and composer; b. London, Nov. 7, 1836; d. Jersey City, N.J., April 9, 1900. He studied at Oxford Univ. (Mus.Bac., 1859; Mus.Doc., 1864). In 1872 he settled in America; taught vocal music at Columbia College in N.Y.: also at the Peabody Inst. in Baltimore. He wrote an opera, *La Belle Américaine;* dramatic oratorio, *Celestial Visions;* church cantata, *The Psalm of Praise;* piano pieces; songs; compiled *A Pocket Dictionary of Musical Terms* in 21 languages (N.Y., 1889).

Pears, Sir Peter, English tenor; b. Farnham, June 22, 1910. He studied at the Royal College of Music in London; during the season of 1936–37 toured the U.S. as a member of the New English Singers. In 1937 he joined Benjamin Britten in a series of recitals devoted mainly to contemporary English composers, with Britten acting as his accompanist. In 1948 he was a co-founder, with Britten, of the Aldeburgh Festival. Pears sang leading tenor parts in almost all of Britten's operas: *Peter Grimes, The Rape of Lucretia, Albert Herring, Billy Budd, Gloriana, The Turn of the Screw,* and *Death in Venice;* he also sang the tenor solo part in Britten's *War Requiem.* He made his debut at the Metropolitan Opera in N.Y. on Oct. 18, 1974, as Aschenbach in *Death in Venice.* He was made a Commander of the Order of the British Empire in 1957, and was knighted by Queen Elizabeth II in 1978.

Pearsall, Robert Lucas de, English composer; b. Clifton, March 14, 1795; d. Wartensee, on Lake Constance, Aug. 5, 1856. He studied law and music; as a boy of 13 wrote a cantata, *Saul and the Witch of Endor.* He lived many years in Germany, where he publ. many of his compositions; was in London on several extended visits; in 1842, purchased a castle on Lake Constance, and remained there for the rest of his life. As a composer, he was at his best in many ingenious madrigals; particularly popular were his part-songs, *Sir Patrick Spens, The Hardy Norseman,* and *O who will o'er the downs so free;* he edited old church music in Germany; publ. an *Essay on Consecutive Fifths and Octaves in Counterpoint.*

BIBLIOGRAPHY: W. Barclay Squire, "Letters of R.L. Pearsall," *Musical Quarterly* (April 1919).

Pechner, Gerhard, German baritone; b. Berlin, April 15, 1903; d. New York, Oct. 21, 1969. He made his first appearance as an opera singer in Berlin in 1927; was compelled to leave Germany in 1933; from 1933 till 1939 he was on the staff of the German Opera House in Prague. In 1940 he was engaged by the San Francisco Opera, and on Nov. 27, 1941, made his debut at the Metropolitan Opera in N.Y.; remained there until 1947. He particularly distinguished himself in Wagnerian roles.

Pederzini, Gianna, noted Italian mezzo-soprano; b. Vò di Avio, Feb. 10, 1903. She studied with De Lucia in Naples; made her debut in 1923 in Messina; in 1930 she joined La Scala in Milan, where she sang until 1943; also appeared in Rome (1939–52), at Covent Garden, London (1931), and at the Teatro Colón in Buenos Aires (1937–39; 1946–47). She returned to La Scala in 1956–57, creating the role of the Prioress in Poulenc's *Dialogues des Carmélites.* She was an outstanding interpreter of roles in Rossini's operas; was also greatly admired for her interpretation of Carmen.

Pedrell, Carlos, Uruguayan composer; b. Minas, Uruguay, Oct. 16, 1878; d. Montrouge, near Paris, March 3, 1941. He studied in Madrid with his uncle, **Felipe Pedrell;** later went to Paris, where he took lessons with Vincent d'Indy and Bréville at the Schola Cantorum. Returning to South America, he was inspector of music in the Buenos Aires schools; lectured at the Univ. of Tucumán; in 1921 he went to Paris, where he remained for the rest of his life. His works are cast in the French style, but the rhythmic elements are related to Spanish and South American sources; his songs, with richly developed accompaniments, are the best among his works.

WORKS: Operas: *Ardid de Amor* (Buenos Aires, June 7, 1917); *Cuento de Abril; La Guitare* (Madrid, 1924); ballets: *La Rose et le gitan* (Antwerp, 1930) and *Alleluia* (Buenos Aires, 1936); for Orch.: *Une Nuit de Schéhérazade* (1908); *Danza y canción de Aixa* (1910); *En el estrado de Beatriz* (1910); *Fantasia Argentina* (1910); *Ouverture catalane* (1912); *Pastorales* for Voice and Orch. (Paris, 1928); choruses; songs.

BIBLIOGRAPHY: A. Suarès, "Carlos Pedrell," *Revue Musicale* (June 1931).

Pedrell, Felipe, eminent Spanish musicologist and composer; b. Tortosa, Feb. 19, 1841; d. Barcelona, Aug. 19, 1922. A chorister in the Cathedral of Tortosa, he was guided in his musical studies by J.A. Nin y Serra. His prolific literary career began in 1867, with articles in various musical reviews; his first opera, *El último Abencerrage,* was produced at Barcelona in 1874. After a visit to Italy and a sojourn in Paris, he settled in Barcelona (1881), where he founded the *Salterio Sacro-Hispano* for the publication of contemporary religious music, and the weekly review *Notas Musicales y Literarias,* both of which ceased publication in 1883. In 1888 he founded the *Ilustración Musical Hispano-Americana,* which he edited until its demise in 1896. In 1889–91 he composed his great dramatic trilogy, *Los Pirineos,* and as a sort of introduction to this work he wrote his famous pamphlet *Por nuestra música,* a plea for the creation of a national lyric drama on the basis of the national folk song. In 1891–92, he was a critic for the *Diario de Barcelona;* in 1894 he went to Madrid, where he was made a member of the Royal Academy of Fine Arts; he also was a prof. at the Madrid Cons. (1895–1903) and a lecturer on music history at the Madrid Ateneo. He was invited to direct the reform of religious music in Spain; edited the review *Música Religiosa* in 1896–99. At the end of 1904 he returned to Barcelona as artistic director for the publishing firm of Vidal y Llimona, which revived the *Salterio Sacro-Hispano.* There he spent the rest of his life, writing, teaching, and composing. Among his pupils were Albéniz, Granados, Manuel de Falla, and Gerhard. Though Pedrell was highly praised by contemporary critics, his music has not obtained recognition outside Spain; but the importance of his achievement in bringing to light the treasures of Spain's musical past is universally recognized, and he is considered the leading spirit of the modern Spanish nationalist revival in music. On his 70th birthday he was honored by the publication of a Festschrift, *Al Maestro Pedrell: Escritos heortásticos,* with contributions from the foremost musical scholars throughout the world.

WORKS: OPERAS: *El último Abencerrage* (Barcelona, April 14, 1874); *Quasimodo* (Barcelona, April 20, 1875); the one-act operas *Mazeppa* and *Tasse à Ferrare,* both to French texts (Madrid, 1881); *Cléopâtre,* 4-act opera to a French text (Madrid, 1881); *Los Pirineos,* his most ambitious effort, a trilogy consisting of a Prologue and the 3 dramas *El Conde de Foix, Rayo de luna,* and *La jornada de Panissars* (the Prologue produced separately in Venice, March 12, 1897; the entire work, Barcelona, Jan. 4, 1902); *La Celestina* (1904; not produced); *Matinada* (really a dramatic cantata; produced scenically, Barcelona, Oct. 27, 1905). FOR ORCH.: Symph. poems: *Excelsior* (after Longfellow) and *El Conde Aranau* and *Glosa* (both with Chorus); *Cant de la Montanya,* "symph. scenes"; *I Trionfi,* suite after Petrarch; *Marcia a Mistral.* VOCAL WORKS: *Canço latina* for Chorus and Orch.; *Messa di Gloria* for Soli, Chorus, Organ, and Orch.; Requiem a cappella; *Hymne à Ste. Thérèse;* motets and antiphons; songs (from V. Hugo's *Les Orientales,* T. Gauthier's *Consolations,* etc.). Also String Quartet, etc.; 302 opus numbers in all. He edited the collections *Hispaniae Schola musica sacra,* works of Morales, Guerrero, Victoria, Cabezón, Ginés Pérez, Diego Ortiz (8 vols.); *Teatro lírico español anterior al siglo XIX* (5 vols., 1897–98); *Salterio Sacro-Hispano* (1905); *Antología de organistas clásicos de España* (2 vols., 1905,

1908); the complete works of Victoria (8 vols., 1903–13; with biography in vol. VIII); *Cancionero popular español* (4 vols., Barcelona, 1919–20; new ed., 2 vols., 1936).

WRITINGS: *Diccionario técnico de la música* (1894); *Teatro lírico español anterior al siglo XIX* (5 vols. in one; 1897–98); *Prácticas preparatorias de instrumentación* (1902); *Emporio científico e histórico de organografía musical antigua española* (1901); *Musicalerías* (1906); *Catàlech de la Biblioteca musical de la Diputació de Barcelona* (2 vols., 1908, 1909); *Jean I. d'Aragon, compositeur de musique* (1909; in Riemann-Festschrift); *Tomás Luis de Victoria* (1918; reprinted from vol. VIII of collected works); *P. Antonio Eximeno* (1921). Of a valuable *Diccionario biográfico y bibliográfico de músicos y escritores de música españoles, portugueses y hispano-americanos antiguos y modernos*, only vol. I appeared (A–G; 1894–97). He publ. a book of reminiscences, *Jornadas de Arte* (Paris, 1911). His collected essays and critical writings were publ. in Paris in 3 vols., *Orientaciones, Musiquerías, Lírica nacionalizada* (1911–13). A complete list of Pedrell's works was publ. by A. Reiff in *Archiv für Musikwissenschaft*, III/1 (1921).

BIBLIOGRAPHY: G. Tebaldini, *Felipe Pedrell ed il dramma lirico spagnuolo* (Turin, 1897); R. Mitjana, *La música contemporanea en España y Felipe Pedrell* (Málaga, 1901); H. de Curzon, *Felipe Pedrell et "Les Pyrénées"* (Paris, 1902); "Felipe Pedrell," *La Nouvelle Revue* (Jan. 1912); A. Reiff, "Felipe Pedrell," *Zeitschrift für Musikwissenschaft* (Feb. 1921); Manuel de Falla, "Felipe Pedrell," *Revue Musicale* (Feb. 1923); E. Istel, "Felipe Pedrell," *Musical Quarterly* (April 1925); F. Bonastre, *Felipe Pedrell: Acotaciones a una idea* (Tarragona, 1977).

Pedrollo, Arrigo, Italian composer; b. Montebello, near Vicenza, Dec. 5, 1878; d. Vicenza, Dec. 23, 1964. He studied at the Milan Cons. (1891–1900); at his graduation, wrote a symph., which was performed by Toscanini. He was the director of the Istituto Musicale in Vicenza (1920–30); then a prof. of composition at the Milan Cons. (1930–41); from 1942 to 1959 was director of the Vicenza Cons. In 1914 he won the Sonzogno competition with his opera *Juana.* His other operas include *Terra promessa* (Cremona, 1908); *La Veglia* (Milan, Jan. 2, 1920); *L'Uomo che ride* (Rome, March 6, 1920); *Maria di Magdala* (Milan, 1924); *Delitto e castigo,* after Dostoyevsky's *Crime and Punishment* (La Scala, Milan, Nov. 16, 1926); *L'Amante in trappola* (Verona, Sept. 22, 1936); *Il Giglio di Ali* (1948).

Pedrotti, Antonio, Italian conductor and pedagogue; b. Trento, Aug. 14, 1901; d. there, May 16, 1975. He was a student of Respighi in composition at the Santa Cecilia Cons. in Rome; in 1929 returned to Trento, his native town, where he became director of the local Cons. He conducted the Augusteum Orch. in Rome from 1938 to 1944.

Pedrotti, Carlo, Italian composer and conductor; b.

Verona, Nov. 12, 1817; d. there (suicide), Oct. 16, 1893. He studied with Domenico Foroni; obtained excellent success with his opera *Lina* (Verona, May 2, 1840); was then engaged as conductor of the Italian Opera at Amsterdam (1841–45), and wrote 2 operas there, *Mathilde* (Spring 1841) and *La Figlia del Arciere* (Feb. 29, 1844); returned to Verona in 1845 and presented there his operas *Romea di Monfort* (Feb. 19, 1846), *Fiorina* (Nov. 22, 1851), *Il Parrucchiere della reggenza* (May 5, 1852), and *Tutti in maschera* (Nov. 4, 1856; his principal work). The following operas were staged in Milan: *Gelmina* (Nov. 3, 1853); *Genoveffa del Brabante* (March 20, 1854), and *La guerra in quattro* (May 25, 1861). Other operas were *Isabella d'Arragona* (Turin, Feb. 7, 1859); *Mazeppa* (Bologna, Dec. 3, 1861); *Marion Delorme* (Trieste, Nov. 16, 1865); *Il Favorito* (Turin, March 15, 1870); *Olema la schiava* (Modena, May 4, 1872).

Peellaert, Augustin-Philippe-Marie-Ghislain, Baron de, Belgian composer; b. Bruges, March 12, 1793; d. Brussels, April 16, 1876. He studied in Paris with Momigny; in 1832, became a member of the executive board of the Brussels Cons. He wrote masses and other sacred works; chamber music; songs; several operas, of which the following were produced in Brussels: *L'Heure du rendez-vous* (1821); *Agnès Sorel* (Aug. 30, 1823); *Le Barmècide* (1824); *Teniers ou La Noce flamande* (Feb. 21, 1825); *L'Exilé* (1827); *Faust* (1834); *Le Coup de pistolet* (1836); *Louis de Male* (1838); publ. an autobiography, *Cinquante ans de souvenirs* (Brussels, 1867).

Peerce, Jan (real name, **Jacob Pincus Perelmuth**), American tenor; b. New York, June 3, 1904. He played the violin in dance bands, and sang at various entertainment places in N.Y. In 1933 he was engaged as a singer at Radio City Music Hall in N.Y.; made his operatic debut in Philadelphia as the Duke in *Rigoletto* (May 14, 1938), and gave his first solo recital in N.Y. on Nov. 7, 1939. His lyrical voice attracted attention, and he was engaged by the Metropolitan Opera Co.; made his debut there as Alfredo in *La Traviata* on Nov. 29, 1941; sang also the parts of Cavaradossi in *Tosca,* Rodolfo in *La Bohème,* and Faust in Gounod's opera; remained on the staff of the Metropolitan until 1966, appearing again in 1967–68.

BIBLIOGRAPHY: Alan Levy, *The Bluebird of Happiness: The Memoirs of Jan Peerce* (N.Y., 1977).

Peeters, Flor, outstanding Belgian organist, pedagogue, and composer; b. Antwerp, July 4, 1903. He studied organ with Depuydt and Gregorian chant with van Nuffel at the Lemmens Inst. in Molines; he succeeded Depuydt as prof. of organ playing there in 1925, holding this position until 1952. He became a prof. of organ at the Antwerp Cons. in 1948, and was its director from 1952–68. He was elevated to the peerage as Baron Peeters by King Baudoin in 1971. He composed nearly 500 works for organ alone, and also wrote much sacred choral music. His works for organ include *Passacaglia and Fugue*

(1938); *Sinfonia* (1940); *Organ Concerto* (1944); *Lied Symphony* (1948); *30 Short Chorale Preludes* (1959); *213 Hymn Preludes for the Liturgical Year* (in 24 installments, 1959–67); *6 Lyrical Pieces* (1966). He also publ. *Anthologia pro organo* (4 vols., Brussels, 1949–59); *Ars organi* (3 vols., Brussels, 1952–54); *Little Organ Book* (Boston, 1957); etc.

BIBLIOGRAPHY: Piet Visser, *Flor Peeters, Organist* (Turnhout, 1950); J. Lade, "The Organ Music of Flor Peeters," *Musical Times,* CIX (1968); J. Hofmann, *Flor Peeters: His Life and His Organ Works* (Fredonia, 1978).

Peiko, Nicolai, Russian composer; b. Moscow, March 25, 1916. He studied with Litinsky, Rakov, and Miaskovsky at the Moscow Cons. (1933–40). After graduation he was commissioned to collect folksong materials in the remote Yakutsk district of Siberia, and produced *Suite on a Yakutsk Theme* for Orch. (1941); then investigated Bashkir folk music and composed a Bashkir opera, *Aikhylu* (1943). Returning to Moscow, he was appointed to the faculty of the Moscow Cons. (1942–59); also taught at the Gnessin Musical Inst. in Moscow. His music faithfully follows the precepts of socialist realism, national in thematic derivation and realistic in social content. His 1st and 5th symphs. are inspired by the heroism and suffering of the war of 1941–45; his 4th Symph. depicts the glory of the 1917 Soviet Revolution.

WORKS: For the stage: Opera, *Aikhylu,* on a Bashkir subject (1943, revised 1953); 2 ballets: *Spring Winds,* on a Tatar subject (1950) and *Jeanne d'Arc* (1957). For Orch.: *Suite on Yakutsk Themes* (1941); Piano Concerto (1943; revised 1954); 7 symphs.: No. 1 (1945); No. 2 (1946); No. 3 (1957); No. 4 (1965); No. 5 (1968); No. 6 (1972); No. 7, for Russian Folk Instruments (1977); *From Russia's Remote Past,* suite (1949); *Moldavian Suite* (1950; Moscow, Dec. 14, 1950); *Festive Overture* on Kabardin themes (1951); 2 *Concert Fantasies* for Violin and Orch., on Finnish themes (1953, 1965); *Symphonic Ballad* (1959); *Concerto-Symphony* (1974); *In the Throes of War,* 5 symph. tableaux (1975); *Concerto-Poem* for Clarinet, Balalaika, and Orch. (1979). Chamber music: Piano Quintet (1961); 3 string quartets (1964, 1965, 1966); *Decimet* for 10 Instruments (1971); Violin Sonata (1976). For Piano: 2 sonatinas (1942, 1957); *Sonatina Fairy Tale* (1943); 2 sonatas (1951, 1975).

BIBLIOGRAPHY: G. Grigorieva, *N. Peiko* (Moscow, 1965).

Peinemann, Edith, German violinist; b. Mainz, March 3, 1937. She learned the rudiments of music from her father, who was concertmaster of the City Orch. in Mainz. At the age of 19 she won an international violin competition of the German radio networks. She then played with many of the major German orchs.; also gave duo recitals with the noted Austrian pianist Jörg Demus. In 1962 she made her first tour of America.

Peixinho, Jorge, avant-garde Portuguese compos-

er; b. Montijo, Jan. 20, 1940. He studied piano at the Lisbon Cons. (1951–58); then went to Italy, where he took lessons with Goffredo Petrassi at the Santa Cecilia Academy in Rome (1959–61) and with Luigi Nono in Venice; later attended the seminars of Boulez and Stockhausen at the Basel Cons. (1962–63); in addition, worked at the electronic studio in Ghent, Belgium (1972–73). In 1974 he was appointed to the music faculty at the New Univ. of Lisbon.

WORKS: *Alba* for Soprano, Contralto, Female Chorus, and 11 Instruments (1959); *Fascinação* for Soprano, Flute, and Piano (1959); *Políptico* for Chamber Orch. (1960); *Sobreposições* for Orch. (1960); *Episodes* for String Quartet (1960); Saxophone Concerto (1961); *Sucessões simétricas* for Piano (1961); *Collage I* for 2 Pianos (1962); *Diafonia* for Harp, Celesta, Piano, Harpsichord, Metal Percussion, and 12 Strings (1963); *Morfocromia* for 2 Instrumental Groups (1963); *Dominó* for Flute and Percussion Groups (1964); *Sequência* for Flute in G, Celesta, Vibraphone, and Percussion (1964); *Kinetofonias* for 25 Strings (1965); *Situação 66* for Flute, Clarinet, Trumpet, Harp, and Viola (1966); *Harmónicos* for Piano and 2 Tapes (1967); *Nomos* for Orch. (1967); *Eurídice Reamada* for 5 Soloists, Chorus, and Orch. (1968); *As Quatro Estações* for Trumpet, Cello, Harp, Piano, and Tape (1968); *CDE* for Clarinet, Violin, Cello, and Piano (1970); *A Idade do Ouro* for Clarinet, Violin, Harp, Piano, Organ, and Tape (1970); *A Lira Destemperada* for Soprano, Trombone, and Percussion (1972); *Voix* for Soprano and Chamber Orch. (1972); *Morrer em Santiago* for 6 Percussionists (1973); *Elegia a Amilcar Cabral* for 4-track Tape (1973); incidental and film music.

Pekov, Mihail, Bulgarian composer; b. Vidin, Aug. 6, 1941. He studied composition with Veselin Stoyanov at the Bulgarian State Cons., graduating in 1967; then went to Leningrad, where he took courses with Salmanov at the Leningrad Cons.

WORKS: Piano Concerto (1965); Violin Concerto (1965); Concerto for Orch. (1970); *Double Concerto* for Violin, Cello, and Orch. (1970); *Music for Chamber Ensemble No. 1* (1970) and *No. 2* (1973); *Partita* for Flute, Viola, Harp, and Harpsichord (1971); 3 string quartets (all 1973); Symph. (1974); Overture (1975).

Pelemans, Willem, Belgian composer; b. Antwerp, April 8, 1901. He studied music history at the Cons. of Malines; then engaged in music journalism. A highly prolific composer, he adopted an attractive idiom of writing music in a Romantic manner.

WORKS: Comic opera, *De mannen van Smeerop* (1952; Brussels, 1963); 3 chamber operas: *La Rose de Bakawali* (1938); *Le Combat de la vierge et du diable* (1949); *De nozem en de nimf* (1960); musical tale, *Het tinnen soldaatje (Le Petit Soldat de plomb),* after Andersen (1945); lyrical drama, *Floris en Blancefloer* (1947); 3 ballets: *Miles gloriosus* (1945); *Herfstgoud (Autumnal;* 1959); *Pas de quatre* (1969); oratorio, *De wandelende jood* (1929); cantatas: *Diederik en Katrina* (1957); *De vogel van sneeuw* (1964); *Piet en de pijp (Pierre et la pipe;*

1963; for children); 't Pelske (1976); 6 symphs. (1936, 1937, 1937, 1938, 1938, 1939); 8 ballades for Orch. (1933–35); 5 concertinos for Chamber Orch. (1948; 1949; 1950; for Strings, 1958; 1966); Schetsen voor een buffa-opera for Chamber Orch. (1952); Ouvertura buffa for Orch. (1959); Petite suite for Orch. (1962); concertos: 5 for Orch. (1948, 1955, 1957, 1961, 1966); 3 for Piano (1945, 1950, 1967); one each for Harpsichord (1931); for Violin (1954); for Viola (1963); for 2 Trumpets, with Strings (1963); for Organ (1965); for 2 Pianos (1973); for Saxophone (1976); Concertino for Cello and Strings (1961); Sextet for Brasses (1968); Petite suite for String Sextet (1967); 2 wind quintets (1948, 1968); Quintet for Flute, Clarinet, Violin, Viola, and Cello (1950); Quintet for Harp, Flute, Violin, Viola, and Cello (1962); 8 string quartets (1942, 1943, 1943, 1943, 1944, 1955, 1961, 1970); 2 quartets for Clarinets (1961, 1976); Saxophone Quartet (1965); Wind Quartet (1965); Piano Quartet (1967); 3 piano trios (1932, 1942, 1972); Pas de trois for Piano Trio; 3 trios for Oboe, Clarinet, and Bassoon (1940, 1941, 1960); 2 sonatas for Flute, Oboe, and Piano (1955, 1956); String Trio (1945); Trio for 2 Violins and Piano (1957); Brass Sonata for Trumpet, Horn, and Trombone (1955); Trio for 2 Oboes and English Horn (1971); 3 violin sonatas (all 1942); Solo Violin Sonata (1955); Viola Sonata (1945); Walssonate for Viola and Piano (1949); Cello Sonata (1959); Solo Cello Sonata (1947); Sonata for Cello and Bassoon (1946); Sonata for Flute, and Harpsichord or Piano (1959); Sonata for Flute and Harp (1967); Clarinet Sonata (1961); Clarinet Sonatina (1961); Concertstuk for Clarinet and Piano (1967); Suite for Trumpet and Piano (1944); Sonata for 2 Guitars (1967); Suite for 2 Guitars (1968); 6 Etudes for 2 Guitars (1974); 6 Nocturnes for Harpsichord (1930); 7 personages van James Ensor for Harpsichord (1933); Studie for Harpsichord (1966). For Piano: 19 sonatas (1935–69); Sonata for 4 hands (1961); 3 toccatas (1948, 1951, 1951); 4 suites (1932–33); 10 Banalities (1944); 2 sonatas for 2 Pianos (1947, 1954). For Voice: 3 Liederen for Vocal Quartet and Wind Quintet (1944); Japanese verzen for Soprano, Alto, Baritone, and Piano (1958); Haikai for Middle Voice, Flute ad lib., and Harp (1967). Among his publications are the brochures Architectonische muziek (1927); Muziek beluisteren (1932); Geest en Klank (1943); De Vlaamse muziek en P. Benoit (1971).

Pelissier, Victor, horn virtuoso and composer. His name appears first in 1792 on Philadelphia concert programs as "first horn of the Theatre in Cape François." In 1793 he went to N.Y., where he lived for many years, and became the principal horn player, also composer and arranger, of the Old American Co.
WORKS: Operas: Edwin and Angelina or The Banditti (John Street Theater, N.Y., Dec. 19, 1796); Ariadne Abandoned by Theseus in the Isle of Naxos (N.Y., 1797); Sterne's Maria or The Vintage (1799); incidental music to about 18 plays performed in N.Y. (mostly in 1794–96), including Fourth of July or Temple of American Independence (1799), Castle of Otranto (adaptation of Sicil-

ian Romance), etc.; various pantomimes performed in Philadelphia; a quartet; and a few separate pieces. In 1811 he publ. the collection Columbian Melodies, which contains 3 songs from Sterne's Maria.
BIBLIOGRAPHY: O.G. Sonneck, Early Opera in America (N.Y., 1915); J.T. Howard, Our American Music (4th ed., N.Y., 1965); Sammelbände der Internationalen Musik-Gesellschaft, VI, 475.

Pellegrini, Vincenzo, Italian composer and organist; b. Pesaro, late 16th century; d. Milan, 1636. He was a canon at Pesaro (1603) and maestro di cappella at the Cathedral of Milan (1611–31). His extant works include Canzoni da intavolatura d'organo fatte alla francese (Venice, 1599); Missarum a 4 e 5 voci (Venice, 1603); sacred vocal pieces with organ accompaniment, publ. under the title Concerti ecclesiastici da 1, 2, 3, 5 e 6 voci (Venice, 1619); other compositions are in the collections Parnassus musicus Ferdinandoeus (Venice, 1615); 2 canzone (La Serpentina and La Capricciosa) in Torchi's L'arte musicale in Italia (vol. III).

Pelletier, (Louis) Wilfred, noted Canadian conductor and music educator; b. Montreal, June 20, 1896; d. New York, April 9, 1982. His father, a baker by trade, was an amateur musician who gave Pelletier his primary instruction; at the age of 14 he played piano in the orch. of the National Theatre in Montreal; in 1915 he won the Prix d'Europe and went to Paris, where he studied piano with Isidor Philipp, composition with Charles-Marie Widor, and opera repertoire with Camille Bellaigue. In 1917 he returned to America and was engaged as rehearsal pianist at the Metropolitan Opera in N.Y.; in 1921 he was appointed an assistant conductor there; then directed its Sunday Night Concert series; from 1928–50 he was a principal conductor there, specializing in the French repertoire; in 1936 he founded the popular series Metropolitan Opera Auditions of the Air. He also was active as a conductor in Canada; from 1935–51 he was conductor of the Société des Concerts Symphoniques de Montréal, and from 1951–66, of the Orch. Symphonique de Québec. From 1943–61 he served as director of the Cons. de Musique in Montreal. In 1968 he was made a Companion of the Order of Canada. He was married consecutively to 2 sopranos: **Queena Mario** (1925–36) and (from 1937) **Rose Bampton.** He publ. an autobiographical sketch, Une Symphonie inachevée (Quebec, 1972).

Pelton-Jones, Frances, American harpsichordist; b. Salem, Oreg., Dec. 6, 1863; d. New York, April 24, 1946. She studied piano with Carl Faelten at the New England Cons. in Boston; organ with Dudley Buck and William C. Carl in N.Y.; became interested in harpsichord playing and attained considerable proficiency at it; presented a special series of harpsichord recitals in N.Y. under the name Salons Intimes, which she continued for 20 years.

Pembaur, Joseph, Jr., Austrian pianist, son of **Jo-**

seph **Pembaur, Sr.;** b. Innsbruck, April 20, 1875; d. Munich, Oct. 12, 1950. He was a pupil of his father; then studied with Rheinberger and Thuille at the Munich Academy of Music; was a prof. of piano at the Munich Musikschule (1897–1900); subsequently was on the faculty of the Leipzig Cons. (1902–21); in 1921, was appointed a prof. at the Munich Academy of Music. He wrote a Violin Sonata; a number of songs; publ. *Von der Poesie des Klavierspiels* (1910; 2nd ed., 1911).

BIBLIOGRAPHY: C. Werner, *Joseph Pembaur zum 60. Geburtstag* (Berlin, 1935).

Pembaur, Joseph, Sr., Austrian composer and teacher; b. Innsbruck, May 23, 1848; d. there, Feb. 19, 1923. He studied at the Vienna Cons. with Bruckner and in Munich with Rheinberger and others. In 1874 he was appointed director of the Innsbruck Music School; retired in 1918.

WORKS: Opera, *Der Bauer von Langwall* (Innsbruck, May 2, 1898); symph. tableau, *In Tirol;* Requiem (in memory of the Tyrolese fallen in World War I; 1916); Organ Sonata; numerous male choruses a cappella; he also publ. *Harmonie- und Modulatinonslehre* (1910) and *Über das Dirigieren* (1892).

Pembaur, Karl Maria, Austrian organist and conductor, son of **Joseph Pembaur, Sr.;** b. Innsbruck, Aug. 24, 1876; d. Dresden, March 6, 1939. He studied with his father; then with Rheinberger at the Munich Academy of Music. In 1901 he went to Dresden, where he became court organist and choral conductor; also conducted at the Dresden Opera. He wrote the singspiel *Seien Sie vorsichtig; Geistliche Sonette* for 5 Solo Voices and Piano; *Bergbilder* for Woodwind Quintet and Piano; marches; songs; publ. *Drei Jahrhunderte Kirchenmusik am sächsischen Hofe* (Dresden, 1920).

Peña Costa, Joaquín, Spanish musicologist; b. Barcelona, March 1, 1873; d. there, June 25, 1944. He studied law at the Univ. of Barcelona, but devoted himself mainly to musical journalism; he translated librettos of Wagner's operas into Catalan; arranged vocal scores of *Tristan und Isolde, Lohengrin, Tannhäuser,* and *Die Meistersinger;* edited 5 vols. of songs of Beethoven, Schubert, Fauré, etc., under the title *Canconer selecte.* In 1940 he began work on a large music dictionary in Spanish; it was completed by H. Anglès, and publ. as *Diccionario de la música labor* (2 vols., Barcelona, 1954; of limited value owing to a multitude of errors).

Peña y Goñi, Antonio, Spanish writer on music; b. San Sebastian, Nov. 2, 1846; d. Madrid, Nov. 13, 1896. He studied at the Madrid Cons; for 30 years was music critic of the periodical *Imparcial,* in which he carried on earnest propaganda for Wagner, whom he knew personally. He composed a cantata, *Viva Hernani* (Madrid, Dec. 21, 1875), and some minor choral and piano works; publ. the important historical book *La opera española y la música dramática en España en el siglo XIX* (1881); also *La*

obra maestra de Verdi (1875); *Impressiones musicales* (1878); *Charles Gounod* (1879); guides to Wagner's operas; etc.

Peñalosa, Francisco de, important Spanish composer; b. Talavera de la Reina, c.1470; d. Seville, April 1, 1528. In 1498 he became a singer in the chapel choir of Ferdinand V; the King obtained a canonry (in absentia) for him in 1505 at the Seville Cathedral; in 1506 the Cathedral authorities revoked the appointment, but by 1510 he was able to fulfill the residence requirement. In 1511 the King made him maestro de capilla to his grandson. In 1512 he went to the royal monastery of S. Pedro de Cardeña, near Burgos. In 1516 he returned to Seville, where he assumed administrative duties at the Cathedral. In 1517 he became chamberlain and singer at the papal chapel; in 1518 he resigned his canonry at Seville Cathedral to become archdeacon of Carmona. In 1521 he resumed his canonry at Seville Cathedral, where he remained until his death. Peñalosa was one of the most important composers of his era, a master of polyphonic sacred and secular music. His sacred works include masses, Magnificats, motets, and hymns. Some of them are found in H. Eslava y Elizondo, ed., *Lira sacro-hispaña* (first series, vol. I, Madrid, 1869).

BIBLIOGRAPHY: G. Reese, *Music in the Renaissance* (N.Y., 1954; 2nd revised ed., 1959); R. Stevenson, *Spanish Music in the Age of Columbus* (The Hague, 1960).

Penderecki, Krzysztof, foremost Polish composer of the 20th-century avant-garde; b. Debica, Nov. 23, 1933. (His name is pronounced Kzhýshtov Penderétskee, not Penderekee.) He studied privately with F. Skolyszewski; then took courses in theory with Arthur Malawski and Stanislaw Wiechowicz at the Superior School of Music in Cracow (1955–58); after graduation he taught there (1958–66); went to West Germany and taught at the Folkwang Hochschule für Musik in Essen (1966–68); in 1973 became a part-time member of the faculty at Yale Univ.; also gave courses at Aspen, Colo. (1977). He rapidly acquired a reputation as one of the most original composers of his generation. In 1975 he was made an honorary member of the Royal Academy of Music in London, the Arts Academy of West Berlin, the Arts Academy of the German Democratic Republic, and the Royal Academy of Music in Stockholm. After a few works of an academic nature, he developed a hyper-modern technique of composition in a highly individual style, in which no demarcation line is drawn between consonances and dissonances, tonal or atonal melody, traditional or innovative instrumentation; an egalitarian attitude prevails toward all available resources of sound. While Penderecki's idiom is naturally complex, he does not disdain tonality, even in its overt triadic forms. In his creative evolution, he has bypassed orthodox serial procedures; his music follows an athematic course, in constantly varying metrical and rhythmic patterns. He utilizes an entire spectrum of modern sonorities, expanding the domain of tone to unpitched elements, making use of such effects as shouting, hissing, and verbal ejaculations in vocal parts, at times reaching a climax of aleatory glossolalia; tapping, rubbing, or snapping the fingers against the body of an instrument; striking the piano strings by mallets, etc. For this he designed an optical notation, with symbolic ideograms indicating the desired sound; thus a black isosceles triangle denotes the highest possible pitch; an inverted isosceles triangle, the lowest possible pitch; a black rectangle for a sonic complex of white noise within a given interval; vertical lines tied over by an arc for arpeggios below the bridge of a string instrument; wavy lines of varying amplitudes for extensive vibrato; curvilinear figures for aleatory passages; dots and dashes for repetitions of a pattern; sinusoidal oscillations for quaquaversal glissandos; etc. He applies these modern devices to religious music, including masses in the orthodox Roman Catholic ritual.

WORKS: *Psalmy Dawida (Psalms of David)* for Chorus, 2 Pianos, Celesta, Harp, 4 Double Basses, and Percussion (1958; Cracow, June 26, 1962); *Emanacje (Emanations)* for 2 Orchs. of String Instruments (1958–59); *Strofy (Strophes)* for Soprano, Narrator, and 10 Instruments (1959; Warsaw, Sept. 17, 1959); *3 Miniatures* for Violin and Piano (1959); *Anaklasis* for 42 Strings and Percussion (1959–60; Baden-Baden, Oct. 16, 1960); *Wymiary czasu i ciszy (Dimensions of Time and Silence)* for Wordless Chorus, Strings, and Percussion (1960; Warsaw, Sept. 18, 1960); *Tren pamieci ofiarom Hiroszimy (Threnody in Memory of Victims of Hiroshima)* for 52 String Instruments (1959–60; Warsaw Radio, May 31, 1961; Penderecki's most impressive and most frequently perf. work, rich in dynamic contrasts and ending on a tone cluster of 2 octavefuls of icositetraphonic harmony); String Quartet No. 1 (1960); *Fonogrammi* for 3 Flutes, Strings, and Percussion (1961); *Psalmus*, electronic music (1961); *Polymorphia* for 48 String Instruments (1961; Hamburg, April 16, 1962; perf. as a ballet under the title *Noctiphobie*, Amsterdam, 1970); *Stabat Mater* for 3 Choruses a cappella (1962; an independent section of the *St. Luke Passion*); *Kanon* for 52 String Instruments and Tape (1962; Warsaw, Sept. 20, 1962); *Fluorescences* for Orch. (1962; Baden-Baden, Oct. 21, 1962); *Cantata in honorem almae matris Universitatis Jagellonicae* for Chorus and Orch. (1964); *Mensura Sortis* for 2 Pianos (1964); Sonata for Cello and Orch. (1964); *Capriccio* (No. 1) for Oboe and 11 Strings (1965); *Passio et mors Domini Nostri Jesu Christi secundum Lucam (Passion According to St. Luke)* for Narrator, Soprano, Baritone, Bass, Boys' Chorus, 3 Mixed Choruses, and Orch. (1962–65; Cathedral in Münster, West Germany, March 30, 1966; a specially commissioned work); *De natura sonoris* (No. 1) for Orch. (1965–66; Royan, France, April 7, 1966); *Dies irae*, oratorio for Soprano, Tenor, Bass, Chorus, and Orch. (1966–67; Cracow, April 14, 1967; also perf. 2 days later as a commemorative service at the site of the Nazi concentration camp at Oświecim-Brzezinka), Concerto for Violino Grande and Orch. (1967; Östersund, Sweden, July 1, 1967; revised version, Hanover, N.H., Aug. 4, 1968; the solo instrument is specially constructed with 5

strings); *Capriccio* (No. 2) for Violin and Orch. (1967; Donaueschingen, Oct. 22, 1967); *Pittsburgh Overture* for Wind Ensemble (1967; commissioned by the American Wind Symph. Orch. in Pittsburgh); *Capriccio per Siegfried Palm* for Solo Cello (1968); String Quartet No. 2 (1968); *De natura sonoris No. 2* for Winds, Percussion, and Strings (1968; Juilliard School of Music, N.Y., Dec. 3, 1971); a 3-act opera, *Die Teufel von Loudon (The Devils of Loudon)*, dealing with a *furor uterinus* among nuns of Loudun struck by a multifutuent incubus personified by a neighboring monastic youth (1968–69; Hamburg, June 20, 1969); *Utrenja (Morning Prayer)* in 2 parts (1969–71): *Grablegung Christi (The Entombment of Christ)* for Soprano, Contralto, Tenor, Bass, Basso Profundo, 2 Choruses, and Orch., to a text in old Slavonic (Altenberg Cathedral, April 8, 1970), and *Auferstehung Christi (Resurrection of Christ)* for the same Soloists, Boys' Chorus, 2 Mixed Choruses, and Orch. (Münster Cathedral, May 28, 1971); *Kosmogonia* for Soprano, Tenor, Bass, Chorus, and Orch., commissioned by the United Nations and performed for the first time at its N.Y. headquarters building (1970; Oct. 24, 1970); *Actions* for Jazz Ensemble (1971; Donaueschingen, Oct. 17, 1971); *Prélude* for Winds, Percussion, and Double Basses (1971; Holland Festival, Amsterdam, July 4, 1971); *Partita*, concerto for Harpsichord, 4 other Electronically Amplified Solo Instruments, and Chamber Orch. (1971; Eastman School of Music, Rochester, N.Y., Feb. 11, 1972); Cello Concerto (1972; Baltimore, Md., March 8, 1972); *Ecloga VIII* for 6 Male Voices a cappella (1972; Edinburgh Festival, Aug. 21, 1972); *Ekecheireia* for Tape (1972); *Canticum canticorum Salomonis (Song of Songs)* for 16-voice Chorus, Chamber Orch., and ad libitum Dance Pair (1970–73; Lisbon, June 5, 1973); Symph. No. 1 (1973; London, July 19, 1973); *Intermezzo* for 24 Strings (1973); Magnificat for Bass Solo, Vocal Group, 2 Choruses, Boys' Chorus, and Orch. (1973–74; Salzburg, Aug. 17, 1974); *Als Jakob erwachte* for Voices, Orch., and 12 Ocarinas (1974; Monte Carlo, Aug. 14, 1974); Violin Concerto (1976; Basel, April 27, 1977); opera, *Raj utracony (Paradise Lost)*, after Milton (1976–78; Chicago, Nov. 29, 1978); *De profundis* for Chorus and Orch. (1977; Graz, Oct. 16, 1977); Te Deum for Soloists, Chorus, and Orch. (1980; Assisi, Italy, Sept. 27, 1980); Symph. No. 2, *Christmas Symphony* (1979–80; N.Y. Phil., May 1, 1980); Cello Concerto No. 2 (1981–82; West Berlin, Jan. 11, 1983); Viola Concerto (1982–83).

BIBLIOGRAPHY: K. Lisicki, *Szkice o Krzysztof Pendereckim* (Warsaw, 1973); W. Schwinger, *Penderecki: Begegnungen, Lebensdaten, Werkkommentare* (Stuttgart, 1979); R. Robinson, *Krzysztof Penderecki* (1983); idem, "Krzysztof Penderecki," *Ovation* (Nov. 1983; an interview).

Penfield, Smith Newell, American organist and teacher; b. Oberlin, Ohio, April 4, 1837; d. New York, Jan. 7, 1920. After preliminary study of the piano in N.Y., he went to Leipzig, where he took lessons from Moscheles, Reinecke, Plaidy, and Papperitz (piano), Richter (organ), and Hauptmann (theory). Returning to America, he conducted various choral societies; from 1882 was active in N.Y. as a church organist and teacher. He wrote a Piano Sonata, subtitled *Poem of Life;* some sacred music; songs; piano pieces.

Penherski, Zbigniew, Polish composer; b. Warsaw, Jan. 26, 1935. He studied composition with Poradowski and Szeligowski at the Warsaw Cons., graduating in 1959.

WORKS: Opera, *The Waning of Perin* (1971–72; Poznan, Oct. 6, 1974); *Studies in Color* for Piano (1961); *Musica humana* for Baritone, Chorus, and Orch. (1963); *Chamber Primer* for Instrumental Ensemble (1964); *Street Music* for Clarinet, Trumpet, Percussion, Accordion, and 4 Pianists on 2 Pianos (1966); *Missa abstracta* for Narrator, Tenor, Chorus, and Orch. (1966); String Quartet (1966); *3 recitativi* for Soprano, Piano, and Percussion (1968); *Hymnus laudans* for Chorus and Orch. (1970; Wroclaw, Feb. 24, 1972); *Incantations* for Percussion Sextet (1972); *Mazurian Chronicles* for Orch. and Tape (1973); *Radio Symphony* for Flute and Percussion (1974); *Anamnesis* for Orch. (1975).

Penn, Arthur, English-born American composer; b. London, Feb. 13, 1875; d. New London, Conn., Feb. 6, 1941. He received his primary education in England; in 1903 he emigrated to America and was active as a teacher in New London. He composed several comic operas, for which he wrote his own librettos: *Yokohama Maid, Your Royal Highness, The Lass of Limerick Town, Captain Crossbones, Mam'zelle Taps, The China Shop;* he also wrote a number of songs in a popular manner, among them *Carissima, The Magic of Your Eyes,* and *Sunrise and You.*

Penna, Lorenzo, Italian composer; b. Bologna, 1613; d. there, Oct. 31, 1693. He studied at the Univ. of Ferrara. In 1630 he entered the Carmelite monastery of S. Martino in Bologna; became maestro di cappella at S. Illario in Casale Monferrato (1656); in 1665 received his doctorate in theology; was then maestro di cappella at S. Cassiano in Imola (1667–69); in 1669 entered the Carmelite Order in Mantua, remaining until 1672; subsequently was director of music at the Carmelite church in Parma (1672–73). In 1676 he became a member of the Accademia dei Filarmonici in Bologna, where he remained until his death.

WORKS: *Messe e salmi concertati* in 5 Voices (1656); *Psalmorum totius anni modulatio* in 4 and 5 Voices (1669); *Correnti francesi a quattro,* with String Instruments (1673; designated as "Sonate" in the dedication); *Il sacro Parnaso delli salmi festivi* for 4 to 8 Voices (1677); *Reggia del sacro Parnaso* for 4 to 8 Voices (1677); *Galeria del sacro Parnaso* for 4 to 8 Voices, with Instrumental Accompaniment ad libitum (1678); he also publ. didactic eds.: *Li primi albori musicali per li principianti della musica figurata* (1672); *Albori musicali per li studiosi della musica figurata* (1678); *Direttorio del canto fermo* (Modena, 1689).

BIBLIOGRAPHY: J.-H. Lederer, *Lorenzo Penna und seine Kontrapunkttheorie* (Diss., Univ. of Graz, 1970).

Pennario, Leonard, brilliant American pianist; b. Buffalo, July 9, 1924. He was taken to California as a child and studied piano there; appeared in public at the age of 7, and was a soloist with the Los Angeles Phil. at 15. He then took piano lessons with Guy Maier; served in the U.S. Army Air Corps during World War II; then resumed his career; was the pianist with Heifetz and Piatigorsky in trio concerts; made several European tours; also was active as a teacher.

Penniman, Richard, black American apostle of rock known as **Little Richard,** extolled by his followers as "King of Rock'n'Roll"; b. Macon, Ga., Dec. 5, 1932. Possessed by religious fervor, he sang in local church choirs, then switched to a traveling medicine show. He won a talent contest in Atlanta at the age of 19, recorded "demo" (demonstration) records, and hit the proverbial jackpot with *Tutti Frutti* (1956). Some of his hits were focused on girls, some with first-name titles: *Lucille, Jenny, Jenny,* and *The Girl Can't Help It* (which was the title song of a film he appeared in). Other smash hits were *Keep a-Knockin', Good Golly, Miss Molly, Long Tall Sally,* and *Slippin' and Slidin'.* He was the harbinger of the unrestrained but puissant manner of American music that produced such individuals as Mick Jagger, Jerry Lee Lewis, James Brown, and Jimi Hendrix. Then, in the midst of his popular and commercial successes, he suddenly hit the religion trail, went to college in Alabama to study theology, embraced the ministry, toured the gospel circuit, and denounced rock'n'roll as the tool of the devil. Still, he put out an autobiographical album entitled *The King of Rock and Roll* before abandoning the sinful world for God. His personal hosannas survived in his early albums, *Here's Little Richard, Fabulous Little Richard,* and (more to the point) *Wild and Frantic Little Richard.*

Penny, George Barlow, American organist and composer of sacred music; b. Haverstraw, N.Y., June 30, 1861; d. Rochester, N.Y., Nov. 15, 1934. He studied in N.Y. with Dudley Buck (organ) and Percy Goetschius (composition); from 1890 to 1911 filled various positions as a teacher and an organist in Kansas; in 1911 was appointed director of the Rochester Cons., connected with the Eastman School of Music there. He made 9 tours of Europe and 2 of the Orient as an organist, lecturer, and conductor; publ. several services for the Episcopal Church, and other sacred music.

Pente, Emilio, Italian violinist and music editor; b. Padua, Oct. 16, 1860; d. Sachsa, Germany, May 14, 1929. He studied at the Milan Cons.; did research on Tartini and recovered about 40 Tartini MSS, which he arranged for publication in Germany; from 1909 to 1928 he taught at the Guildhall School of Music in London; then went to Germany. He edited and arranged a number of violin works by Tartini, and also pieces by Albinoni, Geminiani, Giardini, Nardini, and Vivaldi. He himself composed 17 opus numbers of violin music.

Pentenrieder, Franz Xaver, German composer; b. Kaufbeuren, Bavaria, Feb. 6, 1813; d. Munich, July 17, 1867. He studied with Kalcher and Stunz; became conductor at the Munich Court Opera; wrote a successful opera, *Die Nacht zu Paluzzi* (Munich, Oct. 2, 1840; perf. widely in Germany); a comic opera, *Das Haus ist zu verkaufen* (Leipzig, 1846); a number of church works; songs. As a result of an accident, he became insane, and spent the last few years of his life in an asylum.

Pentland, Barbara, Canadian composer; b. Winnipeg, Jan. 2, 1912. After taking piano lessons at a Montreal boarding school, she went to N.Y., and studied with Frederick Jacobi and Bernard Wagenaar at the Juilliard School of Music (1936–39); also took summer courses with Aaron Copland at the Berkshire Music Center in Tanglewood (1941 and 1942). She was an instructor at the Toronto Cons. (1943–49) and with the music dept. of the Univ. of British Columbia in Vancouver (1949–63). In her compositions she adopts a pragmatic method of cosmopolitan modernism, employing dissonant linear counterpoint and dodecaphonic melodic structures within the framework of Classical forms.
WORKS: Chamber opera, *The Lake* (1952; Vancouver, March 3, 1954); ballet-pantomime, *Beauty and the Beast,* for 2 Pianos (1940); *Concert Overture* (1935); *2 Pieces* for Strings (1938); *Lament* for Orch. (1939); *Holiday Suite* for Chamber Orch. (1941); *Arioso and Rondo* for Orch. (1941); Concerto for Violin and Small Orch. (1942); 4 symphs.: No. 1 (1945–48); No. 2 (1950; Toronto, Feb. 9, 1953); No. 3, *Symphony in 10 Parts,* for Chamber Ensemble (1957; Vancouver, Sept. 18, 1959); No. 4 (1959); *Colony Music* for Piano and Strings (1947); *Variations on a Boccherini Theme* for Orch. (1948); Concerto for Organ and Strings (1949); *Ave atque vale* for Orch. (1951); *Ricercar* for Strings (1955); Concerto for Piano and String Orch. (1956); *Strata* for String Orch. (1964); *Ciné scene* for Chamber Orch. (1968); *News,* to a text from the news media, for Virtuoso Voice and Orch. (1970); *Variations concertante* for Piano and Small Orch. (1970); *Res musica* for String Orch. (1975); Piano Quartet (1939); Cello Sonata (1943); 3 string quartets (1944, 1953, 1969); *Vista* for Violin and Piano (1945); Violin Sonata (1946); Wind Octet (1948); *Weekend Overture* for Resort Combo of Clarinet, Trumpet, Piano, and Percussion (1949); Solo Violin Sonata (1950); Solo Flute Sonatina (1954); Duo for Viola and Piano (1960); *Canzona* for Flute, Oboe, and Harpsichord (1961); Piano Trio (1963); *Variations* for Solo Viola (1965); *Trio con Alea* for String Trio (1966); Septet for Horn, Trumpet, Trombone, Violin, Viola, Cello, and Organ (1967); *Reflections* for Solo Free-bass Accordion (1971); *Interplay* for Accordion and String Quartet (1972); *Mutations* for Cello and Piano (1972); *Occasions* for Brass Quintet (1974); *Disasters of the Sun*

for Mezzo-soprano, 9 Instruments, and Tape (1976); songs. For Piano: *Studies in Line* (1941); Variations (1942); Sonata (1945); *Sonata Fantasy* (1947); 2 sonatinas (1951); *Mirror Study* (1952); 2-piano Sonata (1953); *Toccata* (1958); *3 Duets after Pictures by Paul Klee* (1959); *Fantasy* (1962); *Puppet Show* (1964); *Shadows* (1964); *Signs* (1964); *Suite borealis* (1966); *Space Studies* (1967); *Arctica* for Young Pianists (1971–73); *Vita brevis* (1973).
BIBLIOGRAPHY: S. Eastman and T. McGee, *Barbara Pentland* (Toronto, 1983).

Pépin, Clermont, Canadian composer; b. St.-Georges-de-Beauce, May 15, 1926. He studied piano in Quebec, and harmony in Montreal with Claude Champagne. In 1941 he went to Philadelphia, where he studied composition with Rosario Scalero. From 1949 to 1955 he lived in Paris and took composition lessons with Jolivet, Honegger, and Messiaen. Returning to Canada, he joined the staff of the Montreal Cons. (1955–64; director, 1967–72).
WORKS: 3 ballets: *Les Portes de l'enfer* (1953); *L'Oiseaux-Phénix* (1956); *Le Porte-rêve* (1957–58); 2 piano concertos (1946, 1949); *Variations symphoniques* for Orch. (1947); 5 symphs.: No. 1 (1948); No. 2 (Montreal, Dec. 22, 1957); No. 3, *Quasars* (Montreal, Feb. 7, 1967); No. 4, *La Messe sur le monde,* for Narrator, Chorus, and Orch. (1975); No. 5, *Implosion* (Montreal, Sept. 13, 1983); *Guernica,* symph. poem after Picasso's painting (Quebec, Dec. 8, 1952); *Le Rite de soleil noir,* symph. poem (1955; Luxembourg, Sept. 1955); *Hymne au vent du nord,* cantata (1960); *Monologue* for Chamber Orch. (1961); *Nombres* for 2 Pianos and Orch. (Montreal, Feb. 6, 1963); *Monade* for String Orch. (1964); *Prismes et cristaux* for String Orch. (Montreal, April 9, 1974); *Monade* for Violin and Orch. (1972); *Chroma* for Orch. (Guelph, Ontario, May 5, 1973); Piano Sonata (1947); 5 string quartets (1948, 1955, 1956, 1960, 1976); *Cycle Eluard* for Soprano and Piano (1949); *Musique pour Athalie* for Woodwinds and Brass (1956); Suite for Piano Trio (1958); *Sequences* for Flute, Oboe, Violin, Viola, and Cello (1972); *Réseaux* for Violin and Piano (1973–74); piano pieces; incidental music.
BIBLIOGRAPHY: *34 Biographies of Canadian Composers* (Canadian Broadcasting Co., Montreal, 1964).

Pepöck, August, Austrian operetta composer; b. Gmunden, May 10, 1887; d. there, Sept. 5, 1967. He studied in Vienna with Heuberger and R. Fuchs; then was active as a conductor of theater music in various provincial towns in Germany; subsequently lived mostly in Vienna. He scored great success with his operettas *Mädel ade!* (Vienna, Oct. 5, 1930) and *Der Reiter de Kaiserin* (Vienna, April 30, 1941). He also wrote some chamber music, and songs.

Pepper, Art, American jazz saxophone virtuoso; b. Gardena, Calif., Sept. 1, 1925; d. Los Angeles, June 15, 1982. His father was of German origin; his mother was Italian. He played jazz clarinet and alto saxophone in school bands; got married at 17; was drafted into the U.S. Army; after discharge he joined Stan Kenton's band (1946–52). His darkly emotional temperament led him to develop a passionate manner of shaping music which became known as "West Coast Style." He began making records, sometimes under the punning pseudonym **Art Salt,** but his highly promising career was ruined by his demonic addiction to heroin and other narcotic drugs. He squandered his earnings and, besotted by need of expensive drugs, he descended into thievery and brawls. He was busted in 1952 on narcotics charges, and served time in the Los Angeles County jail; was paroled to the U.S. Public Health Service Hospital at Fort Worth (1953–54), but got in trouble again, and was sentenced to jail in Los Angeles, where he served from 1954 to 1956 and again in 1960–61. Unable to control his habits, he was arrested as a recidivist and sent to San Quentin, where he served from 1961 till 1964 and, after another transgression, in 1965–66. Finally freed, he played with Buddy Rich's Big Band (1968–69). In 1977 and 1978 he completed 2 highly successful tours of Japan. He publ. an astonishingly frank autobiography, based on his own tape recordings and edited by his 3rd wife, Laurie, under the title *Straight Life: The Story of Art Pepper* (N.Y., 1979); it is a shocking but fascinating chronicle of the nether world of the American artistic scene. A film documentary on Pepper's life was presented at the Berlin Film Festival in 1982.

Pepping, Ernst, German composer; b. Duisburg, Sept. 12, 1901; d. Berlin, Feb. 1, 1981. He studied in Berlin with Gmeindl; became a teacher at the Church Music School in Berlin-Spandau in 1934, remaining there throughout his career; from 1953 to 1968 was a prof. of composition at the Berlin Hochschule für Musik. By virtue of his lifelong association with Lutheran Church culture, he acquired a profound understanding of German polyphonic music, both sacred and secular, and is generally regarded as the most significant representative of modern German choral writing; he also made arrangements of German folk songs. A Festschrift was publ. in his honor in 1971.
WORKS: *Deutsche Choralmesse* (1930); *Choralbuch* (1931); *Spandauer Chorbuch,* a collection of choral works for the entire church year, in 20 vols. (1934–41); *Te Deum* (1956); *Grosses Orgelbuch* in 3 parts (1939); *Kleines Orgelbuch* (1940); *Das Weltgericht* for 4 Voices (1958); *Die Weihnachtsgeschichte des Lukas,* set for 4–7 Voices (1959); numerous Psalms and motets, of which the most significant are the "Adventmotettes" *Aus hartem Weh die Menschheit klagt* for 3–4 Voices (1964); *Deines Lichtes Glanz* for 4–6 Voices (1967); 3 symphs. (1939, 1943, 1947); *Partita* for Orch. (1934); *Suite* for Trumpet, Saxophone, and Trombone (1926); Piano Concerto (1951); 2 string quartets; String Trio; 4 piano sonatas; numerous secular works for chorus; 33 folk songs for Children's Voices (1947). He publ. an important collection, *Der polyphone Satz,* in 2 vols. (1943, 1957). A complete list of his works is included in the Festschrift presented to him on his 70th

birthday (Berlin, 1971).
BIBLIOGRAPHY: Karl Laux, "Ernst Pepping," in *Musik und Musiker der Gegenwart* (Essen, 1949; pp. 193–201).

Pepusch, John Christopher (Johann Christoph), German-English opera composer; b. Berlin, 1667; d. London, July 20, 1752. He was taught by Klingenberg (theory) and Grosse (organ). He had a position at the Prussian court in 1681–97; then went to the Netherlands and (in 1700) to London; joined the Drury Lane orch. as a violinist; later as cembalist and composer, adapting Italian airs to English operas and adding recitatives and songs. In 1710 he founded (with Needler, Gates, Galliard, and others) the Academy of Ancient Music, famous for the revival of 16th-century compositions; in 1712, he was organist and composer to the Duke of Chandos, preceding Handel; in 1713, received his Mus.Doc. degree from Oxford. For many years he served as director of Lincoln's Inn Theatre, for which he wrote the masques *Venus and Adonis* (1715), *Apollo and Daphne* (1716), *The Death of Dido* (1716), and *The Union of the 3 Sister-Arts* (1723), and arranged music to the ballad-operas *The Beggar's Opera, Polly,* and *The Wedding.* In 1730 a fortune brought him by marriage with the singer **Marguerite de l'Epine** rendered him independent. From 1737 until his death he was organist of the Charterhouse. Pepusch was a learned, though conservative, musician who enjoyed high renown in England. He publ. a *Treatise on Harmony* (1731; reprinted Hildesheim, 1970); his various odes and cantatas, and his instrumental concertos and sonatas are of slight importance, and his name is preserved in music history mainly for his original music and some arranged numbers in *The Beggar's Opera.*
BIBLIOGRAPHY: *Dictionary of National Biography* (vol. 44); F. Kidson, *"The Beggar's Opera," Its Predecessors and Successors* (Cambridge, 1922; reprinted N.Y., 1969); C.W. Hughes, "J.C. Pepusch," *Musical Quarterly* (Jan. 1945); M. Boyd, "English Secular Cantatas in the 18th Century," *Music Review* (May 1969); D. Cook, "Venus and Adonis; An English Masque 'After the Italian Manner,' " *Musical Times* (Sept. 1980).

Perabo, (Johann) Ernst, German-American pianist; b. Wiesbaden, Nov. 14, 1845; d. Boston, Oct. 29, 1920. The family moved to N.Y. in 1852. He studied with his father; then at the Leipzig Cons. with Moscheles (piano), Reinecke (composition), and others. Returning to America in 1865, he established himself as a concert pianist, and a highly successful teacher in Boston; had nearly 1,000 pupils, among them well-known musicians (Mrs. H.H.A. Beach was one of his pupils). He publ. a number of piano pieces: *Moment musical; Scherzo; Prelude; Waltz; Pensées; Circumstance, or Fate of a Human Life; Prelude, Romance, and Toccatina.*

Peragallo, Mario, Italian composer; b. Rome, March 25, 1910. He was a student of Alfredo Casella, and in his early works followed the line of the Italian Baroque, characterized by modern but euphonious polyphony; later he adopted a radical quasi-dodecaphonic idiom, with frequent reversions to diatonic structures.

WORKS: Operas: *Ginevra degli Almieri* (Rome, Feb. 13, 1937); *Lo stendardo di S. Giorgio* (1941); *La Gita in campagna* (La Scala, Milan, March 24, 1954); scenic cantata, *La collina* (1947); Concerto for Orch. (1940); 2 piano concertos (1949, 1951); Violin Concerto (1954); *Forme sovrapposte* for Orch. (1959); *Vibrazioni* for Flute, "Tiptofono," and Piano (1960); 3 string quartets; Piano Quartet; numerous choral works and songs.

Perahia, Murray, outstanding American pianist of Spanish-Jewish parentage; b. New York, April 19, 1947. He studied piano with J. Haien (1953–64); then entered the Mannes College of Music, where he studied conducting and composition (B.S., 1969); he also continued his piano studies with Artur Balsam and Mieczyslaw Horszowski. In 1968 he made his Carnegie Hall debut; in 1972 he became the first American to win (by a unanimous vote of the jury) the Leeds International Pianoforte Competition; in 1975 he was awarded the first Avery Fisher Prize, sharing it with the cellist Lynn Harrell. He appeared as soloist with the leading orchs. of the U.S. and Europe; also gave many recitals in the U.S. and abroad. In 1982 he was appointed co-artistic director of the Aldeburgh Festival. He excels in classical music; mastered all of Mozart's concertos, often conducting from the keyboard; he is praised also for his congenial interpretation of the standard concert repertoire.

Perceval, Julio, Argentine composer; b. Brussels, July 17, 1903; d. (in a traffic accident) Santiago, Chile, Sept. 7, 1963. He studied organ at the Brussels Cons.; subsequently with Marcel Dupré in Paris. Emigrating to Argentina in 1926, he became active as an organist in Buenos Aires; then was a prof. of organ playing at the Univ. of Cuyo (1939–59). In 1959 he went to Chile, where he taught at the National Cons. of Santiago. He composed a number of songs and organ pieces; also some chamber music.

Pereira-Salas, Eugenio, Chilean musicologist; b. Santiago, May 19, 1904; d. there, Nov. 17, 1979. He studied at the Univ. of Chile in Santiago; in 1926 he went to Europe and took courses at the Sorbonne in Paris and at the Univ. of Berlin; later enrolled at the Univ. of Calif. at Berkeley on a Guggenheim fellowship (1933–34). Returning to Chile, he was a lecturer in geography and history at the Univ. of Chile; in 1938 he organized there a dept. of Chilean folklore. He publ. a number of informative books on Chilean music, among them *Los origines del arte musical en Chile* (Santiago, 1941); *La canción nacional de Chile* (Santiago, 1941); *Juegos y alegrías coloniales de Chile* (Santiago, 1947); *Historia de la música en Chile* (Santiago, 1957).

Peress, Maurice, American conductor; b. New York, March 18, 1930. He studied music at N.Y. Univ.

(B.A., 1951) and at the Mannes College of Music, N.Y. (1955–57); was a member of the faculty of N.Y. Univ. (1957–61) and then assistant conductor of the N.Y. Phil. (1961–62). His other engagements were as music director of the Corpus Christi (Texas) Symph. Orch. (1962–75) and of the Austin (Texas) Symph. Orch. (1970–73). He was music director of the Kansas City Phil. from 1974–80. In 1981 he became president of the Conductors' Guild of the American Symph. Orch. League. In 1971 he conducted the world premiere of Leonard Bernstein's *Mass* at the Kennedy Center in Washington, D.C.; he also conducted the first European performance of the work at the Vienna State Opera in 1981.

Pérez, David, Italian composer of operas; b. Naples (of Spanish parents), 1711; d. Lisbon, Oct. 30, 1778. He was a pupil of Galli (violin) and Mancini (theory) at the Cons. di Loreto in Naples; presented his first opera, *La nemica amante,* at the Teatro San Carlo in Naples on Nov. 4, 1735, followed by *Li travestimenti amorosi* (Naples, July 10, 1740) and *Siroe* (Naples, Nov. 4, 1740); in 1741 went to Palermo as maestro of the court orch., remaining there until 1748. He then lived the life of a traveling composer, visiting various cities in Italy, until 1752, when he was engaged as maestro di cappella at the royal chapel in Lisbon. In 1755 he visited London. Among his best operas are *Alessandro nell'Indie* (Genoa, Carnival 1744); *Demetrio* (Venice, Spring 1751); and *Solimano* (Lisbon, 1757; his most important dramatic work). As an opera composer, he was considered a worthy rival of Jommelli. He also wrote several masses; a Miserere for 5 Voices, with Bassoons obbligati and Organ; *Mattutino de' morti* for Chorus and Orch. (London, 1774); etc.

BIBLIOGRAPHY: E. Soares, *David Pérez, Subsídios para a biografía do célebre mestre* (Lisbon, 1935); H. Kretzschmar, *Geschichte der Oper* (Leipzig, 1919; pp. 188–89); P. Jackson, *The Operas of David Pérez* (Diss., Stanford Univ., 1967).

Pérez Casas, Bartolomeo, Spanish conductor and composer; b. Lorca, near Murcia, Jan. 24, 1873; d. Madrid, Jan. 15, 1956. He studied at the Madrid Cons.; played the clarinet in various military bands; also was a bandmaster. He then established himself in Madrid as a teacher at the Cons.; from 1915 to 1936, conducted the Orquesta Filarmónica de Madrid. He wrote a lyric drama in one act, *Lorenzo;* an orch. suite, *A mi tierra* (an early work, which became fairly popular); a String Quartet; pieces for band.

Perfall, Karl von, German composer and conductor; b. Munich, Jan. 29, 1824; d. there, Jan. 14, 1907. He took music lessons with Hauptmann in Leipzig (1848–49); became conductor of the Munich Liedertafel (1850); founded the Oratorio Society (1854); in 1864 was appointed Intendant of the court music and abandoned his activities as a conductor. From 1867 to 1893 he was Intendant of the Court Theater in Munich. Of his operas (all produced in Munich), *Raimondin* (March 27, 1881) and *Junker Heinz*

(April 9, 1886) were successful. He publ. *25 Jahre Münchener Hoftheater-Geschichte* (1892; covering the period from 1867); *Ein Beitrag zur Geschichte des königlichen Theaters in München* (1894); *Die Entwickelung des modernen Theaters* (1899).

Pergament, Moses, Finnish-born Swedish composer and conductor; b. Helsinki, Sept. 21, 1893; d. Gustavsberg, near Stockholm, March 5, 1977. He studied violin at the St. Petersburg Cons. and conducting at Berlin. In 1915 he settled in Sweden; from 1923 to 1966 was active as a music critic in Swedish newspapers; he publ. 4 books on music. His musical style was initially circumscribed by Russian paradigms; later he was influenced by Sibelius; still later he adopted some modernistic procedures. Several of his compositions reflect an ancestral strain of Jewish melos.

WORKS: Chamber opera, *Himlens hemlighet* (*The Secret of Heaven;* 1952); radio opera, *Eli* (1958; Swedish Radio, March 19, 1959); opera-oratorio, *Abrams Erwachen* (1970–73); ballets: *Vision* (1923) and *Krelantems and Eldeling* (1920–28); *Romance* for Violin and Orch. (1914); *Adagio* for Clarinet and Strings (1915); *Rapsodia ebraica* for Orch. (1935); *Concerto romantico* for Strings (1935); *Dibbuk,* fantasy for Violin and Orch. (1935); *Almquistiana,* 2 suites for Orch. (1936, 1938); *Nedanförmänskliga visor (Subhuman Songs)* for Narrator, Soli, Chorus, and Orch. (1936); *Swedish Rhapsody* for Orch. (1941); *Den judiska sången (The Jewish Song),* choral symph. (1944); Violin Concerto (1948); *Kol Nidré* for Cello and Orch. (1949); Piano Concerto (1951); Concerto for 2 Violins and Orch. (1954); Cello Concerto (1955); *Canto lirico* for Violin and Orch. (1956); *Pezzo intimo* for 16 Solo Cellos (1957); *De sju dödssynderna (The 7 Deadly Sins),* oratorio (1963); Viola Concerto (1964–65); *4 Poems by Edith Södergran* for Soprano and Orch. (1965–66); *Årstider,* 4 songs for Baritone and Orch. (1968); *Drömmen om mullen och vindarna (The Dream of the Earth and the Winds)* for Baritone and Orch. (1969); *Fantasia differente* for Cello and Strings (1970); Piano Trio (1912–13; revised 1940); Violin Sonata (1918–20); 3 string quartets (1922, 1952, 1956); Solo Violin Sonata (1961); Flute Sonata (1968); *Little Suite* for Woodwinds (1970); Sonatina for Flute and String Orch. (1973); *Biblical Cantata* for Chorus and Orch. (1974); over 100 solo songs; theater and film music.

Perger, Richard von, Austrian composer and conductor; b. Vienna, Jan. 10, 1854; d. there, Jan. 11, 1911. He studied cello and theory; was in the Austrian army during the campaign in Bosnia (1878); then received a stipend, and took lessons with Brahms (1880–82); was director of the Cons. of Rotterdam in the Netherlands (1890–95); returning to Vienna, he conducted the Gesellschaftskonzerte; from 1899 to 1907 was director of the Vienna Cons. His music bears unmistakable evidence of the profound influence of Brahms.

WORKS: Text and music of a comic opera, *Der Richter von Granada* (Cologne, 1889); singspiel, *Die 14 Nothhelfer* (Vienna, 1891); musical fairy tale, *Das stählerne Schloss* (Vienna, 1904); Violin Concerto; some chamber music; songs. He publ. a biography of Brahms (1908; new ed. by Hernried, 1934); his *Geschichte der K. K. Gesellschaft der Musikfreunde in Wien* was publ. posthumously (1912).

Pergolesi, Giovanni Battista, remarkable Italian composer; b. Jesi, near Ancona, Jan. 4, 1710; d. Pozzuoli, March 16, 1736. The family's original name was **Draghi;** the surname Pergolesi was derived from the town of Pergola, where Pergolesi's ancestors lived. He was the only surviving child of his parents, 3 children having died in their infancy. He studied music with Francesco Santi, choir director at Jesi Cathedral; was given a stipend by the Marchese Cardolo Pianetti, which enabled him to enter the Cons. dei Poveri at Naples; there he was a pupil of Domenico de Matteis (violin) and Gaetano Greco (theory); later also studied with Durante and Feo. He became proficient as a violinist, and played on various occasions during the carnivals. His first performed work was an oratorio, *La conversione di S. Guglielmo d'Aquitania* (which included a comic section in the Neapolitan dialect), presented at the monastery of S. Agnello Maggiore in Naples in the summer of 1731; another oratorio, *La Fenice sul rogo,* was performed in the same year; this was followed by a serious opera, *Salustia,* and an opera buffa, *Lo Frate 'nnamorato* (Naples, Sept. 23, 1732). In Dec. 1732 he was commissioned by the municipal authorities of Naples to write a solemn Mass as a votive offering after a series of severe earthquakes. On Aug. 28, 1733, Pergolesi presented a serious opera, *Il Prigioniero superbo;* it contained a comic intermezzo, *La Serva padrona,* which was to become his most celebrated work. After a brief sojourn in Rome (May 1734) to conduct his Mass at the San Lorenzo Church, he returned to Naples; there his new opera, *Adriano in Siria,* was produced, on Oct. 25, 1734, with an intermezzo, *Livietta e Tracollo* (perf. at various times under different titles: *La Contadina astuta, La finta Polacca,* etc.). During another trip to Rome he performed his serious opera *L'Olimpiade* (Jan. 8, 1735), directing from the harpsichord, but it had little success. His last opera was a comic play, *Il Flaminio* (Naples, Autumn 1735). At that time his health was undermined by consumption; early in 1736 he went to Pozzuoli, where he died at the age of 26; he was buried in the common grave. His last completed work was a masterpiece of sacred music, *Stabat Mater.* Several dramatic works ascribed to Pergolesi and publ. under his name, notably *Il Maestro di musica* and *Il Geloso schernito,* are spurious. The revival of his comic intermezzo *La Serva padrona* in Paris in 1752 precipitated the so-called *querelle des bouffons* between the supporters of the Italian and the French factions. Pergolesi's instrumental music is less known, and there are grave doubts as to the authenticity of many of these works publ. under his name: 14 trio sonatas (of these, 3 were ed. by Riemann, Berlin, 1900); 6 concertini for Strings (publ. in London as works by Carlo Ricciotti; recently established as the works of Count Unico Wilhelm van Wassenaer); 3 "sinfonie" (string quartets); 2 concertos for Flute and Strings; Sonata for Violin and Strings; 5 harpsichord sonatas. Stravinsky used some of these instrumental works for his ballet *Pulcinella*, but most of the borrowed material is not by Pergolesi. *La Serva padrona* was publ. in new editions by Abert (1911), Karl Geiringer, and others; *Flaminio* was edited by Mortari (1942); the spurious *Il Maestro di musica* (which is in reality a pasticcio publ. in Paris in 1753) was orchestrated and edited by Schering (1924); the intermezzo *La finta Polacca* was issued by Radiciotti (1914); the *Stabat Mater* was publ. by Eulenburg in Alfred Einstein's edition. Among other extant works attributed to Pergolesi are the oratorios *Il Pentimento*, *La Morte d'Abel*, and *Septem verba;* 10 chamber cantatas; at least 5 masses; still doubtful is the authenticity of many arias, including the popular *Tre giorni son che Nina*. A complete edition of Pergolesi's works, *Opera omnia*, was brought out in Rome (1940–42) in 5 vols. (148 works, of which 129 publ. for the first time; many are spurious). The chaotic entanglement of spurious and authentic works is marvelously unraveled in M. Paymer's *Pergolesi: A Thematic Catalogue of the Opera Omnia* (N.Y., 1977).

BIBLIOGRAPHY: P. Boyer, "Notices sur la vie et les ouvrages de Pergolèse," *Mercure de France* (July 1772); Marchese di Villarosa, *Lettera biografica intorno alla patria ed alla vita di G.B. Pergolesi* (Naples, 1831; 2nd ed., 1843); F. Villars, *La Serva padrona, Son apparition à Paris en 1752, son influence, son analyse* (Paris, 1863); A. Gianandrea, *Pergolesiana* (Jesi, 1885); E. Faustini-Fasini, *G.B. Pergolesi attraverso i suoi biografi e le sue opere* (Milan, 1900); G. Radiciotti, *G.B. Pergolesi; Vita, opere ed influenza su l'arte* (Rome, 1910; 2nd ed., Milan, 1935; in German, Zürich, 1954); A. Della Corte, "G.B. Pergolesi," in *L'opera comica italiana nel 1700* (vol. I, pp. 49–75; Bari, 1923); G. Radiciotti, "Tre giorni," *Musica d'Oggi* (July 1925); A. Della Corte, *Pergolesi* (Turin, 1936); R. Giraldi, *G.B. Pergolesi* (Rome, 1936); G. de Saint-Foix, "Le Deuxième Centenaire de Pergolesi," *Revue de Musicologie* (1936); special issues of *Rassegna Musicale* (1936) and *Musica d'Oggi* (1936); L. Reichenburg, *Contribution à l'histoire de la Querelle des Bouffons* (Philadelphia, 1937; a complete list of pamphlets publ. in Paris during the *querelle des bouffons*); H. Claydon, "Three String Quartets Attributed to Pergolesi," *Music & Letters* (Oct. 1938); F. Schlitzer, *G.B. Pergolesi* (Turin, 1940); S.A. Luciani, *G.B. Pergolesi: Note e documenti* (Siena, 1942); E.J. Luin, *Fortuna e influenza della musica di Pergolesi in Europa* (Siena, 1943); F. Walker, "Two Centuries of Pergolesi Forgeries and Misattributions," *Music & Letters* (Oct. 1949); C.L. Cudworth, "Notes on the Instrumental Works Attributed to Pergolesi," ibid.; F. Walker, "Pergolesi Legends," *Monthly Musical Record* (1952); idem, "*Orazio:* The History of a Pasticcio," *Musical Quarterly* (July 1952); A. Loewenberg, *Annals of Opera* (Cambridge, 1943; new ed., 1955); H. Hucke, "Die musikalischen Vorlagen zu Igor Stravinskys *Pulcinella*," in W. Stauder et al., eds., *Frankfurter musikhistorische Studien* (Ost-

hoff Festschrift; Tutzing, 1969); M. Paymer, *The Instrumental Music Attributed to G.B. Pergolesi: A Study in Authenticity* (Diss., City Univ. of N.Y., 1977); A. Dunning, *Count Unico Wilhelm van Wassenaer (1692–1766); A Master Unmasked; or, The Pergolesi–Ricciotti Puzzle Solved* (Büren, 1980).

Peri, Jacopo, Italian composer, called **"Il Zazzerino"** for his abundant hair; b. Rome, Aug. 20, 1561; d. Florence, Aug. 12, 1633. Of a noble family, he studied at Lucca under Cristoforo Malvezzi; was maestro at the court of Ferdinando I and Cosimo II de' Medici, and from 1601 at the court of Ferrara. A participant in the Florentine circle at the houses of Counts Bardi and Corsi, where the revival of ancient Greek musical declamation was planned, Peri set to music Rinuccini's text of *Dafne* (1597). It was first performed at Corsi's palace in Florence, and played again at Pitti's palace. Peri followed it with a setting of Rinuccini's *Euridice* for the wedding of Maria de' Medici with Henry IV of France (produced Oct. 6, 1600; publ. Florence, 1600; reprinted in *Monuments of Music and Music Literature in Facsimile*, I/8). *Dafne* was the first "opera" or drama set to music in monodic style (i.e., vocal soli supported by instruments); this style was termed *stile rappresentativo*. In 1608 Peri wrote for Mantua the recitatives of *Ariadne* (text by Rinuccini), while Monteverdi composed the arias. In the same year he submitted in Mantua the opera *Tetide* (text by Cini), which, however, was not produced. With Grazie, Signorini, and del Turco he wrote *Guerra d'amore* (Florence, 1615). No records are available showing that *Adone* (text by Cicognini), composed in 1620, ever had a public performance. *La precedenza delle dame* was produced at Florence in 1625, and Peri also collaborated with Gagliano on *La Flora* (Florence, Oct. 11, 1628). He publ. in 1609 *Le varie musiche* in one to 3 parts, some to be sung with harpsichord or chitarrone, others to be played on the organ. Kiesewetter printed 3 madrigals *a* 4 in *Schicksale und Beschaffenheit des weltlichen Gesanges* (1841). Fragments from *Euridice* are in several histories of music; a complete edition was publ. by Guidi in Florence, and by Torchi in vol. VI of *L'arte musicale in Italia;* a facsimile reprint was publ. in Milan in 1934; A. Schering's *Geschichte der Musik in Beispielen* contains 3 excerpts (nos. 171a–c).

BIBLIOGRAPHY: G.O. Corazzini, "Commemorazione della Riforma melodrammatica," in the annual report of the Reale Istituto di Musica (Florence, 1895); A. Solerti, *Le origini del melodramma* (3 vols., Florence, 1905); O.G. Sonneck, "Dafne, the First Opera," *Sammelbände der Internationalen Musik-Gesellschaft*, 15 (1913); M. Mila, "J. Peri," *Rassegna Musicale*, 4 (1933). For details of productions of Peri's operas, see A. Loewenberg, *Annals of Opera* (Cambridge, 1943; 3rd ed., 1978).

Peričić, Vlastimir, Serbian composer and musicologist; b. Vršac, Dec. 7, 1927. He studied in Vienna with Uhl; became active as a pedagogue in Belgrade; publ. manuals on harmony and form.

WORKS: String Quartet (1950); *Symphonic Movement* (Belgrade, Oct. 14, 1952); *Fantasia quasi una sonata* for Violin and Piano (1954); Sinfonietta for Strings (Zagreb, Nov. 13, 1957); piano pieces. He compiled a valuable reference work on Serbian composers, *Muzički Stvaraoci u Srbiji* (Belgrade, 1969).

Périer, Jean, French tenor; b. Paris, Feb. 2, 1869; d. there, Nov. 3, 1954. He studied at the Paris Cons., obtaining first prize for singing (1892); made his debut at the Opéra-Comique as Monostatos in *Die Zauberflöte* on Dec. 16, 1892; was engaged there until 1894, and again from 1900 to 1920. He created the role of Pelléas at the premiere of Debussy's opera (1902), and sang the leading tenor parts in several other premieres of French operas; sang at the Metropolitan Opera House in N.Y. in 1908. A talented comedian, he also appeared in variety shows in Paris. He publ. an instructive album, *Mes exercises, tirés des chansons populaires de France* (Paris, 1917).

Perinello, Carlo, Italian music editor; b. Trieste, Feb. 13, 1877; d. Rome, Jan. 6, 1942. He studied music in Trieste and Leipzig; then taught at the Trieste Cons. (1904–14) and at the Milan Cons. He served on the staff of the Istituto Editoriale Italiano, and collaborated in the preparation of its publications.

Perisson, Jean-Marie, French conductor; b. Arcachon, July 6, 1924. He studied harmony with Hugon and counterpoint with Noël Gallon at the Paris Cons., graduating in 1951; then took lessons in conducting with Jean Fournet at the Ecole Normale de Musique and with Igor Markevitch at the Salzburg Mozarteum. He was subsequently engaged as conductor of Radio Strasbourg (1955–56); from 1956 to 1965 was music director in Nice. In 1965–69 he was a conductor at the Paris Opéra; later was appointed chief conductor of the Orch. National de Monte Carlo (1969–71). He also appeared as a guest conductor with the San Francisco Opera Co. In 1972 he was appointed music director of the State Orch. in Ankara, Turkey.

Perkins, Carl, American country-music singer, instrumentalist, and songwriter; b. Jackson, Tenn., April 9, 1932. He began his career as an entertainer at country dances and honky-tonks with the group known as the Perkins Brothers; became a favorite at the Grand Ole Opry in Nashville, Tenn.; later toured in the U.S. and abroad with his own band, which he founded with his sons. In 1956 he wrote the song *Blue Suede Shoes,* which became a hit in various renditions by popular singers of the day.

Perkins, Charles Callahan, American musician and painter; b. Boston, March 1, 1823; d. Windsor, Vt., Aug. 25, 1886. He was educated at Harvard Univ.; also studied in Italy and in Paris. In 1850 he became the head of the Handel and Haydn Society, in which position he exercised considerable influence on musical affairs in Boston; compiled (with John S. Dwight) vol. I of *History of the Handel and Haydn Society of Boston* (Boston, 1883).

Perkins, Francis Davenport, American music critic; b. Boston, Nov. 18, 1897; d. New York, Oct. 8, 1970. He studied at the New England Cons., at Trinity College, Cambridge, England, and at Harvard Univ. (B.A. cum laude, 1918). In 1919 he became exchange editor (later music editor) of the *N.Y. Tribune;* contributed numerous articles to various musical publications.

Perkins, Henry Southwick, American vocal teacher; b. Stockbridge, Vt., March 20, 1833; d. Chicago, Jan. 20, 1914. He studied voice at the Boston Music School (graduated in 1861). He filled various administrative and educational posts in Iowa, Kansas, and Illinois; in 1890 founded the Chicago National College of Music; was active as a director of music festivals and conventions across the country, from Maine to California. He was one of the organizers of the Music Teachers National Assoc. in 1876; edited 30 songbooks, hymnbooks, class books, etc.; composed vocal quartets and songs.

Perkins, John MacIvor, American composer and pedagogue; b. St. Louis, Aug. 2, 1935. He studied music at Harvard Univ. (B.A., 1958) and at Brandeis Univ. (M.F.A., 1962); also took lessons with Nadia Boulanger in Paris and with Roberto Gerhard and Edmund Rubbra in London. He was an instructor of music at the Univ. of Chicago (1962–64) and a lecturer on music at Harvard Univ. (1965–70). In 1970 he was appointed head of the music dept. of Washington Univ. in his native St. Louis. WORKS: *Canons* for 9 Instruments (1957); *3 Miniatures* for String Quartet (1960); *Variations* for Flute, Clarinet, Trumpet, Piano, and Percussion (1962); *Music for 13 Players* (1964); *Music for Orchestra* (1965); choral works and piano pieces.

Perkins, (David) Walton, American pianist and music critic; b. Rome, N.Y., Nov. 16, 1847; d. Chicago, Feb. 6, 1929. He was a pupil of Theodor Kullak and Anton Rubinstein in Berlin; upon his return to America, he settled in Chicago; with William H. Sherwood, organized the Sherwood Music School in Chicago (1897); was its director until 1901. He composed piano pieces and songs; edited collections of choruses, and composed choral works.

Perkins, William, American composer; b. Dallas, April 28, 1941. He studied at the Univ. of Colorado in Boulder with Cecil Effinger (B.A., 1971) and at the New England Cons. of Music in Boston (M.M., 1974). WORKS: *Textures* for Musical Saw and Percussion (1970); *Twilight Music* for Musical Saw and Harpsichord (1970); *Chamber Symphony* (1971); *Contrast* for Woodwind Trio and Percussion (1972); 2 preludes for Vibraphone and Electric Guitar (1973); String Quartet (1974).

Perkins, William Oscar, American vocal teacher and composer, brother of **Henry Southwick Perkins;** b. Stockbridge, Vt., May 23, 1831; d. Boston, Jan. 13, 1902. He studied voice in Milan; lived in Boston as a teacher; publ. about 40 collections of songs, anthems, etc., including many of his own pieces.

Perkowski, Piotr, Polish composer; b. Oweczacze, Ukraine, March 17, 1901. He studied composition with Statkowski at the Warsaw Cons. (1923–25); then took private lessons with Szymanowski in Warsaw and with Albert Roussel in Paris. He subsequently devoted himself to teaching; was director of the Toruń Cons. (1936–39); taught composition at the Warsaw Cons. (1947–51, 1955–73); was artistic director of the Cracow Phil. (1949–51) and dean of the Music Academy in Wroclaw (1951–55); served as councilor for cultural development for the city of Warsaw (1965–74). In his earlier years he followed the fashionable cosmopolitan trend of absolute music without reference to national or general programmatic subjects, but under the influence of social changes he began introducing concrete, historic, and pictorial representations.
WORKS: Opera, *Garlands* (Warsaw, 1962); 5 ballets: *Swantewit* (1930; revised 1945–47; Poznan, June 19, 1948); *Clémentine* (1960–63); *Rhapsody* (1949); *Fantasia* (1950); *Balladyna* (1960–64; Warsaw, 1965); 2 symphs.: No. 1, with Chorus (1925; score lost; reconstructed 1955), and No. 2 (1949); *Geometric Suite* for Orch. (1930); 2 violin concertos (1933, 1960); *Warsaw Overture* (1954); *Sinfonia drammatica* (1963); *Scottish Impressions* for Orch. (1968); 5 cantatas: *Wisla* (1951); *Epitaphe pour Nicos Belojannis* (1952); *Suita weselna (Merry Suite)* for Soprano, Tenor, Chorus, and Orch. (1952); *Suita epicka* (1953); *Alexiares,* with Narrator and Tape (1966–69); *Niebo w plomieniach (The Sky in Flames),* song cycle, with Orch. (1969); String Quartet (1930); *Elegia* for Cello and Organ (1945); Trumpet Sonatina (1954); Flute Sonata (1954); piano pieces.

Perle, George, American composer and theorist; b. Bayonne, N.J., May 6, 1915, of Russian-Jewish immigrant parents. He studied composition with Wesley La Violette at DePaul Univ. in Chicago (1935–38), and also took private lessons with Ernst Krenek (1939–41); obtained his degree of M.Mus. from the American Cons. of Music in Chicago in 1942; received his Ph.D. in 1956 from N.Y. Univ. with the dissertation *Serial Composition and Atonality* (publ. in Berkeley, 1962; 4th ed., 1977); also wrote *Twelve-Tone Tonality* (Berkeley, 1977). He held teaching posts at the Univ. of Louisville in Kentucky (1949–56) and at the Univ. of Calif. at Davis (1957–61); in 1961 he joined the faculty of Queens College in N.Y. He received Guggenheim fellowships in composition in 1966–67 and 1974–75, as well as several other grants. He contributed numerous analytic essays on the works of Schoenberg, Berg, and Webern. He is co-founder and director of the International Alban Berg Society at the City Univ. of N.Y.

WORKS: FOR ORCH.: 2 symphs.; *Rhapsody* (1953; Louisville, Jan. 16, 1954); *3 Movements* (1960; International Society for Contemporary Music Festival, Amsterdam, June 14, 1963); *6 Bagatelles* (1965; Long Island Symph., Nov. 18, 1977); Cello Concerto (1966); *Songs of Praise and Lamentation* for Solo Voices, Chorus, and Orch. (1974; N.Y., Feb. 18, 1975); Concertino for Piano, Winds, and Timpani (Chicago, April 27, 1979); *A Short Symphony* (Boston Symph., Tanglewood, Mass., Aug. 16, 1980); *Serenade III* for Piano and Chamber Orch. (N.Y., Dec. 14, 1983). CHAMBER MUSIC: 3 wind quintets (1959, 1960, 1967); 7 string quartets (1938–73); *Sonata quasi una fantasia* for Clarinet and Piano (1972); Sonata for Solo Viola (1942); Sonata for Solo Clarinet (1943); Sonata for Solo Cello (1947); 2 sonatas for Solo Violin (1959, 1963); *Monody I* for Solo Flute (1960); *Monody II* for Double Bass (1962); *Serenade I* for Viola and Chamber Ensemble (1962); *Serenade II* for Chamber Ensemble (1968); *Solo Partita* for Violin and Viola (1965). FOR PIANO: *Short Sonata* (1964); *Toccata* (1969); *Dodecatonal Suite* (1970); *6 Etudes* (1973–76); *Ballade* (1981). FOR VOICE: *2 Rilke Songs* for Voice and Piano; *13 Dickenson Songs* for Soprano and Piano (1978).
BIBLIOGRAPHY: L. Kraft, "The Music of George Perle," *Musical Quarterly* (July 1971); David Ewen, *American Composers* (N.Y., 1982).

Perlea, Jonel, Rumanian-American conductor and composer; b. Ograda, Dec. 13, 1900; d. New York, July 29, 1970. He studied piano and composition in Munich (1918–20) and conducting in Leipzig (1920–23). He made his conducting debut in Bucharest in 1919; held posts as a conductor in Leipzig (1922–23) and Rostock (1923–25); then returned to Rumania and conducted the Bucharest Opera (1929–32, 1934–36) and the Bucharest Radio Orch. (1936–44), of which he was a founder. He led conducting classes at the Bucharest Cons. (1941–44); during the last year of World War II he was interned in a German concentration camp. After the war he conducted opera in Rome (1945–47); in 1950 conducted at La Scala in Milan. He made his American debut at the Metropolitan Opera in N.Y., on Dec. 1, 1949, conducting *Tristan und Isolde;* appeared at the San Francisco Opera and the Lyric Opera of Chicago; from 1955 to 1970 was conductor of the Conn. Symph. Orch. He taught conducting at the Manhattan School of Music from 1952 until shortly before his death; became a naturalized U.S. citizen in 1960. He suffered a heart attack in 1957 and a stroke in 1958, as a result of which he lost the use of his right arm, but he continued to conduct with his left hand.
WORKS: *2 Sketches* for Orch. (1919); Piano Sonata; String Quartet (1921); *Symphonic Variations on an Original Theme* (1930); *Don Quixote,* symph. poem (1946); *Symphony Concertante* for Violin and Orch. (1968); *3 Studies* for Orch. (1969).

Perlemuter, Vlado, pianist and teacher; b. Kaunas, Lithuania, May 26, 1904 (of Polish parents). He was taken to Paris as a child; studied at the Paris Cons. with Alfred Cortot. After graduation, he joined the faculty of the Cons.; later toured in England and Japan; also served as a visiting prof. at the Royal Northern College of Music in Manchester. He acquired a fine reputation as a congenial interpreter of French piano music.

Perlman, Itzhak, brilliant Israeli-American violinist; b. Tel Aviv, Aug. 31, 1945. He was stricken with polio when he was 4, which left his legs paralyzed; for the rest of his life he had to walk on crutches. Despite this ghastly handicap, he began to play the violin and gave regular recitals at Tel Aviv. In 1958 he was discovered in Israel by Ed Sullivan, the TV producer, and appeared on his show on Feb. 15, 1959. Perlman's courage and good humor endeared him to the public at once. He remained in N.Y., where his parents soon joined him, and was accepted as a scholarship student in the classes of Ivan Galamian and Dorothy DeLay at the Juilliard School of Music. He made his professional American debut on March 5, 1963, playing with the National Orch. Assoc. in N.Y. In 1964 he won first prize in the Leventritt Competition, which carried, besides the modest purse ($1,000), a significant bonus—an appearance with the N.Y. Phil. It also brought about a lasting friendship with Isaac Stern, who promoted him with all the enthusiasm of a sincere admirer. Perlman's career was no longer a problem: he toured the U.S. from coast to coast in 1965–66 and toured Europe in 1966–67. He also began to teach, and in 1975 was appointed to the faculty of Brooklyn College. He seemed to be overflowing with a genuine love of life; he played not only so-called serious stuff but also rag music and jazz; with Isaac Stern and Pinchas Zukerman he indulged in public charivari on television to which he furnished enjoyable commentaries like a regular stand-up (but necessarily sit-down) comedian. And he became quite a habitué of the White House, being particularly popular with Ronald Reagan, who savored Perlman's show-biz savvy; his being a Jew and a handicapped person only added to the public appreciation of his TV appearances in the center of American power. On Jan. 5, 1967, Perlman married Toby Lynn Friedlander. They had children, too.

BIBLIOGRAPHY: David Ewen, *Musicians since 1900* (N.Y., 1978).

Perlongo, Daniel, American composer; b. Gaastra, Mich., Sept. 23, 1942. He studied composition with Bassett and Finney at the Univ. of Michigan (M.M., 1966); then took a course in composition with Petrassi at the Santa Cecilia Academy in Rome (1966–68); as a winner of the American Prix de Rome, he spent useful time at the American Academy in Rome (1970–72). Returning to the U.S., he devoted himself mainly to teaching; was for many years prof. of music at Indiana Univ. of Pa.

WORKS: For Orch.: *7 Pieces* (1966); *Myriad* (Rome, June 1968); *Changes* for Wind Ensemble (1970; Indiana, Pa., April 11, 1973); *Ephemeron* (Rome, Dec. 1972); *Variations* for Chamber Orch. (Indiana, Pa., Nov. 9, 1973); *Voyage* for Chamber Orch. (1975); Concertino for Chamber Orch.

(Omaha, May 2, 1981). Chamber music: *Episodes* for Solo Double Bass (1966); *Movement* for 8 Players (1967); *Intervals* for String Trio (1967); *For Bichi* for Percussion Quartet (1968); *Movement in Brass* for 12 Brasses (1969); *Process 7, 5, 3 for 6 in 12* for Flute, Oboe, Clarinet, and 3 Percussionists (1969); 2 string quartets: No. 1, *Semblance* (1969–70); No. 2 (1983); *Tre Tempi* for Flute, Clarinet, Horn, Violin, and Cello (1971); *Solo* for Violin (1971); *Fragments* for Flute and Cello (1972); *Semblance, Structure and Tune* for Tuba and Percussion (1973); *Ricercar* for Wind Trio (1976); *Summer Music* for Brass Quintet (1978); *Aureole* for Saxophone Quartet (1979); *Soliloquy* for Solo Bass Clarinet (1980). For Piano: Sonata (1965); *Serenade* (1977). For Organ: *Tapestry* (1981).

Perne, François Louis, French music scholar; b. Paris, Oct. 4, 1772; d. Laon (Aisne), May 26, 1832. He studied with Abbé d'Haudimont at the maîtrise of St.-Jacques-de-la-Boucherie; was a chorus singer at the Paris Opéra from 1792, and double-bass player in the orch. there (1799–1816). His profound skill in composition was illustrated by his writing a triple fugue, to be sung backward on reversing the page; his knowledge of old music was extraordinary. In 1813 he became a prof. of harmony at the Paris Cons., as successor to Catel; he became inspector-general of the Cons. in 1816, and librarian in 1819. In 1822 he went into retirement, at an estate near Laon; returned to Paris shortly before his death. He publ. *Exposition de la séméiographie, ou Notation musicale des Grecs* (1815); *Cours d'harmonie et d'accompagnement* (1822); *Chansons du Châtelain de Coucy* (1830); and a great number of articles on Greek and medieval music publ. in vols. I–IX of the *Revue Musicale*, edited by Fétis. He also wrote several pieces of sacred music.

Pernet, André, French bass; b. Rambervillers, Jan. 6, 1894; d. Paris, June 23, 1966. He studied at the Paris Cons. with Gresse; made his debut in 1921 in Nice; was a principal member of the Paris Opéra (1928–45); appeared there again in 1948. His most notable roles included Don Giovanni, Boris Godunov, and Méphistophélès; he also sang in many contemporary operas.

Perosi, Don Lorenzo, distinguished Italian composer of church music; b. Tortona, Dec. 21, 1872; d. Rome, Oct. 12, 1956. He studied at the Milan Cons. (1892–93); also took courses at Haberl's School for Church Music at Regensburg (1893); became maestro di cappella at Imola, and then at San Marco in Venice. He was ordained a priest in 1895; in 1898 became music director of the Sistine Chapel and leader of the papal choir; he resigned this post in 1915 owing to a severe mental disturbance; spent some time in a sanatorium (1922–23). Regaining his health after treatment, he returned to active service as a choral conductor and composer. Shortly after his 80th birthday, he led a performance of his oratorio *Il natale del Redentore* at the Vatican, before Pope Pius XII (Dec. 28, 1952). He was a self-denying and scholarly worker for the cause of the cultivation of a pure church style, both in composition and in performance, and was esteemed above all others as a church musician at the Vatican. His magnum opus, the sacred trilogy *La Passione di Cristo* (I, *La Cena del Signore;* II, *L'Orazione al monte;* III, *La morte del Redentore*), was produced in Milan, Dec. 2, 1897, at the Italian Congress for Sacred Music, and had numerous performances elsewhere in Europe and America. Other oratorios are *La Trasfigurazione del Nostro Signore Gesù Cristo* (Venice, March 20, 1898); *La Risurrezione di Lazaro* (Venice, July 27, 1898; in La Fenice Theater, by special permission); *La Risurrezione di Cristo* (Rome, Dec. 13, 1898); *Il natale del Redentore* (Como, Sept. 12, 1899); *L'entrata di Cristo in Gerusalemme* (Milan, April 25, 1900); *La strage degli innocenti* (Milan, May 18, 1900); *Mosè* (Milan, Nov. 16, 1901); *Dies iste* (Rome, Dec. 9, 1904); *Transitus animae* (Rome, Dec. 18, 1907); *In patris memoriam* (Naples, May 15, 1919); *Giorni di tribulazione* (Milan, Oct. 1916). He wrote further some 40 masses, with Organ; a Requiem, with Instrumental Accompaniment; a *Stabat Mater* for Solo Voices, Chorus, and Orch.; *Vespertina oratio* for Solo Voices, Chorus, and Orch.; about 150 motets, Psalms, etc.; 2 symph. poems: *Dovrei non piangere* and *La festa del villaggio;* a series of 8 orch. pieces, each named after an Italian city: *Roma, Firenze, Milano, Venezia, Messina, Tortona, Genoa, Torina;* other orch. works; a Piano Concerto; a Violin Concerto; chamber music; many organ works.

BIBLIOGRAPHY: I. Seytre, *L'Abbé Perosi: Sa biographie, son œuvre* (Nice, 1901); Romain Rolland, "Don Lorenzo Perosi," in *Musiciens d'aujourd'hui* (Paris, 1914; in Eng., N.Y., 1915); A. Damerini, *Lorenzo Perosi* (Rome, 1924); A. Della Corte, *Lorenzo Perosi* (Turin, 1936); A. Paglialunga, *Lorenzo Perosi* (Rome, 1952); M. Glinski, *Lorenzo Perosi* (Milan, 1953); M. Rinaldi, *Lorenzo Perosi* (Rome, 1967).

Perotin (called **Perotinus Magnus**), celebrated composer of the 12th century; putative dates of life are: b. between 1155 and 1160; d. between 1200 and 1250. He was the greatest master (after Leonin) of the Notre Dame School, representing the flowering of the Ars Antiqua. He was maître de chapelle at Beatae Mariae Virginis (before the erection of Notre-Dame) in Paris. Among his extant works are organa in 2, 3, and 4 parts. His melodic writing differs from the practice of Leonin in that he employs triadic progressions; there is also a suggestion of rudimentary canonic procedures. His most famous quadruple organum, *Sederunt principes*, was publ. by R. Ficker in 1930, and appears in several collections of medieval music. Other works are in Coussemaker's *L'Art harmonique au XIIᵉ et XIIIᵉ siècles;* vol. I of *Oxford History of Music;* Y. Rokseth, *Motets du XIIIᵉ siècle* (1936); Davison and Apel, *Historical Anthology of Music* (vol. 1, 1946). A complete edition is edited by E. Thurston (N.Y., 1970).

BIBLIOGRAPHY: R. Ficker, in *Neue Musikzeitung,* 2 (1928); J. Handschin, in *Schweizerisches Jahrbuch für Musikwissenschaft,* 2; F. Ludwig, in the Riemann-Festschrift (1909), the *Archiv für Musikwissenschaft,* 3, the *Zeitschrift für Musikwissenschaft,* 5, Guido Adler's *Handbuch der Musikgeschichte* (1930), and the Adler-Festschrift (Vienna, 1930); H. Besseler, *Die Musik des Mittelalters und der Renaissance* (Potsdam, 1931–35); G. Reese, *Music in the Middle Ages,* chapter 11 (N.Y., 1940); Hans Tischler, *The Motet in 13th-Century France* (New Haven, 1942); J. Chailley, *Histoire musicale du moyen-âge* (Paris, 1950); W. Waite, *The Rhythm of Twelfth-Century Polyphony* (New Haven, 1954).

Perrault, Michel, Canadian composer; b. Montreal, July 20, 1925. He studied harmony, oboe, and timpani at the Montreal Cons. (1943–46); went to Paris, where he took lessons with Honegger and Nadia Boulanger (1946–47). Returning to Canada, he was a percussion player and assistant conductor of the Montreal Symph. Orch. (1957–60); then became associated with the Minute Opera Co. He founded in Montreal a jazz organization, La Société de Concerts de Musique de Chambre Noire, and his own publishing house, Publications Bonart.

WORKS: 3 ballets: *Commedia del arte* (1958); *Sea Gallows* (1958); *Suite canadienne* (1965); *Les Trois Cones* for Cello and Orch. (1949); *La Belle Rose* for Cello and Orch. (1952); *Fête et parade* for Trumpet and Orch. (1952); *Esquisses en plein air* for Soprano and String Orch. (1954); *Monologues* for String Orch. (1954); *Margoton* for Harp and Orch. (1954); *Le Saucisson canadien* for 4 Saxophones and String Orch. (1955); *Pastiche espagnol* for Trumpet and Orch. (1956); *Pastiche tzigane* for 2 Trumpets and Orch. (1957); *Berubée* for Piano and Orch. (1959); *Jeux de quartes* for Harp and Orch. (1961); *Serenata per tre fratelli* for 3 Horns and Orch. (1962); Doublebass Concerto (1962); *Homage,* overture (1966); Concerto for Horn and Orch. without Brasses (1967); Violin Sonata (1946); Saxophone Quartet (1953); Piano Trio (1954); Sextet for Clarinet, Harp, and String Quartet (1955); incidental music; works for jazz ensemble; songs.

Perrin, Harry Crane, British organist and pedagogue; b. Wellingborough, Aug. 19, 1865; d. Exeter, Nov. 6, 1953. He was a pupil in Dublin of Sir R. Stewart, Dr. C.W. Pearce, and Dr. F. Bates; received a degree of Mus.Bac. from the Univ. of Dublin, 1890; F.R.C.O., 1892; Mus.Doc., 1901. In 1892–98 he held the positions of organist and choirmaster at St. Michael's in Coventry; in 1898–1908, held similar positions at Canterbury Cathedral, and was conductor of the Cathedral Musical Society; in 1908–30 he was a prof. of music and director of the Cons. at McGill Univ. in Montreal (from 1920, dean of the faculty there); in 1930, retired as dean emeritus, and returned to England. He composed cantatas; Overture and Suite for Orch.; numerous church services and anthems; song cycles, part-songs, etc.

Perrin, Pierre, French poet; b. Lyons, c.1620; d. Paris, April 25, 1675. He was the author of the librettos for the first French operas (so called): Cambert's *La*

Pastorale (1659), *Pomone* (1671), and *Ariane* (1672). The privilege obtained from Louis XIV by Perrin and Cambert to organize the Académie de Musique (1668) was revoked in Lully's favor (1672).

BIBLIOGRAPHY: A. Pougin, *Les Vrais Créateurs de l'opéra français, Perrin et Cambert* (Paris, 1881); H. Prunières, "Lully and the Académie de Musique et de Danse," *Musical Quarterly* (Oct. 1925).

Perron (real name, **Pergamenter**), **Karl,** noted German bass-baritone; b. Frankenthal, June 3, 1858; d. Dresden, July 15, 1928. He studied with Hey in Berlin, Hasselbasch in Munich, and Stockhausen in Frankfurt; made his debut as Wolfram in 1884 in Leipzig, where he sang until 1891; then joined the Dresden Court (later State) Opera, remaining on its roster until 1924; during his tenure there, he created the roles of Jochanaan in *Salome,* Orest in *Elektra,* and Baron Ochs in *Der Rosenkavalier;* also appeared at the Bayreuth Festivals (1889–1904), where he was acclaimed for his fine performances of Wotan and King Marke.

Perry, Edward Baxter, American pianist; b. Haverhill, Mass., Feb. 14, 1855; d. Camden, Maine, June 13, 1924. He became nearly blind in childhood, but was able to go to Germany, where he took lessons with Kullak, Pruckner, and also Clara Schumann and Liszt. Returning to America, he originated an innovative type of "lecture-recital," with which he traveled all over the U.S.; he also did some teaching, composed a number of semi-attractive piano pieces, and publ. *Descriptive Analyses of Piano Works* (1902) and *Stories of Standard Teaching Pieces* (1910).

Perry, George, English composer; b. Norwich, 1793; d. London, March 4, 1862. He was a choirboy at the Cathedral of Norwich; moved to London in 1822, and became director of the music at the Haymarket Theatre; then organist of the Quebec Chapel; from 1832 to 1848 served as concertmaster of the Sacred Harmonic Society Orch.

WORKS: Oratorios: *The Death of Abel* (Norwich, 1816); *Elijah and the Priests of Baal* (Norwich, March 12, 1819); *The Fall of Jerusalem* (London, Feb. 20, 1832); *Belshazzar's Feast* (London, Feb. 10, 1836); *Hezekiah* (1847); 2 operas: *Morning, Noon and Night* (London, Sept. 9, 1822) and *Family Jars* (London, Aug. 26, 1822); overture to *The Persian Hunters* (London, Aug. 3, 1817); anthems; songs; piano pieces.

Perry, Julia, black American composer; b. Lexington, Ky., March 25, 1924; d. Akron, Ohio, April 29, 1979. After studying at the Westminster Choir College in Princeton, N.J. (1943–48), she took a course in composition with Dallapiccola at Tanglewood in the summer of 1951; then took composition lessons, intermittently, in Europe with Nadia Boulanger in Paris and again with Dallapiccola in Italy (1952–56); she also attended classes in conducting in Siena (1956–58). She received 2 Guggenheim fellowships and an award from the National Inst. of Arts and Letters.

WORKS: 3 operas: *The Cask of Amontillado* (Columbia Univ., Nov. 20, 1954); *The Selfish Giant* (1964); *The Bottle;* 12 symphs., some with Chorus and others for Band, many having subtitles, such as *Children's Symphony, Simple Symphony, Soul Symphony* (1959–73); *Stabat Mater* for Alto and String Orch. (1951); *Short Piece* for Orch. (1952; revised 1955 and 1965); *Homage to Vivaldi,* a Requiem for Orch. (N.Y., March 13, 1959); *Pastoral* for Flute and Strings (1959); *Homunculus, C.F.* for 10 Percussionists (1960); Violin Concerto (1963); *Frammenti dalle lettere de Santa Caterina* for Soprano, Chorus, and Orch.; *7 Contrasts* for Baritone and Chamber Ensemble; *Episode* for Orch.; *Venus Moon* for Band (1971); *Module* for Orch. (1975); 2 piano concertos; Violin Sonata and other chamber pieces; songs.

Persen, John, Norwegian composer; b. Porsanger, Norwegian Lapland, Nov. 9, 1941. He studied composition with Finn Mortensen at the Norwegian State Academy of Music in Oslo (1968–73); in 1974–76 was president of Ny Musikk, the Norwegian section of the International Society for Contemporary Music; in 1976–82 served as a member of the board of the Norwegian Music Information Center. His music follows the lines of the cosmopolitan avant-garde, with a mixture of jazz, rock, sonorism, and special effects (*CSV* requires 2 pistol shots to be heard at the end of the work). Persen is a nationalistic Lapp from the extreme Polar North; some titles of his compositions are political in their allusions.

WORKS: *Øre-Verk* for Orch. (1972; the title suggests both "earache" and "aural work"); *Orkesterwerk II* (1974; Oslo, May 4, 1974); *Sámesiidat—CSV* for Chorus a cappella (1976; based on a "joik," a Lapp folk song); *CSV* for Orch. (1976; Oslo, March 22, 1977; the ambiguous acronym of the title means either "Dare to show that you are a Lapp" or "the secret Lapp host"); *Stykket har ingen tittel* (i.e., *This Piece Has No Name*), subtitled *Dreietoner for Orchestra* (1976; Trondheim, Jan. 20, 1977); *Music for Resting Marching Band* for Brass Band (1977); *Under Kors og Krone (Under Cross and Crown),* opera (1978–82; based on a revolt of the Lapp population against the authorities in the late 19th century).

Persiani (née **Tacchinardi**), **Fanny,** Italian coloratura soprano; b. Rome, Oct. 4, 1812; d. Neuilly-sur-Seine, France, May 3, 1867. Her father, the tenor **Nicola Tacchinardi,** was her teacher. After a successful debut at Livorno in 1832, she sang in the principal cities of Italy; in 1837–47 she appeared in London and Paris with brilliant success; also visited the Netherlands and Russia, but returned to Paris in 1858. In 1830 she married the composer **Giuseppe Persiani.**

BIBLIOGRAPHY: G. Tebaldini, "Giuseppe Persiani e Fanny Tacchinardi, Memorie ed appunti," *Rivista Musicale Italiana,* 12 (1905).

Persiani, Giuseppe, Italian opera composer; b.

Persichetti

Recanati, Sept. 11, 1799; d. Paris, Aug. 13, 1869. As a youth he played violin in theater orchs. in Rome and Naples, where he studied with Zingarelli. In 1830 he married the singer **Fanny Tacchinardi,** who became known as "La Persiani"; her illustrious name completely eclipsed his; yet he was a notable composer whose dramatic opera *Ines de Castro,* produced in Naples on Jan. 27, 1835, scored great success and was performed all over Europe; the celebrated soprano Malibran sang the title role, and Czerny wrote a piano paraphrase on themes of the opera. Persiani's other operas are *Attila* (Parma, Jan. 31, 1827); *Il Solitario* (Milan, April 26, 1829); *Il Fantasma* (Paris, Dec. 14, 1843); *Eufemio di Messina* (Lucca, Sept. 20, 1829; perf. also under the alternative titles *La distruzione di Catania* and *I Saraceni a Catania*).

BIBLIOGRAPHY: G. Tebaldini, "Giuseppe Persiani e Fanny Tacchinardi, Memorie ed appunti," *Rivista Musicale Italiana,* 12 (1905).

Persichetti, Vincent, outstanding American composer; b. Philadelphia, June 6, 1915. He studied piano, organ, double bass, tuba, theory, and composition as a youth; began his career as a professional musician when he was only 11 years old; became a church organist at 15. He took courses in composition with Russell King Miller at the Combs College of Music (Mus.B., 1935); then served as head of the theory and composition dept. there; concurrently studied conducting with Fritz Reiner at the Curtis Inst. of Music (diploma, 1938) and piano with Olga Samaroff at the Philadelphia Cons. (Mus.D., 1945); also studied composition with Roy Harris at Colorado College. From 1941 to 1947 he was head of the theory and composition dept. of the Philadelphia Cons.; in 1947 joined the faculty of the Juilliard School of Music in N.Y.; in 1963 was named chairman of the composition dept. there. In 1952 he became director of music publishing of Elgan-Vogel, Inc. With F. Schreiber, he wrote a biography of William Schumann (N.Y., 1954); publ. a valuable manual, *Twentieth Century Harmony: Creative Aspects and Practice* (N.Y., 1961). His music is remarkable for its polyphonic skill in fusing the ostensibly incompatible idioms of Classicism, Romanticism, and stark modernism, while the melodic lines maintain an almost Italianate diatonicism in a lyrical manner.

WORKS: Operas: *Parable XX,* in 2 acts (1976), and *Sibyl* (1984). For Orch.: 9 symphs.: No. 1 (1942; Rochester, N.Y., Oct. 21, 1947); No. 2 (1942); No. 3 (1946; Philadelphia, Nov. 21, 1947); No. 4 (1951; Philadelphia, Dec. 17, 1954); No. 5, *Symphony for Strings* (1953; Louisville, Ky., Aug. 28, 1954); No. 6, *Symphony for Band* (St. Louis, April 16, 1956); No. 7 (1958; St. Louis, Oct. 24, 1959); No. 8 (Berea, Ohio, Oct. 29, 1967); No. 9, *Sinfonia: Janiculum* (1970; Philadelphia, March 5, 1971); Concertino for Piano and Orch. (1941; Rochester, Oct. 23, 1945); *Dance Overture* (1942; Tokyo, Feb. 7, 1948); *Fables* for Narrator and Orch. (1943; Philadelphia, April 20, 1945); *The Hollow Men* for Trumpet and String Orch. (1944; Germantown, Pa., Dec. 12, 1946); *Divertimen-*

to for Band (N.Y., June 16, 1950); *Fairy Tale* for Orch. (1950; Philadelphia, March 31, 1951); Concerto for Piano, 4-hands (Pittsburgh, Nov. 29, 1952); *Pageant* for Band (Miami, May 7, 1953); Piano Concerto (1962; Hanover, N.H., Aug. 2, 1964); *Introit* for Strings (1964; Kansas City, May 1, 1965); *Masquerade* for Band (1965; Berea, Ohio, Jan. 23, 1966); *Night Dances* for Orch. (Kiamesha Lake, N.Y., Dec. 9, 1970); *A Lincoln Address* for Narrator and Orch. (1972; based on excerpts from Lincoln's 2nd inaugural address; originally scheduled for perf. at President Richard Nixon's inaugural concert on Jan. 19, 1973, but canceled because of the ominous threat in the text of the "mighty scourge of war" to be brought down on the unyielding foe, which might have been misinterpreted in the light of the then-raging war in Vietnam; the work was eventually perf. by the St. Louis Symph. Orch. at Carnegie Hall in N.Y., on Jan. 25, 1973; also a version for Band, 1973); Concerto for English Horn and String Orch. (N.Y., Nov. 17, 1977); a series of works, each entitled *Serenade:* No. 1 for 10 Wind Instruments (1929); No. 2 for Piano (1929); No. 3 for Violin, Cello, and Piano (1941); No. 4 for Violin and Piano (1945); No. 5 for Orch. (Louisville, Nov. 15, 1950); No. 6 for Trombone, Viola, and Cello (1950); No. 7 for Piano (1952); No. 8 for Piano, 4-hands (1954); No. 9 for Soprano and Alto Recorders (1956); No. 10 for Flute and Harp (1957); No. 11 for Band (1960; Ithaca, N.Y., April 19, 1961); No. 12 for Solo Tuba (1961); No. 13 for 2 Clarinets (1963); No. 14 for Solo Oboe (1984); a series of works, each entitled *Parable:* I for Solo Flute (1965); II for Brass Quintet (1968); III for Solo Oboe (1968); IV for Solo Bassoon (1969); V for Carillon (1969); VI for Organ (1971); VII for Solo Harp (1971); VIII for Solo Horn (1972); IX for Band (1972; Des Moines, Iowa, April 6, 1973); X actually his String Quartet No. 4 (1972); XI for Solo Alto Saxophone (1972); XII for Solo Piccolo (1973); XIII for Solo Clarinet (1973); XIV for Solo Trumpet (1973); XV for Solo English Horn (1973); XVI for Solo Viola (1974); XVII for Solo Double Bass (1974); XVIII for Solo Trombone (1975); XIX for Piano (1975); XX, an opera in 2 acts (1976); XXI for Solo Guitar (1978); XXII for Solo Tuba (1981); XXIII for Violin, Cello, and Piano (1981); XXIV for Harpsichord (1982); 4 string quartets (1939; 1944; 1959; 1972, also listed as *Parable X*); 12 piano sonatas (1939–80); 6 piano sonatinas (1950–54); 8 harpsichord sonatas (1951–84); Suite for Violin and Cello (1940); Sonata for Solo Violin (1940); Concertato for Piano and String Quartet (1940); Sonatine for Organ, Pedals Alone (1940); *Fantasy* for Violin and Piano (1941); *Pastoral* for Woodwind Quintet (1943; Philadelphia, April 20, 1945); *Vocalise* for Cello and Piano (1945); *King Lear,* septet for Woodwind Quintet, Timpani, and Piano (1948; perf. under the title *The Eye of Anguish* by the Martha Graham Dance Co., Montclair, N.J., Jan. 31, 1949); Sonata for Solo Cello (1952); Quintet for Piano and Strings (1954; Washington, D.C., Feb. 4, 1955); *Little Recorder Book* (1956); *Infanta Marina* for Viola and Piano (1960); *Shimah B'koli* (Psalm 130) for Organ (1962); *Masques* for Violin and Piano (1965); *Do Not Go Gentle* for Organ, Pedals Alone (1974); *Auden Variations for Organ* (1977); *Reflective Keyboard*

Studies (1978); *Little Mirror Book for Piano* (1978); *4 Arabesques for Piano* (1978); *3 Toccatinas for Piano* (1979); *Mirror Etudes for Piano* (1979); *Dryden Liturgical Suite for Organ* (1980); *Song of David* for Organ (1981); *Little Harpsichord Book* (1983); many choral works, including *Proverb* for Mixed Chorus (1948); *Hymns and Responses for the Church Year* (1955; Philadelphia, Oct. 7, 1956); *Song of Peace* for Male Chorus and Piano (1959); *Mass for Mixed Chorus,* a cappella (1960; N.Y., April 20, 1961); *Stabat Mater* for Chorus and Orch. (1963; N.Y., May 1, 1964); *Te Deum* for Chorus and Orch. (1963; Philadelphia, March 15, 1964); *Spring Cantata* for Women's Chorus and Piano (1963; Boston, April 1, 1964); *Winter Cantata* for Women's Chorus, Flute, and Marimba (1964; Troy, N.Y., April 9, 1965); *Celebrations* for Chorus and Wind Ensemble (River Falls, Wis., Nov. 18, 1966); *The Pleiades* for Chorus, Trumpet, and String Orch. (1967; Potsdam, N.Y., May 10, 1968); *The Creation* for Soprano, Alto, Tenor, Baritone, Chorus, and Orch. (1969; N.Y., April 17, 1970); *Flower Songs* (Cantata No. 6) for Mixed Chorus and String Orch. (1983; Philadelphia, April 20, 1984); a number of songs, including the major cycle for Soprano and Piano entitled *Harmonium,* after poems of Wallace Stevens (1951; N.Y., Jan. 20, 1952).
BIBLIOGRAPHY: R. Evett, "The Music of Vincent Persichetti," *Juilliard Review* (Spring 1955).

Persinger, Louis, eminent American violinist and teacher; b. Rochester, Ill., Feb. 11, 1887; d. New York, Dec. 31, 1966. He was a student of Hans Becker at the Leipzig Cons., where he made his debut on March 23, 1904; then undertook further study with Ysaÿe in Brussels and Thibaud in Paris. He toured Germany, Austria, and Scandinavia as a concert violinist; served as concertmaster of the Berlin Phil. (1914–15); returning to the U.S., he was director of the Chamber Music Society of San Francisco (1916–28); then devoted himself mainly to teaching; in 1930 he joined the staff of the Juilliard School of Music in N.Y. He achieved a great reputation as a teacher who subordinated technical demands to the paramount considerations of formal balance and expressiveness of the melodic line. Among his pupils were Yehudi Menuhin, Ruggiero Ricci, and Isaac Stern.

Perti, Giacomo (Jacopo) Antonio, greatly significant Italian composer; b. Crevalcore, near Bologna, June 6, 1661; d. Bologna, April 10, 1756. He began to study music with his uncle, Lorenzo Perti, and with Rocco Laurenti; later took lessons in counterpoint with Petronio Franceschini. As early as 1678 he had a Mass performed at the church of S. Tomaso al Mercato. In 1679 he collaborated on the opera *Atide,* to which he contributed the score for the 3rd act. In 1681 he was elected a member of the Accademia Filarmonica, of which he was 5 times the *principe* (in 1719 was named *censor*). He then went to Parma, where he continued his studies with Giuseppe Corso. In 1689 he had his opera *Dionisio Siracusano* performed in Parma, and another opera, *La Rosaura,* in Venice. In 1690 he succeeded his uncle as maestro di cappella at the Cathedral of S. Pietro in Bologna. In 1696 he became maestro di cappella of S. Petronio, a position he held until his death. He also held similar positions at S. Domenico (1704–55; deputized for Alberti from 1734) and at S. Maria in Galliera (1706–50). Emperor Charles VI made him a royal councillor in 1740. His students included G.B. Martini and Giuseppe Torelli.
WORKS: OPERAS: *Atide* (Bologna, June 23, 1679; incomplete; in collaboration with others); *Marzio Coriolano* (Venice, Jan. 20, 1683; not extant); *Oreste in Argo* (Modena, Carnival 1685); *L'incoronazione di Dario* (Bologna, Jan. 13, 1686; not extant); *La Flavia* (Bologna, Feb. 16, 1686); *Dionisio Siracusano* (Parma, Carnival 1689; not extant); *La Rosaura* (Venice, 1689); *Brenno in Efeso* (Venice, 1690; not extant); *L'inganno scoperto per vendetta* (Venice, Carnival 1690 or 1691); *Il Pompeo* (Genoa, Carnival 1691; not extant); *Furio Camillo* (Venice, Carnival 1692); *Nerone fatto Cesare* (Venice, 1693); *La forza della virtù* (Bologna, May 25, 1694; not extant); *Laodicea e Berenice* (Venice, 1695; not extant); *Penelope la casta* (Rome, Jan. 25, 1696; not extant); *Fausta restituita all'impero* (Rome, Jan. 19, 1697; not extant); *Apollo geloso* (Bologna, Aug. 16, 1698; not extant); *Ariovisto* (Milan, Sept. 1699; in collaboration with others; not extant); *La prosperità di Elio Sejano* (Milan, Carnival 1699; in collaboration with others; not extant); *Dionisio rè di Portogallo* (Pratolino, Sept. 1707; not extant); *Il fratricida innocente* (Bologna, May 19, 1708; not extant); *Ginevra principessa di Scozia* (Pratolino, Fall 1708; not extant); *Berenice regina d'Egitto* (Pratolino, Sept. 1709; not extant); *Rodelinda regina de' Longobardi* (Pratolino, Fall 1710; not extant); *Lucio vero* (Bologna, Spring 1717; not extant); *Rosinde ed Emireno* (undated). ORATORIOS: *S. Serafina* [*I due gigli porporati nel martirio de S. Serafina e S. Sabina*] (Bologna, 1679); *Abramo vincitore* (Venice, 1683); *Mosè* (Modena, 1685); *Oratorio della passione di Cristo* (Bologna, 1685); *La beata Imelde Lambertini* (Bologna, 1686); *Agar* (Bologna, 1689); *La passione del Redentore* (Bologna, 1694); *S. Galgano* (Bologna, 1694); *Cristo al limbo* (Bologna, 1698); La sepoltura di Cristo (Bologna, 1704); *S. Giovanni* (Bologna, 1704); *Gesù al sepolcro* (Bologna, 1707); *S. Petronio* (Bologna, 1720); *L'amor divino* [*I conforti di Maria vergine addolorata*] (Bologna, 1723); also several undated oratorios. Additional sacred works include *Messa e salmi concertati* for 4 Voices, Instruments, and Chorus (Bologna, 1735) and 7 *canzonette in aria marmoresca sopra le 7 principali feste di Nostra Signora* (Bologna, 1780); also 120 Psalms, 54 motets, 28 masses; about 150 secular cantatas; also *Cantate morali e spirituali* for One and 2 Voices, with Violin (Bologna, 1688).
BIBLIOGRAPHY: L. Mancini, *J.A. Perti* (Bologna, 1813); G. Atti, *Orazione in lode di I.A. Perti* (1844); an extended biography of Perti is found in L. Busi's *Il Padre Giambatt. Martini* (Bologna, 1891; vol. I, p. 61 et seq.); F. Giegling, "G.A. Perti," *Die Musikforschung,* IV (1955); M. Fabbri, "Giacomo Antonio Perti," in *Musicisti Lombardi ed Emiliani,* Chigiana, XV (1958); G. Vecchi, ed., *La musica barocca a Bologna . . . G.A. Perti* (Bologna, 1961); J.

Berger, "The Sacred Works of Giacomo Antonio Perti," *Journal of the American Musicological Society,* XVII (1964).

Pertile, Aureliano, Italian operatic tenor; b. Montagnana, Nov. 9, 1885; d. Milan, Jan. 11, 1952. He studied with Oregice and Fugazzola; made his debut in *Martha* at Vicenza in 1911; was for a season (1921–22) a member of the Metropolitan Opera in N.Y.; then was at La Scala in Milan (1922–37); also sang in London. After retirement, he settled down in Milan as a voice teacher.

Perusso, Mario, Argentine composer; b. Buenos Aires, Sept. 16, 1936. He began his music career by singing in an opera chorus at the Teatro Colón in Buenos Aires; then began to compose. His one-act opera *La voz del silencio* was produced at the Teatro Colón, on Nov. 23, 1969. Other works include *3 Symphonic Movements* (1954); *Elegía* for Orch. (1964); *Invenzioni* for String Quartet (1967); *La eternidad y el viento* for Orch. (1968).

Pesko, Zoltan, Hungarian conductor; b. Budapest, Feb. 15, 1937. He studied at the Franz Liszt Academy of Music in Budapest; later took courses in conducting with Sergiu Celibidache, Franco Ferrara, and Pierre Boulez. He then went to West Berlin, serving as an assistant conductor to Lorin Maazel at the Deutsche Oper; also served on the faculty of the Berlin Hochschule für Musik (1969–72). In 1974 he became chief conductor of the Teatro Communale in Bologna; in addition, he conducted opera at La Scala in Milan.

Pessard, Emile-Louis-Fortuné, French composer; b. Paris, May 29, 1843; d. there, Feb. 10, 1917. He studied at the Paris Cons. with Bazin (harmony), Laurent (piano), Benoist (organ), and Carafa (composition); won the first harmony prize in 1862, and the Grand Prix de Rome in 1866 with the cantata *Dalila* (1867). In 1881 he was appointed prof. of harmony at the Paris Cons. He enjoyed considerable regard as a composer of fine songs. As a student, Debussy copied Pessard's song *Chanson d'un fou,* and the MS in Debussy's handwriting was publ. erroneously as Debussy's own.
    WORKS: Operas (all produced in Paris): *La Cruche cassée* (Feb. 1870); *Don Quichotte* (Feb. 13, 1874); *Le Char* (Jan. 18, 1878); *Le Capitaine Fracasse* (July 2, 1878); *Tabarin* (Jan. 12, 1885); *Tartarin sur les Alpes* (Nov. 17, 1888); *Les Folies amoureuses* (April 15, 1891); *Une Nuit de Noël* (1893); *Mam'zelle Carabin* (Nov. 3, 1893); *L'Armée des vierges* (Oct. 15, 1902); *L'Épave* (Feb. 17, 1903).

Pestalozzi, Heinrich, Swiss composer; b. Wädenswil, near Zürich, Aug. 26, 1878; d. Zürich, Aug. 9, 1940. He studied theology and music in Berlin; was a singing teacher there (1902–12); then a pastor in Arosa, Switzerland; in 1917 was appointed voice teacher at the Zürich Cons. His many songs and choral works have enjoyed great popularity in Switzerland; a full list is found in Refardt's *Musikerlexikon der Schweiz.* Pestalozzi publ. several manuals on singing: *Individuelle Stimmbildung; Kehlkopfgymnastik; Die deutsche Bühnenaussprache im Gesang; Geheimnisse der Stimmbildung; Der Weg zu einer schönen Stimme.*

Petchnikov, Alexander, Russian violinist; b. Elets, Jan. 20, 1873; d. Buenos Aires, Nov. 3, 1949. He was a pupil of Hřimalý at the Moscow Cons., where he won the Gold Medal; subsequently lived in Germany; from 1913 to 1921 taught at the Royal Academy in Munich; founded a string quartet in Berlin in 1924, and taught at the Stern Cons. there. After the advent of the Nazi regime, he was compelled to leave Germany, and in 1936 went to Argentina.

Peter, Johann Friedrich (John Frederick), American Moravian organist and composer; b. Heerendijk, the Netherlands (of German parentage), May 19, 1746; d. Bethlehem, Pa., July 13, 1813. He was educated in the Netherlands and Germany; came to America in 1770. He served the Moravian Church in various capacities in Nazareth, Bethlehem, and Lititz, Pa., and (from 1779–89) in Salem, N.C., where he married. He spent the rest of his life mostly in Bethlehem as organist of the church. He is widely considered the greatest of the American Moravian composers. His collection of copies of instrumental works by Stamitz, J.C.F. Bach, J.C. Bach, Abel, Boccherini, and Haydn (preserved in the Archives of the Moravian Church) proves his knowledge of contemporary music. He began to compose in 1770. While at Salem he wrote (in 1789) a set of 6 quintets for 2 Violins, 2 Violas, and Cello (his only secular works), which appear to be the oldest preserved examples of chamber music composed in America; they were publ., under the editorship of H.T. David, in 1955, for the N.Y. Public Library series Music of the Moravians in America. His solo arias and choral anthems (more than 100) for strings and organ, or with woodwinds, strings, and organ, are well written, often quite expressive, and evidently constitute the finest and most elaborate concerted church music written in America at that time. Those preserved in the Archives of the Moravian Church at Bethlehem are listed in A.G. Rau and H.T. David's *A Catalogue of Music by American Moravians* (Bethlehem, Pa., 1938).
    BIBLIOGRAPHY: A.G. Rau, "J.F. Peter," *Musical Quarterly* (July 1937); H.T. David, "Musical Life in the Pennsylvania Settlements of the *Unitas Fratrum,*" *Transactions of the Moravian Historical Society* (1942; reprinted as Moravian Music Foundation Publication No. 6, 1959); E. Nolte, "The Paradox of the Peter Quintets," *Moravian Music Foundation Bulletin* (Fall 1967); W. Schnell, *The Choral Music of Johann Friedrich Peter* (Diss., Univ. of Illinois, 1973); J.S. Ingram, "Reflections of the Salem *Collegium Musicum,*" *Moravian Music Foundation Bulletin* (Spring–Summer 1975).

Peter, Simon, American Moravian composer, brother of **Johann Friedrich Peter;** b. Heerendijk, the

Netherlands (of German parentage), April 2, 1743; d. Salem, N.C., May 29, 1819. With his brother, he was educated at the Moravian Brethren's schools in the Netherlands and Germany; came to America in 1770. His ministry was spent in both the Northern and Southern Provinces of the Moravian Church (i.e., both Pennsylvania and North Carolina). From 1784 to 1819 he lived in North Carolina as pastor of several congregations, and was a member of the governing board of the Church. He composed only a few sacred anthems, but one of these, *O Anblick, der mirs Herze bricht,* may well be one of the most expressive of all Lenten songs written in America.

BIBLIOGRAPHY: H.T. David, "Musical Life in the Pennsylvania Settlements of the *Unitas Fratrum,*" *Transactions of the Moravian Historical Society* (1942).

Peters, Carl Friedrich, German music publisher; b. Leipzig, March 30, 1779; d. Sonnenstein, Bavaria, Nov. 20, 1827. In 1814 Peters purchased Kühnel & Hoffmeister's Bureau de Musique (established in 1800; Hoffmeister left the firm in 1805; Kühnel was the sole owner from 1805 to his death in 1813). The firm was thenceforward known as C.F. Peters, Bureau de Musique. Its rich catalogue contained the first edition of collected works of J.S. Bach; it also included music by Beethoven, who entrusted to the Bureau de Musique the publication of his First Symph.; Piano Concerto, op. 19; Septet, op. 20; Piano Sonata, op. 22; and other works. Later C.F. Peters acquired works by Weber, Spohr, Czerny, Chopin, Schumann, Wagner, Liszt, and Brahms. In more recent times the works of Mahler, Grieg, Hugo Wolf, Max Reger, Richard Strauss (his 7 symph. poems), and others were publ. From 1868, classical works were publ. in the inexpensive and reliable Edition Peters. Its large and important musical library was opened to the public in 1893 as the Bibliothek Peters. Scholarly annual books (*Peters Jahrbuch*), containing articles by eminent musicologists, current bibliography, etc., were publ. until 1941. Dr. Max Abraham was sole proprietor from 1880 to 1900. After his death in 1900, his nephew Heinrich Hinrichsen (b. Hamburg, Feb. 5, 1868; d. Auschwitz concentration camp, Sept. 30, 1942) became head of the firm; from 1927 to 1932 he shared the ownership with his son Max Hinrichsen (b. Leipzig, July 6, 1901; d. London, Dec. 17, 1965); soon afterward, 2 other sons joined the firm—in 1933 Walter Hinrichsen (b. Leipzig, Sept. 23, 1907; d. New York, July 21, 1969), and in 1934 Hans Hinrichsen (b. Leipzig, Aug. 22, 1909; d. Perpignan (France) concentration camp, Sept. 18, 1940). The Litolff catalogue was acquired by Peters in 1938. Heinrich Hinrichsen was still in charge in 1939, when the Nazi regime finally forced him into exile, and Johannes Petschull was appointed manager in his stead. After World War II the firm was divided into 3 separate but closely affiliated companies: Peters Edition, London, under the direction of Max Hinrichsen; C.F. Peters Corp., N.Y., owned by Walter Hinrichsen; and the German firm, since 1950 in Frankfurt, under the management of Johannes Petschull. The original firm in Leipzig was taken over by the German Democratic Republic in 1949–50.

BIBLIOGRAPHY: B. Pachnicke, *Edition Peters, 1800/1975: Daten zur Geschichte des Musikverlags Peters* (Leipzig, 1975).

Peters, Reinhard, German conductor; b. Magdeburg, April 2, 1926. He studied violin in Paris with Georges Enesco and Jacques Thibaud; also took piano lessons with Alfred Cortot. In 1952 he became a conductor at the City Opera in Berlin; in 1957 he joined the opera in Düsseldorf; from 1961 to 1970 he was Generalmusikdirektor in Münster. In 1975 he was named chief conductor of the Philharmonia Hungarica in Marl, a post he held until 1979.

Peters (Petermann), Roberta, outstanding American soprano; b. New York, May 4, 1930. She studied voice with William Pierce Hermann; at the age of 20 she made her operatic debut with the Metropolitan Opera in N.Y. as Zerlina in *Don Giovanni* on Nov. 17, 1950, as a substitute on short notice; she subsequently remained on its roster for more than 30 years. She also sang with the opera companies of San Francisco and Chicago, at Covent Garden in London, at the Salzburg Festivals, and at the Vienna State Opera. She was briefly married to the American baritone **Robert Merrill.** With Louis Biancolli, she wrote *A Debut at the Met,* which was publ. in 1967.

Petersen, Wilhelm, German composer; b. Athens, March 15, 1890; d. Darmstadt, Dec. 18, 1957. He studied in Germany and worked as a theater conductor; served in the German army during World War I; in 1922 settled in Darmstadt as a teacher. He wrote the opera *Der goldne Topf* (Darmstadt, March 29, 1941); 5 symphs. (1921, 1923, 1934, 1941, 1957); 3 violin sonatas; 3 string quartets and other chamber music; several sacred choruses and songs. He was highly regarded in Darmstadt as a musician and pedagogue. In 1972 a Wilhelm Petersen Society was founded to memorialize his work.

BIBLIOGRAPHY: A. Petersen, *Wilhelm Petersen, Skizze seines Wesens und Lebens* (Darmstadt, 1962).

Petersilea, Carlyle, American pianist and teacher; b. Boston, Jan. 18, 1844; d. Tropico, near Los Angeles, June 11, 1903. He studied at the Leipzig Cons. with Moscheles, Reinecke, and others, winning a prize. After a tour in Germany, he returned to Boston; established there the Petersilea Academy of Music (1871); after 15 years, he closed his own school to become a teacher at the New England Cons. (1886); in 1892, went to California. He spent the spring of 1884 with Liszt at Weimar. He publ. technical studies and various pieces for piano.

Peterson, Oscar (Emmanuel), black Canadian jazz pianist; b. Montreal, Aug. 15, 1925. He studied piano; made appearances on Canadian radio; also played with the orch. of Johnny Holmes. In 1949 he went to N.Y., and soon established himself as one of the finest jazz pianists of the day. He made numerous tours, often appearing with a guitarist and bass player as fellow musicians (he later replaced the guitar with drums); he also was successful as a guest artist with American orchs.

Peterson-Berger, (Olof) Wilhelm, Swedish composer; b. Ullånger, Feb. 27, 1867; d. Frösön, Dec. 3, 1942. He studied with J. Dente and O. Bolander at the Stockholm Cons. (1886–89); then in Dresden with Scholtz (piano) and Kretschmar (composition); eventually settled in Stockholm, where he became active as a pedagogue and music critic of *Dagens Nyheter* (1896). A symposium of articles was publ. in Stockholm on the occasion of his 70th birthday (1937).

WORKS: *Sveagaldrar,* a festival play for the silver jubilee of the accession of Oscar II (1897); fairy opera, *Lyckan* (*Luck;* Stockholm, March 27, 1903); music dramas (all produced in Stockholm): *Ran* (1899–1900; May 20, 1903); *Arnljot* (1907–9; April 13, 1910); *Domedagsprofeterna* (*The Prophets of Doom;* 1912–17; Feb. 21, 1919); *Adils och Elisiv* (1921–24; Feb. 27, 1927); 5 symphs. with programmatic subtitles: No. 1, *Baneret* (1889–1903; Stockholm, Feb. 23, 1904); No. 2, *Sunnanfärd* (1910; Göteborg, March 22, 1911); No. 3, *Same Ätnam* (1913–15; Stockholm, Dec. 11, 1917); No. 4, *Holmia* (1929; Stockholm, April 9, 1930); No. 5, *Solitudo* (1932–33; Stockholm, April 11, 1934); *Romance* for Violin and Orch. (1915); Violin Concerto (1928; Stockholm, Feb. 6, 1929); orch. suites: *I Somras* (1903); *Earina* (1917); *Italiana* (1922); cantatas: *Norrbotten* (1921); *Operakantaten* (1922; revised 1935–36); *Soluppgång* (1929); 2 violin sonatas (1887, 1910); *Suite* for Violin and Piano (1896); 40 songs for mixed choir; nearly 100 solo songs; over 100 piano pieces.

WRITINGS: *Svensk Musikkultur* (1911); *Richard Wagner som kulturföreteelse* (*Wagner as a Phenomenon of Civilization;* 1913; in German as *Richard Wagner als Kulturerscheinung,* 1917). A selection of his essays was publ. in Stockholm in 2 vols. (1923); another, in one vol., in Östersund (1951). His reminiscences were publ. posthumously (Uppsala, 1943).

BIBLIOGRAPHY: B. Carlberg, *Peterson-Berger* (Stockholm, 1950); S. Beite, *Wilhelm Peterson-Berger: En känd och okänd tondiktare* (Östersund, 1965).

Petin, Nikola, Serbian composer; b. Belgrade, Dec. 19, 1920. He studied with Slavenski and others; became a teacher at Novi Sad. His music is Romantically colored. Among his works are *3 Symphonic Portraits: Hamlet, Ophelia, Polonius; Symphonia brevis; Ballade* for Bassoon and Piano; incidental music for the theater.

Petit, Raymond, French music critic and composer; b. Neuilly-sur-Seine, July 6, 1893. He studied music with Tournemire in Paris; lived there most of his life; contributed numerous articles on modern music to the *Revue Musicale* and criticism to *Le Ménestrel,* as well as to some American publications.

WORKS: Opera, *La Sulamithe; Suite grave* for Orch. (1920); *2 méditations* for String Quartet (1921); *Dialogue* for 2 Violins; *Hymnus* for Voice and Flute (1924); *Il cantico del sole* for Voice and Wind Instruments (Frankfurt Festival of the International Society for Contemporary Music, July 3, 1927); songs.

Petkov, Dimiter, Bulgarian composer and conductor; b. Smolyan, May 4, 1919. He studied composition with Veselin Stoyanov at the Bulgarian State Cons., graduating in 1950; then went to Moscow for postgraduate studies in music theory at the Moscow Cons. (1952–54). Returning to Bulgaria, he became director of the National Opera Theater in Sofia (1954–62 and again from 1975).

WORKS: Musical comedy, *Restless Hearts* (1960; Sofia, 1976); children's operetta, *The Winding Path* (1956; Michailovgrad, Oct. 29, 1975); oratorio, *Rozhan Comes Down from Rhodopa* (1965); 5 cantatas: *September Legend* (1953); *Communists* (1956); *Requiem for a Sailor* (1967); *Cantata about Paissy* (1973); *Festive Cantata* (1974); *The Sparks of October,* suite for Soloists, Children's Chorus, and Orch. (1967); *3 Polyphonic Pieces* for Flute, Clarinet, and Bassoon (1953); choruses; arrangements of folk songs.

Petra-Basacopol, Carmen, Rumanian composer; b. Sibiu, Sept. 5, 1926. She studied with P. Constantinescu, Jora, Ciortea, and Rogalski at the Bucharest Cons. (1949–56); then taught at her alma mater. Her music is lyrical; her instrumentation is colorful and effective.

WORKS: Ballet, *Fata şi masca* (1969); Symph. No. 1 (1955); *Land of the Stone,* symph. poem (1959); Piano Concerto (1961); *Symphonic Triptych* (1962); 2 violin concertos (1963, 1965); *The Death of the Doe,* ballad for Solo Baritone, Clarinet, Piano, Strings, and Percussion (1966); *Song of the Supreme Sacrifices and of the Light,* cantata (1967); *Suite* for Flute and Piano (1950); Cello Sonata (1952); Violin Sonata (1954); *3 Sketches* for Oboe and Bassoon (1956); Piano Trio (1958); Sonata for Flute and Harp (1960); Concertino for Harp, Wind Quintet, Double Bass, and Xylophone (1969); *Elegy* for Violin and Piano (1971); *Primavera,* poem for Soprano, Clarinet, and Piano (1971); *Impressions of the Village Museum,* concert suite for Piano (1960); songs.

Petrassi, Goffredo, outstanding Italian composer; b. Zagarolo, near Rome, July 16, 1904. He worked as a clerk in a music store in Rome, studying musical compositions in his leisure time; began taking regular lessons in composition with Vincenzo di Donato and with Alessandro Bustini at the Santa Cecilia Academy in Rome; in 1939 was appointed to the faculty at the Santa Cecilia Cons. in 1939–59; then was a prof. at the Santa Cecilia Academy from 1959. In 1956 he conducted composition classes at the Berkshire Music Center in Tanglewood. Despite the late beginning, Petrassi acquired a solid technique of composition; the chief influence in his music was that of Casella; later he became interested in 12-tone procedures.

WORKS: OPERAS: *Il Cordovano* (1944–48; La Scala, Milan, May 12, 1949) and *La morte dell'aria* (1949–50; Rome, Oct. 24, 1950). BALLETS: *La follia di Orlando* (1942–43; La Scala, Milan, April 12, 1947) and *Il ritratto di Don Quixote* (1945; Paris, Nov. 21, 1947). FOR ORCH.: *Divertimento* (1930); *Ouverture da concerto* (1931); *Passacaglia* (1931); *Partita* (1932; Rome, April 2, 1933); 8 concertos for Orch.: No. 1 (1933–34; Rome, March 31, 1935); No. 2 (1951; Basel, Jan. 24, 1952); No. 3, *Récréation concertante* (1952–53; Aix-en-Provence Festival, July 23, 1953); No. 4, for String Orch. (1954; Rome, April 28, 1956); No. 5 (1955; Boston, Dec. 2, 1955); No. 6, *Invenzione concertata*, for Brass, Strings, and Percussion (1956–57; London, Sept. 9, 1957); No. 7 (1961–64; Bologna, March 18, 1965); No. 8 (1970–72; Chicago, Sept. 28, 1972); Piano Concerto (1936–39; Rome, Dec. 10, 1939, Walter Gieseking, soloist); Flute Concerto (1960; Hamburg, March 7, 1961); *Estri*, chamber symph. for 15 Performers (1966–67; Dartmouth College, Hanover, N.H., Aug. 2, 1967; as a ballet, Spoleto, July 11, 1968). VOCAL WORKS: *3 Choruses*, with Small Orch. (1932); *Psalm IX* for Chorus, Strings, Brass, 2 Pianos, and Percussion (1934–36); Magnificat for Soprano, Chorus, and Orch. (1939–40); *Coro di morti*, dramatic madrigal for Male Chorus, Brass, Double Basses, 3 Pianos, and Percussion (1940–41; Venice, Sept. 28, 1941); *2 liriche di Saffo* for Voice, and Piano or 11 Instruments (1941); *Quattro inni sacri* for Tenor, Baritone, and Organ (1942; version with Orch., Rome, Feb. 22, 1950); *Noche oscura*, cantata (1950–51; Strasbourg, June 17, 1951); *Nonsense*, to words by Edward Lear, for Chorus a cappella (1952); *Propos d'Alain* for Baritone and 12 Performers (1960); *Sesto non-senso*, after Lear, for Chorus a cappella (1964); *Mottetti per la Passione* for Chorus a cappella (1966); *Beatitudines*, chamber oratorio in memory of Martin Luther King, Jr., for Baritone and 5 Instruments (1969; Fiuggi, July 17, 1969); *Orationes Christi* for Chorus, Brass, 8 Violins, and 8 Cellos (1974–75; Rome, Dec. 6, 1975). CHAMBER MUSIC: *Sinfonia, Siciliana e Fuga* for String Quartet (1929); *Siciliana e marcetta* for 2 Pianos (1930); *Introduzione e allegro* for Violin and Piano (1933; also with 11 Instruments); *Toccata* for Piano (1933); *Preludio, Aria e Finale* for Cello and Piano (1933); *Invenzioni* for 2 Pianos (1944); *Sonata da camera* for Harpsichord and 10 Instruments (1948); *Dialogo angelico* for 2 Flutes (1948); *Musica a 2* for 2 Cellos (1952); String Quartet (1958); *Serenata* for Flute, Viola, Double Bass, Harpsichord, and Percussion (1958); String Trio (1959); *Serenata II*, trio for Harp, Guitar, and Mandolin (1962); *Musica di Ottoni* for Brass and Timpani (1963); *3 per 7* for 3 Performers on 7 Wind Instruments (1966); *Ottetto di Ottoni* for 4 Trumpets and 4 Trombones (1968); *Souffle* for One Performer on 3 Flutes (1969); *Elogio per un'Ombra* for Solo Violin (1971); *Nunc* for Solo Guitar (1971); *Ala* for Flute and Harpsichord (1972); *4 odi* for String Quartet (1973–75); *Oh les beaux jours!* for Piano (1976); *Fanfare* for 3 Trumpets (1944–76); *Petite pièce* for Piano (1976).

BIBLIOGRAPHY: J. Weissman, *Goffredo Petrassi* (Milan, 1957; in Eng.; 2nd ed., 1980); Claudio Annibaldi, *Goffredo Petrassi; A Catalogue of Works* (Milan, 1971); Giuliano Zosi, *Ricerca e sintesi nell'opera di Goffredo Petrassi* (Rome, 1978).

Petrauskas, Kipras, Lithuanian tenor; b. Vilna, Nov. 23, 1885; d. there, Jan. 17, 1968. He studied with his brother, the composer **Mikas Petrauskas**; appeared in his brother's opera *Birute* (Vilna, Nov. 6, 1906); then became a singer at the Imperial Opera in St. Petersburg (1911–20); also appeared in Berlin, Paris, and Milan, and made a tour of the U.S. He returned to Lithuania before World War II, and remained there; in 1950 he received the Stalin Prize.

Petrauskas, Mikas, Lithuanian composer; b. Kaunas, Oct. 19, 1873; d. there, March 23, 1937. He studied organ with his father; was a church organist at the age of 15; then went to St. Petersburg, where he studied with Rimsky-Korsakov at the Cons. During the abortive revolution of 1905 he became implicated in various political activities and was imprisoned; he was briefly in Vilna, where he produced his opera *Birute* (Nov. 6, 1906); in 1907 he emigrated to America; settled in Boston in 1914, and founded the Lithuanian Cons. in South Boston; with the aid of a Lithuanian chorus there, he produced his operas *The Devil Inventor* (3 acts; South Boston, May 20, 1923) and *Egle, Queen of the Snakes* (6 acts; South Boston, May 30, 1924; Petrauskas himself sang the part of the King of the Snakes); cantatas; etc. The Lithuanian Cons. publ. the piano scores of his operas *The King of the Forest* (1918) and *Egle;* he also publ. arrangements of Lithuanian songs in the periodical *Kankles* (Boston, 1917–21); further publ. a brief dictionary of musical terms in Lithuanian (Boston, 1916) and an album of Lithuanian songs (Boston, 1922). In 1930 he went back to Lithuania.

Petrella, Clara, Italian soprano; b. Milan, March 28, 1914. She studied in Milan with her sister, **Micaela Petrella;** made her debut in 1939 in Alessandria; then sang in several provincial Italian theaters. She made her first appearance at La Scala in Milan in 1941, becoming a principal member of the company in 1947; also sang in Rome and Naples; in addition, appeared in concerts. She was particularly noted for her performances of contemporary operas by Italian composers.

Petrella, Errico, Italian opera composer; b. Palermo, Dec. 10, 1813; d. Genoa, April 7, 1877. He studied at the Naples Cons. (Collegio di S. Sebastiano) as a pupil of Costa, Bellini, Ruggi, and Zingarelli. His first theatrical attempt was the 2-act opera buffa *Il Diavolo color di rosa* (Naples, July 1829). Being successful, it was followed by some 20 operas, both comic and serious; *Le Miniere di Freinbergh* (Naples, Feb. 16, 1839) was his first buffo work; *Elnava, o L'assedio di Leida* (Milan, March 4, 1856), the best in the serious style. *Marco Visconti* (Naples, Feb. 9, 1854) obtained immediate popularity in Italy, and

La Contessa d'Amalfi (Turin, March 8, 1864) also had a notable success. Other operas were *Ione,* after Bulwer-Lytton's novel *The Last Days of Pompeii* (Milan, Jan. 26, 1858); *Giovanni II di Napoli* (Naples, Feb. 27, 1869); *I promessi sposi* (Lecco, Oct. 2, 1869); and *Bianca Orsini* (Naples, April 4, 1874). During a quarter of a century he vied with Verdi in Italian favor, but his lack of a true sense of dramatic development and his dependence on Bellini and Donizetti as models caused his operas to appear old-fashioned without a redeeming freshness. Despite his many productions, he died in poverty.

BIBLIOGRAPHY: F. Guardione, *Di Errico Petrella e della traslazione della salma da Genova a Palermo* (Palermo, 1908); G. Siciliano, *Di Errico Petrella, Musicista palermitano* (Palermo, 1913).

Petrelli (née **Wigström**), **Eleanora,** Swedish soprano; b. Simtuna, April 9, 1835; d. Chicago, Feb. 21, 1904. While touring Finland as a member of a small theatrical company, she married a wealthy Russian named Petrov, and Italianized her married name to Petrelli. She studied in Milan with Lamperti, and in Paris with Mme. Viardot-García. After her husband died in 1869, she virtually abandoned the stage, but continued to give concerts in Russia, Germany, and Scandinavian countries. In 1886 she settled in Stockholm, but soon went to Chicago, where she established a school for vocal culture. She publ. a number of songs.

Petri, Egon, distinguished pianist; b. Hannover, Germany, March 23, 1881; d. Berkeley, Calif., May 27, 1962. He was educated in a musical family; his father was the Dutch violinist **Henri Wilhelm Petri** (1856–1914). He studied violin before he began to take piano lessons with Teresa Carreño. As a boy he played 2nd violin in a string quartet organized by his father in Dresden. He then went to Berlin, where he became a pupil of Busoni, who influenced Petri's own conception of piano playing as the fullest representation, by a single instrument, of the sonorities of an orch.; he played with Busoni in London in 1921, in a concert for 2 pianos; made an extensive tour in Russia in 1923. He established himself as an eminent pedagogue in Europe; was a teacher of piano at the Hochschule für Musik in Berlin (1921–26); presented a series of concerts in the U.S. (American debut, N.Y., Jan. 11, 1932); then taught at Cornell Univ. (1940–46) and at Mills College in Oakland, Calif.

Petrić, Ivo, Slovenian composer; b. Ljubljana, June 16, 1931. He studied composition with Skerjanc and conducting with Švara at the Ljubljana Music Academy (1953–58). In 1962 he became the artistic leader of a group dedicated to the promotion of new music; in 1969 was appointed to the secretariat of the Union of Slovenian Composers. His compositions are Romantic in their inspiration, and agreeably modernistic in technical presentation.
WORKS: 3 symphs. (1954, 1957, 1960); *Concerto Grosso* for String Orch. (1955); *Divertimento* for Orch. (1956); Concerto for Flute and Chamber Orch.

(1955–57); Concerto for Clarinet and Chamber Orch. (1958); *Concertante Suite* for Bassoon and Strings (1959); *Concertante Overture* (1960); *Concertante Music* for Wind Quintet, Timpani, and Strings (1962); *Croquis sonores* for Harp and Chamber Ensemble (Warsaw Festival, Sept. 27, 1963); *Mosaics* for Clarinet and Chamber Ensemble (1964); *Symphonic Mutations* (1964); *Epitaph* for Harp, Clarinet, Violin, Cello, Strings, and Percussion (1965); *Integrali v barvah (Integrals in Colors)* for Orch. (1968); *Burlesque pour les temps passés* for Trombone and Orch. (1969); *Music Concertante* for Piano and Orch. (1970); *Dialogues concertants* for Cello and Orch. (1972); *3 Images* for Violin and Orch. (1973); *Nocturnes and Games* for Orch. (1973); *Fresque symphonique* for Orch. (1973); *Episodes lyriques* for Oboe and Orch. (1974); *Gemini Concerto* for Violin, Cello, and Orch. (1975); cantata, *Pierre de la mort (Stone of Death;* 1962); 2 wind quintets (1953, 1959); Bassoon Sonata (1954); Oboe Sonata (1955); Flute Sonata (1955); Clarinet Sonata (1956–57); *3 Sketches* for Flute and String Quartet (1961); Horn Sonatina (1961); *3 Contrasts* for Violin and Piano (1961); *7 Movements* for 7 Instruments (1963); *Jeux à 3* for Cello, Percussion, and Harp (1965); *Jeux à 4* for Flute, Piano, Harp, and Cello (1966); *Little Chamber Concerto* for Solo Oboe, English Horn, Bass Clarinet, Horn, Harp, Piano, and String Quartet (1966); *5 Movements* for Oboe, and Harp or String Quartet (1967); *Intarzije (Inlaid Work)* for Wind Trio, Horn, Trumpet, Trombone, Percussion, and String Quintet (1968); *Lirizmi* for Horn and Piano (1969); *Quatuor 69* for String Quartet (1969); *Gemini Music* for Cello and Piano (1971); *Les Paysages,* poetic sketches for Piano (1972); *Mosaïques* for Percussion (1973); *Capriccio* for Solo Cello and Small Ensemble (1974).

Petridis, Petro, eminent Greek composer; b. Nigdé, Asia Minor, July 23, 1892; d. Athens, Aug. 17, 1977. He took courses at the American College in Constantinople and at the Univ. of Paris; took part in the Balkan war of 1911–12 as a member of the Greek army; then returned to Paris, where he took lessons in music theory with Albert Wolff and Albert Roussel; lived in Paris until 1939, when he returned to Athens. A man of great culture, he was conversant with classical literatures, and could recite Homer from memory. His own music reveals a similar cultural quality. He often used ancient modalities, adorned with modern harmonies.
WORKS: Opera, *Zemphyra* (1923–25); oratorio, *St. Paul* (Athens, June 29, 1951, composer conducting); *A Byzantine Requiem* (1952); 5 symphs. (1928, 1940, 1941, 1943, 1951); Concerto for 2 Pianos and Orch. (1972); Violin Concerto (1972); *Panighiri,* suite of Greek tableaux for Orch.; *Suite grecque; Suite ionienne;* Piano Concerto; chamber music; a number of songs.

Petrov, Andrei, Soviet composer; b. Leningrad, Sept. 2, 1930. He studied composition at the Leningrad Cons. with Evlakhov, graduating in 1954. In 1957 he joined the Communist party. In his music he follows the general precepts of socialist realism, ethnic in thematic material, euphonious in harmony, energetic in rhythm, stimulating in modalities, optimistic in contemporary philosophy, realistic in treatment.

WORKS: For the stage: Opera, *Peter the First* (Leningrad, 1975); 5 ballets: *The Magic Apple Tree* (Leningrad, Nov. 8, 1953), *The Station Master,* after Pushkin (Leningrad, May 9, 1955), *The Shore of Hope* (1959), *The Creation of the World* (1971), and *Pushkin* (1979); musical, *We Want to Dance* (1967). For Orch.: *Pioneer Suite* (1951); *Sport Suite* (1953); *Radda and Lioko,* symph. poem (1954); *Festive Overture* (1955); *Songs of Today,* symph. cycle (1965); *Poem,* in memory of those fallen in the siege of Leningrad, for Strings, Organ, 4 Trumpets, 2 Pianos, and Percussion (1965). For Voice: *The Poem of a Young Pioneer* for Soprano, Mezzo-soprano, and Orch. (1959); *Poème pathétique* for Baritone, 2 Pianos, and Percussion, commemorating the centennial of Lenin's birth (1970), to words by Soviet poets; *Pushkin,* vocal-poetic symph. for Narrator, Mezzo-soprano, Chorus, 2 Harps, and Orch. (1978).

BIBLIOGRAPHY: A. Kenigsberg, *Andrei Petrov* (Moscow, 1959); L. Markhasev, *Andrei Petrov, Familiar and Unfamiliar* (Leningrad, 1974).

Petrov, Ivan, Russian operatic bass; b. Irkutsk, Feb. 29, 1920. He studied with A. Mineyev at the Glazunov Music College in Moscow (1938–39); then joined the Kozlovsky opera group; became a soloist with the Moscow Phil. in 1941. In 1943 he joined the staff of the Bolshoi Theater in Moscow; his most celebrated interpretation was in the title role of *Boris Godunov,* inviting comparisons with Chaliapin. He made several tours as a member of the Opera of the Bolshoi Theater in Europe, Japan, and the U.S.

BIBLIOGRAPHY: I. Nazarenko, *Ivan Petrov* (Moscow, 1957).

Petrov, Osip, celebrated Russian basso; b. Elizavetgrad, Nov. 15, 1807; d. St. Petersburg, March 11, 1878. In 1830 the intendant of the Imperial Opera accidentally heard him singing with an inferior company at a fair in Kursk, and immediately engaged him. Petrov made his debut in St. Petersburg as Sarastro in *The Magic Flute.* The enormous compass of his voice, its extraordinary power and beautiful quality, combined with consummate histrionic skill, secured for him recognition as one of the greatest of Russian bassos; this place he held throughout his long career (he appeared on the stage for the last time March 10, 1878, on the eve of his death). He created the roles of Susanin in Glinka's *Life for the Tsar* (1836), Ruslan in *Ruslan and Ludmila* (1842), the Miller in Dargomyzhsky's *Rusalka* (1856), and Varlaam in Mussorgsky's *Boris Godunov* (1874).

BIBLIOGRAPHY: *Recollections of the 50th Anniversary of O.A. Petrov* (St. Petersburg, 1876); V. Stasov, *O.A. Petrov,* in vol. III of his collected works (St. Petersburg, 1894); A. Kompaneisky, "A Great Russian Singer," *Russkaya Muzykalnaya Gazeta,* 9

(1903); E. Lastotchkina, *Osip Petrov* (Moscow, 1950).

Petrović, Radomir, Yugoslav composer; b. Belgrade, May 13, 1923. He studied in Belgrade, and subsequently became active as a teacher there. His works are in a classical tradition, but he often makes use of national thematic elements; his *Moto sinfonico* (Belgrade, March 3, 1959) is his most successful work.

Petrovics, Emil, Serbian-born Hungarian composer; b. Nagybecskerek (now Zrenjanin), Feb. 9, 1930. He lived in Belgrade until 1941; came to Budapest; studied at the Cons. there with Sugár (1949–51), Viski (1951–52), and Farkas (1952–57). He was music director of the Petőfi Theater in Budapest (1960–64); then taught at the Academy of Dramatic Arts.

WORKS: Satirical one-act opera, *C'est la guerre* (1961; Budapest Radio, Aug. 17, 1961; first stage perf., Budapest, March 11, 1962; highly successful; was awarded the Kossuth Prize in 1966); *Lysistrate,* comic opera after Aristophanes (1962); opera, *Bűn és bűnhődés (Crime and Punishment),* after Dostoyevsky (1969; Budapest, Oct. 26, 1969); 2 oratorios: *Jónás könyve (The Book of Jonah;* 1966), and *Ott essem el én (Let Me Die There)* for Male Chorus and Orch. (1972); Flute Concerto (1957); Symph. for String Orch. (1962); *Cassazione* for Brass (1953); String Quartet (1958); *4 Self-Portraits in Masks* for Harpsichord (1958); Wind Quintet (1964); *Passacaglia in Blues* for Bassoon and Piano (1964; as a ballet, Budapest, 1965).

Petrucci, Ottaviano dei, Italian music publisher, the first to print a complete collection of part-songs from movable type; b. Fossombrone, June 18, 1466; d. there, May 7, 1539. In 1498 he received from the Council of the Republic of Venice the privilege of printing music by this new method for 20 years, and worked there industriously from 1501–11, then ceding the business to A. Scotto and N. da Rafael, and removing to Fossombrone, with a 15-year privilege for printing within the Papal States. His editions, printed with great neatness, are rare and highly prized specimens of early presswork. In Fossombrone he labored from 1513–23. His publications appeared at the most flourishing epoch of the Netherlands School; his first work, *Odhecaton A* (1501; modern ed. by Helen Hewitt, Cambridge, Mass., 1942), contains 96 numbers by famous composers before 1501; *Canti B.* (1502) and *Canti C.* (1504), 49 and 137, respectively. Petrucci's last publications were 3 books of masses (1520–23), printed in folio as chorus books. Books I and IV of the 9 books of *frottole* publ. in Venice from 1504–8 by Petrucci were ed. by R. Schwartz in Jg. 8 of Th. Kroyer's *Publikationen älterer Musik* (Leipzig, 1933–35).

BIBLIOGRAPHY: A. Schmid, *O. d. Petrucci* (Vienna, 1845; contains full list of works known at the time; in Italian, by B. Revel, in *Bollettino Bibliografico Musicale,* 1931–33); A. Vernarecci, *O. d. Petrucci* (Bologna; 2nd ed., 1882); J.B. Weckerlin, *Petrucci harmonice musices odhecaton* (Paris, 1885); E. Vogel, "Der erste Notendruck für Figuralmusik," *Jahrbuch Peters* (1895; full list of contents of *Odhecaton*); M. Cauchie, "L'Odhecaton, Recueil de musique instrumentale," *Revue de Musicologie* (Nov. 1925) and "A propos des trois receuils instrumentaux de la série de l'Odhecaton," ibid. (May 1928); J. Marix, "Harmonice Musices Odhecaton A," ibid. (Nov. 1935); K. Jeppesen, "Die neuentdeckten Bücher der Lauden des O. d. Petrucci," *Zeitschrift für Musikwissenschaft* (Nov. 1929); G. Reese, "The First Printed Collection of Part-Music: The *Odhecaton*," *Musical Quarterly* (Jan. 1934); A. Catelani, "Due stampe ignote di O. Petrucci" (1856; reprinted in *Bollettino Bibliografico Musicale*, 1932); C. Sartori, "A Little-known Petrucci Publication," *Musical Quarterly* (April 1948); C. Sartori, *Bibliografia delle opere musicali stampate da O. Petrucci* (Florence, 1948). A facsimile ed. of the *Odhecaton A* was publ. by the *Bollettino Bibliografico Musicale* (1932).

Petrushka, Shabtai, German-born Israeli composer; b. Leipzig, March 15, 1903. He studied at the Inst. of Technology in Berlin-Charlottenburg, and received an engineering diploma; studied music at the Leipzig Cons. He was an orch. leader in various theaters in Berlin (1928–33); after the advent of the Nazis in 1933 he was a member of the orch. of the Jewish *Kulturbund*, for which he wrote incidental music. He emigrated to Palestine in 1938; served as an arranger and conductor of the Palestine Broadcasting Service (1938–48); then was assistant director of music of the Israel Broadcasting Service (1948–58) and head of the music division of the Israel Broadcasting Authority (1958–68); in 1970 he joined the faculty of the Rubin Academy of Music in Jerusalem.

WORKS: *The Broken Blackboard,* musical for children (1969); String Trio (1939); *4 Movements* for Symph. Band (1953); *5 Oriental Dances* for Orch. (1954); *Piccolo Divertimento* for Symph. Band (1970); *3 Jewish Melodies* for 2 Flutes and 3 Clarinets (1972); *Hebrew Melodies* for Wind Quintet (1974); Wind Quartet (1975); *Jewish Melodies* for Brass Quintet (1974); *3 Sephardic Songs* for Female Chorus (1976).

Petrželka, Vilém, noted Czech composer and music pedagogue; b. Královo Pole, near Brno, Sept. 10, 1889; d. Brno, Jan. 10, 1967. He studied with Janáček at the Brno Organ School (1905–8) and in 1910 became Janáček's assistant at the school; subsequently took private lessons in Prague with Vítězslav Novák; taught at the Phil. Society School in Brno (1914–19) and in 1919 became a prof. at the newly formed Brno Cons. In his compositions he continued the national tradition of modern Moravian music; he was mainly influenced by Janáček, but expanded his resources and on occasion made use of jazz rhythms, quarter-tones, and other modernistic procedures.

WORKS: Opera, *Horník Pavel (The Miner Paul;* 1935–38); cantata, *Modlitba k slunci (A Prayer to the Sun;* 1921; Brno, Feb. 13, 1922); symph. drama, *Námořník Mikuláš (Mariner Nicholas)* for Narra-

tor, Soli, Chorus, Organ, Jazz Band, and Orch., employing quarter-tones (1928; Brno, Dec. 9, 1930); *Věčný návrat (Eternal Return),* symph. poem (1922–23; Brno, Feb. 10, 1924); *Suite* for String Orch. (1924–25); *Dramatic Overture* (1932; Brno, March 26, 1933); *Partita* for String Orch. (1934); one-movement Sinfonietta (1941; Brno, Jan. 22, 1942); Violin Concerto (1943–44; revised 1946); *Pastoral Sinfonietta* (1951–52); Symph. (1956); 2 song cycles, with Orch.: *Živly (The Elements;* 1917) and *Cesta (The Way;* 1924; also with Piano); 5 string quartets (1909; 1914–15; *Fantasy,* op. 19, 1927; *Suite,* 1932; 1947; *Z intimnich chvil (From Intimate Moments)* for Violin and Piano (1918); *Štafeta (The Courier),* 4 songs for Voice and String Quartet (1926–27); Solo Cello Sonata (1930); Violin Sonata (1932); Piano Trio (1936–37); *4 Impromptus* for Violin and Piano (1939–40); *Divertimento* for Wind Quintet (1941); *Serenade* for Nonet or Chamber Orch. (1945); *2 Pieces* for Cello and Piano (1947); Violin Sonatina (1953); *Miniatures* for Wind Quintet (1953); *2 Pieces* for Viola and Piano (1959); *Fantasy* for String Quartet, op. 59 (1959); *Suite* for String Trio (1961); Piano Sonata (1908); *Songs of Poetry and Prose* for Piano (1917); *Suite* for Piano (1930); *5 nálad (5 Moods)* for Piano (1954); a number of choruses, of which the patriotic part-song for male chorus *To je má zem (This Is My Land),* written and performed in 1940, is well known; also arrangements of folk songs.

BIBLIOGRAPHY: L. Firkušný, *Vilém Petrželka* (Prague, 1946).

Pettersson, Gustaf Allan, remarkable sui generis Swedish composer; b. Västra Ryd, Sept. 19, 1911; d. Stockholm, June 20, 1980. His father was a blacksmith; his mother was a devout woman who could sing; the family moved to Stockholm, and lived in dire poverty. Pettersson sold Christmas cards and bought a violin from his meager returns. He also practiced keyboard playing on a church organ. In 1931 he entered the Stockholm Music Academy, studying violin and viola with J. Ruthström and music theory with H.M. Melchers. From 1940 to 1951 he played viola in the Stockholm Concert Society Orch., and also studied composition with Otto Olsson, Tor Mann, and Blomdahl. In his leisure hours he wrote poetry; he set 24 of his poems to music. In 1951 he went to Paris to study with Honegger and René Leibowitz. Returning to Sweden, he devoted himself to composition in large forms. His music is permeated with dark moods, and he supplied deeply pessimistic annotations to his symphs. and other works. In 1963 he began suffering from painful rheumatoid arthritis; he stubbornly continued to compose while compulsively proclaiming his misfortunes in private and in public print. He described himself as "a voice crying out, drowned in the noise of the times." The Stockholm Orch. played several of his symphs., but when his 7th Symph., originally scheduled for the American tour of the Stockholm Orch., was taken off the program, Pettersson, wrathful at this callous defection, forbade performance of any of his music in Sweden. Stylistically, Pettersson's music is related to Mahler's symph.

manner, in the grandiosity of design and in the passionate, exclamatory dynamism of utterance. Most of his symphs. are cast in single movements, with diversity achieved by frequent changes of mood, tempo, meter, and rhythm. Characteristically, they all, except No. 10, are set in minor keys.

WORKS: 16 SYMPHS.: No. 1 (1950–51; withdrawn with instructions to perform it only posthumously); No. 2 (1952–53; Swedish Radio, Stockholm, May 9, 1954); No. 3 (1954–55; Göteborg, Nov. 21, 1956); No. 4 (1958–59; Stockholm, Jan. 27, 1961); No. 5 (1960–62; Stockholm, Nov. 8, 1963); No. 6 (1963–66; Stockholm, Jan. 21, 1968); No. 7 (1966–67; Stockholm, Oct. 13, 1968); No. 8 (1968–69; Stockholm, Feb. 23, 1972); No. 9 (1970; Göteborg, Feb. 18, 1971); No. 10 (1971–72; Swedish Television, filmed Dec. 16, 1973, for delayed broadcast of Jan. 14, 1974); No. 11 (1971–73; Bergen, Norway, Oct. 24, 1974); No. 12, *De döda på torget (The Dead on the Square)*, with Mixed Chorus, to words by Pablo Neruda (1973–74; Stockholm, Sept. 29, 1977); No. 13 (1976; Bergen, June 7, 1978); No. 14 (1978; first perf. posthumously, Stockholm, Nov. 26, 1981); No 15 (1978; posthumous, Stockholm, Nov. 19, 1982); No. 16, originally designed as Concerto for Alto Saxophone and Orch., written for the American saxophonist Fred Hemke; posthumous, Stockholm, Feb. 24, 1983; Hemke, soloist); 3 concertos for String Orch.: No. 1 (1949–50; Stockholm, April 6, 1952); No. 2 (1956; Stockholm, Dec. 1, 1968); No. 3 (1956–57; Stockholm, March 14, 1958); Concerto No. 1 for Violin and String Quartet (1949; Stockholm, March 10, 1951); Concerto No. 2 for Violin and Orch. (1977–78; Stockholm, Jan. 25, 1980; Ida Haendel, soloist); *Symphonic Movement* (1976; as *Poem,* Swedish Television, Stockholm, Dec. 24, 1976).

VOCAL MUSIC: 6 songs for Voice and Piano (1935); *24 Barfotasånger (24 Barefoot Songs),* to Pettersson's own text, for Voice and Piano (1943–45); *Vox humana,* 18 songs for Soprano, Alto, Tenor, Baritone, Mixed Chorus, and String Orch., to texts by American Indians (1974; Stockholm, March 19, 1976).

CHAMBER MUSIC: *2 Elegies* for Violin and Piano (1934); *Fantasy Piece* for Viola Solo (1936); *4 Improvisations* for Violin, Viola, and Cello (1936); *Andante espressivo* for Violin and Piano (1938); *Romanza* for Violin and Piano (1942); *Fugue in E* for Oboe, Clarinet, and Bassoon (1948); 7 sonatas for 2 Violins (1951–52).

BIBLIOGRAPHY: L. Aare, *Allan Pettersson* (Stockholm, 1978); P. Rapoport, *Opus Est: 6 Composers from Northern Europe* (London, 1978; N.Y., 1979; pp. 108–32 and 199–200); idem, *Allan Pettersson,* a brochure publ. by the Swedish Music Information Centre (Stockholm, 1981).

Pettiford, Oscar, black–American Indian jazz bass player; b. on an Indian reservation, Okmulgee, Okla., Sept. 30, 1922; d. Copenhagen, Sept. 8, 1960. He played in his father's band; at the age of 11 he took up the piano, then the bass at 14; left the family band in 1941 to begin his own career, making appearances with Charlie Barnet, Roy Eldridge, and

Dizzy Gillespie. He also worked with Coleman Hawkins, Jimmy Blanton, and Duke Ellington. A master of the string bass, he was also a good cellist.

Petyrek, Felix, Czech composer; b. Brno, May 14, 1892; d. Vienna, Dec. 1, 1951. He studied piano with Godowsky and Sauer; composition with Schreker at the Univ. of Vienna (graduated in 1919). He taught piano at the Salzburg Mozarteum (1919–21); then at the Berlin Hochschule für Musik (1921–23); lived in Italy (1923–26); taught composition at the Odeon Athenon in Athens (1926–30); from 1930 to 1939, taught at the Stuttgart Akademie für Musik; after 1945, he settled in Vienna. Among modern composers, he occupied a fairly advanced position; in his melodic writing, he adopted the scale of alternating whole tones and semitones as a compromise between tonality and atonality.

WORKS: *Der Garten des Paradieses,* opera after Andersen (1923–41; Leipzig, Nov. 1, 1942); *Die arme Mutter und der Tod,* fairy play after Andersen, with Small Orch. (Winterthur, 1923); pantomimes: *Tahi* and *Komödie; Die Litanei* for Boys' Chorus, 2 Trumpets, 2 Harps, and Percussion (Zürich Festival of the International Society for Contemporary Music, June 21, 1926); Sinfonietta; Divertimento for 8 Wind Instruments; Piano Trio; *Tänze* for 2 Flutes; Sextet for Clarinet, String Quartet, and Piano (Donaueschingen Festival, July 30, 1922); Piano Trio; songs; piano pieces.

Petz (Pez), Johann Christoph, German composer; b. Munich, Sept. 9, 1664; d. Stuttgart, Sept. 25, 1716. He was a chorister in Munich (1676–86); then resided in Liège and in Bonn (until 1705); in 1706 was appointed court conductor at Stuttgart, where he remained until his death. He publ. a set of 12 sonatas (Augsburg, 1696) under the title *Duplex Genius sive Gallo-italus Instrumentorum Concentus;* also a Psalm. Two of his operas were produced in Bonn. Instrumental and vocal works were publ. by B.A. Wallner in Denkmäler der Tonkunst in Bayern, 35 (27/28).

Petzel, Johann Christoph. See **Pezel, Johann Christoph.**

Petzet, Walter, German pianist, composer, and music editor; b. Breslau, Oct. 10, 1866; d. Dresden, Aug. 13, 1941. He studied with Kleffel in Augsburg; later at the Munich Academy with Rheinberger and others; in 1887 went to Minneapolis, where he taught piano until 1890; from 1891 to 1896 taught piano at the Scharwenka Cons.; in 1896 succeeded Busoni as a prof. at the Helsinki Cons.; from 1898 to 1910, was a prof. at the Cons. of Karlsruhe; subsequently taught at the Weimar Cons. (1910–13), at the Klindworth-Scharwenka Cons. in Berlin (1913–16), and at the Dresden Cons. (1917–21); lived mostly in Dresden. He wrote 2 piano concertos, numerous piano pieces, etc.; wrote music criticism for the *Signale für die Musikalische Welt.*

Petzold, Rudolf, English composer and teacher; b.

Liverpool (of a German father and English mother), July 17, 1908. He studied composition with Jarnach at the Cologne Hochschule für Musik (1930–33); taught there in 1937–38, and at the Frankfurt Hochschule für Musik in 1941–42; then rejoined the faculty of the Cologne Hochschule für Musik (1946–70), and was its deputy director in 1960–69. He wrote a number of instrumental and choral works in a compact polyphonal style, among them 3 symphs. (1942, 1953, 1956); 4 string quartets (1932, 1948, 1955, 1972); Concerto for Violin and String Orch. (1960); Piano Trio (1961); Cello Sonata (1964); Sonata for Violin Unaccompanied (1965); Piano Sonata (1967); Violin Sonata (1969); several sacred cantatas and other choral music.

Petzoldt, Richard, German musicologist; b. Plauen, Nov. 12, 1907; d. Leipzig, Jan. 14, 1974. He studied at the Univ. of Berlin, where his teachers were Abert, Schering, Moser, Sachs, Hornbostel, Schünemann, and Blume; received his Dr.Phil. with the dissertation *Die Kirchenkompositionen und weltlichen Kantaten Reinhard Keisers* (Düsseldorf, 1935). He edited the *Allgemeine Musikalische Zeitung* (1935–39) and the periodical *Musik in der Schule* (1949–54); was a prof. of music history at the Univ. of Leipzig (1952–67). He publ. a number of informative books and other editions mainly concerned with classical German music. His publications include *Beethoven* (1938); *Schubert* (1940); *Schumann* (1941); *Mozart* (1948); *J.S. Bach und Leipzig* (1950); *Die Oper in ihrer Zeit* (1956); he compiled iconographies of Bach (1950), Schubert (1953), Beethoven (1953), Tchaikovsky (1953), Handel (1955), Glinka (1955), Schumann (1956), and Mozart (1956); for Beethoven's bicentennial he publ. the pictorial vol. *Ludwig van Beethoven* (Leipzig, 1970; 2nd ed., 1973); also publ. a pictorial book on Schütz, *Heinrich Schütz und seine Zeit in Bildern* (Kassel, 1972).

Peuerl (Peurl, Bäwerl, Bäurl, Beurlin), Paul, Austrian organist; b. Stuttgart (baptized, June 13), 1570; d. after 1625. He was an organist at Horn, Lower Austria (from 1602), and of the Protestant church school in Steyer (1609–25). He is generally acknowledged to be the originator of the German variationsuite; following the example of the lutenists, he expanded the earlier combination of pavane and galliard into a new 4-movement suite form for strings. He was also an organ builder. He edited the following (all publ. in Nuremberg): *Newe Padouan, Intrada, Däntz und Galliarda* (1611); *Weltspiegel, das ist: Neue teutsche Gesänge* (1613); *Ettliche lustige Padouanen, Intrada, Galliard, Couranten und Däntz sampt zweyen Canzon zu 4 Stimmen* (1620); *Gantz neue Padouanen, Auffzüg, Balletten, Couranten, Intraden und Däntz* (1625). Selections from his works, ed. by Karl Geiringer, appear in Denkmäler der Tonkunst in Österreich, 70 (36.ii). BIBLIOGRAPHY: E. Noack, "Ein Beitrag zur Geschichte der älteren deutschen Suite," *Archiv für Musikwissenschaft,* II/2 (1920); P. Nettl, "Zur Lebensgeschichte Paul Peuerls," *Bulletin de la Société "Union Musicologique,"* V (1925); K. Geiringer, "Paul Peuerl," *Studien zur Musikwissenschaft,* vol. XVI (Vienna, 1929; pp. 32–69); E. Mohr, *Die Allemande* (Zürich, 1932; pp. 70ff.); H.J. Moser, *Die Musik im frühevangelischen Österreich* (Kassel, 1953; pp. 37ff.).

Pevernage, Andries, Flemish composer; b. Harelbeke, near Courtrai, 1543; d. Antwerp, July 30, 1591. He was a boy chorister in Courtrai. On Feb. 11, 1563, he became choirmaster at St. Salvator in Bruges; on Oct. 17, 1563, he was appointed choirmaster of Notre Dame in Courtrai; due to religious upheavals, he fled to Antwerp in 1578; he returned to Courtrai to resume his post in 1584. On Oct. 29, 1585, he took the oath as choirmaster of Notre Dame in Antwerp. He was greatly honored there, and was buried in the Cathedral.
WORKS: 6 *Missae* for 5 to 7 Voices (Antwerp, 1602); 39 *Cantiones aliquot sacrae* for 6 to 8 Voices, *quibus addita sunt* [29] *elogia nonnulla* (Douai, 1578); 14 motets, *Laudes vespertinae B. Mariae Virginis* (Antwerp, 1604); etc. *Chansons ... livre premier, contenant chansons spirituelles* for 5 Voices (Antwerp, 1589); *Chansons ... livre second* for 5 Voices (Antwerp, 1590); *Chansons ... livre troisième* for 5 Voices (Antwerp, 1590); *Chansons ... livre quatrième* for 6 to 8 Voices (Antwerp, 1591); *Chansons ... tant spirituelles que prophanes* for 5 Voices (Antwerp, 1606–7); etc.
BIBLIOGRAPHY: J. Stellfeld, *Andries Pevernage: Zijne leven, zijne werken* (Louvain, 1943).

Peyser, Herbert Francis, American music critic; b. New York, Aug. 6, 1886; d. there, Oct. 19, 1953. He studied in Germany and France; returning to America, he was assistant to Henry T. Finck on the *N.Y. Evening Post* and (from 1924 to 1940) associate music critic of the *N.Y. World Telegram.* He collaborated with L. Biancolli on the book *Masters of the Orchestra* (N.Y., 1953).

Peyser, Joan, American musicologist, editor, author, and journalist; b. New York, June 12, 1931. She played piano in public at 13; majored in music at Barnard College (B.A., 1951); studied musicology with Paul Henry Lang at Columbia Univ. (M.A., 1956); then devoted herself mainly to musical journalism; enlivened the music pages of the Sunday *N.Y. Times* with book reviews and breezy colloquies with composers; wrote scripts for the television series "The World of Music"; acted as musical adviser to the N.Y. City Board of Education. She publ. the popular book *The New Music: The Sense behind the Sound* (N.Y., 1971); created considerable excitement in the music world with her biography *Boulez: Composer, Conductor, Enigma* (N.Y., 1976); trying to penetrate the eponymous enigma, she undertook a journey to the interior of France, where she interviewed family and friends of her subject, with a fervor suggesting that Boulez was indeed the 4th B of music. From 1977 to 1983 she was editor of the *Musical Quarterly,* the first woman to occupy this position; during her tenure she attempted to veer away from the prevalent musicological sesquipedalianism toward plain diction.

Pezel (Petzold, Petzel, Pezelius, etc.), **Johann Christoph,** German musician; b. Calau, 1639; d. Bautzen, Oct. 13, 1694. He was made 4th Kunstgeiger in the Leipzig town band in 1664, and in 1670 was promoted to Stadtpfeifer. Because of the plague, he left Leipzig in 1681 for Bautzen, where he remained until his death. He publ. several collections of pieces for wind instruments: *Musica vespertina Lipsica* (1669); *Hora decima* (1670); *Intraden* (1676); *Deliciae musicales* (1678); etc. His most interesting work is *Fünffstimmigte blasende Musik* (Frankfurt, 1685; 3 pieces arranged for modern brass ensemble by Robert D. King, and publ. in Wakefield, Mass.). Selections from various of his works, ed. by A. Schering, are in Denkmäler Deutscher Tonkunst, 63.

Pfannstiehl, Bernhard, German organist; b. Schmalkalden, Dec. 18, 1861; d. Freiberg, Oct. 21, 1940. He became blind in infancy, and was educated at the Inst. for the Blind in Leipzig; studied piano at the Leipzig Cons.; was thrice winner of the Mendelssohn Prize. Following Liszt's advice, he made a specialty of the organ; was a church organist in Leipzig (1896–1903), in Chemnitz (1903–11), and at the Kreuzkirche in Dresden (1912–34). He enjoyed a great reputation as an interpreter of Bach.
BIBLIOGRAPHY: K. Hasse, "Bernhard Pfannstiehl," *Die Orgel* (1910).

Pfatteicher, Carl Friedrichs, American specialist in church music and pedagogue, of German parentage; b. Easton, Pa., Sept. 22, 1882; d. Philadelphia, Sept. 29, 1957. He studied theology in Germany and at Harvard Univ. (Th.D., 1912); taught Latin and German at various schools; then was a prof. of music at Philips Academy in Andover, Mass. (1912–47); from 1949 on he was a lecturer in musicology at the Univ. of Pa. He publ. a number of useful school manuals and collections of sacred music, among them *The Christian Church Year in Chorals* (1917); *The Christian Church Year in Part Songs* (1915); *Thesaurus musicae sacrae* (1920); *The Oxford American Hymnal* (1930); was co-editor of *The Office Hymns of the Church in Their Plainsong Settings* and *The Church Organist's Golden Treasury.*

Pfeiffer, Georges-Jean, French composer; b. Versailles, Dec. 12, 1835; d. Paris, Feb. 14, 1908. He began his career as a pianist; then was active as a music critic in Paris; was a member of the Paris firm Pleyel, Wolff et Cie., piano makers.
WORKS: Operetta, *Capitaine Roche* (1862); one-act opera, *L'Enclume* (Paris, 1884); comic opera, *Le Légataire universel* (Paris, July 6, 1901); oratorio, *Hagar;* symph. poem, *Jeanne d'Arc; Légende,* symph. fantasy for Piano and Orch.; many pieces of chamber music; also piano pieces.

Pfeiffer, Theodor, German pianist and pedagogue;

b. Heidelberg, Oct. 20, 1853; d. Baden-Baden, Nov. 9, 1929. He studied piano with Hans von Bülow at the Raff Cons. in Frankfurt. In 1889 he settled in Baden-Baden as a private teacher. He publ. a number of valuable studies: *Studien nach Kreutzerschen Violin-Etüden gebildet; Tonleiterschule; Virtuosen-Studien* (in part, preparatory studies for Bülow's eds.); also wrote a Mass; songs; men's choruses; and piano pieces (*Albumblatt, Dryadenspiel, Mazurka-Caprice, Konzert-Etüde,* etc.). His recollections of Bülow's remarks in teaching specific works were publ. as *Studien bei Hans von Bülow* (1894; 6th ed., 1909).

Pfitzner, Hans Erich, eminent German composer; b. Moscow (of German parents), May 5, 1869; d. Salzburg, May 22, 1949. He studied piano with James Kwast and composition with Iwan Knorr at the Hoch Cons. in Frankfurt; in 1899 he abducted Kwast's daughter and took her to England, where he married her. In 1892–93 he taught piano and theory at the Cons. of Coblenz; then served as assistant conductor of the Municipal Theater in Mainz (1894–96); from 1897–1907 he was on the faculty of the Stern Cons. in Berlin; concurrently he conducted at the Theater Westens (1903–6). During the 1907–8 season he led the renowned Kaim Concerts in Munich. From 1908–18 he was in Strasbourg as municipal music director and also served as dean at the Strasbourg Cons.; from 1910–16 he conducted at the Strasbourg Opera. During the 1919–20 season he filled conducting engagements at the Munich Konzertverein; from 1920–29 he led a master class at the Berlin Academy of Arts; from 1929–34 he taught composition at the Akademie der Tonkunst in Munich. Being of certified German stock, though born in Russia, he was favored by the Nazi authorities, and became an ardent supporter of the Third Reich; he reached the nadir of his moral degradation in dedicating an overture, *Krakauer Begrüssung,* to Hans Frank, the murderous Gauleiter of occupied Poland in 1944. After the collapse of Hitler's brief millennium, Pfitzner had to face the Denazification Court in Munich in 1948; owing to his miserable condition in body and soul, he was exonerated. He was taken to a home for the aged in Munich, and later was transferred to Salzburg, where he died in misery. Eventually, his dead body was honorably laid to rest in a Vienna cemetery.
In his better days, Pfitzner was hailed in Germany as a great national composer. He presented a concert of his works in Berlin on May 12, 1893, with excellent auguries. After the premiere of his opera *Der arme Heinrich* in Mainz on April 2, 1895, the critics, among them the prestigious Humperdinck, praised the work in extravagant terms. Even more successful was his opera *Palestrina,* making use of Palestrina's themes, written to his own libretto, which was conducted by Bruno Walter at its first performance on June 12, 1917, in Munich. The Pfitzner Society was formed in Munich as early as 1904, and a Hans Pfitzner Assoc. was established in Berlin in 1938, with Furtwängler as president. Althought Pfitzner's music is traditional in style and

conservative in harmony, he was regarded as a follower of the modern school, a comrade-in-arms of his close contemporary Richard Strauss. Very soon, however, his fame began to dwindle; there were fewer performances of his operas and still fewer hearings of his instrumental works; he himself bitterly complained of this lack of appreciation of his art. It was a miserable end for a once important and capable musician.

WORKS: OPERAS: *Der arme Heinrich* (1891–93; Mainz, April 2, 1895); *Die Rose vom Liebesgarten* (1897–1900; Elberfeld, Nov. 9, 1901); *Das Christ-Elflein* (1906; Munich, Dec. 11, 1906); *Palestrina* (1911–15; Munich, June 12, 1917, conducted by Bruno Walter); *Das Herz* (1930–31; Berlin and Munich, Nov. 12, 1931). INCIDENTAL MUSIC: *Das Fest auf Solhaug*, after Ibsen (Mainz, Nov. 28, 1890); *Das Käthchen von Heilbronn*, after Kleist (1905; Berlin, Oct. 19, 1905). FOR ORCH.: Scherzo in C minor (1887; Frankfurt, Nov. 8, 1888); *3 Preludes*, symph. excerpts from the opera *Palestrina* (1917); Piano Concerto (1921; Dresden, March 16, 1921; Walter Gieseking, soloist); Violin Concerto (1923; Nuremberg, June 4, 1924, under Pfitzner's direction); Symph. in C-sharp minor, after the 2nd String Quartet (1932; Munich, March 23, 1933, composer conducting); Cello Concerto No. 1 (Frankfurt, 1935); *Duo* for Violin, Cello, and Chamber Orch. (1937; Frankfurt, Dec. 3, 1937, composer conducting); *Kleine Symphonie* (1939; Berlin, Nov. 19, 1939, Furtwängler conducting); Symphony in C (1940; Frankfurt, Oct. 11, 1940); *Elegie und Reigen* (1940; Salzburg, April 4, 1941); *Krakauer Begrüssung* (1944; written in honor of Hans Frank, Nazi governor of Poland); Cello Concerto No. 2 (1944; Solingen, April 23, 1944, composer conducting); *Elegie* (1947). CHAMBER MUSIC: Cello Sonata (1890); Piano Trio (1896); 4 string quartets (1886, 1903, 1925, 1942); Piano Quintet (1908); Violin Sonata (1918); *5 Klavierstücke* (1941); *6 Studien* for Piano (1943); *Sextet* for Clarinet, Violin, Viola, Cello, Double Bass, and Piano (1945). VOCAL MUSIC: *Von deutscher Seele*, romantic cantata after J. von Eichendorff (1921; Berlin, Jan. 27, 1922); *Das dunkle Reich* for Solo Voices and Orch. (1929; Cologne, Oct. 21, 1930); *Fons salutatis* for Chorus and Orch. (1941); *Kantate*, after Goethe (1948–49; left unfinished; completed by R. Rehan); 106 lieder (1884–1931).

WRITINGS: *Gesammelte Schriften* (2 vols., Augsburg, 1926; new ed. in 3 vols., Munich, 1929), containing Pfitzner's vicious pamphlets against modern ideas about music, including *Futuristengefahr*, directed against Busoni (1917), and *Neue Aesetik der musikalischen Impotenz*, denouncing the critic Paul Bekker; *Über musikalische Inspiration* (Berlin, 1940); *Philosophie und Dichtung in meinem Leben* (Berlin, 1944); *Eindrücke und Bilder meines Lebens* (Hamburg, 1947); *Reden, Schriften, Briefe* (posthumous; ed. by W. Abendroth, Berlin, 1955).

BIBLIOGRAPHY: P.N. Cossmann, *Hans Pfitzner* (Munich, 1904); R. Louis, *Hans Pfitzners "Die Rose vom Liebesgarten"* (Munich, 1904); R. Louis, *Hans Pfitzner* (Leipzig, 1907); A. Berrsche, *Hans Pfitzner "Der arme Heinrich"* (1910); A. Seidl, *Hans Pfitzner* (1921); C. Wandrey, *Hans Pfitzner, Seine geistige* *Persönlichkeit und das Ende der Romantik* (1922); W. Lütge, *Hans Pfitzner* (1924); E. Kroll, *Hans Pfitzner* (1924); Pfitzner-Festschrift (1930); W. Abendroth, *Hans Pfitzner* (1935); E. Valentin, *Hans Pfitzner: Werk und Gestalt eines Deutschen* (Regensburg, 1939); J. Müller-Blattau, *Hans Pfitzner* (Potsdam, 1940; 2nd ed., revised, 1969); H. Lindlar, *Hans Pfitzners Klavierlied* (Würzburg, 1940); W. Abendroth, *Hans Pfitzner: Sein Leben in Bildern* (Leipzig, 1941); J. Bahle, *Hans Pfitzner und der geniale Mensch* (Constance, 1949); Hans Rutz, *Hans Pfitzner: Musik zwischen den Zeiten* (Vienna, 1949); a symposium of articles, *Hans Pfitzner zum 75. Geburtstag* (Cologne, 1944); *Hans Pfitzner, Ein Bild in Widmungen, anlässlich seines 75. Geburtstags*, ed. by W. Abendroth (Leipzig, 1944); *In Memoriam Hans Pfitzner* (Vienna, 1950); J. Müller-Blattau, *Hans Pfitzner: Lebensweg und Schaffensernte* (Frankfurt, 1969); *Festschrift aus Anlass des 100 Geburtstag*, ed. by W. Abendroth (Munich, 1969).

Pflüger, Gerhard, German conductor; b. Dresden, April 9, 1907. He studied conducting with Kurt Striegler and Fritz Busch at the Dresden Staatskapelle; then was a conductor in Tilsit (1927–30); held the post of first conductor in Stralsund (1930–32), Gotha-Sondershausen (1932–35), and Altenburg (1938–40); was then music director in Meiningen (1940–44) and Generalmusikdirektor in Rostock (1946–49). In 1949 he became chief conductor of the Leipzig Radio Symph. Orch.; in 1957 he was appointed Generalmusikdirektor of the Nationaltheater in Weimar, a post he held until 1973; was also on the faculty of the Hochschule für Musik in Weimar.

Pflughaupt, Robert, German pianist; b. Berlin, Aug. 4, 1833; d. Aix-la-Chapelle, June 12, 1871. He studied with Dehn in Berlin, Henselt in St. Petersburg, and Liszt in Weimar. He wrote a number of agreeable piano pieces (*Petite valse, Mazurka, Galop de concert, Invitation à la polka*, etc.). His wife, **Sophie Pflughaupt** (née **Shtchepin**; b. Dvinsk, Russia, March 15, 1837; d. Aix-la-Chapelle, Nov. 10, 1867), was also an excellent pianist and also a pupil of Henselt and Liszt.

Pfohl, Ferdinand, German writer on music; b. Elbogen, Bohemia, Oct. 12, 1862; d. Bergedorf, near Hamburg, Dec. 16, 1949. He studied law in Prague; in 1885 went to Leipzig, where he took private lessons in music with Oscar Paul. In 1892 he became the music critic of the influential *Hamburger Nachrichten*, holding this important post until his retirement in 1932; also taught music theory at the Vogt Cons. in Hamburg.

WRITINGS: *Die moderne Oper* (1894); *Die Nibelungen in Bayreuth* (1897); *Arthur Nikisch als Mensch und Künstler* (Leipzig, 1900; 2nd ed., 1925); *Karl Grammann. Ein Künstlerleben* (Berlin, 1910); *Richard Wagner. Sein Leben und Schaffen* (1911; 4th ed., 1924); *Beethoven* (1922); also descriptions of African music: *Quer durch Afrika* (1891) and *West-Östliche Fahrten* (1902); publ. guides to Wagner's operas. His original compositions include the symph. poems *Die versunkene Glocke, Pierrot lunaire,* and *Frau Holle;* a symph. fantasy, *Das Meer;* piano pieces.

Pfordten, Hermann Ludwig von der, German writer on music; b. Munich, July 5, 1857; d. there, Nov. 16, 1933. He was the son of a Bavarian minister; studied in Munich and in Leipzig; became a prof. of music history at the Univ. of Munich; he specialized in writing about Wagner's music.
WRITINGS: *Handlung und Dichtung der Bühnenwerke Richard Wagners* (1893; 8th ed., 1922); *Musikalische Essays* (2 vols., 1897, 1899); *Deutsche Musik* (1917; 3rd ed., 1922); *Der Musikfreund,* an introductory book on music (1923; 8th ed., 1928); *Einführung in Wagners Werke und Schriften* (3rd ed., 1925); popular biographies of Beethoven (1907; 4th ed., 1922), Mozart (1908; 3rd ed., 1926), Schubert (1916; 3rd ed., 1928), Weber (1919), Schumann (1920), and Robert Franz (1923).

Pfrogner, Hermann, Austrian musicologist; b. Graz, Jan. 17, 1911. He studied law at the Univ. of Vienna; held various positions in financial institutions; studied musicology with E. Schenk (1945–47); in 1948 settled in Stuttgart. He contributed numerous articles on modern harmony to various periodicals; publ. a fundamental essay dealing with 12-tone composition, *Die Zwölfordnung der Töne* (Zürich, 1953); also *Musik, Geschichte ihrer Deutung* (Freiburg, 1954); *Lebendige Tonwelt: Zum Phänomen Musik* (Munich, 1976).

Pfundt, Ernst Gotthold Benjamin, celebrated German timpani player; b. Dommitzsch, near Torgau, June 17, 1806; d. Leipzig, Dec. 7, 1871. He studied theology, and at the same time developed an extraordinary ability as a drummer; was invited by Mendelssohn in 1835 to join the Gewandhaus Orch. in Leipzig, and remained there as drummer until his death; achieved legendary fame for his rhythmic skill. He was the inventor of the pedal kettledrums; publ. a method for drums (1849; 3rd ed., enlarged by H. Schmidt, 1894).

Phalèse, Pierre (Petrus Phalesius), Flemish music publisher; b. Louvain, c.1510; d. there, c.1573. He established a music publishing business in 1545; the printing was done elsewhere, and it was not until 1553 that Phalèse began to print on the premises in Louvain. From 1570 he worked in association with Jean Bellère of Antwerp. After the death of Pierre Phalèse, the business was moved to Antwerp (1581), and was managed by his sons, Pierre Jr. and Corneille; it continued under the management of the heirs until about 1674. Two compositions by Pierre Phalèse the elder are found in A. Schering's *Geschichte der Musik in Beispielen* (no. 134).
BIBLIOGRAPHY: A. Goovaerts, *Notice biographique sur Phalèse* (1869); idem, *Histoire et bibliographie de la typographie musicale dans le Pays-Bas* (1880).

Phelps, Ellsworth C., American organist and composer; b. Middletown, Conn., Aug. 11, 1827; d. Brooklyn, N.Y., Nov. 29, 1913. Self-taught in music, he became an organist in New London at the age of 19; settled in Brooklyn in 1857; held various positions as an organist, and taught in the public schools. He wrote several symph. works in a programmatic genre, usually on American subjects: *Hiawatha* (1878) and *Emancipation* (1880); pieces for military band (perf. by Gilmore and Sousa); etc.; more than 200 pieces in all.

Phile (Fyles, Pfeil, Phyla), Philip, violinist and teacher; b. Germany, c.1734; d. Philadelphia, between Aug. 1 and Nov. 9, 1793, in a yellow-fever epidemic. He served in the Pa. German Regiment during the Revolutionary War; was transferred in July 1778 to the Invalid Regiment; was discharged on Jan. 4, 1783; a pension was granted to him on July 11, 1785. He was active in Philadelphia and N.Y.; gave concerts; played in theater orchs.; conducted the orch. of the Old American Co. of Comedians. He was probably the composer of the music of the *President's March,* to which Joseph Hopkinson (son of Francis Hopkinson) wrote the words *Hail Columbia.* He also wrote a piece entitled *Harmony Music* for the series of summer concerts at Gray's Gardens in Philadelphia.
BIBLIOGRAPHY: O.G. Sonneck, *Report on the "Star Spangled Banner," "Hail Columbia," etc.* (Washington, D.C., 1909).

Philidor (real name, **Danican**), famous family of French musicians. (1) **Jean Danican-Philidor;** b. c.1620; d. Paris, Sept. 8, 1679, as "Fifre de la Grande Ecurie" (piper in the King's military band). (2) **André Philidor** (*l'aîné*), son of Jean; d. Dreux, Aug. 11, 1730. As a youth he played the cromorne in the King's military band; later played the oboe, bassoon, and trompette marine, in addition to the cromorne, in the King's private band. He served as a librarian of the Royal Music Library at Versailles, and accumulated a collection of MSS of old instrumental pieces performed at the French court since the time of François I; the bulk of this collection, numbering some 350 MS vols., is at St. Michael's College, Tenbury, Worcester; 59 vols. are in the library of the Paris Cons., 35 vols. in the city library of Versailles, and 35 vols. in the collection of the Library of Congress in Washington, D.C. Among his publ. works are *Mascarade des Savoyards* (1700); *Mascarade du roi de la chine* (1700); *Suite de danses pour les violons et hautbois* (1699); *Pièces à 2 basses de viole, basse de violon et basson* (1700); *Marches et batteries de tambour avec les airs de fifres et de hautbois.* (3) **Jacques** (*le cadet*), brother of André (*l'aîné*); b. Paris, May 5, 1657; d. Versailles, May 27, 1708. He was a bassoonist in the Royal Chapel and later chamber musician to Louis XIV. (4) **Anne Danican-Philidor,** son of André (*l'aîné*); b. Paris, April 11, 1681; d. there, Oct. 8, 1728. A flute player, he composed pastoral operas (*L'Amour vainqueur,* 1697; *Diane et Endymion,* 1698; *Danaë,* 1701), and music for flutes, violins, and oboes. He was the founder of the famous Paris concert series the Concert Spirituel (1725). (5) **Pierre Danican-Philidor,** son of Jacques (*le cadet*); b. Paris, Aug. 22, 1681; d. there, Sept. 1, 1731. He was a flute player; publ. 3 books of suites for 2 transverse flutes (1717, 1718), and flute trios. (6) **François André Danican-Philidor,** the last and greatest in the line of musicians in the family, the youngest son of André (*l'aîné*); b. Dreux, Sept. 7, 1726; d. London, Aug. 31, 1795. He achieved distinction not only in music but in chess; a famous chess opening was named after him. He defeated a number of celebrated chess masters of his time; brought out a fundamental treatise on chess, *L'Analyse des échecs* (London, 1749; new ed., under the title *Analyse du jeu des échecs,* 1777; altogether there were more than 100 eds. of this famous book). As a member of the London Chess Club, he was guaranteed a sum of money in exchange for his availability to play with other members of the club. In 1756 he began a surprisingly successful career as a composer for the theater. His first stage work was *Le Diable à 4,* a *comédie en vaudevilles,* which was the predecessor of opéra-comique; it was produced at the Opéra-Comique on Aug. 19, 1756. His next production was a ballet with music by Charpentier for which Philidor made some revisions, and which was produced under the title *Le Retour du printemps.* These were succeeded by several one-act pieces: *Blaise le savetier* (1759); *L'Huitre et les plaideurs* (1759); *Le Quiproquo ou Le Volage fixé* (1760); *Le Soldat magicien* (1760); *Le Jardinier et son seigneur* (1761). But his most successful production of this period was *Le Maréchal ferrant,* in 2 acts (1761), which was performed more than 200 times; there followed a group of one-act pieces: *Sancho Pança* (1762); *Le Bûcheron, ou Les 3 Souhaits* (1763); *Le Sorcier,* in 2 acts (Jan. 2, 1764); and *Tom Jones,* in 3 acts (Feb. 27, 1765), which enjoyed great success, and incidentally contained an interesting novelty, a vocal quartet a cappella. Philidor's finest production, the grand opera *Ernelinde, Princesse de Norvège,* was staged on Nov. 24, 1767; it was revised in 1769 and produced under the title *Sandomir, Prince de Danemark,* but was revived in 1773 under its original title. Continuing his successful opera productions, Philidor staged *Le Jardinier de Sidon* (1768); *L'Amant déguisé* (1769); *La Nouvelle Ecole des femmes* (1770); *Le Bon Fils* (1773). His next opera, *Sémire et Mélide,* was given at Fontainebleau on Oct. 30, 1773, but it was publ. under the title *Mélide ou Le Navigateur.* There followed *Berthe* (Brussels, 1775); *Les Femmes vengées* (1775); and *Le Puits d'Amour* (1779), a play adapted from a novel originally publ. in 1765, for which Philidor composed 6 ariettes, which were publ. with the novel and then were used in the production of the play. Further works were *Persée* (1780); *L'Amitié au village* (1785); *Thémistocle* (first given at Fontainebleau on May 23, 1786, and then produced the following year at the Paris Opéra); *La Belle Esclave* (1787); and *Le Mari comme il les faudrait tous* (1788). A posthumous opera, *Bélisaire,* completed by Berton, was produced in 1796.

François André Philidor eclipsed his famous rivals Grétry and Monsigny in richness of harmony and skill in orchestration, but he yielded to Grétry, if not to Monsigny, in power of dramatic expression and melodic invention. Philidor was greatly admired by the Parisians, but his love for chess often distracted him from Paris in favor of frequent trips to London to play at the chess club there. Apart from his operas, he wrote church music and chamber pieces, among them quartets for 2 violins, oboe, and continuo. He set to music Horace's *Carmen saeculare,* a sort of secular oratorio that enjoyed notable success; in alternation with Jean-Claude Trial, he issued a series of publications, 12 Ariettes Périodiques.

BIBLIOGRAPHY: J. Lardin, *Philidor peint par lui-même* (Paris, 1847); G. Allen, *The Life of Philidor, Musician and Chess Player* (Philadelphia, 1858; reprint, N.Y., 1971); A. Pougin, "Philidor," *Chronique Musicale* (1874–75); Ch. Piot, "Particularités inédites concernant les œuvres musicales de Gossec et de Philidor," *Bulletins de l'Académie Royale de Belgique* (Brussels, 1875); G.E. Bonnet, "L'Œuvre de Philidor," *Revue Musicale* (Oct. 1921); idem, *Philidor et l'évolution de la musique française au XVIIIᵉ siècle* (1921); *Dictionary of National Biography,* XLV. For details of productions of Philidor's operas, consult A. Loewenberg's *Annals of Opera.*

Philip, Achille, French composer; b. Arles, Oct. 12, 1878; d. Béziers (Hérault), Oct. 12, 1959. He studied at the Paris Cons. with Guilmant (organ) and Vincent d'Indy (composition); from 1905 to 1950 taught organ at the Schola Cantorum in Paris. He wrote an opera, *L'Or du Menhir* (Rouen, 1934); symph. poems: *Les Djinns* (1913); *Dans un parc enchanté* (1917); *Nymphes et Naiades* (1920); also, a number of sacred works; chamber music; songs.

Philipp, Isidor, eminent French pianist; b. Budapest, Sept. 2, 1863; d. Paris, Feb. 20, 1958 (as a result of injuries received from a fall in the Paris Métro). He was brought to Paris as an infant; studied piano with Georges Mathias at the Paris Cons., winning first prize in 1883; then took lessons with Saint-Saëns, Stephen Heller, and Ritter. His concert career was brief, but he found his true vocation in teaching; in 1903 he was appointed prof. of piano at the Paris Cons.; many famous musicians, among them Albert Schweitzer, were his pupils. In Paris he continued to perform, mostly in chamber music groups; formed a concert trio with Loeb and Berthelier, with which he gave a number of successful concerts. After the outbreak of World War II he went to the U.S.; arrived in N.Y. in 1941; despite his advanced age he accepted private students, not only in N.Y., but also in Montreal. At the age of 91, he played the piano part in Franck's Violin Sonata (N.Y., March 20, 1955); then returned to France. He publ. some technical studies for piano, among them *Exercises journaliers; Ecole d'octaves; Problèmes techniques; Etudes techniques basées sur une nouvelle manière de travailler; La Gamme chromatique;* made arrangements for 2 pianos of works by Bach, Mendelssohn, Saint-Saëns, and others; also brought out *La Technique de Liszt* (2 vols., Paris, 1932).

BIBLIOGRAPHY: Henry Bellamann, "Isidor Philipp," *Musical Quarterly* (Oct. 1943).

Philippe de Vitry. See **Vitry, Philippe de.**

Philippot, Michel, French composer; b. Verzy, Feb. 2, 1925. He first took courses in mathematics; then studied music at the Paris Cons. (1945–47); also took private lessons with René Leibowitz (1945–49); was a sound engineer at the French Radio-Television Network (1949–59); became its president in 1973.
WORKS: 2 Piano Sonatas (1946, 1973); Overture for Chamber Orch. (1948); Piano Trio (1953); Variations for 10 Instruments (1957); *3 compositions* for Piano (1958); *Composition* for String Orch. (1959); *Composition* for Double Orch. (1959); *Pièce pour 10* for Chamber Ensemble; *Transformations triangulaires* for 12 Instruments (1962); *Pieces* for Solo Violin (1967); Organ Sonata (1971); Scherzo for Solo Accordion (1972); *Commentariolus Copernicae* for Flute, Clarinet, Bassoon, Horn, Trumpet, Violin, Cello, Piano, and Percussion (1972; Paris, Oct. 22, 1973); *Trio inachevé* for Flute, Clarinet, and Trombone (1973); Octet (1974).

Philips, Peter, important English composer and organist; b. 1561; d. Brussels, 1628. He belonged to a Catholic family; was probably a chorister at St. Paul's Cathedral; was befriended by a Catholic almoner, Sebastian Westcote, and received a bequest upon the latter's death in 1582. In that year, Philips left England; on Aug. 18, 1582, he arrived at Douai, where he presented himself at the English College; then proceeded to Rome, where he entered the service of Cardinal Alessandro Farnese; also was for 3 years organist at the English College in Rome (1582–85). In the autumn of 1585 Philips joined the household of Lord Thomas Paget in Rome, and subsequently traveled with him through Spain, France, and the Netherlands. From early 1587 until June 1588, Philips was with Paget in Paris; then went to Antwerp, remaining there until early 1589; also made visits to Brussels. After Paget's death in 1590, Philips settled in Antwerp, and was active there as a teacher of keyboard playing. In 1593 he went to Amsterdam, where he met Sweelinck. On his return trip to Antwerp, he was detained at Middelburgh, was charged with planning the assassination of Queen Elizabeth, and was alleged to have participated with Lord Paget in the act of burning the Queen in effigy in Paris. He stood trial in The Hague in Sept. 1593, but was released for lack of evidence. Late in 1593 he was back in Antwerp. In 1597 he moved to Brussels, entering the service of the Archduke Albert, as organist of the Royal Chapel. After Albert's marriage to Isabella of Spain (1599) Philips was officially designated as "Organist to Their Serene Highnesses the Archduke Albert and Isabella." On March 9, 1610, he received a canonry at Soignies, but continued to reside in Brussels. On Jan. 5, 1621, he exchanged his title at Soignies for a chaplainship at Tirlemont; in 1623 he is also described as canon of Béthune. However, he continued to be designated canon of Soignies for many

years afterward, even in posthumous editions of his works, possibly because he was best known in that nominal post. Philips was highly esteemed in his day, and his works were printed in many collections; his music shows mixed Italian and Netherlandish characteristics; he excelled in madrigals and motets; his pieces for the virginal reveal a kinship with Sweelinck.
WORKS: 4 madrigals in *Melodia Olympica di diversi eccellentissimi musici* (Antwerp, 1591); 2 vols. of madrigals for 6 Voices (1596, 1603); one vol. of madrigals for 8 Voices (1598); motets for 5 Voices (1612); motets for 8 Voices (1613); *Gemmulae sacrae* for 2–3 Voices, with Continuo (1613); *Les Rossignols spirituels* for 2–4 Voices (1616); *Deliciae sacrae* for 2–3 Voices (1622); litanies for 4–9 Voices (1623); *Paradisus sacris cantionibus conditus* (1628); other works listed in the catalogue of the library of King João IV of Portugal, publ. by Vasconcellos in 1873. W.B. Squire edited the madrigals *Amor che vuoi* for 4 Voices (London, 1890) and *Dispiegate guancie amate* for 8 Voices in *Ausgewählte Madrigale* (Leipzig, 1906); the motets *Hodie Sanctus Benedictus* for 5 Voices (London, 1899) and *Ego sum panis vivus* (London, 1902); Sir Richard Terry, who contributed greatly to a revival of the music by Philips, publ. 4 motets for 5 Voices in the collection *Downside Motets* (London, 1904–5); 19 keyboard pieces are included in the *Fitzwilliam Virginal Book,* vol. 1 (1889); other keyboard pieces are found in various anthologies.
BIBLIOGRAPHY: P. Bergmans, *L'Organiste des archiducs Albert et Isabelle, Peter Philips* (Ghent, 1903); C. Hughes, "Peter Philips: An English Musician in the Netherlands," *Papers of the American Musicological Society, 1940* (1946).

Phillipps, Adelaide, English contralto; b. Stratford-upon–Avon, Oct. 26, 1833; d. Karlsbad, Oct. 3, 1882. Her family took her to America as a child; she was trained as a dancer, and made her first appearance at the Tremont Theater in Boston on Jan. 12, 1842, in a variety show. She also displayed an early gift as a vocalist, and was introduced to Jenny Lind, who encouraged her to study singing; accordingly she was sent to London, where she took lessons with Manuel García; made her professional debut in Milan as Rosina (Dec. 17, 1854). Returning to Boston in 1855, she sang light opera in English; her first appearance on the grand opera stage in America was as Azucena in Verdi's *Il Trovatore* (N.Y., March 17, 1856). After a long and successful tour in Europe she joined the Boston Ideal Opera Co. in 1879–80. She was advised to go to Karlsbad for her health in 1882, but died shortly after her arrival there. During her European engagements she sang under the name **Signorina Filippi.**
BIBLIOGRAPHY: A.C.L. Waterston, *Adelaide Phillipps* (Boston, 1883); V.F. Yellin, in *Notable American Women,* III (N.Y., 1971).

Phillips, Burrill, American composer; b. Omaha, Nov. 9, 1907. He studied music with Edwin Stringham in Denver; then with Howard Hanson and Bernard Rogers at the Eastman School of Music in Rochester, N.Y. After graduation he held numerous teaching posts: at the Eastman School of Music (1933–49, and again in 1965-66); at the Univ. of Illinois in Urbana (1949–64); and as guest lecturer at the Juilliard School of Music in N.Y. (1968–69) and at Cornell Univ. (1972–73). His music is cast in a neo-Classical style.

WORKS: Ballets: *Play Ball* (Rochester, April 29, 1938) and *Step into My Parlor* (1941). For Orch.: *Selections from McGuffey's Reader* (Rochester, May 3, 1934); *Sinfonia concertante* (Rochester, April 3, 1935); *American Dance* for Bassoon and Strings (Rochester, April 25, 1940); *3 Satiric Fragments* (Rochester, May 2, 1941); Piano Concerto (1943); *Scherzo* (1944); *Tom Paine Overture* (N.Y., May 15, 1947); *La piñata* (1960); *Perspectives in a Labyrinth* for 3 String Orchs. (1963). Chamber music: Trio for Trumpets (1937); 2 string quartets (1939, 1959); Violin Sonata (1942); Cello Sonata (1946); *Partita* for Violin, Viola, Cello, and Piano (Rochester, May 7, 1948); *4 Figures in Time* for Flute and Piano (1953); *5 Pieces* for Woodwind Quintet (1965); Quartet for Oboe and Strings (1966); 4 piano sonatas; *9 by 9,* a set of 9 variations, each one in a meter of 9 beats (1942); *Toccata* (1944); *3 Informalities* (1945); *3 Divertimenti* (1946); *5 Various and Sundry* (1961). Also organ pieces; several choruses; opera, *Don't We All* (Rochester, May 9, 1949).

Phillips, Harvey, American tuba player; b. Aurora, Mo., Dec. 2, 1929. He played the sousaphone in high school; after attending the Univ. of Missouri (1947–48), he joined the Ringling Brothers and Barnum & Bailey Circus Band; then took general music courses at the Juilliard School of Music (1950–54) and at the Manhattan School of Music (1956–58); concurrently he played in various ensembles there, including the N.Y. City Ballet Orch., the N.Y. City Opera Orch., the Goldman Band, and the Symph. of the Air; he also was a founding member of the N.Y. Brass Quintet. From 1967–71 he held an administrative position at the New England Cons. of Music. In 1971 he became a prof. of music at the Indiana Univ. School of Music; was named a distinguished prof. of music there in 1979. He commissioned works for tuba from Gunther Schuller, Robert Russell Bennett, Alec Wilder, and Morton Gould.

Phillips, John, American hippie-style folk singer; b. Parris Island, S.C., Aug. 30, 1935. He played guitar and sang folk songs in his soft baritone voice in Greenwich Village. In 1965 he formed a group dubbed The Mamas and The Papas with Denny Doherty (b. Halifax, Nova Scotia, Nov. 29, 1941), Cass Elliot (real name Ellen Cohen, b. Baltimore, Sept. 19, 1941; d. Los Angeles, July 24, 1974), and Michelle Gilliam (b. Long Beach, Calif., June 4, 1945), whom he married (and divorced in 1970). The Mamas and The Papas spawned such hits as *California Dreamin',* *I Saw Her Again, Words of Love, Dedicated to the One I Love* and the hippie smash *San Francisco (Be Sure to Wear Flowers in Your Hair).* In 1967 Phillips, together with the music manager Lou

Adler, produced the eventful Monterey Pop Festival, which catapulted into the limelight such rockers as Jimi Hendrix, Janis Joplin, and The Who. But by dint of begetting the careers of others, The Mamas and The Papas exhausted their own seminal fluid, and by 1968 gave up the ghost. They reunited briefly in 1971 to record the album *People Like Us.* Cass Elliot died of a heart attack in her Los Angeles home, and in 1980, John Phillips served 30 days in jail on drug charges in N.Y.

Phillips, Karen, American pianist and composer; b. Dallas, Oct. 29, 1942. She studied piano at the Eastman School of Music, and theory at the Juilliard School in N.Y.; she also took lessons in viola playing, and gave recitals both as a violist and a pianist. She wrote 4 symphs., a Cello Concerto, some chamber music, and piano pieces.

Phillips, Montague Fawcett, English composer and pedagogue; b. London, Nov. 13, 1885; d. Esher, Jan. 4, 1969. He studied with F. Corder at the Royal Academy of Music in London; subsequently taught there. He wrote a light opera, *The Rebel Maid* (London, March 12, 1921), which enjoyed some success, also numerous choral works and orch. overtures, mostly on subjects from British history; during World War II he wrote *Empire March* for Orch. (1941) and an overture, *In Praise of My Country* (1944).

Phillips, Philip, American hymn-tune writer; b. on a farm in Chautauqua County, N.Y., Aug. 13, 1834; d. Delaware, Ohio, June 25, 1895. He sang in a choir as a child; was a cheesemaker by trade; then traveled as an itinerant singer; publ. gospel songbooks. His best-known hymn is *Home of the Soul.*

BIBLIOGRAPHY: R.G. McCutchan, *Our Hymnody* (N.Y., 1937).

Piaf, Edith, French chanteuse; b. Paris, Dec. 19, 1915; d. there, Oct. 11, 1963. Her real name was **Giovanna Gassion;** she took her first name from Edith Cavell, a Belgian nurse shot by the Germans in World War I. Her childhood was tragic; she was abandoned by her mother, an Italian café singer and professional prostitute; traveled with her father, a circus contortionist, taking part in his act as a shill for his street-corner acrobatics. She became a street singer in Paris, earning the nickname Piaf (Parisian argot for "sparrow") on account of her ragged and emaciated appearance. She was befriended by a cabaret owner; when he was murdered, she was held by the French police as a material witness. During the war and German occupation she entertained French prisoners in Germany; as a result, she was accused of collaboration, but was exonerated. In 1954 she made her first American tour. Although untutored, she developed a type of ballad singing that was infused with profound sentiment and expressive artistry, eliciting an enthusiastic response from nightclub audiences and sophisticated music critics alike. She composed chansonettes, among which *La Vie en rose* became popular; publ. a book of memoirs, *Au bal de la chance* (Paris, 1958; in Eng. as *The Wheel of Fortune*, 1965). A film on the early years of her life was produced in Paris in 1982.

Piastro, Josef, Russian-American violinist; b. Kerch, Crimea, March 1, 1889; d. Monrovia, Calif., May 14, 1964. He studied with Leopold Auer at the St. Petersburg Cons.; came to the U.S. in 1920; was concertmaster of the Los Angeles Phil., and conducted children's concerts in Hollywood. In America he assumed the pseudonym **Borissoff,** to avoid confusion with his brother, also a violinist, **Michel Piastro.** He composed *Crimean Rhapsody* for Violin and Piano (1920).

Piastro, Michel, Russian-American violinist, brother of **Josef Piastro;** b. Kerch, Crimea, July 1, 1891; d. New York, April 10, 1970. Like his brother, he studied with Leopold Auer at the St. Petersburg Cons.; in 1920 came to the U.S.; was concertmaster of the San Francisco Symph. Orch. (1925–31) and of the N.Y. Phil. under Toscanini (1931–43). In 1941 he conducted a radio series, "Longines Symphonette," sponsored by the Longines-Wittnauer Watch Co.

Piatigorsky, Gregor, great Russian cellist; b. Ekaterinoslav, April 17, 1903; d. Los Angeles, Aug. 6, 1976. He received his first music lessons from his father, a violinist; then took cello lessons with Alfred von Glehn; played in various orchs. in Moscow. In 1921 he left Russia and proceeded to Berlin, where he took cello lessons with Julius Klengel. From 1924 to 1928 he was first cellist of the Berlin Phil.; then devoted himself entirely to his concert career. He played the solo part in *Don Quixote* by Richard Strauss under the composer's direction many times in Europe, and was probably unexcelled in this part; Strauss himself called him "mein Don Quixote." He went to America in 1929 and made his American debut at Oberlin, Ohio, on Nov. 5, 1929; played the Dvořák Concerto with the N.Y. Phil., eliciting great praise (Dec. 29, 1929). He was regarded as the world's finest cello player after Casals; continued giving solo recitals and appearing with major European and American orchs. for many years; gave first performances of several cello concertos commissioned by him to Hindemith, Dukelsky, Castelnuovo-Tedesco, and others. He taught advanced classes at the Curtis Inst. in Philadelphia and later at the Univ. of Southern Calif., Los Angeles; presented a series of trio concerts with Heifetz and Pennario. He was the recipient of honorary D.Mus. degrees from Temple Univ., Columbia Univ., the Univ. of Calif. at Los Angeles, etc. He publ. an autobiographical vol., *Cellist* (N.Y., 1965).

Piatti, Alfredo Carlo, Italian cellist and composer; b. Borgo Canale, near Bergamo, Jan. 8, 1822; d. Crocetto di Mozzo, July 18, 1901. He received his primary musical education from his father, the violinist **Antonio Piatti;** then studied cello at the Milan Cons.; began his concert career in 1838, and in 1843 played with Liszt in Munich; obtained excellent success in England, where he gave annual concerts; from 1859 to 1898 he was a regular performer in the Saturday Popular Concerts of chamber music in London. He combined an excellent technical skill with profound musicianship; in the cello world he occupied a position of artistry and authority comparable with that of Joachim among violinists. He wrote 2 cello concertos, 6 cello sonatas, and a number of solo pieces for cello; also ed. 6 string sonatas by Boccherini and Locatelli and brought out editions of cello methods by Kummer and others.

BIBLIOGRAPHY: M. Latham, *Alfredo Piatti* (London, 1901).

Piccaver, Alfred, English tenor; b. Long Sutton, Lincolnshire, Feb. 15, 1884; d. Vienna, Sept. 23, 1958. He studied at the Metropolitan School in N.Y.; made his operatic debut in Prague in 1907; then continued his studies there and in Milan. In 1910 he deputized at the Vienna court opera in the Italian season; remained in Vienna as a leading lyric tenor until 1937. His repertoire included Don José, Florestan, Walther, Lensky, and Andrea Chenier; he also took part in the first Austrian performance of *La Fanciulla del West* in 1913. He appeared in Chicago (1923–25); in 1924 he sang Cavaradossi and the Duke of Mantua at Covent Garden in London. From 1937–55 he taught voice in London; then returned to Vienna to attend the opening of the new building of the Staatsoper; he remained in Vienna as a voice teacher until his death.

Picchi, Mirto, Italian tenor; b. Florence, March 15, 1915; d. there, Sept. 25, 1980. He studied in Florence; made his operatic debut as Radames in the summer season of 1946 at La Scala in Milan. He subsequently acquired a fine reputation as a singer in a wide repertoire, which included not only the Italian standard operas, but also modern roles, such as Peter Grimes in Britten's opera and Tom Rakewell in Stravinsky's *The Rake's Progress.*

Picchi, Silvano, Argentine composer; b. Pisa, Italy, Jan. 15, 1922. His family emigrated to Argentina while he was a child; he studied composition with Constantino Gaito, Alberto Ginastera, Arturo Luzzatti, Gilardo Gilardi, and Floro M. Ugarte in Buenos Aires. He is the music critic of *La Prensa* in Buenos Aires.

WORKS: *Suite irreverente* for Orch. (1949); *Música para caballos* for Orch. (1952); Piano Concerto (Buenos Aires, July 23, 1967); Violin Concerto (Buenos Aires, Aug. 12, 1968); *Discantus* for Guitar and Bassoon (1968); *Euè,* funeral chant for String Orch. on an African theme (Buenos Aires, March 18, 1969); *Sinfonia breve* (1970); *Mozartiana* for Strings (1971); 2 trios for Oboe, Violin, and Piano; guitar pieces; songs.

Piccinni (Piccini), Niccolò, Italian opera composer; b. Bari, Jan. 16, 1728; d. Paris, May 7, 1800. Piccinni's father was a violinist at the Basilica di San Nicola in Bari, and his maternal uncle, **Gaetano Latilla** (1713–83), a well-known operatic composer.

The innate ability of young Piccinni attracted the attention of the Archbishop of Bari, Muzio Gaeta, who arranged for him to enroll at the Cons. di Sant' Onofrio in Naples; there, at the age of 14, he began studying under the celebrated masters Leo and Durante; he continued as a student for 13 years, and then became an instructor at the same Cons. His first work, *Le Donne dispettose,* an opera buffa in the style made popular in Naples by Logroscino, was produced at the Teatro dei Fiorentini in 1754. He wrote 139 operas; in 1761 alone he produced 10 operas; 7 more followed in 1762. An instinct for the theater made him select librettos rich in dramatic content; his melodic invention was fresh, and his arias were written in a pleasing style eminently suitable to the voice; he elaborated the conventional climactic scenes so that dramatic interest was sustained to the end; he varied the tempos and the harmonies in the ensembles, which further contributed to the general effect. After modest successes in Naples with *Le Gelosie* (1755) and *Il Curioso del proprio danno* (1756), he went to Rome, where he produced his opera *Alessandro nelle Indie* (Jan. 21, 1758); later wrote another setting to the same subject (Naples, Jan. 12, 1774). Piccinni's greatest success in Rome was his comic opera *La buona figliuola,* to Goldoni's libretto, based on Richardson's *Pamela* (Feb. 6, 1760; also produced in Italy as *La Cecchina nubile*); Piccinni wrote a sequel to it, *La buona figliuola maritata* (Bologna, June 10, 1761). Other operas produced in Rome were *Le Contadine bizarre* (Feb. 10, 1763); *Gli Stravaganti* (Jan. 1, 1764; also perf. under the title *La Schiava riconosciuta*); *Il Barone di Torreforte* (Jan. 10, 1765); *La Pescatrice* (Jan. 9, 1766); *Antigone* (1770); *Le finte gemelle* (Jan. 2, 1771). His fortunes declined with the rising popularity in Rome of a powerful rival, Anfossi; not wishing to compete, Piccinni returned to Naples, where he staged his opera *I Viaggiatori* with excellent success. Piccinni's historical role was destined to be played on the international scene in Paris, where he went with his family in Dec. 1776. His arrival in Paris precipitated one of the most famous controversies in music history, the "querelle célèbre," which was in essence a continuation of the "guerre des bouffons" of 1752. In the later case, the Parisian public was sharply divided into 2 warring factions, one supporting the Italian operatic art as practiced by Piccinni, and the other championing the operatic realism of Gluck. Piccinni himself had the highest regard for Gluck, and never encouraged the frenzied outbursts of the "Piccinnistes." Gluck left Paris in 1780; at his death in Vienna (1787) Piccinni made plans to organize annual concerts in Paris in Gluck's memory, but failed to find financial support for his project. Piccinni's first opera in French, *Roland* (Jan. 27, 1778), had considerable success; he continued to use French librettos, producing several operas in close succession, of which the following were fairly well received: *Le Fat méprisé* (Paris, May 16, 1779); *Atys* (Paris, Feb. 22, 1780); *Iphigénie* (Paris, Jan. 23, 1781; fairly successful, despite the fact that Gluck's masterpiece on the same subject was produced 2 years

before); *Didon* (Fontainebleau, Oct. 16, 1783; his most enduring work; separate arias have been reprinted many times); *Le Dormeur éveillé* (Paris, Nov. 14, 1783); *Le Faux Lord* (Paris, Dec. 6, 1783); *Pénélope* (Fontainebleau, Nov. 2, 1785). In 1778 Piccinni became director of the Italian troupe in Paris; in 1784 he was appointed *maître de chant* at the newly founded Ecole Royale de Chant et de Déclamation Lyrique in Paris, but lost this position after the Revolution and returned to Naples, where he subsisted on a small pension granted him by the King of Naples; in 1798 went back to Paris, where he was received with public honors and given a purse of 5,000 francs for immediate necessities; an honorary position of 6th inspector was granted to him by the Paris Cons. (formerly the Ecole Royale de Chant). But Piccinni was too ill for active life; he retired to Passy, where he spent the last months of his life. *La Cecchina* was revived in Bari on his bicentenary, Feb. 7, 1928. A complete list of Piccinni's operas is given by A. Cametti under the title "Saggio cronologico delle opere teatrali di Niccolò Piccinni," in *Rivista Musicale Italiana,* 8 (also separately, Turin, 1901).

BIBLIOGRAPHY: Ph. Coquéau, *Entretiens sur l'état actuel de l'opéra de Paris* (Paris, 1779; a discussion of the relative merits of Piccinni and Gluck in dialogue form); P.L. Ginguené, *Notice sur la vie et les ouvrages de Nicolas Piccinni* (Paris, 1800); G. Desnoiresterres, *Gluck et Piccinni* (Paris, 1872); E. Thoinan, *Notes bibliographiques sur la guerre musicale des Gluckistes et Piccinnistes* (Paris, 1878); H. Curzon, *Les Dernières Années de Piccinni à Paris* (Paris, 1890); H. Abert, "Piccinni als Buffokomponist," *Jahrbuch Peters* (1913); G. de Napoli, "Nicola Piccinni nel secondo centenario della nascità," *Rivista Musicale Italiana* (1928); A. Parisi, "Intorno al soggiorno di Nicola Piccinni in Francia," ibid. (1928); A. Della Corte, *Piccinni* (Bari, 1928); P. La Rotella, *Niccolò Piccinni* (Bari, 1928); N. Pascazio, *L'Uomo Piccinni e la "Querelle célèbre"* (Bari, 1951). See also A. Loewenberg, *Annals of Opera*.

Pichl, Wenzel, Bohemian violinist and composer; b. Bechin, Sept. 23, 1741; d. Vienna, Jan. 23, 1805. He studied violin with Pokorny and composition with Seeger in Prague. In 1777 he was appointed chamber composer to Archduke Ferdinand at Milan; went with him to Vienna in 1796; also supplied musical entertainment to Viennese noblemen; he died during a concert at the palace of Prince Lobkowitz. He wrote about 700 works, including 13 operas; some 20 masses; 89 symphs. (of which 66 were publ.); 13 serenades (3 of which were publ.); a great number of concertos for violin and other instruments, with orch.; 7 octets; 7 septets; 6 sextets; 21 quintets; 172 string quartets (of which 163 were publ.); 148 works for baryton; piano pieces; etc. His 6 fugues with a fugal prelude for violin alone became fairly popular (reprint, ed. by Kocian and Gardavsky, Prague, 1951).

BIBLIOGRAPHY: R. Kolisko, *Wenzel Pichls Kammermusik* (Diss., Univ. of Vienna, 1918).

Pick-Mangiagalli, Riccardo, Italian composer; b. Strakonice, Bohemia, July 10, 1882; d. Milan, July 8, 1949. He was of mixed Italian and Bohemian parentage; studied at the Cons. Giuseppe Verdi in Milan with Appiani (piano) and Ferroni (composition). He began his career as a successful concert pianist, but later turned exclusively to composition. In 1936 he succeeded Pizzetti as director of the Cons. Giuseppe Verdi, and held this post until his death. WORKS: OPERAS: *Basi e Bote* (Rome, March 3, 1927); *Casanova a Venezia* (La Scala, Milan, Jan. 19, 1929; an orch. suite from it, entitled *Scene carnevalesche,* was perf. in Milan, Feb. 6, 1931); *L'Ospite inatteso* (Milan-Turin-Genoa Radio network, Oct. 25, 1931; the first opera to be given a world premiere by radio anywhere); *Il notturno romantico* (Rome, April 25, 1936). FOR THE DANCE: *Il salice d'oro,* mimo-drama (Milan, Sept. 18, 1918); *Sumitra* (Frankfurt, 1922); *Mahit,* ballet-fable with singing (La Scala, Milan, March 20, 1923); *La Berceuse* (San Remo, Feb. 21, 1933); *Variazioni coreografiche* (San Remo, April 13, 1935). FOR ORCH.: *Sortilegi,* symph. poem for Piano and Orch. (Milan, Dec. 13, 1917); *Notturno e rondo fantastico* (Milan, May 6, 1919); *2 preludi* (Rome, March 1, 1921); *4 poemi* (Milan, April 24, 1925); *Piccola suite* (Milan, June 12, 1927); *Preludio e fuga* (Rome, March 11, 1928); *Preludio e scherzo sinfonico* (Milan, Oct. 22, 1938); Violin Sonata; String Quartet; piano pieces; songs. BIBLIOGRAPHY: G.M. Gatti, *Musicisti moderni d'Italia e di fuori* (2nd ed., Bologna, 1925).

Picka, František, Czech organist, conductor, and composer; b. Strašice, near Hořovice, May 12, 1873; d. Prague, Oct. 18, 1918. Of a musical family, he received a solid education in Prague; held several posts as a chorus master and opera conductor. His opera, *Malíř Reiner (The Painter Reiner),* was produced in Prague (April 28, 1911); the bulk of his works consists of church music, including 9 masses and many other works in an effective contrapuntal style.

Picken, Laurence (Ernest Rowland), English zoologist, biologist, musicologist, and ethnomusicologist; b. Nottingham, July 16, 1909. He studied the natural sciences at Trinity College in Cambridge (B.A., 1931; M.A., 1935; Ph.D., 1935; D.Sc., 1952). In 1944 he became a Fellow at Jesus College; from 1966 to 1976 was engaged at the Faculty of Oriental Studies. In 1944 he went to China as a member of the British Council Scientific Mission; studied the *ch'in* there with Hsü Yuan-Pai and Cha Fu-Hsi; in 1951 took lessons in Turkish music from Nejdet Senvarol in Istanbul. In 1962 he became editor of the *Journal of the International Folk Music Council;* in 1959 was a visiting prof. of zoology at Washington Univ. in Seattle. He publ. the comprehensive study *Folk Musical Instruments of Turkey* (London, 1975); also edited, with E. Dal, *A Select Bibliography of European Folk Music* (Prague, 1966), and publ., with K. Pont, *Ancient Chinese Tunes* (London, 1973).

Picker, Tobias, American composer; b. New York, July 18, 1954. He studied composition with Charles Wuorinen, Elliott Carter, and Milton Babbitt at Columbia Univ. He held the Charles Ives Scholarship from the National Academy of Arts and Letters and a Guggenheim fellowship, as well as 2 grants from the National Endowment for the Arts. Despite his mental involvement with serial music, he refused to abandon tonality, and his first symph. is defiantly described as in C. The rhythms in most of his music are co-functional with melodic progressions. His works include *When Soft Voices Die* for Piano (1977); *Romance* for Violin and Piano (1978); 4 sextets; an Octet (1979); Piano Concerto (1980); Violin Concerto (1981); *Nova* for Piano and Orch. (San Francisco, Dec. 19, 1981); and *Symphony,* in 2 movements, *Rhapsody* and *Variations* (San Francisco, April 23, 1983).

Pierné, (Henri-Constant-) Gabriel, French composer, conductor, and organist; b. Metz, Aug. 16, 1863; d. Ploujean, near Morlaix, July 17, 1937. He studied at the Paris Cons. (1871-82), where his teachers were Marmontel (piano), César Franck (organ), and Massenet (composition); he won first piano prize (1879), first prize for counterpoint and fugue (1881), and first prize for organ (1882); was awarded the Grand Prix de Rome (1882) with the cantata *Edith;* succeeded César Franck as organist at Ste.-Clotilde (1890), where he remained until 1898. In 1903 he was appointed assistant conductor to Colonne, and in 1910 his successor (until 1934); was elected a member of the Académie des Beaux-Arts in 1925. He was a prolific composer, but of his many works only the oratorio *La Croisade des Enfants* and the piano piece *Marche des petits soldats de plomb* became popular. WORKS: OPERAS: *La Coupe enchantée* (Royan, Aug. 24, 1895; revised version, Opéra-Comique, Paris, Dec. 26, 1905); *Vendée* (Lyons, March 11, 1897); *La Fille de Tabarin* (Opéra-Comique, Paris, Feb. 20, 1901); *On ne badine pas avec l'amour* (Opéra-Comique, Paris, May 30, 1910); *Sophie Arnould,* one-act lyric comedy, based on episodes from the life of the famous singer (Opéra-Comique, Feb. 21, 1927). BALLETS AND PANTOMIMES: *Le Collier de saphirs* (1891); *Les Joyeuses Commères de Paris* (1892); *Bouton d'or* (1893); *Le Docteur Blanc* (1893); *Salomé* (1895); *Cydalise et le chèvre-pied* (1919; Paris Opéra, Jan. 15, 1923; as an orch. suite, 1926); *Impressions de Music-Hall,* "ballet à l'Américaine" (Opéra, April 6, 1927); *Giration* (1934); *Fragonard* (1934); *Images,* "divertissement sur un thème pastoral" (Opéra, June 19, 1935); oratorios: *La Croisade des enfants* for Mixed Choir of Children and Adults (Paris, Jan. 18, 1905); *Les Enfants à Bethléem* for Soloists, Children's Chorus, and Orch. (Amsterdam, April 13, 1907); *Les Fioretti de St. François d'Assise* (1912). FOR ORCH.: *Suite de concert* (1883); *Première suite d'orchestre* (1883); *Ouverture symphonique* (1885); *Marche solennelle* (1889); *Pantomime* (1889); *Ballet de cour* (1901); *Paysages franciscains* (1920);

Gulliver au pays de Lilliput (Paris Festival of the International Society for Contemporary Music, June 23, 1937); Piano Concerto (1887); *Scherzo-Caprice* for Piano and Orch. (1890); *Poème symphonique* for Piano and Orch. (1901); *Konzertstück* for Harp and Orch. (1901); *L'An mil,* symph. poem, with Chorus (1897). CHAMBER MUSIC: *Pastorale variée dans le style ancien* for Wind Instruments (also for Piano); *Berceuse* for Violin and Piano; *Caprice* for Cello and Piano; *Canzonetta* for Clarinet and Piano; *Solo de concert* for Bassoon and Piano; *Variations libres et Finale* for Flute, Violin, Viola, Cello, and Harp. FOR PIANO: *15 pièces* (1883); *Etude de concert; Album pour mes petits amis* (containing the famous *Marche des petits soldats de plomb); Humoresque; Rêverie; Ariette dans le style ancien; Pastorale variée; Sérénade à Colombine; Sérénade vénitienne; Barcarolle* for 2 Pianos. SONG CYCLES: *Contes* (1897); *3 Adaptations musicales* (1902); *3 mélodies* (1904); 38 other songs; harp music; folksong arrangements; etc. He contributed the section "Histoire de l'instrumentation" to Lavignac's *Encyclopédie de la musique.*
BIBLIOGRAPHY: W. Weber, *Gabriel Pierné;* H. Eymieu, "Gabriel Pierné," *Revue Illustrée* (Paris, March 15, 1897); L. Schneider, "Gabriel Pierné," *Le Théâtre* (Paris, March, 1901); O. Séré, *Musiciens français d'aujourd'hui* (Paris, 1921).

Pierné, Paul, French composer, cousin of **Gabriel Pierné;** b. Metz, June 30, 1874; d. Paris, March 24, 1952. He studied at the Paris Cons. with Lenepveu and Caussade; wrote a number of works, which were occasionally performed in Paris: the operas *Le Diable galant* (1913), *Emilde,* and *Mademoiselle Don Quichotte;* a ballet, *Le Figurinai;* 2 symphs.; several symph. poems of a programmatic nature (*Jeanne d'Arc, Cléopâtre, De l'ombre à la lumière, Nuit évocatrice, Rapsodie Lorraine,* etc.); choral works; organ pieces; a song cycle, *Schéhérazade;* piano pieces.

Pierpont, James, American composer; b. Boston, 1822; d. Winter Haven, Fla., 1893. In 1857 he publ. a ballad entitled *One Horse Open Sleigh* (composed in 1850); in 1859 it was publ. under the title *Jingle Bells, or The One Horse Open Sleigh* (the original music is reprinted in facsimile in Richard Jackson's *Popular Songs of 19th-Century America,* N.Y., 1976); however, while the original words and the music to the verse are the same as those known today, the original music to the chorus is different. This song did not acquire its wide popularity as a Christmas song until the 20th century; during the 19th century, Pierpont's most popular works were *The Little White Cottage, or Gentle Nettie Moore* (1857); *We Conquer or Die* (1861); and *Strike for the South* (1863); the last 2 of these were rallying songs for the Confederacy during the Civil War (his father, in contrast, was a fiery abolitionist minister). He was the uncle of the millionaire financier John Pierpont Morgan.
BIBLIOGRAPHY: F.W. Lovering, "Jingle Bells: Its Author Was a Rover," *Musical Courier* (Dec.

1959).

Pierre, Constant, French writer on music; b. Paris, Aug. 24, 1855; d. there, Feb. 12, 1918. He was a pupil at the Paris Cons.; played the bassoon in various Paris orchs.; from 1881 devoted himself mainly to musical journalism; was for many years editor of *Le Monde Musical.*
WRITINGS: Essays on *Les Noëls populaires* (1866) and *La Marseillaise* (1887); *La Facture instrumentale à l'Exposition universelle de 1889* (1890); *Les Facteurs d'instruments de musique, les luthiers* (1893); *L'Ecole de chant de l'Opéra (1672–1807)* (1895); *B. Sarrette et les origines du Conservatoire national de musique et de déclamation* (1895); *Notes inédites sur la musique de la Chapelle Royale (1532–1790)* (1899); *Le Conservatoire national de musique et de déclamation* (1900); *Le Concert Spirituel 1725–1790* (compiled in 1900, but left in MS form until publ. in Paris in 1975; very valuable); *Les Hymnes et chansons de la Révolution* (1904); compiled *Musique des fêtes et cérémonies de la Révolution française* (1899; of documentary value).

Pierson (Pearson), Henry Hugh, English composer; b. Oxford, April 12, 1815; d. Leipzig, Jan. 28, 1873. He was educated at Cambridge; in 1839 went to Germany, where he studied music with Tomaschek and Reissiger; entered the circle of Mendelssohn in Leipzig; after a brief term as a prof. of music at the Univ. of Edinburgh (1844), he returned to Germany, where he remained for the rest of his life; married **Caroline Leonhardt,** who wrote the German librettos for his operas. He changed his name from the original form Pearson to Pierson in order to secure proper pronunciation by Germans; used the pen name **Edgar Mansfeldt** for his publ. music.
WORKS: Operas: *Leila* (Hamburg, Feb. 22, 1848) and *Contarini oder Die Verschwörung zu Padua* (Hamburg, April 16, 1872; revived in Dessau, April 24, 1883, under the title *Fenice);* oratorio, *Jerusalem* (Norwich Festival, Sept. 23, 1852); incidental music to the 2nd part of Goethe's *Faust;* overtures to Shakespeare's *Macbeth, As You Like It,* and *Romeo and Juliet.* His music was totally submerged in Mendelssohn's style.
BIBLIOGRAPHY: H.G. Sear, "*Faust* and Henry Hugh Pierson," *Music Review* (1949).

Pietri, Giuseppe, Italian composer; b. Sant'Ilario, Elba, May 6, 1886; d. Milan, Aug. 11, 1946. He studied at the Cons. of Milan and became a successful composer of operettas; the most popular among them were *Addio giovinezza* (Livorno, 1915); *Acqua cheta* (Rome, 1920); *La Donna perduta* (Rome, 1923); *Primarosa* (Milan, 1926); and *Casa mia* (Rome, 1930).
BIBLIOGRAPHY: R. Carli, *Giuseppe Pietri, Cantore dei goliardi* (Livorno, 1956).

Pijper, Willem, renowned Dutch composer; b. Zeist, Sept. 8, 1894; d. Leidschendam, March 18, 1947. He received a rudimentary education from his father, an amateur violinist; then went to the Toon-kunst School of Music in Utrecht, where he studied composition with Johan Wagenaar and piano with Mme. H.J. van Lunteren-Hansen (1911–16); from 1918 to 1923, was music critic of *Utrecht Dagblad,* and from 1926 to 1929, co-editor of the monthly *De Muziek.* He taught theory at the Amsterdam Cons. (from 1918) and was a prof. of composition there from 1925 to 1930; served as director of the Rotterdam Cons. from 1930 until his death. In his music Pijper continued the Romantic tradition of Mahler, and also adopted the harmonic procedures of the modern French School. He postulated a "germ-cell theory," in which an opening chord or motif is the source of all succeeding harmonic and melodic development; he also cultivated the scale of alternating whole tones and semitones, regarding it as his own, not realizing that it was used abundantly by Rimsky-Korsakov (in Russian reference works it is termed the Rimsky-Korsakov scale); the "Pijper scale," as it became known in the Netherlands, was also used by Anton von der Horst and others. During the German bombardment of Rotterdam in May 1940, nearly all of Pijper's MSS were destroyed by fire, including the unpubl. reduced scoring of his large 2nd Symph. (restored in 1961 by Pijper's student Karel Mengelberg); also destroyed was the unpubl. *Divertimento* for Piano and String Orch.

WORKS: FOR THE STAGE: 2 operas ("symphonic dramas"): *Halewijn* (1932–33; Amsterdam, June 13, 1933; revised 1934) and *Merlijn* (1939–45; incomplete; produced posthumously, Rotterdam, June 7, 1952). INCIDENTAL MUSIC: To Sophocles' *Antigone* (1920; revised 1922 and 1926); Euripides' *Bacchantes* (1924) and *The Cyclops* (1925); Shakespeare's *The Tempest* (1930); Vondel's *Phaëton* (1937). FOR ORCH.: 3 symphs.: No. 1, *Pan* (1917; Amsterdam, April 23, 1918); No. 2, for Large Orch. (1921; Amsterdam, Nov. 2, 1922; reduced scoring accomplished by Karel Mengelberg, 1961); No. 3 (1926; Amsterdam, Oct. 28, 1926; his most frequently perf. work); *6 Symphonic Epigrams* (1928; Amsterdam, April 12, 1928); *6 Adagios* (1940; posthumous, Utrecht, Nov. 14, 1951); *Orchestral Piece with Piano* (1915; Utrecht, Dec. 11, 1915; Pijper originally titled this "Piano Concerto No. 1," which caused confusion with his later and only Piano Concerto [1927; Amsterdam, Dec. 22, 1927], which in turn was sometimes incorrectly referred to as "Piano Concerto No. 2" in some catalogues); Cello Concerto (1936; Amsterdam, Nov. 22, 1936; revised 1947); Violin Concerto (1938–39; Amsterdam, Jan. 7, 1940). CHAMBER MUSIC: 2 piano trios (1913–14, 1921); 5 string quartets (1914; 1920; 1923; 1928, 1946, unfinished); Septet for Wind Quintet, Double Bass, and Piano (1920); Sextet for Wind Quintet and Piano (1922-23); Trio for Flute, Clarinet, and Bassoon (1926–27); Wind Quintet (1928–29); 2 violin sonatas (1919, 1922); 2 cello sonatas (1919, 1924); Flute Sonata (1925); Sonata for Solo Violin (1931). FOR PIANO: *Theme with 5 Variations* (1913); *3 Aphorisms* (1915); 3 sonatinas (1917, 1925, 1925); *3 Old Dutch Dances* (1926); Sonata (1930); 2-piano Sonata (1935). FOR VOICE AND ORCH.: *Fêtes galantes,* after Verlaine, with Mezzo-soprano (1916; Schweningen, Aug. 2, 1917); *Romance sans paroles,* after

Verlaine, with Mezzo-soprano (1919; Amsterdam, April 15, 1920); *Hymne,* after Boutens, with Bass-baritone (1941–43; Amsterdam, Nov. 1945). FOR VOICE AND PIANO: *8 vieilles chansons de France* (1918); *8 Noëls de France* (1919); *8 Old Dutch Love Songs* (1920; revised 1943); *8 Old Dutch Songs,* in 2 sets (1924, 1935). FOR A CAPPELLA CHORUS: *Heer Halewijn* (1920) and *Heer Danielken* (1925). He also wrote a *Passepied* for Carillon (1916) and made orchestrations and arrangements of Haydn, Mozart, etc.; publ. 2 collections of articles: *De Quinten-Cirkel* (Amsterdam, 1929) and *De Stemvork* (Amsterdam, 1930).

BIBLIOGRAPHY: M.D. Calvocoressi, "Willem Pijper," *Monthly Musical Record* (1924); Cor Backers, *Nederlandse Componisten van 1400 tot op onze tijd* (The Hague, 1941; new ed., 1948; pp. 123–31); A.L. Ringer, "Willem Pijper and the Netherlands School of the 20th Century," *Musical Quarterly* (Oct. 1955); W.C.M. Kloppenburg, *Thematisch-bibliografische Catalogus van de Werken van Willem Pijper* (Amsterdam, 1960); J. Wouters, "Willem Pijper," *Sonorum Spectrum,* 30 (Spring 1967); H. Ryker, *The Symphonic Music of Willem Pijper* (Diss., Univ. of Washington, 1971); M. Flothuis, "Willem Pijper: An Unharmonious Figure in an Unharmonious Age," *Key Notes,* 3 (1976).

Piket, Frederick, American composer; b. Constantinople, Jan. 6, 1903; d. Long Island, N.Y., Feb. 28, 1974. He was a son of an Austrian physician resident in Turkey; attended the Vienna State Cons. and later studied in Berlin with Franz Schreker. In 1940 he emigrated to America, settling in N.Y. WORKS: Overture, *Curtain Raiser for an American Play* (Minneapolis, Dec. 30, 1948); Piano Concerto; Violin Concerto; Saxophone Concerto; Concerto for String Orch.: orch. suite, *The Funnies* (after "Superman" and "Little Orphan Annie"); *Sea Charm* for Chorus a cappella; *Legend and Jollity* for 3 Clarinets; *Reflection and Caprice* for 4 Clarinets; Woodwind Trio; numerous choral works for the Jewish service.

Pilarczyk, Helga, German soprano; b. Schöningen, March 12, 1925. She studied piano and aspired to a concert career; then took voice lessons and sang in operetta. She found her true vocation in opera; made her debut at Braunschweig in 1951; was a member of the Hamburg State Opera from 1953 until 1968. She made a specialty of modern music; sang Schoenberg's dramatic monologue *Erwartung,* and the leading parts in Alban Berg's *Wozzeck* and *Lulu* as well as in works by Stravinsky, Prokofiev, Dallapiccola, Honegger, Krenek, and others. She appeared as a guest artist at the Bavarian State Opera in Munich, the Vienna State Opera, La Scala in Milan, the Paris Opéra, Covent Garden in London, and the Metropolitan Opera in N.Y. (debut, Feb. 19, 1965, as Marie in *Wozzeck*); publ. an interesting essay, *Kann man die moderne Oper singen?* (Hamburg, 1964).

Pilati, Mario, Italian composer; b. Naples, Oct. 16,

1903; d. there, Dec. 10, 1938. He studied at the Naples Cons.; was an instructor there (1930–38).

WORKS: *Notturno* for Orch. (1923); *La sera* for Women's Voices and Orch. (1926); Flute Sonata (1926); *Il battesimo di Cristo* for Soli, Chorus, and Orch. (1927); Piano Quintet (1928); Violin Sonata (1929); Cello Sonata (1929); String Quartet (1930); piano pieces; also transcriptions for piano of works by Pizzetti and Casella.

BIBLIOGRAPHY: G. Gavazzeni, "M. Pilati," in his *Il suono è stanco* (Bergamo, 1950).

Pilkington, Francis, English composer; b. c.1570; d. Chester, 1638. He received a B.Mus. degree at Lincoln College, Oxford, in 1595. He became a lay clerk (or conduct) at Chester Cathedral in 1602, and then a minor canon in 1612. After taking Holy Orders, he was made a "full minister" on Dec. 18, 1614. He was active in the Cathedral choir, and was precentor there from 1623 until his death. He also held other curacies in Chester, including his principal charge at St. Bridget's from 1616.

WORKS: *The First Booke of Songs or Ayres of 4. Parts: with tableture for the lute or orpherian, with the violl de gamba* (London, 1605; the versions for 4 voices with lute were publ. in *The Old English Edition*, XVIII–XX, London, 1897–98; the versions for voice and lute were publ. in E.H. Fellowes, ed., *The English School of Lutenist Song Writers*, London, 1920–32; revised by T. Dart, 1971, in *The English Lute-Songs*); *The First Set of Madrigals and Pastorals of 3. 4. and 5. parts* (London, 1613–14; ed. by E.H. Fellowes in *The English Madrigal School, A Guide to Its Practical Use*, London, 1926; revised by T. Dart, 1959, in *The English Madrigalists*); *The Second Set of Madrigals, and Pastorals, of 3. 4. 5. and 6. Parts: apt for violls and voyces* (London, 1624; ed. by E.H. Fellowes in *The English Madrigal School . . .*, London, 1926; revised by T. Dart, 1958, in *The English Madrigalists*. See also B. Jeffery, ed., *Francis Pilkington: Complete Works for Solo Lute* (London, 1970). He also contributed 2 songs to Sir William Leighton's collection *The Teares or Lamentacions of a Sorrowful Soule* (1614).

BIBLIOGRAPHY: E.H. Fellowes, *English Madrigal Verse, 1588–1632* (London, 1920; 3rd ed., revised and enlarged, 1967); idem, *The English Madrigal Composers* (London, 1921; 2nd ed., 1948); R. Newton, "The Lute Music of Francis Pilkington," *Lute Society Journal*, I (1958).

Pillois, Jacques, French-American composer and pedagogue; b. Paris, Feb. 14, 1877; d. New York, Jan. 3, 1935. He was a student of Widor and Vierne at the Paris Cons.; upon graduation, taught at various schools in Paris. In 1927 he went to the U.S. and was on the faculty of N.Y. Univ. (1927–30) and later of Smith College. He wrote some attractive pieces of chamber music and songs, under the pen name **Jacques Desky.**

Pimsleur, Solomon, American pianist and composer; b. Paris (of Austrian-Jewish parents), Sept. 19, 1900; d. New York, April 22, 1962. He was taken to the U.S. as a child in 1903; studied piano privately; took music courses at Columbia Univ., but graduated in English literature (M.A., 1923); also studied with Rubin Goldmark. He gave numerous piano recitals in the U.S. His compositions, in a Romantically flavored and technically competent idiom, include *Ode to Intensity,* a "symphonic ballad" (N.Y., Aug. 14, 1933); *Overture to Disillusionment; Meditative Nocturne* for Orch.; 3 string quartets; Piano Trio; Piano Quintet; Violin Sonata; Cello Sonata; many piano pieces with imaginative titles (*Impulsive Sonata; Tranquil Sonata; Reflective Sonata; Mournful Prelude and Melodious Fugue;* etc.); *Shakespearean Sonnet Symphony* for Chorus and Orch. His projected opera, *Diary of Anne Frank,* remains unfinished.

Pincherle, Marc, noted French musicologist; b. Constantine, Algiers, June 13, 1888; d. Paris, June 20, 1974. He studied music in Paris with Pirro, Laloy, and Rolland; served in both world wars; was taken prisoner of war in June 1940 and was interned in Germany until March 1941. He taught the history of violin playing at the Ecole Normale; was artistic director of the Société Pleyel (1927–55) and president of the Société Française de Musicologie (1948–56). As a musicologist, he devoted his energy mainly to the history of violin music.

WRITINGS: *Les Violonistes compositeurs et virtuoses* (Paris, 1922); *Feuillets d'histoire du violon* (Paris, 1927; 2nd ed., 1935); *Corelli* (Paris, 1933); *Les Musiciens peints par eux-mêmes* (160 letters of famous composers from his own autograph collection; Paris, 1939); *Antonio Vivaldi et la musique instrumentale* (2 vols., Paris, 1948); *Les Instruments du quatuor* (Paris, 1948; 3rd ed., 1970); *L'Orchestre de chambre* (Paris, 1948); *Jean-Marie Leclair l'aîné* (Paris, 1952); *Petit lexique des termes musicaux d'usage courant* (Paris, 1953; 2nd ed., 1973); *Corelli et son temps* (Paris, 1954; Eng. trans. as *Corelli, His Life, His Work,* N.Y., 1956); *Vivaldi* (Paris, 1955; Eng. trans., N.Y., 1957); *Fritz Kreisler* (Geneva, 1956); *Albert Roussel* (Geneva, 1957); *Histoire illustrée de la musique* (Paris, 1959; 2nd ed., 1962; in Eng., N.Y., 1959); *Le Monde des virtuoses* (Paris, 1961; in Eng., N.Y., 1963; also in German, Rumanian, and Japanese); *Musical Creation* (Washington, D.C., 1961); *L'orchestra da camera* (Milan, 1963); *Le Violon* (Paris, 1966; 2nd updated ed., 1974).

Pingoud, Ernest, Russian-born Finnish composer; b. St. Petersburg, Oct. 14, 1888; d. Helsinki, June 1, 1942. He studied piano in St. Petersburg with Siloti; then went to Leipzig, where he took courses in music history with Hugo Riemann and in composition with Max Reger. In 1918 he settled in Finland, where he served as managing director of the Helsinki Phil. Orch. (1924–42). In his music he was influenced by the Russian modern school, particularly by Scriabin, from whom he acquired his predilection for mystical titles, often in French (*La Flamme éternelle, Le Chant d'espace,* etc.).

WORKS: For Orch.: *Prologue* (1916); *Confessions*

(1916); *La Dernière Aventure de Pierrot* (1916); *Diableries galantes "Le fétiche"* (1917); 3 piano concertos (1917, 1921, 1922); *Hymnejä yölle* (*Hymns to the Night;* 1917); *Kuolemantanssi* (*Danse macabre*) for Chorus and Orch. (1918); 5 *Sonnets* for Chamber Orch. (1918); *Ritari peloton ja moitteeton* (*The Knight without Fear or Reproach*), an "adventure" for Orch. (1918); *Mysterium* (1919); *Flambeaux éleints* (1919); *Chantecler* (1919); *Le Sacrifice* (1919); 3 symphs. (1920, 1920, 1923–27); *Profeetta* (*The Prophet;* 1921); *Cor ardens* (1927); *Narcissos* (1930); *Le Chant d'espace* (1931; revised 1938); *Suurkaupungin kasvot* (*The Face of the Big City*), ballet for Piano and Orch. (1936); *La Flamme éternelle* (1938–39); *Epäjumala* (*The Idol*), ballet; chamber music; piano works; songs.
BIBLIOGRAPHY: A. Rudnev, "Ernest Pingoud," in *Suomen Saveltajia* (Helsinki, 1945; pp. 487–500).

Pini-Corsi, Antonio, Italian baritone; b. Zara, June 1858; d. Milan, April 22, 1918. He made his debut in Cremona in 1878; then sang throughout Italy; Verdi chose him to create the role of Ford in *Falstaff* at La Scala in Milan in 1893. He also sang at Covent Garden in London (1894–96, 1902–3). On Dec. 25, 1899, he made his N.Y. Metropolitan Opera debut as Dr. Bartolo in *Il Barbiere di Siviglia;* remained on its roster until 1901; returned for the 1909–14 seasons. He was one of the great buffo singers of his day, being famous for his portrayals of Dr. Bartolo, Leporello, Don Pasquale, and others.

Pinkham, Daniel, American composer; b. Lynn, Mass., June 5, 1923. He studied organ and music theory at Phillips Academy in Andover (1937–40) and at Harvard Univ. with A. Tillman Merritt, Walter Piston, and Archibald T. Davison (A.B., 1943; M.A., 1944); had harpsichord lessons with Putnam Aldrich and Wanda Landowska, and studied organ with E. Power Biggs; took summer courses in composition at the Berkshire Music Center in Tanglewood, with Aaron Copland, Arthur Honegger, and Nadia Boulanger; subsequently was music director of King's Chapel in Boston and a member of the faculty of the New England Cons. of Music. The formal design of his music is compact and contrapuntally cohesive; the rhythmic element is propulsive; now and then he astutely applies modernistic devices without disrupting the tonal fabric of the music. WORKS: FOR ORCH.: Piano Concertino (Cambridge, Mass., May 3, 1950); Concertante No. 1 for Violin and Harpsichord Soli, Strings, and Celesta (Boston, Dec. 16, 1954); Concerto for Celesta and Harpsichord Soli (N.Y., Nov. 19, 1955); Violin Concerto No. 1 (Falmouth, Mass., Sept. 8, 1956); Concertante No. 2 for Violin and Strings (Boston, May 9, 1958); Symph. No. 1 (1961); Symph. No. 2 (Lansing, Mich., Nov. 23, 1963); *Signs of the Zodiac* for Orch. and Optional Narrator (1965); Violin Concerto No. 2 (1968); Organ Concerto (1970); *Serenades* for Trumpet and Symphonic Wind Orch. (1979); also *Catacoustical Measures,* composed to test the acoustics at Lincoln Center's Phil. Hall in N.Y. (1962). FOR

CHORUS AND ORCH.: *Wedding Cantata* (Cambridge, Mass., Sept. 22, 1956); *Easter Cantata* (1957); *Christmas Cantata* (*Sinfonia Sacra;* Boston, Dec. 10, 1957); Requiem (1963); Stabat Mater (1964); St. Mark Passion (1965); *Ascension Cantata* for Orch. of Winds and Percussion (1970); *The Passion of Judas* (1976); *The Descent into Hell* (1979); *When God Arose* (1979); *Hezekiah* (1979); *Before the Dust Returns* (1981); *The Conversion of Saul* (1981); various instrumental pieces for piano, organ, harpsichord, etc.; several dozens of adroit instrumental arrangements of Christmas songs.
BIBLIOGRAPHY: W. Smith, "Daniel Pinkham," *American Composers Alliance Bulletin,* VIII (1959); M. Corzine, *The Organ Works of Daniel Pinkham* (Diss., Eastman School of Music, 1979).

Pinnock, Trevor, English harpsichordist; b. Canterbury, Dec. 16, 1946. He was educated at the Royal College of Music in London. In 1966 he organized the Gailliard Harpsichord Trio; also toured Europe with the Academy of St. Martin-in-the-Fields. In 1973 he founded the English Concert, an ensemble specializing in performances of early music on original instruments or their modern copies. He was artist-in-residence at Washington Univ. in St. Louis, Mo., in 1976, 1978, and 1981; also gave solo recitals.

Piños, Alois Simandl, Czech composer; b. Vyškov, Oct. 2, 1925. He studied forestry at the Univ. of Brno (graduating in 1953), music with Petrželka at the Brno Cons. (1948–49) and at the Janáček Academy of Music with Kvapil and Schaeffer (1949–53); attended the summer courses of new music at Darmstadt (1965) and an electronic music seminar in Munich (1966). In 1953 he joined the faculty of the Janáček Academy of Music in Brno. In 1967 he founded in Brno a modern music group, with which he produced a number of works by the local avantgarde, some composed collectively. WORKS: Chamber opera, *The Criers* (1970); audio-visual works: *The Lattice* for Piano and Film (1970); *The Genesis* for Chamber Orch. and Film (1970); *Static Music for Tape,* with Slides (1970); *Czech Dances* for Orch. (1951); *Wedding Suite* for Orch. (1952); Horn Concerto (1953); Concertino for Orch. (1963); *Abbreviations,* 10 pieces for Orch. (1963); Concerto for Orch. and Tape (1964); *Double Concerto* for Cello, Piano, Winds, and Percussion (1965–66; Prague, March 7, 1967); *Chamber Concerto* for Strings (1967); cantata, *Ars amatoria* (1967); *Concerto on the Name B-A-C-H* for Bass Clarinet, Cello, Piano, Strings, and Percussion (1968); symph., *Apollo XI* (1970); *Symphonic Diptych* (1973–74); Cello Sonata (1950); 2 wind quintets (1951, 1959); Sonata for Viola and Cello (1960); Piano Trio (1960); Suite for String Trio (1961); *Monologues* for Solo Bass Clarinet (1962); *Caricatures* for Flute, Bass Clarinet, and Piano (1962); String Quartet (1962); *Hunting Music* for Baritone and 4 Horns (1963); *Conflicts* for Violin, Bass Clarinet, Piano, and Percussion (1964); *2 Lyrical Sketches* for Narrator, Flute, and Violin (1964); *4 Lyrical Sketches* for Narrator, Flute, Bass Clarinet, and Piano (1965); *3 Pieces* for Bass Clarinet and Piano (1965); *Pulsus intermissi* for Solo Percussionist (1965); *Ludus floralis,* 5 songs for Baritone, Female Chorus, Percussion, and Tape (1966); *Hyperboles,* 7 pieces for Solo Harp (1966); *Gesta Machabaeorum* for Chorus, Flute, Trumpet, Harp, and Percussion (1967–68); *16 January 1969* for Piano Quintet and Kettledrums (1969); *Dialogues* for Solo Bass Clarinet (1969); *2 campanari* for Bass Clarinet, Piano, and Ringing Instruments (1971); *Be Beaten* for Solo Percussionist (1972); *Sonata Concertante* for Cello and Piano (1974); *Power of Love* for Baritone and String Quartet (1974); *Composition for 3* for Flute, Clarinet, and Marimbaphone (1975); *Acquaintance,* to advertising texts, to poems for Soprano, Bass-baritone, and Guitar or Harpsichord (1975); *Paradoxes* for Piano (1965); *2–3–1,* 3 pieces for Piano (1969); *Esca* for Prepared Piano (1971); several tape pieces, including *Home* (1972–73) and *Speleophony* (1976); songs; choruses. Piños publ. *Tónové skupiny* (*The Tone Groups;* Prague, 1971; contains a German-language résumé), intended as a preamble to a projected work, *Composition and Tone Groups.*

Pinsuti, Ciro, celebrated Italian singing teacher and composer; b. Sinalunga, near Florence, May 9, 1829; d. Florence, March 10, 1888. His talent developed so rapidly that at 11 he was elected an honorary member of the Accademia Filarmonica of Rome. Taken to England soon after by Henry Drummond, he studied the piano under C. Potter, and the violin under Blagrove; returned to Bologna in 1845, and studied at the Liceo, also privately with Rossini, soon becoming assistant teacher of a piano class. In 1848 he went back to England; was appointed a prof. of singing at the Royal Academy of Music in 1856. He divided his time between London and Italy; brought out an opera, *Il Mercante di Venezia,* at Bologna (Nov. 9, 1873); another, *Mattia Corvino,* at Milan (1877); and a 3rd, *Margherita,* at Venice (1882). In 1871 he represented Italy at the opening of the London Exhibition, for which he composed the hymn *O people of this favoured land.* As a recipient of the order of the Italian Crown, he was styled "Cavaliere" Pinsuti. Besides his operas, he wrote some 200 songs to Eng. and Italian texts.

Pinto, Alfredo, Italian-Argentine composer; b. Mantua, Oct. 22, 1891; d. Buenos Aires, May 26, 1968. He studied piano with Longo and composition with De Nardis in Naples; then went to Buenos Aires, where he became active as a pianist and conductor. He wrote the operas *La última esposa, o Sheherazade* and *Gualicho* (Buenos Aires, 1940); symph. poems: *Nostalgias* (1929); *Eros* (1930); *Rebelión* (1939); numerous piano pieces, choruses, and songs.

Pinto, Octavio, Brazilian composer; b. São Paulo, Nov. 3, 1890; d. there, Oct. 31, 1950. He was trained as an architect; built apartment houses in Brazil; also studied piano with Isidor Philipp. In 1922 he married the Brazilian pianist **Guiomar Novães;** Villa-Lobos wrote his suite *Prole do bébé* for their chil-

dren. Pinto publ. a number of effective piano miniatures, of which *Scenas infantis* (1932) and *Children's Festival* (1939) are best known.

Pinza, Ezio (baptismal name, **Fortunio**), celebrated Italian bass; b. Rome, May 18, 1892; d. Stamford, Conn., May 9, 1957. The family moved to Ravenna when he was an infant; he studied engineering; also was active in sports. He began to study voice at the age of 18 with Ruzza and Vizzani, at the Cons. of Bologna; served in the Italian artillery during World War I; made his opera debut as Oroveso in *Norma* in Soncino (1914); then sang for 3 seasons at La Scala in Milan; was selected by Toscanini for the leading part in the world premiere of Boito's *Nerone* (May 1, 1924). He made his American debut at the Metropolitan Opera House as Pontifex Maximus in Spontini's *La Vestale* (Nov. 1, 1926) and remained on its staff until 1947; appeared also in San Francisco, Chicago, etc.; sang in Europe and in South America; his most celebrated roles were Méphistophélès in Gounod's *Faust,* Don Giovanni, and Boris Godunov. In 1949 he appeared as a musical comedy star in *South Pacific,* and immediately became successful in this new career; also appeared in films. R. Magidoff edited *Ezio Pinza: An Autobiography* (N.Y., 1958).

Pipelare, Matthaeus, Flemish composer; b. c.1450; d. c.1512. He was active in Antwerp; was engaged as master of the choirboys in 's-Hertogenbosch (1498–1500). His style has a certain affinity with that of Pierre de la Rue. His extant works include 9 masses and a number of motets and chansons.

BIBLIOGRAPHY: R. Cross, "The Life and Works of Matthaeus Pipelare," *Musica Disciplina* (1963).

Pipkov, Lubomir, noted Bulgarian composer; b. Lovec, Sept. 19, 1904; d. Sofia, May 9, 1974. He studied piano at the Bulgarian State Cons. in Sofia (1923–26); then took courses in composition with Nadia Boulanger and Paul Dukas at the Ecole Normale de Musique in Paris (1926–32). Returning to Bulgaria, he occupied several administrative posts, including the directorship of the Sofia Opera Theater (1944–47). His style of composition is determined by the inherent asymmetry of Bulgarian folk songs; there is a similarity in his compositions with those of Bartók, resulting from common sources in Balkan and Macedonian music; his harmonic investiture is often polytonal or polymodal.

WORKS: 3 operas: *The 9 Brothers of Yanina* (1932; Sofia, Sept. 19, 1937); *Momchil* (1939–44; Sofia, April 24, 1948); *Antigone 43* (1961–62; Ruse, Dec. 23, 1963); *Oratorio for Our Time* (1959; Plovdiv, Dec. 18, 1959); 2 cantatas: *The Wedding* (1934) and *Cantata of Friendship* (1958); Concerto for Winds, Percussion, and Piano (1930); 4 symphs.: No. 1 (1939–40); No. 2 (1954); No. 3 for Strings, Trumpet, 2 Pianos, and Percussion (1965); No. 4 for String Orch. (1970); *Heroic Overture* (1950); *Journey through Albania,* variations for String Orch. (1950); Violin Concerto (1951); Piano Concerto (1954); *Symphony-Concerto* for Cello and Orch. (1963; Moscow, April 20, 1964);

Concerto for Clarinet and Chamber Orch. (1966); *The Partisan's Grave* for Trombone and String Orch. (1970); 3 string quartets (1928, 1948, 1966); 2 violin sonatas (1929, 1969); Piano Trio (1930); Piano Quartet (1939); Sonata for Solo Violin (1969); *Tableaux et études métrorythmiques* for Piano (1972); *Suggestions printanières* for Piano (1972); choruses; songs.

BIBLIOGRAPHY: K. Iliev, *Lubomir Pipkov* (Sofia, 1958).

Pirani, Eugenio, Italian pianist and composer; b. Bologna, Sept. 8, 1852; d. Berlin, Jan. 12, 1939. A pupil of Colinelli at the Bologna Liceo Musicale, he graduated in 1869; then studied in Berlin with Th. Kullak (piano) and Kiel (composition); taught in Kullak's Academy, 1870–80; also toured Italy (1873, 1876), England, Germany, France, and Russia. He lived in Heidelberg till 1895, then settled in Berlin. He publ. concert studies and many pieces for piano solo; songs; duets; etc.; also *Die Hochschule des Klavierspiels*, op. 88 (in German and Eng.) and *Secrets of the Success of Great Musicians* (Philadelphia, 1922).

Pires, Filipe, Portuguese composer; b. Lisbon, June 26, 1934. He studied piano with Mendes and composition with Croner de Vasconcelos at the Lisbon Cons. (1946–54); then went to Germany, where he attended classes at the College of Music and Theater in Hannover (1957–60). Returning to Portugal, he taught composition at the Oporto Cons. (1960–70) and at the Lisbon Cons. (1972–75); subsequently worked in an electronic studio in Paris under the direction of Pierre Schaeffer. His own music hews resolutely to the tenets of the cosmopolitan avant-garde.

WORKS: String Quartet (1958); Piano Trio (1960); *Eternal Return* for Baritone and Orch. (1961); *Perspectivas* for 3 groups of Instruments (1965); *Metromonie* for Flute, Viola, and Harp (1966); *Portugaliae Genesis* for Baritone, Chorus, and Orch. (1968; Lisbon, May 21, 1969); *Homo sapiens* for Magnetic Tape (1972); *Dialogues* for 8 Instrumentalists and Tape (1975). He publ. a school manual, *Elementos teóricos de contraponto e cânon* (Lisbon, 1968).

Pirogov, Alexandr, Russian bass; b. Riazan, July 4, 1899; d. Bear's Head island, on the Oka River, June 26, 1964. He studied voice at the Moscow Phil. Inst. and simultaneously attended classes in history and philology at Moscow Univ. In 1924 he joined the Bolshoi Theater, remaining on its roster until 1954. He specialized in the Russian operatic repertoire; his performance of the role of Boris Godunov received a prize in 1949; also notable were his interpretations of Méphistophélès in *Faust* and Don Basilio in *Il Barbiere di Siviglia*. His 2 brothers, Grigori (1885–1931) and Mikhail (1887–1933), were also bass singers.

Pironkov, Simeon, Bulgarian composer; b. Lom, June 18, 1927. He studied composition with Veselin Stoyanov and Khadzhiev at the Bulgarian State Cons. in Sofia, graduating in 1953; in 1961 was appointed director of the Theater for Youth in Sofia. His music is rhythmically animated, harmonically tense, melodically modal, and instrumentally coloristic.

WORKS: Opera after Brecht, *The Good Man from Sechwan* (1967); Sinfonietta (1952); Symph. for String Orch. (1961); *The Apology of Socrates* for Solo Bass, String Orch., and Percussion (1966); *Movements* for 13 Strings (1967); *Requiem for an Unknown Young Man* for 13 Strings (1968); *Night Music* for Orch. (1968); *3 Songs to Ancient Greek Lyrics* for Voice and Orch. (1971); *Ballet Music in Memory of Igor Stravinsky* for Chamber Orch. (1972); *Music* for 2 Pianos and Orch. (1973; Nuremberg, Jan. 17, 1974); Trio for Flute, Clarinet, and Piano (1949); String Trio (1950); Solo Violin Sonata (1955); 2 string quartets (1960, 1966); *16 Preludes* for Piano (1949).

Pirro, André, distinguished French musicologist; b. St.-Dizier, Haute-Marne, Feb. 12, 1869; d. Paris, Nov. 11, 1943. He was a pupil of his father, an organist; from 1896 he was a prof. at the Schola Cantorum; was also a member of its board of directors; from 1904 he was also a lecturer on the history of music theory at the Ecole des Hautes Etudes Sociales; in 1912 he succeeded R. Rolland as prof. of music history at the Sorbonne.

WORKS: *L'Orgue de J.-S. Bach* (1897; won prize of the Académie des Beaux-Arts; preface by Widor; Eng. trans. by J.W. Goodrich, N.Y., 1902); *J.S. Bach* (1906; 6th ed., 1924; Eng. trans., N.Y., 1957); *Descartes et la musique* (1907); *L'Esthétique de J.-S. Bach* (1907; a most valuable work); *Dietrich Buxtehude* (1913); *Heinrich Schütz* (1913); *Les Clavecinistes* (1925); *La Musique à Paris 1380–1422* (Strasbourg, 1930); "Leo X and Music," *Musical Quarterly* (Jan. 1935); *Histoire de la musique de la fin du XIVᵉ siècle à la fin du XVIᵉ* (Paris, 1940). For Guilmant's *Archives des maîtres de l'orgue* he wrote a number of biographies of early French organists (Titelouze, Daquin, Couperin, Marchand, etc.); contributed valuable essays to various musical publications.

Pirrotta, Nino, eminent Italian musicologist; b. Palermo, June 13, 1908. He studied at the Cons. V. Bellini in Palermo and at the Univ. of Florence; served as librarian and lecturer in music history at the Cons. of Palermo (1936–48) and chief librarian at the Santa Cecilia Academy in Rome. He then went to the U.S.; was a visiting prof. at Princeton Univ. (1954–55), Columbia Univ. (1956), and Harvard Univ. (1956–72); was subsequently on the staff of the Univ. of Rome. His principal fields of research are Renaissance polyphony and Baroque opera; his publications include *Il Sacchetti e la tecnica musicale del trecento italiano* (with E. Li Gotti; Florence, 1935); *Il Codice Estense lat. 568 e la musica francese in Italia al principio dell '400* (Palermo, 1946); *Li due Orfei. Da Poliziano a Monteverdi* (Turin, 1969); "Gesualdo, Ferrara e

Venezia" and "Monteverdi e i problemi dell'opera," in *Studi sul teatro veneto fra Rinascimento ed età barocca* (Florence, 1971).

Pisa, Agostino, Italian music scholar; flourished in Rome c.1600, in which year he was Dr.Jur. there. He publ. the earliest known treatise on conducting, *Breve dichiariazione della battuta musicale* (Rome, 1611); a 2nd augmented edition was publ. in the same year, also in Rome, as *Battuta della musica dichiarata.*
BIBLIOGRAPHY: R. Schwartz, "Zur Geschichte des Taktschlagens," *Jahrbuch Peters* (1907); G. Schünemann, *Geschichte des Dirigierens* (Leipzig, 1913).

Pisador, Diego, Spanish lutenist; b. Salamanca, c.1509; d. after 1557. In 1526 he took minor orders; in 1552 he publ. in Salamanca *Libro de música de vihuela,* containing madrigals, a set of Spanish ballads, and transcriptions of secular and sacred works by Josquin Des Prez and others; the collection is reprinted by A. Morphy in *Les Luthistes espagnols du XVIe siècle.*

Pisari (Pizari), Pasquale, Italian composer; b. Rome, 1725; d. there, March 27, 1778. He was a pupil of Giovanni Biordi; in 1752 was taken into the papal chapel, being a fine bass singer; he wrote most of his sacred works for it, and the MSS are preserved in the archives of the papal chapel; they include several masses, motets, 2 Te Deums for 8 Voices, one Te Deum for 4 Voices (his most remarkable work); also a *Dixit* in 16 parts, for 4 Choirs, and a series of motets for the entire year, written for the Lisbon Court. Padre Martini called Pisari the "Palestrina of the 18th century."

Pischna, Josef, famous Bohemian pianist and pedagogue; b. Erdischowitz, June 15, 1826; d. Prague, Oct. 19, 1896. He was a pupil at the Prague Cons.; taught for many years in Moscow; then at the Prague Cons. His pedagogical work for piano, *60 Exercises,* became a standard method in Europe and has been reprinted in many editions.

Pisendel, Johann Georg, German violinist and composer; b. Kadolzburg, Dec. 26, 1687; d. Dresden, Nov. 25, 1755. He studied violin with Torelli at Ansbach, and music theory with Pistocchi; later (1716) took lessons in Venice from Vivaldi, who dedicated several works to him. In 1710 he succeeded Melchior Hoffmann as leader of the Collegium Musicum in Leipzig; then held the post of violinist in the Dresden court chapel orch. (1712); traveled with the Elector of Saxony to Paris, Berlin, Italy, and Vienna (1714–18); in 1728 became concertmaster in Dresden; in 1731 was appointed to a similar post in the orch. of the Dresden Opera. It seems certain that Bach wrote his partitas for unaccompanied violin for Pisendel. In his own works, Pisendel combined characteristics of German, French, and Italian music. Many of his MSS are extant in the Dresden ar-

chives, among them 8 violin concertos; 3 concertos for Oboes and String Orch.; 2 concerti grossi; a Symph.; 2 solo pieces for Violin, with Bass. A Violin Concerto is reprinted in Denkmäler Deutscher Tonkunst, 29/30.
BIBLIOGRAPHY: A. Moser, *Geschichte des Violinspiels* (Berlin, 1923; 2nd ed., revised and enlarged, 1966–67); H.R. Jung, "Johann Georg Pisendel: Zur 200. Wiederkehr seines Todestages am 25. November," *Musica,* IX (1955); idem, *Johann Georg Pisendel (1687–1755): Leben und Werk* (Diss., Univ. of Jena, 1956).

Pisk, Paul Amadeus, Austrian-American composer, pedagogue, and musicologist; b. Vienna, May 16, 1893. He studied piano with J. Epstein, composition with Schoenberg, orchestration with Hellmesberger, musicology with Guido Adler; received his D.Mus. with the dissertation *Das Parodieverfahren in den Messen des Jacobus Gallus* (1916). From 1922 to 1934 he taught at the Volkshochschule Volksheim in Vienna; in 1925–26 was instructor in music theory at the New Vienna Cons.; in 1931–33 lectured at the Austro-American Cons. in Mondsee, near Salzburg. He also wrote music criticism for the Socialist newspaper *Wiener Arbeiterzeitung;* with Paul Stefan he founded the progressive music journal *Musikblätter des Anbruch.* He was closely associated with Schoenberg, Alban Berg, and Anton von Webern, and espoused the tenets of the New Vienna School, adopting in many of his own works the methods of composition with 12 tones related only to one another. As the dark cloud of ignorance and barbarity fell on Germany and approached Austria, Pisk left Vienna and emigrated to the U.S., in 1936. He occupied with great honor several teaching posts in America; at the Univ. of Redlands, Calif. (1937–51), the Univ. of Texas in Austin (1951–62), and Washington Univ. in St. Louis (1963–72); he also gave courses at summer sessions at the Univ. of Calif., Los Angeles (1966), the Univ. of Cincinnati (1969), and Dartmouth College (1972). In 1973 he settled in Los Angeles; his 90th birthday was celebrated by his many disciples and admirers in 1983. He continued to compose prolifically, accumulating an impressive catalogue of works, mostly for chamber music. He wrote (with Homer Ulrich) *History of Music and Musical Style* (N.Y., 1963); edited masses by Jacobus Gallus for Denkmäler der Tonkunst in Österreich. A Festschrift, *Paul A. Pisk, Essays in His Honor,* edited by J. Glowacki, was published by the Univ. of Texas Press, Austin, in 1966.
WORKS: *Schattenseite,* monodrama, (1931); *American Suite,* ballet (Redlands, Calif., Feb. 19, 1948); *Die neue Stadt,* "cantata for the people" (Vienna, Nov. 1926; on the occasion of completion of a workers' settlement); *Der grosse Regenmacher,* scenic ballad for Narrator and Orch. (1931); *Requiem* for Baritone and Orch. (1942). FOR ORCH.: *Partita* (Prague Festival of the International Society for Contemporary Music, May 17, 1925); *Suite on American Folksongs* for 24 Instruments (1944); *Bucolic Suite* for String Orch. (Saratoga Springs, Sept. 10, 1946); *Rococo Suite,* for Viola and Orch.

(1953); *Baroque Chamber Concerto* for Violin and Orch. (1953); *Canzona* for Chamber Orch. (1954); *3 Ceremonial Rites* (1957–58); *Elegy* for String Orch. (1958); *Sonnet* for Chamber Orch. (1960). CHAMBER MUSIC: *3 Songs with String Quartet* (Salzburg, Aug. 10, 1922); String Quartet (1924); 4 violin sonatas (1921, 1927, 1939, 1977); *Fantasy* for Clarinet and Piano (1925); *Rondo* for Violin and Piano (1932); *Variations on a Waltz by Beethoven* for Violin, Viola, and Guitar (1933); Piano Trio (1933–35); *Moresca Figures* for Violin, Clarinet, and Piano (1934); *Berceuse slave* for Oboe and Piano (1939); *Bohemian Dance Rondo* for Bassoon and Piano (1939); Suite for 4 Clarinets (1939); *Shanty-Boy Fantasy* for Oboe and Piano (1940); *Variations on an Old Trumpet Tune* for Brass Sextet (1942); *Little Woodwind Music* (1945); *Cortege* for Brass Choir (1945); *Variations and Fugue on an American Theme* for Violin and Cello (1946); Clarinet Sonata (1947); Suite for Oboe and Piano (1947); *Introduction and Rondo* for Flute and Piano (1948); *First Suite* for Flute Solo (1950); *Intermezzo* for Clarinet and Piano (1950); *Elegy and Scherzino* for Oboe, 2 Clarinets, and Bassoon (1951); Quartet for 2 Trumpets, Horn, and Trombone (1951); Sonata for Horn and Piano (1953); *Suite* for 2 Flutes (1953); Flute Sonata (1954); *Suite* for Oboe, Clarinet, and Piano (1955); *Eclogue* for Violin and Piano (1955); *Idyll* for Oboe and Piano (1957); String Trio (1958); Woodwind Quintet (1958); Woodwind Trio (1960); *Music* for Violin, Clarinet, Cello, and Bassoon (1962); *Envoi* for 6 Instruments (1964); Duo for Clarinet and Bassoon (1966); *Perpetuum mobile* for Organ and Brass Quartet (1968); *2nd Suite* for Flute Solo (1969); *Suite* for Woodwind and Piano (1970); *Variables* for Clarinet and Piano (1973); *Discussions* for Oboe, Clarinet, Bassoon, Viola, and Cello (1974); Brass Quintet (1976); Sonata for Violin and Piano (1977); *Three Vignettes* for Clarinet and Bassoon (1977); *3 Movements* for Violin and Piano (1978); Trio for Oboe, Clarinet, and Bassoon (1979); *Music* for Oboe and Piano (1982); *Suite* for Solo Cello (1983); also piano pieces; songs.

Pistocchi, Francesco Antonio, founder of the famous School of Singing at Bologna; b. Palermo, 1659; d. Bologna, May 13, 1726. Taken to Bologna while very young, he publ. his first work there in 1667, when he was but 8 years old: *Capricci puerili saviamente composti e passeggiati in 40 modi sopra un Basso da un balletto, per il clavicembalo ed altri instrumenti.* His teacher in theory was G.A. Perti; he studied singing under Padre Vastamigli and B. Monari. As a lad he became maestro at the church of San Giovanni in Monte; later a priest in the Oratorian order; was in the service of the Parma court (1686–95); in 1696–99 was Kapellmeister at the court of Ansbach; and returned to Bologna, via Vienna and Venice, about 1700. There he founded, soon after his return, the first school of music in which vocal instruction was given systematically in the several classes. In this school were trained many eminent singers (Bernacchi, Bertolino da Faenza, Minelli, Pio Fabri, etc.); similar institutions soon sprang up in other Italian cities. Pistocchi was twice elected president of the Accademia Filarmonica (1708, 1710).

Piston, Walter (Hamor), outstanding American composer; b. Rockland, Maine, Jan. 20, 1894; d. Belmont, Mass., Nov. 12, 1976. The family name was originally Pistone; his paternal grandfather was Italian. He received his primary education in Boston; studied painting at the Mass. Normal Art School, graduating in 1916; then took piano lessons with Harris Shaw and studied violin with Fiumara, Theodorowicz, and Winternitz; played in restaurants and places of public entertainment as a youth. During World War I he was in the U.S. Navy; after the Armistice he entered Harvard Univ., graduating in musical subjects summa cum laude in 1924; while at Harvard he conducted concerts of the univ. orch., the Pierian Sodality. For a time he was employed as a draftsman for Boston Elevated Railway. In 1924 he went to Paris on a John Knowles Paine Fellowship, and became a student of Nadia Boulanger; also took courses with Paul Dukas at the Ecole Normale de Musique (1925); returning to the U.S. in 1926, he was appointed to the faculty of Harvard Univ.; in 1944 became a prof. of music; was named prof. emeritus in 1960. As a teacher he was greatly esteemed, not only because of his consummate knowledge of music and pedagogical ability, but also because of his immanent humanity in instructing students whose esthetics differed from his own; among his grateful disciples was Leonard Bernstein. As a composer, Piston followed a cosmopolitan course, adhering to classical forms while extending his harmonic structures toward a maximum of tonal saturation; he was particularly expert in contrapuntal writing. Beginning about 1965, Piston adopted, for the first time, a modified system of 12-tone composition, particularly in initial thematic statements; his Symph. No. 8 and *Variations* for Cello and Orch. are explicitly dodecaphonic. Piston rejected the narrow notion of ethnic Americanism in his music, and stated once that an artist could be as American working in the Library of the Boston Atheneum as roaming the Western prairie; yet he employed upon occasion the syncopated rhythms of jazz. He received Pulitzer Prizes for his Symph. No. 3 and Symph. No. 7, and N.Y. Music Critics Circle Awards for his Symph. No. 2, Viola Concerto, and String Quartet No. 5. He held the degree of D.Mus. *honoris causa* from Harvard Univ.; was elected a member of the National Inst. of Arts and Letters, the American Academy of Arts and Letters, and the American Academy of Arts and Sciences. He traveled little and declined invitations to go to South America and to Russia under the auspices of the State Dept., preferring to live in his house in suburban Belmont, near Boston. His working habits were remarkably methodical; he rarely altered or revised his music once it was put on paper, and his handwriting was calligraphic. With 2 exceptions, he never wrote for voices.

WORKS: FOR THE STAGE: Ballet, *The Incredible Flutist* (Boston Pops, May 30, 1938, Arthur Fiedler conducting; very popular as an orch. suite, first perf.

in Pittsburgh, Nov. 22, 1940, Reiner conducting). FOR ORCH.: *Symphonic Piece* (1927; Boston, March 23, 1928, Koussevitzky conducting); 2 suites: No. 1 (1929; Boston, March 28, 1930, composer conducting) and No. 2 (1947–48; Dallas, Feb. 29, 1948, Dorati conducting); Concerto for Orch. (1933; Cambridge, Mass., March 8, 1934, composer conducting); *Prelude and Fugue* (1934; Cleveland, March 12, 1936); 8 symphs.: No. 1 (1937; Boston, April 8, 1938, composer conducting); No. 2 (1943; Washington, D.C., March 5, 1944; received the N.Y. Music Critics Circle Award, 1945); No. 3 (1947; Boston, Jan. 9, 1948, Koussevitzky conducting; received the Pulitzer Prize, 1948); No. 4 (1950; Minneapolis, March 30, 1951, Dorati conducting); No. 5 (1954; commissioned by the Juilliard School of Music in N.Y. for its 50th anniversary and perf. there, Feb. 24, 1956); No. 6 (1955; for the 75th anniversary of the Boston Symph. and perf. by it, Nov. 25, 1955, Munch conducting); No. 7 (1960; Philadelphia, Feb. 10, 1961, Ormandy conducting; won the Pulitzer Prize, 1961); No. 8 (1964–65; Boston, March 5, 1965, Leinsdorf conducting); Concertino for Piano and Chamber Orch. (CBS Radio, N.Y., June 20, 1937, composer conducting); 2 violin concertos: No. 1 (1939; N.Y., March 18, 1940) and No. 2 (Pittsburgh, Oct. 28, 1960); Sinfonietta (1940–41; Boston, Zighera Chamber Orch., March 10, 1941); *Fanfare for the Fighting French* for Brass Ensemble and Percussion (1942); *Prelude and Allegro* for Organ and Strings (CBS Radio, Boston, Aug. 8, 1943; E. Power Biggs, organist); *Fugue on a Victory Tune* (N.Y., Oct. 21, 1944); *Toccata* (Orch. National de France, Munch conducting, Bridgeport, Conn., Oct. 14, 1948); *Fantasy* for English Horn, Harp, and Strings (1952; Boston, Jan. 1, 1954, Munch conducting); *Serenata* (Louisville, Oct. 24, 1956); Viola Concerto (1957; Boston, March 7, 1958; received the N.Y. Music Critics Circle Award, 1959); Concerto for 2 Pianos and Orch. (1959; Dartmouth Community Orch., Hanover, N.H., July 4, 1964); *3 New England Sketches* (Detroit Symphony Orch. at the Worcester [Mass.] Music Festival, Oct. 23, 1959, Paray conducting); *Symphonic Prelude* (Cleveland, April 20, 1961, Szell conducting); *Lincoln Center Festival Overture* (Philadelphia Orch., inauguration week of Lincoln Center, N.Y., Sept. 25, 1962); *Capriccio* for Harp and String Orch. (1963; First Festival of American and Spanish Music, Madrid, Oct. 19, 1964; Zabaleta, soloist); *Variations on a Theme by E.B. Hill* (1963); *Pine Tree Fantasy* (Portland, Maine, Nov. 16, 1965); *Variations* for Cello and Orch. (1966; London Symph. Orch., N.Y., March 2, 1967; Rostropovich, soloist; Rozhdestvensky conducting); Clarinet Concerto (Dartmouth College, Hanover, N.H., Aug. 6, 1967); *Ricercare* (1967; N.Y., March 7, 1968); *Fantasia* for Violin and Orch. (1970; Dartmouth College, March 1973); Flute Concerto (1971; Boston, Sept. 21, 1972); *Bicentennial Fanfare* (1975); Concerto for String Quartet, Wind Ensemble, and Percussion (Portland, Oct. 26, 1976). FOR BAND: *Tunbridge Fair: Intermezzo* (1950). CHAMBER MUSIC: *3 Pieces* for Flute, Clarinet, and Bassoon (1926); Flute Sonata (1930); *Suite* for Oboe and Piano (1931); 5 string quartets (1933, 1935, 1947, 1951, 1962; No. 5 received the N.Y. Music Critics Circle Award, 1964);

2 piano trios (1935, 1966); Violin Sonata (1939); *Interlude* for Viola and Piano (1942); Quintet for Flute and Strings (1942); *Partita* for Violin, Viola, and Organ (1944); Sonatina for Violin, and Harpsichord or Piano (1945); *Divertimento* for 9 Instruments (N.Y., May 18, 1946); Duo for Viola and Cello (1949); Piano Quintet (1949); Wind Quintet (1956); Sextet for Strings (1964); Piano Quartet (1964); *Souvenir* for Flute, Viola, and Harp (1967); *Ceremonial Fanfare* for Brass Ensemble (1969; for the Metropolitan Museum of Art); Duo for Cello and Piano (1972); *3 Counterpoints* for Violin, Viola, and Cello (1973). FOR VOICE: *Carnival Song* for Men's Chorus and 11 Brasses (1938; Harvard Glee Club, Cambridge, Mass., March 7, 1940); *Psalm and Prayer of David* for Chorus, Flute, Clarinet, Bassoon, Violin, Viola, Cello, and Double Bass (1958). FOR PIANO: Sonata (1926); *Passacaglia* (1943); *Improvisation* (1945). FOR ORGAN: *Chromatic Study on B.A.C.H.* (1940).

WRITINGS: *Principles of Harmonic Analysis* (Boston, 1933); *Harmony* (N.Y., 1944; 4th ed., 1978); *Counterpoint* (N.Y., 1947); *Orchestration* (N.Y., 1955).

BIBLIOGRAPHY: N. Slonimsky, "Walter Piston," in Henry Cowell's *American Composers on American Music* (1933); Israel Citkowitz, "Walter Piston—Classicist," *Modern Music* (Jan.–Feb. 1936); Elliott Carter, "Walter Piston," *Musical Quarterly* (July 1946); Madeleine Goss, *Modern Music Makers* (N.Y., 1952); W. Austin, "Piston's Fourth Symphony," *Music Review* (May 1955); Oliver Daniel and others, *Walter Piston* (N.Y., 1964); David Ewen, *American Composers* (N.Y., 1982); Linda I. Solow, ed., *The Boston Composers Project: A Bibliography of Contemporary Music* (Cambridge, Mass., 1983).

Pitfield, Thomas Baron, English composer; b. Bolton, April 5, 1903. He studied at the Royal Manchester College of Music; was an instructor there from 1947 to 1973; also studied engineering and painting; was a book illustrator; wrote verse. In his music, he adopts a simple style, in a folk-song manner. His works include a cantata, *The Rhyming Shopman;* a Piano Concerto; various pieces of chamber music; a set of piano pieces under the general title *Ballet in Education;* also various pieces of humorous content, among them *Planibestiary,* "a zoological sequence in space" for Voices, Piano, and Percussion (1966); *Adam and the Creatures,* "Morality with Music" for Speaker, Chorus, Organ, and Percussion (1968).

BIBLIOGRAPHY: A.K. Holland, "T.B. Pitfield," *Monthly Musical Record* (May 1939); D. Ellis, "Thomas B. Pitfield at 80," *Musical Times* (April 1983).

Pitoni, Giuseppe Ottavio, Italian composer of church music; b. Rieti, March 18, 1657; d. Rome, Feb. 1, 1743. He began music studies at 5, under Pompeo Natale in Rome; at 8 was chorister at S. Giovanni de' Fiorentini, later at the SS. Apostoli, and studied counterpoint under Foggia. In 1673 he was maestro di cappella at Terra di Rotondo; in 1674, at Assisi; in 1676, at Rieti; finally, in 1677, he became maestro at the Collegio di S. Marco in Rome, retaining this post until death, though simultaneously engaged at S. Apollinare (1686), S. Lorenzo in Damaso (1686), S. Giovanni in Laterano (1708–19), and St. Peter's (1719); also in some minor Roman churches. He was an excellent teacher, and taught after the same method by which he himself rose to eminence as a composer, e.g., the writing out in score of Palestrina's works to study his style. Durante, Leo, and Feo were his greatest pupils. As a composer, he cultivated a distinct feature of the Roman school, the writing in many parts.

WORKS: His finest works are a *Dixit a* 16 for 4 Choirs, still sung yearly at St. Peter's during Holy Week, and 3 masses based on popular airs: *Li Pastori a Maremme, Li Pastori a Montagna,* and *Mosca.* He composed over 40 masses and Psalms *a* 12 for 3 Choirs and over 20 *a* 16 for 4 Choirs; Psalms and motets *a* 24 and 36; and left an unfinished Mass *a* 48. He also wrote for St. Peter's a set of masses, vespers, etc., for the entire year, besides motets *a* 3–8, hymns, etc. Only one book of motets, *a* 2, was publ. (Rome, 1697) during his lifetime, probably because he insisted that music written for one church should not be performed in any other. Proske, in his *Musica divina* (1855–61), printed a Mass, a Requiem, 6 motets, a Psalm, a hymn, and a *Christus factus est.* In the Vatican Library is a MS work by Pitoni, *Notizie dei maestri di cappella sì di Roma che oltramontani, 1500–1700;* and a fragmentary *Guida armonica* (108 printed pages).

BIBLIOGRAPHY: M. Tiberti, "G.O. Pitoni," *Musica d'Oggi* (1941); S. Gmeinwieser, "Giuseppe Ottavio Pitoni (1657–1743)," *Allgemeine Musikzeitung,* XXXII (1975); idem, *Giuseppe Ottavio Pitoni: Thematisches Werkverzeichnis* (Wilhelmshaven, 1976).

Pitt, Percy, English conductor and composer; b. London, Jan. 4, 1870; d. there, Nov. 23, 1932. He studied in Germany with Jadassohn and Reinecke at the Leipzig Cons. and with Rheinberger at the Akademie der Tonkunst in Munich. Returning to England in 1893, he became active primarily as a theater conductor; was conductor of the Beecham Opera Co. (1915–18), artistic director of the British National Opera Co. (1920–24), and music director of the British Broadcasting Corp. (1922–30). He wrote some instrumental music; his *Ballade* for Violin and Orch. (1900) was performed by Ysaÿe.

BIBLIOGRAPHY: J.D. Chamier, *Percy Pitt of Covent Garden and the BBC* (London, 1938).

Pittaluga, Gustavo, Spanish composer; b. Madrid, Feb. 8, 1906. He studied law at the Univ. of Madrid and composition with Oscar Esplá; was a member of the Grupo de los 8 in Madrid and of the Paris group of modern musicians, Triton (1935); from 1936 to 1939 was a member of the staff of the Spanish Embassy in Washington, D.C. (for the Loyalist government); then remained in the U.S.; was in charge of the film library at the Museum of Modern Art in N.Y. (1941–43).

WORKS: *La Romería de los Cornudos,* ballet after F.G. Lorca (Madrid, 1933); zarzuela, *El Loro* (Madrid, 1933); *Concerto militaire* for Violin and Orch. (Barcelona, 1933); *Petite suite* for 10 Instruments (Paris, 1935; also for Piano as *3 pièces pour une espagnolade*); *Capriccio alla romantica* for Piano and Orch. (Paris, 1936); *6 danses espagnoles en suite* for Piano (1935); *Vocalise-étude* for Voice and Piano (1932); *Berceuse* for Violin and Piano (1935); *Ricercare* for Violin, Clarinet, Bassoon, and Trumpet (1934); *5 canciones populares* for Chorus and 10 Instruments (1939); *Habanera* for Violin and Piano (1942); *Lament for Federico García Lorca* for Narrator and Orch. (1942).

Pittrich, George Washington, German composer; b. Dresden, Feb. 22 (Washington's birthday; hence the selection of Christian names), 1870; d. Nuremberg, April 28, 1934. He studied at the Dresden Cons. with Draeseke and others; was active as a conductor in Dresden (1890–98), Hamburg (1898), Cologne (1899–1901), Frankfurt (1901–4), Dresden (1904–12), and Berlin (from 1912). He wrote a one-act opera, *Marga* (Dresden, Feb. 8, 1894); incidental music to Shakespeare's *As You Like It* and to several classical German plays; Christmas musical plays: *Der Stern von Bethlehem, Der Zauberschleier, Mäusekönigin;* Clarinet Concerto; Fantasia for Piano, with String Orch.; many songs.

Pitz, Wilhelm, German conductor; b. Breinig, Aug. 25, 1897; d. Aachen, Nov. 21, 1973. He studied violin; then became a member of the Städtisches Orch. in Aachen in 1913; in 1933 he was appointed chorus master of the Stadttheater in Aachen, and also held the post of first conductor there from 1947 to 1960; from 1951 served as chorus master of the Bayreuth Festivals; from 1957 led the Philharmonia Chorus of London; retired from his various choral posts in 1971. He was made an honorary Officer of the Order of the British Empire in 1970.

Pitzinger, Gertrude, Bohemian contralto; b. Mährisch-Schönberg, Aug. 15, 1904. She studied music with Joseph Marx at the Vienna Singakademie, and voice with various teachers. After several concert tours in central Europe she went to the U.S., and gave a N.Y. recital on Jan. 17, 1938, with excellent success; she specialized in German lieder; her repertoire included some 400 songs. She taught singing at the Hochschule für Musik in Frankfurt (1960–73) before retiring.

Piutti, Karl, German composer; b. Elgersburg, April 30, 1846; d. Leipzig, June 17, 1902. He studied at the Leipzig Cons.; in 1880 became organist at the Thomaskirche. He wrote a great number of organ works, including a *Hochzeit Sonata;* about 200 organ preludes; Psalms and motets a cappella; songs. He also publ. *Regeln und Erläuterungen zum Studium der Musiktheorie.*

Pixis, Johann Peter, German pianist; b. Mannheim, Feb. 10, 1788; d. Baden-Baden, Dec. 22, 1874. Of a musical family (his father and his brother were good musicians), he received his primary education at home; went to Munich in 1809, and to Paris in 1823; established himself as a teacher, and was greatly esteemed in the Paris musical world. In 1840 he settled in Baden-Baden, where he continued to teach.

WORKS: Operas: *Almazinde, oder Die Höhle Sesam* (Vienna, April 11, 1820); *Bibiana, oder Die Kapelle im Walde* (Aachen, Oct. 8, 1829); etc.; Piano Concerto; Piano Quartet; Piano Quintet; String Quintet; 7 piano trios; sonatas, variations, transcriptions, etc., for piano solo; altogether about 150 opus numbers. Together with Liszt, Chopin, Thalberg, Czerny, and Herz, he wrote *Hexaméron* (a series of brilliant variations on the march from Bellini's opera *I Puritani*).

BIBLIOGRAPHY: R. Batka, "Aus J.P. Pixis Memoiren," in *Kranz. Gesammelte Blätter über Musik* (Leipzig, 1903).

Pizzetti, Ildebrando, eminent Italian composer; b. Parma, Sept. 20, 1880; d. Rome, Feb. 13, 1968. He studied piano with his father, Odvardo Pizzetti, in Parma and composition with Tebaldini at the Cons. of Parma, graduating in 1901; then devoted himself to composition and teaching; was on the faculty of the Cons. of Parma (1907–8); then on the Cons. of Florence (1908–24), where he became director in 1917; in 1924–36 was director of the Milan Cons.; then taught at the Santa Cecilia Academy in Rome (1936–58); from 1947 to 1952 was also its president. In 1914 he founded (with G. Bastianelli) in Florence a modernistic periodical, pointedly named *Dissonanza*, to promote the cause of new music. In 1930 he made a trip to the U.S. to attend the performance of his *Rondo veneziano*, conducted by Toscanini with the N.Y. Phil.; in 1931 Pizzetti conducted his opera *Fra Gherardo* at the Teatro Colón in Buenos Aires. Pizzetti's music represents the Romantic trend in modern Italy; in his many works for the theater, he created the modern counterpart of medieval mystery plays; the mystical element is very strong in his own texts for his operas. He employed astringent chromatic harmony, but the mainstream of his melody flows along pure diatonic lines.

WORKS: OPERAS: *Fedra* (Milan, March 20, 1915); *Debora e Jaele* (1915–21; Milan, Dec. 16, 1922); *Lo Straniero* (1922–25; Rome, April 29, 1930); *Fra Gherardo* (1925–27; Milan, May 16, 1928; Metropolitan Opera, N.Y., March 21, 1929; his most famous work); *Orsèolo* (Florence, May 5, 1935); *L'Oro* (1938–42; Milan, Jan. 2, 1947); *Vanna Lupa* (Florence, May 4, 1949); *Ifigenia* (1950; Turin Radio, Oct. 3, 1950; first stage perf., Florence, May 9, 1951); *Cagliostro* (La Scala, Milan, Jan. 24, 1953); *La Figlia di Jorio* (Naples, Dec. 4, 1954); *Assassinio nella cattedrale*, after T.S. Eliot's *Murder in the Cathedral* (La Scala, Milan, March 1, 1958; highly acclaimed); *Il calzare d'argento*, sacred play (La Scala, Milan, March 23, 1961); *Clitennestra*, music drama (La Scala, Milan, March 1, 1965). INCIDENTAL MUSIC: To Gabriele d'Annunzio's tragedy *La Nave* (1905) and *La Pisanella* (Paris, June 11, 1913); to *La sacra rappresentazione di Abram e d'Isaac,* mystery play (Florence, 1917; expanded and produced in Turin, March 11, 1926); to *Agamemnon* by Aeschylus (Greek Theater, Syracuse, 1930); to *The Trachiniae* by Sophocles (Greek Theater, Syracuse, 1936); to *As You Like It* by Shakespeare (Florence, May, 1938). CHORAL WORKS: *Requiem* (1922); *De profundis* (1938); *Cantico di gloria* for Treble Chorus, 24 Wind Instruments, 2 Pianos, and Percussion (1948). FOR ORCH.: *Ouverture per una farsa tragica* (1911); *Concerto dell'estate* (N.Y., Feb. 28, 1929, Toscanini conducting); *Rondo veneziano* (N.Y., Feb. 27, 1930; as a ballet, La Scala, Milan, Jan. 8, 1931); Cello Concerto (Venice, Sept. 11, 1934); Symph. in A (1940); Violin Concerto (Rome, Dec. 9, 1945); *Canzone di beni perduti* (Venice, Sept. 4, 1950). CHAMBER MUSIC: 2 string quartets (1906, 1933); Piano Trio (1925); Violin Sonata (1919); Cello Sonata (1921). FOR PIANO: *Da un autunno già lontano* (1911; 3 pieces); *Sonata 1942;* songs: *Tre liriche* (1904); *Sera d'inverno* (1906); *I Pastori*, to a poem by Gabriele d'Annunzio (1908; his most remarkable song); *La Madre al figlio lontano* (1910); *Erotica* (1911); *2 canti popolari greci* (1912); *3 sonetti di Petrarca* (1922); *E il mio dolore io canto* (1940). Also, transcriptions of madrigals by Gesualdo, of Veracini's sonatas for violin and continuo, etc.

WRITINGS: *La musica dei Greci* (Rome, 1914); *Musicisti contemporanei* (Milan, 1914); *Intermezzi critici* (Florence, 1921); *Paganini* (Turin, 1940); *Musica e dramma* (Rome, 1945); *La musica italiana dell' 800* (Turin, 1946); numerous articles in Italian magazines.

BIBLIOGRAPHY: R. Fondi, *I. Pizzetti e il dramma musicale italiano d'oggi* (Rome, 1919); G.M. Gatti, "I. Pizzetti," *Musical Quarterly* (Jan., April 1923); M. Pilati, *"Fra Gherardo" di Pizzetti* (Milan, 1928); M. Rinaldi, *L'arte di Pizzetti e "Lo Straniero"* (Rome, 1930); G. Tebaldini, *I. Pizzetti* (Parma, 1931); G.M. Gatti, *I. Pizzetti* (Turin, 1934; in Eng., London, 1951; a basic biography, with a list of works; new Italian ed., 1955); G. Bastianelli, "Pizzetti," *Il Convegno* (March–April 1921); M. Castelnuovo-Tedesco, "I. Pizzetti e la sua musica corale," *Il Pianoforte* (Aug. 15, 1921; a Pizzetti issue); G. Gavazzeni, *Tre studi su Pizzetti* (Como, 1937); a special Pizzetti number of the *Rassegna Musicale* (Oct. 1940); M. Castelnuovo-Tedesco, "I. Pizzetti," in David Ewen's *The Book of Modern Composers* (N.Y., 1942); a symposium, *Firenze a I. Pizzetti* (Florence, 1947); M. LaMorgia, *La città d'annunziana a Ildebrando Pizzetti: Saggi e note* (Milan, 1958); B. Pizzetti, ed., *Ildebrando Pizzetti: Cronologia e bibliografia* (Parma, 1980).

Pizzi, Emilio, Italian composer; b. Verona, Feb. 1, 1861; d. Milan, Nov. 27, 1940. He studied at the Instituto Musicale at Bergamo and at the Cons. of Milan (with Ponchielli and Bazzini); received first prize for his opera *Lina* (1885); in 1897, was appointed director of the Instituto Musicale at Bergamo; from 1900 lived for some time in London.

WORKS: Operas: *Guglielmo Ratcliff* (Bologna, Oct. 31, 1889); *Gabriella* (world premiere, Boston,

Nov. 25, 1893, with Adelina Patti in the title role); *La Rosalba* (Turin, May 31, 1899); *Vendetta* (in German, Cologne, Dec. 1, 1906; in Italian, as *Ivania,* Bergamo, Sept. 14, 1926); comic opera in Eng., *Bric-à-Brac Will* (London, 1895); *Messa solenne* for Soli, Chorus, and Orch.; Requiem; violin pieces; piano pieces; songs.

Pizzini, Carlo Alberto, Italian composer; b. Rome, March 22, 1905. He studied electrical engineering; then took a course in composition with Respighi at the Santa Cecilia Academy in Rome, graduating in 1929. In 1938 he became a member of the staff of Italian Radio, and was inspector of auditions in 1968–70. He wrote an opera, *Dardanio* (Rome, 1928), and several orch. works, among them *Sinfonia in istile classico* (1930); *Il poema delle Dolomiti* (1931); *Strapaese,* symph. suite (1932); *Al Piemonte,* symph. triptych (1941); *Grotte di Postumia,* divertimento in variation form (1941); *Concierto para tres hermanas* for Guitar and Orch. (1969); also chamber music and piano pieces.

Plaidy, Louis, famous German piano teacher; b. Wermsdorf, Nov. 28, 1810; d. Grimma, March 3, 1874. He began his professional career as a violinist, and performed in public in Dresden and Leipzig; at the same time he took piano lessons from Agthe, and became greatly proficient as a pianist, so that Mendelssohn engaged him in 1843 as a piano teacher at the Leipzig Cons. Plaidy concentrated on the technical problems of piano pedagogy; taught at the Leipzig Cons. until 1865; then continued to give private lessons. He publ. a number of instructive piano studies which are still widely used; his *Technische Studien für das Pianoforte-Spiel* is a standard manual; he also publ. a booklet, *Der Klavierlehrer* (1874; British ed. as *The Pianoforte Teacher's Guide;* American ed., trans. by J.S. Dwight, as *The Piano-Teacher*).

Plamenac, Dragan, eminent Croatian-American musicologist; b. Zagreb, Feb. 8, 1895; d. Ede, the Netherlands, March 15, 1983. He studied jurisprudence at the Univ. of Zagreb and the Univ. of Vienna; then took courses in composition with Franz Schreker at the Vienna Academy of Music and with Vítězslav Novák in Prague. In 1919 he went to Paris and attended lectures at the Sorbonne given by André Pirro; then had a seminar with Guido Adler at the Univ. of Vienna, receiving his Ph.D. there in 1925 with the dissertation *Johannes Ockeghem als Motetten- und Chansonkomponist.* From 1928–39 he taught at the Univ. of Zagreb; after the outbreak of World War II, he came to the U.S., becoming a naturalized American citizen in 1946. In 1947 he received a Guggenheim fellowship; then taught at the Univ. of Illinois, Urbana (1955–63). Plamenac's chief accomplishment was his painstaking and fruitful research into the sources of the music of the Renaissance. He prepared a major edition of the works of Ockeghem in the *Publikationen älterer Musik,* Jg. I/2 (Leipzig, 1927); a 2nd ed., revised in 1959, was publ. in N.Y. as *Masses I–VIII* in the Col-

lected *Works,* I; *Masses and Mass Sections IX–XVI* appeared as vol. II (N.Y., 1947; 2nd ed., 1966).
BIBLIOGRAPHY: G. Reese and R. Snow, eds., *Essays in Musicology in Honor of Dragan Plamenac on his 70th Birthday* (Pittsburgh, 1969).

Planchet, Dominique-Charles, French composer and pedagogue; b. Toulouse, Dec. 25, 1857; d. Versailles, July 19, 1946. He studied at the Ecole Niedermeyer in Paris; was for many years organist at the Cathedral in Versailles; in 1898 was appointed organist at the Ste.-Trinité in Paris; taught at the Ecole Niedermeyer; was active as general secretary of the Société des Compositeurs; in 1905, won the Prix Chartier for chamber music. He wrote an opera, *Le Fils du Croisé* (privately perf. in Versailles, 1885); 2 cello concertos; *Esclavage africain,* cantata for Male Voices; much sacred music; organ pieces; a Piano Trio; a Violin Sonata; songs; contributed the section "L'Art du maître de chapelle" to Lavignac's *Encyclopédie de la musique.* On his chamber music, see the entry in *Cobbett's Cyclopedic Survey of Chamber Music* (London, 1930).

Plançon, Pol (-Henri), famous French bass; b. Fumay, June 12, 1851; d. Paris, Aug. 12, 1914. He was destined by his parents for a commercial career in Paris, but showed a natural vocal ability, and began to study singing with Sbriglia and Duprez; made his operatic debut in Lyons (1877); then appeared in Paris (Feb. 11, 1880); after a season in Monte Carlo, he made a highly successful appearance at the Paris Opéra as Méphistophélès in Gounod's *Faust* (June 25, 1883); sang that role more than 100 times during his 10 seasons at the Opéra, and was regarded as unrivaled in his dramatic delivery and vocal power. On June 3, 1891, he sang Méphistophélès in London; his American debut took place at the Metropolitan Opera House on Nov. 29, 1893, as Jupiter in Gounod's *Philemon et Baucis.* He then resigned from the Paris Opéra and remained a member of the Metropolitan Opera until his retirement in 1908. He had an imposing physique, mobile features, and an innate acting ability. His repertoire consisted of about 50 roles in French, Italian, German, and Eng. In some operas he sang more than one part, as in *Roméo et Juliette* (Capulet and Friar), *Aida* (Ramfis and the King), *Les Huguenots* (St.-Bris and Marcel), etc. Of Wagnerian roles, he sang the Landgrave, King Henry, and Pogner.

Planquette, Jean-Robert, French composer of operettas; b. Paris, July 31, 1848; d. there, Jan. 28, 1903. He studied at the Paris Cons. with Duprato; wrote chansonnettes and "saynètes" for cafés-concerts in Paris; then composed a one-act operetta, *Paille d'avoine* (March 12, 1874), and others. He achieved his first great success with the production of *Les Cloches de Corneville,* a comic opera in 3 acts, at the Folies-Dramatiques (April 19, 1877); it was performed for the 1,000th time there in 1886, and became one of the most popular works of its genre; in Eng., it was given as *The Chimes of Normandy* (N.Y., Oct. 22, 1877; London, Feb. 23, 1878). Other operettas were *Le Chevalier Gaston* (Monte Carlo, Feb. 8, 1879); *Rip Van Winkle* (London, Oct. 14, 1882; very successful); *Nell Gwynne* (London, Feb. 7, 1884); *Surcouf* (Oct. 6, 1887; in Eng. as *Paul Jones*); *La Cocarde tricolore* (Paris, Feb. 12, 1892); *Le Talisman* (Paris, Jan. 20, 1893); *Panurge* (Paris, Nov. 22, 1895); *Mam'zelle Quat'Sous* (Paris, Nov. 5, 1897). A posthumous operetta, *Le Paradis de Mahomet* (orchestrated by Louis Ganne), was produced at the Variétés in Paris on May 15, 1906.

Plantade, Charles-Henri, French composer; b. Pontoise, Oct. 14, 1764; d. Paris, Dec. 18, 1839. As a child, he studied singing and the cello in the Royal School for the "pages de musique"; afterward he took lessons with Honoré Langlé (theory), Hüllmandel (piano), and Petrini (harp). In 1797 he became a singing teacher at the Campan Inst. at St.-Denis, where Hortense de Beauharnais, the future Queen of the Netherlands, was his pupil. He subsequently was in the service of Queen Hortense as her representative in Paris; was a prof. at the Paris Cons. from 1799 to 1807, and again in 1815–16 and 1818–28. From 1812 to 1815 he also held the post of maître de chambre at the Paris Opéra. He received the ribbon of the Legion of Honor from Louis XVIII (1814); from 1816 was music master of the Royal Chapel. Losing his various positions after the revolution of 1830, he retired to Batignolles. He wrote several operas, of which *Le Mari de circonstances* (Opéra-Comique, March 18, 1813) was the most successful; other operas include *Les 2 Sœurs* (May 22, 1792); *Les Souliers mordores* (May 18, 1793); *Au plus brave la plus belle* (Oct. 5, 1794); *Palma, ou Le Voyage en Grèce* (Aug. 22, 1797); *Romagnesi* (Sept. 3, 1799); *Le Roman* (Nov. 12, 1800); *Zoé, ou La Pauvre Petite* (July 3, 1800); *Lisez Plutarque* (Spring 1800); *Bayard à la ferté, ou Le Siège de Mezières* (Oct. 13, 1811). He further composed masses, motets, etc., for the Chapelle Royale; publ. 20 sets of *romances*, 3 books of vocal duets (nocturnes), and a Harp Sonata.

Planté, Francis, French pianist; b. Orthez, Basses-Pyrénées, March 2, 1839; d. St. Avit, near Mont-de-Marsan, Dec. 19, 1934. From 1849 he was a pupil of Marmontel at the Paris Cons.; won first prize after 7 months' tuition. After a course in harmony in Bazin's class (1853), he retired for private study for 10 years, and then reappeared as a pianist of finished technique and style. About 1900 he suddenly vanished from concert life, vowing that he would "never be seen again in public." He created a sensation in 1915 when he was heard again in several concerts in Paris; but, in order to keep his strange vow, he was hidden from the view of the audience by a screen.
BIBLIOGRAPHY: O. Comettant, *Francis Planté* (Paris, 1874); A. Dandelot, *Francis Planté* (Paris, 1920; 3rd ed., 1930); A. Lenoir and Jean de Nahuque, *Francis Planté: Doyen des pianistes* (Paris, 1931).

Plaschke, Friedrich (original name, **Bedřich Plaške**), Czech bass-baritone; b. Jaroměr, Jan. 7, 1875; d. Prague, Feb. 4, 1952. He studied with Leontine von Dotscher and Ottilie Sklenář-Mala in Prague, and then with Karl Scheidemantel in Dresden; made his debut with the Dresden Court (later State) Opera as the Herald in *Lohengrin* in 1900; was on its roster until 1937; during his tenure there, he created the following roles in operas by Richard Strauss: Pöschel in *Feuersnot*, the first Nazarene in *Salome*, Altair in *Die aegyptische Helena*, Waldner in *Arabella*, and Sir Morosus in *Die schweigsame Frau.* He made many guest appearances at Vienna and Munich; also sang at Bayreuth, at Covent Garden in London, and in the U.S. with the German Opera Co. in 1923–24.

Plass, Ludwig, German trombonist and historian of military music; b. Osterode, March 13, 1864; d. Berlin, Sept. 16, 1946. He studied trombone at the Hochschule für Musik in Berlin; in 1893 became solo trombonist of the Royal Chapel; in 1905, court bandleader; collected materials on military music in Germany; wrote 28 pieces for wind instruments; publ. interesting historical essays on the German post horn; also *Bachs Clarintrompeter* (1927); *Was bliesen unsere Reiter?* (1934); etc.

Plasson, Michel, French conductor; b. Paris, Oct. 2, 1933. He studied conducting at the Paris Cons. with Bigot; in 1962 he won first prize at the International Conducting Competition held in Besançon; he then continued his studies with Charles Munch, Leopold Stokowski, Leonard Bernstein, and Erich Leinsdorf. In 1968 he was appointed music director of the Théâtre du Capitole in Toulouse; also made guest conducting appearances in London, N.Y., Tokyo, and other music centers.

Platania, Pietro, Italian composer; b. Catania, April 5, 1828; d. Naples, April 26, 1907. He studied with P. Raimondi at the Naples Cons.; was director of the Palermo Cons. (1863); later maestro di cappella at Milan (1882), and director of the Royal College of Music at Naples (1888).
WORKS: Operas: *Matilde Bentivoglio* (Palermo, 1852); *Piccarda Donati* (Palermo, March 3, 1857); *La vendetta slava* (Palermo, Feb. 4, 1865); *Spartaco* (Naples, March 29, 1891); symph.; *L'Italia;* festival symph., with choruses, to welcome King Umberto in 1878; *Pensiero sinfonico;* Requiem; Psalm 67 for Chorus and Orch.; etc.; publ. *Trattato d'Armonia* (1872).
BIBLIOGRAPHY: F. Guardione, *Pietro Platania* (Milan, 1908).

Plath, Wolfgang, German musicologist; b. Riga, Latvia, Dec. 27, 1930. He studied musicology at the Free Univ. of Berlin with Gerstenberg, and later at Tübingen Univ. (Ph.D., 1958, with the dissertation *Das Klavierbüchlein für Wilhelm Friedemann Bach*). In 1960 he was named co-editor (with Wolfgang Rehm) of the *Neue Mozart-Ausgabe*. His studies of Mozart autographs and texts are valuable; he contributed important articles for the *Mozart-Jahrbuch*.

Plato, great Greek philosopher (427–347 B.C.). He formulated in his *Timaeus* a system of musical harmony, eruditely interpreted by Th.-Henri Martin in his *Études sur le Timée de Platon* (Paris, 1841). Also see R. von Westphal, in his *Harmonik und Melopöie der Griechen* (Leipzig, 1865); von Jan in "Die Harmonie der Sphären" (in *Philogus*, vol. LII); and H. Abert's *Die Lehre vom Ethos in der griechischen Musik* (Leipzig, 1899). Plato's thoughts on music are collected in an essay by Deyk in Weber's *Cäcilia* (1828). Plato likened the movements of music to those of the soul, whose development may therefore be influenced by musical art.
BIBLIOGRAPHY: J. Regner, *Platos Musik-Theorie* (Halle, 1923).

Platti, Giovanni, Italian composer; b. Padua, July 9, 1697; d. Würzburg, Jan. 11, 1763. He was attached to the Würzburg court from 1724 to 1761; was active there as a tenor, violinist, composer, and teacher; was regarded by some music historians as the first composer to employ the classical sonata form, but this contention is debatable.
WORKS: 12 keyboard sonatas by Platti were ed. by L. Hoffmann-Erbrecht (Leipzig, 1953–54); one is included in W.S. Newman, *13 Keyboard Sonatas of the 18th and 19th Centuries* (Chapel Hill, N.C., 1947); a *Miserere* was transcribed by Molinari and performed in Rome (March 15, 1936); a Flute Sonata was ed. by Jarnach (1936).
BIBLIOGRAPHY: F. Torrefranca, "La Creazione della sonata drammatica moderna rivendicata all'Italia: Giovanni Platti, il grande," *Rivista Musicale Italiana*, 17; O. Kaul, *Geschichte der Würzburger Hofmusik im 18. Jahrhundert* (Würzburg, 1924); Fausto Torrefranca, *G.B. Platti e la sonata moderna* (Milan, 1963).

Playford, Henry, English music publisher, son of **John Playford;** b. London, May 5, 1657; d. there, c.1707. He continued his father's trade; his most important publications were *The Theatre of Musick* (with R. Carr; 4 books, 1685–87, described as "the newest and best songs"); *Banquet of Music* (6 books, 1688–92); Purcell's *Orpheus Britannicus* (1698–1702) and his *Ten Sonatas,* with a *Te Deum* and *Jubilate* for St. Cecilia's Day (1697); Blow's *Amphion Anglicus* (1700); and an ode on Purcell's death (1695).

Playford, John, English music publisher; b. Norfolk, 1623; d. London, Nov. 1686. He was in business for 37 years (1647–84); his publishing firm was responsible for the most important music editions of the 17th century; he publ. *The Dancing Master* (1651; 12th ed., 1703; modern ed. by M. Dean-Smith, London, 1958); Hilton's *Catch that catch can* (1652); *Musick's Recreation on the Lyra-Violl* (1652; facsimile ed. by N. Dolmetsch, London, 1960); *Select Musical Ayres and Dialogues* (1653); *Briefe Introduction to the Skill of Musick for Song and Violl* (1654; enlarged ed., 1655, with an essay on "The Art of Descant" by Dr. Thomas Campion, which was revised by Purcell in the 10th ed. of 1683; this very popular work, written by John Playford himself, ran through 19 numbered eds. up to 1730, besides 6 unnumbered eds.); *Psalms and Hymns in Solemn Musick of four parts* (1671); *The Whole Book of Psalms, with the usual Spiritual Song* (1673; 20th ed., 1757); *The Musical Companion* (1673; Book I, catches and rounds; Book II, dialogues, glees, ayres, and songs); *Choice Ayres, Songs and Dialogues to be sung to the theorbo* (5 books, 1676–84); *Musick's Delight on the Cithern* (1666); *The Division-Violin* (variations for violin over a basso ostinato; 2nd ed., 1685).
BIBLIOGRAPHY: F. Kidson, "John Playford and 17th-Century Music Publishing," *Musical Quarterly* (Oct. 1918): J. Pulver, "John Playford," *Music News and Herald* (May 1927); C.L. Day and Eleanor Murrie, *English Song-Books, 1651–1702, and Their Publishers* (London, 1936; reprinted from *Transactions of the Bibliographical Society,* March 1936).

Plaza, Juan Bautista, Venezuelan composer; b. Caracas, July 19, 1898; d. there, Jan. 1, 1964. He went to Rome in 1920 to study at the Pontifical Inst. of Sacred Music; upon returning to Venezuela, became organist of the Cathedral of Caracas. He wrote a number of sacred choral works; also symph. poems: *El picacho abrupto, Vigilia, Campanas de Pascua, Las horas,* etc.; *Fuga criolla* for Orch.; *Sonatina venezolana* for Piano; songs.

Plé-Caussade, Simone, French composer and pianist; b. Paris, Aug. 14, 1897. She studied piano at the Paris Cons. with Alfred Cortot and composition with Georges Caussade, whom she later married; in 1928 she was appointed prof. of harmony and counterpoint at the Paris Cons.; among her students were Gilbert Amy and Betsy Jolas. She wrote a number of orch. and chamber music works in a fine impressionistic manner.

Pleasants, Henry, American music critic; b. Wayne, Pa., May 12, 1910. He studied voice and piano at the Philadelphia Academy of Music and at the Curtis Inst. In 1930 he joined the *Philadelphia Evening Bulletin* as its music critic. He served in the U.S. Army during World War II; then was in the Foreign Service. In 1967 he settled in London, and wrote articles for the *International Herald Tribune.* In 1955 he publ. an acerbic book titled *The Agony of Modern Music,* in which he damned in no uncertain terms all contemporary music as an ear-rasping collection of unpleasant noises produced by arrogant people lacking musical talent. Curiously enough, he found salvation in jazz as a form of folk music. Even more astringent was his 2nd book, *Death of Music? The Decline of the European Tradition and the Rise of Jazz,* publ. in 1961. Both books aroused predictable commotion in the press, which quickly subsided, however, after the sensational element contained in them was exhausted. His subsequent publications purported to convey information and as such were of some validity: *The Great Singers from the Dawn of Opera to Our Own Time* (N.Y., 1966); *Serious Music, and All That Jazz*

(London, 1969); *The Great American Popular Singers* (N.Y., 1974).

Pleshakov, Vladimir, American pianist; b. Shanghai (of Russian parents), Oct. 4, 1934. He studied piano with Russian teachers in Shanghai; in 1949 went to Sydney, Australia, where he took piano lessons with Alexander Sverjensky. In 1955 he emigrated to the U.S. and studied medicine at the Univ. of Calif., Berkeley (A.B., 1958). Turning back to music, he entered Stanford Univ. in the graduate school of music (Ph.D., 1973). He made a special study of piano manufacture in Beethoven's era, and performed on reconstructed pianos at his concerts of classical music.

Plessis, Hubert du, South African composer; b. Malmesbury, Cape Province, June 7, 1922. He studied music with W.H. Bell at Gordonsbai (1942–44) and later at the Rhodes Univ. College in Cape Town; in 1951 he went to London and took courses in composition with Alan Bush and Ferguson at the Royal Academy of Music; returning to South Africa in 1955, he was a lecturer on music at the College of Music in Cape Town and, from 1958, at the Univ. of Stellenbosch. As a composer, he cultivates mainly vocal music; many of his songs are based on South African motifs; among them are the cycles *In den ronde* (1948) and *Die vrou* (1960; to words in Afrikaans, Dutch, and German); he also wrote *Suid-Afrik, Nag en daeraad* for Chorus and Orch. (1966; in Afrikaans).

Pleyel, Camille, French pianist, son of **Ignaz Pleyel;** b. Strasbourg, Dec. 18, 1788; d. Paris, May 4, 1855. He was a pupil of his father; had some success as a composer, but is chiefly noteworthy as a piano manufacturer, entering his father's firm in 1815. Kalkbrenner was his partner for a time; Auguste Wolff, his successor. His wife, **Marie-Félicité-Denise** (b. Paris, Sept. 4, 1811; d. St.-Josse-ten-Noode, March 30, 1875), was also a pianist; she was a pupil of Henri Herz, Moscheles, and Kalkbrenner. In her 15th year, as Mlle. Moke, her virtuosity created a sensation in Belgium, Austria, Germany, and Russia. Before her marriage, Berlioz was in love with her (1830). In 1848–72 she was a prof. of piano at the Brussels Cons.

Pleyel, Ignaz Joseph, remarkable pianist, composer, and piano manufacturer; b. Ruppertsthal, near Vienna, June 18, 1757; d. on his estate near Paris, Nov. 14, 1831. He was the 24th of 38 children in the impoverished family of a schoolteacher; however, he received sufficient education, including music lessons, to qualify for admittance to the class of Wanhal; thanks to the generosity of a princely patron he was apprenticed to Haydn, with whom he lived for 5 years, and was later enabled to go to Rome. In 1783 he became 2nd Kapellmeister at the Strasbourg Cathedral; was advanced to the rank of first Kapellmeister in 1789 but lost his position during the turbulent times of the French Revolution. He conducted the "Professional Concerts" in London during the 1791–92 season, and honored his teacher Haydn by playing a work of Haydn at his opening concert (Feb. 13, 1792). After several years he returned to Strasbourg to liquidate his estate; in 1795 he went to Paris, where he opened a music store which was in business until 1834, and in 1807 founded a piano factory, which manufactured famous French pianos; the firm eventually became known as Pleyel et Cie., and continued to prosper for over a century and a half. The name Pleyel is mainly known through his piano manufacture, but he was a prolific and an extremely competent composer. His productions are so close in style to those of Haydn that specialists are still inclined to attribute certain works in Haydn's catalogues to Pleyel. He composed fully 60 symphs., of which 33 were publ.; more than 60 string quartets, 8 instrumental concertos, and numerous duos, trios, and quintets for strings, as well as 6 quartets for flute and strings, a number of piano and violin sonatas, some songs, and 2 operas: *Ifigenia in Aulide* (produced in Naples on May 30, 1785) and *Die Fee Urgele* for puppet theater, staged in Eszterháza in Nov. 1776. The attribution of Haydn's *6 Feldpartien* to Pleyel remains moot. As a music publisher, Pleyel brought out an Eng. trans. of J.L. Dussek's *Klavierschule,* under the title *Instructions on the Art of Playing the Pianoforte or Harpsichord* (London, 1796); in French as *Méthode pour piano-forte par Pleyel et Dussek;* a German edition appeared in Leipzig in 1804 under Pleyel's name.

BIBLIOGRAPHY: L. de Fourcaud, *La Salle Pleyel* (Paris, 1893); Rita Benton, "A la recherche de Pleyel perdu," *Fontes Artis Musicae* (1970); idem, *Ignace Pleyel: A Thematic Catalogue of His Compositions* (N.Y., 1977).

Plishka, Paul (Peter), American bass; b. Old Forge, Pa., Aug. 28, 1941. He studied at Montclair, N.J., State College; from 1961–65 was a member of the Paterson (N.J.) Lyric Opera; in 1965 he joined the Metropolitan Opera National Co. and sang with it on tour. On June 27, 1967, he made his Metropolitan Opera debut in a concert performance at the Botanical Gardens in the Bronx as the Uncle-Priest in *Madama Butterfly;* he first sang on the Metropolitan's stage as the Monk in *La Gioconda* on Sept. 21, 1967; remained on its roster for many years.

Plonsky, Peter, intransigent American composer and singer of the uncompromising avant-garde; b. Brooklyn, April 23, 1943. He studied composition with Morton Feldman and Earle Brown, who inculcated in him the ultramodern notions of musical indeterminacy within static harmony and relentless monotony. In search of musical timelessness he studied Eastern instruments; traveled in Europe and America collecting symbolic souvenirs; took a handful of earth from the grave of Anton von Webern. At his audiovisual séances, held usually in claustrophiliac emporia, he practiced mental arts; in 1970 he knocked a small radio station off the air by telekinesis of thunderclouds; explored the inner space of his organism to bring about calculated epilepsy by producing a variety of groans, moans, sneezes, wheezes, and tongue clicks; he calls these exhibitions "Mind Emission Vocal Trances" operating "within the astral causality."

WORKS: *Innards* for 9 Performers and 9 Colored Cans of Spray Paint (1963); *Ear Rub,* performed by rubbing the ears to produce sound (1973); autokinetic and hyperkinetic actions.

Plotnikov, Eugene, Russian conductor; b. Odessa, Aug. 29, 1877; d. New York, Sept. 28, 1951. He studied at the Moscow Cons.; was coach and assistant conductor at the Moscow Opera; also conducted at the Paris Opéra (1921). In 1922 he settled in the U.S.; conducted Russian operas in N.Y. and other American cities.

Plowright, Rosalind, English soprano; b. Worksop, May 21, 1949. She studied at the Royal Manchester College of Music; in 1979 she won the International Competition for young singers in Sofia, Bulgaria. She made her debut as Miss Jessel in Britten's opera *The Turn of the Screw* with the English National Opera in 1979; later sang Desdemona and Elisabeth in *Mary Stuart* there. She made her Covent Garden debut as Ortlinde in 1980, and then sang Donna Elvira there in 1983. She subsequently sang Abigaille in Sofia, Bulgaria; Ariadne and Alceste in Bern; Aida, Amelia, and Lenora in Frankfurt; Donna Anna in Munich; and Suor Angelica at La Scala in Milan. She made her American debut with Riccardo Muti and the Philadelphia Orch. in 1982, and then sang in *Il Corsaro* in San Diego.

Plüddemann, Martin, German composer; b. Kolberg, Sept. 29, 1854; d. Berlin, Oct. 8, 1897. He studied at the Leipzig Cons.; later took singing lessons with Hey in Munich; in 1889 was engaged as a singing teacher at the Styrian Music School in Graz. He wrote a number of popular male choruses and ballads; publ. pamphlets of a Wagnerian tendency.

BIBLIOGRAPHY: R. Batka, *M. Plüddemann und seine Balladen* (Prague, 1896); L. Schemann, *M. Plüddemann und die deutsche Ballade* (1930).

Plutarch, famous Greek writer; b. Chaeronea, Boeotia, A.D. 50; d. there, 120. Among his treatises ("Moralia"), one, *De musica,* contains important, historical data concerning music (Latin trans. by R. Volkmann; German trans., with parallel Greek text, and commentary by R. Westphal, 1865; also by Weil and Reinach, with commentary, 1900).

Pocci, Franz, Graf von, composer; b. (of an old Italian noble family) Munich, March 7, 1807; d. there, May 7, 1876. Possessing versatile talents, he wrote plays with music for a puppet theater in Munich, for which he also designed the scenery. He was at his best in pieces for children (*Blumenlieder, Bildertöne für Klavier, Soldatenlieder, Jägerlieder, Alte und neue Kinderlieder,* etc.). His 2 piano sonatas were praised by Schumann for their

poetic expression and fine Romantic spirit. An opera, *Der Alchemist,* was produced in Munich (1840); his grandson F. Pocci publ. a collection, *Franz Poccis Lustiges Komödienbüchlein* (Munich, 1921).

BIBLIOGRAPHY: K. Pastor, *Franz Pocci als Musiker* (Munich, 1932); L. Hirschberg, "F. Pocci, der Musiker," *Zeitschrift für Musikwissenschaft* (1918).

Pochon, Alfred, Swiss violinist; b. Yverdon, July 30, 1878; d. Lutry, Feb. 26, 1959. He made his first public appearance at the age of 11; then went to Liège to study with César Thomson, who engaged him as 2nd violin in his string quartet. In 1902 the philanthropist E. de Coppet asked Pochon to organize a string quartet, later to become famous as the Flonzaley Quartet, so named after Coppet's summer residence near Lausanne; Pochon remained a member, playing 2nd violin, until it was disbanded in 1929. In 1938 Pochon returned to Switzerland; was director of the Cons. of Lausanne until 1957, when he retired. He publ. *A Progressive Method of String-Quartet Playing* (N.Y., 1924).

Podéšť, Ludvík, Czech composer; b. Dubňany, Dec. 19, 1921; d. Prague, Feb. 27, 1968. He studied composition with Jaroslav Kvapil at Brno Univ., graduating in 1948; worked at Brno Radio (1947–51); was music director of the Vit Nejedlý Army Artistic Ensemble (1953–56) and of the music dept. of Czech Television (1958–60).

WORKS: 2 operas: *Tři apokryfy (3 Apocryphas),* to Čapek short stories (1957–58; No. 1, *Staré zlaté časy;* No. 2, *Svatá noc;* No. 3, *Romeo a Julie*), and *Hrátky s čertem (Frolics with the Devil;* 1957–60: Liberec, Oct. 12, 1963); *Smrt (Death),* cantata (1942); *Písně z koncentráku (Songs from the Concentration Camp)* for Baritone and Orch. (1946); *Měsíce (Months)* for Soprano and Orch. (1948; revised 1957–58); Symph. (1947–48; revised 1964); *Raymonda Dienová,* symph. poem (1950–51); 4 suites for Orch. (1951, 1954, 1956, 1960); 2 piano concertos (1951–53, 1958–59); *Jarní Serenáda,* violin concerto (1953); *Advent Rhapsody* for Orch. (1956–57); Concertino for Cimbalom and Orch. (1963); *The Seconds of a Day,* symph. variations (1965); Concertino for 2 Cellos and Chamber Orch. (1965); *Partita* for Strings, Guitar, and Percussion (1967); 2 string quartets (1942); *5 Spring Days* (1948); *Litanie* for String Quartet (1944); Wind Quintet (1946); Violin Sonata (1947); Cello Sonata (1947); *Hojačky* for 2 Clarinets and Piano (1947); *Suite* for Viola and Piano (1955–56); Piano Sonatina (1945); Piano Sonata (1946).

Podešva, Jaromír, Czech composer; b. Brno, March 8, 1927. He studied composition with J. Kvapil at the Janáček Academy in Brno (1947–55); on an American visit attended classes of Aaron Copland at the Berkshire Center in Tanglewood; then had lessons with Dutilleux in Paris; wrote a book of impressions. In 1969 he was appointed to the staff of the Cons. of Ostrava. His music is marked by contrapuntal density and dynamic intensity.

WORKS: Opera, *Opuslíš-li mne (If You Leave*

Me; 1962–63); opera-buffa, *Bambini di Praga* (1968); Piano Concerto (1949); 7 symphs.: No. 1 (1950–51); No. 2 for Strings and Flute (1960–61); No. 3, *Kulmi-nace—Perla na dně: Dvě symfonické paralely myšlenek M. Kundery a B. Hrabala (Culmina-tion—The Pearl at the Bottom: 2 Symphonic Paral-lels to Ideas by M. Kundera and B. Hrabal;* 1966); No. 4 for Chamber Orch. (1966); No. 5, after poems by Yevtushenko and Halas, for Voices and Orch. (1967); No. 6 (1970); No. 7 (1982–83); *Cesta vlasti (Throughout My Homeland;* 1952–53), a 3-part cy-cle of symph. poems: *Kounicovy koleje (Kounic College;* Brno site of a Nazi concentration camp), *V kraj vešla Rudá armáda (The Red Army Enters the Country),* and *Veliký pochod (Great March); Set-kání mládeže (Meeting of Youth)* for Orch. (1956); *Triple Concerto* for Violin, Cello, Piano, and Orch. (1956–57); *Suita notturna* for Orch. (1957); Sin-fonietta for String Orch. (1959); *Slavnost l'Huma-nité,* overture for Strings and Brasses in celebration of the Paris organ of the Communist Party (1961); Flute Concerto (1965); *Dotazník srdce,* chamber cantata for Narrator, Baritone, and 9 Instruments (1965); Concerto for String Quartet and Orch. (1971); Piano Concerto (1973); *Hommage à L. Janá-ček* for Orch. (1977); *Fêtes des perce-neige* for Orch. (1979–80); 5 string quartets (1950; *You Shall Live in Peace,* 1951; 1955; *From the Life of Contemporary Man,* 1959–60; 1965); Clarinet Sonatina (1947–48); 2 violin sonatas (1948, 1958); Piano Trio (1948); Sextet for 2 Violins, Viola, Cello, Clarinet, and Horn (1949); *Poetic Trio* for Violin, Cello, and Piano (1954); *O štastných dětech (Happy Children),* a nonet (1955); Cello Sonatina (1960); Cornet Sonatina (1960); *3 Sonata Studies* for Flute and Piano (1964); Sonata for Soprano and Piano (1967); *5 Pieces* for Violin and Piano (1968); *Suite* for Viola and Piano (1969); Wind Quintet No. 1 (1969–70); *How the Flood Came to Earth* for 5 Children's Choirs, Flute, Trumpet, Cel-lo, and Piano (1971); 2 piano sonatas (1951; *Březen, 1953,* 1953); *4 Miniatures* for Piano (1953); *Rhap-sodiettas* for Piano (1955); numerous a cappella cho-ruses, including *Long Live the Universe,* a quasi sinfonietta (1959–60), and *Sinfonietta to Nature* (1962).

Poglietti, Alessandro, Italian composer. From 1661 he was court organist in Vienna; was killed by the Turks in July 1683 at the siege of Vienna. His compositions include 12 ricercari, suites for harpsi-chord (*On the Hungarian Rebellion, Nightingale Suite,* etc.), and other instrumental pieces, some of which appear in *Toccates et Suites,* publ. by Roger (Amsterdam); also church music. H. Botstiber publ. some reprints in Denkmäler der Tonkunst in Öster-reich, 27 (13.ii); his 12 ricercari are publ. in *Die Or-gel,* II/5–6 (Lippstadt, 1957).

BIBLIOGRAPHY: A. Koczirz, "Zur Lebensge-schichte Alexander Pogliettis," *Studien zur Musik-wissenschaft* (1916).

Pogorelich, Ivo, talented Yugoslav pianist; b. Bel-grade, Oct. 20, 1958. He was sent to Moscow to study; was a student of **Aliza Kezeradze** at the Moscow

Cons.; they were married in 1980. In 1978 he won the Casa Grande Competition in Terni, Italy, and in 1980 won a prize at the International Music Compe-tition in Montreal. He became the center of interna-tional controversy when he was eliminated by the jury of the Chopin Competition in Warsaw before the final rounds; one of the members of the jury, Martha Argerich, resigned in protest and declared that Pogorelich was a "genius"; the Warsaw Music Society awarded him a special prize, and his career skyrocketed. In 1981 he played in London and N.Y., where curiosity enhanced his undoubted merits; his playing reflects his Russian education, particularly in his uninhibited romantic élan, and a most im-pressive technical mastery of the music.

Pohl, Carl Ferdinand, German writer on music; b. Darmstadt, Sept. 6, 1819; d. Vienna, April 28, 1887. During his stay in London (1863–66) he gathered all available facts concerning the residence there of Mozart and Haydn, embodying this information in his publication *Mozart und Haydn in London* (2 vols., 1867). Pohl also began an extended biography of Haydn, but publ. only one vol. (in 2 parts, 1875, 1882; the work was finished by Hugo Botstiber. Oth-er publications: *International Exhibition of 1862. Cursory Notices on the History of the Glass Har-monica* (London, 1862); an interesting historical re-view, *Die Gesellschaft der Musikfreunde ... und ihr Conservatorium* (1871); *Denkschrift aus Anlass des 100 jährigen Bestehens der Tonkünstler-Sozie-tät in Wien* (1871); *Bibliographie der Musiksam-melwerke des 16. und 17. Jahrhunderts* (with R. Eitner and A. Lagerberg; 1877).

Pohl, Richard, German writer on music; b. Leipzig, Sept. 12, 1826; d. Baden-Baden, Dec. 17, 1896. He studied natural sciences and philosophy in Karls-ruhe, Göttingen, and Leipzig; in 1854 went to Wei-mar, where he established a personal friendship with Liszt, and became an ardent advocate of the new German school of music. After Liszt's tempo-rary absence from Weimar, Pohl went to Baden-Baden, where he remained until his death. He was the joint editor of the *Neue Zeitschrift für Musik,* to which he contributed a number of articles under the pseudonym **Hoplit.** He also publ. *Bayreuther Erinnerungen* (1877); *Autobiographisches* (1881); *Franz Liszt* (1883); *Hector Berlioz, Studien und Erinnerungen* (1884); *Die Höhenzüge der musika-lischen Entwickelung* (1888). He possessed a fine literary gift and wrote some poetry; when his first wife, Johanna, a harpist, died in 1870, he wrote a heartfelt memoir, *Meiner theuren Gattin zum Ge-dächtnis;* then married again; his 2nd wife, Luise, compiled Pohl's materials on Berlioz and publ. *Hec-tor Berlioz Leben und Werke* (1900); also a fictional life of Wagner under the title *Richard Wiegand. Episoden aus dem Leben eines grossen Meisters* (1904).

Pohlig, Karl, German conductor; b. Teplitz, Feb. 10, 1858; d. Braunschweig, June 17, 1928. A pupil of Liszt in Weimar, Pest, and Rome, he began his career as a pianist, touring Germany, Austria, Russia, Scandinavia, and Italy; became first Kapellmeister at Graz, then assistant conductor to Mahler at the Vienna Court Opera, and conductor at Covent Garden (1897, 1898); until 1900, was first Kapellmeister at the Hoftheater in Coburg; from 1900–1907, occupied the same post at the Hoftheater in Stuttgart, and was conductor of the symph. concerts; in 1907, was engaged as conductor of the Philadelphia Orch.; directed it for 5 seasons, emphasizing the German repertoire, and particularly Wagner, of whom he was an impassioned admirer.

Poirée, (Elie-Emile-) Gabriel, French writer on music; b. Villeneuve-St.-Georges, near Paris, Oct. 9, 1850; d. Paris, May 25, 1925. He was librarian of the Ste. Geneviève library.
WRITINGS: *L'Evolution de la musique* (1884); an essay on *Tannhäuser* (1895; with Alfred Ernst); *Essais de technique et d'esthétique musicales* (No. 1, Wagner's *Meistersinger*, 1898; No. 2, *Etude sur le discours musical,* 1899; new ed., 1922); *Le Chant gnostico-magique des sept voyelles* (1901; with Ch.-E. Ruelle); *Une Nouvelle Interprétation du second hymne delphique* (1901); *Chopin* (1907); *Wagner* (1921); he also publ. a String Quartet (1908).

Poise, (Jean Alexandre) Ferdinand, French composer of comic operas; b. Nîmes, June 3, 1828; d. Paris, May 13, 1892. He studied at the Paris Cons. with A. Adam and Zimmerman, taking the 2nd Grand Prix de Rome in 1852.
WORKS: Light operas, all produced in Paris: *Bonsoir, voisin* (Sept. 18, 1853); *Le Thé de Polichinelle* (March 4, 1856); *Le Roi Don Pèdre* (Sept. 30, 1857); *Le Jardinier galant* (March 4, 1861); *Le Corricolo* (Nov. 28, 1868); *Les 2 Billets* (Feb. 19, 1870); *Les 3 Souhaits* (Oct. 29, 1873); *La Surprise de l'amour* (Oct. 31, 1877); *L'Amour médicin* (Dec. 20, 1880); *Joli Gilles* (Oct. 10, 1884).

Poissl, Johann Nepomuk, German composer; b. Haukenzell, Bavaria, Feb. 15, 1783; d. Munich, Aug. 17, 1865. He was a pupil of Danzi in Munich; from 1823 to 1847 was in charge of the court music. He wrote about 13 operas; of these the following had a modicum of success: *Athalia* (Munich, June 3, 1814); *Der Wettkampf zu Olympia* (Munich, April 21, 1815); and *Nittetis* (Darmstadt, June 29, 1817); also several oratorios, a Mass, and other works for the church.
BIBLIOGRAPHY: E. Reipschläger, *Schubaur, Danzi und Poissl* (Berlin, 1911); L. Schrott in *Die Musik* (1940; pp. 299–303).

Pokorný, Franz Xaver, Czech composer; b. Königstadt (Mestec Kralove), Dec. 20, 1728; d. Regensburg, July 2, 1794. He joined the court orch. in Oettingen-Wallerstein in 1753; then went to Mannheim, where he studied with Stamitz, Holzbauer, and Richter, returning to Wallerstein after a few months. In 1766 he became a court musician in Thurn and Taxis. In the light of recent research, Pokorný appears as a pioneer in symph. writings; fully 165 symphs. have

been discovered that are probably his; they are all written in the characteristic style of the Mannheim School. The Symph. in E-flat, often credited to G.M. Monn, has been definitely identified as a work by Pokorný.
BIBLIOGRAPHY: J. Murray Barbour, "Pokorný Vindicated," *Musical Quarterly* (Jan. 1963).

Pokrass, Dimitri, Russian composer of popular music; b. Kiev, Nov. 7, 1899. He studied piano at the St. Petersburg Cons. (1913–17); in 1919 he joined the Soviet cavalry during the Civil War, and wrote the song *The Red Cavalry.* This was the first of a series of many songs that have acquired great popularity, among them *If War Comes Tomorrow* (1938), *March of the Tank Brigade, Farewell,* etc. He also wrote music for films.

Polacco, Giorgio, Italian conductor; b. Venice, April 12, 1873; d. New York, April 30, 1960. He studied at first in St. Petersburg, continued in Venice at the Liceo B. Marcello, and graduated from the Cons. G. Verdi in Milan. After conducting in various Italian cities, he was 4 seasons at the Teatro Colón in Buenos Aires, and 7 in Rio de Janeiro. On Nov. 11, 1912, he made his debut at the Metropolitan Opera House; following Toscanini's resignation (1915), Polacco was principal conductor of Italian, French, and Russian works at the Met until 1917; in 1918–30 he was chief conductor of the Italian repertoire of the Chicago Opera Co.

Poldini, Ede (Eduard), Hungarian composer; b. Budapest, June 13, 1869; d. Corseaux, Switzerland, June 28, 1957. He studied at the Budapest Cons., and later with Mandyczewski (theory) and Julius Epstein (piano) in Vienna. In 1908 he went to live at Vevey. In 1935 he received the order of the Hungarian Cross; in 1948 was awarded the Hungarian Pro Arte Prize.
WORKS: Comic operas: *The Vagabond and the Princess* (Budapest, Oct. 17, 1903); *The Carnival Marriage* (Budapest, Feb. 16, 1924; produced in London under the title *Love Adrift,* 1926); *Himfy* (Budapest, 1938). He wrote in all 156 opus numbers, most of them for piano; his *Poupée valsante* became an international favorite; other popular piano pieces are *Arlequinades, Morceaux pittoresques, Images, Moments musicaux, Marionnettes,* etc.

Poldowski (pen name of **Irene Regine Wieniawska;** by marriage, **Lady Dean Paul**), Polish-English composer; b. Brussels, March 18, 1879; d. London, Jan. 28, 1932. She was a daughter of the Polish violinist **Henryk Wieniawski;** her mother was an Englishwoman. She studied at the Brussels Cons. with Gevaert, and later in London with Percy Pitt; married Sir Aubrey Dean Paul; took additional courses in composition with Gédalge and Vincent d'Indy in Paris; began writing songs to French words, in the impressionist style; set to music 21 poems by Paul Verlaine, and 8 poems by others; her songs have been frequently performed at recitals. She also composed *Caledonian Market,* a suite of 8 pieces for Piano; *Berceuse de* *l'enfant mourant* for Violin and Piano; *Tango* for Violin and Piano; *Suite miniature de chansons à danser* for Woodwind Instruments; 2 symph. sketches (*Nocturnes* and *Tenements*); and an operetta, *Laughter*.

Pole, William, English writer on music; b. Birmingham, April 22, 1814; d. London, Dec. 30, 1900. He was a prof. of civil engineering at Univ. College, London; also a student of music at Oxford (Mus.Doc., 1864), and examiner in music for London Univ., 1876–90. He publ. *Philosophy of Music* (1879; 6th ed., 1924); was a contributor to the original edition of *Grove's Dictionary.*

Polgar, Tibor, Hungarian-born Canadian composer and conductor; b. Budapest, March 11, 1907. He studied with Kodály at the Liszt Academy in Budapest, graduating in 1925; lived in West Germany in 1962–64; then emigrated to Canada, and in 1966 became a staff member of the Univ. of Toronto's opera dept.
WORKS: 4 operas: *Kérök* (*The Suitors;* 1954); *A European Lover,* satire (1965); comic operas, *The Troublemaker* (1968); *The Glove,* comic opera for Coloratura Soprano, Tenor, Baritone, Actress-dancer, Actor-dancer, and Piano (1973); *Improvisazione* for 4 Horns (1962); *In Private* for Violin and Viola (1964); cantata, *The Last Words of Louis Riel* (1966–67); *Variations on a Hungarian Theme* for Solo Harp, or for Harp, Strings, and Timpani (1969); *Ilona's 4 Faces* for Saxophone and Piano (1970); Sonatina for 2 Flutes (1971); *Notes on Hungary* for Concert Band (1971); *How Long Shall the Ungodly Triumph?,* Psalm for 6 Voices and Organ (1974); *Annabel Lee* for Voice, Flute, and Harp (1974); arrangements for children's choir and orch.; songs.

Polignac, Armande de, French composer; b. Paris, Jan. 8, 1876; d. Neauphle-le-Vieux (Seine-et-Oise), April 29, 1962. She studied with Gabriel Fauré and Vincent d'Indy; composed the operas *Morgane* and *L'Hypocrite sanctifié;* a dramatic scene, *Judith de Béthulie* (Paris Opéra, March 23, 1916); *La Source lointaine,* Persian ballet (Paris, 1913); *Les 1,001 Nuits,* Arabian ballet (Paris, 1914); *Chimères,* Greek ballet (Paris Opéra, June 10, 1923); *Urashima,* Japanese ballet; also a Chinese ballet for Small Orch., *La Recherche de la vérité; Petite suite pour le clavecin* (1939).

Polin, Claire, American flutist and composer; b. Philadelphia, Jan. 1, 1926. She studied flute with William Kincaid and composition with Vincent Persichetti in Philadelphia, Peter Mennin at the Juilliard School of Music in N.Y., and Roger Sessions and Lukas Foss at the Berkshire Music Center in Tanglewood; held the degrees of B.Mus. (1948), M.Mus. (1950), and D.Mus. (1955); from 1949 to 1964 taught flute playing and composition at the Philadelphia Musical Academy, and from 1958, at Rutgers Univ. A versatile scholar, she wrote and lectured on her ancestral Welsh music, traveled and played flute in distant lands, including Israel,

Russia, and Japan; advanced bold theories, suggesting, for example, a link between Hebrew and Welsh legends, and composed industriously in a cogently modernistic manner, often with recursive ancient modalities.
WORKS: 2 symphs.: No. 1 (1961) and No. 2, "Korean" (1976); *Amphion* for Orch. (1978); 3 string quartets (1953, 1959, 1969); Flute Sonata (1954); *Structures* for Solo Flute (1964); *Consecutivo* for Flute, Clarinet, Violin, Cello, and Piano (1964); *Cader Idris* for Brass Quintet (1970); *The Journey of Owain Madoc* for Brass Quintet and Percussion (1971); *Margoa* for Solo Flute (1972); *Scenes from Gilgamesh* for Flute and String Orch. (1972); *Makimono I* for Flute, Clarinet, Violin, Cello, and Piano (1972); *Makimono II* for Brass Quintet (1972); Sonata for Flute and Harp (1972); *Aderyn Pur* for Flute, Alto Saxophone, and Bird Tape (1973); *Tower Sonata* for Flute, Clarinet, and Bassoon (1974); *Death of Procris* for Flute and Tuba (1974); *Serpentine* for Solo Viola (1974); *Telemannicon* for Solo Oboe and Self-Tape (1975); *Klockwork* for Alto Saxophone, Horn, and Bassoon (1977); *Synaulia* for Flute, Clarinet, and Piano (1977); *Vigniatures* for Harp and Violin (1980); *Felina* for Harp and Violin (1981); *Georgics* for Solo Flute (1982); *Res naturae* for Woodwind Quintet (1982); *Kuequenaku-Cambriola* for Piano and Percussion (1982); *Mythos* for Harp and Strings (1982); *Welsh Bardic Odes* for Soprano, Flute, and Piano (1956); *Canticles* for Male Voices (1959); *Lorca Songs* for Voices and Piano (1965); *Summer Settings* for Solo Harp (1967); *Infinito* for Alto Saxophone, Soprano, Chorus, and Narrator (1973); *Biblical Madrigals* for Chorus (1974); *Windsongs* for Soprano and Guitar (1977); *Isaiah Syndrome* for Chorus (1980); *Out of Childhood* for Solo Piano (1972); *Laissez sonner!* for Solo Piano (1976).

Poliński, Alexander, Polish music historian; b. Wlostow, June 4, 1845; d. Warsaw, Aug. 13, 1916. He was a pupil of Noskowski, Zelenski, and Minchejmer in Warsaw; in 1899 became music critic for the *Warsaw Courier;* from 1904, was a prof. of music history at the Warsaw Cons. He publ. (in Polish) *Concerning Church Music and Its Reform* (1890); *The Song "Bogarodzica" from the Viewpoint of Music* (1903); *History of Polish Music* (1907).

Polívka, Vladimír, Czech pianist and composer; b. Prague, July 6, 1896; d. there, May 11, 1948. He studied piano at the Prague Cons. and took lessons in composition from Vitězslav Novák at the Master School there (1912–18); traveled in Europe, America, and Japan with the violinist Jaroslav Kocián; from 1923 to 1930 taught piano in Chicago. In 1938 he returned to Prague and taught at the Cons.; was chairman of Přítomnost, an association for contemporary music.
WORKS: Chiefly for piano, including *Dni v Chicagu* (*Days in Chicago;* 1926); *3 Impromptus* (1930); *Merry Musik* (1932–33); a tragically colored piano suite, *Krajiny z let okupace* (*Landscapes in the Years of Occupation;* 1941); opera, *Polobůh*

(*The Demi-God;* 1930); melodrama, *A Ballad of a Deaf-Mute* (1936); symph. poem, *Jaro (Spring;* 1918); *Little Symphony* (1921); *Suite* for Viola and Small Orch. (1934); Concerto for Piano and Small Orch. (1934); *Overture* (1942); 2 violin sonatas (1918, 1919); *Suite* for Viola and Wind Quintet (1934); String Quartet (1937); *Divertimento* for Wind Quintet (1939); *Giacona* for Viola and Piano (1944); Viola Sonata (1945); choruses; songs; incidental music. He publ. several collections of children's pieces, collaborated on a book about Smetana (Prague, 1941), and wrote a book of travels, describing his world tour (Prague, 1945).

Polko (née **Vogel**), **Elise,** German singer; b. Leipzig, Jan. 13, 1822; d. Munich, May 15, 1899. She studied with Manuel García in Paris; married a railway engineer, Eduard Polko, under whose name she became professionally known. She publ. a number of semifictional stories about music which became astonishingly popular in Germany during her lifetime.
WRITINGS: *Musikalische Märchen* (3 vols., 1852; also trans. into Eng.); *Faustina Hasse,* a novel about the famous singer (2 vols., 1860); *Alte Herren,* about Bach's predecessors at the Thomaskirche in Leipzig (1865); *Verklungene Akkorde* (1868; several eds.); *Erinnerungen an Felix Mendelssohn-Bartholdy* (1868; in Eng., 1869); *Nicolò Paganini und die Geigenbauer* (1876); *Vom Gesange* (1876); *Aus der Künstlerwelt* (1878); *Der Klassiker der Musik* (1880); *Meister der Tonkunst* (1897).

Pollack, Ben, American drummer and bandleader; b. Chicago, June 22, 1903; d. (suicide by hanging) Palm Springs, Calif., June 7, 1971. He was a drummer with a New Orleans band; in 1924 he organized his own group, with 16-year-old Benny Goodman as clarinetist and Glenn Miller as trombonist and arranger; later he engaged Harry James as trumpeter; he himself presided at the drums. With this stellar personnel he cut a deep swath through jazzland and was dubbed "The Father of Swing." When his career declined, he entered the entertainment business; ran a restaurant in Hollywood; later managed a nightclub in Palm Springs. He left a suicide note, explaining his act as prompted by despondency over personal and financial problems.

Pollak, Egon, Czech-born Austrian opera conductor; b. Prague, May 3, 1879; d. there (of a heart attack during a performance), June 14, 1933. He studied with Knittl at the Prague Cons.; then was engaged in a lifelong career as an opera conductor; from 1901 to 1905 he was assistant to Leo Blech at the Prague Opera; then was principal conductor at the Bremen Opera (1905–10) and at the Leipzig Opera (1910–12). In 1912 he was appointed principal conductor at the Frankfurt Opera. In May and June of 1914 he conducted Wagner's repertoire in Paris and London; in 1915 went to the U.S., where he presented complete cycles of the *Ring des Nibelungen* at the Chicago Lyric Opera during 2 seasons, 1915–17. In 1917 he was able to leave the U.S. with the Austrian diplomatic legation as America entered the war. From 1917 to 1931 he served as Generalmusikdirektor at the Hamburg Opera. In 1928 he conducted German opera in Rio de Janeiro and at the Teatro Colón in Buenos Aires. In 1929–32 he led 2 seasons at the Chicago Opera for 13 weeks during each season. In the winter of 1932 he filled guest engagements in Russia; in 1933 conducted the opera season in Cairo and Alexandria with the ensemble of the Vienna State Opera. On June 14, 1933, he led a performance of *Fidelio,* with Elisabeth Rethberg in the title role, at the Prague Spring Festival, but collapsed and died during the first act.

Pollak, Robert, Austrian violinist; b. Vienna, Jan. 18, 1880; d. Brunnen, Switzerland, Sept. 7, 1962. He studied violin with Carl Flesch and Henri Marteau. In 1906 he went to Geneva, where he taught violin; at the outbreak of World War I he happened to be in Russia, and was interned as an enemy alien. After the war he taught violin at the Moscow Cons.; in 1926 went to the U.S. and taught at the San Francisco Cons.; then went to Japan and taught violin at the Imperial Cons. of Tokyo (1930–37); in 1937 he returned to California and in 1943 became an American citizen.

Pollarolo, (Giovanni) Antonio, Italian composer, son of **Carlo Francesco Pollarolo;** b. Brescia (baptized, Nov. 12), 1676; d. Venice, May 30, 1746. He studied with his father, and became his assistant at San Marco in Venice in 1702; in 1723 he was 2nd maestro di cappella there; in 1740, first maestro. He wrote the operas *Aristeo* (Venice, 1700; not extant) and *Leucippo e Teonoe* (1719), among others.

Pollarolo, Carlo Francesco, Italian organist and composer; b. Brescia, 1653; d. Venice, Feb. 7, 1723. He was a pupil of Legrenzi. In 1665 he became a chorister at San Marco in Venice; in 1690, 2nd organist; in 1692, 2nd maestro di cappella.
WORKS: Oratorios: *Jefte, La Rosinda,* and *Jesabel;* over 85 operas, among them: *La forza della virtù* (1693); *Ottone* (1694); *Gl'Inganni felici* (1696); *Il Faramondo* (1699); *Semiramide* (1713); *Ariodante* (1716). His *Sonata per organo o cembalo* is reprinted in Torchi's *L'arte musicale in Italia* (vol. III).
BIBLIOGRAPHY: O. Termini, *Carlo Francesco Pollarolo: His Life, Time, and Music with Emphasis on the Operas* (Diss., Univ. of Southern Calif., 1970); idem, "Carlo Francesco Pollarolo: Follower or Leader in Venetian Opera?," *Studi Musicali,* VIII (1979).

Pollikoff, Max, American violinist, conductor, and music director; b. Newark, N.J., 1902; d. New York, May 13, 1984. He made his debut as a concert violinist in 1923, in a conventional program, but later devoted himself to contemporary music; he organized the series "Music of Our Time" in 1954, giving periodic concerts at the 92nd Street Y in N.Y.; the series continued until 1974; its programs included works by Charles Ives, Leonard Bernstein, Roger Sessions, Norman Dello Joio, and John Cage.

Pollini, Bernhard (real name, **Baruch Pohl**), German impresario; b. Cologne, Dec. 16, 1838; d. Hamburg, Nov. 27, 1897. A tenor, he made his debut at Cologne in 1858, as Arturo in Bellini's *I Puritani;* later sang baritone roles in an Italian opera troupe, of which he subsequently became manager and artistic director. He then undertook the management of the Italian opera at St. Petersburg and Moscow. In 1874 he became director of the Hamburg City Theater; in 1876 he also became manager of the Altona Theater and in 1894 of the Thalia Theater in Hamburg.

Pollini, Cesare, Cavaliere de', Italian writer on music; b. Padua, July 13, 1858; d. there, Jan. 26, 1912. After legal studies at the Univ. of Padua, he took a 2-year course in music with Bazzini in Milan (1881–83); in 1883–85 he was director of the chief cons. at Padua; resigned to devote himself to writing and composition. He publ. *Terminologia musicale tedesco-italiana; Teoria generale della musica; La musica italiana nelle sue principali fasi storiche;* etc.
 BIBLIOGRAPHY: G. Sacerdoti, *C. Pollini* (Padua, 1912); S. Leoni, *C. Pollini nella vita e nell'arte* (Padua, 1917).

Pollini, Francesco (Giuseppe), Austrian pianist; b. Laibach (Ljubljana), of Italian parents, March 25, 1762; d. Milan, Sept. 17, 1846. He was a pupil of Mozart (who dedicated a violin rondo to him) at Vienna; later of Zingarelli at Milan, where he was appointed a prof. of piano shortly after the opening of the Cons. (1809). He was the first to write piano music on 3 staves, a method imitated by Liszt, Thalberg, and others; a specimen of this style is one of his *32 Esercizi in forma di toccata* (op. 42), a central melody surrounded by passagework for both hands. He publ. a method and many pieces for piano; wrote an opera buffa, *La cassetta nei boschi* (Milan, Feb. 25, 1798).

Pollini, Maurizio, greatly talented Italian pianist; b. Milan, Jan. 5, 1942. He began to study piano as a child at the Verdi Cons. in Milan with Carlo Vidusso and Lonati; gave his first public recital when he was 11; won 2nd prize at the Geneva International Competition when he was 15. In 1960, at the age of 18, he won first prize at the International Chopin Competition in Warsaw, the youngest of 89 contestants. Returning to Italy, he took lessons with Benedetti Michelangeli. On Nov. 1, 1968, he made his U.S. debut in a concert at Carnegie Hall in N.Y.; subsequently appeared with several American orchs.; also gave solo recitals. Because of his signal success in winning the Warsaw Prize, he became known as a Chopin specialist, but he later enlarged his repertoire to include also the moderns. What distinguishes Pollini is his total dedication to music; he seems devoid of a personal desire to excel; his technical equipment is of the highest caliber, but he does not make virtuosity a goal in itself. He is a paragon of modern intellectual pianism.

Pollitt, Arthur W., English organist; b. Liverpool, Nov. 27, 1878; d. there, Feb. 3, 1933. He studied at the Royal College of Music in Manchester, where he became assistant organist at the Cathedral; in 1900–17 was organist at the Liverpool Church and at the School for the Blind; in 1918, became chorus director of the Liverpool Phil. Society. He publ. *The Necessity of Music in a School Curriculum; The Self-reliant Musician; The Enjoyment of Music;* etc.

Pollock, Robert, American composer; b. New York, July 8, 1946. He studied at Swarthmore College and at Princeton Univ. In 1972 he received a Guggenheim Foundation grant. He adopted the serial method of composition early in the game, and became particularly interested in correlating the duration of a note with its pitch; this is the principle on which he built his *Geometrics* for String Quartet and other pieces with abstract titles.

Pololánik, Zdeněk, Czech composer; b. Tišnov, Oct. 25, 1935. He studied organ with J. Černocký and composition with Petrželka and Theodor Schaefer at the Brno Cons. (1957–61). Much of his music represents a curious revival of medieval polyphonic forms, made astringent by abrasive dissonance.
 WORKS: FOR THE STAGE: Opera-oratorio, *Sheer hush-sheereem (Song of Songs;* 1969); 2 ballets: *Mechanism* (1964) and a puppet ballet, *Popelka (Cinderella;* 1966). FOR ORCH.: Sinfonietta (1958); *Toccata* for Double Bass, Brass, Percussion, 2 Harps, Harpsichord, and Piano (1959); *Divertimento* for String Orch. and 4 Horns (1960); 5 symphs.: No. 1 (1961); No. 2 for 11 Wind Instruments (1962); No. 3 for Organ and Percussion Orch. (1963); No. 4 for Strings (1963); No. 5 for Chamber Orch. (1968); *Concentus resonabilis* for 19 Solo Instruments and Tape (1963); *Concerto grosso* for Flute, Guitar, Harpsichord, and String Orch. (1966); Piano Concerto (1966). CHAMBER MUSIC: Sonatina for Cello and Double Bass (1956); *Suite* for Violin and Piano (1957); String Quartet (1958); Double-bass Sonata (1959); *Scherzo contrario* for Violin, Bass Clarinet, and Xylophone (1961); *Little Mythological Exercises* for Narrator and String Quartet (1961); *Musica spingenta I* for Double Bass and Wind Quintet (1961), *II* for Harpsichord and String Quartet (1962), and *III* for Bass Clarinet and 13 Percussion Instruments (1962); *Musica concisa* for Flute, Bass Clarinet, Harpsichord, Piano, and Percussion (1963); *Sonata eccentrica* for Solo Violin (1963); *Preludii dodici (12 Preludes)* for 2 Pianos and Organ (1963); Horn Sonata (1965); *Musica transcurata* for Bass Clarinet and Harpsichord (1967); *Pulsazione* for Percussion (1967). FOR VOICE: Mass for Chorus, Brasses, Harp, and Organ (1956); *Nebuchadnezzar* for Chorus, 3 Trumpets, and 4 Timpani (1960); *Song of the Dead Children* for Chorus, 3 Trumpets, and Percussion (1963); *Vávra* for Children's Chorus and Piano (1964); *Rumor letalis* for Chorus a cappella (1966); *Cantus psalmorum* for Bass, Organ, Harp, and Percussion (1966; Northwestern Univ., Evanston, Ill., April 13, 1969); *Missa brevis* for Children's

Chorus and Organ (1970); songs. FOR PIANO: *Preludes* (1957) and *Variations on 2 Moravian Songs* (1957). FOR ORGAN: *Sonata bravura* (1959); *Sonata gaudia* (1962); *Allegro affanato* (1963).

Polovinkin, Leonid, Russian composer; b. Kurgan, Aug. 13, 1894; d. Moscow, Feb. 8, 1949. He studied at the Moscow Cons. with Glière and Vassilenko; began his career as a composer by writing theater music in Moscow after the Revolution of 1917; adopted a modernistic idiom; emphasized the element of humor. Later he devoted more time to abstract instrumental music; wrote 9 symphs., 4 string quartets, 2 piano trios, several overtures on folk themes, 5 piano sonatas, 24 postludes for Piano, songs.

Pommier, Jean-Bernard, French pianist; b. Bézier, Aug. 17, 1944. He studied piano with Mini Kosloff, Yves Nat, Pierre Sancan, and Eugene Istomin; graduated from the Paris Cons. in 1961 with the first prize; in 1961 he received the first diploma of honor at the International Tchaikovsky Competition in Moscow; then began an international career as a soloist with the major orchs. of the world.

Ponc, Miroslav, Czech violinist, conductor, and composer; b. Vysoké Mýto, Dec. 2, 1902; d. Prague, April 1, 1976. He studied organ with Wiedermann at the Prague Cons. (1920–22) and quarter-tone composition with Alois Hába (1922–24); then went to Berlin and took lessons with Schoenberg. Upon returning to Prague, he studied violin with Josef Suk at the Cons., graduating in 1930; subsequently took lessons in conducting with Scherchen in Strasbourg (1933). After the war he was active mainly as a theater conductor in Prague; wrote a number of scores of incidental music for plays. WORKS: *5 Polydynamic Compositions* for Piano, Xylophone, and String Quartet (1923); song cycles: *A Bad Dream* (1925) and *A Black Swan* (1926); *3 Merry Pieces* for Wind Quintet (1929); *Little Pieces* for Flute or Cello, and Piano (1930); Piano Concertino (1930); *Overture to an Ancient Tragedy,* with the application of quarter-tones in the Greek enharmonic mode (Prague, Feb. 18, 1931); Nonet (1932); *Osudy (The Fates),* 2 antique ballet pictures (1935); *Suite* for Piano with 2 manuals tuned in quarter-tones (1935); String Trio (1937); *3 Intermezzi* from Molière's play *Le Malade imaginaire* (1938).

Ponce, Manuel María, distinguished Mexican composer; b. Fresnillo, Dec. 8, 1882; d. Mexico City, April 24, 1948. He studied piano with his older sister; in 1904 went to Europe, where he took lessons in composition with Enrico Bossi at Bologna and in piano with Martin Krause in Berlin. Upon his return to Mexico, he taught piano at the National Cons. He gave a concert of his compositions in Mexico on July 7, 1912, which included a Piano Concerto. During World War I he lived in N.Y. and in Havana; then went to Paris for additional study, and took lessons with Paul Dukas. His contact with French music wrought a radical change in his style of composition; his later works are more polyphonic in structure and more economical in form. He possessed a great gift of melody; one of his songs, *Estrellita,* became a universal favorite, and was often mistaken for a folk song. In 1941 he made a tour in South America, conducting his own works. He was the first Mexican composer of the 20th century to employ an identifiably modern musical language; his place in the history of Mexican music is a very important one. His works are often performed in Mexico; a concert hall was named after him in the Instituto de Bellas Artes.
WORKS: FOR ORCH.: *Estampas nocturnas* (1923); *Canto y danza de los antiguos Mexicanos* (1933); *Chapultepec,* symph. triptych (Mexico City, Aug. 25, 1929; revised version, Mexico City, Aug. 24, 1934); *Suite en estilo antiguo* (1935); *Poema elegiaco* (Mexico City, June 28, 1935); *Ferial* (Mexico City, Aug. 9, 1940); *Concierto del Sur* for Guitar and Orch. (Montevideo, Oct. 4, 1941); Violin Concerto (Mexico City, Aug. 20, 1943); Piano Trio (1911); *4 miniaturas* for String Quartet (1929); *Pequeña suite en estilo antiguo* for Violin, Viola, and Cello (1933); Sonata for Violin and Viola (1935); Cello Sonata (1922); numerous piano pieces, some based on Mexican rhythms; about 30 songs; 34 arrangements of Mexican folk songs. A collection of his articles was publ. posthumously in 1948.
BIBLIOGRAPHY: Otto Mayer-Serra, *Música y músicos de Latino-América* (Mexico City, 1947; vol. 2, pp. 782–86); D. López Alonso, *Manuel M. Ponce: Ensayo biográfico* (Mexico City, 1950); J.C. Romero, "Efemérides de Manuel Ponce," *Nuestra Música,* 2 (1950).

Ponchielli, Amilcare, celebrated Italian composer; b. Paderno Fasolaro, Cremona, Aug. 31, 1834; d. Milan, Jan. 16, 1886. He studied at the Milan Cons. (1843–54); his first dramatic work (written with 3 other students) was the operetta *Il Sindaco Babbeo* (Milan, March 3, 1851). Leaving the Cons., he was organist at S. Ilario in Cremona; then became a bandmaster. In 1880 he became a prof. at the Milan Cons. Puccini and Mascagni were among his pupils. He brought out the opera *I promessi sposi* at Cremona (Aug. 30, 1856), followed by *La Savoiarda* (Cremona, Jan. 19, 1861; revised as *Lina,* Milan, Nov. 17, 1877) and *Roderico, Re de' Goti* (Piacenza, Dec. 26, 1863). His first striking success was achieved with a revised version of *I promessi sposi* (Milan, Dec. 5, 1872); continuous good fortune attended the production of his operas *I Lituani* (La Scala, Milan, March 7, 1874; revised and revived in 1884 as *Aldona*); *La Gioconda* (Milan, April 8, 1876; his most famous work); *Il Figliuol prodigo* (Milan, Dec. 26, 1880); and *Marion Delorme* (Milan, March 17, 1885). An unfinished opera, *I Mori di Venezia,* in the orchestration by A. Cadore, was produced posthumously in Monte Carlo (March 17, 1914). Ponchielli also brought out a musical farce, *Il Parlatore eterno* (Lecco, Oct. 18, 1873), and the ballets *Le 2 gemelle* and *Clarina* (both 1873); a cantata in honor of Donizetti; a funeral march, *Il 29 Maggio,* for

Manzoni; a fine patriotic hymn, *Inno in memoria di Giuseppe Garibaldi.* Of his operas, *La Gioconda* established itself in the repertoire everywhere; the ballet number from it, *Dance of the Hours,* is extremely popular at concerts of light orch. music. Ponchielli also wrote sacred music, for use at the Cathedral of Bergamo, where he was maestro di cappella from 1881 to 1886.

BIBLIOGRAPHY: A. Mandelli, *Le Distrazioni di A. Ponchielli* (Cremona, 1897); G. Cesari, *A. Ponchielli nell'arte del suo tempo* (Cremona, 1934); G. de Napoli, *A. Ponchielli* (Cremona, 1936); A. Damerini, *A. Ponchielli* (Turin, 1940).

Pond, Sylvanus Billings, American music publisher and composer; b. Milford, Vt., April 5, 1792; d. Brooklyn, March 12, 1871. He was a prominent musician of his time; conducted the N.Y. Sacred Musical Society and the N.Y. Academy of Sacred Music; wrote songs for Sunday school; edited and publ. *Union Melodies* (1838), *The U.S. Psalmody* (N.Y., 1841), and *The Book of Praise,* for the Reformed Dutch Church in America (N.Y., 1866); composed the hymn tunes *Armenia* (1835) and *Franklin Square* (1850). Early in life, he went to Albany; established a piano workshop; from 1820, was partner of the publishing house of Meacham and Pond there; in 1832 he joined Firth & Hall of N.Y., and the firm's name became Firth, Hall & Pond; in 1848 it was reorganized as Firth, Pond & Co.; it was one of the principal publishers of Stephen Foster's songs. In 1850 Pond retired, and his son, **William A. Pond,** became the owner; upon the withdrawal of Firth in 1863, the firm became known as William A. Pond & Co.; W.A. Pond's eldest son, **William A. Pond, Jr.,** was taken into partnership, but died in 1884; William A. Pond Sr. died the following year, and his 2 other sons, **Albert Edward** and **George Warren Pond,** succeeded him. In 1934 Joseph Fletcher acquired the catalogue; in 1946 it was purchased by Carl Fischer, Inc. For the dealings of Firth, Pond & Co. with Stephen Foster, see J.T. Howard, *Stephen Foster, America's Troubadour* (N.Y., 1931; 4th ed., 1965); consult also H. Dichter and E. Shapiro, *Early American Sheet Music, Its Lure and Its Lore, 1768–1889* (N.Y., 1941).

Poné, Gundaris, Latvian-American composer and conductor; b. Riga, Oct. 17, 1932. In 1944 his family went to Germany, where he attended a school in Augsburg and studied violin. In 1950 he emigrated to the U.S., becoming an American citizen in 1956. He studied violin and composition at the Univ. of Minnesota (B.A., 1954; M.A., 1956; Ph.D., 1962); served in the U.S. armed forces in 1956–58. Between 1967 and 1982 he appeared as a guest conductor in his own works in America, Sweden, Germany, Italy, Belgium, and Russia. In 1982 he was appointed a teacher of composition at the State Univ. of N.Y. at New Paltz. In his own music he maintains an equilibrated modern style, often complex in contrapuntal involutions and even venturing into the murky realm of aleatory serialism, but never darkening the immanent sense of tonality. His programmatic works reflect his varied interests in science, politics, history, and philosophy; thus, he entitled a piano trio *On Black Holes,* and in 1968 began an opera on the life of the slain German communist Rosa Luxemburg. He is the recipient of many helpful monetary grants, prestigious commissions, and honorary mentions.

WORKS: *Rosa Luxemburg,* opera in progress (begun in 1968); Sonata for Solo Viola (1959); Violin Concerto (1959); *Quattro temperamenti d'amore* for Baritone and Orch. (1960); *Daniel Propheta,* oratorio (1962); String Quartet (1963); *Serie-Alea* for 4 Woodwinds and Piano (1965); Sonata for Solo Cello (1966); *Montage-Demontage* for Piano and Assistant (1967); *Composizione per quattro orchestre* (1967–69); *San Michele della Laguna* for Instrumental Ensemble (1969); *Oltre questa porta geme la terra* for 3 Pianos (1969); *Junius Broschüre* for 6 Instrumental Groups, 18 Voices, and 4 Speakers (1970); *Vivos voco, mortuos plango* for Orch. (1972); *De mundo magistri Ioanni* for Chamber Ensemble (1972); *Diletti dialettici* for 9 Virtuosos (1973); *Avanti!* for Orch. (Washington, D.C., Oct. 2, 1982; received first prize at the Kennedy Center Friedheim Awards); *5 American Songs* for Soprano and Chamber Orch. (1976); Horn Concerto (1976); *Eisleriana* for 11 Players (1978); *Ely,* 7 studies in nature for 5 Players (1978); *On Black Holes* for Violin, Cello, and Piano (1979); *Woodland Elegies* for Clarinet, Marimba, and Double Bass (1980); *La Serenissima,* "sette ritratti veneziani" for Orch. (Trieste, Sept. 25, 1982, composer conducting; received first prize of Città di Trieste, of 3 million lire); *Di gran maniera* for Solo Violin (1981); *6 Propositions* for Woodwinds and Piano (1982); *Cyprian Reflections* for Clarinet, Cello, and Piano (1982); *5 American Portraits* for Orch. (1983).

Pongrácz, Zoltán, Hungarian composer; b. Dió-szeg, Feb. 5, 1912. He studied with Kodály at the Budapest Academy of Music (1930–35); then took lessons in conducting from Rudolf Nilius in Vienna and Clemens Krauss in Salzburg. During World War II he served as director of the music dept. of Hungarian Radio (1943–44); after the war conducted the Phil. Orch. in Debrecen (1946–49); later taught at the Cons. there (1954–64); in 1968 was appointed a supervisor of vocal music in Budapest, and in 1975 became prof. of electronic composition at the Budapest Academy of Music.

WORKS: Opera, *Odysseus and Nausikaa* (1949–50; Debrecen, 1960); ballet, *The Devil's Present* (1936); *Christmas Cantata* (1935); *St. Stephen Oratorio* (1938); cantata, *Apollo musagètes* (1958); *Negritude* for Speaking Chorus, Chorus, and Percussion (1962); *Ispirazioni* for Chorus, Orch., and Tape (1965); *Music from Nyírség* for Soloists, Chorus, and Folk Orch. (1965); *Pastorale* for Clarinet, Organ, 6 Winds, and Percussion (1941); *Javanese Music,* on a South Asiatic motif, for Chamber Ensemble (1942); Symph. (1943); *Ballo ongaro* for Youth Orch. (1955); *3 Orchestral Etudes* (1963); *Hangok és zörejek (Tones and Noises),* aleatory music for Orch. (1966); *Színek és vonalak (Colors and*

Lines) for Youth Orch. (1971); *Music* for 5 Cellos (1954); Wind Quintet (1956); *Toccata* for Piano (1957); *3 Small Pieces* for Orff Ensemble (1966); *Phonothèse* for Tape (1966); *Sets and Pairs,* electronic variations for Piano and Celesta (1968); *3 Improvisations* for Piano, Percussion, and 3 Tape Recorders (1971); *3 Bagatelles* for Percussion (1972); *Zoophonia,* concrete music synthesized from animal sounds (1973); incidental music for magnetic tape.

Poniatowski, Josef (Michal Xawery Franciszek Jan), Prince of Monte Rotondo, Polish composer; b. Rome, Feb. 20, 1816; d. Chislehurst, England, July 3, 1873. He was a member of the Polish nobility; his uncle was a marshal in Napoleon's army. He studied in Florence, and appeared on the stage as a tenor; then wrote operas (to Italian and French librettos); in 1848 he went to Paris and was elevated to the rank of Senator by Napoleon III; after the fall of the 2nd Empire, he went to England. WORKS: OPERAS: *Giovanni da Procida* (Florence, Nov. 25, 1838); *Don Desiderio* (Pisa, Dec. 26, 1840); *Ruy Blas* (Lucca, Sept. 2, 1843); *Malek-Adel* (Genoa, June 26, 1846); *Esmeralde* (Florence, June 26, 1847); *Pierre de Médicis* (Paris, March 9, 1860); *Au travers du mur* (Paris, May 9, 1861); *L'Aventurier* (Paris, Jan. 26, 1865); *La Contessina* (Paris, April 28, 1868); *Gelmina* (London, June 4, 1872).

Poniridis, Georges, distinguished Greek composer and violinist; b. Constantinople, of Greek parents, Oct. 8, 1892. He studied violin with Ysaÿe at the Brussels Cons. and composition with Vincent d'Indy and Albert Roussel at the Schola Cantorum in Paris, where he remained until the outbreak of World War II; then returned to Athens and served in the Music Division of the Greek Ministry of Education (1954–58). In his music he makes use of authentic Greek motifs, at times endeavoring to emulate the simple monody of ancient Greek chants and the rhythms of classical prosody. WORKS: *Triptyque symphonique* (Athens, Nov. 22, 1937); 2 symphs. (1935, 1942); *3 Symphonic Preludes* (1938); Chamber Symph. for Strings and Percussion; *Petite symphonie* (1956); Flute Sonata (1956); String Quartet (1959); Clarinet Sonata (1962); Quartet for Oboe, Clarinet, Bassoon, and Xylophone (1962); Trio for Xylophone, Clarinet, and Bassoon (1962); Trio for Flute, Oboe, and Clarinet (1962); Piano Concerto (1968); Violin Concerto (1969); 2 violin sonatas; Viola Sonata (1967); Cello Sonata (1967); 3 piano sonatas; scores of incidental music to ancient Greek plays; arrangements of Greek folk songs.

Ponnelle, Jean-Pierre, French opera designer and producer; b. Paris, Feb. 19, 1932. He received his training in Paris; gained early recognition for his staging of Henze's *Boulevard Solitude* at its premiere in Hannover in 1952; worked mostly in German opera houses. In 1962 he began to produce opera. He also distinguished himself in motion picture productions.

Pons, Charles, French composer; b. Nice, Dec. 7, 1870; d. Paris, March 16, 1957. He studied organ, and earned his living as a church organist in his youth; then turned to theater music, and produced a long series of operas: *L'Epreuve* (Nice, 1904); *Laura* (Paris, 1906); *Mourette* (Marseilles, 1909); *Le Voile du bonheur* (Paris, April 26, 1911); *Françoise* (Lyons, 1913); *Loin du bal* (Paris, 1913); *Les Fauves* (Paris, 1917); *Le Drapeau* (Paris, 1918); *Le Passant de Noël* (Nice, 1935); *L'Envol de la Marseillaise* (Marseilles, 1947); overture, *Pyrrhus;* symph. poem, *Heures vendéennes; Symphonie tragique;* several orch. suites; oratorio, *La Samaritaine* (Nice, 1900); other vocal works, with Orch.: *La Mort de Démosthène* (Paris, 1928) and *Dans la forêt normande* (1934); chamber music; songs.

Pons, Lily (baptismal names, **Alice Joséphine**), glamorous French coloratura soprano; b. Draguignan, April 12, 1898; d. Dallas, Texas, Feb. 13, 1976. She studied piano as a child; took voice lessons with Albert di Gorostiaga. She made her debut as an opera singer in Mulhouse in 1927 in the title role in *Lakmé;* sang in provincial theaters in France; then was engaged at the Metropolitan Opera in N.Y. and sang Lucia at her debut there on Jan. 3, 1931, with excellent success; she remained on its roster until 1944 (again from 1945–58; on Dec. 14, 1960, made a concert appearance there). While in N.Y., she continued her vocal studies, with Maria Gay and Giovanni Zenatello. Her fame as an extraordinary dramatic singer spread rapidly; she was engaged to sing at the Grand Opéra and the Opéra-Comique in Paris, at Covent Garden in London, the Teatro Colón in Buenos Aires, in Mexico, and in Cuba. She went to Hollywood and appeared in motion pictures, among them *That Girl from Paris* (1936) and *Hitting a New High* (1938). During World War II she toured the battlefronts of North Africa, India, China, and Burma; received numerous honors. So celebrated did she become that a town in Maryland was named Lillypons in her honor. She was married twice (divorced both times), to August Mesritz, a publisher, and to the conductor **André Kostelanetz.** She possessed an expressive coloratura voice, which she used with extraordinary skill.

Ponse, Luctor, Swiss-born Dutch composer; b. Geneva, Oct. 11, 1914. He studied at the Cons. in Valenciennes, France, winning the Prix d'Excellence for theory in 1930 and for piano in 1932; after further study in Geneva (1933–35), he went to the Netherlands, and in 1964 became a member of the staff of the Inst. of Sonology at Utrecht Univ.; also taught at the Groningen Cons. WORKS: *Divertissement* for String Orch. (1946); Piano Concerto (1951–55); 3 sinfoniettas (1952, 1959, 1961); 2 symphs. (1953, 1957); *Feestgericht,* ballet for Orch. (1957); 2-Piano Concerto (1961–62); *Concerto da camera* for Oboe and String Orch. (1962); 2 violin concertos (1963, 1965); Trio for Flute, Clarinet, and Piano (1940–41); 2 string quartets (1941, 1947); 2 cello sonatas (1943, 1950); *2 Pieces* for Wind Quintet (1943); Duo for Violin and Cello (1946); Violin Sonata (1948); Quintet for Flute, Oboe, Violin, Viola, and Cello (1956); *2 Caprices* for Flute and Piano (1956); Sextet for Flute, Oboe, Violin, Viola, Cello, and Harpsichord (1958); *Variations* for Flute and Harpsichord (1962); *Euterpe Suite* for 11 Instruments (1964); piano pieces.

Ponselle (real name, **Ponzillo**), **Carmela,** American mezzo-soprano, sister of **Rosa Ponselle;** b. Schenectady, N.Y., June 7, 1892; d. New York, June 13, 1977. She began to study singing rather late in life; made her professional debut in 1923; her first appearance at the Metropolitan Opera House was as Amneris in *Aida* (Dec. 5, 1925); she remained on its roster until 1928; was reengaged for the seasons 1930–35; then devoted most of her time to teaching.

Ponselle, Rosa, brilliant American soprano; b. Meriden, Conn., Jan. 22, 1897; d. in her mansion at Green Spring Valley, Md., May 25, 1981. Her parents, who emigrated to the U.S. from southern Italy, gave her, with a prescient hope, the middle name Melba. Her father owned a grocery store in Meriden; she studied music with her mother, an amateur singer, and sang in a local church choir. Her older sister, Carmela Ponselle, also learned to sing, and the 2 sisters, billed under their real name, **Ponzillo,** as "Italian Girls," sang in vaudeville shows in Pittsburgh and in N.Y. Later she took voice lessons in N.Y. with William Thorner, who became her manager; he introduced her to Caruso, who in turn arranged for her to audition at the Metropolitan Opera. She made a fine impression and was engaged for a debut on Nov. 15, 1918, in the role of Leonora in *La forza del destino,* opposite Caruso, who sang the male lead of Don Alvaro. She was immediately successful, and the critics, including the usually skeptical James Huneker, praised her. She subsequently sang at the Metropolitan a rich assortment of Italian opera roles. She was equally successful in London when she appeared at Covent Garden as Norma (May 28, 1929). In 1936 she was married to Carl Jackson, son of the former mayor of Baltimore, who built for her a magnificent villa at Green Spring Valley, near Baltimore; she divorced him in 1950. She made her last appearance at the Metropolitan Opera in N.Y. as Carmen, on Feb. 15, 1937. Altogether, she appeared with the Metropolitan 258 times in N.Y. and 107 times on tour, in 22 roles. After her retirement she became active in social affairs. Her 80th birthday was celebrated in 1977 at her estate, with a multitude of friends and itinerant celebrities in attendance.
BIBLIOGRAPHY: O. Thompson, *The American Singer* (N.Y., 1937; pp. 335–46); T. Villella, in *Le Grand Baton* (Sept. 1975); David Ewen, *Musicians since 1900* (N.Y., 1978).

Pontécoulant, Louis-Adolphe le Doulcet, Marquis de, French writer on music; b. Paris, 1794; d. Bois-Colombe, near Paris, Feb. 20, 1882. After an adventurous career, he began the study of music history and the construction of instruments; publ. *Essai sur la facture musicale considérée dans ses rapports avec l'art, l'industrie, et le commerce* (1857; 2nd augmented ed., as *Organographie* in 2 parts, 1861); *Musée instrumental du Conservatoire de musique* (1864); *La Musique à l'Exposition universelle de 1867* (1868); and *Les Phénomènes de la musique* (1868).

Ponti, Michael, American pianist; b. Freiburg, Germany, Oct. 29, 1937. He was brought to America as a child. He studied piano with Gilmour MacDonald; in 1955 he returned to Germany to continue his studies at the Frankfurt Hochschule für Musik. In 1964 he won first prize in the Busoni Competition, which launched him on a successful career. In his programs he specialized in bringing out neglected or forgotten piano masterpieces of the sonorous Romantic past.

Pontoglio, Cipriano, Italian composer; b. Grumello del Piano, Dec. 25, 1831; d. Milan, Feb. 22, 1892. He was a pupil of Antonio Cagnoni in Milan, and P. Serrao in Naples; then opened a music school in Milan. He composed 5 operas: *Lamberto Malatesta* (Pavia, 1857); *Tebaldo Brusato* (Brescia, 1865; rewritten as *L'Assedio di Brescia,* Rome, June 15, 1872); *La Schiava greca* (Bergamo, 1868); *La notte di natale* (Bergamo, Aug. 29, 1872); *Edoardo Stuart* (Milan, May 21, 1887); publ. songs, piano pieces, etc.

Ponty, Jean-Luc, French jazz violinist; b. Arranches, Sept. 29, 1942. He studied piano and violin with his parents; was a member of the Concerts Lamoureux until a successful appearance at the Antibes Jazz Festival encouraged him to embark upon a career as a jazz musician. He quickly established himself as a master of the idiom, and subsequently gained success in his appearances with rock musicians, including Frank Zappa and the Mothers of Invention.

Poole, Elizabeth, English mezzo-soprano; b. London, April 5, 1820; d. Langley, Buckinghamshire, Jan. 14, 1906. She made her debut at Drury Lane in London in 1834; sang in Italian opera in the U.S. (appearing with Malibran). Until her retirement in 1870 she was immensely popular as a ballad singer. Balfe wrote for her *'Tis gone, the past is all a dream,* which she introduced into *The Bohemian Girl.*

Poot, Marcel, remarkable Belgian composer; b. Vilvoorde, near Brussels, May 7, 1901. He received his first musical training from his father; then studied at the Brussels Cons. with Sevenants, Lunssens, and de Greef (1916–20), and at the Flemish Cons. of Antwerp with Lodewijk Mortelmans (1921–23); in the interim he also received guidance from Paul Gilson. In 1925, with 7 other Gilson pupils (René Bernier, Gaston Brenta, Francis de Bourguignon, Theodore Dejoncker, Robert Otlet, Maurice Schoemaker, and Jules Strens), he founded the Groupe des Synthétistes, dedicated to propaganda of new musical ideas (the group disbanded in 1930). Also in

1925, Poot was co-founder, with Gilson, of *La Revue Musicale Belge*, to which he contributed until its dissolution in 1938. He was on the staff of the Brussels Cons. from 1938 to 1966, and was its director from 1949 until his retirement. The most striking element of his music is its rhythmic vivacity; his harmony is well within the tonal sphere.

WORKS: FOR THE STAGE: Chamber opera, *Moretus* (1943; Brussels, 1944); radio plays (1933–36); 3 ballets: *Pâris et les 3 divines* (1933); *Camera* (1937); *Pygmalion* (1952); 2 oratorios: *Le Dit du routier* (1943) and *Icare* (1945). FOR ORCH.: *Variations en forme de danses* (1923); *Charlot*, 3 sketches inspired by Charlie Chaplin films (1926); *Rondo* for Piano and Small Orch. (1928); *Capriccio* for Oboe and Orch. (1928); 6 symphs. (1929; *Triptyque symphonique*, 1938; 1952; 1970; 1974; 1978); *Poème de l'espace*, symph. poem inspired by Lindbergh's flight (1929; Liège ISCM Festival, Sept. 4, 1930); *Jazz Music* (1930; Brussels, Feb. 21, 1932); *Fugato* (1931); *Ouverture joyeuse* (1934); *Allegro symphonique* (1935); *Fantaisie rythmique* (1936); *Danse laudative* (1937); *Ballade* for String Quartet and Orch. (1937); *Impromptu en forme de rondo* (1937); *Légende épique* for Piano and Orch. (1938); *Suite* for Small Orch. (1940); *Ballade* for Clarinet and Orch. (1941); *Concertstück* for Cello and Orch. (1942); *Fantasia* (1944); *3 Danses* (1945); Sinfonietta (1946; Chicago, Oct. 22, 1946); *Musique légère* (1946); *Mouvement symphonique* for Wind Orch. (1946); *Rhapsodie* (1947); *Divertimento* for Small Orch. (1952); *Ouverture rhapsodique* for Wind Orch. (1952); *Mouvement perpétuel* (1953); *Ballade* for Violin and Orch. (1955); *Rondo diabolique*, scherzo (1958); Piano Concerto (1959; Brussels, May 25, 1960; compulsory work for finalists of 1960 Queen Elisabeth piano competition, won by Malcolm Frager); *2 mouvements symphoniques* (1960); *Suite en forme de variations* (1962); *Concertstück* for Violin and Orch. (1962); *Concerto Grosso* for 11 Strings (1962); *Music* for String Orch. (1963); *Suite anglaise* (1966); *Concerto Grosso* for Piano Quartet and Orch. (1969); Cello Concertino (1971); Oboe Concertino (1972); Trumpet Concerto (1973). CHAMBER MUSIC: Viola Sonatina (1926); Piano Quartet (1932); *3 Pièces en trio* for Piano Trio (1935); *5 Bagatelles* for String Quartet (1939); *Scherzo* for 4 Saxophones (1941); *Divertimento* for Oboe, Clarinet, and Bassoon (1942); Octet for Winds and Strings (1948); String Quartet (1952); *Sarabande* for Horn and Piano (1953); *Ballade* for Oboe, Clarinet, and Bassoon (1954); *Fantaisie* for 6 Clarinets (1955); Concertino for Wind Quintet (1958); *Légende* for Horn and Piano (1958); Concertino for Flute, Violin, and Cello (1963); Concertino for 4 Saxophones (1963); *Musique* for Wind Quintet (1964); *Legende* for 4 Clarinets or Saxophones (1967); Quartet for 4 Horns (1969); *Mosaïque* for 8 Winds (1969); *Musique de chambre* for Piano Trio (1971); several *Ballades* and other pieces for Solo Instruments, with Piano. FOR PIANO: Sonata (1927); *6 petites pièces* (1927); *6 petites pièces faciles* (1936); *6 petites pièces récréatives* (1937); *Suite* (1942); Sonatina (1945); *Variations* (1952); choral works and songs; film music.

Popov, Alexander, Bulgarian composer; b. Kolarovgrad, July 14, 1927. He studied composition with Veselin Stoyanov at the Bulgarian State Cons., graduating in 1954; played viola in the orch. of the National Opera in Sofia; is a member of the Sofia Soloists chamber ensemble.

WORKS: 2 cantatas: *Cantata about the April Uprising* (1952) and *Land of Songs* (1969); *Suite* for Orch. (1956); *Native Land*, variations for Orch. (1958); *The Artist*, suite for String Quartet and String Orch. (1961); Sinfonietta (1964); *Concerto Grosso* for String Orch. (1966); *Prelude and Dance* for Orch. (1972); *Adagio* for Orch. (1973); *Variants* for 13 Strings (1973); 2 string quartets; choruses; songs.

Popov, Gavriil, outstanding and original Russian composer; b. Novocherkassk, Sept. 12, 1904; d. Repino, near Leningrad, Feb. 17, 1972. He studied at the St. Petersburg Cons. with Nikolayev (piano) and Vladimir Shcherbachev (composition). From his student days, he adopted the procedures of modern music; his Septet (Moscow, Dec. 13, 1927) was written in a system of dissonant counterpoint then fashionable in Western Europe; his First Symph. (1927–34) was in a similar vein. When modern music became the target of attack in Russia, Popov modified his style toward a more popular conception, following the tenets of "socialist realism"; he wrote several film scores, among them *Communist Youth Union, Leader of Electrification* (1932); other works: Symph. No. 2, subtitled *Fatherland* (Moscow, Feb. 15, 1944); Symph. No. 3 for String Orch., on Spanish themes (Moscow, Jan. 31, 1947); Symph. No. 4, *Glory Be to the Fatherland* (1949); Symph. No. 5 (1965); Symph. No. 6 (Moscow, Jan. 23, 1970); Organ Concerto (1970).

Popovici, Doru, Rumanian composer and musicologist; b. Reşiţa (Banat), Feb. 17, 1932. He studied at the Bucharest Cons. with P. Constantinescu, Negrea, Andricu, Rogalski, Jora, and Vancea (1950–55); attended the annual international summer courses in new music at Darmstadt; in 1968 was appointed director of Rumanian Radio and Television.

WORKS: 2 one-act operas: *Prometeu* (*Prometheus;* 1958; Bucharest, Dec. 16, 1964) and *Mariana Pineda*, after García Lorca (1966; Bucharest, Dec. 22, 1966); 3 cantatas: *Porumbeii morţii* (1957); *Noapte de August* for Baritone and Orch. (1959); *Omagiu lui Palestrina* for Female Chorus and Orch. (1966); *Triptyque* for Orch. (1955); *2 Symphonic Sketches* (1955); Concertino for String Orch. (1956); Concerto for Orch. (1960); 4 symphs.: No. 1 (1962); No. 2, *Spielberg* (1966); No. 3, *Bizantina*, for Chorus and Orch. (1968); No. 4 for Chorus and Orch. (1973); *Poem bizantin* for Orch. (1968); *Codex Cajoni* for String Orch. (1968); Cello Sonata (1952); Violin Sonata (1963); String Quartet No. 1 (1954; revised 1964); *Fantasy "Orphée"* for String Trio (1955); Sonata for 2 Cellos (1960); Sonata for 2 Violas (1965); *Omagiu lui Tuculescu*, quintet for Piano, Violin, Viola, Cello, and Clarinet (1967); *Musique solen-*

Popp – Porfetye

nelle for Violin and Piano (1969); Piano Sonatina (1953); choruses; songs. He publ. 6 books, all in Bucharest: *Muzica corală românească* (1966); *Începuturile muzicii culte românești* (with Miereanu; 1967); *Gesualdo di Venosa* (1969); *Muzica românească contemporană* (1970); *Cîntec flamand. Școala muzicală neerlandeză* (1971); *Muzica elisabethană* (1972).

Popp, Lucia, Czech soprano; b. Uhorská Ves, Nov. 12, 1939. She studied at the Academy of Music in Bratislava (1959–63), then sang at the Opera there. In 1963 Herbert von Karajan invited her to sing at the Vienna State Opera; within a few seasons, she became one of its principal members. Also in 1963 she appeared at the Salzburg Festival; in 1966 she sang at Covent Garden in London. On Feb. 19, 1967, she made her American debut at the Metropolitan Opera in N.Y. as the Queen of the Night in *Die Zauberflöte;* in 1969 she toured Australia. She was equally expert in coloratura parts and in lyrico-dramatic roles.

Popper, David, famous Czech cellist and composer; b. Prague, Dec. 9, 1843; d. Baden, near Vienna, Aug. 7, 1913. He studied cello with Goltermann at the Prague Cons.; began his career with a tour in 1863; then had a highly successful appearance as a soloist at the Karlsruhe Music Festival on March 29, 1865; from 1868 to 1873 he was first cellist of the Vienna Court Orch. In 1872 he married the famous pianist **Sophie Menter,** but they were divorced 14 years later. From 1896 until his death he taught cello at the Budapest Cons. He wrote a number of extremely attractive and marvelously idiomatic pieces for the cello, which remained in the international repertoire, among them *Sérénade orientale, Gavotte, Tarentelle, Elfentanz, Im Walde, Ungarische Rhapsodie;* also a *Requiem* for 3 Cellos (perf. by him, with Delsart and Howell, in London, Nov. 25, 1891); he also publ. the cello studies *Hohe Schule des Violoncellspiels* (40 studies) and, as a preparatory book of easy pieces, *10 mittelschwere grosse Etüden.*

Poradowski, Stefan, Polish composer and music pedagogue; b. Wloclawek, Aug. 16, 1902; d. Poznan, July 9, 1967. He studied composition with Opieński at the Poznan Cons. (1922–26); then took private lessons with Reznicek in Berlin (1929). Returning to Poland, he taught composition and theory at the Poznan Cons. (1930–39, 1945–67); also gave courses (after 1956) at the Cons. in Wroclaw.
WORKS: Opera, *Flames* (1966); Passion play, *Odkupienie (Redemption)* for Mezzo-soprano, Chorus, and Orch. (1941); *Koń Światowida (The Horse of Sviatovid),* fantastic poem for Tenor, Baritone, Chorus, and Orch. (1931); *Spring Song,* cantata (1926); Sinfonietta (1925); *Concerto antico* for Viola d'Amore and Orch. (1925); *Triptych* for String Orch. (1926); 7 symphs. (1928, 1930, 1932, 1934, 1938, 1952, 1958); Double-bass Concerto (1929); *Capriccio on a Theme by Kreutzer* for String Orch. (1930); *Serenada klasyczna* for String Orch. (1949); *Rapsodia pol-*

ska for Violin and Orch. (1944); *Ratusz poznański (The Town Hall of Poznan),* symph. poem (1950); Concerto for Flute, Harp, and String Orch. (1954); 4 string quartets (1923, 1923, 1936, 1947); Violin Sonata (1925); 5 trios: *I* and *II* for Violin, Viola, and Double Bass (1929, 1930); *III* for String Trio (1935); *IV* for 3 Double Basses (1952); *V* for String Trio (1955). He publ. the textbooks *Nauka harmonii (Science of Harmony;* Poznan, 1931; 5th ed., Warsaw, 1964); *Sztuka pisania kanonów (Art of Writing Canons;* Poznan, 1965).

Porcelijn, David, Dutch composer; b. Achtkarspelen, Friesland, Jan. 7, 1947. He studied flute with Frans Vester (1964–68) and composition with Kees van Baaren and Jan van Vlijmen (1966–70) at the Royal Cons. of The Hague; later took lessons in conducting with Michel Tabachnik in Geneva. A modernist par excellence, Porcelijn makes explorations in every direction; his music ranges from the infra-classical to ultramathematical.
WORKS: *4 Interpretations* for Various Instruments (1967–69); *Continuations* for 11 Wind Instruments (1968); *Combinations* for 26 Solo Instruments (1969–70); *Requiem,* in memory of Varèse, for Percussion Ensemble (1969–70); *Zen* for Solo Flute (1970); *1,000 Frames* for 1 + Wind Instruments and/or 1 + Pianos (1970); *Confrontation and Indoctrinations* for Jazz Band and 19 Instruments (Scheveningen, June 23, 1972); *Cybernetic Object* for Orch. (The Hague, June 18, 1971); *Amoeba* for x Flutes (1971); *Pole,* ballet for 26 Instruments (1971–72); *10-5-6-5(a)* for 2 String Quartets, Wind Quintet, and 2 Vibraphones (1972); *Pulverizations I* for 52 Strings (1972); *Pulverizations* for Wind Quintet (1972); *Pulverizations II* for Alto Saxophone, 22 Winds, 5 Percussion Groups, and 52 Strings (1973); Concerto for Flute, Harp, and Orch. (1973); Flute Concerto (1975); *Shades* for Flute, Violin, and Viola (1975); *Rhythm Song* for Male Chorus and Percussion (1976); *Into the Earth* for 14 Brass and 2 Percussionists (1976).

Porfetye, Andreas, Rumanian composer; b. Zădăreni, July 6, 1927. He studied with Drăgoi, P. Constantinescu, Rogalski, and Vancea at the Bucharest Cons. (1948–54); was editor of the Rumanian revue *Muzica* (1954–69); after 1969, taught at the Bucharest Cons.
WORKS: 3 symphs.: Symph. in C (1955); No. 2 (1965) No. 3, *La Dramatique* (1970); *Partita* for String Orch. (1958); Organ Concerto (1962, revised 1967); *Sinfonia-Serenata* (1964); Violin Concerto (1966); *Sonata* for Orch. (1971); *Cantata de camera* for Mezzo-soprano, Solo Cello, and Chamber Orch. (1959); Cantata No. 2, *Comunistul,* for Mezzo-soprano, Chorus, and Orch. (1962); *In memorian Mihail Sadoveanu,* Requiem for Soprano, Tenor, and Orch. (1962); Horn Sonata (1956); Wind Quintet (1957); *Piccola sonata* for Violin and Organ (1962); Sonata for Cello and Organ (1963); *6 Pieces* for Clarinet and Harp (1965); Sonata No. 1 for Violin and Piano (1967); String Quartet No. 2 (1969); Piano Sonata (1963); Piano Sonatina (1965). For Solo Or-

gan: *Passacaglia and Fugue* (1955), *Toccata, Chorale, and Fugue* (1957), 3 sonatas (1960–68), *Toccata* (1966), and *Fantasy* (1968).

Porges, Heinrich, writer on music; b. Prague, Nov. 25, 1837; d. Munich, Nov. 17, 1900. He was a pupil of Cölestin Müller (piano) and Zwonař (theory). In 1863 he became co-editor (with Brendel) of the *Neue Zeitschrift für Musik,* and was in close contact with Wagner; in 1867 he was called to Munich by King Ludwig II, for whom he had written a study on *Tristan und Isolde* (publ. 1906 by Hans von Wolzogen).
WRITINGS: *Die Aufführung von Beethovens 9. Symphonie unter Richard Wagner in Bayreuth* (1872); *Die Bühnenproben zu den 1876er Festspielen* (1877); and other essays on Wagner in German periodicals.

Porpora, Nicola Antonio, famous Italian composer and singing teacher; b. Naples, Aug. 17, 1686; d. there, March 3, 1768. The son of a bookseller, he entered the Cons. dei Poveri at Naples at the age of 10 and studied with Gaetano Greco, Matteo Giordano, and Ottavio Campanile. Porpora's first opera, *Agrippina,* was presented at the Royal Palace of Naples (Nov. 4, 1708); Cardinal Grimani attended the performance and wrote a libretto on the same subject for Handel. This episode gave rise to the incorrect statement (by Fétis and others) that Handel heard Porpora's opera in Rome in 1710. Porpora produced in Naples 2 more operas: *Flavio Anicio Olibrio* (1711) and *Basilio, re d'oriente* (June 24, 1713). From 1711 until 1725, he held the title of maestro di cappella to Philip, Landgrave of Hesse-Darmstadt. He gained a great reputation as a singing teacher, and numbered among his pupils the famous castrati Farinelli, Caffarelli, Antonio Uberti (who called himself "Porporino" out of respect for his teacher), and Salimbeni. Metastasio, who wrote librettos for several of Porpora's operas, was also his pupil. Porpora's career as a singing teacher was divided between Naples and Venice. In Naples he taught at the conservatories of Sant' Onofrio (1715–22, 1760–61) and Santa Maria di Loreto (1739–41, 1760–61); in Venice he gave lessons at the Ospedali degli Incurabili (1726–33, 1737–38), the Ospedali della Pietà (1742–46), and the Ospedaletto (1746–47). In 1718 Porpora collaborated with Domenico Scarlatti in the writing of the opera *Berenice, regina d'Egitto,* produced in Rome (1718). At about this time he succeeded in obtaining support from the Austrian court. His opera *Temistocle* was produced in Vienna on the Emperor's birthday (Oct. 1, 1718); his next opera, *Faramondo,* was staged in Naples (Nov. 19, 1719). He continued to write operas for theaters in Naples and Rome: *Eumene* (Rome, 1721); *Adelaide* (Rome, 1723); *Semiramide, regina dell'Assiria* (Naples, 1724); *Didone abbandonata* (his first opera to a libretto by Metastasio; Reggio, 1725). In 1726 he settled in Venice. He wrote the following operas during the next 8 years: *Meride e Selinunte* (Venice, 1726); *Siroe, re di Persia* (Milan, 1726); *Semiramide riconosciuta* (Venice, 1729); *Mi-*

tridate (Rome, 1730); *Tamerlano* (Turin, 1730); *Poro* (Turin, 1731); *Germanico in Germania* (Rome, 1732); *Issipile* (Rome, 1733). In 1733 he applied for the post of maestro di cappella at San Marco in Venice, but failed to obtain it. In the same year he was engaged by the directors of the Opera of the Nobility in London (organized as a rival company to that of Handel). For this venture Porpora wrote 5 operas: *Arianna in Nasso* (Dec. 29, 1733); *Enea nel Lazio* (May 11, 1734); *Polifemo* (Feb. 1, 1735); *Ifigenia in Aulide* (May 3, 1735); *Mitridate* (Jan. 24, 1736; a different score from the earlier opera of the same title). For a while he competed successfully with Handel, but soon the Opera of the Nobility began to falter, and Porpora left London on the eve of the company's collapse. From 1747 to 1751, he was in Dresden as singing teacher to the Electoral Princess. There he became Hasse's competitor for the position of music director. Although Hasse himself conducted Porpora's "pastoral drama" *Filandro* (Dresden, July 18, 1747), their relationship was made difficult by the intrigues of Hasse's wife, the singer Faustina Bordoni. In 1751 Porpora left Dresden for Vienna, where he became the teacher of Haydn, who paid for his lessons by serving Porpora as accompanist and personal helper. Porpora returned to Naples in 1758. His last stage work, *Il trionfo di Camilla* (Naples, May 30, 1760; a revision and adaptation to a new text of an earlier opera of the same title produced in Naples on Jan. 20, 1740), was unsuccessful. He wrote, all told, 44 operas, 11 oratorios, and numerous masses and motets. His instrumental music includes 6 *sinfonie da camera* (London, 1735), 12 violin sonatas (Vienna, 1754), a Cello Concerto, and a Cello Sonata. The fugues in Clementi's *Practical Harmony* are from Porpora's violin sonatas, some of which have been publ. by A. Schering, F. David, D. Alard, and A. Moffat. A Trio Sonata was publ. in Riemann's *Collegium Musicum* (no. 23).
BIBLIOGRAPHY: Marchese di Villarosa, *Memorie dei compositori di musica del regno di Napoli* (Naples, 1840); F. Clément, *Les Musiciens célèbres depuis le XVIe siècle* (Paris, 1868); S. Fassini, *Il melodramma italiano a Londra* (Turin, 1914); S. di Giacomo, *I quattro antiche Conservatorii di musica di Napoli* (Palermo, 1925); F. Walker, *A Chronology of the Life and Works of Nicola Porpora,* in *Italian Studies* (Cambridge, 1951; vol. 6); U. Prota-Giurleo, "Per una esatta biografia di Nicolo Porpora," *La Scala* (Jan. 1957; establishing for the first time Porpora's dates of birth and death); A. Mayeda, *Nicola Antonio Porpora als Instrumentalkomponist* (Diss., Univ. of Vienna, 1967; with thematic catalogue); F. Degrada, "Le musiche strumentali di Nicolò Porpora," *Chigiana,* XXV (1968); M. Robinson, "Porpora's Operas for London, 1733–1736," *Soundings,* II (1971–72); E. Sutton, *The Solo Vocal Works of Nicola Porpora: An Annotated Thematic Index* (Diss., Univ. of Minnesota, 1974); C. Vitali, "Un concerto per violoncello attribuito a Porpora," *Studi Musicali,* VIII (1979).

Porrino, Ennio, Italian composer; b. Cagliari, Sardinia, Jan. 20, 1910; d. Rome, Sept. 25, 1959. He studied at the Santa Cecilia Academy in Rome with Mulè, and later took a course with Respighi (1932–35). He subsequently taught in Rome, Venice, and Naples; in 1956, became director of the Cons. in his hometown in Sardinia.

WORKS: 3 operas: *Gli orazi* (Milan, 1941); *L'organo di bambù* (Venice, 1955); *I shardana* (Naples, 1959); 4 ballets: *Proserpina* (Florence, 1938); *Altair* (Naples, 1942); *Mondo tondo* (Rome, 1949); *La bambola malata* (Venice, 1959); *Tartatin de Tarascon,* overture (Rome, 1933); *Sardegna,* symph. poem, based on Sardinian folk themes (Rome, 1933; his most popular work); Trumpet Concertino (1934); *La visione di Ezechiele* for Orch. (1935); *Sinfonia per una fiaba* (1936); *Notturna e Danza* for Orch. (1936); *3 canzoni italiane* for Chamber Orch. (1937); *Preludio in modo religioso e ostinato* for Orch. or Piano (1942); *Sinfonietta dei fanciulli* (1947); *Sonata drammatica* for Piano and Orch. (1947); *Ostinato* for Strings and Piano (1951; Milan, Feb. 3, 1952); *Nuraghi,* 3 primitive dances for Orch. (1952); *Concerto dell'Argentarola* for Guitar and Orch. (1953); *Sonar per musici* for Harpsichord and Strings (1959); *I canti dell'esilio,* 15 songs for Voice and Chamber Orch. (1947); *Il processo di Cristo,* oratorio (1949); chamber pieces, including *Preludio, Aria e Scherzo* for Trumpet and Piano (1942); songs.

Porro, Pierre-Jean, famous French guitar virtuoso; b. Béziers, 1750; d. Montmorency, May 31, 1831. Through his influence the guitar became a fashionable instrument in Paris; he had a class of pupils there; also was editor and publisher of *Journal de Guitarre* (1787–1803). He publ. a guitar method, *Tableau méthodique;* numerous divertissements, sonatas, canzonets, for guitar solo and with other instruments; also *Collection de musique sacrée* for 4 Mixed Voices and Organ.

BIBLIOGRAPHY: F. Donnadieu, *Porro, Compositeur et éditeur de musique* (Béziers, 1897).

Porsile, Giuseppe, Italian composer; b. Naples, May 5, 1680; d. Vienna, May 29, 1750. He studied in Naples at the Cons. dei Poveri di Gesù Cristo with Usino, Giordano, and Greco. He then served as vice-maestro di cappella at the Spanish chapel in Naples. In 1695 he went to Spain to organize the music chapel of King Charles II in Barcelona; he subsequently served Charles III. When Charles III was elected Holy Roman Emperor as Charles VI, with the seat in Vienna, Porsile followed him there. On Dec. 17, 1720, he became court composer. He continued to serve the court after Charles VI died in 1740, being granted an honorary stipend; he was pensioned on April 1, 1749. Most of his stage works were written for the court of Vienna.

WORKS: OPERAS: *Il ritorno di Ulisse alla patria* (Naples, 1707); *Il giorno natalizio dell'imperatrice Amalia Wilhelmina* (Vienna, April 21, 1717); *La Virtù festeggiata* (Vienna, July 10, 1717); *Alceste,* festa teatrale (Vienna, Nov. 19, 1718); *Meride e Selinunte,* dramma per musica (Vienna, Aug. 28, 1721); *Il tempo fermato,* componimento da camera (Vien-

na, Oct. 15, 1721); *La Virtù e la Bellezza in lega,* serenata (Vienna, Oct. 15, 1722); *Il giorno felice,* componimento da camera (Vienna, Aug. 28, 1723); *Componimento a due voci* (Vienna, Aug. 28, 1725); *Spartaco,* dramma per musica (Vienna, Feb. 21, 1726); *Il tempio di Giano, chiuso da Cesare Augusto,* componimento per musica (Vienna, Oct. 1, 1726); *La clemenza di Cesare,* servizio di camera (Vienna, Oct. 1, 1727); *Telesilla,* festa teatrale (Vienna, Nov. 19, 1729); *Scipione Africano, Il maggiore,* festa di camera (Vienna, Oct. 1, 1730); *Dialogo tra il Decoro e la Placidezza,* festa di camera (Vienna, July 26, 1732); *Dialogo pastorale a cinque voci* (Vienna, Aug. 28, 1732); *Dialogo tra la Prudenza e la Vivacità,* festa di camera (Vienna, Oct. 15, 1732); *La Fama accresciuta dalla Virtù,* festa di camera (Vienna, Oct. 15, 1735); *Sesostri, re d'Egitto, ovvero Le feste d'Iside,* dramma per musica (Vienna, Carnival 1737); *Il giudizio rivocato,* festa di camera (Vienna, Oct. 15, 1737). ORATORIOS: *Sisara* (Vienna, March 23, 1719); *Tobia* (Vienna, March 14, 1720); *Il zelo di Nathan* (Vienna, 1721); *L'anima immortale creata e redenta per il cielo* (Vienna, Feb. 26, 1722); *Il trionfo di Giuditta* (Vienna, Feb. 18, 1723); *Il sacrifizio di Gefte* (Vienna, March 9, 1724); *Mosè liberato dal Nilo* (Vienna, March 1, 1725); *Assalone nemico del padre amante* (Vienna, March 14, 1726); *L'estaltazione de Salomone* (Vienna, March 6, 1727); *L'ubbidienza a Dio* (Vienna, March 9, 1730); *Due re, Roboamo e Geroboamo* (Vienna, Feb. 23, 1731); *Giuseppe riconosciuto* (Vienna, March 12, 1733); *La madre de' Maccabei* (Vienna, March 14, 1737). He also composed chamber cantatas, duets, and instrumental pieces.

BIBLIOGRAPHY: U. Prota-Giurleo, "Giuseppe Porsile e la Real cappella di Barcellona," *Gazzetta Musicale di Napoli,* II, no. 10 (1956); O.E. Deutsch, "Das Repertoire der höfischen Oper, der Hof- und der Staatsoper," *Österreichische Musikzeitschrift,* XXIV (1969).

Porta, Costanzo, important Italian composer; b. Cremona, c.1529; d. Padua, May 19, 1601. He studied with Willaert in Venice; was chorus master at Osimo, near Ancona, from 1552 to 1564. In 1565 he became choirmaster at the Basilica of St. Anthony in Padua; in 1567 received a similar post at the Cathedral of Ravenna; in 1575 was in Loreto, returning to Padua in 1585. He was highly esteemed as a master contrapuntist; wrote not only sacred music but also madrigals; combined great technical skill with a characteristic Italian grace of melodic line.

WORKS: Books of motets *a* 4 (1559), *a* 5 (1555), *a* 6 (1585), *a* 4–8 (1580); one book of masses for 4, 5, 6 Voices (1578); 2 books of introits for 5 Voices (1566, 1588); 4 books of madrigals for 4, 5 Voices (1555–85); hymns for 4 Voices (posthumous, 1602); vesper Psalms and canticles for 8 Voices (1605); in MS are various madrigals, Lamentations, a treatise on counterpoint, etc. Reprints are in Torchi's *L'arte musicale in Italia* (vol. 1), Einstein's *The Golden Age of the Madrigal* (N.Y., 1942), etc.

BIBLIOGRAPHY: G. Reese, *Music in the Renais-*

sance (N.Y., 1954); A. Garbelotto, *Il Padre Costanzo Porta da Cremona* (Rome, 1955; a documented biography).

Porter, Andrew, brilliant writer on music; b. Cape Town, South Africa, Aug. 26, 1928. He studied music at Diocesan College in Cape Town; then went to England; continued his education at Univ. College, Oxford; became a proficient organist. In 1949 he joined the staff of the *Manchester Guardian;* then wrote music criticism for the *Financial Times* of London (1953–74); also served as editor of the *Musical Times* of London (1960–67). In 1972 he became the music critic of the *New Yorker.* A polyglot, a polymath, and an uncommonly diversified intellectual, Andrew Porter expanded his interests far beyond the limited surface of purely musical studies; he mastered German, Italian, and French; made an exemplary trans. into Eng. of the entire text of *Der Ring des Nibelungen,* taking perspicuous care for the congenial rendition of Wagner's words and melodic inflections; his trans. was used to excellent advantage in the performance and recording of the cycle by the conductor Reginald Goodall with the English National Opera. Porter also trans. texts of Verdi's operas, Mozart's *Die Zauberflöte,* and some French operas. His mastery of English prose and his unostentatious display of arcane erudition make him one of the most remarkable music critics writing in the English language. Selections from his reviews have been publ. in *A Musical Season* (N.Y., 1974) and *Music of 3 Seasons, 1974 to 1977* (N.Y., 1978).

Porter, Cole, remarkable American composer of popular music; b. Peru, Ind., June 9, 1891; d. Santa Monica, Calif., Oct. 15, 1964. He was educated at Yale Univ. (B.A., 1913); then took academic courses at Harvard Law School, and later at the Harvard School of Music. While at Yale, he wrote football songs (*Yale Bull Dog Song, Bingo Eli Yale,* etc.); also composed music for college functions. His first production in N.Y. was *See America First* (1916). There followed a cascade of musical comedies for which he wrote both the lyrics and the music, which placed him in the front rank of the American musical theater. He was a master of subtle expression without sentimentality, a kinetic dash without vulgarity, and a natural blend of word poetry with the finest of harmonious melodies. WORKS: *Kitchy-Koo* (1919); *50 Million Frenchmen* (1929); *Gay Divorcee* (1932); *Anything Goes* (1934); *Jubilee* (1935); *Red Hot and Blue* (1936); *Leave It to Me* (1938); *Dubarry Was a Lady* (1939); *Panama Hattie* (1940); *Let's Face It* (1941); *Something for the Boys* (1943); *Mexican Hayride* (1944); *Kiss Me, Kate* (1948); *Out of This World* (1950); *Can-Can* (1954); *Silk Stockings* (1955). Of his many songs, at least half a dozen became great favorites: *Begin the Beguine; It's De-Lovely; Night and Day; My Heart Belongs to Daddy; Don't Fence Me In; Wunderbar.* BIBLIOGRAPHY: G. Eells, *The Life That Late He Led. A Biography of Cole Porter* (N.Y., 1967); R.

Kimball and B. Gill, *Cole* (a pictorial biography; N.Y., 1971); L. Siebert, *Cole Porter: An Analysis of 5 Musical Comedies and a Thematic Index of the Complete Works* (Diss., City Univ. of N.Y., 1975); Charles Schwartz, *Cole Porter* (N.Y., 1977; a "candid" biography; conclusively debunks the story that Cole Porter ever served in the French army, let alone the French Foreign Legion, as was claimed for him). *Night and Day,* a motion picture musical biography of Cole Porter, starring Cary Grant in the role of Porter, was produced by Warner Bros. in 1946.

Porter, Quincy, significant American composer; b. New Haven, Conn., Feb. 7, 1897; d. Bethany, Conn., Nov. 12, 1966. He was brought up in an intellectual atmosphere; his father and his grandfather were profs. at Yale Univ. He studied with David Stanley Smith and Horatio Parker at the Yale School of Music (B.Mus., 1921); submitted a violin concerto for the American Prix de Rome and received an honorable mention; also won the Steinert and Osborne prizes. After graduation he went to Paris, where he took courses with Lucien Capet (violin) and Vincent d'Indy (composition). Returning to America in 1922, he earned a living as a violinist in theater orchs. in N.Y. while taking a course in composition with Ernest Bloch. He taught at the Cleveland Inst. of Music (1922–28, 1931–32); played the viola in the Ribaupierre String Quartet there; spent 3 years in Paris on a Guggenheim fellowship (1928–31); was a prof. at Vassar College and conductor of the Vassar Orch. (1932–38); in 1938 succeeded Frederick Converse as dean of the New England Cons. in Boston; from 1942 to 1946, was its director; from 1946 to 1965, was a prof. at Yale Univ. His music is built on strong contrapuntal lines, with incisive rhythms; his harmonic procedures often reach stridently polytonal sonorities, while the general idiom of his works combines elements of both the modern German and the modern French styles of composition. WORKS: *Ukrainian Suite* for String Orch. (Rochester, N.Y., May 1, 1925); Suite in C minor for Orch. (1926); *Poem and Dance* for Orch. (Cleveland, June 24, 1932, composer conducting); 2 symphs.: No. 1 (1934; N.Y., April 2, 1938, composer conducting) and No. 2 (1961–62; Louisville, Ky., Jan. 14, 1964); *Dance in Three-Time* for Chamber Orch. (St. Louis, July 2, 1937); *Music for Strings* (1941); *Fantasy on a Pastoral Theme* for Organ and String Orch. (1942); Viola Concerto (Columbia Univ. Festival, N.Y., May 16, 1948); *Fantasy* for Cello and Small Orch. (1950); *The Desolate City* for Baritone and Orch. (1950); *Concerto Concertante* for 2 Pianos and Orch. (1952–53; Louisville, March 17, 1954; awarded the Pulitzer Prize for 1954 under its original title, *Concerto for 2 Pianos and Orchestra*); *New England Episodes,* symph. suite (commissioned for the Inter-American Music Festival, Washington, D.C., April 18, 1958); Harpsichord Concerto (1959; New Haven, Jan. 19, 1960; Ralph Kirkpatrick, soloist); Concerto for Wind Orch. (1960); 10 string quartets (1923, 1925, 1930, 1931, 1935, 1937, 1943, 1950, 1958, 1965); *In Monasterio* for String Quartet (1927); Piano Quintet

(1927); Clarinet Quintet (1929); *Quintet on a Child-hood Theme* for Flute and Strings (1940); String Sextet on Slavic folk tunes (1947); Divertimento for Wind Quintet (1960); Oboe Quintet (1966); 2 violin sonatas (1925, 1929); *Little Trio* for Flute, Violin, and Viola (1928); Suite for Solo Viola (1930); Horn Sonata (1946); 4 pieces for Violin and Piano (1947); Duo for Violin and Viola (1954); Duo for Flute and Harp (1957); Piano Sonata (1930); *Canon and Fugue* for Organ (1941); *6 Miniatures* for Piano (1943); *Day Dreams* for Piano (1957); several songs.

BIBLIOGRAPHY: H. Ewell, "Quincy Porter," *Modern Music*, XXIII/1 (Winter 1946); H. Boatwright, "Quincy Porter," *American Composers Alliance Bulletin* (1957); *Composers of the Americas*, vol. 4 (Washington, D.C., 1958; reprinted 1962); H. Boatwright, "Quincy Porter," *Perspectives of New Music*, V/No. 2 (1966–67; pp. 162–65); David Ewen, *American Composers* (N.Y., 1982).

Portugal (Portogallo), Marcos Antonio da Fonseca (real name, **Ascenção**), Portuguese composer; b. Lisbon, March 24, 1762; d. Rio de Janeiro, Feb. 7, 1830. A pupil at the ecclesiastical seminary at Lisbon, he continued his musical education with composition lessons from João de Souza Carvalho. Between 1784 and 1791 he wrote for Lisbon 17 stage works, mostly ephemeral. His reputation was made in Italy, where, with the exception of a short visit to Lisbon, he lived from 1792 to 1800, bringing out 22 Italian operas. From 1800 to 1810 he acted as conductor at the San Carlos Theater in Lisbon, producing Italian and Portuguese operas. His *Il Filosofo seducente, ossia Non irritar le donne* (Venice, Dec. 27, 1798) was selected by Napoleon for opening the Théâtre-Italien at Paris in 1801. In 1807 the royal family fled to Brazil before the French invasion; Portugal remained until the San Carlos Theater was closed in 1810, and then followed the court to Rio de Janeiro, where he was made general music director in 1811. The royal theater of São João, after its inauguration in 1813, produced several new operas by him. In that year he became director of the new Cons. at Vera Cruz, jointly with his brother **Simão**; he visited Italy in 1815, returned to Rio de Janeiro, and passed his last years there as an invalid. His masterpiece is generally assumed to be *Fernando nel Messico* (Venice, Jan. 16, 1798; written for the famous English singer Elizabeth Billington; produced in London, in Italian, March 31, 1803); other Italian operas that had a favorable reception were *Demofoonte* (Milan, Feb. 8, 1794) and *Le Donne cambiate* (Venice, Oct. 22, 1797); of Portuguese operas, *A Castanheira (The Chestnut Seller),* produced in Lisbon in 1790, enjoyed considerable popular success. He further wrote about 100 sacred works.

BIBLIOGRAPHY: Manoel Carvalhães, *Marcos Portugal na sua musica dramatica* (Lisbon, 1910).

Porumbescu, Ciprian, Rumanian composer; b. Sipote, Oct. 14, 1853; d. Stupca, Bukovina, June 6, 1883. After preliminary studies in Rumania, he went to Vienna, where he became a student of Bruckner; publ. a collection of "social songs of Rumanian students" (Vienna, 1880); composed an operetta, *Cral nou (The New Moon;* 1882), to a Rumanian libretto, and many songs. His death at the age of 29 deprived Rumania of the country's first national composer, but he is greatly revered as such. The town of Stupca, where he died, has been renamed Ciprian Porumbescu, and his name is attached to the official designation of several Rumanian conservatories. V. Cosma has edited the complete works (2 vols., Bucharest, 1954 and 1958).

BIBLIOGRAPHY: V. Cosma, *Ciprian Porumbescu* (Bucharest, 1957).

Pospíšil, Juraj, Slovak composer; b. Olomouc, Jan. 14, 1931. He first studied music in his hometown; then with Petrželka at the Janáček Academy in Brno and later with Alexander Moyzes and Cikker at the Bratislava Music Academy.

WORKS: *Mountains and People,* symph. poem (1955); *Margita and Besná,* ballad for Soloists, Chorus, and Orch. (1955); Cello Sonata (1956); 2 symphs.: No. 1 (1957) and No. 2, *Nebula in Andromeda* (1963); Sonata for Strings (1961); Trombone Concerto (1962); *Passacaglia and Fugue* for Organ (1962); *Mikropoviedky (Micro-stories)* for Soprano, Flute, Violin, and Cello (1963); *Glosy (Marginal Notes)* for Wind Quintet (1964); *Protirečenia (Contradictions)* for Piano Quartet (1964); *Music* for 12 Strings (1965); Double-bass Sonata (1966); Solo Violin Sonata (1966); *Trojveršia (3 Verses)* for 9 Instruments (1966); String Quartet (1970); Flute Quartet (1971); *Bagatelles* for Trombone and Piano (1972); *Concerto Eroico* for Horn and Orch. (1975); *Fragment* for Orch. (Košice, Oct. 4, 1976); *Symphonic Fresco* (1976); *Little Pieces* for Clarinet and Piano (1976).

Posselt, Ruth, American violinist; b. Medford, Mass., Sept. 6, 1914. She studied with Emanuel Ondricek; has given numerous recitals in America and Europe; gave the world premieres of violin concertos by Walter Piston, Vladimir Dukelsky, Edward Burlingame Hill, and others. On July 3, 1940, she married **Richard Burgin.**

Postnikova, Viktoria, Russian pianist; b. Moscow, Jan. 12, 1944. She studied at the Moscow Central Music School and later at the Moscow Cons., graduating in 1967. In 1966 she received 2nd prize at the International Piano Competition in Leeds, England; then embarked upon a major career, appearing widely in recitals and concerts. She is married to the noted Russian conductor **Gennadi Rozhdestvensky.**

Poston, Elizabeth, English pianist and composer; b. Highfield, Hertfordshire, Oct. 24, 1905. She studied piano with Harold Samuel; during World War II was in charge of music in the European Service of the BBC in London. She has a strong predilection for the Elizabethan period; her stylizations of old song patterns are adroitly made and preserve an authentic modality of the originals.

WORKS: *The Holy Child* for Chorus, Vocal Soloists, and String Orch. (1950); *Concertino da Camera on a Theme of Martin Peerson* for Ancient Instruments (1950); *The Nativity* for Chorus, Vocal Soloists, and String Orch. or Organ (1951); Trio for Flute, Clarinet or Viola, and Piano (1958); *Peter Halfpenny's Tunes* for Recorder and Piano (1959); *Lullaby* and *Fiesta,* 2 pieces for Piano (1960); *Magnificat* for 4 Solo Voices and Organ (1961); *3 Scottish Carols* for Chorus, and Strings or Organ (1969); *Harlow Concertante* for String Quartet and String Orch. (1969); *An English Day Book* for Mixed Voices and Harp (1971); Sonatina for Cello and Piano (1972); she also compiled several books of hymn tunes and Christmas carols.

Pothier, Dom Joseph, learned authority on Gregorian chant; b. Bouzemont, near Saint-Dié, Dec. 7, 1835; d. Conques, Belgium, Dec. 8, 1923. He became a Benedictine monk in 1860 at Solesmes; in 1862, sub-prior; in 1866, prof. of theology at the Solesmes Monastery; in 1893, prior at the Benedictine monastery of Ligué; in 1898, abbot at St.-Wandrille. When the religious orders were banned from France, he moved to Belgium. In 1904 he was appointed by Pius X president of the publication committee of the *Editio Vaticana.*
WRITINGS: *Les Mélodies grégoriennes* (highly important sourcebook, based on the study of original MSS; Tournai, 1880; 3rd ed., 1890; in German, 1881; in Italian, 1890); *Méthode du chant grégorien* (Paris, 1902). He was a chief editor of *Liber gradualis* (Tournai, 1883); *Hymni de tempore et de sanctis* (Solesmes, 1885); *Processionale monasticum* (Solesmes, 1888); *Liber antiphonarius* (Solesmes, 1891); *Liber responsorialis* (Solesmes, 1895); *Cantus mariales* (Paris, 1902); contributed many valuable articles to the *Revue du Chant Grégorien.*
BIBLIOGRAPHY: F. Velluz, *Etude bibiographique sur les mélodies grégoriennes de Dom Joseph Pothier* (Grenoble, 1881); N. Rousseau, *L'Ecole grégorienne de Solesmes* (Tournai, 1911); L. David, *Dom Joseph Pothier, abbé de Saint-Wandrille, et la restauration grégorienne* (St.-Wandrille, 1943); A. Le. Guennant, *Précis de rythmique grégorienne d'après les principes de Solesmes* (Paris, 1948); M. Blanc, *L'Enseignement musical de Solesmes* (Paris, 1953; chapter 2); P. Combe, *Histoire de la restauration du chant grégorien d'après des documents inédits* (Solesmes, 1969).

Potter, (Philip) Cipriani (Hambly), English pianist and composer; b. London, Oct. 2, 1792; d. there, Sept. 26, 1871. He studied music first with his father, then with Attwood, Callcott, and Crotch; also took piano lessons with Woelffl during the latter's sojourn in England. In 1817 he went to Vienna, where he studied composition with Aloys Förster; he met Beethoven, who gave him good advice. He traveled in Germany and Italy; returned to London in 1821; the following year he became a piano teacher at the Royal Academy of Music; succeeded Crotch as principal in 1832; retired in 1859. From 1855 to 1870 he was conductor of the Madrigal Society. He fre-

quently appeared in London as a pianist; introduced 3 of Beethoven's concertos (Nos. 1, 3, 4) to England. He publ. a number of piano pieces, including a set of variations under the title *The Enigma,* comprising "variations in the style of 5 eminent artists." This early anticipation of the famous work by Elgar was not known to Elgar himself. He wrote 10 symphs., 4 overtures, 3 piano concertos, 4 piano sonatas, and other pieces. Wagner conducted one of Potter's symphs. during his engagement with the London Phil. Society in 1855. Potter edited for Novello a series of Mozart's piano works.
BIBLIOGRAPHY: *Dictionary of National Biography* (vol. 46); G. Macfarren, "Cipriani Potter: His Life and Work," *RAM Magazine,* no. 1 (1901); P. Peter, *The Life and Work of Cipriani Potter (1792–1871)* (Diss., Northwestern Univ., 1972).

Poueigh, Jean (Marie-Octave-Géraud), French composer and writer on music; b. Toulouse, Feb. 24, 1876; d. Olivet (Loiret), Oct. 14, 1958. After music study in his native city, he entered the Paris Cons. as a student of Caussade, Lenepveu, and Gabriel Fauré; also received advice from Vincent d'Indy; settled in Paris. He harmonized and edited a number of folk songs of Languedoc and Gascogne in *Les Chansons de France* (1907–8), *3 Chansons des Pays d'Oc,* and *14 Chansons anciennes;* also edited the collection *Chansons populaires des Pyrénées françaises* (vol. 1, 1926). His original compositions include the operas *Les Lointains* (1903); *Le Meneur de louves* (1921); *Perkin,* a Basque legend (Bordeaux, Jan. 16, 1931); *Le Roi de Camargue* (Marseilles, May 12, 1948); *Bois-brûlé* (1956); ballets: *Fünn* (1906); *Frivolant* (Paris Opéra, May 1, 1922); a Moroccan ballet, *Chergui;* a symph. tableau, *La Basilique aux vainqueurs;* piano pieces and songs. Under the pen name of **Octave Séré** he publ. *Musiciens français d'aujourd'hui* (Paris, 1911; 7th ed., 1921); contributed numerous articles to various French periodicals.

Pougin, Arthur (pen name of **François-Auguste-Arthur Paroisse-Pougin**), French writer and critic; b. Châteauroux, Indre, Aug. 6, 1834; d. Paris, Aug. 8, 1921. He was a pupil of Alard (violin) and Reber (harmony) at the Paris Cons.; in 1855 was conductor of the Théâtre Beaumarchais; in 1856–59, assistant conductor of the Folies-Nouvelles; from 1860–63, violinist in the Opéra-Comique orch.; then devoted himself to musical journalism; in his articles he fulminated against Debussy and other "anarchistes de musìque," as he described the modern French composers; but he was brilliant even in his most outrageous stolidity of judgment. He was music critic for *Le Ménestrel, Le Soir, La Tribune, L'Evénement,* and the *Journal Officiel.* He started the *Revue de la Musique* in 1876, but it ran for only 6 months; publ. many biographical sketches and essays: *André Campra* (1861); *Gresnick* (1862); *Dezèdes* (1862); *Floquet* (1863); *Martini* (1864); *Devienne* (1864); the preceding 6 are collected as *Musiciens français du XVIIIᵉ siècle;* also, *Verdi* (1886; in Eng., 1887); edited an *Almanach de la* *musique* (1866, 1867, 1868, the last 2 with necrological supplements); *Dictionnaire historique et pittoresque théâtre* (1885); *Méhul* (1889; 2nd ed., 1893); *L'Opéra-Comique pendant la Révolution* (1891); *Essai historique sur la musique en Russie* (1896; 2nd ed., 1904; in Eng., 1915); *J.-J. Rousseau, Musicien* (1901); *Musiciens du XIXᵉ siècle* (1911); *Marie Malibran* (in Eng., 1911); *Marietta Alboni* (1912); *Massenet* (1914); *Giuseppina Grassini* (1920); *Le Violon, les violonistes, et la musique de violon du XVIᵉ au XVIIIᵉ siècle* (posthumous, 1924). Pougin wrote for Larousse's *Grand dictionnaire universel* all the articles on music. He also edited the supplement to Fétis's *Biographie universelle* (2 vols., 1878–80), and the new eds. of the *Dictionnaire lyrique, ou Histoire des opéras* of Félix Clément and P. Larousse (Paris, 1898; with supplement up to 1904).

Poulenc, Francis, brilliant French composer; b. Paris, Jan. 7, 1899; d. there, Jan. 30, 1963. His mother taught him music in his childhood; at 16 he began taking formal piano lessons with Ricardo Viñes. A decisive turn in his development as a composer occurred when he attracted the attention of Erik Satie, the arbiter elegantiarum of the arts and social amenities in Paris. Deeply impressed by Satie's fruitful eccentricities in the then-shocking manner of Dadaism, Poulenc joined an ostentatiously self-descriptive musical group called the Nouveaux Jeunes. In a gratuitous parallel with the Russian Five, the French critic Henri Collet dubbed the "New Youths" Le Groupe de Six, and the label stuck under the designation Les Six. The 6 musicians included, besides Poulenc: Auric, Durey, Honegger, Milhaud, and Tailleferre. Although quite different in their styles of composition and artistic inclinations, they continued collective participation in various musical events. Poulenc served in the French army (1918–21), and then began taking lessons in composition with Koechlin (1921–24). An excellent pianist, Poulenc became in 1935 an accompanist to the French baritone Pierre Bernac, for whom he wrote numerous songs. Compared with his fortuitous comrades-in-six, Poulenc appears a classicist. He never experimented with the popular devices of "machine music," asymmetrical rhythms, and polyharmonies as cultivated by Honegger and Milhaud. Futuristic projections had little interest for him; he was content to follow the gentle neo-Classical formation of Ravel's piano music and songs. Among his other important artistic contacts was the ballet impresario Diaghilev, who commissioned him to write music for his Ballets Russes. Apart from his fine songs and piano pieces, Poulenc revealed himself as an inspired composer of religious music, of which his choral works *Stabat Mater* and *Gloria* are notable. He further wrote remarkable music for the organ, including a concerto that became a minor masterpiece. A master of artificial simplicity, he pleases even sophisticated listeners by his bland triadic tonalities, spiced with quickly passing diaphonous discords.

WORKS: OPERAS: 2-act opéra-bouffe, *Les Ma-melles de Tirésias* (*The Breasts of Tiresias;* 1944; Opéra-Comique, June 3, 1947; U.S. premiere, Waltham, Mass., June 13, 1953, Bernstein conducting); 3-act religious opera, *Dialogues des Carmélites* (1953–56; La Scala, Milan, Jan. 26, 1957; U.S. premiere, San Francisco, Sept. 22, 1957); one-act monodrama for Soprano Solo, *La Voix humaine*, after Cocteau (1958; Opéra-Comique, Feb. 6, 1959; U.S. premiere, N.Y., Feb. 23, 1960).

BALLETS: *La Baigneuse de Trouville* and *Discours de Général,* 2 movements for *Les Mariés de la Tour Eiffel,* a ballet-farce by Cocteau (Champs-Elysées, June 18, 1921; other movements by members of Les Six, except for Durey, who had already permanently left the group); *Les Biches (The Does),* with Chorus (1923; Monte Carlo, Jan. 6, 1924); *Pastourelle,* 9th movement of an 11-movement collective ballet, *L'Eventail de Jeanne* (1927; first perf. of orch. version, Paris Opéra, March 4, 1929; movements by Roussel, Ravel, Ibert, Milhaud, and others); *Aubade,* choreographic concerto for Piano and 18 Instruments (1929; private perf., Paris, June 18, 1929; public perf., London, Dec. 19, 1929); *Les Animaux modèles,* after fables by La Fontaine (1940–41; Paris Opéra, Aug. 8, 1942).

FOR ORCH.: *Concert champêtre* for Harpsichord or Piano, and Orch. (1927–28; Paris, May 3, 1929); Concerto for 2 Pianos and Orch. (1932; Venice, Sept. 5, 1932); *2 marches et un intermède* for Chamber Orch. (1937; Paris World Exhibition, 1937); Concerto for Organ, String Orch., and Timpani (1938; private perf., Paris, June 21, 1939; first public perf., Paris, June 10, 1941); Sinfonietta (1947; London, Oct. 24, 1948); Concerto for Piano and Orch. (1949; Boston, Jan. 6, 1950); *Matelote provençale,* movement from a collective work of 7 composers, *La Guirlande de Campra* (1952); *Bucolique,* movement from a collective work of 8 composers, *Variations sur le nom de Marguerite Long* (1954).

CHAMBER MUSIC: Sonata for 2 Clarinets (1918; revised 1945); Sonata for Clarinet and Bassoon (1922); Sonata for Horn, Trumpet, and Trombone (1922; revised 1945); Trio for Oboe, Bassoon, and Piano (1926); Sextet for Piano and Wind Quintet (1930–32; revised 1939); *Suite française* for 9 Winds, Percussion, and Harpsichord (1935); Violin Sonata (1942–43; revised 1949); Cello Sonata (1948); Flute Sonata (1956); *Elégie,* to the memory of Dennis Brain, for Horn and Piano (1957); *Sarabande* for Solo Guitar (1960); Clarinet Sonata (1962); Oboe Sonata (1962).

CHORAL WORKS: Chanson à boire for a cappella Male Chorus (1922); *7 chansons* for a cappella Mixed Chorus (1936); *Litanies à la vierge noire* for Female Chorus and Organ (1936); Mass in G for a cappella Mixed Chorus (1937; Paris, May 1938); *Sécheresses (Dryness),* cantata, after texts by Edward James, for Chorus and Orch. (1937; Paris, 1938); *4 motets pour un temps de pénitence* for Mixed Chorus a cappella (1938–39); *Exultate Deo* for Mixed Chorus a cappella (1941); *Salve regina* for Mixed Chorus a cappella (1941); *Figure humaine,* cantata for Double Mixed Chorus (1943); *Un Soir de neige,* chamber cantata for 6 Voices a cappella (1944); 2 books of traditional French songs, arranged for Chorus a cappella (1945); *4 petites* prières de Saint François d'Assise for Male Chorus a cappella (1948); *Stabat Mater* for Soprano, Chorus, and Orch. (1950; Strasbourg Festival, June 13, 1951); *4 motets pour le temps de Noël* for Chorus a cappella (1951–52); *Ave verum corpus* for Female Chorus a cappella (1952); *Laudes de Saint Antoine de Padove* for Male Chorus a cappella (1957–59); *Gloria* for Soprano, Chorus, and Orch. (1959; Boston, Jan. 20, 1961); *7 répons des ténèbres* for Boy Soprano, Boys' and Men's Chorus, and Orch. (1961; posthumous, N.Y., April 11, 1963).

FOR VOICE AND INSTRUMENTS: *Rapsodie nègre* for Baritone, String Quartet, Flute, Clarinet, and Piano (1917; Paris, Dec. 11, 1917; revised 1933); *Le Bestiaire (The Bestiary)*, after Apollinaire, for Mezzosoprano, String Quartet, Flute, Clarinet, and Bassoon (1918–19); *Cocardes,* after Cocteau, for Voice, Violin, Cornet, Trombone, Bass Drum, and Triangle (1919); *Le Bal masqué (The Masked Ball)*, after surrealist verses of Max Jacob, for Voice, Oboe, Clarinet, Bassoon, Violin, Cello, Percussion, and Piano (1932); *La Dame de Monte Carlo*, monologue for Soprano and Orch. (1961; Paris, Dec. 5, 1961).

FOR VOICE AND PIANO: *Histoire de Babar le petit éléphant (History of Babar the Small Elephant)* for Narrator and Piano (1940–45; orchestrated by Jean Francaix, 1962); song cycles: *Le Bestiaire* (1919; arrangement); *Cocardes* (1919; arrangement); *Poèmes de Ronsard* (1924–25; later orchestrated); *Chansons gaillardes* (1925–26); *Airs chantés* (1927–28); *8 chansons polonaises* (1934); *4 chansons pour enfants* (1934); *5 poèmes* after Eluard (1935); *Tel jour, telle nuit* (1936–37); *3 poèmes* after de Vilmorin (1937); *2 poèmes* after Apollinaire (1938); *Miroirs brûlants* (1938–39); *Fiançailles pour rire* (1939); *Banalités* (1940); *Chansons villageoises* (1942; orchestrated 1943); *Métamorphoses* (1943); *3 chansons* after Lorca (1947); *Calligrammes* (1948); *La Fraîcheur et le feu* (1950); *Parisiana* (1954); *Le Travail du peintre* (1956); *2 mélodies* (1956); *La Courte Paille* (1960); separate songs: *Toréador* (1918; revised 1932); *Vocalise* (1927); *Epitaphe* (1930); *A sa guitare,* after Ronsard (1935); *Montparnasse* (1941–45); *Hyde Park* (1945); *Paul et Virginie* (1946); *Le Disparu* (1947); *Mazurka* (1949); *Rosemonde* (1954); *Dernier poème* (1956); *Une Chanson de porcelaine* (1958); others.

FOR PIANO: Sonata, 4-hands (1918); *3 mouvements perpétuels* (1918); *Valse* (1919); *Suite in C* (1920); *6 impromptus* (1920); *Promenades* (1921); *Napoli*, suite of 3 pieces (1921–25); *2 novelettes* (1928); *3 pièces* (1928); *Pièce brève sur la nom d'Albert Roussel* (1929); *8 nocturnes* (1929–38); *15 improvisations* (1932–59); *Villageoises* (1933); *Feuillets d'album* (1933); *Les Soirées de Nazelles* (1930–36); *Mélancolie* (1940); *Intermezzo* (1943); *L'Embarquement pour Cythère* for 2 Pianos (1951); *Thème varié* (1951); Sonata for 2 Pianos (1952–53); *Elégie* for 2 Pianos (1959); *Novelette sur un thème de Manuel de Falla* (1959).

WRITINGS: He wrote a monograph on Chabrier (Paris, 1961); his reminiscences, *Moi et mes amis,* were publ. posthumously (Paris, 1963); another posthumous publ. was *Journal de mes mélodies* (Paris, 1964).

BIBLIOGRAPHY: A Schaeffner, "Francis Poulenc, musicien français," *Contrepoints,* 1 (1946); C. Rostand, *Francis Poulenc: Entretiens avec Claude Rostand* (Paris, 1954); Henri Hell, *Poulenc, musicien français* (Paris, 1958); Jean Roy, *Francis Poulenc* (Paris, 1964); Pierre Bernac, *Francis Poulenc: The Man and His Songs* (London, 1977); Keith W. Daniel, *Francis Poulenc: His Artistic Development and Musical Style* (N.Y., 1982).

Poulet, Gaston, French violinist and conductor; b. Paris, April 10, 1892; d. Draveil (Essonne), April 14, 1974. He studied violin at the Paris Cons., gaining first prize; organized a string quartet and gave concerts in Europe; from 1927 to 1936 conducted the Concerts Poulet at the Théâtre Sarah-Bernhardt in Paris; also taught at the Paris Cons.; in 1932–44 served as director of the Cons. of Bordeaux and conducted the Phil. Orch. there; from 1940 to 1945 conducted the Concerts Colonne in Paris; was a guest conductor with the London Symph. (1947) and in Germany (1948); also in South America. He played the violin in the first performance of Debussy's Violin Sonata, with Debussy himself at the piano. He was a prof. of chamber music at the Paris Cons. in 1944–62; in 1948 founded the famous Besançon Festival.

Poulet, Gérard, French violinist, son of **Gaston Poulet;** b. Bayonne, Aug. 12, 1938. He entered the Paris Cons. at the age of 11 in the class of André Asselin, and won first prize at 12; in the same year (1950) he played 3 violin concertos with the Orch. Colonne, under his father's direction; then appeared with other Paris orchs.; subsequently gave concerts and played with orchs. in England, Germany, Italy, Austria, and the Netherlands. In 1956 he won first Grand Prix at the Paganini competition of Genoa, and was given the honor of performing on Paganini's own violin, the famous Guarneri del Jesù.

Pouplinière. See **La Pouplinière.**

Pourtalès, Guy de (complete name, **Guido James de Pourtalès**), French writer on music; b. Berlin, Aug. 4, 1881; d. Lausanne, June 12, 1941. He studied in Bonn, Berlin, and Paris; was in the French army during World War I; then settled in Paris as a music critic. He publ. a number of successful biographies of composers: *La Vie de Franz Liszt* (1925); *Chopin, ou Le Poète* (1927; 2nd ed., 1946; in Eng. as *Chopin: A Man of Solitude,* London, 1930); *Wagner, Histoire d'un artiste* (1932; revised and augmented ed., 1942); *Berlioz et l'Europe romantique* (1939).

Pousseur, Henri, Belgian composer of the ultramodern school; b. Malmédy, June 23, 1929. He studied at the Liège Cons. (1947–52) and the Brussels Cons. (1952–53); had private lessons in composition from André Souris and Pierre Boulez; until 1959, worked in the Cologne and Milan electronic music studios, where he came in contact with Stockhausen and Berio; was a member of the avant-garde group of composers "Variation" in Liège. He taught music in various Belgian schools (1950–59); was founder (1958) and director of the Studio de Musique Electronique APELAC in Brussels, now a part of the Centre de Recherches Musicales in Liège; gave lectures at the summer courses of new music in Darmstadt (1957–67), Cologne (1962–68), Basel (1963–64), the State Univ. of N.Y. in Buffalo (1966–69), and the Cons. in Liège. In his music he tries to synthesize all the expressive powers of which man, as a biological species, *Homo sapiens* (or even *Homo insipiens*), is capable in the domain of art (or non-art); the technological resources of the subspecies *Homo habilis* (magnetic tape, electronics/synthesizers, aleatory extensions, the principle of indeterminacy, glossolalia, self-induced schizophasia) all form part of his rich musical (or non-musical) vocabulary for multimedia (or nullimedia) representations. The influence of his methods (or non-methods) of composition (or non-composition) is pervasive.

WORKS: Piano Sonatina (1949); *3 chants sacrés* for Soprano and String Trio (1951); *Seismogrammes* for Tape (1953); *Symphonies* for 15 Solo Instruments (1954–55); *Quintet to the Memory of Webern* for Violin, Cello, Clarinet, Bass Clarinet, and Piano (1955); *Exercices* for Piano: *Variations I* and *Impromptu et Variations I* (1956); *Scambi* for Tape (1957); *Mobile* for 2 Pianos (1956–58); *Madrigal I* for Solo Clarinet (1958); *Madrigal II* for Flute, Violin, Viola da Gamba, and Harpsichord (1961); *Madrigal III* for Clarinet, Violin, Cello, 2 Percussionists, and Piano (1962); *Rimes pour différentes sources sonores* for 3 Orch. Groups and Tape (1958–59; Donaueschingen Festival, Oct. 17, 1959); *Electre, "musical action"* (1960); *Répons* for 7 Musicians (1960; revision with Actor added, 1965); *Ode* for String Quartet (1960–61); *Caractères* for Piano (1961); *3 visages de Liège* and *Prospective* for Tape (1961); *Votre Faust,* an aleatory "fantasy in the manner of an opera" for 5 Actors, Vocal Quartet, 12 Musicians, and Tapes, for which the audience decides the ending (in collaboration with Michel Butor; 1961–67; Milan, 1969; concert version, titled *Portail de Votre Faust,* for 4 Voices, Tape, and 12 Instruments); *Trait* for 15 Strings (1962); *Miroir de Votre Faust* for Piano, and Soprano ad libitum (*Caractères II,* 1964–65); *Caractères madrigalesques* for Solo Oboe (*Madrigal IV* and *Caractères III,* 1965); *Apostrophe et 6 réflexions* for Piano (1964–66); *Phonèmes pour Cathy* for Solo Voice (*Madrigal V,* 1966); *Echoes I* for Solo Cello (1967); *Echoes II, de Votre Faust* for Mezzo-soprano, Flute, Cello, and Piano (1969); *Couleurs croisées (Crossed Colors)* for Orch., a series of crypto-musical variations on the civil rights song *We Shall Overcome* (1967; Brussels Radio, Dec. 20, 1968); *Mnemosyne I,* monody, after Hölderlin, for Solo Voice, or Unison Chorus, or one Instrument (1968); *Mnemosyne II,* an instrumental re-creation of *Mnemosyne I,* with ad libitum scoring (1969); *Croisées des couleurs croisées (Crosses of Crossed Colors;* an intensified sequel to *Couleurs croisées*) for Female Voice, 2–5 Pianos, Tape Recorders, and 2 Radio Receivers dialed aleatorily, to texts from Indian and Negro materials and political

speeches (N.Y., Nov. 29, 1970); *Icare apprenti* for an undetermined number of Instruments (1970); *Les Ephémerides d'Icare 2* for Piano and Instruments (Madrid, April 20, 1970); *Invitation à l'Utopie* for Narrator, 2 Female Voices, 4-voice Chorus, and Instruments (Brussels Radio, Jan. 25, 1971); *L'Effacement de Prince Igor,* scene for Orch. (Brussels, Feb. 28, 1972); *Le Temps des paraboles* (1972); *Die Erprobung des Petrus Herbraïcus,* chamber opera (Berlin Festival, Sept. 12, 1974); *Vue sur les jardins interdits* for Organ or Saxophone Quartet (1974); *19 √ 8/4* for Solo Cello (1975). He publ. *Fragments théoriques I. Sur la musique experimentale* (Brussels, 1970).

Powell, (Earl) "Bud," black American jazz pianist; b. New York, Sept. 27, 1924; d. there, Aug. 1, 1966. After dropping out of school at the age of 15, he began playing with local groups in N.Y. Following the zeitgeist, he adopted the bop style, and in 1943 joined Cootie Williams and his band; he also played concerts with Dizzy Gillespie, Sid Catlett, and John Kirby, achieving recognition as a fine bop pianist. He was a frequent participant in the formative jazz sessions at Minton's Playhouse. He gradually discarded the prevalent "stride" piano style with its regular beat, and emancipated the left-hand rhythm by introducing a contrapuntal line with asymmetrical punctuation. His brief career was periodically interrupted by mental eclipses caused by immoderate use of hallucinogenic drugs.

Powell, John, American pianist, composer, and ethnomusicologist; b. Richmond, Va., Sept. 6, 1882; d. Charlottesville, Va., Aug. 15, 1963. His father was a schoolteacher, his mother an amateur musician; he received his primary musical education at home; then studied piano with F.C. Hahr, a pupil of Liszt; subsequently entered the Univ. of Virginia (B.A., 1901) and then went to Vienna, where he studied piano with Leschetizky (1902–7) and composition with Navrátil (1904–7); gave successful piano recitals in Paris and London; returning to the U.S., he toured the country as a pianist, playing some of his own works. His most successful piece was *Rapsodie nègre,* inspired by Joseph Conrad's *Heart of Darkness,* for Piano and Orch.; Powell was the soloist in its first performance with the Russian Symph. Orch. (N.Y., March 23, 1918). The titles of some of his works disclose a whimsical propensity; perhaps his most important achievement lies in ethnomusicology; he methodically collected rural songs of the South; was the organizer of the Virginia State Choral Festivals and of the annual White Top Mountain Folk Music Festivals. A man of versatile interests, he was also an amateur astronomer, and discovered a comet.

WORKS: Symph. in A (Detroit, April 23, 1947); 2 piano concertos; Violin Concerto; *Rapsodie nègre* for Piano and Orch.; *In Old Virginia,* overture (1921); *Natchez on the Hill,* 3 Virginian country dances for Orch. (1932); *A Set of 3* for Orch. (1935); *Virginia Symphony* (Richmond, Nov. 5, 1951); String Quartet; *Sonate Virginianesque* for Violin and Piano (1919); 3 piano sonatas: *Sonate psychologique, Sonate noble, Sonata Teutonica;* piano suite, *In the South;* piano suite (also for Orch.), *At the Fair; In the Hammock* for 2 Pianos, 8-hands; opera, *Judith and Holofernes.*

Powell, Laurence, British-American composer and conductor; b. Birmingham, England, Jan. 13, 1899. He studied at Ratcliffe College, Leicester (1909–15), and Ushaw College, Durham (1915–17); was in the British army and the Royal Air Force during World War I; then studied music at the Birmingham and Midland Inst. School of Music (1919–22) under Sir Granville Bantock; his examiner was Sir Donald Francis Tovey. While there, he won a full scholarship to Birmingham Univ., where he carried on his studies concurrently with Bantock, gaining a Mus.Bac. degree with first-class honors. In 1923 he went to the U.S.; became a naturalized citizen in 1936; took courses at the Univ. of Wisconsin (M.A., 1926); subsequently held various teaching positions: at the Univ. of Wisconsin (1924–26), the Univ. of Arkansas (1926–34), and Little Rock Junior College (1934–39); was organist at St. Mary's Church in Victoria, Texas (1947–52); organist and choirmaster at St. Francis Cathedral in Santa Fe (1952–68); a choir director and organist at Assumption Church in Albuquerque (1968–70); organist and choirmaster at Our Lady of Victory Church in Victoria, Texas (1970–75); upon retirement in 1975, was honored by a plaque inscribed "for Laurence Powell for demonstrating beauty in God and man through music and song." As a conductor, he was the organizer and music director of the Little Rock Symph. Orch. (1934–39); conductor of the Grand Rapids (Mich.) Federal Symph. (1939–41); founder and conductor of the Santa Fe Orch., later renamed Rio Grande Symph. (1953–55).
WORKS: For Orch.: *The Ogre of the Northern Fastness* (1921); *Keltic Legend* (Bournemouth, England, Aug. 27, 1924, composer conducting; revised version, Madison, Wis., May 20, 1931); *Charivari,* suite (1925); 2 symphs. (1929, 1943); *Deirdre of the Sorrows* (1933; Little Rock, March 18, 1937, composer conducting); *The County Fair,* suite (1936); *Suite for String Orch.* (1931; Grand Rapids, May 9, 1940, composer conducting); *Picnic,* an "Arkansas pastoral" for String Orch. (Oklahoma City, March 21, 1936); *Variations* (Rochester, N.Y., Oct. 28, 1941); *Duo concertante* for Recorders and Orch. (1941); *The Santa Fe Trail* for Baritone, Narrator, and Orch. (Rio Grande Symph. Orch., Santa Fe, April 22, 1958); *Penny Overture* (1960); *Overture on French Folk Tunes* (1970); *Oracle* for Orch. (1975); *Halcyone,* dramatic poem for Chorus and Orch. (1923); *Alleluya,* cantata for Chorus and Orch. (1926); *The Seasons* (after poems by Blake) for Chorus a cappella (1928); Piano Quartet (1933); Quartet for Clarinets (1936); 3 sonatinas for Recorders Unaccompanied, one each for Soprano, Alto, and Tenor (1977); several masses; songs. All of his works are deposited in the Library of the Univ. of Arkansas at Fayetteville.

Powell, Maud, American violinist; b. Peru, Ill., Aug. 22, 1868; d. Uniontown, Pa., Jan. 8, 1920. She received her primary instruction at home; then went to Europe, where she took violin lessons with Schradieck in Leipzig and theory with Charles Dancla in Paris. Returning to the U.S. in 1885, she gave concerts and acquired a sort of automatic celebrity, since the female species among violinists was a *rara avis* in her time. Thus, when the Arion Society of N.Y. rigged a musical expedition to Germany in 1892 for the quadricentennial of the discovery of America, she went along as a "representative American violinist." She also played at the Chicago World's Fair in 1893.
BIBLIOGRAPHY: Article by A.R. Coolidge in *Notable American Women,* III (N.Y., 1971).

Powell, Mel, remarkable American composer; b. New York, Feb. 12, 1923. He began his career in popular music, and acquired quite a reputation as a jazz pianist for the Benny Goodman Band; concurrently, he took lessons with Bernard Wagenaar and Joseph Schillinger in N.Y. (1937–39); later also had some instruction in composition with Ernst Toch in Los Angeles (1946–48). In 1948 he entered Hindemith's class at the Yale School of Music (B.M., 1952). From 1957–69 he was on the faculty of Yale Univ.; from 1969–75 he served as dean of music at the Calif. Inst. of the Arts. As a composer, he revealed versatile talents, being technically at home in an incisive jazz idiom, in a neo-Classical manner faithfully emulating his teacher Hindemith, tangentially shadowing Stravinsky, in an expressionist mood of Schoenberg, in the stark, microphonic, dodecaphonic, canonic universe of Anton von Webern, and finally in electronic sonorism. In all these avatars, Powell somehow succeeded in projecting his own personality in most curious quaquaversal ways; thus, while absorbed in atonal composition, he was able to turn out an occasional march tune. In all this, he manages to cultivate the minutiae of rhythmic and intervallic units, with quick changes of tonal and temporal articulation, without venturing into the outer space of musical entropy.
WORKS: *Recitative and Toccata Percossa* for Harpsichord (1952); *6 Love Songs* for Unaccompanied Chorus (1952); *Capriccio* for Concert Band (1953); *Divertimento* for Violin and Harp (1954); *Divertimento* for Flute, Clarinet, Oboe, Bassoon, and Trumpet (1955); Piano Trio (1955–56); *Stanzas* for Orch. (1957); *Miniatures* for Baroque Ensemble (1957); *Filigree Setting* for String Quartet (1959); *Haiku Settings* for Soprano and Piano (1960); *Setting* for Cello and Orch. (1961); *Improvisation* for Clarinet, Viola, and Piano (1962); *Events* for Electronic Tape (1963); *2 Prayer Settings* for Tenor, Oboe, Violin, Viola, and Cello (1963); *Immobiles* for Orch. and Electronic Tape (1966); *Cantilena* for Soprano, Violin, and Electronic Tape (1970); *Machine-Music Variations* (1974–75); *Settings* for Soprano and Chamber Group (1979); *Little Companion Pieces* for Soprano and String Quartet (1980); String Quartet (1982).
BIBLIOGRAPHY: Leslie Thimmig, "The Music of

Mel Powell," *Musical Quarterly* (Jan. 1969).

Power, Lionel (**Lionel** or **Leonell Polbero** or **Powero,** etc.), English composer; date of birth unknown; d. Canterbury, June 5, 1445. He was a contemporary of Dunstable, whose style he so closely approximated that authorship of works of the 2 composers has often been confused (some authorities claim, without foundation, that Power and Dunstable were identical). He wrote a treatise, "Upon the Gamme" (c.1450; transcribed by J. Wylde, in the British Museum; reprinted by Hawkins in *History of the Science and Practice of Music,* vol. 2; also by S.B. Meech in *Speculum,* July 1935, pp. 242–58; and in part by M. Bukofzer, *Geschichte des englischen Diskants und des Fauxbourdons,* 1936).
WORKS: 2 *Ave Reginas,* a *Salve Regina,* a *Mater ora filium,* and 21 pieces (mostly parts of masses) for 3–4 voices appear in Denkmäler der Tonkunst in Österreich, 14/15 (7); *Sammelbände der Internationalen Musik-Gesellschaft* (vol. 2, p. 378); Stainer's *Early Bodleian Music;* and *The Old Hall Manuscript* (3 vols., ed. by A. Ramsbotham; Burnham, Buckinghamshire, 1933–38). See also A. Schering, *Geschichte der Musik in Beispielen* (no. 37) and Davison and Apel, *Historical Anthology of Music* (vol. 1, no. 63). Other pieces preserved in MS at Bologna, Modena, Oxford, Vienna, and London (British Museum) include a *Missa Rex Saeculorum* (with *Kyrie*), a 4-voiced *Ave Regina,* and part of a *Kyrie*. 2 masses attributed to Power were publ. in Documenta Polyphoniae Liturgicae S. Ecclesiae Romanae (series 1, nos. 2 and 9). The *Complete Works,* ed. by C. Hamm, was issued by the American Inst. of Musicology (1969).
BIBLIOGRAPHY: H. Riemann, *Geschichte der Musiktheorie,* (p. 143); W. Korte, *Die Harmonik des 15. Jahrhunderts* (1929; p. 23); C. Hamm, "The Motets of Lionel Power," in H.S. Powers, *Studies in Music History: Essays for Oliver Strunk* (Princeton, N.J., 1968).

Pownall, Mary Ann, English actress and singer; b. 1751; d. Charleston, S.C., Aug. 11, 1796. She was known first as **Mrs. Wrightson** (her first husband was a prompter in a London theater); made her debut in 1770 in *The Recruiting Officer,* in London; from 1776 to 1788 was a Vauxhall favorite. In 1792 she first appeared in Boston with the Old American Co., of which she was a leading artist; later sang in subscription concerts in N.Y., and joined John Henry's N.Y. Co. She composed the text and music of numerous songs, including *Advice to the Ladies of Boston, Washington* (in honor of George Washington), and *Primroses;* some of these appeared in a book of songs that she compiled with J. Hewitt (publ. in N.Y.). Her 2nd husband was A. Pownall.
BIBLIOGRAPHY: J.T. Howard, *Our American Music* (N.Y., 1931, and later eds.).

Pozdro, John (Walter), significant American composer and pedagogue; b. Chicago, Aug. 14, 1923. He was of Polish extraction on his paternal line (*po-zdro* means, approximately, "your health") and

of German origin on his mother's side; his father was a master cabinetmaker and an unsung artist (he sang and played the violin). Pozdro took piano lessons with Nina Shafran; then studied music theory at the American Cons. in Chicago and Northwestern Univ.; later entered the Eastman School of Music at Rochester, N.Y., as a student in composition of Howard Hanson and Bernard Rogers, graduating in 1958 with a Ph.D. He subsequently joined the music faculty at the Univ. of Kansas in Lawrence, became its director of music theory and composition in 1961; from 1958 to 1968 was chairman of the Annual Symposium of Contemporary American Music at the Univ. of Kansas. His music is inherently pragmatic, with tertian torsion resulting in the formation of tastefully enriched triadic harmony, and with asymmetric rhythms enhancing the throbbing pulse of musical continuity.
WORKS: FOR THE STAGE: *Malooley and the Fear Monster,* "family opera" in one act (1976; Lawrence, Kans., Feb. 6, 1977); *Hello, Kansas!,* musical play in observance of the 100th anniversary of the statehood of Kansas (1961; Lawrence, June 12, 1961). FOR ORCH.: *Overture* (1948; Evanston, Ill., Nov. 30, 1949); Symph. No. 1 (1949); *A Cynical Overture* (1952; Univ. of Texas, March 24, 1953); Symph. No. 2 (1957; Rochester, N.Y., May 4, 1958); Symph. No. 3 (1960; Oklahoma City, Dec. 12, 1960); *Waterlow Park* for Orch. (Lawrence, May 8, 1972); *Rondo giocoso* for String Orch. (1964); *Music for a Youth Symphony* (1969). CHAMBER MUSIC: Quintet for Woodwinds and Piano (1947); Sextet for Flute and Strings (1948); 2 string quartets (1947, 1952); *Elegy* for Trumpet and Piano (1953); *Trilogy* for Clarinet, Bassoon, Trumpet, and Piano (1960); Sonata for Brass Instruments and Percussion (1966); Violin Sonata (1971); *Impressions* for Flute, Oboe, Clarinet, Bassoon, and Piano (1984). FOR PIANO: 6 sonatas (1947, 1963, 1964, 1976, 1979, 1982); 8 preludes (1950–74); *Ballade-Fantasy* (1981). VOCAL MUSIC: *All Pleasant Things* for Chorus (1960); *They that Go Down to the Sea* for Chorus (1967); *The Creation* for Children's Voices (1967); *Alleluia* for Chorus (1979); *King of Glory* for Chorus, Organ, and Piano (1983). FOR CARILLON: *Landscape I* (1954); *Landscape II* (1969); *Rustic Landscape* (1981); *Variation on a Slavonic Theme* (1982).

Pozniak, Bronislaw, German pianist and pedagogue; b. Lwow, Aug. 26, 1887; d. Halle, April 20, 1953. He studied at the Cons. of Cracow; then in Berlin with Barth; established a trio, and traveled in Germany; then settled in Breslau as a piano teacher; in 1946 moved to Leipzig, and eventually to Halle. He publ. *ABC des Klavierspielers* (1939; 2nd ed., 1948); *Praktische Anweisungen für das Studium der Chopinschen Werke* (Halle, 1949); was editor of a new edition of Chopin's piano works for Peters.

Praetorius, Ernst, German musicologist; b. Berlin, Sept. 20, 1880; d. Ankara, March 27, 1946. He studied violin in Breslau and Halle; history and theory in Berlin with Friedlaender, Fleischer, and Stumpf; in

1905, received his Dr.Phil. with the dissertation *Die Mensuraltheorie des Franchinus Gafurius* (Leipzig, 1905); in 1906, was appointed director of the famous Heyer Museum in Cologne; held this post until 1909, when he joined the staff of the Cologne Opera. Subsequently, he held similar positions in Bochum (1912), Leipzig (1913), Lübeck (1914), Breslau (1915), and Berlin (1922). From 1924 until 1933 he was Generalmusikdirektor in Weimar; in 1934 went to Turkey, where he was active in the educational field and on the radio; remained in Ankara until his death.

Praetorius (Latinized from **Schulz** or **Schulze**), **Hieronymus,** German composer; b. Hamburg, Aug. 10, 1560; d. there, Jan. 27, 1629. He studied with his father, **Jacobus Schulze,** organist of the Jacobikirche; then in Cologne. He became town cantor in Erfurt in 1580, assistant organist to his father in 1582, and his successor in 1586. He brought out a *Hamburger Melodeyen-Gesangbuch* (1604; with his son **Jacobus,** J. Decker, and D. Scheidemann). His works were publ. in 5 collections in 1622–25, under the general title *Opus musicum novum et perfectum:* I, *Cantiones sacrae a* 5–12; II, *Magnificats a* 8–12; III, *Liber missarum,* 6 masses *a* 5–8; IV, *Cantiones variae, a* 5–20, containing Latin and German motets; V, *Cantiones novae officiosae, a* 5–15, also containing Latin and German motets. A selection of his works (a Mass, a Magnificat, and some motets) was publ. by Hugo Leichtentritt in Denkmäler Deutscher Tonkunst, 23.

BIBLIOGRAPHY: Hugo Leichtentritt, *Geschichte der Motette* (1908; pp. 309ff.); B. Friedrich, *Der Vokalstil des Hieronymus Praetorius* (Hamburg, 1932).

Praetorius, Jacobus, German composer and organist, son of **Hieronymus Praetorius;** b. Hamburg, Feb. 8, 1586; d. there, Oct. 22, 1651. He studied with Sweelinck in Amsterdam; in 1603 was appointed organist at the Peterskirche in Hamburg. He contributed several motets to his father's collection *Hamburger Melodeyen-Gesangbuch.*

Praetorius, Michael, great German musician, composer, and theorist; b. Kreuzberg, Thuringia, Feb. 15, 1571; d. Wolfenbüttel, Feb. 15, 1621. His real family name was **Schultheiss** (German for "magistrate," or "praetor"), which he Latinized as Praetorius. He was the son of a preacher; attended the Latin school of Torgau; studied organ in Frankfurt; then was in the service of the Duke of Braunschweig (from 1604); was also prior of the Ringelheim monastery, although without actual residence there. In 1612 he succeeded Mancinus as Kapellmeister in Wolfenbüttel, and remained there until his death.

WORKS: *Musae Sioniae,* a collection of 1,244 vocal numbers in 9 parts, in note-against-note counterpoint (1605–10; 2nd ed. of Part IX, as *Bicinia et tricinia,* 1611); *Musarum Sioniarum motetae et psalmi 4–16 vocae* (1607); *Eulogodia Sionia* (1611); 60 motets *a* 2–8 for the "close of the Divine Service";

Missodia Sionia (1611); *Hymnodia Sionia* (1611; hymns *a* 2–8); *Megalynodia* (1611; madrigals and motets *a* 5–8); *Terpsichore* (1612; dance pieces *a* 4–6, by Praetorius and some French composers); *Polyhymnia caduceatrix et panegyrica* (1619; songs of peace and rejoicing *a* 1–21); *Polyhymnia exercitatrix* (1620; *a* 2–8); *Uranodia* or *Uranochordia* (1613; 19 songs *a* 4); *Kleine und grosse Litaney* (1613); *Epithalamium* (1614); *Puericinium* (1621; 14 church songs *a* 3–12). REPRINTS: Organ works by W. Gurlitt, in the *Archiv für Musikwissenschaft* (1921); also by K. Matthäi (Braunschweig, 1930); *Psalm 116,* by R. Holle (Mainz, 1933); 2 pieces by A. Schering in *Geschichte der Musik in Beispielen* (nos. 161, 162); various numbers reprinted by G. Tucher, L. Schöberlein, F. Riegel, K. Ameln, etc.

WRITINGS: *Syntagma musicum,* his major work, of which 3 vols. were printed: Vol. I, part 1 (Wolfenbüttel, 1614; in 2 parts), is a historical and descriptive treatise in Latin on ancient and ecclesiastical music, and ancient secular instruments. Vol. II (Wolfenbüttel, 1618; Appendix, 1620), written in German, in 5 parts and an Appendix, is the most important extant source of information on musical instruments of the period, describing their form, compass, tone quality, etc., the organ in particular being treated at great length; the Appendix contains 42 woodcuts of the principal instruments enumerated (vol. II has been reprinted as vol. XIII of the publications of the Gesellschaft für Musikforschung; facsimile reprint, with introduction by W. Gurlitt, Kassel, 1929). Vol. III (Wolfenbüttel, 1618) contains a valuable and interesting account of secular composition at that time, and a treatise on solmisation, notation, etc.; a reprint of vol. III was publ. by E. Bernouilli (1916). A complete edition of Praetorius's works was issued in 21 vols. under the editorship of Friedrich Blume (1928–41).

BIBLIOGRAPHY: W. Gurlitt, *Michael Praetorius (Creuzburgensis), Sein Leben und sein Werke* (Leipzig, 1915); F. Blume, *Michael Praetorius Creuzburgensis* (Wolfenbüttel, 1929); P. Zimmermann, "Zur Biographie des Michael Praetorius," *Braunschweigischer Geschichtsverein Jahrbuch* (1930); R. Unger, *Die mehrchörige Aufführungspraxis bei Michael Praetorius und die Feiergestaltung der Gegenwart* (Wolfenbüttel, 1941); G. Ilgner, *Die lateinischen liturgischen Kompositionen von Michael Praetorius Creuzburgensis* (Kiel, 1944).

Pratella, Francesco Balilla, Italian composer and writer of radical tendencies; b. Lugo di Romagna, Feb. 1, 1880; d. Ravenna, May 17, 1955. He studied with Ricci-Signorini, then at the Liceo Rossini in Pesaro with Cicognani and Mascagni; taught in Cesana (1908–9); was director of the Istituto Musicale in Lugo (1910–29), and of the Liceo Musicale G. Verdi in Ravenna (1927–45). He joined the Italian futurist movement in 1910 (Russolo's manifesto of 1913 was addressed to "Balilla Pratella, grande musicista futurista"), and in 1913 wrote his first composition in a "futurist" idiom, the choral *Inno alla vita.* His other works are the operas *Lilia* (won honorable mention in the Sonzogno Contest, 1903;

perf. in Lugo, Nov. 13, 1905); *La Sina d'Vargöun,* to his own libretto (Bologna, Dec. 4, 1909); *L'Aviatore Dro,* also to his own libretto (Lugo, Nov. 4, 1920); *La ninnananna della bambola,* children's opera (Milan, May 21, 1923); *Dono primaverile,* comedy with music (Bologna, Oct. 17, 1923); *Fabiano* (Bologna, Dec. 9, 1939); incidental music; for Orch.: *Romagna, La guerra, 5 poemi musicali;* chamber music; etc.

WRITINGS: *Cronache e critiche* (1905–17); *Evoluzione della musica* (1910–18); *Saggio di gridi, canzoni, cori e danze del popolo italiano* (1919); *Il Canzioniere dei canterini romagnoli* (1923); *Scritti vari di pensiero, di arte e di storia musicale* (Bologna, 1932); *Luci ed ombre* (1933); *Il vino e la musica* (1937); *Linee di storia della musica* (1946).

BIBLIOGRAPHY: A. Toni, "*La Sina d'Vargöun* di F.B. Pratella," *Rivista Musicale Italiana* (1910); G. Bastianelli, *Musicisti d'oggi e di ieri* (Milan, 1914); G.M. Gatti, *Musicisti moderni d'Italia e di fuori* (Bologna, 1920); A. Ghigi, *F.B. Pratella* (Ravenna, 1929); *F.B. Pratella, Appunti biografici e bibliografici* (Ravenna, 1931).

Pratt, Silas Gamaliel, American composer; b. Addison, Vt., Aug. 4, 1846; d. Pittsburgh, Oct. 30, 1916. Both his parents were church singers. The family moved to Chicago when he was a child, and he received his primary music education there; at 22 he went to Berlin, where he studied piano with Kullak and theory with Kiel (1868–71). He then returned to Chicago, where he served as organist of the Church of the Messiah; in 1872, established the Apollo Club. In 1875 he went to Germany once more; studied orchestration with Heinrich Dorn, and also took some piano lessons with Liszt. On July 4, 1876, he conducted in Berlin his *Centennial Overture,* dedicated to President Grant; also conducted at the Crystal Palace in London, when President Grant was visiting there; another work that he presented in London was *Homage to Chicago March.* Returning to Chicago, he conducted his opera *Zenobia, Queen of Palmyra* (to his own libretto) in concert form, on June 15, 1882 (stage perf., Chicago, March 26, 1883; N.Y., Aug. 21, 1883). The opera was received in a hostile manner by the press, partly owing to the poor quality of the music, but mainly as a reaction to Pratt's exuberant and immodest proclamations of its merit in advance of the production. Undaunted, Pratt unleashed a vigorous campaign for native American opera; he organized the Grand Opera Festival of 1884, which had some support. The following year he visited London again, and conducted there his symph. work *The Prodigal Son* (Oct. 5, 1885). Returning to Chicago, he revised his early lyric opera *Antonio,* renamed it *Lucille,* and produced it on March 14, 1887. In 1888 he moved to N.Y.; there he presented, during the quadricentennial of the discovery of America, his opera *The Triumph of Columbus* (in concert form, Oct. 12, 1892); also produced a scenic cantata, *America,* subtitled *4 Centuries of Music, Picture, and Song* (Nov. 24, 1894; with stereopticon projections). Other works: *Lincoln Symphony;* symph. poem, *The Tragedy of the Deep* (1912; inspired by the *Titanic* disaster);

cantata, *The Last Inca;* he also publ. a manual, *Pianist's Mental Velocity* (N.Y., 1903). In 1906 he settled in Pittsburgh; established there the Pratt Inst. of Music and Art, and remained its director until his death. Pratt was a colorful personality; despite continuous and severe setbacks, he was convinced of his own significance. The story of his salutation to Wagner at their meeting—"Herr Wagner, you are the Silas G. Pratt of Germany"—may be apocryphal, but is very much in character.

BIBLIOGRAPHY: E.E. Hipsher, *American Opera and Its Composers* (Philadelphia, pp. 361–63); *Dictionary of American Biography* (vol. 15).

Pratt, Waldo Selden, distinguished American music historian and pedagogue; b. Philadelphia, Nov. 10, 1857; d. Hartford, Conn., July 29, 1939. He studied at Williams College and at Johns Hopkins Univ., specializing in classical languages; was practically self-taught in music. After completing his studies, he was assistant director of the Metropolitan Museum of Art in N.Y. (1880–82); in 1882 he was appointed to the faculty of the Hartford Theological Seminary, where he taught hymnology; remained there until his retirement in 1925; he also taught music history at Smith College (1895–1908), and later at the Inst. of Musical Art in N.Y. He publ. a manual, *The History of Music* (1907; 3rd ed., 1935); *Musical Ministries in the Church* (1901; 4th ed., 1915); *The Music of the Pilgrims* (1921, commenting on Ainsworth's Psalter as brought to Plymouth in 1620, with the tunes in full; reprinted, N.Y., 1971); *The Music of the French Psalter of 1562* (N.Y., 1939; reprint, 1966).

BIBLIOGRAPHY: Otto Kinkeldey, "Waldo Selden Pratt," *Musical Quarterly* (April 1940); J.T. Howard, in *Dictionary of American Biography,* Supplement II.

Prausnitz, Frederik (Frederick), German-born American conductor; b. Cologne, Aug. 26, 1920. He came to the U.S. in his youth; studied at the Juilliard School of Music in N.Y.; later served on its faculty (1947–61); then was conductor of the New England Cons. Symph. Orch. (1961–69). He was music director of the Syracuse (N.Y.) Symph. Orch. from 1971–74. In 1976 he joined the Peabody Cons. of Music in Baltimore as conductor of its Symph. Orch. and Opera; from 1980 he acted as director of its conducting program and conductor of its Contemporary Music Ensemble.

Predieri, Luca Antonio, Italian composer; b. Bologna, Sept. 13, 1688; d. there, Jan. 3, 1767. He was of a musical family; served as maestro di cappella at S. Paolo in Bologna (1725–29) and at S. Pietro (1729–31). In 1737 he went to Vienna as Kapellmeister, remaining there until 1765; then returned to Bologna. His opera *Il sogno di Scipione* was performed at the Emperor's palace in Laxenburg, near Vienna, on Oct. 1, 1735; of about 30 operas, only a few are extant; he also wrote oratorios and instrumental works for festive occasions.

BIBLIOGRAPHY: R. Ortner, *Luca Antonio Pre-*

dieri und sein Wiener Opernschaffen (Vienna, 1971).

Preger, Leo, Corsican composer; b. Ajaccio, Jan. 27, 1907; d. there, Dec. 25, 1965. He studied with Nadia Boulanger in Paris, and acquired considerable mastery of antique counterpoint; subsequently devoted himself mainly to sacred choral music. He wrote the choral works *La Reine Isaure, Cantate de l'arc, Arrestation de Jésus, Cantique de St. Jean de la Croix;* Psalms, etc.

Preindl, Joseph, Austrian composer; b. Marbach, Jan. 30, 1756; d. Vienna, Oct. 26, 1823. He studied with Albrechtsberger; served as organist at the church of Maria am Gestade in 1775, at the Carmelite church of Vienna-Leopoldstadt (1783), and at St. Michael's (1787–93); in 1793 became Kapellmeister at St. Peter's, and in 1795, Vice-Kapellmeister at St. Stephen's; in 1809 succeeded Albrechtsberger there as Kapellmeister. He publ. about 14 masses and other church works; brought out a *Gesanglehre* (singing manual) and a book of old melodies by German composers. His method, *Wiener Tonschule,* was publ. after his death, edited by Seyfried (Vienna, 1827; 2nd ed., 1832).

Preiss, Cornelius, Austrian writer on music; b. Troppau, May 20, 1884; d. Linz, April 1, 1944. He studied in Olmütz and Graz (Dr.Phil., 1907); taught in Graz (1908–24) and Linz (from 1924). He publ. the valuable survey *Zur Geschichte der Operette* (1908); monographs: *K. Millöcker* (1905); *L.C. Seydler* (1908); *Meyerbeer-Studien* (1907–14); *J. Drechsler* (1910); *R. Volkmann* (1912); *R. Stöhr* (1914); *K. Zeller* (1928); *F.X. Süssmayr* (1933); a collection of Austrian folk songs, *Österreichischer Liederquell* (3 vols., 1930–32); the manual *Sing- und allgemeine Musiklehre* (1933). Preiss was also a composer; he wrote mainly vocal music.

Preobrazhensky, Anton, Russian specialist in Russian sacred music; b. Syzran, Feb. 28, 1870; d. Leningrad, Feb. 17, 1929. He studied at the Kazan Seminary; upon graduation went to Moscow, where he taught at the Synod School (1898–1902); then was librarian at the Court Chapel in St. Petersburg; from 1920 to his death, he taught the history of Russian church music at the Cons. of Leningrad. He publ. a number of valuable reference works on Russian hymnody: *Dictionary of Russian Hymns* (Moscow, 1896); *Bibliography of Hymns* (Moscow, 1900); *The Monodic Hymn in the Russian Church of the 17th Century* (St. Petersburg, 1904); *Liturgic Music in Russia* (1924); also a biography of Lvov (St. Petersburg, 1908).

Presley, Elvis, fantastically popular American rock-'n'-roll singer and balladeer; b. Tupelo, Miss., Jan. 8, 1935; d. Memphis, Aug. 16, 1977. He was employed as a mechanic and furniture repairman in his early youth; picked up guitar playing in his leisure hours; sang cowboy ballads at social gatherings. With the advent of rock 'n' roll, he revealed himself as the supreme genius of the genre; almost effortlessly he captivated multitudes of adolescents by the hallucinogenic monotone of his vocal delivery, enhanced by rhythmic pelvic gyrations (hence the invidious appellation "Elvis the Pelvis"); made recordings that sold millions of albums. He made America conscious of the seductive inanity of rock ballads; he aroused primitive urges among his multitudinous admirers with his renditions of such songs, among them *Don't Be Cruel, Hound Dog, Love Me Tender, All Shook Up, Jailhouse Rock, Heartbreak Hotel, Rock around the Clock, It's Now or Never;* his audience responded by improvising songs about him: *My Boy Elvis, I Wanna Spend Christmas with Elvis,* and *Elvis for President.* He also appeared as an actor in sentimental motion pictures. His art was the prime inspiration for the famous Liverpudlian quartet The Beatles. An International Elvis Presley Appreciation Society was organized by 1970. Elvis Presley was indeed The King of Kings of rock. His death (of cardiac arrhythmia aggravated by an immoderate use of tranquilizers and other drugs) precipitated the most extraordinary outpouring of public grief over an entertainment figure since the death of Rudolph Valentino. His entombment in the family mausoleum in Memphis was the scene of mob hysteria, during which 2 people were run over and killed by an automobile; 2 men were arrested for an alleged plot to spirit away his body and hold it for ransom. Entrepreneurs avid for gain put out a mass of memorial literature, souvenirs, and gewgaws, sweat shirts emblazoned with Presley's image in color, Elvis dolls, and even a life-size effigy, as part of a multimillion-dollar effort to provide solace to sorrowing humanity; the only discordant note was sounded by Presley's own bodyguards, who authored a book provocatively titled *Elvis, What Happened?,* with murky insinuations that the King of Rock was a drug addict. Presley's home, turned into a sanctuary at suburban Whitehaven, in Memphis, was opened to the public on June 7, 1982, and was visited by mobs, not only by drug-besotted local rock fans, but by delegations from fan clubs in civilized nations (even the U.K.). Souvenirs included an "Always Elvis" brand of wine; license plates of out-of-town motorists bore the legend ELVIS-P. A bill was submitted in Congress for declaring Presley's nativity day, Jan. 8, a national day.

BIBLIOGRAPHY: T. Saville, compiler, *The International Elvis Presley Appreciation Society Handbook* (Heanor, Derbyshire, England, 1970); J. Hopkins, *Elvis, A Biography* (N.Y., 1971); A. Hand, compiler, *Elvis Special* (Manchester, England, 1973); G. Peellaert, N. Cohn and L. Schober, *Rock Dreams, Die Geschichte der Popmusik* (Munich, 1973); Jerry Hopkins, *Elvis: The Final Years* (N.Y., 1980); A. Goldman, *Elvis* (a damning biography in repulsive detail; N.Y., 1981); John A. Whisler, *Elvis Presley: Reference Guide and Discography* (Metuchen, N.J., 1981); posthumous publications, put out in 1977, include such contemptible maculature as *The Boy Who Dared Rock; Starring Elvis; The Illustrated Elvis;* and *Elvis Presley Scrapbook.*

Presser, Theodore, American music publisher; b. Pittsburgh, July 3, 1848; d. Philadelphia, Oct. 27, 1925. He studied music at the New England Cons. in Boston with S. Emery, G.E. Whiting, J.C.D. Parker, and B. Lang; then at the Leipzig Cons. with Zwintscher and Jadassohn; in 1883 he founded in Philadelphia the *Etude,* a well-known music monthly of which he was editor until 1907; James F. Cooke was its editor from 1908 to 1949; it discontinued publication in 1957. Shortly after the foundation of the *Etude,* Presser established a publishing house, Theo. Presser Co., for music and books about music, which has come to be one of the important firms in the U.S. In 1906 he founded the Presser Home for Retired Music Teachers, which in 1908 moved to fine new quarters in Germantown (accommodations for 65 guests). In 1916 he established the Presser Foundation to administer this Home, to provide relief for deserving musicians, and to offer scholarships in more than 75 colleges and univs. in the U.S. James Francis Cooke was president of the Foundation from 1918. Presser wrote instructive pieces and studies for piano; was a co-founder of the Music Teachers National Assoc. (1876).

BIBLIOGRAPHY: *Dictionary of American Biography* (vol. 15).

Pressler, Menahem, German-born American pianist; b. Magdeburg, Dec. 16, 1923. He was taken to Palestine by his family after the Hitlerization of Germany; he studied piano with Eliah Rudiakow and Leo Kestenberg; then played with the Palestine Symph. In 1946 he won the Debussy Prize at the piano competition in San Francisco. In 1955 he became a member of the School of Music at Indiana Univ.; that year he became pianist in the Beaux Arts Trio, with which he made several tours; he also continued his career as a soloist.

Preston, Simon, English organist; b. Bournemouth, Aug. 4, 1938. He was educated at the Royal Academy of Music in London; then was an organ scholar at King's College, Cambridge. He made his debut at the Royal Festival Hall in London in 1962; was suborganist at Westminster Abbey (1962–67); then organist and lecturer at Christ Church, Oxford, from 1970. In 1981 he became organist of Westminster Abbey; also made several successful tours of Europe and America.

Prêtre, Georges, French conductor; b. Waziers, Aug. 14, 1924. He studied music at the Douai Cons.; then attended courses at the Paris Cons.; also took lessons in conducting with André Cluytens. He made his debut as conductor at the Marseilles Opera in 1946; subsequently had guest engagements in Lille, Toulouse, and other provincial French cities. In 1955 he was engaged as conductor of the Opéra-Comique in Paris; in 1959 was appointed to the staff of the Paris Opéra. He made his American debut with the Chicago Lyric Opera in 1959. On Oct. 17, 1964, he made his first appearance at the Metropolitan Opera in N.Y., conducting *Samson et Dalila.* His European engagements included those at Covent Garden in London, La Scala in Milan, the Vienna State Opera, and the Salzburg Festivals. In 1965 he made an American tour, which included a guest appearance with the Philadelphia Orch. Prêtre is by temperament a Romantic conductor; externally he produces an impression of bodily eloquence, projecting musical rhetorics with an imperious hand; yet he can be superlatively restrained in conducting the classics.

Previn, André, brilliant American pianist, composer, and conductor; b. Berlin, April 6, 1929, of Russian-Jewish descent; the original spelling of his surname was **Prewin.** He showed an unmistakable musical gift as a child; his father, a lawyer, was an amateur musician who gave him his early training; they played piano, 4–hands, together at home. At the age of 6, he was accepted as a pupil at the Berlin Hochschule für Musik, where he studied piano with Prof. Breithaupt; as a Jew, however, he was compelled to leave school in 1938. The family then went to Paris; he continued his studies at the Paris Cons., Marcel Dupré being one of his teachers. In 1939 the family emigrated to America, settling in Los Angeles, where his father's cousin, Charles Previn, was music director at Universal Studios in Hollywood. He took lessons in composition with Joseph Achron, Ernst Toch, and Mario Castelnuovo-Tedesco. He became an American citizen in 1943. Even before graduating from high school, he obtained employment at MGM; he became an orchestrator there and later one of its music directors; he also became a fine jazz pianist. He served in the U.S. Army (1950–52); stationed in San Francisco, he took lessons in conducting with Pierre Monteux, who was music director of the San Francisco Symph. Orch. at the time. During these years he wrote much music for films; he received Academy Awards for his arrangements of *Gigi* (1958), *Porgy and Bess* (1959), *Irma la Douce* (1963), and *My Fair Lady* (1964). Throughout this period he continued to appear as a concert pianist. In 1962 he made his formal conducting debut with the St. Louis Symph. Orch., and conducting soon became his principal vocation. From 1967–69 he was conductor-in-chief of the Houston Symph. Orch. In 1968 he assumed the post of principal conductor of the London Symph. Orch., retaining it with distinction until 1979; then was made its conductor emeritus. In 1976 he became music director of the Pittsburgh Symph. Orch.; in 1982 he was also appointed music director of the Royal Phil. Orch. of London, effective with the 1985–86 season. During his years as director of the London Symph. Orch., he took it on a number of tours to the U.S., as well as to Russia, Japan, South Korea, and Hong Kong. He also took the Pittsburgh Symph. Orch. on acclaimed tours of Europe in 1978 and 1982. He continued to compose popular music, including the scores for the musicals *Coco* (1969) and *The Good Companions* (1974); with words by Tom Stoppard, he composed *Every Good Boy Deserves Favour* (1977), a work for Actors and Orch. His other compositions include Symph. for Strings (1962); *Overture to a Comedy* (1963); Violin Sonata

(1964); Flute Quartet (1964); *Elegy* for Oboe and Strings (1967); Cello Concerto (1967); Horn Concerto (1968); Guitar Concerto (1972); *Principals* for Orch. (1980); *Reflections* for Orch. (1981); *Divertimento* for Orch. (1982); piano pieces; songs. He edited the book *Orchestra* (Garden City, N.Y., 1979). He was married four times (and divorced thrice): to the jazz singer **Betty Bennett,** to the jazz poet **Dory Langdon** (who made a career of her own as composer and singer of pop songs of lament), to the actress Mia Farrow, and in 1982 to Heather Hales.

BIBLIOGRAPHY: E. Greenfield, *André Previn* (N.Y., 1973); M. Bookspan and R. Yockey, *André Previn: A Biography* (Garden City, N.Y., 1981); also a "profile" in the *New Yorker* (Jan. 10 and 17, 1983).

Previtali, Fernando, Italian conductor; b. Adria, Feb. 16, 1907. He studied cello, piano, and composition at the Cons. of Turin; from 1936 to 1953 conducted the Rome Radio Orch.; from 1953 to 1973 was artistic director of the Santa Cecilia Academy. In 1971 he was appointed music director of the Teatro Regio in Parma. He made several appearances as a guest conductor in the U.S. (made his debut with the Cleveland Orch., Dec. 15, 1955); also conducted in Russia. He wrote a ballet, *Allucinazioni,* and other music; publ. an instructive manual, *Guida allo studio della direzione d'orchestra* (Rome, 1951).

Prévost, André, Canadian composer; b. Hawkesburg, Ontario, July 30, 1934. He studied piano and bassoon at the Montreal Cons. (1951–60); composition with Pépin and Papineau-Couture; then went to Paris, where he studied with Messiaen and Dutilleux. In 1964 he returned to North America and took summer courses at the Berkshire Music Center in Tanglewood under the direction of Schuller, Copland, and Kodály; in 1964 he joined the staff of the music faculty of the Univ. of Montreal.

WORKS: *Poème de l'infini,* symph. poem (1960); *Scherzo* for String Orch. (1960); *Fantasmes* for Orch. (1963; Montreal, Nov. 22, 1963; posthumously dedicated to John F. Kennedy); *Pyknon,* pièce concertante for Violin and Orch. (1966); *Célébration* for Orch. (1966); *Terre des hommes (Man and His World)* for 2 Narrators, 3 Choirs, and Orch. (1967; Montreal, April 29, 1967; opening of Expo '67); *Diallèle* for Orch. (1968; Toronto, May 30, 1968); *Evanescence* for Orch. (1970; Ottawa, April 7, 1970); *Hommage (à Beethoven)* for 14 Strings (1970–71); *Psaume 148* for Chorus, Brass, and Organ (1971; Guelph, Canada, May 1, 1971); *Chorégraphie I (... Munich, September 1972 ...)* for Orch. (1972–73; Toronto, April 22, 1975; inspired by the Munich Olympics tragedy); *Chorégraphie II (E = MC²)* for Orch. (1976); *Chorégraphie III* for Orch. (1976); Cello Concerto (1976); *Pastorale* for 2 Harps (1955); *Fantasie* for Cello and Piano (1956); 2 string quartets (1958; *Ad pacem,* 1971–72); *Mobiles* for Flute, Violin, Viola, and Cello (1959–60); Violin Sonata (1960–61; arranged as a ballet under the title *Primordial,* 1968); Cello Sonata (1962; arranged for Violin, and Piano or Ondes Martenot, 1967); *Triptyque* for Flute, Oboe, and Piano (1962); *Mouvement* for

Brass Quintet (1963); *Ode au St. Laurent* for optional Narrator and String Quartet (1965); *Suite* for String Quintet (1968); *Missa de profundis* for Chorus and Organ (1973); *4 Preludes* for 2 Pianos (1961); *5 Variations sur un thème grégorien* for Organ (1956); songs; choruses.

Prévost, Eugène-Prosper, French conductor and composer; b. Paris, April 23, 1809; d. New Orleans, Aug. 19, 1872. He studied at the Paris Cons. with Lesueur, winning the Grand Prix de Rome in 1831 with the cantata *Bianca cappello.* He conducted theatrical music in Le Havre (1835–38); then went to New Orleans, where he conducted until 1862; was active in Paris (1862–67) before returning to New Orleans as a singing master. He produced several operas in Paris, of which *Cosimo* (Opéra-Comique, Oct. 13, 1835) was the most successful; another, *Blanche et René,* was given in New Orleans in 1861; he also wrote oratorios and masses.

Prey, Claude, French composer; b. Fleury-sur-Andelle, May 30, 1925. He studied at the Paris Cons. with Milhaud and Messiaen; then with Mignone in Rio de Janeiro and with Frazzi in Siena; completed studies at the Laval Univ. in Quebec in 1958.

WORKS: Opera, *Le Phénix* (1957); "opéra épistolaire," *Lettres perdues* (1960); *La Dictée,* lyrical monodrama (1961); chamber opera after Edgar Allan Poe, *Le Cœur révélateur (The Tell-Tale Heart;* 1962); opera in 12 variations, *L'Homme occis* (1963); *Métamorphose d'Echo,* 9 variations for Female Voice and 24 Strings (1965); *Les Mots croisés (Jeu concertante)* for Contralto, Tenor, and 2 Instrumental Groups (1965); *Donna Mobile,* theater-music piece for 8 Actresses and 3 Instrumentalists (1965; Avignon Festival, July 15, 1972); "opéra-test," *La Noirceur du lait* (Strasbourg, 1967); opera-oratorio, *Jonas* (1966; scenic version, Lyons, Dec. 2, 1969); opera-parody in 2 trials, *On veut la lumière? Allons-y!* for 5 Cast Members and 8 Instruments (1967; Angers, 1968); *Fêtes de la faim,* opera for 5 Comedians, Cello, and 2 Percussionists (Avignon, 1969); short opera, *Le Jeu de l'oie* (Paris, 1970); *Théâtrophonie* for 12 Voices and Piano (1971).

Prey, Hermann, outstanding German baritone; b. Berlin, July 11, 1929. He was about to be drafted into the dwindling Nazi battalions during the last days of the war, when was only 15 years old, but emerged unscathed and began to study voice with Günther Baum at the Hochschule für Musik in Berlin. In 1952 he won first prize in a vocal contest organized by the U.S. army of occupation; made his opera debut in Wiesbaden, and then received an engagement to sing in America. Returning to Germany, he joined the Hamburg State Opera (1953–60), with which he performed roles in modern operas by Liebermann, Dallapiccola, and Henze. In 1956 he sang Wolfram in *Tannhäuser* at the Bayreuth Festival. He also was a guest performer at the Bavarian State Opera in Munich, at the Städtische Oper in Berlin, at the Vienna State Opera, at La Scala in Milan, and at Covent Garden in London. On Dec. 17, 1960, he appeared for the first time at the Metropolitan Opera in N.Y., as Wolfram; he returned to the Metropolitan to sing the role of Count Almaviva on Dec. 2, 1964, and, one of his finest roles, that of Papageno in *Die Zauberflöte*. On April 2, 1973, he sang Figaro in *Il Barbiere di Siviglia* at the Metropolitan Opera. He also proved himself a remarkable singer of German lieder, excelling in the cycles of Schubert's songs but also showing an extraordinary verve in performing vocal parts in the works of Schoenberg and Berg. In Germany he became popular as master of ceremonies, speaker, and singer in his own television show in Munich. His extramusical interests are confined to parapsychology. He received the West German Cross of Merit in 1974.

BIBLIOGRAPHY: David Ewen, *Musicians since 1900* (N.Y., 1978).

Preyer, Carl Adolph, German pianist, composer, and teacher; b. Pforzheim, Baden, July 28, 1863; d. Lawrence, Kans., Nov. 16, 1947. He studied at the Stuttgart Cons.; then with Navrátil in Vienna, and with H. Urban and H. Barth in Berlin. In 1893 he settled in the U.S.; became a piano teacher at the School of Fine Arts of the Univ. of Kansas, and remained with that institution throughout his life. He publ. several instructive collections for piano: *20 Progressive Octave Studies, Melodious Pieces in the Form of Etudes, 12 Wrist Studies, 12 Etudes for the Left Hand;* also some character pieces.

BIBLIOGRAPHY: Howard F. Gloyne, *Carl A. Preyer: The Life of a Kansas Musician* (Lawrence, 1949).

Preyer, Gottfried von, Austrian organist and composer; b. Hausbrunn, March 15, 1807; d. Vienna, May 9, 1901. He studied with Sechter; in 1835 became organist of the Lutheran Church in Vienna; in 1838, prof. of music theory at the Vienna Cons., of which he was director from 1844 to 1848. In 1853 he became music director at St. Stephen's; was pensioned in 1876. He wrote 3 operas; the oratorio *Noah* (often perf. in Vienna); a Symph.; several masses and other church music.

Prianishnikov, Ippolit, Russian baritone; b. Kerch, Aug. 26, 1847; d. Petrograd, Nov. 11, 1921. He joined the Russian Imperial Navy; later began to study voice, first at the St. Petersburg Cons. (1873–75), then in Italy, where he became a student of Ronconi; made his debut in Milan in 1876. Returning to Russia, he joined the Maryinsky Theater in St. Petersburg in 1878, remaining there until 1886; then went to Tiflis (1886–89) and Moscow (1892–93), where he sang and produced opera; in later years he also taught voice. Among his students were Bolshakov, Nicolai Figner, and Mravina.

Pribyl, Vilem, Czech tenor; b. Nachod, April 10, 1925. He worked as an engineer and sang with amateur companies before joining the Opera in Ústí nad Labem in 1960. His first signal success came when he sang the role of Dalibor with the Prague National Theater at the Edinburgh Festival of 1964.

Since then he appeared at the Holland, Salzburg, and Vienna festivals, and at the Royal Opera in Covent Garden, London. His repertoire included Radames, Lohengrin, and Otello, as well as roles in operas by Martinů, Prokofiev, and Shostakovich; he is perhaps best known for his performances in the operas of Janáček.

Price, Enrique (Henry), English conductor; b. London, May 5, 1819; d. New York, Dec. 12, 1863. He settled in Colombia, and established the Phil. Orch. of Bogotá (Nov. 11, 1846); was its first conductor.

Price, Florence B. (née **Smith**), black American pianist and composer; b. Little Rock, Ark., April 9, 1888; d. Chicago, June 3, 1953. She studied with Chadwick and Converse at the New England Cons. in Boston, graduating in 1906. She had been publishing her compositions since she was 11 (1899); in 1928 she won a prize from G. Schirmer for *At the Cotton Gin* for Piano; around this time she was also writing musical jingles for radio commercials. Her first notable success came in 1932 with her Symph. in E minor (winner of the Wanamaker Award; perf. by the Chicago Symph. at the Century of Progress Exhibition in 1933); she became known as the first black woman to write symphs. She also wrote *Concert Overture on Negro Spirituals; Piano Concerto in One Movement* (many perfs.); *Negro Folk Songs in Counterpoint* for String Quartet; for Piano: *Arkansas Jitter; 3 Little Negro Dances;* the suite *From the Canebrakes;* many other works for piano and for organ.

BIBLIOGRAPHY: B.G. Jackson, "Florence Price, Composer," *Black Perspective in Music* (Spring 1977).

Price, Jorge Wilson, Colombian musician, son of **Enrique Price;** b. Bogotá, May 20, 1853; d. there, Oct. 9, 1953 (at the age of 100). He was educated in N.Y.; returning to Colombia, he founded the National Academy (1882) and taught violin.

BIBLIOGRAPHY: J.I. Perdomo Escobar, *Historia de la música en Colombia* (Bogotá, 1945).

Price, Leontyne (Mary Violet), remarkably endowed black American soprano; b. Laurel, Miss., Feb. 10, 1927, of working-class parents, a carpenter and a midwife. She was taught piano by a local woman, and also learned to sing. On Dec. 17, 1943, she played piano and sang at a concert in Laurel. She went to Oak Park High School, graduating in music in 1944; then enrolled in the College of Education and Industrial Arts in Wilberforce, Ohio, where she studied voice with Catherine Van Buren; received her B.A. degree in 1948 and then was awarded a scholarship at the Juilliard School of Music in N.Y.; there she received vocal training from Florence Page Kimball, and also joined the Opera Workshop under the direction of Frederic Cohen. Virgil Thomson heard her perform the role of Mistress Ford in Verdi's opera *Falstaff* and invited her to sing in the revival of his opera *4 Saints in 3 Acts* in 1952. She subsequently performed the responsible part of Bess in Gershwin's *Porgy and Bess* on a tour of the U.S. (1952–54) and in Europe (1955). On Nov. 14, 1954, she made a highly acclaimed debut as a concert singer in N.Y. On Dec. 3, 1954, she sang at the first performance of Samuel Barber's *Prayers of Kierkegaard* with the Boston Symph., conducted by Charles Munch. On Jan. 23, 1955 she performed Tosca on television, creating a sensation both as an artist and as a member of her race taking up the role of an Italian diva. Her career was soon assured without any reservations. In 1957 she appeared with the San Francisco Opera; on Oct. 18, 1957 she sang Aida, a role congenial as to both race and her passionate artistry. In 1958 she sang Aida with the Vienna State Opera under the direction of Herbert von Karajan; on July 2, 1958, she sang this role at Covent Garden in London; and again as Aida she appeared at La Scala in Milan in 1959, the first black woman to sing with that most prestigious and most fastidious opera company. On Jan. 27, 1961, she made her first appearance with the Metropolitan Opera in N.Y. in the role of Leonora in *Il Trovatore*. A series of highly successful performances at the Metropolitan followed: Aida on Feb. 20, 1961; Madama Butterfly on March 3, 1961; Donna Anna on March 25, 1961; Tosca on April 1, 1962; Pamina on Jan. 3, 1964; Cleopatra in the premiere of Samuel Barber's opera *Antony and Cleopatra* at the opening of the new Metropolitan Opera House at Lincoln Center in N.Y. on Sept. 16, 1966. On Sept. 24, 1973, she sang Madama Butterfly at the Metropolitan once more. On Feb. 7, 1975, she appeared there in the title role of *Manon Lescaut;* and on Feb. 3, 1976, she sang Aida. She was married in 1952 to the baritone **William Warfield** (who sang Porgy at her performances of *Porgy and Bess)*, but separated from him in 1959; they were legally divorced in 1973. Leontyne Price received many honors and honorary doctorates. On July 4, 1964, she was awarded the Presidential Medal of Freedom.

BIBLIOGRAPHY: H.L. Lyon, *Leontyne Price: Highlights of a Prima Donna* (N.Y., 1973); David Ewen, *Musicians since 1900* (N.Y., 1978).

Price, Margaret, British operatic soprano; b. Tredegar, Wales, April 13, 1941. She studied at the Trinity College of Music in London; made her debut in 1962 at the Welsh National Opera as Cherubino in *Le nozze di Figaro,* and in 1963 sang the same role at Covent Garden in London. She established herself as a foremost performer of soprano roles in Mozart's operas, excelling as Donna Anna in *Don Giovanni,* the Countess in *Le nozze di Figaro,* and Pamina in *Die Zauberflöte;* also distinguished herself as Desdemona in Verdi's *Otello.* She made appearances, invariably successful, with the operas at Cologne, Munich, Hamburg, Chicago, and San Francisco. She joined the cast of the Paris Opéra during its American tour in 1976, eliciting extraordinary praise from the public and critics. Her voice is essentially a lyric soprano, but is capable of technically brilliant coloratura.

Price, (Noble) Ray, American singer of country music; b. Perryville, Texas, Jan. 12, 1926. He studied at North Texas Agricultural College in Arlington (1946–49); then embarked on a career as a country music singer; made numerous recordings, including *Crazy Arms, Heartaches by the Number, Release Me, Danny Boy, For the Good Times,* and many others; also sang on the radio.

Pride, Charley, black American country-music singer; b. on a cotton farm near Sledge, Miss., March 18, 1938. He learned to play the guitar but, bent on a career in baseball, he played in the minor leagues (1954–64); also tried his luck as a singer. He subsequently appeared with the Grand Ole Opry in Nashville, becoming the first black country-music singer to gain admission to this shrine of populist entertainment.

Prieberg, Fred K., German writer on music; b. Berlin, June 3, 1928. He took music courses at the Univ. of Freiburg in Breisgau (1950–53); from 1953 to 1969 lived in Baden-Baden. He publ. a number of informative books on modern music, among them *Musik unterm Strich* (Freiburg, 1956); *Musik des technischen Zeitalters* (Zürich, 1956); *Lexikon der neuen Musik* (Freiburg, 1958); *Musica ex machina* (Berlin, 1960); *Musik in der Sowjetunion* (Cologne, 1965); *Musik im anderen Deutschland* (Cologne, 1968).

Priestman, Brian, English conductor; b. Birmingham, Feb. 10, 1927. He studied at the Univ. of Birmingham (M.A., 1952); served as music director of the Royal Shakespeare Theatre, Stratford-upon-Avon (1960–63); then conducted the Edmonton Symph. in Alberta, Canada (1964–68), and the Baltimore Symph. (1968–69). From 1970 to 1978 he was music director of the Denver Symph. Orch. and was also principal conductor of the New Zealand National Orch. (1973–76). From 1977 to 1980 he was music director of the Florida Phil., and subsequently was music adviser of the Cape Town Symph. in South Africa; while there he was also appointed, in 1980, prof. at the Univ. of Cape Town and director of the South African College of Music.

Prigozhin, Lucian, Soviet composer; b. Tashkent, Aug. 15, 1926. His father was a legal consultant; his mother, a pharmaceutical worker; the family moved to Samarkand, where Prigozhin spent his earliest childhood; they returned to Tashkent in 1934. When Germany invaded Russia in 1941, the entire faculty of the Leningrad Cons. was evacuated to Tashkent, and Prigozhin had an opportunity to study piano and theory with its members. At the end of the war Prigozhin went to Leningrad and enrolled in the class of Vladimir Shcherbachev; later studied with Evlakhov and Kochurov at the Leningrad Cons. His early works followed the precepts of the Russian national school; to this period belong his oratorio *Stenka Razin* and First Symph. Upon his graduation from the Leningrad Cons., Prigozhin became interested in modern techniques; he introduced a concept of "supplementary tones" in the

12-tone method of composition by allowing the members of the tone-row to permutate freely. However, he preserved the basic tonality even when he no longer used the key signature.

WORKS: FOR THE STAGE: *Doctor Aybolit (Ay! It Hurts!),* radio opera for children (1956); *Malchish-Kibalchish,* radio opera for children (1969); *Robin Hood,* opera (1972); ballet, *Circie of Hades* (1964); incidental music for films. ORATORIOS: *Stenka Razin,* vocal-symph. tableau for 2 Soloists and Orch. (1949); *Song of Bread,* cantata (1959); *Prometheus Unbound* for Chorus and Orch., after Aeschylus (1959–60); *The Chronicle of Igor's Campaign* for Mezzo-soprano, Bass, Mixed Choir, and Chamber Ensemble (1966); *Snowstorm,* chamber oratorio, after Alexander Blok's poem *The Twelve* (1968); *Precursors,* chamber cantata for 2 Soloists, Alto Flute, Clarinet, Double Bass, and Percussion (1970); *In Memory of the Great Battle* for Bass, Chorus, and Orch. (1975); *Sun and Stones,* chamber cantata for Mezzo-soprano, Flute, String Quartet, and Piano (1975); *From Horace,* chamber cantata for Baritone, Chorus, Clarinet, Trombone, and Percussion (1976). FOR ORCH.: Sinfonietta (1953); Symph. No. 1 (1955; revised 1975); Symph. No. 2 (1960; revised 1963); Symph. No. 3 (1970); *Music* for Strings and Flute (1961); Symph. Suite from the ballet *Circle of Hades* (1965). CHAMBER MUSIC: Sonata No. 1 for Violin and Piano (*Sonata-burlesque;* 1967); Sonata No. 2 for Violin and Piano (1969); 2 string quartets (1970, 1979); *Musica rustica* for Wind Quintet (1973); Sonata for Horn and Piano (1973). FOR VOICE: *5 Songs* to words by Burns and Shakespeare (1955); *Whirlwind* for Chorus a cappella, to words by Alexander Blok (1973). FOR PIANO: Sonatina (1973); Sonata (1973); *Calendar of Nature,* 12 pieces (1974).

BIBLIOGRAPHY: E. Ruchyevskaya, *Lucian Prigozhin* (Moscow, 1977).

Příhoda, Váša, noted Czech violinist; b. Vodnany, Aug. 22, 1900; d. Vienna, July 26, 1960. He received his first instruction from his father, a professional violinist; made his public debut at the age of 12 in Prague; in 1920 went on an Italian tour; in 1921 appeared in the U.S., and in 1927 played in England; then gave recitals throughout Europe. He continued to concertize after the absorption of Austria and Czechoslovakia into the Nazi Reich, and was briefly charged with collaboration with the occupying powers. He eventually became a prof. at the Vienna Academy of Music.

BIBLIOGRAPHY: J. Vratislavský, *Váša Příhoda* (Prague, 1970).

Prill, Emil, eminent German flutist, brother of **Karl** and **Paul Prill;** b. Stettin, May 10, 1867; d. Berlin, Feb. 28, 1940. He studied with his father; finished his musical education at the Hochschule für Musik in Berlin; in 1888 taught in Kharkov, Russia; then played first flute with the Hamburg Phil.; in 1892 became first flutist at the Berlin Opera; in 1903 was appointed an instructor at the Hochschule. He publ. the methods *Schule für die Böhm-Flöte* and *Flötenschule;* also a valuable practical collection of flute

passages from orch. works, *Orchesterstudien* (7 books).

Prill, Karl, German violinist, brother of **Emil** and **Paul Prill;** b. Berlin, Oct. 22, 1864; d. Vienna, Aug. 18, 1931. He studied violin with Joachim at the Berlin Hochschule für Musik; played in various orchs., including that of the Gewandhaus (1891–97); in 1897 became concertmaster of the Court (later State) Opera in Vienna; also of the Vienna Phil. until 1925; also taught violin at the Vienna Academy of Music. He organized the Prill String Quartet, which was famous in his day.

Prill, Paul, German cellist and conductor, brother of **Emil** and **Karl Prill;** b. Berlin, Oct. 1, 1860; d. Bremen, Dec. 21, 1930. He studied with Manecke (cello) and Sturm (theory); was solo cellist in various German orchs.; conducted opera in Rotterdam (1886–89), Hamburg (1889–92), and Nuremberg (1901–6); conducted the Mozart Orch. in Berlin (1906–8); then settled in Munich as conductor of the Konzertverein.

Prima, Louis, black American jazz trumpeter and bandleader; b. New Orleans, Dec. 7, 1911; d. there, Aug. 24, 1978. He played the violin and the trumpet; in 1934, went to N.Y., where he led his own band with much success. He composed the hit song *Sing, Sing, Sing* (1940) for Benny Goodman. He was for a while (1952–61) married to the singer **Keely Smith.**

Primrose, William, preeminent Scottish viola virtuoso; b. Glasgow, Aug. 23, 1903; d. Provo, Utah, May 1, 1982. He studied violin in Glasgow with Camillo Ritter; then had lessons in Belgium (1925–27) with Eugène Ysaÿe, who advised him to take up viola so as to avoid the congested violin field. He became the violist in the London String Quartet (1930–35), with which he made several tours. In 1937 he settled in the U.S., and was engaged as the principal viola player in the NBC Symph. Orch. in N.Y. under Toscanini, holding this post until 1942. In 1939 he established his own string quartet. On Feb. 24, 1953, he was named a Commander of the Order of the British Empire; in 1956 he became violist in the Festival Quartet. He also became active as a teacher; was on the faculty of the Univ. of Southern Calif. in Los Angeles (1961–65) and at the School of Music of Indiana Univ. in Bloomington (1965–74). In 1972 he inaugurated a master class at the Tokyo Univ. of Fine Arts and Music. Returning to the U.S., he taught at Brigham Young Univ. in Provo, Utah. Primrose was greatly esteemed as a viola virtuoso; he gave first performances of viola concertos by several modern composers. He commissioned a viola concerto from Béla Bartók, but the work was left unfinished at the time of Bartók's death, and the task of reconstructing the score from Bartók's sketches remained to be accomplished by Bartók's friend and associate Tibor Serly; Primrose gave its first performance with the Minneapolis Symph. on Dec. 2, 1949. He publ. *A Method for Violin and Viola Players* (London, 1960).

Pringsheim, Klaus, German conductor and composer; b. Feldafing, near Munich, July 24, 1883; d. Tokyo, Dec. 7, 1972. A scion of a highly cultured family, he studied mathematics with his father, a prof. at Munich Univ., and physics with Röntgen, the discoverer of X-rays. His twin sister, Katherine, was married to Thomas Mann. In Munich, Pringsheim took piano lessons with Bernard Stavenhagen, a student of Liszt, and composition with Ludwig Thuille. In 1906 he went to Vienna and was engaged as assistant conductor of the Vienna Opera, under the tutelage of Gustav Mahler, who took him as a pupil in conducting and composition, a relationship that developed into profound friendship. Mahler recommended him to the management of the German Opera in Prague; Pringsheim conducted there from 1909 to 1914; then was engaged as conductor and stage director at the Opera of Bremen (1915–18) and music director of the Max Reinhardt theaters in Berlin (1918–25). In 1923–24 he conducted in Berlin a Mahler cycle of 8 concerts, featuring all of Mahler's symphs. and songs with orch. In 1927 he became the music critic of the socialist newspaper *Vorwärts*. A turning point in Pringsheim's life came in 1931 with an invitation to teach music at the Imperial Academy of Music in Tokyo, where he taught until 1937; several of his Japanese students became prominent composers. From 1937 to 1939 Pringsheim served as music adviser to the Royal Dept. of Fine Arts in Bangkok, Thailand. In 1939 he returned to Japan; was briefly interned in 1944 as an opponent of the Axis policies. In 1946 he went to California; after some intermittent activities, he returned to Japan in 1951; was appointed director of the Musashino Academy of Music in Tokyo; continued to conduct; also wrote music reviews for English-language Tokyo newspapers. As a composer, Pringsheim followed the neo-Romantic trends, deeply influenced by Mahler. His compositions include a Concerto for Orch. (Tokyo, Oct. 13, 1935); Japanese radio opera, *Yamada Nagasama* (1953); Concertino for Xylophone and Orch. (1962); *Theme, Variations and Fugue* for Wind Orch. (his last composition, 1971–72); and a curious album of 36 2-part canons for piano (1959). A chapter from his theoretical work *Pythagoras, die Atonalität und wir* was publ. in *Schweizerische Musikzeitung* (1957). His reminiscences, "Mahler, My Friend," were publ. posthumously in the British periodical *Composer* (1973–74). Pringsheim was a signatory of a letter of protest by surviving friends of Mahler against the motion picture *Death in Venice*, after a novelette of Thomas Mann, in which the central character, a famous writer who suffers a homosexual crisis, was made to resemble Mahler.

Printz, Wolfgang Caspar, German composer and writer; b. Waldthurn, Oct. 10, 1641; d. Sorau, Oct. 13, 1717. Originally a theological student, he later led a roving life, and then was cantor successively at Promnitz, Triebel, and (from 1665) Sorau. He brought out *Historische Beschreibung der edelen Sing- und Kling-Kunst* (Dresden, 1690), a work of some importance for the history of music of the 17th century. His other theoretical writings include *Anweisung zur Singkunst* (1666; 2nd ed., 1671; 3rd ed., 1685); *Compendium ad Oden componendam* (1668); *Musica modulationis vocalis* (1678); *Exercitationes ... de concordantiis* (1687–89); also a curious satire on music theory, *Phrynis Mytilenaeus oder Satyrischer Componist* (1676–77; 2nd ed., 1696); also wrote 3 musical stories, characterizing different types of musicians. According to his own statement, the MSS of his numerous compositions were destroyed in a fire. A complete edition of his works, in 3 vols., was initiated in 1974, with the publication of *Musikerromane* (Berlin, 1974).

BIBLIOGRAPHY: E. Schmitz, "Studien über W. Printz als Musikschriftsteller," *Monatshefte für Musik-Geschichte* (1904); H. Heckmann, *Wolfgang Caspar Printz und seine Rhythmuslehre* (Diss., Univ. of Freiburg, 1952).

Pritchard, Sir John, distinguished English conductor; b. London, Feb. 5, 1921. He took private lessons in conducting; then entered on a long and fruitful association with the Glyndebourne Festival Opera, eventually succeeding Vittorio Gui as music director (1969–77). In the meantime, he served as music director of the Royal Liverpool Phil. Orch. (1957–63); from 1962 to 1966 he led the London Phil., which he also conducted on tours in Germany, Austria, and France (1966–67) and in Japan (1969–70). In 1971 he made his American debut conducting the Metropolitan Opera in N.Y.; he was also a guest conductor with the Pittsburgh Symph. Orch. In 1978 he was appointed chief conductor of the Cologne Opera, and in 1979, chief guest conductor of the BBC Symp. Orch. In 1981 he became joint music director (with Sylvain Cambreling) of the Théâtre Royal de la Monnaie in Brussels. He was knighted in 1983.

Proch, Heinrich, Austrian conductor, composer, and singing teacher; b. Böhmisch-Leipa, July 22, 1809; d. Vienna, Dec. 18, 1878. He studied law and at the same time took violin lessons; became conductor of the Josephstadt Theater in Vienna in 1837; from 1840 to 1870 conducted at the Vienna Opera. He wrote many songs that were popular for a time; his set of variations for coloratura soprano, with flute obbligato, was particularly well known; he also brought out in Vienna a comic opera, *Ring und Maske* (Dec. 4, 1844), and 3 one-act operas: *Die Blutrache* (Dec. 5, 1846); *Zweiter und dritter Stock* (Oct. 5, 1847); *Der gefährliche Sprung* (Jan. 5, 1849).

Procházka, Rudolf, Bohemian writer on music and composer; b. Prague, Feb. 23, 1864; d. there, March 24, 1936. He studied violin with Wittich and composition with Fibich; then devoted himself mainly to music education; in 1911 he organized a commission for the licensing of music teachers in Bohemia. He publ. several monographs: *Dei böhmischen Musikschulen* (1890); *Mozart in Prag* (1892; very valuable; revised by Paul Nettl in 1939 as *Mozart in Böhmen*); *Robert Franz* (1894); *Arpeggien: Musikalisches aus alten und neuen Tagen* (1897; 2nd ed. as *Musikalische Streiflichter,* 1901);

Johann Strauss (1900; 2nd ed., 1903); *Das romantische Musik-Prag* (1914); *Der Kammermusikverein in Prag* (1926). He also was a composer; wrote an allegorical opera, *Das Glück* (Prague, 1898); some orch. pieces; *Deutsch-böhmische Reigen* for Piano, 4-hands; solo piano pieces; many choruses and songs.

BIBLIOGRAPHY: C. Hunnius, *Rudolf von Procházka, Ein deutscher Tondichter Böhmens* (Leipzig, 1902); E. Janetschek, "Rudolf von Procházka," *Neue Zeitschrift für Musik* (Dec. 1915).

Procter, Alice McElroy, American pianist; b. Albany, N.Y., April 18, 1915. She studied composition at Smith College and at the Eastman School of Music in Rochester, N.Y., where she received her Ph.D. Subsequently, she taught piano in Boston and its environs. She publ. some ingratiating teaching pieces for piano, among them *Jumping Cat* and *Footsteps in the Night*. She is the wife of the composer **Leland Procter**.

Procter, Leland, American composer and teacher; b. Newton, Mass., March 24, 1914. He studied composition at the Eastman School of Music in Rochester, N.Y., with Howard Hanson and Bernard Rogers, and later at the Univ. of Oklahoma. Returning to Boston, he taught at the New England Cons. He publ. some teaching pieces for piano and wrote symph. works. He is the husband of the pianist **Alice McElroy Procter**.

Procter, Norma, English contralto; b. Cleethorpes, Feb. 15, 1928. She studied voice with Roy Henderson and Alec Redshaw; made her debut in Handel's *Messiah* at Southwark Cathedral in 1948; soon established herself as an outstanding concert singer; in 1961 she made her operatic debut at Covent Garden as Orpheus in Gluck's opera.

Prod'homme, Jacques-Gabriel, industrious French librarian and music critic; b. Paris, Nov. 28, 1871; d. there, June 17, 1956. He studied philology and music history at the Ecole des Hautes Etudes Sociales (1890–94); then became a writer on musical and other subjects in the socialist publications, among them *La Revue Socialiste, Droits de l'Homme,* and *Messidor.* An ardent believer in the cause of peace, he edited in Munich the *Deutsch-französische Rundschau,* dedicated to the friendship between the French and German peoples (1897–1900). His hopes for peace were shattered by 2 devastating wars within his lifetime.

WRITINGS: Among his publications are *Le Cycle Berlioz,* in 2 vols.: *La Damnation de Faust* (1896) and *L'Enfance du Christ* (1898); *Hector Berlioz. Sa vie et ses œuvres* (1905); *Les Symphonies de Beethoven* (1906; 15th ed., 1938; awarded a prize by the French Academy); *Paganini* (1907; in Eng., 1911); *Ecrits de musiciens* (1912); *La Jeunesse de Beethoven* (1921); *Richard Wagner et la France* (1921); *L'Opéra, 1669–1925* (1925); *Pensées sur la musique et les musiciens* (1926); *Beethoven raconté par ceux qui l'ont vu* (1927); *Mozart raconté par ceux qui l'ont vu* (1928); *Schubert raconté par ceux qui l'ont vu* (1928); *Wagner raconté par ceux qui l'ont vu* (1929); *Les Sonates pour piano de Beethoven* (1937); *L'Immortelle bien-aimée de Beethoven* (1946); *Gluck* (1948); *Gossec* (1949); he also contributed a number of articles to the *Musical Quarterly.* In collaboration with Ch. Bertrand, he publ. *Guide musical et étude analytique de la Götterdämmerung* (1902); with A. Dandelot, *Gounod. Sa vie et ses œuvres d'après des documents inédits* (2 vols., 1911); with E. Crauzat, *Les Menus plaisirs du roi; L'Ecole royale et le Conservatoire de Paris* (1929). Together with Fr. Holl, F. Caille, and L. van Vassenhove, he trans. Wagner's prose works in 13 vols. (1908–25).

Profe, Ambrosius, German organist and music editor; b. Breslau, Feb. 12, 1589; d. there, Dec. 27, 1661. He studied theology at Wittenburg; then was cantor in Jauer, Silesia (1617–29); from 1633 to 1649 he was a church organist in Breslau. He edited important collections of German sacred music: *Geistliche Concerte und Harmonien* for 1–7 Voices (1641–46); *Corollarium geistlicher Collectaneorum* (a supplement to the previous vol.; 1649); a collection of Christmas songs, *Cunis solennibus Jesuli recens-nati sacra genethliaca* (1646); also brought out Heinrich Albert's *Arien* (1657).

Profeta, Laurenţiu, Rumanian composer; b. Bucharest, Jan. 12, 1925. He studied with P. Constantinescu, A. Mendelsohn, and Chirescu at the Bucharest Cons. (1945–49); later took courses at the Moscow Cons. (1954–56). He served as director of music for the Ministry of Culture (1952–60) and secretary of the Rumanian National Committee of the International Music Council (1960–70). His music is marked by rhapsodic expansiveness in Romantically rich harmonies.

WORKS: 3 ballets: *Soţia căpitanului (The Captain's Wife;* 1946); *Prinţ şi cereşor (The Prince and the Beggar;* 1963–66); *Marinarul visător (The Dreaming Sailor;* 1972); *Cîntece de tabără (Songs of Bivouac),* suite for Soloists, Children's Chorus, and Orch. (1957); *Intîmplarea din grădină (The Adventures of the Gardener),* oratorio (1958); *Cantaţa patriei (Cantata of the Fatherland)* for Narrator, Mezzo-soprano, Chorus, and Orch. (1959); *Brăduţul singuratic (The Singular Spruce Tree),* musical tale (1960); *6 Humorous Pieces* for Children Soloists, Children's Chorus, and Orch. (1966); *Suite for Marionettes* for Chamber Orch. (1951); *Poemul patriei* for Orch. (1952); *Zile de vacanţă (Vacation Days),* symph. suite (1956); *Carnival* for 2 Pianos (1957); film music; choruses; songs.

Prohaska, Carl, Austrian composer; b. Mödling, near Vienna, April 25, 1869; d. Vienna, March 28, 1927. He studied piano with Anna Assmayr in Vienna and with Eugen d'Albert in Berlin; composition with Franz Krenn; musicology with Mandyczewski in Vienna. In 1908 he joined the faculty of the Akademie der Tonkunst in Vienna, where he taught piano and theory. He wrote an opera, *Madeleine*

Guinard; an oratorio, *Frühlingsfeier* (1913); String Quartet; Piano Trio; Quintet for 2 Violins, Viola, Cello, and Double Bass; a group of piano pieces.

Prohaska, Felix, Austrian conductor, son of **Carl Prohaska;** b. Vienna, May 16, 1912. He received his primary music education at home with his father; then studied piano with Steuermann, and theory with Egon Kornauth and Hanns Gál. He served as chorus conductor at the Graz Opera (1936–39); conducted opera in Duisburg (1939–41) and in Strasbourg (1941–43); then was principal conductor at the Vienna State Opera (1945–55) and at the Frankfurt Opera (1955–61); returned to Vienna (1964–67); conducted at the opera in Hannover (1965–74) and also served as director of the Hochschule für Musik there in 1961–75; from 1975 he conducted in Kiel; also filled guest engagements in Europe and South America.

Prohaska, Jaro, Austrian bass-baritone; b. Vienna, Jan. 24, 1891; d. Munich, Sept. 28, 1965. He sang in the Wiener Sängerknaben; studied voice with Otto Müller in Vienna; made his operatic debut in Lübeck in 1922; then sang in Nuremberg (1925–32). In 1932 he joined the Berlin State Opera, remaining on its roster until 1953; also made many appearances at the Bayreuth Festivals (1933–42), where he excelled in such roles as Hans Sachs, Wotan, and the Dutchman; from 1947 he taught voice at the Berlin Hochschule für Musik.

Prokofiev, Sergei, great Russian composer; b. Sontzovka, near Ekaterinoslav, April 27, 1891 (according to the newly found birth certificate); d. Moscow, March 5, 1953. His mother was an amateur pianist, and he received his first training from her. He improvised at the piano; in June 1900, at the age of 9, he completed the piano score of an opera, *The Giant;* then wrote an overture and 3 tableaux for an opera entitled *On Desert Island* (1902); in 1904 he embarked on the composition of another opera, *Ondine,* which he completed in 1907. He then went to Moscow, where he began taking regular lessons from Glière, under whose guidance he composed a Symph. in G and the opera *Feast during the Plague,* after Pushkin (1903). At the age of 13 he entered the St. Petersburg Cons., where he studied composition with Rimsky-Korsakov, Wihtol, and Liadov; piano with Mme. Essipova; and conducting with Nicolas Tcherepnin. He graduated from the Cons. in 1914; received the Anton Rubinstein Prize (a grand piano) as a pianist-composer for his First Piano Concerto. Even before graduation, he appeared before various modern music societies in St. Petersburg, playing his own piano pieces, and soon earned a reputation as a youthful "futurist." He developed a novel piano idiom, explicitly demonstrated in his *Sarcasms* and *Visions fugitives,* percussive and sharp, yet not without a lyric charm. Grotesquerie and irony animated Prokofiev's early works; he also felt a strong attraction toward subjects of elemental or primitive character. His first important orch. composition, the *Scythian Suite,* or *Ala and Lolly,*

draws upon the ancient Russian sun-worship. While a parallel with Stravinsky's *Le Sacre du printemps* may exist, there is no similarity between the styles of the 2 works. Another score, primitivistic in its inspiration, was *Seven, They Are Seven,* an incantation from an old Sumerian ritual. During the same period, Prokofiev wrote his famous *Classical Symphony,* which he completed at the age of 26. In it he successfully re-created the formal style of the 18th century; while the structure was indeed classical, the sudden modulatory shifts and a subtle element of grotesquerie betrayed a 20th-century hand. He conducted the first performance of the *Classical Symphony* in the spring of 1918, and then left Russia, proceeding through Siberia and Japan to America; gave concerts of his music in N.Y., Chicago, and other cities. In 1920 he went to Paris, where he became associated with Diaghilev, who produced Prokofiev's ballets *Chout* (French transliteration of the Russian word for "buffoon"), *Le Pas d'acier,* and *L'Enfant prodigue.* Koussevitzky, who became Prokofiev's publisher, commissioned several works from him for his concerts in Paris, and subsequently in Boston. In 1921 Prokofiev again visited the U.S., for the production by the Chicago Opera Co. of his opera *Love for 3 Oranges.* In 1927 he played a series of concerts in Russia; visited Russia again in 1929; then after a stay in Paris and other European cities, he went to Russia in December 1932 and remained permanently, with the exception of concert engagements in Europe and America. He had never relinquished Soviet citizenship, and was not officially an émigré. He visited the U.S. for the last time in 1938. In Russia he wrote some of his most popular works: the symph. fairy tale *Peter and the Wolf* (for a children's theater in Moscow); the cantata *Alexander Nevsky* (originally for a film); the ballet *Romeo and Juliet;* the opera *War and Peace;* the 5th, 6th, and 7th symphs.; several piano sonatas; songs; etc. Although Prokofiev was a target of sharp criticism on the part of the Soviet press for his "decadent" practices in adopting certain modernistic procedures, his status on the whole remained very high; virtually all of his works were publ.; his music became a major influence on the young generation of Soviet composers. Outside Russia, too, Prokofiev enjoyed enduring fame; his *Classical Symphony,* his 3rd Piano Concerto, *Peter and the Wolf,* the march from *Love for 3 Oranges,* the suite from *Lieutenant Kijé,* and many of the piano works have become repertoire pieces all over the world. Prokofiev never departed from the tonal system despite occasional excursions into modernistic practices (polytonality, atonality). He had an innate sense of sharp rhythm, often in asymmetrical patterns; in his melodic writing he was equally adept in simple lyricism, along modal lines, and in a modern manner spanning large intervals; he was a master of instrumentation, developing an individual method of treating orchestral sonorities. Above all, his music shows a professional care for the performer, never reaching beyond the practicable limits of execution. In 1923 he married **Lina Llubera,** a Spanish soprano. Her real name was **Carlina Codina;** she was born in Madrid in 1898, Catalan on her father's side, and Polish and French on her mother's side. She assumed the stage name Lina Llubera; made her debut in Milan as Gilda in *Rigoletto.* About 1940 Prokofiev went to live with Myra Mendelson, a young Komsomol writer, but was not legally divorced from Lina Llubera. In 1946, the latter was sent to a concentration camp in Central Asia on a political charge, and spent 8 years there. She left Russia in 1976, and in 1977 was in the U.S.

WORKS: OPERAS: *Magdalena* (1913); *The Gambler,* after Dostoyevsky (1915–16; revised 1927; premiere, Brussels, April 29, 1929); *Love for 3 Oranges,* after Carlo Gozzi (Chicago, Dec. 30, 1921, composer conducting); *The Flaming Angel* (1919; 2 fragments perf. at a Koussevitzky concert, Paris, June 14, 1928; complete perf. in concert form was given in Paris on Nov. 25, 1954; its stage premiere was given in Venice on Sept. 14, 1955); *Simeon Kotko* (1939; Moscow, June 23, 1940); *Betrothal in a Convent,* after Sheridan's *Duenna* (1940; Leningrad, Nov. 3, 1946); *War and Peace,* after Tolstoy (1941–52; first version, Leningrad, June 12, 1946; 2nd version, Leningrad, April 1, 1955); *A Tale about a Real Man* (1947–48; privately perf., Leningrad, Dec. 3, 1948; severely censured by Soviet critics and not produced in public; revived posthumously at the Bolshoi Theater in Moscow on Oct. 8, 1960).

BALLETS: *A Tale of a Buffoon Who Outwitted 7 Buffoons* (usually perf. outside Russia as *Chout;* 1920; Paris, May 17, 1921); *Le Pas d'acier* (1924; Paris, June 7, 1927); *L'Enfant prodigue* (1928; Paris, May 21, 1929); *Sur le Borysthène* (1930; Paris, Dec. 16, 1932); *Romeo and Juliet* (1935–36; Leningrad, Jan. 11, 1940); *Cinderella* (1940–44; Moscow, Nov. 21, 1945); *A Tale of the Stone Flower* (1948–50; Moscow, Feb. 12, 1954).

INCIDENTAL MUSIC: To *Egyptian Nights,* op. 61 (1933); *Boris Godunov* (1936); *Eugene Onegin* (1936); *Hamlet* (1937–38; first perf. in connection with the opening of the Leningrad Theater, May 15, 1938). Film music: *Lieutenant Kijé* (1933); *The Queen of Spades* (1938); *Alexander Nevsky* (1938); *Lermontov* (1941); *Tonya* (1942); *Kotovsky* (1942); *Partisans in the Ukrainian Steppes* (1942); *Ivan the Terrible* (1942–45).

CHORAL WORKS: 2 poems for Women's Chorus, with Orch.: *The White Swan* and *The Wave* (1909); *Seven, They Are Seven,* cantata for Tenor, Chorus, and Orch. (1917–18; Paris, May 29, 1924); cantata for the 20th anniversary of the October Revolution, for 2 Choruses, Military Band, Accordions, and Percussion, to texts by Marx, Lenin, and Stalin (1937; not perf. at the time; was finally brought to a perf. in Moscow on April 5, 1966, but not in its entirety; the section which used a text from Stalin was eliminated); *Songs of Our Days,* op. 76, suite for Solo Voices, Mixed Chorus, and Orch. (Moscow, Jan. 5, 1938); *Alexander Nevsky,* cantata for Mezzo-soprano, Mixed Chorus, and Orch. (Moscow, May 17, 1939); *Salute,* cantata for Mixed Chorus and Symph. Orch., for Stalin's 60th birthday (Moscow, Dec. 21, 1939); *Ballad of a Boy Who Remained Unknown,* cantata for Soprano, Tenor, Chorus, and Orch. (Moscow, Feb. 21, 1944); *Hymn to the Soviet Union* (1943; submitted to the competition for a new Soviet

anthem but failed to win; a song by Alexander Alexandrov was selected); *Flourish, Powerful Land,* cantata for the 30th anniversary of the October Revolution (Moscow, Nov. 12, 1947); *Winter Bonfire,* suite for Narrators, Boys' Chorus, and Symph. Orch. (Moscow, Dec. 19, 1950); *On Guard for Peace,* oratorio for Mezzo-soprano, Narrators, Mixed Chorus, Boys' Chorus, and Symph. Orch. (Moscow, Dec. 19, 1950).

FOR ORCH.: Sinfonietta (1914; Petrograd, Nov. 6, 1915; new version, 1929; Moscow, Nov. 18, 1930); *Rêves,* symph. tableau (St. Petersburg, Dec. 5, 1910); *Autumn,* symph. tableau (Moscow, Aug. 1, 1911); First Piano Concerto (Moscow, Aug. 7, 1912, composer, soloist); 2nd Piano Concerto (Pavlovsk, Sept. 5, 1913, composer, soloist; 2nd version, Paris, May 8, 1924, composer, soloist); First Violin Concerto (1916–17; Paris, Oct. 18, 1923); *Scythian Suite* (1914; Petrograd, Jan. 29, 1916); *Chout,* symph. suite from the ballet (Brussels, Jan. 15, 1924); *Classical Symphony* (1916–17; Petrograd, April 21, 1918, composer conducting); 3rd Piano Concerto (1917–21; Chicago, Dec. 16, 1921, composer, soloist); *Love for 3 Oranges,* symph. suite from the opera (Paris, Nov. 29, 1925); Symph. No. 2 (1924; Paris, June 6, 1925; 2nd version, not completed); *Le Pas d'acier,* symph. suite from the ballet (1926; Moscow, May 27, 1928); Overture for Chamber Orch. (Moscow, Feb. 7, 1927; also for Large Orch., 1928; Paris, Dec. 18, 1930); *Divertissement* (1925–29; Paris, Dec. 22, 1929); Symph. No. 3 (1928; Paris, May 17, 1929); *L'Enfant prodigue,* symph. suite from the ballet (1929; Paris, March 7, 1931); Symph. No. 4 (Boston, Nov. 14, 1930; a new version, radically revised, 1947); *4 Portraits,* symph. suite from the opera *The Gambler* (1931; Paris, March 12, 1932); *On the Dnieper,* symph. suite from the ballet (1933); 4th Piano Concerto, for Left Hand Alone (1931; Berlin, Sept. 5, 1956); 5th Piano Concerto (Berlin, Oct. 31, 1932, composer, soloist); *Symphonic Song* (Moscow, April 14, 1934); First Cello Concerto (1933–38; Moscow, Nov. 26, 1938; revised and perf. for the first time in Moscow on Feb. 18, 1952, as Cello Concerto No. 2, but later retitled *Sinfonia-Concertante;* this final version was perf. posthumously in Copenhagen on Dec. 9, 1954); *Lieutenant Kijé,* symph. suite from film music (1934; Paris, Feb. 20, 1937, composer conducting); *Egyptian Nights,* symph. suite (1934; Moscow, Dec. 22, 1938); 2nd Violin Concerto (1935; Madrid, Dec. 1, 1935); *Romeo and Juliet,* first suite from the ballet (Moscow, Nov. 24, 1936); *Romeo and Juliet,* 2nd suite from the ballet (Leningrad, April 15, 1937); *Peter and the Wolf,* symph. fairy tale (Moscow, May 2, 1936); *4 Marches* for Military Band (1935–37); *Russian Overture* (Moscow, Oct. 29, 1936); *Symphonic March* (1941); *The Year 1941* (1941; Sverdlovsk, Jan. 21, 1943); *March* for Military Orch. (Moscow, April 30, 1944); Symph. No. 5 (1944; Moscow, Jan. 13, 1945); *Romeo and Juliet,* 3rd suite from the ballet (Moscow, March 8, 1946); *Ode on the End of the War* for 8 Harps, 4 Pianos, Military Band, Percussion Ensemble, and Double Basses (1945; Moscow, Nov. 12, 1945); *Cinderella,* 3 suites from the ballet (1946); *Waltzes,* suite for Orch. (1946; Moscow, May 13, 1947); Symph. No. 6 (1945–47; Leningrad, Oct. 11,

1947); *Festive Poem* (Moscow, Oct. 3, 1947); *Ivan the Terrible,* suite for Orch. (1942–45); *Pushkin Waltzes* (1949); *Summer Night,* symph. suite on themes from the opera *Betrothal in a Convent* (1950); *Wedding Scene,* suite from the ballet *A Tale of the Stone Flower* (Moscow, Dec. 12, 1951); *Gypsy Fantasy,* from the ballet *A Tale of the Stone Flower* (Moscow, Nov. 18, 1951); *Ural Rhapsody,* from the ballet *A Tale of the Stone Flower* (1951); *The Mistress of the Copper Mountain,* suite from the ballet *A Tale of the Stone Flower* (incomplete); *The Meeting of the Volga with the Don River* (for the completion of the Volga-Don Canal; 1951; Moscow, Feb. 22, 1952); Symph. No. 7 (1951–52; Moscow, Oct. 11, 1952); Concertino for Cello and Orch. (1952; unfinished); Concerto for 2 Pianos and String Orch. (1952; incomplete).

CHAMBER MUSIC: *Humorous Scherzo* for 4 Bassoons (1912; London, Sept. 2, 1916); *Ballade* for Cello and Piano (1912); *Overture on Hebrew Themes* for Clarinet, 2 Violins, Viola, Cello, and Piano (N.Y., Jan. 26, 1920); Quintet for Oboe, Clarinet, Violin, Viola, and Double Bass (1924; Moscow, March 6, 1927); First String Quartet (Washington, D.C., April 25, 1931); Sonata for 2 Violins (Moscow, Nov. 27, 1932); First Violin Sonata (1938–46; Moscow, Oct. 23, 1946); 2nd String Quartet (1941; Moscow, Sept. 5, 1942); Sonata for Flute and Piano (Moscow, Dec. 7, 1943); 2nd Violin Sonata (transcription of the Flute Sonata; Moscow, June 17, 1944); Sonata for Violin Unaccompanied (1947); Cello Sonata (1949; Moscow, March 1, 1950).

PIANO MUSIC: 9 sonatas: No. 1 (1909); No. 2 (1912); No. 3 (1917); No. 4 (1917); No. 5 (1923); No. 6 (1940); No. 7 (1942); No. 8 (1944); No. 9 (1947); No. 10 remains in sketches (1953); 2 sonatinas (1931–32); 4 Etudes (1909); 4 Pieces (1911); 4 Pieces (1912); Toccata (1912); 10 Pieces (1913); *Sarcasms,* suite of 5 pieces (1912–14); *Visions fugitives,* suite of 20 pieces (1915–17); *Tales of an Old Grandmother,* 4 pieces (1918); *Schubert's Waltzes,* transcribed for 2 Pianos (1911); March and Scherzo from the opera *Love for 3 Oranges* (1922); *Things in Themselves* (1928); 6 Pieces (1930–31); 3 Pieces (1934); *Pensées* (1933–34); *Children's Music,* 12 easy pieces (1935); *Romeo and Juliet,* 10 pieces from the ballet (1937); 3 pieces from the ballet *Cinderella* (1942); 3 Pieces (1941–42); 10 pieces from the ballet *Cinderella,* op. 97 (1943); 6 pieces from the ballet *Cinderella* (1944).

SONGS: *2 Poems* (1911); *The Ugly Duckling,* after Andersen (1914); *5 Poems* (1915); *5 Poems* (1916); *5 Songs without Words* (1920; also for Violin and Piano); *5 Poems* (1921); *6 Songs* (1935); *3 Children's Songs* (1936); *3 Poems* (1936); 3 songs from the film *Alexander Nevsky* (1939); *7 Songs* (1939); *7 Mass Songs* (1941–42); 6 transcriptions of folk songs (1944); 2 duets (1945); *Soldiers' March Song* (1950).

BIBLIOGRAPHY: M. Montagu-Nathan, "S. Prokofiev," *Musical Times* (Oct. 1916); idem, "Prokofiev's First Pianoforte Concerto," ibid. (Jan. 1917); idem, *Contemporary Russian Composers* (N.Y., 1917); L. Sabaneyev, *Modern Russian Composers* (N.Y., 1927); Nicolas Slonimsky, "S. Prokofiev," *Quarterly on the Soviet Union* (N.Y., April 1939); Gerald Abraham, *8 Soviet Composers* (London, 1943); S. Prokofiev, "The War Years," *Musical Quarterly* (Oct. 1944); I. Nestyev, *S. Prokofiev* (Moscow, 1946; in Eng., N.Y., 1946; enlarged Russian ed., Moscow, 1957; in Eng. with a foreword by N. Slonimsky, Stanford, Calif., 1961); Rena Moisenko, *Realist Music: 25 Soviet Composers* (London, 1949; pp. 173–87); N. Nabokov, *Old Friends and New Music* (Boston, 1951; pp. 141–83); S. Schlifstein, ed., *S. Prokofiev, Materials, Documents, Reminiscences* (Moscow, 1956; of prime documentary value; contains Prokofiev's autobiography and a complete catalogue of Prokofiev's works, with exhaustive commentaries and dates); F. Streller, *Prokofiev* (Leipzig, 1960); C. Samuel, *Prokofiev* (Paris, 1960); L. Gakkel, *Piano Works of S. Prokofiev* (Moscow, 1960); I.V. Nestyev and G. Edelman, eds., *Sergey Prokofiev, Articles and Materials* (Moscow, 1962); L. Berger, ed., *Traits of Prokofiev's Style* (Moscow, 1962); M. Hofmann, *Prokofiev* (Paris, 1963); L. and E. Hanson, *Prokofiev, The Prodigal Son* (London, 1964); S. Slonimsky, *The Symphonies of Prokofiev* (Leningrad, 1964); S. Schlifstein, ed., *Prokofiev,* album of pictures annotated in Russian and Eng. (Moscow, 1965); V. Serov, *S. Prokofiev, A Soviet Tragedy* (N.Y., 1968); V.M. Blok, *Cello Works by Prokofiev* (Moscow, 1973); D. Appel, ed., and G. Daniels, trans., *Prokofiev by Prokofiev: A Composer's Memoir* (Garden City, N.Y., 1979); C. Bennett, "Prokofiev and Eugene Onegin," *Musical Times* (April 1980); V. Blok, ed., *Sergei Prokofiev: Materials, Articles, Interviews* (London, 1980). A complete text of Prokofiev's autobiography was publ. in Moscow in 1973.

Proksch, Josef, Bohemian pianist and pedagogue; b. Reichenberg, Aug. 4, 1794; d. Prague, Dec. 20, 1864. He studied with Koželuch; in 1811 he lost his eyesight, but still learned Logier's system, and in 1830 founded a "Musikbildungsanstalt" (school of piano playing) in Prague. He publ. a useful piano manual, *Versuch einer rationellen Lehrmethode im Pianofortespiel;* also *Musikalisches Vademecum; Aphorismen über katholische Kirchenmusik; Allgemeine Musiklehre;* made for his pupils transcriptions, for 2, 3, 4, and even 8 pianos, of orch. works; composed a Concerto for 3 Pianos, sonatas, and other works; also vocal music. His son, **Theodor Proksch** (1843–76), and a daughter, **Marie Proksch** (1836–1900), managed the school after his death; the last director of the Proksch school was **Robert Franz Proksch,** a great-grandnephew of Josef Proksch; he died in 1933.

BIBLIOGRAPHY: R. Müller, *Josef Proksch* (Prague, 1874); H.P. Kraus, *Musikbibliothek Josef Proksch* (Vienna, 1934).

Prony, Gaspard-Claire-François-Marie-Riche, Baron de, French harpist and music theorist; b. Chamelot, Rhône, July 12, 1755; d. Paris, July 29, 1839. As a member of the Académie, he was in charge of educational information; he publ. a report on Erard's double-pedal harp, *Rapport sur la nouvelle harpe à double mouvement* (1815); other reports are: *Note sur les avantages du nouvel établissement d'un professorat d'harpe à l'école* *royale de musique* (1825); *Instruction élémentaire sur les moyens de calculer les intervalles musicaux* (1832; employing Euler's system of logarithms).

Prošev, Toma, Macedonian composer; b. Skopje, Nov. 10, 1931. He studied with Škerjanc at the Zagreb Academy of Music, graduating in composition in 1961; then made a musical pilgrimage to Nadia Boulanger in Paris (1964); thus musically replenished, he returned to Zagreb and devoted himself to teaching. His music is moderately modern.
WORKS: 2 operas: (*Paučina* (*The Cobweb;* 1957) and *Mali princ* (*The Little Prince;* 1964); 2 ballets: *Okviri i odjeci* (*Frames and Echoes;* 1961) and *Pjesma nad pjesmama* (*Song of Songs;* 1967); 3 oratorios: *Jama* (*The Pit;* 1961); *Skopje* (1965); *Sonce na prastarata zemja* (*Sun of the Ancient Country;* 1967); Piano Concertino (1958); *Makete (Dummies)* for Orch. (1960); *Concertante Music* for Cello and String Orch. (1960); *Improvisations concertante* for Violin and String Orch. (1962); 2 symphs. (1962, 1963); 2 violin concertos (1963, 1964); *Tempera I–IV* for Strings (1963–70); *Metastasis* for Orch. (1963); Concerto for Ondes Martenot and Orch. (1964); *Relations* for Orch. (1964); *Morphographie* for Chamber Orch. (1965); *Diametry* for Voice and Chamber Orch. (1966); *3 Movements* for Clarinet and String Orch. (1966); *Colors* for 6 Solo Voices and Ensemble (1967); *Chamber Music* (1971); *Intergrali* for Piano and Chamber Ensemble (1971); Violin Sonata (1953); String Quartet (1959); *Intima* for Piano (1962).

Proske, Carl, German authority on sacred music; b. Gröbnig, Feb. 11, 1794; d. Regensburg, Dec. 20, 1861. He was a medical student, served in the medical corps during the war of 1813–15; took the degree of M.D. at Halle in 1817, and practiced at Oberglogau and Oppeln. In 1823 he renounced medicine for theology, and studied at Regensburg; was ordained in 1826; became vicar-choral in 1827, and canon and Kapellmeister of the Church of Our Lady at Regensburg in 1830. After diligent research in Germany and Italy, he began his lifework, the publication of sacred classics, the first being Palestrina's *Missa Papae Marcelli* (Palestrina's original version, and arrangements by Anerio *a* 4 and Suriano *a* 8), followed by the famous collection *Musica divina,* containing chiefly Italian masterworks of the 16th–17th centuries: vol. I, 12 masses *a* 4 (1853); vol. II, motets for the entire church year (1855); vol. III, fauxbourdons, Psalms, Magnificats, hymns, and antiphons (1859); vol. IV, Passions, Lamentations, responses, Te Deums, litanies (1863; ed. by Wesselack); its publication was continued by Schrems and Haberl. Proske also publ. *Selectus novus missarum a* 4–8 (1855–59). His valuable library was purchased for the Episcopal Library at Regensburg; in 1909, when Dr. Karl Weinmann was appointed librarian, it was opened to musicians and music students.
BIBLIOGRAPHY: Dom. Mettenleiter, *Carl Proske* (Regensburg, 1868; 2nd ed., 1895); K. Weinmann, *Carl Proske, der Restaurator der klassischen Kir-*

chenmusik (Regensburg, 1909); idem, "Die Proskesche Musikbibliothek in Regensburg," in the Riemann Festschrift (Leipzig, 1909); A. Scharnagl, "Dr. Carl Proske: Leben und Werk," *Der Zwiebelturm,* XVII (1962).

Prosniz, Adolf, Austrian pianist and pedagogue; b. Prague, Dec. 2, 1829; d. Vienna, Feb. 23, 1917. He was a pupil of Proksch and Tomaschek; in 1869–1900 was a prof. of piano at the Vienna Cons.; then retired and lived in Vienna.
WRITINGS: *Kompendium der Musikgeschichte* (vol. I, 1889; 3rd ed., 1920; vol. II, 1900; vol. III, 1915); *Handbuch der Klavierliteratur* (vol. I [1450–1830], 1884; 2nd ed., 1908; vol. II [1830–1904], 1907); *Elementarmusiklehre* (6 eds.); *Historische Klavierliteratur aus dem 16., 17. und 18. Jahrhundert. Ausgewählte Beispiele zu jedem Handbuch der Klavierliteratur* (9 vols.).

Prota-Giurleo, Ulisse, Italian musicologist; b. Naples, March 13, 1886; d. Perugia, Feb. 9, 1966. At first an art critic, he took up the study of musicology, and devoted himself chiefly to Neapolitan music. His publications (all printed in Naples) are valuable for their documentation.
WRITINGS: *Musicisti napoletani alla corte di Portogallo* (1923); *Musicisti napoletani in Russia* (1923); *Paisiello ed i soui primi trionfi a Napoli* (1923); *Nicola Logroscini, "il dio dell'opera buffa"* (1927); *La grande orchestra del R. Teatro San Carlo nel settecento* (1927); *La famiglia e la giovinezza di Salvator Rosa* (containing 52 unpubl. documents; 1929); "Notizie sul musicista belga Jean Macque," *Report of the First Congress of the International Society for Musical Research* (Burnham, 1930); *Sacchini non nacque a Pozzuoli* (1952); *Nouvi contributi alla biografia di Domenico Cimarosa* and *Nuovi contributi alle biografie di Nicola Porpora e Giuseppe Porsile* (both publ. serially in *La Scala* during 1955–56); *I Teatri di Napoli nel '600; La commedia e le maschere* (Naples, 1962); numerous essays publ. in the Italian periodicals *Samnium, Vita Musicale Italiana, Nostro Tempo,* etc.

Protheroe, Daniel, American conductor and composer; b. Cwmgiedd, near Ystradgynlais, South Wales, Nov. 5, 1866; d. Chicago, Feb. 24, 1934. In 1884–86 he was conductor of the Choral Society at Ystradgynlais; in 1886–94, a choral conductor in Scranton, Pa.; in 1894–1909, a singer and teacher in Milwaukee; then lived in Chicago as music director of the Central Church. He wrote a symph. poem, *In the Cambrian Hills;* a String Quartet; works for men's chorus; songs; a *Course in Harmony and Choral Conducting.*

Prout, Ebenezer, eminent English music theorist and teacher; b. Oundle, Northamptonshire, March 1, 1835; d. London, Dec. 5, 1909. Excepting some piano lessons as a boy, and later a course with Charles Salaman, he was wholly self-taught. His father had him trained to be a schoolteacher, and he took the degree of B.A. at London Univ. in 1854; but in 1859 he went over definitely to music; was organist at Union Chapel in Islington in 1861–73; a prof. of piano at the Crystal Palace School of Art in 1861–85; a prof. of harmony and composition at the National Training School from 1876; he took Sullivan's class at the Royal Academy of Music in 1897; also conducted the Hackney Choral Assoc. in 1876–90, bringing it to a high state of efficiency. He edited the *Monthly Musical Record* in 1871–74; was critic on the *Academy* in 1874–79 and on the *Athenaeum* in 1879–89. In 1894 he was called to Dublin Univ. as prof. of music, succeeding Sir R. Stewart; in 1895 both Dublin and Edinburgh univs. conferred on him the degree of Mus.Doc. *honoris causa.* His valuable theoretical works are the following: *Instrumentation* (Novello primer, 1876; 3rd ed., 1904); *Harmony, Its Theory and Practice* (1889; 20th ed., entirely rewritten, 1903); *Counterpoint, Strict and Free* (1890); *Double Counterpoint and Canon* (1891); *Fugue* (1891); *Fugal Analysis* (1892); *Musical Form* (1893); *Applied Forms* (1895); all of these have passed through many editions. He also publ. *The Orchestra* (2 vols., 1898–99; in German, 1905–6) and *Some Notes on Bach's Church-Cantatas* (1907). He was a competent composer of useless works, among them 4 symphs.; 2 overtures; 2 organ concertos; a Piano Quintet; 2 string quartets; 2 piano quartets; Clarinet Sonata; the cantatas *Hereward, Alfred,* and *The Red Cross Knight;* a considerable amount of church music; *Freedom,* ode for Baritone Solo and Orch.; organ arrangements.

Provenzale, Francesco, one of the founders of the Neapolitan Opera School; b. Naples, 1627; d. there, Sept. 6, 1704. From 1663 he was maestro at the Cons. di Santa Maria di Loreto; in 1673–1701, director of the Cons. della Pietà de' Turchini; c.1680, associate conductor of the Royal Chapel; in 1686–99, conductor at the Tesoro di San Gennaro in Naples. Romain Rolland believed him to be identical with Francesco della Torre.
WORKS: Operas (all perf. in Naples): *Ciro* (1653); *Serse* (1655); *Artemisia* (1657); *Teseo o L'Incostanza triofante* (1658); *L'Eritrea* (1659); *Lo Schiavo di sua moglie* (1671); *La Stellidaura vendicata o Diffendere l'offensore* (1674); *Candaule re di Lidia* (1679); also oratorios; motets; a 9-voiced hymn with instrumental accompaniment, *Pange lingua;* cantatas.
BIBLIOGRAPHY: R. Rolland, *Histoire de l'opéra avant Lully et Scarlatti* (1895); H. Riemann, *Handbuch der Musikgeschichte,* II, 2, pp. 385ff.; H. Goldschmidt, "F. Provenzale als Dramatiker," *Sammelbände der Internationalen Musik-Gesellschaft,* VII/4; G. Pannain, "F. Provenzale e la lirica del suo tempo," *Rivista Musicale Italiana* (1925).

Prudent, Emile, French pianist; b. Angoulême, Feb. 3, 1817; d. Paris, May 13, 1863. Early orphaned, he was adopted by a piano tuner; studied at the Paris Cons. with Zimmerman (piano) and Laurent (harmony), taking first prize in 1833. He made tours as a pianist in France, Belgium, England, and Germany; then settled in Paris, and was greatly esteemed there as a teacher. He wrote a number of piano works; contemporary critics ranked him between Thalberg and Döhler; his paraphrase of *Lucia di Lammermoor* enjoyed considerable success; he publ. *6 études de salon,* and other effective piano pieces (*L'Hirondelle, La Berceuse, Chanson sicilienne, Le Réveil des fées,* etc.).

Pruett, James W., American librarian and music educator; b. Mount Airy, N.C., Dec. 23, 1932. He studied music and comparative literature at the Univ. of North Carolina Chapel Hill (B.A., 1955; M.A., 1957; Ph.D., 1962). After serving as music librarian at the Univ. (1955–76), assistant prof. of music (1963–74), and prof. of music (1974–76), he was appointed chairman of the music dept. there in 1976; in 1974–77 he was the editor of *Notes,* the quarterly journal of the Music Library Association. His specialties are the music of the late Italian Renaissance and American musical biography; he contributed valuable papers on musical bibliography to various scholarly journals; publ. an interesting essay, "Charles Butler: Musician, Grammarian, Apiarist," in the *Musical Quarterly* (1963).

Prüfer, Arthur, German musicologist; b. Leipzig, July 7, 1860; d. Würzburg, June 3, 1944. He was a law student; then turned to music; studied at the Leipzig Cons. (1887–88), also attending the lectures on musicology of Paul and Kretzschmar at the Univ.; studied further in Berlin (1888–89) with Spitta and Bargiel; took the degree of Dr.Phil. (Leipzig, 1890) with the dissertation *Über den ausserkirchlichen Kunstgesang in den evangelischen Schulen des 16. Jahrhunderts;* qualified in 1895 as a lecturer at the Univ. of Leipzig with the essay *Johann Hermann Schein;* in 1902, qualified as an associate prof. with the lecture *J.S. Bach und die Tonkunst des 19. Jahrhunderts.* Further publications: *Die Bühnenfestspiele in Bayreuth* (1899; 2nd ed., completely rewritten and greatly enlarged, as *Das Werk von Bayreuth,* 1909); *Joh. Herm. Schein und das weltliche deutsche Lied des 17. Jahrhunderts* (1908); *R. Wagner in Bayreuth* (1910); *Die Musik als tönende Faust-Idee* (1920); *Tristan und Isolde* (3rd ed., 1928); *Deutsches Leben im Volkslied und Wagners Tannhäuser* (1929); *Tannhäuser und der Sängerkrieg* (1930). He edited the first collected edition of Schein's works, publ. 1901–23 by Breitkopf & Härtel (8 vols. appeared); publ. separately selections of 20 "weltliche Lieder" and instrumental pieces of Schein.

Prumier, Antoine, French harpist; b. Paris, July 2, 1794; d. there, Jan. 20, 1868. He studied at the Paris Cons.; played the harp in the orch. of the Opéra-Comique (from 1835); succeeded Nadermann as prof. of harp at the Cons. He wrote for harp about 100 fantasies, rondos, and airs with variations. His son **Ange-Conrad Prumier** (b. Paris, Jan. 5, 1820; d. there, April 3, 1884) succeeded him at the Opéra-Comique, and became a prof. at the Cons. in 1870. He publ. études for harp; nocturnes for harp and horn; sacred songs.

Prunières, Henry, eminent French musicologist; b. Paris, May 24, 1886; d. Nanterre, April 11, 1942. He studied music history with R. Rolland; received his doctorat ès lettres from the Univ. of Paris in 1913 with the dissertation *L'Opéra italien en France avant Lulli* (publ. in Paris, 1913); in 1909–14, was an instructor at the Ecole des Hautes Etudes Sociales in Paris; in 1920, founded the important journal *La Revue Musicale*, of which he was editor in chief until 1939; in 1921, he organized the concerts at the Théâtre du Vieux Colombier; was head of the French section of the International Society for Contemporary Music.

WRITINGS: *Lully* (1910; 2nd ed., 1927); *La Musique de la chambre et de l'écurie* (Paris, 1912); *Le Ballet de cour en France avant Benserade et Lully* (Supplementary Diss., 1913; publ. in Paris, 1914); *Monteverdi* (1924; enlarged 1926; 2nd ed., 1931; also in Eng., N.Y., 1926; reprint, 1972); *La Vie illustre et libertine de J.-B. Lully* (1929); *Cavalli et l'opéra vénitien au XVIIᵉ siècle* (1931); *Nouvelle histoire de la musique* (2 vols., 1934, 1936; in Eng., one vol., 1943; reprint, N.Y., 1972); also the following valuable essays: "La Musique de la chambre et de l'écurie sous le règne de François I," *Année Musicale*, 1 (1911); "Jean de Cambeford, Surintendant de la musique de la chambre de roy," ibid., 2 (1913). He was general editor of a complete ed. of Lully's works (10 vols., Paris, 1930–39).

BIBLIOGRAPHY: Special issue of *La Revue Musicale* (1952–53), dedicated to Prunières.

Prüwer, Julius, Austrian conductor; b. Vienna, Feb. 20, 1874; d. New York, July 8, 1943. He studied piano with Friedheim and Moriz Rosenthal, and theory with R. Fuchs and Krenn; also profited greatly by his friendly association with Brahms. He studied conducting with Hans Richter; began his career as a conductor in Bielitz; then conducted at the Cologne Opera (1894–96) and at the Municipal Theater in Breslau (1896–1923), where he distinguished himself by conducting numerous new works. From 1924 to 1933 he conducted popular concerts of the Berlin Phil. After 1933 he was compelled to leave Germany owing to the barbarous racial laws of the Nazi regime; he conducted in Russia and in Austria; eventually reached N.Y., where he remained until his death.

Pryor, Arthur (Willard), American trombonist, bandleader, and composer of band music; b. St. Joseph, Mo., Sept. 22, 1870; d. Long Branch, N.J., June 18, 1942. He began his professional career in 1889 as a performer on the slide trombone. When J.P. Sousa formed his own band in 1892, he hired Pryor as his trombone soloist; from 1895 until he left to form his own band in 1903, Pryor was assistant conductor for Sousa. Pryor's Band gave its first major concert at the Majestic Theatre in N.Y. on Nov. 15, 1903, but beginning in 1904 it initiated series of summer outdoor concerts at Asbury Park, Coney Island, and other amusement parks. From 1903 to 1909 it made 6 coast-to-coast tours. Unlike Sousa, who would have nothing to do with "canned music," Pryor was quick to take advantage of the developing record industry; he made some 1,000 acoustic records before 1930. He also entered upon a series of commercial radio broadcasts. He composed about 300 works, including operettas, ragtime and cakewalk tunes, and novelties such as *The Whistler and His Dog,* Pryor's best-known work. He was a charter member of ASCAP in 1914 and of the American Bandmasters Assoc. in 1929. In 1933 he retired to Long Branch.

BIBLIOGRAPHY: *Dictionary of American Biography* (Supplement II, pp. 610–11).

Przybilski, Bronislaw, Polish composer; b. Lodz, Dec. 11, 1941. He studied music theory with Kiesewetter at the Lodz Cons.; then joined its faculty. In his music he experiments with mathematical notions, except in straightforward Polish pieces.

WORKS: *Circulus* for Percussion (1971); *Canon enigmaticus per fiati* for 2 to 50 arbitrarily selected Wind Instruments (1971); *Rotazioni per 3* for 3 selected Instruments (1971); *Polish Dance Suite* for Orch. (1971); *Omaggio a Nicolaus Copernicus* for Orch. (1972; Lodz, May 25, 1973); *Scherzi musicali* for String Ensemble (1973); *Voices* for 3 Narrators and Instrumental Ensemble (1974); *Polish Symphony* (1974).

Ptaszyńska, Marta, Polish composer and percussionist; b. Warsaw, July 29, 1943. She studied piano and timpani at the Music Lyceum in Warsaw (1957–62); then took courses in composition with Dobrowolski and Rudziński at the Warsaw Cons. (1962–68) and worked out problems of electronic music with Kotoński in his studio; had supplementary practice in percussion at the Cons. of Poznan (1963–67); in 1969 traveled to Paris, where she, like everybody, had lessons with Nadia Boulanger. In 1972 she received a grant from the Kosciuszko Foundation to travel to the U.S., and studied percussion at the Cleveland Inst. of Music (1972–74). From 1974 till 1977 she taught percussion at Bennington College in Vermont; in 1977 became an instructor in composition at the Univ. of Calif., Berkeley. She played with the "Percussions de Strasbourg"; was a composer and percussionist at the Claremont Music Festival in California, and at the 4th N.Y. Festival of Contemporary American Music. Her music is entirely free of any strictures, whether academically traditional or fashionably modern. Being a virtuoso drummer, she naturally gives a prominent place to percussion in her scores; she also makes use of stereophony by spatial separation of players or groups of instruments.

WORKS: *Oscar from Alva,* opera for television, with libretto by the composer, based on Byron's poem, scored for a Large Ensemble, including a Raucous Rock Group (1972); *Improvisations* for Orch. (1968; Cracow, March 26, 1971); oratorio, *Chant for All the People on Earth* (1969); *Helio, Centricum, Musicum,* multimedia spectacle for Voices, Dancers, and Instrumentalists (1973); *Spectri sonori* for Orch. (1973; Cleveland, Jan. 22, 1974); *Crystallites* for Orch. (1973; Bydgoszcz, Poland, Jan.

24, 1975); Concerto for Percussion Quartet and Orch. (1974; Bennington College, Vt., Oct. 20, 1974); *Chimes, Bells, Wood, Stones* for Wind and String Instruments and Percussion (Bennington College, June 9, 1977); *Preludes* for Vibraphone and Piano (1965); *Variations* for Solo Flute (1967); *Scherzo* for Xylophone and Piano (1967; received the Polish State Prize); *A Tale of Nightingales* for Baritone and 6 Instruments (1968); *Projections sonores* for Chamber Ensemble (1970); *Madrigals,* in memory of Stravinsky, for Wind Instruments, String Quartet, Trumpet, Trombone, and Gong (1971); *Space Model* for Solo Percussion (1971); *Sonospheres No. 1* for Clarinet, Trombone, Cello, and Piano (1971); *Sonospheres No. 2* for 8 Instruments (1971); *Cadenza* for Flute and Percussion (1971–72); *Sonospheres No. 3* for Flute, Clarinet, Trombone, Cello, Piano, and Percussion (1972); *Siderals* for 2 Percussion Quintets, with Light Projections (Univ. of Illinois, Urbana, Nov. 21, 1974); *Recitative, Arioso, Toccata* for Solo Violin (1969–75); *2 Poems* for Solo Tuba (1973–75); *Mobile* for 2 Percussion Players (1975); *Ornaments in Wood* for Flute, Clarinet, Bass Clarinet, and Bassoon (1975); *Classical Variations* for 4 Timpani and String Quartet (1976); *Quodlibet* for Solo Double Bass (1976); *Epigrams* for 20 Women's Voices, Flute, Harp, Piano, and Percussion (1976–77); *Inventions* for Solo Percussionists (1972–77); *Linear Constructions in Space* for Percussion Quartet (1977); *Un Grand Sommeil noir* for Soprano, Flute, and Harp, to words by Verlaine (1977; Pontino, Italy, June 1979); *Soirée snobe chez la Princesse,* instrumental theater (1979); *Dream Lands, Magic Spaces* for Violin, Piano, and Percussion (1979); *3 Interludes* for 2 Pianos (1969); *Touracou* for Harpsichord (1974); *Farewell Souvenir* for Piano (1975); *2 Sonnets to Orpheus* for Mezzo-soprano and Chamber Orch. (1980–81); percussion music for children.

Ptolemy, Claudius, great Alexandrian astronomer, geographer, and mathematician who flourished early in the 2nd century A.D. He wrote an important treatise on music, a poor Latin version of which was made by Gogavinus (1562); Wallis publ. the original Greek text in 1682; O. Paul gives a fragment in Greek, with German trans., in his *Boëtius.* A new edition of this work was publ. by Ingemar Düring (Göteborg, 1930), with excellent commentary and explanation.
BIBLIOGRAPHY: I. Düring, *Ptolemaios und Porphyrios über die Musik* (Göteborg, 1934); M. Shirlaw, "Claudius Ptolemy as Musical Theorist," *Music Review* (Aug. 1955).

Puccini, Giacomo, celebrated Italian composer; b. Lucca, Dec. 22, 1858; d. Brussels, Nov. 29, 1924. Beginning with his great-great-grandfather, Giacomo (1712–81), all of his ancestors in the direct line were musicians of local prominence: **Antonio** (1747–1832), **Domenico** (1771–1815), **Michele** (1813–64). As a child Puccini showed neither inclination nor special talent for music; but his mother, determined to continue family tradition, sent him to the Istituto Musicale of Lucca (founded by Pacini), where Carlo Angeloni, a pupil of Michele Puccini, became his teacher. After Angeloni's untiring patience had aroused interest, and then enthusiasm, in his pupil, progress was rapid and Puccini soon was a good pianist and organist. About 1875 he became organist at the church in a nearby village, Mutigliano, and soon after was also appointed organist at San Pietro in Somaldi. In 1877 he submitted a cantata, *Juno,* to a competition held at Lucca, but failed to win the prize. Nevertheless, he produced the work, which won considerable local success, so that the young composer brought out, also with success, a motet for the feast of Santa Paolina. These successes fired his ambition, and when he became acquainted about that time with *Aida,* he resolved to win laurels as a dramatic composer. Assistance from a grand-uncle and a stipend granted by Queen Margherita enabled him to enter the Milan Cons., where he spent 3 years (1880–83) in serious study with Antonio Bazzini and Amilcare Ponchielli. For his graduation he wrote a *Capriccio sinfonico,* which at its performance at one of the Cons. concerts, and later by Faccio, elicited unstinting praise from the critics. In the same year Ponchielli introduced Puccini to the librettist Fontana, who furnished him the text of a one-act opera; in a few weeks the score was finished and sent to the Sonzongo competition. It did not win the prize, but on May 31, 1884, *Le villi* was produced at the Teatro dal Verme in Milan, with gratifying success. Ricordi, who was present, considered the work sufficiently meritorious to commission the young composer to write a new opera for him; but 5 years elapsed before this work, *Edgar* (3 acts; text by Fontana), was produced at La Scala (April 21, 1889), scoring only a moderate success. By this time Puccini had become convinced that, in order to write a really effective opera, he needed a better libretto than Fontana had provided. Accordingly, he commissioned Domenico Oliva to write the text of *Manon Lescaut;* during the composition, however, Puccini and Ricordi practically rewrote the entire book, and in the publ. score Oliva's name is not mentioned. With *Manon Lescaut* (4 acts), first produced at the Teatro Regio in Turin on Feb. 1, 1893, Puccini won a veritable triumph, which was even surpassed by the next work, *La Bohème* (4 acts; text by Illica and Giacosa), produced at the same theater on Feb. 1, 1896. These 2 works not only carried their composer's name throughout the world, but also have found and maintained their place in the repertoire of every opera house. With fame came wealth, and in 1900 he built at Torre del Lago, where he had been living since 1891, a magnificent villa. The next opera, *Tosca* (3 acts; text by Illica and Giacosa), produced at the Teatro Costanzi in Rome on Jan. 14, 1900, is Puccini's most dramatic work; it has become a fixture of the standard repertoire, and contains some of Puccini's best-known arias. At its premiere at La Scala on Feb. 17, 1904, *Madama Butterfly* (2 acts; text by Illica and Giacosa) was hissed. Puccini thereupon withdrew the score and made some slight changes (division into 3 acts, and addition of the tenor aria in the last scene). This revised version was greeted with frenzied applause in Brescia on May 28 of the same year. Puccini was now the acknowledged ruler of the Italian operatic stage, his works rivaling those of Verdi in the number of performances. The first performance of *Madama Butterfly* at the Metropolitan Opera House (Feb. 11, 1907) took place in the presence of the composer, whom the management had invited especially for the occasion. It was then suggested that he write an opera on an American subject, the premiere to take place at the Metropolitan. He found his subject when he witnessed a performance of Belasco's *The Girl of the Golden West;* he commissioned C. Zangarini and G. Civinini to write the libretto, and in the presence of the composer the world premiere of *La Fanciulla del West* occurred, amid much enthusiasm, at the Metropolitan on Dec. 10, 1910; while it never equaled the success of Puccini's *Tosca* or *Madama Butterfly,* it returned to favor in the 1970s as a period piece. Puccini then brought out *La Rondine* (3 acts; Monte Carlo, March 27, 1917) and the 3 one-act operas *Il Tabarro* (after Didier Gold's *La Houppelande), Suor Angelica,* and *Gianni Schicchi* (all perf. at the Metropolitan Opera House, Dec. 14, 1918). His last opera, *Turandot* (after Gozzi), was left unfinished; the final scene was completed by Franco Alfano and the work performed at La Scala in Milan on April 25, 1926; it was also given at the Metropolitan on Nov. 16, 1926. Puccini died of cancer of the larynx. All of his operas have been performed in the U.S.: *Le villi* (Metropolitan, Dec. 17, 1908); *Manon Lescaut* (Hinrichs Co., Philadelphia, Aug. 29, 1894); *La Bohème* (Los Angeles, Oct. 18, 1897); *Tosca* (Metropolitan, Feb. 4, 1901); *Madama Butterfly* (Washington, D.C., Oct. 15, 1906).

BIBLIOGRAPHY: M. Virgilio, *Della Decadenza dell'opera in Italia* (Milan, 1900); A. Brüggemann, *Madama Butterfly e l'arte di G. Puccini* (Milan, 1904); Wakeling Dry, *G. Puccini* (London, 1906); F. Torrefranca, *G. Puccini e l'opera internazionale* (Turin, 1912); D.C. Parker, "A View of G. Puccini," *Musical Quarterly* (Oct. 1917); A. Weismann, *G. Puccini* (Munich, 1922); A. Cœuroy, *La Tosca* (Paris, 1924); A. Bonaventura, *G. Puccini: L'Uomo, l'artista* (Livorno, 1924); A. Fraccaroli, *La vita di G. Puccini* (Milan, 1925; also in German); G. Marotti and F. Pagni, *G. Puccini intimo* (Florence, 1926); G. Adami, letters of Puccini (Milan, 1928; in Eng., London, 1931); A. Neisser, *Puccini* (Leipzig, 1928); F. Salerno, *Le Donne pucciniane* (Palermo, 1928); G.M. Gatti, "The Works of G. Puccini," *Musical Quarterly* (Jan. 1928); R.C. Merlin, *Puccini* (Milan, 1930); R. Specht, *Puccini* (Berlin, 1931; in Eng., N.Y., 1933); W. Maisch, *Puccinis musikalische Formgebung* (Neustadt, 1934); G. Adami, *Puccini* (Milan, 1935; in German, 1943); M. Carner, "The Exotic Element in Puccini," *Musical Quarterly* (Jan. 1936); K.G. Fellerer, *G. Puccini* (Potsdam, 1937); V. Seligman, *Puccini among Friends* (correspondence; N.Y., 1938); G. Marotti, *G. Puccini intimo* (Florence, 1942); F. Thiess, *Puccini, Versuch einer Psychologie seiner Musik* (Berlin, 1947); A. Bonaccorsi, *G. Puccini e i suoi antenati musicali* (Milan, 1950); G. Marek, *Puccini: A Biography* (N.Y., 1951); Dante del Fiorentino, *Immortal Bohemian: An Intimate Memoir of G. Puccini* (N.Y., 1952); V. Terenzio, *Ritratto di Puccini* (Bergamo, 1954); A. Machard, *Une Vie d'amour: Puccini* (Paris, 1954); L. Ricci, *Puccini interprete di se stesso* (Milan, 1954); E. Greenfield, *Puccini: Keeper of the Seal* (London, 1958); C. Sartori, *Puccini* (Milan, 1958); M. Carner, *Puccini* (London, 1958); C. Paladini, *G. Puccini* (Florence, 1961); W. Sandelewski, *Puccini* (Cracow, 1963); C. Hopkinson, *A Bibliography of the Works of G. Puccini* (N.Y., 1968); S. Jackson, *Monsieur Butterfly: The Story of G. Puccini* (1974); *Letters of G. Puccini* (London, 1974); W. Ashbrook, *The Operas of Puccini* (N.Y., 1968); D. Amy, *G. Puccini* (Paris, 1970); A. Monnosi, *Puccini a tu per tu* (Pisa, 1970); G. Tarozzi, *Puccini: La fine del bel canto* (Milan, 1972); M. Carner, *Puccini* (London, 1974); N.A. Galli, *Puccini e la sua terra* (Lucca, 1974); G. Magri, *Puccini e le sue rime* (Milan, 1974); I. Lombardi, *Puccini, ancora da scoprire* (Lucca, 1976); E. Siciliani, *Puccini* (Milan, 1976); W. Weaver, *Puccini: The Man and His Music* (N.Y., 1977); C. Casini, *Giacomo Puccini* (Turin, 1978); L. Pinzauti, *Puccini* (Milan, 1978); H. Greenfield, *Puccini* (N.Y., 1980).

Puchalsky, Vladimir, Russian pianist and composer; b. Minsk, April 2, 1848; d. Kiev, Feb. 23, 1933. He studied at the St. Petersburg Cons. with Leschetizky (piano) and Zaremba (theory); in 1876 was appointed an instructor at the Kiev Cons.; he remained in Kiev until his death. He wrote an opera, *Valeria;* piano pieces and songs.

Puchat, Max, German composer and pianist; b. Breslau, Jan. 8, 1859; d. (killed in a fall in the Karwendel Alps) Aug. 12, 1919. He studied with Kiel in Berlin, winning the Mendelssohn Prize in 1884. From 1886 to 1903 he was active as a choral conductor in the German provinces; then went to Milwaukee, where he conducted the local Musikverein (1903–5); in 1910, settled in Breslau, where he established his own music school. He wrote several symph. works: *Euphorion* (1888); *Leben und Ideal* (1892); *Tragödie eines Künstlers* (1894); *Ouvertüre über ein nordisches Thema;* etc.; Piano Concerto; String Quartet; songs.

Pucitta, Vincenzo, Italian composer; b. Civitavecchia, 1778; d. Milan, Dec. 20, 1861. He studied with Fenaroli in Naples; traveled through Europe; and was successful as an opera composer in Italy, Austria, France, and England; wrote about 30 operas, of which the best were *La burla fortunata* (Venice, April 9, 1804) and *La Vestale* (London, May 3, 1810).

Puente, Giuseppe Del, baritone; b. Naples, Jan. 30, 1841; d. Philadelphia, May 25, 1900. He first studied cello at the Naples Cons. but later began to cultivate his voice, making his operatic debut at Jassy; was then engaged for the Teatro San Carlo in Naples, and for appearances in France, Germany, Russia, Spain, and England (made his Covent Garden debut in 1873, and became very popular there). His first American engagement was under Strakosch at the

N.Y. Academy of Music in 1873–74; he became a member of the first Metropolitan Opera Co. and sang the role of Valentin in the inaugural performance of *Faust* on Oct. 22, 1883; remained on its roster for the seasons of 1883–84, 1891–92, and 1894–95. In 1885 he returned to the N.Y. Academy of Music under Mapleson's management, taking part in the American premiere of *Manon* on Dec. 23 of that year; he was also a member of the opera troupes of Patti and Hinrichs; with the latter's company he sang in the American premiere of *Cavalleria rusticana* (Philadelphia, Sept. 9, 1891). He married the mezzo-soprano **Helen Dudley Campbell.**

Puget, Paul-Charles-Marie, French composer; b. Nantes, June 25, 1848; d. Paris, March 14, 1917. He studied at the Paris Cons. with Marmontel (piano) and Massé (composition); won first Grand Prix de Rome in 1873 with the cantata *Mazeppa;* wrote much theater music; his opera *Beaucoup de bruit pour rien,* after Shakespeare (Paris, March 24, 1899), had a moderately good reception.

Pugnani, (Giulio) Gaetano (Gerolamo), celebrated Italian violinist and composer; b. Turin, Nov. 27, 1731; d. there, July 15, 1798. He studied violin with G.B. Somis; when he was 10, he was allowed to play in the last chair of the 2nd violins in the orch. of Turin's Teatro Regio; he officially became a member of the orch. on April 19, 1748. In 1749, on a royal stipend, he went to Rome to study with Ciampi; later toured in Europe as a concert violinist. His own style of composition approximated that of Tartini. Fritz Kreisler publ. an arrangement for violin and piano of a piece, purportedly by Pugnani, titled *Preludio e Allegro e Tempo di Minuetto,* but this proved to be by Kreisler himself. Pugnani was particularly successful in London, where he played concerts with J.C. Bach; from 1767–69 he also served as conductor at the King's Theatre, where he brought out his successful opera *Nanetta e Lubino* (April 8, 1769). He then returned to Turin, where he was appointed concertmaster of the King's Music and of the orch. of the Teatro Regio in 1770. He was named general director of instrumental music in 1776; in 1786 he served as supervisor of military music. He made, from 1780–82, a concert tour of Europe, which included a visit to Russia. He was also active as a teacher of the violin. His students included Viotti, Conforti, Bruni, and Polledro.

WORKS: FOR THE STAGE: *Nanetta e Lubino,* opera buffa (London, April 8, 1769); *Issea,* favola pastorale (Turin, 1771); *Tamas Kouli-Kan nell'India,* dramma per musica (Turin, Feb. 1, 1772; not extant); *Aurora,* festa per musica (Turin, 1775; not extant); *Adone e Venere,* opera seria (Naples, Nov. 1784); *Achille in Sciro,* dramma per musica (Turin, Jan. 15, 1785); *Demofoonte,* dramma per musica (Turin, Dec. 26, 1787); *Demetrio a Rodi,* festa per musica (Turin, 1789); also *Correso e Calliroe,* balletto eroico (1792; not extant); ballet music to Gluck's *Orfeo* (not extant); oratorio, *Betulia liberata;* several cantatas. FOR ORCH.: Violin Concerto, sinfonias, overtures, etc.; 40 trio sonatas; 6 string quartets; sonatas for Violin; duets for 2 Violins; about 20 sonatas for Violin and Basso Continuo.

BIBLIOGRAPHY: G. Rangoni, *Essai sur le goût de la musique . . . Saggio sul gusto della musica col carattere de' tre celebri sonatori di violino i signori Nardini, Lolli, e Pugnani* (Livorno, 1790); F. Fayolle, *Notices sur Corelli, Tartini, Gaviniès, Pugnani et Viotti* (Paris, 1810); A. Bertolotti, *Gaetano Pugnani e altri musici alla corte di Torino nel secolo XVIII* (Milan, 1892); D. Carutti, "Della famiglia di Gaetano Pugnani," *Miscellanea di storia italiana,* III/2 (Turin, 1896); A. Moser, *Geschichte des Violinspiels* (Berlin, 1923; 2nd ed., revised and enlarged, 1966–67); S. Cordero di Pamparato, "Gaetano Pugnani, violinista torinese," *Rivista Musicale Italiana,* XXXVII (1930); A. Della Corte, *Notizie di Gaetano Pugnani* (Turin, 1931); A. Della Corte, "Due inedite opere teatrali di Gaetano Pugnani," *Musica d'Oggi,* XIII (1931); E.M. von Zschinsky-Troxler, *Gaetano Pugnani* (Berlin, 1939; with thematic catalogue); A. Müry, *Die Instrumentalwerke Gaetano Pugnanis* (Diss., Univ. of Basel, 1941); G. Barblan, "Ansia preromantica in Gaetano Pugnani," *Chigiana,* XVI (1959); W. Newman, *The Sonata in the Classic Era* (Chapel Hill, 1963; 2nd ed., revised, 1972); S. McVeigh, *The Violinist in London's Concert Life, 1750–1784: Felice Giardini and His Contemporaries* (Diss., Oxford Univ., 1980).

Pugni, Cesare, Italian composer; b. Genoa, May 31, 1802; d. St. Petersburg, Jan. 26, 1870. He studied violin with Alessandro Rolla and composition with Asioli at the Cons. of Milan; began his career as a composer for the stage with the ballet *Elerz e Zulmida* (Milan, May 6, 1826) and the opera *Il Disertore svizzero* (Milan, May 28, 1831), followed by several other operas: *La vendetta* (Milan, Feb. 11, 1832); *Ricciarda di Edimburgo* (Trieste, Sept. 29, 1832); *Il Contrabbandiere* (Milan, June 13, 1833); *Un episodio di S. Michele* (Milan, June 14, 1834); etc.; he also wrote an ingenious *Sinfonia a canone* for 2 orchs. playing the same music, but with the 2nd orch. coming in one measure later than the first (this musical legerdemain amused Meyerbeer); he then lived in Paris, where he produced the ballets *La Fille de marbre* (Oct. 20, 1847), *Le Violon du diable* (Jan. 19, 1849), etc. In 1851 he was appointed ballet composer for the Imperial Theater in St. Petersburg; wrote about 300 ballet scores; of these, *Esmeralda* (originally produced in Milan, 1845) and *Konyok-Gorbunok* (*Le Cheval enchanté;* St. Petersburg, 1864) still retain their popularity in Russia.

Pugno, Raoul, celebrated French pianist; b. (of an Italian father) Montrouge, Seine, June 23, 1852; d. (while on a concert tour) Moscow, Jan. 3, 1914. He studied at the Paris Cons. with G. Mathias (piano) and Ambroise Thomas (composition). He became music director of the Paris Opéra in 1871; then served as organist at the St.-Eugène Church in 1872; became choirmaster there in 1878–92; then taught harmony at the Paris Cons. (1892–96) and subsequently was a prof. of piano there (1896–1901). In the meantime he gave numerous recitals, and gradually rose to the rank of a great virtuoso; he appeared in England in 1894; in America in 1897–98. He was equally remarkable as an ensemble player; his sonata recitals with Ysaÿe became world famous. Pugno was also a composer; he wrote several operas: *Ninetta* (Paris, Dec. 23, 1882); *Le Sosie* (Oct. 7, 1887); *Le Valet de cœur* (April 19, 1888); *Le Retour d'Ulysse* (Paris, Feb. 1, 1889); *La Vocation de Marius* (March 29, 1890); etc.; ballet, *La Danseuse de corde* (Paris, Feb. 5, 1892); piano pieces; songs. His score for *La Ville morte* (after Gabriele d'Annunzio), left incomplete at his death, was finished by Nadia Boulanger.

Pujol, Francesc, Catalan composer; b. Barcelona, May 15, 1878; d. there, Dec. 24, 1945. He studied at the Barcelona Cons., also with Millet; was assistant conductor (1900–41), then music director (1941–45), of the Orfeó Catalá in Barcelona. He wrote many sardanas; church music; orch. works; etc.; publ. valuable studies on Catalan songs: *Chant de la Sibila; L'Œuvre du "Chansonnier populaire de la Catalogne"* (Report of the International Musicological Congress, Vienna, 1927); *Observacions, apéndix i notes al Romancerillo catalán de Manuel Milá y Fontanals* (with Joan Punti; 1927—); Catalan folk songs, with piano accompaniment (Madrid, 1921).

Pujol, Juan, Catalan church musician; b. Barcelona, c.1573; d. there, May 1626. From 1593 to 1595 he was maestro de canto in Tarragona; in 1596–1612, was maestro at Nuestra Señora del Pilar in Saragossa; then at the Barcelona Cathedral until his death. His masses, motets, Passions, Psalms, and villancicos are preserved in MS. A collected edition of Pujol's works was undertaken by H. Anglès, of which 2 vols. appeared (1926, 1932).

Puliti, Leto, Italian music scholar; b. Florence, June 29, 1818; d. there, Nov. 15, 1875. He publ. the valuable historical account *Cenni storici della vita del serenissimo Ferdinando de' Medici* (1884), with information on Cristofori, the inventor of the piano.

Pulver, Jeffrey, English violinist and musicologist; b. London, June 22, 1884. He studied with Ševčik (Prague), Heermann (Frankfurt), Marteau (Geneva), and A. Moser (Berlin). He made a speciality of old English music, and played the viola d'amore, the tenor viola, and other old string instruments. WRITINGS: *A Dictionary of Musical Terms* (1913); *A Dictionary of Old English Music and Musical Instruments* (1923); *Johannes Brahms* (1926); *A Biographical Dictionary of Old English Music* (1927); *Paganini, the Romantic Virtuoso* (London, 1936; reprint, N.Y., 1970); *The Ancient Dance Forms* (2 parts; 1912, 1914); *The Intermezzi of the Opera* (1917); *The Viols in England* (1920); *The Music of Ancient Egypt* (1921); etc.

Puppo, Giuseppe, Italian violinist; b. Lucca, June 12, 1749; d. Florence, April 19, 1827. He was a successful violin virtuoso at an early age; traveled in Spain; was in England from 1777 until 1783, when he settled in Paris; was a fashionable teacher there; in 1811, abandoned his family in Paris; went to Naples and then to Florence, where he died in poverty. He publ. 3 violin concertos, 8 études for violin, and 6 piano fantasias.

Purcell, Daniel, brother of **Henry Purcell;** b. London, c.1660; d. there (buried, Nov. 26), 1717. He became organist of Magdalen College, Oxford, in 1688; took his brother's place as a dramatic composer in 1695, and was organist of St. Andrew's, Holborn, from 1713.
WORKS: Incidental music to 30 dramas; several odes (e.g., funeral ode for his brother); *The Psalm Tunes set full for the Organ or Harpsichord* appeared posthumously (London, 1718).

Purcell, Henry, one of the greatest of English composers; b. London (?), c.1659; d. Dean's Yard, Westminster, Nov. 21, 1695. Until recently it was believed that his father was Henry Purcell (d. 1664), Gentleman of the Chapel Royal and Master of the choristers at Westminster Abbey. But the latest evidence indicates that he was the son of Henry's brother, Thomas Purcell, who was also a Gentleman of the Chapel Royal and held other important posts at the court. From 1669 Henry Purcell was a chorister of the Chapel Royal under Cooke and Humfrey, also receiving instruction from Dr. Blow. When his voice broke in 1673, he was appointed Assistant Keeper of the Instruments. In 1677 he was appointed composer to the King's band, and in 1679 he succeeded Blow as organist of Westminster Abbey. In 1682 he became one of the 3 organists of Chapel Royal as Lowe's successor; in 1683, Keeper of the King's Wind Instruments. His first printed composition is a song in vol. I (1675) of Playford's *Choice Ayres;* vol. II (1679) contains several other songs, and an elegy on the death of Matthew Locke. In 1680 Purcell wrote the first of 29 "odes" and "welcome songs." His first publ. chamber music dates from 1683: *Sonatas of III Parts: two violins and bass: to the Organ or Harpsichord* (with engraved portrait), 12 numbers, based on Italian models, each having an adagio, a canzone (fugue), a slow movement, and an air. *The Yorkshire Feast Song,* called by D'Urfey, the author, "one of the finest compositions he ever made," was composed and produced in 1690. This is one of 29 "welcome songs," which Purcell wrote (on an average of 2 annually) in his capacity of "composer-in-ordinary." Although the texts are almost invariably stupid or bombastic, Purcell wrote some of his finest music for these occasional odes. During his last 5 years he developed extraordinary activity in theatrical composition, to which he had given some attention since 1680, when he began to write some incidental dances and occasional airs for various dramas. In spite of this close connection with the stage, he wrote only one opera, *Dido and Aeneas,* produced in 1689. He lies in the north aisle of Westminster Abbey, and his burial tablet well expresses contemporary estimation of his worth: "Here lyes Henry Purcell, Esq.; who left this life, and is gone to that blessed place where only his harmony can be exceeded." His church music shows him to be an original melodist, and a master of form, harmony, and all contrapuntal devices; his music for the stage is equally rich in invention, dramatic instinct, and power of characterization; his chamber works surpass those of his predecessors and contemporaries.

WORKS: Besides the compositions mentioned, there were publ. during Purcell's life a theoretical treatise, *The Art of Descant*, in the 10th ed. of Playford's *Briefe Introduction of the Skill of Musick* (1683); Playford also publ. several airs and "symphonies" (written for various dramas) in *The Theatre of Musick* (1685), anthems and sacred songs in *Harmonia Sacra* (1688), and pieces for harpsichord in *Musick's Handmaid* (part II, 1689); of the incidental music to plays there appeared *Amphitryon* (1690; the airs in the text, the instrumental pieces in *Ayres for the Theatre*), *Dioclesian* (1691), and "Select ayres" from the *Fairy Queen* (1692). The stage pieces for which Purcell wrote music include the following: Lee's *Theodosius* (1680); D'Urfey's *The Virtuous Wife* (1694); Tate's arrangement of Shakespeare's *Richard II*, D'Urfey's *Sir Barnaby Whigg* (1681); Beaumont and Fletcher's *The Double Marriage* (1682 or 1685); Davenant's *Circe* and Lee's *Sophonisba* (1685); D'Urfey's *A Fool's Preferment* (1688); Betterton's *Dioclesian*, Settle's *Distressed Innocence*, Southerne's *Sir Anthony Love*, Dryden's *Amphitryon*, Lee's *The Massacre of Paris* (1689); Dryden's *King Arthur, The Gordian Knot Untyed* (author unknown), Dryden's *The Indian Emperor*, Southerne's *The Wives' Excuse* (1691); Dryden's *Cleomenes, The Fairy Queen* (an arrangement of the *Midsummer Night's Dream*), D'Urfey's *The Marriage-hater Matched*, Crowne's *Regulus*, Shadwell's *The Libertine*, Bancroft's *Henry II*, Dryden's *Aureng-Zebe*, Dryden, Lee's *Oedipus* (1692); Congreve's *The Old Bachelor*, D'Urfey's *The Richmond Heiress*, Southerne's *The Maid's Last Prayer*, Wright's *The Female Virtuosos* (after Molière), Congreve's *The Double Dealer*, Shadwell's *Epsom Wells*, Fletcher's *Rule a Wife and Have a Wife* (1693); D'Urfey's *Don Quixote* (part I), Dryden's *Love Triumphant*, Crowne's *The Married Beau*, Southerne's *The Fatal Marriage*, Ravenscroft's *The Canterbury Guests*, D'Urfey's *Don Quixote* (part II), Shadwell's arrangement of *Timon of Athens*, Dryden's *The Spanish Friar*, Dryden's *Tyrannic Love* (1694); Behn's *Abdelazer*, Beaumont and Fletcher's *Bonduca*, Howard and Dryden's *Indian Queen*, Scott's *The Mock Marriage*, Norton's *Pausanias*, Gould's *The Rival Sisters*, Southerne's *Oroonoko*, Davenant and Dryden's arrangement of *The Tempest*, D'Urfey's *Don Quixote* (part III) (1695). In this list only *Dioclesian, The Fairy Queen, The Indian Queen*, and *King Arthur* are provided with sufficient music to be possibly classed as "semi-operas"; the music for other dramas usually includes overtures, airs, and instrumental dances. Purcell's widow, who survived him till 1706, publ. *A Choice Collection of Lessons for the Harpsichord or Spinet* (1696), *Ten Sonatas in Four Parts* (1697),

Orpheus Britannicus: A Collection of the choicest Songs... with Symphonies for Violins or Flutes... (Part I, 1698; 2nd ed., 1706; Part II, 1702; 2nd ed., 1711; both parts in one vol., with the addition of several new numbers, 1721). Many compositions were publ. in Playford's *Harmonia Sacrae* (1688–93); Walsh's *The Catch Club*, or *Merry Companions* (c.1730); Boyce's *Cathedral Music* (3 vols., 1760–73); Arnold's continuation of the same (4 vols., 1790); Page and Sexton's *Harmonia Sacra* (3 vols., 1800). Vincent Novello collected all services, anthems, hymns, and sacred songs, and publ. them as *Purcell's Sacred Music* (4 vols., 1829–32; very inaccurate). The Musical Antiquarian Society publ. *Dido and Aeneas* (ed., G.A. Macfarren, 1840); *Bonduca* (ed., E.F. Rimbault, 1842; with historical sketch of dramatic music in England); *King Arthur* (ed., E. Taylor, 1843); *Ode for St. Cecilia's Day* (ed., E.F. Rimbault, 1847). In 1876 the Purcell Society was formed in London for the purpose of publishing the first complete ed. of Purcell's works; 26 vols. were brought out from 1878–1928; in 1957 publication resumed, with the set being extended to 32 vols. by 1977. The Purcell Society also began to publ. a *Popular Edition of Selected Works* (vol. 1: *15 Songs and Airs;* London, 1939). Various selections have been publ. by P. Warlock (*Fantasias* in 3, 4, and 5 parts; some publ. for the first time; London, 1927); G. Jensen, A. Egidi, A. Moffat, and H. David (trio sonatas); W. Barclay Squire (harpsichord pieces); A. Schering in *Geschichte der Musik in Beispielen* (nos. 246–48a); F. Blume in *Das Chorwerk* (5 sacred choruses); E. Dent (*Let the Dreadful Engines*); W. Gillies Whittaker (22 sonatas; Eds. de l'Oiseau-Lyre, Paris); etc. The so-called *Trumpet Voluntary*, ascribed to Purcell, and made popular through an orch. transcription by Sir Henry Wood, is not by Purcell but by Jeremiah Clarke; for details, see C.L. Cudworth, "Some New Facts about the Trumpet Voluntary," *Musical Times* (Sept. 1953).

BIBLIOGRAPHY: W.H. Cummings, *Purcell* (London, 1881; 3rd ed., 1911; abridged ed., 1923); W. Barclay Squire, "Purcell's Dramatic Music," *Sammelbände der Internationalen Musik-Gesellschaft*, V/4 (1904); J.F. Runciman, *Purcell* (London, 1909); G.E. Arkwright, "Purcell's Church Music," *Musical Antiquary* (July 1910); P.A. Scholes, "H. Purcell: Sketch of a Busy Life," *Musical Quarterly* (July 1916); W. Barclay Squire, "Purcell's *Dido and Aeneas*," *Musical Times* (June 1918); H. Dupré, *Purcell* (Paris, 1927; in Eng., N.Y., 1928); D. Arundell, *H. Purcell* (London, 1927; in German, 1929); E. Dent, *Foundations of the English Opera* (1928); A.K. Holland, *H. Purcell, the English Musical Tradition* (London, 1932); F. de Quervain, *Der Chorstil H. Purcells* (Leipzig, 1935); J.A. Westrup, *Purcell* (London, 1937; revised ed., 1980); S. Favre-Lingorow, *Der Instrumentalstil von Purcell* (Bern, 1950); S. Demarquez, *Purcell* (Paris, 1951); G. van Ravenzwaaÿ, *Purcell* (Haarlem, 1954); R. Sietz, *Henry Purcell: Zeit, Leben, Werk* (Leipzig, 1955); Imogen Holst, ed., *Henry Purcell, 1659–1695; Essays on His Music* (London, 1959); F.B. Zimmerman, *Henry Purcell: An Analytical Catalogue of His Music* (N.Y., 1963); idem, *Henry Purcell, His Life and Times*

(N.Y., 1967); idem, *Henry Purcell, Melodic and Intervallic Indexes to His Complete Works* (1975); A. Hutchings, *Purcell* (London, 1982); M. Laurie, "Purcell's Extended Solo Songs," *Musical Times* (Jan. 1984).

Puschmann, Adam, German meistersinger; b. Görlitz, 1532; d. Breslau, April 4, 1600. He was a pupil of Hans Sachs; brought out *Gründlicher Bericht des deutschen Meistergesanges* (1571; new ed., Halle, 1888); his songs were publ. by Georg Münzer in 1906. His brother **Zacharias Puschmann** (with whom he is often confused) was a cantor in Görlitz.

Pustet, Friedrich, German publisher; b. Hals, near Passau, Feb. 25, 1798; d. Munich, March 6, 1882. In 1826 he founded a music publishing firm, mainly for church music, in Regensburg; for 30 years he had the exclusive right of printing, with the privilege of the Holy See, the chant books according to the Editio Medicaea, which, however, was superseded by the newer Vaticana Edition. In 1921 Pustet's firm merged with the publishing house of Kösel, retaining, however, the original name; the firm thus lasted through 5 generations of the family, and was directed in the 1970s, still in Regensburg, by **Friedrich Pustet** (b. Munich, Nov. 26, 1927). Pustet publ. Proske's *Musica divina;* Peter Wagner's *Elemente des gregorianischen Gesanges;* Johner's *Cantus ecclesiastici; Kirchenmusikalisches Jahrbuch* (from its founding in 1886 through the vol. for 1935); etc. A Festschrift was compiled by H. Bohatta on the centenary of the foundation of the firm (Regensburg, 1926).

Putnam, Ashley, American soprano; b. New York, Aug. 10, 1952. She studied flute at the Univ. of Michigan, eventually turning to voice (B.M., 1974; M.M., 1975). After graduating, she was an apprentice with the Santa Fe Opera Co. In 1976 she made her operatic debut in the title role of Donizetti's *Lucia di Lammermoor* with the Virginia Opera Assoc. in Norfolk; subsequently sang with the St. Louis Opera, San Diego Opera, Houston Opera, and Miami Opera. Her first appearance with the N.Y. City Opera in 1978 brought her critical accolades.

Puyana, Rafael, Colombian harpsichordist; b. Bogotá, Oct. 14, 1931. He studied piano at the New England Cons. of Music in Boston, and harpsichord with Wanda Landowska in N.Y.; had his general musical training at the Hartt College of Music in Hartford, Conn. He made his N.Y. recital debut in 1957; then embarked upon an international career. He became favorably known for his performances of Baroque music.

Pyamour, John, English composer; date of birth unknown; d. 1431. He was a clerk of the Chapel Royal in 1419, and Master of Children in 1420; was commissioned to find boys with good voices for the royal service; traveled with King Henry V and the chapel on the Continent, and probably remained in Normandy for several years. His motet *Quam pulchra es* is extant in MS.
BIBLIOGRAPHY: John Harvey, *Gothic England* (London, 1947).

Pycard, English singer and composer who flourished c.1400. The *Old Hall Manuscript* contains 6 works by him; his contrapuntal skill was out of the ordinary, and he used complicated canonic forms in sections of the Mass.
BIBLIOGRAPHY: M. Bukofzer, *Studies in Medieval and Renaissance Music* (N.Y., 1950).

Pylkkänen, Tauno Kullervo, Finnish composer; b. Helsinki, March 22, 1918; d. there, March 13, 1980. He studied composition with Palmgren and Madetoja at the Sibelius Academy in Helsinki, while also attending the Helsinki Cons. (1937–41). He subsequently worked at the Finnish Broadcasting Co. (1942–61) and was artistic director of the Finnish National Opera (1960–70); then lectured in opera history at the Sibelius Academy. He is primarily an opera composer; his idiom is basically Romantic, with sporadic excursions into modernity.
WORKS: Operas: *Bathsheba Saarenmaalla* (*Bathsheba at Saarenmaa;* 1940; revised 1958); *Mare ja hänen poikansa* (*Mare and Her Son;* 1943); *Simo Hurtta* (1948); *Sudenmorsian* (*The Wolf's Bride),* radio opera (1950); *Varjo* (*The Shadow;* 1952); *Opri and Oleksi* (1957); *Ikaros* (1956–60); *Vangit* (*The Prisoners;* 1964); *Tuntematon sotilas* (*The Unknown Soldier;* 1967); ballet, *Kaarina Maununtytär* (*Kaarina, Maunu's Daughter;* 1960); for Orch.: *Introduction and Fugue* (1940); *Lapin kesä* (*Summer in Lapland;* 1941); *Kullervon sotaanlähtö* (*Kullervo Leaves for War;* 1942); Sinfonietta (1944); Symph. No. 1 (1945); *Suite* for Oboe and Strings (1946); *Marathon,* overture (1947); *Symphonic Fantasy* (1948); *Ultima Thule* (1949); Cello Concerto (1950); *Symphonic Prelude* (1952); chamber music: *Notturno* for Violin and Piano (1943); String Quartet (1945); *Fantasia appassionata* for Cello and Piano (1954); *Trittico* for Clarinet, Violin, Viola, and Cello (1978); several cantatas and songs.
BIBLIOGRAPHY: *Suomen Säveltäjiä* (Helsinki, 1945; pp. 726–31).

Pyne, James Kendrick, English organist; b. Bath, Feb. 5, 1852; d. Ilford, Essex, Sept. 3, 1938. He was a pupil of his father, **James K. Pyne** (for 53 years organist at Bath Abbey); then of Dr. S.S. Wesley, organist at Winchester Cathedral. He was church organist at the Manchester Cathedral (1876–98); in 1877 became organist of the Town Hall Corp. in Manchester; celebrated his 50 years of tenure (1927) by giving 3 organ recitals on the jubilee day. He composed organ music; also a Communion Service and sacred works.
BIBLIOGRAPHY: S. Lucas, "J.K. Pyne," *Musical Opinion* (Nov. 1927).

Pythagoras, Greek philosopher and mathematician; b. Samos, c.582 B.C.; d. Metapontum, c.500 B.C.

His doctrines on the musical ratios are preserved in the writing of his followers, no books by Pythagoras himself having come down to us. The Pythagoreans (Archytas, Didymos, Eratosthenes, Euclid, Ptolemy, etc.) reckoned only the fifth and octave as pure consonances (the fourth being the fifth below); their system recognized only intervals reached by successive skips of pure fifths, the major third being the 4th fifth above (ratio 64:81, instead of the modern 64:80, or 4:5), their minor third the 3rd fifth below; etc. Their thirds and sixths were, consequently, dissonant intervals.

BIBLIOGRAPHY: Klaus Pringsheim, "Pythagoras, die Atonalität und wir," *Schweizerische Musikzeitung* (1957); I. Focht, "La Notion pythagoricienne de la musique," *Esthetics and Sociology of Music,* 3 (1972).

Quadri, Argeo, Italian conductor; b. Como, March 23, 1911. He studied piano, composition, and conducting at the Milan Cons.; then conducted opera throughout Italy. In 1956 he became a conductor at the Covent Garden Opera in London; in 1957 was appointed to the Vienna State Opera.

Quagliati, Paolo, Italian composer and excellent cembalist; b. Chioggia, c.1555; d. Rome, Nov. 16, 1628. He publ. *Carro di fedeltà d'amore,* one of the earliest music dramas, containing not only monodies, but ensemble numbers up to 5 voices (Rome, 1611); also motets and "dialogues" *a* 2–8 (3 vols.; 1612, 1620, 1627); etc. Reprints are in H. Riemann's *Musikgeschichte in Beispielen* and in L. Torchi's *L'arte musicale in Italia,* III.
    BIBLIOGRAPHY: A. Cametti, "Paolo Quagliati, organista e compositore," *Rassegna Dorica* (Dec. 20, 1930; pp. 28–34).

Quaile, Elizabeth, American piano pedagogue; b. Omagh, Ireland, Jan. 20, 1874; d. South Kent, Conn., June 30, 1951. She came early to N.Y. and studied with Franklin Robinson; then devoted herself to teaching; from 1916 to 1919 she was head of the piano dept. of the David Mannes School; then went to Paris, where she studied piano with Harold Bau-

er. Returning to N.Y. in 1921, she founded, with Angela Diller, the Diller-Quaile School of Music. She publ. a number of highly successful piano teaching materials, some written by her alone (*First Book of Technical Exercises, A Pre-Czerny Book,* etc.), and some in collaboration with Angela Diller. The books proved to be standard guides for piano students.

Quantz, Johann Joachim, famous German flutist and composer; b. Oberscheden, Hannover, Jan. 30, 1697; d. Potsdam, July 12, 1773. Naturally musical, at 8 he played the double bass at village festivals. His father died when he was but 10, and Quantz was apprenticed to an uncle, then "Stadtmusikus" at Merseburg, in 1708, learning various instruments, among them the harpsichord with Kiesewetter. His apprenticeship ended, he went to Radeburg, Pirna, and in 1716 joined the town orch. of Dresden, under Heine. In 1717, during 3 months' leave of absence, he studied counterpoint with Zelenka and Fux at Vienna; in 1718 he became oboist in the Royal Polish orch. of Warsaw and Dresden, but soon took up the flute, which he studied under Buffardin. In 1724 he was sent to Italy in the suite of the Polish ambassador; he studied counterpoint under Gasparini at Rome; went to London via Paris in 1726; and returned to Dresden in 1727, resuming his position as orch. flute player in 1728. That year he played before Frederick the Great (then Crown Prince) at Berlin, and so pleased him that he engaged Quantz to teach him the flute, and to make 2 long visits to Berlin annually for that purpose. Frederick ascended the throne in 1740, and the following year called Quantz to Berlin and Potsdam as chamber musician and court composer at a salary of 2,000 thalers, besides an honorarium for each composition furnished, and 100 ducats for each flute supplied by Quantz. Here he remained until his death.

WORKS: He left in MS 300 concertos for one and 2 flutes, and some 200 other flute pieces (solos, duets, trios, and quartets). He publ. *Sei sonate* with Bass (1734); *Sei duetti* (1759); *Neue Kirchenmelodien* (1760; settings of 22 odes by Gellert as chorales); *Versuch einer Anweisung, die Flöte traversiere zu spielen* (1752; this famous flute method also contains valuable information on 18th-century performance practices; 2nd and 3rd eds., 1780, 1789; French, 1752; Dutch, 1755; Eng. trans. by E.R. Reilly, N.Y., 1966); *Application pour la flûte traversière à deux clefs* (an account of his invention of a 2nd key applied to the flute for just intonation, and also of the tuning barrel for the instrument).

BIBLIOGRAPHY: Quantz's autobiography is in Marpurg's *Historisch-kritische Beyträge zur Aufnahme der Musik* (Berlin, 1755; reprinted in Willi Kahl, *Selbstbiographien deutscher Musiker des XVIII. Jahrhunderts,* Cologne, 1948); A. Quantz, *Leben und Werke des Flötisten J.J. Quantz* (Berlin, 1877); R. Schäfke, "Quantz als Ästhetiker. Eine Einführung in die Musikästhetick des galanten Stils," *Archiv für Musikwissenschaft,* VI/2 (1924); Everett Helm, *Music at the Court of Frederick the Great* (Norman, Okla., 1960); E.R. Reilly, *Quantz and His "Versuch." Three Studies* (American Musicological Society Studies and Documents, 5, 1971).

Quarenghi, Guglielmo, Italian cellist; b. Casalmaggiore, Oct. 22, 1826; d. Milan, Feb. 3, 1882. He was a pupil at the Milan Cons. (1839–42); from 1850, was first cello at La Scala Theater; in 1851, became a prof. of cello at the Cons.; from 1879 to 1881, was maestro di cappella at the Milan Cathedral.

WORKS: An excellent cello method, and original pieces and transcriptions for cello; also church music, and an opera, *Il dì di S. Michele* (Milan, 1863).

Quarles, James Thomas, American organist and educator; b. St. Louis, Nov. 7, 1877; d. Saugus, Calif., March 4, 1954. He studied organ with local teachers; then with Widor in Paris. He was a church organist in St. Louis (1897–1913); then taught at Cornell Univ. (1913–23) and at the Univ. of Missouri (1923–43). He gave nearly 1,000 organ recitals in various parts of the U.S.; composed anthems, organ pieces, and songs.

Quatremère de Quincy, Antoine-Chrysostome, French writer; b. Paris, Oct. 25, 1755; d. there, Dec. 28, 1849. He was secretary of the Académie des Arts; publ. *De la nature des opéras bouffons italiens* (Paris, 1789; a pamphlet) and eulogies of Catel, Boieldieu, Gossec, Méhul, Monsigny, Paisiello, and other deceased members of the Académie (in *Recueil de notices historiques,* 1834–37, 2 vols.; also printed separately).

Quef, Charles, French organist and composer; b. Lille, Nov. 1, 1873; d. there, July 2, 1931. He studied at the Lille Cons. and at the Paris Cons. with Guiraud, Théodore Dubois, Guilmant, and Widor (in 1898, won first prize for organ and improvisation); was organist in Paris at Ste. Marie, St. Laurent, and (from 1901) of La Trinité, succeeding Guilmant; concertized in France and England. He publ. sacred choruses and other works.

Queler, Eve, American conductor; b. New York, Jan. 1, 1936. Her maiden name was **Rabin;** in 1956 she married Stanley Queler, a law student. She studied piano at the Mannes College of Music and the Hebrew Union School of Sacred Music. While still a student, she served as studio accompanist for the baritone Martial Singher in Marlboro, Vt.; also had a fellowship at the Berkshire Center in Tanglewood. Fascinated by the art of conducting as a supreme means of musical self-expression, she took lessons with the noted opera conductor Carl Bamberger; then studied for two years with Joseph Rosenstock, onetime conductor of the Metropolitan Opera. In 1970 she won an award to study with Walter Susskind at the American Inst. of Orch. Conducting. By arduous application, she developed a fine career conducting operas in concert version. She made her debut leading a performance of *Cavalleria rusticana* in N.Y. in 1967; then served for 5 seasons as assistant conductor to Julius Rudel at the N.Y. City Opera; very early in her career she decided to promote works not often played; she conducted, with her Opera Orch. of N.Y., Respighi's *Belfagor* in 1971; Zandonai's *Francesca da Rimini* in 1973; Donizetti's *Parisina d'Este* in 1974; Massenet's *Le Cid* in 1976; Smetana's *Dalibor* in 1977; and a number of works by early Baroque composers. She was also able to raise funds to secure excellent casts for her performances. As a rule her orch. presents three productions of operas in concert form each season. She has also had guest engagements with American symph. orchs. Consistently, she began receiving enthusiastic reviews of her concerts. In the process, she rated a number of "firsts" of her gender: first woman conductor to lead a concert at Lincoln Center; first woman to be a guest conductor of the Philadelphia Orch., the Montreal Symph., the New Jersey Symph., etc.; as well as being the first woman to be appointed associate conductor of the Fort Wayne Phil. She is also credited with the first and finest American performance of an early and insignificant opera by Puccini, *Edgar,* which she conducted in N.Y. on April 13, 1977. And she made several feminine "firsts" in Europe, including a concert performance of *Tristan und Isolde* in London (July 20, 1978).

Querol Gavaldá, Miguel, Spanish musicologist; b. Ulldecona, Tarragona, April 22, 1912. He studied music at the Benedictine Monastery of Monserrat (1926–36) and later in Barcelona with Juan Lamote de Grignon. He publ. *La música en las obras de Cervantes* (Barcelona, 1948); *La escuela estética catalana contemporánea* (Diss., Univ. of Madrid, 1953); edited the *Cancionero musical de la casa de Medinaceli* (2 vols.; Barcelona, 1949–50); *Breve historia de la música* (Madrid, 1955); also wrote some church music; chamber music; *Sonata romántica catalana* for Piano; etc.

Quilico, Louis, Canadian baritone; b. Montreal, Jan. 14, 1925. He studied voice in N.Y. with Martial Singher. After winning several vocal competitions, he appeared with the N.Y. City Opera in 1955; made his European debut in 1959; subsequently sang at Covent Garden in London, the Paris Opéra, and the Teatro Colón in Buenos Aires. On Feb. 10, 1972, he made his Metropolitan Opera debut as Golaud in Debussy's *Pelléas et Mélisande;* remained on its roster, singing mostly in French and Italian operas.

Quilter, Roger, English composer; b. Brighton, Nov. 1, 1877; d. London, Sept. 21, 1953. He received his primary education at Eton College; then went to Germany, where he studied with Iwan Knorr. He is particularly noted for his fine settings of Shakespeare's poems.

WORKS: Incidental music for Shakespeare's play *As You Like It* (1922); *The Sailor and His Lass* for Soprano, Baritone, Chorus, and Orch. (1948); numerous song cycles, among them *7 Elizabethan Lyrics, 3 Songs of the Sea, 4 Shakespeare Songs,* etc. He also wrote a light opera, *Julia* (London, Dec. 3, 1936).

BIBLIOGRAPHY: L. Woodgate, "Roger Quilter," *Musical Times* (Nov. 1953).

Quinault, Jean-Baptiste-Maurice, French singer and actor; b. Verdun, Sept. 9, 1687; d. Gien, Aug. 30, 1745. He was an actor at the Théâtre Français, in Paris (1712–28) and at the Comédie Française until 1734. He set to music about 20 *intermèdes,* ballets, etc., and also produced a grand ballet, *Les Amours des déesses* (Paris, Aug. 9, 1729).

Quinault, Philippe, French dramatic poet; b. Paris, June 3, 1635; d. there, Nov. 26, 1688. He was Lully's librettist.

BIBLIOGRAPHY: G.A. Crapelet, *Notice sur la vie et les ouvrages de Quinault* (Paris, 1824); E. Richter, *Philippe Quinault. Sein Leben, seine Tragödien, seine Bedeutung für das Theater Frankreichs und des Auslandes* (Leipzig, 1910); Etienne Gros, *Philippe Quinault, Sa vie et son œuvre* (Paris, 1926); J.B.A. Buijtendorp, *Philippe Quinault, Sa vie, ses tragédies et ses tragi-comédies* (Amsterdam, 1928).

Quinet, Fernand, Belgian cellist, conductor, and composer; b. Charleroi, Jan. 29, 1898; d. Liège, Oct. 24, 1971. He studied music theory in Charleroi; then enrolled at the Brussels Cons., where he studied cello with Edouard Jacobs and composition with Léon Dubois. After graduation he devoted his time to teaching and conducting. He served as director of the Cons. in Charleroi (1924–38); in 1938 he succeeded François Rasse as director of the Liège Cons., and held this post until 1963; in 1948 he founded the Liège Symph. Orch., and was its principal conductor until 1965. He composed relatively little.

WORKS: Songs: *Recueillement, Les chevaux de bois; 4 mélodies; En bateau; La Légende de sœur Béatrice,* cantata (1920); *La Guerre,* cantata (1921; received the Belgian Grand Prix de Rome); Violin Sonata (1923); *Charade,* 4 pieces for Piano Trio (1927); Viola Sonata (1928); *Moralités-non-légendaires* for Voice and 18 Instruments (1930); *L'Ecole buissonnière* for String Quartet (1930); *3 Symphonic Movements* (London Festival of the International Society for Contemporary Music, July 28, 1931); *Suite* for 3 Clarinets (1930).

Quinet, Marcel, Belgian composer; b. Binche, July 6, 1915. He studied at the conservatories of Mons and Brussels with Léon Jongen, Raymond Moulaert, and Marcel Maas (1934–42); also took private composition lessons with Jean Absil (1940–45). He then devoted himself to music pedagogy; was on the staff of the Brussels Cons. (from 1943) and also taught at the Chapelle Musicale Reine Elisabeth (1956–59 and 1968–71). His music is moderately modernistic in the amiable manner of the French school, with some euphoniously dissonant excrescences.

WORKS: *La Vague et le Sillon,* cantata (1945; Belgian Grand Prix de Rome, 1945); *3 esquisses concertantes* for Violin and Orch. (1946); *Divertissement* for Orch. (1946); *3 pièces* for Orch. (1951; perf. at the Salzburg International Festival of the Society for Contemporary Music, June 21, 1952); Sinfonietta (1953); *Variations élégiaques sur un thème de Rolland de Lassus* (Paris, 1955); 3 piano concertos (1955, 1964, 1966); Variations for Orch. (1956); *Serenade* for String Orch. (1956); *Impressions symphoniques* (1956); *Allegro de concert* for Orch. (1958); *Divertimento* for Chamber Orch. (1958); Concertino for Flute, Celesta, Harp, and Strings (1959); Symph. (1960); Concertino for Oboe, Clarinet, Bassoon, and String Orch. (1960); *Ballade* for Clarinet and String Orch. (1961); Viola Concerto (1962–63); *Concerto grosso* for 4 Clarinets and Strings (1964); *Les 2 Bavards,* chamber opera (1966); *Overture for a Festival* (1967); *La Nef des fous,* ballet (1969); *Music* for Strings and Timpani (1971); *Mouvements* for Chamber Orch. (1973); *Lectio pro Feria Sexta,* cantata (1973); *Esquisses symphoniques* (1973); *Gorgone* for Orch. (1974); *Croquis,* 8 piano pieces (1946); *8 petites pièces* for Wind Quintet (1946); 2 string trios (1948, 1969); *2 impromptus* for Piano (1949); Wind Quintet (1949); Violin Sonatina (1952); *Passacaille* for Piano (1954); Piano Quartet (1957); String Quartet (1958); *Petite Suite* for 4 Clarinets (1959); *Toccata* for Piano (1961); *Sonate à 3* for Trumpet, Horn, and Trombone (1961); *Hommage à Scarlatti* for Piano (1962); *Ballade* for Violin and Wind Quintet (1962); Wind Quartet (1964); Sonata for 2 Violins and Piano (1964); *Partita* for Piano (1965); *Ballatella* for Trumpet or

Horn or Trombone, and Piano (1966); *Pochades* for 4 Saxophones (1967); Trio for Oboe, Clarinet, and Bassoon (1967); Flute Sonata (1968); *3 Preludes* for Piano (1970); *Polyphonies* for 3 Performers on 8 Wind Instruments (1971); *Novelettes* for 2 Pianos (1973); *Dialogues* for 2 Pianos and Chamber Orch. (1975); *Tableautins* for Piano (1974); songs.

Quintanar, Hector, Mexican composer and conductor; b. Mexico City, April 15, 1936. He had lessons in music theory with Carlos Chávez, Rodolfo Halffter, and Galindo at the National Cons. in Mexico City (1959–64); also worked on problems of electronic music in N.Y. (1964), Paris (1967), and Mexico City (1968). Upon his return to Mexico, he supervised the construction of the country's first electronic laboratory, at the National Univ. (1968). In his compositions he employs traditional instruments as well as electronic sound.

WORKS: 3 symphs. (1961, 1962, 1964); *Sinfonia modal* (1961–62); *El viejo y el mar,* symph. poem after Hemingway (1936); *Fábula* for Chorus and Orch. (1964); Double Quartet for String Quartet and Wind Quartet (1964–65); String Trio (1965–66); Violin Sonata (1967); *Aclamaciones* for Chorus, Tape, and Orch. (1967); Sonata for 3 Trumpets (1967); *Galaxias* for Orch. (1968; Mexico City, July 7, 1968); *Sideral I* for Tape (1968), *Sideral II* for Orch. (1969; Mexico City, July 7, 1969), *Sideral III* for Tape (1971); *Solutio?* for Soprano and Piano (1969); *Símbolos* for Violin, Clarinet, Saxophone, Horn, Trumpet, Trombone, Piano, Tape, Optical Slides, and Lights (1969); *Ilapso* for Clarinet, Bassoon, Trumpet, Trombone, Percussion, Violin, and Double Bass (1970); *Voz* for Soprano and Tape (1971); Quintet for Piano, Violin, Double Bass, Flute, and Trumpet (1973); *Diálogos* for Piano and Tape (1973).

Quiroga, Manuel, Spanish violinist; b. Pontevedra, April 15, 1890; d. there, April 19, 1961. He studied at the Royal Cons. in Madrid and at the Paris Cons.; toured in Europe and in the U.S. with great success. He suffered a street accident in N.Y. in 1937 during one of his American tours, and was compelled to abandon public appearances; returned to Spain and retired to Pontevedra. He composed some violin pieces and a "sainete," *Los amos del barrio* (Madrid, Sept. 7, 1938).

Quittard, Henri Charles Etienne, French musicologist; b. Clermont-Ferrand, May 13, 1864; d. Paris, July 21, 1919. He was a student of César Franck, but did not elect to pursue a career as a composer or a performer; instead, he wrote music criticism in *Le Matin* and *Le Figaro;* in 1912 he was appointed archivist at the Paris Opéra.

WRITINGS: *Henry du Mont: Un musicien en France au XVIIᵉ siècle* (1906); *Les Couperins* (1913); also contributed articles on 17th-century French music to various scholarly publications.

Quivar, Florence, black American mezzo-soprano; b. Philadelphia, March 3, 1944. She studied at the Philadelphia Academy of Music; was a member of the Juilliard Opera Theater in N.Y.; subsequently launched a successful concert career, appearing as soloist with the N.Y. Phil., the Cleveland Orch., the Philadelphia Orch., the Chicago Symph., and the Boston Symph. Orch. She joined the Metropolitan Opera in N.Y. in 1979, in the roles of Jocasta in *Oedipus Rex,* Isabella in *L'Italiana in Algeri,* and Fides in *Le Prophète.* In 1982 she made her London debut with the London Phil.; during the summer of 1983 she toured the major European music festivals with Zubin Mehta and the Israel Phil.

R

Raabe, Peter, German conductor and writer on music; b. Frankfurt an der Oder, Nov. 27, 1872; d. Weimar, April 12, 1945. He studied with Bargiel at the Hochschule für Musik in Berlin; in 1894 began a career as a theater conductor; in 1899 was appointed conductor of the Netherlands Opera in Amsterdam; then conducted the Kaim Orch. in Munich (1903–6) and the newly established Kaim Orch. in Mannheim (1906–7); in 1907 he became principal conductor in Weimar; in 1910 he was appointed custodian of the Liszt Museum in Weimar; from 1920 to 1934 he conducted the Municipal Orch. in Aachen. In 1935 he became head of the Reichsmusikkammer and the Deutscher Tonkünstlerverein; in these offices he was called upon to perform administrative tasks for the Nazi regime, including the racial restrictions of musicians. His co-workers presented him with an honorary *Festschrift zu Peter Raabes 70. Geburtstag* (Leipzig, 1942). Raabe died just before the total collapse of the Third Reich, which he tried to serve so well. He left some scholarly and valuable writings, among them: *Grossherzog Karl Alexander und Liszt* (Leipzig, 1918); *Franz Liszt: Leben und Schaffen* (Stuttgart, 1931; 2 vols., with an annotated catalogue of Liszt's works; revised ed. by his son Felix, 1968); *Die Musik im dritten Reich* (Berlin, 1935; an exposition of the musical ideology of the Third Reich); *Kulturwille im deutschen Musikleben* (Berlin, 1936); *Deutsche Meister* (Berlin, 1937); *Wege zu Weber* (Regensburg, 1942); *Wege zu Liszt* (Regensburg, 1943); *Wege zu Bruckner* (Regensburg, 1944).

Raaff, Anton, German singer, a friend of Mozart; b. Gelsdorf, near Bonn (baptized, May 6), 1714; d. Munich, May 28, 1797. He studied with Ferrandini in Munich and Bernacchi in Bologna; sang in Italy; then in Bonn, in Vienna, and at various German courts (1742–52); in Lisbon (1753–55), Madrid (1755–59), and Naples, returning in 1770 to Germany, where he was attached to the court of the Elector Karl Theodor at Mannheim. In 1778 he went to Paris with Mozart; in 1779 was in Munich. Mozart wrote the role of Idomeneo for him, and also the aria *Se al labbro mio non credi,* K. 295.
BIBLIOGRAPHY: H. Freiberger, *Anton Raaff (1714–1797): Sein Leben und Wirken* (Cologne, 1929); P. Petrobelli, "The Italian Years of Anton Raaff," *Mozart Jahrbuch* (1973–74).

Raalte, Albert van, Dutch conductor; b. Amsterdam, May 21, 1890; d. there, Nov. 23, 1952. He studied at the Cologne Cons. with Bram Eldering (violin) and Waldemar von Baussnern (theory); later in

Leipzig with Nikisch and Max Reger; was a theater conductor in Brussels (1911) and Leipzig (1912); conducted Wagner's operas at the Municipal Opera in Leipzig (1914–15), then at the Dutch National Opera in The Hague (1915–22); formed his own opera enterprise there. He remained in the Netherlands during the German occupation; conducted the radio orch. at Hilversum; was sent to a concentration camp as a person with Jewish associations; after the liberation in 1945, he returned to his post at Hilversum, building the radio orch. to a high degree of efficiency.

Raasted, Niels Otto, Danish organist and composer; b. Copenhagen, Nov. 26, 1888; d. there, Dec. 31, 1966. He studied at the Copenhagen Cons. (1909–12); then at the Cons. of Leipzig, with Max Reger, Karl Straube, and R. Teichmüller (1913–14); returning to Denmark, he became a cathedral organist; also conducted the Bach Society (1925–46).
WORKS: 3 symphs. (1914, 1938, 1944); several orch. suites, among them *Pictures from Finland* (1928) and *Hans Christian Andersen Suite* (1940); *Sinfonia da chiesa* (1944); 3 string quartets (1914, 1918, 1920); 5 violin sonatas; 6 organ sonatas; an oratorio, *Saul* (1923); cantatas (all perf. on Copenhagen Radio): *Sangen om København* (June 27, 1934); *Thylands pris* (May 12, 1941); *Kong Vaar* (Oct. 20, 1947).

Rääts, Jaan, Estonian composer; b. Tartu, Oct. 15, 1932. He studied with Heino Eller at the Tallinn Cons. (1952–57); was director of the music division of the Estonian Radio (1955–66); then served as music director of Estonian Television. His music possesses firm thematic lines animated by a motoric pulse.
WORKS: 7 symphs. (1957, 1958, 1959, 1959, 1966, 1967, 1973); Concerto for String Orch. (1961); Violin Concerto (1963); a "declamatorio," *Karl Marx* (Tallinn, June 6, 1964); Nonet (1966); *24 Preludes* for Piano (1968); 3 piano quintets; Piano Sextet (1972); 5 string quartets; 4 piano sonatas.

Rabaud, Henri, eminent French composer and conductor; b. Paris, Nov. 10, 1873; d. there, Sept. 11, 1949. The son of Hippolyte Rabaud (1839–1900), prof. of cello at the Paris Cons., he was a pupil of Gédalge and Massenet; won the Premier Grand Prix de Rome in 1894 with his cantata *Daphné;* in 1908 he became conductor at the Paris Opéra and at the Opéra-Comique; from 1914 to 1918 he was director of the Opéra. In 1918 he was engaged to conduct the Boston Symph. Orch., succeeding Karl Muck; conducted only one season (1918–19) and was followed by Pierre Monteux; returned to Paris and was appointed director of the Paris Cons. in 1922 (following Gabriel Fauré's resignation); he held this post until 1941.
WORKS: Operas: *La Fille de Roland* (Opéra-Comique, March 16, 1904); *Le Premier Glaire* (Béziers, 1908); *Marouf, Savetier du Caire* (Opéra-Comique, May 15, 1914; his most successful opera); *Antoine et Cléopâtre,* after Shakespeare (1916–17); *L'Appel de la mer* (one act; Opéra-Comique, April

10, 1924; in German, Leipzig, May 6, 1927); *Le Miracle des loups* (Opéra-Comique, Nov. 14, 1924); *Rolande et le mauvais garçon* (Paris Opéra, May 28, 1934); *Le Jeu de l'Amour et du Hasard* (1948; produced posthumously at Monte Carlo, 1954); oratorio, *Job* (1900); Psalm 4 for Soli, Chorus, and Orch.; *Hymne à la France éternelle* (1916); *L'Eté* for 4-voice Choir; for Orch.: 2 symphs.; *La Procession nocturne,* symph. poem after Lenau's *Der nächtliche Zug* (first perf. Paris, Jan. 15, 1899; his most famous orch. work); *Eglogue,* "poème virgilien"; *Divertissement sur des chansons russes; Suite anglaise* for String Quartet; Concertino for Cello and Piano; *Allegro de concert* for Cello and Piano; piano pieces; songs; etc.
BIBLIOGRAPHY: Max d'Ollone, *Henri Rabaud: Sa vie et son œuvre* (Paris, 1958).

Rabe, Folke, Swedish composer; b. Stockholm, Oct. 28, 1935. He studied composition with Blomdahl and Lidholm at the Royal College of Music in Stockholm (1957–64); also took lessons with Ligeti (1961–64). In 1965 he worked at the Tape Music Center in San Francisco; in 1968 he joined the staff of the Swedish Foundation for Nationwide Concerts. An accomplished jazz musician, he was a founder, with Jan Bark, of the Culture Quartet of 4 trombones. He experimented with multimedia techniques; produced pieces of "vocal theater" with non-semantic texts.
WORKS: *Notturno* for Mezzo-soprano, Flute, Oboe, and Clarinet (1959); *7 Variations* for Piano (1957–60); *Pièce* for Speaking Chorus, with nonsense verses by Lasse O'Månsson (1961); *Impromptu* for Clarinet, Trombone, Cello, Piano, and Percussion (1962); 2 works for the Culture Quartet, composed in collaboration with Jan Bark: *Bolos* (1962) and *Polonaise* (1965); *Medea,* theater music for Speaking or Singing Female Chorus, Oboe, Prepared Piano, and Percussion (1963; Stockholm, March 22, 1963); *Pajazzo* for 8 Jazz Musicians, Conductor, and Audience (1963); *Rondes-fragment* for Chorus (1964); *Hep-Hep* for Orch. (1966); *Hommage à Mesmer,* electronic music; *Joe's Harp* for Chorus (1970).

Rabich, Ernst, German choral conductor and composer; b. Herda, May 5, 1856; d. Gotha, Feb. 1, 1933. After study with local teachers, he became in 1880 a church organist and conductor of the Liedertafel (900 singers) in Gotha; He was the editor from 1897 of *Blätter für Haus- und Kirchenmusik* and later of the *Musikalisches Magazin* (a large collection of excellent monographs to which he contributed); retired in 1918. He composed several choral works, with Orch.: *Die Martinswand; Die Frühlingsfeier; Des Volkes Gruss; Das hohe Lied der Arbeit; Dornröschen;* etc.; brought out *Psalter und Harfe,* a collection of motets (5 books); *Thüringer Liederkranz.*

Rabin, Michael, American violinist; b. New York, May 2, 1936; d. there, Jan. 19, 1972. He was of a musical family; his father was a violinist in the N.Y. Phil., his mother a pianist. He studied with Ivan

Galamian in N.Y. and made excellent progress; in his early youth he appeared as a soloist with a number of American orchs.; made several European tours as a concert violinist, and also played in Australia. His sudden death at the age of 35 was a shock to American music-lovers.

Rabinof, Benno, American violinist; b. New York, of Russian-Jewish parents, Oct. 11, 1910; d. Brevard, N.C., July 2, 1975. He studied privately with Victor Küzdö, Franz Kneisel, and Leopold Auer; made his debut in 1927, playing the Tchaikovsky Violin Concerto with members of the N.Y. Phil., conducted by Leopold Auer. In 1930 he played Glazunov's Violin Concerto, with Glazunov himself leading the Boston Symph. Orch. as guest conductor. With his wife, the pianist **Sylvia Smith-Rabinof,** he traveled extensively in Europe and America.

Rabinovich, David, Russian musicologist; b. Kharkov, Aug. 8, 1900. He studied piano at the St. Petersburg Cons. with Essipova, and first performed in public at the age of 13; then entered classes in composition with Glière and piano with Igumnov at the Moscow Cons., graduating in 1930. He subsequently abandoned his career as a concert pianist, and devoted himself to musicology, specializing in monographs on Soviet composers. He publ. *D. Shostakovich, Composer* (Moscow, 1959, in an Eng. trans.); *Portraits of Pianists* (Moscow, 1962); numerous articles in Soviet music periodicals.

Rabl, Walter, Austrian conductor and composer; b. Vienna, Nov. 30, 1873; d. Klagenfurt, July 14, 1940. He was a pupil of J.F. Hummel, and later of Navratil in Vienna; studied musicology with Guido Adler in Prague (Dr.Phil., 1897). He conducted at the Düsseldorf Opera (1903–6), and at the municipal theaters in Essen, Dortmund, and Magdeburg (1915–24); wrote an opera, *Liane* (Strasbourg, 1903); Symph.; Quartet for Clarinet, Violin, Cello, and Piano; Violin Sonata; several song cycles.
BIBLIOGRAPHY: A. Eccarius-Sieber, "Walter Rabl," in vol. II of *Monographien moderner Musiker* (Leipzig, 1907).

Rachmaninoff, Sergei, great Russian composer and superb pianist; b. on his father's estate at Oneg, district of Novgorod, April 1, 1873; d. Beverly Hills, Calif., March 28, 1943. He was of a musical family; his grandfather was an amateur pianist, a pupil of John Field; his father also played the piano; Rachmaninoff's *Polka* was written on a theme improvised by his father. After financial setbacks, the family estate was sold, and in 1882 Rachmaninoff was taken to St. Petersburg; became a piano pupil of Demiansky at the Cons. there (1882–85); acting on the advice of his cousin, the well-known pianist and conductor Alexander Siloti, Rachmaninoff went to Moscow and studied piano with Zverev (1885–88) at the Moscow Cons.; in 1888 he began to study piano with Siloti and composition with Taneyev and Arensky. He met Tchaikovsky, who appreciated Rachmaninoff's talent and gave him friendly ad-

vice. At the age of 19 he wrote his Prelude in C-sharp minor, which became one of the most celebrated piano pieces in the world. He graduated as a pianist in 1891, and as a composer in 1892, receiving the gold medal for his opera in one act, *Aleko,* after Pushkin (1892). His First Symph. was given in Moscow in 1897, with little success. Discouraged, Rachmaninoff destroyed the MS; however, the orch. parts were preserved, and after Rachmaninoff's death the score was restored and performed in Moscow (1945). He toured with the Italian violinist Teresina Tua in Russia (1895); gave his own piano recitals, and soon became known as a piano virtuoso; in 1899 he gave a concert of his orch. works with the Phil. Society of London. He continued to compose for orch., for piano, and for voice; in 1901 he gave the first performance of his 2nd Piano Concerto in Moscow, at a concert conducted by Siloti; this concerto became the most celebrated work of its genre written in the 20th century, and its singular charm has never abated since; it is no exaggeration to say that it became a model for piano concertos by a majority of modern Russian composers, and also of semi-popular virtuoso pieces for piano and orch. written in America. On April 29, 1902, Rachmaninoff married his cousin Natalie Satina; they spent some months in Switzerland, then returned to Moscow. Rachmaninoff was engaged to conduct opera at the Bolshoi Theater for 2 seasons (1904–6), and proved himself a very efficient conductor. From 1906 to 1909 he lived mostly in Dresden; spent the summers in his Russian country home near Novgorod. In 1909 he made his first American tour; his initial public appearance in the U.S. took place at Smith College in Northampton, Mass., on Nov. 4, 1909. His fame was such that the Boston Symph. Orch. offered him the post of permanent conductor, but he declined; the offer was repeated in 1918, but then, too, Rachmaninoff decided against acceptance. From 1910 to 1917 he lived in Moscow; conducted the Phil. Society Orch. there (1911–13). After the October Revolution of 1917, he left his native country, never to return; lived on his small estate on Lake Lucerne in Switzerland; made annual tours in Europe and in the U.S.; in 1935 made N.Y. his home; later settled in Los Angeles. He became an American citizen a few weeks before his death.

Among Russian composers Rachmaninoff occupies a very important place. The sources of his inspiration lie in the Romantic tradition of 19th-century Russian music; the link with Tchaikovsky's lyrical art is very strong; melancholy moods prevail and minor keys predominate in Rachmaninoff's compositions, as in Tchaikovsky's; but there is an unmistakable stamp of Rachmaninoff's individuality in the broad, rhapsodic sweep of the melodic line, and particularly in the fully expanded sonorities and fine resonant harmonies of his piano writing; its technical resourcefulness is unexcelled since Liszt. Despite the fact that Rachmaninoff was an émigré and stood in avowed opposition to the Soviet regime (until the German attack on Russia in 1941 impelled him to modify his stand), his popularity never wavered in Russia; after his death Russian musicians paid spontaneous tribute to him.

Rachmaninoff's music is much less popular in Germany, France, and Italy; on the other hand, in England and America it constitutes a potent factor on the concert stage.

WORKS: OPERAS: *Aleko,* after Pushkin's *The Gypsies* (Moscow, May 9, 1893); *The Miserly Knight* (Moscow, Jan. 24, 1906, composer conducting); *Francesca da Rimini* (Moscow, Jan. 24, 1906, composer conducting). FOR ORCH.: Symph. No. 1 (St. Petersburg, March 27, 1897); Symph. No. 2 (St. Petersburg, Feb. 8, 1908, composer conducting); Symph. No. 3 (Philadelphia, Nov. 6, 1936); *Andante and Scherzo for String Orch.* (Moscow, Feb. 24, 1891); *Prince Rostislav,* symph. poem (1891); *Intermezzo* (Moscow, Oct. 31, 1892); *The Rock,* symph. fantasy (1893; Moscow, March 20, 1896); *Caprice bohémien* for Orch. (1894); *The Isle of the Dead,* symph. poem, inspired by Böcklin's painting (Moscow, May 1, 1909, composer conducting); *Symph. Dances* (Philadelphia, Jan. 3, 1941); 4 piano concertos: No. 1, in F-sharp minor (1890–91; revised 1917); No. 2, in C minor (Moscow, Nov. 9, 1901, composer soloist; one of his most famous works); No. 3, in D minor (N.Y., Nov. 28, 1909, composer soloist); No. 4, in G minor (Philadelphia, March 18, 1927); *Rhapsody on a Theme by Paganini* for Piano and Orch. (Philadelphia Orch., Baltimore, Nov. 7, 1934, composer soloist). CHAMBER MUSIC: *Trio élégiaque,* in memory of Tchaikovsky (1893); *Romance* and *Danse hongroise* for Violin and Piano (1893); Cello Sonata (1901). CHORAL WORKS: *The Spring* for Baritone, Chorus, and Orch. (Moscow, March 24, 1902); *Liturgy of St. John Chrysostom* for Chorus a cappella (Moscow, Nov. 25, 1910); *The Bells,* after Edgar Allan Poe, for Orch., Chorus, and Soloists (St. Petersburg, Dec. 13, 1913, composer conducting); Vesper Mass for Chorus a cappella (Moscow, March 10, 1915); *3 Russian Songs* for Chorus and Orch. (Philadelphia, March 18, 1927). FOR PIANO: *5 morceaux de fantaisie,* op. 3: *Elégie, Prélude* (the famous one, in C-sharp minor), *Mélodie, Polichinelle, Sérénade* (1892); *7 morceaux de salon,* op. 10 (1894); *6 moments musicaux,* op. 16 (1896); *Variations on a Theme by Chopin,* op. 22 (1903); 10 Preludes, op. 23 (1904); Sonata No. 1, in D minor, op. 28 (1907); 13 Preludes, op. 32 (1910); *6 études-tableaux,* op. 33 (1911); *Polka V.R.,* on a theme by the composer's father, Vasily Rachmaninoff (1911); Sonata No. 2, in B-flat minor (1913); *9 études-tableaux,* op. 39 (1916–17; orchestrated by Respighi, 1931); *Variations on a Theme by Corelli* for Piano, op. 42 (1931); 6 Duets for Piano, 4-hands, op. 11 (1894); *Fantasy* (Suite No. 1) for 2 Pianos, op. 5 (1893); Suite No. 2, op. 17 (1901); arrangements for Piano of *Prelude, Gavotte,* and *Gigue* from Bach's Violin Partita in E major, of Mendelssohn's *Scherzo* from *A Midsummer Night's Dream,* of Mussorgsky's *Hopak,* of Rimsky-Korsakov's *Flight of the Bumble-Bee,* of Fritz Kreisler's *Liebesfreude* and *Liebeslied,* and of his own song, *Lilacs.* SONGS: (all written before 1916): 6 Songs, op. 4; 6 Songs, op. 8; 12 Songs, op. 14, of which *Spring Waters* is best known; 12 Songs, op. 21 (including *Fate,* on Beethoven's 5th Symph., and *Lilacs*); 15 Songs, op. 26 (including *Christ Is Risen*); 14 Songs, op. 34 (including *Vocalise*); 6 Songs, op. 38.

BIBLIOGRAPHY: Ivan Lipayev, *S. R.* (Saratov, 1913, in Russian); V. Belaiev, *R.* (Moscow, 1924); V. Belaiev, "S. R.," *Musical Quarterly* (July 1927); Oskar von Riesemann, *R.'s Recollections* (N.Y., 1934; reprint, 1970); Watson Lyle, *R.: A Biography* (London, 1939); Alfred and Katherine Swan, "*R.:* Personal Reminiscences," *Musical Quarterly* (Jan. and April 1944); A. Gronowicz, *S. R.* (N.Y., 1946); Sophie Satin, ed., *In Memory of R.* (N.Y., 1946, in Russian); Igor Boelza, ed., *R. and Russian Opera* (Moscow, 1947); A. Solovtsov, *S. R.* (Moscow, 1947); J. Culshaw, *S. R.* (London, 1949); J. Andriessen, *R.* (Amsterdam, 1950); V. Seroff, *R.* (N.Y., 1950; in French, Paris, 1954); A. Alexeyev, *S. R.* (Moscow, 1954); S. Bertensson and J. Leyda, *S. R.* (N.Y., 1956); Z. Apetian, ed., *Reminiscences about R.* (Moscow, 1957); R. Threlfall, *S. R., His Life and Music* (London, 1973); R. Walker, *R.: His Life and Times* (Tunbridge Wells, 1980); R. Threlfall and G. Norris, *A Catalogue of the Compositions of S. R.* (London, 1982).

Rachmilovich, Jacques, Russian conductor; b. Odessa, Oct. 8, 1895; d. on board the S.S. *Giacomo* en route to Italy, Aug. 7, 1956, and was buried at sea. He studied at the St. Petersburg Cons.; emigrated to America in 1925 and settled in California, where he organized the Santa Monica Symph. Orch. (1945). He made numerous appearances as a guest conductor, specializing in modern music.

Radecke, Ernst, German musicologist, son of **Robert Radecke;** b. Berlin, Dec. 8, 1866; d. Winterthur, Switzerland, Oct. 8, 1920. He studied music with his father; then took courses in musicology at the univs. of Jena, Munich, and Berlin; received his Dr.Phil. at the Univ. of Berlin with his dissertation *Das deutsche weltliche Lied in der Lautenmusik des 16. Jahrhunderts* (publ. Leipzig, 1891). In 1893 he went to Winterthur, and devoted himself mainly to teaching; in 1908 became a lecturer on musicology at the Univ. of Zürich. He publ. a number of analytic essays on Classical works.

Radecke, Robert, German conductor and composer; b. Dittmannsdorf, Oct. 31, 1830; d. Wernigerode, June 21, 1911. He was a brother of the conductor **Rudolf Radecke;** studied at the Leipzig Cons., with Ferdinand David (violin) and Moscheles (piano); also took a course in composition with Hauptmann; appeared first as a violinist; then went to Berlin, where he conducted the Court Opera (1863–87); also taught at the Royal Inst. for Church Music there (1892–1907). He wrote a "Liederspiel," *Die Mönkgüter* (Berlin, May 1, 1874); several overtures; 2 piano trios; choruses and piano works; but became known to the general public mainly for his song *Aus der Jugendzeit,* which obtained extraordinary popularity in Germany and was commonly mistaken for a folk song.

Radecke, Rudolf, German conductor, pedagogue, and composer, brother of **Robert Radecke;** b. Dittmannsdorf, Sept. 6, 1829; d. Berlin, April 15, 1893. He studied at the Leipzig Cons.; in 1859 went to Berlin, where he organized the Radecke Choral Society (1868) and a music school (1869); also taught music at the Stern Cons. (1864–71). He wrote a number of part-songs.

Radenković, Milutin, Serbian composer; b. Mostar, April 6, 1921. He studied at the Belgrade Music Academy, where he subsequently became a teacher; was also active as a music critic. His works are couched in a neo-Classical idiom; the most significant are Concertino for Piano and Orch. (1958) and *Dramatic Overture* (1960); he also composed chamber music; 2 piano sonatas; piano études and preludes; song cycles.

Radford, Robert, English bass; b. Nottingham, May 13, 1874; d. London, March 3, 1933. He was educated at the Royal Academy of Music, taking voice lessons with Alberto Randegger. He made his operatic debut at Covent Garden in London in 1904 as the Commendatore in *Don Giovanni;* later sang the bass roles Hagen and Hunding in the Wagner productions conducted by Hans Richter in London. In 1921 he became a founder, with Beecham, of the British National Opera Co.; later became its director. In 1929 he was appointed to the faculty of his alma mater, the Royal Academy of Music. His fame as an opera singer was great in England, but he never sang with any foreign opera companies.

Radić, Dušan, Serbian composer; b. Sombor, April 10, 1929. He studied at the Music Academy of Belgrade; then went to Paris, where he had private lessons with Milhaud and Messiaen. His music follows the cosmopolitan modernistic manner, Baroque in formal structure, dissonant in contrapuntal intricacies, and hedonistic in its utilitarian appeal.
WORKS: *Symphoniette* (1954); *Spisak (Inventory),* song cycle of 13 numbers for 13 Performers (2 Female Voices and 11 Instruments; Belgrade, March 17, 1954); *Balada o mesecu lutalici (Ballad of the Errant Moon),* ballet (Belgrade, Oct. 19, 1960); Concertino for Clarinet and Strings (1956); *Sinfonia* (1965–66); Piano Quintet; several cantatas; songs; theater music.
BIBLIOGRAPHY: V. Peričić, *Muzički Stvaraoci u Srbiji* (Belgrade, 1969; pp. 407–21).

Radica, Ruben, Croatian composer; b. Split, May 19, 1931. He studied with Kelemen in Zagreb, with Frazzi in Siena, and with Leibowitz in Paris. In 1963 he was appointed to the faculty of the Music Academy in Zagreb. He belongs to the avant-garde of Slovenian music; in 1961 he adopted the 12-tone method of composition.
WORKS: *Concerto grosso* (1957); *4 Dramatic Epigrams* for Piano and String Quartet (1959); *Concerto abbreviato* for Cello and Orch. (1960); *Lyrical Variations* for Strings (1961); *Formacije (Formations)* for Orch. (1963); *19 and 10, Interferences* for Narrator, Chorus, and Orch. (1965); *Sustajarnje (Prostration)* for Electric Organ and Orch. (1967); *Composition* for Ondes Martenot and Chamber

Orch. (Graz, Sept. 26, 1968); *Extensio* for Piano and Orch. (1973).

Radiciotti, Giuseppe, Italian writer on music; b. Jesi, Le Marche, Jan. 25, 1858; d. Tivoli, April 4, 1931. He was a music pupil of his uncle, G. Faini; after finishing a course of studies at the Univ. of Rome, he taught in secondary schools there; in 1895 he was appointed prof. at the Liceo in Tivoli.
WRITINGS: *Teatro, musica e musicisti in Sinigaglia* (1893); *Contributi alla storia del teatro e della musica in Urbino* (1899); *Il teatro e la musica in Rome nel secondo quarto del secolo XIX* (1904); *Teatro, musica e musicisti in Recanati* (1904); *L'arte musicale dei Marchigiani* (1905); *L'Arte musicale in Tivoli nei secoli XVI, XVII e XVIII* (1907); *G.B. Pergolesi* (1910; 2nd ed., 1935; in German, 1954); *Rossini* (1914); *La Cappella musicale del duomo di Pesaro* (1914); *G. Rossini: Vita documentata, opere ed influenza sul'arte* (a monumental biography in 3 vols., 1927–29; 2nd ed., 1941); *Aneddoti rossiniani autentici* (Rome, 1929); also numerous essays in various journals.
BIBLIOGRAPHY: L. Parigi, "G. Radiciotti," in *Critica Musicale* (1918); V. Scotti, "G. Radiciotti," in the *Bollettino Bibliografico Musicale* (1931); A. Belardinelli, *Giuseppe Radiciotti* (Jesi, 1933).

Radnai, Miklós, Hungarian composer; b. Budapest, Jan. 1, 1892; d. there, Nov. 4, 1935. He studied violin, piano, and composition at the Academy of Music; in 1925 was appointed director of the Budapest Opera. He wrote a ballet, *The Birthday of the Infanta,* after Oscar Wilde (Budapest, April 26, 1918); *Symphony of the Magyars* for Chorus and Orch.; Violin Concerto; some chamber music; a textbook of harmony; contributed critical essays to Hungarian publications.

Radó, Aladár, Hungarian composer; b. Budapest, Dec. 26, 1882; killed in battle near Belgrade, Sept. 7, 1914. He studied in Budapest and Berlin; wrote 2 operas: *The Black Knight* (1911) and *Golem* (1912); Symph. (1909); *Hungarian Concerto* for Cello and Orch. (1909); 2 string quartets; String Quintet; publ. several albums of piano pieces and song cycles.

Radoux, Charles, Belgian composer, writer on music, and pedagogue, son of **Jean-Théodore Radoux;** b. Liège, July 30, 1877; d. there, April 30, 1952. He studied with his father; in 1907 received the Belgian Prix de Rome with the cantata *Geneviève de Brabant;* in 1911 was appointed prof. at the Liège Cons.; wrote music criticism for the *Journal de Liège;* was active in folk-song research; served as inspector of music education from 1930 to 1942.
WORKS: Operas: *Les Sangliers des Ardennes* (Liège, 1905) and *Oudelette* (Brussels, April 11, 1912); choral compositions, with Orch.: *Adieu-Absence-Retour, Chanson d'Halewyn, Les Fées;* orch. sketches: *Danse tzigane, Burlesque, Vision, Triptique champêtre; Scène grecque* for Cello and Orch.; *Variations* for Violin and Orch.; *Lamentation* (on a Bach prelude) for English Horn and

Piano; piano pieces; folk-song albums (*5 noëls liégeois, 7 chansons populaires de l'ancien Hainaut, Cramignons liégeois,* etc.). He used the surname **Radcux-Rogier** in his works.

Radoux, Jean-Théodore, Belgian composer and pedagogue; b. Liège, Nov. 9, 1835; d. there, March 20, 1911. He studied bassoon with Daussoigne-Méhul at the Cons. of Liège, where he became a teacher of bassoon in 1856; won the Belgian Prix de Rome with the cantata *Le Juif errant* (1859); then went to Paris for additional study with Halévy. In 1872 he was appointed director of the Cons. of Liège.
WORKS: Operas: *Le Béarnais* (Liège, March 14, 1866) and *La Coupe enchantée* (Brussels, 1872); oratorio, *Cain* (1877); symph. poems: *Ahasvère* and *Le Festin de Balthasar;* patriotic overture, *Epopée nationale;* church music; publ. a monograph, *Vieuxtemps. Sa vie, ses œuvres* (1891).

Radovanović, Vladan, Serbian composer; b. Belgrade, Sept. 5, 1932. He studied at the Music Academy in Belgrade. His early works are set in a neo-Classical style; later he annexed ultramodern techniques, including electronic effects. His *Urklang* for Mezzo-soprano and Chamber Orch. (Belgrade, March 14, 1962) deploys a counterpoint of instrumental colors, with the soloist singing wordlessly. Similarly wordless is his suite *Chorales, Intermezzi e Fuga* for Women's Chorus (Belgrade, May 16, 1962). His experimental period includes such innovative works as *Sphaeroön* in 26 vocal parts, singing detached vowels (Belgrade, March 14, 1962), and *Pentaptych,* suite for Voice and 6 Instruments (Belgrade, April 22, 1964).
BIBLIOGRAPHY: V. Peričić, *Muzički Stvaraoci u Srbiji* (Belgrade, 1969; pp. 422–29).

Radziwill, Prince Anton Heinrich, Polish music amateur and patron of the arts; b. Vilna, June 13, 1775; d. Berlin, April 7, 1833. He played the cello and possessed a fine singing voice; he also wrote incidental music for Goethe's *Faust,* but his name is retained in music history solely because of his associations with Beethoven and Chopin. Beethoven dedicated to him his *Namensfeier* overture, op. 115, and Chopin inscribed to him his op. 8.

Rae, Allan, Canadian composer; b. Blairmore, Alberta, July 3, 1942. He studied arranging and music theory at the Berkeley School of Music in Boston, graduating in 1965; then took courses in electronic music at the Royal Cons. in Toronto (1970–73); subsequently joined its faculty as an instructor in electronic music.
WORKS: 2 string quartets (1966, 1967); *A Day in the Life of a Toad* for Brass Quintet (1970); *Trip* for Orch. (1970); *Impressions* for Wind Quintet (1971); *Sleep Whispering* for Vibraphone, Flute, and Piano (1971); *Wheel of Fortune* for Winds and Strings (1971); *Symphony, In the Shadow of Atlantis* (1972); *The Hippopotamus* for Orch. (1972); *Like Gods, Like Gods among Them,* dance drama (1973); *Listen to the Wind,* suite for Chorus and Orch.

(1973); *Poems for Trio* for Piano Trio (1974); *A Crack in the Cosmic Turtle* for Jazz Group and Orch. (1975); 4 brass quartets for 2 Trumpets and 2 Trombones (1975); *Image* for Orch. (1975); *Rainbow Sketches* for Flute, Oboe, Violin, Piano, and 2 Percussionists (1976); Sonata for Brass Clarinet and String Orch. (1976); Harp Concerto (1976); Concerto for Double Bass and String Orch., to 4 Dali paintings (1977).

Raeli, Vito, Italian musical journalist; b. Tricase, July 8, 1880; d. there, May 7, 1970. He studied music privately; in 1905 he moved to Rome; in 1920 he founded the *Rivista Nazionale di Musica,* which he edited until it discontinued publication in 1943. He publ. numerous valuable monographs and essays on Italian composers, among them *Da V. Ugolini a O. Benevoli: Nella cappella, 1603–1646* (Rome, 1920) and *Maestri compositori pugliesi* (Tricase, 1928).

Raff, Joseph Joachim, greatly renowned German composer and pedagogue; b. Lachen, near Zürich, May 27, 1822; d. Frankfurt, June 24, 1882. He was educated at the Jesuit Lyceum in Schwyz; then became a schoolteacher; at the same time he studied music; in 1843 he sent some of his piano pieces to Mendelssohn, who was sufficiently impressed to recommend them for publication by Breitkopf & Härtel. Mendelssohn's early death made it necessary for Raff to seek other associations; in 1850–56 he was Liszt's assistant at Weimar and became an ardent propagandist of the new German school. Liszt produced Raff's opera *König Alfred* (Weimar, March 9, 1851). In 1854 Raff publ. a highly partisan pamphlet, *Die Wagnerfrage,* in which he took up the cause of Wagner, then a center of fierce debate. In 1859 he married the actress Doris Genast. Raff's 2nd opera, *Dame Kobold,* was produced in Weimar on April 9, 1870; 4 other operas were never staged. In 1877 he was appointed director of the Hoch Cons. in Frankfurt; his teaching was extremely successful; musicians from many countries enrolled in his classes; among them was MacDowell. Raff was a composer of prodigious fecundity, a master of all technical aspects of composition. He wrote 214 opus numbers which were publ., and many more that remained in MS. In spite of his fame, his music fell into lamentable desuetude after his death; some examples of his contrapuntal skill are quoted in school manuals. He wrote 11 symphs., some of them furnished with Romantic subtitles indicating the nature of the music: No. 1, *An das Vaterland,* op. 96; No. 2, op. 140; No. 3, *Im Walde,* op. 153; No. 4, op. 167; No. 5, *Leonore,* op. 177; No. 6, *Gelebt, gestrebt; gelitten, gestritten; gestorben, umworben* (an epigraph that might well be applied to Raff's own destiny); No. 7, *In den Alpen,* op. 201; No. 8, *Frühlingsklange,* op. 205; No. 9, *Im Sommer,* op. 208; No. 10, *Zur Herbstzeit,* op. 213; No. 11, *Der Winter,* op. 214 (left unfinished; completed by M. Erdmannsdörfer); *Symphonietta* for 8 Woodwinds and 2 Horns; Piano Concerto; 2 violin concertos; Cello Concerto; 8 string quartets; 3 piano trios; 5 violin sonatas; about 120 piano pieces of various descriptions and 9 pieces for Piano, 4-hands; numerous transcriptions of orch. and other works.

BIBLIOGRAPHY: A. Schäfer, *Chronologisch-systematisches Verzeichnis der Werke Joachim Raffs* (Wiesbaden, 1888); Helen Raff, *Joachim Raff. Ein Lebensbild* (Regensburg, 1925); J. Kälin and A. Marty, *Leben und Werk des Komponisten Joachim Raff* (Zürich, 1972).

Rago, Alexis, Venezuelan composer; b. Caracas, May 25, 1930. He studied in Caracas and later at the Peabody Cons. in Baltimore; then went for further studies to Vienna and Rome, where he took courses in piano and composition. Returning to Venezuela, he became director of the Cons. of the state of Aragua.

WORKS: *3 escenas de ritos prohibidos* for Piano (1959); *Autantepuy,* symph. poem (1962); *5 instantes* for Orch. (1968); *Mítica de sueños y cosmogonías* for Wind Quintet (commissioned by the 4th Inter-American Festival in Washington, D.C., and perf. there on June 25, 1968); *Guri,* symph. poem on indigenous themes (1968); *Sincronismos, audiosonorrítmicos* (1969); several piano suites; songs.

Rahlwes, Alfred, German conductor and composer; b. Wesel, Oct. 23, 1878; d. Halle, April 20, 1946. He studied with Wüllner, G. Hollaender, and W. Hess at the Cologne Cons.; upon graduation, was active as a choral conductor in Halle. He wrote an opera, *Frau Potiphar* (Essen, 1907); numerous men's choral pieces; chamber music; songs.

BIBLIOGRAPHY: M. Soupe, "Alfred Rahlwes zum Gedächtnis," in *Handel Festival Program Book* (Halle, 1956).

Raichev, Alexander, Bulgarian composer; b. Lom, April 11, 1922. He studied composition with Vladigerov and orchestration with Goleminov at the Sofia Cons. (1943–47); later took courses at the Budapest Cons. (1949–50); returning to Bulgaria, he was appointed to the faculty of the Sofia Cons. His music is marked by Balkan melorhythms and asymmetrical time periods.

WORKS: 3 operas: *The Bridge* (Ruse, Oct. 2, 1965); *Your Presence* (1968); *Alarm* (1974); operetta-revue, *The Orchid's Glory* (1962; Sofia, March 6, 1963); 3 oratorios: *Friendship* (1954); *Dimitrov Is A Live* (1954); *October 50* (1967); *September Requiem* (1973); Piano Concerto (1947); 5 symphs. and Orch. (1955); *Bright Day,* overture (1966); *Leninist Generations,* symph. eulogy (1970); *Flaming Dawn,* overture (1971); *Academic Overture* (1973); *Festival Overture* (1975); chamber music; songs; choruses.

Raichl, Miroslav, Czech composer; b. Náchod, Feb. 2, 1930. He studied composition with Bořkovec at the Prague Academy of Music, graduating in 1953; subsequently devoted himself mainly to teaching and administrative work in the Union of Czechoslovak Composers.

WORKS: *Fuente Ovejuna,* opera after Lope de Vega (1957; Prague, 1959); 2 symphs. (1955, 1960); Cello Concerto (1956); *Revolutionary Overture*

(1958); *Someone Was Playing on the Oboe* for Female Chorus a cappella (1970).

Raida, Karl Alexander, German composer; b. (of German parents) Paris, Oct. 4, 1852; d. Berlin, Nov. 26, 1923. He studied at the conservatories of Stuttgart and Dresden; was Kapellmeister from 1878–92 at the Viktoria Theater in Berlin, where he founded the Akademie für Dramatischen Gesang (1882) and the Gesellschaft der Opernfreunde (1887); in 1895–97 he served as director of the new Deutsches Theater in Munich. He was a successful composer of light operas, operettas, ballets, farces, etc.

Raimann, Rudolf, Hungarian composer; b. Veszprem, May 7, 1861; d. Vienna, Sept. 26, 1913. He entered the service of Prince Esterházy as music director; wrote an opera, *Enoch Arden,* after Tennyson (Budapest, May 8, 1894), and about a dozen operettas, produced in Vienna: *Das Waschermädel* (April 19, 1905); *Paula macht alles* (March 27, 1909); *Die Frau Gretl* (April 7, 1911); *Unser Stammhalter* (Nov. 15, 1912); etc.

Raimondi, Gianni, Italian tenor; b. Bologna, April 17, 1923. He made his debut in 1947 in Bologna; appeared at La Scala in Milan as Alfredo in *La Traviata,* with Maria Callas as Violetta. In 1957 he made his first American tour; on Sept. 29, 1965, appeared as Rodolfo in *La Bohème* at the Metropolitan Opera in N.Y.; among his other parts were Cavaradossi in *Tosca,* the Duke in *Rigoletto,* and Faust in Gounod's opera; he remained with the Metropolitan until 1969.

Raimondi, Ignazio, Italian composer; b. Naples, c.1737; d. London, Jan. 14, 1813. He left Italy about 1770; conducted concerts in Amsterdam (1762); then went to Paris, and eventually (1780) to London, where he remained until the end of his life.

WORKS: Symph., *Les Aventures de Télémaque* (Amsterdam, Jan. 15, 1777); opera, *La Muta* (Paris, Nov. 12, 1789); symph., *The Battle* (1785; very popular in England); several string quartets; string trios; various other instrumental pieces.

Raimondi, Pietro, inventive Italian composer; b. Rome, Dec. 20, 1786; d. there, Oct. 30, 1853. He studied with La Barbara and Tritto at the Cons. della Pietà de' Turchini in Naples; in 1807 brought out an opera buffa, *Le bizzarie d'amore,* at Genoa; it was followed by about 60 other dramatic works and 21 ballets, for whose production he traveled from place to place (Florence, Naples, Rome, Messina, Milan, etc.); was director of the royal theaters at Naples (1824–32) and a prof. at the Palermo Cons. (1833–52); in 1852 became maestro di cappella at St. Peter's in Rome. Raimondi was a contrapuntist of remarkable skill; he publ. 4 fugues *a 4,* which could be combined as a quadruple fugue *a 16;* 6 fugues *a 4,* to be combined as a sextuple fugue *a 24;* in the *24 fughe a 4, 5, 6 e 8 voci* publ. by Ricordi, there is one such quadruple fugue *a 16,* and a quintuple fugue *a*

20; further, 6 fugues *a* 4, performable as a sextuple fugue *a* 24; and a fugue *a* 64, for 16 Chowever, was the sacred trilogy *Giuseppe* (Joseph), comprising 3 oratorios (*Potifar, Giuseppe, Giacobbe*), performed at the Teatro Argentina in Rome, Aug. 7, 1852, at first separately, and then simultaneously, the ensemble of 400 musicians on the stage and in the orch. presenting a most striking effect and arousing great curiosity among professional musicians.

BIBLIOGRAPHY: F. Cicconetti, *Memorie intorno a Pietro Raimondi* (Rome, 1867); Cecil Gray, "Pietro Raimondi," *Music Review* (Jan. 1940).

Raimondi, Ruggero, Italian bass; b. Bologna, Oct. 3, 1941. He was educated at the Santa Cecilia Academy in Rome; made his debut in Spoleto in 1964; in 1968 sang at La Scala in Milan. On Sept. 14, 1970, he made his Metropolitan Opera debut as Silva in *Ernani.* His other signal appearances were at the Paris Opéra, at the State Opera in Munich, and at the Deutsche Oper in Berlin. He was distinguished in the role of Don Giovanni and was also praised for his dramatic rendition of Boris Godunov.

Rainey, Gertrude ("Ma"), black American blues singer; b. Columbus, Ga., April 26, 1886; d. Rome, Ga., Dec. 22, 1939. She made her first appearance in public in Columbus when she was 12; after touring with the Rabbit Foot Minstrels and Tolliver's Circus, she organized her own Georgia Jazz Band; retired in 1933. Her style of blues singing influenced Bessie Smith.

Rainger, Ralph, American composer of popular songs, pianist, and arranger; b. New York, Oct. 7, 1901; d. Beverly Hills, Oct. 23, 1942. He received solid training in music, and even attended Schoenberg's lectures at the Univ. of Calif. in Los Angeles. He became a professional accompanist; in 1930 went to Hollywood, where he prospered as a film composer. Among the many songs he wrote, *Thanks for the Memories* received an Academy Award in 1938 and became a perennial favorite as the theme song of the comedian Bob Hope.

Rainier, Priaulx, South African-born English composer; b. Howick, Natal, Feb. 3, 1903. She studied violin at the South African College of Music; in 1920 went to London, where she studied violin and took courses with McEwen at the Royal Academy of Music; studied briefly with Nadia Boulanger in Paris (1939); in 1943–61 was a prof. at the Royal Academy of Music.

WORKS: *Incantation* for Clarinet and Orch. (1933); *3 Greek Epigrams* for Soprano and Piano (1937); String Quartet (1939); *Suite* for Clarinet and Piano (1943); *Sinfonia da camera* for String Orch. (1947; revised version, London, Feb. 21, 1958); *Dance of the Rain* for Tenor and Guitar (1948); *Barbaric Dance Suite* for Piano (1949); *Ballet Suite* for Orch. (1950); *Cycle for Declamation* for Solo Soprano, Tenor, or Baritone (1953); *6 Pieces* for Wind Quintet (1954); *Requiem* for Solo Tenor and Chorus (1955–56); *Trio-Suite* for Piano Trio (1959); *Pastoral Trip-*

tych for Solo Oboe (1960); *Dance Concerto "Phalaphala"* for Orch. (1960–61; London, Jan. 17, 1961); *Quanta* for Oboe Quartet (1961–62); *Suite* for Solo Cello (1963–65); Cello Concerto (1963–64; London, Sept. 3, 1964); String Trio (1965–66); *Aequora lunae (The Seas of the Moon)* for Double Orch., Percussion, and Solo Winds (1966–67; Cheltenham Festival, July 18, 1967); *Trios and Triads* for 10 Trios and Percussion (1969–73); *The Bee Oracles,* after Sitwell, for Tenor or Baritone Solo, Flute, Oboe, Violin, Cello, and Harpsichord (1970); *Quinque* for Harpsichord (1971); *Requiem* for Chorus and Orch. (BBC, London, Nov. 29, 1971); *Ploërmel* for Winds and Percussion (1973; London, Aug. 13, 1973); *Prayers from the Ark* for Tenor and Harp (1976); *Canti e Finale* for Violin and Orch. (1976–77; Edinburgh Festival, Sept. 8, 1977); *Concertante* for Oboe, Clarinet, and Orch. (1977–80; London, Aug. 7, 1981); *Grand Duo* for Cello and Piano (1980–82; London, May 30, 1983); songs.

Rains, Leon, American operatic bass; b. New York, Oct. 1, 1870; d. Los Angeles, June 11, 1954. He studied with Saenger in N.Y. (1891–96) and with Bouhy in Paris; made a concert tour with Melba in the U.S. (1898); then was a member of the court opera at Dresden (from 1899); made his first appearance with the Metropolitan Opera Co. on Feb. 24, 1909, as Hagen in *Götterdämmerung;* then returned to Dresden, and continued to sing there for several years, eventually returning to America.

Raisa, Rosa, soprano; b. Bialystok, Poland, May 23, 1893; d. Los Angeles, Sept. 28, 1963. In order to escape the horrors of anti-Semitic persecutions, she fled to Naples at the age of 14; on Lombardi's advice she entered the Cons. San Pietro a Majella, where she studied under Barbara Marchisio; made her debut at Parma on Sept. 6, 1913, in Verdi's *Oberto, Conte di San Bonifacio* (revived for the Verdi centenary); then sang 2 seasons at the Costanzi in Rome; in 1913–14 (and again in 1916–32 and 1933–36) with the Chicago Opera Co.; in 1914 at Covent Garden; sang with increasing success in Rio de Janeiro, Montevideo, São Paulo, and Milan; on her reappearance with the Chicago company she scored a triumph as Aida (Nov. 13, 1916); she retired in 1937.

Raison, André, French composer and organist, active in Paris 1687–1719. He received instruction at Nanterre; was organist of the Jacobins and at the church of Ste. Geneviève in Paris; publ. 2 books of organ pieces (1688, 1714), of which the first was reprinted by Guilmant in *Archives des maîtres de l'orgue,* 2 (Paris, 1899).

Raitio, Väinö, Finnish composer; b. Sortavala, April 15, 1891; d. Helsinki, Sept. 10, 1945. He studied in Helsinki with Melartin and Furuhjelm and in Moscow with Ilyinsky; also in Berlin (1921) and Paris (1925–26). His music is programmatic in the Romantic manner, but there is a more severe strain in his pieces derived from Finnish legends.

WORKS: 5 operas to Finnish librettos: *Jeftan ty-*

tär (*Jephtha's Daughter;* 1929; Helsinki, 1931); *Prinsessa Cecilia* (1933; Helsinki, 1936); *Väinämöisen kosinta* (*Väinämöisen's Courtship;* 1935); *Lyydian kuningas* (*The King of Lydia;* 1937; Helsinki, 1955); *Kaksi kuningatarta* (*2 Queens;* Helsinki, 1945); Piano Concerto (1915); *Poem* for Cello and Orch. (1915); *Symphonic Ballad* (1916); Symph. (1918–19); *Joutsenet* (*The Swans*) for Orch. (1919); *Fantasias estatica,* symph. poem (1921); *Antigone* for Orch. (1921–22); *Kuutamo Jupiterissa* (*Moonlight on Jupiter*), symph. tableau (1922); *Fantasia poetica,* symph. poem (1923); *Pyramid* for Chorus and Orch. (1924–25); *Vesipatsas* (*Waterspout*), ballet (1929); *Felis domestica,* scherzo for Orch. (1935); Concerto for Violin, Cello, and Orch. (1936); *Nocturne* for Violin and Orch. (1938); *Fantasy* for Cello, Harp, and Orch. (1942); *Le Ballet grotesque* (1943); String Quartet; Piano Quintet; Violin Sonata; works for piano and organ.

BIBLIOGRAPHY: Sulho Ranta, ed., *Suomen Säveltäjiä* (Helsinki, 1945; pp. 514–21).

Raitt, John (Emmet), American singer of popular music and actor; b. Santa Ana, Calif., Jan. 29, 1917. He studied at the Univ. of Southern Calif. and the Univ. of Redlands; began his career as a singer in light opera; also appeared in recitals. He then went to N.Y., where he sang in the Broadway production of *Oklahoma* and in *Carousel;* subsequently starred in other musicals, including *Pajama Game* and *Annie Get Your Gun;* also appeared in films and on television. In later years he devoted much of his efforts to theatrical productions.

Rajičić, Stanojlo, Serbian composer; b. Belgrade, Dec. 16, 1910. He studied music in Vienna and Berlin; upon returning to Serbia, he joined the faculty of the Belgrade Academy of Music (1945). His early compositions are set in a radical idiom of atonal music, verging on dodecaphony, but later he adopted a national style derived from melorhythms of Serbian folk songs.

WORKS: 2 operas: *Simonida* (1956; Sarajevo, May 24, 1957) and *Karadjordje* (1973); ballet, *Pod zemljom* (*Under the Earth;* 1940); 6 symphs. (1935, 1941, 1944, 1946, 1959, 1967); 3 piano concertos (1940, 1942, 1950); 3 violin concertos (1941, 1946, 1950); 2 clarinet concertos (1943, 1962); Cello Concerto (1949); Bassoon Concerto (1969); *Magnovenja* (*Moments*), song cycle for Mezzo-soprano and Orch. (1964); Piano Trio (1934); 2 string quartets (1938, 1939); piano pieces.

BIBLIOGRAPHY: V. Peričić, *Muzički Stvaraoci u Srbiji* (Belgrade, 1969; pp. 430–52).

Rajna, Thomas, Hungarian-English pianist and composer; b. Budapest, Dec. 21, 1928. He studied composition and piano at the Franz Liszt Academy of Music in Budapest (1944–47), where his teachers were Kodály, Veress, and Weiner; in 1947 he came to London on a scholarship to study with Howells and others at the Royal College of Music, graduating in 1952. He taught at the Guildhall School of Music (1963–70) and the Univ. of Surrey (1967–70),

and in 1970 was appointed a lecturer in piano at the Univ. of Cape Town in South Africa. As a pianist he excels in performances of 20th-century music. His own works assume a classical mold, with distinctly modern contents in harmony and counterpoint.

WORKS: *Dialogues* for Clarinet and Piano (1947); String Quartet (1948); *Rhapsody* for Clarinet and Orch. (1948–50); *Music* for Cello and Piano (1950); *Suite* for Strings (1952–54); *Music* for Violin and Piano (1956–57); *Serenade* for 10 Winds, Percussion, Harpsichord, and Piano (1958); Piano Concerto (1960–62; first public perf., London, March 18, 1966); *Movements* for Strings (1962); *Cantilenas & Interludes* for Orch. (1968; London, Feb. 7, 1968); *2 Hebrew Prayers* for Chorus a cappella (1972–73); *4 Traditional African Lyrics* for Voice and Piano (1976).

Rajter, Ludovít, Czech conductor; b. Pezinok, July 30, 1906. He studied piano and cello in Bratislava; then went to Vienna to study at the Academy of Music (1924–29); took lessons in conducting with Clemens Krauss and in Budapest with Dohnányi; in Budapest he conducted the Radio Orch. (1933–45) and taught conducting at the Academy of Music (1938–45). He then was conductor of the Radio Orch. in Bratislava (1945–49); subsequently led the Slovak Phil. Orch. there (1949–61). In 1968 he was appointed principal conductor of the Radio Orch. in Bratislava.

Rakov, Nicolai, Russian composer; b. Kaluga, March 14, 1908. He studied violin in Moscow and composition at the Moscow Cons. with Glière; in 1935 joined its staff as a teacher of orchestration. He was also active as a violinist and conductor. In his compositions he pursues the Romantic and nationalistic line of Russian music.

WORKS: 2 symphs. (1940, 1957); Sinfonietta (1958); *Little Symphony* for Strings (1962); 2 violin concertos (1944, 1955); Concertino for Violin and String Orch. (1959); Violin Sonata (1951); Oboe Sonata (1951); Flute Sonata (1970); 2 piano sonatinas; numerous pieces for Russian folk instruments.

BIBLIOGRAPHY: A. Solovtsov, *Nicolai Rakov* (Moscow, 1958).

Raksin, David, remarkable American composer for films; b. Philadelphia, Aug. 4, 1912. He learned to play piano and woodwind instruments from his father, who was a bandleader; when barely past puberty, organized his own jazz band. In 1934 he entered the Univ. of Pa.; studied composition privately with Isadore Freed (1934–35). In 1935 he went to Hollywood and was engaged by Charlie Chaplin to arrange and orchestrate the music for his film *Modern Times;* this provided Raksin a wonderful companionship with a great comedian who could not read or write music, and he bore with fortitude Chaplin's periodic outbursts of petulance. Raksin wrote a delectable piece of reminiscences, "Life with Charlie," in the *Quarterly Journal of the Library of Congress* (Summer 1983). When Chaplin was forced into exile by the red-baiters of the U.S. Congress for his alleged radical activities and was also pursued by the authorities for his undeniable proclivities in the field of moral turpitude, Raksin struck out on his own; he also profited by his sojourn in California to attend the classes of Schoenberg at the Univ. of Calif. (1937–38). He wrote more than 100 film scores, some of which obtained great popularity in symph. arrangements; his greatest success was the theme song *Laura,* ingratiatingly melodious in its sinuous and convoluted pattern; it generated some 300 different versions. Apart from his activity as a composer, in his early years he filled in several minor parts as an actor in sound movies and television films. Using material from his film music, he composed several symph. suites, among them *Forever Amber* and *The Bad and the Beautiful.* Other coruscating scores were *The Secret Life of Walter Mitty, Carrie,* and *Separate Tables.* He also wrote much incidental music for the theater, as well as purely symph. and choral pieces, including a madrigal, *Simple Symmetries.* His orchestral *Toy Concertino* for Orch. became a favorite; he also made an orchestration of Stravinsky's *Circus Polka* for George Balanchine's production with the Barnum and Baily Circus. In 1956 he was appointed lecturer in composition at the Univ. of Calif. at Los Angeles; also served as adjunct prof. of music at the Univ. of Southern Calif. In 1979 he received the first Max Steiner Award for Career Achievement from the National Film Society. In 1983 he wrote the musical score for the popular television production *The Day After,* presenting a vision of the devastating effects of a nuclear attack on Kansas City.

Ralf, Richard, German composer; b. Karlsruhe, Sept. 30, 1897. He studied piano as a child with his father, the choirmaster at the Karlsruhe Opera; later attended the Scharwenka Cons. in Berlin, graduating in 1914. Drafted into the German army, he suffered severe shell shock at the French front; returning to Berlin, he studied composition with Hugo Kaun. In 1946 he emigrated to the U.S., eventually settling in Los Angeles. His music follows the florid and emotional trend of post-Wagnerian Romanticism.

WORKS: *Transcendental,* ballet (1921); Violin Sonata (1923); String Quartet (1924); Violin Concerto (1925); *Brothers Arise,* cantata (1959); *Symphonic Songs* for Mezzo-soprano and Orch. (1968).

Ralf, Torsten, Swedish tenor; b. Malmö, Jan. 2, 1901; d. Stockholm, April 27, 1954. He studied at the Stockholm Cons. and in Berlin; made his debut as Cavaradossi in Stettin (1930); then sang in Frankfurt (1933–35), Dresden (1935–44), London (1935–39), N.Y. (Metropolitan Opera House, 1945–47), and Buenos Aires (1946).

Ramann, Lina, German writer on music; b. Mainstockheim, near Kitzingen, June 24, 1833; d. Munich, March 30, 1912. She was a pupil of Franz and Frau Brendel at Leipzig; founded (1858) a music seminary for women teachers, at Glückstadt, Holstein; in 1865, with Ida Volkmann, a music school at

Nuremberg, which they sold in a most flourishing condition to August Göllerich in 1890; from then until her death she lived in Munich, devoting herself entirely to literary work.

WRITINGS: *Die Musik als Gegenstand der Erziehung* (1868); *Aus der Gegenwart* (1868); *Allgemeine Erzieh- und Unterrichtslehre der Jugend* (1869; 3rd ed., 1898); *Bach und Händel* (1869); *Fr. Liszts Oratorium "Christus"; Eine Studie zur zeit- und musikgeschichtlichen Stellung desselben* (1880); *Franz Liszt als Künstler und Mensch* (3 vols., 1880–94; vol. 1 in Eng., 1882); *Franz Liszt als Psalmensänger* (1886); she trans. and ed. Liszt's literary works, *Gesammelte Schriften* (6 vols., 1880–83); wrote a *Grundriss der Technik des Klavierspiels,* in 12 books. She also composed 4 sonatinas (op. 9) and other piano music; ed. *Liszt-Pädagogium* (5 vols. of Liszt's piano compositions with Liszt's own changes, additions, remarks, etc.).

BIBLIOGRAPHY: M. Ille-Beeg, *Lina Ramann* (1914).

Ramboušek, Joseph, Czech double-bass virtuoso and pedagogue; b. Mníšek, Nov. 16, 1845; d. Moscow, March 10, 1901. He studied with Josef Hrabět at the Prague Cons.; then was in Stuttgart and Göteborg, and finally went to Moscow, where he was engaged as a double-bass player at the Moscow Opera. He taught at the Phil. Inst. in Moscow; among his pupils was Koussevitzky.

Rameau, Jean-Philippe, great French composer, the creator of the modern science of harmony; b. Dijon, Sept. 25, 1683; d. Paris, Sept. 12, 1764. Of a musical family, he learned to play the harpsichord as a small child; from age 10 to 14 he attended the Jesuit College at Dijon, then devoted himself to music; in 1701 was sent to Italy; after a brief stay at Milan he joined the orch. of a traveling French opera troupe as violinist. In 1702 he was assistant organist at Notre-Dame in Avignon; in June of that year he became organist at Clermont-Ferrand. In 1706 he publ. his first *Livre de pièces de clavecin* in Paris, where he probably had been living since the spring of 1705. Until 1708 he remained in Paris as a church organist. In 1709 he became his father's successor at the Cathedral in Dijon; in July 1713 he became an organist in Lyons; in 1715–23 he was organist of the Cathedral at Clermont-Ferrand, where he wrote his famous *Traité de l'harmonie* (Paris, 1722). This epoch-making work, though little understood at the time, attracted considerable attention and roused opposition, so that when he settled definitely in Paris (1723) he was by no means unknown. The fact that he failed in 1727 in a competition for the position of organist at St.-Vincent-de-Paul did not injure his reputation, for it was generally known that Marchand (probably out of jealousy) had exerted his powerful influence in favor of Daquin, who was in every respect inferior to Rameau. In 1732 he became organist at Ste.-Croix-de-la-Bretonnerie, and soon was recognized as the foremost organist in France. In 1726 appeared his *Nouveau système de musique théorique,* an introduction to the *Traité*. The leading ideas of his system of harmony are (1) chord-building by thirds; (2) the classification of a chord and all its inversions as one and the same, thus reducing the multiplicity of consonant and dissonant combinations to a fixed and limited number of root chords; and (3) his invention of a fundamental bass (*basse fondamentale*), which is an imaginary series of root tones forming the real basis of the varied chord progressions employed in a composition. The stir that these novel theories occasioned, and his reputation as the foremost French organist, by no means satisfied Rameau's ambition; his ardent desire was to bring out a dramatic work at the Opéra. He had made a modest beginning with dramatic music in 1723, when he wrote some dances and divertissements for Alexis Piron's fairy burlesque *L'Endriague,* which was produced at the Théâtre de la Foire St.-Germain. In 1726 he brought out at the same theater 2 light operas by the same poet, *L'Enrôlement d'Arlequin* (Feb. 28) and *La Robe de dissension, ou Le Faux Prodigue* (autumn). He then became music master to the wife of the "fermier-général" La Pouplinière, and the latter obtained from Voltaire a libretto for *Samson,* which Rameau set to music; but it was rejected on account of its biblical subject. A 2nd libretto, by Abbé Pellegrin, was accepted, and *Hippolyte et Aricie* was produced at the Opéra in 1733; its reception was cool, despite undeniable superiority over the operas of Lully and his following in the rich and varied harmony and instrumentation, and Rameau almost renounced dramatic composition. But the persuasions of his friends, who also influenced public opinion in his favor, were effective; in 1735 he brought out the successful opera-ballet *Les Indes galantes,* and in 1737 his masterpiece, *Castor et Pollux,* a work that for years held its own beside the operas of Gluck. A career of uninterrupted prosperity commenced; he was recognized as the leading theorist of the time, and his instruction was eagerly sought; for the next 30 years his operas dominated the French stage; he was named composer of the King's chamber music, and just before his death he was granted a patent of nobility. From the beginning of his dramatic career Rameau roused opposition, and at the same time found ardent admirers. The first war of words was waged between the "Lullistes" and the "Ramistes." This had scarcely been ended by a triumphant revival of *Pygmalion* in 1751, when the production of Pergolesi's *La Serva padrona* (1752) caused a more prolonged and bitter controversy between the adherents of Rameau and the "Encyclopédistes," a struggle known as "La Guerre des Bouffons," in which Rameau participated by writing numerous essays defending his position. Practically the same charges were made against him as would be made a century later against Wagner: unintelligible harmony, lack of melody, preponderance of discords, noisy instrumentation, etc. But when 25 years later the war between Gluckists and Piccinnists was raging, Rameau's works were praised as models of beauty and perfection. It is a matter for regret that Rameau was indifferent to the quality of his librettos; he relied so much upon his musical inspiration that he never could be brought to a realization of the importance of a good text; hence the inequality of his operas. Nevertheless, his operas mark a decided advance over Lully's in musical characterization, expressive melody, richness of harmony, variety of modulation, and expert and original instrumentation.

WRITINGS: *Traité de l'harmonie* (1722; Eng. trans. with commentary by P. Gossett, 1971); *Nouveau système de musique théorique* (1726); *Plan abrégé d'une nouvelle méthode d'accompagnement* (1730); *Les Différentes Méthodes d'accompagnement pour le clavecin ou pour l'orgue* (1732); *Génération harmonique* (1737); *Démonstration du principe de l'harmonie* (1750); *Nouvelles réflexions de M. Rameau sur sa démonstration du principe de l'harmonie* (1752); *Réflexions sur la manière de former la voix* (1752); *Observations sur notre instinct pour la musique* (1754); *Code de musique pratique* (1760). The publications of 1722, 1726, 1737, 1750, 1752, 1754, and 1760 have been reissued in the series Monuments of Music and Music Literature in Facsimile; E. Jacobi ed. *Jean-Philippe Rameau: Complete Theoretical Writings* (Rome, 1967–72).

WORKS: FOR THE STAGE: Theatrical entertainments to which Rameau contributed music: *L'Endriague* (Paris, Feb. 3, 1723); *L'Enrôlement d'Arlequin* (Paris, Feb. 1726); *La Robe de dissension* (Paris, Sept. 7, 1726); *Les Jardins de l'Hymen ou La Rose* (1726; Paris, March 5, 1744); *Les Courses de Tempé* (Paris, Aug. 30, 1734); *Aruéris* (Paris, Dec. 15, 1762). Operas and opera-ballets: *Samson* (1733; unperf.); *Hippolyte et Aricie* (Paris, Oct. 1, 1733); *Les Indes galantes,* "ballet-héroïque" (Paris, Aug. 23, 1735); *Castor et Pollux* (Paris, Oct. 24, 1737; revised version, June 1754); *Les Fêtes d'Hébé,* opéra-ballet (Paris, May 21, 1739); *Dardanus,* tragédie en musique (Paris, Nov. 19, 1739); *La Princesse de Navarre,* comédie-ballet (Versailles, Feb. 23, 1745); *Platée,* comédie-lyrique (Versailles, March 31, 1745); *Les Fêtes de Polymnie,* opéra-ballet (Paris, Oct. 12, 1745); *Le Temple de la Gloire,* opéra-ballet (Versailles, Nov. 27, 1745); *Les Fêtes de l'Hymen et de l'Amour,* "ballet-héroïque" (Versailles, March 15, 1747); *Zaïs,* "pastorale-héroïque (Paris, Feb. 29, 1748); *Pygmalion,* ballet (Paris, Aug. 27, 1748); *Les Surprises de l'Amour,* divertissement (Versailles, Nov. 27, 1748); *Naïs,* "pastorale-héroïque" (Paris, April 22, 1749); *Zoroastre* (Paris, Dec. 5, 1749); *La Guirlande,* ballet (Paris, Sept. 21, 1751); *Acante et Céphise,* "pastorale-héroïque" (Paris, Nov. 18, 1751); *Daphnis et Eglé,* "pastorale-héroïque" (Fontainebleau, Oct. 30, 1753); *Les Sybarites,* ballet (Fontainebleau, Nov. 13, 1753); *La Naissance d'Osiris,* ballet (Fontainebleau, Oct. 12, 1754); *Anacréon,* ballet (Fontainebleau, Oct. 23, 1754; revised version to different text, Paris, May 31, 1757); *Les Paladins,* comédie-ballet (Paris, Feb. 12, 1760); 3 ballets, *Nélée et Myrthis, Zéphyre,* and *Io,* have not been publicly performed; the tragédie-lyrique *Les Boréades* (1764) was not performed until April 19, 1975, in a concert in London; stage premiere took place in Aix-en-Provence on July 21, 1982. SECULAR CANTATAS: *Thétis* (1718); *Aquilon et Orinthie* (1719); *Les Amants trahis* (1721); *Orphée* (1721); *L'Impatience* (1721); *Le*

Berger fidèle (1728). SACRED VOCAL: 4 Psalm settings for Mixed Chorus, Soloists, and Instrumental Ensemble: *Deus noster refugium* (1716); *In convertendo* (1718); *Quam dilecta* (1720); *Laboravi* (1722). Most of the above were publ. in short score (voice, violin, and bass, with the ritornelli in full). Other publ. music: *Premier livre de pièces de clavecin* (1706); *Pièces de clavecin avec une méthode pour la mécanique des doigts* (n.d.; with important notes); *Pièces de clavecin avec une table pour les agréments* (1731); *Nouvelles suites de pièces pour clavecin avec des remarques sur les différents genres de musique* (n.d.; Farrenc publ. these last 2 in his *Trésor des pianistes*, 1861); *Pièces de clavecin en concerts* (1741; with accompaniment of Violin, Flute, and Viola or 2nd Violin); detached numbers of the above are in Pauer's *Old French Composers* and *Popular Pieces by Rameau;* Hugo Riemann ed. a complete edition of the clavecin compositions (publ. by Steingräber). In 1895 Durand & Cie. began the publication of a monumental edition under the editorship of C. Saint-Saëns and Ch. Malherbe; after the latter's death (1911) his part of the work was divided between M. Emmanuel and M. Teneo; 18 vols. appeared up to 1924: I, *Pièces de clavecin;* II, *Musique instrumentale;* III, *Cantates;* IV, *Motets* (first series); V, *Motets* (2nd series); VI, *Hippolyte et Aricie;* VII, *Les Indes galantes;* VIII, *Castor et Pollux;* IX, *Les Fêtes d'Hébé;* X, *Dardanus;* XI, *La Princesse de Navarre, Les Fêtes de Ramire, Nélée et Myrthis, Zéphire;* XII, *Platée;* XIII, *Les Fêtes de Polymnie;* XIV, *Le Temple de la Gloire;* XV, *Les Fêtes de l'Hymen et de l'Amour;* XVI, *Zaïs;* XVII, in 2 parts: Part I, *Pygmalion, Les Surprises de l'Amour;* Part II, *Anacréon, Les Sybarites;* XVIII, *Naïs;* the complete ed. was never completed. A new ed., under the joint auspices of the Assoc. pour la Publication des Œuvres de Rameau in Paris and the Broude Trust of N.Y., with N. Zaslaw as general ed. and F. Lesure as managing ed., began publication in 1983.

BIBLIOGRAPHY: BIOGRAPHY: C. Poisot, *Notice biographique sur J.-P. Rameau* (Paris, 1864); T. Nisard, *Monographie de J.-P. Rameau* (Paris, 1867); A. Pougin, *Rameau* (Paris, 1876); R. Garraud, *Rameau* (Paris, 1876); H. Grigne, *Rameau* (Dijon, 1876); M. Brenet, "Notes et croquis sur J.-P. Rameau," *Guide Musical* (1899) and "La Jeunesse de Rameau," *Rivista Musicale Italiana* (1902–3); H. Quittard, "Les Années de jeunesse de Rameau," *Revue d'Histoire et de Critique Musicale* (1902); L. de La Laurencie, *Quelques documents sur J.-P. Rameau et sa famille* (Paris, 1907) and *Rameau* (Paris, 1908); L. Laloy, *Rameau* (Paris, 1908); L. de la Laurencie, "Rameau et ses descendants," *Sammelbände der Internationalen Musik-Gesellschaft* (1911); M.M. Mayer, *J.-P. Rameau; J.S. Bach* (Chambéry, 1946); Y. Tiénot, *J.-P. Rameau, Esquisse biographique* (Paris, 1954); H. Charlier, *J.-P. Rameau* (Lyons, 1955); P. Berthier, *Réflexions sur l'art et la vie de J.-P. Rameau (1683–1764)* (Paris, 1957); C. Girdlestone, *J.-P. Rameau: His Life and Work* (London, 1957; 2nd ed., revised, 1969); J. Malignon, *Rameau* (Paris, 1960). CRITICISM AND HISTORY: L. Danjou, *Rameau, Son influence sur l'art musical* (Paris, 1866); J. Carlez, *Grimm et la musique de son temps* (Paris, 1872); R. de Récy, "La Critique musicale au siècle dernier; Rameau et les Encyclopédistes," *Revue des Deux Mondes* (July 1886); A. Jullien, *La Musique et les philosophes au XVIIIe siècle* (Paris, 1873); E. Newman, *Gluck and the Opera* (London, 1895); H. Imbert, "L'Œuvre de J.-P. Rameau," *Guide Musical* (1896); H. Riemann, *Geschichte der Musiktheorie* (2nd ed., 1921; pp. 459ff.); E. Dacier, "L'Opéra au XVIIIe siècle," *Revue Musicale* (1902); E. Hirschberg, *Die Encyklopädisten und die französische Oper im 18. Jahrhundert* (Leipzig, 1903); R. Rolland, *Musiciens d'autrefois* (Paris, 1908); A. Jullien, *Musiciens d'hier et d'aujourd'hui* (Paris, 1910); P.-M. Masson, "Lullistes et Ramistes," *L'Année Musicale* (1911); J. Rivière, *Etudes* (Paris, 1911); J.-G. Prod'homme, *Ecrits de musiciens, XVe au XVIIIe siècle* (Paris, 1912); L. Striffling, *Le Goût musical en France au XVIIIe siècle* (Paris, 1913); G. Cucuel, *La Pouplinière et la musique de chambre au XVIIIe siècle* (Paris, 1913); M. Shirlaw, *The Theory of Harmony* (London, 1917); J. Tiersot, "Rameau," *Musical Quarterly* (Jan. 1928); P. Lasserre, *Philosophie de goût musical* (Paris, 1928; new ed., 1931); P.M. Masson, *L'Opéra de Rameau* (1930; 2nd ed., 1932); "Rameau et Beethoven," in the Liège *Kongressbericht* (1930), and "Rameau and Wagner," *Musical Quarterly* (Oct. 1939); G. Migot, *Rameau et le génie de la musique française* (Paris, 1930); J. Gardien, *J.-P. Rameau* (Paris, 1949); P.M. Masson, "Les Deux Versions du *Dardanus* de Rameau," *Acta Musicologica* (Jan.–July 1954); J. Malignon, *Rameau* (Paris, 1960); H. Charlier, *J.-P. Rameau* (Lyons, 1960); Sr. M.M. Keane, *The Theoretical Writings of J.-P. Rameau* (Washington, 1961); G. Sadler, "Nais, Rameau's Opéra pour la Paix,'" *Musical Times* (July 1980); M. Cyr, "Towards a Chronology of Rameau's Cantatas," *Musical Times* (Sept. 1983).

Ramey, Samuel, American bass; b. Colby, Kans., March 28, 1942. He attended Kansas State Univ.; then went to Wichita State Univ., where he studied voice with Arthur Newman; later sang with the Grass Roots Opera Co. in Raleigh, N.C. In 1973 he made his professional debut as Zuñiga in *Carmen* with the N.Y. City Opera; in 1976 he sang at the Glyndebourne Festival. In 1978 he had engagements with the Netherlands Opera and the Hamburg State Opera; in 1981 he performed at La Scala in Milan and the Vienna State Opera. He excels in lyrico-dramatic roles, such as Don Giovanni and Mefistofele in Boito's opera, and also in buffo roles, such as Leporello and Figaro.

Ramin, Günther, distinguished German organist, conductor, composer, and pedagogue; b. Karlsruhe, Oct. 15, 1898; d. Leipzig, Feb. 27, 1956. As a boy he sang in the Thomanerchor in Leipzig; he then studied organ with Karl Straube, piano with Robert Teichmüller, and theory with Stephan Krehl at the Leipzig Cons. In 1918 he was appointed organist of the Thomaskirche in Leipzig; he also was organist of the Gewandhaus concerts and a teacher at the Leipzig Cons. During the season 1933–34 he toured the U.S. as an organ virtuoso. He was also active as a conductor; he led the Lehrergesangverein in Leipzig (1922–35) and the Gewandhaus Choir (1933–34 and 1945–51); from 1935–43 he conducted the Phil. Choir in Berlin. In 1940 he became cantor of the Thomaskirche, where he sought to preserve the integrity of the Thomanerchor after the establishment of the German Democratic Republic. His compositions include an *Orgelchoral-Suite* and many other organ pieces, as well as chamber music and songs. He edited several collections of organ works and publ. the manual *Gedanken zur Klärung des Orgelproblems* (Kassel, 1929; new ed., 1955). A vol. of his essays on Bach was edited by D. Hellman (Wiesbaden, 1973).

BIBLIOGRAPHY: L. von Koerber, *Der Thoma nerchor und sein Kantor* (Hamburg, 1954); E. Hasse, *Erinnerungen an Günther Ramin* (Berlin, 1958); C. Ramin, *Günther Ramin* (Freiburg, 1958).

Ramírez, Luis Antonio, Puerto Rican composer; b. San Juan, Feb. 10, 1923. He studied piano and harmony with Alfredo Romero in San Juan (1954–57); then went to Spain and studied composition with Cristóbal Halffter and Daniel Bravo, and piano with Juan Molinari at the Madrid Cons. (1957–60). Returning to San Juan, he taught at the Univ. of Puerto Rico.

WORKS: *Sonata elegiaca* for Cello and Piano (1970); *Fantasia sobre un Mito Antillano* for Double Bass, Guitar, Horn, Percussion, and Strings (1970); *3 piezas breves* for Horn, 2 Trumpets, Trombone, Piano, Percussion, and Strings (1972); *Fragmentos* for Orch. (1973).

Ramos (Ramis) de Pareja, Bartolomé, Spanish theorist; b. Baeza, c.1440; d. after 1491. After lecturing at the Univ. of Salamanca, he went to Bologna in 1472; publ. in 1482 his Latin treatise *Musica practica* (modern ed. by J. Wolf, Leipzig, 1901; extract in Eng. in O. Strunk, *Source Readings in Music History*, N.Y., 1950), one of the important landmarks in the science of harmony. In 1484 he was in Rome. He established the mathematical ratios 4:5 and 5:6 for the intervals of the major and minor third, thus completing the definition of the consonant triad and laying the basis of our harmonic system. He was also the first to set forth the theory of equal temperament, probably based on the practice of the early Spanish guitarists (*vihuelistas*), since the frets on the guitar were placed a semitone apart.

BIBLIOGRAPHY: J. Haar, "Roger Caperon and Ramos de Pareia," *Acta Musicologica* (1969).

Ramous, Gianni, Italian pianist and composer; b. Milan, April 12, 1930. He studied piano with Carlo Zecchi; autodidact in composition. In 1964 he became a member of the faculty at the Cons. of Genoa. He wrote *Polimorfia* for Orch. (1966); Piano Concerto (1964); *Prismi* for Solo Violin, Winds, and Drums (1969); 3 string quartets (1948, 1949, 1959); oratorio, *La Crucifissione* (1961); cantata, *Lettera alla madre* (1963); comic opera-farce, *Le fatiche del guerriero* (Trieste, Nov. 23, 1963).

Ramovš, Primož, Slovenian composer; b. Ljubljana, March 20, 1921. He studied composition with Slavko Osterc at the hometown Academy of Music (1935–41), with Vito Frazzi in Siena (1941), and privately with Casella and Petrassi in Rome (1941–43). Since 1945 he has worked at the library of the Slovene Academy of Sciences and Art (director since 1952); also taught at the Ljubljana Cons. (1948–64). The framework of his style of composition is neo-Classical, distinguished by great contrapuntal skill and ingenious handling of rich, dissonant sonorities; dodecaphony and aleatorality are sometimes employed.

WORKS: 3 numbered symphs. (1940, 1943, 1948); 3 divertimentos for Orch. (1941, 1942, 1944); Piano Concerto (1946); Concertino for Piano and String Orch. (1948); Concerto for 2 Pianos and String Orch. (1949); *Suite* for 2 Violins, Cello, and String Orch. (1950); Sinfonietta (1951); *Musique funèbre* for Orch. (1955); *Chorale and Toccata* for Orch. (1955); *Adagio* for Cello and String Orch. (1958); *Concerto piccolo* for Bassoon and String Orch. (1958); Trumpet Concertino (1960); *7 Compositions* for Strings (1960); Concerto for Violin, Viola, and Orch. (1961); *Koncertantza glasba (Concertante Music)* for Percussion and Orch. (1961; his most remarkable work); *Intrada* for Orch. (1962); *Profiles* for Orch. (1964); *Vzporedja (Parallels)* for Piano and String Orch. (1965); *Odmevi (Echoes)* for Flute and Orch. (1965); *Antiparallels* for Piano and Orch. (1966; Zagreb, May 15, 1967); *Finale* for Orch. (1966); *Portret* for Harp, Winds, Strings, and Percussion (1968); *Symphony 68* (1968; Ljubljana, Oct. 27, 1968); *Nasprotja (Contrasts)* for Flute and Orch. (1969); Symph. for Piano and Orch. (1970). Chamber music: Quartet for 4 Horns (1939); Wind Trio (1942); Trio for Flute, Trumpet, and Bassoon (1952); Sonatina for Clarinet, Piano, and Trumpet (1953); *Kontrasti* for Piano Trio (1961); *Aphorisms* for Viola and Piano (1961); *Zvučna slika* for Horn and Piano (1962); *Eneafonia* for 9 Instruments (1963); *Fluctuations* for Chamber Ensemble (1964); *Prolog—Dialog—Epilog* for Flute, Clarinet, and Bassoon (1966); *Nihanja (Oscillations)* for Solo Flute, Harp, Percussion, and Strings (1969); *Con sordino* for Trumpet, Trombone, and Piano (1969); *Siglali* for Piano and 8 Instruments (1973); many compositions for solo instruments; piano pieces; choruses; songs.

Rampal, Jean-Pierre, eminent French flutist; b. Marseilles, Jan. 7, 1922. He took flute lessons with his father, Joseph Rampal; attended courses in medicine; then enrolled in the Paris Cons. He played flute in the orch. of the Vichy Opera (1947–51) and later was first flutist at the Paris Opéra. In 1968 he was appointed prof. at the Paris Cons. At the peak of his career, he combined his pedagogical activities with worldwide tours as a soloist with major orchs. and in recitals, achieving extraordinary success, considering that flute recitals rarely attract large audiences. His playing is remarkable for its virtuoso technique and an uncanny ability to graduate subtle dynamics of flute sonorities in all registers. Several French composers, among them Poulenc and Jolivet, wrote special works for him.

Ramsey, Robert, English organist and madrigalist; b. c.1595. He took his B.Mus. at Cambridge in 1616; was organist of Trinity College (1628–44) and Master of the Children (1637–44). He wrote numerous church services, anthems, and madrigals, which remained in MS until 1962, when an *Evening Service* and some madrigals were publ. in England; more recently E. Thompson ed. *Robert Ramsey: English Sacred Music,* in *Early English Church Music,* VII (London, 1967), and *Robert Ramsey: Latin Sacred Music,* in *Early English Church Music,* XX (London, 1978); see also I. Spink, ed., *English Songs 1625–1660,* in *Musica Britannica,* XXXIII (London, 1971).
BIBLIOGRAPHY: E. Thompson, "Robert Ramsey," *Musical Quarterly* (April 1963).

Ran, Shulamit, Israeli composer; b. Tel Aviv, Oct. 21, 1949. She studied piano; took composition lessons from Paul Ben-Haim (1960–63). A scholarship enabled her to go to the U.S., where she enrolled in the Mannes College of Music in N.Y. (1963–67), studying piano with Nadia Reisenberg and composition with Dello Joio; in 1963 she attended the seminars of Aaron Copland and Lukas Foss at the Berkshire Music Center in Tanglewood. In 1973 she joined the faculty of the Univ. of Chicago. WORKS: *Capriccio* for Piano and Orch. (N.Y., Nov. 30, 1963, composer soloist); *Symphonic Poem* for Piano and Orch. (Jerusalem, Oct. 17, 1967, composer soloist); *10 Children's Scenes* for Piano, 4-hands (1967); *Structures* for Piano (1968); *7 Japanese Love Poems* for Voice and Piano (1969); *O the Chimneys,* after poems by Sachs, for Voice, Flute, Clarinet, Bass Clarinet, Cello, Percussion, Piano, and Tape (N.Y., Jan. 19, 1970); *Concert Piece* for Piano and Orch. (1971; Tel Aviv, July 12, 1971, composer soloist); *3 Fantasy Pieces* for Cello and Piano (1972); *Ensembles for 17* for High Female Voice and 16 Instrumentalists (Chicago, April 11, 1975); *Sonata brevis* for Harpsichord (1975); *Double Vision* for 2 Quintets and Piano (Chicago, Jan. 21, 1977); Piano Concerto (1977); *For an Actor: Monolog for Clarinet* (1978); *Apprehensions* for Violin, Clarinet, and Piano (1979); *Private Game* for Clarinet and Cello (1979); *Fantasy-variations* for Solo Cello (1980); *Excursions* for Clarinet, Cello, and Piano (1980); *A Prayer* for Horn and 4 Instruments (1982); *Verticals* for Solo Piano (1983); *Sonata-Waltzer* for Piano (1983).

Ranczak, Hildegard, Czech soprano; b. Vitkovice, Dec. 20, 1895. She studied at the Vienna Cons.; made her debut in Düsseldorf in 1918; remained there until 1923; then sang in Cologne (1923–25) and Stuttgart (1925–27); in 1927 she joined the Bavarian State Opera in Munich, where she appeared until 1944; sang there again from 1946 to 1949; also sang at Covent Garden in London, the Paris Opéra, the Rome Opera, and the Berlin State Opera. She created the role of Clairon in Richard Strauss's *Capriccio* in 1942.

Randall, James, American composer; b. Cleveland, June 16, 1929. He studied at Columbia Univ. (B.A., 1955), at Harvard Univ. (M.A., 1956), and at Princeton (M.F.A., 1958); in 1957 he was appointed to the music faculty of Princeton Univ. WORKS: *Pitch-derived Rhythm: 5 Demonstrations* (1961); *Mudgett: Monologues of a Mass Murderer* for Tape (1965); *Lyric Variations* for Violin and Computer (1968). He dabbled in mathematics; the structure of much of his music shows an interrelation between seemingly unrelated categories, such as pitch and rhythm, much in the manner that the transcendental number *pi* is mathematically placed in relation with an imaginary number *i* and the transcendental base of natural logarithms.

Randegger, Alberto, Jr., Italian violinist and composer, nephew of **Alberto Randegger, Sr.;** b. Trieste, Aug. 3, 1880; d. Milan, Oct. 7, 1918. He accompanied his uncle to London and appeared as a violinist at an orch. concert conducted by the latter; took courses at the Royal Cons. of Music; then returned to Italy and lived in Milan. He composed a short opera, *L'ombra di Werther* (Trieste, 1899); a Violin Concerto; piano pieces and songs.

Randegger, Alberto, Sr., Italian conductor; b. Trieste, April 13, 1832; d. London, Dec. 18, 1911. He studied piano and composition in Italy; in 1854 went to England and became successful as a singing teacher. In 1868 he was appointed prof. of singing at the Royal Academy of Music in London. From 1879 to 1885 he conducted the Carl Rosa Co.; then was opera conductor at Drury Lane and Covent Garden (1887–98).

Randegger, Giuseppe Aldo, Italian pianist and pedagogue; b. Naples, Feb. 17, 1874; d. New York, Nov. 30, 1946. He studied in Naples; in 1893 he went to America and was active mainly as a teacher; he composed an opera, *The Promise of Medea,* and a number of songs.

Randolph, David, American conductor; b. New York, Dec. 21, 1914. He studied at City College, N.Y. (B.S., 1936) and Teachers College, Columbia Univ. (M.A., 1941); from 1943–47 was assistant director of music of the U.S. Office of War Information. In 1943 he organized the Randolph Singers, which he conducted until 1972. In 1955 he founded the Masterwork Chorus and Orch.; also led the St. Cecilia Chorus and Orch. and, beginning in 1981, the Masterwork Chamber Orch. He taught conducting at the Dalcroze School (1947–50); was a prof. of music at the State Univ. of N.Y. College at New Paltz (1970–72), at Fordham Univ. (1972–73), and at Montclair State College (from 1973). He was also active as a radio music commentator. He publ. the book *This Is Music* (N.Y., 1964); also edited The David Randolph Madrigal Series.

Randolph, Harold, American pianist and music educator; b. Richmond, Va., Oct. 31, 1861; d.

Rands – Rangström

Northeast Harbor, Maine, July 6, 1927. He studied at the Peabody Cons. in Baltimore; in 1898 he succeeded Asger Hamerik as director there, and enjoyed an excellent reputation as a teacher and administrator.

BIBLIOGRAPHY: D. Leedy, "Harold Randolph, the Man and Musician," *Musical Quarterly* (April 1944).

Rands, Bernard, remarkable English-born American composer; b. Sheffield, March 2, 1934. He studied piano and organ at home; at the age of 18 he entered the Univ. of Wales, majoring in music and English literature. He also developed a passion for Celtic lore; in his student days he became a sort of polyglot, delving into the linguistic mysteries of Welsh, Irish, and Scottish vocables, and on the way acquiring a fluency in French, Italian, and Spanish. He also immersed himself in the hypergrammatical and ultrasyntactic glossolalia of James Joyce. After graduating from the Univ. of Wales (B.Mus., 1956; M.Mus., 1958), he went to Italy, where he took lessons in musicology with Roman Vlad in Rome and studied composition with Luigi Dallapiccola in Florence (1958–60); also attended the International Teaching Festivals in Darmstadt, taking part in the seminars in composition and conducting with Pierre Boulez and Bruno Maderna; later he consulted Luciano Berio in Milan on problems of electronic music. On a grant from the Arts Council of Great Britain, he traveled to Sydney, Australia, in 1972 and accompanied the BBC Symph. Orch. on its European tour in 1974. From 1968 to 1975 he was an instructor in the music dept. of York Univ.; he also held the appointment of Fellow in Creative Arts at Brasenose College, Oxford Univ. In 1976 he was engaged as a prof. of music at the Univ. of Calif. at San Diego; he found the musical atmosphere there congenial to his innovative ideas, and he eventually became a permanent resident of the U.S.; he was appointed a visiting prof. at the Calif. Inst. of the Arts in Valencia in 1984–85 while retaining his San Diego post.

The sources of his music are astonishingly variegated, drawing upon religious, mystical, mathematical, and sonoristic premises. At one time he was preoccupied with Hinduism; these interests are reflected in his work *Aum (Om),* a mantric word interpreted as having 3 sounds representing the triune stasis of Brahma, Vishnu, and Siva. Despite the complex nature of his compositions, Rands seems to encounter little resistance on the part of performers and audiences; his music possesses the rare quality of immediate communication. Each work reflects a message; thus his *Metalepsis 2* is described by him as a "non-denominational Mass for all who suffer at the hands of tyrants." Several works reflect the scientific bent of his mind, as exemplified by *Formants;* there are mundane references in the titles of such works as *Memos* and *Agenda;* other sets contain references to sports, as in *Wildtrack.* Then there are in his catalogue educational pieces, such as *Sound Patterns,* designed to be interpreted by children and professional performers alike. His *Canti lunatici* penetrate the inner recesses of the human mind in a state of turbulence. Rands received the Pulitzer Prize in 1984 for his *Canti del sole* for Tenor and Orch.

WORKS: For Orch.: *Refractions* for 24 Players (1961); *Wildtrack 1* (1969), *2* (1973), and *3* (1975); *Mesalliance* for Piano and Orch. (1972); *Ology* for Jazz Orch. (1973); *Aum* for Harp and Orch. (London, April 17, 1974). For Youth Orch.: *Per Esempio* (1968); *Sound Patterns 1, 2, 3, 4, 5* for children's performance (1967–69); *Agenda* (1970). For Various Ensembles: *Actions for 6* for Flute, Harp, Viola, Cello, and 2 Percussion Players (1963); *Formants 2 (Labyrinth)* for Harp and Chamber Group (1970); *Tableau* for Flute, Clarinet, Viola, Cello, Piano, and Percussion (1970); *As All Get Out* (1972); *Scherzi* for Clarinet, Violin, Cello, and Piano (1975); *Cuaderno* for String Quartet (1975). For Solo Instruments: *Formants 1 (Les Gestes)* for Harp Solo (1965); *Memo 1* for Double Bass (1971), *2* for Trombone (1972), *3* for Cello (1973), and *4* for Tuba (1974); *Serenata* for Flute and Chamber Group (1975). For Piano: *Espressioni 1, 2, 3, 4, 5* (1970–75). For Voices and Instruments: *5 Ballads* (1970–75); *Flickering Shadows* (1971); *Metalepsis* (1971); *Canti lunatici* for Soprano and Chamber Ensemble (1971); *Déjà 2* for Soprano and Chamber Ensemble (1972); *Serena* for Singing Actor, Mime, Trumpet, and Tape (1972); *Canti del sole* for Tenor and Orch. (1983; received the Pulitzer Prize).

Rangström, Ture, remarkable Swedish composer; b. Stockholm, Nov. 30, 1884; d. there, May 11, 1947. He studied singing in Berlin and Munich with Julius Hey (1905–7), then composition with Lindegren in Stockholm and Pfitzner in Munich. Returning to Sweden, he became music critic of the *Stockholms Dagblad* (1910–14) and the *Svenska Dagbladet* (1907–9, and after 1927). From 1922 to 1925 he was conductor of the Göteborg Symph. Orch.; then became stage director at the Stockholm Opera. His music is permeated with a lyrical sentiment, and his forms are rhapsodic; in his symphs. he achieves great intensity by a concentrated development of the principal melodic and rhythmic ideas; his songs are also appreciated.

WORKS: Operas: *Kronbruden (The Crown Bride),* after Strindberg (premiere, Stuttgart, in German, as *Die Kronbraut,* Oct. 21, 1919); *Middelalderlig* (Stockholm, 1921); *Gilgamesh* (left incomplete; finished and orchestrated by John Fernström; Stockholm, Nov. 20, 1952; 4 symphs.: No. 1, *In memoriam A. Strindberg* (1915); No. 2, *My Country* (1919); No. 3, *Song Under the Stars* (1931); No. 4, *Invocatio* (1936); symph. poems: *Dithyramb* (1909; revised in 1949 by Atterberg); *En höstsang (Ode to Autumn;* 1912); *Havet sjunger (The Sea Sings;* 1914); *Gamla Stockholm* (1939); *Festpreludium 1944,* for the 50th anniversary of the Stockholm Opera Theater (1944); *Divertimento elegiaco* for Strings (1918); *Un Petit Rien* for String Orch. (1937); *Ballad* for Piano and Orch. (1937); *Poem-Capriccio amoroso* for Violin and Orch. (1944); *Ein Nachtstück in E.T.A. Hoffmanns Manier* for String Quartet (1909);

other chamber music; piano pieces; about 60 fine songs, to Swedish texts.

BIBLIOGRAPHY: The special issue of *Musik-revy*, 25 (1970).

Ránki, Dezsö, Hungarian pianist; b. Budapest, Sept. 8, 1951. He studied piano with Klára Máthé, and at the Franz Liszt Academy of Music, with Pál Kadosa and Ferenc Rados. In 1969 he won the International Schumann Competition in Zwickau, and from that time toured with notable success. His repertoire encompasses the classics and the moderns; he particularly excels in the works of Béla Bartók.

Ránki, György, Hungarian composer; b. Budapest, Oct. 30, 1907. He studied composition with Kodály at the Budapest Academy of Music (1926–30); won the Erkel Prize twice (1952, 1967) and the Kossuth Prize (1954); in 1963 was awarded the title "Merited Artist of the Hungarian People's Republic." His music derives its inspiration chiefly from Hungarian folk songs.

WORKS: *Hóemberek* (*Snow Men;* London, 1939); musical comedy, *A csendháborító* (*The Rioter;* 1950; Budapest Radio, 1950; stage version, Budapest, 1959); opera, *Pomádé király új ruhája* (after Andersen's *The Emperor's New Clothes;* Budapest, June 6, 1953); children's musical comedy, *A gyöztes ismeretlen* (*The Winner Is Unknown;* 1961); operetta, *Hölgyválasz* (*Spoon Dance;* 1961); children's opera, *Muzsikus Péter új kalandjai* (*New Adventures of Peter Musician;* 1962); symph. dance drama, *Cirkusz* (*The Circus;* 1965); opera, *The Tragedy of Man* (Budapest, Dec. 4, 1970); 4 cantatas: *A város peremén* (*At the Outskirts of the City;* 1947); *In the Year 1848* (1948); *Freedom Song* (1950); *Battle in Peace* (1951); 2 oratorios: *1944* (1967) and *Cantus Urbis* (1972); *Kardtánc* (*Sword Dance*) for Orch. (1949; version for Violin and Piano, 1957); *Hungarian Dances from the 16th Century* for Orch. (1950); *1514,* fantasy for Piano and Orch. depicting the Hungarian peasant uprising of 1514 (1959; version for 2 Pianos and Percussion, 1962); *Don Quijote and Dulcinea,* 2 miniatures for Oboe and Small Orch. (1960; version for Oboe and Piano, 1961); *Aurora tempestuosa,* prelude for Orch. (1967); *Aristophanes,* suite for Violin and Piano (1947); Sonata for Recorder and Cimbalom (1948); *Serenata all'antiqua* for Violin and Piano (1956); *Pentaerophonia* for Wind Quintet (1958); *Lament,* in memoriam Kodály, for Voices, Chorus, and Cimbalom (1971); piano pieces; music for radio plays and some 80 motion pictures.

Rankin, Nell, American mezzo-soprano; b. Montgomery, Ala., Jan. 3, 1926. She studied voice with Jeanne Lorraine at the Birmingham Cons. of Music; in 1945 went to N.Y., where she continued her vocal training with Karin Branzell (1945–49). She then traveled to Europe, and in 1950 made her operatic debut as Ortrud in *Lohengrin* at the Zürich State Opera, of which she later became an active member; in 1950–51 she sang at the Basel State Opera,

and in 1951 appeared at La Scala, Milan. In 1951 she won the Metropolitan Opera Audition and made her operatic debut there on Nov. 22, 1951, as Amneris; she then sang at Covent Garden in London (1953–54) and at the San Francisco Opera, on Sept. 27, 1955. Subsequently she appeared at the Teatro Colón in Buenos Aires and in many other opera houses, in Mexico, in Naples, and in Vienna. Her best roles are Carmen, Azucena, Ortrud, Santuzza, and Maddalena.

Rankl, Karl, Austrian conductor and composer; b. Gaaden, near Vienna, Oct. 1, 1898; d. Salzburg, Sept. 6, 1968. He was a pupil of Schoenberg and Anton von Webern in Vienna; from them he acquired a fine understanding of the problems of modern music. He occupied various positions as a chorus master and an opera coach in Vienna; served as assistant to Klemperer at the Kroll Opera House in Berlin (1928–31); then conducted opera in Graz (1932–37) and at the German Theater in Prague (1937–39). At the outbreak of war he went to England; was music director consecutively at Covent Garden Opera (1946–51), of the Scottish National Orch. in Glasgow (1952–57), and of the Elizabethan Opera Co. in Sydney, Australia; eventually returned to Austria. He composed an opera, *Deirdre of the Sorrows,* which received a prize at the Festival of Britain in 1951; other works include 8 symphs., an oratorio, *Der Mensch;* and many other choral works.

BIBLIOGRAPHY: Donald Brook, *International Gallery of Conductors* (London, 1951; pp. 140–44).

Ranta, Sulho, eminent Finnish composer and writer on music; b. Peräseinäjoki, Aug. 15, 1901; d. Helsinki, May 5, 1960. He studied at the Helsinki Cons. with Melartin, and later in Germany, France, and Italy. Returning to Finland, he taught at the Sibelius Academy in Helsinki (1934–56); was also active as a music critic. He was editor of a comprehensive biographical dictionary of 90 Finnish composers, *Suomen Säveltäjiä* (Helsinki, 1945), and of a general biographical survey of performers, *Sävelten Taitureita* (Helsinki, 1947).

WORKS: 4 symphs.: *Sinfonia programmatica* (1929–31); *Sinfonia piccola* (1931–32); *Sinfonia semplice* (1936); *Sinfonia dell'arte* (1947); *Oratorio volgare* for Solo Voices, Chorus, and Orch. (1951); *Tuntematon maa* (*The Unknown Land*) for Piano and Orch. (1930); Concertino No. 1 for Piano and Strings (1932); *Kainuun kuvia* (*Images boréales*), suite for Orch. (1933); Concertino No. 2 for Flute, Harp, Viola, and Strings (1934); Concerto for Orch. (1938); *Kansansatu* (*Folk Story*), symph. variations (1940); *Sydärnen tie* (*The Way of the Heart*), cantata (1945–46); *Eksyneitten legioonalaisten rukous* (*Prayer of the Lost Legionnaires*) for 8 Soloists, Chorus, and Orch. (1956); Piano Trio (1923); *Suite symphonique* for Flute, Clarinet, Horn, String Quartet, and Piano (1926–28); Concertino for String Quartet (1935); piano pieces.

Rapee, Erno, conductor; b. Budapest, June 4, 1891; d. New York, June 26, 1945. He studied piano with

Emil Sauer at the National Academy in Budapest; gave concerts as a pianist; appeared as a conductor with various European orchs.; in 1912 came to America as an accompanist; in 1913 was engaged as music director of the Hungarian Opera Co. in N.Y.; then became conductor for S.L. Rothafel (Roxy) at his motion picture theaters in N.Y.; after several years at the Roxy Theater (1926–31) he became music director of the NBC Symph. Orch.; then at Radio City Music Hall, again under Rothafel's management. He introduced classical works into his prograrms, mostly in the form of potpourris, but upon occasion also in full version; brought out a collection of music to accompany silent movies, *Motion Picture Moods for Pianists and Organists, Adapted to 52 Moods and Situations* (N.Y., 1924; reprint, 1974), containing pieces of light music by famous and obscure composers depicting the emotions and excitements of joy, melancholy, passion, frustration, and also typical movie scenes, such as love-making within permissible limits (kisses not to exceed 7 seconds in duration), costumed bacchanalia, fights to the death, etc.

Rapf, Kurt, Austrian composer; b. Vienna, Feb. 15, 1922. He studied piano, organ, and composition at the Vienna Academy of Music (1936–42). In 1945 he formed a chamber music ensemble, Collegium Musicum Wien, and conducted it until 1956. From 1953 to 1960 he served as city music director in Innsbruck; in 1970 he became president of the Austrian Composers' Union. He wrote mostly instrumental music in an approved neo-Baroque idiom. WORKS: *4 Impressions* for 9 Players (1966); *6 Pieces* for Wind Quintet (1963); Quintet for Harp and 4 Wind Instruments (1968); *Aphorismen* for Orch. (1968); Violin Concerto (1971); *Toccata, Adagio and Finale* for Organ (1972); choruses; piano pieces.

Raphael, Günther, German composer; b. Berlin, April 30, 1903; d. Herford, Oct. 19, 1960. He was the son of the organist **Georg Raphael;** studied in Berlin with Max Trapp (piano), Walter Fischer (organ), and Robert Kahn (composition). He then taught at the Leipzig Cons. (1926–34). Suspected of fractional Jewish ancestry, he was deprived of the right to teach by the Nazi regime, and went to Sweden. After the war he taught at Laubach (1945–48), at the Duisburg Cons. (1949–53), and at the Mainz Cons. (1956–58); finally was a prof. at the Hochschule für Musik in Cologne from 1957 until his death. WORKS: 5 symphs. (1926, 1932, 1942, 1947, 1953); 2 violin concertos (1928, 1960); *Symphonic Fantasy* for Violin and Orch. (1940); Concertino for Saxophone and Orch. (1951); Concertino for Flute and Orch. (1956); *Zoologica,* character study for Orch. (1958); numerous pieces of chamber music. BIBLIOGRAPHY: *In memoriam Günther Raphael* (Wiesbaden, 1961).

Raphling, Sam, American composer; b. Fort Worth, Texas, March 19, 1910. He studied piano in Chicago and, as an exchange fellowship student, in Germany. Returning to the U.S., he was active in Chicago as a teacher and pianist; publ. a number of compositions in various genres: *Abraham Lincoln Walks at Midnight* for Orch.; *Cowboy Rhapsody* for Violin and Orch.; *American Album* for 2 Pianos (1946); Sonatina for 2 Clarinets (1948); *Prelude and Toccata* for Trumpet and Trombone (1949); *Lyric Prelude* for Trombone and Piano (1950); *Dance Suite* for 2 Trumpets (1950); *Variations* for 2 Flutes Unaccompanied (1955; also for Flute and Clarinet); Sonatina for 2 Trombones (1955; also for 2 Bassoons); *Sonata, Variations, Introduction and Workout* for French Horn Unaccompanied (1955); *Nocturnal Prelude* for Piano (1955); *Duograms* for 2 Oboes (1955); Trio for 3 Oboes (1955); *Pastorale* for Oboe and Piano (1955); operas; symphs.; concertos; etc.

Rappold, Marie (née **Winterroth**), English dramatic soprano; b. London, of German parents, c.1873; d. North Hollywood, Calif., May 12, 1957. The family moved to America when she was a child. She studied with Oscar Saenger in N.Y.; made her opera debut at the Metropolitan Opera on Nov. 22, 1905; remained on its roster until 1909; then went to Europe. She was married to Dr. Julius Rappold, but divorced him and married the tenor **Rudolf Berger.** She had another period of singing at the Metropolitan Opera (1910–20); then settled in Los Angeles as a singer.

Rappoldi, Eduard, Austrian violinist and composer; b. Vienna, Feb. 21, 1831; d. Dresden, May 16, 1903. He studied at the Vienna Cons.; then played violin in opera orchs. in Vienna and Rotterdam; conducted opera in Lübeck and Prague; was 2nd violinist in the Joachim Quartet in Berlin (1871–77); concertmaster of the Court Opera in Dresden (1878–98); from 1893 till his death, a prof. of violin at the Dresden Cons. He publ. 2 violin sonatas; chamber music; piano pieces; songs. His wife, **Laura Rappoldi-Kahrer** (b. Mistelbach, near Vienna, Jan. 14, 1853; d. Dresden, Aug. 2, 1925), was an excellent pianist, a pupil of Liszt; from 1890 taught piano at the Dresden Cons.

Rasbach, Oscar, American composer; b. Dayton, Ky., Aug. 2, 1888; d. Pasadena, Calif., March 24, 1975. He studied academic subjects in Los Angeles; music with Ludwig Thomas, Julius Jahn, José Anderson, and A.J. Stamm. He was first engaged in business; then went to Vienna, where he took piano lessons with Leschetizky and studied theory with Hans Thornton. He returned to the U.S. in 1911 and settled in San Marino, Calif. He wrote 2 operettas, *Dawn Boy* and *Open House,* and a number of songs, of which *Trees,* to Joyce Kilmer's dendrological poem, became enormously popular.

Rascher, Sigurd M., German-American saxophone virtuoso; b. Elberfeld, May 15, 1907. He studied at the Stuttgart Cons., and became proficient on the saxophone. In 1939 he went to the U.S., where he developed a fine concert career playing works written especially for him by celebrated composers, among them Jacques Ibert, Frank Martin, and (most important) Glazunov, who composed a Saxophone Concerto for him in 1934.

Raselius (Rasel), Andreas, German composer and theorist; b. Hahnbach, near Amberg, c.1563; d. Heidelberg, Jan. 6, 1602. He was the son of a Lutheran preacher; from 1581 to 1583 studied at Heidelberg Univ.; then became a teacher at the Heidelberg Academy; subsequently was appointed cantor at the Gymnasium in Regensburg (1584); remained there till 1600, when he returned to Heidelberg as Hofkapellmeister to the Elector Palatine Frederick IV. In 1589 he publ. a music instruction book, *Hexachordum seu Quaestiones musicae practicae.* Other publ. works: *Teutsche Sprüche* (2 vols.: *a* 5, 1594; *a* 5–9, 1595); *Regensburgischer Kirchenkontrapunkt* (5-voiced Lutheran chorales; 1599); in MS: motets and Magnificats. A selection of his Latin and German motets was ed. by L. Roselius in Denkmäler der Tonkunst in Bayern, 36 (29/30).
BIBLIOGRAPHY: J. Auer, *A. Raselius* (1892); L. Roselius, *A. Raselius als Motettenkomponist* (Berlin, 1924).

Raskin, Judith, noted American soprano; b. New York, June 21, 1928. She studied at Smith College, graduating in 1949; took private voice lessons with Anna Hamlin in N.Y. Her stage career received an impetus on July 7, 1956, when she sang the title role in Douglas Moore's folk opera *The Ballad of Baby Doe,* produced at Central City, Colorado. In 1957 she became a member of the NBC-TV Opera; in 1959 joined the N.Y. City Opera. She made her Metropolitan Opera debut in N.Y. on Feb. 23, 1962, as Susanna in *Le nozze di Figaro.* In 1975 she was appointed to the faculty of the Manhattan School of Music.

Rasmussen, Karl Aage, Danish composer; b. Kolding, Dec. 13, 1947. He studied composition with Norgaard and Gudmundsen-Holmgreen at the Aarhus Cons., graduating in 1970. In 1972 he was appointed editor of the weekly program "Resonance" at Danish Radio. His music follows the cosmopolitan trends of pragmatic hedonism within neo-Classical formal structures.
WORKS: *Jefta,* opera for 9 Singers, 7 Musicians, and Tape (1976); *Crapp's Last Tape,* radio opera after Beckett, for Baritone, Solo Instruments, and Chamber Orch. (Aarhus, Nov, 1, 1968); *Canto serioso* for String Quartet (1965); *Mass* for Chorus, Solo Horn, and Bell Chimes (1966); *This Moment* for 3 Sopranos, Flute, and Percussion (1966); *Coralis Constantinus* for Chamber Orch. (1967); *Symphony for Young Lovers,* 6 movements for Orch. (1967); *Repriser—Fristelser og eventyr (Recapitulations—Temptations and Fairy Tales)* for Orch. (1968); *Symphonie classique* for Chamber Orch. (1969); *Afskrift (Transcript)* for Flute, Violin, Viola, Cello, and Piano (1971); *Protokol og Myte* for Accordion, Electric Guitar, and Percussion (1971); *Als kind (As a Child)* for String Quartet (1972); *Music* for Solo Accordion (1972); *Genklang (Echo)* for Piano, 4-hands, Prepared Piano, Mistuned ("honky-tonk")

Piano, and Celesta (1972); *Anfang und Ende (Beginning and End)* for Orch. (1970–73; Aarhus, Feb. 11, 1976); *Love Is in the World* for Soprano, Guitar, and Percussion (1974); *Lullaby* for Flute and Piano (1976); *Berio-Mask,* palimpsest for Chamber Ensemble (1977); *Le Tombeau de Père Igor* for Clarinet, Cello, and Piano (1977); *Vladimir Mayakovsky,* "Konzertstück" for a stage performance (1977); *Schein,* polyphony for Orch. (1977).

Rasse, François, Belgian composer; b. Helchin, near Ath, Jan. 27, 1873; d. Brussels, Jan. 4, 1955. He studied violin with Eugène Ysaÿe at the Brussels Cons., winning the Belgian Grand Prix de Rome in 1899; from 1925 to 1938 was director of the Liège Cons.
WORKS: Operas: *Déidamia* (1905) and *Sœur Béatrice* (1938); ballet, *Le Maître à danser* (1908); for Orch.: *Symphonie romantique* (1901); *Symphonie mélodique* (1903); *Symphonie rythmique* (1908); tone poems: *Douleur* (1911); *Joie* (1925); *Aspiration* (1946); Violin Concerto (1906); *La Dryade* for Clarinet and Orch. (1943); *Lamento* for Cello and Orch. (1952); 2 string quartets (1906, 1950); Piano Quartet (1941); numerous piano pieces; choral works; songs. A catalogue of his works was publ., with a biographical sketch, by the Centre Belge de Documentation Musicale (1954).

Rastrelli, Joseph, German composer and conductor; b. Dresden, April 13, 1799; d. there, Nov. 15, 1842. He was a pupil of his father, the Italian musician Vincenzo Rastrelli (1760–1839); then studied with Mattei in Bologna. In 1830 he was appointed court conductor in Dresden; was Wagner's predecessor in this post. His opera, *Salvator Rosa, oder Zwey Nächte in Rom* (Dresden, July 22, 1832), was the first new German opera produced in Dresden after the disbanding of the Italian Opera Co. there.

Rasumovsky. See **Razumovsky.**

Ratez, Emile-Pierre, French composer; b. Besançon, Nov. 5, 1851; d. Lille, May 19, 1934. He studied at the Paris Cons. with Bazin and Massenet (1872–81); played the viola in the orch. of the Opéra-Comique; in 1891 was appointed director of the Lille branch of the Paris Cons.; also conducted popular concerts there (1893–1906). He wrote the operas *Lydéric* (Lille, 1895) and *Paula* (Besançon, 1904); a ballet, *La Guivre* (Paris, 1925); a cantata, *Scènes héroïques* (1899); chamber music; publ. *Traité élémentaire de contrepoint et de fugue* and *Traité d'harmonie théorique et pratique.*

Rath, Felix vom, German composer; b. Cologne, June 17, 1866; d. Munich, Aug. 25, 1905. He studied piano with Reinecke in Leipzig and composition with Thuille in Munich, where he settled. A composer of more than ordinary abilities, he publ. a Piano Concerto, a Piano Quartet, a Violin Sonata, and a number of piano pieces.

Rathaus, Karol, Polish-American composer; b. Tarnopol, Sept. 16, 1895; d. New York, Nov. 21, 1954. He studied composition at the Vienna Academy of Music (1913–19, 1919–21; Ph.D., 1922) and in Berlin (1920–21, 1922–23); in 1932 went to Paris, and in 1934 to London. In 1938 he settled in the U.S., becoming an American citizen in 1946. After a brief stay in Hollywood in 1939, during which he wrote some film scores, he settled in N.Y.; in 1940 he was appointed to the faculty of Queens College. He was highly respected as a teacher of composition. His own music, however, never attracted large audiences; always noble in purpose and design and masterly in technique, it reveals a profound feeling for European neo-Romanticism.

WORKS: FOR THE STAGE: Opera, *Fremde Erde* (Berlin, Dec. 10, 1930; a symph. interlude is publ. separately and was revised in 1950); 2 ballets: *Der letzte Pierrot* (1926; Berlin, May 7, 1927) and *Le Lion amoureux* (London, 1937). FOR ORCH.: 3 symphs. (1921–22, 1923, 1942–43); *4 Dance Pieces* (1924); Piano Concertino (1925); *Overture* (1927); Suite for Violin, and Chamber Orch. or Piano (1929); *Uriel Acosta,* incidental music (1930; as an orch. suite, 1933; revised 1947); Suite (Liège Festival of the International Society for Contemporary Music, Sept. 6, 1930); *Allegro concertante* for Strings and Trumpet Obbligato (1930); Serenade (1932); *Symphonic Movement* (1933); *Contrapuntal Triptych* (1934); *Jacob's Dream,* a nocturne (1938; posthumous, Liverpool, 1961); Piano Concerto (1939; Berkeley, Calif., Festival of the International Society for Contemporary Music, Aug. 1, 1942); *Prelude and Gigue* (1939); *Music for Strings* (1941); *Polonaise symphonique* (1943; N.Y., Feb. 26, 1944); *Vision dramatique* (1945; Tel Aviv, April 4, 1948); *Salisbury Cove Overture* (1949); *Sinfonia concertante* (1950–51); *Intermezzo giocoso* for Woodwinds, Brass, and Percussion (1950–51; separate work from *Sinfonia concertante*); *Prelude* (1953; Louisville, Ky., June 5, 1954). FOR VOICE: *Song without Words* and *Fugue,* both for Chorus and Chamber Orch. (1928); *3 Calderon Songs* for Low Voice, and Orch. or Piano (1931); *XXIII Psalm* for Tenor, Women's Chorus, and Orch. or Piano (1945); *O Juvenes,* academic cantata (1947); *Lament from "Iphigenia in Aulis" by Euripides* for Chorus and Horn (1947); *Diapason,* after Dryden and Milton, for Baritone, Chorus, and Orch. (1950); a cappella choruses; songs. In 1952 he revised and edited the orch. score to Mussorgsky's *Boris Godunov* on a commission from the Metropolitan Opera, which gave the new version on March 6, 1953. CHAMBER MUSIC: 5 string quartets (1921, 1925, 1936, 1946, 1954); 2 violin sonatas (1924, 1938); Clarinet Sonata (1927); *Little Serenade* for Clarinet, Bassoon, Trumpet, Horn, and Piano (1927); Trio for Violin, Clarinet, and Piano (1944); Piano Quintet (1948; unfinished); *Dedication and Allegro* for Violin and Piano (1949); *Rapsodia notturna* for Viola or Cello, and Piano (1950); *Trio Serenade* for Piano Trio (1953); *Divertimento* for 10 Woodwinds (1954; unfinished). FOR PIANO: 4 sonatas (1920; 1920–24, revised 1928; 1927; 1946); numerous pieces. FOR ORGAN: *Prelude and Toccata* (1933). MUSIC FOR FILMS: 17 scores, including those for *The Brothers*

Karamazov (1931), *The Dictator* (1934), *Dame de pique* (1937), *Let Us Live* (1939), and *Out of Evil* (1950).

BIBLIOGRAPHY: Boris Schwarz, "Karol Rathaus," *Musical Quarterly* (Oct. 1955).

Rathburn, Eldon, Canadian composer; b. Queenstown, New Brunswick, April 21, 1916. He studied composition with Willan, organ with Peaker, and piano with Godden at the Royal Cons. in Toronto; in 1947 was appointed a staff composer with the National Film Board of Canada and supplied musical scores for many notable documentaries, including *The Romance of Transportation* (1952), *City of Gold* (1957), and *Labyrinth* (1967); in 1972 became an instructor at the Univ. of Ottawa. His music is extremely amiable, aiming to please everybody.

WORKS: *Symphonette* (1943; revised 1946); 2 *Cartoons* for Orch. (1944, 1946); *Images of Childhood* for Orch. (1949–50); *Overture to a Hoss Opera* (1952); *Nocturne* for Piano and Small Orch. (1953); *Overture burlesca* (1953); *Milk Maid Polka* for Orch. (1956); *Gray City* for Orch. (1960); *City of Gold,* suite for Orch. from music to the film (1967); *Aspects of Railroads* for Orch. (1969); *3 Ironies* for Solo Brass Quintet and Orch. (Hamilton, Ontario, Oct. 15, 1975); *Steelhenge,* concerto for Steel Band and Orch. (1975); *5 Short Pieces* for differing combinations of Winds, each piece having a separate title (1949–56); *Bout* in 3 rounds, for Guitar and Double Bass (1971); *The Metamorphic 10* for Accordion, Mandolin, Banjo, Guitar, Double Bass, Harp, Piano, Celesta, and 3 Percussionists (1971); 2 *Interplays* for Saxophone Quartet (1972); *Rhythmette* for 2 Pianos and Rhythm Band (1973); *The Nomadic 5,* brass quintet (1974); *Silhouette* for 2 Pianos (1936); *Black and White* for Piano (1970); songs.

Rațiu, Adrian, Rumanian composer; b. Bucharest, July 28, 1928. He studied with Paul Constantinescu, Negrea, and Rogalski at the Bucharest Cons. (1950–56); attended the summer courses in new music at Darmstadt (1969). He was editor of the Rumanian music journal *Muzica* (1959–63); in 1962 was appointed to the staff of the Bucharest Cons. His music is pleasantly atonal and euphoniously dissonant.

WORKS: Symph. No. 1 (1956; revised 1961); Concerto for Oboe, Bassoon, and String Orch. (1963); *Diptych* for Orch. (1965); *Studi* for Strings (1968); 6 *Images* for Cello and Orch. (1971); *Poem* for Cello and Orch. (1972); Piano Concerto (1973); *Oda păcii (Ode to Peace),* cantata (1959); String Quartet (1956); *Viziune nocturnă* for Viola and Piano (1964); *Partita* for Wind Quintet (1966); *Concertino per la "Musica Nova"* for Clarinet, Violin, Viola, Cello, and Piano (1967; Musica Nova is a Rumanian chamber ensemble); *Impresii* for Chamber Ensemble (1969); *Diaphonie* for 2 Flutes (1972); *Improvisation* for Oboe and Piano (1972); *Sonata a 5* for 2 Trumpets, Horn, Trombone, and Tuba (1973); *Monosonata I* and *II* for Piano (1968, 1969); *Constelațuii (Constellations)* for Piano (1970); choruses; songs.

Ratner, Leonard Gilbert, American musicologist

and composer; b. Minneapolis, July 30, 1916. He studied composition with Arnold Schoenberg at the Univ. of Calif., Los Angeles, and musicology with Manfred Bukofzer and Albert Elkus at Berkeley (Ph.D., 1947). He also had composition lessons with Ernest Bloch and Frederick Jacobi. In 1947 he was appointed to the staff of Stanford Univ.; held a Guggenheim fellowship in 1962–63.

WORKS: Chamber opera, *The Necklace;* Symph.; overture, *Harlequin;* 2 string quartets; Violin Sonata; Cello Sonata; Piano Sonata; etc.

WRITINGS: *Music: The Listener's Art* (N.Y., 1957); *Harmony: Structure and Style* (N.Y., 1962); *Classic Music: Expression, Form, and Style* (N.Y., 1979).

Rattenbach, Augusto, Argentinian composer; b. Buenos Aires, Feb. 5, 1927. After a study of elementary music theory in Argentina, he went to Hamburg, where he learned modern techniques. Most of his mature compositions are in a serial idiom, with the formative elements determined in advance.

WORKS: Piano Concerto (1956); *Passacaglia* (1957); Wind Quintet (1957); ballet, *Un episodio vulgar* (1961); *Serenata* for Flute, Clarinet, Trumpet, and Cello (1962); *Obstinaciones* for Orch. (1965); a series of *Microvariaciones* for various Ensembles.

Rattle, Simon, brilliant English conductor; b. Liverpool, Jan. 19, 1955. He studied piano and also played percussion with the Royal Liverpool Phil. He took lessons in conducting with Pierre Boulez; he was 16 when he won a scholarship to the Royal Academy of Music in London, and launched a remarkably youthful career when, in 1974, he won first prize in the International Conductor's Competition; was then named assistant conductor of the Bournemouth Symph. In 1976 he made his first appearance in America during the tour of the London Symph. Orch. In 1977 he became associate conductor of the Royal Liverpool Phil. and assistant conductor of the BBC Scottish Symph. He made his first appearance with an American orch. conducting the Los Angeles Phil. in 1979; also in 1979 was named principal conductor of the London Choral Society. In 1980 he became principal conductor and artistic adviser of the City of Birmingham Symph. Orch.; in 1981 was appointed (with Michael Tilson Thomas) principal guest conductor of the Los Angeles Phil. Orch. His last name inspired jokes among orch. players, but this handicap (if it was a handicap) soon turned to his advantage, as did his tousled hair and youthful vim.

Ratzenberger, Theodor, German pianist; b. Grossbreitenbach, April 14, 1840; d. Wiesbaden, March 8, 1879. He was a pupil of Liszt (piano) and Cornelius (composition); publ. some salon pieces for piano.

Rauchenecker, Georg Wilhelm, German violinist and composer; b. Munich, March 8, 1844; d. Elberfeld, July 17, 1906. He studied violin with Joseph Walter; filled various posts as a theater violinist in France; then lived in Switzerland. In 1889 he established a music school in Elberfeld, and conducted an orch. society there until his death.

WORKS: Operas (all produced in Elberfeld): *Die letzten Tage von Thule* (1889); *Ingo* (1893); *Don Quixote* (1897); *Sanna* (1898); *Zlatorog* (1903); *Der Florentiner* (posthumous; Strasbourg, 1910); Symph.; *Orientalische Fantasie* for Solo Violin, with String Quintet; 6 string quartets; String Sextet; Octet for Woodwind Instruments.

Raudenbush, George King, American violinist and conductor; b. Jersey Shore, Pa., March 13, 1899; d. San Diego, Calif., May 26, 1956. He studied in Detroit and in Boston, where he was a pupil of Chadwick; made his debut as a violinist in N.Y., in 1921; then played the violin in the N.Y. Symph. Orch.; in 1929 he founded the Harrisburg Symph. Orch. and conducted it until 1950.

Raugel, Félix, French musicologist; b. St.-Quentin, Nov. 27, 1881; d. Paris, Dec. 30, 1975. While attending the Lycée at Lille he studied music with C. Queste and F. Lecocq; continued his studies in 1900 in Paris with H. Libert and at the Schola Cantorum with Vincent d'Indy. Together with E. Borrel he founded in 1908 the Société Haendel for the cultivation of early music.

WRITINGS: *Les Orgues de l'abbaye de St. Mihiel* (1919); *Recherches sur quelques maîtres de l'ancienne facture d'orgues française; Le Cantique français* (Tourcoing, 1920); *Les Organistes* (1923); *Les Grandes Orgues des églises de Paris et du département de la Seine* (1927); *Palestrina* (1930); *Les Grandes Orgues de Notre Dame* (1934); *Le Chant choral* (1948); *L'Oratorio* (1948); ed. organ works of Handel, Scarlatti, Buxtehude, etc.

Rautavaara, Einojuhani, Finnish composer; b. Helsinki, Oct. 9, 1928. He studied composition with Merikanto at the Sibelius Academy in Helsinki (1948–54); in N.Y. and at Tanglewood with Copland, Persichetti, and Sessions (1955–56); in Switzerland for dodecaphonic studies with Vogel (1957); and in Cologne with Rudolf Petzold (1958). In 1966 he was appointed to the faculty of the Sibelius Academy in Helsinki. He adopted in his works an eclectic modern idiom, with occasional dodecaphonic excursions. In 1975 he began a series of chamber operas based on the *Kalevala,* the Finnish national epic.

WORKS: FOR THE STAGE: Opera, *Kaivos (The Mine;* 1958–61; Finnish Television, 1963); ballet, *Kiusaukset (The Temptations;* 1969; Helsinki, Feb. 8, 1973); comic opera, *Apollo contra Marsyas* (1970; Helsinki, Aug. 30, 1973); *Runo 42, "Sammon ryosto,"* opera (1974–81); *Marjatta matala neita,* mystery play in one act (1975); *Late One Night,* opera (1975–76). VOCAL WORKS: *Die Liebenden (The Lovers)* for Voice and Orch. (1959); *Itsenäisyys-kantaatti (Independence Cantata;* 1967); *Daughter of the Sea* for Soprano, Chorus, and Orch. (Helsinki, Dec. 4, 1971); *Vigilia (The Mass)* for Soloists and Chorus (1971); *True and False Unicorn* for Chorus, Tape, and Chamber Ensemble (1971); *The Water Circle* for Chorus, Piano, and Orch. (Copenhagen, Dec. 4, 1972). FOR ORCH.: 4 symphs. (1956, 1957, 1961, 1964–70); *Arabescata* (1963); *Anadyomene* (1968); *Sotilasmessu (Soldier's Mass)* for Winds and Percussion (1968); Cello Concerto (1968); Piano Concerto (1969); *Dithyrambos* for Violin and Orch. (1970); *Regular Sets of Elements in a Semiregular Situation* for 3 Flutes, 3 Horns, Trumpet, Percussion, Piano, 4 Violins, and 4 Cellos (1971); *Cantus Arcticus,* concerto for Birds (on tape) and Orch. (Oulu, May 26, 1972); *A Portrait of the Artist at a Certain Moment* for Strings (Jyvskyla, May 28, 1972); Flute Concerto (1973); *Ballad* for Harp and Strings (1973); *Annunciations,* concerto for Organ, Brass Quintet, and Symph. Wind Orch. (1976–77); Violin Concerto (1977); *Angels and Visitations* (1978); *Angel of Dusk,* concerto for Double Bass (1980); *Hommage* for Strings (1982). CHAMBER MUSIC: 4 string quartets (1952, 1958, 1965, 1975); *A Requiem in Our Time* for 13 Brasses and Percussion (1953); *2 Preludes and Fugues* for Cello and Piano (1955); Wind Octet (1964); Quartet for Oboe and String Trio (1965); Bassoon Sonata (1965–68); *Sonetto* for Clarinet and Piano (1969); Solo Cello Sonata (1969); *Music* for Upright Piano and Amplified Cello (1976); *Playgrounds for Angels* for 10 Brasses (1981). PIANO MUSIC: *Pelimannit (The Fiddlers),* suite (1952); *Ikonit (Icons),* suite (1956); *Partita* (1958); *Etudes* (1969); 2 sonatas: No. 1, *Christus und die Fischer* (1969), and No. 2, *The Fire Sermon* (1970); *Toccata* for Organ (1971); solo songs.

Rautio, Matti, Finnish composer; b. Helsinki, Feb. 25, 1922. He studied composition and piano at the Sibelius Academy in Helsinki; from 1966 until 1970 was director of the school music dept. of the Sibelius Academy; then became a lecturer on music theory there. In his works he follows a median line of modern music, programmatic and utilitarian in the use of advanced techniques.
    WORKS: *Divertimento 1* for Cello, and Orch. or Piano (1955); *Sininen haikara (The Blue Heron),* suite from the ballet (1957); *Tanhumusiikkia (Folk Dance Music)* for Soprano, Baritone, Chorus, and Orch. (1960); Piano Concerto (1968–71); *Divertimento 2* for Cello and Piano (1972).

Ravanello, Oreste, Italian composer; b. Venice, Aug. 25, 1871; d. Padua, July 2, 1938. He studied with Agostini and Girardi in Venice; in 1893 became an organist at San Marco; in 1898 was appointed maestro di cappella at San Antonio in Padua; in 1914 became director of the Istituto Musicale. He composed about 30 masses; numerous pieces for organ; publ. several useful guides for organ playing, among them *Cento studi ed esercizi per il organo.*
    BIBLIOGRAPHY: A. Garbelotto and M. Cicogna, *Oreste Ravanello* (Padua, 1939).

Ravasenga, Carlo, Italian composer; b. Turin, Dec. 17, 1891; d. Rome, May 6, 1964. He studied violin, piano, and composition in Turin; then became active as a teacher and music editor. He wrote the operas *Una tragedia fiorentina,* after Oscar Wilde

(Turin, 1916), and *Il giudizio di Don Giovanni* (1916); orch. suite, *Un giorno di festa* (1916); symph. suite, *Giuditta e Oloferno; Variazioni pittoresche* for String Quartet; *Contrasto burlesco-sentimentale* for Piano; Violin Sonata; Piano Sonata.

Ravel, Maurice (Christian names, **Joseph Maurice**), great French composer; b. Ciboure, Basses-Pyrénées, March 7, 1875; d. Paris, Dec. 28, 1937. His father was a Swiss engineer, and his mother of Basque origin. The family moved to Paris when he was an infant. He began to study piano at the age of 7 with Henri Ghis and harmony at 12 with Charles-René. In 1889 he entered the Paris Cons.; studied piano with Anthiome; won first medal in 1891, and passed to the advanced class of Charles de Bériot; studied harmony with Emile Pessard. While still a student he wrote and publ. a *Menuet antique* for Piano and *Habanera* for 2 Pianos (later included in the *Rapsodie espagnole* for Orch.); these pieces, written at the age of 20, already reveal great originality in the treatment of old modes and of Spanish motifs; however, he continued to study; in 1897 he entered the class of Gabriel Fauré (composition) and Gédalge (counterpoint and fugue); his well-known *Pavane pour une infante défunte* for Piano was written during that time (1899). On May 27, 1899, he appeared in public as a conductor, in a performance of his overture *Shéhérazade* with the Société Nationale in Paris; some elements of the work were incorporated in Ravel's song cycle of the same title (1903). In 1901 he won the 2nd Prix de Rome with the cantata *Myrrha;* but ensuing attempts to win the Grand Prix de Rome were unsuccessful; at his last try (1905) he was eliminated in the preliminaries, and so was not allowed to compete; the age limit then set an end to his further effort to enter. Since 6 prizes all went to pupils of Lenepveu, suspicion of unfair discrimination was aroused; Jean Marnold publ. an article, "Le Scandale du Prix de Rome," in the *Mercure de France* (June 1905) in which he brought the controversy into the open; this precipitated a crisis at the Paris Cons.; its director, Théodore Dubois, resigned, and Gabriel Fauré took his place. By that time, Ravel had written a number of his most famous compositions, and was regarded by most French critics as a talented disciple of Debussy. No doubt Ravel's method of poetic association of musical ideas paralleled that of Debussy; his employment of unresolved dissonances and the enhancement of the diatonic style into pandiatonicism were techniques common to Debussy and his followers; but there were important differences: whereas Debussy adopted the scale of whole tones as an integral part of his musical vocabulary, Ravel resorted to it only occasionally; similarly, augmented triads appear much less frequently in Ravel's music than in Debussy's; in his writing for piano Ravel actually anticipated some of Debussy's usages; in a letter addressed to Pierre Lalo and publ. in *Le Temps* (April 9, 1907) Ravel pointed out that at the time of the publication of his piano piece *Jeux d'eau* (1902) Debussy had brought out only his suite *Pour le piano,* which had contained little that was novel. In Paris, elsewhere in France, and soon in England and other European countries, Ravel's name became well known, but for many years he was still regarded as an ultramodernist. A curious test of audience appreciation was a "Concert des Auteurs Anonymes" presented by the Société Indépendante de Musique on May 9, 1911; the program included Ravel's *Valses nobles et sentimentales,* a set of piano pieces in the manner of Schubert; yet Ravel was recognized as the author. Inspired evocation of the past was but one aspect of Ravel's creative genius; in this style are written the *Pavane pour une infante défunte, Le Tombeau de Couperin,* and *La Valse;* luxuriance of exotic colors marks his ballet *Daphnis et Chloé,* his opera *L'Heure espagnole,* the song cycles *Shéhérazade* and *Chansons madécasses,* and his virtuoso pieces for Piano *Miroirs* and *Gaspard de la nuit;* other works are deliberately austere, even ascetic, in their pointed classicism: the piano concertos, the Piano Sonatina, and some of his songs with piano accompaniment. His association with Diaghilev's Ballets Russes was most fruitful; for Diaghilev he wrote one of his masterpieces, *Daphnis et Chloé;* another ballet, *Boléro,* commissioned by Ida Rubinstein and performed at her dance recital at the Paris Opéra on Nov. 22, 1928, became Ravel's most spectacular success as an orch. piece.

Ravel never married, and lived a life of semi-retirement, devoting most of his time to composition; he accepted virtually no pupils, although he gave friendly advice to Vaughan Williams and to others; he was never on the faculty of any school. As a performer, he was not brilliant; he appeared as a pianist only in his own works, and often accompanied singers in programs of his songs; although he accepted engagements as a conductor, his technique was barely sufficient to secure a perfunctory performance of his music. When the war broke out in 1914, he was rejected for military service because of his frail physique, but he was anxious to serve; his application for air service was denied, but he was received in the ambulance corps at the front; his health gave way, and in the autumn of 1916 he was compelled to enter a hospital for recuperation. In 1922 he visited Amsterdam and Venice, conducting his music; in 1923 he appeared in London; in 1926 he went to Sweden, England, and Scotland; in 1928 he made an American tour as a conductor and pianist; in the same year he received the degree of D.Mus. *honoris causa* at Oxford Univ. In 1929 he was honored at his native town of Ciboure by the inauguration of the Quai Maurice Ravel. Shortly afterward, he began to experience difficulties in muscular coordination, and suffered from attacks of aphasia, symptoms indicative of a cerebral malady; a brain operation was performed on Dec. 19, 1937, but was not successful, and he died 9 days later.

WORKS: FOR THE STAGE: One-act opera, *L'Heure espagnole,* to text by Franc-Nohain (Paris, Opéra-Comique, May 19, 1911; Chicago, Jan. 5, 1920); "fantaisie lyrique," *L'Enfant et les sortilèges,* libretto by Colette (Monte Carlo, March 21, 1925); ballets: *Daphnis et Chloé* (Paris, June 8, 1912); *Adélaide ou*

Le Langage des fleurs, after the *Valses nobles et sentimentales* (Paris, April 22, 1912); *Ma Mère l'Oye,* elaborated from the piano suite (Théâtre des Arts, Paris, Jan. 21, 1912); *Le Tombeau de Couperin,* choreographic poem from the orch. suite (Ballets Suédois, Paris, Nov. 8, 1920); *La Valse* (Paris, Dec. 12, 1920); *Boléro* (Ida Rubinstein's dance recital, Paris, Nov. 22, 1928). FOR ORCH.: Overture, *Shéhérazade* (1898; Paris, May 27, 1899; publ. Paris, 1975); *Pavane pour une infante défunte* (1899; Paris, Dec. 25, 1910); *Alborado del gracioso* (1905; Paris, May 17, 1919); *Rapsodie espagnole* (Paris, March 15, 1908); *Daphnis et Chloé,* 2 suites from the ballet (1909–11); *Ma Mère l'Oye,* after the piano duet (1912); *Le Tombeau de Couperin* (1917; Paris, Feb. 28, 1920); *La Valse* (Paris, Dec. 12, 1920); *Tzigane* for Violin and Orch. (also with Piano Accompaniment; Paris, Dec. 7, 1924); *Boléro* (1928; first American perf., N.Y., Nov. 14, 1929); Piano Concerto in D for Left Hand Alone, written for the one-armed pianist Paul Wittgenstein, who gave its first performance (Vienna, Nov. 27, 1931); Piano Concerto in G (Paris, Jan. 14, 1932; composer conducting; Marguerite Long, pianist). CHAMBER MUSIC: Sonata in one movement for Violin and Piano (1897; publ. Paris, 1975); String Quartet in F (1903); *Introduction et Allegro* for Harp, String Quartet, Flute, and Clarinet (Paris, Feb. 22, 1907); Piano Trio (1914); Sonata for Violin and Cello (1920–22); *Berceuse sur le nom de Fauré* for Violin and Piano (1922); Violin Sonata (1923–27); *Tzigane* for Violin and Piano (London, April 26, 1924; Jelly d'Aranyi, violinist; Ravel at the piano, in a concert of Ravel works). VOCAL WORKS: 3 cantatas, written for the Prix de Rome: *Myrrha, Alcyone,* and *Alysse* (1901–3); *Shéhérazade,* song cycle for Solo Voice and Orch. (Paris, May 17, 1904); *3 poèmes de Mallarmé* for Voice, Piano, 2 Flutes, 2 Clarinets, and String Quartet (1913; Paris, Jan. 14, 1914); *3 chansons* for Mixed Chorus a cappella (1916); *Chansons madécasses* for Voice, Flute, Cello, and Piano (1926); *Don Quichotte à Dulcinée,* 3 songs, with Orch. Accompaniment (Paris, Dec. 1, 1934). Songs: *Ballade de la Reine morte d'aimer* (1894); *Un Grand Sommeil noir* (1895); *Sainte* (1896); *2 épigrammes de Clément Marot* (1896); *Si morne* (1898; publ. Paris, 1975); *Manteau de fleurs* (1903); *Le Noël des jouets,* text by Ravel (1905); *5 mélodies populaires grecques* (1905; another Greek melody was publ. in the *Revue Musicale,* Dec. 1938); *Les Grands Vents venus d'outre-mer* (1906); *Histoires naturelles* (1906); *Sur l'herbe* (1907); *Vocalise en forme d'habanera* (1907); *4 chants populaires* (1910); *2 mélodies hébraïques* (1914); *Ronsard à son âme* (1924); *Rêves* (1927). FOR PIANO: *Sérénade grotesque menuet antique* (1895); *Pavane pour une infante défunte* (1899); *Jeux d'eau* (1901); *Miroirs* (5 pieces): *Noctuelles, Oiseaux tristes, Une Barque sur l'océan, Alborada del Gracioso, La Vallée des cloches* (1905); *Sonatine* (1903–5); *Gaspard de la nuit: Ondine, Le Gibet, Scarbo* (1908); *Menuet sur le nom d'Haydn* (1909); *Valses nobles et sentimentales* (1911); *Prélude* (1913); *A la manière de ... Borodine, Chabrier* (1913); *Le Tombeau de Couperin* (1914–17); *Sites auriculaires* for 2 Pianos (1895–97): *Habanera* and *Entre cloches; Ma Mère l'Oye,* 5 "pièces enfantines" for Piano, 4-hands, written for Christine Verger, age 6, and Germaine Durant, age 10, and performed by them (Paris, April 20, 1910); *Frontispiece* for 2 Pianos, 5-hands (1918). Ravel was commissioned by Koussevitzky to make an orchestration of Mussorgsky's *Pictures at an Exhibition;* it was first performed by Koussevitzky at one of his concerts (Paris, Oct. 19, 1922) and subsequently became one of the most popular orch. suites; Ravel also orchestrated Chabrier's *Menuet pompeux,* arranged Debussy's *Prélude à l'après-midi d'un faune* for 2 Pianos, etc.

BIBLIOGRAPHY: O. Séré, *Musiciens français d'aujourd'hui* (1911); Roland-Manuel, *Maurice Ravel et son œuvre* (1914; revised ed., 1926; in Eng., London, 1941); M.O. Morris, "Maurice Ravel," *Music & Letters* (July 1921); A. Cœuroy, *La Musique française moderne* (1922); E. Vuillermoz, *Musiques d'aujourd'hui* (1923); E.B. Hill, *Modern French Music* (N.Y., 1924); F.H. Shera, *Debussy and Ravel* (London, 1925); special Ravel issue of *Revue Musicale* (April 1925); Cecil Gray, *A Survey of Contemporary Music* (London, 1925); Roland-Manuel, *Ravel et son œuvre dramatique* (1928); M.D. Calvocoressi, *Music and Ballet* (London, 1933); Roland-Manuel, *A la gloire de Ravel* (1938); special Ravel issue of *Revue Musicale* (Dec. 1938); V. Jankélévitch, *Maurice Ravel* (Paris, 1939; 2nd ed., 1956; in Eng., 2nd ed., 1959); R. Wild, ed., *Ravel par quelques-uns de ses familiers* (Paris, 1939); P. Landormy, "Maurice Ravel," *Musical Quarterly* (Oct. 1939); M. Goss, *Bolero: The Life of Maurice Ravel* (N.Y., 1940); M.D. Calvocoressi, "Ravel's Letters to Calvocoressi," *Musical Quarterly* (Jan. 1941); K. Akeret, *Studien zum Klavierwerk von Maurice Ravel* (Zürich, 1941); H. Jourdan-Morhange, *Ravel et nous* (Geneva, 1945); A. Machabey, *Maurice Ravel* (Paris, 1947); N. Demuth, *Ravel* (London, 1947); Roland-Manuel, *Ravel* (Paris, 1948; a new work); W.L. Landowski, *Maurice Ravel, Sa vie, son œuvre* (Paris, 1950); L. La Pegna, *Ravel* (Brescia, 1950); José Bruyr, *Maurice Ravel, ou Le Lyrisme et les sortilèges* (Paris, 1950); W. Tappolet, *Maurice Ravel: Leben und Werk* (Olten, 1950); V. Perlemuter, *Ravel d'après Ravel* (Lausanne, 1953); V. Seroff, *Maurice Ravel* (N.Y., 1953); Marcelle Gerar and René Chalupt, eds., *Ravel au miroir de ses lettres* (Paris, 1956); R. de Fragny, *Maurice Ravel* (Lyons, 1960); R.H. Myers, *Ravel: Life and Works* (London, 1960); H.H. Stuckenschmidt, *Maurice Ravel: Variationen über Person und Werk* (Frankfurt, 1966; in Eng., Philadelphia, 1968); Arbie Orenstein, "L'Enfant et les sortilèges: Correspondence inédit de Ravel et Colette," *Revue de Musicologie,* LII/2 (1966); A. Orenstein, "Maurice Ravel's Creative Process," *Musical Quarterly* (Oct. 1967); R. Petit, *Ravel* (Paris, 1970); A. Orenstein, "Some Unpublished Music and Letters by Maurice Ravel," *Music Forum,* 3 (1973); Arbie Orenstein, *Ravel, Man and Musician* (N.Y., 1975; contains an amplified list of works, including early unpubl. compositions); R. Nichols, *Ravel* (London, 1977); H. MacDonald, "Ravel's Unknown Choruses," *Musical Times* (Dec. 1983).

Ravenscroft, John (Giovanni), English composer; b. London; d. there, c.1708. In 1695 he was in Rome, where he publ. a set of "sonate a trè" under the Italianized name Giovanni Ravenscroft. He apparently was a pupil of Corelli, whose style he imitated. His op. 2, containing 6 sonatas for 2 Violins, with Continuo, was publ. posthumously in London.

BIBLIOGRAPHY: W.S. Newman, "Ravenscroft and Corelli," *Music & Letters* (Oct. 1957).

Ravenscroft, Thomas, English composer and music editor; b. c.1590; d. c.1633. He was a chorister at St. Paul's Cathedral under Edward Pearce; in 1605 received his B.Mus. at Cambridge; from 1618 to 1622 he was music master at Christ's Hospital in London.

WORKS: *Pammelia: Musick's Miscellanie: or Mixed Varietie of Pleasant Roundelayes and Delightful Catches of 3–10 Parts in one* (1609; the first collection of rounds, catches, and canons printed in England; 2nd ed., 1618); *Deuteromelia: or the Second Part of Musick's Melodie* (1609); *Melismata: Musicall Phansies, Fitting the Court, Citie, and Countrey Humours, to 3, 4 and 5 Voyces* (1611); *A Briefe Discourse of the true (but neglected) use of Charact'ring the Degrees by their Perfection, Imperfection, and Diminution in Mensurable Musicke: Harmony of four voyces concerning the pleasure of five usuall recreations, 1. Hunting, 2. Hawking, 3. Dancing, 4. Drinking, 5. Enamouring* (1614); and *The Whole Booke of Psalmes: With the Hymnes Evangelicall and Songs Spirituall Composed into 4 parts by Sundry Authors* (1621; 2nd ed., newly corrected and enlarged, 1633; his best-known and most valuable work, containing numbers by 15 leading British composers, and some by Ravenscroft himself).

Ravina, Jean-Henri, French composer; b. Bordeaux, May 20, 1818; d. Paris, Sept. 30, 1906. He studied at the Paris Cons. with Zimmerman (piano) and Laurent (theory); taught at the Cons. (1834–36); then made a concert tour as pianist in Russia (1858); later traveled in Spain; lived chiefly in Paris. He wrote elegant and attractive salon pieces for piano, which enjoyed considerable vogue, and eventually became part of the piano repertoire: *Nocturne; Douce pensée; Jour de bonheur; Petit boléro; Câlinerie;* also *Etudes de style et de perfectionnement; Etudes harmonieuses;* etc.; a Piano Concerto. He made 4-hand arrangements of all of Beethoven's symphs.

Rawls, Lou (Louis Allen), black American singer of popular music; b. Chicago, Dec. 1, 1936. After serving in the U.S. Army (1956–58), he joined the choral gospel group The Pilgrim Travelers; after the group disbanded in 1959, he launched a career as a nightclub entertainer in Los Angeles. From 1960 on he toured in Europe, Australia, and Japan; also appeared on special television shows and issued many recordings; his record album *Stormy Monday* was a best-seller.

Rawsthorne, Alan, important English composer; b. Haslingden, May 2, 1905; d. Cambridge, July 24, 1971. He went to a dentistry school; did not begin to study music until he was 20, when he entered the Royal Manchester College of Music; later studied piano with Egon Petri in Berlin (1930–31). After returning to England in 1932, he occupied various teaching posts; then devoted himself mainly to composition, and succeeded brilliantly in producing music of agreeable, and to some ears even delectable, music. In 1961 he was made a Commander of the Order of the British Empire. His music is essentially a revival of the contrapuntal style of the past, without much harmonic elaboration; but the rhythms are virile and the melodies fluid, emanating from a focal point of tonality.

WORKS: Ballet, *Madame Chrysanthème* (London, April 1, 1955); Concerto for Clarinet and Strings (1936); *Symphonic Studies* (1938; International Society for Contemporary Music Festival, Warsaw, April 21, 1939); 2 piano concertos: No. 1 (originally for Strings and Percussion, 1939; rescored for Full Orch., 1942; London, 1942) and No. 2 (1951; London, June 17, 1951); 4 overtures: *Street Corner* (1944); *Cortèges*, fantasy overture (1945); *Hallé*, for the centennial of the Hallé Orch. (1958); *Overture for Farnham* (1967); 2 violin concertos: No. 1 (1940; sketches lost in an air raid; reconstructed 1943–48; Cheltenham Festival, July 1, 1948) and No. 2 (London, Oct. 24, 1956); Concerto for Oboe and Strings (1947); Concerto for String Orch. (1949); 3 symphs.: No. 1 (1950; London, Nov. 15, 1950); No. 2, *Pastoral*, with Solo Soprano (1959; Birmingham, Sept. 29, 1959); No. 3 (1964; Cheltenham Festival, July 8, 1964); *Concertante Pastorale* for Flute, Horn, and Strings (1951); *A Canticle of Man*, chamber cantata for Baritone, Chorus, Flute, and Strings (1952); *Practical Cats*, an entertainment for children, after T.S. Eliot, for Narrator and Orch. (Edinburgh, Aug. 26, 1954); *Improvisations on a Theme of Constant Lambert* for Orch. (1960); Concerto for 10 Instruments (1962); *Medieval Diptych* for Baritone and Orch. (1962); *Divertimento* for Chamber Orch. (1962); *Carmen Vitale*, cantata (1963; London, Oct. 16, 1963); *Elegiac Rhapsody* for Strings (1964); Cello Concerto (London, April 6, 1966); *The God in the Cave* for Chorus and Orch. (1967); Concerto for 2 Pianos and Orch. (1968); *Theme, Variations and Finale* for Orch. (1968); *Triptych* for Orch. (1970); Trio for Flute, Oboe, and Piano (1936); *Theme and Variations* for 2 Violins (1937); Viola Sonata (1938); *Theme and Variations* for String Quartet (1939); 3 string quartets (1939, 1954, 1965); Clarinet Quartet (1948); Cello Sonata (1949); Violin Sonata (1959); Piano Trio (1962); *Concertante* for Violin and Piano (1935–62); Quintet for Piano, Oboe, Clarinet, Horn, and Bassoon (1963); *Tankas of the 4 Seasons* for Tenor, Oboe, Clarinet, Bassoon, Violin, and Cello (1965); Quintet for Piano and Strings (1968); Oboe Quartet (1970); *Suite* for Flute, Viola, and Harp (1970); Quintet for Piano, Clarinet, Horn, Violin, and Cello (1971); *Elegy* for Solo Guitar (1971; completed from composer's sketches by Julian Bream); *Bagatelles* for Piano (1938); *The Creel* for 2 Pianos (1940); Piano Sonatina (1948); *4 Romantic Pieces* for Piano (1953); *Ballade* for Piano (1967); *Theme with 4 Studies* for Piano (1971); choruses; several song cycles, to French and English words.

BIBLIOGRAPHY: K. Avery, "Alan Rawsthorne," *Music & Letters* (Jan. 1951); A.E.F. Dickinson, "The Progress of Alan Rawsthorne," *Music Review* (May 1951); A. Frank, *Modern British Composers* (London, 1954; pp. 74–79); F. Routh, *Contemporary British Music: The Twenty-five Years from 1945 to 1970* (London, 1972; pp. 44–55); F. Routh, "Rawsthorne's Instrumental Style," *Musical Times* (March 1984).

Raxach, Enrique, Spanish-born Dutch composer; b. Barcelona, Jan. 15, 1932. He studied composition with Nuri Aymerich; in 1958 he moved to Paris; then lived in Zürich, Munich, and Cologne. From 1959–66 he attended the summer courses in Darmstadt given by Messiaen, Boulez, Maderna, and Stockhausen. In 1962 he settled in the Netherlands; in 1969 he became a Dutch citizen. In his music he explores purely structural potentialities; the idiom of his composition is influenced by Varèse and Xenakis.

WORKS: FOR ORCH.: *Polifonias* for String Orch. (1953–54); *Metamorphose I* (1956); *Promethus* (1957); *Metamorphose II* (1958); *Metamorphose III* (1959); *Fluxion* (1962–63); *Syntagma* (1964–65); *6 Movements* (1965); *Textures* (1965–66); *Equinoxial* (1967–68); *Inside Outside* (1969); *Figuren in einer Landschaft* (1974); *Ad marginem* (1975); *Erdenlicht* (1975). CHAMBER MUSIC: String Quartet No. 1 (1961); *Estrofas* for Clarinet, Violin, Cello, Double Bass, and Percussion (1962); *Summer Music* for Flute, Cello, and Piano (1967); *Imaginary Landscape* for Flute and Percussion (1968); *Scattertime* for Instruments (1971); String Quartet No. 2 (1971); *Chimaera* for Bass Clarinet and Stereophonic Magnetic Tape (1974); *Aubade* for Percussion Quartet (1978). VOCAL MUSIC: Cantata for Tenor and Chamber Orch. (1952); *Vocalise-Etude* for Bass and Piano (1967); *Paraphrase* for Mezzo-soprano and 11 Players (1969); *Interface* for Chorus, Percussion, Organ, and Double Bass (1972); *Sine nomine* for Soprano and Orch. (1973); *Grand duo concertant* for Soprano and Double Bass (1975); *Soirée musicale* for Bass Clarinet, Women's Choir, and Orch. (1978).

Ray, Don Brandon, American conductor and composer; b. Santa Maria, Calif., June 7, 1926. He studied composition with John Vincent at the Univ. of Calif., Los Angeles (B.A., 1948), and with Ernst Kanitz at the Univ. of Southern Calif.; conducting with Roger Wagner and Richard Lert. In 1960 he was engaged as conductor of the Committee on the Arts (COTA) Symph. Orch. and Chorale in the San Fernando Valley. He composed orch. pieces, Protestant church services, incidental music to theatrical plays; *Symrock* (symph. rock) for Orch. (1978).

Rayner, Sydney, American tenor; b. New Orleans, 1895; d. East Patchogue, Long Island, N.Y., Sept. 14, 1981. He studied singing in Italy; made his debut in Rome in 1927. He sang at the Opéra-Comique in Paris and at the State Opera in Berlin; made his first appearance at the Metropolitan Opera in N.Y. in 1936 as Don José, and remained with the company for several years. His best roles were Radames and Faust.

Razumovsky, Count (from 1815, **Prince**) **Andrei,** Russian diplomat and music-lover; b. St. Petersburg, Nov. 2, 1752; d. Vienna, Sept. 23, 1836. He was the Russian ambassador at Vienna from 1793 to 1809; from 1808 to 1816 he maintained the celebrated Razumovsky Quartet (first violin, Schuppanzigh; 2nd violin, Louis Sina, whose part was occasionally taken over by Razumovsky; viola, Weiss; cello, Lincke), later known as the Schuppanzigh Quartet (without Razumovsky). Razumovsky's name was immortalized through the dedication to him of Beethoven's 3 string quartets, op. 59, and (with Prince Lobkowitz) 5th and 6th Symphs. He was a munificent and prodigal patron of art, but after the destruction by fire of his Vienna palace (Dec. 31, 1814) he gave up the quartet, and disappeared from musical history.

Razzi, Fausto, Italian composer; b. Rome, May 4, 1932. He studied composition with Goffredo Petrassi at the Santa Cecilia Academy in Rome; then devoted himself to teaching. Among his works is a String Quartet (1958); *Movimento* for Piano and Orch. (1966); *Improvvisazione* for Viola, 18 Wind Instruments, and Timpani (1966); *4 invenzioni* for 7 Instruments (1968); *Musica* for 10 Wind Instruments (1969).

Rea, John, Canadian composer; b. Toronto, Jan. 14, 1944. He studied composition with Ruth Wylie at Wayne State Univ. in Detroit and with Weinzweig at the Univ. of Toronto (M.M., 1959); then took a postgraduate course at Princeton Univ.
WORKS: Opera, *The Prisoner's Play* (Univ. of Toronto, May 22, 1973); ballet, *Les Jours* (1969; ballet suite, Toronto, July 11, 1974); *Jeux de scène: Fantasie-Hommage à Richard Wagner,* musical-theater work for 6 Performers on Blacksmith's Anvil, English Horn, Oboe, Cello, Piccolo, Flute, Piano, Marimba, and 3 Glockenspiels (1976; Vancouver, Feb. 27, 1977); Clarinet Sonatina (1965); *Sestina* for Flute, Clarinet, Trumpet, Cello, Harpsichord, and Percussion (1968); *Prologue, Scene and Movement* for Soprano, Viola, and 2 Pianos (1968); *Tempest* for any combination of Voices and/or Instruments (1969); *What You Will,* set of 12 single pieces of 6 polytonal duets for Piano (1969); *Fantaisies et allusions* for Saxophone Quintet (1969); 4 pieces of miscellaneous instrumentation, each named *Anaphora* (1970–75).

Read, Daniel, American composer; b. Attleboro, Mass., Nov. 16, 1757; d. New Haven, Dec. 4, 1836. He worked on a farm as a youth; studied mechanics, and was employed as a surveyor at 18; began to compose at 19. He served in the Continental Army as a private; at 21 he settled at New Stratford; later went to New Haven. In 1782–83 he maintained a singing school on the North River. He also was a comb maker. At his death, he left a collection of some 400 tunes by him and other composers. He publ. *The American Singing Book, or a New and Easy Guide to the Art of Psalmody, devised for the use of Singing Schools in America* (New Haven, 1785; subsequent eds., 1786, 1792, 1793, 1795); the *American Musical Magazine* (containing New England church music; compiled with Amos Doolittle, New Haven, 12 numbers, May 1786 to Sept. 1787; reprinted, Scarsdale, N.Y., 1961); *Supplement to The American Singing Book* (New Haven, 1787); *The Columbian Harmonist,* in 3 books: no. 1 (New Haven, 1793), no. 2 (New Haven, 1794; 2nd ed., with numerous additions, 1798; 3rd ed., with further additions, 1801), no. 3 (New Haven, 1795); all 3 books in one vol. (New Haven, 1795; 2nd ed., completely revised, Dedham, 1804; 3rd ed., Boston, 1807; 4th ed., Boston, 1810). Shortly before his death he completed the compilation *Musica Ecclesia, or Devotional Harmony,* but it remained unpubl. Many of his tunes—e.g., *Sherburne, Windham,* and *Lisbon—* achieved great popularity.
BIBLIOGRAPHY: G. Hood, "Daniel Read," *Musical Herald* (N.Y., Oct. 1882); F.J. Metcalf, *American Composers and Compilers of Sacred Music* (N.Y., 1925); I. Lowens, "Daniel Read's World," *Notes* (March 1952); *Dictionary of American Biography.*

Read, Gardner, outstanding American composer and erudite music scholar; b. Evanston, Ill., Jan. 2, 1913. He studied theory at the Northwestern Univ. School of Music; conducting with Bakaleinikoff, and composition at the Eastman School of Music in Rochester, N.Y., with Paul White, Bernard Rogers, and Howard Hanson (B.Mus., 1936; M.M., 1937); he studied with Aaron Copland at the Berkshire Music Center in Tanglewood; taught composition at the St. Louis Inst. of Music (1941–43), at the Kansas City Cons. of Music (1943–45), and at the Cleveland Inst. of Music (1945–48); was appointed composer-in-residence and prof. of composition at Boston Univ. College of Music in 1948; retired in 1978. A composer of extraordinary fecundity, he excels in instrumental music; his idiom of composition is basically Romantic, but the harmonic and contrapuntal textures are intense and dense with polytonal encounters.
WORKS: OPERA: *Villon* (1967). FOR ORCH.: *The Lotus-Eaters* (Interlochen, Mich., Aug. 12, 1932); *Sketches of the City,* symph. suite after Carl Sandburg (Rochester, April 18, 1934); *The Painted Desert* (Interlochen, July 28, 1935); Symph. No. 1 (1936; N.Y., Nov. 4, 1937; awarded first prize in the American Composer's Contest sponsored by the N.Y. Phil.); *Fantasy* for Viola and Orch. (Rochester, April 22, 1937); *Prelude and Toccata* (Rochester, April 29, 1937); *Suite* for String Orch. (N.Y., Aug. 5, 1937); *Passacaglia and Fugue* (Chicago, June 30, 1938); *The Golden Journey to Samarkand* for Chorus, Soloists, and Orch. (1936–39); *Pan e Dafni* (1940); *American Circle* (Evanston, March 15, 1941); *First Overture* (Indianapolis, Nov. 6, 1943); Symph. No. 2 (awarded first prize of the Paderewski Fund Competition, 1942; Boston, Nov. 26, 1943, composer conducting); *Night Flight,* tone poem after Antoine de St.-Exupéry (Rochester, April 27, 1944); Cello Concerto (1945); *Threnody* for Flute and Strings

(Rochester, Oct. 21, 1946); *A Bell Overture* (Cleveland, Dec. 22, 1946); *Partita* for Small Orch. (Rochester, May 4, 1947); *Pennsylvaniana Suite* (Pittsburgh, Nov. 21, 1947); Symph. No. 3 (1948); *Quiet Music for Strings* (Washington, D.C., May 9, 1948); *Dance of the Locomotives* (Boston, June 26, 1948); *Sound Piece* for Brass and Percussion (Boston, May 11, 1949); *The Temptation of St. Anthony,* dance-symph. after Flaubert (Chicago, April 9, 1953); *Toccata giocosa* (Louisville, Ky., March 13, 1954); *Vernal Equinox* (Brockton, Mass., April 12, 1955); Symph. No. 4 (1958; Cincinnati, Jan. 30, 1970); *Jeux des timbres* for Orch. (1963); Piano Concerto (1977). VOCAL WORKS: *4 Nocturnes* for Voice and Orch. (Rochester, April 3, 1935); *From a Lute of Jade* for Voice and Orch. (Rochester, March 15, 1937); *Songs for a Rainy Night* for Voice and Orch. (Rochester, April 27, 1942); *The Prophet,* oratorio after Kahlil Gibran (1960; Boston, Feb. 23, 1977); *The Reveille* for Chorus, Winds, Percussion, and Organ (1962); *Chants d'Auvergne* for Chorus and Instruments (1962); *The Hidden Lute* for Soprano, Flute, Harp, and Percussion (1979); many songs and choruses. CHAMBER MUSIC: *Suite* for String Quartet (1936); Piano Quintet (1945); *Sonata brevis* for Violin and Piano (1948); *9 by 6* for Wind Sextet (1951); String Quartet No. 1 (1957); *Sonoric Fantasia No. 1* for Celesta, Harp, and Harpsichord (1958); *Sonoric Fantasia No. 2* for Violin and Orch. (1965); *Sonoric Fantasia No. 3* for Viola and Small Orch. (1970); *Sonoric Fantasia No. 4* for Organ and Percussion (1975–76); *Los dioses aztecos,* suite of 7 movements for Percussion Ensemble (1959); *Petite suite* for Recorders and Harpsichord (1963); *Invocation* for Trombone and Organ (1977); *Galactic Novae* for Organ and Percussion (1978). FOR ORGAN: *Passacaglia and Fugue* (1937); *Suite for Organ* (co-winner, first prize of Pa. College for Women, Pittsburgh, 1950); *8 Preludes on Old Southern Hymns* (1951). FOR PIANO: *3 Satirical Sarcasms* (1941); *Driftwood Suite* (1943); *Dance of the Locomotives* (1944); *Sonata da chiesa* (1948); *Touch Piece* (1949); *5 Polytonal Studies* (1964). PUBLICATIONS: *Thesaurus of Orchestral Devices* (Westport, Conn., 1953; 2nd ed., 1969); *Music Notation: A Manual of Modern Practice* (Boston, 1964; 2nd ed., 1971); *Style and Orchestration* (N.Y., 1975); *Contemporary Instrumental Techniques* (N.Y., 1976); *Modern Rhythmic Notation* (Bloomington, Ind., 1978).

Reading, John, English organist; b. c.1645; d. Winchester, 1692. He was lay vicar of Lincoln Cathedral in 1667 and Master of the Choristers in 1670; served as organist of Winchester Cathedral from 1675–81, then of Winchester College, for which he composed the well-known song *Dulce Domum* (publ. in Hayes's *Harmonia Wiccamica*).

Reading, John, son of the preceding; b. c.1685; d. London, Sept. 2, 1764. He was Chorister of the Chapel Royal under Blow until 1699; organist of Dulwich College from 1700–2; lay vicar at Lincoln Cathedral in 1702, and Master of the Choristers in 1703; later organist in several London churches. He publ. *A Book of New Anthems* and *A Book of New Songs with Symphonies and a Thorough Bass fitted to the Harpsichord.*

Reardon, John, American baritone; b. New York, April 8, 1930. He studied at Rollins College (B.Mus., 1952); then took voice lessons with Martial Singher and Margaret Harshaw. He made his first appearance with the N.Y. City Opera on Oct. 16, 1954, as Falke in *Die Fledermaus.* He made his Metropolitan Opera debut in N.Y. on Sept. 28, 1965, as Count Tomsky in Tchaikovsky's *Queen of Spades.* He mastered an extensive repertoire, which included several roles in modern operas.

Rebel, François, French composer; b. Paris, June 19, 1701; d. there, Nov. 7, 1775. He became an excellent violinist under the tutelage of his father, Jean-Féry Rebel. He was in charge of the "24 violins" of the King and master of the royal chamber music. From 1757 to 1767 Rebel and his lifelong friend and collaborator, François Francœur, were directors of the Académie Royale de Musique (the Opéra). The operas composed jointly by Rebel and Francœur and produced at Paris include *Pirame et Thisbé* (Oct. 17, 1726) and *Scanderberg* (Oct. 27, 1735).

BIBLIOGRAPHY: L. de La Laurencie, "Une Dynastie de musiciens aux XVIIᵉ et XVIIIᵉ siècles: Les Rebel," *Sammelbände der Internationalen Musik-Gesellschaft,* 7.

Rebello, João Lourenço (João Soares), Portuguese composer; b. Caminha, 1610; d. Apélacao (now a part of Lisbon), Nov. 16, 1661. He was maestro to King John IV of Portugal, who dedicated to Rebello his *Defensa de la música moderna* (1649). Psalms *a* 16, Magnificats, Lamentations, and Misereres by Rebello were publ. in Rome (1657).

Reber, (Napoléon-) Henri, French composer; b. Mulhouse, Alsace, Oct. 21, 1807; d. Paris, Nov. 24, 1880. He studied with Reicha and Le Sueur at the Paris Cons.; became a prof. of harmony in 1851; succeeded Halévy as prof. of composition in 1862 (being succeeded in turn by Saint-Saëns in 1880), and was also inspector of the branch conservatories from 1871.

WORKS: Ballet, *Le Diable amoureux* (Sept. 23, 1840); comic operas (all produced at the Opéra-Comique): *La Nuit de Noël* (Feb. 9, 1848); *Le Père Gaillard* (Sept. 7, 1852); *Les Papillottes de M. Benoist* (Dec. 28, 1853); *Les Dames capitaines* (June 3, 1857); 4 symphs.; chamber music; piano pieces for 2 and 4 hands; 33 songs; vocalises for Soprano or Tenor (op. 16), etc.; and a *Traité d'harmonie* (1862, and several later eds.).

BIBLIOGRAPHY: Saint-Saëns, *Notice sur N. Henri Reber* (Paris, 1881).

Řebiček, Josef, Czech conductor and composer; b. Prague, Feb. 7, 1844; d. Berlin, March 24, 1904. He studied violin at the Prague Cons.; was violinist in the court orch. in Weimar; then played in theater orchs. in Prague and Wiesbaden; conducted opera in Warsaw, Budapest, etc.; from 1897 till 1903 was guest conductor of the Berlin Phil., succeeding Franz Mannstädt. He wrote *Huldigungsfestklänge* (on old Dutch themes) for Orch.; a Symph.; a Violin Sonata; many pieces for violin.

Rebikov, Vladimir, Russian composer; b. Krasnoyarsk, Siberia, May 31, 1866; d. Yalta, Aug. 4, 1920. He studied at the Moscow Cons. with Klenovsky; then in Berlin and Vienna. He then went to Odessa, where his first opera, *In the Thunderstorm,* was produced in 1894. In 1898 he moved to Kishinev, Bessarabia, where he organized a branch of the Imperial Russian Musical Society. In 1901 he settled in Moscow, remaining there until 1919; he spent his last year of life in the Crimea. His early works were under the influence of Tchaikovsky, but beginning with *Esquisses* for Piano he made a decisive turn toward a modern style; he became particularly fond of the whole-tone scale and its concomitant, the augmented triad; claimed priority in this respect over Debussy and other European composers; his piano piece *Les Démons s'amusent* is based entirely on the whole-tone scale. He declared that music is a language of emotion and therefore could not be confined to set forms, or to arbitrarily defined consonances. An entirely new departure is represented by his *Mélomimiques,* short lyric pieces for Piano, in which mimicry and suggestion are used in an impressionistic manner. He also wrote several vocal "melomimics," 3 "rhythmo-declamations" for Piano (op. 32), and 20 for Voice and Piano. In these compositions he abandoned cohesive form in favor of a free association of melodic and rhythmic phrases, sparingly harmonized; prevalence of esthetic theories over musical substance made his experiments ephemeral. A melodious waltz from his children's opera, *The Christmas Tree,* is his most popular composition.
WORKS: Operas: *In the Thunderstorm* (Odessa, Feb. 27, 1894) and *The Christmas Tree,* children's opera (Moscow, Nov. 1, 1903); musico-psychological pantomime, *Little Snow White* (Tiflis, 1909); 2-act fairy opera, *Prince Charming;* scenic fables after Krylov: *The Grasshopper and the Ant, A Dinner with a Bear, The Ass and the Nightingale, The Funeral, The Liar* (Moscow, Dec. 27, 1903); several "musico-psychological tableaux": *Slavery and Freedom, Songs of the Harp, The Nightmare,* etc.; numerous piano pieces (*Scènes bucoliques, Silhouettes, Dans la forêt, Chansons blanches, Idylles, Les Danses, Les Démons s'amusent,* etc.). He publ. numerous articles on musical esthetics, particularly relating to modern music; translated into Russian Gevaert's *Traité d'instrumentation.*
BIBLIOGRAPHY: M. Montagu-Nathan, *Contemporary Russian Composers* (N.Y., 1917); N. Nabokov, *Old Friends and New Music* (Boston, 1951; pp. 148–50).

Rebling, Gustav, German organist; b. Barby, July 10, 1821; d. Magdeburg, Jan. 9, 1902. He was a pupil of F. Schneider at Dessau (1836–39); in 1847 became organist of the French church in Magdeburg; in 1858, of the Johanniskirche; retired in 1897. He wrote pieces for organ and piano; choruses and songs; 2 cello sonatas; other chamber music.

Rebner, Adolf, Austrian violinist; b. Vienna, Nov. 21, 1876; d. Baden-Baden, June 19, 1967. He was a pupil of Grün at the Vienna Cons.; settled in Frankfurt in 1896, and after 1904 taught violin at the Hoch Cons. In 1921 he organized the Rebner String Quartet, with Hindemith as the violist, and gave numerous concerts with it, obtaining excellent success; with the advent of the Nazi regime in Germany he went to Vienna; after the Anschluss, lived briefly in the U.S.; eventually returned to Europe and lived in Baden-Baden.

Rebner, Wolfgang Edward, German pianist, son of **Adolf Rebner;** b. Frankfurt, Dec. 20, 1910. He studied at the Hoch Cons. in Frankfurt; served as accompanist to the cellist Feuermann in the U.S. (1935–37) and South America. In 1955 he returned to Germany, and taught at the Richard Strauss Cons. in Munich. He composed some excellent chamber music and the orch. suites *Persönliche Noten* (1961) and *Aus Südamerika* (1964).

Rechberger, Herman, Austrian-born Finnish composer; b. Linz, Feb. 14, 1947. He had early musical training in Linz, Zürich, and Brussels; in 1970 he went to Finland, where he studied composition with Sallinen and electronic music with Osmo Lindeman at the Sibelius Academy in Helsinki (1971–77). From 1975 to 1979 he was an instructor in a children's workshop in Helsinki; in 1979 became a producer for contemporary music at the Finnish Broadcasting Company. In his own music he employs the full arsenal of contemporary resources, experimenting in multimedia spectacles, with ample use of electronics.
WORKS: FOR THE STAGE: *The Singer,* after Francis Mann's "The Devil in a Convent," for Actors, Singers, Orch., and Electronic Tape (1976); *Naula (The Nail)* for Actors, Dancers, and Instruments (1975–76); *A Midsummer Night's Dream,* after Shakespeare, for Instrumental Ensemble (1980–81); *Spoon River* for various Sound Environments plus a Solitary Harmonium (1981–82); *... ismo,* a satirical play, for Actor, Sound Objects, Slide Projectors, Kinetic Wall, Videotape, and 5 Instruments (1982). FOR ORCH.: Concerto for Guitar and Strings (1971); *Kaamos* for Strings and Timpani (1973); *Music for Under-developed Film* (1973); *La macchina capriciosa* for Double Bassoon, Slides, and Chamber Orch. (1974–75); *Consort Music 1* for Recorders, Orch., and Electronic Tape (1974–75); *Consort Music 2* for Renaissance Instruments, Treble Recorder, and Chamber Orch. (1977); *Consort Music 4* for Chamber Orch. (1980); *Himojen puutarha (The Garden of Delights),* after the Bosch painting (1976–77). CHAMBER MUSIC: *Ode to a Steam Locomotive* for Flute, Clarinet, Viola and Cello (1971); *Ways* for Flute and 2 Guitars (1975); *Textures* for Percussion

(1975); *The King's Hunt* for Horn Solo (1977); *Charmeaux* for Trumpet and Percussion (1977); *Rotazioni* for Solo Violin and Viola (1970); *fragebogen* for Double Bassoon and Pedal Sounds (1979); *Consort Music 3* for 9 Brasses (1980–81); *About 4 Seasons* for String Quartet (1981); *Szene am . . .* for Bass Clarinet and Piano (1981); *pp* for Prepared Tenor Recorder (1982); choruses.

Redding, Otis, black American rhythm-and-blues and soul singer and songwriter; b. Dawson, Ga., Sept. 9, 1941; d. in an airplane crash, near Madison, Wis., Dec. 10, 1967. He sang in church, took part in revival meetings, and adopted the "shouting" manner of projection. His early record *Shout Bamalama* is a fair example of this technique. He then progressed toward a more refined type of gospel and soul singing, and in 1966 issued an album called *Dictionary of Soul.* His death at 26 was mourned and commemorated in a posthumous album, *The Immortal Otis Redding.* His most successful hits, sung in a powerful baritone voice, included *Respect, (Sittin' on) The Dock of the Bay,* and *Try a Little Tenderness.*

Redel, Kurt, German flutist and conductor; b. Breslau, Oct. 8, 1918. In 1939 he became a member of the Salzburg Mozarteum Orch.; in 1941 he joined the orch. of the Bavarian State Opera in Munich. From 1946 to 1953 he taught at the Music Academy in Detmold. In 1953 he founded the Pro Arte Orch. of Munich; made several tours with it, performing programs of works of the Baroque period.

Redford, John, English organist, composer, and poet; d. London, 1547. He was one of the vicars-choral of St. Paul's Cathedral in London. His works are found in D. Stevens, ed., *The Mulliner Book,* in *Musica Britannica,* I (1951); J. Caldwell, ed., *Early Tudor Organ Music* I: *Music for the Office,* in *Early English Church Music,* VI (1966) and D. Stevens, ed., *Early Tudor Organ Music* II: *Music for the Mass,* in *Early English Church Music,* X (1969).
    BIBLIOGRAPHY: C.F. Pfatteicher, *John Redford* (Kassel, 1934); *Grove's Dictionary* (6th ed., 1980).

Redhead, Richard, English composer of church music; b. Harrow, March 1, 1820; d. Hallingley, April 27, 1901. He served as organist in various churches in London; wrote much vocal music; edited the collections *Cathedral and Church Choir Book, Parochial Church Tune Book,* and *The Universal Organist.*

Redlich, Hans Ferdinand, distinguished Austrian musicologist and conductor; b. Vienna, Feb. 11, 1903; d. Manchester, England, Nov. 27, 1968. He studied piano and conducting, but devoted his energies mainly to writing biographical and analytical books on composers; he was only 16 when he publ. an essay on Mahler. After taking courses at the univs. of Vienna and Munich, he obtained his Dr.Phil. at the Univ. of Frankfurt with the dissertation *Das Prob-*

lem des Stilwandels in Monteverdis Madrigalwerk (publ. Leipzig, 1931; revised ed., Berlin, 1932). He conducted opera at the Municipal Theater of Mainz (1925–29); then lived in Mannheim. In 1939 he emigrated to England; from 1941 to 1955 he conducted the Choral and Orch. Society in Letchworth; also was a lecturer at the Extra Mural Board of the Univ. of Cambridge (1941–55); from 1955 to 1962 he was a lecturer at the Reid School of Music at the Univ. of Edinburgh; then was at the Univ. of Manchester. He publ. *Gustav Mahler: Eine Erkenntnis* (Nuremberg, 1919); *Richard Wagner: Tristan und Isolde, Lohengrin, Parsifal* (London, 1948; 3rd ed., 1951); *Claudio Monteverdi: Leben und Werk* (Olten, 1949; in Eng., London, 1952); *Bruckner and Mahler* (London, 1955; revised ed., 1963); *Alban Berg: The Man and His Music* (London, 1957; a fundamental work).

Redman, Don(ald Matthew), black American jazz instrumentalist, composer-arranger, and bandleader; b. Piedmont, W.Va., July 29, 1900; d. New York, Nov. 30, 1964. He began his studies on trumpet as a child; eventually mastered all the wind instruments; became an arranger for Fletcher Henderson's band (1924–27); then worked with Louise Armstrong; also was an arranger for Paul Whiteman, Ben Pollack, and others. He toured Europe with his own band (1946–47); then appeared on television and served as music director for Pearl Bailey. His arrangement of *Deep Purple* for Jimmy Dorsey became a major hit.

Redman, Harry Newton, American organist and composer; b. Mount Carmel, Ill., Dec. 26, 1869; d. Boston, Dec. 26, 1958. He studied organ and composition with Chadwick; from 1897 taught at the New England Cons. in Boston. He wrote 2 string quartets, 2 violin sonatas, an *Octave Method,* and studies for piano; 2 albums of songs; etc. About 1925 he abandoned music and devoted himself chiefly to painting; exhibited in Boston as late as 1957.

Rée, Anton, Danish pianist and pedagogue; b. Aarhus, Oct. 5, 1820; d. Copenhagen, Dec. 20, 1886. He studied with Karl Krebs in Hamburg; had a few lessons with Chopin in Paris. In 1842 he returned to Denmark and settled in Copenhagen as a teacher. He publ. *Musikhistoriske Momenter* and a book of exercises, *Bidrag til Klavierspillets Teknik; Danses caractéristiques* for Piano; etc.

Rée, Louis, pianist, cousin of **Anton Rée;** b. Edinburgh, Oct. 15, 1861; d. Vienna, Feb. 28, 1939. He was a pupil of Leschetizky in Vienna; settled there as a teacher; gave duo-piano concerts with his wife, **Susanne Pilz-Rée** (1865–1937). He wrote a Concerto for 2 Pianos (1925); publ. transcriptions for 2 pianos and various other works.

Reed, Alfred, American composer and arranger; b. New York, Jan. 25, 1921. He studied harmony with John Sacco; enlisted in the U.S. Air Force during the war and was assigned to the Army Air Force Band;

upon discharge from military service, he enrolled at the Juilliard School of Music in N.Y. as a student of Vittorio Giannini. In 1948 he was appointed staff composer and arranger with NBC; later served in the same capacity with ABC. In 1953 he became conductor of the Baylor Symph. Orch. at Baylor Univ. in Waco, Texas. In 1966 he joined the music faculty at the Univ. of Miami, where he developed a unique music merchandising program. He composed a great number of band pieces; also wrote a multitude of 3-minute musical sequences for soundtrack library recordings. He holds an honorary Mus.D. degree from the Cons. of Music in Lima, Peru.

Reed, Herbert Owen, American composer and educator; b. Odessa, Mo., June 17, 1910. He studied with Howard Hanson and Bernard Rogers at the Eastman School of Music in Rochester, N.Y. (Ph.D., 1939); upon graduation, he was appointed to the faculty of Michigan State Univ., retiring in 1976.
WORKS: "Folk opera," *Michigan Dream* (East Lansing, Mich., May 13, 1955); short opera-legend, *Earth Trapped* (East Lansing, Feb. 24, 1962); ballet-pantomime, *The Mask of the Red Death,* after Edgar Allan Poe (1936); *Butterfly Girl and Mirage Boy,* chamber dance-opera on an Indian spirit legend (1980); symph. poem, *Evangeline* (Rochester, March 30, 1938); Symph. No. 1 (Rochester, April 27, 1939); Cello Concerto (1949); *La fiesta mexicana* for Concert Band (1949); *The Turning Mind* for Orch. (1968); oratorio, *A Tabernacle for the Sun* (1963); chamber opera-dance, *Living Solid Face* (South Dakota Univ., Brookings, Nov. 28, 1976); chamber music; piano pieces; choruses; solo songs. He publ. several teaching manuals: *A Workbook in the Fundamentals of Music* (N.Y., 1946); *Basic Music* (N.Y., 1954); *Composition Analysis Chart* (N.Y., 1958); *Basic Contrapuntal Technique* (with P. Harder; N.Y., 1964); *Scoring for Percussion* (with J.T. Leach, Englewood Cliffs, N.J., 1969; revised ed., 1979); with R. Sidnell, *The Materials of Music Composition* (2 vols., 1978, 1980).

Reed, Jerry, American country-music singer, guitarist, and songwriter; b. Atlanta, March 20, 1937. He labored in cotton mills as a youth while pursuing his career as a singer in local haunts in Atlanta; when he was 18, he was hired as a songwriter for Capitol Records, and wrote such hits as *Amos Moses, Georgia Sunshine,* and *Alabama Wild Man.* In 1971 he scored a signal success when he brought out the song *When You're Hot, You're Hot.*

Reed, Lou, musically educated American proponent of avant-garde rock style; b. New York, March 2, 1944. He studied piano with reputable teachers, read books, wrote poetry, essayed journalism, vocalized to guitar accompaniment, and finally found his proper niche improvising variously with such psychedelically inclined groups as The Primitives and The Warlocks. In 1966 he recruited a British musician of a similarly educated background, John Cale, and together they formed a sodality inexplicably named The Velvet Underground, projecting bizarre stage behavior and playing sophisticated numbers in dissonant harmony. They attracted the surrealist artist Andy Warhol, who hired them for his "total environment" show "The Exploding Plastic Inevitable." Under Warhol's nihilistic influence, The Velvet Underground revived the dadaistic, surrealistic type of old European modernism, superadded with the screeching, screaming, sadomasochistic electronic sound to Lou Reed's demoralizing anarchistic lyrics openly extolling the psychedelic advantages of narcotics and totally emancipated sex play in such songs as *Heroin* and *Venus in Furs.* Reed left the group in 1970, and put out such invitations to anarchy as *Walk on the Wild Side* and *Metal Music Machine,* in which electronic bleeps and hisses accompanied the shouted homicidal orders *Live . . . Take No Prisoners.*

Reed, Peter Hugh, American music critic and journalist; b. Washington, D.C., June 14, 1892; d. Wingdale, N.Y., Sept. 25, 1969. He studied voice in Italy, preparing for an operatic career, which was frustrated when he entered the U.S. Army in World War I and was gassed. His speaking voice was, however, unimpaired; he became a pioneer of radio reviews of phonograph records. In 1935 he founded the *American Music Lover,* a monthly magazine devoted to serious music on records; in 1944 the name was changed to the *American Record Guide.* Reed remained its editor and publisher until 1957.

Reed, Thomas German, versatile English musician; b. Bristol, June 27, 1817; d. London, March 21, 1888. Under the guidance of his father, he appeared in Bath as a child of 10 in the various capacities of singer, pianist, and actor. In 1844 he married **Priscilla Horton** (b. Birmingham, Jan. 1, 1818; d. Bexley Heath, March 18, 1895), an actress and a singer. Together they started the celebrated series "Mr. and Mrs. German Reed's Entertainment" (1855), which included productions of operettas by Offenbach, Balfe, Clay, Sullivan, etc. These entertainments enjoyed great success, and were continued by his son **Alfred German Reed,** who died in London on March 10, 1895, a few days before the death of his mother.

Reed, William Henry, English violinist and composer; b. Frome, July 29, 1876; d. Dumfries, July 2, 1942. He studied at the Royal Academy of Music in London; was a violinist in the London Symph. Orch. at its foundation in 1904; then taught violin at the Royal College of Music; was concertmaster of the London Symph. Orch. from 1912 to 1935. He was a close friend of Elgar, and publ. a book, *Elgar As I Knew Him* (1936). His works include the orch. sketches *The Lincoln Imp* (Hereford Festival, 1921) and *Aesop's Fables* (Hereford Festival, 1924); Violin Concerto; *Rhapsody* for Violin and Orch.; 5 string quartets; violin pieces; songs; etc.

Reed, William Leonard, English composer; b. London, Oct. 16, 1910. He studied at the Guildhall School of Music in London (1917–26), at Oxford Univ. (1929–33), and at the Royal College of Music (1934–36), where his teachers were Constant Lambert and Howells. He traveled to Scandinavia and the U.S., where he stayed for several years.

WORKS: Operas: *The Vanishing Island* (Santa Barbara, Calif., 1955) and *The Crowning Experience* (Detroit, 1958); operettas: *Annie* (London, 1967) and *High Diplomacy* (London, 1969); several orch. pieces in a light vein; various pieces of chamber music; choruses; piano works. He publ. *The Golden Book of Carols* (London, 1947); *The Treasury of Christmas Music* (London, 1950); *Music of Britain* (London, 1952); *The Treasury of Eastern Music* (London, 1963); *The Treasury of English Church Music* (with G. Knight, 5 vols., London, 1965); *The Second Treasury of Christmas Music* (London, 1967).

Reese, Della, black American singer of gospel and popular music; b. Detroit, July 6, 1932. Her real name was **Delloreese Patricia Early.** She studied at Wayne State Univ. in Detroit; concurrently formed Meditations, a gospel group; later toured with Mahalia Jackson (1945–49) and other gospel singers; from 1954 she turned to popular music, and became successful as a vocalist; appeared extensively in nightclubs and on radio and television.

BIBLIOGRAPHY: *Current Biography* (Sept. 1971).

Reese, Gustave, eminent American musicologist; b. New York, Nov. 29, 1899; d. Berkeley, Calif., Sept. 7, 1977. At N.Y. Univ. he studied jurisprudence (LL.B., 1921) and music (Mus.Bac., 1930); subsequently joined its faculty, teaching there during the periods 1927–33, 1934–37, and 1945–74; concurrently he worked with G. Schirmer, Inc., publishers (1924–45; from 1940 to 1945 was director of publications); was director of publications for Carl Fischer, music publishers (1944–55). From 1933 to 1944 he was associate editor, and in 1944–45 editor, of the *Musical Quarterly*. In 1934 he was a co-founder of the American Musicological Society; was its president from 1950 to 1952, and remained its honorary president until his death. He gave numerous lectures at American univs.; also gave courses at the Juilliard School of Music in N.Y. An entire generation of American music scholars numbered among his students; he was widely regarded as a founder of American musicology as a science. He held a chair at the Graduate School of Arts and Science at N.Y. Univ., which gave him its "Great Teacher Award" in 1972 and its presidential citation on his retirement from active teaching in 1974; he then became a visiting prof. at the Graduate Center of the City Univ. of N.Y. He died while attending the congress of the International Musicological Society in Berkeley. Gustave Reese contributed a great number of informative articles to various American and European publications and music encyclopedias, but his most lasting achievement lies in his books, *Music in the Middle Ages* (N.Y., 1940; also in Italian, Florence, 1960) and *Music in the Renaissance* (N.Y.,

1954; revised 1959), which have become classics of American music scholarship; he also brought out an interesting book that describes selected early writings on music not available in English, *Fourscore Classics of Music Literature* (N.Y., 1957). On his 65th birthday, he was honored with an offering of a collection of articles by his colleagues and students, *Aspects of Medieval and Renaissance Music,* edited by Jan LaRue (N.Y., 1966; 2nd ed., 1978).

Reeve, William, English composer; b. London, 1757; d. there, June 22, 1815. He was a pupil of Richardson; served as organist at Totness, Devon, from 1781–83; returned to London, and composed operettas, pantomimes, and incidental music for plays, for Astley's Circus and Covent Garden (1791); in 1792 he became organist of St. Martin's, Ludgate Hill; from 1802, part-proprietor of Sadler's Wells Theatre. Besides music to some 40 plays, he composed glees and songs; the song *I am a friar in orders grey,* in the play *Merry Sherwood,* was very popular.

Reeves, David Wallace, American bandmaster; b. Oswego, N.Y., Feb. 14, 1838; d. Providence, R.I., March 8, 1900. As a boy he began to play cornet in circus and minstrel bands; later was in Union Army bands; his career as a bandmaster began in 1866, when he became the leader of the American Band of Providence, which is said to trace its roots back to the War of 1812; during its 35 years under the direction of Reeves it became a model of excellence among American municipal bands; Reeves succeeded in standardizing the instrumentation of the ordinary parade and outdoor-concert band; he wrote some 80 marches, of which the best is *The 2nd Connecticut Regiment March,* known to have been a favorite of Charles Ives. Reeves was a great friend of Patrick Sarsfield Gilmore, conductor of the band of the N.Y. 22nd Regiment, and it was Gilmore who popularized Reeves's marches. Upon Gilmore's death, Reeves took over the 22nd Regiment Band for the 1892–93 season, until it was taken over by Victor Herbert in the fall of 1893. J.P. Sousa called Reeves "the father of band music in America."

Reeves, Martha, rhythm-and-blues artist; b. Detroit, July 18, 1941. She worked as a clerk at Motown Records, and stepped in as a substitute at a recording session. She liked singing, and the Motown mogul Berry Gordy, Jr. liked her singing, too. She recruited two of her high-school friends to do a trio in 1963, making a hit with the song *Heat Wave,* under the moniker Martha and the Vandellas. Adapting the kinetic Motown style, they scored again with *Nowhere to Run;* becoming raunchier in their feministic affirmative action, they put out *I'm Ready for Love* and *My Baby Loves Me.* There were personnel changes, and the Vandellas finally disintegrated. Martha Reeves continued to make records alone, producing such autobiographical albums as *The Rest of My Life* and *Gotta Keep Moving.*

Reeves, (John) Sims, English tenor; b. Shooter's

Hill, Kent, Sept. 26, 1818; d. Worthing, London, Oct. 25, 1900. Learned to play several instruments; had lessons with J.B. Cramer (piano) and W.H. Callcott (harmony); he made his debut (as a baritone) at in the role of Rodolfo (*Sonnambula*), on Dec. 14, 1838; studied further and sang minor tenor parts at Drury Lane, 1841–43; studied in Paris under Bordogni, and in Milan under Mazzucato, appearing at La Scala in 1846 as Edgardo (*Lucia*). He retired in 1891, but reappeared in concerts in 1893, and even made a successful tour in South Africa in 1896. He publ. *Sims Reeves; His Life and Recollections Written by Himself* (London, 1888); *My Jubilee, or Fifty Years of Artistic Life* (London, 1889); *Sims Reeves on the Art of Singing* (1900).

BIBLIOGRAPHY: H.S. Edwards, *The Life and Artistic Career of Sims Reeves* (London, 1881); C.E. Pearce, *Sims Reeves: Fifty Years of Music in England* (1924); *Modern English Biography*, vol. VI.

Refardt, Edgar, eminent Swiss musicologist and bibliographer; b. Basel, Aug. 8, 1877; d. there, March 3, 1968. He studied law; obtained the degree of Dr.Jur. in 1901; in 1915 was appointed librarian and cataloguer of the musical collection of the Municipal Library of Basel; publ. valuable bibliographical works on Swiss music; also essays on various literary and musical subjects.

WRITINGS: *Verzeichnis der Aufsätze zur Musik in den nichtmusikalischen Zeitschriften der Universitätsbibliothek Basel* (Leipzig, 1925); *Historisch-biographisches Musikerlexikon der Schweiz* (Zürich, 1928; basic source of information on Swiss music and musicians); *Hans Huber: Leben und Werk eines Schweizer Musikers* (1944; definitive biography of Huber; supersedes Refardt's previous writings on Huber); *Johannes Brahms, Anton Bruckner, Hugh Wolf: Drei Wiener Meister des 19. Jahrhunderts* (1949); *Musik in der Schweiz* (1952; collection of articles); *Thematischer Katalog der Instrumentalmusik des 18. Jahrhunderts in den Handschriften der Universitätsbibliothek Basel*, ed. by Hans Zehntner (Basel, 1957); etc.

Refice, Licinio, Italian composer of sacred music; b. Patrica, near Rome, Feb. 12, 1883; d. Rio de Janeiro, Sept. 11, 1954 (while conducting his mystery play, *Santa Cecilia*). He studied with Falchi and Renzi at Santa Cecilia Academy in Rome; in 1910 became a teacher of church music at the Scuola Pontifica Superiore di Musica Sacra, remaining at this post until 1950. In 1947 he toured the U.S. as director of the Roman Singers of Sacred Music (99 concerts).

WORKS: Operas: *Cecilia* (Rome, 1934) and *Margherita da Cortona* (Milan, 1938); cantatas: *La Vedova di Naim* (1912); *Maria Magdalena* (Rome, 1917); *Il Martirio di S. Agnese* (Rome, 1919); *Stabat Mater* (1917); *Te Deum* (1918); *Missa Jubilaei* (1925); *Missa Italica* (1944); choral symph. poems: *Dantis poetae transitus* (Ravenna, 1921) and *Il trittico francescano* (Assisi, 1925); a Requiem; sacred play, *Santa Cecilia* (Rome, Feb. 15, 1934); oratorios: *Cananea* and *La Samaritana;* hymns; motets; etc.

Regamey, Constantin, Russian-born Swiss composer; b. Kiev, Jan. 28, 1907; d. Lausanne, Dec. 27, 1982. He went to Poland in 1920 and took piano lessons with Turczyński (1921–25); then turned to linguistics and took courses in Sanskrit at the Univ. of Warsaw and later at L'Ecole des Hautes Etudes in Paris, graduating in 1936. Returning to Poland, he taught Sanskrit at the Univ. of Warsaw (1937–39); concurrently he edited periodicals on contemporary music. He was interned by the Germans during the war, but was allowed to go to Switzerland. He received an appointment to teach Slavic and oriental languages at the Univ. of Lausanne; also gave courses in Indo-European linguistics at the Univ. of Freiburg. However, he did not abandon his musical activities; he served as co-editor of *Feuilles Musicales* (1954–62); was president of the Assoc. of Swiss Composers (1963–68) and a member of the executive board of the International Society for Contemporary Music (1969–73). In 1978 he became partially paralyzed; he dictated the last pages of his last work, *Visions,* to Jean Balissat, a fellow composer, who also orchestrated the work. As a composer, he adopted free serial methods, without a doctrinaire adherence to formal dodecaphony. In 1963 he moderated his modernity and wrote music using free, often composite, techniques.

WORKS: Fairy-tale opera, *Mio, mein Mio,* after Bächli and Lindgren (1973). For Orch.: *Variazioni e tema* (1948); *Music* for Strings (1953); *Autographe* for Chamber Orch. (1962–66); *4 × 5,* concerto for 4 Quintets (1964; Basel, May 28, 1964); *Lila,* double concerto for Violin, Cello, and Chamber Orch. (1976). Chamber music: Quintet for Clarinet, Bassoon, Violin, Cello, and Piano (1944); Sonatina for Flute, and Piano or Harpsichord (1944); String Quartet (1948). For Voice: *7 chansons persanes,* after Omar Khayyám, for Baritone and Chamber Orch. (1942); *5 études* for Female Voice and Orch. (1955–56); *5 poèmes de Jean Tardieu* for Chorus a cappella (1962); *Symphonie des Incantations* for Soprano, Baritone, and Orch. (1967); *3 Lieder des Clowns* for Baritone and Orch. (1968; excerpted from the incomplete opera *Don Robott*); *Unidentity and Infinity* for Silent Narrator, Female Voice, and an unidentified number of Instruments (1969); *Alpha,* cantata for Tenor and Orch., to a Hindu text (1970); *Visions,* after the life of the prophet Daniel, for Baritone, Chorus, Orch., and Organ (1978–79; orchestrated by Jean Balissat).

WRITINGS: A survey, *Musique du XXe siècle: Présentation de 80 œuvres pour orchestre de chambre* (Lausanne and Paris, 1966).

BIBLIOGRAPHY: H. Jaccard, *Initiation à la musique contemporaine: Trois compositeurs vaudois: Raffaele d'Alessandro, Constantin Regamey, Julien-François Zbinden* (Lausanne, 1955); B. Schäffer, *Leksykon kompozytorów XX wieku M–Z* (Cracow, 1965).

Reger, Max, preeminent German composer; b. Brand, Bavaria, March 19, 1873; d. Leipzig, May 11, 1916. In 1874 his father, a schoolteacher and good organist (d. 1905 in Munich), removed to Weiden, where Reger attended the Realschule. Although he was intended for the schoolmaster's career, he received thorough instruction on the piano and harmonium from his father, and on the organ and in theory from Lindner. At an early age he began to write piano pieces and chamber music; after hearing *Die Meistersinger* and *Parsifal* in Bayreuth (1888), he gave expression to the emotions created in him by those masterpieces in an ambitious symph. poem, *Héroïde funèbre.* In 1889 he passed the entrance examination for the teachers' seminary. But by that time music had taken such complete possession of him that he submitted a number of his MSS to Hugo Riemann, who immediately recognized Reger's exceptional talent. Accordingly, Reger became Riemann's pupil at the Sondershausen Cons. in April 1890, and in 1891 followed him to the Wiesbaden Cons., where he continued his studies till 1895, and also taught piano and organ (till 1896). After serving a year in the army, he settled in Weiden as a composer, writing the works up to about op. 50. However, he did not attract general attention until 1901, when he removed to Munich, whence he undertook pianistic tours through Germany, Austria, and Switzerland. During the academic year of 1905–6 he was a prof. of counterpoint at the Königliche Akademie der Tonkunst, and conductor of the Gesangsverein; in 1907 he was called to Leipzig as music director at the Univ. (also conductor of the Univ. chorus St. Pauli) and a prof. of composition at the Cons.; the former post he resigned in 1908, but the latter he retained till his death in 1916; he was made Dr.Phil. *honoris causa* from the Univ. of Jena; in 1911, Hofrat; in 1913, Generalmusikdirektor; in 1911–15, Hofkapellmeister in Meiningen; then in Jena and Leipzig. He died suddenly of paralysis of the heart. A German Max Reger Society was founded in 1920, with branches in many cities; society was established in Austria. The Max Reger Archives (containing most of his MSS) are at Weimar. A complete edition of Reger's works was begun in 1954 by Breitkopf & Härtel, reaching 38 vols. by 1977. W. Altman publ. a catalogue of Reger's works (1917; 2nd ed., 1926); Fritz Stein edited a thematic catalogue: *Thematisches Verzeichnis der im Druck erschienen Werke von Max Reger* (Leipzig, 1934; 1953).

WORKS: FOR ORCH.: *Symphoniesatz* in D minor (1890; posthumous, Dortmund Reger Festival, 1960); op. 50, *2 Romanzen* for Violin and Orch. (1900); op. 90, *Sinfonietta* (Essen, Oct. 8, 1905); op. 93, *Suite im alten Stil* (originally for Violin and Piano, 1906; orchestrated 1916); op. 95, *Serenade* (1905–6); op. 100, *Variationen und Fuge über ein lustiges Thema von J.A. Hiller* (Cologne, Oct. 15, 1907); op. 101, Violin Concerto in A (Leipzig, Oct. 13, 1908); op. 108, *Symphonischer Prolog zu einer Tragödie* (1908); op. 114, Piano Concerto in F minor (Leipzig, Dec. 15, 1910; U.S. premiere, Minneapolis, Nov. 16, 1945; Serkin, soloist); op. 120, *Ein Lustspielouvertüre* (1911); op. 123, *Konzert in alten Stil* (1912); op. 125, *Romantische Suite* (1912); op. 128, *4 Tondichtungen nach Böcklin* (Essen, Oct. 12, 1913); op. 130, *Ballet-Suite* (1913); op. 132, *Variationen und Fuge über ein Thema von Mozart* (1914; Berlin, Feb. 5, 1915); op.

140, *Eine vaterländische Ouvertüre* (1914); op. 147, *Sinfonische Rhapsodie* for Violin and Orch. (unfinished; completed by Florizel von Reuter).

VOCAL WORKS: With Orch.: Op. 21, *Hymne an den Gesang* for Men's Chorus; op. 71, *Gesang der Verklärten* for Mixed Chorus *a* 5; op. 106, *Psalm 100* for Mixed Chorus and Organ; op. 112, *Die Nonnen* for Mixed Chorus and Organ; op. 119, *Die Weihe der Nacht* for Alto Solo and Mixed Chorus; op. 124, *An die Hoffnung* for Alto Solo; op. 126, *Römischer Triumphgesang* for Men's Chorus; mixed choruses a cappella, opp. 6, 39 (*a* 6); men's choruses a cappella, opp. 38, 83; women's choruses a cappella, op. 111b; duets, opp. 14, 111a; about 300 songs, opp. 3, 4, 5, 12, 15, 23, 31, 35, 37, 43, 48, 51, 55, 62, 66, 68, 70, 75, 76 (60 *Schlichte Weisen*), 88, 97, 98, 104; op. 19, *Zwei geistliche Gesänge;* op. 61, *Leicht ausführbare Kompositionen zum gottesdienstlichen Gebrauch in der katholischen Kirche* (38 motets for Mixed Voices); op. 105, *Zwei geistliche Lieder;* op. 110, Motets for Mixed Chorus a cappella (*a* 5); op. 137, *Zwölf geistliche Lieder; Der evangelische Kirchenchor* (I, 40 mixed choruses for all festivals [4 series]; II, cantata, *O wie selig,* for Mixed Chorus, String Orch., and Organ; III, cantata, *O Haupt voll Blut und Wunden,* for Alto and Tenor Soli, Mixed Chorus, Violin and Oboe Soli, and Organ); men's and mixed choruses; and songs (sacred and secular), without opus numbers.

CHAMBER MUSIC: Op. 118, String Sextet in F; op. 64, Piano Quintet in C minor; op. 113, Piano Quartet in D minor; 5 string quartets: op. 54 (G minor and A), op. 74 (D minor), op. 109 (E-flat), op. 121 (F-sharp minor); 2 piano trios: op. 2 (B minor, for Piano, Violin, and Viola) and op. 102 (E minor); op. 77a, *Serenade* for Flute, Violin, and Viola; op. 77b, Trio for Flute, Violin, and Viola; op. 103a, *Suite* for Violin and Piano (A minor); 9 violin sonatas: op. 1 (D minor), op. 3 (D), op. 41 (A), op. 72 (C), op. 84 (F-sharp minor), op. 103b (*2 kleine Sonaten,* D minor and A), op. 122 (E minor), op. 139 (C minor); op. 93, *Suite im alten Stil* for Violin and Piano; 4 cello sonatas: op. 5 (F minor), op. 28 (G minor), op. 78 (F), op. 116 (A minor); 3 clarinet sonatas: op. 49 (A-flat major and F-sharp minor) and op. 107 (B-flat); op. 42, 4 sonatas for Violin Solo; op. 117, *Präludien und Fugen* for Violin Solo; op. 131, 3 suites for Cello Solo; op. 91, 7 sonatas for Unaccompanied Violin; op. 131a, 6 preludes and fugues for Unaccompanied Violin; op. 131b, 3 duos for 2 Violins; op. 133, Piano Quartet in A minor; op. 141a, *Serenade* in G major for Flute, Violin, and Cello; op. 141b, Trio in D minor for Violin, Viola, and Cello; op. 143, *Träume am Kamin,* 12 pieces for Piano Solo; op. 146, Clarinet Quintet in A major without opus number; Piano Quintet in C minor.

FOR ORGAN: Op. 16, *Suite* in E minor; op. 27, Fantasy on *Ein' feste Burg;* op. 29, *Fantasie und Fuge* in C minor; op. 30, Fantasy Sonata on *Freu dich sehr, o meine Seele;* op. 33, Sonata in F-sharp minor; op. 40, 2 fantasies, on *Wie schön leucht' uns der Morgenstern* and *Straf mich nicht in deinem Zorn;* op. 46, *Fantasie und Fuge über BACH;* op. 52, 3 fantasies, on *Alle Menschen müssen sterben, Wachet auf! ruft uns die Stimme,* and *Hallelujah! Gott zu loben;* op. 57, *Symphonische Phantasie und Fuge;* op. 60, Sonata in D minor; op. 67, *52 Vorspiele* to the chorales in general use; op. 73, *Variationen und Fuge über ein Originalthema;* op. 92, *Suite* in G minor; op. 127, *Introduktion, Passacaglia und Fuge* in E minor; numerous minor pieces: opp. 7, 56, 59, 63, 65, 69, 79, 80, 85, 129; also organ transcriptions of Bach clavier pieces.

FOR PIANO: 4 hands: op. 9, *Walzer-Capricen;* op. 10, *Deutsche Tänze;* op. 22, *Sechs Walzer;* op. 34, *5 pièces pittoresques;* op. 58, *Sechs Burlesken;* op. 94, *Sechs Stücke;* for 2 Pianos: op. 86, *Variatonen und Fuge über ein Thema von Beethoven,* and op. 96, *Introduktion, Passacaglia und Fuge;* for Piano Solo: op. 17, *Aus der Jugendzeit* (20 pieces); op. 18, *Improvisationen* (8 pieces); op. 20, *5 Humoresken;* op. 24, *6 morceaux;* op. 25, *Aquarellen;* op. 26, *7 Fantasiestücke;* op. 32, *7 Charackterstücke;* op. 36, *Bunte Blätter* (9 pieces); op. 44, *Zehn kleine Vortragsstücke;* op. 45, *6 Intermezzi;* op. 53, *Silhouetten* (7 pieces); op. 81, *Variationen und Fuge über ein Thema von Bach;* op. 82, *Aus meinem Tagebuche* (35 pieces); op. 89, *4 Sonatinen* (E minor, D, F, A minor); op. 99, *6 Präludien und Fugen;* op. 115, *Episoden* (2 books); op. 134, *Variationen und Fuge über ein Thema von Ph. Telemann;* 2 books of canons in all major and minor keys; 4 *Spezialstudien für die linke Hand allein;* minor pieces. Transcriptions for Piano, 4-hands: Bach's Prelude and Fugue in D, Toccata and Fugue in D minor, Fantasia in G, Prelude and Fugue in G, Prelude and Fugue in A minor, Fantasia and Fugue in G minor, Toccata and Fugue in E, Prelude and Fugue in E minor; Bach's orch. suites and *Brandenburg Concertos;* Hugo Wolf's symph. poem *Penthesilea* and the overture *Italienische serenade;* songs of Jensen, Brahms, Hugo Wolf, and Richard Strauss.

BIBLIOGRAPHY: R. Braungart, *Max Reger,* in vol. II of *Monographien Moderner Musiker* (Leipzig, 1907); G. Robert-Tornow, *Max Reger und Karl Straube* (Göttingen, 1907); V. Junk, *Max Reger als Orchesterkomponist* (Leipzig, 1910); W. Fischer, *Über die Wiedergabe der Orgelkompositionen Max Regers* (Cologne, 1911); M. Hehemann, *Max Reger. Eine Studie über moderne Musik* (Munich, 1911; 2nd ed., 1917); F. Rabich, *Regerlieder: Eine Studie* (Langensalza, 1914); H. Grace, "The Late Max Reger as Organ Composer," *Musical Times* (June 1916); H. Poppen, *Max Reger* (1917); E. Isler, *Max Reger* (Zürich, 1917); R. Würz, *Max Reger: Eine Sammlung von Studien* (4 vols., Munich, 1920–23); H. Unger, *Reger* (1921 and 1924); K. Hasse, *Max Reger* (1921); E. Segnitz, *Max Reger* (1922); E. Brennecke, "The Two Reger-Legends," *Musical Quarterly* (July 1922); A. Lindner (his teacher), *Max Reger, Ein Bild seines Jugendlebens und künstlerischen Werdens* (Stuttgart, 1922; 3rd ed., 1938); G. Bagier, *Reger* (Stuttgart, 1923); A. Spemann, *Max Reger-Brevier* (1923); H. Unger, *Max Reger* (Bielefeld, 1924); E. Gatscher, *Die Fugentechnik Regers in ihrer Entwicklung* (Stuttgart, 1925); S. Kallenberg, *Max Reger* (1929); E.C. Ebert-Stockinger, *Max Reger* (1930); G.R. Dejmek, *Der Variationszyklus bei Max Reger* (Essen, 1930); Elsa Reger (his widow), *Mein Leben für und mit Max Reger* (1930); P. Coenen, *Max Re-*

gers Variationsschaffen (Berlin, 1935); R. Huesgen, *Der junge Max Reger und seine Orgelwerke* (Schramberg, 1935); H.E. Rahner, *Regers Choralfantasien für die Orgel* (Kassel, 1936); E. Brand, *Max Reger im Elternhaus* (Munich, 1938); F.W. Stein, *Max Reger* (Potsdam, 1939); idem, *Max Reger. Sein Leben in Bildern* (1941); E.H. Müller von Asow, *Max Reger und sein Welt* (Berlin, 1945); K. Hasse, *Max Reger: Entwicklungsgang eines deutschen Meisters* (Leipzig, 1946); H.M. Poppen, *Max Reger* (Leipzig, 1947); R. Braungart, *Freund Reger; Erinnerungen* (Regensburg, 1949); A. Kalkoff, *Das Orgelschaffen Max Regers* (Kassel, 1950); *Max Reger. Festschrift* (contains articles about Reger; Leipzig, 1953); special Reger issue of the *Zeitschrift für Musik* (March 1953); G. Wehmeyer, *Max Reger als Liederkomponist* (Regensburg, 1955); E. Otto, *Max Reger: Sinnbild einer Epoche* (Wiesbaden, 1957); Reger-Festkomitee, ed., *Max Reger; Beiträge zur Regerforschung* (Meiningen, 1966); O. Schreiber and G. Sievers, eds., *Max Reger zum 50. Todestag* (Bonn, 1966); G. Sievers, *Die Grundlagen Hugo Riemanns bei Max Reger* (Wiesbaden, 1967); E. Brand-Selter, *Max Reger; Jahre der Kindheit* (Wilhelmshaven, 1968); H. Wirth, *Max Reger in Selbstzeugnissen und Bilddokumenten* (Reinleh, 1973); K. Röhring, ed., *Max Reger: Ein Synposion* (Wiesbaden, 1974).

Regis, Johannes, noted Flemish composer and organist; b. Flanders, c.1430; d. Soignies, c.1485. He was "magister puerorum" at the Cathedral of Antwerp (1463–64); then was clerk to Dufay at Cambrai (1464–74), and finally canon and scholasticus in Soignies (1481–82). He wrote 2 masses on the melody of *L'Homme armé;* a 5-part motet, *O admirabile commercium,* and other choral pieces. His collected works were publ. in 2 vols. by the American Inst. of Musicology in Rome (1956), under the editorship of C.W.H. Lindenburg.

BIBLIOGRAPHY: C.W.H. Lindenburg, *Het Leven en de werken van Johannes Regis* (Amsterdam, 1938).

Regli, Francesco, Italian lexicographer; b. Milan, 1802; d. Turin, March 10, 1866. He founded a theatrical publication, *Il Pirata,* in 1835; publ. a *Dizionario biografico dei più celebri poeti ed artisti melodrammatici che fiorirono in Italia dal 1800 al 1860* (Turin, 1860); *Storia del violino in Piemonte* (Turin, 1863); *Elogio a G. Rossini* (Turin, 1864); *Elogio a Felice Romani* (Turin, 1865).

Regnart, Jacob, one of 5 brothers active as musicians; b. probably in or near Douai, France, c.1540; d. Prague, Oct. 16, 1599. He was trained as a chorister; was alumnus at the Imperial Chapel in Vienna, and was a tenor there from 1560; in 1568–70 he was in Italy; from 1579 he was 2nd Kapellmeister at the Imperial Court in Prague; in 1585–95, Vice Kapellmeister to Archduke Ferdinand of Innsbruck, and then in Prague again as Vice Kapellmeister (from Nov. 1596); publ. (1574–1611) a great number of masses, motets, canzone, villanelle, and German songs (many books of these last went through 7 eds.; in a collection of 1590 are some songs by his brothers, **Franz, Karl,** and **Pascasius**). In the *Monatshefte für Musikgeschichte* (vol. XII, p. 97) is a list of his works; W. Pass edited *Thematischer Katalog Sämtlicher Werke Jacob Regnarts* (Vienna, 1969), and the *Opera omnia,* in Corpus Mensurabilis Musicae, LXII/4–6 (1972–75).

BIBLIOGRAPHY: H. Osthoff, *Die Niederländer und das deutsche Lied* (Berlin, 1938; pp. 343–422).

Regt, Hendrik de, Dutch composer; b. Rotterdam, July 5, 1950. He studied composition with Otto Ketting in The Hague (1968–72).

WORKS: *Canzoni e Scherzi* for Soprano, Flute, and Harp (1972); *Proteus,* music for Flute, Viola, and Harp (1974); *Metamorfosen* for Oboe and English Horn (1974); *Silenus en Bacchanten* for Flute, Oboe, and Guitar (1974); *Pastorale* for Flute and Oboe (1974–75); *Circe* for Clarinet, Violin, and Piano (1975); *Mond im Zenit verharrend,* after Goethe, for Chorus and Orch. (1976); about 30 works, each entitled *Musica,* written for different instrumental combinations: for Wind Quintet (1969); Oboe, Cello, Harp, and Percussion (1970); 4 Saxophones (1971); Flute, Percussion, and Narrator (1970–72); Flute, Viola, Cello, Guitar, and Percussion (1972); 2 Trumpets, Horn, and Trombone (1971–72); Flute, Guitar, and Percussion (1972); 4 Clarinets (1972–73); 4 Horns (1974).

Rehberg, Walter, Swiss pianist and writer; b. Geneva, May 14, 1900; d. Zürich, Oct. 22, 1957. He studied with his father, Willy Rehberg (1863–1937); then in Berlin with Ernst Toch and Eugen d'Albert; began a career as a pianist; in 1934 was appointed prof. at the Music Academy in Zürich. He publ. (with his wife, Paula Rehberg) popular biographies of Brahms (1944), Schubert (1946), Chopin (1949), and Schumann (1954).

Rehfuss, Heinz, German-born Swiss bass-baritone; b. Frankfurt, May 25, 1917. He studied with his father, **Carl Rehfuss** (1885–1946), a singer and teacher, and with his mother, **Florentine Rehfuss-Peichert,** a contralto. The family moved to Neuchâtel, Switzerland, and Heinz Rehfuss became a Swiss citizen. He made his professional debut in opera at Biel-Solothurn in 1938; then sang with the Stadttheater in Lucerne (1938–39) and at the Zürich Opera (1940–52). He subsequently was active in America; taught voice at the Montreal Cons. in 1961; in 1965 was on the faculty of the State Univ. of N.Y. at Buffalo; in 1970 was a visiting prof. at the Eastman School of Music in Rochester, N.Y. He also toured in Asia, giving vocal recitals in India and Indonesia. He was successful mainly in dramatic roles, such as Don Giovanni and Boris Godunov.

Rehm, Wolfgang, German musicologist; b. Munich, Sept. 3, 1929. He studied musicology with Gurlitt and Zenck at Freiburg Univ. (Ph.D., 1952, with the dissertation *Das Chansonwerk von Gilles Binchois*); also studied theory and piano at the Hoch-

schule für Musik in Freiburg. In 1954 he joined the publ. firm of Bärenreiter in Kassel, eventually becoming chief editor. In 1960 he was named co-editor (with Wolfgang Plath) of the *Neue Mozart-Ausgabe.*

Reich, Steve, American composer of sui generis hypnopompic music; b. New York, Oct. 3, 1936. He studied philosophy at Cornell Univ. (B.A., 1957), where he became fascinated with the irrationally powerful theories of Ludwig Wittgenstein (a brother of the amputated pianist Paul Wittgenstein), who enunciated the famous tautological formula "Whereof one cannot speak thereof one must be silent." Reich in his music confuted this dictum by speaking loudly of tonalities and modalities which had remained in limbo for a millennium. He had a normal childhood; took piano lessons, but also studied drumming with Roland Koloff, a virtuoso timpanist; synchronously, he became infatuated with jazz and Bach by way of Stravinsky's stylizations. In N.Y. he took private composition lessons with Hall Overton and earned his living by driving a taxicab. From 1958 to 1961 he took courses with William Bergsma and Vincent Persichetti at the Juilliard School of Music; later went to California, where he entered Mills College in the classes of Darius Milhaud and Luciano Berio (M.A., 1963); in 1965 he returned to N.Y. In 1966 he organized his own ensemble, called Steve Reich and Musicians, which began as a trio with Arthur Murphy and Jon Gibson and eventually expanded into a duo-de-viginti multitude. In the summer of 1970 Reich traveled to Ghana, where he practiced under the tutelage of indigenous drummers. In 1973 he studied the Balinese gamelan with a native teacher at the American Society for Eastern Arts Summer Program at the Univ. of Washington in Seattle. Becoming conscious of his ethnic heredity, he went to Jerusalem in 1976 to study the traditional forms of Hebrew cantillation. In 1974 he received grants from the National Endowment for the Arts and from the N.Y. State Council on the Arts; he was also invited to Berlin as an artist-in-residence. In 1975 he received a grant from the Rockefeller Foundation, and in 1976 a 2nd grant from the National Endowment for the Arts. In 1978 he was awarded a Guggenheim fellowship. Thus reinforced, he was able to abandon taxicab driving and other menial ways of earning money; soon his music became popular enough to enable him to exist as an independent artist. Slowly but surely he rose to fame; his group was invited to perform at the Holland Festival and at the radio stations of Frankfurt and Stuttgart. His music was astoundingly audacious; rather than continue in the wake of obsolescent modernism, inexorably increasing in complexity, he deliberately reduced his harmonic and contrapuntal vocabulary and defiantly explored the fascinating potentialities of repetitive patterns. This kind of technique has been variously described as minimalist (for it was derived from a minimum of chordal combinations), phase music (because it shifted from one chord to another, a note at a time), modular (because it was built on symmetric modules), and pulse music (because it derived from a series of measured rhythmic units). Another definition is simply "process," suggesting tonal progressions in flux. Etiologically, this type of composition is hypnopompic, for it creates a subliminal state between a strong dream and a sudden reality. Analytically, it represents a paradox, for it is uncompromisingly modern in its use of exotic instruments, infinitely challenging in its obdurate continuity, and yet elemental in the deliberate limitations of its resources. This system of composition is akin to serialism in its application of recurrent melodic progressions and periodic silences. Despite its apparent disregard for musical convention, or indeed for public taste, Reich likes to trace his musical ancestry to the sweetly vacuous homophony of the Ars Antiqua, with particular reference to the opaque works of the great master of the Notre Dame School of Paris, Perotin. He deliberately avoids fanciful titles in his works, preferring to define them by names of instruments, or numbers of musical parts. The extraordinary aspect of Reich's career is that by rejecting the conventional way of music-making, and by thus infuriating the academics, he finds a direct avenue to the hearts, minds, and ears of the young.

WORKS: *Pitch Charts* for Instrumental Ensemble (1963); *Music for Piano and Tapes* (1964); *Livelihood* for Tape (1965); *It's Gonna Rain* for Tape (1965); *Come Out* for Tape (1966); *Melodica* for Tape (1966); *Reed Phase* for a Reed Instrument and Tape (1966); *Piano Phase* for 2 Pianos or 2 Marimbas (1967); *My Name Is* for Several Performers, Tape Recorders, and Audience (1967); *Violin Phase* for Violin and Tape (1967); *Pendulum Music* for Microphone, Amplifiers, Speakers, and Performers (1968); *Pulse Music* for the Phase-shifting Pulse Gate, an electronic device built by Reich (1969); *4 Log Drums* for 4 Log Drums and Phase-shifting Pulse Gate (1969); *4 Organs* for 4 Electric Organs and Maracas (1970); *Drumming* for 8 small tuned Drums, 3 Marimbas, 3 Glockenspiels, 2 Female Voices, Whistling, and Piccolo (1971); *Clapping Music* for 2 Musicians clapping hands in an interlocking rhythmic pattern (1972); *Music for Pieces of Wood* (1973); *Music for Mallet Instruments, Voice and Organ* (1973); *6 Pianos* (1973); *Music for 18 Musicians* for Violin, Cello, 2 Clarinets, 4 Pianos, 4 Female Voices, 3 Marimbas, 2 Xylophones, and Metallophone (1975; N.Y., April 24, 1976); *Music for a Large Ensemble* (1978; Holland Festival, June 1979); *Variations for Winds, Strings and Keyboards* (1979; with Chamber Orch., N.Y., Feb. 19, 1980; full orch. version, San Francisco, May 14, 1980); *Octet* for String Quartet, 2 Pianos, and 2 Clarinets doubling on Bass Clarinet and Flute (Radio Frankfurt, June 21, 1979); *Tehillim* (*Psalms,* in Hebrew) for 4 Sopranos, Percussion, Woodwinds, Electric Organs, and String Quartet (Houston, Nov. 21, 1981; N.Y. Phil., Sept. 16, 1982); *Vermont Counterpoint* for 11 Flutes, 10 of them recorded on Tape (N.Y., Oct. 1, 1982). He also publ. a book, *Writing about Music* (N.Y., 1974; French ed., *Ecrits et entretiens sur la musique,* Paris, 1981).

Reich, Willi, Austrian writer on music; b. Vienna, May 27, 1898; d. Zürich, May 1, 1980. He studied at the Univ. of Vienna, receiving his Ph.D. (1934) with the dissertation *Padre Martini als Theoretiker und Lehrer;* also studied privately with Alban Berg; edited a modern music magazine, *23.* In 1938 he settled in Switzerland; in 1948, became music critic of the *Neue Zürcher Zeitung.*

WRITINGS: *Alban Berg* (Vienna, 1937; basic biography); *Bekenntnis zu Mozart* (Lucerne, 1945); *Joseph Haydn* (Lucerne, 1946); *Hugo Wolf-Rhapsodie* (Zürich, 1947); *Richard Wagner* (Olten, 1948); *Anton Bruckner: Ein Bild seiner Persönlichkeit* (Basel, 1953); ed. *Arthur Honegger Nachklang: Schriften, Photos, Dokumente* (Zürich, 1957); *Gustav Mahler im eigenen Wort, im Wort der Freunde* (Zürich, 1958); *Felix Mendelssohn im Spiegel eigener Aussagen und zeitgenössischer Dokumente* (Zürich, 1970).

Reicha, Anton, Czech composer; b. Prague, Feb. 26, 1770; d. Paris, May 28, 1836. He was a nephew and pupil of **Joseph Reicha** (*recte* **Rejcha;** composer and violinist, leader and later Kapellmeister, of the Electoral orch. at Bonn). From 1785, he was a flutist in the Bonn orch. in which Beethoven was a viola player; from 1794–99 he taught piano in Hamburg, wrote an opera, and traveled to Paris in hopes of producing it; but had to content himself with the successful performance of 2 symphs. From 1801 to 1808 he lived in Vienna, was intimate with Beethoven, and associated with Haydn, Albrechtsberger, and Salieri. After the French invasion he went to Paris; brought out the moderately successful comic operas *Cagliostro* (Nov. 27, 1810), *Natalie* (July 13, 1816), and *Sapho* (Dec. 16, 1822); also was held in high esteem as a theorist and teacher (among his pupils were Liszt, Elwart, Gounod, Lefebvre, and Dancla), and as an instrumental composer. Among his best works are 4 sets of 6 woodwind quintets each (opp. 88, 91, 99, 100). In 1818 he succeeded Méhul as prof. of counterpoint and fugue at the Paris Cons.; was naturalized in 1829; succeeded to Boieldieu's chair in the Académie Française in 1835.

WRITINGS: *Etudes ou théories pour le pianoforte, dirigées d'une manière nouvelle* (1800); *Traité de mélodie, abstraction faite de ses rapports avec l'harmonie* (1814; 2nd ed., 1832); *Cours de composition musicale* (1818); *Traité de haute composition musicale* (2 vols., 1824, 1826; ed. 1834 by Czerny, together with the *Cours de composition musicale,* in German as *Vollständiges Lehrbuch,* 4 vols.); *Art du compositeur dramatique* (1833); *Petit traité d'harmonie pratique* (n.d.).

BIBLIOGRAPHY: J.A. Delaire, *Notice sur Reicha* (Paris, 1837); E. Bücken, *Anton Reicha; Sein Leben und Kompositionen* (Munich, 1912) and "Beethoven und A. Reicha," *Die Musik* (March 1913); A. Hnilička, *Portraite* (Prague, 1922); J.G. Prod'homme, "From the Unpublished Autobiography of A. Reicha," *Musical Quarterly* (July 1936); M. Emmanuel, *A. Reicha* (Paris, 1937); O. Šotolová, *Antonín Rejcha* (Prague, 1977; with thematic catalogue).

Reichardt, Johann Friedrich, German composer and writer; b. Königsberg, Nov. 25, 1752; d. Giebichenstein. near Halle, June 27, 1814. A pupil of C.G. Richter (piano and composition) and Veichtner (violin), he later studied philosophy at the univs. of Königsberg and Leipzig; in 1775 obtained the post of Kapellmeister to Frederick the Great. He founded (1783) the Concerts Spirituels for the performance of new works, for which he wrote short analytical programs. Dismissed in 1794 because of his sympathy with the French Revolution, Reichardt lived in Altona till 1797; was then appointed inspector of the saltworks at Giebichenstein. The French invasion drove him to Danzig in 1806, and on Jerome Bonaparte's threat to confiscate his property Reichardt joined him at Kassel, and became his court conductor; he left Kassel in 1808, then settled in Giebichenstein. For Berlin and Potsdam Reichardt composed numerous Italian and German operas, incidental music to plays, and German singspiels, the latter exercising considerable influence on the development of German opera. As a song composer (cf. Lindner, *Geschichte des deutschen Liedes*), he ranks high (he set about 60 of Goethe's lyrics to music); his instrumental music includes 7 symphs., 14 piano concertos, 2 piano quartets, 6 string trios, a Violin Concerto, 11 violin sonatas, 12 piano sonatas, etc. An extremely diligent writer, he edited a number of musical periodicals and publ. several books: *Über die deutsche komische Oper* (1774); *Über die Pflichten des Ripienviolinisten* (1776); *Briefe eines aufmerksamen Reisenden, die Musik betreffend* (2 parts, 1774, 1776); *Schreiben über die Berlinische Musik* (1775); *Vertraute Briefe aus Paris* (3 parts, 1804, 1805); *Vertraute Briefe, geschrieben auf einer Reise nach Wien* (2 vols., 1810). His autobiography is in the *Berlinische musikalische Zeitung,* nos. 55–89 (1805). His wife, **Juliane** (née **Benda;** b. Potsdam, May 4, 1752; d. there, May 11, 1783), was a fine pianist, who also publ. a number of songs.

BIBLIOGRAPHY: H.M. Schletterer, *J.F. Reichardt. Sein Leben und seine musikalische Tätigkeit* (Augsburg, 1865; only vol. I publ.); C. Lange, *J.F. Reichardt* (Halle, 1902); W. Pauli, *J.F. Reichardt. Sein Leben und seine Stellung in der Geschichte des deutschen Liedes* (Berlin, 1902); M. Faller, *Reichardt und die Anfänge der musikalischer Journalistik* (Kassel, 1929); P. Sieber, *Reichardt als Musikästhetiker* (Strasbourg, 1930); H. Dennerlein, *Reichardt und seine Klavierwerke* (Münster, 1930); J. Müller-Blattau, "Musik zur Goethezeit," *Euphorion* (1930); F. Flössner, *Beiträge zur Reichardt-Forschung* (Frankfurt, 1933); E. Neuss, *Das Giebichensteiner Dichterparadies; J.F. Reichardt und die Herberge der Romantik* (Halle, 1949); W. Salmen, *Johann Friedrich Reichardt* (Freiburg, 1963); R. Pröpper, *Die Bühnenwerke Johann Friedrich Reichardts* (Bonn, 1965); N. Reich, *A Translation and Commentary of Selected Writings of Johann Friedrich Reichardt* (Diss., N.Y. Univ., 1973).

Reichardt, Luise, daughter of **Johann Reichardt;** b. Berlin, April 11, 1779; d. Hamburg, Nov. 17, 1826. She composed a number of songs, of which selections were publ. by G. Rheinhardt (Munich, 1922) and N. Reich (N.Y., 1978).

BIBLIOGRAPHY: M.G.W. Brandt, *Leben der Luise Reichardt* (Karlsruhe, 1858; 2nd ed., 1865).

Reichel, Friedrich, German composer; b. Oberoderwitz, Jan. 27, 1833; d. Dresden, Dec. 29, 1889. He studied with Wieck and Rietz in Dresden. Chief among his 32 publ. works is a *Frühlingssymphonie;* he also wrote an operetta, *Die geängsteten Diplomaten;* part-songs for men's voices; and some motets.

Reicher-Kindermann, Hedwig, German dramatic soprano; b. Munich, July 15, 1853; d. Trieste, June 2, 1883. She was a daughter of the baritone **August Kindermann** (1817–91); began her career as a contralto but later sang soprano. She first sang in the chorus of the Munich Court Opera (1870–71); made her debut at Karlsruhe in 1871; sang at the opening of Bayreuth in 1876; then sang in Hamburg (1877). The Wagnerian impresario Neumann engaged her for his Wagner troupe in Leipzig from 1880, and she successfully performed the roles of Fricka and Brünnhilde. She was married to the playwright Emanuel Reicher, and adopted the hyphenated name Reicher-Kindermann in her professional activities. Her early death was lamented.

BIBLIOGRAPHY: A. Neumann, *Erinnerungen an Richard Wagner* (Leipzig, 1907; in Eng., N.Y., 1908).

Reichert, Arno Julius, German writer on music; b. Dresden, May 31, 1866; d. there, Feb. 10, 1933. After studying at the Dresden Cons., he was appointed teacher of music at the Freimaurer-Institut in Dresden; in 1894–1904 taught at R.L. Schneider's Musikschule; from 1904 was head of the music division of the Dresden Royal Library. He arranged about 450 folk songs for chorus; publ. *50 Jahre Sinfonie-Konzerte* (a record of the works produced in Dresden from 1858–1908) and *Die Original-Musik-Handschriften der sächsischen Landesbibliothek* (Leipzig, 1923).

Reichert, Johannes, German conductor and composer; b. Dresden, June 19, 1876; d. Teplitz, Feb. 15, 1942. He was a pupil of Draeseke (1893), and of Nicode and Buchmayer (1894–98); in 1896–1900 was conductor of the orch. class at the Dresden Musikschule; in 1902–6, also répétiteur at the court theater; founded in 1899 the Volkssingakademie (a mixed chorus recruited exclusively from the working classes); from 1905–13 was the private teacher of the crown prince of Saxony; in 1906–22, municipal music director in Teplitz-Schönau; then lived in retirement in Teplitz.

Reichmann, Theodor, German baritone; b. Rostock, March 15, 1849; d. Marbach, on Lake Constance, May 22, 1903. He studied voice with Lamperti in Milan; returning to Germany, he made his operatic debut in Magdeburg in 1869; subsequently sang in Rotterdam, Strasbourg, Hamburg, and Munich; also made guest appearances at the Metropolitan Opera in N.Y. (1889–91) and at Covent Garden Opera in London. In 1893 he was engaged at the Court Opera in Vienna and remained there until his death.

Reichwein, Leopold, Austrian conductor; b. Breslau, May 16, 1878; d. (suicide) Vienna, April 8, 1945. He was a theater conductor in Breslau, Mannheim, and Karlsruhe; then was on the staff of the Vienna Opera (1913–21), and music director of the Gesellschaft der Musikfreunde in Vienna (1921–26), and music director in Bochum (1926–38); he returned to Vienna in 1938; conducted at the State Opera, and taught conducting at the Vienna Academy of Music. He committed suicide at the end of the war when he was accused of Nazi affiliations. He was also a composer; wrote the operas *Vasantasena* (Breslau, 1903) and *Die Liebenden von Kandahar* (Breslau, 1907); incidental music to Goethe's *Faust;* songs.

Reid, General John, b. Straloch, Perthshire, Feb. 13, 1721; d. London, Feb. 6, 1807. A musical amateur, he left $52,000 to found a chair of music at Edinburgh Univ., also providing that an annual concert of his own compositions should be given. The chair was founded in 1839; the following have been "Reid" profs.: John Thomson; Sir Henry Bishop, 1842; Henry Hugh Pearson, 1844; John Donaldson, 1845; Sir Herbert Stanley Oakeley, 1865; Frederick Niecks, 1891; and Donald Francis Tovey, from 1914 until his death in 1940.

Reif, Paul, Czech-American composer; b. Prague, March 23, 1910; d. New York, July 7, 1978. He played violin as a child; studied composition in Vienna with Richard Stöhr and Franz Schmidt, and conducting with Franz Schalk and Bruno Walter; also had lessons with Richard Strauss. In 1941 he emigrated to the U.S., and in 1942 joined the U.S. Intelligence Corps; while with the U.S. Army in North Africa he set to music the soldiers' song *Dirty Gertie from Bizerte,* which was introduced by Josephine Baker in Algiers in April 1943. Upon his discharge in 1945 he was awarded the Croix de Guerre and the Purple Heart. Returning to the U.S., he was active as an arranger in Hollywood; wrote a number of lightweight pieces (*Petticoat Waltz, Dream Concerto,* etc.); also several song cycles, among them *5 Finger Exercises,* to poems by T.S. Eliot; *Reverence for Life* and *Monsieur le Pélican* as a tribute to Albert Schweitzer; etc.
WORKS: *Triple City* for Chorus and Brass Ensemble (N.Y., April 16, 1963); *Requiem to War* for Mixed Chorus and Percussion (N.Y., May 20, 1963); *Birches,* to Robert Frost's words, for Voice and Orch. (N.Y., Feb. 2, 1965); *Letter from a Birmingham Jail* for Mixed Chorus and Piano, to words by Martin Luther King, Jr. (Howard Univ., Washington, D.C., March 2, 1965); *Philidor's Defense* for Chamber Orch., inspired by the famous Philidor

chess opening: 1. P-K4, P-K4; 2. N-KB3, P-Q3 (N.Y., April 10, 1965); operas: *Mad Hamlet* (1965) and *Portrait in Brownstone* (N.Y., May 15, 1966); *Pentagram* for Piano (1969); *The Artist* (N.Y., April 17, 1972); *The Curse of Mauvais-Air* (N.Y., May 9, 1974); *5 Divertimenti* for 4 Strings (1969); *Episodes* for String Orch. (1972); Quintet for Clarinet, Viola, Piano, Percussion, and Folksinger (1974); *Duo for 3* for Clarinet, Cello, and Mezzo-soprano (1974); *America 1776–1876–1976* for Orch., Solo Guitar, Banjo, Electric Guitar, and Vocal Quartet (Metropolitan Museum, N.Y., Jan. 24, 1976).

Reimann, Aribert, German pianist and composer; b. Berlin, March 4, 1936. He studied with Blacher and Pepping; then took music courses at the German Academy in Rome; subsequently became active as an accompanist. He composed *Quasimodo Cantata;* an opera, *Traumspiel,* after Strindberg (Kiel, June 20, 1965); 2 piano concertos: No. 1 (Berlin, Oct. 26, 1962) and No. 2 (Nuremberg, Jan. 12, 1973); Cello Concerto (1959); *Nenia* for Women's Voices (Sprechstimme) and Orch. (1968); *Inane,* monologue for Soprano and Orch. (Berlin, Jan. 8, 1969); *Loqui* for Orch. (Saarbrücken, Dec. 5, 1969); *Vogelscheuchen,* ballet (Berlin, Oct. 7, 1970); *Melusine,* opera (Schwetzinger, April 29, 1971); *Lear,* opera after Shakespeare (Munich, July 9, 1978); *Requiem* (Kiel, June 26, 1982).

Reimann, Heinrich, German writer on music, son of **Ignaz Reimann;** b. Rengersdorf, Silesia, March 14, 1850; d. Berlin, May 24, 1906. He studied music with his father; conducted singing societies in Silesia; in 1887 went to Berlin, where he was engaged as a librarian, organ teacher, and music critic. He publ. several biographical monographs: *Johannes Brahms* (Berlin, 1897; several subsequent printings); *Hans von Bülow* (posthumous; Berlin, 1909); *Johann Sebastian Bach* (posthumous; Berlin, 1912; completed by Schrader); also brought out an informative memoir, *Musikalische Rückblicke* (2 vols., Berlin, 1900); publ. a valuable collection of old German songs, arranged for concert performance, *Das deutsche Lied* (4 vols.); the collection *Internationales Volksliederbuch* (3 vols.); *Das deutsche geistliche Lied* (6 vols.).

Reimann, Ignaz, German church composer; b. Albendorf, Silesia, Dec. 27, 1820; d. Rengersdorf, June 17, 1885. He publ. 18 masses, 4 Requiems, 3 Te Deums, 48 offertories, 40 graduals; many other works, including instrumental works, in MS.

Reimers, Paul, German tenor; b. Lunden, Schleswig-Holstein, March 14, 1878; d. New York, April 14, 1942. He studied with Georg Henschel in England; made his stage debut as Max in *Der Freischütz* in Hamburg (1903), but did not pursue his operatic career and sang mainly in oratorio. In 1913 he went to America; gave several concerts in programs of German lieder, and also performed songs of the modern French school.

Rein, Walter, German composer and pedagogue; b. Stotternheim, near Erfurt, Dec. 10, 1893; d. Berlin, June 18, 1955. He studied composition with Erwin Lendvai; joined the Jöde youth movement in music, and wrote many instructive choral works; in 1935 became a prof. at the Hochschule für Musik-Erziehung in Berlin (until 1945). His folk-song arrangements were publ. in Jöde's *Musikant* and the *Lobeda-Chorbuch.*

Reina, Domenico, Italian tenor; b. Lugano, 1797; d. there, July 29, 1843. He studied with Boile in Milan; made his debut in 1829 at La Scala in Milan as Ilio in Rossini's *Zelmira;* while there, he created Arturo in Bellini's *La Straniera;* also Tamas in Donizetti's *Gemma di Vergy.* He was greatly admired for his performances of the lyrico-dramatic tenor parts in the operas of Rossini, Bellini, and Donizetti.

Reinach, Théodore, French musicologist; b. St. Germain-en-Laye, July 3, 1860; d. Paris, Oct. 28, 1928. He studied jurisprudence and philology, specializing particularly in Greek studies; was editor of the *Revue des Etudes Grecques* (1888–1907); his investigations into the nature of Greek music are of importance. He publ. *La Musique grecque* (Paris, 1926); brought out Plutarch's treatise on music (with H. Weil; Paris, 1900) and *Le Second Hymne delphique à Apollon* (with L. Boëllmann; Paris, 1897).

Reinagle, Alexander, important American musician; b. Portsmouth, England (of Austrian parents), baptized April 23, 1756; d. Baltimore, Sept. 21, 1809. He studied in Edinburgh with Raynor Taylor, and in London for a time; also visited Lisbon and other continental cities. From his correspondence he appears to have been an intimate friend of C.P.E. Bach. He came to N.Y. early in 1786, settling in the same year in Philadelphia, where he taught, managed subscription concerts (also in N.Y.), and was active as a singer, pianist, conductor, and composer; in 1787, introduced 4-hand piano music to America; was associated, possibly as harpsichordist, with the Old American Co., and most likely took part in their 1788–89 season in N.Y.; in 1793 he was engaged as music director of a stock company for the production of plays and comic operas, with Thomas Wignell as general director; also built the New Theatre, which opened on Feb. 2, 1793, with Reinagle acting as composer, singer, and director; later also managed a company in Baltimore. WORKS: *Collection of Most Favorite Scots Tunes with Variations for Harpsichord* (London; probably issued in Glasgow); *6 Sonatas with Accompaniment for Violin* (London, c.1780); *Miscellaneous Quartets* (Philadelphia, 1791); *Concerto on the Improved Pianoforte with Additional Keys* (1794); *Preludes* (1794); accompaniments and incidental music to *The Sicilian Romance* (1795), *The Witches of the Rock,* pantomime (1796), and various English plays; *Masonic Overture* (1800); 4 piano sonatas (in Library of Congress, Washington, D.C.; Sonata No. 2 publ. in abridged form by J.T. Howard in *A Program of Early American Piano-Music,* N.Y., 1931; see also S.R. Duer, *An Annotated Edition of 4 Sonatas by Alexander Reinagle* [Peabody Cons., 1976]); *Collection of Favorite Songs;* music to Milton's *Paradise Lost* (incomplete).

BIBLIOGRAPHY: J.R. Parker, "Musical Reminiscences," *Euterpeiad* (Jan. 19, 1822); O.G. Sonneck, *Early Concert Life in America* (Leipzig, 1907; in Eng.); idem, *Early Opera in America* (N.Y., 1915); E.C. Krohn, "A. Reinagle as Sonatist," *Musical Quarterly* (Jan. 1932); J.T. Howard, *Our American Music* (N.Y., 1939, and later eds.); O.G. Sonneck and W.T. Upton, *Bibliography of Early Secular American Music* (Washington, 1945); *Sammelbände der Internationalen Musik-Gesellschaft,* 11; *Dictionary of American Biography;* C.A. Horton, *Serious Art and Concert Music for Piano in the 100 Years from Alexander Reinagle to Edward MacDowell* (Univ. of North Carolina, 1965).

Reinecke, Carl (Heinrich Carsten), renowned German pianist, composer, and conductor; b. Altona, June 23, 1824; d. Leipzig, March 10, 1910. He was a pupil of his father, a music teacher. His first concert tour was to Denmark and Sweden in 1843; he then went to Leipzig, learned much through meetings with Mendelssohn and Schumann, made a 2nd tour through North Germany, and was from 1846–48 court pianist to Christian VIII at Copenhagen. Then, after spending some years in Paris, he became a teacher at the Cologne Cons. in 1851; was music director at Barmen (1854–59) and Breslau (1859–60), and (1860–95) conductor of the Gewandhaus Concerts at Leipzig. At the same time he was a prof. of piano playing and free composition at the Leipzig Cons. An eminent pianist, he excelled as an interpreter of Mozart, made concert tours almost yearly, and was enthusiastically welcomed in England, the Netherlands, Scandinavia, Switzerland, and throughout Germany; among his pupils were Grieg, Riemann, Sinding, Arthur Sullivan, Karl Muck, and Cosima Wagner. As a composer and a teacher of composition, Reinecke was the leader in Leipzig for a quarter of a century; his numerous works, in every genre, are classic in form and of refined workmanship.

WORKS: Operas: *König Manfred* (Wiesbaden, July 26, 1867); *Ein Abenteuer Händels* (Schwerin, 1874); *Auf hohen Befehl* (Hamburg, Oct. 1, 1886); *Der Gouverneur von Tours* (Schwerin, 1891); several musical fairy tales for Solos, Chorus, and Piano: *Nussknacker und Mausekönig, Schneewittchen, Dornröschen, Aschenbrödel, Die wilden Schwäne, Glückskind und Pechvogel,* etc.; oratorio, *Belsazar;* several choral works, with Orch.: *Sommertagsbilder, Schlachtlied, Der deutsche Sang,* etc.; numerous choruses for Mixed Voices; for Orch.: 3 symphs., 9 overtures, smaller works; 4 piano concertos; Violin Concerto; Cello Concerto; Harp Concerto; Flute Concerto; chamber music: Octet for Wind Instruments; Sextet for Wind Instruments; 6 string quartets; Piano Quintet; 2 piano quartets; 6 piano trios; Trio for Piano, Oboe, and Horn; Trio for Piano, Clarinet, and Horn; Violin Sonata; 3 violin sonatinas; 3 cello sonatas; Sonata for Flute and Piano; numerous character pieces for Piano; Sonata for Piano, Left Hand; a suite, *Biblische Bilder;* 3 sonatas for 2 Pianos; altogether about 300 opus numbers. He wrote cadenzas to 42 movements of piano concertos by Bach, Mozart, Beethoven, and Weber; some of these cadenzas are often used. He also wrote the following books: *Was sollen wir spielen?* (1886); *Zur Wiederbelebung der Mozartschen Klavierkonzerte* (1891); *Die Beethovenschen Klaviersonaten* (1896; 9th ed., 1924; in Eng., 1898); *Und manche liebe Schatten steigen auf* (1900); *Meister der Tonkunst* (1903); *Aus dem Reich der Töne* (1907).

BIBLIOGRAPHY: J. von Wasielewski, *Carl Reinecke. Ein Künstlerbild* (Leipzig, 1892); E. Segnitz, *Carl Reinecke* (Leipzig, 1900); M. Steinitzer, *Das Leipziger Gewandhaus im neuen Heim unter Carl Reinecke* (Leipzig, 1924); N. Topusov, *Carl Reinecke; Beiträge zu seinem Leben* (Diss., Univ. of Berlin, 1943).

Reiner, Fritz, eminent Hungarian conductor; b. Budapest, Dec. 19, 1888; d. New York, Nov. 15, 1963. He studied piano with Thomán and composition with Koessler at the Music Academy in Budapest; concurrently took courses in jurisprudence. He was conductor of the People's Opera in Budapest (1911–14) and of the Court Opera in Dresden (1914–21); subsequently conducted in Hamburg, Berlin, Vienna, Rome, and Barcelona. In 1922 he was engaged as music director and conductor of the Cincinnati Symph. Orch.; held this position until 1931, when he became a prof. of conducting at the Curtis Inst. of Music in Philadelphia; among his students were Leonard Bernstein, Lukas Foss, and several other well-known American musicians. In 1936–37 he made guest appearances at Covent Garden Opera in London; between 1935 and 1938 was guest conductor at the San Francisco Opera; from 1938 to 1948 he was conductor and music director of the Pittsburgh Symph. Orch.; in the interim filled engagements at the Metropolitan Opera in N.Y. He achieved the peak of his success as a conductor with the Chicago Symph. Orch., which he led from 1953 to 1962, and which he brought up to the point of impeccably fine performance, both in Classical and modern music. His striving for perfection created for him the reputation of a ruthless master of the orch.; he was given to explosions of temper, but musicians and critics agreed that it was because of his uncompromising drive toward the optimum of orch. playing that the Chicago Symph. Orch. achieved a very high rank among American symph. organizations.

BIBLIOGRAPHY: H. Schonberg, *The Great Conductors* (N.Y., 1967; pp. 335–37).

Reiner, Karel, prominent Czech composer and pianist; b. Žatec, June 27, 1910; d. Prague, Oct. 17, 1979. He studied law in Prague (Dr.Jur., 1933); then attended classes in quarter-tone and sixth-tone composition with Alois Hába at the Prague Cons. (1934–35); was associated with E.F. Burian's improvisa-

tional theater in Prague (1934–38). Unable to leave Central Europe when the Nazis invaded Czechoslovakia, he was detained at Terezín, and later sent to the dread camps of Dachau and Auschwitz, but survived, and after liberation resumed his activities as a composer and pianist. His earliest works were atonal and athematic; in 1935–36 he wrote a *Suite* and a *Fantasy* for quarter-tone piano, and a set of 5 quarter-tone songs; after 1945 he wrote mostly traditional music; then returned to ultramodern techniques.

WORKS: 2 operas: *Pohádka o zakleté písen (Tale of an Enchanted Song,* 1949) and *Schustermärchen (The Cobbler's Tale* or *The Horrible Dragon, the Princess and the Cobbler),* fairy-tale opera for puppets, 5 Singers and Chamber Ensemble (1972); ballet, *Jednota (Unity,* 1933); cantata, *Bylo jim tisíc let (It Was a Thousand Years since Then,* 1962); Piano Concerto (1932); Violin Concerto (1937); *Concertante Suite* for Winds and Percussion (1947); *Divertimento* for Clarinet, Harp, Strings, and Percussion (1947); *3 Czech Dances* for Orch. (1949); *Spring Prelude* for Orch. (1950); *Motýli tady nežijí (Butterflies Don't Live Here Anymore),* 6 Pictures for Orch., based on music to the film (1959–60; depicts the fate of Jewish children in the Terezín concentration camp); Symph. (1960); *Symphonic Overture* (1964); Concerto for Bass Clarinet, Strings, and Percussion (1966); *Concertante Suite* for Orch. (1967); Bassoon Concertino (1969); *Promluvy (Utterances)* for Chamber Orch. (1975); *Music* for Strings (1975); *Introduction and Allegro (Diptych* No. 2) for Orch. (1976); *Diptych* No. 1 for Orch. (1977); 3 Symph. Movements (1978); 3 string quartets (1931, 1947, 1951); *7 Miniatures* for Wind Quintet (1931); *Dvanáct (The Twelve),* suite for Piano and Wind Quintet (1931); 2 nonets (Concerto, 1933; *Preambule,* 1974); *Sonata Brevis* for Cello and Piano (1946); *4 Compositions* for Clarinet and Piano (1954); *3 Compositions* for Oboe and Piano (1955); *Elegie and Capriccio* for Cello and Piano (1957); Double-bass Sonata (1957); Violin Sonata (1959); *Small Suite* for 9 Wind Instruments (1960); *6 Bagatelles* for Trumpet and Piano (1962); *2 Compositions* for Oboe and Harp (1962); *4 Compositions* for Solo Clarinet (1963); *6 Studies* for Flute and Piano (1964); Trio for Flute, Bass Clarinet, and Percussion (1964); Piano Trio (1965); *Suite* for Bassoon and Piano (1965); *Music* for 4 Clarinets (1965); *Crty (Sketches)* for Piano Quartet (1966–67); *Concert Studies* for Solo Cymbalom (1967); *2 Compositions* for Saxophone and Piano (1967); *Concertante Sonata* for Percussion (1967); *Prolegomena* for String Quartet (1968); *4 Abbreviations* for Brass Quintet (1968); *Dua,* 5 compositions for 2 Flutes, 2 Oboes, 2 Clarinets, and 2 Trumpets, in any combination (1969); *Volné listy (Loose Leaves)* for Clarinet, Cello, and Piano (1969); *Formulas* for Trombone and Piano (1970); *Recordings* for Solo Bassoon (1970); *Drawings* for Clarinet, Horn, and Piano (1970); *Maxims* for Flute Quartet (1970); *Tercetti* for Oboe, Clarinet, and Bassoon (1971); *Talks* for Wind Quintet (1971–72); *Akrostichon a Allegro* for Bass Clarinet and Piano (1972); *Duo* for 2 Quarter-tone Clarinets (1972); *Replicas* for Flute, Viola, and Harp (1973); *Sujets* for Solo

Guitar (1973); *Overtura ritmica* for Solo Guitar (1974); *Strophes* for Viola and Piano (1975); *Portraits*, suite for String Trio (1977); *Dialogues* for 2 Flutes (1978); *Panels*, sextet for Brasses (1979); *Talks* for Baritone, Saxophone, and Flute (1979); *9 Merry Improvisations* for Piano (1928–29); *5 Jazz Studies* for Piano (1930); 3 piano sonatas (1931, 1942, 1961); *Minda-Minda*, 7 compositions for Piano (1937); songs.

Reinhardt, Delia, German soprano; b. Elberfeld, April 27, 1892; d. Arlesheim, near Basel, Oct. 3, 1974. She studied with Hedwig Schako at the Hoch Cons. in Frankfurt; made her debut in Breslau in 1913. In 1916 she joined the Munich Court (later Bavarian State) Opera, where she sang until 1923. She made her debut at the Metropolitan Opera in N.Y. on Jan. 27, 1923, as Sieglinde; then sang at the Berlin State Opera (1924–33); also made guest appearances at Covent Garden in London (1924–29). Among her outstanding roles were Desdemona, Elsa, and Eva.

Reinhardt, Django (Jean Baptiste Reinhardt), Belgian jazz guitarist; b. Liberchies, Jan. 23, 1910; d. Fontainebleau, May 16, 1953. He began his career in Paris in 1922; gained recognition through his recordings with the singer Jean Sablon and violinist Stephane Grappelli; in 1934 he formed the Quintette du Hot Club de France with Grappelli. After World War II, he toured the U.S.; appeared with Duke Ellington in N.Y. He was an innovative figure in the early jazz movement in Europe; in later years he utilized electrical amplification in his performances.
BIBLIOGRAPHY: C. Delaunay, *Django Reinhardt: Souvenirs* (Paris, 1954; Eng. ed., 1961); M. Abrams, *The Book of Django* (Los Angeles, 1973).

Reinhardt, Heinrich, Austrian operetta composer; b. Pressburg, April 13, 1865; d. Vienna, Jan. 31, 1922. He studied with Bruckner and Mocker in Vienna; was music critic for several papers.
WORKS: Operettas: *Das süsse Mädel* (Vienna, Oct. 25, 1901; his greatest success); *Der liebe Schatz* (Vienna, Oct. 30, 1902); *Der General-Konsul* (Vienna, Jan. 28, 1904); *Krieg im Frieden* (Vienna, Jan. 20, 1906); *Die süssen Grisetten* (Vienna, 1907); *Ein Märchen für alles* (Munich, 1908); *Die Sprudelfee* (Vienna, 1909); *Napoleon und die Frauen* (Vienna, April 28, 1911); *Prinzessin Gretl* (Berlin, 1914); *Des Königs Gäste* (Vienna, 1916); *Die erste Frau* (Munich, 1918); 2 operas: *Die Minnekönigin* and *Der Schuster von Delft.* He also is the author of *Die Entwicklung der Operette* and *Virtuosentum und Künstlerschaft.*

Reinhold, Hugo, Austrian composer; b. Vienna, March 3, 1854; d. there, Sept. 4, 1935. He studied piano with Julius Epstein and composition with Bruckner at the Vienna Cons., graduating in 1874; then was engaged as a piano teacher at the Akademie der Tonkunst in Vienna. He composed a number of attractive piano pieces, a Violin Sonata, and songs.

Reining, Maria, Austrian soprano; b. Vienna, Aug. 7, 1903. She studied at a business school, and was employed in the foreign exchange dept. of a Vienna bank before taking up singing. In 1931 she made her debut at the Vienna State Opera, remaining on its roster until 1933; then sang in Darmstadt (1933–35) and at the Munich State Opera (1935–37). In 1937 she rejoined the Vienna State Opera, continuing on its roster, with interruptions, until 1956. In 1937 she appeared at the Salzburg Festival; Toscanini engaged her to sing Eva in *Die Meistersinger* in Salzburg under his direction in 1937; she also sang the role of the Marschallin in *Der Rosenkavalier* and the title role in *Arabella* by Richard Strauss. She was equally successful in soubrette roles and as a dramatic soprano. In 1938 she appeared with the Covent Garden Opera in London and with the Chicago Opera; in 1949, as the Marschallin with the N.Y. City Opera. She also sang at La Scala in Milan, and toured as a concert singer. In 1962 she became a prof. of singing at the Mozarteum in Salzburg.

Reinken (Reincken), Jan Adams, famous organist and composer; b. April 26, 1623; d. Hamburg, Nov. 24, 1722 (at the age of 99). The place of his birth has not been determined; he may have been born in Wilshausen, Alsace, Wildeshausen near Bremen, or in a Dutch village of similar name. By 1654 he was in Hamburg, where he studied with Heinrich Scheidemann, the organist of the Katharinenkirche. In 1657 he became organist of the Berghkercke in Deventer, the Netherlands. In 1658 he returned to Hamburg as assistant organist to Scheidemann at the Katharinenkirche; in 1663 he succeeded his teacher as organist, a position he held with great distinction for 60 years. Reinken was one of the most celebrated organ virtuosos of his time. In 1720 Bach played at the Katharinenkirche, and Reinken, then 97 years old, was in attendance. Reinken was a consultant on organ building, and a noted teacher of the organ; his students included **Andreas Kneller** (later his son-in-law) and G.D. Leiding. He composed several virtuoso organ pieces, and also 6 instrumental suites publ. as *Hortus musicus.*
WORKS: For Keyboard: *An den Wasserflüssen Babylon; Ballet* in E minor; *Fuga* in G minor; *Partite diverse sopra l'Aria "Schweiget mir von Weiber nehmen," altrimente chiamata "La Meyerin";* 3 suites, in C major, E minor, and G major; *Toccata* in C major; *Was kann uns kommen an für Noth.* His complete works for keyboard may be found in K. Beckmann, *J.A. Reincken: Sämtliche Orgelwerke* (Wiesbaden, 1974). Chamber music: *Hortus musicus,* 6 suites for 2 Violins, Viola da Gamba, and Basso Continuo (Hamburg, 1687; later ed., by J.C.M. van Riemsdijk, Amsterdam, 1888). Vocal music: *Geistlich Konzert "auf Michael": Und es erhub sich ein Streit* for 4 Voices, 2 Violins, Viola, 2 Trumpets, Timpani, and Basso Continuo.
BIBLIOGRAPHY: J. Mattheson, *Critica musica,* I (Hamburg, 1722); J. Mattheson, *Grundlage einer Ehren-Pforte ...* (Hamburg, 1740; new ed. by M. Schneider, Berlin, 1910); J.C.M. van Riemsdijk, "Jean Adam Reincken," *Tijdschrift van de Vereni-*

ging voor Nederlandse muziekgeschiedenis, II/1 (1887); M.E. Houck, "J(e)an Adam(s) Reincken," *Tijdschrift van de Vereniging voor Nederlandse muziekgeschiedenis*, VI/2 (1899); W. Stahl, "Zur Biographie J.A. Reinckens," *Archiv für Musikwissenschaft*, III (1920–21); A. Pirro, "Notes pour servir, éventuellement, à la biographie de Reincken," *Gedenkboek aangeboden aan Dr. D.F. Scheurleer* (The Hague, 1925); A. Pirro, "Reincken et la musique en Alsace au XVII siècle," in *Annuaire* of the Club Vosgien (vol. 3, Strasbourg, 1935); W. Apel, "Neu aufgefundene Clavierwerke von Scheidemann, Tunder, Froberger, Reincken und Buxtehude," *Acta Musicologica*, XXXIV (1962); G. Sharp, "Jan Adam Reincken, 1623–1722," *Musical Times*, CXIV (1973).

Reinmar (original name, **Wochinz**), **Hans**, distinguished Austrian baritone; b. Vienna, April 11, 1895; d. Berlin, Feb. 7, 1961. He studied at the Vienna Academy of Music and in Milan; made his debut in 1919 in Olomouc; then sang in Nuremberg, Zürich, Dresden, and Hamburg; was a member of the Berlin Städtische Oper (1928–45, 1952–61), the Bavarian State Opera in Munich (1945–46, 1950–57), the Berlin State Opera (1948–52), and the Berlin Komische Oper (1952–61); also sang at the festivals in Bayreuth and Salzburg. He excelled in dramatic roles in Italian operas.

Reinthaler, Karl (Martin), German composer; b. Erfurt, Oct. 13, 1822; d. Bremen, Feb. 13, 1896. He studied with G.A. Ritter and Marx in Berlin, and for 3 years in Rome; taught singing at the Cologne Cons. (1853); from 1857, was municipal music director in Bremen.
WORKS: 2 operas: *Edda* (Bremen, 1875) and *Käthchen von Heilbronn* (Frankfurt, 1881); oratorio, *Jephtha*, repeatedly performed in Germany and elsewhere; the famous *Bismarck Hymne;* choral works; a Symph.; songs; Psalms.

Reisenauer, Alfred, German pianist and composer; b. Königsberg, Nov. 1, 1863; d. (on a concert tour) Libau, Latvia, Oct. 3, 1907. He was a pupil of Liszt, with whom he was on friendly terms in Rome. He traveled as a concert pianist in almost every region of the globe, including Siberia; publ. a number of attractive songs to words by Heine, Uhland, and Goethe.
BIBLIOGRAPHY: J. Schwerin, *Erinnerungen an Alfred Reisenauer* (Königsberg, 1909).

Reisenberg, Nadia, Russian-born American pianist; b. Vilna, July 14, 1904; d. New York, June 10, 1983. She studied piano with Leonid Nikolayev at the St. Petersburg Cons. In 1922 she emigrated to America, and continued taking piano lessons with Alexander Lambert and later with Josef Hofmann at the Curtis Inst. in Philadelphia. She began her career as a concert pianist in Russia; gave recitals in Europe and America; appeared as soloist with Barbirolli, Rodzinski, and Damrosch in N.Y. and with Koussevitzky in Boston; gave sonata recitals with the cellist Joseph Schuster, played piano parts in trios, quartets, and quintets with members of the Budapest String Quartet; made a specialty of appearing on radio hours; performed all 27 piano concertos of Mozart on weekly radio broadcasts in N.Y. She was also a noted teacher; taught at the Curtis Inst., at Queens College, at the Mannes College of Music, and at the Juilliard School of Music; also gave master classes in Jerusalem. She recorded all the nocturnes and mazurkas of Chopin, as well as works by Tchaikovsky, Mussorgsky, and Rachmaninoff. She possessed a faultless technique, particularly in pearly scale passages, and a fine lyrical form of expression.

Reiser, Alois, Czech-American composer; b. Prague, April 6, 1887; d. Hollywood, April 4, 1977. He studied composition with Dvořák; also took cello lessons and toured Europe; later emigrated to the U.S. and played cello with the Pittsburgh Symph. Orch. and the N.Y. Symph. From 1918 to 1929 he was engaged as a theater conductor in N.Y.; in 1929 he settled in Hollywood, where he worked as a composer and conductor at the Hollywood film studios. His works adhere to the established style of European Romanticism; typical of these are *Slavic Rhapsody,* which he conducted in Los Angeles on March 8, 1931, and *Erewhon,* which he conducted there on Jan. 24, 1936. He also composed a Cello Concerto, which he performed in Los Angeles on March 23, 1933; and a considerable amount of chamber music. He wrote an opera, *Gobi,* in which he painted in tones the great Asian desert; it had its first and last performance in N.Y. on July 29, 1923, and even then only in concert excerpts.

Reiss, Albert, German dramatic tenor; b. Berlin, Feb. 22, 1870; d. Nice, June 19, 1940. He was an actor before making his debut as a singer in Königsberg as Ivanov in *Zar und Zimmermann* (Sept. 28, 1897); then sang in various German towns; on Dec. 23, 1901, made his American debut at the Metropolitan Opera House in the minor roles of the Sailor and the Shepherd in *Tristan und Isolde;* then sang more important parts in Wagner's operas. In 1919 he returned to Berlin; in 1938 retired from the stage and lived in Nice.

Reiss, Józef Wladyslaw, Polish musicologist; b. Debica, Aug. 4, 1879; d. Cracow, Feb. 22, 1956. He studied musicology with Guido Adler at the Univ. of Vienna; received his Dr.Phil. with a dissertation on the Polish composer Gomólka (1910); in 1922 he went to Cracow, where he was a prof. of music at Cracow Univ., remaining at that post until 1939; he resumed it after the war, retiring in 1953. He wrote (in Polish): *The Problem of Meaning in Music* (Cracow, 1915; 2nd ed., enlarged, 1922); *A Concise History of Music* (Warsaw, 1920; 3rd ed., revised, 1931); *Beethoven* (Warsaw, 1920); *Henryk Wieniawski* (Warsaw, 1931; 3rd ed., 1970); *An Almanac of Music in Cracow, 1780–1914* (Cracow, 1939); *Violins and Violinists* (Cracow, 1955); *Short Encyclopedia of Music* (Warsaw, 1960); also a manual on form, *Formenlehre,* which appeared in German (Leipzig,

1917).

Reisserová, Julie, Czech composer; b. Prague, Oct. 9, 1888; d. there, Feb. 25, 1938. She studied with J.B. Foerster; also with Albert Roussel in Paris. Among her works are *Pastorale maritime* for Orch. (1933); *Esquisses* for Piano; several albums of songs.

BIBLIOGRAPHY: J. Vacková, *Julie Reisserová* (Prague, 1948).

Reissiger, Carl Gottlieb, German composer; b. Belzig, near Wittenberg, Jan. 31, 1798; d. Dresden, Nov. 7, 1859. He studied with Schicht at the Thomasschule in Leipzig from 1811; went to Vienna in 1821 and thence to Munich (1822), pursuing his studies of composition under Winter; taught at the Berlin Royal Inst. for Church Music, and in 1826 he succeeded Marschner as music director of the German Opera at Dresden; soon after was appointed court Kapellmeister as Weber's successor. Reissiger was a prolific composer (over 200 opus numbers), writing with great facility but with little originality. The waltz for Piano, *Weber's Last Thought,* long misattributed to Weber, was proved to be a composition by Reissiger; many of his songs also became popular.

BIBLIOGRAPHY: H. Pfiel, *C.G. Reissiger* (1879); K. Kreiser, *C.G. Reissiger* (Dresden, 1918).

Reissmann, August, German writer on music; b. Frankenstein, Silesia, Nov. 14, 1825; d. Berlin, July 13, 1903. He studied in Breslau; in 1850 he went to Weimar, where he became a student and an associate of Liszt. He then devoted himself mainly to musical commentary; lived in Berlin (1863–80), where he gave lectures on music history at the Stern Cons.

WRITINGS: *Von Bach bis Wagner* (1861); *Das deutsche Lied in seiner historischen Entwicklung* (Kassel, 1861); *Robert Schumann* (1865; in Eng., 1886); *Felix Mendelssohn-Bartholdy* (1867); *Schubert* (1873); *Joseph Haydn* (1879); *J.S. Bach* (1881); *Händel* (1882); *Gluck* (1882); *Weber* (1886); contributed to German music encyclopedias. He was also a composer; wrote 3 operas: *Gudrun* (Leipzig, 1871); *Die Bürgermeisterin von Schorndorf* (Leipzig, 1880); *Gralspiel* (Düsseldorf, 1895); several cantatas; a Violin Concerto; chamber music; many songs.

BIBLIOGRAPHY: J. Göllrich, *August Reissmann als Schriftsteller und Komponist* (Leipzig, 1884).

Reiter, Josef, Austrian composer; b. Braunau, Jan. 19, 1862; d. Bad Reichenhall, June 2, 1939. He received his first instruction in music from his father, a town organist; in 1886 went to Vienna, where he became active as a choral conductor; then was director of the Mozarteum in Salzburg (1908–11). He wrote 4 operas: *Der Bundschuh* (Troppau, 1894); *Klopstock in Zürich* (Linz, 1894); *Der Totentanz* (Dessau, 1908); *Der Tell* (Vienna, 1917); also numerous choruses and solo songs. He was an inspired Hitlerite; composed a cantata in honor of the Anschluss in 1938; and even before the reification of the Hitler magic in concrete murderous terms, dedicated his *Goethe-Symphonie* to his beloved Führer (1931).

BIBLIOGRAPHY: M. Morold, *Josef Reiter* (Vienna, 1904); L. Etzmannsdorfer, *Josef Reiter* (Vienna, 1924).

Reizenstein, Franz, German pianist and composer; b. Nuremberg, June 7, 1911; d. London, Oct. 15, 1968. He studied piano with Leonid Kreutzer and composition with Hindemith at the Hochschule für Musik in Berlin (1930–34); with the advent of the anti-Semitic Nazi regime he went to England; entered the Royal College of Music in London and studied with Lambert and Vaughan Williams (1934–36); also took private piano lessons with Solomon (1938–40). He was then an instructor in piano at the Royal Academy (1958–64), and from 1964 to his death, at the Royal Manchester College. He wrote music of fine neo-Romantic quality.

WORKS: 2 radio operas: *Men against the Sea* (1949) and *Anna Kraus* (1952); *Genesis,* oratorio (1958); *Voices of Night,* cantata (1950–51); Cello Concerto (1936); *Prologue, Variations and Finale* for Violin and Orch. (1938; originally for Violin and Piano); 2 piano concertos: No. 1 (1941) and No. 2 (1956–61; London, June 7, 1961, composer soloist); *Cyrano de Bergerac,* overture (1951); *Serenade in F* for Wind Ensemble and Double Bass, or for Small Orch. (1951); Violin Concerto (1953); Concerto for String Orch. (1966–67; London, Jan. 17, 1969); Sonata for Cello Solo (1931; revised 1967); *Theme, Variations and Fugue* for Clarinet Quintet (1932; revised 1960); Wind Quintet (1934); *Divertimento* for String or Brass Quartet (1936–37); Oboe Sonatina (1937); *Partita* for Flute and String Trio (1938); Violin Sonata (1945); Cello Sonata (1947); Piano Quintet (1948); Trio for Flute, Oboe, and Piano (1949); *Fantasia Concertante* for Violin and Piano (1956); Trio for Flute, Clarinet, and Bassoon (1963); *Concert Fantasy* for Viola and Piano (1956); Sonata for Viola Solo (1967); Sonata for Violin Solo (1968); 2 piano sonatas (1944, 1964).

Rekašius, Antanas, Lithuanian composer; b. Pauvandene, Telsiu, July 24, 1928. He studied composition with Juzeliunas at the Lithuanian State Cons. in Vilnius (1954–59); taught at the J. Gruodis Music School in Kaunas (1959–69). His music is cast in a highly advanced idiom incorporating aleatory and sonoristic techniques.

WORKS: For the stage: Opera-oratorio, *The Ballad of Light* (1969), 4 ballets: *The Light of Happiness* (1959), *The Smouldering Cross* (1963), *Passions* (1968), and *A Little Humming Fly* (1969; for children). For Orch.: *Dramatic Poem* (1958); 5 symphs.: No. 1 (1962); No. 2 (1968); No. 3 (1969); No. 4 (1970); No. 5, *Segments* (1981); Concerto for Flute and Chamber Orch. (1971); *Metafonia* for Violin and Orch. (1972); *Diafonia* for Cello and Orch. (1972); *Sonnets* for Chamber Orch. (1974); *Epitaph and Poem* for Strings (1975); *Emanations,* concerto for Electric Cello and Chamber Ensemble (1981). Chamber music: 4 string quartets (1954, 1974, 1976,

1980); 4 wind quintets (1974, 1976, 1978, 1980); 2 capriccios for Flute and Oboe (1974, 1976); Solo Flute Sonata (1975); Solo Oboe Sonata (1976); Solo Clarinet Sonata (1976); Solo Horn Sonata (1976); song cycles; children's choruses.

Relfe, John, English music theorist and composer; b. Greenwich, 1763; d. London, c.1837. He was a member of the King's Band in 1810; also an esteemed teacher of piano and harmony.

WORKS: Airs, sonatas, lessons, divertimentos, etc., for harpsichord or piano; songs; *Guida Armonica* (3 parts, 1798; 2nd ed. as *The Principles of Harmony,* 1817); *Remarks on the Present State of Musical Instruction* (1819); *Lucidus ordo* (1821). He proposed a reformed thoroughbass figuring, marking the root chord *r.,* and the inversions ' and *S'.

Rellstab, Johann Karl Friedrich, German writer on music; b. Berlin, Feb. 27, 1759; d. there, Aug. 19, 1813. He was a pupil of Agricola and Fasch; succeeded his father as head of a printing establishment, adding a music printing and publ. dept. and a circulating library of music; founded short-lived amateur concerts in 1787; lost his property in the war of 1806, and gave music lessons, lectured on harmony, and wrote criticism for the *Vossische Zeitung.* His compositions are unimportant.

WRITINGS: *Versuch über die Vereinigung der musikalischen und oratorischen Deklamation* (Vienna, 1785); *Anleitung für Klavierspieler, den Gebrauch der Bach'schen Fingersetzung, die Manieren und den Vortrag betreffend* (1790); a polemical pamphlet, *Über die Bemerkungen eines Reisenden* [Reichardt], *die Berlinischen Kirchenmusiken, Konzerte, Opern und die königliche Kammermusik betreffend* (1789).

BIBLIOGRAPHY: O. Guttmann, *J.K.F. Rellstab* (Berlin, 1910).

Rellstab, (Heinrich Friedrich) Ludwig, the noted novelist, son of **Johann Karl Friedrich Rellstab;** b. Berlin, April 13, 1799; d. there, Nov. 27, 1860. He was an artillery officer and a teacher of mathematics and history in the Brigade School in Berlin; retired from the army in 1821, and lived as a writer in Berlin from 1823; was editor and music critic of the *Vossische Zeitung* (1826–48). He publ. the satirical pamphlets *Henriette, oder Die schöne Sängerin, Eine Geschichte unserer Tage von Freimund Zuschauer* (1826; on Henriette Sontag's triumphs) and *Über mein Verhältniss als Critiker zu Herrn Spontini als Componisten und General-Musikdirector in Berlin, nebst einem vergnüglichen Anhang* (1827; directed against Spohr's truckling to virtuosity in *Agnes von Hohenstaufen*), for each of which he suffered a period of imprisonment, though his opinions were eventually upheld in official circles and by the public. Between 1830 and 1841 Rellstab edited the musical periodical *Iris im Gebiet der Tonkunst;* he also contributed to several other papers. In his *Gesammelte Schriften* are biographies of Liszt, Ludwig Berger, Bernhard Klein, Nanette Schechner, and others; vol. I contains criticisms on opera and concert which came out in the *Vossische Zeitung* between 1826 and 1848. He wrote an autobiography, *Aus meinem Leben* (2 vols., 1861).

BIBLIOGRAPHY: L.R. Blengert, *L. Rellstab* (Leipzig, 1918); W. Franke, *Der Theaterkritiker Ludwig Rellstab*

Remedios, Alberto, English tenor; b. Liverpool, Feb. 27, 1935. He studied in Liverpool with Edwin Francis and later in London with Clive Carey at the Royal College of Music. In 1955 he joined the Sadler's Wells Opera; sang at Covent Garden in London in 1966. He was a member of the Frankfurt Opera in 1968–70; made his U.S. debut with the San Francisco Opera in 1973. He was highly successful in Wagner's operas as Lohengrin, Siegfried, and Siegmund; showed fine lyrical talent as Faust in Gounod's opera, and a dramatic flair in Verdi's *Otello.*

Remenkov, Stefan, Bulgarian composer; b. Silistra, April 30, 1923. He studied piano with Nenov and composition with Pantcho Vladigerov and Veselin Stoyanov at the Bulgarian State Cons. in Sofia, graduating in 1950; later took a course with Khachaturian at the Moscow Cons.

WORKS: Operetta, *The Errors Are Ours* (1966); 2 children's operettas: *Ghanem* (1967) and *The Prince and the Pauper* (1973); ballet, *The Unvanquished* (1960); 2 piano concertos (1953, 1970); *Prelude and Dance* for String Orch. (1957); 4 symphs.: No. 1, *Children's Symphony* (1961); No. 2, *Symphony in the Classical Style* (1962); No. 3 (1965); No. 4 (1968); Cello Concerto (1964); Concertino for Flute and String Orch. (1973); *Fantasy* for Violin and Orch. (1974); Violin Sonata (1955); Nonet; 3 piano sonatas (1944, 1948, 1949).

Reményi, Eduard (né **Hoffmann**), eminent Hungarian violinist; b. Miskolc, Jan. 17, 1828; d. San Francisco, May 15, 1898. He studied with Böhm at the Vienna Cons. (1842–45). Banished from Austria for participation in the Hungarian Revolution of 1848, he began the career of a wandering violinist in America; returned to Europe in 1852, and in 1854 became solo violinist to Queen Victoria. In 1860 he was amnestied, and appointed solo violinist to the Austrian Court; in 1865, he commenced a brilliant tour, visiting Paris, Germany, Belgium, and the Netherlands; then proceeded to London in 1877, and to America in 1878, traveling in the U.S., Canada, and Mexico; in 1886 he began a new concert tour around the world, visiting Japan, China, and South Africa. Some notes on his trip to the Far East are in the N.Y. Public Library. He collapsed suddenly while playing the pizzicato from the *Sylvia* suite of Delibes at a San Francisco concert, and died of apoplexy. His technique was prodigious; in vigor, passion, and pathos he was unexcelled. He made skillful transcriptions of Chopin's waltzes, polonaises, and mazurkas, and pieces by Bach, Schubert, etc.; these are united under the title of *Nouvelle école du violin.* He was also a natural performer of Gypsy music; Liszt profited very much by his help in supplying and arranging authentic Gypsy tunes. He composed a Violin Concerto and some solos for violin.

BIBLIOGRAPHY: G. Kelley and G. Upton, *Eduard Reményi. Musician, Littérateur, and Man* (Chicago, 1906); E. Sas, *Reményi* (Budapest, 1934).

Remoortel, Edouard van, Belgian conductor; b. Brussels, May 30, 1926; d. Paris, May 16, 1977. He studied at the Brussels Cons., and took a course in conducting with Josef Krips. From 1951 on he was the principal conductor of the Belgian National Orch.; in 1958 was appointed music director and conductor of the St. Louis Symph. Orch., retaining this post until 1962. In 1965 he went to Monte Carlo as artistic consultant to the Orch. National de l'Opéra of Monaco.

Rémusat, Jean, French flutist; b. Bordeaux, May 11, 1815; d. Shanghai, Sept. 1, 1880. He studied with Tulou. After successful concert giving, he became first flutist at the Queen's Theatre in London; from 1853 was flutist at the Théâtre-Lyrique in Paris. He publ. a flute method and solo pieces for flute.

Remy, Alfred, American music lexicographer; b. Elberfeld, Germany, March 16, 1870; d. New York, Feb. 26, 1937. He emigrated to the U.S. in 1882; studied piano and violin; lectured on music history and on languages at various schools in N.Y. and Brooklyn; from 1906 to 1915 was on the music staff of Columbia Univ. He contributed articles to various American reference works and was editor in chief of the 3rd edition of *Baker's Biographical Dictionary of Musicians* (N.Y., 1919).

Rémy, Guillaume, Belgian violinist; b. Ougrée, Aug. 26, 1856; d. Nantes, France, June 16, 1932. He studied at the Cons. of Liège; graduated in 1873, sharing the first prize with Ysaÿe; continued his studies under Massart at the Paris Cons.; was awarded first prize in 1878. Settling in Paris, he became concertmaster of the Colonne Orch., frequently appearing as a soloist. From 1885 to 1930 he was a prof. at the Paris Cons.; played recitals with Saint-Saëns and Gabriel Fauré at the piano. He also formed a string quartet. During the last years of his life he was head of the violin dept. of the American Cons. at Fontainebleau.

Renaud, Maurice, French baritone; b. Bordeaux, July 24, 1861; d. Paris, Oct. 16, 1933. He studied in Paris and Brussels; sang at the Théâtre de la Monnaie in Brussels (1883–90), at the Opéra-Comique in Paris (1890–91), and at the Paris Opéra (1891–1902). He made his American debut in New Orleans, on Jan. 4, 1893. From 1906 till 1909 he sang at the Manhattan Opera House, where he became a favorite; then appeared in Chicago for a season, and at the Metropolitan Opera House (1910–12); thereafter, was active chiefly in France. He sang baritone and bass parts in some 60 operas.

Renié, Henriette, eminent French harpist and composer; b. Paris, Sept. 18, 1875; d. there, March 1, 1956. She studied with Alphonse Hasselmans at the Paris Cons.; received first prize for harp at the age of 11; then entered the classes of Lenepveu and Dubois in harmony and composition. She performed her own Concerto for Harp and Orch. at the Concerts Lamoureux in Paris on March 24, 1901; further wrote *Pièce symphonique* for Harp and Orch.; *Légende et Danse caprice* for Harp and Orch.; publ. numerous pieces for Harp Solo: *Promenades matinales, Feuilles d'automne, Ballade fantastique, Légende, Contemplation, Défile lilliputien, Danse des lutins,* etc.; Trio for Harp, Violin, and Cello; Trio for Harp, Flute, and Bassoon; several songs. She taught for many years at the Paris Cons.; among her students was Marcel Grandjany.

Renner, Josef, German choral conductor; b. Schmatzhausen, near Landshut, Bavaria, April 25, 1832; d. Regensburg, Aug. 11, 1895. He received his primary music education from his father; was a choral conductor in Regensburg (1858–92) and organized the Regensburg Madrigal Quartet with the purpose of reviving authentic performances of German part-songs of the Renaissance. He publ. several valuable collections of German madrigals: *Auswahl deutscher Madrigale von Meistern des 16. Jahrhundert, Neue Regensburger Sängerhalle, Regensburger Oberquartette, Mutter Donau,* and *Männerquartette von der Donau* (242 numbers in all).

Rennert, Günther, leading German opera producer and administrator; b. Essen, April 1, 1911; d. Munich, July 31, 1978. He was educated in Munich, Berlin, and Halle. From 1935 to 1939 he worked in Wuppertal, in Frankfurt (with Walter Felsenstein), and in Mainz; then in Königsberg (1939–42) and at the Städtische Oper in Berlin. In 1946 he became Intendant of the Hamburg State Opera, a post he held until 1956; then worked as a guest producer with several major opera houses, including La Scala in Milan and the Metropolitan Opera in N.Y. From 1967 to 1976 he was Intendant of the Bavarian State Opera in Munich. Through the consistent successes of his operatic productions in several cities under changing circumstances, Rennert acquired a reputation as one of the most competent members of his profession.

BIBLIOGRAPHY: W.E. Schäfer, *Günther Rennert, Regisseur in dieser Zeit* (Bremen, 1962).

Resinarius, Balthasar, German composer; b. Tetschen, c.1486; d. Böhmisch-Leipa, April 12, 1544. He was a choirboy in the court chapel of Emperor Maximilian; then studied at the Univ. of Leipzig; subsequently became Bishop of Leipa, Bohemia. He was one of the most important early Protestant composers of sacred music. He brought out 118 "Responsories" (Wittenberg, 1543; 80 printed by Rhaw and reprinted by Bärenreiter and Concordia, 1957); 30 choral pieces in Rhaw's *Neue deutsche geistliche Gesenge für die gemeinen Schulen* (1544; ed. by J. Wolf in *Denkmäler deutscher Tonkunst,* 39); 4 motets in *Offices* collected by Rhaw; 3 bicinia in Roten-bucher's *Diphona amoena et florida* (Nuremberg, 1549).

BIBLIOGRAPHY: I.M. Schröder, *Die Responsorienvertonungen des Balthasar Resinarius* (Kassel, 1954).

Resnik, Regina, American soprano; b. New York, Aug. 30, 1922. She studied in N.Y.; made her concert debut at the Brooklyn Academy of Music (Oct. 27, 1942); sang in opera in Mexico (1943); won an annual audition at the Metropolitan Opera in 1944, and appeared there in *Il Trovatore* (Dec. 6, 1944); sang the leading part in Beethoven's *Fidelio* (March 17, 1945). In 1953 she appeared in Bayreuth as Sieglinde. Later she sang mezzo-soprano parts; appeared as Marina in *Boris Godunov* at the Metropolitan Opera on Feb. 15, 1956; remained there until 1974. She married Harry W. Davis, a lawyer, in N.Y. on July 16, 1946.

Respighi, Ottorino, eminent Italian composer; b. Bologna, July 9, 1879; d. Rome, April 18, 1936. He studied violin with F. Sarti at the Liceo Musicale of Bologna; composition with L. Torchi and G. Martucci. In 1900 he went to Russia, and played first viola in the orch. of the Imperial Opera in St. Petersburg; there he took lessons with Rimsky-Korsakov, which proved a decisive influence in Respighi's coloristic orchestration. From 1903 to 1908 he was active as a concert violinist; also played the viola in the Mugellini Quartet of Bologna. In 1913 he was engaged as a prof. of composition at the Santa Cecilia Academy in Rome; in 1924, was appointed its director, but resigned in 1926, retaining only a class in advanced composition; subsequently devoted himself to composing and conducting. He was elected a member of the Italian Royal Academy on March 23, 1932. In 1925–26 and again in 1932 he made tours of the U.S. as a pianist and a conductor.

His style of composition is a highly successful blend of songful melodies with full and rich harmonies; he was one of the best masters of modern Italian music in orchestration. His power of evocation of the Italian scene and his ability to sustain interest without prolixity is incontestable. Although he wrote several operas, he achieved his greatest success with 2 symph. poems, *Le fontane di Roma* and *I pini di Roma,* each consisting of 4 tone paintings of the Roman landscape; a great innovation for the time was the insertion of a phonograph recording of a nightingale in the score of *I pini di Roma.*
WORKS: OPERAS: *Re Enzo* (Bologna, March 12, 1905); *Semirama,* lyric tragedy in 3 acts (Bologna, Nov. 20, 1910); *La bella addormentata nel bosco,* musical fairy tale (Rome, April 13, 1922, perf. by Vittorio Podrecca's marionettes, Teatro dei Piccoli, with singers off stage); *Belfagor,* lyric comedy (Milan, April 26, 1923); *La campana sommersa,* after Hauptmann's *Die versunkene Glocke* (Hamburg, Nov. 18, 1927); *Maria Egiziaca,* mystery play in one act (N.Y., March 16, 1932); *La fiamma* (Rome, Jan. 23, 1934); a free transcription of Monteverdi's *Orfeo* (Milan, March 16, 1935); *Lucrezia* (posthumous, Mi-

lan, Feb. 24, 1937). BALLETS: *La Boutique Fantasque,* on themes by Rossini (London, June 5, 1919); *Scherzo veneziano* (Rome, Nov. 27, 1920); *Belkis, Regina di Saba* (Milan, Jan. 23, 1932). FOR ORCH.: *Notturno* (1905); *Sinfonia drammatica* (1915); *Le fontane di Roma,* symph. poem in 4 movements (Rome, March 11, 1917); *Antiche arie e danze per liuto,* 3 sets, the 3rd for String Orch. (1916, 1923, 1931); *Ballata delle gnomidi* (Rome, April 11, 1920); *I pini di Roma,* symph. poem in 4 movements (Rome, Dec. 14, 1924); *Rossiniana,* suite from Rossini's piano pieces (1925); *Vetrate di chiesa,* symph. impressions in 4 movements (Boston, Feb. 25, 1927); *Impressioni brasiliane,* symph. suite (1927; composed for Respighi's Brazilian tour and conducted by him for the first time in São Paulo, June 16, 1928); *Trittico Botticelliano* for Chamber Orch. (commissioned by E.S. Coolidge; 1927); *Gli Uccelli,* suite for Small Orch. on themes by Rameau, B. Pasquini, and others (1927); *Feste romane,* symph. poem in 4 movements (N.Y. Phil., Toscanini conducting, Feb. 21, 1929); *Metamorphoseon modi XII,* theme and variations (commissioned by the Boston Symph.; Boston, Nov. 7, 1930); *Concerto gregoriano* for Violin and Orch. (Rome, Feb. 5, 1922); *Concerto in modo misolidio* for Piano and Orch. (N.Y., Dec. 31, 1925, composer soloist); *Concerto a 5* for Violin, Oboe, Trumpet, Double Bass, Piano, and Strings (1932). CHORAL WORKS: *La Primavera,* cantata for Soloists, Chorus, and Orch. (Rome, March 4, 1923); *Lauda per la Natività del Signore* for Soloists, Chorus, and Orch. (1930). CHAMBER MUSIC: 11 pieces for Violin and Piano (1904–7); String Quartet in D major (1907); *Quartetto dorico* for String Quartet (1924); *Il tramonto,* after Shelley, for Mezzo-soprano and String Quartet (1917); Violin Sonata (1917). Also *Huntingtower Ballad* for Band (Sousa memorial concert, Washington, D.C., April 17, 1932); 45 songs; 3 vocalises without words; arrangements of works by Monteverdi, Vitali, Pergolesi, Cimarosa, Marcello, etc., and of several *Etudes tableaux* by Rachmaninoff; he was co-author, with S.A. Luciani, of *Orpheus: Iniziazione musicale, storia della musica* (Florence, 1925).

His wife, **Elsa Olivieri Sangiacomo Respighi** (b. Rome, March 24, 1894), was his pupil; wrote a fairy opera, *Fior di neve;* the symph. poem *Serenata di maschere;* and numerous songs; was also a concert singer herself. She publ. Respighi's biography, *Ottorino Respighi: Dati biografici ordinati* (Milan, 1954; in Eng., London, 1962).

BIBLIOGRAPHY: S.A. Luciani, in the *Bolletino Bibiliografico Musicale* (1926); M. Saint-Cuy, "Ottorino Respighi," in *Musicisti contemporanei* (1932); M. Mila, "Probleme di gusto ed arte in Ottorino Respighi," *Rassegna Musicale* (1933); R. de Rensis, *Ottorino Respighi* (Turin, 1935); Elsa Respighi, *Ottorino Respighi* (Milan, 1962).

Restori, Antonio, Italian musicologist; b. Pontremoli, Massa Carrara, Dec. 10, 1859; d. Genoa, June 30, 1928. He studied philology at the Univ. of Bologna, and taught in secondary schools in various Italian cities; from 1897 he was a prof. of Romance languages at the Univ. of Messina. He publ. *Notazione musicale dell'antichissima Alba bilingue* (1892); *Musica allegra di Francia nei secoli XII e XIII* (1893); *La Gaîté de la Tor, aubade del secolo XIII* (1904); "La Musique des chansons françaises," in Juleville's *Histoire de la langue et de la littérature françaises* (1895).

Reszke, Edouard de. See **De Reszke, Edouard.**

Reszke, Jean de. See **De Reszke, Jean.**

Rethberg, Elisabeth (real name, **Elisabeth Sättler**), German soprano; b. Schwarzenberg, Sept. 22, 1894; d. Yorktown Heights, N.Y., June 6, 1976. She studied piano and voice in Dresden; joined the Dresden Court Opera at the age of 21, and was on its staff from 1915 to 1922; then went to the U.S. and made her American debut as Aida at the Metropolitan Opera in N.Y. (Nov. 22, 1922), remaining on its staff until 1942. She subsequently embarked on a grand concert tour with Ezio Pinza in the U.S., Europe, and Australia; their close association resulted in a lawsuit for alienation of affection brought by Ezio Pinza's wife against her, but the court action was not pursued. Elisabeth Rethberg was married twice: first to Ernst Albert Dormann, from whom she was divorced, and then to **George Cehanovsky,** the singer, whom she married in 1956.
BIBLIOGRAPHY: H. Henschel and E. Friedrich, *Elisabeth Rethberg* (Schwarzenberg, 1928).

Réti, Rudolf, outstanding American composer and theorist; b. Užice, Serbia, Nov. 27, 1885; d. Montclair, N.J., Feb. 7, 1957. He studied at the Cons. of Vienna; took early interest in new music and was one of the founders of the International Society for Contemporary Music (Salzburg, 1922). In 1938 he came to the U.S.; in 1943 married the Canadian pianist **Jean Sahlmark;** in 1950 they settled in Montclair, N.J. His compositions are marked by precise structure and fine stylistic unity. Among his works are *Symphonia mystica* (1951); *Triptychon* for Orch. (1953); Concertino for Cello and Orch. (1953); 2 piano concertos; Violin Sonata; several choruses and solo songs; piano pieces. An original music analyst, he publ. several books which contributed to the development of logical theory of modern music: *The Thematic Process in Music* (N.Y., 1952); *Tonality, Atonality, Pantonality* (posthumous; N.Y., 1958); *Thematic Patterns in Sonatas of Beethoven* (posthumous; brought out by D. Cooke, London, 1965).

Rettich, Wilhelm, German composer and conductor; b. Leipzig, July 3, 1892. He studied at the Leipzig Cons. with Max Reger; was in the German army in World War I and was taken prisoner by the Russians; sent to Siberia, he made his way to China after the Russian Revolution and eventually returned to Leipzig; occupied various posts as a theater conductor; was music director of the local synagogue until 1933, when the advent of the Nazi regime forced him to leave Germany; he went to the

Netherlands and became a naturalized Dutch citizen. In 1964 he returned to Germany and lived in Baden-Baden. As a composer, he excelled in symph. and chamber music; wrote 3 symphs.; Violin Concerto; Piano Concerto; much chamber music for various combinations; piano pieces and songs.

Reubke, Adolf, German organ builder at Hausneindorf, near Quedlinburg; b. Halberstadt, Dec. 6, 1805; d. Hausneindorf, March 3, 1875. He built the great organ in the Cathedral of Magdeburg, with 88 stops, and one at the Jacobikirche with 53 stops. His son **Emil Reubke** (1836–85) inherited his firm and introduced various improvements, such as pneumatic tubes. Another son of Adolf Reubke, **Julius** (b. Hausneindorf, March 23, 1834; d. Pillnitz, June 3, 1858), was a fine pianist and a favorite pupil of Liszt; his death at the age of 24 was a great loss to music. His few compositions show considerable talent; his Organ Sonata is still played. **Otto Reubke,** (b. Hausneindorf, Nov. 2, 1842; d. Halle, May 18, 1913), the youngest son of Adolf Reubke, was a pupil of Hans von Bülow; for many years he directed the Robert Franz Singakademie in Halle (1867–1911).

Reuchsel, Amédée, French organist; b. Lyons, March 21, 1875; d. Montereau (Loire), July 10, 1931. He studied organ with J. Dupont and harmony with A. Mailly and E. Tinel at the Brussels Cons.; then went to Paris, where he became a student of Gabriel Fauré. He publ. *Théorie abrégée de la musique* and *L'Education musicale populaire,* and edited the collection *Solfège classique et moderne* for the Paris Cons. (18 books).

Reuchsel, Maurice, French violinist and composer, brother of **Amédée Reuchsel;** b. Lyons, Nov. 22, 1880; d. there, July 12, 1968. He studied with his father; after concerts in France and Italy, he returned to Lyons, where he taught violin. He publ. *La Musique à Lyon* (1903), *L'Ecole classique du violon* (1905), and *Un Violoniste en voyage* (1907).

Reuling, (Ludwig) Wilhelm, German conductor and composer; b. Darmstadt, Dec. 22, 1802; d. Munich, April 19, 1879. He studied with Rinck and Seyfried; was a theater conductor in Vienna (1829–54). He composed 37 operas and operettas, and 17 ballets, produced mostly in Vienna; in addition, he wrote overtures, chamber music, and songs. A complete list of his operas produced in Vienna, with dates of premieres, is found in Anton Bauer, *Opern und Operetten in Wien* (Vienna, 1955).

Reusner (Reussner), Esajas, German lute player and composer; b. Löwenberg, Silesia, April 29, 1636; d. Berlin, May 1, 1679. He was a pupil of his father, a lutenist, and at the age of 15 was engaged as musician to Countess Radziwill in Breslau; at 19 he was lutenist at Brieg; in 1674 became lutenist at the court of the Elector of Brandenburg in Berlin. He publ. several suites for the lute: *Deliciae testudinis* (1667; new ed., 1697, as *Erfreuliche Lautenlust*);

Neue Lautenfrüchte (1676); a book of 100 religious melodies arranged for the lute, and publ. in tablature (1678). Reprints of suites and chorale settings by Reusner are in the *Reichsdenkmale,* vol. 12.

BIBLIOGRAPHY: G. Sparmann, *Esaias Reusner und die Lautensuite* (Diss., Univ. of Berlin, 1926); K. Koletschka, "E. Reussner der Jüngere und seine Bedeutung für die deutsche Lautenmusik des XVII. Jahrhunderts," *Studien zur Musikwissenschaft* (1928).

Reuss, August, German composer; b. Liliendorf, Moravia, March 6, 1871; d. Munich, June 18, 1935. He was a pupil of L. Thuille in Munich; after a brief activity as Kapellmeister in Augsburg (1906) and Magdeburg (1907), he lived in Berlin; then in Munich; in 1927 he was co-director of the Trapp Music School; in 1929, a prof. at the Akademie der Tonkunst. His works include a comic opera, *Herzog Philipps Brautfahrt* (Graz, 1909); a Piano Concerto; a String Quartet; etc.

Reuss, Eduard, German music pedagogue and critic; b. New York, Sept. 16, 1851; d. Dresden, Feb. 18, 1911. He went to Germany as a child, and became a student of Liszt in Weimar; also studied composition with Savard in Paris (1876–77); from 1880 to 1896 he was a music teacher at Karlsruhe, and from 1896 to 1902 in Wiesbaden. He was married to the singer **Luise Reuss-Belce,** whom he accompanied on her American tour during the season 1902–3; then returned to Dresden. He publ. several books on Liszt: *Franz Liszt. Ein Lebensbild* (1898); *Liszts Lieder* (1906); *Franz Liszt in seinen Briefen* (1911).

Reuss, Wilhelm Franz, German conductor, son of **Eduard Reuss** and **Luise Reuss-Belce;** b. Karlsruhe, March 17, 1886; d. in a Russian prisoner-of-war camp, Königsberg, May 15, 1945. He studied music theory with Draeseke and Max von Schillings; filled in conducting engagements in Berlin (1923–27) and Kassel (1927–33); in 1935 went to Königsberg.

Reuss-Belce, Luise, Austrian soprano; b. Vienna, Oct. 24, 1860; d. Aibach, Germany, March 5, 1945 (was found dead in a refugee train during the last months of the war). She studied voice in Vienna; made her debut as Elsa in *Lohengrin* in Karlsruhe (1881); then sang in Bayreuth (1882) and in Wiesbaden (1896–99); her subsequent appearances were at Covent Garden in London (1900) and at the Metropolitan Opera House in N.Y., where she sang Wagner parts (1902–3); from 1903 to 1911 she was an opera singer in Dresden. In 1885 she married **Eduard Reuss;** after his death in 1911 she moved to Berlin, where she established a singing school. In 1913 she was appointed stage manager at the festival opera performances in Nuremberg; she was the first woman to occupy such a post in Germany.

Reuter, Florizel von, American composer and violinist; b. Davenport, Iowa, Jan. 21, 1890. He studied violin with César Thomson in Brussels and Henri Marteau in Geneva; after a brief concert career, he settled in Munich (1934). His opera *Postmaster Wynn,* after Pushkin's tale, was produced in Berlin in 1947. He eventually returned to America, where he was active as a composer and writer; among his works are a *Rumanian Rhapsody* for Orch. (1966) and some chamber music. He publ. a manual, *Führer durch die Solo-Violinmusik* (Berlin, 1926), and *Psychical Experiences of a Musician* (London).

Reuter, Rolf, German conductor; b. Leipzig, Oct. 7, 1926. He studied at the Academy for Music and Theater in Dresden. He conducted in Eisenach (1951–55); then was Generalmusikdirektor in Meiningen (1955–61). In 1961 he became a conductor at the Leipzig Opera, and subsequently served as its Generalmusikdirektor (1963–78). From 1979–81 he was chief conductor of the Weimar State Orch. In 1981 he was appointed chief conductor and music director of the Komische Oper in East Berlin.

Reutter, (Johann Adam Karl) Georg von, Jr., Austrian composer, son of **Georg von Reutter, Sr.;** b. Vienna, April 6, 1708; d. there, March 11, 1772. He studied with his father, and upon the latter's death (1738), succeeded him as Kapellmeister at St. Stephen's Cathedral in Vienna. He became 2nd court Kapellmeister in 1747 (the first being Antonio Predieri), and acting first Kapellmeister in 1769 (after Predieri's retirement). In 1740 he was ennobled by Maria Theresa with the title "Edler von Reutter." He wrote several operas, oratorios, and much church music; a Mass, a Requiem, etc. are in Denkmäler der Tonkunst in Österreich, 88; a symph., *Servizio di tabula,* in vol. 31 (15.ii). Reutter was the choir leader who engaged young Haydn as a chorister at St. Stephen's and who, according to some accounts, treated him harshly.

BIBLIOGRAPHY: N. Hofer, *Die beiden Reutter als Kirchenkomponisten* (Vienna, 1915).

Reutter, Georg von, Sr., Austrian organist and composer; b. Vienna, (baptized, Nov. 3) 1656; d. there, Aug. 29, 1738. He was a pupil of Johann Casper Kerll; in 1686, became organist at St. Stephen's Cathedral in Vienna; from 1697 to 1703 was a theorbo player at the Imperial Court Chapel. In 1700 he became court and chamber organist, and in 1715, first Kapellmeister at St. Stephen's Cathedral, a post that he held until his death. The ricercar and 6 capriccios publ. under his name in Denkmäler der Tonkunst in Österreich, 27 (13.ii) are really by Strungk.

BIBLIOGRAPHY: N. Hofer, *Die beiden Reutter als Kirchenkomponisten* (Vienna, 1915); G. Frotscher, *Geschichte des Orgelspiels* (Berlin, 1934–35; vol. I).

Reutter, Hermann, outstanding German composer; b. Stuttgart, June 17, 1900. He studied piano and cello in Stuttgart and singing and composition at the Munich Academy of Arts; in 1923 began a concert career as a pianist; made numerous concert tours with the singer Sigrid Onegin (1930–40), including 7 separate tours in the U.S. Returning to Germany, he dedicated himself to composition and teaching. He was for many years (1932–66) a prof. of composition at the Hochschule für Musik in Stuttgart; conducted a seminar in song composition; gave similar courses in Scandinavia. In 1971 he traveled as a visiting prof. in the U.S. and Japan. In appreciation of his service to music he received a "Festschrift der Freunde," *Hermann Reutter, Werk und Wirken* (Mainz, 1965), on his 65th birthday. As a composer, Reutter follows the traditional line of German neo-Classicism, in which the basic thematic material, often inspired by German folk music, is arranged along strong contrapuntal lines, wherein a dissonant intervallic fabric does not disrupt the sense of immanent tonality.

WORKS: OPERAS: *Saul* (Baden-Baden, July 15, 1928); *Der verlorene Sohn,* after André Gide (Stuttgart, March 20, 1929); *Doktor Johannes Faust* (Frankfurt, May 26, 1936); *Odysseus* (Frankfurt, Oct. 7, 1942); *Der Weg nach Freundschaft,* subtitled *Ballade der Landstrasse* (Göttingen, Jan. 25, 1948); *Don Juan und Faust* (Stuttgart, June 11, 1950); *The Bridge of San Luis Rey,* after Thornton Wilder's novel (Frankfurt Radio, June 20, 1954); *Die Witwe von Ephesus* (Cologne, June 23, 1954); *Der Tod des Empedokles,* scenic concerto in one act (Schwetzingen, May 29, 1966); *Hamlet* (Stuttgart, 1980). VOCAL WORKS: Oratorio, *Der grosse Kalender* (1933); *Der glückliche Bauer,* cantata (1944); *Pandora* (1949); *Die Rückkehr des verlorenen Sohnes,* chamber oratorio after André Gide, being a new version of the opera *Der verlorene Sohn* (Munich, Feb. 15, 1952); *Spanischer Totentanz* for 2 Voices and Orch., after García Lorca (1953); *Ein kleines Requiem* for Bass, Cello, and Piano (1961); triptychon, *St. Sebastian* (1968); *Der Himmlische Vagant,* a lyrical portrait of François Villon for 2 Voices and Instruments (Donaueschingen Music Festival, Oct. 6, 1951). FOR ORCH.: *Prozession* for Cello and Orch. (Wiesbaden, Dec. 6, 1957); 5 piano concertos; Violin Concerto; String Quartet; Violin Sonata; Cello Sonata; *Fantasia apocalyptica* for Piano; *Antagonismus* for 2 Pianos; 3 vols. of Russian songs, arranged and harmonized; other minor pieces. He brought out an anthology of contemporary art songs, *Das zeitgenössische Lied* (4 vols., Mainz, 1969).

BIBLIOGRAPHY: Karl Laux, *Musik und Musiker der Gegenwart* (Essen, 1949; pp. 203–15).

Revelli, William D., American bandleader and prime developer of modern U.S. univ. bands; b. Spring Gulch, near Aspen, Colo., Feb. 12, 1902. The family moved to Southern Illinois, near St. Louis, when he was an infant; he began to study the violin at the age of 5; later he was a pupil of Dominic Sarli. He was graduated from the Chicago Musical College in 1919. After playing violin professionally in the Chicago area, he became in 1925 the leader of the Hobart, Ind., High School Band, which he in time built to national prominence, winning the high school band championship for 6 consecutive years. In 1935 he was made director of the Univ. of Michigan Band at Ann Arbor, and was also in charge of its Wind Instruments Dept. Over the next 36 years he developed his band into 7 independent groups of players and the Wind Dept. into a body of 14 specialist teachers. Revelli's Symph. Band toured the country many times and made several trips abroad under State Dept. auspices, most notably a 16-week tour in early 1961 that took it to the Soviet Union, Bulgaria, Turkey, Egypt, and other countries in the Middle East. In 1971 Revelli became director emeritus of the Univ. of Michigan Bands. As an instructor and promoter of bands within the U.S. academic system, Revelli continued the tradition of Fillmore and A.A. Harding. He was the recipient of many awards, and was active as an editor, adviser, and administrator of the various undertakings in the American band field; he was also founder of the College Band Directors National Assoc. (1941) and was its honorary life president; received honorary doctoral degrees from 5 American univs.

Révész, Géza, Hungarian specialist in musical psychology; b. Siófek, Dec. 9, 1878; d. Amsterdam, Aug. 19, 1955. He studied experimental psychology at the Univ. of Göttingen (Dr.Phil., 1905); taught psychology at the Univ. of Budapest (1910–20). In 1921 he settled in the Netherlands, where he became director of the Psychological Inst. of the Univ. of Amsterdam.

WRITINGS: *Zur Grundlegung der Tonpsychologie* (Leipzig, 1913); *Das frühzeitige Auftreten der Begabung und ihre Erkennung* (Leipzig, 1921); *Musikgenuss bei Gehörlosen* (with prof. Katz; Leipzig, 1926); *Inleiding tot de muziekpsychologie* (Amsterdam, 1944; in German, Bern, 1946; in Eng. as *Introduction to the Psychology of Music,* N.Y., 1953). The book that attracted the most attention, and also put in doubt the efficacy of the author's method, was *Erwin Nyiregyházi. Psychologische Analyse eines musikalisch hervorragenden Kindes* (Leipzig, 1916; in Eng. as *The Psychology of a Musical Prodigy,* London, 1925), which analyzes the case of a talented Hungarian child pianist who had perfect pitch, could transpose at sight and commit to memory short musical phrases instantly; but examples cited in the book do not go beyond the capabilities of thousands of other musically gifted children.

Revueltas, Silvestre, remarkable Mexican composer; b. Santiago Papasquiaro, Dec. 31, 1899; d. Mexico City, Oct. 5, 1940. He studied violin at the Mexico Cons.; in the U.S., studied with Felix Borowski in Chicago (1916) and with Ševčik in N.Y. (1922); conducted theater orchs. in Texas (1926–28); in 1929 returned to Mexico City and became assistant conductor to Carlos Chávez of the Orquesta Sinfónica de Mexico; only then did he begin to compose. In 1937 he went to Spain, where he was active in the cultural affairs of the Loyalist government during the Civil War. His health was ruined by exertions and an irregular life-style, and he died of pneumonia. His remains were deposited in the Rotonda de los Hombres Ilustres in Mexico City on March 23, 1976, to the music of his *Redes* and the funeral march from Beethoven's *Eroica.* He possessed an extraordinary natural talent and an intimate understanding of Mexican music, so that despite a lack of academic training in composition, he succeeded in creating works of great originality, melodic charm, and rhythmic vitality.

WORKS (all premiered in Mexico City unless noted otherwise): BALLETS: *El Renacuajo paseador* (1933; Oct. 4, 1940) and *La Coronela* (left unfinished at his death; completed by Galindo and Huízar; produced posthumously, Nov. 20, 1941). FOR ORCH.: *Cuauhnahuac* (1931–32; June 2, 1933); *Esquinas* for Small Orch. (1931; Nov. 20, 1931; for Large Orch., 1933); *Ventanas* (*Windows;* 1931; Nov. 4, 1932); *Alcancías* (*Penny Banks;* 1932); *Colorines* for Small Orch. (1932; Aug. 30, 1932); *Ocho por Radio* for Small Orch. (1933; Oct. 13, 1933); *Janitzio* (1933; Oct. 13, 1933; revised 1936); *Caminos* (*Paths;* 1934; July 17, 1934); *Planos,* "geometric dance" (1934; Nov. 5, 1934); *Redes* (*Waves),* concert suite from the film score, for Small Orch. (1935; Barcelona, Oct. 7, 1937); *Homenaje a Federico García Lorca* for Small Orch. (1935; Madrid, Sept. 22, 1937); *Sensemayá,* based on an Afro-Cuban legend, for Voice and Small Orch. (1937; revised for Large Orch. alone, 1938; Dec. 15, 1938); *Música para charlar* (*Music for Chatter),* concert suite from the film scores *El Indio* and *Ferro-carriles de Baja California* (1938; Dec. 15, 1938); *Hora de junio* for Narrator and Orch. (1938); *La noche de los Mayas,* concert suite from the film score (1939); *Itinerarios* (1939); *Paisajes* (1940); *Parias* for Soprano, Chorus, and Small Orch. (1940); *Troka* (1940). CHAMBER MUSIC: 3 string quartets: No. 1 (1930); No. 2, *Magueyes* (1931); No. 3, *Música de feria* (1931); *3 Pieces* for Violin and Piano (1932); *Tocata sin fuga* for Violin and 7 Winds (1933); *Canto de guerra de los frentes leales* (*War Song of the Loyalist Front)* for 3 Trumpets, 3 Trombones, 2 Tubas, Percussion, and Piano (1938); *3 sonetas* for Chamber Ensemble (1940); *3 Little Serious Pieces* for Piccolo, Oboe, Trumpet, Clarinet, and Saxophone (1940). He also wrote many songs.

BIBLIOGRAPHY: O. Mayer-Serra, "Silvestre Revueltas," *Musical Quarterly* (April 1941); N. Slonimsky, *Music of Latin America* (N.Y., 1945; reprinted 1972; pp. 247–51); G. Contreras, *S. Revueltas* (Mexico, 1954). A complete catalogue of his works can be found in *Composers of the Americas,* vol. 1 (Washington, D.C., 1955).

Revutsky, Lev, Ukrainian composer; b. Irshavetz, near Poltava, Feb. 20, 1889; d. Kiev, March 31, 1977. He studied in Kiev with Glière; then was as an instructor at the Musico-Dramatic Inst. in Kiev (1924–41). During the occupation of Kiev by the Germans he went to Tashkent; in 1944 returned to Kiev; in 1957 he was elected to the Ukrainian Academy of Sciences. His works include 2 symphs. (1915, 1926); 2 piano concertos (1914, 1934); a number of choral pieces to Ukrainian words.

BIBLIOGRAPHY: G. Kisselev, *Lev Revutsky* (Kiev, 1949); V. Klein, *Lev Revutsky, Composer, Pianist* (Kiev, 1972).

Rey, Cemal Reshid, Turkish composer; b. Constantinople (later Istanbul), Oct. 25, 1904. Of a distinguished family (his father was a poet and also served twice as Minister of the Interior in the Turkish government), he studied in Paris with Laparra (composition) and Marguerite Long (piano); returning to Constantinople in 1923, he taught at the Cons.; from 1949 to 1969 he was principal conductor of the Istanbul Radio Orch. His music is imbued with Turkish melorhythms; many of his works are written on Turkish subjects.

WORKS: Operas: *Yann Marek* (1922); *Sultan Cem* (1923); *Zeybek* (1926); *Tchelebi* (1945); *Benli Hürmüz* (1965); operetta, *Yaygara* (1969); 3 symphs. (1941, 1950, 1968); *La Légende du Bebek* for Orch. (Paris, Dec. 15, 1929); *Karagueuz,* symph. poem (Paris, Feb. 14, 1932, composer conducting); *Scènes turques* for Orch. (Paris, March 6, 1932); *Concerto chromatique* for Piano and Orch. (Paris, March 12, 1933, composer soloist); Violin Concerto (1939); *L'Appel,* symph. poem (Paris, April 3, 1952, composer conducting); *Fatih* for Orch. (1956); 3 symph. scherzos (1958); *Colloque instrumental* for Flute, 2 Horns, Harp, and Strings (1957); *Variations on an Istanbul Folksong* for Piano and Orch. (1966); numerous arrangements of Turkish folk songs for various instrumental combinations; choruses; piano pieces.

Rey, Jean-Baptiste, French conductor and composer; b. Tarn-et-Garonne, Dec. 18, 1734; d. Paris, July 15, 1810. He studied at Toulouse and became a theater conductor in the provinces. In 1776 he was appointed court musician to Louis XVI, as "surintendant de la chapelle." He conducted the Concerts Spirituels (1782–86); then was in charge of the musical performances at the Paris Opéra. In 1799 he became a prof. at the Paris Cons. He taught according to the principles of Rameau and became embroiled in an academic controversy with the followers of the more modern method of Catel. He played an important role in producing operas by Gluck, Grétry, and others; wrote some stage music himself.

Rey, Louis Charles Joseph, French composer and cellist, brother of **Jean-Baptiste Rey;** b. Lauzerte, Oct. 26, 1738; d. Paris, May 12, 1811. He was trained as a cellist, and was in the orch. of the Paris Opéra from 1766 until 1806; composed music for cello and other instruments.

Reyer, Louis-Etienne-Ernest, French composer; b. Marseilles, Dec. 1, 1823; d. Le Lavandou, near Hyères, Jan. 15, 1909. An ardent admirer of Wagner, he added the German suffix -*er* to his real name **Rey.** He studied in the free municipal school of music; then took a place in the government financial bureau at Algiers, and while there composed a Solemn Mass (for the arrival of the French governor in Algiers; perf. 1847) and publ. several songs. He definitely embarked upon a musical career in 1848, studying at Paris with his aunt, **Louise Dumont,** the wife of Aristide Farrenc. In 1866 he became librarian at the Opéra, and followed d'Ortigue as music critic of the *Journal des Débats;* his collected essays were publ. in 1875 as *Notes de musique;* also in *Quarante ans de musique* (posthumous, 1909). He was elected to David's chair in the Institut in 1876; was made a Chevalier of the Legion of Honor in 1862; received the Grande-Croix in 1906. Although Reyer was an avowed admirer of Wagner, his music does not betray specific Wagnerian influences; both in form and in harmonic progressions, Reyer adheres to the Classical French school of composition, with a certain tendency toward exoticism in his choice of librettos.

WORKS: *Le Sélam,* to a text by Gautier (labeled a "symphonie orientale," but actually a 4-act opera, Paris, April 5, 1850); *Maître Wolfram,* one-act opera (Paris, May 20, 1854); *Sacountale,* ballet pantomime (Paris, July 14, 1858); *La Statue,* opera in 3 acts (Paris, April 11, 1861; recast in 5 acts, Feb. 27, 1903); *Erostrate,* opera (Baden-Baden, Aug. 21, 1862, by the Paris Opéra troupe); *Sigurd,* opera (Brussels, Jan. 7, 1884; his most popular work; 300 perfs. up to 1925 in Paris, and many abroad); *Salammbô,* opera (Brussels, Feb. 10, 1890); cantata, *Victoire* (1859); hymn, *L'Union des arts* (1862); men's choruses: *L'Hymne de Rhin, Le Chant du paysan, Chœur des buveurs, Chœur des assiégés;* dramatic scene, *La Madeleine au désert* (1874); also some church music.

BIBLIOGRAPHY: A. Jullien, *E. Reyer* (Paris, 1909); H. Roujon, *Notice sur la vie et les travaux de E. Reyer* (Paris, 1911); H. de Curzon, *E. Reyer, Sa vie et ses œuvres* (Paris, 1923).

Reynolds, Anna, English mezzo-soprano; b. Canterbury, Oct. 4, 1931. She studied piano at the Royal Academy of Music in London; then went to Italy for vocal lessons; she made her operatic debut in Parma in 1960 as Suzuki; subsequently sang in Vicenza (1961), Rome (1964), Spoleto (1966), Trieste (1967), Venice (1969), and at La Scala in Milan (1973). She made her first appearance in England at Glyndebourne in 1962; sang at Covent Garden in 1967; also sang at Bayreuth (1970–76). She made her Metropolitan Opera debut in N.Y. as Flosshilde in *Das Rheingold* on Nov. 22, 1968.

Reynolds, Roger, American composer; b. Detroit, July 18, 1934. At the Univ. of Michigan he studied engineering (B.S.E., 1957) and composition (M.M., 1961); spent a year in Cologne on a Fulbright grant for work on electronic music (1962); was in Paris in 1963, and in Italy on a Guggenheim fellowship in 1964–65. In his early scores he used serial methods, but later expanded his resources to include the entire spectrum of multimedia expression, enhanced by the mathematical concepts of sets and matrices and Gestalt psychology. In 1960 he was one of the founders of the avant-garde festival ONCE in Ann Arbor, Mich. In 1966 he went to Japan at the invitation of the Inst. of Current World Affairs. In 1969 he staged there the Cross Talk Intermedia festival, featuring experimental works by Japanese and American composers. In 1970 he joined the faculty of the Univ. of Calif. in San Diego. Reynolds uses graphic notation in his scores, suggesting the desired sounds by pictorial shapes.

WORKS: *Epigram and Evolution* for Piano (1959); *Sky,* song cycle for Soprano, Alto Flute, Bassoon, and Harp, to Japanese Haiku poems (1960); *Wedge* for Chamber Orch. (1961); *Acquaintances* for Flute, Double Bass, and Piano (1961); 4 Etudes for Flute Quartet (1961); *Mosaic* for Flute and Piano (1962); *The Emperor of Ice Cream,* his major work, to a poem of Wallace Stevens, scored for 8 Voices, Piano, Percussion, and Double Bass (1962); *A Portrait of Vanzetti* for Narrator, Wind Instruments, Percussion, and Magnetic Tape (1963); *Graffiti* for Orch. (1964); *Fantasy* for Pianists (1964); *Quick Are the Mouths of Earth* for Chamber Orch. (1965); *Ambages* for Solo Flute (1965); *Masks* for Orch. and Mixed Chorus, to a text by Melville (1965); *Blind Men* for Mixed Choir, Brass, Percussion, and Slide Projection, to a text by Melville (1966); *Threshold* for Orch. (1967); ... *between* ... for Chamber Orch. and Electronics (1968); *Traces* for Piano, Flute, Cello, Tapes, and Electronics (1969); *Ping,* inspired by a story of Samuel Beckett, scored for Flute (multiphonic), Piano (motorized by agitating strings), Harmonium, Bowed Cymbal and Tam-tam, Electronic Sound Distribution, Film, Ring Modulator, 35 Slides, and Magnetic Tape (1969); *I/O* (for "In and Out") for 9 Female Vocalists, 9 Male Mimes, 2 Flutes, Clarinet, Electronics, and Projections (1969), based on a concept of Buckminster Fuller with relation to the synergetic antonyms of the opposite sexes; *Compass,* a collage of Video Projections, Taped Voices, Cello, and Double Bass, to words by Jorge Luis Borges (1973); *Promises of Darkness* for 11 Instruments (N.Y., Jan. 8, 1976); *Fiery Winds* for Orch. (N.Y., Feb. 13, 1978); *Transfigured Wind II* for Orch. (N.Y., June 4, 1984).

BIBLIOGRAPHY: G. Chase, *Roger Reynolds: Profile of a Composer* (N.Y., 1982).

Reynolds, Verne, American horn player and composer; b. Lyons, Kans., July 18, 1926. He studied violin, piano, and French horn; took courses in composition at the Cincinnati Cons. of Music (B.M., 1950) and at the Univ. of Wisconsin as a student of Cecil Burleigh (M.M., 1951); then went to London, where he enrolled at the Royal College of Music in the class of Herbert Howells. Returning to the U.S., he taught at the Univ. of Wisconsin (1950–53) and at Indiana Univ. (1954–59). In 1959 he joined the faculty of the Eastman School of Music in Rochester, N.Y., as a teacher of horn playing. He also played horn in the Cincinnati Symph. Orch. (1947–50), and was principal horn player of the Rochester Phil. Orch. (1959–68).

WORKS: Violin Concerto (1951); overture, *Saturday with Venus* (1953); *The Hollow Men* for Baritone, Male Chorus, Brass Choir, and Percussion (1954); *Music for 5 Trumpets* (1957); *Serenade* for 13 Winds (1958); 48 études for Horn (1959); *Celebration Overture* for Orch. (1960); *Partita* for Horn and Piano (1961); Sonata for Flute and Piano (1962); *Suite* for 4 Horns (1962); *Suite* for Brass Quintet (1963); Woodwind Quintet (1964); *Serenade* for Horn and Strings (1966); String Quartet (1967); *Concertare I* for Brass Quintet and Percussion (1968); *Con-*

certare II for Trumpet and Strings (1968); Sonata for Tuba and Piano (1968); *Concertare III* for Woodwind Quintet and Piano (1969); Sonata for Horn and Piano (1970); 48 études for Trumpet (1970); Violin Sonata (1970); *Concertare IV* for Brass Quintet and Piano (1971); *Scenes* for Wind Instruments and Percussion (1971); *Ventures* for Orch. (1975); *Concertare V* for Chamber Ensemble (1976); *Scenes Revisited* for Wind Ensemble (1977); *Festival and Memorial Music* for Orch. (1977); Concerto for Band (1980); Sonata for Cello and Piano (1983).

Řezáč, Ivan, Czech composer; b. Řevnice, Nov. 5, 1924; d. Prague, Dec. 26, 1977. He studied piano with Rauch and composition with Šín, Janeček, and Dobiáš at the Prague Academy, graduating in 1953; later he joined its faculty, becoming its dean in 1961. In his music he follows the type of optimistic lyricism made popular by Shostakovich.
WORKS: 3 piano concertos (1955, 1964, 1972); 2 symphs. (1958, 1961); *Návrat (The Return)* for Cello and Orch. (1962); 2 string quartets (1955, 1971); Cello Sonata (1956); Piano Trio (1958); *Nocturnes* for Violin and Piano (1959); *Torso of a Schumann Monument* for Viola and Piano (1963); Duo for Violin and Piano (1965); *6 Tales* for Cello and Guitar (1973); *Musica da camera* for Flute, Oboe, Violin, Viola, and Cello (1973); opera, *Mr. Theodor Mundstock* (1974); *Quadrature of the Heart* for String Quartet and Orch. (1975); *Vivace* for 67 Musicians (1977); *Montage* for Orch. (1977); 2 piano sonatas (1954, 1957); 2 piano sonatinas (1959, 1966); *Dry Points* for Piano (1962); *Sisyfona Neděle (Sisyphus Sunday)* for Piano (1972).

Reznicek, Emil Nikolaus von, Austrian composer; b. Vienna, May 4, 1860; d. Berlin, Aug. 2, 1945. He studied law at Graz and music with Wilhelm Mayer (W.A. Rémy); later took a brief course with Reinecke and Jadassohn at the Leipzig Cons. He was subsequently engaged as a theater conductor in Graz, Zürich, Berlin, Jena, Mainz, Stettin, and Weimar; was Kapellmeister at the court theater in Mannheim (1896–99). After a short residence in Wiesbaden, he settled in Berlin, and in 1902 established there a very successful series of concerts for chamber orch., Orchester-Kammerkonzerte; in 1906 he was appointed prof. at the Scharwenka Cons. in Berlin; conducted the Warsaw Opera from 1906 to 1909; then became the conductor of the Komische Oper in Berlin (1909–11); from 1920 to 1926, he taught at the Hochschule für Musik in Berlin.
WORKS: Operas: *Donna Diana,* to his own libretto (Prague, Dec. 16, 1894; very successful; the overture frequently perf. in concerts); *Till Eulenspiegel* (Karlsruhe, Jan. 12, 1902); *Ritter Blaubart* (Darmstadt, Jan. 29, 1920); *Holofernes* (Berlin, Oct. 27, 1923); *Spiel oder Ernst* (Dresden, Nov. 11, 1930); *Der Gondoliere des Dogen* (Stuttgart, Oct. 29, 1931); 5 symphs.; 3 symph. poems; *Symphonietta* (also known as the *Ironische Symphonie;* Berlin, March 30, 1905, composer conducting); Violin Concerto (Berlin, Feb. 26, 1925); *Nachtstück* for Cello, Harp,

4 Horns, and String Quartet; piano pieces; songs.
BIBLIOGRAPHY: O. Taubmann, *Emil Nikolaus von Reznicek* (Leipzig, 1907); Max Chop, *E.N. von Reznicek: Sein Leben und seine Werke* (Vienna, 1920); R. Specht, *E.N. von Reznicek: Eine vorläufige Studie* (Leipzig, 1923).

Rhaw (Rhau), Georg, German publisher and composer; b. Eisfeld, Franconia, 1488; d. Wittenberg, Aug. 6, 1548. He studied at the Univ. of Wittenberg (1512–14); was then cantor of the Thomaskirche and of the Thomsschule in Leipzig, from 1518 to 1520, bringing out a Mass *a* 12 and a Te Deum at the disputation of Luther and Eck; then settled in Eisleben as a schoolmaster; later, went to Hildburghausen; in 1523 went to Wittenberg, where he established a publishing business, issuing many first editions of Luther's writings and numerous collections of musical works, mostly Protestant, including *Sacrorum Hymnorum Liber Primus* (1542; modern ed. by R. Gerber in *Das Erbe deutscher Musik,* vols. 21, 25); *Newe deutsche Gesenge für die gemeinen Schulen* (1544; reprinted by J. Wolf as vol. 34 of Denkmäler Deutscher Tonkunst); *Bicinia gallica, latina et germanica* (1545; contains the earliest known version of the *Ranz des vaches;* selections were republ. in F. Jöde's *Musikantengilde,* 1926; also ed. by K. Ameln, Kassel, 1934); etc. He was the author of an *Enchiridion musices,* in 2 parts (1517, 1520).
BIBLIOGRAPHY: W. Wölbing, *Georg Rhaw* (Berlin, 1922); H. Albrecht, ed., *Georg Rhaw* Musikdrucke *aus den Johren 1538 bis 1545* (5 vols. Kassel, 1955–70).

Rheinberger, Joseph (Gabriel), eminent German organist, composer, and pedagogue; b. Vaduz, Liechtenstein, March 17, 1839; d. Munich, Nov. 25, 1901. He played piano and organ as a child; then took regular lessons in organ playing with J.G. Herzog, piano with J.E. Leonhard, and composition with J.J. Maier, at the Munich Cons.; subsequently studied composition with Franz Lachner while earning his living as a piano accompanist at the Munich Gesangverein. From 1864 to 1877 he served as principal conductor of the Munich Oratorio Society. In 1859 he succeeded his teacher Leonhard as prof. of piano at the Munich Cons., and also taught composition there. His loyalty to the cultural and musical institutions in Munich earned him many honors from the Bavarian government; King Ludwig II made him Knight of St. Michael; toward the end of his life, in 1894, he was given the rank of "Zivilverdienstorden," the equivalent of nobility; in 1899 he was made Dr.Phil. *honoris causa* by the Univ. of Munich. Rheinberger's reputation as a teacher of organ was without equal during his lifetime; students flocked to him from all parts of the world. As a composer, he created a number of works remarkable for their dignity, formal perfection, and consummate technical mastery, if not their inventive power. His organ sonatas are unquestionably among the finest productions of organ literature.
WORKS: Romantic opera, *Die sieben Raben* (Mu-

nich, 1869); comic opera, *Des Türmers Töchterlein* (Munich, 1873); *Florentiner Symphonie;* symph. poem, *Wallenstein;* Piano Concerto; oratorio, *Der Stern von Bethlehem;* 12 masses; 3 Requiems; motets and hymns; 2 organ concertos; 20 organ sonatas; Nonet; 2 string quintets; Piano Quintet; 4 piano trios; Violin Sonata; Cello Sonata; Horn Sonata; for Piano: *Symphonische Sonata; Romantische Sonata;* numerous lieder.

BIBLIOGRAPHY: P. Molitor, *Joseph Rheinberger und seine Kompositionen für die Orgel* (Leipzig, 1904); T. Kroyer, *Joseph Rheinberger* (Regensburg, 1916); Harvey Grace, *The Organ Works of Rheinberger* (London, 1925); Hans-Josef Irmen, *Joseph Rheinberger als Antipode des Cäcilanismus* (Regensburg, 1970); H.-J. Irmen, *J. Rheinberger. Thematisches Verzeichnis* (Regensburg, 1974).

Rhené-Baton (real name, **René Baton**), French conductor; b. Courseulles-sur-Mer, Calvados, Sept. 5, 1879; d. Le Mans, Sept. 23, 1940. He studied piano at the Paris Cons. and music theory privately with Gédalge. He began his conducting career as a chorus director at the Opéra-Comique in Paris; then conducted various concert groups in Angers and Bordeaux; from 1916 to 1932 he was principal conductor of the Concerts Pasdeloup. He composed orch. pieces, chamber music, and a number of songs.

BIBLIOGRAPHY: D. Sourdet, *Douze chefs d'orchestre* (Paris, 1924).

Rhodes, Willard, American pianist, opera conductor, and music educator, and a foremost ethnomusicologist; b. Dashler, Ohio, May 12, 1901. He earned his A.B. and B.Mus. degrees from Heidelberg College in Tiffin, Ohio, both in 1922; then studied at the Mannes School of Music in N.Y. (1923–25) and at Columbia Univ. (M.A., 1925); went to Paris, where he took lessons in piano with Alfred Cortot and in composition with Nadia Boulanger (1925–27). From 1927 to 1935 he served as conductor with the American Opera Co., the Cincinnati Summer Opera Co., and with his own Rhodes Chamber Opera Co. He then turned to educational music; was director of music in the public schools of Bronxville, N.Y. (1935–37). In 1937 he was appointed to the faculty at Columbia Univ.; became prof. emeritus in 1969. He held the post of music consultant to the U.S. Bureau of Indian Affairs beginning in 1937, and was a founding member (1953) and first president (1956–58) of the Society for Ethnomusicology. It was in this connection that he accumulated a most valuable collection of Amerindian folk music, both notated and recorded (many pressings released by the Library of Congress). In 1961 he was elected president of the Society for Asian Music, and in 1968 of the International Folk Music Council; also was a Fellow of the African Studies Assoc. and numerous other ethnomusicological organizations. He did field work in Rhodesia and Nyasaland (1957–58) and in South India (1965–66); was visiting prof. at the Juilliard School of Music in N.Y., Brigham Young Univ. in Utah, the Univ. of Hawaii, and Ahmadu Bello Univ. in Nigeria. In 1978 he accepted an appointment as visiting prof. at the Univ. of Arizona.

BIBLIOGRAPHY: *Ethnomusicology,* special issue dedicated to Rhodes, with lists of his publ. writings and recordings (May 1969).

Riadis, Emile, Greek composer; b. Salonica, May 13, 1885; d. there, July 17, 1935. He studied in Munich with Felix Mottl; in 1910 went to Paris, where he appeared as a composer under the name Riadis, formed from the ending of his mother's maiden name, Elefteriadis (his father's real name was **Khu**). In 1915 he became a piano teacher at the Cons. of Salonica. He wrote a number of songs, distinguished by an expressive melodic line, somewhat oriental in its intervallic pattern; his harmonizations are in the French manner.

WORKS: Byzantine Mass; orch. suite, *Biblical Dances;* symph. poem, *Sunset in Salonica;* String Quartet; Piano Quartet; Cello Sonata; *3 Greek Dances* for Piano; and several sets of songs: *Jasmins et minarets, Les Etranges Pèlerinages,* etc.

Riaño, Juan Facundo, an authority on old Spanish and Moorish musical notation; b. Granada, Spain, Nov. 24, 1828; d. Madrid, Feb. 27, 1901. He was the founder and director of the Museo de Reproducciones Artísticas. He publ. (in Eng.) *Critical and Bibliographical Notes on Early Spanish Music* (London, 1887), a valuable work containing many reproductions of old Spanish instruments. He developed the theory that the neumes of the Mozarabic notation were derived from the characters of the Visigothic alphabet.

Ribári, Antal, Hungarian composer; b. Budapest, Jan. 8, 1924. He studied composition at the Budapest Academy of Music (1943–47); later took lessons with Ferenc Szabó.

WORKS: 2 operas: *Lajos Király Válik (The Divorce of King Louis;* 1959) and *Liliom* (1960); ballet, *Fortunio* (1969); 6 cantatas: *The Wounded Pigeon and the Fountain* (1962); *The Well of Tears* (1964); *Hellas* (1964); *Clown* (1967); *Dylan Thomas* (1971); *Requiem for the Lover,* after Blake, Shelley, and Swinburne (1973); Sinfonietta (1956); Cello Concerto (1958); 3 symphs. (1960, 1964, 1970); *Musica per archi* (1961); *Pantomime* for Orch. (1962); Violin Concertino (1965); *Metamorphosis* for Soprano, 3 Woodwinds, Piano, Vibraphone, 3 Bongos, 3 Gongs, and Strings (1966); *Dialogues* for Viola and Orch. (1967); *Sinfonia festiva* (1972); 3 violin sonatas (1953, 1954, 1972); 2 string quartets (1955, 1969); String Quintet (1956); Viola Sonata (1958); 2 cello sonatas (1948, revised 1973; 1968); *9 Miniatures* for String Quartet (1966); *5 Miniatures* for Wind Trio (1969); *Chamber Music* for 5 Instruments (1970); *Dialogues* for Flute and Piano (1971); *Fantasia* for String Trio (1971); *All'antica,* suite for Piano (1968); 2 piano sonatas (1947, 1971); songs.

Ribera (Maneja), Antonio, Spanish conductor; b. Barcelona, May 3, 1873; d. Madrid, March 4, 1956. He studied with Riemann and Mottl in Leipzig and Munich; conducted the Wagner Society in Barcelona (1901–4); then was a theater conductor in Lemberg (1905–12), again in Barcelona (1912–25), and finally in Madrid (from 1925).

Ribera (y Tarragó), Julián, Spanish scholar and musicologist; b. Carcagente, near Valencia, Sept. 19, 1858; d. there, May 2, 1934. He was for many years a prof. of Hispanic-Arabic literature at the Univ. of Madrid. His magnum opus is *La música de las cantigas. Estudio sobre su origen y naturaleza* (Madrid, 1922; in Eng. as *Music in Ancient Arabia and Spain,* London, 1929), in which he maintains that the famous cantigas of Alfonso the Wise are derived from the metrical forms of the Arabs; he further publ. *La música andaluza medieval en las canciones de trovadores, troveros y minnesinger* (3 vols., Madrid, 1923–25); *Historia de la música árabe medieval y su influencia en la española* (Madrid, 1927; in Eng. as *Music in Ancient Arabia and Spain,* London, 1929; reprint, N.Y., 1970); *La música de la jota aragonesa* (1928).

BIBLIOGRAPHY: H. Spanke, "Die Theorie Riberas über Zusammenhänge zwischen frühromanischen Strophenformen und andalusisch-arabischer Lyrik des Mittelalters," in *Volkstum und Kultur der Romanen,* III (pp. 258–78); V. Castañeda, "Don J. Ribera y Tarragó," *Boletín de la Academia de la Historia,* 104 (Madrid, 1934; pp. 401–16).

Ricci, Corrado, Italian librettist; b. Ravenna, April 18, 1858; d. Rome, June 5, 1934. From 1906 to 1919 he served as general director of the dept. of fine arts in the Italian Ministry of Education in Rome; he was instrumental in having a concert hall established at the Augusteo. Besides several librettos, he publ. *Figure e figuri del mondo teatrale* (Milan, 1920); *Arrigo Boito* (Milan, 1919); *Burney, Casanova e Farinelli in Bologna* (Milan, 1890).

Ricci, Federico, Italian composer, brother of **Luigi Ricci;** b. Naples, Oct. 22, 1809; d. Conegliano, Dec. 10, 1877. He studied with Zingarelli and Raimondi. In collaboration with his elder brother he produced 4 operas: *Il Colonnello* (Naples, March 14, 1835); *Il Disertore per amore* (Naples, Feb. 13, 1836); *L'Amante di richiamo* (Turin, June 13, 1846); *Crispino e la comare* (Venice, Feb. 28, 1850). He had excellent success with his own operas *La Prigione d'Edimburgo* (Trieste, March 13, 1838) and *Corrado d'Altamura* (La Scala, Milan, Nov. 16, 1841). In 1853 he received the appointment as music director of the Imperial theaters in St. Petersburg, Russia; upon his return he produced another successful opera, *Una follia a Roma* (Paris, Jan. 30, 1869); he retired in 1876.

BIBLIOGRAPHY: F. de Villars, *Notice sur Luigi et Federico Ricci* (Paris, 1866); L. de Rada, *I Fratelli Ricci* (Florence, 1878).

Ricci, Luigi, Italian composer, brother of **Federico Ricci;** b. Naples, July 8, 1805; d. Prague, Dec. 31, 1859. He wrote about 30 operas, at least 4 of them in collaboration with his brother Federico. He was only 18 when his first opera, *L'Impresario in angustie,* was performed at the Cons. di S. Sebastiano, where he was a student (1823). In 1836 he was appointed maestro di cappella of the Cathedral at Trieste and chorus master at the city theater there. In 1844 he married Lidia Stolz, of Prague; in 1855, when he was about 50, he developed symptoms of insanity, and was committed to an asylum in Prague, where he died.

WORKS: Operas: *Il colombo* (Parma, June 27, 1829); *L'Orfanella di Ginevra* (Rome, Sept. 9, 1829); *Chiara di Rosemberg* (Milan, Oct. 11, 1831); *Il nuovo Figaro* (Parma, Feb. 15, 1832); *Chi dura vince* (Rome, Dec. 26, 1834); *Il Birraio di Preston* (Florence, Feb. 4, 1847); *Crispino e la comare* (in collaboration with his brother Federico; Venice, Feb. 28, 1850; Metropolitan Opera, N.Y., Jan. 18, 1919); *La festa di Piedigrotta* (Naples, June 23, 1852); *Il Diavolo a 4* (Trieste, May 15, 1859). His son (by his wife's identical twin sister, Francesca Stolz), **Luigi Ricci, Jr.** (b. Trieste, Dec. 27, 1852; d. Milan, Feb. 10, 1906), was also a composer of operas.

BIBLIOGRAPHY: F. de Villars, *Notice sur Luigi et Frederico Ricci* (Paris, 1866); L. de Rada, *I Fratelli Ricci* (Florence, 1878); C. de Incontrera, *Luigi Ricci* (Trieste, 1959).

Ricci, Ruggiero, celebrated American violinist; b. San Francisco, July 24, 1918. His musical education was lovingly fostered by his father, along with 6 of his siblings, every one of whom started out as a musician, and 2 of whom, the cellist **Giorgio Ricci** and the violinist **Emma Ricci,** achieved the rank of professional performer. Ruggiero Ricci studied violin with Louis Persinger, and made a sensational appearance at a public concert in San Francisco on Nov. 15, 1928, when he was 10 years old, with his teacher accompanying him at the piano. On Oct. 20, 1929, he played in N.Y.; he embarked on an international concert tour in 1932. He successfully negotiated the perilous transition from child prodigy to serious artist; he accumulated a formidable repertoire of about 60 violin concertos, including all the violin works of Paganini; edited the newly discovered MS of Paganini's early Violin Concerto, presumed to have been composed c.1815, and gave its first N.Y. performance with the American Symph. Orch. on Oct. 7, 1977; he also gave the first performances of violin concertos by several modern composers, among them Alberto Ginastera (1963) and Gottfried von Einem (1970). During World War II he served as "entertainment specialist" with the U.S. Army Air Force. After the end of the war, he returned to the concert stage; made several world tours, which included South America, Australia, Japan, and Russia; he also gave master courses at the North Carolina School of the Arts, Indiana Univ., and the Juilliard School of Music in N.Y. He owns a 1734 Guarnerius del Gesù violin. In 1978 he celebrated a "Golden Jubilee," marking half a century of his professional career.

Ricciarelli, Katia, Italian soprano; b. Rovigo, Jan.

18, 1946. She studied voice at the Venice Cons.; made her debut in Mantua in 1969; then sang in Venice and Rome, and at La Scala in Milan. On April 11, 1975, she made her American debut as Mimi in *La Bohème* at the Metropolitan Opera in N.Y.

Riccitelli, Primo, Italian composer; b. Campli, Aug. 9, 1875; d. Giulianova, March 27, 1941. He was a pupil of Mascagni at the Liceo Rossini in Pesaro; wrote operas: *Maria sul Monte* (1911; Milan, July 8, 1916); *I Compagnacci* (one act; Rome, April 10, 1923; Metropolitan Opera, N.Y., Jan. 2, 1924); *Madone Oretta* (Rome, Feb. 3, 1932); also songs.

Riccius, August Ferdinand, German composer; b. Bernstadt, Feb. 26, 1819; d. Karlsbad, July 5, 1886. He was conductor of the Euterpe Concerts in Leipzig (from 1849); then at the City Theater there (1854–64); in 1864 went to Hamburg, where he conducted opera and wrote music criticism for the *Hamburger Nachrichten*. He composed an overture to Schiller's *Braut von Messina*; a cantata, *Die Weihe der Kraft*; piano music; choruses; songs.

Riccius, Karl August, German violinist, conductor, and composer, nephew of **August Ferdinand Riccius**; b. Bernstadt, July 26, 1830; d. Dresden, July 8, 1893. He studied in Dresden with Wieck, and in Leipzig with Mendelssohn, Schumann, and Ferdinand David. In 1847 he became violinist in the Dresden Court Orch., and later also conductor. He wrote a comic opera, *Es spukt* (Dresden, 1871); several ballets; music to various plays; publ. piano pieces and songs.

Rice, William Gorham, American writer on music; b. Albany, N.Y., Dec. 23, 1856; d. there, Sept. 10, 1945. His writings include *Carillons of Belgium and Holland; The Carillon in Literature;* "Tower Music of Belgium and Holland," *Musical Quarterly* (April 1915); etc.

Rich, Alan, American music critic of an uncommonly bellicose disposition tempered by prejudice toward favorites; b. Boston, June 17, 1924. He muddled through a premedical course at Harvard Univ. (A.B., 1945) but made a *salto mortale* to grab a chance at a little dinky job as a secondary music critic of the moribund *Boston Herald,* at which he served from 1944–47; moving ahead, he wrote for various insolvent papers, such as the *New York Sun* (1947–48). Turning serious, he took a course in musicology with Manfred Bukofzer and Joseph Kerman at the Univ. of Calif. at Berkeley (M.A., 1952); spent a season in Vienna on an Alfred Hertz Memorial Traveling Fellowship in Music (1952–53), where he was guided musicographically by the grand man of scholarly research, Otto Erich Deutsch; and incidentally learned the rudiments of conducting with Walter Gmeindl. Returning to the U.S., he wrote for the *American Record Guide* (1948–61), *Musical America* (1955–61), the *N.Y. Times* (1961–63), the *N.Y. Herald Tribune* (1963–66), and its ephemeral

successor, the *N.Y. World-Journal-Tribune* (1966–67), as well as for the prosperously extant weekly *New York* magazine (1968–81). Afflicted with acute Mehtaphobia he went back West after Zubin Mehta abandoned Los Angeles for N.Y.; became a bicoastal writer, working for *New York* and its Western clone, *California* magazine. In 1979 he began producing documentaries for Public Radio; taught music criticism at the Univ. of Southern Calif. and the Calif. Inst. of the Arts; in 1983 became the music critic for *Newsweek* magazine. He won 4 Deems Taylor-ASCAP writing awards; publ. *Careers and Opportunities in Music* (N.Y., 1964); *Music, Mirror of the Arts* (N.Y., 1969); and 3 vols. of the *Simon & Schuster Listeners Guide to Music* (1980). Virgil Thomson described Alan Rich as "our only musical muckraker."

Rich, "Buddy" (Bernard Rich), American jazz drummer and bandleader; b. New York, June 30, 1917. His parents were vaudeville performers; he began to tour with them at the age of 6 as "Traps the Drum Wonder"; then played with the bands of Bunny Berigan, Harry James, Tommy Dorsey, and others. He formed his own band in 1945; later appeared again with Dorsey and Harry James; also made tours in the U.S. and Europe. In 1966 he organized his own big band and toured widely with it.

Rich, Charlie, American country-music singer; b. Colt, Ark., Dec. 12, 1932. He took up the saxophone in his youth; during service in the U.S. Air Force, he played in a jazz group; after his discharge, he made a successful career as a singer.

Richafort, Jean, Flemish composer; b. c.1480; d. c.1548. Probably a pupil of Josquin, he was chapel master at St. Rombaut, in Mechlin, from 1507 to 1509; in 1531 he was in the service of Mary of Hungary, regent of the Netherlands; in 1542–47, chapel master at St. Gilles in Bruges. Surviving are masses, Magnificats, motets, and chansons.

BIBLIOGRAPHY: G. Van Doorslaer, "Jean Richafort," *Bulletin de l'Académie Royale d'Archéologie de Belgique* (1930; pp. 103ff.); G. Reese, *Music in the Renaissance* (N.Y., 1954); M.E. Kabis, *The Works of Jean Richafort, Renaissance Composer* (Diss., 2 vols., N.Y. Univ., 1957).

Richard, Keith, English rock musician, b. Dartford, Kent, Dec. 18, 1943. His real surname was **Richards.** He met his exact contemporary Mick Jagger in London and did some experimental jamming with him, later joining a rhythm-and-blues club circuit, eventually forming one of the most successful rock groups, The Rolling Stones. Their concerts in England and America outgrew the dimensions of mere musical events and achieved the distinction of a social movement, complete with hallucinogenic drugs, homicidal eruptions, and sexual extravagance. Keith Richard, the most reckless of the group, was busted for possession and, much worse, trafficking in heroin, but the British law was lenient to him, and he escaped *durance vile* in a gaol. He was busted again in Toronto in 1977, but was sentenced only to the penalty of giving a benefit concert. He maintained close relationships with Mick Jagger and the Rolling Stones, weathering such blows as a boycott by a feminist organization that accused the group of violent sexism and racism in the song *Brown Sugar*, containing obscene unprintable verses. His strength as the lead guitar, combined with his lurid lyrics (composed with Mick Jagger), provided The Rolling Stones with their most outrageous successes, including *Satisfaction, 19th Nervous Breakdown, Street Fighting Man, Sympathy for the Devil, Sister Morphine*, and *Let's Spend the Night Together*.

Richards, (Henry) Brinley, British composer and pianist; b. Carmarthen, Wales, Nov. 13, 1817; d. London, May 1, 1885. He was a pupil of the Royal Academy of Music; resided in London, and was highly esteemed as a concert pianist and teacher. He wrote the popular hymn *God bless the Prince of Wales* (1862).

Richards, Lewis Loomis, American pianist and music educator; b. St. Johns, Mich., April 11, 1881; d. East Lansing, Mich., Feb. 15, 1940. He studied at the Brussels Cons.; in 1927 became head of the dept. of music at Michigan State College; was also director of the Michigan State Inst. of Music and Allied Arts.

Richardson, Alfred Madeley, English organist; b. Southend-on-Sea, Essex, June 1, 1868; d. New York, July 23, 1949. He received his classical education at Keble College, Oxford (A.M., 1892), and studied at the Royal College of Music under Sir C.H.H. Parry, Sir W. Parratt, and E. Pauer; then went to the U.S., and in 1912 was appointed instructor in theory at the Inst. of Musical Art in N.Y. He publ. *The Psalms; Their Structure and Musical Rendering* (1903); *Church Music* (1904); *The Choir-Trainer's Art* (1914); *Extempore Playing* (1922); *The Medieval Modes* (1933); *Fundamental Counterpoint* (1936).

Richault, Charles-Simon, French publisher; b. Chartres, May 10, 1780; d. Paris, Feb. 20, 1866. In 1805 he founded a music publishing house, the first issues of which were Mozart's concertos and Beethoven's symphs. in score. His sons **Guillaume-Simon** (1806–77) and **Léon** (1839–95) carried on the business, publishing works by French composers and also excellent editions of German classics. In 1898 the stock was bought by the publisher Costallat of Paris.

Richter, Alfred, German pedagogue, son of **Ernst Friedrich Richter;** b. Leipzig, April 1, 1846; d. Berlin, March 1, 1919. He was trained by his father and became a competent music teacher; was a member of the faculty of the Leipzig Cons. (1872–82); then lived in London, but returned to Germany in 1897. He brought out a number of music school manuals, among them a supplement to his father's *Lehrbuch der Harmonie* (Leipzig, 1853); *Aufgabenbuch* (1879;

went through 64 eds. before 1952; in Eng. as *Additional Exercises;* N.Y., 1882); *Die Elementarkenntnisse der Musik* (1895; 6th ed., 1920); *Die Lehre von der thematischen Arbeit* (1896); *Das Klavierspiel für Musikstudierende* (1898; 2nd ed., 1912); *Die Lehre von der Form in der Musik* (1904; 2nd ed., 1911). He also composed piano pieces, songs, and choruses.

Richter, Ernst Friedrich (Eduard), eminent German theorist and composer; b. Gross-Schönau, Oct. 24, 1808; d. Leipzig, April 9, 1879. A son of a schoolmaster, he was educated in Zittau; matriculated in 1831 as a student of theory at the Univ. of Leipzig; when the Leipzig Cons. was founded in 1843, he became Hauptmann's co-adjutor as teacher of harmony; conducted the Leipzig Singakademie (1843–47); was organist of the Petrikirche (from 1851) and the Neukirche (from 1862); in 1868 became music director of the Nikolaikirche and cantor of the Thomaskirche. He composed several sacred cantatas, masses, Psalms, etc., and also wrote chamber music, piano pieces, and organ compositions. But he became primarily known as the compiler of practical and useful manuals on harmony, counterpoint, and fugue, which went into numerous editions and translations into all European languages, among them *Lehrbuch der Harmonie* (Leipzig, 1853; 36th ed., 1953; in Eng., N.Y., 1867; newly trans. by Theodore Baker from the 25th German ed. N.Y., 1912; also in Swedish, Russian, Polish, Italian, French, Spanish, and Dutch); *Lehrbuch des einfachen und doppelten Kontrapunkts* (Leipzig, 1872; 15th ed., 1920; in Eng., London, 1874, and N.Y., 1884; also in French and Russian); *Lehrbuch der Fuge* (Leipzig, 1859; in Eng., London, 1878; also in French); these 3 manuals were brought out together as *Die praktischen Studien zur Theorie der Musik* (Leipzig, 1874–76); Richter's son, **Alfred Richter,** compiled a supplement to the *Lehrbuch der Harmonie* as *Aufgabenbuch,* which also went into a number of editions.

Richter, Ferdinand Tobias, Austrian organist and composer; b. Würzburg (baptized, July 22), 1651; d. Vienna, Nov. 3, 1711. He was court organist in Vienna from 1683; enjoyed a great reputation as a theorist and teacher. The following works are extant in Vienna in MS: 2 stage pieces: *L'Istro ossequioso* (Vienna, Jan. 6, 1694) and *Le promesse degli dei* (Vienna, June 9, 1697); *5 sepulcri* (a special type of Viennese oratorio perf. in semi-operatic manner during Holy Week); an oratorio; Sonata for 7 Instruments; 2 sonatas for 8 Instruments. Modern reprints of his suites, toccatas, and versets are found in *Denkmäler der Tonkunst in Österreich,* 27 (13. ii).

Richter, Francis William, American organist, nephew of **Hans Richter;** b. Minneapolis, Feb. 5, 1888; d. Los Angeles, Dec. 25, 1938. He became blind at the age of 3; showed musical ability, and was sent to Vienna, where he studied with the blind pianist Joseph Labor; also took lessons with Leschetizky (piano) and Karl Goldmark (theory); subsequently studied organ with Guilmant in Paris. Returning to the U.S., he was active as a church organist and teacher. In 1930 he settled in Portland, Oreg.; then moved to Los Angeles.

Richter, Franz Xaver, German composer; b. Holleschau, Moravia, Dec. 1, 1709; d. Strasbourg, Sept. 12, 1789. In 1740 he was Vice-Kapellmeister at the chapel of the Prince-Abbot at Kempten; in 1747 he joined the electoral orch. at Mannheim; from 1769 till his death, he was Kapellmeister at Strasbourg Cathedral. A prolific composer of decided originality, he was one of the chief representatives of the new instrumental style of the Mannheim school.
WORKS: In the library of Strasbourg Cathedral are the MSS of 28 masses, 2 Requiems, 16 Psalms, 38 motets, 2 cantatas, 2 Passions, Lamentations for Holy Week, etc. (the greater part with Orch.). An oratorio, *La deposizione della Croce,* was produced in Mannheim (April 12, 1748). Publ. works: 69 symphs. (4 reprinted by Riemann in Denkmäler der Tonkunst in Bayern, 4 and 13 [3.i and 7.ii]; 6 string quartets (reprinted in vol. 27 [15]; 8 trios for Flute (or Violin), Cello, and Piano (G minor reprinted in vol. 28 [16]; A in *Collegium musicum);* 12 trio sonatas for 2 Violins, with Basso Continuo; 6 duets for Flute; 6 sonatas for Flute, with Basso Continuo; 6 piano concertos with String Orch. Almost all the chamber music was originally publ. in London. A treatise, *Harmonische Belehrung oder gründliche Anweisung zur musikalischen Tonkunst* (MS in library of the Brussels Cons.), was publ. in translation by C. Kalkbrenner as *Traité d'harmonie et de composition* (1804).
BIBLIOGRAPHY: F.X. Mathias, "Thematischer Katalog der im Strassburger Münsterarchiv aufbewahrten kirchenmusikalischen Werke Fr.X. Richters," in Reimann Festschrift (Leipzig, 1909); W. Barth, *Die Messenkompositionen Franz Xaver Richters* (1709–89) (Diss., Univ. of Munich, 1941); W. Gässler, *Die Sinfonien von Franz Xaver Richter* (Diss., Univ. of Munich, 1942); R. Schmitt, "Franz Xaver Richter," *Caecilia, LXXII* (1964).

Richter, Hans, eminent German conductor; b. Raab, Hungary, April 4, 1843; d. Bayreuth, Dec. 5, 1916. He studied theory with Sechter, violin with Heissler, and French horn with Kleinecke at the Vienna Cons.; from 1862 to 1866 he was employed as horn player in the orch. at the Kärnthnertor-Theater in Vienna. The turning point in his career was his contact with Wagner at Triebschen in 1866, when Wagner asked him to make a fair copy of the score of *Die Meistersinger;* obviously satisfied with Richter's work, Wagner recommended him to Hans von Bülow as a chorus master at the Munich Opera (1867); in 1868–69 Richter was also given an opportunity to assist von Bülow as conductor of the court orch. in Munich. Subsequently Richter became a favorite conductor of Wagner and prepared rehearsals of Wagner's operas, among them the Brussels performance of *Lohengrin* (March 22, 1870). From 1871 to 1875 he was conductor of the Pest National Theater; then conducted the Imperial Opera

in Vienna and became its first principal conductor in 1875; concurrently he conducted the concerts of the Vienna Phil. (1875–82 and again in 1883–97). He was selected by Wagner to conduct the entire *Ring des Nibelungen* at the Bayreuth Festival in 1876; received the Order of Maximilian from the King of Bavaria and the Order of the Falcon from the Grand Duke of Weimar. When Wagner went to London in 1877, he took Richter along with him and let him conduct several concerts of the Wagner Festival in Albert Hall. In May 1879 Richter conducted a 2nd Wagner Festival in London, which led to the establishment of an annual series of May concerts known as "Orchestral Festival Concerts" and later simply "Richter Concerts," which he conducted regularly until 1897; then he was engaged as conductor of the Hallé Orch. in Manchester. He was also regular conductor of the Birmingham Festival (1885–1909) and of the Wagner operas at Covent Garden (1903–10). He conducted his farewell concert with the Manchester Symph. Orch. on April 11, 1911. His popularity in England was immense; his corpulent, bearlike figure and imposing Germanic beard imparted an air of authority; his technique was flawless. Besides Wagner's music, Richter gave repeated performances of symphs. of Brahms; among English composers he favored Elgar.
BIBLIOGRAPHY: F. Klickmann, "Dr. Hans Richter," *Windsor Magazine* (Sept. 1896); L. Karpath, *Wagners Briefe an Hans Richter* (Vienna, 1924); Heinrich Kralik, *The Vienna Opera House* (Vienna, 1955); H. Schonberg, *The Great Conductors* (N.Y., 1967; pp. 177–84).

Richter, Karl, distinguished German organist and conductor; b. Plauen, Oct. 15, 1926; d. Munich, Feb. 15, 1981. He studied organ, harpsichord, and conducting at the Dresden Kreuzschule; then took courses at the Leipzig Cons. with Rudolf Mauersberger, Günther Ramin, and Karl Straube. In 1946 he became choirmaster of the Christuskirche in Leipzig; in 1947 was named organist of Leipzig's Thomaskirche. In 1951 he settled in Munich; organized the Munich Bach Orch. and Choir, which brought him great acclaim; made many tours and numerous recordings with them; also appeared as a guest conductor in Europe, including several concerts conducted in Russia. In 1965 he brought his Munich Bach Orch. and Choir to the U.S., making his American debut in Carnegie Hall in N.Y. on April 18, 1965; he made his last American conducting appearance in N.Y. on June 13, 1980.
BIBLIOGRAPHY: D.K. McIntire, "Karl Richter (1926–1981)," *Le Grand Baton* (March 1981).

Richter, Marga, American composer; b. Reedsburg, Wis., Oct. 21, 1926. She was prepared for a musical career by her mother, **Inez Chandler-Richter,** an American-born soprano; studied at the MacPhail School of Music in Minneapolis; in 1943 entered the Juilliard School of Music in N.Y., where she studied piano with Roslyn Tureck and composition with Persichetti and Bergsma, graduating in 1949 (M.S., 1951). She received 14 ASCAP awards since 1966 and 2 grants from the National Endowment for the Arts (1977, 1979). Her compositions reflect a pragmatic modern trend without rigid adherence to any particular doctrine or technique; the overriding concern is aural.

WORKS: 2 ballets: *Abyss* (1964; Cannes, Feb. 5, 1965) and *Bird of Yearning* (1967; as *Der Türm,* Cologne, Oct. 30, 1969; version for Piano, 1976). For Orch.: Concerto for Piano, with Violas, Cellos, and Basses (1955); *Lament* for String Orch. (1956); *Aria and Toccata* for Viola and Strings (1956–57); *Variations on a Sarabande* (1959); *8 Pieces* (1961; originally for Piano); *Landscapes of the Mind I,* Concerto No. 2 for Piano and Orch. (1968–74; Tucson, March 19, 1976; Masselos, soloist); *Fragments* (1976); *Country Auction* for School Band (1976); *Blackberry Vines and Winter Fruit* (1976; North Bennington, Vt., Oct. 17, 1976); *Music for 3 Quintets and Orchestra* (1978–80); *Düsseldorf Concerto* for Solo Flute, Solo Viola, Harp, Percussion, and String Ensemble (1981–82; Düsseldorf Ensemble, Salzburg, May 20, 1982). Chamber music: *One for 2 and 2 for 3* for Trombone Duet and Trio (1947; revised 1974); 2 string quartets: No. 1 (1950; withdrawn) and No. 2 (1958); *Ricercare* for Brass Quartet (1958); *Darkening of the Light* for Solo Viola (1961; version for Solo Cello, 1976); *Suite* for Violin and Piano (1964); *Landscapes of the Mind II* for Violin and Piano (1971); *Pastorale* for 2 Oboes (1975); *Landscapes of the Mind III* for Piano Trio (1979); *Sonora* for 2 Clarinets and Piano (1981). For Piano: Sonata (1954–55); *Melodrama* for 2 Pianos (1958); *Variations on a Theme by Latimer* for Piano, 4-hands (1964); *Remembrances* (1971); *Requiem* (1976). Songs; choruses; a vocal sextet, *Do Not Press My Hands* (1981).

Richter, Nico Max, Dutch composer; b. Amsterdam, Dec. 2, 1915; d. there, Aug. 16, 1945. He studied conducting with Scherchen; directed a student orch.; in February 1942 he was arrested by the Nazis as a member of the Dutch Resistance, and spent 3 years in the Dachau concentration camp, which fatally undermined his health; he died shortly after liberation. WORKS: *Amorijs,* chamber opera; *Kannitverstan,* ballet; *Serenade,* sinfonietta for Flute, Oboe, Guitar, and Strings (1931–34); Concertino for Clarinet, Horn, Trumpet, Piano, and 2 Violins (1935); Trio for Flute, Viola, and Guitar (1935); *Sinfonia* for Chamber Orch. (1936); *Serenade* for Flute, Violin, and Viola (1945; 2 extant movements reconstructed by Lex van Delden).

Richter, Sviatoslav, outstanding Russian pianist; b. Zhitomir, March 20, 1915. Both his parents were pianists; the family moved to Odessa when he was a child. He was engaged as a piano accompanist at the Odessa Opera, and developed exceptional skill in playing orch. scores at sight. He made his debut as a concert pianist at the Sailors' Collective Circle in Odessa in 1935. In 1937 he entered the Moscow Cons., where he studied piano with Neuhaus, graduating in 1947; was awarded the Stalin Prize in 1949. During the Russian tour of the Philadelphia Orch.

in 1958, Richter was soloist, playing Prokofiev's 5th Piano Concerto in Leningrad; he made several international concert tours, including visits to China (1957) and the U.S. (1960). Both in Russia and abroad he earned a reputation as a piano virtuoso of formidable attainments; was especially praised for his impeccable sense of style, with every detail of the music rendered with lapidary perfection.

Richter-Haaser, Hans, German pianist; b. Dresden, Jan. 6, 1912; d. Dec. 16, 1980. He studied in Dresden; then went to Detmold, where he conducted the municipal orch. (1946–47). He then began his career as a pianist; for many years (1947–63) taught piano at the North West German Music Academy in Detmold. He made several tours in Europe and America; gave his first American concert in N.Y. in 1959; last played in N.Y. in 1974.

Rickenbacher, Karl Anton, Swiss conductor; b. Basel, May 20, 1940. He studied at the Städtisches Cons. in West Berlin (1962–66); then was engaged as an assistant conductor at the Zürich Opera (1966–69); subsequently was a conductor in Freiburg (1969–74). In 1976 he became principal conductor of the Westphalian Symph. Orch.; also held a similar post with the BBC Scottish Symph. Orch. in Glasgow (1977–80).

Ricketts, Frederick J., English bandmaster and composer who used the pseudonym **Kenneth J. Alford;** b. London, Feb. 21, 1881; d. Redgate, Surrey, May 15, 1945. Trained first as an organist, Ricketts graduated from Kneller Hall, the school for British bandmasters, afterward serving his longest stint as bandmaster of the Royal Marines (1928–44). In February 1914 he publ., under his pseudonym "Alford" (not to be confused with the American bandmaster and composer Harry L. Alford), his popular march *Col. Bogey,* epitomizing the steadily swinging and moderately paced English military march. *Col. Bogey* reached its height of fame when it was introduced into the motion picture *The Bridge on the River Kwai* (1958).

Ricordi & Co., G., famous music publishing firm of Milan, founded by **Giovanni Ricordi** (b. Milan, 1785; d. there, March 15, 1853). As first violinist and conductor at the old Fiando theater, he also earned small sums as a music copyist, and in 1807 went to Leipzig to learn music engraving in Breitkopf & Härtel's establishment. On returning, he opened a little shop and began publishing in 1808, engraving the first works himself. He was an intimate of Rossini, whose operas he publ.; also recognized Verdi's genius when the latter was still unknown. His son **Tito Ricordi** (b. Milan, Oct. 29, 1811; d. there, Sept. 7, 1888) succeeded to the business. In 1845 he established the *Gazzetta Musicale,* one of the most important Italian musical papers; also introduced the Edizioni Economiche, and under his administration the house became the largest music publishing firm in Italy. He was on terms of intimate friendship with Verdi, whose works (especially *Aida*) made a fortune for both publisher and author. Owing to ill health, he withdrew from active management in 1887. His successor was his son **Guilio Ricordi** (b. Milan, Dec. 19, 1840; d. there, June 6, 1912), a man of extraordinary business ability, who continued the policy of expansion. In 1888 he bought, and consolidated with his own, the important firm of Francesco Lucca. It was he who discovered Puccini. A trained musician, he publ., under the pseudonym of **J. Burgmein,** much elegant salon music (160 opus numbers). He was editor of the *Gazzetta Musicale* until his death, upon which the magazine ceased publication. His son **Tito** (b. May 17, 1865; d. Milan, March 30, 1933), a remarkable pianist, was the subsequent head of the house; he retired in 1919, and control of the firm left the family; it became a limited company in 1952. The catalogue contains over 120,000 numbers, and in the archives are the autograph scores of more than 550 operas by the most famous Italian composers. The firm has branches in N.Y., Canada, Australia, and South America.

BIBLIOGRAPHY: E. di S.M. Valperga, *Ricordi,* (Rome, 1943); G. Adami, *G. Ricordi, L'Amico dei musicisti italiani* (Milan, 1945); O. Vergani, *Piccolo viaggio in un archivio* (Milan, 1953); C. Sartori, *Casa Ricordi, 1808–1958: Profilo storico* (Milan, 1958).

Ridder, Anton de, Dutch tenor; b. Amsterdam, Feb. 13, 1929. He studied voice at the Amsterdam Cons. with Hermann Mülder (1947–49) and with Jan Keyzer (1951–56). From 1956 to 1962 he was on the roster of the Karlsruhe Opera; then sang at the Gärtnerplatz Theater in Munich (1962–66). He subsequently was a member of the Cologne Opera; in 1965 joined the Komische Oper in West Berlin. In 1969 he took part in the Salzburg Festival; also sang in Vienna and Hamburg. He was equally adept at lyric and dramatic tenor parts.

Ridderbusch, Karl, German bass; b. Recklinghausen, May 29, 1932. He studied at the Duisburg Cons.; then won the Rudolf Schock Competition and continued his studies at the Essen Folkwangschule. He made his debut at the City Theater in Münster in 1961; then sang in Essen, Düsseldorf, Vienna, Milan, Berlin, Hamburg, and Paris. He made his Metropolitan Opera debut on Nov. 21, 1967, as Hunding in *Die Walküre;* in 1971 he sang at Covent Garden in London. He excels in Wagnerian roles.

Riddle, Nelson, American composer-arranger of popular music and orch. leader; b. Hackensack, N.J., June 1, 1921. He took up the trombone at the age of 14; played in the bands of Charlie Spivak and Tommy Dorsey. After military service, he studied with Mario Castelnuovo-Tedesco in Los Angeles; then became an enormously successful arranger in Hollywood, preparing scores for numerous films and television programs; worked with Judy Garland, Frank Sinatra, Nat King Cole, Ella Fitzgerald, and others. He won an Academy Award for his score for the film *The Great Gatsby* (1974).

Rider-Kelsey, Mme. Corinne, American soprano; b. on a farm near Batavia, N.Y., Feb. 24, 1877; d. Toledo, Ohio, July 10, 1947. She attended Oberlin College; then studied voice in Chicago and N.Y.; made her professional debut in Handel's *Messiah* (St. Louis, Nov. 24, 1904); made her first operatic appearance as Micaëla in *Carmen,* at Covent Garden in London on July 2, 1908. In 1926 she married the violinist **Lynell Reed,** who wrote her biography under the title *Be Not Afraid* (N.Y., 1955). See V.L. Scott in *Notable American Women,* III (N.Y., 1971).

Řídký, Jaroslav, eminent Czech composer, conductor, and teacher; b. Františkov, near Liberec, Aug. 25, 1897; d. Poděbrady, Aug. 14, 1956. He took courses in composition at the Prague Cons. with Jaroslav Křička and E.B. Foerster; simultaneously studied the harp; was first harpist in the Czech Phil. (1924–38); later became conductor of its choir (1925–30). He taught theory at the Prague Cons. (1928–48); in 1948 was appointed prof. of composition at the Music Academy in Prague, remaining at this post until his death.

WORKS: 7 symphs: No. 1 (1924); No. 2, with Cello obbligato (1925); No. 3 (1927); No. 4, with Chorus (1928); No. 5 (1930–31); No. 6, *The Year 1938* (1938; unfinished); No. 7 (1955); Sinfonietta for Full Orch. (1923); Violin Concerto (1926); *Overture* (1928–29); 2 cello concertos (1930, 1940); 2 cantatas: *A Winter Fairytale* (1936) and *To My Fatherland* (1941); *Serenade* for String Orch. (1941); Chamber Sinfonietta (1944–45); Piano Concerto (1952); *Slavonic March* for Orch. (1954); 2 cello sonatas (1923, 1947–48); Clarinet Quintet (1926); 5 string quartets (1926, 1927, 1931, 1933, 1937); *Serenata appassionata* for Cello and Piano (1929); 2 nonets (1933–34, 1943); Wind Quintet (1945); *Joyous Sonatina* for Violin and Piano (1947); Piano Trio (1950–51); piano pieces; choruses.

Ridout, Godfrey, Canadian composer; b. Toronto, May 6, 1918. He studied piano, organ, conducting, and composition at the Toronto Cons. and at the Univ. of Toronto, where he became a member of the faculty in 1948. His music is tuneful and winsome. In 1963–64 he reconstructed a comic opera, *Colas et Colinette,* the earliest known North American work in this form, composed by the French-Canadian musician Joseph Quesnel in 1788, for which only vocal parts and a 2nd violin part were extant.

WORKS: Television opera, *The Lost Child* (1975); ballet, *La Prima Ballerina* (1966; Montreal Expo '67; *Ballade* for Viola and String Orch. (1938; Toronto, May 29, 1939); *Festal Overture* (1939); *Comedy Overture* (1941); *Dirge* for Orch. (1943); *2 Etudes* for String Orch. (1946; revised 1951); *Esther,* dramatic symph. for Soprano, Baritone, Chorus, and Orch. (1951–52; Toronto, April 29, 1952); *Cantiones Mysticae:* No. 1, after Donne, for Soprano and Orch. (1953; N.Y., Oct. 16, 1953, Stokowski conducting); No. 2, *The Ascension,* for Soprano, Trumpet, and Strings (1962; Toronto, Dec. 23, 1962); No. 3, *The Dream of the Rood,* for Baritone or Tenor, Chorus, Orch., and Organ (1972); *Music for a Young Prince,* suite for

Orch. (1959); *Fall Fair* for Orch. (perf. at the United Nations on U.N. Day, Oct. 24, 1961); *4 Sonnets* for Chorus and Orch. (1964); *In Memoriam Anne Frank* for Soprano and Orch. (Toronto, March 14, 1965); *When Age and Youth Unite* for Chorus and Orch. (1966); *4 Songs of Eastern Canada* for Soprano and Orch. (1967); *Partita academica* for Concert Band (1969); *Frivolités canadiennes,* based on melodies by Joseph Vézina, for Small Orch. (1973); *Jubilee* for Orch. (1973); *Concerto Grosso* for Solo Piano, Solo Violin, and String Orch. (1974; Toronto, Jan. 18, 1975); *George III His Lament,* variations on an old British tune, for Small Orch. (1975); *Tafelmusik* for Wind Ensemble (1976); *Folk Song Fantasy* for Piano Trio (1951); *Introduction and Allegro* for Flute, Oboe, Clarinet, Bassoon, Horn, Violin, and Cello (1968); choruses; songs.

Riechers, August, German violin maker; b. Hannover, March 8, 1836; d. Berlin, Jan. 4, 1893. He was trained by Bausch of Leipzig in the making and repairing of violins; Joachim entrusted his violins to Riechers's hands. He publ. a valuable pamphlet, *Die Geige und ihr Bau* (1893; in Eng. as *The Violin and the Art of Its Construction; A Treatise on the Stradivarius Violin,* 1895), with 4 plates of full-size diagrams exhibiting the structure and exact dimensions of the model Stadivarius violin.

Riedel, Karl, German choral conductor; b. Kronenberg, near Elberfeld, Oct. 6, 1827; d. Leipzig, June 3, 1888. He was a silk-dyer by trade; owing to revolutionary perturbations of 1848, he abandoned his trade and decided to study music; took lessons with Carl Wilhelm at Krefeld; then enrolled in the Leipzig Cons. In 1854 he organized a singing society which he named (after himself) the Riedelverein, which specialized in programs of old church music; it became extremely successful and continued its activities long after Riedel's death. In 1868 Riedel was elected president of the Allgemeiner Deutscher Musikverein, and founded its Leipzig branch; he also became president of the Wagnerverein. He publ. the collections *Altböhmische Hussiten- und Weihnachtslieder* and *12 altdeutsche Lieder;* made a skillful reduction of Schütz's 4 Passions to one; edited Schütz's *Sieben Worte,* J.S. Franck's *Geistliche Melodien,* Eccard's *Preussische Festlieder,* and Praetorius's *Weihnachtslieder.*
BIBLIOGRAPHY: A. Göhler, *Der Riedelverein zu Leipzig* (Leipzig, 1904; includes a brief biographical sketch of Riedel).

Riedt, Friedrich Wilhelm, German flutist; b. Berlin, Jan. 24, 1710; d. there, Jan. 5, 1783. He studied with Graun; in 1741 became chamber musician to Frederick the Great; in 1749, director of the "Musikübende Gesellschaft" in Berlin. He wrote 6 trios for 2 Flutes and Continuo; sonatas for 2 Flutes; Sonata for Flute and Cello; publ. *Versuch über die musikalischen Intervalle* (Berlin, 1753); contributed various articles (critical and polemical) to Marpurg's *Historisch-kritische Beyträge zur Aufnahme der Musik.*

Riegel (Rigel), Heinrich (Henri) Joseph, French composer; b. Wertheim, Franconia, Feb. 9, 1741; d. Paris, May 2, 1799. He was of German extraction; studied with F.X. Richter in Mannheim and with Jommelli in Stuttgart. In 1767 he went to Paris; from 1783 to 1786, belonged to a group of composers associated with the Concert Spirituel. On the title page of several of his works publ. in Paris his name appears as Rigel, and this gallicized form was adopted by his son **Henri-Jean,** who was born in Paris. Riegel was one of the earliest composers to write ensemble music with piano, publ. as "symphonies" for 2 Violins, Cello, 2 Horns, and Piano. He was a fairly voluminous composer; wrote several short operas in the manner of the German singspiel, all of which were produced in Paris: *Le Savetier et le financier* (1778); *L'Automat* (1779); *Rosanie* (1780); *Blanche et vermeille* (1781); *Lucas* (1785); *Les Amours du Gros-Caillou* (1786); *Alix de Beaucaire* (1791). His other works include 6 symphs.; 5 piano concertos; 6 string quartets; several *Sonates de clavecin en quattuor;* a number of piano sonatas, some with Violin obbligato; and 3 *Sonates en symphonies* for Piano. During the revolutionary period in France he composed various pieces celebrating the events. A "symphonie" in D was republ. by R. Sondheimer (1923). A Sonata is included in W.S. Newman's *Six Keyboard Sonatas from the Classical Era* (1965).
BIBLIOGRAPHY: G. de Saint-Foix, "Rigel," *Revue Musicale* (June 1925); R. Sondheimer, "H.J. Rigel," *Music Review* (Aug. 1956).

Riegel, Kenneth, American tenor; b. Womelsdorf, Pa., April 29, 1938. He studied at the Manhattan School of Music in N.Y. and also at the Metropolitan Opera Studio. He made his operatic debut as the Alchemist in Henze's opera *König Hirsch* with the Santa Fe Opera in 1965; then sang with the Cincinnati Opera, the Houston Opera, the N.Y. City Opera, and others. On Oct. 22, 1973, he made his debut with the Metropolitan Opera in N.Y. as Iopas in *Les Troyens.*

Rieger, Fritz, German conductor; b. Oberaltstadt, June 28, 1910; d. Bonn, Sept. 29, 1978. He was educated at the Prague Academy of Music, taking courses in piano with Langer, composition with Finke, and conducting with Szell. From 1931 to 1938 he conducted at the German Opera Theater in Prague; from 1939 to 1941 was conductor of the Bremen Opera; from 1947 to 1949, at the Mannheim National Theater. From 1949 to 1966 he was Generalmusikdirektor of the Munich Phil.; also conducted at the Bavarian State Opera. In 1972–73 he was chief conductor of the Melbourne Symph.; he also gave guest performances in Japan. In his programs he gave considerable prominence to modern music.

Riegger, Wallingford, outstanding American composer; b. Albany, Ga., April 29, 1885; d. New York, April 2, 1961. He received his primary education at home: his mother was a pianist; his father a violinist. The family moved to N.Y. in 1900, and

Riegger began serious study with Percy Goetschius (theory) and Alwin Schroeder (cello) at the Inst. of Musical Art; after graduation (1907), he went to Berlin, where he took courses at the Hochschule für Musik; conducted opera in Würzburg and Königsberg (1915–16); also led the Bluethner Orch. in Berlin (1916–17). He returned to America in 1917 and taught theory and cello at Drake Univ., Des Moines (1918–22); in 1922 received the Paderewski Prize for his Piano Trio; in 1924 was awarded the E.S. Coolidge Prize for his setting of Keats's *La Belle Dame sans merci;* in 1925 he was given the honorary degree of D.Mus. by the Cincinnati Cons. He taught at the Inst. of Musical Art in N.Y. (1924–25) and at the Ithaca Cons. (1926–28); then settled in N.Y., where he became active as a composer and a participant in various modern music societies; took part in the development of electronic instruments (in association with Theremin), and learned to play an electric cello. His music is of a highly advanced nature; a master craftsman, he wrote in disparate styles with an equal degree of proficiency; used numerous pseudonyms for certain works (**William Richards, Walter Scotson, Gerald Wilfring Gore, John H. McCurdy, George Northrup, Robert Sedgwick, Leonard Gregg, Edwin Farell, Edgar Long,** etc.). After a long period of neglect on the part of the public and the critics, he began to receive recognition; his 3rd Symph. was the choice of the N.Y. Music Critics Circle in 1948.

WORKS: FOR THE STAGE: Several works for the dance groups of Martha Graham, Doris Humphrey, and others, scored for various instrumental ensembles: *Bacchanale* (N.Y., 1931); *Frenetic Rhythms* (N.Y., 1933); *Evocation* (Toronto, 1933); the trilogy *Theatre Piece, With My Red Fires,* and *New Dance* (1934; orchestrated 1936; N.Y., July 2, 1936); *Chronicle* (N.Y., 1936); *The Cry* (N.Y., 1935); *Candide* (N.Y., 1937); *Case History No. . . .* (N.Y., 1937); *Trojan Incident* (N.Y., 1938); *Machine Ballet* (Toronto, 1938); *Pilgrim's Progress* (N.Y., 1941). FOR ORCH.: *American Polonaise* (1922; retitled *Triple Jazz*); *Rhapsody* (1926; N.Y., Oct. 29, 1931); *Fantasy and Fugue* for Organ and Orch. (1930–31); *Dichotomy* for Chamber Orch. (1931–32; Berlin, March 10, 1932); *Scherzo* (1932; N.Y., Jan. 30, 1933); *New Dance,* finale of dance trilogy, in 7 different instrumentations (1934; orch. version in 1936, revised 1940–41; Pittsburgh, Jan. 30, 1942, Reiner conducting); *Canon and Fugue* for Orch. or String Orch. (1941); *Passacaglia and Fugue* (1942; Berkeley, Calif., Aug. 1, 1942); *Processional: Funeral March* for Orch. or Concert Band (1943); 4 symphs.: Nos. 1 and 2 for School Orch. (1943, 1944; both withdrawn); No. 3 (1946–47; N.Y., May 16, 1948; revised 1956); No. 4 (1956–57; Univ. of Illinois, April 12, 1957); *Music for Orchestra* (1939; revised 1951; Cleveland, March 22, 1956); *Variations* for Piano and Orch. (1952–53; Louisville, Ky., Feb. 13, 1954; versions for 2 Pianos and Orch., and for 2 Solo Pianos); *Suite for Young Orchestras* for varying combinations of Strings and Winds (1954); *Romanza* for Strings (1954); *Dance Rhythms* (Atlanta, March 4, 1955); *Overture* (1955); *Preamble and Fugue* (1955); *Festival Overture* (1957); *Variations* for Violin and Orch. (1958; Louisville, April 1,

1959); *Quintuple Jazz* (1958; Univ. of Iowa, May 20, 1959); Sinfonietta (1959); *Duo* for Piano and Orch. (1960); *Introduction and Fugue* for Cello, Wind Orch., and Timpani (1960). FOR VOICE: *La Belle Dame sans merci* for 4 Solo Voices and Chamber Orch. (Pittsfield, Mass., Sept. 19, 1924); *Eternity,* after Dickinson, for Women's Voices, Flute, 2 Horns, and Double Bass (1940); *Who Can Revoke?* for Chorus and Piano (1948); *In Certainty of Song,* cantata (1950); *The Dying of the Light,* after Dylan Thomas, for Chorus, and Orch. or Piano (1954). CHAMBER MUSIC: Piano Trio (1919–20); *Whimsey* for Cello and Piano (1920); *Study in Sonority* for 10 Violins, or multiples of 10 (1927); *Suite* for Solo Flute (1929); *3 Canons* for Flute, Oboe, Clarinet, and Bassoon (1931); *Divertissement* for Flute, Harp, and Cello (1933); 2 string quartets (1938–39, 1948); *Duos* for Flute, Oboe, and Clarinet (1943); Violin Sonatina (1947); *Music for Brass Choir* (1948–49); Piano Quintet (1951); Nonet for Brass (1951); Wind Quintet (1952); Concerto for Piano and Wind Quintet (1952); *Variations* for Violin and Viola (1956); *Movement* for 2 Trumpets, Trombone, and Piano (1957); *Prelude and Fugue* for 4 Cellos (1957); *Cooper Square* for Solo Accordion (1958). FOR PIANO: *Blue Voyage* (1927); *Scherzo* (1932); *New and Old,* 12 study pieces (1944).

BIBLIOGRAPHY: H. Cowell, ed., *American Composers on American Music* (Stanford, Calif., 1933; reprinted in N.Y., 1962); R.F. Goldman, "The Music of Wallingford Riegger," *Musical Quarterly* (Jan. 1950); M. Goss, *Modern Music-Makers* (N.Y., 1952; pp. 117–27); *Composers of the Americas,* vol. 7 (Washington, D.C., 1961; contains a complete list of works); Stephen Spackman, *Wallingford Riegger. Two Essays in Musical Biography* (N.Y., 1982).

Riehl, Wilhelm Heinrich von, German writer on music; b. Biebrich-on-Rhine, May 6, 1823; d. Munich, Nov. 16, 1897. He studied at the Univ. of Munich, where he became (1854) a prof. of political economy; also lectured on music history. He publ. the valuable compendium *Musikalische Charakterköpfe* (3 vols., 1853–61; 6th ed., 1879; 3rd vol. contains the essays "Die Kriegsgeschichte der deutschen Oper" and "Die beiden Beethoven") and 2 vols. of original songs, *Hausmusik* (1856, 1877). Posthumous publications: *Zur Geschichte der romantischen Oper* (Berlin, 1928); *Musik im Leben des Volkes,* a collection of Riehl's articles, compiled and ed. by J. Müller-Blattau (Kassel, 1936).

BIBLIOGRAPHY: H. Simonsfeld, *Heinrich Riehl als Kulturhistoriker* (Munich, 1899); V. von Geramb, *W. H. Riehl, Leben und Wirken* (Salzburg, 1954).

Riem, Friedrich Wilhelm, German organist and composer; b. Kölleda, Thuringia, Feb. 17, 1779; d. Bremen, April 20, 1857. He was a pupil of J.A. Hiller in Leipzig; organist at the Thomaskirche (1807–14), then in Bremen. He wrote an oratorio, *Der Erlöser;* String Quintet; Piano Quartet; 3 string quartets; 4 violin sonatas; 6 piano sonatas; also publ. a collection of organ pieces for concert and church.

Riemann, (Carl Wilhelm Julius) Hugo, preeminent German musicologist; b. Gross-Mehlra, near Sondershausen, July 18, 1849; d. Leipzig, July 10, 1919. He was trained in theory by Frankenberger at Sondershausen; studied piano with Barthel and Ratzenberger; took the gymnasial course in the Rossleben Klosterschule (1865–68) and studied first law, then philosophy and history, at Berlin and Tübingen; then entered the Leipzig Cons. In 1873 he took the degree of Dr.Phil. at Göttingen with the dissertation *Musikalische Logik;* was active as a conductor and teacher at Bielefeld until 1878, when he qualified as univ. lecturer on music at Leipzig; taught music at Bromberg (1880–81), then at the Hamburg Cons. till 1890, at the Sondershausen Cons. for a short time, and at the Wiesbaden Cons. until 1895, when he resumed his lectures at Leipzig. In 1905 he was made prof.; in 1908, director of the newly established Collegium Musicum; and in 1914, also director of the newly established Forschungsinstitut für Musikwissenschaft. He was made Mus.Doc. *honoris causa* by the Univ. of Edinburgh (1899). On his 60th birthday he was honored by the publication of a Festschrift (ed., Karl Mennicke) containing contributions from the world's foremost scholars, many of whom were Riemann's pupils. The 2nd Riemann Festschrift was publ. after his death in 1919.

The mere bulk of Riemann's writings, covering every branch of musical science, constitutes a monument of indefatigable industry, and is proof of enormous concentration and capacity for work. When one takes into consideration that much of this work is the result of painstaking research and of original, often revolutionary, thinking, one must share the great respect and admiration in which Riemann was held by his contemporaries. Although many of his ideas are now seen in a different light, his works treating of harmony were considered to constitute the foundation of modern music theory. His researches in the field of music history have solved a number of vexing problems, and thrown light on others. And, finally, in formulating the new science of musicology, the labors of Riemann have been a most important factor.

WRITINGS: THEORY: *Musikalische Syntaxis* (1877); *Skizze einer neuen Methode der Harmonielehre* (1880; rewritten as *Handbuch der Harmonielehre,* 1887; 8th ed., 1920); *Elementarmusiklehre* (1883); *Neue Schule der Melodik* (1883); *Vergleichende Klavierschule* (1883); *Musikalische Dynamik und Agogik* (1884); *Praktische Anleitung zum Phrasierung* (1886; rewritten as *Vademecum der Phrasierung,* 1900); *Systematische Modulationslehre . . .* (1887); *Lehrbuch des einfachen, doppelten und imitierenden Kontrapunkts* (1888; 6th ed., 1921; in Eng., 1904); *Die Elemente der musikalischen Ästhetik* (1900); *Grosse Kompositionslehre* (vol. I, *Der homophone Satz,* 1902; vol. II, *Der polyphone Satz,* 1903; vol. III, *Der Orchestersatz und der dramatische Gesangstil,* 1913); *System der musikalischen Rhythmik und Metrik* (1903); *Grundriss der Musikwissenschaft* (1908; 4th ed., edited by J. Wolf, 1928); *L. van Beethovens Sämtlich Klavier-Solosonaten, Ästhetische und formal-technische*

Analyse mit historischen Notizen (Berlin, 1918–19). HISTORY: *Studien zur Geschichte der Notenschrift* (1878); *Die Entwickelung unserer Notenschrift* (1881); *Die "Martyriai" der byzantinischen liturgischen Notation* (1882); "Notenschrift und Notendruck," in *Röder Festschrift* (1896); *Geschichte der Musiktheorie im IX.–XIX. Jahrhundert* (1898); *Epochen und Heroen der Musikgeschichte* (1900); *Geschichte der Musik seit Beethoven (1800–1900)* (1901); *Handbuch der Musikgeschichte* (5 vols., 1904–13); as supplement to this, *Musikgeschichte in Beispielen* (1912; a collection of 150 compositions, 13th–18th century; 4th ed., with introduction by A. Schering, 1929); *Die byzantinische Notenschrift im 10.–15. Jahrhundert* (vol. I, 1909; vol. II, 1915); *Kompendium der Notenschriftkunde* (1910); *Folkloristische Tonalitätsstudien* (1916). LEXICOGRAPHY: *Musik–Lexikon,* one of the standard reference works on music; publ. in Leipzig, 1882; following eds. appeared in 1884, 1887, 1894, 1900, 1905, 1909, 1916; the 9th, 10th, and 11th eds. were brought out in 1919, 1922, and 1929, under the editorship of Alfred Einstein; the 12th ed., under Wilibald Gurlitt, was publ. in 3 vols. (Mainz, 1959, 1961, 1967; to these was added a supplement in 2 vols. (Mainz, 1972, 1975), ed. by Carl Dahlhaus; Dahlhaus and Eggebrecht were co-editors of the *Brockhaus-Riemann Musiklexikon* (1978); *Opern-Handbuch* (Leipzig, 1887; supplement, 1893). Riemann contributed to Schlesinger's *Meisterführer* analyses of Beethoven's string quartets (vol. XII, 1903), and some of the orch. works of Brahms (vol. III, 1908), Schumann (vol. XIII, 1911), and Tchaikovsky (vol. XIV, 1911); revised Marx's *Lehre von der musikalischen Komposition* (4 vols., 1887–88); ed. vols. IV (1907) and V (1908) of Deiters's trans. of Thayer's *Beethoven,* and revised vols. II and III (1910, 1911). He publ. in various journals innumerable articles and essays; of these some were collected and publ. as *Präludien und Studien* (3 vols., 1895, 1900, 1901); ed. works of early composers in Denkmäler Deutscher Tonkunst in Bayern and in Denkmäler Deutscher Tonkunst; also the collections *Alte Kammermusik* (4 vols.), *Collegium musicum* (50 books), *Hausmusik aus alter Zeit* (96 madrigals, canzone, etc., of the 14th and 15th centuries), etc. He composed many instructive piano pieces; also chamber music, choruses, and songs.

BIBLIOGRAPHY: Biographical sketch by K. Mennicke in the Riemann-Festschrift (Leipzig, 1909); R. Heuler, "Dr. H. Riemann als Volksschulgesangpädagog," *Sonde* (Würzburg, 1910); Riemann issue of the *Zeitschrift für Musikwissenschaft* (July 1919); H. Grabner, *Die Funktionstheorie Hugo Riemanns* (Munich, 1923); H.L. Denecke, *Die Kompositionslehre Hugo Riemanns* (Kiel, 1937); W. Gurlitt, "Hugo Riemann: 1849–1919," *Abhandlungen der Akademie der Wissenschaft und der Literatur Mainz* (Wiesbaden, 1951).

Riemann, Ludwig, German writer on music; b. Lüneburg, March 25, 1863; d. Essen, Jan. 25, 1927. He was a pupil of his father; also of O. von Königslöw and H. Schröder (violin), H. Grüters and A. Löschhorn (piano), J. Alsleben, A. Haupt, and W. Bargiel (composition) at the Königliche Institut für Kirchenmusik in Berlin; from 1889 he was a teacher of singing at the Gymnasium in Essen; in 1918 he was made prof.

WRITINGS: *Populäre Darstellung der Akustik in Beziehung zur Musik* (1896); *Über eigentümliche, bei Natur- und orientalischen Kulturvölkern vorkommende, Tonreihen und ihre Beziehungen zu den Gesetzen der Harmonie* (1899); *Das Wesen des Klavierklanges und seine Beziehungen zum Anschlag* (1911; valuable); *Das Erkennen der Ton- und Akkordzusammenhänge in Tonstücken klassischer und moderner Literatur* (1925); *Kurzgefasste praktische Modulationsübungen* (2nd ed., 1924); etc.

Riemenschneider, Albert, American organist and music editor; b. Berea, Ohio, Aug. 31, 1878; d. Akron, July 20, 1950. He studied at Baldwin-Wallace College (B.A., 1899) and in Cleveland; then went to Vienna, where he took lessons with R. Fuchs and H. Reinhold; proceeded to Paris, where he continued his organ study with Widor and Guilmant. Returning to America in 1905, he became a choral director of Baldwin-Wallace Cons., and later president of the College. His main contribution to American musicology is a number of fine editions of Bach's vocal works, among them *Liturgical Year* (the *Orgelbüchlein;* 1933); *Chorales* (120 chorales in original clefs and with the original orch. parts; 2 vols., 1939; with C.N. Boyd); *371 Harmonized Chorales and 69 Chorale Melodies with Figured Bass* (1941).

Riepel, Joseph, Austrian theorist; b. Hörschlag, Jan. (baptized, Jan. 22) 1709; d. Regensburg, Oct. 23, 1782. He studied in Linz; then took a course with Zelenka in Dresden (1740–45); in 1751 he settled in Regensburg. He publ. several vols. dealing with theory, harmony, and rhythm, which are valuable from the historical point of view: *De rhythmopoeia oder von der Tactordnung* (Augsburg, 1752); *Harmonisches Sylbenmass* (Regensburg, 1776); etc.; also composed symphs., piano concertos, violin concertos, and sacred choral music.

BIBLIOGRAPHY: W. Twittenhoff, *Die musiktheoretischen Schriften J. Riepels* (Halle, 1935); E. Schwarzmaier, *Die Takt- une Tonordnung J. Riepels* (Wolfenbüttel, 1936); J. Markl, *J. Riepel als Komponist* (Kallmünz, 1937).

Ries, Ferdinand, German pianist and composer; b. Bonn, Nov. 28, 1784; d. Frankfurt, Jan. 13, 1838. He was the son of **Franz Anton Ries,** "der alte Ries," a close friend of Beethoven; thanks to this relationship, Ferdinand Ries was accepted by Beethoven as a piano pupil and studied with him in Vienna from 1801 to 1804; also in Vienna he took a course in music theory with Albrechtsberger. He made successful tours as a concert pianist in Germany, Scandinavia, and Russia; then went to London, where he remained from 1813 to 1824, and acquired prominence as a piano teacher. From 1827 he stayed mainly in Frankfurt. He was an excellent pianist and a prolific composer.

WORKS: Operas: *Die Räuberbraut* (Frankfurt, 1828) and *Liska* (produced in London, 1831, under the title *The Sorceress*); 2 oratorios; 8 symphs.; 8 piano concertos; chamber music; 52 piano sonatas and other pieces for his instrument. His music reflects both the spirit and the technique of composition of Beethoven, the fateful distance between them being that of genius, which Ries never possessed. His reminiscences of Beethoven were publ. posthumously under the title *Biographische Notizen über L. von Beethoven* (Koblenz, 1828; numerous later eds. in all European languages; the work was partly dictated by Ries to Wegeler during the last years of Ries's life, and inevitably contains stories that could not be trusted).

BIBLIOGRAPHY: L. Überfeldt, *Ferdinand Ries' Jugendentwicklung* (Bonn, 1915); D. McArdle, "Beethoven and Ferdinand Ries," *Music & Letters,* XLVI (1965); C. Hill, *The Music of Ferdinand Ries: A Thematic Catalogue* (Armidale, New South Wales, 1977).

Ries, Franz, German publisher, son of **Hubert Ries;** b. Berlin, April 7, 1846; d. Naumberg, June 20, 1932. He studied violin with his father and later with Massart at the Paris Cons. His career as a concert violinist was brief, and in 1875 he entered the music publishing business; from 1881 to 1924 was director of the firm Ries & Erler in Berlin; in 1924 his son **Robert Ries** became the proprietor; after the death of Robert Ries the firm was taken over by his 2 daughters.

Ries, Franz Anton, German violinist; b. Bonn, Nov. 10, 1755; d. Godesberg, Nov. 1, 1846. He was known as "der alte Ries," to distinguish him from his son **Ferdinand.** Franz Anton Ries was music director of the Margrave Max Franz of Cologne and Bonn, and was a close friend of Beethoven in Bonn.

Ries, Hubert, German violinist, brother of **Ferdinand Ries;** b. Bonn, April 1, 1802; d. Berlin, Sept. 14, 1886. He studied at Kassel under Spohr (violin) and Hauptmann (composition); in 1836, was concertmaster of the royal orch. in Berlin; in 1851 a teacher at the Royal Theaterinstrumentalschule; pensioned in 1872. He publ. excellent instructive works for violin: *Violinschule* (also in Eng.); *Erzählungen aus alter Zeit* (30 instructive duets); *15 Violinstudien von mässiger Schwierigkeit,* op. 26; *30 Violinstudien für den ersten Unterricht,* op. 28; *50 Intonationsübungen, 12 Violinstudien in Form von Konzertstücken,* op. 9; duets, exercises, etc.; also 2 violin concertos (opp. 13 and 16).

Riesemann, Oscar, Russian-German musicologist; b. Reval, Estonia, Feb. 29, 1880; d. St. Niklausen, near Lucerne, Switzerland, Sept. 28, 1934. He studied music theory with Sandberger and Thuille at the Royal Academy in Munich; then took courses in philology and jurisprudence at the Univ. of Moscow; subsequently went to Germany again and took courses with Friedlaender in Berlin and with Hugo

Riemann in Leipzig, where he obtained his Dr.Phil. with the dissertation *Die Notation des alt-russischen Kirchengesanges* (publ. in Moscow, in German, 1908). He then was active as a music critic in Moscow, and during World War I served on the Russian side in the sanitary corps, but made his way to Germany once more during the Russian Revolution; he described this turbulent period in an autobiographical publication, *Fluchten* (Stuttgart, 1925). He subsequently lived in Munich and then in Switzerland. He publ. a monograph on Mussorgsky (Munich, 1926; in Eng., N.Y., 1929), and *Rachmaninoff's Recollections* (N.Y., 1934; in Eng.), a loyal but not always accurate account, which was gently repudiated by Rachmaninoff himself.

Rieter-Biedermann, Jakob Melchior, Swiss publisher; b. Winterthur, May 14, 1811; d. there, Jan. 25, 1876. He founded a successful music publishing house in 1849 in Winterthur, with a branch at Leipzig in 1862, which gradually became more important than the original house, so that the latter was dissolved in 1884. After the death of proprietor Robert Astor (d. Leipzig, April 14, 1917), the firm was bought by C.F. Peters. Brahms was the most famous composer in their catalogue.

Rieti, Vittorio, Italian-American composer; b. Alexandria, Egypt, Jan. 28, 1898. He studied with Frugatta in Milan; then took courses with Respighi and Casella in Rome, where he lived until 1940, when he emigrated to the U.S. (became an American citizen June 1, 1944). He taught at the Peabody Cons. in Baltimore (1948–49), Chicago Musical College (1950–53), Queens College in N.Y. (1958–60), and Hunter College in N.Y. (1960–64). His style of composition represents an ingratiating synthesis of cosmopolitan modern tendencies.
WORKS: Operas: *Orfeo,* lyric tragedy (1928); *Teresa nel bosco* (Venice Festival, Sept. 15, 1934); *Don Perlimplin* (Univ. of Illinois, Urbana, March 30, 1952); *The Pet Shop* (N.Y., April 14, 1958); *The Clock* (1960); *Maryam the Harlot* (1966); ballets: *L'Arca di Noè* (1922); *Barabau,* with Chorus (Ballets Russes, London, Dec. 11, 1925); *Le Bal* (Monte Carlo, 1929); *David triomphant* (Paris, 1937); *Waltz Academy* (Boston, 1944); *The Mute Wife,* on themes by Paganini (N.Y., 1944); *Trionfo di Bacco e Arianna* (N.Y., 1948); *Unicorn* (1950); oratorio, *Viaggio d'Europa* (Rome, 1954); for Orch.: 6 symphs.: of these, No. 4 is subtitled *Sinfonia tripartita* (St. Louis, Dec. 16, 1944) and No. 6 was first perf. in N.Y., Dec. 11, 1974; *Concerto du Loup* (named after the Loup River in Southern France) for Chamber Orch. (Los Angeles, Aug. 8, 1942); Concerto for 5 Wind Instruments and Orch. (Prague Festival, May 31, 1924); 3 piano concertos (1926, 1937, 1960); Violin Concerto (1928); Harpsichord Concerto (1930); 2 cello concertos; Concerto for 2 Pianos and Orch. (Cincinnati, 1952); Sonata for Flute, Oboe, Bassoon, and Piano (1924); 4 string quartets (1926, 1942, 1953, 1960); Woodwind Quartet (1958); *Madrigal* for 12 Instruments; *5 Fables of La Fontaine* for Orch. (1968); Triple Concerto for Violin, Viola, Piano, and Orch.

(1971); Octet for Flute, Oboe, Piano, Bassoon, Viola, Violin, Cello, and Piano (1971); Piano Trio (1972); Concerto for String Quartet and Orch. (N.Y., Feb. 1, 1978). See *Notes* (Dec. 1972) for a list of his works.

Rietsch, Heinrich, Czech musicologist and composer; b. Falkenau-on-Eger, Sept. 22, 1860; d. Prague, Dec. 12, 1927. He studied in Vienna under Krenn and R. Fuchs (composition) and Hanslick (music history). In 1900 he became an instructor at the German Univ. in Prague. He edited Muffat's *Florilegium* for Denkmäler der Tonkunst in Österreich; also J.J. Fux's *Concentus musico-instrumentalis* (ibid.). He publ. *Die Tonkunst in der 2 Hälfte des 19. Jahrhunderts* (Leipzig, 1900); *Die deutsche Liedweise* (Leipzig, 1904); *Die Grundlagen der Tonkunst* (Leipzig, 1907); several of his publications were reprinted. His autobiographical sketch was publ. in *Neue Musikzeitung* (1915).
BIBLIOGRAPHY: Paul Nettl, "Verzeichnis der wissenschaftlichen und künstlerischen Arbeiten von Rietsch bis 1920," *Zeitschrift für Musikwissenschaft,* II (p. 736).

Rietschel, Georg Christian, German organist and theologian; b. Dresden, May 10, 1842; d. Leipzig, June 13, 1914. After filling several pastorates in various German cities, he became a prof. of theology at Leipzig Univ. (1899). He publ. *Die Aufgabe der Orgel im Gottesdienste bis in das 18. Jahrhundert* (1892) and *Lehrbuch der Liturgik* (2 vols., 1900, 1909).

Rietz, Julius, German conductor and editor; b. Berlin, Dec. 28, 1812; d. Dresden, Sept. 12, 1877. He was of a musical family: his father was a court musician, and his brother was a friend of Mendelssohn. Julius Rietz studied cello and played in theater orchs. in Berlin. In 1834 he became 2nd conductor of the Düsseldorf Opera; from 1847 to 1854 he was a theater conductor in Leipzig; in 1848–60 served as conductor of the Gewandhaus Concerts; later he was appointed artistic director of the Dresden Cons. A scholarly musician and competent orch. conductor, Rietz was also an excellent music editor; he prepared for publication the complete edition of Mendelssohn's works for Breitkopf & Härtel (1874–77), and also edited Mozart's operas and symphs., Beethoven's overtures, etc. As a composer, he followed the musical style of Mendelssohn.
BIBLIOGRAPHY: "Pauline Viardot-Garcia to Julius Rietz, Letters of Friendship," *Musical Quarterly* (July 1915 to Jan. 1916); H. Zimmer, *Julius Rietz* (Diss., Univ. of Berlin, 1943).

Riezler, Walter, German musicologist; b. Munich, Oct. 2, 1878; d. there, Jan. 22, 1956. He studied music with Max Reger and Felix Mottl (1904–6). He was first interested principally in art; he was director of the Stettin Museum of Fine Arts from 1910–33; in 1934 he returned to Munich; after 1946 taught music history at the Univ. of Munich. He publ. an excellent monograph on Beethoven (1936), which went through 7 German editions up to 1951 and was also translated into English (N.Y., 1938).

Rifkin, Joshua, American musicologist, pianist, and conductor; b. New York, April 22, 1944. He studied with Persichetti at the Juilliard School of Music in N.Y. (B.S., 1964); with Gustave Reese at N.Y. Univ. (1964–66); at the Univ. of Göttingen (1966–67); and later with Mendel, Lockwood, Babbitt, and Oster at Princeton Univ. (M.F.A., 1969). He also worked with Stockhausen at Darmstadt (1961, 1965). In 1970 he joined the faculty of Brandeis Univ. He is noted for his research in the field of Renaissance and Baroque music, but he became popular as a performer and explicator of ragtime.

Rigel, Henri-Jean, French composer, son and pupil of **Heinrich Joseph Riegel** (he changed his name from its German form to French); b. Paris, May 11, 1772; d. Abbeville, Dec. 16, 1852. He conducted the French Opera in Cairo (1798–1800); in 1808 was attached to Napoleon's court as a chamber musician. He wrote the operas *Les 2 Meuniers* (Cairo, 1799) and *Le Duel nocturne* (Dec. 23, 1805); 4 piano concertos and numerous minor piano pieces.

Righini, Vincenzo, Italian composer; b. Bologna, Jan. 22, 1756; d. there, Aug. 19, 1812. He was a pupil of Bernacchi (singing) and Padre Martini (counterpoint); made his stage debut as a tenor at Parma in 1775; in 1776 went to Prague, where he also began composing; in 1780 he became singing master to the Archduchess Elisabeth at Vienna, and conductor of the Italian Opera; from 1787 to 1793 he was Electoral Kapellmeister at Mainz; in 1793, after the successful production of his opera *Enea nel Lazio* at Berlin, he was appointed Kapellmeister at the Court Opera. WORKS: Some 20 operas, including *Il Convitato di pietra* (Vienna, Aug. 21, 1777; one of the early settings of the *Don Giovanni* story) and *Gerusalemme liberata* and *La selva incantata* (a single work consisting of 2 2-act operas; Berlin, Jan. 7, 1803); a series of fine vocal exercises (1806).

Rignold, Hugo, English conductor; b. Kingston-on-Thames, May 15, 1905; d. London, May 30, 1976. His father was a theatrical conductor, his mother an opera singer. He was taken to Canada as a child, and studied violin in Winnipeg; in 1920 he returned to England on a scholarship to the Royal Academy of Music. During World War II he was stationed in Cairo, where he trained a radio orch. in performances of symph. music. Returning to England, he was a ballet conductor at Covent Garden (1947); from 1948 to 1954 was conductor of the Liverpool Phil.; in 1957–60 served as music director of the Royal Ballet; then became music director of the Birmingham Symph. Orch. (1960–68).
BIBLIOGRAPHY: Donald Brook, *International Gallery of Conductors* (Bristol, 1951; pp. 151–54).

Rihm, Wolfgang, German composer; b. Karlsruhe, March 13, 1952. He studied theory and composition with Eugene Velte at the Hochschule für Musik in Karlsruhe (1968–72) and also attended courses given by Humphrey Searle; then went to Cologne, where he enrolled in the seminars of Stockhausen (1972–73); also audited classes of Klaus Huber in Freiburg (1973); in addition, received counseling from Wolfgang Fortner. From 1973–78 he taught at the Hochschule für Musik in Karlsruhe. His own music thrives on calculated unpredictability; but he does not shrink from producing shockingly euphonious and startlingly pleasurable sounds.
WORKS: FOR THE STAGE: Opera-in-progress, *Harlekin* (1977—); 2 chamber operas: No. 1, *Faust und Yorick* (1976), and No. 2, *Jakob Lenz* (1977–78; Hamburg, March 8, 1979). FOR ORCH.: 3 symphs.: No. 1 (1969); No. 2 (1975); No. 3, after Nietzsche and Rimbaud, for Soprano, Baritone, Chorus, and Orch. (1976–77); *Trakt* (1971); *Morphonie, Sektor IV* for String Quartet and Orch. (1972); *Magma* (1974); *Dis-Kontur* (1974); *Sub-Kontur* (1974–75; Donaueschingen, Oct. 26, 1976); *Konzertarie,* a "telepsychogramm" based on a telegram King Ludwig II sent to Wagner, for Mezzo-soprano and Orch. (1975); *O Notte* for Baritone and Small Orch. (1975); *Cuts and Dissolves,* concerto for 29 Players (1976); *Nachtordnung,* 7 pieces for 15 Strings (1976); *Lichtzwang,* music for Violin and Orch., in memory of Paul Celan (1975–76); *Hölderlin-Fragmente* for Voice, and Orch. or Piano (1977); *La Musique creuse le ciel,* music for 2 Pianos and Orch. (1977–79; Cologne, Nov. 14, 1980); *Abgesangsszene* No. 1 for Orch. (1979; Kassel, Nov. 8, 1979), No. 2, after Nietzsche and Novalis, for Voice and Orch. (1979; Karlsruhe, Oct. 5, 1980), No. 3, after Huchel, for Baritone and Orch. (1980), No. 4, after Nietzsche, for Voice and Orch. (1979–80), and No. 5 for Orch. (1979; Kiel, Jan. 12, 1981); *Walzer* (1979–81); *Doppelgesang* No. 1 for Viola, Cello, and Orch. (1980) and No. 2 for Clarinet or Bass Clarinet, Cello, and Orch. (1981–83; Hitzacker, Aug. 7, 1983); *Lenz-Fragmente,* 5 songs for Voice, and Orch. or Piano (1980); *Tutuguri,* subtitled *Ballet nach Artaud,* a series of 7 works inspired by the writings of Antonin Artaud: *I* (1981), *II* (1981–82; Chicago Symph., March 3, 1982), *III* for 6 Percussionists and Orch. (1981; Karlsruhe, Dec. 5, 1981), *IV* (1982; Saarbrücken, May 20, 1982), *V* (1981; in progress), *VI* for 6 Percussionists (1981), and *VII* for 7 Voices and Orch. (1981; in progress); Viola Concerto (1980–83; West Berlin, March 13, 1983); *Wölfli-Liederbuch* for Baritone, and Orch. or Piano (1981–82); *Chiffre I* for Piano and 7 Instruments (1982; Saarbrücken, April 22, 1983) and *II, Silence to Be Beaten,* for Percussion and Orch. (1983); *Gebild* for Piccolo Trumpet, 2 Percussionists and 20 Strings (1983; Zürich, May 15, 1983); *Monodram* for Cello and Orch. (1983; Graz, Austria, Oct. 9, 1983). CHAMBER MUSIC: 5 string quartets: No. 1 (1968); No. 2 (1970); No. 3, *Im Innersten* (1976); No. 4 (1979–81); No. 5 (1981); *Paraphrase* for Cello, Piano, and Percussion (1972); *Deploration* for Flute, Cello, and Percussion (1973); *Hervorgedunkelt,* 5 songs after Celan, for Mezzo-soprano, Flute, Harp, Vibraphone, Cello, Organ, and Percussion (1974); *Music for 3 Strings* for Violin, Viola, and Cello (1977); *Erscheinung,* sketch after

Schubert, for 9 Strings (1978); *Ländler* for 13 Strings or Piano (1979); *Music Hall Suite* for Clarinet, Alto and Tenor Saxophones, Trumpet, Violin, Double Bass, Piano, and Percussion (1979); *Nature Morte* for 13 Strings (1979–80); *Nietzsche-Fragmente* for Mezzo-soprano, Baritone, Chorus, and Flute (1981); *Canzona* for 4 Violas (1982); *Fremde Szene* for Piano Trio (1982). SOLO SONGS: *Alexanderlieder* for Mezzo-soprano, Baritone, and 2 Pianos (1975–76); *Neue Alexanderlieder* for Baritone and Piano (1979). FOR PIANO: *Klavierstück* No. 4 (1974), No. 5, *Tombeau* (1975), No. 6, *Bagatellen* (1977–78), and No. 7 (1980); *Ländler* (1979; also for Strings). FOR ORGAN: *Contemplatio* (1967); *3 Fantasies* (1967); *Fantasy* (1968); *Siebengestalt* for Organ, with Tamtam (1974); *Bann, Nachtschwärmerei* (1980).

Riisager, Knudåge, prominent Danish composer; b. Port Kunda, Estonia, March 6, 1897; d. Copenhagen, Dec. 26, 1974. He attended courses in political science at the Univ. of Copenhagen (1916–21); concurrently studied music with Peter Gram, Peter Møller, and Otto Malling (1915–18); then went to Paris and took private lessons with Albert Roussel and Paul Le Flem (1923–24); subsequently studied counterpoint with Hermann Grabner in Leipzig (1932). He held a position in Denmark's Ministry of Finance (1925–47); was chairman of the Danish Composers' Union (1937–62) and director of the Royal Danish Cons. (1956–67). A fantastically prolific composer, he wrote music in quaquaversal genres, but preserved a remarkable structural and textural consistency while demonstrating an erudite sense of modern polyphony. He also had a taste for exotic and futuristic subjects.

WORKS: (all premieres are in Copenhagen unless stated otherwise): FOR THE STAGE: Opera buffa, *Susanne* (1948; Royal Danish Opera, Jan. 7, 1950); 14 ballets: *Benzin* (1927; Dec. 26, 1930); a "ballet-bouffonnerie," *Cocktails-Party* (1929); *Tolv med Posten* (*Twelve by the Mail*), after H.C. Andersen (1939; Feb. 21, 1942); *Slaraffenland* (*Fool's Paradise;* 1940; Feb. 21, 1942; originally an orch. piece, 1936); *Qarrtsiluni,* on Eskimo themes (1942; Feb. 21, 1942; originally an orch. piece, 1938); *Fugl fønix* (*Phoenix;* 1944–45; May 12, 1946); *Etude,* based on Czerny's studies (1947; Jan. 15, 1948); *Månerenen* (*The Moon Reindeer;* 1956; Nov. 22, 1957); *Stjerner* (1958); *Les Victoires de l'Amour* (1958; March 4, 1962); *Fruen fra havet* (*Lady from the Sea;* 1959; N.Y., April 20, 1960); *Galla-Variationer* (1966; March 5, 1967); *Ballet Royal* (May 31, 1967); *Svinedrengen* (*The Swineherd;* Danish Television, March 10, 1969). FOR ORCH.: *Erasmus Montanus,* overture (1920; Göteborg, Sweden, Oct. 15, 1924); *Suite Dionysiaque* for Chamber Orch. (1924); 5 symphs.: No. 1 (1925; July 17, 1926); No. 2 (1927; March 5, 1929); No. 3 (1935; Nov. 21, 1935); No. 4, *Sinfonia gaia* (1940; Oct. 24, 1940); No. 5, *Sinfonia serena* for Strings and Percussion (1949–50; Nov. 21, 1950); *Introduzione di traverso,* overture (1925); *Variations on a Theme of Mezangean* (1926); *T-DOXC,* "poème mécanique" (1926; Sept. 3, 1927); *Klods Hans* (1929); *Fastelavn* (*Shrovetide),* overture (1929–30); *Suite* for Small Orch.

(1931); Concerto for Orch. (1931; Dec. 7, 1936); Concertino for Trumpet and String Orch. (1933; March 2, 1934); *Primavera,* overture (1934; Jan. 31, 1935); *Slaraffenland,* 2 suites (1936, 1940; as a ballet, 1940); *Sinfonia concertante* for Strings (1937); *Partita* (1937); *Basta* (1938); *Qarrtsiluni* (1938; as a ballet, 1940); *Torgutisk dans* (1939); *Tivoli-Tivoli!* (1943; Aug. 15, 1943); *Sommer-Rhapsodi* (1943; Jan. 30, 1944); *Bellman-Variationer* for Small Orch. (1945); Sinfonietta (1947; Stockholm, Oct. 1, 1947); *Chaconne* (1949); *Archaeopteryx* (1949); *Variations on a Sarabande of Charles, Duke of Orleans, 1415* for String Orch. (1950); Violin Concerto (1950–51; Oct. 11, 1951); *Toccata* (1952); *Pro fistulis et fidibus* for Woodwinds and String Orch. (1952; March 2, 1953); *Rondo giocoso* for Violin and Orch. (1957; June 18, 1957); *Burlesk ouverture* (1964); *Entrada-Epilogo* (May 19, 1971); *Bourrée,* ballet-variations (Danish Radio, March 7, 1972); *Trittico* for Woodwinds, Brass, Double Bass, and Percussion (Danish Radio, March 3, 1972); *Apollon* (Nov. 11, 1973); incidental music. FOR VOICE: *Dansk Salme* for Chorus and Orch. (1942; April 13, 1943); *Sang til Solen* for Mezzo-soprano, Baritone, Chorus, and Orch. (1947; Sept. 25, 1947); *Sangen om det Uendelige (Canto dell'Infinito)* for Chorus and Orch. (1964; Sept. 30, 1965); *Stabat Mater* for Chorus and Orch. (1966; Danish Radio, Nov. 9, 1967); choruses; songs. CHAMBER MUSIC: 2 violin sonatas (1917, 1923); 6 string quartets (1918, 1920, 1922, 1925–26, 1932, 1942–43); Sonata for Violin and Viola (1919); Wind Quintet (1921); *Variations* for Clarinet, Viola, and Bassoon (1923); Sinfonietta for 8 Wind Instruments (1924); *Divertimento* for String Quartet and Wind Quintet (1925); Sonata for Flute, Violin, Clarinet, and Cello (1927); *Music* for Wind Quintet (1927); *Conversazione* for Oboe, Clarinet, and Bassoon (1932); Concertino for 5 Violins and Piano (1933); *Serenade* for Flute, Violin, and Cello (1936); Quartet for Flute, Oboe, Clarinet, and Bassoon (1941); *Divertimento* for Flute, Oboe, Horn, and Bassoon (1944); Sonatina for Piano Trio (1951); 2-Violin Sonata (1951); String Trio (1955). FOR PIANO: *4 épigrammes* (1921); Sonata (1931); *2 morceaux* (1933); Sonatina (1950); *4 Børneklaverstykker* (1964). He publ. a collection of essays, *Det usynlige mønster* (*The Unseemly Monster;* Copenhagen, 1957), and a somewhat self-deprecatory memoir, *Det er sjovt at være lille* (*It Is Amusing to Be Small;* Copenhagen, 1967).

BIBLIOGRAPHY: Sigurd Berg, *Knudåge Riisagers Kompositioner,* an annotated catalogue of works (Copenhagen, 1967).

Riley, John, American composer and cellist; b. Altoona, Pa., Sept. 17, 1920. He studied cello and composition in the U.S., and also in London; received his Mus.B. at the Eastman School of Music in Rochester, N.Y., in 1951; studied composition on a Fulbright grant with Arthur Honegger in Paris (1952–53); at Yale Univ. with Quincy Porter (Mus.M., 1955). His works include *Rhapsody* for Cello and Orch. (1951); *Apostasy* for Orch. (1954); *Fantasy* for Oboe and String Orch. (1955); Sinfonietta (1955); 2 string quartets (1954, 1959).

Riley, Terry, American composer of the avant-garde; b. Colfax, Calif., June 24, 1935. He studied at the Univ. of Calif. at Berkeley with Seymour Shifrin, William Denny, and Robert Erickson, obtaining his M.A. in composition in 1961; went to Europe and played piano and saxophone in cabarets in Paris and in Scandinavia. In 1970 he was initiated in San Francisco as a disciple of Pandit Pran Nath, the North Indian singer, and followed him to India. In his music Riley explores the extremes of complexity and gymnosophistical simplicity. His ascertainable works include *Spectra* for 6 Instruments (1959), String Trio (1961), and *In C* for Orch., notated in fragments to be played any number of times at will in the spirit of aleatory latitudinarianism, all within the key of C major, with an occasional F sharp providing a *trompe l'oreille* effect; it was first performed in San Francisco, May 21, 1965. His other compositions include *Poppy Nogoods Phantom Band* (1966); *A Rainbow in Curved Air* (1968); *Genesis '70*, a ballet (1970); *Sunrise of the Planetary Dream Collector* for String Quartet (1981); *The Medicine Wheel* for String Quartet (1983). Riley's astrological signs are Sun in Cancer (euphemistically known in Southern California as Moon Children so as to exorcise middle-aged fear of malignancy), Scorpio Rising, and Aries Moon.

Rilling, Helmuth, noted German organist, conductor, and pedagogue; b. Stuttgart, May 29, 1933. He studied at the Hochschule für Musik in Stuttgart and later took a course in organ playing with Fernando Germani at the Santa Cecilia Academy in Rome. He taught choral conducting and organ at the Kirchenmusikschule in Berlin-Spandau (1963–66); in 1966 he was appointed to the faculty of the Frankfurt Hochschule für Musik; in 1969 he succeeded Kurt Thomas as conductor of the Frankfurter Kantorei. He was also in charge of the Stuttgart Bach Choir (Gaeschinger Kantorei) and led it during his first American tour; he conducted the summer Bach festivals of the Univ. of Oregon in Eugene. On Jan. 21, 1982, he appeared as a guest conductor with the Los Angeles Phil. He is recognized as an authority on choral music of the Baroque era.

Rimbault, Edward Francis, English writer and editor; b. London, June 13, 1816; d. there, Sept. 26, 1876. He was the son of **Stephen Francis Rimbault,** organist and composer (1773–1837); was a pupil of his father, of Samuel Wesley, and of Dr. Crotch; was organist of the Swiss Church, Soho, in 1832. He began giving lectures on English musical history in 1838; in 1840 he founded, with E. Taylor and W. Chappell, the Musical Antiquarian Society; received the degree of Dr.Phil. from Göttingen. He composed various songs, of which *Happy Land* became a popular favorite.

WRITINGS: *Bibliotheca Madrigaliana* (1847; English poetry and compositions publ. during the reigns of Elizabeth and James I); *The Organ, Its History and Construction* (1855 and other eds.; it is the first part of the Appendix to Hopkins's *The Organ: Its History*); *The Pianoforte: Its Origin, Progress and Construction* (1860); *The Early English Organ-builders and Their Works* (1864); *J.S. Bach* (after Hilgenfeldt and Forkel; 1869); *Singing Tutor* (after Lablache); etc. He edited collections of sacred and secular music, particularly those by English composers of the 16th, 17th, and 18th centuries.

Rimsky-Korsakov, Andrei, son of **Nicolai Rimsky-Korsakov;** b. St. Petersburg, Oct. 17, 1878; d. Leningrad, May 23, 1940. He studied philology at the Univ. of St. Petersburg and later at Strasbourg and Heidelberg (Dr.Phil., 1903); returning to Russia, he devoted his energies to Russian music history. In 1915 he began the publication of an important magazine, *Musikalny Sovremennik (The Musical Contemporary),* but the revolutionary events of 1917 forced suspension of its publication. He edited the first 4 vols. of the complete biography of his father, *N.A. Rimsky-Korsakov; Life and Works* (Moscow, 1933, 1935, 1936, 1937; an additional vol., No. 5, was completed and edited by his younger brother **Vladimir Rimsky-Korsakov**); also publ. *M.P. Mussorgsky, Letters and Documents* (1932; extremely valuable); edited and annotated his father's *Chronicle of My Musical Life* (Moscow, 1935); compiled the catalogue, *Musical Treasures of the Manuscript Dept. of the Leningrad Public Library* (1938). He was married to the composer **Julia Weissberg.**

Rimsky-Korsakov, Georgi, grandson of **Nicolai Rimsky-Korsakov** and nephew of **Andrei Rimsky-Korsakov;** b. St. Petersburg, Dec. 26, 1901; d. Leningrad, Oct. 10, 1965. He studied at the St. Petersburg Cons.; in 1923, founded a society for the cultivation of quarter-tone music; composed some works in that system; publ. the articles "Foundations of the Quarter-Tone System" (Leningrad, 1925) and "The Deciphering of the 'Luce' Part in Scriabin's Prometheus," in the Russian magazine *De Musica* (1927); then became active in work on electronic musical instruments; was co-inventor of the "Emeriton" (1930), capable of producing a complete series of tones at any pitch and of any chosen or synthetic tone color; wrote solo pieces for it; also an Octet for 2 Emeritons, 2 Clarinets, Bassoon, Violin, Viola, and Cello (1932). From 1927 to 1962 he was on the faculty of the Cons. of Leningrad.

Rimsky-Korsakov, Nicolai, great Russian composer; b. Tikhvin, near Novgorod, March 18, 1844; d. Liubensk, near St. Petersburg, June 21, 1908. He remained in the country until he was 12 years old; in 1856 he entered the Naval School in St. Petersburg, graduating in 1862. He took piano lessons as a child with provincial teachers, and later with a professional musician, Théodore Canillé, who introduced him to Balakirev; he also met Cui and Borodin. In 1862 he was sent on the clipper *Almaz* on a voyage that lasted 2½ years; returning to Russia in the summer of 1865, he settled in St. Petersburg, where he remained most of his life. During his travels he maintained contact with Balakirev, and continued to report to him the progress of his musical composition. He completed his First Symph. (which was also the earliest work in this form by a Russian composer), and it was performed under Balakirev's direction on Dec. 31, 1865, at a concert of the Free Music School in St. Petersburg. In 1871 Rimsky-Korsakov was engaged as a prof. of composition and orchestration at the St. Petersburg Cons., even though he was aware of the inadequacy of his own technique. He remained on the faculty until his death, with the exception of a few months in 1905, when he was relieved of his duties as prof. for his public support of the rebellious students during the revolution of that year. As a music educator, Rimsky-Korsakov was of the greatest importance to the development and maintenance of the traditions of the Russian national school; among his students were Glazunov, Liadov, Arensky, Ippolitov-Ivanov, Gretchaninov, Nicolas Tcherepnin, Maximilian Steinberg, Gnessin, and Miaskovsky. Igor Stravinsky studied privately with Rimsky-Korsakov from 1903 on.

In 1873 Rimsky-Korsakov abandoned his naval career, but was appointed to the post of inspector of the military orchs. of the Russian navy, until it was abolished in 1884. From 1883 to 1894 he was also assistant director of the Court Chapel and led the chorus and the orch. there. Although he was not a gifted conductor, he gave many performances of his own orch. works; made his debut at a charity concert for the victims of the Volga famine, in St. Petersburg, March 2, 1874; the program included the first performance of his 3rd Symph. From 1886 until 1900 he conducted the annual Russian Symph. concerts organized by the publisher Belaieff; in June 1889 he conducted 2 concerts of Russian music at the World Exposition in Paris; in 1890 he conducted a concert of Russian music in Brussels; led a similar concert there in 1900. His last appearance abroad was in the spring of 1907, when he conducted in Paris 2 Russian historic concerts arranged by Diaghilev; in the same year he was elected corresponding member of the French Academy, to succeed Grieg. These activities, however, did not distract him from his central purpose as a national Russian composer. His name was grouped with those of Cui, Borodin, Balakirev, and Mussorgsky as the "Mighty Five," and he maintained an intimate friendship with most of them; at Mussorgsky's death he collected his MSS and prepared them for publication; he also revised Mussorgsky's opera *Boris Godunov;* it was in Rimsky-Korsakov's version that the opera became famous. Later some criticism was voiced against Rimsky-Korsakov's reduction of Mussorgsky's original harmonies and melodic lines to an academically acceptable standard. He had decisive influence in the affairs of the Belaieff publishing firm and helped publish a great number of works by Russian composers of the St. Petersburg group; only a small part of these sumptuously printed scores represents the best in Russian music, but culturally Rimsky-Korsakov's solicitude was of great importance. Although he was far from being a revolutionary, he freely expressed his disgust at the bungling administration of Czarist Russia; he was particularly indignant about the attempts of

the authorities to alter Pushkin's lines in his own last opera, *Le Coq d'or,* and refused to compromise; he died, of angina pectoris, with the situation still unresolved; the opera was produced posthumously, with the censor's changes; the original text was not restored until the Revolution of 1917.

Rimsky-Korsakov was one of the greatest masters of Russian music. His source of inspiration was Glinka's operatic style; he made use of both the purely Russian idiom and coloristic oriental melodic patterns; such works as his symph. suite *Scheherazade* and *Le Coq d'or* represent Russian orientalism at its best; in the purely Russian style, the opera *Snow Maiden* and the *Russian Easter Overture* are outstanding examples. The influence of Wagner and Liszt in his music was small; only in his opera *The Legend of the Invisible City of Kitezh* are there perceptible echoes from *Parsifal.* In the art of orchestration Rimsky-Korsakov had few equals; his treatment of instruments, in solo passages and in ensemble, was invariably idiomatic. In his treatise on orchestration he selected only passages from his own works to demonstrate the principles of practical and effective application of registers and tone colors. Although an academician in his general esthetics, he experimented boldly with melodic progressions and ingenious harmonies that pointed toward modern usages. He especially favored the major scale with the lowered submediant and the scale of alternating whole tones and semitones (which in Russian reference works came to be termed as "Rimsky-Korsakov's scale"; in the score of his opera-ballet *Mlada* there is an ocarina part tuned in this scale); in *Le Coq d'or* and *Kashchei the Immortal* he applied dissonant harmonies in unusual superpositions; but he set for himself a definite limit in innovation, and severely criticized Richard Strauss, Debussy, and Vincent d'Indy for their modernistic practices.

WORKS: OPERAS: *Pskovityanka* (*The Maid of Pskov;* 1868–72; revised 1891; St. Petersburg, Jan. 13, 1873; last version, St. Petersburg, April 18, 1895); *Maiskaya noch* (*May Night;* St. Petersburg, Jan. 21, 1880); *Snegurotchka* (*Snow Maiden;* St. Petersburg, Feb. 10, 1882); *Mlada* (St. Petersburg, Nov. 1, 1892); *Noch pered Rozhdestvom* (*Night before Christmas;* St. Petersburg, Dec. 10, 1895); *Sadko* (Moscow, Jan. 7, 1898; Metropolitan Opera, N.Y., Jan. 29, 1929); *Mozart i Salieri,* on Pushkin's play dealing with Salieri's supposed poisoning of Mozart (Moscow, Dec. 7, 1898); *Boyarynia Vera Sheloga* (Moscow, Dec. 27, 1898; originally written as a prologue to *Pskovityanka;* N.Y., May 9, 1922); *Tsarskaya neviesta* (*The Tsar's Bride;* Moscow, Nov. 3, 1899); *Tsar Saltan* (Moscow, Nov. 3, 1900); *Servilia* (St. Petersburg, Oct. 14, 1902); *Kashchei Bezsmertny* (*Kashchei the Immortal;* Moscow, Dec. 25, 1902); *Pan Voyevoda* (*The Commander;* St. Petersburg, Oct. 16, 1904); *Skazanie o nevidimom grade Kitezhe* (*The Legend of the Invisible City of Kitezh;* St. Petersburg, Feb. 20, 1907); *Zolotoy pietushok* (*The Golden Cockerel;* usually perf. under the French title *Le Coq d'or;* posthumous; Moscow, Oct. 7, 1909; the only opera of Rimsky-Korsakov often produced abroad).

FOR ORCH.: Op. 1, Symph. No. 1, in E minor (originally in E-flat minor; later rewritten and transposed); op. 5, *Sadko,* symph. poem (1867; revised 1869 and 1891); op. 6, *Fantasy on Serbian Themes* (1867; revised 1888); op. 9, Symph. No. 2, *Antar* (1868; revised 1876 and 1897; also as a symph. suite); op. 28, *Overture on Russian Themes* (1866; revised 1880); op. 29, *Conte féerique* (1880); op. 30, Piano Concerto in C-sharp minor (1882–83); op. 31, *Symphoniette in A minor* (on Russian themes; 1879); Op. 32, Symph. No. 3, in C major (1873–74; revised 1885–86); op. 33, *Fantaisie de concert sur des thèmes russes* for Violin and Orch. (1886); op. 34, *Capriccio espagnol* (1887); op. 35, *Scheherazade,* symph. suite (St. Petersburg, Nov. 3, 1888); op. 36, *Grande pâque russe* (*Russian Easter Overture;* 1888); suite from the opera *Tsar Saltan* (1903; includes the famous musical tableau *The Flight of the Bumblebee*); op. 59, *Pan Voyevoda,* suite from the opera (1903); op. 61, *Nad mogiloï* (*At the Grave;* in memory of Belaieff; 1904); op. 62, *Chanson russe* (*Dubinushka;* 1905, with Chorus ad lib.); without opus numbers: *Night on Mount Triglav,* from the opera *Mlada* (1907); suite from the opera *Le Coq d'or* (1907).

CHAMBER MUSIC: Op. 12, String Quartet in F (1875); op. 37, *Serenade* for Cello and Piano (1903); without opus numbers: String Sextet in A (1876); Quintet in B-flat for Flute, Clarinet, Horn, Bassoon, and Piano (1876); first movement of a String Quartet on B-la-f (Belaieff; other movements by Liadov, Borodin, and Glazunov; 1886); String Quartet in G (1897); Trio in C minor for Violin, Cello, and Piano (1897).

VOCAL WORKS, WITH ORCH.: Op. 20, *Stikh ob Alexeye* (*Poem about Alexis),* folk song for Mixed Chorus (1877); op. 21, *Slava* (*Glory)* for Mixed Chorus (1876–80); op. 44, *Svitezyanka,* cantata for Soprano and Tenor Solo and Mixed Chorus (1897); op. 53, *Strekozy* (*Dragonflies)* for Women's Voices (1897); op. 58, *Piesnia o veshchem Olegye* (*Poem of Oleg the Wise)* for Men's Chorus; op. 60, *From Homer* for Women's Voices (1899); op. 49, *Anchar* (*The Upas Tree)* and *Prorok* (*The Prophet),* 2 ariosos for Bass, (1897); choruses a cappella, opus 13, 14, 16, 18, 19, 23; 77 songs; 5 vocal duets; a Vocal Trio.

PIANO PIECES: Op. 10, 6 *Variations on BACH;* op. 11, 4 pieces; op. 15, 3 pieces; op. 17, 6 fugues.

ARRANGEMENTS AND EDITIONS: He edited a collection of 100 Russian folk songs, op. 24 (1876); harmonized 40 folk songs. After Dargomyzhsky's death, he orchestrated his posthumous opera *Kamennyi gost* (*The Stone Guest);* also orchestrated Borodin's *Prince Igor;* his greatest task of musical reorganization was the preparation for publication and performance of Mussorgsky's works; he reharmonized the cycle *Songs and Dances of Death* and the symph. picture *Night on Bald Mountain;* orchestrated the opera *Khovanshchina;* revised *Boris Godunov* (in melody and harmony, as well as in orchestration).

WRITINGS: Among his pedagogical works, the book on harmony (St. Petersburg, 1884; numerous subsequent eds. in Russian; in Eng., N.Y., 1930) is widely used in Russian music schools; publ. *Foundations of Orchestration* (2 vols., St. Petersburg, 1913; ed. by Maximilian Steinberg; also available in French and in Eng.); collected articles were publ. in 1911, edited by M. Gnessin. His autobiographical book, *The Chronicle of My Musical Life* (posthumous, 1909; 5th ed. by his son Andrei, supplemented and annotated, 1935), is a valuable document of the most important period of Russian music; it is publ. also in English (N.Y., 1924; new ed., 1942), in French (Paris, 1938), etc. A complete edition of Rimsky-Korsakov's works was begun in 1946; 49 vols. were publ. by 1970.

BIBLIOGRAPHY: V. Yastrebtzev, *R.-K.* (1900; 2nd ed. with a complete list of works, 1908); N. Findeisen, *R.-K.* (1908); I. Lapshin, *Philosophical Motives in the Works of R.-K.* (1911); N. van Gilse van der Pals, *R.-K.* (Leipzig, 1914); M. Montagu-Nathan, *History of Russian Music* (London, 1915; pp. 179–236); Rosa Newmarch, *The Russian Opera* (London, 1915; pp. 281–333); M. Montagu-Nathan, *R.-K.* (London, 1916); Igor Glebov, *R.-K.* (1922); E. Istel, "*R.-K.,* the Oriental Wizard," *Musical Quarterly* (July 1929); N. van Gilse van der Pals, *R.-K.s Opernschaffen* (Leipzig, 1929); A. Rimsky-Korsakov, *R.-K., Life and Works* (fundamental biography; 5 fascicles; Moscow, 1933, 1935, 1936, 1937, 1946; last vol. ed. by Vladimir Rimsky-Korsakov); Igor Markevitch, *R.-K.* (Paris, 1935); G. Abraham and M.D. Calvocoressi, *Masters of Russian Music* (London, 1936); A. Solovtzov, *R.-K.* (Moscow, 1948; 2nd ed., 1957); G. Abraham, *R.-K.; A Short Biography* (London, 1949); M.O. Yankovsky, *R.-K. and the Revolution of 1905* (Moscow, 1950); V. Kisselev, *R.-K.; Documents* (Moscow, 1951); D. Kabalevsky, ed., *R.-K., Materials and Letters* (Moscow, 2 vols., 1953 and 1954); M.F. Gnessin, *Reflections and Reminiscences about N.A. R.-K.* (Moscow, 1956); I. Kunin, *R.-K.* (Moscow, 1964); S. Evseyev, *R.-K. and Russian National Songs* (Moscow, 1970); numerous monographs on individual operas and other works.

Rinaldo di Capua, Italian opera composer; b. Capua, c.1710; d. Rome, after 1770. He came from the vicinity of Naples and seems to have been active chiefly in Rome, where Burney knew him in 1770, and where most of his operas were given (others were produced in Florence, Venice, London, and Paris). His career as a dramatic composer probably began in 1737. Thereafter he produced about 30 theatrical works with varying success, among them *Ciro riconosciuto* (Rome, Jan. 19, 1737), *Vologeso re de' Parti* (Rome, 1739), and *La Zingara* (Paris, June 19, 1753; his best work). He also composed *Cantata per la Natività della Beata Vergine* (1747).

BIBLIOGRAPHY: Charles Burney, *Present State of Music in France and Italy* (1771); P. Spitta's study of Rinaldo di Capua in *Vierteljahrsschrift für Musikwissenschaft,* III (1887); G. Radiciotti, in *Musica d'Oggi* (July 1925); A. Loewenberg, *Annals of Opera* (Cambridge, 1943); R.L. Bostian, *The Works of Rinaldo di Capua* (Diss., Univ. of North Carolina, Chapel Hill, 1961; 2 vols.).

Rinck, Johann Christian Heinrich, famous German organist; b. Elgersburg, Feb. 18, 1770; d. Darmstadt, Aug. 7, 1846. He studied under Bach's pupil Kittel in Erfurt (1786–89); was town organist at Giessen (1790) and at Darmstadt (1805); became court organist there in 1813, and chamber musician in 1817. One of the foremost players of the time, he made frequent concert tours. He wrote many organ works.

BIBLIOGRAPHY: His *Selbstbiographie* (Breslau, 1833); M.J. Fölsing, *Züge aus dem Leben und Wirken des Dr. C.H. Rinck* (Erfurt, 1848); F. Clément, *Musiciens célèbres* (Paris, 1868; 4th ed., 1887); F.W. Donat, *C.H. Rinck und die Orgelmusik seiner Zeit* (1933).

Ringbom, Nils-Eric, Finnish violinist and composer; b. Turku, Dec. 27, 1907. He studied at the Turku Academy, and took private lessons with Leo Funtek; played violin in the municipal orch. of Turku; then moved to Helsinki and became director of the annual Sibelius Festival (1951–60) and managing director of the Helsinki Phil. (1942–70).

WORKS: *Little Suite* for Orch. (1933); *Till livet (To Life)* for Chorus and String Orch. (1936); 5 symphs. (1939, 1944, 1948, 1962, 1970); *Vandrerska (The Wanderer)* for Soprano and Orch. (1942); Duo for Violin and Viola (1945); *Hymn to Helsinki* for Chorus and Orch. (1949); Wind Sextet (1951; first work by a Finnish composer ever perf. at the International Festival for Contemporary Music, Salzburg, 1952). He publ. *Helsingfors Orkesterföretag* (a history of the Helsinki Orch., 1932; in Swedish and Finnish); *Sibelius* (in Swedish and Finnish, Helsinki, 1948; also publ. in German and Eng.).

Ringer, Alexander L., American musicologist; b. Berlin, Feb. 3, 1921, of Dutch parentage. He attended the Hollander Cons. in Berlin; in 1939 went to Amsterdam, where he studied composition with Henk Badings. In 1946 he emigrated to the U.S.; was on the staff of the City College of N.Y. (1948–52) and the Univ. of Pa. (1952–55); received his Ph.D. from Columbia Univ. in 1955; also taught at the Univ. of Calif., Berkeley (1955–56), and the Univ. of Oklahoma (1956–58). In 1958 he was appointed to the faculty of the Univ. of Illinois, Urbana; also was a regular guest lecturer at the Hebrew Univ. in Jerusalem.

WRITINGS: *The Chasse: Historical and Analytical Bibliography of a Musical Genre* (Diss., Columbia Univ.; Ann Arbor, Michigan Univ. Microfilm, 1955); *An Experimental Program in the Development of Musical Literacy among Musically Gifted Children in the Upper Elementary Grades* (Washington, D.C., 1970).

Ringwall, Rudolph, American conductor; b. Bangor, Maine, March 19, 1891; d. Cleveland, Jan. 26, 1978. He studied at the New England Cons. of Music, graduating in 1913; until 1920 he served as a violinist with the Boston Symph. Orch. In 1926 he was appointed assistant conductor of the Cleveland Orch., and from 1934 until his retirement in 1956 was its associate conductor. He led numerous concerts for young people in Cleveland and on tour.

Rinuccini, Ottavio, great Italian poet and librettist; b. Florence, Jan. 20, 1563; d. there, March 28, 1621. He wrote several librettos for the Florentine creators of opera: the text of the intermezzo *Apollo e il pitone*, set to music by Marenzio in 1589; and subsequently the famous *La favola di Dafne*, set to music by Peri in 1597, a work that is usually regarded as the first true opera. Rinuccini's *Euridice*, with music by Peri, was performed in 1600; another setting, by Caccini, in 1602. He also wrote the libretto of Monteverdi's *Arianna* (1608). These texts were republ. by A. Solerti in vol. II of *Gli albori del melodramma* (Milan, 1905) and by A. Della Corte, *Drammi per musica dal Rinuccini allo Zeno* (Turin, 1958).

BIBLIOGRAPHY: F. Meda, *Ottavio Rinuccini* (Milan, 1894); A. Civita, *Ottavio Rinuccini ed il sorgere del melodramma in Italia* (Mantua, 1900); F. Raccamadoro-Ramelli, *Ottavio Rinuccini, Studio biografico e critico* (1900); A. Solerti, *Le origini del melodramma* (Turin, 1903); idem, *Musica, ballo e drammatica alla corte medicea dal 1600 al 1637* (Florence, 1905); O.G. Sonneck, "Dafne, The First Opera," *Sammelbände der Internationalen Musik-Gesellschaft* (1913); A. Della Corte, *Ottavio Rinuccini librettista* (Turin, 1925); U. Rolandi, "Didascalie sceniche in un raro libretto dell'Euridice del Rinuccini," *Rivista Musicale Italiana* (1926); M. Schild, *Die Musikdramen Ottavio Rinuccinis* (Würzburg, 1933).

Riotte, Philipp Jakob, German conductor and composer; b. St. Wendel, Saar, Aug. 16, 1776; d. Vienna, Aug. 20, 1856. He studied with André in Offenbach; in 1808 settled in Vienna, where he conducted at the Theater an der Wien; produced there 48 works of his own, including operas, ballets, and minor pieces; also wrote a Symph., 9 piano sonatas, 6 violin sonatas, etc. He was the author of the "tone picture" *Die Schlacht bei Leipzig (The Battle of Leipzig)* for Piano, which achieved extraordinary popularity in Germany.

BIBLIOGRAPHY: G. Spengler, *Der Komponist P.J. Riotte* (Diss., Univ. of Saarbrücken, 1973).

Ripa, Alberto da (called **Alberto Mantovano**), Italian lutenist; b. Mantua, c.1480; d. Paris, 1551. Little is known about his life, except that he was in the service of Francis I of France from 1529. His *Tablature de luth* was brought out posthumously by his pupil Guillaume Morlaye (6 books, Paris, 1553–62); individual pieces by him are found in the publications of Phalèse (1546 and 1574) and also in Francesco da Forli's *Intavolatura di liuto* (1536); J.-M. Vaccaro edited *Alberto da Rippe: Œuvres*, in *LeChœur des muses, Corpus des luthistes français* (1972–75).

BIBLIOGRAPHY: J.G. Prod'homme, "Guillaume Morlaye, Editeur d'Albert de Ripe," *Revue de Musicologie* (1925); L. Nordstrom, "Albert de Rippe, Joueru de luth du roy," *Early Music,* VII (1979).

Rischbieter, Wilhelm Albert, German music theorist and pedagogue; b. Braunschweig, July 20, 1834; d. Dresden, Feb. 11, 1910. He studied with Hauptmann; was a violinist in Leipzig, Bremen, Nuremberg, and Liegnitz. In 1862 he was appointed teacher of harmony and composition at the Dresden Cons.

and held this position for nearly 40 years, until 1900. He publ. *Über Modulation, Quartsextakkord und Orgelpunkt* (1879); *Erläuterungen und Aufgaben zum Studium des Kontrapunkts* (1885); *Die Gesetzmässigkeit der Harmonik* (1888).

Riseley, George, English organist and conductor; b. Bristol, Aug. 28, 1845; d. there, April 12, 1932. He was a chorister at the Bristol Cathedral from the age of 7, and studied with Cathedral organist John Davis Corfe; in 1876 succeeded him at that post; in 1877 he organized a series of orch. concerts in Bristol which contributed greatly to Bristol's musical life; also conducted the Bristol Festival (1896–1911). In 1898 he was appointed conductor of the Queen's Hall Choral Society in London. He wrote a Jubilee Ode (Bristol, 1887), part-songs, and pieces for organ. For an account of his career see the *Musical Times* (Feb. 1899).

Risler, Edouard, French pianist; b. Baden-Baden (of a German mother and Alsatian father), Feb. 23, 1873; d. Paris, July 22, 1929. He studied piano with Diémer at the Paris Cons. and continued his studies with Klindworth, Stavenhagen, and Eugène d'Albert in Germany. In 1923 he was appointed prof. of the Paris Cons. He gave concert recitals all over Europe and acquired a high reputation as a fine musician as well as a virtuoso pianist; he made a specialty of presenting cycles of one composer's works; he played Beethoven's 32 sonatas, Chopin's complete piano works, and both books of Bach's *Well-tempered Clavier.*

Rist, Johann, German poet and composer; b. Ottensen, near Hamburg, March 8, 1607; d. Wedel-on-Elbe, Aug. 31, 1667. He studied theology at the univs. of Hamburg and Bremen; later became a pastor in Mecklenburg and Wedel. In 1644 he was made poet laureate by the Emperor, and in 1653 was elevated to the rank of nobleman. He organized in Hamburg a Liederschule, for which he secured the cooperation of many important composers of the day, among them Schiedemann and Thomas Selle. He has been described as the "organizer of the German Parnassus," and indeed his role in the development of a purely national type of secular song, of German folk inspiration, was historically significant. He also wrote a number of sacred songs—*O Ewigkeit, du Donnerwort; O Traurigkeit; O Herzeleid; Werde munter, mein Gemüte;* etc.—which are still sung in Lutheran churches in Germany. He compiled valuable collections of German sacred songs; a modern edition was brought out by E. Mannack, *J. Rist: Sämtliche Werke* (Berlin, 1967—).
BIBLIOGRAPHY: T. Hansen, *Johann Rist und seine Zeit* (Halle, 1872; reprint, Leipzig, 1973); W. Krabbe, *Johann Rist und das deutsche Lied* (Bonn, 1910); O. Kern, *Johann Rist als weltlicher Lyriker* (Marburg, 1919); O. Heins, *Johann Rist und das niederdeutsche Drama des 17. Jahrhunderts* (1930).

Ristenpart, Karl, German conductor; b. Kiel, Jan. 26, 1900; d. Lisbon, Dec. 24, 1967. He studied music in Berlin and Vienna. In 1932 he became conductor of the Berlin Chamber Orch.; also led concerts with the Radio Orch. in Berlin. In 1946 he was named conductor of the Chamber Orch. of RIAS (Radio in the American Sector of Berlin). In 1953 he became conductor of the Chamber Orch. of the Saar, a noted ensemble of the Saarland Radio in Saarbrücken; made many tours and recordings with this group.

Ristić, Milan, Serbian composer; b. Belgrade, Aug. 31, 1908. He studied in Belgrade with Slavenski and in Prague with Alois Hába. A prolific composer, he writes mostly instrumental music; his style ranges from neo-Romantic grandiosity to economic neo-Classicism, from epically declamatory diatonicism to expressionistically atonal melos. Some of his works are written in an explicit dodecaphonic technique; in some, he makes use of quarter-tones.
WORKS: 6 symphs. (1941, 1951, 1961, 1966, 1967, 1968); Violin Concerto (1944); Piano Concerto (1954); *Suite giocosa* for Orch. (1956); *Symphonic Variations* (1957); *Burleska* for Orch. (1957); *7 Bagatelles* for Orch. (1959); Concerto for Orch. (1963); Clarinet Concerto (1964); 2 string quartets; Wind Quintet; Septet; Violin Sonata; Viola Sonata; 24 fugues for various instrumental combinations; Suite for 4 Trombones in quarter-tones.
BIBLIOGRAPHY: V. Peričić, *Muzički Stvaraoci u Srbiji* (Belgrade, 1969; pp. 453–73).

Ristori, Giovanni Alberto, Italian composer; b. Bologna, 1692; d. Dresden, Feb. 7, 1753. He received his education from his father, a violinist in an Italian opera company; with him he went to Dresden (1715) and obtained the post of director of the Polish chapel there; then was appointed chamber organist to the court of Saxony (1733), church composer (1746), and assistant conductor (1750). He wrote a number of operas for the Italian Opera in Dresden. His *Calandro,* staged at Pillnitz, near Dresden, on Sept. 2, 1726, was one of the earliest Italian comic operas produced in Germany, and so possesses historical significance beyond its intrinsic worth; other operas produced in Dresden and in court theaters near Dresden were *Cleonice* (Aug. 15, 1718); *Un pazzo ne fa cento, ovvero Don Chisciotte* (Feb. 2, 1727); *Arianna* (Aug. 7, 1736); *Le Fate* (Aug. 10, 1736); etc. He also wrote 3 oratorios, 16 cantatas, 11 masses; some instrumental music; many of his MSS were destroyed during the siege of Dresden (1760).
BIBLIOGRAPHY: C.R. Mengelberg, *G.A. Ristori* (Leipzig, 1916).

Ritter, Alexander, German composer and poet; b. Narva, Estonia (of German parents), June 27, 1833; d. Munich, April 12, 1896. He was taken to Dresden in 1841; there he studied violin with Franz Schubert (namesake of the great composer), who was concertmaster of the Dresden Opera; then studied at the Leipzig Cons. (1849–51) with Ferdinand David (violin) and E.F. Richter (theory). In 1854 he married Wagner's niece **Franziska Wagner** and settled in Weimar, where he entered into a close association with Liszt, Bülow, Cornelius, Raff, and others.

He was conductor at the opera in Stettin (1856–58), where his wife was engaged as a soprano; he then lived in Dresden (1858–60), Schwerin (1860–62), and Würzburg (1863–82). When Bülow became conductor at the Hofkapelle in Meiningen (1882), Ritter settled there and played the violin in the orch.; after Bülow's departure from Meiningen in 1886, Ritter moved to Munich. He wrote 2 operas, *Der faule Hans* (Munich, Oct. 15, 1885) and *Wem die Krone?* (Weimar, June 8, 1890), to his own librettos, and several symph. poems in an intensely Romantic manner (*Seraphische Phantasie, Erotische Legende, Karfreitag und Frohnleichnam,* and *Kaiser Rudolfs Ritt zum Grabe*); a String Quartet; about 60 songs; piano pieces. Ritter's significance derives, however, not from these well-made but ephemeral compositions, but from his profound influence on young Richard Strauss; it was Ritter who encouraged Strauss in the creation of a new type of philosophical tone poem along the lines of "Musik als Ausdruck" (music as expression), a modern development of the art of Liszt, Wagner, and Berlioz. Ritter wrote the poem printed in the score of *Tod und Verklärung.*

BIBLIOGRAPHY: S. von Hausegger, *Alexander Ritter. Ein Bild seines Charakters und Schaffens* (Berlin, 1907).

Ritter, August Gottfried, German organist; b. Erfurt, Aug. 25, 1811; d. Magdeburg, Aug. 26, 1885. He was a pupil of Fischer at Erfurt, Hummel at Weimar, and Rungenhagen at Berlin; filled various posts as organist at Erfurt, Merseburg, and Magdeburg; edited the *Urania* (1844–48); was co-editor of the *Orgelfreund* and *Orgelarchiv;* publ. a valuable book, *Zur Geschichte des Orgelspiels im 14. bis zum Anfange des 18. Jahrhunderts* (1884), and *Die Kunst des Orgelspiels* (2 vols., in Eng., N.Y., 1874); also organ pieces; 4 books of chorales; a Piano Concerto, a Piano Quartet, 2 symphs., 3 overtures, etc.

Ritter, Frédéric Louis, German-American music historian and choral conductor; b. Strasbourg, June 22, 1826; d. Antwerp, July 4, 1891. He was of Spanish extraction, his original family name being Caballero, which was translated into German as Ritter ("knight"). He studied in Strasbourg with Schletterer and in Paris with J.G. Kastner. In 1856 he went to Cincinnati, where he organized the Phil. Orch., but left for N.Y. in 1861; was active mainly as a choral conductor; in 1867 became a prof. of music at Vassar College. He publ. several manuals and music histories: *History of Music* (2 vols., Boston, 1870, 1874; 2nd ed., 1880); *Music in England* (N.Y., 1883); *Music in America* (N.Y., 1883; 3rd ed., 1893); *Music in Its Relation to Intellectual Life* (N.Y., 1891); etc. His wife, **Fanny Raymond Ritter** (b. Philadelphia, 1840; d. Poughkeepsie, N.Y., Oct. 26, 1890), was the author of *Woman as a Musician: An Art-Historical Study* (1876); *Some Famous Songs* (1878); etc.

Ritter, Hermann, German violist, inventor of the viola alta; b. Wismar, Sept. 16, 1849; d. Würzburg, Jan. 22, 1926. He studied at the Hochschule für Musik in Berlin; attended courses at the Univ. of Heidelberg; turning his attention to musical instruments, he began a series of experiments for the purpose of improving the muffled tone of the ordinary viola; profiting by some practical hints in A. Bagatella's book *Regole per la costruzione di violini* (Padua, 1786), he constructed a slightly larger model possessed of better resonance and a more brilliant tone. Exhibiting this new "viola alta" in 1876, he attracted the attention of Wagner, who invited his cooperation for the Bayreuth Festival; after that engagement he made successful tours of all Europe as a viola virtuoso; from 1879, he was a prof. of viola and music history at the Musikschule in Würzburg; in 1905 he founded the "Ritterquartett" (violin, W. Schulze-Prisca; viola alta, Ritter; viola tenore, E. Cahnbley; viola bassa, H. Knöchel).

WRITINGS: *Die Geschichte der Viola alta und die Grundsätze ihres Baues* (Leipzig, 1876; 2nd ed., 1877; reprinted, Wiesbaden, 1969); *Repetitorium der Musikgeschichte* (1880); *Aus der Harmonielehre meines Lebens* (1883); *Elementartheorie der Musik* (1885); *Ästhetik der Tonkunst* (1886); *Studien und Skizzen aus Musik-und Kulturgeschichte, sowie Musikästhetik* (Dresden, 1892); *Katechismus der Musikästhetik* (2nd ed., 1894); *Katechismus der Musikinstrumente* (1894); *Volksgesang in alter und neuer Zeit* (1896); *Schubert* (1896); *Haydn, Mozart, Beethoven* (1897); *Die fünfsaitige Geige und die Weiterentwicklung der Streichinstrumente* (1898); *Allgemeine illustrierte Encyklopädie der Musikgeschichte* (6 vols., 1901–2). He publ. numerous original compositions and transcriptions for viola and piano, and *Elementartechnik der Viola alta.*

BIBLIOGRAPHY: G. Adema, *Hermann Ritter und seine Viola alta* (Würzburg, 1881; 2nd ed., 1894).

Ritter, Peter, German composer; b. Mannheim, July 2, 1763; d. there, Aug. 1, 1846. He studied violin and cello with his father; completed his theoretical studies under Abbé Vogler. He entered the Mannheim court orch. as a cellist in 1783; later became its concertmaster and, in 1803, conductor. He brought out in Mannheim his first opera, *Der Eremit auf Formentera* (Dec. 14, 1788; text by the celebrated poet A. von Kotzebue), which attained considerable vogue in Germany; some 20 more operas and singspiels followed, but were not successful. In 1787 he married the famous actress Katharina Baumann (to whom Schiller had proposed); in 1790 both were employed at the Hoftheater; his wife retired on a pension in 1819, and Ritter himself in 1823. Besides his operas, he wrote a fine chorale, *Grosser Gott dich loben wir* (1792); an oratorio, *Das verlorene Paradies;* and much chamber music (selections publ. by Riemann in vol. 28 [16], of *Denkmäler der Tonkunst in Bayern*). Twenty-four autograph scores, including 2 symphs., several concertos, etc., are in the Library of Congress in Washington, D.C.

BIBLIOGRAPHY: W. Schulze, *Peter Ritter* (Berlin, 1895); G. Schmidt, *Peter Ritter* (Diss., Univ. of Munich, 1924); M. Gilveath, *The Violoncello Concertos of Peter Ritter* (Diss., Univ. of North Carolina, Chapel Hill, 1961).

Ritter (real name, **Bennet**), **Théodore,** French pianist and composer; b. near Paris, April 5, 1841; d. Paris, April 6, 1886. He was a pupil of Liszt; made successful European tours; publ. numerous solo pieces for Piano, of which *Les Courriers* was a favorite; his operas, *Marianne* (Paris, 1861) and *La Dea risorta* (Florence, 1865), were unsuccessful.

Rivé-King, Julie, American pianist; b. Cincinnati, Oct. 30, 1854; d. Indianapolis, July 24, 1937. She received her primary instruction from her mother; then studied in N.Y. with William Mason and in Leipzig with Reinecke; also was for a time a pupil of Liszt. She played Liszt's Piano Concerto No. 1 at her American debut, with the N.Y. Phil. (April 24, 1875); this was the beginning of an active career; she gave about 4,000 concerts in the U.S., retiring only a year before her death. In 1876 she married Frank King of Milwaukee. From 1905 till 1936 she was a piano instructor at the Bush Cons. in Chicago. She wrote some attractive piano pieces (*Impromptu, Polonaise héroïque, Bubbling Spring,* etc.). See A.R. Coolidge in *Notable American Women* (N.Y., 1971).

Rivier, Jean, French composer; b. Villemomble, July 21, 1896. He was in the French army in World War I, and did not begin his musical studies until 1918, when he entered the Paris Cons. and studied with Caussade; participated in various modern music societies in Paris; formed a style of composition that combined the elements of French Classicism and Impressionism. He was also esteemed as a teacher; was on the faculty of the Paris Cons. from 1947 to 1966.
WORKS: Opera, *Vénitienne* (Paris, July 8, 1937); 7 symphs.: No. 1 (Paris, Jan. 29, 1933); No. 2 for Strings (1937); No. 3 (1937; Paris, Nov. 25, 1940); No. 4 (Paris, 1947); No. 5 (Strasbourg, June 24, 1951); No. 6, *Les Présages* (Paris, Dec. 11, 1958); No. 7, *Les Contrastes* (Paris, Jan. 9, 1962); Piano Concerto (1941); Violin Concerto (1942); *3 pastorales* (Paris, Feb. 7, 1929); *Adagio* for String Orch. (Paris, March 1, 1931); *Ouverture pour une opérette imaginaire* (Paris, Dec. 13, 1931); Concertino for Viola and Orch. (Paris, Feb. 15, 1936); *Jeanne d'Arc à Domrémy,* symph. tableau (Paris, Jan. 31, 1937); *Ballade des amants désespérés* for Orch. (1945); *Rapsodie provençale* (Aix-en-Provence, July 22, 1949); *Résonances* (1965); *Brillances* for 7 Woodwind Instruments (1971); *Triade* for String Orch. (1967); *Climats* for Celesta, Vibraphone, Xylophone, Piano, and Strings (1968); Clarinet Concerto (1960); Bassoon Concerto (1965); Oboe Concerto (1966); Trumpet Concerto (1972); Duo for Flute and Clarinet (1968); 2 string quartets; violin pieces; piano pieces; song cycles; choruses.

Roach, Max(well), black American jazz drummer; b. New York, Jan. 10, 1925. He first played with Charlie Parker; after working with Coleman Hawkins, Dizzy Gillespie, and Benny Carter, he estab-

lished himself as an outstanding bop drummer; subsequently led his own groups on many successful tours. Of an intellectual turn of mind, he read books, and in 1972 became a prof. of music at the Univ. of Mass. at Amherst.

Robbins, Marty, American country-western singer; b. Glendale, Ariz., Sept. 26, 1925; d. Nashville, Dec. 8, 1982. He enlisted in the navy in 1944, and was stationed in the Pacific; after the end of the war he worked as a ditchdigger in Phoenix, Ariz., and began to play the guitar and sing songs of his own invention; his unassuming, happy-go-lucky way of singing country songs soon won him a following; he took part in the broadcasts from the Grand Ole Opry in Nashville and in 1953 produced his first hit, *Singin' the Blues.* Other hits followed: *El Paso, Tonight Carmen, Devil Woman, Teen-age Dream, A White Sport Coat and a Pink Carnation, Up to My Shoulders in a Headache,* etc. He became a successful country-music balladeer. In 1970 he was elected to the Nashville Songwriters' Hall of Fame. In 1979 the National Cowboy Hall of Fame gave him its Golden Trustee Award for his gunfighter ballads. He was also inducted into the Country Music Hall of Fame. A passionate stock-car racer, he providentially survived a number of theoretically fatal accidents. He used to say that he was in the song business because he despised honest labor. His songs extolled the beauty of a loving heart, but when his own heart had to undergo quadruple coronary bypass surgery, he died.

Roberton, Sir Hugh S., Scottish composer and choral conductor; b. Glasgow, Feb. 23, 1874; d. there, Oct. 7, 1952. In 1906 he founded the Glasgow Orpheus Choir, which contributed to a large extent to the cultivation of choral music in Scotland. He disbanded it in 1951. He publ. about 300 vocal pieces, including *The Faux Bourdon Series of Psalm Tunes; Songs of the Isles;* and *Concert Edition of Scottish Songs;* also a pamphlet, *Prelude to the Orpheus* (London, 1947).

Roberts, Megan, American composer of the avant-garde; b. Hempstead, N.Y., Oct. 12, 1952. She was taken to California as a babe in arms, and flourished there; took lessons with Robert Ashley at Mills College in Oakland, and with Emma Lou Diemer at the Univ. of Calif., Santa Barbara. She experimented with unimedia arts of audio, video, dance and theater; then switched to rock 'n' roll. Her most mind-boggling contribution to the unichoreovideoelectrobiosonic School of California Calisthenics is *Suite for a Small Chamber* (1976), in which the movements of dancers trigger electronic devices and tape-loop playback machines. In her video piece *Factory* (1976) she utilizes the technique of strobosonic photophonoscopy. On Jan. 14, 1977, she presented in San Francisco a multimedia study in violence free of moral redeeming value. Her major work, *I Could Sit Here All Day* (1976), is scored for birds, drums, and disembodied human voices, and tends to represent the ante-human and anti-human predecessors of rock 'n' roll.

Robertson, Leroy, American composer; b. Fountain Green, Utah, Dec. 21, 1896; d. Salt Lake City, July 25, 1971. He studied in Provo; then in Boston with Chadwick and Converse at the New England Cons.; subsequently went to Europe, where he took courses with Ernest Bloch in Switzerland and with Hugo Leichtentritt in Berlin. Returning to America, he became an instructor of music at Brigham Young Univ. at Provo; in 1948, was appointed head of the music dept. of the Univ. of Utah (retiring in 1963). In 1947 his symph. work *Trilogy* received the first prize of $25,000 in a contest sponsored by Henry H. Reichhold of Detroit; it was performed by the Detroit Symph. Orch. on Dec. 11, 1947, but despite the attendant publicity, the work was not successful, and there were few subsequent performances. Other works: *The Book of Mormon,* oratorio (Salt Lake City, Feb. 18, 1953); *Prelude, Scherzo, Ricercare* for Orch. (1940); *Rhapsody* for Piano and Orch. (1944); *Punch and Judy Overture* (1945); Violin Concerto (1948); Piano Concerto (Salt Lake City, Nov. 30, 1966); Piano Quintet (1933); String Quartet (1940; N.Y. Music Critics Circle Award, 1944); *American Serenade* for String Quartet (1944); other chamber music; piano pieces; songs.

Robertson, Rae, pianist; b. Ardersier, Scotland, Nov. 29, 1893; d. Los Angeles, Nov. 4, 1956. He studied with F. Niecks at Edinburgh Univ.; then at the Royal Academy of Music in London with Matthay and F. Corder; married the pianist **Ethel Bartlett,** and the 2 gave numerous concerts in Europe and America as duo-pianists. With her he edited an Oxford Univ. Press series of works for 2 pianos.

Robeson, Lila, American contralto; b. Cleveland, April 4, 1880; d. Euclid, Ohio, Dec. 7, 1960. She studied singing with Isidor Luckstone and Oscar Saenger in N.Y.; made her operatic debut as Ortrud with the Aborn Opera Co. (Boston, April 4, 1911); from 1912 till 1920 she was a member of the Metropolitan Opera Co.; then devoted herself mainly to teaching; in 1953 taught voice at Case Western Reserve Univ. in Cleveland.

Robeson, Paul, great black American bass; b. Princeton, N.J., April 9, 1898; d. Philadelphia, Jan. 23, 1976. He first studied law (B.A., 1919, Rutgers Univ.; LL.B, 1923, Columbia Univ.); when his talent for singing and acting was discovered, he appeared in plays in the U.S. and England; acted the part of Emperor Jones in Eugene O'Neill's play and of Porgy in the Negro folk play by Du Bose and Dorothy Heyward. In 1925 he gave his first Negro spiritual recital in N.Y.; then toured in Europe. In 1930 he appeared in the title role of Shakespeare's *Othello* in London. Returning to the U.S., he continued to give recitals, but his radical political beliefs interfered with the success of his career. In 1952 he was awarded the International Stalin Peace Prize ($25,000). During the summer of 1958 he made an extensive European tour.

BIBLIOGRAPHY: E.G. Robeson, *Paul Robeson, Negro* (N.Y., 1930); S. Graham, *Paul Robeson* (N.Y., 1946); Marie Seton, *Paul Robeson* (London, 1958); autobiography, *Here I Stand* (London, 1958); E.P. Hoyt, *Paul Robeson* (London, 1967); Dorothy Butler Gilliam, *Paul Robeson, All American* (N.Y., 1977); *Pictorial Biography of Paul Robeson,* subtitled *The Whole World in His Hands,* compiled by Robeson's granddaughter Susan Robeson (N.Y., 1981).

Robin, Mado, French soprano; b. Yseures-sur-Creuse, near Tours, Dec. 29, 1918; d. Paris, Dec. 10, 1960. She studied voice with Giuseppe Podestà; then began her career as a concert artist; made her operatic debut in 1945 as Gilda at the Paris Opéra; also sang at the Opéra-Comique; made guest appearances in Brussels, Liège, and San Francisco. She was best known for her performances in the roles of Lakmé and Lucia.

Robinson, Earl, American composer; b. Seattle, July 2, 1910; studied at the Univ. of Washington (B.M., 1933); then took lessons with Aaron Copland. In 1934 he joined the Federal Theater Project, for which he wrote incidental music for several plays; his *Ballad for Americans* from the revue *Sing for Your Supper* became nationally famous (1939).

Robinson, Faye, black American soprano; b. Houston, Nov. 2, 1943. She studied at Bennett College in Greensboro, N.C., at Texas Southern Univ. in Houston, and at North Texas State Univ. in Denton. She received first prize in the San Francisco Opera Auditions; made her operatic debut with the N.Y. City Opera in 1972 as Micaela in *Carmen;* also sang opera in Hamburg, Houston, Washington, D.C. and Aix-en-Provence.

Robinson, Forbes, English bass; b. Macclesfield, May 21, 1926. He studied in Manchester; then went to Italy and took courses at the La Scala Opera School in Milan. He made his professional debut at Covent Garden in London in 1954; later sang at the Aldeburgh Festival and the Edinburgh Festival, and with the English Opera Group, the English National Opera, the Teatro Colón in Buenos Aires, and the Zürich Opera. He had an extensive repertoire; his roles included Figaro, Boris Godunov, and Don Giovanni.

Robinson, Franklin Whitman, American organist and teacher; b. New York, June 27, 1875; d. Northeast Harbor, Maine, Sept. 16, 1946. He studied with MacDowell and Rybner at Columbia Univ. (M.A., 1907); in 1908 became an instructor at the Inst. of Musical Art in N.Y.; publ. *Anthems and Chant Forms* (1908–14) and *Aural Harmony* (N.Y., 1914; revised ed., 1936).

Robinson, Ray, American writer on music and choral conductor; b. San Jose, Calif., Dec. 26, 1932. He learned to play the viola; studied at San Jose State College (B.A., 1956) and at Indiana Univ. in

Bloomington (M.M., 1958; D.Mus.Ed., 1969, with the dissertation *A History of the Peabody Conservatory*). He was subsequently an associate prof. of music and chairman of the division of fine arts at Cascade College in Portland, Oreg. (1959–63). From 1963–66 he was dean of the Peabody Cons. of Music in Baltimore; then was its associate director (1966–69). In 1969 he became president of Westminster Choir College in Princeton, N.J. His books include *The Choral Experience* (with A. Winold; 1976); *Choral Music: A Norton Historical Anthology* (1978); *Krzysztof Penderecki: A Guide to His Works* (1983); and *A Study of the Penderecki St. Luke Passion* (with A. Winold; 1983).

Robinson, "Smokey" (William Robinson, Jr.), black American singer and songwriter of popular music; b. Detroit, Feb. 19, 1940. He grew up in a Detroit ghetto; formed a pop group dubbed the Matadors, renamed the Miracles in 1954; it produced such hits as *Bad Girl, Shop Around, The Tracks of My Tears,* and *Tears of a Clown.* Robinson also pursued a solo career; his sweet soul style made his renditions of *Castles Made of Sand, So in Love,* and *Let Me Be the Clock* major hits.

Robinson, Stanford, English conductor; b. Leeds, July 5, 1904. He played piano in hotel orchs. in London before entering the Royal College of Music; there he studied conducting under Sir Adrian Boult; organized the London Wireless Chorus for the BBC in 1924; was conductor of the BBC Theatre Orch. in 1932–36; then became director of music productions there; served as associate conductor of the BBC Symph. Orch in 1946–49; then conducted the BBC Opera Orch. for broadcasting symph. music (1949–52); subsequently served as staff conductor at the BBC until 1966.
BIBLIOGRAPHY: Donald Brook, *International Gallery of Conductors* (Bristol, 1951; pp. 155–58).

Robison, Paula, American flutist; b. Nashville, June 8, 1941. She studied at the Univ. of Southern Calif.; then took flute lessons with Julius Baker at the Juilliard School of Music in N.Y.; also studied at the Aspen Music School. In 1961 she made her recital debut in N.Y.; in 1966 she became the first American flutist to win the Geneva International Competition. She made numerous appearances as a soloist with American orchs. and chamber groups.

Robles, Daniel Alomias, Peruvian composer and folk-song collector; b. Huánuco, Jan. 3, 1871; d. Chosica, near Lima, July 17, 1942. He was of Indian blood; traveled through Indian villages of Peru, Bolivia, and Ecuador and collected many hundreds of melodies, of which the *Himno al sol* was notated by him as sung by a 117-year-old Indian. From 1919 to 1934 he lived mostly in the U.S.; then returned to Lima. He had no formal education and little musical technique; his melodic and rhythmic material was arranged by various composers for performances. In this manner he brought out an operetta, *El condor pasa;* several orch. suites (*El resur-*

gimiento de los Andes, El Indio, Danza huanca, etc.). Five melodies collected by Robles are reproduced in *La Musique des Incas et ses survivances* by Raoul and Marguerite d'Harcourt (Paris, 1925).
BIBLIOGRAPHY: N. Slonimsky, *Music of Latin America* (N.Y., 1945; p. 275).

Robyn, Alfred George, American pianist, organist, and composer; b. St. Louis, April 29, 1860; d. New York, Oct. 18, 1935. He studied with his father, an organist; traveled with Emma Abbott at the age of 16 as pianist and accompanist; filled numerous posts as church organist in N.Y. He wrote light operas: *The Yankee Consul* (1903); *The Gypsy Girl* (1905); *The Yankee Tourist* (1907); *Fortune Land* (1907); *All for the Ladies* (1912); etc.; oratorios: *The Ascension; Love Unending; Praise and Thanksgiving;* symph. poem, *Pompeii;* Piano Concerto; Piano Quintet; 4 string quartets; numerous piano pieces; songs. Some of his songs and piano pieces sold extremely well.

Rocca, Lodovico, Italian composer; b. Turin, Nov. 29, 1895. He studied with Orefice at the Cons. of Milan; also attended the Univ. of Turin; from 1940 to 1966 he was director of the Cons. of Turin.
WORKS: Operas: *In terra di leggenda* (Milan, Sept. 28, 1933); *Il Dibuc* (Milan, March 24, 1934); *La morte di Frine* (Milan, April 24, 1937); *Monte Ivnor* (Rome, Dec. 23, 1939); *L'uragano* (Milan, Feb. 8, 1952); for Orch: *Contrasti* (1919); *Aurora di morte* (1920); *La foresta delle samodive* (1921); *L'alba del malato* (1922); *Le luci* (1923); *Chiaroscuri* (1924); *La cella azzurra* (1925); *Biribù, Occhi di rana* for Voice and String Quartet (1937); *Schizzi francescani* for Tenor and 8 Instruments (1942); *Antiche iscrizioni* for Soloists, Chorus, and Orch. (1952; Rome, Feb. 6, 1953).
BIBLIOGRAPHY: G. Bas, in *Musica d'Oggi* (1925 and 1927); M. Castelnuovo-Tedesco in *Il Pianoforte* (1925); A. Damerini, ibid. (1927); F. Lunghi, "Lodovico Rocca," *Santa Cecilia,* III/2 (Rome, 1954); M. Bruni, *Lodovico Rocca* (Milan, 1963).

Rochberg, George, significant American composer; b. Paterson, N.J., July 5, 1918. He studied theory and composition with George Szell in N.Y. (1939–41); served in the U.S. military forces during World War II; after the war, enrolled in composition classes at the Curtis Inst. with Rosario Scalero and Gian Carlo Menotti (B. Mus., 1947). In 1950 he was in Rome on a Fulbright fellowship; in 1951 was appointed music editor for the Theodore Presser Co.; also taught classes at the Curtis Inst.; in 1960 he joined the music faculty of the Univ. of Pa. In his style he pursues the ideal of tonal order and logically justifiable musical structures; the most profound influence he experienced was that of Schoenberg and Anton von Webern; many of his works follow the organization in 12 different notes; at the same time he does not deny himself the treasures of the sanctified past, and even resorts to overt quotations in his works of recognizable fragments from music by composers as mutually unrelated as Schütz,

Bach, Mahler, and Ives, treated by analogy with the "objets trouvés" in modern painting and sculpture. WORKS: *Capriccio* for 2 Pianos (1949); Symph. No. 1 (Philadelphia, March 28, 1958); *Night Music* (1952; won the George Gershwin Memorial Award); *Cantio sacra* for Chamber Orch. (1953); *Fantasia* for Violin and Piano (1955); *Sinfonia fantasia* (1956); *Waltz Serenade* for Orch. (Cincinnati, Feb. 14, 1958); *Cheltenham Concerto* (1958); Symph. No. 2 (Cleveland, Feb. 26, 1959); *Time-Span*, symph. movement (St. Louis, Oct. 22, 1960); Symph. No. 3 for Solo Voices, Chamber Chorus, Double Chorus, and Orch. (using quotations from works by Schütz, Bach, Mahler, and Ives; N.Y., Nov. 24, 1970); Violin Concerto (Pittsburgh, April 4, 1975); Symph. No. 4 (Seattle, Nov. 15, 1976); Oboe Concerto (N.Y., Dec. 13, 1984); *Dialogues* for Clarinet and Piano (1958); String Quartet No. 1 (1952); String Quartet No. 2, with Soprano (1961); String Quartet No. 3 (1972); *Concord Quartets* (Nos. 4, 5, and 6; Philadelphia, Jan. 20, 1979); *Black Sounds* for Wind Instruments and Percussion (1965); *Contra mortem et tempus* for Violin, Flute, Clarinet, and Piano; containing phrases from works by Boulez, Varèse, and Ives (1965); *Tableaux* for Soprano and 11 Players (1968); Piano Quintet (1975); opera, *The Confidence Man*, after Melville's novel (Santa Fe, July 31, 1982); a number of piano pieces and songs. He publ. a theoretical essay, *The Hexachord and Its Relation to the 12-Tone Row* (Bryn Mawr, 1955), and several magazine articles dealing with 12-tone techniques. BIBLIOGRAPHY: A.L. Ringer, "The Music of George Rochberg," *Musical Quarterly* (Oct. 1966).

Roche, Jerome, English musicologist; b. Cairo, May 22, 1942. He studied at St. John's College, Cambridge (B.A., 1962; Mus.B., 1963); received his Ph.D. from Cambridge Univ. in 1968 with the dissertation *North Italian Liturgical Music in the Early 17th Century*. In 1967 he became a lecturer at the Univ. of Durham. He publ. the books *Palestrina* (London, 1972) and *The Madrigal* (London, 1972); with his wife, Elizabeth, he brought out a useful reference source, *A Dictionary of Early Music from the Troubadours to Monteverdi* (London, 1981).

Rochlitz, Johann Friedrich, German writer on music; b. Leipzig, Feb. 12, 1769; d. there, Dec. 16, 1842. A pupil of Doles at the Thomasschule, he entered the Univ. of Leipzig as a theological student; publ. some novels and sketches; his 2 pamphlets, *Blicke in das Gebiet der Kunst* and *Einige Ideen über Anwendung des guten Geschmacks* (both 1796), treat in part of music. In 1798 he founded the *Allgemeine Musikalische Zeitung,* which he edited till 1818 and contributed to until 1835. From 1805 he was a director of the Gewandhaus Concerts. His best-known work is *Für Freunde der Tonkunst* (4 vols., 1824–32; 3rd ed., 1868), which contains biographies, essays, analyses of compositions, etc.; vol. IV has an outline, *Geschichte der Gesangmusik,* which Rochlitz supplemented by a *Sammlung vorzüglicher Gesangstücke* in 3 vols., from Dufay to Vallotti. Müller-Blattau compiled Rochlitz's essays on Bach un-

der the title *Wege zu Bach* (1926). Rochlitz composed songs for men's chorus; also a setting of the 23rd Psalm; wrote texts for operas, oratorios, cantatas, etc. BIBLIOGRAPHY: Ernst Rychnovsky, *L. Sphor und F. Rochlitz* (Prague, 1904); J. Gensel, *Aus Rochlitzs Briefen an Henriette Voigt* (Leipzig, 1906); H. Ehinger, *J.F. Rochlitz als Musikschriftsteller* (Leipzig, 1929).

Rockstro (real name, **Rackstraw**), **William Smyth,** English music scholar; b. North Cheam, Surrey, Jan. 5, 1823; d. London, July 2, 1895. He studied at the Leipzig Cons. under Mendelssohn, Plaidy, and Hauptmann. Returning to London, he taught piano and singing; wrote a popular ballad, *Queen and Huntress;* publ. piano arrangements of numerous operas; devoted himself to a close study of ecclesiastical music, and became an acknowledged authority on plainchant; became a Roman Catholic in 1876. WRITINGS: *History of Music for Young Students* (1879); *Practical Harmony* (1881); *Rules of Counterpoint* (1882); *Life of G.F. Handel* (1883); *Mendelssohn* (1884); *General History of Music* (1886; 3rd ed., 1897); *Jenny Lind, the Artist* (1891; with Canon Scott Holland); *Jenny Lind, Her Vocal Art and Culture* (1894; with Otto Goldschmidt); also publ. *Festival Psalter, Adapted to the Gregorian Tones; Accompanying Harmonies to the Ferial Psalter;* and *Harmonies for Additional Chants and the Ambrosial Te Deum.*

Rodan, Mendi, Rumanian-born Israeli conductor; b. Isai, April 17, 1929. He studied violin and conducting at the Bucharest Academy of Music; after leading various ensembles in Rumania, he settled in Israel in 1961. In 1963 he became chief conductor of the Israel Broadcasting Symph. Orch. in Jerusalem, a post he held until 1972. He also founded the Jerusalem Chamber Orch. in 1965 and led it until 1969; made tours with it to Europe, the U.S., and the Far East. In 1962 he joined the faculty of the Rubin Academy of Music in Jerusalem; was made a prof. there in 1973.

Roda y López, Cecilio de, Spanish writer on music; b. Albuñol, near Granada, Oct. 24, 1865; d. Madrid, Nov. 27, 1912. From 1904 he was president of the music division of the Ateneo in Madrid; elected member of the Academy in 1906. He was the author of *Los instrumentos, las danzas y las canciones en el Quijote* (1905); *La evolución de la música* (1906); *Un quaderno di autografi di Beethoven del 1825* (Turin, 1907); etc.

Rode, (Jacques-) Pierre (Joseph), French violinist; b. Bordeaux, Feb. 16, 1774; d. Château-Bourbon, near Damazan, Nov. 25, 1830. He was a pupil of Fauvel; from 1787, of Viotti at Paris; made his debut in 1790 in a concerto by Viotti at the Théâtre Feydeau; after tours in the Netherlands and Germany and a short visit to London, he was appointed prof. of violin at the newly opened Paris Cons. (1795).

During a visit to Spain in 1799 he met Boccherini, who wrote concertos for him. In 1800 he was court violinist to Napoleon; from 1803 to 1808 was in Russia with Boieldieu; became first violinist to the court of Alexander I; then spent 3 years in Paris, after which he toured Germany and Austria (at Vienna Beethoven wrote for him the G major Sonata, op. 96, which Rode perf. with Archduke Rudolph in Vienna, on Dec. 29, 1812); lived for a time in Berlin, where he married in 1814; then retired and lived in Bordeaux.

WORKS: 13 violin concertos; the famous *24 caprices en forme d'études, dans les 24 tons de la gamme;* 12 études; 3 books of violin duos; etc.; and a *Méthode du violon* (with Baillot and Kreutzer).

BIBLIOGRAPHY: A. Pougin, *Notice sur Rode* (Paris, 1874); H. Ahlgrimm, *Pierre Rode* (Vienna, 1929).

Rode, Wilhelm, German bass-baritone; b. Hannover, Feb. 17, 1887; d. Icking, near Munich, Sept. 2, 1959. He studied in Hannover; made his debut in 1908 as the Herald in *Lohengrin* in Erfurt; then sang in Bremerhaven, Breslau, and Stuttgart; was a leading member of the Bavarian State Opera in Munich (1922–34); made guest appearances in Vienna, Paris, Berlin, Dresden, Budapest, and Prague. In 1934 he was appointed Intendant of the Deutsches Opernhaus in Berlin, where he also continued to appear as a singer; he retired in 1944. He was reputed to be one of the finest performers of bass-baritone roles in Wagner's operas.

Rodeheaver, Homer Alvan, American composer of hymn tunes who described himself as a "musical missionary"; b. Union Furnace, Ohio, Oct. 4, 1880; d. New York, Dec. 18, 1955. Taken to Jellicoe, Tenn., as a child, he grew up helping in his father's lumber business and learning to play the trombone from a local musician. During the Spanish-American War he enlisted as trombonist in the 4th Tennessee Regimental Band. After the war he became interested in gospel songs and evangelism; accompanied the evangelist Billy Sunday on his tours (1910–30), leading the singing with his trombone. He composed the music for many gospel songs, of which the best known is *Then Jesus Came.* His theme song was *Brighten the Corner,* composed by Charles H. Gabriel. Rodeheaver was the founder of the Summer School of Sacred Music at Winona Lake, Ind., and was connected with the Rodeheaver-Hall-Mack Music Publishing Co. there. Besides a dozen or so collections of hymn poems and homilies, he publ. *Song Stories of the Sawdust Trail* (N.Y., 1917), *20 Years with Billy Sunday* (Nashville, 1936), and *Letter from a Missionary in Africa* (Chicago, 1936). With his predecessor Ira D. Sankey, he was a leading figure in American musical evangelism.

Röder, Carl Gottlieb, German printer of music; b. Stötteritz, near Leipzig, June 22, 1812; d. Gohlis, Oct. 29, 1883. He founded the great Leipzig establishment for engraving and printing music; starting in 1846 with one engraver's apprentice, the business

became one of the largest in the world. A book printing dept. was added later. In 1872 Röder's sons-in-law C.L.H. Wolff and C.E.M. Rentsch became partners in the firm; Röder himself retired in 1876. After Rentsch's death (Feb. 19, 1889) his heirs withdrew from the firm, but a son-in-law of Wolff, Karl Johannes Reichel (b. Aug. 15, 1853; d. Leipzig, Sept. 9, 1927), became a partner, and after Wolff's death (1915), head of the firm. On the 50th anniversary of its foundation the firm issued a Festschrift, to which Hugo Riemann contributed a valuable essay, *Notenschrift und Notendruck;* a 2nd Festschrift (on the 75th anniversary) took the form of a study by W. von zur Westen entitled *Musiktitel aus 4 Jahrhunderten* (1921). The firm became a joint stock company in 1930; after World War II it was nationalized by the German Democratic Republic.

Röder, Martin, German composer and singing teacher; b. Berlin, April 7, 1851; d. Boston, June 7, 1895. After studying music in Berlin, he went to Milan, where he organized the Società del Quartetto Corale (1875), giving performances of vocal quartets; then occupied various posts as singing teacher in Berlin (1881–87), Dublin (1887–92), and finally at the New England Cons. in Boston (1892). He wrote 3 operas, of which only one, *Vera,* was performed (Hamburg, 1881); 2 symph. poems, *Azorenfahrt* and *Leonore;* the overture *Attila;* chamber music; publ. *Studi, critici, raccolti* (Milan, 1881) and *Dal Taccuino di un direttore di orchestra* (1881; in German as *Aus dem Tagebuche eines wandernden Kapellmeisters,* 1884).

Rodgers, Jimmie, American singer of country music; b. Mendoza, Miss., Sept. 8, 1897; d. New York, May 26, 1933. Known as "the Singing Brakeman" because he worked on the railroad, he made early recordings in a western style of country music in the 1920s, but his career was dogged by tuberculosis and an inability to control his spendthrift life-style. In 1961 his name was the first to be placed in the Country Music Hall of Fame in Nashville, and in 1977 a U.S. postage stamp was issued to commemorate the 80th anniversary of his birth.

Rodgers, Richard, celebrated American composer of popular music; b. Hammels Station, Long Island, N.Y., June 28, 1902; d. New York, Dec. 30, 1979. He studied at Columbia Univ. (1919–21) and at the Inst. of Musical Art in N.Y. (1921–23). He collaborated for 18 years with the lyricist Lorenz Hart in a series of inspired and highly popular musical comedies: *The Girl Friend* (1926); *A Connecticut Yankee* (1927); *On Your Toes* (1936); *Babes in Arms* (1937); *I Married an Angel* (1938); *The Boys from Syracuse* (1942). *The Rodgers and Hart Song Book* (N.Y., 1951) contains their most famous songs. After Hart's death in 1943 Rodgers became associated with Oscar Hammerstein II. Together they wrote the greatly acclaimed musical *Oklahoma!* (1943; Pulitzer Prize, 1944), followed by a number of no less successful productions: *Carousel* (1945); *Allegro* (1947); *South Pacific* (1948; Pulitzer Prize, 1950);

The King and I (1951); *Me and Juliet* (1953); *Pipe Dream* (1955); *The Flower Drum Song* (1958); *The Sound of Music* (1959). After Hammerstein's death in 1960, Rodgers wrote his own lyrics for his next musical, *No Strings* (1962); then followed *Do I Hear a Waltz* (1965) to the lyrics of Stephen Sondheim. Rodgers wrote the music for the television shows *Victory at Sea* (1952) and *Winston Churchill: The Valiant Years* (1960). Individual songs from his musical comedies have become perennial favorites: *Some Enchanted Evening, Getting to Know You, Do-Re-Mi*, etc., etc., etc.

BIBLIOGRAPHY: Deems Taylor, *Some Enchanted Evenings: The Story of Rodgers and Hammerstein* (N.Y., 1953); David Ewen, *Richard Rodgers* (N.Y., 1957; 2nd ed., N.Y., 1963); *Richard Rodgers Fact Book* (N.Y., 1965; new ed. with supplement, 1968); Rodgers publ. *Musical Stages: An Autobiography* (N.Y., 1975).

Rodio, Rocco, contrapuntist of the early Neapolitan school; b. Bari, Apulia, c.1530; d. c.1615. He publ. *Regole per far contrapunto solo e accompagnato nel canto fermo* (first ed., 1600; 3rd ed., 1626); also a collection (Naples, 1580) of 9 masses; the last, *Missa de Beata Virgine* (*a* 5) is remarkable, because it can also be sung by 4 or 3 voices, by omitting the *quintus,* the *quintus* and *superius* (soprano), or the *quintus* and *bassus.*

Rodolphe, Jean Joseph, French composer; b. Strasbourg, Oct. 14, 1730; d. Paris, Aug. 18, 1812. He studied the French horn with his father; then the violin with Leclair (*l'aîné*) in Paris; composition with Traetta in Parma, and with Jommelli in Stuttgart; wrote ballet music for Jommelli's productions there. In 1764 he was in Paris once more; brought out his first opera, *Le Mariage par capitulation* (Comedie-Italienne, Dec. 3, 1764); another opera, *L'Aveugle de Palmyre* (Comédie-Italienne, March 5, 1767), obtained considerable success. The famous balletmaster Noverre produced several of Rodolphe's ballets at the Paris Opéra. Mozart met Rodolphe in Paris in 1778, and spoke of him highly. Three of Rodolphe's ballets are printed in the *Denkmäler deutscher Tonkunst,* 43/44. From 1784 to 1802 Rodolphe taught composition and solfège at the Paris Cons.; publ. the manuals *Solfèges* and *Théorie d'accompagnement.*

Rodrigo, Joaquín, Spanish composer; b. Sagunto, Valencia, Nov. 22, 1901. He lost his sight as a child; revealed an innate talent for music and was sent to Paris, where he studied with Paul Dukas; in 1939 he returned to Spain. His music is profoundly imbued with Spanish melorhythms; his *Concierto de Aranjuez* for Guitar and Orch. (Barcelona, Nov. 9, 1940) became famous. He further composed *Juglares* for Orch. (1923); *Concierto heroico* for Piano and Orch. (Lisbon, April 5, 1943); *Concierto de estio* for Violin and Orch. (Lisbon, April 11, 1944); *Concierto in modo galante* for Cello and Orch. (Madrid, Nov. 4, 1949); Concerto for Harp and Orch. (1954); *Fantasia para un gentilhombre* for Guitar and Orch. (1955);

Sones en la Giralda for Harp and Orch. (1963); *Concierto Andaluz* for 4 Guitars (1967); *Concierto-madrigal* for 2 Guitars and Orch. (1968); *Sonata Pimpante* for Violin and Piano (1966); *Sonata a la española* for Guitar (1969); *Pájaros de primavera* for Guitar (1972); choruses; piano pieces.

BIBLIOGRAPHY: F. Sopeña, *Joaquín Rodrigo* (Madrid, 1946; 2nd ed., revised, 1970); A. Iglesias, *Joaquín Rodrigo* (Orense, 1965); V. Vaya Pia, *Joaquín Rodrigo: Su vida y su obra* (Madrid, 1977).

Rodrigo de Ledesma, Mariano, Spanish composer; b. Zaragoza, Dec. 14, 1779; d. Madrid, March 28, 1848. He served as a chorister at the Cathedral of Zaragoza; was organist and chorus master at Vinaroz (1799–1802); then tenor in Madrid; in 1807 he was appointed conductor of the Madrid opera theater, but the French invasion forced him to flee, and he took refuge in Seville. In 1812 he was in Cádiz; there he composed an anti-Bonaparte hymn, *En tan fausto día,* while Joseph Bonaparte was king of Spain; fled to England, where he established himself as a singing teacher in London. With the restoration of legitimate monarchy in Spain, he returned there, and received a court appointment; publ. *40 ejercicios de vocalización* (Madrid, 1820; Paris, 1827; also in Eng.). He was again in England from 1823 to 1831; heard Weber conduct his operas in London, and was profoundly impressed; thenceforth he tried to emulate Weber, writing music in a Romantic manner. Back in Spain once more, he became maestro to Queen María Cristina. He wrote chiefly church music: 3 Solemn Masses, 9 Lamentations, a Stabat Mater; also some secular songs and instrumental pieces. Eslava reprinted 5 motets for 4 Voices and Orch. by Rodrigo in the *Lira sacro-hispana.*

BIBLIOGRAPHY: R. Mitjana, *El Maestro Rodrigo de Ledesma y sus Lamentaciones de Semana Santa* (Málaga, 1909).

Rodriguez, Augusto, Puerto Rican composer; b. San Juan, Feb. 9, 1904. He studied literature at the Univ. of Puerto Rico; music at Harvard with E.B. Hill and Walter Piston; since 1934, has been a prof. at the Univ. of Puerto Rico; organized a chorus, which achieved a high degree of excellence; gave a concert with it in N.Y. in 1949. He publ. several songs and dance suites.

Rodriguez, Felipe, Spanish composer; b. Madrid, May 1, 1759; d. there, May 1814. He was a member of the Monserrat School; in 1778 was ordained priest; served as organist in Madrid. He wrote organ pieces, some of which are printed in *Música instrumental,* edited by D. Pujol (vol. 2, Montserrat, 1946), and church music; his *Rondo* for Piano is printed by J. Nín in the collection *17 sonates et pièces anciennes d'auteurs espagnols* (Paris, 1929).

Rodriguez, Robert Xavier, American composer; b. San Antonio, Texas, June 28, 1946. He studied with Hunter Johnson at the Univ. of Texas in Austin, with Halsey Stevens at the Univ. of Southern Calif., with Jacob Druckman at Tanglewood, and with Nadia Boulanger in Paris; also attended master classes with Bruno Maderna and Elliott Carter. WORKS: For the stage: *Le Diable amoureux,* one-act opera (1978); *Canto,* cantata (1978). For Orch.: *Adagio* for Small Orch. (1967); *Lyric Variations* for Oboe, 2 Horns, and Strings (1970); Concerto for Piano, 13 Wind Instruments, Percussion, and Strings (1974); *Sinfonia Concertante* (1974); *Favola Concertante* for Violin, Cello, and Strings (1977); *Discantus I* (1979); *Discantus II* (1979). Chamber music: 2 piano trios (1970, 1971); Concerto II for Piano and 7 Instruments (1972); Sonata for Soprano Saxophone and Piano (1972); Variations for Violin and Piano (1976); Toccata for Guitar Quartet (1975). Vocal music: *Lyrics for Autumn* for Soprano and Cello (1972); *5 poemas de García Lorca* for Mezzo-soprano, Tenor, and Piano (1975); *Praline and Fudge,* to texts from cookbooks, for Bass and Piano (1979).

Rodríguez, Vicente, Spanish organist and composer; b. Valencia, c.1685; d. there, (buried Dec. 16) 1760. He was a cleric; served as organist of the Valencia Cathedral from 1716 to his death; wrote several masses; also keyboard music; his Sonata in F (1744), printed by Joaquín Nín in his collection *17 sonates et pièces anciennes d'auteurs espagnols* (Paris, 1929), is in the style of Domenico Scarlatti.

Rodríguez de Hita, Antonio, Spanish composer; b. 1724; d. Madrid, Feb. 21, 1787. From 1740 to 1757 he was chorus master at the Cathedral of Palencia, where he publ. a book of advice to his pupils, *Consejos que a sus discípulos da don Antonio Rodriguez de Hita.* Then he became music director at the Convent of the Incarnation in Madrid. From 1768 he collaborated with the dramatist Ramón de la Cruz in a series of notable stage works impregnated with Spanish atmosphere; the best are the comic operas (zarzuelas) *Las segadoras de Vallecas* (Madrid, Sept. 3, 1768) and *Las labradoras de Murcia* (Madrid, Sept. 16, 1769). He also composed the Spanish opera *La Briseida* (Madrid, July 11, 1768); various hymns for 4 and 8 Voices; etc. BIBLIOGRAPHY: E. Cotarelo y Mori, *Don Ramón de la Cruz* (Madrid, 1899, with music examples); E. Cotarelo y Mori, *Historia de la zarzuela* (Madrid, 1934).

Rodzinski, Artur, eminent Polish conductor; b. Spalato, Dalmatia, Jan. 1, 1892; d. Boston, Nov. 27, 1958. He studied jurisprudence at the Univ. of Vienna; at the same time took piano lessons with Emil Sauer, composition with Schreker, and conducting with Schalk. He made his conducting debut in Lwow in 1921; subsequently conducted Polish operas in Warsaw. In 1926 he was appointed assistant conductor to Leopold Stokowski with the Philadelphia Orch.; in 1929 he was appointed permanent conductor of the Los Angeles Phil.; after 4 seasons there he was engaged as conductor of the Cleveland Orch., where he introduced the novel custom of presenting operas in concert form; on Jan. 31, 1935, he conducted the American premiere of Shostakovich's controversial opera *Lady Macbeth of the District of Mtzensk.* In 1943 he received his most prestigious appointment as conductor and music director of the N.Y. Phil., but his independent character and temperamental ways of dealing with the management forced him to resign amid raging controversy in the middle of his 4th season (Feb. 3, 1947); almost immediately he was engaged as conductor and music director of the Chicago Symph. Orch., but there, too, a conflict rapidly developed, and the management announced after a few months of the engagement that his contract would not be renewed, stating as a reason that his operatic ventures using the orch. were too costly. After these distressing American experiences Rodzinski conducted mainly in Europe; in the autumn of 1958 he received an invitation to conduct at the Lyric Opera in Chicago, but a heart ailment forced him to cancel his plans, and he died in a Boston hospital. BIBLIOGRAPHY: His widow, Halina Rodzinski, publ. a scrupulously documented and startlingly candid biography, *Our Two Lives* (N.Y., 1976). See also Donald Brook, *International Gallery of Conductors* (Bristol, 1951; pp. 159–64).

Roeckel, August, Austrian writer on music; b. Graz, Dec. 1, 1814; d. Budapest, June 18, 1876. He studied music with his father, Joseph August Roeckel (1783–1870), who was a singer and impresario; he also took lessons with J.N. Hummel, who was his uncle. He served as a theater conductor in Weimar (1838–43) and music director in Dresden (1843–49); became involved in the revolutionary activities in Saxony in 1848 and was arrested and sentenced to death; however, his sentence was commuted and he spent 13 years in the prison in Waldheim; upon release he engaged in literary activities. He maintained an active correspondence with Wagner, whose music and ideas he admired; Wagner's letters to him were publ. by La Mara, *Richard Wagners Briefe an August Roeckel* (Leipzig, 1894; in Eng., Bristol, 1897).

Roesgen-Champion, Marguerite, Swiss harpsichord player and composer; b. Geneva, Jan. 25, 1894; d. Paris, June 30, 1976. She studied composition with Ernest Bloch and Jaques-Dalcroze at the Cons. of Geneva, but devoted herself mainly to harpsichord playing, giving numerous recitals in Europe. Her own works are couched in the neo-Romantic vein; she wrote *Faunesques* for Orch. (Paris, 1929); *Concerto moderne* for Harpsichord and Orch. (Paris, Nov. 15, 1931, composer soloist); symph. suite, *Aquarelles* (Paris, Nov. 26, 1933); Harp Concerto (Paris, March 28, 1954); 5 concertos for Harpsichord and Orch. (1931–59); *Concerto romantique* for Piano and Orch. (1961); a number of pieces for flute in combination with the harpsichord and other instruments; a curious piece for Piano, 4-hands, entitled *Spoutnik* (1971).

Rogalski, Theodor, Rumanian composer and conductor; b. Bucharest, April 11, 1901; d. Zürich, Feb. 2,

1954. He studied at the Bucharest Cons. with Castaldi and Cuclin; at the Leipzig Cons. with Karg-Elert (1920–23); and in Paris with Vincent d'Indy (1924–26). Returning to Rumania, he was music director of Bucharest Radio (1939–44) and chief conductor of Bucharest State Phil. (1950–54). His music is permeated with the spirit of Rumanian folklore, while his harmony and orchestration reveal impressionistic traits.

WORKS: *3 dansuri romîneşti* (*3 Rumanian Dances;* Bucharest, May 27, 1951; attained great popularity and had numerous perfs. in Europe and America); *2 caprieci* for Orch. (1932); String Quartet (1925); violin pieces and songs.

Rogatis, Pasqual de. See **De Rogatis, Pascual.**

Rogé, Pascal, Franch pianist; b. Paris, April 6, 1951. He studied at the Paris Cons. In 1971 he won first prize in the Long-Thibaud Competition in Paris; then gave concerts throughout France. He acquired a fine reputation playing in programs of French music.

Rogel, José, Spanish composer of light opera; b. Orihuela, Alicante, Dec. 24, 1829; d. Cartagena, Feb. 25, 1901. At a very early age he was taught music by the organist J. Cascales, and at 10 composed a Mass, which he conducted himself. After he finished his law studies in Valencia, he studied counterpoint with Pascual Pérez; subsequently conducted at various theaters in Madrid, and in 1854 began his unusually successful career as composer of zarzuelas, of which he wrote about 75 (some in collaboration). Among the best are *El Joven Telémaco, Las Amazones del Tormes, El Rey Midas, Los Infiernos de Madrid, Genoveva de Brabante, Pablo y Virginia.*

Roger, Gustave-Hippolyte, famous French tenor; b. La Chapelle St.-Denis, near Paris, Dec. 17, 1815; d. Paris, Sept. 12, 1879. He was a pupil of Morin at the Paris Cons.; made his debut at the Opéra-Comique in 1838; then at the Paris Opéra, where he created the role of the Prophète in Meyerbeer's opera (1849); later toured in Germany. While hunting in the fall of 1859, the accidental discharge of his gun injured his right arm so severely that it had to be amputated. An artificial arm proved ineffective, and he was obliged to retire from the stage in 1861. From 1868 until his death he was a prof. of singing at the Cons. He publ. his memoirs as *Le Carnet d'un Ténor* (Paris, 1880).

BIBLIOGRAPHY: A. Laget, *G.-H. Roger* (Paris, 1865).

Roger, Victor, French composer of operettas; b. Montpellier, July 21, 1854; d. Paris, Dec. 2, 1903. He studied at the Ecole Niedermeyer; wrote light music; composed some 30 operettas, of which the following were brought out in Paris with considerable success: *Joséphine vendue par ses sœurs* (March 20, 1886); *Oscarine* (Oct. 15, 1888); *Le Fétiche* (March 13, 1890); *Samsonnet* (Nov. 26, 1890); *Miss Nicol-*

Nick (Jan. 23, 1895); *Le Voyage de Corbillon* (Jan. 30, 1896); *Sa Majesté l'Amour* (Dec. 23, 1896); *Les Fêtards* (Oct. 28, 1897); *L'Auberge du Tohu-Bohu* (Feb. 10, 1897); *L'Agence Crook & Co.* (Jan. 22, 1898); *La Petite Tâche* (March 26, 1898); *Poule blanche* (Jan. 13, 1899); *Le Jockey malgré lui* (Dec. 4, 1902). After his death 3 completely finished scores were found: *La Fille de Fra Diavolo, La Princesse de Babylone,* and *Adélaïde.*

Roger-Ducasse, Jean-Jules Aimable, French composer; b. Bordeaux, April 18, 1873; d. Le-Taillan-Médoc, near Bordeaux, July 19, 1954. He studied at the Paris Cons. with Fauré (composition), Pessard (harmony), Gédalge (counterpoint), and de Bériot. In 1902 he won the 2nd Prix de Rome for the cantata *Alcyone;* in 1909 was appointed inspector of singing in the Paris schools; subsequently was a prof. of ensemble at the Paris Cons.; from 1935 to 1945 taught composition there; then retired to Bordeaux. His first work to be played in public was a *Petite suite* for Orch. (Paris, March 5, 1898). He adopted a pleasing style of Impressionism; his symph. pieces enjoyed considerable success, without setting a mark for originality.

WORKS: Comic opera, *Cantegril* (Opéra-Comique, Feb. 9, 1931); mimodrama, *Orphée* (St. Petersburg, Jan. 31, 1914); for Orch.: *Variations plaisantes sur un thème grave* (Paris, Jan. 24, 1909); *Suite française* (1909); *Prélude d'un ballet* (1910); *Le Joli Jeu de furet,* orch. scherzo (1911); *Nocturne de printemps* (Paris, Feb. 14, 1920); *Symphonie sur la Cathédrale de Reims* (never completed); *Le Petit Faune* (Bordeaux, May 22, 1954); etc.; *Sarabande,* symph. poem with Voices (1911); *Au Jardin de Marguerite* for Soloists, Chorus, and Orch. (1901–5); *Sur quelques vers de Virgile* for Chorus and Orch.; Piano Quartet (1899–1912); String Quartet (1900–9); songs (*Le Cœur de l'eau, Noëls des roses, 7 préludes,* études, arabesques, etc.); pedagogical works (*Solfèges,* 3 vols.; *Dictée musicale,* 4 vols.; *Exercises de piano,* 3 vols.; etc.). His autobiography was publ. in *L'Ecran des musiciens* (1930).

BIBLIOGRAPHY: L. Ceillier, *Roger-Ducasse* (Paris, 1920); A. Cœuroy, *La Musique franéaise moderne* (Paris, 1922); *Catalogue de l'œuvre de Roger-Ducasse* (Bordeaux, 1955).

Rogers, Bernard, American composer; b. New York, Feb. 4, 1893; d. Rochester, N.Y., May 24, 1968. He studied architecture before devoting himself to music. His first teacher was Arthur Farwell; he subsequently studied with Ernest Bloch in Cleveland. His symph. composition *To the Fallen* was performed by the N.Y. Phil. on Nov. 13, 1919; on the strength of it, he won a Pulitzer Traveling Scholarship and went to Europe for further study; in 1927 he received a Guggenheim fellowship; took courses with Nadia Boulanger in Paris and Frank Bridge in London. When he returned from Europe in 1929, he was engaged as an instructor at the Eastman School of Music in Rochester, N.Y.; remained there until 1967, teaching orchestration and composition.

WORKS: Operas: *The Marriage of Aude* (Rochester, May 22, 1931); *The Warrior* (to the story of Samson and Delilah; N.Y., Jan. 11, 1947); *The Veil* (Indiana Univ., Bloomington, Ind., May 18, 1950). For Orch.: *The Faithful* (1918); *Adonais* (Rochester, April 29, 1927); *Prelude to Hamlet* (1928); Symph. No. 2 (Rochester, Oct. 24, 1930); *3 Japanese Dances* (Rochester, May 3, 1934); *Once upon a Time,* 5 fairy tales for Small Orch. (Rochester, April 4, 1935); *The Supper at Emmäus* (Rochester, April 29, 1937); Symph. No. 3 (Rochester, Oct. 27, 1937); *The Colors of War* (Rochester, Oct. 25, 1939); *The Song of the Nightingale* (Cincinnati, March 21, 1940); *The Dance of Salome* (Rochester, April 25, 1940); *The Plains,* "landscapes for orch." (N.Y., May 3, 1941); *Invasion* (N.Y., Oct. 17, 1943); *Characters from Hans Christian Andersen* (Rochester, April 28, 1945); *In Memory of Franklin Delano Roosevelt* (N.Y., April 11, 1946); *Amphitryon,* symph. overture (N.Y., March 10, 1947); Symph. No. 4 (Rochester, May 4, 1948); *Dance Scenes* (Louisville, Ky., Oct. 28, 1953); *Fantasy* for Flute, Viola, and Orch. (Rochester, April 25, 1938); Symph. No. 5, *Africa* (Cincinnati, Jan. 30, 1959); *Soliloquy* for Bassoon and String Orch. (Rochester, Oct. 18, 1938); *The Silver World* for Flute, Oboe, and Strings (1950); *Leaves from the Tale of Pinocchio,* suite for Narrator and Small Orch. (1950). Vocal works: *The Passion,* oratorio in 6 scenes for Soloists, Mixed Chorus, and Orch. (Cincinnati, May 12, 1944; his most significant work); *Apparitions* for Orch. (1967); *The Raising of Lazarus* for Soloists, Chorus, and Orch. (1928); *The Exodus,* sacred poem for Soloists, Chorus, and Orch. (1932); *Fantasia* for Horn, Kettledrums, and String Orch. (Rochester, Feb. 20, 1955); a String Quartet and other chamber music. He publ. a valuable manual, *The Art of Orchestration* (N.Y., 1951).

BIBLIOGRAPHY: E.E. Hipsher, *American Opera and Its Composers* (Philadelphia, 1934; pp. 369–70); David Diamond, "Bernard Rogers," *Musical Quarterly* (April 1947).

Rogers, Clara Kathleen (née **Barnett**), English soprano; b. Cheltenham, Jan. 14, 1844; d. Boston, March 8, 1931. She was the daughter of the composer **John Barnett;** studied at the Leipzig Cons. with Moscheles and Plaidy (piano), Papperitz and Richter (theory), David and Rietz (ensemble playing); singing with Goetz in Berlin and with Sangiovanni in Milan. She made her debut in Turin (1863) as Isabella in *Robert le Diable* (stage name, **"Clara Doria"**); came to America in 1871 with the Parepa-Rosa Co.; debut, N.Y., in *Bohemian Girl* (Oct. 4, 1871); later settled in Boston as a teacher; from 1902 was a prof. of singing at the New England Cons.; married a Boston lawyer, Henry M. Rogers, in 1878. She publ. *The Philosophy of Singing* (1893); *Dreaming True* (1899); *My Voice and I* (1910); *English Diction in Song and Speech* (1912); *The Voice in Speech* (1915); *Memories of a Musical Career* (Boston, 1919) and its sequel, *The Story of Two Lives* (Norwood, Mass., 1932); songs.

Rogers, Francis, American baritone; b. Roxbury, Mass., April 14, 1870; d. New York, May 15, 1951. He

studied singing with W.L. Whitney in Boston, Vannuccini in Florence, Bouhy in Paris, and Luckstone in N.Y.; from 1924 was a member of the faculty of the Juilliard Graduate School in N.Y. He publ. *Some Famous Singers of the 19th Century* (N.Y., 1914).

Rogers, James Henderson, American organist and song composer; b. Newark, N.Y., 1852; d. St. Petersburg, Fla., May 30, 1933. He studied music in N.Y.; was a church organist; composed a quantity of anthems and other church pieces, later collected in a book under the title *The Church Chorus Series.*

Rogers, James Hotchkiss, American organist and composer; b. Fair Haven, Conn., Feb. 7, 1857; d. Pasadena, Calif., Nov. 28, 1940. He studied with Clarence Eddy in Chicago; in Berlin under Loeschhorn and Ehrlich (piano), Rohde (theory), and Haupt (organ); in Paris under Fissot (piano), Guilmant (organ), and Widor (theory). Returning to the U.S., he settled in Cleveland (1883) as organist; eventually retired to California. He publ. about 150 works: a Lenten cantata, *The Man of Nazareth;* an Easter cantata, *The New Life;* anthems, secular part-songs, songs, piano pieces, studies for piano and organ. Among his most popular songs are *The Star* and *At Parting.*

Rogers, Kenny (Kenneth Ray Rogers), American country-music singer; b. Houston, Aug. 21, 1939. After attending the Univ. of Houston for a brief time, he left academic pursuits to join the Bobby Doyle Jazz Trio; later he became a member of The New Christy Minstrels, the popular folksinging group; finally, he sang with The First Edition, a pop-rock outfit. With this varied background, he decided to make a solo career as a country-music singer when The First Edition disbanded in 1975; his spectacular success began in 1977 with his recording of *Lucille,* which won him a Grammy. He subsequently starred in the television movie *The Gambler,* based on his recording. His rough, bearded manhood, with a touch of gray, and his carefree lifestyle, combined with the macho image projected on the podium and on the television tube, contributed greatly to his star status among prematurely faded female fans in the subculture of California and adjacent territories.

Rogers, "Shorty" (Milton), American jazz trumpeter, bandleader, and composer; b. Great Barrington, Mass., April 14, 1924. He studied the trumpet at the High School of Music and Art in N.Y.; then went to California and played with Red Norvo, Woody Herman, and Stan Kenton; was also successful as an arranger. After 1954 he led his own bands.

Roget, Henriette, French composer and organist; b. Bastia, Corsica, Jan. 9, 1910. She studied organ with Marcel Dupré and composition with Henri Busser at the Paris Cons.; received the Premier 2nd Prix de Rome in 1933. She was director in charge of voice training at the Paris Opéra until 1959; served as organist at the Oratoire du Louvre and prof. of piano accompanying and score reading at the Paris Cons. She wrote a great number of piano books for children, among them *Adroits petits doigts* (1957), *Abécédaire* (1958), and *Méthode* (1970).

WORKS: *Montanyas del Rosello* for Organ and Orch. (Paris, April 6, 1933, composer soloist); *Sinfonia andorrana* for Orch. (1936); *Concerto classique* for Cello and Orch. (1944); *Concerto sicilien* for Piano and Orch. (1943); *Symphonie pour rire* (1947); *Cathérinettes*, ballet (1937); *Hymne à l'aviation* (1937; awarded a prize at the Paris Exhibition); *3 Ballades françaises* for Orch. (Paris, Jan. 11, 1936); *Rythmes* for Orch. (Paris, Jan. 23, 1937); a number of effective organ pieces.

BIBLIOGRAPHY: A. Machabey, *Portraits de trente musiciens français* (Paris, 1949).

Rogg, Lionel, outstanding Swiss organist; b. Geneva, April 21, 1936. He studied organ with Pierre Segond and piano with Nikita Magaloff at the Geneva Cons. and won prizes playing both instruments. In 1961 he gave a series of recitals in Geneva devoted to the complete works for organ by Bach; subsequently he made tours of Europe and America. In 1960 he was appointed to the faculty of the Geneva Cons.; in addition, he gave master classes in organ. As a virtuoso on the organ, he possesses a remarkable gift for improvisation.

Rogister, Jean, Belgian violist and composer; b. Liège, Oct. 25, 1879; d. there, March 20, 1964. He studied violin, viola, horn, and composition at the Liège Cons.; played viola in local orch. groups. His style of composition followed the precepts of César Franck, but upon occasion he introduced into his music some modernistic impressionistic sonorities.

WORKS: Lyric drama, *Lorsque minuit sonna* (1930); *Requiem* (1944; with Orch. and Full Chorus, Liège, March 24, 1946); *The Bells*, oratorio after Edgar Allan Poe, for Soprano and 8 Instruments (1924); 3 symphs.: No. 1 (1927); No. 2, *Symphonie wallonne* (1931–32); No. 3, with Solo String Quartet (1942–43); *Symphonie intime* for String Quartet, Double Bass, Flute, Clarinet, and Bassoon (1929); *Fantaisie concertante* for Viola and Orch. (1910); Viola Concerto (1914); Cello Concerto (1917); Trombone Concerto (1919); *Poème* for Violin and Orch. (1920); *Impression de mai* for Violin and Orch. (1935); *Suite* for Flute and Chamber Orch. (1949); symph. poems: *Destin* (1919); *La Fiancée du lutin* (1920); *Nuit d'Avril* (1921); *Paysage* (1923); *Fantaisie burlesque sur un thème populaire* (1928); *La Lune et les peupliers* (1932); *Jeux symphoniques* (1952); *Hommage à César Franck* (1955); *Adagio* for 2 String Ensembles (1960); 8 string quartets (1902, 1914, 1921, 1926, 1927, 1928, 1931, 1940); *Esquisse dramatique* for String Quartet (1935); Quintet for Ancient Instruments (Clavecin, 2 Quintons, Viola d'Amore, and Viola da Gamba, 1934); Wind Quintet (1947); choruses; songs.

Rögner, Heinz, German conductor; b. Leipzig, Jan. 16, 1929. He studied piano with Hugo Steuer, viola with Gutschlicht, and conducting with Egon Böl-

sche at the Hochschule für Musik in Leipzig; was a conductor at the German National Theater in Weimar (1951–54); then led the opera school at the Hochschule für Musik in Leipzig (1954–58). From 1958 to 1962 he was chief conductor of the Great Radio Orch. in Leipzig; from 1962 to 1973 he was Generalmusikdirektor of the German State Opera in East Berlin. In 1973 he became chief conductor of the East Berlin Radio Symph., and in 1974 led its Radio Choir. He made appearances as a conductor of opera and symph. in East Germany, West Germany, Rumania, and Hungary.

Rogowski, Ludomir, Polish composer; b. Lublin, Oct. 3, 1881; d. Dubrovnik, Yugoslavia, March 14, 1954. Of a musical family, he received his early training at home; in 1906 went to Leipzig and took a course with Hugo Riemann. Returning to Poland, he conducted the Vilna Symph. Orch., which he founded (1910); in 1911 was in Paris; from 1912 to 1914, was a theater conductor in Warsaw. He was again in France (1917–19), then in Poland (1919–26), finally settling in Dubrovnik (1927), where he remained for the rest of his life, with only occasional engagements as a conductor in Warsaw (1935 and 1938).

WORKS: Operas: *Tamara* (1918); *Un Grand Chagrin de la petite Ondine* (1919); *La Sérénade inutile* (1921); *Królewicz Marko* (1930); ballets: *Bajka* (1922) and *Kupala* (1925); 7 symphs.: No. 1, *Offering* (1921); No. 2, *Rejoicing* (1936); No. 3 (1940); No. 4 (1943); No. 5 (1947); No. 6 (1949); No. 7 (1951); other symph. works: *Images ensoleillées* (1918); *Villafranca* (1919); *Les Saisons* (1933); *Les Sourires* (1933); *Poéme du travail* (1936); *Fantômes* (1937); 4 rhapsodies on Slavonic themes (1945); *Dubrovnik Impressions* (1950); 6 works for Violin and Orch.; 2 string quartets; short pieces for various instruments; numerous arrangements of Slavonic songs for Chorus. In some of his works he made use of the so-called Slavonic scale (Lydian mode with the lowered 7th) and the scale of alternating whole tones and semitones, known as Rimsky-Korsakov's scale.

Roguski, Gustav, Polish composer and pedagogue; b. Warsaw, May 12, 1839; d. there, April 5, 1921. He studied in Germany with Kiel; then went to Paris, where he became a pupil of Berlioz. Returning to Warsaw in 1873, he was appointed prof. at the Cons. He wrote a Symph., 2 string quartets, a Quintet for Wind Instruments and Piano, many piano pieces, choruses, and songs; publ. a manual of harmony in Polish (with L. Zelenski). He was greatly esteemed as a teacher of composition; Paderewski was his pupil.

Rohde, (Friedrich) Wilhelm, Danish violinist and composer; b. Altona, Dec. 11, 1856; d. Gentofte, near Copenhagen, April 6, 1928. He was a pupil at the Leipzig Cons. of H. Schradieck and F. David (violin), J. Röntgen (piano), E.F. Richter (composition), and H. Kretzschmar. He lived in Chicago (1878–85); after one season as violist in the Boston Symph. Orch. he returned to Germany; lived in Schwerin; from

1914, in Copenhagen. He composed several symph. poems; a Serenade for Strings; *Höller-Galopp* for Violin, Cello, Flute, Horn, and Piano; a number of male choruses; piano pieces.

Rohloff, Ernst, German music historian; b. Graudenz, April 17, 1899. He studied in Leipzig with Straube (organ) and with Schering and Abert (musicology); received his Dr.Phil. for the dissertation *Studien zum Musiktraktat des Johannes de Grocheo* (Leipzig, 1926); settled in Weissenfels as a teacher and organist. He publ. several valuable papers on medieval music.

Röhr, Hugo, German conductor and composer; b. Dresden, Feb. 13, 1866; d. Munich, June 7, 1937. He studied composition with Wüllner at the Dresden Cons.; began his career as conductor in Augsburg; after filling several engagements in Breslau, Prague, and Mannheim, he was appointed conductor at the court opera in Munich (1896); from 1924 to 1934 he taught conducting at the Munich Academy of Music. He wrote several short operas: *Das Vaterunser* (Munich, 1904); *Frauenlist* (Leipzig, 1917); *Cœur-Dame* (1927); *Ekkehard*, a dramatic poem for Soli, Chorus, and Orch.; chamber music; songs.

Röhrig, Emil, German composer; b. Rettert, Oct. 31, 1882; d. Aachen, July 22, 1954. After studying violin in Chemnitz, he became engaged as violinist and conductor in Krefeld and Aachen. He wrote much music for brass; also concertos for double bass, viola, trumpet, etc.; cantatas and other choral works.

Roig, Gonzalo, Cuban conductor and composer; b. Havana, July 20, 1890; d. there, June 13, 1970. He played violin in theater orchs.; in 1922 organized the Orquesta Sinfónica de la Habana. He also wrote zarzuelas, among which *Cecilia Valdés* enjoyed considerable success. In 1912 he wrote the song *Quiereme mucho,* which became a popular hit.

Rojo, Casiano, Spanish authority on Gregorian chant; b. Acinas, near Burgos, Aug. 5, 1877; d. at the monastery of Santo Domingo de Silos, Burgos, Dec. 4, 1931. He was employed as organist and chorus leader; received his training in the proper interpretation of Gregorian chant from Dom Pothier; publ. a valuable manual, *Método de canto gregoriano* (Valladolid, 1906); *Antiphonarium Mozarabicum de la Catedral de León* (with G. Prado; León, 1928); and *El Canto mozárabe* (with G. Prado; Barcelona, 1929).

Rokseth, Yvonne (née **Rihouët**), French musicologist and organist; b. Maisons-Laffitte, near Paris, July 17, 1890; d. Strasbourg, Aug. 23, 1948. She studied at the Paris Cons.; with d'Indy and Roussel at the Schola Cantorum; and with Pirro at the Sorbonne; received her doctorat ès lettres with the dissertation *La Musique d'orgue au XVe siècle et au début du XVIe* (Paris, 1930); held various positions as organist in Paris (1920–25); was later librarian at the

Paris Cons. and a prof. of musicology at the Univ. of Strasbourg (from 1937); publ. a biography of Grieg (Paris, 1933); edited *Deux livres d'orgue parus chez P. Attaingnant en 1531,* in the series Publications de la Société Française de Musicologie (1925); *Polyphonies du XIIIe siècle: Le Manuscrit Montpellier H 196* (facsimile, transcription, and commentary, 4 vols., 1935–39); also organ works of Marc Antonio da Bologna of 1523; etc.; co-editor of *Trois Chansonniers français du XVe siècle* (Paris, 1927).

BIBLIOGRAPHY: G. Thibault, "Yvonne Rokseth," *Revue de Musicologie* (1948).

Roland, Claude-Robert, Belgian composer, organist, and conductor; b. Pont-de-Loup, Dec. 19, 1935. He studied composition at the Music Academy in Châtelet and at the conservatories of Mons, Liège, Paris, and Brussels with Froidebise, C. Schmit, R. Bernier, Messiaen, and Defossez; also took a course in conducting with Scherchen. He was an organist in churches in various Belgian cities (1955–67); director of the Music Academy at Montignies-le-Tilleul (1966–75); in 1972 was appointed to the staff of the Brussels Cons.

WORKS: *Sonance* for String Quartet (1956); 2 *Sonances* for Piano (1956, 1960); *Recherche* for Orch. (1956); *Indicatif 1* for 12 Strings (1957); *Sonance* for Clavichord (1959); *Sinfonia scolastica pour les bouffons de la Reine* (1961); *Serenade* for Chamber Orch. (1961); *Chansons et reveries* for Violin and Piano (1962); Organ Concerto (1963); *Ballade* for Violin and Piano (1966); *Prelude, Fugue et Rondo a 5* for Wind Quintet (1967); *Sonancelle* for Solo Guitar (1967); *Rossignolet du bois* for Orch. (1971); *Prélude, Fugue et Commentaires* for 4 Clarinets (1971).

Roland-Manuel, Alexis (real name, **Roland Alexis Manuel Lévy**), French composer and writer; b. Paris, March 22, 1891; d. there, Nov. 1, 1966. He was a pupil of Albert Roussel and Vincent d'Indy; also studied privately with Ravel. In 1947 he became a prof. at the Paris Cons. In his compositions he adopted the French neo-Classical style, close to Roussel's manner; however, it is not as a composer but as a perspicacious critic that he became chiefly known. He publ. 3 books on Ravel: *Maurice Ravel et son œuvre* (1914), *Maurice Ravel et son œuvre dramatique* (1928), *Maurice Ravel* (1938; in Eng., London, 1947); also monographs on Honegger (1925) and Manuel de Falla (1930).

WORKS: *Isabelle et Pantalon,* opéra-bouffe (Paris, Dec. 11, 1922); *Le Diable amoureux,* light opera (1929); *L'Ecran des jeunes filles,* ballet (Paris Opéra, May 16, 1929); *Elvire,* ballet on themes of Scarlatti (Paris Opéra, Feb. 8, 1937); Piano Concerto (1938); *Cantique de la sagesse* for Chorus and Orch. (1951); oratorio, *Jeanne d'Arc* (1937).

Rolandi, Gianna, gifted American soprano; b. New York, Aug. 16, 1952. Her first contact with opera came through her mother, herself a singer, and by the age of 15 she had already become acquainted with much of the operatic repertoire. She then enrolled at the Curtis Inst. of Music in Philadelphia and, while still a student, was awarded a contract to sing at the N.Y. City Opera, with which she made an impressive debut in 1975. On Dec. 26, 1979, she sang with the Metropolitan Opera in N.Y. as Sophie in *Der Rosenkavalier*. In 1982 she sang the title role in a televised production of *Lucia di Lammermoor* with the N.Y. City Opera, receiving flattering notices from the press.

Roldán, Amadeo, Cuban violinist and composer; b. Paris (of Cuban parents), July 12, 1900; d. Havana, March 2, 1939. He studied violin at the Madrid Cons. with Fernández Bordas, graduating in 1916; won the Sarasate Violin Prize; subsequently studied composition with Conrado del Campo in Madrid and with Pedro Sanjuán. In 1921 he settled in Havana; in 1924, became concertmaster of the Orquesta Filarmónica there; in 1925, assistant conductor; in 1932, conductor. In his works he employed with signal success the melorhythms of Afro-Cuban popular music; as a mulatto, he had an innate understanding of these elements.
WORKS: *La Rebambaramba,* a ballet, employing a number of Cuban percussion instruments in the score; a suite from this ballet (Havana, Aug. 12, 1928); *Obertura sobre témas cubanos* (Havana, Nov. 29, 1925); *El Milagro de Anaquillé* (Havana, Sept. 22, 1929); *Danza negra* for Voice and 7 Instruments (1929); *Motivos de son* for Voice and 9 Instruments (1930); 3 *Toques* for Chamber Orch. (1931); 6 *Rítmicas*: Nos. 1–4 for Piano and Wind Quintet, Nos. 5 and 6 for Percussion Ensemble.

Rolfe Johnson, Anthony, English tenor; b. Tackley, Nov. 5, 1940. He studied voice in London at the Guildhall School of Music. His first major role was with the English Opera Group in 1973. He subsequently established himself as a leading concert singer; also sang opera with the English National Opera and the Welsh National Opera, and periodically at the Glyndebourne Festivals. He handles a varied operatic repertoire with assurance and taste.

Rolla, Alessandro, Italian violinist, Paganini's teacher; b. Pavia, April 6, 1757; d. Milan, Sept. 15, 1841. He was a pupil of Renzi and Conti; from 1782 till 1802 he was concertmaster of the ducal orch. in Parma; Paganini studied with him there. He served as first violinist and director of the orch. at La Scala in Milan from 1803 to 1833; in 1805 was appointed violinist to the French Viceroy Eugène Beauharnais, in Milan; he was a prof. at the Cons. of Milan from its foundation in 1808 until 1835.
WORKS: Ballets: *Adelasia* (Milan, 1779); *Iserbeck* (Padua, 1802); *Eloisa e Roberto* or *Il Conte d'Essex* (Rome, 1805); *Pizzarro* (Milan, 1807); *Abdul* (Vienna, 1808); *Achilles auf Skyros* (Vienna, 1808); symphs.; 3 violin concertos; 4 viola concertos; 6 string quartets; trios for Violin, Viola, and Cello, also for 2 Violins and Cello; other chamber music.
BIBLIOGRAPHY: G. Zampieri, *L'epoca e l'arte di Alessandro Rolla* (Pavia, 1941).

Rolla, Antonio, Italian violinist, son of **Alessandro**

Rolla; b. Parma, April 18, 1798; d. Dresden, May 19, 1837. He studied with his father; was concertmaster of the orch. of the Italian Opera Co. in Dresden (1823–35); composed a number of violin pieces.

Rolland, Romain, famous French author and musicologist; b. Clamecy, Nièvre, Jan. 29, 1866; d. Vézelay, Yonne, Dec. 30, 1944. He was educated at the Ecole de Rome; received his doctorat ès lettres from the Univ. of Paris in Sorbonne (1895) with 2 theses, *Cur ars picturae apud Italos XVI saeculi deciderit* and the very valuable *Les Origines du théâtre lyrique moderne* (*Histoire de l'opéra en Europe avant Lully et Scarlatti;* 4th ed., 1936); the latter was awarded the Prix Kastner-Bourgault by the Academy in 1896, and at the same time won him the professorship in the history of music at the Ecole Normale. In 1900 he organized the first international congress for the history of music in Paris, and read a paper on *Les Musiciens italiens en France sous Mazarin et "l'Orfeo" de Luigi Rossi* (publ. 1901); with J. Combarieu he edited the transactions and the papers read as *Documents, mémoires et vœux* (1901). In Oct. 1901 he founded, with J. Combarieu (editor), P. Aubry, M. Emmanuel, L. Laloy, and himself as principal contributors, the fortnightly *Revue d'Histoire et Critique Musicales.* In 1903 the Univ. of Paris commissioned him to organize the music section of the newly founded Ecole des Hautes Etudes Sociales, of which he was the first president, and where he lectured on the history of music; resigned in 1909, devoting his entire time to literary work. From 1913 he resided in Switzerland, but in 1938 returned to France and took up his residence at Vézelay.

Rolland's writings exhibit sound scholarship, broad sympathy, keen analytical power, well-balanced judgment, and intimate acquaintance with the musical milieu of his time. The book by which he is most widely known is *Jean-Christophe,* a musical novel remarkable for its blending of historical accuracy, psychological and esthetic speculation, subtle psychological analysis, and romantic interest; for it he received the Nobel Prize (1915). The first vol. was publ. in 1905, the last (10th) in 1912 (Eng. trans., N.Y., 1910–13). Rolland's other works include *Paris als Musikstadt* (1904; in Strauss's series Die Musik; rewritten and publ. in French as *Le Renouveau* in *Musiciens d'aujourd'hui*); *Beethoven* (Paris, 1903; 3rd ed., 1927, as *La Vie de Beethoven;* Eng. trans., 1969); *La Vie de Haendel* (Paris, 1906; 2nd ed., 1910; Eng. trans., 1916; revised and enlarged by F. Raugel, 1974); *Voyage musical au pays du passé* (1920; in Eng., 1922); *Beethoven: Les Grandes Époques créatrices* (4 vols., Paris, 1928–45; Eng. trans., 1964); *Goethe et Beethoven* (1930; in Eng., 1931); *Beethoven: Le Chant de la Résurrection* (1937; on the *Missa solemnis* and the last sonatas); essays in various journals he collected and publ. in 2 vols. as *Musiciens d'autrefois* (1908; 6th ed., 1919; in Eng., 1915) and *Musiciens d'aujourd'hui* (1908; 8th ed., 1947; in Eng., 1914); *Essays on Music* (a selection from some of the above books; N.Y., 1948).
BIBLIOGRAPHY: P. Seippel, *Romain Rolland:*

L'Homme et l'œuvre (Paris, 1913); Stefan Zweig, *Romain Rolland: Der Mann und das Werk* (Frankfurt, 1921; in Eng., N.Y., 1921); J. Bonnerot, *Romain Rolland, Sa vie, son œuvre* (Paris, 1921); E. Lerch, *Romain Rolland und die Erneuerung der Gesinnung* (Munich, 1926); M. Lob, *Un Grand Bourguignon, Romain Rolland* (Auxerre, 1927); C. Sénéchal, *Romain Rolland* (Paris, 1933); M. Doisy, *Romain Rolland* (Brussels, 1945); R. Argos, *Romain Rolland* (Paris, 1950); W.T. Starr, *A Critical Bibliography of the Published Writings of Romain Rolland* (Evanston, Ill., 1950); J. Robichez, *Romain Rolland* (Paris, 1961); E. Bondeville, *Romain Rolland à la recherche de l'homme dans la création artistique* (Paris, 1966); *Richard Strauss and Romain Rolland: Correspondence,* ed. by R. Myers (London, 1968).

Rolle, Johann Heinrich, German composer; b. Quedlinburg, Dec. 23, 1716; d. Magdeburg, Dec. 29, 1785. He was an organist in Magdeburg (1732–36); played violin and later viola in the Berlin court orch. (1741–47); then returned to Magdeburg as organist at the Johanniskirche; in 1751 became his father's successor as town music director there. He wrote 6 Passions, 23 oratorios, several church services for the entire year; *Odes of Anacreon* for Voice and Harpsichord; etc.
BIBLIOGRAPHY: W. Kawerau, *J.H. Rolle. Ein musikalisches Characterbild* (Magdeburg, 1885); H. von Hase, "J.H. Rolle," *Zeitschrift für Musikwissenschaft,* 2; R. Kaestner, *J.H. Rolle* (Kassel, 1932).

Röllig, Carl Leopold, Austrian composer and inventor; b. Hamburg, c.1735; d. Vienna, March 4, 1804. He was a harmonica player; invented the "Orphika" and "Xänorphika" (pianos with bows instead of hammers), and made many tours, in an attempt to popularize them. In 1791 he settled in Vienna. He wrote a comic opera, *Clarisse* (Hamburg, Oct. 10, 1771); publ. the pamphlets *Über die Harmonika* (1787) and *Über die Orphika* (1795).

Rollin, Jean, French composer; b. Paris, Aug. 3, 1906; d. France, Aug. 30, 1977. He studied composition at the Paris Cons. with Noël Gallon, and musicology with Pirro and Masson. His works include a Concerto for Piano and Strings (1947); a Violin Concerto (1950); a Concerto for Double Bass and Orch. (1951); 2 symphs. (1953, 1958); the opera *Gringouê* (1965); chamber music; songs.

Rollins, "Sonny" (Theodore Walter Rollins), black American jazz tenor saxophonist; b. New York, Sept. 7, 1929. He first worked with Babs Gonzales, Bud Powell, and Fats Navarro; then went to Chicago, where he studied with Ike Day. After making recordings with Miles Davis, he made appearances with Charlie Parker, Thelonious Monk, and other leading jazz musicians; also served as a member of the Modern Jazz Quartet. At the height of his career, he ranked among the foremost masters of the tenor saxophone.

Rolón, José, Mexican composer; b. Ciudad Guzmán, Jalisco, June 22, 1883; d. Mexico City, Feb. 3, 1945. He studied in Paris with Moszkowski, and later with Nadia Boulanger and Dukas. In Mexico he was active as a teacher. He composed a symph. poem, *Cuauhtémoc* (Mexico City, Jan. 10, 1930); symph. suite, *Zapotlán* (Mexico City, Nov. 4, 1932); Piano Concerto (Mexico City, Sept. 4, 1942); many effective piano pieces.

Roman, Johan Helmich, significant Swedish composer; b. Stockholm, Oct. 26, 1694; d. Haraldsmala, near Kalmar, Nov. 20, 1758. He was of Finnish ethnic origin; began playing the violin as a mere child, and at 16 was already a member of the court orch., where his father, **Johan Roman,** was concertmaster. In 1715 he traveled to England, where he took lessons with Ariosti and Pepusch in London; returned to Stockholm in 1721. In 1727 he was appointed conductor of the court orch.; from 1735 to 1737 he traveled in Europe; in 1740 he was named a member of the Swedish Academy, and in 1745 retired from active work. Roman was the first Swedish composer to write instrumental and choral music that could compare favorably with German and Italian works, and was for that reason called "the father of Swedish music." His style shows the influence of Handel, with whom he became personally acquainted in England.
WORKS: Two sets of Roman's numerous compositions were publ. during his lifetime, *12 sonate a flauto traverso, violone e cembalo* (1727) and *Assaggio a violino solo* (1740). A great number of his works in MS are preserved in various Swedish libraries, among them 21 *sinfonie,* 2 *sinfonie da chiesa,* 6 overtures, 5 suites, 2 concerti grossi, 5 violin concertos, about 20 violin sonatas, 17 trio sonatas, etc.; of these several were publ. in modern times; an edition of his collected works was begun in Stockholm in 1965 in the series Monumenta Musicae Svecicae; I. Bengtsson ed. *Mr. Roman's Spuriosity Shop: A Thematic Catalogue of 503 Works . . . from ca. 1680–1750* (Stockholm, 1976).
BIBLIOGRAPHY: P. Vretblad, *J.H. Roman Svenska musikens fader* (2 vols., Stockholm, 1914; vol. II contains complete thematic catalogue); C.A. Moberg, *J.H. Roman* (Stockholm, 1944); I. Bengtsson, *J.H. Roman och hans Instrumentalmusik* (Uppsala, 1955); G. Carleberg, *Buxtehude, Telemann och Roman* (Stockholm, 1965).

Roman, Stella (original name, **Florica Vierica Alma Stela Blasu**), Rumanian soprano; b. Cluj, March 25, 1904. She studied in Cluj, Bucharest, and Milan; made her debut in Piacenza in 1932; then sang at the Rome Opera and at La Scala in Milan. On Jan. 1, 1941, she made her Metropolitan Opera debut in N.Y. as Aida; she remained on its roster until 1950. She was best known for her roles in Italian operas.

Romani, Carlo, Italian composer; b. Avelino, May 24, 1824; d. Florence, March 4, 1875. He studied with Palafuti (piano) and Picchianti (composition); completed his studies under his uncle, **Pietro Romani;** set to music the recitatives of *Der Freischütz* for its first Italian performance (Florence, Feb. 3, 1843); wrote operas (all produced at Florence): *Tutti amanti* (1847); *Il Mantello* (1852; successful); *I Baccanali di Roma* (1854); *Ermellina ossia Le Gemme della corona* (1865); an oratorio, *San Sebastiano* (1864); various patriotic songs.

Romani, Felice, renowned Italian librettist; b. Genoa, Jan. 31, 1788; d. Moneglia, Jan. 28, 1865. He wrote about 100 librettos for Mayr, Winter, Vaccai, Rossini, Bellini, Donizetti, Pacini, Ricci, etc.

BIBLIOGRAPHY: F. Regli, *Elogio a Felice Romani* (Turin, 1865); L. Lianovosani, *Saggio bibliografico relativo ai melodrammi di Felice Romani* (Milan, 1878); E. Branca (Romani's wife), *Felice Romani ed i più riputati maestri di musica del suo tempo* (Turin, 1882); C. Paschetto, *Felice Romani* (Turin, 1907); M. Rinaldi, *Felice Romani* (Rome, 1965).

Romani, Pietro, Italian composer; b. Rome, May 29, 1791; d. Florence, Jan. 11, 1877. He studied with Fenaroli; became conductor at the Teatro della Pergola in Florence; taught singing at the Istituto Musicale there. He wrote 2 operas, *Il Qui pro quo* (Rome, 1817) and *Carlo Magno* (Florence, 1823); also ballet music; he is remembered chiefly for his aria *Manca un foglio,* for Bartolo in *Il Barbiere de Siviglia,* which he wrote for the production of the opera in Florence in 1816 as a substitute for Rossini's original aria *A un dottor della mia sorte,* which presented some vocal difficulties. Romani's aria was long retained in many productions of the opera.

Romberg, Andreas (Jacob), German violinist and composer; b. Vechta, near Münster, April 27, 1767; d. Gotha, Nov. 10, 1821. He was the son of the clarinetist and music director **Gerhard Heinrich Romberg** (1745–1819); played in public at 7; in 1784 made a concert tour with his cousin **Bernhard Romberg** through the Netherlands and France, remaining in Paris as soloist for the Concert Spirituel during that season. From 1790 to 1793 he played in the Electoral orch. at Bonn with Bernhard; toured in Italy with him; lived many years in Hamburg (1801–15), and then succeeded Spohr as court Kapellmeister at Gotha.

WORKS: Operas: *Der Rabe* (Hamburg, April 7, 1794); *Die Ruinen zu Paluzzi* (Hamburg, Dec. 27, 1811); *Die Grossmut des Scipio* (Gotha, 1816); singspiels; choral works, with Orch.; church music; 10 symphs.; 23 violin concertos; 33 string quartets; 8 flute quintets, with Strings; Clarinet Quintet; 2 string quintets; Piano Quartet; 3 violin sonatas; 11 rondos and caprices for Violin; Concertante for Violin and Cello, with Orch.; etc. His *Toy Symphony* was popular for a time, as was his setting of Schiller's *Lied von der Glocke.*

BIBLIOGRAPHY: J.F. Rochlitz, *Für Freunde der Tonkunst* (vol. 1, Leipzig, 1824); K. Stephenson, *Andreas Romberg* (Hamburg, 1938).

Romberg, Bernhard, German cellist and composer; b. Dinklage, Nov. 11, 1767; d. Hamburg, Aug. 13, 1841. He was the son of **Bernhard Anton Romberg,** famous bassoonist (1742–1814), who took him to Paris in 1781; he remained there for 2 years; played in the court orch. at Bonn (1790–93); then traveled in Spain; was the constant companion of his cousin **Andreas Romberg;** in 1796 they played at a concert with Beethoven in Vienna. Romberg was appointed prof. of cello playing at the Paris Cons. in 1801, but resigned in 1803. He was then in Hamburg and Berlin; in 1807 toured in Russia; paid a visit to England (1814); then was court Kapellmeister in Berlin (1815–19); was subsequently in Vienna (1822–25) and again in Russia (1825); lived in Paris (1839–40) before retiring to Hamburg.

WORKS: For the cello he wrote 9 concertos, 3 concertinos, a Fantasia with Orch., 4 sets of Russian airs with Orch., caprices and fantasias on Swedish, Spanish, and Rumanian airs, and polonaises. In Berlin he publ. a cello method (1840); also brought out several operas: *Ulysses und Circe* (Berlin, July 27, 1807); *Rittertreue* (Berlin, Jan. 31, 1817); *Alma* (Copenhagen, May 15, 1824); etc.; 11 string quartets; other chamber music.

BIBLIOGRAPHY: H. Schäfer, *Bernhard Romberg* (Münster, 1931).

Romberg, Sigmund, famous operetta composer; b. Nagy Kaniza, Hungary, July 29, 1887; d. New York, Nov. 9, 1951. He studied at the Univ. of Bucharest and in Vienna (with Heuberger); in 1909 came to the U.S. as an engineer, later turning to composition; settled in N.Y. in 1913. He composed over 70 operettas, including *The Midnight Girl* (Feb. 23, 1914; his first success); *The Blue Paradise* (with E. Eysler; N.Y., Aug. 5, 1915); *Maytime* (N.Y., Aug. 16, 1917); *Blossom Time* (on Schubert's melodies; N.Y., Sept. 29, 1921); *The Rose of Stamboul* (March 7, 1922); *The Student Prince* (N.Y., Dec. 2, 1924); *The Desert Song* (N.Y., Nov. 30, 1926); *My Maryland* (N.Y., Sept. 12, 1927); *The New Moon* (Sept. 19, 1928); *Up in Central Park* (N.Y., Jan. 27, 1945).

BIBLIOGRAPHY: E. Arnold, *Deep in My Heart* (a biography in the form of a novel, N.Y., 1949). See R. Crawford in *Dictionary of American Biography,* Supplement V.

Romero, Mateo (real name, **Matthieu Rosmarin**), Spanish composer; b. Liège, 1575; d. Madrid, May 10, 1647. He was a soldier and was often called "El Maestro Capitán." After serving with the Spanish army in Flanders, he became cantor of the Chapel Royal in Madrid (1593), and was maestro de capilla in 1598–1634; in 1609 he was ordained a priest. In 1638 he went to Portugal as emissary to the Duke of Braganza (the future Emperor João IV). He enjoyed a reputation as one of the finest composers of both sacred and secular music of his time. Twenty–two works by Romero for 3–4 Voices are included in the *Cancionero de Sablonara* (modern ed. by J. Arcoa, Madrid, 1918); other compositions are found in Diego Pizarro's collection *Libro de tonos humanos* and in Pedrell's *Teatro lírico español,* III (La Coruña, 1896–98); a motet, *Libera me,* was included by Eslava in his collection *Lira sacro-hispana.*

BIBLIOGRAPHY: R.A. Pelinski, *Die weltliche Vokalmusik Spaniens am Anfang des 17. Jahrhunderts, der Cancionero de la Sablonara* (Tutzing, 1971).

Romeu, Luis, Spanish composer; b. Vich, near Barcelona, June 21, 1874; d. there, Sept. 23, 1937. A priest, he was first choirmaster, then organist, at the Cathedral in Vich. His works, which show the influence of Catalan folk song, include a Mass for the *Mare de Deu de Nuria* and *Cants catequistics et Marianes* (3 collections). He publ. a book on Catalan church music, *La Versio auténtica dels Goigs del Roser de tot l'any* (vol. I of *Obra del Cançoner popular de Catalunya;* Barcelona, 1928). The total number of his works, secular and sacred, is 331.

Römhildt, Johann Theodor, German organist and composer; b. Salzungen, Sept. 23, 1684; d. Merseburg, Oct. 26, 1756. He studied with Johann Jakob Bach in Ruhla; in 1697 entered the Thomasschule in Leipzig, where he was a pupil of Schelle and Kuhnau; subsequently served as cantor at Spremberg, Freystadt, and Merseburg; in 1731 was appointed court musician in Merseburg, and in 1735 Cathedral organist there. He composed 238 church cantatas, 19 secular cantatas, 2 oratorios, 2 masses, a *St. Matthew Passion* (which was publ. in 1921 in Leipzig), motets and some instrumental works.
BIBLIOGRAPHY: Karl Paulke, "J.T. Römhildt," *Archiv für Musikwissenschaft* 1 (1919).

Ronald, Sir Landon (real name, **L.R. Russell**), English conductor; b. London, June 7, 1873; d. there, Aug. 14, 1938. He was a son of the composer **Henry Russell, Sr.** and brother of the impresario **Henry Russell, Jr.** He entered the Royal College of Music, where he studied composition with Sir Charles Parry and also attended the classes of Sir Charles Stanford and Sir Walter Parratt. He first embarked on a concert career as a pianist, but soon turned to conducting light opera and summer symph. concerts. In 1909 he was appointed conductor of the New Symph. Orch. in London (later named Royal Albert Hall Orch.); from 1910 until his death he was principal of the Guildhall School of Music. He was knighted in 1922. He composed an operetta, *A Capital Joke;* a ballet, *Britannia's Realm* (1902; for the coronation of King Edward VII); and a scenic spectacle, *Entente cordiale* (1904; to celebrate the triple alliance of Russia, France, and England); about 300 songs. He publ. 2 autobiographical books: *Variations on a Personal Theme* (London, 1922) and *Myself and Others* (London, 1931).

Roncaglia, Gino, Italian musicologist; b. Modena, May 7, 1883; d. there, Nov. 27, 1968. He studied with Sinigaglia; devoted himself to musical biography.
WRITINGS: *Giuseppe Verdi* (Naples, 1914); 2nd ed., revised, 1940, as *L'ascensione creatice di Giuseppe Verdi;* 3rd ed., 1951); *La Rivoluzione musicale italiana* (Milan, 1928); *Rossini l'Olimpico* (Milan, 1946; 2nd ed., 1953); *Invito alla musica* (Milan, 1947; 4th ed., 1958); *Invito all' opera* (Milan, 1949;

4th ed., 1958); *La Cappella musicale del Duomo di Modena* (Florence, 1957); *Galleria verdiana: Studi e figure* (Milan, 1959).

Ronconi, Domenico, famous Italian tenor and singing teacher; b. Lendinara, July 11, 1772; d. Milan, April 13, 1839. He was a successful opera tenor; sang in Italy, France, Germany, and Russia. In 1829 he opened a singing school in Milan; publ. vocal exercises that were widely used. His son, **Giorgio Ronconi** (b. Milan, Aug. 6, 1810; d. Madrid, Jan. 8, 1890), was a well-known baritone; spent some years in N.Y. (from 1867).

Ronga, Luigi, eminent Italian musicologist; b. Turin, June 19, 1901. He studied at the Univ. of Turin and in Dresden; in 1926 became a prof. at the Cons. of Palermo; later joined the faculty of the Santa Cecilia Academy in Rome (1930); became a lecturer at the Univ. of Rome in 1938, and was a prof. there from 1950–71.
WRITINGS: He publ. an excellent monograph on Frescobaldi (Turin, 1930); also one on Rossini (Florence, 1939) and essays on other Italian composers; *Bach, Mozart, Beethoven; Tre problemi critici* (Venice, 1956); *Arte e gusto nella musica, dell'ars nova a Debussy* (Milan, 1956); *The Meeting of Poetry and Music* (N.Y., 1956); *La musica nell'età barocca* (Rome, 1959); *Il linguaggio musicale romantico* (Rome, 1960); *La musica europea nella seconda metà dell'Ottocento* (Rome, 1961).

Rongé, Jean-Baptiste, Belgian composer and translator; b. Liège, April 1, 1825; d. there, Oct. 28, 1882. He was a pupil at the Liège Cons.; won the 2nd Belgian Prix de Rome (1851); wrote occasional cantatas and other pieces; a meeting with the poet André van Hasselt directed his interests toward literary work; in collaboration they translated into French the librettos of *Don Giovanni, Zauberflöte, Freischütz, Barbiere di Siviglia,* and other famous operas. After van Hasselt's death (1874), Rongé returned to composing, producing a comic opera, *La Comtesse d'Albany* (Liège, 1877); also wrote some choruses and songs, and 24 *Etudes rythmiques* (for Voice).

Ronnefeld, Peter, German composer and conductor; b. Dresden, Jan. 26, 1935; d. Kiel, Aug. 6, 1965. He studied with Blacher in Berlin and Messiaen in Paris; was chorus conductor at the Vienna State Opera (1958–61); served as chief conductor at the Theater der Stadt Bonn (1961–63); then was Generalmusikdirektor in Kiel from 1963 until his death. As a conductor, he specialized in modern music, but he also excelled in the Romantic repertoire; his own opera, *Die Ameise* (Düsseldorf, Oct. 21, 1961), had a fine reception. He further wrote Concertino for Flute, Clarinet, Horn, Bassoon, and String Orch. (1950); *Sinfonie '52* (1952); *Rondo* for Orch. (1954); 2 *Episodes* for Chamber Orch. (1956); cantata, *Quartär* (1958); ballet, *Die Spirale* (1961). His early death was lamented.

Ronstadt, Linda, spectacular American pop singer; b. Tucson, Ariz., July 15, 1946. She filled jobs singing with her brother Pete and sister Suzi in local pizza parlors in Tucson; after a semester at the Univ. of Arizona she went to Los Angeles, where she formed a group, The Stone Poneys, and soon began singing for discs. In her song selection, she ranges from country-western through resurrected Motown classics to "new wave"; in 1972 she put out an album, ambitiously announced as *Linda Ronstadt*. In 1973 she toured with Neil Young. Several hits followed, and it became clear to her and her public that she had a magic touch; she sang at President Carter's inauguration. In 1980 she hit the front pages when Gov. Jerry Brown of California took her on an African safari trip; also in 1980, she expanded her repertoire to include the Broadway stage by appearing in the role of Mabel in the centennial anniversary production of Gilbert and Sullivan's *Pirates of Penzance*. Her greatest hits included *Different Drum* (recorded with The Stone Poneys); *Love Has No Pride, Faithless Love, Blue Bayou, I Never Will Marry,* and *Alison.*

Röntgen, Julius, important German-Dutch composer; b. Leipzig, May 9, 1855; d. Bilthoven, near Utrecht, Sept. 13, 1932. He studied music with his father, Engelbert Röntgen (1829–97); later with Plaidy and Reinecke in Leipzig and F. Lachner in Munich. In 1877–1925 he taught in Amsterdam; was conductor of the Society for the Promotion of Music (1886–98); was a co-founder (1884) of the Amsterdam Cons., and its director from 1914 to 1924. He was a friend of Brahms and Grieg; edited the letters of Brahms to T. Engelmann (1918); publ. a biography of Grieg (1930). An astonishingly industrious composer, he wrote an enormous amount of music in every genre, cast in an expansive Romantic style: 12 symphs.; 3 piano concertos; 3 operas (*Agnete, Samum,* and *Der lachende Kavalier*); much chamber music; etc.; edited old Dutch keyboard compositions (vol. 37 of the *Vereeniging voor Nederlandsche Muziekgeschiedenis*) and 14 songs by Adrianus Valerius. His correspondence was publ. by his widow (1934).

Rooley, Anthony, English lutenist; b. Leeds, June 10, 1944. He studied guitar at the Royal Academy of Music in London, but was self-taught as a lutenist. In 1969 he organized (with James Tyler) the Consort of Musicke, an ensemble devoted to the performance of Renaissance music. He was the editor of *The Penguin Book of Early Music* (Harmondsworth, 1980).

Roos, Robert de, Dutch composer; b. The Hague, March 10, 1907; d. March 18, 1976. He studied composition with Johan Wagenaar at his local Royal Cons.; then went to Paris, where he studied composition with Koechlin, Roland-Manuel, and Milhaud, piano with Isidor Philipp, and conducting with Monteux (1926–34); returning to the Netherlands, he worked with Sem Dresden. He served as a cultural attaché at the Netherlands Embassy in Paris (1947–56); then was First Secretary for Press and Cultural Affairs in Caracas (1957–62), London (1962–67), and Buenos Aires (1967).
WORKS: Chamber oratorio after Omar Khayyám (1928); *5 Etudes* for Piano and Small Orch. (1929); *Mouvement symphonique* (1930); ballet, *Kaartspel (Card Game;* 1934); dance pantomime, *Landelijke Comedie (Pastoral Comedy)* for Orch. (1937–39); *Lyrische suite* for Chorus and Small Orch. (1938); Violin Concertino (1939); *Danses* for Flute and Small Orch. (1940); Viola Concerto (1941–42); Sinfonietta (1943); *Sinfonia romantica (Museum-Symphonie)* for Chamber Orch. (1943); Piano Concerto (1943–44); *Adam in ballingschap* for 2 Narrators, 2 Flutes, 2 Horns, and Strings (1944); *Quo Vadis,* suite for Orch. (1947); *Variations sérieuses sur un thème ingénu* for Orch. (1947); *De getemde Mars* for Chorus and Orch. (1948); 2 violin concertos (1949–50, 1956–58); Sinfonia No. 2 (1952); *Suggestioni* for Orch. (1961); *Composizioni* for Orch. (1962); *Sinfonia in 2 moti* for String Orch. (1968); *Postrema Verba,* cantata for Baritone, Chorus, and 25 Instruments (1969); *2 Songs* for Baritone and Instruments (1971); *Musica* for Violins, Cellos, and Double Basses (1971); *Rapsodie e Danza* for 2 Flutes and Orch. (1972–73); *3 Romantic Songs* for Soprano and Orch. (1975); Sextet for Piano and Winds (1935); 7 string quartets (1941; 1942; 1944–45; 1945–49; 1951; 1969–70; *Quartettino,* 1971); Solo Violin Sonata (1943); *Introduction, Adagio and Allegro* for 2 Violins (1945); Violin Sonata (1946); *Capriccio* for Clarinet and Piano (1952); *Distrazioni* for Violin and Piano (1953); *3 pezzi senza nome* for Piano Quartet (1958); Trio for 2 Violins and Cello (1965); *4 per 2* for Oboe and Viola (1966); *Incidenze* for Flute, Cello or Viola da Gamba, and Harpsichord (1966–67); *Incontri* for Wind Quintet (1966); Piano Trio (1968); *2 moti lenti* for 2 Violins and Cello (1970); *4 pezzi* for Wind Trio (1970–71); incidental music for Classical dramas.

Root, Frederick Woodman, American organist and writer on music, son of **George Frederick Root;** b. Boston, June 13, 1846; d. Chicago, Nov. 8, 1916. He was taught by his father, then by Dr. B.C. Blodgett and William Mason in N.Y. In 1863 he became organist of the 3rd Presbyterian Church in Chicago; in 1865, of the Swedenborgian Church; in 1869–70 traveled in Europe, studying singing with Vannuccini in Florence. He publ. *The Technic and Art of Singing, Methodical Sight-Singing, Introductory Lessons in Voice Culture, The Polychrome Lessons in Voice Culture, Resources of Musical Expression, A Study of Musical Taste, The Real American Music;* composed anthems, cantatas, songs.

Root, George Frederick, American composer and publisher; b. Sheffield, Mass., Aug. 30, 1820; d. Bailey's Island, Maine, Aug. 6, 1895. He was a pupil of George J. Webb in Boston; then lived in N.Y.; was organist of the Church of the Strangers. Going to Chicago in 1859, he joined the music publishing firm of Root and Cady, established in 1858 by his elder brother, Ebenezer Towner Root, and Chauncey Marvin Cady; it was dissolved in 1871. He wrote many popular songs (*Battlecry of Freedom; Tramp, tramp, tramp; Just before the battle, Mother*); publ. numerous collections of church music and school songs. For some of his earlier compositions he used the German translation of his name, **Friedrich Wurzel,** as a pseudonym.

BIBLIOGRAPHY: His autobiography, *The Story of a Musical Life* (Cincinnati, 1891); D.J. Epstein, "Music Publishing in Chicago before 1871: The Firm of Root and Cady, 1858–1871," *Notes* (June 1944 through June 1946; reprinted in one vol., *Detroit Studies in Music Bibliography*, 14, Detroit, 1969).

Rootham, Cyril Bradley, English organist and composer; b. Bristol, Oct. 5, 1875; d. Cambridge, March 18, 1938. He studied music with his father, Daniel Rootham (1837–1922); won classical and musical scholarships at St. John's College (Mus.Bac., 1900; A.M., 1901; Mus.Doc., 1910); finished at the Royal College of Music under Sir Charles Stanford and Sir Walter Parratt. From 1901 till his death he was organist at St. John's College, Cambridge; also conductor of the Univ. Musical Society there (1912–36).

WORKS: His career as a composer was also bound with the musical life in Cambridge; he brought out there his opera *The 2 Sisters,* on Feb. 14, 1922; *For the Fallen* for Chorus and Orch. (1919); *Brown Earth* (perf. by the musical societies of Oxford and Cambridge Univs., Albert Hall, London, March 14, 1923). His 2nd Symph. (with a choral ending) was performed posthumously by the BBC, March 17, 1939. Other works include *Pan,* rhapsody for Orch. (1912); String Quintet (1909); String Quartet (1914); Septet for Viola, Flute, Oboe, Clarinet, Bassoon, Horn, and Harp (1930); Piano Trio (1931).

Ropartz, (Joseph) Guy (Marie), French composer; b. Guingamp, Côtes-du-Nord, June 15, 1864; d. Lanloup-par-Plouha, Côtes-du-Nord, Nov. 22, 1955. He entered the Paris Cons. as a pupil of Dubois and Massenet; then took lessons in organ and composition from César Franck, who remained his chief influence in composition; from 1894 until 1919, was director of the Cons. and conductor of the symph. concerts at Nancy; from 1919 to 1929 conducted the Municipal Orch. in Strasbourg; after that lived in retirement in Lanloup-par-Plouha.

WORKS: FOR THE STAGE: 3-act opera, *Le Pays* (Nancy, Feb. 1, 1912; Paris Opéra, April 14, 1913; his most important stage work); incidental music for Pierre Loti's *Pêcheur d'Islande* (1889–91) and *Le Mystère de Saint Nicolas,* a legend in 13 scenes (1905). FOR ORCH.: 5 symphs.: No. 1 (1895); No. 2 (1900); No. 3, with Chorus (1906); No. 4 (1910); No. 5 (1945); *La Cloche des morts* (1887); *Les Landes* (1888); *Marche de Fête* (1888); *5 pièces brèves* (1889); *Carnaval* (1889); *Sérénade* (1892); *Dimanche breton* (1893); *A Marie endormie* (1912); *La Chasse du prince Arthur* (1912); *Soir sur les Chaumes* (1913); *Divertissement* (1915); *Sérénade champêtre* (Paris, Feb. 24, 1934); *Pastorale et Danse* for Oboe and Orch. (1907); *Romanza e Scherzino* for Violin and Orch. (1926); *Rapsodie* for Cello and Orch. (Paris, Nov. 3, 1928). SACRED MUSIC FOR CHORUS: 5 motets a cappella (1900); 3 masses; Requiem for Soloists, Chorus, and Orch. (Paris, April 7, 1939); *De Profundis* for Solo Voice, Chorus, and Orch. (1942); etc. CHAMBER MUSIC: 6 string quartets (1893, 1912, 1925, 1934, 1940, 1951); Piano Trio (1918); String Trio (1935); 3 violin sonatas; 2 cello sonatas. FOR PIANO: *Dans l'ombre de la montagne* (1913); *Musiques au jardin* (1917); *Croquis d'été* (1918); *Croquis d'automne* (1929); *Jeunes filles* (1929); *3 nocturnes;* etc.; many organ pieces. SONGS: *Chrysanthèmes, La Mer, Paysage, Tes yeux, De tous les temps, Poème d'adieu, En mai, Chanson de bord, Il pleut, Au bord d'un ruisseau, Douloureux mensonge, La Vieille Maison,* etc. PEDAGOGIC WORKS AND OTHER WRITINGS: *Enseignement du Solfège, Leçons d'harmonie,* etc.; *Notations artistiques* (essays; Paris, 1891); also 3 vols. of poems and a play, *La Batte.*

BIBLIOGRAPHY: A. Cœuroy, *La Musique française moderne* (1922); M. Boucher, "Guy Ropartz," *Revue Musicale* (1924); F. Lamy, *J.G. Ropartz, L'Homme et l'œuvre* (Paris, 1948); L. Kornprobst, *J.G. Ropartz* (Strasbourg, 1949); *Livre du centenaire de J.G. Ropartz* (Paris, 1966).

Rore, Cipriano (Cyprian) de, celebrated composer; b. Mechlin or Antwerp, 1516; d. Parma, 1565. He was a pupil of Willaert, maestro at San Marco in Venice; in 1542 publ. his first book of madrigals *a* 5. From about 1547 to 1558 he was in the service of the Duke of Ferrara, Ercole II; visited Antwerp in 1558, and in 1561 was appointed maestro di cappella to Duke Ottavio Farnese at Parma. Upon Willaert's death in 1562, Rore was appointed his successor as maestro di cappella at San Marco, but soon resigned and returned to the court of Parma (July 1564).

WORKS: Publications: 8 books of madrigals, 3 of motets, a Passion according to St. John, *Fantasie e ricercari.* Motets and madrigals are in collections by Susato, Phalèse, and others. In MS (Munich Library) are 3 masses: *Vivat Felix Hercules a 5, Praeter rerum seriem a 7,* and *Missa a note nere a 5;* also motets and madrigals. Reprints in A. Einstein's *The Italian Madrigal* (5 madrigals in vol. 3); A. Schering's *Vier Meister-Madrigale aus dem 16. Jahrhundert* (Leipzig, 1916); Davison and Apel's *Historical Anthology of Music* (vol. 1, no. 131); F. Blume's *Das Chorwerk* (madrigals ed. by W. Wiora in vol. 5; 1930); Madrigals *a* 3 and *a* 4, ed. by Gertrude P. Smith (Northampton, Mass., 1943); G. Tagliapietra's *Antologia di musica antica e moderna per pianoforte* (Milan, 1931); P. de Monte's complete works: vols. 4 (1928), 8 (1929), 23 (1933); A. Schering's *Geschichte der Musik in Beispielen* (no. 106); A. Einstein's *The Golden Age of the Madrigal* (1942); reprints of motets by Commer, Burney, Hawkins, Kiesewetter, Dehn, etc. The *Opera Omnia,* ed. by B. Meier, is issued by The American Inst. of Musicology: motets, vols. 1, 6, and 8; madrigals, vols. 2, 3, and 4; masses, vol. 7; Magnificats and chansons, vol. 8.

BIBLIOGRAPHY: R. van Aerde, *Notice sur la vie et les œuvres de Cipriano de Rore* (Mechlin, 1909);

J. Musiol, *Cipriano de Rore, Ein Meister der venezianischen Schule* (Breslau, 1932); A. Einstein, *The Italian Madrigal* (Princeton, 1949; vol. 1, pp. 384ff.); A. Johnson, "The Masses of Cipriano de Rore," *Journal of the American Musicological Society* (Fall 1953); B. Meier, "Staatskompositionen von Cyprian de Rore," *Tijdschrift van de Vereniging voor Nederlandse Musiekgeschiedenis*, XXI/2 (1969); D. Harrán, "Rore and the *Madrigale Cromatico*," *Music Review* (Feb. 1973).

Rorem, Ned, brilliant American composer; b. Richmond, Ind., Oct. 23, 1923. He received his musical training in Chicago, where he studied with Leo Sowerby at the American Cons.; subsequently attended Northwestern Univ. (1940–42), the Curtis Inst. in Philadelphia (1943), and the Juilliard School of Music in N.Y. (1946); in N.Y. he also took lessons with Virgil Thomson and Aaron Copland. From 1949 to 1951 he lived in Morocco; then moved to Paris, where he stayed until 1957; he entered the circle of modern Parisian composers, and the French influence, particularly in his songs, remains the most pronounced characteristic of his music. Returning to the U.S., he was composer-in-residence at the Univ. of Buffalo (1959–61) and at the Univ. of Utah (1966–67); in 1980 he joined the faculty of the Curtis Inst. of Music. Rorem is regarded as one of the finest song composers in America; he has a natural feeling for the vocal line and for the prosody of the text. A born linguist, he has mastered the French language to perfection; he is also an elegant stylist in English. He publ. a succession of personal journals, recounting with gracious insouciance his encounters in Paris and N.Y.

WORKS: Operas: *A Childhood Miracle* for 6 Voices and 13 Instruments (N.Y., Punch Opera Co., May 10, 1955); *The Robbers* (N.Y., April 15, 1958); *Miss Julie* (N.Y., Nov. 4, 1965); *Bertha* (N.Y., Nov. 26, 1973); Symph. No. 1 (Vienna, 1951); Symph. No. 2 (La Jolla, Calif., Aug. 5, 1956); Symph. No. 3 (N.Y., April 19, 1959); *Design* for Orch. (Louisville, Ky., May 28, 1955); 3 piano concertos (1950, 1951, 1970); *Sinfonia* for Woodwinds and Percussion (Pittsburgh, July 14, 1957); *The Poets' Requiem* for Chorus, Soprano Solo, and Orch., on 8 contemporary poems (N.Y., Feb. 15, 1957); *Eagles,* symph. poem (Philadelphia, Oct. 23, 1959); Trio for Flute, Cello, and Piano (1960); *Lovers,* a "narrative" for Harpsichord, Oboe, Cello, and Percussion (1964); *Sun* for Orch. (N.Y., July 1, 1967); *Assembly and Fall,* symph. poem (1975); *Air Music,* a Bicentennial commission from the Cincinnati Symph. Orch. (Cincinnati, Dec. 5, 1975; received the Pulitzer Prize, 1976); *Book of Hours* for Flute and Harp (1976); 8 piano études (1976); *Serenade* for Voice, Viola, Violin, and Piano (1976); *Sky Music* for Solo Harp (1976); *Women's Voices,* a set of songs (1976); *Romeo and Juliet* for Flute and Guitar (1977); 2 string quartets; 3 piano sonatas; *A Quiet Afternoon,* a set of 9 piano pieces; *Sicilienne* for 2 Pianos; *From an Unknown Past,* a cycle of 7 choruses; *5 Prayers for the Young* for Chorus; organ suite, *A Quaker Reader* (N.Y., Feb. 2, 1977); Double Concerto for Violin, Cello, and Orch. (Cincinnati,

May 16, 1979); *Sunday Morning,* symph. suite (N.Y., Feb. 5, 1981); many songs.

WRITINGS: *Paris Diary* (N.Y., 1966); *New York Diary* (N.Y., 1967); *Critical Affairs* (N.Y., 1970); *The Final Diary* (N.Y., 1974); *Pure Contraption: A Composer's Essays* (N.Y., 1974); *Essays and a Diary* (N.Y., 1983).

Ros-Marbá, Antonio, Spanish conductor; b. Barcelona, April 2, 1937. He was educated at the Barcelona Cons.; studied conducting with Sergiu Celibidache in Siena. He conducted in Europe, Israel, and Mexico. In 1977 he was named chief conductor of the Orquesta Nacional de España in Madrid; in 1979 he also assumed the post of principal conductor of the Netherlands Chamber Orch.

Rosa, Carl (real name, **Karl Rose**), famous opera impresario; b. Hamburg, March 22, 1842; d. Paris, April 30, 1889. At 12 he made tours as a violinist in England, Denmark, and Germany; studied further in the conservatories of Leipzig (1859) and Paris; was concertmaster at Hamburg (1863–65); gave a concert at the Crystal Palace in London (March 10, 1866), and toured in the U.S. with Mr. Bateman, meeting the singer **Euphrosyne Parepa** and marrying her in N.Y. in 1867. They organized an English opera company and toured America until 1871; then returned to London. After his wife's death in 1874, he produced opera in English in various London theaters, forming the Carl Rosa Opera Co., which under various managements continued to be an important factor in English musical life for many years.

Rosa, Salvatore, Italian painter, poet, and musician; b. Arenella, near Naples, June 21, 1615; d. Rome, March 15, 1673. He studied music and became an expert lute player; from 1635 to 1640 he divided his time between Rome and Naples, and from 1640 to 1649 was court painter to the Medici at Florence; then lived in Rome. The pieces credited to Rosa by Burney and others have been proved to be spurious; it is doubtful whether Rosa ever composed music. His *Satire,* written about 1640 and containing sharp criticism of Italian church music of his day, was publ. posthumously in 1695, and was reprinted several times; Mattheson attacked Rosa's views in his *Mithridat, wider den Gift einer welschen Satyre des Salvator Rosa* (1749).

BIBLIOGRAPHY: N. d'Arienzo, "S. Rosa musicista," *Rivista Musicale Italiana* (1894); D. Battesti, *Saggio sulla vita e le satire di Salvatore Rosa* (Bourges, 1913); F. Gerra, *Salvatore Rosa e la sua vita romana dal 1650 al 1672...* (a summary of 200 letters written by Rosa; Rome, 1937); Frank Walker, "Salvatore Rosa and Music," *Monthly Musical Record* (Oct. 1949 and Jan.–Feb. 1950).

Rosand, Aaron, American violinist; b. Hammond, Ind., March 15, 1927. Reared as a certified child prodigy, he played the Mendelssohn Violin Concerto at the age of 10 with the Chicago Symph. Orch.; then enrolled at the Curtis Inst. in Philadelphia as a pupil of Efrem Zimbalist; in 1948 made a successful adult debut in N.Y. He then went to Europe, where he soon established himself as a charismatic performer of pleasurable Romantic music, which included works, not often played, by Ysaÿe, Enesco, Spohr, and Szymanowski. He concertized in South America, Asia, and Russia before returning to the U.S. in 1980 for a series of concerts.

Rosbaud, Hans, eminent Austrian conductor; b. Graz, July 22, 1895; d. Lugano, Dec. 29, 1962. He studied at the Hoch Cons. in Frankfurt; was director of the City Hochschule für Musik in Mainz (1921–30); also conducted the City Orch. there; served as first Kapellmeister of the Frankfurt Radio and of the Museumgesellschaft concerts (1928–37); then became Generalmusikdirektor in Münster (1937–41) and later in Strasbourg (1941–44); subsequently was appointed Generalmusikdirektor of the Munich Phil. (1945). In 1948 he became chief conductor of the Symph. Orch. of the Southwest Radio in Baden-Baden, and in 1957, music director of the Tonhalle Orch. in Zürich. He particularly distinguished himself as a conductor of modern works. He conducted the first stage performances of Schoenberg's *Moses und Aron* (Zürich, 1957).

Rösch, Friedrich, German composer; b. Memmingen, Dec. 12, 1862; d. Berlin, Oct. 29, 1925. He was a law student at Munich; studied music with Rheinberger; lived in Berlin, St. Petersburg, and Munich. In 1898 he, with Hans Sommer and Richard Strauss, organized the Genossenschaft deutscher Tonsetzer (dissolved in 1937).
WORKS: *Antonius,* a burlesque oratorio; numerous choral pieces in a humorous vein; 4-part madrigals for Men's Chorus; songs; a book, *Musikästhetische Streitfragen* (Leipzig, 1897).

Rosé, Arnold (Josef), distinguished violinist; b. Jassy, Rumania, Oct. 24, 1863; d. London, Aug. 25, 1946. He studied under Karl Heissler at the Vienna Cons.; made his professional debut at the Gewandhaus in Leipzig, Oct. 30, 1879; in 1881 was appointed concertmaster of the Vienna Phil. and Opera orch.; held this post, intermittently, for 57 years, until 1938, when he was forced to leave Vienna; spent his last years in London. In 1882 he founded the Rosé quartet, which won a high reputation throughout Europe; the Quartet made its American debut at the Library of Congress in Washington, D.C., on April 28, 1928. In 1902 Rosé married Justine Mahler, a sister of Gustav Mahler.

Rose, Leonard, brilliant American cellist; b. Washington, D.C., July 27, 1918. He enrolled at the Miami Cons. when he was 11, and studied cello there with Walter Grossman; then went to N.Y. to study with his cousin, **Frank Miller;** received a scholarship to the Curtis Inst. of Music in Philadelphia in the class of Felix Salmond (1934–38). He then played in the NBC Symph. Orch. under Toscanini (1938–39); subsequently was first cellist of the Cleveland Orch. (1939–43) and the N.Y. Phil. (1943–51). From 1951 he

pursued a career as a soloist. With Isaac Stern and Eugene Istomin he organized a trio which gave regular concerts. He taught at the Juilliard School of Music in N.Y. from 1947 to 1951 and again from 1962, and at the Curtis Inst. from 1951 to 1962. Several of his students became successful artists in their own right; among them were Stephen Kates, Lynn Harrell, and Yo-Yo Ma.

Roseingrave, Thomas, English organist and composer; b. Winchester, 1690; d. Dunleary, June 23, 1766. He was the son and pupil of the organist **Daniel Roseingrave** (1650–1727); went to Italy in 1710 on a stipend from the Chapter of St. Patrick's Cathedral in Dublin, and at Venice met Alessandro and Domenico Scarlatti; traveled with the latter to Rome and Naples. In 1720 he was at London, where he produced Domenico Scarlatti's opera *Narciso;* from 1725 to 1737 he was organist at St. George's, Hanover Square; then lived at Hampstead, and about 1749 returned to Dublin.
WORKS: *15 Voluntarys and Fugues, made on Purpose for the Organ or Harpsichord* (1730); *12 Solos for the German Flute, with a Thorough Bass for the Harpsichord; 8 Suites of Lessons for Harpsichord; 6 Double Fugues* for Organ or Harpsichord (1750); etc.
BIBLIOGRAPHY: V. Butcher, "Thomas Roseingrave," *Music & Letters* (July 1938).

Rösel, Artur, German violinist and composer; b. Münchenbernsdorf, Aug. 23, 1859; d. Weimar, April 3, 1934. He studied violin and composition in Weimar; was violinist in various theater orchs. in Hamburg, Lugano, and Rotterdam. In 1888 he became concertmaster of the Weimar court orch. He wrote a "lyric stage play," *Halimah* (Weimar, 1895); symph. poem, *Frühlingsstürme;* 2 violin concertos; Viola Concerto; 2 string quartets; violin pieces.

Rösel, Peter, outstanding German pianist; b. Dresden, Feb. 2, 1945. In 1963 he won 2nd prize in the International Schumann Competition in Zwickau; he was then chosen by the German Democratic Republic's Ministry of Culture for further training at the Moscow Cons., where he studied with Dmitri Bashkirov and Lev Oborin, graduating in 1969. In 1978 he made a highly successful tour of the U.S. as piano soloist with the Gewandhaus Orch. of Leipzig. Apart from a brilliant technique, Rösel has a Romantic sensitivity characteristic of the Russian mode of instrumental playing; his repertoire is comprehensive, ranging from Mozart to Prokofiev.

Roselius, Ludwig, German composer and musicologist; b. Kassel, Aug. 2, 1902; d. Bremen, Feb. 6, 1977. He studied in Berlin; took courses in composition with Georg Schumann at the Prussian Academy of the Arts, and musicology with H. Abert and J. Wolf at the Univ. of Berlin; received his Dr.Phil. for his dissertation *Andreas Raselius als Motettenkomponist* (1924); he also edited motets by Raselius for Denkmäler der Tonkunst in Bayern, 36 (29/30). He served as rehearsal conductor for the chorus of the

German Opera House in Berlin (1921–23); lived in Berlin and Bremen (1928–40); remained in Bremen as a music critic. He wrote the operas *Doge und Dogaressa* (Dortmund, Nov. 14, 1928); *Godiva* (Nuremberg, Aug. 17, 1933); *Gudrun* (Graz, April 29, 1939); also many choruses for schools.

Rosell, Lars-Erik, Swedish composer; b. Nybro, Aug. 9, 1944. He studied composition (with Lidholm) and organ at the State College of Music in Stockholm (1968–72). In his music, he often requires improvisation from performers.

WORKS: *Moments of a Changing Sonority* for Harpsichord, Hammond Organ, and Strings (1969); *Terry Riley* for 3 Pianos (1970); *Twilight* for Chamber Ensemble (1970); *Dorian Mode* for Piano, Vibraphone, Clarinet, Cello, and Trombone (1971); *3 Psaltarpsalmer* for Chorus and Instruments (1971); *Poem in the Dark,* after Sachs, for Mezzo-soprano, Flute, Trombone, Double Bass, and Percussion (1972); *Efter syndafallet,* dramatic scene after Arthur Miller's play *After the Fall,* for Soprano, Alto, Baritone, and Instrumental Ensemble (Stockholm, Feb. 15, 1973); chamber opera, *Nattesang* (1974; Copenhagen, Dec. 15, 1974); *Visiones prophetae,* biblical scene for Soloists, 3 Choruses, Wind Orch., Harp, Organ, and 2 Double Basses (Lund, June 27, 1974); *Musik* for Cello and String Orch. (Stockholm, March 4, 1975); *Expando* for Orch. (1976).

Rosellen, Henri, French pianist and composer; b. Paris, Oct. 13, 1811; d. there, March 18, 1876. He studied at the Paris Cons. with Zimmerman (piano) and Halévy (composition); later became a pupil of Henri Herz, under whose influence he began to compose salon music for piano. His *Rêverie* was fantastically popular for many years; he further composed *Nocturne et Tarentelle; 12 Etudes brillantes; 76* fantasias on operatic airs; variations for Piano; chamber music. He was a highly successful teacher in Paris, and publ. a *Manuel des pianistes.*

Rosen, Charles, erudite American pianist and musicologist; b. New York, May 5, 1927. He studied piano with Moriz Rosenthal and music theory with Karl Weigl; then took a course in music history at Princeton Univ., receiving his B.A. summa cum laude in 1947 and his M.A. in 1949; also holds the degree of Ph.D. in French literature (1951). He made his N.Y. debut as pianist in 1951; was assistant prof. in modern languages at the Mass. Inst. of Technology (1953–55); in 1971 was appointed prof. of music at the State Univ. of N.Y. at Stony Brook; was the Ernest Bloch Prof. of Music at the Univ. of Calif., Berkeley, in 1976–77. He is equally adept as a virtuoso pianist, particularly in the modern repertoire, and as a brilliant writer on musical, philosophical, and literary subjects. In 1972 he received the National Book Award for his vol. *The Classical Style: Haydn, Mozart, Beethoven* (N.Y., 1971); also publ. *Sonata Forms* (N.Y., 1980).

Rosen, Jerome, American composer; b. Boston, July 23, 1921. He studied composition with William Denny at the Univ. of Calif., Berkeley (M.A., 1949); also had sessions with Sessions there; then went to Paris, where he obtained a diploma as a clarinetist (1950). Upon his return to the U.S., he became a prof. of music at the Univ. of Calif., Davis (1952). He wrote a Sonata for Clarinet and Cello (1954); String Quartet (1955); Saxophone Concerto (Sacramento, Jan. 24, 1958); Clarinet Quintet (1959); *Petite suite* for 4 Clarinets (1962); *Elegie* for Percussion (1967); *5 Pieces* for Violin and Piano (1970); songs.

Rosen, Jerome, American violinist, pianist, poet, physicist, and polymath nonpareil; b. Detroit, Nov. 16, 1939. He began to play the violin at the age of 5, and the piano at 6; studied violin with Josef Gingold in Cleveland and Ivan Galamian at the Curtis Inst. of Music in Philadelphia (1955–58); took piano lessons with Arthur Loesser in Cleveland; composition with Herbert Elwell and Marcel Dick in Cleveland and Wallingford Riegger in Stockbridge, Mass.; studied chamber music playing with Alexander Schneider and conducting with George Szell, Louis Lane, and James Levine in Cleveland. He subsequently worked in the Cleveland Orch. as violinist and pianist (1959–66); then played violin in the Detroit Symph. Orch. (1968–72). In 1972 he joined the Boston Symph. as a violinist and in 1974 as a pianist, harpsichordist, and celesta player. Concurrently he gave violin recitals in Detroit, N.Y., and other American cities, and played chamber music. He also took a hand in conducting, in Detroit and Cleveland; in 1973–77 was conductor of the Boston Univ. Repertoire Orch. He taught chamber music playing at the Berkshire Music Center (1973–74 and 1977); served as rehearsal pianist for Seiji Ozawa, Rostropovich, Casals, and George Szell. Besides music, he took courses in physics and mathematics at Case Western Reserve Univ.; wrote heavy and light poetry. He is not related to his namesake, Jerome Rosen, the composer, or Charles Rosen, the pianist.

Rosen, Max, American violinist; b. Dorohoi, Rumania, April 11, 1900; d. New York, Dec. 17, 1956. He was brought to the U.S. as an infant and studied with David Mannes in N.Y. In 1912 he went to Germany, where he had lessons with Leopold Auer; made his concert debut in Dresden, Nov. 16, 1915, and his American debut as soloist with the N.Y. Phil. (Jan. 12, 1918); he subsequently settled in N.Y. as a violin teacher.

Rosen, Nathaniel, American cellist; b. Altadena, Calif., June 9, 1948. He studied at the Univ. of Southern Calif. with Gregor Piatigorsky; later served as his assistant; eventually joined the Pittsburgh Symph. Orch. In 1978 he won the Gold Medal of the Tchaikovsky Competition in Moscow, the first American cellist to be so honored. This prestigious award instantly propelled him into the precious outer sanctum of Tchaikovsky medalists and secured for him a plethora of concert engagements not commonly vouchsafed to unanointed cellists.

Rosenberg, Hilding (Constantin), eminent Swedish composer; b. Bosjökloster, June 21, 1892. He studied organ and served as church organist in the provinces. In 1914 he enrolled at the Royal Academy of Music in Stockholm, where he took courses in composition with Ellberg and Stenhammar, and studied piano with Andersson; entered the Cons. in 1915. In 1920 he obtained a stipend for further studies; took courses in piano with Buchmayer in Dresden, and attended classes in conducting with Striegler and Scherchen. Returning to Sweden, he became an assistant conductor at the Stockholm Opera (1932–34). In 1948 he visited the U.S. and conducted the first American performance of his Fourth Symph. His music continues the traditional lines of Scandinavian Romanticism, but injects a strong element of neo-Classical polyphony. In his string quartets Nos. 8–12 he makes use of the 12-tone technique. His imposing mastery of composition contributed to his stature as one of the most prestigious figures in modern Swedish music. As a pedagogue, he formed an important group of disciples.

WORKS: FOR THE STAGE: 7 operas: *Resan till Amerika* (*Journey to America;* Stockholm, Nov. 24, 1932; also an orch. suite); *Marionetter* (*Marionettes;* 1937–38; Stockholm, Feb. 14, 1939; also an orch. suite); *De 2 Konungadöttrarna* (*The 2 Princesses;* Swedish Radio, Sept. 19, 1940); *Lycksalighetens ö* (*The Isle of Bliss;* Stockholm, Feb. 1, 1945); chamber opera, *Kaspers fettisdag* (*Kasper's Shrove Tuesday;* 1953; Stockholm, Jan. 28, 1954); radio opera, *Porträttet* (*The Portrait*), after Gogol's short story (1955; Swedish Radio, March 22, 1956); lyric comedy, *Hus med dubbel ingång* (*The House with 2 Doors;* libretto after Calderón's *Casa con dos puertas;* Stockholm, May 24, 1970); 4-part opera-oratorio, *Josef och hans bröder* (*Joseph and His Brothers*), based on Thomas Mann's novel (1945–48; last part of the oratorio perf. in Stockholm, March 23, 1948; shortened version for concert perf., 1951); 6 ballets: *Yttersta domen* (*The Last Judgment;* 1929; also an orch. suite); *Orfeus i stan* (*Orpheus in Town;* 1938; Stockholm, 1938; also an orch. suite); *Eden* (1961; produced by Birgit Cullberg from *Music for String Orchestra,* 1946); *Salome* (1963; Stockholm, Feb. 28, 1964); *Sönera* (*The Sons;* 1963–64); *Babels Torn* (*The Tower of Babel;* 1966; Swedish TV, Jan. 8, 1968). FOR ORCH.: 9 symphs.: No. 1 (1917; revised 1919; first perf. in Göteborg, April 5, 1921; a 2nd revision, in progress since 1922, first perf. in Stockholm, May 18, 1974); No. 2, *Sinfonia Grave* (1928; revised 1935; Göteborg, March 27, 1935); No. 3 (1939; Swedish Radio, Dec. 11, 1939), originally a symph. drama for radio subtitled *De 4 livsåldrarna* (*The 4 Ages of Man*), with words from Romain Rolland's *Jean Christoph* read before each movement; text and subtitle were later discarded; No. 4, *Johannes uppenbarelse* (*The Revelation of St. John*), with Baritone and Chorus (1940; Swedish Radio, Dec. 6, 1940); No. 5, *Örtagårdsmästaren* (*The Gardener*), with Contralto and Chorus (1944; Swedish Radio, Oct. 17, 1944); No. 6, *Sinfonia semplice* (1951; Gävle, Jan. 24, 1952); Symph. for Wind Orch. and Percussion (the same music as his ballet *Babels Torn;* first concert perf., Göteborg, Oct. 27, 1972); No. 7 (1968; Swedish Radio, Sept. 29, 1968); No. 8, with Chorus, subtitled *In candidum*

(1974; Malmö, Jan. 24, 1975); *Sinfonia da chiesa* Nos. 1 and 2 (1923, 1924); 2 violin concertos (1924, 1951); *Suite* for Strings (1927); Trumpet Concerto (1928); *Suite* for Violin and Orch. (1929); *5 Pieces* for Piano and Strings (1933; revised 1965); *Sinfonia concertante* for Violin, Viola, Oboe, Bassoon, and Orch. (1935); *Bergslagsbilder* (*Pictures from Bergslagen;* 1937); *Taffel-musik* (*Table Music;* 1939); 2 cello concertos (1939, 1953); *Djufar,* suite (1942); Viola Concerto (1942); *Overtura bianca-nera* for Strings (1946); Concerto No. 1 for String Orch. (1946); Concerto No. 2 (1949); Piano Concerto (1950); Concerto No. 3, *Louisville Concerto* (1954; Louisville, Ky., March 12, 1955); *Riflessioni* Nos. 1–3 for String Orch. (1959–60); *Metamorfosi I–III* (1963–64). VOCAL WORKS: *Den heliga natten* (*The Holy Night*), a Christmas oratorio (1936); *Huvudskalleplats* (*Calvary*), a Good Friday oratorio (1938; revised 1965); *14 Chinese Poems* for Soprano and Piano (1945–51); *Åt Jordgudinnan* (*To the Earth Goddess*) for Mezzo-soprano, Flute, Clarinet, Violin, Viola, Cello, and Lute (1959); *Dagdrivaren,* 6 songs for Baritone and Orch. (1962–63); small solo songs; motets. CHAMBER MUSIC: 12 string quartets: Nos. 1–7 (1920, 1924, 1926, 1939, 1949, 1953, 1956); Nos. 8–12 (1957); Trio for Flute, Violin, and Viola (1921); 3 solo violin sonatas (1921; revised 1966, 1953, 1963); 2 violin sonatas (1926, 1941); Trio for Oboe, Clarinet, and Bassoon (1927); Wind Quintet (1959; revised 1965); Solo Flute Sonata (1959); Solo Clarinet Sonata (1960); *6 moments musicaux* for String Quartet (1972). FOR PIANO: 4 sonatas: No. 1 (1923); No. 2 (1925; Stockholm, Sept. 4, 1970); No. 3 (1926); No. 4 (1927); *11 Studies* (1924); *Improvisations* (1939–41); *Theme and Variations* (1941); *6 Polyphonic Studies* (1945); Sonatina (1949). FOR ORGAN: *Fantasia e Fuga* (1941); *Preludio e Fuga* (1948); *Toccata, Aria Pastorale e Ciaconna* (1952). He also publ. *Toner från min ottagård* (Malmo, 1978). P. Lyne edited *Hilding Rosenberg: Catalogue of Works* (Stockholm, 1970).

BIBLIOGRAPHY: M. Pergament, *Hilding Rosenberg: A Giant of Modern Swedish Music* (Stockholm, 1956).

Rosenbloom, Sydney, British pianist and composer; b. Edinburgh, June 25, 1889; d. East London, South Africa, July 22, 1967. He studied at the Royal Academy of Music in London; after teaching in the English provinces, he went to South Africa (1920); in 1921 was appointed prof. at the Harrison Cons. in Johannesburg. In 1930 he visited the U.S., and gave piano recitals in California. Upon returning to South Africa, he settled in East London. His works are mostly for piano, written in an ingratiating and highly pianistic manner, along Romantic lines: *Caprice Impromptu, Valse-Etude, 3 Concert Studies, 6 Preludes, 2 Scherzos, Romance triste, Etchings, From My Sketch Book, Falling Snow,* etc.

Rosenboom, David, American composer of the avant-garde; b. Fairfield, Iowa, Sept. 9, 1947. He studied piano with his mother; also played violin, viola, trumpet, and drums. He attended the Univ. of Illinois, where he took courses in composition with

Salvatore Martirano and Gordon Binkerd; worked with Lejaren Hiller in the Experimental Music Studio there (1965–67). In 1968–69 he served as artistic coordinator for the Electric Ear mixed-media series at the Electric Circus in N.Y. In 1970 he participated in research in neurophysics and biofeedback systems at the State Univ. of N.Y. at Stony Brook. With this esthetic background, his music was bound to be experimental in nature; however, he also composed in classical forms. His scores are notated in diagrams and engineering blueprints, with special symbols for dynamics, tempi, etc. WORKS: *Contrasts* for Violin and Orch. (1963); Septet for Strings, Brass, and Piano (1964); Sextet for Bassoon, Flute, and String Quartet (1965); Trio for Clarinet, Trumpet, and String Bass (1966); *Caliban upon Setebos,* after Robert Browning, for Orch. (1966); *The Thud, Thud, Thud, of Suffocating Blackness* for Saxophone, Electric Cello, Piano, Celesta, Percussion, Tape, and Lights (1966); *mississippippississim* for 33 Musicians, Speaker, and Tape (1968); *How Much Better If Plymouth Rock Had Landed on the Pilgrims* for Electronic and Traditional Instruments (1969); *Ecology of the Skin,* a demonstration in biofeedback experience with audience participation (1970). His zodiac sign is Virgo.

Rosenfeld, Gerhard, German composer; b. Königsberg, Feb. 10, 1931. He studied music theory at the Hochschule für Musik in East Berlin (1952–57); had private lessons in composition with Wagner-Régeny (1955–57), Hanns Eisler (1958–60), and Leo Spies (1960–61). WORKS: *Divertimento* for Chamber Orch. (1962); Sinfonietta (1964); 2 violin concertos (1964, 1973); Nonet (1967); Cello Concerto (1967–69); Piano Concerto (1969); 2 *Quartettinos* for String Quartet (1969, 1973); *Fresken* for Orch. (1969); Piano Sonata (1969); *Sonatine* for Orch. (1971); Concerto for Harp, Double Bass, and Orch. (1971); *Reger-Variationen* for String Quartet, Wind Quintet, 3 Trumpets, 3 Trombones, Tuba, Percussion, and String Orch. (1973).

Rosenfeld, Leopold, Danish composer and writer on music; b. Copenhagen, July 21, 1850; d. there, July 19, 1909. He studied at the Copenhagen Cons. and was for some years music critic of *Musikbladet;* wrote several choral works with Orch., of which *Henrik og Else* (Copenhagen, Feb. 7, 1885) had considerable success; he also publ. a number of piano pieces and about 200 songs to German and Danish texts.

Rosenfeld, Paul, American author and music critic; b. New York, May 4, 1890; d. there, July 21, 1946. He studied at Yale Univ. (B.A., 1912) and at Columbia Univ. School of Journalism (Litt.B., 1913). He then associated himself with progressive circles in literature and music; wrote music criticisms for *The Dial* (1920–27); contributed also to other literary and music magazines. Although not a musician by training, Rosenfeld possessed a penetrating in-

sight into musical values; he championed the cause of modern American music. He collected the most significant of his articles in book form: *Musical Portraits* (on 20 modern composers; 1920); *Musical Chronicle,* covering the N.Y. seasons 1917–23 (1923); *An Hour with American Music* (1929); *Discoveries of a Music Critic* (1936). Analects from his articles were publ. as *Musical Impressions* (N.Y., 1969). BIBLIOGRAPHY: J. Mellquist and L. Wiese, ed., *Paul Rosenfeld, Voyager in the Arts* (N.Y., 1948); H.A. Leibowitz, "Remembering Paul Rosenfeld," *Salmagundi* (Spring 1969); B. Mueser, *The Criticism of New Music in N.Y.: 1919–1929* (City Univ. of N.Y., 1975).

Rosenhain, Jacob (Jacques), German pianist and composer; b. Mannheim, Dec. 2, 1813; d. Baden-Baden, March 21, 1894. He was a child prodigy; made his first public appearance at the age of 11 in Mannheim; studied there with Schmitt, and in Frankfurt with Schnyder von Wartensee. In 1837 he went to Paris and London; continued to travel until 1870, when he settled as a teacher in Baden-Baden. His brother **Eduard Rosenhain** (b. Mannheim, Nov. 16, 1818; d. Frankfurt, Sept. 6, 1861) was also a noteworthy pianist and teacher; he wrote a Serenade for Cello and Piano, and piano pieces. WORKS: Operas: *Der Besuch im Irrenhause* (Frankfurt, Dec. 29, 1834); *Le Démon de la nuit* (Paris, March 17, 1851); *Le Volage et jaloux* (Baden-Baden, Aug. 3, 1863); 3 symphs.; 3 string quartets; 4 piano trios; many piano pieces; *12 études caractéristiques* for Piano; etc. He publ. *Erinnerungen an Paganini* (1893). BIBLIOGRAPHY: E. Kratt-Harveng, *Jacques Rosenhain* (Baden-Baden, 1891).

Rosenman, Leonard, American composer; b. Brooklyn, Sept. 7, 1924. He studied with local teachers; later took courses with Roger Sessions, Luigi Dallapiccola, and briefly with Arnold Schoenberg. His main mundane occupation is that of a movie composer; he wrote the scores for such commercially notable films as *East of Eden, Rebel without a Cause,* and *The Chapman Report* (dealing with sexual statistics); also compiled music for television programs, among them *The Defenders* and *Marcus Welby, M.D.* But he is also the composer of a number of highly respectable and even elevated musical works, among them a Violin Concerto and the challenging score *Foci* for 3 orchs. His *Threnody on a Song of K. R.* (written to the memory of his wife, Kay Rosenman), a set of orch. variations on her original melody, was performed by the Los Angeles Phil., under the composer's direction, May 6, 1971.

Rosenmüller, Johann, German composer; b. Ölsnitz, c.1619; d. Wolfenbüttel, Sept. 10, 1684. He graduated from the Univ. of Leipzig in 1640; from 1642 was master at the Thomasschule; later deputy cantor for Tobias Michael; in 1651 he was appointed organist of the Nikolaikirche. Imprisoned for a moral offense in 1655, he escaped and fled to Hamburg, thence to Venice (1658); became composer at the Ospedale della Pieta there in 1678; in 1682 was appointed ducal Kapellmeister at Wolfenbüttel.

WORKS: *Kernsprüche mehrenteils aus Heiliger Schrift,* for 3 to 7 parts, with Continuo (2 vols., 1648, 1652); *Studentenmusik mit 3 und 5 Violen* (dance music; 1654); *12 sonate da camera a 5 stromenti* (Venice, 1670; reprinted by Karl Nef in Denkmäler Deutscher Tonkunst, 18); *Sonate a 2–5 stromenti d'arco* (Nuremberg, 1682); 6 mass sections; 2 Magnificats; many sacred choruses. Rosenmüller's setting of *Welt ade* was used by Bach in his church cantata No. 27, *Wer weiss wie nahe mir mein Ende.*

BIBLIOGRAPHY: A. Horneffer, *Johann Rosenmüller* (Berlin, 1898); F. Hamel, *Die Psalmkompositionen Johann Rosenmüllers* (Strasbourg, 1933).

Rosenshein, Neil, American tenor; b. New York, Nov. 27, 1947. He studied voice in N.Y.; made his operatic debut as Count Almaviva in *Il Barbiere di Siviglia* with the Opera Assoc. of Florida in 1973; subsequently sang with the Opera Co. of Boston, the San Francisco Opera, the Houston Opera, the Santa Fe Opera, and in Europe with the Netherlands Opera, the Scottish Opera, and the Geneva Opera. He also toured in the U.S. in recitals.

Rosenstock, Joseph, Polish-American conductor; b. Cracow, Jan. 27, 1895. He studied at the Cracow Cons.; then with Schreker in Vienna; graduated from the Vienna Academy of Music in 1920; conducted opera in Darmstadt (1922–25), Wiesbaden (1925–27), and Mannheim (1930–33); his American debut was at the Metropolitan Opera, conducting *Die Meistersinger* (Oct. 30, 1929); in 1933 he was disqualified in Germany as a Jew; conducted operatic performances of the Jewish Kulturbund in Berlin until 1936, when he was appointed conductor of the Nippon Phil. Orch. in Tokyo; was successful there until 1941; then went to the U.S.; conducted in Tokyo again in 1945–46; from 1948 to 1955 he was conductor and music director of the N.Y. City Opera. In 1965 he settled in Salt Lake City, conducting occasional concerts and teaching.

Rosenthal, Harold, English music editor and critic; b. London, Sept. 30, 1917. He received his B.A. degree from the Univ. of London in 1940; served as a noncombatant in the British army during World War II; in 1950 launched, with the Earl of Harewood, the magazine *Opera* and became its editor in 1953; also issued *Opera Annuals* (1954–60). He was archivist of the Royal Opera House (1950–56); contributed to many European and American music journals. His publications include *Sopranos of Today* (London, 1956), *Two Centuries of Opera at Covent Garden* (London, 1958), *The Concise Oxford Dictionary of Opera* (with John Warrack; London, 1964; 2nd ed., 1979; revised 1980), and *Covent Garden, A Short History* (London, 1967). He edited *The Opera Bedside Book* (London, 1965) and *The Mapleson Memoirs* (revised ed., London, 1966); revised Loewenberg's *Annals of Opera* (1978). He contributed a number of biographical articles on singers for *The New Grove;* also publ. an autobiography, *My Mad World of Opera* (1982).

Rosenthal, Manuel, French composer and conductor; b. Paris, June 18, 1904, of a Russian mother and French father. He studied violin and composition at the Paris Cons., graduating in 1924; also took some lessons with Ravel. He was mobilized in 1939, and taken prisoner of war; remained in Germany for a year, returning to France in March 1941. After conducting various orchs. in Europe, he made a tour of the U.S. in the autumn of 1946; in 1948, was appointed instructor in composition at the College of Puget Sound in Tacoma, Wash. In 1949 he was engaged as conductor of the Seattle Symph. Orch.; was dismissed summarily for moral turpitude in Oct. 1951 (the soprano who appeared as soloist with the Seattle Symph. Orch. under the name of Mme. Rosenthal was not his legal wife). In 1962 he was appointed prof. of orch. conducting at the Paris Cons.; was conductor of the Liège Symph. Orch. (1964–67). He composed a number of works in an entertaining manner, expertly orchestrated.

WORKS: *Bootleggers,* a satirical operetta (Paris, May 2, 1933); *La Poule noire,* one-act operetta (Paris, 1937); *Les Petits Métiers* for Orch. (St. Louis, March 3, 1936); *La Fête du vin,* choreographic poem (1937; N.Y., Dec. 5, 1946, composer conducting); *St. Francis of Assisi* for Chorus, Orch., and Vibraphone (Paris, Nov. 1, 1944, composer conducting); *Musique de table,* symph. suite (N.Y., Oct. 10, 1946); *Aeolus* for Wind Quintet and Strings (1970); *2 études en camaïeu* for Strings and Percussion (1971). He arranged for L. Massine, choreographer, a ballet, *Gaîté Parisienne* (based on music from various Offenbach operettas; Monte Carlo, April 5, 1938; highly successful).

Rosenthal, Moriz, famous Polish pianist; b. Lwow, Dec. 17, 1862; d. New York, Sept. 3, 1946. He studied piano at the Lwow Cons. with Karol Mikuli, who was a pupil of Chopin; in 1872, when he was 10 years old, he played Chopin's Rondo in C for 2 Pianos with his teacher in Lwow. The family moved to Vienna in 1875, and Rosenthal became the pupil of Joseffy, who inculcated in him a passion for virtuoso piano playing, which he taught according to Tausig's method. Liszt accepted Rosenthal as a student during his stay in Weimar and Rome (1876–78). After a hiatus of some years, during which Rosenthal studied philosophy at the Univ. of Vienna, he returned to his concert career in 1884, and established for himself a reputation as one of the world's greatest virtuosos; was nicknamed (because of his small stature and great pianistic power) "little giant of the piano." Beginning in 1888 he made 12 tours of the U.S., where he became a permanent resident in 1938. He publ. (with L. Schytte) a *Schule des höheren Klavierspiels* (Berlin, 1892). His wife, **Hedwig Kanner-Rosenthal,** was a distinguished piano teacher.

Rosetti, Francesco Antonio (real name, **Franz Anton Rösler**), Bohemian composer; b. in the region of Leitmeritz, c.1750; d. Ludwigslust, June 30, 1792. For many years Rosetti was confused with a Bohemian cobbler named Rösler, who was born in Niemes in 1746 and whose date of birth was erroneously listed as that of Rosetti. He was a theological student; was engaged as a string player in court orchs.; in 1789 he became music director in Ludwigslust. He was a prodigiously fertile composer who wrote in the manner of Haydn and Boccherini, and was even dubbed "a German Boccherini." He wrote 3 Requiems; one of these was composed in memory of Mozart; it was performed in Prague shortly after Mozart's death in 1791; its score is unfortunately lost. His other works include an opera, *Das Winterfest der Hirten* (1789), and nearly 90 "symphonies"; 9 string quartets; 4 flute concertos; 5 oboe concertos; 3 clarinet concertos; 4 bassoon concertos; 5 horn concertos; 5 concertos for 2 Horns; etc., etc. Oskar Kaul publ. 5 symphs. in vol. 22 (12.i) and chamber music in vol. 33 (25) of the *Denkmäler der Tonkunst in Bayern.*

BIBLIOGRAPHY: Oskar Kaul, *Die Vokalwerke Anton Rosettis* (Munich, 1911); S. Murray, "The Rösler-Rosetti Problem: A Confusion of Pseudonym and Mistaken Identity," *Music & Letters,* LVII (1976).

Rosier, Carl, Netherlandish organist and composer; b. Liège, Dec. 26, 1640; d. Cologne, Dec., 1725. He served as organist at the Cologne Cathedral and City Hall (1699–1725); wrote much sacred music; publ. 14 sonatas for Oboe, with Violins (Amsterdam, 1700).

BIBLIOGRAPHY: Ursel Niemöller, *Carl Rosier, Kölner Dom- und Ratskapellmeister* (Cologne, 1957).

Rosing, Vladimir, Russian-American tenor and opera director; b. St. Petersburg, Jan. 23, 1890; d. Los Angeles, Nov. 24, 1963. He studied voice with Jean de Reszke; made his debut as a tenor in St. Petersburg in 1912; gave a successful series of song recitals in programs of Russian songs in London between 1913 and 1921. In 1923 he was appointed director of the opera dept. at the Eastman School of Music in Rochester, N.Y.; founded an American Opera Co., which he directed in a series of operatic productions in the English language. In 1939 he went to Los Angeles as organizer and artistic director of the Southern Calif. Opera Assoc. He staged several pageants: *The California Story* in Hollywood Bowl in 1950; *The Oregon Story* in 1959; *The Kansas Story* in 1960.

Roslavetz, Nicolai, remarkable Russian composer; b. Suray, near Chernigov, Jan. 5, 1881; d. Moscow, Aug. 23, 1944. He studied violin with Jan Hřimalý, and composition with Ilyinsky and Vassilenko, at the Moscow Cons., graduating in 1912; won the Silver Medal for his cantata *Heaven and Earth,* after Byron. A composer of advanced tendencies, he publ. in 1913 an atonal Violin Sonata, the first of its kind by a Russian composer; his 3rd String Quartet exhibits 12-tone properties. He edited a short-lived journal, *Muzykalnaya Kultura,* in 1924, and

became a leading figure in the modern movement in Russia. But with a change of Soviet cultural policy toward socialist realism and nationalism, Roslavetz was subjected to severe criticism in the press for persevering in his aberrant ways. To conciliate the authorities, he tried to write operettas; then was given an opportunity to redeem himself by going to Tashkent to write ballets based on Uzbek folk songs; he failed in all these pursuits. But interest in his music became pronounced abroad, and posthumous performances were arranged in West Germany.

WORKS: Symph. (1922); symph. poems: *Man and the Sea,* after Baudelaire (1921), and *End of the World,* after Paul Lafargue (1922); Cello Sonata (1921); Violin Concerto (1925); cantata, *October* (1927); *Nocturne* for Harp, Oboe, 2 Violas, and Cello (1913); 3 string quartets (1913, 1916, 1920); 3 piano trios; 4 violin sonatas; *3 Dances* for Violin and Piano (1921); Cello Sonata (1921); 5 piano sonatas.

BIBLIOGRAPHY: D. Gojowy, "N.A. Roslavetz, Ein früher Zwölftonkomponist," *Die Musikforschung* (1969; includes a detailed list of the location, dates of publication, etc., of extant works).

Rösler, Franz Anton. See **Rosetti, Francesco.**

Rösler, Johann Josef, Hungarian composer; b. Chemnitz, Aug. 22, 1771; d. Prague, Jan. 29, 1813. He served as Kapellmeister for Prince Lobkowitz in Prague; brought out an opera, *Elisene, Prinzessin von Bulgarien* (Prague, Oct. 18, 1807), which was the first original stage work to be produced at the German Opera Theater in Prague; wrote a great amount of instrumental music. A movement from one of his piano concertos was erroneously attributed to Beethoven.

BIBLIOGRAPHY: H. Engel, "Der angeblich Beethovensche Klavierkonzertsatz," *Neues Beethovenjahrbuch* (1925).

Rosner, Arnold, American composer; b. New York, Nov. 8, 1945. He studied mathematics at the State Univ. of N.Y. at Buffalo, and composition with Leo Smit, Allen Sapp, and Lejaren Hiller (Ph.D., 1972). He subsequently taught at various schools, including Wagner College in Staten Island and Kingsborough Community College. His music is couched formally in a neo-Classical idiom, but he freely admits melodic, harmonic, and contrapuntal methods of the modern school of composition.

WORKS: Opera: *The Chronicle of 9* (1984); 6 symphs. (1961, 1961, 1963, 1964, 1973, 1976); *A MyLai Elegy* for Orch. (1971); *5 Ko-ans* for Orch. (1977); *Nocturne* for Orch. (1978); 5 string quartets (1962, 1963, 1965, 1972, 1977); *5 Mystical Pieces* for English Horn, Harp, and Strings (1967; later revised as *5 Meditations*); *6 Pastoral Dances* for Woodwinds and Strings (1968); *A Gentle Musicke* for Flute and Strings (1969); 2 concerti grossi for Orch. (1974, 1979); *Responses, Hosanna and Fugue* for Harp and String Orch. (1977); Sonata for Flute and Cello (1962); Wind Quintet (1964); Concertino for Harp, Harpsichord, Celesta, and Piano (1968); Cello Sonata (1968); Sonata for Oboe or Violin, and Piano

(1972); 3 piano sonatas (1963, 1970, 1978); *Musique de clavecin* for Harpsichord (1974); Sonata for Horn and Piano (1979); choral works: masses (1967, 1971, 1974); Requiem (1973); Magnificat (1979); *Let Them Praise* for Boys' Choir (1984); songs: *3 Elegiac Songs* (1973); *Nightstone* (1979).

Rosowsky, Solomon, Jewish-American music scholar and composer; b. Riga, Latvia, March 27, 1878; d. New York, July 30, 1962. He studied law at the Univ. of Kiev, and composition at the St. Petersburg Cons. with Liadov, Rimsky-Korsakov, and Glazunov. He was a co-founder of the Society for Jewish Folk Music in St. Petersburg in 1909; in 1920 he went back to Riga, and organized there the first Jewish Cons. of Music; in 1925 he emigrated to Palestine. He settled in N.Y. in 1947, devoting himself mainly to the music of biblical times, culminating in the publication of an important vol., *The Cantillation of the Bible* (N.Y., 1957). His compositions include a Piano Trio (1909) and several scores of incidental music for plays in Yiddish.

Ross, Diana, black American pop artist; b. Detroit, March 26, 1944. She sang for social events in Detroit; then organized a female trio whose other members were her close contemporaries Florence Ballard and Mary Wilson, assuming the grandiose name of The Supremes. Florence Ballard dropped out in 1967 and was replaced by Cindy Birdsong, and the group thenceforth was called Diana Ross and The Supremes. Their hits included *Come See about Me, Stop! In the Name of Love, Baby Love, You Can't Hurry Love, I Hear a Symphony,* ad infinitum. The Supremes, and Diana Ross as their top singer, broke the curse of drugs and alcohol besetting so many pop singers by campaigning for virtue and love sans narcotics. In 1970 Diana Ross left The Supremes and started on a highly successful career as a solo singer, in cabarets, in nightclubs, on the radio, on television, in Las Vegas, on Broadway, and in the movies, where she starred in a film biography of Billie Holiday, *Lady Sings the Blues.* As a soloist she hit the top of the charts with an anti-drug number, *Reach Out and Touch,* and capped it with her logo song *Ain't No Mountain High Enough;* she recorded the eponymous albums *Diana! An Evening with Diana Ross,* the generic song *Why Do Fools Fall in Love,* and a duet with Lionel Richard, *Endless Love.*

Ross, Hugh, choral conductor and organist; b. Langport, England, Aug. 21, 1898. He studied at the Royal College of Music, where he won first prize in organ and was made a Fellow in 1915; went to Canada; became conductor of the Winnipeg Male Voice Choir (1921); organized and conducted the Winnipeg Symph. Orch. (1923–27); in 1927, was appointed conductor of the Schola Cantorum in N.Y.; conducted many modern works.

Ross, Walter, American composer; b. Lincoln, Nebr., Oct. 3, 1936. He studied music at the Univ. of Nebraska, receiving an M.M.A. in 1962; then composition with Robert Palmer and conducting with Husa at Cornell Univ. (D.M.A., 1966). In 1967 he was appointed to the music faculty of the Univ. of Virginia. Much of his music is inspired by American themes.

WORKS: One-act chamber opera, *In the Penal Colony* (1972); *The Silent Firefly* for Mezzo-soprano and Instruments (1965); Concerto for Brass Quintet and Orch. (1966); *Cryptical Triptych* for Trombone and Piano (1968); *5 Dream Sequences* for Percussion Quartet and Piano (1968); *Old Joe's Fancy* for Saxophone Quartet and Concert Band (1969); 3 trombone concertos (1971, 1977, 1982); Trombone Quartet (1972); *Fancy Dances* for 3 Bass Tubas (1972); Concerto for Tuba and Concert Band (1973); *Divertimento* for Wind Quintet (1974); *Concerto basso* for Tuba and Euphonium Ensemble (1974); *Piltdown Fragments* for Tuba and Tape (1975); *A Jefferson Symphony* for Chorus and Orch. (Charlottesville, April 13, 1976); Concerto for Wind Quintet and String Orch. (1977); String Trio (1978); *Nocturne* for String Orch. (1980); *Trio Giocondo* for Clarinet, Violin, and Piano (1980); Sonata for Violin and Piano (1981); Suite No. 1 for Chamber Ensemble (1983); Bassoon Concerto (1983).

Rosseau, Norbert, Belgian composer; b. Ghent, Dec. 11, 1907; d. there, Nov. 1, 1975. He played violin as a child; his family emigrated to Italy in 1921, and he studied piano with Silvestri and composition with Respighi. His early works are cast in a traditional style of European modernism; later he half-heartedly experimented with dodecaphony and electronics; some of his works bear pseudo-scientific titles, as, for example, the symph. poem entitled $H_2O.$

WORKS: FOR THE STAGE: 2 operas: *Sicilenne* (1947) and *Les Violons du prince* (1954); *Juventa,* ballet (1957). VOCAL MUSIC: *Inferno,* oratorio after Dante (1940); *L'An mille,* dramatic ode (1946); *Incantations,* cantata (1951); *Maria van den Kerselare,* Flemish oratorio (1952); *Zeephellen,* chamber cantata, with Children's Chorus (1958); *Il Paradiso terrestre,* oratorio after Dante (1968). FOR ORCH.: *Suite Agreste* (1936); $H_2O,$ symph. poem (1938; Liège, June 24, 1939); 2 concertos for Orch. (1948, 1963); 2 symphs.: No. 1 (1953) and No. 2, *Sinfonia sacra,* for Soloists, Chorus, and Orch. (1960–63); *Suite concertante* for String Quintet, Winds, Harpsichord, and Timpani (1959); Concerto for Wind Quintet and Orch. (1961); *Variations* for Orch. (1963); Viola Concerto (1964); *Sonata a 4* for 4 Violins and Strings (1966); Horn Concerto (1967). CHAMBER MUSIC: Violin Sonatina (1949); *3 jouets* for Oboe, Clarinet, and Bassoon (1955); Wind Quintet (1955); Clarinet Sonatina (1956); String Quartet (1956); Trio for Flute, Cello, and Piano (1956); *Rapsodie* for Flute, Bassoon, and Piano (1958); *Serenade à Syrinx* for Flute, Violin, Cello, and Harp (1959); Concertino for Piano, Double String Quartet, and Double Bass (1963); *Pentafonium* for Viola, Cello, Flute, Oboe, and Harpsichord (1964); *Diptique* for String Quartet (1971); *Dialogue* for Flute, Oboe, Viola, and Piano (1971); Piano Quartet (1975).

Rossellini, Renzo, Italian composer; b. Rome, Feb. 2, 1908; d. Monte Carlo, May 14, 1982. He studied composition in Rome with Setaccioli and Sallustio; also took courses in orchestration with Bernardino Molinari. In 1940 he was appointed prof. of composition at the Rome Cons., and in 1956 became a member of the Santa Cecilia Academy. In 1973 he was named artistic director at the Opera at Monte Carlo.

WORKS: Operas: *Alcassino e Nicoletta* (1928–30); *La guerra,* to his own libretto (Rome, Feb. 25, 1956); *Il vortice* (Naples, Feb. 8, 1958); *Uno sguardo del ponte,* after Arthur Miller's play (Rome, March 11, 1961); *L'Avventuriere* (Monte Carlo, Feb. 2, 1968); *La Reine morte* (Monte Carlo, 1973). Ballets: *La danza di Dâssine* (San Remo, Feb. 24, 1935); *Poemetti pagani* (Monte Carlo, 1963); *Il Ragazzo e la sua ombra* (Venice, 1966). For Orch.: *Suite in 3 tempi* (1931); *Ut unum sint* (Miami, Oct. 20, 1963); *Stornelli della Roma bassa* (1946); film music. He publ. 2 books of autobiographical content, *Pagine di un musicista* (Bologna, 1964) and *Addio del passato* (Milan, 1968).

Rossi, Abbate Francesco, Italian composer; b. Bari, c.1645; d. date unknown. He was a canon in Bari in 1680. He composed the operas *Bianca di Castiglia* (Milan, 1674); *Il Sejano moserno della Tracia* (Venice, 1680); *La pena degli occhi* and *La Clorilda* (both Venice, 1688); *Mitrane* (Venice, 1689); oratorio, *La Caduta degli angeli;* Requiem; Psalms; etc.

Rossi, Giovanni Gaetano, Italian composer; b. Borgo S. Donnino, Parma, Aug. 5, 1828; d. Genoa, March 30, 1886. He studied at the Milan Cons.; from 1852 was concertmaster at the Teatro Regio in Parma; also court organist and (1864–73) director of the Istituto Musicale. From 1873 to 1879 he conducted at the Teatro Carlo Felice in Genoa; was also director of the Liceo Musicale from 1874. He composed 4 operas; an oratorio, *Le 7 parole;* overture, *Saulo;* a Requiem; 3 masses; etc.

Rossi, Giulio, Italian bass; b. Rome, Oct. 27, 1865; d. Milan, Oct. 9, 1931. He had a tenor voice until he was 19, when an unintentional plunge into the Tiber in December induced an illness, after which his voice lowered to the range of *basso profondo.* He then began vocal study under Oreste Tomassoni; made his debut at Parma, Oct. 20, 1887. In 1889 he toured South America with Adelina Patti, and made 2 tours of Mexico and California with Luisa Tetrazzini; from 1908 till 1919 sang at the Metropolitan Opera. His repertoire included about 80 Italian operas.

Rossi, Lauro, Italian dramatic composer; b. Macerata, Feb. 19, 1810; d. Cremona, May 5, 1885. He was a pupil of Furno, Zingarelli, and Crescentini at Naples, bringing out a comic opera, *Le Contesse villane,* there (1829) with fair success. He became maestro at the Teatro Valle in Rome (1831–33); with his 10th opera, *La casa disabitata o I falsi monetari,* produced at La Scala, Milan, Aug. 11, 1834, he won a veritable triumph; it made the rounds of Italy and was given in Paris. In 1835 he went to Mexico as conductor and composer to an Italian opera troupe; when it folded, he set up his own opera company, becoming its director in 1837, and going to Havana (1840) and New Orleans (1842), returning to Italy in 1843. He brought out a new opera, *Il Borgomastro di Schiedam* (Milan, June 1, 1844), with indifferent success; his opera *Il Domino nero* (Milan, Sept. 1, 1849) fared a little better. His most successful opera was *La Contessa di Mons* (Turin, Jan. 31, 1874). He wrote 29 operas in all. In 1850 he was given the post of director of the Milan Cons.; in 1870 he succeeded Mercadante as director of the Naples Cons.; resigned in 1878, and retired to Cremona in 1882.

BIBLIOGRAPHY: F. Florimo, *La Scuola musicale di Napoli* (1882).

Rossi, Luigi (Latinized as **Aloysius Rubeus**), Italian composer and singer; b. Torremaggiore, Foggia, 1598; d. Rome, Feb. 19, 1653. He studied in Naples with G. de Macque; then went to Rome, where his opera *Il palazzo d'Atlante incantato* was produced (Feb. 22, 1642). In 1646 he was called by Mazarin to Paris with 20 other singers, and there staged his most important work, *Orfeo* (March 2, 1647), the first Italian opera expressly written for a Paris production. He wrote besides the oratorio *Giuseppe* and some 100 cantatas; reprints of some of these appear in Gevaert's *Les Gloires de l'Italie,* Riemann's *Kantatenfrühling,* and Landshoff's *Alte Meister des Bel Canto.* Riemann also publ. several da capo arias by Rossi in the *Handbuch der Musik-Geschichte* (vol. II/2).

BIBLIOGRAPHY: A. Wotquenne, *Etude bibliographique sur Luigi Rossi* (Brussels, 1909); Henry Prunières, "Notes sur la vie de Luigi Rossi," *Sammelbände der Internationalen Musik-Gesellschaft,* 12; idem, "Les Représentations du Palazzo d'Atlante," and A. Cametti, "Alcuni documenti inediti su la vita di Luigi Rossi," *Sammelbände der Internationalen Musik-Gesellschaft,* 14; Henry Prunières, "Notes bibliographiques sur les cantates de Luigi Rossi au Conservatoire de Naples," *Zeitschrift der internationalen Musik-Gesellschaft,* 14; idem, *L'Opéra italien en France avant Lulli* (Paris, 1913; pp. 86–150); Romain Rolland, "Le Premier Opéra joué à Paris: L'Orféo de Luigi Rossi," *Musiciens d'autrefois* (1912); A. Cametti, "Luigi Rossi: Organista a S. Luigi dei Francesi," *La Critica Musicale* (1919); A. Ghislanzoni, *Luigi Rossi* (Rome, 1954); E. Caluori, *The Cantatas of Luigi Rossi* (Diss., Brandeis Univ., 1972).

Rossi, Mario, eminent Italian conductor; b. Rome, March 29, 1902. He studied at the Santa Cecilia Academy in Rome; then taught conducting there (1931–36). He subsequently led performances at the Florence May Festival (1936–44). In 1946 he was appointed chief conductor of the RAI Orch. in Turin; also appeared as a guest conductor with the Berlin Phil., Vienna Phil., Concertgebouw Orch., etc. He retired in 1969.

Rossi, Michel Angelo, Italian composer; b. Genoa, 1602; d. Rome (buried July 7), 1656. He was a pupil of Frescobaldi; in 1638 was attached to the court of the Duke of Este in Modena; in 1640 he went to Rome. Among his works are an opera, *Erminia sul Giordano* (Rome, Feb. 2, 1633), and a set of *Toccate e Correnti per organo o cembalo* (2nd ed., Rome, 1657). The complete keyboard works of Rossi were publ. by A. Toni (Milan, 1920); the 1657 edition of *Toccate e Correnti* is included in L. Torchi, *L'arte musicale in Italia,* and 10 *correnti* were publ. by F. Boghen (Milan, 1923); 2 toccatas and 3 *correnti* were edited by Béla Bartók (N.Y., 1930).

BIBLIOGRAPHY: Alceo Toni, "Michel Angelo Rossi," *Bollettino Bibliografico Musicale* (June 1927); J. Peterson, *The Keyboard Works of Michelangelo Rossi* (Diss., Univ. of Illinois, 1975).

Rossi, Salomone (Salamone), Italian composer of Jewish origin (called himself **Ebreo**); b. Mantua, 1570; d. there, c.1630. Nothing is known of the circumstances of his life, except that he was in the service of the court of Mantua, and publ. 13 books of madrigals and instrumental works. He also wrote some synagogue music. As composer of instrumental works, he demonstrated technical procedures in advance of his time; particularly notable are his variations on popular Italian melodies.

WORKS: Canzonettas for 3 Voices (1589); madrigals (5 books; 1600, 1602, 1603, 1610, 1622); sonatas (4 books: I, II, *Sinfonie e gagliarde,* 1607, 1608; III, IV, *Varie sonate, sinfonie, gagliarde, brandi e corrente;* 2nd ed. of III publ. in 1623; IV publ. in 1622, and reprinted in 1636); madrigals for 4–5 Voices (1614); *cantici,* Psalms, hymns, and *laudi* for 3–8 Voices (1620); *madrigaletti* for 2–3 Voices, with Basso Continuo (1628). His *Salmi e Cantici ebraici* was publ. under its original Hebrew title, *Hashirim asher lish'lomo,* in Venice, 1623. He also wrote an intermezzo to the drama *L'Idropica* (1608) and music to a sacred play, *Maddalena.* Naumbourg and Vincent d'Indy prepared a new ed. of selected sacred and secular works by Rossi (2 vols., Paris, 1877); examples of Rossi's instrumental music appear in Riemann's *Alte Kammermusik, Musikgeschichte in Beispielen* (no. 81) and *Handbuch der Musikgeschichte* (II/2); 6 duets are reprinted in Landshoff's *Alte Meister des Bel Canto;* F. Rikko and J. Newman ed. *Sinfonie, Gagliarde, Canzone* (N.Y., 1965). Lazare Saminsky remodeled Rossi's *Adon Olam* in conformity with modern choral sonorities, retaining his harmonic texture, as part of his *Sabbath Evening Service* (N.Y., 1930). The *Complete Works* were begun in 1967, ed. by Fritz Rikko (N.Y.). A complete list of works, locations of MSS and 17th century publications, reprints, etc., are included in J. Newman and F. Rikko, *A Thematic Index to the Works of Salomon Rossi* (Music Indexes and Bibliographies, 6, Hackensack, N.J., 1972).

BIBLIOGRAPHY: D. Maggid, *Die Dreihundertjahrfeier des Salomon de Rossi* (1887); E. Birnbaum, "Jüdische Musiker am Hofe zu Mantua von 1542–1628," in *Kalendar für Israeliten für das Jahr 5654* (Vienna, 1893); Paul Nettl, *Alte jüdische Spielleute und Musiker* (Prague, 1923); B. Selwyn, *The Gonzaga Lords of Mantua* (London, 1927); A. Einstein, "S. Rossi as Composer of Madrigals," *Hebrew Union College Annual,* 23 (Cincinnati, 1950/51); N. Zaslaw, "Synagogue Music Rediscovered. I. Salomon Rossi: The Songs of Solomon," *American Choral Review* (April 1972).

Rossi-Lemeni, Nicola, Italian bass; b. Istanbul, Nov. 6, 1920, of an Italian father and a Russian mother. He was educated in Italy; studied law and planned a diplomatic career. In 1943 he decided to become a professional singer, but the war interfered with his plans, and his debut did not take place until 1946, in Venice. He first appeared in America as Boris Godunov, with the San Francisco Opera (Oct. 2, 1951); also sang Mefistofele (Boito), William Tell, etc.; in 1947, he was engaged at La Scala in Milan; sang at the Metropolitan Opera in N.Y. in 1953–54. In 1980 he joined the faculty of Indiana Univ. in Bloomington. He married the soprano **Virginia Zeani.** Besides the regular operatic repertoire, he sang a number of parts in modern works, such as Wozzeck.

Rossignol, Felix Ludger. See Joncières, Victorin de.

Rossini, Gioachino (Antonio), great Italian opera composer possessing an equal genius for shattering melodrama in tragedy and for devastating humor in comedy; b. Pesaro, Feb. 29, 1792; d. Paris, Nov. 13, 1868. He came from a musical family; his father served as town trumpeter in Lugo and Pesaro, and played brass instruments in provincial theaters; his mother sang opera as *seconda donna.* When his parents traveled, Gioachino Rossini was usually boarded in Bologna. After the family moved to Lugo, his father taught him to play the French horn; he also had a chance to study singing with a local canon. Later the family moved to Bologna, where he studied singing, harpsichord, and music theory with Padre Tesei; also learned to play the violin and viola. Soon he acquired enough technical ability to serve as maestro al cembalo in local churches and at occasional opera productions. He studied voice with Matteo Babbini, a local tenor. In 1806 he was accepted as a student at the Liceo Musicale in Bologna; there he studied singing and solfeggio with Gibelli, cello with Cavedagna, piano with Zanotti, and counterpoint with Padre Mattei. He also began composing. On Aug. 11, 1808, his cantata *Il pianto d'Armonia sulla morte d'Orfeo* was performed at the Liceo Musicale in Bologna and received a prize. About the same time he wrote his first opera, *Demetrio e Polibio;* in 1810 he was commissioned to write a work for the Teatro San Moisè in Venice; he submitted his opera *La cambiale di matrimonio,* which won considerable acclaim. His next production was *L'equivoco stravagante,* produced in Bologna in 1811. There followed a number of other operas: *L'inganno felice* (Venice, 1812), *Ciro in Babilonia* (Ferrara, 1812), and *La scala di seta* (Venice, 1812). In 1812 he obtained a commission from La

Rossini

Scala of Milan; the resulting work, *La pietra del paragone*, became a fine success. In 1813 Rossini produced 3 operas for Venice: *Il Signor Bruschino, Tancredi,* and *L'Italiana in Algeri;* the last became a perennial favorite. The next 3 operas, *Aureliano in Palmira* (produced in Milan in 1813), *Il Turco in Italia* (staged in Milan in 1814), and *Sigismondo* (perf. in Venice in 1814), were unsuccessful. By that time Rossini, still a very young man, had been approached by the famous impresario Barbaja, the manager of the Teatro San Carlo and the Teatro Fondo in Naples, with an offer for an exclusive contract, under the terms of which Rossini was to supply 2 operas annually for Barbaja. The first opera Rossini wrote for him was *Elisabetta, regina d'Inghilterra,* produced at the Teatro San Carlo in Naples; the title role was entrusted to the famous Spanish soprano Isabella Colbran, who was Barbaja's favorite mistress. An important innovation in the score was Rossini's use of *recitativo stromentato* in place of the usual *recitativo secco.* His next opera, *Torvaldo e Dorliska,* produced in Rome in 1815, was an unfortunate failure. Rossini now determined to try his skill in composing an opera buffa, based on the famous play by Beaumarchais *Le Barbier de Seville;* it was an audacious decision on Rossini's part, since an Italian opera on the same subject by Paisiello, *Il Barbiere di Siviglia,* originally produced in 1782, was still playing with undiminished success. To avoid confusion, Rossini's opera on this subject was performed at the Teatro Argentina in Rome under a different title, *Almaviva, ossia L'inutile precauzione.* Rossini was only 23 years old when he completed the score, which proved to be his own greatest accomplishment and a standard opera buffa in the repertoire of theaters all over the world. Rossini himself conducted its first performance in Rome on Feb. 20, 1816, but if contemporary reports and gossip can be trusted, the occasion was marred by various stage accidents which moved the unruly Italian audience to interrupt the spectacle with vociferous outcries of derision; however, the next performance scored a brilliant success. For later productions Rossini used the title *Il Barbiere di Siviglia.* Strangely enough, the operas he wrote immediately afterward were not uniformly successful: *La Gazzetta,* produced in Naples in 1816, passed unnoticed; the next opera, *Otello,* also produced in Naples in 1816, had some initial success but was not retained in the repertoire after a few sporadic performances. There followed *La Cenerentola* and *La gazza ladra,* both dated from 1817, which fared much better. But the following 7 operas, *Armida, Mosè in Egitto, Ricciardo e Zoraide, Ermione, La Donna del lago, Maometto II,* and *Zelmira,* produced in Naples between 1817 and 1822, were soon forgotten; only the famous Prayer in *Mosè in Egitto* saved the opera from oblivion. The *prima donna assoluta* in all these operas was **Isabella Colbran;** after a long association with Barbaja, she went to live with Rossini, who finally married her on March 16, 1822. This event, however, did not result in a break between the impresario and the composer; Barbaja even made arrangements for a festival of Rossini's

works in Vienna at the Kärnthnertortheater, of which he became a director. In Vienna Rossini met Beethoven. Returning to Italy, he produced a fairly successful mythological opera, *Semiramide* (Venice, 1823), with Colbran in the title role. Rossini then signed a contract for a season in London with Giovanni Benelli, director of the Italian opera at the King's Theatre. Rossini arrived in London late in 1823 and was received by King George IV. In London Rossini conducted several of his operas, and was also a guest at the homes of the British nobility, where he played piano as an accompanist to singers, at very large fees. In 1824 he settled in Paris, where he became director of the Théâtre-Italien. For the coronation of King Charles X he composed *Il viaggio a Reims,* which was performed in Paris under his direction on June 19, 1825. He used parts of this *pièce d'occasion* in his opera *Le Comte Ory.* In Paris he met Meyerbeer, with whom he established an excellent relationship. After the expiration of his contract with the Théâtre-Italien, he was given the nominal titles of "Premier Compositeur du Roi" and "Inspecteur Général du Chant en France" at an annual salary of 25,000 francs. He was now free to compose for the Paris Opéra; there, on Oct. 9, 1826, he produced *Le Siège de Corinthe,* a revised French version of *Maometto II.* Later he also revised the score of *Mosè in Egitto* and produced it at the Paris Opéra in French as *Moïse et Pharaon* on March 26, 1827. There followed *Le Comte Ory* (Aug. 20, 1828). In May 1829 Rossini was able to obtain an agreement with the government of King Charles X guaranteeing him a lifetime annuity of 6,000 francs. In return he promised to write more works for the Paris Opéra. On Aug. 3, 1829, his *Guillaume Tell* was given its premiere at the Opera; it became immensely popular. And then, at the age of 37, Rossini stopped writing operas. The French revolution of July 1830, which dethroned King Charles X, invalidated Rossini's contract with the French government. Rossini contemplated suing the government of King Louis Philippe, the successor to the throne of Charles X, for the continuation of his annuity; the incipient litigation was settled in 1835. In 1832 Rossini met Olympe Pélissier, who became his mistress; in 1837 Rossini legally separated from Colbran. She died in 1845, and on Aug. 16, 1846, Rossini married Pélissier. From 1836 to 1848 they lived in Bologna, where Rossini served as consultant to the Liceo Musicale. In 1848 they moved to Florence; in 1855 he decided to return to Paris, where he was to remain for the rest of his life. His home in the suburb of Passy became the magnet of the artistic world. Rossini was a charming, affable, and gregarious host; he entertained lavishly; he was a great gourmet, and invented recipes for Italian food that were enthusiastically adopted by French chefs. His wit was fabulous, and his sayings were eagerly reported in the French journals. He did not abandon composition entirely during his last years of life; in 1867 he wrote a *Petite messe solennelle;* as a token of gratitude to the government of the Second Empire he composed a *Hymne à Napoleon III et à son vaillant peuple;* of great interest are the numerous piano pieces, songs, and instrumental works which he called *Péchés de vieillesse (Sins of Old Age)*, a collection containing over 150 pieces.

What were the reasons for Rossini's decision to stop writing operas? Rumors flew around Paris that he was unhappy about the cavalier treatment he received from the management of the Paris Opéra, and he spoke disdainfully of yielding the operatic field to "the Jews" (Meyerbeer and Halévy), whose operas captivated the Paris audiences. The report does not bear the stamp of truth, for Rossini was friendly with Meyerbeer until Meyerbeer's death in 1864. Besides, Rossini was not in the habit of complaining; he enjoyed life too well. He was called "Le Cygne de Pesaro" ("The Swan of Pesaro," his birthplace). The story went that a delegation arrived from Pesaro with a project of building a monument to Rossini; the town authorities had enough money to pay for the pedestal, but not for the statue itself. Would Rossini contribute 10,000 francs for the completion of the project? "For 10,000 francs," Rossini was supposed to have replied, "I would stand on the pedestal myself." *Se non è vero è ben trovato.* Rossini had a healthy sense of self-appreciation, but he invariably put it in a comic context. While his mother was still living, he addressed his letters to her as "Mother of the Great Maestro."

The circumstance that Rossini was born on a leap-year day was the cause of many a bon mot on his part. On Feb. 29, 1868, he decided to celebrate his 19th birthday, for indeed, there had been then only 19 leap years since his birth. He was superstitious; like many Italians, he stood in fear of Friday the 13th. He died on Nov. 13, 1868, which was a Friday. In 1887 his remains were taken to Florence for entombment in the Church of Santa Croce.

Rossini's melodies have been used by many composers as themes for various works: Respighi utilized Rossini's *Quelques riens* in his ballet *La Boutique fantasque,* and other themes in his orch. suite *Rossiniana.* An opera entitled *Rossini in Neapel* was written by Bernhard Paumgartner. Benjamin Britten made use of Rossini's music in his orch. suites *Soirées musicales* and *Matinées musicales.* The most famous arrangement of any of Rossini's compositions is the Prayer from *Mosè in Egitto,* transcribed for violin by Paganini.

A complete edition of the works of Rossini, the *Quaderni rossiniani, a cura della Fondazione Rossini,* began publication in Pesaro in 1954.

WORKS: OPERAS: *Demetrio e Polibio,* opera seria (1808; Teatro Valle, Rome, May 18, 1812); *La cambiale di matrimonio,* farsa (Teatro San Moisè, Venice, Nov. 3, 1810); *L'equivoco stravagante,* opera buffa (Teatro del Corso, Bologna, Oct. 26, 1811); *L'inganno felice,* farsa (1811; Teatro San Moisè, Venice, Jan. 8, 1812); *Ciro in Babilonia, ossia La caduta di Baldassare,* dramma con cori or oratorio (Teatro Municipale, Ferrara, March 1812); *La scala di seta,* farsa (Teatro San Moisè, Venice, May 9, 1812); *La pietra del paragone,* melodramma giocoso or opera buffa (Teatro alla Scala, Milan, Sept. 26, 1812); *L'occasione fa il ladro, ossia Il cambio della valigia,* burletta per musica (Teatro San Moisè, Venice, Nov. 24, 1812); *Il Signor Bruschino, ossia Il Figlio*

per azzardo, farsa giocosa (1812; Teatro San Moisè, Venice, Jan. 1813); *Tancredi,* opera seria or melodramma eroico (1812–13; Teatro La Fenice, Venice, Feb. 6, 1813); *L'Italiana in Algeri,* melodramma giocoso (Teatro San Benedetto, Venice, May 22, 1813); *Aureliano in Palmira,* opera seria or dramma serio (Teatro alla Scala, Milan, Dec. 26, 1813); *Il Turco in Italia,* opera buffa or dramma buffo (Teatro alla Scala, Milan, Aug. 14, 1814); *Sigismondo,* opera seria or dramma (Teatro La Fenice, Venice, Dec. 26, 1814); *Elisabetta, regina d'Inghilterra,* dramma (Teatro San Carlo, Naples, Oct. 4, 1815); *Torvaldo e Dorliska,* dramma semiserio (Teatro Valle, Rome, Dec. 26, 1815); *Il Barbiere di Siviglia,* opera buffa or commedia (first perf. as *Almaviva, ossia L'inutile precauzione,* Teatro Argentina, Rome, Feb. 20, 1816); *La Gazzetta, ossia Il matrimonio per concorso* (subtitle does not appear in the first printed libretto), opera buffa (Teatro dei Fiorentini, Naples, Sept. 26, 1816); *Otello, ossia Il Moro di Venezia,* opera seria or dramma (Teatro del Fondo, Naples, Dec. 4, 1816); *La Cenerentola, ossia La bontà in trionfo,* dramma giocoso (1816–17; Teatro Valle, Rome, Jan. 25, 1817); *La gazza ladra,* melodramma or opera semiseria (Teatro alla Scala, Milan, May 31, 1817); *Armida,* opera seria or dramma (Teatro San Carlo, Naples, Nov. 11, 1817); *Adelaide di Borgogna, ossia Ottone, re d'Italia,* dramma (Teatro Argentina, Rome, Dec. 27, 1817); *Mosè in Egitto,* azione tragico-sacra or oratorio (Teatro San Carlo, Naples, March 5, 1818); *Adina, o Il Califfo di Bagdad,* farsa (1818; Teatro São Carlos, Lisbon, June 22, 1826); *Ricciardo e Zoraide,* dramma, opera seria, or opera semiseria (Teatro San Carlo, Naples, Dec. 3, 1818); *Ermione,* azione tragica (Teatro San Carlo, Naples, March 27, 1819); *Eduardo* [later *Edoardo*] *e Cristina,* dramma (Teatro San Benedetto, Venice, April 24, 1819); *La Donna del lago,* melodramma or opera seria (Teatro San Carlo, Naples, Sept. 24, 1819); *Bianca e Falliero, ossia Il consiglio dei tre,* opera seria (Teatro alla Scala, Milan, Dec. 26, 1819); *Maometto II,* dramma or opera seria (Teatro San Carlo, Naples, Dec. 3, 1820); *Matilde Shabran* [later *Matilde di Shabran*]*, ossia Bellezza e Cuor di Ferro,* opera semiseria (1820–21; Teatro Apollo, Rome, Feb. 24, 1821); *Zelmira,* dramma or opera seria (1821–22; Teatro San Carlo, Naples, Feb. 16, 1822); *Semiramide,* melodramma tragico or opera seria (1822–23; Teatro La Fenice, Venice, Feb. 3, 1823); *Il viaggio a Reims, ossia L'albergo del Giglio d'Oro,* cantata scenica (Théâtre-Italien, Paris, June 19, 1825); *Le Siège de Corinthe,* grand opera (revision of *Maometto II;* Opéra, Paris, Oct. 9, 1826); *Moïse et Pharaon, ou Le Passage de la Mer Rouge,* grand opera (revision of *Mosè in Egitto;* Opéra, Paris, March 26, 1827); *Le Comte Ory,* opéra-comique (utilizing numbers from *Il viaggio a Reims;* Opéra, Paris, Aug. 20, 1828); *Guillaume Tell,* grand opera (1828–29; Opéra, Paris, Aug. 3, 1829).

CANTATAS: *Il pianto d'Armonia sulla morte d'Orfeo* (Bologna, Aug. 11, 1808); *La morte di Didone* (1811; Venice, May 2, 1818); *Dalle quete e pallid'ombre* (1812); *Egle ed Irene* (1814); *L'Aurora* (Rome, Nov. 1815); *Le nozze di Teti e di Peleo* (Naples, April 24, 1816); Cantata con cori ("Omaggio Umiliato

. . . ''; also known as *Corifea, Partenope,* or *Igea;* Naples, Feb. 20, 1819); *Cantata a tre voci con cori* ("Cantata . . . 9 Maggio 1819''; Naples, May 9, 1819); *La riconoscenza* (Naples, Dec. 27, 1821); *L'augurio felice* (1822); *La Santa Alleanza* (Verona, Nov. 24, 1822); *Il vero omaggio* (Verona, Dec. 3, 1822); *Il Bardo* (1822); *Omaggio pastorale* (Treviso, April 1, 1823); *Il pianto delle muse in morte di Lord Byron* (London, June 9, 1824); *Cantata per il battesimo del figlio del banchiere Aguado* (Paris, July 16, 1827); *Giovanna d'Arco* (1832; revised 1852); *Cantata ad Onore del Sommo Pontefice Pio IX* (Bologna, Aug. 16, 1846).

OTHER VOCAL MUSIC: 3 early masses (the first contains 3 sections only by Rossini for a composite score composed by students of the Liceo Musicale in 1808 and perf. in Bologna, June 2, 1808; 1808; 1809); *Messa solenne* (Naples, March 19, 1820); *Tantum ergo* (1824); *Soirées musicales* (1830–35); *Stabat Mater* (first version, 1831–32; orch. version, 1841; Paris, Jan. 7, 1842); *Tantum ergo* (Bologna, Nov. 28, 1847); *O salutaris Hostia* (1857); *Laus Deo* (1861); *Petite messe solennelle* (1863; Paris, March 14, 1864; orch. version, 1867; Paris, Feb. 24, 1869).

FOR ORCH.: Overture in D major (1808); 3 sinfonias: D major (1808); E-flat major (1809; later revised for use as the overture to *La cambiale di matrimonio*); A major (discovered by P. Ingerslev-Jenson and called the "Odense"); *Variazioni in fa maggiore per più strumenti obbligati con accompagnamento di orchestra* (1809); *Variazioni in do maggiore per clarinetto obbligato con accompagnamento di orchestra* (1810); marches.

CHAMBER MUSIC: 6 *sonate a quattro* (1804); 5 string quartets (1806–8); 5 duets (1806); *Tema con variazione per quattro strumenti a fiato* for Flute, Clarinet, Horn, and Bassoon (1812); *Rondeau fantastique* for Horn and Piano (1856).

BIBLIOGRAPHY: A valuable source is the *Bollettino del Centro Rossiniano di Studi* (Pesaro, 1955–60; 1967—). G. Righetti-Giorgi, *Cenni di una donna già cantante sopra il maestro R.* (Bologna, 1823); G. Carpani, *Le Rossiniane, ossia Lettere musico-teatrali* (Padua, 1824); Stendhal, *Vie de R.* (Paris, 1824; many subsequent eds. and translations; in Eng. as *Life of R.,* trans. and ed. by R. Coe, London and N.Y., 1956; 2nd ed., 1970); J.A. Wendt, *R.'s Leben und Treiben* (Leipzig, 1824); J.-L. d'Ortigue, *De la guerre des dilettanti, ou De la Révolution opérée par R. dans l'opéra français, et des rapports qui existent entre la musique, la littérature et les arts* (Paris, 1830); A. Zanolini, *Biografia di G. R.* (Paris, 1836; also later eds.); H. Blaze de Bury, "R.: Sa vie et ses œuvres," *Revue des Deux Mondes* (May–June 1854); L. and M. Escudier, *R.: Sa vie et ses œuvres* (Paris, 1854); E. de Mirecourt, *R.* (Paris, 1855); A. Aulagnier, *G. R.: Sa vie et ses œuvres* (Paris, 1864); A.-J. Azevedo, *G. R.: Sa vie ses œuvres* (Paris, 1864); F. Hiller, *Plaudereien mit R.,* vol. II of *Aus dem Tonleben unserer Zeit* (Leipzig, 1868); R. Wagner, "Eine Erinnerung an R.," *Allgemeine Zeitung* (Augsburg, Dec. 17, 1868); H. Edwards, *Life of R.* (London, 1869; reissued in a condensed version as *R. and His School,* London, 1881); C. Montrond, *R.: Etude biographique* (Lille, 1870); F. Mordani, *Della*

vita privata di G. R.: Memorie inedite (Imola, 1871); A. Pougin, *R.: Notes, impressions, souvenirs, commentaires* (Paris, 1871); G. Vanzolini, *Della vera patria di G. R.* (Pesaro, 1873); L. Silvestri, *Della vita e delle opere di G. R.* . . . (Milan, 1874); C. Magnico, *R. e Wagner, o La musica italiana e la musica tedesca* (Genoa, 1875); G. de Sanctis, *G. R.: Appunti di viaggio* (Rome, 1878); J. Sittard, *G.A. R.* (Leipzig, 1882); C. Thrane, *R. og operaen* (Copenhagen, 1885); V. Camaiti, *G. R.: Notizie biografiche, artistiche e aneddotiche* (Florence, 1887); R. Gandolfi, *G. R.* (Florence, 1887); G. Mazzatinti, *Lettere inedite di G. R.* (Imola, 1890); A. Allmaÿer, *Undici lettere di G. R. pubblicate per la prima volta* . . . (Siena, 1892); A. Kohut, *R.* (Leipzig, 1892); G. Mazzatinti, *Lettere inedite e rare di G. R.* (Imola, 1892); E. Michotte, *Souvenirs: Une Soirée chez R. à Beau-Sejour (Passy) 1858* . . . (Brussels, n.d. [after 1893]; Eng. trans. by H. Weinstock, Chicago, 1968); E. Checchi, *R.* (Florence, 1898); A. Maffei, *R.* (Florence, 1898); G. Tebaldini, "Da R. a Verdi," *Aversa a Domenico Cimarosa* (Naples, 1901); G. Mazzatinti and F. and G. Manis, *Lettere di G. R.* (Florence, 1902); L. Dauriac, *R.: Biographie critique* (Paris, 1906); E. Michotte, *Souvenirs: La Visite de R. Wagner à R. (Paris, 1860): Détails inédits et commentaires* (Paris, 1906; Eng. trans. by H. Weinstock, Chicago, 1968); E. Corradi, *G. R.* (Rome, 1909); F. Cowen, *R.* (London and N.Y., 1912; G. Fara, *Genio e ingegno musicale: G. R.* (Turin, 1915); N. Morini, *La casa di R. in Bologna* (Bologna, 1916); L. Neretti, *I due inni patriottici di G. R.* (Florence, 1918); F. Vatielli, *R. e Bologna* (Bologna, 1918); H. de Curzon, *R.* (Paris, 1920; 2nd ed., 1930); G. Radiciotti, " 'Il Signor Bruschino' ed il 'Tancredi,' " *Rivista Musicale Italiana* (1920); V. du Bled, "Le Salon de R.," *La Revue Musicale* (1921); H. Prunières, "Stendhal and R.," *Musical Quarterly* (Jan. 1921); R. Fauchois, *R.* (Lyons, 1922); G. Radiciotti, *Il Barbiere di Siviglia: Guida attraverso la commedia e la musica* (Milan, 1923); idem, "Stendhal e R.," *Il Pianoforte* (Dec. 1923); G. Pannain, "R. nel 'Guglielmo Tell,' " *Rivista Musicale Italiana* (1924); G. Radiciotti, "R. à Londres," *La Revue Musicale* (Feb. 1, 1924; Eng. trans. in *Sackbut,* April 1924); idem, "L'Italiana in Algeri' di G. R.," *Il Pianoforte* (Nov. 1925); G. Gatti, *Le "Barbier de Séville" de R.* (Paris, 1926); G. Biamonti, *"Il Barbiere di Siviglia" di G. R.* (Rome, 1929); idem, *Guglielmo Tell* (Rome, 1929); J. Cooke, *R.: A Short Biography* (Philadelphia, 1929); H. Peyser, "The 'Cenerentola' of R.," *Musical America* (June 1929); G. Radiciotti, *G. R.: Vita documenta, opere ed influenza su l'arte* (the standard Italian biography; 3 vols., Tivoli, 1927–29); idem, *Aneddoti rossiniani autentici* (Rome, 1929); H. de Curzon, *Une Heure avec R.* (Paris, 1930); A. Bonaventura, *R.* (Florence, 1934); G. Derwent, *R. and Some Forgotten Nightingales* (London, 1934); H. Gerigk, *R.* (Potsdam, 1934); F. Toye, *R.: A Study in Tragi-Comedy* (London and N.Y., 1934); H. Faller, *Die Gesangskoloratur in R.s Opern und ihre Ausführung* (Berlin, 1935); G. Monaldi, *Gli Uomini illustri: G. R. nell'arte, nella vita, negli aneddoti* (Milan, n.d. [1936]); L. D'Amico, *R.* (Turin, 1939); R. Bacchelli, *G. R.* (Turin, 1941; 2nd ed., 1945); F. Bonavia, *R.* (London, 1941); A. Fraccaroli, *R.* (Milan,

1941; 4th ed., 1944); G. Pannain, "Personalità di R.," *Musica,* I (1942); L. Ronga, "Vicende del gusto rossiniano nell'Ottocento," ibid.; idem, "Svolgimento del gusto rossiniano fino al Novecento," *Musica,* II (1943); G. Roncaglia, *R. l'olimpico* (Milan, 1946; 2nd ed., 1953); G. Brigante Colonna, *Vita di R.* (Florence, 1947); K. Pfister, *Das Leben R.s: Gesetz und Triumph der Oper* (Vienna and Berlin, 1948); C. van Berkel, *G. R.* (Haarlem, 1950); P. Ingerslev-Jensen, "An Unknown R. Overture: Report of a Discovery in Odense," *Music Review* (Feb. 1950); *La Rassegna Musicale,* special issue devoted to Rossini and his works (July–Sept. 1954); F. Bonafé, *R. e son œuvre* (Le-Puy-en-Velay, 1955); U. Gozzano, *R.: Il romanzo dell'opera* (Turin, 1955); B. Riboli, "Malattia di G. R. secondo una relazione medica del 1842," *Note e Riviste di Psichiatria* (July and Dec. 1955); L. Rognoni, *R., con un'appendice comprendente lettere, documenti, testimonianze* (Parma, 1956; 3rd ed., 1977); F. Schlitzer, *Rossiniana: Contributo all'epistolario di G. R., Quaderni dell'Accademia chigiana,* XXXV (1956); idem, *R. a Siena e altri scritti rossiniani (con lettere inedite), Quaderni dell'Accademia chigiana,* XXXIX (1958); R. Bacchelli, *R. e esperienze rossiniane* (Milan, 1959); P. Ingerslev-Jensen, *R.* (Copenhagen, 1959); F. Schlitzer, *Un piccolo carteggio inedito di R. con un impresario italiano a Vienna* (Florence, 1959); A. Porter, "A Lost Opera by R.," *Music & Letters* (Jan. 1964); D. Schwartz, "R.: A Psychoanalytic Approach to the Great Renunciation," *Journal of the American Psychoanalytic Society,* XIII (1965); V. Viviani, ed., *I libretti di R.* (Milan, 1965); A. Bonaccorsi, ed., *G. R.* (Florence, 1968); F. d'Amico, *L'opera teatrale di G. R.* (Rome, 1968); H. Weinstock, *R.: A Biography* (the outstanding modern biography; N.Y., 1968); P. Gossett, *The Operas of R.: Problems of Textual Criticism in Nineteenth-Century Opera* (Diss., Princeton Univ., 1970); N. Till, *R.: His Life and Times* (Tunbridge Wells, 1983).

Rössl-Majdan, Hildegard, Austrian singer; b. Moosbierbaum, Jan. 21, 1921. She was educated at the Vienna Academy of Music. In 1951 she joined the Vienna State Opera; in later years she taught voice in Graz.

Rössler, Ernst Karl, German organist and composer; b. Pyritz, Pomerania, Oct. 18, 1909; d. Königsfeld, Aug. 19, 1980. He studied organ and was active mainly in organ building and church music. He lectured on composition for organ in Lübeck and Freiburg im Breisgau; publ. *Klangfunktion und Registrierung* (Kassel, 1952) and several other papers concerning organ registration. He composed some sacred choruses and numerous organ pieces.

Rostand, Claude, French writer on music; b. Paris, Dec. 3, 1912; d. Villejuif, Oct. 9, 1970. He studied with N. Dufourcq. In 1958 he organized a modern music society in Paris, Musique d'Aujourd'hui.

WRITINGS: *L'Œuvre de Gabriel Fauré* (Paris, 1945); *Richard Strauss* (Paris, 1949); *La Musique française contemporaine* (Paris, 1952); dialogues with Milhaud, Poulenc, Markevitch, and others; biographies of Brahms (2 vols., Paris, 1954–55), Liszt (Paris, 1960), Hugo Wolf (Paris, 1967), and Webern (1969); *Dictionnaire de la musique contemporaine* (Lausanne, 1970).

Rostropovich, Leopold, Russian cellist, father and teacher of **Mstislav Rostropovich;** b. Voronezh, March 9, 1892; d. Orenburg, July 31, 1942. He studied cello with his father, Vitold Rostropovich; gave concerts; from 1925 to 1931 was a prof. at the Cons. of Azerbaijan in Baku; then lived in Moscow; after the outbreak of the Nazi-Soviet war in 1941 he moved to Orenburg.

Rostropovich, Mstislav, eminent Russian cellist and conductor; b. Baku, March 27, 1927. His father and grandfather were cello players; he took lessons with his father; in 1937 entered the Moscow Cons., where he studied with Kozolupov, and took courses in composition with Shebalin; graduated in 1948 and joined the faculty of the Moscow Cons.; concurrently taught classes at the Leningrad Cons. In 1950 he won the International Competition of Cellists in Prague; then embarked on a highly successful career as a cello virtuoso, achieving a high rank among master cellists, next to Casals and Piatigorsky. Prokofiev, Shostakovich, Benjamin Britten, Walter Piston, Lukas Foss, and others wrote special works for him. He also revealed himself as an excellent pianist, and played accompaniments (from memory) to his wife, the singer **Galina Vishnevskaya.** Still another achievement in his versatile career was that of a fine conductor, both in opera and in symph. concerts. He received the Lenin Prize in 1963. But despite all these distinctions and official honors, he began having difficulties with the Soviet authorities, owing chiefly to his spirit of uncompromising independence; he let the dissident author Solzhenitsyn stay at his *dacha* near Moscow; also dared to criticize the bureaucrats of the Soviet Ministry of Culture, which was in charge of handling artistic engagements. As a result, he found himself hampered in his professional activities and was denied the opportunity to play and conduct as often as he wished. In 1974 he decided to take a leave of absence and went abroad, while still keeping his Soviet citizenship. His wife and 2 daughters followed him to the U.S. In 1975 he accepted the offer to conduct the National Symph. Orch. in Washington, D.C., and made a brilliant debut with it on March 5, 1975. In March 1978 he and his wife were stripped of their citizenship by the Soviet government as "ideological renegades." He organized the first Rostropovich International Cello Competition in Paris in 1981.

BIBLIOGRAPHY: Tatiana Gaidamovich, *Mstislav Rostropovich* (Moscow, 1969); "The Magnificent Maestro," *Time* (Oct. 24, 1977; the cover story).

Roswaenge, Helge, Danish tenor; b. Copenhagen (of German parents), Aug. 29, 1897; d. Munich, June 19, 1972. He studied engineering and took voice lessons; then made a grand tour through Scandinavia,

Germany, and Austria in concert and in opera. From 1929 to 1945, and again from 1949, he was attached principally to the Berlin State Opera; also sang at the Vienna State Opera (1936–58), and in Bayreuth and Salzburg. In his prime, his voice was often compared in quality of bel canto with that of Caruso. He publ. 3 booklets of an autobiographical nature: *Skratta Pajazzo* (*Ridi, Pagliaccio;* Copenhagen, 1945); *Mach es besser, mein Sohn* (Leipzig, 1962); *Leitfaden für Gesangsbeflissene* (Munich, 1964).

BIBLIOGRAPHY: F. Tassie, *Helge Rosvaenge* (Augsburg, 1975).

Rota, Nino, brilliant Italian composer; b. Milan, Dec. 3, 1911; d. Rome, April 10, 1979. He was a precocious musician; at the age of 11 he wrote an oratorio which had a public performance, and at 13 composed a lyric comedy in 3 acts, *Il Principe porcaro,* after Hans Christian Andersen. He then undertook a serious study of composition with Alfredo Casella and Ildebrando Pizzetti at the Santa Cecilia Academy in Rome, graduating in 1930; later went to the U.S., and enrolled in the Curtis Inst. of Philadelphia, studying composition with Rosario Scalero and conducting with Fritz Reiner. Returning to Italy, he entered the Univ. of Milan to study literature, gaining a degree in 1937. Turning definitely to music, he joined the faculty of the Liceo Musicale in Bari; later became its director (1950–78). His musical style demonstrates a great facility, and even felicity, with occasional daring excursions into the forbidding territory of dodecaphony. However, his most durable compositions are related to his music for the cinema; he composed the sound tracks of a great number of films of the Italian director Federico Fellini covering the period from 1950 to 1979.

WORKS: OPERAS: *Il Principe porcaro* (1925); *Ariodante* (Parma, Nov. 5, 1942); *Torquemada* (1943; revised version, Naples, Jan. 24, 1976); radio opera, *I 2 timidi* (Italian Radio, 1950; stage version, London, March 17, 1952); *Il cappello di paglia di Firenzi* (*Florentine Straw Hat;* 1946; Palermo, April 2, 1955); *La scuola di guida* (Spoleto, 1959); *Lo scoiattolo in gamba* (Venice, Sept. 16, 1959); opera buffa, *La notte di un nevrastenico* (concert version, Turin, July 9, 1959; stage version, Milan, Feb. 8, 1960); *Aladino e la lampada magica* (Naples, Jan. 14, 1968); *La visita meravigliosa,* after H.G. Wells (Palermo, Feb. 6, 1970); *Napoli milionaria,* to a libretto dealing with the American occupation of Naples in 1945 (produced in Spoleto, June 22, 1977). BALLETS: *La rappresentazione di Adamo ed Eva* (Perugia, Oct. 5, 1957); *La strada* (after the 1954 Fellini film of the same name; Milan, 1965; revised 1978); *La Molière imaginaire* (Paris, 1976). FOR ORCH.: *Balli* (1932); *Serenata* (1932); 3 symphs. (1936–39, 1938–43, 1957); *Sinfonia sopra una canzone d'amore* (1947–72); Harp Concerto (1948); *Variazioni sopra un tema gioviale* (1954); *Concerto festivo* (1958); Piano Concerto (1960); *Concerto soirée* for Piano and Orch.; *Fantasia sopra 12-note del "Don Giovanni" di Mozart* for Piano and Orch.

(1961); Concerto for String Orch. (1964); Trombone Concerto (1968); *Divertimento concertante* for Double Bass and Orch. (1968–69); Cello Concerto (1973); *Castel del Monte* for Horn and Orch. (1975–76); Bassoon Concerto (1974–77); *The Godfather Suite* (from the films; Buffalo, Nov. 5, 1976); *Piccolo mondo antico,* concerto for Piano and Orch. (1979). FOR VOICE: Oratorios: *L'infanzia di S. Giovanni Battista* (1923); *Mysterium Catholicum* (1962); *La vita di Maria* (1970); *Roma capomunni* (1972); *Rabelaisiana* (1978); 3 masses (1960–62); songs. CHAMBER MUSIC: *Invenzioni* for String Quartet (1933); Viola Sonata (1934); *Canzona* for 11 Instruments (1935); Quintet for Flute, Oboe, Viola, Cello, and Harp (1935); Violin Sonata (1937); Sonata for Flute and Harp (1937); Trio for Flute, Violin, and Piano (1958); Nonet (1958); Elegy for Oboe and Piano (1959); Sonata for Organ and Brass (1968). FOR PIANO: *Variazioni e fuga sul nome B-A-C-H* (1950); *15 Preludes* (1964). FOR ORGAN: Organ Sonata (1965). FILM SCORES: For films by Fellini, including *Lo sceicco bianco* (*The White Sheik;* 1950); *I vitelloni* (1953); *La strada* (1954); *Il bidone* (1955); *Notti di Cabiria* (1957); *La dolce vita* (1959); part of *Boccaccio 70* (1962); *Otto de mezza* (*8 ½;* 1963); *Giulietta degli spiriti* (*Juliet of the Spirits;* 1965); *Satyricon* (1969); *The Clowns* (1971); *Fellini Roma* (1972); *Amarcord* (1974); *Casanova* (1977); *Orchestra Rehearsal* (1979). His scores for other directors include Cass's *The Glass Mountain* (1950); De Filippo's *Napoli milionaria* (1950); Vidor's *War and Peace* (1956); Visconti's *Le notti bianche* (1957), *Rocco e i suoi fratelli* (1960), and *Il gattopardo* (*The Leopard;* 1963); Zeffirelli's *The Taming of the Shrew* (1966) and *Romeo e Giulietta* (1968); Bondarchuk's *Waterloo* (1969); Coppola's *The Godfather I* (1972) and *II* (1974); Harvey's *The Abdication* (1974); Wertmuller's *Love and Anarchy* (1974); Guillermin's *Death on the Nile* (1978); Monicelli's *Caro Michele* (1978); and Troell's *Hurricane* (1979).

BIBLIOGRAPHY: Dorle Soria, "Artist Life," *High Fidelity/Musical America* (Nov. 1975; pp. MA5+); Derek Elley, "Nino Rota: A Tribute," *Records and Recording* (June 1979).

Roters, Ernst, German composer; b. Oldenburg, July 6, 1892; d. Berlin, Aug. 25, 1961. He studied at the Klindworth-Scharwenka Cons. in Berlin with Moritz Mayer-Mahr (piano), Hugo Leichtentritt (theory), and Georg Schumann (composition); was in the German army during World War I; then worked in the films; was again in the German army during the last year of World War II (1944–45); after the cessation of hostilities, he returned to Berlin, where he conducted the Deutsches Theater (1945–47). A highly prolific composer (150 opus numbers before 1955), he wrote an opera, *Die schwarze Kammer* (Darmstadt, 1928); incidental music for 15 plays; about 50 radio works; 3 piano concertos; numerous pieces of chamber music and songs.

Roth, Bertrand, Swiss pianist; b. Degersheim, Feb. 12, 1855; d. Bern, Jan. 25, 1938. He studied at the

Leipzig Cons. and later in Weimar with Liszt; from 1884 to 1900, taught at the Cons. of Dresden; in 1901 he established there the Musiksalon Bertrand Roth, Sunday matinées at which works by contemporary composers were performed.

Roth, Feri, eminent Hungarian violinist; b. Zvolen, Czechoslovakia, July 18, 1899; d. Los Angeles, May 7, 1969. He studied at the State Academy in Budapest; organized a string quartet with which he toured Europe and Africa; then emigrated to the U.S. and formed the Roth Quartet (with Jenö Antal, Ferenc Molnar, and Janos Scholz), which made an American debut at the Pittsfield Music Festival, Sept. 21, 1928. In 1946 he was appointed prof. of violin and chamber ensemble at the Univ. of Calif. at Los Angeles, a post he held until his death.

Roth, Herman, German musicologist; b. Hornberg, Baden, Feb. 15, 1882; d. Berlin, Feb. 1, 1938. He studied philology and philosophy; then took courses in music with Philipp Wolfrum in Heidelberg (1902) and Hugo Riemann in Leipzig (1905). He was music critic in Leipzig (1907–10) and Munich (1910–21); taught at the Cons. of Baden (1921–24) and at the Hochschule für Musik at Stuttgart (1925–32); then settled in Berlin. He publ. the books *Heinrich Kasper Schmid* (Munich, 1921) and *Elemente der Stimmführung* (Stuttgart, 1926); edited works by Bach, Handel, etc.

Rothenberger, Anneliese, German lyric soprano; b. Mannheim, June 19, 1924. After vocal study in Mannheim, she made her operatic debut in Koblenz in 1943. From 1946 to 1957 and again in 1958–73 she was a member of the Hamburg State Opera; also had engagements in Düsseldorf, Salzburg, Edinburgh, and Aix-en-Provence. In 1958 she joined the Vienna State Opera; also sang at La Scala in Milan and in Munich. On Nov. 18, 1960, she made a notable debut at the Metropolitan Opera in N.Y. as Zdenka in *Arabella,* by Richard Strauss. She was one of the most versatile singers of her generation, capable of giving congenial renditions of soprano parts in operas of Mozart and Verdi; she also gave an excellent performance of the challenging role of Marie in Alban Berg's opera *Wozzeck.* She further distinguished herself in the even more demanding role of Lulu in Alban Berg's opera, which she sang with the Hamburg Opera. She publ. an autobiography, *Melodie meines Lebens* (Munich, 1972).

Rother, Artur, German conductor; b. Stettin, Oct. 12, 1885; d. Aschau, Sept. 22, 1972. He studied piano and organ with his father; also attended the univs. of Tübingen and Berlin. He conducted in Wiesbaden; was also an assistant at the Bayreuth Festivals (1907–14); from 1927 to 1934 was Generalmusikdirektor in Dessau; in 1938 went to Berlin as a conductor at the Deutsches Opernhaus, where he remained until 1958. He was also a composer of stage music.

Rothier, Léon, French bass; b. Rheims, Dec. 26, 1874; d. New York, Dec. 6, 1951. He studied at the Paris Cons. with Crosti (singing), Lhérie (opéra-comique), and Melchissedec (opera), winning first prizes in all 3 classes upon graduation. He made his operatic debut as Jupiter in Gounod's *Philémon et Baucis* at the Opéra-Comique, where he remained until 1903; then was active at Marseilles (1903–7), Nice (1907–9), and Lyons (1909–10). On Dec. 10, 1910, he made his American debut at the Metropolitan Opera in N.Y. as Méphistophélès; after retirement (1939), he remained in N.Y. as a teacher.

Rothmüller, Marko, Yugoslav baritone; b. Trnjani, Dec. 31, 1908. He studied in Zagreb; then took lessons in singing with Franz Steiner in Vienna, and also had lessons in composition with Alban Berg. He made his operatic debut as Ottokar in *Der Freischütz* at the Schiller Theater in Hamburg-Altona in 1932; was a member of the opera in Zagreb (1932–34) and Zürich (1935–47); then was with the Covent Garden Opera in London (1948–52). He sang for a season with the N.Y. City Opera (1948–49); then sang at Glyndebourne (1949–55); made his debut at the Metropolitan Opera in N.Y. on Jan. 22, 1959, as Kothner in *Die Meistersinger;* remained there until 1964; also taught voice in N.Y. He then joined the faculty of Indiana Univ. School of Music in Bloomington; retired there in 1979. He was distinguished in Wagner roles; also sang leading roles in modern works, including Wozzeck in Alban Berg's opera. He wrote some chamber music and songs; publ. an interesting vol., *Die Musik der Juden* (Zürich, 1951; in Eng., London, 1953; 2nd ed., revised, 1967).

Rothwell, Evelyn, English oboist; b. Wallingford, Jan. 24, 1911. She studied at the Royal College of Music with Leon Goossens; in 1931 she joined the Covent Garden Opera touring orch.; then was a member of the Scottish Orch. in Glasgow (1933–36) and of the London Symph. Orch. (1935–39); also played in the Glyndebourne Festival Orch. (1934–39). In 1939 she married the conductor **Barbirolli.** In 1971 she became a prof. of oboe at the Royal Academy of Music.
BIBLIOGRAPHY: H. Atkins and P. Cotes, *The Barbirollis: A Musical Marriage* (London, 1983).

Rothwell, Walter Henry, British-American conductor; b. London, Sept. 22, 1872; d. Santa Monica, Calif., March 12, 1927. He studied at the Vienna Cons. (1881–88) with J. Epstein (piano), R. Fuchs (theory), and Bruckner (composition); took further courses in Munich with Thuille and Schillings. In 1895 he became assistant conductor to Mahler at the Hamburg Opera; then conducted the German opera in Amsterdam (1903–4) and (1904–8) the Savage Opera Co. in the U.S., with which he gave performances of *Parsifal* in English. He then was conductor of the St. Paul Symph. Orch. (1908–14); after several years in N.Y. as a teacher, he was engaged (1919) to organize and conduct the Los Angeles Phil. Orch., which he led until his death. He was married (Sept. 10, 1908) to the soprano **Elisabeth Wolff.**

Rottenberg, Ludwig, Austrian conductor and composer; b. Czernowitz, Bukovina, Oct. 11, 1864; d. Frankfurt, May 6, 1932. He studied music with A. H římalý, R. Fuchs, and E. Mandyczewski in Vienna; was Kapellmeister at the Stadttheater in Brünn (1891–92) and at the Frankfurt opera (1893–1926); retired in 1927. In 1912 and 1913 he conducted the Wagner performances at Covent Garden in London. He publ. a collection of 30 songs, a Violin Sonata, and piano variations; his opera, *Die Geschwister,* was produced in Frankfurt on Nov. 30, 1915. Rottenberg was the father-in-law of **Paul Hindemith.**

Rotzsche, Hans-Joachim, German tenor and choral conductor; b. Leipzig, April 25, 1929. He studied at the Leipzig Hochschule für Musik, where his principal teachers were Günther Ramin, Amadeus Webersinke, and Johannes Weyrauch; also studied voice with Fritz Polster. In 1961 he joined the faculty of the Leipzig Hochschule für Musik; in 1963 he became director of the choral program at the Univ. of Leipzig. He was named cantor of the Thomaskirche of Leipzig in 1972; also conducted the Neues Bachisches Collegium Musicum.

Rouart-Lerolle & Cie., French publishing house, founded in 1905 at Paris by **Alexander Rouart** (1869–1921), through the purchase of the firms of Meuriot and Baudoux. When, in 1908, **Jacques Lerolle,** son of the famous painter, became his associate, the firm acquired the catalogue of the publ. house of Gregh (founded in 1840). After the death of Rouart in 1921, Lerolle became director; Mme. Rouart, the founder's widow, a partner; and François Hepp (1887–1965), son-in-law of Rouart, co-director. In 1942 the entire stock of Rouart-Lerolle & Cie. was sold to Salabert.

Rouget de l'Isle, Claude-Joseph, composer of the *Marseillaise;* b. Lons-le-Saulnier, Jura, May 10, 1760; d. Choisy-le-Roy, June 27, 1836. He composed the famous national hymn in 1792, while stationed in Strasbourg as a military engineer. The original title of the *Marseillaise* was *Le Chant de guerre de l'armée du Rhin,* and it was designed to be a patriotic song at the time of the war with Austria; it was taken up by the Marseilles soldiers marching toward Paris, and so assumed its universally known title. Rouget de l'Isle was himself not a revolutionary; he was in fact imprisoned for refusing to take the oath against the crown. He went to Paris after Robespierre's downfall, and composed a *Hymne dithyrambique sur la conjuration de Robespierre* (1794), *Chant des vengeances* (1798), and a *Chant du combat* for the army in Egypt (1800). He publ. 50 *Chants français* in 1825; wrote several opera librettos. Maurice de La Fuye and Emile Guéret, in their book *Rouget de l'Isle, Inconnu* (Paris, 1943), argued that he wrote only the words and not the music of the *Marseillaise,* and suggested that the composer was Ignace Pleyel. A. Loth, in his pamphlet *Le Chant de la Marseillaise* (Paris, 1886), claimed that the composer was one Grisons.
BIBLIOGRAPHY: J. Tiersot, *Rouget de l'Isle: Son œuvre, sa vie* (Paris, 1892); A. Köckert, *Rouget de l'Isle* (Leipzig, 1898); A. Lanier, *Rouget de l'Isle* (Besançon, 1907); J. Tiersot, *Histoire de la Marseillaise* (Paris, 1915); R. Brancour, *La Marseillaise et le Chant du départ* (1916); E. Istel, "Is the Marseillaise a German Composition?" *Musical Quarterly* (April 1922); V. Helfert, "La Marseillaise," *Rivista Musicale Italiana* (1922); A. Becker, *La Marseillaise* (Braunschweig, 1930); G. de Froidcourt, *Grétry, Rouget de Lisle et la Marseillaise* (Liège, 1945); F. Chailley, "La Marseillaise: Etude critique sur ses origines," *Annales historiques de la Révolution française,* XXXII (1960).

Rouse, Christopher, American composer; b. Baltimore, Feb. 15, 1949. He studied with Richard Hoffmann at the Oberlin Cons. (1967–71); later took private lessons with George Crumb (1970–73); then entered Cornell Univ. in the class of Karel Husa (M.M., D.M., 1977); subsequently taught at the Univ. of Michigan (1978–81) and at the Eastman School of Music in Rochester, N.Y.
WORKS: *Kabir Padavali* for Soprano and Orch. (1972); *Subjectives VIII* for Trumpet, Percussion, and Tape (1972–73); *Love Songs* for Bass-baritone and Orch. (1973); *Vulcan* for Concert Band (1975); *Alloeidea* for Orch. (1978); *Mitternachtlieder* for Bass-baritone and Chamber Ensemble (1979); *Thor* for Wind Ensemble (1979); *Liber Daemonum* for Organ (1980); *The Infernal Machine* for Orch. (Univ. of Michigan Symph., Evian Festival, France, May 9, 1981); String Quartet (1982); *Rotae Passionis* for Chamber Ensemble (1982); *Gorgon* for Orch. (1983–84).

Roussakis, Nicolas, American composer of Greek ancestry; b. Athens, June 14, 1934. He emigrated to the U.S. in 1949; attended Columbia College (B.A., 1956) and the Graduate Faculties of Columbia Univ. (M.A., 1960), where he attended courses of Otto Luening, Jack Beeson, Henry Cowell, Ben Weber, Ralph Shapey, and Philipp Jarnach. To earn a living, he played the clarinet; received a Fulbright grant for study in Germany (1961–63); attended seminars of Boulez, Berio, Ligeti, and Stockhausen in Darmstadt. Upon his return to the U.S., he became active with contemporary music groups. In 1977 he was appointed to the faculty at Rutgers Univ. He was co-founder, with Francis Thorne, of the American Composers Orch. His own works are marked by an aggressive modernity of idiom, but are satisfyingly playable and surprisingly pleasurable even to untutored ears. They include *Night Speech* for Chorus and Percussion (1968); *Short Pieces* for 2 Flutes (1969); *Concertino* for Percussion and Woodwinds (1973); *Ode and Cataclysm* for Orch. (1975); *Ephemeris* for String Quartet (1979); piano pieces; choruses.

Rousseau, Jean-Jacques, great philosopher and author; b. Geneva, June 28, 1712; d. Ermenonville, near Paris, July 2, 1778. Without other musical training besides desultory self-instruction, Rousseau made his debut as a music scholar at the age of 29, reading a paper before the Académie in Paris (1724), which was received and publ. as a *Dissertation sur la musique moderne* (1743). His opera *Les Muses galantes* had only one private representation, at the house of La Pouplinière in 1745; his revision of the intermezzo *La Reine de Navarre* (by Voltaire and Rameau) was a failure in Paris; but his opera *Le Devin du village* (Fontainebleau, Oct. 18, 1752; Paris Opéra, March 1, 1753) was very successful and remained in the repertoire for 75 years. In the meantime, his musical articles for the *Encyclopédie* had evoked scathing criticism from Rameau and others; improved by revision and augmentation, they were republ. as his *Dictionnaire de musique* (Geneva, 1767; the existence of this ed. cannot be proved; first known ed., Paris, 1768). In 1752 commenced the dispute, known as the "guerre des bouffons," between the partisans of French and Italian opera; Rousseau sided with the latter, publishing a *Lettre à M. Grimm au sujet des remarques ajoutées à sa lettre sur Omphale* (1752), followed by the caustic *Lettre sur la musique française* (1753; to which the members of the Opéra responded by burning him in effigy and excluding him from the theater) and *Lettre d'un symphoniste de l'Académie royale de musique à ses camarades* (1753). He wrote 2 numbers for the melodrama *Pygmalion* (1770; Paris, Oct. 30, 1775). Publ. posthumously were 6 new arias for *Le Devin du village,* and a collection of about 100 *romances* and duets, *Les Consolations des misères de ma vie* (1781), and fragments of an opera, *Daphnis et Chloé* (1780). All his writings on music have been often republ. in eds. of his *Collected Works* (1782; many subsequent eds.).

BIBLIOGRAPHY: A. Jensen, *J.-J. R. Fragments inédits, recherches biographiques* (Paris, 1882); A. Jansen, *J.-J. R. als Musiker* (Berlin, 1884); A. Pougin, *J.-J. R., Musicien* (Paris, 1901); E. Istel, *J.-J. R. als Komponist seiner lyrischen Szene "Pygmalion"* (Leipzig, 1901); F. Hellouin, "J.-J. R. et la psychologie de l'orchestre," in *Feuillets d'histoire musicale française* (Paris, 1903); E. Schütte, *J.-J. R. Seine Persönlichkeit und sein Stil* (Leipzig, 1910); J. Tiersot, *J.-J. R.* (Paris, 1912); E. Faguet, *Rousseau artiste* (Paris, 1913); A.L. Sells, *The Early Life of Rousseau: 1712–40* (London, 1929); R. Gérin, *J.-J. R.* (Paris, 1930); M. Moffat, *Rousseau et le théâtre* (Paris, 1930); J. Tiersot, "Concerning J.-J. R., the Musician," *Musical Quarterly* (July 1931); H.V. Somerset, "J.-J. R. as a Musician," *Music & Letters* (1936); L. Richebourg, *Contributions à l'histoire de la "querelle des bouffons"* (Paris, 1937); A. Pochon, *J.-J. R., Musiciens et le critique* (Montreux, 1940); E. Kisch, "Rameau and Rousseau," *Music & Letters* (1941); A.R. Oliver, *The Encyclopaedists as Critics of Music* (N.Y., 1947); Jean Senelier, *Bibliographie générale des œuvres de J.-J. R.* (Paris, 1949); A. Lowenberg, *Annals of Opera* (Cambridge, 1943; 3rd ed., 1978). *Correspondance générale de J.-J. R.,* ed. by Dufour and Plan, was publ. in 20 vols. (Paris, 1924–34). The Institut du Musée Voltaire brought out the *Correspondance complète de J.-J. R.,* ed. by R.A. Leigh (18 vols., Geneva, 1965–73).

Rousseau, Marcel (-Auguste-Louis), French

composer; b. Paris, Aug. 18, 1882; d. there, June 11, 1955. He studied with his father, **Samuel Rousseau;** then entered the Paris Cons. as a student of Lenepveu; won the Deuxième Premier Grand Prix de Rome with the cantata *Maia* (1905). Later in his professional career he added his father's first name to his own, and produced his works as **Samuel-Rousseau.**

WORKS: Operas (all produced in Paris): *Tarass Boulba,* after Gogol (Nov. 22, 1919); *Le Hulla* (March 9, 1923); *Le Bon Roi Dagobert* (Dec. 5, 1927; his most successful work); *Kerkeb* (April 6, 1951); ballets: *Promenade dans Rome* (Paris, Dec. 7, 1936) and *Entre 2 rondes* (Paris, April 27, 1940); orch. tableaux: *Solitude triste* and *Impression dolente;* etc. In 1947 he was elected to the Académie des Beaux-Arts.

Rousseau, Samuel-Alexandre, French composer, father of **Marcel Samuel-Rousseau;** b. Neuve-Maison, Aisne, June 11, 1853; d. Paris, Oct. 1, 1904. He studied at the Paris Cons. with César Franck (organ) and Bazin (composition); won the Grand Prix de Rome with the cantata *La Fille de Jephté* (1878); also the Prix Cressent with the one-act comic opera *Dianora* (Opéra-Comique, Dec. 22, 1879). His opera *Mérowig* was awarded the Prize of the City of Paris, and was performed in concert form at the Grand Théâtre there on Dec. 12, 1892. In 1892 he was appointed conductor at the Théâtre-Lyrique; was for 10 years chorus master at the Société des Concerts du Cons.; also taught harmony at the Paris Cons. On June 8, 1898, his lyric drama *La Cloche du Rhin* was staged at the Paris Opéra with considerable success, but had only 9 performances in all; this was followed by the music dramas *Milia* (Opéra-Comique, 1904) and *Léone* (Opéra-Comique, March 7, 1910).

Roussel, Albert (Charles Paul Marie), outstanding French composer; b. Tourcoing, Département du Nord, April 5, 1869; d. Royan, Aug. 23, 1937. Orphaned as a child, he was educated by his grandfather, mayor of his native town, and after the grandfather's death, by his aunt. He studied academic subjects at the Collège Stanislas in Paris; music with the organist Stoltz; then studied mathematics in preparation for entering the Naval Academy; at the age of 18 he began his training in the navy; from 1889 to Aug. 1890 he was a member of the crew of the frigate *Iphigénie,* sailing to Indochina. This voyage was of great importance to Roussel, since it opened for him a world of oriental culture and art, which became one of the chief sources of his musical inspiration. He later sailed on the cruiser *Dévastation;* received a leave of absence for reasons of health, and spent some time in Tunis; was then stationed in Cherbourg, and began to compose there. In 1893 he was sent once more to Indochina. He resigned from the navy in 1894 and went to Paris, where he began to study music seriously with Eugène Gigout. In 1898 he entered the Schola Cantorum in Paris as a pupil of Vincent d'Indy; continued this study until 1907, when he was already 38 years old, but at the same time he was entrusted with a class in counterpoint, which he conducted at the Schola Cantorum from 1902 to 1914; among his students were Erik Satie, Stan Golestan, Paul Le Flem, Roland-Manuel, Guy de Lioncourt, and Varèse. In 1909 Roussel and his wife, Blanche Preisach-Roussel, undertook a voyage to India, where he became acquainted with the legend of the queen Padmâvatî, which he selected as a subject for his famous opera-ballet. His choral symph. *Les Evocations* was also inspired by this tour. At the outbreak of war in 1914, Roussel applied for active service in the navy but was rejected and volunteered as an ambulance driver. After the Armistice of 1918, he settled in Normandy and devoted himself to composition. In the autumn of 1930 he visited the U.S.

Roussel began his work under the influence of French Impressionism, with its dependence on exotic moods and poetic association. However, the sense of formal design asserted itself in his symph. works; his *Suite en fa* (1927) signalizes a transition toward neo-Classicism; the thematic development is vigorous, and the rhythms are clearly delineated, despite some asymmetrical progressions; the orchestration, too, is in the Classical tradition. Roussel possessed a keen sense of the theater; he was capable of fine characterization of exotic or mythological subjects, but also knew how to depict humorous situations in lighter works. An experiment in a frankly modernistic manner is exemplified by his *Jazz dans la nuit* for Voice and Piano.

WORKS: FOR THE STAGE: *Le Marchand de sable qui passe,* incidental music (Le Havre, Dec. 16, 1908); *Le Festin de l'araignée,* ballet-pantomime in one act (Paris, April 3, 1913); *Padmâvatî,* opera-ballet in 2 acts (1914–18; Paris, June 1, 1923); *La Naissance de la lyre,* lyric opera in one act (Paris, July 1, 1925); *Bacchus et Ariane,* ballet in 2 acts (Paris, May 22, 1931); *Le Testament de la tante Caroline,* opéra-bouffe (1932–33; Olomouc, Czechoslovakia, Nov. 14, 1936; Paris, March 11, 1937); *Aeneas,* ballet with Chorus, in one act (Brussels, July 31, 1935). FOR ORCH.: 4 symphs.: No. 1, *Le Poème de la forêt* (1904–6; Brussels, March 22, 1908); No. 2, *Symphonie en si bémol* (1919–21; Paris, March 4, 1922); No. 3, *Symphonie en sol mineur* (commissioned by the Boston Symph. Orch.; perf. there by Koussevitzky, Oct. 24, 1930); No. 4, *Symphonie en la majeur* (1934; Paris, Oct. 19, 1935); *Suite en fa* (Boston, Jan. 21, 1927); *Sinfonietta* for Strings (Paris, Nov. 19, 1934); *Résurrection,* symph. poem (Paris, May 17, 1904); *Evocations,* suite in 3 movements (Paris, May 18, 1912); *Pour une fête de printemps* (Paris, Oct. 29, 1921); *Rapsodie flamande* (Brussels, Dec. 12, 1935); *Concert pour petit orchestre* (Paris, May 5, 1927); *Petite suite pour orchestre* (Paris, Feb. 6, 1930); Piano Concerto (Paris, June 7, 1928); Concertino for Cello and Orch. (Paris, Feb. 6, 1937); *Le Bardit de Francs* for Male Chorus, Brass, and Percussion (Strasbourg, April 21, 1928); *Psaume LXXX* for Tenor, Chorus, and Orch. (Paris, April 25, 1929); symph. suites from theater works: *Le Festin de l'araignée* (1912); *Padmâvatî* (1914–18); *La Naissance de la lyre* (1922–24); *Bacchus et Ariane* (1930). CHAMBER MUSIC: Piano Trio (1902); *Divertissement* for Flute, Oboe, Clari-

net, Bassoon, Horn, and Piano (1906); *Sérénade* for Flute, Violin, Viola, Cello, and Harp (1925); Trio for Flute, Viola, and Cello (1929); String Quartet (1932); Trio for Violin, Viola, and Cello (1937); 2 violin sonatas (1908, 1924); *Joueurs de flûte,* suite for Flute and Piano (1924); *Andante et Scherzo* for Flute and Piano (1934). FOR PIANO: *Des heures passant,* a cycle of 4 pieces (1898); *Rustiques,* a cycle of 3 pieces (1904–6); suite of 3 pieces (1910); Sonatina (1912); *Petit canon perpétuel* (1913); *Prélude et fugue (Hommage à Bach);* etc. SONGS: *Adieux* (1907); *Jazz dans la nuit* (1928); *2 idylles* (1931); 3 sets of *Poèmes chinois* (1908, 1927, 1932); etc. A complete catalogue of works, with a biographical notice and annotations, was publ. in Paris in 1947 and constitutes a primary source of information.

BIBLIOGRAPHY: Roland-Manuel, "A. R.," *Revue Musicale* (Nov. 1922); L. Vuillemin, *A. R. et son œuvre* (Paris, 1924); Roussel issue of *Revue Musicale* (May–June 1929); H. Prunières, "A. R. and the 80th Psalm," *Musical Quarterly* (Jan. 1930); R. Dumesnil, "L'Œuvre symphonique de A. R.," *Musique Française* (Feb. 1933); R. Petit, "A. R.," *Modern Music* (Nov.–Dec. 1937); A. Hoérée, *A. R.* (Paris, 1938); P. Landormy, "A. R.," *Musical Quarterly* (Oct. 1938); N. Demuth, *A. R.: A Study* (London, 1947); R. Bernard, *A. R.: Sa vie, son œuvre* (Paris, 1948); Marc Pincherle, *A. R.* (Paris, 1957); Basil Deane, *Albert Roussel* (London, 1961); Dom Angelico Surchamp, *Albert Roussel: L'Homme et son œuvre* (Paris, 1967).

Rousselière, Charles, French tenor; b. St. Nazaire, Jan. 17, 1875; d. Joue-les-Tours, May 11, 1950. He studied at the Paris Cons.; made his debut in 1900 as Samson at the Paris Opéra, where he sang until 1912; also sang with the Monte Carlo Opera (1905–14), creating roles in Mascagni's *Amica,* Saint-Saëns's *L'Ancêtre,* and Fauré's *Pénélope;* also sang the role of Julien in Charpentier's opera at its first performance at the Opéra-Comique in Paris. He made his debut at the Metropolitan Opera in N.Y. as Romeo on Nov. 26, 1906, but remained on its roster for only one season. He made guest appearances at La Scala in Milan, the Teatro Colón in Buenos Aires, in Palermo, etc. He was at his best in the roles of Radames, Manrico, Siegmund, and Loge.

Roussier, Abbé Pierre-Joseph, French writer on music; b. Marseilles, 1716; d. as canon at Ecouis, Normandy, Aug. 18, 1792.

WRITINGS: *Observations sur différents points d'harmonie* (1765); *Traité des accords, et de leur succession* (1764; supplemented by *L'Harmonie pratique,* 1775); *Mémoire sur la musique des anciens* (1770); *Notes et observations sur le mémoire du P. Amiot concernant la musique des chinois* (1779); *Mémoire sur la nouvelle harpe de M. Cousineau* (1782); *Mémoire sur le clavecin chromatique* (1782); *Lettre sur l'acceptation des mots "basse fondamentale"* (1783; *Journal Encyclopédique,* vol. I); etc.

BIBLIOGRAPHY: R. Osborne, *The Theoretical Writings of Abbé Pierre-Joseph Roussier* (Diss.,

Ohio State Univ., 1966).

Rovelli, Pietro, Italian violinist; b. Bergamo, Feb. 6, 1793; d. there, Sept. 8, 1838. He studied with R. Kreutzer; then played in various orchs. in Italy; was concertmaster of the court orch. in Munich (1815–19); then taught and conducted in Bergamo. He publ. excellent études and caprices for Violin; also *Variazioni* for Violin and Orch.

Rovere, Agostino, Italian bass; b. Monza, 1804; d. New York, Dec. 10, 1865. He studied in Milan; made his debut in 1826 in Pavia; was a leading singer at La Scala in Milan (1831–44, 1846–47, 1856–57); also appeared in Vienna (1839, 1842–45), where he created the role of Boisfleury in Donizetti's *Linda di Chamounix;* also sang at Covent Garden in London (1847–48). He was most famous for his buffo roles; excelled as Leporello, Bartolo, and Dulcamara.

Rowbotham, Rev. John Frederick, British music historian; b. Edinburgh, April 18, 1854; d. Sutton-Cheney, Oct. 20, 1925. He studied music in Oxford, Berlin, Dresden, Paris, and Vienna; held various appointments as vicar and rector until 1910, when he founded the *Bard,* of which he was editor. He traveled on the Continent to collect materials for his *History of Music,* publ. in 3 vols. (London, 1885–87); also publ. *How to Write Music Correctly* (1889); *A Short History of Music* (1891); *Private Life of the Great Composers* (1892); *The Troubadours, and the Courts of Love* (1895); *A History of Music to the Time of the Troubadours* (1899); *Story Lives of Great Musicians* (1908); etc.

Rowen, Ruth Halle, American musicologist and educator; b. New York, April 5, 1918. She studied at Horace Mann High School (graduated 1935), at Barnard College (B.A., 1939), and at the Columbia Univ. Graduate Faculties (William Mason Scholar, M.A., 1941; Clarence Barker Scholar, Ph.D., 1948), where she took courses with William John Mitchell, Paul Henry Lang, Erich Hertzmann, and Douglas Stuart Moore; in 1954–63 directed the education dept. of Carl Fischer, Inc.; in 1963 was appointed musicologist at the inception of the M.A. program in music at the City College of N.Y. (chairman 1966–75); in 1967 became one of the 12 original faculty members of the Ph.D. program in music at the Graduate School of the City Univ. of N.Y. She served as musicianship chairman of the National Federation of Music Clubs (1962–74). She wrote *Early Chamber Music* (N.Y., 1949; new preface and supplementary bibliography, 1974); *Music through Sources and Documents* (Englewood Cliffs, N.J., 1978); co-author of *Hearing—Gateway to Music* (Evanston, Ill., 1959); co-composer of *Choral Program Favorites* (N.Y., 1956).

Rowicki, Witold, Russian-born Polish conductor and composer; b. Taganrog, Feb. 26, 1914. He studied violin with Malawski and composition with Piotrowski at the Cracow Cons., graduating in 1938; during the war he was in Germany, where he took private conducting lessons with Paul Hindemith's brother, Rudolf (1942–44). After the war he was a founder of the Katowice Radio Symph. Orch. (1945–50) and of the Warsaw Phil. (1950–55); became its music director in 1958; subsequently directed the Wielki Theater Opera Center in Warsaw (1965–70). He achieved a fine reputation for his promotion of modern Polish music. He is also a composer; his works include a Symph. (1957) and a *Warsaw Concerto* for Orch. (Warsaw, Nov. 6, 1976).
BIBLIOGRAPHY: L. Terpilowski, *Witold Rowicki* (Cracow, 1961).

Rowley, Alec, English composer; b. London, March 13, 1892; d. Weybridge, Surrey, Jan. 12, 1958. He studied at the Royal Academy of Music; upon graduation, became a teacher. Among his works are a pantomime, *The Princess Who Lost a Tune;* 2 piano concertos; *Rhapsody* for Viola and Orch.; Concerto for Oboe and Orch.; *Phyllis and Corydon* for String Quartet; *From Faerie* for String Quartet; *Little Jesus* for Voice, Piano, and String Quartet; *Watercolours* for Piano, Violin, Viola, and Cello; *Pastel Portraits* for Piano, Violin, and Cello; 3 little trios for Piano, Violin, and Cello; *The Puppet Show, 4 Contrasts, A Short Suite;* also piano pieces for children.

Roy, Klaus George, Austrian-born American composer, writer, and program annotator; b. Vienna, Jan. 24, 1924. He came to the U.S. in 1940; studied at Boston Univ. with Karl Geiringer (B.Mus., 1947) and at Harvard Univ. with Archibald T. Davison, Otto Kinkeldey, Arthur Tillman Merritt, and Walter Piston (M.A., 1949). In 1945–46 he served as an officer in education and information with U.S. Army General Headquarters in Tokyo. From 1948–57 he was employed as a librarian and instructor at Boston Univ.; concurrently he wrote music criticism for the *Christian Science Monitor.* In 1958 he was appointed director of publicity and program book editor of the Cleveland Orch.; also made broadcasts of comments during intermission. As a composer, he was extraordinarily prolific, considering the multitude of his external jobs. He wrote theater pieces, choruses, anthems, hymns, Christmas songs, etc., all extremely pleasing to the ear.
WORKS: *Tripartita* for 11-part Brass Choir (1950); *St. Francis' Canticle of the Sun* for Mixed Chorus with Solo Viola (Boston, Nov. 5, 1951); *Sterlingman,* one-act chamber opera (Boston, April 18, 1957); *40 Bars for 40 Fingers,* teaching pieces for 2 Pianos, 8-hands (1965); *Serenade* for Cello Solo (1968); *Chorale-Variants* on the Appalachian ballad tune *Jimmy Randal* (Cleveland, April 3, 1966).

Royce, Edward, American composer and teacher; b. Cambridge, Mass., Dec. 25, 1886; d. Stamford, Conn., July 7, 1963. He studied at Harvard Univ. (B.A., 1907), later at the Stern Cons. in Berlin; in 1913 founded the music dept. at Middlebury College in Vermont; was head of the theory dept. at the Ithaca Cons. (1916–21); from 1923 till 1947 was a prof. of theory at the Eastman School of Music in Rochester, N.Y.

WORKS: He composed 2 tone poems: *The Fire Bringers* (Rochester, April 23, 1926) and *Far Ocean* (Rochester, June 3, 1929); piano pieces, songs.

Royer, Etienne, French composer; b. Grenoble, April 12, 1882; d. Paris, March 2, 1928. He studied with Vincent d'Indy and Sérieyx at the Schola Cantorum in Paris; was a cello pupil of L. Revel; wrote music criticism and publ. pedagogical works. He composed *Danse mystique* for Orch.; *Cantus memorialis* for Violin and Orch.; *Pour le temps de la moisson* and *Pour les fêtes de mai,* for String Quartet (based on French folk tunes); songs; piano pieces; etc.

Royer, Joseph-Nicolas-Pancrace, French composer; b. Turin, c.1705; d. Paris, Jan. 11, 1755. He was a native of Burgundy, and settled in Paris in 1725. In 1739 he became a member of the court orch.; in 1748, lessee and director of the Concert Spirituel; in 1753, inspector of the Paris Opéra and "maître de musique de la chambre du roy."

WORKS: Operas: *Pyrrhus* (Paris, Oct. 26, 1730); *Zaïde* (Sept. 3, 1739); *Le Pouvoir de l'amour* (April 23, 1743); *Almasis* (Versailles, Feb. 26, 1748); *Myrtil* (Versailles, June 20, 1750); *Pandore,* after Voltaire (not produced). He publ. sonatas and a book of pieces for the clavecin.

BIBLIOGRAPHY: M. Brenet, *Les Concerts en France sous l'ancien régime* (Paris, 1900).

Rôze, Marie-Hippolyte (née **Roze-Ponsin**), famous French soprano; b. Paris, March 2, 1846; d. there, June 21, 1926. She studied at the Paris Cons. with Mocker and later with Auber, winning 2 prizes in 1865; made her debut at the Opéra-Comique in the title role of Hérold's *Marie* (Aug. 16, 1865); sang there for 3 seasons; then appeared at the Paris Opéra as Marguerite in Gounod's *Faust* (Jan. 2, 1879); made her London debut as Marguerite (1872); continued to sing in England for many years. She visited America twice, in 1877–78 and 1880–81. In 1874 she married an American bass, **Julius E. Perkins,** who died the following year; later she married the impresario **J.H. Mapleson, Jr.,** but the marriage ended in divorce. In 1890 she settled in Paris as a teacher.

Rôze, Raymond (J.H. Raymond Rôze-Perkins), English composer, son of **Marie Rôze;** b. London, 1875; d. there, March 31, 1920. He studied at the Brussels Cons., where he won first prize; wrote overtures and incidental music to many plays. In 1913 he organized at Covent Garden a season of opera in English, during which he conducted his own opera *Joan of Arc* (Oct. 31, 1913); another opera by him, *Arabesque,* was produced at the Coliseum in London in 1916.

Rozhdestvensky, Gennadi, eminent Soviet conductor; b. Moscow, May 4, 1931. He studied piano with Oborin and conducting with Anosov at the Moscow Cons.; graduated in 1954. From 1951 to 1960 he served as assistant conductor at the Bolshoi Theater in Moscow, and from 1965 to 1970 was its principal conductor. From 1961 to 1974 he was music director and conductor of the U.S.S.R. State Radio Orch.; in 1976 he was appointed prof. of the Moscow Cons. From 1974 to 1977 he was the principal conductor of the Stockholm Phil. Orch.; in 1978 he became chief guest conductor of the BBC Orch. in London. He made numerous guest appearances in the U.S. with major orchs. In 1981 he was appointed chief conductor of the Vienna Symph. Orch. He is distinguished by his encompassing interest in new music; he conducted notable performances of works by Soviet composers, particularly Prokofiev and Shostakovich, as well as by Stravinsky, Schoenberg, Berg, Milhaud, Honegger, and Poulenc. He publ. a technical treatise, *Technique of Conducting* (Leningrad, 1974), and a collection of essays, *Thoughts about Music* (Moscow, 1975).

Rozkošný, Josef Richard, Czech composer; b. Prague, Sept. 21, 1833; d. there, June 3, 1913. He studied painting and music in Prague; his teachers were Tomaschek (piano) and Kittl (composition). His songs and choruses became popular, and he successfully attempted the composition of operas to Czech librettos; 8 operas were produced in Prague, among them: *Svatojanské proudy* (*The Rapids of St. John;* Oct. 3, 1871); *Popelka* (*Cinderella;* May 31, 1885); *Černé jezero* (*The Black Lake;* Jan. 6, 1906). He also publ. a number of piano pieces.

Rózsa, Miklós, brilliant Hungarian-American composer; b. Budapest, April 18, 1907. He studied piano and composition in Leipzig, with Hermann Grabner; musicology with Theodor Kroyer. In 1931 he settled in Paris, where he became successful as a composer; his works were often performed in European music centers. In 1935 he went to London as a writer for the films; in 1940 emigrated to the U.S., and settled in Hollywood. His orch. and chamber music is cast in the advanced modern idiom in vogue in Europe between the 2 wars; neo-Classical in general content, it is strong in polyphony and incisive rhythm; for his film music, he employs a more Romantic and diffuse style, relying on a Wagnerian type of grandiloquence.

WORKS: For Orch.: *Nordungarische Bauernlieder und Tänze* (1929); Symph. (1930); *Serenade* for Small Orch. (1932); *Scherzo* (1933); *Thema, Variationen und Finale* (1933); *Capriccio, Pastorale e Danza* (1938); *Variations on a Hungarian Peasant Song* (N.Y., Nov. 14, 1943); Concerto for String Orch. (Los Angeles, Dec. 28, 1944); Violin Concerto (Dallas, Jan. 5, 1956; Jascha Heifetz, soloist); *Sinfonia concertante* for Violin, Cello, and Orch. (1966); Piano Concerto (Los Angeles, April 6, 1967); Cello Concerto (1969); *Tripartita* for Orch. (1973); Viola Concerto (Pittsburgh, May 4, 1984; Pinchas Zukerman, soloist). He has won Oscars for 3 film scores: *Spellbound* (1945), *A Double Life* (1947), and *Ben Hur* (1959); other notable film scores are *Quo Va-*

dis? (1951), *Ivanhoe* (1952), *Julius Caesar* (1953), *Lust for Life* (1956), and *El Cid* (1961).

BIBLIOGRAPHY: Christopher Palmer, *Miklós Rózsa: A Sketch of his Life and Work* (with a foreword by Eugene Ormandy; N.Y., 1975); *Double Life: The Autobiography of Miklós Rózsa* (London, 1983).

Rozsnyai, Zoltán, Hungarian conductor; b. Budapest, Jan. 29, 1927. He was educated at the Franz Liszt Academy of Music, where his teachers included Bartók, Kodály, and Dohnányi; also took courses at the Technical Univ. and at the Pazmany Peter Univ. of Sciences in Budapest; completed his musical training at the Univ. of Vienna. He was conductor of the Phil. Orch. in Miskolc (1948–50); then conducted the Debrecen Opera (1950–53); later led several Hungarian orchs. He left Hungary after the abortive revolution of 1956 and went to the U.S. In 1957 he organized the Philharmonia Hungarica; toured with it in 1958. He was an assistant conductor of the N.Y. Phil. (1962–63); then was music director of the Cleveland Phil. (1965–68) and the San Diego Symph. (1967–71). In 1976 he became music director of the Golden State Opera Co. in Los Angeles; in 1978, became music director of the Knoxville (Tenn.) Orch.

Różycki, Ludomir, Polish composer; b. Warsaw, Nov. 6, 1884; d. Katowice, Jan. 1, 1953. He studied piano with his father, a teacher at the Warsaw Cons.; theory with Noskowski at the Cons., graduating with honors in 1903. He then went to Berlin, where he took lessons with Humperdinck; in 1908 he was appointed conductor of the opera theater in Lwow; then undertook a European tour; settled in Berlin, where he remained through the years of World War I. In 1920 he returned to Warsaw; after 1945, lived mostly in Katowice. He was highly regarded in Poland as a national composer of stature; his style of composition was a successful blend of German, Russian, and Italian ingredients, yet the Polish characteristics were not obscured by the cosmopolitan harmonic and orch. dress.

WORKS: Operas: *Boleslaw smialy* (*Boleslaw the Bold;* Lwow, Feb. 11, 1909); *Meduza* (Warsaw, Oct. 22, 1912); *Eros und Psyche* (Breslau, March 10, 1917; in German); *Casanova* (Warsaw, June 8, 1923); *Beatrice Cenci* (Warsaw, Jan. 30, 1927); *Mlyn diabelski* (*The Devilish Mill;* Poznan, Feb. 21, 1931); *Lili chce spiewac,* comic opera (Poznan, March 7, 1933); ballets: *Pan Twardowski* (Warsaw, May 9, 1921; his most successful work; more than 800 perfs. in Warsaw) and *Apollon et la belle* (1937); symph. poems: *Stanczyk* (1903); *Anhelli* (1909); *Warszawianka* (1910); *Mona Lisa Gioconda* (1910); *Pietà* (1942); *Warszawa wyzwolona* (*Warsaw Liberated;* 1950); 2 piano concertos (1918, 1942); Violin Concerto (1944); Piano Quintet (1913); String Quartet (1916); Violin Sonata (1903); Cello Sonata (1906); a number of piano pieces; several song cycles.

BIBLIOGRAPHY: A. Wieniawski, *Ludomir Różycki* (Warsaw, 1928); M. Kaminski, *Ludomir Różycki* (Katowice, 1951).

Rubbra, Edmund, notable English composer; b. Northampton, May 23, 1901. His parents were musical, and he was taught to play the piano by his mother. He left school as a young boy and was employed in various factories; at the same time he continued to study music by himself, and attempted some composition; organized a concert devoted to the works of his favorite composer, Cyril Scott (Northampton, 1918); subsequently took lessons from him in London; in 1919 he studied with Holst; his other teachers in composition were John Ireland, Eugene Goossens, and Vaughan Williams. He compensated for a late beginning in composition by an extremely energetic application to steady improvement of his technique; finally elaborated a style of his own, marked by sustained lyricism and dynamic Romanticism; his harmonic language often verges on polytonality. He taught at Oxford Univ. (1947–68), and at Guildhall School of Music from 1961.

WORKS: One-act opera, *Bee-Bee-Bei* (1933); ballet, *Prism* (1938); for Orch.: *Double Fugue* (1924); *Triple Fugue* (1929); Symph. No. 1 (London, April 30, 1937); Symph. No. 2 (London, Dec. 16, 1938); Symph. No. 3 (Manchester, Dec. 15, 1940); Symph. No. 4 (London, Aug. 14, 1942); Symph. No. 5 (London, Jan. 26, 1949); Symph. No. 6 (London, Nov. 17, 1954); Symph. No. 7 (Birmingham, Oct. 1, 1957); Symph. No. 8 (London, Jan. 5, 1971); Symph. No. 9, *The Resurrection,* for Soloists, Chorus, and Orch. (1973); Symph. No. 11 (London, Aug. 20, 1980); Chamber Symph. (Middlesborough, Jan. 8, 1975); *Sinfonia concertante* for Piano and Orch. (London, Aug. 10, 1943); *Soliloquy* for Cello and Orch. (London, Jan. 1, 1945); Viola Concerto (London, April 15, 1953); chamber music: *Fantasy* for 2 Violins and Piano (1925); *Lyric Movement* for Piano Quintet (1929); 2 string quartets (1933, 1952); Piano Trio (1950); 2 violin sonatas (1925, 1931); Cello Sonata (1946); choral works: *The Sacred Hymnody* (1921); *La Belle Dame sans merci* (1925); *The Morning Watch* (1941); *Te Deum* (1951); a number of madrigals and motets for Unaccompanied Chorus; songs with Orch. (*Ballad of Tristram, 4 Medieval Latin Lyrics, 5 Sonnets,* etc.); songs with Piano; miscellaneous pieces for various instruments. He publ. *Counterpoint. A Survey* (London, 1960).

BIBLIOGRAPHY: Edwin Evans, "Edmund Rubbra," *Musical Times* (Feb.–March 1945; with a list of works); Colin Mason, "Rubbra's 4 Symphonies," *Music Review* (Jan. 1941); Alan Frank, *Modern British Composers* (London, 1953; pp. 53–57).

Rubens, Paul Alfred, English composer of light music; b. London, April 29, 1875; d. Falmouth, Feb. 5, 1917. He was educated at Oxford; in 1899 he contributed some numbers to the famous musical revue *Floradora,* and this success induced him to devote himself to the composition of light operas. The following stage works by him were produced: *Lady Madcap* (1904); *Miss Hook of Holland* (1907); *My Mimosa Maid* (1908); *Dear Little Denmark* (1909); *The Balkan Princess* (1910); *The Sunshine Girl* (1912); he also wrote numerous songs and ballads.

Rubenson, Albert, Swedish composer; b. Stockholm, Dec. 20, 1826; d. there, March 2, 1901. He studied at the Leipzig Cons. (1844–48) with Ferdinand David (violin), Hauptmann (counterpoint), and Gade (composition). Returning to Stockholm, he wrote music criticism; in 1872 became inspector at the Stockholm Cons., and from 1888 till his death was its director. He wrote an overture, *Julius Caesar;* a Symph.; several orch. suites; a String Quartet; many songs. His style was derived from Mendelssohn and Schumann, but he attempted to inject some elements of Swedish folk song into his music, and in doing so contributed to the rise of musical nationalism in Sweden.

Rubin, Marcel, Austrian composer; b. Vienna, July 7, 1905. He studied piano with Richard Robert, theory of composition with Richard Stöhr, and counterpoint and fugue with Franz Schmidt at the Vienna Academy of Music; simultaneously attended courses in law. In 1925 he went to Paris, where he took private lessons with Darius Milhaud. He was back in Vienna in 1931 to complete his studies in law, and in 1933 received his degree of Dr.Juris. After the Nazi Anschluss of Austria in 1938, Rubin, being a non-Aryan, fled to Paris, but was interned as an enemy alien in France; after France fell in 1940, he made his way to Marseilles. Convinced that only the Communists could efficiently oppose Fascism, he became a member of the illegal Austrian Communist party in exile; in 1942 he went to Mexico and remained there until 1946; he returned to Vienna in 1947. His music follows the modernistic models of Parisianized Russians and Russianized Frenchmen, with a mandatory hedonism in "new simplicity." Although Rubin studied works of Schoenberg, Berg, and Anton von Webern with great assiduity and wrote articles about them, he never adopted the method of composition with 12 tones in his own music.
WORKS: Comic opera, *Kleider machen Leute* (Vienna Volksoper, Dec. 14, 1973); "dance piece," *Die Stadt* (1948); 6 symphs. (1927–28, 1937, 1939, 1945, 1965, 1974); Concerto for Double Bass and Orch. (1970); Trumpet Concerto (1972); *Ballade* for Orch. (1948); *Rondo-Burleske* for Orch. (1960); *3 Komödianten* for Orch. (1963); Sonatina for Orch. (1965); Sinfonietta for String Orch. (1966); *Pastorale* for Strings (1970); 3 piano sonatas (1925, 1927, 1928); String Quartet (1926; revised 1961); String Trio (1927; revised 1962); Sonatina for Oboe and Piano (1927); Cello Sonata (1928); *Divertimento* for Piano, Violin, and Cello (1967); *Serenade* for Flute, Oboe, Clarinet, Horn, and Bassoon (1971); Violin Sonata (1974); oratorio, *Die Albigenser* (1957–61); song cycles to poems by Clément Marot, Guillaume Apollinaire, Rimbaud, Goethe, François Villon, etc.
BIBLIOGRAPHY: Hartmut Krones, *Marcel Rubin* (Vienna, 1975).

Rubini, Giovanni Battista, celebrated Italian tenor; b. Romano, near Bergamo, April 7, 1794; d. there, March 3, 1854. His teacher was Rosio of Bergamo; after an auspicious debut in Pavia (1814), he sang for a time in Naples; there he married (1819) a singer, **Mlle. Chomel,** known under the professional name of **La Comelli.** On Oct. 6, 1825, he sang in Paris, where he scored his first triumphs in Rossini's operas at the Théâtre-Italien; his performances of the leading parts in the operas of Bellini and Donizetti were also very successful, and there is reason to believe that Rubini's interpretations greatly contributed to the rising fame of both of those composers. Between 1831 and 1843 he sang in Paris and London; in 1843 he undertook a tour with Liszt, traveling with him in the Netherlands and Germany; in the same year he sang in Russia with tremendous acclaim; visited Russia again in 1844; then returned to Italy, bought an estate near his native town, and remained there until his death; for some years he gave singing lessons. He publ. *12 lezioni di canto moderno per tenore o soprano* and an album of 6 songs, *L'Addio.*
BIBLIOGRAPHY: C. Traini, *G.B. Rubini* (Romano, 1954).

Rubinstein, Anton, celebrated Russian composer and pianist, brother of **Nicolai Rubinstein;** b. Vykhvatinetz, Podolia, Nov. 28, 1829; d. Peterhof, near St. Petersburg, Nov. 20, 1894. He was of a family of Jewish merchants who became baptized in Berdichev in July 1831. His mother gave him his first lessons in piano; the family moved to Moscow, where his father opened a small pencil factory. A well-known Moscow piano teacher, Alexandre Villoing, was entrusted with Rubinstein's musical education, and was in fact his only piano teacher. In 1839 Villoing took him to Paris, where Rubinstein played before Chopin and Liszt; remained in Paris until 1841; then made a concert tour in the Netherlands, Germany, Austria, England, Norway, and Sweden, returning to Russia in 1843. Since Anton's brother Nicolai evinced a talent for composition, the brothers were taken in 1844 to Berlin, where, on Meyerbeer's recommendation, Anton too studied composition, with Dehn; subsequently he made a tour through Hungary with the flutist Heindl. He returned to Russia in 1848 and settled in St. Petersburg. There he enjoyed the enlightened patronage of the Grand Duchess Helen, and wrote 3 Russian operas: *Dmitri Donskoy* (1852); *Sibirskie Okhotniki* (*The Siberian Hunters;* 1853); and *Fomka Durachok* (*Thomas the Fool;* 1853). In 1854, with the assistance of the Grand Duchess, Rubinstein undertook another tour in Western Europe. He found publishers in Berlin, and gave concerts of his own works in London and Paris, exciting admiration as both composer and pianist; on his return in 1858, he was appointed court pianist and conductor of the court concerts. He assumed the direction of the Russian Musical Society in 1859; in 1862 he founded the Imperial Cons. in St. Petersburg, remaining its director until 1867. For 20 years thereafter he held no official position; from 1867 until 1870 he gave concerts in Europe, winning fame as a pianist 2nd only to Liszt. During the season of 1872–73, he made a triumphant American tour, playing in 215 concerts, for which he was paid lavishly; appeared as a soloist and jointly with the violinist Wieniawski. He produced a sensation by playing without notes, a novel procedure at the time. Returning to Europe, he elaborated a cycle of historical concerts, in programs ranging from Bach to Chopin; he usually devoted the last concert of a cycle to Russian composers. In 1887 he resumed the directorship of the St. Petersburg Cons., resigning again in 1891, when he went to Dresden (until 1894). He returned to Russia shortly before his death.

In 1890 Rubinstein established the Rubinstein Prize, an international competition open to young men between 20 and 26 years of age. Two prizes of 5,000 francs each were offered, one for composition, the other for piano playing. Quinquennial competitions were held in St. Petersburg, Berlin, Vienna, and Paris.

Rubinstein's role in Russian musical culture is of the greatest importance. He introduced European methods into education, and established high standards of artistic performance. He was the first Russian musician who was equally prominent as composer and interpreter. According to contemporary reports, his playing possessed extraordinary power (his octave passages were famous) and insight, revealed particularly in his performance of Beethoven's sonatas. His renown as a composer was scarcely less. His *Ocean Symphony* was one of the most frequently performed orch. works in Europe and in America; his piano concertos were part of the standard repertoire; his pieces for Piano Solo, *Melody in F, Romance, Kamennoi Ostrow,* became perennial favorites. After his death, his orch. works all but vanished from concert programs, as did his operas (with the exception of *The Demon,* which is still perf. in Russia); his Piano Concerto No. 4, in D minor, is occasionally heard.

WORKS: FOR THE STAGE: Operas: *Dmitri Donskoy* (St. Petersburg, April 30, 1852); *Sibirskie okhotniki* (*The Siberian Hunters;* 1853); *Fomka Durachok* (*Thomas the Fool;* St. Petersburg, May 23, 1853); *Die Kinder der Heide,* 5-act German opera (Vienna, Feb. 23, 1861); *Feramors,* after the poem *Lalla Rookh* of T. Moore (Dresden, Feb. 24, 1863); *The Demon,* after Lermontov (St. Petersburg, Jan. 25, 1875); *Die Makkabäer* (Berlin, April 17, 1875); *Nero* (Hamburg, Nov. 1, 1879); *Kupets Kalashnikov* (*The Merchant Kalashnikov;* St. Petersburg, March 5, 1880); *Sulamith* and *Unter Räubern* (both perf. Hamburg, Nov. 8, 1883); *Der Papagei* (*The Parrot;* Hamburg, 1884); *Goriusha* (St. Petersburg, Dec. 3, 1889); ballet, *Die Rebe* (*The Vine;* 1885). VOCAL WORKS: Oratorios: *Paradise Lost* (Weimar, 1858; revised and arranged as a sacred opera, Düsseldorf, 1875); *The Tower of Babel* (Königsberg, 1870); *Moses* (1892); *Christus* (1893); 2 cantatas: *Die Nixe* for Alto Solo and Female Chorus, and *Der Morgen* for Male Chorus; scene and aria for Soprano, *E dunque ver?;* 2 scenes for Alto and Orch.: *Hecuba* and *Hagar in der Wüste;* about 100 songs (of these, *Asra* is popular). FOR ORCH.: 6 symphs. (No. 2, *Ocean;* No. 4, *Dramatic;* No. 5, *Russian*); *Ouverture triomphale; Ouverture de concert;* 3 "character pictures":

Faust, Ivan the Terrible, Don Quixote; a "morceau symphonique," *La Russie;* 5 piano concertos; *Fantaisie* for Piano and Orch.; *Konzertstück* for Piano and Orch.; Violin Concerto; 2 cello concertos. CHAMBER MUSIC: Octet for Piano, Strings, and Winds; Sextet for Strings; Quintet for Piano, Flute, Clarinet, Horn, and Bassoon; String Quintet; Piano Quintet; 10 string quartets; Piano Quartet; 5 piano trios; 2 violin sonatas; 2 cello sonatas. FOR PIANO: 4 sonatas; *Kamennoi Ostrow; Soirées à St. Petersburg; Album de Péterhof; Soirées musicales;* 6 *Barcarolles; Sérénade russe;* polkas, mazurkas, etc.

WRITINGS: *Memoirs* (St. Petersburg, 1889; in Eng. as *Autobiography of Anton Rubinstein,* Boston, 1890); *Music and Its Representatives* (Moscow, 1891; in Eng., N.Y., 1892; also publ. as *A Conversation on Music*); *Leitfaden zum richtigen Gebrauch des Pianoforte-Pedals* (posthumous; Leipzig, 1896; in French, Brussels, 1899); *Gedankenkorb, Litterarischer Nachlass* (posthumous; Stuttgart, 1896); *Die Meister des Klaviers* (posthumous; Berlin, 1899).

BIBLIOGRAPHY: A. McArthur, *A. Rubinstein* (London, 1889); E. Zabel, *A. Rubinstein* (Leipzig, 1892); A. Soubies, *A. Rubinstein* (Paris, 1895); I. Martinov, *Episodes de la vie de Rubinstein* (Brussels, 1895); J. Rodenberg, "Meine persönlichen Erinnerungen an A. Rubinstein, nebst Briefen," *Deutsche Rundschau,* 21 (Berlin, 1895; in Eng. in *Music,* 8, Chicago, 1905); E. Wessel, *Some Explanations, Hints and Remarks of A. Rubinstein from His Lessons in the St. Petersburg Cons.* (St. Petersburg, 1901; in German, Leipzig, 1904); N. Findeisen, *A. Rubinstein* (Moscow, 1907); La Mara, *A. Rubinstein,* in the series, Musikalische Studienköpfe (vol. 3, 7th ed., Leipzig, 1909; separately, Leipzig, 1911); N. Bernstein, *A. Rubinstein* (Leipzig, 1911); A. Hervey, *A. Rubinstein* (London, 1913); K. Preiss, *A. Rubinsteins pianistische Bedeutung* (Leipzig, 1914); Igor Glebov, *A. Rubinstein in His Musical Activities and Opinions of His Contemporaries* (Moscow, 1929); C.D. Bowen, *"Free Artist": The Story of Anton and Nicholas Rubinstein* (N.Y., 1939; fictionalized account, but accurate as to actual events; with a complete list of works and a detailed bibliography, compiled by Otto E. Albrecht); O. Bennigsen, "The Brothers Rubinstein and Their Circle," *Musical Quarterly* (Oct. 1939); L. Barenboym, *A.G. Rubinstein,* vol. I (Moscow, 1957).

Rubinstein, Artur, celebrated cosmopolitan pianist of Jewish-Polish origin; b. Lodz, Poland, Jan. 28, 1887; d. Geneva, Dec. 20, 1982. He was a product of a merchant family with many children, of whom he alone exhibited musical propensities. He became emotionally attached to the piano as soon as he saw and heard the instrument; at the age of 7, on Dec. 14, 1894, he played pieces by Mozart, Schubert, and Mendelssohn at a charity concert. His first regular piano teacher was one Adolf Prechner. He was later taken to Warsaw, where he had piano lessons with Alexander Różycki. A significant *gradus ad Parnassum* was a trip to Berlin, where Rubinstein played for the famous violinist Joachim. Funds were raised for his stay in Berlin, where he was taught piano by Heinrich Barth, a pupil of Liszt, and by Robert Kahn. He also had some theory lessons with Max Bruch. He made his formal debut in Berlin when he was 13, playing a Mozart concerto at the Berlin Hochschule für Musik, with Joachim conducting. Recitals in Dresden and Hamburg followed. In 1902 he was a soloist with the Warsaw Symph., directed by Emil Mlynarski (Rubinstein's future father-in-law). In the summer of 1903, he took regular lessons with Paderewski in Switzerland. He soon was able to support himself, and went to Paris, where he played with the Lamoureux Orch. and met Ravel, Paul Dukas, and Jacques Thibaud. He also played the G minor Piano Concerto by Saint-Saëns in the presence of the composer, who commended him. The ultimate plum of artistic success came when Rubinstein received an American contract. He made his debut at Carnegie Hall, in N.Y., on Jan. 8, 1906, as soloist with the Philadelphia Orch. in his favorite Saint-Saëns concerto. His American tour was not altogether successful, and he returned to Europe for further study. In 1915 he appeared as soloist with the London Symph. Orch. During the season 1916–17, he gave numerous recitals in Spain, a country in which he was to become extremely successful; from Spain he went to South America, where he also became a great favorite; he developed a flair for Spanish and Latin American music, and his renditions of the piano works of Albéniz and Manuel de Falla were models of authentic Hispanic modality. The Brazilian composer Villa-Lobos dedicated to Rubinstein his *Rudepoema,* regarded as one of the most difficult piano pieces ever written. Symbolic of his cosmopolitan career was the fact that he maintained apartments in N.Y., Beverly Hills, Paris, and Geneva. He was married to Aniela Mlynarska in 1932. Of his 4 children, one was born in Buenos Aires, one in Warsaw, and 2 in America. In 1946 he became an American citizen. On June 11, 1958, Rubinstein gave his first postwar concert in Poland; in 1964 he played in Moscow, Leningrad, and Kiev. In Poland and in Russia he was received with tremendous emotional acclaim. But he forswore any appearances in Germany, having been horrified by reports of German atrocities during World War II and enraged by the Nazi crimes against the Jewish people. German admirers of his playing had to be satisfied with his recordings, which sold millions of copies around the world.

Rubinstein was one of the finest interpreters of Chopin's music, to which his fiery temperament and poetic lyricism were particularly congenial. His style of playing tended toward bravura in Classical compositions, but he rarely indulged in mannerisms; his performances of Mozart and Beethoven were inspiring. In his characteristic spirit of robust humor, he made jokes about the multitude of notes he claimed to have dropped, but asserted that a worse transgression against music would be pedantic inflexibility in tempo and dynamics. He was a bon vivant, an indefatigable host at parties, and a fluent, though not always grammatical, speaker in most European languages, including Russian and his native Polish. In Hollywood, he played on the sound tracks for the motion pictures *I've Always Loved You* (1946), *Song of Love* (1947), and *Night Song* (1947). He also appeared as a pianist, representing himself, in the films *Carnegie Hall* (1947) and *Of Men and Music* (1951). A film documentary entitled *Artur Rubinstein, Love of Life* was produced in 1975; a 90-minute television special, *Rubinstein at 90,* was broadcast to mark his entry into that nonagenarian age; and he spoke philosophically about the inevitability of dying. He was the recipient of numerous international honors: a membership in the French Académie des Beaux Arts and the Légion d'Honneur, and the Order of Polonia Restituta of Poland; he held the Gold Medal of the Royal Phil. Society of London and several honorary doctorates from American institutions of learning. He was a passionate supporter of Israel, which he visited several times. In 1974 an international piano competition bearing his name was inaugurated in Jerusalem. On April 1, 1976, he received the U.S. Medal of Freedom, presented by President Ford. In 1976 he was forced to curtail, and finally to cease, concert activities when he was afflicted with retinitis pigmentosa, which led to his total blindness; but even then he never renounced his joie de vivre. He once said that the slogan "wine, women, and song" as applied to him was 80% women and only 20% wine and song. And in a widely publicized interview he gave at the age of 95 he declared his ardent love for Annabelle Whitestone, the Englishwoman who was assigned by his publisher to help him organize and edit his autobiography. He slid gently into death in his Geneva apartment, as in a pianissimo ending of a Chopin nocturne, ritardando, morendo ... Rubinstein had expressed a wish to be buried in Israel; his body was cremated in Switzerland; the ashes were flown to Jerusalem to be interred in a separate emplacement at the cemetery, since the Jewish law does not permit cremation.

BIBLIOGRAPHY: Bernard Gavoty, *Artur Rubinstein* (Geneva, 1955; in Eng., 1956); an autobiography in 2 vols., *My Young Years* (N.Y., 1973) and *My Many Years* (N.Y., 1980); David Even, *Musicians since 1900* (N.Y., 1978).

Rubinstein, Beryl, American pianist and composer; b. Athens, Ga., Oct. 26, 1898; d. Cleveland, Dec. 29, 1952. He studied piano with his father and Alexander Lambert; toured the U.S. as a child (1905–11); then went to Berlin to study with Busoni and Vianna da Motta. He was appointed to the faculty of the Cleveland Inst. of Music in 1921; became its director in 1932. He wrote an opera, *The Sleeping Beauty,* to a libretto by John Erskine (Juilliard School of Music, N.Y., Jan. 19, 1938); 32 piano studies; 3 dances for Piano; transcriptions from Gershwin's *Porgy and Bess.* He conducted his orch. *Scherzo* with the Cleveland Orch. on March 17, 1927; performed his Piano Concerto in C with the same orch. on Nov. 12, 1936.

Rubinstein, Joseph, Russian pianist; b. Starokonstantinov, Feb. 8, 1847; d. (committed suicide) Lucerne, Sept. 15, 1884. He studied in Vienna with

Dachs; later took lessons with Liszt in Weimar. He was an ardent admirer of Wagner, whom he knew personally; in 1874 he was the pianist at the preliminary rehearsals of *Der Ring des Nibelungen* at Bayreuth; made piano transcriptions of it and also of *Parsifal.*

Rubinstein, Nicolai, Russian pianist and pedagogue, brother of **Anton Rubinstein;** b. Moscow, June 14, 1835; d. Paris, March 23, 1881. He began to study piano with his mother at the age of 4, when his brother, 6 years older than he, was already on the road to fame as a child prodigy; was taken to Berlin with his brother, and there studied with Kullak (piano) and Dehn (composition). The brothers met Mendelssohn and Meyerbeer; returning to Moscow in 1846, he began to take lessons with Alexandre Villoing. He also studied law, and received a degree from the Univ. of Moscow (1855); subsequently was a minor functionary in the government; earned his living by giving private lessons. In 1858 he began his concert career; appeared in Russia, and also in London. In 1859, when he was only 24 years old, he became head of the Moscow branch of the Russian Music Society; in 1866 this society opened the Moscow Cons., of which Nicolai Rubinstein was director until his death. From 1860 he was the regular conductor of the Moscow concerts of the Imperial Russian Musical Society. In 1878 he conducted 4 Russian concerts at the Paris Exposition; at the first and the 4th of the series he performed Tchaikovsky's Piano Concerto No. 1 (which he had criticized so sharply when Tchaikovsky first submitted it to him in 1874). Anton Rubinstein declared that Nicolai was a better pianist than himself, but this generous appreciation was not accepted by the public. As an educator, however, Nicolai Rubinstein played perhaps a greater role than his famous brother. Among his pupils were Taneyev, Siloti, and Emil Sauer.

BIBLIOGRAPHY: N. Findeisen, "Nicolai Rubinstein," *Russkaya Muzÿkalnaya Gazeta,* 10 (1901); C. D. Bowen, *"Free Artist": The Story of Anton and Nicholas Rubinstein* (N.Y., 1939); O. Bennigsen, "The Brothers Rubinstein and Their Circle," *Musical Quarterly* (Oct. 1939).

Rubio Piqueras, Felipe, Spanish musicologist; b. Valera de Arriba, Sept. 13, 1881; d. Toledo, 1936. He was ordained priest in 1904, and served as organist at the Cathedral of Badajoz until 1917; then went to Toledo as a church organist. He publ. valuable works on music in Toledo: *Códices polifónicos toledanos* and *Música y músicos toledanos* (1923); also wrote some church music.

Rübner, Cornelius. See **Rybner, Cornelius.**

Rübsam, Wolfgang, German organist; b. Giessen, Oct. 16, 1946. He studied at Southern Methodist Univ. (M.Mus., 1970); took lessons with Helmut Walcha at the Frankfurt Staatliche Hochschule für Musik, where he graduated with an artist diploma in 1971; subsequently studied with Marie-Claire

Alain in Paris (1971–74). In 1974 he joined the faculty of Northwestern Univ.

Rubsamen, Walter (Howard), renowned American musicologist; b. New York, July 21, 1911; d. Los Angeles, June 19, 1973. He studied flute with Georges Barrère in N.Y.; musicology at Columbia Univ. with Paul Henry Lang (B.A., 1933); then went to Germany, where he attended classes of Otto Ursprung and Rudolph von Ficker at the Univ. of Munich; received his doctorate there with the dissertation *Pierre de la Rue als Messenkomponist* (1937). Returning to the U.S., he was appointed to the music faculty at the Univ. of Calif., Los Angeles, obtaining a full professorship in 1955; in 1965 he was appointed chairman of the music dept. there, remaining in this capacity until his death.

WRITINGS: *Literary Sources of Secular Music in Italy c.1500* (Berkeley, Calif., 1943; reprint, N.Y., 1972); *Chanson and Madrigal, 1480–1530* (with D. Heartz and H.M. Brown; Cambridge, Mass., 1964); "Mr. Seedo, Ballad Opera and the Singspiel," in *Miscelánea en homenaje a Mons. Higinio Anglés* (Barcelona, 1958–61); he edited *Opera Omnia* of Pierre de La Rue for the American Inst. of Musicology and brought out a German 16th-century *Magnificat on Christmas Carols* (N.Y., 1971); contributed a number of informative articles on ballad opera in England and on Renaissance composers to various American and European publications.

Rückauf, Anton, outstanding composer of German songs; b. Prague, March 13, 1855; d. Schloss Alt-Erla, Austria, Sept. 19, 1903. He studied with Proksch in Prague and with Nottebohm and Nawrátil in Vienna; publ. about 80 songs, which were made popular by the singer Gustav Walter at his recitals, with Rückauf himself at the piano; he also wrote an opera, *Die Rosenthalerin,* which was produced in Dresden in 1897.

Ruckers, Hans, known as "the eldest" of the family of celebrated Flemish harpsichord makers; b. Mechlin, c.1550; d. Antwerp, c.1598. He was the first of the family to make instruments; in 1579 was admitted to the Guild of St. Luke. His 2nd son, **Hans Ruckers,** also known as **Jean** (baptized, Antwerp, Jan. 15, 1578; d. there, April 24, 1643), was greatly esteemed by his contemporaries, and was exempted from Civic Guard duties in appreciation of his artistry. **Andreas Ruckers** the elder (baptized, Antwerp, Aug. 30, 1579; d. c.1654) manufactured harpsichords between 1601 and 1644. **Andreas Ruckers** the younger, son of the elder Andreas (baptized, Antwerp, March 31, 1607; d. after 1667), made instruments between 1637 and 1667. Another member of the same family was **Christoffel Ruckers,** who flourished c.1600. He constructed 2 virginals.

BIBLIOGRAPHY: For a list of surviving instruments and other particulars, see Donald H. Boalch, *Makers of the Harpsichord and Clavichord, 1440 to 1840* (N.Y., 1956); also, Georg Kinsky, "Die Familie Ruckers," *Zeitschrift für Musikwissenschaft,* IV; André M. Pols, *De Ruckers en de klavierbouw in*

Vlaanderen (Antwerp, 1942); J. Lambrechts-Douillez, "Documents Dealing with the Ruckers Family and Antwerp Harpsichord-Building," in E.M. Ripin, *Keyboard Instruments* (Edinburgh, 1971); G. O'Brien, "Ioannes and Andreas Ruckers," *Early Music,* VII (1979).

Rüdel, Hugo, German horn player and choral conductor; b. Havelberg, Feb. 7, 1868; d. Berlin, Nov. 27, 1934. He studied in Berlin, and was engaged as horn player in the orch. of the Berlin Opera; in 1906 he became choral conductor at the Bayreuth Festivals; in 1909 he took over the famous Domchor in Berlin; also conducted other singing societies.

Rudel, Julius, outstanding Austrian-American conductor; b. Vienna, March 6, 1921. He studied at the Vienna Academy of Music; in 1938 emigrated to the U.S. (naturalized citizen, 1944) and continued his studies at the Mannes School of Music in N.Y. On Nov. 25, 1944, he made his American debut as conductor of the N.Y. City Opera; in 1957 became its music director. He also appeared as guest conductor of the Philadelphia Orch. and of several operatic companies; received numerous awards from American cultural organizations. In 1961 the Austrian government bestowed on him honorary insignia for arts and sciences. He championed the cause of American opera; gave first performances of several new stage works by American composers. In 1979 he resigned his post with the N.Y. City Opera and became music director of the Buffalo Phil. Orch.

BIBLIOGRAPHY: *Current Biography* (July 1965).

Ruders, Poul, Danish composer; b. Ringsted, March 27, 1949. He studied organ with Finn Reiff and composition with Ib Nørholm at the Royal Danish Music Cons. in Copenhagen; later was active mostly as a church organist. In his own compositions he follows a neo-Baroque movement.

WORKS: For Orch.: *Pavane* (1971); *Etudes* (1974); *Capriccio pian' e forte* (Odense, Sept. 5, 1978); *Recitatives and Arias,* piano concerto (1978; State Univ. of N.Y. at Buffalo, April 1, 1979); Violin Concerto (1981; Copenhagen, Oct. 16, 1982). Chamber music: 3 string quartets (1972–79); *Zerstörte Horizonten* for 2 Electric Organs, Baby Grand Piano, Flute, Guitar, and Trombone (1973); *Medieval Variations* for 8 Instruments (1974); *Bravour Studium* for Cello and Piano (1976); *Rondeau* for 7 Musicians (1976); *Wind-Drumming* for Wind Quintet and Percussion (1979); *4 Compositions* for Flute, Clarinet, Horn, Piano, and String Quintet (1980); *Greeting Concerto* for Chamber Ensemble (1982). For Voice: *Stabat Mater* for Chorus, Piano, and Organ (1973); *Pest-sange* for Soprano, Guitar, and Piano (1975); *Gloria* for Chorus and 12 Brasses (1981; Copenhagen, Nov. 12, 1982). For Piano: *3 Letters from the Unknown Soldier* (1967); 2 sonatas: No. 1, *Dante Sonata* (1970), and No. 2 (1982); *Recitatives* (1977). For Organ: *Requiem* (1969); *Antiquitäten* (1972); *Symphonies* (1978).

Rudersdorff, Hermine, Russian dramatic soprano; b. Ivanovsky, Ukraine, Dec. 12, 1822; d. Boston, Feb. 26, 1882. A pupil of Bordogni at Paris and of de Micherout at Milan, she sang at first in Germany (1840–54), then in London (1854–65). Engaged at the Boston Jubilee of 1869, she settled in Boston, becoming renowned as a teacher (Emma Thursby was her pupil). In 1844 she married Dr. Küchenmeister, from whom she was divorced, then married in 1850 an English merchant, Maurice Mansfield. Their son was the famous actor Richard Mansfield (1857–1907).

Rudhyar, Dane, American composer, painter, and mystical philosopher; b. Paris, March 23, 1895. His parental name was **Daniel Chennevière;** he changed it in 1917 to Rudhyar, derived from an old Sanskrit root conveying the sense of dynamic action and the color red, astrologically related to the Zodiacal sign of his birth and the red-colored planet Mars. He studied philosophy at the Sorbonne, in Paris, receiving his baccalauréat in 1911, and took music courses at the Paris Cons. In composition he was largely self-taught; he also achieved a certain degree of proficiency as a pianist; developed a technique which he called "orchestral pianism." In 1913 the French publisher Durand commissioned him to write a short book on Debussy, with whom he briefly corresponded. At the same time he joined the modern artistic circles in Paris. In 1916 he went to America; became a naturalized American citizen in 1926. His "dance poems" for Orch., *Poèmes ironiques* and *Vision végétale,* were performed at the Metropolitan Opera House, N.Y., April 4, 1917. In 1918 he visited Canada; in Montreal he met the pianist Alfred Laliberté, who was closely associated with Scriabin, and through him Rudhyar became acquainted with Scriabin's theosophic ideas. In Canada he also publ. a collection of French poems, *Rapsodies* (Toronto, 1918). In 1920 he went to Hollywood to write scenic music for *Pilgrimage Play, The Life of Christ,* and also acted the part of Christ in the prologue of the silent film version of *The Ten Commandments* produced by Cecil B. DeMille. In Hollywood he initiated the project of "Introfilms," depicting inner psychological states on the screen through a series of images, but it failed to receive support and was abandoned. Between 1922 and 1930 he lived part-time in Hollywood and part-time in N.Y.; he was one of the founding members of the International Composers Guild in N.Y. In 1922 his orch. tone poem *Soul Fire* won the $1,000 prize of the Los Angeles Phil.; in 1928 his book *The Rebirth of Hindu Music* was publ. in Madras, India. After 1930 Rudhyar devoted most of his time to astrology. His first book on the subject, *The Astrology of Personality,* was publ. in 1936 and became a standard text in the field; it was described by Paul Clancy, the pioneer in the publishing of popular astrological magazines, as "the greatest step forward in astrology since the time of Ptolemy." A new development in Rudhyar's creative activities took place in 1938 when he began to paint, along nonrepresentational symbolistic lines; the titles of his paintings (*Mystic*

Tiara, Cosmic Seeds, Soul and Ego, Avatar, etc.) reflect theosophic themes. His preoccupations with astrology left him little time for music; about 1965 he undertook a radical revision of some early compositions, and wrote several new ones; in 1984 he lived in Palo Alto, Calif., and continued an active schedule of lecturing.

The natural medium for Rudhyar's musical expression is the piano; his few symph. works are mostly orchestrations of original piano compositions. In his writing for piano Rudhyar builds sonorous chordal formations supported by resonant pedal points, occasionally verging on polytonality; a kinship with Scriabin's piano music is clearly felt, but Rudhyar's harmonic idiom is free from Scriabin's Wagnerian antecedents. Despite his study of oriental religions and music, Rudhyar does not attempt to make use of Eastern modalities in his own music.

WORKS: FOR ORCH.: *3 poèmes ironiques* (1914); *Vision végétale* (1914); *The Warrior,* symph. poem for Piano and Orch. (1921; perf. 55 years later, Palo Alto, Dec. 10, 1976); *Sinfonietta* (1927); *Syntonies* in 4 sections: *To the Real* (1920); *The Surge of Fire* (1921); *Ouranos* (1927); *The Human Way* (1927); *Tripthong* for Piano and Orch. (1948; revised 1977); *Thresholds* (1954) *Dialogues* for Chamber Orch. (1977; San Francisco, May 23, 1982); *Cosmic Cycle* (1981). CHAMBER MUSIC: *3 Melodies* for Flute, Cello, and Piano (1919); *3 Poems* for Violin and Piano (1920); *Solitude* for String Quartet (1950); Piano Quintet (1950); *Barcarolle* for Violin and Piano (1955) *Alleluia* for Carillon (1976); *Nostalgia* for Flute, Piano, and Strings (1977); 2 string quartets: No. 1, *Advent* (1978), and No. 2, *Crisis and Overcoming* (1979). SONGS: *3 chansons de Bilitis* (1919); *3 poèmes tragiques* (1918); *3 invocations* (1939). FOR PIANO: *3 poèmes* (1913); *Mosaics,* a tone cycle in 8 movements on the life of Christ (1918); *Syntony* (1919–34; revised 1967); *3 Paeans* (1925); *Granites* (1929); *9 Tetragrams* (1920–67); *Pentagrams* (1924–26); *Transmutation* (1976); *Theurgy* (1976); *Autumn* and *3 Cantos* (1977); *Epic Poem* (1979); *Rite of Transcendence* (1981).

WRITINGS: *Claude Debussy* (Paris, 1913); *Art as Release of Power* (N.Y., 1930); *The Astrology of Personality* (N.Y., 1936; revised 1970); *The Practice of Astrology* (Amsterdam, 1967; N.Y., 1970); *The Planetarization of Consciousness* (Amsterdam, 1970; N.Y., 1972); *The Astrological Houses* (N.Y., 1972); *Culture, Crisis and Creativity* (Wheaton, Ill., 1977); *The Astrology of Transformation* (Wheaton, 1980); *The Magic of Tone and the Art of Music* (Boulder, 1982); *The Rhythm of Wholeness* (Wheaton, 1983).

BIBLIOGRAPHY: Paul Rosenfeld, *An Hour with American Music* (N.Y., 1929; pp. 71–78); A. Morang, *Dane Rudhyar, Pioneer in Creative Synthesis* (N.Y., 1939); *Dane Rudhyar. A Brief Biography* (Berkeley, Calif., 1972); a special issue of *Human Dimensions,* dedicated to Rudhyar (Buffalo, N.Y., 1975).

Rüdinger, Gottfried, German composer; b. Lindau, Aug. 23, 1886; d. Gauting, near Munich, Jan. 17, 1946.

He was a student in theology; at the same time he took courses in composition with Max Reger at the Leipzig Cons. (1907–9); in 1910 he settled in Munich and began teaching privately; taught at the Academy there from 1920. He composed industriously in many genres; brought out a "peasant play-opera," *Tegernseer im Himmel,* and the children's operas *Benchtesgadener Sagenspiel, Musikantenkomödie, König Folkwart,* etc.; wrote much choral and chamber music; his pieces for small brass ensembles, in the style of old town piper music, are especially attractive; he also brought out a number of instructive piano pieces.

Rudnick, Wilhelm, German organist and composer; b. Damerkow, Dec. 30, 1850; d. there, Aug. 7, 1927. He studied at Kullak's Akademie der Tonkunst in Berlin; subsequently occupied various posts as church organist in Landsberg and Liegnitz; was also active as choral conductor. He wrote numerous organ works of excellent quality; a fantasy on *Ein' feste Burg, Trinitatis-Sonate, Pfingsten-Sonate, Konzert-Phantasie, Choralvorspiele;* vocal works.

Rudnicki, Marian Teofil, Polish conductor and composer; b. Cracow, March 7, 1888; d. Warsaw, Dec. 31, 1944. He conducted operetta in Cracow (1916–19) and later at the Warsaw Municipal Opera. He wrote mostly theater music; also composed choral works and solo songs.

Rudnytsky, Antin, Polish pianist, conductor, and composer; b. Luka, Galicia, Feb. 7, 1902; d. Toms River, N.J., Nov. 30, 1975. He studied piano with Schnabel and Petri in Berlin, composition with Schreker, and musicology with Curt Sachs; received his Dr.Phil. at the Univ. of Berlin in 1926. In 1927 he went to Russia, where he conducted opera in Kharkov and Kiev; then was again in Poland, as conductor of the Muncipal Opera in Lwow (1932–37). In 1937 he emigrated to the U.S.; toured with his wife, the singer **Maris Sokil,** as her piano accompanist. He composed 3 symphs. (1936, 1941, 1942); a Cello Concerto (1942); an opera, *Dovbush* (1937); some ballet music; miscellaneous pieces for instrumental ensembles; piano works.

Rudolf, Max, eminent German conductor; b. Frankfurt, June 15, 1902. He studied piano with Eduard Jung and composition with Bernhard Sekles at the Hoch Cons. in Frankfurt; was employed as a coach and a conductor in various provincial opera houses in Germany; then was active as a conductor in Prague (1929–35); in 1935 he went to Göteborg, Sweden, where he served as a regular guest conductor with the Göteborg Symph. Orch. and the Swedish Broadcasting Co., and director of the Oratorio Society. In 1940 he emigrated to the U.S.; became naturalized as an American citizen in 1946. In 1945 he joined the conductorial staff of the Metropolitan Opera Co. in N.Y., and a year later became a member of its management; gave many distinguished performances of standard operas. In 1958 he was appointed principal conductor and music director of the Cincinnati Symph. Orch.; took it on a world tour in 1966, and on a European tour in 1969; in 1963 and from 1967 to 1970 was the music director of the Cincinnati May Festival; in 1970 he moved to Philadelphia, where he conducted the opera class at the Curtis Inst. of Music (until 1973); then was principal conductor of the Dallas Symph. (1973–74). In 1976 he was appointed music adviser to the New Jersey Symph. Orch. He publ. *The Grammar of Conducting* (N.Y., 1950), which also appeared in a Japanese translation.

Rudorff, Ernst Friedrich Karl, German pianist; b. Berlin, Jan. 18, 1840; d. there, Dec. 31, 1916. He studied with Bargiel in Berlin and with Moscheles, Plaidy, and Reinecke in Leipzig. After a few years of teaching in Cologne (1865–68), he was appointed head of the piano dept. at the Hochschule für Musik in Berlin, and held this post for 41 years (1869–1910). He was a friend of Brahms, whose letters to him were publ. in vol. III of the Brahms correspondence (Berlin, 1907); Rudorff's correspondence with Joachim was publ. in vol. III of *Briefe von und an Joseph Joachim* (1913). He composed 3 symphs.; piano pieces.
BIBLIOGRAPHY: Elisabeth Rudorff, ed., *Aus den Tagen der Romantik, Bildnis einer deutschen Familie* (Leipzig, 1938).

Rudziński, Witold, Polish composer; b. Siebież, Lithuania, March 14, 1913. He studied piano at the Cons. of Vilna (1931–36); went to Paris, where he took composition lessons with Nadia Boulanger and Charles Koechlin (1938–39); upon his return, he taught at the Vilna Cons. (1939–42) and the Lodz Cons. (1945–47); settled in Warsaw and became active mainly as a musical administrator and pedagogue; in 1957 became a member of the faculty of the Superior School of Music in Warsaw.
WORKS: 5 operas: *Janko muzykant (Janko the Musician;* 1948–51; Bytom, June 20, 1953); *Komendant Paryza (The Commander of Paris;* 1955–58; Poznan, 1960); *Odprawa posłów greckich (The Departure of Greek Emissaries;* Cracow, 1962); *Sulamita (The Shulamite;* 1964); *Chlopi (The Peasants;* 1972; Warsaw, June 30, 1974); 2 oratorios: *Gaude Mater Polonia* for Narrator, 3 Soloists, Chorus, and Orch. (1966) and *Lipce* for Chorus and Chamber Orch. (1968); cantata, *Chlopska droga (Peasants' Road;* 1952); *Dach świata (The Roof of the World)* for Narrator and Orch. (1960); *The Nike of the Vistula,* war ballads and scenes for Narrator, 4 Soloists, Chorus, and Orch. (1973); Piano Concerto (1936); 2 symphs. (1938, 1944); *Divertimento* for String Orch. (1940); *Uwertura baltycka (Baltic Overture;* 1948); *Parades,* suite for Orch. (1958); *Musica Concertante* for Piano and Chamber Orch. (1959); *Musica profana* for Flute, Clarinet, Trumpet, and Strings (1960); *Obrazy Swiętokrzyskie (Pictures from the Holy-Cross Mountains)* for Orch. (1965); Concerto Grosso for Percussion and 2 String Orchs. (1970; Poznan, March 29, 1973); *Uwertura góralska (Mountain Overture)* for Orch. (1970); Trio for Flute, Oboe, and Piano (1934); Clarinet

Sonatina (1935); 2 string quartets (1935, 1943); Violin Sonata (1937); Viola Sonata (1946); Nonet (1947); Quintet for Flute and Strings (1954); *2 portraits de femmes* for Solo Voice and String Quartet (1960); *Variations and Fugue* for Percussion (1966); *Preludes* for Clarinet, Viola, Harp, and Percussion (1967); *Polonaise-Rapsodie* for Cello and Piano (1969); *Fantazja góralska (Mountain Fantasia)* for Guitar (1970); *To Citizen John Brown,* concertino for Soprano, Flute, Horn, Cello, Piano, and Percussion (1972); *Proverbia latina* for Harpsichord (1974); *Suite* for 2 Pianos (1937); songs. He publ. a biography of Moniuszko in 2 vols. (Cracow, 1955, 1961) and *The Technique of Béla Bartók* (Cracow, 1965).

Rudziński, Zbigniew, Polish composer; b. Czechowice, Oct. 23, 1935. He studied composition with Perkowski at the Warsaw State College of Music (1956–62); traveled to Paris on a French government grant (1965–66); upon his return to Poland, was music director of the Warsaw Documentary Film Studio (1960–67).
WORKS: Sonata for 2 String Quartets, Piano, and Kettledrums (1960); *4 Songs* for Baritone and Chamber Ensemble (1961); *Epigrams* for Flute, 2 Female Choruses, and 6 Percussionists (1962); *Contra Fidem* for Orch. (1964); String Trio (1964); *Study in C* for Variable Ensemble (1964); *Moments musicaux I, II,* and *III,* for Orch. (1965, 1967, 1968); *Impromptu* for 2 Pianos, 3 Cellos, and Percussion (1966); Symph. for textless Bass, Chorus, and Orch., with Strings (1969); Quartet for 2 Pianos and Percussionists (1969); *Muzyka noca (Night Music)* for Chamber Orch. (1970); *Requiem* for Narrator, Chorus, and Orch. (1971); *Tutti e solo* for Soprano, Flute, Horn, and Piano (1973); Piano Sonata (1975); *Campanella* for Percussion Ensemble (1977); *Tritons* for Percussion Ensemble (1980).

Ruelle, Charles Emile, French musicologist, authority on Greek music; b. Paris, Oct. 24, 1833; d. there, Oct. 15, 1912. He was chief librarian of the Bibliothèque de Ste.-Geneviève, Paris, from 1898 to 1905; translated into French the treatises of Aristoxenus (1871), Nicomachus (1881), etc.; publ. the valuable treatises *Etudes sur l'ancienne musique grecque* (1875 and 1900); *Le Monocorde* (1891); *Sextus Empiricus* (1899); *De la musique des Grecs modernes et en particulier de leur musique ecclésiastique* (1876); contributed to the *Dictionnaire des antiquités grecques.*

Rufer, Josef, Austrian music scholar; b. Vienna, Dec. 18, 1893. He studied composition with Zemlinsky and Schoenberg in Vienna (1919–22); later was assistant to Schoenberg at the Prussian Academy of Arts in Berlin; from 1929 was also active as a music critic. From 1947 to 1950 he edited (with Stuckenschmidt) the monthly music magazine *Stimmen;* then was a teacher of theory and 12-tone method of composition at the Hochschule für Musik in Berlin (1956–69). He publ. a number of valuable books dealing with 12-tone music: *Die Komposition* *mit zwölf Tönen* (Berlin, 1952; Eng. trans. by Humphrey Searle as *Composition with 12 Notes Related Only to One Another,* London, 1954); *Musiker über Musik* (Darmstadt, 1955); and, most important, an annotated catalogue of Schoenberg's works, *Das Werk Arnold Schönbergs* (Kassel, 1959; in Eng., *The Works of Arnold Schoenberg,* London, 1962).

Rüfer, Philippe (-Barthélemy), German pianist and composer; b. Liège (of German parents), June 7, 1844; d. Berlin, Sept. 15, 1919. He studied at the Cons. of Liège; in 1871, settled in Berlin, where he taught piano at the Stern Cons., Kullak's Akademie der Tonkunst, and (from 1881) the Scharwenka Cons. He wrote the operas *Merlin* (Berlin, Feb. 28, 1887) and *Ingo* (Berlin, Feb. 1896); a Symph.; 3 overtures; piano music; songs.
BIBLIOGRAPHY: P. Magnette, *Philippe Rüfer. Etude biographique et critique* (Liège, 1910).

Ruff, Willie, American jazz musician; b. Sheffield, Ala., Jan. 9, 1931. He studied at Yale Univ. (M.M., 1954); played the French horn and string bass. He formed a duo with pianist Dwike Mitchell, and together they filled a series of highly successful engagements in intellectual nightclubs. In 1959 they gave a series of jazz concerts in Russia, triumphantly overriding Soviet scruples regarding the allegedly decadent nature of jazz, and scoring a popular success. They were equally triumphant as part of President Johnson's goodwill entourage to Mexico in April 1966.

Ruffo, Titta, famous Italian baritone; b. Pisa, June 9, 1877; d. Florence, July 5, 1953. His real name was **Ruffo Cafiero Titta,** but he found it convenient to transpose his first and last names for professional purposes. He studied with Persichini at the Santa Cecilia Academy in Rome, then with Cassini in Milan. He made his operatic debut in Rome as the Herald in *Lohengrin* (1898); then sang in Rio de Janeiro; returning to Italy, he appeared in all the principal theaters; also sang in Vienna, Paris, and London. He made his American debut in Philadelphia as Rigoletto (Nov. 4, 1912) with the combined Philadelphia-Chicago Opera Co.; his first appearance with the Metropolitan Opera was as Figaro in *Il Barbiere di Siviglia* (N.Y., Jan. 19, 1922). He left the Metropolitan in 1928 and returned to Rome. In 1937 he was briefly under arrest for opposing the Mussolini regime; then went to Florence, where he remained until his death. He publ. a book of memoirs, *La mia parabola* (Milan, 1937).
BIBLIOGRAPHY: M.A. Barrenechea, *Titta Ruffo; Notas de psicología artística* (Buenos Aires, 1911).

Ruggi, Francesco, Italian composer; b. Naples, Oct. 21, 1767; d. there, Jan. 23, 1845. He studied at the Cons. di S. Loreto in Naples under Fenaroli; became a prof. of composition at the Cons. di San Pietro in Majella. He wrote the operas *L'ombra di Nino* (Naples, 1795), *La Guerra aperta* (Naples, 1796), and *Sofì tripponi* (Milan, 1804); much sacred music.

Ruggles, Carl (real Christian names, **Charles Sprague**), remarkable American composer; b. Marion, Mass., March 11, 1876; d. Bennington, Vt., Oct. 24, 1971. He learned to play violin as a child; then went to Boston, where he took violin lessons with Felix Winternitz and theory with Josef Claus; later enrolled as a special student at Harvard Univ., where he attended composition classes of John Knowles Paine. Impressed with the widely assumed supremacy of the German school of composition (of which Paine was a notable representative), Ruggles germanized his given name from Charles to Carl. In 1907 he went to Minnesota, where he organized the Winona Symph. Orch. and conducted it for several years (1908–12). In 1917 he went to N.Y., where he became active in the promotion of modern music; was a member of the International Composers Guild and of the Pan American Assoc. of Composers. He wrote relatively few works, which he was in the habit of constantly revising and rearranging, and they were mostly in small forms. He did not follow any particular modern method of composition, but instinctively avoided needless repetition of thematic notes, which made his melodic progressions atonal; his use of dissonances, at times quite strident, derived from the linear proceedings of chromatically inflected counterpoint. A certain similarity with the 12-tone method of composition of Schoenberg resulted from this process, but Ruggles never adopted it explicitly. In his sources of inspiration, he reached for spiritual exaltation with mystic connotations, scaling the heights and plumbing the depths of musical expression. Such music could not attract large groups of listeners and repelled some critics; one of them remarked that the title of Ruggles's *Sun-Treader* ought to be changed to *Latrine-Treader.* Unable and unwilling to withstand the prevailing musical mores, Ruggles removed himself from the musical scene; he went to live on his farm in Arlington, Vt., and devoted himself exclusively to his avocation, painting; his pictures, mostly in the manner of Abstract Expressionism, were occasionally exhibited in N.Y. galleries. In 1966 he moved to a nursing home in Bennington, where he died at the age of 95. A striking revival of interest in his music took place during the last years of his life, and his name began to appear with increasing frequency on the programs of American orchs. and chamber music groups. His MSS were recovered and publ.; virtually all of his compositions have been recorded.
WORKS: *Men and Angels,* symph. suite for 5 Trumpets and Bass Trumpet (N.Y., Dec. 17, 1922; revised for Brass Instruments or Strings and renamed *Angels;* Miami, April 24, 1939); *Men and Mountains,* symph. suite in 3 movements: *Men, Lilacs, Marching Mountains* (N.Y., Dec. 7, 1924; revised for Large Orch., N.Y., March 19, 1936); *Portals* for String Orch. (N.Y., Jan. 24, 1926); *Sun-Treader,* after Browning, for Large Orch. (Paris, Feb. 25, 1932, Slonimsky conducting); *Polyphonic Composition* for 3 Pianos (1940); *Evocations,* piano suite (1945; an orch. version was perf. in N.Y., Feb. 3, 1971); *Organum* for Large Orch. (N.Y., Nov. 24, 1949); song cycle, *Vox clamans in deserto,* for Voice

and Chamber Orch. (1923); *Exaltation* for "congregation in unison" and Organ (1958). *Symphonia dialectica* for Orch., begun in 1923, remained unfinished.

BIBLIOGRAPHY: Paul Rosenfeld, *An Hour with American Music* (N.Y., 1929; pp. 101–6); Charles Seeger, "Carl Ruggles," *Musical Quarterly* (Oct. 1932); Lou Harrison, "Carl Ruggles," *Score* (June 1955); idem, *About Carl Ruggles* (Yonkers, N.Y., 1946); John Kirkpatrick, "The Evolution of Carl Ruggles. A Chronicle Largely in His Own Words," *Perspectives of New Music* (1967/68); T. Peterson, *The Music of Carl Ruggles* (Diss., Univ. of Washington, 1967); N. Archbal, *Carl Ruggles: Composer and Painter* (Diss., Univ. of Minnesota, 1975).

Rugolo, Pete, Italian-born American jazz orch. leader and composer; b. San Pietro, Patti, Sicily, Dec. 25, 1915. He was brought to the U.S. as a child; obtained a B.A. at San Francisco State College and an M.A. at Mills College, where he studied composition with Darius Milhaud. In 1945 he became an arranger for Stan Kenton; after 1949 he pursued his career as an orch. leader and composer for films and television. He wrote music in a light classical idiom touched with jazz.

Rühlmann, Frans, Belgian conductor; b. Brussels, Jan. 11, 1868; d. Paris, June 8, 1948. He studied at the Cons. of Brussels; filled engagements as conductor at the Théâtre de la Monnaie in Brussels, and also in Liège, Antwerp, etc. In 1905 he was engaged at the Opéra-Comique in Paris; in 1914 conducted at the Paris Opéra; also led a series of popular concerts in Antwerp.

Rühlmann, Franz, German musicologist; b. Chemnitz, Dec. 7, 1896; d. in a camp for prisoners of war, Landsberg (Gorzów Wielkopolski, in northwestern Poland), June 15, 1945. He was in the German army in both wars; studied in Leipzig with Kiel; received his Dr.Phil. in 1924 with the dissertation *Richard Wagner und die deutsche Opernbühne;* was an instructor of theater music at the Hochschule für Musik in Berlin (from 1933). He brought out vocal scores of *Der Freischütz,* Mozart's *Requiem,* Gluck's operas, etc.

Rühlmann, (Adolf) Julius, German writer on music; b. Dresden, Feb. 28, 1816; d. there, Oct. 27, 1877. He played the trombone in the court orch. of Dresden; founded the Dresden Tonkünstlerverein (1855); taught piano and music history at the Dresden Cons. He prepared a valuable *Geschichte der Bogeninstrumente,* which was publ. posthumously by his son, Richard Rühlmann (1882); he also wrote *Die Urform der Bogeninstrumente* (1874).

Ruiter, Wim de, Dutch composer and organist; b. Heemstede, Aug. 11, 1943. He studied organ with Piet Kee in Amsterdam (1963–69) and composition with Ton de Leeuw there (1968–74); taught 20th-century music theory at the Cons. in Zwolle (1973–77)

and at the Sweelinck Cons. (formerly Amsterdam Cons.) since 1973. With another Dutch organist he gave successful concerts of duo-organ music, 4-hands, 4-feet.

WORKS: *Solo* for Flute (1969); *Music* for 2 Double Basses (1969); Quartet for 2 Violas and 2 Cellos (1970); Quartet for Flute, Bass Clarinet, Vibraphone, and Piano (1970); *2 Quartets Together* (1970; a joining together of the previous 2 quartets); *Situations* for 16 Voices (1970); 2 string quartets (1972, 1974); *Hoplopoia* for Chorus and Orch. (1973); *Re* for Orch. (Utrecht, Sept. 14, 1975); *Thick & Thin* for Organ, 4-hands, 4-feet (1975); *Tall & Small* for Treble Recorder (1975); *Off & On* for 4 Bass Clarinets (1976); *To Be or Not to Be* for 12 Wind Instruments and Vibraphone (1976); Quintet for 5 Flutes and Tape (1976; in collaboration with Jacques Bank); Quartet for Recorders (1977); *3 Pieces* for Orch. (1977).

Rummel, Christian, German composer and conductor; b. Brichsenstadt, Nov. 27, 1787; d. Wiesbaden, Feb. 13, 1849. He was an able performer on the piano, violin, and clarinet; served as municipal conductor in Wiesbaden from 1815 until 1841; publ. a Clarinet Concerto, 2 quintets, etc. His son **Joseph Rummel** (b. Wiesbaden, Oct. 6, 1818; d. London, March 25, 1880) was court pianist to the Duke of Nassau, and publ. piano music; another son, **August Rummel** (b. Wiesbaden, Jan. 14, 1824; d. London, Dec. 14, 1886), also was a good pianist.

Rummel, Franz, pianist, son of **Joseph Rummel** and grandson of **Christian Rummel;** b. London, Jan. 11, 1853; d. Berlin, May 2, 1901. He studied with Louis Brassin at the Brussels Cons., winning first prize in 1872; toured in America 3 times (1878, 1886, 1898). He married a daughter of S.F.B. Morse, inventor of the telegraph.

Rummel, Walter Morse, distinguished pianist, son of **Franz Rummel** and grandson of S.F.B. Morse, inventor of the telegraph; b. Berlin, July 19, 1887; d. Bordeaux, May 2, 1953. He studied piano with Leopold Godowsky, and composition with Hugo Kaun. In 1908 he went to Paris, where he became acquainted with Debussy, and devoted himself to promoting Debussy's piano works, of which he became a foremost interpreter. He was married twice, to the pianist **Thérèse Chaigneau,** with whom he appeared in duo-piano recitals (later divorced), and to Sarah Harrington (also divorced).

Runciman, John F., English music critic; b. 1866; d. London, April 7, 1916. He was a church organist before he joined the staff of the *Saturday Review* in London (1894) as a music critic; held this position till his death; also was editor of the *Chord* (quarterly) and the *Musician's Library.* His critical reviews were remarkable for their unabashed violence in denouncing composers and performers whom he did not like; on some occasions he became involved in libel suits. He publ. selected essays in 1899 under the title of *Old Scores and New Readings,* a biographical study of Haydn (1908), one of Purcell (1909), and *Richard Wagner, Composer of Operas* (1913).

Rung, Frederik, Danish composer, son of **Henrik Rung;** b. Copenhagen, June 14, 1854; d. there, Jan. 22, 1914. He studied with his father; became conductor at the Copenhagen Opera (1884); also led the Cecilia Society (founded by his father); taught at the Copenhagen Cons. from 1881 till 1893.
WORKS: Operas: *Det hemmelige Selskab* (*The Secret Party;* Copenhagen, Feb. 9, 1888) and *Den trekantede Hat* (*The 3-cornered Hat;* Copenhagen, Nov. 7, 1894); Symph.; Rhapsody for Orch.; *Danse des papillons* for Orch.; Serenade for 9 Instruments; Piano Quintet; 2 string quartets; Violin Sonata; piano pieces; songs.

Rung, Henrik, Danish conductor and composer, father of **Frederik Rung;** b. Copenhagen, March 3, 1807; d. there, Dec. 13, 1871. He founded the Cecilia Society in 1891; wrote a number of choral works and popular songs.
BIBLIOGRAPHY: C. Thrane, *Caeciliaföreningen og dens Stifter* (Copenhagen, 1901).

Runge, Paul, German musicologist; b. Heinrichsfeld, Posen, Jan. 2, 1848; d. Colmar, Alsace, July 4, 1911. He studied with J. Schneider and at the Royal Inst. for Church Music in Berlin; lived from 1873 as an organist and a teacher in Colmar. His writings, which are of importance especially in connection with the music of the Minnesingers and Mastersingers, are *Die Sangesweisen der Colmarer Handschrift und die Liederhandschrift Donaueschingen* (1896); *Die Lieder und Melodien der Geissler des Jahres 1349* (1900); *Die Lieder des Hugo von Montfort mit den Melodien des Burk Mangolt* (1906); "Die Notation des Meistergesanges" (1907; in the report of the Basel Congress of the Internationale Musik-Gesellschaft); with R. Batka he publ. *Die Lieder Mülichs von Prag* (1905).

Rungenhagen, Carl Friedrich, German conductor and composer; b. Berlin, Sept. 27, 1778; d. there, Dec. 21, 1851. He was a pupil of Benda; in 1815 became 2nd conductor of the Singakademie, succeeding Zelter in 1833 as first conductor; was a member of the Berlin Academy, and a teacher in the School of Composition. He composed 4 operas, 3 oratorios, a Te Deum, 30 motets, 30 4-part songs, over 100 sacred and 1,000 secular songs; also symphs., quartets, etc.

Runolfsson, Karl Otto, Icelandic composer; b. Reykjavik, Oct. 24, 1900; d. there, Nov. 29, 1970. He played the trumpet in the radio orch. in Reykjavik; in 1939 was appointed teacher at the Cons. there. He wrote a set of Icelandic songs for Voice and Orch. (1938); Symph. (1968); choral works on Icelandic themes; Trumpet Sonata; Violin Sonata.

Runze, Maximilian, German writer on music and editor; b. Woltersdorf, Pomerania, Aug. 8, 1849; d.

Berlin, May 9, 1931. He studied philosophy and theology at the univs. of Greifswald and Berlin; from 1882 was rector of St. Johannis-Moabit in Berlin and a lecturer at the Humboldt-Akademie. His writings on the life and works of Karl Loewe are valuable: *Karl Loewe, Eine ästhetische Beurteilung* (1884); *Loewe redivivus* (1888); *Ludwig Giesebrecht und Karl Loewe* (1894); *Goethe und Loewe* (1901); *Karl Loewe* (1905; a biography); also *Die musikalische Legende* (1902); *Volkslied und Ballade* (1907). He ed. *Arien aus ungedruckten Opern und Oratorien Loewes* (3 vols., 1892); *Loewe-Hohenzollern Album* (2 vols., 1898); *Gesamtausgabe der Balladen, Legenden und Gesänge Loewes* (17 vols., 1899-1903).

Ruolz-Montchal, Henri (-Catherine-Camille), Comte de, French composer; b. Paris, March 5, 1808; d. there, Sept. 30, 1887. He was a pupil of Berton, Lesueur, Paër, and Rossini; won some success as a composer, but the loss of his family fortune in 1840 induced him to abandon music and devote himself to the more practical study of chemistry.
WORKS: Operas: *Attendre et courir* (with F. Halévy; 1830); *Lara* (Naples, Nov. 22, 1835; was highly praised by Alexandre Dumas in the *Gazette Musicale de Paris*); *La Vendetta* (Paris, 1839); *La Jolie Fille de Perth; Manfred;* a Requiem; *Cantate en honneur de Jeanne d'Arc;* String Quartet; 2 piano trios; motets; songs.

Rupnik, Ivan, Serbian composer; b. Belgrade, Aug. 29, 1911. He studied in Ljubljana; later in Vienna with Alban Berg. His early works are in a neo-Romantic vein, with expressionistic overtones; later he abjured modern devices and began writing music for the masses, in conformity with socialist ideology. His cantata, *Song of the Dead Proletarians,* which he conducted in Belgrade on Dec. 14, 1947, is an epitome of programmatic realism. He further wrote 2 symphs., several overtures (*Romantic Overture, Youth Overture*), ethnic symph. works (*Musical Impressions from Istria, A Peasant Evening Party*), and a *Hymn of Peace.*

Rusca, Francesco, Italian composer of church music; was Maestro di Cappella of the Como Cathedral from 1659 until 1699. He wrote about 100 masses, Psalms, cantatas, etc., in a highly developed polyphonic style, containing as many as 16 independent vocal and instrumental parts. His 5 keyboard toccatas are included in vol. III of *I classici* (Como, 1961).

Rusconi, Gerardo, Italian composer; b. Milan, Feb. 1, 1922; d. there, Dec. 23, 1974. He studied at the Cons. of Parma; began his career as a composer by writing light music for the stage, radio, and the films; then undertook more serious genres of music. He composed *La moglie di Lot* for Soprano, Horn, and Piano (1962); *Concerto breve* for Horn and Strings (1965); *3 musiche* for Flute and Piano (1967); *Moments* for Orch. in memory of Martin Luther King (1968); *L'appuntamento,* one-act opera (1971);

numerous transcriptions and harmonizations of popular songs.

Rush, Loren, American composer; b. Fullerton, Calif., Aug. 23, 1935. He studied piano, bassoon, and double bass; played the bassoon in the Oakland Symph. and the double bass in the Richmond Symph.; also was a drummer. He studied composition with Robert Erickson at San Francisco State College (B.A., 1957); upon graduation, organized the Loren Rush Jazz Quartet; enrolled at the Univ. of Calif. at Berkeley, studying composition with Andrew Imbrie, Seymour Shifrin, William Denny, and Charles Cushing (M.A., 1960). He applies a whole spectrum of modern techniques, including serialism, spatial distribution, controlled improvisation, and pointillistic exoticism.

WORKS: *5 Japanese Poems* for Soprano, Flute, Clarinet, Viola, and Piano (1959); *Serenade* for Violin and Viola (1960); *Mandala Music*, improvisation for a group, inspired by the oriental geometrization of the cosmos and an important symbol in Jungian psychology (1962); *Hexahedron* for Piano, notated on all 6 surfaces of a large cube (1964); *Nexus 16* for Chamber Orch. (1964); *soft music, HARD MUSIC* for 2 Amplified Pianos (1969); *The Cloud Messenger* for Orch. (1970).

Rushing, James Andrew ("Jimmy"), black American blues singer; b. Oklahoma City, Aug. 26, 1903; d. New York, June 8, 1972. He was reared in a musical family; learned to play the violin and the piano, then began to make appearances as a singer; he later worked with Bennie Moten (1929–35) and Count Basie (1935–48); subsequently appeared as a guest artist with Benny Goodman, Harry James, and Eddie Condon. He was affectionately dubbed "Mr. Five by Five."

Russell, Charles Ellsworth ("Pee Wee"), American jazz clarinetist; b. Maple Wood, Mo., March 27, 1906; d. Alexandria, Va., Feb. 15, 1969. He played violin, piano, and drums; later studied clarinet with Charlie Merrill; then attended the Univ. of Missouri; eventually made his way to N.Y., where he played in the bands of Red Nichols, Bobby Hackett, Eddie Condon, and others. In later years he embarked upon an ambitious solo career; appeared at the leading jazz festivals with the Newport All Stars.

Russell, George, American jazz pianist and composer; b. Cincinnati, June 23, 1923. He took up the drums in his youth; then turned to composition, and later developed a modal technique which he called the Lydian Chromatic Concept of Tonal Organization; he conducted classes in his theory of composition at the New England Cons. of Music in Boston.

Russell, George Alexander, American organist and song composer; b. Franklin, Tenn., Oct. 2, 1880; d. Dewitt, N.Y., Nov. 24, 1953. The son of a Presbyterian minister, he studied at home; his mother, Felicia Putnam Russell (a direct descendant of General Israel Putnam of Revolution fame), taught him piano; the family moved to Texas, where he studied academic subjects; entered the College of Fine Arts of Syracuse Univ., studying organ with George A. Parker and composition with William Berwald; subsequently studied in Europe with Leopold Godowsky and Harold Bauer (piano), and with Widor (organ). Returning to America in 1908, he toured as accompanist to various artists; in 1910 he became director of the Auditorium concerts at Wanamaker's in N.Y.; in 1917 was appointed prof. in the newly founded chair of music at Princeton Univ.; assembled the famous Rodman Wanamaker Collection of old Italian string instruments. He wrote the songs *Sunset, The Sacred Fire, In Fountain Court, Lyric from Tagore, Expectation, Puer Redemptor,* etc.; the piano pieces *Theme and Variations, Contrapuntal Waltz,* etc.

BIBLIOGRAPHY: J.T. Howard, *Alexander Russell* (N.Y., 1925).

Russell, Henry, English singer and composer; b. Sheerness, Dec. 24, 1812; d. London, Dec. 8, 1900. He studied in Italy as a young boy; took a few lessons from Rossini in Naples; was in London in 1828; then in Canada (1833); served as organist of the First Presbyterian Church of Rochester, N.Y. (1833–41). He returned to England in 1841 and became extremely popular there as a composer and singer of dramatic and topical songs, of which *Woodman, Spare That Tree* attained immense popularity; other songs were *Old Arm Chair; Oh, Weep Not!; A Life on the Ocean Wave* (official march of the Royal Marines); *Cheer, Boys, Cheer; Ivy Green; The Gambler's Wife; Old Bell; The Maniac;* etc. He publ. a book of reminiscences, *Cheer, Boys, Cheer* (London, 1895), and *L'Amico dei cantanti,* a treatise on singing. He was the father of **Henry Russell,** the impresario, and of **Sir Landon Ronald,** the composer and conductor, whose real name was **L.R. Russell.**

BIBLIOGRAPHY: J. Stevens, *Henry Russell in America: Chutzpah and Huzzah* (Diss., Univ. of Illinois, 1975).

Russell, Henry, English impresario, son of **Henry Russell,** the singer and composer; b. London, Nov. 14, 1871; d. there, Oct. 11, 1937. He studied singing at the Royal College of Music, and devised an original method of vocal instruction, which attracted the attention of Mme. Melba, who sent him a number of her good pupils. Owing to his wide acquaintance with singers, he was invited in 1904 to manage a season of opera at Covent Garden; in 1905 he brought his company to the U.S., where Boston was the principal field of his operations; his success there resulted, in 1909, in the formation of the Boston Opera Co., of which he was general manager until its dissolution in 1914. Just before the outbreak of World War I, he had taken the entire Boston troupe to Paris, where he gave a successful spring season at the Théâtre des Champs-Elysées. He then lived mostly in London. He publ. a book of memoirs, *The Passing Show* (London, 1926).

Russell, Leon, American country-rock musician; b. Lawton, Okla., April 2, 1941. He played piano and trumpet; then learned to play guitar. He moved to Los Angeles in 1959, did recording gigs with Frank Sinatra, Bobby Darin, and others, and began recording his own songs, among them *Delta Lady* and *Hummingbird.* Apart from regular pop numbers, Russell also put out an album of country-and-western songs; he toured widely and successfully. He clandestinely married the vocalist Mary McCreary in 1976 and put out *The Wedding Album.* His solo releases included the albums *Leon Russell, The Shelter People, Carney,* and *Leon Live.* His use of a honky-tonk piano imparted to his songs a distinct country-and-western flavor, which contributed to the success of his duo with Willie Nelson, *One for the Road.* His other hits were *A Song for You, Tight Rope,* and *Magic Mirror.*

Russell, Louis Arthur, American organist and pianist; b. Newark, N.J., Feb. 24, 1854; d. there, Sept. 5, 1925. He studied singing with William Shakespeare and George Henschel in London. Returning to America in 1878, he was active as a church organist in Newark; founded the College of Music there (1885) and organized the Newark Symph. Orch. (1893). He publ. several instructive books: *The Embellishments of Music; How to Read Modern Music; Problems of Time and Tune; Development of Artistic Pianoforte Touch;* etc.

Russell, William, American composer; b. Canton, Mo., Feb. 26, 1905, of German-American parents. His complete name was **Russell William Wagner,** but when he began to study music he eliminated his patronymic as possibly invidious, and placed his first Christian name as a surname. He was fascinated with the sounds of drums, and wrote music almost exclusively for percussion instruments; his first important work in this category was the *Fugue for 8 Percussion Instruments* (1932). Another work of importance was *3 Dance Movements,* composed in 1933 and performed for the first time in N.Y. on Nov. 22, 1933. The scoring is for tone clusters and piano strings activated with a fork, and a cymbal sounded by drawing the teeth of a saw across its edge; the ensemble also includes a bottle which must be broken at the climax. In 1940 he went to New Orleans and became active as an administrator of festivals and other social events. Eventually, he gave up composition.

Russo, William Joseph, American composer; b. Chicago, June 25, 1928. He played trombone in various jazz bands, including the Stan Kenton Band (1950–54), for which he also became a composer-arranger; studied privately in Chicago with John Becker (1953–55) and Karel Jirák (1955–57). He then went to N.Y., where he organized his own band (1958–61); proceeded to London and conducted a jazz orch. (1962–65). Returning to America, he was affiliated with the Center for New Music in Chicago (1965–76), where he directed the Chicago Jazz Ensemble and the Free Theater, for which he composed 4 rock cantatas; subsequently moved to San Francisco, where he found a congenial environment for his type of sophisticated jazz and blues. Learned counterpoint lends distinction to his own compositions even when they reach the never-never land of decibel-laden rock.

WORKS: *John Hooton,* opera for Jazz Orch., Soloists, Strings, Piano, and Chorus (1961); *Antigone,* opera for 4 Soloists and Chamber Orch. (1967); *Aesop's Fables,* rock opera for 6 to 10 Soloists and Rock Band (1971); 2 comic operas: *Isabella's Fortune* (1974) and *Pedrolino's Revenge* (N.Y., Sept. 11, 1974); ballet, *Les Deux Errants (The Seekers;* 1955); 4 rock cantatas: *The Civil War* (1968); *David* (in collaboration with Robert Perrey; 1968); *Liberation* (1969); *Joan of Arc* (1970); *The English Suite* for Jazz Orch. (1955); 2 symphs.: No. 1 (1955) and No. 2, *Titans* (1957; N.Y. Phil., April 19, 1959); Concerto Grosso for Saxophone Quartet and Concert Band (1960); *Variations on an American Theme* for Orch. (1961); Cello Concerto (1962); *The Island* for 6 Soloists and Jazz Orch. (1963); *The English Concerto* for Violin and Orch. (1963; Bath Festival, June 1963; Yehudi Menuhin, soloist); *In Memoriam* for 2 Soloists, Small Chorus, and Jazz Orch. (1966); *America 1966,* concerto grosso for Jazz Orch. (1966); *3 Pieces* for Blues Band and Orch. (1967–68; Ravinia Festival, Chicago Symph., July 7, 1968); *Songs of Celebration* for 5 Soloists, Chorus, and Orch. (1971); *Song of Songs* for 6 Soloists, Chorus, and modified Jazz Band-Orch. (1972); *Carousel Suite* for Narrator, Dancers, and Chamber Orch. (1975); *Street Music,* blues concerto for Piano, Harmonica, and Orch. (1975). He wrote the books *Composing for the Jazz Orchestra* (Chicago, 1961) and *Jazz Composition and Orchestration* (Chicago, 1968).

Russolo, Luigi, Italian futurist composer; b. Portogruaro, May 1, 1885; d. Cerro, Feb. 4, 1947. In 1909 he joined the futurist movement of Marinetti; formulated the principles of "art of noises" in his book, *L'arte dei rumori* (Milan, 1916); constructed a battery of noise-making instruments ("intonarumori"), with which he gave concerts in Milan (April 21, 1914) and Paris (June 18, 1921), creating such a commotion in the concert hall that on one occasion a group of outraged concertgoers mounted the stage and physically attacked Russolo and his fellow noisemakers. The titles of his works sing the glory of the machine and of urban living: *Convegno dell'automobili e dell'aeroplani, Il Risveglio di una città, Si pranza sulla terrazza dell'Hotel.* In his "futurist manifesto" of 1913 the noises are divided into 6 categories, including shrieks, groans, clashes, explosions, etc. In 1929 he constructed a noise instrument which he called "Russolophone." Soon the novelty of machine music wore out, the erstwhile marvels of automobiles and airplanes became commonplace, and the future of the futurists turned into a yawning past; Russolo gradually retreated from cultivation of noise and devoted himself to the most silent of all arts, painting. His pictures, influenced by the modern French school, and remarkable for their vivid colors, had several successful exhibitions in Paris and N.Y. The text of Russolo's manifesto is reproduced, in an English translation, in N. Slonimsky's *Music since 1900*.

Rust, Friedrich Wilhelm, German violinist and composer; b. Wörlitz, near Dessau, July 6, 1739; d. Dessau, Feb. 28, 1796. He was a pupil of the violinist Höckh at Zerbst and (1763) of Franz Benda at Berlin, under the patronage of Prince Leopold III of Anhalt-Dessau, whom he accompanied to Italy (1765–66), and who appointed him court music director in 1775. He brought out several stage pieces, wrote incidental music to plays and considerable instrumental music. Davis Singer and Wilhelm Rust publ. several of his violin pieces. His son, **Wilhelm Karl Rust** (b. Dessau, April 29, 1787; d. there, April 18, 1855), was an organist at Vienna (1819–27), then a teacher in Dessau; publ. pieces for piano and organ.
BIBLIOGRAPHY: W. Hosäus, *F.W. Rust und das Dessauer Musikleben* (Dessau, 1882); E. Prieger, *F.W. Rust* (Cologne, 1894; with list of works); R. Czach, *F.W. Rust* (Essen, 1927).

Rust, Wilhelm, German organist and editor; b. Dessau, Aug. 15, 1822; d. Leipzig, May 2, 1892. He was a pupil of his uncle, **W.K. Rust** (piano and organ); later of F. Schneider (1840–43). He went to Berlin in 1849, taught there, and entered the Singakademie; joined the Leipzig Bach-Verein in 1850; played in numerous concerts; became organist of St. Luke's in 1861; was conductor of the Berlin Bach-Verein from 1862–74, "Royal Music Director" in 1864; in 1870 became a teacher of theory and composition at the Stern Cons.; in 1878, organist of the Thomaskirche at Leipzig, and a teacher in the Cons. there; in 1880 he succeeded Richter as cantor of the Thomasschule. As editor of several vols. of the Bach edition prepared by the Bach-Gesellschaft, he displayed great erudition.

Ruthardt, Adolf, German piano pedagogue and music editor; b. Stuttgart, Feb. 9, 1849; d. Leipzig, Sept. 12, 1934. He studied music with his father, Friedrich Ruthardt; then enrolled at the Stuttgart Cons.; subsequently was active as a piano teacher, first in Geneva (1868–85) and then at the Leipzig Cons. (1887–1914). He wrote a number of attractive piano pieces and useful student exercises, among them *Trillerstudien, Oktavenstudien, Terzen-Etüden, Sexten-Etüden*, etc.; also publ. an *Elementär-Klavierschule*. He brought out a selection of Cramer's *Studies* (1909), a collection of *Old Dances* (2 vols., 1913), and *Klavierbuch nordischer Komponisten* (2 vols., 1913); further publ. *Das Klavier: Ein geschichtlicher Abriss* and ed. various manuals of piano literature.

Ruthström, (Bror Olaf) Julius, Swedish violinist; b. Sundsvall, Dec. 30, 1877; d. Stockholm, April 2, 1944. He studied at the Stockholm Cons. (1894–99) and the Berlin Hochschule für Musik (1901–3); was a pupil of A. Moser, J. Joachim, and W. Burmester; toured Scandinavia and Central Europe; publ. valuable pedagogic works for the violin: *Mechanics of Passage-Playing* (1914); *The Art of Bowing* (1921); *Double-Note Studies* (1924); *Violin School* (1928).

Rutz, Ottmar, German singing teacher; b. Fürth, July 15, 1881; d. Garmisch, Sept. 8, 1952. He was the son of Josef Rutz and Klara Rutz, vocal teachers in Munich, whose ideas on various physiological aspects of singing (especially as regards the position of pectoral muscles in singing different types of songs) he expounded in several books: *Neue Entdeckungen von der menschlichen Stimme* (Munich, 1908); *Musik, Wort und Körper als Gemütsausdruck* (Leipzig, 1911); *Typenstimmbildung, zugleich die neue Ausdruckskunst für Bühne und Konzert* (with Klara Rutz; 1920); *Menschheitstypen und Kunst* (1921); *Vom Ausdruck des Menschen* (1926).

Ruygrok, Leo (Leonard Petrus), Dutch cellist, conductor, and composer; b. Utrecht, May 8, 1889; d. Hilversum, Jan. 3, 1944. He studied composition with Johan Wagenaar and cello with Ed. Ferrée; was active as a cellist; then was a conductor at Arnhem (1915–19) and in The Hague (1919–40). He wrote 2 symphs., 4 overtures, and cello pieces.

Ruyneman, Daniel, Dutch composer; b. Amsterdam, Aug. 8, 1886; d. there, July 25, 1963. He began his study of music relatively late; took composition lessons with Zweers at the Amsterdam Cons. (1913–16); in 1918 was co-founder of the Society of Modern Dutch Composers; in 1930, organized the Netherlands Society for Contemporary Music, serving as president until 1962; edited its magazine, *Tijdschrift voor Hedendaagse Muziek* (1930–40), until it was suppressed during the Nazi occupation of the Netherlands. Ruyneman made a special study of Javanese instruments and introduced them in some of his works. He was naturally attracted to exotic subjects with mystic connotations and coloristic effects; also worked on restoration of old music; in 1930 he orchestrated fragments of Mussorgsky's unfinished opera *The Marriage*, and added his own music for the missing acts of the score.
WORKS: FOR THE STAGE: Opera, *The Brothers Karamazov* (1928); music for the "psycho-symbolic" play *De Clown*, for Vocal and Instrumental Orch. (1915). FOR ORCH.: 2 symphs.: No. 1, *Symphonie brève* (1927), and No. 2, *Symphony 1953* (1953; Utrecht, March 14, 1956); *Musica per orchestra per una festa Olandese* (1936); Concerto for Orch. (1937); Piano Concerto (1939); Violin Concerto (1940; Amsterdam, Feb. 23, 1943); *Partita* for String Orch. (1943); *Amphitryon,* overture (1943); *Amatarasu (Ode to the Sun Goddess),* on a Japanese melody, for Chamber Ensemble (1953); *Gilgamesj,* Babylonian epos for Orch. (1962). VOCAL WORKS: *Sous le pont Mirabeau* for Female Chorus, Flute, Harp, and String Quartet (1917); *De Roep (The Call),* a color spectrum of wordless vowel sounds for 5-part a cappella Mixed Chorus (1918); *Sonata,* on wordless vowel sounds, for Chamber a cappella Chorus (1931); *4 Liederen* for Tenor and Small Orch. (1937);

Die Weise von Liebe und Tod des Kornets Christoph Rilke for Narrator and Piano (1946; orchestrated 1951); *Ancient Greek Songs* for Baritone or Bass, Flute, Oboe, Cello, and Harp (1954); *5 Melodies* for Voice and Piano (1957); *3 chansons de Maquisards condamnés* for Alto or Baritone, and Orch. (1957); *Réflexions I* for Soprano, Flute, Guitar, Viola, Vibraphone, Xylophone, and Percussion (1958–59). CHAMBER MUSIC: *Réflexions: II* for Flute, Viola, and Guitar (1959); *III* for Flute, Violin, Viola, Cello, and Piano or Harpsichord (1960–61; reconstructed by Rob du Bois); *IV* for Wind Quintet (1961); 3 violin sonatas (No. 2, 1914; No. 3, 1956); *Klaaglied van een Slaaf* for Violin and Piano (1917); *Hiëroglyphs* for 3 Flutes, Celesta, Harp, Cup-bells, Piano, 2 Mandolins, and 2 Guitars (1918; the unique cup-bells, which some claim were cast by J. Taylor & Co., Loughborough, England, and which others claim were found by the composer in a London junk shop, were destroyed in a Rotterdam air raid in 1940, and perfs. of the work since then have substituted a vibraphone); Sonata for Violin (1925); *Divertimento* for Flute, Clarinet, Horn, Violin, and Piano (1927); Clarinet Sonata (1936); *4 tempi* for 4 Cellos (1937); *Sonatina in modo antiquo* for Cello and Piano (1939); *Sonata da camera* for Flute and Piano (1942); String Quartet (1946); *Nightingale Quintet* for Winds (1949); *4 chansons Bengalies* for Flute and Piano (1950); Sonatina for Flute, and Piano or Harpsichord (1951); Oboe Sonatina (1952); *3 Fantasies* for Cello, and Piano or Harpsichord (1960). FOR PIANO: *3 Pathematologieën* (1915); 2 sonatinas (1917, 1954); Sonata (1931); *Kleine Sonata* (1938); *5 sonatines mélodiques pour l'enseignement moderne du piano* (1947).

BIBLIOGRAPHY: A. Petronio, *Daniel Ruyneman et son œuvre* (Liège, 1922); C. Bérard, "Daniel Ruyneman," *Chesterian* (1928); A. Hoérée, "Daniel Ruyneman," *Revue Musicale* (March 1949); Wouter Paap, "Daniel Ruyneman," *Mens en Melodie,* 5 (1962); Jos Wouters, "Daniel Ruyneman," *Sonorum Speculum,* 11 (1962); Rob du Bois, "Daniel Ruyneman: On the Barricades," *Key Notes* (1976).

Ruzicka, Peter, German composer; b. Düsseldorf, July 3, 1948. He studied piano, oboe, and counterpoint at the Hamburg Cons. (1963–68); then took lessons in composition with Henze in Rome and Otte in Bremen. Ruzicka's admiration for Mahler is revealed through frequent use of material from Mahler's symphs. in his music.

WORKS: *3 Szenen* for Solo Clarinet (1967); *Esta noche,* funeral music for the victims of war in Vietnam, for Alto Flute, English Horn, Viola, and Cello (1967); Concerto for Beat Band and Orch. (1968); *desfuge,* scene with text by Paul Celan, for Alto and Cello Sonata (1969); 2 string quartets (1969, 1970); *Antifone-strofe* for 25 Solo Strings and Percussion (1970); *Metastrofe,* subtitled "an attempt at a break-out," for 87 Instruments (Berlin, May 4, 1971); *Epigenesis* for Orch. (1971); *Sinfonia* for Solo Strings, 16 Vocalists, and Percussion (1970–71); *Experience,* musical theater (1971–72); *In processo di tempo,* an "anti-cello concerto" for 26 Instruments and Non-

anticello (Hilversum, Sept. 11, 1972); *Torso* for Orch. (1973); *Versuch,* 7 pieces for String Orch. (Utrecht, Sept. 19, 1975); *Emanzione,* variations for Flute and Orch. (Berlin, Jan. 13, 1976); *Gestalt und Abbruch sieben Fragmente* for Voices (Baden-Baden, Oct. 21, 1979).

Růžička, Rudolf, Czech composer; b. Brno, April 25, 1941. He studied at the Janáček Academy of Music in Brno; then taught electronic music there. In 1967 he, along with A. Parsch and M. Štědroň, joined a composing collective group originally founded by Alois Piňos, and named, in English, "Teamwork." It was modeled after the Soviet "Production Collective" (Procoll) of 1925; together, the "Teamwork" produced some pieces of utilitarian music. Růžička's individual compositions include a *Sonata aleatorica* for Organ and Percussion (1964); *Melodrama I* and *II* for 3 Narrators, Chorus, and 7 Instruments (1965); *Elektronika A* for Alto, Chamber Orch., and Electronic Sound (1965); *Elektronika B* for Chamber Orch. and Electronic Sound (1966) and *C* for Tape (1967); *Musica à 5* for Viola, Bass Clarinet, Harpsichord, Flute, and Percussion (1966); *Timbres* for Wind Quintet and Tape (1968); *Deliciae* for Double Bass and *musique concrète* (1969); *Conteminationi* for Bass Clarinet and Piano (1969); *Sonata nuova* for Cello and Piano (1970); *Cantata ai ai a* (1970); 2 tape pieces, *Discordia* and *Mavors* (both 1970); *Sinfonia cosmica* for Orch. and Organ (1971); *Sonate triste* for Trombone and Piano (1971); 2 string quartets.

Růžičková, Zuzana, Czech harpsichordist; b. Plzeň, Jan. 14, 1928. She studied at the Prague Cons.; in 1956 won the Munich International Competition; was also a member of the Prague Chamber Soloists (1962–67), which she co-founded with the conductor Vaclav Neumann. In 1962 she joined the faculty of the Prague Academy of Music. She is married to **Viktor Kalabis.**

Ryan, Thomas, American musician; b. Ireland, 1827; d. New Bedford, Mass., March 5, 1903. He settled in the U.S. in 1844, and in 1849 was a co-founder of the Mendelssohn Quintette Club, playing the viola (and upon occasion, the clarinet), with August Fries (first violin), Francis Riha (2nd violin), Eduard Lehmann (viola and flute), and Wulf Fries (cello). With this club he traveled all over the U.S., doing missionary work in bringing good music to remote communities; he also acted as its manager; arranged Classical sonatas and other works for it; after half a century, Ryan was the sole remaining original member of the organization. He publ. his memoirs, *Recollections of an Old Musician* (N.Y., 1899).

Ryba, Jan Jakub, Czech composer; b. Přeštice, Oct. 26, 1765; d. Rožmitál, April 8, 1815. He studied academic subjects in Prague; in 1788 was appointed rector at a school in Rožkmitál; remained there until his death (suicide). A very prolific composer, he left about 120 masses, 100 motets, 30 pastorals

(Christmas cantatas to Latin and Czech texts); also many songs to Czech words; of these last, 2 albums were publ. during his lifetime; other works were a Symph., several string quartets, sonatas. There is a growing realization in Czechoslovakia of Ryba's importance as an early representative of the national art song.

BIBLIOGRAPHY: J. Němeček, *Jan Jakub Ryba* (Prague, 1947; 2nd ed., 1963).

Rybner, (Peter Martin) Cornelius, pianist, conductor, and composer; b. Copenhagen, Oct. 26, 1855; d. New York, Jan. 21, 1929. His original name was **Rübner,** but he changed it to Rybner about 1920. He studied at the Copenhagen Cons. with Gade and J.P. Hartmann; then at the Leipzig Cons. with Ferdinand David (violin) and Reinecke (piano); finished his pianistic studies under Hans von Bülow and Anton Rubinstein. After a series of concerts in Europe as pianist, he settled in Karlsruhe; succeeded Mottl in 1892 as conductor of the Phil. Society there, and held this position until 1904, when he emigrated to the U.S., succeeding MacDowell as head of the music dept. at Columbia Univ. (1904–19). His works include a ballet, *Prinz Ador* (Munich, 1902); a symph. poem, *Friede, Kampf und Sieg;* a Violin Concerto; numerous choruses; piano pieces; songs; also some chamber music.

Rychlík, Jan, Czech composer; b. Prague, April 27, 1916; d. there, Jan. 20, 1964. He studied with Jaroslav Řídký at the Prague Cons. A practical musician, he played in dance orchs., experimented with modern techniques, and was active as a music critic; he wrote a book on jazz and one on valveless brass instruments.

WORKS: *Symphonic Overture* (1944); *Suite* for Wind Quintet (1946); *Concert Overture* (1947); *Partita Giocosa* for Wind Orch. (1947); Trio for Clarinet, Trumpet, and Bassoon (1948); *Divertimento* for 3 Double Basses (1951); *Etudes* for English Horn and Piano (1953); String Trio (1953); *4 Partitas* for Solo Flute (1954); *Chamber Suite* for String Quartet (1954); *Arabesques* for Violin and Piano (1955); *Burlesque Suite* for Solo Clarinet (1956); *Serenade* for Wind Octet (1957); Wind Quintet (1960); *Hommagi gravicembalistici* for Harpsichord (1960); *African Cycle I–V* for 8 Winds and Piano (1961; first complete perf., Prague, June 29, 1962); *Relazioni* for Alto Flute, English Horn, and Bassoon (1964); music for 55 films and 8 plays.

Rychlik, Józef, Polish composer; b. Cracow, May 12, 1946. He graduated in composition from the Cracow High School of Music. He composed *Symphonic Music I* for 2 String Quartets and 2 Pianos (1969); *Symphonic Music II* for Chamber Ensemble (1969); *Ametrio* for Flute, Violin, and Cello (1971); *Spatial Sequences* for 22 Players (1971); *"000"* for Chamber Group and any Wind Instrument Solo (1972); *Sketches* for Organ and Orch. (1972); *Plenitudo temporis* for Orch. (1974); *Peut-être,* graphic composition for any Solo Instrument, or Voice, or Dancer, or Ballet Group, with ad lib. Tape (1974).

Rychnovsky, Ernst, Czech music critic; b. Janovice, June 25, 1879; d. Prague, April 25, 1934. He studied law in Prague; then music with Rietsch; became music critic of the *Prager Tageblatt.* He publ. monographs on Spohr and Rochlitz (1904), Kittl (2 vols., 1904, 1905), Blech (1905), Haydn (1909), Schumann (1910), Liszt (1911), Smetana (1924), etc.; compiled a bibliography on German intellectual life in Bohemia (1906-9).

Ryder, Arthur Hilton, American organist and composer; b. Plymouth, Mass., April 30, 1875; d. Newton, Mass., July 18, 1944. He studied at Harvard Univ. with Walter Spalding (theory) and J.K. Paine (composition); subsequently was church organist and choir director in Boston and neighboring towns. In 1935 he developed a system of "Radical Harmony" which he taught at extension courses at Boston Univ.; also composed songs and organ pieces.

Ryder, Thomas Philander, American organist and composer; b. Cohasset, Mass., June 29, 1836; d. Somerville, Mass., Dec. 2, 1887. He was for many years organist at Tremont Temple in Boston; publ. a number of piano pieces in a light vein.

Rydman, Kari, Finnish composer; b. Helsinki, Oct. 15, 1936. He attended music classes at the Univ. of Helsinki; then developed energetic activities as a composer, music critic, and schoolteacher. In his music he reveals himself as a blithe spirit, writing ultramodern pieces, but also turning out some fetching Finnish pop tunes.

WORKS: 5 string quartets (1959, 1963, 1964, 1964, 1966); Piano Quintet (1960); Trio for Violin, Cello, and Percussion (1961); *Sonata 1* for 3 Violins, Viola, Cello, Piano, and Percussion (1962); *Sonata 2* for Violin, Viola, Guitar, and Percussion (1962); *Sonata 4* for Violin, Clarinet, Guitar, and Percussion (1963); *Sonata 6* for Cello and Percussion (1964); *Khoros 1* for 3 Flutes, Oboe, Percussion, Harp, Violin, Viola, Cello, and Double Bass (1964); *Khoros 2* for Orch. (1966); *Rondeaux des nuits blanches d'été* for Orch. (1966); *Sonata 8* for Viola and Harpsichord (1967); *Symphony of the Modern Worlds,* commissioned by the Swedish Broadcasting Corp. (1968), which contains blues, beat rhythms, political songs, and the Chinese Communist anthem, *Dong Fang Hong (The East Is Red);* Sonata 9 for Small Orch. (1969); *DNA* for Orch. and Electronic Organ (1970); *Suite* for Narrator and Orch. (1971).

Ryelandt, Joseph, Belgian composer; b. Bruges, April 7, 1870; d. there, June 29, 1965. He studied composition with Edgar Tinel. Thanks to a personal fortune (he was a Baron), he did not have to earn a living by his music, but he taught at the Cons. of Ghent (1929–39) and served as director of the Municipal Cons. in Bruges (1924–45). He lived a very long life (*obiit aet.* 95) and composed much music. WORKS: *La Parabole des vierges,* spiritual drama (1894); *Sainte Cécile,* lyrical drama (1902); 5 oratorios: *Purgatorium* (1904); *De Komst des Heren* (*The Coming of the Lord;* 1906–7); *Maria* (1910); *Ag-*

nus Dei (1913–15); Christus Rex (1921–22); Te Deum for Soli, Chorus, and Orch. (1927); 5 symphs. (1897, 1904, 1908, 1913, 1934); Gethsemani, symph. poem (1908); Patria, overture (1917); 11 piano sonatas; 4 string quartets; Horn Sonata (1897); 2 piano quintets; 2 piano trios; 7 violin sonatas; 3 cello sonatas; Viola Sonata; 7 cantatas; organ pieces; songs.

Rysanek, Leonie, Austrian soprano; b. Vienna, Nov. 14, 1926. She studied at the Academy of Music and Dramatic Art in Vienna with **Rudolf Grossmann,** whom she later married. She made her debut at Innsbruck in 1949; then sang at Saarbrücken (1950–52) and at the Munich State Opera (1952–54). In 1954 she joined the staff of the Vienna State Opera; in subsequent years also sang at La Scala in Milan, at Covent Garden in London, and at the Paris Opéra. She made a spectacular American appearance at the Metropolitan Opera House in N.Y. on Feb. 5, 1959, when she replaced Maria Callas in the role of Lady Macbeth in Verdi's opera on short notice; she remained on its staff until 1973, and again in 1975–76 and subsequent seasons, and sang the roles of Aida, Desdemona, and Tosca, as well as several Wagner parts (Elsa in Lohengrin, Elisabeth in Tännhauser, Sieglinde in Die Walküre). She received the Lotte Lehmann Ring from the Vienna State Opera in 1979. Her younger sister **Lotte Rysanek** (b. Vienna, March 18, 1928) attained a fine reputation in Vienna as a lyric soprano.

Rytel, Piotr, Polish composer; b. Vilna, Sept. 20, 1884; d. Warsaw, Jan. 2, 1970. He studied with Michalowski and Noskowski at the Warsaw Cons.; in 1911, was appointed a prof. of piano, and in 1918 a prof. of harmony there. In 1948 he conducted at the Warsaw Opera House. He was the director of Sopot State College of Music, 1956–61.
WORKS: Operas: Ijola (1927; Warsaw, Dec. 14, 1929); Koniec Mesjasza (1935–36); Krzyzowcy (1940–41); Andrzej z Chelmna (1942–43); ballet, Śląski pierścień (The Silesian Ring; 1956); symph. poems: Grazyna (1908; revised 1954); Poemat (1910); Korsarz, after Byron (The Corsair; 1911); Sen Dantego (The Dream of Dante; 1911); Legenda o św. Jerzym (The Legend of St. George; 1918); 3 symphs.: No. 1 (1909); No. 2, Mickiewiczowska (in honor of the Polish poet Mickiewicz) for Tenor, Chorus, and Orch. (1949); No. 3 for Tenor and Orch. (1950–51); Piano Concerto (1907); Violin Concerto (1950); Sinfonia concertante for Flute, Clarinet, Horn, Harp, and Orch. (1960); Romance for Clarinet and Piano (1948); Variations for Clarinet and Piano (1957).

Ryterband, Roman, Polish pianist and composer; b. Lodz, Aug. 2, 1914; d. Palm Springs, Calif., Nov. 17, 1979. After a period of study in Poland, he lived mostly in Switzerland; eventually settled in America, becoming a citizen in 1964. His works reflect Polish motifs; his harmonic idiom is mildly modernistic. His works include an "opera grotesque," Fantômes rebelles; a music drama, A Border Incident; Sonata for 2 Flutes and Harp; Quintet for 2 Flutes, Viola, Cello, and Harpsichord; Russian Rhapsody for Orch.; Suite polonaise for Piano; and assorted pieces for various instrumental combinations.

Rzewski, Frederic, American avant-garde composer; b. Westfield, Mass., April 13, 1938, of Polish parentage. He attended Harvard Univ. (1954–58) and Princeton Univ. (1958–60); was active (1960–62) in modern music circles in Italy, where he stayed on a Fulbright scholarship; subsequently he received a Ford Foundation grant, which enabled him to spend 2 years in Berlin (1963–65); while in Rome, he organized, with other similarly futuroscopic musicians, the MEV (Musica Elettronica Viva). In the interim he played concerts with the topless cellist Charlotte Moorman. From 1971 he lived mostly in N.Y. As a composer, he pursues the shimmering distant vision of optimistic, positivistic anti-music. He is furthermore a granitically overpowering piano technician, capable of depositing huge boulders of sonoristic material across the keyboard without actually wrecking the instrument.
WORKS: For Violin for Violin Solo (1962); Nature morte for Instruments and Percussion Groups (1965); Composition for 2 (1964); Zoologischer Garten (1965); Spacecraft (his magnum opus; 1967; "plan for spacecraft" publ. in Source, 3, 1968); Impersonation, audiodrama (1967); Requiem (1968); Symphony for Several Performers (1968); Last Judgement for Trombone (1969); Falling Music for Piano and Tape (1971); Coming Together for Speaker and Instruments (1972); Piano Variations on the song No Place to Go But Around (1974); The People United Will Never Be Defeated, a set of 36 variations for Piano on the Chilean song ¡El pueblo unido jamás será vencido! (1975); 4 Piano Pieces (1977); Song and Dance for Flute, Bass Clarinet, Vibraphone, and Electric Bass (1977); Satyrica for Jazz Band (River Falls, Wis., April 27, 1983).

S

Saar, Louis Victor (Franz), Dutch pianist and teacher; b. Rotterdam, Dec. 10, 1868; d. St. Louis, Nov. 23, 1937. He studied with Rheinberger in Munich (1886–89); lived in Vienna, Leipzig, and Berlin; in 1894 he went to the U.S.; taught music at various schools in N.Y.; was a member of the faculty at the Cincinnati College of Music (1906–17), at the Chicago Musical College (1917–33), and from 1934 until his death, at the St. Louis Inst. of Music. He was also a composer; wrote about 150 opus numbers, including musico-geographic orch. pieces such as *From the Mountain Kingdom of the Great Northwest* (1922) and *Along the Columbia River* (1924); publ. arrangements of folk songs for men's chorus, and *Album of Church Classics*.

Sabaneyev, Leonid, Russian writer on music; b. Moscow, Oct. 1, 1881; d. Antibes, France, May 3, 1968. He studied with Taneyev at the Moscow Cons.; also took a course in mathematics at the Univ. of Moscow. In 1920 he joined the board of the newly organized Moscow Inst. of Musical Science. In 1926 he left Russia and lived in France. He was an energetic promoter of modern music, and a friend of Scriabin, about whom he wrote a monograph, which would have been important if his account of Scriabin's life and ideology could be trusted; he compromised himself when he wrote a devastating review of Prokofiev's *Scythian Suite* at a concert that never took place.

WRITINGS (all in Russian): *Richard Wagner and the Synthesis of Arts* (1913); *The Development of the Harmonic Idea* (1913); *Medtner* (1913); *Scriabin* (1916; 2nd revised ed., 1923); *History of Russian Music* (Moscow, 1924; also in German, 1926); *Modern Russian Composers* (in Eng., N.Y., 1927); *Sergei Taneyev* (in Russian; Paris, 1930); *Music for the Films* (in Eng., London, 1935). He wrote 2 piano trios (1907, 1923), a Violin Sonata, and some other music.

Sabata, Victor de. See **De Sabata, Victor.**

Sabbatini, Galeazzo, Italian composer and theorist; b. Pesaro, c.1595; d. there, Dec. 6, 1662. He studied with Vincenzo Pellegrini, canon of Pesaro Cathedral. Sabbatini was subsequently appointed canon there (1626–30); then was maestro di cappella to the Duke of Mirandola (1630–39); again served as canon at Pesaro Cathedral (from 1641). His last publ. work appeared in Venice in 1639. Among his other publications was a treatise on basso continuo, *Regola facile e breve per sonare sopra il basso continuo* (Venice, 1628; 3rd ed., Rome, 1669). He publ. 2 books of madrigals *a* 2–4 (1625, 1626); 2 books of

Sacrae laudes a 2–5 (1637, 1641); one with Organ (1642); 3 books of *Madrigali concertati a* 2–5 (with Instruments; 1627, 1630, 1636); Hymns to the Virgin Mary *a* 3–6 (1638); *Sacri laudi e motetti a voce sola* (1639).

Sabbatini, Luigi Antonio, Italian music theorist; b. Albano Laziale, near Rome, Oct. 24, 1732; d. Padua, Jan. 29, 1809. He studied with Padre Martini in Bologna, and Vallotti in Padua. He was maestro di cappella at the basilica of S. Barnaba in Marino (1767–72); in 1772 was appointed to the Franciscan basilica of the 12 Holy Apostles in Rome; in 1786 he took over the duties of maestro di cappella at the Antonius Basilica, succeeding Agostino Ricci, who was in turn the successor of Vallotti. He publ. *Elementi teorici della musica colla pratica de' medesimi in duetti, e terzetti a canone* (1789; trans. in part into French by Choron); *La vera idea delle musicali numeriche segnature* (1799; gives an epitome of Vallotti's system); *Trattato sopra le fughe musicali* (1802; contains musical examples by Vallotti); and *Notizie sopra la vita e le opere del R.P.Fr.A. Vallotti* (1780).

Sabin, Robert, American music critic and editor; b. Rochester, N.Y., Feb. 21, 1912; d. New York, May 17, 1969. He studied at the Eastman School of Music in Rochester before going to N.Y.; was editor of *Musical America* (1945–50); edited the 9th edition of Oscar Thompson's *International Cyclopedia of Music and Musicians* (1964).

Sabin, Wallace Arthur, English organist; b. Culworth, Dec. 15, 1860; d. Berkeley, Calif., Dec. 8, 1937. He studied with M.J. Monk at Banbury and T.W. Dodds at Oxford; emigrated to the U.S. and settled in San Francisco, where he was organist at St. Luke's (1894–1906), at Temple Emanu-El (from 1895), and at the First Church, Scientist (from 1906). His settings of the Hebrew liturgy were publ. in Stark's Service Book. He composed many part-songs for men's voices.
BIBLIOGRAPHY: R.R. Rinder, *Tribute to W.A. Sabin* (San Francisco, 1938).

Sacchetti, Liberius, Russian writer on music and pedagogue; b. Kenzar, near Tambov, Aug. 30, 1852; d. Petrograd, March 10, 1916. He studied with Rimsky-Korsakov and others at the St. Petersburg Cons.; in 1878 was appointed to its faculty as a lecturer on musical esthetics. He publ. an *Outline of General Music History* (St. Petersburg, 1882); *A Brief Anthology of Musical History* (St. Petersburg, 1896); manuals on esthetics for use at the St. Petersburg Cons.; etc. He was highly regarded as a scholar and teacher in Russia.

Sacchi, Don Giovenale, Italian scholar; b. Barzio, Como, Nov. 22, 1726; d. Milan, Sept. 27, 1789. He was a member of the Barnabite monastic order, and an assiduous student of ancient music; also was distinguished as a biographer.

WRITINGS: *Del numero e delle misure delle corde musiche e loro corrispondenze* (1761); *Della divisione del tempo nella musica, nel ballo e nella poesia* (1770); *Della natura e perfezione dell'antica musica de' Greci* (1778); *Della quinte successive nel contrappunto e delle regole degli accompagnamenti* (1780); *Vita del Cav. Don Carlo Broschi, detto Farinelli* (1784); *Don Placido, Dialogo dove cercasi se lo studio della musica al religioso convenga o disconvenga* (1786); etc.; he also trans. Cardinal Fontana's *Vita di Benedetto Marcello* (1788).

Sacchini, Antonio (Maria Gasparo Gioacchino), Italian opera composer; b. Florence, June 14, 1730; d. Paris, Oct. 6, 1786. He entered the Cons. of Santa Maria di Loreto at Naples as a pupil of Francesco Durante (composition), Nicola Fiorenza (violin), and Gennaro Manna (singing). His intermezzo *Fra Donato* was performed at the Cons. in 1756; he subsequently wrote music for various stage productions in Naples; then proceeded to Rome, where his opera *Semiramide* was successfully produced in 1762. This success marked the beginning of his career as an operatic composer; thereafter he produced operas every year: *Olimpiade* (Padua, July 9, 1763); *Alessandro nell'Indie* (Venice, 1763); *Lucio Vero* (Naples, Nov. 4, 1764); *La Contadina in corte* (Rome, 1765); *L'isola d'amore* (Rome, 1766). In 1768 he succeeded Traetta as director of the Cons. dell'Ospedaletto in Venice; his oratorio *Caritas omnia vincit* was brought out there on April 16, 1769. He then went to Munich and produced there his operas *L'Eroe cinese* (1769) and *Scipione in Cartagena* (Jan. 8, 1770). In 1772 he traveled to London with Venanzio Rauzzini, and while there presented the following operas: *Tamerlano* (May 6, 1773); *Montezuma* (Feb. 7, 1775); *Erifile* (Feb. 7, 1778); *L'Amore soldato* (May 5, 1778); *Il Calandrino e l'avaro deluso* (Nov. 24, 1778); *Enea e Lavinia* (March 25, 1779). In 1781 he received an invitation from Marie Antoinette, through the "intendant des menus-plaisirs," to come to Paris. His name was already known in France, since his opera *L'isola d'amore,* arranged as *La Colonie* ("comic opera imitated from the Italian"), had been produced in Paris on Aug. 16, 1775. He arrived in Paris in August 1781, and was forthwith commissioned to write 3 works at a fee of 10,000 francs each. For this purpose he adapted his Italian opera *Armida e Rinaldo* (Milan, 1772) to a French text as *Renaud,* "tragédie lyrique" in 3 acts (produced at the Académie Royale de Musique, Feb. 25, 1783), and his opera *Il cidde* (Rome, 1764) as *Chimène* (Fontainebleau, Nov. 18, 1783); the 3rd opera, *Dardanus,* was a new work; it was staged at the Trianon at Versailles, Sept. 18, 1784, in the presence of Louis XVI and Marie Antoinette. In Paris Sacchini found himself in unintended rivalry with Piccinni as a representative of Italian music in the famous artistic war against the proponents of the French operas of Gluck; Sacchini's most successful opera, however, was to the French text *Œdipe à Colonne,* first presented at Versailles (Jan. 4, 1786) and produced at the Paris Opéra (Feb. 1, 1787) after Sacchini's death. It held the stage for half a century, and there were sporadic revivals later on. His last opera, also to a French libretto, *Arvire et Evelina,* was left unfinished, and was produced posthumously (Paris Opéra, April 29, 1788; 3rd act added by J.B. Rey). Sacchini's music is a typical product of the Italian operatic art of his time. It possesses melodious grace, but lacks dramatic development. The undistinguished style of Sacchini's productions is probably the reason for the disappearance of his operas from the active repertoire; Piccinni fared much better in comparison.

BIBLIOGRAPHY: A. Jullien, *La Cour et l'opéra sous Louis XVI: Marie Antoinette et Sacchini* (Paris, 1878); J.-G. Prod'homme, *Ecrits de musiciens des XVe–XVIIIe siècles* (Paris, 1912); idem, "Un Musicien napolitain à la cour de Louis XVI," *Le Ménestrel* (Dec. 11 and Dec. 18, 1925); V. Morelli, "Antonio Sacchini," *Vita Musicale Italiana,* 7–8 (1926); U. Prota-Giurleo, *Sacchini non nacque a Pozzuoli* (Naples, 1952, proving that Sacchini was born in Florence and not in the vicinity of Naples); F. Schlitzer, *Antonio Sacchini: Schede e appunti per una sua storia teatrale* (Siena, 1955); A. Loewenberg, *Annals of Opera* (Cambridge, 1943; 2nd ed., Geneva, 1955).

Sacco, P. Peter, American composer of Italian descent; b. Albion, N.Y., Oct. 25, 1928. Virtually his whole family consisted of tenors: his father, a brother, and couple of uncles. Peter Sacco followed the family tradition and became a tenor himself. He also studied piano and exhibited himself in public as a keyboard prodigy; he also studied trumpet and tuba. After 3 years of preparatory school in music in Rochester, N.Y., he entered Fredonia State Univ. (B.M., 1950); he was drafted into the U.S. Army, and was stationed in Frankfurt, Germany (1950–52); there he studied music theory with a local teacher and also played church organ and piano programs for the officer's club. In 1953 he enrolled in the Eastman School of Music in Rochester as a student of Bernard Rogers and Howard Hanson (M.M., 1954). He continued to perform as a tenor; sang in various school performances of classical operas and oratorios. In 1959 he was appointed to the music faculty of San Francisco State Univ.; in 1970–71 he was a visiting prof. at the Univ. of Hawaii, where he taught composition and gave vocal recitals. As a composer, he adheres to traditional harmony, but has diversified into ingenious chromatic developments, approximating a euphonious type of dodecaphony.

WORKS: Opera, *Mr. Vinegar* (Redding, Calif., May 12, 1967); oratorio, *Jesu* (Grand Rapids, Mich., Dec. 3, 1956, composer conducting); oratorio, *Midsummer Dream Night* (San Francisco, June 25, 1961, composer conducting); *Solomon,* oratorio (San Francisco, Dec. 12, 1976, composer as tenor soloist); Symph. No. 1 (Oklahoma City, Dec. 17, 1958); Symph. No. 2, *The Symphony of Thanksgiving* (San Francisco, March 23, 1976); Symph. No. 3, *The Convocation Symphony* (Redding, June 1, 1968); *Moab Illuminations* for Orch. (1972); Piano Concerto (1964; San Francisco, April 4, 1968); Violin Concerto

(1969; Walnut Creek, Calif., April 24, 1974).

Sacher, Paul, Swiss conductor; b. Basel, April 28, 1906. He studied with Karl Nef (music theory) and Weingartner (conducting). In 1926 he founded the Kammer Orchester in Basel; commissioned special works from a number of celebrated contemporary composers (among them Richard Strauss, Hindemith, Honegger, etc.) and presented them for the first time with his ensemble; in 1933 he founded the Schola Cantorum Basiliensis; from 1941, was leader of the Collegium Musicum in Zürich. His Schola Cantorum Basiliensis was amalgamated with Basel's Cons. and Musikschule to form the Musikakademie der Stadt Basel, which he directed from 1954–69. He publ. *Alte und neue Musik* (Zürich, 1951) and an annotated catalogue of the 25 years of the Basel Kammer Orchester. Sacher made his American debut in N.Y. on April 3, 1955, conducting a concert of the Collegiate Chorale at Carnegie Hall. A Festschrift was publ. in his honor in Basel in 1976.

BIBLIOGRAPHY: *30 Jahre Collegium musicum* (Zürich, 1972).

Sachs, Curt, eminent German musicologist and authority on musical instruments; b. Berlin, June 29, 1881; d. New York, Feb. 5, 1959. While attending the Gymnasium in Berlin, he studied piano and composition with L. Schrattenholz and clarinet with Rausch; entered Berlin Univ.; studied music history with Oskar Fleischer, and also art history (Dr.Phil., 1904); after some years as an art critic, he turned to musicology, and studied with Kretzschmar and Joh. Wolf; specialized in the history of musical instruments; in 1919 was appointed curator of the Museum of Musical Instruments in Berlin, and in 1920, prof. of the National Academy of Music there; also was a prof. at the Univ. of Berlin. In 1933 he was compelled to leave Germany; went to Paris as Chargé de Mission at the Musée de l'Homme; was a visiting prof. at the Sorbonne. In 1937 he settled in the U.S.; was a lecturer at the Graduate School of Liberal Arts of N.Y. Univ. (1937–38); consultant to the N.Y. Public Library (1937–52); adjunct prof., Columbia Univ. (from 1953); president of the American Musicological Society (1948–50). In 1956, he was made a Dr.Phil. (*honoris causa*) of West Berlin Univ.

WRITINGS: *Musikgeschichte der Stadt Berlin bis zum Jahre 1800* (1908); *Musik und Oper am kurbrandenburgischen Hof* (1910); *Reallexikon der Musikinstrumente* (1913; very valuable); *Handbuch der Musikinstrumentenkunde* (1920; 2nd ed., 1930; very valuable); *Die Musikinstrumente des alten Ägyptens* (1921); *Katalog der Staatlichen Instrumentensammlung* (1922); *Das Klavier* (1923); *Die modernen Musikinstrumente* (1923); *Geist und Werden der Musikinstrumente* (1929); *Vergleichende Musikwissenschaft in ihren Grundzügen* (1930); *Eine Weltgeschichte des Tanzes* (1933; in Eng. as *World History of the Dance*, N.Y., 1937); *Les Instruments de musique de Madagascar* (Paris, 1938); *The History of Musical Instruments* (N.Y., 1940); *The Rise of Music in the Ancient World*

(N.Y., 1943); *The Commonwealth of Art* (N.Y., 1946); *Our Musical Heritage* (N.Y., 1948; 2nd ed., 1955); *Rhythm and Tempo: A Study in Music History* (N.Y., 1953); valuable essays in various European and American periodicals; he also compiled and ed. *The Evolution of Piano Music* (N.Y., 1944).

BIBLIOGRAPHY: E. Hertzmann, "Alfred Einstein and Curt Sachs," *Musical Quarterly* (April 1941); K. Hahn, "Verzeichnis der wissenschaftlichen Arbeiten von Curt Sachs," *Acta Musicologica,* 29; G. Reese and R. Brandel, eds., *The Commonwealth of Music, in Honor of Curt Sachs* (N.Y., 1965).

Sachs, Hans, foremost poet of the Meistersinger; b. Nuremberg, Nov. 5, 1494; d. there, Jan. 19, 1576. He wrote over 4,000 poems (*Meisterschulgedichte*), 1,700 tales, etc., and 208 dramatic poems; also invented numerous melodies (*Weisen*). He is the central figure in Wagner's opera *Die Meistersinger von Nürnberg.* The original melodies of a large number of the poems are preserved in *Das Singebuch des Adam Puschmann* (ed. by G. Münzer, 1907).

BIBLIOGRAPHY: C. Schweitzer, *Un Poète allemand au XVIᵉ siècle: Etude sur la vie et les œuvres de H. Sachs* (Nancy, 1889); K. Drescher, *Studien zu H. Sachs* (Marburg, 1891); R. Genée, *H. Sachs und seine Zeit* (Leipzig, 1894; 2nd ed., 1901); B. Suphan, *H. Sachs: Humanitätszeit und Gegenwart* (Weimar, 1895); K. Drescher, *Nürnberger Meistersingerprotokolle von 1575–1689* (2 vols., Tübingen, 1898); K. Mey, *Der Meistergesang* (1901); H. Holzschuher, *H. Sachs in seiner Bedeutung für unsere Zeit* (Berlin, 1906); E. Mummenhoff, *Musikpflege und Musikaufführungen im alten Nürnberg* (Leipzig, 1908); H. Nutzhorn, *Meistersangeren H. Sachs* (Copenhagen, 1911); F.H. Ellis, *H. Sachs Studies* (Bloomington, Ind., 1941); idem, *The Early Meisterlieder of Hans Sachs* (Bloomington, Ind., 1974); B. Könneker, *Hans Sachs* (Stuttgart, 1971); N. Holzberg, *Hans-Sachs-Bibliographie* (Nuremberg, 1976); K. Wedler, *Hans Sachs* (Leipzig, 1976).

Sachs, Léo, composer; b. Frankfurt, Germany, April 3, 1856; d. Paris, Nov. 13, 1930. He was active in the field of modern music in Paris; composed several symph. poems (*Retour des cloches; Sur l'eau; Lamento*); a Piano Quintet; 2 string quartets; a Piano Trio; 3 violin sonatas; a Viola Sonata; a Cello Sonata; *Petite suite* for String Quartet; 24 preludes for piano. His total output amounts to nearly 200 opus numbers. His style of composition was mildly modernistic.

Sachse, Leopold, opera stage director; b. Berlin, Jan. 5, 1880; d. Englewood, N.J., April 4, 1961. He studied at the Cons. of Cologne; then in Vienna; in 1902 joined the Strasbourg Opera as a baritone; in 1907 became general manager of the Stadttheater in Münster; in 1913 organized the Sachse Opera in Berlin; from 1922 to 1933 was with the Hamburg Staatsoper. In 1935 he was engaged as stage director of Wagner's operas at the Metropolitan Opera House in N.Y., retiring in 1943; in 1945 became stage director of the N.Y. City Opera; in 1951 organized the Opera in English Co. at Cooper Union in N.Y. From 1936 to 1943 he taught stage technique at the Juilliard Graduate School in N.Y.

Sack, Erna, German coloratura soprano; b. Spandau-Berlin, Feb. 6, 1898; d. Mainz, March 2, 1972. She studied in Prague and in Berlin; made her first operatic appearance at the Municipal Theater in Bielefeld; sang in Austria at the Salzburg festivals, in Italy, and in England; made her first American appearance as a concert singer in 1937–38, and revisited the U.S. in 1954. In 1953 she gave a series of concerts in Australia.

Sacks, Stuart, American composer; b. Albany, N.Y., Feb. 28, 1941. He studied at Boston Univ. with Hugo Norden; developed a neo-Romantic style couched in emotional tonality. The CBS television network presented on April 11, 1965, in N.Y., performances of his *Saul* for Mezzo-soprano, Oboe, Percussion, and Strings and *Poème* for Violin and Piano. His other works include an overture; *Arioso* for Strings; *Divertissement* for Winds and Strings; *Elegy* for Solo Cello and Orch.

Sacrati, Francesco (Paolo), Italian composer; b. Parma (baptized, Sept. 17), 1605; d. Modena, May 20, 1650. He was one of the earliest composers for the opera theaters that opened in Venice after 1637; was also a pioneer of opera buffa before the rise of the Neapolitan school. He wrote an opera, *La Delia,* for the opening of the Teatro Crimani dei Santi Giovanni e Paolo in Venice (Jan. 20, 1639); there followed *La finta pazza* (Teatro Novissimo, Venice; Jan. 14, 1641); this was also one of the earliest Italian operas performed in Paris (Salle du Petit Bourbon, Dec. 14, 1645); other operas by Sacrati were: *Bellerofonte* (1642); *Ulisse errante* (1644); *L'isola d'Alcina* (Bologna, 1648). In 1649 he was appointed maestro di cappella at the court of Modena, but he died a few months after the appointment.

BIBLIOGRAPHY: Henry Prunières, *L'Opéra italien en France avant Lully* (Paris, 1913); A. Loewenberg, *Annals of Opera* (Cambridge, 1943; 2nd ed., 1955).

Sadai, Yizhak, Bulgarian-born Israeli composer; b. Sofia, May 13, 1935. He emigrated to Israel in 1949; studied with Haubenstock-Ramati and Roscovich at the Tel Aviv Academy of Music (1951–56); then devoted himself to teaching; in 1966 joined the music staff of the Univ. of Tel Aviv.

WORKS: *Divertimento* for Alto, Flute, Viola, and Piano (1954); 3 cantatas: *Ecclesiastes* (1956); *Hazvi Israel* (1957); *Psychoanalysis* (1958); *Ricercare symphonique* for Orch. (1956); *Serenade* for Winds (1956); *Interpolations* for Harpsichord and String Quartet (1960); *Nuances* for Chamber Orch. (1964); *Aria da Capo* for 6 Instruments and 2 Tape Recorders (1965); *Registers* for Violin and Piano (1967); *Préludes a Jérusalem* for Voice and Instruments (1968); *From the Diary of a Percussionist* for Percussion Player and Tape (1971); *La Prière interrompue* for

Tape (1975).

Sadie, Stanley, eminent English writer on music and lexicographer; b. London, Oct. 30, 1930. He studied music privately with Bernard Stevens (1947–50) and then with R.T. Dart, P.A.S. Hadley, and C.L. Cudworth at Cambridge (B.A. and Mus.B., 1953; M.A., 1957; Ph.D., 1958, with the dissertation *British Chamber Music, 1720–1790*). He was on the staff of Trinity College of Music in London (1957–65); from 1964–81 was a music critic on the staff of the *Times* of London. In 1967 he became the editor of the *Musical Times*. A distinguished scholar, he wrote the following monographs: *Handel* (London, 1962); *Mozart* (London, 1966); *Beethoven* (London, 1967; 2nd ed., 1974); *Handel* (London, 1968); and *Handel Concertos* (London, 1972); also publ. numerous articles in British and American music journals. With Arthur Jacobs he edited *The Pan Book of Opera* (London, 1964; revised ed. as *Opera: A Modern Guide*, N.Y., 1972; new ed., 1983). In 1969 he was entrusted with the formidable task of preparing for publication, as editor in chief, a completely new edition of *Grove's Dictionary of Music and Musicians;* after 11 years of labor, *The New Grove Dictionary of Music and Musicians* was publ. in London in 1980; this 6th ed., in 20 vols., reflected the contributions of more than 2,400 scholars throughout the world, and was accorded a premier place of honor among the major reference sources of its kind. He also edited *The New Grove Encyclopedia of Musical Instruments* (London, 1984) and was co-editor, with H. Wiley Hitchcock, of *The New Grove Dictionary of Music in the United States* (scheduled for publication in 1985). He has served as editor of the Master Musicians series since 1976. In 1981 he received the honorary degree of D.Litt. from the Univ. of Leicester and was made an honorary member of the Royal Academy of Music, London. In 1982 he was made a Commander of the Order of the British Empire.

Saenger, Gustav, American music editor and arranger; b. New York, May 31, 1865; d. there, Dec. 10, 1935. He studied violin with Leopold Damrosch and others; was an orch. violinist; then conducted theater orchs. in N.Y.; in 1897 was engaged as an arranger for Carl Fischer, Inc., and in 1909 became editor in chief of Fischer's publications; also edited the Fischer periodicals *Metronome* (from 1900) and the *Musical Observer* (1904–29). Besides a vast number of arrangements, he publ. pieces for violin and piano (*5 Silhouettes; 3 Concert Miniatures;* etc.); also *New School of Melody.*

Saenger, Oscar, American singing teacher; b. Brooklyn, Jan. 5, 1868; d. Washington, D.C., April 20, 1929. He sang in church as a boy; studied voice with J. Bouhy at the National Cons. in N.Y., and taught there from 1889 to 1897; made his debut with the Hinrichs Grand Opera Co. in 1891; after a brief tour in Germany and Austria he returned to America and devoted himself entirely to teaching. Among his students were many well-known singers (Marie Rappold, Paul Althouse, Mabel Garrison, etc.).

Saenz, Pedro, Argentine composer; b. Buenos Aires, May 4, 1915. He studied piano with Alberto Williams, and theory with Arturo Palma. In 1948 he went to Paris, where he took lessons with Arthur Honegger, Darius Milhaud, and Jean Rivier. Returning to Buenos Aires, he occupied numerous teaching and administrative posts in educational institutions.
WORKS: *Movimentos sinfónicos* for Orch. (1963); Piano Quintet (1942); String Trio (1955); *Divertimento* for Oboe and Clarinet (1959); *Capriccio* for Harpsichord and String Quartet (1966); numerous piano pieces and songs.

Saerchinger, César, German-American editor and writer; b. Aachen, Oct. 23, 1884; d. Washington, D.C., Oct. 10, 1971. He studied singing with his mother (a pupil of G.B. Lamperti); settled in America in 1902, and continued his musical education in N.Y. While still a young man, he began writing biographical articles for various American encyclopedias; was managing editor and contributor to *The Art of Music* (14 vols., 1915–17); from 1919 to 1930 was a foreign correspondent of the *N.Y. Evening Post* and the *Musical Courier;* lived in Berlin (1920–25) and London (1925–37); then returned to N.Y. He edited *International Who's Who in Music and Musical Gazetteer* (N.Y., 1918); publ. *Voice of Europe* (N.Y., 1937) and *Artur Schnabel* (London, 1957).

Saeverud, Harald, prominent Norwegian composer; b. Bergen, April 17, 1897. He studied music theory at the Bergen Music Academy with B. Holmsen (1915–20) and with F.E. Koch at the Hochschule für Musik in Berlin (1920–21); took a course in conducting with Clemens Krauss in Berlin (1935). In 1953 he received the Norwegian State Salary of Art (a government life pension for outstanding artistic achievement). He began to compose very early, and on Dec. 12, 1912, at the age of 15, conducted in Bergen a program of his own symph. pieces. His music is permeated with characteristically lyrical Scandinavian Romanticism, with Norwegian folk melos as its foundation; his symph. compositions are polyphonic in nature and tonal in essence, with euphonious dissonant textures imparting a peculiarly somber character to the music.
WORKS: Ballet, *Ridder Blåskjeggs mareritt* (*Bluebeard's Nightmare;* 1960; Oslo, Oct. 4, 1960); 9 symphs.: No. 1, in 2 symph. fantasias (1916–20; first complete perf., Bergen, 1923); No. 2 (1922; Bergen, Nov. 22, 1923; revised 1934; Oslo, April 1, 1935); No. 3 (1925–26; Bergen, Feb. 25, 1932); No. 4 (1937; Oslo, Dec. 9, 1937); No. 5, *Quasi una fantasia* (1941; Bergen, March 6, 1941); No. 6, *Sinfonia dolorosa* (1942; Bergen, May 27, 1943); No. 7, *Salme* (*Psalm;* 1944–45; Bergen, Sept. 1, 1945); No. 8, *Minnesota* (1958; Minneapolis, Oct. 18, 1958); No. 9 (1965–66; Bergen, June 12, 1966); *Ouverture Appassionata* (1920; retitled 2nd fantasia of his First Symph., often played independently); *50 Small Variations* for Orch. (1931); *The Rape of Lucretia,* incidental music for Shakespeare's play (1935; also a *Lucretia Suite* for Orch., 1936); Oboe Concerto (1938); *Divertimento No. 1* for

Flute and Strings (1939); *Syljetone (The Bride's Heirloom Brooch)* for Chamber Orch. or Piano (1939); *Rondo amoroso* for Chamber Orch. or Piano (1939); *Gjaetlevise-Variasjoner (Shepherd's Tune Variations)* for Chamber Orch. (1941); *Siljuslåtten (Countryside Festival Dance;* 1942; also for Piano); *Galdreslåtten (The Sorcerer's Dance;* 1942); *Romanza* for Violin, and Orch. or Piano (1942); *Kjempeviseslåtten (Ballad of Revolt;* 1943; also for Piano); *Peer Gynt,* incidental music to a revised production of Ibsen's verse drama (1947; Oslo, March 2, 1948; also exists as 2 orch. suites and as a piano suite); *Olav og Kari,* dance scene for 2 Singers, Chorus, and Orch. (1948); Piano Concerto (1948–50); Violin Concerto (1956); *Vade mors (Get Thee Behind Me, Death;* 1955); *Allegria (Sinfonia concertante;* 1957); Bassoon Concerto (1963); *Mozart-Motto-Sinfonietta* (1971); *5 Capricci* for Piano (1918–19); Piano Sonata (1921); *Tunes and Dances from "Siljustøl,"* 5 vols. for Piano (1943–45); 6 piano sonatinas (1948–50); *20 Small Duets* for Violins (1951); 3 string quartets (1970, 1975, 1978); *Fabula gratulatorum* for Piano (1973); *Pastorale (Indian Summer)* for Solo Cello (1978).

BIBLIOGRAPHY: C. Baden, *Harald Saeverud 80 år* (Oslo, 1977).

Saeverud, Ketil. See **Hvoslef, Ketil.**

Safonov, Vasili, eminent Russian pianist, conductor, and pedagogue; b. Ishcherskaya, Caucasus, Feb. 6, 1852; d. Kislovodsk, Feb. 27, 1918. He studied at the Cons. of St. Petersburg with Leschetizky and Brassin (piano) and Zaremba (theory); made his debut as pianist with the Imperial Russian Music Society in St. Petersburg, on Nov. 22, 1880; then taught piano at the St. Petersburg Cons. (1881–85); in 1885 was appointed to the piano faculty of the Moscow Cons., and in 1889 became its director, resigning in 1905; among his pupils were Scriabin and Medtner. He conducted the symph. concerts of the Imperial Russian Music Society in Moscow; was the first modern conductor to dispense with the baton; achieved international fame as a forceful and impassioned interpreter of Russian music; conducted in almost all the capitals of Europe; on March 5, 1904, was engaged as guest conductor of the N.Y. Phil., obtaining sensational success; as a consequence, was appointed regular conductor for 3 seasons (1906–9; was succeeded by Gustav Mahler); at the same time he was also director of the National Cons. in N.Y. After his return to Russia, he was appointed permanent conductor of the Imperial Russian Music Society in St. Petersburg. He publ. *A New Formula for the Piano Teacher and Piano Student* (Moscow, 1916; in Eng.).

BIBLIOGRAPHY: *V. Safonov* (Moscow, 1959).

Safranek-Kavić, Lujo, Croatian composer; b. Zagreb, Oct. 12, 1882; d. there, July 18, 1940. He wrote a symph. suite for Violin and Orch., *Guslar* (inspired by the playing of the gusle, the South Slav national instrument); 2 operas (*Hasanaginica* and *The Queen of Medvedgrad*); chamber music; songs.

Sagaev, Dimiter, Bulgarian composer; b. Plovdiv, Feb. 27, 1915. He studied composition with Stoyanov and Vladigerov at the Bulgarian State Cons. in Sofia, graduating in 1940; then became an instructor at the Bulgarian Cons. His music is Romantic in essence and is national in its thematic resources with its rhythmical pulse derived from Bulgarian folk songs.

WORKS: 2 operas: *Under the Yoke* (1965) and *Samouil* (1975); ballet, *The Madara Horseman* (1960); oratorio, *In the Name of Freedom* (1969); cantata-poem, *The Shipka Epic* (1977; commemorating the centennial of the crucial battle between the Russian and the Turkish forces in the Balkans); *Youth Suite* for Orch. (1952); *Sofia,* symph. poem (1954); *3 Bulgarian Symphonic Dances* (1956); 2 violin concertos (1963, 1964); Viola Concerto (1963); Oboe Concerto (1964); Symph. No. 1 for Narrator, Singer, 2 Female Choruses, and Orch. (1964); Bassoon Concerto (1973; Burgas, March 26, 1974); Flute Concerto (1974); 7 string quartets (1945, 1962, 1962, 1963, 1966, 1967, 1968); 2 wind quintets (1961, 1962); Trio for Flute, Violin, and Piano (1974); Quartet for Flute, Viola, Harp, and Piano (1975); songs; incidental music. Sagaev publ. several theoretical texts, including *Textbook of Wind Orchestration* (Sofia, 1957), *How to Work with Student Brass Bands* (Sofia, 1962), and *A Practical Course of Symphony and Orchestration* (Sofia, 1966).

Sagittarius. See **Schütz, Heinrich.**

Saikkola, Lauri, Finnish composer; B. Viipuri (Vyborg), March 31, 1906. He studied violin at the Viipuri School of Music (1919–28) and then took private composition lessons from Akimov and Funtek (1930–34); was a violinist in the Viipuri Phil. (1923–34) and the Helsinki Phil. Orch. (1934–65). His music is rooted in the Romantic tradition.

WORKS: 2 operas: *Ristin* (Helsinki, 1959) and *The Master's Snuff Box,* chamber opera (1970); *3 Symphonic Scenes* (1932); *1500-Meter Race,* a parody for Orch. (1933); *Partita* for Orch. (1935); *Pastorale* for Orch. (1936); 5 symphs.: No. 1, *Sinfonia campale* (1938); No. 2, *Sinfonia tragica* (1946); No. 3 (1949); No. 4 (1951); No. 5 (1958); *Karelian Scenes* for Orch. (1940); *Karelia in Flames* for Orch. (1940); *Nocturno* for Cello and Orch. (1944); *Taivaaseen menijä (Going to Heaven),* folk story for Narrator, Soloists, Chorus, and Orch. (1950); Violin Concerto (1952); *Concerto di miniatura* for Cello and Chamber Orch. (1953); *Concerto da camera* for Piano and Chamber Orch. (1957); *Pezzi* for Strings (1965); *Musica sinfonica* (1966); *The Well of Dreams* for Baritone, Chorus, and Chamber Orch. (1968); Clarinet Concerto (1969); *Raasepori fantasia* for Orch. (1971); 3 string quartets (1931–68); *Divertimento* for Wind Quartet (1949); Wind Quintet (1968); 2 suites for Clarinet and Piano (1955, 1968); *Suite* for Oboe and Piano (1968); Viola Sonatina.

Saint-Foix, Georges (du Parc Poullain, Comte) de, eminent French musicologist, specialist in Mozart research; b. Paris, March 2, 1874; d. Aix-en-

Provence, May 26, 1954. He studied jurisprudence, and also attended classes in music theory with Vincent d'Indy at the Schola Cantorum in Paris. His principal, and most important, publication was *W.A. Mozart, Sa vie musicale et son œuvre de l'enfance à la pleine maturité* (2 vols., 1912, with T. de Wyzewa; 3rd vol., by Saint-Foix alone, 1937; 4th vol., 1940; 5th vol., 1946); of no less importance is his book *Les Symphonies de Mozart* (Paris, 1932; 2nd ed., 1948; in Eng., London, 1947; reprint, N.Y., 1968). He contributed a number of informative articles dealing with Mozart's contemporaries, in several instances in collaboration with T. de Wyzewa and L. de La Laurencie.

Saint-George, George, notable player on the viola d'amore; b. (of English parents) Leipzig, Nov. 6, 1841; d. London, Jan. 5, 1924. He studied piano, violin, and theory in Dresden and Prague; his violin teacher, Moritz Mildner of Prague, had a fine viola d'amore, which he lent to Saint-George for practicing; he made such progress on this little-used instrument that he decided to adopt it as a specialty. About 1862 he settled in London and became a manufacturer of string instruments; gave performances on the Welsh crwth for the "Hon. Soc. Cymmrodorion"; also played the viola d'amore in duos with his son, **Henry Saint-George,** who assisted him on the viola da gamba.

Saint-George, Henry, son of **George Saint-George;** b. London, Sept. 26, 1866; d. there, Jan. 30, 1917. He studied the violin with his father, with whom he subsequently gave concerts, playing works for early instruments; was editor of *The Strad* for 4 years; publ. *The Bow: Its History, Manufacture and Use* (1895; 3rd ed., 1922); *The Place of Science in Music* (1905); *Fiddles: Their Selection, Preservation and Betterment* (1910).

Saint-Georges, Joseph Boulogne, Chevalier de, West Indian composer and violinist; b. near Basse Terre, Guadeloupe, 1739, the son of a wealthy Frenchman and a Negro slave; d. Paris, June 10, 1799. He was raised in Santo Domingo; went to Paris with his father in 1749 (his mother joined them in 1760); as a youth he studied boxing and fencing, and became one of the leading fencers of Europe; he also studied music, with Jean-Marie Leclair *l'aîné*, and with François Gossec (1763–66); the latter dedicated his op. 9 string trios to Saint-Georges. In 1771 Saint-Georges became concertmaster of the Concerts des Amateurs in Paris, led by Gossec; in 1772 he appeared as violin soloist in his 2 violin concertos, op. 2; in 1773, succeeded Gossec as director of the Concerts des Amateurs. He continued his activities as a fencer, and in this capacity went to London twice, in 1785 and 1789; in 1792 he became colonel of a Negro regiment, the Légion Nationale des Américains et du Midi (among his 1,000 troops was the father of Dumas *père*); he left the service in 1797 and spent the last 2 years of his life in Paris. WORKS: Operas (perf. at the Comédie Italienne, Paris): *Ernestine* (July 19, 1777); *La Chasse* (Oct. 12,

1778); *L'Amant anonyme* (March 8, 1780); *La Fille Garçon* (Aug. 18, 1787); *La Marchand des marrons* (Théâtre des Petits Comédiens, Paris, 1789); *Le Droit du seigneur* (1789); *Guillaume tout Cœur* (1790); 10 violin concertos; 6 *symphonies concertantes* for 2 Violins and Orch.; 2 symphs.; 6 string quartets (1778); 3 violin sonatas (1781); 118 songs, with keyboard accompaniment; other instrumental and vocal music.

BIBLIOGRAPHY: Roger de Beauvoir, *Le Chevalier de Saint-Georges* (Paris, 1810); L. de La Laurencie, "The Chevalier de Saint-Georges, Violinist," *Musical Quarterly,* 5 (1919); idem, *L'École française de violon* (vol. 2, 1923; reprint, Geneva, 1971); B.S. Brook, *La Symphonie française dans la seconde moitié du XVIIIᵉ siècle* (Paris, 1962); E. Derr, *Joseph Boulogne, Chevalier de Saint-Georges: Black Musician and Athlete in Galant Paris* (Ann Arbor, 1972); D.-R. de Lerma, "Two Friends within the Saint-Georges Songs," *Black Perspective in Music* (Fall 1973); idem, "The Chevalier de Saint-Georges," *Black Perspective in Music* (Spring 1976).

Saint-Huberty, Antoinette, French soprano; b. Strasbourg, Dec. 15, 1756; d. London, July 21, 1813. She sang in Berlin and Strasbourg; created the role of Melissa in Gluck's *Armide* in Paris in 1777; was a leading singer at the Paris Opéra (1781–90); while there, she sang in the premieres of Piccini's *Didone,* Sacchini's *Chimère,* and Salieri's *Danaides.*

BIBLIOGRAPHY: E. de Goncourt, *Mme. Saint-Huberty* (1885).

Saint-Lubin, Léon de, violinist and composer; b. Turin, July 5, 1805; d. Berlin, Feb. 13, 1850. After filling various positions as a theater violinist, he pursued further studies with Spohr; was concertmaster at the Josephstadt Theater in Vienna (1823–30); then held a similar position at the Königstadt Theater in Berlin (1830–47). He composed 2 operas, *König Branors Schwert* and *Der Vetter des Doctor Faust;* 5 violin concertos; 2 string quintets, 2 piano trios, a Violin Sonata, and 19 string quartets.

Saint-Marcoux, Micheline Coulombe, Canadian composer; b. Notre-Dame-de-la-Doré, Quebec, Aug. 9, 1938. She studied with François Brassard in Jonquière; in Montreal with Claude Champagne at the École Vincent d'Indy, graduating in 1962, and later with Gilles Tremblay and Clermont Pépin at the Cons. there (1963–67). She went to Paris in 1969 and studied composition with Gilbert Amy and Jean-Paul Guézec and electronic music with members of the Groupe de Recherches Musicale; she was a co-founder in Paris of the Groupe International de Musique Electroacoustic, along with 5 other composers from different countries. She returned to Montreal in 1971; became active as a teacher. WORKS: Flute Sonata (1964); *Kaléidoscope* for Piano, left-hand (1964); String Quartet (1965–66); *Equation I* for 2 Guitars (1967); *Modulaire* for Orch. (1967; Montreal, March 31, 1968); *Séquences* for 2 Ondes Martenots and Percussion (1968); *Assemblages* for Piano (1969); *Doréanes* for Piano (1969);

Hétéromorphie for Orch. (Montreal, April 14, 1970); *Bernavir* for Tape (1970); *Trakadie* for Tape and Percussion (1970); *Makazoti* for 8 Voices and Instrumental Group (1971); *Arksalalartôq* for Tape (1971); *Contrastances* for Tape (1971); *Moustières* for Tape (1971); *Zones* for Tape (1972); *Alchéra* for Mezzo-soprano, Flute, Clarinet, Trombone, Violin, Cello, Percussion, Harpsichord or Hammond Organ, and Tape (1973); *Ishuma* for Soprano, Instrumental Group, Ondes Martenot, and Synthi A (1973–74); *Genesis* for Wind Quintet (1975); *Miroirs* for Tape and Harpsichord (1975); *Moments* for Soprano, Flute, Viola, and Cello (1977).

Saint-Requier, Léon, French composer, conductor, and music editor; b. Rouen, Aug. 8, 1872; d. Paris, Oct. 1, 1964. He studied with Vincent d'Indy, Guilmant, and Charles Bordes; taught harmony at the Schola Cantorum (1900–34) and at the Ecole César Franck (1934–44); was active as a choral conductor at various Paris churches; edited the collection *Palestrina* (sacred songs of the 16th, 17th, and 18th centuries). He composed a Christmas motet, *Il est né le divin enfant*, using some folk melodies (1924); the oratorio *La Mort du doux Jésus* (1932); *Messe de grande louange* (1946); *Le Sermon sur la montagne* (1949); *Messe de St. Jean Apôtre* (1957); other religious works.

Saint-Saëns, (Charles-) Camille, celebrated French composer; b. Paris, Oct. 9, 1835; d. Algiers, Dec. 16, 1921. His widowed mother sent him to his great-aunt, Charlotte Masson, who taught him to play piano. He proved exceptionally gifted, and gave a performance in a Paris salon before he was 5; at 6 he began to compose; at 7 he became a private pupil of Stamaty; so rapid was his progress that he made his pianistic debut at the Salle Pleyel on May 6, 1846, playing a Mozart concerto and a movement from Beethoven's C minor Concerto, with Orch. After studying harmony with Pierre Maleden, he entered the Paris Cons., where his teachers were Benoist (organ) and Halévy (composition). He won the 2nd prize for organ in 1849, and the first prize in 1851. In 1852 he competed unsuccessfully for the Grand Prix de Rome, and failed again in a 2nd attempt in 1864, when he was already a composer of some stature. His *Ode à Sainte Cécile* for Voice and Orch. was awarded the first prize of the Société Sainte-Cécile (1852). On Dec. 11, 1853, his First Symph. was performed; Gounod wrote him a letter of praise, containing a prophetic phrase regarding the "obligation de devenir un grand maître." From 1853 to the end of 1857 Saint-Saëns was organist at the church of Saint-Merry in Paris; in 1857 he succeeded Lefébure-Wély as organist at the Madeleine. This important position he filled with distinction, and soon acquired a great reputation as virtuoso on the organ and a master of improvisation. He resigned in 1876, and devoted himself entirely to composition and conducting; also continued to appear as a pianist and organist. From 1861 to 1865 he taught piano at the Ecole Niedermeyer; among his pupils were André Messager and Gabriel Fauré.

Saint-Saëns was one of the founders of the Société Nationale de Musique (1871), established for the encouragement of French composers, but withdrew in 1886 when Vincent d'Indy proposed to include works by foreign composers in its program. In 1875 he married Marie Truffot; their 2 sons died in infancy; they separated in 1881, but were never legally divorced; Madame Saint-Saëns died in Bordeaux on Jan. 30, 1950, at the age of 95. In 1891 Saint-Saëns established a museum in Dieppe (his father's birthplace), to which he gave his MSS and his collection of paintings and other art objects. On Oct. 27, 1907, he witnessed the unveiling of his own statue (by Marqueste) in the court foyer of the opera house in Dieppe. He received many honors: In 1868 he was made a Chevalier of the Legion of Honor; in 1884, Officer; in 1900, Grand-Officer; and in 1913, Grand-Croix (the highest rank). In 1881 he was elected to the Institut de France; was also a member of many foreign organizations; received an honorary Mus.D. degree at Cambridge Univ. He visited the U.S. for the first time in 1906; was a representative of the French government at the Panama-Pacific Exposition in 1915 and conducted his choral work *Hail California* (San Francisco, June 19, 1915), written for the occasion. In 1916, at the age of 81, he made his first tour of South America; continued to appear in public as conductor of his own works almost to the time of his death. He took part as conductor and pianist in a festival of his works in Athens in May 1920. He played a program of his piano pieces at the Saint-Saëns museum in Dieppe on Aug. 6, 1921. For the winter he went to Algiers, where he died.

The position of Saint-Saëns in French music was very important. His abilities as a performer were extraordinary; he aroused the admiration of Wagner during the latter's stay in Paris (1860–61) by playing at sight the entire scores of Wagner's operas; curiously, Saint-Saëns achieved greater recognition in Germany than in France during the initial stages of his career. His most famous opera, *Samson et Dalila*, was produced in Weimar (in 1877) under the direction of Edouard Lassen, to whom the work was suggested by Liszt; it was not performed in France until nearly 13 years later, in Rouen. He played his first and 3rd piano concertos for the first time at the Gewandhaus in Leipzig. Solidity of contrapuntal fabric, instrumental elaboration, fullness of sonority in orchestration, and a certain harmonic saturation are the chief characteristics of his music, qualities that were not yet fully exploited by French composers at the time, and the French public preferred the lighter type of music. However, Saint-Saëns overcame this initial opposition, and toward the end of his life was regarded as an embodiment of French traditionalism. The shock of the German invasion of France in World War I made him abandon his former predilection for German music, and he wrote virulent articles against German art. He was unalterably opposed to modern music, and looked askance at Debussy; he regarded later manifestations of musical modernism as outrages, and was outspoken in his opinions. That Saint-Saëns possessed a fine sense of musical characterization, and true Gallic wit, is demonstrated by his ingenious suite *Carnival of the Animals,* which he wrote in 1886 but did not allow to be publ. during his lifetime. He also publ. a book of elegant verse (1890).

WORKS: FOR THE THEATER: Operas: *La Princesse jaune* (Paris, June 12, 1872); *Le Timbre d'argent* (Paris, Feb. 23, 1877); *Samson et Dalila* (Weimar, Dec. 2, 1877; Paris Opéra, Nov. 23, 1892; Metropolitan Opera, N.Y., Feb. 8, 1895); *Etienne Marcel* (Lyons, Feb. 8, 1879); *Henry VIII* (Paris, March 5, 1883); *Proserpine* (Paris, March 16, 1887); *Ascanio* (Paris, March 21, 1890); *Phryné* (Paris, May 24, 1893); *Les Barbares* (Paris, Oct. 23, 1901); *Hélène* (Monte Carlo, Feb. 18, 1904); *L'Ancêtre* (Monte Carlo, Feb. 24, 1906); *Déjanire* (Monte Carlo, March 14, 1911). Incidental music: *Antigone* (Paris, Nov. 21, 1893); *Andromaque,* by Racine (Paris, Feb. 7, 1903); *On ne badine pas avec l'amour,* by Alfred de Musset (Paris, Feb. 8, 1917). Ballet, *Javotte* (Lyons, Dec. 3, 1896).

FOR ORCH.: Symph. in A major (1850); Symph. No. 1 (Paris, Dec. 18, 1853); Symph. in F major, subtitled "Urbs Roma" (Paris, Feb. 15, 1857); Symph. No. 2 (Leipzig, Feb. 20, 1859); Symph. No. 3, with Organ (London, May 19, 1886); *Le Rouet d'Omphale,* symph. poem (1869; Paris, Jan. 9, 1872); *Marche héroïque* (Paris, Dec. 10, 1871); *Phaéton,* symph. poem (Paris, Dec. 7, 1873); *Danse macabre,* symph. poem (Paris, Jan. 24, 1875; one of his most successful works); *La Jeunesse d'Hercule,* symph. poem (Paris, Jan. 28, 1877); *Suite algérienne* (Paris, Dec. 19, 1880); *Une Nuit à Lisbonne* (Paris, Jan. 23, 1881); *Le Carnaval des animaux* (contains, as its 13th section, the popular *Swan;* Paris, Feb. 26, 1922); 5 piano concertos (all first perf. by Saint-Saëns): No. 1, in D (Leipzig, Oct. 26, 1865); No. 2, in G minor (Paris, May 6, 1868); No. 3, in E-flat (Leipzig, Nov. 25, 1869); No. 4, in C minor (Paris, Oct. 31, 1875); No. 5, in F (Paris, June 3, 1896); 3 violin concertos: No. 1, in A major (*Concertstück;* Paris, April 4, 1867); No. 2, in C (1858; Paris, Feb. 13, 1880); No. 3, in B minor (Paris, Jan. 2, 1881); *Introduction et Rondo capriccioso* for Violin and Orch. (1863; arranged for Violin and Piano by Bizet, and perf. for the first time in Paris, Nov. 6, 1913); 2 cello concertos: No. 1, in A minor (Paris, Jan. 19, 1873; still extremely popular), and No. 2, in D minor (Paris, Feb. 5, 1905); *Africa,* fantasy for Piano and Orch. (Paris, Oct. 25, 1891).

CHAMBER MUSIC: Piano Quintet (1858); 2 piano trios (1869, 1892); Piano Quartet (1875); Septet for Trumpet, Strings, and Piano (1881); 2 string quartets (1899, 1919); 2 violin sonatas (1885, 1896); 2 cello sonatas (1873, 1905); Oboe Sonata (1921); Clarinet Sonata (1921); Bassoon Sonata (1921).

VOCAL WORKS: *Oratorio de Noël* (1863); *Le Déluge,* oratorio (Paris, March 5, 1876); *Hail California* for Chorus and Orch. (1915); *Hymne à la Paix* for Chorus and Orch. (1919); numerous choruses a cappella; song cycles: *Mélodies persanes* (1870) and *La Cendre rouge* (1915); about 100 other songs; *La Fiancée du timbalier* for Voice and Orch. (Paris, Feb. 19, 1888); also a Requiem.

FOR PIANO: Etudes and various other pieces; also duets for piano, 4-hands and for 2 pianos.

ARRANGEMENTS: He completed Guiraud's opera *Frédégonde* (Paris Opéra, Dec. 18, 1895); publ. numerous arrangements of works by Classical and Romantic composers; edited Gluck's *Armide, Orphée,* and *Echo et Narcisse* in the Pelletan edition (1875–1902), the Durand edition of Rameau's works (from 1895), and Mozart's piano sonatas (1915).

Durand publ. *Catalogue général et thématique des œuvres de C. S.-S.* (1897; revised ed., 1907).

WRITINGS: *Notice sur H. Reber* (1881); *Matérialisme et musique* (1882); *Harmonie et mélodie* (1885; a collection of essays, chiefly on Wagner); *Notes sur les décors de théâtre dans l'antiquité romaine* (1886); *Ch. Gounod et le Don Juan de Mozart* (1894); *Problèmes et mystères* (1894); *Portraits et souvenirs* (1899); *Essai sur les lyres et cithares antiques* (1902); *Ecole buissonnière* (1913; in Eng. as *Musical Memories,* N.Y., 1919; reprint, N.Y., 1969 and 1971); *Au Courant de la vie* (1914); *Germanophilie* (1916); *Les Idées de M. Vincent d'Indy* (1919); *Outspoken Essays on Music* (London and N.Y., 1922; trans. of assorted articles; reprint, Westport, Conn., 1969).

BIBLIOGRAPHY: C. Kit and P. Loanda, *Musique savante. Sur la musique de M. S.-S.* (Lille, 1889); Blondel, *C. S.-S. et son cinquantenaire artistique* (Paris, 1896); C. Bellaigue, *C. S.-S.* (Paris, 1899); E. Solenière, *C. S.-S.* (Paris, 1899); O. Neitzel, *C. S.-S.* (Berlin, 1899); P. Locard, *Les Maîtres contemporains de l'orgue* (Paris, 1900); special S.-S. issue of *Le Monde Musical* (Oct. 31, 1901); A. Hervey, *French Music in the 19th Century* (London, 1903); E. Baumann, *Les Grandes Formes de la musique: L'Œuvre de S.-S.* (Paris, 1905; new ed., 1923); special *S.-S.* issue of *Musica* (June 1907); L. Aubin, *Le Drame lyrique* (Tours, 1908); R. Rolland, *Musiciens d'aujourd'hui* (Paris, 1908; Eng. trans., 1914); A. Jullien, *Musiciens d'hier et d'aujourd'hui* (Paris, 1910); O. Séré, *Musiciens français d'aujourd'hui* (revised ed., 1921); J. Bonnerot, *C. S.-S.* (Paris, 1914; 2nd ed., 1922); L. Augé de Lassus, *S.-S.* (Paris, 1914); J. Montargis, *C. S.-S.* (Paris, 1919); *Funerailles de S.-S.* (collection of speeches, Paris, 1921); J. Chantavoine, *L'Œuvre dramatique de C. S.-S.* (Paris, 1921); A. Hervey, *S.-S.* (London, 1921); W. Lyle, *C. S.-S., His Life and Art* (London, 1923); G. Servières, *S.-S.* (Paris, 1923; 2nd ed., 1930); L. Laloy, *Cinquante ans de musique française, 1874–1923* (1924); A. Dandelot, *S.-S.* (Paris, 1930); J. Handschin, *C. S.-S.* (Zürich, 1930); J. Normand, *S.-S.* (1930); L. Schneider, *Une Heure avec S.-S.* (1930); J. Langlois, *C. S.-S.* (Moulins, 1934); R. Dumanine, *Les Origines normandes de C. S.-S.* (Rouen, 1937); René Fauchois, *La Vie et l'œuvre prodigieuse de C. S.-S.* (Paris, 1938); D. Brook, *Five Great French Composers* (London, 1946); J. Chantavoine, *C. S.-S.* (Paris, 1947); James Harding, *S.-S. and His Circle* (London, 1965); S. Ratner, *The Piano Works of C. S.-S.* (Diss., Univ. of Michigan, 1972); D. Fallon, *The Symphonies and Symphonic Poems of C. S.-S.* (Diss., Yale Univ., 1973); E. Harkins, *The Chamber Music of S.-S.* (Diss., N.Y. Univ., 1976).

Sainton, Prosper, violinist; b. Toulouse, June 5, 1813; d. London, Oct. 17, 1890. He was a pupil of Habeneck at the Paris Cons., winning first prize for violin in 1834; was a prof. at the Cons. of Toulouse

(1840–44); went to England in 1844; was appointed prof. at the Royal Academy of Music in 1845; became concertmaster of the London Phil. (1846–54), at Covent Garden (1847–71), and at Her Majesty's Theatre (1871–80). In 1860 he married **Charlotte Helen Dolby,** a contralto (b. London, May 17, 1821; d. there, Feb. 18, 1885). Sainton wrote 2 violin concertos and several violin solos; his wife composed some songs and choruses.

Saito, Hideo, Japanese cellist, conductor, and music educator; b. Tokyo, May 23, 1902; d. there, Sept. 18, 1974. He went to Germany for music study; was a cello student of Julius Klengel in Leipzig (1923–27) and of Feuermann in Berlin (1930). Returning to Japan, he played cello in the Nihon Symph. Orch., and studied conducting with Rosenstock, then resident in Japan. He was a co-founder of the Toho Music School in Tokyo, where he taught cello, conducting, and academic music courses. Among his students was Seiji Ozawa, who came to regard Saito's influence as a major factor in his own career.

Sakač, Branimir, Croatian composer; b. Zagreb, June 5, 1918; d. 1979. He graduated in composition from the Zagreb Music Academy in 1941; later taught there. In his music he adopted a purely structural method, using highly dissonant contrapuntal combinations within strict neo-Classical forms.
WORKS: *Serenade* for String Orch. (1947); *Simfonija o mrtvom vojniku (Symphony of the Dead Soldiers;* 1951); Chamber Symph. (1953); Solo Violin Sonata (1953); *3 sintetskim poemama (3 Synthetic Poems;* 1959); *Aleatory Prelude* for Piano and Tape (1961); *2 Miniatures* for Flute, Harp, and Percussion (1963); *Episode* for Orch. and Tape (1963); *Study I* for Piano and Percussion (1963); *Study II* for Piano (1964); *Structure I* for Chamber Ensemble (1965); *Prostori (Spaces)* for Orch; *Solo I* for Violin and Chamber Orch.; *Doppio* for String Quartet; *Canto dalla Commedia,* after Dante, for Solo Violin, Percussion, and Chorus (1969); *Turm-Musik (Tower Music)* for Orch. (1970); *Ad litteram* for Piano (1970); *Barasou (Ballad of Rats and Mice)* for Voice and Chamber Ensemble (1971); *Matrix Symphony* for 3 Voices and Orch. (1972); *Syndrome* for Chamber Ensemble (1974); tape pieces.

Sala, Nicola, Italian composer and theorist; b. Tocco-Gaudio, near Benevento, April 7, 1713; d. Naples, Aug. 31, 1801. He was a pupil of Fago, Abos, and Leo at the Cons. della Pietà de' Turchini in Naples; apparently was not engaged as a teacher there until his old age; was appointed 2nd maestro when he was 74, in 1787, and first maestro 6 years later; continued to teach until 1799. It was during his tenure at the Cons. that he publ. his most celebrated theoretical work, *Regole del contrappunto prattico* (3 vols., 1794; reprinted by Choron in Paris, 1808, as *Principii di composizione delle scuole d'Italia).* He brought out several operas: *Vologeso* (Rome, 1737); *Zenobia* (Naples, Jan. 12, 1761); *Demetrio* (Naples, Dec. 12, 1762); *Merope* (Naples,

Aug. 13, 1769); an oratorio, *Giuditta* (1780); masses; litanies; other religious works.

Salabert, Francis, French music publisher; b. Paris, July 27, 1884; d. in an airplane accident at Shannon, Ireland, Dec. 28, 1946. The Editions Salabert was founded by his father, **Edouard Salabert,** in 1896; at the latter's death in 1903, Francis Salabert took over the management. A professional musician and composer in his own right, he made a series of practical arrangements for small orch. of numerous classical and modern works, which were widely used. Editions Salabert expanded greatly through the purchase of the stock of orch. and other music of the firms Gaudet (1927), Mathot (1930), Senart (1941), Rouart-Lerolle (1942), and Deiss (1946). On the death of Francis Salabert, his widow assumed the directorship.

Salaman, Charles Kensington, English pianist; b. London, March 31, 1814; d. there, June 23, 1901. He studied with Charles Neate in London and with Henri Herz in Paris. Returning to London, he took an active part in musical affairs; in 1853 he founded, with Lucas Blagrove and others, the Concerti da Camera; from 1837 to 1855 was an associate of the Phil. Society; in 1849 he was a founder of an amateur choral society in London; was a co-founder, in 1858, of the Musical Society of London; one of the founders of the Musical Assoc. in 1874. He wrote a comic opera, *Pickwick* (London, 1889); about 100 choral works for the synagogue; many anthems, part-songs, piano pieces; also many songs to Eng., Latin, Greek, and Hebrew texts.

Salas Viu, Vicente, Spanish-Chilean musicologist; b. Madrid, Jan. 29, 1911; d. Santiago, Chile, Sept. 2, 1967. He studied academic subjects at the Univ. of Madrid; music with Rodolfo Halffter; wrote for various literary and musical publications until 1939, when he emigrated to Chile; he settled in Santiago. He publ. a very valuable book, *La creación musical en Chile 1900–1951* (Santiago, 1952), in 2 sections, embracing a general account of musical activities in Chile and detailed biographies of 40 Chilean composers; also *La última luz de Mozart* (Santiago, 1949); *Momentos decisivos en la música* (Buenos Aires, 1957).

Salas y Castro, Esteban, Cuban composer; b. Havana, Dec. 25, 1725; d. Santiago de Cuba, July 14, 1803. He studied organ and theology; in 1764 became maestro de capilla in Santiago, retaining this position until his death. He wrote mostly sacred music.
BIBLIOGRAPHY: P. Hernández Balaguer, "La capilla de música de la catedral de Santiago de Cuba," *Revista Musical Chilena* (1964).

Salazar, Adolfo, eminent Spanish musicologist; b. Madrid, March 6, 1890; d. Mexico City, Sept. 27, 1958. He studied with Manuel de Falla and Pérez Casas. In 1914 he became editor in chief of the *Revista Musical Hispano-Americana* (until 1918); from

1973

1918 to 1936 was music critic of the influential Madrid daily *El Sol;* was founder and later secretary of the Sociedad Nacional de Música (1915–22). During the final period of the Spanish Civil War he was cultural attaché at the Spanish embassy in Washington (1938–39); then settled in Mexico City as a writer and teacher.

WRITINGS: *Música y músicos de hoy* (Madrid, 1928); *Sinfonía y ballet* (Madrid, 1929); *La música contemporánea en España* (Madrid, 1930); *La música actual en Europa y sus problemas* (Madrid, 1935); *El siglo romántico* (Madrid, 1935; new ed. as *Los grandes compositores de la época romántica,* 1955); *La música en el siglo XX* (Madrid, 1936); *Música y sociedad en el siglo XX* (Mexico City, 1939); *Las grandes estructuras de la música* (Mexico City, 1940); *La rosa de los vientos en la música europea* (Mexico City, 1940; reissued in 1954 as *Conceptos fundamentales en la historia de la música*); *Forma y expresión en la música: Ensayo sobre la formación de los géneros en la música instrumental* (Mexico City, 1941); *Introducción en la música actual* (Mexico City, 1941); *Los grandes periodos en la historia de la música* (Mexico City, 1941); *Poesía y música en lengua vulgar y sus antecedentes en la edad media* (Mexico City, 1943); *La música en la sociedad europea* (4 vols., Mexico City, 1942–46; a monumental work covering the entire period of music history until modern times); *La música moderna* (Buenos Aires, 1944; in Eng. as *Music in Our Time,* N.Y., 1946); *Música, instrumentos y danzas en las obras de Cervantes* (Mexico City, 1948); *La danza y el ballet* (Mexico City, 1949); *La música, como proceso histórico de su invención* (Mexico City, 1950); *J.S. Bach* (Mexico City, 1951); *La música de España* (Buenos Aires, 1953); several other smaller works, brochures, and pamphlets on a variety of subjects. Salazar was also a composer; wrote 3 symph. works: *Paisajes, Estampas,* and *Don Juan de los Infernos;* songs to words by Verlaine; piano pieces.

Saldoni, Baltasar, Spanish composer and lexicographer; b. Barcelona, Jan. 4, 1807; d. Madrid, Dec. 3, 1889. He was a pupil of Mateo Ferrer at Montserrat and of Carnicer in Madrid. In 1826 he produced in Madrid his light opera *El Triunfo del amor* and the Italian operas *Saladino e Clotilde* (1833), *Ipermestra* (Jan. 20, 1838), and *Cleonice regina di Siria* (Jan. 24, 1840); he also wrote the zarzuelas *La corte de Mónaco* (Feb. 16, 1857) and *Los maridos en las máscaras* (Barcelona, Aug. 26, 1864). In 1830 he was appointed prof. of singing at the Madrid Cons. His magnum opus as a scholar was the *Diccionario biográfico-bibliográfico de efemérides de músicos españoles,* in 4 vols. (Madrid, 1868–81), to which was added a supplementary vol. in the form of a chronology of births and deaths of Spanish musicians, day by day and year by year, with exhaustive biographical notes. This monumental compilation, upon which Saldoni worked nearly 40 years, contains (inevitably) a number of errors, but in the absence of other musicographical works on Spanish musicians, it still retains considerable documentary value.

Sales, Pietro Pompeo, Italian composer; b. Brescia, 1729; d. Hanau, Germany, Nov. 21, 1797. Little is known about his early life; when a devastating earthquake destroyed his home in Italy, he went to Germany; served as director of the court chapel of Prince-Bishop Joseph, landgrave of Hesse-Darmstadt, in Augsburg and Dillingen (1756–68); then was in Stuttgart; from 1770 was director of the court chapel of the Trier Elector Clemens Wenzeslaus at Ehrenbreitstein-am-Rhein; moved with the Elector to Koblenz, where Charles Burney met him in 1772. After the French invasion of 1797 he fled to Hanau, where he died shortly afterward. He also visited London. His operas had performances in Germany and Italy, as well as in London; he also composed oratorios, church music, and instrumental works; a piano sonata is reprinted in Haffner's *Raccolta Musicale.*

BIBLIOGRAPHY: F. Collignon, *Pietro Pompeo Sales* (Bonn, 1923).

Saleski, Gdal, Russian cellist; b. Kiev, Feb. 11, 1888; d. Los Angeles, Oct. 8, 1966. He sang in a Kiev synagogue; then went to Germany, where he took lessons in cello with Julius Klengel at the Leipzig Cons.; also played in the cello section of the Gewandhaus Orch. under Nikisch; subsequently was in Scandinavia (1915–21); then went to the U.S.; played cello in the NBC Symph. Orch. under Toscanini (1937–48). He publ. the compilation *Famous Musicians of a Wandering Race* (N.Y., 1927; revised ed. under the title *Famous Musicians of Jewish Origin,* N.Y., 1949); biographical data in it are often inaccurate; both editions include Bizet, Ravel, and Saint-Saëns, in the mistaken belief that since they wrote music on Jewish subjects, they must have been Jews.

Saléza, Albert, French tenor; b. Bruges, near Bayonne, Oct. 18, 1867; d. Paris, Nov. 26, 1916. He studied at the Paris Cons.; made his debut at the Opéra-Comique on July 19, 1888, as Mylio in *Le Roi d'Ys* by Lalo; then sang at Nice (1892–94) and at Monte Carlo (1894–97), returning to the Paris Opéra in 1897; sang at the Théâtre de la Monnaie, Brussels (1898–99); made his American debut at the Metropolitan Opera, N.Y., on May 10, 1898; returned to sing in Paris in 1901. In 1911 he became a prof. of singing at the Paris Cons.

BIBLIOGRAPHY: H. de Curzon, *Croquis d'artistes* (Paris, 1898).

Salieri, Antonio, illustrious Italian composer; b. Legnago, near Verona, Aug. 18, 1750; d. Vienna, May 7, 1825. He studied music with his brother, Francesco, who was a violinist, and also took lessons from the organist Simoni. His father died in 1765, and Salieri was taken to Venice by a wealthy patron; there he studied harmony with Pescetti and singing with Pacini. Gassmann, the Viennese composer, who was in Venice at the time, took Salieri to Vienna in 1766, and provided for his education there.

While Gassmann was in Rome (1770), Salieri took his place as conductor at the Burg Theater in Vienna, and brought out there his first opera, *Le Donne letterate,* with marked success. From that time until 1774 he produced 9 more operas of his own, all in the Italian style, the last being *La calamità dei cuori.* When Gassmann died in 1774, Salieri became his successor as court composer. He began a serious study of Gluck's style under the master's own direction; Gluck recommended Salieri to the administration of the Académie de Musique in Paris for the composition of a French opera; this was produced in Paris as *Les Danaïdes,* based on an Italian libretto, *Ipermestra,* by Calzabigi; the opera was advertised as composed by Gluck in collaboration with Salieri, but after the 12th performance Gluck declared that the work was entirely by Salieri; it remained in the repertoire of the Paris Opéra for many years. Salieri then returned to Vienna, where he produced a comic opera, *La grotta di Trofonio* (Oct. 12, 1785), with much success. His French opera *Les Horaces* was produced in Paris on Dec. 7, 1786, and proved a failure, but his next French opera, *Tarare* (Paris Opéra, June 8, 1787), made a sensation, and was performed on all the principal stages in Europe; Lorenzo Da Ponte made a revised Italian version of it as *Axur, Re d'Ormus,* which was produced in Vienna on Jan. 8, 1788, with enormous acclaim. In 1788 Salieri succeeded Bonno as court Kapellmeister at Vienna, retaining this post until 1824, but he did not conduct operatic performances after 1790, confining himself to the concerts of the Hofsängerkapelle; was also conductor of the Tonkünstler-Societät (founded in 1771 by Gassmann) until 1818. In Vienna he enjoyed great renown as a teacher; Beethoven studied with him, and acknowledged himself willingly as Salieri's pupil; Schubert and Liszt were also his pupils. Salieri was undoubtedly a master of the Italian method of composition, and his technique in harmony and counterpoint was of the highest. He had a reputation for intrigue, and this gave rise to the fantastic story of his poisoning of Mozart (Pushkin publ. a drama, *Mozart and Salieri,* based on this story, and Rimsky-Korsakov set it to music). In all, Salieri wrote 39 operas, of which 6 remained unproduced; 11 cantatas; 6 masses; 4 Te Deums; a Requiem; many other pieces of church music; 2 symphs.; 2 piano concertos; various other instrumental works.

BIBLIOGRAPHY: I. von Mosel, *Über das Leben und die Werke des Anton Salieri* (Vienna, 1827); A. von Hermann, *Antonio Salieri* (Vienna, 1897); C. Serini, "Antonio Salieri," *Rivista Musicale Italiana* (1926); R. Nützlader, "Salieri als Kirchenmusiker," *Studien zur Musikwissenschaft,* 14 (Vienna, 1927); G. Magnani, *Antonio Salieri* (Legnago, 1934); A. Della Corte, *Un Italiano all'estero, Antonio Salieri* (Turin, 1936); E.J. Juin, "Documenti inediti sul Salieri come maestro di F. Liszt e di altri," *Rivista Musicale Italiana* (1936); R. Angermüller, *Antonio Salieri* (3 vols.; vol. 1, Salzburg, 1970; vol. 3, Munich, 1971).

Salinas, Francisco de, Spanish organist and theorist; b. Burgos, March 1, 1513; d. Salamanca, Jan. 13, 1590. He became blind at the age of 10; was taught organ playing, and studied languages at the Univ. of Salamanca. In 1538 he was taken to Italy by Cardinal Sarmiento; in 1553–58, was organist to the Duke of Alba at the vice-regal court of Naples, where Diego Ortiz was maestro. In 1561 Salinas returned to Spain, and from 1567 until his death was a prof. of music at the Univ. of Salamanca. He wrote the theoretical treatise *De musica libri septem* (Salamanca, 1577), chiefly valuable for the examples of Spanish folk music it contains. It was to Salinas that Luis de León dedicated his famous *Ode to Music.*

BIBLIOGRAPHY: Otto Kinkeldey, *Orgel und Klavier in der Musik des 16. Jahrhunderts* (Leipzig, 1910); F. Pedrell, *Lírica nacionalizada* (Paris, 1913; pp. 211–63; contains musical examples); J.B. Trend, "Francisco de Salinas," *Music & Letters* (Jan. 1927); A.M. Daniels, *The De musica libri VII of Franciscus de Salinas* (Diss., Univ. of Southern Calif., 1962; contains Eng. trans.).

Sallinen, Aulis, Finnish composer; b. Salmi, April 9, 1935. He studied under Aarre Merikanto and Joonas Kokkonen at the Sibelius Academy (1955–60); was managing director of the Finnish Radio Symph. (1960–70); taught at the Sibelius Academy (1963–76); was appointed Arts Professor by the Finnish state for the years 1976–81. In his music he uses modern techniques, with a prevalence of euphonious dissonance and an occasional application of serialism.

WORKS: 3 operas: *Ratsumies (The Horseman;* 1973–74; Savonlinna Opera Festival, July 17, 1975); *Punainen viiva (The Red Line;* 1976–78; Helsinki, Nov. 30, 1978); *The King Goes Forth to France* (Savonlinna Opera Festival, July 7, 1984); ballet, *Variations sur Mallarmé* (1967; Helsinki, 1968); *2 Mythical Scenes* for Orch. (1956); Concerto for Chamber Orch. (1959–60); *Variations* for Cello and Orch. (1960–61); *3 Lyrical Songs about Death* for Baritone, Male Chorus, and Orch. (1962); orch. elegy, *Mauermusik (Wall Music),* subtitled "In memory of a certain young German" killed at the Berlin Wall (1962); *14 Juventas Variations* for Orch. (1963); *Metamorphoses* for Piano and Chamber Orch. (1964); Violin Concerto (1968); *Chorali* for 32 Wind Instruments, Percussion, Harp, and Celesta (1970); 4 symphs.: No. 1 (1970–71); No. 2, *Symphonic Dialogue,* for Solo Percussionist and Orch. (1972); No. 3 (1974–75); No. 4 (1979); *Suita grammaticale* for Children's Choir, Strings, Kantele, and School Instruments (1971–72); *Chamber Music I* for Chamber String Orch. (1975); *Chamber Music II* for Alto Flute and Chamber String Orch. (1975–76); Cello Concerto (1976); 4 string quartets: No. 1 (1958); No. 2, *Canzona* (1960); No. 3, *Some Aspects of Peltoniemi Hintrik's Funeral March* (1969); No. 4, *Quiet Songs* (1971); *Serenade* for 2 Wind Quartets (1963); *Elegy for Sebastian Knight* for Solo Cello (1964); *Quattro per 4* for Violin, Cello, Oboe, and Harpsichord (1964–65); *4 Etudes* for Violin and Piano (1970); *Chaconne* for Organ (1970); Solo Cello

Sonata (1971); *Metamorfora* for Cello and Piano (1974); *Canto and Ritornello* for Solo Violin (1975); *4 Dream Songs* for Solo Voice and Piano (1972); *Dies irae* (1978).

BIBLIOGRAPHY: J. Parsons, "Aulis Sallinen," *Musical Times* (Nov. 1980).

Salmanov, Vadim, Russian composer; b. St. Petersburg, Nov. 4, 1912; d. Leningrad, Feb. 27, 1978. He studied piano with his father; theory with Akimenko. He studied composition with Gnessin at the Leningrad Cons. in 1941, then served in the army (1941–45); was leader of the composition dept. of the Leningrad Cons. (1947–51) and taught composition and orchestration there after 1951, becoming a prof. in 1965. His early works are marked by broad Russian melodism, with the harmonic structure following the models of Prokofiev and Shostakovich; after 1960 he adopted more advanced techniques, including dodecaphony.

WORKS: Ballet, *The Man* (1960); oratorio, *The 12,* to the text by Alexander Blok (1957); 2 cantatas: *Ode to Lenin* (1970) and *Skify,* after Blok (*The Scythians;* 1973); symph. poem, *Soja,* for Voice and Orch. (1951); *Little Symphony* for String Orch. (1941); *The Forest,* symph. picture (1948); *Russian Capriccio* for Orch. (1950); *Slavic Dance* for Orch. (1952); 4 symphs. (1952, 1959, 1963, 1976); *Children's Symphony* (1962); *Poetic Pictures,* symph. suite (1955); Sonata for Piano and String Orch. (1961); 2 violin concertos (1964, 1974); *Nights in the Big City* for Violin and Chamber Orch. (1969); *Monologue* for Cello and Chamber Orch. (1972); 6 string quartets (1945; 1947, revised 1958; 1961; 1968; 1971;); 2 violin sontas (1945, 1962); 2 piano trios (1946, 1949); Piano Quartet (1947); *Spain Is in My Heart* for Mezzo-soprano and Piano (1962) and other songs; choruses.

Salmenhaara, Erkki, Finnish composer; b. Helsinki, March 12, 1941. He studied at the Sibelius Academy with Kokkonen; then went to Vienna, where he took lessons with Ligeti (1963). He joined the faculty of the Univ. of Helsinki in 1963. His music is often inspired by literary works; he favors unusual combinations of instruments, including electronics; makes use of serial techniques in dense, fastidious sonorities.

WORKS: Opera, *Portugalin nainen (The Woman of Portugal;* 1972; Helsinki, Feb. 4, 1976); *9 Improvisations,* concerto for Piano, Strings, and Timpani; Symph. No. 1; Symph. No. 2 (1963, revised 1966); Symph. No. 3 (1964); *Le Bateau ivre,* after Rimbaud, for Orch. (1966); *BFK-83* for Orch. (1967); *La Fille en mini-jupe,* poem for Orch. (1967); *Suomi-Finland,* an "unsymphonic poem" for Orch. (1967); *Requiem profanum* for Soprano, Alto, Baritone, Strings, and Piano (1968–69); *Illuminations,* after Rimbaud, poem for Orch. (1971); Symph. No. 4, *Nel mezzo del cammin di nostra vita,* after Dante (1971); Horn Concerto (Oslo, Oct. 3, 1974); *Intrada* for Orch. (1975); Concerto for 2 Violins and Orch. (Helsinki, Sept. 21, 1982); Cello Sonata (1960); String Trio (1961); *La Clarté vibrante,* cantata for

Soprano, 4 Cellos, and Percussion; *Pan and Echo* for 4 Suspended Cymbals, Tam-tam, and Amplifier; Concerto for 2 Violins, with Amplifiers and Loudspeakers; *Composition* for String Quartet (1963); *Elegia I* for 3 Flutes, 2 Trumpets, and Double Bass (1963); *Elegia II* for 2 String Quartets (1963); *Composition 3* for Violin, Clarinet, Guitar, and Percussion (1963); Wind Quintet (1964); *Elegia III* for Cello (1965); 3 Piano Sonatas (1966, 1973, 1975); *Elegia IV* for Viola (1967); *Etude* for Harpsichord (1969); *Trois scènes de nuit* for Violin and Piano (1970); *Quartetto* for Flute, Violin, Viola, and Cello (1971); *Prelude, Pop Tune and Fugue* for Flute; *And the Fire and the Rose Are One* for 2 Violins (1972); songs.

Salmhofer, Franz, Austrian composer; b. Vienna, Jan. 22, 1900; d. there, Sept. 2, 1975. He was a chorister at the Admont Monastery in Styria until 1914; then studied composition with Schreker at the Vienna Academy of Music and musicology with Guido Adler at the Univ. of Vienna. In 1923 he married the pianist **Margit Gál.** In 1929 he became conductor at the Hofburg Theater, for which he composed incidental music, ballets, and operas; he resigned in 1939; from 1945 to 1955 he was director at the Vienna State Opera; then director of the Volksoper, 1955–63.

WORKS: Operas: *Dame in Traum* (Vienna, Dec. 26, 1935); *Iwan Sergejewitsch Tarassenko* (Vienna, March 9, 1938); *Das Werbekleid* (Vienna, June 25, 1946); ballets: *Das lockende Phantom, Der Taugenichts in Wien, Weihnachtsmärchen, Österreichische Bauernhochzeit;* 2 symphs. (1947, 1955); overtures: *Der Ackermann und der Tod* and *Heroische Ouvertüre;* Trumpet Concerto; Cello Concerto; *Der geheimnisvolle Trompeter,* symph. poem for Narrator and Orch., after Walt Whitman's *The Mystic Trumpeter* (1924); *Kammersuite* for 16 Instruments (Vienna, May 10, 1923); String Quartet; Piano Quartet; Viola Sonata; Cello Sonata; songs; piano pieces.

Salminen, Matti, Finnish bass; b. Turku, July 7, 1945. After vocal studies in Finland, he made his operatic debut at the Helsinki Opera as King Philipp in *Don Carlos* in 1969; he then toured in Europe, appearing in Cologne, Zürich, Hamburg, Munich, and Stuttgart, at Covent Garden in London, and at the Bayreuth Festival. He particularly distinguished himself in the great basso roles in operas by Mozart, Wagner, and Verdi.

Salmon, Albert Glover, American pianist and composer; b. Southold, N.Y., Sept. 28, 1868; d. (suicide by swallowing poison), Boston, Sept. 17, 1917. He studied at the New England Cons., graduating in 1888; also took private lessons with B.J. Lang and Otto Bendix in Boston, and with Percy Goetschius and MacDowell in N.Y. He then went to Russia, where he took composition lessons with Glazunov in St. Petersburg and became deeply interested in Russian music; he collected a valuable library of works by Russian composers (about 3,000 vols.), as well as autographs. His own compositions were mostly for piano, in a salon manner (*Valse arabesque, Scherzo, Novelette, Fileuse, Impromptu, Tarentelle fantastique*, etc.).

Salmond, Felix, distinguished English cellist; b. London, Nov. 19, 1888; d. New York, Feb. 19, 1952. He studied at the Royal College of Music with W.E. Whitehouse, and in Brussels with Edouard Jacobs; made his debut in London (1909), accompanied at the piano by his mother, Mrs. Norman Salmond. He gave the world premiere of Elgar's Cello Concerto, under Elgar's direction, on Oct. 27, 1919; after a European tour, he settled in America (debut, N.Y., March 29, 1922); was head of the cello dept. at the Curtis Inst. of Music in Philadelphia (1925–42) and taught cello at the Juilliard Graduate School of Music in N.Y. from its opening in 1924. He enjoyed a reputation as a fine chamber music player and an excellent teacher.

Salò, Gasparo da. See **Gasparo da Salò.**

Saloman, Siegfried, composer; b. Tondern, Schleswig, Oct. 2, 1816; d. Stockholm, July 22, 1899. He studied composition with J.P. Hartmann in Copenhagen, and violin with Lipinski in Dresden. He lived in Copenhagen for many years and produced 2 operas there, *Tordenskjold I Dynekilen* (May 23, 1844) and *Diamantkorset* (*The Diamond Cross;* March 20, 1847); toured Russia and the Netherlands (1847–50); married the singer **Henriette Nissen,** and traveled with her; in 1859, settled in Russia; one of his operas, to a German libretto, was produced in Russian as *Karpatskaya roza* in Moscow, Jan. 7, 1868; several other operas were produced in Stockholm, where he went in 1879 after the death of his wife. Some of his violin pieces and songs have been publ.

Salomon (Salomonis). See **Elias, Salomon.**

Salomon, Johann Peter, German violinist, composer, and impresario; b. Bonn (baptized, Feb. 20), 1745; d. London (following a riding accident; buried in Westminster Abbey), Nov. 25, 1815. He was a member of the Electoral orch. at Bonn (1758–62); after a successful concert tour he was engaged as concertmaster and composer to Prince Heinrich of Prussia at Rheinsberg (1764). When the orch. was disbanded, Salomon went to Paris and then to London, where he settled in 1781; made himself known as a violinist and conductor; introduced symphs. by Haydn and Mozart in a series of concerts he gave in 1786. In 1790 he went to Italy to engage singers for the Italian Opera in London, and from there went to Vienna, where he saw Haydn and persuaded him to accept an engagement in London. At Salomon's behest Haydn wrote the works familiarly known as his "Salomon Symphonies"; it is through his association with Haydn's 2 visits to England, in 1790–91 and 1794–95, that Salomon's name remains in the annals of music. He was a founder of the Phil. Society in London (1813); conducted its first concert, on March 8, 1813. His own works are of merely an-

tiquarian interest; they include the operas *Les Recruteurs* (Rheinsberg, 1771); *Le Séjour du bonheur* (Berlin, March 5, 1773); *Titus* (Rheinsberg, 1774); *La Reine de Golconde* (Rheinsberg, 1776); *Windsor Castle,* or *The Fair Maid of Kent* (Covent Garden, April 6, 1795); also violin sonatas.
BIBLIOGRAPHY: "Memoir of Johann Peter Salomon," *Harmonicon* (London, Feb. 1830).

Salonen, Esa-Pekka, Finnish composer and conductor; b. Helsinki, June 30, 1958. He studied French-horn playing at the Sibelius Academy in Helsinki (1973–77); took composition courses with Rautavaara and conducting classes with Panula; he then traveled to Italy, where he studied with Donatoni in Siena and Castiglioni in Milan (1979–81). Returning to Finland, he engaged in theater conducting. In his music he tends toward pragmatic aural accessibility, employing fairly modern techniques while preserving the formal centrality of traditional tonality.
WORKS: For Orch.: *Aubades* for Flute, Soprano, and Strings (1977–78); *Apokalyptische Phantasie* for Brass Band and Electronic Tape (1978); *Boutade* for Violin, Cello, Piano, and Orch. (1979); *. . . auf den ersten Blick und ohne zu wissen* (a quotation from Kafka's *The Trial*) for Alto Saxophone and Orch. (1980–81); *Giro* (1981). Chamber music: *Horn Music I* for Horn and Piano (1976); *Horn Music II* for 6 Horns, Percussion, and Electronic Tape (1979); Cello Sonata (1976–77); *Nachtlieder* for Clarinet and Piano (1978); *Sets* for Brass Quintet (1978); *Prologue* for Oboe, Violin, Cello, and Percussion (1979); *Goodbye* for Violin and Guitar (1979–80); *Meeting* for Clarinet and Harpsichord (1982); Wind Quintet (1982).

Salonen, Sulo, Finnish composer; b. Pyhtää, Jan. 27, 1899; d. Porvoo, May 21, 1976. He was a pupil of Furuhjelm and Palmgren; devoted himself mainly to the composition of sacred music; structurally, they continue the tradition of Lutheran services of the 19th century.
WORKS: *Passion Cantata* (1942); *Viisauden ylistys (In Praise of Wisdom)* for Narrator, Voices, and Instruments (1961); *Requiem* (1962); Wind Quintet (1962); String Trio (1971); 2 string quartets (1971, 1972); *Cum jubilo* for Chorus, Organ, and Percussion (Helsinki, Jan. 24, 1974); about 50 motets; numerous organ pieces.

Salter, Lionel (Paul), English conductor, pianist, harpsichordist, and writer on music; b. London, Sept. 8, 1914. He studied at the Royal College of Music and at Cambridge Univ. with Dent and Ord (B.A., 1935; B.Mus., 1936); then returned to the Royal College of Music, where he studied conducting with Lambert and piano with Benjamin. He began his career working in radio and television in London; in 1945 he became assistant conductor of the BBC Theatre Orch.; from 1948 he held administrative posts with the BBC; retired in 1974. His books include *Going to a Concert* (London, 1950), *Going to the Opera* (London, 1955), *The Musician and His World* (London, 1963), and *Music and the 20th-Century Media* (with J. Bornoff; Florence, 1972); he also compiled a useful *Gramophone Guide to Classical Music and Recordings.*

Salter, Mary Elizabeth Turner (Mrs. Sumner Salter), American soprano; b. Peoria, Ill., March 15, 1856; d. Orangeburg, N.Y., Sept. 12, 1938. She studied in Burlington, Iowa, and in Boston; from 1874 to 1893, sang in churches in Boston and N.Y.; she married **Sumner Salter** in 1881, and settled with him in Williamstown, Mass.

WORKS: She publ. a number of song cycles, and was still composing at the age of 80 (*Christmas Song,* 1936). Song cycles: *Love's Epitome, A Night in Naishapur, Lyrics from Sappho, From Old Japan;* about 80 songs publ. separately (*The Cry of Rachel, The Pine Tree, Für Musik, Die stille Wasserrose,* etc.); duets, some part-songs, and church music.

Salter, Sumner, American organist and arranger; b. Burlington, Iowa, June 24, 1856; d. New York, March 5, 1944. After graduating from Amherst College, he studied at the New England Cons.; then taught at various schools in Boston and elsewhere; from 1905 to 1923, was director of music at Williams College; then retired. He edited *The Pianist and Organist* (official organ of the American Guild of Organists) from 1895 to 1898; publ. church music and numerous organ arrangements of various works. In 1881 he married **Mary E. Turner,** the singer and composer.

Saltzmann-Stevens, Minnie, American soprano; b. Bloomington, Ill., March 17, 1874; d. Milan, Jan. 25, 1950. She studied voice with Jean De Reszke in Paris; made her operatic debut as Brünnhilde in the English version of the *Ring des Nibelungen* at London's Covent Garden in 1909; she continued to sing there until 1913; also appeared at the Bayreuth Festivals of 1911 and 1913; from 1911–14 she sang with the Chicago Opera.

Salva, Tadeáš, Slovak composer; b. Lúčky, near Ruzomberok, Oct. 22, 1937. He studied with Ján Zimmer in Bratislava; then with Cikker and A. Moyzes in Prague and with Szabelski and Lutoslawski in Warsaw (1960–65); was manager of the music dept. of the radio at Košice (1965–68); then was a dramaturgist for the television studio in Bratislava. He occasionally uses jazz elements.

WORKS: Television opera, *Margita a besné* (*Margaret and the Wild;* 1972); *Cantiliniae* for Chamber Chorus (1961); *Canticum Zachariae* (1963); Concerto for Clarinet, Narrator, 4 Voices, and Percussion (1965); *Symfónia lásky* (*Symphony of Love*) for Narrator, Chorus, 3 Oboes, Horn, Double Bass, Piano, and Percussion (1965); *Requiem* for 3 Narrators, 3 Choruses, Brass, 6 Kettledrums, Percussion, and Organ (1966); Concerto for Cello and Chamber Orch. (1967); *Mša glagolskaja* (*Glagolitic Mass*) for Solos, Chorus, 2 Harps, 3 Oboes, Brass, Percussion, and Organ (1969); *Aliquoten* for Tape (1971); Nonet (1971); *Music per archi* (1971); *War and the World,*

poem for Baritone, Women's Chorus, Double Bass, Organ, and Chamber Orch. (1972); *Ballad-Fantasy* for Soprano, Piano, and Orch. (1972); *Burlesque* for Violin and Chamber Orch. (1972); *Elegies* for Narrator, Soprano, Chorus, and Chamber Orch. (Bratislava, Oct. 5, 1974); *Ballad* for 2 Clarinets (1974); 3 string quartets; other chamber music songs.

Salvayre, (Gervais-Bernard-) Gaston, French composer; b. Toulouse, June 24, 1847; d. St. Ague, near Toulouse, May 17, 1916. He was a pupil at the Cons. of Toulouse; then entered the Paris Cons., studying organ with Benoist and composition with Ambroise Thomas. After failing to win the Prix de Rome for 5 consecutive years, he finally obtained it in 1872 with the cantata *Calypso.* He was subsequently chorus master at the Opéra-Populaire in 1877.

WORKS: Operas: *Le Bravo* (Paris, April 18, 1877); *Richard III* (St. Petersburg, Dec. 21, 1883); *Egmont* (Paris, Dec. 6, 1886); *La Dame de Monsoreau* (Paris, Jan. 30, 1888); *Solange* (Paris, March 10, 1909); ballets: *Le Fandango* (Paris, Nov. 26, 1877); *La Fontaine des fées* (Paris, 1899); *L'Odalisque* (Paris, 1905); for Orch.: *Le Jugement dernier* (Paris, Dec. 3, 1876, under the title *La Résurrection*); *Ouverture symphonique* (Paris, March 22, 1874); *Air et Variations* for String Orch. (1877).

Salvi, Lorenzo, Italian tenor; b. Ancona, May 4, 1810; d. Bologna, Jan. 16, 1879. He made his debut at the Teatro San Carlo in Naples in 1830; then sang at La Scala in Milan (1839–42); during his tenure there, he created the title role in Verdi's *Oberto;* also the role of Riccardo in *Giorno di regno;* made guest appearances at Covent Garden in London (1847–50) and in N.Y.

Salvini-Donatelli, Fanny, Italian soprano; b. Florence, 1815; d. Milan, June 1891. She made her debut at the Teatro Apollo in Venice as Rosina in 1839; then sang throughout Italy; also appeared in Vienna (1842) and in London at Drury Lane (1858). She created Violetta in *La Traviata* in 1853 in Venice.

Salviucci, Giovanni, Italian composer; b. Rome, Oct. 26, 1907; d. there, Sept. 4, 1937. He studied with Respighi and Casella; developed a fine style of instrumental writing; his works were performed by Italian orchs. with increasing frequency, but his early death cut short his promising career. His *Ouverture* in C-sharp minor (1932) received a national prize.

WORKS: Symph. poem, *La tentazione e la preghiera* (1931); *Sinfonia italiana* (1932; Rome, Feb. 25, 1934); *Introduzione, Passacaglia e Finale* (1934); *Serenata* for 9 Instruments (1937); *Psalm of David* for Soprano and Chamber Orch. (Rome, 1935); *Alcesti,* after Euripides, for Chorus and Orch. (1937).

BIBLIOGRAPHY: F. Ballo, "Giovanni Salviucci," *Rassegna Musicale* (Jan. 1937); G. Arledler, *Prospettive critiche su Giovanni Salviucci* (Diss., Univ. of Bologna, 1974).

Salzedo (originally, **Léon Carlos Salzédo**), **Carlos,** eminent harpist and composer; b. Arcachon, France, April 6, 1885; d. Waterville, Maine, Aug. 17, 1961. He studied at the Cons. of Bordeaux (1891–94), winning first prize in piano; then entered the Paris Cons., where his father, **Gaston Salzédo,** was a prof. of singing; studied with Charles de Bériot (piano), gaining first prize in 1901, and with Hasselmans (harp), also receiving first prize. He began his career as a concert harpist upon graduation; traveled all over Europe (1901–5); was solo harpist of the Association des Premiers Prix de Paris in Monte Carlo (1905–9); in 1909 settled in N.Y.; was first harpist in the orch. of the Metropolitan Opera Co. (1909–13). In 1913 he formed the Trio de Lutèce (from Lutetia, the ancient name for Paris), with Georges Barrère (flute) and Paul Kéfer (cello). In 1921 he was co-founder, with Edgar Varèse, of the International Composers' Guild in N.Y., with the aim of promoting modern music; this organization presented many important contemporary works; in the same year he founded a modern music magazine, *Eolian Review,* later renamed *Eolus* (discontinued in 1933). He became an American citizen in 1923; was elected president of the National Assoc. of Harpists; held teaching positions at the Inst. of Musical Art in N.Y., and the Juilliard Graduate School of Music; organized and headed the harp dept. at the Curtis Inst. of Music in Philadelphia. In 1931 he established the Salzedo Harp Colony at Camden, Maine, for teaching and performing during the summer months. Salzedo introduced a number of special effects, and publ. special studies for his new techniques; designed a "Salzedo Model" harp, capable of rendering novel sonorities (Eolian Flux, Eolian chords, gushing chords, percussion, etc.). His own compositions are rhythmically intricate and contrapuntally elaborate and require a virtuoso technique.

WORKS: *Terres enchantées* for Orch., with Harp Solo (perf. under the title *The Enchanted Isle* by Salzedo with the Chicago Symph. Orch., Nov. 28, 1919); *5 Poetical Studies* for Harp Solo (1918); *3 Poems* for Soprano, 6 Harps, and 3 Wind Instruments (1919); *Bolmimerie* for 7 Harps (1919); *4 Preludes to the Afternoon of a Telephone* for 2 Harps (1921); *Sonata* for Harp and Piano (1922); *3 Poems by Mallarmé* for Soprano, Harp, and Piano (1924); Concerto for Harp and 7 Wind Instruments (N.Y., April 17, 1927, composer soloist); *Pentacle,* 5 pieces for 2 Harps (1928); *Préambule et Jeux* for Harp, 4 Wind Instruments, and 5 String Instruments (Paris, 1929); *Scintillation* for Harp Solo (1936); *Panorama,* suite for Harp Solo (1937); *10 Wedding Presents* for Harp Solo (1946–52); etc.; many transcriptions for harp of various works by Bach, Corelli, Rameau, Haydn, Brahms, etc. He publ. *Modern Study of the Harp* (N.Y., 1921); *Method for the Harp* (N.Y., 1929); *The Art of Modulating* (in collaboration with Lucile Lawrence; N.Y., 1950).

Salzer, Felix, distinguished Austrian-American theorist and pedagogue; b. Vienna, June 13, 1904. He studied theory and composition with Schenker and Weise; musicology with Guido Adler; in 1926 received his Dr.Phil. at the Univ. of Vienna; then taught at the New Vienna Cons.; emigrated to the U.S. in 1939; became a naturalized citizen in 1945. He was on the faculty of the Mannes College of Music in N.Y. (1940–56); in 1956 was appointed to the faculty of Queens College of the City Univ. of N.Y. He is a leading "Schenkerian" theorist and was instrumental in bringing the views of Heinrich Schenker to the attention of American musicians; his own contribution has been in the expansion and application of Schenker's concepts—previously restricted to a narrow range of tonal music—to Renaissance, medieval, and some 20th-century music. He publ. a number of important books on music theory: *Sinn und Wesen der abenländischen Mehrstimmigkeit* (Vienna, 1935); *Structural Hearing* (2 vols., N.Y., 1952; new ed., N.Y., 1962); *Counterpoint in Composition: The Study of Voice Leading* (with C. Schachter; N.Y., 1969); edited (with William Mitchell) *Music Forum* (N.Y., 1967—), a hardcover periodical.

Salzman, Eric, American composer and musicologist; b. New York, Sept. 8, 1933. He studied composition at Columbia Univ., with Otto Luening, Vladimir Ussachevsky, William Mitchell, and Jack Beeson (B.A., 1954), and at Princeton Univ. with Roger Sessions and Milton Babitt (M.F.A., 1956); in addition, he took courses in musicology with Oliver Strunk, Arthur Mendel, and Nino Pirotta. In 1957 he went to Europe on a Fulbright fellowship to study with Goffredo Petrassi in Rome; also attended courses of Karlheinz Stockhausen at Darmstadt. Returning to the U.S., he became a music critic for the *N.Y. Times* (1958–62) and for the *N.Y. Herald Tribune* (1963–66). He taught at Queens College in N.Y. (1966–68); then was director of "New Images of Sounds," a series of concerts given at Hunter College in N.Y. He founded the Quog Music Theater in 1970 with the aim of creating a new music theater for contemporary performing arts. In 1984 he was appointed editor of the *Musical Quarterly.* In his compositions he follows the most advanced techniques in mixed media.

WORKS: String Quartet (1955); Flute Sonata (1956); *Partita* for Solo Violin (1958); *Inventions* for Orch. (1959); *The Owl and the Cuckoo* for Soprano, Guitar, and Chamber Ensemble (1963); *Verses and Cantos* for 4 Voices and Instruments with electronic extensions (N.Y., Nov. 30, 1967); *Larynx Music,* magnetic tape piece for dance (1968); *Feedback,* "environment piece" for Magnetic Tape and Film (1968); *The Nude Paper Sermon* for Actor, Renaissance Consort, Chorus, and Electronics (1968–69); *The Conjurer,* multimedia spectacle (1975; with Michael Sahl); *Civilization and Its Discontents,* opera buffa for radio (N.Y., 1977; with Sahl); *Noah,* spectacle (N.Y., Feb. 10, 1978); *The Passion of Simple Simon* (N.Y., 1979); aleatory pieces for Electronic and Mixed Media under the general title *The Electric Ear,* for perf. at the Electric Circus in Greenwich Village in N.Y. He publ. *Twentieth Century Music: An Introduction* (Englewood Cliffs, N.J., 1967); also (with Sahl) a book on vernacular harmony, *Making Changes* (N.Y., 1976).

Samara, Spiro, Greek composer; b. Corfu, Nov. 29, 1861; d. Athens, March 25, 1917. He was a pupil of Enrico Stancampiano in Athens; later of Léo Delibes at the Paris Cons. He won considerable success with his first opera, *Flora mirabilis* (Milan, May 16, 1886), and devoted himself almost exclusively to dramatic compositions. Other operas were *Medgè* (Rome, 1888); *Lionella* (Milan, 1891); *La Martire* (Naples, May 23, 1894); *La Furia domata* (Milan, 1895); *Storia d'amore* (Milan, 1903; in Gotha, 1906, as *La Biondinetta*); *Mademoiselle de Belle-Isle* (Genoa, Nov. 9, 1905); *Rhea* (Florence, April 11, 1908); *La guerra in tempo di guerra* (Athens, 1914). He publ. *Scènes orientales,* suite for Piano, 4-hands; many pieces for piano solo; songs.

Samaroff, Olga (née **Hickenlooper**), American pianist and educator; b. San Antonio, Texas, Aug. 8, 1882; d. New York, May 17, 1948. She studied as a child with her mother and grandmother (Mrs. L. Grünewald, a former concert pianist); subsequently studied in Paris (with Delaborde), Baltimore (with Ernest Hutcheson), and Berlin (with Ernst Jedliczka). She made her concert debut in N.Y. (Jan. 18, 1905) with the N.Y. Symph. Society; appeared with other orchs. in the U.S. and Europe; gave joint recitals with Fritz Kreisler, Zimbalist, and other violinists. In 1911 she married **Leopold Stokowski;** they divorced in 1923. For 2 seasons she was music critic for the *N.Y. Evening Post* (1927–29); taught at the Juilliard Graduate School and at the Philadelphia Cons. of Music; from 1930, gave master courses in N.Y.; lectured extensively on music appreciation.
WRITINGS: *The Layman's Music Book* (N.Y., 1935); *The Magic World of Music* (N.Y., 1936); *A Music Manual* (N.Y., 1937); *An American Musician's Story* (N.Y., 1939; autobiography); *The Listener's Music Book* (N.Y., 1947; enlarged and revised ed. of *The Layman's Music Book*).
BIBLIOGRAPHY: *Notable American Women,* III (Cambridge, Mass., 1971).

Samazeuilh, Gustave, French composer; b. Bordeaux, June 2, 1877; d. Paris, Aug. 4, 1967. He studied music with Chausson and at the Schola Cantorum with Vincent d'Indy; also took some lessons from Paul Dukas. In his music he absorbed the distinct style of French Impressionism, but despite the fine craftsmanship of his work, performances were few and far between.
WORKS: For Orch.: *Etude symphonique* (1907); *Nuit* (Paris, March 15, 1925); *Naïades au soir* (Paris, Oct. 18, 1925); *L'Appel de la danse* (1946); for Orch., with Chorus: *Le Sommeil de Canope* (1908); *Chant d'Espagne* (Paris, Jan. 10, 1926); *Le Cercle des heures* (Paris, Feb. 17, 1934); String Quartet (1911); *Suite en trio* for Strings (1938); etc.; many transcriptions for piano of orch. works by d'Indy, Debussy, Franck, and Fauré. He was known also as a writer on musical subjects; publ. *Un Musicien français: Paul Dukas* (Paris, 1913; augmented ed., 1936); *Musiciens de mon temps: Chroniques et souvenirs* (Paris, 1947).

Saminsky, Lazare, Russian-American composer, conductor, and writer on music; b. Valegotsulova, near Odessa, Nov. 8, 1882; d. Port Chester, N.Y., June 30, 1959. He studied mathematics and philosophy at the Univ. of St. Petersburg; composition with Rimsky-Korsakov and Liadov, conducting with Nicolas Tcherepnin at the St. Petersburg Cons. (graduated, 1910). He emigrated to the U.S. in 1920, settling in N.Y.; in 1923 was a co-founder of the League of Composers; in 1924 was appointed music director of Temple Emanu-El in N.Y.; established an annual Three-Choir Festival there in 1936, presenting old and new music. In his compositions he followed the Romantic tradition; Hebrew subjects and styles play an important part in some of his music. He was married to an American writer, Lillian Morgan Buck, who died in 1945; in 1948 he married the American pianist **Jennifer Gandar.**
WORKS: Operas: *Gagliarda of a Merry Plague,* chamber opera (N.Y., Feb. 22, 1925); *The Daughter of Jephta* (1929); *Julian, the Apostate Caesar* (1923–38); 5 symphs.: No. 1, *Of the Great Rivers,* in "E-Frimoll" (free minor mode; Petrograd, Feb. 25, 1917, composer conducting; No. 2, *Symphonie des sommets* (1918; Amsterdam, Nov. 16, 1922); No. 3, *Symphony of the Seas* (Paris, June, 1925, composer conducting); No. 4 (Berlin, April 19, 1929, composer conducting); No. 5, *Jerusalem, City of Solomon and Christ,* with Chorus (1929–30; perf. many years later, N.Y., April 29, 1958); *Vigiliae,* symph. triptych (Moscow, Feb. 20, 1913, composer conducting); *Lament of Rachel,* suite from a ballet (Boston, March 3, 1922); *Litanies of Women* for Voice and Chamber Orch. (Paris, May 21, 1926); *Venice,* a "poem-serenade" for Chamber Orch. (Berlin, May 9, 1928); *Ausonia,* orch. suite (Florence, Feb. 24, 1935); *3 Shadows,* poems for Orch. (N.Y., Feb. 6, 1936); *Pueblo, A Moon Epic* (Washington, D.C., Feb. 17, 1937); *Stilled Pageant* for Orch. (Zürich, Aug. 1938); *Eon Hours,* suite of 4 rondos for 4 Voices and 4 Instruments (N.Y., Nov. 28, 1939); *Requiem,* in memory of Lillian M. Saminsky (N.Y., May 20, 1946); *A Sonnet of Petrarch* for 3 Voices and 3 Instruments (1947); *To a New World* for Orch. (1932; N.Y., April 16, 1951); several Hebrew services; piano pieces.
PUBLICATIONS: *Music of Our Day* (N.Y., 1932); *Music of the Ghetto and the Bible* (N.Y., 1934); *Living Music of the Americas* (N.Y., 1949); *Essentials of Conducting* (N.Y., 1958); *Physics and Metaphysics of Music and Essays on the Philosophy of Mathematics* (The Hague, 1957).
BIBLIOGRAPHY: *Lazare Saminsky, Composer and Civic Worker,* a collection of essays by Domenico de Paoli, Leigh Henry, L. Sabaneyev, Joseph Yasser, and Léon Vallas (N.Y., 1930); Wayne Shirley, *Modern Music ... Analytic Index,* ed. by W. and C. Lichtenwanger (N.Y., 1976; pp. 183–84).

Sammarco, (Giuseppe) Mario, Italian baritone; b. Palermo, Dec. 13, 1868; d. Milan, Jan. 24, 1930. He studied singing with Antonio Cantelli, making a successful debut in Palermo, 1888, in *Faust;* then sang in Brescia, Madrid, Lisbon, Brussels, Moscow, Warsaw, Berlin, and Vienna. After his London appearance as Scarpia in *Tosca* at Covent Garden (Oct. 19, 1905), he sang there every season until the outbreak of World War' I. He made his American debut as Tonio (Feb. 1, 1908) at the Manhattan Opera House in N.Y.; in 1910 joined the Chicago Opera Co. He sang in Russian, Spanish, Italian, French, and Eng. He retired from the stage in 1919.

Sammartini (San Martini), Giovanni Battista, significant Italian composer, younger brother of **Giuseppe Sammartini;** b. Milan, 1701; d. there, Jan. 15, 1775. He served as a church organist in Milan; in 1728 was appointed maestro di cappella at the Santissimo Entierro in Milan; in 1768 held a similar position at S. Gottardo. His historical significance lies not so much in his own music as in his authority as a teacher; Gluck was his student between 1737 and 1741. His own works are important mainly in the evolution of the sonata form, in which he introduced extensive thematic development; but the claim that he anticipated Haydn in the formulation of symph. form cannot be sustained; a chamber symph. in 4 movements, supposedly written by Sammartini in 1734 and often cited as the earliest work in symph. form, is apparently nonexistent. But Sammartini was a prodigiously industrious composer; among his works are 3 operas, of which 2 were produced in Milan: *L'ambizione superata dalla virtù* (1734) and *Agrippina* (1743); an oratorio, *Gesù bambino adorato;* about 20 symphs.; 6 trio sonatas for flute, 2 violins, and bass; string quartets; harpsichord sonatas; sacred and secular church music. Four symphs. were brought out by N. Jenkins (*Collegium musicum,* VI, New Haven, 1963); other symphs. were edited by B.D. Churgin (Harvard Publications in Music, vol. 1, *The Early Symphonies,* Cambridge, Mass., 1968); several concertos were brought out by H. Töttcher (Hamburg, 1968) and by H. Illy (Kassel, 1971).
BIBLIOGRAPHY: Fausto Torrefranca, "Le origini della Sinfonia," *Rivista Musicale Italiana* (1913); G. de Saint-Foix, "La Chronologie de l'œuvre instrumentale de Giovanni Sammartini," *Sammelbände der Internationalen Musik-Gesellschaft* (1914); R. Sondheimer, "G.B. Sammartini," *Zeitschrift für Musikwissenschaft* (1920); H.G. Mishkin, "5 Autograph String Quartets by G.B. Sammartini," *Journal of the American Musicological Society* (Summer 1953); idem, "The Published Instrumental Works of G.B. Sammartini," *Musical Quarterly* (1959); W.S. Newman, *The Sonata in the Classical Era* (Chapel Hill, N.C., 1963); N. Jenkins and B. Churgin, *Thematic Catalogue of the Works of G.B. Sammartini* (1976).

Sammartini (San Martini), Giuseppe, called "il Londinese" (because he lived in London), to distinguish him from his brother, **Giovanni Battista Sammartini;** b. Milan, Jan. 6, 1695; d. London, Nov. 1750. In 1727 he went to London; played the oboe at the King's Theatre; then became director of chamber music in the household of the Prince of Wales. He gave concerts with Arrigoni at Hickford's Rooms in 1732; Burney heard him play in 1744. He contributed a "sinfonia" and an aria to an oratorio, *La calumnia delusa* (1724), a pasticcio by several Italian composers. He further wrote sonatas for 2 flutes, 12 *concerti grossi,* 12 violin sonatas, 8 overtures, harpsichord pieces, etc. A sonata was edited by Riemann in his *Collegium musicum.*

Sammons, Albert Edward, English violinist and composer; b. London, Feb. 23, 1886; d. Southdean, Sussex, Aug. 24, 1957. He studied with his father and other teachers in London; began his professional career at the age of 11; made his solo debut in 1906. He was first violinist of the London String Quartet (1907–16); also concertmaster of the London Phil.; edited the Violin Concerto by Delius; composed a *Phantasy Quartet* for Strings and other works; taught violin at the Royal College of Music. He was made a Commander of the Order of the British Empire in 1944.

Samosud, Samuil, Russian opera conductor; b. Odessa, May 14, 1884; d. Moscow, Nov. 6, 1964. He conducted opera in Leningrad (1917–36); then moved to Moscow, conducting at the Bolshoi Theater (1936–43) and at the Stanislavsky Musical Theater (1943–50); also appeared as a symph. conductor.

Sampson, George, English organist and conductor; b. Clifton, July 24, 1861; d. Brisbane, Australia, Dec. 23, 1949. He studied with George Riseley and Harford Lloyd; was an organist at various churches in Bristol; in 1898, went to Australia; in 1907 he organized and conducted there the Sampson Orch., which later became the Queensland State and Municipal Orch. His works include a *Berceuse* for Organ and Strings, church music, and a *Romance* for Violin and Piano. He was also the author of *The Pianoforte; Rhythm; Elements of Music; Queensland Manual of Music; A Day with Felix Mendelssohn* (1910); *Seven Essays* (Cambridge, 1947).

Sams, Eric, English music critic; b. London, May 3, 1926. He was educated at Cambridge Univ.; became active in broadcasting and in musical journalism; contributed regularly to the *Musical Times;* publ. valuable monographs: *The Songs of Hugo Wolf* (London, 1961) and *Songs of Robert Schumann* (London, 1969; 2nd ed., 1975).

Samuel, Adolphe, Belgian composer; b. Liège, July 11, 1824; d. Ghent, Sept. 11, 1898. He was educated at the Cons. of Liège and the Brussels Cons., winning the Belgian Grand Prix de Rome (1845); taught harmony at the Brussels Cons. (1850–70); in 1871 was appointed director of the Ghent Cons. He founded the Brussels Popular Concerts in 1865; in 1869 organized the first annual musical festivals, with an orch. of 450 and a chorus of 1,200.
WORKS: 5 operas: *Il a rêvé* (1845); *Giovanni da Procida* (1848); *Madeleine* (1849); *Les Deux Préten-*

dants (1851); *L'Heure de la retrainte* (1852); 7 symphs.; overtures; string quartets; piano pieces; publ. *Cours d'harmonie pratique et de basse chiffrée; Livre de lecture musicale* (400 national airs).

BIBLIOGRAPHY: E.L.V. Mathieu, *Notice sur Adolphe Samuel* (1922).

Samuel, Gerhard, German-American conductor and composer; b. Bonn, April 20, 1924. He studied violin as a child; his family emigrated to America in 1938. He performed menial jobs as a dishwasher and shoe salesman in N.Y. before winning a scholarship at the Eastman School of Music in Rochester, N.Y.; there he studied conducting with Hermann Gerhard and composition with Howard Hanson (B.S., 1945); also played violin with the Rochester Phil. (1941–45). In 1945 he enrolled at Yale Univ., studying composition with Paul Hindemith (M.M., 1947); attended for 2 summers the conducting sessions with Koussevitzky at the Berkshire Music Center in Tanglewood. From 1949 to 1959 he was a violinist with and assistant conductor of the Minneapolis Symph. Orch.; from 1959 to 1970 he conducted the Oakland Symph. Orch.; then was associate conductor of the Los Angeles Phil. Orch. In 1976 he was appointed to the faculty of Cincinnati College. He composed a number of choral and symph. works in a fine modernistic idiom, inter alia, *12 on Death and No* for Tenor, Small Chorus, and Orch. (1968); *Looking at Orpheus Looking* for Orch. (1971); *To an End* for Chorus and Orch. (1972); *Into Flight From* for Orch. (1973); *Requiem for Survivors* for Orch. (1974).

Samuel, Harold, famous English pianist; b. London, May 23, 1879; d. there, Jan. 15, 1937. He studied at the Royal College of Music with Dannreuther (piano) and Stanford (composition); later was on its faculty. He was particularly distinguished as an interpreter of Bach; in 1921 gave 6 successive Bach recitals in London and a similar cycle in N.Y.; toured the U.S. regularly from 1924. He wrote a musical comedy, *Hon'ble Phil,* and some piano pieces.

Samuel-Rousseau, Marcel. See **Rousseau, Marcel.**

Sanborn, (John) Pitts, American music critic; b. Port Huron, Mich., Oct. 19, 1879; d. New York, March 7, 1941. He studied at Harvard Univ. (B.A., 1900; M.A., 1902); was music editor of the *N.Y. Globe* (1905–23), *N.Y. Evening Mail* (1924–31), and *N.Y. World Telegram* (from 1931). He publ. *Prima Donna—A Novel of the Opera* (London, 1929); *The Metropolitan Book of the Opera* (with Emil Hilb; N.Y., 1937); a pamphlet, *Beethoven and His Nine Symphonies* (1939); etc.

Sánchez de Fuentes, Eduardo, important Cuban composer and educator; b. Havana, April 3, 1874; d. there, Sept. 7, 1944. He studied music with Ignacio Cervantes and Carlos Anckermann. He occupied an influential position in the artistic affairs of Cuba; wrote 6 operas and many other works, but is known outside Cuba chiefly by his popular song *Tú,* which he publ. at the age of 18.

WORKS: Operas (all produced in Havana): *El Náufrago,* after Tennyson's *Enoch Arden* (Jan. 31, 1901); *Dolorosa* (April 23, 1910); *Doreya* (Feb. 7, 1918); *Kabelia,* to his own libretto after a Hindu legend (June 22, 1942); *Bocetos cubanos* for Orch., Women's Chorus, and Soprano Solo (Barcelona, 1922); *Temas del patio,* symph. prelude; songs (*Mírame así,* etc.); piano pieces; publ. *El Folk-lore en la música cubana* (1923); *Folklorismo* (1928); *Viejos ritmos cubanos* (1937); etc.

BIBLIOGRAPHY: O. Martínez, *Eduardo Sánchez de Fuentes: In Memoriam* (Havana, 1944); M. Guiral, *Un grand musicógrafo y compositor cubano: Eduardo Sánchez de Fuentes* (Havana, 1944); A. Carpentier, *La música en Cuba* (Mexico, 1946; pp. 213–17).

Sandberg, Mordecai, American composer; b. Rumania, Feb. 4, 1897; d. North York, Ontario, Dec. 28, 1973. He studied in Vienna; from 1922 to 1938 he lived in Jerusalem; in 1940 emigrated to America. A musician of grandiose visions, he set out to write a musical score for the entire Bible, and composed a tetralogy, *Shelomo,* for Soloists, Chorus, and Orch.; other works are 2 oratorios: *Ruth* (N.Y., May 22, 1949) and *Ezkerah* (N.Y., April 22, 1952); 2 symphs.; chamber music and piano pieces.

Sandberger, Adolf, eminent German musicologist; b. Würzburg, Dec. 19, 1864; d. Munich, Jan. 14, 1943. He studied composition in Würzburg and Munich; musicology at the Univ. of Berlin, with Spitta; obtained his Dr.Phil. in 1887; in 1889 he was appointed custodian of the music dept. of the Munich Library; also lectured at the Univ. of Munich (1894–1930). He was editor of Denkmäler der Tonkunst in Bayern and of Breitkopf & Härtel's monumental edition of the complete works of Roland de Lassus. Sandberger was one of the most important teachers of musicology in Germany, who formulated the basic principles of contemporary musical bibliography. He was also a composer; he wrote an opera, *Ludwig der Springer;* 2 string quartets; Piano Trio; Violin Sonata; various piano pieces; choruses; songs. Among his writings were *Leben und Werke des Dichtermusikers Peter Cornelius* (Diss., Univ. of Berlin, 1887); *Beiträge zur Geschichte der bayerischen Hofkapelle unter Orlando di Lasso* (planned in 3 vols.; vol. I, 1894; vol. III, 1895; vol. II was not publ.); *Zur Geschichte des Haydnschen Streichquartetts* (1899); *Lasso und die geistigen Strömungen seiner Zeit* (Munich, 1926). His collected essays were issued in 3 vols.: I, Biography of Lassus (1921); II, Beethoven (1924); III, History of Opera (1934). A Sandberger Festschrift was publ. in his honor in 1918, edited by Kroyer; a 2nd Festschrift appeared in 1929.

BIBLIOGRAPHY: L. Schiedermair, "Adolf Sandberger," *Zeitschrift für Musikwissenschaft* (Jan. 1935); E.I. Luin, "In memoria di Adolf Sandberger,"

Rivista Musicale Italiana (1943; pp. 418–23).

Sandby, Herman, Danish cellist and composer; b. Kundby, near Holbaek, March 21, 1881; d. Copenhagen, Dec. 14, 1965. He studied cello with Hugo Becker and composition with Iwan Knorr in Frankfurt (1895–1900); gave concerts in Scandinavia, England, and Germany; in 1912 settled in America as first cellist of the Philadelphia Orch.; moved to N.Y. in 1916; returned to Denmark in 1930.
WORKS: Cello Concerto (Philadelphia, Feb. 5, 1916); *The Woman and the Fiddler,* symph. suite; 3 symphs. (1930, 1938, 1942); *Serenade* for Strings (1940); 3 string quartets; String Sextet; String Quintet; Piano Quintet; Piano Trio; etc.

Sanderling, Kurt, eminent German conductor; b. Arys, Sept. 9, 1912. He went to Russia after the advent of the Nazis, and conducted the Moscow Radio Orch. (1936–41) and the Leningrad Phil. (1941–60). He then was chief conductor of the (East) Berlin Symph. Orch. (1960–77). From 1964 to 1967 he was chief conductor of the Dresden State Opera. He also filled a number of engagements as a guest conductor in Western Europe and America.

Sanders, Paul F., Dutch composer; b. Amsterdam, Dec. 21, 1891. He studied with Sem Dresden and Willem Pijper; contributed to various Dutch publications; was co-founder (with Pijper) of the magazine *De Muziek;* in 1947 was N.Y. correspondent of Dutch newspapers.
WORKS: *Pierrot aan de lantaarn,* ballet for Recitation and Chamber Orch. (1923); *Rataplan,* ballet for Chamber Orch. (1925); *Mara* for Chorus and Orch.; String Quartet; Sonata for Solo Violin (1933); *Little Suite* for Piano, 4-hands; songs; etc. He publ. *De Piano* (Amsterdam, 1926); *Moderne Nederlandsche Componisten* (The Hague, 1933).

Sanders, Robert L., American composer; b. Chicago, July 2, 1906; d. Delray Beach, Fla., Dec. 26, 1974. He studied at the Bush Cons. of Music (later named Chicago Cons.; Mus.B., 1924; Mus.M., 1925); in 1925 went to Rome on a fellowship of the American Academy there, and studied composition with Respighi; later was in Paris, where he took lessons with Guy de Lioncourt. Returning to America in 1929, he joined the faculty of the Chicago Cons.; was also organist at the First Unitarian Church; from 1938 to 1947 he was dean of the School of Music at Indiana Univ. in Bloomington; from 1947 to 1973 taught at the Brooklyn College of Music. He wrote a number of orch. and other pieces, among them a choreographic suite for Orch., *Scenes of Poverty and Toil* (perf. under the title *The Tragic Muse,* Chicago, Jan. 30, 1936, composer conducting); 3 "little symphonies" (1939, 1954, 1963); Symph. in A (1954–55); *The Mystic Trumpeter* for Baritone, Speaker, Chorus, and Speaking Chorus, to texts by Walt Whitman (1941); *Song of Myself,* cantata, to words by Walt Whitman (Brooklyn, April 19, 1970); other choral works; chamber music; *Variations on an Original Theme* for Pipe Organ,

pedals only (1956).

Sanderson, Sibyl, American soprano; b. Sacramento, Calif., Dec. 7, 1865; d. Paris, May 15, 1903. She was educated in San Francisco, where her musical talent attracted attention; taken to Paris by her mother at the age 19, she studied at the Cons. with Massenet; also with Sbriglia and Mathilde Marchesi. Massenet was charmed with her voice and her person; wrote the leading part in *Esclarmonde* for her; she created it at the Opéra-Comique, on May 14, 1889; the role of Thaïs (Paris Opéra, March 16, 1889) was also written by Massenet for her. Other French composers were equally enchanted with her; Saint-Saëns wrote *Phryné* for her (1893). She made her American debut at the Metropolitan Opera in N.Y. as Manon (Jan. 16, 1895), but had little success with the American public. In 1897 she married a wealthy Cuban, Antonio Terry, who died in 1900.
BIBLIOGRAPHY: J. Massenet, *Mes Souvenirs* (Paris, 1912); T. Wilkins, in *Notable American Women,* III (Cambridge, Mass., 1971).

Sandi, Luis, Mexican composer; b. Mexico City, Feb. 22, 1905. He studied violin with Rocabruna (1923–30) and composition with Campa and Mejía (1925–31) at the National Cons. of Mexico City. He conducted a chorus at the Cons. (1922–35); in 1937 he founded the Coro de Madrigalistas and conducted it until 1965. He was a prof. of music in primary schools (1924–32) and chief of the Music Section of the Secretariat of Public Education (1933–65).
WORKS: 2 operas: *Carlota* (Mexico City, Oct. 23, 1948) and *La señora en su Balcón* (1964); 3 ballets: *Día de Difuntos* (*Day of the Dead,* 1938); *Bonampak* (1948; Mexico City, Nov. 2, 1951); *Coatlicue* (1949); *El venado* for Orch. (1932; Mexico City, Oct. 28, 1938); *Sonora* for Orch. (1933); *Suite banal* for Small Orch. (1936); *Norte* for Orch. (Mexico City, Aug. 15, 1941); Concertino for Flute and Orch. (1944); *Tema y Variaciones* for Orch. (1944); *Esbozos sinfónicos* (1951); *4 Miniatures* for Orch. (1952); *América,* symph. poem (1965); *Las Troyanas* for Chorus and Instruments (1936); *Gloria a los héroes,* cantata (1940); *La suave patria,* cantata (1951); String Quartet (1938); *La hoja de plata* for Instruments (1939); *Fátima,* suite for Guitar (1948); *Cuatro momentos* for String Quartet (1950); *Hoja de album* for Cello and Piano (1956); Cello Sonatina (1958); Quintet (1960); Sonatina for Solo Violin (1967); Violin Sonata (1969); *4 piezas* for Recorders (1977); numerous choruses; songs; piano pieces. He publ. a booklet, *De música y otras cosas* (Mexico City, 1969).
BIBLIOGRAPHY: Carlos Chávez, "Luis Sandi," *Nuestra Música* (July 1949); a list of works is found in vol. 14 of *Compositores de América* (Washington, D.C., 1968).

Sándor, Arpád, Hungarian pianist; b. Budapest, June 5, 1896; d. there, Feb. 10, 1972. He studied there with Bartók and Kodály at the Royal Academy, graduating in 1914; after several years in Berlin, he toured the U.S. as an accompanist in 1922; then returned to Germany, and wrote art criticism in the *Berliner Tageblatt*. In 1933 he settled permanently in the U.S.; was accompanist to Jascha Heifetz, Lily Pons, and other celebrated artists. He became an American citizen in 1943.

Sándor, György, Hungarian pianist; b. Budapest, Sept. 21, 1912. He studied at the Royal Academy of Music in Budapest with Bartók (piano) and Kodály (composition). After a series of concerts in Europe (1930–38), he settled in the U.S. in 1939; was soloist in the premiere of Bartók's posthumous Piano Concerto No. 3, with the Philadelphia Orch. (Feb. 8, 1946); traveled in Australia in 1951. He made brilliant transcriptions of several modern orch. works, including *L'Apprenti sorcier* by Paul Dukas; also publ. *On Piano Playing: Motion, Sound, and Expression* (N.Y., 1981).

Sandoval, Miguel, pianist, conductor, and composer; b. Guatemala City, Nov. 22, 1903; d. New York, Aug. 24, 1953. He settled in the U.S. in 1925; was active as a conductor and pianist; wrote a symph. poem, *Recueridos en un paseo,* and publ. numerous piano works and songs in a Latin American vein.

Sandström, Sven-David, Swedish composer; b. Motala, Oct. 30, 1942. He studied general subjects at Stockholm Univ. (1963–67); attended theory classes with Lidholm at the State College of Music (1968–72); also took special courses in advanced techniques of composition with Nørgaard and Ligeti. In 1980 he joined the faculty of the State College of Music in Stockholm. In his own works he pursues the techniques of enhanced serialism, making use of fractional tones and occasionally resorting to aleatory procedures; some of his applications are aggressively oxymoronic and deliberately offensive; thus, his *Requiem,* dedicated to the memory of child victims of war and racism, has a text in Swedish and English by the poet Tobias Berggren, replete with sadistic obscenities and pornographic proclamations.
WORKS: FOR THE STAGE: Church opera, *Stark såsom döden (Strong like Death),* after B.V. Wall (Stockholm, April 18, 1978); chamber opera, *Hasta o älskade brud (Hasta, O Beloved Bride,* 1978); music drama *Kejsaren Jones (Emperor Jones),* after O'Neill's play (1980); incidental music for *Ett drömspel (The Dreamplay),* after Strindberg, for Chorus, Brasses, Percussion, Organ, and String Quartet (1980).
FOR ORCH.: *Bilder (Pictures)* for Percussion and Orch. (Norrköping, April 17, 1969); *Intrada* for Wind Instruments, Strings, and Percussion (1969); *17 Bildkombinationen (17 Picture Combinations)* for Wind Instruments, Percussion, and Strings (1969); *In the Meantime* for Chamber Orch. (1970); *Sounds* for 14 Strings (1970); *To You* (Arvika, Aug. 15, 1970); *Around a Line* for Wind Instruments, Piano, Percussion, and Strings (1971); *Through and Through* (1972; Stockholm, Feb. 1, 1974); *Con tutta forza* for 41 Wind Instruments and 6 Percussionists

(Stockholm, Oct. 28, 1976); *Culminations* (Swedish Radio, Feb. 22, 1977); *Agitato* for Piano and Orch. (1978); *The Rest Is Dross* for String Orch. (1979); Flute Concerto (1980; Stockholm, Oct. 24, 1983); Guitar Concerto (Malmö, May 18, 1983).
CHAMBER MUSIC: *Music* for 5 String Instruments (1968); Sonata for Flute Solo (1968); *Combinations* for Solo Clarinet (1960); *Concertato* for Clarinet, Trombone, Cello, and Percussion (1969); String Quartet (1969); *Disturbances* for 6 Brasses (1970); *Disjointing* for Solo Trombone (1970); *Jumping Excursions* for Clarinet, Cello, Trombone, and Cymbal (1970); *Mosaic* for String Trio (1970); *Under the Surface* for 6 Trombones (1971); *Concentration* for 8 Wind Instruments and 4 Double Basses (1971); *Closeness* for Solo Clarinet (1973); *... And All the Flavors Around,* 6 pieces for Violin, Piano, Clarinet, and Flute (with variable accompaniment; 1973); *6 Character Pieces* for Flute, Oboe, Bassoon, 2 Violins, Double Bass, and Percussion (1973); *Convergence* for Solo Bassoon (1973); *Inside* for Bass Trombone and Piano (1974); *Metal, Metal* for 4 Percussionists (1974); *In the Shadow of ...* for Piano, Cello, and Percussion (1974); *Ratio* for Tuba and Bass Drum (1974); *Utmost* for Wind Quintet, Trumpet, Trombone, Tuba, and Percussion (1975; London, Nov. 10, 1975, Pierre Boulez conducting); *Effort* for Solo Cello (1977); *Break This Heavy Chain That Does Freeze My Bones Around* for 2 Bassoons (1979); *Within* for 8 Trombones and ad lib Percussion (1979); *Drums* for Timpani and 4 Percussionists (1980).
FOR VOICE: *Invention* for 16 Voices (1969); *Lamento* for 3 Choral Groups and 4 Trombones (1971); *Visst?* for Soprano, 2 Choruses, Wind Instruments, Pop Orch., and Violin Group (1971; Mellerud, April 23, 1972); *Just a Bit* for Soprano, Bassoon, Violin, and Harp (1972); *Birgitta-Music I* for Speaking and Singing Groups, Orch., Renaissance Ensemble, Organ, and Folk Musicians and Dancers (Vadstena, June 23, 1973); *Dilecte mi (Canticum canticorum),* motet for Female Choir and Male Choir (1974); *Expression* for Amplified Mezzo-soprano, Cello, Piano, 4-hands, and Tape (1976); *A Cradle Song/The Tyger,* 2 poems after Blake, for Chorus a cappella (1978); *Spring—Introduction—Earth's Answer,* 3 poems after Blake, for Chorus a cappella (1978); *Tystnaden (Silence)* for Tenor, Narrator, and 14 String Instruments (1979); *Requiem: De ur alla minnen fallna (Requiem: Mute the Bereaved Memories Speak)* for 4 Soloists, Mixed Chorus, Children's Chorus, Orch., and Tape (1979; Stockholm, Feb. 19, 1982); *Agnus Dei* for Chorus a cappella (1980).
FOR PIANO: *Concentration II* for 2 Pianos (1972); *High Above* (1972); *5 Duets* for One Piano (1973). FOR ORGAN: *The Way* (1973); *Openings* (1975); *Libera me* (1980).

Sandt, Maximilian van de, Dutch pianist and composer; b. Rotterdam, Oct. 18, 1863; d. Cologne, July 14, 1934. He was a pupil of Liszt in the last year of the master's life; toured in Europe with conspicuous success; was on the faculty of the Cons. of Cologne (1896–1906); from 1910 taught at Bonn. He composed many brilliant piano pieces in a Romantic vein.

Sandvik, Ole Mörk, Norwegian musicologist; b. Hedemarken, May 9, 1875; d. Holmenkollen, near Oslo, Aug. 5, 1976, at the age of 101. He studied theology; taught liturgy at the Theological Seminary of the Univ. of Oslo (1916–45). He continued his activities as a writer and lecturer, working at the Oslo Library on various research projects until a very old age.

WRITINGS: *Norsk kirkemusic* (1918); *Folkemusikk i Gudbrandsdalen* (1919; 2nd ed., 1948); *Norsk folkemusikk* (1921); *Norges musikkhistorie* (1921, with G. Schjelderup); *Norsk koralhistorie* (1930); *Østerdalsmusikken* (1943); *Gregoriansk sang* (1945); a centennial biography of Agathe Backer-Gröndahl (1948); a monograph on L.M. Lindeman (1950); he compiled the Gradual for the Norwegian Church; publ. albums of regional folk songs; etc. A symposium of articles in his honor was publ. on the occasion of his 70th birthday (Oslo, 1945).

Sanford, Harold Bryant, American conductor and arranger; b. Florence, Mass., Sept. 5, 1879; d. Springfield, Mass., Jan. 19, 1945. He studied violin with Emil Mollenhauer in Boston, and theory with Goetschius; was employed as a violinist, conductor, and arranger by Victor Herbert in N.Y. (1906–24); conducted recordings for various phonograph companies; also on the radio.

Sanford, Samuel Simons, American pianist; b. Bridgeport, Conn., 1849; d. New York, June 6, 1910. He studied with William Mason; in 1868 went to Europe, where he took lessons with Anton Rubinstein, who had a high opinion of Sanford's abilities. However, Sanford did not undertake a pianistic career; in 1894 he became a prof. of applied music at Yale Univ., developing the music dept. in collaboration with Horatio Parker.

Sangiovanni, Antonio, celebrated Italian singing teacher; b. Bergamo, Sept. 14, 1831; d. Milan, Jan. 6, 1892. He studied at the Cons. of Milan; in 1854 was appointed prof. of singing there, and acquired considerable fame as a builder of voices. Two generations of Italian and foreign singers were his pupils.

Sanjuán, Pedro, Spanish composer and conductor; b. San Sebastian, Nov. 15, 1886; d. Washington, D.C., Oct. 18, 1976. He studied composition with Turina; after conducting in Europe, he went to Havana, where he organized the Havana Phil. (1926); was also a teacher of composition there; Roldán, Caturla, and other Cuban composers were his pupils. In 1932 he went back to Spain; was in Madrid in 1932–36; from 1939 until 1942, he was again conductor of the Havana Phil.; in 1942 was appointed prof. of composition at Converse College in Spartanburg, S.C.; became an American citizen in 1947.

WORKS: *Rondo fantástico* (Havana, Nov. 29, 1926); *Castilla,* suite for Orch. (Havana, June 12, 1927); *Sones de Castilla* for Small Orch.; *La Macumba,* a "ritual symphony" (St. Louis, Dec. 14, 1951, composer conducting); *Antillean Poem* for Band (N.Y., Aug. 11, 1958, composer conducting); *Symphonic Suite* (Washington, D.C., May 9, 1965); choral works; piano pieces.

Sankey, Ira David, American composer of gospel songs and evangelical singer; b. Edinburgh, Pa., Aug. 28, 1840; d. Brooklyn, Aug. 13, 1908. As a youth of 17, he became choir leader in the Methodist Church of New Castle, Pa.; served for a year with the N.Y. 12th Infantry Regiment at the time of the Civil War. In 1870 he was a delegate to the YMCA convention at Indianapolis, where his forceful singing attracted the attention of the evangelist preacher Dwight L. Moody. He joined Moody as music director and remained at this post for some 30 years, until approaching blindness forced his retirement in 1903. Of his many gospel tunes, the most popular has proved to be *The Ninety and Nine,* which he improvised at a moment's notice during a service in Edinburgh, Scotland. His chief publications were *Sacred Songs and Hymns* (London, 1873) and 6 vols. of *Gospel Hymns* issued between 1875 and 1891. He also publ. *My Life and the Story of the Gospel Hymns and of the Sacred Songs and Solos* (Philadelphia, 1907). He is not to be confused with another gospel song writer, Ira Allan Sankey, a lesser light than Ira David Sankey.

BIBLIOGRAPHY: E.J. Goodspeed, *A Full History of the Wonderful Career of Moody and Sankey, in Great Britain and America* (1876; reprint, N.Y., 1971); G.C. Stebbins, *Reminiscences and Gospel Hymn Stories* (N.Y., 1924; reprint, N.Y., 1971); R.G. McCutchan, *Our Hymnody* (N.Y., 1937).

San Martini. See **Sammartini.**

Sanromá, Jesús María, brilliant Puerto Rican pianist; b. Carolina, Puerto Rico (of Catalonian parents), Nov. 7, 1902. At the age of 14 he was sent to the U.S. by the governor of Puerto Rico; studied piano with Antoinette Szumowska at the New England Cons.; in 1920, won the Mason & Hamlin piano prize; then went to Europe, where he studied with Alfred Cortot (in Paris) and Artur Schnabel (in Berlin); from 1926 till 1944 he was pianist of the Boston Symph. Orch.; taught at the New England Cons.; gave annual concerts in the U.S., Canada, and South America; also played in Europe. In 1951 he was appointed chairman of the music dept. at the Univ. of Puerto Rico. He excels particularly in the works of modern composers, and has given several world premieres of contemporary concertos (by Hindemith, etc.).

BIBLIOGRAPHY: E.S. Belava, *El Niño Sanromá* (San Juan, Puerto Rico, 1952).

San Sebastián, Padre José Antonio de. See **Donostia, Jose Antonio de.**

Santa Cruz (Wilson), Domingo, foremost Chilean composer; b. La Cruz, near Quillota, July 5, 1899. He studied jurisprudence at the Univ. of Chile; then entered diplomatic service; was 2nd secretary of the Chilean legation in Spain (1921–24); received his musical training with Enrique Soro in Santiago and with Conrado del Campo in Madrid. Returning to Chile, he devoted himself to musical administration, teaching, and composition; in 1928 he became a prof. at the National Cons. in Santiago, and was dean of the faculty of fine arts at the Univ. of Chile in 1933–51 and again in 1962–68. His role in the promotion of musical culture in Chile was of great importance; he traveled in Europe and the U.S. as a lecturer. In his works he follows the cosmopolitan traditions of neo-Classical music, and made use of identifiable Chilean melodies in but a few of his compositions.

WORKS: *Cantata de los rios de Chile* for Chorus and Orch. (Santiago, Nov. 27, 1942); *5 piezas breves* for String Orch. (Santiago, May 31, 1937); *Variaciones* for Piano and Orch. (Santiago, June 25, 1943); *Sinfonia concertante* for Flute, Piano, and Strings (Santiago, Nov. 29, 1945); Symph. No. 1 for Strings, Celesta, and Percussion (Santiago, May 28, 1948); Symph. No. 2 for Strings (Santiago, Nov. 26, 1948); *Egloga* for Soprano, Chorus, and Orch. (Santiago, Nov. 24, 1950); *Cantares de la Pascua* for Chorus a cappella (Santiago, Dec. 7, 1950); *Canciones del mar,* song cycle (1955); *Endechas* for Tenor and 8 Instruments (1957); 3 string quartets; Symph. No. 3, with Contralto Solo (Washington, D.C., May 9, 1965); Symph. No. 4 (1968); *Oratorio Ieremieae prophetae* (1969); many songs and choruses; piano pieces.

BIBLIOGRAPHY: Otto Mayer-Serra, *Música y músicos de latinoamérica* (Mexico City, 1947; vol. 2, pp. 892–99); special issue of the *Revista Musical Chilena* (Dec. 1951); Vicente Salas Viú, *La creación musical en Chile 1900–1951* (Santiago, 1951; pp. 367–422).

Santa María, Fray Tomás de, important Spanish organist and composer; b. Madrid, c.1510; d. Ribadavia, 1570. He publ. *Libro llamado Arte de tañer fantasía* (Valladolid, 1565), a treatise on playing fantasias on keyboard instruments and on the guitar or lute (German trans., with critical and biographical introduction, by E. Harich-Schneider and R. Boadella, Leipzig, 1937).

BIBLIOGRAPHY: F. Pedrell, *Hispaniae schola musica sacra* (vol. 6); Villalba, *Antología de organistas clásicos españoles,* I; O. Kinkeldey, *Orgel und Klavier in der Musik des 16. Jahrhunderts* (Leipzig, 1910; with musical examples); H. Collet, *Le Mysticisme musical espagnol au XVIᵉ siècle* (Paris, 1913); J. Bonnet, *Historical Organ Recitals,* VI (1940); G. Reese, *Music in the Renaissance* (N.Y., 1954); W. Hultberg, *Sancta Maria's "Libro llamado Arte de tañer fantasia": A Critical Evaluation* (Diss., Univ. of Southern Calif., 1964).

Santana, Carlos, Mexican-American guitarist; b. Jalisco, July 20, 1947. He took up clarinet and violin, switching to guitar at 14. In 1962 the family moved to San Francisco. In 1967 he formed The Santana Blues Band, and played the honky-tonk circuit. His appearance at the Woodstock Festival in 1969 was marked by a performance of a long, specially composed work, *Soul Sacrifice,* for band, which mesmerized the multitudes assembled there. His album *Abraxas* included the Latin American hits *Samba Pa Ti* and *Oye Como Va* by Tito Puente, and Peter Green's *Black Magic Woman.* The band began to disintegrate in 1972, when Santana saw the light in the bearded visage of a traveling guru, went berserk, and assumed the pseudo-Hindu name Devadip. He found other converts to the new faith among disenchanted Americans, but by 1976 returned to his Latin roots and put out several successful albums, including the hit *She's Not There,* and culminating with the exclamatory *Zebop!* in 1981.

Santelmann, William Henry, German-American violinist and band conductor; b. Offensen, Sept. 24, 1863; d. Washington, D.C., Dec. 17, 1932. He studied at the Leipzig Cons.; in 1887 settled in America; played the baritone in the U.S. Marine Band in Washington (1887–95); was its conductor from 1898 until 1927, when he retired. He wrote the suite *Pocahontas* for Band; marches and dances; made numerous transcriptions.

Santi, Padre Angelo de, Italian Jesuit priest and music scholar; b. Trieste, July 12, 1847; d. Rome, Jan. 28, 1922. He took a leading part in the reform of Catholic church music, his views being embodied in the *Motu proprio* of Pius X on sacred music (1903). He founded the Schola Cantorum of the Vatican Seminary. He publ. *Il Maestro Filippo Capocci e le sue composizioni per organo* (1888); *L'origine delle feste natalizie* (1907); also articles in *Rassegna Gregoriana,* etc.

Santi, Nello, Italian conductor; b. Adria, Sept. 22, 1931. He studied in Padua; made his debut at the Opera there in 1951; then made appearances at many of the opera houses in Italy; also conducted at Covent Garden in London and at the Metropolitan Opera in N.Y.; subsequently made appearances at the major houses in Germany and Austria. In 1958 he was appointed a regular conductor at the Zürich Opera.

Santini, Abbate Fortunato, Italian music scholar and composer; b. Rome, Jan. 5, 1778; d. there, Sept. 14, 1861. He was noted as the collector of one of the finest music libraries ever formed; was ordained priest in 1801; as early as 1820 he publ. a catalogue of the MSS then in his possession, *Catalogo della musica antica, sacra e madrigalesca,* listing 1,000 titles by more than 700 composers. His original compositions include a Requiem; a *Stabat Mater;* many motets.

BIBLIOGRAPHY: V. Stassov, *L'Abbé Santini et sa collection musicale à Rome* (Florence, 1854; biography and summary of Santini's own catalogue); Mendelssohn's *Reisebriefe* (Leipzig, 1861; 5th ed., 1882; Eng. trans. by Lady Wallace as *Letters from Italy and Switzerland,* London, 1862); J. Killing,

Kirchenmusikalische Schätze der Bibliothek des Abbate F. Santini (Düsseldorf, 1910); K. Fellerer, "Verzeichnis der kirchenmusikalischen Werke der santinischen Sammlung," *Kirchenmusikalisches Jahrbuch* (Regensburg, 1931).

Santini, Gabriele, Italian conductor; b. Perugia, Jan. 20, 1886; d. Rome, Nov. 13, 1964. He studied in Perugia and Bologna; then conducted opera in Rio de Janeiro, Buenos Aires, N.Y., and Chicago. From 1925 to 1929 he was Toscanini's assistant at La Scala in Milan; conducted at the Rome Opera from 1944 to 1947; his active career continued for many years.

Santley, Sir Charles, English baritone; b. Liverpool, Feb. 28, 1834; d. Hove, near London, Sept. 22, 1922. He studied with Nava in Milan; then with Garcia in London; made his professional debut as Adam in Haydn's *Creation* on Nov. 16, 1857. His stage debut was in Pavia in 1857 as Dr. Grenville in *La Traviata;* his Covent Garden debut, on Oct. 1, 1859, was as Hoël in *Dinorah;* he remained at Covent Garden until 1863; joined the Carl Rosa Co. in 1875, and toured with it for several years; visited America in 1871 and 1891, and Australia in 1889–90. In 1887 he was made a Commander of the Order of St. Gregory by Pope Leo XIII; in 1907, was knighted. His songs were publ. under the pseudonym **Ralph Betterton;** he also publ. *Student and Singer* (London, 1892; a vol. of reminiscences); *The Singing Master* (2 parts, London, 1900); *The Art of Singing and Vocal Declamation* (London, 1908); *Reminiscences of My Life* (London, 1909).
BIBLIOGRAPHY: J.J.M. Levien, *Sir Charles Santley* (London, 1930).

Santoliquido, Francesco, Italian composer; b. San Giorgio a Cremano, Naples, Aug. 6, 1883; d. Anacapri, Italy, Aug. 26, 1971. He studied at the Santa Cecilia in Rome; graduated in 1908; in 1912 he went to live in Hammamet, a village in Tunisia, spending part of each year in Rome; in 1933 made his home in Anacapri. Many of his compositions contain melodic inflections of Arabian popular music.
WORKS: Operas: *La Favola di Helga* (Milan, Nov. 23, 1910); *Ferhuda* (Tunis, Jan. 30, 1919); *La Bajadera dalla maschera gialla* (Rome, 1923); *La porte verde,* musical tragedy in 4 acts (Bergamo, Oct. 15, 1953); for Orch.: *Crepuscolo sul mare* (Nuremberg, Jan. 19, 1909, composer conducting); *Il profumo delle oasi sahariane* (Tunis, April 17, 1918; also in Rome, March 5, 1922); *Acquarelli* (Rome, April 11, 1923); Symph. in F (1924); *La sagra dei morti,* heroic elegy for the victims of World War I (Rome, 1929); *3 miniature per i piccoli* (1933); *Preludio e Burlesca* for String Orch. (Rome, 1938); *Alba di gloria,* symph. prelude (Rome, Nov. 13, 1940); *Grotte di Capri,* 5 pieces for Orch. (1943); *Santuari asiatici,* symph. sketches (Naples, 1952); String Quartet; Violin Sonata; *Aria antica* for Cello and Piano; *Chiarità lunare* for Violin and Piano; *2 pezzi* for 5 Wind Instruments; *Piccola ballata* for Piano; *2 Acquaforti tunisine* for Piano; a cycle of songs to words by Pierre Louys; *Messa facile* for Chorus; publ. *Il Dopo-Wagner; Claudio Debussy e Richard Strauss* (Rome, 1909); also books of verse; wrote short stories in Eng.

Santoro, Claudio, important Brazilian composer and conductor; b. Manáos, Nov. 23, 1919. He studied at the Cons. of Rio de Janeiro and later in Paris with Nadia Boulanger. Returning to Brazil, he taught music in various schools; conducted concerts in South America and Europe, including Russia. He wrote music in an advanced idiom as a youth, mostly in the 12-tone style; but later he decided to compose works accessible to the masses, and this attitude was strengthened by his acceptance of the Russian tenets of socialist realism in art; however, he returned to the avant-garde type of composition (including aleatory practices) in his music of the 1960s. In 1970 he went to Germany and became a prof. of composition at the Hochschule für Musik in Heidelberg; he returned to Brazil in 1978.
WORKS: Ballets: *A fábrica (The Factory;* 1947); *Anticocos* (1951); *O café* (1953); *Icamiabas* (1959); *Zuimaaluti* (1960); *Prelúdios* (1962); *Ode to Stalingrad* for Chorus and Orch. (1947); 8 symphs.: No. 1 (1940); No. 2 (1945); No. 3 (Rio de Janeiro, Dec. 20, 1949); No. 4, *Da paz (Symphony of Peace;* Rio de Janeiro, Oct. 30, 1945); No. 5 (Rio de Janeiro, March 28, 1956); No. 6 (Paris, May 1, 1963); No. 7, *Brasilia* (1960); No. 8 (1963); *Variations on a 12-tone Row* for Orch. (1945); *Chôro* for Saxophone and Orch. (Rio de Janeiro, June 20, 1952); *Ponteio* for String Orch. (Rio de Janeiro, June 19, 1945); *Abertura tragica* for Orch. (1958); 2 violin concertos (1951, 1958); 3 piano concertos (1953, 1959, 1960); Cello Concerto (1961; Washington, D.C., May 12, 1965); 7 string quartets (1943–65); 5 violin sonatas (1940–57); 4 cello sonatas (1943–63); String Trio (1941); Flute Sonata (1941); Oboe Sonata (1943); Trumpet Sonata (1946); *Diagrammas cíclicos* for Piano and Percussion (1966); 6 pieces for various Instruments, entitled *Mutations* (1968–72); *Antistruktur* for Harp and Cello (1970); 25 preludes for Piano (1957–63); oratorio, *Berlin, 13 de agôsto* for Narrator, Chorus, and Orch. (1962); *Agrupamento à 10* for Voice and Chamber Orch. (1966); *Aleatorius I–III,* in graphic notation (1967). For a list of works prior to 1963, consult vol. 9 of *Composers of America* (Washington, D.C., 1963).

Santos, (Jóse Manuel) Joly Braga, Portuguese composer; b. Lisbon, May 14, 1924. He studied composition with Luís de Freitas Branco at the Lisbon Cons. (1934–43), then conducting with Scherchen at the Venice Cons. (1948), electronic music at the Gavessano (Switzerland) Acoustic Experimental Stadium (1957–58) and composition with Mortari at the Rome Cons. (1959–60). He conducted the Oporto Radio Symph. Orch. (1955–59); in 1961 joined the staff, as conductor. His music represents a felicitous fusion of Portuguese Renaissance modalities and folk rhythms.
WORKS: 3 operas: radio opera, *Viver ou morrer* (*To Live or to Die,* 1952); *Mérope* (Lisbon, May 15, 1959); *Trilogia das Barcas* (1969; Lisbon, May, 1970);

3 ballets: *Alfama* (1956); *A nau Catrineta* (1959); *Encruzilhada* (1968); 3 symph. overtures (1945, 1947, 1954); 6 symphs.: No. 1 (1946); No. 2 (1948); No. 3 (1949); No. 4 (1950); No. 5, *Virtus Lusitaniae* (1966); No. 6, with Solo Soprano and Chorus (1972); *Nocturno* for String Orch. (1947); Concerto for String Orch. (1951); *Variações sinfónicas sobre un theme de l'Alentejano* (1952); Viola Concerto (1960); *Divertimento* for Chamber Orch. (1961); *3 esboços sinfónicos* (*3 Symphonic Sketches;* 1962); Sinfonietta for String Orch. (1963); *Double Concerto* for Violin, Cello, String Orch., and Harp (1965); *Variações concertantes* for String Orch. and Harp (1967); Piano Concerto (1973); *Variações* for Orch. (1976); *Requiem à memória de Pedro de Freitas Branco* for Soloists, Chorus, and Orch. (1964); *Ode à música* for Chorus and Orch. (1965); *Nocturno* for Violin and Piano (1942); 2 string quartets (1944, 1956); Violin Sonata (1945); Piano Quartet (1957); choruses.

Santucci, Marco, Italian composer; b. Camajore, Tuscany, July 4, 1762; d. Lucca, Nov. 29, 1843. He was Anfossi's successor (1797–1808) as maestro at S. Giovanni in Laterano, Rome; in 1808 was appointed canon at the Cathedral of Lucca. A motet *a* 16 for 4 choirs received a prize from the Accademia Napoleone in 1806 because of the "entirely new and original" combination of voices. Baini publ. an energetic protest against this award, pointing out that such polyphonic writing was common in works by Italian composers of the 16th and 17th centuries. Santucci also wrote masses, motets, Psalms, canons in up to 7 parts, symphs., organ sonatas, etc.; publ. the treatise *Sulla melodia, sull'armonia e sul metro* (1828).
  BIBLIOGRAPHY: G. Rinuccini, *Biografia di Marco Santucci* (Milan, 1851).

Sanz, Gaspar, Spanish 17-century guitarist; b. Calanda (Aragón). He studied at Salamanca Univ., taking degrees in theology and philosophy; became maestro to the Spanish Viceroy at Naples. He was guitar teacher to Don Juan of Austria, for whom he wrote an *Instrucción de música sobre la guitarra española* (Zaragoza, 1674; 2nd ed., 1697), containing examples of contemporary Spanish dance music and folk songs.
  BIBLIOGRAPHY: R. de Zayas, "Gaspar Sanz: A Transcription of His Complete Works for the Guitar," *Consort,* XXXI (1975).

Sanzogno, Nino, Italian conductor and composer; b. Venice, April 13, 1911; d. Milan, May 4, 1983. He studied composition with Malipiero in Venice; took conducting lessons with Scherchen in Brussels in 1935; after playing violin in a string quartet, he was appointed opera conductor at the Teatro La Fenice in Venice in 1937; he first conducted at La Scala in Milan in 1939; was a regular conductor there in succeeding years; also toured in South America. He became favorably known as an excellent conductor of modern opera in Italy; he also gave courses on conducting in Darmstadt. He composed a Viola Concerto, Cello Concerto, Octet for Strings and Woodwinds, and some orch. pieces.

Sapelnikov, Vasili, Russian pianist; b. Odessa, Nov. 2, 1867; d. San Remo, March 17, 1941. He was a pupil of L. Brassin and Sophie Menter at the St. Petersburg Cons.; in 1888, made his debut at Hamburg with Tchaikovsky's First Piano Concerto, under the composer's direction; then made tours throughout Europe; lived chiefly in Germany, also for a time in Florence; in 1916, returned to Russia, remaining there until 1922; from 1923, was again in Germany and Italy. He wrote an opera, *Der Khan und sein Sohn,* and pieces for piano (*Petite mazourka, Danse des elfes, Valse-Caprice, Impromptu, Solitude*).

Saperstein, David, American composer; b. New York, March 6, 1948. He studied at the Juilliard School of Music in N.Y.: took courses with Elliott Carter, Walter Piston, and Vincent Persichetti at the Dartmouth College Summer Sessions (1963–64), and with Milton Babbitt at Princeton Univ., receiving his A.B. degree there in 1969. His works, written in an advanced idiom, include Wind Quintet (1963); Duo for Violin and Percussion (1965); Brass Quartet (1966); *Etudes* for Piano (1967); *Variations* for 8 Instruments (1969); Sextet (1970).

Saperton, David, American pianist; b. Pittsburgh, Oct. 29, 1889; d. Baltimore, July 5, 1970. He received his first instruction on the piano from his grandfather, a former tenor at the Brünn Opera, while his father, a physician and former concert bass, superintended his theoretical studies. At the age of 10 he made his first public appearance with an orch. in Pittsburgh; in 1905 he gave a recital in N.Y.; in 1910–12, toured Germany, Austria, Hungary, Italy, Russia, and Scandinavia; then returned to the U.S.; in 1924, joined the piano faculty of the Curtis Inst. in Philadelphia.

Sapio, Romualdo, Italian singing teacher; b. Palermo, Sept. 8, 1858; d. New York, Sept. 22, 1943. He studied at the Palermo Cons.; made his debut as a conductor in Milan (1883); conducted Patti's tours of North and South America; also operatic and concert tours of Albani and Nordica; in 1892 settled in N.Y. as a teacher of singing; the same year he married the concert singer **Clementine de Vere.**

Saporiti, Teresa, Italian soprano; b. c.1763; d. Milan, March 17, 1869 (!). She was a member of Pasquale Bondini's Italian company and gave performances with it in Leipzig, Dresden, and Prague, often obliged to appear in male costume and take on castrati roles. The success of Bondini's production of *Le nozze di Figaro* in Prague in 1786 prompted him to request an opera from Mozart for the following year; the part of Donna Anna in *Don Giovanni* was written with Saporiti's voice in mind: the taxing coloratura in her aria in the 2nd act indicates that Mozart had a high opinion of her ability. Saporiti later appeared in Venice and at La Scala, in operas by Guglielmi and Bianchi. By 1795 she was prima buffa assoluta in Gennaro Astarita's company in St. Petersburg; sang in Astarita's own comic operas, as well as in revivals of Cimarosa's *Italiana in Londra* and Paisiello's *Il Barbiere di Siviglia*. She fell into total oblivion; if the dates of her life can be verified, she lived to the age of 105.

Sapp, Allen Dwight, American composer; b. Philadelphia, Dec. 10, 1922. After studying music with local teachers, he entered Harvard Univ., where he studied composition with Walter Piston and orchestration with E.B. Hill (A.B., 1942; A.M., 1949); he also did graduate work there with A.T. Davison, A.T. Merritt, and Randall Thompson; then attended classes of Aaron Copland and Nadia Boulanger in Cambridge, Mass. (1942–43). He subsequently had numerous teaching jobs: at Harvard Univ. (1949–58), Wellesley College (1958–61), the State Univ. of N.Y. at Buffalo (1961–76), and Florida State Univ. (1976–78). In 1978 he joined the faculty of the Univ. of Cincinnati. His music is cast in a neo-Classical idiom, with contrapuntal elements coalescing in a florid design.
WORKS: *The Double Image* for Orch. (1957); *The Septagon* for Orch. (1957); *Colloquies* for Piano and Orch. (1963); *Imaginary Creatures* for Harpsichord and Chamber Orch. (1981); *Colloquies IV* for Orch. (1983); *The Cheektowaga and Tonawanda Divisions* for Wind Orch. (1983); *Crennelations* for Tenor and Orch., after Ezra Pound's *Marvoil* (1982); *Illusions and Affirmations* for Bass Voice and Strings (1982). Chamber music: 4 violin sonatas (1943, 1949, 1960, 1981); 7 piano sonatas (1940, 1956, 1957, 1980, 1981, 1981); 4 string quartets (1951, 1981, 1981, 1982); Viola Sonata (1949); Piano Trio (1950); String Trio (1956); 3 piano sonatas, 4-hands (1944, 1981, 1981); *Nocturne* for Cello (1978); *Colloquies III* for Piano and 10 Wind Instruments (1982); *Colloquies II* for Piano, Flute, and Viola (1983); *The Companion of Sirius: The Serious Companion* for Tuba and Piano (1984).

Sárai, Tibor, Hungarian composer; b. Budapest, May 10, 1919. He studied composition with Pál Kadosa; taught at the Béla Bartók Cons. (1953–59) and at the Budapest Academy of Music. In his compositions he adheres to the national Hungarian tradition, enhanced by a free use of euphonious dissonances.
WORKS: Oratorio, *Variations on the Theme of Peace* (1961–64); *Serenade* for String Orch. (1946); *Tavaszi concerto (Spring Concerto)* for Flute, Viola, Cello, and String Orch. (1955); *6 Scenes* from the dance play "János vitéz" (1956–57); Symph. No. 1 (1965–67); Symph. No. 2, with Soprano Solo (1972–73); *Diagnosis '69* for Tenor and Orch. (1969); *Musica* for 45 Strings (1970–71); *Jövöt faggató ének (Future Questioning)* for Alto, Baritone, Male Chorus, and Orch. (1971); 2 string quartets (1958, 1971); *Lassú és friss* for Violin and Piano (1958); Quartet for Flute, Violin, Viola, and Cello (1961–62); *Studio* for Flute and Piano (1964); *De profundis*, solo cantata for Tenor and Wind Quintet (1968); Piano Sonatina (1959); *8 Small Piano Pieces* (1965).

Saran, Franz Ludwig, German writer on music; b.

Altranstädt, near Lützen, Oct. 27, 1866; d. Erlangen, April 24, 1931. He studied languages in Halle, Leipzig, and Freiburg; in 1896 he became an instructor in German language and literature at the Halle Univ.; in 1905, a prof.; from 1913, a prof. at the Univ. of Erlangen. His works having to do with music include revising and editing R. Westphal's *Aristoxenos von Tarent Melodik und Rhythmik* (2 vols., 1893) and editing and transcribing the famous Jena MS of *Minnelieder* (2 vols., with G. Holz and E. Bernoulli, 1901; vol. 2 includes a systematic treatise on the rhythm of medieval songs); he also publ. *Der Rhythmus des französischen Verses* (1904).

Sarasate, Pablo de (Pablo Martín Melitón Sarasate y Navascuez), celebrated Spanish violin virtuoso; b. Pamplona, March 10, 1844; d. Biarritz, Sept. 20, 1908. He studied at the Paris Cons. under Alard, taking first prize in the violin class in 1857, and a "premier accessit" in 1859. In 1866 he acquired a Stradivarius violin. His playing was noted for its extraordinary beauty of tone, impeccable purity of intonation, perfection of technique, and grace of manner; but his repertoire consisted almost exclusively of fantasies on operatic airs (mostly arranged by himself). Later his taste changed, and he turned to the masterpieces of violin literature. His tours, extending through all Europe, North and South America, South Africa, and the Orient, were an uninterrupted succession of triumphs. He bequeathed to his native city the gifts that had been showered upon him by admirers throughout the world; the collection was placed in a special museum. For him Saint-Saëns wrote his *Rondo capriccioso;* Lalo, his *Symphonie espagnole;* Bruch, the *Schottische Fantasie;* Mackenzie, the *Pibroch* suite. Sarasate's compositions, exclusively for violin, are pleasing and effective.
WORKS: For Violin and Orch., *Zigeunerweisen* (his best and most popular work); *Navarra* for 2 Violins; *Jota de San Fermín* for Orch.; Spanish dances for Violin and Piano; etc.
BIBLIOGRAPHY: M.L. van Vorst, "Sarasate," *Scribner's Magazine* (March 1896); Julio Altadill, *Memorias de Sarasate* (Pamplona, 1909); A. Hartmann, "The Perfect Virtuoso," *Musical America* (March 25, 1940); León Zárate, *Sarasate* (Barcelona, 1945); G. Woolley, "Pablo Sarasate: His Historical Significance," *Music & Letters* (July 1955); Angel Sagardia, *Pablo Sarasate* (Palencia, 1956).

Sargeant, Winthrop, American music critic; b. San Francisco, Dec. 10, 1903. He studied violin in San Francisco with Arthur Argiewicz and with Lucien Capet in Paris; took composition lessons with Albert Elkus in San Francisco and with Karl Prohaska in Vienna. He played the violin in the San Francisco Symph. Orch. (1922–24), in the N.Y. Symph. (1926–28), and in the N.Y. Phil. (1928–30). He then devoted himself to musical journalism; was on the editorial staff of *Musical America* (1931–34); was music critic of the *Brooklyn Daily Eagle* (1934–36); served as music editor of *Time* magazine (1937–39); also wrote essays on various subjects for *Time*

(1939–45); subsequently was roving correspondent for *Life* magazine (1945–49) and music critic for the *New Yorker* (1947–72); from 1972 reviewed records for it. He evolved a highly distinctive manner of writing: professionally solid, stylistically brilliant, and ideologically opinionated; he especially inveighed against the extreme practices of the cosmopolitan avant-garde. He publ. *Jazz: Hot and Hybrid* (N.Y., 1938; 3rd ed., N.Y., 1975); *Geniuses, Goddesses, and People* (N.Y., 1949); *Listening to Music* (N.Y., 1958); *In Spite of Myself: A Personal Memoir* (N.Y., 1970); *Divas: Impressions of Today's Sopranos* (N.Y., 1973).

Sargent, Sir (Harold) Malcolm (Watts), eminent English conductor; b. Stamford, Lincolnshire, April 29, 1895; d. London, Oct. 3, 1967. He studied organ at the Royal College of Organists in London; then was articled to Dr. Keeton, organist of Peterborough Cathedral (1912–14); served in the infantry during World War I. He made his first major conducting appearance on Feb. 3, 1921, in Leicester, leading the Queen's Hall Orch. of London in his own composition, *Allegro impetuoso: An Impression on a Windy Day.* He then went to London, where he conducted the D'Oyly Carte Opera Co. and Diaghilev's Ballets Russes; from 1928 he was conductor-in-chief of the Royal Choral Society. From 1929 to 1940 he was conductor of the Courtauld-Sargent Concerts in London. He toured Australia in 1936, 1938, and 1939, and Palestine in 1937. Later he was conductor-in-chief and musical adviser of the Hallé Orch. of Manchester (1939–42); then was principal conductor of the Liverpool Phil. Orch. (1942–48). In 1945 he made his American debut with the NBC Symph. Orch. in N.Y.; then made appearances in Europe, Australia, and Japan. He was knighted in 1947. From 1950 to 1957 he was chief conductor of the BBC Symph. Orch.; led this ensemble on several European tours. From 1948 to 1966 he also served as chief conductor of the London Promenade Concerts. He took the London Phil. Orch. on an extensive Far Eastern tour in 1962; also led the Royal Phil. Orch. to the Soviet Union and the U.S. in 1963. His performances of the standard repertoire were distinguished for their precision and brilliance; he championed the music of Elgar, Vaughan Williams, Walton, and other English composers throughout his career. A commemorative stamp with his portrait was issued by the Post Office of Great Britain on Sept. 1, 1980.

Sargon, Simon, American pianist and composer; b. Bombay, India, April 6, 1938, of mixed Sephardic, Russian-Jewish, and Indian parentage. He took private lessons with Mieczyslaw Horszowski; studied music theory at Brandeis Univ. (B.A., 1959) and composition with Vincent Persichetti at the Juilliard School of Music in N.Y. (M.S., 1962); also took a course with Darius Milhaud at the Aspen School of Music. He was subsequently active as a teacher at Sarah Lawrence College (1965–68); at the Rubin Academy of Music in Jerusalem (1971–74), where he served as head of the voice dept.; and synchronously at Hebrew Univ. in Jerusalem (1973–74). In 1974 he was appointed music director at Temple Emanu-El in Dallas, Texas.
WORKS: Chamber opera, *Thirst,* after a play of Eugene O'Neill (Jerusalem, Dec. 17, 1972); oratorio, *Not by Might,* based on the Books of the Maccabees (Dallas, Dec. 16, 1979); cantatas: *Elul: Midnight* (Dallas, Sept. 17, 1976); *Visions of Micah* (Dallas, April 30, 1980); *Flame of the Lord* (Dallas, May 31, 1977); a musical play for children, *A Voice Still and Small* (Dallas, Dec. 6, 1981); temple services; songs.

Sari, Ada (real name, **Jadwiga Szajerowa**), Polish soprano; b. Wadowice, near Cracow, June 29, 1886; d. Ciechocinek, July 12, 1968. She studied in Milan; after appearances in Rome, Naples, Trieste, and Parma, she joined the staff of the Warsaw Opera; made extensive tours in Europe, in South America, and in the U.S. Eventually she returned to Warsaw, devoting herself mainly to teaching.

Sárközy, István, Hungarian composer; b. Pesterzsébet, Nov. 26, 1920. He studied composition with Kodály, Farkas, and Viski at the Budapest Academy of Music; in 1959 was appointed to its faculty.
WORKS: Cantatas: *Ode to Stalin* (1949); *Julia Songs* (1958); *The Earthquake Approaches* (1958); comedy oratorio, *"Y" War,* for 10 Solo Voices, Vocal Quintet, and 8 Instruments (1971); *Concerto grosso* (1943–44; revised with an added subtitle, *Ricordanze I,* 1969); *Small Suite* for Orch. (1951); *Fantasy and Dance* for Gypsy Orch. (1952); *To Youth,* overture (1953); *Sinfonia concertante* for Clarinet and Orch. (1963); *Concerto semplice (Ricordanze II)* for Violin and Orch. (Budapest, Oct. 11, 1974); *12 Variations* for Piano (1945); Sonatina for 2 Pianos (1950); *Sonata da camera* for Flute and Piano (1964); *Ciaccona* for Solo Cello (1967); *Chamber Sonata* for Clarinet and Piano (1969); *Psaume et Jeu,* quartet for Wind Instruments (1970); *4 Etudes* for Solo Clarinet (1972); *Ricordanze III* for String Quartet (1977); scores of incidental music; songs.

Sarly, Henry, Belgian composer; b. Tirlemont, Dec. 28, 1883; d. Brussels, Dec. 3, 1954. He studied with his father and with Huberti, Tinel, Gilson, and Du Bois at the Brussels Cons.; in 1921 became inspector of musical education in Belgian schools. He composed a number of attractive pieces, among them *Scènes brabançonnes* for Orch.; Piano Quintet; *Poème* for Piano Trio; Violin Sonata; numerous piano pieces and songs. He also publ. a manual, *Cours théorique et pratique d'harmonie.*

Sarnette, Eric Antoine Joseph André, French inventor of musical instruments; b. Tarbes, Hautes-Pyrénées, Nov. 28, 1898. He studied at Marseilles, and later at the Paris Cons.; also took lessons with Adolphe Sax, the son of the inventor of the saxophone. He became interested in acoustical problems; was active on the staff of the French Radio; manufactured new musical instruments (the sax trumpet, alto clarinet, etc.); publ. *La Musique et le* *micro* (Paris, 1934) and *L'Orchestre moderne à la Radio* (Paris, 1940).

Saro, J. Heinrich, German bandmaster and composer; b. Jessen, Jan. 4, 1827; d. Berlin, Nov. 27, 1891. In 1859 he became a bandmaster in Berlin; in 1867 his band won the international competition at the Paris Exposition; in 1872 he was awarded a gold medal for his performance at the Boston Jubilee. He wrote a number of brilliant pieces of military music, and also some symph. works; publ. *Lehre vom musikalischen Wohlklang und Tonsatz* and *Instrumentationslehre für Militärmusik.*

Sarrette, Bernard, founder of the Paris Cons.; b. Bordeaux, Nov. 27, 1765; d. Paris, April 11, 1858. A captain in the national guard at Paris, he brought together, after the 13th of July, 1789, 45 musicians to form the nucleus of the Parisian band of the national guard. In 1790 the City of Paris assumed the expenses of this band, which was increased to 70 members, among them artists of distinction. In 1792 the financial embarrassments of the Commune led to the suspension of payment; but Sarrette held the band together and, with the aid of the municipality, established a free school of music employing all the members as teachers. From this school came the musicians employed in the 14 armies of the Republic. Its energetic principal had it converted into a national Inst. of Music, in a decree of Nov. 8, 1793; and it was definitely organized as the Paris Cons. in a decree of Aug. 3, 1795. Sarrette, having gained his end, assumed the captaincy of the 103rd Regiment; but the board of directors (5 inspectors and 4 profs.) proved so incompetent that he was recalled to the directorship of the Cons. in 1796. By introducing advanced methods of instruction and establishing the school of declamation, the concert hall, the grand library, etc., he raised the Cons. to an institution of the first rank. At the Restoration in 1814 he was deprived of his position; nor would he accept it after the revolution of 1830, not wishing to oust his friend Cherubini.
BIBLIOGRAPHY: Pierre Constant, *B. Sarrette et les origines du Conservatoire national de musique et de déclamation* (Paris, 1895).

Sarti, Giuseppe, noted Italian composer; nicknamed **"Il Domenichino";** b. Faenza, (baptized, Dec. 1) 1729; d. Berlin, July 28, 1802. He took music lessons in Padua with Valotti; when he was 10, he went to Bologna to continue his studies with Padre Martini. Returning to Faenza, he was organist at the Cathedral from 1748 to 1752; in 1752 he was appointed director of the theater in Faenza; that same year his first opera, *Pompeo in Armenia,* was performed. His next opera, *Il re pastore,* was staged in Venice in 1753 with great success. Toward the end of 1753 he went to Copenhagen as a conductor of Pietro Mingotti's opera troupe. His work impressed the King of Denmark, Frederik V, and in 1755 he was named court Kapellmeister. He subsequently was made director of the Italian Opera, but it was closed in 1763; he then was appointed director of

court music. In 1765 he was sent by the King to Italy to engage singers for the reopening of the Opera, but Frederik's death aborted the project. Sarti remained in Italy, where he served as maestro di coro at the Pietà Cons. in Venice (1766–67). In 1768 he returned to Copenhagen, where he resumed his duties as director of the royal chapel; from 1770 to 1775 he was conductor of the court theater. He then returned to Italy with his wife, the singer **Camilla Passi,** whom he had married in Copenhagen. He became director of the Cons. dell'Ospedaletto in Venice in 1775. In 1779 he entered the competition for the position of maestro di cappella at Milan Cathedral, winning it against a number of competitors, including Paisiello. By this time his prestige as a composer and as a teacher was very high. Among his numerous pupils was Cherubini. In 1784 he was engaged by Catherine the Great as director of the Imperial chapel in St. Petersburg. On his way to Russia he passed through Vienna, where he was received with honors by the Emperor Joseph II; he also met Mozart, who quoted a melody from Sarti's opera *Fra i due litiganti* in *Don Giovanni.* His greatest success in St. Petersburg was *Armida e Rinaldo* (Jan. 26, 1786), remodeled from an earlier opera, *Armida abbandonata,* originally performed in Copenhagen in 1759; the leading role was sung by the celebrated Portuguese mezzo-soprano Luiza Todi, but she developed a dislike of Sarti, and used her powerful influence with Catherine the Great to prevent his reengagement. However, he was immediately engaged by Prince Potemkin, and followed him to southern Russia and Moldavia during the military campaign against Turkey; on the taking of Ochakov, Sarti wrote an ode to the Russian liturgical text of thanksgiving, and it was performed in January 1789 at Jassy, Bessarabia, with the accompaniment of cannon shots and church bells. Potemkin offered him a sinecure as head of a singing school in Ekaterinoslav, but Sarti did not actually teach there. After Potemkin's death in 1791, his arrangements with Sarti were honored by the court of St. Petersburg; in 1793 Sarti was reinstated as court composer and was named director of a conservatory. Sarti's operas enjoyed considerable success during his lifetime but sank into oblivion after his death. He was an adept contrapuntist, and excelled in polyphonic writing; his *Fuga a otto voci* on the text of a *Kyrie* is notable. He was also astute in his adaptation to political realities. In Denmark he wrote singspiels in Danish; in Russia he composed a Requiem in memory of Louis XVI in response to the great lamentation at the Russian Imperial Court at the execution of the French king (1793). He also composed an offering to the Emperor Paul, whose daughters studied music with Sarti. After Paul's violent death at the hands of the palace guard, Sarti decided to leave Russia, but died in Berlin on his way to Italy. In 1796 Sarti presented to the Russian Academy of Sciences an apparatus to measure pitch (the so-called St. Petersburg tuning fork).
WORKS: *Pompeo in Armenia,* dramma per musica (Faenza, Carnival 1752); *Il re pastore,* dramma per musica (Venice, Carnival 1753); *Vologeso,*

dramma per musica (Copenhagen, Carnival 1754); *Antigono,* dramma per musica (Copenhagen, Oct. 14, 1754; some arias by other composers); *Ciro riconosciuto,* dramma per musica (Copenhagen, Dec. 21, 1754); *Arianna e Teseo,* dramma per musica (Copenhagen, Carnival 1756); *Anagilda,* dramma per musica (Copenhagen, Fall 1758); *Armida abbandonata,* dramma per musica (Copenhagen, 1759; later version as *Armida e Rinaldo,* St. Petersburg, Jan. 26, 1786); *Achille in Sciro,* dramma per musica (Copenhagen, 1759); *Andromaca,* dramma per musica (Copenhagen, 1759?); *Filindo,* pastorale eroica (Copenhagen, 1760); *Astrea placata,* festa teatrale (Copenhagen, Oct. 17, 1760); *Nitteti,* dramma per musica (Copenhagen, Oct. 12, 1760); *Issipile,* dramma per musica (Copenhagen, 1760?); *Alessandro nell'Indie,* dramma per musica (Copenhagen, 1761); *Semiramide,* dramma per musica (Copenhagen, Fall 1762); *Didone abbandonata,* dramma per musica (Copenhagen, Winter 1762); *Narciso,* dramma pastorale (Copenhagen, Carnival 1763); *Cesare in Egitto,* dramma per musica (Copenhagen, Fall 1763); *Il naufragio di Cipro,* dramma pastorale (Copenhagen, 1764); *Il gran Tamerlano,* tragedia per musica (Copenhagen, 1764); *Ipermestra,* dramma per musica (Rome, Carnival 1766); *La giardiniera brillante,* intermezzo (Rome, Jan. 3, 1768); *L'asile de l'amour,* dramatic cantata (Copenhagen, July 22, 1769); *La Double Méprise, ou, Carlile et Fany,* comédie mêlée d'ariettes (Copenhagen, July 22, 1769); *Soliman den Anden,* singspiel (Copenhagen, Oct. 8, 1770); *Le Bal,* opéra comique (Copenhagen, 1770); *Il tempio d'eternità,* festa teatrale (Copenhagen, 1771); *Demofoonte,* dramma per musica (Copenhagen, Jan. 30, 1771); *Tronfølgen i Sidon,* lyrisk tragicomedia (Copenhagen, April 4, 1771); *Il re pastore,* dramma per musica (Copenhagen, 1771; a different score from the one of 1753); *La clemenza di Tito,* dramma per musica (Padua, June 1771); *Deucalion og Pyrrha,* singspiel (Copenhagen, March 19, 1772); *Aglae, eller Støtten,* singspiel (Copenhagen, Feb. 16, 1774); *Kierlighedsbrevene,* singspiel (Copenhagen, March 22, 1775); *Farnace,* dramma per musica (Venice, 1776); *Le gelosie villane (Il feudatario),* dramma giocoso (Venice, Nov. 1776); *Ifigenia,* dramma per musica (Rome, Carnival 1777); *Medonte Re di Epiro,* dramma per musica (Florence, Sept. 8, 1777); *Il militare bizzarro,* dramma giocoso (Venice, Dec. 27, 1777); *Olimpiade,* dramma per musica (Florence, 1778); *Scipione,* dramma per musica (Mestre, Fall 1778); *I contratempi,* dramma giocoso (Venice, Nov. 1778); *Adriano in Siria,* dramma per musica (Rome, Dec. 26, 1778); *L'ambizione delusa,* intermezzo (Rome, Feb. 1779); *Mitridate a Sinope,* dramma per musica (Florence, Fall 1779); *Achille in Sciro,* dramma per musica (Florence, Fall 1779); *Siroe,* dramma per musica (Turin, Dec. 26, 1779); *Giulio Sabino,* dramma per musica (Venice, Jan. 1781); *Demofoonte,* dramma per musica (Rome, Carnival 1782; a different score from the one of 1771); *Didone abbandonata,* dramma per musica (Padua, June 1782; a different score from the one of 1762); *Alessandro e Timoteo,* dramma per musica (Parma, April 6, 1782); *Fra i due litiganti il terzo gode,* dramma giocoso (Milan, Sept. 14, 1782; subsequently perf. under various titles); *Attalo Re di Bitinia,* dramma per musica (Venice, Dec. 26, 1782); *Idalide,* dramma per musica (Milan, Jan. 8, 1783); *Erifile,* dramma per musica (Pavia, Carnival 1783); *Il trionfo della pace,* dramma per musica (Mantua, May 10, 1783); *Olimpiade,* dramma per musica (Rome, 1783; a different score from the one of 1778); *Gli amanti consolati,* dramma giocoso (St. Petersburg, 1784); *I finti eredi,* opera comica (St. Petersburg, Oct. 30, 1785); *Armida e Rinaldo,* dramma per musica (St. Petersburg, Jan. 26, 1786; based upon *Armida abbandonata* of 1759); *Castore e Polluce,* dramma per musica (St. Petersburg, Oct. 3, 1786); *Zenoclea,* azione teatrale (1786; not performed); *Alessandro nell'Indie,* dramma per musica (Palermo, Winter 1787; a different score from the one of 1761); *Cleomene,* dramma per musica (Bologna, Dec. 27, 1788); *The Early Reign of Oleg,* Russian opera to a libretto by Catherine the Great (St. Petersburg, Oct. 22, 1790; in collaboration with V. Pashkevich); *Il trionfo d'Atalanta* (1791; not performed); *Andromeda,* dramma per musica (St. Petersburg, Nov. 4, 1798); *Enea nel Lazio,* dramma per musica (St. Petersburg, Oct. 26, 1799); *La famille indienne en Angleterre,* opera (St. Petersburg, 1799); *Les Amours de Flore et de Zéphire,* ballet anacréontique (Gatchina, Sept. 19, 1800); also several secular cantatas, masses, Requiems, Te Deums, etc.; instrumental works, including symphs. and chamber music.

BIBLIOGRAPHY: G. Pasolini, *Giuseppe Sarti* (Faenza, 1883); C. Thrane, "Sarti in Kopenhagen," *Sammelbände der Internationalen Musik-Gesellschaft,* III (1901–2); A. Untersteiner, "Giuseppe Sarti," *Gazzetta Musicale di Milano,* LVII (1902); C. Rivalta, *Giuseppe Sarti, Musicista faentino del secolo XVIII* (Faenza, 1928); F. Samory, *A Giuseppe Sarti nel 2° centenario di sua nascita* (Faenza, 1929); G. Fesetchko, "Giuseppe Sarti," *Sovietskaya Muzyka* (Dec. 1950); R.A. Mooser, *Annales de la musique et des musiciens en Russie au XVIIIᵉ siècle* (vol. II, Geneva, 1951; pp. 415–50 and 463–79); D. Lehmann, "Zwischen Sarti und Rasumowski, Mozart im russischen Musikleben des 18. Jahrhunderts," *Acta Mozartiana,* II/2–3 (1955); H. O'Douwes, "De russische jaren van Giuseppe Sarti," *Mens en melodie,* XII (1957); M. Selden, "Laurels for Catherine the Great (The Early Reign of Oleg)," *Opera News,* XXIII/20 (1959); R. Jones, *A Performing Edition and Discussion of G. Sarti's Te Deum in D* (Diss., Stanford Univ., 1966); W. Mitchell, "Giuseppe Sarti and Mozart's Quartet K421," *Current Musicology,* no. 9 (1969).

Sartori, Claudio, eminent Italian music scholar and bibliographer; b. Brescia, April 1, 1913. He received an arts degree in 1934 from the Univ. of Pavia with a thesis in music history; then studied with Gérold at the Univ. of Strasbourg and with Vittadini at the Pavia Cons. He served as an assistant librarian at the Bologna Cons. (1938–42); in 1943 he was appointed prof. of Italian literature there; in 1967 he assumed a similar professorship at the Milan Cons. He founded and became director of the

Ufficio Ricerche Musicali in 1965; its aim was to conduct a thorough codification of Italian musical sources, providing information on all MSS and publ. music in Italy before 1900, on all publ. librettos in Italy down to 1800, and on all literature on music in Italy. In addition to this invaluable compilation, he also served as editor in chief of *Dizionario Ricordi della musica e dei musicisti* (Milan, 1959).
WRITINGS: *Il R. Conservatorio di Musica G.B. Martini di Bologna* (Florence, 1942); *Bibliografia delle opere musicali stampate da Ottaviano Petrucci* (Florence, 1948; later continued as "Nuove conclusive aggiunte alla 'Bibliografia del Petrucci,'" *Collectanea Historiae Musicae*, I, 1953); *Bibliografia della musica strumentale italiana stampata in Italia fino al 1700* (2 vols., Florence, 1952 and 1968); *Monteverdi* (Brescia, 1953); *Catalogo delle musiche della Cappella del Duomo di Milano* (Milan, 1957); *Riccardo Malipiero* (Milan, 1957); *Casa Ricordi 1808–1958* (Milan, 1958); *Dizionario degli editori musicali italiani* (Florence, 1958); *Giacomo Puccini a Monza* (Monza, 1958); *Puccini* (Milan, 1958); editor of *Puccini Symposium* (Milan, 1959); *Assisi: La Cappella della Basilica di S. Francesco: Catalogo del fondo musicale nella Biblioteca comunale di Assisi* (Milan, 1962); editor of *L'enciclopedia della musica* (Milan, 1963–64); *Commemorazione di Ottaviano de' Petrucci* (Fossombrone, 1966); *Giacomo Carissimi: Catalogo delle opere attribuite* (Milan, 1975); editor, with F. Lesure, of *Bibliografia della musica italiana vocale profana pubblicata dal 1500 al 1700* (Geneva, 1978).

Sartorio, Antonio, important Italian composer of operas; b. Venice, 1630; d. there, Dec. 30, 1680. His first opera, *Gl'amori infruttuosi di Pirro,* was performed in Venice on Jan. 4, 1661; his second opera, *Seleuco* (Venice, Jan. 16, 1666), established his reputation. In 1666 he went to Germany to take up the post of Kapellmeister to Duke Johann Friedrich of Braunschweig-Lüneburg, who maintained his court in Hannover. He held this post until 1675, but continued to make regular visits to Venice to oversee productions of his operas. It was in Venice that he brought out his most famous opera, *L'Adelaide,* on Feb. 19, 1672. He returned to Venice permanently in 1675; in 1676 he was appointed vice-maestro di cappella at San Marco, a position he held until his death. Sartorio was a leading representative of the Venetian school of opera; his operas are notable for their arias, which he composed in a varied and effective manner.
WORKS: Operas: *Gl' amori infruttuosi di Pirro* (Venice, Jan. 4, 1661); *Seleuco* (Venice, Jan. 16, 1666); *La prosperità d'Elio Seiano* (Venice, Jan. 15, 1667); *La caduta d'Elio Seiano* (Venice, Feb. 3, 1667); *L'Ermengarda Regina de' Longobardi* (Venice, Dec. 26, 1669); *L'Adelaide* (Venice, Feb. 19, 1672); *L'Orfeo* (Venice, Dec. 14, 1672); *Massenzio* (Venice, Jan. 25, 1673); *Alcina* (c.1674; not performed); *Giulio Cesare in Egitto* (Venice, Dec. 17, 1676); *Antonino e Pompeiano* (Venice, 1677); *L'Anacreonte tiranno* (Venice, 1677); *Ercole su' l Termodonte* (Venice, 1678); *I

duo tiranni al soglio (Venice, Jan. 15, 1679); *La Flora* (music completed by M.A. Ziani; Venice, Carnival 1681). Sartorio also composed a number of cantatas and sacred vocal works; publ. *23 Salmi a due chori ma accomodati all' uso della serenissima cappella ducale di S. Marco* for 8 Voices (Venice, 1680).
BIBLIOGRAPHY: H.C. Wolff, *Die Venezianische Oper in der zweiten Hälfte des 17. Jahrhunderts* (Berlin, 1937); S.T. Worsthorne, *Venetian Opera in the 17th Century* (Oxford, 1954).

Sartorius, Paul, German organist and composer; b. Nuremberg, Nov. 16, 1569; d. Innsbruck, Feb. 28, 1609. His real name was **Schneider,** Sartorius being its Latin trans. ("tailor"). He studied with Lechner in Nuremberg; then went to Rome for further study; was organist at the court chapel of Duke Maximilian II of Austria in Mergentheim (1594–1602); in 1602 he went to Innsbruck. He publ. *Missae tres octonis v. decantandae* (Munich, 1599); *Madrigali a cinque voci* (Venice, 1600); *Sonetti spirituali a sei voci* (Nuremberg, 1601); *Neue Teutsche Liedlein mit vier Stimmen nach art der Welschen Canzonette* (Nuremberg, 1601); *Sacrae cantiones sive motecta* (Venice, 1602); he further wrote masses and motets in a polyphonic style similar to Palestrina's, and some choral works to German texts.
BIBLIOGRAPHY: W. Senn, *Musik und Theater am Hof zu Innsbruck* (Innsbruck, 1954).

Sáry, László, Hungarian composer; b. Györ, Jan. 1, 1940. He studied at the Budapest Academy with Endre Szervánszky; after graduation in 1966, he joined the Budapest New Music Studio. In his music he strives to attain the ultimate "total sound."
WORKS: 3 vocal quintets: *Lamento 65* (1965); *3 Madrigals* (1966); *Incanto* (1969); *Variations* for Clarinet and Piano (1966); *Catacoustics* for 2 Pianos (1967); *Cantata No. 1* for Soprano, Chamber Chorus, and Chamber Ensemble (1967–68; the middle movement is often played separately as *Quartetto* for Soprano, Flute, Violin, and Cimbalom); *Musica da camera* for Flute and Percussion (1968); *Fluttuazioni* for Violin and Piano (1968–69); *Versetti* for Organ and Percussion (1966–69); *Hommage aux ancêtres* for Vocal Sextet (1969); *Improvisations '69* for Vocal Sextet and Chamber Ensemble (1969); *Pezzo concertato* for Flute and Piano (1969–70); 3 *Sonanti:* No. 1 for Harpsichord, No. 2 for Flute and Percussion, and No. 3 for Cimbalom (all 1970); *Canzone solenne* for Orch. (1971); *Immaginario No. 1* for Orch. (1971); *Psalmus* for Voice and 2 String Instruments plucked with a plectrum (1972); Trio for Flute, Piano, and Gongs (1972); *Pentagram* for 5 Instrumental Ensembles, with Mixed Voices and 6 Articulators (1972); *Image* for Clarinet, Cello, and Piano (1972); *Sounds* for any Soloist or any kind of Ensemble or Orch. (1972–73); *String* for one or more Keyboard Instruments or Chamber Ensemble (1973); *Drop by Drop,* in 2 versions: No. 1 for String Orch., and No. 2 for 2 Prepared Pianos (1975); *Snowdrops* for optional Instruments (1975).

Sás, Andrés, Peruvian composer; b. Paris, April 6, 1900, of French-Belgian parents; d. Lima, Peru, July 25, 1967. He studied at the Brussels Cons. with Marchot (violin), Ernest Closson (music history), and Maurice Imbert (counterpoint). In 1924 he was engaged by the Peruvian government to teach violin at the National Academy of Music in Lima; in 1928 he returned temporarily to Belgium; the following year, settled in Lima permanently; married the Peruvian pianist **Lily Rosay,** and with her established the Sás-Rosay Academy of Music. He became profoundly interested in Peruvian folk music, and collected folk melodies; made use of many of them in his own compositions.

WORKS: Incidental music to Molière's *Le Malade imaginaire* (1943); ballets: *La señora del pueblo* (Viña del Mar, Chile, Jan. 20, 1946) and *El hijo prodigo* (1948); for Orch.: *Canción India* (1927); *3 estampas del Perú* (1936); *Poema Indio* (1941); *Sueño de Zamba* (1943); *Danza gitana* (1944); *La patrona del pueblo* (1945); *La parihuana* (1946); *Las seis edades de la Tía Conchita* (1947); *La leyenda de la Isla de San Lorenzo* (1949); *Recuerdos* for Violin and Piano (also for Orch.; 1927); *Rapsodia peruana* for Violin and Piano (also for Orch.; 1928); *Sonata-Fantasía* for Flute and Piano (1934); String Quartet (1938); *Cantos del Perú* for Violin and Piano (1941); for Piano: *Aires y Danzas del Perú* (2 albums, 1930 and 1945); *Suite peruana* (1931); *Himno y Danza* (1935); *Sonatina peruana* (1946); *Fantasía romántica* for Trumpet and Orch. (1950); numerous choruses and songs.

BIBLIOGRAPHY: N. Slonimsky, *Music of Latin America* (N.Y., 1945; pp. 275–76).

Saslavsky, Alexander, Russian-American violinist; b. Kharkov, Russia, Feb. 8, 1876; d. San Francisco, Aug. 2, 1924. He studied in his native town with local violin teachers; then with Jakob Grün in Vienna; after a Canadian tour in 1893 he joined the N.Y. Symph. Orch.; in 1903 became its concertmaster; in 1919, became concertmaster of the newly organized Los Angeles Phil.

BIBLIOGRAPHY: *Dictionary of American Biography.*

Sass, Marie, Belgian soprano; b. Ghent, Jan. 26, 1838; d. Auteuil, near Paris, Nov. 8, 1907. Her real Belgian name was **Saxe.** She studied voice in Paris; became known, albeit adversely, in the role of Elisabeth in the highly controversial Paris production of *Tannhäuser* in 1861; she also sang the role of Selika in the premiere of *L'Africaine* (Paris, April 28, 1865), but lived too long to maintain even a minimal subsistence, and died in abject poverty.

Sass, Sylvia, Hungarian soprano; b. Budapest, July 12, 1951. She was educated at the Franz Liszt Academy of Music in Budapest; upon graduation, she joined the Hungarian State Opera; later sang in Vienna, Salzburg, and Hamburg. In 1976 she made her first appearance at Covent Garden in London; on March 17, 1977, she made her Metropolitan Opera debut in N.Y. as Tosca; also gave recitals.

Sassòli, Ada, Italian harpist; b. Bologna, Sept. 25, 1886; d. Rome, Dec. 3, 1946. She studied at the Cons. of Bologna; then entered the class of A. Hasselmans at the Paris Cons., winning first prize for harp playing in 1902. She toured with Mme. Melba in England and Australia (1904–5); made several tours of the U.S.; appeared as a soloist with the Boston Symph. and other American orchs.; returned to Europe in 1916; was appointed prof. of harp at the Santa Cecilia in Rome, and lived there until her death.

Satie, Erik (Alfred-Leslie), celebrated French composer who elevated his eccentricities and verbal virtuosity to the plane of high art; b. Honfleur, May 17, 1866; d. Paris, July 1, 1925. He received his early musical training from a local organist, Vinot, who was a pupil of Niedermeyer; at 13 he went to Paris, where his father was a music publisher, and attended the Paris Cons. (1879–86); took organ lessons with Guilmant, but soon relinquished systematic study of music; played in various cabarets in Montmartre; in 1884 he publ. a piano piece which he numbered, with malice aforethought, op. 62. His whimsical ways and Bohemian manner of life attracted many artists and musicians; he met Debussy in 1891; joined the Rosicrucian Society in Paris in 1892 and began to produce short piano pieces with eccentric titles intended to ridicule modernistic fancies and Classical pedantries alike. Debussy thought highly enough of him to orchestrate 2 numbers from his piano suite *Gymnopédies* (1888). Satie was 40 years old when he decided to learn something about the technique of composition, and entered the Schola Cantorum in Paris, in the classes of Vincent d'Indy and Albert Roussel. In 1898 he moved to Arcueil, a suburb of Paris; there he held court for poets, singers, dancers, and musicians, among whom he had ardent admirers. Milhaud, Sauguet, and the conductor Desormière organized a group, which they called only half-facetiously "Ecole d'Arcueil," in honor of Satie as master and leader. But Satie's eccentricities were not merely those of a Parisian poseur; rather, they were adjuncts to his esthetic creed, which he enunciated with boldness and total disregard for professional amenities (he was once brought to court for sending an insulting letter to a music critic). Interestingly enough, he attacked modernistic aberrations just as assiduously as reactionary pedantry, publishing "manifestos" in prose and poetry. Although he was dismissed by most serious musicians as an uneducated person who tried to conceal his ignorance of music with persiflage, he exercised a profound influence on the young French composers of the first quarter of the 20th century; moreover, his stature as an innovator in the modern idiom grew after his death, so that the avant-garde musicians of the later day accepted him as inspiration for their own experiments; thus "space music" could be traced back to Satie's *musique d'ameublement,* in which players were stationed at different parts of a hall playing different pieces in different tempi. The instruction in his piano piece *Vexations,* to play it 840 times in succession, was carried out literally in N.Y.

on Sept. 9, 1963, by a group of 5 pianists working in relays overnight, thus setting a world's record for duration of any musical composition. When critics accused Satie of having no idea of form, he publ. *Trois morceaux en forme de poire,* the eponymous pear being reproduced in color on the cover; other pieces bore self-contradictory titles, such as *Heures séculaires et instantanées* and *Crépuscule matinal de midi;* other titles were *Pièces froides, Embryons desséchés, Prélude en tapisserie, Préludes flasques (Pour un chien), Descriptions automatiques,* etc. In his ballets he introduced jazz for the first time in Paris; at the performance of his ballet *Relâche* (Paris, Nov. 29, 1924), the curtain bore the legend "Erik Satie is the greatest musician in the world; whoever disagrees with this notion will please leave the hall." Other ballets were *Parade* (Paris, May 18, 1917, produced by Diaghilev's Ballets Russes), and *Mercure* (Paris, June 15, 1924); other works were the symph. drama *Socrate* for 4 Sopranos and Chamber Orch. (Paris, Feb. 14, 1920); incidental music to Péladan's *Le Fils des étoiles* (1891; prelude orchestrated by Ravel) and for *Le Prince de Byzance* (1891); stage music to H. Mazel's *Le Nazaréen* (1892), to J. Bois's *La Porte héroïque au ciel* (1893), and to M. de Féraudy's *Pousse l'Amour* (1905); many pieces were produced posthumously, as *Jack in the Box* and the mockingly titled *Cinq grimaces pour le "Songe d'une nuit d'été,"* orchestrated by Milhaud, etc. In 1912 Erik Satie publ. a facetious autobiographic notice, *Mémoirs d'un amnésique.*

BIBLIOGRAPHY: G. Jean-Aubry, *La Musique française d'aujourd'hui* (Paris, 1916); Carl van Vechten, "Erik Satie," in *Interpreters and Interpretations* (N.Y., 1917); R.D. Chennevière, "Erik Satie and the Music of Irony," *Musical Quarterly* (Oct. 1919); A. Cœuroy, *La Musique française moderne* (Paris, 1922); W.W. Roberts, "The Problem of Satie," *Music & Letters* (Oct. 1923); 2 special issues of the *Revue Musicale* (March 1924; June 1925); G.M. Gatti, *Musicisti moderni d'Italia e di fuori* (Bologna, 1925); W. Dankert, "Der Klassizismus Erik Saties und seine geistesgeschichteliche Stellung," *Zeitschrift für Musikwissenschaft* (Nov. 1929); P.-D. Templier, *Erik Satie* (Paris, 1932); D. Milhaud, "Notes sur Erik Satie," in *Les Œuvres nouvelles* (vol. 6, N.Y., 1946); W.H. Mellers, *Studies in Contemporary Music* (London, 1947); Rollo H. Myers, *Erik Satie* (London, 1948); Anne Rey, *Erik Satie* (Paris, 1974); Grete Wehmeyer, *Erik Satie* (Berlin, 1974); N. Wilkins, trans. and ed., *The Writings of Erik Satie* (London, 1980).

Sato, Keijirō, Japanese composer; b. Tokyo, June 6, 1927. He studied medicine; music became his avocation. Most of his works are modernistic miniatures for piano or strings, e.g., a group of pieces under the generic title *Calligraphy* for 9, 10, and 11 String Instruments (1962–65); he also wrote *Electronic Raga* (1967).

Satter, Gustav, pianist and composer; b. Vienna, Feb. 12, 1832; d. Savannah, Ga., 1879. He studied in Vienna and Paris; undertook a pianistic tour in the U.S. and Brazil (1854–60) with surprising success; went back to Paris, where Berlioz warmly praised his music; then lived in Vienna, Dresden, Hannover, and Stockholm.

WORKS: Opera, *Olanthe;* overtures: *Lorelei, Julius Cæsar, An die Freude;* 2 symphs.; symph. poem, *George Washington;* much chamber music; 3 sonatas, studies, waltzes, etc., for piano; about 160 opus numbers in all.

BIBLIOGRAPHY: *The Life and Works of Gustav Satter* (by an anonymous ex-Confederate admirer; Macon, Ga., 1879).

Sattler, Heinrich, German organist and teacher; b. Quedlinburg, April 3, 1811; d. Oct. 17, 1891. He devoted himself mainly to teaching; from 1861, was on the staff of the Oldenburg Seminary. He publ. a treatise, *Die Orgel* (5 eds.); a book, *Erinnerung an Mozarts Leben und Werke* (1856); composed an oratorio, *Die Sachsentaufe;* 2 cantatas, *Triumph des Glaubens* and *Pfingstkantate;* sacred works; chamber music; many organ pieces.

Satz, Ilya, Russian composer; b. Tchernobyl, Kiev district, April 30, 1875; d. St. Petersburg, Dec. 12, 1912. He studied cello in Kiev; then took lessons in composition with Taneyev in Moscow; his general education was desultory. He traveled in Europe in 1900; then made a tour as a cellist through Siberia. He returned to Moscow in 1903; in 1905 became music director of the Studio of the Moscow Art Theater, and wrote incidental music for new plays, including Maeterlinck's *Blue Bird* and Andreyev's *A Man's Life;* also composed ballet music for Salome's dance; the ballet *The Goat-Footed (The Dance of the Satyrs)* was reorchestrated and prepared for performance by Glière. Satz had a talent for the grotesque; a lack of technique prevented his development into a major composer. A memorial volume, *Ilya Satz,* with articles by Glière and several members of the Moscow Art Theater, was publ. at Moscow in 1923.

Sauer, Emil von, eminent pianist; b. Hamburg, Oct. 8, 1862; d. Vienna, April 27, 1942. He studied with Nicolai Rubinstein in Moscow (1879–81), and Liszt in Weimar (1884–85); made numerous European tours; played in the U.S. in 1898–99 and 1908. From 1901 till 1907, and again from 1915, he was a prof. at the Meisterschule für Klavierspiel in Vienna; from 1908 till 1915 he lived in Dresden; appeared in concerts until 1936, and then retired to Vienna. He wrote 2 piano concertos, 2 piano sonatas, many studies for piano; edited the complete works of Brahms and pedagogical works of Pischna, Plaidy, Kullak, etc. He publ. an autobiography, *Meine Welt* (1901).

Sauguet, Henri, French composer; b. Bordeaux, May 18, 1901. His real name is **Henri-Pierre Poupard;** he assumed his mother's maiden name, Sauguet. He was a pupil of Joseph Canteloube; in 1922 he went to Paris, where he studied with Koechlin; became associated with Erik Satie, and formed a group designated as the Ecole d'Arcueil (from the locality near Paris where Satie lived). In conformity with the principles of utilitarian music, he wrote sophisticated works in an outwardly simple manner; his first conspicuous success was the production of his ballet *La Chatte* by Diaghilev in 1927.

WORKS: Operas: *Le Plumet du colonel* (Paris, April 24, 1924); *La Contrebasse,* after Chekhov (Paris, 1932); *La Chartreuse de Parme* (Paris, March 16, 1939); *La Gageure imprévue* (Paris, July 4, 1944); *Les Caprices de Marianne* (Aix-en-Provence, July 20, 1954); ballets: *La Chatte* (Monte Carlo, April 30, 1927); *Paul et Virginie* (Paris, April 15, 1943); *Les Mirages* (Paris, Dec. 15, 1947); *Cordelia* (Paris, May 7, 1952); *L'As de cœur* (1960); *Paris* (1964); *L'Imposteur ou Le Prince et le mendiant* (1965); for Orch.: *Les Saisons et les jours,* "allegoric symph." (Paris, Dec. 15, 1946); *Symphonie expiatoire,* in memory of innocent war victims (Paris, Feb. 8, 1948); Symph. No. 2 (1955); *Symphonie des marches* (Paris, June 4, 1966); Symph. No. 4, *Troisième âge* (1971); 3 Piano Concertos (1933, 1948, 1963); *Orphée* for Violin and Orch. (Aix-en-Provence, July 26, 1953); *Mélodie concertante* for Cello and Orch. (1963); *The Garden Concerto* for Harmonica and Orch. (1970); oratorio, *Chant pour une ville meurtrie* (1967); *Alentours saxophoniques* for Alto Saxophone, Wind Ensemble, and Piano (1976); 2 string quartets (1926, 1948); piano pieces; songs.

BIBLIOGRAPHY: M. Schneider, *Henri Sauguet* (Paris, 1959); F.-Y. Bril, *Henri Sauguet* (Paris, 1967).

Saunders, Arlene, American soprano; b. Cleveland, Oct. 5, 1935. She studied at Baldwin-Wallace College; after making her operatic debut in 1958, she sang at Milan's Teatro Nuovo, the Cincinnati Opera, the N.Y. City Opera, the Hamburg State Opera, the Vienna State Opera, the Bavarian State Opera in Munich, the Rome Opera, and the Paris Opéra; also appeared at the Edinburgh and Glyndebourne festivals. She made her debut at the Metropolitan Opera in N.Y. as Eva in *Die Meistersinger* on April 2, 1976.

Sauret, Emile, French violinist; b. Dun-le-Roi (Cher), May 22, 1852; d. London, Feb. 12, 1920. He studied with Vieuxtemps at the Paris Cons. and with Bériot in Brussels; was a child prodigy, and made his London debut at the age of 14. He was 20 when he was engaged for an American tour (1872); gave concerts in America again in 1874, 1876, 1877, and 1895. From 1903 till 1906 he taught at the Chicago Musical College; returning to Europe, he lived in Geneva and Berlin; was at various times a prof. of violin in London and Berlin. In 1873 he married the pianist **Teresa Carreño** (divorced in 1876). He was a typical representative of the French school of violin playing, distinguished by grace, elegance, and excellent taste.

WORKS: For Violin and Orch.: *Souvenir de Moscou, Rapsodie russe, Rapsodie suédoise, Farfalla,* and *Elégie et Rondo;* for Violin and Piano: *Feuilles d'album, Pensées fugitives, Scènes champêtres,* 20

grandes études, 12 études artistiques, 24 études-caprices; he publ. a method, *Gradus ad Parnassum du violoniste* (in 4 parts, with annotations in French and German); also made about 25 transcriptions.

Sauveur, Joseph, French acoustician; b. La Flèche, March 24, 1653; d. Paris, July 9, 1716. A deaf-mute, learning to speak in his 7th year, he became a remarkable investigator in the realm of acoustics; in 1696, became a member of the Académie. He was the first to calculate absolute vibration numbers, and to explain scientifically the phenomenon of overtones.

WRITINGS (all publ. in the *Mémoires* of the Académie): *Principes d'acoustique et de musique* (1700–1); *Application des sons harmoniques à la composition des jeux d'orgue* (1702); *Méthode générale pour former des systèmes tempérés . . .* (1707); *Table générale des systèmes tempérés* (1711); *Rapports des sons des cordes d'instruments de musique aux flèches des cordes* (1713).

BIBLIOGRAPHY: H. Scherchen, *Vom Wesen der Musik,* chap. I (Zürich, 1946; in Eng. as *The Nature of Music,* Chicago, 1950).

Sauzay, (Charles-) Eugène, French violinist and composer; b. Paris, July 14, 1809; d. there, Jan. 24, 1901. He studied with Baillot at the Paris Cons., and was a member of Baillot's string quartet; taught violin at the Paris Cons. from 1860 to 1892. He publ. *Symphonie rustique; Etudes harmoniques* for Violin; numerous transcriptions; also the books *Haydn, Mozart, Beethoven, Etude sur le quatuor* (Paris, 1861; 2nd ed., 1884) and *L'Ecole de l'accompagnement* (Paris, 1869).

Savage, Henry Wilson, American impresario; b. New Durham, N.H., March 21, 1859; d. Boston, Nov. 29, 1927. He started in business as a real estate operator in Boston, where he built the Castle Square Theater; later went into theatrical enterprise himself and in 1897 opened a season of opera in English. His Castle Square Opera Co. flourished, and he undertook tours of other cities. In 1900 he formed the English Grand Opera Co. and engaged several artists from the Carl Rosa Co. of London. In 1904–5 he organized a special troupe, producing *Parsifal* in English in the principal cities of the East and Midwest; in 1906–7 the same company made a tour with Puccini's *Madama Butterfly;* he also produced light opera with another company, which, among other operettas, introduced Lehár's *The Merry Widow* to the U.S. (1906).

BIBLIOGRAPHY: *Dictionary of American Biography.*

Savard, (Marie-Gabriel-) Augustin, French music educator; b. Paris, Aug. 21, 1814; d. there, June 7, 1881. He studied with Leborne and Bazin; in 1843 he was appointed prof. of solfège at the Paris Cons., and later taught harmony and thoroughbass. He was an excellent teacher; among his many foreign students was MacDowell. He publ. the manuals *Cours complet d'harmonie théorique et pratique* (2 vols., Paris, 1853, 1856) and *Principes de la musique* (Paris, 1861; very popular; 14th ed., 1913); its abridged version, *Premières notions de musique* (Paris, 1866), also went into numerous editions.

Savard, Marie-Emmanuel-Augustin, French composer and pedagogue, son of **Marie-Gabriel-Augustin Savard;** b. Paris, May 15, 1861; d. Lyons, Dec. 6, 1942. He studied at the Paris Cons. with Durand, Taudou, and Massenet; won the Prix de Rome in 1886 with the cantata *La Vision de Saul;* in 1892–93 was chorus master at the Opéra; was director of the Cons. in Lyons from 1902 until 1921, when he retired.

WORKS: Lyric drama, *La Forêt* (Paris Opera, 1910); 2 symphs.; an overture, *Roi Lear; Poème* for Voice and Orch.; String Quartet; Violin Sonata; etc.

Savart, Félix, French acoustician; b. Mézières, June 30, 1791; d. Paris, March 16, 1841. He was a prof. of acoustics at the Collège de France; in 1821, was elected a member of the Académie.

WRITINGS (publ. in the *Annales de Physique et de Chimie*): *Mémoire sur la construction des instruments à cordes et à archet* (1819, separate reprint; in German, 1844); *Sur la communication des mouvements vibratoires entre les corps solides* (1820); *Sur les vibrations de l'air* (1823); *Sur la voix humaine* (1825); *Sur la communication des mouvements vibratoires par les liquides* (1826); *Sur la voix des oiseaux* (1826); etc.

Saville, Frances, American soprano; b. San Francisco, Jan. 6, 1863; d. Burlingame, Calif., Nov. 8, 1935. She went early to Australia, where she made her debut in oratorio; continued her studies in Paris with Marchesi; in 1892 made her operatic debut in Brussels; also appeared with the Carl Rosa Co. in England, at the Opéra-Comique in Paris, and in Vienna, Berlin, St. Petersburg, Warsaw, etc.; on Nov. 18, 1895, she made her debut as Juliette (with Jean de Reszke) at the Metropolitan Opera House in N.Y., on whose roster she remained through that season and again in 1899–1900; later she appeared at the Vienna Opera; then lived in retirement in California.

Savín, Francisco, Mexican conductor and composer; b. Mexico City, Nov. 18, 1929. He studied piano in Mexico City with José Velásquez (1944–53) and took conducting lessons with Scherchen and composition with Rodolfo Halffter (1955–56). He then went to Europe; studied at the Music Academy in Prague, and composition with Karel Janeček (1957–59). Returning to Mexico, he was an assistant conductor of the Mexican National Symph. Orch. (1959–62) and principal conductor of the Xalapa Symph. Orch. (1963–67); was then director of the National Cons. of Music in Mexico City (1967–70); in 1973 was appointed director of the conducting workshop at the National Cons.

WORKS: *Quetzalcoátl,* symph. poem for 2 Narrators and Orch. (1957); *Metamorfosis* for Orch. (1962); *2 formas plásticas* for Wind Quintet (1964,

1965); *3 líricas* for Mezzo-soprano, Flute, Clarinet, Viola, Percussion, and Piano (1966); *Concreción* for Electronic Organ and Orch. (1969); *Monología de las Delicias* for 4 Female Voices and Orch. (1969); *Quasar 1* for Electronic Organ, Tape, and Percussion (1970).

Savine, Alexander, American conductor, composer, and voice teacher; b. Belgrade, April 26, 1881; d. Chicago, Jan. 19, 1949. He studied in Belgrade with S. Mokranjac, and later studied voice at the Vienna Cons. with Pauline Lucca. He then was engaged as an opera conductor in Berlin (1905–7); taught voice at the Musical Academy in Winnepeg, Canada (1908–12); later settled in the U.S.; was director of the opera dept. at the Inst. of Musical Art in N.Y. (1922–24); in 1929 moved to Chicago. He married in 1914 the soprano **Lillian Blauvelt.** He wrote the opera *Xenia* (Zürich, May 29, 1919); 4 symph. poems; choruses; songs.

Sawallisch, Wolfgang, German conductor; b. Munich, Aug. 23, 1923. He studied piano and composition at the Munich Cons., graduating in 1946. He made his conducting debut in Augsburg in 1947; subsequently occupied posts as music director in Aachen (1953–57), Wiesbaden (1957–59), and Cologne (1959–63); served as Generalmusikdirektor of the Hamburg Phil. (1961–73). He was chief conductor of the Vienna Symph. (1960–70), with which he toured the U.S. in 1964; concurrently he served as chief conductor of the Orch. de la Suisse Romande of Geneva, resigning at the close of the 1977–78 season. Specializing in opera, he has achieved some of his finest successes in the Wagnerian repertoire, conducting in Bayreuth since 1957.

Sax, (Antoine-Joseph-) Adolphe, inventor of the saxophone; b. Dinant, Belgium, Nov. 6, 1814; d. Paris, Feb. 4, 1894. He was the son of **Charles-Joseph Sax,** the instrument maker, and acquired great skill in manipulating instruments from his early youth; his practical and imaginative ideas led him to undertake improvements of the clarinet and other wind instruments. He studied the flute and clarinet at the Brussels Cons.; in 1842 he went to Paris with a wind instrument of his invention, which he called the "saxophone," made of metal, with a single-reed mouthpiece and conical bore. He exhibited brass and woodwind instruments at the Paris Exposition of 1844, winning a silver medal; his father joined him in Paris, and together they continued the manufacture of new instruments; evolved the saxhorn (improved over the bugle-horn and ophicleide by replacing the keys with a valve mechanism) and the saxo-tromba, a hybrid instrument producing a tone midway between the bugle and the trumpet. Conservative critics and rival instrument makers ridiculed Sax's innovations, but Berlioz and others warmly supported him; he also won praise from Rossini. His instruments were gradually adopted by French military bands. Sax won a gold medal at the Paris Industrial Exposition of 1849. Financially, however, he was unsuccessful, and was compelled to go into bankruptcy in 1852. He exhibited his instruments in London (1862) and received the Grand Prix in Paris (1867) for his improved instruments. In 1857 the Paris Cons. engaged him as instructor of the saxophone; with some interruptions, saxophone instruction was continued at the Paris Cons. for a century. He publ. a method for his instrument. Although Wieprecht, Červený, and others disputed the originality and priority of his inventions, legal decisions gave the rights to Sax; the saxophone became a standard instrument; many serious composers made use of it in their scores (Bizet's *L'Arlésienne*, etc.). The instrument fell into desuetude after Sax's death; but about 1918 a spectacular revival of the saxophone took place, when it was adopted in jazz bands; its popularity became worldwide; numerous methods were publ. and special schools established; and there appeared saxophone virtuosos for whom many composers wrote concertos.

BIBLIOGRAPHY: O. Comettant, *Histoire d'un inventeur au XIXᵉ siècle* (Paris, 1860); T. Lajarte, *Instruments Sax et fanfares civiles* (Paris, 1876); J. Kool, *Das Saxophone* (Leipzig, 1931); Albert Remy, *La Vie tourmentée d'Adolphe Sax* (Brussels, 1939); L. Kochnitzky, *Adolphe Sax and His Saxophone* (N.Y., 1949); M. Perrin, *Le Saxophone, Son histoire, sa technique et son utilisation dans l'orchestre* (Paris, 1955); J.M. Londeix, *125 ans de musique pour saxophone* (Paris, 1971); M. Haine, *Adolphe Sax: Sa vie, son œuvre, ses instruments de musique* (Brussels, 1980); W. Horwood, *Adolphe Sax, Life and Legacy* (Bramley, 1980).

Sax, Charles-Joseph, Belgian instrument maker; b, Dinant-sur-Meuse, Feb. 1, 1791; d. Paris, April 26, 1865. He established an instrument factory at Brussels in 1815, manufacturing not only wind instruments, but also pianos, harps, and guitars; his specialty, however, was brass instruments. He joined his son **Adolphe Sax** in Paris, and helped him to launch his revolutionary inventions.

Sayão, Bidú (Balduina) (de Oliveira), noted Brazilian soprano; b. Niteroi, near Rio de Janeiro, May 11, 1902. She studied with Elena Theodorini in Rio de Janeiro, and then with Jean de Reszke in Vichy and Nice. Returning to Brazil, she gave her first professional concert in Rio de Janeiro in 1925; in 1926 she sang the role of Rosina in *The Barber of Seville* at the Teatro Municipal there. She made her American debut on Dec. 29, 1935, in a recital in N.Y. On Feb. 13, 1937, she sang Manon with the Metropolitan Opera in N.Y., earning enthusiastic reviews in the press. She remained on the roster of the Metropolitan Opera until 1952; her finest performances were in lyric roles in bel canto operas; especially memorable were her interpretations of Violetta in *La Traviata,* Gilda in *Rigoletto,* and Mimi in *La Bohème.* She also showed her versatility in coloratura parts, such as Lakmé; in France, she was described as "a Brazilian nightingale." She also sang vocal parts in several works of her great compatriot Villa-Lobos. She was a recipient of numerous honors from European royalty, and of the

Palmes Académiques from the French government; in 1972 she was decorated a Commandante by the Brazilian government.

BIBLIOGRAPHY: David Ewen, *Musicians since 1900* (N.Y., 1978).

Saygun, Ahmed Adnan, Turkish composer; b. Izmir, Sept. 7, 1907. He studied composition in Paris with Le Flem and Vincent d'Indy at the Schola Cantorum. Returning to Turkey in 1931, he was active as a teacher and composer; in 1946 he was appointed a prof. at the Cons. of Ankara. He visited the U.S. in 1950 and in 1957–58.

WORKS: 3 operas on Turkish themes: *Tas Bebek* (Ankara, Dec. 27, 1934); *Kerem* (Ankara, March 1, 1953); *Köroglu* (Ankara, 1973); oratorio, *Yunus Emre* (Ankara, May 25, 1946); Piano Concerto (1956); 4 symphs. (1953, 1955, 1961, 1973); Violin Concerto (1967); Wind Quintet (1968); 3 string quartets (1947, 1958, 1967); Quartet for Clarinet, Saxophone, Percussion, and Piano; orch. suite of national dances, *Zeybek, Interlude and Horon* (Ankara, April 14, 1951); Cello Sonata; Violin Sonata; songs.

Saylor, Bruce, American composer and musicologist; b. Philadelphia, April 24, 1946. He studied composition with Hugo Weisgall and Roger Sessions (B.M., 1968; M.S., 1969); then went to Italy, where he took courses at the Santa Cecilia Academy with Petrassi and Evangelisti (1969–70); returning to the U.S., he enrolled at the City Univ. of N.Y. Graduate School as a composition student of Weisgall and Perle (Ph.D., 1978). He subsequently held teaching posts as lecturer at Queens College (1970–76) and instructor at N.Y. Univ. (1976–79). In 1979 he was appointed associate prof. at Queens College. In 1982–83 he was awarded a Guggenheim fellowship. Apart from his compositions, he publ. a monograph, *The Musical Thought of Henry Cowell* (Brooklyn, 1978), and contributed articles on several American composers to *The New Grove.*

WORKS: *Cantilena* for String Orch. (1965); Woodwind Quartet (1965); 5 songs to Walt Whitman's words, for Soprano and String Quartet (1965–67); Suite for Viola Solo (1967); *To Winter* and *To Autumn* for Soloists, Chorus, and Orch. (1968); *Notturno* for Piano and Orch. (1969); Duo for Violin and Viola (1970); *Conductus* for Winds, Strings, and Percussion (1970); *Lyrics* for Soprano and Violin (1971); *Loveplay* for Mezzo-soprano, Flute, and Viola (1975); *My Kinsman, Major Molineux,* one-act opera after Nathaniel Hawthorne (Pittsburgh, Aug. 28, 1976); *Turns and Mordents* for Flute and Orch. (Yale Univ., March 6, 1977); *Cycle,* choreographic poem for Voice and Instruments (1978); *Inner World Out,* dance score for Clarinet, Violin, Viola, and Cello (1978); *Wildfire,* dance score for 2 Flutes and 2 Harps (1979); *Firescreen* for Flute, Cello, and Piano (1979); *St. Ulmo's Fire* for Flute and Harp (1980); *Songs from Water Street* for Mezzo-soprano, Viola, and Piano (1980); *Paeans to Hyacinthus* for Orch. (Houston, Texas, Feb. 6, 1981); *The Waves,* dramatic monologue for Voice, Flute, Clarinet, Viola, and Cello, to a text by Virginia Woolf (1981);

Saltarello for Piano (1981); *State Trumpets* for Organ (1982); *Te Deum* for Chorus and Organ (1982); choruses; psalms.

Sayn-Wittgenstein-Berleburg, Count Friedrich Ernst, German composer; b. Castle Sannerz, Fulda, June 5, 1837; d. Meran, April 16, 1915. He pursued a military career; also studied music with Julius Rietz in Leipzig; publ. *Szenen aus der Frithjofsage* for Voice and Orch.; also songs; wrote 2 operas: *Die Wolfenbraut* (Graz, 1879) and *Antonius und Kleopatra* (Graz, 1883).

Sayve, Lambert de, Flemish composer; b. Sayve, near Liège, 1549; d. Linz, Feb. 1614. As a youth he went to Vienna, where he became a singer in the Imperial chapel in 1562; in 1569 he became choirmaster at the monastery of Melk, near Linz, a post he retained until 1577 (made a trip to Spain in 1570). In 1582 he entered the service of the Archduke Charles in Graz; in 1583 he joined the retinue of Archduke Matthias, King of Bohemia, and lived in Prague. He publ. during his lifetime *Il primo libro delle canzoni a la Napolitana a 5 voci* (Vienna, 1582); *Teutsche Liedlein mit 4 Stimmen* (Vienna, 1602); and (his most important works) the collection *Sacrae symphoniae* (1612), containing 141 pieces *a* 4 to 16 in 12 books. Modern reprints by F. Blume are in *Das Chorwerk*, 51; by A. Einstein in Denkmäler der Tonkunst in Österreich, 77 (41). Six masses by Sayve (*a* 5 to 16) are in Austrian libraries.
BIBLIOGRAPHY: R. Bragard, *Lambert de Sayve* (Liège, 1934); H. Osthoff, *Die Neiderländer und das deutsche Lied* (Berlin, 1938); H. Federhofer, "L. de Sayve an der Grazer Hofkapelle," *Revue Belge de Musicologie,* 3 (1949); G. Rebscher, *Lambert de Sayve als Motettenkomponist* (Diss., Univ. of Frankfurt, 1959).

Sbriglia, Giovanni, celebrated singing teacher; b. Naples, June 23, 1832; d. Paris, Feb. 20, 1916. He sang as a tenor at the San Carlo Theater in Naples; was heard in Italy by Maretzek, the impresario, who engaged him for a season at the Academy of Music in N.Y., where Sbriglia appeared with Adelina Patti (1860); he then made a grand tour of the U.S. with Parodi and Adelaide Phillipps; also sang in Mexico and Havana. He returned to Europe in 1875 and settled in Paris, where he became a highly successful vocal teacher. Jean, Joséphine, and Edouard de Reszke studied with him when they were already professional artists; Sbriglia trained the baritone voice of Jean de Reszke, enabling him to sing tenor roles. Pol Plançon, Nordica, and Sibyl Sanderson were among his pupils.

Scacciati, Bianca, Italian soprano; b. Florence, July 3, 1894; d. Brescia, Oct. 15, 1948. She studied in Milan; made her debut there as Marguerite in *Faust* in 1917. She rapidly asserted herself as one of the most impressive dramatic sopranos in Italy; sang for many seasons at La Scala in Milan; also made successful appearances at Covent Garden in London, at the Paris Opéra, and at the Teatro Colón in Buenos Aires. She was particularly noted for her interpretation of the title role of Puccini's *Turandot.*

Scala, Francis Maria, Italian-born American bandleader, first leader of the U.S. Marine Band so designated; b. Naples, 1819 (or 1820); d. Washington, D.C., April 18, 1903. Beginning his musical career on the clarinet, he enlisted in the U.S. Navy as a musician 3rd-class on the frigate *Brandywine* when it was anchored at Naples in 1841. Following the ship's return to Washington, Scala left the navy for the Marine Corps, and in 1843 was designated fifemajor of the fife corps associated with Marine Corps headquarters. On Sept. 9, 1855, he became de facto the leader of the Marine Band; in 1861 he was made "Principal Musician," and on Sept. 4, 1868, was for the first time, referred to as "Leader of the Band." John Philip Sousa was one of his apprentice bandsmen. Retiring in 1871, Scala continued to reside in Washington until his death. In Sept. 1945 his son Norman P. Scala made the first of several gifts to the Library of Congress honoring his father; these materials contain a large amount of MSS and printed music, chiefly band arrangements made by or for Scala, that represent in essence the library of the Marine Band during the Civil War; included is a note in the hand of Abraham Lincoln, then Scala's Commander-in-Chief.

Scalchi, Sofia, celebrated Italian mezzo-soprano; b. Turin, Nov. 29, 1850; d. Rome, Aug. 22, 1922. She studied with Boccabati; made her debut at Mantua in 1866 as Ulrica in Verdi's *Ballo in maschera;* then sang throughout Italy; appeared in concert in London (Sept. 16, 1868) and at Covent Garden (Nov. 5, 1868) as Azucena, obtaining enormous success. She visited the U.S. for the first time in 1882 with Mapleson's opera company; sang in the opening season of the Metropolitan Opera (1883–84) and again in 1891–92 and 1893–96. She then toured with unfailing success in Russia, Austria, Spain, and South America. She married Count Luigi Lolli in 1875; in 1896 she retired to her estate in Turin; in 1921 went to Rome, where she remained until her death. Her voice had a range of 2½ octaves; it was essentially a contralto voice, but with so powerful a high register that she successfully performed soprano parts.

Scalero, Rosario, eminent Italian pedagogue and composer; b. Moncalieri, near Turin, Dec. 24, 1870; d. Settimo Vittone, near Turin, Dec. 25, 1954. He studied violin with Sivori in Genoa, and in London with Wilhelmj; general subjects with Mandyczewski in Vienna. In 1896 he was engaged as a violin teacher in Lyons, France; then was an instructor at Santa Cecilia in Rome, and examiner at the Naples Cons. and later at the Cons. of Parma. In 1919 he came to the U.S., and was head of the composition classes at the David Mannes School in N.Y.; in 1928 joined the faculty of the Curtis Inst. of Music in Philadelphia; among his students there were Samuel Barber, Gian Carlo Menotti, and Lukas Foss. He wrote a Violin Concerto; *Neapolitan Dances* for Violin and Piano; chamber music; sacred songs; etc.

Scaria, Emil, Austrian bass; b. Graz, Sept. 18, 1838; d. Blasewitz, near Dresden, July 22, 1886. He studied with Netzer at Graz, with Lewy in Vienna, and with García in London. After singing in opera in Dessau (1862), Leipzig (1863), and Dresden (1864), he acquired a fine reputation; in 1872–73, Scaria was a guest artist at the Vienna Court Opera, becoming a member in 1873, and remaining on its roster until 1886. He excelled in Wagner's operas; created the role of Gurnemanz in *Parsifal*. Scaria suffered a mental breakdown in 1882; he resumed his career by touring the U.S. in 1884; suffered a relapse in 1886 and subsequently died, without having recovered his sanity.

BIBLIOGRAPHY: A. Neumann, *Erinnerungen an Richard Wagner* (Leipzig, 1907; Eng. trans., N.Y., 1908).

Scarlatesco, Ion, Rumanian composer; b. Bucharest, 1872; d. there, Sept. 19, 1922. A versatile musician, he began his career as a pianist; also wrote plays and was active as a music critic and harmony teacher. He composed about 50 ballads for Voice and Piano; a String Quartet; *Rumanian Rhapsody* for Orch.; several other pieces in the Rumanian style, among which *Bagatelle* for Violin became popular.

Scarlatti, Alessandro, founder of the "Neopolitan School" of music; b. Palermo, May 2, 1660; d. Naples, Oct. 22, 1725. He was brought to Rome in 1672, and was a pupil there of Carissimi; in 1679 he conducted his first known opera, *L'errore innocente,* at Rome; then followed a performance there of *L'onestà negli amori* at the palace of Queen Christina of Sweden (Feb. 6, 1680); on the score of another opera, *Il Pompeo* (Rome, Jan. 25, 1683), he is styled maestro di cappella to the Queen. In 1694 he was maestro to the Viceroy at Naples. In 1703 he became assistant maestro to Foggia at S. Maria Maggiore in Rome, and succeeded him as first maestro in 1707, resigning in 1709 and returning to Naples, where he subsequently became maestro of the royal chapel. He also taught music; was briefly engaged at the Cons. di Santa Maria di Loreto in Naples (1689), but never had prolonged tenure; among his private pupils was Hasse, who studied with him in 1724. Scarlatti wrote approximately 115 operas (about 50 are extant); *La Rosaura* (Rome, 1690), edited by Eitner, was printed by the *Gesellschaft für Musikforschung,* vol. XIV; in *Teodora Augusta* (Rome, Jan. 3, 1693) he used an incipient *recitativo obbligato,* accompanied by the entire orch.; also several arias with the first part sung *da capo,* a style that was later generally adopted by opera composers. An aria and a duet from *Laodicea e Bernice* (Naples, 1701) have been publ. by J.J.C. Maier, also a terzet and quartet from *La Griselda* (Rome, 1721), with German trans. by Wolzogen; in *Il Tigrane,* his most celebrated opera, marked in the libretto as his 106th work for the stage (Naples, Feb. 16, 1715), the orch. comprises violins, violas, cellos, double basses, 2 flutes, 2 oboes, 2 bassoons, and 2 horns; *Il trionfo dell'onore,* his only comic opera (Naples, Nov. 26, 1718), was trans. into Eng. by Geoffrey Dunn (London, July 23, 1937). Other important operas are: *Olimpia vendicata* (Naples, Dec. 23, 1685); *La Statira* (Rome, Jan. 5, 1690); *Pirro e Demetrio* (Naples, Jan. 28, 1694); *Il Prigioniero fortunato* (Naples, Dec. 14, 1698). Fourteen oratorios are also known; he is said to have written over 200 masses (up to 10 parts), besides much other sacred music (*Concerti sacri,* motets a 1–4, with 2 Violins, Viola, and Organ, were publ. at Amsterdam as opp. 1 and 2; a few separate numbers are in the collections of Choron, the Prince of Moskowa, Commer [a *Tu es Petrus*], Dehn, Proske, and Rochlitz; Choron also publ. a Requiem, and Proske a Mass); his secular vocal music includes madrigals (one *a 4* is in Padre Martini's *Esempli di contrappunto fugato*), serenatas, duets, and some 800 cantatas. He also composed 12 symphs. (concertos) for Small Orch.; String Quartet; Sonata for 3 Flutes; Sonata for 2 Flutes, 2 Violins, and Continuo; Sonata for Flute, 2 Violins, and Continuo; 2 suites for Flute and Harpsichord; variations on Corelli's *La Follia;* toccatas for harpsichord; etc. Some of his works have been publ. by G. Bas and F. Nekes (a 4-voiced *Missa ad voces aequales*), Lenzewski (concertos for strings and continuo), Tebaldini (Sonata for Flute and Strings), J.S. Shedlock (toccatas for harpsichord; 9 vols.), Tagliapietra, Longo (keyboard compositions), etc. In 1974 Harvard Publications in Music began issuing a series of the operas, edited by D.J. Grout.

BIBLIOGRAPHY: E.J. Dent, "The Operas of A. S.," *Sammelbände der Internationalen Musik-Gesellschaft,* IV/1; idem, *A. S. His Life and Works* (London, 1905; new ed. with preface and notes by F. Walker, London, 1960); C. Van den Borren, *A. S. et l'esthétique de l'opéra napolitain* (1922); A. Lorenz, "A. S.s Opern in Wien," *Zeitschrift für Musikwissenschaft,* IX/2 (1926); idem, *A. S.s Jugendopern* (2 vols., Augsburg, 1927); E. Jaloux, *Sur un air de S.* (Maastricht, 1928); A. Cametti, in *Musica d'Oggi* (Feb. 1931); P. Fienga, "La Véritable Patrie et la famille d'A. S.," *Revue Musicale* (Jan. 1929); *Gli Scarlatti* (Siena, 1940); O. Tiby, *La famiglia Scarlatti: Nuove ricerche e documenti* (Rome, 1947); M. Fabbri, *A. S. e il principe Ferdinando de' Medici* (Florence, 1961); R. Pagano & L. Bianchi, *A. S. Catalogue of Works* (Turin, 1972).

Scarlatti, (Giuseppe) Domenico, famous Italian composer and harpsichordist, son of **Alessandro Scarlatti;** b. Naples, Oct. 26, 1685; d. Madrid, July 23, 1757. A pupil of his father, he was named organist and composer at the royal chapel in Naples when he was 16; 2 years later his first operas, *Ottavia restituita al trono* and *Il Giustino,* were produced in Naples (Dec. 19, 1703). In 1705 he was sent by his father to Venice, where he studied with Gasparini. In 1709 he was back in Rome, where he engaged in a friendly contest with Handel, who was adjudged his superior on the organ, while Scarlatti held his own on the harpsichord. From 1709–14 he was maestro di cappella to Queen Maria Casimira of Poland, for whose private theater (in her palace in Rome) he composed 7 operas and an oratorio. He had been appointed in 1713 assistant to Bai, maestro di cappella at the Vatican, and upon the latter's death in 1714 succeeded him as maestro; resigned in 1719. During this time he was also maestro to the Portuguese Ambassador to the Holy See. There is no evidence that Scarlatti went to London in 1720, as is usually stated. But in that year his opera *Amor d'un ombra e gelsoia d'un'aura* (rewritten as *Narciso*) was produced there at the Haymarket Theatre under Roseingrave's direction (May 30), and his brother **Francesco** gave a concert there in September. Scarlatti went to Lisbon c.1719, where he was engaged as maestro of the royal chapel and music teacher to the Princess Maria Barbara, for whom he composed his famous *Esercizi per gravicembalo*, of which the first were publ. in 1738. In 1729 the princess married the heir to the Spanish throne, and Scarlatti accompanied her to Madrid, where he spent the rest of his life. When Maria Barbara became queen in 1746, he was appointed her *maestro de cámara*. After leaving Italy he returned only twice, once for a brief visit to his father at Naples in 1724, and the other time to marry Maria Catalina Gentili on May 15, 1728, in Rome. In Madrid, Scarlatti does not appear to have composed operas, but he founded an instrumental school in Spain, the chief representative being P. Antonio Soler, his pupil. He composed over 600 sonatas and pieces for harpsichord, besides operas, cantatas, and sacred music (2 Misereres *a* 4; a Stabat Mater; a Salve Regina for Soprano and Strings [1756], his last work); the MS of his *Fuga estemporanea per orchestra* is in the library of the Univ. of Münster. The principal MS source for the harpsichord works of Scarlatti is the collection of the Biblioteca Marciana at Venice, which belonged originally to the Queen of Spain and at her death was brought to Italy by Farinelli. Domenico Scarlatti's special claim to renown rests upon his harpsichord music; he studied the characteristics of the instrument, and adapted his compositions to them, being one of the finest writers in the "free style" (a homophonic style with graceful ornamentation, in contrast to the former contrapuntal style). He also obtained effects by the frequent crossing of the hands; runs in thirds and sixths; leaps wider than an octave; broken chords in contrary motion; tones repeated by rapidly changing fingers; etc. During Scarlatti's lifetime some of his keyboard pieces were printed in various editions in London and Paris. Later editions include a collection by Czerny, of 200 pieces; Breitkopf, 60; Pauer, 50; Köhler, 12 sonatas and fugues; Tausig, 3 sonatas; Bülow, 18 pieces in suite form; Schletterer, 18; André, 28; Banck, 30; Farrenc, 100 (in *Trésor des pianistes*); Sauer, 25; Barth, 70; Gerstenberg, 5 sonatas (not included in the Longo ed.); Buonamici, 22 (in Schirmer's Library, vol. 73). Ricordi publ. Scarlatti's "complete" harpsichord works, edited by A. Longo, in 11 vols. (one vol. as supplement; pp. 1906ff.), also a thematic index (Milan, 1937); 60 sonatas edited by Ralph Kirkpatrick were publ. by G. Schirmer. A complete edition of the sonatas is in vols. 31–41 of the Le Pupitre series; the *Complete Keyboard Works*, in a fine facsimile edition of 18 vols., was put out by Ralph Kirkpatrick in 1971.

BIBLIOGRAPHY: E.J. Dent, in the *Monthly Musical Record* (1906), and in *Auftakt* (1922); A. Longo, *D. Scarlatti e la sua figura nella storia della musica* (Naples, 1913); G.F. Malipiero, "D. Scarlatti," *Musical Quarterly* (July 1927); F. Torrefranca, *Le origini italiane del romanticismo musicale* (Turin, 1930); W. Gerstenberg, *Die Klavierkompositionen D. Scarlattis* (1933); S. Sitwell, *A Background for D. Scarlatti* (London, 1935); U. Rolandi, "Per una biobibliografia di Scarlatti," *Bolletino dei Musicisti* (Nov. 1935); C. Valabrega, *D. Scarlatti, Il suo secolo, la sua opera* (with 233 musical examples; Modena, 1937); S.A. Luciani, "D. Scarlatti" (biographical and bibliographical notes; valuable), *Rassegna Musicale* (Dec. 1938; Jan. and Feb. 1939; also reprinted separately); *Gli Scarlatti* (Siena, 1940); A. Solar Quintes, "Documentos sobre la familia de Domenico Scarlatti," *Anuario Musical* (Barcelona, 1949); H. Keller, *D. Scarlatti* (Leipzig, 1957); G. Pestelli, *Le Sonate di Domenico Scarlatti: Proposta di un ordinamento cronologico* (Turin, 1967); R. Kirkpatrick, "Who Wrote the Scarlatti Sonatas?" *Notes* (March 1973). The most important publication dealing with his life and works is *Domenico Scarlatti* by Ralph Kirkpatrick, publ. in Princeton, N.J., and London in 1953. Apart from clearing up biographical data, Kirkpatrick gives a new chronological numbering of works, which has been widely accepted and has superseded Longo's catalogue.

Scarlatti, Giuseppe, Italian composer, grandson of **Alessandro Scarlatti,** nephew of **Domenico Scarlatti;** b. Naples, c.1718; d. Vienna, Aug. 17, 1777. He was in Rome in 1739, and later in Lucca, where he married **Barbara Stabili,** a singer (1747). He went to Vienna in 1757, and remained there for 20 years until his death. He wrote 31 operas, produced in Rome, Florence, Lucca, Turin, Venice, Naples, Milan, and Vienna; of these the most successful was *L'isola disabitata* (Venice, Nov. 20, 1757). Another Giuseppe Scarlatti (a nephew of Alessandro Scarlatti), whose name appears in some reference works, was not a musician.

BIBLIOGRAPHY: H. Springer, "Das Partitur-Autograph von Giuseppe Scarlattis bisher verschollener Clemenza di Tito," *Beiträge zum Bibliotheks-und Buchwesen* (1913); *Gli Scarlatti* (Siena, 1940); O. Tiby, *La famiglia Scarlatti: Nuove ricerche e documenti* (Rome, 1947); Frank Walker, "Some Notes on the Scarlattis," *Music Review* (Aug. 1951).

Scarmolin, (Anthony) Louis, American conductor and composer; b. Schio, Italy, July 30, 1890; d. Union City, N.J., July 13, 1969. He came to the U.S. as a boy; graduated from the N.Y. College of Music in 1907; served in the U.S. Army during World War I; then lived in Union City, N.J. He wrote 6 operas and several symph. poems and overtures; also *Miniature Symphony* (Cleveland, Feb. 7, 1940); altogether he composed some 200 opus numbers.

Scarpini, Pietro, Italian pianist; b. Rome, April 6, 1911. He studied at the Santa Cecilia Cons. in Rome;

made his concert debut in 1936; then gave recitals in Europe and in the U.S.; from 1940 to 1967 he taught at the Cons. of Florence; in 1967 joined the faculty of the Milan Cons. He specializes in the modern repertoire of piano music; wrote a Piano Concerto and a Piano Quintet; also made an arrangement for 2 pianos of Mahler's 10th Symph.

Scelsi, Giacinto, remarkable Italian composer; b. La Spezia, Jan. 8, 1905. He studied composition with Respighi and Casella in Rome; then went to Vienna, where he became interested in the Schoenbergian method of writing music outside the bounds of traditional tonality; at the same time he became deeply immersed in the study of the musical philosophy of the East, in which the scales and rhythms are perceived as functional elements of the human psyche. As a result of these multifarious absorptions of ostensibly incompatible ingredients, Scelsi formulated a style of composition that is synthetic in its sources and pragmatic in its artistic materialization.

WORKS: FOR ORCH.: *Rotative* for 3 Pianos, Wind Instruments, and Percussion (1930); *Rapsodia romantica* (1931); Sinfonietta (1932); *Preludio e fuga* (1938); *Balata* for Cello and Orch. (1945); *La nascità del verbo* (1948; International Festival for Contemporary Music, Brussels, June 28, 1950); *4 pezzi su una nota sola* (1959); *Hurqualia* for Orch. and Amplified Instruments (1960); *Aion* (1961); *Nomos* for 2 Orchs. and Organ (1963); *Chukrim* for String Orch. (1963); *Amahit* for Violin and 18 Instruments (1965); *Anagamin* for 12 String Instruments (1965); *Ohoi* for 16 String Instruments (1966); *Uaxuctum* for Chorus, Orch., and Ondes Martenot (1966); *Natura renovatur* for 11 String Instruments (1967); *Konx-om-pax* for Chorus, Orch., and Organ (1969); *Pfhat* for Chorus and Orch. (1974). CHAMBER MUSIC: 4 string quartets (1944, 1961, 1963, 1964); *Piccola Suite* for Flute and Clarinet (1953); *Hyxos* for Alto Flute, Gong, and Bells (1955); String Trio (1958); *Elegia* for Viola and Cello (1958); *Rucke di Guck* for Piccolo and Oboe (1958); *I presagi* for 10 Instruments (1958); *Kya* for Solo Clarinet and 7 Instruments (1959); *Khoom* for Soprano and 6 Instruments (1962); *Duo* for Violin and Cello (1965); *Ko-lho* for Flute and Clarinet (1966); *Okanagon* for Harp, Tam-tam, and Double Bass (1968); *Duo* for Violin and Double Bass (1977); *5 Divertimenti* for Violin Solo (1952–56); *Pwill* for Flute Solo (1954); *Coelocanth* for Viola Solo (1955); *3 Studies* for Viola Solo (1956); *Trilogy,* 3 pieces for Cello Solo (1957–65); *Ko-Tha* for Guitar Solo (1967); *Praham II* for 9 Instruments (1973); *3 pezzi* for Clarinet; *3 pezzi* for Trumpet; *3 pezzi* for Saxophone; *3 pezzi* for French Horn; *3 pezzi* for Trombone; other pieces for solo instruments. VOCAL WORKS: *Taiagaru,* 5 invocations for Soprano Solo (1962); *20 canti del Capricorno* for Solo Voice (1962–72); *Manto per 4* for Voice, Flute, Trombone, and Cello (1972); *Praham I* for Voice, 12 Instruments, and Tape (1972). FOR PIANO: 24 preludes (1936–40); *Hispania* (1939); 10 suites; 3 sonatas.

Schaab, Robert, German organist and composer; b. Rötha, near Leipzig, Feb. 28, 1817; d. Leipzig, March 18, 1887. He studied with C.F. Becker and Mendelssohn; became organist of the Johanniskirche in Leipzig; publ. a great number of works for organ; his 60 *Choralvorspiele* (opp. 118, 119, 121) are valuable.

Schaaf, Edward Oswald, American composer; b. Brooklyn, Aug. 7, 1869; d. Newark, N.J., June 25, 1939. He was a physician (M.D., Bellevue Hospital Medical College, N.Y., 1894); studied at the Univ. of Vienna (1894–96); was musically an autodidact, through intensive study of classical masterworks. He wrote a grand opera, 8 smaller operas, 2 symphs., 4 string quartets, 2 masses, 70 songs, 20 military band pieces, and 90 works for player-piano. He publ. *A Study of Modern Operatic Art; The Art of Playing Piano Transcriptions;* etc.; lived most of his life in Newark.

Schachner, Rudolf Joseph, German pianist and composer; b. Munich, Dec. 31, 1821; d. Reichenhall, Aug. 15, 1896. He was a pupil of J.B. Cramer; appeared in concert in Vienna, Paris, Leipzig, etc.; in 1853, settled in London as a teacher; later went to Vienna. He composed 2 piano concertos and a number of pieces for piano solo: *Poésies musicales, Romance variée, Ombres et rayons, La Chasse,* etc.

Schacht, Matthias Henriksen, Danish music lexicographer; b. Visby, Jütland, April 29, 1660; d. Kerteminde, Aug. 8, 1700. He was a pedagogue; served as rector; left in MS a music dictionary, *Bibliotheca musica* (publ. by G. Skjerne as *Musicus danicus,* Copenhagen, 1928), which Gerber utilized for his lexicon.

Schacht, Theodor von, German pianist, composer, and conductor; b. Strasbourg, 1748; d. Regensburg, June 20, 1823. He studied piano with Küffner and harmony with Riepel in Regensburg (1756–66); then took lessons in composition with Jommelli in Stuttgart (1766–71). Returning to Regensburg in 1771, he became music director of the town theater; in 1773 was appointed court music Intendant. From 1786–1805 he led the court orch. He then went to Vienna; in 1812 he returned to Germany. He was a prolific musician; wrote a number of operas and theater pieces to German and Italian texts, as well as competently crafted symphs., concertos, and chamber music. He was a minor master of contrapuntal arts; his series of 84 canons, dedicated to members of "the fair sex," quite amusing and even daring for his time, was publ. in Baden in 1811 under the title *Divertimento del bel sesso nel soggiorno di Baden.*

BIBLIOGRAPHY: S. Färber, *Das Regensburger fürstlich Thurn und Taxissche Hoftheater und seine Oper* (Regensburg, 1936).

Schack (Žak), Benedikt, Bohemian tenor and composer; b. Mirotitz (baptized, Feb. 7), 1758; d. Munich, Dec. 10, 1826. He studied in Prague and Vienna; made his operatic debut in Salzburg (1786); became acquainted with Mozart's librettist Schikaneder, and through him met Mozart in Vienna (1789 and became friendly with him; he was the singer (if contemporary reports are to be trusted) who sang passages from the Requiem for the dying composer. Mozart wrote piano variations (K. 613) on an aria from Schack's opera *Die verdeckten Sachen.* Among Schack's theatrical pieces the following were performed in Vienna: *Der dumme Gärtner aus dem Gebirge* (July 12, 1789); *Die wiener Zeitung* (Jan. 12, 1791); *Die Antwort auf die Frage* (Dec. 16, 1792); *Die beiden Nannerin* (July 26, 1794).

Schad, Joseph, German pianist and composer; b. Steinach, March 6, 1812; d. Bordeaux, July 4, 1879. He studied at the Würzburg Cons. and later with Aloys Schmitt at Frankfurt. In 1834 he became an organist at Morges, Switzerland; in 1847, settled in Bordeaux, where he gained high repute as a piano teacher. He publ. a great number of melodious piano pieces which enjoyed some success during his lifetime: *Le Soupir, La Gracieuse, La Rose des Alpes, Fleur des Alpes, Tarentelle,* etc.; fantasias, transcriptions.

Schadewitz, Carl, German composer; b. St. Ingbert, Jan. 23, 1887; d. Reppendorf, near Kitzingen, March 27, 1945. He studied in Würzburg, and lived there most of his life as a choral conductor and teacher. He was a prolific composer; his works include a musical fairy tale, *Johannisnacht;* a "Romantic" oratorio, *Kreislers Heimkehr;* an opera, *Laurenca;* a tone poem, *Heldengedenken* (1943); a number of songs, of which the cycle *Die Heimat* (1934) is outstanding; much chamber music; choruses.
BIBLIOGRAPHY: A. Maxsein, *Carl Schadewitz* (Würzburg, 1954).

Schaefer, Karl Ludolf, German physiologist, physicist, and acoustician; b. Rostock, July 2, 1866; d. Berlin, Feb. 12, 1931. He obtained his M.D. diploma in 1889; then studied with Carl Stumpf; taught vocal physiology at the Berlin Hochschule. He publ. *Musikalische Akustik* (1902; 2nd ed., 1912); *Einführung in die Musikwissenschaft auf physikalischer, physiologischer und psychologischer Grundlage* (Leipzig, 1915); numerous other studies on acoustics and tone psychology.

Schaefer, Theodor, Czech composer; b. Telč, Jan. 23, 1904; d. Brno, March 19, 1969. He studied with Jaroslav Kvapil at the Brno Cons. (1922–26) and with Novák at the Prague Cons. (1926–29). Upon graduation he taught at the Palacký Univ. at Olomouc, the Brno Cons., and, until his death, at the Janáček Academy in Brno. He was an advocate of a so-called diathematic principle of constructing themes using fragments of preceding thematic units.
WORKS: Children's opera, *Maugli* (1932); ballet, *Legenda o štěstí* (*Legend of Happiness;* 1952); 2 unnumbered symphs. (1926, 1955–61); Violin Concerto

(1932–33); *Wallachian Serenade* for Orch. (1936); Piano Concerto (1937–43); *Jánošík,* balladic overture (1939); *Winter Cantata* for Soprano, Chorus, and Orch. (1943–45); *Diathema* for Viola and Orch. (1955–56); *The Barbarian and the Rose* for Piano and Orch. (1957–58); *Diathema* for Orch. (1957–58); *Rhapsodic Reportage* for Orch. (1960); 3 string quartets (1929, 1941, 1944–45); Wind Quintet (1935–36); *Divertimento mesto* for Wind Quintet and String Trio (1946); *Cikánovy housle (Gypsy Violin);* 4 movements for Violin and Piano (1960); *Etudes* for Piano (1936–37); *Theme with Variations* for Piano (1936); choruses; songs, including *Milostné balady (Love Ballads),* for voice and piano, commemorating the destruction of the village of Lidice by the Nazis (1943); *Bithematikon* for Baritone and Piano (1967).

Schaeffer (Schäffer), Boguslaw (Julien), remarkable Polish composer and music theoretician of great originality; b. Lwow, June 6, 1929. He studied violin at Opole, composition with Artur Malawski at the State High School of Music in Cracow, and musicology with Jachimecki at the Jagiello Univ. in Cracow (1949–53); in 1959 he took a course in advanced techniques with Luigi Nono. In 1963 he was appointed a prof. of composition at the Cons. of Cracow; in 1967 he began publishing a periodical devoted to new music, *Forum Musicum.* Schaeffer's early works were inspired by the melorhythms of Polish folk songs, but he made a decisive turn in 1953 with his *Music for Strings: Nocturne,* which became the first serial work by a Polish composer; he devised a graphic and polychromatic optical notation indicating intensity of sound, proportional lengths of duration, and position of notes in melodic and contrapuntal lines, with the components arranged in binary code; he also wrote music in the "third stream" style, combining jazz with classical procedures; he further experimented in "antigenic" or "decomposed" techniques. He is married to **Mieczyslawa Janina Hanuszewska** (b. Borszów, Oct. 1, 1929), a learned musicographer.
WORKS: Concerto for 2 Pianos (1951); *3 Short Pieces* for Chamber Orch. (1951); Sonatina for Piano (1952); *2 Studies* for Solo Flute (1953); *Music for String Quartet* (1954); *Composition* for Piano (1954); *2 Studies* for Solo Saxophone (1954); Sonata for Solo Violin (1955); *Study in Diagram* for Piano (1956); *Permutations* for 10 Instruments (1956); 10 *Models* for Piano (1954, 1957, 1961, 1963, 1965, 1970, 1971, 1972, 1976, 1977); *Extremes* for 10 Instruments, a score without notes (1957); 4 string quartets (1957, 1964, 1971, 1973); *4 movimenti* for Piano and Orch. (1957); *Tertium datur,* treatise for Harpsichord and Chamber Orch. (1958; Warsaw, Sept. 19, 1960); *8 Pieces* for Piano (1954–58); *Variations* for Piano (1958); *Monosonata* for 6 String Quartets subdivided into 3 uneven groups (1959; International Society for Contemporary Music Festival, Darmstadt, June 19, 1961); *Equivalenze sonore,* concerto for Percussion Chamber Orch. (1959); *3 Studies, Articulation,* and *Linear Construction* for Piano (1959); *Concerto breve* for Cello and Orch. (1959); Concerto for String

Quartet (1959); *Joint Constructions* for Strings (1960); *Negatives* for Solo Flute (1960); *Montaggio* for 6 Players (1960); *Topofonica* for 40 Instruments (1960); *Little Symphony: Scultura* (1960; Warsaw, Sept. 29, 1965); *Configurations, Points of Departure,* and *Non-Stop* for Piano (1960; *Non-Stop* was first perf. by a relay team of 2 pianists at the first Polish Happening in Cracow, Aug. 27–28, 1964, with a total duration of 8 hours); *Concerto per sei e tre* for a changing Solo Instrument (Clarinet, Saxophone, Violin, Cello, Percussion, and Piano) and 3 Orchs. (1960; Katowice, Nov. 7, 1962); *Musica* for Harpsichord and Orch. (Venice, April 25, 1961); *Kody (Codes)* for Chamber Orch. (Warsaw, Sept. 19, 1961); *Azione a due* for Piano and 11 Instruments (1961; Stuttgart, Dec. 4, 1970); *Imago musicae* for Violin and 9 Interpolating Instruments (1961); *Sound Forms* for Solo Saxophone (1961); *3 Compositions for MJQ* (Modern Jazz Quartet), 3rd-stream music (1961); *Constructions* for Solo Vibraphone (1962); *4 Pieces* for String Trio (1962); *Course "J"* for Jazz Ensemble and Chamber Symph. Orch. (Warsaw, Oct. 28, 1962); *Musica ipsa* for an Orch. of Deep Instruments (Warsaw, Sept. 20, 1962); *TIS-MW-2,* metamusical audio-visual spectacle for Actor, Mime, Ballerina, and 5 Musicians (1962–63; Cracow, April 25, 1964); *Expressive Aspects* for Soprano and Flute (1963); *Contours* for Piano (1963); *Collage and Form* for 8 Jazz Musicians and Orch. (1963; Urbana, Ill., March 19, 1967); Violin Concerto (1961–63); *TIS GK,* stage work (1963); *Scenario* for a nonexistent but possible instrumental Actor (1963); *Music for MI* for Voice, Vibraphone, 6 Narrators, Jazz Ensemble, and Orch. (1963); *S'alto* for Saxophone and Chamber Orch. of Soloists (1963; Zagreb, May 13, 1963); *Audiences I–V* for various Performers (1964); *Sfumato* for Solo Harpsichord (1964); *2 Pieces* for Violin and Piano (1964); *Collage* for Chamber Orch. (1964); Quartet for 2 Pianists and 2 Optional Performers (1965); *Przeslanie (Transmissions)* for Cello and 2 Pianos (1965); *Symphony: Electronic Music* for Tape (1964–66); *Howl,* monodrama, after Allen Ginsberg's poem, for Narrator, 2 Actors, Ensemble of Instrumentalists, and Ensemble of Performers (1966); *Visual Music* for 5 Optional Performers (1966); Trio for Flute, Harp, Viola, and Tape (1966); Quartet for Oboe and String Trio (1966); *Composition* for Harp and Piano (1966); *Decet* for Harp and 9 Instruments (1966); *Assemblage* for Tape (1966); *4H/1P* for Piano, 4-hands (1966); Quartet for 4 Actors (1966; ISCM Festival, Athens, Sept. 15, 1979); Piano Concerto (1967); *Hommage à Strzeminski* for Tape (1967); *Media* for Voices and Instruments (1967); *Symfonia: Muzyka orkiestrowa* (1967); *Quartet SG* (1968); *Lecture* for 6 Performers (1968); *Fragment* for 2 Actors and Cello Player (1968); *Jazz Concerto* for Jazz Ensemble of 12 Instruments and an Orch. of Flutes, Bassoons, Trumpets, Trombones, and Low Strings (1969; ISCM Festival, Boston, Oct. 30, 1976); Piano Trio (1969); *Scena otwarta* for 3 Players (1969); *Heraklitiana* for 10 various Solo Instruments and Tape (1970); *Synectics* for 3 Performers (1970); *Comunicazione audiovisiva* for 5 Players (1970); *Algorithms* for 7 Performers (1970); *Thema* for Tape (1970); *Texts* for Orch. (1971); *Mare,*

concertino for Piano and 9 Instruments (1971); *Estratto* for String Trio (1971); *15 Elements* for 2 Pianos (1971); *Experimenta* for Pianist (on 2 pianos) and Orch. (1971; Poznan, April 27, 1972); *Variants* for Solo Oboe (1971); *Variants* for Wind Quintet (1971); *Sgraffito* for Flute, Cello, Harpsichord, and 2 Pianos (1971); *Contract* for Soprano, Cello, and Percussion (1971); *Confrontations* for Solo Instrument and Orch. (1972); *Conceptual Music* (1972); *Interview* for Solo Violin (1972); Concerto for 3 Pianos (1972); *Free Form* No. 1 for 5 Instruments (1972) and No. 2, *Evocazioni,* for Solo Double Bass (1972); *blueS No. 1* for 2 Pianos and Tape (1972); *blueS No. 2* for Instrumental Ensemble (1972); *blueS No. 3* for 2 Pianos (1978); *blueS No. 4* for 2 Pianos and Tape (audiovisual; 1980); *Bergsoniana* for Soprano, Flute, Piano, Horn, Double Bass, and Piano (1972); *Dreams of Schäffer,* after Ionesco, for an Ensemble of Performers (1972; Cracow, April 14, 1975); *Hommage à Czyzewski* for an Ensemble of Stage and Musical Performers (1972); *19 Micropieces* for Cello and 6 Concurrent Performers (1972); *Negative Music* for any Instrument (1972); *Neues* for 3 Violins (1972); *21 VI 1972, Twilight,* situational composition (1972); Symph. in 9 movements for Large Orch. and 6 Solo Instruments (1973; Wroclaw, April 21, 1977, composer at the piano as one of the soloists); *Tentative Music* for 159 Instruments (1973); *aSa* for Harpsichord (1973); *aDieu* for Trombone Solo (1973); *Synthistory* for Tape (1973); *Open Music,* emotiographs for any Voice or Instrument (1975); *4 Dispositions* for Piano (1960, 1965, 1970, 1975); *Warsaw Overture: Harmonies and Counterpoints No. 1* for Orch. (1975); *Antiphona,* choral-concrete sketch for Tape (1975); *Missa elettronica* for Boys' Choir and Electronic Tape (1975; Warsaw, Sept. 24, 1976); *Romuald Traugutt: Harmonies and Counterpoints No. 2* for Orch. (1976; Warsaw, Sept. 20, 1977); *Iranian Set* for an Ensemble of Performers (Shiraz, July 12, 1976); *Spinoziana,* action music for an Ensemble of Performers (1977); *Minimal Art* for Tuba and Piano (1977); *Gravesono* for an Orch. of Wind and Percussion Instruments (1977); *Self-expression* for Solo Cello (1978); *Vaniniana* for an Ensemble of Performers (1978–80); *Poetries,* to poems by Carol Adler, for Quadro-tape (1978); *Matan* for 3 Percussionists (1978; version for 5 Percussionists, 1980); *Kesukaan* for 13 String Instruments (1978); *Miserere* for Soprano, Choir, Orch., and Tape (1978); *Heideggeriana* for an Ensemble of Performers (1979); *Tsiyur* for Organ and Tape (1979); *Jangwa* for Double Bass and Orch. (1979); *Te Deum* for Voices and Orch. (1979); *Maah* for Orch. and Tape (1979); *Cantata: Electronic Music* (1979–80); *Berlin '80* for Piano and Electronic Sources (1980); *Out of tune, No. 2* for Soprano, Cello, and Piano (1980).

WRITINGS: *Almanach wspólczesnych kompozytorów polskich* (*Almanach of Modern Polish Composers;* Cracow, 1956; 3rd ed., with Mieczyslawa Hanuszewska, 1980); *Maly informator muzyki XX wieku* (*Little Lexicon of Music of the 20th Century;* Cracow, 1958; new ed., 1975); *Nowa muzyka, Problemy wspólczesnej techniki kompozytorskiej* (*New Music, Problems of Contemporary Technique in Composing;* Cracow, 1958; new ed., 1969); *Klasycy dodekafonii (Classics of Dodecaphonic Music;* 2 vol., Cracow, 1961, 1964); *Leksykon kompozytorów XX wieku (Lexicon of 20th-century Composers;* 2 vols., Cracow, 1963, 1965); *W kręgu nowej muzyki (In the Sphere of New Music;* Cracow, 1967); *Dzwieki i znaki (Sounds and Signs: Introduction to Contemporary Composition;* Warsaw, 1969); *Muzyka XX wieku (Music of the 20th Century;* Cracow, 1975); *Wstęp do kompozycji (Introduction to Composition;* Cracow, 1976; in Polish and Eng.); *Historia muzyki. Style i twórcy (History of Music, Styles and Authors;* Poznan, 1979).

BIBLIOGRAPHY: Jadwiga Hodor and Bohdan Pociej, *Boguslaw Schäffer and His Music* (Glasgow, 1975); Jadwiga Hodor, "Twórczość kompozytorska Boguslawa Schäffera," a comprehensive study, in *Miesiecznik Literacki,* IX (1979).

Schaeffer, Pierre, French acoustician, composer, and novelist; b. Nancy, Aug. 14, 1910. Working in a radio studio in Paris, he conceived the idea of arranging a musical montage of random sounds, including outside noises. On April 15, 1948, he formulated the theory of *musique concrète,* which was to define such random assemblages of sounds. When the magnetic tape was perfected, Schaeffer made use of it by rhythmic acceleration and deceleration, changing the pitch and dynamics and modifying the nature of the instrumental timbre. He made several collages of elements of "concrete music," among them *Concert de bruits* (1948) and (with Pierre Henry) *Symphonie pour un homme seul* (1950); also created an experimental opera, *Orphée 53* (1953). He incorporated his findings and ideas in the publication *A la recherche de la musique concrète* (Paris, 1952) and in *Traité des objects sonores* (Paris, 1966). Eventually he abandoned his acoustical experimentations and turned to literature. He publ. both fictional and quasi-scientific novels, among them *Traité des objets musicaux* (1966); *Le Gardien de volcan* (1969); *Excusez-moi si je meurs* (1981); *Prélude, Chorale et Fugue* (1983).

BIBLIOGRAPHY: Marc Pierret, *Entretiens avec Pierre Schaeffer* (Paris, 1969); S. Brunet, *Pierre Schaeffer* (Paris, 1970).

Schaeffner, André, French writer on music; b. Paris, Feb. 7, 1895; d. there, Aug. 11, 1980. He studied composition with Vincent d'Indy at the Schola Cantorum, and took a course in ethnography at the Institut d'Ethnologie in Paris. In 1931 he founded an ethnological dept. at the Musée de l'Homme in Paris, which he headed until 1965. Between 1931 and 1958 he led 6 scientific excursions in Africa. In 1958–67 he was president of the Société Française de Musicologie. He also took great interest in modern music and in lexicography; he was editor of the French edition of Riemann's *Musiklexikon (Dictionnaire de musique,* Paris, 1931). He compiled *Le Jazz* (with Cœuroy; Paris, 1926) and a monograph on Stravinsky (Paris, 1931), as well as *Origines des instruments de musique* (Paris, 1936; reprint with additional bibliography, The Hague, 1968). He further publ. numerous treatises on various aspects of modern and primitive music, among them *Les Kissi, Une Société noire et ses instruments de musique* (Paris, 1951).

Schäfer, Dirk, eminent Dutch composer, pianist, and pedagogue; b. Rotterdam, Nov. 23, 1873; d. Amsterdam, Feb. 16, 1931. He studied in Rotterdam and Cologne; after a European concert tour he settled in Amsterdam, where he was active as a pianist and teacher; he composed several piano works on exotic themes; also *Rapsodie javanaise* for Orch. (1904); 2 violin sonatas; Piano Quintet; Cello Sonata; songs. A book of reminiscences about him, *Herinnering aan Dirk Schäfer,* was publ. in Amsterdam the year after his death.

BIBLIOGRAPHY: Cor Backers, *Nederlandse Componisten van 1400 tot op onze tijd* (Amsterdam, 1942; pp. 110–12).

Schafer, R. Murray, Canadian composer; b. Sarnia, Ontario, July 18, 1933. He studied at the Royal Cons. of Music in Toronto with John Weinzweig (1954–55); went to Vienna in 1956 and then on to England as a journalist. Returning to Canada in 1961, he became associated with the Canadian Broadcasting Corp.; explored the nature of physical sound for an "inventory of world soundscapes." He developed a sui generis system of topological transmutation, exemplified by his satire/tribute for orch. and tape *The Son of Heldenleben* (Montreal, Nov. 13, 1968), in which he systematically distorted the thematic materials of *Ein Heldenleben* by Richard Strauss, retaining the essential motivic substance of the original score.

WORKS: 2 operas: *Loving/Toi,* with Electronic Sound (stage premiere, Toronto, March 11, 1978), and *Patria,* a trilogy-in-progress, of which *Patria II* is complete (Stratford, Ontario, Aug. 23, 1972); *Jonah,* musical-dramatic work for Actors, Singers, Chorus, and Instruments (1979); Concerto for Harpsichord and 8 Wind Instruments (1954); *Minnelieder* for Mezzo-soprano and Wind Quintet (1956); *Protest and Incarceration,* 2 songs for Mezzo-soprano and Orch. (1960); *St. Jean de Brebeuf,* cantata for Baritone and Orch. (1961); *Canzoni for Prisoners* for Orch. (1961–62); *5 Studies on Texts by Prudentius* for Soprano and 4 Flutes (1962); 2 educational works of variable duration for Youth Orch.: *Invertible Material* (1963) and *Statement in Blue,* in aleatory notation (1964); *Untitled Composition* for Orch. (1963); *Requiems for the Party Girl* for Soprano and 9 Instruments (1966); *Threnody* for 5 Young Narrators, Youth Chorus, and Orch., with Tape (1966); *Gita,* piece for Chorus, Brass Ensemble, and Tape (Lenox, Mass., Aug. 10, 1967); *From the Tibetan Book of the Dead* for Soprano, Chorus, Flute, Clarinet, and Tape (1968); *The Son of Heldenleben* (1968); *No Longer Than 10 Minutes* for Orch. (1970; the title derives from the stipulation of the maximum length of the piece; Toronto, Feb. 16, 1971); *Sappho* for Mezzo-soprano, Harp, Piano, Guitar, and Percussion (1970); String Quartet (1970);

Okeanos for Tape (1971); *Enchantress* for Soprano, Flute, and 8 Cellos (1971); *In Search of Zoroaster* for Male Voice, Chorus, Percussion (played by chorus members), and Organ (1971); *East* for Orch. (1972); *Tehillah* for Chorus and Percussion (1972); *Arcana* for Voice and Instruments (1972); the trilogy *Lustro* (1969–72; premiere as a trilogy, Toronto, May 31, 1973) consisting of 3 separately composed works: *Divan i Shams i Tabriz* for 7 Singers, Tape, and Orch. (1969), *Music for the Morning of the World* for Voice and Tape (1970), and *Beyond the Great Gate of Light* for 7 Singers, Tape, and Orch. (1972); *North/White* for Orch. (1973; Vancouver, Aug. 17, 1973; a protest of government and industry's "rape of the Canadian North"); String Quartet No. 2, *Waves* (1976); *Train* for Youth Orch. (1976); *Adieu Robert Schumann* for Contralto and Orch., derived from Clara Schumann's diaries chronicling Schumann's madness (1976; Ottawa, March 14, 1978); *Apocalypsis* for 500 Professional and Amateur Performers (1976); first complete perf., London, Ontario, Nov. 28, 1980); *Beauty and the Beast* for Voice and String Quartet (1980); *Apocalypsis* for Soloist, Chorus, and Orch., allegorical spectacle about the destruction of the world according to St. John the Divine (1980; Ontario, Nov. 28, 1980); *RA,* multimedia work with audience participation, based on the myth of the Egyptian sun god (Toronto, dawn-to-dusk, May 6, 1983). WRITINGS: *British Composers in Interview* (London, 1963); *The Composer in the Classroom* (Toronto, 1965); *Ear Cleaning* (Toronto, 1967); *The New Soundscape* (Toronto, 1969); *When Words Sing* (N.Y., 1971); *E.T.A. Hoffmann and Music* (Toronto, 1975); *The Tuning of the World* (N.Y., 1977); *Ezra Pound and Music: The Complete Criticism* (N.Y., 1977).

Schäffer, August, German composer; b. Rheinsberg, Aug. 25, 1814; d. Baden-Baden, Aug. 7, 1879. He was a pupil, from 1833, of Mendelssohn in Berlin, where he spent most of his life. His humorous duets and quartets won great popularity; he also composed symphs., string quartets, piano pieces, etc., and produced a few operas: *Emma von Falkenstein* (Berlin, 1839); *José Riccardo* (Hannover, 1857); *Junker Habakuk* (Hannover, 1861).

Schäffer, Julius, German choral conductor and writer; b. Krevese, near Osterburg, Sept. 28, 1823; d. Breslau, Feb. 10, 1902. He studied theology at Halle, where friendship with Franz, and musicians in the nearby city of Leipzig, won him over to music. In 1850 he went to Berlin to study under Dehn; in 1855, to Schwerin, where he founded and conducted the Schlosskirchenchor, modeled after the Berlin cathedral choir. In 1860 he became conductor of the Singakademie, in Breslau. He publ. chorale books (1866, 1880); songs and part-songs. In defense of Franz's "additional accompaniments" to scores by Bach and Handel, Schäffer wrote, *versus* Chrysander, *Zwei Beurteiler Robert Franzs* (1863); *Fr. Chrysander in seinen Klavierauszugen zur deutschen Händel-Ausgabe* (1876); and *R. Franz in seinen Bearbeitungen älterer Vokalwerke* (1877); also *Die Breslauer Singakademie* (1875).
BIBLIOGRAPHY: E. Bonn, *Julius Schäffer* (Breslau, 1903).

Schaffrath, Christoph, German composer; b. Hohenstein-on-Elbe, 1709; d. Berlin, Feb. 17, 1763. As a harpsichordist, he entered the service of Frederick the Great in 1735 (while the latter was still Crown Prince) at Rheinsberg, and in 1740 followed that monarch to Berlin. He wrote concertos and sonatas for harpsichord, chamber music, etc.

Schafhäutl, Karl Franz Emil von, German acoustician; b. Ingolstadt, Feb. 16, 1803; d. Munich, Feb. 25, 1890. Among other occupations he was a prof. of mining and custodian of the state geological collections. He was also a student of acoustics, and worked in close cooperation with Theobald Böhm, whom he advised and aided in the construction of his instruments.
WRITINGS: "Theorie gedackter, zylindrischer und konischer Pfeifen und der Querflöten," and "Über Schall, Ton, Knall und einige andere Gegenstände der Akustik," both in *Neue Annalen der Chemie* (1833, 1834; both also separately printed); *Über Phonometrie* (1854); *Abt Georg Jos. Vogler; Sein Leben, Charackter und musikalisches System* (1888); also, in the *Allegemeine Musikalische Zeitung,* 1879, investigations into the phenomena of *Klangfarbe* (tone color), with results at variance with Helmholtz's theory.
BIBLIOGRAPHY: "Errinerungen an K. Ett und K. von Schafhäutl," *Kirchenmusikalisches Jahrbuch* (1891).

Schalk, Franz, Austrian conductor; b. Vienna, May 27, 1863; d. Edlach, Sept. 2, 1931. He studied with Bruckner; in 1888 was Kapellmeister in Reichenbach; in 1889–95, in Graz; in 1895–98, in Prague; was a guest conductor at Covent Garden in London in 1898, 1907, and 1911; succeeded Seidl in 1898 as conductor at the Metropolitan Opera House in N.Y.; in 1899, he was conductor of the Berlin Royal Opera; from 1900 at the Vienna Hofoper; in 1904–21 he was also conductor of the Vienna Gesellschaft der Musikfreunde and a prof. of conducting at the Royal Academy of Music; during the 1907–8 season he was conductor of the Vienna Phil., with which he made guest appearances beginning in 1903; also appeared as a guest conductor after the completion of his regular tenure; from 1918 he was director of the Vienna State Opera (succeeded Gregor; in 1919–24, was co-director with R. Strauss; thereafter sole director). A tireless worker, he contributed much to the high artistic standards of the Vienna Opera. His book *Briefe und Betrachtungen* was brought out posthumously (Vienna, 1935).

Schalk, Josef, Austrian pianist and writer on music, brother of **Franz Schalk;** b. Vienna, March 24, 1857; d. there, Nov. 7, 1900. He studied with Bruckner and Epstein; was a piano teacher at the Vienna Cons. His arrangements of the Bruckner symphs.

for piano, 4-hands, did much to make these works known, and his book, *Anton Bruckner und die moderne Musikwelt* (1885), effectively upheld Bruckner's music. He was also a friend of Hugo Wolf, whom he championed.

Schall, Claus, Danish composer; b. Copenhagen, April 28, 1757; d. there, Aug. 9, 1835. He was a violinist and theater conductor; wrote many instrumental pieces and 7 operas to Danish librettos, of which the following (all produced in Copenhagen) were the most successful: *Claudine af Villa Bella* (Jan. 29, 1787); *Kinafarerne* (March 2, 1792); *Domherren i Milano* (March 16, 1802); *De tre Galninger* (March 19, 1816).

Scharfe, Gustav, German singing teacher; b. Grimma, Saxony, Sept. 11, 1835; d. Dresden, June 25, 1892. He was a baritone at the Dresden Court Opera for 11 years, a teacher of singing at the Cons. (1874), and a prof. (1880). He wrote *Die methodische Entwickelung der Stimme,* a standard work; also choruses and songs.

Scharfenberg, William, German-American music editor; b. Kassel, Feb. 22, 1819; d. Quogue, Long Island, N.Y., Aug. 8, 1895. He studied with Hummel at Weimar; played 2nd violin in Spohr's quartet in Kassel; in 1838 went to N.Y., where he became a popular piano teacher. He was successively secretary, vice-president, treasurer, and president of the N.Y. Phil. Society; for many years he served as music editor and adviser to the firm of G. Schirmer, and did excellent editorial work in this capacity.

Scharrer, August, German composer and conductor; b. Strasbourg, Aug. 18, 1866; d. Weiherhof, near Fürth, Oct. 24, 1936. He studied music in Strasbourg and Berlin; then became a theater conductor in Karlsruhe (1897–98) and Regensburg (1898–1900); then was 2nd conductor of the Kaim Orch. (1900–1904); from 1914 to 1931 he conducted the Phil. Society of Nuremberg. He wrote an opera, *Die Erlösung* (Strasbourg, Nov. 21, 1895); several orch. overtures; some chamber music, choruses, and songs.

Scharrer, Irene, English pianist; b. London, Feb. 2, 1888; d. there, Jan. 11, 1971. She studied with Tobias Matthay at the Royal Academy of Music; toured as a concert pianist in the U.S.; returning to London, she taught at the Matthay School.

Scharwenka, (Ludwig) Philipp, German composer and pedagogue; b. Samter, Posen, Feb. 16, 1847; d. Bad Nauheim, July 16, 1917. He studied with Wüerst and Dorn at the Kullak Academy of Music in Berlin; in 1868 was appointed teacher of composition there; with his brother **Xaver** he founded in 1881 the Scharwenka Cons. in Berlin; together they made an American trip in 1891; in 1893 the Scharwenka Cons. was amalgamated with the Klindworth Cons.; the resulting Klindworth-Scharwenka Cons. ac-

quired an excellent reputation for its teaching standards. He was an excellent composer in a Romantic vein, greatly influenced by Schumann; his *Arkadische Suite* for Orch., the symph. poem *Frühlingswogen,* and the orch. *Dramatische Fantasie* were performed many times until they inevitably lapsed into innocuous desuetude; he also wrote a Symph., a Violin Concerto, much chamber music, and piano pieces.

Scharwenka, (Franz) Xaver, German pianist, composer, and pedagogue, brother of **Philipp Scharwenka;** b. Samter, Posen, Jan. 6, 1850; d. Berlin, Dec. 8, 1924. He studied with Kullak and Wüerst at the Kullak Academy of Music in Berlin, graduating in 1868; then joined its faculty. Apart from teaching, he established an annual series of chamber music concerts in Berlin; in 1881, he founded with his brother the Scharwenka Cons.; in 1891 he went to the U.S. and opened a N.Y. branch of his Cons.; appeared as soloist in his own Piano Concerto (N.Y., Jan. 24, 1891). Returning to Berlin in 1898, he became co-director of the newly amalgamated (1893) Klindworth-Scharwenka Cons.; in 1914 established his own course of master classes for piano. As a composer, he was undoubtedly superior to his brother, although both were faithful imitators of Schumann and other German Romantics. He wrote an opera, *Mataswintha* (Weimar, Oct. 4, 1896; Metropolitan Opera, N.Y., April 1, 1907); 4 piano concertos; numerous effective piano pieces, of which his *Polish Dances* became favorites with American piano teachers and students. He also publ. technical studies for piano, *Beiträge zur Fingerbildung; Studien im Oktavenspiel;* a collection of famous études, arranged according to progressive difficulty, under the title *Meisterschule des Klavierspiels; Methodik des Klavierspiels* (1907; with A. Spanuth); and a book of memoirs, *Klänge aus meinem Leben: Erinnerungen eines Musikers* (Leipzig, 1922).

Schat, Peter, Dutch composer; b. Utrecht, June 5, 1935. He studied composition with Kees van Baaren and piano with Jaap Callenbach at The Hague Cons.; then traveled to England and took private lessons with M. Seiber; also received instruction with Boulez in Zürich. Upon returning to the Netherlands, he became active in connection with the Studio for Electro-Instrumental Music in Amsterdam. From his earliest steps in composition, he adopted the serial method; also experimented with electronic sonorities. With Louis Andriessen and Misha Mengelberg, he organized in 1968 a series of Political-Demonstrative Experimental Concerts and also formed the Amsterdam Electric Circus, an itinerant troupe of musicians.

WORKS: His most notorious production was *Labyrinth,* a "total theater" spectacle in mixed media (1961–65; Amsterdam, June 23, 1966), which spawned a series of excerpts: *Choirs from the "Labyrinth"* for Chorus and Orch. (1962–63); *Voices from the "Labyrinth"* for 3 Voices and Orch. (1962–63); *Dances from the "Labyrinth"* for Orch. (1962); *Scenes from the "Labyrinth"* for Speaking Voices,

Soprano, Tenor, Bass, Chorus, and Orch. (1961–64); *Improvisations from the "Labyrinth"* for 3 Voices, Bass Clarinet, Double Bass, Piano, and Percussion (1964); *Tapes from the "Labyrinth"* for 4 Tapes (1964–65). OTHER WORKS: A "circus opera," *Houdini* (1974–76; Amsterdam, Sept. 29, 1977); *Introduction and Adagio in Old Style* for String Quartet (1955); Septet for Flute, Oboe, Horn, Bass Clarinet, Piano, Cello, and Percussion (1957); *2 Pieces* for Flute, Violin, Trumpet, and Percussion (1959); Wind Octet (1959); *Inscripties* for Piano (1959); *Mosaics* for Orch. (1959); *Crytogamen* for Baritone and Orch. (1959); *Concerto da camera* for 2 Clarinets, Piano, Strings, and Percussion (1960); *Improvisations and Symphonies* for Wind Quintet (1960); *The Fall*, after James Joyce, for Chorus a cappella (1960); *Entelechie I* for 5 Instrumental Groups (1961); *Entelechie II*, scenes for 11 Musicians (1961); *Signalement* for 6 Percussionists and 3 Double Basses (1961); *Sextet,* fragment for 3 Actors and 3 Musicians (1961); *First Essay on Electrocution* for Violin, Guitar, and Metal Guitar (1966); *Clockwise and Anti-clockwise* for 16 Wind Instruments (1967); *Anathema* for Piano (1968); *On Escalation* for 6 Solo Percussionists and Orch. (Amsterdam, May 30, 1968); *Hypothema* for Recorders (1969); *Thema* for Solo Electrified Oboe, 4 Electric Guitars, Hammond Organ, and 18 Wind Instruments (Amsterdam, July 5, 1970); *To You* for Solo Voice, 6 Guitars, 3 Bass Guitars, 4 Pianos, 2 Hammond Organs, 6 Humming Tops, and Electronics (1970–72; Amsterdam, June 20, 1972); *Canto General,* dedicated to the memory of the slain socialist president of Chile, Salvador Allende, for Mezzo-soprano, Violin, and Piano (1974); *May 75,* a song of liberation for 2 Soloists, Chorus, and Orch. (1975); 10th scene from the opera *Houdini*); *Houdini Symphony* for 4 Soloists, Chorus, and Orch. (1976); *Houdini,* a circus opera for 7 Soloists, Dancers, Escape Artists, Acrobats, and Orch., commissioned by Hans de Roo and the Netherlands Opera Foundation (1976). He also collaborated with Louis Andriessen, Reinbert de Leeuw, Misha Mengelberg, and Jan van Vlijmen on the anti-imperialist opera *Reconstructie* (1968–69; Holland Festival, Amsterdam, June 29, 1969).

BIBLIOGRAPHY: Reinbert de Leeuw, "Labyrinth: An Opera of Sorts," *Sonorum Speculum,* 27 (Summer 1966); "Peter Schat about *To You*," *Sonorum Speculum,* 55 (1974); "Interview with Peter Schat," *Key Notes,* 4 (1976/2).

Schatz, Albert, German music collector; b. Rostock, May 19, 1839; d. there, Oct. 18, 1910. From his early youth he became interested in the history of opera and began to collect materials on this subject. He made an extensive trip to America and spent 7 years in San Francisco; returning to Rostock in 1873, he purchased the music business of Ludwig Trutschel. In 1908 he sold his valuable collection of librettos and the accompanying card catalogues and other records to the Library of Congress in Washington, D.C., where the whole collection is retained as a separate unit and is made available on positive microfilm.

BIBLIOGRAPHY: O.G. Sonneck, ed., *Catalogue of Opera Librettos Printed before 1800* (2 vols., Washington, 1914).

Schaub, Hans Ferdinand (properly, **Siegmund Ferdinand**), German composer, conductor, and teacher; b. Frankfurt, Sept. 22, 1880; d. Hanstedt, near Marburg, Nov. 12, 1965. He studied at the Frankfurt Hoch Cons. with Iwan Knorr (theory) and Carl Friedberg (piano), with Arnold Mendelssohn in Darmstadt, and with Humperdinck in Berlin; also took lessons with Richard Strauss. He then became an instructor at the Cons. of Breslau (1903–6); in 1906, settled in Berlin as a teacher at Benda's Cons. and editor of the *Deutsche Musikerzeitung.* In 1916 he moved to Hamburg as a music critic and pedagogue. After 1951 he lived in Hanstedt.

WORKS: *Passacaglia* for Orch. (1928); *3 Intermezzi* for Small Orch.; *Capriccio* for Violin and Piano; cantata, *Den Gefallenen* (1940); oratorio, *Deutsches Te Deum* (1942).

Schauffler, Robert Haven, American writer on music; b. Brünn, Moravia (of American parents), April 8, 1879; d. New York, Nov. 24, 1964. He was educated at Princeton Univ., and also took courses at the Univ. of Berlin; studied cello with B. Steindel, A. Schroeder, and A. Hekking.

WRITINGS: *The Musical Amateur* (Boston, 1911); *Fiddler's Luck. The Gay Adventures of a Musical Amateur* (Boston, 1920); *Beethoven: The Man Who Freed Music* (N.Y., 1929; abridged ed., 1932, as *The Mad Musician;* new ed., 1937); *The Unknown Brahms* (N.Y., 1933); *The Magic of Music; An Anthology* (N.Y., 1935); *Fiddler's Folly and Encores* (N.Y., 1942); *Florestan: The Life and Work of Robert Schumann* (N.Y., 1945); *Franz Schubert: The Ariel of Music* (N.Y., 1949); various smaller publications.

Schaum, John W., American piano pedagogue; b. Milwaukee, Jan. 27, 1905. He studied at Milwaukee State Teachers College, at Marquette Univ. (B.M., 1931), and at Northwestern Univ. (M.M., 1934). He established a successful piano teaching class in Milwaukee and publ. several piano methods and many collections of piano pieces that sold an enormous number of copies: *The Schaum Piano Course* (9 vols.); *The Schaum Adult Piano Course* (3 vols.); *The Schaum Duet Albums* (2 vols.); also theory books: *The Schaum Theory Lessons* (2 vols.) and *The Schaum Note Spellers* (2 vols.).

Schebek, Edmund, Bohemian writer on music; b. Petersdorf, Moravia, Oct. 22, 1819; d. Prague, Feb. 11, 1895, as Imperial councillor and secretary of the Chamber of Commerce. He wrote the official Austrian report on the musical instruments at the Paris Exposition of 1855 (separate reprint, 1858); *Der Geigenbau in Italien und sein deutscher Ursprung* (1875; in Eng., London, 1877); *Zwei Briefe über J.J. Froberger* (1874).

Schebest, Agnese, Austrian mezzo-soprano; b.

Vienna, Feb. 10, 1813; d. Stuttgart, Dec. 22, 1869. She studied at Dresden, and sang in the opera there; publ. an autobiography, *Aus dem Leben einer Künstlerin* (1857).

Schech, Marianne, German soprano; b. Geitau, Jan. 18, 1914. She was educated in Munich; made her operatic debut in Koblenz in 1937; then sang in Munich (1939–41) and Düsseldorf (1941–44), and at the Dresden State Opera (1944–51); also sang with the Bavarian State Opera in Munich. In 1956 she was named a Kammersängerin. On Jan. 22, 1957, she made her debut at the Metropolitan Opera in N.Y. as Sieglinde in *Die Walküre;* also made guest appearances in London, Vienna, and Hamburg. She retired from the stage in 1970 and devoted herself mainly to teaching.

Scheel, Fritz, German conductor; b. Lübeck, Nov. 7, 1852; d. Philadelphia, March 13, 1907. His grandfather and father were orch. conductors, and at 10 the boy played the violin in his father's orch.; in 1864–69 he was a pupil of F. David in Leipzig. At 17 he began his career as a concertmaster and conductor at Bremerhaven; in 1873 he was solo violinist and conductor of the summer concerts in Schwerin; succeeded Hans Sitt in 1884 as conductor of the Chemnitz municipal orch.; in 1890–93 was conductor of orch. concerts in Hamburg. He came to America in 1893, and after conducting some orch. concerts in N.Y., went to Chicago in 1894 as conductor of the Trocadero concerts at the Columbian Exposition; in 1895 he established the San Francisco Symph. Orch., which he conducted for 4 seasons; then accepted an engagement to conduct a series of summer concerts at Woodside Park in Philadelphia. His playing of Beethoven's symphs. induced influential music-lovers to organize the Philadelphia Orchestral Assoc., which established in the fall of 1900 the Philadelphia Orch., of which Scheel was conductor until his death.
BIBLIOGRAPHY: Frances A. Wister, *25 Years of the Philadelphia Orchestra 1900–1925* (Philadelphia, 1925); John H. Mueller, *The American Symphony Orchestra* (Bloomington, Ind., 1951; pp. 125–27); H. Kupferberg, *Those Fabulous Philadelphians* (N.Y., 1969; pp. 15–26); *Dictionary of American Biography,* XVI.

Scheff, Fritzi, Austrian soprano; b. Vienna, Aug. 30, 1879; d. New York, April 8, 1954. She studied singing with her mother, Hortense Scheff, of the Vienna Opera, and adopted her last name, having previously appeared under her father's name, **Yager.** She made her operatic debut in Frankfurt (1896); appeared at the Metropolitan Opera in N.Y. as Marzelline in *Fidelio* (Dec. 28, 1900), and continued for 3 seasons as a member of the company. Later she shifted to light opera, and it was in this field that she became famous. She created the role of Fifi in Victor Herbert's operetta *Mlle. Modiste* (Trenton, N.J., Oct. 7, 1905); her singing of Fifi's waltz song *Kiss Me Again* became a hallmark of her career. Her 3 marriages (to Baron Fritz von Bardeleben, the

American writer John Fox, Jr., and the singer George Anderson) ended in divorce.

Scheffler, Siegfried, German composer; b. Ilmenau, May 15, 1892; d. Hamburg, June 5, 1969. He studied with his father; then took courses at the Leipzig Cons. with Max Reger, Stephan Krehl, Hans Sitt, and others; also attended classes in musicology at the Univ. of Leipzig with Hugo Riemann and Arnold Schering, and in Berlin with Humperdinck and Kretzschmar. In 1924 he settled in Hamburg; wrote music criticism and supervised music programs at the Hamburg Radio. He composed *Wunderhorn Lieder* (1914); *Rokoko-Novelle* for Orch. (1923); incidental music for various plays. He publ. *Richard Wagner* (2 vols., Hamburg, 1928) and *Melodie der Welle* (Berlin, 1933).

Scheibe, Johann Adolf, German theorist and composer; b. Leipzig, May 3, 1708; d. Copenhagen, April 22, 1776. He studied law at Leipzig, but on his father's death had recourse to his musical training to support himself; failing to obtain the post of organist at the Nicolaikirche in Leipzig in the competition (1729; adjudicated by Bach, among others) with Görner, he traveled for a time, and settled in Hamburg; publ. a paper, *Der Critische Musicus* (1737–40; No. 6 contains a sharp attack on Bach). In 1739 he became Kapellmeister to the Margrave of Brandenburg-Culmbach; on Dec. 1, 1740, he became court conductor at Copenhagen; was pensioned in 1747. In 1745 he had reprinted in Leipzig the previous issues of *Der Critische Musicus,* with the addition of polemical exchanges that ensued in the interim. A large portion of his MSS are no longer extant.
WORKS: Danish opera, *Thusnelda* (Copenhagen, 1749); tragic cantatas *a* 2, with Clavier; songs; *Musikalische Erquickungstunden* (6 sonatas for Flute, with Continuo); 3 sonatas for Flute, with Harpsichord. In MS he left 2 oratorios, about 200 church works, 150 flute concertos, 30 violin concertos, etc. He also wrote *Abhandlung vom Ursprung und Alter der Musik, insonderheit der Vocalmusik* (1754; maintains that part-songs originated with Northern peoples); *Abhandlung über das Recitativ* (1764–65); *Über die musikalische Composition* (only vol. 1, of the 4 projected, was publ. in 1773); etc.
BIBLIOGRAPHY: E. Riechel, "Gottsched und J.A. Scheibe," *Sammelbände der Internationalen Musik-Gesellschaft,* 2 (1901); E. Rosenkaimer, *J.A. Scheibe als Verfasser seines "Critischen Musicus"* (Diss., Univ. of Bonn, 1923); K.A. Storch, *J.A. Scheibes Anschauungen von d. musikalischen Historie, Wissenschaft und Kunst* (Diss., Univ. of Leipzig, 1923); I. Willheim, *Johann Adolf Scheibe: German Musical Thought in Transition* (Diss., Univ. of Illinois, 1963); G. Buelow, "In Defence of J.A. Scheibe against J.S. Bach," *Proceedings of the Royal Musical Association,* CI (1974–75).

Scheibler, Johann Heinrich, inventor and writer on music; b. Montjoie, near Aix-la-Chapelle, Nov. 11, 1777; d. Krefeld, Nov. 20, 1837. A silk manufacturer at Krefeld, he became interested in acoustic phenomena and invented an apparatus, consisting of 56 tuning forks, for tuning fixed-tone instruments according to the equally tempered scale. He publ. several pamphlets to explain his invention: *Der physikalische und musikalische Tonmesser* (1834); *Anleitung, die Orgel vermittelst der Stösse (vulgo Schwebungen) und des Metronoms correct gleichschwebend zu stimmen* (1834); etc.; all of these were united as *Schriften über physikalische und musikalische Tonmessung* (1838). His system is more clearly explained by Töpfer (1842), Vincent (1849), and Lecomte (1856). At the Stuttgart Congress of physicists in 1834, Scheibler proposed the pitch of $a^1 = 440$ (vibrations) at 69° F, which was adopted (hence called the "Stuttgart pitch").

BIBLIOGRAPHY: J.J. Löhr, *Über die Scheibler'sche Erfindung überhaupt und dessen Pianoforte- und Orgel-Stimmung insbesondere* (Krefeld, 1836).

Scheidemann, Heinrich, important German organist, composer, and pedagogue; b. Wöhrden, Holstein, c.1595; d. Hamburg, 1663. He studied with Sweelinck in Amsterdam from 1611 to 1614; in 1629 he succeeded his father as organist at the Katharinenkirche in Hamburg, and held that post until his death. Among his students was J.A. Reinken, who became his assistant in 1658, and his successor at his death. Scheidemann excelled especially as a composer of organ music.

BIBLIOGRAPHY: W. Breig, *Die Orgelwerke von Heinrich Scheidemann* (Wiesbaden, 1967).

Scheidemantel, Karl, German baritone; b. Weimar, Jan. 21, 1859; d. there, June 26, 1923. He was a pupil of Bodo Borchers, and sang at the court theater in Weimar (1878–86); also studied voice with Julius Stockhausen in the summers of 1881–83. He was a member of the Dresden Court Opera from 1896–1911; in 1911–20, a prof. at the Grossherzogliche Musikschule in Weimar; in 1920–23, director of the Landesoper in Dresden. In 1909 the Dresden Opera brought out Mozart's *Così fan tutte* with an entirely new text by Scheidemantel (as *Dame Kobold*). His new trans. of *Don Giovanni* won the prize of the Deutscher Bühnenverein (1914). He publ. *Stimmbildung* (1907; 4th ed. as *Gesangsbildung,* 1913; in Eng., 1910); also edited a collection of songs, *Meisterweisen* (1914; 6 parts).

BIBLIOGRAPHY: P. Trede, *K. Scheidemantel* (Dresden, 1911).

Scheidt, Samuel, important German organist and composer; b. Halle, (baptized, Nov. 3) 1587; d. there, March 24, 1654. He studied at the Gymnasium in Halle; from c.1603 to 1608 he was organist at the Moritzkirche in Halle, and then went to Amsterdam to study with Sweelinck. He returned to Halle in 1609, and was appointed court organist to Margrave Christian Wilhelm of Brandenburg; in late 1619 he also assumed the post of court Kapellmeister; when the margrave left for Denmark in 1625 to support the Protestant cause in the Thirty Years' War, Scheidt retained his post even though without

emolument, eking out a modest living by teaching. In 1628 he was named music director of the Marktkirche, the principal church in Halle, continuing in this employment until 1630. In 1638 he resumed his post as court Kapellmeister and served until his death. Scheidt was highly esteemed as an organist; he was consulted on the building of organs as an inspector; he was also a noted organ teacher. As a composer, Scheidt excelled in both keyboard and sacred vocal works.

WORKS: FOR KEYBOARD: *Tabulatura nova continens variationes aliquot psalmorum, fantasiarum, cantilenarum, passamezzo et canones* (Hamburg, 1624); *Pars secunda tabulaturae continens fugarum, psalmorum, cantionum et echus, tocatae, variationes varias omnimodas pro quorumvis organistarum captu et modulo* (Hamburg, 1624); *III. et ultima pars tabulaturae continens Kyrie Dominicale, Credo in unum Deum, Psalmum de Coena Domini sub communione, hymnos praecipuorum festorum totius anni, Magnificat . . . & Benedicamus* (Hamburg, 1624); *Tabulatur-Buch hundert geistlicher Lieder und Psalmen* (Görlitz, 1650); additional instrumental works include *Paduana, galliarda, courante, alemande, intrada, canzonetto, ut vocant, in gratiam musices studiosorum, potissimum violistarum, a 4, 5,* and Basso Continuo (Hamburg, 1621); *Ludorum musicorum secunda pars continens paduan, galliard, alemand, canzon, et intrad, a 4, 5, 7,* and Basso Continuo (Hamburg, 1622); *Ludorum musicorum tertia pars continens paduanas, cour. et canzon., a 3, 4, 7, 8,* and Basso Continuo (Hamburg, 1624; not extant); *Ludorum musicorum quarta pars, a 3, 4,* and Basso Continuo (Hamburg, 1627); *LXX Symphonien auff Concerten manir: Vornemlich auff Violinen zu gebrauchen durch die gewöhnliche Tonos, und die 7 Claves, a 2* and Basso Continuo (Leipzig, 1644); also canons in *Tabulatura nova continens variationes aliquot psalmorum, fantasiarum, cantilenarum, passamezzo et canones* (Hamburg, 1624). VOCAL CHURCH MUSIC: *Cantiones sacrae* for 8 Voices (Hamburg, 1620); *Pars prima concertuum sacrorum, adiectis symphoniis et choris instrumentalibus* for 2 to 5, 8, and 12 Voices and Basso Continuo (Hamburg, 1622); *Newe geistliche Concerten . . . prima pars* for 2 and 3 Voices and Basso Continuo (Halle, 1631); *Geistlicher Concerten . . . ander Theil* for 2 to 6 Voices and Basso Continuo (Halle, 1634); *Geistlicher Concerten . . . dritter Theil* for 2 to 6 Voices and Basso Continuo (Halle, 1635); *Liebliche Krafft-Blümlein aus des Heyligen Geistes Lustgarten abgebrochen und zum Vorschmack dess ewigen Lebens im zweystimmichten Himmels-Chor versetzet* for 2 Voices and Basso Continuo (Halle, 1635); *Geistlicher Concerten . . . vierter Theil* for 2 to 6 Voices and Basso Continuo (Halle, 1640). A collected edition of his works was begun by G. Harms and continued by others; 13 vols. were publ. in Hamburg from 1923–62, and additional vols. have been publ. in Leipzig since 1971.

BIBLIOGRAPHY: C. Mahrenholz, *Samuel Scheidt: Sein Leben und sein Werk* (Leipzig, 1924); R. Hünicken, *Samuel Scheidt: Ein althallischer Musikus* (Halle, 1934); W. Serauky, *Samuel Scheidt in seinen Briefen* (Halle, 1937); a Festschrift in honor of his 350th birthday (Wolfenbüttel, 1937); A. Adrio, "Zu Samuel Scheidts Vokalmusik," *Musik und Kirche*, XXIV (1954); C. Mahrenholz, "Samuel Scheidt und die Orgel," *Musik und Kirche*, XXV (1955); E. Gessner, *Samuel Scheidts geistliche Konzerte: Ein Beitrag zur Geschichte der Gattung* (Berlin, 1961); W. Braun, "Samuel Scheidts Bearbeitungen alter Motetten," *Archiv für Musikwissenschaft*, XIX–XX (1962–63); W. Breig, "Zu den handschriftlich überlieferten Liedvariationen von Samuel Scheidt," *Die Musikforschung*, XXII (1969); A. Adrio, "Samuel Scheidts Cantiones Sacrae Octo Vocum von 1620: Beobachtungen und Anmerkungen," in *Kerygma und Melos: Christhard Mahrenholz 70 Jahre* (Kassel, 1970); F. Krummacher, *Die Choralbearbeitung in der protestantischen Figuralmusik zwischen Praetorius und Bach* (Kassel, 1978).

Schein, Johann Hermann, important German composer; b. Grünhain, near Annaberg, Jan. 20, 1586; d. Leipzig, Nov. 19, 1630. His father was a pastor; upon his death, Schein moved to Dresden, where he entered the Hofkapelle of the Elector of Saxony as a boy soprano; received instruction from the Kapellmeister, Rogier Michael; continued his studies in music at Pforta, an electoral school near Naumburg, from 1603–7; his teachers were Bartholomäus Scheer and Martin Roth. In 1607 he returned to Dresden; in 1608 he received an electoral scholarship to study jurisprudence and liberal arts at the Univ. of Leipzig, where he remained until 1612. In 1613 he became Hausmusikmeister to Gottfried von Wolffersdorff in Weissenfels, and served as praeceptor to his children. In 1615 he was appointed Kapellmeister to Duke Johann Ernst the Younger in Weimar. In 1616 he was named cantor at the Thomasschule in Leipzig, as successor to Calvisius. His duties in Leipzig inlcuded directing the choral music at the Thomaskirche and the Nicolaikirche, and teaching singing and Latin grammar and syntax at the Thomasschule. Schein was one of the earliest German composers to introduce into Lutheran church music the Italian techniques of madrigal, monody, and concerto. In the alliterative parlance of learned German writers, Schein became known as the chronologically second of the glorious trio of near-contemporaneous German masters, Schütz (b. 1585), Schein (b. 1586), and Scheidt (b. 1587). But Schütz, the oldest of them, outlived Schein by 42 years; he visited him at his deathbed and brought him, as a friendly offering, a 6-part motet of his composition on Schein's favorite passage from the New Testament.

WORKS: SACRED VOCAL MUSIC: *Cymbalum Sionium sive Cantiones sacrae,* for 5 to 12 Voices (Leipzig, 1615); *Opella nova, geistlicher Concerten ... auff italiänische Invention componirt* for 3 to 5 Voices and Basso Continuo (Leipzig, 1618; 2nd ed., 1626); *Fontana d'Israel, Israelis Brünlein, auserlesener Krafft-Sprüchlin altes und Newen Testaments ... aufeiner ... Italian madrigalische Manier* for 5 and 6 Voices and Basso Continuo (Leipzig, 1623; 2nd ed., 1651); *Opella nova, ander Theil, geistlicher Concerten* for 3 to 6 Voices, Instruments, and Basso Continuo (Leipzig, 1626); *Cantional oder Gesangbuch Augspurgischer Confession* for 4 to 6 Voices (Leipzig, 1627; 2nd ed., enlarged, 1645). SECULAR VOCAL MUSIC: Texts by Schein: *Venus Kräntzlein ... oder Newe weltliche Lieder* for 5 Voices, *neben etzlichen Intraden, Gagliarden und Canzonen* (Wittenberg, 1609); *Musica boscareccia, oder Wald-Liederlein auff italian-villanellische Invention ... mit lebendiger Stimm ... auch auff musicalischen Instrumenten zu spielen* for 3 Voices (Leipzig, 1621; 6th ed., 1643; *Ander Theil* [Leipzig, 1628; 6th ed., 1641] *Dritter Theil* [Leipzig, 1628; 5th ed., 1643]; also publ. with revised text as *Musica boscareccia sacra* [3 vols., Erfurt, 1644–51]); *Diletti pastorali, Hirten Lust* for 5 Voices and Basso Continuo, *auff Madrigal-Manier componirt* (Leipzig, 1624); *Studenten-Schmauss a 5: Einer löblischen Compagni de la Vinobiera* (Leipzig, 1626). INSTRUMENTAL MUSIC: *Banchetto musicale newer ... Padouanen, Gagliarden, Courenten und Allemanden a 5, auff allerley Instrumenten* (Leipzig, 1617); other works are found in several of his vocal collections. A collected edition of his works, edited by A. Prüfer, was publ. by Breitkopf und Härtel (7 vols., Leipzig, 1901–23); the *Neue Ausgabe sämtlicher Werke,* ed. by A. Adrio, began publ. in Kassel in 1963 by Bärenreiter.

BIBLIOGRAPHY: A. Prüfer, *Johann Hermann Schein* (Leipzig, 1895); A. Prüfer, "Zur Familiengeschichte des Leipziger Thomas-Kantors Johann Hermann Schein," *Monatshefte für Musikgeschichte,* XXX (1898); A. Prüfer, *Johann Hermann Schein und das weltliche deutsche Lied des 17. Jahrhunderts* (Leipzig, 1908); W. Brauer, "Jakob Regnart, J.H. Schein und die Anfänge der deutschen Barocklyrik," *Deutsche Vierteljahrsschrift für Literaturwissenschaft und Geistersgeschichte,* XVII (1939); I. Hueck, *Die künstlerische Entwicklung Johann Hermann Scheins, dargestellt an seinen geistlichen Werken* (Diss., Univ. of Freiburg, 1945); H. Redlich, "Schein and the German Madrigal," *The Listener,* LIII (1959); A. Adrio, *Johann Hermann Schein* (Berlin, 1959); H. Rauhe, *Dichtung und Musik im weltlichen Vokalwerk Johann Hermann Scheins* (Diss., Univ. of Hamburg, 1959); W. Reckziegel, *Das Cantional von Johann Hermann Schein: Seine geschichtlichen Grundlagen* (Berlin, 1963); F. Peterson, *Johann Hermann Schein's Cymbalum Sionium: A Liturgico-musical Study* (Diss., Harvard Univ., 1966); S. Sorensen, "Johann Hermann Scheins *Opella nova,*"in *Renaissance muziek 1400–1600: Donum natalicium René Bernard Lenaerts* (Louvain, 1969); F. Krummacher, *Die Choralbearbeitung in der protestantischen Figuralmusik zwischen Praetorius und Bach* (Kassel, 1978).

Scheinpflug, Paul, German violinist, conductor, and composer; b. Loschwitz, near Dresden, Sept. 10, 1875; d. Memel, March 11, 1937. He studied violin with Rappoldi and composition with Draeseke at the Dresden Cons.; in 1898 went to Bremen as concertmaster of the Phil. and conductor of the Liederkranz; then was conductor of the Musikverein in

Königsberg (1909–14); conducted the Blüthner Orch. in Berlin (1914–19); was music director in Duisburg (1920–28); in 1929 he became conductor of the Dresden Phil., holding this post until 1933.

WORKS: Symph. poem, *Frühlung; Ouvertüre zu einem Lustspiel;* Piano Quartet; String Quartet; violin sonatas; many male choruses; *Worpswede,* song cycle for Voice, Piano, Violin, and English Horn; many song albums.

BIBLIOGRAPHY: F. Dubitzky, *Paul Scheinpflug* (Leipzig, 1907).

Schelble, Johann Nepomuk, German singer and pedagogue; b. Hüfingen, Black Forest, May 16, 1789; d. there, Aug. 6, 1837. He studied with Weisse in Donaueschingen, with Volger in Darmstadt, and with Krebs in Stuttgart. From 1814 to 1816 he was in Vienna and became an intimate friend of Beethoven; then settled in Frankfurt, where he founded the famous Cäcilien-Verein (1818), and sang at the Frankfurt theater (1817–19). His methods for teaching the musical rudiments and training the sense of absolute pitch were much admired; he enjoyed the esteem of many musicians of his time; Mendelssohn paid tribute to him in his correspondence.

BIBLIOGRAPHY: K. Lanz, *Die Gehörsentwicklungs-Methode von Schelble* (Braunschweig, 1873); O. Bormann, *J.N. Schelble* (Diss., Univ. of Frankfurt, 1926).

Schelle, Johann, significant German composer of Protestant church music; b. Geising, Thuringia, (baptized, Sept. 6) 1648; d. Leipzig, March 10, 1701. He received his early musical trainig from his father, who was a schoolmaster; in 1655 he was sent to Dresden to sing in the chori of the electoral chapel, which was directed by Schütz; in 1657 he went to Wolfenbüttel, where he sang in the choir of the ducal court. In 1665 he became a student at the Thomasschule in Leipzig under Knüpfer; subsequently studied at the Univ. of Leipzig, becoming cantor in Eilenburg in 1670. In 1677 he succeeded Knüpfer as cantor of the Thomaskirche in Leipzig; also served as director chori musici for the city and acted as director of music for the Nicolaikirche. He taught music at the Thomasschule; he was succeeded by his cousin, **Johann Kuhnau.** Schelle's importance as a composer rests upon his settings of the sacred Gospel cantata to German texts (in place of the traditional Latin texts) for Protestant liturgical use in Leipzig. He extended this practice to the chorale cantata as well. See A. Schering's edition in the Denkmäler deutscher Tonkunst, LVIII–LIX (1918).

BIBLIOGRAPHY: B.F. Richter, "Zwei Funeralprogramme auf die Thomaskantoren Sebastian Knüpfer und Joh. Schelle," *Monatshefte für Musikgeschichte,* XXXIII (1901) and XXXIV (1902); F. Graupner, *Das Werk des Thomaskantors Johann Schelle* (Berlin, 1929); R. Murray, *The German Church Music of Johann Schelle* (Diss., Univ. of Michigan, 1971).

Schelle, Karl Eduard, German music critic; b. Biesenthal, near Berlin, May 31, 1816; d. Vienna, Nov. 16, 1882. In 1864 he succeeded Hanslick as music critic for the Vienna *Presse;* also lectured on music history at the Vienna Cons. He publ. *Der Tannhäuser in Paris* (1861) and a valuable monograph, *Die papstliche Sängerschule in Rom, genannt die Sixtinische Kapella* (1872).

Schelling, Ernest (Henry), American conductor, composer, and pianist; b. Belvidere, N.J., July 26, 1876; d. New York, Dec. 8, 1939. He first appeared in public as a child prodigy, playing the piano at the age of 4½ at the Academy of Music in Philadelphia. He was then sent to Paris, where he studied, while still a small child, with Mathias (a pupil of Chopin) and also with Moszkowski; his other teachers were Leschetizky, Hans Huber, Barth, and finally Paderewski at Morges, Switzerland (1898–1902). Extended tours in Europe (from Russia to Spain) followed; he also toured in South America; returned permanently to the U.S. in 1905, and devoted most of his energies to conducting and composing. He conducted young people's symph. concerts in N.Y. (from 1924), in Philadelphia, Boston, Cincinnati, Los Angeles, San Francisco, etc.; for 2 seasons (1936–38) he was regular conductor of the Baltimore Symph. Orch.; also made frequent appearances as a conductor in Europe.

WORKS: *A Victory Ball,* orch. fantasy after the poem by Alfred Noyes (first perf. by Stokowski with the Philadelphia Orch., Feb. 23, 1923; his most successful work); *Légende symphonique* (Philadelphia, Oct. 31, 1913); *Suite fantastique* for Orch. (Amsterdam, Oct. 10, 1907); *Impressions from an Artist's Life,* symph. variations for Piano and Orch. (Boston, Dec. 31, 1915, composer soloist; first work by an American ever conducted by Toscanini; N.Y., March 14, 1929); Violin Concerto (Boston Symph., Providence, R.I., Oct. 17, 1916; Fritz Kreisler, soloist); *Morocco,* symph. tableau (N.Y., Dec. 19, 1927, composer conducting). For further details see William Lichtenwanger, *Dictionary of American Biography,* Supplement II.

Schenck, Jean (Johann), German virtuoso on the viola da gamba; b. Amsterdam, (baptized, June 3) 1660; d. c.1715. He became chamber musician to the Elector-Palatine at Düsseldorf in 1696; later at Amsterdam, where he publ. *Kunst-Oeffeningen;* 15 sonatas for Gamba, with Continuo (1688); *Il giardino armonico,* sonatas for 2 Violins, Gamba, and Continuo (1692); *Scherzi musicali* for Gamba; 18 sonatas for Violin, with Continuo (1693); etc.; also *Sang-Arien van d'opera Ceres en Bacchus.*

BIBLIOGRAPHY: A. Einstein, *Zur deutschen Literatur für Viola da Gamba im 16. und 17. Jahrhundert* (Leipzig, 1905; pp. 32–35); K.H. Pauls, *Die Musikforschung* (1962, pp. 157–71; 1966, pp. 288–89); idem, ed., *Gambenkompositionen von Johannes Schenk und Conrad Höffler,* in Das Erbe Deutscher Musik, First Series, LXVII (1973).

Schenck, Pyotr, Russian composer; b. St. Petersburg, Feb. 28, 1870; d. Perkiarvy, Finland, July 5, 1915. He studied piano and theory at the St. Petersburg Cons.; gave concerts as a pianist; then devoted himself to conducting; appeared in several European countries. His music was entirely under the influence of Tchaikovsky.

WORKS: 2 operas: *Acteya*, from Etruscan life, which had a concert performance, conducted by the composer, in St. Petersburg (Dec. 3, 1899), and *The Miracle of Roses* (St. Petersburg, Oct. 7, 1913); also ballet music; 3 symphs.; an orch. fantasy, *Dukhy (Ghosts)*; a symph. poem, *Hero and Leander*; instrumental pieces; choruses; songs.

Schenk, Erich, eminent Austrian musicologist; b. Salzburg, May 5, 1902; d. Vienna, Oct. 11, 1974. He studied theory and piano at the Mozarteum in Salzburg; then went to Munich, where he enrolled as a student of Sandberger in musicology at the Univ. of Munich; received his Ph.D. in 1925 with the dissertation *Giuseppe Antonio Paganelli: Sein Leben und seine Werke* (publ. in Salzburg, 1928); he completed his Habilitation at the Univ. of Rostock in 1929 with *Studien zur Triosonate in Deutschland nach Corelli*; he subsequently founded its musicology dept. (1936). From 1940 until his retirement in 1971 he was a prof. of musicology at the Univ. of Vienna. He was particularly esteemed for his studies of Baroque and Classical music. In 1947 he revived the Denkmäler der Tonkunst in Österreich series, overseeing its progress until 1972. In 1955 he also took over the valuable *Studien zur Musikwissenschaft*. Festschrifts honored him on his 60th (Vienna, 1962) and 70th (Kassel, 1975) birthdays.

WRITINGS: *Johann Strauss* (Potsdam, 1940); *Musik in Kärnten* (Vienna, 1941); *Beethoven zwischen den Zeiten* (Bonn, 1944); *950 Jahre österreichische Musik* (Vienna, 1946); *Kleine wiener Musikgeschichte* (Vienna, 1946); *W.A. Mozart: Eine Biographie* (Vienna, 1955; in Eng., 1960, as *Mozart and His Time*; 2nd German ed., augmented, 1975, as *Mozart: Sein Leben, seine Welt*); *Ausgewählte Aufsätze: Reden und Vorträge* (Vienna, 1967); ed., *Beethoven-Studien* (Vienna, 1970).

Schenk, Johann, Austrian composer; b. Wiener-Neustadt, Nov. 30, 1753; d. Vienna, Dec. 29, 1836. He studied with Wagenseil in Vienna. In 1778 he had a Mass performed, which made his reputation; it was followed by other pieces of sacred music; then he began composing light operas, some of which enjoyed great popularity. It was from Schenk that Beethoven took surreptitious lessons while studying with Haydn.

WORKS: Operettas (all produced in Vienna): *Die Weinlese* (Oct. 12, 1785); *Die Weihnacht auf dem Lande* (Dec. 14, 1786); *Im Finstern ist nicht gut tappen* (Oct. 12, 1787); *Das unvermutete Seefest* (Dec. 9, 1789); *Das Singspiel ohne Titel* (Nov. 4, 1790); *Der Erntekranz* (July 9, 1791); *Achmet und Almanzine* (July 17, 1795); *Der Dorfbarbier* (Vienna, Oct. 30, 1796; his most popular work; originally staged as a comedy, June 18, 1785); *Die Jagd* (May 7, 1799); *Der Fassbinder* (Dec. 17, 1802). In 1819 he wrote his last works, the cantatas *Die Huldigung* and *Der Mai*. He also wrote 6 symphs., string quar-

tets, string trios, and songs. The score of *Der Dorfbarbier* was publ. by R. Haas in Denkmäler der Tonkunst in Österreich, 66 (34).

BIBLIOGRAPHY: F. Staub, *Johann Schenck. Eine Skizze seines Lebens* (Vienna, 1901). A short biographical sketch is publ. in *Studien zur Musikwissenschaft* (1924); F. Rieger, *Johann Schenk, Ein Altmeister des deutschen Singspiels* (St. Pölten, 1944).

Schenker, Heinrich, outstanding Austrian music theorist; b. Wisniowczyki, Galicia, June 19, 1868; d. Vienna, Jan. 13, 1935. He studied jurisprudence at the Univ. of Vienna (Dr.Jur., 1890); concurrently entered the class of Anton Bruckner at the Vienna Cons. He composed some songs and piano pieces; Brahms liked them sufficiently to recommend Schenker to his publisher Simrock. For a while Schenker served as accompanist of the baritone Johannes Messchaert; then returned to Vienna and devoted himself entirely to the development of his theoretical research; gathered around himself a group of enthusiastic disciples who accepted his novel theories, among them Otto Vrieslander, Hermann Roth, Hans Weisse, Anthony van Hoboken, Oswald Jonas, Felix Salzer, and John Petrie Dunn. He endeavored to derive the basic laws of musical composition from a thoroughgoing analysis of the standard masterworks. The result was the contention that each composition represents a horizontal integration, through various stages, of differential triadic units derived from the overtone series. By a dialectical manipulation of the thematic elements and linear progressions of a given work, Schenker succeeded in preparing a formidable system in which the melody is the "Urlinie" (basic line), the bass is "Grundbrechung" (broken ground), and the ultimate formation is the "Ursatz" (background). The result seems as self-consistent as the Ptolemaic planetary theory of epicycles. Arbitrary as the Schenker system is, it proved remarkably durable in academia; some theorists even attempted to apply it to modern works lacking in the triadic content essential to Schenker's theories.

WRITINGS: *Ein Beitrag zur Ornamentik als Einführung zu Ph.E. Bachs Klavierwerke* (Vienna, 1904; 2nd ed., revised, 1908; Eng. trans. in *Music Forum*, IV, 1976); *Neue musikalische Theorien und Fantasien*: I. *Harmonielehre* (Stuttgart, 1906; in Eng., ed. by O. Jonas, Chicago, 1954); II. *Kontrapunkt* in 2 vols., *Cantus Firmus und zweistimmiger Satz* (Vienna, 1910) and *Drei- und mehrstimmiger Satz, Übergänge zum freien Satz* (Vienna, 1922); III. *Der freie Satz* (Vienna, 1935; new ed. by O. Jonas, 1956; Eng. trans. by E. Oster, 1979); monographs on Beethoven's 9th Symph. (Vienna, 1912) and 5th Symph. (Vienna, 1925); *Der Tonwille* (a periodical containing articles and analyses by Schenker and appearing at irregular intervals from 1921–24); *Das Meisterwerk in der Musik* (a continuation of *Der Tonwille* in the form of an annual; 3 vols., Vienna, 1925, 1926, 1930); *Fünf Urlinie-Tafeln* (Vienna, 1932; 2nd ed., revised, 1969 by F. Salzer); *Johannes Brahms: Oktaven und Quinten*

(Vienna, 1933).

BIBLIOGRAPHY: W. Riezler, "Die Urlinie," *Die Musik* (April 1930); I. Citkowitz, "The Role of H. Schenker," *Modern Music*, 11 (1933); O. Jonas, *Das Wesen des musikalischen Kunstwerkes: Eine Einführung in die Lehre H. Schenkers* (Vienna, 1934); R. Sessions, "H. Schenker's Contribution," *Modern Music*, 12 (1953); A.T. Katz, "H. Schenker's Method of Analysis," *Musical Quarterly* (July 1935); A. Waldeck and N. Broder, "Musical Synthesis as Expounded by H. Schenker," *Musical Mercury* (Dec. 1935); A.T. Katz, *Challenge to Musical Tradition* (N.Y., 1945); F. Salzer, *Structural Hearing* (N.Y., 1952; 2nd ed., 1962; a development of the Schenker theories); F. Salzer and C. Schachter, *Counterpoint in Composition. The Study of Voice Leading* (N.Y., 1969; a textbook based on Schenkerian principles); L. Laskowski, ed., *H. Schenker: An Annotated Index to His Analyses of Musical Works* (N.Y., 1978); A. Whittall, "Schenker and the Prospects for Analysis," *Musical Times* (Sept. 1980); A. Forte and S. Gilbert, *An Introduction to Schenkerian Analysis* (London, 1983). A periodical that places heavy emphasis on the application of Schenker's ideas is the *Music Forum* (1967—). See also "Schenker System" in W. Apel, *Harvard Dictionary of Music* (Cambridge, Mass., 1944–69).

Scherchen, Hermann, eminent German conductor; b. Berlin, June 21, 1891; d. Florence, June 12, 1966. He was self-taught in music; played the viola in the Berlin Phil. (1907–10); in 1911–12, toured with Arnold Schoenberg. In 1914 he obtained an engagement as a symph. conductor in Riga; at the outbreak of World War I he was interned in Russia; after the Armistice he returned to Berlin; founded and directed the Neue Musikgesellschaft there (1918); edited the music periodical *Melos* (1920–21); conducted numerous concerts at modern music festivals in Donaueschingen, Frankfurt, etc.; conducted symph. concerts of the Collegium Musicum in Winterthur, Switzerland from 1922 to 1947 (with interruptions); from 1928 until 1933 was in charge of the music of the Königsberg Radio. In 1933 he left Germany; edited the periodical *Musica Viva* in Brussels (1933–36); conducted at music festivals in Barcelona (1936) and Paris. On Oct. 30, 1964, he conducted the Philadelphia Orch. in his long-awaited U.S. debut concert. He distinguished himself as a scholarly exponent of modern music; conducted many world premieres of ultramodern works; publ. a valuable manual on conducting, *Lehrbuch des Dirigierens* (Leipzig, 1929; in Eng. as *Handbook of Conducting*, London, 1933; 6th ed., 1949); *Vom Wesen der Musik* (Zürich, 1946; in Eng. as *The Nature of Music*, London, 1947; Chicago, 1950); *Musik für Jedermann* (Winterthur, 1950).

Scheremetiev, Alexander. See **Sheremetiev, Alexander.**

Schering, Arnold, eminent German music historian; b. Breslau, April 2, 1877; d. Berlin, March 7, 1941. His father was a merchant; the family moved to Dresden, where Schering began to take violin lessons with Blumner. In 1896 he enrolled in a Berlin music school, where he studied violin with Joachim, hoping to start a concert career; he organized a tour with the pianist Hinze-Reinhold, but soon gave up virtuoso aspirations, and in 1898 entered classes in musicology with Fleischer and Stumpf; then took courses with Sandberger at the Univ. of Munich and with Kretzschmar at the Univ. of Leipzig, obtaining his degree of Dr.Phil. with the dissertation *Geschichte des Instrumentalkonzerts* (Leipzig, 1902; amplified in vol. I of the series Kleine Handbücher der Musikgeschichte, 1905; 2nd ed., 1927). He completed his Habilitation at the Univ. of Leipzig with the dissertation *Die Anfänge des Oratorium* (1907; greatly expanded in 1911 and publ. as *Geschichte des Oratoriums*). He then devoted himself to teaching and musical journalism; from 1904–39 was editor of the Bach-Jahrbuch. From 1909–23 he taught at the Leipzig Cons.; in 1920 was named prof. of the Univ. of Halle; in 1928 he was appointed president of the German Musicological Society. In his voluminous publications he strove to erect an infallible system of esthetic principles derived from musical symbolism and based on psychological intuition, ignoring any contradictions that ensued from his axiomatic constructions. In his book *Beethoven in neuer Deutung*, publ. in 1934, at the early dawn of the Nazi era, Schering even attempted to interpret Beethoven's music in terms of racial German superiority, alienating many of his admirers. But in his irrepressible desire to establish an immutable sequence of historic necessity, he compiled an original and highly informative historical tabulation of musical chronology, *Tabellen zur Musikgeschichte*, which was originally publ. in 1914 and went through several editions. He advanced the idea that in order to understand new developments in the language of music it is necessary to study the music of the past, and conversely, that the understanding of old music can be enhanced by a study of new music. This thesis, obvious and possibly circular in its formulation, which Schering propounded with great solemnity at the opening of the first congress of the German Musicological Society in Leipzig in 1925, remains nevertheless a worthwhile restatement of the obvious. Schering's other theories, speculations, and declarations left no influence on sober musical thought of later generations.

PUBLICATIONS: *Geschichte des Instrumentalkonzerts bis auf die Gegenwart* (Leipzig, 1905; 2nd enlarged ed., 1927; reprint, Wiesbaden, 1965); *Geschichte des Oratoriums* (Leipzig, 1911; reprint, 1966); *Musikalische Bildung und Erziehung zum musikalischen Hören* (Leipzig, 1911; 4th ed., 1924); *Tabellen zur Musikgeschichte* (Leipzig, 1914; 4th ed., 1934; 5th ed., brought up to the modern period by H.J. Moser, Wiesbaden, 1962); *Aufführungspraxis alter Musik* (Berlin, 1931; reprint, Wiesbaden, 1969); *Geschichte der Musik in Beispielen* (Leipzig, 1931; 2nd ed., 1954; Eng. trans., 1950); *Beethoven in neuer Deutung* (Berlin, 1934); *Beethoven und die Dichtung* (Berlin, 1936); *J.S. Bachs Leipziger Kirchenmusik* (Leipzig, 1936; 2nd ed., 1954); *Von grossen*

Meistern der Musik (Berlin, 1940); *Das Symbol in der Musik* (Berlin, 1941); *Über Kantaten J.S. Bachs* (posthumous; Berlin, 1942; 2nd ed., 1950); *Vom musikalischen Kunstwerk* (posthumous; Berlin, 1949; 2nd ed., 1951); numerous eds. of works by German composers, among them Hasse, Quantz, and Schütz.

BIBLIOGRAPHY: *Festschrift Arnold Schering zum 60. Geburtstag* (Berlin, 1937).

Scherman, Thomas K., American conductor; b. New York, Feb. 12, 1917; d. there, May 14, 1979. He was a son of Harry Scherman, founder and president of the Book-of-the-Month Club; attended Columbia Univ. (B.A., 1937); then studied piano with Isabelle Vengerova, theory with Hans Weisse, and conducting with Carl Bamberger, Max Rudolf, and Otto Klemperer, whose assistant he became in conducting a chamber orch. composed of European refugees at The New School in N.Y. (1939–41). He subsequently served in the U.S. Army (1941–45), reaching the rank of captain in the Signal Corps. In 1947 he organized in N.Y. the Little Orch. Society for the purposes of presenting new works, some of them specially commissioned, and of reviving forgotten music of the past; he also gave performances of operas in concert versions. He terminated the seasons of the Little Orch. Society in 1975, but organized the New Little Orch. Society to present children's concerts; these he continued to lead until his death.

Schermerhorn, Kenneth DeWitt, American conductor; b. Schenectady, N.Y., Nov. 20, 1929. He studied music at the New England Cons. (graduated, 1950), and opera conducting there with Boris Goldovsky. His first important engagement was as conductor of the American Ballet Theater (1956–65); he subsequently conducted the New Jersey Symph. Orch. (1962–68); in 1968 he was appointed conductor of the Milwaukee Symph. Orch., a post he retained until 1980. He thrice conducted the Hong Kong Phil.; also conducted opera at Long Beach, Calif. In 1982 he was appointed general music director of the American Ballet Theater in N.Y.; he was appointed music director of the Nashville Symph. Orch. in 1983.

Scherzer, Otto, German violinist and composer; b. Ansbach, March 24, 1821; d. Stuttgart, Feb. 23, 1886. After studying with Molique, he became a violinist in the Stuttgart Court Orch. (1838–54); was music director at Tübingen Univ. (1860–77); publ. a number of songs and piano pieces.

BIBLIOGRAPHY: Anon., *Otto Scherzer. Ein Künstlerleben* (Stuttgart, 1897).

Schetky, Johann Georg Christoph, German cellist and composer; b. Darmstadt, Aug. 19, 1737; d. Edinburgh, Nov. 29, 1824. The original family name was **Von Teschky**; Schetky's ancestors were from Transylvania. He traveled in Germany; in 1768 was in Hamburg; in 1772, settled in Edinburgh, where he was first cellist of the concerts in St. Cecilia's Hall.

He married Maria Anna Teresa Reinagle, sister of Alexander Reinagle. He publ. 6 string quartets; 6 string trios; 6 duos for violin and cello; 6 cello sonatas, with bass; 6 flute duos; 6 cello duos; 6 sonatas for violin and cello; harpsichord sonatas; songs. In MS he left 3 symphs., 4 cello concertos, and an oratorio. His son **J. George Schetky** (b. Edinburgh, June 1, 1776; d. Philadelphia, Dec. 11, 1831) was the 2nd of 11 children; he emigrated to America in 1787; was naturalized in Philadelphia on Nov. 19, 1806. He appeared as a cellist in Philadelphia; c.1800 he entered into partnership with Benjamin Carr in the music publishing business; was a co-founder of the Musical Fund Society in Philadelphia. His arrangement for military band of Kotzwara's *Battle of Prague* was much played.

BIBLIOGRAPHY: Madeira, *Music in Philadelphia* (Philadelphia, 1896); O.G. Sonneck, *Bibliography of Early American Secular Music* (Washington, D.C., 1905); idem, *Early Concert Life in America* (Leipzig, 1907; in Eng.); Laurance Oliphant Schetky, *The Schetky Family; A Compilation of Letters, Memoirs and Historical Data* (privately publ., Portland, Oreg., 1942; of great documentary value, establishing correct factual data from family archives; the author was a grandson of J. George Schetky).

Scheurleer, Daniel François, Dutch musicologist; b. The Hague, Nov. 13, 1855; d. there, Feb. 6, 1927. Although a banker, he took an active part in musical affairs; was president, for many years, of the Vereeniging voor Nederlandsche Muziekgeschiedenis; was made Dr.Phil. *honoris causa* by the Univ. of Leyden in 1910; he was the owner of a valuable musical library (catalogue publ. in 1885; 2 supplements, 1903 and 1910) and collection of instruments (catalogue publ. 1885 and 1887; now in the Museum of The Hague); in 1921 he founded the Union Musicologique. He publ. *Het Muziekleven in Nederland in de tweede helft der 18ᵉ eeuw* (The Hague, 1909) and other studies; edited Fruytier's *Ecclesiasticus* (1563), etc.

BIBLIOGRAPHY: *Gedenkboek aangeboden aan Dr. D.F. Scheurleer op zijn 70sten Verjaardag* (1925; contains a complete bibliography of his works).

Schibler, Armin, Swiss composer; b. Kreuzlingen, Nov. 20, 1920. He studied with Willy Burkhard in Zürich; since 1944 he has been music director at the Kanton Gymnasium there. Much of his music is cast in neo-Classical forms; some works employ a modified form of the 12-tone technique.

WORKS: OPERAS: *Der spanische Rosenstock* (Bern, April 9, 1950); *Der Teufel im Winterpalais* (1950–53); *Das Bergwerk von Falun* (1953); *Die Füsse im Feuer* (Zürich, April 25, 1955; aroused considerable interest); *Blackwood & Co.,* burlesque opera (Zürich, June 3, 1962); symph. oratorio, *Media in vita* (Zürich, April 26, 1963). FOR ORCH.: Concertino for Piano and Chamber Orch. (1943); *Fantasy* for Viola and Small Orch. (1945); *Fantasy* for Oboe, Harp, and Small Orch. (1946); Symph. No. 1 (1946); *Passacaglia* (1949); *Symphonic Variations* (1950);

Concertante fantasie for Cello and Orch. (1951); Symph. No. 2 (1953); *Concerto for Amateur Orchestra* (1953); Symph. No. 3 (Winterthur, Nov. 13, 1957); *Metamorphoses Ebrietatis,* symph. poem (Montreux, Sept. 6, 1966); Horn Concerto (1956); Trombone Concerto (1957); *Concerto breve* for Cello and Orch. (1958–59); Violin Concerto (1960); Trumpet Concerto (1960–61); Concerto for Percussion and Orch. (Zürich, Jan. 6, 1961); Piano Concerto (1962–68); Concerto for Piano, Percussion, and String Orch. (1963); Double Concerto for Flute, Harp, and Chamber Orch. (1966); Bassoon Concerto (1967); *6 Pieces* for Orch. (1969). CANTATAS: *Die Hochzeit* (1946); *Gefährten* (1946); *Weil Alles erneut sich begibt* (1949); *Mondlicht* (1950). CHAMBER MUSIC: Solo Sonata for Flute (1944); Suite for Cello Alone (1945); *Little Concerto* for Viola Alone (1947); 4 string quartets (1945, 1951, 1958, 1960); *Trio concertante* for Trumpet, Violin, and Piano (1948); *Duo concertante* for Violin and Piano (1950); *Dodecaphonic Studies* for Piano; several works for speaking and singing voices.
BIBLIOGRAPHY: K.H. Wörner, *Armin Schibler; Werk und Persönlichkeit* (Amriswil, 1953).

Schicht, Johann Gottfried, German composer; b. Reichenau, Saxony, Sept. 29, 1753; d. Leipzig, Feb. 16, 1823. In 1776, already well trained as an organist and pianist, he matriculated at Leipzig as a law student, but became a pianist at Johann Adam Hiller's Liebhaber-Konzerte, and at the Gewandhaus Concerts evolved from them in 1781, succeeding Hiller as conductor in 1785. In 1810 he became cantor at the Thomasschule.
WORKS: Oratorios: *Die Feier der Christen auf Golgotha, Moses auf Sinai,* and *Das Ende des Gerechten;* masses, motets, Te Deums, the *100th Psalm;* several chorale-motets (*Nach einer Prüfung kurzer Tage, Jesus meine Zuversicht, Herzlich lieb hab' ich dich, o Herr,* etc.); 9 settings of Leo's Miserere *a* 4–8; an excellent book of chorales (1819; of 1,285 melodies, 306 are original); a concerto, sonatas, caprices, etc., for piano; and *Grundregeln der Harmonie* (Leipzig, 1812).
BIBLIOGRAPHY: P. Langer, *Chronik der Leipziger Singakademie* (Leipzig, 1902).

Schick, George, American conductor; b. Prague, April 5, 1908. He studied at the Prague Cons.; was assistant conductor at the Prague Opera from 1927 until 1938. He settled in the U.S. in 1939; was conductor of the San Carlo Opera (1943); then conducted in Chicago; from 1948 to 1950 was conductor of the Little Symph. of Montreal; from 1950 to 1956 was associate conductor of the Chicago Symph. Orch. He was a conductor at the Metropolitan Opera (1958–69); then served as president of the Manhattan School of Music in N.Y. (1969–76).

Schick (née **Hamel**), **Margarete Luise,** noted German soprano; b. Mainz, April 26, 1773; d. Berlin, April 29, 1809. She studied with Steffani at Würzburg, and later with Righini at Mainz, where her stage debut took place in 1791. Her favorite roles were Susanna (*Figaro*) and Zerlina (*Don Giovanni*). She was in Berlin from 1793 as a chamber and theater singer to the court; at the National Theater there from 1794. From 1794 she sang at the Royal Opera in Berlin, having great success in operas by Gluck. Her contemporaries regarded her as the equal of the famous Mara. In 1791 she married the violinist **Ernst Schick.**
BIBLIOGRAPHY: K. Levezow, *Leben und Kunst der Frau Margarete Luise Schick* (Berlin, 1809).

Schickele, Peter, American composer; b. Ames, Iowa, July 17, 1935. He studied at the Juilliard School of Music, with Vincent Persichetti and William Bergsma. After quaquaversal professional gyrations, he rocketed to fame in the rollicking role of the roly-poly character P.D.Q. Bach, the mythical composer of such outrageous travesties as *The Civilian Barber, Gross Concerto for Divers Flutes* (featuring a Nose Flute and a Wiener Whistle to be eaten during the perf.), *Concerto for Piano vs. Orchestra, Iphigenia in Brooklyn, The Seasonings, Pervertimento for Bagpipes, Bicycles & Balloons, No-No Nonette, Schleptet, Fuga Meshuga, Missa Hilarious, Sanka Cantata, Fantasie-Shtick,* etc., all perpetrated in a clever pseudo-Baroque style. On April 24, 1984, his opera, *The Abduction of Figaro,* was premiered in Minneapolis. He publ. *The Definitive Biography of P.D.Q. Bach (1807–1742?)* (N.Y., 1976).

Schidlowsky, León, Chilean composer; b. Santiago, July 21, 1931. He studied philosophy and psychology at the Univ. of Chile (1948–52) and had private lessons in composition with Free Focke and in harmony with Juan Allende; then went to Germany for further studies (1952–55). Returning to Chile, he organized the avant-garde group Tonus for the propagation of new techniques of composition; was a music teacher at the Hebrew Inst. in Santiago (1955–61), director of the music archives of the Inst. of Musical Extension of the Univ. of Chile (1961–65), and director of the Inst. and a member of the faculty of the Cons. Nacional de Música in Santiago (1965–69). In 1969 he emigrated to Israel, where he was appointed to the faculty of the Rubin Academy in Tel Aviv. In his music he adopts a serial technique, extending it into fields of rhythms and intensities; beginning in 1964 he superadded aleatory elements, using graphic notation.
WORKS: Opera, *Die Menschen* (1970); *Requiem* for Soprano and Chamber Orch. (1954); *Caupolicán,* epic narrative for Narrator, Chorus, 2 Pianos, Celesta, and Percussion Orch. (1958); *Tríptico* for Orch. (1959); *Oda a la tierra* for 2 Narrators and Orch. (1958–60); *La Noche de Cristal,* symph. for Tenor, Male Chorus, and Orch., commemorating the martyrdom of Jews on the Nazi "crystal night" (1961); *Eróstrato* for Percussion Orch. (1963); *Invocación* for Soprano, Narrator, Percussion, and String Orch. (1964); *Nueva York* for Orch., dedicated to "my brothers in Harlem" (1965; 3rd Inter-American Music Festival, Washington, D.C., May 9, 1965); *Jeremias* for 8 Mixed Voices and String Orch.

(1966); *Kadish* for Cello and Orch. (1967); *Epitaph for Hermann Scherchen* for Orch. (1967); *Babi Yar* for String Orch., Piano, and Percussion (1970); *Serenata* for Chamber Orch. (1970); *Arcanas* for Orch. (1971); *Constellation II* for String Orch. (1971); *Rabbi Akiba,* scenic fantasy for Narrator, 3 Soloists, Children's and Mixed Chorus, and Orch. (1972); *Amereida* (consisting of *Memento, Llaqui,* and *Ecce Homo*) for Narrator and Orch. (1965–72); *2 Psalms* for Contralto, Clarinet, Bass Clarinet, Violin, and Cello (1954); *6 Japanese Songs* for Soprano and 9 Instruments (1954); *Cantata negra* for Contralto, Piano, Xylophone, and 3 Percussionists (1957); *Amatorias* for Tenor and Instrumental Ensemble (1962–63); *De profundis* for Soprano, Contralto, Tenor, Flute, Oboe, Bass Clarinet, Saxophone, Trumpet, Trombone, and Strings (1963); *Lament* for Chorus a cappella (1966); *Requiem* for 12 Soloists a cappella (1968); *Espergesia* for Tenor and Percussion (1968); *Monodrama* for Actress and Percussion (1970); *In memoriam* for Narrator, Flute, Oboe, Clarinet, Cello, and Percussion (1971); *Canticas* for 2 Sopranos, Countertenor, Tenor, Baritone, and Brass (1971); *Verrà la morte* for Solo Soprano (1972); *Hommage à Picasso,* to a text by Gertrude Stein, for Soprano, Alto, Tenor, and Bass (1973); *Elegía* for Clarinet and String Quartet (1952); Trio for Flute, Cello, and Piano (1955); *Cuarteto mixto* for Flute, Clarinet, Violin, and Cello (1956); Concerto for 6 Instruments (1957); *In memoriam* for Clarinet and Percussion (1957); *4 Miniatures* for Flute, Oboe, Clarinet, and Bassoon (1957); *Soliloquios* for 8 Instruments (1961); *Visiones* for 12 Strings (1967); String Quartet (1967); Wind Quintet (1968); *Eclosión* for 9 Instruments (1967); *6 Hexáforos* for 6 Percussionists (1968); Sextet (1970); *Kolot* for Solo Harp (1971); *Meshulash (Triangle)* for Piano Trio (1971). For Piano: *6 Miniatures,* to paintings by Klee (1952); *8 Structures* (1955); *5 Pieces* (1956); *Actus* (1972).

BIBLIOGRAPHY: M.E. Grebe, "León Schidlowsky, síntesis de su trayectoria creativa," *Revista Musical Chilena* (1968; contains a list of works); W. Elias, *Léon Schidlowsky* (Tel Aviv, 1978).

Schiedermair, Ludwig, eminent German musicologist; b. Regensburg, Dec. 7, 1876; d. Bensberg, near Cologne, April 30, 1957. He studied in Munich with Sandberger and Beer-Walbrunn; received his Dr.Phil. in 1901 for the dissertation *Künstlerische Bestrebungen am Hofe des Kurfürsten Ferdinand Maria von Bayern;* studied further with Riemann in Leipzig and with Kretzschmar in Berlin. In 1906 he became an instructor of musicology at the Univ. of Marburg; in 1912, a lecturer at the Univ. of Bonn (1920, prof.). In 1927, on the occasion of the Beethoven centennial, he was appointed director of the Beethoven-Haus Research Inst. in Bonn. He retired from the Univ. of Bonn in 1945.

WRITINGS: *Gustav Mahler* (Leipzig, 1901); *Beiträge zur Geschichte der Oper um die Wende des 18. und 19. Jahrhunderts (Simon Mayr)* (2 vols., Leipzig, 1907, 1910); *Bayreuther Festspiele im Zeitalter des Absolutismus* (Leipzig, 1908); *Die Briefe*

Mozarts und seiner Familie (5 vols., Munich, 1914; vol. 5 is an iconography); *W.A. Mozarts Handschrift* (Bückeburg, 1919; facsimiles); *Einführung in das Studium der Musikgeschichte* (Munich, 1918; new ed., Bonn, 1947); *Mozart* (Munich, 1922; 2nd ed., Bonn, 1948); *Der junge Beethoven* (Leipzig, 1925; 4th ed., 1970); *Beethoven: Beiträge zum Leben und Schaffen* (Leipzig, 1930; 3rd ed., 1943); *Die deutsche Oper* (Leipzig, 1930); *Die Gestaltung weltanschaulicher Ideen in der Vokalmusik Beethovens* (Leipzig, 1934); *Musik am Rheinstron* (Cologne, 1947); *Musikalische Begegnungen; Erlebnis und Erinnerung* (Cologne, 1948); *Deutsche Musik im Europäischen Raum* (Münster, 1954). A Festschrift, *Beethoven und die Gegenwart,* was publ. in honor of Schiedermair's 60th birthday (Berlin, 1937); a 2nd Festschrift appeared in Cologne in 1956.

BIBLIOGRAPHY: J. Schmidt-Görg, "Ludwig Schiedermair," *Die Musikforschung,* 2 (1957).

Schiedermayer, Johann Baptist, German composer; b. Pfaffenmünster, Bavaria, June 23, 1779; d. Linz, Austria, Jan. 6, 1840, as Cathedral organist. He wrote the singspiels *Wellmanns Eichenstämme* (Linz, 1815), *Das Glück ist kugelrund* (Linz, 1816), *Die Rückkehr ins Vaterhaus* (Linz, 1816); 16 masses and much other sacred music; also symphs., string trios, organ pieces, etc.; *Theoretisch-praktische Choralehre zum Gebrauch beim katholischen Kirchenritus* (1828); an abridged ed. of Leopold Mozart's violin method.

Schiedmayer, the name of 2 well-known firms of piano makers in Stuttgart: Schiedmayer & Söhne and Schiedmayer Pianofortefabrik. **Balthasar Schiedmayer** (1711–81) began manufacturing musical instruments in Erlangen c.1740; at his death in 1781, his son **Johann David Schiedmayer** (1753–1805) assumed the management; he was succeeded by his 19-year-old son, **Johann Lorenz Schiedmayer** (1786–1860), with whom he had moved (c.1800) from Erlangen to Nuremberg. Johann Lorenz ended the business at Nuremberg after 2 years, and went to Vienna for a brief time; in 1809 he was in Stuttgart, where he set up business in partnership with a young piano maker, Karl Dieudonné (d. 1825); from 1825, he carried on the business alone, until 1845, when his eldest sons, **Adolf Schiedmayer** (1819–90) and **Hermann Schiedmayer** (1820–61), entered the firm, which was then called J.L. Schiedmayer & Söhne. In 1853 Johann Lorenz Schiedmayer provided his 2 younger sons, **Julius** (1822–78) and **Paul** (1829–90), with their own separate factory, producing harmoniums. After their father's death they turned to piano making, and their business became known as Schiedmayer Pianofortefabrik. Upon Paul Schiedmayer's death in 1890, his son, **Max Julius,** became head of the firm.

BIBLIOGRAPHY: A. Eisenmann, *Schiedmayer und Söhne* (Stuttgart, 1909); *150 Jahre Schiedmayer und Söhne* (Stuttgart, 1959).

Schiff, Andras, Hungarian pianist; b. Budapest, Dec. 21, 1953. He studied at the Liszt Academy of

Music in Budapest and in London with George Malcolm; made his debut in Budapest in 1972; was a prizewinner at the International Tchaikovsky Competition in Moscow in 1974 and at the Leeds International Competition in 1975; subsequently was a soloist with the leading orchs. in America; toured in Japan. He excels in the Romantic repertoire but is also a fine interpreter of Bach's works.

Schiff, Heinrich, gifted Austrian cellist; b. Gmunden, Nov. 18, 1951. He first studied piano; then took cello lessons with Tobias Kuhne in Vienna and later with André Navarra in Detmold. After winning prizes in competitions in Geneva, Vienna, and Warsaw, he was a soloist with the Vienna Phil., the Concertgebouw Orch. in Amsterdam, the Stockholm Phil., the BBC Symph., and the Royal Phil. in London; also concertized in Toronto and Montreal. In 1978 he toured Australia, and in 1979 played in Japan. His playing is marked by assured technical resources and mellowness of tone.

Schifrin, Lalo (Boris), American composer; b. Buenos Aires, June 21, 1932. He studied music at home with his father, who was concertmaster at the Teatro Colón; took composition lessons with Argentine dodecaphonist Juan Carlos Paz. In 1950 he went to Paris, where he attended the classes of Olivier Messiaen. He became interested in jazz and represented Argentina at the International Jazz Festival in Paris in 1955; returning to Buenos Aires, he formed his own jazz band, adopting the bebop style. In 1958 he went to N.Y. as arranger for Xavier Cugat; then was pianist with Dizzy Gillespie's band (1960–62); composed for it several exotic pieces, such as *Manteca, Con Alma,* and *Tunisian Fantasy,* based on Gillespie's *Night in Tunisia.* In 1963 he wrote a ballet, *Jazz Faust.* In 1964 he went to Hollywood, where he rapidly found his métier as composer for the films and television; among his motion picture scores are *The Liquidator, The Fox,* and *The Cincinnati Kid.* He also experimented with applying the jazz idiom to religious texts, as, for instance, in his *Jazz Suite on Mass Texts* (1965). He achieved his greatest popular success with the theme-motto for the television series *Mission: Impossible,* in 5/4 time, for which he received 2 Grammy awards. His adaptation of modern techniques into mass media placed him in the enviable position of being praised by professional musicians. His oratorio *The Rise and Fall of the Third Reich,* featuring realistic excerpts and incorporating an actual recording of Hitler's speech in electronic amplification, was brought out at the Hollywood Bowl on Aug. 3, 1967. His other works include a Suite for Trumpet and Brass Orch. (1961); *The Ritual of Sound* for 15 Instruments (1962); *Pulsations* for Electronic Keyboard, Jazz Band, and Orch. (Los Angeles, Jan. 21, 1971); *Madrigals for the Space Age,* in 10 parts, for Narrator and Chorus (Los Angeles, Jan. 15, 1976); Capriccio for Clarinet and Strings (Los Angeles, Nov. 5, 1981).

Schikaneder, Emanuel (Johann), Mozart's librettist; b. Straubing, Sept. 1, 1751; d. Vienna, Sept. 21, 1812. His baptismal names were Johannes Joseph; he assumed the name Emanuel later in life. He was a member of a troupe of itinerant players when he met Mozart at Salzburg in 1780. In 1783 he reached Vienna, where he was an actor and an impresario. He was not successful until he persuaded Mozart to set to music his play *Die Zauberflöte,* which recouped his fortunes; it was produced on Sept. 30, 1791, shortly before Mozart's death; Schikaneder himself took the part of Papageno. He wrote 55 theater pieces and 44 librettos for operas, and singspiels; with Zitterbarth he was the manager of the Theater an der Wien, which he directed from its foundation (1801) until 1806. He died insane after a series of financial setbacks.
BIBLIOGRAPHY: O.E. Deutsch, *Das Freihaustheater auf der Wieden, 1787–1801* (Vienna, 1937); Egon von Komorzynski, *Der Vater der Zauberflöte: Emanuel Schikaneders Leben* (Vienna, 1948); idem, *Emanuel Schikaneder: Ein Beitrag zur Geschichte des deutschen Theaters* (Vienna, 1951). For a complete list of his librettos see Anton Bauer, *Opern und Operetten in Wien* (Vienna, 1955).

Schilhawsky, Paul, Austrian pianist, conductor, and educator; b. Salzburg, Nov. 9, 1918. He studied piano at the Salzburg Mozarteum; also took courses in musicology at the Univ. of Munich and received instruction in conducting with Clemens Krauss; then appeared as a piano soloist and accompanist. In 1945 he was engaged as a conductor at the Salzburg Landestheater; in 1948 he became a prof. of piano at the Salzburg Mozarteum and director of the opera school; from 1958 he taught the classes there for lieder singing and accompanying; from 1971 to 1979 he was rector of the Hochschule für Musik in Salzburg; from 1972 served as director of the International Summer Academy there.

Schiller, Friedrich von, great German poet; b. Marbach, Nov. 10, 1759; d. Weimar, May 9, 1805. Many musicians have turned to his works for inspiration.
BIBLIOGRAPHY: M. Berendt, *Schiller bis Wagner* (Berlin, 1901); J. Baltz, *Beethoven und Schiller* (Arnsberg, 1905); A. Kohut, *F. Schiller in seinen Beziehungen zur Musik* (Stuttgart, 1905); H. Knudsen, *Schiller und die Musik* (Greifswald, 1908); G. Adler, *Schiller und Schubert* (Vienna, 1910).

Schilling, Gustav, German musical lexicographer; b. Schwiegershausen, near Hannover, Nov. 3, 1805; d. Crete, Nebr., March 1880. He studied theology at Göttingen and Halle; in 1857 he emigrated to America; lived in N.Y.; later was in Montreal; finally settled in Nebraska.
WRITINGS: His most important work was the *Enzyklopädie der gesammten musikalischen Wissenschaften oder Universal-Lexikon der Tonkunst* (6 vols., 1835–38; 2nd ed., 7 vols., 1840–42). Other publications are *Versuch einer Philosophie des Schönen in der Musik* (1838); *Lehrbuch der allgemeinen Musikwissenschaft* (1840); *Geschichte der heutigen oder modernen Musik* (1841); *Die musikalische*

Europa (1842); *Musikalische Dynamik; oder, Die Lehre vom Vortrage in der Musik* (1843); *Der Pianist* (1843); *Franz Liszt* (1844); *Sicher Schlüssel zur Klaviervirtuosität* (1844); *Die schöne Kunst der Töne* (1847); *Musikalische Didaktik* (1851); *Allgemeine Volksmusiklehre* (1852); *Akustik oder die Lehre vom Klange* (2nd ed., 1856).

Schillinger, Joseph, Russian composer and theorist; b. Kharkov, Aug. 31, 1895; d. New York, March 23, 1943. He studied at the St. Petersburg Cons. with Tcherepnin, Wihtol, and others; from 1918 to 1922, taught at the State Academy of Music in Kharkov; also conducted an orch. there; from 1922 to 1928 was active in Leningrad as a teacher and composer. In 1928 he came to America, settling in N.Y.; taught at The New School for Social Research; then established private classes, teaching his own system of composition, based on rigid mathematical principles. He became highly successful as an instructor; George Gershwin took lessons from him; many other composers of popular music became his students. After Schillinger's death, Lyle Dowling and Arnold Shaw edited and publ. his magnum opus, under the title *The Schillinger System of Musical Composition* (2 vols., N.Y., 1946); this was followed by *The Mathematical Basis of the Arts* (N.Y., 1947); a short vol. of musical patterns, *Kaleidophone,* was publ. previously (N.Y., 1940). Schillinger was also a composer in his own right; his works include *March of the Orient* for Orch. (Leningrad, May 12, 1926); *First Airphonic Suite* for Theremin, with Orch. (Cleveland, Nov. 28, 1929; Leo Theremin, inventor of the instrument, as soloist); piano pieces; etc.

BIBLIOGRAPHY: Frances Schillinger, *Joseph Schillinger: A Memoir by His Wife* (N.Y., 1949); Vernon Duke, "Gershwin, Schillinger, and Dukelsky," *Musical Quarterly* (Jan. 1947).

Schillings, Max von, renowned German composer and conductor; b. Düren, April 19, 1868; d. Berlin, July 24, 1933. While attending the Gymnasium at Bonn he studied violin with O. von Königslöw, and piano and composition with K.J. Brambach. He then entered the Univ. of Munich, where he studied law, philosophy, literature, and art. He became associated with Richard Strauss, and under his influence decided to devote himself entirely to music. In 1892 he was engaged as assistant stage director at the Festival Theater in Bayreuth; in 1902 he became chorus master; in 1908 he moved to Stuttgart, becoming Generalmusikdirektor in 1911; on the occasion of the inauguration of the new opera theater there, he was given the rank of nobility, and added the nobiliary particle "von" to his name; he remained in Stuttgart until 1918; was Intendant of the Berlin State Opera (1919–25). He made several visits as a conductor to the U.S. In 1923 he married the soprano **Barbara Kemp.** As a composer, he trailed in the path of Wagner, barely avoiding direct imitation.

WORKS: Operas: *Ingwelde* (Karlsruhe, Nov. 13, 1894); *Der Pfeifertag* (Schwerin, Nov. 26, 1899); *Moloch* (Dresden, Dec. 8, 1906); *Mona Lisa* (Stuttgart,

Sept. 26, 1915; enjoyed considerable success; produced by the Metropolitan Opera, N.Y., March 1, 1923); incidental music to the *Oresteia* of Aeschylus (1900) and to Part I of Goethe's *Faust;* a symph. prologue to the *Oedipus Rex* of Sophocles; also several melodramas with Orch.: *Kassandra, Das eleusische Fest, Das Hexenlied,* and *Jung Olaf;* 2 symph. fantasies: *Meergruss* and *Seemorgen;* Violin Concerto; String Quartet; String Quintet; pieces for violin and piano; men's choruses a cappella; songs; piano pieces. A complete catalogue of his works, compiled by J. Beck, was publ. at Berlin in 1934.

BIBLIOGRAPHY: R. Louis, *Max Schillings* (Leipzig, 1909); A. Richard, *Max Schillings* (Munich, 1922); W. Raupp, *Max von Schillings* (Hamburg, 1935); J. Geuenich and K. Strahn, eds., *Gedenkschrift Max von Schillings zum 100. Geburtstag* (Düren, 1968).

Schimon, Adolf, Austrian singing teacher and composer; b. Vienna, Feb. 29, 1820; d. Leipzig, June 21, 1887. He studied with Berton, Halévy, and others at the Paris Cons.; studied the Italian method in Florence, bringing out his opera *Stradella* there in 1846; was *maestro al cembalo* at Her Majesty's Theatre in London (1850–53), then at the Italian Opera in Paris (1854–59). In 1858 Flotow brought out Schimon's comic opera *List um List* at Schwerin. His works further included Italian and French songs; German lieder; 2 string quartets; Piano Trio; Violin Sonata; piano music; etc. He was married to the soprano **Anna Regan (Schimon-Regan).**

Schimon-Regan, Anna, distinguished German soprano; b. Aich, near Karlsbad, Sept. 18, 1841; d. Munich, April 18, 1902. In 1859 she had her first singing lessons from Mme. Schubert in Karlsbad; the next year her aunt, the famous **Caroline Unger,** took her to Florence and taught her until 1864; she was then engaged at the court opera in Hannover (1864–67); during the winter of 1867–68 she sang in Berlioz's concerts in St. Petersburg. She made her first visit to England in 1869, appearing in concerts with Caroline Unger; gave song recitals there every winter until 1875. In 1872 she married **Adolf Schimon,** and settled in Munich.

Schindelmeisser, Ludwig (Louis), German composer; b. Königsberg, Dec. 8, 1811; d. Darmstadt, March 30, 1864. He studied with A.B. Marx in Berlin and also with Dorn in Leipzig, where he met Wagner and became friendly with him. He worked as an opera conductor in Berlin, Budapest, Frankfurt, and Hamburg, and himself wrote several operas: *Peter von Szapáry* (Budapest, Aug. 8, 1839); *Malvina* (Budapest, 1841); *Der Rächer,* after Corneille's *Le Cid* (Budapest, April 4, 1846); *Melusine* (Darmstadt, 1861); a ballet, *Diavolina;* orch. overtures: *Rule Britannia* and *Loreley;* numerous piano pieces and songs.

Schindler, Anton Felix, violinist and conductor, historically significant as amanuensis, close associate, and early biographer of Beethoven; b. Meedl,

Moravia, June 13, 1795; d. Bockenheim, near Frankfurt, Jan. 16, 1864. He studied violin with his father; went to Vienna in 1813 to study law. In 1814 he met Beethoven, soon becoming his secretary, his social mediator, and, to some extent, his business manager; for some years he held the position of concertmaster of the orch. of the Josephstadttheater. Beethoven's stormy temper created inevitable difficulties; during one such outburst, Beethoven even accused his faithful helper of mishandling the financial receipts from the ticket sales for the premiere of the 9th Symph. However, Schindler had enough modesty and intelligence to disregard such personal misunderstandings, and continued to serve Beethoven. After Beethoven's death, Schindler obtained possession of valuable MSS, documents, papers, and about 400 of the biographically important conversation books, which recorded Beethoven's dialogues with friends and visitors. In a misguided attempt to protect Beethoven's reputation, Schindler apparently destroyed some of these materials, at least the parts that reflected Beethoven's pettiness and complaints. More reprehensible is the indication that some of Beethoven's conversation books, invaluable in their biographical content, were altered by Schindler, as appears from the painstaking handwriting analysis conducted on these books in 1977 by Dagmar Beck and Gritat Herre. In 1846 Schindler sold most of his Beethoven collection to the Royal Library in Berlin. He served as music director in Münster (1831–35) and Aachen (1835–37). In 1848 he moved to Frankfurt and supported himself mainly by teaching. In 1856 he settled in Bockenheim, where he remained until his death. No matter what criticism can be raised against Schindler as a man of limited endowments unable to grasp the dimension of Beethoven's genius, the fact remains that it was Schindler who became the prime source of information about Beethoven's life, a witness to the musical greatness that Beethoven embodied. His fundamental book, *Biographie von Ludwig van Beethoven,* was publ. in Münster in 1840; the 2nd edition, containing the valuable supplement *Auszüge aus Beethovens Konversationsheften,* appeared in 1845; the English translation of the original edition, made by Moscheles, was publ. in London in 1841. The 3rd edition of Schindler's biography appeared in 1860 and was translated into English by Donald MacArdle under the title *Beethoven as I Knew Him* (London, 1966). Of interest are also Schindler's diaries (1841–43), which were edited by M. Becker (Frankfurt, 1939).

BIBLIOGRAPHY: E. Hüffer, "Anton Felix Schindler, Der Biograph Beethovens" (Diss., Münster, 1909); W. Nohl, "Die Beziehungen Anton Schindlers zu Beethoven," *Die Musik,* XVII (1925); D. MacArdle, "Anton Felix Schindler, Friend of Beethoven," *Music Review,* XXIV (1963); E. Doernberg, "Anton Schindler," *Musical Quarterly* (April 1965); D. Beck and G. Herre, "Einige Zweifel an der Überlieferung der Konversationshefte," *Internationaler Beethoven-Kongress: Berlin 1977;* P. Stadlen, "Schindler's Beethoven Forgeries," *Musical Times* (July 1977); D. Beck and G. Herre, "Anton Schindlers fingierte Eintragungen in den Konversa-tionsheften," in H. Goldschmidt, ed., *Zu Beethoven: Aufsätze und Annotationen* (Berlin, 1979).

Schindler, Kurt, German conductor and music editor; b. Berlin, Feb. 17, 1882; d. New York, Nov. 16, 1935. He studied piano with Ansorge and composition with Bussler and others in Berlin; took additional theory lessons in Munich with Thuille. He then was briefly assistant conductor to Richard Strauss in Berlin and to Mottl in Munich; in 1904 he emigrated to America and, after serving as an assistant chcrus master at the Metropolitan Opera House, was engaged as a reader and music editor for G. Schirmer, Inc. In 1909 he founded in N.Y. the MacDowell Chorus, which became in 1910 the Schola Cantorum. Schindler conducted it until 1926 in programs including his choral arrangements of folk songs of various nations. His editions of arrangements of folk songs are valuable; among them are *6 Old French Christmas Carols* (1908); *Century of Russian Song from Glinka to Rachmaninov* (50 songs, with Eng. trans.; 1911); *The Developement of Opera* (examples of various periods; 1912); *Songs of the Russian People* (1915); *10 Student Songs of Finland* (1915); *A Cappella Choruses from the Russian Liturgy* (1913–17); *Masters of Russian Song* (2 vols., 1917); *Old Spanish Sacred Motets* (1918); *Modern Spanish Choral Works* (1918); *60 Russian Folk-Songs* (3 vols., 1918–19); *Folk Music and Poetry of Spain and Portugal* (N.Y., 1941; posthumous; about 1,000 musical examples; text in Eng. and Spanish).

Schiøler, Victor, prominent Danish pianist; b. Copenhagen, April 7, 1899; d. there, Feb. 17, 1967. He studied with his mother, Augusta Schiøler (1868–1946); then with Ignaz Friedman and Artur Schnabel; made his piano debut in 1914; from 1919 toured in Europe; made his first American tour in 1948–49. He was also active as a conductor in Denmark.

Schiøtz, Aksel, famous Danish tenor and pedagogue; b. Roskilde, Sept. 1, 1906; d. Copenhagen, April 19, 1975. His father was an architect, and he urged Schiøtz to follow an academic career; accordingly, he enrolled at the Univ. of Copenhagen in language studies, obtaining a master's degree in 1929. He also studied singing, first at the Danish Royal Opera School in Copenhagen, and later with John Forsell in Stockholm. He made his operatic debut at the Royal Danish Theater in Copenhagen in 1939 as Ferrando in *Così fan tutte.* He became known as a fine interpreter of Mozart's tenor roles and a superb lieder singer. In 1946 he made appearances in England; in 1948 visited the U.S. His career was tragically halted when he developed a brain tumor, which led to an impairment of his speech; however, he regained his capacities as a singer and gave concerts as a baritone. From 1955 to 1958 he taught voice at the Univ. of Minnesota; from 1958 to 1961 was a prof. of voice at the Royal Cons. of Music and the Univ. of Toronto, and from 1961 to 1968, at the Univ. of Colorado. He returned to Copenhagen in 1968 and joined the faculty of the Royal Danish School of Educational Studies. He died of leukemia and intestinal cancer. In 1977 a memorial fund was formed in the U.S. to preserve his memory by granting scholarships in art songs. He publ. *The Singer and His Art* (N.Y., 1969).

BIBLIOGRAPHY: G. Schiøtz, *Kunst og Kamp: Gerd og Aksel Schiøtz* (Copenhagen, 1951); David Ewen, *Musicians since 1900* (N.Y., 1978).

Schipa, Tito (baptismal names, **Raffaele Attilio Amadeo**), famous Italian tenor; b. Lecce, Jan. 2, 1888; d. New York, Dec. 16, 1965. He studied composition with A. Gerunda, and began his career as a composer of piano pieces and songs; then turned to singing, and in 1910 made his debut at Vercelli in *La Traviata*. After numerous appearences in Europe, he was engaged by the Chicago Civic Opera (1919–32); made his first appearance with the Metropolitan Opera on Nov. 23, 1932, as Nemorino in *L'elisir d'amore;* continued to sing with the Metropolitan until 1935, then again in 1940–41, making appearances throughout the season. Schipa made extensive tours of Europe and South America, as well as in the U.S.; lived in California until 1941, when he went back to Italy. On Sept. 28, 1946, he married Teresa Borgna of São Paulo, Brazil. He toured the U.S. again in 1947. He retired from opera in 1954, but continued to give solo concerts until late in life. He wrote an operetta, *La Principessa Liana* (1935); a Mass (1929); several songs; also wrote a book, *Si confessi* (Genoa, 1961).

Schipper, Emil, Austrian bass-baritone; b. Vienna, Aug. 19, 1882; d. there, July 20, 1957. He studied in Vienna and Milan; made his debut at the German Theater in Prague in 1904 as Telramund; then sang in Linz (1911) and at the Vienna Volksoper (1912–15); was a member of the Bavarian State Opera in Munich (1916–22); joined the Vienna State Opera in 1922, remaining on its roster until 1940; also made guest appearances at Covent Garden in London (1924–28) and in Chicago (1928–29). He was married to the mezzo-soprano **Maria Olczewska.**

Schippers, Thomas, greatly gifted American conductor; b. Kalamazoo, Mich., March 9, 1930; d. New York, Dec. 16, 1977. He played piano in public at the age of 6, and was a church organist at 14. He studied piano at the Curtis Inst. of Music in Philadelphia (1944–45) and privately with Olga Samaroff (1946–47); subsequently attended Yale Univ.; there he took some composition lessons from Paul Hindemith. In 1948 he won 2nd prize in the contest for young conductors organized by the Philadelphia Orch. He then took a job as organist at the Greenwich Village Presbyterian Church in N.Y.; joined a group of young musicians in an enterprise called the Lemonade Opera, and conducted this group for several years. On March 15, 1950, he conducted in N.Y. the premiere of Menotti's opera *The Consul;* also conducted the television premiere of his *Amahl and the Night Visitors* (N.Y., Dec. 25, 1951). In 1951 he became a staff member of the N.Y. City Opera Co. On March 26, 1955, he led the N.Y. Phil. as guest conductor, the youngest musician ever to conduct the orch. In the fall of 1955 he made his debut as an opera conductor at the Metropolitan Opera in N.Y., also the youngest to do so; in 1955 he was a guest conductor at La Scala in Milan. From 1958 to 1976 he was associated with Menotti in the Spoleto Festival of Two Worlds. Other engagements included appearances with the N.Y. Phil., which he accompanied in 1959 to the Soviet Union as an alternate conductor with Leonard Bernstein. In 1962 he conducted at La Scala the world premiere of Manuel de Falla's cantata *Atlantida;* in 1964 he conducted at the Bayreuth Wagner Festival. He was a favorite conductor for new works at the Metropolitan Opera; conducted the first performance of Menotti's opera *The Last Savage* and the opening Metropolitan production of Samuel Barber's *Antony and Cleopatra* (Sept. 16, 1966); he also conducted the first production at the Metropolitan of the original version of Mussorgsky's *Boris Godunov* (1974). In 1970 he was appointed conductor and music director of the Cincinnati Symph. Orch., one of the few American-born conductors to occupy a major symph. orch. post. There was an element of tragedy in his life. Rich, handsome, and articulate, he became a victim of lung cancer, and was unable to open the scheduled season of the Cincinnati Orch. in the fall of 1977; in a grateful gesture the management gave him the title of conductor laureate; he bequeathed a sum of $5,000,000 to the orch. He was happily married, but his wife died of cancer in 1973. When he conducted a production of *La forza del destino* at the Metropolitan Opera on March 4, 1960, the baritone Leonard Warren collapsed and died on the stage.

Schirmer, the family of music publishers. The first of the family to be connected with music was **Johann Georg Schirmer,** who settled in Sondershausen and was married there on July 18, 1781. He was a cabinet-maker, a native of Gäuroden, and made musical instruments. His son, **Ernst Ludwig Rudolf Schirmer** (b. Sondershausen, May 8, 1784), emigrated to N.Y. with his wife and children in 1840. There his son **(Friedrich) Gustav (Emil) Schirmer** (b. Königsee, Thuringia, Sept. 19, 1829; d. Eisenach, Aug. 5, 1893) found employment in the music store of Scharfenberg & Luis, and after several years entered the employ of Kerksieg & Breusing, music dealers, becoming manager in 1854. In 1861 he took over the business with a partner, and acquired sole control in 1866, establishing the firm that was to become **G. Schirmer, Inc.** He was an enlightened and progressive publisher; he entered into personal relations with noted European composers, and was among the original patrons of Wagner's Bayreuth Festival. He was an amateur pianist and had a real love for music. The diary of Tchaikovsky's visit to N.Y. in 1891 makes repeated mention of Schirmer and his family. Schirmer married an American, Mary Fairchild, by whom he had 5 daughters and 2 sons. The younger of these sons, **Gustave Schirmer** (b. New York, Feb. 18, 1864; d. Boston, July 15, 1907), organized in 1885 the Boston Music Co., which gained prominence especially through the publication of

Schirmer — G. Schirmer, Inc.

Ethelbert Nevin's music. Shortly afterward, with his brother **Rudolph Edward Schirmer** (b. New York, July 22, 1859; d. Santa Barbara, Calif., Aug. 19, 1919), he became a partner in the firm founded by their father in N.Y., and after the latter's death in 1893 he managed the business jointly with his brother, retaining independent control of the Boston Music Co. Rudolph was educated in N.Y. public schools, and from 1873 to 1875 lived at Weimar with his mother, brother, and 4 sisters; studied violin and piano there with Helene Stahl and came in contact with the Liszt circle; in 1876 entered the College of New Jersey (later Princeton Univ.), and after graduation in 1880 studied law for 4 years at Columbia College, being admitted to the bar in 1884. In 1885 he took the place of his brother Gustave in his father's music publishing business. Later he was rejoined by Gustave, and upon their father's death in 1893, Rudolph became president of the firm, assuming sole control from 1907. In 1915 he founded the *Musical Quarterly.* He was a director of the N.Y. Oratorio Society and the N.Y. Symph. Society, and a trustee of the Inst. of Musical Art in N.Y. **Gustave Schirmer, 3rd** (b. Boston, Dec. 29, 1890; d. Palm Beach, Fla., May 28, 1965), son of Gustave Schirmer and grandson of the founder of G. Schirmer, Inc., inherited the Boston Music Co. from his father and acquired the Willis Music Co. of Cincinnati. He was president of G. Schirmer, Inc. in 1919–21 and 1944–57. Rudolph E. Schirmer's son, also named **Rudolph Edward Schirmer** (b. Santa Barbara, Calif., June 8, 1919), was vice-president of G. Schirmer, Inc., from 1949 to 1965; he was then chairman of the board, from 1965 to 1979.

Schirmer, Ernest Charles, American music publisher; b. Mt. Vernon, N.Y., March 15, 1865; d. Waban, Mass., Feb. 15, 1958. His father, Edward Schirmer (1831–85), a native of Thuringia, Saxony, was a brother of the famous music publisher **Gustav Schirmer** (with their family the 2 brothers emigrated to the U.S. in 1840). Ernest Schirmer entered apprenticeship in the music store of Gustav Schirmer in N.Y. in 1878. In Oct. 1891, he became business manager of the Boston Music Co.; was admitted to partnership in Jan. 1902. In 1917 he withdrew from the Boston Music Co., and in 1921 founded the E.C. Schirmer Music Co., with the stated purpose of promoting good music. In 1956 he was still active in the affairs of the company. The publications of the firm include the Concord Series, the Choral Repertory of the Harvard Univ. Glee Club, Radcliffe, Vassar, and Wellesley College Choral Music, the Polyphonic and "A Cappella" Libraries, the St. Dunstan Edition of Sacred Music, and treatises on harmonic analysis, musical theory, and music appreciation. The firm enjoys a world market for its publications, with agencies in London and Berlin.

G. Schirmer, Inc., one of the greatest music publishing houses in America. It was an outgrowth of the business founded in N.Y. in 1848 by Kerksieg & Breusing, of which **Gustav Schirmer** became manager in 1854. With another employee, Bernard Beer, Schirmer took over the business in 1861, and the firm became known as "Beer & Schirmer." In 1866 Schirmer became the sole owner, establishing the house of "G. Schirmer, Music Publishers, Importers and Dealers." Until 1880 the business was located at 701 Broadway in N.Y.; then it was moved to 35 Union Square, and in 1909 was transferred to a 7-story building at 3 East 43rd St. It remained at that address until 1960, when it was moved to 609 5th Ave., and its retail store relocated at 4 East 49th St. In 1969 G. Schirmer, Inc. was acquired by Macmillan Inc., and in 1973 the executive offices were moved to 866 3rd Ave. In 1973 Schirmer Books was founded as a division of Macmillan Publishing Co., Inc., taking over the publication of books on music for college, trade, and professional/reference markets, while G. Schirmer continued publication of musical works. The N.Y. firm also maintained branches in Cleveland (until 1962) and in Los Angeles (until 1967). After the death of the founder, Gustav Schirmer, in 1893, the firm was incorporated under the management of his sons, **Rudolph Edward Schirmer** and **Gustave Schirmer.** Rudolph Schirmer died in 1919 and was succeeded by his nephew **Gustave Schirmer, 3rd,** who was president until 1921. Then W. Rodman Fay became president, with O.G. Sonneck as vice-president. On May 7, 1929, Carl Engel was made president and continued in that office (except for one year, 1933, when his place was taken by Hermann Irion) until his death in 1944, when **Gustave Schirmer, 3rd,** became president again, retiring in 1957. He was succeeded by Rudolph Tauhert, who was president from 1957 to 1972. John Santuccio is currently (1984) president and Bruce MacCombie is vice-president and director of publications. In 1892 the firm began publication of the Library of Musical Classics, notable for careful editing and general typographical excellence; with its didactic Latin motto, "Musica laborum dulce lenimen," it became a familiar part of musical homes. In the same year was launched the Collection of Operas, a series of vocal scores with original text and Eng. trans.; another series, The Golden Treasury, was begun in 1905. Schirmer's Scholastic Series, containing pedagogical works, began publication in 1917. Among other laudable initiatives was the American Folk-Song Series, offering authentic folk material. An expansion into the field of lexicography followed with the publication of *Baker's Biographical Dictionary of Musicians,* first issued in 1900 under the editorship of its original author, Theodore Baker; its 6th edition was publ. in 1978, edited by Nicolas Slonimsky, who also took care of the 5th edition in 1958. Theodore Baker also compiled and edited *A Dictionary of Musical Terms* (G. Schirmer, N.Y., 1895; many reprints) and *Pronouncing Pocket-Manual of Musical Terms* (1905; more than a million copies sold). In 1915 the *Musical Quarterly* was founded under the editorship of O.G. Sonneck; its subsequent editors have been Carl Engel (1929–44), Gustave Reese (1944–45), Paul Henry Lang (1945–72), and Christopher Hatch (1972–77); in 1977 its editorship was entrusted to Joan Peyser. The *Musical Quarterly* has publ. through the years articles by the foremost scholars of Europe and America; it occupies the preeminent place among music journals in the English language. The music catalog of G. Schirmer, Inc. comprises tens of thousands of publications, ranging from solo songs to full orch. scores. Particularly meritorious is the endeavor of the publishers to promote American music; the firm has publ. works by Ernest Bloch, Charles Loeffler, Charles Griffes, Walter Piston, Roy Harris, William Schuman, Samuel Barber, Gian Carlo Menotti, Paul Creston, Leonard Bernstein, Elliott Carter, Henry Cowell, Norman Dello Joio, Morton Gould, Virgil Thomson, Milton Babbitt, Gunther Schuller, and many others; it also took over some works of Charles Ives. Among European composers, the works of Arnold Schoenberg, Gustav Holst, and Benjamin Britten are included in the Schirmer catalogue, as well as a number of works by Soviet composers.

Schiske, Karl, significant Austrian composer; b. Györ (Raab), Hungary, Feb. 12, 1916; d. Vienna, June 16, 1969. He studied music theory privately with Ernst Kanitz in Vienna (1932–38) and musicology with Orel and Schenk at the Univ. of Vienna (Dr.Phil., 1942). In 1952 he was appointed to the faculty of the Vienna Academy of Music; in 1967 he received the Great Austrian State Prize. In 1966–67 he was a visiting prof. at the Univ. of Calif., Riverside. His technique of composition is curiously synthetic, and yet invariably logical, containing elements of medieval counterpoint and the serial methods of composition.
WORKS: *Vorspiel* for Orch. (1938); Piano Concerto (1938–39); 2 concertos for String Orch. (1941, 1945); 5 symphs. (1941–42, 1947–48, 1950–51, 1955, 1965); *Tanzrondo* for Orch. (1942); *Kammerkonzert* for Chamber Orch. (1949); Violin Concerto (1952); *Divertimento* for Chamber Orch. or 10 Instruments (1963); 2 string quartets (1936, 1945); Sextet for Clarinet, String Quartet, and Piano (1937); Wind Quintet (1945); Violin Sonata (1943–48); *Musik* for Clarinet, Trumpet, and Viola (1948); *3 Pieces for Gloria* for Solo Violin (1951); *Synthese* for "4 x 4" Instruments (1958); *Reitjagd,* cantata for Baritone, Chorus, and Orch. (1938); *Vom Tode,* oratorio (1946); *Candada,* 4 pieces for Soprano, Chorus, and Small Orch. (1956; posthumous, Vienna, March 9, 1972); Sonata for Piano, 4-hands (1949); Piano Sonatina (1953); other piano pieces; organ pieces; choruses.

Schiuma, Alfredo, Argentine composer; b. Buenos Aires, July 1, 1885; d. there, July 24, 1963. He studied with Romaniello in Buenos Aires, and later established his own music school there. He wrote several operas in a singable Italianate idiom; the following were produced in Buenos Aires: *Amy Robsart,* based on Walter Scott's novel *Kenilworth* (April 24, 1920); *La Sirocchia* (April 23, 1922); *Tabaré* (Aug. 6, 1925); *Las virgenes del sol* (June 20, 1939); *La infanta* (Aug. 12, 1941); 4 symphs. (1928–57); symph. tableau, *Pitunga* (Buenos Aires, March 31, 1929); symph. sketch, *Los Incas* (Buenos Aires, April 26, 1931); also choruses, chamber music, and songs.

Schjelderup, Gerhard, Norwegian composer and writer; b. Christiansand, Nov. 17, 1859; d. Benediktbeuren, Bavaria, July 29, 1933. He went to Paris in 1878, and studied with Franchomme (cello) and Massenet (composition); in 1888 settled in Germany; lived in Dresden (from 1896); then moved to Benediktbeuren, where he remained till his death. He wrote music influenced partly by Wagner, partly by Grieg.
WORKS: Operas: *Sonntagmorgen* (Munich, May 9, 1893); *Norwegische Hochzeit* (Prague, March 17, 1900); *Frühlingsnacht* (Dresden, May 1, 1908; in Norwegian as *Vaarnat,* Oslo, Aug. 31, 1915); *Sturmvögel* (Schwerin, Sept. 19, 1926); musical fairy tale, *Sampo; Weihnacht-Suite* for Orch.; 2 symph. poems: *Eine Sommernacht auf dem Fjord* and *Brand* (after Ibsen); *In Baldurs Hain* for Violin and Piano; *Fantasiestück* for Cello and Piano; songs. He publ. a biography of Grieg (in Norwegian, 1903; German ed., with Walter Niemann, 1908) and a monograph on Wagner (in Norwegian, 1908; in German, 1913).
BIBLIOGRAPHY: O.M. Sandvik, "G. Schjelderup," *Schweizerische Musikzeitung* (Oct. 1948).

Schladebach, Julius, German physiologist and musician; b. Dresden, 1810; d. Kiel, Sept. 21, 1872. He publ. vol. 1 of a *Neues Universal-Lexikon der Tonkunst* (1854), completed by Bernsdorf; also *Die Bildung der menschlichen Stimme zum Gesang* (1860).

Schläger, Hans, Austrian composer; b. Felskirchen, Dec. 5, 1820; d. Salzburg, May 17, 1885. He was a pupil of Preyer at Vienna; chorus master of the Männergesangverein (1844–61); then Kapellmeister of the Salzburg Cathedral, and director of the Mozarteum, resigning on his marriage to Countess Zichy in 1867. He wrote the operas *Heinrich und Ilse* (Salzburg, 1869) and *Hans Haidekukuk* (Salzburg, 1873); the symph. tone picture *Waldmeisters Brautfahrt;* symphs.; string quartets; etc.

Schlegel, Leander, Dutch composer; b. Oegstgeest, near Leiden, Feb. 2, 1844; d. there, Oct. 20, 1913. He studied at the Cons. in The Hague; then went to Leipzig, where he was a student of Reinecke; toured with Wilhelmj as his accompanist; then returned to the Netherlands; was director of a music school in Haarlem (1870–98); in 1898 he moved to Overveen, where he continued to teach. He was a composer of solid attainments; in his music he tried to emulate Brahms; wrote a Symph., a Piano Quartet, a String Quartet, and a number of piano pieces in a Romantic mood; also many melodious songs.

Schleinitz, Heinrich Conrad, German musician; b. Zschaitz, near Döbeln, Oct. 1, 1803; d. Leipzig, May 13, 1881. He studied at the Thomasschule in Leipzig; then became a member of the Gewandhaus managing board, and was instrumental in engaging Mendelssohn as conductor and director of the Leipzig Cons.; after Mendelssohn's death, he took over the administration of the school.

Schlesinger, Adolph Martin, German music publisher; b. Sülz, Silesia, Oct. 4, 1769; d. Berlin, Nov. 11, 1838. About 1795 he founded a music store in Berlin; it became known under the name of Schlesinger'-sche Buch- und Musikalienhandlung in 1821. He was one of Beethoven's German publishers. The firm was carried on after his death by his son, **Heinrich Schlesinger,** who began publishing in 1851 the influential music periodical *Echo*. In 1864 the business was sold to R. Lienau (1838–1920), whose sons took it over after his death. The firm was further enlarged and enriched by the acquisition of several other music publishing firms, among them Haslinger of Vienna (1875), Krentzlin of Berlin (1919), Vernthal of Berlin (1925), and Köster of Berlin (1928). Schlesinger was the original publisher of *Der Freischütz* by Carl Maria von Weber; Beethoven's opp. 108–11, 132, 135; also works by Mendelssohn, Chopin, Liszt, and Berlioz.

Schlesinger, Kathleen, British musicologist; b. Hollywood, near Belfast, Ireland, June 27, 1862; d. London, April 16, 1953. She was educated in Switzerland; then settled in England; became interested in musical instruments; publ. *The Instruments of the Modern Orchestra* (2 vols., London, 1910). Her chief work is *The Greek Aulos* (London, 1939), not only containing a description of ancient Greek instruments, but also propounding an original theory of the formation of Greek modes, which aroused much controversy; the weight of learned opinion inclined against her hypotheses.

Schlesinger, Maurice, music publisher, son of **Adolph Martin Schlesinger;** b. Berlin, Oct. 3, 1797; d. Baden-Baden, Feb. 25, 1871. He moved to Paris in 1819, and was at first engaged in book selling. In July 1821 he established a music publishing business, and launched the publication of the *Gazette Musicale,* soon united with the *Revue Musicale* (continued publication until 1880). He became one of the most important Paris publishers; publ. full scores of operas by Meyerbeer, Donizetti, and others; also Berlioz's *Symphonie fantastique* and much of Chopin's music. In 1846 he sold the catalogue to Brandus and Dufour; later it was acquired by Joubert.

Schlesinger, Sebastian Benson, German composer; b. Hamburg, Sept. 24, 1837; d. Nice, Jan. 8, 1917. He went to the U.S. at the age of 13; studied music in Boston, chiefly under Otto Dresel; was for 17 years German consul in Boston; then lived for a time in London, and during his last years in Paris. He was a gifted composer; publ. about 120 songs, which received praise from Max Bruch and Robert Franz; wrote several piano pieces in a Romantic vein (*Novelette, Albumblatt, Impromptu-Caprice,* etc.).

Schletterer, Hans Michel, German conductor and writer on music; b. Ansbach, May 29, 1824; d. Augsburg, June 4, 1893. He studied with Spohr in Kassel and Ferdinand David in Leipzig. After filling a number of teaching posts in provincial towns, he taught at the Univ. of Heidelberg (1854–58); then was a choral conductor and singing teacher in Augsburg, where he founded an oratorio society and a music school. He publ. 17 books of choral music a cappella; a selection of Lutheran church music, *Musica sacra* (2 vols., 1887; 3rd ed., 1927); *Das deutsche Singspiel* (1863); *J.Fr. Reichardt* (1865); *Geschichte der geistlichen Dichtung und kirchlichen Tonkunst* (1869); *Studien zur Geschichte der französischen Musik* (3 vols., 1884–85; mostly borrowed from Castil-Blaze); etc.

Schlick, Arnolt, the elder, blind organist and lutenist; b. in or near Heidelberg, c.1460; d. Heidelberg, c.1525. He was organist to the Count Palatine at Heidelberg from 1485; since he bore the title of Imperial organist, he may have also served at one time at the court of Friedrich III.
    WORKS: *Tablaturen etlicher Lobgesang und Lidlein uff die Orgeln und Lauten* (1512; new ed. by G. Harms, 1924; 2nd ed., 1957; reprints by R. Eitner in *Monatshefte für Musik-Geschichte*, 1869; A.G. Ritter, *Zur Geschichte des Orgelspiels*, II/96, 1884; and W. Tappert, *Sang und Klang aus alter Zeit,* Berlin, 1906).
    WRITINGS: *Spiegel der Orgelmacher und Organisten* (1511; reprinted by R. Eitner as a supplement to *Monatshefte für Musik-Geschichte,* 1869; by E. Flade, 1932; by P. Smets, 1937, and Flade again, 1951; publ. in facsimile and an Eng. trans., Buren, 1978).
    BIBLIOGRAPHY: R. Eitner, in *Monatshefte für Musik-Geschichte,* XXI; F. Stein, *Zur Geschichte der Musik in Heidelberg* (containing index of *Spiegel der Orgelmacher;* 1912; 2nd ed., 1921); A. Pirro, "Orgues et organistes de Haguenau," *Revue de Musicologie* (1926); R. Kendall, "Notes on A. Schlick," *Acta Musicologica* (1939); A. Mendel, "Pitch in the 16th and Early 17th Centuries," *Musical Quarterly* (Jan. 1948); H.H. Lenneberg, "The Critic Criticized: Sebastian Virdung and His Controversy with A. Schlick," *Journal of the American Musicological Society* (Spring 1957).

Schlieder, Frederick William, American organist and composer; b. Foreston, Ill., Jan. 22, 1873; d. New York, Jan. 13, 1953. He studied at Syracuse Univ. (M.M., 1895); later took organ lessons in Paris with Guilmant; returning to America in 1905, he was active as a concert organist; from 1910 until 1923, was organist at the Collegiate Church of St. Nicholas in N.Y.; also taught harmony at the Philadelphia Cons. He publ. *Lyric Composition through Improvisation: First Year's Training in Formal Self-expression* (Boston, 1927); a sequel was publ. by the Schlieder Book Foundation, Decatur, Ill. (1946); he further publ. *Beyond the Tonal Horizon of Music,* a collection of aphorisms (Decatur, 1948).

Schloezer, Boris de, renowned Russian-French writer on music; b. Vitebsk, Dec. 8, 1881; d. Paris, Oct. 7, 1969. He studied music in Brussels and Paris; returning to Russia, he devoted himself to a profound study of philosophy, esthetics, and music the-

ory. His sister, Tatiana Schloezer, was the 2nd wife of Scriabin, and Schloezer became an intimate friend of Scriabin, who confided to him his theosophic and musical ideas. In 1920 he emigrated to France, where he continued his literary activities in the Russian émigré press and in French literary magazines. He publ. a monograph on Scriabin (vol. 1, Berlin, 1923, in Russian; vol. 2 was planned but not completed; vol. 1, covering Scriabin's ideology and commentary on his music, was publ. in a French trans., with an introduction by Scriabin's daughter Marina, Paris, 1975); other publications in French: *Igor Stravinsky* (Paris, 1929); *Introduction à J.S. Bach* (Paris, 1947; in Spanish, Buenos Aires, 1961; in German under the title *Entwurf einer Musikasthetik*, Hamburg, 1964). Schloezer also wrote a philosophical fantasy, *Mon nom est personne (My Name Is Nobody)* and *Rapport secret*, depicting a distant planet whose inhabitants achieved immortality and divinity through science.
BIBLIOGRAPHY: *Boris de Schloezer*, collection of articles by 10 authors (Paris, 1981).

Schlögel, Xavier, Belgian composer; b. Brillonville, Famène, July 14, 1854; d. Ciney, near Namur, March 23, 1889. He studied with Ledent at the Liège Cons. He composed *Scènes champêtres* for Orch.; *Ballade des épées* for Voice and Orch.; *Messe solennelle* for Male Chorus, Organ, and Orch.; string quartets and piano trios.

Schlösser, (Karl Wilhelm) Adolf, German pianist, son and pupil of **Louis Schlösser;** b. Darmstadt, Feb. 1, 1830; d. Great Bookham, England, Nov. 10, 1913. He made his debut at Frankfurt in 1847; after concert tours in Germany, France, and England, he settled in London (1854); taught (until 1903) at the Royal Academy of Music. He composed a Piano Quartet; Piano Trio; 24 studies and many other pieces for piano.

Schlösser, Louis, German composer; b. Darmstadt, Nov. 17, 1800; d. there, Nov. 17, 1886. He was pupil of Rinck at Darmstadt, of Seyfried, Mayseder, and Salieri at Vienna, and of Le Sueur and Kreutzer at the Paris Cons.; was court conductor in Darmstadt.
WORKS: About 70 opus numbers publ., including the operas *Granada* (Vienna, 1826); *Das Leben ein Traum* (1839); *Die Jugend Karls II. von Spanien* (1847); *Die Braut des Herzogs* (1847); *Benvenuto Cellini;* operetta, *Kapitän Hector;* melodrama, *Die Jahreszeiten;* music to *Faust;* ballets; entr'actes; symphs.; overtures; string quartets; Concertino for Horn, with Orch.; piano pieces; songs; etc.

Schlosser, Max, distinguished German tenor; b. Amberg, Oct. 17, 1835; d. Utting am Ammersee, Sept. 2, 1916. He sang in Zürich, St. Gallen, and Augsburg, but then decided to become a baker. Still, he did not abandon hopes for a stage career; he met Hans von Bülow, who entrusted him with the role of David at the premiere of *Die Meistersinger von Nürnberg* in Munich in 1868; he remained a member of the Munich Court Opera until his retirement in 1904. He

also sang at Bayreuth and made guest appearances with Neumann's traveling opera company. He was principally known for his fine performances of the Wagnerian repertoire.

Schlottmann, Louis, German pianist and composer; b. Berlin, Nov. 12, 1826; d. there, June 13, 1905. He studied with Taubert and Dehn; gave successful concerts in London and elsewhere, and settled in Berlin as a teacher.
WORKS: Overtures to *Romeo and Juliet* and *Wallensteins Lager; Trauermarsch, Rezitativ und Finale,* symph. scene for Orch.; *Concertstück* for Piano; chamber music; piano pieces (*3 Capricettes; Polonaise de concert; Andantino; Jugendspiegel*); choruses and songs.

Schlusnus, Heinrich, eminent German baritone; b. Braubach am Rhein, Aug. 6, 1888; d. Frankfurt, June 18, 1952. He studied voice in Frankfurt and Berlin; made his operatic debut as the Herald in *Lohengrin* at the Hamburg Opera on Jan. 1, 1914; was then on its roster for the 1914–15 season; he subsequently sang at the Nuremberg Opera (1915–17). In 1917 he joined the Berlin State Opera, remaining there until 1945. In 1927–28 he sang with the Chicago Civic Opera. He was renowned as a lieder singer, and made several American tours.
BIBLIOGRAPHY: E. von Naso and A. Schlusnus, *Heinrich Schlusnus, Mensch und Sänger* (Hamburg, 1957).

Schmedes, Erik, Danish tenor; b. Gentofte, near Copenhagen, Aug. 27, 1868; d. Vienna, March 21, 1931. He studied piano, then turned to singing; studied with Mme. Artôt in Paris; made his operatic debut as a baritone in Wiesbaden (Jan. 11, 1891), as the Herald in *Lohengrin;* then sang baritone roles in Nuremberg and Dresden (1894–97). After a course of study with A. Iffert in Dresden, he developed a definite tenor voice, and appeared as Siegfried at the Vienna Opera (Feb. 11, 1898); remained as a tenor with the Vienna Opera until 1924. He was a member of the Metropolitan Opera Co. in N.Y. during the season 1908–9; made his debut there as Siegmund (Nov. 18, 1908).

Schmelzer, Johann Heinrich, Austrian composer; b. Scheibbs, c.1623; d. Prague, 1680. In 1649–70, he was a violinist at the Vienna court chapel; in 1671, assistant conductor; in 1679, first conductor. He may have been the teacher of the famous violinist Heinrich Biber. Schmelzer composed valuable chamber music, including *Duodena selectarum sonatarum* (12 trio sonatas, 1659; reprint in Denkmäler der Tonkunst in Österreich, 105); *Sacro-profanus concentus musicus* (sonatas for 2–8 instruments, 1662; reprint, ibid., vols. 111/112); *Sonate unarum fidium* (6 solo violin sonatas, 1664; reprint, ibid., vol. 93; also one reprinted in the supplement to G. Beckermann's *Das Violinspiel in Deutschland vor 1700*); also the trumpet fanfares to Bertali's Festspiel *La Contesa dell'aria* (1667), publ. as *Arie per il balletto a cavallo* (ed. by P. Nettl in Denkmäler der Tonkunst in Österreich, 56 [28.ii]) and a *Missa nuptialis* (ed. by G. Adler in Denkmäler der Tonkunst in Österreich, 49). Other MSS of vocal and instrumental works by Schmelzer are in Vienna, Kromeriz, Paris, and Uppsala.

BIBLIOGRAPHY: E. Wellesz, *Die Ballett-Suiten von J.H. und A.A. Schmelzer* (Vienna, 1914); A. Moser, *Geschichte des Violinspiels* (pp. 126ff.); P. Nettl, in *Studien zur Musikwisenschaft*, VIII.

Schmelzl (Schmeltzl, Schmaelzl), Wolfgang, Austrian musician; b. Kennath, c.1500; d. St. Lorenz at Steinfeld, c.1561. He was a Protestant cantor at Amberg; then, c.1540, a teacher in Vienna and singer at the S. Salvator Chapel; and finally a Catholic priest at St. Lorenz at Steinfeld, near Vienna, where he died. He is known for a collection of 4- to 5-voiced quodlibets and folk songs of the period, publ. in 1544 (reprint by Schering in *Geschichte der Musik in Beispielen*, no. 111).

BIBLIOGRAPHY: Elsa Bienenfield, "W. S., Sein Liederbuch (1544) und das Quodlibet des XVI. Jahrhunderts," *Sammelbände der Internationalen Musik-Gesellschaft*, VI/1 (1904); R. Eitner, in *Monatshefte für Musik-Geschichte*, III.

Schmid, Adolf, Austrian conductor and arranger; b. Hannsdorf, Nov. 18, 1868; d. Englewood, N.J., Feb. 12, 1958. He studied at the Vienna Cons.; in 1901 went to London, where he became music director of His Majesty's Theatre; in 1915 he emigrated to the U.S.; conducted ballet performances, including the Pavlova Ballet Russe (1916–18); then became an arranger for radio and schools; also wrote some picturesque music for orch., such as *Caravan Dance, A Bacchanal Dance,* etc. He publ. *The Language of the Baton* (N.Y., 1937).

Schmid, Anton, Austrian writer on music; b. Pihl, near Leipa, Bohemia, Jan. 30, 1787; d. Salzburg, July 3, 1857. After serving as a choirboy, he went to Vienna, where he was employed as a librarian (1819) and custodian (1844) at the Vienna Library. He publ. the valuable monographs *Ottaviano dei Petrucci da Fossombrone, der erste Erfinder des Musiknotendruckes mit beweglichen Metalltypen, und seine Nachfolger in 16. Jahrhundert* (1845); *J. Haydn und N. Zingarelli* (1847; to prove that Haydn composed *Gott erhalte Franz den Kaiser*); *Christoph Willibald, Ritter von Gluck* (1854); and "Beiträge zur Literatur und Geschichte der Tonkunst" (in Dehn's *Cäcilia*, 1842–46).

Schmid, Erich, Swiss conductor; b. Balsthal, Jan. 1, 1907. He studied at the Hoch Cons. in Frankfurt and took composition lessons with Arnold Schoenberg in Berlin. He returned to Switzerland in 1933; was Generalmusikdirektor in Glarus until 1949, when he became chief conductor of the Zürich Tonhalle Orch. From 1957 to 1972 he was chief conductor of the Zürich Radio Orch. and served as a prof. of conducting at the Basel Music Academy (1963–73). He then went to America and conducted the Birmingham (Ala.) Symph. Orch. (1979–81). He became known as a champion of modern music; brought to performance numerous works by Swiss composers.

Schmid, Ernst Fritz, eminent German musicologist; b. Tübingen, March 7, 1904; d. Augsburg, Jan. 20, 1960. He studied violin, viola, and viola d'amore at the Munich Academy; took private lessons in music theory and conducting; then studied musicology at the univs. of Munich (with Sandberger), Freiburg (with Gurlitt), Tübingen (with Hasse), and Vienna (with Haas, Orel et al.); received his Ph.D. from the Univ. of Tübingen with the dissertation *Carl Philipp Emanuel Bach und seine Kammermusik* (publ. in Kassel, 1931); completed his Habilitation as a Privatdozent in musicology at the Univ. of Graz in 1934 with his *Joseph Haydn: Ein Buch von Vorfahren und Heimat des Meisters* (publ. in Kassel, 1934). He became a prof. at the Univ. of Tübingen in 1935; also founded the Schwäbisches Landesmusikarchiv; he left Tübingen in 1937 to devote himself to private research; during World War II, he served in the German army; in 1948 he founded the Mozartgemeinde, and in 1951 the German Mozartgesellschaft. In 1954 he became academic director of the Neue Mozart Ausgabe; from 1955 he oversaw the publication of the new critical edition of Mozart's complete works, the *Neue Ausgabe Sämtlicher Werke.* In addition to his valuable research on Mozart, he discovered the private music collection of Emperor Franz II in Graz in 1933; this important collection is now housed in Vienna's Nationalbibliothek.

WRITINGS: *Wolfgang Amadeus Mozart* (Lübeck, 1934; 3rd ed., 1955); *Die Orgeln der Abtei Amorbach* (Buchen, 1938); ed. of *Ein schwäbisches Mozartbuch* (Lorch and Stuttgart, 1948); *Musik am Hofe der Fürsten von Löwenstein-Wertheim-Rosenberg, 1720–1750* (Würzburg, 1953); *Musik an den schwäbischen Zollernhöfen der Renaissance* (Kassel, 1962).

BIBLIOGRAPHY: W. Fischer et al., eds., *In memoriam Ernst Fritz Schmid, 1904–1960: Ein Gedenkblatt für seine Angehörigen und Freunde* (Recklinghausen, 1961).

Schmid, Heinrich Kaspar, German composer; b. Landau, Sept. 11, 1874; d. Munich, Jan. 8, 1953. He studied with Thuille and Bussmeyer at the Munich Academy; in 1903 he went to Athens, where he taught music at the Odeon; in 1905 returned to Munich and was on the faculty of the Munich Academy until 1921; then was director of the Karlsruhe Cons. (1921–24) and of the Augsburg Cons. (1924–32). His eyesight failed him and he was totally blind during the last years of his life. As a composer, he followed the Romantic tradition of the Bavarian School; he wrote a great number of lieder, and composed singspiels in a folklike manner, as well as choruses and chamber music.

BIBLIOGRAPHY: H. Roth, *H.K. Schmid* (Munich, 1921); W. Zentner, "H.K. Schmid," *Neue Musikzeitschrift* (Aug.–Sept. 1949).

Schmid, Otto, German music editor and critic; b.

Dresden, May 6, 1858; d. there, Sept. 12, 1931. He studied music privately with Kretschmer in Dresden; taught music history at the Dresden Cons. (1912–24) and wrote music criticism. Among his publications are monographs on Koschat (1887) and Kretschmer (1890); publ. a valuable history of music in Dresden: *Die Heimstätten der Sächsischen Landestheater* (Dresden, 1919); *Richard Wagners Opern und Musikdramen in Dresden* (Dresden, 1919); *Der Mozart-Verein zu Dresden* (Dresden, 1921); etc.; he edited the important collections *Musik am sächsischen Hofe* (10 vols.; compositions by Hasse, J.C. Schmidt, J.A. and C.S. Binder, Naumann, Petzold, etc., and members of the royal house); *Orgelwerke altböhmischer Meister* (2 vols.).

Schmidl, Carlo, Italian music publisher and lexicographer; b. Trieste, Oct. 7, 1859; d. there, Oct. 7, 1943. He was the son and pupil of the Hungarian composer **Antonio Schmidl** (1814–80). In 1872 he entered the employ of the music publisher Vicentini, and in 1889 he established his own business at Trieste; also directed the Leipzig branch of the Ricordi Co. (1901–6). He compiled and publ. an important biographical music dictionary, *Dizionario universale dei musicisti* (Milan, 1887–89; 2nd ed., 1926–29; supplement, 1938), containing scrupulously accurate data on Italian musicians, exact dates of performance of major works, and other information testifying to independent research. Schmidl also wrote biographies of Schumann (1890) and G.S. Mayr (1901).

Schmidt, Arthur Paul, German-American music publisher; b. Altona, Germany, April 1, 1846; d. Boston, May 5, 1921. He settled in Boston in 1866, and entered the music firm of George D. Russell & Co. In 1876 he established a business of his own; for some years maintained branches in N.Y. and Leipzig. Henry R. Austin became president of the firm in 1949. The A.P. Schmidt Co. won prominence by publication of the works of MacDowell; it brought out virtually the complete output of Arthur Foote (more than 150 items); also works by Chadwick, Hadley, Paine, Mrs. Beach, and other composers of the "New England School."

Schmidt, Franz, important Austrian composer; b. Pressburg, Dec. 22, 1874; d. Perchtoldsdorf, near Vienna, Feb. 11, 1939. He studied organ, piano, and cello at the Vienna Cons.; was a pupil of Anton Bruckner (composition) and Robert Fuchs (theory); also took piano lessons with Leschetizky. From 1896 to 1911 he played cello in the Vienna Phil. Orch.; also taught at the Cons. of the Gesellschaft der Musikfreunde in 1901–8 (both cello and piano). He became a prof. of piano at the Vienna Academy of Music in 1914; a prof. of counterpoint and composition there from 1922; director there, 1925–27; from 1927 to 1931, was rector of the Hochschule für Musik; retired in 1937. While engaged in pedagogical activities he continued to compose; his music is steeped in Viennese Romanticism, and the influence of Bruckner is particularly pronounced. Although he is regarded in Austria as a very important symph. composer, his music is almost totally unknown elsewhere.

WORKS: Operas: *Notre Dame* (Vienna, April 1, 1914; an orch. suite from it, entitled *Zwischenspiel aus einer unvollständigen romantischen Oper,* was perf. by the Vienna Phil., Dec. 6, 1903) and *Fredigundis* (Berlin, Dec. 19, 1922); oratorio, *Das Buch mit sieben Siegeln* (Vienna, June 15, 1938); 4 symphs.: No. 1 (Vienna, Jan. 25, 1902); No. 2 (Vienna, Dec. 3, 1913); No. 3 (Vienna, Dec. 2, 1928); No. 4 (Vienna, Jan. 10, 1934); *Konzertante Variationen über ein Thema von Beethoven* (Piano Concerto No. 1) for Piano, left-hand, and Orch. (Vienna, Feb. 2, 1924; Paul Wittgenstein, soloist); Piano Concerto No. 2, left-hand alone (Vienna, Feb. 10, 1935; Wittgenstein, soloist); *Chaconne* for Orch. (Vienna, Jan. 29, 1933); 2 string quartets; Piano Quintet; 2 clarinet quintets; several works for organ.

BIBLIOGRAPHY: Andreas Liess, *Franz Schmidt. Leben und Schaffen* (Graz, 1951); Carl Nemeth, *Franz Schmidt. Ein Meister nach Brahms und Bruckner* (Vienna, 1957); R. Scholz, *Franz Schmidt als Orgelkomponist* (Vienna, 1971); N. Tschulik, *Franz Schmidt* (Vienna, 1972).

Schmidt, Gustav, German conductor and composer; b. Weimar, Sept. 1, 1816; d. Darmstadt, Feb. 11, 1882. He studied with Mendelssohn in Leipzig; subsequently pursued an active career as an opera conductor in theaters in Brünn (1841–44)), Würzburg (1845), Frankfurt (1846; 1851–61), Wiesbaden (1849), and Leipzig (1864–76). In 1876 he was named court Kapellmeister in Darmstadt. He was a determined champion of Wagner's operas, and he himself composed a number of operas, of which the following enjoyed some transient productions: *Prinz Eugen* (Frankfurt, 1847); *Die Weiber von Weinsberg* (Weimar, 1858, conducted by Liszt); *La Réole* (Breslau, 1863); *Alibi* (Weimar, 1880). He also composed ballads and male choruses.

Schmidt, Heinrich, German music editor; b. Kirchenlamitz, near Bayreuth, April 30, 1861; d. Bayreuth, May 23, 1923. He was a pupil of Rheinberger, Kellermann, and Riehl at the Königliche Akademie der Tonkunst in Munich; received his Dr.Phil. from the Univ. of Munich in 1897 with the dissertation *Joh. Mattheson, Ein Förderer der deutschen Tonkunst, im Lichte seiner Werke* (Leipzig, 1897); from 1898 he was a teacher at the seminary in Bayreuth. He edited *Streichorchester für Mittelschulen* (8 vols.; selections of classical pieces); *Der Männerchor auf natürlicher Grundlage* (1913); *Der Chorgesang für Mittelschulen* (1918); and a new edition of Hohmann's *Violinschule.* He publ. *Die Orgel unserer Zeit in Wort und Bild* (1904; 2nd ed., 1922) and *Richard Wagner in Bayreuth* (1909; with U. Hartmann).

Schmidt, Johann Philipp Samuel, German composer; b. Königsberg, Sept. 8, 1779; d. Berlin, May 9, 1853. He wrote operas for Königsberg and Berlin; many cantatas; 9 oratorios and masses; symphs.;

quintets and quartets for strings; etc.; also contributed to musical periodicals of Berlin and Leipzig.

Schmidt, John Henry, German organist, composer, and singing teacher; lived in Radevormwald, near Düsseldorf, until Dec. 1783, when he arrived in Gouda, the Netherlands; was appointed organist of the Cathedral of St. John at Schiedam on Oct. 23, 1785; held this office until 1790, when he sailed for Rio de Berbice, British Guiana. In 1796 he arrived in N.Y.; in June 1796 he appeared in Charleston and advertised as a singing teacher and piano manufacturer; toward the end of 1796 he settled in Philadelphia, where he became organist of St. Peter's Church (1797); also announced concerts in Baltimore (1796) and Albany (1797). He composed a *Sonata for Beginners.*
  BIBLIOGRAPHY: O.G. Sonneck, *Bibliography of Early Secular American Music* (Washington, D.C., 1905); idem, *Early Concert Life in America* (Leipzig, 1907; in Eng.).

Schmidt, Joseph, Rumanian tenor; b. Bavideni, Bukovina, March 4, 1904; d. Zürich, Nov. 16, 1942. He studied at the Berlin Cons.; in 1928 began his career as a radio singer and won great popularity in Germany. In 1933 he went to Belgium; in 1938 was briefly in America; then settled in Switzerland. His voice was regarded as of great lyric expressiveness, but being almost a dwarf (he stood only 4 feet 10 inches in height), he was unable to appear in opera.

Schmidt, Karl, German music scholar; b. Friedberg (Hesse), July 10, 1869; d. there, Feb. 28, 1948. He studied in Leipzig; was active in school music in Laubach and Friedberg; publ. the valuable paper *Quaestiones de musicis scriptoribus romanis imprimis Cassiodoro et Isidoro* (Leipzig, 1898).

Schmidt, Leopold, German writer on music; b. Berlin, Aug. 2, 1860; d. there, April 30, 1927. He studied philosophy at the Univ. of Berlin, and at the same time attended music courses at the Royal Hochschule. He subsequently held numerous positions as a theater conductor in Berlin and in the provinces; then taught at the Klindworth-Scharwenka Cons. in Berlin and wrote music criticism for the *Berliner Tageblatt.* He publ. a number of competently written monographs on Meyerbeer (1898), Haydn (1898; 3rd ed., 1914), Mozart (1909), and Beethoven (1914); also wrote several analytic guides for classical and modern operas; edited *Beethovenbriefe* in 2 vols. (1909, 1922) and *Brahms Briefwechsel* (1910). His collected criticism was publ. in 3 vols. (1909, 1913, 1922).

Schmidt, Ole, Danish conductor and composer; b. Copenhagen, July 14, 1928. He attended the Royal Danish Cons.; had conducting lessons from Albert Wolff, then with Rafael Kubelik and Sergui Celibidache. He made his conducting debut at the Copenhagen Academy of Music in 1955; was conductor of the Royal Danish Opera and Ballet (1959–65) and guest conductor of the Hamburg Symph. Orch. (1970–71); also was a guest conductor of the Danish Radio Symph. (1971). In 1975 he received the Carl Nielsen Prize; became chief conductor of the Aarhus Symph. in 1979. His music follows the vigor and lyrical sentiment of Scandinavian Romanticism, while sustaining the Classical symmetry of form.
  WORKS: Opera, *Edstillingen* (*The Exhibition;* Copenhagen, Dec. 5, 1969); ballet, *Fever* (Copenhagen, Oct. 18, 1957); Symph. No. 1 (1955); *Chamber Concerto* for Piano and Strings (1955); *Pièce concertante* for Trumpet, Trombone, Harp, Piano, Celesta, Percussion, and Strings (1956); *Chamber Symphony* for Wind Quintet and Strings (1958); *Symphonic Fantasy and Fugue* for Accordion and Chamber Orch. (1959); *Pastel* for Chamber Orch. (1961); *Briol,* symph. sketch (1962); Concerto No. 2 for Accordion, Wind Orch., and Percussion (1963–64); Horn Concerto (Copenhagen, Sept. 8, 1966); Violin Concerto (Dortmund, May 19, 1971); Tuba Concerto (1973); *Divertimento* for Violin, Viola, Cello, and Piano (1957); 5 string quartets (1962–77); *Improvisation* for Piano, Double Bass, and Drums (1961); *Painting and Plugging* for Harp, Strings, and Piano (1963); Brass Quintet (1977); *Sinfonietta for 3 Quintets* for Brass, Woodwinds, and Strings (1977).

Schmidt, Trudeliese, German contralto; b. Saarbrücken, Nov. 7, 1943. She studied in her native city; made her debut there in 1965; then sang in Wiesbaden and Düsseldorf. From 1971 she made regular appearances in Munich and Hamburg; sang at the Bayreuth Festival in 1975; also made a concert tour in Japan.

Schmidt, William, American composer; b. Chicago, March 6, 1926. He moved to Los Angeles in 1952 and studied composition with Halsey Stevens and Ingolf Dahl at the Univ. of Southern Calif.; at the same time, was active as a jazz arranger. He composed *Concerto Breve for Brass and Band* (1957); pieces for orch. and numerous works for various chamber ensembles; 6 bassoon duets (1957); *Serenade* for Tuba and Piano (1958); *Rondino* for Trombone and Piano (1959); *Viola Sonata* (1959); Woodwind Quintet (1959); *Percussive Rondo* for Percussion Quartet (1957); etc.

Schmidt-Görg, Joseph, German musicologist; b. Rüdinghausen, near Dortmund, March 19, 1897; d. Bonn, April 3, 1981. He studied musicology with Schiedermair; received a Dr.Phil. (1926) from the Univ. of Bonn. On the centennial of Beethoven's death, in 1927, Schmidt-Görg was appointed Schiedermair's assistant in the Beethoven Archives; later served as director of the archives (1945–72); concurrently lectured on musicology at the Univ. of Bonn (1930–65). On his 70th birthday he was presented with a Festschrift under the friendly Latin title *Colloquium amicorum* (Bonn, 1967), containing a catalogue of his writings. He publ. numerous books, treatises, and monographs connected with Beethoveniana: *Unbekannte Manuskripte zu Beethovens* *weltricher und geistlicher Gesangsmusik* (Bonn, 1928); *Katalog der Handschriften des Beethoven-Hauses und Beethoven-Archivs* (Bonn, 1935); *Ludwig van Beethoven* (with H. Schmidt; Bonn, 1969; in Eng., London, 1970; in Italian, Rome, 1970). He also publ. a comprehensive survey, *Die Messe* (Cologne, 1967; in Eng. as *History of the Mass*, N.Y., 1968), and a compendious monograph, *Nicolas Gombert: Leben und Werk* (Tutzing, 1971); also edited works by Renaissance composers.

Schmidt-Isserstedt, Hans, German conductor; b. Berlin, May 5, 1900; d. Hamburg, May 28, 1973. He studied composition with Franz Schreker; then devoted himself mainly to conducting. After a series of appointments as an opera conductor in Germany he was engaged at the Hamburg State Opera in 1935; was conductor of the Staatsoper in Berlin in 1943; conducted at Glyndebourne in 1958, and in London, at Covent Garden, in 1962. In 1963 he made his American debut as a symph. conductor. In 1945 he founded the North German Radio Symph. of Hamburg; retired in 1971.

Schmieder, Wolfgang, noted German music librarian; b. Bromberg, May 29, 1901. He studied musicology with Kroyer and Moser, German philology and literature with F. Panzer and F. von Waldberg, and art history with C. Neumann at the Univ. of Heidelberg; received his Ph.D. there in 1927 with the dissertation *Zur Melodiebildung in Liedern von Neidhart von Reuental.* He was an assistant lecturer in the musicology dept. of the Univ. of Heidelberg (1927–30); then studied library science with M. Bollert at the Sächsischen Landesbibliothek in Dresden and with O. Glauning at the Univ. of Leipzig Library. He was librarian of the Technische Hochschule in Dresden (1931–33); then went to Leipzig as head of the archives of Breitkopf & Härtel (1933–42). In 1946 he founded the music dept. of the City and Univ. Library in Frankfurt, which he headed until 1963. He was presented a Festschrift on his 70th birthday in 1971, *Quellenstudien zur Musik,* edited by K. Dorfmüller and G. von Dadelsen. Of his numerous publications, of fundamental importance is his exhaustive *Thematisch-systematisches Verzeichnis der musikalischen Werke von Johann Sebastian Bach: Bach-Werke-Verzeichnis* (Leipzig, 1950; 3rd ed., 1961; 4th ed., 1966); also valuable is *Musikalische alte Drücke bis etwa 1750* (with G. Hartweig; 2 vols., Wolfenbüttel, 1967).

Schminke, Oscar Eberhard, American organist and composer; b. New York, Dec. 12, 1881; d. Liberty, N.Y., Feb. 22, 1969. He suffered from partial deafness since childhood, and after taking piano lessons decided against making music his profession; entered the N.Y. College of Dentistry, graduating in 1903; however, he continued to study music; took organ lessons with Gaston Déthier in N.Y. He publ. several works for organ (*Marche russe, Poème exotique,* etc.); piano pieces (*Chameleon, Moods,* etc.); about a dozen songs.

Schmitt, Aloys, German pianist and composer; b. Erlenbach, Aug. 26, 1788; d. Frankfurt, July 25, 1866. He studied composition with André at Offenbach; in 1816 went to Frankfurt, where he remained all his life. He composed 4 operas: *Der Doppelgänger* (Hannover, 1827); *Valeria* (Mannheim, 1832); *Das Osterfest zu Paderborn* (Frankfurt, 1843); *Die Tochter der Wüste* (Frankfurt, 1845); 2 oratorios: *Moses* and *Ruth;* church music; etc. But he is principally known and appreciated for his numerous piano compositions, including 4 piano concertos, several piano quartets, piano trios, a number of attractive character pieces for piano, and studies for school.
BIBLIOGRAPHY: H. Henkel, *Leben und Wirken von Dr. Aloys Schmitt* (Frankfurt, 1873).

Schmitt, Camille, Belgian composer; b. Aubange, March 30, 1908; d. Limelette, May 11, 1976. He studied at the Brussels Cons. (1928–37); was an organist in France and Belgium (1923–48), a prof. at the Liège Cons. (1947–66), and director of the French Section of the Brussels Cons. (1966–73). His wife was the composer **Jacqueline Fontyn.**
WORKS: *Triptyque angevin* for Orch. (1941); *Psaume* for Orch. (1942); Sinfonietta (1943); *Rapsodie* for Orch. (1944); *Préludes joyeux* for Orch. (1945; International Society for Contemporary Music Festival, Copenhagen, June 2, 1946); Piano Concerto (1955); *Métamorphoses* for Orch. (1963); *Contrepoints* for Orch. (1965); *Polyphonies* for Orch. (1966); *Alternances* for Orch. (1970); Wind Quintet (1943); Trio for Oboe, Clarinet, and Bassoon (1945); String Quartet (1948); *Prélude* for Clarinet and Piano (1952); *Dialogue* for Violin and Piano (1953); *Métamorphoses* for Cello and Piano (1961); Quartet for 4 Clarinets (1964); *Burlesques* for Flute, Oboe, Clarinet, and Bassoon (1965); *Contrepoints* for Wind Quintet (1965); *Polyphonies* for Wind Quintet (1969); *Polyphonies* for Saxophone Quartet (1970); *Psautier* for Alto, Piano, Oboe, Clarinet, and Bassoon (1946); *La Halte des heures,* cantata for Solo Voice and Piano (1959); *Polyphonies* for Piano (1966); *Histoire pour Pierre* for Piano (1970); choruses.

Schmitt, Florent, outstanding French composer; b. Blâmont, Sept. 28, 1870; d. Neuilly, near Paris, Aug. 17, 1958. He had his first music lessons from H. Hess (piano) and G. Sandré (harmony) in Nancy. In 1889 he went to Paris, where he studied harmony with Dubois and Lavignac and composition with Massenet and Fauré. He won the 2nd Prix de Rome in 1897 with the cantata *Frédégonde* and the first prize in 1900 with the cantata *Sémiramis,* which was performed at a Colonne concert on Dec. 11, 1900. He spent the years 1901–4 in the Villa Medicis in Rome, sending to the Académie several important instrumental and choral works; then spent 2 years traveling in Germany, Austria, Hungary, and Turkey. In 1906 he settled permanently in Paris, devoting himself entirely to composition. He served as a member of the executive committee of the Société Musicale Indépendante from its foundation in 1909; was also a member of the Société Nationale de Musique. His formative years were spent in the ambience of French symbolism in poetry and Impressionism in music, and he followed these directions in his programmatically conceived orch. music; but he developed a strong, distinctive style of his own, mainly by elaborating the contrapuntal fabric of his works and extending the rhythmic design to intricate asymmetrical combinations; he also exploited effects of primitivistic percussion, in many respects anticipating the developments of modern Russian music. The catalogue of his works is very long; he continued to compose until his death at the age of 87; attended the premiere of his Symph., given at the Strasbourg Festival of the International Society for Contemporary Music on June 15, 1958. He visited the U.S. in 1932 as soloist in his *Symphonie concertante* with the Boston Symph. He was an influential music critic, writing regularly for *Le Temps* (1919–39).

WORKS: BALLETS: *La Tragédie de Salomé* (Paris, Nov. 9, 1907); *Le Petit Elfe Ferme-l'œil*, after Hans Christian Andersen (Opéra-Comique, Feb. 29, 1924); *Oriane la sans-égale* (Paris Opéra, Jan. 7, 1938); incidental music to *Antoine et Cléopâtre*, after Shakespeare (Paris Opéra, June 14, 1920); *Reflets* (Opéra-Comique, May 20, 1932). VOCAL MUSIC, WITH ORCH.: *Musique sur l'eau* (1898); *Psaume XLVII* for Soprano, Chorus, Orch., and Organ (1904; Paris, Dec. 27, 1906); *Danse des Devadasis* for Solo Voice, Chorus, and Orch. (1900–8); *Tristesse au Jardin* (1897–1908); *Chant de guerre* for Tenor, Male Chorus, and Orch. (1914); *Kerob-Shal* for Tenor and Orch. (1920–24); *Fête de la lumière* for Soprano, Chorus, and Orch. (1937); *L'Arbre entre tous* for Chorus and Orch. (1939); *A contre-voix* for Mixed Chorus (1943); motets and choruses a cappella. FOR ORCH.: *En été* (1894); *Feuillets de voyage* (1903–13); *Reflets de l'Allemagne*, suite of waltzes (1905); *Puppazzi*, suite in 8 movements (1907); *Musiques de plein-air* (1897–99); *Sélamlik*, symph. poem for Military Band (1906); *Le Palais hanté*, symph. study after Poe (1900–4); *3 rapsodies* (1903–4); *Scherzo vif* for Violin and Orch. (1903–10); *La Tragédie de Salomé*, from the ballet of the same title (Paris, Jan. 8, 1911); *Légende* for Viola or Saxophone, and Orch. (1918); *Mirages: Tristesse de Pan, La Tragique Chevauchée* (1921); *Fonctionnaire MCMXII: Inaction en musique* (1924; Paris, Jan. 16, 1927); *Danse d'Abisag* (1925); *Salammbô*, 6 symph. episodes after Flaubert, from film music (1925); *Ronde burlesque* (1927; Paris, Jan. 12, 1930); *Chançunik* (humorous phonetic spelling of *Sens unique*, i.e., "one-way street"; Paris, Feb. 15, 1930); *Symphonie concertante* for Piano and Orch. (Boston, Nov. 25, 1932, composer soloist); *Suite sans esprit de suite* (Paris, Jan. 29, 1938); *Branle de sortie* (Paris, Jan. 21, 1939); *Janiana*, subtitled "Symphony for Strings," score entitled Symph. No. 2 (1941; Paris, May 1, 1942); *Habeyssée* for Violin and Orch. (phonetic representation of "ABC," as pronounced in French; Paris, March 14, 1947); Symph. (1957; Strasbourg, June 15, 1958). CHAMBER MUSIC: *Scherzo-pastorale* for Flute and Piano (1889); *4 pièces* for Violin and Piano (1901); *Andante et Scherzo* for Harp and String

Quartet (1906); Piano Quintet (1901–8); *Lied et Scherzo* for Double Wind Quintet (1910); *Sonate libre en deux parties enchaînées* for Violin and Piano (1919); *Suite en rocaille* for Flute, Violin, Viola, Cello, and Harp (1934); *Sonatine en trio* for Flute, Clarinet, and Harpsichord (1935); *Minorités* for Flute, Violin, and Piano (1938); *Hasards* for Violin, Viola, Cello, and Piano (1939); *A tours d'anches* for Flute, Clarinet, Bassoon, and Piano (1939); Quartet for Saxophones (1941); String Trio (1944); Quartet for Flutes (1944); String Quartet (1945–48). FOR PIANO: *Soirs* (10 preludes); *Ballade de la neige* (1896); *Musiques intimes* (2 sets, 1890–1900 and 1898–1904); *Nuits romaines* (1901); *Puppazzi*, 8 pieces (1907; also for Orch.); *Pièces romantiques* (6 pieces, 1900–8); *3 danses* (1935; also for Orch.); *Feuillets de voyage* (1903; also for Orch.); *Suite sans esprit de suite* (1938; also for Orch.); *Clavecin obtempérant*, suite (1945); etc.; *Reflets de l'Allemagne*, 8 waltzes for Piano, 4-hands (1905; also for Orch.). SONGS: *Soir sur le lac* (1898); *4 lieds* to words by Richepin, Maeterlinck, etc.; *Kerob-Shal*, 3 songs (also for Voice and Orch.).

BIBLIOGRAPHY: M.D. Calvocoressi, "Œuvres de Florent Schmitt," *L'Art Moderne* (Jan. 6, 1907); O. Séré, *Musiciens français d'aujourd'hui* (revised ed., Paris, 1921); G. Jean-Aubry, *La Musique française d'aujourd'hui* (Paris, 1916); A. Cœuroy, *La Musique française moderne* (Paris, 1922); P.O. Ferroud, *Autour de Florent Schmitt* (Paris, 1927); Eric Blom, "Florent Schmitt," *Chesterian* (March 1932); Yves Hucher, *Florent Schmitt, L'Homme et l'artiste* (Paris, 1953). A catalogue and bibliography was issued by Y. Hucher and M. Raveaux as *L'Œuvre de Florent Schmitt* (Paris, 1960).

Schmitt, Georg Aloys, German pianist, conductor, and composer, son and pupil of **Aloys Schmitt;** b. Hannover, Feb. 2, 1827; d. (suddenly, during a rehearsal) Dresden, Oct. 15, 1902. He studied music theory with Vollweiler in Heidelberg; then went on a European tour as a pianist; subsequently devoted himself mainly to theatrical conducting; he was court conductor at Schwerin (1857–92); in 1893 was appointed director of the Mozartverein in Dresden, which had a multitudinous choral ensemble (some 1,400 members) and its own orch. Schmitt wrote the opera *Trilby;* several concert overtures; much chamber music, and piano pieces. He orchestrated keyboard works of Handel and Mozart.

Schmitt, Hans, piano teacher; b. Koben, Bohemia, Jan. 14, 1835; d. Vienna, Jan. 14, 1907. He was at first an oboist at Bucharest and Vienna, but throat trouble compelled him to give up that instrument, and he studied the piano under Dachs at the Vienna Cons. (1860–62), taking the silver medal, and being appointed teacher at the Cons. His instructive works for piano include *300 Studies without Octave-stretches; Vademecum; Fundament der Klaviertechnik; Zirkelübungen in Skalen und Akkorden; 120 kleine Vortragsstücke; Repertoirestudien; Das Pedal des Klaviers* (1875, after Louis Köhler; in Eng., 1893).

Schmitt, Jacob (Jacques), German pianist, brother and pupil of **Aloys Schmitt;** b. Obernburg, Bavaria, Nov. 2, 1803; d. Hamburg, May 24, 1853. He was a reputable piano teacher, and composed about 370 piano pieces; among his works are sonatinas for 2 and 4 hands, and numerous studies, rondos, and nocturnes; especially useful is his *Musikalisches Schatzkästlein,* a collection of 133 short piano pieces.

Schmitt-Walter, Karl, German baritone; b. Gernersheim am Rhein, Dec. 23, 1900. He studied in Nuremberg and Munich; made his debut in 1921 in Oberhausen; then sang in Nuremberg, Saarbrücken, and Dortmund; was a member of the Wiesbaden Opera (1929–34). In 1934 he went to Berlin, where he sang at the Deutsche Oper until 1950; was subsequently a member of the Bavarian State Opera in Munich (1950–61); also sang at Bayreuth and Salzburg. In 1957 he became a prof. of voice at the Munich Academy of Music.

Schmitz, Arnold, German musicologist; b. Sablon, near Metz, July 11, 1893. He studied with Schiedermair in Bonn; then took courses in Munich and Berlin with Kaun and Beer-Walbrunn; was on the faculty of the univs. of Bonn (1921–28) and Breslau (1929–39); during World War II he was in the German army; from 1947 to 1961 he was a prof. at the Univ. of Mainz; in 1965–67 he occupied the chair of musicology at the Univ. of Basel. He publ. *Beethovens "zwei Prinzipe"* (Berlin, 1923); *Das romantische Beethovenbild* (Berlin, 1927); *Die Bildlichkeit der wortgebundenen Musik J.S. Bachs* (Mainz, 1950).

Schmitz, Elie Robert, eminent French pianist; b. Paris, Feb. 8, 1889; d. San Francisco, Sept. 5, 1949. He studied at the Paris Cons. with Diémer, winning first prize in piano; in 1908 toured as accompanist of Slezak, Emma Eames, and other celebrated singers; in 1912, organized in Paris the Assoc. des Concerts Schmitz, which he led until 1914; in 1919 toured the U.S. as a pianist; in 1920 founded the Franco-American Music Society in N.Y. (incorporated in 1923 as Pro Musica), of which he was president from its inception; toured again in the U.S. and Europe (1921–29), and in the Orient (1929–30, 1932–33); eventually settled in San Francisco as a teacher. He publ. a book on his system of piano study, *The Capture of Inspiration* (N.Y., 1935; 2nd ed., 1944), and a valuable technical analysis with commentary, *The Piano Works of Claude Debussy* (N.Y., 1950).

Schmitz, Eugen, German musicologist; b. Neuburg, Bavaria, July 12, 1882; d. Leipzig, July 10, 1959. He studied musicology with Sandberger and Kroyer at the Univ. of Munich; obtained his Dr.Phil. in 1905 with the dissertation *Der Nürnberger Organist Johann Staden: Beiträge zur Würdigung seiner musikgeschichtlichen Stellung* (extracts publ. in Leipzig, 1906). He wrote music criticism in Dresden; taught music at the Dresden Technische Hochschule (1916–39). From 1939 to 1953 he was director

of the Musikbibliothek Peters in Leipzig. Among his publications are *Hugo Wolf* (Leipzig, 1906); *Richard Strauss als Musikdramatiker* (Munich, 1907); *Richard Wagner* (Leipzig, 1909; 2nd ed., 1918); *Harmonielehre als Theorie* (Munich, 1911); *Geschichte der Kantate und des geistlichen Konzerts* (Leipzig, 1914; 2nd ed., 1955); *Palestrina* (Leipzig, 1914; 2nd ed., 1954); *Musikästhetik* (Leipzig, 1915; 2nd ed., 1925); *Orlando di Lasso* (Leipzig, 1915; 2nd ed., 1954); *Klavier, Klaviermusik und Klavierspiel* (Leipzig, 1919); *Richard Wagner: Wie wir ihn heute sehen* (Dresden, 1937); he was an editor for Denkmäler der Tonkunst in Bayern, 12 and 14 (7.i and 8.i).

Schmuller, Alexander, violinist; b. Mozyr, Russia, Dec. 5, 1880; d. Amsterdam, March 29, 1933. He was a pupil of Ševčik, Hřimaly, and Auer; from 1908 he taught at the Stern Cons. in Berlin, and from 1914 at the Amsterdam Cons. For several years he gave concerts with Max Reger, whose music he was one of the first to champion; made many concert tours in Europe and the U.S.

Schnabel, Artur, celebrated Austrian pianist and pedagogue; b. Lipnik, April 17, 1882; d. Morschach, Canton Schwyz, Switzerland, Aug. 15, 1951. After taking lessons for 2 years from Hans Schmitt, he studied in Vienna with Leschetizky (1891–97); appeared in public as a child prodigy; lived many years in Berlin, where he gave joint recitals with the violinist Carl Flesch; formed in 1912 a trio with A. Wittenberg (violin) and A. Hekking (cello); from 1925 until 1933 he taught at the Hochschule für Musik in Berlin; after the advent of the Nazi regime he went to Switzerland, where he organized his famous master classes during summer seasons. He made his American debut in 1921, and revisited the U.S. several times; lived in N.Y. after 1939, and became an American citizen in 1944; but eventually returned to Europe. It was as an interpreter of Beethoven that he reached his greatest heights; he was distinguished also in his performances of the piano music of Brahms. His pedagogical method was strict in the observance of every detail of the music, but at the same time he inspired his pupils by encouraging an individual treatment in the matter of dynamics and formal concept. Schnabel was also a composer; in his works he pursued an uncompromisingly modernistic idiom, thriving on dissonance and tracing melodic patterns along atonal lines. WORKS: Symph. No. 1 (1938–40; Minneapolis, Dec. 13, 1946); *Rhapsody* for Orch. (Cleveland, April 15, 1948); Piano Concerto; chamber music. PUBLICATIONS: *Reflections on Music* (Manchester, 1933; N.Y., 1934); *Music and the Line of Most Resistance* (Princeton, 1942); *My Life and Music* (London, 1961); edited the piano sonatas of Beethoven. BIBLIOGRAPHY: César Saerchinger, *Artur Schnabel* (London, 1957); K. Wolff, *The Teaching of Artur Schnabel* (London, 1972).

Schnabel, Joseph Ignaz, German composer of sacred music; b. Naumburg-on-Queiss, Silesia, May

24, 1767; d. Breslau, June 16, 1831. He was appointed Kapellmeister at the Cathedral of Breslau (1804) and remained in Breslau for the rest of his life; from 1812 taught at the Roman Catholic Seminary and was director of the Royal Inst. for Church Music. He wrote many sacred works; publ. 5 masses, 4 graduals, 2 offertories, hymns; also wrote marches for military band; Quintet for Guitar and Strings; Clarinet Concerto. His brother, **Michael Schnabel** (b. Naumburg, Sept. 23, 1775; d. Breslau, Nov. 6, 1842), founded a piano factory in Breslau (1814); his son, **Karl Schnabel** (b. Breslau, Nov. 2, 1809; d. there, May 12, 1881), an excellent pianist and composer of operas and piano music, carried on the business after Michael Schnabel's death.

BIBLIOGRAPHY: H.E. Guckel, *Joseph Ignaz Schnabel,* part 2 of *Katholische Kirchenmusik in Schlesien* (Leipzig, 1912).

Schnabel, Karl Ulrich, German pianist and composer, son of **Artur Schnabel;** b. Berlin, Aug. 6, 1909. He studied piano with Leonid Kreutzer and composition with Paul Juon in Berlin; after a series of appearances as a soloist in Europe, including Russia, he made an American tour (debut, N.Y., Feb. 23, 1937); played duo-piano recitals with his father; also gave duo-piano concerts (4 hands at one piano) with his wife, **Helen Fogel.**

Schneerson, Grigori, eminent Russian musicologist; b. Eniseisk, Siberia, March 13, 1901; d. Moscow, Feb. 6, 1982. He was the son of a political exile under the tsarist regime; went to Moscow as a youth and studied piano at the Moscow Cons. with Medtner and Igumnov. From 1939 to 1948 he was in charge of the music dept. of the Society for Cultural Relations with Foreign Nations; from 1948 to 1961 was head of the foreign section of the monthly *Sovietskaya Muzyka,* and from 1954 to 1966 edited the bibliographic series Foreign Literature of Music. A remarkably gifted linguist, he mastered several European languages and undertook a study of Chinese. In his polemical writings he displayed wit and sarcasm in attacking the extreme manifestations of Western modernism, but preserved scholarly impartiality in analyzing the music of all genres and styles. He was a Member Correspondent of the Academy of the Arts of the German Democratic Republic (1968), Honorary Member of the Accademia di Scienze, Lettere, Arti (1976), and a recipient of the Bernier Prize of the Académie des Beaux-Arts, Paris (1976).

WRITINGS (all publ. in Moscow): *Musical Culture in China* (1952); *Aram Khachaturian* (1957; also in Eng., 1959); *Music, Living and Dead* (in praise of the state of music in the nations of the socialist bloc, and in condemnation of Western trends; 1960; revised and mitigated, 1964); *Ernst Busch* (1962; revised 1964); *French Music of the 20th Century* (1964; revised 1970); *Music and Times* (1970); *Articles on Foreign Music: Essays, Reminiscences* (1974); *American Song* (1977); *Portraits of American Composers* (1977); ed. *D. Shostakovich: Articles and Materials* (1976).

Schnéevoigt, Georg Lennart, Finnish conductor; b. Viborg, Nov. 8, 1872; d. Malmö, Nov. 28, 1947. He studied cello with Karl Schröder in Sondershausen and Julius Klengel in Leipzig; appeared as a cellist; in 1900 began his career as a conductor; from 1904 to 1908 conducted the Kaim Orch. in Munich; in 1908–9, the Kiev Symph.; in 1909–14, the Riga Symph.; in 1912–14, the Helsinki Symph.; the last merged with Kajanus's Helsinki Phil. in 1914 to form the City Orch.; Kajanus and Schnéevoigt were joint conductors from 1916–32; Schnéevoigt then succeeded Kajanus and continued until 1941; from 1915 to 1924 he also led the Konsertförening in Stockholm; in 1919 founded the Oslo Phil. Orch., and led it until 1927; also conducted in Germany; conducted the Los Angeles Phil. (1927–29); was general director of the National Opera in Riga (1929–32); then went to Malmö, Sweden. In 1907 he married the pianist **Sigrid Sundgren.**

Schneider, Alexander, Russian-American violinist; b. Vilna, Oct. 21, 1908. He went to study in Germany as a youth; took violin lessons with Adolf Rebner at the Frankfurt Cons. and with Carl Flesch in Berlin; served as concertmaster of the Orch. der Museumgesellschaft. Upon the advent of the anti-Semitic Nazi regime, he emigrated to the U.S.; joined the Budapest Quartet as 2nd violin, and made a world tour with it. In 1950 he established, with Pablo Casals, annual summer music festivals in Prades, France, and was a close collaborator with Casals in arranging the spring music festivals in Puerto Rico. He took part, in association with Rudolf Serkin, in the Marlboro (Vt.) music festivals. In 1945 he received the Elizabeth Sprague Coolidge medal for eminent services to chamber music. He also appeared as a conductor with world orchs. (Israel Phil., Los Angeles Phil., as well as the Casals orch. in Puerto Rico); was active as a teacher; played sonata recitals with Eugene Istomin and other pianists.

Schneider, Edward Faber, American pianist, composer, and pedagogue; b. Omaha, Nebr., Oct. 3, 1872; d. Santa Clara, Calif., July 1, 1950. He studied piano with Xaver Scharwenka in N.Y. during the latter's residence there; then went to Germany, where he took piano lessons with Heinrich Barth in Berlin; eventually settled in San Francisco; taught piano at Mills College for 25 years. He wrote several unnecessary symph. pieces in a mandatory Romantic vein (*In Autumn Time; Sargasso Sea; Thus Spake the Deepest Stone;* all perf. in San Francisco for the first and last time); some quite acceptable piano pieces; and, inevitably, songs.

Schneider, Friedrich, German organist and composer; b. Alt-Waltersdorf, Saxony, Jan. 3, 1786; d. Dessau, Nov. 23, 1853. He was a son and pupil of **Johann Gottlob Schneider;** being brought up in a musical atmosphere, he began composing early in life, and publ. 3 piano sonatas at the age of 17; in 1820 he wrote an oratorio, *Das Weltgericht,* that was extremely successful; the following year he was called to Dessau as court Kapellmeister; there he founded a celebrated school of music, which he directed from 1829 to his death; it attracted pupils from all over Germany. Besides *Das Weltgericht*, he wrote oratorios: *Die Sündflut* (1823); *Das verlorene Paradies* (1824); *Das befreite Jerusalem* (1835); also a series of oratorios tracing the life of Jesus from birth to crucifixion; he further wrote 25 cantatas; 7 operas; 23 symphs.; numerous pieces of chamber music; choruses; piano sonatas for 2 and 4 hands. He also publ. theoretical works: *Elementarbuch der Harmonie und Tonsetzkunst* (1820; in Eng., etc., 1828); *Vorschule der Musik* (1827); *Handbuch des Organisten* (1829–30; in 4 parts).

BIBLIOGRAPHY: F. Kempe, *Friedrich Schneider als Mensch und Künstler* (Dessau, 1859; 2nd ed., Berlin, 1864); K. Hoede, *Friedrich Schneider und die Zerbster Liedertafel zur Hundertjahrfeier 1927* (Zerbst, 1927).

Schneider, Georg Abraham, German horn virtuoso and composer; b. Darmstadt, April 19, 1770; d. Berlin, Jan. 19, 1839. He was a member of the royal orch. at Berlin; from 1820 was Kapellmeister of the court opera and "Musikmeister" of all regiments of the Guards.

WORKS: Operettas: *Der Orakelspruch; Aucassin und Nicolette; Die Verschworenen; Der Traum; Der Währwolf;* 13 ballets; music to numerous plays, melodramas, etc.; 2 oratorios; cantatas; orch. masses; 54 entr'actes for orch.; overtures; concertos for horn, flute, oboe, english horn, bassoon, etc.; quintets, quartets, and other chamber music.

Schneider, Johann, outstanding German organist, son of **Johann Gottlob Schneider** and brother of **Friedrich Schneider;** b. Alt-Gersdorf, near Zittau, Oct. 28, 1789; d. Dresden, April 13, 1864. He studied jurisprudence and organ; in 1812 became a church organist at Görlitz, and in 1825 was appointed court organist at Dresden. He was praised by Mendelssohn as one of the finest organ virtuosos of the period; he was also greatly renowned as a teacher. He composed a number of organ pieces and songs with organ obbligato.

Schneider, Johann Gottlob, German organist and composer; b. Alt-Waltersdorf, Saxony, Aug. 1, 1753; d. Gersdorf, May 3, 1840. He was apprenticed as a weaver but subsequently decided to study music; his principal achievement consists of giving a fine musical upbringing to his sons, **Friedrich Schneider** and **Johann Schneider.**

Schneider, Julius, German organist and composer; b. Berlin, July 6, 1805; d. there, April 3, 1885. He studied composition with Bernhard Klein; organ and piano with various teachers in Berlin. In 1829 he became organist of the Friedrichwerder church in Berlin, and in 1854 was appointed teacher of organ at the Berlin Inst. of Church Music. He composed a variety of organ pieces; a Piano Concerto; some chamber music.

Schneider, Karl Ernst, German writer on music; b. Aschersleben, Dec. 29, 1819; d. Dresden, Oct. 25, 1893. He wrote *Das musikalische Lied in geschichtlicher Entwickelung* (3 vols., 1863–65); *Zur Periodisierung der Musikgeschichte* (1863); *Musik, Klavier und Klavierspiel* (1872).

Schneider, Louis, French writer on music; b. Lyons, June 23, 1861; d. Grenoble, Aug. 21, 1934. He settled in Paris; wrote music criticism; publ. several books on music: *Schumann, Sa vie et ses œuvres* (1905; in collaboration with Mareschal); *Massenet* (1908; 2nd ed., 1926); *Monteverdi* (1921); *Offenbach, Hervé, Charles Lecocq, Maîtres de l'opérette française* (2 vols., 1924); also humorous musical chronicles under the pen name "Le Pompier de service."

Schneider, Marius, Alsatian musicologist; b. Hagenau, July 1, 1903. He studied in Strasbourg, Paris, and Berlin; was a member of the staff at the Ethnological Museum in Berlin (1931–39); lived in Barcelona between 1944 and 1951; returned to Germany and became a member of the faculty of the Univ. of Cologne (1955–68). His publications include *Die Ars nova des 14. Jahrhunderts in Frankreich und Italien* (Diss., Univ. of Berlin, 1930; publ. in Wolfenbüttel, 1931); *Geschichte der Mehrstimmigkeit* (2 vols., Berlin, 1934, 1935); *El origen musical de los animales-símbolos en la mitología y la escultura antigua* (Barcelona, 1946); *La danza de espadas y la tarantela* (Barcelona, 1948); *Singende Steine* (Kassel, 1955); *Il significato della musica* (Rome, 1970); numerous valuable contributions to ethnomusicology, philosophy of music, and history of musical structures. A Festschrift was publ. in his honor in Regensburg in 1977.

Schneider, Max, eminent German musicologist; b. Eisleben, July 20, 1875; d. Halle, May 5, 1967. He studied musicology at the Leipzig Cons. with Riemann and Kretzschmar and harmony and composition with Jadassohn. Upon graduation he was librarian at the Univ. of Berlin (1904–7); then served in the music division of the Royal Library (1907–14); subsequently taught at the Univ. of Breslau (1915–28); then was a prof. at the Univ. of Halle (1928–60). He did useful work in compiling miscellaneous biobibliographical materials in music; publ. *Die Anfänge des Basso continuo* (Diss., Univ. of Berlin, 1917; publ. in Leipzig, 1918; reprint, Farmborough, 1971); *Beiträge zu einer Anleitung Clavichord und Cembalo zu spielen* (Strasbourg, 1934); *Beiträge zur Musikforschung* (vol. I, Halle, 1935). He edited numerous important bibliographical surveys; also edited the works of Heinrich Schütz. He enjoyed a well-merited reputation in Germany as a thorough scholar. He was honored 3 times by Festschrifts: *Festschrift Max Schneider zum 60. Geburtstag* (Halle, 1935); *Festschrift Max Schneider zum 80. Geburtstag* (Leipzig, 1955); *Festschrift Max Schneider zum 85. Geburtstag* (Leipzig, 1960).

Schneider, Theodor, German cellist and conductor, son of **Friedrich Schneider;** b. Dessau, May 14,

1827; d. Zittau, June 15, 1909. He studied with his father, and with Drechsler (cello); in 1845 was cellist in the Dessau Court Orch.; in 1854, cantor and choir director of the court and city churches; from 1860–96 served as cantor and music director at the Jakobikirche in Chemnitz; was also conductor of the Singakademie and of a Männergesangverein, which he founded in 1870. He retired in 1898.

Schneider-Trnavsky, Mikuláš, Slovak composer; b. Trnava, May 24, 1881; d. Bratislava, May 28, 1958. He studied in Budapest, Vienna, and Prague; returned to Bratislava in 1918, and served as inspector of music schools in Slovakia. He publ. several valuable collections of Slovak folk songs, arranged with piano accompaniment: *Sbierka slovenských ludových piesní* (2 vols., 1905–10); *Sbierka slovenských národných piesní* (5 sections, Bratislava, 1930; new ed., Prague, 1935–40); *50 Slovakische Volkslieder* (Bratislava, 1943). He publ. a book of memoirs, *Usmevy a slzy (Smiles and Tears;* Bratislava, 1959). In 1956 he received the title of National Artist from the government of Czecholovakia.
WORKS: Operetta, *Bellarosa* (Bratislava, 1941); *Dumka and Dance* for Orch. (1905); *Comedy Overture* (1930–31); *Symphony of Recollections* (1956); Violin Sonata (1905); *Slovak Sonatina* for Piano (1938); church music, including several masses.

Schneiderhan, Wolfgang (Eduard), Austrian violin virtuoso and pedagogue; b. Vienna, May 28, 1915. He studied violin mainly in Prague, with Ševčik and Pisek. Returning to Vienna, he became concertmaster of the Vienna Symph., then of the Vienna State Orch., and finally of the Vienna Phil. (1938–49). From 1938–50 he was a prof. of violin at the Vienna State Academy. From 1938–51 he led the Schneiderhan Quartet; from 1949–60 he also was a member of a trio, with the eminent pianist Edwin Fischer and the cellist Enrico Mainardi. In 1956 he and the Swiss violinist and conductor Rudolf Baumgartner founded in Lucerne the Festival Strings. These activities as a chamber music player never detracted from Schneiderhan's virtuoso career as a concert violinist. He was married to the German soprano **Irmgard Seefried.**
BIBLIOGRAPHY: F. Fassbind, *Wolfgang Schneiderhan, Irmgard Seefried: Eine Künstler- und Lebensgemeinschaft* (Bern, 1960).

Schneidt, Hanns-Martin, German organist and conductor; b. Kitzingen, Dec. 6, 1930. He studied at the Thomasschule in Leipzig with Günther Ramin; also took courses in choral music in Munich and served as a church organist there. In 1955 he became director of the Church Music School in Berlin; was also conductor of the Berlin Bach-Collegium and Choir, as well as cantor and organist at the Church of St. John the Evangelist. In 1971 he became a prof. of conducting at the Hochschule für Musik in Hamburg; in 1975 was appointed Generalmusikdirektor of Wuppertal. He wrote a number of choral works.

Schneitzhoeffer, Jean, French composer; b. Toulouse, Oct. 13, 1785; d. Paris, Oct. 4, 1852. He studied with Catel at the Paris Cons.; after serving as timpanist at the Paris Opéra (1815–23), he was appointed *chef du chant* there; from 1831 to 1850 he was in charge of choral classes at the Paris Cons. He composed several ballet scores for the Paris Opéra; of these, *La Sylphide* (1832), which he wrote for the famous dancer Maria Taglioni, became a perennial favorite. His other ballets are *Proserpine* (1818); *Zémire et Azor* (1824); *Mars et Vénus;* he also wrote *Sinfonia dei gatti,* several concert overtures, and a Requiem.

Schnerich, Alfred, Austrian musicologist; b. Tarvis, Carinthia, Oct. 22, 1859; d. Vienna, April 29, 1944. He studied art history at the Institut für Österreichisches Geschichtsforschung in Vienna; obtained his Dr.Phil. in 1888; from 1889 he was librarian at the Univ. of Vienna; in 1921 he became Hofrat; retired in 1923. He was a member of the editorial commission of Denkmäler der Tonkunst in Österreich.
WRITINGS: *Der Messentypus von Haydn bis Schubert* (1892); *Messe und Requiem seit Haydn und Mozart* (1909); *Jos. Haydn und seine Sendung* (1922; 2nd ed., 1926); *Die kirchliche Tonkunst* (1927).

Schnitger (Schnitker), Arp, German organ builder; b. Schmalenfleth, Golzwarden, Oldenburg, July 2, 1648; d. Neuenfelde, July 24, 1719. His organs are in Hamburg, Bremen, Magdeburg, Berlin, etc. His son **Franz Kaspar** (d. 1729) worked with an elder brother at Zwolle in the Netherlands, building the organ at Zwolle (63 stops) and that at Alkmar (56 stops).
BIBLIOGRAPHY: P. Rubardt, *Arp Schnitger* (Freiberg, 1928); G. Fock, *Schnitger und seine Schule* (Kiel, 1931); W. Sumner, "Arp Schnitger and His Organs," *Organ,* XVII (1938); G. Fock, *Arp Schnitger und seine Schule* (Kassel, 1975).

Schnittke, Alfred, Russian composer of avantgarde tendencies; b. (of German origin) Engels, in the German Volga Republic, near Saratov, Nov. 24, 1934. He had his first piano lessons in Vienna (1946–48), where his father was stationed as a correspondent of a German-language Soviet newspaper. Returning to Moscow, he studied composition with Golubev and instrumentation with Rakov at the Moscow Cons. (1953–58); in 1961 was appointed to its faculty. After writing in a conventional manner, he became acutely interested in the new Western techniques, particularly in serialism and "sonorism," in which dynamic gradations assume thematic significance; soon he became known as one of the boldest experimenters in modernistic composition in Soviet Russia.
WORKS: FOR ORCH.: 4 symphs.: No. 1 (1972); No. 2, *St. Florian,* with Chorus (London, April 23, 1980); No. 3 (Leipzig, Nov. 5, 1981); No. 4 (Moscow, April 12, 1984); 4 violin concertos: No. 1 (1957); No. 2 (1966); No. 3 (1978; Moscow, Jan. 29, 1979); No. 4 (1982; West

Berlin, Sept. 11, 1984); Piano Concerto (1960); Concerto for Piano and String Orch. (Leningrad, Dec. 9, 1979); *Poem about Cosmos* (1961); *Music* for Piano and Chamber Orch. (1964); *. . . pianissimo . . .* (Donaueschingen, Oct. 19, 1969); Concerto for Oboe, Harp, and String Orch. (1977); Concerto Grosso No. 1 for 2 Violins, Piano, Harpsichord, and Strings (1977), and No. 2 for Violin, Cello, and Orch., for the centennial of the West Berlin Phil. Orch. (1982); *Passacaglia* (1979–80). CHAMBER MUSIC: 2 Violin Sonatas (1963, 1968); *Dialogues* for Cello and 7 Instrumentalists (1965); 3 string quartets (1966, 1981, 1984); *Serenade for 5 Musicians* for Clarinet, Violin, Double Bass, Percussion, and Piano (1968); *Canon in memoriam Igor Stravinsky* for String Quartet (1971); *Hymnus I* for Cello, Piano, and Percussion (1974), *II* for Cello and Double Bass (1974), and *III* for Violin, Recorder, Celesta, and Bells (1974); *Praeludium in memoriam Dmitri Shostakovich* for Violin and Tape (1975); Piano Quintet (1976; also for Orch., Moscow, Dec. 29, 1979); *Suite in the Old Style* for Violin and Piano (1977); Cello Sonata (1978); *Lebenslauf* for 4 Metronomes, Piano, and Percussion (1982); *Moz-Art* for 2 Violins (1983). FOR CHORUS: 2 oratorios: *Nagasaki* (1958) and *Songs of War and Peace,* with thematic materials from contemporary Russian folk songs (1959); *3 Poems* for Mezzo-soprano and Piano (1965); *Der gelbe Klang,* scenic composition after the poetic drama by the abstract painter Wassily Kandinsky, for 9 Instruments, Tape, Chorus, Pantomime, and Light Projection (1973); *Requiem* for Chorus, Organ, Piano, Electric Bass, Electric Guitar, Brass, Percussion, and Celesta (1975; Budapest, Oct. 8, 1977); *3 Madrigals* for Soprano, Violin, Viola, Double Bass, Harpsichord, and Vibraphone (Moscow, Nov. 11, 1980); *Minnesang* for 48 Voices a cappella (1981); *Seid nüchtern und wachet . . . ,* based on the version of the Faust legend publ. in 1587 under the title *Historia von Doktor Johann Fausten,* commissioned by the Vienna Choral Academy on the occasion of its 125th anniversary (Vienna, June 19, 1983; first Moscow perf., Oct. 23, 1983); also, *Variations on a Chord* for Piano (1966); an electronic *Study* (1969).

Schnoor, Hans, German writer on music; b. Neumünster, Oct. 4, 1893; d. Bielefeld, Jan. 15, 1976. He studied with H. Riemann and A. Schering at the Univ. of Leipzig, where he received his Ph.D. with the dissertation *Das Buxheimer Orgelbuch* in 1919; became a music critic in Dresden and Leipzig (1922–26); then music editor of the *Dresdner Anzeiger* (1926–45); in 1949 settled in Bielefeld. WRITINGS: *Musik der germanischen Völker im XIX. und XX. Jahrhundert* (Breslau, 1926); *Weber auf dem Weltheater* (Dresden, 1942; 4th ed., 1963); *Weber: Ein Lebensbild aus Dresdner Sicht* (Dresden, 1947); *400 Jahre deutscher Musikkultur; Zum Jubiläum der Staatskapelle und zur Geschichte der Dresdner Oper* (Dresden, 1948); *Geschichte der Musik* (1953); *Weber; Gestalt und Schöpfung* (Dresden, 1953; 2nd ed., revised, 1974); *Oper, Operette, Konzert; Ein praktisches Nachschlagsbuch* (Gutersloh, 1955); *Harmonie und Chaos* (Munich, 1962);

Die Stunde des Rosenkavalier (Munich, 1969).

Schnorr von Carolsfeld, Ludwig, German tenor; b. Munich, July 2, 1836; d. Dresden, July 21, 1865. He was the son of the noted painter; he studied with J. Otto in Dresden, and at the Leipzig Cons.; then he was a pupil of Eduard Devrient at Karlsruhe, where he made his debut, followed by an engagement in 1858. From 1860 he was the leading tenor at Dresden. He created the role of Tristan in Wagner's *Tristan und Isolde* at Munich, June 10, 1865 (his wife, **Malwine Schnorr von Carolsfeld,** singing Isolde). He died shortly afterward, of heart failure, at the age of 29.
BIBLIOGRAPHY: R. Wagner, *Meine Erinnerungen an Ludwig Schnorr von Carolsfeld,* in vol. VIII of *Gesammelte Schriften und Dichtungen;* C.H.N. Garrigues, *Ein ideales Sängerpaar, Ludwig Schnorr von Carolsfeld und Malwine Schnorr von Carolsfeld* (Copenhagen, 1937).

Schnorr von Carolsfeld (née **Garrigues**), **Malwine,** soprano, wife of **Ludwig Schnorr von Carolsfeld;** b. Copenhagen, Dec. 7, 1825; d. Karlsruhe, Feb. 8, 1904. She created Isolde on June 10, 1865, in Munich, her husband singing Tristan; after his death she sang in Hamburg, and later in Karlsruhe; after her retirement from the stage she taught. In 1867 she publ. a vol. of poems by her husband and herself.
BIBLIOGRAPHY: C.H.N. Garrigues, *Ein ideales Sängerpaar, Ludwig Schnorr von Carolsfeld und Malwine Schnorr von Carolsfeld* (Copenhagen, 1937).

Schnyder von Wartensee, Xaver, composer; b. Lucerne, April 18, 1786; d. Frankfurt, Aug. 27, 1868. He was a pupil at Vienna of J.C. Kienlen; joined the campaign against the French in 1815; taught at the Pestalozzian Inst. in Yverdun; in 1817 settled in Frankfurt. His works include 3 symphs.; No. 2 is entitled *Erinnerung an Joseph Haydn* (Frankfurt, Oct. 20, 1837); No. 3 is entitled *Militärsymphonie* (Frankfurt, Jan. 18, 1850); he also wrote cantatas; sacred and secular songs; Swiss songs for men's chorus; etc.; *System der Rhythmik* (posthumous publication by B. Widmann).
BIBLIOGRAPHY: *Lebenserinnerungen von X. Schnyder von Wartensee* (Zürich, 1887; contains an autobiography and a complete list of works; new ed. by Willi Schuh, Berlin, 1940).

Schoberlechner, Franz, pianist and composer; b. Vienna, July 21, 1797; d. Berlin, Jan. 7, 1843. He studied with Hummel and E.A. Förster at Vienna, and at 10 played in public Hummel's 2nd Concerto, written for him. On a pianistic tour to Italy he produced his opera *I Virtuosi teatrali* at Florence (1814), and the next year became maestro di cappella to the Duchess of Lucca, producing there a 2nd opera, *Gli Arabi nelle Gallie* (1816); in 1820 returned to Vienna, where he brought out an opera in German, *Der junge Onkel* (Jan. 14, 1823); made a trip to Russia in 1823, and there married the singer **Sophie dall'Occa** (1807–63), with whom he made further tours to Italy

Schobert – Schoemaker

and Vienna. He purchased a villa in Florence in 1831, and retired to it some years later. Besides his operas, he composed overtures, string quartets, a Piano Trio, and many piano pieces (sonatas, variations, fantasias, etc.).

Schobert, Johann, important composer; b. probably in Silesia, c.1740; d. Paris, Aug. 28, 1767 (with his entire family, except one child, from eating poisonous mushrooms). From 1760, he was chamber musician to the Prince de Conti in Paris. His works show the general characteristics of the Mannheim School, although it cannot be proved that he ever was in that city. The slow movement of Mozart's Clavier Concerto, K. 39, is based on music by Schobert.
WORKS: Opp. 1, 2, 3, sonatas for Clavecin and Violin; opp. 4, 5, 16, 17, sonatas for Clavecin Solo; opp. 6, 8, clavecin trios; opp. 9, 10, 11, 12, 18, clavecin concertos; op. 13, *Concerto pastoral* for Clavecin; opp. 14, 15, 6 symphs. for Clavecin, Violin, and 2 Horns. (The same works are reprinted by Hummel in Amsterdam with different opus numbers.) A singspiel, *Le Garde-chase et le braconnier*, was produced in Paris (1765) with little success. A selection of Schobert's works (with thematic catalogue) was publ. by H. Riemann in vol. 39 of Denkmäler Deutscher Tonkunst (1909).
BIBLIOGRAPHY: G. de Saint-Foix, "J. Schobert," *Revue Musicale*, III/10 (1922); K. Schalscha, *Zur Würdigung Schoberts* (1923); H.T. David, *J. Schobert als Sonatenkomponist* (1928); H. Turrentine, *Johann Schobert and French Clavier Music from 1700 to the Revolution* (Diss., Univ of Iowa, 1962).

Schoeck, Othmar, eminent Swiss composer and conductor; b. Brunnen, Sept. 1, 1886; d. Zürich, March 8, 1957. He was the son of a painter; studied at the Zürich Cons. with Nägeli and Freund; later, with Reger in Leipzig; from 1909 to 1915, conducted the men's chorus "Aussersihl" in Zürich; from 1917 to 1944 led the symph. concerts at St. Gall. Schoeck is acknowledged as a foremost song composer of Switzerland.
WORKS: Operas: *Don Ranudo de Colibrados* (Zürich, April 16, 1919); *Das Wandbild,* pantomime (libretto by Busoni; Halle, Jan. 2, 1921); *Venus* (Zürich, May 10, 1922); *Penthesilea* (Dresden, Jan. 8, 1927); *Massimilla Doni* (Dresden, March 2, 1937); *Das Schloss Dürande* (Berlin, April 1, 1943). For Orch.: Violin Concerto (1911–12); Cello Concerto (1947); Horn Concerto (1951); *Festlicher Hymnus* (1950); etc. Chamber music: 2 string quartets; 2 violin sonatas; etc. Song cycles: Op. 36, *Elégie* for Voice and Chamber Orch. (1924); op. 38, *Gaselen* for Voice and Chamber Orch.; op. 40, *Lebendig begraben* for Bass and Large Orch (1927); op. 45, *Wanderung im Gebirge* for Voice and Piano (1930); op. 47, *Notturno* for Bass and String Quartet; over 120 songs. A thematic index of his works was publ. by W. Vogel (Zürich, 1956).
BIBLIOGRAPHY: W. Schuh, "Der harmonische Stil O. Schoecks," *Neue Musikzeitung* (1928); E. Isler, *Führer durch "Penthesilea"* (1928); H. Corrodi,

O. Schoeck (Frauenfeld, 1931; new ed., much enlarged, 1936); W. Schuh, *O. Schoeck* (Zürich, 1934); also articles in the *Schweizerische Musikzeitung* (special Schoeck issue, March 1943); *Festgabe der Freunde zum 50. Geburtstag,* ed. by W. Schuh (Erlenbach-Zürich, 1936); W. Vogel, *Wesenszüge von Othmar Schoecks Liedkunst* (Zürich, 1950). The Schoeck Society, organized for the purpose of making his music better known, issued a valuable annotated catalogue of his works (Bern, 1961); W. Vogel publ. 2 companion vols., *Othmar Schoeck im Wort* (St. Gall, 1957) and *Othmar Schoeck im Gespräch* (Zürich, 1965); F. Kienberger, *Othmar Schoeck: Eine Studie* (Zürich, 1975); S. Tiltmann-Fuchs, *Othmar Schoecks Liederzyklen für Singstimme und Orchester* (Regensburg, 1976); W. Vogel, *Othmar Schoeck: Leben und Schaffen im Spiegel der Selbstzeugnissen und Zeitgenossenberichten* (Zürich, 1976); D. Puffet, *The Song Cycles of Othmar Schoek* (Stuttgart and Bern, 1982).

Schœlcher, Victor, French statesman and music amateur; b. Paris, July 21, 1804; d. Houilles, Dec. 24, 1893. During the 2nd Empire he lived in England because of his radical politics, and became an enthusiastic admirer of Handel's music; publ. *The Life of Handel* (1857) in an inadequate Eng. trans. (the first 4 chapters in the original French were publ. in *La France Musicale*, 1860–62; the entire MS was bought for the library of the Paris Cons. in 1881). Schœlcher accumulated a fine collection of Handel materials, which he donated to the Paris Cons.

Schoemaker, Maurice, Belgian composer; b. Anderlecht, near Brussels, Dec. 27, 1890; d. Brussels, Aug. 24, 1964. He studied theory with Théo Ysaÿe, Martin Lunssens, and Paul Gilson; was one of 8 Gilson pupils to form, in 1925, the Groupe des Synthétistes, whose aim was to promote modern music. He held administrative posts in various Belgian musical organizations.
WORKS: Operas: *Swane* (1933); *Arc-en-ciel* (1937); *De Toverviool* (1954); 3 radio plays: *Sire Halewijn* (1935); *Médée la magicienne* (1936); *Philoctetes* (1942); 2 ballets: *Breughel-Suite* (1928) and *Pan* (1937); *Le Facétieux Voyage* for Orch. (1914); *Récit, Aria et Final* for Violin and Orch. (1920); *Pan,* prelude for Orch. (1921); *Feu d'artifice* for Wind Orch. (1922); *2 fantasques* for Orch. (1924); *Sinfonia da camera* (1929); *Légende de Sire Halewijn,* symph. poem (1930); *Rapsodie flamande* for Orch. (1931); *Variations on a Popular Song* for Orch. (1937); *Sinfonia breve* (1938); *Pièce concertante* for Trombone and Orch. (1939); *Variazioni* for Horn and Orch. (1941); *Mouvement symphonique* (1942); *Scènes espagnoles* for Orch. (1943); *2 danses flamandes* for Orch. (1944); Symph. (1946); Bassoon Concerto (1947); *Ouverture romane* (1947); *Marillac l'Epée,* dramatic prologue (1949); Piano Trio (1934); Piano Sonata (1934); Solo Cello Sonata (1940); *Suite champêtre* for Oboe, Clarinet, and Bassoon (1940); String Quartet (1945); *Varia-*

tions miniatures for String Trio (1949); *Morceau de concert* for Trombone and Piano (1949); *Tombeau de Chopin* for 2 Pianos (1949); *Sonata du souvenir* for Cello and Piano (1953); *La Cage des oiseaux (Birdcage)* for 4 Clarinets (1961).

Schoen-René, Anna E., noted German singer and teacher; b. Coblenz, Jan. 12, 1864; d. New York, Nov. 13, 1942. She studied singing with Pauline Viardot-García, and sang in opera before coming to America in 1895; she devoted herself to teaching in the U.S., first in Minneapolis and then in N.Y., where she joined the faculty of the Juilliard School of Music. She publ. a book of memoirs, *America's Musical Heritage* (N.Y., 1941).

Schoenberg (Schönberg), Arnold (Franz Walter), great Austrian-American composer whose new method of musical organization in 12 different tones related only to one another profoundly influenced the entire development of modern techniques of composition; b. Vienna, Sept. 13, 1874; d. Los Angeles, July 13, 1951. He studied at the Realschule in Vienna; learned to play the cello, and also became proficient on the violin. His father died when Schoenberg was 16; he took a job as a bank clerk to earn a living; an additional source of income was arranging popular songs and orchestrating operetta scores. Schoenberg's first original work was a group of 3 piano pieces which he wrote in 1894; it was also about that time that he began to take lessons in counterpoint from Alexander Zemlinsky, whose sister he married in 1901. He also played cello in Zemlinsky's instrumental group, Polyhymnia. In 1897 Schoenberg wrote his first String Quartet, in D major, which achieved public performance in Vienna on March 17, 1898. About the same time he wrote 2 songs with piano accompaniment which he designated as op. 1. In 1899 he wrote his first true masterpiece, *Verklärte Nacht,* set for string sextet, which was first performed in Vienna by the Rosé Quartet and members of the Vienna Phil., on March 18, 1902. It is a fine work, deeply imbued with the spirit of Romantic poetry, with its harmonic idiom stemming from Wagner's modulatory procedures; it remains Schoenberg's most frequently performed composition. About 1900, Schoenberg was engaged as conductor of several amateur choral groups in Vienna and its suburbs; this increased his interest in vocal music. He then began work on a choral composition, *Gurre-Lieder,* of monumental proportions, to the translated text of a poem by the Danish writer Jens Peter Jacobsen. For grandeur and opulence of orchestral sonority, it surpassed even the most formidable creations of Mahler or Richard Strauss; it calls for 5 solo voices, a speaker, 3 male choruses, an 8-part mixed chorus, and a very large orch. Special music paper of 48 staves had to be ordered for the MS. Schoenberg completed the first 2 parts of *Gurre-Lieder* in the spring of 1901, but the composition of the remaining section was delayed by 10 years; it was not until Feb. 23, 1913, that Franz Schreker was able to arrange its complete performance with the Vienna Phil. and its choral forces.

In 1901 Schoenberg moved to Berlin, where he joined E. von Wolzogen, F. Wedekind, and O. Bierbaum in launching an artistic cabaret, which they called Überbrettl. Schoenberg himself composed a theme song for it with trumpet obbligato, and conducted several shows. He met Richard Strauss, who helped him to obtain the Liszt Stipendium and a position as a teacher at the Stern Cons. Schoenberg returned to Vienna in 1903 and formed friendly relations with Gustav Mahler, who became a sincere supporter of Schoenberg's activities; Mahler's power in Vienna was then at its height, and he was able to help Schoenberg in his career as a composer. In March 1904 Schoenberg organized with Alexander Zemlinsky the Vereinigung Schaffender Tonkünstler for the purpose of encouraging performances of new music. Under its auspices Schoenberg conducted on Jan. 26, 1905, the first performance of his symph. poem *Pelleas und Melisande;* in this score occurs the first use of a trombone glissando. There followed a performance on Feb. 8, 1907, of Schoenberg's *Kammersymphonie,* op. 9, with the participation of the Rosé Quartet and the wind instrumentalists of the Vienna Phil.; the work produced much consternation in the audience and among critics because of its departure from traditional tonal harmony, with chords built on fourths and nominal dissonances used without immediate resolution. About the same time, Schoenberg turned to painting, which became his principal avocation. In his art, as in his music, he adopted the tenets of Expressionism, that is, freedom of personal expression within a self-defined program. Schoenberg's reputation as an independent musical thinker attracted to him such progressive-minded young musicians as Alban Berg, Anton von Webern, and Egon Wellesz, who followed Schoenberg in their own development. Schoenberg's 2nd String Quartet, composed in 1908, which included a soprano solo, was his last work that carried a definite key signature, if exception is made for his *Suite* for Strings, ostentatiously marked as in G major, which he wrote for school use in America in 1934. On Feb. 19, 1909, Schoenberg completed his piano piece op. 11, no. 1, which became the first musical composition to dispense with all reference to tonality. In 1910 Schoenberg was appointed to the faculty of the Vienna Academy of Music; in 1911 he completed his important theory book *Harmonielehre,* dedicated to the memory of Mahler; it comprises a traditional exposition of chords and progressions, but also offers illuminating indications of possible new musical developments, including fractional tones and melodies formed by the change of timbre on the same note. In 1911 he went again to Berlin, where he became an instructor at the Stern Cons. and also taught composition privately. In 1912 he brought out a work that attracted a great deal of attention: *5 Orchesterstücke,* which was performed for the first time not in Germany, not in Austria, but in London, under the direction of Sir Henry Wood, who conducted it there on Sept. 3, 1912; the critical reception was that of incomprehension, with a considerable measure of curiosity. The score was indeed revolutionary in nature, each movement representing an experiment in musical organization. In the same year Schoenberg produced another innovative work, a cycle of 21 songs with instrumental accompaniment, entitled *Pierrot Lunaire,* and consisting of 21 "melodramas," to German texts translated from verses by the Belgian poet Albert Giraud. Here Schoenberg made systematic use of *Sprechstimme,* with a gliding speech-song replacing precise pitch (not an entire innovation, for Engelbert Humperdinck had applied it in his incidental music to Rosmer's play *Königskinder* in 1897). The work was given, after some 40 rehearsals, in Berlin on Oct. 16, 1912, and the reaction was startling, the purblind critics drawing upon the strongest invective in their vocabulary to condemn the music.

Meanwhile, Schoenberg made appearances as conductor of his works in various European cities (Amsterdam, 1911; St. Petersburg, 1912; London, 1914). During World War I he was sporadically enlisted in military service; after the Armistice he settled in Mödling, near Vienna. Discouraged by his inability to secure performances for himself and his associates in the new music movement, he organized in Vienna, in Nov. 1918, the Verein für Musikalische Privataufführungen (Society for Private Musical Performances), from which critics were demonstratively excluded, and which ruled out any vocal expression of approval or disapproval. The organization disbanded in 1922. About that time Schoenberg began work on his *Suite* for Piano, op. 25, which was to be the first true 12-tone piece consciously composed in that idiom. In 1925 he was appointed prof. of a master class at the Prussian Academy of Arts in Berlin. With the advent of the beastly Nazi regime, the German Ministry of Education dismissed him from his post as a Jew. As a matter of record, Schoenberg had abandoned his Jewish faith in Vienna on March 21, 1898, and in a spirit of political accommodation converted to Catholicism, which was the principal faith in Austria; 35 years later, horrified by the hideous persecution of Jews at the hands of the Nazis, he was moved to return to his ancestral faith and was reconverted to Judaism in Paris on July 24, 1933. With the rebirth of his hereditary consciousness, he turned to specific Jewish themes in works such as *Survivor from Warsaw* and *Moses und Aron.* Although Schoenberg was well known in the musical world, he had difficulty obtaining a teaching position; he finally accepted the invitation of Joseph Malkin, founder of the Malkin Cons. of Boston, to join its faculty. He arrived in the U.S. on Oct. 31, 1933. After teaching in Boston for a season, he moved to Hollywood. In 1935 he became a prof. of music at the Univ. of Southern Calif., and in 1936 accepted a similar position at the Univ. of Calif. in Los Angeles, where he taught until 1944, when he reached the mandatory retirement age of 70. He experienced considerable financial difficulties and applied for a Guggenheim fellowship but, incredibly, was turned down. On April 11, 1941, he became an American citizen. In 1947 he received the Award of Merit for Distinguished Achievements from the National Inst. of Arts and Letters. In the U.S. he changed the original spelling of his name from Schönberg to Schoenberg.

In 1924 Schoenberg's creative evolution reached the all-important point at which he found it necessary to establish a new governing principle of tonal relationship, which he called the "method of composing with 12 different notes related entirely to one another." This method was adumbrated in Schoenberg's music as early as 1914 and is used partially in his *5 Klavierstücke,* op. 23, and in his *Serenade,* op. 24; it was employed for the first time in its integral form in the piano *Suite,* op. 25 (1924); in it, the thematic material is based on a group of 12 different notes arrayed in a certain pre-arranged order; such a tone row was henceforth Schoenberg's mainspring of thematic invention; development was provided by the devices of inversion, retrograde, and retrograde inversion of the basic series; allowing for transposition, 48 forms were obtainable in all, with counterpoint and harmony, as well as melody, derived from the basic tone row. Immediate repetition of thematic notes was admitted; the realm of rhythm remained free. As with most historic innovations, the 12-tone technique was not the creation of Schoenberg alone but was, rather, a logical development of many currents of musical thought. Josef Matthias Hauer rather unconvincingly claimed priority in laying the foundations of the 12-tone method; among others who had elaborated similar ideas at about the same time with Schoenberg was Jef Bolyscheff, a Russian émigré who expounded his theory in a publication entitled "12 Tondauer-Musik." Instances of themes consisting of 12 different notes are found in the *Faust Symphony* of Liszt and in the tone poem *Also sprach Zarathustra* of Richard Strauss in the section on Science. Schoenberg's great achievement was the establishment of the basic 12-tone row and its changing forms as foundations of a new musical language; using this idiom, he was able to write music of great expressive power. In general usage, the 12-tone method is often termed "dodecaphony," from Greek *dodeca,* "12," and *phone,* "sound." The tonal composition of the basic row is devoid of tonality; an analysis of Schoenberg's works shows that he avoided using major triads in any of their inversions, and allowed the use of only the 2nd inversion of a minor triad. Schoenberg deprecated the term "atonality" that was commonly applied to his music. He suggested, only half in jest, the term "atonicality," i.e., absence of the dominating tonic. The most explicit work of Schoenberg couched in the 12-tone idiom was his *Klavierstück,* op. 33a, written in 1928–29, which exemplifies the clearest use of the tone row in chordal combinations. Other works that present a classical use of dodecaphony are *Begleitungsmusik zu einer Lichtspielszene,* op. 34 (1929–30); Violin Concerto (1934–36); and Piano Concerto (1942). Schoenberg's disciples Alban Berg and Anton von Webern followed his 12-tone method in general outlines but with some personal deviations; thus, Berg accepted the occasional use of triadic harmonies, and Webern built tone rows in symmetric groups. Other composers who made systematic use of the 12-tone method were Egon Wellesz, Ernst Krenek, René Leibowitz, Roberto Gerhard, Humphrey Searle, and Luigi Dallapiccola. As time went on, dodecaphony became a lingua franca of universal currency; even in Russia, where Schoenberg's theories were for many years unacceptable on ideological grounds, several composers, including Shostakovich in his last works, made use of 12-tone themes, albeit without integral development. Ernest Bloch used 12-tone subjects in his last string quartets, but he refrained from applying inversions and retrograde forms of his tone rows. Stravinsky, in his old age, turned to the 12-tone method of composition in its total form, with regrograde, inversion, and retrograde inversion; his conversion was the greatest artistic vindication for Schoenberg, who regarded Stravinsky as his most powerful antagonist, but Schoenberg was dead when Stravinsky saw the light of dodecaphony.

Schoenberg's personality was both heroic and egocentric; he made great sacrifices to sustain his artistic convictions, but he was also capable of engaging in bitter polemics when he felt that his integrity was under attack. He strongly opposed the claims of Hauer and others for the priority of the 12-tone method of composition, and he vehemently criticized in the public press the implication he saw in Thomas Mann's novel *Doktor Faustus,* in which the protagonist was described as the inventor of the 12-tone method of composition; future historians, Schoenberg argued, might confuse fiction with facts, and credit the figment of Mann's imagination with Schoenberg's own discovery. He was also subject to superstition in the form of triskaidecaphobia, the fear of the number 13; he seriously believed that there was something fateful in the circumstance of his birth on the 13th of the month. Noticing that the title of his work *Moses und Aaron* contained 13 letters, he crossed out the 2nd "a" in Aaron to make it 12. When he turned 76 and someone remarked facetiously that the sum of the digits of his age was 13, he seemed genuinely upset, and during his last illness in July 1951 he expressed his fear of not surviving July 13; indeed, he died on that date. Schoenberg placed his MSS in the Music Division of the Library of Congress in Washington, D.C.; the remaining materials were deposited after his death at the Schoenberg Inst. at the Univ. of Southern Calif. in Los Angeles. Schoenberg's centennial in 1974 was commemorated worldwide. A *Journal of the Schoenberg Institute* began publication in 1976, under the editorship of Leonard Stein.

WORKS: FOR THE STAGE: *Erwartung,* monodrama, op. 17 (1909; Prague, June 6, 1924, Zemlinsky conducting); *Die glückliche Hand,* drama with music, to Schoenberg's own libretto, op. 18 (1910–13; Vienna, Oct. 14, 1924, Stiedry conducting); *Von Heute auf Morgen,* opera in one act, op. 32 (1928–29; Frankfurt, Feb. 1, 1930, W. Steinberg conducting); *Moses und Aron,* biblical drama, to Schoenberg's own libretto (2 acts composed 1930–32; 3rd act begun in 1951, but not completed; radio perf. of Acts 1 and 2, Hamburg, March 12, 1954; stage perf., Zürich Festival of the International Society for Contemporary Music, June 6, 1957, Rosbaud conducting).

FOR ORCH.: *Pelleas und Melisande,* symph. poem after Maeterlinck, op. 5 (1902–3; Vienna, Jan. 26, 1905, Schoenberg conducting); *Kammersymphonie* No. 1, for 15 Instruments, op. 9 (1906; Vienna, Feb. 8, 1907; arranged for Orch., 1922; new version for Orch., op. 9b, 1935); *5 Orchester-Stücke,* op. 16 (1909; London, Sept. 3, 1912, Henry Wood conducting; revised 1922 and 1949); *3 Little Pieces* for Chamber Orch. (1911; Berlin, Oct. 10, 1957); *Variations,* op. 31 (1926–28; Berlin, Dec. 2, 1928, Furtwängler conducting); *Begleitungsmusik zu einer Lichtspielszene (Accompaniment to a Cinema Scene),* op. 34 (1929–30; Berlin, Nov. 6, 1930, Klemperer conducting); Suite in G major for Strings (1934; Los Angeles, May 18, 1935, Klemperer conducting); Violin Concerto, op. 36 (1934–36; Philadelphia, Dec. 6, 1940; Krasner, violinist; Stokowski conducting); 2nd Chamber Symph., op. 38a (1906–16 and 1939; N.Y., Dec. 15, 1940, Stiedry conducting; op. 38b is an arrangement for 2 Pianos, 1941–42); Piano Concerto, op. 42 (1942; N.Y., Feb. 6, 1944; Steuermann, pianist; Stokowski conducting); *Theme and Variations* for Wind Band, op. 43a (1943; arranged for Orch., op. 43b, Boston, Oct. 20, 1944, Koussevitzky conducting).

FOR CHORUS: *Gurre-Lieder* for Soli, Mixed Chorus, and Orch. (1900–3 and 1910–11; Vienna, Feb. 23, 1913, Schreker conducting); *Friede auf Erden,* op. 13 (1907); 4 pieces for Mixed Chorus, op. 27 (1925); *3 Satires,* op. 28 (1925); 3 German folk songs (Vienna, Nov. 1929); 6 pieces for Men's Chorus, op. 35 (1929–30); *Kol Nidre* for Speaker, Chorus, and Orch., op. 39 (Los Angeles, Oct. 4, 1938); *A Survivor from Warsaw* for Narrator, Chorus, and Orch., op. 46 (1947; Albuquerque, Nov. 4, 1948); 3 German folk songs for Chorus a cappella, op. 49 (1948); *Dreimal tausend Jahre* for Mixed Chorus a cappella, op. 50a (Fylkingen, Sweden, Oct. 29, 1949); *De Profundis* for Chorus a cappella, to a Hebrew text, op. 50b (1950; Cologne, Jan. 29, 1954). The oratorio *Die Jakobsleiter,* begun in 1917, was left unfinished; a performing version was prepared by Winfried Zillig, and given for the first time in Vienna on June 16, 1961.

CHAMBER MUSIC: String Quartet in D major (perf. in Vienna in 1897, but not heard again until it was revived at the Library of Congress in Washington, D.C., on Feb. 8, 1952); *Verklärte Nacht (Transfigured Night),* sextet for Strings, op. 4 (1899; Vienna, March 18, 1902; arranged for String Orch., 1917; revised 1943); String Quartet No. 1, in D minor, op. 7 (1904–5; Vienna, Feb. 5, 1907); String Quartet No. 2, in F-sharp minor, op. 10, with Voice (1907–8; Vienna, Dec. 1908); Serenade for Clarinet, Bass Clarinet, Mandolin, Guitar, Violin, Viola, and Cello, op. 24 (4th movement with a sonnet by Petrarch for Baritone; 1920–23; Donaueschingen, July 20, 1924); Quintet for Flute, Oboe, Clarinet, Horn, and Bassoon, op. 26 (1923–24; Vienna, Sept. 13, 1924); Suite for 2 Clarinets, Bass Clarinet, Violin, Viola, Cello, and Piano, op. 29 (1925–26; Paris, Dec. 15, 1927); String Quartet No. 3, op. 30 (Vienna, Sept. 19, 1927); String Quartet No. 4, op. 37 (1936; Los Angeles, Jan. 9, 1937); *Ode to Napoleon,* after Byron, for String Quartet, and Reciter (1942; also in version with String Orch., N.Y., Nov. 23, 1944); String Trio, op. 45 (1946; Cambridge, Mass., March 1947); *Phantasy* for Violin, with Piano Accompaniment (Los Angeles, Sept. 13, 1949).

SONGS: 2 songs, op. 1 (1898); 4 songs, op. 2 (1899); 6 songs, op. 3 (1899–1903); 8 songs, op. 6 (1903–5); 6 songs, op. 8 (with Orch.; 1903–5); 2 ballads, op. 12 (1907); 2 songs, op. 14 (1907–8); cycle of 15 poems from Stefan George's *Das Buch der hängenden Gärten* (1908–9; Vienna, Jan. 14, 1910); *Herzgewächse*, after Maeterlinck, for Soprano, with Celesta, Harmonium, and Harp, op. 20 (1911); *Pierrot Lunaire*, 21 poems by Albert Giraud, for Sprechstimme with Piano, Flute (interchangeable with Piccolo), Clarinet (interchangeable with Bass Clarinet), Violin (interchangeable with Viola), and Cello, op. 21 (Berlin, Oct. 16, 1912); 4 songs, op. 22 (with Orch.; 1913–16; Frankfurt, Feb. 21, 1932); 3 songs, op. 48 (1933).

FOR KEYBOARD: Piano: *3 Klavierstücke*, op. 11 (1909; revised 1924); *6 kleine Klavierstücke*, op. 19 (1911); *5 Klavierstücke*, op. 23 (1920–23); *Suite*, op. 25 (1921–23); *Klavierstück*, op. 33a (1928–29); *Klavierstück*, op. 33b (1931); organ: *Variations on a Recitative*, op. 40 (1941).

ARRANGEMENTS AND TRANSCRIPTIONS: 2 chorale preludes by Bach, for Large Orch.: No. 1, *Komm, Gott, Schöpfer, Heiliger Geist*, and No. 2, *Schmücke dich, O liebe Seele* (1922); *Prelude and Fugue* in E-flat major for Organ by Bach, for Large Orch. (1928); Piano Quartet No. 1, in G minor, op. 25, by Brahms, for Orch. (1937); also a Cello Concerto, transcribed from a Harpsichord Concerto by G.M. Monn (1932–33); Concerto for String Quartet and Orch. after Handel's Concerto Grosso, op. 6, No. 7 (1933); etc.

WRITINGS: *Harmonielehre* (Vienna, 1911,; 3rd ed., revised, 1922; abridged Eng. trans. as *Theory of Harmony*, N.Y., 1947; complete Eng. trans., 1978); *Models for Beginners in Composition* (N.Y., 1942; 3rd ed., revised, 1972, by L. Stein); *Style and Idea* (N.Y., 1950; enlarged ed. by L. Stein, London, 1975); *Structural Functions of Harmony* (N.Y., 1954; 2nd ed., revised, 1969, by L. Stein); *Preliminary Exercises in Counterpoint*, ed. by L. Stein (London, 1963); *Fundamentals of Musical Composition*, ed. by L. Stein (London, 1967); also numerous essays in German and American publications.

BIBLIOGRAPHY: COLLECTED WORKS, SOURCE MATERIAL: J. Rufer et al. are preparing a complete ed. of his works, *Arnold Schönberg: Sämtliche Werke* (Mainz, 1966—). Rufer has also compiled an annotated catalogue, *Das Werk Arnold Schönbergs* (Kassel, 1959; Eng. trans., 1962; 2nd German ed., revised, 1975). I. Vojtěch has ed. vol. I of the *Gesammelte Schriften* (Frankfurt, 1976).

See also the following: Special issue of *Der Merker*, II/17 (1911); *A. S.: Mit Beiträgen von Alban Berg, Paris von Gutersloh . . .* (essays by 11 admirers; Munich, 1912); E. Wellesz, "S. and Beyond," *Musical Quarterly* (Jan. 1916); idem, *A. S.* (Leipzig, 1921; Eng. trans., revised, London, 1925); C. Gray, "A. S., A Critical Study," *Music & Letters* (Jan. 1922); E. Stein, *Praktischer Leitfaden zu S.s Harmonielehre* (Vienna, 1923); P. Stefan, *A. S.: Wandlung, Legende, Erscheinung, Bedeutung* (Vienna, 1924); *A. S. zum 60. Geburtstag* (articles by friends and pupils; Vienna, 1934); H. Wind, *Die Endkrise der bürgerlichen*

Musik und die Rolle A. S.s (Vienna, 1935); R. Hill, "S.'s Tone-Rows and the Tonal System of the Future," *Musical Quarterly* (Jan. 1936); M. Armitage, ed., *A. S.* (contains essays by Sessions, Krenek, E. Stein, C. Engel, Klemperer, P. Pisk, P. Stefan et al.; also 2 by Schoenberg: "Tonality and Form" and "Problems of Harmony"; N.Y., 1937); H. Jalowetz, "On the Spontaneity of S.'s Music," *Musical Quarterly* (Oct. 1944); D. Milhaud, "To A. S. on His Seventieth Birthday: Personal Recollections," ibid.; R. Sessions, "S. in the United States," *Tempo*, no. 9 (1944; revised in *Tempo*, no. 103, 1972); P. Gradenwitz, "The Idiom and Development in S.'s Quartets," *Music & Letters*, XXVI (1945); R. Leibowitz, *S. et son école* (Paris, 1947; Eng. trans., 1949); D. Newlin, *Bruckner, Mahler, S.* (N.Y., 1947; revised ed., 1978); W. Rubsamen, "S. in America," *Musical Quarterly* (Oct. 1951); H. Stuckenschmidt, *A. S.* (Zürich, 1951; 2nd ed., revised, 1957; Eng. trans., 1959); G. Perle, "S.'s Later Style," *Music Review*, XIII (1952); J. Rufer, *Die Komposition mit zwölf Tönen* (Berlin, 1952; Eng. trans. as *Composition with 12 Notes Related to One Another*, London, 1954); L. Rognoni, *Espressionismo e dodecafonia* (Turin, 1954; 2nd ed., revised, 1966, as *La scuola musicale di Vienna*); H. Keller, "S.'s 'Moses and Aron,'" *Score*, no. 21 (1957); T. Tuttle, "S.'s Compositions for Piano Solo," *Music Review*, XVIII (1957); K. Wörner, *Gotteswort und Magie* (Heidelberg, 1959; Eng. trans., revised, 1963, as *S.'s "Moses and Aron"*); M. Kassler, *The Decision of A. S.'s Twelve-Note-Class-System and Related Systems* (Princeton, 1961); H. Pauli, "Zu S.s 'Jakobsleiter,'" *Schweizerische Musikzeitung/Revue Musicale Suisse*, CII (1962); G. Perle, *Serial Composition and Atonality: An Introduction to the Music of S., Berg and Webern* (Berkeley, 1962; 5th ed., revised, 1982); W. Rogge, *Das Klavierwerke A. S.s* (Regensburg, 1964); P. Friedheim, "Rhythmic Structure in S.'s Atonal Compositions," *Journal of the American Musicological Society*, XIX (1966); J. Meyerowitz, *A. S.* (Berlin, 1967); B. Boretz and E. Cone, eds., *Perspectives on S. and Stravinsky* (Princeton, 1968); G. Krieger, *S.s Werke für Klavier* (Göttingen, 1968); A. Payne, *S.* (London, 1968); W. Reich, *A. S., oder Der konservative Revolutionär* (Vienna, 1968; Eng. trans., 1971); R. Brinkmann, *A. S.: Drei Klavierstücke Op. 11* (also includes bibliography of publ. writings; Wiesbaden, 1969); R. Leibowitz, *S.* (Paris, 1969); D. Rexroth, *A. S. als Theoretiker der tonalen Harmonik* (Bonn, 1971); J. Maegaard, *Studien zur Entwicklung des dodekaphonen Satzes bei A. S.* (Copenhagen, 1972); A. Whittall, *S. Chamber Music* (London, 1972); E. Freitag, *A. S. in Selbstzeugnissen und Bilddokumenten* (Reinbek, 1973); J. Samson, "S.'s 'Atonal' Music," *Tempo*, no. 109 (1974); E. Steiner, "S.'s Quest: Newly Discovered Works from His Early Years," *Musical Quarterly* (Oct. 1974); H. Stuckenschmidt, *S.: Leben, Umwelt, Werk* (Zürich, 1974; Eng. trans. as *S.: His Life, World and Work*, London, 1976); C. Rosen, *A. S.* (N.Y., 1975); G. Schubert, *S.s frühe Instrumentation* (Baden-Baden, 1975); M. Macdonald, *S.* (London, 1976); D. Newlin, *S. Remembered: Diaries and Recollections (1938–76)* (N.Y., 1980).

Schoenefeld, Henry, American pianist and composer; b. Milwaukee, Oct. 4, 1857; d. Los Angeles, Aug. 4, 1936. He studied at the Leipzig Cons.; upon his return to America he conducted a German male chorus in Chicago (1891–1902) and subsequently conducted various German choral societies in California. He merits consideration in American music because he was one of the earliest American composers to use authentic Indian musical sources. The result of his striving in this direction was a "grand opera," *Atala, or The Love of 2 Savages* (which was never produced); *Suite caractéristique* for String Orch. (based on Indian themes); *Wachicanta,* an Indian pantomime; *2 Indian Legends* for Orch.; *Rural Symphony* (won a $500 prize offered by the National Cons. of N.Y., 1892); *Danse américaine* for Piano; many other piano pieces in the salon style (*Little Soldier's March, Valse élégante, Mystics of the Woods, Valse noble,* etc.).

BIBLIOGRAPHY: Rupert Hughes, *Contemporary American Composers* (Boston, 1900; pp. 128–35).

Schöffler, Paul, German operatic bass; b. Dresden, Sept. 15, 1897; d. Amersham, England, Nov. 21, 1977. He studied in Dresden and Berlin; in 1925 made his debut at the Dresden State Opera; in 1937 became a member of the Vienna State Opera. He made his American debut with the Metropolitan Opera in N.Y. on Jan. 26, 1950, as Jokanaan in *Salome;* continued there, with some interruptions, until 1956; returned to the Metropolitan in 1963 to sing the role of Hans Sachs in *Die Meistersinger* (Jan. 14, 1963); he remained on its roster until 1965, when he went to England.

Scholes, Percy Alfred, eminent English writer on music; b. Leeds, July 24, 1877; d. Vevey, Switzerland, July 31, 1958. (He pronounced his name "Skoles.") He took his B.Mus. at Oxford in 1908, and later the M.A., D.Litt., and Hon.D.Mus., as also the Hon.Litt.D., at Leeds; received his doctorat ès lettres from the Univ. of Lausanne (1934); was an organist at various churches until 1905; was an extension lecturer at the univs. of Oxford, Cambridge, London, and Manchester; in 1908 founded the Home Music Study Union, and until 1921 edited its publications, the *Music Student* and *Music and Youth;* toured the U.S. as a lecturer in 1915 and on 4 later occasions; was music critic of the *London Evening Standard* and the *Observer* (1920–27), and for the BBC (1923–29); from 1925–30 edited the Audiographic Series of Pianola and Duo Art Rolls; in 1928 organized the Anglo-American Music Education Conferences (Lausanne, 1931, 1933); was music editor of *Radio Times* (1932–36); lived in Oxford, and for periods in Switzerland, where he later settled permanently. A writer of great literary attainments and stylistic grace, he succeeded in presenting music "appreciation" in a manner informative and stimulating to the layman and professional alike. His *Oxford Companion to Music* was unique in the lexicographical field in its vividness of presentation and its comprehensiveness. His scholarly biographies of Burney and Hawkins are among the finest of the genre.

WRITINGS: *Everyman and His Music* (1917); *An Introduction to British Music* (1918); *The Listener's Guide to Music* (1919; 10th ed., 1942); *Music Appreciation: Why and How?* (1920; 4th ed., 1925); *The Book of the Great Musicians* (3 vols., 1920; many eds.); New Works by Modern British Composers (2 series, 1921, 1924); *The Beginner's Guide to Harmony* (1922; several further eds.); *The Listener's History of Music* (3 vols., 1923–28; 4th ed., 1933); *Crotchets* (1924); *Learning to Listen by Means of the Gramophone* (1925); *Everybody's Guide to Broadcast Music* (1925); *The Appreciation of Music by Means of the Pianola and Duo Art* (1925); *A Miniature History of Music* (1928); *The Columbia History of Music through Eye and Ear* (5 albums of records with accompanying booklets; 1930–39; eds. in Japanese and Braille); *Music and Puritanism* (Vevey, 1934); *The Puritans and Music in England and New England* (London, 1934); *Music: The Child and the Masterpiece* (1935; American ed., *Music Appreciation: Its History and Technics*); *Radio Times Music Handbook* (1935; 3rd ed., 1936; American ed. as *The Scholes Music Handbook,* 1935); *The Oxford Companion to Music* (encyclopedia; London and N.Y., 1938; 9th completely revised ed., 1955; contains a glossary of pronunciation and over 1,100 portraits and pictures; the 10th ed. was edited by John Owen Ward, N.Y., 1970); *God Save the King: Its History and Romance* (London, 1942; new ed. as *God Save the Queen! The History and Romance of the World's First National Anthem,* London, 1954); *The Mirror of Music, 1844–1944, A Century of Musical Life in Britain as Reflected in the Pages of the "Musical Times"* (London, 1947); *The Great Dr. Burney* (2 vols., London, 1948); *Sir John Hawkins: Musician, Magistrate, and Friend of Johnson* (London, 1952); *The Concise Oxford Dictionary of Music* (London, 1952); *The Oxford Junior Companion to Music* (London, 1954); various pamphlets, e.g., *Song of Supper,* publ. by the London Vegetarian Society (1948); innumerable articles in the musical press; contributions to encyclopedias and dictionaries; etc.

Schollum, Robert, Austrian composer, musicologist, and critic; b. Vienna, Aug. 22, 1913. He studied piano and organ at the Vienna Academy of Music; composition with Joseph Marx. After World War II he settled in Linz as an organist and educator. In 1959 he was appointed prof. of singing at the Vienna Academy of Music. In 1961 he received the Austrian State Prize for composition, and in 1971 obtained the prize of the City of Vienna.

WORKS: 5 symphs. (1955, 1959, 1962, 1967, 1969); Violin Concerto (1961); 2 string quartets (1949, 1966); *Mosaik* for Oboe, Percussion, and Piano (1967); *Die Ameisen* for Cello and Piano (1974). He publ. several books: *Musik in der Volksbildung* (Vienna, 1962); *Egon Wellesz* (Vienna, 1964); *Die Wiener Schule. Entwicklung und Ergebnis* (Vienna, 1969); *Das kleine Wiener Jazzbuch* (Salzburg, 1970); *Singen als menschliche Kundgebung* (Vienna, 1970).

Scholtz, Herrmann, German pianist and composer; b. Breslau, June 9, 1845; d. Dresden, July 13, 1918. He studied in Breslau, with Plaidy in Leipzig, and with Hans von Bülow and Rheinberger in Munich; taught at the Munich Hochschule für Musik (1870–75); then went to Dresden. He was an accomplished pianist and a fine teacher; also wrote a number of piano pieces in a fashionable style: *Albumblätter, Mädchenlieder, Lyrische Blätter, Stimmungsbilder, Ballade,* etc. He edited Chopin's works for Peters; also edited the Piano Concerto, op. 15, of Brahms.

Scholz, Bernhard E., German conductor and composer; b. Mainz, March 30, 1835; d. Munich, Dec. 26, 1916. He studied with Ernst Pauer in Mainz and with Dehn in Berlin; after teaching in Munich, he was engaged as assistant court Kapellmeister in Hannover (1859–65); then conducted the Cherubini Society in Florence (1865–66); led the concerts of the Breslau Orch. Society (1871–82), and in the spring of 1883 succeeded Raff as director of the Hoch Cons. in Frankfurt; retired in 1908.
WORKS: Operas: *Carlo Rosa* (Munich, 1858); *Ziethen'sche Husaren* (Breslau, 1869); *Morgiane* (Munich, 1870); *Golo* (Nuremberg, 1875); *Der Trompeter von Säkkingen* (Wiesbaden, 1877); *Die vornehmen Wirte* (Leipzig, 1883); *Ingo* (Frankfurt, 1898); *Anno 1757* (Berlin, 1903); *Mirandolina* (Darmstadt, 1907); a great many choral works, with orch.; 2 symphs.; Piano Concerto; 2 string quartets; String Quintet; Piano Quartet; 2 piano trios; 3 violin sonatas; 5 cello sonatas; numerous piano pieces and songs.
WRITINGS: *Lehre vom Kontrapunkt und der Nachahmung* (1897); *Wohin treiben wir?* (1897; collection of essays); *Musikalisches und Persönliches* (1899); *Verklungene Weisen* (1911); ed. Dehn's *Lehre vom Kontrapunkt, dem Kanon und der Fuge* (1859; 2nd ed., 1883).

Schönbach, Dieter, German composer of the avant-garde; b. Stolp-Pommern, Feb. 18, 1931. He studied at the Freiburg Hochschule für Musik with Wolfgang Fortner; in 1959 he was appointed music director at the municipal theater in Bochum; he left Bochum in 1973. His style of composition is quaquaversal. He wrote the first genuine multimedia opera, *Wenn die Kälte in die Hütten tritt, um sich bei den Frierenden zu wärmen, weiss einer "Die Geschichte von einem Feuer"* (Kiel, 1968); a multimedia show, *Hymnus 2* (Munich, 1972); *Farben und Klänge,* in memory of Kandinsky, for Orch. (1958); Piano Concerto (1958); *Kammermusik* for 14 Instruments (1964); *Hoquetus* for 8 Wind Instruments (1964); 4 chamber music pieces, each titled *Canzona da sonar* (1966–67); *Atemmusik* for Fifes, Whistles, and some other "breath" Instruments (1969); also several liturgical cantatas to Latin texts. His *Canticum Psalmi Resurrectionis* was performed at the International Festival of Contemporary Music in Rome on June 13, 1959.

Schönberg, Arnold. See Schoenberg, Arnold.

Schonberg, Harold C., American music critic; b. New York, Nov. 29, 1915. He studied at Brooklyn College (B.A., 1937) and at N.Y. Univ. (M.A., 1938). He served in the army (1942–46); then was on the staff of the *N.Y. Sun* (1946–50); he was appointed to the music staff of the *N.Y. Times* in 1950; was senior music critic from 1960 until 1980. In 1971 he received the Pulitzer Prize "for distinguished criticism." In his concert reviews and feature articles he reveals a profound knowledge of music and displays a fine journalistic flair without assuming a posture of snobbish aloofness or descending to colloquial vulgarity. His intellectual horizon is exceptionally wide; he is well-versed in art, and can draw and paint; is a chess aficionado and covered knowledgeably the Spassky-Fischer match in Reykjavik in 1972 for the *N.Y. Times.* He publ. *Chamber and Solo Instrument Music* (N.Y., 1955); *The Collector's Chopin and Schumann* (N.Y., 1959); *The Great Pianists* (N.Y., 1963); *The Great Conductors* (N.Y., 1967); *Lives of the Great Composers* (N.Y., 1970; 2nd ed., N.Y., 1981); *Facing the Music* (N.Y., 1981).

Schönberg, Stig-Gustav, Swedish composer; b. Norrköping, May 13, 1933. He studied organ at the Royal College of Music in Stockholm (1953–60) and later with Flor Peeters in Belgium; took courses in composition with Larsson, Blomdahl, and Erland von Koch.
WORKS: *Toccata concertante* Nos. 1–4 for Organ (1954, 1968, 1970, 1972); *Intermezzo* for Orch. (1958); *Introduction and Allegro* for String Orch. (1958–59); *Lacrimae Domini* for Organ (1958); *5 Pieces* for Clarinet and Cello (1959); *Dialogues* for Flute and Clarinet (1960); 6 string quartets (1961, 1963, 1968, 1969, 1970, 1971–72); Concerto for Organ and String Orch. (Linköping, June 28, 1963); *Il dolce piano,* 10 preludes for Piano (1964); *Sinfonia aperta* (1965; revised 1971); 3 concertinos for String Orch. (1966); *Impressions* for Piano (1966); *Madeleine och Konrad,* ballet (1967; revised 1972); *Partita* for Clarinet and Piano (1968); *Concitatio* for Orch. (1968; revised 1971); *Impromptu visionario* for Orch. (1972); *Regina coeli* for Soprano, Chorus, Orch., and Organ (1973); *Sonate pastorale* for Oboe and Organ (1973); *Cantata gloriae* (1974).

Schönberger, Benno, pianist and composer; b. Vienna, Sept. 12, 1863; d. Wisborough Green, Sussex, March 9, 1930. He studied piano with Anton Door and composition with Bruckner and Volkmann at the Vienna Cons.; then took lessons with Liszt. After a European concert tour he went to London, where he taught at the Royal Academy of Music and appeared in chamber music concerts. For piano he wrote 3 sonatas, 3 rhapsodies, a Bolero, a Polonaise, and about 40 songs.

Schondorf, Johannes, German choral conductor and composer; b. Röbel, July 1, 1833; d. Güstrow, Oct. 4, 1912. He studied at the Stern Cons. in Berlin; then was a singing teacher at the Cathedral School in Güstrow; also conducted a choral society there. He publ. *Vaterländische Gesänge* for Mixed Voices; many school songs; also piano pieces.

Schöne, Lotte (original name, **Charlotte Bodenstein**), Austrian soprano; b. Vienna, Dec. 15, 1891; d. Paris, Dec. 22, 1977. She studied in Vienna; made her debut at the Vienna Volksoper in 1912; then sang at the Vienna Court (later State) Opera (1917–26); also at the Berlin Städtische Oper (1926–33); made many appearances at the Salzburg Festivals (1922–35). After leaving Germany in 1933, she went to Paris, became a French citizen, and made guest appearances at the Opéra and the Opéra-Comique; she retired from the stage in 1953. She was particularly successful in soubrette roles.

Schönstein, Karl, Austrian singer and government official; b. Ofen, June 26, 1797; d. Vienna, July 16, 1876. Before he assumed office, he had a career as a concert singer; was one of the earliest interpreters of Schubert's songs; Schubert's song cycle *Die schöne Müllerin* is dedicated to him.

Schönzeler, Hans-Hubert, German conductor and musicologist; b. Leipzig, June 22, 1925. He went to Australia as a youth, and studied conducting with Eugene Goossens at the New South Wales Cons. of Music in Sydney; later traveled in Europe, where he received further instruction in conducting with Rafael Kubelik, with Carlo Zecchi in Hilversum, the Netherlands, and with Paul van Kempen in Siena, Italy. He eventually made his home in London, where he led the 20th-Century Ensemble (1957–62). In 1967 he was appointed deputy chief conductor of the West Australian Symph. Orch. in Perth, while continuing his appearances as guest conductor in Western Europe. He publ. a biography of Bruckner (London and N.Y., 1970; revised ed., 1978) and composed piano pieces, a Viola Sonata, and songs.

Schoop, Paul, Swiss-American composer; b. Zürich, July 31, 1909; d. Los Angeles, Jan. 1, 1976. He studied piano in Paris with Alfred Cortot and Robert Casadesus, and in Berlin with Artur Schnabel; composition with Paul Dukas and with Hindemith and Schoenberg in the U.S. He settled in Los Angeles, and wrote music for films; also composed a comic opera, *The Enchanted Trumpet;* a symph. poem, *Fata Morgana;* and a number of ballet scores for productions of his sister, a modern dancer, Trudi Schoop.

Schopenhauer, Arthur, great German philosopher; b. Danzig, Feb. 22, 1788; d. Frankfurt, Sept. 21, 1860. Although his excursions into the realm of music are neither remarkable nor very valuable, they are stimulating, and have inspired a number of valuable contributions by modern investigators, especially in the field of musical esthetics. Wagner was influenced to a considerable extent by Schopenhauer's philosophical system.
BIBLIOGRAPHY: K. Fuchs, *Präliminarien zu einer Kritik der Tonkunst* (Greifswald, 1870); F. von Hausegger, *Richard Wagner und Arthur Schopenhauer* (Leipzig, 1878; 2nd ed., 1892); H. Dinger, *Die Weltanschauung Wagners in den Grund-* *gedanken ihrer Entwickelung* (Leipzig, 1893; traces especially the influence of Hegel and Schopenhauer); M. Seydel, *Arthur Schopenhauers Metaphysik der Musik* (Leipzig, 1895); E. Zoccoli, *L'estetica di Schopenhauer* (Milan, 1901); G. Melli, *La filosofia di Schopenhauer* (Florence, 1905; treats the relations between Schopenhauer and Wagner); Th. Lessing, *Schopenhauer, Wagner, Nietzsche* (Munich, 1906); A. Mäcklenburg, "Schopenhauer und seine Stellung zur Musik," *Die Musik* (Dec. 1908); F.J. Wagner, *Beiträge zur Würdigung der Musiktheorie Schopenhauers* (Diss., Univ. of Bonn, 1910); A. von Gottschalk, *Beethoven und Schopenhauer* (Blanckenburg, 1912); L. Dunton Green, "Schopenhauer and Music," *Musical Quarterly* (April 1930).

Schorr, Friedrich, baritone; b. Nagyvárad, Hungary, Sept. 2, 1888; d. Farmington, Conn., Aug. 14, 1953. He studied law at the Univ. of Vienna, and also took private lessons in singing; appeared with the Chicago Opera Co. (1911–12); then was a member of the opera companies in Graz (1912–16), Prague (1916–18), and Cologne (1918–23), and of the Berlin State Opera (1923–31). He sang Wolfram at the Metropolitan Opera in N.Y. on Feb. 14, 1924, and continued as a member until the season 1942–43; sang Wotan at the Bayreuth Festivals in 1925, 1927, 1928, and 1930; specialized in Wagnerian opera. He sang the leading roles of the American premieres at the Metropolitan of Krenek's *Jonny Spielt Auf* (1929) and Weinberger's *Schwanda* (1931).

Schott, Anton, German tenor; b. Castle Staufeneck, June 24, 1846; d. Stuttgart, Jan. 6, 1913. He was in the Prussian army; after the Franco-Prussian War, he sang at the Munich Opera (1871) and the Berlin Opera (1872–75); then in London and in Italy; made his American debut at the Metropolitan Opera in N.Y. as Tannhäuser (Nov. 17, 1884); remained on its roster until 1885, and again in 1886–87. He excelled as an interpreter of Wagnerian roles. He publ. a polemical brochure, *Hie Welf, hie Waibling* (1904).

Schott, Bernhard, the founder of the German music publishing firm **B. Schotts Söhne;** b. Eltville, Aug. 10, 1748; d. Sandholf, near Heidesheim, April 26, 1809. His firm was founded in 1770; after his death the business was carried on by his sons **Johann Andreas Schott** (1781–1840) and **Johann Joseph Schott** (1782–1855) under the firm name of B. Schotts Söhne. The 2 sons of Johann Andreas Schott, **Franz Philip Schott** (b. July 30, 1811; d. May 8, 1874) and **Peter Schott** (d. Paris, Sept. 20, 1894), succeeded to the business; Peter Schott was manager of the Paris and Brussels branches; subsequently **Peter Schott, Jr.,** took over the directorship, together with Ludwig Strecker and Franz von Landwehr. B. Schotts Söhne publ. the journals *Cäcilia* (1824–48), *Süddeutsche Musikzeitung* (1852–69), and *Melos* (1920–34 and from 1946). Dr. Ludwig Strecker, son of the director of the same name (d. in 1978), and Heinz Schneider Schott, Dr. Strecker's son-in-law, became the directors (1952). Arno Volk was chairman of the board of directors in 1974–77. The main office is at Mainz, and a principal branch is at London. (Schott Frères at Brussels is now an entirely different firm.) The Schott catalogue is one of the richest in the world; it includes works by Beethoven (last quartets, 9th Symph.), operas by Donizetti, Rossini, etc.; Wagner's *Meistersinger, Ring des Nibelungen,* and *Parsifal;* virtually all works by Hindemith, and a great number of other contemporary works. Schott is the publisher of the Riemann Musik-Lexikon.

BIBLIOGRAPHY: W. Altmann, *Richard Wagners Briefwechsel mit seinen Verlegern* (Leipzig, 1911; vol. II contains correspondence with Schott); L. Strecker, *Richard Wagner als Verlagsgefährte* (Mainz, 1951); *Der Musikverlag B. Schott* (Mainz, 1954).

Schouwman, Hans, Dutch pianist and composer; b. Gorinchem, Aug. 8, 1902; d. The Hague, April 8, 1967. He was a pupil of Peter van Anrooy; developed a singing voice and gave recitals, accompanying himself on the piano. WORKS: *3 danswijzen (3 Dance Tunes)* for Voice, 2 Flutes, Strings, and Percussion (1938); *5 Sketches* for Clarinet and Small Orch. (1942); *Friesland,* 4 songs for Voice and Orch. (1945); *Memento mori* for Alto, Chorus, and Small Orch. (1947); *Suite* for Amateur Orch. (1958); *De Prinses op de erwt* for Orch. (1965); 2 oboe sonatinas (1940, 1944); *Aubade en Barcarolle* for Clarinet and Piano (1944); Trio for Clarinet, Bassoon, and Piano (1944); *Romance en Humoreske* for Bassoon and Piano (1944); *4 Pieces* for Flute and Piano (1944); *2 Legends* for Horn and Piano (1944); *Notturno* for Mezzo-soprano, Cello, and Piano (1949); *Nederlandse suite* for Wind Quintet (1953); *Om de kribbe* for Soprano, Contralto, Female Chorus, and Piano (1952); *3 Preludes* for Piano, left-hand (1959); 2 series of old Dutch songs, with string accompaniment; arrangements of folk songs for various instruments; vocal duets; solo songs.

Schrade, Leo, eminent German musicologist; b. Allenstein, Dec. 13, 1903; d. Spéracédès (Alpes-Maritimes), Sept. 21, 1964. He studied with Hermann Halbig at the Univ. of Heidelberg (1923–27), with Adolf Sandberger at the Univ. of Munich, and with Theodor Kroyer at the Univ. of Leipzig, obtaining his Dr.Phil. in 1927 with the dissertation *Die ältesten Denkmäler der Orgelmusik* (publ. in Münster, 1928); held teaching positions in music at the Univ. of Königsberg (1928–32), then at the Univ. of Bonn (from 1932). In 1937 he emigrated to the U.S.; was on the faculty of Yale Univ. (1938–58), where he taught music history; in 1958 he was appointed to the music faculty of the Univ. of Basel. During the academic season 1962–63 he was Charles Eliot Norton Lecturer at Harvard; his lectures were publ. under the title *Tragedy in the Art of Music* (Cambridge, Mass., 1964). He publ. a number of books and articles of prime documentary value, promulgating some important musico-historical theories. WRITINGS: *Die handschriftliche Überlieferung der ältesten Instrumentalmusik* (Habilitations-

schrift, Univ. of Königsberg, 1929; publ. in Lahr, 1931); *Beethoven in France* (New Haven and London, 1942); *Monteverdi* (N.Y., 1950; 2nd ed., 1964); *Bach: The Conflict between the Sacred and the Secular* (N.Y., 1954); *W.A. Mozart* (Bern, 1964). He ed. Luis Milán's *Libro de música de vihuela* (Leipzig, 1927); Virdung's *Musica getutscht* (Kassel, 1931); other collections. His edition of the complete *Polyphonic Music of the 14th Century* began to appear in 1956; at his death the first 4 vols. were publ.: I: *The "Roman de Fauvel"; The Works of Philippe de Vitry; French Cycles of the "Ordinarium Missae";* II–III: *The Works of Guillaume de Machaut;* IV: *The Works of Francesco Landini.* Schrade's "Commentary Notes" to these vols. were publ. in Monaco. By 1978, 8 more vols. had appeared under the editorship of Frank Lloyd Harrison, W. Thomas Marrocco, Kurt von Fischer, F. Alberto Gallo, and Ernest H. Sanders, with 12 more vols. announced as in progress under the editorship of Kurt von Fischer. Schrade was honored with a Festschrift: *Music and History: Leo Schrade on the Occasion of His 60th Birthday* (Cologne, 1963; London, 1965).

Schrader, Barry, American composer; b. Johnstown, Pa., June 26, 1945. He enrolled in the Univ. of Pittsburgh in English literature (B.A., 1967) and in musicology (M.A., 1970); also served as an organist at Heinz Chapel. In 1969–70 he studied electroacoustic techniques with Morton Subotnick. In 1970 he moved to Los Angeles and attended the Calif. Inst. of the Arts (M.F.A. in composition, 1971); later joined its faculty. From 1975 to 1978 he also taught at Calif. State Univ. at Los Angeles. He organized a series of electro-acoustic music programs under the name "Currents," held in Los Angeles from 1973 to 1979; also participated in the Australian International Electronic Music Festival, the Biennale de Paris, and the Tokyo Gakugei Univ. Exhibition of Electronic Music. Most of his music is for electronic sound; in his *Bestiary* (1972–74), Schrader explored the potentialities of synthesizing new timbres; in his *Trinity* (1976) he transmuted given timbres to more complex sonorities. In his *Lost Atlantis* he essayed a programmatic use of electronic sound. He also experimented in combining live music with electronic resources, as in his work *Moon-Whales and other Moon Songs* (1982–83). He publ. *Introduction to Electro-Acoustical Music* (Englewood Cliffs, N.J., 1982). He was the founder and director of the Electro-Acoustical Music Marathon, an annual festival held at the Calif. Inst. of the Arts. WORKS: *Signature for Tempo* for Soprano and Piano (1966); *Serenade* for Electronic Tape (1969); *Incantation* for Electronic Tape (1970); *Sky Ballet* for Sound Environment (1970); *Elysium* for Harp, Dancers, Electronic Tape, and Pictorial Projections (1971); *Besitary* for Electronic Tape (1972–74); *Death of the Red Planet,* film score (1973); *Heavy Light,* film score (1973); *Exploratorium,* film score (1975); *Trinity* for Electronic Tape (1976); *Lost Atlantis* for Electronic Tape (1977); *Mobiles,* film score (1978); *Along the Way,* film score (1980); *Galaxy of Terror,* film score (1981); *Moon-Whales* *and Other Moon Songs* for Soprano and Electronic Tape (1982–83).

Schradieck, Henry, German-American violinist; b. Hamburg, April 29, 1846; d. Brooklyn, March 25, 1918. He studied violin as a child with Léonard in Brussels (1854–58), and later with Ferdinand David in Leipzig (1859–61). He then served as concertmaster of the Phil. Concerts in Hamburg (1868–74) and of the Gewandhaus Orch. in Leipzig (1874–82). In 1883 he emigrated to America, where he was active as a violin teacher in Cincinnati and N.Y. He publ. valuable technical studies for the violin: *25 grosse Studien für Geige allein; Scale-studies; Technical Studies; Guide to the Study of Chords; Finger Exercises; Schule der Violintechnik* (3 parts; also adapted for viola).

Schramm, Margit, German operetta soprano; b. Dortmund, July 21, 1935. She was educated at the Dortmund Cons. and made her debut at Saarbrücken in 1956. She sang in Koblenz (1957–58), in Munich at the Gärtnerplatz Theater (1959–64), in Berlin at the Theater des Westens (1965–66), and in the municipal theaters in Dortmund (1967). In 1968 she joined the ensemble of the State Theater in Wiesbaden. Her repertoire of German and Austrian operettas is vast and impressive.

Schramm, Rudolf, German-American musician; b. Grieffenberg, Silesia, July 9, 1902; d. Westwood, N.J., April 6, 1981. He studied in Breslau and Leipzig; in 1925 he emigrated to the U.S., where he became active as an arranger and compiler of educational music; wrote songs in a semiclassical manner and composed music for 86 documentary films.

Schreck, Gustav, German composer and teacher; b. Zeulenroda, Sept. 8, 1849; d. Leipzig, Jan. 22, 1918. He studied at the Leipzig Cons. with Plaidy, Papperitz, and Jadassohn; after a few years of teaching in Finland, he returned to Leipzig and joined the faculty of the Cons. there in 1887. His works are mostly vocal; he wrote an oratorio, *Christus der Auferstandene,* and other sacred works; also Sonata for Bassoon and Piano; Sonata for Oboe and Piano; *Divertimento* for 9 Woodwinds; piano pieces; songs.

Schreiber, Frederick C., Austrian-American organist and composer; b. Vienna, Jan. 13, 1895. He studied piano, cello, and composition in Vienna; was on the faculty of the Vienna Cons. of Music (1927–38). In 1939 he emigrated to the U.S. and settled in N.Y., where he served as chorus director and organist at the Reformed Protestant Church (1939–58). A prolific composer, he wrote a great number of works in various genres, among them 7 symphs. (1927–57); *The Beatitudes,* a symph. trilogy for Orch. and Chorus (1950); *Christmas Suite* for Orch. (1967); *Images* for Orch. (1971); *Contrasts* for Orch. (1972); 2 piano concertos; Cello Concerto; 2 violin concertos; *Variations on a German Folksong* (1974); numerous choral pieces; chamber music, in-

cluding 2 string quintets, 7 string quartets, Piano Quartet, and 3 piano trios; a great many organ compositions.

Schreiber, Friedrich Gustav, German organ teacher and composer; b. Bienstedt, Aug. 5, 1817; d. Mühlhausen, July 14, 1889. He studied with E. Kast and L. Gebhardt in Erfurt; taught organ in Prague (1840–47); settled at Erfurt in 1851 as municipal music director and cantor at St. Balsius's; founded and conducted a choral society, with which he produced oratorios. Among his works are *Borussia* for Male Chorus and Orch.; *Pestalozzi-Kantate* and *Der deutsche Geist* for Soli, Male Chorus, and Orch.; songs.

Schreier, Peter, noted German tenor; b. Meissen, July 29, 1935. He studied at the Hochschule für Musik in Dresden (1956–59). In 1961 he was engaged at the Dresden State Opera, and in 1963 joined the State Opera of Berlin. He then appeared at the Vienna State Opera, the Salzburg Festival, La Scala in Milan, the Teatro Colón in Buenos Aires, and the Metropolitan Opera in N.Y. He also sang in oratorios and in lieder recitals. He further became a choral conductor, and brought out on records several works by Bach, including the B-minor Mass, and by Mozart.

Schreker, Franz, eminent composer and teacher; b. Monaco, March 23, 1878; d. Berlin, March 21, 1934. He spent his early childhood in Monaco, where his father, a native of Austria, was court photographer. He was 10 when his father died and the family moved to Vienna; there he studied violin with Rosé and theory with Robert Fuchs. In 1908 he organized the Vienna Phil. Chorus and conducted many new works with it. In 1912 he was appointed prof. of composition at the Akademie der Tonkunst. In 1920 he went to Berlin, where he was director of the Hochschule für Musik (until 1932); there he had many talented pupils who later became well-known composers (Krenek, Rathaus, Alois Hába, and others). In 1932 he became prof. of a class for advanced students at the Prussian Academy of Arts, but lost this post with the advent of the Nazi regime (1933), when he was forced to resign; he died a year later. As a composer, he led the neo-Romantic movement in the direction of Expressionism, emphasizing psychological conflicts in his operas; in his harmonies he expanded the basically Wagnerian sonorities to include many devices associated with Impressionism. He exercised considerable influence on the German and Viennese schools of his time, but with the change of direction in modern music toward economy of means and away from mystical and psychological trends, Schreker's music suffered a decline after his death. However, a retrospective of his works was the focal point of the 1976 annual Styrian Autumn Festival held in Graz, Austria; and in 1978 his last unperformed opera, *Christophorus,* was finally premiered. WORKS: FOR THE STAGE: 9 operas (all to his own librettos, except for *Flammen*): *Flammen* (1901;

piano reduction, Vienna, 1902); *Der ferne Klang* (*The Distant Sound;* 1901–10; Frankfurt, Aug. 18, 1912); *Das Spielwerk und die Prinzessin* (*The Chime Box and the Princess;* 1909–12; Frankfurt and Vienna, March 15, 1913; revised 1916; produced as a mystery play, *Das Spielwerk,* Munich, Oct. 30, 1920); *Die Gezeichneten* (*The Stigmatized;* 1913–15; Frankfurt, April 25, 1918); *Der Schatzgräber* (*The Treasure Digger;* 1915–18; Frankfurt, Jan. 21, 1920); *Irrelohe* (1919–24; Cologne, March 27, 1924); *Der singende Teufel* (*The Singing Devil;* 1924–28; Berlin, Dec. 10, 1928); *Christophorus* (1925–29; Freiburg, Oct. 1, 1978; original premiere, set for Freiburg in 1933, canceled by the Nazis); *Der Schmied von Gent* (*The Blacksmith of Ghent;* 1929–32; Berlin, Oct. 29, 1932). Ballet: *Der Geburtstag der Infantin,* after Oscar Wilde, for String Orch. (Vienna, 1908; revised for Full Orch. in 1923 and retitled *Spanisches Fest*); *Ein Tanzspiel* (1908; orchestrated 1920; also known as *Rokoko* and *4 Pieces in the Old Style*). Pantomime: *Der Wind* for Violin, Viola, Cello, Clarinet, and Piano (1908). FOR ORCH.: *Andante* for Strings (1896); *Ekkehard,* overture for Orch. and Organ (1901–2); *Romantische Suite,* a "Nachtspiel" (1902); *Phantastische Ouvertüre* (1902); *Vorspiel zu einem Drama* (1913; used as a prelude to his opera *Die Gezeichneten*); *Kammersymphonie* for 23 Solo Instruments (1916; Vienna, March 12, 1917); *Kleine Suite* for Small Orch. (Breslau, Jan. 17, 1929); *Vorspiel zu einer grossen Oper* (1933; Baden-Baden, March 11, 1958; symph. fragments from an uncompleted opera, *Memnon*). FOR VOICE: *Psalm 116* for Female Chorus, Orch., and Organ (1896); *Der Holdstein* for Soloists, Chorus, and Orch. (1899); *Schwanengesang* for Chorus and Orch. (1902); *5 Songs,* after Ronsperger, for Middle Voice and Orch. (1909; instrumented 1920); *Vom ewigen Leben,* lyrical songs, after Whitman, for Soprano and Orch. (1924; instrumented 1929); many motets and songs. He also wrote a Violin Sonata (1897).

Schrems, Joseph, German music scholar and choral leader; b. Warmensteinach, Oct. 5, 1815; d. Regensburg, Oct. 25, 1872. He was appointed Kapellmeister of the Cathedral at Regensburg in 1839, and held this position almost until his death; revived much early church music in performance; succeeded Proske as editor of *Musica Divina.* Through his efforts the library of the Regensburg Cathedral became one of the largest collections of early church music in existence.

Schröder, Alwin, cellist, brother of **Carl** and **Hermann Schröder;** b. Neuhaldensleben, June 15, 1855; d. Boston, Oct. 17, 1928. He studied piano with his father, and violin with De Ahna; then devoted himself to the cello; became successor to his brother Carl as first cellist in the Gewandhaus Orch. in Leipzig. In 1891 he went to America; joined the Boston Symph. Orch. (until 1925). He was also for a time the cellist in the Kneisel Quartet. His publications include *Violoncello Studies, Technical Studies, New Studies in Scale-playing,* as well as collections of classical pieces adapted for cello.

Schröder, Carl, German cellist and composer, brother of **Alwin** and **Hermann Schröder;** b. Quedlinburg, Dec. 18, 1848; d. Bremen, Sept. 22, 1935. He studied with Drechsler and Kiel; in 1871 he formed a string quartet with his brothers **Hermann, Franz,** and **Alwin.** He was solo cellist in the Gewandhaus Orch. in Leipzig (1874–81); afterward held 8 successive posts as conductor in Germany and the Netherlands, finally settling in Berlin as cello teacher at the Stern Cons. (1911–24). He then retired and lived in Bremen. Among his works are 2 operas: *Aspasia* (1892) and *Asket* (1893); 2 string quartets; other chamber music. He compiled 3 pedagogical manuals: *Katechismus des Dirigierens und Taktierens* (1889); *Katechismus des Violinspiels* (1889); *Katechismus des Violoncellspiels* (1890); these were also publ. in Eng. (1893, 1895, 1896). His collections of classical works for the cello, especially *Vortragstudien* (60 pieces), are of value.

Schröder, Hanning, German composer; b. Rostock, July 4, 1896. He was a medical student; concurrently he took violin lessons with Havemann in Berlin and composition with Weismann in Freiburg im Breisgau; then took a course in musicology with W. Gurlitt. In 1929 he married the musicologist **Cornelia Auerbach** (b. Breslau, Aug. 24, 1900); they remained in Germany under the Nazi regime, but were barred from professional work for their act of human charity in giving shelter to a Jewish couple in their Berlin apartment. After the war, they took up residence in West Berlin. WORKS: *Musik* for Recorder Solo (1954), and similar works for Solo Viola, Solo Cello, Solo Violin, and Solo Bassoon; *Hänsel und Gretel,* singspiel for children (Berlin, Dec. 23, 1952); *Divertimento* for 5 Wind Instruments (1957); *Divertimento* for Viola and Cello (1963); *Metronome 80* for Violin Solo (1969); Nonet for Wind Quintet, Violin, Viola, Cello, and Double Bass (1970); *Varianten* for Solo Flute and Orch. (1971).

Schröder, Hermann, German violinist and composer, brother of **Carl** and **Alwin Schröder;** b. Quedlinburg, July 28, 1843; d. Berlin, Jan. 30, 1909. He studied with A. Ritter at Magdeburg; from 1885 was a teacher at the Royal Inst. for Church Music in Berlin; also had a music school of his own. He publ. *Untersuchung über die sympathischen Klänge der Geigeninstrumente* (1891); *Die symmetrische Umkehrung in der Musik* (1902); *Ton und Farbe* (1906); chamber music for instructive purposes: *6 instruktive Quartette, 3 kleine Trios,* etc.; a violin method, *Die Kunst des Violinspiels* (1887); etc.

Schröder, Jaap, distinguished Dutch violinist and pedagogue; b. Amsterdam, Dec. 31, 1925. He studied violin at the Amsterdam Cons. and in Paris; also attended classes in musicology at the Sorbonne. He then returned to the Netherlands; served as concertmaster of the Hilversum Radio Chamber Orch., and was a member of the Netherlands String Quartet. In 1975 he founded the Quartetto Esterhazy, which gave performances of music from the Classical era on period instruments; it was dissolved in 1981. He subsequently served as music director and concertmaster of the Academy of Ancient Music in London. In 1982 he was appointed visiting music director of the Smithsonian Chamber Players in Washington, D.C.

Schrøder, Jens, conductor; b. Bielsko, Poland, Nov. 6, 1909. He was educated at the Prague Academy of Music; then conducted in Copenhagen and other Danish cities. In 1942 he became chief conductor of the Aalborg Symph. Orch., a post he held until 1980; was also chief conductor of the Municipal Theater there (1942–75) and a guest conductor with the Danish Radio Symph. and the Royal Danish Orch., as well as a conductor with the Jutland Opera (from 1974). In 1980 Queen Margrethe II made him a Knight of the Dannebrog Order (First Grade) in appreciation of his many contributions to the musical life of Denmark.

Schröder-Devrient, Wilhelmine, celebrated German soprano; b. Hamburg, Dec. 6, 1804; d. Coburg, Jan. 26, 1860. She received early training for the stage from her father, a baritone, and from her mother, Antoinette Sophie Bürger, a well-known actress; she herself played children's parts and was an actress until her 17th year. After the death of her father in 1818, she followed her mother to Vienna, where she studied with Mazatti; made her debut at the Kärnthnertortheater in Vienna on Jan. 20, 1821, as Pamina in Mozart's *Zauberflöte;* then sang Agathe in *Der Freischütz* under the direction of Weber himself (Vienna, March 7, 1822). When *Fidelio* was revived in Vienna in 1822, she sang Leonore in the presence of Beethoven. In 1823 she was engaged at the court opera in Dresden; there she married the actor Karl Devrient (divorced, 1828). She sang in Paris in 1830; then again in 1831 and 1832 with spectacular success; in the summer of 1832 she appeared in London. She returned to Germany in 1837; continued to sing in Dresden until 1847; also appeared as a concert singer, evoking praise from critics and musicians alike; Wagner expressed his admiration for her; she created the roles of Adriano Colonna in *Rienzi* (Oct. 20, 1842), Senta in *Der fliegende Holländer* (Dresden, Jan. 2, 1843), and Venus in *Tannhäuser* (Dresden, Oct. 19, 1845). She contracted 2 more marriages: to Döring (divorced) and von Bock (1850).

BIBLIOGRAPHY: C. von Glümer, *Erinnerungen an Wilhelmine Schröder-Devrient* (Leipzig, 1862; reprinted in Reclam's ed., 1905); A. von Wolzogen, *Wilhelmine Schröder-Devrient* (Leipzig, 1863); G. Bonacci, "G. Schröder-Devrient e Gasparo Spontini," in *Nuova Antologia* (Rome, 1903); C. Hagemann, *Wilhelmine Schröder-Devrient* (Berlin, 1904); E. Schuré, *Précurseurs et revoltés* (Paris, 1904). A purported autobiography, publ. anonymously in many eds. since about 1870 as *Aus den Memoiren einer Sängerin* or *Memoires d'une chanteuse allemande,* is in fact a pornographic fantasy whose real author is unknown. A novel based on her life by Eva von Baudissin, *Wilhelmine Schröder-Devrient: Der Schicksalsweg einer grossen Künstlerin,* was publ. in Berlin in 1937. See also Richard Wagner's *Über Schauspieler und Sänger* (dedicated to her memory), in vol. IX of his *Gesammelte Schriften und Dichtungen,* and his numerous references to her in *Mein Leben.*

Schröder-Feinen, Ursula, German dramatic soprano; b. Gelsenkirchen, July 21, 1936. She studied voice with Maria Helm and at the Essen Folkwangschule. She sang in the chorus of the Gelsenkirchen Opera, made her operatic debut there in 1961, and remained on its roster until 1968; then sang with the Düsseldorf Opera. On Dec. 4, 1970, she made her first American appearance as Chrysothemis in *Elektra* at the Metropolitan Opera in N.Y.; also sang at Bayreuth, Salzburg, Milan, and Berlin. A versatile singer, her repertoire includes major dramatic roles in German and Italian opera.

Schröter, Christoph Gottlieb, German organist and music theorist; b. Hohnstein, near Schandau in Saxony, Aug. 10, 1699; d. Nordhausen, May 20, 1782. He served as a chorister in Dresden; in 1717 he went to Leipzig, where he studied theology, but turned to music when he became Lotti's copyist in Dresden; then traveled in Germany, the Netherlands, and England; returning to Saxony, he obtained the position of lecturer at Jena Univ.; then served as organist in Minden (1726–32); in 1732 he was appointed organist at Nordhausen, and he held this position for half a century until his death. He wrote mainly choral sacred music; composed 7 sets of church cantatas for the entire church year; a Passion, *Die sieben Worte Jesu,* for which he wrote the verses; also instrumental music, including overtures, concertos, and sonatas, as well as fugues and preludes for organ. He claimed priority for the invention of a hammer action for keyed string instruments, anticipating Cristofori's invention of the pianoforte; his argument is expounded with polemical passion in his paper "Umständliche Beschreibung eines neuerfundenen Clavierinstruments, auf welchem man in unterschiedenen Graden stark und schwach spielen kann," which was publ. in 1763 in Marpurg's *Kritische Briefe;* however, music historians rejected his arguments as choronologically invalid. In the field of music theory he publ. an important paper, *Deutliche Anweisung zum Generalbass in beständiger Veränderung des uns angebohrnen harmonischen Dreyklanges* (1772), in which he expounds the thesis that the major and minor triads are the sole fundamental chords in harmony; he also publ. *Letzte Beschäftigung mit musikalischen Dingen; Nebst sechs Temperatur-Planen und einer Notentafel* (1782) and some other theoretical articles in an egotistically assertive vein.

Schröter, Corona (Elisabeth Wilhelmine), celebrated German soprano; b. Guben, Jan. 14, 1751; d. Ilmenau, Aug. 23, 1802. She was trained in music by her father, **Johann Friedrich Schröter,** who was an oboe player. She continued her studies with Hiller in Leipzig. In 1765 she appeared in a "grand concert" in Leipzig and was engaged there until 1771. On Nov. 23, 1776, she sang at the court of Weimar, and was appointed Kammersängerin to the Dowager Duchess of Weimar. She was also active on the dramatic stage; Goethe esteemed her highly as an actress. She composed some songs, publ. in 2 vols. (1786 and 1794), among them the first setting of Goethe's *Erlkönig.*

BIBLIOGRAPHY: R. Keil, *Corona Schröter. Eine Lebensskizze* (Leipzig, 1875); H. Düntzer, *Charlotte von Stein und Corona Schröter* (Ilmenau, 1902); H. Stümcke, *Corona Schröter* (Bielefeld, 1904).

Schröter, Johann Samuel, pianist and composer, brother of **Corona Schröter;** b. Guben(?), between 1750 and 1753; d. London, Nov. 1, 1788. He traveled with his father and sister to London, where they gave concerts together. He remained in London, and in 1782 was appointed successor of John (Johann) Christian Bach as music master to the Queen. Twelve piano concertos and 7 trios were publ. in London, also in Paris. His widow became attached to Haydn during the latter's stay in London (1790–91) and sent him many impassioned letters, of which copies made by Haydn are extant.

BIBLIOGRAPHY: Konrad Wolff, "Johann Samuel Schroeter," *Musical Quarterly* (July 1958).

Schröter, Leonhart, German contrapuntist; b. Torgau, c.1532; d. Magdeburg, c.1601. From 1561 to 1576 he was cantor at Saalfeld; from 1572–73, librarian at Wolfenbüttel; from 1576–95, cantor of the Old Latin School in Magdeburg. He was an important composer of Lutheran church music; publ. *55 geistliche Lieder* (1562); a German Te Deum for 8 Voices (1571; publ. 1576; reprinted by Kade in vol. V of Ambros's *Geschichte der Musik*); also a Latin Te Deum (1584); 16 *Weihnachtsliedlein* for 4–8 Voices (1587; reprinted by Engelke in 1914 for Peters); 28 *Hymni sacri* (1587). Four *Weihnachtsliedlein* are found in Schlesinger's *Musica sacra* (no. 11), other pieces in Jöde's *Das Chorbuch*, I and IV; further reprints by W. Ehmann (Göttingen, 1932), G. Hormann (1933), and E. Lendvai (1934).

BIBLIOGRAPHY: G. Hofmann, *Leonhart Schröter, Ein lutherischer Kantor zu Magdeburg* (Diss., Univ. of Altdorf, 1934).

Schryock, Buren, American composer and conductor; b. Sheldon, Iowa, Dec. 13, 1881; d. San Diego, Jan. 20, 1974. At the age of 7 he moved to West Salem, Oreg., where he studied music and played organ in a church; occupied various teaching posts in Michigan, Texas, Nebraska, and California; was conductor of the San Diego Symph. Orch. (1913–20) and of the San Diego Opera Co. (1920–36); then settled in National City, near San Diego.

WORKS: 5 operas to his own librettos: *Flavia* (1930–46); *Mary and John* (1948); *Nancy and Arthur* (1951); *Malena and Nordico* (1954); *Tanshu and Sanchi* (1955); a Symph.; chamber music; piano pieces.

Schub, André-Michel, outstanding French-born American pianist; b. Paris, Dec. 26, 1952. He was brought to N.Y. by his parents as an infant and was taught piano by his mother; then became a pupil of Jascha Zayde. After attending Princeton Univ. for a year, he went to the Curtis Inst. of Music in Philadelphia to study with Rudolf Serkin. In 1974 he won first prize in the Naumburg International Piano Competition; in 1981 he received first prize at the prestigious Van Cliburn Piano Competition, which launched him on a highly successful career. He was a soloist with the Boston Symph. Orch., Chicago Symph. Orch., Cleveland Orch., N.Y. Phil., and Philadelphia Orch. His brilliant virtuoso technique is matched by a sensitive temperament; he shines in the Classic and Romantic repertoire.

Schubart, (Christian Friedrich) Daniel, German poet and musician; b. Obersontheim, Swabia, March 24, 1739; d. Stuttgart, Oct. 10, 1791. He was an organist at Geisslingen in 1763–69; then at Ludwigsburg, being forced out in 1773 for dissolute conduct; then went to Augsburg, where he founded a paper, the *Deutsche Chronik*, in 1774; from 1777–87 he was imprisoned at Hohenasperg for political reasons. After his release, he was made music director of the Stuttgart theater and court poet. He was the author of the words of Schubert's famous song *Die Forelle.* His own compositions are unassuming, but he was historically important in contributing to the creation of the German lied of the folk type; his song *Schlaf wohl, du Himmelsknabe du* rivaled real folk songs in popularity. He also wrote piano pieces. His son, **Ludwig Schubart,** edited his philosophical disquisition, *Ideen zu einer Aesthetik der Tonkunst* (1806; new ed., 1924), written in the extravagant vein characteristic of Schubart's whole life.

BIBLIOGRAPHY: *Schubarts Leben und Gesinnungen von ihm selbst, im Kerker, aufgesetzt* (2 vols., Stuttgart, 1791–93); F.D. Strauss, *Schubarts Leben in seinen Briefen* (2 vols., Berlin, 1849); G. Hauff, *Schubart in seinen Leben und seinen Werken* (Stuttgart, 1885); H. Solcher, *Schubart der Gefangene auf dem Hohenasperg* (Bamberg, 1895); E. Holzer, *Schubart als Musiker* (Stuttgart, 1905); H. Hesse and K. Isenberg, *Schubart: Dokumente seines Lebens* (Berlin, 1927); R. Hammerstein, *Schubart, Ein Dichter-Musiker der Goethe-Zeit* (Freiburg im Breisgau, 1943); E. Thorn, *Genius in Fesseln: Schubarts Leben* (2nd ed., Geislingen, 1956); D. Ossenkip, *Christian Friedrich Daniel Schubart's Writings on Music* (Diss., Columbia Univ., 1960).

Schubaur, Johann Lukas, German composer; b. Lechfeld, Dec. (baptized, Dec. 23) 1749; d. Munich, Nov. 15, 1815. While studying medicine in Vienna, he earned his livelihood by giving music lessons; began to practice in 1775 in Neuburg but soon moved to Munich, where he became physician to the court and president of the medical commission. He was one of the earliest and most successful composers of German singspiels. The following were produced in Munich: *Melida* (1781); *Die Dorfdeputierten* (1783); *Das Lustlager* (1784); *Die treuen Köhler* (1786); also composed *Psalm 107* and a cantata, *Il Sacrifizio.*

BIBLIOGRAPHY: E. Reipschläger, *Schubaur, Danzi und Poissl als Opernkomponisten* (Berlin, 1911).

Schubert, Ferdinand, brother of the great composer **Franz Schubert;** b. Lichtenthal, near Vienna, Oct. 18, 1794; d. Vienna, Feb. 26, 1859, as director of the Normal School of St. Anna. He was devoted to his gifted brother, and inherited the latter's literary remains. He composed a *Tantum ergo;* a *Regina coeli;* a German Requiem *a* 4, with Organ; part-songs; etc.; wrote much other church music, a Requiem for Franz, 2 children's operas, etc. (most in MS).

Schubert, Franz, German violinist; b. Dresden, July 22, 1808; d. there, April 12, 1878. He was son and pupil of the Konzertmeister **Franz Anton Schubert** (1768–1827); also took lessons with Rottmeier and L. Haase; then went to Paris, where he studied with Lafont. Upon returning to Dresden, he joined the royal orch. (1823) and in 1861 succeeded Lipinski as first Konzertmeister. He was often confused with his great namesake, much to his distress, for he regarded himself as superior. He wrote a celebrated violin piece, *L'Abeille;* also composed violin études; a Fantasia for Violin, with Orch.; numerous other violin pieces.

Schubert, Franz (Peter), great Austrian composer, supreme melodist, inspired master of Romantic lieder; b. Himmelpfortgrund (then a suburb of Vienna and now a part of that city), Jan. 31, 1797; d. Vienna, Nov. 19, 1828. He studied violin with his father, a schoolmaster, and received instruction on the piano from his brother Ignaz; in addition, he took lessons in piano, organ, singing, and theory with Holzer, the choirmaster. In 1808 he became a member of the Vienna Imperial Court chapel choir and also entered the Stadtkonvict, a training school for court singers, where he studied music with the Imperial Court organist Wenzel Ruzicka and with the famous court composer Salieri. He played violin in the school orch. and conducted it whenever an occasion called for it. He began composing in school; wrote a *Fantasie* for Piano, 4-hands, several chamber music works, orch. overtures, and the unfinished singspiel *Der Spiegelritter.* His first song, *Hagars Klage,* is dated March 30, 1811. In 1813 he left the Stadtkonvict, but Salieri, evidently impressed by his talent, continued to give him instruction. He further attended a training college for teachers in Vienna, and then became an instructor at his father's school. Although very young, he began writing works in large forms; between 1813 and 1816 he composed 5 symphs., 4 masses, several string quartets, and also some stage music. He also wrote his first opera, *Des Teufels Lustschloss.* It was then that he wrote some of his most famous lieder. He was only 17 years old when he wrote *Gretchen am Spinnrade,* and only 18 when he composed the overpowering dramatic song *Erlkönig.* The prodigious facility that Schubert displayed is without equal; during the year 1815 he composed about 140 songs; on a single day, Oct. 15, he wrote 8 lieder. From Schubert's sketches it is possible to follow his method of composition; he would write the melody first, indicate the harmony, and then write out the song in full; often he subjected the finished work to several revisions. He became friendly with the poets Johann Mayrhofer and Franz von Schober, and set a number of their poems to music. In 1817 he lodged with Schober and his widowed mother, arranging to pay for his keep from his meager resources. It was then that he met the noted baritone singer Johann Michael Vogl, who put many of Schubert's songs on his concert programs. Outstanding lieder from this period include the *3 Harfenspieler, Der Wanderer, Der Tod und das Mädchen, Ganymed, An die Musik,* and *Die Forelle.* During the summer of 1818 Schubert served as music tutor to the family of Count Esterházy at Zélesz in Hungary. On March 1, 1818, his Overture in C major, "in the Italian style," became his first orch. work to be accorded a public performance in Vienna. On June 14, 1820, his singspiel *Die Zwillingsbrüder* was performed at the Kärnthnertortheater in Vienna. On Aug. 19, 1820, a score of his incidental music for the play *Die Zauberharfe* was heard at the Theater an der Wien; this score contains an overture that became subsequently popular in concert performances under the name *Rosamunde Overture,* although it was not composed for the score to the play *Rosamunde, Fürstin von Zypern,* which was produced at the Theater an der Wien more than 3 years later, on Dec. 20, 1823. Although Schubert still had difficulties in earning a living, he formed a circle of influential friends in Vienna, and appeared as a pianist at private gatherings; sometimes he sang his songs, accompanying himself at the keyboard; he was also able to publ. some of his songs. A mystery is attached to his most famous work, begun in 1822, the Symph. in B minor, known popularly as the "Unfinished" Symph. Only 2 movements are known to exist; only a few initial bars of the 3rd movement, a Scherzo, remained in sketches. What prevented him from finishing it? Speculations are as rife as they are worthless, particularly since Schubert was usually careful in completing a work before embarking on another composition. A hundred years after Schubert's death, an enterprising phonograph company arranged a contest for the completion of the "Unfinished" Symph.; prizes were given, but the products delivered, even some signed by well-known composers, were spectacularly poor. In 1823 Schubert completed his masterly song cycle *Die schöne Müllerin;* in 1824 he once again spent the summer as a private tutor in Count Esterházy's employ in Zélesz. In 1827 Schubert wrote another remarkable song cycle, *Die Winterreise.* On March 26, 1828, he presented in Vienna a public concert of his works. From that year, which proved to be his last, date such masterpieces as the piano sonatas in C minor, A major, and B-flat major; the String Quintet in C major; and the 2 books of songs collectively known as the *Schwanengesang.* His health was frail, and he moved to the lodgings of his brother Ferdinand. On the afternoon of Nov. 19, 1828, Schubert died, at the age of 31. Probably the most plausi-

Schubert

ble account of Schubert's illness is given by D. Kerner in his *Krankheiten grosser Musiker* (Stuttgart, 1973); a further discussion is found in the *Musical Times*, in E. Sams's "Schubert's Illness Re-examined" (Jan. 1980). There is no substantial evidence that Schubert died of syphilis; from all accounts of his daily life, he was never promiscuous, and was not known to engage in unseemly liaisons.

Schubert is often described as the creator of the genre of strophic lieder; this summary description is chronologically untenable; Zelter wrote strophic lieder a generation before Schubert. Goethe, whose poems were set to music by Zelter, Beethoven, and Schubert, favored Zelter's settings. What Schubert truly created was an incomparably beautiful florilegium of lieder typifying the era of German Romantic sentiment and conveying deeply felt emotions, ranging from peaceful joy to enlightened melancholy, from philosophic meditation to throbbing drama; the poems he selected for his settings were expressive of such passing moods. He set to music 72 poems by Goethe, 47 by Mayrhofer, 46 by Schiller, 44 by Wilhelm Müller, 28 by Matthison, 23 by Hölty, 22 by Kosegarten, 13 by Körtner, 12 by Schober, and 6 by Heine.

In a sense, Schubert's *Moments musicaux, Impromptus,* and other piano works are songs without texts; on several occasions he used musical material from his songs for instrumental works, as in the great *Wanderer Fantasia* for Piano, based on his song *Der Wanderer,* and the "Forellen" Piano Quintet, in which the 4th movement is a set of variations on the song *Die Forelle.* His String Quartet in D minor includes a set of variations on Schubert's song *Der Tod und das Mädchen* in its 2nd movement. But Schubert was not given to large theater works and oratorios. Even his extended works in sonata form are not conceived on a grand scale but, rather, are constructed according to the symmetry of recapitulations; his music captivates the listeners not by recurring variety but by the recalled felicities; time and again in his MSS he simply indicates the repetition of a group of bars by number. Therein lies the immense difference between Schubert and Schumann, both Romantic poets of music: where Schubert was satisfied with reminding the listener of a passage already heard, Schumann variegates. Schubert was indeed the most symmetrical composer in the era of free-flowing musical prose and musical poetry.

Much confusion exists in the numbering of Schubert's symphs., of which he wrote 8, the last being listed in most catalogues as No. 9; the missing uncounted symph. is No. 7, which exists as a full draft, in 4 movements, of which the first 110 bars are fully scored; several "completions" exist, the first by John Francis Barnett, made in 1883; the 2nd by Felix Weingartner, manufactured in 1934; and the 3rd, and perhaps the most Schubertomorphic, constructed with artful imitation of Schubert's ways and means, by Brian Newbould, in 1977. The "Unfinished" Symph. is then No. 8. There remains the mysterious "Gastein" Symph., so named because Schubert was supposed to have written it in Gastein, in the Tyrol, in 1825. It was long regarded as irretrieva-

bly lost, but was eventually identified with No. 9, the great C major Symph. Incredibly, as late as 1978 there came to light in a somehow overlooked pile of music in the archives of the Vienna Stadtsbibliothek a sketch of still another Schubert symph., composed during the last months of his life; this insubstantial but magically tempting waft of Schubert's genius was completed by Brian Newbould; if admitted into the Schubert treasure box, it will have to be numbered as his 10th.

The recognition of Schubert's greatness was astonishingly slow. Fully 40 years elapsed before the discovery of the MS of the "Unfinished" Symph. Posthumous performances were the rule for Schubert's symph. premieres, and the publication of his symphs. was exceedingly tardy. Schumann, ever sensitive to great talent, was eager to salute the kindred genius in Schubert's symphs., about whose "Heavenly length" he so admiringly complained. But it took half a century for Schubert to become firmly established in music history as one of the great Sch's (with Chopin phonetically counted in).

WORKS: In the list of Schubert's works given below, the D. numbers are those established by O. Deutsch (with D. Wakeling) in his *Schubert: Thematic Catalogue of All His Works in Chronological Order* (London, 1951; in German as *Franz Schubert: Thematisches Verzeichnis seiner Werke in chronologischer Folge . . .*, publ. in the *Neue Ausgabe sämtlicher Werke* of Schubert in a revised ed. in 1978).

FOR THE STAGE: *Der Spiegelritter,* D. 11, singspiel (1811–12; unfinished; only the Overture and Act I completed; first perf. by the Swiss Radio, Dec. 11, 1949); *Des Teufels Lustschloss,* D. 84, opera (1813–15; 2 versions; Vienna, Dec. 12, 1879); *Adrast,* D. 137, opera (1817–19; unfinished; Vienna, Dec. 13, 1868); *Der vierjährige Posten,* D. 190, singspiel (1815; Dresden, Sept. 23, 1896); *Fernando,* D. 220, singspiel (1815; Vienna, April 13, 1907); *Claudine von Villa Bella,* D. 239, singspiel (1815; unfinished; only the Overture and Act I completed; Vienna, April 26, 1913); *Die Freunde von Salamanka,* D. 326, singspiel (1815; Halle, May 6, 1928); Die Bürgschaft, D. 435, opera (1816; unfinished; only Acts I and II completed; Vienna, March 7, 1908); *Die Zauberharfe,* D. 644, melodrama (1820; Theater an der Wien, Vienna, Aug. 19, 1820); *Die Zwillingsbrüder,* D. 647, singspiel (1819; Kärnthnertortheater, Vienna, June 14, 1820); *Sakuntala,* D. 701, opera (1820; only sketches for Acts I and II; these first perf. in Vienna, June 12, 1971); Duet and Aria for Hérold's *Das Zauberglöckchen (La Clochette),* D. 723 (1821; Vienna, June 20, 1821); *Alfonso und Estrella,* D. 732, opera (1821–22; Weimar, June 24, 1854); *Die Verschworenen (Der häusliche Krieg),* D. 787, singspiel (1823; Vienna, March 1, 1861); *Rüdiger,* D. 791, opera (1823; sketches only; these first perf. in Vienna, Jan. 5, 1868); *Fierabras,* D. 796, opera (1823; Karlsruhe, Feb. 9, 1897); *Rosamunde, Fürstin von Zypern,* D. 797, incidental music to the play by H. von Chézy (1823; Theater an der Wien, Vienna, Dec. 20, 1823); *Der Graf von Gleichen,* D. 918, opera (1827; sketches only); *Der Minnesänger,* D. 981, singspiel (date unknown; unfinished; not extant).

CHURCH MUSIC: *Salve Regina* in F major for Soprano, Organ, and Orch., D. 27 (1812); *Kyrie* in D minor for Soprano, Tenor, Choir, Organ, and Orch., D. 31 (1812); *Kyrie* in B-flat major for Choir, D. 45 (1813); *Kyrie* in D minor for Soprano, Alto, Bass, Choir, and Orch., D. 49 (1813); *Kyrie* in F major for Choir, Organ, and Orch., D. 66 (1813); Mass No. 1, in F major, for 2 Sopranos, Alto, 2 Tenors, Bass, Choir, Organ, and Orch., D. 105 (1814); *Salve Regina* in B-flat major for Tenor, Organ, and Orch., D. 106 (1814); *Totus in corde langueo,* offertory in C major for Soprano or Tenor, Clarinet or Violin, Organ, and Orch., D. 136 (1815); Mass No. 2, in G. major, for Soprano, Tenor, Bass, Choir, Organ, and Strings, D. 167 (1815); *Stabat Mater* in G minor for Choir, Organ, and Orch., D. 175 (1815); *Tres sunt,* offertory in A minor for Choir, Organ, and Orch., D. 181 (1815); *Benedictus es, Domine,* gradual in C major for Choir, Organ, and Orch., D. 184 (1815); *Dona nobis pacem* in F major for Bass, Choir, Organ, and Orch., D. 185 (alternative movement for D. 105; 1815); *Salve Regina* (offertorium) in F major for Soprano, Organ, and Orch., D. 223 (2 versions, 1815 and 1823); Mass No. 3, in B-flat major, for Soprano, Alto, Tenor, Bass, Choir, Organ, and Orch., D. 324 (1815); *Deutsches Salve Regina (Hymne an die heilige Mutter Gottes)* in F major for Choir and Organ, D. 379 (1816); *Stabat Mater* (oratorio) in F major/F minor for Soprano, Tenor, Bass, Choir, and Orch., D. 383 (1816); *Salve Regina* in B-flat major for Choir, D. 386 (1816); Mass No. 4, in C major, for Soprano, Alto, Tenor, Bass, Choir, Organ, and Orch., D. 452 (1816); *Tantum ergo* in C major for Soprano, Choir, Organ, and Orch., D. 460 (1816); *Tantum ergo* in C major for Soprano, Alto, Tenor, Bass, Choir, and Orch., D. 461 (1816); Magnificat in C major for Soprano, Alto, Tenor, Bass, Choir, Organ, and Orch., D. 486 (1815); *Auguste jam coelestium* in G major for Soprano, Tenor, and Orch., D. 488 (1816); *Deutsches Requiem (Deutsche Trauermesse)* in G minor for Soprano, Alto, Tenor, Bass, Choir, and Organ, D. 621 (1818); *Salve Regina* (offertorium) in A major for Soprano and Strings, D. 676 (1819); Mass No. 5, in A-flat major, for Soprano, Alto, Tenor, Bass, Choir, Organ, and Orch., D. 678 (2 versions, 1819–22); *Tantum ergo* in B-flat major for Soprano, Alto, Tenor, Bass, Choir, Organ, and Orch., D. 730 (1821); *Tantum ergo* in C major for Choir, Organ, and Orch., D. 739 (1814); *Tantum ergo* in D major for Choir, Organ, and Orch., D. 750 (1822); *Salve Regina* in C major for 2 Tenors and 2 Basses, D. 811 (1824); *Deutsche Messe* for Choir and Organ, or Choir, Organ, and Orch., D. 872 (1827); Mass No. 6, in E-flat major, for Soprano, Alto, Tenor, Bass, Choir, and Orch., D. 950 (1828); Benedictus in A minor for Soprano, Alto, Tenor, Bass, Choir, Organ, and Orch., D. 961 (alternative movement for D. 452; 1828); *Tantum ergo* in E-flat major for Soprano, Alto, Tenor, Bass, Choir, and Orch., D. 962 (1828); *Intende voci,* offertory in B-flat major for Tenor, Choir, and Orch., D. 963 (1828); etc.

OTHER VOCAL MUSIC: *Quell' innocente figlio,* D. 17 (many versions, 1812); *Entra l'uomo allor che nasce,* D. 33 (many versions, 1812); *Te solo adoro* for Soprano, Alto, Tenor, and Bass, D. 34 (1812); *Serbate, o dei custodi,* D. 35 (2 versions, 1812); *Die Advokat-*en for Men's Voices and Piano, D. 37 (1812); *Totengräberlied* for Men's Voices, D. 38 (1813); *Dreifach ist der Schritt der Zeit* for Men's Voices, D. 43 (1813); *Dithyrambe,* D. 47 (1813; fragment only); *Unendliche Freude* for Men's Voices, D. 51 (1813); *Vorüber die stöhnende Klage* for Men's Voices, D. 53 (1813); *Unendliche Freude,* canon for Men's Voices, D. 54 (1813); *Selig durch die Liebe* for Men's Voices, D. 55 (1813); *Hier strecket der wallende Pilger* for Men's Voices, D. 57 (1813); *Dessen Fahne Donnerstürme wallte* for Men's Voices, D. 58 (1813); *Hier umarmen sich getreue Gatten* for Men's Voices, D. 60 (1813); *Ein jugendlicher Maienschwung,* D. 61 (1813); *Thronend auf erhabnem Sitz* for Men's Voices, D. 62 (1813); *Wer die steile Sternenbahn* for Men's Voices, D. 63 (1813); *Majestätsche Sonnenrosse* for Men's Voices, D. 64 (1813); *Schmerz verzerret ihr Gesicht,* canon, D. 65 (1813; sketch only); *Frisch atmet des Morgens lebendiger Hauch* for Men's Voices, D. 67 (1813); *Dreifach ist der Schritt der Zeit,* D. 69 (1813); *Dreifach ist der Schritt der Zeit (Ewig still steht die Vergangenheit),* canon for Men's Voices, D. 70 (1813); *Die zwei Tugendwege* for Men's Voices, D. 71 (1813); *Trinklied (Freunde, sammelt euch im Kreise)* for Bass, Men's Voices, and Piano, D. 75 (1813); *Zur Namensfeier meines Vaters* for Men's Voices and Guitar, D. 80 (1813); *Verschwunden sind die Schmerzen,* canon for Men's Voices, D. 88 (1813); *Wer ist gross?* for Bass, Men's Voices, and Orch., D. 110 (1814); *Mailied (Grüner wird die Au)* for Men's Voices, D. 129 (1815); *Der Schnee zerrinnt,* canon, D. 130 (1815); *Lacrimoso son io,* canon, D. 131 (2 versions, 1815); *Lied beim Rundetanz,* D. 132 (1815?); *Lied im Freien,* D. 133 (1815?); *Klage um Ali Bey* for Men's Voices, D. 140 (1815); *Bardengesang* for Men's Voices, D. 147 (1816); *Trinklied (Brüder! unser Erdenwallen)* for Tenor, Men's Voices, and Piano, D. 148 (1815); *Nun lasst uns den Leib begraben (Begrabnislied)* for Choir and Piano, D. 168 (1815); *Osterlied* for Choir and Piano, D. 168a (originally D. 987; 1815); *Trinklied vor der Schlacht* for 2 Unison Choruses and Piano, D. 169 (1815); *Schwertlied* for Voice, Unison Chorus, and Piano, D. 170 (1815); *Trinklied (Ihr Freunde und du gold'ner Wein)* for Voice, Unison Chorus, and Piano, D. 183 (1815); *An die Freude* for Voice, Unison Chorus, and Piano, D. 189 (1815); *Mailied (Grüner wird die Au)* for 2 Voices, D. 199 (1815); *Mailied (Der Schnee zerrinnt)* for 2 Voices, D. 202 (1815); *Der Morgenstern* for 2 Voices, D. 203 (1815); *Jägerlied* for 2 Voices, D. 204 (1815); *Lützows wilde Jagd* for 2 Voices, D. 205 (1815); *Hymne an den Unendlichen* for Choir and Piano, D. 232 (1815); *Das Abendrot* for Men's Voices and Piano, D. 236 (1815); *Trinklied im Winter* for Men's Voices, D. 242 (1815); *Frühlingslied (Die Luft ist blau)* for Men's Voices, D. 243 (1815); *Willkommen, lieber schöner Mai,* canon for 3 Voices, D. 244 (2 versions, 1815); *Punschlied: Im Norden zu singen* for 2 Voices, D. 253 (1815); *Trinklied (Auf! jeder sei nun froh)* for Men's Voices and Piano, D. 267 (1815); *Bergknappenlied* for Men's Voices and Piano, D. 268 (1815); *Das Leben,* D. 269 (2 versions, 1815); *Punschlied (Vier Elemente, innig gesellt)* for Men's Voices and Piano, D. 277 (1815); *Namensfeier für*

Schubert

Franz Michael Vierthaler (Gratulations Kantate) for Soprano, Tenor, Bass, Chorus, and Orch., D. 294 (1815); *Das Grab,* D. 329a (1815; sketch only); *Das Grab* for 4 Voices and Piano, D. 330 (1815); *Der Entfernten* for Men's Voices, D. 331 (1816?); *Die Einsiedelei* for Men's Voices, D. 337 (1816?); *An den Frühling* for Men's Voices, D. 338 (1816?); *Amors Macht,* D. 339 (1816?); *Badelied,* D. 340 (1816?); *Sylphen,* D. 341 (1816?); *Trinklied (Funkelnd im Becher)* for Men's Voices, D. 356 (1816); *Gold'ner Schein,* canon for 3 Voices, D. 357 (1816); *Fischerlied* for Men's Voices, D. 364 (1816?); *Das Grab* for Men's Voices and Piano, D. 377 (1816); *Die Schlacht,* D. 387 (1816; sketch only); *Beitrag zur fünfzig jährigen Jubelfeier des Herrn Salieri* for Tenor, Men's Voices, and Piano, D. 407 (1816); *Naturgenuss* for Men's Voices and Piano, D. 422 (1822?); *Andenken (Ich denke dein, wenn durch den Hain)* for Men's Voices, D. 423 (1816); *Erinnerungen (Am Seegestad)* for Men's Voices, D. 424 (1816); *Lebensbild* for Men's Voices, D. 425 (1816; not extant); *Trinklied (Herr Bacchus ist ein braver Mann)* for Men's Voices, D. 426 (1816; not extant); *Trinklied im Mai* for Men's Voices, D. 427 (1816); *Widerhall (Auf ewig dein)* for Men's Voices, D. 428 (1816); *An die Sonne* for Choir and Piano, D. 439 (1816); *Chor der Engel* for Choir, D. 440 (1816); *Das grosse Halleluja* for Chorus and Piano, D. 442 (1816); *Schlachtlied* for Chorus and Piano, D. 443 (1816); *Prometheus,* cantata for Soprano, Bass, Chorus, and Orch., D. 451 (1816; not extant); *Kantate zu Ehren von Josef Spendou* for 2 Sopranos, Bass, Choir, and Orch., D. 472 (1816); *Der Geistertanz* for Men's Voices, D. 494 (1816); *La pastorella al prato* for Men's Voices and Piano, D. 513 (1817?); *Jagdlied* for Unison Voices and Piano, D. 521 (1817); *Gesang der Geister über den Wassern* for Men's Voices, D. 538 (1817); *Das Grab* for Unison Voices and Piano, D. 569 (1817); *Lied im Freien* for Men's Voices, D. 572 (1817); *Das Dörfchen,* D. 598 (originally D. 641; 1817; sketch only); *Die Geselligkeit (Lebenslust)* for Choir and Piano, D. 609 (1818); *Leise, leise lasst uns singen* for Men's Voices, D. 635 (1819?); *Viel tausend Sterne prangen* for Choir and Piano, D. 642 (1812?); *Das Grab* for Choir, D. 643a (1819); *Sehnsucht (Nur wer die Sehnsucht kennt)* for Men's Voices, D. 656 (1819); *Ruhe, schönstes Gluck der Erde* for Men's Voices, D. 657 (1819); *Kantate zum Geburtstag des Sängers Johann Michael Vogl (Der Frühlingsmorgen)* for Women's and Men's Voices and Piano, D. 666 (1819); *Lazarus, oder Die Feier der Auferstehung,* oratorio for 3 Sopranos, 2 Tenors, Bass, Choir, and Orch., D. 689 (1820; unfinished); *Der 23. Psalm* for Women's Voices and Piano, D. 706 (1820); *Frühlingsgesang* for Men's Voices, D. 709 (1822); *Im Gegenwärtigen Vergangenes* for Men's Voices and Piano, D. 710 (1821); *Gesang der Geister über den Wassern* for Men's Voices, 2 Violas, 2 Cellos, and 2 Double Basses, D. 714 (originally D. 704 as a sketch; 1820–21); *Die Nachtigall* for Men's Voices and Piano, D. 724 (1821); *Frühlingsgesang* for Men's Voices and Piano, D. 740 (1822); *Geist der Liebe (Der Abend schleiert Flur und Hain)* for Men's Voices and Piano, D. 747 (1822); *Am Geburtstag des Kaisers,* cantata for Soprano, Alto, Tenor, Bass, Choir, and Orch., D. 748 (1822); *Gott in der Natur* for Women's Voices and Piano, D. 757 (1822); *Des Tages Weihe* for Choir and Piano, D. 763 (1822); *Ich hab' in mich gesogen,* D. 778b (1823?; sketch only); *Gondelfahrer* for Men's Voices and Piano, D. 809 (1824); *Gebet* for Choir and Piano, D. 815 (1824); *Lied eines Kriegers* for Bass, Unison Voices, and Piano, D. 822 (1824); *Wehmut* for Men's Voices, D. 825 (1826); *Ewige Liebe* for Men's Voices, D. 825a (1826); *Flucht* for Men's Voices, D. 825b (1825); *Der Tanz* for Choir and Piano, D. 826 (1828); *Bootgesang* for Men's Voices and Piano, D. 835 (1825); *Coronach (Totengesang der Frauen und Mädchen)* for Women's Voices and Piano, D. 836 (1825); *Trinklied aus dem 16. Jahrhundert* for Men's Voices, D. 847 (1825); *Nachtmusik* for Men's Voices, D. 848 (1825); *Widerspruch* for Men's Voices and Piano, D. 865 (1826?); *Canon* for 6 Voices, D. 873 (1826?, sketch only); *Nachklänge* for Men's Voices, D. 873a (1826?; sketch only); *Die Allmacht* for Choir and Piano, D. 875a (1826; sketch only); *Mondenschein* for Men's Voices and Piano, D. 875 (1826); *Nachthelle* for Tenor, Men's Voices, and Piano, D. 892 (1826); *Grab und Mond* for Men's Voices, D. 893 (1826); *Wein und Liebe* for Men's Voices, D. 901 (1827); *Zur guten Nacht* for Baritone, Men's Voices, and Piano, D. 903 (1827); *Schlachtlied* for Men's Voices, D. 912 (1827); *Nachtgesang im Walde* for Men's Voices and 4 Horns, D. 913 (1827); *Frühlingslied* for Men's Voices, D. 914 (1827); *Das stille Lied* for Men's Voices, D. 916 (1827; sketch only); *Ständchen,* D. 920 (originally D. 921; 2 versions, 1827); *Der Hochzeitsbraten* for Soprano, Tenor, Bass, and Piano, D. 930 (1827); *Kantate für Irene Kiesewetter* for 2 Tenors, 2 Basses, Choir, and Piano, 4-hands, D. 936 (1827); *Hymnus an den Heiligen Geist,* D. 941 (now listed as D. 948; 2 versions, 1828); *Mirjams Siegesgesang* for Soprano, Choir, and Piano, D. 942 (1828); *Der 92. Psalm: Lied für den Sabbath* for Soprano, Alto, Tenor, Baritone, Bass, and Choir, D. 953 (1828); *Glaube, Hoffnung und Liebe* for 2 Tenors, 2 Basses, Choir, and Wind Instruments or Piano, D. 954 (1828); *Gott im Ungewitter* for Choir and Piano, D. 985 (1827?); *Gott der Weltschopfer* for Choir and Piano, D. 986 (1827?); *Liebe säuseln die Blätter,* canon for 3 Voices, D. 988 (1815?).

SONGS (author of text precedes date of composition): Sketch for a song, D. 1a (no text; 1810?); *Hagars Klage,* D. 5 (Schücking; 1811); *Des Mädchens Klage,* D. 6 (Schiller; 1811?); *Leichenfantasie,* D. 7 (Schiller; 1811?); *Der Vatermörder,* D. 10 (Pfeffel; 1811); *Der Geistertanz,* D. 15 and 15a (fragments only; Matthisson; 1812?); *Quell' innocente figlio,* D. 17 (Metastasio; 1812); *Klaglied,* D. 23 (Rochlitz; 1812); *Der Jüngling am Bache,* D. 30 (Schiller; 1812); *Entra l'uomo allor che nasce,* D. 33 (Metastasio; 1812); *Serbate, o dei custodi,* D. 35 (Metastasio; 1812); *Lebenstraum,* D. 39 (Baumberg; 1810?); *Misero pargoletto,* D. 42 (several versions; Metastasio; 1813?); *Totengräberlied,* D. 44 (Hölty; 1813); *Die Schatten,* D. 50 (Matthisson; 1813); *Sehnsucht,* D. 52 (Schiller; 1813); *Verklärung,* D. 59 (Pope; Herder, trans.; 1813); *Thekla: Eine Geisterstimme,* D. 73 (Schiller; 1813); *Pensa, che questo istante,* D. 76 (2 versions; Metastasio; 1813); *Der Taucher,* D. 77 (2 versions; 2nd version originally D. 111; Schiller; first version, 1813–14; 2nd version, 1815); *Son fra l'onde,* D. 78 (Metastasio; 1813); *Auf den Sieg der Deutschen,* D. 81, with 2 Violins and Cello (Schubert?; 1813); *Zur Namensfeier des Herrn Andreas Siller,* D. 83, with Violin and Harp (1813); *Don Gayseros,* D. 93 (3 versions: *Don Gayseros, Don Gayseros; Nächtens klang die süsse Laute; An dem jungen Morgenhimmel;* F. de la Motte Fouqué; 1815?); *Adelaide,* D. 95 (Matthisson; 1814); *Trost: An Elisa,* D. 97 (Matthisson; 1814); *Erinnerungen,* D. 98 (2 versions; Matthisson; 1814); *Andenken,* D. 99 (Matthisson; 1814); *Geisternähe,* D. 100 (Matthisson; 1814); *Erinnerung,* D. 101 (Matthisson; 1814); *Die Betende,* D. 102 (Matthisson; 1814); *Die Befreier Europas in Paris,* D. 104 (3 versions; Mikan; 1814); *Lied aus der Ferne,* D. 107 (2 versions; Matthisson; 1814); *Der Abend,* D. 108 (Matthisson; 1814); *Lied der Liebe,* D. 109 (Matthisson; 1814); *An Emma,* D. 113 (3 versions; Schiller; 1814); *Romanze,* D. 114 (2 versions; Matthisson; 1814); *An Laura, als sie Klopstocks Auferstehungslied sang,* D. 115 (Matthisson; 1814); *Der Geistertanz,* D. 116 (Matthisson; 1814); *Das Mädchen aus der Fremde,* D. 117 (Schiller; 1814); *Gretchen am Spinnrade,* D. 118 (Goethe; 1814); *Nachtgesang,* D. 119 (Goethe; 1814); *Trost in Tränen,* D. 120 (Goethe; 1814); *Schäfers Klagelied,* D. 121 (2 versions; Goethe; 1814); *Ammenlied,* D. 122 (Lubi; 1814); *Sehnsucht,* D. 123 (Goethe; 1814; *Am See,* D. 124 (2 versions; Mayrhofer; 1814); *Szene aus Goethes Faust,* D. 126, with 4 Voices (2 versions; Goethe; 1814); *Ballade,* D. 134 (Kenner; 1815?); *Rastlose Liebe,* D. 138 (2 versions; Goethe; first version, 1815; 2nd version, 1821); *Der Mondabend,* D. 141 (Kumpf; 1815); *Geistes-Gruss,* D. 142 (6 versions; Goethe; 1815?); *Genügsamkeit,* D. 143 (Schober; 1815); *Romanze,* D. 144 (unfinished; F. Graf zu Stolberg-Stolberg; 1816); *Der Sänger,* D. 149 (2 versions; Goethe; 1815); *Lodas Gespenst,* D. 150 (Ossian; E. Baron de Harold, trans.; 1816); *Auf einen Kirchhof,* D. 151 (Schlechta; 1815); *Minona,* D. 152 (Bertrand; 1815); *Als ich sie erröten sah,* D. 153 (Ehrlich; 1815); *Das Bild,* D. 155 (1815); *Die Erwartung,* D. 159 (2 versions; Schiller; 1816); *Am Flusse,* D. 160 (Goethe; 1815); *An Mignon,* D. 161 (2 versions; Goethe; 1815); *Nähe des Geliebten,* D. 162 (2 versions; Goethe; 1815); *Sängers Morgenlied,* D. 163 (Körner; 1815); *Liebesrausch,* D. 164 (fragment only; Körner; 1815); *Sängers Morgenlied,* D. 165 (Körner; 1815); *Amphiaraos,* D. 166 (Körner; 1815); *Trinklied vor der Schlacht,* D. 169, for 2 Unison Choruses (Körner; 1815); *Schwertlied,* D. 170, with Unison Chorus (Körner; 1815); *Gebet während der Schlacht,* D. 171 (Körner; 1815); *Der Morgenstern,* D. 172 (fragment only; Körner; 1815); *Das war ich,* D. 174 (2 versions; Körner; first version, 1815; 2nd version, 1816); *Die Sterne,* D. 176 (Fellinger; 1815); *Vergebliche Liebe,* D. 177 (Bernard; 1815); *Liebesrausch,* D. 179 (Körner; 1815); *Sehnsucht der Liebe,* D. 180 (2 versions; Körner; 1815; 2nd version not extant); *Die erste Liebe,* D. 182 (Fellinger; 1815); *Trinklied,* D. 183, with Unison Chorus (Zettler; 1815); *Die Sterbende,* D. 186 (Matthisson; 1815); *Stimme der Liebe,* D. 187 (Matthisson; 1815); *Naturgenuss,* D. 188 (Matthisson; 1815); *An die Freude,* D. 189, with Unison Chorus (Schiller;

1815); *Des Mädchens Klage,* D. 191 (2 versions; Schiller; 1815); *Der Jüngling am Bache,* D. 192 (Schiller; 1815); *An den Mond,* D. 193 (Hölty; 1815); *Die Mainacht,* D. 194 (Hölty; 1815); *Amalia,* D. 195 (Schiller; 1815); *An die Nachtigall,* D. 196 (Hölty; 1815); *An die Apfelbäume, wo ich Julien erblickte,* D. 197 (Hölty; 1815); *Seufzer,* D. 198 (Hölty; 1815); *Auf den Tod einer Nachtigall,* D. 201 (fragment only; Hölty; 1815); *Das Traumbild,* D. 204a (Hölty; 1815; not extant); *Liebeständelei,* D. 206 (Körner; 1815); *Der Liebende,* D. 207 (Hölty; 1815); *Die Nonne,* D. 208 (2 versions; Hölty; first version, fragment only, 1815; 2nd version, originally D. 212, 1815); *Der Liedler,* D. 209 (Kenner; 1815); *Die Liebe (Klärchens Lied),* D. 210 (Goethe; 1815); *Adelwold und Emma,* D. 211 (Bertrand; 1815); *Der Traum,* D. 213 (Hölty; 1815); *Die Laube,* D. 214 (Hölty; 1815); *Jägers Abendlied,* D. 215 (Goethe; 1815); *Meerestille,* D. 215a (Goethe; 1815); *Meerestille,* D. 216 (Goethe; 1815); *Kolmas Klage,* D. 217 (Ossian; 1815); *Grablied,* D. 218 (Kenner; 1815); *Das Finden,* D. 219 (Kosegarten; 1815); *Der Abend,* D. 221 (Kosegarten; 1815); *Lieb Minna,* D. 222 (Stadler; 1815); *Wandrers Nachtlied,* D. 224 (Goethe; 1815); *Der Fischer,* D. 225 (Goethe; 1815); *Erster Verlust,* D. 226 (Goethe; 1815); *Idens Nachtgesang,* D. 227 (Kosegarten; 1815); *Von Ida,* D. 228 (Kosegarten; 1815); *Die Erscheinung,* D. 229 (Kosegarten; 1815); *Die Täuschung,* D. 230 (Kosegarten; 1815); *Das Sehnen,* D. 231 (Kosegarten; 1815); *Geist der Liebe,* D. 233 (Kosegarten; 1815); *Tischlied,* D. 234 (Goethe; 1815); *Abends unter der Linde,* D. 235 (Kosegarten; 1815); *Abends unter der Linde,* D. 237 (Kosegarten; 1815); *Die Mondnacht,* D. 238 (Kosegarten; 1815); *Huldigung,* D. 240 (Kosegarten; 1815); *Alles um Liebe,* D. 241 (Kosegarten; 1815); *Die Bürgschaft,* D. 246 (Schiller; 1815); *Die Spinnerin,* D. 247 (Goethe; 1815); *Lob des Tokayers,* D. 248 (Baumberg; 1815); *Die Schlacht,* D. 249 (Schiller; 1815; fragment only); *Das Geheimnis,* D. 250 (Schiller; 1815); *Hoffnung,* D. 251 (Schiller; 1815); *Das Mädchen aus der Fremde,* D. 252 (Schiller; 1815); *Punschlied: Im Norden zu singen,* D. 253 (Schiller; 1815); *Der Gott und die Bajadere,* D. 254 (Goethe; 1815); *Der Rattenfänger,* D. 255 (Goethe; 1815); *Der Schatzgräber,* D. 256 (Goethe; 1815); *Heidenröslein,* D. 257 (Goethe; 1815); *Bundeslied,* D. 258 (Goethe; 1815); *An den Mond,* D. 259 (Goethe; 1815); *Wonne der Wehmut,* D. 260 (Goethe; 1815); *Wer kauft Liebesgötter?,* D. 261 (Goethe; 1815); *Die Fröhlichkeit,* D. 262 (Prandstetter; 1815); *Cora an die Sonne,* D. 263 (Baumberg; 1815); *Der Morgenkuss,* D. 264 (2 versions; Baumberg; 1815); *Abendständchen: An Lina,* D. 265 (Baumberg; 1815); *Morgenlied,* D. 266 (Stolberg; 1815); *An die Sonne,* D. 270 (Baumberg; 1815); *Der Weiberfreund,* D. 271 (Cowley; Ratschky, trans.; 1815); *An die Sonne,* D. 272 (Tiedge; 1815); *Lilla an die Morgenröte,* D. 273 (1815); *Tischlerlied,* D. 274 (1815); *Totenkranz für ein Kind,* D. 275 (Matthisson; 1815); *Abendlied,* D. 276 (Stolberg; 1815); *Ossians Lied nach dem Falle Nathos,* D. 278 (2 versions; Ossian; Harold, trans.; 1815); *Das Rosenband,* D. 280 (Klopstock; 1815); *Das Mädchen von Inistore,* D. 281 (Ossian; Harold, trans.; 1815); *Cronnan,* D. 282 (Ossian; Harold, trans.; 1815); *An den Frühling,* D. 283 (Schiller; 1815); *Lied,* D. 284 (Schiller?; 1815);

Furcht der Geliebten (An Cidli), D. 285 (2 versions; Klopstock; 1815); *Selma und Selmar,* D. 286 (2 versions; Klopstock; 1815); *Vaterlandslied,* D. 287 (2 versions; Klopstock; 1815); *An sie,* D. 288 (Klopstock; 1815); *Die Sommernacht,* D. 289 (2 versions; Klopstock; 1815); *Die frühen Gräber,* D. 290 (Klopstock; 1815); *Dem Unendlichen,* D. 291 (3 versions; Klopstock; 1815); *Shilric und Vinvela,* D. 293 (Ossian; Harold, trans.; 1815); *Hoffnung,* D. 295 (2 versions; Goethe; 1816?); *An den Mond,* D. 296 (Goethe; 1816?); *Augenlied,* D. 297 (2 versions; Mayrhofer; 1817?); *Liane,* D. 298 (Mayrhofer; 1815); *Der Jüngling an der Quelle,* D. 300 (Salis-Seewis; 1817?); *Lambertine,* D. 301 (Stoll; 1815); *Labetrank der Liebe,* D. 302 (Stoll; 1815); *An die Geliebte,* D. 303 (Stoll; 1815); *Wiegenlied,* D. 304 (Körner; 1815); *Mein Gruss an den Mai,* D. 305 (Kumpf; 1815); *Skolie,* D. 306 (Deinhardstein; 1815); *Die Sternewelten,* D. 307 (Jarnik; Fellinger, trans.; 1815); *Die Macht der Liebe,* D. 308 (Kalchberg; 1815); *Das gestörte Glück,* D. 309 (Körner; 1815); *Sehnsucht,* D. 310 (2 versions; Goethe; 1815); *An den Mond,* D. 311 (1815; fragment only); *Hektors Abschied,* D. 312 (2 versions; Schiller; 1815); *Die Sterne,* D. 313 (Kosegarten; 1815); *Nachtgesang,* D. 314 (Kosegarten; 1815); *An Rosa,* D. 315 (Kosegarten; 1815); *An Rosa,* D. 316 (2 versions; Kosegarten; 1815); *Idens Schwanenlied,* D. 317 (2 versions; Kosegarten; 1815); *Schwangesang,* D. 318 (Kosegarten; 1815); *Luisens Antwort,* D. 319 (Kosegarten; 1815); *Der Zufriedene,* D. 320 (Reissig; 1815); *Mignon,* D. 321 (Goethe; 1815); *Hermann und Thusnelda,* D. 322 (Klopstock; 1815); *Klage der Ceres,* D. 323 (Schiller; 1815–16); *Harfenspieler,* D. 325 (Goethe; 1815); *Lorma,* D. 327 (Ossian; Harold, trans.; 1815; fragment only); *Erlkönig,* D. 328 (4 versions; Goethe; 1815); *Die drei Sänger,* D. 329 (Bobrik; 1815; fragment only); *Das Grab,* D. 330 (Salis-Seewis; 1815); *An mein Klavier,* D. 342 (Schubart; 1816?); *Am Tage aller Seelen (Litanei auf das Fest aller Seelen),* D. 343 (2 versions; Jacobi; *Am ersten Maimorgen,* D. 344 (Claudius; 1816?); *Der Entfernten,* D. 350 (Salis-Seewis; 1816?); *Fischerlied,* D. 351 (Salis-Seewis; 1816); *Licht und Liebe (Nachtgesang)* D. 352, for Soprano and Tenor (Collin; 1816?); *Die Nacht,* D. 358 (Uz; 1816); *Sehnsucht,* D. 359 (Goethe; 1816); *Lied eines Schiffers an die Dioskuren,* D. 360 (Mayrhofer; 1816); *Am Bach im Frühlinge,* D. 361 (Schober; 1816); *Zufriedenheit,* D. 362 (Claudius; 1816?); *An Chloen,* D. 363 (Uz; 1816; fragment only); *Der König in Thule,* D. 367 (Goethe; 1816); *Jägers Abendlied,* D. 368 (Goethe; 1816); *An Schwager Kronos,* D. 369 (Goethe; 1816); *Klage,* D. 371 (1816); *An die Natur,* D. 372 (Stolberg-Stolberg; 1816); *Lied,* D. 373 (Fouqué; 1816); *Der Tod Oskars,* D. 375 (Ossian; Harold, trans.; 1816); *Lorma,* D. 376 (Ossian; Harold, trans.; 1816; fragment only); *Morgenlied,* D. 381 (1816); *Abendlied,* D. 382 (1816); *Laura am Klavier,* D. 388 (2 versions; Schiller; 1816); *Des Mädchens Klage,* D. 389 (Schiller; 1816); *Entzuckung an Laura,* D. 390 (Schiller; 1816); *Die vier Weltalter,* D. 391 (Schiller; 1816); *Pflügerlied,* D. 392 (Salis-Seewis; 1816); *Die Einsiedelei,* D. 393 (Salis-Seewis; 1816); *An die Harmonie,* D. 394 (Salis-Seewis; 1816); *Lebensmelodien,* D. 395 (Schlegel; 1816); *Gruppe aus dem Tartarus,* D. 396 (Schiller; 1816; fragment only); *Ritter Toggenburg,* D. 397 (Schiller; 1816); *Frühlingslied,* D. 398 (Hölty; 1816); *Auf den Tod einer Nachtigall,* D. 399 (Hölty; 1816); *Die Knabenzeit,* D. 400 (Hölty; 1816); *Winterlied,* D. 401 (Hölty; 1816); *Der Flüchtling,* D. 402 (Schiller; 1816); *Lied,* D. 403 (4 versions; Salis-Seewis; 1816); *Die Herbstnacht,* D. 404 (Salis-Seewis; 1816); *Der Herbstabend,* D. 405 (2 versions; Salis-Seewis; 1816); *Abschied von der Harfe,* D. 406 (Salis-Seewis; 1816); *Die verfehlte Stunde,* D. 409 (Schlegel; 1816); *Sprache der Liebe,* D. 410 (Schlegel; 1816); *Daphne am Bach,* D. 411 (Stolberg-Stolberg; 1816); *Stimme der Liebe,* D. 412 (2 versions; Stolberg-Stolberg; 1816); *Entzückung,* D. 413 (Matthisson; 1816); *Geist der Liebe,* D. 414 (Matthisson; 1816); *Klage,* D. 415 (Matthisson; 1816); *Lied in der Abwesenheit,* D. 416 (Stolberg-Stolberg; 1816; fragment only); *Stimme der Liebe,* D. 418 (Matthisson; 1816); *Julius an Theone,* D. 419 (Matthisson; 1816); *Minnelied,* D. 429 (Hölty; 1816); *Die frühe Liebe,* D. 430 (2 versions; Hölty; 1816; 2nd version not extant); *Blumenlied,* D. 431 (Hölty; 1816); *Der Leidende,* D. 432 (2 versions; 1816); *Seligkeit,* D. 433 (Hölty; 1816); *Erntelied,* D. 434 (Hölty; 1816); *Klage,* D. 436 (2 versions; Hölty; 1816; 2nd version originally D. 437); *Das grosse Halleluja,* D. 442 (Klopstock; 1816); *Schlachtlied,* D. 443 (Klopstock; 1816); *Die Gestirne,* D. 444 (Klopstock; 1816); *Edone,* D. 445 (Klopstock; 1816); *Die Liebesgötter,* D. 446 (Uz; 1816); *An den Schlaf,* D. 447 (1816); *Gott im Frühlinge,* D. 448 (2 versions; Uz; 1816); *Der gute Hirt,* D. 449 (Uz; 1816); *Fragment aus dem Aeschylus,* D. 450 (2 versions; Aeschylus; Mayrhofer, trans.; 1816); *Grablied auf einen Soldaten,* D. 454 (Schubart; 1816); *Freude der Kinderjahre,* D. 455 (Köpken; 1816); *Das Heimweh,* D. 456 (Winkler; 1816); *An die untergehende Sonne,* D. 457 (Kosegarten; 1816–17); *Aus Diego Manazares (Ilmerine),* D. 458 (Schlechta; 1816); *An Chloen,* D. 462 (Jacobi; 1816); *Hochzeit-Lied,* D. 463 (Jacobi; 1816); *In der Mitternacht,* D. 464 (Jacobi; 1816); *Trauer der Liebe,* D. 465 (2 versions; Jacobi; 1816); *Die Perle,* D. 466 (Jacobi; 1816); *Pflicht und Liebe,* D. 467 (Gotter; 1816); *An den Mond,* D. 468 (Hölty; 1816); *Mignon,* D. 469 (Goethe; 1816; fragments only); *Liedesend,* D. 473 (2 versions; Mayrhofer; 1816); *Lied des Orpheus, als er in die Hölle ging,* D. 474 (2 versions; Jacobi; 1816; first version unfinished); *Abschied (nach einer Wallfahrtsarie),* D. 475 (Mayrhofer; 1816); *Rückweg,* D. 476 (Mayrhofer; 1816); *Alte Liebe rostet nie,* D. 477 (Mayrhofer; 1816); *Harfenspieler I (Gesänge des Harfners No. 1),* D. 478 (2 versions; Goethe; first version, 1816; 2nd version, 1822); *Harfenspieler II (Gesänge des Harfners No. 3),* D. 479 (2 versions; Goethe; first version, 1816 and 2nd version, 1822); *Harfenspieler III (Gesänge des Harfners No. 2),* D. 480 (3 versions; Goethe; first and 2nd versions, 1816; 3rd version, 1822); *Sehnsucht,* D. 481 (Goethe; 1816); *Der Sänger am Felsen,* D. 482 (Pichler; 1816); *Lied,* D. 483 (Pichler; 1816); *Gesang der Geister über den Wassern,* D. 484 (Goethe; 1816; fragment only); *Der Wanderer,* D. 489 (3 versions; Lübeck; 1816; 2nd version originally D. 493b; and 3rd version originally D. 493a); *Der Hirt,* D. 490 (Mayrhofer; 1816); *Geheimnis,* D. 491 (Mayrhofer; 1816); *Zum Punsche,* D. 492 (Mayrhofer; 1816; *Abendlied der Fürstin,* D. 495

(Mayrhofer; 1816); *Bei dem Grabe meines Vaters,* D. 496 (Claudius; 1816); *Klage um Ali Bey,* D. 496a (Claudius; 1816); *An die Nachtigall,* D. 497 (Claudius; 1816); *Wiegenlied,* D. 498 (1816); *Abendlied,* D. 499 (Claudius; 1816); *Phidile,* D. 500 (Claudius; 1816); *Zufriedenheit,* D. 501 (2 versions; Claudius; 1816); *Herbstlied,* D. 502 (Salis-Seewis; 1816); *Mailied,* D. 503 (Hölty; 1816); *Am Grabe Anselmos,* D. 504 (2 versions; Claudius; 1816); *Skolie,* D. 507 (Matthisson; 1816); *Lebenslied,* D. 508 (Matthisson; 1816); *Leiden der Trennung,* D. 509 (2 versions; Metastasio; Collin, trans.; 1816; first version, fragment only); *Vedi quanto adoro,* D. 510 (Metastasio; 1816); *Nur wer die Liebe kennt,* D. 513a (Werner; 1817?; sketch only); *Die abgeblühte Linde,* D. 514 (Széchényi; 1817?); *Der Flug der Zeit,* D. 515 (Széchényi; 1817?); *Sehnsucht,* D. 516 (Mayrhofer; 1816?); *Der Schäfer und der Reiter,* D. 517 (2 versions; Fouqué; 1817); *An den Tod,* D. 518 (Schubart; 1817?); *Die Blumensprache,* D. 519 (Platner?; 1817?); *Frohsinn,* D. 520 (2 versions; Castelli; 1817); *Jagdlied,* D. 521 (Werner; 1817); *Die Liebe,* D. 522 (Leon; 1817); *Trost,* D. 523 (1817); *Der Alpenjäger,* D. 524 (3 versions; Mayrhofer; 1817); *Wie Ulfru fischt,* D. 525 (2 versions; Mayrhofer; 1817); *Fahrt zum Hades,* D. 526 (Mayrhofer; 1817); *Schlaflied (Abendlied; Schlummerlied),* D. 527 (2 versions; Mayrhofer; 1817); *La pastorella al prato,* D. 528 (Goldoni; 1817); *An eine Quelle,* D. 530 (Claudius; 1817); *Der Tod und das Mädchen,* D. 531 (Claudius; 1817); *Das Lied vom Reifen,* D. 532 (Claudius; 1817; fragment only); *Täglich zu singen,* D. 533 (Claudius; 1817); *Die Nacht,* D. 534 (Ossian; Harold, trans.; 1817); *Lied,* D. 535, with Small Orch. (1817); *Der Schiffer,* D. 536 (2 versions; Mayrhofer; 1817); *Am Strome,* D. 539 (Mayrhofer; 1817); *Philoket,* D. 540 (Mayrhofer; 1817); *Memnon,* D. 541 (Mayrhofer; 1817); *Antigone und Oedip,* D. 542 (Mayrhofer; 1817); *Auf dem See,* D. 543 (2 versions; Goethe; 1817); *Ganymed,* D. 544 (Goethe; 1817); *Der Jüngling und der Tod,* D. 545 (2 versions; Spaun; 1817); *Trost im Liede,* D. 546 (Schober; 1817); *An die Musik,* D. 547 (2 versions; Schober; 1817); *Orest auf Tauris,* D. 548 (Mayrhofer; 1817); *Mahomets Gesang,* D. 549 (Goethe; 1817; fragment only); *Die Forelle,* D. 550 (5 versions; Schubart; 1817?-21); *Pax vobiscum,* D. 551 (Schober; 1817); *Hänflings Liebeswerbung,* D. 552 (2 versions; Kind; 1817); *Auf der Donau,* D. 553 (Mayrhofer; 1817); *Uraniens Flucht,* D. 554 (Mayrhofer; 1817); sketch for a song, D. 555 (no text; 1817); *Liebhaber in allen Gestalten,* D. 558 (Goethe; 1817); *Schweizerlied,* D. 559 (Goethe; 1817); *Der Goldschmiedsgesell,* D. 560 (Goethe; 1817); *Nach einem Gewitter,* D. 561 (Mayrhofer; 1817); *Fischerlied,* D. 562 (Salis-Seewis; 1817); *Die Einsiedelei,* D. 563 (Salis-Seewis; 1817); *Gretchen im Zwinger (Gretchen; Gretchens Bitte),* D. 564 (Goethe; 1817; fragment only); *Der Strom,* D. 565 (1817); *Das Grab,* D. 569, for Unison Chorus (Salis-Seewis; 1817); *Iphigenia,* D. 573 (Mayrhofer; 1817); *Entzückung an Laura,* D. 577 (2 versions; Schiller; 1817; fragments only); *Abschied,* D. 578 (Schubert; 1817); *Der Knabe in der Wiege (Wiegenlied),* D. 579 (2 versions; Ottenwalt; 1817; 2nd version, fragment only); *Vollendung,* D. 579a (originally D. 989; Matthisson; 1817); *Die Erde,* D. 579b (originally D. 989a;

Matthisson; 1817); *Gruppe aus dem Tartarus,* D. 583 (Schiller; 1817); *Elysium,* D. 584 (Schiller; 1817); *Atys,* D. 585 (Mayrhofer; 1817); *Erlafsee,* D. 586 (Mayrhofer; 1817); *An den Frühling,* D. 587 (2 versions; Schiller; 1817; 2nd version originally D. 245); *Der Alpenjäger,* D. 588 (2 versions; Schiller; 1817; first version, fragment only); *Der Kampf,* D. 594 (Schiller; 1817); *Thekla: Eine Geisterstimme,* D. 595 (2 versions; Schiller; 1817); *Lied eines Kindes,* D. 596 (1817; fragment only); *Auf der Riesenkoppe,* D. 611 (Körner; 1818); *An den Mond in einer Herbstnacht,* D. 614 (Schreiber; 1818); *Grablied für die Mutter,* D. 616 (1818); a vocal exercise for 2 Voices and Figured Bass, D. 619 (no text; 1818); *Einsamkeit,* D. 620 (Mayrhofer; 1818); *Der Blumenbrief,* D. 622 (Schreiber; 1818); *Das Marienbild,* D. 623 (Schreiber; 1818); *Blondel zu Marien,* D. 626 (1818); *Das Abendrot,* D. 627 (Schreiber; 1818); *Sonett I,* D. 628 (Petrarch; Schlegel, trans.; 1818); *Sonett II,* D. 629 (Petrarch; Schlegel, trans.; 1818); *Sonett III,* D. 630 (Petrarch; Gries, trans.; 1818); *Blanka (Das Mädchen),* D. 631 (Schlegel; 1818); *Vom Mitleiden Mariä,* D. 632 (Schlegel; 1818); *Der Schmetterling,* D. 633 (Schlegel; 1819?); *Die Berge,* D. 634 (Schlegel; 1821?); *Sehnsucht,* D. 636 (3 versions; Schiller; 1821?); *Hoffnung,* D. 637 (Schiller; 1819?); *Der Jüngling am Bache,* D. 638 (2 versions; Schiller; 1819?); *Widerschein,* D. 639 (2 versions; Schlechta; 1819?; 2nd version originally D. 949); *Abend,* D. 645 (Tieck; 1819; fragment only); *Die Gebüsche,* D. 646 (Schlegel; 1819); *Der Wanderer,* D. 649 (Schlegel; 1819); *Abendbilder,* D. 650 (Silbert; 1819); *Himmelsfunken,* D. 651 (Silbert; 1819); *Das Mädchen,* D. 652 (2 versions; Schlegel; 1819); *Bertas Lied in der Nacht,* D. 653 (Grillparzer; 1819); *An die Freunde,* D. 654 (Mayrhofer; 1819); *Marie,* D. 658 (Novalis; 1819); *Hymne I,* D. 659 (Novalis; 1819); *Hymne II,* D. 660 (Novalis; 1819); *Hymne III,* D. 661 (Novalis; 1819); *Hymne IV,* D. 662 (Novalis; 1819); *Der 13. Psalm,* D. 663 (M. Mendelssohn, trans.; 1819; fragment only); *Beim Winde,* D. 669 (Mayrhofer; 1819); *Die Sternennächte,* D. 670 (Mayrhofer; 1819); *Trost,* D. 671 (Mayrhofer; 1819); *Nachtstück,* D. 672 (2 versions; Mayrhofer; 1819); *Die Liebende schreibt,* D. 673 (Goethe; 1819); *Prometheus,* D. 674 (Goethe; 1819); *Strophe aus Die Götter Griechenlands,* D. 677 (2 versions; Schiller; 1819); *Über allen Zauber Liebe,* D. 682 (Mayrhofer; 1820?; fragment only); *Die Sterne,* D. 684 (Schlegel; 1820); *Morgenlied,* D. 685 (Werner; 1820); *Frühlingsglaube,* D. 686 (3 versions; Uhland; first and 2nd versions, 1820; 3rd version, 1822); *Nachthymne,* D. 687 (Novalis; 1820); *4 Canzonen: Non t'accostar all'urna* (Vitorelli), *Guarda, che bianca luna* (Vitorelli), *Da quel sembiante appresi* (Metastasio), *Mio ben ricordati* (Metastasio), D. 688 (all 1820); *Abendröte,* D. 690 (Schlegel; 1823); *Die Vögel,* D. 691 (Schlegel; 1820); *Der Knabe,* D. 692 (Schlegel; 1820); *Der Fluss,* D. 693 (Schlegel; 1820); *Der Schiffer,* D. 694 (Schlegel; 1820); *Namenstagslied,* D. 695 (Stadler; 1820); *Des Fräuleins Liebeslauschen (Liebeslauschen),* D. 698 (Schlechta; 1820); *Der entsühnte Orest,* D. 699 (Mayrhofer; 1820); *Freiwilliges Versinken,* D. 700 (Mayrhofer; 1820); *Der Jüngling auf dem Hügel,* D. 702 (Hüttenbrenner; 1820); *Der zürnenden Diana,* D. 707 (2 versions; Mayrhofer; 1820); *Im Walde*

(Waldesnacht), D. 708 (Schlegel; 1820); *Lob der Tränen*, D. 711 (2 versions; Schlegel; 1818); *Die gefangenen Sänger*, D. 712 (Schlegel; 1821); *Der Unglückliche*, D. 713 (2 versions; Pichler; 1821); *Versunken*, D. 715 (Goethe; 1821); *Grenzen der Menschheit*, D. 716 (Goethe; 1821); *Suleika*, D. 717 (1821?); *Geheimes*, D. 719 (Goethe; 1821); *Suleika*, D. 720 (2 versions; 1821); *Mahomets Gesang*, D. 721 (Goethe; 1821; fragment only); *Linde Lüfte wehen*, D. 725 (1821; fragment only); *Mignon*, D. 726 (Goethe; 1821); *Mignon*, D. 727 (Goethe; 1821); *Johanna Sebus*, D. 728 (Goethe; 1821; fragment only); *Der Blumen Schmerz*, D. 731 (Mayláth; 1821); *Ihr Grab*, D. 736 (Engelhardt; 1822?); *An die Leier*, D. 737 (Bruchmann; 1822?); *Im Haine*, D. 738 (Bruchmann; 1822?); *Sei mir gegrüsst*, D. 741 (Rückert; 1821?); *Der Wachtelschlag*, D. 742 (Sauter; 1822); *Selige Welt*, D. 743 (Senn; 1822); *Schwanengesang*, D. 744 (Senn; 1822); *Die Rose*, D. 745 (2 versions; Schlegel; 1822); *Am See*, D. 746 (Bruchmann; 1822?); *Herrn Josef Spaun, Assessor in Linz (Sendschreiben an den Assessor Spaun in Linz)*, D. 749 (Collin; 1822); *Die Liebe hat gelogen*, D. 751 (Platen-Hallermünde; 1822); *Nachtviolen*, D. 752 (Mayrhofer; 1822); *Heliopolis*, D. 753 (Mayrhofer; 1822); *Heliopolis*, D. 754 (Mayrhofer; 1822); *Du liebst mich nicht*, D. 756 (2 versions; Platen-Hallermünde; 1822); *Todesmusik*, D. 758 (Schober; 1822); *Schatzgräbers Begehr*, D. 761 (2 versions; Schober; 1822); *Schwestergruss*, D. 762 (Bruchmann; 1822); *Der Musensohn*, D. 764 (2 versions; Goethe; 1822); *An die Entfernte*, D. 765 (Goethe; 1822); *Am Flusse*, D. 766 (Goethe; 1822); *Willkommen und Abschied*, D. 767 (2 versions; Goethe; 1822); *Wandrers Nachtlied*, D. 768 (Goethe; 1824); *Drang in die Ferne*, D. 770 (Leitner; 1823); *Der Zwerg*, D. 771 (Collin; 1822?); *Wehmut*, D. 772 (Collin; 1822?); *Auf dem Wasser zu singen*, D. 774 (Stolberg-Stolberg; 1823); *Dass sie hier gewesen*, D. 775 (Rückert; 1823?); *Du bist die Ruh*, D. 776 (Rückert; 1823); *Lachen und Weinen*, D. 777 (Rückert; 1823?); *Greisengesang*, D. 778 (2 versions; Rückert; 1823); *Die Wallfahrt*, D. 778a (Rückert; 1823?); *Der zürnende Barde*, D. 785 (Bruchmann; 1823); *Viola*, D. 786 (Schober; 1823); *Lied (Die Mutter Erde)*, D. 788 (Stolberg-Stolberg; 1823); *Pilgerweise*, D. 789 (Schober; 1823); *Vergissmeinnicht*, D. 792 (Schober; 1823); *Das Geheimnis*, D. 793 (Schiller; 1823); *Der Pilgrim*, D. 794 (2 versions; Schiller; 1823); *Die schöne Müllerin*, song cycle, D. 795 (Müller; 1823; 1, *Das Wandern;* 2, *Wohin?;* 3, *Halt!;* 4, *Danksagung an den Bach;* 5, *Am Feierabend;* 6, *Der Neugierige;* 7, *Ungeduld;* 8, *Morgengruss;* 9, *Des Müllers Blumen;* 10, *Tränenregen;* 11, *Mein!;* 12, *Pause;* 13, *Mit dem grünen Lautenbande;* 14, *Der Jäger;* 15, *Eifersucht und Stolz;* 16, *Die liebe Farbe;* 17, *Die böse Farbe;* 18, *Trockne Blumen;* 19, *Der Müller und der Bach;* 20, *Des Baches Wiegenlied*); *Romanze zum Drama Rosamunde*, D. 797 (Chézy; 1823); *Im Abendrot*, D. 799 (Lappe; 1824?); *Der Einsame*, D. 800 (2 versions; Lappe; 1825); *Dithyrambe*, D. 801 (Schiller; 1826); *Der Sieg*, D. 805 (Mayrhofer; 1824); *Abendstern*, D. 806 (Mayrhofer; 1824); *Auflösung*, D. 807 (Mayrhofer; 1824); *Gondelfahrer*, D. 808 (Mayrhofer; 1824); *Lied eines Kriegers*, D. 822, with Unison Chorus (1824); *Nacht und Träume*, D. 827 (2 versions; Collin; 1823); *Die junge Nonne*, D. 828 (Craigher de Jachelutta; 1825); *Abschied*, D. 829 (Pratobevera; 1826); *Lied der Anne Lyle*, D. 830 (MacDonald; 1825); *Gesang der Norna*, D. 831 (Scott; Spiker, trans.; 1825); *Des Sängers Habe*, D. 832 (Schlechta; 1825); *Der blinde Knabe*, D. 833 (2 versions; Cibber; Craigher, trans.; 1825); *Im Walde*, D. 834 (2 versions; Schulze; 1825); *Ellens Gesang*, D. 837 (Scott; Storck, trans.; 1825); *Ellens Gesang*, D. 838 (Scott; Storck, trans.; 1825); *Ellens Gesang (Hymne an die Jungfrau)*, D. 839 (Scott; Storck, trans.; 1825); *Totengräbers Heimwehe*, D. 842 (Craigher; 1825); *Lied des gefangenen Jägers*, D. 843 (Scott; Storck, trans.; 1825); *Normans Gesang*, D. 846 (Scott; Storck, trans.; 1825); *Das Heimweh*, D. 851 (2 versions; Felsö-Eör; 1825); *Die Allmacht*, D. 852 (2 versions; Pyrker; 1825); *Auf der Bruck*, D. 853 (2 versions; Schulze; 1825); *Fülle der Liebe*, D. 854 (Schlegel; 1825); *Wiedersehn*, D. 855 (Schlegel; 1825); *Abendlied für die Entfernte*, D. 856 (Schlegel; 1825); *2 Szenen aus dem Schauspiel Lacrimas*, D. 857: 1, *Lied der Delphine;* 2, *Lied des Florio* (Schütz; 1825); *An mein Herz*, D. 860 (Schulze; 1825); *Der liebliche Stern*, D. 861 (Schulze; 1825); *Um Mitternacht*, D. 862 (2 versions; Schulze; first version, 1825; 2nd version, 1826); *An Gott*, D. 863 (Hohlfeld; 1827; not extant); *Das Totenhemdchen*, D. 864 (Bauernfeld; 1824; not extant); *Widerspruch*, D. 865 (Seidl; 1826?); *4 Refrainlieder*, D. 866 (Seidl; 1828): 1, *Die Unterscheidung;* 2, *Bei dir allein;* 3, *Die Männer sind méchant;* 4, *Irdisches Glück; Wiegenlied*, D. 867 (Seidl; 1826?); *Totengräber-Weise*, D. 869 (Schlechta; 1826); *Der Wanderer an den Mond*, D. 870 (Seidl; 1826); *Das Zügenglöcklein*, D. 871 (2 versions; Seidl; 1826); *O Quell, was strömst du rasch und wild*, D. 874 (Schulze; 1826; fragment only); *Im Jänner 1817 (Tiefes Leid)*, D. 876 (Schulze; 1826); *Gesänge aus Wilhelm Meister*, D. 877: 1, *Mignon und der Harfner;* 2, 3, and 4, *Lied der Mignon* (Goethe; 1826); *Am Fenster*, D. 878 (Seidl; 1826); *Sehnsucht*, D. 879 (Seidl; 1826); *Im Freien*, D. 880 (Seidl; 1826); *Fischerweise*, D. 881 (2 versions; Schlechta; 1826); *Im Frühling*, D. 882 (Schulze; 1826); *Lebensmut*, D. 883 (Schulze; 1826); *Über Wildemann*, D. 884 (Schulze; 1826); *Trinklied (Come, thou monarch of the vine)*, D. 888 (Shakespeare; Grünbühel and Bauernfeld, trans.; 1826); *Standchen (Hark, hark the lark)*, D. 889 (Shakespeare; Schlegel, trans.; 1826); *Hippolits Lied*, D. 890 (Gerstenberg; 1826); *Gesang (An Sylvia; Who Is Sylvia)*, D. 891 (Shakespeare; Bauernfeld, trans.; 1826); *Fröhliches Scheiden*, D. 896 (Leitner; 1827–28; sketch only); *Sie in jedem Liede*, D. 896a (Leitner; 1827–28; sketch only); *Wolke und Quelle*, D. 896b (Leitner; 1827–28; sketch only); *3 Gesänge*, D. 902 (1827): 1, *L'incanto degli occhi (Die Macht der Augen);* 2, *Il Traditor deluso (Der getäuschte Verräter);* 3, *Il modo di prender moglie (Die Art, ein Weib zu nehmen); Alinde*, D. 904 (Rochlitz; 1827); *An die Laute*, D. 905 (Rochlitz; 1827); *Der Vater mit dem Kind*, D. 906 (Bauernfeld; 1827); *Romanze des Richard Löwenherz*, D. 907 (2 versions; Scott; Müller, trans.; 1826); *Jägers Liebeslied*, D. 909 (Schober; 1827); *Schiffers Scheidelied*, D. 910 (Schober; 1827); *Die Winterreise*, song cycle, D. 911 (Müller; 1827; Book I: 1, *Gute Nacht;* 2, *Die Wetterfahne;* 3, *Ge-*

frorne Tränen; 4, *Erstarrung;* 5, *Der Lindenbaum;* 6, *Wasserflut* [2 versions]; 7, *Auf dem Flusse;* 8, *Rückblick;* 9, *Irrlicht;* 10, *Rast* [2 versions]; 11, *Frühlingstraum;* 12, *Einsamkeit* [2 versions]; Book II: 13, *Die Post;* 14, *Der greise Kopf;* 15, *Die Krähe;* 16, *Letzte Hoffnung;* 17, *Im Dorfe;* 18, *Der stürmische Morgen;* 19, *Täuschung;* 20, *Der Wegweiser;* 21, *Das Wirthaus;* 22, *Mut* [2 versions]; 23, *Die Nebensonnen* [2 versions]; 24, *Der Leiermann* [2 versions]; sketch for a song, D. 916a (no text; 1827); *Das Lied im Grünen,* D. 917 (Reil; 1827); *Frühlingslied,* D. 919 (Pollak; 1827); *Heimliches Lieben,* D. 922 (2 versions; 1827); *Eine altschottische Ballade,* D. 923 (3 versions; first and 3rd for 2 Voices; Eng. author unknown; Herder, trans.; 1827); *Das Weinen,* D. 926 (Leitner; 1827–28); *Vor meiner Wiege,* D. 927 (Leitner; 1827–28); *Der Wallensteiner Lanzknecht beim Trunk,* D. 931 (Leitner; 1827); *Der Kreuzzug,* D. 932 (Leitner; 1827); *Des Fischers Liebesglück,* D. 933 (Leitner; 1827); *Lebensmut,* D. 937 (Rellstab; 1828; fragment only); *Der Winterabend,* D. 938 (Leitner; 1828); *Die Sterne,* D. 939 (Leitner; 1828); *Auf dem Strom,* D. 943, with Horn or Cello obbligato (Rellstab; 1828); *Herbst,* D. 945 (Rellstab; 1828); *Glaube, Hoffnung und Liebe,* D. 955 (Kuffner; 1828); *Schwanengesang,* D. 957 (1828; Book I: 1, *Liebesbotschaft [Rellstab];* 2, *Kriegers Ahnung [Rellstab];* 3, *Frühlingssehnsucht [Rellstab];* 4, *Ständchen [Rellstab];* 5, *Aufenthalt [Rellstab];* 6, *In der Ferne [Rellstab];* Book II: 7, *Abschied [Rellstab];* 8, *Der Atlas [Heine];* 9, *Ihr Bild [Heine];* 10, *Das Fischermädchen [Heine];* 11, *Die Stadt [Heine];* 12, *Am Meer [Heine];* 13, *Der Doppelgänger [Heine];* 14, *Die Taubenpost [Seidl];* *Der Hirt auf dem Felsen,* D. 965, with Clarinet obbligato (Müller; 1828); *Der Graf von Habsburg,* D. 990 (Schiller; 1815?); *Kaiser Maximilian auf der Martinswand,* D. 990a (Collin; 1815?); *Augenblicke in Elysium,* D. 990b (originally D. 582; Schober; not extant); *Das Echo,* D. 990c (originally D. 868; Castelli); *Die Schiffende,* D. 990d (Hölty; not extant); *L'incanto degli occhi,* D. 990e (Metastasio); *Il Traditor deluso,* D. 990f (Metastasio; not extant); *Mein Frieden,* D. AI/30 (Heine; 1815?).

For orch.: Overture in D major, D. 2a (originally D. 996; 1811?; fragment only); Symph. in D major, D. 2b (originally D. 997; 1811?; fragment of first movement only); Overture in D major, to Albrecht's comedy *Der Teufel als Hydraulicus,* D. 4 (1812?); Overture in D major, D. 12 (1811?); Overture in D major, D. 26 (1812); 3 minuets and trios, D. 39a (1813; not extant); orch. fragment in D major, D. 71c (originally D. 966a; 1813); Symph. No. 1, in D major, D. 82 (1813); orch. fragment in B-flat major, D. 94a (1814?); Symph. No. 2, in B-flat major, D. 125 (1814–15); Symph. No. 3, in D major, D. 200 (1815); Concerto (Concertstück) in D major for Violin and Orch., D. 345 (1816); Symph. No. 4, in C minor, D. 417, "Tragic" (1816); Rondo in A major for Violin and Strings, D. 438 (1816); Overture in B-flat major, D. 470 (1816); Symph. No. 5, in B-flat major, D. 485 (1816); Overture in D major, D. 556 (1817); Polonaise in B-flat major for Violin and Orch., D. 580 (1817); Symph. No. 6, in C major, D. 589 (1817–18); Overture in D major, D. 590, "im italienischen Stile" (1817); Overture in C major, D. 591, "im italienischen Stile"

(1817); Symph. in D major, D. 615 (piano sketches for 2 movements only; 1818); Overture in E minor, D. 648 (1819); Symph. in D major, D. 708a (sketches only; date unknown); Symph. (No. 7) in E major, D. 729 (1821; sketched in score; performing version arranged by Weingartner); Symph. No. 8, in B minor, D. 759, "Unfinished" (1822; 2 movements and an unfinished scherzo); "Gmunden" or "Gastein" Symph., D. 849 (now believed to be identical with D. 944); Symph. in D major, D. 936a (1828; sketches only); Symph. No. 9, in C major, D. 944, "Great" (probably begun in 1825; completed in 1826).

For piano: Fantasie in C minor, D. 2e (originally D. 993; 1811); Fugue in D minor, D. 13 (1812?); Overture, D. 14 (1812?; sketch only; not extant); 6 variations in E-flat major, D. 21 (1812; not extant); 7 variations in F major, D. 24 (1812; fragment only; not extant); Fugue in C major, D. 24a (1812); Fugue in G major, D. 24b (1812); Fugue in D minor, D. 24c (1812); Fugue in C major, D. 24d (1812; fragment only); Fugue in F major, D. 25c (1812; fragment only); Andante in C major, D. 29 (1812); fugal sketches in B-flat major, D. 37a (originally D. 967; 1813?); Fugue in E minor, D. 41a (1813; fragment only); Fugue in E minor, D. 71b (1813; fragment only); Allegro in E major, D. 154 (sketch of D. 157; 1815); 10 variations in F major, D. 156 (1815); Sonata in E major, D. 157 (1815; unfinished); Adagio in G major, D. 178 (1815); Sonata in C major, D. 279 (1815); Allegretto in C major, D. 346 (1816?; fragment only); Allegretto moderato in C major, D. 347 (1813?; fragment only); Andantino in C major, D. 348 (1816; fragment only); Adagio in C major, D. 349 (1816?; fragment only); Sonata in F major, D. 459 (1816; fragment only); *5 Klavierstücke,* D. 459a (first 2 from preceding work; 1816?); Adagio in D-flat major, D. 505 (original slow movement of D. 625; 1818); Rondo in E major, D. 506 (1817); Sonata in A minor, D. 537 (1817); Sonata in A-flat major, D. 557 (1817); Sonata in E minor, D. 566 (1817); Sonata in D-flat major, D. 567 (unfinished; first version of D. 568; 1817); Sonata in E-flat major, D. 568 (1817); Scherzo in D major and Allegro in F-sharp minor, D. 570 (unfinished; 1817); Sonata in F-sharp minor, D. 571 (1817; fragment only); Sonata in B major, D. 575 (1817); 13 variations on a theme by Anselm Hüttenbrenner, in A minor, D. 576 (1817); 2 scherzos in B-flat major and D-flat major, D. 593 (1817); Andante in A major, D. 604 (1816?); Fantasia in C major, D. 605 (1821–24; fragment only); Fantasy in C major, D. 605a, "Grazer Fantasie" (1818?); March in E major, D. 606 (1818?); Adagio in E major, D. 612 (1818); Sonata in C major, D. 613 (2 movements; 1818); Sonata in F minor, D. 625 (2 movements; 1818); Sonata in C-sharp minor, D. 655 (1819; fragment only); Sonata in A major, D. 664 (1819?); Variations on a Waltz by Diabelli, in C minor, D. 718 (1821); Overture to *Alfonso und Estrella,* in D major, D. 759a (an arrangement of the D. 732 overture; 1822); Fantasy in C major, D. 760, "Wanderfantasie" (1822); Sonata in E minor, D. 769a (originally D. 994; 1823?; fragment only); 6 *Momens musicals* [sic] in C major, A-flat major, F minor, C-sharp minor, F minor, A-flat major, D. 780 (1823–28); Sonata in A minor, D. 784 (1823); *Ungarische Melodie* in B mi-

Schubert

nor, D. 817 (1824); Sonata in C major, D. 840, *Reliquie* (unfinished; 1825); Sonata in A minor, D. 845 (1825); Sonata in D major, D. 850 (1825); Sonata in G major, D. 894 (originally known as the *Fantasie, Andante, Menuetto und Allegretto;* 1826); 4 impromptus, in C minor, E-flat major, G-flat major, and A-flat major, D. 899 (1827); Allegretto in C minor, D. 900 (1820?; fragment only); Allegretto in C minor, D. 915 (1827); sketch for a piano piece in C major, D. 916b (1827); sketch for a piano piece in C minor, D. 916c (1827); 4 impromptus, in F minor, A-flat major, B-flat major, and F minor, D. 935 (1827); 3 Klavierstücke, in E-flat minor, E-flat major, and C major, D. 946 (1828); Sonata in C minor, D. 958 (1828); Sonata in A major, D. 959 (1828); Sonata in B-flat major, D. 960 (1828); March in G major, D. 980f (date unknown).

FOR PIANO, FOUR-HANDS: Fantasie in G major, D. 1 (1810); Fantasie in G major, D. 1b (1810?; fragment only); Sonata in F major, D. 1c (1810; unfinished); Fantasie in G minor, D. 9 (1811); Fantasie in C minor, D. 48, "Grande sonate" (2 versions; 1813); Overture in D major, D. 592, "im italienischen Stile" (an arrangement of D. 590; 1817); Overture in C major, D. 597, "im italienischen Stile" (an arrangement of D. 591; 1817); 4 polonaises, in D minor, B-flat major, E major, and F major, D. 599 (1818); 3 *marches héroïques,* in B minor, C major, and D major, D. 602 (1818?); Rondo in D major, D. 608 (2 versions; 1818); Sonata in B-flat major, D. 617 (1818); Deutscher in G major, with 2 trios and 2 Ländler, in E major, D. 618 (1818); Polonaise and Trio, D. 618a (sketch only; 1818); 8 variations on a French song, in E minor, D. 624 (1818); Overture in G minor, D. 668 (1819); Overture in F major, D. 675 (1819); 3 *marches militaires,* in D major, G major, and E-flat major, D. 733 (1818); Overture to *Alfonso und Estrella,* D. 773 (an arrangement of the D. 732 overture; 1823); Overture to *Fierabras,* D. 798 (an arrangement of the D. 796 overture; 1823); Sonata in C major, D. 812, "Grand duo" (1824); 8 variations on an original theme, in A-flat major, D. 813 (1824); 4 Ländler, in E-flat major, A-flat major, C minor, and C major, D. 814 (1824); *Divertissement à l'hongroise* in G minor, D. 818 (1824); 6 *grandes marches,* in E-flat major, G minor, B minor, E-flat minor, and A-flat major, D. 819 (1824); *Divertissement sur des motifs originaux français* in E minor, D. 823: 1, *Marche brillante;* 2, *Andantino varié;* 3, *Rondeau brillant* (1825?); 6 polonaises, in D minor, F major, B-flat major, D major, A major, and E major, D. 824 (1826); *Grande marche funèbre* in C minor, D. 859 (on the death of Alexander I of Russia; 1825); *Grande marche héroïque* in A minor, D. 885 (for the coronation of Nicholas I of Russia; 1826); 8 variations on a theme from Hérold's *Marie,* in C major, D. 908 (1827); March in G major, D. 928, "Kindermarsch" (1827); Fantasie in F minor, D. 940 (1828); Allegro in A minor, D. 947, Lebensstürme (1828); Rondo in A major, D. 947 (1828); Fugue in E minor, D. 952 (1828); Allegro moderato in C major and Andante in A minor (Sonatine), D. 968 (1818?); Introduction, 4 variations on an original theme, and Finale, in B-flat major, D. 968a (originally D. 603; 1824?); 2 *marches caractéristiques* in C major, D. 968b (originally D.

886; 1826?).

DANCES FOR PIANO: Waltzes and March, D. 19b (1812?; not extant); 12 minuets with trios, D. 22 (1812; not extant); 30 minuets with trios, D. 41 (1813; 10 not extant); 2 minuets, in D major and A major, both with 2 trios, D. 91 (1813; 2 other minuets lost); 12 Wiener Deutsche, D. 128 (1812?); Deutscher in E major, with trio, D. 135 (1815); Deutscher in C-sharp minor, with trio, D. 139 (1815); 12 waltzes, 17 Ländler, and 9 écossaises, D. 145 (1815–21); 20 waltzes (*Letzte Walzer*), D. 146 (Nos. 1 and 3–11, 1815; Nos. 2 and 12–20, 1823); Ecossaise in D minor/F major, D. 158 (1815); Minuet in A minor, with trio, D. 277a (1815); 12 écossaises, D. 299 (1815); Minuet in A major, with trio, D. 334 (1815?); Minuet in E major, with 2 trios, D. 335 (1813?); 36 Originaltänze (*Erste Walzer*), D. 365 (1816–21); 17 Ländler, D. 366 (1816–24); 8 Ländler, D. 378 (1816); 3 minuets, in E major, A major, and C major, each with 2 trios, D. 380 (1816); 12 Deutsche, D. 420 (1816); 6 écossaises, D. 421 (1816); Ecossaise in E-flat major, D. 511 (1817?); 8 écossaises, D. 529 (1817); Minuet in C-sharp minor, D. 600 (1814?); Trio in E major, D. 610 (1818); Deutscher in C-sharp minor and Ecossaise in D-flat major, D. 643 (1819); 12 Ländler, D. 681 (1815?; Nos. 1–4 not extant); 6 écossaises, D. 697 (1820); Deutscher in G-flat major, D. 722 (1821); 16 Ländler and 2 écossaises (*Wiener-Damen Ländler*), D. 734 (1822?); Galop and 8 écossaises, D. 735 (1822?); 2 Deutsche, in A major and D major, D. 769 (No. 1, 1824; No. 2, 1823); 34 *Valses sentimentales,* D. 779 (1823?); 12 écossaises, D. 781 (1823); Ecossaise in D major, D. 782 (1823?); 16 Deutsche and 2 écossaises, D. 783 (1823–24); 12 Deutsche (Ländler), D. 790 (1823); 3 écossaises, D. 816 (1824); 6 Deutsche, D. 820 (1824); 2 Deutsche, in F major and G major, D. 841 (1825); Waltz in G major (*Albumblatt*), D. 844 (1825); 12 Grazer Walzer, D. 924 (1827); Grazer Galopp in C major, D. 925 (1827); Deutscher, D. 944a (1828; not extant); 12 waltzes (*Valses nobles*), D. 969 (1826); 6 Ländler, D. 970 (date unknown); 3 Deutsche, in A minor, A major, and E major, D. 971 (1822); 3 Deutsche, in D-flat major, A-flat major, and A major, D. 972 (date unknown); 3 Deutsche, in E major, E major, and A-flat major, D. 973 (date unknown); 2 Deutsche, both in D-flat major, D. 974 (date unknown); Deutscher in D major, D. 975 (date unknown); Cotillon in E-flat major, D. 976 (1825); 8 écossaises, D. 977 (date unknown); Waltz in A-flat major, D. 978 (1825); Waltz in G major, D. 979 (1826); 2 waltzes, in G major and B minor, D. 980 (1826); 2 dance sketches, in A major and E major, D. 980a (originally D. 640; date unknown); 2 Ländler, both in E-flat major, D. 980b (originally D. 679; date unknown); 2 Ländler, both in D-flat major, D. 980c (originally D. 680; fragment only; date unknown); Waltz in C major, D. 980d (1827); 2 dance sketches, in G minor and F major, D. 980c (date unknown).

CHAMBER MUSIC: String Quartet, D. 2c (originally D. 998; 1811?; fragment only); 6 minuets, D. 2d (originally D. 995; 1811); sketch for a trio of a minuet, in C major, D. 2f (1811); String Quartet in C major, D. 3 (1812; fragment only); Overture in C minor, D. 8 (1811); Overture in C minor, D. 8a (an arrangement of D. 8; 1811); String Quartet in G minor/B-flat major, D. 18 (1810?); String Quartet, D. 19 (1810?; not extant); String Quartet, D. 19a (1810?; not extant); Overture in B-flat major, D. 20 (1812; not extant); Trio (Sonata in one movement) in B-flat major, D. 28 (1812); String Quartet in C major, D. 32 (1812); String Quartet in B-flat major, D. 36 (1812–13); String Quartet in C major, D. 46 (1813); String Quartet in B-flat major, D. 68 (1813; 2 movements only); Wind Octet in F major, D. 72 (1813); Allegro in F major, D. 72a (1813; unfinished); String Quartet in D major, D. 74 (1813); Wind Nonet in E-flat minor, D. 79, "Franz Schuberts Begräbnis-Feyer" (*Eine kleine Trauermusik*) (1813); Minuet in D major, D. 86 (1813); String Quartet in E-flat major, D. 87 (1813); Andante in C major, D. 87a (1813); 5 minuets and 6 trios, D. 89 (1813); 5 Deutsche and 7 trios, with coda, D. 90 (1813); String Quartet in D major, D. 94 (1811?); 5 minuets and 6 Deutsche, with trios, D. 94b (1814; not extant); Trio in G major, for Schubert's arrangement of Matiegka's *Notturno,* op. 21, D. 96 (1814); String Quartet in C minor, D. 103 (1814; fragments, Grave, and Allegro extant); String Trio in B-flat major, D. 111a (1814; not extant); String Quartet in B-flat major, D. 112 (1814); String Quartet in G minor, D. 173 (1815); String Quartet in E major, D. 353 (1816); 4 komische Ländler in D major, D. 354 (1816); 8 Ländler in F-sharp minor, D. 355 (1816); 9 Ländler in D major, D. 370 (1816); 11 Ländler in B-flat major, D. 374 (1816); Sonata (Sonatina) in D major, D. 384 (1816); Sonata (Sonatina) in A minor, D. 385 (1816); Sonata (Sonatina) in G minor, D. 408 (1816); String Trio in B-flat major, D. 471 (1816; unfinished); Adagio and Rondo concertante in F major, D. 487 (1816); Sonata (Duo) in A major, D. 574 (1817); String Trio in B-flat major, D. 581 (1817); Variations in A major, D. 597a (1817; not extant); Overture in B-flat major, D. 601 (an arrangement of the D. 470 overture; 1816?; fragment only); Piano Quintet in A major, D. 667 (*Die Forelle*) (1819); String Quartet in C minor, D. 703 (*Quartettsatz*) (1820); Introduction and variations on *Trockne Blumen* from *Die schöne Müllerin,* in E minor/E major, D. 802 (1824); Octet in F major, D. 803 (1824); String Quartet in A minor, D. 804 (1824); String Quartet in D minor, D. 810, "Der Tod und das Mädchen" (1824); Sonata in A minor, D. 821, "Arpeggione" (1824); String Quartet in G major, D. 887 (1826); Rondo in B minor (*Rondo brillant*) (1826); Piano Trio movement in E-flat major, D. 897, "Notturno" (1828?); Piano Trio in B-flat major, D. 898 (1828?); Piano Trio in E-flat major, D. 929 (1827); Fantasy in C major, D. 934 (1827); String Quintet in C major, D. 956 (1828); Fugue in C major, D. A1/3 (1812; fragment only).

BIBLIOGRAPHY: COLLECTED EDITIONS, SOURCE MATERIAL: The first complete critical ed. of his works, *Franz Schuberts Werke: Kritisch durchgesehene Gesamtausgabe,* ed. by E. Mandyczewski (assisted by Brahms, Brüll, Hellmesberger, J.N. Fuchs et al.), was publ. by Breitkopf & Härtel (40 vols. in 21 series, Leipzig, 1884–97). A new and exhaustive critical ed., *Franz Schubert: Neue Ausgabe sämtlicher Werke,* ed. by W. Dürr, A. Feil, C. Landon et al., is being publ. under the sponsorship of the Internationalen Schubert-Gesellschaft (Kassel,

1964––). The standard thematic catalogue is by O. Deutsch and D. Wakeling, *Schubert: Thematic Catalogue of All His Works in Chronological Order* (London, 1951; in German as *Franz Schubert: Thematisches Verzeichnis seiner Werke in chronologischer Folge . . . ,* publ. in the *Neue Ausgabe sämtlicher Werke* of Schubert in a revised ed. in 1978). See also R. van Hoorickx, "Thematic Catalogue of Schubert's Works: New Additions, Corrections and Notes," *Revue Belge de Musicologie,* XXVIII–XXX (1974–76).

Other sources include the following: O. Deutsch, ed., *F. S.s Briefe und Schriften* (Munich, 1919; Eng. trans., 1928; 4th German ed., 1954); *Bericht über den Internationalen Kongress für Schubertforschung: Wien 1928* (essays on source material and collections; Augsburg, 1929); O. Deutsch, ed., *F. S.s Tagebuch* (facsimile and transcription; Vienna, 1928; Eng. trans., 1928); R. Lachmann, "Die S.-Autographen der Staatsbibliothek zu Berlin," *Zeitschrift für Musikwissenschaft,* XI (1928); J.-G. Prod'homme, "Les Manuscrits de S. à la Bibliothèque du Conservatoire de Paris," *Revue Musicale,* XII (1928); W. Kahl, *Verzeichnis des Schrifttums über F. S.: 1828–1928* (Regensburg, 1938); H. Werlé, ed., *F. S. in seinen Briefen und Aufzeichnungen* (Leipzig, 1948; 4th ed., 1955); M.J.E. Brown, "Recent S. Discoveries," *Music & Letters,* XXXII (1951); idem, "New, Old and Rediscovered S. Manuscripts," ibid., XXXVII (1957); R. van Hoorickx, "About Some Early S. Manuscripts," *Music Review,* XXX (1969); C. Landon, "Neue S.-Funde," *Österreichische Musikzeitschrift,* XXIV (1969; Eng. trans. in *Music Review,* XXXI, 1970); R. Klein, *S.-Stätten* (Vienna, 1972); R. van Hoorickx, "Some Unknown S. Manuscripts," *Musical Times,* CXVIII (1977); E. Hilmar, *Verzeichnis der S.-Handschriften in der Musiksammlung der Wiener Stadt- und Landesbibliothek* (Kassel, 1978).

ICONOGRAPHY: A. Trost, "F. S.s Bildnisse," *Berichte und Mittheilungen des Alterthums-Vereines zu Wien,* XXXIII/2 (1898); O. Deutsch, *Die historischen Bildnisse F. S.s in getreuen Nachbildungen* (Vienna, 1922); A, Orel, *F. S., 1797–1828: Sein Leben in Bildern* (Leipzig, 1939); R. Petzoldt, *F. S.: Sein Leben in Bildern* (Leipzig, 1953); E. Hilmar and O. Brusatti, eds., *F. S.* (exhibition catalogue; Vienna, 1978); E. Badura-Skoda, "A S. Life Mask," *Musical Times,* CXX (1979).

BIOGRAPHICAL: H. Kreissle von Hellborn, *F. S., Eine biographische Skizze* (Vienna, 1861; 2nd ed., greatly enlarged as *F. S.,* 1865; Eng. trans., London, 1866); A. Reissmann, *F. S.: Sein Leben und seine Werke* (Berlin, 1873); H. Frost, *F. S.* (London, 1881; 2nd ed., 1923); M. Friedlaender, *Beiträge zur Biographie F. S.s* (Berlin, 1887; new ed. as *F. S.: Skizze seines Lebens und Wirken,* Leipzig, 1928); A. Niggli, *S.* (Leipzig, 1890); H. Ritter, *F. S.* (Bamberg, 1896); R. Heuberger, *F. S.* (Berlin, 1902; 3rd ed., revised, 1920, by H. von der Pforten); M. Zenger, *F. S.s Wirken und Erdenwallen* (Langensalza, 1902); O. Deutsch, *S.-Brevier* (Berlin, 1905); W. Klatte, *S.* (Berlin, 1907); L.-A. Bourgault-Ducoudray, *S.* (Paris, 1908; new ed., 1926); H. Antcliffe, *S.* (London, 1910); W. Dahms, *S.* (Berlin, 1912); O. Deutsch, ed., *F. S.: Die Dokumente seines*

Lebens und Schaffens (in collaboration, first with L. Scheibler, then with W. Kahl and G. Kinsky, it was planned as a comprehensive work in 3 vols. containing all known documents, pictures, and other materials, arranged in chronological order, with a thematic catalogue; only 2 vols. publ.: vol. III, *Sein Leben in Bildern*, Munich, 1913; vol. II, part 1, *Die Dokumente seines Lebens*, Munich, 1914, which appeared in an Eng. trans. by Eric Blom as *S.: A Documentary Biography*, London, 1946, and in an American ed. as *The S. Reader: A Life of F. S. in Letters and Documents*, N.Y., 1947; a 2nd German ed., enlarged, was publ. in the *Neue Ausgabe sämtlicher Werke* of Schubert in 1964); K. Kobald, *S. und Schwind* (Zürich, 1921); O. Bie, *F. S.: Sein Leben und sein Werk* (Berlin, 1925; Eng. trans., 1928); E. Bethge, *F. S.* (Leipzig, 1928); H. Eulenberg, *S. und die Frauen* (Hellerau, 1928); N. Flower, *F. S.* (London and N.Y., 1928; new ed., 1949); A. Glazunov, *S.* (Leningrad, 1928); K. Kobald, *F. S. und seine Zeit* (Zürich, 1928; Eng. trans., 1928; new German ed., 1948); G. Kruse, *F. S.* (Bielefeld, 1928); P. Landormy, *La Vie de S.* (Paris, 1928); J.-G. Prod'homme, *S.* (Paris, 1928); idem, *S. raconté par ceux qui l'ont vu* (Paris, 1928); P. Stefan, *F. S.* (Berlin, 1928; new ed., Vienna, 1947); A. Weiss, *F. S.* (Vienna, 1928); R. Bates, *F. S.* (London, 1934); W. Vetter, *F. S.* (Potsdam, 1934); A. Schünemann, *Erinnerungen an S.* (Berlin, 1936); A. Orel, *Der junge S.* (Vienna, 1940); A. Kolb, *F. S., Sein Leben* (Stockholm, 1941); K. Höcker, *Wege zu S.* (Regensburg, 1942); B. Paumgartner, *F. S.* (Zürich, 1943; 2nd ed., 1947); R. Tenschert, *Du holde Kunst: Ein kleiner S.-Spiegel* (Vienna, 1943); A. Hutchings, *S.* (London, 1945; 4th ed., revised, 1973); W. and P. Rehberg, *F. S.* (Zürich, 1946); C. Weingartner, *F. S.* (Alten, 1947); R. Schauffler, *F. S.: The Ariel of Music* (N.Y., 1949); A. Einstein, *S.: A Musical Portrait* (N.Y., 1951; German ed., 1952); H. Rutz, *S., Dokumente seines Lebens und Schaffens* (Munich, 1952); H. Goldschmidt, *F. S.* (Berlin, 1954; 5th ed., 1964); P. Mies, *F. S.* (Leipzig, 1954); O. Deutsch, ed., *S.: Die Erinnerungen seiner Freunde* (Leipzig, 1957; Eng. trans. as *S.: Memoirs by His Friends*, N.Y., 1958; 3rd German ed., 1974); M.J.E. Brown, *S.: A Critical Biography* (London, 1958; 2nd ed., 1961); F. Hug, *F. S.: Leben und Werk eines Frühvollendeten* (Frankfurt, 1958); L. Kusche, *F. S.: Dichtung und Wahrheit* (Munich, 1962); K. Kobald, *F. S.* (Vienna, 1963); A. Kolb, *S.* (Gütersloh, 1964); J. Bruyr, *F. S.: L'Homme et son œuvre* (Paris, 1965); F. de Eaubonne and M.-R. Hofmann, *La Vie de S.* (Paris, 1965); W. Marggraf, *F. S.* (Leipzig, 1967); J. Reed, *S.: The Final Years* (London, 1972); J. Wechsberg, *S.* (N.Y., 1977); H. Fröhlich, *S.* (Munich, 1978); H. Osterheld, *F. S.: Schicksal und Persönlichkeit* (Stuttgart, 1978); E. Sams, "S.'s Illness Re-examined," *Musical Times* (Jan. 1980); P. Gammond, *S.* (London, 1982).

CRITICAL, ANALYTICAL: J. Rissé, *F. S. in seinen Liedern* (2 vols., Hannover, 1872); H. de Curzon, *Les Lieder de F. S.* (Brussels, 1899); M. Gallet, *S. et le Lied* (Paris, 1907); O. Wissig, *F. S.s Messen* (Leipzig, 1909); M. Bauer, *Die Lieder F. S.s* (Leipzig, 1915); H. von der Pfordten, *S. und das deutsche Lied* (Leipzig, 1916; 2nd ed., 1920); W. Kahl, "Das lyrische Klavierstück S.s," *Archiv für Musikwissenschaft*, 3 (1921);

R. Krott, *Die Singspiele S.s* (Diss., Univ. of Vienna, 1921); O. Deutsch, *Die Originalausgaben von S.s Goethe-Liedern* (Vienna, 1926); H. Költzsch, *F. S. in seinen Klaviersonaten* (Leipzig, 1927); F. von Kraus, *Beiträge zur Erforschung des malenden und poetisierenden Wesens in der Begleitung von F. S.s Liedern* (Mainz, 1927); R. Capell, *S.'s Songs* (London, 1928; 3rd ed., revised, 1973, by M. Cooper); F. Damian, *F. S.s Liederkreis, Die schöne Müllerin* (Leipzig, 1928); F. Günther, *S.s Lied* (Stuttgart, 1928); K. Huschke, *Das 7 Gestirn der grossen S. 'schen Kammermusikwerke* (Pritzwalk, 1928); K. Kobald, *Der Meister des deutschen Liedes, F. S.* (Vienna and Leipzig, 1928); C. Lafite, *Das Schubertlied und seine Sänger* (Vienna, 1928); P. Mies, *S., Der Meister des Liedes* (Berlin, 1928); F. Weingartner, *S. und sein Kreis* (Zürich, 1928); H. Biehle, *S.s Lieder als Gesangsproblem* (Langensalza, 1929); H. Bosch, *Die Entwicklung des Romantischen in S.s Liedern* (Leipzig, 1930); H. Therstappen, *Die Entwicklung der Form bei S.* (Leipzig, 1931); E. Laaff, *F. S.s Sinfonien* (Wiesbaden, 1933); T. Archer, "The Formal Construction of *Die schöne Müllerin*," *Musical Quarterly* (Oct. 1934); E. Porter, *The Songs of S.* (London, 1937); E. Schaeffer, "S.'s *Winterreise*," *Musical Quarterly* (Jan. 1938); O. Deutsch, "The Chronology of S.'s String Quartets," *Music & Letters*, XXIV (1943); G. Abraham, ed., *The Music of S.* (N.Y., 1947); O. Deutsch, "The Discovery of S.'s Great C Major Symphony: A Story in 15 Letters," *Musical Quarterly* (Oct. 1952); M.J.E. Brown, "S.'s *Winterreise*, Part I," ibid. (April 1953); W. Vetter, *Der Klassiker S.* (2 vols., Leipzig, 1953); E. Schmitz, *S.s Auswirkung auf die deutsche Musik bis zu Hugo Wolf und Bruckner* (Leipzig, 1954); H. Haas, *Über die Bedeutung der Harmonik in den Liedern F. S.s* (Bonn, 1957); H.-M. Sachse, *F. S.s Streichquartette* (Munich, 1958); M. Chusid, *The Chamber Music of F. S.* (Diss., Univ. of Calif., Berkeley, 1961); E. Porter, *S.'s Song-technique* (London, 1961); E. Norman-McKay, *The Stage-works of S., Considered in the Framework of Austrian Biedermeier Society* (Diss., Oxford Univ., 1962–63); A. Bell, *The Songs of S.* (Lowestoft, 1964); R. Stringham, *The Masses of F. S.* (Diss., Cornell Univ., 1964); S. Kunze, *F. S.: Sinfonie h-moll: Unvollendete* (Munich, 1965); M.J.E. Brown, *Essays on S.* (London, 1966); idem, *S. Songs* (London, 1967); T. Georgiades, *S.: Musik und Lyrik* (Göttingen, 1967); P. Radcliffe, *S. Piano Sonatas* (London, 1967); D. Weekley, *The One-piano, Four-hand Compositions of F. S.: Historical and Interpretative Analysis* (Diss., Indiana Univ., 1968); J. Westrup, *S. Chamber Music* (London, 1969); M.J.E. Brown, *S. Symphonies* (London, 1970); H. Gal, *F. S. oder Die Melodie* (Frankfurt, 1970; Eng. trans. as *F. S. and the Essence of Melody*, London, 1974); M. Citron, *S.'s Seven Complete Operas: A Musico-dramatic Study* (Diss., Univ. of North Carolina, 1971); R. Coolidge, "Form in the String Quartets of F. S.," *Music Review*, XXXII (1971); D. Fischer-Dieskau, *Auf den Spuren der S.-Lieder; Werden–Wesen–Wir* (Wiesbaden, 1971; Eng. trans. as *S.: A Biographical Study of the Songs*, London, 1976); R. Weber, *Die Sinfonien F. S.s im Versuch einer Strukturwissenschaftlichen Darstellung und Untersuchungen*

(Diss., Univ. of Münster, 1971); G. Cunningham, *F. S. als Theaterkomponist* (Diss., Univ. of Freiburg, 1974); G. Moore, *The S. Song Cycles, with Thoughts on Performance* (London, 1975); J. Reed, "How the 'Great' C major Was Written," *Music & Letters*, LVI (1975); R. Winter, "S.'s Undated Works, A New Chronology," *Musical Times*, CXIX (1978); C. Brauner, "Irony in the Heine Lieder of S. and Schumann," *Musical Quarterly* (April 1981); R. van Hoorickx, "An Unknown S. Letter," *Musical Times* (May 1981); L. Minchin, *S. in English* (London, 1982).

Schubert, Louis, German violinist; b. Dessau, Jan. 27, 1828; d. Dresden, Sept. 17, 1884. He went to St. Petersburg at the age of 17; then was concertmaster of the City Theater in Königsberg for 6 years; eventually settled in Dresden and became a singing teacher. He produced the operettas *Aus Sibirien* (Königsberg, 1865); *Die Rosenmädchen* (Königsberg, 1860); *Die Wahrsagerin* (Dresden, 1864); *Die beiden Geizigen* (Altenburg, 1879); *Faustina Hasse* (Altenburg, 1879); publ. a method for violin and a *Gesangschule in Liedern.*

Schuberth, Carl, German cellist; b. Magdeburg, Feb. 25, 1811; d. Zürich, July 22, 1863. He studied in Magdeburg and Dessau; after a European tour, which included Russia (1835), was engaged as a court musician in St. Petersburg, and remained there for 20 years; then went to Switzerland. He publ. 2 cello concertos; Variations for Cello, with Orch.; String Octet; 2 string quintets; 4 string quartets; Cello Sonata.

Schuberth, Julius (Ferdinand Georg), founder of the firm J. Schuberth & Co. of Leipzig and N.Y.; b. Magdeburg, July 14, 1804; d. Leipzig, June 9, 1875. He established the Hamburg business in 1826; opened a branch in Leipzig in 1832, and in N.Y. in 1850. His brother, **Fritz Wilhelm** (1817–90), took over the Hamburg house in 1853 (firm name, "Fritz Schuberth"). Julius Schuberth publ. the *Kleine Hamburger Musikzeitung* (1840–50), the *New Yorker Musikzeitung* (from 1867), and *Schuberth's kleine Musikzeitung* (1871–72). In 1872 he founded the music library at Weimar known as the Liszt-Schuberth-Stiftung. In 1891 the business was purchased by Felix Siegel (d. Leipzig, July 4, 1920), the originator of the *Musikalische Universalbibliothek.* In 1943 the entire stock of the Schuberth Publishing House was destroyed in an air raid; after World War II it was reestablished in Wiesbaden.

Schubiger, Anselm (baptismal names, **Josef Allis**), learned Swiss writer on music; b. Uznach, March 5, 1815; d. at the Monastery of Einsiedeln, March 14, 1888. He took Holy Orders in 1839 and assumed the clerical name Anselm. He wrote *Die Sängerschule St. Gallens* (Einsiedeln, 1858); *Die Pflege des Kirchengesanges und der Kirchenmusik in der deutschen katholischen Schweiz* (Einsiedeln, 1873); *Musikalische Spicilegien* (Berlin, 1876; a collection of miscellaneous essays on medieval music); also various papers publ. in journals.

Schuch, Ernst von, eminent Austrian conductor; b. Graz, Nov. 23, 1846; d. Kötzschenbroda, near Dresden, May 10, 1914. He studied violin; in 1867 he became a theater conductor in Breslau; then conducted in Würzburg, Graz, and Basel; in 1872 he obtained a position with Pollini's Italian Opera House in Dresden, and in 1873 was engaged as court conductor, remaining with the Dresden Court Opera for 40 years. In 1897 he was given the rank of hereditary nobility, which entitled him to add the nobiliary particle "von" to his name. He was a worthy successor to the traditions established in Dresden by Weber and Wagner, and earned a reputation as one of the finest opera conductors. He was moreover a man of great general culture and of progressive ideas. He brought out about 50 new operas, and conducted the world premiere of the operas *Feuersnot, Salome, Elektra,* and *Der Rosenkavalier* by Richard Strauss; also included in his repertoire operas by Puccini, which were new to Germany at the time. He seldom left Dresden; his most extensive journey was a trip to N.Y. to conduct 3 orch. concerts in 1900. In 1875 he married the opera singer **Klementine Proska** (real name, **Procházka**; b. Ödenburg, Feb. 12, 1850; d. Kötzschenbroda, June 8, 1932), who was the principal coloratura soprano during Schuch's tenure at the Dresden Opera until her retirement in 1904. Their daughter **Liesel von Schuch** (b. Dresden, Dec. 12, 1891) was also a coloratura soprano at the Dresden Opera from 1914 to 1935; then taught voice at the Dresden Hochschule für Musik (until 1967).
BIBLIOGRAPHY: L. Hartmann, "Ernst Schuch und das moderne Kapellmeistertun," *Nord und Süd* (May 1896; Breslau); P. Sakolowski, *Ernst von Schuch* (Leipzig, 1901); F. von Schuch, *Richard Strauss, Ernst von Schuch und Dresdens Oper* (2nd ed., Leipzig, 1953).

Schucht, Jean F., German writer on music; b. Holzthalleben, Thuringia, Nov. 17, 1822; d. Leipzig, March 30, 1894. He studied with Hauptmann and Spohr at Kassel; from 1868 was in Leipzig as a critic for the *Neue Zeitschrift für Musik.* He publ. *Wegweiser in der Tonkunst* (1859); *Kleines Lexikon der Tonkunst; Partiturenkenntniss; Meyerbeers Leben und Bildungsgang* (1869); *Grundriss einer praktischen Harmonielehre* (1876); a biography of Chopin (1880); wrote piano pieces and songs.

Schüchter, Wilhelm, German conductor; b. Bonn, Dec. 15, 1911; d. Dortmund, May 27, 1974. He studied conducting with Hermann Abendroth and composition with Philipp Jarnach at the Cologne Hochschule für Musik. He then conducted opera at Würzburg (1937–40) and served as assistant to Herbert von Karajan in Aachen (1940–42); also conducted at the Berlin Städtische Oper (1942–43). In 1947 he became first conductor of the North German Radio Symph. Orch. in Hamburg. From 1958 to 1961 he was chief conductor of NHK (Japan Broadcasting Corp.); in 1962 returned to Germany as Generalmusikdirektor in Dortmund, a post he held until his death.

Schudel, Thomas, American-born Canadian composer; b. Defiance, Ohio, Sept. 8, 1937. He studied composition and bassoon at Ohio State Univ. (1955–59), receiving an M.A. in both subjects there in 1961; then joined the composition classes of Bassett and Finney at the Univ. of Michigan (1961–64). He subsequently was principal bassoonist with the Regina (Canada) Symph. Orch. (1964–74) and taught at the Univ. of Regina (1964–67, 1972–78); became a Canadian citizen in 1974. WORKS: *4 Movements* for Flute, Bassoon, and Percussion (1963); *4 Movements* for Cello and Piano (1964); *Set No. 1* for Violin, Cello, Flute, Oboe, and Percussion (1965); *Set No. 2* for Wind Quintet and Brass Quintet (1966); Violin Sonata (1966); String Quartet (1967); Symph. No. 1 (1971; Trieste, Italy, Oct. 20, 1972; won the Trieste International Competition for symph. composition); *Mosaic* for Flute, 3 Percussionists, and Tape (1974); *Variations* for Orch. (1976–77); *Nocturne and Dance* for Oboe and Piano (1977); *The Dream* for Piano (1977).

Schuecker, Edmund, Austrian harpist; b. Vienna, Nov. 16, 1860; d. Bad Kreuznach, Nov. 9, 1911. After studying with Zamara at the Vienna Cons., he played the harp in various orchs.; taught at the Leipzig Cons. (1884). In 1891 he went to America as harpist of the newly organized Chicago Symph.; was a member of the Pittsburgh Symph. (1903–4) and of the Philadelphia Orch. (1904–9). He wrote pieces for harp, of which a *Mazurka* became popular; also publ. harp manuals: *Etüden- und Melodien-Album* (4 books); *Etüdenschule* (3 books); *6 Virtuosenetüden, Orchestra-Studies* (5 books); *The Most Important Parts from Wagner's Operas* (2 books).

Schuecker, Heinrich, Austrian-American harpist, brother of **Edmund Schuecker;** b. Vienna, Nov. 25, 1867; d. Boston, April 17, 1913. He studied at the Vienna Cons. (1878–84) with Zamara. In 1885 he was engaged as first harpist of the Boston Symph. Orch., and held this position until his death. He also taught harp at the New England Cons. in Boston.

Schuecker, Joseph E., harpist, son of **Edmund Schuecker;** b. Leipzig, May 19, 1886; d. Los Angeles, Dec. 9, 1938. He studied with his father, and later at the Vienna Cons. with Zamara. From 1904 to 1909 he was first harpist of the Pittsburgh Symph. Orch.; in 1909 succeeded his father as harpist in the Philadelphia Orch.; in 1915–20 taught at the Carnegie Inst. at Pittsburgh; in 1926–30, again played in the Pittsburgh Symph.; then lived in California. He was the author of a *History of the Harp.*

Schueller, Rudolf, Austrian conductor; b. Böhmisch-Leipz, July 31, 1884; d. Cleveland, Aug. 1, 1949. He studied at the Univ. of Prague; conducted opera in Berlin (1909–14); after World War I was engaged at the Rumanian Opera at Cluj (1920–24); in 1925 he settled in America; was head of the Opera School of the Cleveland Inst. of Music; wrote operas and orch. works.

Schuh, Willi, eminent Swiss music critic and musicologist; b. Basel, Nov. 12, 1900. He studied music in Aarau with Kutschera and Wehrli, in Bern with Papst, and in Munich with Courvoisier and Beer-Walbrunn. He took courses in art history and musicology in Munich with Sandberger and in Bern with Kurth; in 1927 he received his Ph.D. from the Univ. of Bern with the dissertation *Formprobleme bei Heinrich Schütz* (publ. in Leipzig, 1928). In 1928 he was engaged as music critic of the *Neue Zürcher Zeitung;* was its music editor from 1944 until 1965; was also editor in chief of the *Schweizerische Musikzeitung* (from 1941 until 1968). He also taught music history and harmony in Winterthur, in St. Gall, and at the Zürich Cons. He was made an honorary member of the Schweizerischer Tonkünstlerverein in 1969 and of the Schweizerische Musikforschende Gesellschaft in 1971. He was one of the editors of the *Schweizer Musikerlexikon* (Zürich, 1964). Several of his writings were republ. in *Kritiken und Essays* (4 vols.: vol. 1, *Über Opern von Richard Strauss,* Zürich, 1947; vol. 2, *Zeitgenössische Musik,* Zürich, 1947; vol. 3, *Schweizer Musik der Gegenwart,* Zürich, 1948; vol. 4, *Von neuer Musik,* Zürich, 1955); also *Umgang mit Musik: Über Komponisten, Libretti und Bilder* (Zürich, 1970; 2nd ed., 1971). He was the editor of *Die Briefe Richard Wagners an Judith Gautier* (Zürich, 1936); *Ferruccio Busoni: Briefe an seine Frau* (Zürich, 1936); Hugo von Hofmannsthal's *Beethoven* (Vienna, 1937; 2nd ed., 1949); with H. Ehinger and E. Refardt, *Schweizer Musikbuch* (Zürich, 1939); *Richard Strauss: Betrachtungen und Erinnerungen* (Zürich, 1949; Eng. trans., 1955; 2nd Swiss ed., revised, 1957); *Hugo von Hofmannsthal: Briefwechsel* (Zürich, 1952; Eng. trans., 1961; 4th Swiss ed., revised, 1970); *Richard Strauss: Briefe an die Eltern* (Zürich, 1954); *Igor Strawinsky: Leben und Werk, von ihm selbst* (Zürich and Mainz, 1957); *Richard Strauss und Stefan Zweig: Briefwechsel* (Frankfurt, 1957; in Eng. as *A Confidential Matter: The Letters of Richard Strauss and Stefan Zweig 1931–1935,* Berkeley, Calif., 1977); with G. Kende, *Richard Strauss und Clemens Krauss: Briefwechsel* (Munich, 1963; 2nd ed., 1964); *Richard Strauss und Willi Schuh: Briefwechsel* (Zürich, 1969). His publ. writings include *Othmar Schoeck* (Zürich, 1934); *In memoriam Richard Strauss* (Zürich, 1949); *Danae oder Die Vernunftheirat* (Frankfurt, 1952); *Renoir und Wagner* (Zürich, 1959); *Ein paar Erinnerungen an Richard Strauss* (Zürich, 1964); *Hugo von Hofmannsthal und Richard Strauss: Legende und Wirklichkeit* (Munich, 1964); *Der Rosenkavalier: Vier Studien* (Olten, 1968); *Richard Strauss: Jugend und frühe Meisterjahre: Lebenschronik 1864–98* (the authorized biography; Zürich, 1976; in Eng. as *Richard Strauss: A Chronicle of the Early Years 1864–98,* Cambridge, 1982). BIBLIOGRAPHY: J. Stenzl, "Willi Schuh zum 75. Geburtstag," *Schweizerische Musikzeitung/Revue*

Musicale Suisse, CXV (1975).

Schüler, Johannes, German conductor; b. Vietz, Neumark, June 21, 1894; d. Berlin, Oct. 3, 1966. He studied at the Berlin Hochschule für Musik; then conducted opera in Gleiwitz (1920–22), Königsberg (1922–24), and Hannover (1924–28); served as music director in Oldenburg (1928–32); also conducted in Halle (1932); later was music director in Essen (1933–36). In 1936 he joined the roster of the Berlin State Opera; in 1949 he became Generalmusikdirektor in Hannover, a post he held until 1960.

Schulhoff, Erwin, Czech composer and pianist, great-grandnephew of **Julius Schulhoff;** b. Prague, June 8, 1894; d. in a concentration camp, Wülzburg, Bavaria, Aug. 18, 1942. He studied music in Prague and Vienna; then went to Leipzig, where he studied piano with Teichmüller and composition with Max Reger (1908–10); continued his studies in Cologne (1910–14). Returning to Prague, he was active as a piano teacher; traveled as a concert pianist in Russia and France. He was an eager propagandist of modern music; together with Alois Hába, he worked on the problems of quarter-tone music. In 1933 he was a delegate at the International Congress of Revolutionary Musicians in Moscow. Convinced of the necessity of social revolution, he became a member of the Communist party; after the Nazi occupation of Czechoslovakia in 1939, he was granted Soviet citizenship to protect him from arrest; however, after the Nazi invasion of Russia in 1941, he was taken to the concentration camp, where he died the following year. As a composer, he followed the modern trends of the period between the 2 wars, including the European species of jazz. He was the first to set to music the original German text of the Communist Manifesto of 1848; the MS disappeared, but was eventually retrieved, and the work was finally performed in Prague on April 5, 1962. WORKS: FOR THE STAGE: *Ogelala,* ballet (Dessau, Nov. 21, 1925); *La Somnambule,* ballet dance-grotesque (1925; Oxford International Society for Contemporary Music Festival, July 24, 1931); *Bartipanu,* ballet scenes for Molière's *Le Bourgeois Gentilhomme* (1926; also an orch. suite); *Plameny (Flames),* opera (1927–28; Brno, Jan. 27, 1932). FOR ORCH.: 2 piano concertos (1913, 1923); *32 Variations on an Original Theme* (1919); *Suite* for Chamber Orch. (1921); 8 symphs.: No. 1 (1925); No. 2 (1932; Prague, April 24, 1935); No. 3 (1935); No. 4, *Spanish,* for Baritone and Orch. (1936–37); No. 5 (1938); No. 6, *Symphony of Freedom,* with choral finale (1940–41; Prague, May 5, 1946); No. 7, *Eroica* (1941; unfinished); No. 8 (1942; unfinished); *Double Concerto* for Flute, Piano, String Orch., and 2 Horns (Prague, Dec. 8, 1927); Concerto for String Quartet and Wind Orch. (1930; Prague, Nov. 9, 1932). CHAMBER MUSIC: 2 violin sonatas (1913, 1927); Cello Sonata (1915); *5 Pieces* for String Quartet (1923); String Sextet (1924); 2 string quartets (1924, 1925); Duo for Violin and Cello (1925); *Concertino* for Flute, Viola, and Double Bass (1925); *Divertissement* for Oboe, Clari-

net, and Bassoon (1926); Sonata for Solo Violin (1927); Flute Sonata (1927); *Hot Sonata* for Saxophone and Piano (1930). VOCAL MUSIC: *Landschaften (Landscapes),* vocal symph. for Mezzo-soprano and Orch. (1918); *Menschheit (Humanity),* vocal symph. for Alto and Orch. (1919); *H.M.S. Royal Oak,* jazz oratorio (radio perf., Brno, Feb. 12, 1935); *The Communist Manifesto,* cantata to the German text of the famous declaration of Marx and Engels (1932; Prague, April 5, 1962); *1917,* cycle of 12 songs (1933). FOR PIANO: *Variations on an Original Theme* (1913); 5 *Grotesken* (1917); 4 sonatas (1918, 1924, 1926, 1927); 5 *Arabesken* (1919); *Ironies* (1920); *Rag Music* (1922); *Partita* (1922); *Ostinato* (1923); 5 *Etudes de Jazz* (1926); 6 *Esquisses de Jazz* (1927); *Hot Music* (1928); *Suite dansante en Jazz* (1931).
BIBLIOGRAPHY: *E. Schulhoff, Vzpomniky, studie a dokumenty* (collection of articles and documents; Prague, 1958).

Schulhoff, Julius, noted pianist and composer; b. Prague, Aug. 2, 1825; d. Berlin, March 13, 1898. He studied in Prague; proceeded to Paris, where he gave concerts under the patronage of Chopin, to whom he dedicated his first composition, an *Allegro brillant.* He made a long tour through Austria, England, Spain, and Southern Russia; returning to Paris, he was a successful teacher; after the outbreak of the Franco-Prussian War (1870) he settled in Dresden; moved to Berlin shortly before his death. He publ. excellent salon music for piano; his *Galop di bravura* and *Impromptu Polka* were great favorites.

Schuller, Gunther, significant American composer, conductor, and educator; b. New York, Nov. 22, 1925. He was of a musical family; his paternal grandfather was a bandmaster in Germany before emigrating to America; his father was a violinist with the N.Y. Phil. Schuller was sent to Germany as a child for a thorough academic training; returning to the U.S., he was enrolled at the St. Thomas Church Choir School, where he studied music theory with T. Tertius Noble and took French-horn lessons with Robert Schulze at the Manhattan School of Music. He played horn with the N.Y. Phil. in 1942; in 1943 he became principal French-horn player with the Cincinnati Symph. Orch. On April 16, 1945, at the age of 19, he appeared as soloist in his first Concerto for Horn and Orch. with the Cincinnati Symph. At the same time he became fascinated with jazz; he played the French horn in a combo conducted by Miles Davis; he also began to compose jazz pieces. From 1945 to 1959 he played horn in the orch. of the Metropolitan Opera in N.Y.; from 1950 to 1963 he taught horn at the Manhattan School of Music; then was engaged to teach composition at the School of Music at Yale Univ. (1964–65). In 1966 he was appointed president of the New England Cons. in Boston, holding this post until 1977; concurrently he was chairman of the composition dept. at the Berkshire Music Center in Tanglewood, Mass.; he became its artistic director in 1969 and full director in 1972. In 1975 he founded Margun Music Inc., intended for a broad range of publications. He publ. a manual, *Horn Technique* (N.Y., 1962), and a very valuable study, *Early Jazz: Its Roots and Musical Development* (N.Y., 1968). In his multiple activities he tried to form a link between serious music and jazz; he popularized the style of "cool jazz" (recorded as *Birth of the Cool*). In 1957 he launched the slogan "third stream" to designate the combination of classical forms with improvisatory elements of jazz as a synthesis of disparate, but not necessarily incompatible, entities, and wrote fanciful pieces in this synthetic style; in many of these he worked in close cooperation with John Lewis of the Modern Jazz Quartet. As part of his investigation of the roots of jazz, he became interested in early ragtime and formed, in 1972, the New England Cons. Ragtime Ensemble; its recordings of Scott Joplin's piano rags in band arrangement were instrumental in bringing about the "ragtime revival." In his own works he freely applied serial methods, even when his general style was dominated by jazz. Schuller received honorary doctorates in music from Northwestern Univ. (1967), the Univ. of Illinois (1968), Williams College (1975), the New England Cons. (1978), and Rutgers Univ. (1980).

WORKS: FOR THE STAGE: 2 operas: *The Visitation,* in 3 acts (on a U.S. racial theme, freely adapted by Schuller from Kafka's *The Trial;* 1965–66; Hamburg, Oct. 12, 1966; U.S. premiere by the Hamburg company, N.Y., June 28, 1967), and *The Fisherman and His Wife,* one-act children's opera, to a libretto by John Updike from the Grimm fairy tale (Boston, May 7, 1970); *Variants,* jazz ballet for Jazz Quartet and Orch. (1960; N.Y., Jan. 4, 1961).

FOR ORCH.: 2 horn concertos: No. 1 (1943–44; Cincinnati, April 6, 1945, composer soloist) and No. 2 (1978); *Suite* for Chamber Orch. (1945); Cello Concerto (1945); *Vertige d'Eros,* symph. poem (1945; Madison, Wis., Oct. 15, 1967); *Symphonic Study* (1947–48); *Fantasia concertante* for 3 Trombones, and Orch. or Piano (1947); Symph. for Brass and Percussion (1949–50; revised 1964); *Dramatic Overture* (1951); *Recitative and Rondo* for Violin, and Orch. or Piano (1953–55); *Contours* for Chamber Orch. (1955–58); *Spectra* (1956–58; N.Y., Jan. 14, 1960); *7 Studies on Themes of Paul Klee* (1959; Minneapolis, Nov. 27, 1959); *Capriccio* for Tuba and Chamber Orch. (1960); *Contrasts* for Woodwind Quintet and Orch. (1961; Donaueschingen, Oct. 22, 1961; first U.S. work ever perf. at this annual German festival); *Movements* for Flute and Strings (1961); 2 piano concertos: No. 1 (1962; Cincinnati, Oct. 29, 1962) and No. 2 (1981); *Composition in 3 Parts* (1962; Minneapolis, March 29, 1963); *Threnos* for Oboe and Orch. (1963); *Meditation* for Concert Band (1963); *5 Bagatelles* (1964; Fargo, N.Dak., March 22, 1964); Symph. No. 1 (1964; Dallas, Feb. 8, 1965); *American Triptych: 3 Studies in Textures* (1964; New Orleans, March 9, 1965); 2 concertos for Orch.: No. 1 (1965; Chicago, Jan. 20, 1966; originally titled *Gala Music*) and No. 2 (1975; Washington, D.C., Oct. 12, 1976); *Colloquy* for 2 Pianos and Orch. (1966); *5 Etudes* for Youth Orch. (1966); *Diptych* for Brass Quintet and Orch. (1966; Boston, March 31, 1967); *Triplum I* (1967; N.Y., June 28, 1967) and *II*

(1974; Baltimore, Feb. 26, 1975); *Fanfare for St. Louis* (1967); Double-bass Concerto (1968; N.Y., June 27, 1968); *Shapes and Designs* (1968); *Consequents* (1970); *Museum Piece* for Renaissance Instruments and Orch. (1970; Boston, Dec. 11, 1970); *Capriccio stravagante* (1972); *3 invenzione* for Chamber Ensemble (1972; Tanglewood, Aug. 8, 1972); *3 Nocturnes* (1972); *4 Soundscapes—Hudson Valley Reminiscences* (1974; Poughkeepsie, N.Y., March 7, 1975); Violin Concerto (1975–76; Lucerne, Aug. 25, 1976); *Deaï* for 3 Orchs. (1977–78; Tokyo, March 17, 1978; U.S. premiere, Tanglewood, Aug. 4, 1979); Double-bassoon Concerto (1978; Washington, D.C., Jan. 16, 1979; first concerto ever written for this instrument); Trumpet Concerto (1979); *In Praise of Winds* for Wind Orch. (1981); Saxophone Concerto (1983; Pittsburgh, Jan. 18, 1984).

CHAMBER MUSIC: Sonata for Clarinet, Horn, and Piano (1941); *Suite* for Woodwind Quintet (1945); *3 hommages* for Horn and Piano (1942–46); *Fantasia concertante* for 3 Oboes and Piano (1946); Cello Sonata (1946); *Fantasia concertante* for 3 Trombones and Piano (1947; also with Orch.); Quartet for 4 Double Basses (1947); *Perpetuum mobile* for 4 Muted Horns, and Bassoon or Tuba (1948); Trio for Oboe, Horn, and Viola (1948); Oboe Sonata (1948–51); *Duo Sonata* for Clarinet and Bass Clarinet (1949); *Fantasy* for Solo Cello (1951); *5 Pieces* for 5 Horns (1952); *2 Movements* for Flute and String Trio (1952); *Recitative and Rondo* for Violin and Piano (1954; orchestrated 1955); *Music* for Violin, Piano, and Percussion (1957); 2 string quartets (1957, 1966); Woodwind Quintet (1958); *Fantasy Quartet* for 4 Cellos (1959); *Fantasy* for Solo Harp (1959); *Lifelines,* film score for Flute, Guitar, and Percussion (1960); *Lines and Contrasts* for 16 Horns (1960); *Double Quintet* for Woodwind and Brass Quintets (1961); *Music* for Brass Quintet (1961); *Fanfare* for 4 Trumpets and 4 Trombones (1962); *Little Brass Music* for 4 Brasses (1962); *Music for Carillon* (1962); *Automation,* music for a real or imaginary film score, for 9 Instruments (1963); *Studies* for Solo Horn (1963); *Episodes* for Solo Clarinet (1964); *Aphorisms* for Flute and String Trio (1967); *Concerto da camera* for 9 Instruments (1971); *5 Moods* for 4 Tubas (1973); *Sonata serenata* for Clarinet, Violin, Cello, and Piano (1978); Octet (1978).

THIRD-STREAM MUSIC: *Blues* for Brass Quintet, Double Bass, and Drums (1945); *Atonal Jazz Study* for 12 Instruments (1948); *Symphonic Tribute to Duke Ellington* for Jazz Orch. (1955); *12 by 11* for 11 Instruments (1955); *Transformation* for 11 Instruments (1956); *Conversations* for Jazz Quartet and String Quartet (1959); Concertino for Jazz Quartet and Orch. (1959); *Abstraction* for 9 Instruments (1959); *Variants,* jazz ballet for Jazz Quartet and Orch. (1960; N.Y., Jan. 4, 1961); *Variants on a Theme of John Lewis* for 12 Performers (1960; based on Lewis's tune *Django*); *Variants on a Theme of Thelonius Monk* for 13 Performers (1960; based on Monk's tune *Criss-Cross*); *Journey into Jazz* for Narrator, Jazz Quintet, and Orch. (1962; Washington, D.C., May 30, 1962); *Night Music* for Jazz Quintet (1962); *Densities No. 1* for Jazz Quartet (1963);

Music from "Yesterday in Fact" for Jazz Quintet, Flute, Bass Clarinet, Horn, Violin, and Cello (1963; music for a Polish-made film); *Tear Drop* for 9 Instruments (1967).

FOR VOICE: *6 Early Songs* for Soprano and Piano (1943–44; orchestrated 1973); *Meditations* for Soprano and Piano (1960); *6 Renaissance Lyrics* for Tenor and 7 Instruments (1962); *5 Shakespearean Songs* for Baritone and Orch. (1964); *Sacred Cantata* for Chorus and Orch. (1966); *The Power within Us,* oratorio for Baritone, Narrator, Chorus, and Orch. (1971); *Poems of Time and Eternity,* to words by Emily Dickinson, for Chorus and 9 Instruments (1972).

BIBLIOGRAPHY: David Ewen, *American Composers* (N.Y., 1982).

Schulthess, Walter, Swiss conductor and composer; b. Zürich, July 24, 1894; d. there, June 23, 1971. He studied with Andreae in Zürich, with Courvoisier in Munich, with Ansorge in Berlin; in 1918 settled in Zürich. As a composer, he excelled in lyric songs, in a style resembling Othmar Schoeck's. He also wrote 2 violin sonatas; *Variationen* for Cello and Orch.; Concertino for Piano and Orch.; piano pieces. He was married to the violinist **Stefi Geyer** (1888–1956).

Schultz, Edwin, German baritone and song composer; b. Danzig, April 30, 1827; d. Tempelhof, near Berlin, May 20, 1907. He studied singing with Brandstätter in Berlin; conducted choral societies and concerts. In 1880 the Prussian Ministry of War commissioned him to compile a book of soldiers' songs. He publ. many male choruses, songs, duets, and the collection *Meisterstücke für Pianoforte.*

Schultz, Helmut, German musicologist; b. Frankfurt, Nov. 2, 1904; killed in battle at Waldenburg, April 13, 1945. He studied musicology with Kroyer in Leipzig; in 1933 was appointed to the faculty of the Univ. of Leipzig. He publ. several books: *Johann Vesque von Püttlingen* (Regensburg, 1930); *Instrumentenkunde* (Leipzig, 1931); *Das Madrigal als Formideal* (Leipzig, 1939); edited (with Robert Haas) the works of Hugo Wolf; also was editor of works by Haydn, Rosetti, etc.

Schultz, Svend, Danish composer and choral conductor; b. Nykøbing, Dec. 30, 1913. He studied at the Royal Cons. in Copenhagen (1933–38); became active as a piano teacher and choral conductor; was music critic of *Politiken,* the Copenhagen newspaper (1942–49). In his music, he evolved a neo-Classical style characterized by simplicity of form and a cumulative rhythmic drive.

WORKS: 10 operas: *Bag kulisserne* (*Behind the Scenes;* 1946; Copenhagen, May 26, 1949); *Solbadet* (*The Sunbath;* 1947; Aarhus, Nov. 26, 1949); *Kaffehuset* (*The Coffee House;* 1948); *Høst* (*Harvest;* 1950); *Bryllupsrejsen* (*The Honeymoon;* 1951); *Tordenvejret* (*The Thunderstorm;* 1954); *Hosekraemmeren* (*The Stocking Peddler;* 1955); *Dommer Lynch* (*Judge Lynch;* 1959); comic television opera, *Konen i muddergrøften* (*The Woman in the Mud-*

dy Ditch; 1964; Danish Television, April 18, 1965); children's opera, *Lykken og forstanden* (1973); 2 marionette operas: *Hyrdinden og skorstensfejeren* (*The Shepherdess and the Chimney-Sweep;* 1953) and *The Marionettes* (1957); chamber operetta, *Den kåde Donna* (Copenhagen, Aug. 30, 1957); musical church play, *Eva* (1968); oratorio, *Job* (1945); *Sankt Hans Nat* for Soloists, Chorus, and Orch. (1953); *Hymn* for Chorus and Orch. (Copenhagen, March 13, 1957); *Hr. Mortens klosterrov* (*Morten's Pillage of the Monastery)* for Soloists, Chorus, and Chamber Orch. (1958; Copenhagen, Oct. 13, 1960); *3 Pastorales* for Soloists, Chorus, and Orch. (Danish Radio, May 28, 1962); *The 4 Temperaments* for Female and Male Choruses, and Orch. (Hillerød, Nov. 15, 1974); *Serenade* for String Orch. (1940); 5 symphs.: No. 1, *Sinfonia piccola* (1941); No. 2 (1949); No. 3 (1955); No. 4 (1958); No. 5 (1962); Piano Concerto (1943); *Storstrømsbroen (The Storstroem Bridge),* symph. vision (1951); *Introduction and Rondo* for Piano and Orch. (Danish Radio, Nov. 8, 1964); *2 Variations: Nocturne and Aubade* for Orch. (1965); *Sinfonia piccola No. 2* (1973); *Northern Overture* (1975); 5 string quartets (1939, 1940, 1960, 1961, 1962); Flute Quartet (1961); *Romantic Trio* for Piano Trio (1961); Quartet for Flute, Violin, Viola, and Cello (1962); 2 piano trios (1942, 1963); Clarinet Quintet (1965); *Music for Wind Players* for Flute, Trumpet, Clarinet, Percussion, Vibraphone, and Piano (1966); Piano Sonata (1931); 2 piano sonatinas (1940, 1950).

Schultze, Norbert, German composer; b. Braunschweig, Jan. 26, 1911. He studied music and theatrical arts in Cologne and Munich, and took lessons in piano and composition; during the season 1931–32 he acted in a student cabaret, *Vier Nachrichter,* under the name of **Frank Norbert;** then was a theater conductor, arranger, and composer in Munich. He wrote several operas: *Schwarzer Peter* (Hamburg, 1936); *Das kalte Herz* (Leipzig, 1943); television opera, *Peter der dritte* (1964); operetta, *Regen in Paris* (Nuremberg, 1957); pantomimes: *Struwwelpeter* (Hamburg, 1937); *Max und Moritz* (Hamburg, 1938); *Maria im Walde* (Vienna, 1940); but his chief claim to fame was a sentimental song, *Lili Marleen,* which he wrote in 1938, and which became immensely popular after it was broadcast from the German-occupied Belgrade in 1941; it became a hit throughout the war, not only on the German side but also among Allied soldiers on all fronts; it was trans. into 27 languages.

Schulz, August, German violinist, conductor, and composer; b. Lehre, near Braunschweig, June 15, 1837; d. Braunschweig, Feb. 12, 1909. He studied violin with Joachim; was violinist in the court orch. at Braunschweig; then concertmaster at Detmold; returned to Braunschweig as a conductor of symph. concerts and choral societies. He wrote an opera, *Der wilde Jäger* (Braunschweig, 1887); for Chorus and Orch.: *Eine Sommernacht, Prinzessin Ilse,* etc.; many male choruses; altogether, nearly 200 opus numbers.

Schulz, Ferdinand, German choral conductor and composer; b. Kossar, near Krossen, Oct. 21, 1821; d. Berlin, May 27, 1897. He was a pupil of A.W. Bach and Dehn in Berlin; after serving as chorister, he became conductor of the Cäcilien-Verein in 1856. He wrote motets and other church music; publ. male choruses, songs, and piano pieces.

Schulz, Johann Abraham Peter, German composer; b. Lüneburg, March 31, 1747; d. Schwedt, June 10, 1800. He studied with Kirnberger in Berlin; from 1768 to 1773 was music master to a Polish princess; from 1776 to 1778 was music director of the French theater in Berlin; then was Kapellmeister to Prince Heinrich at Rheinsberg (1780–87); from 1787 to 1795 he was court conductor at Copenhagen; finally returned to Germany, where he was director of an opera troupe.
WORKS: A song composer of marked ability, he publ. in 1779 *Gesänge am Clavier*, in 1782 *Lieder im Volkston*, both printed together, with augmentations, as *Lieder im Volkston* in 1785; a 3rd book was publ. in 1790. His sacred songs are *Uzens lyrische Gedichte* (1784) and *Religiöse Oden und Lieder* (1786). *Chansons italiennes* (1782), *4 Lieder* with Piano, and a *Rundgesang* (round) for Mixed Voices were also publ. Among his stage works are: *Das Opfer der Nymphen* (Berlin, 1774); operetta, *La Fée Urgèle* (1782; in German as *Was den Damen gefällt*); operetta, *Clarisse, oder Das unbekannte Dienstmädchen* (Berlin, 1775); tragic melodrama, *Minona* (publ. 1786); *Le Barbier de Séville* (Hamburg, 1786); opera, *Aline, Reine de Golconde* (Rheinsberg, 1787); the following were produced in Copenhagen: *Høstgildet* (*The Harvest Home*; Sept. 16, 1790); *Indtoget* (*Entry*; Feb. 26, 1793); *Peters Bryllup* (*Peter's Wedding*; Dec. 12, 1793). He further wrote church music, small instrumental works, a Piano Sonata, and various other pieces for Piano (*Musikalische Belustigung, Musikalische Badinage, Musikalischer Luftball*, etc.); publ. *Entwurf einer neuen und leichtverständlichen Musiktablatur…* (1786; merely the old organ tablature) and *Gedanken über den Einfluss der Musik auf die Bildung eines Volks* (1790); claimed authorship of *Wahre Grundsätze zum Gebrauch der Harmonie* (1773; publ. as Kirnberger's).
BIBLIOGRAPHY: K. Klunger, *J.A.P. Schulz in seinen volkstümlichen Liedern* (Leipzig, 1909); O.K. Riess, *J.A.P. Schulz Leben* (Diss., Univ. of Leipzig, 1913); J.F. Reichardt, *J.A.P. Schulz* (new ed., Kassel, 1948).

Schulz, Johann Philipp Christian, German conductor and composer; b. Langensalza, Feb. 1, 1773; d. Leipzig, Jan. 30, 1827. He studied with Schicht at Leipzig; from 1810 was conductor of the Gewandhaus concerts. He publ. overtures to *Faust* and *Die Jungfrau von Orleans;* dances interpolated into *Faust* (arranged for Piano); *Salvum fac regem* for 4 Voices, with Brass; marches, etc.; songs with piano.

Schulz, Leo, German-American cellist; b. Posen, March 28, 1865; d. La Crescenta, Calif., Aug. 12, 1944.

He was a child prodigy, and appeared in public at the age of 5; then studied at the Hochschule für Musik in Berlin; was first cellist with the Berlin Phil. (1885) and the Gewandhaus Orch. in Leipzig (1886–89); then settled in America; was first cellist of the Boston Symph. (1889–98), then of the N.Y. Phil. (1899–1906); taught in various schools; wrote overtures, string quartets, and some cello music; edited *Cello Classics* (2 vols.), *Cello Album* (2 books), and *Cello Composers* (2 vols.).

Schulz-Beuthen, Heinrich, German composer; b. Beuthen, June 19, 1838; d. Dresden, March 12, 1915. He was destined for a career as civil engineer; while a student at the Univ. of Breslau, he learned to play the piano and attempted composition; produced a singspiel, *Fridolin* (Breslau, 1862); then went to study at the Leipzig Cons., with Moscheles (piano) and Hauptmann (composition). In 1866 he went to Zürich, where he remained until 1880; then lived in Dresden (1880–93) and Vienna (1893–95); finally settled in Dresden, where he became a prof. at the Cons. He was an ardent disciple of Liszt and Wagner; during his lifetime he was regarded as a significant composer.
WORKS: 8 symphs.: No. 1, *Dem Andenken Haydns;* No. 2, *Frühlingsfeier;* No. 3, *Sinfonia maestosa;* No. 4, *Schön Elsbeth;* No. 5, *Reformationssymphonie* (with Organ); No. 6, *König Lear* (with Male Chorus); No. 7 (expanded from a string quartet); No. 8, *Siegessymphonie;* symph. poems: *Mittelalterliche Volksszene, Des Meeres und der Liebe Wellen, Beethoven-Hymnus, Ein Pharaonenbegräbnis, Wilhelm Tell, Sturmesmythe;* overtures; orch. suites; *Symphonisches Konzert* for Piano and Orch.; String Quintet; Wind Octet; String Trio; etc.; a number of piano works (*Heroische Sonata, Erinnerung an die Jugendzeit, Präludium und Fuge*); several sacred choral works; opera, *Aschenbrödel* (Zürich, 1879; text by Mathilde Wesendonk); 4 other operas.
BIBLIOGRAPHY: K. Mey, *H. Schulz-Beuthen* (Leipzig, 1909); A. Zosel, *H. Schulz-Beuthen* (Würzburg, 1931).

Schulz-Dornburg, Rudolf, German conductor; b. Würzburg, March 31, 1891; d. Gmund-am-Tegernsee, Aug. 16, 1949. He studied in Cologne, where he became a choral director; then conducted opera in Mannheim, Münster, and Essen; in 1934 settled in Berlin as a radio conductor; from 1945 to 1948 was Generalmusikdirektor in Lübeck.

Schulz-Evler, Andrei, Polish pianist; b. Radom, Dec. 12, 1852; d. Warsaw, May 15, 1905. He studied at the Warsaw Cons., and later with Tausig in Berlin; was a prof. of piano at the Kharkov Music School (1888–1904); publ. 52 piano pieces and songs; his transcription of the *Blue Danube Waltz* was very popular with pianists for a time.

Schulz-Schwerin, Karl, German pianist; b. Schwerin, Jan. 3, 1845; d. Mannheim, May 24, 1913. He studied at the Stern Cons. in Berlin (1862–65) with

Hans von Bülow, Stern, and Weitzmann. He was court pianist to the Grand Duke of Mecklenburg; then taught at the Stern Cons. (1885–1901); from 1901 lived in Mannheim. He composed a Symph.; overtures to *Torquato Tasso* and *Die Braut von Messina; Serenata giocosa, In Memoriam,* and *Jubiläums-Festmarsch* for Orch.; *Sanctus, Osanna, Benedictus, Ave Maria,* etc., for soli, chorus, and orch.; piano pieces.

Schuman, William Howard, eminent American composer, educator, and music administrator; b. New York, Aug. 4, 1910. He studied harmony with Max Persin; then took lessons in composition with Charles Haubiel; in 1933 he entered Teacher's College at Columbia Univ. (B.S., 1935; M.A., 1937); attended the Mozarteum Academy in Salzburg during the summer of 1935; returning to N.Y., he became an instructor at Sarah Lawrence College; took composition lessons with Roy Harris at a summer session of the Juilliard School of Music in 1936; on March 27, 1936, he married Frances Prince. He attracted the attention of Koussevitzky, who gave the first performance of Schuman's *American Festival Overture* with the Boston Symph. Orch. in 1939, and later conducted his 3rd and 5th symphs.; his 4th Symph. was performed by Rodzinski in Cleveland in 1942, and the Coolidge String Quartet gave a performance of Schuman's String Quartet in 1940. He continued to teach at Sarah Lawrence until 1945; then served as director of publications for G. Schirmer, Inc. (1945–52); in 1945, also, he was appointed president of the Juilliard School of Music, a post he held until 1962. Continuing his astonishing advance as an executive, he became president of Lincoln Center in N.Y., serving from 1962 to 1969; his career in this respect was unique among American composers. He was the first recipient of the Pulitzer Prize in music in 1943; received the Composition Award of the American Academy of Arts and Letters; also held 2 successive Guggenheim fellowship awards (1939, 1940). His music is characterized by great emotional tension, which is maintained by powerful asymmetric rhythms; the contrapuntal structures in his works reach a great degree of complexity and are saturated with dissonance without, however, losing the essential tonal references. In several of his works he employs American melorhythms, but his general style of composition is cosmopolitan, exploring all viable techniques of modern composition. WORKS: "Baseball opera," *The Mighty Casey* (Hartford, Conn., May 4, 1953; revised as a cantata, retitled *Casey at the Bat,* and produced in this version in Washington, D.C., April 6, 1976). BALLETS: *Undertow* (choreographer: Antony Tudor; N.Y., April 10, 1945); *Night Journey* (Martha Graham; Cambridge, Mass., May 3, 1947); *Judith,* choreographic poem for Orch. (Martha Graham; Louisville, Ky., Jan. 4, 1950). FOR ORCH.: Symph. No. 1 (N.Y., Oct. 21, 1936); Symph. No. 2 (N.Y., May 25, 1938); Symph. No. 3 (Boston, Oct. 17, 1941); Symph. No. 4 (Cleveland, Jan. 22, 1942); Symph. No. 5, *Symphony for Strings* (Boston, Nov. 12, 1943); Symph.

No. 6 (Dallas, Feb. 27, 1949); Symph. No. 7 (Boston, Oct. 21, 1960); Symph. No. 8 (N.Y., Oct. 4, 1962); *To Thee Old Cause* for Oboe, Brass, Timpani, Piano, and Strings, after Walt Whitman, dedicated to the memories of Martin Luther King and Robert F. Kennedy (N.Y., Oct. 3, 1968); Symph. No. 9, subtitled *Le Fosse Ardeatine,* in memory of Italian civilians murdered by the Germans in a cave in Rome in retaliation for resistance activities (Philadelphia, Jan. 10, 1969); Symph. No. 10, subtitled *American Muse,* dedicated to the U.S. Bicentennial (Washington, April 6, 1976); *American Festival Overture* (Boston, Oct. 6, 1939); Concerto for Piano and Small Orch. (N.Y., Jan. 13, 1943); *Prayer in Time of War* (Pittsburgh, Feb. 26, 1943); *William Billings Overture* (N.Y., Feb. 17, 1944); *Circus Overture* (Philadelphia, July 20, 1944); Violin Concerto (1947; Boston, Feb. 10, 1950; Isaac Stern, soloist; revised 1954 and 1958); *Credendum* (Cincinnati, Nov. 4, 1955); *New England Triptych* (Miami, Oct. 28, 1956); *A Song of Orpheus* for Cello and Orch. (Indianapolis, Feb. 17, 1962); *In Praise of Shahn,* canticle for Orch., in memory of the American painter Ben Shahn (N.Y., Jan. 30, 1970); *Voyage for Orchestra* (1971; Rochester, N.Y., Oct. 27, 1972). FOR BAND: *Newsreel* (1941); *George Washington Bridge* (1950); *Chester,* overture (1956). CHORAL WORKS: *4 Canonic Choruses* (original title, *Chorale Canons*) for Mixed Voices (1932–33); *Pioneers!* for 8-part Mixed Chorus, after Walt Whitman (1937); *Choral Etude* for Mixed Chorus (1937); *Prologue* for Mixed Chorus and Orch. (1939); *Prelude* for Women's Voices (1939); *This Is Our Time,* secular cantata for Mixed Chorus and Orch. (1940); *Requiescat* for Women's Chorus (1942); *Holiday Song* for Mixed Chorus (1942); *A Free Song,* secular cantata for Mixed Chorus and Orch., after Walt Whitman (Boston, March 26, 1943; won the first Pulitzer Prize awarded for a musical work); *Truth Shall Deliver* for Men's Voices (1946); *4 Rounds on Famous Words* (1957); *The Lord Has a Child,* hymn (1957); Concerto on Old English Rounds for Viola, Women's Chorus, and Orch. (Boston, Nov. 29, 1974); *The Young Dead Soldiers* for Soprano, Horn, Woodwinds, and Strings, to a text of Archibald MacLeish (Washington, April 6, 1976); *The Earth Is Born,* music for a film (1957); 4 string quartets (1936, 1937, 1939, 1950); *Quartettino* for 4 Bassoons (1939); *3-Score Set* for Piano (1943); *Voyage,* a cycle of 5 pieces for Piano (1953); songs.

BIBLIOGRAPHY: N. Broder, "The Music of William Schuman," *Musical Quarterly* (Jan. 1945); F.R. Schreiber and V. Persichetti, *William Schuman* (N.Y., 1954). See also *Modern Music ... Analytic Index,* compiled by Wayne Shirley, ed. by W. and C. Lichtenwanger (N.Y., 1976; p. 196); C. Rouse, *William Schuman Documentary* (N.Y., 1981).

Schumann, Camillo, German organist and composer, brother of **Georg Schumann;** b. Königstein, March 10, 1872; d. Gottleuba, Dec. 29, 1946. He learned the rudiments of music from his father; then studied with Jadassohn and Reinecke at the Leipzig Cons. After further study with Adolf Bargiel in Berlin (1894–96) he became organist at the church in Eisenach. For some years before his death he lived in retirement at Gottleuba. He was a prolific composer, especially noted for his organ works; he also wrote 6 cantatas, 3 piano trios, 5 cello sonatas, 2 clarinet sonatas, 2 violin sonatas, and 30 albums of piano pieces.

Schumann, Clara (née **Wieck**), famous pianist, wife of **Robert Schumann;** b. Leipzig, Sept. 13, 1819; d. Frankfurt, May 20, 1896. She was the daughter of **Friedrich Wieck;** was trained by her father from her 5th year; played in public for the first time on Oct. 20, 1828; made tours from 1832, and during a sojourn in Vienna (1836) received the title of Imperial Chamber Virtuoso. At Paris she had great success in 1839. On Sept. 12, 1840, she was married to Schumann, despite the stubborn opposition of her father to this union. With Schumann she made a tour of Russia as a pianist (1844); appeared with Jenny Lind in Vienna (1846). After Schumann's death (1856) she went with her children to Berlin, living for some years with her mother, who had been divorced from Wieck and had married the music teacher Adolf Bargiel (d. Feb. 4, 1841). From 1856 to 1888 she played regularly in England. In 1863 she moved to Lichtenthaler, near Baden-Baden. In 1878–79 she taught piano at the Hoch Cons. at Frankfurt. She was a masterly and authoritative interpreter of Schumann's compositions; later she became an equally admirable interpreter of Brahms, her lifelong friend. She was completely free of all mannerisms, and impressed her audiences chiefly by the earnestness of her regard for the music she played. She was a composer in her own right; wrote a Piano Concerto and numerous character pieces for piano; also some songs; Schumann made use of her melodies in several of his works. She wrote cadenzas to Beethoven's concertos in C minor and G major; edited the Breitkopf & Hartel edition of Schumann's works, and some of his early correspondence; also edited finger exercises from Czerny's piano method.
BIBLIOGRAPHY: A. von Meichsner, *Friedrich Wieck und seine Töchter Clara und Marie* (Leipzig, 1875); La Mara, *Clara Schumann,* in vol. V of *Musikalische Studienköpfe* (Leipzig, 1882; 3rd ed., 1902); B. Litzmann, *Clara Schumann, Ein Künstlerleben nach Tagebüchern und Briefen* (3 vols., Leipzig, 1902–8; Eng. trans. in 2 vols., abridged, London, 1913); W. Kleefeld, *Clara Schumann* (Bielefeld, 1910); Florence May, *The Girlhood of Clara Schumann* (London, 1912); F. Schumann, "Brahms and Clara Schumann," *Musical Quarterly* (Oct. 1916); Eugenie Schumann, *Erinnerungen* (1925; Eng. trans., 1927); B. Litzmann, *Letters of Clara Schumann and Johannes Brahms* (2 vols., Leipzig, 1927; Eng. trans., N.Y., 1927); K. Höcker, *Clara Schumann* (1938); J.N. Burk, *Clara Schumann* (N.Y., 1940); A. De Lara, "Clara Schumann's Teaching," *Music & Letters* (Jan. 1945); L. Henning, *Die Freundschaft Clara Schumanns mit Johannes Brahms* (Zürich, 1952); W. Quednau, *Clara Schumann* (Berlin, 1955); Margaret and Jean Alley, *A Passionate Friendship; Clara Schumann and Brahms* (London, 1956; con-

tains a selection of letters); R. Pitron, *Clara Schumann* (Paris, 1961); K. Stephenson, *Clara Schumann: 1819–1896* (Bonn, 1969); P. Susskind Pettler, "Johannes Brahms and Clara Schumann: Clara's Influence as Critic, Advisor and Friend," *International Brahms Congress: Detroit 1980;* J. Chissell, *Clara Schumann* (London, 1983). See also the bibliography under Robert Schumann.

Schumann, Elisabeth, celebrated German soprano; b. Merseburg, June 13, 1888; d. New York, April 23, 1952. She studied in Dresden, Berlin, and Hamburg; made her debut at the Hamburg Opera on Sept. 2, 1909, as the Shepherd in *Tannhäuser;* remained on its roster until 1919. In the meantime, she made her American debut at the Metropolitan Opera in N.Y. on Nov. 20, 1914, as Sophie in *Der Rosenkavalier,* one of her most famous roles; sang there only one season (1914–15). From 1919 to 1938 she was a principal member of the Vienna State Opera; in 1921 made a concert tour of the U.S. with Richard Strauss; after 1938 she settled in the U.S.; taught at the Curtis Inst. of Music in Philadelphia; gave many recitals; became a U.S. citizen in 1944. She publ. *German Song* (London, 1948). In opera, she succeeded in giving congenial interpretations of works by composers as far apart as Mozart and Richard Strauss; she was also a fine performer of German lieder.

Schumann, Georg (Alfred), German composer and choral conductor; b. Königstein, Oct. 25, 1866; d. Berlin, May 23, 1952. He studied with his father, the town music director, and with his grandfather, a cantor; then took courses in Dresden and at the Leipzig Cons. with Reinecke and Jadassohn; received the Beethoven Prize in 1887. He conducted a choral society in Danzig (1890–96) and the Bremen Phil. Orch. (1896–99). In 1900 he became conductor of the Singakademie in Berlin; in 1934 he was elected president of the Berlin Akademie der Künste.
WORKS: For Orch.: *Zur Karnevalszeit,* suite; *Liebesfrühling,* overture; *Lebensfreude,* overture; 2 symphs.; also, 2 violin sonatas; 2 piano quintets; Cello Sonata; Piano Trio; Piano Quartet; oratorio, *Ruth* (1909); other choral works, with Orch.: Amor und Psyche, Totenklage, Sehnsucht, Das Tränenkrüglein; numerous songs; for Piano: *Stimmungsbilder, Traumbilder, Fantasie-Etüden, Harzbilder.*
BIBLIOGRAPHY: P. Hielscher, *Georg Schumann,* in vol. 1 of *Monographien moderner Musiker* (Leipzig, 1906); H. Biehle, *Georg Schumann* (Münster, 1925).

Schumann, Robert Alexander, German composer of surpassing imaginative power whose music expressed the deepest spirit of the Romantic era; b. Zwickau, June 8, 1810; d. Endenich, near Bonn, July 29, 1856. He was the 5th and youngest child of a Saxon bookseller, who encouraged his musical inclinations. At the age of 10 he began taking piano lessons from J.G. Kuntzsch, organist at the Zwickau Marienkirche. In 1828 he enrolled at Leipzig Univ., as *studiosus juris,* although he gave more attention to philosophical lectures than to law. In Leipzig he became a piano student of Friedrich Wieck, his future father-in-law. In 1829 he went to Heidelberg, where he applied himself seriously to music; in 1830 he returned to Leipzig and lodged in Wieck's home; he also took a course in composition with Heinrich Dorn. His family life was unhappy; his father died at the age of 53 of a nervous disease not distinctly diagnosed; his sister Emily committed suicide at the age of 19. Of his 3 brothers, only one reached late middle age. Schumann himself became absorbed in the Romantic malaise of Weltschmerz; his idols, the writers and poets Novalis, Kleist, Byron, Lenau, and Hölderin, all died young, and in tragic circumstances. He hoped to start his music study with Carl Maria von Weber, who also died unexpectedly. Schumann wrote plays and poems in the Romantic tradition and at the same time practiced his piano playing in the hope of becoming a virtuoso pianist. He never succeeded in this ambition; ironically, it was his beloved bride, Clara, who became a famous concert pianist, and Schumann himself was often introduced to the public at large as merely her husband. His own piano study was halted when he developed an ailment in the index and middle fingers of his right hand. He tried all the fashionable remedies of the period, allopathy, homeopathy, and electrophysical therapy; in addition, he used a mechanical device to lift the middle finger of his right hand, but it only caused him harm. His damaged fingers exempted him from military service; the medical certificate issued in 1842 stated that the index and middle fingers of his right hand were affected so that Schumann was unable to pull the trigger of a rifle. Schumann had a handsome appearance; he liked the company of young ladies, and enjoyed beer, wine, and strong cigars; this was in sharp contrast with his inner disquiet; as a youth he confided to his diary a fear of madness. He had auditory hallucinations which caused insomnia; he also suffered from acrophobia. When he was 23 years old, he noted sudden onsets of inexpressible angst, momentary loss of consciousness, and difficulty in breathing. He called his sickness a pervasive melancholy, a popular malaise of the time. He thought of killing himself. What maintained his spirits then was his great love for **Clara Wieck,** 9 years his junior; he did not hesitate to confess his psychological perturbations to her. Her father must have surmised the unstable character of Schumann, and resisted any thought of allowing Clara to become engaged to him; the young couple had to go to court to overcome Wieck's objections, and were finally married on Sept. 12, 1840, the day before Clara turned 21. In 1843, when Schumann and Clara already had 2 daughters, Wieck approached him with an offer of reconciliation. Schumann gladly accepted the offer, but the relationship remained only formal.

Whatever inner torment disturbed Schumann's mind, it did not affect the flowering of his genius as a composer; some psychologists have even expressed the belief that madness is a necessary attribute of genius, and that poetry, art, and music are but external aspects of a delusion. However that might be, Schumann as a young man wrote music full of natural beauty, harmonious and melodious in its flow; his compositions are remarkably free from the somber and dramatic qualities that characterize the music of Beethoven and his Romantic followers. One of the most extraordinary features of Schumann's artistic imagination was his fanciful way of personifying his friends and intimates through musical notes; thus his Platonic love for Ernestine von Fricken, who came from the little town of Asch in Bohemia, inspired Schumann to use the notes A, E-flat (Es), C, and B-natural (H), or A-flat (As), C, and B (H), spelling Asch, as themes for his most famous piano pieces, *Papillons* and *Carnaval.* Schumann's very first opus number was a set of variations on the notes A, B, E, G, G, which spelled the name of Countess Meta von Abegg, to whom Schumann was also poetically attached. And, incidentally, it was Ernestine's adoptive father, an amateur flutist, who gave him the theme for his remarkable set of variations for Piano titled *Etudes symphoniques.*

As Schumann's talent for music grew and he became recognized as an important composer, he continued his literary activities. In 1834 he founded, with J. Knorr, L. Schunke, and Wieck, a progressive journal, *Neue Zeitschrift für Musik,* in which he militated against the vapid mannerisms of fashionable salon music and other aspects of musical stagnation. He wrote essays, signing them with the imaginary names of Florestan, Eusebius, or Meister Raro. (Eusebius was the name of 3 Christian saints; etymologically, it is a compound of the Greek components *eu,* "good," and *sebiai,* "to worship." Florestan is obviously "one in a state of flowering"; Raro is "rare"; Schumann also noticed that the juxtaposition of the names Clara and Robert would result in the formation of Raro: ClaRARObert.) As early as 1831, Schumann, in the guise of Eusebius, hailed the genius of Chopin in an article containing the famous invocation "Hut ab, ihr Herren, ein Genie!" The article appeared in the *Allgemeine Musikalische Zeitung;* it was signed only by Schumann's initials; in an editorial note he was identified merely as a young student of Prof. Wieck; but the winged phrase became a favorite quotation of biographers of both Chopin and Schumann, cited as Schumann's discovery of Chopin's talent. Actually, Chopin was a few months older than Schumann, and had already started on a brilliant concert career, while Schumann was an unknown. One of the most fanciful inventions of Schumann was the formation of an intimate company of friends which he named Davidsbündler, to describe the sodality of David, dedicated to the mortal struggle against Philistines in art and to the passionate support of all that was new and imaginative. Schumann immortalized this society in his brilliant piano work *Davidsbündlertänze.* Another characteristically Romantic trait was Schumann's attachment to nocturnal moods, nature scenes, and fantasies; the titles of his piano pieces are typical: *Nachtstücke, Waldszenen,* and *Fantasiestücke,* the last including the poetic *Warum?* and the explosive *Aufschwung.* A child at heart himself, Schumann created in his piano set of exquisite miniatures, *Kinderszenen,* a marvelous musical nursery which included the beautifully sentimental dream piece *Träumerei*. Parallel with his piano works, Schumann produced some of his finest lieder, including the song cycles to poems by Heine (op. 24) and Eichendorff (op. 39), *Die Frauenliebe und Leben* (op. 42), and *Dichterliebe*, to Heine's words (op. 48). In 1841, in only 4 days, he sketched out his First Symph., in B-flat major, born, as he himself said, in a single "fiery hour." He named it the *Spring* symph. It was followed in rapid succession by 3 string quartets (op. 41), the Piano Quintet (op. 44), and the Piano Quartet (op. 47). To the same period belongs also his impassioned choral work *Das Paradies und die Peri*. Three more symphs. followed the *Spring* symph. within the next decade, and also a Piano Concerto, a masterpiece of a coalition between the percussive gaiety of the solo part and songful paragraphs in the orch.; an arresting hocketus occurs in the finale, in which duple meters come into a striking conflict with the triple rhythm of the solo part.

In 1843 Schumann was asked by Mendelssohn to join him as a teacher of piano, composition, and score reading at the newly founded Cons. in Leipzig. In 1844 Schumann and Clara undertook a concert tour to Russia; in the autumn of 1844 they moved to Dresden, remaining there until 1850. To this period belong his great C major Symph. (1846), the Piano Trio (1847), and the opera *Genoveva* (1848). In 1847 he assumed the conducting post of the Liedertafel, and in 1848 organized in Dresden the Chorgesang-Verein. In 1850 he became town music director in Düsseldorf, but his disturbed condition began to manifest itself in such alarming ways that he had to resign the post. He continued to compose, however. In 1853 he completed a Violin Concerto. Joachim, in whose care Schumann left the work, thought it was not worthy of Schumann's genius, and ruled that it should not be performed until the centennial of Schumann's death. In the 1930s an eccentric Hungarian violinist, Jelly d'Aranyi, declared that Schumann's ghost had appeared before her at a spiritualistic séance, revealed to her the place where the MS was kept (it was no secret, anyway; the MS was where it was supposed to be, on the shelf of the Prussian Library in Berlin), and urged her to perform it. She was cheated out of the prize, however, and the concerto was first performed by another violinist in Berlin, on Nov. 26, 1937. Jelly d'Aranyi had to be satisfied with giving its first British performance.

Schumann's condition continued to deteriorate. On Feb. 27, 1854, he threw himself into the Rhine, but was rescued. On March 4, 1854, he was placed, at his own request, in a sanatorium at Endenich, near Bonn, remaining there until the end of his life. Strangely enough, he did not want to see Clara, and there were months when he did not even inquire about her and the children. But Brahms was a welcome visitor, and Schumann enjoyed his company during his not infrequent periods of lucidity; in Feb. 1855 Brahms played piano, 4-hands, with him. The common assumption that Schumann's illness was syphilitic in origin remains moot, but cumulative symptomology and clearly observed cyclothymic sudden changes of moods point to tertiary syphilis and final general paresis. The doctor who treated him was inclined to diagnose his condition as the result of a sclerosis of the brain; other physicians described it as dementia praecox. Schumann had 7 children; 3 daughters lived to a very old age, but one son suffered from mental disease. A detailed account of Schumann's illness is contained in Dr. Dieter Kerner's book *Krankheiten grossen Musiker,* publ. in Stuttgart in 1973.

WORKS: FOR THE STAGE: *Der Corsar,* opera (1844; unfinished; only a chorus and sketch for an air completed); *Genoveva,* opera, op. 81 (1847–49; Leipzig, June 25, 1850); *Manfred,* incidental music to Byron's play, op. 115 (1848–49; Leipzig, June 13, 1852).

VOCAL MUSIC: For various voices: *Psalm CL* for Soprano, Alto, Piano, and Orch. (1822); Overture and chorus (*Chor von Landleuten*), with Orch. (1822); *6 Lieder* for Men's Voices, op. 33 (1840): 1, *Der träumende See* (Mosen); 2, *Die Minnesänger* (Heine); 3, *Die Lotosblume* (Heine); 4, *Der Zecher als Doktrinär* (Mosen); 5, *Rastlose Liebe* (Goethe); 6, *Frühlingsglocken* (Reinick); *Tragödie* for Chorus and Orch. (Heine; 1841); *Das Paradies und die Peri* for Solo Voices, Chorus, and Orch., op. 50 (adaptation of Moore's *Lalla Rookh;* 1843; Leipzig, Dec. 4, 1843); *Szenen aus Goethes Faust* for Solo Voices, Chorus, and Orch. (Goethe; 1844–53; Cologne, Jan. 13, 1862); *5 Lieder* for Mixed Voices, op. 55 (R. Burns; 1846): 1, *Das Hochlandmädchen;* 2, *Zahnweh;* 3, *Mich zieht es nach dem Dörfchen hin;* 4, *Die alte, gute Zeit;* 5, *Hochlandbursch; 4 Gesänge* for Mixed Voices, op. 59 (1846): 1, *Nord oder Süd!* (K. Lappe); 2, *Am Bodensee* (Platen); 3, *Jägerlied* (Mörike); 4, *Gute Nacht* (Rückert); also a 5th song added later, *Hirtenknaben-Gesang* (Droste-Hulshoff); *3 Gesänge* for Men's Voices, op. 62 (1847): 1, *Der Eidgenossen Nachtwache* (Eichendorff); 2, *Freiheitslied* (Rückert); 3, *Schlachtgesang* (Klopstock); *Ritornelle in canonischen Weisen* for Men's Voices, op. 65 (Rückert; 1847): 1, *Die Rose stand im Tau;* 2, *Lasst Lautenspiel und Becherklang;* 3, *Blüt' oder Schnee!;* 4, *Gebt mir zu trinken!;* 5, *Zürne nicht des Herbstes Wind;* 6, *In Sommertagen rüste den Schlitten;* 7, *In Meeres Mitten ist ein offener Laden;* 8, *Hätte zu einem Traubenkerne; Beim Abschied zu singen* for Chorus and Wind Instruments, op. 84 (Feuchtersleben; 1847); *Zum Anfang* for Men's Voices (Rückert; 1847); *3 Freiheitsgesänge* for Men's Voices, with Wind Instruments ad libitum (1848): 1, *Zu den Waffen* (Ullrich); 2, *Schwarz-Rot-Gold* (Freiligrath); 3, *Deutscher Freiheitsgesang* (Furst); *Romanzen und Balladen* for Mixed Voices, op. 67, I (1849): 1, *Der König von Thule* (Goethe); 2, *Schön-Rohtraut* (Mörike); 3, *Heidenröslein* (Goethe); 4, *Ungewitter* (Chamisso); 5, *John Anderson* (Burns); *Romanzen und Balladen* for Mixed Voices, op. 75, II (1849): 1, *Schnitter Tod* (*Des Knaben Wunderhorn;* Brentano); 2, *Im Walde* (Eichendorff); 3, *Der traurige Jäger* (Eichendorff); 4, *Der Rekrut* (Burns); 5, *Vom verwundeten Knaben* (Herder's Volkslieder); *Romanzen* for Women's Voices and Piano ad libitum, op. 69, I (1849): 1, *Tamburinschlägerin* (Alvaro de Ameida; Eichendorff, trans.); 2, *Waldmädchen* (Eichendorff); 3, *Klosterfräulein* (Kerner); 4, *Sol-*

datenbraut (Mörike); 5, *Meerfey* (Eichendorff); 6, *Die Kapelle* (Uhland); *Romanzen* for Women's Voices and Piano ad libitum, op. 91, II (1849): 1, *Rosmarien (Des Knaben Wunderhorn);* 2, *Jäger Wohlgemut (Des Knaben Wunderhorn);* 3, *Der Wassermann* (Kerner); 4, *Das verlassene Mägdelein* (Mörike); 5, *Der Bleicherin Nachtlied* (Reinick); 6, *In Meeres Mitten* (Rückert); *Verzweifle nicht im Schmerzenstal,* motet for Double Chorus and Organ ad libitum, op. 93 (Rückert; 1852; orchestrated 1852); *Requiem für Mignon* for Solo Voices, Chorus, and Orch., op. 98b (Goethe; 1849; Düsseldorf, Nov. 21, 1850); *5 Gesänge aus H. Laubes Jagdbrevier* for Men's Voices and Piano, 4-hands, ad libitum, op. 137 (Laube; 1849): 1, *Zur hohen Jagd;* 2, *Habet acht!;* 3, *Jagdmorgen;* 4, *Frühe;* 5, *Bei der Flasche; 4 doppelchörige Gesänge* for Mixed Voices, op. 141 (1849): 1, *An die Sterne* (Rückert); 2, *Ungewisses Licht* (Zedlitz); 3, *Zuversicht* (Zedlitz); 4, *Talismane* (Goethe); *Romanzen und Balladen* for Mixed Voices, op. 145, III (1849–51): 1, *Der Schmidt* (Uhland); 2, *Die Nonne* (anonymous); 3, *Der Sänger* (Uhland); 4, *John Anderson* (Burns); 5, *Romanze vom Gänsebuben* (Malsburg); *Romanzen und Balladen* for Mixed Voices, op. 146, IV (1849–51): 1, *Brautgesang* (Uhland); 2, *Der Bänkelsänger Willie* (Burns); 3, *Der Traum* (Uhland); 4, *Sommerlied* (Rückert); *Das Schifflein,* with Flute and Horn (Uhland); *Nachtlied* for Chorus and Orch., op. 108 (Hebbel; 1849; Düsseldorf, March 13, 1851); *Der Rose Pilgerfahrt* for Solo Voices, Chorus, and Orch., op. 112 (Horn; 1851; Düsseldorf, Feb. 5, 1852); *Der Königssohn* for Solo Voices, Chorus, and Orch., op. 116 (Uhland; 1851); *Des Glockentürmers Töchterlein* for Mixed Voices (Rückert; 1851); *Fest-Ouverture* for Tenor, Chorus, and Orch., op. 123 (Müller and Claudius; 1852–53; Düsseldorf, May 17, 1853); *Des Sängers Fluch* for Solo Voices, Chorus, and Orch., op. 139 (Pohl, after Uhland; 1852); *Vom Pagen und der Königstochter* for Solo Voices, Chorus, and Orch., op. 140 (Geibel; 1852); *Das Glück von Edenhall* for Solo Voices, Chorus, and Orch., op. 143 (Hasenclever, after Uhland; 1853); *Bei Schenkung eines Flügels* for Mixed Voices and Piano (Schumann; 1853); *Neujahrslied* for Chorus and Orch., op. 144 (Rückert; 1849–50; Düsseldorf, Jan. 11, 1851); *Mass* for Chorus and Orch., op. 147 (1852–53); *Requiem* for Chorus and Orch., op. 148 (1852).

SONGS: *Verwandlung* (Schulze; 1827); *Lied* (Schumann; 1827); *Sehnsucht* (Schumann; 1827); *Die Weinende* (Byron; 1827); *Erinnerung* (Jacobi; 1828); *Kurzes Erwachen* (Kerner; 1828); *Gesanges Erwachen* (Kerner; 1828); *An Anna,* I (Kerner; 1828); *An Anna,* II (Kerner; 1828); *Im Herbste* (Kerner; 1828); *Hirtenknabe* (Schumann; 1828); *Der Fischer* (Goethe; 1828); *Vom Reitersmann* (date unknown); *Maultreiberlied* (1838; not extant); *Ein Gedanke* (Ferrand; 1840); *Patriotisches Lied* for Voice, Chorus, and Piano (N. Becker; 1840); *Der Reiter und der Bodensee* (Schwab; 1840; fragment only); *Die nächtliche Heerschau* (Zedlitz; 1840; fragment only); *Liederkreis,* op. 24 (Heine; 1840): 1, *Morgens steh ich auf und frage;* 2, *Es treibt mich hin;* 3, *Ich wandelte unter den Bäumen;* 4, *Lieb Liebchen;* 5, *Schöne Wiege meiner Leiden;* 6, *Warte, warte,*

wilder Schiffmann; 7, *Berg und Burgen schaun herunter;* 8, *Anfangs wolit ich fast verzagen;* 9, *Mit Myrten und Rosen; Myrthen,* op. 25 (1840): 1, *Widmung* (Rückert); 2, *Freisinn* (Goethe); 3, *Der Nussbaum* (Mosen); 4, *Jemand* (Burns); 5, *Lieder aus dem Schenkenbuch im Divan,* I (Goethe); 6, *Lieder aus dem Schenkenbuch im Divan,* II (Goethe); 7, *Die Lotosblume* (Heine); 8, *Talismane* (Goethe); 9, *Lied der Suleika* (Goethe; attributed to Marianne von Willemer); 10, *Die Hochländer-Witwe* (Burns); 11, *Lieder der Braut aus dem Liebesfrühling,* I (Rückert); 12, *Lieder der Braut aus dem Liebesfrühling,* II (Rückert); 13, *Hochländers Abschied* (Burns); 14, *Hochländisches Wiegenlied* (Burns); 15, *Aus den hebräischen Gesängen* (Byron); 16, *Rätsel* (C. Fanshawe); 17, *2 Venetianische Lieder,* I (Moore); 18, *2 Venetianische Lieder,* II (Moore); 19, *Hauptmanns Weib* (Burns); 20, *Weit, weit* (Burns); 21, *Was will die einsame Träne?* (Heine); 22, *Niemand* (Burns); 23, *Im Westen* (Burns); 24, *Du bist wie eine Blume* (Heine); 25, *Aus den östlichen Rosen* (Rückert); 26, *Zum Schluss* (Rückert); *Lieder und Gesänge,* op. 27, I (1840): 1, *Sag an, o lieber Vogel* (Hebbel); 2, *Dem roten Röslein* (Burns); 3, *Was soll ich sagen?* (Chamisso); 4, *Jasminenstrauch* (Rückert); 5, *Nur ein lächelnder Blick* (G.W. Zimmermann); *3 Gedichte,* op. 29 (Geibel; 1840): 1, *Ländliches Lied* for 2 Sopranos; 2, *Lied* for 3 Sopranos; 3, *Zigeunerleben* for Soprano, Alto, Tenor, and Bass, and Triangle and Tambourine ad libitum; *3 Gedichte,* op. 30 (Geibel; 1840): 1, *Der Knabe mit dem Wunderhorn;* 2, *Der Page;* 3, *Der Hidalgo; 3 Gesänge,* op. 31 (1840): 1, *Die Löwenbraut* (Chamisso); 2, *Die Kartenlegerin* (Chamisso, after Béranger); 3, *Die rote Hanne,* with Chorus ad libitum (Chamisso, after Béranger); *4 Duette* for Soprano and Tenor, op. 34 (1840): 1, *Liebesgarten* (Reinick); 2, *Liebhabers Ständchen* (Burns); 3, *Unterm Fenster* (Burns); 4, *Familien-Gemälde* (A. Grün); *12 Gedichte,* op. 35 (Kerner; 1840): 1, *Lust der Sturmnacht;* 2, *Stirb, Lieb und Freud!;* 3, *Wanderlied;* 4, *Erstes Grün;* 5, *Sehnsucht nach der Waldgegend;* 6, *Auf das Trinkglas eines verstorbenen Freundes;* 7, *Wanderung;* 8, *Stille Liebe;* 9, *Frage;* 10, *Stille Tränen;* 11, *Wer machte dich so krank?;* 12, *Alte Laute; 6 Gedichte,* op. 36 (Reinick; 1840): 1, *Sonntags am Rhein;* 2, *Ständchen;* 3, *Nichts schöneres;* 4, *An den Sonnenschein;* 5, *Dichters Genesung;* 6, *Liebesbotschaft; 12 Gedichte aus "Liebesfrühling,"* op. 37 (Rückert; 1840; Nos. 2, 4, and 11 by Clara Schumann): 1, *Der Himmel hat ein' Träne geweint;* 2, *O ihr Herren;* 5, *Ich hab in mich gesogen;* 6, *Liebste, was kann denn uns scheiden?* for Soprano and Tenor; 7, *Schön ist das Fest des Lenzes* for Soprano and Tenor; 8, *Flügel! Flügel! um zu fliegen;* 9, *Rose, Meer und Sonne;* 10, *O Sonn, o Meer, o Rose;* 12, *So wahr die Sonne scheinet* for Soprano and Tenor; *Liederkreis,* op. 39 (Eichendorff; 1840): 1, *In der Fremde;* 2, *Intermezzo;* 3, *Waldesgespräch;* 4, *Die Stille;* 5, *Mondnacht;* 6, *Schöne Fremde;* 7, *Auf einer Burg;* 8, *In der Fremde;* 9, *Wehmut;* 10, *Zwielicht;* 11, *Im Walde;* 12, *Frühlingsnacht; 5 Lieder,* op. 40 (1840): 1, *Märzveilchen* (H.C. Andersen); 2, *Muttertraum* (Andersen); 3, *Der Soldat* (Andersen); 4, *Der Spielmann* (Andersen); 5, *Verratene Liebe* (Chamisso);

Frauenliebe und -leben, op. 42 (Chamisso; 1840): 1, *Seit ich ihn gesehen;* 2, *Er, der Herrlichste von allen;* 3, *Ich kann's nicht fassen, nicht glauben;* 4, *Du Ring an meinem Finger;* 5, *Helft mir, ihr Schwestern;* 6, *Süsser Freund, du blickest;* 7, *An meinem Herzen, an meiner Brust;* 8, *Nun hast du mir den ersten Schmerz getan; 3 zweistimmige Lieder,* op. 43 (1840): 1, *Wenn ich ein Vöglein wär (Das Knaben Wunderhorn);* 2, *Herbstlied* (S.A. Mahlmann); 3, *Schön Blümelein* (Reinick); *Romanzen und Balladen,* op. 45, I (1840): 1, *Der Schatzgräber* (Eichendorff); 2, *Frühlingsfahrt* (Eichendorff); 3, *Abends am Strand* (Heine); *Dichterliebe,* op. 48 (Heine; 1840): 1, *Im wunderschönen Monat Mai;* 2, *Aus meinen Tränen spriessen;* 3, *Die Rose, die Lilie, die Taube, die Sonne;* 4, *Wenn ich in deine Augen seh;* 5, *Ich will meine Seele tauchen;* 6, *Im Rhein, im heiligen Strome;* 7, *Ich grolle nicht;* 8, *Und wüssten's die Blumen, die kleinen;* 9, *Das ist ein Flöten und Geigen;* 10, *Hör' ich das Liedchen klingen;* 11, *Ein Jüngling liebt ein Mädchen;* 12, *Am leuchtenden Sommermorgen;* 13, *Ich hab' im Traum geweinet;* 14, *Allnächtlich im Traume;* 15, *Aus alten Märchen;* 16, *Die alten, bösen Lieder; Romanzen und Balladen,* op. 49, II (1840): 1, *Die beiden Grenadiere* (Heine); 2, *Die feindlichen Brüder* (Heine); 3, *Die Nonne* (A. Fröhlich); *Lieder und Gesänge,* op. 51, II: 1, *Sehnsucht* (Geibel; 1840); 2, *Volksliedchen* (Rückert; 1840); 3, *Ich wandre nicht* (C. Christern; 1840); 4, *Auf dem Rhein* (K. Immermann; 1846); 5, *Liebeslied* (Goethe; 1850); *Romanzen und Balladen,* op. 53, III (1840): 1, *Blondels Lied* (Seidl); 2, *Loreley* (W. Lorenz); 3, *Der arme Peter* (Heine); *Belsatzar,* op. 57 (Heine; 1840); *Romanzen und Balladen,* op. 64, IV: 1, *Die Soldatenbraut* (Mörike; 1847); 2, *Das verlassne Mägdelein* (Mörike; 1847); 3, *Tragödie* (Heine; 1841); *Spanisches Liederspiel,* op. 74 (Geibel, after Spanish poets; 1849): 1, *Erste Begegnung* for Soprano and Alto; 2, *Intermezzo* for Tenor and Bass; 3, *Liebesgram* for Soprano and Alto; 4, *In der Nacht* for Soprano and Tenor; 5, *Es ist verraten* for Soprano, Alto, Tenor, and Bass; 6, *Melancholie* for Soprano; 7, *Geständnis* for Tenor; 8, *Botschaft* for Soprano and Alto; 9, *Ich bin geliebt* for Soprano, Alto, Tenor, and Bass; 10, *Der Kontrabandiste* for Baritone; *Lieder und Gesänge,* op. 77, III: 1, *Der frohe Wandersmann* (Eichendorff; 1840); 2, *Mein Garten* (Hoffmann von Fallersleben; 1850); 3, *Geisternähe* (Halm; 1850); 4, *Stiller Vorwurf* (O. Wolff?; 1840); 5, *Aufträge* (C. L'Egru; 1850); *Soldatenlied* (Hoffmann von Fallersleben; 1844); *Das Schwert* (Uhland; 1848); *Der weisse Hirsch* (Uhland; 1848; sketches only); *Die Ammenuhr (Des Knaben Wunderhorn;* 1848); *4 Duette* for Soprano and Tenor, op. 78 (1849): 1, *Tanzlied* (Rückert); 2, *Er und Sie* (Kerner); 3, *Ich denke dein* (Goethe); 4, *Wiegenlied* (Hebbel); *Sommerruh,* duet (C. Schad; 1849); *Lieder-Album für die Jugend,* op. 79 (1849): 1, *Der Abendstern* (Hoffmann von Fallersleben); 2, *Schmetterling* (von Fallersleben); 3, *Frühlingsbotschaft* (Hoffmann von Fallersleben); 4, *Frühlingsgruss* (von Fallersleben); 5, *Vom Schlaraffenland* (von Fallersleben); 6, *Sonntag* (von Fallersleben); 7, *Zigeunerliedchen* (Geibel); 8, *Des Knaben Berglied* (Uhland); 9, *Mailied,* duet ad libitum (C. Overbeck); 10,

Das Käuzlein (Des Knaben Wunderhorn); 11, *Hinaus ins Freie!* (von Fallersleben); 12, *Der Sandmann* (Kletke); 13, *Marienwürmchen (Des Knaben Wunderhorn);* 14, *Die Waise* (von Fallersleben); 15, *Das Glück,* duet (Hebbel); 16, *Weihnachtslied* (Andersen); 17, *Die wandelnde Glocke* (Goethe); 18, *Frühlingslied,* duet ad libitum (von Fallersleben); 19, *Frühlings Ankunft* (von Fallersleben); 20, *Die Schwalben,* duet *(Des Knaben Wunderhorn);* 21, *Kinderwacht* (anonymous); 22, *Des Sennen Abschied* (Schiller); 23, *Er ist's* (Mörike); *Spinnelied,* trio ad libitum (anonymous); *Des Buben Schützenlied* (Schiller); 26, *Schneeglöckchen* (Rückert); 27, *Lied Lynceus des Türmers* (Goethe); 28, *Mignon* (Goethe); *3 Gesänge,* op. 83 (1850): 1, *Resignation* (Buddeus); 2, *Die Blume der Ergebung* (Rückert); 3, *Der Einsiedler* (Eichendorff); *Der Handschuh,* op. 87 (Schiller; 1850); *6 Gesänge,* op. 89 (W. von der Neun; 1850): 1, *Es stürmet am Abendhimmel;* 2, *Heimliches Verschwinden;* 3, *Herbstlied;* 4, *Abschied vom Walde;* 5, *Ins Freie;* 6, *Röselein, Röselein!; 6 Gedichte,* op. 90 (Lenau; 1850): 1, *Lied eines Schmiedes;* 2, *Meine Rose;* 3, *Kommen und Scheiden;* 4, *Die Sennin;* 5, *Einsamkeit;* 6, *Der schwere Abend;* 7, *Requiem; 3 Gesänge,* op. 95 (Byron; 1849): 1, *Die Tochter Jephthas;* 2, *An den Mond;* 3, *Dem Helden; Lieder und Gesänge,* op. 96, IV (1850): 1, *Nachtlied* (Goethe); 2, *Schneeglöckchen* (anonymous); 3, *Ihre Stimme* (Platen); 4, *Gesungen!* (Neun; Schöpff); 5, *Himmel und Erde* (Neun; Schöpff); *Lieder und Gesänge aus Wilhelm Meister,* op. 98a (Goethe; 1849): 1, *Kennst du das Land;* 2, *Ballade des Harfners;* 3, *Nur wer die Sehnsucht kennt;* 4, *Wer nie sein Brot mit Tränen ass;* 5, *Heiss mich nicht reden;* 6, *Wer sich der Einsamkeit ergibt;* 7, *Singet nicht in Trauertönen;* 8, *An die Türen will ich schleichen;* 9, *So lasst mich scheinen; Minnespiel,* op. 101 (Rückert; 1849): 1, *Meine Töne still und heiter* for Tenor; 2, *Liebster, deine Worte stehlen* for Soprano; 3, *Ich bin dein Baum* for Alto and Bass; 4, *Mein schöner Stern!* for Tenor; 5, *Schön ist das Fest des Lenzes* for Soprano, Alto, Tenor, and Bass; 6, *O Freund, mein Schirm, mein Schutz!* for Alto or Soprano; 7, *Die tausend Grüsse* for Soprano and Tenor; 8, *So wahr die Sonne scheinet* for Soprano, Alto, Tenor, and Bass; *Mädchenlieder* for Soprano and Alto or 2 Sopranos, op. 103 (Kulmann; 1851): 1, *Mailied;* 2, *Frühlingslied;* 3, *An die Nachtigall;* 4, *An den Abendstern; 7 Lieder,* op. 104 (Kulmann; 1851): 1, *Mond, meiner Seele Liebling;* 2, *Viel Glück zur Reise, Schwalben!;* 3, *Du nennst mich armes Mädchen;* 4, *Der Zeisig;* 5, *Reich mir die Hand, o Wolke;* 6, *Die letzten Blumen starben;* 7, *Gekämpft hat meine Barke; Schön Hedwig,* declamation, op. 106 (Hebbel; 1849); *6 Gesänge,* op. 107 (1851–52): 1, *Herzeleid* (Ullrich); 2, *Die Fensterscheibe* (Ullrich); 3, *Der Gärtner* (Mörike); 4, *Die Spinnerin* (Heyse); 5, *Im Wald* (Müller); 6, *Abendlied* (Kinkel); *3 Lieder* for 3 Women's Voices, op. 114 (1853): 1, *Nänie* (Bechstein); 2, *Triolett* (L'Egru); 3, *Spruch* (Rückert); *4 Husarenlieder* for Baritone, op. 117 (Lenau; 1851): 1, *Der Husar, trara!;* 2, *Der leidige Frieden;* 3, *Den grünen Zeigern;* 4, *Da liegt der Feinde gestreckte Schar; 3 Gedichte,* op. 119 (G. Pfarrius; 1851): 1, *Die Hütte;* 2, *Warnung;* 3, *Der Bräutigam und die*

Birke; 2 *Balladen,* declamations, op. 122 (1852–53): 1, *Ballade vom Haideknaben* (Hebbel); 2, *Die Flüchtlinge* (Shelley); 5 *heitere Gesänge,* op. 125 (1850–51): 1, *Die Meerfee* (Buddeus); 2, *Husarenabzug* (C. Candidus); 3, *Jung Volkers Lied* (Mörike); 4, *Frühlingslied* (Braun); 5, *Frühlingslust* (Heyse); *5 Lieder und Gesänge,* op. 127: 1, *Sängers Trost* (Kerner; 1840); 2, *Dein Angesicht* (Heine; 1840); 3, *Es leuchtet meine Liebe* (Heine; 1840); 4, *Mein altes Ross* (Moritz, Graf von Strachwitz; 1850); 5, *Schlusslied des Narren* (Shakespeare; 1840); *Frühlingsgrüsse* (Lenau; 1851); *Gedichte der Königin Maria Stuart,* op. 135 (1852): 1, *Abschied von Frankreich;* 2, *Nach der Geburt ihres Sohnes;* 3, *An die Königin Elisabeth;* 4, *Abschied von der Welt;* 5, *Gebet; Spanische Liebeslieder,* op. 138 (Geibel; 1849): 1, *Vorspiel* for Piano, 4-hands; 2, *Tief im Herzen trag ich Pein* for Soprano; 3, *O wie lieblich ist das Mädchen* for Tenor; 4, *Bedeckt mich mit Blumen* for Soprano and Alto; 5, *Flutenreicher Ebro* for Baritone; 6, *Intermezzo* for Piano, 4-hands; 7, *Weh, wie zornig ist das Mädchen* for Tenor; 8, *Hoch, hoch sind die Berge* for Alto; 9, *Blaue Augen hat das Mädchen* for Tenor and Bass; 10, *Dunkler Lichtglanz* for Soprano, Alto, Tenor, and Bass; from *Des Sängers Fluch,* op. 139 (Pohl, after Uhland; 1852): 4, *Provenzalisches Lied;* 7, *Ballade; 4 Gesänge,* op. 142 (1840): 1, *Trost im Gesang* (Kerner); 2, *Lehn deine Wang* (Heine); 3, *Mädchen-Schwermut* (Bernhard); 4, *Mein Wagen rollet langsam* (Heine); *Mailied,* duet (1851); *Liedchen von Marie und Papa,* duet (Schumann; 1852); *Glockentürmers Töchterlein* (Rückert); *Das Käuzlein (Des Knaben Wunderhorn); Deutscher Blumengarten,* duet (Rückert).

FOR ORCH.: Piano Concerto in E-flat major (1828; unfinished); Piano Concerto in F major (1829–31; unfinished); *Introduction and Variations on a Theme of Paganini* (1831); Symph. in G minor (1832–33; first movement perf. Zwickau, Nov. 18, 1832; first complete perf., Schneeberg, Feb. 12, 1833; 3 movements only with a sketch for a 4th movement); Piano Concerto in D minor (1839; one movement only); Symph. in C minor (1840–41; sketches for 4 movements; some of the music used in Symph. No. 2, in C major, op. 61); Symph. No. 1, in B-flat major, op. 38, *Spring* (Leipzig, March 31, 1841); *Ouvertüre, Scherzo, und Finale* in E major, op. 52 (Leipzig, Dec. 6, 1841; revised 1845); Piano Concerto in A minor, op. 54 (first movement composed as the *Fantasie* for Piano and Orch., 1841; movements 2–3, 1845; Leipzig, Jan. 1, 1846); Symph. No. 2, in C major, op. 61 (1845–46; Leipzig, Nov. 5, 1846); *Conzertstück* in F major for 4 Horns, op. 86 (1849; Leipzig, Feb. 25, 1850); *Introduction and Allegro Appassionato, Conzertstück,* op. 92 (1849; Leipzig, Feb. 14, 1850); Symph. No. 3, in E-flat major, op. 97, *Rhenish* (1850; Düsseldorf, Feb. 6, 1851); *Die Braut von Messina,* overture in C minor, to Schiller's play, op. 100 (1850–51; Düsseldorf, March 13, 1851); Symph. No. 4, in D minor, op. 120 (originally his Symph. No. 2; Leipzig, Dec. 6, 1841; revised as his Symph. No. 4, 1851; Düsseldorf, Dec. 30, 1852); *Julius Cäsar,* overture in F minor, to Shakespeare's play, op. 128 (1851; Düsseldorf, Aug. 3, 1852); Cello Concerto in A minor, op. 129 (1850; Leipzig, June 9, 1860); *Fantasie* in C major

for Violin, op. 131 (1853; Hannover, Jan. 1854); *Introduction and Allegro* in D minor/D major for Piano, op. 134 (1853; Utrecht, Nov. 26, 1853); *Hermann und Dorothea,* overture in B minor, to Goethe's poem, op. 136 (1851); Violin Concerto in D minor (1853; first perf. in Berlin, Nov. 26, 1937).

CHAMBER MUSIC: Quartet in C minor for Violin, Viola, Cello, and Piano (1828–30); Quartet in F minor (1829); Quartet in B major for Violin, Viola, Cello, and Piano (1831–32; unfinished); Quartet (1838; not extant); sketches for 2 string quartets: D major and E-flat major (1839); 3 string quartets, op. 41: A minor, F major, A major (1842); Quintet in E-flat major for 2 Violins, Viola, Cello, and Piano, op. 44 (1842); Quartet in E-flat major for Violin, Viola, Cello, and Piano, op. 47 (1842); *Andante and Variations* for 2 Pianos, 2 Cellos, and Horn (1843; original version of op. 46); Trio No. 1, in D minor, for Violin, Cello, and Piano, op. 63 (1847); *Adagio and Allegro* for Horn and Piano, with Violin or Cello ad libitum, in A-flat major, op. 70 (1849); *Phantasiestücke* for Clarinet and Piano, with Violin or Cello ad libitum, op. 73 (1849); Trio No. 2, in F major, for Violin, Cello, and Piano, op. 80 (1847); *Phantasiestücke* for Violin, Cello, and Piano, op. 88 (1842); 3 *Romanzen* for Oboe and Piano, with Violin or Clarinet ad libitum, op. 94 (1849); 5 *Stücke im Volkston* for Cello and Piano, with Violin ad libitum, op. 102 (1849); Sonata No. 1, in A minor, for Violin and Piano, op. 105 (1851); Trio No. 3, in G minor, for Violin, Cello, and Piano, op. 110 (1851); *Märchenbilder* for Viola and Piano, with Violin ad libitum, op. 113 (1851); Sonata No. 2, in D minor, for Violin and Piano, op. 121 (1851); *Märchenerzählungen* for Clarinet, Viola, and Piano, with Violin ad libitum, op. 132 (1853); Sonata for Violin and Piano, F. A. E. [based on the thematic motto of Joachim, *Frei aber einsam,* "Free but alone"] (1853; 2nd and 4th movements by Schumann; first movement by Dietrich; 3rd movement by Brahms); Sonata No. 3, in A minor, for Violin and Piano (1853; incorporates Schumann's 2 movements composed for the F. A. E. sonata); 5 *Romanzen* for Cello and Piano (1853; not extant).

FOR PIANO: 8 polonaises for Piano, 4-hands (1828); *Variations on a Theme of Prince Louis Ferdinand of Prussia* for Piano, 4-hands (1828); *Romanze* in F minor (1829; unfinished); 6 *Walzer* (1829–30); *Thème sur le nom Abegg varié pour le pianoforte,* op. 1 (1829–30); *Variations on a Theme of Weber,* from *Preziosa* (1831); *Valse* in E-flat major (1831; unfinished); *Valse pour Friedrich Wieck* (1831–32; unfinished); Sonata in A-flat major (1831–32; first movement and Adagio); *Andante with Variations on an Original Theme* in G major (1831–32); *Prelude and Fugue* (1832); *Papillons,* op. 2 (1829–31); 6 *Studien nach Capricen von Paganini,* op. 3, I (1832; formerly op. 2); 6 *Intermezzos,* op. 4 (1832; formerly known as *Pièces phantastiques,* op. 3); *Phantasie satyrique* (1832; fragments only); *Fandango* in F-sharp minor (1832); *Exercice fantastique* (1832; formerly op. 5; not extant); *Rondo* in B-flat major (1832; unfinished); 12 *Burlesken* (1832); *Fugue* in D minor (1832); *Fugue* No. 3 (1832); 5 pieces (1832–33; 1, 4, and 5 unfinished); *Sehnsuchts-walzer Variationen: Scènes musicales sur un thème connu* (1832–33); 10

Impromptus über ein Thema von Clara Wieck, op. 5 (1833); *Etüden in Form freier Variationen über ein Beethovensches Thema* (1833); *Variations sur un nocturne de Chopin* (1834); movement for a Sonata, in B-flat major (1836); Sonata No. 4, in F minor (1836–37; unfinished); *Davidsbündlertänze,* 18 character pieces, op. 6 (1837); *Toccata* in C major, op. 7 (1829–32; formerly op. 6); Allegro in B minor, op. 8 (1831); *Carnaval: Scènes mignonnes sur quatre notes,* op. 9 (1833–35); 6 *Konzert-Etüden nach Capricen von Paganini,* op. 10, II (1833); Sonata No. 1, in F-sharp minor, op. 11 (1832–35); *Phantasiestücke,* op. 12 (1832?–37); *Symphonische Etüden,* op. 13 (1834–37); *Concert sans orchestre,* in F minor, op. 14 (1835–36; revised as Sonata No. 3, 1853); *Scherzo* (1836; from op. 14); *Kinderszenen,* op. 15 (1838); *Kreisleriana,* op. 16 (1838; revised 1850); *Phantasie* in C major, op. 17 (1836–38); *Arabeske* in C major, op. 18 (1838); *Blumenstück* in D-flat major, op. 19 (1839); *Humoreske* in B-flat major, op. 20 (1838); 8 *Novelletten,* op. 21 (1838); Sonata No. 2, in G minor, op. 22 (1833–38; new finale, 1838); *Nachtstücke,* 4 pieces, op. 23 (1839); *Allegro* in C minor (1839; not extant); *Faschingsschwank aus Wien: Phantasiebilder,* op. 26 (1839–40); 3 *Romanzen,* op. 28: B-flat minor, F-sharp major, B major (1839); *Klavierstücke,* op. 32 (1838–39); Sonatina in B-flat major (1840; not extant); *Andante and Variations* in B-flat major, op. 46, for 2 Pianos (1843); *Studien für den Pedal-Flügel,* op. 56 (1845); *4 Skizzen für den Pedal-Flügel,* op. 58 (1845); *6 Fugues on B-A-C-H,* op. 60, for Pedal Piano or Organ (1845); *Bilder aus Osten: 6 Impromptus,* op. 66, for Piano, 4-hands (1848); *Album für die Jugend,* op. 68 (1848); *4 Fugues,* op. 72: D minor, D minor, F minor, F major (1845); *4 Marches,* op. 76: B-flat major, G minor, B-flat major (Lager-Scene), E-flat major (1849); *Waldszenen,* op. 82 (1848–49); *12 vierhändige Klavierstücke für kleine und grosse Kinder,* op. 85 (1849); *Bunte Blätter,* op. 99 (1838–49); *Ballszenen,* op. 109, for Piano, 4-hands (1851); *Phantasiestücke,* 3 pieces, op. 111: C minor, A-flat major, C minor (1851); *3 Clavier-Sonaten für die Jugend,* op. 118: G major, D major, C major (1853); *Albumblätter,* op. 124 (1854); *7 Klavierstücke in Fughettenform,* op. 126 (1853); *Kinderball,* op. 130, for Piano, 4-hands (1853); 5 *Gesänge der Frühe,* op. 133 (1853); *Canon on F. Himmel's An Alexis send ich dich,* in A-flat major (1854); *Thema* in E-flat major (1854); *Variations on an Original Theme* (1854).

BIBLIOGRAPHY: COLLECTED WORKS, SOURCE MATERIAL: A complete ed. of his works, *Robert Schumann: Werke,* was ed. by Clara Schumann et al. and publ. by Breitkopf & Härtel (34 vols., Leipzig, 1881–93; supplement ed. by Brahms, 1893). His *Gesammelte Schriften über Musik und Musiker* is a collection of his articles from *Neue Zeitschrift für Musik* (4 vols., Leipzig, 1854; Eng. trans., London, 1877; 5th German ed., revised by M. Kreisig, 1914). A judicious selection from the complete writings, ed. by H. Simon, was publ. under the same title as the original ed. (3 vols., Leipzig, 1888–89). A selection of Schumann's critical reviews, trans. into Eng. by P. Rosenfeld, was publ. in N.Y. in 1946. The Robert-Schumann-Gesellschaft began the publication

of the *Sammelbände der Robert-Schumann-Gesellschaft* in Leipzig in 1961. See also H. Drinker, *Texts of the Vocal Works of Robert Schumann in English Translation* (N.Y., 1947), and L. Minchin, *Schumann in English: Four Famous Song-Cycles in Singable English Verse* (London, 1981).

A thematic catalogue was prepared by A. Dörffel, *Thematisches Verzeichniss sämmtlicher in Druck erschienenen Werke Robert Schumanns* (Leipzig, 1860; 4th ed., 1868). See also K. Hofmann, *Die Erstdrucke der Werke von Robert Schumann* (Tutzing, 1979).

Other sources include: F. Kerst, *S.-Brevier* (Berlin, 1905); A. Schumann, ed., *Der junge S.: Dichtungen und Briefe* (Leipzig, 1910); E. Bienenfeld, "Die Stammtafel der Familie R. S.s: Ahnen und Nachkommen eines Genies," *Archiv für Rassen- und Gesellschaftsbiologie,* XXVI (1932); W. Boetticher, *R. S. in seinen Schriften und Briefen* (Berlin, 1942); G. Eismann, *R. S.: Ein Quellenwerk über sein Leben und Schaffen* (2 vols., Leipzig, 1956); P. Mies, "Literatur um R. S.: Ein Beitrag zu seinem 100. Todestag," *Musikhandel,* VII (1956); R. Münnich, *Aus R. S.s Briefen und Schriften* (Weimar, 1956); C. Eismann, "Bemerkenswertes zur Genealogie R. S.s," *Die Musikforschung,* XXII (1969); F. Munte, *Verzeichnis des deutschsprachigen Schrifttums über R. S. 1856–1970* (Hamburg, 1972).

CORRESPONDENCE AND DIARIES: C. Schumann, ed., *S.s Jugendbriefe. Nach den Originalen mitgeteilt* (Leipzig, 1885; Eng. trans., London, 1888; 4th German ed., 1910); F. Jansen, ed., *R. S.s Briefe: Neue Folge* (Leipzig, 1886; Eng. trans., London, 1890; 2nd German ed., augmented, 1904); H. Erler, *R. S.s Leben: Aus seinen Briefen geschildert* (2 vols., Berlin, 1886–87; 3rd ed., 1927); "Aus S.s Kreisen," *Die Musik,* 14 (1914; unpubl. letters from and to S.); G. Eismann, ed., *R. S.: Tagebücher, Vol. I (1827–38)* (Leipzig, 1971).

BIOGRAPHICAL: W. von Wasielewski, *R. S.* (Dresden, 1858; Eng. trans., Boston, 1871; augmented German ed., 1906); A. Reissmann, *R. S.: Sein Leben und seine Werke* (Berlin, 1865; 3rd ed., 1879; in Eng., London, 1886); A. Niggli, *R. S.* (Basel, 1879); P. Spitta, *Ein Lebensbild R. S.s* (Leipzig, 1882); W. von Wasielewski, *Schumanniana* (Bonn, 1883); J. Fuller-Maitland, *S.* (London, 1884; new ed., 1913); H. Reimann, *R. S.s Leben und Werke* (Leipzig, 1887); R. Batka, *S.* (Leipzig, 1893); H. Abert, *R. S.* (Berlin, 1903; 3rd ed., 1918); A. Paterson, *S.* (London, 1903; revised ed., 1934); L. Schneider and M. Mareschal, *S.: Sa vie et ses œuvres* (Paris, 1905); C. Mauclair, *S.* (Paris, 1906); P. Möbius, *Über R. S.s Krankheit* (Halle, 1906); M.D. Calvocoressi, *S.* (Paris, 1912); M. Wieck, *Aus dem Kreise Wieck-S.* (Dresden, 1912; 2nd ed., 1914); W. Dahms, *S.* (Berlin, 1916); F. Nussbaum, *Der Streit um R. S.s Krankheit* (Diss., Univ. of Cologne, 1923); F. Niecks, *R. S.: A Supplementary and Corrective Biography* (London, 1925); R. Pitrou, *La Vie intérieure de R. S.* (Paris, 1925); E. Schumann, *Erinnerungen* (Stuttgart, 1925; Eng. trans., London, 1927); V. Basch, *S.* (Paris, 1926); idem, *La Vie douloureuse de S.* (Paris, 1928; Eng. trans., N.Y., 1931); H. Tessmer, *R. S.* (Stuttgart, 1930); E. Schumann, *R. S.: Ein Lebensbild meines Vaters* (Leipzig, 1931); M. Beaufils,

S. (Paris, 1932); C. Valabrega, *S.* (Modena, 1934); W. Gertler, *R. S.* (Leipzig, 1936); W. Korte, *R. S.* (Potsdam, 1937); E. Bücken, *R. S.* (Cologne, 1940); W. Boetticher, *R. S.: Einführung in Persönlichkeit und Werk* (Berlin, 1941); H. Kleinebreil, *Der kranke S.: Untersuchungen über Krankheit und Todesursache R. S.s* (Diss., Univ. of Jena, 1943); R. Schauffler, *Florestan: The Life and Work of R. S.* (N.Y., 1945); J. Chissell, *S.* (London, 1948; 2nd ed., revised, 1967); R. Sutermeister, *R. S.: Sein Leben nach Briefen, Tagebüchern und Erinnerungen des Meisters und seiner Gattin* (Zürich, 1949); K. Wörner, *R. S.* (Zürich, 1949); A. Cœuroy, *R. S.* (Paris, 1950); E. Müller, *R. S.* (Olten, 1950); M. Brion, *S. et l'âme romantique* (Paris, 1954; in Eng. as *S. and the Romantic Age,* London, 1956); P. and W. Rehberg, *R. S.: Sein Leben und sein Werk* (Zürich, 1954); G. Eismann, *R. S.: Eine Biographie in Wort und Bild* (Leipzig, 1956; 2nd ed., augmented, 1964; Eng. trans., 1964); H. Moser and E. Rebling, eds., *R. S.: Aus Anlass seines 100. Todestages* (Leipzig, 1956); R. Petzold and E. Crass, *R. S.: Sein Leben in Bildern* (Leipzig, 1956); A. Boucourechliev, *S.* (Paris, 1957; Eng. trans., 1959); P. Young, *Tragic Muse: The Life and Works of R. S.* (London, 1957; 2nd ed., enlarged, 1961); E. Sams, "S.'s Hand Injury," *Musical Times* (Dec. 1971 and May 1972); K. Laux, *R. S.* (Leipzig, 1972); R. Henson and H. Urich, "S.'s Hand Injury," *British Medical Journal,* no. 1 (1978); T. Dowley, *S.: His Life and Times* (Tunbridge Wells, 1982); G. Nauhau, *R. S.: Haushaltbücher* (2 vols., Leipzig, 1982); R. Taylor, *R. S.: His Life and Work* (London, 1982). CRITICAL, ANALYTICAL: A. Ambros, "R. S.s Tage und Werke," *Kultur-historische Bilder aus dem Musikleben der Gegenwart* (Leipzig, 1860); H. Deiters, "S. als Schriftsteller," *Allgemeine Musikalische Zeitung,* 47–49 (1865); L. Mesnard, *Un Successeur de Beethoven: Etude sur R. S.* (Paris, 1876); S. Bagge, "S. und seine Faustszenen," *Sammlung musikalischer Vorträge,* no. 4 (Leipzig, 1879); P. Graf von Waldersee, "Über S.s *Manfred,*" ibid., no. 13 (Leipzig, 1880); F. Jansen, *Die Davidsbündler. Aus R. S.s Sturm- und Drangperiode* (Leipzig, 1883); B. Vogel, *R. S.s Klaviertonpoesie* (Leipzig, 1886); M. Friedlaender, *Textrevision zu R. S.s Liedern* (Leipzig, 1887); V. Joss, *Friedrich Wieck und sein Verhältniss zu R. S.* (Dresden, 1900); H. Kretzschmar, "R. S. als Asthetiker," *Jahrbuch der Musikbibliothek Peters 1906;* H. Abert, "R. S.s Genoveva," *Zeitschrift der Internationalen Musik-Gesellschaft,* XI (1909); M. Katz, *Die Schilderung des musikalischen Eindrucks bei S.* (Giessen, 1910); L. Hirschberg, *R. S.s Tondichtungen balladischen Charakters* (Langensalza, 1913); E. Wolff, *R. S. Lieder in ersten und späteren Fassungen* (Leipzig, 1914); O. Karsten, *Die Instrumentation R. S.s* (Diss., Univ. of Vienna, 1922); F. Schnapp, *Heinrich Heine und R. S.* (Hamburg, 1924); P. Frenzel, *R. S. und Goethe* (Leipzig, 1926); G. Minotti, *Die Enträtselung des Schumannschen Sphinx-Geheimnisses* (Leipzig, 1926); J. Fuller-Maitland, *S.'s Pianoforte Works* (London, 1927); G. Minotti, "Die Enträtselung des Schumannschen Abegg-Geheimniss," *Zeitschrift für Musik* (July–Aug. 1927); M. Cohen, *Studien zur Sonataform bei R. S.* (Diss., Univ. of Vienna, 1928);

K. Wagner, *R. S. als Schüler und Abiturient* (Zwickau, 1928); J. Fuller-Maitland, *S.'s Concerted Chamber Music* (London, 1929); M. Ninck, *S. und die Romantik in der Musik* (Heidelberg, 1929); R. Goldenberg, *Der Klaviersatz bei S.* (Diss., Univ. of Vienna, 1930); H. Rosenwald, *Geschichte des deutschen Liedes zwischen Schubert und S.* (Berlin, 1930); W. Gertler, *R. S. in seinen früheren Klavierwerken* (Wolfenbüttel, 1931); M. Schweiger, *Die Harmonik in den Klavierwerken R. S.s* (Diss., Univ. of Vienna, 1931); W. Schwarz, *S. und die Variation: Mit besonderer Berücksichtigung der Klavierwerke* (Kassel, 1932); H. Kötz, *Der Einfluss Jean Pauls auf R. S.* (Weimar, 1933); G. Wilcke, *Tonalität und Modulation im Streichquartett Mendelssohns und S.s* (Leipzig, 1933); G. Minotti, *Die Geheimdokumente der Davidsbündler* (Leipzig, 1934); G. Abraham, "The Three Scores of S.'s D minor Symphony," *Musical Times,* LXXXI (1940); R. Felber, "S.'s Place in German Song," *Musical Quarterly* (July 1940); R. Hernried, "Four Unpublished Compositions by R. S.," ibid. (Jan. 1942); P. Kehm, *Die "Neue Zeitschrift für Musik" unter S.s Redaktion: 1834–44* (Diss., Univ. of Munich, 1943); I. Forger, *R. S. als Kritiker: Ein Beitrag zur Geschichte der musikalischen Kritik und zum S.-Problem* (Diss., Univ. of Münster, 1948); W. Edelmann, *Über Text und Musik in R. S.s Sololieder* (Diss., Univ. of Münster, 1950); G. Abraham, "S.'s 'Jugendsinfonie' in G minor," *Musical Quarterly* (Jan. 1951); G. Abraham, ed., *S.: A Symposium* (London, 1952); H. Homeyer, *Grundbegriffe der Musikanschauung R. S.s: Ihr Wesen, ihre Bedeutung und Funktion in seinem literarischen Gesamtwerk* (Diss., Univ. of Münster, 1956); H. Pleasants, *The Musical World of R. S.* (N.Y., 1965); A. Zlotnik, "Die beiden Fassungen von S.s D-Moll Symphonie," *Österreichische Musikzeitschrift,* XXI (1966); L. Plantinga, *S. As Critic* (New Haven, 1967); T. Brown, *The Aesthetics of R. S.* (N.Y., 1968); A. Gebhardt, *R. S. als Symphoniker* (Regensburg, 1968); E. Sams, *The Songs of R. S.* (London, 1969; 2nd ed., revised, 1975); S. Walsh, *The Lieder of S.* (London, 1971); J. Chissell, *S. Piano Music* (London, 1972); A. Desmond, *S. Songs* (London, 1972); A. Walker, ed., *R. S.: The Man and His Music* (London, 1972; 2nd ed., revised, 1976); L. Siegel, "A Second Look at S.'s *Genoveva,*" *Music Review,* XXXVI (1975); W. Boetticher, *R. S.s Klavierwerke: Entstehung, Urtext, Gestalt: Untersuchungen anhand unveröffentlicher Skizzen und biographischer Dokumente* (Wilhelmshaven, 1976—); R. Hallmark, *The Genesis of S.'s "Dichterliebe": A Source Study* (Ann Arbor, Mich., 1979); C. Becker, "A New Look at S.'s Impromptus," *Musical Quarterly* (Oct. 1981); C. Brauner, "Irony in the Heine Lieder of Schubert and S.," ibid. (April 1981); G. Moore, *"Poet's Lore" and Other S. Cycles and Songs* (London, 1981); B. Turchin, "S.'s Conversion to Vocal Music: A Reconsideration," *Musical Quarterly* (July 1981).

Schumann, Walter, American composer of applied music; b. New York, Oct. 8, 1913; d. Minneapolis, Aug. 21, 1958. He studied law and music at the Univ. of Southern Calif. in Los Angeles; became associated with radio shows and composed music for films; wrote an opera, *John Brown's Body* (Los Angeles, Sept. 21, 1953). He contributed the famous ominously syncopated theme to the television serial *Dragnet,* based on the initial 3 notes of the minor scale.

Schumann-Heink, Ernestine (née **Rössler**), famous contralto; b. Lieben, near Prague, June 15, 1861; d. Hollywood, Calif., Nov. 17, 1936. Her father was an officer in the Austrian army; her mother, an Italian amateur singer. In 1872 she was sent to the Ursuline Convent in Prague, where she sang in the church choir; after lessons from Marietta von Leclair in Graz, she made her first public appearance, singing the contralto solo in Beethoven's 9th Symph. (1876); made her opera debut at the Dresden Court Opera (Oct. 15, 1878) as Azucena; continued her studies with Karl Krebs and Franz Wüllner. In 1883 she was engaged to sing at the Hamburg City Opera; when the company was taken to Covent Garden in London in 1892, she sang Erda; subsequently specialized in the Wagnerian roles; took part in the Bayreuth Festivals from 1896 until 1903, and in 1905 and 1906; also sang with the Berlin Opera. She made her American debut as Ortrud on Nov. 7, 1898, in Chicago; appeared in the same role with the Metropolitan Opera in N.Y. on Jan. 9, 1899; canceled her contract with the Berlin Opera in order to remain a member of the Metropolitan Opera Co. (until 1903; then appeared intermittently until 1932); created the role of Klytemnestra in *Elektra* (Dresden, Jan. 25, 1909); made her last operatic appearance as Erda at the Metropolitan on March 11, 1932. She became an American citizen in 1908. During the last years of her life she was active mainly as a teacher. Her operatic repertoire included about 150 parts; her voice, of an even quality in all registers, possessed great power, making it peculiarly suitable to Wagnerian roles. She was married in 1882 to Ernst Heink of Dresden, from whom she was later divorced; in 1893 she married the actor Paul Schumann in Hamburg; he died in 1904; she assumed the names of both Schumann and Heink. Her 3rd husband was a Chicago lawyer, William Rapp, Jr., whom she married in 1905 (divorced, 1914).

BIBLIOGRAPHY: M. Lawton, *Schumann-Heink, The Last of the Titans* (N.Y., 1928). See also A.T. Zwart in *Notable American Women* (Cambridge, Mass., 1971).

Schünemann, Georg, eminent German musicologist and music educator; b. Berlin, March 13, 1884; d. there (suicide), Jan. 2, 1945. He studied at the Stern Cons. in Berlin; played flute in various orchs. in Berlin; then took courses in musicology with Kretzschmar, Friedländer, Wolf, and others at the Univ. of Berlin; also studied German literature and philosophy there, receiving his Ph.D. in 1907 (Diss. *Geschichte des Dirigierens,* publ. in Leipzig, 1913). In 1919 he joined the faculty of the Univ. of Berlin; was appointed deputy director of the Berlin Hochschule für Musik in 1920, and director in 1932; later held the post of director of the State Musical Instrument

Collections. In 1935 he was appointed director of the music division of the Prussian State Library. He took his own life during the darkest stages of the war.

WRITINGS: *Das Lied der deutschen Kolonisten in Russland* (Berlin, 1923); *Die Musica des Listhenius* (Berlin, 1927); *Geschichte der deutschen Schulmusik* (Leipzig, 1928; 2nd ed., 1931); *Die Musikerziehung,* I: *Die Musik in Kindheit und Jugend, Schule und Volk* (Leipzig, 1930); *C.F. Zelter, der Begründer der preussischen Musikpflege* (Berlin, 1932); *Führer durch die deutsche Chorliteratur* (2 vols., Wolfenbüttel, 1935–36). He ed. *Musiker-Handschriften von Bach bis Schumann* (facsimile ed., Berlin, 1936; revised and publ. in an Eng. trans. by W. Gerstenberg and M. Hürimann, 1968); *C.F. Zelter, Der Mensch und sein Werk* (Berlin, 1937); *Die Violine* (Hamburg, 1940); *Geschichte der Klaviermusik* (Hamburg, 1940; 2nd ed., revised by H. Gerigk, 1953; 3rd ed., 1956); *Die Singakademie zu Berlin* (Regensburg, 1941); also ed. *Ludwig van Beethovens Konversationshefte* (not complete; 3 vols., Berlin, 1941–43); wrote numerous essays in German music magazines.

BIBLIOGRAPHY: E. Preussner, "Georg Schünemann," *Die Musikforschung,* I (1948).

Schunke, Karl, German pianist; b. Magdeburg, 1801; d. Paris (suicide), Dec. 16, 1839. He studied music with his father, the horn player **Michael Schunke** (1778–1821); then took some lessons with Ferdinand Ries, whom he accompanied to London. In 1828 he went to Paris, where he became a fashionable piano teacher; nevertheless, he suffered from some sort of malaise and killed himself. He composed a number of brilliant salon pieces à la mode and transcriptions of operatic arias for piano.

Schunke, Ludwig, German pianist; b. Kassel, Dec. 21, 1810; d. Leipzig, Dec. 7, 1834. He was a cousin of **Karl Schunke;** studied with his father, **Gottfried Schunke** (1777–1861), who was, like Karl Schunke's father, a horn player; also like his cousin, he went to Paris, where he studied piano with Kalkbrenner and Reicha; settled in Leipzig in 1833 and became an intimate friend of Schumann, of whom he was an exact contemporary, and with whom he became associated in founding the *Neue Zeitschrift für Musik.* His early death at not quite the age of 24 was greatly mourned, for his piano pieces were full of promise; among them were a Sonata, a set of variations, *2 Caprices,* and a set of *Charakterstücke.* Schumann wrote a heartfelt appreciation of Schunke's talent, which was reprinted in his *Gesammelte Schriften.*

Schuppanzigh, Ignaz, Austrian violinist, friend of Beethoven; b. Vienna, Nov. 20, 1776; d. there, March 2, 1830. He learned to play the violin and the viola; in 1795 became conductor of the Augarten concerts and from about 1798 was manager. Beethoven played several times at these concerts. In 1794–95 he was first violinist in the quartet that played regularly for Prince Lichnowsky. In 1808 he founded the private quartet of Prince Razumovsky (with Mayseder, Linke, and Weiss), interpreting the Beethoven quartets under the master's eye, and also playing quartets of Haydn and Mozart. After a fire in Razumovsky's palace (Dec. 31, 1814) he left Vienna, returning in 1823. Schuppanzigh then became a member of the court orch.; also was director of the German Opera in 1828. He publ. a *Solo brillant* for Violin, with String Quartet; solo variations on a Russian theme; 9 variations for 2 violins.

BIBLIOGRAPHY: G. Kinsky, "Beethoven und das Schuppanzigh-Quartette," *Rheinische Musik- und Theater-Zeitung*, XXI (pp. 235ff.). See also the literature on Beethoven.

Schuré, Edouard, Alsatian writer on music; b. Strasbourg, Jan. 21, 1841; d. Paris, April 7, 1929. He studied law and philology in Strasbourg; lived in Bonn, Berlin, and Munich; in 1867 settled in Paris. In his writings (in French) he was an avowed propagandist of German music, and particularly Wagner. WRITINGS: *Histoire du Lied; ou, La Chanson populaire en Allemagne* (Paris, 1868; new ed. with the study *Le Réveil de la poésie populaire en France*, 1903); *Le Drame musical* (Paris, 1875; 12th ed., 1914; German trans. by Hans von Wolzogen as *Das musikalische Drama;* 3rd ed., 1888; part II is devoted to an appreciation of Wagner); *Souvenirs sur Richard Wagner* (Paris, 1900); *Précurseurs et révoltés* (Paris, 1904); *The Musical Idea in Wagner* (Eng. trans. from French, Hampstead, 1910).

BIBLIOGRAPHY: J. Mainor, *Edouard Schuré* (Angers, 1905); A. Roux and R. Veyssié, *Edouard Schuré, Son œuvre et sa pensée* (Paris, 1913); R.A. Schuler, *Edouard Schuré à travers son écriture* (Paris, 1928); A. Roux, *In memoriam Schuré* (Paris, 1931).

Schuricht, Carl, distinguished German conductor; b. Danzig, July 3, 1880; d. Corseaux-sur-Vevey, Switzerland, Jan. 7, 1967. He studied at home, his father being an organ manufacturer and his mother a pianist. He then took lessons with Humperdinck at the Hochschule für Musik in Berlin, and later in Leipzig with Max Reger. He subsequently conducted theater orchs. in Germany; in 1912 he became municipal music director in Wiesbaden, and held this post until 1944, when he moved to Switzerland; in 1946 he reopened the Salzburg Festival; continued to conduct there and in France; in 1956 brought the Vienna Phil. to America for its first American tour. In 1957 he conducted at the Ravinia Festival with the Chicago Symph. and at Tanglewood with the Boston Symph.; in subsequent years, regularly conducted the Berlin and Vienna phil. orchs.; also was a frequent guest conductor of the Stuttgart Radio Symph. He composed some piano music and an orch. suite, *3 Herbststücke.*

BIBLIOGRAPHY: B. Gavoty, *Carl Schuricht* (Geneva, 1955).

Schurig, Arthur, German writer on music; b. Dresden, April 24, 1870; d. there, Feb. 15, 1929. He studied in Dresden, Berlin, and Leipzig; followed a military career; upon retirement, devoted much of his leisure to writing on music; publ. an excellent biography of Mozart, *W.A. Mozart; Sein Leben und sein Werk* (2 vols., 1913; 2nd ed., 1923); edited Leopold Mozart's *Reise-Aufzeichnungen* (1920) and Constanze Mozart's *Briefe, Aufzeichnungen, Dokumente* (1922).

Schurig, Volkmar (Julius Wilhelm), German organist and composer; b. Aue-on-the-Mulde, March 24, 1822; d. Dresden, Jan. 31, 1899. He studied in Dresden, where he played organ in the English Church (1844–56); subsequently filled various other posts as an organist, singing teacher, and cantor. He publ. organ fantasias; organ preludes; sacred choruses to English texts; children's songs; brought out a useful collection, *Liederperlen deutscher Tonkunst.*

Schürmann, Georg Caspar, German composer; b. Idensen, near Hannover, c.1672; d. Wolfenbüttel, Feb. 25, 1751. He was a singer (alto-falsetto) at the Hamburg Opera (1693–97); was then engaged as court Kapellmeister to the Duke of Braunschweig in Wolfenbüttel; traveled in Italy for further study; from 1703 to 1706 was court Kapellmeister in Meiningen; returned to Wolfenbüttel in 1707 and remained there most of his life. He wrote about 40 operas for the Duke of Braunschweig, produced in Wolfenbüttel and Hamburg; only 3 appear to have survived in their entirety; his church music is also lost. The following were produced in Braunschweig: *Heinrich der Vogler* (part I, Aug. 1, 1718; part II, Jan. 11, 1721); *Die getreue Alceste* (1719); *Ludovicus Pius* (1726); this last opera, under the German title, *Ludwig der Fromme,* is partly reproduced in Eitner's *Publikationen älterer Musikwerke;* a suite from *Alceste* and 3 books of arias was publ. by G.F. Schmidt (Wolfenbüttel, 1934).

BIBLIOGRAPHY: G.F. Schmidt, *Die frühdeutsche Oper und die musikdramatische Kunst G.C. Schürmanns* (2 vols., Regensburg, 1933–34; expanded from his dissertation, Univ. of Munich, 1913).

Schurmann (Schürmann), (Eduard) Gerard, greatly significant composer and conductor with Dutch and Hungarian biological antecedents and of geographically Indonesian birth; b. Kertosono, Java, Jan. 23, 1924. He traces his paternal ancestry to the 18th-century German composer **Georg Caspar Schürmann,** who sang alto-falsetto parts at the Hamburg Opera, served as Kapellmeister at the court of the Duke of Braunschweig, and wrote 40-odd operas. Gerard Schurmann's father was an employee at a sugar factory in Java; his mother was a professional pianist who had studied with Béla Bartók at the Budapest Academy of Music. As war clouds gathered over Southeastern Asia, Schurmann was sent to England in 1937; he went to school in London, and after matriculation, joined the Royal Air Force, serving in aircrews on active flying duty. While still in uniform, he gave piano recitals; took piano lessons with Kathleen Long and composition with Alan Rawsthorne. During his travels in

Italy he took lessons in conducting with Franco Ferrara. The government of the Netherlands offered him the position of cultural attaché at the Dutch Embassy in London; being fluent in the Dutch language, which was his mother tongue in Indonesia, he accepted. Later he moved to the Netherlands and worked in the radio studios in Hilversum. He developed a successful career in London as a pianist, conductor, and composer. In 1981 he decided to move to the U.S., and settled in Hollywood, where he became active as a movie composer. Apart from that financially helpful activity, he traveled, conducting guest engagements in France, Italy, Switzerland, Ireland, Scotland, Czechoslovakia, Vienna, and London; his repertoire was comprehensive, ranging from Mozart to Bartók, from Haydn to Schoenberg and Webern, from Tchaikovsky to Shostakovich; his own pieces also figured on his programs. In America he dropped the ancestral umlaut on the 4th letter of his last name. The structure of Schurmann's music is asymptotic toward tonality; melodic progressions are linear, with the fundamental tonic and dominant often encasing the freely atonal configurations, while dodecaphony assumes the adumbrative decaphonic lines, with 2 notes missing in the tone row. The harmonic texture is acrid, acerbic, and astringent; the styptic tendency is revealed in Schurmann's predilection for dissonant minor seconds and major sevenths treated as compound units; yet after the needed tension is achieved, the triadic forms are introduced as a sonic emollient. Thanks to this versatility of application, Schurmann achieves a natural felicity in dealing with exotic subjects; his proximity to gamelan-like pentatonicism during his Indonesian adolescence lends authentic flavor to his use of pentatonic scales; remarkable in his congenial treatment is the set *Chuench'i,* to Eng. translations of 7 Chinese poems. On the other hand, his intimate knowledge of Eng. music and history enables him to impart a true archaic sentiment to his opera-cantata based on the medieval poem *Piers Plowman.* Schurmann is self-critical in regard to works of his which he deems imperfect; thus, he destroyed his Piano Concerto, which he had played under prestigious auspices with the London Symph. Orch., conducted by Adrian Boult in Cambridge in April 1944.

WORKS: *Piers Plowman,* opera-cantata in 2 acts, to the poem of William Langland (Three Choirs Festival, Gloucester Cathedral, Aug. 22, 1980). For Orch.: *6 Studies of Francis Bacon,* comprising *Figures in a Landscape, Popes, Isabel, Crucifixion, George and the Bicycle,* and *Self-Portrait* (Dublin, Jan. 7, 1969); *Variants* (Guildford Festival, March 8, 1971); *Attack and Celebration* (1971); Piano Concerto (Portsmouth, Nov. 21, 1973; John Ogdon, soloist); Violin Concerto (Liverpool, Sept. 26, 1978; Ruggiero Ricci, soloist). Chamber music: Violin Sonata (1943); String Quartet No. 1 (1943); String Quartet No. 2 (1946); *Duo* for 2 Violins (1950); Wind Quintet (1964); *Fantasia* (1968); Sonatina for Flute and Piano (1968); *Serenade* for Solo Violin (1969); *Duo* for Violin and Piano (1984). For Piano: Sonata (1943); *Rotterdam,* suite for 2 Pianos (1944); *Bagatelles* (1945); *Contrasts* (1973); *Leotaurus* (1975); 2

Ballades (1981–83). For Voice: *Pacific,* 3 songs (1943); *5 Facets* (London, Jan. 20, 1946; Peter Pears, tenor; Benjamin Britten, pianist); 9 poems of William Blake (1956); *Chuench'i,* cycle of 7 songs from the Chinese (1966; also for Voice and Orch.; Harrogate, Aug. 10, 1969); *Summer Is Coming,* madrigal, unaccompanied (1970); *The Double Heart,* cantata for Voices Unaccompanied (1976).

Schuster, Bernhard, German publisher and composer; b. Berlin, March 26, 1870; d. there, Jan. 13, 1934. He studied piano, organ, and violin; was active for a time as a theater conductor. In 1901 he founded the fortnightly review *Die Musik,* which from its inception ranked with the foremost musical journals of Germany; was its editor in chief until 1933. In 1905 he founded the publishing house "Schuster und Loeffler" (Berlin and Leipzig), which brought out a number of important works on music (the business was acquired by the Stuttgart Deutsche Verlags-Anstalt in 1922). Schuster publ. 2 books of songs; also composed the operas *Der Jungbrunnen* (Karlsruhe, 1920) and *Der Dieb des Glücks* (Wiesbaden, March 10, 1923); a Symph.; a String Quartet; sacred choruses.

Schuster, Josef, German composer; b. Dresden, Aug. 11, 1748; d. there, July 24, 1812. He spent 4 years in Italy (1765–69) for study, and after 5 years in Dresden, went to Italy again; took lessons with Padre Martini at Bologna; wrote Italian operas, and was made honorary maestro to the King of Naples; after another 2 years in Dresden, he made a 3rd visit to Italy (1778–81), finally establishing himself in Dresden as a theatrical conductor; from 1787 he was associated with Seydelmann as court Kapellmeister. He composed a number of operas, mostly to Italian texts; also cantatas, oratorios, symphs., etc.; publ. piano pieces for 2- and 4-hands, divertissements for piano and violin, etc.

BIBLIOGRAPHY: R. Engländer, "Die Opern Josef Schusters," *Zeitschrift für Musikwissenschaft* (1928); R. Engländer, "Les Sonates de violon de Mozart et les 'Duetti' de J. Schuster," *Revue de Musicologie* (1939).

Schuster, Joseph, cellist; b. Constantinople, May 23, 1903; d. Los Angeles, Feb. 16, 1969. He studied at the St. Petersburg Cons. and later at the Hochschule für Musik in Berlin; was first cellist in the Berlin Phil. (1926–31); emigrated to America in 1934; made his concert debut in N.Y. on March 15, 1935; from 1936 to 1944 was first cellist of the N.Y. Phil.

Schütt, Eduard, Russian-born Austrian pianist and composer; b. St. Petersburg, Oct. 22, 1856; d. Obermais, near Merano, Italy, July 26, 1933. After studying piano at the St. Petersburg Cons., he went to Germany, where he took courses with Richter, Jadassohn, and Reinecke at the Leipzig Cons.; then proceeded to Vienna, where he became a private pupil of Leschetizky. He wrote the comic opera *Signor Formica* (Vienna, Nov. 19, 1892); 2 piano concertos; Piano Quartet; 2 piano trios; numerous character pieces for piano, some of which retained popularity for a long time (*Scènes de bal, Thème varié et Fugato, Silhouetten-Portraits, Poésies d'automne, Carnaval mignon,* etc.).

Schütz, Franz, Austrian organist; b. Vienna, April 15, 1892; d. there, May 19, 1962. He was on the staff of the Cons. of the Gesellschaft der Musikfreunde in Vienna from 1921; gave organ recitals; composed organ pieces.

Schütz (Sagittarius), Heinrich, great German composer; b. Köstritz, Oct. 8, 1585; d. Dresden, Nov. 6, 1672. He was born into a prosperous family of innkeepers; in 1590 the family settled in Weissenfels, where his father became burgomaster. He was trained in music by Heinrich Colander, the town organist. In 1599 he became a choirboy in the court chapel of Landgrave Moritz of Hessen-Kassel; in Kassel he pursued his academic studies with Georg Otto, the court Kapellmeister. On Sept. 27, 1608, he entered the Univ. of Marburg to study law; an opportunity to continue his musical education came in 1609 when Landgrave Moritz offered to send him to Venice to take lessons with the renowned master Giovanni Gabrieli. Under Gabrieli's tutelage, he received a thorough training in composition, and he also learned to play the organ. In 1611 he brought out a book of 5-voice madrigals, which he dedicated to his benefactor, Landgrave Moritz. After Gabrieli's death in 1612 Schütz returned to Kassel, serving as second organist at the court chapel. In 1615 the Elector invited him to Dresden as Saxon Kapellmeister; Praetorius was also active at the Dresden court for special occasions at this time. In 1616 Landgrave Moritz asked the Elector to allow Schütz to return to Kassel, but the Elector declined; in 1617 Schütz assumed fully his duties as Saxon Kapellmeister, being granted an annual salary of 400 florins from 1618. In addition to providing music for court occasions, he was responsible for overseeing the functions of the court chapel. In 1619 he publ. his first collection of sacred music, the *Psalmen Davids sampt etlichen Moteten und Concerten.* On June 1, 1619, he married Magdalena Wildeck, the daughter of a court official in Dresden. They had 2 daughters. She died on Sept. 6, 1625, and Schütz remained a widower for the rest of his life. During a court visit to Torgau, Schütz produced the first German opera, *Dafne,* set to Opitz's translation and adaptation of Rinuccini's libretto for Peri's opera; it was presented at Hartenfels Castle on April 13, 1627, to celebrate the wedding of the Princess Sophia Eleonora of Saxony to Landgrave Georg II of Hesse-Darmstadt. In 1628 he was granted a leave of absence, and went to Italy. There he had an occasion to study the new operatic style of Monteverdi; he adopted this new style in his *Symphoniae sacrae* (publ. in Venice, 1629). He returned to his post in Dresden in 1629. When Saxony entered the Thirty Years' War in 1631, conditions at the Dresden court chapel became difficult. In 1633 Schütz accepted an invitation to go to Copenhagen, where he obtained the post of Kapellmeister to King Christian IV. In

June 1634 he returned to Dresden. His *Musicalische Exequien,* composed for the interment of Prince Heinrich Posthumus, appeared in 1636. He also publ. 2 vols. of *Kleine geistliche Concerte* (1636 and 1639). He composed the music for the opera-ballet *Orpheus und Euridice,* which was performed in Dresden on Nov. 20, 1638, to celebrate the marriage of Prince Johann Georg of Saxony and Princess Magdalena Sybilla of Brandenburg. In late 1639 Schütz obtained another leave of absence to serve as Kapellmeister to Georg of Calenberg, who resided in Hildesheim. After a year's stay in Dresden, in 1641–42, he set out once more for Copenhagen, where he again served as Kapellmeister, until April 1644. Returning to Germany, he lived mostly in Braunschweig (1644–45), and was active at the court of nearby Wolfenbüttel. In 1645 he returned to Dresden; the Elector declined his request for retirement but did allow him to live a part of each year in Weissenfels. Schütz continued to compose industriously during these years. The second book of his *Symphoniae sacrae* appeared in 1647, followed by his *Geistliche Chor-Music* in 1648. In succeeding years Schütz repeatedly asked to be pensioned, but his requests were ignored. Finally, when Johann Georg II became Elector in 1657, Schütz was allowed to retire on a pension with the title of Chief Kapellmeister. His Passions *St. Luke, St. John,* and *St. Matthew* all date from these last years, as does his *Christmas Oratorio.* About 1670 he returned to Dresden to settle his affairs and await his end, which came peacefully in 1672, in his 87th year.

The importance of Schütz in music history resides in his astute adaptation of the new Italian styles to German music. He was extraordinarily productive, but not all of his works survived; the majority of his extant compositions are vocal works of a sacred nature. The most important collection of Schütz's MSS is housed in the Hessische Landesbibliothek in Kassel. The first major edition of his works, edited by Philipp Spitta, was publ. by Breitkopf und Härtel (16 vols., Leipzig, 1885–94; supplementary vols. were publ. in 1909 and 1927). A 2nd edition of his works, the *Neuen Schütz-Gesellschaft* edition, began to appear in 1955 in Kassel. A 3rd edition, the *Stuttgarter Schütz-Ausgabe,* began publication in 1971. A catalogue of his works, edited by W. Bittinger, is found in his *Schütz-Werke-Verzeichnis (SWV): Kleine Ausgabe* (Kassel, 1960).

WORKS: *Il primo libro de madrigali* (Venice, 1611); *Die Wort Jesus Syrach ... auff hochzeitlichen Ehrentag des ... Herrn Josephi Avenarii* (perf. in Dresden, April 21, 1618; publ. in Dresden, 1618); *Concert mit 11 Stimmen: Auff des ... Herrn Michael Thomae ... hochzeitlichen Ehren Tag,* (perf. in Leipzig, June 15, 1618; publ. in Dresden, 1618); *Psalmen Davids sampt etlichen Moteten und Concerten* (Dresden, 1619); *Der 133. Psalm ... auff die hochzeitliche Ehrenfrewde Herrn Georgii Schützen* (perf. in Leipzig, Aug. 9, 1619; publ. in Leipzig, 1619; not extant); *Syncharma musicum* (perf. in Breslau, Nov. 3, 1621; publ. in Breslau, 1621; not extant); *Historia der frölichen und siegreichen Aufferstehung unsers einigen Erlösers und Seligmachers Jesu Christi* (Dresden, 1623); *Kläglicher*

Schütz

Abschied von der churfürstlichen Grufft zu Frey-
bergk (perf. in Freiberg, Jan. 28, 1623; publ. in Freiberg, 1623); *Cantiones sacrae* (Freiberg, 1625); *De*
vitae fugacitate: Aria ... bey Occasion des ...
Todesfalles der ... Jungfrawen Anna Marien Wil-
deckin (perf. in Dresden, Aug. 15, 1625; publ. in Freiberg, 1625); *Ultima verba psalmi 23 ... super ...*
obitu ... Jacobi Schultes (perf. in Leipzig, July 19,
1625; publ. in Leipzig, 1625); *Psalmen Davids, hiebe-*
vorn in teutzsche Reimen gebracht, durch D. Cor-
nelium Beckern, und an jetzo mit ein hundert und
drey eigenen Melodeyen ... gestellet (Freiberg,
1628; 2nd ed., 1640; 3rd ed., revised and enlarged,
Dresden, 1661); *Symphoniae sacrae* (Venice, 1629);
Verba D. Pauli ... beatis manibus Dn. Johannis-
Hermanni Scheinii ... consecrata (perf. in Leipzig,
Nov. 19, 1630; publ. in Dresden, 1631; not extant); *An*
hoch printzlicher Durchläuchtigkeit zu Dennen-
marck ... Beylager: Gesang der Venus-Kinder in
der Invention genennet Thronus Veneris (perf. in
Copenhagen, Oct. 1634; publ. in Copenhagen, 1634);
Musicalische Exequien ... dess ... Herrn Heinri-
chen dess Jüngern und Eltisten Reussen (perf. in
Gera, Feb. 4, 1636; publ. in Dresden, 1636; not ex-
tant); *Erster Theil kleiner geistlichen Concerten*
(Leipzig, 1636); *Anderer Theil kleiner geistlichen*
Concerten (Dresden, 1639); *Symphoniarum sac-*
rarum secunda pars (Dresden, 1647); *Danck-Lied:*
Für die hocherwiesene fürstl. Gnade in Weymar
(perf. in Weimar, Feb. 12, 1647; publ. in Gotha, 1647);
Musicalia ad chorum sacrum, das ist: Geistliche
Chor-Music ... erster Theil (Dresden, 1648); *Sym-*
phoniarum sacrarum tertia pars (Dresden, 1650);
Zwölff geistliche Gesänge (Dresden, 1657); *Can-*
ticum B. Simeonis ... nach dem hochseligsten Hin-
tritt ... Johann Georgen (perf. in Dresden, Oct. 8,
1657; publ. in Dresden, 1657); *Historia, der freuden-*
und gnadenreichen Geburth Gottes und Marien
Sohnes, Jesu Christi (Dresden, 1664; includes the
Christmas Oratorio, which was lost until discovered by Schering, 1908); *Die sieben Wortte unsers*
lieben Erlösers und Seeligmachers Jesu Christi
(date not determined); *Historia des Leidens und*
Sterbens unsers Herrn und Heylandes Jesu Christi
nach dem Evangelisten S. Matheum (perf. in Dresden, April 1, 1666); *Historia des Leidens und Ster-*
bens ... Jesu Christi nach dem Evangelisten St.
Lucam (perf. in Dresden, April 8, 1666); *Historia des*
Leidens und Sterbens ... Jesu Christi nach dem
Evangelisten St. Johannem (perf. in Dresden, April
13, 1666); *Königs und Propheten Davids hundert*
und neunzehender Psalm ... nebenst dem An-
hange des 100. Psalms ... und eines deutschen Mag-
nificats (Dresden, 1671).

BIBLIOGRAPHY: *Heinrich Schütz: Autobiogra-*
phie (Memorial 1651) (facsimile ed., Leipzig, 1972);
M. Geier, *Kurtze Beschreibung des ... Herrn Hein-*
rich Schützens ... Lebens-Lauff (Dresden, 1672; reprint, 1935); J. Mattheson, *Grundlage einer Ehren-*
Pforte ... (Hamburg, 1740; new ed. by M. Schneider,
Berlin, 1910); M. Fürstenau, *Beiträge zur Ge-*
schichte der königl sächsischen musikalischen
Kapelle (Dresden, 1849); W. Schäfer, "Einige Beiträge zur Geschichte der kurfürstlichen musikalischen Capelle oder Cantorei unter den Kurfürsten
August, Christian I. u. II. u. Johann Georg I.," Sachsen-Chronik, I (1854); W. Schäfer, "Heinrich Schütz:
Kurfürstlich sächsischer Kapellmeister, 1617 bis
1672," Sachsen-Chronik, I (1854); M. Fürstenau, *Zur*
Geschichte der Musik und des Theaters am Hofe zu
Dresden (vol. I, Dresden, 1861); F. Chrysander, "Geschichte der Braunschweig-Wolfenbüttelschen Capelle und Oper vom 16. bis zum 18. Jahrhundert,"
Jahrbuch für musikalische Wissenschaft (Vol. I,
1863); F. Spitta, *Die Passionen nach den vier Evan-*
gelisten von Heinrich Schütz (Leipzig, 1886); P.
Spitta, "Schütz, Heinrich," in the *Allgemeine deut-*
sche Biographie; revised as "Heinrich Schütz' Leben und Werke," in *Musikgeschichtliche Aufsätze,*
(Berlin, 1894); P. Spitta, "Händel, Bach und Schütz,"
Zur Musik (Berlin, 1892); P. Spitta, *Die Passions-*
musiken von Sebastian Bach und Heinrich Schütz
(Hamburg, 1893); M. Seiffert, "Anecdota Schütz-
iana," *Sammelbände der Internationalen Musik-*
Gesellschaft, I (1899–1900); A. Schering, "Ein wied-
eraufgefundenes Werk von Heinrich Schütz," *Zeit-*
schrift der Internationalen Musik-Gesellschaft, X
(1908–9); A. Pirro, *Schütz* (Paris, 1913; 2nd ed., 1924);
E.H. Müller von Asow, *Heinrich Schütz: Leben und*
Werke (Berlin and Dresden, 1922); J.M. Müller-Blat-
tau, ed., *Die Kompositionslehre Heinrich Schütz-*
ens in der Fassung seines Schülers Christoph Bern-
hard (Leipzig, 1926; 2nd ed., 1963); H. Spitta,
Heinrich Schütz' Orchester- und unveröffentlichte
Werke (Diss., Univ. of Göttingen, 1927); W. Schuh,
Formprobleme bei Heinrich Schütz (Leipzig, 1928);
R. Gerber, *Das Passionsrezitativ bei Heinrich*
Schütz und seine stilgeschichtlichen Grundlagen
(Gütersloh, 1929); E.H. Müller von Asow, ed., *Hein-*
rich Schütz: Gesammelte Briefe und Schriften (Re-
gensburg, 1931); M. Schneider, "Zum Weihnachts-
oratorium von Heinrich Schütz," in *Theodor*
Kroyer: Festschrift zum sechzigsten Geburtstage
(Regensburg, 1933); A. Heller, *Der Deutsche Hein-*
rich Schütz in seinen italienischen Madrigalen
(Diss., Univ. of Prague, 1934); W. Kreidler, *Heinrich*
Schütz und der Stile concitato von Claudio Mon-
teverdi (Kassel, 1934); A.A. Abert, *Die stilistischen*
Voraussetzungen der "Cantiones sacrae" von Hein-
rich Schütz (Wolfenbüttel and Berlin, 1935); F.
Blume, "Heinrich Schütz 1585–1672," in *Die grossen*
Deutschen (vol. I, Berlin, 1935); K. Gudewill, *Das*
sprachliche Urbild bei Heinrich Schütz (Kassel,
1936); H.J. Moser, *Heinrich Schütz: Sein Leben und*
Werk (Kassel, 1936; 2nd ed., revised, 1954; Eng.
trans. as *Heinrich Schütz: His Life and Work* by C.
Pfatteicher, St. Louis, 1959); L. Reitter, *Doppelchor-*
technik bei Heinrich Schütz, (Derendingen, 1937);
H. Hoffmann, *Heinrich Schütz und Johann Sebas-*
tian Bach: Zwei Tonsprachen und ihre Bedeutung
für die Aufführungspraxis (Kassel, 1940); H.J. Moser, *Kleines Heinrich-Schütz-Buch* (Kassel, 1940;
3rd ed., 1952; Eng. trans., 1967); C. Roskowski, *Die*
"Kleinen geistlichen Konzerte" von Heinrich
Schütz (Diss., Univ. of Münster, 1947); J. Piersig,
Das Weltbild des Heinrich Schütz (Kassel, 1949); G.
Toussaint, *Die Anwendung der musikalisch-rheto-*
rischen Figuren in den Werken von Heinrich
Schütz (Diss., Univ. of Mainz, 1949); G. Weizsäcker,
Heinrich Schütz: Lobgesang eines Lebens (Stutt-

gart, 1952; 2nd ed., 1956); articles in *Bekenntnis zu Heinrich Schütz* (Kassel, 1954); articles in *Festschrift zur Ehrung von Heinrich Schütz (1585–1672)* (Weimar, 1954); L. Schrade, "Heinrich Schütz and Johann Sebastian Bach in the Protestant Liturgy," *The Musical Heritage of the Church* (Valparaiso, Ind., 1954); C. Agey, *A Study of the "Kleine geistliche Konzerte" and "Geistliche Chormusik" of Heinrich Schütz* (Diss., Florida State Univ., 1955); J. Heinrich, *Stilkritische Untersuchungen zur "Geistlichen Chormusik" von Heinrich Schütz* (Diss., Univ. of Göttingen, 1956); W. Gurlitt, "Heinrich Schütz 1585–1672," in *Die grossen Deutschen* (Vol. V, Berlin, 2nd ed., 1957); H.H. Eggebrecht, *Heinrich Schütz: Musicus poeticus* (Göttingen, 1959); G. Kirchner, *Der Generalbass bei Heinrich Schütz* (Kassel, 1960); W. Haacke, *Heinrich Schütz: Eine Schilderung seines Lebens und Wirkens* (Königstein, 1960); A. Rowley, *A Bibliography of Heinrich Schütz* (Diss., Univ. of London, 1960); W. Huber, *Motivsymbolik bei Heinrich Schütz* (Basel, 1961); L. Schrade, *Das musikalische Werk von Heinrich Schütz in der protestantischen Liturgie* (Basel, 1961); D. McCulloch, "Heinrich Schütz (1585–1672) and Venice," *Church Music*, II, no. 20 (1967); H. Wichmann-Zemke, *Untersuchungen zur Harmonik in den Werken von Heinrich Schütz* (Diss., Univ. of Kiel, 1967); R. Tellart, *Heinrich Schütz: L'Homme et son œuvre* (Paris, 1968); H. Drude, *Heinrich Schütz als Musiker der evangelischen Kirche* (Diss., Univ. of Göttingen, 1969); H.H. Eggebrecht, *Schütz und Gottesdienst: Versuch über das Selbstverständliche* (Stuttgart, 1969); J.P. Larsen, "Schütz und Dänemark," *Sagittarius*, II (1969); D. Manicke, "Heinrich Schütz als Lehrer," *Sagittarius*, II (1969); W. Breig, "Neue Schütz-Funde," *Archiv für Musikwissenschaft*, XXVII (1970); R. Bray, "The 'Cantiones sacrae' of Heinrich Schütz Re-examined," *Music & Letters*, LIII (1971); D. Arnold, "Schütz in Venice," *Music and Musicians*, XXI/1 (1972); O. Brodde, *Heinrich Schütz: Weg und Werk* (Kassel, 1972); R. Petzoldt and D. Berke, *Heinrich Schütz und seine Zeit in Bildern* (Kassel, 1972); W. Siegmund-Schultze, ed., *Heinrich Schütz 1585–1672: Festtage 1972* (Gera, 1972); R. Grunow, ed., *Begegnungen mit Heinrich Schütz: Erzählungen über Leben und Werk* (Berlin, 1974); A. Skei, *Heinrich Schütz: A Guide to Research* (N.Y. and London, 1981).

Schützendorf, 4 brothers, all baritones: (1) **Gustav** (b. Cologne, 1883; d. Berlin, April 27, 1937), the best known, studied singing in Milan; sang at the Munich Opera, in Berlin, and in Leipzig; made his American debut as Faninal in *Der Rosenkavalier* at the Metropolitan Opera in N.Y., Nov. 17, 1922, and remained on its roster until 1935; then returned to Germany; in 1929 he married the soprano **Grete Stückgold.** (2) **Alfons** (b. Vught, the Netherlands, May 25, 1882; d. Weimar, Aug. 1946) was distinguished as a Wagnerian singer, and took part in the Bayreuth Festivals; in 1932 settled in Berlin as a singing teacher. (3) **Guido** (b. Vught, near Hertogenbosch, the Netherlands, April 22, 1880; d. Germany,

April 1967) sang with the German Opera Co. on its tour in the U.S. in 1929–30. (4) **Leo** (b. Cologne, May 7, 1886; d. Berlin, Dec. 18, 1931) was a member of the Berlin State Opera from 1920 to 1929, and made numerous appearances abroad.

Schuyler, Philippa Duke, black American pianist and composer; b. New York, Aug. 22, 1932; d. (in a helicopter crash in Danang Bay, Vietnam) May 9, 1967. A precocious musician, she wrote an orchestral work at the age of 12 and appeared as piano soloist with the N.Y. Phil. at Lewisohn Stadium when she was 14, on the same program with her "fairy-tale symphony," *Rumpelstiltskin*. Under the auspices of the State Dept., she traveled to Africa and played command performances for Emperor Haile Selassie of Ethiopia and the Queen of Malaya. Mayor Fiorello La Guardia of N.Y. declared June 19, 1940, as Philippa Schuyler Day at the N.Y. World's Fair. A product of an interracial marriage (her mother was a white Texas heiress), she was a founder of the Amerasian Foundation to aid mothers of illegitimate children fathered by American soldiers in Vietnam. She wrote a number of works based on African themes, including *The Nile Fantasy* for Orch.; and on the lighter side, a "Cockroach Ballet," inspired by some unexterminable cockroaches encountered in many hotels and apartments during her travels. *Time* magazine publ. a story about her, "Harlem Prodigy," in its issue of June 22, 1936.

Schuyt (Schuijt), Cornelis, Netherlandish composer; b. Leyden, 1557; d. there (buried, June 12), 1616; studied at first with his father, an organist, and then in Italy. In 1593 was appointed organist in his native city. He publ. madrigals *a* 5 (1600) and *a* 6 (1611); 12 pavans and galliards in the 12 modes; and 2 *canzone alla francese* (1611). The 5-part madrigals were reprinted by A. Smijers (2 vols., 1937–38).

BIBLIOGRAPHY: M. Seiffert, "Cornelis Schuijt," *Tijdschrift der Vereeniging voor Noord-Nederlands Musiekgeschiedenis*, 5 (1897); A. Annegarn, *Floris en Cornelis Schuyt: Muziek in Leiden van de vijftiende tot het begin van de zeventiende eeuw* (Utrecht, 1973).

Schuyt, Nicolaas (Nico), Dutch composer; b. Alkmaar, Jan. 2, 1922. He studied piano with Jacob van Domselaar and Eberhard Rebling; composition with Bertus van Lier. In 1964 he joined the Foundation Donemus for publication of contemporary Dutch music in Amsterdam. He composed many pieces for performance by youth groups.

WORKS: School opera, *De Varkenshoeder (The Little Pig Boy;* 1951); ballet, *De Kast van de oude chinees (The Old Chinese Cupboard);* a cantata for student performance, *Wij zullen een muur bouwen* (1952); Concerto for Youth Orch. (1952–53); *Sonata a tre* for Oboe, Bassoon, and Piano (1953–54); *5 Dramatic Nocturnes* for Flute and Piano (1954); *Sonatina in due pezzi* for Piano (1955); *Réveil* for Orch. (1955); *Corteggio* for Orch. (1958); *Sinfonia divertente* for Small Orch. (1958); Sonatina for Youth Chamber Orch. (1961); *Quatuor de ballet* for Clarinet, Trumpet, Percussion, and Piano (1962); *De belevenissen van Strip-Thijs* for Clarinet, Trumpet, Percussion, and Piano (1962); Sonata for Orch. (1964); *Discorsi capricciosi* for Small Orch. (1965); *Allegro and Passacaglia* for Violin and Piano (1965); *Arkadia* for Mezzo-soprano, Viola, and Cello (1966); *Hymnus* for Small Orch. (1966); *Naar de maan (To the Moon)* for Female Chorus, Mixed Chorus, and Orch. (1967–68); *Greetings from Holland* for Small Orch. (1970); *Alla notturna* for 2 Oboes, Oboe d'Amore, and English Horn (1971); *Quasi in modo de valzer* for Orch. (1973); *3 Preludes* for Strings and Piano (1973); *Furies for 4,* piano quartet (1975).

Schwalb, Mikloš, Hungarian-American pianist; b. Budapest, Feb. 20, 1903; d. Boston, Oct. 2, 1981. He was a piano student of Dohnányi, and appeared with the Budapest Phil. as soloist at the age of 17. He went to America in 1935 and established himself as a teacher in Boston, making occasional appearances in solo piano recitals.

Schwalm, Oskar, German music critic and composer; b. Erfurt, Sept. 11, 1856; d. Berlin, Feb. 11, 1936. He studied at the Leipzig Cons. with Reinecke, Jadassohn, and others; was engaged in music publishing; wrote an overture, *König Drosselbart;* piano pieces; etc.; publ. collections of school songs.

Schwalm, Robert, German composer, brother of **Oskar Schwalm;** b. Erfurt, Dec. 6, 1845; d. Königsberg, March 6, 1912. He studied at the Leipzig Cons.; in 1875 settled in Königsberg, where he conducted several choral societies.
WORKS: Opera, *Frauenlob* (Leipzig, 1885); male choruses, with Orch.: *Morgengrauen, Bismarck-Hymne, An Deutschland, Mila, Wikingerfahrt, Gotenzug, Festgesang, Der Goten Todesgesang, Abendstille am Meer, Thermopylae,* etc.; several biblical cantatas; piano pieces; songs.

Schwanenberg, Johann Gottfried, German composer; b. c.1740; d. Braunschweig, March 29, 1804. He was educated in Italy; upon returning to Germany, he produced 12 operas to Italian librettos; wrote concertos for piano and violin; 3 piano sonatas; etc.; also wrote several critical papers on music theory, in one of which he argued for the deletion of H from the German musical scale.

Schwann, William, American organist and musicographer; b. Salem, Ill., May 13, 1913. He studied at the Louisville (Ky.) School of Music at the Univ. of Louisville (A.B., 1935). He began his musical career as an organist and choir director in Louisville churches (1930–35); then went to Boston, where he studied organ with E. Power Biggs; also attended classes of Hugo Leichtentritt, Wallace Woodworth, and A.T. Merritt at Harvard Univ.; wrote music criticism. In 1939 he set up a retail shop of phonograph records in Cambridge; in 1949 he launched

his *Schwann Record Catalog.* In 1953 the title was changed to *Schwann Long Playing Record Catalog.* In 1971 he added 8-track cartridge tape and cassette tape listings under the new title *Schwann Record and Tape Guide.* He also publishes a semiannual *Supplementary Record & Tape Guide,* an annual *Children's Record Catalog,* an annual *Country and Western Record & Tape Catalog,* and a quadrennial *Artist Issue,* which lists classical music indexed alphabetically by the names of performing artists. The *Schwann Catalog* is generally regarded as the most authoritative and the most comprehensive compilation of its kind.

Schwartz, Arthur, American composer of popular music; b. Brooklyn, Nov. 25, 1900; d. Kintnersville, Pa., Sept. 3, 1984. He was educated at Columbia Univ.; taught English in high schools and practiced law before engaging in composition. Among his most successful shows was the revue *The Band Wagon,* to lyrics by Howard Dietz (1931), containing the hit song *Dancing in the Dark;* the show was made into a movie musical (1953).

Schwartz, Elliott, American composer, teacher, and commentator; b. Brooklyn, Jan. 19, 1936. He studied composition with Otto Luening and Jack Beeson at Columbia Univ., and privately with Paul Creston; also attended classes of Varèse, Wolpe, Henry Brant, and others at the Bennington Composers Conference in Vermont (summers, 1961–66). He was an instructor in music at the Univ. of Mass., Amherst (1960–64); in 1964, was appointed to the faculty of Bowdoin College in Brunswick, Maine. He publ. *The Symphonies of Ralph Vaughan Williams* (Amherst, 1964); edited (with Barney Childs) *Contemporary Composers on Contemporary Music* (N.Y., 1967); also publ. *Electronic Music: A Listener's Guide* (N.Y., 1973) and *Music: Ways of Listening* (N.Y., 1982). In his compositions he develops the Satiesque notions of unfettered license in music leading to their completely unbuttoned state.
WORKS: *Texture* for Chamber Orch. (1966); *Dialogue* for Double Bass (1967); *Elevator Music* for anybody riding in an elevator (1967); *Signals* for Trombone and Double Bass (1968); *Magic Music* for Piano and Orch. (1968); *Music for Napoleon and Beethoven* for Trumpet, Piano, And Tape (1969); *Music for Soloists and Audience,* a free-for-all with 4 Conductors (1970); *Eclipse I* for 10 Players (1971); *Dream Overture* for Orch. and Recorded Music (1972); *Eclipse III* for Chamber Orch. (1975); *The Harmony of Maine* for Solo Synthesizer and Orch. (1975); all kinds of miscellaneous pieces, involving toys, music boxes, and various noisemakers.

Schwartz, Francis, American composer; b. Altoona, Pa., March 10, 1940. He studied at the Juilliard School of Music (B.S., 1961; M.S., 1962); piano with Lonny Epstein, music theory with Vittorio Giannini, and chamber music with Louis Persinger. In 1966 he was appointed to the music faculty of the Univ. of Puerto Rico in San Juan. In his works he cultivates multimedia compositions, in which music, stage, and electronics are combined. The most dramatic theater work was *Auschwitz*, staged in San Juan on May 15, 1968. Other works are *Yo protesto* (Casals Festival, San Juan, March 23, 1974); *Caligula* (N.Y., March 3, 1975); and *Time, Sound, and the Hooded Man* (Buenos Aires, July 16, 1975).

Schwartz, Rudolf, German musicologist; b. Berlin, Jan. 20, 1859; d. Halle, April 20, 1935. He studied philosophy at the Univ. of Berlin, where he also took courses in musicology with Philipp Spitta; he graduated from Leipzig Univ. (Dr.Phil., 1892). In 1901 he became librarian of the *Musikbibliothek Peters* and editor of the *Peters Jahrbuch,* to which he contributed numerous valuable essays. A memorial issue of the *Jahrbuch* of 1936 contains a complete list of his writings.

Schwarz, Boris, eminent Russian-born American violinist, conductor, musicologist, writer, and educator; b. St. Petersburg, March 26, 1906; d. New York, Dec. 31, 1983. He went to Berlin as a youth; at the age of 14 he made his concert debut as a violinist in Hannover, accompanied at the piano by his father, **Joseph Schwarz.** He took violin lessons with Carl Flesch in Berlin and with Jacques Thibaud and Lucien Capet in Paris; attended courses in musicology with Curt Sachs, Arnold Schering, and Johannes Wolf at the Univ. of Berlin. In 1936 he settled in the U.S., where he was engaged as concertmaster of the Indianapolis Symph. Orch. (1937–38) and later played first violin in the NBC Symph. Orch. under Toscanini. He also studied musicology at Columbia Univ., earning his Ph.D. in 1950. From 1941–76 he was on the faculty of Queens College of the City Univ. of N.Y., where he organized the Queens College Orch. Society, conducting annual concerts of symph. and choral music. In 1962 he was an exchange prof. of music in Moscow. He was trilingual as a writer, being equally fluent in Russian, German, and English; contributed numerous articles, mostly on Russian music, to *The New Grove Dictionary of Music and Musicians.* His book *Music and Musical Life in Soviet Russia, 1917–1970* (N.Y., 1972; 2nd ed., 1983), highly critical of certain aspects of the musical situation in Russia, attracted a great deal of attention, and won an award from the American Society of Composers, Authors and Publishers as the best book on music criticism. His second book, *Great Masters of the Violin,* publ. shortly before his death, was valuable for its accuracy of documentation.

Schwarz, Gerard, American trumpet player and conductor; b. Weehawken, N.J., July 19, 1947. He studied at the High School of Music and Art and at the Juilliard School of Music; then played trumpet in the American Brass Quintet and the N.Y. Phil.; subsequently he devoted himself mainly to conducting. In 1978 he became music director of the Los Angeles Chamber Orch.; made several tours with it, earning merited encomiums for his natural musicianship sans irruptive ostentation.

Schwarz, Rudolf, Austrian conductor; b. Vienna, April 29, 1905. He studied piano and violin; played viola in the Vienna Phil.; then conducted opera in Düsseldorf and Karlsruhe. With the advent of the Nazi regime in 1933 he was, as a Jew, forbidden to engage in professional activities, and became music director of the Jüdischer Kulturbund in Berlin. He was sent to the Belsen concentration camp but survived, and after liberation went to England; was conductor of the Bournemouth Municipal Orch. (1947–50), Birmingham Orch. (1950–57), and BBC Symph. Orch. (1957–62); then was principal conductor of the Northern Sinfonia Orch. in Newcastle upon Tyne in 1964–67, and its artistic director in 1967–73. He was made a Commander of the Order of the British Empire in 1973.

Schwarz, Vera, Austrian soprano; b. Zagreb, July 10, 1889; d. Vienna, Dec. 4, 1964. She studied voice and piano in Vienna; appeared in operettas there; went to Hamburg in 1914 and to Berlin in 1917; toured in South America. In 1939 she went to Hollywood, where she became a vocal instructor; in 1948 she returned to Austria; gave courses at the Mozarteum in Salzburg. Her best roles were Carmen and Tosca.

Schwarz, Wilhelm, German singing teacher; b. Stuttgart, May 11, 1825; d. Berlin, Jan. 4, 1878. He taught singing in Hannover and Berlin; publ. *System der Gesangkunst nach physiologischen Gesetzen* (1857) and *Die Musik als Gefühlssprache im Verhältniss zur Stimm- und Gesangbildung* (1860).

Schwarzkopf, Elisabeth, celebrated German soprano; b. Jarotschin, near Poznan, Poland, Dec. 9, 1915. She studied at the Berlin Hochschule für Musik, and privately with Maria Ivogün; made her debut at the Deutsche Oper in Berlin in 1938; later sang also at the Vienna State Opera and gave numerous performances at the Salzburg Festivals; she acquired renown as a fine Mozart singer. On March 1, 1940, she was registered as a member of the German Nazi Party, under No. 7548960; membership was mandatory for artists employed by national theaters; she was cleared by the Allied Denazification Commission and was able to resume her career. In 1951 Furtwängler invited her to participate in the reopening celebrations at the Bayreuth Festival; on Sept. 11, 1951, she sang the part of Anne Trulove in the world premiere of Stravinsky's *The Rake's Progress* in Venice. She gave her first American recital at Carnegie Hall in N.Y. on Oct. 25, 1953; her American opera debut took place in San Francisco on Sept. 20, 1955; she appeared with the Metropolitan Opera in N.Y. on Oct. 13, 1964, in the role of the Marschallin in *Der Rosenkavalier;* remained on its roster until 1966. In 1975 she made a farewell tour of the U.S. as a lieder singer; in 1976 gave a master class in vocal interpretation at the Juilliard School of Music with her husband, **Walter Legge;** then lived mostly in Zürich. She edited a memoir of Walter Legge, *On and Off the Record* (N.Y., 1982).

Schwedler, (Otto) Maximilian, German flutist; b. Hirschberg, March 31, 1853; d. Leipzig, Jan. 16, 1940. He studied in Dresden; played flute in various German orchs.; in 1881 joined the Gewandhaus Orch. in Leipzig; also taught at the Leipzig Cons. He was the inventor of the "Schwedler flute" (1885), fully described in his *Katechismus der Flöte und des Flötenspiels* (Leipzig, 1897); made numerous transcriptions for flute, and publ. a flute method.

Schweitzer, Albert, great humanitarian, physician, and organist, and an authority on Bach; b. Kaysersberg, Alsace, Jan. 14, 1875; d. in his jungle hospital at Lambaréné, Gabon, Sept. 4, 1965, at the age of 90. He was the son of a Günsbach vicar; studied organ with Eugen Münch at Mulhouse, with Ernst Münch at Strasbourg, and with Widor in Paris (from 1893); was organist of the Bach Concerts in Strasbourg from 1896; studied theology and philosophy at the univs. of Strasbourg, Paris, and Berlin; in 1902 joined the faculty of the Univ. of Strasbourg; while teaching there he completed the full medical course (M.D., 1912), with the intention of becoming a medical missionary in Africa, to which task he subsequently devoted most of his time and energy, making occasional concert tours as an organist in Europe to raise funds for his hospital work among the African natives. In 1952 he was awarded the Nobel Peace Prize, the only professional musician to hold this prestigious award. His philosophical and theological writings had established his reputation as one of the foremost thinkers of our time. In the field of music he distinguished himself as the author of one of the most important books on Bach, greatly influencing the interpretation of Bach's music, and contributing to the understanding of Bach's symbolic treatment of various musical devices. In 1906 he became organist of the Société J.S. Bach in Paris; in 1909 he presided over the conferences on organ building at the Congress of the International Music Society in Vienna, which led to the adoption of international regulations, and read a paper, "Die Reform unseres Orgelbaues," urging the simplification of the modern organ to correct faulty tone quality caused by extreme wind pressure (full report in the *Wiener Kongressbericht der Internationalen Musik-Gesellschaft,* 1909; pp. 581–679). With Widor he edited the first 5 vols. of the Schirmer critico-practical edition of Bach's organ works (eds. in Eng., French, and German), and with Edouard Nies-Berger, the remaining 3 vols. He held the degrees of Dr.Theol. and Dr.Phil.; also the honorary degrees of D.D. (Oxon.) and Litt.D. (St. Andrews).
WRITINGS: *Deutsche und französische Orgelbaukunst und Orgelkunst* (Leipzig, 1906; 2nd ed., 1927); *Jean Sébastien Bach, Le Musicien-poète* (Paris, 1905; German enlarged ed., 1908; Eng. trans. by Ernest Newman, Leipzig, 1911; reissued, 1923); publ. an autobiography, *Aus meinem Leben und Denken* (Leipzig, 1931; Eng. trans. as *My Life and Thought,* London, 1933; revised ed. as *Out of My Life and Thought,* N.Y., 1949; selections in German publ. as a school textbook, with an introduction in Eng., N.Y., 1949); also *African Notebook* (N.Y.,

1939); *On the Edge of the Primeval Forest* (combined ed. of various previous vols. in German and Eng., N.Y., 1948). See also C.R. Joy, ed., *Music in the Life of A. S.* (selections from his writings; N.Y., 1951); R. Grabs, ed., *Gesammelte Werke* (5 vols., Munich, 1974).
BIBLIOGRAPHY: C.T. Campion, *A. S.: Philosopher, Theologian, Musician, Doctor* (N.Y., 1928); Jan Eigenhuis, *A. S.* (Haarlem, 1929); H. Christaller, *A. S.* (1931); John D. Regester, *A. S.: The Man and His Work* (N.Y., 1931); Magnus C. Ratter, *A. S.* (London, 1935: revised ed., 1950); A.A. Roback, ed., *The A. S. Jubilee Book* (Cambridge, Mass., 1946; a collection of essays); G. Seaver, *A. S.: The Man and His Mind* (London, 1947); O. Kraus, *A. S.: His Work and His Philosophy* (N.Y., 1947); H. Hagedorn, *Prophet in the Wilderness: The Story of A. S.* (N.Y., 1947); R. Grabs, *A. S.: Weg und Werk eines Menschenfreundes* (Berlin, 1953); R. Sonner, *S. und die Orgelbewegung* (Colmar, 1955); Werner Picht, *The Life and Thought of A. S.* (N.Y., 1965).

Schweitzer, Anton, German composer; b. Coburg (baptized, June 6), 1735; d. Gotha, Nov. 23, 1787. He was a chorister and later viola player in Hildburghausen; in 1764 went to Italy for serious study; returning to Germany, he was appointed (in 1766) music director of the ducal theater in Weimar; in 1769 became conductor of Seyler's operatic troupe, which was engaged by the Duke of Weimar in 1772. After the destruction by fire of the Weimar Theater in 1774, Schweitzer went to Gotha; there he was appointed court conductor in 1778. Schweitzer was one of the earliest composers to write serious operas to German texts. He produced in Weimar his operas *Die Dorfgala* (June 30, 1772) and *Alceste* (May 28, 1773; libretto by Wieland); there followed another opera, *Rosamunde* (Mannheim, Jan. 20, 1780); Mozart expressed appreciation of Schweitzer's operas. But it was as a composer of singspiels that Schweitzer achieved popularity in his day; he was also important historically as the first composer of a melodrama in German, after Rousseau's *Pygmalion* (Weimar, May 13, 1772; however, it is not extant).
BIBLIOGRAPHY: J. Maurer, *Anton Schweitzer als dramatischer Komponist* (Leipzig, 1912); A. Loewenberg, *Annals of Opera* (1943; 2nd ed., 1955).

Schwencke, Christian Friedrich Gottlieb, German composer, son of the bassoonist **Johann Gottlieb Schwencke** (1744–1823); b. Wachenhausen, Harz, Aug. 30, 1767; d. Hamburg, Oct. 27, 1822. He studied with Marpurg and Kirnberger; succeeded C.P.E. Bach as town cantor and music director at the Katharinenkirche in Hamburg, in 1788. He wrote cantatas, sacred and secular; 2 oratorios; church music; 6 organ fugues; 3 violin sonatas; piano sonatas. He rescored Handel's *Messiah* and Bach's *Mass in B minor;* wrote for the Leipzig *Allgemeine Zeitung.*

Schwencke, Friedrich Gottlieb, pianist and organist, son and pupil of **Johann Friedrich Schwencke;** b.

Hamburg, Dec. 15, 1823; d. there, June 11, 1896. He gave organ concerts in Paris (1855); succeeded his father in 1852 as organist of the Nikolaikirche in Hamburg. He wrote 3 fantasies for organ, trumpet, trombone, and kettledrums; sacred songs for female chorus, with organ; in 1886 he publ. a new and unabridged edition of his father's chorale preludes.

Schwencke, Johann Friedrich, German organist and composer, son and pupil of **Christian Friedrich Gottlieb Schwencke;** b. Hamburg, April 30, 1792; d. there, Sept. 28, 1852. He became organist at the Nikolaikirche in Hamburg in 1829; composed numerous cantatas; over 500 chorale preludes and postludes for organ; a Septet for 5 Cellos, Double Bass, and Kettledrums; harmonized about 1,000 chorales and 73 Russian folk songs; publ. the popular *Hamburgisches Choralbuch;* made many transcriptions; orchestrated Beethoven's *Adelaide,* and various works by other composers.

Schwerké, Irving, American writer on music; b. Appleton, Wis., July 21, 1893; d. there, Nov. 3, 1975. He received his education at the Univ. of Wisconsin; in 1921 went to Paris; was music correspondent for the *Chicago Tribune* and the *Musical Courier* (1921–40); during the war he lived in Switzerland; then returned to his hometown of Appleton. He wrote the books *Kings Jazz and David* (Paris, 1927); *Tansman, Compositeur polonais* (Paris, 1931); *Views and Interviews* (Paris, 1936).

Schwieger, Hans, German conductor; b. Cologne, June 15, 1906. He studied in Cologne; was assistant conductor at the Berlin State Opera (1927–30), at the Kassel Opera (1930–31), in Mainz (1932–43), and in Danzig (1936–37). In 1937 he went to Japan, where he conducted the Tokyo Symph. Orch. In 1938 he settled in the U.S.; organized and conducted the Southern Symph. Orch. at Columbia, S.C. (1938–41); then was conductor of the Fort Wayne Phil. (1944–48). From 1948 to 1971 he was conductor of the Kansas City Phil.; then filled engagements as a guest conductor in Europe.
BIBLIOGRAPHY: Hope Stoddard, *Symphony Conductors of the U.S.A.* (N.Y., 1957; pp. 182–89).

Schytte, Ludvig (Theodor), Danish composer; b. Aarhus, April 28, 1848; d. Berlin, Nov. 10, 1909. He was a pharmacist as a young man; then began to study piano with Anton Rée and composition with Gade, finishing under Taubert in Berlin and Liszt in Weimar. He settled in Vienna in 1887 as a teacher; moved to Berlin in 1907; taught there at the Stern Cons. A master of the miniature forms, he wrote a number of attractive piano pieces, some of which became extremely popular; about 200 were publ.
WORKS: For Piano: *Promenades musicales, Rapsodie norwégienne, Aus froher Kinderzeit, Spanische Nächte, Valse piquante, Waldbilder, Aus der Heimat und Fremde;* numerous piano studies (*6 brillante Vortragsetüden, Melodische Spezialetüden, Studien in Ornamentik und Dynamik*); for

Piano, 4-hands: *Bajaderntänze, Kindersymphonie, Musikalische Wandelbilder, Reiseblätter, Kindersuite,* etc.; also a one-act opera, *Hero* (Copenhagen, Sept. 25, 1898); operetta, *Der Mameluk* (Vienna, Dec. 22, 1903); Piano Concerto; chamber music; a song cycle, *Die Verlassene.*

Sciammarella, Valdo, Argentine composer; b. Buenos Aires, Jan. 20, 1924. He studied composition with Julián Bautista; subsequently engaged in pedagogy. In 1965 he was appointed head of the music dept. at the National School of Fine Arts in Buenos Aires. He wrote a one-act lyric comedy, *Marianita Limena* (Buenos Aires, Nov. 11, 1957); *Variaciones concertantes* for Piano and Orch. (1952); *Scherzino* for Oboe, Clarinet, and Bassoon (1956); *Galeria humana,* chamber ballet (1962); piano pieces.

Scimone, Claudio, Italian conductor, musicologist, and educator; b. Padua, Dec. 23, 1934. He studied conducting with Dimitri Mitropoulos and Franco Ferrara. In 1959 he founded the noted chamber orch. I Solisti Veneti (in Padua) and made numerous tours with it, presenting works from the Baroque to the avant-garde. He also acquired a fine reputation as a scholar specializing in Italian music; supervised a modern edition of the works of Giuseppe Tartini and prepared a complete edition of Rossini. In addition to numerous articles for various music journals, he publ. *Segno, Significato, Interpretazione* (1970). In 1974 he became director of the Cons. of Music in his native Padua.

Sciutti, Graziella, Italian soprano; b. Turin, April 17, 1927. She studied singing in Rome, and became particularly successful in soubrette roles; made her debut at Aix-en-Provence in 1951. She was associated with the Glyndebourne Festivals in England between 1954 and 1959; later sang at the Piccola Scala in Milan.

Scontrino, Antonio, Italian composer and teacher; b. Trapani, May 17, 1850; d. Florence, Jan. 7, 1922. He studied at the Palermo Cons.; was a virtuoso on the double bass and gave concerts; went to Munich for a special study of German music at the Musikschule (1872–74); after various engagements as an orch. player and teacher, he settled in Florence in 1892 and taught composition at the Istituto Musicale there.
WORKS: 5 operas: *Matelda* (Milan, June 19, 1879); *Il Progettista* (Rome, Feb. 8, 1882); *Il sortilegio* (Turin, June 21, 1882); *Gringoire* (Milan, May 24, 1890); *La Cortigiana* (Milan, Jan. 30, 1896); incidental music to Gabriele d'Annunzio's *Francesca da Rimini; Sinfonia marinaresca; Sinfonia romantica;* Concerto for Double Bass and Orch.; 3 string quartets; church music; songs.
BIBLIOGRAPHY: A biographical brochure, *Antonio Scontrino nella vita e nell'arte,* was publ. in his native town of Trapani in 1935. A detailed analysis of his instrumental works is found in Cobbett's *Cyclopedic Survey of Chamber Music.*

Scott, Charles Kennedy, English choral conductor and composer; b. Romsey, Nov. 16, 1876; d. London, July 2, 1965. He studied organ at the Brussels Cons., taking first prize (1897). In 1898 he settled in London; in 1904 he established the Oriana Madrigal Society there, in 1919 the Phil. Choir, and in 1922 the Euterpe String Players. He publ. *Madrigal Singing* (London, 1907; new enlarged ed., 1931); a vocal method, *Word and Tone* (2 vols., London, 1933); *The Fundamentals of Singing* (N.Y., 1954); edited old carols and choral music of the 16th century.
BIBLIOGRAPHY: S. de B. Taylor, "C.K. Scott," *Musical Times* (Nov. 1951).

Scott, Cyril (Meir), remarkable English composer; b. Oxton, Cheshire, Sept. 27, 1879; d. Eastbourne, Dec. 31, 1970. He was a scion of a cultural family; his father was a classical scholar, his mother a fine amateur musician. Having displayed a natural penchant for music as a child, he was sent to Frankfurt, where he studied piano and theory with Iwan Knorr; returning to England in 1898, he continued to study music and began to compose. In 1900 Hans Richter conducted in Liverpool and Manchester Scott's *Heroic Suite;* also in 1900, his First Symph. was played in Darmstadt; his overture *Pelléas and Mélisande* was performed in Frankfurt. His 2nd Symph. was given at a Promenade Concert in London on Aug. 25, 1903. (It was later converted into *3 Symphonic Dances.*) His setting of Keats's *La Belle Dame sans merci* for Chorus and Orch. was produced in London in 1916, and revived at the Leeds Festival in 1934. His opera *The Alchemist,* for which he wrote his own libretto, was produced in Essen, Germany, on May 28, 1925. In 1920 Scott traveled to the U.S. and played his First Piano Concerto with the Philadelphia Orch. under Stokowski (Nov. 5, 1920). But he acquired fame mainly as a composer of some exotically flavored piano pieces, of which *Lotus Land* became a perennial favorite; Fritz Kreisler arranged it for violin and piano and played it repeatedly at his concerts. Other popular piano pieces were *Danse nègre, Chinese Serenade, Russian Dance, Sphinx, Autumn Idyll, Berceuse, Little Russian Suite, Indian Suite, Spanish Dance,* and most particularly the ingratiating suite *Impressions of the Jungle Book,* after Kipling. He also wrote over 100 songs. In all these pieces, Scott showed himself a master of musical miniature; he wrote in a distinctly modern idiom, very much in the style of French Impressionism; employed sonorous parallel progressions of unresolved dissonant chords; made frequent use of the whole-tone scale. His writing for piano is ingratiating in its idiomatic mastery; his harmonious modalities exude an aura of perfumed euphony. Among his other works are: *Christmas Overture* (London, Nov. 13, 1906); *La Princesse Maleine,* symph. poem (London, Aug. 22, 1907); 2 piano concertos (1915, 1950); Violin Concerto (Birmingham, Jan. 27, 1928); Cello Concerto (1937); Concerto for Oboe and String Orch. (London, Sept. 13, 1948); Symph. No. 3, subtitled *The Muses* (1939); *Neopolitan Rhapsody* for Orch. (1960); 4 string quartets; 2 string trios; 2 piano trios; *Rapso-die arabesque* for Flute, Violin, Viola, Cello, and Harp; Clarinet Quintet (1951); *Sonata melodica* for Violin and Piano (1951); Piano Quintet; Piano Quartet; 4 violin sonatas; Trio for Flute, Cello, and Piano; Flute Sonata; *Rondo serioso* for Viola d'Amore. From his early youth Cyril Scott was attracted to occult sciences and was a believer in the reality of the supernatural; he publ. books and essays on music as a divinely inspired art and inveighed violently against jazz as the work of Satan. He publ. the following books: *My Years of Indiscretion* (London, 1924); *The Philosophy of Modernism in Its Connection with Music* (London, 1917); *The Influence of Music on History and Morals: A Vindication of Plato* (London, 1928); *Music: Its Secret Influence throughout the Ages* (London, 1933; 5th ed., 1952); *An Outline of Modern Occultism* (N.Y., 1935); *The Christian Paradox* (N.Y., 1942); an autobiographical vol., *Bone of Contention* (London, 1969); 2 publications on medical matters: *Medicine, Rational and Irrational* (London, 1946) and *Cancer Prevention* (London, 1968).
BIBLIOGRAPHY: Arthur Eaglefield Hull, *Cyril Scott: Composer, Poet and Philosopher* (London, 1918; 3rd ed., 1921).

Scott, Francis George, Scottish composer; b. Hawick, Roxburghshire, Jan. 25, 1880; d. Glasgow, Nov. 6, 1958. He studied humanities at the Univ. of Edinburgh; later at Durham Univ. (B.M., 1909); also took theory lessons with a local organist. As a composer, he cultivated Scottish art music; publ. a number of songs at his own expense; of these the most significant are *Scottish Lyrics* (5 vols., 1921–39). His more ambitious works include *The Ballad of Kynd Kittok* for Baritone and Orch.; *Lament for the Heroes* for String Orch.; and a concert overture, *Renaissance* (Glasgow, Jan. 14, 1939). Scott had a number of ardent admirers in England, among them the poet Hugh MacDiarmid and the composer Kaikhosru Sorabji, who in their exuberant encomiums place him in the ranks of Schubert and Schumann as a songwriter.

Scott, Hazel, American jazz pianist; b. Port of Spain, Trinidad, June 11, 1920; d. New York, Oct. 2, 1981. She was taken to the U.S. as a child and was musically nurtured by her mother, who led an all-female band. She enrolled in the Juilliard School of Music in N.Y., but soon abandoned all academic ambitions and effloresced in nightclubs. In 1938 she sang in the Broadway show *Sing Out the News;* she also appeared in several films, among them *Broadway Rhythm* and *Rhapsody in Blue.* From 1939 to 1945 she performed at Cafe Society Downtown, a Greenwich Village club in N.Y. In 1945 she married the black Harlem congressman Adam Clayton Powell, Jr., but divorced him in 1960 as he got into messy political, financial, and personal troubles that led to his expulsion from Congress; they had a child, who became a television executive. Her 2nd marriage also failed. She went to Paris, where she became quite a vedette at fashionable watering holes of French habitués of such places; in 1967 she came back to N.Y. and continued to perform until a few weeks before she died of cancer of the pancreas.

Scott, Marion Margaret, English writer on music; b. London, July 16, 1877; d. there, Dec. 24, 1953. She studied at the Royal College of Music in London. In 1911 she organized, with Gertrude Eaton, the Society of Women Musicians. She specialized in Haydn research and compiled a complete catalogue of Haydn string quartets, which she publ. in *Music & Letters* (July 1930). She also publ. the monographs *Beethoven* (London, 1934; revised ed., 1951) and *Mendelssohn* (London, 1938).

Scott, Tom (Thomas Jefferson), American folk-singer and composer; b. Campbellsburg, Ky., May 28, 1912; d. New York, Aug. 12, 1961. He studied violin with an uncle; played in dance bands; wrote songs; then went to Hollywood, where he took theory lessons with George Antheil; subsequently studied with Harrison Kerr and Wallingford Riegger.
WORKS: Opera, *The Fisherman* (1956); for Orch.: *Song with Dance* (1932); *Plymouth Rock* (1938); *Hornpipe and Chantey* (1944); Symph. No. 1 (Rochester, N.Y., Oct. 22, 1946); *From the Sacred Harp* (1946); *Ballad of the Harp Weaver* for Narrator, Harp, Chorus, and String Quartet (N.Y., Feb. 22, 1947); *Johnny Appleseed* (N.Y., March 1, 1948); *Lento* for Saxophone and Strings (1953); chamber music: 2 string quartets (1944, 1956); *Emily Dickinson Suite* for Violin and Harp (1955); chanteys for chorus; a number of solo songs; arrangements of folk songs; etc.
BIBLIOGRAPHY: J. Ringo, "Some Notes on Tom Scott's Music," *American Composers Alliance Bulletin* (Winter 1957; with a list of works).

Scotti, Antonio, celebrated Italian baritone; b. Naples, Jan. 25, 1866; d. there, Feb. 26, 1936. He studied with Francesco Lamperti; made his debut in Naples (March 1889) as Cinna in Spontini's *La Vestale;* then sang elsewhere in Italy, and in Russia, Spain, and South America; made his London debut at Covent Garden on June 8, 1899, as Don Giovanni, and appeared in the same role with the Metropolitan Opera in N.Y. (Dec. 27, 1899). He remained with the Metropolitan for 33 years; made his farewell appearance on Jan. 20, 1933. He also toured in America with his own company. He possessed great histrionic ability, and was especially noted for his dramatic roles (Scarpia, Rigoletto, Falstaff, Don Giovanni).

Scotto, Renata, famous Italian soprano; b. Savona, Feb. 24, 1934. She studied piano and voice in Savona; made her debut at the Teatro Nuovo in Milan as Violetta in *La Traviata;* from 1957 sang at La Scala in Milan; subsequently sang at Covent Garden in London and at the Vienna State Opera with brilliant success. She made her American debut at the Lyric Opera in Chicago on Nov. 2, 1960; her debut at the Metropolitan Opera in N.Y. was on Oct. 13, 1965.

Scotus (Scot), Joannes (called **Erigena**), noted philosopher; b. c.815; d. c.881. His work *De divisione naturae* contains a definition of music, with a description of musical practice in his day.
BIBLIOGRAPHY: J. Handschin, "Die Musikanschauung des Johannes Scotus (Erigena)," *Deutsche Vierteljahrsschrift für Literaturwissenschaft und Geistesgeschichte,* V/2; D.M. Cappuyns, *Jean Scot Erigène* (Brussels, 1964).

Scovotti, Jeanette, American soprano; b. New York, Dec. 5, 1936. She studied in N.Y. at the High School of Music and Art, and at the Juilliard School of Music. She first made appearances as a concert singer; on Nov. 15, 1962, she sang Adele in *Die Fledermaus* at her debut at the Metropolitan Opera; also sang in Chicago, San Francisco, Buenos Aires, Hamburg, and Munich.

Scriabin, Alexander, remarkable Russian composer whose solitary genius had no predecessors and left no disciples; b. Moscow, Jan. 6, 1872; d. there, April 27, 1915. His mother died when he was a child, and his father remarried; he received his musical education from his aunt; at the age of 12 he began to take regular piano lessons with George Conus and with Zverev. In 1885 he studied composition with Taneyev. He entered the Moscow Cons. in 1888 as a piano student of Safonov. He practiced assiduously, but never became a virtuoso pianist; at his piano recitals he performed mostly his own works. Graduating with a gold medal from Safonov's class, Scriabin remained at the Moscow Cons. to study fugue with Arensky, but failed to pass the required test and never received a diploma for composition. By that time he had already written several piano pieces in the manner of Chopin; the publisher Belaieff heard him play and offered him a contract; he also financed Scriabin's European tour; on Jan. 15, 1896, Scriabin gave a concert of his own music in Paris. Returning to Russia, he completed his first major work, a Piano Concerto, and was soloist in its first performance on Oct. 23, 1897, in Odessa. In the same year he married the pianist **Vera Isakovich.** They spent some time abroad; on Jan. 31, 1898, they gave a joint recital in Paris in a program of Scriabin's works. From 1898 to 1903 Scriabin taught piano classes at the Moscow Cons. His first orch. work, *Reverie,* was conducted in Moscow by Safonov on March 24, 1899; he also conducted the first performance of Scriabin's First Symph. (March 29, 1901). Scriabin's 2nd Symph. was brought out by Liadov in St. Petersburg (Jan. 25, 1902). After the death of his original publisher, Belaieff, in 1904, Scriabin received an annual grant of 2,400 rubles from the wealthy Moscow merchant Morosov, and went to Switzerland, where he began work on his 3rd Symph., *Le Poème divin;* it had its first performance in Paris on May 29, 1905, under the direction of Arthur Nikisch. At that time Scriabin separated from Vera Isakovich and established a household with Tatiana Schloezer, sister of the music critic Boris de Schloezer, who subsequently became Scriabin's close friend and biographer. In December 1906, Scriabin went to America at the invitation of Modest Altschuler, who at that time had organized the Russian Symph. Society in N.Y.; Scriabin appeared as soloist at Altschuler's concerts in N.Y. and also gave piano recitals of his own works in N.Y., Chicago, Detroit, and other American music centers. Tatiana Schloezer joined him in N.Y. in January 1907, but they were warned by friends familiar with American mores of the time that charges of moral turpitude might be brought against them, since Scriabin had never obtained a legal divorce from his first wife and Tatiana Schloezer was his common-law wife. There was no evidence that such charges were actually contemplated, but to safeguard themselves against such a contretemps, they left America in March 1907 and went to Paris. In the meantime, Altschuler continued to express interest in Scriabin's music, and on Dec. 10, 1908, he gave the world premiere, with his Russian Symph. Orch., of Scriabin's great work *Le Poème de l'extase;* the first Russian performance of this work came later in St. Petersburg (Feb. 1, 1909). In the spring of 1908 Scriabin met Serge Koussevitzky, who became one of his most ardent supporters, both as a conductor and as a publisher. He gave Scriabin a 5-year contract with his newly established publishing firm Editions Russes, with a generous guarantee of 5,000 rubles annually. In the summer of 1910 Koussevitzky engaged Scriabin as soloist on a tour in a chartered steamer down the Volga River, with stopovers and concerts at all cities and towns of any size along the route. Scriabin wrote for Koussevitzky his most ambitious work, *Promethée,* or *Poème du feu,* with an important piano part, which Scriabin performed at the world premiere of the work in Moscow on March 15, 1911. The score also included a color keyboard (*clavier à lumière* or, in Italian, *luce*) intended to project changing colors according to the scale of the spectrum, which Scriabin devised (for at that time he was deeply immersed in the speculation about parallelism of all arts in their visual and auditory aspects). The construction of such a color organ was, however, entirely unfeasible at the time, and the world premiere of the work was given without *luce.* A performance with colored lights thrown on a screen was attempted by Altschuler at Carnegie Hall in N.Y. on March 20, 1915, but it was a total failure. Another attempt was made in Moscow by Safonov after Scriabin's death, but that, too, was completely unsuccessful. The crux of the problem was that the actual notes written on a special staff in the score had to be translated into a color spectrum according to Scriabin's visualization of corresponding colors and keys (C major was red, F-sharp major was bright blue, etc.). Perhaps the nearest approximation to Scriabin's scheme was the performance of *Promethée* by the Iowa Univ. Symph. Orch. on Sept. 24, 1975, under the direction of James Dixon, with a laser apparatus constructed by Lowell Cross; previously, the American pianist Hilde Somer made use of the laser to accompany her solo piano recitals of Scriabin's works, without attempting to follow the parallelism of sounds and colors envisioned by Scriabin, but nonetheless conveying the idea underlying the scheme. The unique collaboration between Scriabin and Koussevitzky came to an unfortunate end soon after the production of *Promethée;* Scriabin regarded Koussevitzky as the chief apostle of his messianic epiphany, while Koussevitzky believed that it was due principally to his promotion that Scriabin reached the heights in musical celebrity; to this collision of 2 mighty egotisms was added a trivial disagreement about financial matters. Scriabin left Koussevitzky's publishing firm and in 1912 signed a contract with the Moscow publisher Jurgenson, who guaranteed him 6,000 rubles annually. In 1914 Scriabin visited London and was soloist in his Piano Concerto and in *Prometheus* at a concert led by Sir Henry Wood (March 14, 1914); he also gave a recital of his own works there (March 20, 1914). His last public appearance was in a recital in Petrograd on April 15, 1915; upon his return to Moscow an abscess developed in his lip, leading to blood poisoning; he died after a few days' illness. His 3 children (of the union with Tatiana Schloezer) were legitimized at his death. His son **Julian,** an exceptionally gifted boy, was accidentally drowned at the age of 11 in the Dnieper River at Kiev (June 22, 1919); Julian's 2 piano preludes, written in the style of the last works of his father, were publ. in a Scriabin memorial vol. (Moscow, 1940). His daughter **Marina** is a scholar and composer.

Scriabin was a genuine innovator in harmony. After an early period of strongly felt influences (Chopin, Liszt, and Wagner), he gradually evolved in his own melodic and harmonic style, marked by extreme chromaticism; in his piano piece *Désir,* op. 57 (1908), the threshold of polytonality and atonality is reached; the key signature is dispensed with in his subsequent works; chromatic alterations and compound appoggiaturas create a harmonic web of such complexity that all distinction between consonance and dissonance vanishes. Building chords by fourths rather than by thirds, Scriabin constructed his "mystic chord" of 6 notes (C, F-sharp, B-flat, E, A, and D), which is the harmonic foundation of *Promethée.* In his 7th Piano Sonata (1913) appears a chordal structure of 25 notes (D-flat, F-flat, G, A, and C, repeated in 5 octaves) which was dubbed "a 5-story chord." These harmonic extensions were associated in Scriabin's mind with theosophic doctrines; he aspired to a universal art in which the impressions of the senses were to unite with religious experience. He made plans for the writing of a "Mysterium," which was to accomplish such a synthesis, but only the text of a preliminary poem (*L'Acte préalable*) was completed at his death. Scriabin dreamed of having the "Mysterium" performed as a sacred action in the Himalayas, and actually made plans for going to India; the outbreak of World War I in 1914 put an end to such a project. Scriabin's fragmentary sketches for *L'Acte préalable* were arranged in 1973 by the Soviet musician Alexander Nemtin, who supplemented this material with excerpts from Scriabin's 8th Piano Sonata, *Guirlandes,* and Piano Preludes, op. 74; the resulting synthetic score was performed in Moscow on March 16, 1973, under the title *Universe;* a species of color keyboard was used at the performance, projecting colors according to Scriabin's musical spectrum.

WORKS: FOR ORCH.: Concerto for Piano and Orch., op. 20 (1897); *Rêverie,* op. 24 (1899); Symph. No. 1, op. 26 (1900); Symph. No. 2, op. 29 (1901); Symph. No. 3 (*The Divine Poem*), op. 43 (1905); *The Poem of Ecstacy,* op. 54 (1908); *Prometheus (The Poem of Fire),* op. 60 (1911). FOR PIANO: 10 sonatas (opp. 6, 19, 23, 30, 53, 62, 64, 66, 68, 70); 79 preludes in 15 sets (opp. 11, 13, 15, 16, 17, 22, 27, 31, 33, 35, 37, 39, 48, 67, 74); 24 études in 4 sets (opp. 2, 8, 42, 65); 6 impromptus (opp. 10, 12, 14); 21 mazurkas (opp. 3, 25, 40); 2 nocturnes (op. 5); *Prelude and Nocturne* for Left Hand Alone (op. 9); *Polonaise* (op. 21); *Fantaisie* (op. 28); *Poème tragique* (op. 34); *Poème satanique* (op. 36); *3 morceaux* (op. 49); *4 morceaux* (op. 51); *3 morceaux* (op. 52); *4 morceaux* (op. 56); *2 morceaux* (op. 57); *Feuillet d'album* (op. 58); *2 morceaux* (op. 59); *Poème-Nocturne* (op. 61); *2 poèmes* (op. 63); *Vers la flamme* (op. 72); *2 danses* (op. 73).

BIBLIOGRAPHY: A.E. Hull, *Modern Harmony* (London, 1914; chapter IV has an exposition of Scriabin's principles); *Musikalnyi Sovremennik,* special Scriabin number (Petrograd, 1915); J.L. Dunk, *Hyperacoustics* (London, 1916; discusses Scriabin's harmonic principles); L. Sabaneyev, *S.* (Moscow, 1916; 2nd ed., 1923); A.E. Hull, *S.* (London, 1916); idem, "A Survey of the Pianoforte Works of S.," *Musical Quarterly* (Oct. 1916); idem, "The Pianoforte Sonatas of S.," *Musical Times* (Nov.–Dec. 1916); M. Montagu-Nathan, *A Handbook of the Pianoforte Works of S.* (Boston, 1916); idem, *Contemporary Russian Composers* (London, 1917); A.E. Hull, "S.'s Scientific Derivation of Harmony Versus Empirical Methods," *Proceedings of the Musical Association* (London, 1917); Paul Rosenfeld, *Musical Portraits* (N.Y., 1920); Igor Glebov, *S.* (Petrograd, 1921); Boris de Schloezer, "A. S.," *Revue Musicale* (1921); O. von Riesemann, "A. S. im Lichte eigener Jugendbriefe," *Die Musik* (1923); Boris de Schloezer, *S.* (Berlin, 1923; in Russian; vol. 1 only; in French, Paris, 1975); A.J. Swan, *S.* (London, 1923); C. Gray, *A Survey of Contemporary Music* (London, 1924); V. Yakovlev, *S.* (Moscow, 1925); Georg Rimsky-Korsakov, "The Deciphering of the 'Lumière' Part in Scriabin's *Promethus,*" *De Musica* (Leningrad, 1927; in Russian); R.H. Hill, "A. S.," *Fortnightly Review* (1928); A.J. Swan, *Music 1900–1930* (N.Y., 1929); L. Sabaneyev, "S. and the Idea of Religious Art," *Musical Times* (1931); P. Dickenmann, *Die Entwicklung der Harmonik bei A. S.* (Leipzig, 1935); M.D. Calvocoressi and G. Abraham, *Masters of Russian Music* (N.Y., 1936); *S.: Symposium on the 25th Anniversary of His Death* (Moscow, 1940); N. Slonimsky, "A. S.," in *Great Modern Composers,* ed. by O. Thompson (N.Y., 1941); D. Brook, *Six Great Russian Composers* (London, 1946); L. Danilevich, *S.* (Moscow, 1953); Faubion Bowers, *Scriabin: A Biography of the Russian Composer* (2 vols., Palo Alto, 1969); S. Pavchinsky and V. Zuckerman, eds., *A.N. S.,* collection of essays (Moscow, 1973); Faubion Bowers, *The New S.: Enigma and Answers* (N.Y., 1975); G. Eberle, *Zwischen Tonalität und Atonalität: Studien zur Harmonik A. S.* (Munich, 1978); M. Kelkel, *A. S., Sa vie, l'esoterisme et la langage musical dans son œuvre* (Paris, 1978); O. Kolleritsch, ed., *A. S.* (Graz, 1980). Scriabin's correspondence, ed. by L. Sabaneyev, was publ. in Moscow, 1923.

Scriabine, Marina, Russian-French music scholar and composer, daughter of **Scriabin;** b. Moscow, Jan. 30, 1911. After her father's death, she lived with her mother in Kiev and Moscow; when her mother died, she went to Belgium to live with her maternal grandmother; in 1927 she settled in Paris. She studied at the Ecole Nationale des Arts Décoratifs and designed art posters; studied music theory with René Leibowitz. In 1950 she joined the Radiodiffusion Française and worked in electronic techniques; composed a *Suite radiophonique* (1951); also a ballet, *Bayalett* (1952), and some chamber music. In 1967 she received a doctorate in esthetics for her thesis *Représentation du temps et de l'intemporalité dans les arts plastiques figuratifs.* She publ. *Problèmes de la musique moderne* (in collaboration with her uncle, Boris de Schloezer; Paris, 1959; also in Spanish, 1960); *Le Langage musical* (Paris, 1963); *Le Miroir du temps* (Paris, 1973). She contributed the biographical entry on Scriabin for the *Encyclopédie de la musique* publ. by Fasquelle (Paris, 1961); wrote an introduction to Schloezer's book on Scriabin, in French (Paris, 1975).

Scribe, Eugène, famous French dramatist and author of many opera librettos; b. Paris, Dec. 25, 1791; d. there, Feb. 21, 1861. He was the writer of the finest librettos set to music by Auber (*La Muette de Portici, Fra Diavolo, Le Domino noir,* etc.) and Meyerbeer (*Robert le Diable, Les Huguenots, Le Prophète, L'Africaine*). For Boieldieu he wrote *La Dame blanche;* for Halévy, *Manon Lescaut* and *La Juive;* he also wrote for less celebrated composers. In the complete edition of his *Œuvres dramatiques* (76 vols., Paris, 1874–85), 26 vols. are filled by his opera librettos.

BIBLIOGRAPHY: J.G. Prod'homme, "Wagner, Berlioz and Monsieur Scribe," *Musical Quarterly* (July 1926).

Scribner, Norman, American choral conductor; b. Washington, D.C., Feb. 25, 1936. He studied at the Peabody Inst. of Johns Hopkins Univ. (B.Mus., 1961). In 1960 he was appointed director of music of St. Alban's Episcopal Church in Washington, D.C.; was also a staff keyboard artist with the National Symph. Orch. (1963–67). In 1965 he founded the all-volunteer Choral Arts Society of Washington, D.C.; in 1971 he founded the Norman Scribner Choir. He served on the faculties of American Univ. (1960–63) and George Washington Univ. (1963–69). He also composed; among his works are Sextet for Winds and Piano (1975); *The Nativity,* choral cantata (1975); *The Tide Pool,* song cycle for Mezzo-soprano and Orch. (1977); *Laudate Dominum,* choral cantata (1979); *I Hear America Singing,* choral suite (1979); *Nicholas,* musical show (1980).

Scruggs, Earl (Eugene), American country-music

singer and banjo player; b. Flint Hill, N.C., Jan. 6, 1924. He took up the banjo as a child and developed such a mastery of the instrument that he made a hit as a member of Bill Monroe's Blue Grass Boys; he then teamed up with Lester Flatt, the guitarist, and they organized their own band, The Foggy Mountain Boys, which quickly assumed a prominent place in country-music circles. Scruggs's 3-finger banjo style was artistically complemented by Flatt's accomplished guitar playing. After they dissolved their partnership in 1969, Scruggs formed his own group, the Earl Scruggs Revue; with it he cultivated the country-rock genre. He starred in the movie *Banjo Man* in 1975. The Flatt-Scruggs partnership resulted in such successful songs as *Roll in My Sweet Baby's Arms, Old Salty Dog Blues, The Ballad of Jed Clampett* (from the insipid television comedy series "The Beverly Hillbillies"), and *Foggy Mountain Breakdown* (the theme song of the film *Bonnie and Clyde*). He publ. the book *Earl Scruggs and the 5-String Banjo* (N.Y., 1968).

Scudo, Pierre, French music critic; b. Venice, June 8, 1806; d. Blois, Oct. 14, 1864. He was brought up in France; studied at Choron's school in Paris; was for a time an opera singer; played clarinet in military bands; then turned to journalism; publ. several political pamphlets; became music critic of the influential *Revue des Deux Mondes*. A writer of considerable talent, he held reactionary views; violently attacked Berlioz, Liszt, and Wagner. He became deranged and died in an insane asylum. His articles were publ. in book form: *Critique et littérature musicale* (2 series, 1850, 1859); *L'Art ancienne et l'art moderne* (1854); *L'Année musicale, ou Revue annuelle des théâtres lyriques et des concerts* (3 vols., 1860–62); etc. He also wrote a musical novel, *Le Chevalier Sarti* (1857; not connected with the composer Giuseppe Sarti); its sequel, *Frédérique,* was publ. in the *Revue des Deux Mondes*. He publ. some songs (*Le Fil de la Vierge, La Baigneuse,* etc.).

Sculthorpe, Peter, eminent Australian composer; b. Launceston, Tasmania, April 29, 1929. He studied at the Univ. of Melbourne Cons. of Music (B.Mus., 1950); then went to England and took courses from Egon Wellesz and Edmund Rubbra at Wadham College, Oxford Univ. (1958–60); returning to Australia, he was appointed lecturer in music at the Univ. of Sydney in 1963; was composer-in-residence at Yale Univ. while on a Harkness Fellowship (1965–67), and a visiting prof. of music at the Univ. of Sussex (1971–72); in 1969 was appointed reader in music at the Univ. of Sydney. In 1970 he was made a Member of the Order of the British Empire, and in 1977, an Officer of the Order of the British Empire; in 1982 he was awarded an honorary doctorate of letters from the Univ. of Tasmania. In his music, Sculthorpe rejects European techniques such as serialism in favor of a typically Australian approach to music. He thus looked to Asia, in particular Japan, Indonesia, and Tibet, for both literary and musical inspiration. As a result, his music is often a battleground for European Expressionism and native ritualism. Sculthorpe was also influenced by the physical environment of Australia, as in *Sun Music I–IV* for Orch., and in his utilization of birdcalls and insect sounds.

WORKS: FOR THE STAGE: Opera, *Rites of Passage* (1971–73); ballet, *Sun Music Ballet* (Sydney, 1968; incorporates music from the 4 separate *Sun Music* pieces). FOR ORCH.: *The 5th Continent* for Speaker and Orch. (1963; uses narrated selections from D.H. Lawrence's novel *Kangaroo*); 4 works titled *Sun Music: I* (1965), *II* (1969), *III* (1966), and *IV* (1967); *Overture for a Happy Occasion* (1970); *Love 200* for Rock Band and Orch. (Sydney, Feb. 14, 1970); *Music for Japan* (1970); *Rain* (1970); *Port Essington* for String Orch. (1977); *Mangrove* (Sydney, April 28, 1979); Piano Concerto (1983). CHAMBER MUSIC: 10 string quartets: No. 1 (1947); No. 2 (1948); No. 3 (1949); No. 4 (1950); No. 5, *Irkanda II* (1959); No. 6 (1964–65); No. 7, previously titled *Red Landscape* (1966); No. 8, previously titled *String Quartet Music* (1969); No. 9 (1975); No. 10 (1982); *The Loneliness of Bunjil* for String Trio (1954; revised 1960); 4 works titled *Irkanda* (aboriginal for "a remote and lonely place"): *I* for Solo Violin (1955), *II* (String Quartet No. 5; 1959), *III* for Piano Trio (1961), and *IV* for Solo Violin, Strings, and Percussion (1961); *Tabuh Tabuhan* for Wind Quintet and Percussion (1968); *Dream* for any number of Performers (1970); *How the Stars Were Made* for Percussion Ensemble (1971); *Song of Tailitnama* for Soprano, 6 Cellos, and Percussion (1974); *Alone* for Solo Violin (1976); *Lament for Strings* (1976); *Landscape II* for Piano Quartet (1978); *Requiem* for Solo Cello (1979). VOCAL MUSIC: *Sun Music for Voices and Percussion* (1966); *Night Piece* for Chorus and Piano (1966); *Morning Song for the Christ Child* for 4-part Chorus a cappella (1966); *The Stars Turn* for Voice and Orch. (1970); *Ketjak* for 6 Male Voices and Tape Feedback (1972); *Eliza Fraser Sings* for Soprano, Flute, and Piano (1978). FOR PIANO: Sonatina (1954); *Left Bank Waltz* (1962; revised 1971); *Night* (1965; revised 1970); *Landscape* for Piano and prerecorded Tape (1971); *Snow, Moon and Flowers* (1971); *Stars* (1971); *Koto Music I* for Piano and prerecorded Tape (1973); *Koto Music II* for Piano and prerecorded Tape (1976); *Mountains* (1981); also incidental music for films, plays, radio; choruses.

BIBLIOGRAPHY: Michael Hannan, *Peter Sculthorpe* (Brisbane, 1982).

Seagle, Oscar, American baritone; b. Chattanooga, Tenn., Oct. 31, 1877; d. Dallas, Dec. 19, 1945. He sang in concerts in the U.S. from 1896 until 1905; then went to Paris for further study, with Jean de Reszke; made his Paris debut in 1907, and also sang in England; returned to America at the outbreak of World War I in 1914 and settled in N.Y. as a singing teacher.

Seaman, Christopher, English conductor; b. Faversham, Kent, March 7, 1942. He was educated at King's College, Cambridge; studied music at the Guildhall School of Music in London; then joined the London Phil. as timpanist in 1964. In 1968 he became assistant conductor of the BBC Scottish Symph. Orch. in Glasgow; was its principal conductor from 1971 to 1977; was also principal conductor and artistic director of the Northern Sinfonia Orch. in Newcastle upon Tyne from 1974 to 1979. In 1979 he was named principal guest conductor of the Utrecht Symph. Orch., and in 1980, of the Gelders Orch. in Arnhem.

Searle, Humphrey, significant English composer; b. Oxford, Aug. 26, 1915; d. London, May 12, 1982. He studied classical literature at Oxford Univ. and music at the Royal College of Music in London, where his teachers were John Ireland and R.O. Morris. In 1937 he went to Vienna, where he took private lessons with Anton von Webern; this study proved to be a decisive influence in Searle's own compositions, which are imbued with the subtle coloristic processes peculiar to the modern Vienna School of composition. He served in the British army during World War II, and was stationed in Germany in 1946. Returning to London, he engaged in various organizations promoting the cause of modern music. Although his own method of writing includes some aspects of the 12-tone method, he does not renounce tonal procedures, and sometimes applies purely national English melodic patterns. He publ. a manual, *Twentieth-Century Counterpoint* (London, 1954), and contributed numerous articles to British, American, and German publications. He was honorary secretary of the Liszt Society (1950–62); acted as an adviser in music for the Sadler's Wells Royal Ballet in England (1946–57). In 1964–65 he was composer-in-residence at Stanford Univ. in California; then occupied a similar post at the Univ. of Southern Calif., Los Angeles (1976–77); from 1965 to 1976 he was a prof. at the Royal College of Music in London. WORKS: 2 suites for Strings (1942, 1944); 2 piano concertos (1944, 1955); Quintet for Bassoon and Strings (1945); *Intermezzo* for 11 Instruments (1946); *Put Away the Flutes* for Tenor and 6 Instruments (1947; in memory of Anton von Webern); *Fuga giocosa* for Orch. (1948); Quartet for Violin, Viola, Clarinet, and Bassoon (1948); *Gold Coast Customs,* to Edith Sitwell's poem, for Speakers, Men's Chorus, and Orch. (1948); *The Shadow of Cain,* to Edith Sitwell's poem, for Speakers, Men's Chorus, and Orch. (1952); 5 symphs.: No. 1 (1953); No. 2 (1958); No. 3 (Edinburgh, Sept. 3, 1960); No. 4 (Birmingham, Nov. 8, 1962); No. 5 (Manchester, Oct. 7, 1964); *Passacaglietta in nomine Arnold Schoenberg* for String Quartet (1949); *Gondoliera* for English Horn and Piano (1950); Suite for Clarinet and Piano (1956); *3 Cat Poems* for Speaker, Flute, Cello, and Guitar (1953); *Burn-Up* for Speaker and Instruments (1962); *Scherzi* for Orch. (1964); *Zodiac Variations* for Orch. (1973); *3 Movements* for String Quartet (1959); *Sinfonietta* for 9 Instruments (1969); *Jerusalem* for Speaker, Tenor, Chorus, and Orch. (1970); *Counting the Beats* for Voice and Piano (1963); 2 ballets: *Dualities* (1963) and *The Great Peacock* (1958); *Oxus* for Voice and Orch. (1967); operas: *The Diary of a Madman,* after Gogol

(Berlin Music Festival, Oct. 3, 1958); *The Photo of the Colonel* (Frankfurt, June 3, 1964); *Hamlet,* to a German libretto (Hamburg, March 5, 1968); *Labyrinth* for Orch. (1971); *Les Fleurs du mal* for Tenor, Horn, and Piano (1972). WRITINGS: *The Music of Liszt* (London, 1954; 2nd ed., N.Y., 1966); *Twentieth-Century Counterpoint* (London, 1954); *Ballet Music: An Introduction* (London, 1958). BIBLIOGRAPHY: M. Schafer, *British Composers in Interview* (London, 1963).

Seashore, Carl Emil, American psychologist and musician; b. Mörlunda, Sweden, Jan. 28, 1866; d. Lewiston, Idaho, Oct. 16, 1949. He was brought to the U.S. as a child; studied at Yale Univ. (Ph.D., 1895); taught psychology at Yale (until 1902), then at Iowa State Univ.; was dean of the Graduate College there in 1908–37, then again in 1942–46. He devised a widely used method for measuring musical talent ("Seashore Test") through special measurements of his own invention (audiometer, tonoscope, chronograph, etc.). WRITINGS: *The Voice Tonoscope* (1903); *Localisation of Sound* (1903); *A Sound Perimeter* (1903); *The Tonoscope and Its Use in the Training of the Voice* (1906); *The Measure of a Singer* (1912); *Seeing Yourself Sing* (1916); *Vocational Guidance in Music* (1916); *The Measurement of Musical Memory* (1917); *The Psychology of Musical Talent* (1919); *Psychology of the Vibrato* (1936); *Psychology of Music* (1938); *Pioneering in Psychology* (1942); *In Search of Beauty in Music* (N.Y., 1947); etc. BIBLIOGRAPHY: The special Seashore issue of *University of Iowa Studies in Psychology,* 21 (1928).

Sebastian, Georges (original name, **György Sebestyén**), Hungarian conductor; b. Budapest, Aug. 17, 1903. He studied composition with Leo Weiner and Kodály at the State Academy of Music in Budapest, graduating in 1921; then took private lessons in conducting with Bruno Walter in Munich (1922–23); subsequently was active as an opera coach, at the Munich State Opera, the Metropolitan Opera in N.Y., and the Hamburg Municipal Opera, and in Leipzig and Berlin. In 1931 he went to Russia, where he conducted at the Moscow Radio. In 1938 he went to the U.S.; was conductor of the Scranton Phil. Orch (1940–45). In 1946 he went back to Europe, and lived mainly in Paris; continued to fill orch. and operatic engagements in Europe.

Sebastian, John, American pop musician; b. New York, March 17, 1944. His father, a famous classical harmonica player, taught him music. He played a variety of instruments as a child before turning to guitar. He formed a group called The Lovin' Spoonful, which began to produce one "good-time" hit after another. A crisis came in 1967 when his vocalist was busted in San Francisco on drug charges. The group survived momentarily, but folded in 1969. Sebastian embraced radical politics and counterculture, and made a spectacular hit at the notorious gathering of acidheads at the Woodstock Festival in

1969. Among The Lovin' Spoonful's best successes were *Do You Believe in Magic* and *Summer in the City.* Also successful were *Younger Girl, Did You Ever Have to Make Up Your Mind,* and *Darling, Be Home Soon.* The band created sound-track albums for the films *What's Up, Tiger Lily* and *You're a Big Boy Now.*

Sebastiani, Johann, German composer; b. Weimar, Sept. 30, 1622; d. Königsberg, 1683. He was in the service of the Elector of Brandenburg at Königsberg; was appointed Kapellmeister to the palace church in 1663 and pensioned in 1679. He wrote a Passion, *Das Leiden und Sterben Jesu Christi* (1672), employing a 5-part chorus with 6 instruments. It is noteworthy for the devotional chorales therein introduced, as in Bach's Passions. It was reprinted by Zelle in vol. 17 of Denkmäler Deutscher Tonkunst. Sebastiani's *Parnass-Blumen, Geistliche und weltliche Lieder* were publ. in Hamburg in 2 vols. (1672, 1675); 13 funeral songs for several voices were issued separately at Königsberg between 1664 and 1680.

Sebök, György, Hungarian pianist; b. Szeged, Nov. 2, 1922. He first studied piano in Szeged; then went to the Franz Liszt Academy of Music in Budapest, where he studied composition with Kodály and chamber music with Leo Weiner. In 1949 he was appointed to the faculty of the Bartók Cons. in Budapest; in 1952 he won the Liszt Prize. During the Hungarian turmoil in 1956 he went to Paris, and later settled in the U.S. In 1962 he was appointed prof. of piano at the Indiana Univ. School of Music in Bloomington; continued to travel widely, visiting South Africa and Japan as a pianist and pedagogue.

Šebor, Karl, Bohemian conductor and composer; b. Brandeis, Aug. 13, 1843; d. Prague, May 17, 1903. He was a pupil of Kittl; was conductor of the National Opera (1864–67), and military bandmaster in Vienna (from 1871). He wrote Czech operas (all produced in Prague): *The Templars in Moravia* (Oct. 19, 1864); *Drahomira* (1867); *The Hussite's Bride* (Sept. 28, 1868); *Blanka* (1870); *The Frustrated Wedding* (Oct. 25, 1879); cantatas; overtures; songs.

Sechter, Simon, Austrian composer and teacher; b. Friedberg, Bohemia, Oct. 11, 1788; d. Vienna, Sept. 10, 1867. He studied with Koželuh and Hartmann in Vienna; in 1810 he obtained the position of piano and singing instructor at the Vienna Inst. for the Blind until 1825, the year he became active as principal court organist; in 1851 he became a prof. of harmony and composition at the Vienna Cons.; retired in 1863. The excellence of his teaching attracted to him a number of students from all over Europe, among them Henselt, Bruckner, Nottebohm, Vieuxtemps, Thalberg, and Pauer. So great was his renown, even before he held an official teaching position, that Schubert, some weeks before his death (1828), expressed a desire to study with him. He was a master contrapuntist and wrote a vast amount of church music; publ. many fugues and preludes for organ; several intricate piano pieces (Dances in Counterpoint; 12 Contrapuntal Pieces; 4 books of amusing fugues for 4-hands on national and operatic airs; etc.); string quartets; songs. He also wrote an opera, *Ali Hitsch-Hatsch,* which was produced in Vienna on Nov. 12, 1844. His most important pedagogical work is the treatise *Die Grundsätze der musikalischen Komposition* (3 vols., Vienna, 1853–54), on the lines of Rameau's "basse fondamentale"; the first vol. was publ. in Eng. trans. (N.Y., 1871; 12th ed., 1912). He also publ. a *Generalbass-Schule* and a new edition of Marpurg's *Abhandlung von der Fuge.*

BIBLIOGRAPHY: K.F. Pohl, *Simon Sechter* (Vienna, 1868); G. Capellen, *Ist des System S. Sechters ein geeigneter Ausgangspunkt für die theoretische Wagnerforschung?* (Leipzig, 1902); E. Tittel, *Simon Sechter als Kirchenkomponist* (Diss., Univ. of Vienna, 1935); H. Kier, "Simon Sechter (1788–1867): zum 100. Todestag der österreichischen Kirchenmusikers und Theoretikers," Musica Sacra, LXXXVIII/1 (1968).

Seckendorff, Carl Siegmund von, German composer; b. Erlangen, Nov. 26, 1744; d. Ansbach, April 26, 1785. He was an officer in the Austrian and Sardinian armies (1761–74), then in the diplomatic service in Weimar (1776–84); shortly before his death he was appointed Prussian ambassador in Ansbach (1784). At Weimar he was on intimate terms with Goethe, who allowed him to write music for a number of his poems before their publication (*Der Fischer, Der König in Thule,* etc.); in these songs Seckendorff caught the characteristic inflections of folk melodies. He publ. 3 collections of *Volk- und andere Lieder* (1779–82); wrote 12 string quartets; 8 divertimentos for violin and piano; 3 piano trios; 2 piano sonatas for 3 hands (probably the earliest example of such trimanual settings); 3 singspiels: *Lila* (1776); *Proserpine* (1778); *Jery und Bätely* (1780).

BIBLIOGRAPHY: V. Knab, *K.S. von Seckendorff* (Ansbach, 1914); Max Friedlaender, *Gedichte von Goethe in Kompositionen seiner Zeitgenossen* (1896 and 1916); E. Herrmann, *Das Weimarer Lied in der 2. Hälfte des 18. Jahrhunderts* (Diss., Univ. of Leipzig, 1925).

Secunda, Sholom, Jewish-American composer; b. Alexandria, near Kherson, Russia, Sept. 4, 1894; d. New York, June 13, 1974. The family came to the U.S. in 1907. He took music lessons with Percy Goetschius and Ernest Bloch at the Inst. of Musical Art in N.Y., graduating in 1917; became a naturalized American citizen in 1923. In 1932 he became a founder of the Society of Jewish Composers, Publishers and Songwriters, which was absorbed by Broadcast Music Incorporated in 1940. Virtually all his life, from 1916–73, he was associated with the Yiddish Theater in N.Y., for which he wrote over 40 operettas; most of these hardly made any impression outside ethnic circles, but one song, "Bei mir bist du schön," from the operetta *I Would if I Could,* produced in 1933, made an unexpected splash even among gentiles, and was sung, in the original Yiddish, by the Andrews Sisters, Rudy Vallee, July Garland, and Kate Smith, becoming one of the most popular songs worldwide. Secunda sold the copyright in 1937 for $30; he regained it in 1961, but never made any appreciable sum of money from it; a legal hassle with the author of the lyrics, Jacob Jacobs, further depleted Secunda's income. Other songs from his operettas were often taken as traditional; among these, "Dona, Dona, Dona," from Secunda's operetta *Esterke* (1940), was recorded by Joan Baez. Secunda also wrote some Jewish service music.

BIBLIOGRAPHY: Victoria Secunda, *Bei Mir Bist Du Schön: The Story of Sholom Secunda* (N.Y., 1982).

Seedo (Sydow), German musician active in London between 1720 and 1736; d. Potsdam, c.1754. He was one of the earliest composers of English ballad-operas in London; contributed airs to a number of operatic and choreographic productions at Drury Lane in London (*The Boarding-School, The Devil of a Duke, The Judgment of Paris, The Lottery,* etc.).

BIBLIOGRAPHY: Walter H. Rubsamen, "Mr. Seedo, Ballad Opera, and the Singspiel," in *Miscelánea en Homenaje a Monseñor Higinio Anglés,* vol. II (Barcelona, 1958–61); E. Roberts, "Mr. Seedo's London Career, and His Work with Henry Fielding," *Philological Quarterly,* XLV (1966).

Seefried, Irmgard, outstanding German soprano; b. Köngetried, Bavaria, Oct. 9, 1919. She received her early musical instruction from her father; then studied voice at the Augsburg Cons., graduating in 1939. Herbert von Karajan subsequently engaged her for the Aachen Opera season of 1940–41; on May 2, 1943, she made her debut at the Vienna State Opera under Karl Böhm as Eva in *Die Meistersinger;* in 1944 Richard Strauss chose her for the role of the Composer in *Ariadne auf Naxos* at his 80th-birthday celebration. She subsequently sang in Salzburg, Edinburgh, Berlin, Paris, London, and Buenos Aires. On Nov. 20, 1953, she made her Metropolitan Opera debut in N.Y. as Susanna in *Le nozze di Figaro.* She was made a Kammersängerin of the Vienna State Opera in 1947; was named an honorary member in 1969. She married the noted Austrian violinist **Wolfgang Schneiderhan.** Apart from her operatic achievements, she was also a distinguished concert and lieder singer.

BIBLIOGRAPHY: F. Fassbind, *Wolfgang Schneiderhan, Irmgard Seefried; Eine Künstler- und Lebensgemeinschaft* (Bern, 1960).

Seeger, Charles, eminent American ethnomusicologist, composer, and teacher; b. (of American parents) Mexico City, Dec. 14, 1886; d. Bridgewater, Conn., Feb. 7, 1979. He studied at Harvard Univ., graduating in 1908; then taught music at the Univ. of Calif. (1912–19), at the Inst. of Musical Arts in N.Y. (1921–33), and at The New School for Social Research in N.Y. (1931–35); was assistant director of the Federal Music Project, W.P.A. (1938–40); chief music director, Pan American Union, Washington,

D.C. (1941–53); a visiting prof. at Yale Univ. (1949–50); lecturer, Univ. of Calif., Los Angeles (1957–61); member of the Society of Ethnomusicology (1960; honorary president, 1972); holder of various honorary degrees; in 1972 received the Chilean decoration of Commander al Mérito. His work in the field of ethnomusicology is of the greatest significance; no less important was his work as a pedagogue; among his students was Henry Cowell. His 2nd wife was the renowned American composer **Ruth Crawford; Pete Seeger** is the son of his first marriage. His 90th birthday was celebrated in several sessions presented at the Univ. of Calif., Berkeley, in Aug. 1977. His publications include (in collaboration with E.G. Stricklen) *An Outline Course in Harmonic Structure and Musical Invention* (1913) and *Harmonic Structure and Elementary Composition* (1916). A collection of his articles, *Studies in Musicology 1935–1975,* was publ. in Berkeley (1977).

BIBLIOGRAPHY: Henry Cowell, ed., *American Composers on American Music* (Stanford, Calif., 1933).

Seeger, Horst, German musicologist; b. Erkner, near Berlin, Nov. 6, 1926. He studied musicology at Humboldt Univ. in Berlin; received his Ph.D. in 1958 with the dissertation *Komponist und Folklore in der Musik des 20. Jahrhunderts.* He was chief dramaturge of the East Berlin Komische Oper (1960–73); in 1973 became Intendant of the Dresden State Opera. His books include *Wolfgang Amadeus Mozart* (Leipzig, 1956); *Joseph Haydn* (Leipzig, 1961); *Der kritische Musikus: Musikkritiken aus zwei Jahrhunderten* (Leipzig, 1963); *Wir und die Musik* (Berlin, 1968); also edited *Musiklexikon* (Leipzig, 1966); *Opern-Lexikon* (Berlin, 1978).

Seeger (also known as **Seegr, Segert, Zeckert,** etc.), **Joseph,** Bohemian organist; b. Repin, March 21, 1716; d. Prague, April 22, 1782. He was a pupil of Czernohorsky and Franz Benda in Prague; played the violin in a Prague church before being appointed organist at the Kreuzherrenkirche (1745); retained this position until his death. He was greatly esteemed as a teacher; among his pupils were J.A. Koželuh, Kuchar, Mašek, Myslivecek, etc. His most celebrated organ works, *8 Toccatas and Fugues,* were publ. posthumously (1793); his organ preludes were included in Guilmant's collection *Ecole classique de l'orgue.*

Seeger, Pete, American folksinger, son of **Charles Seeger** and nephew of the poet Alan Seeger; b. New York, May 3, 1919. After a brief study of social sciences at Harvard Univ., he became a traveling singer; formed 2 folk-song groups, the Almanac Singers and the Weavers; served in the U.S. Army in 1942–45, and entertained U.S. troops in the Pacific. In 1963 he undertook a worldwide tour, visiting Australia and many countries in Europe, including Russia, where he was spectacularly successful. He publ. a manual, *How to Play the 5-String Banjo* (1948), and compiled several songbooks.

Seeger, Ruth Crawford. See **Crawford, Ruth Porter.**

Seeling, Hans, Bohemian pianist; b. Prague, 1828; d. there, May 26, 1862. He went to Italy in 1852; then traveled in the East, returning to Europe in 1857; was in Paris in 1859; then in Germany; finally went back to Prague. He publ. many salon pieces which were successful (*Barcarolle, Lorelei,* etc.).

Segal, Uri, Israeli conductor; b. Jerusalem, March 7, 1944. He studied violin; then went to London and enrolled at the Guildhall School of Music; afterward studied conducting in Siena. In 1969 he won first prize in the Mitropoulos Competition in N.Y.; served as Leonard Bernstein's assistant with the N.Y. Phil. (1969–70); subsequently developed a fine career conducting major orchs. in Europe and America. In 1980 he became principal conductor of the Bournemouth Symph. Orch.

Segerstam, Leif, Finnish conductor and composer; b. Vaasa, March 2, 1944. He studied composition in Helsinki with Fougstedt, Kokkonen, and Englund; took violin, piano, and conducting at the Sibelius Academy in Helsinki, graduating in 1963. He then went to the U.S.; enrolled at the Juilliard School of Music, N.Y., and studied violin with Louis Persinger, composition with Hall Overton and Vincent Persichetti, and conducting with Jean Morel (1963–65); also attended a summer conducting course in 1964 at Aspen, Colo., with Walter Susskind. Returning to Europe, he was a conductor at the Finnish National Opera and Ballet (1965–68); in 1969 joined the staff of the Stockholm Royal Opera. In 1972 he went to West Berlin, where he became conductor at the Deutsche Oper; then served as principal conductor of the Austrian Radio Orch. (1975–82); concurrently served as chief conductor of the Finnish Radio Orch. He describes his own music as being "freely pulsative."
WORKS: FOR ORCH.: *A Legend* for String Orch. (1960); *Divertimento* for String Orch. (1963); *Pandora,* essay (1967; also a one-act ballet); *Concerto Serioso* for Violin and Orch. (1967); *Capriccio* for Solo Sopranino and Small Orch. (1967); *Seven Red Moments* for Trumpet and Orch. (1967); *Patria* (1973; Stockholm, April 27, 1974); *Two; onwards: inwards, outwards, (upwards, downwards)... aroundwards...towards ....* for 2 Pianos and Orch., with 2 String Sections (1974; Helsinki, April 29, 1975); *Screams & Visions* (1975); *Visions of Inner Time* for Piano and String Orch. (1976); *Concerto-Fantasia* for Violin, Piano, and Small Orch. (1977); piano concertos: No. 1, *Thoughts 1978* (1977), and No. 2, *Orchestral Diary Sheet No. 11d* (1981); 5 symphs.: No. 1, *Orchestral Diary Sheets Nos. 33, 34 & 36* (1977–78); No. 2, *Orchestral Diary Sheet No. 22* (1980); No. 3, *Orchestral Diary Sheet No. 23* (1981); No. 4, *Orchestral Diary Sheets Nos. 24, 25 & 26* (1981); No. 5, *Orchestral Diary Sheets Nos. 11 & 12* (1981–83); *Plays* for 2 Amplified Cellos, Percussion, and Small Orch. (1978; Vienna, Feb. 1, 1978); *Orchestral Diary Sheet No. 11a,* Cello Concerto No. 1 (1981), *11b,* Violin Concerto No. 2 (1981), *11c,* with Violin and Cello Obbligato (1981), *11d,* Piano Concerto No. 2 (1981), *11e,* with Organ Solo (1981), *11f,* with Trombone Solo (1981), *11g,* with Clarinet Solo (1981), *11h,* with Alto Saxophone Solo (1981); *Chamber Symphony* (1982–83).
FOR VOICE: *3 American Songs,* after Frost and Pound, for Voice and Piano (1964–65); *3 Leaves of Grass,* after Whitman, for Voice and Piano (1966); *Youth Cantata* (1967); *Seitsemän punaista hetkeä (7 Red Moments),* after Viola Renwall and Gunnar Björling, for Soprano and Orch. (1967); *Tre plus eller fyra Nnnuuu-r (3 plus or 4 Nnnows),* after Björling, for Mezzo-soprano and Chamber Orch. (1968); *3 Pictures* for Chamber Chorus, Flute, Bass Clarinet, Viola, Vibraphone, and Glockenspiel (1970); *6 Songs of Experience,* after Blake and Auden, for Soprano and stereophonically placed Orch. without Conductor (1970–71; Stockholm, April 27, 1974); *3 Songs of Parting,* after Whitman, for Bass Voice and Piano (1971–72); *Prolonged Moments* for 3 Sopranos, Wind Ensemble, and Percussion (Stockholm, Oct. 14, 1973); *Visions of Inner Time,* after Björling, for Voice and Piano (1975); *3 Last Songs,* after Philip Martin, for Voice and Piano (1979).
CHAMBER MUSIC: 25 string quartets: No. 1 (1962); No. 2 (1964); No. 3 (1965–66); No. 4 (1966); No. 5, *Lemming Quartet (1970); Nos. 6–9 (1974–76); No. 10, A Contemplation of a Serious Matter,* homage to Ives (1976); Nos. 11–15 (1977–78); Nos. 16–19 (1979); Nos. 20–23 (1980); Nos. 24–25 (1982); *Improvisation* for Solo Violin (1965); *Myriasm* for 2 Violins (1965); *Poem* for Violin or Cello, and Piano (1966); *3 Moments of Parting* for Various Instruments and Piano (1973); *A Nnnnooooowwws* for Wind Quintet (1973); *At the Border* for a String Instrument and Piano (1974); *Another of Many Nnnnooooowwws* for Wind Quintet (1975); *Moments kept Remaining* for Flute and Cello or Violin and Clarinet, and Piano (1975); *Visions of Inner Time* for Violin, Viola, Cello, and Piano (1976); 2 piano trios (1976, 1977); *Tranquil Traumas* Nos. 1, 4 & 5 for 2 Violins (1976–77) and Nos. 2 & 3 for 2 Double Basses (1976); *Music for 4 Friends* for Violin, Trumpet, Horn, and Percussion (1976); *7 Noëms* for Violin or Cello, and Piano (1977–80); *Epitaph* No. 1 for Solo Cello (1977), No. 2a for Violin and Piano (1977), No. 2b for Cello and Piano (1977), No. 2c for Saxophone and Piano (1977), and No. 2d for Bass Clarinet and Piano (1977); 3 string trios (1977–78); *Signature* for 3 Trumpets (1978); *A Moment of Brasstime* for 2 Trumpets and 2 Trombones (1978); 22 *Episodes* for various instrumental combinations (1978–81).
FOR PIANO: *3 Meditations* (1965); *7 Questions to Infinity* (1970); *Tensions* (1976).
FOR ORGAN: *Thoughts 1977.*

Seghers, François-Jean-Baptiste, Belgian violinist; b. Brussels, Jan. 17, 1801; d. Margency, near Paris, Feb. 2, 1881. He studied in Brussels with Gensse, and at the Paris Cons. with Baillot; founded in Brussels the Société Ste.-Cécile in 1848, and conducted it until 1854. Its concerts of orch. and choral works were famous; after the founder's death it rapidly declined and was soon dissolved.

Segnitz, Eugen, German musicologist; b. Leipzig, March 5, 1862; d. Berlin, Sept. 25, 1927. He studied privately with Papperitz; wrote music criticism; publ. valuable biographical studies: *Carl Reinecke* (1900); *Wagner und Leipzig* (1901); *Liszt und Rom* (1901); *Goethe und die Oper in Weimar* (1908); *Franz Liszts Kirchenmusik* (1911); *Arthur Nikisch* (1920); *Max Reger* (1922).

Segovia, Andrés, illustrious Spanish guitar virtuoso; b. Linares, near Jaen, Feb. 21, 1893. He received his first instruction on the guitar at age 6 from a traveling flamenco guitarist; although he later studied briefly with Miguel Llobet, he was basically self-taught. He made his formal debut in Granada in 1909 at the age of 16; then played in Madrid in 1912 and in Barcelona in 1916; toured South America in 1919. He made his Paris debut on April 7, 1924; his program included a work written especially for him by Albert Roussel, entitled simply *Segovia.* He then played throughout Europe; made his U.S. debut at Town Hall in N.Y. on Jan. 8, 1928; traveled all over the world, arousing admiration for his artistry wherever he went. He did much to reinstate the guitar as a concert instrument capable of a variety of expression; made many transcriptions for the guitar, including one of Bach's *Chaconne* from the Partita No. 2 for Violin. He also commissioned several composers to write works for him, including Ponce, Turina, Castelnuovo-Tedesco, Moreno-Torroba, Villa-Lobos, and Tansman. He continued to give concerts at an advanced age; made appearances in 1984 in celebration of the 75th anniversary of his professional debut. He received many honors during his long career; a commemorative plaque was affixed in 1969 to the house where he was born, honoring him as the "hijo predilecto de la ciudad." He wrote *Andrés Segovia: An Autobiography of the Years 1893–1920* (N.Y., 1976).
BIBLIOGRAPHY: V. Bobri, *The Segovia Technique* (N.Y., 1972); G. Wade, *Segovia: A Celebration of the Man and His Music* (London, 1983); A. Kozinn, "Andrés Segovia," *Ovation* (April 1984).

Seiber, Mátyás, significant Hungarian-born English composer; b. Budapest, May 4, 1905; d. in an automobile accident, Kruger National Park, Johannesburg, South Africa, Sept. 24, 1960. Of a musical family, he learned to play the cello at home; later entered the Budapest Academy of Music, where he studied with Kodály (1919–24). During the following years he traveled as a member of a ship's orch. on a transatlantic liner; visited Russia as a music journalist. From 1926 to 1933 he taught composition at the Frankfurt Cons.; was the cellist in the Lenzewski Quartet, which specialized in modern music; then was again in Budapest. The catastrophic events in Central Europe and the growing Nazi influence in Hungary forced him to emigrate to England, where he quickly acquired a group of loyal disciples; was co-founder of the Society for the Promotion of New Music; in 1942 was appointed to the faculty of Morley College. His early music followed the national trends of the Hungarian School; later he expanded his melodic resources to include oriental modes and also jazz, treated as folk music; by the time he arrived in England he had added dodecaphony to his oeuvre, though he used it in a very personal, lyrical manner, as in his cantata *Ulysses* and his 3rd String Quartet.
WORKS: Opera, *Eva spielt mit Puppen* (1934); 2 operettas; *Besardo Suite* No. 1 for Orch. (1940); *Besardo Suite* No. 2 for String Orch. (1941); *Transylvanian Rhapsody* for Orch. (1941); *Pastorale and Burlesque* for Flute and String Orch. (1941–42); *Fantasia concertante* for Violin and String Orch. (1943–44; London, Dec. 3, 1945); *Notturno* for Horn and String Orch. (1944); cantata, *Ulysses,* after Joyce, for Tenor, Chorus, and Orch. (1946–47; London, May 27, 1949); *4 French Folksongs* for Soprano and Strings (1948); *Faust* for Soprano, Tenor, Chorus, and Orch. (1949); *Cantata secularis* for Chorus and Orch. (1949–51); Concertino for Clarinet and String Orch. (1951; London, May 11, 1954); *Elegy* for Viola and Small Orch. (1955); *3 Pieces* for Cello and Orch. (1956); chamber cantata, *3 Fragments from "A Portrait of the Artist as a Young Man,"* after Joyce, for Narrator, Wordless Chorus, and Instrumental Ensemble (1957); *Improvisations* for Jazz Band and Symph. Orch. (in collaboration with Johnny Dankworth, 1959; London, June 2, 1959); ballet *The Invitation* (1960; posthumous, London, Dec. 30, 1960); 3 string quartets (1924; 1934–35; *Quartetto Lirico,* 1948–51); *Sarabande and Gigue* for Cello and Piano (1924); *Sonata da camera* for Violin and Cello (1925); *Serenade* for 2 Clarinets, 2 Bassoons, and 2 Horns (1925); *Divertimento* for Clarinet and String Quartet (1928); 2 *Jazzolettes* for 2 Saxophones, Trumpet, Trombone, Piano, and Percussion (1929, 1933); *4 Hungarian Folksongs* for 2 Violins (1931); *Fantasy* for Cello and Piano (1940); *Fantasia* for Flute, Horn, and String Quartet (1945); *Andantino and Pastorale* for Clarinet and Piano (1949); *Concert Piece* for Violin and Piano (1953–54); *Improvisation* for Oboe and Piano (1957); *More Nonsense,* after E. Lear, for Baritone, Violin, Guitar, Clarinet, and Bass Clarinet (1957); *Permutazioni a cinque* for Wind Quintet (1958); Violin Sonata (1960); *Rhythmical Studies* for Piano (1933); *Scherzando capriccioso* for Piano (1944); arrangements of folk songs; songs with instrumental or orch. accompaniment. He also wrote scores for over 25 films, including that for Orwell's *Animal Farm,* England's first feature-length animated film (1954); wrote a handbook on jazz percussion playing, *Schule für Jazz-Schlagzeug* (1929), and publ. *The String Quartets of Béla Bartók* (London, 1945).
BIBLIOGRAPHY: H. Keller, "Mátyás Seiber," *Musical Times* (Nov. 1955); H. Wood, "The Music of Mátyás Seiber," ibid. (Sept. 1970).

Seidel, Friedrich Ludwig, German organist and composer; b. Treuenbrietzen, June 1, 1765; d. Charlottenburg, May 5, 1831. He studied with Benda in Berlin; served as organist of the Marienkirche; was music director of the royal orch. (1808) and court

Kapellmeister (1822). He composed the operas *Der Dorfbarbier* (1817) and *Lila* (1818); incidental music to dramas; an oratorio, *Die Unsterblichkeit* (1797); masses, motets, songs, piano music.

Seidel, Jan, Czech composer; b. Nymburk, Dec. 25, 1908. He was first attracted to architecture and graphic art; attended Alois Hába's classes in quarter-tone composition at the Prague Cons. (1936–40); then took private lessons in music theory with J.B. Foerster for a more traditional musical training. He was a composer, conductor, and pianist in E.F. Burian's Theater (1930–45); acted as artistic adviser to the recording firm Esta (1938–45) and the Gramophone Corp. (1945–53); was chief of the Opera of the National Theater (1958–64); then served as dramatic adviser there. His String Quartet No. 2 is in the quarter-tone system, but most of his music is based on folk-song tradition according to the doctrine of socialist realism.
WORKS: Opera, *Tonka Šibenice* (1964); *Symphonic Prologue* (1942); Symph. No. 1 (1943); 2 oboe concertos (1955); 2 orch. suites from the film *The Piper of Strakonice* (1956, 1958); *Lovecká sinfonietta (Hunting Sinfonietta)* for Horn and Small Orch. (1965–66; Prague, March 14, 1973); Concerto for Flute, Strings, and Piano (1966); *Giocosa* for Chamber Orch. (1972); cantatas: *Call to Battle* (1946); *May Prelude* (1952); *Message to the Living* (1953); 4 string quartets: No. 1, with Solo Soprano (1930); No. 2, with Narration (1940); No. 3, *Chrysanthemums* (1943); No. 4 (1944); 2 wind quintets (1941, 1946); Violin Sonata (1950); numerous patriotic choruses and songs.

Seidel, Johann Julius, German organist; b. Breslau, July 14, 1810; d. there, Feb. 13, 1856. He was organist at St. Christopher's Church; publ. *Die Orgel und ihr Bau* (Breslau, 1843; 4th ed. by B. Kothe, 1885; reprinted with an appendix by H. Schmidt, 1907; in Eng., London, 1852).

Seidel, Toscha, Russian violinist; b. Odessa, Nov. 17, 1899; d. Rosemead, Calif., Nov. 15, 1962. He began to play the violin as a small child; took lessons from Max Fiedelmann in Odessa; subsequently became a pupil of Leopold Auer at the St. Petersburg Cons. (graduated in 1912); then went to America (debut, N.Y., April 14, 1918); made many tours in Europe and the U.S.; also played in Australia. He suffered an irreversible mental illness and was confined to a sanatorium in California for several years before his death.

Seidl, Anton, famous Hungarian conductor; b. Pest, May 7, 1850; d. New York, March 28, 1898. He studied at the Leipzig Cons.; then was engaged by Hans Richter as chorus master at the Vienna Opera; Richter in turn recommended him to Wagner to assist in preparing the score and parts of the *Ring* tetralogy for the forthcoming Bayreuth Festival; Seidl worked in Bayreuth until 1879, when he went to Leipzig as a conductor at the Opera. In 1882 he was engaged by the impresario Angelo Neumann for a grand tour of Wagner's operas. After Wagner's death in 1883 he conducted the Bremen Opera; in 1885 was engaged to conduct the German opera repertoire at the Metropolitan Opera House in N.Y. He made his American debut with *Lohengrin* (N.Y., Nov. 23, 1885); also conducted the American premieres of *Die Meistersinger* (Jan. 4, 1886) and *Tristan und Isolde* (Dec. 1, 1886). During the week of March 4–11, 1889, he conducted in N.Y. the entire *Ring des Nibelungen*. In 1891 he was engaged as permanent conductor of the N.Y. Phil., and led it until his sudden death (of ptomaine poisoning). Seidl was an excellent technician of the baton and established a standard of perfection rare in American orch. playing of that time; he introduced many unfamiliar works by German composers and conducted the world premiere of Dvořák's symph. *From the New World* (1893).
BIBLIOGRAPHY: H.E. Krehbiel, *Anton Seidl* (N.Y., 1898); H.T. Finck, ed., *Anton Seidl. A Memorial by His Friends* (N.Y., 1899).

Seidl, Arthur, German writer on music; b. Munich, June 8, 1863; d. Dessau, April 11, 1928. He studied with Spitta and Bellermann; received his Dr.Phil. from the Univ. of Leipzig in 1887 with the dissertation, *Vom Musikalisch-Erhabenen. Prolegomena zur Ästhetik der Tonkunst* (1887; 2nd ed., 1907). From 1890 to 1893 he was in Weimar; from 1893 to 1897, in Dresden. In 1899 he went to Munich as critic for the *Neueste Nachrichten*. From 1903 to his death, was active mostly at Dessau.
WRITINGS: *Zur Geschichte des Erhabenheitsbegriffs seit Kant* (1889); *Hat Richard Wagner eine Schule hinterlassen?* (1892); *Richard Strauss. Eine Charakterstudie* (with W. Klatte; 1896); *Moderner Geist in der deutschen Tonkunst* (1901; 2nd ed., 1913); *Wagneriana* (3 vols., 1901–2); *Moderne Dirigenten* (1902); *Kunst und Kultur* (1902); *Die Hellerauer Schulfeste und die "Bildungsanstalt Jaques-Dalcroze"* (1912); *Straussiana* (1913); *Ascania. Zehn Jahre in Anhalt* (1913); *Richard Wagners "Parsifal"* (1914); *Neue Wagneriana* (3 vols., 1914); *Hans Pfitzner* (1921); *Neuzeitliche Tondichter und zeitgenössische Tonkünstler* (2 vols., Regensburg, 1926).
BIBLIOGRAPHY: L. Frankenstein, *Arthur Seidl* (Regensburg, 1913); B. Schuhmann, ed., *Musik und Kultur. Festschrift zum 50. Geburtstag Arthur Seidls* (1913).

Seifert, Uso, German organist and composer; b. Römhild, Feb. 9, 1852; d. Dresden, June 4, 1912. He studied with Wüllner and Nicodé at the Dresden Cons.; taught there for 25 years, and was later organist of the Reformed Church. He publ. a piano method; numerous piano pieces (*Capriccietto, Valse-Impromptu, Polacca graziosa, Polonaise,* etc.); choruses; organ works (*Präludium und Doppelfuge, Einleitung und Doppelfuge, 20 Orgelvorspiele,* etc.); edited classic instructive works.

Seiffert, Max, eminent German musicologist; b. Beeskow-on-Spree, Feb. 9, 1868; d. Schleswig, April

13, 1948. He studied musicology with Philipp Spitta at the Univ. of Berlin; took the degree of Dr.Phil. with the dissertation *J.P. Sweelinck und seine direkten deutschen Schüler* (Leipzig, 1891). In 1914 he was elected a member of the Prussian Academy of the Arts. He devoted himself chiefly to the editing of works by German composers; publ. *Geschichte der Klaviermusik* (Berlin, 1899–1901; nominally the 3rd ed. of Weitzmann's history, but actually a new and valuable book); compiled numerous catalogues of keyboard works; edited materials for the Denkmäler Deutscher Tonkunst, Denkmäler der Tonkunst in Bayern, and Denkmäler der Tonkunst in Österreich, and edited the complete works of Sweelinck for the *Vereeniging voor Nederlandsche Muziekgeschiedenis;* also prepared many works by Bach and Handel for modern performance. A Festschrift for him was publ. for his 70th birthday (1938), and another for his 80th (1948).

Seifriz, Max, German violinist and composer; b. Rottweil, Württemberg, Oct. 9, 1827; d. Stuttgart, Dec. 20, 1885. He served as court Kapellmeister to Prince Hohenzollern in Löwenberg (1854–69); then moved to Stuttgart and was active there as a municipal music director. He publ., with E. Singer, a *Grosse theoretisch-praktische Violinschule* (2 vols., 1884–97); composed a number of choruses and a Symph.

Seinemeyer, Meta, German soprano; b. Berlin, Sept. 5, 1895; d. Dresden, Aug. 19, 1929. She studied voice with Ernst Grenzebach; was on the staff of the German Opera in Berlin from 1918 to 1925. In 1926 she toured South America; then sang at the Vienna Opera in 1927, and at Covent Garden in London in 1929. She died of a rare blood disease; on her deathbed she married the conductor **Frieder Weissmann.** Her voice possessed a silken quality and a natural expressiveness which was particularly effective in the Romantic repertoire.

Seiss, Isodor (Wilhelm), German composer and teacher; b. Dresden, Dec. 23, 1840; d. Cologne, Sept. 25, 1905. He studied piano with Friedrich Wieck and music theory with J. Otto. In 1870 he was appointed to the faculty of the Cons. of Cologne, where he conducted the concerts of the Musikalische Gesellschaft (1873–1900); among his students was Willem Mengelberg. He publ. a number of useful piano studies in the bravura style (*Bravourstudien, Fantasie in Form einer Tokkata,* etc.). He also composed an opera, *Der vierjährige Posten.*

Seitz, Robert, German music publisher and piano manufacturer; b. Leipzig, April 8, 1837; d. there, Sept. 26, 1889. He was a music publisher from 1866 to 1878; then, selling out, he established a piano factory, which failed in 1884, when his interesting paper, *Das Musikalische Centralblatt,* ceased to appear.

Seixas, (José Antonio) Carlos de, important Portuguese composer of keyboard music; b. Coimbra, June 11, 1704; d. Lisbon, Aug. 25, 1742. He received his primary musical education from his father, a church organist; then became himself a church organist in Lisbon. He wrote a great number of keyboard sonatas (sometimes designated as "toccatas"), of which 88 are preserved. He knew Domenico Scarlatti personally, but was not demonstrably influenced by the Italian style of keyboard composition. Eighty keyboard sonatas by Seixas were brought out in a modern edition by Santiago Kastner, in the series Portugaliae Musica (Lisbon, 1965); an overture and a sinfonia were publ. in the same series in 1969, edited by P. Salzmann.

BIBLIOGRAPHY: Santiago Kastner, *Carlos de Seixas* (Coimbra, 1947); K. Heimes, *Carlos de Seixa's Keyboard Sonatas* (Diss., Univ. of South Africa, 1967).

Séjan, Nicolas, French composer and organist; b. Paris, March 19, 1745; d. there, March 16, 1819. He was a pupil of Forqueray; organist of St.-André-des-Arts in 1760, of Notre Dame in 1772, of St.-Sulpice in 1783; in 1789, of the royal chapel, and teacher at the Ecole Royale de Chant. He lost his post in the Revolution, but in 1807 became organist at Les Invalides, and in 1814 (after the restoration of the monarchy) of the royal chapel. He publ. 6 violin sonatas, piano sonatas, 3 piano trios, and music for piano and for organ.

BIBLIOGRAPHY: C. Bouvet, "Nicolas Séjan et G.-F. Couperin, Organistes de l'Opéra," *Musique et Théâtre* (1926).

Šejna, Karel, Czech conductor; b. Zálezly, Nov. 1, 1896. He studied the double bass at the Prague Cons. (1914–20); also took private lessons in composition with K.B. Jirák. In 1921 he joined the Czech Phil. Orch. as principal double bass; later appeared as a conductor with it; in 1937 he was appointed 2nd conductor of the Czech Phil.; was its artistic director in 1949–50; then 2nd conductor again from 1950 until his retirement in 1965. He was particularly esteemed for his congenial interpretations of Czech music.

Sekles, Bernhard, German conductor, composer, and teacher; b. Frankfurt, March 20, 1872; d. there, Dec. 8, 1934. He studied with Iwan Knorr at the Hoch Cons. in Frankfurt, where he became a prof. of theory in 1896; from 1923 to 1933 he was director of the Cons.

WORKS: 2 operas: *Scheherazade* (Mannheim, Nov. 2, 1917) and *Die zehn Küsse* (Frankfurt, 1926); ballets: *Der Zwerg und die Infantin,* after Oscar Wilde (Frankfurt, 1913), and *Die Hochzeit des Faun* (Wiesbaden, 1921); symph. poem, *Aus den Gärten der Semiramis; Serenade* for 11 Solo Instruments; *Kleine Suite* for Orch.; *Passacaglia und Fuge* for String Quartet; Trio for Clarinet, Cello, and Piano; Violin Sonata; several albums of piano music.

Selby, Bertram Luard, English organist, composer, and teacher; b. Ightham, Kent, Feb. 12, 1853; d.

Winterton, Dec. 26, 1918. He studied with Reinecke and Jadassohn at the Leipzig Cons.; filled various organ positions in London; was organist at the Rochester Cathedral.

WORKS: 2 operas: *The Ring* (1886) and *Adela* (1888); operetta ("duologue"), *Weather or no* (London, Aug. 10, 1896; very successful; also produced in Germany as *Das Wetterhäuschen*); 2 piano quintets; a Violin Sonata; piano pieces; organ works.

Selby, William, organist and composer; b. England, c.1738; d. Boston, Dec. 12, 1798. In 1760 he was appointed organist at Holy Sepulcher Church in London; from 1765 to 1770 he publ. both sacred music and secular music there. He settled in the U.S. in 1771, becoming organist at King's Chapel in Boston; in 1773–74 was organist at Trinity Church in Newport, R.I.; in 1776 returned to Boston as organist at Trinity Church, and from 1778, at the Stone Chapel (formerly King's Chapel). He led an extremely active musical life in Boston as an organist and conductor, giving many concerts of secular music as well as religious, and generally raising the musical standards of the area. He composed and publ. 9 Psalms and hymns for solo voice; 8 religious and secular choral works; 6 songs; 9 pieces for guitar and 3 for keyboard.

BIBLIOGRAPHY: O.G. Sonneck, *Bibliography of Early Secular American Music* (1905; 2nd ed., revised by W.T. Upton, 1945); D. McKay, "William Selby, Musical Emigré in Colonial Boston," *Musical Quarterly* (Oct. 1971).

Selig, Robert Leigh, American composer; b. Chicago, Jan. 29, 1939; d. Cambridge, Mass., Jan. 15, 1984. He studied at Northwestern Univ., and later (1966–67) took doctoral courses at Boston Univ., where he studied with Gardner Read. He held Guggenheim fellowships twice, in 1971 and in 1977. In 1968 he was appointed to the faculty at the New England Cons. of Music in Boston.

WORKS: *Mirage* for Trumpet and String Orch. (1967); *Variations* for Brass Quintet (1967); *Islands* for Chorus and Chamber Orch. (1968); Concerto for Rock Group and Orch. (1969); *Rhapsody* for Flute, Violin, and Clarinet (1970); *Orestes: Flight into Fury* for Trumpet and Piano (1970); Quartet for Voice, Flute, Cello, and Percussion (1971); Symph. for Woodwind Quintet (1971); *Chocorua,* opera for Voice, Chorus, and Chamber Orch. (1972); *Pometacomet, 1676* for Band (1974–75); *Survival Fragments* for Soprano and Piano (1976); Sonata: *3 Cryptic Portraits* for Piano (1977); Music for Brass Instruments (1977); *Reflections from a Back Window* for Piano (1980); *After the Ice* for Soprano and Piano (1981).

Seligmann, Hippolyte-Prosper, French cellist; b. Paris, July 28, 1817; d. Monte Carlo, Feb. 5, 1882. He studied at the Paris Cons., taking first prize in 1836; made extensive tours. He publ. *6 études caractéristiques,* fantasies, caprices, etc., for cello, with piano; 2 albums of songs.

Selle, Thomas, German composer; b. Zörbig, March 23, 1599; d. Hamburg, July 2, 1663. He was a rector in Wesselburen (1625), cantor in Itzehoe (1634), cantor at the Johanneum, and music director of the 5 principal churches in Hamburg (from 1641). He publ. sacred and secular songs (including settings of poems by Rist), and left in MS numerous madrigals, motets, and Passions. He was an early member of the Hamburg school of German songwriting. His collections include: *Concertatio Castalidum* (1624); *Deliciae pastorum Arcadiae* (1624); *Hagiodecamelhydrion* (1627–31); *Deliciorum juvenilium decas* (1634); *Monophonetica* (1636). His *Johannes-Passion* of 1642 was brought out in a modern edition by R. Gerber (1934); reprints of separate songs were publ. by H.J. Moser.

BIBLIOGRAPHY: A. Arnheim, "Thomas Selle als Schulkantor in Itzehoe und Hamburg," in the Liliencron Festschrift (1910); H.J. Moser, "Aus der Frühgeschichte der deutschen Generalbasspassion," *Jahrbuch Peters* (1920); L. Krüger, *Die Hamburgische Musikorganisation im 17. Jahrhundert* (1933; pp. 64ff.); S. Günther, *Die geistliche Konzertmusik von Thomas Selle nebst einer Biographie* (Giessen, 1935).

Sellner, Joseph, German oboe player and teacher; b. Landau, Bavaria, March 13, 1787; d. Vienna, May 17, 1843. He played the oboe in an Austrian army regiment; then at Prague in Weber's orch. (from 1811); from 1817 at the Vienna Court Opera. He taught at the Vienna Cons. from 1821, and conducted the student concerts there until 1838. His *Theoretischpraktische Oboen-Schule* is a fine method for oboe; he also publ. a Concerto and 3 concertinos for oboe, with orch.; and a Concerto for 2 Oboes.

Selmer, Johan Peter, Norwegian composer; b. Christiania, Jan. 20, 1844; d. Venice, July 22, 1910. After studying law in Norway, he went to Paris, where he took a course under Ambroise Thomas at the Paris Cons. (1868–70); later studied at the Leipzig Cons. with Richter (1871–74). From 1883 to 1886 he conducted the Oslo Phil. He was greatly influenced by Berlioz and Wagner; his symph. pieces bear the imprint of late Romanticism; like Grieg, he made use of Norwegian folk material.

WORKS: For Orch. (all perf. in Oslo): *Scène funèbre* (Sept. 30, 1871); *Alastor,* after Shelley (Oct. 24, 1874); *Karneval in Flandern* (Nov. 8, 1890); *In den bergen,* suite (1892); *Prometheus,* symph. poem (Oct. 29, 1898; his most important work); choral works, with Orch.: *Nordens aand (The Spirit of the North); Hilsen til Nidaros,* cantata; *Nogle politiske sange og andre viser (Some Political Songs and Other Airs)* for chorus in unison, and orch.; numerous male choruses a cappella; arrangements for folk melodies; songs for solo voice, with piano.

BIBLIOGRAPHY: P. Merkel, *Der norwegische Komponist Johan Selmer. Ein Lebensbild* (Leipzig, 1904).

Selva, Blanche, French pianist and teacher; b. Brive, Jan. 29, 1884; d. St. Amand, Tallende, Puy-de-

Dome, Dec. 3, 1942. She studied piano at the Paris Cons., and took courses in composition with Vincent d'Indy at the Schola Cantorum, where she became a teacher. She was one of the strongest propagandists of modern French music early in the century; she presented programs of piano works by Debussy, Ravel, and other masters of modern French music at the time when they were not yet universally recognized. She also publ. several books dealing with piano technique; her compendium, *L'Enseignement musical de la technique du piano* (4 vols., Paris, 1922) is valuable. She further publ. disquisitions on musical form: *La Sonate* (Paris, 1913); *Quelques mots sur la sonate* (Paris, 1914); *Les Sonates de Beethoven* (Barcelona, 1927); also a monograph on Déodat de Séverac (Paris, 1930).

Selvaggi, Rito, Italian composer and pedagogue; b. Noicattaro di Bari, May 22, 1898; d. Zoagli (Genoa), May 19, 1972. He studied piano and composition at the Liceo Musicale in Pesaro, and later took lessons with Busoni. He devoted himself mainly to teaching; was a prof. at the Cons of Parma (1934–38), then director of the Palermo Cons. (1938–58) and of the Cons. in Pesaro (1959–68). He composed the operas *Maggiolata veneziana* (Naples, 1929) and *Santa Caterina de Siena* (1947); the music drama *Eletta* (1947); the oratorio *Estasi francescana* (1926); a "trittico sinfonico," *La Natività di Gesù* (1935); *Sonata drammatica* for Viola and Piano (1954); *Elegie* for Cello, Chorus, and Orch., in memory of Toscanini (1957); numerous choruses and piano transcriptions of classical symphs.

Sembrich, Marcella (real name, **Praxede Marcellina Kochańska;** Sembrich was her mother's maiden name), famous coloratura soprano; b. Wisniewczyk, Galicia, Feb. 15, 1858; d. New York, Jan. 11, 1935. From the age of 4 she took piano lessons from her father, Kasimir Kochański; violin lessons were soon added. At 10 she appeared in public as a performer on both instruments. At the age of 11 she entered the Lemberg (Lwow) Cons., where she studied with Wilhelm Stengel. In 1874 she played and sang for Liszt, who urged her to train her voice. She then studied singing with Viktor Rokitansky in Vienna, and with G.B. Lamperti, Jr., in Milan. On May 5, 1877, she married her former teacher **Wilhelm Stengel** (b. Lemberg, Aug. 7, 1846; d. New York, May 15, 1917), and with him went to Athens, where she made her operatic debut on June 3, 1877, as Elvira in Bellini's *Puritani;* returning to Vienna, she studied the German repertoire with Richard Lewy. From 1878 to 1880 she sang at Dresden. On June 12, 1880, she made her London debut as Lucia; her American debut was at the Metropolitan Opera House, on Oct. 24, 1883. Thereafter she sang at the principal opera houses of Germany, Austria, France, Spain, Scandinavia, and Russia until 1898, then becoming a regular member of the Metropolitan Opera Co. for that season, and again from 1901–9. Her farewell appearance in opera was at the Metropolitan on Feb. 6, 1909. Her repertoire included 40 operatic parts, of which Violetta was the favorite.

Of Wagnerian roles, she sang only Eva in *Die Meistersinger.* In 1924 she joined the faculty of the newly founded Curtis Inst. in Philadelphia; also taught at the Juilliard School in N.Y.

BIBLIOGRAPHY: G. Armin, *Marcella Sembrich und Herr Prof. Julius Hey* (Leipzig, 1898); H.G. Owen, *A Recollection of Marcella Sembrich* (N.Y., 1950).

Semet, Théophile (-Aimé-Emile), French composer; b. Lille, Sept. 6, 1824; d. Corbeil, near Paris, April 15, 1888. He studied with Halévy; was a percussionist at the Opéra; wrote popular songs before attempting operatic composition. The following operas by Semet were produced in Paris: *Nuits d'Espagne* (Dec. 30, 1857); *Gil Blas* (March 23, 1860); *Ondine* (Jan. 7, 1863); *La Petite Fadette* (Sept. 11, 1869).

Semkow, Jerzy (Georg), Polish conductor; b. Radomsko, Oct. 12, 1928. He studied at the Cracow Cons.; in 1950 was apprenticed to Eugene Mravinsky, conductor of the Leningrad Phil.; also conducted opera at the Bolshoi Theater in Moscow. In the meantime, he continued studies in conducting with Tullio Serafin in Rome and Bruno Walter in Vienna. After serving as conductor of the National Polish Opera in Warsaw, he received the conductorship of the Royal Opera House in Copenhagen. In the interim, he was a guest conductor with numerous European orchs.; toured Japan with the London Phil. Orch. He made his U.S. debut in 1968 with the Boston Symph. Orch.; there followed appearances with the N.Y. Phil., Chicago Symph. Orch., Cleveland Orch., etc. In 1976 he was appointed music director of the St. Louis Symph. Orch., where he remained until 1979, when he was named artistic director of the Orch. Sinfonica di Roma della Radiotelevisione Italiana. A conductor of the Romantic school, he gives impassioned performances of the Vienna classics and of Russian and Polish compositions; he is also adept in precise projections of modern scores.

Semmler, Alexander, German-American composer and arranger; b. Dortmund, Nov. 12, 1900; d. Kingston, N.Y., April 24, 1977. He studied at Munich Univ.; emigrated to the U.S. in 1923; became a naturalized citizen in 1930. A highly competent musician, he readily adapted himself to the demands of the American music market, especially in films, and was able to write film scores of different connotations in various styles. Among his works are *Times Square Overture, American Indian Suite,* and a Piano Trio (1964).

Senaillé (Senaillié), Jean Baptiste, French violinist and composer; b. Paris, Nov. 23, 1687; d. there, Oct. 15, 1730. Although the spelling "Senaillé" is widely used, he signed his name "Senaillié," as did his father; contemporary editions of his music invariably used the form "Senaillié." He studied first with his father, a member of the "24 violons du roi"; later was a pupil of Jean Baptiste Anet; then went to Italy, where he studied with Vitali. He returned to Paris in 1720; gave many performances at the Concert Spirituel. His playing was in the Italian tradition; in his music, also, he was influenced by the Italian school of Corelli and Vitali. He publ. 50 violin sonatas (with continuo) in 5 books (1710–27); modern reprints by Moffat, Jensen, Alard, etc.

BIBLIOGRAPHY: L. de La Laurencie, *L'Ecole française de violon* (Paris, 1922; vol. 1, pp. 165–79); A. Moser, *Geschichte des Violinspiels* (1923; p. 179).

Senart, Maurice, French music publisher; b. Paris, Jan. 29, 1878; d. there, May 23, 1962. In 1908 he founded a music publishing enterprise in partnership with Roudanez; in 1912, became sole head of the firm, which bears his name. Among his early publications was the important collection edited by Henry Expert, *Maîtres musiciens de la Renaissance;* there followed several other collections; many editions of classical music; collected works of Chopin, edited by Alfred Cortot. Senart was also a decided supporter of modern French music; publ. many works by Honegger and Milhaud, and works by composers of other nationalities resident in Paris (Tansman, Harsanyi, etc.). His publishing firm was acquired by Salabert in 1941.

Sendrey, Albert Richard, American composer, son of **Aladár Szendrei;** b. Chicago, Dec. 26, 1911. He studied in Leipzig, Paris, and London; was an arranger for film companies in Paris (1935–37) and London (1937–44) before settling in Hollywood in 1944. Among his original works are *Oriental Suite* for Orch. (1935); 3 symphs.; piano pieces; cello pieces.

Sendrey, Alfred. See **Szendrei, Aladár.**

Senesino, Francesco (real name, **Bernardi;** called Senesino after his birthplace), Italian male mezzo-soprano; b. Siena, c.1680; d. c.1759. He studied in Bologna with Bernacchi; in 1719 was engaged to sing at the court theater in Dresden; Handel heard him there, and engaged him for his Italian opera company in London. He began his London appearances in Bononcini's opera *Astarto* (Nov. 30, 1720), and his success was enormous from the start. For 15 consecutive seasons he enjoyed the favor of the London public; was associated with Handel's company until 1733, when a rival organization, the "Opera of the Nobility," engaged him and several other celebrated Italian singers to sing under the direction of Porpora. In 1736 he returned to Siena; in 1737–39 he was in Florence. It is not known where or exactly when he died.

BIBLIOGRAPHY: F. Haböck, *Die Kastraten und ihre Gesangskunst* (Stuttgart, 1927); A. Heriot, *The Castrati in Opera* (London, 1956, pp. 91ff.).

Senff, Bartholf (Wilhelm), German music publisher and editor; b. Friedrichshall, near Coburg, Sept. 2, 1815; d. Badenweiler, June 25, 1900. As a young man he entered Kistner's music publishing house in Leipzig, advancing to the position of managing clerk; here he already began publishing the *Signale für die Musikalische Welt,* a trial number appearing in Dec. 1842; the first regular number was issued on Jan. 1, 1843. This was one of the most important German music periodicals of the 19th century; it includes reports of musical events, special articles, and correspondence from the music centers of the world; many celebrated musicians contributed to it, among them Hans von Bülow. Senff remained editor of the *Signale* until his death, and publication continued (with a brief interruption in 1917–18) until 1941. He founded his own publishing business in 1847; his catalogue included original publications of works by Schumann, Liszt, Anton Rubinstein, Raff, Franz, etc. His niece, Marie Senff, managed the firm until 1907, when she sold it and the *Signale* to Simrock of Berlin.

Senfl, Ludwig, important church composer of the Renaissance; b. Basel, c.1486; d. Munich, c.1543. His father was a singer from Freiburg im Breisgau; the family name may have been **Senffl, Sänftli, Sänfly, Senfel,** etc., and the ultimate origin undoubtedly German, although Ludwig Senfl was known under the appellation "Schweizer" (the Swiss). As a small child, from 1496, he sang in the imperial court chapel; in 1507–9 he was in Constance, where he was a pupil of Isaac; he was Isaac's assistant at St. Ann's Church in Augsburg, and also sang in the court chapel of Maximilian I; after Isaac's death (1517), Senfl completed his teacher's *Choralis Constantinus* and became his successor as chamber composer; remained in Augsburg for some time after Maximilian's death (1519), and received a stipend from Charles V; edited the historically important *Liber selectarum cantionum* (1520), which was one of the earliest books with musical notation publ. in Germany. In 1523 he settled in Munich as "intonator" at the Bavarian court chapel; his fame grew; he was referred to by an early contemporary as "prince of all German music." There is extant a letter written to Senfl by Martin Luther, dated Oct. 4, 1530, containing high praise of the composer (reprinted in F.A. Beck's *Dr. M. Luthers Gedanken über die Musik,* Berlin, 1828).

WORKS: *5 Salutationes Domini nostri Hiesu Christi,* motets in 4 voices (Nuremberg, 1526); *Varia carminum genera, quibus tum Horatius tum alii egreii poetae harmoniis composita* for 4 Voices (Nuremberg, 1534; 9 odes are in P. Hofhaimer's *Harmonie poeticae,* 1539); *Magnificat octo tonorum* for 4–5 Voices (Nuremberg, 1537). Eighty-one numbers by Senfl are in the collection *121 newe Lieder* (Nuremberg, 1534), and 64 numbers in *115 guter newer Liedlein* (Nuremberg, 1544); single compositions in various collections of the period (for a list, see Eitner's *Bibliographie,* Berlin, 1877, and vol. IV of the *Publikationen älterer Musikwerke*); Magnificats and a selection of 12 motets are in Denkmäler der Tonkunst in Bayern, 5 (3.ii). Many MSS (sacred and secular vocal works) are in the Munich Library. Some songs have been publ. in Jöde's *Chorbuch,* and in Denkmäler Deutscher Tonkunst (vol. 34, ed. by J. Wolf); *Weltliche Lieder* for 4-part Mixed

Chorus were publ. by Willi Schuh (Zürich, 1929); motets are in Schering's *Geschichte der Musik in Beispeilen* (nos. 74, 84–86); etc.; 7 masses were edited by E. Löhrer and O. Ursprung for the *Reichsdenkmale deutscher Musik* (Leipzig, 1936), and this was taken over the following year by the Schweizerische Musikforschende Gesellschaft as vol. I of the collected works of Senfl; as of 1977, there were 11 vols.

BIBLIOGRAPHY: Th. Kroyer, *Ludwig Senfl und sein Motettenstil* (Munich, 1902); H.J. Moser, "Instrumentalismen bei Ludwig Senfl," in the J. Wolf Festschrift (1929); idem, "Der Altmünchner Tonmeister Ludwig Senfl," *Süddeutsche Monatshefte* (1930); E. Löhrer, *Die Messen von Ludwig Senfl* (Lichtensteig, 1938); H. Birtner, "Sieben Messen von Ludwig Senfl," *Archiv für Musikforschung* (1942); G. Reese, *Music in the Renaissance* (N.Y., 1954); M. Bente, *Neue Wege der Quellenkritik und die Biographie Ludwig Senfls* (Wiesbaden, 1968).

Senilov, Vladimir, Russian composer; b. Viatka, Aug. 8, 1875; d. Petrograd, Sept. 18, 1918. He was a student of jurisprudence at the Univ. of St. Petersburg; went to Leipzig, where he studied with Hugo Riemann (1895–1901); returning to Russia, he studied composition with Rimsky-Korsakov and Glazunov at the St. Petersburg Cons., graduating in 1906. His works include a lyric drama, *Vasili Buslayev;* one-act opera, *Hippolytus,* after Euripides; *In Autumn,* symph. poem; *Mtziri,* symph. poem after Lermontov; *Pan,* symph. poem; *The Scythians,* symph. poem; 3 string quartets; choral pieces; songs.

Serafin, Tullio, eminent Italian conductor; b. Rottanova de Cavarzere, Venice, Sept. 1, 1878; d. Rome, Feb. 2, 1968. He studied at the Cons. in Milan; made his conducting debut in Ferrara in 1898. In 1901 Toscanini engaged him as one of his assistant conductors at La Scala. Later he was principal conductor of La Scala (1909–14, 1917–18); from 1924 to 1934 he was a conductor at the Metropolitan Opera in N.Y. In 1934 he became chief conductor and artistic director of the Rome Opera, a post he retained until 1943; after the war he was engaged as artistic director of La Scala (1946–47). From 1956 to 1958 he conducted at the Chicago Lyric Opera; in 1962 he was named artistic adviser of the Rome Opera. He was especially authoritative in the Italian operatic repertoire. As an artistic adviser, he helped launch the careers of Maria Callas and several other noted artists. He publ. (with A. Toni) 2 vols. on the history of Italian opera, *Stile, tradizioni e convenzioni del melodramma italiano del Settecento e dell'Ottocento* (Milan, 1958–64).

Serafino, Santo, celebrated Italian violin maker; b. Udine, Nov. 1, 1699; d. Venice, c.1758. He was a pupil of Niccolo Amati, and probably worked in Cremona; signed his name on the labels as "Sanctus Seraphinus Nicolai Amati Cremonensis Alumnus." His instruments contained elements characteristic of Stainer and of Niccolo Amati. His nephew **Giorgio Serafino** (b. Venice, c.1726; d. there, Jan. 25, 1775)

worked in Venice in the first half of the 18th century.

Serassi, Giuseppe ("il Vecchio"), the founder of a celebrated house of Italian organ builders; b. Gordano, 1694; d. Crema, Aug. 1, 1760. His son **Andrea Luigi** (1725–99) carried on the business; built the cathedral organs of Crema, Parma, and Fossano. A younger member of the family, **Giuseppe ("il Giovane";** b. Bergamo, Nov. 16, 1750; d. there, Feb. 19, 1817), upheld the reputation of the firm, and built many organs in Lombardy. His catalogue of 1815 lists 345 instruments. He publ. a description of the new organ at Como (1808), with a short history of the organ and good rules for registration; also brought out a pamphlet, *Sugli organi* (1816). The catalogue publ. in 1852 by his sons, **Carlo** and **Giuseppe Serassi,** shows a total of 654 organs constructed.

Serato, Arrigo, Italian violinist; b. Bologna, Feb. 7, 1877; d. Rome, Dec. 27, 1948. He received his musical training from his father, a cellist. He was mainly active as a chamber music player; formed the Trio Bolognese with Federico Sarti and Gustavo Tofano and the Quartetto Bolognese with Sarti, Massarenti, and Angelo Consolini; then settled in Berlin, where he took a course in violin study with Joachim, and was also a member of Joachim's string quartet. He returned to Italy in 1915 and taught master classes in violin at the Santa Cecilia Academy in Rome until his death. Concurrently he resumed his career as a chamber music player; in 1925 he organized a trio with Pizzetti (piano) and Mainardi (cello); also gave recitals with the pianist Ernesto Consolo.

BIBLIOGRAPHY: A. Della Corte, *Arrigo Serato violinista* (Siena, 1950).

Serauky, Walter, eminent German musicologist; b. Halle, April 20, 1903; d. there, Aug. 20, 1959. He studied at Leipzig Univ. with Schering, H.J. Moser, and Prüfer; received his Dr.Phil. at the Univ. of Halle in 1928 with the dissertation *Die musikalische Nachahmungsästhetik im Zeitraum von 1700 bis 1850* (publ. Münster, 1929); joined the faculty of the Univ. of Halle; in 1949 was appointed prof. at the Leipzig Univ. He contributed valuable essays to various German publications; brought out a music history of the city of Halle (5 vols., 1935–43); in 1956 he began publication of an extensive study of Handel, *G.F. Händel; Sein Leben, sein Werk;* also edited works by Handel, Türk, and Reichardt.

Serebrier, José, Uruguayan-American conductor and composer; b. Montevideo, Dec. 3, 1938. He began to conduct at the age of 12; went to the U.S. in 1950; studied composition with Vittorio Giannini at the Curtis Inst. in Philadelphia (1956–58) and conducting with Antal Dorati in Minneapolis; also took conducting lessons with Monteux at his summer residence in Maine. He subsequently conducted guest engagements in the U.S., South America, and Europe; gave the first performance in Poland of the 4th Symph. of Charles Ives. He was composer-in-residence with the Cleveland Orch. (1968–70); concurrently was music director of the Cleveland Phil. (1968–71). He is married to the soprano Carole Farley.

WORKS: Quartet for Saxophones (1955); *Pequeña música* for Wind Quintet (1955); Symph. No. 1 (1956); *Momento psicologico* for String Orch. (1957); *Suite canina* for Wind Trio (1957); Symph. for Percussion (1960); *The Star Wagon* for Chamber Orch. (1967); *Nueve* for Double Bass and Orch. (1970); *Colores mágicos,* variations for Harp and Chamber Orch., with "Synchrona" images (5th Inter-American Music Festival, Washington, D.C., May 20, 1971).

Serendero-Proust, David, Chilean composer and conductor; b. Santiago, July 28, 1934. He studied violin and composition at the National Cons. of Music in Santiago; then went to Germany, where he studied conducting in Stuttgart. From 1967 to 1972 he was appointed conductor of the Orquestra Sinfónica de Chile in Santiago. In 1972 he moved to West Germany, where he became active as a conductor in Wiesbaden.

WORKS: String Trio (1952); *Duo heterogéneo* for Flute and Clarinet (1953); *El ensayo,* a melodrama for Soprano and 14 Instruments (1962); *Estratos* for Orch. (Mexico City, March 28, 1969, composer conducting).

Sereni, Mario, Italian baritone; b. Perugia, March 25, 1928. He studied at the Santa Cecilia Academy in Rome; also in Siena with Mario Basiola; made his debut at the Florence May Festival in 1953, and then sang throughout Italy. In 1956 he sang at the Teatro Colón in Buenos Aires. He made his Metropolitan Opera debut in N.Y. on Nov. 9, 1957, as Gérard in *Andrea Chénier;* also sang in London, Vienna, Milan, Chicago, Houston, Dallas, and other opera centers.

Seress, Rezsö, Hungarian composer of popular songs; b. Budapest, Nov. 3, 1899; d. there, Jan. 12, 1968. He earned his living by playing piano and singing in restaurants and nightclubs; acquired fame in 1936 by his song *Gloomy Sunday,* which was banned in Hungary and several other countries because its morbid tune precipitated a wave of Sunday suicides among the young. Seress himself jumped out of a window from the 2nd floor of his Budapest apartment on Jan. 8, 1968 (a Monday, not a Sunday), and died 4 days later.

Sérieyx, Auguste, French composer and writer on music; b. Amiens, June 14, 1865; d. Montreux, Switzerland, Feb. 19, 1949. He studied in Paris at the Schola Cantorum with Gédalge and Vincent d'Indy; taught composition there (1900–14), and collaborated with d'Indy in his monumental *Cours de composition* (3 vols., Paris, 1897–1933); publ. a biography of d'Indy (Paris, 1913) and a short treatise, *Les Trois Etats de la tonalité* (Paris, 1910). His compositions include *La Voie Lactée* for Solo Voice and Orch.; the cantata *Salvete cedri libani;* Violin Sonata; piano

pieces; songs.

Sering, Friedrich Wilhelm, German composer; b. Fürstenwalde, near Frankfurt an der Oder, Nov. 26, 1822; d. Hannover, Nov. 5, 1901. From 1871 he was head teacher at the Seminary in Strasbourg, where he organized a Gesangverein. He composed an oratorio, *Christi Einzug in Jerusalem; Psalm 72* for Mixed Chorus, with Piano; wrote the manuals *Gesanglehre für Volksschulen* and *Die Choralfiguration, theoretisch-praktisch,* and an elementary violin method.

Serini, Giovanni Battista, Italian composer; b. Cremona, c.1724; date and place of death unknown. He was in the service of Robert d'Arcy, British ambassador in Venice (1744–46); subsequently was court musician in Bückeburg (1750–56). A collection of his instrumental and vocal works was found in the library at York Minster. Three keyboard sonatas are included in vol. 29 of *I classici della musica italiana.*

BIBLIOGRAPHY: Jack Pilgrim, "A Note on G.B. Serini," *Musical Times* (Aug. 1964).

Serkin, Peter, American pianist, son of **Rudolf Serkin;** b. New York, July 24, 1947. He made his public debut at the age of 11; when he was 12, he enrolled at the Curtis Inst. of Music in Philadelphia as a student of his father (graduated in 1965); at the age of 14 appeared with his father in Mozart's Concerto for 2 Pianos and Orch. with the Cleveland Orch. (April 19, 1962); then he started on a brilliant career of his own, specializing in ultramodern music. In 1973 he formed the chamber group Tashi ("good fortune" in Tibetan) with clarinetist Richard Stoltzman, violinist Ida Kavafian, and cellist Fred Sherry; later he also gave virtuoso performances of Romantic music, excelling expecially in Chopin's works.

Serkin, Rudolf, eminent Austrian pianist; b. Eger, Bohemia, March 28, 1903 (of Russian parentage). His father was a Russian singer named Mardko Serkin. In Vienna Rudolf Serkin studied piano with Richard Robert and composition with Joseph Marx and Arnold Schoenberg. After an early debut at the age of 12, he began his serious concert career in 1920; appeared frequently in joint recitals with the violinist Adolf Busch (whose daughter he married); made his American debut with Busch at a Coolidge Festival concert in Washington, D.C. (1933); in 1939 he was appointed to the faculty of the Curtis Inst. in Philadelphia; then served as its director from 1968 until 1976. Subsequently he took the lead in establishing in Marlboro, Vt., a summer center for festivals and schooling. His performances of the Viennese classics are unexcelled in authority, faithfulness of treatment, and technical virtuosity.

Serly, Tibor, American violist, composer, and conductor, of Hungarian extraction; b. Losonc, Hungary, Nov. 25, 1901; d. London, Oct. 8, 1978. His family moved to the U.S. in 1905. He received his early

musical training from his father; then returned to Hungary, where he enrolled in the Royal Academy of Music in Budapest; there he took courses with Koessler, Hubay, Béla Bartók, and Kodály (1922–26). He came back to the U.S. in 1927; played viola in the Cincinnati Symph. and in the Philadelphia Orch. When Béla Bartók came to America in 1940, Serly became his closest friend and adviser; after Bartók's death in 1945, Serly completed the last 17 measures of Bartók's 3rd Piano Concerto and totally reconstructed and orchestrated Bartók's Viola Concerto from 13 unnumbered MS pages. In 1948 he devised a system of composition called Modus Lascivus, as a sequel to his previous theoretical work, which was entitled "A Second Look at Harmony." Although the medieval Modus Lascivus was synonymous with the C-major scale, Serly expanded its connotation to include enharmonic modulation; indeed, his treatise on Modus Lascivus is subtitled "The Road to Enharmonicism." Shortly before his death he arranged Bartók's Viola Concerto for cello and orch.
WORKS: FOR ORCH.: Viola Concerto (1929); Symph. No. 1 (1931; Budapest, May 13, 1935, composer conducting); *Innovations* for 2 Harps and String Orch. (1931–33); Symph. No. 2 for Winds, Brass, and Percussion (1932); *6 Dance Designs* for Orch. (1933–34; Budapest, May 13, 1935); *Transylvanian Suite* for Chamber Orch. (1935); *Sonata Concertante* for String Orch. (1936); *The Pagan City,* symph. poem (1932–38; in collaboration with John Klenner); *Colonial Pageant* and *Alarms and Excursions,* 2 suites for Orch. (1936–37); *Midnight Madrigal* for Trumpet and Orch. (1939); *American Elegy,* based on "Taps," for Orch. (1945); *Rhapsody* for Viola and Chamber Orch. (1946–48; N.Y., Feb. 27, 1948); *Miniature Suite* for 12 Winds and Percussion (1947; revision of a discarded *Rhapsody* of 1927); Trombone Concerto (Chatauqua, Aug. 17, 1952); *Lament* for String Orch. (1955–58); Concerto for Violin and Wind Orch. (1955–58; Portland, Oreg., Nov. 30, 1978); *Symphonic Variations* for Audience and Small Orch. (1957); String Symph. (1956); *Little Xmas Cantata* for Audience and Small Orch. (1957); *American Fantasy of Quodlibets* for Orch. (1959); *Concertino 3 × 3* for Piano and Orch. (1964–65; Syracuse, N.Y., Jan. 13, 1967); *Anniversary Cantata on a Quodlibet* for Voices and Small Orch. (1966); *Canonic Fugue in 10 Voices on 10 Tones* for String Orch. (1972; Portland, Oreg., June 5, 1977); *Music* for 4 Harps and String Orch. (1977). CHAMBER MUSIC: Violin Sonata (1923); String Quartet No. 1 (1924); Sonata for Solo Violin (1947); *Chorale* for 3 Harps (1967); *Stringometrics* for Violin and Harp (1968). BALLETS: *Ex Machina* (1943); *Cast Out* (1973). FOR PIANO: Sonata No. 1 (1946); Concerto for 2 Pianos (1948–52); *40 Piano Etudes in Modus Lascivus* (1946–60; first perf. in their totality by Serly's wife, Miriam Molin, N.Y., May 4, 1977). OTHER VOCAL WORKS: *Consovowels 1–5:* No. 1 for Soprano Solo (1968); Nos. 2 and 3 for Soprano and Clarinet (1970–71); Nos. 4 and 5 for Soprano and Violin (1972); 4 songs from James Joyce's *Chamber Music* for Voice and Chamber Orch. (1926); *Strange Story,* after Wylie's poem, for Mezzo-soprano and Orch. (1927).

Sermilä, Jarmo, Finnish composer; b. Hämeenlinna (Tavastehus), Aug. 16, 1939. He studied under Tauno Marttinen and Joonas Kokkonen in Finland and under František Kovaříček in Czechoslovakia. Returning to Finland, he organized a group of composers of electronic music. In his music he pursues an experimental line, particularly in instrumentation.
WORKS: *Monody* for Horn and Percussion (1970); *Homage* for 3 Trumpets, 3 Trombones, 2 Horns, and Percussion (1971; Helsinki, April 19, 1972); *Pentagram* for Trumpet Solo, 2 Bassoons, 4 Horns, 6 Cellos, 2 Double Basses, and Percussion (1972; Turku, Jan. 18, 1973); *Early Music* for 2 Flutes and Strings (1972); *Tavastonia* for Double Bass and Piano (1973); *Crisis* for Clarinet and String Quartet (1973); 2 electronic works: *The Myth Is Weeping Again* and *A Doll's Cry* (1973); *Electrocomposition* (1976); *The Lions and the Bear* for Soprano and Percussion (1974); *Perception* for 2 Cellos and 2 Flutes (1974); *Mimesis 2* for Orch. (1974; Helsinki, Jan. 27, 1976); *Counterbass* for Double Bass and String Orch. (1975); *Cornologia* for 22 to 44 Horns (1975); *Colors and Contrasts* for Flute, Violin, and Piano (1976); *Love-Chain Songs* for Soprano, Wind Quintet, String Quintet, and 2 Percussionists (1976); *Contemplation 1* for Fluegelhorn and Tape (1976).

Sermisy, Claude (Claudin) de, French composer; b. c.1490; d. Paris, Sept. 13, 1562. In 1508 he was appointed "clerc musicien" of the Sainte-Chapelle in Paris; accompanied Francis I to Italy in 1515; was present at the meeting between Francis and Henry VIII at the Field of the Cloth of Gold (1520). Sermisy composed chansons, motets, and masses, which were printed in collections of the time and frequently republ. after his death, indicating a wide popularity. Attaingnant's *31 chansons* (1529) contains 11 songs by Sermisy, which are reprinted in Expert's *Les Maîtres musiciens;* other modern reprints include 3 chansons in Eitner's *Publikationen älterer Musikwerke* (Leipzig, 1899; vol. 23); 3 chansons in Commer's *Collectio operum musicorum* (vol. 12); 2 chansons in Bordes, *Chansonnier du XIVe siècle;* 4 chansons in Expert's *Anthologie chorale des maîtres musiciens de la Renaissance française.*
BIBLIOGRAPHY: O. Kade, *Die ältere Passionskomposition* (Gütersloh, 1893; deals fully with Sermisy's Passion music); M. Brenet, *Les Musiciens de la Sainte-Chapelle du Palais* (Paris, 1910); G. Reese, *Music in the Renaissance* (N.Y., 1954); G. Allaire, *The Masses of Claude de Sermisy* (Diss., Boston Univ., 1960); I. Cazeaux, *The Secular Music of Claude de Sermisy* (Diss., Columbia Univ., 1961). *Opera omnia,* ed. by G. Allaire and I. Cazeaux, began publication in 1970 in the Corpus Mensurabilis Musicae series.

Serocki, Kazimierz, prominent Polish composer and pianist; b. Toruń, March 3, 1922; d. Warsaw, Jan. 9, 1981. He studied piano in Lodz; also took a course in composition there with Sikorski. In 1947, following the path of many other composers of his generation, he went to Paris to study with the fabled Nadia Boulanger. Returning to Poland, he formed, with Tadeusz Baird and Jan Krenz, the modernistic Group '49, dedicated to the cause of the avant-garde; in 1956 was one of the organizers of the audaciously futuristic "Warsaw Autumn" Festivals. In the interim he toured as a concert pianist. In his early music he fell into the fashionable neo-Classical current strewn with tolerable dissonances and spiked with bristling atonalities; experimented with Webernized dodecaphonies before molding his own style of composition, an amalgam of pragmatic serialism and permissible aleatory procedures, while maintaining an air of well-nigh monastic nominalism in formal strictures and informal structures; in some pieces he makes incursions into the exotic field of American jazz.

WORKS: *Symphonic Scherzo* (1948); *Triptych* for Chamber Orch. (1949); *4 tańce ludowe (4 People's Dances)* for Chamber Orch. (1949); *Romantic Concerto* for Piano and Orch. (1950); 2 symphs.: No. 1 (1952) and No. 2, *Symphony of Songs*, for Soprano, Baritone, Chorus, and Orch. (1953; Warsaw, June 11, 1953); Trombone Concerto (1953); Sinfonietta for 2 String Orchs. (1956); *Musica concertante* for Chamber Orch. (1958); *Episodes* for Strings and 3 groups of Percussion (1958–59); *Segmenti* for 12 Winds, 6 Strings, Piano, Celesta, Harpsichord, Guitar, Mandolin, and 58 Percussion Instruments (1960–61); *Symphonic Frescoes* (1963); *Forte e piano,* music for 2 Pianos and Orch. (1967; Cologne, March 29, 1968); *Dramatic Story* for Orch. (1968–71; Warsaw, Sept. 23, 1971); *Fantasia elegiaca* for Organ and Orch. (1971–72; Baden-Baden, June 9, 1972); Sonatina for Trombone and Orch. (1972–73; Strasbourg, Dec. 19, 1975); *Concerto alla cadenza* for Recorder and Orch. (1975); *Ad Libitum,* 5 pieces for Orch. (1976; Hamburg, Sept. 17, 1977); *Pianophonie* for Piano, Electronic Sound Transformation, and Orch. (1976–78; Metz, West Germany, Nov. 18, 1978); *3 melodie Kurpiowskie (3 Melodies from Kurpie)* for 6 Sopranos, 6 Tenors, and Chamber Orch. (1949); 2 cantatas: *Mazowsze* (1950) and *Murarz warszawski* (1951); *Serce nocy (Heart of the Night),* cycle for Baritone and Piano (1956); *Oczy powietrza (Eyes of the Wind),* cycle for Soprano, and Orch. or Piano (1957–58); *Niobe* for 2 Narrators, Chorus, and Orch. (1966); *Poezje (Poems)* for Soprano and Chamber Orch. (1968–69); *Suite* for 4 Trombones (1953); *Continuum,* sextet for 123 Percussion Instruments manipulated by 6 Multimanual Percussionists (1965–66); *Swinging Music* for Clarinet, Trombone, Cello or Double Bass, and Piano (1970); *Phantasmagoria* for Piano and Percussion (1970–71); *Impromptu fantastique* for 6 Flutes, Mandolins, Guitars, Percussionists, and Piano (1973–74); Piano Sonatina (1952); Piano Sonata (1955); *A piacere* for Piano (1963).

Seroff, Victor, American writer on music; b. Batumi, Caucasus, Oct. 14, 1902; d. New York, May 10, 1979. He studied law at the Univ. of Tiflis; then took piano lessons with Moriz Rosenthal in Vienna and Theodore Szanto in Paris; eventually settled in N.Y.

and became an American citizen.

WRITINGS: *Dmitri Shostakovich: The Life and Background of a Soviet Composer* (N.Y., 1943); *The Mighty Five: The Cradle of Russian National Music* (N.Y., 1948); *Rachmaninoff* (N.Y., 1950); *Maurice Ravel* (N.Y., 1953); *Debussy, Musician of France* (N.Y., 1956); *Hector Berlioz* (N.Y., 1967); *Prokofiev: A Soviet Tragedy* (N.Y., 1968); *Mussorgsky* (N.Y., 1968); *Franz Liszt* (N.Y., 1970). BIBLIOGRAPHY: M.R. Werner, *To Whom It May Concern: The Story of V.I. Seroff* (N.Y., 1931).

Serov, Alexander, important Russian composer; b. St. Petersburg, Jan. 23, 1820; d. there, Feb. 1, 1871. He was trained in a law school; also took cello lessons with Karl Schuberth; became a functionary in the Ministry of Justice; served in St. Petersburg (1840–45); then in Simferopol, Crimea (1845–48); in 1849 turned definitely to music, and abandoned government employ. He never took lessons in composition, except a correspondence course in counterpoint, but achieved a certain mastery in harmony and orchestration by studying the classics. In 1851 he began writing critical articles on music and soon became an important figure in Russian journalism; in 1856 he became editor of the *Musical and Theatrical Monitor.* In 1858 he made his first trip abroad, visiting Germany and Bohemia; the following year made another German visit, and also traveled in Austria and Switzerland; during this journey he met Wagner, whose ardent admirer he became and remained to the end of his career; expounded Wagner's ideas in Russian publications and engaged in bitter polemics with those who did not subscribe to his views, including his old friend and schoolmate Vladimir Stasov. He started very late in the field of composition; inspired by the performance of a biblical play, *Judith,* by an Italian troupe at St. Petersburg in 1861, he resolved to write an opera on this subject, essaying an Italian libretto, but later deciding on a Russian text. *Judith* was produced in St. Petersburg on May 28, 1863, with excellent success, but although Serov intended to emulate Wagner in the music, the style of *Judith* was closer to Meyerbeer. Quite different was Serov's 2nd opera, *Rogneda,* written on a Russian subject, in a distinctly national idiom, with plentiful use of Russian folk songs. *Rogneda* was staged in St. Petersburg on Nov. 8, 1865, and won a spectacular success; the Tsar Alexander II attended a subsequent performance and granted Serov an annual stipend of 1,000 rubles for it. He then began the composition of another Russian opera, *Vrazhya sila (Malevolent Power),* but death (as a result of a sudden heart failure) overtook him when the 5th act was still incomplete; the opera was finished by N.T. Soloviev and produced posthumously in St. Petersburg on May 1, 1871. All 3 operas of Serov retain their popularity in Russia but are unknown elsewhere. Serov wrote further an Ave Maria for Adelina Patti (1868); a Stabat Mater; incidental music to *Nero; Plyaska Zaporozhtsev (Dance of the Zaporozh Cossacks)* for Orch. (1867); *Ouverture d'une comédie* for Piano, 4-hands; and a few other small pieces. A

selection from his writings was publ. in 4 vols. (St. Petersburg, 1892–95). In 1863 Serov married a young Cons. pupil, **Valentina Bergmann** (1846–1924), who was the first Russian woman to compose operas: *Uriel Acosta* (Moscow, 1885) and *Ilya Murometz* (Moscow, March 6, 1899; with Chaliapin in the title role). She helped to edit and publish Serov's posthumous works; wrote essays; publ. a number of piano pieces and a book of memoirs (St. Petersburg, 1914) under the name **Valentina Serova.**
BIBLIOGRAPHY: N. Findeisen, *A.N. Serov. His Life and Work* (St. Petersburg, 1900; 2nd ed., 1904); Valentina Serova, *A.N. Serov* (St. Petersburg, 1914); G. Abraham and M.D. Calvocoressi, *Masters of Russian Music* (N.Y., 1936); G. Khubov, *The Life of A.N. Serov* (Moscow, 1950).

Serpette, Gaston, French composer; b. Nantes, Nov. 4, 1846; d. Paris, Nov. 3, 1904. He studied with Ambroise Thomas at the Paris Cons., taking the Premier Grand Prix de Rome in 1871 with the cantata *Jeanne d'Arc.* From 1874 he produced in Paris a steady progression of light operas, of which the following enjoyed a modicum of success: *La Branche cassée* (Jan. 23, 1874); *Le Manoir du pic tordu* (May 28, 1875); *Le Moulin du vert galant* (April 12, 1876); *La Petite Muette* (Oct. 3, 1877); *Le Petit Chaperon rouge* (Oct. 10, 1885); *Adam et Eve* (Oct. 6, 1886); *Mademoiselle du téléphone* (May 2, 1891); *Shakespeare* (Nov. 23, 1899).

Serrano, Emilio, Spanish composer of light operas; b. Vitoria, March 13, 1850; d. Madrid, April 8, 1939. He studied at the Madrid Cons., and taught piano and composition there for half a century (1870–1920); also conducted symph. concerts in Madrid. He wrote 5 operas: *Mitridates* (Madrid, 1882); *Doña Juana la Loca* (Madrid, 1890); *Irene de Otranto* (Madrid, Feb. 17, 1891); *Gonzalo de Córdoba* (Madrid, Dec. 6, 1898); *La Maja de Rumbo* (Buenos Aires, Sept. 24, 1910).

Serrao, Paolo, Italian composer; b. Filadelfia, Catanzaro, 1830; d. Naples, March 17, 1907. He studied with Mercadante at the Cons. of Naples, and taught there from 1863. His first opera to be performed was *Pergolesi* (July 19, 1857), followed by *La Duchessa di Guisa* (Dec. 6, 1865) and *Il Figliuol prodigo* (April 23, 1868); also composed an oratorio, *Gli Ortonesi in Scio;* a funeral symph. for Mercadante, *Omaggio a Mercadante;* a cantata with Orch., *Le tre ore d'agonia;* much church music.

Serres, Louis (Arnal) de, French composer and teacher; b. Lyons, Nov. 8, 1864; d. Néronde (Loire), Dec. 25, 1942. He studied at the Paris Cons. with Taudou (harmony) and César Franck (organ); joined the faculty of the Schola Cantorum; taught there from 1900; when the institution was reorganized in 1935 as the Ecole César Franck, he became its director. His compositions include *Les Heures claires* for Voice and Orch.; *Les Caresses* for Orch.; choruses, motets, and songs.

Servais, (Adrien-) François, famous Belgian cellist; b. Hal, near Brussels, June 6, 1807; d. there, Nov. 26, 1866. He studied at the Brussels Cons.; played in a theater orch. there; then went to Paris, where he gave a concert in 1834, with brilliant success; on May 25, 1835, he played his own cello concerto with the London Phil.; subsequently made a grand tour of Europe; spent several years in Russia as a concert player, even reaching Siberia. He was appointed prof. at the Brussels Cons. in 1848, and taught many pupils who became distinguished artists. He wrote 3 concertos and 16 fantasias for cello, with orch.; 6 études and 14 duos for cello, with piano (with Gregoir); 3 duos for violin and cello (with Léonard).

Servais, François (Franz), French composer and conductor; b. St. Petersburg, Russia, c.1847; d. Asnières, near Paris, Jan. 14, 1901. It was claimed for him that he was an illegitimate son of Liszt and Princess Carolyne Sayn-Wittgenstein, but nothing in her voluminous correspondence with Liszt indicates that she was an expectant mother. However it might be, he was adopted by **François Servais** and assumed his name. He studied cello with Kufferath at the Brussels Cons., and won the Belgian Prix de Rome in 1873 with the cantata *Le Tasse.* From the outset of his career as a conductor he was a Wagner enthusiast, and gave the first Belgian performances of several Wagner operas, in Brussels. His own opera *Iôn* (originally entitled *L'Apollonide*) was produced in Karlsruhe in 1899.
BIBLIOGRAPHY: E. Michotte, *Au souvenir de François Servais* (Paris, 1907).

Servais, Joseph, Belgian-French cellist, son of **Adrien-François Servais**; b. Hal, near Brussels, Nov. 23, 1850; d. there, Aug. 29, 1885. He was a pupil of his father; made his debut in a joint recital with him in Warsaw (1867); then went to Weimar, where he played in the orch. (1868–70); in 1872 returned to Belgium, where he was a prof. at the Brussels Cons. until his early death.

Servières, Georges, French writer on music; b. Fréjus, Oct. 13, 1858; d. Paris, July 25, 1937. He publ. a number of informative books: *Richard Wagner jugé en France* (1887); *Le "Tannhäuser" à l'Opéra 1861* (1895); *La Musique française moderne* (1897); *Weber* (1906); *Emmanuel Chabrier* (1912); *Episodes d'histoire musicale* (1914); *Saint-Saëns* (1923); *Documents inédits sur les organistes français des XVIIe et XVIIIe siècles* (1923); *Edouard Lalo* (1925); *La Décoration artistique des buffets d'orgues* (1928); *Gabriel Fauré* (1930).

Sessions, Roger, eminent American composer; b. Brooklyn, Dec. 28, 1896. He studied music at Harvard Univ. (B.A., 1915); took a course in composition with Horatio Parker at the Yale School of Music (B.M., 1917); then took private lessons with Ernest Bloch in Cleveland and N.Y.; this association was of great importance for Sessions; his early works were strongly influenced by Bloch's rhapsodic style and rich harmonic idiom verging on polytonality. Sessions taught music theory at Smith College (1917–21); then was appointed to the faculty of the Cleveland Inst. of Music, first as assistant to Ernest Bloch, then as head of the dept. He held 2 consecutive Guggenheim fellowships (1926, 1927), a fellowship of the American Academy in Rome (1928–31), and a Carnegie Fellowship (1931–32). He lived mostly in Europe from 1926 to 1933; in the interim he presented with Aaron Copland a series of concerts of modern music in N.Y. (called Copland-Sessions Concerts) which played an important cultural role at the time. His subsequent teaching posts included Boston Univ. (1933–35), the New Jersey College for Women (1935–37), Princeton Univ. (1935–45), and the Univ. of Calif. at Berkeley (1945–51); taught again at Princeton (1953–65), at Berkeley (1966–67), and at Harvard Univ. (1968–69); also gave courses at the Juilliard School of Music in N.Y. Among American composers who had fruitful sessions with Sessions during his years of professorship were David Diamond, Paul Bowles, Leon Kirchner, Milton Babbitt, and Hugo Weisgall. In his compositions, Sessions evolved a remarkably compact polyphonic idiom, rich in unresolvable dissonances and textural density, and yet permeated with true lyricism. In his later works he adopted a *sui generis* method of serial composition. The music of Sessions is decidedly in advance of his time; the difficulty of his idiom, for both performers and listeners, creates a paradoxical situation in which he is recognized as one of the most important composers of the century, while actual performances of his works are exasperatingly infrequent. In 1974 he received a special citation of the Pulitzer Award Committee "for his life's work as a distinguished American composer." In 1982 he was awarded a 2nd Pulitzer Prize, for his work *Concerto for Orchestra,* composed in 1981.

WORKS: For the stage: *The Black Maskers,* incidental music to Leonid Andreyev's play (Smith College, Northampton, Mass., June 1923); *The Trial of Lucullus,* one-act opera (Berkeley, April 18, 1947); *Montezuma,* 3-act opera (1962; West Berlin, April 19, 1964); 9 symphs.: No. 1 (Boston, April 22, 1927); No. 2 (San Francisco, Jan. 9, 1947); No. 3 (Boston, Dec. 6, 1957); No. 4 (Minneapolis, Jan. 2, 1960); No. 5 (Philadelphia, Feb. 7, 1964); No. 6 (Newark, N.J., Nov. 19, 1966); No. 7 (Ann Arbor, Mich., Oct. 1, 1967); No. 8 (N.Y., May 2, 1968); No. 9 (Syracuse, March 1980); symph. suite from *The Black Maskers* (Cincinnati, Dec. 5, 1930); Violin Concerto (Chicago, Jan. 8, 1940); *Idyll of Theocritus* for Soprano and Orch. (Louisville, Ky., Jan. 14, 1956); Piano Concerto (N.Y., Feb. 10, 1956); 2 string quartets (1936, 1951); Duo for Violin and Piano (1942); Sonata for Solo Violin (1953); String Quintet (1958); *Divertimento* for Orch. (1960); *Psalm 140* for Soprano and Orch. (1963); *6 Pieces* for Cello (1966); *When Lilacs Last in the Door-yard Bloom'd,* cantata for Vocal Soloists, Chorus, and Orch. (1967–70; Univ. of Calif., Berkeley, May 23, 1971); *Rhapsody* for Orch. (Baltimore, March 18, 1970); Concerto for Violin, Cello, and Orch. (1970–71); Concertino for Chamber Orch. (1971–72; Chicago, April 14, 1972); *3 Biblical Choruses* for Chorus and Chamber Orch. (1971); *Concer-*

to for Orchestra (Boston, Oct. 23, 1981; a centennial commission by the Boston Symph. Orch.; awarded a Pulitzer Prize in 1982); 3 piano sonatas (1930, 1946, 1965); *Pages from a Diary* for Piano (1939); *3 Chorale Preludes* for Organ (1925); *Mass* for Unison Chorus and Organ (1956); *5 Pieces* for Piano (1975). Sessions publ. the books *The Musical Experience of Composer, Performer, Listener* (Princeton, 1950); *Harmonic Practice* (N.Y., 1951); *Reflections on the Music Life in the United States* (N.Y., 1956); and *Questions about Music* (Cambridge, Mass., 1970).

BIBLIOGRAPHY: N. Slonimsky, in *American Composers on American Music,* ed. by Henry Cowell (Stanford, Calif., 1933; reprint, N.Y., 1962); Mark Brunswick, "Roger Sessions," *Modern Music* (1933); Aaron Copland, *Our New Music* (N.Y., 1941; pp. 176ff.); M.A. Schubart, "Roger Sessions," *Musical Quarterly* (April 1946); L.A. Wright and A. Bagnall, "Roger H. Sessions: A Selective Bibliography and a Listing of His Compositions," *Current Musicology,* 15 (1973); F. Prausnitz, *Roger Sessions: A Critical Biography* (London, 1983); O. Daniel, "Roger Sessions," *Ovation* (March 1984).

Šesták, Zdeněk, Czech composer; b. Citoliby, Dec. 10, 1925. He studied composition with Hlobil and Krejčí at the Prague Cons. (1945–50) and music history at Charles Univ. (1945–49); in 1970 he joined as an active member the Czech Performing Rights Organization.

WORKS: *To Fallen Warriors,* symph. prelude (1949); *Pantomime* for Orch. (1959); *Rhapsodic Fantasy* for Cello and Orch. (1960); 4 numbered symphs.: No. 1, *Epitaph* (1961); No. 2 (1970); No. 3 (1971); No. 4 for String Orch. (1973); *Vocal Symphony* for Chorus and Orch. (1962); *Balladic Intermezzo* for Orch. (1964); *Symphonic Fantasy,* variations for Orch. (1966); Concerto for String Orch. (1974); *Auschwitz,* melodrama to a text by Quasimodo (1959); *Hommage à Apollinaire* for 12 Mixed Choruses (1972); *The Death of Manon Lescaut,* 4 dramatic fragments for Soprano, Tenor, Chorus, Solo Viola, and Piano (1974); *Cassation* for 5 Wind Instruments (1958); *Suite* for Flute and Piano (1959); *2 Pieces* for Violin and Piano (1960); Concertino for Wind Quintet (1964); *Divertimento concertante* for Wind Quintet (1966); *5 Virtuoso Inventions* for Solo Bassoon (1966); Sonata for 2 Clarinets (1967); *Music for Solo Oboe* (1967); Concertino No. 1 for Horn and Piano (1967); *3 Metamorphoses* for Solo Flute (1968); *Musica partita* for Solo Clarinet (1968); Concertino No. 2 for Horn and Piano (1972); numerous songs; children's pieces.

Setaccioli, Giacomo, Italian composer and teacher; b. Corneto, Tarquinia, Dec. 8, 1868; d. Siena, Dec. 5, 1925. He studied at the Santa Cecilia Academy in Rome; after teaching there (1922–25), he was appointed director of the Cons. Cherubini in Florence. He wrote the operas *La Sorella di Mark* (Rome, May 7, 1896), *L'ultimo degli Abenceragi* (Rome, 1893), and *Il Mantelaccio* (posthumous; Rome, 1954); several symph. pieces; a *Requiem;* chamber music; songs; piano pieces. He publ. *Debussy è un in-*

novatore? (Rome, 1910) and *Studi e conferenze di critica musicale* (Rome, 1923).

Seter, Mordecai, Russian-born Israeli composer; b. Novorossiysk, Feb. 26, 1916. He went to Palestine in 1926; then traveled to Paris and studied composition with Nadia Boulanger and Paul Dukas (1932–37); returning to Palestine, he taught at the Israeli Academy of Music. His own works are marked by the eastern Mediterranean style and techniques of composition.
WORKS: 5 ballets: *Pas de deux* or *Women in Tent* (ballet version of the 1956 *Ricercar*); *Midnight Vigil, Rhapsody on Yemenite Themes* (1958); *The Legend of Judith* (1962); *Part Real, Part Dream* (ballet version of the *Fantasia concertante,* 1964); *Jephthah's Daughter* (ballet version of symph. score, 1965); radiophonic oratorio, *Midnight Vigil* (1962; concert version of the ballet; Jerusalem, July 16, 1963); *Elegy* for Viola or Clarinet, and Orch. or Piano (1954); *Ricercar* for Violin, Viola, Cello, and String Ensemble (1956); *Variations* for Orch. (1959); *Fantasia concertante* for Chamber Orch. (1965); Sinfonietta (1966); *Yemenite Suite* for Chamber Orch., with optional Voice (1966); *Meditation* for Orch. (1967); *Rounds* for Chamber Orch. (1967–68); *Requiem* for Oboe, Piano, and String Orch. (1970); *Sabbath Cantata* for Soloists, Chorus, and String Orch. (1940); *Jerusalem* for Chorus and Orch. (1966); *Sapei,* music for Chorus, Percussion, Piano, and Strings (1968); *Partita* for Violin and Piano (1951); Sonata for 2 Violins (1952); Sonata for Solo Violin (1953); *Diptyque* for Wind Quintet (1955); *Chamber Music 1970,* 6 works for different instrumental combinations (1970); *Concertante* for Violin, Oboe, Horn, and Piano (1973); Piano Trio (1973); Woodwind Trio (1974); Quintet for Violin, Cello, Flute, Horn, and Piano (1975); *Ensemble* for 6 Instruments (1975); *Solo and Tutti* for Clarinet and String Quartet (1976); 4 string quartets (1976–77); 2 piano quartets (1973–81, 1982); Piano Sonata (1982).

Ševčik, Otakar, noted Czech violinist and pedagogue; b. Horaždowitz, March 22, 1852; d. Pisek, Jan. 18, 1934. He studied violin with his father; then at the Prague Cons. with Anton Bennewitz. From 1870 to 1873 he was concertmaster of the Mozarteum in Salzburg; held a similar post in the Theater an der Wien in Vienna. He then went to Russia, where he became a prof. at the Cons. of Kiev (1875); also gave concerts in Russia, achieving great success there. In 1892 he returned to Prague; became head of the violin dept. at the Prague Cons. (1901–6); in 1909 he became head of the master school for violin at the Vienna Academy of Music; from 1919 to 1924 he taught again in Prague; also visited abroad as a teacher in the U.S. (1920, 1924, 1931), London (1932), etc. His method, in contradistinction to the usual diatonic system, is founded on chromatic progressions, especially valuable in securing both accuracy and facility. In various parts of the world he had hundreds of pupils, among them Jan Kubelík, Kocian, Marie Hall, Baloković, Erica Morini, and Efrem Zimbalist. He publ. the following pedagogi-

cal works (in German, Bohemian, French, and Russian; most of them also printed in Eng.): *Schule der Violintechnik* (4 parts); *Schule der Bogentechnik* (6 parts); *Violinschule für Anfänger* (7 parts); *Triller-Vorstudien und Ausbildung des Fingeranschlags* (2 parts); *Lagenwechsel-Übungen; Doppelgriff-Vorstudien;* also *Böhmische Tänze und Weisen* for Violin and Piano.
BIBLIOGRAPHY: Paul Stoeving, *A Key to Ševčik's Works* (London, 1914); V. Nopp, *Otakar Ševčik* (Prague, 1948); J. Dostál, ed., *Otakar Ševčik* (collection of essays on him; Prague, 1953).

Séverac, Déodat de, French composer; b. Saint-Félix-de-Caraman, Lauragais, July 20, 1872; d. Céret, March 24, 1921. He received his first lessons on the piano from his father, a painter and an ardent lover of music. He studied music at the Cons. of Toulouse; in 1896 he entered the Schola Cantorum in Paris, where he remained until 1907, studying with Magnard and Vincent d'Indy. He resided alternately in Paris and in his native town.
WORKS: Operas: *Le Cœur du moulin* (Paris, Dec. 8, 1909) and *Les Princesses d'Hokifari* (not produced); incidental music to L. Damard's *Le Mirage* (1905), E. Sicard's *Héliogabale* (1910), M. Navarre's *Muguetto* (1911), E. Verhaeren's *Hélène de Sparte* (Paris, May 5, 1912); symph. poems: *Nymphes au Crépuscule, Tryptique, Les Grenouilles qui demandent un Roi, Nausikaa; Les Muses sylvestres,* suite for Double String Quintet and Piano; *Le Parc aux cerfs,* suite for Oboe, String Quintet, and Piano; *Suite* in E for Organ; for Piano: *Petite suite; En Languedoc,* suite; *La Nymphe émue ou Le Faune indiscret; En vacances,* album of little pieces; Sonata; several collections of folk songs; solo songs.
BIBLIOGRAPHY: O. Séré, *Musiciens français d'aujourd'hui* (Paris, 1921); L. Moulin, *Déodat de Séverac* (1922); Blanche Selva, *Déodat de Séverac* (Paris, 1930); A. Cortot, *La Musique française de piano* (vol. 2, Paris, 1932); P. Landormy, "Déodat de Séverac," *Musical Quarterly* (April 1934); G. Soula and I. Girard, *Hommage à Déodat de Séverac* (Toulouse, 1952); E. Brody, "Déodat de Séverac: A Mediterranean Musician," *Music Review,* XXIX (1968).

Severinsen, Carl ("Doc"), American jazz trumpeter and bandleader; b. Arlington, Ore., July 7, 1927. He studied cornet with his father, and later with Benny Baker; subsequently played in several jazz bands, including those of Charlie Barnet and Tommy Dorsey; later joined the band of the Johnny Carson "Tonight" show, and eventually became its conductor.

Severn, Edmund, composer and teacher; b. Nottingham, England, Dec. 10, 1862; d. Melrose, Mass., May 14, 1942. In 1866 his father, a violinist, settled in Hartford, Conn.; Severn studied violin with him and with Bernhard Listemann in Boston; composition with Chadwick in Boston and with Philipp Scharwenka in Berlin. His works include 2 symph. poems: *Lancelot and Elaine* (1898) and *Eloise and Abelard* (1915); a suite, *From Old New England* (originally for Violin and Piano, 1912; orchestrated and conducted by the composer at the Springfield [Mass.] Music Festival, May 17, 1919); *Song Celestial* for Orch. (1912); Violin Concerto (N.Y. Phil., Jan. 7, 1916); choral works; songs.

Sevitzky, Fabien, Russian conductor, nephew of **Serge Koussevitzky;** b. Vishny Volochok, Sept. 29, 1891; d. Athens, Greece, Feb. 2, 1967. He began a career as a concert player on the double bass, under his original name, Koussevitzky; his uncle, who was already a celebrated double-bass player himself, suggested that he adopt a truncated form of the last name, and he complied to avoid a family quarrel. He made his appearances as a conductor in Russia under the name Sevitzky; lived in Moscow until 1922; spent a year in Poland as a double-bass player in the Warsaw Phil.; with his wife, a Russian singer, **Maria Koussevitzky** (who retained her legal name), he went to Mexico in 1923; then emigrated to the U.S.; joined the Philadelphia Orch., and in 1925 organized the Philadelphia Chamber String Sinfonietta; he led the People's Symph. Orch. in Boston (1934–36); then was permanent conductor of the Indianapolis Symph. Orch. (1937–55) and music director of the Univ. of Miami Symph. Orch. (1959–65). He died during a guest appearance as a conductor in Athens.

Seybold, Artur, German composer; b. Hamburg, Jan. 6, 1868; d. Weissenfels, near Leipzig, Dec. 15, 1948. He studied at the Hamburg Cons.; traveled as violinist with Laube's orch. in Russia (1888); lived in Hamburg as a teacher and conductor of choral societies (from 1890). His numerous compositions for violin and piano and his male choruses won considerable popularity; he also publ. a violin method, *Das neue System,* and instructive pieces.

Seydelmann, Franz, German composer; b. Dresden, Oct. 8, 1748; d. there, Oct. 23, 1806. He was the son of a player in the court orch., which he joined as a youth; studied in Italy with Josef Schuster (1765–69). In 1772 both he and Schuster were appointed composers of church music to the Elector in Dresden; later both became conductors at the court church, cembalists at the Italian Opera in Dresden, and in 1787, conductors there.
WORKS: 7 Italian operas, and a German opera, *Arsene* (Dresden, March 3, 1779); the piano score of *Arsene* is publ.; also publ. are several numbers from his operas *Il capriccio corretto* and *La villanella di Misnia;* 6 piano sonatas for 4-hands; 3 sonatas for piano solo; 3 flute sonatas; 3 violin sonatas. In MS are the other Italian operas, 36 masses, 40 Psalms, 37 offertories, a Requiem, numerous other vocal works, both sacred and secular.
BIBLIOGRAPHY: R. Cahn-Speyer, *Franz Seydelmann als dramatischer Komponist* (Leipzig, 1909).

Seyffardt, Ernst Hermann, German choral conductor and composer; b. Krefeld, May 6, 1859; d. Partenkirchen, Dec. 1942. He studied at the Cologne Cons. with F. Hiller and G. Jensen, and at the Berlin Hochschule für Musik with Kiel; conducted the Liedertafel in Freiburg (1887–92); in 1892 was appointed conductor of the Neuer Singverein in Stuttgart; also taught at the Stuttgart Cons.; retired in 1929.
WORKS: Dramatic scene, *Thusnelda;* Symph.; Violin Sonata; Piano Quartet; String Quartet; *Schicksalsgesang* for Alto Solo, Chorus, and Orch.; *Zum Gedächtniss* for Baritone Solo, Male Chorus, and Orch.; patriotic cantata, *Aus Deutschlands grosser Zeit;* song cycle, *Vom Schwarzwald bis zum Rhein;* other vocal works. His opera, *Die Glocken von Plurs,* was produced at Krefeld in 1912.

Seyfried, Ignaz Xaver, Ritter von, Austrian composer; b. Vienna, Aug. 15, 1776; d. there, Aug. 27, 1841. He was a close friend of Mozart, and had some piano lessons with him; studied also with Koželuh and Haydn; afterward with Albrechtsberger. In 1797 he became conductor at Schikaneder's theater in Vienna; then at the new Theater an der Wien, when it opened in 1801, retaining this post until 1827. He was an extremely prolific composer, and some of his singspiels were very successful; one of them, *Die Ochsenmenuette,* based on Haydn's music (Vienna, Dec. 31, 1823), gave rise to the well-known anecdote about Haydn's composing an *Ox Minuet* for a butcher and receiving an ox as a gift. Seyfried also wrote the opera *Der Wundermann am Rheinfall* (Vienna, Oct. 26, 1799), which elicited praise from Haydn. He further wrote numerous melodramas, ballets, oratorios, motets, symphs., quartets, etc. He publ. Beethoven's exercises in thoroughbass, counterpoint, and composition (1832), with some unwarranted additions (see Thayer's *Beethoven,* III, 80); edited a complete edition of Albrechtsberger's theoretical works; also edited Preindl's *Wiener Tonschule* (1827; 2nd ed., 1832). For a complete list of Seyfried's theatrical works and dates of performances, see Anton Bauer, *Opern und Operetten in Wien* (Graz, 1955).

Seymour, John Laurence, American composer; b. Los Angeles, Jan. 18, 1893. He studied piano with Fannie Charles Dillon; then went to Europe and took lessons in composition with Pizzetti in Italy and with Vincent d'Indy in Paris. Returning to America, he devoted himself mainly to teaching. He was one of the few American composers to have an opera performed by the Metropolitan Opera House in N.Y.; it was an exotic piece entitled *In the Pasha's Garden* (N.Y., Jan. 24, 1935). Another opera, *Ramona,* was produced at the Brigham Young Univ. in Provo, Utah (Nov. 11, 1970); he further wrote the operas *The Devil and Tom Walker* (1926); *The Snake Woman; The Protégé of the Mistress;* and *The Affected Maids* (after Molière's *Les Précieuses ridicules*); the operettas *The Bachelor Belles, Hollywood Madness,* etc.; a Piano Concerto; sonatas for various instruments, with piano.

Sgambati, Giovanni, celebrated Italian pianist and composer; b. Rome, May 28, 1841; d. there, Dec. 14, 1914. He studied piano with Amerigo Barbieri, and appeared in public at the age of 6; sang in church, and conducted instrumental groups. He then became a pupil of Liszt in Rome; subsequently gave orch. concerts, playing German masterpieces; performed Beethoven's *Eroica* in 1866 for the first time in Rome. Historically, Sgambati's concerts were important as the first systematic attempt to introduce to the Italian public a varied fare of symph. music. Sgambati appeared also as a pianist; after a concert tour in Italy and Germany, he established in 1868 a free piano class annexed to the Santa Cecilia Academy in Rome, which in 1877 was formally recognized by the government as the Liceo Musicale; it became the foremost music school in Italy; Sgambati taught piano there until his death. He was an ardent admirer of Wagner, whom he met in 1876; Wagner recommended Sgambati to his own publishers, Schott of Mainz, who subsequently brought out many of Sgambati's works. As a pianist and teacher, Sgambati enjoyed a very high reputation in Germany and Italy; his own music betrays strong Germanic influence; unlike most Italian composers of his time, he devoted his energies exclusively to instrumental music, avoiding all service to the theater.

WORKS: Symph. in D (Rome, March 28, 1881); Symph. No. 2; *Epitalamio sinfonico* (1887); overtures; Piano Concerto; *Te Deum* for Orch.; *Messa da Requiem;* 2 piano quintets (1876, 1877; his most enduring works); String Quartet (1884); numerous piano pieces: *Fogli volanti, Pièces lyriques, Mélodies poétiques,* 6 nocturnes, etc.; also *Formulario del pianista* (technical exercises); songs.

BIBLIOGRAPHY: Bettina Walker, *My Musical Experiences* (1892; pp. 44–84); R.A. Streatfeild, in *Masters of Italian Music* (1895; pp. 246–56); E. Segnitz, "Sgambatis Klaviermusik," *Musikpädagogische Blätter,* 11, 12 (1911); A. de Angelis, "G. Sgambati," *Rivista Musicale Italiana* (Jan. 1912); A. Bonaventura, "G. Sgambati," *La Nuova Musica* (1914); A. Casella, "G. Sgambati," *Music & Letters* (Oct. 1925); A. Casella, in Cobbett's *Cyclopedic Survey of Chamber Music;* A. Bonaventura, "G. Sgambati," *Musica d'Oggi* (1941).

Shafran, Daniel, remarkable Russian cellist; b. Petrograd (Leningrad), Jan. 13, 1923. He studied cello with his father, Boris Shafran, who was an eminent cellist in his own right, and with Alexander Strimer. Daniel Shafran received first prize at the 1937 Moscow competition for string players and at the Prague competition of 1952. He made several concert tours in Europe, and appeared in the U.S. in 1960, 1964, and 1977, with excellent success.

Shakespeare, William, English tenor and singing teacher; b. Croydon, June 16, 1849; d. London, Nov. 1, 1931. He studied at the Royal Academy of Music with Sterndale Bennett; went to Leipzig for study with Reinecke, but soon left for Milan to cultivate his voice; studied with Lamperti there. From 1875, he appeared in England as a tenor; in 1878 was appointed prof. of singing at the Royal Academy of Music in London; won a high reputation as vocal teacher. His compositions are entirely in the vein of

German Romanticism, his model being Mendelssohn. He publ. *The Art of Singing* (3 parts; 1898–99; several times republ.); *Singing for Schools and Colleges* (1907); *Plain Words on Singing* (1924); and *The Speaker's Art* (1931).

Shanet, Howard, American conductor; b. Brooklyn, Nov. 9, 1918. He studied cello with Evsei Beloussoff; played in the National Orch. Assoc., under the direction of Leon Barzin; later studied conducting with Rudolph Thomas, Fritz Stiedry, and Koussevitzky at the Berkshire Music Center in Tanglewood; took composition lessons with Hans Weisse, Paul Dessau, Martinu, Lopatnikoff, and Arthur Honegger. He completed his academic studies at Columbia Univ. (A.B., 1939; A.M., 1941). He served in the U.S. Army as warrant officer and bandleader (1942–44); taught at Hunter College in N.Y. between 1945 and 1953; was on the staff at the Berkshire Music Center in the summers of 1948 to 1952; in 1953 was appointed to the faculty of Columbia Univ. and as conductor of the Univ. Orch.; in 1972 became chairman of the music dept.; in 1974 initiated an extensive program in music performance, the first of this nature at Columbia Univ.; served as assistant conductor of the N.Y. City Symph. (1947–48), conductor of the Huntington (W.Va.) Symph. Orch. (1951–52), and a guest conductor with the Israel Phil. Orch. (1950) and the N.Y. Phil. (1951, 1959). In 1977 he received the presidential citation of the National Federation of Music Clubs and a certificate of distinguished service at the Inst. of International Education. He composed *A War March* for Military Band (1944); *2 Canonic Pieces* for 2 Clarinets (1947); *Variations on a Bizarre Theme* for Orch. (1960); arranged and reconstructed the score *Night of the Tropics* by Gottschalk (1955). He publ. an "adult education book," *Learn to Read Music* (N.Y., 1956; trans. into Norwegian, 1972, and Italian, 1975); a fundamental documentary vol., *Philharmonic: A History of New York's Orchestra* (N.Y., 1975); edited and wrote a critical introduction for *Early Histories of the New York Philharmonic,* containing reprints of books by Krehbiel, Huneker, and Erskine (N.Y., 1978).

Shankar, Ravi, Indian sitarist and composer; b. Benares, April 7, 1920. He was trained by his brother, Uday Shankar, and began his career as a musician and a dancer; then engaged in a serious study of the Indian classical instrument, the sitar; in time became a great virtuoso on it. As a consequence of the growing infatuation with oriental arts in Western countries in the 1960s, he suddenly became popular, and his concerts were greeted with reverential awe by youthful multitudes. This popularity increased a thousandfold when the Beatles went to him to receive the revelation of Eastern musical wisdom, thus placing him on the pedestal usually reserved for untutored guitar strummers. As a composer, he distinguished himself by several film scores, including the famous *Pather Panchali;* he also wrote the film scores for *Kabulliwallah* and *Anuradha.* For the Tagore centenary he wrote a ballet, *Samanya Kshati,* based on Tagore's poem of the same name; it was produced in New Delhi on May 7, 1961. He also wrote 2 concertos for sitar and orch. (1970, 1976). He publ. a memoir, *My Music, My Life* (N.Y., 1968); Elise B. Barnett edited *Ravi Shankar: Learning Indian Music, A Systematic Approach* (1981; includes cassette tapes).

Shapero, Harold, American composer; b. Lynn, Mass., April 29, 1920. He learned to play piano as a youth; was for several years a pianist in dance orchs.; began serious study in 1936, at the Malkin Cons. in Boston, with Nicolas Slonimsky; then studied with Krenek, with Walter Piston at Harvard Univ., with Paul Hindemith at the Berkshire Music Center in Tanglewood, and with Nadia Boulanger in Cambridge, Mass. He graduated from Harvard Univ. in 1941; received the American Prix de Rome for his *9-Minute Overture* (N.Y., June 8, 1941); held a Guggenheim fellowship in 1946 and 1947; won the Gershwin Prize (1946); etc.; in 1949–50 was in Rome; in 1952 was appointed a prof. at Brandeis Univ. in Waltham, Mass. He married the painter Esther Geller in 1945. In his music Shapero adheres to an austere Classical pattern, without excluding a highly emotional melodic line; his exceptional mastery of contrapuntal technique secures clarity of intermingled sonorities in his chamber music. In some of his early compositions he applied the dodecaphonic method.
WORKS: *Serenade in D* for String Orch. (1945); *Symphony for Classical Orchestra* (Boston, Jan. 30, 1948); *The Travelers,* overture (1948); *Credo* for Orch. (Louisville, Ky., Oct. 19, 1955); Concerto for Orch. (1951–58); *3 Pieces for 3 Pieces* for Flute, Clarinet, and Bassoon (1938); Trumpet Sonata (1939); String Quartet (1940); *4-Hand Piano Sonata* (1941); Violin Sonata (1942); *Partita* for Piano and Chamber Orch. (1960); *3 Improvisations in B flat* (1968) and *3 Studies in C sharp* (1969) for Piano and Synthesizer; *3 Amateur Sonatas* for Piano.
BIBLIOGRAPHY: Madeleine Goss, *Modern Music Makers* (N.Y., 1952; pp. 474–78).

Shapey, Ralph, American conductor and composer; b. Philadelphia, March 12, 1921. He studied violin with Emmanuel Zetlin and composition with Stefan Wolpe. In 1964 he was appointed to the faculty of the Univ. of Chicago and was made conductor of the resident Contemporary Chamber Players. Disappointed at repeated rejections of his works by performers and publishers, Shapey announced in 1969 that he would never again submit any of his works to anyone for performance or publication. But by an extraordinary turn of events, in 1983 he received a munificent cash prize from the MacArthur Foundation in Chicago, with no strings attached. He sprang into action with renewed energy and faith in human fortune. His music employs serialistic but uncongested procedures in acrid counterpoint, while formally adhering to neo-Classical paradigms.
WORKS: *Fantasy* for Orch. (1951); Symph. No. 1 (1952); Concerto for Clarinet and Small Ensemble (1954; Strasbourg Festival, June 9, 1958); *Challenge:*

The Family of Man for Orch. (1955); *Ontogeny* for Orch. (1958); *Invocation-Concerto* for Violin and Orch. (1959; N.Y., May 24, 1968); *Rituals* for Orch. (1959; Chicago, May 16, 1966); *Dimensions* for Soprano and 23 Instruments (1960); *Incantations* for Soprano and 10 Instruments (1961); *Convocation* for Chamber Group (1962); *Chamber Symphony* for 10 Solo Players (1962); *Partita* for Violin and 13 Players (1966); *Partita-Fantasy* for Cello and 16 Players (1967); *Praise,* oratorio for Bass-baritone, Chorus, and Orch. (1961–71; Chicago, Feb. 28, 1976); *The Covenant* for Soprano, 16 Players, and Tape (1976); *Trilogy: Song of Songs I–III* for Soprano, Bass, 14 Instruments, and Tape (1978–80); Double Concerto for Violin, Cello, and Orch. (1982; Juilliard School of Music, N.Y., Jan. 24, 1984, composer conducting); 7 string quartets (1946; 1949; 1950; 1953; 1957; with Voice, 1963; 1972); Piano Quintet (1946); 2 piano sonatas (1946, 1954); *Evocation* for Violin, Piano, and Percussion (1959; N.Y., March 26, 1960); *Soliloquy* for Narrator, String Quartet, and Percussion (1959); *5* for Violin and Piano (1960); *Discourse* for 4 Instruments (1961); *7* for Piano, 4-hands (1963); Brass Quintet (1963); String Trio (1965); *Partita* for Solo Violin (1966); *Mutations No. 2* for Piano (1966); *Deux* for 2 Pianos (1967); *Songs of Ecstasy* for Soprano, Piano, Percussion, and Tape (1967); *Reyem,* a "musical offering" for Flute, Violin, and Piano (1967); *31 Variations* for Piano (1972–73); *21 Variations* for Piano (1978); *Evocation* for Cello, Piano, and Percussion (1979); *Evocation* for Viola and Piano (1981); Concerto Grosso for Wind Quintet (1981); solo songs; piano pieces.
BIBLIOGRAPHY: David Ewen, *American Composers* (N.Y., 1982).

Shapleigh, Bertram, American music theorist; b. Boston, Jan. 15, 1871; d. Washington, D.C., July 2, 1940. He studied at the New England Cons.; went to London in 1899, and remained there until 1916; then lived in N.Y. and Washington. He made a specialty of oriental music, and gave numerous lectures on the subject. The Bertram Shapleigh Foundation was established in Washington after his death.

Shaporin, Yuri, significant Russian composer; b. Glukhov, Ukraine, Nov. 8, 1887; d. Moscow, Dec. 9, 1966. He studied law, and graduated from the Univ. of St. Petersburg in 1913; also studied at the St. Petersburg Cons. with Sokolov (composition), graduating in 1918. He wrote theatrical music in Leningrad; moved to Moscow in 1936.
WORKS: Opera, *The Decembrists* (1930–50; Moscow, June 23, 1953); cantata, *A Tale of the Battle for the Russian Land* (Moscow, April 18, 1944); incidental music to *King Lear, Tartuffe, Boris Godunov,* and Leskov's *The Flea* (also as an orch. suite); Symph. (Moscow, May 11, 1933); symphony-cantata, *On the Field of Kulikovo* (Moscow, Nov. 18, 1939); 2 piano sonatas; several song cycles.
BIBLIOGRAPHY: Gerald Abraham, *Eight Soviet Composers* (London, 1942; pp. 89–98); E.A. Grosheva, *Yuri Shaporin* (Moscow, 1957); S. Levit, *Yuri Shaporin* (Moscow, 1964); Ivan Martynov, *Yuri*

Shaporin (Moscow, 1966).

Sharp, Cecil James, English editor and collector of folk songs; b. London, Nov. 22, 1859; d. there, June 23, 1924. He studied music privately while attending Cambridge Univ.; in 1882 he went to Australia, settling in Adelaide, where he worked in a bank and practiced law, becoming associate to the Chief Justice of Southern Australia; in 1889 he resigned from the legal profession and took up a musical career; was assistant organist of the Adelaide Cathedral, and co-director of the Adelaide College of Music. In 1892 he returned to England; was made music instructor of Ludgrove School (1893–1910) and also principal of the Hampstead Cons. (1896–1905). At the same time he became deeply interested in English folk songs; publ. a *Book of British Songs for Home and School* (1902); then proceeded to make a systematic survey of English villages with the aim of collecting authentic specimens of English songs. In 1911 he established the English Folk Dance Society; also was director of the School of Folk Song and Dance at Stratford-upon-Avon. During World War I he was in the U.S., collecting folk music in the Appalachian Mountains, with a view to establishing their English origin. In 1923 he received the degree of M.M. *honoris causa* from Cambridge Univ. In 1930 the "Cecil Sharp House" was opened in London as headquarters of the English Folk Dance Society (amalgamated with the Folk Song Society in 1932). Sharp publ. many collections of folk songs and dances: *English Folk Carols* (1911); *Folk-Songs from Various Counties* (1912); *English Folk-Chanteys* (1914); *One Hundred English Folk-Songs* (1916); *Folk-Songs of English Origin* (2 vols., 1921–23); *English Folk-Songs from the Southern Appalachians* (1917; new enlarged ed., 2 vols., ed. by Maud Karpeles, posthumous, Oxford, 1932; republ. 1952); *American-English Folk-Songs* (1918–21); *The Morris Book* (in 5 parts; 1907–13); *Morris Dance Tunes* (in 10 parts; 1907–13); *The Country Dance Book* (in 6 parts; 1909–22); *Country Dance Tunes* (in 11 parts; 1909–22); *The Sword Dances of Northern England* (in 5 parts; 1911–13). Books: *English Folk Song* (London, 1907; 3rd ed., revised by Maud Karpeles, London, 1954); *The Dance: An Historical Survey of Dancing in Europe,* with A.P. Oppé (London, 1924). BIBLIOGRAPHY: W.S. Shaw, "Cecil Sharp and Folk Dancing," *Music & Letters* (Jan. 1921); A.H. Fox Strangways and M. Karpeles, *Cecil Sharp* (London, 1933; 2nd ed., London, 1955).

Sharp, Geoffrey (Newton), English music critic; b. Leeds, June 14, 1914; d. Chelmsford (Essex), March 29, 1974. He studied at Trinity College, Cambridge, and also at the Royal College of Music in London. In 1940 he began publication of the quarterly *Music Review* in Cambridge. He also wrote articles on music for various journals.

Sharpe, Herbert Francis, English pianist and composer; b. Halifax, Yorkshire, March 1, 1861; d. London, Oct. 14, 1925. He studied piano at the National Training School in London; joined the faculty of the Royal College of Music in 1884; gave numerous concerts in London and elsewhere; composed many piano pieces and publ. *Pianoforte School* (with Stanley Lucas).

Shattuck, Arthur, American pianist; b. Neenah, Wis., April 19, 1881; d. New York, Oct. 16, 1951. He studied piano with Leschetizky in Vienna (1895–1902); made his home in Paris, touring extensively in many countries, including Iceland and Egypt. Returning to America, he appeared as a soloist with many orchs.

Shaverzashvili, Alexander, Soviet composer; b. Tiflis, Caucasus, July 8, 1919. He studied at the Tiflis Cons. with Andrei Balanchivadze; from 1955 he was a prof. there. He wrote a comic opera, *Grasshopper* (Tiflis, March 18, 1955); Symph. (1945); 2 piano concertos (1946, 1949); Piano Quintet (1955); String Quartet; Piano Trio; Violin Sonata; songs.

Shavitch, Vladimir, American conductor; b. Russia, July 20, 1888; d. Palm Beach, Fla., Dec. 26, 1947. He studied piano with Godowsky and Busoni in Berlin, and composition with Hugo Kaun and Paul Juon (1902–12). Coming to America in 1914, he became conductor of the Syracuse (N.Y.) Symph. Orch.; also conducted in Rochester, N.Y. (1923–27); appeared as a guest conductor in European capitals.

Shaw, Arnold, American composer, writer, editor, lecturer, and music executive; b. Brooklyn, June 28, 1909. He majored in English literature at Columbia Univ. (M.A., 1931); also studied music; composed a number of snappy piano pieces with a sophisticated tilt (*The Mod Muppet, Bubblegum Waltzes, Stabiles Mobiles*) and singable songs (*Dungaree Doll, Woman Is a Five-Letter Word*); edited the mind-boggling books by Joseph Schillinger (*Mathematical Basis of the Arts; Schillinger System of Musical Composition*); lectured at the Juilliard School of Music, New School for Social Research, Univ. of Calif., Los Angeles; as general manager of Edward B. Marks Music Corp., promoted popular singers, among them Rod McKuen, Burt Bacharach, and Elvis Presley. He lives in Las Vegas; in 1973–74 was named Nevada Composer of the Year. WRITINGS: *Lingo of Tin Pan Alley* (N.Y., 1950); *The Money Song,* a novel (N.Y., 1953); *Belafonte: An Unauthorized Biography* (N.Y., 1960); *Sinatra: 20th Century Romantic* (N.Y., 1968); *The Rock Revolution* (N.Y., 1969); *The World of Soul: Black America's Contribution to the Pop Music Scene* (N.Y., 1970); *The Street That Never Slept* (N.Y., 1971); *The Rockin' 50s* (N.Y., 1974); *Honkers and Shouters: The Rhythm & Blues Years* (N.Y., 1978).

Shaw, Artie (real name, **Arthur Arshawsky**), American clarinetist and bandleader; b. New York, May 23, 1910. He played clarinet in bands as a boy; after playing with a variety of radio and dance bands, he formed his own band in 1935, becoming one of the foremost proponents of "big band swing";

his greatest hit, among more than 600 recordings, was that of Cole Porter's song *Begin the Beguine.* But he considered his fabulous commercial successes as artistically unfulfilling, and throughout his career made attempts for recognition as a "serious" musician. In the 1930s he introduced a group consisting of clarinet, string quartet, and a rhythm section; sporadically, from 1939 to 1954, he led small combos of from 5 to 7 players (but always labeled the "Gramercy 5") in experimental jazz attempts, these groups sometimes including celesta or harpsichord; he also performed as soloist in several clarinet concertos in 1949. He was married consecutively to several movie stars (Lana Turner, Ava Gardner, etc.); in between he also wed the sex authoress Kathleen Winsor. He publ. a quasi-autobiographical novel, *The Trouble with Cinderella* (N.Y., 1952), and the novel *I Love You, I Hate You, Drop Dead!* (1965).

BIBLIOGRAPHY: Vladimir Simosko, "Artie Shaw and His Gramercy Fives," *Journal of Jazz Studies* (Oct. 1973).

Shaw, Frank Holcomb, American organist and teacher; b. Paxton, Ill., May 8, 1884; d. Oberlin, Ohio, Sept. 1, 1959. He studied at Oberlin Cons.; then went to Paris, where he took organ lessons with Widor; upon returning to the U.S., he filled various teaching posts; from 1924 to 1949 was director of the Oberlin Cons.

Shaw, George Bernard, famous Irish dramatist; b. Dublin, July 26, 1856; d. Ayot St. Lawrence, England, Nov. 2, 1950. Before winning fame as a playwright, he was active as a music critic in London, writing for the *Star* (under the name of "Corno di Bassetto") during the season of 1888–89, and for the *World* from 1890 to 1894. In 1899 he publ. *The Perfect Wagnerite,* a highly individual socialistic interpretation of the *Ring of the Nibelung.* His criticisms from the *World* were reprinted as *Music in London* in 3 vols. (1932; new ed., 1950); those from the *Star* as *London Music in 1888–89* (London and N.Y., 1937); selected criticisms were publ., edited by Eric Bentley, in N.Y., 1954. Shaw's play *Arms and the Man* was made into an operetta, *The Chocolate Soldier,* by Oskar Straus (1908); his *Pygmalion* was converted into a highly successful musical comedy (1956) under the title *My Fair Lady,* with a musical score by Frederick Loewe.

BIBLIOGRAPHY: W. Irvine, "G.B. Shaw's Musical Criticism," *Musical Quarterly* (July 1946).

Shaw, Martin, English organist and composer; b. London, March 9, 1875; d. Southwold, Sussex, Oct. 24, 1958. He was a pupil at the Royal College of Music in London; played organ in various churches in London. In 1900 he founded the Purcell Society in London; wrote an opera, *Mr. Pepys* (London, Feb. 11, 1926); several masques and ballads; the oratorios *Easter, The Rock* (after T.S. Eliot), and *The Redeemer;* sacred choruses; etc. He publ. *The Principles of English Church Music Composition* (1921); edited *The English Carol Book, Songs of Britain,*

The Motherland Song Book, and (with his brother, Geoffrey Shaw) *The League of Nations Song Book.* He publ. his autobiography, *Up to Now,* in 1929.

Geoffrey Shaw (b. London, Nov. 14, 1879; d. there, April 14, 1943) was an organist and composer; also was active in musical education.

Shaw, Mary (née **Postans**), English contralto; b. London, 1814; d. Hadleigh Hall, Suffolk, Sept. 9, 1876. She studied with Sir George Smart; made her debut in London in 1834, with marked success, as Ismelda in the premiere of Verdi's *Oberto;* in 1838 sang in the Gewandhaus in Leipzig, under Mendelssohn's direction, and in other German cities. She made her operatic debut at La Scala in Milan on Nov. 17, 1839; in 1842 she sang at Covent Garden in London and at the principal festivals in England. In 1844, at the height of her success, her career was suddenly ended when her husband (the painter Alfred Shaw, whom she had married in 1835) became insane (he died in 1847); the shock affected her vocal cords, so that she was unable to sing. Some time later she remarried and went to live in the country.

Shaw, Oliver, blind American organist, composer, and singer; b. Middleboro, Mass., March 13, 1779; d. Providence, Dec. 31, 1848. He was a singing teacher and church organist in Providence from 1807; was a composer of popular psalm tunes and ballads, which he sang in public; some favorites were *Mary's Tears, The Inspiration, Sweet Little Ann,* and *The Death of Perry.* He publ. the collection *The Social Sacred Melodist* (1835).

BIBLIOGRAPHY: T. Williams, *A Discourse on the Life and Death of Oliver Shaw* (Boston, 1851); *Memorial of Oliver Shaw* (Providence, 1884); B.N. Degen, *Oliver Shaw: His Music and Contribution to American Society* (Diss., Univ. of Rochester, 1971).

Shaw, Robert, noted American conductor; b. Red Bluff, Calif., April 30, 1916. He came from a clerical family; his father and his grandfather were clergymen; his mother sang in church choirs. He studied at Pomona College (1934–38), where he conducted its Glee Club; in 1938 Fred Waring asked him to help organize the Fred Waring Glee Club, and Shaw conducted it until 1945. In 1941 he founded his own Collegiate Chorale in N.Y., which he led in diversified programs of choral music, old and new, until 1954. In 1944 he was awarded a Guggenheim fellowship. He taught choral conducting at the Berkshire Music Center at Tanglewood (1942–45) and at the Juilliard School of Music in N.Y. (1946–49). In 1946 he made his debut as a symph. conductor with the Naumburg Orch. in N.Y. In 1948 he founded the Robert Shaw Chorale, which he conducted with notable success for 20 seasons. Eager to acquire more experience as an orch. conductor, he attended conducting sessions with Monteux and Rodzinski in N.Y. in 1950. From 1953 to 1958 he conducted summer concerts of the San Diego Symph. Orch. In 1956 he led the Robert Shaw Chorale through a tour of 15 countries of Europe, including

Russia, and the Middle East, under the auspices of the State Dept. In 1964 the Robert Shaw Chorale gave concerts in South America. For his Chorale, Shaw commissioned several choral works from contemporary composers, including Béla Bartók, Darius Milhaud, Benjamin Britten, Samuel Barber, and Aaron Copland. Beginning in 1956 he was co-director of the Alaska Festival of Music in Anchorage. From 1956 to 1967 he served as associate conductor with Szell and the Cleveland Orch. In 1967 he was engaged as conductor and music director of the Atlanta Symph. Orch., and by dint of talent and perseverance brought it to a high degree of excellence. In 1977 he conducted the Atlanta Symph. at the gala concert for President Jimmy Carter's inauguration in Washington, D.C.

BIBLIOGRAPHY: David Ewen, *Musicians since 1900* (N.Y., 1978); J. Mussulman, *Dear People . . . Robert Shaw: A Biography* (Bloomington, Ind., and London, 1979).

Shaw, (Harold) Watkins, English musicologist and teacher; b. Bradford, April 3, 1911. He studied history at Wadham College, Oxford (B.A., 1932); then took courses in musicology with Colles and R.O. Morris at the Royal College of Music in London (1932–33). In 1949 he was appointed a lecturer at the Worcester College of Education; from 1971 till his retirement in 1980, he served as keeper of the Parry Room Library at the Royal College of Music. He publ. several valuable essays on Handel, including *The Story of Handel's "Messiah"* (London, 1963) and *A Textual and Historical Companion to Handel's "Messiah"* (London, 1965).

Shawe-Taylor, Desmond, eminent British music critic; b. Dublin, May 29, 1907. He was educated at Oriel College, Oxford; through the years he contributed literary and musical criticism to various newspapers and periodicals. After service in World War II, he was engaged as music critic of the *New Statesman* in 1945, retaining his post until 1958; from 1950 to 1958 he also served as phonograph record reviewer for the *Observer.* In 1958 he was named music critic of the *Sunday Times;* also was a guest critic for the *New Yorker* (1973–74). He was made a Commander of the Order of the British Empire in 1965. His writings are notable for their unostentatious display of wide learning. He publ. the vol. *Covent Garden* for the World of Music series (London, 1948); also, with Edward Sackville-West, *The Record Guide* (London, 1951, and later revisions).

Shchedrin, Rodion, brilliant Soviet composer; b. Moscow, Dec. 16, 1932. He studied with Shaporin at the Moscow Cons., graduating in 1955. In his music he developed a richly harmonious idiom, diversified by impulsive rhythms.

WORKS: Opera, *Not Only for Love* (Moscow, 1961); ballets: *The Humpback Horse* (1955; extremely popular in Russia) and *Anna Karenina* (1972); 3 piano concertos (1954, 1966, 1976); Symph. No. 1 (1958); Symph. No. 2 (1962–65; includes a section which artfully imitates the tuning of an orch.); *Ob-*

streperous Street Tunes for Orch. (1963; extremely popular); *Chimes* for Orch., commissioned by the N.Y. Phil. (N.Y., Jan. 11, 1968); *Chamber Orchestra Suite* for 20 Violins, Harp, Accordion, and 2 Double Basses (1961); Piano Quintet (1952); 2 string quartets (1951, 1954); *24 Preludes and Fugues* for Piano (1969–70); *Polyphonic Album* for Piano (1973); oratorio, *Lenin Dwells in the Heart of the People* (1969); *Bureaucratiade* for Voices and Orch., a satirical work (1963); *Poetorium* for Speaker, Chorus, and Orch. (1969); *Musical Offering* for Organ, 3 Flutes, 3 Bassoons, and 3 Trombones (Moscow, Oct. 21, 1983). He made an ingenious arrangement of fragments from Bizet's *Carmen* as a ballet suite, scored for strings and percussion, reducing Bizet's romantic melodies to a coarse but extremely effective ensemble, which he wrote for his wife, the ballerina Maya Plisetskaya (1968).

BIBLIOGRAPHY: N. Rogozhina, *Rodion Shchedrin* (Moscow, 1959).

Shcherbachev, Vladimir, Russian composer; b. Warsaw, Jan. 24, 1889; d. Leningrad, March 5, 1952. He studied at the St. Petersburg Cons. with Maximilian Steinberg and Liadov, graduating in 1914. From 1924 to 1931 he was a prof. of composition at the Leningrad Cons. He wrote an opera, *Anna Kolosova* (1939); 5 symphs.: No. 1 (1914; Petrograd, Nov. 5, 1916); No. 2 (Leningrad, Dec. 14, 1924); No. 3 (Leningrad, Feb. 4, 1932, composer conducting); No. 4, subtitled *History of the Izhorsky Factory* (Leningrad, May 28, 1934, in partial perf.; complete perf., Radio Leningrad, Dec. 23, 1935; public perf., Leningrad, Jan. 21, 1936); No. 5 (Leningrad, Dec. 21, 1948; revised version, Kiev, Oct. 21, 1950); music for films; the orch. suite from one of them, *The Thunderstorm,* became popular in Russia; he further wrote *A Fairy Tale* for Orch. (Petrograd, Dec. 20, 1915); Nonet (1917); numerous piano works.

Shearing, George Albert, English-American jazz pianist; b. London, Aug. 13, 1919. He was blind from birth; learned to read music with Braille notation; for several years he played piano in a blind band; then transferred to the U.S. (naturalized in 1955) and organized a quintet, with vibraphone, guitar, drums, and bass. In the early 1940s he played a typical stride style of the time; in the late 1940s, influenced by the innovations of bebop, he developed a new manner, characterized by surprising, extended harmonies, and a pianistic technique whereby both hands play thick chords in parallel motion ("locked-hand style"). He composed famous tunes, among them *Lullaby of Birdland.*

Shebalin, Vissarion, Russian composer; b. Omsk, June 11, 1902; d. Moscow, May 28, 1963. He studied at the Moscow Cons. with Miaskovsky (1923–28); in 1935, was appointed prof. of composition there; from 1942 to 1948 was its director. On Feb. 10, 1948, by resolution of the Communist Central Committee, he was condemned (along with Shostakovich, Prokofiev, Miaskovsky, and others) for adhering to a "decadent formalism" in composition; but these strictures were removed in a corrective declaration of May 28, 1958, "restoring the dignity and integrity of Soviet composers."

WORKS: Musical comedy, *Bridegroom from the Embassy* (Sverdlovsk, Aug. 1, 1942); operas: *The Taming of the Shrew*, after Shakespeare (concert version, Oct. 1, 1955; stage premiere, Kuibishev, May 25, 1957) and *Sun over the Steppe* (Moscow, June 9, 1958); ballets: *Festival* (1958; unfinished) and *Reminiscences of a Bygone Day* (1961); 5 symphs.: No. 1 (1925; Leningrad, Nov. 13, 1926); No. 2 (1929); No. 3 (1934; Moscow, Feb. 11, 1944); No. 4 (1935; Moscow, Feb. 27, 1936); No. 5 (1962; Moscow, Oct. 9, 1962); *Overture on Mari Themes* (1926); Horn Concertino (1930; revised 1959); Violin Concertino (1931); 3 suites for Orch. (1935; 1935, revised 1961; 1963); *Variations on Russian Folk Songs* for Orch. (1940); Violin Concerto (Leningrad, Oct. 29, 1940); *Russian Overture* (1941); Sinfonietta (1949); Cello Concerto (1950); symph. poem, *Lenin*, with Chorus and Soloists (1931; first complete perf., Leningrad, Jan. 21, 1934; revised 1959); cantata, *Moscow* (Moscow, Dec. 14, 1946); 9 string quartets (1923, 1934, 1939, 1940, 1942, 1943, 1947, 1960, 1963); Piano Trio (1924); Viola Sonata (1954); Violin Sonata (1958); Cello Sonata (1960); Guitar Sonatina (1963); several piano sonatas; choruses and songs. He completed Mussorgsky's unfinished opera *The Fair at Sorotchintsy*, using only Mussorgsky's own material (Leningrad, Dec. 21, 1931; version with supplementary materials, Moscow, March 19, 1952).

BIBLIOGRAPHY: Gerald Abraham, *Eight Soviet Composers* (London, 1943; pp. 61–69); Igor Boelza, *V. Shebalin* (Moscow, 1945).

Shedlock, J(ohn) S(outh), English writer on music; b. Reading, Sept. 29, 1843; d. London, Jan. 9, 1919. After graduating from London Univ. (1864), he studied composition with Lalo in Paris; upon his return to London, he devoted himself to writing; was music critic of the *Academy* (1879–1901) and of the *AthenAum* (1898–1916). He publ. a detailed description of Beethoven's sketchbook purchased by the British Museum (*Musical Times,* June 1892–Jan. 1893); this led him to further investigations of Beethoven memorabilia, and in 1893 he discovered in Berlin a copy of Cramer's studies with notations by Beethoven; publ. his findings as *The Beethoven-Cramer Studies* (1893); also publ. 2 vols. of Beethoven's letters in English translation, a short biography of Beethoven in Bell's *Miniature Series* (1905), and a valuable book, *The Pianoforte Sonata, Its Origin and Development* (London, 1895); edited Kuhnau's *Biblical Sonatas* (1895) and harpsichord pieces by Frescobaldi and Froberger.

Shekhter, Boris, Russian composer; b. Odessa, Jan. 20, 1900; d. Moscow, Dec. 16, 1961. He was graduated from the Odessa Cons. in 1922; then entered the Moscow Cons., studying composition with Vasilenko and Miaskovsky; graduated in 1929. In 1940 he went to Turkestan, and became a prof. at the Cons. of Ashkhabad.

WORKS: Operas: *The Year 1905* (with A. Davi-

denko, 1935) and *Yusup and Akhmed* (Ashkhabad, June 12, 1942); cantatas: *Volga-Don* (1952) and *A House in Shushenskoye* (1955); 5 symphs. (1929, 1943, 1945, 1947, 1951); orch. suite, *Turkmenia,* based on Central Asian themes (1932; Florence Festival of the International Society for Contemporary Music, April 4, 1934; his best work); *Rhapsody* for Orch. (1935); piano pieces; songs.

Shelley, Harry Rowe, American organist and composer; b. New Haven, Conn., June 8, 1858; d. Short Beach, Conn., Sept. 12, 1947. He was a pupil of Dudley Buck and Dvořák in N.Y.; from 1899 was active as a church organist and teacher.

WORKS: 3 operas: *Leila, Romeo and Juliet,* and *Lotus San;* symph. poem, *The Crusaders;* orch. suite, *Souvenir de Baden-Baden;* cantatas: *Vexilla Regis* (N.Y., 1894); *Lochinvar's Ride* (N.Y., 1915); *Death and Life; The Inheritance Divine;* much choral music and some effective piano pieces. His ballads *Minstrel Boy* and *Love's Sorrow* attained considerable success. He also edited the popular collections *Gems for the Organ, The Modern Organist,* and *101 Interludes for Organ.*

Shenshin, Alexander, Russian composer; b. Moscow, Nov. 18, 1890; d. there, Feb. 18, 1944. He studied philology at Moscow Univ.; later took music lessons with Gretchaninov and Glière. He subsequently taught music in Moscow, and also conducted occasional symph. concerts. His music is cast in a style reminiscent of Liadov; the elements of exotic musical patterns are noticeable. He composed an opera, *O T'ao* (1925); ballets: *Ancient Dances* (1933) and *Story of Carmen* (1935); a song cycle, *From Japanese Anthologies;* numerous songs to German poems.

BIBLIOGRAPHY: V. Belaiev, *A.A. Shenshin* (Moscow, 1929; in Russian and German).

Shepard, Frank Hartson, American pianist and pedagogue; b. Bethel, Conn., Sept. 20, 1863; d. Orange, N.J., Feb. 15, 1913. He studied music in Boston; then took courses at the Leipzig Cons. (1886–90) with Jadassohn, Reinecke, and others. Returning to America in 1891, he established the Shepard School of Music at Orange, N.J., of which he was director until his death; also was organist at Grace Church there. He publ. *Piano Touch and Scales; Church Music and Choir Training; How to Modulate; Harmony Simplified; Children's Harmony;* etc.

Shepherd, Arthur, eminent American composer and pedagogue; b. Paris, Idaho, Feb. 19, 1880; d. Cleveland, Jan. 12, 1958. He studied with G. Haessel; in 1892, entered the New England Cons., where he studied piano with Dennée and Carl Faelten, and composition with Goetschius and Chadwick. In 1897 he went to Salt Lake City, where he settled as a teacher and conductor of the Salt Lake Symph. Orch.; returned to Boston in 1908, and became a prof. of harmony and counterpoint at the New England Cons. (until 1917). In 1917 he joined the U.S. Army, and was bandmaster of the 303rd Field Artillery in France. From 1920 to 1926 he was assistant conductor of the Cleveland Orch., and also conducted children's concerts there; was music critic of the Cleveland *Press* (1929–32). In 1927 he became a prof. of music at Case Western Reserve Univ., retiring in 1950; then lived in Boston and Cleveland. A composer of national tendencies, he wrote in a grand Romantic manner, derived from an intense feeling for American melos.

WORKS: FOR ORCH.: Overtures: *The Nuptials of Attila, Ouverture joyeuse* (Paderewski Prize, 1902); *The Festival of Youth* (1915); *Overture to a Drama* (1919; Cleveland, March 27, 1924); *Fantaisie humoresque* for Piano and Orch. (Boston, Feb. 8, 1918); *Horizons,* First Symph. (Cleveland, Dec. 15, 1927); *Choreographic Suite* (Cleveland, Oct. 22, 1931); 2nd Symph. (Cleveland, March 7, 1940); *Fantasy on Down East Spirituals* (Indianapolis, Nov. 2, 1946); Violin Concerto (1946–47); *Theme and Variations* (Cleveland, April 9, 1953); *Hilaritas,* overture for Concert Band (1942). FOR CHORUS: *Song of the Sea Wind* for Women's Voices and Piano (1915); *He Came All So Still* for Women's Voices a cappella (1915); *Deck Thyself My Soul* for Mixed Chorus and Organ (1918); *Ballad of Trees and the Master* for Mixed Chorus a cappella (1935); *Song of the Pilgrims,* cantata for Tenor Solo, Mixed Chorus, and Orch. (1937); *Invitation to the Dance* for Mixed Chorus and Piano (1937); *Grace for Gardens* for Mixed Chorus a cappella (1938); *Build Thee More Stately Mansions* for Women's Voices (1938); *Psalm XLII* for Chorus and Orch. (1944); *Drive On* for Baritone Solo and Mixed Chorus (1946). CHAMBER MUSIC: 2 violin sonatas (1914, 1927); *Triptych* for Voice and String Quartet (1926); 3 string quartets (1935, 1936, 1944); Piano Quintet (1940); *Praeludium salutatorium* for Flute, Oboe, Horn, Bassoon, Violin, Viola, and Cello (1942); *Divertissement* for Flute, Oboe, Clarinet, Bassoon, and Horn (1943). FOR PIANO: 2 sonatas in F minor (1907, 1929); songs. He publ. a valuable handbook, *The String Quartets of Beethoven* (Cleveland, 1937).

BIBLIOGRAPHY: D. Leedy, "Arthur Shepherd," *Modern Music* (1939); W.S. Newman, "Arthur Shepherd," *Musical Quarterly* (April 1950); R. Loucks, *Arthur Shepherd, American Composer* (Provo, Utah, 1980).

Shera, Frank Henry, English writer on music; b. Sheffield, May 4, 1882; d. there, Feb. 21, 1956. He studied at the Royal College of Music in London, where his teachers were Stanford, Parratt, and Walford Davies. He was music director at Malvern College from 1916 to 1926; in 1928 he was appointed prof. of music at Sheffield Univ., retiring in 1948. He publ. *Musical Groundwork* (1922), *Debussy and Ravel* (1925), and *Elgar's Instrumental Works* (1931) in the Musical Pilgrim series.

Sheremetiev, Alexander, Count, Russian nobleman and amateur musician; b. St. Petersburg, March 12, 1859; d. Ste.-Geneviève-des-Bois, near Paris, May 18, 1931. The private choir maintained by his father, Dmitri, attained wide celebrity in St. Petersburg. In 1882 Count Alexander founded a symph. orch. in his own name, and in 1884 a church choir under the direction of Archangelsky. In 1898 he instituted in St. Petersburg a series of symph. concerts at popular prices, conducted by himself and others. Thanks to his inherited wealth, he was able to engage excellent musicians; presented programs of Russian composers, thus contributing to the cause of national music. He also wrote some pieces himself (*Pathetische Fantasie* for Orch.; chamber music; etc.). After the Revolution of 1917 he went to Paris, and died in poverty, in a Russian charity institution near Paris.

Sheridan, Frank, American pianist; b. New York, May 1, 1898; d. there, April 15, 1962. He studied piano with Harold Bauer; made his debut with the N.Y. Phil. at the Lewisohn Stadium in 1924; toured in Europe in 1929–30; joined the faculty of the Mannes Music School in N.Y.; also taught at Columbia Univ.

Sheriff, Noam, Israeli composer; b. Tel Aviv, Jan. 7, 1935. He took private lessons in composition with Ben-Haim (1949–57); studied philosophy at the Hebrew Univ. of Jerusalem (1956–60); then went to Germany and attended classes of Boris Blacher at the Hochschule für Musik in Berlin (1960–62). Returning to Israel, he taught at the Jerusalem Academy of Music and at the National Academy in Tel Aviv. Most of his works are inspired by Jewish folk rhythms and melodic patterns, arranged in modernistic atonal and asymmetrical configurations.

WORKS: *Song of Degrees* for Orch. (1960); *Ashrei (Blessed Is the Man)* for Contralto, Flute, 2 Harps, and 2 Tom-toms (1961); *Destination 5 Minutes* for Brass and Percussion (1962); *Heptaprisms,* ballet music (1965); *Israel Suite* for Orch. (1965); *Confession* for Solo Cello (1966); *Arabesque* for Solo Flute (1966); *3 Inventions:* for Solo Flute (1967), for Horn (1968), and for Harp (1968); *2 Epigrams* for Chamber Orch. (1968); *Cain,* electronic ballet music (1969); String Quartet (1968–69); *A Stone in the Tower of David* for Orch. (1972); numerous arrangements of folk songs for the Israeli Broadcasting Authority.

Sherman, Norman, American-born composer and bassoonist living in Canada; b. Boston, Feb. 25, 1926. He studied composition at Boston Univ. (1946–50); then took lessons with Messiaen in Paris (1950). He was principal bassoonist with the Winnipeg Symph. Orch. (1957–61), The Hague Phil. in the Netherlands (1961–69), National Arts Centre Orch. of Ottawa (1969–73), Radio Symph. Orch. of Israel (1973–74), and (since 1974) Kingston (Ontario) Symph.; also taught bassoon and chamber music at the Queen's Univ. in Kingston.

WORKS: Concerto for Flute, Clarinet, Horn, Bassoon, and Piano (1948); *Traditions* for Wind Quintet (1948); ballet, *The Red Seed* (1950); *Sinfonia concertante* for Bassoon and Strings (1950; Winnipeg, Jan. 19, 1961); *2 Pieces* for Orch. (No. 1, 1953; No. 2, 1963); *Through the Rainbow and/or across the Valley* for Orch. (1967; Rotterdam, April 25, 1968); *The Re-*

union for Flute, Violin, Viola, and Cello (1967–72); *Thesis* for Orch. (1974; Kingston, March 23, 1975); *Canadian Summer* for Orch. (1975); *Quadron* for String Quartet (1976); *Quintessant* for Wind Quintet (1977); *Bouquet* for Piano or Celesta, and Clarinet and 3 Percussionists (1977).

Sherwood, William Hall, American pianist and pedagogue; b. Lyons, N.Y., Jan. 31, 1854; d. Chicago, Jan. 7, 1911. He was the son of Rev. L.H. Sherwood, the founder of the Lyons Music Academy, from whom he received his primary education; spent 5 years in Germany studying with Kullak in Berlin; also took lessons with Liszt in Weimar. He returned to the U.S. in 1876; taught at the New England Cons., and later at the Chicago Cons.; in 1897 established his Sherwood Piano School in Chicago. Among his publ. compositions for piano are 2 suites and 2 sets of *Gypsy Dances.*

Shibata, Minao, Japanese composer; b. Tokyo, Sept. 29, 1916. He attended Tokyo Univ., graduating from the faculty of science in 1939; took private lessons in composition with Saburo Moroi (1940–43); taught at the Tokyo Univ. of Arts (1959–69).
WORKS: Radio opera, *Strada a Roma* (1961); Piano Sonata (1943); 2 string quartets (1943, 1947); *Classical Suite* for Violin and Piano (1947); *Symbology* for Soprano and Chamber Orch. (1953); *Black Portrait* for Soprano and Chamber Orch. (1954); *Musique concrète* for Stereo Tape (1955); 2 *Improvisations* for Piano (1957, 1968); *Black Distance* for Soprano and Chamber Orch. (1958); 3 *Poems on Katsue Kitazono* for Soprano and Chamber Orch. (1954–58); Sinfonia (1960; Tokyo, Dec. 12, 1960); *Michi (The Street)* for Chorus and 4 Percussion Instruments (1960); *Poem Recited in the Night* for Soprano and Chamber Orch. (1963); *Essay* for 3 Trumpets and 3 Trombones (1965); *Improvisation for Electronic Sounds* (1968); *Imagery* for Marimba (1969); *Display '70 I* and *II* for Ryûteki, Marimba, Percussion, and Tape (1969, 1970); *Concerto for 8* for 8 Flutes (1971).

Shield, William, English violinist and composer; b. Whickham, Durham, March 5, 1748; d. Brightling, Sussex, Jan. 25, 1829. He was taught by his father, a singing master, on whose death he was apprenticed to a shipbuilder; at the same time he took lessons in music with Charles Avison at Newcastle upon Tyne; played violin in various small theaters in the neighborhood; in 1772 he settled in London, as violinist at the King's Theatre; from 1773 to 1791 he played the viola there. He produced his first comic opera, *A Flitch of Bacon,* at the Haymarket Theatre on August. 17, 1778; it was followed by a great number of theatrical pieces; he held the post of composer to Covent Garden Theatre from 1778 to 1791; then traveled in France and Italy, returning to Covent Garden in 1792; he retained this position until 1797. He was appointed Master of the King's Music in 1817. He wrote about 40 light operas, pantomines, musical farces, ballad operas, etc., of which only separate numbers were ever publ.; he also wrote 6 string quartets; 6 string trios; 6 duets for 2 violins; other instrumental pieces; publ. *An Introduction to Harmony* (1800) and *Rudiments of Thorough-bass* (c.1815). He had some original ideas, and was not averse to experimentation; e.g., he wrote movements in 5/4 time.
BIBLIOGRAPHY: G. Hauger, "William Shield," *Music & Letters* (Oct. 1950).

Shifrin, Seymour J., American composer; b. Brooklyn, Feb. 28, 1926; d. Boston, Sept. 26, 1979. He studied with Otto Luening at Columbia Univ., graduating in 1947 (M.A., 1949), and privately with Darius Milhaud and William Schuman. He subsequently taught at the Univ. of Calif., Berkeley (1952–66), and at Brandeis Univ. at Waltham, Mass. (1966–79). He was twice a recipient of Guggenheim fellowship grants (1956, 1959) and of Koussevitzky International Recording awards (1970, 1972). He wrote music of high chromatic consistency, with finely delineated contrapuntal lines often resulting in sharp dissonance.
WORKS: *Music for Orchestra* (1948); *Chamber Symphony* (1952–53); *Cantata to Sophoclean Choruses* for Chorus and Orch. (1957–58); *3 Pieces* for Orch. (1958; Minneapolis, Jan. 8, 1960); *Chronicles* for 3 Male Soloists, Chorus, and Orch. (1970); *5 Last Songs,* with Orch. or Piano (1979; his last work); Cello Sonata (1948); 5 string quartets (1949, 1962, 1965–66, 1966–67, 1971–72); *Serenade* for Oboe, Clarinet, Horn, Viola, and Piano (1954); *Concert Piece* for Solo Violin (1959); *Odes of Shang* for Chorus, Piano, and Percussion (1963); *Satires of Circumstance* for Mezzo-soprano, Flute, Clarinet, Violin, Cello, Double Bass, and Piano (1964); *In Eius Memoriam* for Flute, Clarinet, Violin, Cello, and Piano (1967–68); *Duo* for Violin and Piano (1969); Piano Trio (1974); *A Renaissance Garland* for Renaissance Instruments (1975); *The Nick of Time* for Chamber Ensemble (1977–78); piano pieces, including *4 Cantos* (1950), *Composition* (1950), *Trauermusik* (1956), *The Modern Temper* for Piano, 4-hands (1959), *Fantasy* (1961), *Responses* (1973), and *Waltz* (1977); songs; choruses.

Shilkret, Nathaniel, American composer, arranger, and conductor; b. New York, Jan. 1, 1895; d. Franklin Square, Long Island, N.Y., Feb. 18, 1982. He studied composition with Pietro Floridia; played the clarinet in the Russian Symph. Orch. in N.Y., the N.Y. Phil., and the Metropolitan Opera House Orch.; also in the bands led by John Philip Sousa and Edwin Franko Goldman. In 1916 he became music director of the Victor Talking Machine Co. and created the Victor Salon Orch.; held executive posts with Victor until 1935; then went to Hollywood, where he became active as an arranger of movie scores, but continued to spend part of the season in N.Y., where he led a number of radio broadcasts. He wrote a symph. poem, *Skyward* (1928); a Trombone Concerto (1942); and also various descriptive pieces for orch. Perhaps the most memorable contribution he made to music history was his commissioning of Schoenberg, Stravinsky, Toch, Milhaud, Castelnuovo-Tedesco, and Tansman to write a movement each for a biblical cantata, *Genesis,* to which he himself contributed a movement.

Shimizu, Osamu, prolific Japanese composer; b. Osaka, Nov. 4, 1911. He studied composition with Hashimoto and Hosokawa at the Tokyo Music Academy from 1936 to 1939; was active in the music dept. of Tokyo Radio; wrote articles on music.

WORKS: 10 operas: *The Tale of the Mask-Maker Shuzenji* (Osaka, Nov. 4, 1954); *The Charcoal Princess* (Osaka, Nov. 1, 1956); *The Man Who Shoots at the Blue Sky* (Osaka, Nov. 26, 1956); *Gauche, the Violoncellist* (Osaka, Oct. 11, 1957); *The Singing Skeleton* (Osaka, March 15, 1962); *Shunkan, the Exile* (Osaka, Nov. 18, 1964); *The Merciful Poet,* operetta (1965); *Muko Erabi (The Marriage Contest),* comic opera (Los Angeles, Oct. 3, 1968); *Daibutsu-Kaigen (The Great Image of Buddha),* historic opera on the inauguration of the bronze statue of Buddha on April 9, A.D. 752 (Tokyo, Oct. 2, 1970); *Ikuta Gawa (The River Ikuta;* Tokyo, Nov. 10, 1971); ballets: *The Sun* (1955); *The Crane* (1956); *The Earth* (1957); *Araginu* (1958); *Fire in the Field* (1962); *Love Poems* (1966); numerous cantatas, including *Rennyo* (Tokyo, April 8, 1948), *La Paix* (Tokyo, April 22, 1949), and *Hymn to Dengyō-Daishi* (1966); 3 symphs.: No. 1 (Tokyo, Dec. 8, 1951); No. 2 (1957); No. 3 (1961); *Dance Suite on the Themes of Flowers* for Orch. (1944); *Poème* for Flute and Orch. (1950); *4 Movements on Indian Melodies* for Orch. (1950); *Suite* for Orch. (1953); *Taiheiraku,* gagaku for Orch. (1971); String Quartet (1940); *Ballad* for Flute and Piano (1940); *Ballad* for Violin and Orch. (1941); Quartet for Flute, Oboe, Clarinet, and Bassoon (1958); *Olympic Hymn* for the opening of the Olympic Games in Japan (Tokyo, Oct. 10, 1964).

Shimoyama, Hifumi, Japanese composer; b. Aomoriken, June 21, 1930. He studied violin with Hiroshi Narita and composition with Yoritsuné Matsudaira; was a member of the "Group 20.5," with the aim of promoting new music, which included works by Yori-Aki Matsudaira, Kenjiro Ezaki, and others (1956–62).

WORKS: Violin Sonata (1956); String Quartet (1959); Piano Sonata (1960); *Structure* for 4 Players (1961); *Dialog* for Cello and Piano (1962); *Dialog 1* and *2* for 2 Guitarists (1963, 1971); *Reflections* for Strings in 3 groups (1967; Hamburg Festival of the International Society for Contemporary Music, June 27, 1969); *Zone* for 16 Strings (1970); *2 Ceremonies* for Solo Cello (1969, 1971); *Exorcism* for 5 Strings (1970); *Breath* for Chorus, Percussion, Piano, and 3 Horns (1971; Tokyo, Nov. 9, 1972); *MSP* for Violin and Piano (1972); *Wave* for Solo Cello, Strings, Harp, Piano, and Percussion (1972); *Transmigration* for Percussion and Double Bass (1973); *Poem* for Cello, Piano, and Tape (1974).

Shindo, Tak, American composer of Japanese parentage; b. Sacramento, Calif., Nov. 11, 1922. He studied music at the Univ. of Southern Calif., orchestration with Miklós Rózsa. As a musicologist, he specialized in Japanese music. He became active as a composer and arranger in various motion picture studios in Hollywood.

Shinohara, Makota, Japanese composer; b. Osaka, Dec. 10, 1931. He studied composition with Ikenouchi at the Tokyo Univ. of Arts (1952–54); went to France, where he took lessons at the Paris Cons. (1954–60); subsequently traveled to Germany and took courses with B.A. Zimmermann at the Hochschule für Musik in Cologne (1962–64) and with Stockhausen at the Cologne State Cons. (1964–65); later worked at the Electronic Music Studio of Utrecht Univ. (1965–66) and at the Columbia-Princeton Electronic Music Studio in N.Y. (1971–72). Returning to Japan, he joined the staff of Tokyo Radio.

WORKS: Violin Sonata (1958); *3 pièces concertantes* for Trumpet and Piano (1959); *Obsession* for Oboe and Piano (1960); *Solitude* for Orch. (1961); *Alternance* for 6 Percussionists (1961–62); *Tendance* for Piano (1962); *Vision* and *Mémoires* for Tape (1965, 1966); *Consonance* for Flute, Horn, Cello, Harp, Vibraphone, and Marimba (1967); *Personnage* for Solo Male Voice and Stereo Tape, with optional Pantomime and Color Lighting (1968); *Visione II* for Orch. (1970); *Reflexion* for Solo Oboe (1970); *City Visit* for Tape (1971); *Rencontre* for Percussion and Tape (1972); *Tayutai* for Koto (1972); *Kyudo* for Shakuhachi and Harp (1973).

Shira, Francesco, Italian composer and conductor; b. Malta, Aug. 21, 1808; d. London, Oct. 15, 1883. He studied at the Milan Cons. with Basili; brought out his first opera, *Elena e Malvina,* at La Scala in Milan (Nov. 17, 1832); on the strength of his success he was engaged as conductor of the San Carlos Theater in Lisbon (1833–42); also taught at the Lisbon Cons. In 1842, after a brief sojourn in Paris, he became conductor for the English Opera at the Princess's Theatre; then conducted at Drury Lane in London (1844–47); in 1848 he went over to Covent Garden; returned to Drury Lane in 1852; in later years made a high reputation as a singing teacher, without abandoning composition; wrote the operas *Niccolò de' Lapi* (London, 1863), *Selvaggia* (Venice, Feb. 20, 1875), and *Lia* (Venice, 1876).

Shirinsky, Vasili, Russian violinist and composer; b. Ekaterinodar, Jan. 17, 1901; d. Mamontovka, near Moscow, Aug. 16, 1965. He studied violin with D. Krein and composition with Miaskovsky at the Moscow Cons.; then played in orchs.; in 1923 joined the Moscow Cons. Quartet as 2nd violin. Concurrently, he was active as conductor with the Moscow Radio Orch. (1930–32) and the Opera Theater Orch. (1932–36). In 1939 he was appointed prof. of quartet playing at the Moscow Cons. His works include an opera, *Ivan the Terrible* (1954); 2 symphs. (1936, 1938); Harp Concerto (1957); Violin Concerto (1921); 6 string quartets (1923, 1925, 1929, 1940, 1953, 1958); Piano Sonata (1929); 98 fugues for Piano (1937–63); 24 piano preludes (1962); incidental music for theatrical plays; choruses. His music adheres to the principles of socialist conservatism, emphasizing playability and tonal coherence; it was met with appreciation by the Soviet critics, but its performances were few and far between. His brother, **Sergei Shirinsky** (b. Ekaterinodar, July 18, 1903; d. Moscow, Oct. 18, 1974), was a cellist, who promoted in his programs the cause of Soviet music; he also made playable arrangements of various works by Classical and Romantic composers.

Shirley, George, black American tenor; b. Indianapolis, April 18, 1934. He was educated at Wayne State Univ. in Detroit. After winning the Metropolitan Opera Audition of the Air, he made his debut at the Metropolitan in N.Y. on Nov. 13, 1961; then made appearances with other leading American opera houses; in addition, he sang at Glyndebourne, Covent Garden in London, and La Scala in Milan.

Shirley-Quirk, John, English baritone; b. Liverpool, Aug. 28, 1931. (His hyphenated name is composed of the place-name Shirley, in Derbyshire, where his ancestors lived, and the Celtic appellation in the Manx language, used on the channel isle of Man.) He studied voice with Roy Henderson, and at the same time took courses in chemistry and physics at the Univ. of Liverpool; then taught science in a British Air Force station. Benjamin Britten engaged him to sing in his church parables at the Aldeburgh Festivals; he also sang the multiple roles of several characters in Britten's opera *Death in Venice;* made his formal debut at the Glyndebourne Festival in 1961. He sang the part of the Traveler in the Metropolitan Opera production of *Death in Venice* in N.Y., on Oct. 18, 1974. He also gave concert recitals. In 1975 he was named a Commander of the Order of the British Empire.

Shishov, Ivan, Russian composer; b. Novocherkassk, Oct. 8, 1888; d. Moscow, Feb. 6, 1947. He studied composition with Koreshchenko at the Phil. Society in Moscow, and also took courses in choral polyphony with Kastalsky and in form and orchestration with G. Conus, graduating in 1914. He subsequently conducted choral groups and taught at the Moscow Cons. (1925–31). He wrote the opera *Painter Serf* (Moscow, March 24, 1929); 2 symphs.(1925, 1933); a Requiem in memory of Lenin (1925); a symph. poem, *In the Desert* (1920); a festive overture, *Song of Victory* (1942; anticipating the victory over Nazi Germany by 3 years); piano pieces; choruses; more than 300 songs; he also arranged Russian folk songs.

Shnitke, Alfred. See **Schnittke, Alfred.**

Shore, Dinah (real name, **Frances Rose Shore**), famous American singer of popular music and actress; b. Winchester, Tenn., March 1, 1917. She studied sociology at Vanderbilt Univ. (B.A., 1938). However, she soon experienced a plenary inspiration to sing forth, and betook herself to N.Y.; there she auditioned over the radio station WNEW with the song *Dinah,* which soon became her stage name; she often shared the honors as a radio "thrush" with the rising star Frank Sinatra. By 1940 she reached stardom in the radio polls; Eddie Cantor was so taken with her rendition of the song *Yes, My Darling Daughter,* supposedly derived from a Jewish-Ukrainian folk song, that he hired her to sing on his highly successful radio show. Her records, such as *Blues in the Night* and *Buttons and Bows,* sold into the millions.

Shore, John, English trumpeter; b. London, 1662; d. there, Nov. 20, 1752. In 1707 he succeeded his uncle **William Shore** as Sergeant Trumpeter to the English Court; in 1711 he was one of the 24 musicians to Queen Anne, and also a lutenist of the Chapel Royal. He is the reputed inventor of the tuning fork. Purcell wrote for Shore trumpet obbligatos to many of his songs.

Shore, Samuel Royle, English music scholar, editor, and composer; b. Birmingham, April 12, 1856; d. Hindhead, Surrey, Feb. 19, 1946. He studied organ with A.R. Gaul, but was mostly self-educated in composition and music history. He became an authority on church music; edited The Cathedral Series of music of the 16th–17th centuries; wrote numerous ecclesiastical works, among them a Te Deum, 4 Communion Services, a Requiem, anthems, etc.

Short, "Bobby" (Robert Waltrip Short), black American singer and pianist of popular music; b. Danville, Ill., Sept. 15, 1926. He was self-taught in music; appeared in vaudeville as a child; later went to N.Y., where he began his career as a highly successful nightclub entertainer; also appeared in Los Angeles, London, and Paris with equal success. He ultimately garnered a reputation as the leading café singer of his time. He is the POSSLQ of Gloria Vanderbilt.

Shostakovich, Dmitri, preeminent Russian composer of the Soviet generation, whose style and idiom of composition largely defined the nature of new Russian music; b. St. Petersburg, Sept. 25, 1906; d. Moscow, Aug. 9, 1975. He was a member of a cultured Russian family; his father was an engineer employed in the government office of weights and measures; his mother was a professional pianist. Shostakovich grew up during the most difficult period of Russian revolutionary history, when famine and disease decimated the population of Petrograd. Of frail physique, he suffered from malnutrition; Glazunov, the director of the Petrograd Cons., appealed personally to the Commissar of Education, Lunacharsky, to grant an increased food ration for Shostakovich, essential for his physical survival. Shostakovich received his early musical training from his mother, who taught him piano; in 1919 he entered the Petrograd Cons., where he studied piano with Nikolayev and composition with Maximilian Steinberg; graduated in piano in 1923, and in composition in 1925. As a graduation piece, he submitted his First Symph., written at the age of 18; it was first performed by the Leningrad Phil. on May 12, 1926, under the direction of Nicolai Malko, and subsequently became one of Shostakovich's most popular works. His 2nd Symph., composed for the 10th anniversary of the Soviet Revolution, bearing the surname *Dedication to October* and ending with a rousing choral finale, was less successful despite its revolutionary sentiment. He then wrote a satirical opera, *The Nose,* after Gogol's whimsical story about the sudden disappearance of the nose from the face of a government functionary; here Shostakovich revealed his flair for musical satire; the score featured a variety of modernistic devices and included an interlude written for percussion instruments only. *The Nose* was produced in Leningrad on Jan. 12, 1930, with considerable popular acclaim, but was attacked by officious theater critics as a product of "bourgeois decadence," and quickly withdrawn from the stage. Somewhat in the same satirical style was Shostakovich's ballet *The Golden Age* (1930), which included a celebrated dissonant *Polka,* satirizing the current disarmament conference in Geneva. There followed the 3rd Symph., subtitled *May First* (first perf. in Leningrad on Jan. 21, 1930), with a choral finale saluting the International Workers' Day. Despite its explicit revolutionary content, it failed to earn the approbation of Soviet spokesmen, who dismissed the work as nothing more than a formal gesture of proletarian solidarity. Shostakovich's next work was to precipitate a crisis in his career, as well as in Soviet music in general; it was an opera to the libretto drawn from a short story by the 19th-century Russian writer Leskov, entitled *Lady Macbeth of the District of Mtzensk,* and depicting adultery, murder, and suicide in a merchant home under the Czars. It was produced in Leningrad on Jan. 22, 1934, and was hailed by most Soviet musicians as a significant work comparable to the best productions of Western modern opera. But both the staging and the music ran counter to growing Soviet puritanism; a symph. interlude portraying a scene of adultery behind the bedroom curtain, orchestrated with suggestive passages on the slide trombones, shocked the Soviet officials present at the performance by its bold naturalism. After the Moscow production of the opera, *Pravda,* the official organ of the ruling Communist party, publ. an unsigned (and therefore all the more authoritative) article accusing Shostakovich of creating a "bedlam of noise." The brutality of this assault dismayed Shostakovich; he readily admitted his faults in both content and treatment of the subject, and declared his solemn determination to write music according to the then-emerging formula of "socialist realism." His next stage production was a ballet, *The Limpid Brook,* portraying the pastoral scenes on a Soviet collective farm. In this work Shostakovich tempered his dissonant idiom, and the subject seemed eminently fitting for the Soviet theater; but *The Limpid Brook,* too, was condemned in *Pravda,* this time for an insufficiently dignified treatment of Soviet life. Having been rebuked twice for 2 radical-

ly different theater works, Shostakovich abandoned all attempts to write for the stage, and returned to purely instrumental composition. But as though pursued by vengeful fate, he again suffered a painful reverse. His 4th Symph. was placed in rehearsal by the Leningrad Phil., but withdrawn before the performance when representatives of the musical officialdom and even the orch. musicians themselves sharply criticized the piece. Shostakovich's rehabilitation finally came with the production of his 5th Symph. (Leningrad, Nov. 21, 1937), a work of rhapsodic grandeur, culminating in a powerful climax; it was hailed, as though by spontaneous consensus, as a model of true Soviet art, classical in formal design, lucid in its harmonic idiom, and optimistic in its philosophical connotations. The height of Shostakovich's rise to recognition was achieved in his 7th Symph. He began its composition during the siege of Leningrad by the Nazis in the autumn of 1941; he served in the fire brigade during the air raids; then flew from Leningrad to the temporary Soviet capital in Kuibishev, on the Volga, where he completed the score, which was performed there on March 1, 1942. Its symph. development is realistic in the extreme, with the theme of the Nazis, in mechanical march time, rising to monstrous loudness, only to be overcome and reduced to a pathetic drum dribble by a victorious Russian song. The work became a musical symbol of the Russian struggle against the overwhelmingly superior Nazi war machine; it was given the subtitle *Leningrad Symphony,* and was performed during the war by virtually every orch. in the Allied countries. After the tremendous emotional appeal of the *Leningrad Symphony,* the 8th Symph., written in 1943, had a lesser impact; the 9th, 10th, and 11th symphs. followed (1945, 1953, 1957) without attracting much comment; the 12th Symph., dedicated to the memory of Lenin, aroused a little more interest. But it was left for his 13th Symph. (first perf. in Leningrad on Dec. 18, 1962) to create a controversy which seemed to be Shostakovich's peculiar destiny; its vocal first movement for solo bass and male chorus, to words by the Soviet poet Evtushenko, expressing the horror of the massacre of Jews by the Nazis during their occupation of the city of Kiev, and containing a warning against residual anti-Semitism in Soviet Russia, met with unexpected criticism by the then-chairman of the Communist party, Nikita Khrushchev, who complained about the exclusive attention in Evtushenko's poem to Jewish victims, and his failure to mention the Ukrainians and other nationals who were also slaughtered. The text of the poem was altered to meet these objections, but the 13th Symph. never gained wide acceptance. There followed the remarkable 14th Symph., in 11 sections, scored for voices and orch., to words by Federico García Lorca, Apollinaire, Rilke, and the Russian poet Küchelbecker. Shostakovich's 15th Symph., his last (perf. in Moscow under the direction of Shostakovich's son **Maxim Shostakovich** on Jan. 8, 1972), demonstrated his undying spirit of innovation; the score is set in the key of C major, but it contains a dodecaphonic passage and literal allusions to motives from Rossini's *William Tell*

Shostakovich

Overture and the Fate Motif from Wagner's *Die Walküre*. Shostakovich's adoption, however limited, of themes built on 12 different notes, a procedure that he had himself condemned as anti-musical, is interesting both from the psychological and sociological standpoint; he experimented with these techniques in several other works; his first explicit use of a 12-tone subject occurred in his 12th String Quartet (1968). Equally illuminating is his use in some of his scores of a personal monogram, D.S.C.H. (for D, Es, C, H in German notation, i.e., D, E-flat, C, B). One by one, his early works, originally condemned as unacceptable to Soviet reality, were returned to the stage and the concert hall; the objectionable 4th and 13th symphs. were publ. and recorded; the operas *The Nose* and *Lady Macbeth of the District of Mtzensk* (renamed *Katerina Izmailova*, after the name of the heroine) had several successful revivals.

Shostakovich excelled in instrumental music. Besides the 15 symphs., he wrote 15 string quartets, a String Octet, Piano Quintet, 2 piano trios, Cello Sonata, Violin Sonata, Viola Sonata, 2 violin concertos, 2 cello concertos, 24 preludes for piano, 24 preludes and fugues for piano, 2 piano sonatas, several short piano pieces; also choral works and song cycles.

What is remarkable about Shostakovich is the unfailing consistency of his style of composition. His entire oeuvre, from his first work to the last (147 opus numbers in all), proclaims a personal article of faith. His idiom is unmistakably of the 20th century, making free use of dissonant harmonies and intricate contrapuntal designs, yet never abandoning inherent tonality; his music is teleological, leading invariably to a tonal climax, often in a triumphal triadic declaration. Most of his works carry key signatures; his metrical structure is governed by a unifying rhythmic pulse. Shostakovich is equally eloquent in dramatic and lyric utterance; he has no fear of prolonging his slow movements in relentless dynamic rise and fall; the cumulative power of his kinetic drive in rapid movements is overwhelming. Through all the peripeties of his career, he never changed his musical language in its fundamental modalities. When the flow of his music met obstacles, whether technical or external, he obviated them without changing the main direction. In a special announcement issued after Shostakovich's death, the government of the Union of Soviet Socialist Republics summarized his work as a "remarkable example of fidelity to the traditions of musical classicism, and above all, to the Russian traditions, finding his inspiration in the reality of Soviet life, reasserting and developing in his creative innovations the art of socialist realism, and in so doing, contributing to universal progressive musical culture." His honors, both domestic and foreign, were many: the Order of Lenin (1946, 1956, 1966), People's Artist of the U.S.S.R. (1954), Hero of Socialist Labor (1966), Order of the October Revolution (1971), honorary membership in the American Inst. of the Arts (1943), honorary Doctor of Oxford Univ. (1958), Laureate of the International Sibelius Prize (1958), Doctor of Fine Arts from Northwest-

ern Univ. (1973). He visited the U.S. as a delegate to the World Peace Conference in 1949, as a member of a group of Soviet musicians in 1959, and to receive the degree of D.F.A. from Northwestern Univ. in 1973. A postage stamp of 6 kopecks, bearing his photograph and an excerpt from the *Leningrad Symphony*, was issued by the Soviet Post Office in 1976 to commemorate his 70th birthday. The publication of Shostakovich's collected works in 42 vols., to be completed in 1984, was initiated in 1978.

WORKS: STAGE AND DRAMATIC MUSIC: *The Nose* (Leningrad, Jan. 12, 1930); *Lady Macbeth of the District of Mtzensk* (Leningrad, Jan. 22, 1934; under the title *Katerina Izmailova*, Moscow, Jan. 24, 1934; Metropolitan Opera, N.Y., Feb. 5, 1935; score revised, 1962); *Moskva Cheryomushki* (Moscow, Jan. 24, 1959); ballets: *The Golden Age* (Leningrad, Oct. 26, 1930; contains the celebrated dance number *Polka*); *Bolt* (Leningrad, April 8, 1931); *The Limpid Brook* (Leningrad, April 4, 1935). INCIDENTAL MUSIC: Mayakovsky's comedy *The Bedbug* (1929); *Rule Britannia* (1931); *Hamlet* (1932); *The Human Comedy*, after Balzac (1934); *Salud, España* (1936); *King Lear* (1940); *Russian River* (1944). FILM SCORES: *New Babylon* (1929); *Alone* (1930); *Golden Mountains* (1931); *The Stranger* (1932); *Love and Hatred* (1934); *Maxim's Youth* (1935); *Companions* (1935); *Maxim's Return* (1937); *Friends* (1938); *Great Citizen* (1938); *A Man with a Gun* (1938); *Silly Little Mouse* (1939); *Zoya* (1944); *Plain Folks* (1945); *Young Guard* (1948); *Encounter on the Elba River* (1948); *The Fall of Berlin* (1949); *Unforgettable Year 1919* (1951); *Song of the Great Rivers* (1954); *Gadfly* (1955); *The First Echelon* (1956); *5 Days, 5 Nights* (1960); *Sophie Perovskaya* (1967), a tribute to one of the executed conspirators in the assassination of Czar Alexander II of Russia in 1881; *King Lear* (1970).

FOR ORCH.: 15 symphs.: No. 1 (Leningrad, May 12, 1926); No. 2, with a choral ending, dedicated to the October Revolution (Leningrad, Nov. 6, 1927); No. 3, subtitled *May First* (Leningrad, Jan. 21, 1930); No. 4 (1936; Moscow, Jan. 20, 1962); No. 5 (Leningrad, Nov. 21, 1937); No. 6 (Leningrad, Nov. 5, 1939); No. 7, *Leningrad Symphony* (Kuibishev, March 1, 1942; first American perf., NBC Symph., N.Y., Toscanini conducting, July 19, 1942); No. 8 (Moscow, Nov. 4, 1943); No. 9 (Leningrad, Nov. 3, 1945); No. 10 (Leningrad, Dec. 17, 1953); No. 11 (Moscow, Oct. 30, 1957); No. 12, *The Year 1917*, dedicated to the memory of Lenin (Leningrad, Oct. 1, 1961); No. 13 for Orch., Male Chorus, and Solo Bass, to words by Evtushenko (1961; Moscow, Dec. 18, 1962); No. 14 for Soprano, Bass, and Chamber Orch., in 11 sections (Leningrad, Sept. 29, 1969); No. 15 (Moscow, Jan. 8, 1972); Piano Concerto No. 1 for Piano, Trumpet, and Strings (Leningrad, Oct. 15, 1933); *5 Fragments* (1935; Moscow, April 26, 1965); Piano Concerto No. 2 (Moscow, May 10, 1957; Maxim Shostakovich, son of the composer, soloist); Violin Concerto No. 1 (Leningrad, Oct. 29, 1955); Violin Concerto No. 2 (Moscow, Sept. 26, 1967); Cello Concerto No. 1 (Leningrad, Oct. 4, 1959); Cello Concerto No. 2 (Moscow, Sept. 25, 1966).

OTHER WORKS FOR ORCH.: *Scherzo* (1919); *Theme and Variations* (1922); *Tahiti Trot*, orchestration of

Tea for 2 by Youmans (1928); *Technically Killed,* a circus piece (1931); *Suite* for Jazz Orch. (Leningrad, Nov. 28, 1938); orchestration of Mussorgsky's opera *Boris Godunov* (1940); *Festive Overture* (1954); *Overture on Russian and Kirghiz Folk Themes* (1963; Moscow, Oct. 10, 1965); *Funeral and Triumphant Prelude in Memory of the Heroes of the Battle of Stalingrad* (1967); *October,* symph. poem (Moscow, Sept. 26, 1967); *March of Soviet Militia* for Band (1970); 4 ballet suites (1949, 1951, 1952, 1953); also *2 Fables of Krylov,* op. 4 (first perf. Sept. 26, 1981, at a memorial concert in Moscow).

VOCAL WORKS: 6 songs to words by Japanese poets for Voice and Orch. (1932–38); *Leningrad* for Chorus and Orch. (Moscow, Oct. 15, 1942); *Song of the Forests,* cantata (Leningrad, Nov. 15, 1949); *Democratic Vistas,* a cycle of 10 poems by Walt Whitman for Chorus and Orch. (Moscow, Oct. 10, 1951); 4 songs to texts by Pushkin (1936); 6 songs to words by Burns, Shakespeare, and Walter Raleigh (1942); *Song of the Fatherland* for Soloists, Chorus, and Orch. (1947); *From Jewish Folk Poetry,* vocal cycle, with Piano (1948); *The Sun Shines over Our Fatherland,* cantata for Boys' Chorus, Mixed Choir, and Orch. (1952); *4 Monologues* to words by Pushkin for Voice and Piano (1952); *5 Songs* to words by Dolmatovsky for Voice and Piano (1954); *Spanish Songs* (1956); *Satires (Scenes from the Past),* 5 songs for Voice and Piano (1960); *The Death of Stepan Razin* for Orch., Mixed Choir, and Bass, to words by Evtushenko (Moscow, Dec. 28, 1964); *5 Songs* to texts from the Moscow comic magazine *Crocodile* (1965); *Foreword to My Collected Works and a Brief Meditation anent This Foreword* for Bass Voice and Orch. (1966); *7 Songs* to words by Alexander Blok, for Soprano, Violin, Cello, and Piano (1967); *Spring, Spring,* song to words by Pushkin (1967); *Faith,* ballad cycle for Men's Chorus a cappella (1970); *6 Songs* for Contralto and Chamber Orch. by Marina Tsvetayeva (1974); *Suite* for Bass and Piano, to texts by Michelangelo (1974); *4 Songs* to words from Dostoyevsky for Bass and Piano (1975).

CHAMBER MUSIC: Piano Trio No. 1 (1923); *3 Pieces* for Cello and Piano (1924); *2 Pieces* for String Octet (1925); Cello Sonata (1934); 15 string quartets (1938, 1944, 1946, 1949, 1952, 1956, 1960, 1960, 1964, 1964, 1966, 1968, 1970, 1973, 1974); Piano Quintet (1940); 2 piano trios (1923, 1944); Violin Sonata (1968); Viola Sonata (1975).

PIANO MUSIC: *8 Preludes* (1919–20); *3 Fantastic Dances* (1922); *Suite* for 2 Pianos (1922); 2 sonatas (1926, 1942); *Aphorisms* (1927); *24 Preludes* (1932–33); *Children's Album* (1945); *Puppets' Dances* (1946); *24 Preludes and Fugues* (1950–51); Concertino for 2 Pianos (1953).

BIBLIOGRAPHY: N. Slonimsky, "Dmitri Shostakovich," *Musical Quarterly* (Oct. 1942); Victor Seroff, *Dmitri Shostakovitch: The Life and Background of a Soviet Composer* (N.Y., 1943); M. Sahlberg-Vatchadze, *Shostakovich* (Paris, 1945); Ivan Martinov, *Shostakovich* (Moscow, 1946; in Eng., N.Y., 1947); L. Danilevitch, *Dmitri Shostakovich* (Moscow, 1958); D. Rabinovich, *Dmitri Shostakovich* (Foreign Languages Publishing House; in Eng., Moscow, 1959); G. Ordzhonokidze, compiler, *Dmitri* *Shostakovich,* collection of articles (Moscow, 1967); *Dmitri Shostakovich,* articles and materials, ed. by G. Schneerson (Moscow, 1976); M. Sabinina, *Shostakovich the Symphonist* (Moscow, 1976); R. Blokker *The Music of Dmitri Shostakovich* (Rutherford, N.J., 1979); Solomon Volkov, *Testimony* (N.Y., 1980; a highly controversial biography purported to be the accurate transcript of Volkov's conversations with Shostakovich, in which he relates the horrors of Soviet life under Stalin and his own fear of persecution; Shostakovich's family vehemently protested against the views attributed to Shostakovich in the book, and vituperative accounts of *Testimony* appeared in the Soviet press); D. and L. Sollertinsky, *Pages from the Life of Dmitri Shostakovich* (London, 1981); C. Norris, ed., *Shostakovich: The Man and His Music* (London, 1982); E. Roseberry, *Shostakovich: His Life and Times* (Tunbridge Wells, 1982); D. Hulme, *Shostakovich Catalogue* (Muir of Ord, Ross-shire, 1982); J. Devlin, *Shostakovich* (Borough Green, 1983). See also *Modern Music . . . Analytic Index,* compiled by Wayne Shirley, ed. by Wm. and C. Lichtenwanger (N.Y., 1976; pp. 197–99).

Shostakovich, Dmitri, Russian pianist, son of **Maxim Shostakovich** and grandson of **Dmitri Shostakovich;** b. Moscow, Aug. 9, 1961. He studied piano with Elena Khoven; made his debut as a soloist with the State Academy Symph. Orch. in 1978 in Moscow; also toured Italy in 1979. In April 1981 he was soloist with the U.S.S.R. State Radio Orch. during its tour of West Germany, conducted by his father, who then decided not to return to Russia; both applied for resident visas for the U.S., which were granted. In Sept. 1981 he joined his father and Mstislav Rostropovich in a series of concerts with the National Symph. Orch. of Washington, D.C., in celebration of the 75th anniversary of the birth of his grandfather. He also appeared with the Israel Phil., the Oslo Phil., the London Phil., and the Los Angeles Phil.

Shostakovich, Maxim, Russian conductor, son of **Dmitri Shostakovich;** b. Leningrad, May 10, 1938. He studied piano at the Moscow Cons. with Yakov Flier, and conducting with Gauk and Rozhdestvensky. In 1963 he became assistant conductor of the Moscow Symph. Orch., and in 1966, of the U.S.S.R. State Orch. From 1971 to 1981 he was principal conductor and artistic director of the U.S.S.R. State Radio Orch. He made many appearances as a guest conductor in the Soviet Union and in Europe; also toured Japan, Mexico, and Canada; appeared in the U.S. in 1969, conducting the U.S.S.R. State Orch. on its American tour. He gained his reputation mainly by his obviously authentic interpretations of his father's works. During his tour in West Germany with the U.S.S.R. State Radio Orch. in April 1981, he announced his decision not to return to the Soviet Union. His defection aroused a burst of indignation in the Soviet press, and he was denounced as a traitor to his father's legacy. Eventually he and his son, the pianist Dmitri, settled in the U.S. On Memorial Day, 1981, he conducted the National Symph. Orch. of Washington, D.C., in a concert on the West Lawn of the U.S. Capitol. He was subsequently a guest conductor of the Atlanta Symph., the Los Angeles Phil., the Chicago Symph., and other orchs.

BIBLIOGRAPHY: *U.S. News & World Report* (Nov. 9, 1981; interview).

Shtogarenko, Andrei, Ukrainian composer; b. Noviye Kaidaki, near Ekaterinoslav, Oct. 15, 1902. He studied at the Kharkov Cons., graduating in 1936. During World War II he worked in Turkmenia. From 1954 to 1968 he was director of the Kiev Cons.; a prof. of music there from 1960. Virtually all of his music is devoted to Ukrainian subjects.

WORKS: 3 symphs. (1947, 1965, 1968); symph. cantata, *My Ukraine* (1943); cantata, *Moscow,* for the 800th anniversary of its foundation (1948); *Partisan Sketches* for Orch. (1957); *The Dawn of Communism Has Come* for Chorus, Vocal Soloists, and Orch. (1957); choral symph., *Lenin Walks the Planet* (1958); Violin Concerto (1969); choruses; songs; film scores.

BIBLIOGRAPHY: A. Znosco-Borovsky, *Andrei Shtogarenko* (Kiev, 1947).

Shulman, Alan, American composer; b. Baltimore, June 4, 1915. He studied cello at the Peabody Cons. of Music in Baltimore and with Felix Salmond in N.Y.; took a course in composition with Bernard Wagenaar at the Juilliard School of Music, graduating in 1937; during World War II was in the U.S. Maritime Service.

WORKS: For Orch.: *A Laurentian Overture* (N.Y., Jan. 7, 1952); *Waltzes* (1949); *Popocatepetl,* symph. picture (1952); *Theme and Variations* for Viola and Orch. (N.Y., Feb. 17, 1941); *Pastorale and Dance* for Violin and Orch. (N.Y., July 15, 1944); Cello Concerto (1948; N.Y., April 13, 1950); chamber music: *Rendezvous* for Clarinet and Strings (1946); *Threnody* for String Quartet (1950); *Suite Miniature* for Octet of Cellos (1956); *Suite* for Solo Cello (1950); *Top Brass* for 12 Brass Instruments (Portland, Oreg., April 25, 1958); *4 Diversions* for a Pride of Cellos (Philadelphia, April 6, 1975); numerous short works for violin, for cello, for piano, etc.

Shumsky, Oscar, American violinist; b. Philadelphia, March 23, 1917. He began fiddling as a mere toddler; was a minuscule soloist at the age of 8 with the Philadelphia Orch. under Stokowski. He then began to study in earnest, first with Leopold Auer, then at the Curtis Inst. of Music in Philadelphia with Efrem Zimbalist. Soon he became a professional violinist; was a member of the NBC Symph. Orch. (1939–42); then taught at the Peabody Cons. in Baltimore. In 1953 he joined the staff of the Juilliard School of Music in N.Y.; also taught classes at the Curtis Inst. (1961–65) and, from 1975, at the Yale School of Music.

Shure, Leonard, American pianist; b. Los Angeles, April 10, 1910. He studied in Berlin with Artur Schnabel; returning to the U.S. in 1933, he taught at the New England Cons. of Music; then was engaged at the School of Music of the Univ. of Texas in Austin. His manner of playing is sweepingly Romantic and subjective.

Sibelius, Jean (Johan Julius Christian), great Finnish composer whose music, infused with the deeply felt modalities of national folk songs, opened a modern era of Northern musical art; b. Hämeenlinna, Dec. 8, 1865; d. Järvenpää, Sept. 20, 1957. The family name stems from a Finnish peasant named Sibbe, traced back to the late 17th century; the Latin noun ending was commonly added among educated classes in Scandinavia. Sibelius was the son of an army surgeon; from early childhood he showed a natural affinity for music. At the age of 9 he began to study piano; then took violin lessons with Gustaf Levander, a local bandmaster. He learned to play violin well enough to take part in amateur performances of chamber music. In 1885 he enrolled at the Univ. of Helsingfors (Helsinki), to study law, but abandoned it after the first semester. In the fall of 1885 he entered the Helsingfors Cons., where he studied violin with Vasiliev and Csillag; he also took courses in composition with the eminent Finnish musician Wegelius. In 1889 his String Quartet was performed in public, and produced a sufficiently favorable impression to obtain for him a government stipend for further study in Berlin, where he took lessons in counterpoint and fugue with Albert Becker. Later he proceeded to Vienna for additional musical training, and became a student of Robert Fuchs and Karl Goldmark (1890–91). In 1892 he married Aino Järnefelt. From then on, his destiny as a national Finnish composer was determined; the music he wrote was inspired by native legends, with the great Finnish epic *Kalevala* as a prime source of inspiration. On April 28, 1892, his symph. poem *Kullervo,* scored for soloists, chorus, and orch., was first performed in Helsingfors. There followed one of his most remarkable works, the symph. poem entitled simply *En Saga,* that is, "a legend"; in it he displayed to the full his genius for variation forms, based on a cumulative growth of a basic theme adorned but never encumbered with effective contrapuntal embellishments. From 1892 to 1900 he taught theory of composition at the Helsingfors Cons. In 1897 the Finnish Senate granted him an annual stipend of 3,000 marks. On April 26, 1899, he conducted in Helsingfors the premiere of his First Symph., in E minor. He led first performances of all of his symphs., in 1902, 1907, 1911, 1915, 1923, and 1924. On July 2, 1900, the Helsingfors Phil. gave the first performance of his most celebrated and most profoundly moving patriotic work, *Finlandia.* Its melody soon became identified among Finnish patriots with the aspiration for national independence, so that the Czarist government went to the extreme of forbidding its performances during periods of political unrest. In 1901 Sibelius was invited to conduct his works at the annual festival of the Allgemeiner Deutscher Tonkünstlerverein at Heidelberg. In 1904 he settled in his country home at Järvenpää, where he remained for the rest of his life; he traveled rarely. In 1913 he accepted a commission for an orch. work from the American music patron Carl Stoeckel, to be performed at the 28th annual Festival at Norfolk, Conn. For it he contributed a symph. legend, *Aalotaret* (*Nymphs of the Ocean;* it was later revised under the title *The Oceanides*). He took his only sea voyage to America to conduct its premiere on June 4, 1914; on that occasion he received the honorary degree of Mus.Doc. from Yale Univ. Returning to Finland just before the outbreak of World War I, Sibelius withdrew into seclusion, but continued to work. He made his last public appearance abroad in Stockholm, conducting his 7th Symph. there on March 24, 1924. He wrote 2 more works after that, including a score for Shakespeare's *The Tempest* and a symph. poem, *Tapiola;* he practically ceased to compose after 1927. At various times rumors were circulated that he had completed his 8th Symph., but no one had actually seen even any sketches of this work. One persistent story was that Sibelius himself decided to burn his incomplete works. Although willing to receive journalists and reporters, he avoided answering questions about his music. He lived out his very long life as a retired person, absorbed in family interests; in some modest ways he was even a *bon vivant;* he liked his cigars and his beer, and he showed no diminution in his mental alertness. Only once was his peaceful life gravely disrupted; this was when the Russian army invaded Finland in 1940; Sibelius sent an anguished appeal to America to save his country, which by the perverse fate of world politics became allied with Nazi Germany. But after the war Sibelius cordially received a delegation of Soviet composers who made a reverential pilgrimage to his rural retreat.

Honors were showered upon him; festivals of his music became annual events in Helsinki; a postage stamp bearing his likeness was issued by the Finnish government on his 80th birthday; special publications, biographical, bibliographical, and photographic, were publ. in Finland. Artistically, too, Sibelius attained the status of greatness rarely vouchsafed to a living musician; several important contemporary composers paid him homage by acknowledging their debt of inspiration to him, Vaughan Williams among them. Sibelius was the last representative of 19th-century nationalistic Romanticism. He stayed aloof from modern developments, but he was not uninterested in reading scores and listening to performances on the radio of works of such men as Schoenberg, Prokofiev, Bartók, and Shostakovich.

The music of Sibelius marked the culmination of the growth of national Finnish art, in which Pacius was the protagonist, and Wegelius, the teacher of Sibelius, a worthy cultivator. Like his predecessors, Sibelius was schooled in the Germanic tradition, and his early works reflect German lyricism and German dramatic thought. He opened a new era in Finnish music when he abandoned formal conventions and began to write music that seemed inchoate and diffuse but followed a powerful line of development by variation and repetition; a parallel with Beethoven's late works has frequently been

drawn. The thematic material employed by Sibelius is not modeled directly on known Finnish folk songs; rather, he re-created the characteristic melodic patterns of folk music. The prevailing mood is somber, even tragic, with a certain elemental sweep and grandeur. His instrumentation is highly individual, with long songful solo passages, and with protracted transitions that are treated as integral parts of the music. His genius found its most eloquent expression in his symphs. and symph. poems; he wrote relatively little chamber music, and only in his earlier years. His only opera, *The Maid in the Tower* (1896), to a text in Swedish, was never publ. He wrote some incidental music for the stage; the celebrated *Valse triste* was written in 1903 for *Kuolema,* a play by Arvid Järnefelt, brother-in-law of Sibelius.

WORKS: FOR THE STAGE: *Jungfrun i tornet* (*The Maid in the Tower*), opera (1896; Helsinki, Nov. 7, 1896); incidental music: Overture, op. 10, and Suite, op. 11, to *Karelia* (1893; Helsinki, Nov. 13, 1893); *King Kristian II,* op. 27, for a play by A. Paul (1898; Helsinki, Feb. 28, 1898, composer conducting); *Kuolema (Death)* for Strings and Percussion, op. 44, for a play by Arvid Järnefelt (1903; Helsinki, Dec. 2, 1903, composer conducting); *Pelléas et Mélisande,* op. 46, for Maeterlinck's play (1905; Helsinki, March 17, 1905, composer conducting); *Belshazzar's Feast,* op. 51, for a play by H. Procopé (1906; Helsinki, Nov. 7, 1906, composer conducting); *Svanevhit (Swanwhite),* op. 54, for Strindberg's play (1908; Helsinki, April 8, 1908, composer conducting); *Ödlan (The Lizard)* for Solo Violin and String Quintet, op. 8, for a play by M. Lybeck (1909; Helsinki, April 6, 1910, composer conducting); *Jedermann* for Mixed Chorus, Piano, Organ, and Orch., op. 83, for Hofmannsthal's play (1916; Helsinki, Nov. 5, 1916); *The Tempest,* op. 109, for Shakespeare's play (1925; Copenhagen, March 16, 1926); also *Näcken (The Watersprite),* 2 songs with Piano Trio, for a play by Wennerberg (1888); *The Language of the Birds,* a wedding march for A. Paul's play *Die Sprache der Vögel* (1911); *Scaramouche,* op. 71, a "tragic pantomime" after the play by P. Knudsen and M. Bloch (1913; Copenhagen, May 12, 1922).

ORCH. MUSIC: 7 symphs.: No. 1, in E minor, op. 39 (1899; Helsinki, April 26, 1899, composer conducting); No. 2, in D major, op. 43 (1901–2; Helsinki, March 8, 1902, composer conducting); No. 3, in C major, op. 52 (1904–7; Helsinki, Sept. 25, 1907, composer conducting); No. 4, in A minor, op. 63 (1911; Helsinki, April 3, 1911, composer conducting); No. 5, in E-flat major, op. 82 (1915; Helsinki, Dec. 8, 1915, Kajanus conducting; revised 1916; Helsinki, Dec. 14, 1916; revised 1919; Helsinki, Nov. 24, 1919); No. 6, in D minor, op. 104 (1923; Helsinki, Feb. 19, 1923, composer conducting); No. 7, in C major, op. 105 (1924; Stockholm, March 24, 1924, composer conducting). Other works: *Andantino* and *Menuetto* for Clarinet, 2 Cornets, 2 Horns, and Baritone (1890–91); Overture in E major (1890–91); *Scène de ballet* (1891); *Menuetto* (1894); *Skogsrået (The Wood Nymph),* tone poem, op. 15 (1894); *Vårsång (Spring Song),* tone poem, op. 16 (1894; Vaasa, June 21, 1894); *4 Legends,* op. 22 (all 4 first perf. in Helsinki, April

Sibelius

13, 1896, composer conducting): 1, *Lemminkäinen and the Maidens of the Island* (1895; revised 1897 and 1939); 2, *The Swan of Tuonela* (1893; revised 1897 and 1900); 3, *Lemminkäinen in Tuonela* (1895; revised 1897 and 1939); 4, *Lemminkäinen's Homeward Journey* (1895; revised 1897 and 1900); *King Kristian II*, suite from the incidental music, op. 27 (1898); *Scènes historiques*, op. 25, I (1899; revised 1911); *Finlandia*, tone poem, op. 26 (1899; revised 1900; Helsinki, July 2, 1900, Kajanus conducting); *Björneborgarnas March* (1900); *Cortège* (1901); Overture in A minor (1902; Helsinki, March 3, 1902, composer conducting); *Romance* in C major for Strings, op. 42 (1903; Turku, March 1904, composer conducting); Concerto in D minor for Violin and Orch., op. 47 (1903; Helsinki, Feb. 8, 1904; Viktor Nováček, soloist; composer conducting; revised 1905; Berlin, Oct. 19, 1905; Karl Halir, soloist; R. Strauss conducting); *Cassazione*, op. 6 (1904); *Pelléas et Mélisande*, suite from the incidental music, op. 46 (1905); *Pohjola's Daughter*, symph. fantasia, op. 49 (1906; St. Petersburg, Dec. 29, 1906, composer conducting); *Belshazzar's Feast*, suite from the incidental music, op. 51 (1906; Helsinki, Sept. 25, 1907); *Pan and Echo*, dance intermezzo, op. 53 (1906); *Nightride and Sunrise*, tone poem, op. 55 (1907; St. Petersburg, Jan. 1909); *Svanevhit (Swanwhite)*, suite from the incidental music, op. 54 (1908); *In Memoriam*, funeral march, op. 59 (1909; Helsinki, April 3, 1911); *The Dryad*, tone poem (1910), and *Dance Intermezzo* (1907), op. 45; *Rakastava (The Lover)* for Strings and Percussion, op. 14 (1911); *Scènes historiques*, op. 66, II (1912); 2 serenades for Violin and Orch., op. 69: No. 1, in D major (1912), and No. 2, in G minor (1913); *The Bard*, tone poem, op. 64 (1913; revised 1914); *Aallottaret (Nymphs of the Ocean)*, tone poem, op. 73 (1914; 2nd version as *The Oceanides*, 1914; the latter first perf. at the Norfolk [Conn.] Festival, June 4, 1914, composer conducting); 2 pieces for Violin or Cello, and Orch., op. 77 (1914); *2 Humoresques* for Violin and Orch., op. 87 (1917); *4 Humoresques* for Violin and Orch., op. 89 (also numbered as 3–6 in continuation of the preceding; 1917); *Promotiomarssi (Academic March)* (1919); 3 pieces, op. 96: 1, *Valse lyrique* (1920); 2, *Autrefois, Scène pastorale* for 2 Voices and Orch. (1919); 3, *Valse chevaleresque* (1920); *Suite mignonne* for 2 Flutes and Strings, op. 98a (1921); *Suite champêtre* for Strings, op. 98b (1921); *Andante festivo* for Strings and Percussion (1922; also for String Quartet); *Suite caractéristique* for Harp and Strings, op. 100 (1922); *The Tempest*, concert version of the incidental music, op. 109 (1925); *Tapiola*, tone poem, op. 112 (1926; N.Y., Dec. 26, 1926, W. Damrosch conducting).

CHAMBER MUSIC: *Vattendroppar (Water Drops)* for Violin and Cello (1875–76); Quartet in E minor for Piano, 2 Violins, and Cello (1881–82); Piano Trio in A minor (1881–82); Sonata in D minor for Violin and Piano (1881–82); *Andantino* for Cello and Piano (1884); Quartet for Violin, Cello, Harmonium, and Piano (1884?); String Quartet in E-flat major (1885); Suite in G minor for String Trio (1885); Duo for Violin and Viola (1886); *Andante cantabile* for Violin and Piano (1887); Piano Trio, *Korpo* (1887); Piano Trio in C major, *Loviisa* (1888); *Romance and Epilogue* for Violin and Piano, op. 2 (1888; revised 1912); *Fugue* for String Quartet (1888); *Theme and Variations* in C-sharp minor for String Quartet (1888); String Quartet in A minor (1889); Sonata in F major for Violin and Piano (1889); Suite in A major for String Trio (1889); Quintet in G minor for Piano and Strings (1889–90); String Quartet in B-flat major, op. 4 (1890); Octet for Flute, Clarinet, and Strings (1891); Quartet in C major for Piano, 2 Violins, and Cello (1891); Rondo for Viola and Piano (1893); *Kehtolaulu (Lullaby)* for Violin and Kantele (1899); Fantasia for Cello and Piano (1899–1900); *Malinconia* for Cello and Piano, op. 20 (1901); String Quartet in D minor, op. 56, *Voces intimae* (1909); 4 pieces for Violin or Cello, and Piano, op. 78: 1, *Impromptu* (1915); 2, *Romance* (1915); 3, *Religioso* (1919); 4, *Rigaudon* (1915); 6 pieces for Violin and Piano, op. 79: *Souvenir, Tempo di menuetto, Danse caractéristique, Sérénade, Danse idyll,* and *Berceuse* (1915); Sonatina in E major for Violin and Piano, op. 80 (1915); 5 pieces for Violin and Cello, op. 81: *Mazurka, Rondino, Waltz, Aubade,* and *Menuetto* (1915); *Novelette* for Violin and Piano, op. 102 (1923); *5 danses champêtres* for Violin and Piano, op. 106 (1925); 4 pieces for Violin and Piano, op. 115: *On the Heath, Ballade, Humoresque,* and *The Bells* (1929); 3 pieces for Violin and Piano, op. 116: *Scène de danse, Danse caractéristique,* and *Rondeau romantique* (1929); also *Adagio* for String Quartet (date unknown); Piano Sonata in F major, op. 12 (1893); over 25 other pieces for piano composed between 1893 and 1929. For Organ: 2 pieces, op. 111: *Intrada* (1925) and *Surusoitto (Mournful Music;* 1931).

VOCAL MUSIC: *Kullervo*, symph. poem for Soprano, Baritone, Male Chorus, and Orch., op. 7 (1892; Helsinki, April 28, 1892); *Rakastava (The Lover)* for Male Chorus a cappella, op. 14 (1893; Helsinki, April 28, 1894); *Laulu Lemminkäiselle (A Song for Lemminkäinen)* for Male Chorus and Orch., op. 31, No. 1 (1900); *Har du mod? (Have You Courage?)* for Male Chorus and Orch., op. 31, No. 2 (1904); *Atenarnes sång (The Song of the Athenians)* for Male Voices, with Wind Instruments and Percussion, op. 31, No. 3 (1899; Helsinki, April 26, 1899); *Tulen synty (The Origin of Fire)* for Baritone, Male Chorus, and Orch., op. 32 (1902; Helsinki, April 9, 1902, composer conducting; revised 1910); *Vapautettu kuningatar (The Liberated Queen)*, cantata for Mixed Chorus and Orch., op. 48 (1906; Helsinki, May 12, 1906); *Luonnotar (Spirit of Nature)*, tone poem for Soprano and Orch., op. 70 (1910; Gloucester, Sept. 10, 1913); *Oma maa (Our Native Land)*, cantata for Mixed Chorus and Orch., op. 92 (1918); *Jordens sång (Song of the Earth)*, cantata for Mixed Chorus and Orch., op. 93 (1919); *Maan virsi (Hymn of the Earth)*, cantata for Mixed Chorus and Orch., op. 95 (1920; Helsinki, June 1920, composer conducting); *Väinön virsi (Väinö's Song)* for Mixed Chorus and Orch., op. 110 (1926; Helsinki, June 28, 1926, Kajanus conducting); *Masonic Ritual Music* for Male Voices, Piano, and Organ, op. 113 (1927–46; revised 1948); also numerous other choral works, and 95 songs composed between 1891 and 1917.

BIBLIOGRAPHY: K. Flodin, *Finska musiker* (Helsinki, 1900); R. Newmarch, *J. S.: A Finnish Composer* (Leipzig, 1906); E. Furuhjelm, *J. S.: Hans tondikting och drag ur hans liv* (Borgå, 1916); W. Niemann, *J. S.* (Leipzig, 1917); C. Gray, *S.* (London, 1931; 2nd ed., 1945); K. Ekman, *J. S.: En konstnärs liv och personlighet* (Stockholm, 1935; Eng. trans. as *J. S.: His Life and Personality,* Helsinki, 1935; 4th Swedish ed., 1959); C. Gray, *S.: The Symphonies* (London, 1935); A. Meyer, "S.: Symphonist," *Musical Quarterly* (Jan. 1936); B. de Törne, *S.: A Close-Up* (London, 1937); R. Newmarch, *J. S.: A Short History of a Long Friendship* (Boston, 1939; 2nd ed., 1945); H. Askeli, "A Sketch of S. the Man," *Musical Quarterly* (Jan. 1940); B. Sandberg, *J. S.* (Helsinki, 1940); E. Arnold, *Finlandia: The Story of S.* (N.Y., 1941; 2nd ed., 1951); E. Roiha, *Die Symphonien von J. S.: Eine formanalytische Studie* (Jyväskylä, 1941); I. Krohn, *Der Formenbau in den Symphonien von J. S.* (Helsinki, 1942); E. Tanzberger, *Die symphonischen Dichtungen von J. S. (Ein inhalts- und form-analytische Studie)* (Würzburg, 1943); S. Levas, *J. S. ja hänen Ainolansa* (Helsinki, 1945; 2nd ed., 1955); M. Similä, *Sibeliana* (Helsinki, 1945); B. de Törne, *S., i närbild och samtal* (Helsinki, 1945; 2nd ed., 1955); G. Abraham, ed., *S.: A Symposium* (London, 1947; 2nd ed., 1952); I. Hannikainen, *S. and the Development of Finnish Music* (London, 1948); N.-E. Ringbom, *S.* (Stockholm, 1948; Eng. trans., Norman, Okla., 1954); V. Helasvuo, *S. and the Music of Finland* (Helsinki, 1952; 2nd ed., 1957); O. Andersson, *J. S. i Amerika* (Åbo, 1955); S. Parmet, *S. symfonier* (Helsinki, 1955; Eng. trans. as *The Symphonies of S.: A Study in Musical Appreciation,* London, 1959); L. Solanterä, *The Works of J. S.* (Helsinki, 1955); H. Johnson, *J. S.* (N.Y., 1959); E. Tanzberger, *J. S.: Eine Monographie* (Wiesbaden, 1962); F. Blum, *J. S.: An International Bibliography on the Occasion of the Centennial Celebrations, 1965* (Detroit, 1965); R. Layton, *S.* (London, 1965; 2nd ed., revised, 1978); E. Tawaststjerna, *J. S.* (the definitive study; 3 vols., Helsinki, 1965–72; Eng. trans. by R. Layton, 1976—); R. Layton, *The World of S.* (London, 1970); B. James, *The Music of J. S.* (East Brunswick, N.J.; London; and Mississauga, Ontario; 1983).

Siboni, Erik (Anton Waldemar), Danish pianist and composer; b. Copenhagen, Aug. 26, 1828; d. Frederiksberg, Feb. 22, 1892. He was the son of the tenor **Giuseppe Siboni** (b. Forli, Jan. 27, 1780; d. Copenhagen, March 28, 1839, as director of the Opera and Cons.); studied with J.P.E. Hartmann; then with Moscheles and Hauptmann at Leipzig and with Sechter at Vienna; returned to Copenhagen, and in 1865 became organist and prof. of piano at the Royal Academy of Music at Sorö; retired in 1883.
WORKS: Operas: *Loreley* (Copenhagen, 1859) and *Carl II's flugt (Flight of Charles II;* Copenhagen, 1862); 2 symphs.; Piano Quartet; other chamber music; choral works: *Slaget ved Murten (Battle of Murten); Stormen paa København (Storming of Copenhagen);* etc.

Sicilianos, Yorgo, Greek composer; b. Athens, Aug. 29, 1922. He studied composition with Varvoglis (1944–49); then went to Rome, where he took a course with Pizzetti at the Santa Cecilia Academy (1951–53); supplemented his music education at the Paris Cons. (1953–54). On a Fulbright scholarship he traveled to the U.S., where he took a course in composition with Walter Piston at Harvard Univ. and attended the summer class of Boris Blacher at the Berkshire Center in Tanglewood, Mass.; also enrolled for an academic season at the Juilliard School of Music in N.Y., where he studied with Persichetti (1955–56). Upon his return to Greece, he occupied various educational and administrative posts; in 1967 he was appointed to the faculty of Pierce College in Athens. His style of composition is classical in format, pandiatonic in harmony, and intricately polyphonic in contrapuntal and fugal developments.
WORKS: *Prelude and Dance* for Orch. (1948; Athens Radio, Sept. 1, 1948); *The Revelation of the 5th Seal,* symph. poem (1951; Athens, May 11, 1952); 4 string quartets (1951, 1954, 1957–61, 1967); Concertino for 5 Winds and String Orch. (1953; Rome, June 9, 1953); Concerto for Orch. (1953–54; Athens, Nov. 28, 1954); Symph. No. 1 (1955; New York, March 1, 1958); *Tanagra,* ballet for 2 Pianos and Percussion (1958; Athens, April 21, 1958; orch. version, Athens, Feb. 5, 1962); *Bacchantes,* ballet for Women's Chorus and Orch., after Euripides (1959–60; Athens, Jan. 11, 1960); *Synthesis* for Double String Orch. and Percussion (1962; Athens, Nov. 26, 1962); Cello Concerto (1963); *Miniatures* for Piano (1963); *Variations on 4 Rhythmical Patterns* for Orch. (1963); *Stasimon B!* for Women's Chorus, Mezzo-soprano, and Orch. (1965); *Perspectives* for Orch. in 4 groups (1966); *Episodes I,* variations and interludes for Chamber Orch. (1964–67) and *II* for Double Chorus, 3 Performers, and Tape (1971); *Epiklesis II,* after Aeschylus, for Narrator, Male Chorus, 4 Women's Voices, and 12 Instruments (1968); *Epitaph* for Mixed Chorus, Children's Chorus, Narrator and Orch. (1969–71); *Etudes Compositionnelles* for Solo Piano (1972–73; orchestrated for Piano and Orch., 1975); *Medea,* stage music, after Euripides, for Women's Chorus, Flute, Tuba, Percussion, and Tape (1973); *Parable,* choreographic picture for Chorus, Flute, Tuba, Percussion, and Tape (1973); *Etude* for Solo Tuba (1974); *Paysages* for 2 Percussionists (1975); *6 Songs* for Voice and Piano (1975); *Schemata* for 6 Percussionists (1976); *Antiphone* for Brass, Timpani, and Strings (1976); *The Moonlight Lady,* cantata for Mezzo-soprano, Narrator, Clarinet, Viola, and Guitar (1977).

Sidlin, Murry, American conductor; b. Baltimore, May 6, 1940, of Russian-Latvian parents. He studied theory with Elliott Galkin and Louis Cheslock, and trumpet with Harold Rherig, at the Peabody Cons. in Baltimore (B.A., 1962; M.A., 1968). During the summers of 1961 and 1962 he traveled to Italy and studied conducting with Sergiu Celibidache at the Accademia Chigiana in Siena. Returning to the U.S., he took courses with Donald Grout and Karel Husa at Cornell Univ. (1963–65). After completing his academic studies, he devoted himself principally to symph. conducting. In 1971–73 he served as assistant conductor of the Baltimore Symph., and in 1973–77 was resident conductor of the National Symph. Orch. in Washington, D.C.; in 1977 he was engaged as music director of the New Haven Symph. Orch., and in 1980 became conductor of the Long Beach (Calif.) Symph. Orch., which he brought to a considerable degree of excellence. He furthermore was guest conductor of the Gavleborg Orkester of Sweden (1976–77) and had conducting engagements in Pittsburgh, Seattle, Denver, San Antonio, and San Diego, as well as with the Boston Pops Orch.

Sieber, Ferdinand, Austrian singing teacher; b. Vienna, Dec. 5, 1822; d. Berlin, Feb. 19, 1895. He studied with Ronconi; after a brief period of singing in opera, he became a singing teacher in Dresden (1848–54), later settling in Berlin, where he had numerous pupils. He taught in the tradition of the old Italian method. He publ. valuable instructive works: *Die Kunst des Gesangs,* in 2 parts (theoretical and practical studies), with a supplement, *50 Vocalisen und Solfeggien; Vollständiges Lehrbuch der Gesangskunst für Lehrer und Schüler* (1858; 3rd ed., 1878); *Katechismus der Gesangskunst* (1862 and many subsequent eds.); *Die Aussprache des Italienischen im Gesang* (1860; 2nd ed., 1880); and *Handbuch des deutschen Liederschatzes* (1875), containing a catalogue of 10,000 songs arranged according to vocal range; he also wrote many songs.

Siebert, Wilhelm Dieter, German composer; b. Berlin, Oct. 22, 1931. He studied with Rufer in Berlin and with Fortner in Freiburg im Breisgau. About 1957 he devoted himself mainly to experimental music, incorporating the rhythmic resources of jazz and the unlimited sonorities of electronics; in 1963 he joined the Neue Musik group in Berlin.
WORKS: Trio for Flute, Harp, and Percussion (1967); *Paganini Variations* for Flute, Piano, String Trio, and Magnetic Tape (1968); choral music with tape; opera, *The Sinking of the Titanic* (1979).

Siegel, Carl F.W., German music publisher active early in the 19th century; d. Leipzig, March 29, 1869. He founded his firm in 1846, making a specialty of choral music. He was succeeded by Richard Linnemann (b. Leipzig, April 14, 1845; d. there, Dec. 1, 1909), who studied at the Leipzig Cons. and in 1871 acquired control of *Die Sängerhalle* (organ of the German singing society), which continued publication until 1916. Richard Linnemann's sons were Carl Linnemann (b. Leipzig, Sept. 25, 1872; d. there, Dec. 14, 1945) and Richard Linnemann, Jr. (b. Leipzig, Nov. 5, 1874; d. there, April 5, 1932); they entered the business in 1901; bought the stock of E.W. Fritzsch in 1901 and that of K.F. Kistner in 1919. From 1919 to 1927 the firm publ. *Archiv für Musikwissenschaft.*

Siegel, Jeffrey, American pianist; b. Chicago, Nov. 18, 1942. He studied piano with Rudolph Ganz at the Chicago Musical College and later with Rosina Lhévinne and Ilona Kabos at the Juilliard School of Music in N.Y. He won the silver medal at the Queen Elisabeth of Belgium Competition in Brussels; then was a soloist with many of the leading orchs. of the U.S. and Europe, including the Chicago Symph., Boston Symph., N.Y. Phil., London Symph., and London Phil.

Siegel, Rudolf, German conductor and composer; b. Berlin, April 12, 1878; d. Bayreuth, Dec. 4, 1948. He studied with Humperdinck in Berlin and with Thuille in Munich; in 1910 became conductor of a choral society in Munich; then was in Berlin (1912–14) and Königsberg (1914–17). From 1919 until 1930 he was music director at Krefeld; then moved to Berlin; in 1945 he went to Ebing, near Bamberg; eventually moved to Munich. He wrote an opera, *Herr Dandolo* (Essen, 1914); *Apostatenmarsch* for Male Chorus and Orch.; *Heroische Tondichtung* for Orch.; *Dem Vaterlande* for Men's Chorus and Orch.; made arrangements of German folk songs.

Siegl, Otto, Austrian violinist, conductor, and composer; b. Graz, Oct. 6, 1896; d. Vienna, Nov. 9, 1978. He received his first music lessons from his mother, an amateur pianist; then studied violin with a local teacher. In 1915 he was drafted into the Austro-Hungarian army and served as a Tyrol rifleman in World War I. While still in the service he met the musicologist Max Auer, who gave him instruction in the classics. After the Armistice, he was a violinist in the Vienna Symph. Orch. (1921–22) and assistant conductor at the Graz Opera (1922–24); also wrote music criticism. In 1926 he went to Germany, where he worked as a choral conductor in Bielefeld, Essen, and Herford; from 1933 to 1948 he was on the staff of the Cologne Hochschule für Musik; from 1948 to 1967 he was a prof. at the Music Academy in Vienna. In 1957 he was awarded the Great State Prize for Music. A pragmatic musician, he was a master of polyphony; his choral writing is especially meritorious.
WORKS: 2 symphs. (1958, 1959); Cello Concerto (1957); Flute Concerto (1955); Chamber Concerto for Piano and Orch. (1960); Clarinet Concerto with String Orch. (1968); 2 string quintets (1940, 1954); *Quintet-Serenade* for Clarinet, Bassoon, Violin, Viola, and Cello (1961); 5 string quartets (1924–56); Trio for Clarinet, Cello, and Piano (1959); 4 cello sonatas (1923, 1923, 1924, 1967); 2 violin sonatas (1925, 1940); 2 viola sonatas (1925, 1938); 2 clarinet sonatas (1965, 1968); Flute Sonata (1968); Sonata for Clarinet and Cello (1965); oratorio, *Stern des Lebens* (1959); several cantatas; 4 masses; numerous choruses and about 80 lieder.
BIBLIOGRAPHY: W. Trienes, *Otto Siegl* (Mülheim, 1956); Wolfgang Suppan, *Otto Siegl* (Vienna, 1966).

Siegmeister, Elie, significant American composer; b. New York, Jan. 15, 1909. He took piano lessons as a youth with Emil Friedberger; in 1925 entered Columbia Univ. and studied composition there with

Seth Bingham; also took private lessons in counterpoint with Wallingford Riegger. In 1927 he went to Paris, where he studied with Nadia Boulanger; returning to N.Y. in 1932, he taught music at various schools; studied conducting at the Juilliard School of Music, N.Y. (1935–38); in 1939 he organized a vocal ensemble, the American Ballad Singers, for the purpose of performing authentic American folk songs, and traveled as its conductor for several years. He felt strongly that music should express the social values of the people; in his early songs, he selected texts by contemporary American poets voicing indignation at the inequities of the modern world; he also gave lectures and conducted choruses at the revolutionary Pierre Degeyter Club in N.Y. From the outset, he adopted an extremely dissonant harmonic idiom and a quasi-atonal melos, with the intervallic stress on minor seconds, major sevenths, and minor ninths. In his symphs. and chamber music he organized this dissonant idiom in self-consistent modern formulations, without, however, espousing any of the fashionable doctrines of composition, such as dodecaphony. The subject matter of the orch. and vocal compositions of his early period was marked by a strongly national and socially radical character, exemplified by such works as *American Holiday, Ozark Set, Prairie Legend, Wilderness Road,* and *Western Suite,* the last achieving the rare honor of being performed by Toscanini; Siegmeister did not ignore the homely vernacular; his Clarinet Concerto is a brilliant realization of jazz, blues, and swing in a classically formal idiom. Siegmeister achieved an important position as an educator; in 1949 he was appointed to the faculty of Hofstra Univ. in Hempstead, Long Island; he became composer-in-residence there in 1966; prof. emeritus in 1976. In 1978 he received a Guggenheim fellowship award.

WORKS: FOR THE STAGE: *Doodle Dandy of the USA,* play with music, to text by Saul Lancourt (N.Y., Dec. 26, 1942); *Sing Out, Sweet Land,* to text by Walter Kerr (Hartford, Conn., Nov. 10, 1944); *Darling Corie,* one-act opera, libretto by Lewis Allan (1952; Hofstra Univ., Feb. 18, 1954); *Miranda and the Dark Young Man,* one-act opera, libretto by Edward Eager (1955; Hartford, Conn., May 9, 1956); *The Mermaid in Lock No. 7,* one-act opera, libretto by Edward Mabley (Pittsburgh, July 20, 1958); *Dublin Song,* 3-act opera, libretto by Edward Mabley, based on Sean O'Casey's drama *The Plough and the Stars* (1963; St. Louis, May 15, 1963; revised and perf. under the title *The Plough and the Stars,* Baton Rouge, La., March 16, 1969); *Night of the Moonspell,* 3-act opera, libretto by Edward Mabley after Shakespeare's play *Midsummer Night's Dream* (Shreveport, La., Nov. 14, 1976); *Fables from the Dark Wood,* for ballet (Shreveport, April 25, 1976); *The Marquesa of O,* opera (1979–83); film score, *They Came to Cordura* (1959).

FOR ORCH.: *American Holiday* (1933); *Ozark Set* (1943; Minneapolis, Nov. 7, 1944); *Prairie Legend* (1944; N.Y., Jan. 18, 1947); *Wilderness Road* (1944; Minneapolis, Nov. 9, 1945); *Western Suite* (1945; N.Y., Nov. 24, 1945; Toscanini conducting the NBC Symph. Orch.); *Sunday in Brooklyn* (N.Y., July 21,

1946); *Lonesome Hollow* (1946; Columbus, Ohio, 1948); *Summer Night* (1947; N.Y., Sept. 27, 1952); Symph. No. 1 (1947; N.Y., Oct. 30, 1947; revised 1972); *From My Window* (1949); Symph. No. 2 (1950; N.Y., Feb. 25, 1952; revised 1972); *Riversong* (1951; revised 1982; St. Joseph, Mo., Nov. 21, 1982); *Divertimento* (1953; Oklahoma City, March 28, 1954); Concerto for Clarinet and Orch. (Oklahoma City, Feb. 3, 1956); Symph. No. 3 (1957; Oklahoma City, Feb. 8, 1959); Concerto for Flute and Orch. (1960; Oklahoma City, Feb. 17, 1961); *Theater Set,* drawn from the music for the film *They Came to Cordura* (1960; Rochester, N.Y., May 8, 1969); *Dick Whittington and His Cat* for Narrator and Orch. (1966; Philadelphia, Feb. 10, 1968); *5 Fantasies of the Theater* (1967; Hofstra Univ., Oct. 18, 1970); Symph. No. 4 (1970; Cleveland, Dec. 6, 1973); Symph. No. 5, subtitled *Visions of Time* (1971–75; Baltimore, May 4, 1977); Piano Concerto (Denver, Colo., Dec. 3, 1976; Alan Mandel, soloist; revised 1982); *Shadows and Light,* subtitled *Homage to 5 Paintings* (Shreveport, La., Nov. 9, 1975); Double Concerto for Violin, Piano, and Orch. (Columbia, Md., June 25, 1976); Violin Concerto (1977–78) *Fantasies in Line and Color,* subtitled *5 American Paintings* (1981); Symph. No. 6 (Sacramento, Calif., Nov. 4, 1984); Violin Concerto (Oakland, Calif., Jan. 29, 1985).

VOCAL MUSIC: For Voice and Orch.: *Strange Funeral in Braddock* (1933; originally for Voice and Piano; Evergreen, Colo., July 30, 1972); *Abraham Lincoln Walks at Midnight* for Mixed Chorus and Orch., to a text of Vachel Lindsay (1937); *Funnybone Alley* for Voice and String Orch., musical fantasy for children to poems by Alfred Kreymborg (1946); *I Have a Dream* for Mixed Chorus, Baritone, Narrator and Orch., to a text by Edward Mabley based on a speech by Martin Luther King, Jr. (1967; Omaha, Nebr., Oct. 7, 1968); *The Face of War* for Bass Voice and Orch., to poems by Langston Hughes (N.Y., May 24, 1968); *A Cycle of Cities* for Mixed Chorus, Soprano, Tenor, and Orch., to poems by Lawrence Ferlinghetti, Langston Hughes, and Norman Rosten (Wolf Trap, Va., near Washington, D.C., Aug. 8, 1974); *Cantata for FDR,* to a text by Oscar Brand (1981; Denver, May 5, 1982); *Ways of Love* for Soprano and Chamber Ensemble (N.Y., Jan. 15, 1984).

FOR CHORUS: *Heyura, Ding, Dong, Ding* (1935; revised 1970); *John Henry* (1935); *Johnny Appleseed,* to words by Stephen Vincent Benét (1940); *American Ballad Singers Series* (1943); *American Folk Song Choral Series* (1953); *Sing Unto the Lord a New Song* for Chorus and Organ (1981). Songs: *Cortege for Rosenbloom,* to words by Wallace Stevens (1926); *4 Robert Frost Songs* (1930); *The Strange Funeral in Braddock,* to words by Michael Gold (1933); *3 Elegies for García Lorca,* to words by Antonio Machado (1938); *Nancy Hanks,* to words by Rosemary Benét (1941); *Songs of Experience,* to words by William Blake (1966); 11 songs to words by e.e. cummings (1970); *Songs of Innocence,* to words by William Blake (1972); *City Songs,* to words by N. Rosten (1977); *3 Minute Songs,* to words by Langston Hughes (1978); *Brief Introduction to the Problems of Philosophy,* 5 songs to words by Irwin Edman

(1979).

CHAMBER MUSIC: *Nocturne* for Flute and Piano (1927); *Prelude* for Clarinet and Piano (1927); *Contrasts* for Bassoon and Piano (1929); 3 string quartets (1935, 1960, 1973); *Down River* for Alto Saxophone and Piano (1939); 5 violin sonatas (1951, 1965, 1965, 1971, 1972); *Song for a Quiet Evening* for Violin and Piano (1955); *Fantasy and Soliloquy* for Solo Cello (1964); Sextet for Brass and Percussion (1965); *American Harp* for Solo Harp (1966); *Declaration* for Brass and Timpani (1976); *Celebration* for Band (1977; N.Y., June 16, 1982); for Piano: *Theme and Variations No. 1* (1932); *Toccata on Flight Rhythms* (1937); *American Sonata* (1944); *Sunday in Brooklyn* (1946); Sonata No. 2 (1964); *Theme and Variations No. 2* (1967); *On This Ground* (1971); Sonata No. 3 (1979); Sonata No. 4, *Prelude, Blues and Toccata* (1980); *3 Studies* (1982).

WRITINGS: *A Treasury of American Song* (with Olin Downes; N.Y., 1940); *The Music Lover's Handbook* (1943; revised as *The New Music Lover's Handbook*, Irvington-on-Hudson, N.Y., 1973; 3rd ed., 1983) *Work and Sing* (N.Y., 1944); *Invitation to Music* (Irvington-on-Hudson, 1961); *Harmony and Melody* (2 vols.; Belmont, Calif., 1965–66).

BIBLIOGRAPHY: David Ewen, *The World of 20th-Century Music* (Englewood Cliffs, N.J., 1968); Grigory Schneerson, *Portraits of American Composers* (Moscow, 1977, pp. 113–34); autobiographical sketch in *The New Music Lover's Handbook* (Irvington-on-Hudson, N.Y., 1973; pp. 561–69); Arthur Cohn, *Recorded Classical Music* (N.Y., 1982); David Ewen, *American Composers* (N.Y., 1982); Jack Gallagher, *Structural Design and Motivic Unity in the 2nd, 3rd and 4th Symphonies of Elie Siegmeister* (Diss., Cornell Univ., 1982).

Siegmund-Schultze, Walther, German musicologist; b. Schweinitz, July 6, 1916. He studied musicology with Arnold Schmitz at the Univ. of Breslau (Ph.D., 1940, with the dissertation *Mozarts Vokal- und Instrumentalmusik in ihren motivisch-thematischen Beziehungen*); he completed his Habilitation at the Univ. of Halle with his *Untersuchungen zum Brahms Stil und Brahms Bild* in 1951. In 1954 he became a lecturer at the Univ. of Halle; in 1956 he was made a prof. of musicology there, director of the musicological faculty, and dean of the philosophy faculty. He is noted for his studies of 18th-century music; his analysis of the styles of Bach, Handel, and Mozart is interesting as an example of Marxist theories applied to music.

WRITINGS: *Die Musik Bachs* (Leipzig, 1953); *Georg Friedrich Händel: Leben and Werk* (Leipzig, 1954; 3rd ed., 1962); *Mozarts Melodik und Stil: Eine Studie* (Leipzig, 1957); *Lehrbriefe für das Fernstudium: Die Musik der Klassik* (Halle, 1964); *Georg Friedrich Händel: Thema mit 20 Variationen* (Halle, 1965); *Die Hauptvertreter der bürgerlichen Musikkultur im 20. Jahrhundert* (Halle, 1966–67); *Johannes Brahms: Eine Biographie* (Leipzig, 1966; 2nd ed., 1974); *Die Musik der sozialistischen Länder (ausser DDR)* (Halle, 1967); *Ziele und Aufgaben der sozialistischen Musikerziehung* (Leipzig, 1967; 3rd ed., 1975); *Die Bach-Händel-Epoche* (Halle, 1968); *Das Musikschaffen der DDR* (Halle, 1969); *Ludwig van Beethoven: Eine Biographie* (Leipzig, 1975; 2nd ed., 1977); *Johann Sebastian Bach* (Leipzig, 1976).

Siehr, Gustav, German bass; b. Arnsberg, Sept. 17, 1837; d. Munich, May 18, 1896. He studied with Heinrich Dorn and Julius Krause; made his debut in 1863 in Neustrelitz; then sang in Prague (1865–70) and Wiesbaden (1870–81); in 1881 he became a member of the Munich Court Opera, where he remained until his death; also sang at the Bayreuth Festivals, where he created the role of Hagen in *Götterdämmerung* in 1876. He was particularly distinguished as a Wagnerian interpreter.

Siems, Margarethe, outstanding German soprano; b. Breslau, Dec. 30, 1879; d. Dresden, April 13, 1952. She studied with Orgeni in Dresden and Battistini in Milan; made her debut at the German Theater in Prague in 1902; in 1908 she joined the Dresden Court (later State) Opera, where she became a principal member of the company; during her tenure, Richard Strauss chose her to create the roles of Chrysothemis in *Elektra,* Marschallin in *Der Rosenkavalier,* and Zerbinetta in *Ariadne auf Naxos.* After leaving the Dresden Opera in 1919, she continued to make some operatic appearances until her farewell appearance in Breslau in 1925; she taught voice in Berlin, Dresden, and Breslau from 1920 until 1940. In addition to her roles in Strauss's operas, she gained renown for her performances in the operas of Bellini, Donizetti, Verdi, and Wagner.

Siepi, Cesare, Italian bass; b. Milan, Feb. 10, 1923. He made his debut in Schio (Venice) in 1941; in 1946 appeared for the first time at La Scala, Milan. He made his American debut at the Metropolitan Opera, N.Y., on Nov. 6, 1950, in the role of Philip II in *Don Carlos*; remained on its roster until 1973. In 1966 he became a member of the Vienna State Opera; also appeared at Covent Garden in London, in Salzburg, and in other musical centers. His most successful roles were Méphistophélès in Gounod's *Faust* and Figaro in Mozart's *Marriage of Figaro.*

Sieveking, Martinus, Dutch pianist; b. Amsterdam, March 24, 1867; d. Pasadena, Calif., Nov. 26, 1950. He studied piano with his father; began his career as an accompanist; traveled with Adelina Patti on her tour of England (1891–92); then settled in the U.S.; in 1915 established his own piano school in N.Y. and announced a new method which guaranteed to achieve virtuosity in 24 months; not very successful in N.Y., he went to California, where he found a fertile field for his quick road to virtuosity for everybody.

Siface, Giovanni Francesco, famous Italian male soprano; b. Pescia, Feb. 12, 1653; d. Ferrara, May 29, 1697 (murdered by hired assassins). He was a member of the Papal Chapel in 1675–77; was in Modena from 1679 till 1687; later sang at Venice and London.

Sigismondi, Giuseppe, Italian singing teacher and composer; b. Naples, Nov. 13, 1739; d. there, May 10, 1826. He was librarian at the Cons. in Naples (from 1808); wrote an opera, 4 oratorios, vocal music, and pieces for piano and organ; only a few of his works were publ.

Sigtenhorst-Meyer, Bernhard van den, Dutch composer; b. Amsterdam, June 17, 1888; d. The Hague, July 17, 1953. He studied at the Amsterdam Cons.; later in Vienna and Paris; settled in The Hague as a composer and writer.
WORKS: 2 string quartets (1919, 1944); Sonata for Cello Solo (1926); 2 violin sonatas (1926, 1938); *6 Miniatures* for Oboe and Piano (1926–46); 2 piano sonatas (1922, 1925); 3 piano sonatinas (1928, 1930, 1948); other piano pieces: *La Vieille Chine* (1916), *Les Oiseaux* (1917); 2 albums, *Le Monde de contes-bleus* (1926–28). He edited works by Sweelinck; publ. the valuable treatises *Jan P. Sweelinck en zijn in-strumentale muziek* (The Hague, 1934; 2nd ed., 1946) and *De vocale muziek van Jan P. Sweelinck* (The Hague, 1948).
BIBLIOGRAPHY: C. Backers, *Nederlandsche Componisten* (The Hague, 2nd ed., 1948, pp. 131–37); H. Antcliffe, "Sigtenhorst-Meyer: A Personal Impression," *Monthly Musical Record* (Dec. 1953).

Sigurbjörnsson, Thorkell, Icelandic composer; b. Reykjavik, July 16, 1938. He studied violin, piano, organ, theory, and music history at the Reykjavik School of Music (1948–57); then came to the U.S. and studied composition and piano at Hamline Univ. in St. Paul, Minn. (1957–59), and electronic music with Lejaren Hiller and composition with Gaburo at the Univ. of Illinois (1959–61). Returning to Reykjavik, he founded the modern group Musica Nova; was assistant director of music for the Iceland State Broadcasting Service (1966–69) and a music critic. In his music he modernizes traditional modalities by an injection of acrid dissonances and vitalizes the fundamentally placid metrical divisions by disruptive rhythmic asymmetries.
WORKS: *Ballade* for Tenor, Flute, Viola, and Guitar (1960); *Leikar* for Chorus and Orch. (1961); *Flökt (Fluctuations)* for Orch. (1961); *Víxl (Rotation)* for Violin, Clarinet, Cello, and Duplicate Instruments on Tape (1962); chamber opera, *Composition in 3 Scenes* (1964); children's opera, *Apaspil* (1966); *Cadenza and Dance* for Violin and Orch. (1967); children's opera, *Rabbi* (1968); *Hässelby-Quartet,* string quartet (1968); *Ymur* for Orch. (1969); *Kisum* for Clarinet, Viola, and Piano (1970); *Intrada* for Clarinet, Viola, and Piano (1970); *Ys og Thys (Much Ado),* overture (1970); *Laeti* for Orch. and Orch. on Tape (1971); ballet, *Thorgeirsboli (The Bull-man,* 1971); *Happy Music* for Brass Ensemble (1971); *Mistur* for Orch. (1972); *Haflög* for Orch. (1973); *Dáik* for Clarinet, Cello, and Synthesizer (1973); *Hylling (Homage)* for Flute, Cello, Piano, Percussion, Tape, and Audience (1974); *Nídur,* concerto for Double Bass and Orch. (1974); *Búkolla,* concerto for Clari-

net and Orch. (1974); *Four Better or Worse* for Flute, Clarinet, Cello, and Piano (1975); *Albumblatt* for Orch. (1975); *Wiblo* for Horn, Piano, and Strings (1976); *Solstice* for Soprano, Alto, Baritone, Flute, Marimba, and Double Bass (1976); *Ríma* for Orch. (1977); *Copenhagen Quartet* for String Quartet (1977); *The Pied Piper* for Flute and String Trio (1978); *Eurydice* for Flute and Orch. (1978); *Columbine* for Flute and Strings (Falun, Sweden, Dec. 5, 1982).

Sigwart, Botho (real name, **Sigwart Botho, Count of Eulenburg**), German pianist and composer, son of the German diplomat and poet Count Phillip of Eulenburg; b. Berlin, Jan. 10, 1884; d. in Galicia, June 2, 1915 (from wounds received in battle). He studied piano in Vienna and musicology at the Univ. of Munich (Dr.Phil., 1907, with the dissertation *Erasmus Widmann*); completed his studies with Max Reger at Leipzig (1908–9). In 1909 he married the concert singer **Helene Staegemann.** He wrote a number of piano pieces, a String Quartet, and several melodramas.

Siki, Béla, distinguished Hungarian pianist; b. Budapest, Feb. 21, 1923. He studied with Dohnányi and Leo Weiner at the Budapest Academy of Music; later took lessons with Dinu Lipatti in Geneva. In 1947 he won the Concours International d'Exécutions Musicales in Geneva; then made tours of Australia, Japan, South America, and the U.S. In 1965 he became a prof. of piano at the Univ. of Washington in Seattle, and in 1980 at the Univ. of Cincinnati College-Cons. of Music. He wrote *Piano Repertoire: A Guide to Interpretation and Performance* (N.Y., 1981). He became especially known for his authoritative performances of the works of Liszt and Bartók.

Siklós, Albert, Hungarian composer; b. Budapest, June 26, 1878; d. there, April 3, 1942. His real name was **Schönwald,** but he changed it to Siklós in 1910. He studied law, and later took courses with Koessler at the Budapest Academy of Music, graduating in 1901; he taught at the Academy from 1910, and gradually became one of its most respected teachers. He was a prolific composer, but few of his works were publ., and there were virtually no performances outside Hungary. He wrote the opera *The House of the Moons* (Budapest, Dec. 21, 1927), a ballet, *The Mirror* (Budapest, March 28, 1923), and other stage works; 2 symphs. and an interesting *Symphonie aethérique* for 12 Double Basses (1899); Cello Concerto; Violin Concerto; much chamber music; piano pieces. He publ. a number of instructive books; also a music dictionary in Hungarian.

Sikorski, Kazimierz, Swiss-born Polish composer and pedagogue; b. Zürich, June 28, 1895 (of Polish parents). He studied at the College of Music in Warsaw; then took a course in musicology with Chybiński in Lwow; completed his musical studies in Paris (1925–27). He taught at the State Cons. in Lodz (1947–54); at the State College in Warsaw (1951–57);

became its director (1957–66). Many Polish composers of the younger generation were his students, among them Grazyna Bacewicz, Panufnik, Palester, and Serocki.

WORKS: 4 symphs. (1918, 1921, 1953, 1971); *Suite for String Orch.* (1917); Clarinet Concerto (1947); Concerto for Horn and Small Orch. (1948); *Popular Overture* (1954); Flute Concerto (1957); Concerto for Trumpet, String Orch., 4 Timpani, Xylophone, and Tam-tam (1959); *6 Old Polish Dances* for Small Orch. (1963); *Concerto Polyphonique* for Bassoon and Orch. (1965); Oboe Concerto (1967); Trombone Concerto (1973); 3 string quartets; String Sextet; choruses. He publ. 3 books: *Instrumentoznawstwo* (*The Study of Instruments*, Warsaw, 1932; 2nd and 3rd eds., 1950 and 1975; the 3rd ed. includes information on modern percussion); *Harmonia* (*Harmony*, 3 vols., Cracow, 1948–49; 4th ed., 1972); and *Kontrapunkt* (*Counterpoint*, 3 vols., Cracow, 1953–57).

Sikorski, Tomasz, Polish composer and pianist, son of **Kazimierz Sikorski;** b. Warsaw, May 19, 1939. He studied piano with Drzewiecki and composition with his father; then took lessons with Nadia Boulanger in Paris. As a pianist, he emphasizes new music in his programs. His own compositions are also in the advanced idiom.

WORKS: Radio opera, *Przygody Sindbada zeglarza* (*The Adventures of Sinbad the Sailor,* 1971); *Echoes 2 quasi improvvisazione* for One to 4 Pianos, Percussion, and Tape (1961–63); *Antyfony* for Soprano without Text, Piano, Horn, Chimes, 2 Gongs, 2 Tam-tams, and Tape (1963); *Prologues* for Female Chorus, 2 Pianos, 4 Flutes, 4 Horns, and 4 Percussionists (1964); *Architectures* for Piano, Winds, and Percussion (1965); *Concerto breve* for Piano, 24 Winds, and 4 Percussionists (1965); *Sequenza I* for Orch. (1966); *Sonant* for Piano (1967); *Intersections* for 36 Percussion Instruments (1968); *Homophony* for 4 Trumpets, 4 Horns, 4 Trombones, Piano, and 2 Gongs (1968); *Diafonia* for 2 Pianos (1969); *For Strings* for 3 Violins and 3 Violas (1970); *Vox humana* for Chorus, 12 Brasses, 2 Pianos, 4 Gongs, and 4 Tam-tams (1971); *Zerstreutes Hinausschauen* for Piano (1971); *Holzwege* for Orch. (1972); *Etude* for Orch. (1972); *Bez tytulu (Untitled)* for Piano, Clarinet, Trombone, and Cello (1972); *Listening Music* for 2 Pianos (1973); *Music from Afar* for Chorus and Orch. (1974); *Other Voices* for Winds and Percussion (1975).

Silas, Eduard, pianist and composer; b. Amsterdam, Aug. 22, 1827; d. London, Feb. 8, 1909. He studied piano in Frankfurt and Paris; took courses at the Paris Cons. with Halévy; won first prize for organ playing in competition with Saint-Saëns. In 1850 he settled in England as an organist; also taught harmony at the Guildhall School in London. Among his works are 3 symphs., 3 piano concertos, 2 string quintets, 2 piano trios, numerous piano pieces; also an oratorio, *Joash* (Norwich Festival, 1863); and a Mass.

Silbermann, German family of organ and piano makers. (1) **Andreas Silbermann,** b. Klein-Bobritzsch, Saxony, May 16, 1678; d. Strasbourg, March 16, 1734. He settled in Strasbourg in 1702; was in Paris, 1704–6, before making his home in Strasbourg for good; was the builder of the organ of the Strasbourg Münster (1713–16) and of 34 others. (2) **Gottfried Silbermann,** brother of Andreas, b. Klein-Bobritzsch, Jan. 14, 1683; d. Dresden, Aug. 4, 1753. Apprenticed to a bookbinder, he ran away and joined his brother in Strasbourg, working as his helper. He then lived in Freiberg; built 47 organs, the finest of which is in the Freiberg Cathedral (1710–14), having 3 manuals and 44 stops. He owed his fame, however, mainly to the manufacture of pianos in Germany, in which field he was a pioneer; the hammer action in his instruments was practically identical with that of Cristofori, the piano inventor. Silbermann also invented the "cembal d'amour," a clavichord with strings of double length, struck in the middle by the tangents, thus yielding the duplicated octave of the tone of the entire string. He supplied 3 pianos to Frederick the Great for Potsdam, and Bach played on them during his visit there in 1747. (3) **Johann Andreas Silbermann,** eldest son of Andreas; b. Strasbourg, May 26, 1712; d. there, Feb. 11, 1783. He built 54 organs; publ. *Geschichte der Stadt Strassburg* (1775). (4) **Johann Daniel Silbermann,** brother of Johann Andreas; b. Strasbourg, March 31, 1717; d. Leipzig, May 9, 1766. He worked with his uncle Gottfried at Freiberg, and continued the manufacture of pianos after the latter's death. (5) **Johann Heinrich Silbermann,** brother of Johann Andreas and Johann Daniel; b. Strasbourg, Sept. 24, 1727; d. there, Jan. 15, 1799; made pianos at Strasbourg, similar to those of his uncle Gottfried, and introduced them into France. (6) **Johann Friedrich Silbermann,** son of Johann Heinrich; b. Strasbourg, June 21, 1762; d. there, March 8, 1817. He was an organist in Strasbourg; during the Revolution wrote a *Hymne à la Paix;* also composed some German songs.

BIBLIOGRAPHY: L. Mooser, *Gottfried Silbermann* (Langensalza, 1857); G. Zschaler, *Gottfried Silbermann* (1898); E. Flade, *Der Orgelbauer Gottfried Silbermann* (Leipzig, 1926); H. Hullemann, *Die Tätigkeit des Orgelbauers Gottfried Silbermann im Reussenland* (Leipzig, 1937); R. Gärtner, *Gottfried Silbermann der Orgelbauer* (Dresden, 1938); J. Wörsching, *Die Orgelbauer Familie Silbermann in Strassburg* (Mainz, 1941; 2nd ed., 1960); E. Flade, *Gottfried Silbermann. Ein Beitrag zur Geschichte des deutschen Orgel- und Klavierbau im Zeitalter Bachs* (Leipzig, 1953); Donald Boalch, *Makers of the Harpsichord and Clavichord 1440–1840* (London, 1956, pp. 112–14; contains genealogy and list of extant instruments made by members of the family). W. Müller brought out *Gottfried Silbermann: Persönlichkeit und Werk: Eine Dokumentation,* for the 300th anniversary of his birth in 1983.

Silcher, Friedrich, German composer; b. Schnait, Württemberg, June 27, 1789; d. Tübingen, Aug. 26, 1860. He studied with his father and with Auberlen, an organist at Fellbach; lived for some years in Stuttgart; in 1817 was appointed music director at the Univ. of Tübingen, receiving the honorary degree of Dr.Phil. in 1852. He was an influential promoter of German popular singing; publ. several collections of German folk songs, in which he included his own compositions; of the latter, *Lorelei (Ich weiss nicht, was soll es bedeuten,* to words by Heinrich Heine) became so popular that it was often mistaken for a folk song; his other well-known songs are *Ännchen von Tharau, Morgen muss ich fort von hier, Zu Strassburg auf der Schanz,* etc. He also publ. *Choralbuch* for 3 voices; 3 books of hymns for 4 voices; *Tübinger Liedertafel* (male choruses). He wrote the books *Geschichte des evangelischen Kirchengesanges* (1844); *Harmonie- und Kompositionslehre* (1851; 2nd ed., 1859).

BIBLIOGRAPHY: A. Köstlin, *F. Silcher und Weber* (Stuttgart, 1877); A. Prümers, *F. Silcher: Der Meister des deutschen Volkslieds* (Stuttgart, 1910); G. Brügel, "Kritische Mitteilungen zu Silchers Volksliedern," *Sammelbände der Internationalen Musik-Gesellschaft* (1914); A. Bopp, *F. Silcher* (Stuttgart, 1916); idem, *Liederbuch aus Schwaben* (1918); H. Kleinert and H. Rauschnabel, eds., *F. Silcher* (Stuttgart, 1935); A. Lämmle, *F. Silcher* (Mühlacker, 1956).

Silja, Anja, remarkably musical German soprano; b. Berlin, April 17, 1940. She studied voice with her grandfather, **Egon Friedrich Maria Aders van Rijn;** gave a solo recital in Berlin at the age of 10; at 15 she sang Rosina at the State Theater in Braunschweig. In 1958 she appeared at the Württemberg State Theater in Stuttgart, and in 1965 joined its roster. In 1960–63 she sang with the Municipal Theater in Frankfurt; in 1960 and in subsequent years she appeared at the Bayreuth Festivals; in 1968 she had a guest engagement at the Holland Festival. On Feb. 26, 1972, she made her American debut with the Metropolitan Opera in N.Y. as Leonore in *Fidelio;* she also was a guest artist with the Chicago and San Francisco operas. The breadth of her repertoire is commanding. Wagner's grandson Wieland coached her in the Wagnerian roles, among them Elisabeth, Elsa, Eva, and Senta, which she performed at Bayreuth. She also sang the parts of Salome and Elektra in the operas of Richard Strauss, of Marie and Lulu in Alban Berg's operas, and of the sole character in Schoenberg's *Erwartung.* As a matter of course, she mastered the majority of standard soprano parts (Carmen, Donna Anna, etc.). She married the conductor **Christoph von Dohnányi.**

Sills, Beverly (real name, **Belle Miriam Silverman**), celebrated American soprano; b. Brooklyn, May 25, 1929. Her father was an insurance salesman from Rumania and her mother a rather musical person from Odessa. At the age of 3 she appeared on the radio under the cute nickname "Bubbles," and won a prize at a Brooklyn contest as "the most beautiful baby of 1932." At 4, she joined a Saturday morning children's program, and at 7 she sang in a movie. At 10 she had a part on the radio show "Our Gal Sun-

day." Her natural thespian talent and sweet child's voice soon proved to be valuable financial assets. She did a commercial advertising Rinso White soap, and appeared on an early television program, "Stars of the Future." She also scored as the "one most likely to succeed" in Public School 91 in Brooklyn. In 1945 she joined a Gilbert and Sullivan touring company, billed as "the youngest prima donna in captivity." She then engaged in professional voice training with Estella Liebling and also took piano lessons with Paolo Gallico. In 1947 she made her first appearance in opera when she sang the subsidiary role of Frasquita in *Carmen* with the Philadelphia Opera Co. In 1951–52 she toured with the Charles L. Wagner Opera Co., with which she sang Violetta in *La Traviata* and Micaela in *Carmen.* In 1953 she sang with the Baltimore Opera and the San Francisco Opera. On Oct. 29, 1955, she made her debut with the N.Y. City Opera. On Nov. 17, 1956, she married Peter Bulkeley Greenough of Cleveland. She extended her repertoire to embrace modern American operas, her roles in these including the title role of Douglas Moore's *The Ballad of Baby Doe;* she also sang a demanding role in the American premiere of Luigi Nono's avant-garde opera *Intolleranza 1960.* She was a guest singer at the Vienna State Opera and in Buenos Aires in 1967, at La Scala in Milan in 1969, and at Covent Garden in London and the Deutsche Oper in Berlin in 1970. She made her first appearance with the Metropolitan Opera as Donna Anna in a concert production of *Don Giovanni* on July 8, 1966, at the Lewisohn Stadium in N.Y.; her formal debut with the Metropolitan took place at Lincoln Center in N.Y. as Pamira in *Le Siège de Corinthe* by Rossini, on April 7, 1975. At the height of her career she received well-nigh universal praise, not only for the excellence of her voice and her virtuosity in coloratura parts, but also for her intelligence and erudition, rare among the common run of operatic divas. But when she reached the age of 50, she decided to abandon the stage, and in 1979 accepted the role of general director of the N.Y. City Opera; in that capacity she showed an uncommon administrative talent; she also produced a number of television shows dealing with opera and concert singing. In her personal life, she suffered a double tragedy; one of her two children was born deaf, and the other was mentally retarded. In 1972 she accepted the national chairmanship of the Mothers' March on Birth Defects. She publ. an autobiography, *Bubbles: A Self-portrait* (N.Y., 1976; 2nd revised ed., 1981, as *Bubbles: An Encore*). She received (deservedly so) honorary doctorates from Harvard Univ., N.Y. Univ., and the Calif. Inst. of the Arts. On Nov. 22, 1971, she was the subject of a cover story in *Time.*

BIBLIOGRAPHY: David Ewen, *Musicians since 1900* (N.Y., 1978).

Siloti, Alexander, eminent Russian pianist, pedagogue, and conductor; b. on the family estate near Kharkov, Oct. 9, 1863; d. New York, Dec. 8, 1945. He studied piano with Zverev and Nicolai Rubinstein at the Moscow Cons., and music theory with Tchaikovsky (1876–81), winning the gold medal. He made his debut as a pianist in Moscow in 1880; then made a tour in Germany; Liszt accepted him as a student in 1883, and Siloti continued his study with Liszt in Weimar until Liszt's death in 1886. Returning to Russia, he was appointed a prof. of piano at the Moscow Cons. (1888–91); among his students was Rachmaninoff (his first cousin). Between 1891 and 1900 he lived in Germany, France, and Belgium; returned to Russia in 1901 and conducted the concerts of the Moscow Phil. Society during the season 1901–2; in 1903 he organized his own orch. in St. Petersburg, which he conducted until 1913; these concerts acquired great cultural importance; Siloti invited Mengelberg and Mottl as guest conductors, and Rachmaninoff, Casals, and Chaliapin as soloists. In 1915 he began a series of popular free concerts, and in 1916 started a Russian Musical Fund to aid indigent musicians. In 1919 he left Russia; he lived in Finland, Germany, and England; in 1922 he settled in N.Y., where he was active principally as a teacher but continued to appear as a soloist with American orchs.; from 1925 to 1942 he was on the faculty of the Juilliard School of Music. He publ. a collection of piano pieces which he edited, with indications of fingering and pedaling; also arranged and edited concertos by Bach and Vivaldi. He publ. a book of his reminiscences of Liszt (St. Petersburg, 1911; in Eng., Edinburgh, 1913).

BIBLIOGRAPHY: *Dictionary of American Biography*, III.

Silva, Francisco Manuel da, Brazilian composer of the Brazilian national anthem; b. Rio de Janeiro, Feb. 21, 1795; d. there, Dec. 18, 1865. He was a pupil of Marcos Portugal. In 1833 he founded the Sociedade Beneficente Musical; was active mostly as a music teacher and choral conductor. He wrote an opera, *O prestigio da lei,* but he owes his fame to the fact that he was the composer of the Brazilian national anthem, *Ouviram do Ypiranga as margens placidas.*

BIBLIOGRAPHY: A. de Albuquerque, *Ouviram do Ypiranga. Vida de Francisco Manuel de Silva* (Rio de Janeiro, 1959); A. de Andrade, *Francisco Manuel da Silva e seu tempo, 1808–65. Uma fase do passado musical do Rio de Janeiro á luz de novos documentos* (2 vols., Rio de Janeiro, 1967).

Silva, Luigi, American cellist; b. Milan, Nov. 13, 1903; d. New York, Nov. 29, 1961. He was of a musical family; his father was a vocal teacher; his mother a Viennese singer. He studied music at home; then took cello lessons with Arturo Bonucci in Bologna and composition with Respighi in Rome. He played in several string quartets in Italy; in 1939 he emigrated to the U.S.; taught cello and chamber music at the Eastman School of Music in Rochester, N.Y. (1941–49); in 1949 joined the staff of the Juilliard School of Music, N.Y. He made transcriptions for cello of works by Paganini, Boccherini, and other Italian composers; edited Bach's unaccompanied cello suites.

Silva, Oscar da, Portuguese pianist and composer; b. Paranhos, near Oporto, April 21, 1870; d. Oporto, March 6, 1958. He studied at the Lisbon Cons.; in 1892 went to Germany, where he had lessons with Reinecke and Clara Schumann. Returning to Portugal in 1910, he devoted himself mainly to teaching, acquiring a very high reputation as a piano pedagogue. From 1932 to 1952 he lived in Brazil; then returned to Portugal. He wrote an opera, *Dona Mecia* (Lisbon, July 4, 1901); a symph. poem, *Alma crucificada;* and a number of effective piano pieces, among them *Rapsodia portuguesa, Estudos indefinidos, Papillon dans le jardin, Paginas portuguesas;* also some chamber music and a number of songs to French words.

BIBLIOGRAPHY: A. Pinto, *Musica moderna portuguesa e os seus representantes* (Lisbon, 1930, pp. 114–29).

Silva, (David) Poll da, French composer; b. St.-Esprit, near Bayonne, March 28, 1834; d. Clermont, Oise, May 9, 1875. He went to Paris as a youth, and was encouraged by Halévy to study music and compose despite his incipient blindness; his mother, who was an educated musician, wrote out his compositions from dictation. Despite his handicap, he wrote 3 operas, 2 oratorios, 2 symphs., and various other works.

Silver, Charles, French composer; b. Paris, April 16, 1868; d. there, Oct. 10, 1949. He studied with Dubois and Massenet at the Paris Cons., winning the Grand Prix de Rome in 1891 with the cantata *L'Interdit.* He wrote the operas *La Belle au bois dormant* (Marseilles, 1902); *Le Clos* (Paris, 1906); *Myriane* (Nice, 1913); *La Mégère apprivoisée* (Paris, Jan. 30, 1922); *La Grand'-mère* (Oct. 7, 1930); *Quatre-vingt-treize* (Paris, Jan. 24, 1936); also orch. works, songs, etc.

Silver, Horace, black American jazz pianist and composer; b. Norwalk, Conn., Sept. 2, 1928. He served as a member of Stan Getz's quintet (1950–51); then was music director of Art Blakey's Jazz Messengers; in 1956 he organized his own quintet. He was a leading proponent of "funky" jazz, which combined elements of swing and gospel music; he composed several pieces in this style which attained a certain popularity among jazz aficionados.

Silverstein, Joseph, distinguished American violinist and conductor; b. Detroit, March 21, 1932. He received his early instruction in violin playing from his father; then studied with Efrem Zimbalist at the Curtis Inst. of Music in Philadelphia; later took lessons with Josef Gingold and Mischa Mischakoff. He played in the Houston Symph. Orch., Denver Symph. Orch., and Philadelphia Orch. before joining the Boston Symph. Orch. in 1955; from 1962–83 he was its concertmaster; from 1971–83 also served as its assistant conductor. He was further chairman of the violin faculty of the Berkshire Music Center at Tanglewood, and also taught at Boston Univ. He appeared as guest conductor with the St. Louis

Symph., Los Angeles Phil., Houston Symph., San Francisco Symph., National Symph. of Washington, D.C., and other American orchs. In 1979–80 he was interim music director of the Toledo (Ohio) Symph.; from 1981–83 he was principal guest conductor of the Baltimore Symph. Orch. In 1983 he was appointed music director of the Utah Symph. Orch. in Salt Lake City.

Silvestri, Constantin, Rumanian conductor and composer; b. Bucharest, June 13, 1913 (May 31, old style); d. London, Feb. 23, 1969. He studied composition with Jora at the Bucharest Cons.; toured as a concert pianist (1925–46); then was engaged as conductor of the Bucharest Phil. (1946–55); later conducted the Bucharest Opera (1955–57) and the Rumanian Radio Orch. (1958–59); also taught conducting at the Bucharest Cons. (1948–59). In 1961 he went to England, where he became principal conductor of the Bournemouth Symph. Orch. until his death. He composed mostly in small forms in an unpretentious neo-Baroque manner.
WORKS: Concerto Grosso (1941); 2 string quartets (1935, 1947); *Sonatina a 2 voci* for Clarinet and Cello (1938); Oboe Sonata (1939); 2 violin sonatas (1939); piano pieces and songs.

Silvestrov, Valentin, Ukrainian composer; b. Kiev, Sept. 30, 1937. He studied with Liatoshinsky at the Kiev Cons.; began to compose in a boldly experimental idiom of Western provenance; wrote piano pieces in the strict 12-tone technique. Although severely reprimanded in the press, he was not forcibly restrained from continuing to write music in a modernistic manner.
WORKS: For Piano: *Variations* (1958); Sonatina (1959); Sonata (1960); *Signals* (1962); *Serenade* (1962); Piano Quintet (1961); *Quartetto piccolo* for String Quartet (1961); Trio for Flute, Trumpet, and Celesta (1962); Symph. No. 1 (1963); *Mysteries* for Alto Flute and Percussion (1964); *Monodia* for Piano and Orch. (1965); *Projections* for Harpsichord, Vibraphone, and Bells (1965); *Spectrum* for Chamber Orch. (1965); Symph. No. 2 for Flute, Percussion, Piano, and Strings (1965); Symph. No. 3 (1966); *Drama* for Violin, Cello, and Piano (1971); *Meditation* for Cello and Chamber Orch. (1972); String Quartet (1974); Symph. No. 4 for Brass Instruments and Strings (1976); also children's pieces for piano, and songs. Some of his compositions had their world premieres at European festivals of modern music.

Simai, Pavol, Czech composer; b. Levice, June 29, 1930. He studied with Pál Kadosa in Budapest, with Alexander Moyzes and Jan Cikker in Bratislava, and with Paul Dessau in East Berlin. In 1968 he settled in Sweden.
WORKS: Flute Sonatina (1952); *Zuzuka,* ballet (1954–60); *Mother Speaks,* melodrama for Female Speaker, Flute, Clarinet, Bassoon, Guitar, and Percussion (1959); *Victory* for Orch. (1963); *Meditation* for Contralto and String Quartet (1965); *5:10* for Clarinet, Violin, Cello, and Piano (1972); Piano Trio

(1974); *Violoncellen* for Mezzo-soprano, Cello, and Piano (1975).

Simandl, Franz, double-bass player and composer; b. Blatna, Bohemia, Aug. 1, 1840; d. Vienna, Dec. 13, 1912. He was double-bass player in the Vienna Court Orch.; from 1869, taught at the Vienna Cons.; publ. *Neueste Methode des Kontrabass-Spiels* (in 3 parts) and *30 Etüden für Kontrabass; Die hohe Schule des Kontrabass-Spiels,* a collection of concertos, studies, solo pieces, etc. His original compositions include a *Konzertstück, Konzert-Etude,* Concerto, fantasias, and minor pieces for his instrument.

Simeonov, Konstantin, Russian conductor; b. Koznakovo, June 20, 1910. He began a career as a singer; then studied conducting at the Leningrad Cons. with Alexander Gauk; subsequently appeared as a guest conductor throughout the Soviet Union. He served as chief conductor of the Ukrainian Theater of Opera and Ballet in Kiev (1961–66); then occupied a similar post at the Kirov Theater of Opera and Ballet in Leningrad (1966–75); he resumed his Kiev post in 1975. He also filled engagements abroad; conducted opera at La Scala in Milan in 1964.

Simić, Borivoje, Serbian conductor and composer; b. Belgrade, Nov. 1, 1920. He studied in Belgrade and became a choral conductor at Belgrade Radio. His music is modernistic in nature and eclectic in its materials, making use of dissonant counterpoint and jazz. His *Movimento dinamico* (Belgrade, Sept. 30, 1955) is characteristic in this respect.

Similä, Martti, Finnish conductor and composer; b. Oulu (Uleaborg), April 9, 1898; d. Lahti, Jan. 9, 1958. He studied in Finland, then in Paris and London; conducted the Helsinki Opera (1927–44) and the Municipal Orch. of Lahti. He made 2 tours in the U.S. as a pianist, in 1923 and 1926; was again in the U.S. in 1957 to lead a memorial concert of the music of Sibelius with the N.Y. Phil. (Dec. 8, 1957). He wrote a book, *Sibeliana;* also composed orch. music.

Simionato, Giulietta, Italian contralto; b. Forli, May 5, 1910. She studied voice with Guido Palumbo in Milan; made her operatic debut in Florence in 1938; from 1939 till 1959 she was the leading contralto singer at La Scala, Milan. After the war, she made guest appearances in the major opera houses in Europe; also appeared in South America. She made her debut at the Metropolitan Opera in N.Y. on Oct. 26, 1959, as Azucena in *Il Trovatore;* sang there again in 1960 and 1962; in 1966 retired from the stage. Her best roles were Rosina in *The Barber of Seville* and Amneris in *Aida.*

Simmons, Calvin, brilliant black American conductor; b. San Francisco; April 27, 1950, the son of a longshoreman and a gospel singer; drowned in Connery Pond, east of Lake Placid, N.Y., Aug. 21, 1982, when his canoe overturned. He sang in the San Francisco Boys' Choir; then went to the Cincinnati

College-Cons. of Music, where he studied conducting with Max Rudolf; when Rudolf was appointed to the faculty of the Curtis Inst. of Music in Philadelphia, Simmons joined him there; he also took piano lessons with Serkin. Returning to San Francisco, he joined the staff of the San Francisco Opera, eventually becoming assistant conductor; subsequently served in the same capacity with the Los Angeles Phil. (1975–78). In 1978 he conducted a performance of *Hansel and Gretel* at the Metropolitan Opera in N.Y. In 1979 he was appointed music director and conductor of the Oakland (Calif.) Symph. Orch. Endowed with natural musical intelligence and practical ability, Simmons easily overcame the still-lingering doubts that a person with black pigmentation of skin could make classical music. His untimely death deprived his race and American music of a great talent.

Simon, Abbey, American pianist; b. New York, Jan. 8, 1922. He studied with David Saperton and Josef Hofmann at the Curtis Inst. of Music in Philadelphia; also took lessons with Leopold Godowsky in N.Y. He began his concert career at 18, evolving a grand bravura style of pianistic virtuosity in which no technical difficulties seem to exist, no tempi are too fast, no nuance is too subtle. He made successful tours in the U.S., South America, Europe (including Russia), Australia, and Japan.

Simon, Alicia, Polish musicologist; b. Warsaw, Nov. 13, 1879; d. there, May 23, 1957. She studied in Warsaw; then went to Germany, where she attended the classes of Kretzschmar and Johannes Wolf at the Univ. of Berlin. She worked in Berlin (1920–23) and Geneva (1923–24); went to the U.S., and worked on the staff of the Library of Congress in Washington (1924–28); then returned to Poland. She was a prof. at the Univ. of Łodz from 1945 to her death. She publ. some valuable studies on Polish music, among them *Polnische Elemente in der deutschen Musik bis zur Zeit der Wiener Klassiker* (Diss., Univ. of Zürich, 1914; publ. in 1916); *The Polish Songwriters* (in Eng.; Warsaw, 1936; 2nd ed., 1939).

Simon, Anton, French pianist and composer; b. Paris, Aug. 5, 1850; d. St. Petersburg, Feb. 1, 1916. He studied piano at the Paris Cons.; in 1871 went to Russia, where he became active as a piano teacher. He wrote the operas *Rolla* (Moscow, April 29, 1892); *The Song of Triumphant Love* (Moscow, Dec. 14, 1897); *The Fishermen* (Moscow, March 7, 1899); a mimodrama, *Esmeralda* (1902); 2 ballets: *The Stars* (1898) and *Living Flowers* (1900); Piano Concerto; Clarinet Concerto; 22 pieces for brass instruments; numerous piano compositions and songs.

Simon, James, German musicologist; b. Berlin, Sept. 29, 1880; d. in the Auschwitz concentration camp, about Oct. 14, 1944. He studied piano with Ansorge and composition with Max Bruch. From 1907 to 1919 he taught at the Klindworth-Scharwenka Cons. in Berlin. He left Germany shortly after the advent of the Nazi regime, and lived in Zürich; then moved to Amsterdam, where the Hitlerite wave engulfed him after the Nazi invasion of the Netherlands. He was deported to Theresienstadt on April 5, 1944, and from there, on Oct. 12, 1944, was sent to Auschwitz, where he was put to death a few days later. His opera, *Frau im Stein,* was produced in Stuttgart in 1925; he also wrote a Symph.; Piano Concerto; Sextet for Piano and Wind Instruments; choruses; many songs.

Simon, Paul, American lyricist and folk-rock singer; b. Newark, N.J., Oct. 13, 1941. Still in high school in Queens, N.Y., he got together with Art Garfunkel, singing songs of their own. They were just 16 when they recorded a song, *Hey, Schoolgirl;* later Simon got a job as a song promoter with E.B. Marks Publishing Co., and also wrote songs. In 1962 he went to England, where he put out an album, *Paul Simon Song Book.* In 1965 he produced, with Garfunkel, their quintessential hit *Sounds of Silence,* which was issued with a dubbed rock sound, and hit the top of the chart; the album of the same title included the nostalgic song of alienation, *I Am a Rock.* He joined Garfunkel in producing the album *Parsley, Sage, Rosemary, and Thyme.* Their subsequent album, *Bookends,* also scored a hit. They proved their mettle and versatility in writing the sound track for the film *The Graduate.* Simon and Garfunkel became a hyphenated entity as far as the public was concerned, but the difference between them was great. Simon was an introspective intellectual who wrote poetry of surprising excellence, while Garfunkel was adept in practical endeavors, composing little but singing and acting in films. Together they produced *Bridge over Troubled Waters, The 59th Street Bridge Song (Feelin' Groovy), The Boxer, Cecilia,* and *Scarborough Fair/Canticle.* Simon's own productions were the eponymous album *There Goes Rhymin' Simon, Mother and Child Reunion, Me and Julio Down by the School Yard,* and *One-Trick Pony.*

Simon, Stephen, American conductor; b. New York, May 3, 1937. He studied piano with Joel Rosen; then enrolled at the Yale Univ. School of Music; also took courses in choral conducting with Hugh Ross and Julius Herford. In 1963 he became music director of the Westchester Orch. Society; in 1970 he was appointed music director of the Handel Society in N.Y., which produced a number of Handel's little-known works.

Simon-Girard, Juliette, French soprano; b. Paris, May 8, 1859; d. Nice, Dec. 1959, at the age of 100. She made her debut at the Folies-Dramatiques in Paris, where she created the principal role in *Les Cloches de Cornevilles* on April 19, 1877; then sang at the premieres of *La Fille du Tambour-major* (1879), *Fanfan la tulipe* (1882), and many other operettas; she became particularly successful in Offenbach's repertoire. She married the tenor **Nicolas Simon,** known as **Simon-Max** (1855–1923); divorced him in 1894, and married the comedian Huguenet. She then retired and lived in Nice.

Simonds, Bruce, American pianist and pedagogue; b. Bridgeport, Conn., July 5, 1895. After studying at Yale Univ. (A.B., 1917), he attended the Schola Cantorum in Paris (1919–20) and the Matthay School in London (1920–21). He made his debut as a pianist in Europe in 1921; in the same year returned to the U.S. and embarked on a successful career as a concert pianist; also in 1921, he joined the teaching staff at Yale; became a prof. in 1938; was dean of the Yale School of Music from 1941 to 1954.

Simone, Nina, black American jazz singer; b. Tryon, N.C., Feb. 21, 1933. Her real name was **Eunice Waymon.** She studied piano with Vladimir Sokoloff at the Curtis Inst. of Music in Philadelphia (1950–53) and later with Carl Friedberg at the Juilliard School of Music in N.Y. (1974). Relinquishing her academic training, she turned to jazz; made numerous appearances at nightclubs and jazz festivals, in programs of gospel songs, contemporary urban ballads, and African chants; it was as a singer of "soul" songs that she became principally known.

Simoneau, Léopold, Canadian tenor; b. Quebec City, May 3, 1918. He studied singing in N.Y.; made his debut as an opera singer in Montreal in 1943; also sang in Paris, at La Scala in Milan, and in Salzburg. He first sang at the Metropolitan Opera in N.Y. on Oct. 18, 1963, as Ottavio in *Don Giovanni.* He was particularly praised for his performances of Mozart's roles. In 1971 he went to San Francisco, where he taught at the Cons. He is married to the Canadian coloratura soprano **Pierrette Alarie.**

Simonetti, Achille, Italian-British violinist; b. Turin, June 12, 1857; d. London, Nov. 19, 1928. He studied violin with Gamba at the Milan Cons. and with Dancla at the Paris Cons.; toured in England with the singer Marie Rôze and the double-bass virtuoso Bottesini; settled in London in 1891, but made frequent tours on the Continent. He wrote a cadenza for Brahms's Violin Concerto, which he played for the first time in Dresden (Dec. 11, 1896); composed numerous solo pieces for the violin.

Simonis, Jean-Marie, Belgian composer; b. Mol, Nov. 22, 1931. He studied composition with Stekke, Souris, Louel, and Quinet, and conducting with Defossez at the Royal Cons. of Brussels; taught at the Royal Cons. from 1969 and at the Music Academy in Uccles from 1971. WORKS: Radio opera, *Gens de maison* (1962); *3 Motets* for Soprano, Chorus, and Orch. (1961); *Introduction et Danse* for Chamber Orch. (1963); *3 esquisses symphoniques* (1964); *Sinfonia da camera* for String Orch. (1966); *L'Automne,* symph. poem (1967); *Scherzetto* for Chamber Orch. (1968); *3 Pieces* for 4 Clarinets (1965); *Duetti* for Viola and Piano (1968); *Impromptu* for Solo Cello (1968–69); *Séquences* for Clarinet and Piano (1969); *3 Lagu Dolanan* for Soprano and Percussion (1969); *Suggestions* for Flute and 4 Percussionists (1970); *Boutades* for 4 Saxophones (1971); *Mouvements* for 2 Pianos (1971); a number of piano pieces: *Etude de*

Concert (1963); *Historiettes* (1972); *Impromptu* (1973); *2 animations* (1973); *2 pastourelles* (1973); *Evocations* (1974).

Simonov, Yuri, Russian conductor; b. Saratov, March 4, 1941. He studied viola and conducting at the Leningrad Cons.; then was conductor of the Kislovodsk Phil. in the Caucasus (1967–69). In 1969 he won first prize at the international competition of conductors at the Santa Cecilia Academy in Rome; returning to Moscow, he was appointed a conductor of the Bolshoi Theater, and in 1970 was named its chief conductor; showed considerable initiative in staging modern Russian operas.

Simpson (or **Sympson**), **Christopher,** English player of the viola da gamba, writer, and composer; b. Yorkshire, c.1610; d. Scampton, Lincolnshire, between May 5 and July 29, 1669. He fought on the Royalist side in the English civil war (1643) and later entered the service of Sir Robert Bolles as music tutor to the latter's son. Simpson was famous as a composer. WORKS: *The Division Violist or an Introduction to the Playing Upon a Ground: Divided into 2 parts* (London, 1659; 2nd ed., with title and text in Latin and Eng., in 3 parts, London, 1665; 3rd ed., 1712; with 2 sonatas for Viola da Gamba; modern ed. by Nathalie Dolmetsch, London, 1958); *The Principles of Practicle Musick ... either in Singing or Playing upon an Instrument* (London, 1665; enlarged ed. as *Practicall Musick in 5 Parts teaching by a new and easie Method,* London, 1667; modern ed. by P. Lord, Oxford, 1970); he also compiled annotations to Campion's *Art of Discant* (1655). In MS: *Months and Seasons: Fancies, Airs, Galliards* for 2 Basses and a Treble; *Fancies for Viola da Gamba;* etc. BIBLIOGRAPHY: M. Meredith, *Christopher Simpson and the Consort of Viols* (Diss., Univ. of Wales, Cardiff, 1969).

Simpson, George Elliott, American music educator and composer; b. Orange, N.J., Nov. 1, 1876; d. Kansas City, Oct. 8, 1958. He studied with Emil Mollenhauer (violin) in N.Y. (1886–90); then took composition lessons with Carl Busch in Kansas City (1894–1900); subsequently studied at the Leipzig Cons. with Jadassohn and Reinecke (1900–1903). He held various teaching positions in Kansas City and in Texas. His works include *American Symphony* (Kansas City, March 26, 1925); 12 symph. poems; 4 overtures; about 50 piano pieces and 80 songs.

Simpson, Robert, English composer and writer on music; b. Leamington, Warwickshire, March 2, 1921. He studied composition with Howells in London (1941–44); received his Mus.D. from Durham Univ. in 1951; joined the staff of the BBC as a music producer in 1951, resigning in 1980. He publ. a valuable monograph, *Carl Nielsen, Symphonist* (London, 1952; 2nd ed., revised, 1979); also *The Essence of Bruckner* (London, 1966) and 3 BBC booklets: *Bruckner and the Symphony* (1963), *Sibelius and Nielsen*

2135

(1965), and *Beethoven's Symphonies* (1970); also edited *The Symphony* (2 vols., Harmondsworth, 1966 and 1967). He was awarded the Carl Nielsen Gold Medal of Denmark in 1956 for his valiant work in behalf of Nielsen's music. While occupied with writing and directing radio programs, he composed symphs., chamber music, and choruses.

WORKS: 8 symphs.: No. 1, in one movement (1951; Copenhagen, June 11, 1953); No. 2 (1955; Cheltenham Festival, July 16, 1957); No. 3 (1962; Birmingham, March 14, 1963); No. 4 (1970–72; Manchester, April 26, 1973); No. 5 (1972; London, May 3, 1973); No. 6 (1976; London, April 8, 1979); No. 7 (1977); No. 8 (1981; London, Nov. 10, 1982); Violin Concerto (1959; Birmingham, Feb. 25, 1960); Piano Concerto (1967; Cheltenham Festival, July 14, 1967); 9 string quartets (1952, 1953, 1954, 1973, 1974, 1975, 1977, 1979, 1982); *Canzona* for Brass (1958); *Variations and Fugue* for Recorder and String Quartet (1958); Trio for Clarinet, Cello, and Piano (1967); Quartet for Clarinet and Strings (1968); Quartet for Horn, Violin, Cello, and Piano (1975); *Media morte in vita sumus,* motet for Chorus, Brass, and Timpani (1975); Piano Sonata (1946); *Variations and Finale on a Theme by Haydn* for Piano (1948); 2-piano Sonata (1980).

BIBLIOGRAPHY: R. Johnson, *Robert Simpson. 50th Birthday Essays* (London, 1971).

Simpson, Thomas, English composer; b. Milton, Kent (baptized, April 1), 1582; d. after 1625. He went to Germany as a youth; served as a viol player at the Heidelberg court from 1608 to 1611; then was Musicus to the Prince of Holstein-Schaumburg (1616–22) and subsequently was employed in the royal chapel of Copenhagen as a court musician to King Christian IV. An excellent composer of court dances and songs, he brought out *Opusculum newer Pavanen* (Frankfurt, 1610); *Pavanen, Galliarden, Courtanten und Volten* (Frankfurt, 1611; reprinted in 1617 under the title *Opus newer Paduanen, Galliarden, Intraden, Canzonen, etc.*); and *Tafel-Consort, allerhand lustige Lieder von 4 Instrumenten und Generalbass* (Hamburg, 1621).

BIBLIOGRAPHY: G. Oberst, *Englische Orchestersuiten um 1600* (Wolfenbüttel, 1929).

Simrock, Nikolaus, founder of the famous German publishing house in Berlin; b. Mainz, Aug. 23, 1751; d. Bonn, June 12, 1832. He played the horn in the Electoral Orch. in Bonn until 1794. He began dealing in printed music and instruments in 1780; in 1785 opened a music shop in Bonn, selling musical instruments; in 1793 he established there a music publishing house with its own printing press. During Beethoven's lifetime Simrock's catalogue listed 85 of his works, including the *Kreutzer Sonata* and opus numbers 17, 31, 81b, 102, and 107. His son **Peter Joseph Simrock** (b. Bonn, Aug. 18, 1792; d. Cologne, Dec. 13, 1868) succeeded him and greatly increased the prestige of the house by acquiring the early works of Brahms. Peter was succeeded by his son **Friedrich August ("Fritz") Simrock** (b. Bonn, Jan. 2, 1837; d. Ouchy, near Lausanne, Aug. 20, 1901), who transferred the firm to Berlin in 1870, publ. the works of Brahms, and, at the suggestion of Brahms, added the works of Dvořák to his catalogue. His nephew **Johann Baptist ("Hans") Simrock** (b. Cologne, April 17, 1861; d. Berlin, July 26, 1910) reorganized the firm in 1902 as a stock company and established branches in London and Paris. A grandson of Fritz August Simrock, **Fritz Auckenthaler** (b. Zürich, Nov. 17, 1893; d. Basel, April 19, 1973), headed the firm from 1920 to 1929, when it was sold to A.J. Benjamin in Hamburg; in 1951 the Hamburg firm, which also had a branch in London, resumed its original name, N. Simrock Co.

BIBLIOGRAPHY: W. Ottendorf-Simrock, *Das Haus Simrock* (Ratingen, 1954); K. Stephenson, *Johannes Brahms und Fritz Simrock, Weg einer Freundschaft. Briefe des Verlegers an den Komponisten* (Hamburg, 1961).

Sims, Ezra, American composer of innovative music; b. Birmingham, Ala., Jan. 16, 1928. His education was highly diversified; he took courses in mathematics at Birmingham Southern College, obtaining a B.A. in 1947, and concurrently studied with Hugh Thomas and B. Ackley Brower at the Birmingham Cons. (1945–48). He entered Yale Univ. as a student of Quincy Porter (B.M., 1952), and then enrolled in the U.S. Army Language School, where he earned a degree in Mandarin Chinese in 1953. Returning to music, he studied with Darius Milhaud and Leon Kirchner at Mills College (M.A., 1955). He attended Aaron Copland's seminar at the Berkshire Music Center at Tanglewood, Mass., in 1960. To earn a living, he took all kinds of menial jobs, as a mail clerk, steelworker, and display designer. From 1958 to 1962 and again from 1965 to 1974 he was employed as a cataloguer at the music library of Harvard Univ. In 1962 he received a Guggenheim fellowship, and had an opportunity to go to Tokyo, where he put together the electronic portion of the background score for the Japanese play *Sakoku*. In 1978 he again traveled to Japan. He made his permanent home in Cambridge, Mass.; there he founded the whimsically named New England Dinosaur; there was nothing extinct about his concerts there, however; on the contrary, the Dinosaur programs were projections into a distant future rather than a retrospection into a fossilized past. The music Ezra Sims writes himself is microtonal, based on a scale of 18 tones within a larger complex of 72 degrees in equal temperament. Amazingly enough, he found string players in Boston and elsewhere who could perform his microtonal pieces with spectacular ease. In 1977 he developed a polyphonic keyboard providing any tuning whatsoever, in Pythagorean, or just, intonation, as well as in equal temperament that divides the octave into fewer than 37 intervals.

WORKS: *Chamber Cantata on Chinese Poems* (1954); Cello Sonata (1957); String Quartet No. 1 (1959); String Quartet No. 2, in *Sonate concertante* (1961); String Quartet No. 3 (1962); Octet for Strings in quarter-tones and sixth-tones (1964); *Antimatter* for Magnetic Tape Collage (1968); *A Frank Overture: 4 Dented Interludes and Coda* (1969); *Real*

Toads, musique concrète (1970); *Dreams for Sale* for Mezzo-soprano, Baritone, and Piano (1970); Quartet for Oboe and Strings (1971); *Second Thoughts* for Double Bass, microtonal music with quarter-tones and sixth-tones (1974); Quintet for Flute, Clarinet, Violin, Viola, and Cello (1974); *Slow Hiccups* for 2 Recorders (1975); *Elegie nach Rilke* for Soprano, Flute, Clarinet, Violin, and Cello, microtonal music including *Sprechstimme* (Cambridge, Mass., Nov. 16, 1976); *Yr obedt servt* for Small Ensemble (1977); *Aeneas on the Saxophone* for Voices, Clarinet, Horn, Trombone, Viola, and Double Bass, microtonal music to 18-note scale (perf. on the 50th birthday of Ezra Sims, Dinosaur Annex, Boston, Jan. 16, 1978); *And, As I Was Saying* for Viola or Violin, microtonal music (1979); *All Done from Memory* for Violin Solo, microtonal music in an 18-tone scale or equal temperament in 72-tone scale (1980; Dinosaur Annex, Boston, Jan. 18, 1981; Janet Packer, soloist); Sextet for Clarinet, Saxophone, Horn, Violin, Viola, and Cello (1981); *This Way to the Egress-or-Manners Makyth Man* for String Trio (1984).

BIBLIOGRAPHY: David Ewen, *American Composers* (N.Y., 1982); *The Boston Composers Project* (Cambridge, Mass., 1983).

Sims, "Zoot" (John Haley Sims), American jazz tenor-alto saxophonist and clarinetist; b. Inglewood, Calif., Oct. 29, 1925. He began to study clarinet as a child; later mastered the tenor and alto saxophones. He played with Bobby Sherwood's band; then joined Benny Goodman; gained renown as one of the "Four Brothers" saxophone section of Woody Herman's orch. (1947–49); subsequently toured in the U.S. and Europe. In later years he played the soprano saxophone with equal aplomb.

Šín, Otakar, eminent Czech music theorist and composer; b. Rokytno, Moravia, April 23, 1881; d. Prague, Jan. 21, 1943. He studied composition with Vítězslav Novák at the Prague Cons., where he was appointed a prof. of theory in 1919. He publ. the textbooks *Complete Science of Harmony on the Basis of Melodies and Rhythm* (Prague, 1922), *Science of Counterpoint, Imitation and Fugue* (Prague, 1936), and *General Science of Music as a Preparation for the Study of Harmony, Counterpoint and Musical Forms* (completed and publ. posthumously by František and Karel Janeček in Prague, 1949).

WORKS: 2 symph. poems: *Tillotama* (1908) and *King Menkera* (1916–18); *Radio Overture* (1936); *3 Czech Dances* for Orch. (1939; also for Nonet); 2 string quartets (1923, 1926–28); Cello Sonata (1934); *Small Suite* for Violin and Piano (1937); *Hunting,* festive greeting for Horns (1938); numerous piano pieces; choruses; songs.

Sinatra, Frank (Francis Albert), popular American singer; b. Hoboken, N.J., Dec. 12, 1915, of immigrant Italian parents. He sang in a glee club in school; appeared on amateur radio shows. Inspired by the tone production of Tommy Dorsey's trombone playing, he evolved, by convex inhalation from a corner of the mouth, a sui generis "mal can-

to" in *sotto voce* delivery, employing a Caruso-like *coup-de-glotte* at climactic points. This mode of singing, combined with an engagingly slender physique, stirred the young females of the World War II era to fainting frenzy at his performances. Sinatra's press agents were quick to exploit the phenomenon, dubbing him "Swoonlight Sinatra." He eventually overcame his anesthetic appeal and became a successful baritone crooner; like most of his colleagues, he never learned to read music. He revealed an unexpected dramatic talent as a movie actor, eliciting praise from astonished cinema critics. In May 1976, the Univ. of Nevada at Las Vegas conferred on him the honorary degree of Literarum Humanitarum Doctor, in appreciation of his many highly successful appearances in the hotels and gambling casinos of Las Vegas.

BIBLIOGRAPHY: E.J. Kahn, *The Voice: The Story of an American Phenomenon* (N.Y., 1947); A. Shaw, *Sinatra: 20th-Century Romantic* (N.Y., 1968); A.I. Lonstein, *The Compleat Sinatra Discography, Filmography, Television Appearances, Motion Picture Appearances, Radio, Concert, Stage Appearances* (Ellenville, N.Y., 1970); Earl Wilson, *Sinatra: An Unauthorized Biography* (N.Y., 1976; Sinatra instituted a suit for $3 million against the publishers for alleged distortion of his life as "boring and uninteresting").

Sinclair, George Robertson, English organist; b. Croydon, Oct. 28, 1863; d. Birmingham, Feb. 7, 1917. He received his musical education in Dublin; in 1889 was appointed organist of Hereford Cathedral; also conducted the Three Choirs Festivals (1891–1912). He acquired a reputation as a master organist; the 11th variation of Elgar's *Enigma* is inscribed to Sinclair ("G.R.S.") and vividly portrays Sinclair's virtuosity in the use of the organ pedals.

BIBLIOGRAPHY: *Musical Times* (Oct. 1900; March 1906; March 1917).

Sinding, Christian, celebrated Norwegian composer; b. Kongsberg, Jan. 11, 1856; d. Oslo, Dec. 3, 1941. He studied first with L. Lindeman in Norway, then at the Leipzig Cons. with Schradieck (violin), Jadassohn (theory), and Reinecke (orchestration); after 4 years (1877–81) he returned to Norway, and had his Piano Quartet and a symph. performed in Oslo; a government stipend enabled him to continue his studies in Germany, and he spent 2 years (1882–84) in Munich, Berlin, and Dresden; there he wrote his first opera, *Titandros,* much influenced by Wagner. On Dec. 19, 1885, he gave a concert of his works in Oslo; during another stay in Germany, his Piano Quintet was played in Leipzig, with Brodsky and Busoni among the performers (Jan. 19, 1889); Erika Lie-Nissen played his Piano Concerto in Berlin (Feb. 23, 1889). He publ. a number of piano pieces in Germany; of these, *Frühlingsrauschen* became an international favorite. His opera to a German text, *Der heilige Berg* (1914), was not successful. In 1915 he received a life pension of 4,000 crowns "for distinguished service"; on his 60th birthday (1916) the Norwegian government presented him with a purse of 30,000 crowns, a mark of appreciation for "the greatest national composer since Grieg." He was invited by George Eastman to teach at the Eastman School of Music in Rochester, N.Y., during the academic season 1921–22; after this journey, he lived mostly in Oslo. He continued to compose, and toward the end of his life wrote in larger forms; his 3rd Symph. was conducted by Nikisch with the Berlin Phil. in 1921, and his 4th Symph. was performed on his 80th birthday in Oslo (1936). His works aggregate to 132 opus numbers. Most of his music is of a descriptive nature; his lyric pieces for piano and his songs are fine examples of Scandinavian Romanticism, but the German inspiration of his formative years is much in evidence; he was chiefly influenced by Schumann and Liszt.

WORKS: OPERAS: *Titandros* (1884; not produced); *Der heilige Berg* (Dessau, April 19, 1914). FOR ORCH.: Symph. No. 1 (Oslo, March 25, 1882); Symph. No. 2 (Berlin, March 22, 1907); Symph. No. 3 (Berlin, Jan. 10, 1921); Symph. No. 4, subtitled *Vinter og Vaar* (Oslo, Jan. 11, 1936); *Episodes chevaleresques*, op. 35 (1888); *Rondo infinito*, op. 42 (1889; revised 1897); Piano Concerto in D-flat (Berlin, Feb. 23, 1889); 3 violin concertos (1898, 1901, 1917); *Legende* for Violin and Orch., op. 46 (1900); *Romanze* for Violin and Orch., op. 100 (1910); *Abendstimmung* for Violin and Orch., op. 120 (1915). CHAMBER MUSIC: String Quartet, op. 70 (1904); Piano Quintet, op. 5 (1884); 3 piano trios: op. 23 (1893), op. 64 (1902), op. 87 (1908); 4 violin sonatas: op. 12 (1894), op. 27 (1895), op. 73 (1905), op. 99, subtitled *Sonate im alten Stil* (1909); 4 violin suites: op. 10 (1889), op. 14 (1891), op. 96 (1909), op. 123 (1919); *Scènes de la vie* for Violin and Piano, op. 51 (1900); *Cantus doloris*, variations for Violin and Piano, op. 78 (1906); 3 capriccios for Violin and Piano, op. 114 (1913); *Nordische Ballade* for Cello and Piano, op. 105 (1911); etc. For Piano: Sonata, op. 91 (1909); *Fatum*, variations, op. 94 (1909); *5 Stücke*, op. 24 (1894); *7 Stücke*, op. 25 (1895); *6 Stücke*, op. 31 (1896); *6 Stücke*, op. 32 (1896; No. 3 is the celebrated *Frühlingsrauschen*); *6 Charakterstücke*, op. 33 (1896; contains *A la Menuetto* and *Ständchen*); *6 Charakterstücke*, op. 34 (1896; contains *Chanson*); *6 Klavierstücke*, op. 49 (1899; contains *Humoresque*); *Mélodies mignonnes*, op. 52 (1900); *4 morceaux de salon*, op. 54 (1900; contains *Sérénade*); etc. VOCAL WORKS: Songs: *Alte Weisen*, op. 1 (1886); *Lieder und Gesänge*, op. 11 (1888; contains *Viel Träume* and *Ein Weib*); *Galmandssange*, op. 22 (1893; contains *Mainat*); *Nyinger*, op. 90 (1908); etc.; about 250 publ. songs in all; several cantatas and other choral works. A complete list of Sinding's works was publ. by Ö. Gaukstad in *Norsk Musikkgranskning* (1938).

Singelée, Jean-Baptiste, Belgian violinist and composer; b. Brussels, Sept. 25, 1812; d. Ostend, Sept. 29, 1875. He publ. 144 works (2 concertos, many solos for violin, fantasias on operatic airs, etc.).

Singer Edmund, Hungarian violinist; b. Totis, Oct. 14, 1830; d. Stuttgart, Jan. 23, 1912. He studied in Budapest, and later at the Paris Cons.; was a con-certmaster in Weimar (1853–61); later was a prof. at the Stuttgart Cons. He publ. a number of attractive violin pieces: *Tarantella, Rapsodie hongroise, Airs variés*, etc.; wrote cadenzas for the violin concertos of Beethoven and Brahms; edited the études of Rode, Kreutzer, Fiorillo, Rovelli, and Gaviniés; with M. Seifriz, compiled the *Grosse theoretisch-praktische Violinschule* (2 vols., 1884).

Singer, Jacques, conductor; b. Przemyśl, Poland, May 9, 1911; d. New York, Aug. 11, 1980. He emigrated to the U.S.; studied violin at the Curtis Inst. of Music in Philadelphia and the Juilliard School of Music in N.Y. From 1937 to 1942 he was music director of the Dallas Symph.; then conducted the Vancouver Symph. (1947–50), the Corpus Christi Symph. (1955–62), and the Portland (Oreg.) Symph. (1962–73).

Singer, Kurt, German musicologist; b. Berent, Oct. 11, 1885; d. in the Terezin concentration camp, Feb. 7, 1944. He studied musicology with Friedlaender in Berlin; also became a doctor of medicine; wrote criticisms for the socialist newspaper *Vorwärts*. In 1935, deprived of his posts in German organizations, he became music director of the Reichsverband Jüdischer Kulturbünde. He went to the Netherlands in 1939, but was arrested there by the invading Germans, and eventually perished.

WRITINGS: *Richard Wagner* (Berlin, 1913); *Bruckners Chormusik* (Stuttgart, 1924); *Berufskrankheiten der Musiker* (Berlin, 1927; in Eng. as *Diseases of the Musical Profession*, N.Y., 1932); *Heilwirkung der Musik* (Stuttgart, 1927).

Singer, Otto, German pianist and composer; b. Sora, July 26, 1833; d. New York, Jan. 3, 1894. He studied piano with Moscheles in Leipzig; then became a pupil of Liszt in Weimar; emigrated to America in 1867. He wrote several cantatas, including *The Landing of the Pilgrim Fathers* (1876); 2 piano concertos and other piano music. His son, **Otto Singer, Jr.** (b. Dresden, Sept. 14, 1863; d. Leipzig, Jan. 8, 1931), studied music in Munich; was active primarily as a choral conductor in Leipzig and Berlin. Among Singer's compositions are a *Konzertstück* for Violin and Orch.; a Piano Quintet; many choruses. He arranged vocal scores of operas by Wagner and Richard Strauss.

Singer, Peter, Austrian composer and music theorist; b. Häselgehr (Lechthal), July 18, 1810; d. Salzburg, Jan. 25, 1882. He was a Franciscan monk; composed 101 masses, about 600 offertories, etc.; publ. *Cantus choralis in provincia Tirolensi consuetus* (Salzburg, 1862). In 1839 he invented the "Pansymphonikon," a kind of orchestrion with reeds; publ. *Metaphysische Blicke in die Tonwelt, nebst einem neuen System der Tonwissenschaft* (Munich, 1847).

BIBLIOGRAPHY: Pater Hartmann, *Peter Singer* (Innsbruck, 1910).

Singher, Martial, noted French baritone and pedagogue; b. Oloron-Sainte-Marie, Basses-Pyrénées, Aug. 14, 1904. He received his education as a public-school teacher in Dax, and then at the Ecole Normale de Toulouse and the Ecole Normale Supérieure de St. Cloud. He then studied voice with André Gresse at the Paris Cons. (premier prix for singing, 1929; premier prix for opera and opéra-comique singing, 1930; Grand Prix Osiris de l'Institute de France, 1930). He also studied voice with Juliette Fourestier. He made his operatic debut in Amsterdam as Orestes in *Iphigénie en Tauride* on Nov. 14, 1930. He then joined the Paris Opéra, remaining with it until 1941; also sang at the Opéra-Comique. On Jan. 10, 1940, he married Margareta Busch, daughter of the conductor Fritz Busch. He came to the U.S. in 1941; made his Metropolitan Opera debut in N.Y. on Dec. 10, 1943, as Dapertutto in *Les Contes d'Hoffmann;* subsequently sang the roles of the Count in *Le nozze di Figaro,* Lescaut in *Manon,* all 4 baritone roles in *Les Contes d'Hoffmann;* remained on the roster, with some interruptions, until 1959. He also sang with the leading orchs. of the U.S. and appeared widely in song recitals. He was on the faculty of the Mannes College of Music in N.Y. (1951–62) and the Curtis Inst. of Music in Philadelphia (1955–68); then was director of the voice and opera dept. and the opera producer at the Music Academy of the West in Santa Barbara (1962–81). His students have included Donald Gramm, John Reardon, James King, Louis Quilico, Judith Blegen, Benita Valente, and Jeannine Altmeyer. He was a particularly distinguished interpreter of the French operatic and song repertoire.

Singleton, Arthur James ("Zutty"), black American jazz drummer; b. Bunkei, La., May 14, 1898; d. New York, July 14, 1975. He began his career in New Orleans in 1915; in 1929 went to N.Y., where he played with Louis Armstrong, Sidney Bechet, and others; also formed his own jazz groups. He was considered one of the best jazz drummers of his time.

Singleton, Esther, American writer on music; b. Baltimore, Nov. 4, 1865; d. Stonington, Conn., July 2, 1930. She lived most of her life in N.Y.; publ. *A Guide to the Operas* (1899); *A Guide to Modern Opera* (1909); *The Orchestra and Its Instruments* (1917); contributed the chapter on American music to Lavignac's *Encylopédie de la musique* (1915).

Sinico, Francesco, Italian choral conductor and composer; b. Trieste, Dec. 12, 1810; d. there, Aug. 18, 1865. He studied with G. Farinelli; was an organist and conductor in various churches; in 1843 established his own singing school in Trieste, providing excellent training for choral singing. He produced his opera *I Virtuosi di Barcellona* in 1841. His son, **Giuseppe Sinico** (b. Trieste, Feb. 10, 1836; d. there, Dec. 31, 1907), continued the popular singing classes at the Sinico School in Trieste; wrote several operas, which he produced there: *Marinella* (Aug. 26, 1854), *I Moschettieri* (March 26, 1859), *Aurora di Nevers* (March 12, 1861), *Alessandro Stradella*

(Lugo, Sept. 19, 1863), and *Spartaco* (Nov. 20, 1886). He publ. *Breve metodo teoricopratico di canto elementare.*

BIBLIOGRAPHY: *Una famiglia triestina di musicisti "I Sinico"* (Trieste, 1932).

Sinigaglia, Leone, Italian composer; b. Turin, Aug. 14, 1868; d. there, May 16, 1944. He was a pupil at the Turin Cons., studying with Giovanni Bolzoni; later studied in Vienna (1894–1900) with Mandyczewski, and in Prague and Vysoka with Dvořák (1900–1901). His first successful work was a violin concerto (1900) dedicated to Arrigo Serato, who played it with considerable success in the principal cities of Germany. Sinigaglia's early works were much influenced by Brahms and Dvořák; then he turned for inspiration to the music of his native Piedmont, and in this field achieved a lasting reputation. Toscanini conducted in Turin the premiere of Sinigaglia's suite *Danze piemontesi,* on popular themes (May 14, 1905); later Sinigaglia publ. a collection of songs (6 albums), *Vecchie canzoni popolari del Piemonte;* another work in the folk-song manner is the symph. suite *Piemonte* (1909; Utrecht, Feb. 16, 1910); he further wrote *Le Baruffe Chiozzotte,* an overture to Goldoni's comedy (Utrecht, Dec. 21, 1907); *Rapsodia piemontese* for Violin and Orch.; *Romanze* for Violin and Orch.; *Variations on a Theme of Brahms* for String Quartet (1901); *Serenade* for String Trio (1906); Cello Sonata (1923).

BIBLIOGRAPHY: E. Desderi, "L. Sinigaglia," *Rivista Musicale Italiana* (1946); L. Rognoni, "Leone Sinigaglia," *Musicisti piemontesi e liguri,* Chigiana, XVI (1959); C. Mosso and E. Bassi, eds., *Leone Sinigaglia, Torino, 1868–1944: Primo centenario della nascita* (Turin, 1968).

Sinopoli, Giuseppe, Italian conductor and composer; b. Venice, Nov. 2, 1946. He studied at the Benedetto Marcello Cons. in Venice; concurrently enrolled in the medical school at the Univ. of Padua, receiving a diploma in medicine in 1971; subsequently he practiced as a surgeon and a psychiatrist. He then went to Vienna to study conducting with Swarowsky; in 1972 joined the faculty of the Venice Cons.; in 1975 he organized the Bruno Maderna Ensemble (so named after the notable conductor), with which he gave performances of modern music; from 1979 he presented programs of contemporary music with the Berlin Phil. On Jan. 20, 1983, he made his American debut with the N.Y. Phil. In 1983 he was appointed principal conductor of the Philharmonia Society of London. As a composer, he pursues a modern technological trend, making frequent use of electronic sound and computers. In this manner he wrote *25 studi su tre parametri* (1969); *Musica per calcolatori analogici* (1969); *Numquid et unum* for Cembalo and Flute (1970); *Opus Ghimal* for Orch. (1971); *Sunyata* for String Quintet and Soprano (1972); Piano Sonata (1974).

Siohan, Robert, French music theorist, writer, and composer; b. Paris, Feb. 27, 1894. He studied at the

Paris Cons.; in 1929 founded the Concerts Siohan, which he conducted until 1936; was choral conductor at the Paris Opera (1931–46); from 1948 to 1962 he was an instructor in solfège and sight-reading at the Paris Cons.; subsequently served as inspector-general of music in the Ministry of Culture. He received his doctorate at the Sorbonne in 1954 with the thesis *Théories nouvelles de l'homme* (publ. under the title *Horizons sonores,* Paris, 1956). Among his compositions are the opera *Le Baladin de satin cramoisi* (1927); *Cantique au frère soleil* (1928); Violin Concerto; Cello Concerto; Piano Concerto; *Gravitations* for Viola and Piano; Quartet with Soprano part. He publ. a monograph on Stravinsky (Paris, 1959; in Eng., N.Y., 1970); *Histoire du public musical* (Lausanne, 1967); numerous articles in French and German publications.

Sipilä, Eero, Finnish composer; b. Hailuoto, July 27, 1918; d. Kajaani, May 18, 1972. He studied with Merikanto and Madetoja; wrote relatively few works, mostly in Baroque forms, and also sacred choral pieces; the most important are *Partita* for Wind Quartet (1955); *Super flumina Babylonis* and *Miserere,* 2 motets for Chorus (1963); *Te Deum Laudamus* for Alto, Baritone, Chorus, and Orch. (1969); *Composition* for Orch. (Kajaani, May 8, 1973).

Siqueira, José de Lima, Brazilian composer and conductor; b. Conceição, June 24, 1907. He played saxophone and trumpet, taking instruction from his father; then entered the National School of Music in Rio de Janeiro, where he studied with Burle Marx and Francisco Braga. Upon graduation he founded the Orquesta Sinfónica Brasileira (1940), which he conducted until 1948; in 1949 he organized another orch., called Orquesta Sinfónica de Rio de Janeiro; he also filled engagements as a conductor in the U.S. (1944) and in Russia (1955).
WORKS: Opera, *A compadecida* (1959; Rio de Janeiro, Dec. 20, 1961); symph. drama, *Gimba* (1960); *O carnaval Carioca,* festive theater piece to commemorate the centennial of the city of Rio de Janeiro (1965); *Alvorada brasileira,* symph. poem (1936); *4 poemas indígenas* for Orch. (1944); 4 symphs. (1933, 1951, 1954, 1956); 6 orch. pieces, each entitled *Dança brasileira;* 5 symph. suites on Brazilian themes (1955–70); *Candomblé,* oratorio on folkloric texts (Rio de Janeiro, Dec. 20, 1957); *Encantamento da Magia Negra,* a fetishist motet on native themes (1957); Cello Concerto (1952); Piano Concerto (1955); Violin Concerto (1957); 3 string quartets; Piano Trio; 2 violin sonatas; Cello Sonata; numerous songs and piano pieces. A list of his works is found in *Composers of America,* vol. 16 (Washington, D.C., 1970).

Širola, Božidar, Croatian musicologist and composer; b. Žakanj, Dec. 20, 1889; d. Zagreb, April 10, 1956. He studied musicology with Guido Adler in Vienna, receiving his Dr.Phil. in 1921 at the Univ. of Vienna. Returning to Yugoslavia, he was on the faculty of the Zagreb Cons. (1935–41); then was director of the Ethnographic Museum in Zagreb. He wrote the operas *Comedy in Stanac* (1916), *Cittern and Drum* (1930), and *The Village Chaplain* (1940); 8 oratorios; 4 masses; *Symphonie concertante* for Piano and Orch. (1952); Violin Concerto (1953); *Spomen iz Slovenije (Reminiscences of Slovenia)* for Wind Octet (1926); 13 string quartets; Piano Quartet; 3 piano trios; 8 piano sonatas; *24 Inventions* for Piano; publ. (in German) several valuable essays on Croatian music, and (in Croatian) a history of Croatian music (Zagreb, 1922).

Sistermans, Anton, Dutch bass; b. 's Hertogenbosch, Aug. 5, 1865; d. The Hague, March 18, 1926. He studied with Stockhausen in Frankfurt; from 1895 gave concerts in Europe; his only appearance in opera was as Pogner (Bayreuth, 1899). From 1904 to 1915 he taught singing at the Klindworth-Scharwenka Cons. in Berlin; then lived in The Hague.

Sitsky, Larry, Australian pianist and composer; b. Tientsin, China, Sept. 10, 1934 (to Russian émigré parents). The family went to Australia in 1951. Sitsky studied piano with Winifred Burston at the New South Wales Cons. in Sydney (1951–55); then went to San Francisco, where he studied with Egon Petri (1958–61). Returning to Australia, he taught piano at the Queensland State Cons. (1961–65), and since 1966 has taught at the Canberra School of Music. As a concert pianist, he gave recitals at a young age while still in China (1945–51), and has continued concertizing since then throughout Australia.
WORKS: 2 operas: *The Fall of the House of Usher,* after Poe (1965), and *Lenz* (1969–70); ballet, *Sinfonia (The Dark Refuge)* for 10 Players (1964); *Apparitions* for Amateur or School Orch. (1966); *Prelude (Homage to Stravinsky)* for Orch. (1968); Concerto for Violin, Female Chorus, and Orch. (1970); Concerto for Amplified Wind Quintet and Orch. (1970–71; Sydney, April 3, 1971); *Burlesque* for Flute, Oboe, and Piano (1958); Solo Violin Sonata (1959); Solo Flute Sonata (1959); Oboe Sonatina (1962); Woodwind Quartet (1963); Sonata for 2 Guitars (1968); String Quartet (1969); *Sonata formalis* for Piano (1959); *Fantasia (In Memory of Petri)* for Piano (1962); *Dimensions* for Piano and 2 Tapes (1964); *Improvisations* for Harpsichord (1965); Concerto for 2 Solo Pianos (1967); *5 Improvisations* for Chorus and Piano (1961); *Song of Love* for Orch. (1974); *The Legions of Asmodeus* for 4 Theremins (1975); *Narayana* for Piano Trio (1975).

Sitt, Hans, German violinist and composer; b. Prague, Sept. 21, 1850; d. Leipzig, March 10, 1922. He studied at the Prague Cons.; held various positions as a violinist and conductor of theater orchs. in Breslau, Prague, and Chemnitz. In 1881 he settled in Leipzig; organized a series of popular concerts there; was viola player in the Brodsky Quartet; conducted the Bachverein (1885–1903) and other musical societies there. He wrote 3 violin concertos, a Viola Concerto, 2 cello concertos; publ. valuable studies for the violin; also *Praktische Violaschule; Schulausgabe neuerer Violinlitteratur* (5 books);

and (with Reinecke) *Lyrica,* a collection of 30 Classical and Romantic pieces for violin and piano.

Sittard, Alfred, German organist, son of **Josef Sittard;** b. Stuttgart, Nov. 4, 1878; d. Berlin, March 31, 1942. He studied with his father, and later with Wüllner at the Cologne Cons.; was organist at the Kreuzkirche in Dresden (1903–12), and then at St. Michael's in Hamburg (1912–25). In 1925 he was appointed prof. of organ at the Berlin Akademie für Kirchen- und Schulmusik, and in 1933 became Kapellmeister of the Berlin Cathedral chorus. He publ. *3 Choralstudien* for Organ; also wrote *Das Hauptorgelwerk und die Hilfsorgel der Michaeliskirche in Hamburg* (1912).

Sittard, Josef, German music historian; b. Aachen, June 4, 1846; d. Hamburg, Nov. 24, 1903. He studied at the Stuttgart Cons., and later joined its faculty as an instructor in singing and piano; from 1885 was music critic for the Hamburg *Correspondent.* He publ. several valuable papers dealing with German theater music; *Studien und Charakteristiken* (Hamburg, 1889; collected essays); *Geschichte des Musik- und Concertwesens in Hamburg* (Leipzig, 1890); *Zur Geschichte der Musik und des Theaters am Württembergischen Hofe* (2 vols., Stuttgart, 1890, 1891); etc.; also composed some choral works and songs.

Sivori, Camillo, Italian violinist; b. Genoa, Oct. 25, 1815; d. there, Feb. 19, 1894. He was a child prodigy; as a mere infant, was presented to Paganini, who accepted him as a pupil; later he studied with Paganini's own teacher, Giacomo Costa. Sivori played in Paris and London at the age of 12, producing an understandable sensation; toured Germany and Russia, and in 1846–50 made an extensive tour through North and South America. His manner of playing, if not his bizarre behavior, was modeled after Paganini's. He composed 2 violin concertos and numerous character pieces in the virtuoso manner fashionable in his day: *Tarentelle napolitaine, Carnaval de Chili, Carnaval de Cuba, Carnaval américain, Folies espagnoles,* etc.
BIBLIOGRAPHY: E. James, *Camillo Sivori: A Sketch of His Life, Talents, Travels and Successes* (London, 1845); L. Escudier, *Mes souvenirs* (Paris, 1863); A. Pierrottet, *Camillo Sivori* (Milan, 1896).

Sixt, Johann Abraham, German organist and composer; b. Gräfenhausen, Württemberg, Jan. 3, 1757; d. Donaueschingen, Jan. 30, 1797. He was the son of a schoolmaster and organist; received his musical training at home; traveled in Germany; was in Vienna in 1784, and received a recommendation from Mozart. He then settled in Donaueschingen, and remained there for 13 years as a piano teacher and chamber musician to the court, until his death. He wrote piano trios, sonatas, and other instrumental works; of particular interest are his lieder, with long introductions in the accompaniment, setting the mood of the text.

Sixta, Jozef, Slovak composer; b. Jičín, May 12, 1940. He studied with Očenaš at the Cons. in Bratislava (1955–60) and with Alexander Moyzes at the Music Academy there (1960–64); then went to Paris, where he had lessons with Messiaen and Jolivet. Returning to Bratislava, he taught at the Academy of Music there.
WORKS: Quintet for Piano and Winds (1961); *Fantasia* for Piano (1962); Symph. (1964); String Quartet (1965); *Variations* for 13 Instruments (1967); *Synchronia* for String Orch. (1968); *Asynchronia* for String Orch. (1970); Nonet (1970); Quartet for 4 Flutes (1976).

Sjöberg, Svante Leonard, Swedish organist, conductor, and composer; b. Karlskrona, Aug. 28, 1873; d. there, Jan. 18, 1935. He studied at the Stockholm Cons. with Nordquist and Dente, and in Berlin with Max Bruch. Returning to Sweden in 1901, he was organist at the Stadskyrka in Karlskrona, and conductor of the Musikförening there (1901–34). He wrote an overture to *Gustaf Vasa* (1901); some chamber music; songs.

Sjögren, Emil, Swedish composer; b. Stockholm, June 16, 1853; d. there, March 1, 1918. He studied composition at the Stockholm Cons. with H. Berens, in Berlin with Kiel, and in Vienna with Grädener. In 1891 he was appointed organist at St. John's Church in Stockholm. His importance as a composer rests chiefly on his songs, of which he wrote about 200, to texts in Swedish, French, and German; he also wrote a Festival Overture; several choruses; 5 violin sonatas; a Cello Sonata; 2 piano sonatas; several groups of lyric pieces for piano. Nils Brodén compiled an index of all of Sjögren's publ. compositions (Stockholm, 1918). A complete edition of his songs was undertaken by the Swedish Academy in 1950–51.
BIBLIOGRAPHY: S.E. Svensson, "Emil Sjögrens vokala lyrik," *Svensk Tidskrift för Musikforskning* (1935).

Skalkottas, Nikos, greatly talented Greek composer; b. Chalkis, island of Euboea, March 8, 1904; d. (of a strangulated hernia) Athens, Sept. 19, 1949. He studied violin with his father, with his uncle, and with a nonrelated violinist at the Athens Cons. (1914–20). In 1921 he went to Berlin, where he continued his violin studies at the Hochschule für Musik (1921–23); then took lessons in music theory with Philipp Jarnach (1925–27). But the greatest influence on his creative life was Schoenberg, whom he met in Berlin; Schoenberg, in his book *Style and Idea,* mentions Skalkottas as one of his most gifted disciples. Skalkottas eagerly absorbed Schoenberg's instruction in the method of composition with 12 tones related only to one another, but in his own music applied it in a very individual manner, without trying to imitate Schoenberg's style. In Berlin Skalkottas also received some suggestions in free composition from Kurt Weill. He returned to Athens in 1933, when Schoenberg was driven out of Germany by the Nazis; in Athens Skalkottas earned his living by playing violin in local orchs., but continued to compose diligently, until his early death. His music written between 1928 and 1938 reflects Schoenberg's idiom; later works are tonally conceived, and several of them are in the clearly ethnic Greek modalities, set in the typical asymmetric meters of Balkan folk music. After his death a Skalkottas Society was formed in Athens to promote performances and publication of his works; about 110 scores of various genres are kept in the Skalkottas Archives in Athens.

WORKS: FOR ORCH.: *The Mayday Spell,* "fairy drama" for Soprano, Speaker, Dancers, and Orch. (1944–49); 2 ballets: *The Maid and Death* (1938) and *La Mer grecque* (1948); 2 suites for Orch. (1929, 1944); 3 piano concertos: No. 1 (1931); No. 2 (1937–38); No. 3, with 10 Winds and Percussion (1939; London, July 9, 1969; due to the length of the work, a different soloist was used for each movement); *36 Greek Dances* for Orch. (1933–36; also perf. in separate sections); 2-piano Concertino (1937; Oxford, July 1, 1969); Violin Concerto (1938); Concertino for Oboe and Strings (1961 orchestration by P. Guarino of the original for Oboe and Piano, 1939); Concerto for Violin, Viola, and Wind Orch. (1939–40; London, July 7, 1969); *10 Sketches* for String Orch. or String Quartet (1940); Double-bass Concerto (1940); *Little Suite* for String Orch. (1942); *The Return of Ulysses,* symph. in one movement (1944–45; London, June 23, 1969); Concerto for 2 Violins and Orch. (1944–45); *5 Short Greek Dances* for Orch. (1946); *Classical Symphony in A* for Wind Orch. (1947); Sinfonietta (1948); Piano Concertino (1949); *The Unknown Soldier* for Chorus and Orch. (1929). CHAMBER MUSIC: Sonata for Solo Violin (1925); 4 violin sonatinas (1928, 1929, 1935, 1935); 5 string quartets: No. 1 (1928; his first 12-tone work); No. 2 (1929); No. 3 (1935); No. 4 (1940, London, July 13, 1969); *Easy String Quartet* (1929); 2 violin sonatas (1929, 1940); Octet for 4 Woodwinds and String Quartet (1930); *Piece for 8 Winds or Double String Quartet* (1931); Piano Trio (1936); *Scherzo* for Piano and 3 Strings (1936); *March of the Little Soldiers* for Violin and Piano (1936); *Rondo* for Violin and Piano (1936); *Little Chorale and Fugue* for Violin and Piano (1936); *8 Variations on a Greek Folk Tune* for Piano Trio (1938); *Suite* for Cello and Piano (1938); Cello Sonata (1938); *9 Greek Dances* for String Quartet (1938–47; transcribed from the *36 Greek Dances*); *Gavotta* for Violin and Piano (1939); Concertino for Oboe and Piano (1939); Duo for Violin and Viola (1939–40); *Largo* for Cello and Piano (1940); 2 quartets for Piano, Oboe, Bassoon, and Trumpet (1941–43); Concertino for Trumpet and Piano (1941–43); *Sonata concertante* for Bassoon and Piano (1943); 2 *Little Suites* for Violin and Piano (1946, 1949); Duo for Violin and Piano (1947); *Bolero* for Cello and Piano (1948–49); *Little Serenade* for Cello and Piano (1949); Cello Sonatina (1949); *Tender Melody* for Cello and Piano (1949). FOR PIANO: Sonatina (1927); *15 Little Variations* (1927); 4 *Suites* (1936, 1940, 1940, 1940); *32 Pieces* (1940); *4 Etudes* (1940); an unpubl. treatise, in Greek, *The Technique of Orchestration* (1940).

BIBLIOGRAPHY: J. Papaioannou, "Nikos Skal-

kottas," in H. Hartog, ed., *European Music in the Twentieth Century* (N.Y., 1957).

Škerjanc, Lucijan Marija, Slovenian composer; b. Graz, Dec. 17, 1900; d. Ljubljana, Feb. 27, 1973. He studied composition in Vienna with Josef Marx and in Paris with Vincent d'Indy; returning to Yugoslavia, he became a prof. of the Academy of Music in Ljubljana. His music reflects neo-Romantic trends, with some impressionistic colors. His works include 5 symphs.; Clarinet Concerto; Harp Concerto; Horn Concerto; String Quintet; *Concertone* for 4 Cellos; he also publ. a manual on counterpoint.

Škerl, Dane, Slovenian composer; b. Ljubljana, Aug. 26, 1931. He studied with Škerjanc at the Ljubljana Academy of Music, graduating in 1952; then took courses in electronic music in Cologne. He taught at the Music Academy in Sarajevo (1960–70); in 1970 was appointed to the faculty of the Music Academy of Ljubljana.

WORKS: 2 ballets: *Kontrasti* (*Contrasts;* 1967) and *Grozdanin kikot* (1969); Concertino for Violin and String Orch. (1948); *Prelude and Scherzo* for Clarinet and Strings (1948); Concertino for Piano and Strings (1949); 5 symphs. (1951, 1963, 1965, 1970, 1972); *Serenade* for Strings (1952); Concerto for Orch. (1956); *Rolo* for Orch. (1959); *Inventions* for Violin and Strings (1960); *18 Etudes* for Strings (1960); *5 Compositions* for Clarinet and Strings (1961); *Contrasts* for Orch. (1962); Clarinet Concerto (1963); *Little Suite* for Orch. (1965); *7 Bagatelles* for Strings (1966); *Improvvisazione concertante* for Horn, Viola, and Chamber Orch. (1968); Trombone Concerto (1970); cantata, *Moj dom* (*My House;* 1962); *4 Miniatures* for Flute, Bassoon, and Piano (1957); *Prelude and Scherzo* for Violin, Clarinet, and Piano (1959); *Skica* (*Sketch*) for Violin and Piano (1964); *3 Improvisations* for Flute, Cello, and Piano (1966); piano pieces.

Skilton, Charles Sanford, distinguished American composer; b. Northampton, Mass., Aug. 16, 1868; d. Lawrence, Kans., March 12, 1941. He first studied in Germany; after graduating from Yale Univ. (B.A., 1889), he studied in N.Y. with Harry Rowe Shelley (organ) and Dudley Buck (composition); then went to Germany, where he studied with Bargiel at the Hochschule für Musik in Berlin (1891–93). From 1893 to 1896 he was director of music at the Salem Academy and College in North Carolina, and conducted the local orch. there; then filled a similar post at the State Normal School, in Trenton, N.J. (1897–1903); in 1903 he was engaged as a prof. of organ and theory at the Univ. of Kansas, Lawrence, where he remained most of his life. He made a detailed study of Indian music, and introduced Indian motifs into the traditional forms of a suite or a fantasy.

WORKS: Operas: *The Sun Bride* (radio perf., April 17, 1930); *Kalopin* (not produced; received the David Bispham Memorial Medal of the American Opera Society of Chicago, 1930); *The Day of Gayomair* (1936; not produced); for Orch.: *Suite Prime-*

val, on Indian melodies, in 2 parts: *2 Indian Dances* (originally for String Quartet, 1915; Minneapolis, Oct. 29, 1916) and part II (Minneapolis, Nov. 13, 1921); *Autumn Night* (Detroit, Dec. 11, 1930); *Shawnee Indian Hunting Dance* (Detroit, Dec. 11, 1930); *A Carolina Legend,* symph. poem; *Mt. Oread,* overture; *Sioux Flute Serenade* for Small Orch. (1920); cantata, *The Witch's Daughter* (1918); *The Guardian Angel,* oratorio (1925); *From Forest and Stream* (1930); *Midnight* for Women's Voices; *The Fountain* for Women's Voices; String Quartet; Sonatina for Violin and Piano; *Sarabande* for Wind Instruments. He also publ. *Modern Symphonic Forms* (N.Y., 1927).

BIBLIOGRAPHY: J.T. Howard, *Charles Sanford Skilton* (N.Y., 1929).

Skinner, Ernest M., American organ builder; b. Clarion, Pa., Jan. 15, 1866; d. Duxbury, Mass., Nov. 27, 1960. He was the founder of the Ernest M. Skinner Co., organ builders, originally of Dorchester, later of Methuen, Mass. Until 1905 the business was carried on by Skinner himself; it was then incorporated, with Skinner as president. From 1917 to 1932 he was technical director of the Skinner Organ Co., which in 1932 was merged with the Aeolian Co. of Garwood, N.J., and became the Aeolian-Skinner Organ Co. Skinner was especially successful in the construction of organ pipes reproducing the exact tone color of the various woodwind instruments and the French horn; among several important inventions is the "duplex windchest," by means of which the stops of 2 manuals are made interchangeable, and the arrangement of placing the stops on swinging sides. The Skinner Co. built the organ in the National Cathedral at Washington, D.C. Skinner publ. the valuable books *The Modern Organ* (1915; 6th ed., 1945) and *The Composition of the Organ* (1947).

Sklavos, Georges, Greek composer; b. Brailov, Rumania, of Greek parents, Aug. 20, 1888; d. Athens, March 19, 1976. He studied with Armand Marsick at the Athens Cons.; was appointed instructor there in 1913. He devoted himself chiefly to the musical theater.

WORKS: Operas: *Lestenitza* (Athens, March 14, 1947); *Kassiani* (Oct. 30, 1959); *Amphitryon* (1960); symph. poem, *L'Aigle* (1922); ethnically colored orch. pieces: *Fantaisie crétoise; Noces insulaires; Suite arcadienne;* also choruses; songs.

Sköld, (Karl) Yngve, Swedish composer; b. Vallby, April 29, 1899. He studied piano and composition in Stockholm (1915–18), then in Brno (1920–22) and Prague (1922). From 1938 to 1964 he was librarian of the Swedish Composers' Society. His music blends Nordic Romanticism with subdued modernity.

WORKS: 4 symphs. (1915, 1937, 1949, 1966); 3 piano concertos (1917, 1946, 1969); Cello Sonata (1927); 4 string quartets (1930, 1955, 1965, 1974); *Suite concertante* for Viola and Orch. (1936); *Sinfonia di chiesa* for Orch. (1939); Violin Concerto (1941); Cello Concerto (1947); *Double Concerto* for Violin, Cello, and Orch. (1950); *Divertimento* for Orch. (1951); Quintet for 2 Flutes, Cello, and Piano (1958); Sonata for Viola and Organ (1962); Concertino for 5 Winds, Timpani, and Strings (1963); 2 piano sonatas (1963); Piano Sonatina (1970); *Divertimento* for Violin, Viola, and Cello (1971); *Trio domestico* for Piano Trio (1974).

Skriabin, Alexander. See **Scriabin.**

Škroup, Franz (František), Czech composer and conductor; b. Osice, near Pardubice, June 3, 1801; d. Rotterdam, Feb. 7, 1862. He studied law in Prague. In 1827 he became assistant conductor, and from 1837 principal conductor, at the Bohemian Theater, Prague, and remained at that post until 1857; he put into performance several Wagner operas for the first time in Prague. He wrote several operas to Czech librettos, which he conducted at the Bohemian Theater: *Dráteník* (Feb. 2, 1826); *Oldřich a Božena* (Dec. 14, 1828); *Libušin snatek* (*Libusa's Marriage;* 3rd act perf. Nov. 6, 1835; first full perf., April 11, 1850); also the German operas *Drahomira* (Nov. 20, 1848) and *Der Meergeuse* (Nov. 29, 1861). In 1860 Škroup took a position offered to him with a German opera troupe in Rotterdam, and died there after 2 seasons. Besides his operas, he wrote some chamber music and many popular Bohemian songs, of which *Kde domov muj* became so famous that it was mistaken for a folk song and was made into the Czech national anthem.

BIBLIOGRAPHY: J. Plavec, *František Škroup* (Prague, 1946).

Škroup, Jan Nepomuk, Czech composer, brother of **František Škroup;** b. Osice, near Pardubice, Sept. 15, 1811; d. Prague, May 5, 1892. He was a chorus master at the Prague Opera; then served as music director at various churches in Prague and finally at the Cathedral; in 1846, he was appointed teacher of singing at the Theological Seminary. He wrote manuals for church services: *Manuale pro sacris functionibus* and *Musica sacra pro populo;* also a vocal method.

Skrowaczewski, Stanislaw, eminent Polish-born American conductor and composer; b. Lwow, Oct. 3, 1923. His father was a brain surgeon; his mother, a fairly good pianist. A precocious *wunderkind* even for a fabled land of child prodigies, he composed an orch. overture at the age of 8, played a piano recital at 11, and performed Beethoven's 3rd Piano Concerto at 13, conducting the orch. from the keyboard. He enrolled at the Lwow State Cons.; at the same time he took courses in physics, chemistry, and philosophy at the Univ. of Lwow. The oppressive Nazi occupation of Poland interrupted his studies, and an unfortunate bomb exploded in the vicinity of his house, causing an injury to his hands that interfered with his further activities as a concert pianist. After the war, he moved to Cracow, where he took lessons in composition with Palester and conducting with Bierdiajew. In 1947 he received a French government scholarship which enabled him to study composition with Nadia Boulanger and conducting with Paul Kletzki in Paris. He then led the Wroclaw Orch. (1946–47), the State Silesian Phil. in Katowice (1949–54), the Cracow Phil. (1954–56), and the National Phil. Orch. in Warsaw (1956–59). In 1956 he won the first prize in the international conducting competition in Rome. On Dec. 4, 1958, he made his American debut as a guest conductor of the Cleveland Orch., scoring an impressive success which secured for him consideration for a permanent American post. In 1960 he was named music director of the Minneapolis Symph. Orch. (renamed the Minnesota Orch. in 1968), and asserted his excellence both as a consummate technician of the baton and a fine interpreter of the classic and modern repertoire. In 1966 he became an American citizen. In the interim he appeared as a guest conductor in Canada, Mexico, South America, Israel, Hawaii, Australia, and New Zealand. As an opera conductor, he made his Metropolitan Opera debut in N.Y. on Jan. 8, 1970, in *Die Zauberflöte*. In 1979 he resigned as music director of the Minnesota Orch., and was made its conductor emeritus. In 1982 he was appointed principal conductor and musical adviser of the Halle Orch. in Manchester, England.

WORKS: 4 symphs.: No. 1 (1936); No. 2 (1945); No. 3, *Symphony for Strings* (1947); No. 4 (1954); *Overture 1947* (1947); *Ugo and Parisina*, ballet (1949); *Music at Night*, extracts from *Ugo and Parisina* (1949–51); Concerto for English Horn and Orch. (Minneapolis, Nov. 21, 1969); *Ricercari notturni* for Saxophone and Orch. (1977; Minneapolis, Jan. 19, 1978); Concerto for Clarinet and Orch. (1981); Trio for Clarinet, Bassoon, and Piano (1982); also 4 string quartets, 6 piano sonatas, songs, and music for the theater and cinema.

BIBLIOGRAPHY: David Ewen, *Musicians since 1900* (N.Y., 1978).

Skuhersky, František, Czech composer, pianist, and organist; b. Opočno, July 31, 1830; d. České Budějovice, Aug. 19, 1892. He first studied medicine; then had music lessons with Kittl in Prague; from 1854 to 1866 he was in Innsbruck, where he conducted the Musikverein. Returning to Prague, he conducted the court orch., gave music courses at the Czech Univ., and became particularly interested in the problem of Bohemian church music. He publ. several fundamental texts on music theory in the Czech language: *O formách hudebních* (Prague, 1873); *Nauka o hudební komposici* (4 vols., Prague, 1880–84); *Nauka o harmonii* (Prague, 1885). He wrote the operas *Vladimir, Bohuv Zvolenec* (Prague, Sept. 27, 1863), and *Rektor a General* (Prague, March 28, 1873), and a German opera, *Der Liebesring* (Innsbruck, 1861; in Czech under the title *Lora*, Prague, April 13, 1868); a symph. poem, *May;* 4 masses; *30 Orgelvorspiele in den Kirchentonarten* (without accidentals) and a similar set of organ pieces with accidentals; many organ studies; piano pieces and songs.

Slatkin, Felix, American violinist and conductor; b. St. Louis, Dec. 22, 1915; d. Los Angeles, Feb. 8, 1963. He studied violin with Zimbalist and conducting with Reiner at the Curtis Inst. of Music in Philadelphia; then was a member of the St. Louis Symph. Orch. In 1937 he went to Los Angeles, where he played in film studio orchs. In 1947 he organized the Hollywood String Quartet, which gave regular performances until it was dissolved in 1961. He also was active as a conductor, especially in programs of light music. His son, **Leonard Slatkin,** is a noted American conductor.

Slatkin, Leonard, American conductor; b. Los Angeles, Sept. 1, 1944. He was reared in a family of musicians; his father, **Felix Slatkin,** was a violinist and conductor, his mother a cellist. Leonard Slatkin played the violin in infancy; took up the viola at puberty; played piano through adolescence; studied composition with Castelnuovo-Tedesco in Los Angeles. He made his conducting debut at the Aspen Music Festival at the age of 19; then studied conducting with Jean Morel at the Juilliard School of Music (Mus.B., 1968). He subsequently held the posts of associate conductor of the St. Louis Orch. and principal guest conductor of the Minnesota Symph. Orch.; also was a guest conductor with the N.Y. Phil., Chicago Symph. Orch., Philadelphia Orch., and several European orchs., among them the London Symph. and the Concertgebouw Orch. of the Netherlands. In 1977–79 he was conductor of the New Orleans Phil.; then (as of the 1979–80 season) was engaged as conductor of the St. Louis Symph. Orch.

Slaughter, A. Walter, English composer; b. London, Feb. 1860; d. there, April 2, 1908. He was a chorister at St. Andrews on Wells St.; studied with A. Cellier and Jacobi. He was a conductor, successively, of the Royal Theatre, the Olympic, Drury Lane, and St. James's Theatre; wrote a number of musical stage works, among them the 3-act comic opera *Marjorie* (1889), *The Rose and the Ring* (after Thackeray; 1890), and a musical comedy, *The French Maid* (1897).

Slavenski, Josip, outstanding Yugoslav composer; b. Cakovec, May 11, 1896; d. Belgrade, Nov. 30, 1955. His real name was **Stolcer (Stolzer),** but he changed it to the distinctly Slavonic name around 1930, and used it exclusively in his publ. works. He studied with Kodály in Budapest and with Novák in Prague. In 1924 he established himself in Belgrade; in 1945 he became a prof. of composition at the Music Academy there. A musician of advanced ideas, he attempted to combine Slavic melodic and rhythmic elements with modern ingredients; he experimented with nontempered scales and devised a "natural" scale of 53 degrees to the octave. His first such experiment was *Prasimfonia* ("protosymphony"), scored for Orch., Organ, and Piano (1919–26); there followed *Balkanophonia*, suite for Orch. (Berlin, Jan. 25, 1929); an oriental cantata, *Religiophonia* (1934). Other works are a Violin Concerto (1927); 4 string quartets (1923, 1928, 1938, 1940); *Slavenska Sonata* for Violin and Piano (1924); *Sonata religiosa* for Violin and Organ (1925); piano pieces on Balkan themes.

BIBLIOGRAPHY: K. Kovačević, *Hrvatski kompozitori i njihova djela* (Zagreb, 1960).

Slavický, Klement, Czech composer; b. Tovačov, Sept. 22, 1910. He studied composition with Jirák and Suk, and conducting with Dědeček and Talich at the Prague Cons. (1927–31) and then at its Master School there (1931–33); was music director of Czech Radio in Prague (1936–51); then taught privately. WORKS: *Fantasia* for Orch. and Solo Piano (1931); 4 sinfoniettas (1940, 1962, 1972–80, 1982); *Moravian Dance Fantasies* for Orch. (1951); *Rhapsodic Variations* for Orch. (1953; Prague, Feb. 17, 1954); 2 string quartets (1932, 1972); *2 Compositions* for Cello and Piano (1936); Trio for Oboe, Clarinet, and Bassoon (1937); *Suite* for Oboe and Piano (1959); *Partita* for Solo Violin (1962); *Intermezzi mattutini* for Flute and Harp (1965); *Trialogo* for Violin, Clarinet, and Piano (1966); *Capricci* for Horn and Piano (1967); *Musica monologica* for Harp (1968); *Poema a rondo* for Cello and Piano (1973); *Přátelství (Friendship),* violin sonata (1974); *Sentenze* for Trumpet and Piano (1976). For Piano: *3 Compositions* (1947); a sonata subtitled *Zamyšlení nad životem* (*Contemplation of Life;* 1957–58); *In Black and White* (1958); *12 Little Etudes* (1964); *Etudes and Essays,* 7 pieces (1965); *Suite* for Piano, 4-hands (1968); *Cycle* (1970); organ pieces; choruses; songs.

Slavík, Josef, Bohemian violinist; b. Jince, March 26, 1806; d. Budapest, May 30, 1833. He studied with Pixis at the Prague Cons.; went to Vienna in 1826; then went on a concert tour; in 1829 was appointed to the court chapel in Vienna, and became a friend of Schubert, who dedicated to him his *Fantasie* for Violin and Piano, which Slavik performed for the first time in 1828. Among his own compositions are a Violin Concerto (1823) and *Grand Potpourri* for Violin and Orch. (1826).

BIBLIOGRAPHY: J. Pohl, *Josef Slavík* (Prague, 1906); St. Klíma, *Josef Slavík* (Prague, 1956).

Sleeper, Henry Dike, American organist and music educator; b. Patten, Maine, Oct. 9, 1865; d. Winter Park, Fla., Jan. 28, 1948. He studied with J.K. Paine in Boston, and later in London. After teaching at various colleges, he joined the faculty of Smith College in 1898, and was head of the music dept. there from 1904 to 1924. He wrote a number of organ pieces and songs; was co-editor of *The Common Order Choir Book* (1903) and *Hymns of Worship and Service* (college ed.).

Slenczynska, Ruth, American pianist of precocious talent; b. Sacramento, Calif., Jan. 15, 1925. Her father, a violinist, subjected her to severe discipline when her musical talent was revealed in early childhood; she played in public in Berlin when she was 6 years old, and performed with an orch. in Paris at the age of 11. She made a sensation and was acclaimed by European critics as a prodigy of na-

ture; she took lessons with Egon Petri, Artur Schnabel, Alfred Cortot, and others in Europe and America, and even played for Rachmaninoff, who became interested in her destiny. However, she developed psychological difficulties with her father, whose promotion of her career became obsessive, and had to cease public appearances; when she played concerts at the age of 15, the critics characterized her performances as mechanical reproductions of the music, seemingly without any personal projection. She then engaged in teaching; became a prof. of piano at Southern Illinois Univ. in Edwardville. She publ. a book of memoirs (with Louis Biancolli), *Forbidden Childhood* (N.Y., 1957), in which she recounted the troubles of a child prodigy's life; she also brought out a pedagogical edition, *Music at Your Fingertips. Aspects of Pianoforte Technique* (with A.M. Lingg; N.Y., 1961).

Slezak, Leo, famous Austrian tenor; b. Mährisch-Schönberg, Moravia, Aug. 18, 1873; d. Egern-on-the-Tegernsee, Bavaria, June 1, 1946. As a youth, he sang in the chorus of the Brünn Opera; made his debut as Lohengrin there (March 17, 1896); the role became one of his outstanding successes. He was with the Berlin Opera for a season (1898–99); in 1901 became a member of the Vienna Opera, where he was active until 1926; also performed frequently in Prague, Milan, and Munich. Not satisfied with his vocal training, he went to Paris, where he studied with Jean de Reszke. He made his London debut with marked acclaim as Lohengrin, May 18, 1900, at Covent Garden; appeared in America for the first time as Otello, with the Metropolitan Opera Co., N.Y. (Nov. 17, 1909); sang with the Metropolitan during its spring tour of 1910 and its summer season in Paris; remained with the company until 1913; subsequently sang also in Russia; gave recitals presenting distinguished programs, and performed with impeccable taste. He also acted in motion pictures. He was a man of great general culture, and possessed an exceptionally sharp literary wit, which he displayed in his reminiscences, *Meine sämtlichen Werke* (1922) and *Der Wortbruch* (1927); both were later combined in a single vol. (1935; Eng. trans. as *Songs of Motley: Being the Reminiscences of a Hungry Tenor,* London, 1938); he also publ. *Rückfall* (1940). A final book of memoirs, *Mein Lebensmärchen,* was publ. posthumously (1948). His son, the film actor Walter Slezak, publ. Slezak's letters, *Mein lieber Bub. Briefe eines besorgten Vaters* (Munich, 1966), and *What Time's the Next Swan?* (N.Y., 1962), alluding to the possibly apocryphal story of the swan failing to arrive in time in *Lohengrin.*

Slick, Grace, American rock singer and songwriter; b. Chicago, Oct. 30, 1939. She attended Finch College and the Univ. of Miami; then moved to San Francisco and soon became a part of the radical milieu there. With her husband, Jerry Slick, and others, she formed the rock group The Great Society in 1965. In 1966 she joined The Jefferson Airplane, which airlifted her to the stratosphere of rock fame; she rose even higher with its successor, The Jefferson Starship, but in 1978 struck out on her own. Her most successful songs were *White Rabbit, Manhole, Dreams,* and *Welcome to the Wrecking Ball.*

Slobodianik, Alexander, brilliant Soviet pianist; b. Kiev, Sept. 5, 1941. He studied at the Moscow Cons. with Gornostaeva, graduating in 1964. In 1966 he received 4th prize at the Tchaikovsky Competition in Moscow. He subsequently undertook numerous concert tours in Russia and abroad. He was particularly successful during his American tours in the 1970s. Like most Soviet pianists who venture abroad, he astounds by his unlimited technical resources, but he is also appreciated for the romantic élan of his playing.

Slobodskaya, Oda, Russian soprano; b. Vilna, Dec. 10, 1888; d. London, July 29, 1970. She studied at the St. Petersburg Cons.; made her operatic debut as Lisa in *The Queen of Spades* at the Maryinsky Theater in 1919. She also sang the regular repertoire there, including the roles of Marguerite in *Faust* and Aida. She emigrated in 1922; sang in Paris, at La Scala in Milan, and in Buenos Aires; eventually settled in London; sang Venus in *Tannhäuser* at Covent Garden in 1932. She developed an active career in England, establishing herself as an authoritative interpreter of Russian songs in recital; she also joined the faculty of the Guildhall School of Music and proved a sympathetic and effective voice teacher.
    BIBLIOGRAPHY: M. Leonard, *Slobodskaya* (London, 1978).

Slonimsky, Nicolas, Russian-American musicologist; b. St. Petersburg, April 27, 1894. A failed *wunderkind,* he was given his first piano lesson by his illustrious maternal aunt **Isabelle Vengerova,** on Nov. 6, 1900, according to the old Russian calendar. Possessed by inordinate ambition, aggravated by the endemic intellectuality of his family of both maternal and paternal branches (novelists, revolutionary poets, literary critics, university professors, translators, chessmasters, economists, mathematicians, inventors of useless artificial languages, Hebrew scholars, speculative philosophers), he became determined to excel beyond common decency in all these doctrines; as an adolescent, wrote out his future biography accordingly, setting down his death date as 1967, but survived. He enrolled in the St. Petersburg Cons. and studied harmony and orchestration with 2 pupils of Rimsky-Korsakov, Kalafati and Maximilian Steinberg; also tried unsuccessfully to engage in Russian journalism. After the Revolution he made his way south; was a rehearsal pianist at the Kiev Opera, where he took some composition lessons with Glière (1919); then was in Yalta, Crimea (1920), where he earned his living as a piano accompanist to displaced Russian singers, and as an instructor at a dilapidated Yalta Cons.; thence proceeded to Turkey, Bulgaria, and Paris, where he became secretary and piano-pounder to Serge Koussevitzky. In 1923 he came to the U.S.; became coach in the opera dept. of the East-

man School of Music in Rochester, N.Y., where he took an opportunity to study some more composition with the visiting prof. Selim Palmgren, and conducting with Albert Coates; in 1925 was again with Koussevitzky in Paris and Boston, but was fired for insubordination in 1927. He learned to speak polysyllabic English and began writing music articles for the *Boston Evening Transcript* and the *Christian Science Monitor;* ran a monthly column of musical anecdotes of questionable authenticity in *Etude* magazine; taught theory at the Malkin Cons. in Boston and at the Boston Cons.; conducted the Pierian Sodality at Harvard Univ. (1927–29) and the Apollo Chorus (1928–30). In 1927 he organized the Chamber Orch. of Boston with the purpose of presenting modern works; with it he gave first performances of works by Charles Ives, Edgar Varèse, Henry Cowell, and others; became a naturalized American citizen in 1931. In 1931–32 he conducted special concerts of modern American, Cuban, and Mexican music in Paris, Berlin, and Budapest under the auspices of the Pan-American Assoc. of Composers, producing a ripple of excitement; he repeated these programs at his engagements with the Los Angeles Phil. (1932) and at the Hollywood Bowl (1933), which created such consternation that his conducting career came to a jarring halt. In 1945–47 he became, by accident (the head of the dept. had died suddenly of a heart attack), lecturer in Slavonic languages and literatures at Harvard Univ.; in 1962–63 he traveled in Russia, Poland, Yugoslavia, Bulgaria, Rumania, Greece, and Israel under the auspices of the Office of Cultural Exchange at the U.S. State Dept., as a lecturer in native Russian, ersatz Polish, synthetic Serbo-Croatian, Russianized Bulgarian, Latinized Rumanian, archaic Greek, passable French, and tolerable German. Returning from his multinational travels, he taught variegated musical subjects at the Univ. of Calif., Los Angeles; was irretrievably retired after a triennial service (1964–67), ostensibly owing to irreversible obsolescence and recessive infantiloquy; but, disdaining the inexorable statistics of the actuarial tables, continued to agitate and even gave longwinded lecture-recitals in institutions of dubious learning. As a composer, he cultivated miniature forms, usually with a gimmick, e.g., *Studies in Black and White* for Piano (1928) in "mutually exclusive consonant counterpoint," a song cycle, *Gravestones,* to texts from tombstones in an old cemetery in Hancock, N.H. (1945), and *Minitudes,* a collection of 50 quaquaversal piano pieces (1971–77). His only decent orch. work is *My Toy Balloon* (1942), a set of variations on a Brazilian song, which includes in the score 100 colored balloons to be exploded *f f f* at the climax. He also conjured up a *Möbius Strip-Tease,* a perpetual vocal canon notated on a Möbius band to be revolved around the singer's head; it had its first and last performance at the Arrière-Garde Coffee Concert at UCLA, on May 5, 1965, with the composer officiating at the piano nonobbligato. A priority must be conceded to him for writing the earliest singing commercials to authentic texts from the *Saturday Evening Post* advertisements, among them *Make This a Day of Pepsodent,*

No More Shiny Nose, and *Children Cry for Castoria* (1925). More "scholarly," though no less defiant of academic conventions, is his *Thesaurus of Scales and Melodic Patterns* (1947), an inventory of all conceivable and inconceivable tonal combinations, culminating in a mind-boggling "Grandmother Chord" containing 12 different tones and 11 different intervals. Beset by a chronic itch for novelty, he coined the term "pandiatonicism" (1937), which, *mirabile dictu,* took root and even got into reputable reference works, including the 15th edition of the *Encyclopædia Britannica.* In his quest for trivial but not readily accessible information, he blundered into the muddy field of musical lexicography; publ. *Music since 1900,* a chronology of musical events, which actually contains some beguiling serendipities (N.Y., 1937; 4th ed., 1971); took over the vacated editorship (because of the predecessor's sudden death during sleep) of Thompson's *International Cyclopedia of Music and Musicians* (4th to 8th eds., 1946–58), and somehow managed to obtain the editorship of the 5th and 6th editions of the prestigious *Baker's Biographical Dictionary of Musicians* (N.Y., 1958; 1978). Other publications: *Music of Latin America* (N.Y., 1945; several reprints; also in Spanish, Buenos Aires, 1947); *The Road to Music,* ostensibly for children (N.Y., 1947); *A Thing or Two about Music* (N.Y., 1948; inconsequential; also lacking an index); *Lexicon of Musical Invective,* a random collection of pejorative reviews of musical masterpieces (N.Y., 1952); numerous articles for encyclopedias; also a learned paper, *Sex and the Music Librarian,* valuable for its painstaking research; the paper was delivered by proxy, to tumultuous cachinnations, at a symposium of the Music Library Assoc., at Chapel Hill, N.C., Feb. 2, 1968.

BIBLIOGRAPHY: Henry Cowell, "Nicolas Slonimsky," in *American Composers on American Music* (Stanford, Calif., 1933; cf. reciprocally, Nicolas Slonimsky, "Henry Cowell," ibid.). In 1978 he mobilized his powers of retrospection in preparing an autobiography, *Failed Wunderkind,* subtitled *Rueful Autopsy* (in the sense of self-observation, not dissection of the body).

Slonimsky, Sergei, greatly talented Soviet composer, nephew of **Nicolas Slonimsky;** b. Leningrad, Aug. 12, 1932. A member of a highly intellectual family (his father was a well-known Soviet author; his paternal grandfather, an economist, the author of the first book on Karl Marx in the Russian language; his father's maternal uncle was a celebrated Russian editor and literary critic; his father's maternal aunt was the noted piano teacher Isabelle Vengerova), he studied at the Leningrad Cons., taking composition with Boris Arapov and Orest Evlakhov (graduated in 1955) and piano with Vladimir Nilsen (graduated in 1956); he also took courses in musicology with F. Rubtzov (folk music) and N. Uspensky (polyphonic analysis). While a student, he wrote a fairy-tale suite, *Frog-Princess,* and in 1951 composed a string quartet on Russian folk motifs. In 1959 he was appointed to the faculty of the Lenin-

grad Cons. For further study of folk music he traveled into the countryside, in the rural regions of Pskov and Novgorod. Concurrently, he explored the technical modalities of new music, in the tradition of Soviet modernism, evolving a considerable complexity of texture in a framework of dissonant counterpoint, while safeguarding the tonal foundation in triadic progressions. Some of his works, such as his opera *Virineya,* represent a contemporary evolution of the Russian national school of composition, broadly diatonic and spaciously songful; his other works tend toward ultramodern practices, including polytonality, microtonality, dodecaphony, tone-clusters, amplified sound, prepared piano, electronic sonorism, aleatory proceedings, and spatial placement of instruments. His Concerto for Orch. employs electronically amplified guitars and solo instruments; even more advanced is his *Antiphones* for String Quartet, employing non-tempered tuning and an "ambulatory" setting, in which the players are placed in different parts of the hall and then walk, while playing, en route to the podium; the piece is especially popular at modern music festivals. A prolific composer, he is the author of 7 symphs., many pieces of chamber music, choral works, and solo compositions. In 1980 he completed his most significant work, the opera-ballad *Mary Stuart,* which, after its inaugural production in Kuibyshev, had successful performances in Leningrad and, in 1984, in Leipzig. The score utilizes authentic Scottish folk songs, suitably arranged in modern harmonies, as well as original themes in the pentatonic scale. In 1983 he was awarded the prestigious Glinka Prize for *Mary Stuart.* Apart from his work as a composer and teacher, he contributes music criticism to Soviet magazines; publ. a valuable analytic survey, *The Symphonies of Prokofiev* (Leningrad, 1976).

WORKS: OPERAS: *Virineya* (Leningrad, Sept. 30, 1967); *The Master and Margarita,* chamber opera after a novel by Bulgakov (1973; awaiting perf. at an unforeseeable future); *Mary Stuart,* opera-ballad (1978–80; Kuibyshev, Jan. 31, 1981; Leningrad, April 18, 1981; Leipzig, May 26, 1984).

BALLETS: *Icarus* (1962–69; Moscow, May 29, 1971).

FOR ORCH.: 7 symphs.: No. 1 (1958; Leningrad, March 11, 1962); No. 2 (1977; Leningrad, Sept. 21, 1979); No. 3 (1982; Leningrad, Dec. 15, 1982); No. 4, dedicated to the memory of his father (Kuibyshev, Oct. 1, 1983; Leningrad, March 23, 1984); No. 5 (1983); No. 6 (1983); No. 7 (1984); *Carnival Overture* (1957); *Choreographic Miniatures* (1964); *Concerto buffo* (1964–65; Leningrad, April 28, 1966); Concerto for Symph. Orch., 3 Electric Guitars, and Solo Instruments (1973; Leningrad, Feb. 9, 1974); *Dramatic Song* (1974); *Festive Music* for Balalaika, Castanets, and Orch. (1975); *Symphonic Motet* (1976); *Quiet Music* (1981; Leningrad, March 7, 1982); *Concerto primaverile* for Violin and String Orch. (1983; Vilna, Oct. 8, 1983; Sergei Stadler, soloist).

CHAMBER MUSIC: String Quartet on Russian Themes (1951); 2 Pieces for Viola and Piano (1956); Suite for Viola and Piano (1959); Sonata for Violin Solo (1960); *Chromatic Flute and Humoresque* for Flute (1961); 3 Pieces for Cello Solo (1964); *Dia-*

logues for Wind Quintet (1964); *Antiphones* for String Quartet (1968); *Sonatina allegro* for French Horn and Piano (1974); *Monologue and Toccata* for Clarinet and Piano (1974); *Solo espressivo* for Oboe Solo (1975); *Exotic Suite* for 2 Violins, 2 Electric Guitars, Saxophone, and Percussion (1976; Leningrad, Nov. 3, 1978); *Legend* for Domra and Piano (1976); *Merry Rondo* for Domra and Piano (1976); *Novgorod Dance* for Clarinet, Trombone, Cello, Piano, and Percussion (1980); *Rondo,* on a theme by Gounod, for Trumpet and Piano (1980); *Musica lirica* for Flute, Violin, and Harpsichord (1981); *Dithyramb* for Cello Ensemble and Piano (1982); *In the World of Animals,* children's suite for Cello and Piano (1982).

FOR VOICE: *Songs of Freedom,* on Russian folk motifs, for Mezzo-soprano, Baritone, and Piano (1957); *Spring has arrived,* vocal cycle on verses by Japanese poets, for Voice and Piano (1958); *Polish Stanzas,* vocal cycle on works by the Polish poet Anthoni Slonimski, first cousin of the composer's father (1963); *Lyric Stanzas,* vocal cycle for Voice and Piano (1964); *Voice from the Chorus,* cantata to words by Alexander Blok (1964); *Farewell to a Friend* for Voice and Piano (1966); *Monologues* for Soprano, Oboe, French Horn, and Harp (1967); *2 Russian Songs* for Chorus a cappella (1968); *6 Songs* to words by Anna Akhmatova (1969); *Northern Landscapes* for Chorus a cappella (1969); *Merry Songs* for Voice and Piano (1971); *Choral Games* for Children's Chorus, Boy Soloist, and 2 Percussion Instruments (1972); *Evening Music* for Chorus a cappella (1973); *4 Songs* to words by Osip Mandelstam (1974); *10 Songs* to words by Anna Akhmatova (1974); *4 Russian Songs* for Chorus a cappella (1974); *Virineya,* suite-oratorio from the opera of the same name (1974); *Pesnohorka (Sing-Chorus)* for Contralto, Flute, Oboe, Trumpet, Balalaika, Accordion, 3 Electric Guitars, Castanets, and Vibraphone, on Russian folk songs (1975); *Songs of the Troubadours,* vocal cycle on old French ballads for Soprano, Tenor, 4 Recorders, and Lute (1975); *Songs of Songs* for Soprano, Tenor, Chorus, Oboe, French Horn, and Harp (1975); *Bashkir Girl's Song* for Voice, Flute, and 2 Bongos (1977); *Quiet Flows the Don* for Mixed Choir, to words of old Cossack chants, after Sholokhov's novel (1977); *2 Poems* to words by Pushkin, for Chorus a cappella (1979); Suite from the opera *Mary Stuart* for Chorus and Orch. (1980); *2 Songs* to words by Alexander Blok, for Mezzo-soprano and Piano (1980); *White Night* for Chorus a cappella (1980); *Morning Song* for Children's Chorus and Snare Drum (1981); *Strophes of Dhammapada,* after the classic Buddhist epic, for Soprano, Harp, and Percussion (1983; Leningrad, Feb. 21, 1984); *Song of Leningrad* for Bass, Chorus, and Orch. (1983); *Little Triptych* for Chorus a cappella (1983); *2 Vocalises* for Soprano and Mezzo-soprano (1983); *Railroad* for Chorus, Trumpet, Piano, and Percussion (1983); *White Night in Leningrad* for Chorus a cappella (1983); *4 Strophes* from *Oedipus Colonus* of Sophocles, for Chorus (1983).

FOR PIANO: Sonata (1962); *Three Graces,* suite in the form of variations (1964); *Children's Pieces* (1970); *Coloristic Fantasy* (1972); *Tiny Pieces* for

children (1973); *Serenade from a Musical,* street song (1976); *Round Dance and Merry Rumba* (1977); *Charlie Chaplin Whistles On* (1978); *Cat's Lullaby* (1978); *Hungarian March* for Piano, 4-hands (1980); *Intermezzo in Memory of Brahms* (1980); *Travel Suite* (1981); *Romantic Waltz* (1982); *Variations on a Theme by Mussorgsky* (1984); 3 pieces: *Jump Rope; Blues; Metro* (1984). FOR ORGAN: *Pastorale and Toccata* (1961); *Chromatic Poem* (1969); *Round Dance and Fugue* (1976); *Rondo-Humoresque* (1979); also incidental music for theatrical plays; film music.

BIBLIOGRAPHY: A. Milka, *Sergei Slonimsky* (Leningrad, 1976).

Slonimsky, Yuri, eminent Russian writer on ballet; b. St. Petersburg, March 13, 1902; d. there (Leningrad), April 23, 1978. He studied law at St. Petersburg Univ.; at the same time attended the Inst. of Art History; was a co-founder, with Georgi Balanchivadze (George Balanchine), of Young Ballet, a group organized to promote modern dance. A brilliant ballet critic, Yuri Slonimsky achieved a fine reputation for his penetrating analysis of current productions and historical essays on ballet. He publ. *Giselle* (Leningrad, 1926; revised 1969); *Masters of Ballet* (Moscow, 1937); *The Soviet Ballet* (in Eng., N.Y., 1947); *Tchaikovsky and the Ballet Theater of His Time* (Moscow, 1956). He was the author of several ballet librettos, among them *Icarus* by Sergei Slonimsky (no relation).

Slonov, Mikhail, Russian song composer; b. Kharkov, Nov. 16, 1869; d. Moscow, Feb. 11, 1930. He collected Russian folk songs and himself composed a number of songs, some of them popularized by Chaliapin, such as *Farewell.*

Sloper, (Edward Hugh) Lindsay, English pianist and teacher; b. London, June 14, 1826; d. there, July 3, 1887. He studied with Moscheles in London, A. Schmitt in Frankfurt, and Rousselot in Paris; made his debut in London (1846); became a popular concert pianist and teacher there. He wrote many piano pieces; studies and textbooks for piano; songs.

Slovák, Ladislav, Czech conductor; b. Bratislava, Sept. 9, 1919. He studied organ at the Bratislava Music Academy; later took a course in conducting with Talich; then went to Russia as an assistant conductor of the Leningrad Phil. Returning to Czechoslovakia, he served as chief conductor of the Radio Symph. in Bratislava (1955–61); in 1961 was appointed chief conductor of the Slovak Phil. there.

Smallens, Alexander, American conductor; b. St. Petersburg, Russia, Jan. 1, 1889; d. Tucson, Ariz., Nov. 24, 1972. He was brought to the U.S. as a child; studied at the College of the City of N.Y. (B.A., 1909); then took courses at the Paris Cons. (1909). He devoted himself mainly to theatrical conducting; was assistant conductor of the Boston Opera (1911–14); accompanied the Anna Pavlova Ballet Co. on a tour of South America (1915–18); then was on the staff of the Chicago Opera Co. (1919–23) and of the Philadelphia Civic Opera (1924–31); from 1927 to 1934 he was assistant conductor of the Philadelphia Orch., and from 1947 to 1950, was music director at Radio City Music Hall in N.Y. He was the original conductor of Gershwin's opera *Porgy and Bess*, and conducted it on a European tour in 1956.

Smalley, Roger, English composer; b. Swinton, near Manchester, July 26, 1943. He studied at the Royal College of Music in London with Antony Hopkins (piano) and Peter Racine Fricker (composition); later attended courses in new music with Stockhausen in Cologne. In 1967 he became artist-in-residence at King's College, Cambridge. In 1970 he formed a new ensemble, called Intermodulation, to promote socially unacceptable music. In this antagonistic manner he wrote *Strata* for 15 String Players (1970) and *Beat Music* for 55 Players (London, Aug. 12, 1971). But he also composed an austere *Missa brevis* and *Symphony in One Movement* (London, Aug. 25, 1982).

Smallwood, Williams, English organist; b. Kendal, Dec. 31, 1831; d. there, Aug. 6, 1897. He studied with Dr. Camidge and H. Phillips; was organist of the Kendal Parish Church from 1847 till his death. He composed didactic piano pieces and salon music; also anthems, hymns, songs, etc. His *Pianoforte Tutor* had an immense sale.

Smareglia, Antonio, Italian composer; b. Pola, Istria, May 5, 1854; d. Grado, near Trieste, April 15, 1929. He was trained in engineering before turning to music; studied composition with Franco Faccio at the Cons. of Milan. He became totally blind about 1905, but continued to compose by improvising on the piano with a musical amanuensis; lived in Milan until 1921, when he was appointed a prof. of composition at the Tartini Cons. in Trieste.
WORKS: Operas: *Preziosa* (Milan, Nov. 19, 1879); *Bianca da Cervia* (Milan, Feb. 7, 1882); *Re Nala* (Venice, Feb. 9, 1887); *Il Vassallo di Szigeth* (Vienna, Oct. 4, 1889); *Cornelio Schutt* (Prague, May 20, 1893); *Nozze istriane* (Trieste, March 28, 1895; very successful); *La falena* (Venice, Sept. 4, 1897); *Oceana* (Milan, Jan. 22, 1903); *L'abisso* (Milan, Feb. 9, 1914).
BIBLIOGRAPHY: G. Zuccoli, *A. Smareglia* (Trieste, 1923); G.D. Nacamuli, *A. Smareglia* (Trieste, 1930); A. Smareglia, *Vita ed arte di Antonio Smareglia* (Lugano, 1932); Mario Smareglia, *A. Smareglia* (Pola, 1934); Silvio Benco, *Ricordi di Antonio Smareglia* (Duino, 1968).

Smart, Sir George (Thomas), English organist and conductor; b. London, May 10, 1776; d. there, Feb. 23, 1867. He was a chorister in the Chapel Royal under Ayrton; was a pupil of Dupuis (organ) and Arnold (composition). He was knighted in 1811 in Dublin by the Lord Lieutenant after conducting a series of concerts. He was an original member of the Phil. Society and conductor of its concerts

(1813–44), introducing the works of Beethoven and Schumann; also conducted the Lenten oratorios (1813–25). He publ. a collection of glees and canons (1863), 2 vols. of sacred music, 2 piano sonatinas, etc.; edited Orlando Gibbons's madrigals and Handel's "Dettingen" Te Deum.
BIBLIOGRAPHY: H.B. and C.L. Cox, *Leaves from the Journals of Sir George Smart* (London, 1907); C. Maclean, "Sir George Smart, Musician-Diarist," *Sammelbände der Internationalen Musik-Gesellschaft*, X (1909); A. Hyatt King, "The Importance of Sir George Smart," *Musical Times* (Dec. 1950).

Smart, Henry, English organist, son of **Sir George Smart's** brother Henry (1778–1823); b. London, Oct. 26, 1813; d. there, July 6, 1879. He was a pupil of his father and of W.H. Kearns; served as organist at several London churches; finally at St. Pancras, Euston Road, in 1864, his sight failing in that year; he received a government pension in 1879. His opera, *Bertha, or the Gnome of the Hartzberg*, was produced at the Haymarket Theatre, May 26, 1855; the cantatas *The Bride of Dunkerron* (1864), *King René's Daughter* (1871), *The Fishermaidens* (1871), and *Jacob* (1873) appeared after he was blind. He wrote many songs, part-songs, and anthems; an Evening Service; organ music; etc.
BIBLIOGRAPHY: W. Spark, *Henry Smart, His Life and Works* (London, 1881); W.D. Seymour, *Henry Smart* (London, 1881).

Smetáček, Václav, Czech conductor; b. Brno, Sept. 30, 1906. He studied oboe at the Prague Cons.; was first oboist in the Czech Phil. Orch. (1930–33); also studied composition with Jaroslav Křička at Charles Univ. in Prague, receiving his Ph.D. in 1933. In 1934 he embarked on his chief career, as a conductor; led the choral society Hlahol in Prague (1934–36); concurrently was a conductor with Prague Radio, 1934–43; then enlarged his activities into the field of opera and symph. music; has made numerous appearances as a guest conductor all over Europe, in America, and in Japan.

Smetana, Bedřich (Friedrich), great Bohemian composer; b. Leitomischl, March 2, 1824; d. (insane) Prague, May 12, 1884. (His name is pronounced with a stress on the first syllable; Smetana himself said that the rhythm should be identical with the initial phrase in Beethoven's *Fidelio Overture*.) His talent manifested itself very early, but his father's prejudice against music as a profession precluded systematic instruction. However, a friend of his school days, Katharina Kolař, who was studying the piano with Proksch in Prague, introduced Smetana to her master, who accepted him as a pupil (piano and theory). Kittl, the director of the Cons., procured him a position as music teacher in the family of Count Thun. After 4 years of earnest work, Smetana gave up his position and undertook his first concert tour, which resulted in a disastrous financial failure. In despair he turned to Liszt, who helped him open a piano school of his own. This flourished, and a year later (1849) he married **Katharina Kolař,** who had also become a fine pianist. His reputation as a performer, especially as an interpreter of Chopin, grew rapidly, but his first compositions were received coldly. When, therefore, the Phil. Society of Göteborg (Sweden) offered him its conductorship in 1856, he immediately accepted. In his first year there he wrote his first 3 symph. poems, *Richard III, Wallensteins Lager,* and *Hakon Jarl* (after Öhlenschläger). As a conductor and pianist he was highly appreciated. But the cold climate undermined his wife's health. For her sake he spent his vacations regularly in Prague; on the trip there in 1859, she died in Dresden. Meanwhile, important events were evolving at home. Škroup had made a beginning with national opera, whose chief national element was Bohemian texts, the music being practically devoid of national characteristics. The younger musicians and poets sought the establishment of a national art. After Austria had granted political autonomy to Bohemia in 1860, agitation was begun for the erection of a national opera house in Prague. Smetana resigned his post in Göteborg, and returned to Prague in May 1861, assuming a leading role in the new movement. On Nov. 18, 1862, the new opera house was opened, but the dozen Bohemian operas by Škroup, Shuherský, and Šebor could not furnish an important or varied repertoire; consequently, Meyerbeer and the Italians were sung in Bohemian. Smetana therefore turned to opera, and finished his first dramatic work, *Braniboři v Čechách (The Brandenburgers in Bohemia),* in 1863. It was not produced till Jan. 5, 1866; its success, while not overwhelming, was decided. On May 30, 1866, his 2nd opera, *Prodaná nevěsta (The Bartered Bride),* was received with immense enthusiasm. Smetana was appointed first conductor (replacing the Meyerbeer fanatic Mayer), and was acclaimed as Bohemia's greatest composer. This opera has also found success abroad (Austria and Germany, 1892; Scandinavia, 1894; England, 1895; Italy, 1905; Belgium, 1907; U.S., Feb. 19, 1909, at the Metropolitan Opera House). The next opera, *Dalibor* (May 16, 1868), on account of Smetana's employment of leading motifs and more elaborate treatment of the orch., caused several critics to charge the composer with attempting to Wagnerize the national opera. In 1871, when there was talk of crowning Emperor Francis Josef as King of Bohemia, Smetana wrote *Libussa* for the coronation festivities. But no coronation took place, and Smetana's enemies found means of preventing a production at the National Opera. Hoping to duplicate the success of his 2nd work, he selected a comedy, *Dvě vdovy (The 2 Widows),* produced on March 27, 1874, with only moderate success. He returned to the symph. poem, but now found inspiration in national subjects. Thus originated the 6 masterpieces bearing the collective title *Má vlast (My Country):* *Vyšehrad* (the ancient castle of the Bohemian kings) and *Vltava (The Moldau)* in 1874; *Šárka* (a valley north of Prague, named after a mythological character) and *Z českých luhův a hayův (From Bohemia's Meadows and Groves)* in 1875; *Tábor* *(The Camp;* introducing the Hussite war song) in 1878; and *Blaník* in 1879. To this period also belongs

the famous E-minor String Quartet *Z mého života (Aus meinem Leben;* 1876). But Smetana's labors on behalf of national art had already borne fruit; a reaction soon set in, and by the end of 1875 his friends again controlled the opera. Early in 1876 he began a new opera, *Hubička (The Kiss),* produced with gratifying success on Nov. 7, 1876. *Tajemství (The Secret),* staged in Prague on Sept. 18, 1878, was hailed as a 2nd *Bartered Bride,* and won even the opposition party. For the opening (June 11, 1881) of the new National Opera, *Libussa* was unanimously chosen, and created a profound impression. His last opera, *Čertova stěna (The Devil's Wall),* presented on Oct. 29, 1882, was a comparative failure. Meanwhile, an early syphilitic infection affected his hearing, so that he became almost totally deaf and had to cease all public appearances; his brain was affected, he suffered hallucinations, and had to be confined in an asylum. A detailed account of Smetana's illness and death is found in Dieter Kerner's *Krankheiten grosser Musiker* (Stuttgart, 1969; vol. 2, pp. 77–92). Smetana's other works are: *Triumph-Symphonie,* in honor of the marriage of Emperor Franz Josef (1854; contains the Austrian national anthem); *Richard III,* symph. poem (Prague, Jan. 5, 1862, composer conducting); *Hakon Jarl,* symph. poem (Prague, Feb. 24, 1864, composer conducting); *Píseň Česká (Bohemian Song)* for Vocal Quartet and Orch. (1868; Prague, March 29, 1875); *Pražský Karneval (The Carnival of Prague),* symph. poem (Prague, March 2, 1884); *Rybář (The Fisher),* music to a tableau after Goethe, for Harmonium, Harp, and String Quintet (Žofin, April 12, 1869); *Festmarsch* for the Shakespeare tercentenary (1864); String Quartet in D minor; Piano Trio; 2 pieces for Violin and Piano; choruses and songs; piano music (a set of Bohemian dances, 3 sets of polkas, the popular concert étude *Am Seegestade,* etc.).

BIBLIOGRAPHY: B. Wellek, *F. Smetana. Mit einem Anhang von Korrespondenzen Smetanas an Liszt* (Prague, 1895; 2nd ed. as *F. Smetanas Leben und Wirken,* 1899); O. Hostinský, *B. Smetana* (Prague, 1901); R. Batka, *Die Musik in Böhmen* (Berlin, 1906); W. Ritter, *F. Smetana* (Paris, 1907); K. Hoffmeister, *B. Smetana* (Prague, 1914); V. Helfert, *B. Smetana* (Brno, 1924); V. Balthasar, *B. Smetana* (Prague, 1924); E. Rychnovsky, *Smetana* (Stuttgart, 1924); Z. Nejedlý, *B. Smetana,* a monumental biography in 4 vols. (Prague, 1924–33; 2nd ed. in 7 vols., 1950–54); J. Bistron, *F. Smetana* (Vienna, 1924); J. Tiersot, *Smetana* (Paris, 1926); J. Teichmann, *B. Smetana* (Prague, 1944); P. Pražák, *Smetanovy zpěvohry* (on Smetana's operas; 4 vols., Prague, 1948); H. Boese, *Zwei Urmusikanten: Smetana, Dvořák* (Zürich, 1955); Brian Large, *Smetana* (N.Y., 1970); J. Smetana and J. Clapham, "Smetana: A Century After," *Musical Times* (April 1984). Documentary vols. containing various materials on Smetana were publ. in Prague by Mirko Očadlik (1950) and F. Bartoš (9th ed., 1954; in Eng. as *Letters and Reminiscences,* Prague, 1955); numerous monographs on Smetana's individual works have also been publ. in Prague.

Smeterlin, Jan, Polish pianist; b. Bielsko, Feb. 7,

1892; d. London, Jan. 18, 1967. He was a child prodigy; made his first concert appearance at the age of 8; toured widely as a concert pianist, eventually settling in London. He was praised for his congenially Romantic interpretations of Chopin's music.

Smijers, Albert(us Antonius), eminent Dutch musicologist; b. Raamsdonksveer, July 19, 1888; d. Huis ter Heide, near Utrecht, May 15, 1957. He studied music with Averkamp at the Cons. of Amsterdam; was trained for the priesthood; was ordained in 1912; then entered the school for church music at Klosterneuburg; took a course in musicology with Guido Adler at the Univ. of Vienna (1915–19); received the degree of Dr.Phil. with the dissertation *Karl Luython als Motettenkomponist* (1917; publ. in Amsterdam, 1923). Returning to the Netherlands, he taught at Beekvliet Seminary in Amsterdam until 1929, then at the Amsterdam Cons. (1929–33); in 1930 he was appointed prof. of musicology at the Univ. of Utrecht; formed the Inst. of Musicology there. He brought out 7 vols. of the anthology *Van Ockeghem tot Sweelinck* (Amsterdam, 1939–56); in collaboration with Charles Van den Borren and others, he publ. *Algemeene Muziekgeschiedenis* (Utrecht, 1938); began an edition of the collected works of Josquin Des Prez and Obrecht.

Smirnov, Dmitri, outstanding Russian tenor; b. Moscow, Nov. 19, 1882; d. Riga, April 27, 1944. He sang in a church choir as a youth; then studied voice with Dodonov and others in Moscow. In 1904 he was accepted as a member of the Bolshoi Theater, but interrupted his career by traveling to Paris and Milan for further voice training. Returning to Moscow in 1906, he sang again at the Bolshoi Theater; from 1910 appeared also with the Maryinsky Opera Theater in St. Petersburg. During the same period he took part in the famous Russian Seasons in Paris. On Dec. 30, 1910, he made his debut at the Metropolitan Opera in N.Y. in the role of the Duke of Mantua in *Rigoletto,* remaining with the company until 1912; then sang at the Grand Opéra in Paris and at Drury Lane in London, and made guest appearances in Berlin, Madrid, and Rome. Although he lived mostly abroad, he revisited Russia in 1926 and 1928 as a guest artist. In 1935–37 he lived in London; later appeared mostly in solo recitals; was also active as a voice teacher; taught at the Cons. of Athens, and later in Riga, Latvia, where he remained until his death. In Russia he was regarded as one of the finest lyric tenors of his time, often compared to Caruso; as a *bel canto* singer he was praised by Russian and European critics. Apart from the Russian repertoire, in which he excelled, he made a deep impression in such lyrico-dramatic roles as Faust, Don José, Canio, and Rodolfo.

Smirnov, Dmitri, Russian composer; b. Minsk, Nov. 2, 1948. He studied composition with Edison Denisov at the Moscow Cons. Upon graduation in 1972, he was editor of the Leningrad publication *Soviet Composer* (1973–79). His wife, **Elena Firsova** (b. Leningrad, March 21, 1950), is also a composer.

WORKS: For Orch.: 2 piano concertos: No. 1 (1971) and No. 2, with Strings (1978); *Pastorale* (1975); Clarinet Concerto (1974–77); *Triple Concerto* for Saxophone, Piano, Double Bass, Strings, and Percussion (1977); *The 4 Seasons,* symph. (1980). Chamber music: *Monolog* for Solo Clarinet (1968); 2 violin sonatas (1969, 1979); String Trio (1970); *2 Fugues* for Solo Violin (1970); String Quartet (1973); *Lyrical Composition* for Flute, Oboe, Violin, Cello, and Harpsichord (1975); *Solo* for Harp (1976); Bassoon Sonata (1977); Piano Trio (1977); Cello Sonata (1978); *Mirages,* 5 pieces for Saxophone Quartet (1979). For Voice: *6 Songs after Blok* for Voice and Orch. (1972); *6 Haiku* for Voice, Flute, and Piano (1973); *Cantata in Memory of Pablo Neruda* for 2 Solo Voices, Chorus, Strings, and Percussion (1974); *5 songs after Pushkin* for Voice, Flute, Violin, Cello, and Percussion (1976); *Eternal Calm* for Voice, Strings, Organ, and Percussion (1972–77). For Piano: 2 sonatas (1966–67, 1980); *2 Little Pieces* (1968).

Smit, Leo, Dutch composer; b. Amsterdam, May 14, 1900; d. in a concentration camp, probably in Poland, in 1943 or 1944. He studied composition with Sem Dresden at the Amsterdam Cons.; taught at the Cons. (1924–27); then lived in Paris. He returned to Amsterdam in 1937; was arrested by the Nazis in 1943 and sent to the concentration camp at Westerbork in the Netherlands; was removed to an unknown camp (presumably in Poland) and an equally unknown fate. His music was greatly influenced by the contemporary French school of his time.

WORKS: *Introduction to Teirlinck's play "De Vertraagde Film"* for Chamber Orch. (1923); Quintet for Flute, Violin, Viola, Cello, and Harp (1928); *Schemselnihar,* ballet (1929); *Silhouetten,* suite for Orch.; *2 hommages* (Sherlock Holmes and Remington) for Piano (1928–30); Harp Concertino (1933); Sextet for Piano and Wind Quintet (1933); Symph. (1934–36); Concerto for Piano and Wind Orch. (1937); *Forlane en Rondeau* (orchestrated by Godfried Devreese); Concertino for Cello and Small Orch. (1937); *Suite* for Oboe and Cello (1938); Trio for Clarinet, Viola, and Piano (1938); Concerto for Viola and Strings (1940); *Divertimento* for Piano, 4-hands (1940); Flute Sonata (1943).

Smit, Leo, American pianist and composer; b. Philadelphia, Jan. 12, 1921. He studied piano with Isabelle Vengerova at the Curtis Inst. of Music in Philadelphia; took lessons in composition with Nicolas Nabokov. He made his debut as a pianist at Carnegie Hall in N.Y. in 1939; then taught at various schools and colleges. In 1967 he traveled in Latin America and gave concerts of American music there. His own style of composition is neo-Classical, marked by a strong contrapuntal fabric; the influence of Stravinsky, with whom he had personal contact, is particularly pronounced here. He wrote an opera, *The Alchemy of Love,* to a libretto by the astronomer Fred Hoyle (1969); the ballet *Virginia Sampler* (N.Y., March 4, 1947); *The Parcae,* overture (Boston, Oct. 16, 1953); Symph. No. 1 (Boston, Feb. 1, 1957); *Capriccio* for String Orch. (Ojai, Calif., May

23, 1958); Sextet for Clarinet, Bassoon, and Strings (1940); *Academic Graffiti* for Voice, Clarinet, Cello, Piano, and Percussion, to a text by W.H. Auden (1959); Piano Concerto (1968); *In Woods* for Oboe, Harp, and Percussion (1978); choruses and a number of piano pieces.

Smith, Ada Beatrice Queen Victoria Louise Virginia, black American singer, who became popular under the pseudonym **Bricktop;** b. Alderson, W.Va., Aug. 14, 1894; d. New York, Jan. 31, 1984. Fascinated with saloons, she danced and sang in Chicago's cabarets. In 1924 she went to Paris and opened her own club on Rue Pigalle, which she called Chez Bricktop, dispensing chic informality. She met celebrities and taught the Prince of Wales, the future King Edward VIII, the Black Bottom; she was on friendly terms with Hemingway, Evelyn Waugh, Steinbeck, and other habitués of her boîte. Her admirers called her Brickie. Returning to N.Y. at the outbreak of war in 1939, she became a hostess in café society; Cole Porter wrote a song for her, *Miss Otis regrets, she's unable to lunch today.* She went back to Europe in 1951 and opened a club on the Via Veneto in Rome; she also had a club in Mexico. In 1964 she was back in N.Y. In 1973 she made a documentary film, *Honeybaby, honeybaby!* On her last birthday in 1983, when she turned 89, she was presented by N.Y.'s Mayor Koch with a seal of the city and a certificate of appreciation for her "extraordinary talent and indomitable spirit." In 1983 she publ. (with professional assistance) an autobiography, *Bricktop by Bricktop.*

Smith, Alice Mary (Mrs. Meadows White), English composer; b. London, May 19, 1839; d. there, Dec. 4, 1884. She was a pupil of Sterndale Bennett and G.A. Macfarren; married M. White in 1867.
  WORKS: Cantatas: *Rüdesheim* (1865); *Ode to the Northeast Wind* (1878); *Ode to the Passions* (1882); *Song of the Little Baltung* (1883); *The Red King* (1884); Symph. in C minor; 4 overtures: *Endymion, Lalla Rookh, Masque of Pandora,* and *Jason;* 2 piano quartets; 2 string quartets; Piano Trio; Clarinet Concerto; *Introduction and Allegro* for Piano and Orch.; part-songs; etc.

Smith, Bernard (Bernhard Schmidt), called "Father Smith," organ builder; b. in Germany, c.1630; d. London, Feb. 20, 1708. He settled in London in 1660 with 2 nephews; became organ builder to the King and court organ builder to Queen Anne. He built organs for St. Margaret's, Westminster (1675); Durham Cathedral (1683); the Temple (1684); St. Paul's Cathedral (1697); and the Banqueting Hall, Whitehall (1699).
  BIBLIOGRAPHY: A. Freeman, *Father Smith* (London, 1926).

Smith, Bessie (Elizabeth), black American "blues" singer; b. Chattanooga, Tenn., April 15, 1894; d. in an automobile accident, Sept. 26, 1937, on a highway outside Clarksdale, Miss. Born in a wretchedly poor family, she joined Rainey's Rabbit Foot Minstrels (blues pioneer Ma Rainey was her teacher) and developed a style of singing that rapidly brought her fame. Her first record, *Down Hearted Blues,* sold 800,000 copies in 1923, and she was billed as the "Empress of the Blues." She was a large, impressive woman—5'9*S' and weighing over 200 pounds—and had a powerful voice to match; the excellence of her vocal equipment, along with her natural expressive qualities and improvisatory abilities, combined to make her the consummate blues singer of her time.
  BIBLIOGRAPHY: P. Oliver, *Bessie Smith* (London, 1959); Gunther Schuller, *Early Jazz* (N.Y., 1968); Carman Moore, *Somebody's Angel Child* (N.Y., 1969); C. Albertson, *Bessie* (N.Y., 1973); idem, *Bessie Smith. Empress of the Blues* (a collection of her songs, with essays by Albertson and Schuller; N.Y., 1975). See also L. Gara in *Notable American Women,* III (Cambridge, Mass., 1971).

Smith, Carleton Sprague, distinguished American musicologist; b. New York, Aug. 8, 1905. He was educated at Harvard Univ. (M.A., 1928) and at the Univ. of Vienna, where he studied history (Dr.Phil., 1930). Returning to the U.S., he was an instructor in history at Columbia Univ. (1931–35), then at N.Y. Univ. (1939–67); he also served as chief of the Music Division at the N.Y. Public Library (1931–43 and 1946–59); a linguist, he lectured in South America, in Spanish and Portuguese, on the social history of the U.S.; a skillful flutist, he often took part in concerts of old and new music.

Smith, Cecil, American music critic; b. Chicago, July 12, 1906; d. London, May 28, 1956. He studied with H. Levy (piano) and Sowerby (composition) in Chicago; later at Harvard Univ. with Piston. He taught at the Univ. of Chicago (1929–46); was music critic of the *Chicago Tribune* (1936–42) and editor of *Musical America* (1948–51). He went to England in 1951 and wrote for the London *Daily Express;* remained in London until his death. He wrote the books *Musical Comedy in America* (N.Y., 1950) and *Worlds of Music* (Philadelphia, 1952).

Smith, Clarence ("Pine Top"), black American jazz pianist; b. Troy, Ala., June 11, 1904; d. (shot during a disturbance in a dance hall) Chicago, March 14, 1929. After playing in clubs in Pittsburgh, he served as accompanist to Ma Rainey; then went to Chicago, where he became a pioneering figure as a pianist in the boogie-woogie style; his 1928 recording of *Pine Top's Boogie Woogie* secured his fame among jazz enthusiasts.

Smith, David Stanley, American composer and music educator; b. Toledo, Ohio, July 6, 1877; d. New Haven, Conn., Dec. 17, 1949. He studied with Horatio Parker at Yale Univ., graduating in 1900. He then went to Europe, where he took courses in composition with Thuille in Munich and Widor in Paris. Upon his return to the U.S. he obtained a Mus.Bac. degree at Yale (1903) and was appointed an instructor at the Yale School of Music; in 1916 he became a prof. there; in 1920 was appointed dean of the School of Music, retiring in 1946. He was conductor of the New Haven Symph. Orch. from 1920 to 1946. WORKS: Symph. No. 1 (1910); Symph. No. 2 (1917); Symph. No. 3 (Cleveland, Jan. 8, 1931, composer conducting); Symph. No. 4 (Boston, April 14, 1939, composer conducting); *Prince Hal,* overture (New Haven, Dec. 1912); *Impressions,* suite for Orch. (1916); *Fête galante,* fantasy for Flute and Orch. (N.Y., Dec. 11, 1921); *A Satire,* orch. sketch (N.Y., Nov. 15, 1933); *Epic Poem* for Orch. (Boston, April 12, 1935, composer conducting); *Requiem* for Violin and Orch. (1939); *Credo,* symph. poem (1941); 4 Pieces for String Orch. (1943); *The Apostle,* symph. poem (1944); *Flowers,* suite of 4 pieces for 10 Instruments (1924); *Sinfonietta* for String Orch. (1931); choral works: *Rhapsody of St. Bernard* for Mixed Chorus and Orch. (1915); *Visions of Isaiah* for Soprano, Tenor, Chorus, and Orch. (1927); *The Ocean* for Bass Solo, Mixed Chorus, and Orch. (1945); chamber music: 10 string quartets; *Sonata Pastorale* for Oboe and Piano; 2 violin sonatas; Piano Quintet; Cello Sonata; piano works; songs (cycle, *Songs of 3 Ages,* etc.).

BIBLIOGRAPHY: B.C. Tuthill, "David Stanley Smith," *Musical Quarterly* (Jan. 1942).

Smith, Gerrit, American organist and composer; b. Hagerstown, Md., Dec. 11, 1859; d. Darien, Conn., July 21, 1912. He studied music at the Stuttgart Cons.; began his professional career as an organist in Buffalo; settled in N.Y. in 1885 as a church organist. He was one of the founders of the Manuscript Society in N.Y.; wrote a cantata, *King David;* many songs of a lyric inspiration; *25 Song-Vignettes* (for children); and an interesting suite, *Aquarelles,* including 8 songs and 8 piano pieces.

BIBLIOGRAPHY: Rupert Hughes, *Contemporary American Composers* (Boston, 1900; pp. 309–17).

Smith, Hale, black American composer; b. Cleveland, June 29, 1925. He studied piano with Dorothy Price and composition with Marcel Dick at the Cleveland Inst. of Music (1946–50; M.M., 1952); moved to N.Y. in 1958; was active as an arranger for music publishers; in 1963 became a musical consultant for C.F. Peters Corp.; from 1969 was adviser for the Black Music Center of Indiana Univ.; in 1970 joined the music faculty of the Univ. of Conn. He wrote musical scores for Dizzy Gillespie, Ahmad Jamal, Eric Dolphy, and Abby Lincoln, and worked in various capacities for Quincy Jones, Clark Terry, Oliver Nelson, Miriam Makeba, and Hugh Masekela. WORKS: Chamber opera, *Blood Wedding* (Cleveland, 1953); *Orchestral Set* (1952; revised 1968); *Contours* for Orch. (Louisville, Oct. 17, 1961); *By Yearning and By Beautiful* for String Orch. (1964); *Music* for Harp and Orch. (1972); *Ritual and Incantations* for Orch. (1974); *Innerflexions* for Orch. (N.Y., Sept. 2, 1977); Duo for Violin and Piano (1953); Cello Sonata (1955); *Epicedial Variations* for Violin and Piano (1956); *3 Brevities* for Solo Flute (1960); *Introductions, Cadenzas and Interludes* for 8 Players (1974);

Variations for 6 Players (1975); *5 Songs* for Voice and Violin (1956); *2 Love Songs of John Donne* for Soprano and 9 Instruments (1958); *Comes Tomorrow,* jazz cantata for Chorus and Accompaniment (1972; revised 1977); *Toussaint L'Ouverture 1803* for Chorus and Piano (1977); *Evocation* for Piano (1966); *Anticipations, Introspections and Reflections* for Piano (1971).

BIBLIOGRAPHY: M. Breda, *Hale Smith: Biographical and Analytical Study of the Man and His Music* (Diss., Univ. of Southern Mississippi, Harrisburg, 1975).

Smith, Joe, black American jazz trumpeter; b. Ripley, Ohio, June 28, 1902; d. New York, Dec. 2, 1937. He played with jazz groups in St. Louis; then went to N.Y., where he worked with Fletcher Henderson's orch.; also acted as accompanist to Bessie Smith, Ma Rainey, and Ethel Waters; subsequently played in Bennie Moten's band and McKinney's Cotton Pickers until ill health cut short his career.

Smith, John Christopher (Johann Christoph Schmidt), organist and composer; b. Ansbach, Germany, 1712; d. Bath, England, Oct. 3, 1795. His father went to England with Handel in 1716, as his agent; the son followed in 1720 and became Handel's pupil. When Handel's eyesight began to deteriorate, Smith helped him in playing the organ and harpsichord at performances of Handel's oratorios, and continued to supervise performances of Handel's music after Handel's death; Smith presented Handel's MS scores, and other objects left to him by Handel, to King George III in appreciation for a royal pension. He retired about 1770, and settled in Bath. He wrote several English operas, of which 2 Shakespearean pieces, *The Fairies* (Drury Lane, Feb. 3, 1755) and *The Tempest* (Drury Lane, Feb. 11, 1756) were publ.; also wrote the oratorios *Paradise Lost* (Feb. 29, 1760), *Judith, Redemption,* etc.

BIBLIOGRAPHY: W. Coxe, *Anecdotes of G.F. Handel and J.C. Smith* (London, 1799); A. McCredie, "John Christopher Smith as a Dramatic Composer," *Music & Letters,* XLV (1964).

Smith, John Stafford, English organist and composer; b. Gloucester (baptized, March 30), 1750; d. London, Sept. 21, 1836. He studied with his father, Martin Smith, organist at Gloucester Cathedral, and also took lessons with Boyce. In 1784 he was made a Gentleman of the Chapel Royal, and in 1802 succeeded Arnold as organist there; from 1805 to 1817 he was master of the Boy Choristers there; from 1785 served as lay-vicar at Westminster Abbey; was also known as a composer of catches and glees and won several prizes of the Catch Club in London. The importance of John Stafford Smith to American music lies in the fact that he included in his 5th collection of glees, which he issued in 1799, an arrangement of the tune *To Anacreon in Heaven,* to which Francis Scott Key wrote *The Star-Spangled Banner* (1814); but there were several reasons for questioning whether he was the composer; his authorship was doubted by many reputable

American scholars. William Lichtenwanger, in his paper "The Music of *The Star-Spangled Banner:* From Ludgate Hill to Capitol Hill," in the *Quarterly Journal of the Library of Congress* (July 1977), seems to have dispelled these doubts by publishing excerpts from the "Recollections" of Richard John Samuel Stevens, an active member of the Anacreontic Society of London, who states in the rubric for 1777: "The president was Ralph Tomlinson. ... He wrote the Poetry of the Anacreontic Song; which Stafford Smith set to Music." Smith was an excellent musician; he transcribed into modern notation old MSS for the *History of Music* by Sir John Hawkins; edited *Musica antiqua,* containing compositions "from the commencement of the 12th to the 18th century" (2 vols., 1812); publ. *A Collection of Songs of Various Kinds for Different Voices* (1785).

BIBLIOGRAPHY: O.G. Sonneck, *Report on The Star-Spangled Banner* (1914); numerous other publications dealing with Smith and *The Star-Spangled Banner* are superseded by Lichtenwanger's paper.

Smith, Julia, American pianist, composer, and writer on music; b. Denton, Texas, Jan. 25, 1911. She studied piano with Carl Friedberg at the Juilliard School of Music in N.Y.; devoted herself mainly to composition and music criticism. She wrote the operas *Cynthia Parker* (Denton, Feb. 16, 1940); *The Gooseherd and the Goblin* (N.Y., Feb. 22, 1947); *The Stranger of Manzano* (Dallas, May 6, 1947); *Cockcrow* (Austin, April 22, 1954); *The Shepherdess and the Chimney Sweep* (Fort Worth, Dec. 28, 1967); *Daisy* (Miami, Nov. 3, 1973); *Folkways Symphony* (1948); *Remember the Alamo* for Speaker, Chorus, and Wind Orch. (1964); Piano Trio (1955); String Quartet (1964); Piano Concerto (Dallas, Feb. 28, 1976). She publ. the monographs *Aaron Copland* (N.Y., 1955); *Master Pianist. The Career and Teaching of Carl Friedberg* (N.Y., 1963); *A Directory of Women Composers* (Chicago, 1970).

Smith, Kate (Kathryn Elizabeth Smith), American singer of popular music; b. Greenville, Va., May 1, 1909. She first sang in local church choirs; then went to N.Y., where she landed several parts in Broadway musicals, including *Honeymoon Lane* (1926), *Hit the Deck* (1927), and *Flying High* (1930). She rose to prominence on radio and television. It was her custom to include her rendition of *When the Moon Comes over the Mountain* in all of her appearances; she also immortalized Irving Berlin's *God Bless America* in innumerable appearances she made during World War II. In 1982 she received the Presidential Medal of Freedom.

Smith, Lawrence Leighton, American conductor; b. Portland, Oreg., April 8, 1936. He studied piano with Leonard Shure in N.Y. and with Ariel Rubstein in Portland; then enrolled in Portland State Univ. (B.S., 1956) and at the Mannes College of Music in N.Y. (B.M., 1959). In 1964 he received first prize at the Mitropoulos International Conducting Competition in N.Y.; was then assistant conductor at the

Metropolitan Opera (1965–68). He was music director of the Westchester (N.Y.) Symph. Orch. (1967–69); was then principal guest conductor of the Phoenix (Ariz.) Symph. Orch. (1971–73). From 1973–80 he was music director of the Oregon Symph. Orch. in Portland. In 1980 he became music director of the San Antonio Symph. Orch.; was also artistic adviser and principal guest conductor of the North Carolina Symph. Orch. in Raleigh (1980–81).

Smith, Leland, American composer; b. Oakland, Calif., Aug. 6, 1925. He studied composition at Mills College with Darius Milhaud (1941–43) and at the Univ. of Calif., Berkeley, with Roger Sessions (1946–48), obtaining his A.B. and M.A. degrees; also took courses in musicology there with Manfred Bukofzer. He subsequently attended classes of Olivier Messiaen at the Paris Cons. (1948–49). In 1950 he was appointed to the music faculty of the Univ. of Calif. at Berkeley; other posts included Mills College (summer classes between 1951 and 1961) and the Univ. of Chicago (1952–58). In 1958 he joined the faculty at Stanford Univ.; became a prof. in 1968. His style of composition is that of liberal modernism marked by a discriminate application of eclectic idioms, not excluding triadic usages.

WORKS: Sonata for Trumpet and Piano (1947); Trio for Flute, Cello, and Piano (1947); Trio for Violin, Trumpet, and Clarinet (1948); *Divertimento No. 1* for 5 Instruments (1949); Symph. No. 1 (1951); Woodwind Quintet (1951); Sonata for Heckelphone (or Viola) and Piano (1954); *Santa Claus,* opera in 5 scenes on the libretto by e.e. cummings (1955); Concerto for Orch. (1956); Quintet for Bassoon and Strings (1956); *Divertimento No. 2* for Chamber Orch. (1957); *3 Pacifist Songs* (1960); Wind Trio (1960); Quartet for Horn, Violin, Cello, and Piano (1961); *Orpheus* for Guitar, Harp, and Harpsichord (1967); *Machines of Loving Grace* for Computer, Bassoon, and Narrator (1970). He publ. *Handbook of Harmonic Analysis* (Stanford, 1963).

Smith, Moses, American music critic; b. Chelsea, Mass., March 4, 1901; d. Boston, July 27, 1964. He studied law at Harvard Univ. (graduated in 1924) and also music. He was music critic of the *Boston American* (1924–34) and of the *Boston Evening Transcript* (1934–39); then was music director of the Columbia Phonograph Co. (1939–42). In 1947 he publ. a controversial biography of Koussevitzky, who brought a libel suit for $1,000,000 against Smith and his publisher, claiming that the book described him as "generally incompetent, brutal to the musicians and a poseur." The suit, however, was dismissed.

Smith, Patrick J(ohn), American music critic, author, and editor; b. New York, Dec. 11, 1932. He was educated at Princeton Univ. (A.B., 1955); then pursued a career as a music critic, contributing articles to *High Fidelity, Musical America,* the *Musical Quarterly,* and the *Musical Times.* In 1965 he became book editor of *Musical America;* served as N.Y. music correspondent to the *Times* of London;

from 1977–81 was president of the Music Critics Assoc. He wrote the books *The Tenth Muse, A Historical Study of the Opera Libretto* (N.Y., 1970) and *A Year at the Met* (N.Y., 1983).

Smith, Reed, American educator and writer on folklore; b. Washington, N.C., Jan. 16, 1881; d. Pawley's Island, S.C., July 24, 1943. He was educated at the Univ. of South Carolina and at Harvard Univ. (Ph.D., 1909); in 1910, was appointed a prof. of English literature at the Univ. of South Carolina; he publ. *South Carolina Ballads* (1928); also various essays on songs of the South.

Smith, Ronald, English pianist; b. London, Jan. 3, 1922. He studied at the Royal Academy of Music in London; made his debut at a Promenade concert in London in 1942. He later became best known for his interpretations of the massive, programmatic works of Alkan, about whom he has written several books: *Alkan, The Man and His Music* (London, 1975), *Alkan the Enigma* (London, 1976), and *Alkan in Miniature* (London, 1978). He toured Australia as a lecturer and gave talks on the BBC and French Radio. He also composed a number of works, including a Symph. and a Violin Concerto.

Smith, Sydney, English pianist and composer; b. Dorchester, July 14, 1839; d. London, March 3, 1889. He studied piano at the Leipzig Cons. with Moscheles and Plaidy; settled in London in 1859 as a teacher; publ. many salon pieces for piano (*La Harpe éolienne, Le Jet d'eau, The Spinning-wheel,* etc.); also arrangements from operas.

Smith, Warren Storey, American music critic; b. Brookline, Mass., July 14, 1885; d. Boston, Oct. 13, 1971. He studied piano in Boston; in 1922 joined the staff of the New England Cons., where he taught until 1960; was mainly active as a music critic; was music editor of the *Boston Post* (1924–53). He was also a composer; wrote a Piano Trio, piano solo pieces, and several songs.

Smith, William, a.k.a. **"Willie the Lion"** (full name, **William Henry Joseph Berthol Bonaparte Smith**), black American jazz pianist; b. Goschen, N.Y., Nov. 24, 1897; d. New York, April 18, 1973. He attended Howard Univ., and studied music privately with Hans Steinke. After serving in the U.S. Army in World War I, he settled in Harlem, where he established himself as one of the great "stride" pianists. He toured Europe several times, and toured in Africa in 1949. His own compositions (*Fingerbuster, Echoes of Spring,* etc.) had an authenticity that described perfectly the atmosphere of Harlem. His autobiography, *Music on My Mind,* is a personal impression of the Harlem jazz scene. Duke Ellington dedicated his *Portrait of a Lion* to him.

Smith, William O., American composer and jazz clarinetist; b. Sacramento, Calif., Sept. 22, 1926. He began playing clarinet at the age of 10, and at 12 started a grade-school dance band. He then enrolled at the Juilliard School of Music in N.Y. (1945–46) while earning a living by playing in jazz groups. Returning to California, he took courses with Darius Milhaud at Mills College (1946–47) and attended sessions with Sessions at the Univ. of Calif. at Berkeley (M.A., 1952). Intermittently, he played in Dave Brubeck's jazz octet in California (1947–52). In 1957 he was awarded the American Prix de Rome, and in 1960 he received a Guggenheim grant. His scholarly interests were certainly insular in the great mass of innocent jazz practitioners; his own music is omnivorous, ingesting dodecaphony, inhaling electronics, and absorbing by osmosis a variety of quaquaversal elements, while maintaining a dignified formality of organized musical structure.

WORKS: Suite for Clarinet, Flute, and Trumpet (1947); *Serenade* for Flute, Violin, Trumpet, and Clarinet (1947); *Schizophrenic Scherzo* for Clarinet, Trumpet, Alto and Tenor Saxophones, and Trombone (1947); Clarinet Sonata (1948); *"anyone,"* after e.e. cummings, cantata for Soprano, Women's Chorus, and Chamber Orch. (1948); Concertino for Trumpet and Jazz Instruments (1948); Clarinet Quintet (1950); String Quartet (1952); *Capriccio* for Violin and Piano (1952); *Suite* for Violin and Clarinet (1952); *"my father moved through dooms of love,"* after e.e. cummings, cantata for Chorus and Small Orch. (1955); *Divertimento* for Violin, Cello, Clarinet, Bassoon, and Horn (1955); *Divertimento* for Flute, Clarinet, Guitar, Vibraphone, Bass, and Drums (1956); Concerto for Clarinet and Jazz Combo (1957); Trio for Clarinet, Violin, and Piano (1957); Quintet for Clarinet, Violin, Cello, and Piano (1958); *5 Pieces* for Solo Clarinet (1958); *Improvisation* for Clarinet and Recorded Clarinet (1960); *4 Studies* for 2 Pianos (1962); Concerto for Jazz Soloist (Clarinet) and Orch. (1962); *Explorations* for Jazz Combo and Tape (1963); *Variants* for Solo Clarinet (1963); *Interplay* for Jazz Combo and Orch. (1964); *Mosaic* for Clarinet and Piano (1964); *Elegy for Eric* for Jazz Combo (1964; in memory of Eric Dolphy); *Tangents* for Clarinet and Orch. (Rome Radio, July 3, 1965); *Explorations II* for 5 Instruments (1966); *Fancies* for Solo Clarinet (1966); *Quadi* for Jazz Quartet and Orch. (N.Y., Oct. 6, 1968; Modern Jazz Quartet, soloists); *Songs for Myself Alone* for Soprano and Percussion (1970); *Quadrodram* for Clarinet, Trombone, Piano, Percussion, Dancer, and Film (Seattle, Dec. 9, 1970); *Chamber Muse* for Percussion, Clarinet, and Dancer (1970); *Straws* for Flute and Bassoon (1974); *Jazz Set* for Flute and Clarinet (1974); *Agate* for Soloist and Jazz Orch. (1974); *Theona* for Jazz Ensemble and Orch. (1975; Seattle, March 15, 1978); *Chrones* for String Quartet (1975); *Elegia* for Clarinet and String Orch. (Seattle, Nov. 14, 1976); *5* for Brass Quintet (1975); *5 Minutes* for Solo Clarinet (1977); *Ilios* for Chorus and Wind Instruments (1977); *Janus* for Trombone and Jazz Orch. (1977; Univ. of Washington, March 2, 1978); *Ecco!* for Clarinet and Orch. (Seattle, March 15, 1978); *Intermission* for Soprano, Chorus, and Instruments (1978); *9 Studies* for Solo Clarinet (1978); *Webster's Story* for Soprano, Clarinet, and Trombone (1978).

Smith, Wilson George, American pianist and composer; b. Elyria, Ohio, Aug. 19, 1855; d. Cleveland, Feb. 26, 1929. He studied piano with the Scharwenka brothers in Berlin. Returning to the U.S. in 1882, he settled in Cleveland, where he taught piano. He publ. a number of salon pieces for piano, such as *Poème d'amour, Humoresque, Menuet moderne, Romanza appassionata,* and *Babbling Brook;* also about 40 songs. His album of 5 piano pieces, *Hommage à Edvard Grieg,* was commended for its spirit by Grieg himself.

BIBLIOGRAPHY: Rupert Hughes, *Contemporary American Composers* (Boston, 1900; pp. 394–406).

Smither, Howard E., American musicologist and educator; b. Pittsburg, Kans., Nov. 15, 1925. He studied at Hamline Univ. in St. Paul, Minn. (A.B., 1950), and at Cornell Univ. with Donald J. Grout and William W. Austin (M.A., 1952); in 1953 received a senior graduate fellowship, awarded by Cornell for study in Germany; received his Ph.D. from Cornell in 1960; attended classes of Rudolf von Ficker in Munich; in 1965–66 studied in Italy on a Fulbright grant; in 1972 did research in Italy on the history of the oratorio on a fellowship from the National Endowment for the Humanities. He was on the faculties of Oberlin Cons. (1955–60), the Univ. of Kansas (1960–63), and Tulane Univ. (1963–68); in 1968 was appointed a prof. of music at the Univ. of North Carolina at Chapel Hill. He publ. an important study, *A History of the Oratorio* (2 vols., Chapel Hill, 1977); contributed to the 6th edition of *Grove's Dictionary of Music and Musicians* a major article on the oratorio, as well as biographical articles on Italian composers of oratorios. He was president of the American Musicological Society from 1980 to 1982.

Smola, Emmerich, German conductor and double-bass player; b. Bergreichenstein, July 8, 1922. He studied music with his father, and later took lessons in conducting with Theodor Seidl in Prague. In 1946 he joined the Southwest German Radio Orch. as a double-bass player; then served as its conductor (1948–51); later made appearances as a radio conductor in Vienna, Paris, Brussels, and Stockholm.

Smolensky, Stepan, Russian music scholar; b. Kazan, Oct. 20, 1848; d. Vasilsursk, near Nizhny-Novgorod, Aug. 2, 1909. He devoted his efforts mainly to collecting and analyzing Russian MSS of old church music; publ. *A Course of Choral Church Singing* (Kazan, 1885) and numerous papers on specific subjects connected with old Russian musical notation. A list of Smolensky's writings was publ. in a memorial vol. edited by N. Findeisen (St. Petersburg, 1911).

Smolian, Arthur, conductor and writer; b. Riga, Dec. 3, 1856; d. Leipzig, Nov. 5, 1911. He was a pupil of Rheinberger and Wüllner at the Munich Cons.; conducted choruses in Leipzig (from 1884); taught at the Karlsruhe Cons. (1890–1901); in 1901 settled again in Leipzig as a music critic and editor. In his writings he was an ardent proponent of Wagner's ideas. He publ. *Vom Schwinden der Gesangskunst* (1903) and *Stella del Monte* (1903; a free narrative of Berlioz's last years).

Smulders, Charles, Belgian composer; b. Maastricht, May 8, 1863; d. Liège, April 21, 1934. He studied at the Liège Cons.; won the Belgian Prix de Rome in 1889; taught at the Liège Cons. He wrote the symph. poems *Adieu-Absence-Retour; Chant d'amour; Le Jour; Le Crépuscule;* 2 piano concertos; *Hebrew Melodies* for Cello and Orch.; Violin Sonata; Piano Sonata; choruses; songs.

BIBLIOGRAPHY: W. Paap, "C. Smulders en A. Diepenbrock," *Mens en Melodie,* 1 (1946).

Smyth, Dame Ethel (Mary), foremost English woman composer; b. Rectory (Middlesex), April 22, 1858; d. Woking, Surrey, May 8, 1944. She studied at the Leipzig Cons.; then with Heinrich von Herzogenberg, following him to Berlin; her String Quintet was performed in Leipzig in 1884. She returned to London in 1888; presented her orchestral *Serenade* (April 26, 1890) and an overture, *Antony and Cleopatra* (Oct. 18, 1890). Her prestige as a serious woman composer rose considerably with the presentation of her Mass for Solo Voices, Chorus, and Orch. at Albert Hall (Jan. 18, 1893). After that she devoted her energies to the theater. Her first opera, *Fantasio,* to her own libretto in German, after Alfred de Musset's play, was produced in Weimar on May 24, 1898; this was followed by *Der Wald* (Berlin, April 9, 1902), also to her own German libretto; it was produced in London in the same year, and in N.Y. by the Metropolitan Opera on March 11, 1903. Her next opera, *The Wreckers,* was her most successful work; written originally to a French libretto, *Les Naufrageurs,* it was first produced in a German version as *Strandrecht* (Leipzig, Nov. 11, 1906); the composer herself trans. it into Eng., and it was staged in London on June 22, 1909; the score was revised some years later, and produced at Sadler's Wells, London, on April 19, 1939. She further wrote a comic opera, in Eng., *The Boatswain's Mate* (London, Jan. 28, 1916); a one-act opera, described as a "dance-dream," *Fête galante* (Birmingham, June 4, 1923); and *Entente cordiale* (Bristol, Oct. 20, 1926). Other works are a Concerto for Violin, Horn, and Orch. (London, March 5, 1927); *The Prison* for Soprano and Bass Solo, Chorus, and Orch. (London, Feb. 24, 1931); choral pieces (*Hey Nonny No, Sleepless Dreams,* etc.); a group of songs; etc. Her formative years were spent in Germany, and her music never overcame the strong German characteristics, in the general idiom as well as in the treatment of dramatic situations on the stage. At the same time, she was a believer in English national music and its potentialities. She was a militant leader for woman suffrage in England, for which cause she wrote *The March of the Women,* the battle song of the W.S.P.U. After suffrage was granted, her role in the movement was officially acknowledged; in 1922 she was made a Dame of the British Empire. She publ. a number of books, mostly autobiographical in nature: *Impressions That Remained* (2 vols., 1919; new ed., 1945); *Streaks of Life* (1921); *As Time Went On* (1936); *What Happened Next* (1940); also some humorous essays and reminiscences, *A Three-legged Tour in Greece* (1927); *A Final Burning of Boats* (1928); *Female Pipings in Eden* (1934); *Beecham and Pharaoh* (1935).

BIBLIOGRAPHY: R. Boughton, in *Music Bulletin* (Feb. 1923); R. Capell, in *Monthly Musical Record* (July 1923); R.A. Streatfeild, *Musiciens anglais contemporains* (Paris, 1913); Kathleen Dale, "Dame Ethel Smyth," *Music & Letters* (July 1944); C. St. John, *Ethel Smyth: A Biography* (N.Y., 1959).

Snel, Joseph-François, Belgian violinist and composer; b. Brussels, July 30, 1793; d. Koekelberg, near Brussels, March 10, 1861. He studied violin with Baillot at the Paris Cons. In 1818 he founded in Brussels the Académie de Musique et de Chant (with Mees); he popularized in Belgium the instructional singing methods of Galin and Wilhem; held various positions as an inspector of schools. His ballets *Frisac et le page inconstant, L'Enchantement de Polichinelle*, etc., were produced at the Brussels Opera; in 1830, during the Belgian revolution, he wrote the ballet *Barricades.*

Snetzler (Schnetzler), Johann, Swiss organ builder; b. Schaffhausen, April 6, 1710; d. there, Sept. 28, 1785. He went to London in 1746 and established an organ workshop there; built organs for the Moravian churches in London and in Leeds, for Chesterfield Church, and (on the recommendation of Burney) for the Church of King's Lynn. He returned to Switzerland shortly before his death. His London factory was purchased by Ohrmann, Nutt, and Eliot. A list of his organs exported to the U.S is found in W.L. Summer's *The Organ* (London, 1952).

Snoer, Johannes, Dutch harpist; b. Amsterdam, June 28, 1868; d. Vienna, March 1, 1936. He studied with Edmund Schuecker when the latter was in Amsterdam; from 1894 to 1910 was first harpist of the Gewandhaus Orch. in Leipzig; traveled as a soloist in Europe and America in 1905–6. He publ. several practical pieces for the harp, and didactic works: *Praktische Harfenschule, Tägliche Übungen, Studien in Konzertform, Orchesterstudien,* etc.; also *Die Harfe als Orchesterinstrument* (Leipzig, 1898).

Snow, Hank (Clarence Eugene Snow), Canadian-born American singer of country music; b. Brooklyn, Nova Scotia, May 9, 1914. He began his singing career on a radio station in Halifax in 1935; also made recordings and toured extensively throughout Canada and the U.S. as The Singing Ranger. He settled in the U.S. in 1948; became an American citizen in 1957. In 1950 he joined the "Grand Ole Opry" radio program in Nashville, Tenn.; also made tours of Europe and the Far East. He was elected to the Country Music Hall of Fame in 1979.

Sobinov, Leonid, celebrated Russian tenor; b. Yaroslavl, June 7, 1872; d. Riga, Oct. 14, 1934 (buried in Moscow). He was an offspring of a middle-class family with peasant roots (his grandfather was an emancipated serf). He studied law at Moscow Univ., where he also sang in a student choir. In 1892 he began to study voice with Dodonov and soon appeared professionally in a traveling Italian opera company in Moscow without interrupting his univ. study; he graduated in law in 1894, and was appointed assistant advocate to a Moscow lawyer. Turning decisively to singing, he made his debut at the Bolshoi Theater in 1897, and retained his connection with it during almost his entire career. In 1901 he also joined the Imperial Maryinsky Theater in St. Petersburg. His successes on the European stage were no less outstanding; he sang at La Scala in Milan from 1904 to 1906; from 1909 he also appeared in London, Paris, and Berlin. He was eloquent in the roles of Alfredo in *La Traviata,* Des Grieux in *Manon,* and Faust in Gounod's opera. His performance of Lensky in *Eugene Onegin* remained an unsurpassed model of Russian operatic lyricism. In his solo recitals he could squeeze the last fluid ounce out of Tchaikovsky's melancholy songs. No wonder that he was idolized by Russian audiences, particularly among the young and female; a whole tribe of "Sobinovites" appeared, and long queues formed before his concerts, willing to stand in line for hours in the hope of obtaining scarce tickets. During the period of 1918–19 in and around Kiev, his occasional piano accompanist was the editor of the present volume.

BIBLIOGRAPHY: *Leonid Sobinov: Life and Creative Work,* ed. by Y. Boyarsky (Moscow, 1937); M. Lvov, *L. Sobinov* (Moscow, 1951); A. Orfenov, *Creative Work of L. Sobinov* (Moscow, 1965).

Sobolewski, Friedrich Eduard de, German-American composer; b. Königsberg, Oct. 1, 1808, of Polish parents; d. St. Louis, May 17, 1872. He was a pupil of Weber in Dresden; became an opera conductor in Königsberg and Bremen; produced there his operas *Imogen* (1833), *Velleda* (1836), and *Salvator Rosa* (1848); his opera *Komala* was produced by Liszt in Weimar on Oct. 30, 1858. In 1859 he emigrated to the U.S., settling in Milwaukee, then a center of German musical immigrants. There he staged his opera *Mohega,* on Oct. 11, 1859, to his own libretto in German; he selected an American subject dealing with an Indian girl saved by Pulaski from death. Sobolewski subsequently moved to St. Louis; organized a symph. orch. there, which he led from 1860 to 1866. He wrote the oratorios *Johannes der Täufer, Der Erlöser,* and *Himmel und Erde;* 2 symphs.; the symph. poems *Vineta* and *Meeresphantasie;* several male choruses; publ. the pamphlets *Reaktionäre Briefe* (1854), *Oper nicht Drama* (1858), and *Das Geheimnis der neuesten Schule der Musik* (1859).

BIBLIOGRAPHY: E.E. Hipsher, *American Opera and Its Composers* (Philadelphia, 1927; 2nd ed., 1934; pp. 382–85).

Socor, Matei, Rumanian composer and pedagogue; b. Jassy, Sept. 28, 1908. He studied music theory with Castaldi at the Bucharest Cons. (1927–29); then went to Germany and took a course in composition with Karg-Elert at the Leipzig Cons. (1930–33). Returning to Rumania, he dedicated himself to teaching music at various schools in Bucharest and elsewhere.
WORKS: Concerto for Orch. (1939); *Passacaglia* for Cello and Chamber Orch. (1944); Violin Concerto (1955); *Mama,* poem for Mezzo-soprano, Chorus, and Orch. (1949); Wind Sextet (1969); Piano Sonata (1932); choruses; songs.

Söderblom, Ulf, Finnish conductor; b. Turku, Feb. 5, 1930. He studied conducting with Hans Swarowsky at the Vienna Academy of Music, graduating in 1957; then joined the Finnish National Opera in Helsinki as a conductor; he became its chief conductor in 1973. In 1983 he brought the Finnish National Opera to the U.S. for performances of operas by Sallinen and Kokkonen at the Metropolitan Opera in N.Y. He received the Finnish State Award in 1977.

Soderino, Agostino, Italian organist and composer; flourished in the early 17th century. He was a church organist in Milan, where he publ. his *Canzoni a 4 & 8 voci . . . Libri I, Op. 2* (1608); 2 keyboard canzonas from this publication (*La scaramuccia* and *La Ducalina*) are reprinted in L. Torchi, *L'Arte Musicale in Italia* (vol. III).

Söderlind, Ragnar, Norwegian composer; b. Oslo, June 27, 1945. He studied in Oslo with Baden (counterpoint), Hukvari (conducting), and Ulleberg (horn); then studied at the Sibelius Academy in Helsinki with Erik Bergman and Joonas Kokkonen.
WORKS: Chamber opera, *Esther og den blå ro* (1972); *Nocturne* for Orch. (1963); *Prelude* for Orch. (1964); *Pietà* for Mezzo-soprano and String Orch. (1965); *Rokkomborre,* symph. poem (1967); *Polaris,* symph. vision (1967–70); *Trauermusik* for Orch. (1968); *Fantasia borealis* for Chamber Orch. (1969); *Sinfonia minimale* for Amateur Orch. (1971); *International Rhapsody* for Orch. (1971); *Sinfonia* for Orch., with Solo Soprano (1975); *Elegia I* for Solo Cello and *II* for Solo Violin (1966; when played simultaneously, they become *Elegia III*); *Dithyrambe,* sketch for Bassoon and Harp (1967); *Körsbärblommor (Cherry Blossom),* 5 Japanese love poems for Baritone, Flute, English Horn, Cello, and Percussion (1967); *Intermezzo* for Percussionist (1968); *La Mort des pauvres* for Male Chorus, 4 Trombones, and Percussion (1969); *La poema battutta* for 8 Percussionists (1973); *2 Pieces from the Desert* for Oboe and Piano (1973; orchestrated 1974); String Quartet (1975); *Consolation* for Piano (1969); choruses; songs.

Soderlund, Gustav Frederic, Swedish-American music scholar and teacher; b. Göteborg, Jan. 25, 1881; d. Rochester, N.Y., Nov. 28, 1972. He studied piano in Sweden; went to South America in 1908, and taught music at the Cons. of Valparaiso, Chile. In 1916 he settled in the U.S.; was on the faculty of the Univ. of Kansas (1919–27) and at the Eastman School of Music in Rochester, N.Y. (1928–47). He publ. in the Eastman School Series 2 collections of musical examples for use in teaching: *Examples Illustrating the Development of Melodic Line and Contrapuntal Style* (1932) and *Examples of Gregorian Chant* (1937).

Söderman, (Johan) August, Swedish composer; b. Stockholm, July 17, 1832; d. there, Feb. 10, 1876. He studied piano and composition at the Stockholm Academy of Music (1847–50); then, as a composer of operettas, joined a theatrical company on a Scandinavian tour. In 1856 he went to Leipzig, where he studied privately with Richter and acquired an appreciation of German vocal music; he was particularly influenced by the lyric works of Schumann, Wagner, and Liszt, an influence that is combined with Swedish national elements in his theater music.
WORKS: Operettas: *Urdur* (Helsinki, 1852) and *Hin Ondes första lärospan* (*The Devil's First Lesson;* Stockholm, Sept. 14, 1856); incidental music to about 80 plays by Shakespeare, Schiller, and Swedish writers; *Digte og Sange,* part-songs to words by Bjørnson; several songs to Swedish words; a ballad for Solo Voice, Chorus, and Orch., *Die Wallfahrt nach Kevlaar,* after Heine (1859–66); also a *Missa solemnis* (1875).
BIBLIOGRAPHY: G. Jeanson, *A. Söderman: En svensk tondiktares liv och verk* (Stockholm, 1926; includes a complete list of his works).

Sodero, Cesare, conductor; b. Naples, Aug. 2, 1886; d. New York, Dec. 16, 1947. He studied with Alessandro Longo (piano) and Martucci (composition) at the Naples Cons.; in 1907 emigrated to the U.S. and settled in N.Y.; was a music director of the Edison Phonograph Co., the National Broadcasting Co., and the Mutual Broadcasting Co.; conducted the San Carlo Grand Opera Co. and the Philadelphia Grand Opera. He wrote an opera, *Ombre russe* (Venice, June 19, 1930); ballets; chamber music.

Söderström, Elisabeth, Swedish soprano; b. Stockholm, May 7, 1927. She was educated at the Royal Academy of Music in Stockholm; made her operatic debut in 1947 at the Drottningholm Court Theater; then sang at many European music centers. On Oct. 30, 1959, she appeared at the Metropolitan Opera House in N.Y. in the role of Susanna in *Le nozze di Figaro;* remained on its roster until 1964.

Soffredini, Alfredo, Italian composer; b. Livorno, Sept. 17, 1854; d. Milan, March 12, 1923. He studied with Mazzucato and Sangalli at the Milan Cons.; was editor of the influential *Gazzetta Musicale* (Milan) from 1896 to 1912; also taught composition; among his students was Mascagni.
WORKS: 8 operas to his own librettos: *Il Saggio* (Livorno, Feb. 3, 1883); 2-act children's opera, *Il piccolo Haydn* (Faenza, Nov. 24, 1889; Vienna, 1897;

also productions in Russia and elsewhere); *Salvatorello* (Pavia, March 25, 1894); *Tarcisio* (Milan, Nov. 23, 1895); *Aurora* (Pavia, April 21, 1897); *La coppa d'oro* (Milan, Jan. 27, 1900); *Graziella* (Pavia, Nov. 15, 1902); *Il leone* (Cesena, 1914). He publ. *Le opere di Verdi* (Milan, 1901) and contributed essays on Italian music to various publications, as well as to the *Gazzetta Musicale.*

Sofronitzky, Vladimir, Russian pianist; b. St. Petersburg, May 8, 1901; d. Moscow, Aug. 29, 1961. He studied with Nikolayev at the Leningrad Cons., graduating in 1921; then went on a concert tour in Russia, Poland, and France. Returning to Russia, he taught piano at the Leningrad Cons. (1936–42), and at the Moscow Cons. from 1942 until his death. He was greatly praised for his interpretations of Chopin, and particularly Scriabin.
BIBLIOGRAPHY: V. Delson, *Vladimir Sofronitzky* (Moscow, 1959); J. Milstein, *Reminiscences of Sofronitzky* (Moscow, 1970).

Sohn, Joseph, American music critic and writer; b. New York, March 22, 1876; d. there, March 15, 1935. After graduation from the College of the City of N.Y., he went to Berlin for further musical studies; upon his return to N.Y. he became music critic of the *N.Y. American* and the *Forum.* He publ. *Robert Schumann, a Lyrical Poet* (1896); *Lessons of the Opera* (1903); *Music in America and Abroad* (1904); *Joseph Joachim* (1904); *Opera in New York* (1907); *The Mission of Richard Wagner* (1910).

Sojo, Vicente Emilio, Venezuelan composer and pedagogue; b. Guatire, Dec. 8, 1887; d. Caracas, Aug. 11, 1974. He studied music at the Academia de Bellas Artes in Caracas; in 1921 became a prof. of music theory at the Escuela Superior de Música in Caracas. In 1937 he founded the Orquesta Sinfónica Venezuela and the choral ensemble Orfeón Lamas, which became of prime importance in the musical culture of Venezuela. Sojo was also active in national ethnomusicology; he collected and harmonized several hundred Venezuelan folk songs and church hymns of the colonial period. He composed mainly sacred music, motets, and organ pieces.
BIBLIOGRAPHY: Ramón Fernández, *V.E. Sojo* (Caracas, 1968); a list of his works is found in *Compositores de America,* vol. XIV (Washington, D.C., 1968).

Sokalsky, Pyotr, Russian writer on music; b. Kharkov, Sept. 26, 1832; d. Odessa, April 11, 1887. He studied biology and taught school. His significance in Russian music lies in his being an ardent collector of Russian folk songs; his chief work, *The Russian Folk Song; Its Melodic Structure and Harmonic Characteristics,* was publ. posthumously in 1888. He also wrote some piano music and 3 operas: *The Siege of Dubno, Mazeppa,* and *A Night in May.*

Sokola, Miloš, Czech composer; b. Bučovice, Moravia, April 18, 1913; d. Malé-Košice, Sept. 27,

1976. He studied composition with Petrželka, and violin with O. Vávra at the Brno Cons. (1936–38); had further composition studies in Prague with V. Novák (1938–39) and J. Křička (1943–45). From 1942 to 1973 he was a violinist in the Prague National Theater Orch.
WORKS: Opera, *Marnotratný syn* (*The Prodigal Son;* 1948; Olomouc, 1963); *9 Variations on a Theme by Vítežslava Kaprálová* for Orch. (1952; Prague, Feb. 17, 1957; from Kaprálová's *April Preludes*); Violin Concerto (1952); *Devátý květen* (*The Ninth of May),* symph. poem (1960); Concerto for Organ and String Orch. (1971); Piano Concertino (1972); 5 string quartets (1944; with Solo Tenor, 1946; 1955; 1964; 1971); Violin Sonata (1972); Wind Quintet (1973); for Piano: *5 Miniatures* (1931); Sonata (1946); *Valses* (1953); *12 Preludes* (1954); *Suite* for Left Hand (1972); for Organ: *Toccata quasi Passacaglia* (1964); *B-A-C-H Studies* (1972); *Andante cantabile* (1973).

Sokoloff, Nicolai, American conductor; b. near Kiev, Russia, May 28, 1886; d. La Jolla, Calif., Sept. 25, 1965. He was brought to America as a child, and studied violin with Loeffler in Boston; played the violin in the Boston Symph. Orch.; then conducted various symph. groups. In 1918 he became conductor of the newly organized Cleveland Orch., and to the extent of his limited abilities, he discharged his duties at this post in an acceptable fashion until 1933. He served as music director of the Federal Music Project (1935–38); for 2 seasons conducted the Seattle Symph. Orch. (1938–40); then went to live in La Jolla, Calif., occasionally filling in guest conducting engagements.

Sokolov, Nicolai, Russian composer and pedagogue; b. St. Petersburg, March 26, 1859; d. there (Petrograd), March 27, 1922. He was a pupil of Rimsky-Korsakov at the St. Petersburg Cons., graduating in 1884; later taught harmony there for many years, until his death. He was also a prolific composer in the traditional Russian manner; many of his works were publ. by Belaieff, among them music for Shakespeare's play *The Winter's Tale;* 3 string quartets; violin pieces; a great number of songs.

Solano, Francisco Ignacio, Portuguese music theorist; b. Coimbra, c.1720; d. Lisbon, Sept. 18, 1800. He publ. *Nova instrucçao musical* (1764); *Nova arte e breve compendio de musica* (1768; 2nd ed., 1794); *Novo tratado de musica* (1779); *Dissertação sobre o caracter da musica* (1780).

Solares, Enrique, Guatemalan pianist and composer; b. Guatemala City, July 11, 1910. He studied piano with Salvador Ley in Guatemala; composition with Raymond Moulaert in Brussels, Jaroslav Křička in Prague (1936–39), and Alfredo Casella in Rome (1939–42). He returned to Guatemala in 1943; taught piano, then entered the diplomatic service and was a consular officer in Guatemalan embassies in Rome, Brussels, Madrid, and Paris. His compositions are set in Baroque forms; later he experimented with serial techniques.

WORKS: *Ricercare sobre el nombre de BACH* for String Orch. (1941); *Toccatina* for Guitar (1946); *Partita* for String Orch. (1947); Sonata for Solo Violin (1958); *Fantasia* for Guitar (1959); *Idea con 15 Deformaciones* for Piano (1962); *7 Traversuras* for Piano (1969); *12 Microtransparencias* for Piano (1970).

Soldat, Marie, Austrian violinist; b. Graz, March 25, 1863; d. there, Sept. 30, 1955. She first studied in Graz, and from 1879 to 1882 with Joachim at the Hochschule für Musik in Berlin, graduating as winner of the Mendelssohn Prize; made a specialty of the Brahms Violin Concerto, which she performed with great authority. In 1887 she formed in Berlin her own string quartet (all women); in 1899 she married the lawyer Röger, and settled in Vienna, continuing her concert career; there she formed a new string quartet (with Elsa von Plank, Natalie Bauer-Lechner, and Leontine Gärtner); eventually retired in Graz, remaining there until her death at the age of 92.

Solenière, Eugène de, French writer on music; b. Paris, Dec. 25, 1872; d. there, Dec. 4, 1904. After studying music in Germany, he settled in Paris as a writer and lecturer on musical esthetics.

WRITINGS: *La Femme compositeur* (1895); *Rose Caron* (1896); *Notes musicales* (1896); *Massenet; Etude critique et documentaire* (1897); *Musique et religion* (1897); *Camille Saint-Saëns* (1899); *Cent années de musique française 1800–1900* (1901); *Notules et impressions musicales* (1902).

Soler, Padre Antonio, important Spanish composer and organist; b. Olot, Catalonia (baptized, Dec. 3), 1729; d. El Escorial, near Madrid, Dec. 20, 1783. He entered the school of the monastery of Montserrat as a child, and studied organ and harmony there. In 1752 he took Holy Orders at El Escorial, and spent the rest of his life there. For some time between 1752 and 1756 he had an opportunity to take lessons with Domenico Scarlatti, who was then attached to the Spanish court; Scarlatti's influence is apparent in Soler's harpsichord sonatas. Soler was a prolific composer of both sacred and secular music; a catalogue of his MSS at El Escorial contains 428 separate numbers. Fourteen harpsichord sonatas by Soler were publ. by J. Nín in *Classiques espagnols du piano* (2 vols., Paris, 1925, 1929); 100 piano sonatas and a *Fandango,* edited by the pianist F. Marvin, were publ. in N.Y. (1958–59); 6 concertos for 2 Keyboard Instruments were edited by Santiago Kastner (Barcelona, 1952); 6 quintets for Strings and Organ were brought out by Roberto Gerhard for the *Institut d'Estudis Catalans* (Barcelona, 1933, with an introductory essay by H. Anglès); a collection of 27 *Sonatas para Clave* was printed in London by T. Birchall; 6 organ concertos were edited by Padre S. Rubrio (Madrid, 1968).

BIBLIOGRAPHY: J. Nín, "The Bicentenary of Antonio Soler," *Chesterian* (1930); F. Carroll, *An Introduction to Antonio Soler* (Diss., Univ. of Rochester, 1960); K. Heimes, *Antonio Soler's Keyboard Sonatas* (Pretoria, 1969).

Soler, Josep, Catalan composer; b. Barcelona, March 25, 1935. He studied composition with René Leibowitz in Paris (1959) and with Cristòfor Taltabull in Barcelona (1960–64). In 1977 he was appointed to the staff of the Barcelona Cons.

WORKS: 3 operas: *Agamemnon* (1960); *Edipo y Iocasta* (1972; Barcelona, Oct. 30, 1974); *Jesús de Nazaret* (1974–78); *Danae* for String Orch. (1959; revised 1969; Lisbon, June 23, 1977); *Cantata Ioel Prophetae,* chamber cantata (1960); Trio for 2 Violins and Piano (1961); Piano Trio (1964); *Orpheus* for Piano and Orch. (1965; revised 1974); *Quetzalcoatl* for Flute and Chamber Orch. (1966); 2 symphs.: *The Solar Cycle I* and *The Solar Cycle II* (1967; 1969, revised 1977); *Lachrymae* for 11 Instruments (1967); *Diaphonia* for 17 Wind Instruments (1968); String Trio (1968); *Música triste* for Guitar (1968); Piano Concerto (1969); Concerto for Harpsichord, Oboe, English Horn, Bass Clarinet, Viola, and Cello (1969); *Sounds in the Night* for 6 Percussionists (1969); *Inferno* for Chamber Ensemble (1970); 3 string quartets (1966, 1971, 1975); *Tañido de Falsas* for Guitar and Percussion (1971); *Noche oscura* for Organ and Percussion (1971); Cello Concerto (1973); *Requiem* for Solo Percussion and Orch. (1974–75; Kassel, Germany, Sept. 18, 1977); *Apuntava l'alba* for Orch. (1975; Barcelona, Feb. 5, 1976); *3 Erotic Songs* for Chorus a cappella (1976); *Shakespeare Lieder* for Tenor and Orch. (1976–77); *Harmonices mundi,* in 3 vols.: No. 1 for Piano, and Nos. 2 and 3 for Organ (1977); songs.

Solerti, Angelo, Italian historiographer; b. Savona, Sept. 20, 1865; d. Massa Carrara, Jan. 10, 1907. His contributions to the early history of opera are valuable: *Le origini del melodramma* (a collection of contemporary documents and prefaces to the earliest operas; Turin, 1903); *Gli albori del melodramma* (3 vols., Milan, 1904–5); *Musica, ballo e drammatica alla corte medicea dal 1600 al 1637* (Florence, 1905); *Ferrara e la Corte Estense nella second metà del secolo XVI* (contains a chapter on *Musica e canto;* Città di Castello, 1891).

Sollberger, Harvey, American flutist and composer; b. Cedar Rapids, Iowa, May 11, 1938. He studied composition with Philip Bezanson at the Univ. of Iowa and with Jack Beeson and Otto Luening at Columbia Univ. (M.A., 1964). In 1964–72 he was on the staff of Columbia Univ.; then at the Manhattan School of Music. In his music he employs an imaginatively applied serial method.

WORKS: Trio for Flute, Cello, and Piano (1961); *Grand Quartet* for Flutes (1962); *Solos* for Violin and 5 Instruments (1962); *2 Oboes Troping* (1963); *Chamber Variations* for 12 Players and Conductor (1964); *Musica transalpina* for Soprano, Baritone, and 6 Players (1965).

Sollertinsky, Ivan, brilliant Russian music critic; b. Vitebsk, Dec. 3, 1902; d. Novosibirsk, Feb. 11, 1944.

He studied philosophy at the Univ. of Petrograd (1919–24); then became a music critic; he showed profound understanding of the problems of modern music and was one of the earliest supporters of Shostakovich; publ. numerous articles dealing with Soviet music in general; these were assembled in a collection with a biographical sketch and bibliography compiled by M. Druskin (Leningrad, 1946); another collection of his essays was edited by Shostakovich (Leningrad, 1956).

Solomon (real name, **Solomon Cutner**), English pianist; b. London, Aug. 9, 1902. He made a sensational debut as a child prodigy at the age of 8, playing Tchaikovsky's Concerto No. 1 in London (June 30, 1911). Later he was sent to Paris for further study, resuming his career as an adult performer in 1923. He appeared under the single name Solomon, without a patronymic; toured all over the world as a concert pianist; also played with orchs. His interpretation of the classics is particularly fine in that he adheres strictly to the spirit of the music, without superimposing any mannerisms of his own. In 1956 he suffered a stroke, which paralyzed his right arm; as a result, he was forced to withdraw from his concert career; he has since lived in London.

Solomon, Izler, American conductor; b. St. Paul, Minn., Jan. 11, 1910. He took violin lessons with Myron Poliakin in Philadelphia and Michael Press in N.Y.; then took courses at Michigan State College (1928–31). He made his debut as a conductor with the Lansing (Mich.) Civic Orch. on March 17, 1932; then conducted the Illinois Symph. (1936–42) and the Columbus (Ohio) Phil. (1941–49); was guest conductor of the Israel Phil. during its American tour in 1951; also filled in engagements with the Buffalo Phil. Orch., Chicago Symph., Los Angeles Phil., Detroit Symph., Philadelphia Orch., etc. From 1956 to 1975 he was principal conductor and music director of the Indianapolis Symph. Orch.; during his tenure he brought it to a considerable degree of perfection; in his programs he included many works of the modern American school. In 1976 he suffered a stroke, and was unable to continue his career.

Solomon, Maynard (Elliott), American recording executive and writer on music; b. New York, Jan. 5, 1930. He was educated in N.Y. at the High School of Music and Art and at Brooklyn College (A.B., 1950). He was co-founder of the Vanguard Recording Society, Inc., and produced numerous phonograph recordings. As an author, he contributed many articles on Beethoven, Schubert, and other composers to the *Musical Quarterly, Music & Letters, 19th Century Music, Beethoven Studies,* the *Beethoven-Jahrbuch,* and other publications, and also served as associate editor of *American Imago.* He wrote the provocative study *Beethoven* (N.Y., 1977; in German, Munich, 1979), which offers a plausible surmise as to the identity of the mythical "Immortal Beloved." He also edited "Beethoven's Tagebuch 1812–1818," in *Beethoven Studies 3* (London, 1982).

Soloviev, Nicolai, Russian composer; b. Petrozavodsk, May 9, 1846; d. Petrograd, Dec. 27, 1916. After completing his studies in composition at the St. Petersburg Cons., he was appointed a prof. of harmony there (1874). He composed the operas *Cordelia* (St. Petersburg, Nov. 24, 1885) and *Vakula the Smith* (1880), and completed the score of Serov's opera *The Evil Power.* He further wrote a symph. picture, *Russia and the Mongols* (1882); a choral *Prayer for Russia* (1876); a number of songs and piano pieces. He was known in St. Petersburg principally as a music critic.

Soloviev-Sedoy, Vasili, Russian composer; b. St. Petersburg, April 25, 1907; d. Moscow, Dec. 2, 1979. He studied at the Leningrad Cons., graduating in 1936; was active as a pianist, playing improvisations on the radio and accompanying exercises in the Leningrad Studio of Creative Gymnastics. During the war he organized a series of theatrical productions for the Soviet army. He was a member of the Supreme Soviet in the 3rd, 4th, and 5th congresses. In 1975 he was awarded the order of Hero of Socialist Labor. He was regarded in Russia as one of the most expert composers of Soviet songs, some of which acquired immense popularity; one of them, *Evenings at Moscow,* became a musical signature of daily news broadcasts on the Soviet radio. Soloviev-Sedoy was able to synthesize the melos of Russian folk songs with revolutionary ballads and marching rhythms. Among his major works is a ballet, *Taras Bulba,* after Gogol (Leningrad, Dec. 12, 1940). He also composed an operetta, *A Faithful Friend* (Kuibyshev, Oct. 6, 1945). Several monographs have been publ. about his life and works; a notographical index of his songs was issued in 1971.

Solti, Sir Georg (György), eminent Hungarian-born English conductor; b. Budapest, Oct. 21, 1912. He began to study the piano when he was 6, making his first public appearance in Budapest when he was 12; at 13 he enrolled there at the Franz Liszt Academy of Music, studying piano with Dohnányi and, briefly, with Bartók; took composition courses with Kodály. He graduated at the age of 18, and was engaged by the Budapest Opera as a répétiteur; also served as an assistant to Bruno Walter (1935) and Toscanini (1936 and 1937) at the Salzburg Festivals. On March 11, 1938, he made a brilliant conducting debut at the Budapest Opera with Mozart's *Le nozze di Figaro;* the wave of anti-Semitism in Hungary under the reactionary military rule forced him to leave Budapest (he was Jewish). In 1939 he went to Switzerland, where he was active mainly as a concert pianist; in 1942 he won the Concours International de Piano in Geneva; finally, in 1944, he was engaged to conduct concerts with the orch. of the Swiss Radio. In 1946 the American occupation authorities in Munich invited him to conduct *Fidelio* at the Bavarian State Opera; his success led to his appointment as its music director, a position he held from 1946–52. In 1952 he became Generalmusikdirektor in Frankfurt, serving as director of the Opera and conductor of the Museumgesellschaft Concerts. In 1953 he went to America; made his U.S. debut with the San Francisco Opera on Sept. 25, 1953, conducting *Elektra;* he later conducted the Chicago Symph. Orch., the N.Y. Phil. Orch., and the orch. of the Metropolitan Opera in N.Y., where he made his first appearance on Dec. 17, 1960, with *Tannhäuser.* He was then engaged as music director of the Los Angeles Phil. Orch., but the project collapsed when the board of trustees refused to grant him full powers in musical and administrative policy. In 1959 he went to England and conducted opera at Covent Garden in London; in 1961 he assumed the post of music director of the Royal Opera House there, retaining it with great distinction until 1971. In 1969 he was appointed conductor and music director of the Chicago Symph. Orch., and it was in that capacity that he achieved a triumph as an interpreter and orch. builder, so that the "Chicago sound" became a synonym for excellence. He showed himself an enlightened disciplinarian and a master of orch. psychology, so that he could gain and hold the confidence of the players while demanding from them the utmost in professional performance. Under his direction the Chicago Symph. Orch. entered the foremost ranks of American orchs. He took the orch. to Europe in 1971, 1974, and 1978. He held the additional posts of music adviser of the Paris Opéra (1971–73) and music director of the Orch. de Paris (1972–75), which he took on a tour of China in 1974; he served as principal conductor and artistic director of the London Phil. Orch. from 1979–83; was then accorded the title of conductor emeritus. During all these years he retained his post with the Chicago Symph. Orch., while continuing his appearances as a guest conductor with European orchs. In 1983 he conducted the entire *Ring* cycle at the Salzburg Festival, in commemoration of the 100th anniversary of the death of Richard Wagner. In 1968 he was made an honorary Commander of the Order of the British Empire; in 1971 he was named an honorary Knight Commander of the Order of the British Empire. In 1972 he became a British subject and was knighted, assuming the title of Sir Georg. Solti is generally acknowledged as one of the foremost conductors of his time.

BIBLIOGRAPHY: W.B. Furlong, *Season with Solti: A Year in the Life of the Chicago Symphony* (N.Y. and London, 1974); P. Robinson, *Solti* (London, 1979).

Soltys, Adam, Polish composer, son of **Mieczyslaw Soltys;** b. Lwow, July 4, 1890; d. there, July 6, 1968. He studied with his father, and later with Georg Schumann in Berlin; also took courses in musicology at the Univ. of Berlin with Kretzschmar and Johannes Wolf (Dr.Phil., 1921). Returning to Poland, he was a prof. of composition at the Lwow Cons.; was its director from 1930 to 1939, and again after the war. His compositions include 2 symphs. (1927, 1946); the symph. poems *Slowanie* (1949), *O pokaj* (*About Peace;* 1953), and *Z gór i dolin* (*From Mountains and Valleys;* 1960); also numerous teaching pieces for violin and for piano.

Soltys, Mieczyslaw, Polish composer; b. Lwow, Feb. 7, 1863; d. there, Nov. 12, 1929. He studied music in Vienna and Paris; returning to Poland, he was appointed director of the Lwow Cons. in 1899, retaining this post for 30 years, until his death. He wrote the operas *Rzeczpospolita Babinska* (Lwow, April 27, 1905), *Opowiesc ukrainska* (Lwow, March 8, 1910), *Panie Kochanku* (Lwow, May 3, 1924), and *Nieboska komedia* (1925); a symph. poem, *The Fugitive;* Piano Concerto; choruses; piano pieces; songs.

Somary, Johannes, American conductor; b. Zürich, April 7, 1935. Born of American parents, he was brought to the U.S. as a child, and received his musical training at the Yale Univ. School of Music (M.Mus., 1959). In 1961 he founded the Amor Artis Chorale and Orch. in N.Y.; with it he conducted Handel's oratorios *Esther, Susanna,* and *Theodora.* In 1977 he was appointed music director of the Fairfield County Chorale.

Somer, Hilde, American pianist; b. Vienna, Feb. 11, 1930; d. Freeport, Bahamas, Dec. 24, 1979. She studied with her mother; in 1938 the family went to the U.S. and she enrolled at the Curtis Inst. of Music in Philadelphia as a student of Rudolf Serkin; she also took private lessons with Claudio Arrau. As a concert artist, she cultivated modern works; commissioned piano concertos from John Corigliano, Jr. (San Antonio, April 7, 1968) and Antonio Tauriello (Washington, D.C., June 29, 1968), the 2nd Piano Concerto by Albert Ginastera (Indianapolis, March 22, 1973), and a "spatial concerto" by Henry Brant (Tucson, Ariz., Nov. 16, 1978). She also gave a series of concerts of piano music by Scriabin, with color images projected upon the screen to suggest Scriabin's own ideas of a synthesis of sounds and colors.

Somers, Harry Stewart, outstanding Canadian composer and pianist; b. Toronto, Sept. 11, 1925. He studied piano with Reginald Godden (1942–43) and Weldon Kilburn (1945–49) at the Royal Cons. in Toronto; attended classes in composition with Weinzweig at the Toronto Cons.; then went to Paris, where he took private lessons with Darius Milhaud (1949–50); in 1969 he traveled to Rome on a grant from the Canadian Cultural Inst. Returning to Canada, he eked out a meager living as a music copyist, but in 1971 was named a Companion of the Order of Canada, and became active as commentator on new music for Canadian radio and television. His historical opera, *Louis Riel,* was performed at the Kennedy Center in Washington, D.C., on Oct. 23, 1975, as part of America's Bicentennial celebration. His musical idiom is quaquaversal, absorbing without prejudice ancient, national, and exotic resources, from Gregorian chant to oriental scales, from simple folkways to electronic sound, all handled with fine expertise.

WORKS: FOR THE STAGE: *The Fool,* one-act chamber opera for 4 Soloists and Chamber Orch. (1953; Toronto, Nov. 15, 1956); *The Homeless Ones,* television operetta (1955; Canadian Television, Toronto,

Dec. 31, 1955); *The Fisherman and His Soul,* ballet (Hamilton, Nov. 5, 1956); *Ballad,* ballet (1958; Ottawa, Oct. 29, 1958); *The House of Atreus,* ballet (1963; Toronto, Jan. 13, 1964); *Louis Riel,* historical opera (1966–67; Toronto, Sept. 23, 1967; uses electronic sound); *Improvisation,* theater piece for Narrator, Singers, Strings, any number of Woodwinds, 2 Percussionists, and Piano (Montreal, July 5, 1968); *And,* choreography for Dancers, Vocal Soloists, Flute, Harp, Piano, and 4 Percussionists (1969; Canadian Television, Toronto, 1969); *Enkidu,* chamber opera after the epic of Gilgamesh (Toronto, Dec. 7, 1977). FOR ORCH.: *Scherzo* for Strings (1947); 2 piano concertos: No. 1 (Toronto, March, 1949) and No. 2 (Toronto, March 12, 1956); *North Country* for String Orch. (Toronto, Nov. 10, 1948); *Suite* for Harp and Chamber Orch. (Toronto, Dec. 11, 1952); *The Case of the Wayward Woodwinds* for Chamber Orch. (1950); Symph. No. 1 (1951; Toronto, April 27, 1953); *Passacaglia and Fugue* (1954); *Little Suite for String Orchestra on Canadian Folk Songs* (1955); *Fantasia* (Montreal Orch., April 1, 1958); *Lyric* (Inter-American Music Festival, Washington, D.C., April 30, 1961); *5 Concepts* (1961; Toronto, Feb. 15, 1962); *Movement* (1962; Canadian Television, Toronto, March 4, 1962); *Stereophony* (1962–63; Toronto, March 19, 1963); *The Picasso Suite,* light music for Small Orch. (1964; Saskatoon, Feb. 28, 1965); *Those Silent Awe-filled Spaces,* from a saying by the Canadian artist Emily Carr, for Orch. (1977–78; Ottawa, Feb. 2, 1978). FOR VOICE: *5 Songs for Dark Voice* for Contralto and Orch. (Stratford, Ontario, Aug. 11, 1956); *At the Descent from the Cross* for Bass Voice and 2 Guitars (1962); *12 Miniatures* for Soprano, Recorder or Flute, Viola da Gamba, and Spinet (1963); *Crucifixion* for Chorus, English Horn, 2 Trumpets, Harp, and Percussion (1966); *Kuyas* for Soprano, Flute, and Percussion (1967; adapted from *Louis Riel*); *Voiceplay* for Male or Female Singer/ Actor (Toronto, Nov. 14, 1972; Cathy Berberian, soloist); *Kyrie* for Soloists, Chorus, Flute, Oboe, Clarinet, Cello, 3 Trumpets, Piano, and 6 Percussionists (1970–72); *Zen, Yeats and Emily Dickinson* for Female Narrator, Male Narrator, Soprano, Flute, Piano, and Tape (1975); choruses; songs. CHAMBER MUSIC: 3 string quartets (1943, 1950, 1959); *Suite* for Percussion (1947); *Mime* for Violin and Piano (1948); *Rhapsody* for Violin and Piano (1948); Wind Quintet (1948); Trio for Flute, Violin, and Cello (1950); 2 violin sonatas (1953, 1955); *Movement* for Wind Quintet (1957); Sonata for Solo Guitar (1959); *Theme and Variations* for any combination of Instruments (1964); *Music* for Solo Violin (1974). PIANO MUSIC: *Strangeness of Heart* (1942); *Flights of Fancy* (1944); 5 sonatas (*Testament of Youth,* 1945; 1946; 1950; 1950; 1957); *3 Sonnets* (1946); *Solitudes* (1947); *4 Primitives* (1949); *12 × 12,* fugues (1951). BIBLIOGRAPHY: B. Cherney, *Harry Somers* (Toronto, 1975).

Somervell, Sir Arthur, English music educator and composer; b. Windermere, June 5, 1863; d. London, May 2, 1937. He studied the classics at King's College, Cambridge (B.A., 1883), and music with Stanford and Parry at the Royal College of Music; then taught music courses there (1893–1901); subsequently was active as an inspector of music. He was knighted in 1929. He composed *Normandy,* symph. variations; *Highland Concerto* for Piano and Orch.; numerous educational pieces for schools; choruses; song cycles; piano pieces; etc. He edited *Songs of the Four Nations* (50 folk songs of England, Scotland, Ireland, and Wales).

Somfai, László, Hungarian musicologist; b. Jászladány, Aug. 15, 1934. He studied at the Liszt Music Academy in Budapest as a student of Szabolcsi and Bartha; received his Ph.D. there in 1959; served as a music librarian at the National Széchényi Library (1958–62); in 1963 joined the staff of the Bartók Archives (from 1969 known as the Inst. of Musicology of the Hungarian Academy of Sciences); became its director in 1972. He also taught at the Budapest Academy of Music and was editor of the archive series Documenta Bartókiana (from 1972).
WRITINGS: *Haydn als Opernkapellmeister: Die Haydn-Dokumente der Esterházy-Opernsammlung* (with D. Bartha; Budapest and Mainz, 1960); *Joseph Haydn: Sein Leben in zeitgenössischen Bildern* (Budapest and Kassel, 1966; in Eng., 1969); *Anton Webern* (Budapest, 1968).

Somis, Giovanni Battista, Italian violinist and composer; b. Turin, Dec. 25, 1686; d. there, Aug. 14, 1763, as maestro at the court. He was a son and pupil of the court violinist **Francesco Lorenzo Somis** (called "Ardy" or "Ardito"; 1663–1736). In 1696 he entered the orch. of the ducal chapel at Turin, and in 1703–6 was a pupil of Corelli in Rome; he then returned to Turin. In 1733 he appeared as a soloist at the Concert Spirituel in Paris with great success. He was the teacher of Giardini, Guignon, Pugnani, Chabran, and Leclair. He publ. *Trattenimenti per camera,* op. 5 (trio sonatas for 2 Violins and Basso Continuo; Paris, 1733). Sonatas for Violin Solo and other works are in MS.
BIBLIOGRAPHY: G. Fino, "Un grande violinista torinese ed una famiglia di violinisti, G.B. Somis," *Il Momento* (Turin, Oct. 25–26, 1927).

Somis, Lorenzo Giovanni, Italian violinist, brother of **Giovanni Battista Somis;** b. Turin, Nov. 11, 1688; d. there, Nov. 29, 1775. He studied in Bologna; in 1724–70 was 2nd violin in the ducal chapel at Turin. He publ. *8 sonate da camera a violino solo e violoncello o cimbalo,* op. 2 (Paris, 1723), and *6 sonate e tre,* op. 3 (Paris, 1725).

Sommer, Hans (real name, **Zincke**), German composer and writer on music; b. Braunschweig, July 20, 1837; d. there, April 26, 1922. He studied mathematics at the Univ. of Göttingen (Dr.Phil., 1858); later taught mathematics in Braunschweig while taking active part in musical affairs there. In 1885 he married and settled in Berlin; from 1888 till 1898 he lived in Weimar; then was again in Braunschweig. He was one of the original founders of the Genossenschaft Deutscher Tonsetzer (Society of German

Composers), with Richard Strauss, Max Schillings, and Friedrich Rösch.

WORKS: Operas: *Der Nachtwächter* (Braunschweig, Nov. 22, 1865); *Loreley* (Braunschweig, April 11, 1891); *Saint Foix* (Munich, Oct. 31, 1894); *Der Meermann* (Weimar, April 19, 1896); *Rübezahl* (Braunschweig, May 15, 1904; his strongest opera); *Riquet mit dem Schopf* (Braunschweig, April 14, 1907); *Der Waldschratt* (Braunschweig, March 31, 1912). His operas *Augustin, Münchhausen,* and *Das Schloss der Herzen* were not perf. His lyric songs were greatly appreciated in Germany, and often perf. in England; among the best are the cycles *Der Rattenfänger von Hamelin, Der wilde Jäger, Hunold Singuf, Tannhäuser, Sapphos Gesänge, Aus dem Süden, and Eliland;* also *Balladen und Romanzen,* etc.

BIBLIOGRAPHY: E. Stier, "Hans Sommer," in vol. 1 of *Monographien moderner Musiker* (Leipzig, 1906); Erich Valentin, *Hans Sommer* (Braunschweig, 1939).

Sommer, Vladimír, Czech composer; b. Dolní Jiřetín, near Most, Feb. 28, 1921. He studied composition with K. Janeček at the Prague Cons. (1942–46) and with Bořkovec at the Prague Academy of Music (1946–50). He was music director of Radio Prague (1952–53) and secretary of the Guild of Czech Composers (1953–56); taught at the Prague Academy (1953–60), and then at the Charles Univ. in Prague. His music is crafted in a fine functional manner.

WORKS: Sonata for 2 Violins (1948); *Cantata on Gottwald* for Baritone, Chorus, and Orch. (Prague, Nov. 20, 1949); Violin Concerto (Prague, June 13, 1950); 3 string quartets (1950, 1955, 1960–66); Piano Sonata (1954–56); *Antigone,* overture (1956–57); 3 symphs.: No. 1, *Vokální symfonie,* for Narrator, Mezzo-soprano, Chorus, and Orch., to texts by Dostoyevsky, Kafka, and Cesare Pavese (1957–59; revised 1963; Prague, March 12, 1963); No. 2, *Anno mundi ardenti,* for String Orch., Piano, and Timpani (1968); No. 3, *Sinfonia concertante,* for 2 Violins, Viola, Cello, and Chamber Orch. (1968); Cello Concerto (1956–59); *Černý Muž (The Black Man),* symph. poem for Tenor, Bass, and Orch. (1964); songs.

Sommerfeldt, Øistein, Norwegian composer; b. Oslo, Nov. 25, 1919. He studied piano, bassoon, music theory, and composition in Paris with Nadia Boulanger (1950–56); is currently a music critic in Oslo.

WORKS: *3 Suites* for Orch. (1956; based on Grieg's *Dances* for Piano, op. 72); *Miniature Suite* for Orch. (1958; revised 1972); *Miniature Overture* (1960); *Adagio, Scherzo, and Finale* for Orch. (1969); *Hafrsfjord* for Narrator, and Orch. or Military Band (1972); *3 Lyric Scenes* for Tenor or Soprano, and Orch. (1972); *Sinfonia "La Betulla"* (1967–74); 5 piano sonatinas (1956, 1960, 1968, 1970, 1972); *Divertimento* for Flute (1960; revised 1969); *Divertimento* for Bassoon (1960; revised 1973); *Transformation,* audio-visual score for Chamber Group and Tape (1970); *Divertimento* for Trumpet (1971); Violin Sonata (1971); *Elegy* for Trumpet and Organ (1971); *Suite* for Piano Trio (1973); *Divertimento* for Oboe (1974).

Somogi, Judith, American conductor; b. New York, May 13, 1937. She studied violin, piano, and organ at the Juilliard School of Music in N.Y.; attended courses at the Berkshire Music Center in Tanglewood; then served as a musical assistant at the N.Y. City Opera; later was an assistant to Thomas Schippers at the Spoleto Festival and to Leopold Stokowski at the American Symph. Orch. in N.Y. In 1974 she made a successful appearance with the N.Y. City Opera, and subsequently conducted in San Francisco, San Diego, San Antonio, and Pittsburgh. She made her European debut in Saarbrücken in 1979. After filling a successful engagement with the Frankfurt Opera in 1982, she was named to the post of its first conductor.

Somogyi, László, Hungarian conductor; b. Budapest, June 25, 1908. After preliminary studies at the Liszt Academy in Budapest, he took a course in conducting with Hermann Scherchen. In Budapest he founded the Hungarian State Orch. In 1964 he was engaged as conductor of the Rochester (N.Y.) Phil.; he returned to Europe in 1970, and was active mainly as a guest conductor with various ensembles.

Sondheim, Stephen, brilliant American composer and lyricist; b. New York, March 22, 1930. Of an affluent family, he received his academic education in private schools; composed a school musical at the age of 15. He then entered Williams College, where he wrote the book, lyrics, and music for a couple of college shows; graduated magna cum laude in 1950. In quest of higher musical learning, he went to Princeton, where he took lessons in modernistic complexities with Milton Babbitt, and acquired sophisticated techniques of composition. He made his mark on Broadway when he wrote the lyrics for Bernstein's *West Side Story* (1957). His first success as a lyricist-composer came with the Broadway musical *A Funny Thing Happened on the Way to the Forum* (1962), which received a Tony award. His next musical, *Anyone Can Whistle* (1964), proved unsuccessful, but *Company* (1970), for which he wrote both lyrics and music, established him as a major composer and lyricist on Broadway. There followed *Follies* (1971), for which he wrote 22 pastiche songs; it was named best musical by the N.Y. Drama Critics Circle. His next production, *A Little Night Music,* with the nostalgic score harking back to the turn of the century, received a Tony, and its leading song, "Send in the Clowns," was awarded a Grammy in 1976. This score established Sondheim's characteristic manner of treating musicals; it is almost operatic in conception, and the score boldly introduces dissonant counterpoint *à la moderne.* In 1976 he produced *Pacific Overtures,* based on the story of the Western penetration into Japan in the 19th century, and composed in a stylized Japanese manner, modeled after the Kabuki theater; he also wrote the score to the musical *Sunday in the Park with George,* inspired by the painting by Georges Seurat entitled "Sunday Afternoon on the Island of La Grande Jatte" (N.Y., May 1, 1984).

BIBLIOGRAPHY: C. Zadan, *Sondheim & Co.* (N.Y., 1974).

Sondheimer, Robert, German musicologist; b. Mainz, Feb. 6, 1881; d. Hannover, Dec. 7, 1956. He studied with Engelbert Humperdinck at the Cons. of Cologne; then took courses in musicology in Bonn, Berlin, and Basel; in 1933 he settled in London, where he established Sondheimer Edition, incorporating the bulk of Edition Bernoulli, which he had headed previously in Berlin. He brought out numerous editions of works by Haydn and the composers of the Mannheim School. He publ. *Haydn. A Historical and Psychological Study Based on His Quartets* (London, 1951).

Sonneck, Oscar George Theodore, eminent American musicologist; b. Jersey City, N.J., Oct. 6, 1873; d. New York, Oct. 30, 1928. He attended the Gelehrtenschule in Kiel (1883–89) and the Kaiser Friedrich Gymnasium in Frankfurt (1889–93), where he also took piano lessons with James Kwast; in 1893–97 he studied at Munich Univ. (musicology with Sandberger and philosophy with Riehl and Lipps); was a private pupil in composition of M.E. Sachs; in 1897–98, was a pupil of K. Schröder (conducting) at the Sondershausen Cons. and of Iwan Knorr (instrumentation) in Frankfurt; he spent the greater part of 1899 in research work in Italy; then returned to the U.S., continuing his research in the principal libraries. On Aug. 1, 1902, he was appointed chief of the Music Division of the Library of Congress in Washington, D.C.; he resigned on Sept. 5, 1917, to accept a position with the publishing house of G. Schirmer in N.Y. as director of the Publication Dept., managing editor of the *Musical Quarterly* (of which he had been editor since its foundation in 1915), and personal representative of the president, Rudolph E. Schirmer; in 1921 he became vice-president of G. Schirmer. He represented the U.S. government at the international congresses of music held in London and Rome in 1911. He took a leading part in the formation of the Society for the Publication of American Music, and of the Beethoven Assoc. in N.Y. Under Sonneck's administration, the Music Division of the Library of Congress became one of the largest and most important music collections in the world. His writings, exhibiting profound and accurate scholarship and embodying the results of original research, laid a real foundation for the scientific study of music in the U.S.; his elaborate catalogues, issued by the Library of Congress, are among the most valuable contributions to musical bibliography. The Sonneck Society, an organization designed to encourage the serious study of American music in all its aspects, was established in 1975 and named after Sonneck in recognition of his achievements in this area. He was also a composer and a poet; wrote a String Quartet; symph. pieces; *Rhapsody* and *Romanze* for Violin and Piano; some vocal works and piano pieces. He publ. 2 vols. of poems in German: *Seufzer* (1895) and *Eine Totenmesse* (1898).

WRITINGS: *Francis Hopkins and James Lyon. Two Studies in Early American Music* (1905); *Early Concert Life in America (1731–1800)* (1907); *Report on "The Star-Spangled Banner," "Hail Columbia," "America," "Yankee Doodle"* (1909); *A Survey of Music in America* (1913); *The Star-Spangled Banner* (1914); *Early Opera in America* (1915); *Suum Cuique* (1916; collection of essays); *Miscellaneous Studies in the History of Music* (1921); *Beethoven. Impressions of Contemporaries* (1926); *Beethoven Letters in America* (1927); *The Riddle of the Immortal Beloved* (1927). Catalogues: *Classification of Music and Literature of Music* (1904; 2nd ed., revised and augmented, 1917); *Bibliography of Early Secular Music* (1905; 2nd ed., revised and enlarged by W.T. Upton, 1945); *Dramatic Music* (1908); *Orchestral Music* (1912); *Opera Librettos Printed before 1800* (2 vols., 1914); *First Editions of Stephen C. Foster* (1915; with W.R. Whittlesey); *First Editions of Edward MacDowell* (1917).

BIBLIOGRAPHY: H. Putnam and R. Goldmark, "Remarks at the Funeral Services for O.G. Sonneck," *Musical Quarterly* (Jan. 1929); C. Engel, "O.G. Sonneck," in "Adler-Festschrift" (1930); *Musical Quarterly* (Oct. 1933); H. Wiley Hitchcock, *After 100 [!] Years: The Editorial Side of Sonneck* (booklet; contains a bibliography of Sonneck's writings and musical compositions, compiled by I. Lowens; Library of Congress, 1975).

Sonninen, Ahti, Finnish composer; b. Kuopio, July 11, 1914. He studied with Palmgren, Merikanto, Ranta, and Leo Funtek at the Sibelius Academy in Helsinki; from 1938 to 1952 was a choral and orch. director for Finnish Radio. He followed the tenets of international musical modernism in his technique of composition, but also adhered to subjects from Finnish folklore.

WORKS: FOR THE STAGE: *Merenkuninkaan tytär (Daughter of Neptune),* opera (1949); *Pessi and Illusia,* ballet (1952); *Ruususolmu (Wreath of Roses),* ballet (1956); *Karhunpeijaiset (Feast to Celebrate the Killing of a Bear),* ritual opera (1968); *Se (It),* ballet farce (Helsinki, Feb. 24, 1972); *Haavruuva (Lady of the Sea),* opera (1971). VOCAL WORKS: *7 Songs to Hungarian Folk Poems* for Soprano and Orch. (1939–41); *Midsummer Night* for Soprano and Orch. (1946); *El amor pasa* for Soprano, Flute, and Orch. (1953); *Smith of the Heavens* for Baritone and Orch. (1957); *The Karelian Wedding* for Voice, Chorus, Flute, Accordion, Percussion, Harpsichord, and Tape (1965); *Highway Requiem* for Soprano, Baritone, Chorus, and Orch. (1970); *Forging of the Golden Virgin* for Voices, 2 Percussionists, and Tape (1971); *Finnish Messiah* for Soloists, Mixed and Children's Choruses, and Orch. (1972); *In the Court of the Lamb,* suite for Soloists, Chorus, and Orch. (1972); about 15 cantatas and 100 choruses a cappella. FOR ORCH.: *East Karelian Suite* (1942); Violin Concerto (1943–45); Piano Concerto (1944–45); *Symphonic Sketches* (1947); *Preludio festivo* (1953); *Under Lapland's Sky,* suite (1954); *Pezzo pizzicato*

(1954–55); *Rhapsody* (1957); *4 Partitas* for Strings (1958); *Prelude and Allegro* for Trumpet, Trombone, and Orch. (1961); *Reactions* for Chamber Orch. (1961). CHAMBER MUSIC: *Conference* for Clarinet, Horn, Trumpet, and Trombone (1954); *Theses* for String Quartet (1968); *Divertimento* for Wind Quintet (1970). FOR PIANO: Suites: *In the Big City* (1954); *White Pepper* (1970); *Black Pepper* (1970); *Koli* (1970); *3 Characters* (1971); about 70 songs with piano; music for films.

Sonnleithner, Joseph, Austrian music amateur, librettist, and archivist; b. Vienna, March 3, 1766; d. there, Dec. 26, 1835. He was a son of the Austrian composer **Christoph von Sonnleithner,** who taught him music. Joseph Sonnleithner was one of the founders of the Gesellschaft der Musikfreunde, to which he bequeathed his books and musical instruments. He publ. the interesting *Wiener Theateralmanach* (1794, 1795, 1796). He wrote some librettos and adapted others, including *Fidelio* for Beethoven and *Faniska* by Cherubini. In 1827 he discovered the famous Antiphonary of St. Gall of the 9th century, in neume notation, probably a copy of the one sent there by Charlemagne in 790. His nephew was **Leopold von Sonnleither** (b. Vienna, Nov. 15, 1797; d. there, March 4, 1873). The staunch friend of Schubert, he procured the publication of the *Erlkönig* (Schubert's first publ. work); at his father's house, *Prometheus, Gesang der Geister über den Wassern,* the *23rd Psalm,* and other important works by Schubert were performed from MS.
BIBLIOGRAPHY: A. Fareanu, "Leopold von Sonnleithners Erinnerungen an Franz Schubert," *Zeitschrift für Musikwissenschaft* (1919).

Sontag, Henriette (real name, **Gertrud Walpurgis Sonntag**), celebrated German soprano; b. Coblenz, Jan. 3, 1806; d. Mexico City (on a tour), June 17, 1854. She played children's parts on the stage; then studied at the Prague Cons. with Triebensee, Pixis, Bayer, and Frau Czegka; she made her first appearances as a singer in Prague; in 1822 she sang in Italian and German opera at Vienna, and in 1823 created the title role in Weber's *Euryanthe;* on May 7, 1824, she sang in Vienna the soprano solos in Beethoven's *Missa solemnis* and 9th Symph.; made her first Berlin appearance on Aug. 3, 1825, in the part of Isabella in Rossini's *Italiana in Algeri;* her Paris debut as Rosina in *Il Barbiere di Siviglia* at the Théâtre-Italien (May 15, 1826) was an unqualified success, and she was adjudged by many as superior to Catalani; she broke her Berlin contract in order to sing at the Italian Opera in Paris (1827); went to London in 1828, and secretly married the Sardinian ambassador to the Dutch court, Count Rossi; was ennobled by the King of Prussia (as "Fräulein Henriette von Lauenstein"). She then interrupted her career on the stage, and settled with her husband at The Hague; also traveled with him on his diplomatic missions to Germany and Russia. She continued to give concerts as a solo singer, arousing enthusiasm wherever she went. In 1849 she resumed her operatic career; made several tours in England;

in the autumn of 1852 she embarked for the U.S., and gave a number of concerts; then went to Mexico (1854), where she sang opera. She died of cholera during an epidemic there.
BIBLIOGRAPHY: Théophile Gautier, *L'Ambassadrice, Biographie de la comtesse Rossi* (Paris, 1850); J. Gundling, *Henriette Sontag* (2 vols., Leipzig, 1861); W. Berger, *Berühmte Frauen* (Berlin, 1904); H. Stumcke, *Henriette Sontag* (Berlin, 1913); F. Rogers, "Henriette Sontag in New York," *Musical Quarterly* (Jan. 1942); E. Pirchan, *Henriette Sontag* (Vienna, 1946); Frank Russell, *Queen of Song, The Life of Henriette Sontag, Countess de Rossi* (N.Y., 1964).

Sonzogno, Edoardo, Italian music publisher; b. Milan, April 21, 1836; d. there, March 14, 1920. He inherited a printing plant and bookstore founded by his father, and in 1874 began to publ. popular editions of French and Italian music with marked success. In 1883 he inaugurated a series of contests for new operas; the 2nd contest, in 1889, was won by Mascagni (then unknown) with *Cavalleria rusticana.* Sonzogno established his own theater (the Lirico Internazionale) at Milan in 1894. From 1861 until his retirement in 1909 he was sole proprietor of the newspaper *Il Secolo.* He was succeeded by his nephew **Riccardo Sonzogno** (1871–1915); upon the latter's death, the business was taken over by another nephew, **Renzo Sonzogno,** who had previously headed a firm of his own. He died in 1920, and in 1923 control was acquired by a group of Italian industrialists.

Sonzogno, Giulio Cesare, Italian composer; b. Milan, Dec. 24, 1906; d. there, Jan. 23, 1976. He was related to the family of the music publishers Sonzogno. He studied cello and composition in Milan; composed mostly for the stage.
WORKS: Ballet, *L'amore delle tre melarancie (Love for 3 Oranges),* after Carlo Gozzi, on the same subject that Prokofiev used in his famous opera (La Scala, Milan, Feb. 1, 1936); operas: *Regina Uliva* (Milan, March 17, 1949); *I Passeggeri* (Trieste, 1961); *Il denaro del Signor Arne* (1968); *Boule de suif,* after Maupassant (Bergamo, 1970); *Mirra* (1970).

Soot, Fritz, distinguished German tenor; b. Neunkirchen, Aug. 20, 1878; d. Berlin, June 9, 1965. He first pursued a career as an actor; then studied voice with Scheidemantel in Dresden; made his debut with the Dresden Court Opera as Tonio in *La Fille du régiment* in 1908, remaining on its roster until 1918; during his tenure there, he sang in the first performance of *Der Rosenkavalier* as the Italian Singer. His subsequent engagements were in Stuttgart (1918–22), at the Berlin State Opera (1922–44, 1946–52), and at the Berlin Städtische Oper (1946–48). He sang in the premieres of Berg's *Wozzeck,* as well as in works by Pfitzner and Schreker; he excelled in such Wagnerian roles as Tristan, Siegmund, and Siegfried.

Sopeña (Ibáñez), Federico, Spanish writer on

music; b. Valladolid, Jan. 25, 1917. He studied in Bilbao and Madrid; from 1951 to 1956 was director of the Madrid Cons.; was also the founder and publisher of the music magazine *Música*. He publ. a number of useful monographs of Spanish composers: *J. Turina* (1943; revised 1956); *Joaquín Rodrigo* (Madrid, 1946; 2nd ed., 1970); also *Historia de la música en cuadros esquemáticos* (Madrid, 1946; 5th ed., 1974); *La música europea contemporánea* (1953); *Historia de la música española contemporánea* (Madrid, 1958; 2nd ed., 1967).

Sopkin, Henry, American conductor; b. Brooklyn, Oct. 20, 1903. He studied violin in Chicago; taught music in high schools there, and conducted college orchs. In 1944 he was engaged as conductor of the Atlanta Youth Symph., which became the nucleus of a professional symph. orch. there; Sopkin brought it up to a considerable degree of professional efficiency. In 1966 he was appointed music instructor at the Calif. Inst. of the Arts in Los Angeles.

Soproni, József, Hungarian composer; b. Sopron, Oct. 4, 1930. He was a pupil of János Viski at the Budapest Academy of Music (1949–56); then taught at the Béla Bartók Cons. from 1957 and at the Academy from 1963. His music is marked by a strong polyphonic art, but he also employs the technique of sonorism, or sound for sound's sake.
WORKS: Concerto for String Orch. (1953); *4 Bagatelles* for Piano (1957); *Partita* for Harpsichord (1957); Viola Sonatina (1958); 4 string quartets (1958, 1960, 1965, 1971); *Meditatio con Toccata* for Organ (1959); *Requiem on the Death of a Poet* (1960); *Carmina polinaesiana*, cantata for Female Chorus and Chamber Ensemble (1963); *Musica da camera* No. 1 for Piano Trio (1963); *7 Pieces* for Piano (1963); *Ovidii metamorphoses*, cantata for Soprano, Chorus, and Orch., with Solo Violin (1965); Violin Concerto (1967); Cello Concerto (1967); *De aetatibus mundi carmina*, cantata after Ovidius for Soprano, Baritone, Chorus, and Orch. (1968); *Eklypsis* for Orch. (1969); *Incrustations* for Piano (1970); *Invenzioni sul B-A-C-H* for Piano (1971); Flute Sonata (1971); *Concerto da camera* for 12 Performers (1972); Symph. No. 1 (1975; Budapest, May 19, 1977); *Musica da camera* No. 2 for Clarinet, Violin, Cello, and Piano (1976); songs.

Sor (real name, **Sors**), **Fernando,** celebrated Spanish guitar virtuoso; b. Barcelona, Feb. 13, 1778; d. Paris, July 10, 1839. At the age of 11 he entered the school of the monastery of Montserrat, where he studied music under the direction of Anselmo Viola; wrote a Mass; then left the monastery and returned to Barcelona, where he presented his only opera, *Telemaco nella isola di Calipso*, on Aug. 25, 1797. A few years later he went to Madrid; there he joined the French army, earning the rank of captain. When Bonapartist rule was defeated in Spain, in 1813, he fled to Paris. There he met Cherubini, Méhul, and other important composers, who urged him to give concerts as a guitarist, and he soon acquired fame. In Paris he produced 2 ballets, *Cen-*

drillon (London, 1822) and *Le Sicilien, ou L'Amour peintre* (1827). He was summoned to London by the Duke of Sussex in 1815; in 1823 he traveled in Russia; wrote funeral music for the obsequies of Alexander I of Russia (1825). After another stay in London, he returned to Paris, settling there permanently in 1826. He wrote for the guitar a number of fantasies, minuets, and studies, as well as a method; all these works are modeled after the Classical forms, rather than on popular motifs. Selected works by Sor have been edited by G. Meier; his *Complete Works for Guitar* was publ. in 5 vols. (c.1970).
BIBLIOGRAPHY: M. Rocamora, *Fernando Sor* (Barcelona, 1957); G. Marini, "La música per chitarra di Fernando Sor," *Il Convegno Musicale*, I (Jan. 1964; includes list of works); Brian Jeffery, *Fernando Sor, Composer and Guitarist* (London, 1977).

Sorabji, Kaikhosru (real Christian names, **Leon Dudley**), remarkable English composer of unique gifts; b. Chingford, Aug. 14, 1892. His father was a Parsi, his mother of Spanish-Sicilian extraction. He was largely self-taught in music, but through sheer perseverance and an almost mystical belief in his demiurgic powers, he developed an idiom of composition of extraordinary complexity, embodying within the European framework of harmonies the Eastern types of melodic lines and asymmetrical rhythmic patterns, and creating an enormously intricate but architectonically stable edifice of sound. Sorabji's most arresting work is his magisterial *Opus Clavicembalisticum*, completed in 1930, taking about 5 hours to play and comprising 3 parts with 12 subdivisions, including a theme with 49 variations and a passacaglia with 81 variations; characteristically, the score is dedicated to "the everlasting glory of those few men blessed and sanctified in the curses and execrations of those many whose praise is eternal damnation." Sorabji played *Opus Clavicembalisticum* for the first time in Glasgow under the auspices of the Active Society for the Propagation of Contemporary Music on Dec. 1, 1930. Wrathful at the lack of interest in his music, Sorabji issued in 1936 a declaration forbidding any performance of his works by anyone anywhere; since this prohibition could not be sustained for works actually publ., there must have been furtive performances of his piano works in England and the U.S. by fearless pianists. Sorabji eventually mitigated his ban, and in 1975 allowed the American pianist Michael Habermann to perform some of his music; in 1976 he also gave his blessing to the English pianist Yonty Solomon, who included Sorabji's works in a London concert on Dec. 7, 1976; on June 16, 1977, Solomon gave in London the first performance of Sorabji's 3rd Piano Sonata. Gradually, Sorabji's music became the cynosure and the lodestone of titanically endowed pianists. Of these, the most Brobdingnagian was the Australian pianist Geoffrey Madge, who gave the second complete performance in history of *Opus Clavicembalisticum* at the 1982 Holland Festival in Utrecht; he repeated this feat at the first American performance of the work at the Univ. of Chicago on April

24, 1983; 2 weeks later he played it in Bonn. True to his estrangement from the human multitudes and music officials, Sorabji took refuge far from the madding crowd in a castle he owned in England; a notice at the gate proclaims: Visitors Unwelcome. Yet as he approached his 90th birthday, he received at least 2 American musicians who came to declare their admiration, and allowed them to photocopy some of his MSS.

WORKS: FOR ORCH.: 8 indefinitely numbered piano concertos (1915–16; 1916–17; 1917; 1918; 1922; *Simorg-Anka,* 1924; 1924–25; 1927); *Chaleur* (1920); Symph. No. 1 for Orch., Chorus, Organ, and Piano (1921–22); *Opusculum* (1923); *Jāmī,* symph. for Orch., Baritone, Chorus, Organ, and Piano (1942–51); *Symphonic Variations* for Piano and Orch. (1951–55); *Symphonic High Mass* for Orch., Solo Voices, Chorus, Organ, and Piano (1955–61); *Opus Clavisymphonicum* for Piano and Orch. (1957–59); *Opusculum Claviorchestale* for Piano and Orch. (1973–75).

CHAMBER MUSIC: 2 piano quintets: No. 1 (1920); No. 2 (1949–53); *Concertino non Grosso* for 4 Violins, Viola, 2 Cellos, and Piano (1968); *Il tessuto d'Arabeschi* for Flute and String Quartet (1979; Philadelphia, May 2, 1982).

FOR PIANO: 6 piano sonatas: No. 0 (1917); No. 1 (1919); No. 2 (1920); No. 3 (1922); No. 4 (1928–29); No. 5, *Opus Archimagicum* (1934–35); 2 pieces: *In the Hothouse* and *Toccata* (1918, 1920); *Fantaisie espagnole* (1919); *Prelude, Interlude and Fugue* (1920–22); *3 Pastiches:* on Chopin, Bizet, and Rimsky-Korsakov (1922); *Le Jardin parfumé* (1923); *Variations and Fugue on "Dies Irae"* (1923–26); *Valse-Fantaisie (Hommage à Johann Strauss)* (1925); *Fragment* (1926, revised 1937); *Djami,* nocturne (1928); 4 toccatas: No. 1 (1928); No. 2 (1933–34); No. 3 (1957); No. 4 (1964–67); *Opus Clavicembalisticum* (1929–30; Glasgow, Dec. 1, 1930, composer at the keyboard); *Symphonic Variations* (1935–37); 6 symphs. for Piano Solo: No. 1, *Tantrik* (1938–39); No. 2 (1954); No. 3 (1959–60); No. 4 (1962–64); No. 5, *Symphonia Brevis* (1973–75); No. 6, *Symphonia Magna* (1975–76); *Gulistan,* a nocturne (1940); *100 Transcendental Studies* (1940–44); *St. Bertrand de Comminges: "He Was Laughing in the Tower"* (1941); *Concerto per suonare da me solo* (1946); *Sequentia Cyclia on "Dies Irae"* (1949); *Un nido di scatole* (1954); *Passeggiata veneziana* (1956); *Rosario d'arabeschi* (1956); *Fantasiettina* (1961); *Symphonic Nocturne* (1977–78); *Il grido del gallino d'oro* (1978–79); *Evocazione nostalgica—Villa Tasca* (1979); *Opus secretum* (1980–81); *Passeggiata arlecchinesca* (1981–82).

FOR VOICE: *5 sonetti del Michelangelo Buonarroti* for Voice and Chamber Orch. (1923; Toronto, Feb. 2, 1980); songs.

FOR ORGAN: 3 solo symphs.: No. 1 (1924); No. 2 (1929–32); No. 3 (1949–53).

BIBLIOGRAPHY: A.G. Browne, "The Music of Kaikhosru Sorabji," *Music & Letters* (Jan. 1930); E. Rubbra, "Sorabji's Enigma," *Monthly Musical Record* (Sept. 1932); B. Posner, *Sorabji* (Diss., Fordham Univ., N.Y., 1975); P. Rapoport, "Sorabji and the Computer," *Tempo,* no. 117 (1976); P. Rapoport, *Opus Est: 6 Composers from Northern Europe* (London, 1978, and N.Y., 1979; pp. 161–90).

Sörenson, Torsten, Swedish composer; b. Grebbestads, April 25, 1908. He was educated at the Royal College of Music in Stockholm, graduating in 1936; later studied composition with Hilding Rosenberg (1942) and Carl Orff (1949). In 1935 he was appointed a church organist in Göteborg.

WORKS: *Den underbara Kvarnan* for Baritone and Orch. (1936; revised 1958); *Sinfonietta* for String Orch. (1946; revised 1957); 2 trios for Flute, Clarinet, and Oboe (1949, 1959); *Hymn om Kristus,* cantata (1950); Concerto for Organ and String Orch. (1952); Symph. for Chamber Orch. (1956); Sonata for Viola Solo (1956); Piano Sonata (1956); *Sinfonia da chiesa* Nos. 1 and 2 for String Orch. (1958, 1964–69); 3 sonatas for Flute Solo (1962, 1964, 1966); *Hymnarium,* 56 motets for One to 6 Voices, and Instruments (1957–62); *Per quattro archi,* string quartet (1970); Brass Quintet (1970); *Laudate nomen Domini* for Chorus, 17 Winds, and Percussion (1972); *En sang om Herrens boninger* for Soprano, 2 Choruses, and Orch. (1975); *Svart-Vitt (Black and White),* 24 pieces for Piano (1975).

Soresina, Alberto, Italian composer; b. Milan, May 10, 1911. He studied with Paribeni and Bossi at the Milan Cons., graduating in 1933; then took a course in composition in Siena with Frazzi. He subsequently was on the faculty of the Cons. of Milan (1947–60), and later taught singing at the Cons. of Turin (1963–66); in 1967 was appointed a teacher of music theory at the Milan Cons.

WORKS: Operas: *Lanterna rossa* (Siena, 1942); *Cuor di cristallo* (Bergamo, 1942); *L'amuleto* (Bergamo, Oct. 26, 1954); *Tre sogni per Marina* (Lecco, 1967); for Orch.: *Trittico Wildiano* (1939); *Il Santo,* symph. poem (1940); *2 notturni* for Harp and String Orch. (1946); *Divertimento* (1956); chamber music: Concertino per Viola, Cello, and Piano (1953); *Sonatina serena* for violin and piano (1956); several works for voice and orch., including *La Fanciulla mutata in rio* (1939); piano pieces.

Sorge, Georg Andreas, erudite German composer and theorist; b. Mellenbach, Schwarzburg, March 21, 1703; d. Lobenstein, April 4, 1778. While still a youth, he was appointed court organist at Lobenstein (1721), and he retained this position until his death. In middle life, he wrote numerous works for piano and organ; music historians regard him as a typical "little master" of Bach's time. His reverence for Bach is demonstrated by his 3 keyboard fugues on B.A.C.H. Among his works publ. in his lifetime are *Clavierübung aus 18 Sonatinen in 3 Teilen* (1738); *Clavierübung aus 24 Praeludia durch den ganzen Circulum Modorum* and *Clavier-Toccata per omnem Circulum Modorum* (both works in emulation of Bach's *Well-Tempered Clavier*). His masterwork remains *Vorgemach der musicalischen Composition* (3 vols., 1745–47), in which he relates his discovery of combinatorial tones before Tartini.

BIBLIOGRAPHY: M. Frisch, *Georg A. Sorge* (Leipzig, 1954); R. Frisius, *Untersuchungen über den Akkordbegriff* (Göttingen, 1970).

Soriano, Alberto, Uruguayan composer and musicologist; b. Santiago del Estero, Argentina, Feb. 5, 1915. He studied violin in Bahia, Brazil; in 1937 went to Montevideo, where he settled. In his music he makes use of South American melorhythms, while retaining fundamental classical forms. From 1953 to 1969 he was a prof. of enthnomusicology at the Univ. of Montevideo. Among his scholarly publications is *Algunas de las inmanencias etnomusicológicas* (Montevideo, 1967).
WORKS: Piano Concerto (1952); Guitar Concerto No. 1 (1952); *Sinfonietta* for Guitar, Cello, Bassoon, and Flute (1952); *4 rituales sinfónicos* (1953); *Divertimento* for Bassoon and String Orch. (1954); Cello Sonata (1955); Violin Concerto (1956); Guitar Concerto No. 2 (1957); Violin Sonata (1959); Piano Trio (1961); *Canticos sinfónicos a la Revolución de Cuba* (1961); Concertino for Cello and Orch. (1961); *Pastoral de Sibiu* for Flute and Orch. (1962); *Tríptico de Praga* for Orch. (1962); *Tiempo sinfónico para los caidos en Buchenwald* (1962). A list of his works is found in *Compositores de América,* vol. 16 (Washington, D.C., 1970).

Soriano, Francesco. See **Suriano, Francesco.**

Soriano, Gonzalo, Spanish pianist; b. Alicante, March 14, 1913; d. Madrid, April 14, 1972. He studied with Cabiles in Madrid, and later with Cortot and Landowska in Paris. He made his debut in Alicante in 1929; pursued an active career in Europe; also gave concerts in the U.S. and the Far East. He was particularly noted for his congenial performances of Spanish music.

Soriano Fuertes, Mariano, Spanish music historian; b. Murcia, March 28, 1817; d. Madrid, March 26, 1880. He was a pupil of his father (director of the royal chamber music); in 1843 he became a prof. at the Madrid Cons.; from 1844, he was director, successively, of music schools at Córdoba, Seville, and Cádiz; he conducted opera at Barcelona, where he founded the *Gaceta Musical.* He composed some zarzuelas. He was the author of *Música árabe-española* (1853); *Historia de la música española desde la venida de los fenicios hasta el año de 1850* (4 vols., 1855–59; a pioneering work, but quite unscientific and unreliable); *Memoria sobre las sociedades corales en España* (1865); *Calendario histórico musical . . .* (1872).

Sormann, Alfred (Richard Gotthilf), German pianist and composer; b. Danzig, May 16, 1861; d. Berlin, Sept. 17, 1913. He studied at the Hochschule für Musik in Berlin with Barth, Spitta, and Bargiel; in 1885, studied with Liszt. He made his debut in 1886, giving successful concerts in the chief German towns. He composed the operas *Die Sibylle von Tivoli* (Berlin, 1902) and *König Harald* (Stettin,

1909); a Piano Concerto; 2 string quartets; a Piano Trio; concert études and other piano pieces; songs.

Soro, Enrique, significant Chilean composer; b. Concepción, July 15, 1884; d. Santiago, Dec. 2, 1954. He was a son of the Italian composer **José Soro,** and was educated by him; he played in public as a small child. He was granted a stipend by the government of Chile for study in Italy; entered the Cons. of Milan at 14; graduated in 1904, with a grand prize in composition. Returning to Chile in 1905, he was appointed inspector of musical education in primary schools; in 1906 joined the faculty of the Cons. of Santiago; from 1919 to 1928 he was its director. He traveled as a pianist; gave concerts in Europe and South America; also publ. a number of works. In 1948 he was awarded the Premio Nacional de Arte.
WORKS: For Orch.: *Sinfonía romántica* (1920); Piano Concerto (1919); *Suite sinfónica,* No. 1, subtitled *Pensamientos intimos* (1918); *Suite sinfónica,* No. 2 (Santiago, May 9, 1919, composer conducting); *3 preludios sinfónicos* (Santiago, July 18, 1936); *Aires chilenos* for Orch. (Santiago, 1942); *Suite en estilo antiguo* (Santiago, May 28, 1943). Chamber music: Piano Quintet (1919); *Impresiones líricas* for Piano and Strings (1918); String Quartet (1904); Piano Trio (1926); Violin Sonata; Cello Sonata; 3 piano sonatas (1920, 1923, 1942); a number of piano pieces in a salon genre, some of them based on Chilean melorhythms.
BIBLIOGRAPHY: L.G. Giarda, *Analytische Studie über Soros 2. Sonate für Violine und Klavier A moll, das Quartett A dur und das Klavierquintett* (Santiago, 1919); Vicente Salas Viú, *La creación musical en Chile 1900–1951* (Santiago, 1953; pp. 427–52).

Sotin, Hans, German bass; b. Dortmund, Sept. 10, 1939. He studied at the Dortmund Cons.; made his debut with the Essen Opera in 1962; from 1964 sang with the Hamburg State Opera; also at the Bayreuth Festivals from 1971. He made his debut at the Metropolitan Opera on Oct. 26, 1972, as Sarastro in *Die Zauberflöte;* in 1973 he joined the Vienna State Opera. In 1974 he sang at Covent Garden in London; also appeared in concerts. He commended himself as a dramatic singer in operas of Mozart as well as in those of Wagner.

Soto de Langa, Francisco, Spanish composer; b. Langa, c.1534; d. Rome, Sept. 25, 1619. He spent most of his life in Rome, where he was one of the disciples of St. Philip Neri; for Neri's Congregation of the Oratorio he edited 5 books of "laudi spirituali" (publ. between 1583 and 1598; it is not known how much he contributed to them); some specimens are reproduced in Alaleona's *Studi su la storia dell'oratorio musicale in Italia* (Turin, 1908).

Soubies, Albert, French writer on music; b. Paris, May 10, 1846; d. there, March 19, 1918. He studied law and was admitted to the bar; about the same time he became a pupil of Savard, Bazin, and Guilmant at the Paris Cons. In 1876 he became music critic for *Le Soir* and in 1885 began to write for the *Revue de l'Art Dramatique*. In 1874 he revived the famous old *Almanach Duchesne* (publ. between 1752 and 1815), reissuing it as *Almanach des Spectacles* (43 vols. publ. up to 1914).

WRITINGS: *Histoire de la musique* (his principal work; issued in separate sections dealing with music in individual European nations; publ. 1896–1906); *Les Grands Théâtres parisiens*, in 2 parts: *67 ans à l'Opéra: 1826–1893* (1893) and *69 ans à l'Opéra-Comique: 1825–1894* (1894); *Histoire de l'Opéra-Comique* (2 vols., 1892–93; with Charles Malherbe); *Histoire du Théâtre-lyrique 1851–1870* (1899); *L'Œuvre dramatique de Richard Wagner* (1886).

Soubre, Etienne-Joseph, Belgian composer; b. Liège, Dec. 30, 1813; d. there, Sept. 8, 1871. He studied at the Liège Cons., and became its director (1862). He composed the opera *Isoline* (Brussels, 1855); *Symphonie triomphale* (1845); 2 cantatas; a Requiem, with Orch.; *Stabat Mater* and *Ave Verum*, with Orch.; *Hymne à Godefroid de Bouillon* for Male Chorus and Orch.; church music, choruses, overtures, symphs., etc.

Soudant, Hubert, Dutch conductor; b. Maastricht, March 16, 1946. He studied trumpet and French horn at the Maastricht Cons.; then took courses in conducting with Jean Fournet and Franco Ferrara. Having mastered the art, he had engagements as a guest conductor in London, Milan, Paris, Cologne, Manchester, and Munich. In 1978 he made a successful appearance conducting concerts at the Mostly Mozart Festival in N.Y.

Souhaitty, Jean-Jacques, Franciscan monk and music theorist; flourished in the middle of the 17th century; lived in Paris. He was the first to employ number notation, indicating by the numerals 1 to 7 the degrees of the scale, and used this system for popular teaching. He publ. *Nouvelle méthode pour apprendre le plain-chant et la musique* (Paris, 1665; 2nd ed. as *Nouveaux éléments de chant . . .*, 1677) and *Essai du chant de l'église par la nouvelle méthode des chiffres* (Paris, 1679).

Soukupová, Věra, Czech contralto; b. Prague, April 12, 1932. She studied voice in Prague; joined the Pilsen Opera in 1957; then was a member of the National Theater in Prague (1960–63); from that time she began to make regular appearances with many of the leading opera houses of both Eastern and Western Europe; also sang at the major festivals. In 1968 she joined the Hamburg State Opera.

Souliotis, Elena, Greek soprano; b. Athens, May 28, 1943. She was educated in Milan; made her debut at the Teatro San Carlo in Naples in 1964; then made appearances at La Scala in Milan, Covent Garden in London, and the Teatro Colón in Buenos Aires.

Šourek, Otakar, Czech writer on music; b. Prague, Oct. 1, 1883; d. there, Feb. 15, 1956. He was trained as an engineer; was employed in the Prague City Council works dept. (1907–39); music was his avocation. He wrote music criticism for several publications, including Prague's *Venkov* (1918–41). However, it was as an authority on the life and music of Dvořák that he gained distinction; he devoted fully 40 years to Dvořák research, and served as the first editor of the composer's collected works.

WRITINGS: *Život a dílo Antonína Dvořáka* (*The Life and Works of Dvořák;* 4 vols., Prague, 1916–33; vols. I–II, 3rd ed., 1955–56; vols. III–IV, 2nd ed., 1957–58; in German as *Dvořák: Leben und Werk,* one vol., abridged by P. Stefan, Vienna, 1935; in Eng. trans. by Y. Vance as *Anton Dvořák,* N.Y., 1941); *Dvořák's Werke: Ein völlstandiges Verzeichnis in chronologischer, thematischer und systematischer Anordnung* (Berlin, 1917; revised Czech ed., Prague, 1960); *Výlety pana Broučka* (*Mr. Brouček's Excursions;* Prague, 1920); *Dvořákovy symfonie* (Prague, 1922; 3rd ed., 1948; abridged ed. in German in *Antonín Dvořák Werkanalysen I, Orchesterwerke,* Prague, 1954, and in Eng. in *The Orchestral Works of Antonín Dvořák,* Prague, 1956); *Antonín Dvořák* (Prague, 1929; 4th ed., 1947; Eng. trans. as *Antonín Dvořák: His Life and Work,* Prague, 1952); *Dvořákova citanka* (*A Dvořák Reader;* Prague, 1929; 3rd ed., 1946; in Eng., Prague, 1954); *Dvořák ve vzpomínkach a dopisech* (Prague, 1938; 9th ed., 1951; in Eng. as *Dvořák: Letters and Reminiscences,* Prague, 1954; in German, 1955; in Russian, 1964); *Smetanova Má vlast* (Prague, 1940); *Antonín Dvořák přátelům doma* (*Dvořák to His Friends at Home;* 395 letters; Prague, 1941); *Antonín Dvořák a Hans Richter* (letters to Richter; Prague, 1942); *Dvořákovy skladby komorni* (Prague, 1943; 2nd ed., 1949; abridged ed. in German in *Antonín Dvořák Werkanalysen II, Kammermusik,* Prague, 1954, and in Eng. in *The Chamber Music of Antonín Dvořák,* Prague, 1956); *Dvořákovy skladby orchestralni* (2 vols., Prague, 1944 and 1946; abridged ed. in German in *Antonín Dvořák Werkanalysen I, Orchesterwerke,* Prague, 1954, and in Eng. in *The Orchestral Works of Antonín Dvořák,* Prague, 1956); *Komorni skladby Bedřicha Smetany* (Smetana's chamber works; Prague, 1945); *Rudolf Karel* (Prague, 1947).

BIBLIOGRAPHY: F. Oeser, "Otakar Šourek," *Musica* (April 1956).

Souris, André, Belgian composer; b. Marchienne-au-Pont, July 10, 1899; d. Paris, Feb. 12, 1970. He studied at the Brussels Cons. (1911–18) with M. Lunssens (harmony), Closson (music history), and privately with Gilson (composition). In 1925 he began teaching at the Royal Cons. in Brussels; in 1927 he won the Prix Rubens, and traveled to Italy, France, and Austria; conducted the Belgian Radio Orch. (1937–46); in 1949–64 he was a prof. of harmony at the Royal Cons. in Brussels. His first works were in the style of Debussy, but in 1925 he pursued a more advanced quasi-atonal technique of composition. He was the founder of the quarterly music review *Polyphonie* (1947–54).

WORKS: *Scherzo* for Orch. (1923); *Burlesque* for Small Orch. (1931); *Danceries de la Renaissance* for Orch. (1932); *Hommage à Babeuf* for Wind Orch. and Percussion (1934; Paris, June 22, 1927); *Symphonies* for Orch. (1939); *Pastorales Wallonnes* for Vocal Quartet and Small Orch. (1942); *Le Marchand d'images,* rustic cantata on popular Walloon songs, for Soli, Chorus, and Orch. (3 versions, 1944, 1954, and 1965); *5 Laude* for Vocal Quartet, Chorus, and Small Orch. (1961); *Ouverture pour une Arlequinade* for Small Orch. (1962); *3 poèmes japonais* for Soprano, String Quartet, and Piano (1916); *Bagatelles* for Violin and Piano (1923); *Berceuse* for Violin and Piano (1924); *Choral, Marche et Galop* for 2 Trumpets and 2 Trombones (1925); *Avertissement* for 3 Narrators and Percussion (1926); *Quelques airs de clarisse Juranville* for Mezzo-soprano, String Quartet, and Piano (1928); *Fatrasie* for Violin, and Harp or Piano (1934); *Rengaines* for Wind Quintet (1937); *Comptines pour enfants sinistres* for Soprano, Mezzo-soprano, Viola, Clarinet, and Piano (1942); *L'Autre Voix* for Soprano and 5 Instruments; *Triptyque pour un violon* for Narrator, 6 Soli, Organ, and Percussion (1963); *Concert flamand,* suite for 4 Winds (1965); *3 pièces anciennes* for Violin and Viola (1969); film music; songs. He collaborated with René Vannes on the *Dictionnaire des musiciens* (Brussels, 1946).

BIBLIOGRAPHY: Paul Nougé, *André Souris* (1928); R. Wangermee, *La Musique belge contemporaine* (Brussels, 1959; pp. 82–99); A. Fraiken, "Necrologies: André Souris," *La Vie Musicale Belge* (Jan.–Feb. 1970).

Sousa, John Philip, famous American bandmaster and popular composer; b. Washington, D.C., Nov. 6, 1854; d. Reading, Pa., March 6, 1932. He was the son of a Portuguese father and a Bavarian mother. He studied violin with John Esputa and harmony with G.F. Benkert in Washington (1864–67); also acquired considerable proficiency on wind instruments; played in the Marine Band at the age of 13; led an orch. in a vaudeville theater in Washington before he was 18; in 1877 was engaged as violinist in the special orch. in Philadelphia that was conducted by Offenbach during his American tour. In 1880 Sousa was appointed leader of the Marine Band; he resigned on Aug. 1, 1892, and organized a band of his own, with which he gave successful concerts throughout the U.S. and Canada; played at the Chicago World's Fair in 1893 and at the Paris Exposition in 1900; made 4 European tours (1900, 1901, 1903, and 1905), with increasing acclaim, and finally a tour around the world, in 1910–11. His flair for writing band music was extraordinary; the infectious rhythms of his military marches and the brilliance of his band arrangements earned him the sobriquet "The March King"; particularly celebrated is his march *The Stars and Stripes Forever,* which became famous all over the world. During World War I Sousa served as a lieutenant in the Naval Reserve. He continued his annual tours almost to the time of his death. He compiled for the Navy Dept. *National, Patriotic and Typical Airs of All Lands* (1890); publ. an autobiography, *Marching Along* (Boston, 1928); and wrote 5 novels.

WORKS: His publ. compositions aggregate to several hundred, including the comic operas *The Smugglers* (1879); *Désirée* (1884); *The Queen of Hearts* (1886); *El Capitan* (Boston, April 13, 1896; his most brilliant operetta); *The Charlatan* (1897); *The Bride Elect* (1898); *Chris and the Wonderful Lamp* (1900); *The Free Lance* (1906); *The Glass-Blowers* (1911); *The American Maid* (1913); *Victory* (1915); suites for Orch. and Band: *Last Days of Pompeii; 3 Quotations; Sheridan's Ride; At the King's Court; Looking Upward; Impressions at the Movies;* etc.; a symph. poem, *The Chariot Race* (from *Ben Hur*); many waltzes, songs, etc.; and numerous popular military marches: *The Stars and Stripes Forever, El Capitan, The Washington Post, The High School Cadets, Thunderer, Semper Fidelis, Liberty Hall, Manhattan Beach, King Cotton, Hands Across the Sea* (a selection of 24 marches are reprinted in facsimile from the original sheet music in Lester S. Levy's *Sousa's Great Marches* [N.Y., 1975]; he publ. an instruction book for trumpet and drum, and one for violin.

BIBLIOGRAPHY: *Through the Years with Sousa* (excerpts from his writings; N.Y., 1910); Ann M. Lingg, *J.P. Sousa* (N.Y., 1954); R.F. Goldman, "The Great American Composers: John Philip Sousa," *HiFi Stereo Review* (July 1967); J.R. Smart, *The Sousa Band. A Discography* (Washington, D.C., 1970); W.B. Stacy, *John Philip Sousa and His Band Suites: An Analytic and Cultural Study* (Diss., Univ. of Colorado, 1972); P.E. Bierley, *John Philip Sousa: American Phenomenon* (N.Y., 1973); idem, *John Philip Sousa: A Descriptive Catalog of His Works* (Urbana, Ill., 1973); J. Newsom, ed., *Perspectives on John Philip Sousa* (Washington, D.C., 1983).

Souster, Tim, English composer of the extreme avant-garde; b. Bletchley, Buckinghamshire, Jan. 29, 1943. He studied music theory at New College in Oxford (B.A., 1964; B.Mus., 1965); in 1964 attended courses in new music given by Stockhausen and Berio in Darmstadt. Back in England, he became one of the most articulate exponents of serial, aleatory, and combinatorial ideas, in which electronic media are employed in conjunction with acoustical performances by humans; he expounded these ideas in his writings in the *Listener, Tempo,* and other progressive publications. In 1969 he was a co-founder of the Intermodulation Group, with the aim of presenting works by congenial composers and experimenters; it disbanded in 1976; he formed a new group, OdB. In 1969–71 he was composer-in-residence at King's College in Cambridge.

WORKS: *Songs of the Seasons* for Soprano and Viola (1965); *Poem in Depression* for Soprano, Flute, Viola, Cello, and Piano (1965); *Parallels* for 2 Percussion Players (1966); *Metropolitan Games* for Piano Duet (1967); *Titus Groan Music* for Wind Quintet, Electronics, and Magnetic Tape (1969); *Chinese Whispers* for Percussion and 3 Electronic Synthesizers (1970); *Waste Land Music* for Soprano

Saxophone, Modulated Piano, Modulated Organ, and Electronic Synthesizer (London, July 14, 1970); *Triple Music II* for 3 Orchs. (London, Aug. 13, 1970).

Southard, Lucien H., American composer; b. Sharon, Vt., Feb. 4, 1827; d. Augusta, Ga., Jan. 10, 1881. He studied music in Boston. After serving in the Union Army during the Civil War, he conducted the orch. of the Peabody Cons. in Baltimore (1868–71); then lived in Boston (1871–75) and Augusta. He composed an opera, *Omano,* from Indian life, to an Italian libretto (MS score in the Boston Public Library); church music; glees; and organ pieces; publ. a harmony manual (1855); edited collections of sacred music.

BIBLIOGRAPHY: F.J. Metcalf, *American Composers and Compilers of Sacred Music* (1925).

Southern, Eileen, black American musicologist; b. Minneapolis, Feb. 19, 1920. The Norwegian pianist Meda Zarbell Steele supervised her studies at Chicago Musical College and helped her obtain scholarships at the Univ. of Chicago, where she studied with Scott Goldwaite and Sigmund Levarie (B.A., 1940; M.A., 1941, with the thesis *The Use of Negro Folksong in Symphonic Music*). She then taught at Prairie View State College (1941–42), Southern Univ. (1943–45, 1949–51), Alcorn State College (1945–46), Claflin Univ. (1947–49), and secondary schools in N.Y. (1954–60). Simultaneously she pursued her own studies of medieval and Renaissance music; enrolled at N.Y. Univ. in the classes of Gustave Reese and Martin Bernstein, and wrote her dissertation, *The Buxheim Organ Book* (Ph.D., 1961; publ. 1963). She subsequently gave courses in Renaissance music at Brooklyn College (1960–68) and York College (1968–75); also publ. a fundamental study on music, *The Music of Black Americans: A History* (N.Y., 1971), with a companion vol., *Readings in Black American Music* (N.Y., 1971); in 1973 she founded the journal *Black Perspective in Music.* In 1976 she was appointed to the staff of Harvard Univ. as prof. of music and chairman of the dept. of Afro-American studies; in 1982 she publ. the valuable book *Biographical Dictionary of Afro-American and African Musicians* (Westport, Conn.).

Souzay, Gérard (real name, **Gérard Marcel Tisserand**), French baritone; b. Angers, Dec. 8, 1918. His principal voice teacher was Pierre Bernac; he also studied with Claire Croiza, Vanni Marcoux, and Lotte Lehmann. He specialized in French art songs and German lieder; before embarking on a stage career he gave recitals; then went to the U.S. He made his American operatic debut with the N.Y. City Opera in 1960; on Jan. 21, 1965, he appeared at the Metropolitan Opera in N.Y. as Count Almaviva in *Le nozze di Figaro;* subsequently led a master class in singing and interpretation at the Mannes College of Music in N.Y.

Sowande, Fela, Nigerian composer; b. Oyo, May 29, 1905. He studied music in Lagos; then went to London, where he played in a combo in nightclubs; at the same time he took courses at London Univ. and the Trinity College of Music. He served in the Royal Air Force during World War II. In 1944 he composed an *African Suite* for Strings; returned to Nigeria in 1953; in 1957 he received a grant from the State Dept. to travel in the U.S.; was again in the U.S. in 1961, on a Rockefeller grant, and on June 1, 1961, conducted a group of members of the New York Phil. in Carnegie Hall in a program of his own compositions, among them *Nigerian Folk Symphony.* Upon returning to Nigeria, he joined the staff of the Univ. College at Ibadan. In his music he pursues the goal of cultural integration of native folk material with Western art forms.

Sowerby, Leo, remarkable American composer and organist; b. Grand Rapids, Mich., May 1, 1895; d. Fort Clinton, Ohio, July 7, 1968. He studied piano with Calvin Lampert and music theory with Arthur Andersen in Chicago; also had sporadic lessons with Percy Grainger. He learned to play the organ without a teacher, and yet developed a virtuoso technique that enabled him to hold prestigious appointments as a church organist. He was extremely precocious; on Jan. 17, 1917, he presented himself in Chicago in a program grandiloquently billed "Leo Sowerby: His Music," which included such ambitious works as a Piano Concerto, with the composer at the keyboard; a Cello Concerto; and symph. pieces. When the U.S. entered the war, Sowerby served in the army; after the Armistice he returned to his career in music. In 1921 he received the American Prix de Rome, the first of its kind to be awarded for composition; he spent 3 years at the American Cons. in Rome. Returning to Chicago, he was appointed prof. of composition at the American Cons. there; he held this post and, concurrently, that of organist at the St. James Cathedral in Chicago, for 37 years, until 1962. He then went to Washington, D.C., where he organized the College for Church Musicians at the National Cathedral. He received numerous awards of merit; in 1946 he won the Pulitzer Prize for his *Canticle of the Sun.* Sowerby never attempted to discover new ways of making music; his style was eclectic in the positive sense of the word, selecting what appeared to be the best in various doctrines and styles. Hindemith's invidious reference to Sowerby as the 4th B in music, a "sour B," is not appropriate, for Sowerby's music is anything but sour; he certainly knew how to build up sonorous masses, particularly in his vocal compositions.

WORKS: FOR ORCH.: Violin Concerto (1913; revised 1924); *The Sorrow of Mydath,* symph. poem (1915); *Rhapsody on British Folk Tunes* (1915); concert overture, *Comes Autumn Time* (Chicago, Jan. 17, 1917); Cello Concerto No. 1, in A major (Chicago, Jan. 17, 1917); Piano Concerto, with Soprano obbligato (Chicago, Jan. 17, 1917; revised in 1919, without soprano); *The Irish Washerwoman,* an orch. transcription (Chicago, Jan. 17, 1917); *Money Musk,* transcription (1917); *A Set of 4,* subtitled "Suite of Ironies" (Chicago, Feb. 15, 1918); Concerto for Harp and Small Orch. (1919); 5 symphs.: No. 1 (Chicago, April 7, 1922); No. 2 (Chicago, March 29, 1929); No. 3 (Chicago, March 6, 1941); No. 4 (Boston, Jan. 7, 1949, Koussevitzky conducting); No. 5 (1964); *King Estmere*, ballad for 2 Pianos and Orch. (Rome, April 8, 1923); *Rhapsody* for Chamber Orch. (1922); *From the Northland* (Rome, May 27, 1924); *Synconata* and *Monotony* for Jazz Orch. (1924, 1925; Chicago, Oct. 11, 1925); *Medieval Poem* for Organ and Orch. (Chicago, April 20, 1926); *Prairie*, symph. poem (Interlochen, Mich., Aug. 11, 1929); Cello Concerto No. 2, in E minor (1929–34; N.Y., April 2, 1935); *Passacaglia, Interlude and Fugue* (1931–32); 2nd Piano Concerto (1932; Boston, Nov. 30, 1936); Sinfonietta for String Orch. (1933–34); *Theme in Yellow*, piece after the Sandburg poem (1937); Concerto in C for Organ and Orch. (Boston, April 22, 1938; E. Power Biggs, soloist); *Concert Overture* (1941); *Poem* for Viola, and Orch. or Organ (1941); *Fantasy on Hymn Tunes* (1943); *Classic Concerto* for Organ and String Orch. (1944); *Portrait: Fantasy in Triptych* (1946; Indianapolis, Nov. 21, 1953); *Concert Piece* for Organ and Orch. (1951); *All on a Summer's Day* (1954; Louisville, Ky., Jan. 8, 1955); untitled work (Concerto No. 2) for Organ and Orch. (1967–68).

FOR VOICE: *A Liturgy of Hope* for Soprano, Male Chorus, and Organ (1917); an untitled oratorio in 5 parts based on the Book of Psalms (1924); *The Vision of Sir Launfal*, cantata after James Lowell (1925); *Great Is the Lord* for Chorus, Orch., and Organ (1933); *Forsaken of Man* for Chorus and Organ (1939); *Song for America* for Chorus and Orch. (1942); *The Canticle of the Sun*, after St. Francis, for Chorus and Orch. (1944; N.Y., April 16, 1945; won the 1946 Pulitzer Prize); *Christ Reborn*, cantata for Chorus and Organ (1950; Philadelphia, Nov. 1, 1953); *The Throne of God* for Chorus and Orch. (1956; Washington, D.C., Nov. 18, 1957); *The Ark of the Covenant*, cantata for Chorus and Organ (1959); *Solomon's Garden*, cantata for Tenor, Chorus, and Chamber Orch. (1964); *La Corona* for Chorus and Orch. (1967); numerous anthems, songs, etc.

CHAMBER MUSIC: Quartet for Violin, Cello, Horn, and Piano (1911); 3 unnumbered piano trios (in D, undated; 1911; 1953); 5 unnumbered violin sonatas (in E, 1912, revised 1916; in G, undated; in B-flat, 1922; in A, *Fantasy Sonata*, 1944; in D, 1959); 2 unnumbered cello sonatas (1912; in E minor, 1920); Sonata for Solo Violin (1914); Serenade for String Quartet (1916); Wind Quintet (1916); Trio for Flute, Viola, and Piano (1919); 2 string quartets (1923–24, 1934–35; both MSS lost); *Pop Goes the Weasel* for Wind Quintet (1927); *Chaconne* for Trombone and Piano (1936); Clarinet Sonata (1938); *Poem* for Viola and Organ (1941); Trumpet Sonata (1945); *Ballade* for English Horn and Organ (1949); *Fantasy* for Trumpet and Organ (1962); *Suite* for Oboe and Piano (1963); *Triptych of Diversions* for Organ, 2 Violins, Double Bass, Oboe, and Percussion (1962); *Dialog* for Organ and Piano (1967); an undated Horn Trio.

FOR SOLO ORGAN: Sonata (1914–17); Symph. in G major (1930); *Suite* (1934); *Church Sonata* (1956); *Sinfonia brevis* (1965); *Bright, Blithe and Brisk* (1967); *Passacaglia* (1967); pieces.

FOR SOLO PIANO: Sonata in E-flat major (1912); *Florida*, suite (1929); Sonata in D (1948; revised 1964); *Suite* (1959); *Suite* for Piano, 4-hands (1959); pieces.

Sowinski, Wojciech (Albert), Polish pianist; b. Lukaszówka, Podolia, 1803; d. Paris, March 5, 1880. He was a pupil of Czerny and Seyfried in Vienna; toured Italy as a pianist; in 1830 settled in Paris, and was a successful piano teacher there. He publ. the first dictionary of Polish musicians in a Western language, *Les Musiciens polonais et slaves, anciens et modernes. Dictionnaire biographique des compositeurs, chanteurs, instrumentistes, luthiers* (Paris, 1857; in Polish, Paris, 1874), and it is through this publication that his name is remembered. He also wrote 4 operas: *Lenore, Le Modèle, Une Scène sous la ligne,* and *Zlote gody;* an oratorio, *Saint Adalbert;* several motets; a Symph.; overtures on Polish subjects; a Piano Concerto; a Piano Quartet; a Piano Trio; numerous piano pieces in the salon genre.

Soyer, Roger, French bass; b. Paris, Sept. 1, 1939. He studied at the Paris Cons.; made his debut at the Paris Opéra in 1962; then sang at La Scala in Milan, the Salzburg Festival, the Vienna State Opera, and the Bavarian State Opera in Munich. He made his Metropolitan Opera debut in N.Y. as Don Giovanni on Nov. 16, 1972; also appeared as a concert artist.

Spadavecchia, Antonio, Russian composer of Italian descent; b. Odessa, June 3, 1907. He studied with Shebalin at the Moscow Cons., and also took lessons from Prokofiev.

WORKS: Operas: *Ak-Buzat (The Magic Steed;* Ufa, Nov. 7, 1942; in collaboration with Zaimov); *The Inn Hostess,* after Goldoni (Moscow, April 24, 1949); *Pilgrimage of Sorrows,* after Alexei Tolstoi (Perm, Dec. 29, 1953); *The Gadfly* (Perm, Nov. 8, 1957); *Yukki* (1970); ballets: *Enemies* (Moscow, May 20, 1938); *The Shore of Happiness* (Moscow, Nov. 6, 1948); symph. suite, *Dzangar* (1940); *Heroic Overture on Bashkir Songs* (Ufa, Nov. 6, 1942); Piano Concerto (1944); *Romantic Trio* for Violin, Cello, and Piano (1937).

Spaeth, Sigmund, American writer on music; b. Philadelphia, April 10, 1885; d. New York, Nov. 11, 1965. He studied piano and violin with A. Bachmann; then attended Haverford College (M.A., 1906); received a Ph.D. from Princeton Univ. (1910), with the dissertation *Milton's Knowledge of Music* (publ. 1913). He was music editor of the *N.Y. Evening Mail* (1914–18); education director of the American Piano Co. (1920–27); president of the National Assoc. of American Composers and Conductors (1934–37); lectured widely on music; gave popular talks on the radio; was active in musical journalism; held various posts in educational organizations.

WRITINGS: *The Common Sense of Music* (1924); *The Art of Enjoying Music* (1933); *Music for Everybody* (1934); *Great Symphonies* (1936); *Stories be-*

hind the World's Great Music (1937); *Music for Fun* (1939); *Great Program Music* (1940); *At Home with Music* (1945); *A History of Popular Music in America* (N.Y., 1948); *Opportunities in Music* (N.Y., 1950); *Dedication; The Love Story of Clara and Robert Schumann* (N.Y., 1950). He ed. several annotated songbooks: *Barber Shop Ballads* (1925; reprinted 1940); *Read 'em and Weep* (1926; revised 1945); *Weep Some More, My Lady* (N.Y., 1927); *50 Years of Music* (N.Y., 1959).

Spalding, Albert, American violinist; b. Chicago, Aug. 15, 1888; d. New York, May 26, 1953. He was taken to Europe as a child and studied violin in Florence and Paris; made his public debut in Paris on June 6, 1905, and his American debut as a soloist with the N.Y. Symph. Orch. on Nov. 8, 1908. Beginning in 1919 he made annual tours of the U.S. and acquired the reputation of a fine artist, even though not necessarily a contagiously flamboyant one. He wrote a number of pieces for the violin; publ. an autobiography, *Rise to Follow* (N.Y., 1943), and a fictionalized biography of Tartini, *A Fiddle, a Sword, and a Lady* (N.Y., 1953).

Spalding, Walter Raymond, American pedagogue; b. Northampton, Mass., May 22, 1865; d. Cambridge, Mass., Feb. 10, 1962. He was a graduate of Harvard Univ. (B.A., 1887; M.A., 1888, with honors in music); taught classics at St. Mark's School in Southborough, Mass., in 1889–92; from 1892 to 1895 studied music in Paris (with Guilmant and Widor) and in Munich (with Rheinberger); was appointed an instructor of music at Harvard in 1895, became an assistant prof. in 1903, and a prof. in 1912; also was a prof. at Radcliffe College. In 1920–21 he lectured at 8 French univs.
WRITINGS: *Tonal Counterpoint* (1940); *Modern Harmony in Its Theory and Practice* (1905; with Arthur Foote); *Music; An Art and a Language* (1920); *Music at Harvard* (1935).

Spangenberg, Heinrich, German composer; b. Darmstadt, May 24, 1861; d. there, Sept. 27, 1925. He studied at the Hoch Cons. in Frankfurt; in 1881 for a short time was a pupil of N. Rubinstein (piano) in Moscow; then studied with Leschetizky (piano) and Grädener (composition) in Vienna. In 1884 he became Kapellmeister at the Opera and instructor at the Cons. in Mainz; in 1886 he became an instructor at Fredenberg's Cons. in Wiesbaden; in 1888, conductor of the Lehrerverein; about 1890 he founded his own Cons. in Wiesbaden, of which he was director until 1914. He composed 3 operas; piano pieces; songs; numerous choruses for men's voices.

Spani, Hina (original name, **Higinia Tuñon**), Argentinian soprano; b. Puán, Feb. 15, 1896; d. Buenos Aires, July 11, 1969. She studied in Buenos Aires and Milan; made her operatic debut at La Scala in Milan in 1915 as Anna in Catalani's *Loreley;* also sang in Turin, Naples, and Parma; made many appearances at the Teatro Colón in Buenos Aires (1915–40). From 1946 she taught voice in Buenos Aires, and

from 1952 served as director of the School of Music at the Univ. of Buenos Aires. She was highly regarded as a dramatic soprano; her repertoire included more than 70 roles.

Spanier, Francis Joseph ("Muggsy"), American jazz cornetist; b. Chicago, Nov. 9, 1906; d. Sausalito, Calif., Feb. 12, 1967. He began his professional career in 1922 in Chicago, where he worked with several bands; he played with Ted Lewis (1929–36) and Ben Pollack (1936–38); later played with Earl Hines, and eventually made his home in California.

Spanuth, August, German music editor; b. Brinkum, near Hannover, March 15, 1857; d. Berlin, Jan. 9, 1920. He was a pupil of Heymann (piano) and Raff (composition) at the Hoch Cons. in Frankfurt; made his debut as a pianist in 1874; then lived as a concert pianist and teacher in Koblenz and Bremen; toured the U.S. as a pianist in 1886; taught at the Chicago Musical College in 1887–93; from 1893 to 1906 was in N.Y. as a teacher and as music critic of the *Staatszeitung;* settled in Berlin in 1906 as a teacher at the Stern Cons. and (from 1907) as editor of *Signale für die Musikalische Welt.* He publ. *Preparatory Piano Exercises* and *Essential Piano Technics;* songs and piano pieces; with X. Scharwenka he wrote *Methodik des Klavierspiels* (1907).

Spark, William, English organist and composer; b. Exeter, Oct. 28, 1823; d. Leeds, June 16, 1897. He was a chorister in Exeter Cathedral; was a pupil of S.S. Wesley; from 1850–80, was organist at St. George's, Leeds; was founder (1851) of the Leeds Madrigal and Motet Society; became borough organist of Leeds in 1860; received a Mus.Doc. degree from the Univ. of Dublin in 1861; was editor of the *Organist's Quarterly Journal.*
WRITINGS: *Memoir of Dr. S.S. Wesley; Henry Smart, His Life and Works* (London, 1881); *Musical Memories* (1888); *Musical Reminiscences* (1892).

Sparnaay, Harry, prominent Dutch bass-clarinet player; b. Amsterdam, April 14, 1944. He played tenor saxophone in the Bohemia Jazz Quintet and later in the Theo Deken Orch.; studied clarinet at the Amsterdam Cons., where he eventually turned to the bass clarinet. He had over 100 works written for him (as a soloist or for his chamber duo, Fusion Moderne, which was formed in 1971 with the pianist Polo de Haas) by Berio, Goeyvaerts, Hrisanidis, Kunst, Logothetis, Raxach, Straesser, and others; played in contemporary music festivals in Amsterdam, Berlin, Bonn, Frankfurt, and Zagreb.

Spasov, Ivan, Bulgarian composer; b. Sofia, Jan. 17, 1934. He studied composition with Vladigerov at the Bulgarian State Cons. (1951–56) and later with Sikorski and Wislocki at the Warsaw Cons. In 1962 he became music director of the symph. orch. in Pazardjik and also taught at the Plovdiv Cons.
WORKS: *Sonata concertante* for Clarinet and Orch. (1959); 2 symphs. (1960, 1975); *Micro-Suite* for

Chamber Orch. (1963); *Dances* for Orch. (1964); *Episodes* for 4 Instrumental Groups (1965); *Movements I* for 12 Strings (1966) and *II* for 12 Strings and 3 Bagpipes (1968); 2 *Bulgarian Melodies* for Orch. (1968, 1970); *Competition* for 22 Winds (1969; Plovdiv, May 10, 1973); Cello Concerto (1974); *Monologues of a Woman,* monodrama (1975); Piano Concerto (1976); oratorio, *Plakat* (1958); Clarinet Sonata (1959); Viola Sonata (1960); *Bagatelles* for Flute and Harp (1964); *10 Groups* for Hunting Horn and Piano (1965); *Musique pour des amis* for String Quartet and Jazz Quartet (1966); String Quartet No. 1 (1973); *Games* for Piano (1964); *The Art of the Seria* in 3 notebooks (1968, 1969, 1970); songs.

Spazier, Johann Gottlieb Carl, German song composer and scholar; b. Berlin, April 20, 1761; d. Leipzig, Jan. 19, 1805. He was a student of philosophy at Halle and Göttingen; was a prof. at Giessen; settled in Leipzig in 1800. He wrote many songs, some of which became great favorites.
WRITINGS: The autobiographical *Karl Pilgers. Roman seines Lebens* (3 vols., 1792–96); *Freie Gedanken über die Gottesverehrung der Protestanten* (1788); *Etwas über Gluckische Musik und die Oper "Iphigenia in Tauris"* (1795).
BIBLIOGRAPHY: M. Friedlaender, *Das deutsche Lied im 18. Jahrhundert* (1902).

Speaight, Joseph, English pianist and pedagogue; b. London, Oct. 24, 1868; d. there, Nov. 20, 1947. He studied piano with Ernst Pauer and composition with R.O. Morgan at the Guildhall School of Music; taught there from 1894 to 1919; then was on the faculty of Trinity College (1919–39). He wrote 3 symphs., a Piano Concerto, piano pieces, and songs.

Speaks, Oley, American baritone and song composer; b. Canal Winchester, Ohio, June 28, 1874; d. New York, Aug. 27, 1948. He studied singing with Emma Thursby and composition with Max Spicker and W. Macfarlane; sang at various churches in N.Y. (1898–1906); then devoted himself entirely to concert singing and composition. He wrote some of the most popular songs in the American repertoire: *On the Road to Mandalay, Sylvia, The Prayer Perfect, Morning, Life's Twilight, My Homeland, The Lord Is My Light, To You,* etc.

Specht, Richard, Austrian writer on music; b. Vienna, Dec. 7, 1870; d. there, March 18, 1932. Trained as an architect, he turned to music criticism at the suggestion of Brahms and Goldmark, writing at first for *Die Zeit* (a Vienna daily), and in 1908–15 for *Die Musik*. In 1909 he founded *Der Merker,* which he edited until 1919 (at first with R. Batka, later with J. Bittner). In 1914 he became an Officier de l'Académie (France); in 1926, a prof.
WRITINGS: *Kritisches Skizzenbuch* (1900); *Gustav Mahler* (1906; enlarged 1913); *Joh. Strauss* (1909); *Das Wiener Operntheater von Dingelstedt bis Schalk und Strauss* (1919); *Richard Strauss und sein Werk,* in 2 vols. (1921); *Julius Bittner* (1921); *Wilhelm Furtwängler* (1922); *E.N. von Reznicek*

(1923); *Brahms* (1928; in Eng., 1930); *Bildnis Beethovens* (1930; in Eng. as *Beethoven as He Lived,* 1933); *Giacomo Puccini* (1931; in Eng., 1933).

Speer, Daniel, German musician; b. Breslau, July 2, 1636; d. Göppingen, Oct. 5, 1707. He served as a church organist in Stuttgart (1664–66); then was active in Gross Bottwar and Leonberg. In 1668 he settled in Göppingen and taught at the Lateinschule. In 1689 he publ. a pamphlet criticizing the Württemberg authorities for their lack of adequate response to the French invasion; for this he was arrested and imprisoned at the Hohenneuffen fortress. Upon his release in 1693 he returned to Göppingen as Kollaborator and Kantor of the Lateinschule. He publ. (under assumed names and anagrams) several collections of songs of a whimsical and satirical nature; he also wrote some chamber music.
BIBLIOGRAPHY: H.J. Moser, "Daniel Speer," *Acta Musicologica,* 9 (1937); H.J. Moser, "Daniel Speer als Dichter und Musiker," in *Musik in Zeit und Raum* (Berlin, 1960).

Speidel, Wilhelm, German pianist and composer; b. Ulm, Sept. 3, 1826; d. Stuttgart, Oct. 13, 1899. He was a pupil at Munich of Wänner and W. Kuhe, and of Ignaz Lachner (composition); in 1846–48, was a teacher at Thann, Alsatia; in 1848–54, was at Munich; in 1854, bacame music director at Ulm; in 1857, became conductor of the Liederkranz choral group at Stuttgart; he was co-founder, with Lebert and others, of the Stuttgart Cons., and a teacher of piano there until he founded his Künstler- und Dilettantenschule für Klavier in 1874. On Lebert's death (1884), Speidel rejoined the Cons., uniting with it his own school.

Spelman, Timothy Mather, American composer; b. Brooklyn, Jan. 21, 1891; d. Florence, Italy, Aug. 21, 1970. He studied music with H.R. Shelley in N.Y., and with W.R. Spalding and E.B. Hill at Harvard Univ. (1909–13); then went to Europe, where he took a course with Walter Courvoisier at the Munich Cons. (1913–15); he returned to the U.S. in 1915 and was active as director of a military band. After 1918 he went back to Europe with his wife, the poetess Leolyn Everett, settling in Florence. As the specter of a new war loomed, he returned to the U.S.; in 1947 he went back to Florence. His music was performed more often in Europe than in America; indeed, his style of composition is exceedingly European, influenced by Italian Romanticism and French Impressionism.
WORKS: *Snowdrop,* pantomime (Brooklyn, 1911); *The Romance of the Rose,* "wordless fantasy" (Boston, 1913; revised version, St. Paul, Minn., Dec. 4, 1915); *La Magnifica,* short music drama to a libretto by Leolyn Everett-Spelman (1920); *The Sunken City,* opera (1930); *The Courtship of Miles Standish,* opera after Longfellow (1943); for Orch.: *Saint's Days,* suite in 4 movements (one movement, *Assisi, the Great Pardon of St. Francis,* was perf. in Boston, March 26, 1926); *The Outcasts of Poker Flat,*

symph. poem after Bret Harte (1928); Symph. (Rochester, N.Y., Oct. 29, 1936); *Jamboree,* "pocket ballet" (1945); Oboe Concerto (1954); *5 Whimsical Serenades* for String Quartet (1924); *Le Pavillion sur l'eau* for Flute, Harp, and Strings (1925); *Pervigilium Veneris* for Soprano, Baritone, Chorus, and Orch. (Paris, April 30, 1931); a number of choruses and songs.

Spencer, Allen, American pianist and pedagogue; b. Fair Haven, Vt., Oct. 30, 1870; d. Chicago, Aug. 25, 1950. He studied piano in Rochester, N.Y., and Chicago; in 1892 was appointed a teacher at the American Cons. in Chicago; then became its dean (1928–48). He publ. *Foundations of Piano Technique.*

Spencer, Emile-Alexis-Xavier, French composer; b. Brussels, May 24, 1859; d. Nanterre (Seine), May 24, 1921. He studied piano in Brussels; in 1881 went to Paris, where he found his métier as a composer for vaudeville; he was credited with about 4,000 chansonettes, which were popularized by famous singers, among them Yvette Guilbert. His chanson *Jambes de bois* was used by Stravinsky in *Pétrouchka* under the impression that it was a folk song; when Spencer brought an action for infringement on his authorship, Stravinsky agreed to pay him part of the royalties for performances.

Spencer, S. Reid, American pianist and teacher; b. Baltimore, July 30, 1872; d. Brooklyn, July 28, 1945. He studied with P.C. Lutkin at the Northwestern Univ. School of Music, and taught there from 1895 to 1900. After teaching in various conservatories, he established his own music school in Brooklyn (1927). He publ. a textbook on harmony (1915).

Spencer, Vernon, English-American pianist and composer; b. Belmont, Durham, Oct. 10, 1875; d. Los Angeles, Jan. 9, 1949. He studied at the Leipzig Cons., graduating in 1897; in 1903 he settled in the U.S.; was director of the Wesleyan Univ. Cons. of Music at Lincoln, Nebr.; from 1911 taught in Los Angeles. He publ. some songs and character pieces for piano.

Spendiarov, Alexander, Russian-Armenian composer; b. Kakhovka, Crimea, Nov. 1, 1871; d. Erevan, May 7, 1928. He studied violin as a child; in 1896 went to St. Petersburg and took private lessons with Rimsky-Korsakov. In his works he cultivated a type of Russian orientalism in which the elements of folk songs of the peripheral regions of the old Russian Empire are adroitly arranged in the colorful harmonies of the Russian national school. His best work in this manner was an opera, *Almast,* the composition of which he undertook shortly before his death. It was completed and orchestrated by Maximilian Steinberg, and performed posthumously in Moscow on June 23, 1930. Other works are: *The 3 Palm Trees,* a symph. tableau (1905); *Crimean Sketches* for Orch. (1903–12); *2 Songs of the Cri-*

mean Tatars for Voice and Orch. (1915; Moscow, Dec. 25, 1927); *Etudes d'Eriwan,* on Armenian melodies (1925).

BIBLIOGRAPHY: A. Shaverdian, *A. Spendiarov* (Moscow, 1929); G. Tigranov, *A. Spendiarov* (Erevan, 1953); R. Atadjan, *A. Spendiarov* (Erevan, 1971).

Spengel, Julius Heinrich, German composer; b. Hamburg, June 12, 1853; d. there, April 17, 1936. He studied at the Cologne Cons.; later at the Berlin Hochschule für Musik with Rudorff, Joachim, Kiel, and A. Schulze. He settled as a teacher in Hamburg; in 1878 was conductor of the Cäcilienverein there; was organist of the Gertrudenkirche (1886); was made Royal Prof. in 1906.

WORKS: Piano Quintet; *Psalm 39* for 6-part Chorus and Wind Instruments; *Zwiegesang in der Sommernacht* for Chorus and Orch.; *König Alfreds Gesang* for Baritone and Orch.; male and female choruses; songs.

Sperontes (real name, **Johann Sigismund Scholze**), German composer; b. Lobendau, Silesia, March 20, 1705; d. Leipzig, Sept. 27, 1750. Between 1736 and 1745 he brought out a collection of poems and melodies to words by Johann Christian Günther, *Singende Muse an der Pleisse in zweimal 50 Oden;* this became famous, and its success generated many imitations, by composers in Leipzig, Hamburg, and Vienna. There is a reprint (ed. by E. Buhle) in Denkmäler Deutscher Tonkunst, 35 and 36.

BIBLIOGRAPHY: P. Spitta, in *Vierteljahrsschrift für Musikwissenschaft,* 1 (1885); H. von Hase, in *Zeitschrift der Internationalen Musik-Gesellschaft,* XIV/4; A. Schering, "Zwei Singspiele des Sperontes," *Zeitschrift für Musikwissenschaft,* VII/4.

Speyer, Wilhelm, German violinist and composer; b. Frankfurt, June 21, 1790; d. there, April 5, 1878. He studied in Offenbach with F. Fränzl (violin) and A. André (composition); later in Paris with Baillot (violin). After extensive travels as a concert violinist, he returned to Frankfurt and embraced a mercantile career, but continued his association with eminent musicians (Spohr, Mendelssohn, etc.) and began to compose. He wrote a great deal of chamber music; his violin pieces were often played, but he achieved lasting popularity with his ballads written in a characteristically Romantic style; of these, *Der Trompeter* and *Die drei Liebchen* were particularly famous. His son **Edward Speyer** (b. Frankfurt, May 14, 1839; d. Shenley, Hertfordshire, Jan. 8, 1934) lived most of his life in London, where he organized the Classical Concerts Society; he publ. a monograph on his father, *Wilhelm Speyer, der Liederkomponist* (Munich, 1925), and a book of reminiscences, *My Life and Friends* (posthumous, London, 1937).

Spialek, Hans, American arranger and conductor; b. Vienna, April 17, 1894; d. New York, Nov. 20, 1983. He sang in a boys' chorus at the Vienna Opera and took courses at the Vienna Cons. He was drafted into the Austrian army during World War I and taken prisoner by the Russians. In Russia his musical abilities were duly appreciated, and after the Russian Revolution he was given a job at the Bolshoi Theater in Moscow as assistant stage manager (1918–20); later he conducted symph. orchs. in Bessarabia (1920–22). He married a Russian singer, **Dora Boshoer.** In 1923 he went to Germany, and in 1924 reached the U.S. He earned his living as a music copyist, but soon moved several notches higher by arranging for shows; he also supplied orch. interludes and entr'acte music, showing such expertise at organizing the raw materials of American musicals that even before he could master the American tongue he intuitively found the proper instrumentation for the text; and he could work fast to meet the deadlines. Altogether he orchestrated 147 shows, among them 5 by Cole Porter and 11 by Richard Rodgers and Lorenz Hart. With Robert Russell Bennett, he became one of the most reliable arrangers on Broadway. He also composed some orch. works in the approved Broadway style, with such idiosyncratic titles as *The Tall City* and *Manhattan Watercolors.*

Spicker, Max, German-American conductor, composer, and music editor; b. Königsberg, Aug. 16, 1858; d. New York, Oct. 15, 1912. He studied with Louis Köhler (piano), then at the Leipzig Cons. with Reinecke and Richter. In 1882 he settled in N.Y., where he became a reader for G. Schirmer, Inc. He wrote many songs; edited *Aus aller Herren Länder* (a collection of folk songs arranged for male chorus), *Anthology of Sacred Song* (4 vols.), *Operatic Anthology* (5 vols.), *The Synagogical Service* (2 vols.; with W. Sparger), etc.

Spiegel, Laurie, American composer of the avant-garde; b. Chicago, Sept. 20, 1945. She studied the classical guitar with Oscar Ghiglia, Renaissance lute playing with Suzanne Bloch, and composition with Jacob Druckman at the Juilliard School of Music in N.Y. She moved in quaquaversal directions in her own creative output until 1970, when she plugged herself into an electronic outlet, and in 1973 reached the Ultima Thule of scientifically regulated composition with the GROOVE hybrid system, using a digital computer to control analog audio synthesis equipment at the Bell Laboratories in Murray Hill, N.J.; was closely associated with experimental color video in collaboration with Nam June Paik, a pioneer of electronic dislocation of images on television sets. She applied the principles of musical variations to the changes of mandala-shaped visual images; also utilized transcendental meditation technique with a single tone subjected to dynamic amplification or diminution. Among her computer-generated works are *The Expanding Universe* (1975), *Waves* (1975), and *Patchwork* (1976). In several of her compositions she harks back to the polyphonic schools of the Renaissance, applying modal stereophonic hockets.

Spiegelman, Joel, American pianist, harpsichordist, conductor, and composer; b. Buffalo, N.Y., Jan. 23, 1933. He studied at the Yale School of Music (1949–50), the Univ. of Buffalo (1950–53), the Longy School of Music at Cambridge, Mass. (1953–54), and Brandeis Univ., where he attended the classes of Harold Shapero, Irving Fine, and Arthur Berger; in 1956 he went to Paris, where he studied privately with Nadia Boulanger. He returned to the U.S. in 1960 and took courses in musicology at Brandeis. He also studied languages, and became fluent in French and Russian. In 1966 he was appointed a teacher of harpsichord and theory at Sarah Lawrence College, where he was also an instructor in electronic music. In 1977 he organized in N.Y. the new Russian Chamber Orch., composed entirely of Soviet Jews who had left Russia in the 1970s.

WORKS: *Ouverture de Saison 1958* for 2 Harps, 2 Flutes, Piano, and Celesta (1958); *Kusochki (Morsels)* for Piano, 4-hands (1966); *3 Miniatures* for Clarinet and Piano (1972); *Chamber Music* for Piano Quartet and Percussion (1973); *2 Fantasies* for String Quartet (1963, 1974).

Spielter, Hermann, German composer; b. Bremen, April 26, 1860; d. New York, Nov. 10, 1925. He studied with Reinecke and Jadassohn at the Leipzig Cons.; emigrated to the U.S. in 1894 and settled in N.Y. as a teacher. He wrote an operetta, *Die Rajahsbraut* (N.Y., 1910), numerous choral pieces, chamber music, and a Piano Sonata.

Spiering, Theodore, American violinist and conductor; b. St. Louis, Sept. 5, 1871; d. Munich, Aug. 11, 1925. He studied with Schradieck at the Cincinnati College of Music and with Joachim at the Hochschule für Musik in Berlin. Returning to America, he organized his own quartet, with which he toured the U.S. and Canada (1893–1905); then traveled in Germany (1906–9). In 1909 he was appointed concertmaster of the N.Y. Phil. Orch. (under Mahler); during Mahler's last illness Spiering was called upon to conduct 17 concerts of the N.Y. Phil. in the spring of 1911. He publ. *6 Künstler-Etüden* for Violin; with Rudolph Ganz he edited a number of classical and modern violin pieces.

Spies, Hermine, eminent German contralto; b. Löhneberger Hütte, near Weilburg, Feb. 25, 1857; d. Wiesbaden, Feb. 26, 1893. She was a pupil of Stockhausen in Frankfurt; in 1883 began to give song recitals in Germany; in 1889 made an appearance in England with excellent success; also sang in Austria, Denmark, and Russia. She excelled as an interpreter of songs by Brahms, who had a high regard for her. Shortly before her death she married Dr. W.A.F. Hardtmuth of Wiesbaden.

BIBLIOGRAPHY: Marie Spies, *Hermine Spies. Ein Gedenkbuch für ihre Freunde* (Stuttgart, 1894).

Spiess, Meinrad, German composer and theorist; b. Honsolgen, Aug. 24, 1683; d. Yrsee, June 12, 1761. He was a pupil of Giuseppe Antonio Bernabei in Munich; in 1708 he was ordained a priest; from 1712 to 1749 was music director of the monastery of Yrsee, eventually becoming prior. He publ. a number of collections of sacred choruses, motets, etc., with instrumental accompaniment: *Antiphonarium Marianum* (1713); *Cithara Davidis* (1713); *Philomela ecclesiastica* (1718); *Cultus latreuticomusicus* (1719); *Laus Dei in Sanctis ejus* (1723); *Hyperdulia musica* (1726); *Tractatus musicus compositorio-practicus* (1746); also composed instrumental works and a number of organ pieces.

Spilka, František, Czech composer; b. Štěken, Nov. 13, 1887; d. Prague, Oct. 20, 1960. He studied at the Prague Cons. with Stecker, Knittl, and Dvořák; in 1918 was appointed administrative director of the Prague Cons. He established the Prague Teachers' Choral Society in 1908, of which he remained choirmaster until 1921, and gave concerts with it in France and England; later directed the Prague singing ensemble Smetana. Spilka developed, together with Ferdinand Vach, a new approach to choral performance, emphasizing sound color.
WORKS: 2 operas: *Stará práva* (*Ancient Rights;* 1915; Prague, June 10, 1917) and *Cain* or *The Birth of Death* (1917); oratorio, *Jan Hus at the Stake* (1907); cantata, *Miller's Journeyman* (1947); *Rhapsody* for Orch. (1896); *Overture* (1897); *6 Sonnets* for Violin and Piano (1944); *Rhapsodic Sonata* for Cello and Piano (1946); numerous piano pieces; songs and choruses.

Spindler, Fritz, German pianist and composer; b. Wurzbach, Nov. 24, 1817; d. Lössnitz, near Dresden, Dec. 26, 1905. He studied with Friedrich Schneider at Dessau; settled in 1841 at Dresden, where he had great success as a teacher. Most of his works (over 400 opus numbers) are salon pieces and characteristic pieces for piano; he also publ. instructive sonatinas, opp. 157, 290, and 294, and a 4-hand Sonatina, op. 136.

Spinelli, Nicola, Italian composer; b. Turin, July 29, 1865; d. Rome, Oct. 17, 1909. He studied at the Naples Cons., under Serrao. In 1889 his one-act opera, *Labilia,* took the 2nd prize in the famous competition instituted by the publisher Sonzogno, when Mascagni won the first prize with *Cavalleria rusticana;* Spinelli's opera was produced in Rome on May 7, 1890, with indifferent success. His next opera, *A basso porto,* was more fortunate; after its initial production in Cologne on April 18, 1894 (in a German version), it was staged in Rome, in Italian (March 11, 1895), and then in Budapest, St. Petersburg, etc.; it was also produced in the U.S. (St. Louis, Jan. 8, 1900; N.Y., Jan. 22, 1900).

Spisak, Michal, Polish composer; b. Dabrowa Górnicza, Sept. 14, 1914; d. Paris, Jan. 29, 1965. He studied music in Katowice; then took composition with Sikorski in Warsaw and with Nadia Boulanger in Paris, where he lived from 1937 until his death.
WORKS: Opera, *Marynka* (1955); *Serenade* for Orch. (1939); Concertino for String Orch. (1942); *Aubade* for Small Orch. (1943); *Allegro de Voiron*

for Orch. (1943); Bassoon Concerto (1944; International Society for Contemporary Music Festival, Copenhagen, June 2, 1947); *Toccata* for Orch. (1944); *Suite* for String Orch. (1945); Piano Concerto (1947); 2 *Symphonies concertante* (1947, 1956); *Etudes* for Strings (1948); *Divertimento* for 2 Pianos and Orch. (1948); Sonata for Violin and Orch. (1950); Trombone Concertino (1951); *Divertimento* for Orch. (1951); *Andante and Allegro* for Violin and Orch. (1954); *Concerto giocoso* for Chamber Orch. (1957); Oboe Concerto (1962); Violin Concerto (posthumous; Katowice, Jan. 30, 1976); Quartet for Oboe, 2 Clarinets, and Bassoon (1938); Sonatina for Oboe, Clarinet, and Bassoon (1946); Violin Sonata (1946); Wind Quintet (1948); *Duetto concertante* for Viola and Bassoon (1949); String Quartet (1953); *Suite* for 2 Violins (1957); *Improvvisazione* for Violin and Piano (1962); Concerto for 2 Solo Pianos (1942); choruses; piano pieces; songs.

Spitalny, Phil, American conductor of popular music; b. Odessa, Russia, Nov. 7, 1889; d. Miami, Fla., Oct. 11, 1970. He emigrated to the U.S. in 1905; played clarinet in various bands. In 1934 he conceived the idea of organizing an instrumental ensemble consisting only of girls of nubile age and engaging exterior; in 1935 he inaugurated the radio program "Hour of Charm" with his group. In 1937 he won the award of merit of the Radio Committee of the Women's National Exposition of Arts and Industries. With the advent of television, Spitalny's radio program fell into terminal desuetude, and he went to Florida. He was also an amateur composer; made arrangements of amorous songs, among them *The Kiss I Can't Forget.*

Spitta, Friedrich, German theologian and writer on music, brother of **Philipp Spitta;** b. Wittingen, Jan. 10, 1852; d. Göttingen, June 8, 1924. From 1887 to 1918 he was a prof. of theology at Strasbourg Univ., and from 1919, at Göttingen; from 1896 he was also editor (with J. Smend) of *Monatschrift für Gottesdienst und kirchliche Kunst,* in which (Jan.–March 1913) he publ. important facts concerning Benedictus Ducis. He publ. *Liturgische Andacht zum Luther-Jubiläum* (1883); *H. Schütz,* festival oration (1886); *Die Passionen nach den vier Evangelisten von H. Schütz* (1886); *Über Chorgesang im evangelischen Gottesdienste* (1886); *"Ein' feste Burg ist unser Gott." Die Lieder Luthers* (1905); *Studien zu Luthers Liedern* (1907); *Das Deutsche Kirchenlied in seinen charakteristischen Erscheinungen* (vol. I: *Mittelalter und Reformationszeit,* 1912); *H. Schütz* (1925); also a new edition of Mergner's *Paul Gerhardt Lieder* (1918).

Spitta, (Johann August) Philipp, eminent German musicologist; b. Wechold, Hannover, Dec. 27, 1841; d. Berlin, April 13, 1894. He was a student of philology at Göttingen; taught at the Ritter und Domschule in Reval in 1864–66, at the Sondershausen Gymnasium till 1874, and for one year at the Nikolai-Gymnasium in Leipzig, where he was cofounder of the Bach-Verein (1874). In 1875 he became a prof. of music history at Berlin Univ., life-secretary to the Royal Academy of Arts, and a teacher at, and vice-director of, the Hochschule für Musik. As a teacher, he had extraordinary success; among his pupils were O. Fleischer, A. Sandberger, M. Freidlaender, R. Schwartz, M. Seiffert, E. Vogel, K. Krebs, and J. Combarieu. He was one of the leading spirits in organizing the publication of Denkmäler Deutscher Tonkunst.

WRITINGS: *J.S. Bach,* a comprehensive biography carefully and learnedly written, with valuable discussions of the principal works (2 vols., 1873, 1880; in Eng., London, 1884–85; condensed ed., Leipzig, 1935; 5th ed., 1962); also a short sketch of Bach in Waldersee's *Vorträge* (1880); a short biography of Schumann for *Grove's Dictionary,* afterward publ. separately in German (*Vorträge,* 1882); *Händel und Bach,* 2 festival orations (1885); *Zur Ausgabe der Kompositionen Friedrichs des Grossen* (1890); 2 collections of articles, *Zur Musik* (1892; 16 essays) and *Musikgeschichtliche Aufsätze* (Berlin, 1894); an essay, *Die Passionsmusiken von Sebastian Bach und Heinrich Schütz* (Hamburg, 1893); many papers in the *Allgemeine Musikalische Zeitung,* the *Monatshefte für Musikgeschichte,* and, more particularly, in his own periodical, the *Vierteljahrsschrift für Musikwissenschaft,* founded in 1884 with Chrysander and G. Adler. Spitta also edited a critical ed. of Buxtehude's organ works (2 vols., 1875, 1876), with valuable historical notes; the complete ed. of Schütz's works (16 vols.); and vol. I of Denkmäler Deutscher Tonkunst (1892; contains Scheidt's *Tabulatura nova* of 1624). He left in MS an almost completed *Geschichte der romantischen Oper in Deutschland.* Spitta's correspondence with Brahms was publ. in *Brahmsgesellschaft* (vol. 15).

BIBLIOGRAPHY: W. Gurlitt, "Der Musikhistoriker Philipp Spitta," *Musik und Kirche,* XIV (1942).

Spitzmueller, Alexander, Austrian composer; b. Vienna, Feb. 22, 1894; d. Paris, Nov. 12, 1962. He studied jurisprudence; then took lessons in composition with Alban Berg and Hans Apostel. In 1928 he went to Paris, where he became active in radio broadcasting. His early works are in the neo-Classical vein; eventually he followed the method of composition with 12 tones, following its usage by Berg and Webern.

WORKS: *Sinfonietta ritmica* (1934); Symph. for Strings (1955); 2 piano concertos (1938, 1954); *May 40,* satirical suite for Orch. (Amsterdam Festival of the International Society for Contemporary Music, June 12, 1948); *3 hymnes à la Paix* for Orch. (1947); opera, *Der Diener zweier Herren* (1958); ballets: *Le Premier Amour de Don Juan* (1954); *Die Sackgasse* (1957); *Construction humaine* (1959); Violin Sonata; Cello Sonata; *Variations* for Viola and Guitar; String Quartet; Saxophone Quartet; a number of sacred and secular choruses.

Spivacke, Harold, eminent American musicologist and librarian; b. New York, July 18, 1904; d. Washington, D.C., May 9, 1977. He studied at N.Y. Univ. (M.A., 1924) and at the Univ. of Berlin, where he received his Dr.Phil. in 1933, magna cum laude, with the dissertation *Über die objektive und subjektive Tonintensität;* while in Berlin he took private lessons with Eugen d'Albert and Hugo Leichtentritt as an American-German Students Exchange Fellow and an Alexander von Humboldt Stiftung Fellow. Returning to the U.S., he joined the staff of the Music Division of the Library of Congress in Washington, D.C., first as assistant chief (1934–37), then as chief, in which capacity he served for 35 years (1937–72). He also held numerous advisory positions with the Dept. of State, UNESCO, etc. As chief of the Music Division of the Library of Congress, he was responsible for the acquisition of many important MSS by contemporary composers, including a large collection of Schoenberg's original MSS. He also commissioned works from contemporary composers for the Coolidge Foundation at the Library of Congress. He publ. some valuable bibliographical papers, among them *Paganiniana* (Washington, 1945). In 1939 he was chairman of the Organizing Committee of the National Music Council, and until 1972 was Archivist and a member of the Executive Committee of the Council.

BIBLIOGRAPHY: C. Sprague Smith, "Harold Spivacke (1904–1977)," *Musical Quarterly,* LXIII (1977).

Spivak, Charlie, Russian-born American trumpet player and bandleader; b. Trilsey, Feb. 17, 1905; d. Cleveland, March 1, 1982. After settling in the U.S., he played trumpet in the bands of Tommy and Jimmy Dorsey, Jack Teagarden, and Ray Noble; during the big band era of the early 1940s he became a popular bandleader in his own right, and enjoyed popularity until the advent of bebop.

Spivakovsky, Tossy, outstanding Russian-American violinist; b. Odessa, Feb. 4, 1907. He studied with Willy Hess in Berlin; made his concert debut there at the age of 10; toured Europe (1920–33) and Australia (1933–41); then came to the U.S.; appeared with major American orchs.

BIBLIOGRAPHY: G. Yost, *The Spivakovsky Way of Bowing* (Pittsburgh, 1949).

Spohr, Ludwig (Louis), celebrated German violinist, composer, and conductor; b. Braunschweig, April 5, 1784; d. Kassel, Oct. 22, 1859. The family moved to Seesen in 1786. His father, a physician, was an amateur flute player, and his mother, a singer and pianist. In this musical atmosphere Spohr's talent developed very early; at the age of 5 he began taking lessons on the violin with Rector Riemenschneider and Dufour, a French émigré. Spohr then returned to Braunschweig, where he was taught by the organist Hartung and the violinist Maucourt. He had already composed various violin pieces; the Duke himself became interested in the 15-year-old Spohr, admitted him to the ducal orch., and arranged for his further study with the violinist Franz Eck. In 1802 Eck took Spohr with him on a tour to Russia, where he made the acquaintance of Clementi and John Field; he returned to Braunschweig in 1803 and resumed his post in the ducal orch. In 1804 he made his first official tour (his first actual tour to Hamburg in 1799 proved a failure) as a violinist, giving concerts in Berlin, Leipzig, and Dresden; in 1805 he became concertmaster in the ducal orch. at Gotha; married the harp player **Dorette Scheidler,** and toured with her in Germany in 1807. His reputation as a violin virtuoso was established, and he began to give more attention to composition. He wrote oratorios, operas, violin concertos, symphs., and chamber music, which obtained excellent success in Germany. In 1812 he gave a series of concerts in Vienna, and was acclaimed both as a composer and as a violinist; accepted the position of concertmaster in the orch. of the Theater an der Wien, which he held until 1815. He then made a grand tour of Germany and Italy; played a *concertante* of his own with Paganini in Rome. In 1816 Spohr's opera *Faust* was performed by Weber in Prague. After a visit to the Netherlands in 1817, he received the post of opera conductor in Frankfurt, where he produced one of his most popular operas, *Zemire und Azor* (1819). In 1820 he visited England; appeared with his wife at several concerts of the London Phil. Society; this was the first of his 6 tours of England, where he acquired a lasting reputation as a violinist, conductor, and composer; his works continued to be performed in England for many decades after his death. On his way back to Germany he presented several concerts in Paris in 1820, but his reception there failed to match his London successes. He then proceeded to Dresden, and was recommended by Weber for the post of court Kapellmeister in Kassel, originally offered to Weber. Spohr accepted it, and settled there in 1822. It was in Kassel that he produced his masterpiece, the opera *Jessonda* (1823), which held the stage in Europe throughout the 19th century. He conducted its performances in Leipzig and Berlin; also appeared as conductor and composer at various musical festivals (Düsseldorf, 1826; Nordhausen, 1829; Norwich, 1839; Bonn, 1845; etc.). The success of *Jessonda* was followed by the production in Kassel of his oratorio *Die letzten Dinge* (1826) and his symph. *Die Weihe der Töne* (1832), both of which elicited great praise. His wife died in 1834; he married the pianist **Marianne Pfeiffer** in 1836. Spohr made another journey to England in 1847; visited Frankfurt in 1848. Returning to Kassel, he found himself in an increasingly difficult position because of his outspoken radicalism; the Elector of Hesse refused to grant him further leaves of absence, and Spohr decided to ignore the ban, which resulted in litigation with the Kassel court. In 1853 he made his last tour of England, appearing at the New Phil. Concerts in London. He was retired from Kassel in 1857 on a pension; a few months later he broke his left arm, but despite the accident, at an advanced age, he made another appearance (his last) conducting *Jessonda* in Prague (1858).

Spohr's style was characteristic of the transition period between Classicism and Romanticism. He was a master of technical resources; some of his works demonstrate a spirit of bold experimentation (the *Historical Symph.;* Symph. for 2 Orchs.; Quar-

tet Concerto; Nonet; etc.), yet in his esthetics he was an intransigent conservative. He admired Beethoven's early works but confessed his total inability to understand Beethoven's last period; he also failed to appreciate Weber. It is remarkable, therefore, that he was an early champion of Wagner; in Kassel he brought out *Der fliegende Holländer* (1843) and *Tannhäuser* (1853), despite the strenuous opposition of the court. He was a highly esteemed teacher; among his pupils were Ferdinand David and Moritz Hauptmann. His autobiography was publ. posthumously as *Louis Spohrs Selbstbiographie* (2 vols., Kassel, 1860–61; in Eng., London, 1865 and 1878). The Spohr Society was founded in Kassel in 1908, dissolved in 1934, and revived in 1952.

WORKS: OPERAS: *Die Prüfung* (Gotha, 1806); *Alruna, die Eulen-Königin* (1808); *Der Zweikampf mit der Geliebten* (Hamburg, Nov. 15, 1811); *Faust* (Prague, Sept. 1, 1816); *Zemire und Azor* (Frankfurt, April 4, 1819); *Jessonda* (Kassel, July 28, 1823); *Der Berggeist* (Kassel, March 24, 1825); *Pietro von Albano* (Kassel, Oct. 13, 1827); *Der Alchymist* (Kassel, July 28, 1830); *Die Kreuzfahrer* (Kassel, Jan. 1, 1845); oratorios: *Das Jüngste Gericht* (Erfurt, Aug. 15, 1812); *Die letzten Dinge* (Kassel, March 25, 1826); in Eng. as *The Last Judgment*); *Des Heilands letze Stunden* (Kassel, 1835; in Eng. as *Calvary* at the Norwich Festival, 1839); *Der Fall Babylons* (Norwich Festival, 1842). OTHER VOCAL WORKS: *Das befreite Deutschland,* dramatic cantata; a Mass for 5 Voices and Double Chorus; 6 Psalms; hymns, partsongs, etc.; duets; 10 books of German songs; a sonatina for Voice and Piano, *An sie am Klavier.* FOR ORCH.: 10 symphs.: No. 1 (Leipzig, June 11, 1811); No. 2 (London, April 10, 1820); No. 3 (Kassel, April 6, 1828); No. 4, subtitled *Die Weihe der Töne,* a "characteristic tone painting in the form of a symphony" (1832); No. 5 (1837); No. 6 (1839), subtitled *Historische Symphonie,* in 4 movements traversing 4 styles of music in historic sequence (Bach-Handel Period, 1720; Haydn-Mozart, 1780; Beethoven, 1810; and the *Allerneueste* ["the very newest," i.e., Spohr's own style] of the year 1840); No. 7, *Irdisches und Göttliches im Menschenleben,* for Double Orch., in 3 parts portraying the mundane and divine elements in man's life (1842); No. 8 (1847); No. 9, *Die Jahreszeiten,* in 2 parts: 1, *Winter and Spring,* and 2, *Summer and Autumn* (1850); No. 10 (1857); overtures: *Macbeth; Im ernsten Styl;* etc.; 15 violin concertos (among the finest being No. 8, "in modo d'una scena cantante," and No. 9), all ed. by Ferdinand David; *Quartet Concerto* for 2 Violins, Viola, and Cello, with Orch.; 3 clarinet concertos. CHAMBER MUSIC: Nonet for Violin, Viola, Cello, Double Bass, Woodwinds, and Horn; Octet for Violin, 2 Violas, Cello, Double Bass, Clarinet, and 2 Horns; 4 double quartets for Strings; Septet for Piano, Flute, Clarinet, Horn, Bassoon, Violin, and Cello; String Sextet; 7 string quintets; Quintet for Piano, Flute, Clarinet, Horn, and Bassoon; Piano Quintet; 34 string quartets; 5 piano trios; 14 *duos concertants* for 2 Violins; 3 *duos concertantes* for Piano and Violin; 3 *sonates concertants* for Harp and Violin; Piano Sonata; *Rondoletto* for Piano; etc. A new edition of his works (*Neue Auswahl der Werke*), ed. by F. Göthel, was begun in 1963 (Kassel, Verlag der Spohr-Gesellschaft).

BIBLIOGRAPHY: W. Neumann, *L. Spohr. Eine Biographie* (Kassel, 1854); A. Malibran, *L. Spohr. Sein Leben und Wirken* (Frankfurt, 1860); L. Stierlin, *L. Spohr* (2 vols., Zürich, 1862–63); F. Hiller, *M. Hauptmanns Briefe an L. Spohr und andere* (Leipzig, 1876; in Eng., London, 1892); H.M. Schletterer, *L. Spohr* (Leipzig, 1881); L. Nohl, *Spohr* (Leipzig, 1882); C. Robert, *L. Spohr* (Berlin, 1883); La Mara, "Aus Spohrs Leben," in *Klassisches und Romantisches aus der Tonwelt* (Leipzig, 1892); R. Wassermann, *L. Spohr als Opernkomponist* (Rostock, 1910); E. Istel, "5 Briefe Spohrs an Marschner," in "Liliencron-Festschrift" (Leipzig, 1910); F. Göthel, *Das Violinspiel L. Spohrs* (Diss., Univ. of Berlin, 1934); Edith von Salburg, *L. Spohr* (Leipzig, 1936); P. Heidelbach, "Ludwig Spohrs Prozess gegen den Kurfürst von Hessen," *Allgemeine Musikalische Zeitung* (1936); Dorothy M. Mayer, *The Forgotten Master: The Life and Times of Louis Spohr* (London, 1959). For details of perfs. of Spohr's operas see A. Loewenberg, *Annals of Opera* (Cambridge, 1943; 3rd ed., Geneva, 1978); H. Homburg, *Ludwig Spohr: Bilder und Dokumente seiner Zeit* (Kassel, 1968); C. Brown, "Spohr's 'Jessonda,' " *Musical Times* (Feb. 1980); idem, "Spohr, Faust and Leitmotif," ibid. (Jan. 1984).

Spontini, Gaspare (Luigi Pacifico), significant Italian opera composer; b. Majolati, Ancona, Nov. 14, 1774; d. there, Jan. 24, 1851. His father, a modest farmer, intended him for the church and gave him into the charge of an uncle, a priest at Jesi, who attempted to stifle his musical aspirations. Spontini sought refuge at Monte San Vito with another relative, who not only found a competent music teacher for him, but effected a reconciliation so that, after a year, he was able to return to Jesi. In 1793 he entered the Cons. della Pietà de' Turchini in Naples, where his teachers were Tritto (singing) and Sala (composition). He rapidly mastered the conventional Italian style of his time; some of his church music performed in Naples came to the attention of a director of the Teatro della Pallacorda in Rome, who commissioned him to write an opera. This was *I puntigli delle donne,* produced with notable success during Carnival in 1796. In his subsequent opera, *L'eroismo ridicolo* (Naples, 1798), he was helped by Piccinni's practical advice. When the Neapolitan court fled to Palermo before the French invasion, Spontini was engaged as maestro di cappella and wrote 3 operas in quick succession, one for Naples and 2 for the Palermo court theater in 1800. He left Palermo soon afterward and proceeded to Rome (1801), Venice (1802), and Naples and Paris (1803). In Paris he brought out 2 French operas at the Théâtre-Italien, *La Petite Maison* (May 12, 1804) and *Julie, ou Le Pot de fleurs* (March 12, 1805), in sedulous imitation of the Parisian light opera; but the attempt failed completely. Fortunately for Spontini, he met the poet Etienne de Jouy, a writer of superior accomplishments, who influenced him to change his style. The result was the one-act opera *Milton,* produced at the Théâtre Feydeau on Nov. 27, 1804. Its music showed greater expressiveness and a finer taste than Spontini's preceding works. The next libretto offered by Etienne de Jouy to Spontini (after it was rejected by Boieldieu and Méhul) was *La Vestale.* Spontini worked on the score for 3 years, repeatedly revising and rewriting in his desire to attain his best, and the final product became his masterpiece. In the meantime, the Empress Josephine had appointed him her "compositeur particulier," and her appreciation of Spontini increased after the production of his patriotic cantata *L'Eccelsa gara,* celebrating the victory of Austerlitz. Her powerful patronage secured a hearing for *La Vestale,* which was brought out at the Académie Impériale (Grand Opéra), despite virulent open and secret opposition on the part of influential musicians, on Dec. 15, 1807, and won triumphant success. Not only did the public receive it with acclamation; by a unanimous verdict of the judges, Méhul, Gossec, and Grétry, the prize offered by Napoleon for the best dramatic work was awarded to Spontini. Shortly after the equal success of his grand opera *Fernand Cortez* (Nov. 28, 1809), Spontini married the daughter of Jean-Baptiste Erard, and in 1810 became director of the Italian Opera, in which capacity he staged Mozart's *Don Giovanni* in its original form for the first time in Paris. He was dismissed in 1812, on charges of financial irregularity, but in 1814 Louis XVIII appointed him court composer, Spontini having refused reinstatement as operatic director in favor of Catalani. He now wrote stage pieces in glorification of the Restoration: *Pélage, ou Le Roi et la paix* (Aug. 23, 1814); *Les Dieux rivaux* (June 21, 1816); this was followed by *Olympie* (Paris Opéra, Dec. 22, 1819). He then accepted the appointment, by King Friedrich Wilhelm III, of court composer and general music director at Berlin; made his debut there, in the spring of 1820, with his opera *Fernand Cortez,* fairly electrifying his audiences, although, like *Julie, Milton,* and *La Vestale,* it had been heard before in Berlin. Here Spontini's remarkable ability as a conductor had freest scope; besides repeating his earlier works, he wrote for Berlin the festival play *Lalla Rookh* (1821), remodeled as the opera *Nurmahal, oder Das Rosenfest von Kaschmir* (Berlin, May 27, 1822); *Alcidor* (Berlin, May 23, 1825); and *Agnes von Hohenstaufen* (Berlin, June 12, 1829); none of these, however, found favor in other German cities. In spite of his success, and the King's continued favor, Spontini's position in Berlin gradually grew untenable; he had been placed on an equality with the Intendant of the Royal Theater, and there were frequent misunderstandings and sharp clashes of authority, not mitigated by Spontini's jealousies and dislikes, his overweening self-conceit, and his despotic temper. Partly through intrigue, partly by reason of his own lack of self-control, he narrowly escaped imprisonment for *lèse-majesté,* and was finally driven out of the theater by the hostile demonstrations of the audience. He retired in 1841, retaining his titles and full pay, but with his prestige and popularity greatly impaired. Thereafter he was inactive as a composer. He returned to Paris, but met with hostility from the director of the Opéra there. In 1844 he conducted a performance (prepared by Wagner) of *La Vestale* at Dresden. Finally, shattered in health, he retired to his native place and devoted his time to public charities. He was a knight of the Prussian "Ordre pour le Mérite," a member of the Berlin Akademie (1833) and the French Institut (1839), and received from Halle Univ. the degree of Dr.Phil.; in 1844 the Pope gave him the rank and title of "Conte de Sant' Andrea."

BIBLIOGRAPHY: L. de Loménie, *M. Spontini, par un homme de rien* (Paris, 1841); E.M. Oettinger, *Spontini* (Leipzig, 1843); I. Montanari, *Elogio* (Ancona, 1851); Raoul-Rochette, *Notice historique sur la vie et les ouvrages de M. Spontini* (Paris, 1852); C. Robert, *G.L.P. Spontini* (Berlin, 1883); Ph. Spitta, "Spontini in Berlin," in *Zur Musik* (1892); W. Altmann, "Spontini an der Berliner Oper," *Sammelbände der Internationalen Musik-Gesellschaft* (1903); E. Prout, "Spontini's *La Vestale*," *Monthly Musical Record*, 35 (1905); R. Wagner, "Erinnerungen an Spontini," in his *Gesammelte Schriften*, vol. V; A. Pougin, "Les Dernières Années de Spontini," *Rivista Musicale Italiana*, XXXIX (1922); C. Radicotti, *Spontini a Berlino* (Ancona, 1925); C. Bouvet, *Spontini* (Paris, 1930); K. Schubert, *Spontinis italienische Schule* (Strasbourg, 1932); A. Ghislanzoni, *G. Spontini* (Rome, 1951); P. Fragapane, *G. Spontini* (Bologna, 1954); *Atti del primo congresso internazionale di studi Spontiniani 1951* (Fabriano, 1954); F. Schlitzer, *Frammenti biografici di G. Spontini* (Siena, 1955); A. Belardinelli, ed., *Documenti spontiniani inediti* (2 vols., Florence, 1955); letters of Spontini publ. by Radiciotti and Pfeiffer in *Note d'archivio* (1932).

Spoorenberg, Erna, Dutch soprano; b. Djakarta, Indonesia, April 11, 1926. She studied in Hilversum and Amsterdam; made her debut in an appearance with Radio Hilversum in 1947. In 1951–52 she sang with the Vienna State Opera; in 1958 became a leading member of the Netherlands Opera in Amsterdam. She made occasional appearances at various European music centers, but principally was associated with the musical life of the Netherlands.

Sporck, Georges, French composer; b. Paris, April 9, 1870; d. there, Jan. 17, 1943. He studied with Guiraud and Dubois at the Paris Cons., and later with Vincent d'Indy; was Officer of Public Instruction; wrote a number of symph. works of a programmatic nature, often with regional color: *Symphonie vivaraise; Islande; Boabdil; Kermesse; Paysages normandes; Esquisses symphoniques; Préludes symphoniques; Méditation; Orientale;* etc.; Violin Sonata; piano pieces (*Etudes symphoniques, Sonatina*, etc.); 2 books of songs. He also publ. instructive editions of classical works (Bach, Mozart, Beethoven, Mendelssohn, Schumann, etc.).

Spratlan, Lewis, American composer; b. Miami, Sept. 5, 1940. He studied composition with Yehudi Wyner, Gunther Schuller, and Mel Powell at Yale Univ. (1958–65); taught at Bay Path Junior College (1965–67), and at Pa. State Univ. (1967–70), where he was director of the electronic music studio; in 1970 he became a member of the faculty of Amherst College. WORKS: Opera, *Dream* (1976–77); *Missa brevis* for Male Chorus and Instruments (1965); *Flange* for 14 Players (1965); *Unsleeping City* for Dancers, Oboe, Trumpet, Violin, and 3 Percussionists (1966); *Structures after Hart Crane* for Tenor, Piano, and Tape (1968); *Cantata Domino* for Male Chorus, Winds, and Tape (1969); *Moonsong* for Chorus, Flute, Piano, and 2 Percussionists (1969); Wind Quintet (1970); *Serenade* for 6 Instruments (1970); *Trope-Fantasy* for Oboe, English Horn, and Harpsichord (1970); *Summer Music* for Oboe, Horn, Violin, Cello, and Piano (1971); *Diary Music I* for Chamber Ensemble (1971); *Dance Suite* for Clarinet, Violin, Guitar, and Harpsichord (1973); *Night Songs* for Soprano, Tenor, and Orch. (1974); *Fantasy* for Piano and Chamber Ensemble (1974); *3 Ben Jonson Songs* for Soprano, Flute, Violin, and Cello (1975).

Springer, Alois, German conductor; b. Gross Olkowitz, Dec. 20, 1935. He studied violin and piano at the Hochschule für Musik in Frankfurt; took courses in conducting at the Wuppertal Cons. In 1956 he played violin in the Zürich Chamber Orch. and also served as assistant conductor there. He was subsequently engaged as concertmaster of the Municipal Orch. in Trier (1959); conducted in the summers of 1965 and 1966 in Tanglewood; also was engaged as Leonard Bernstein's assistant with the N.Y. Phil. (1967–68). He was a soloist in and assistant conductor of the Orch. of Radio Luxembourg (1965–69); from 1968 to 1975 acted as chief conductor of the Philharmonia Hungarica in Marl, West Germany; also made appearances as a guest conductor, mainly with radio orchs.

Springer, Hermann, German musicologist; b. Döbeln, May 9, 1872; d. Feb. 1945 (killed during the fighting near Landsberg, in East Germany). He studied philology and music history in Leipzig, Berlin, and Paris; obtained his Dr.Phil. in 1894 with the dissertation *Das altprovenzalische Klagelied* (publ. in 1895). He entered the Prussian Library Service in 1899, continuing in this position for nearly 40 years; was a member of various learned societies. He publ. *Beethoven und die Musikkritik* (Vienna, 1927); contributed musicographical papers to German and Austrian publications.

Springer, Max, German writer on music and composer; b. Schwendi, Württemberg, Dec. 19, 1877; d. Vienna, Jan. 20, 1954. He attended the Univ. in Prague, and studied music with Klička. In 1910 he was appointed prof. of Gregorian choral singing and organist in the section for church music of the State Academy at Klosterneuburg, near Vienna, and held this post until his retirement shortly before his death. He publ. *Die Kunst der Choralbegleitung* (1907; Eng. trans., 1908) and manuals on liturgical choral singing; *Graduale Romanum* in modern notation (1930); *Kontrapunkt* (Vienna, 1936). He composed 4 symphs. and a great deal of church music, including 8 masses.

Springsteen, Bruce, seeded American rock artist and songwriter; b. Freehold, N.J., Sept. 23, 1949. He sang and played guitar in honky-tonks in Newark and in Greenwich Village in N.Y. He began recording songs of personal discontent and societal alienation with such titles as *It's Hard to Be a Saint in the City.* He recruited several similarly dissident rock musicians to form the E-Street Band, and in 1975 produced the album *Born to Run,* which struck a sympathetic chord with disillusioned youth, and soon made Springsteen a cult figure. The title song received a certified gold award. His next release was *Darkness on the Edge of Town,* further exploiting the general malaise of American youth. In 1980 he produced his greatest hit, *The River,* an album that glorified, with bitter irony, the automobile as a symbol of the age, with titles such as *Stolen Car. Drive All Night* and *Wreck on the Highway.* Unlike his companions on the rock scene, Springsteen kept off drugs and seemed to lead a decent private life.

Spross, Charles Gilbert, American organist and composer; b. Poughkeepsie, N.Y., Jan. 6, 1874; d. there, Dec. 23, 1961. He studied piano with X. Scharwenka while the latter was in N.Y.; also studied organ with various teachers; for nearly 40 years was an organist at various churches in Poughkeepsie; Paterson, N.J.; N.Y.; etc.; was accompanist to celebrated singers (Fremstad, Schumann-Heink, Nordica, Emma Eames, etc.). He publ. about 250 songs; 5 sacred cantatas; a Violin Sonata; other chamber music. After his retirement in 1952, he lived in Poughkeepsie.

Spry, Walter, American pianist, pedagogue, and composer; b. Chicago, Feb. 27, 1868; d. Spartanburg, S.C., Sept. 25, 1953. He studied with Leschetizky in Vienna (1889–90), and at the Hochschule für Musik in Berlin (1890–93). In 1905 he established his own music school in Chicago; from 1917 to 1933 taught at the Columbia School of Music there, and from 1933 to his death, at the Converse College School of Music (Spartanburg, S.C.). He wrote mostly for piano; also composed songs.

Squarcialupi, Antonio, renowned Italian organist (called "Antonio degli Organi"); b. Florence, March 27, 1416; d. there, July 6, 1480. He was organist in Florence at Orsanmichele from 1431, and then at the church of Santa Maria del Fiore in the same city from 1432, remaining there until his death; he enjoyed the protection of Lorenzo the Magnificent. He was highly esteemed by Dufay (cf. F.X. Haberl, "Dufay," in the *Vierteljahrsschrift für Musikwissenschaft,* 1885; p. 436). Since none of his works has survived, only oblique reports on their excellence can be adduced, but his name was immortalized by the famous "Squarcialupi Codex," a collection of Florentine polyphonic music of the 14th century, preserved in the Biblioteca Medicea-Laurenziana in Florence (Cod. Pal. 87). The collection was edited by Johannes Wolf and publ. in 1955.

BIBLIOGRAPHY: Bianca Becherini, "Un canta in panca fiorentino; Antonio di Guido," *Rivista Musicale Italiana* (July–Dec. 1948); F.A. D'Accone, "Antonio Squarcialupi alla luce di documenti inediti," *Chigiana,* XXIII/3 (1966).

Squire, William Barclay, English musicologist; b. London, Oct. 16, 1855; d. there, Jan. 13, 1927. He received his education in Frankfurt, Germany, and at Pembroke College, Cambridge (B.A., 1879; M.A., 1902). In 1885 he was placed in charge of the printed music in the British Museum, retiring as Assistant Keeper in 1920; compiled catalogues of music for the British Museum (publ. in 1899 and 1912); also the catalogue of the King's Music Library (3 vols., 1927–29). He edited (with J.A. Fuller-Maitland) *The Fitzwilliam Virginal Book* (2 vols., London, 1899; reprint, N.Y., 1963); edited Byrd's masses, Purcell's music for harpsichord, and Elizabethan madrigals.

Squire, William Henry, English cellist and composer; b. Ross, Herefordshire, Aug. 8, 1871; d. London, March 17, 1963. His father was an amateur violinist, and he received his primary music education at home; then studied with Hubert Parry at the Royal College of Music; made his debut as a cellist in London on Feb. 12, 1891, and became a popular recitalist in England; wrote a Cello Concerto and many other cello pieces. He retired in 1941, and lived in London.

Šrámek, Vladimír, Slovak composer; b. Košice, March 10, 1923. He graduated from the Prague Cons.; was active in the music dept. of the National Museum (1953–63).

WORKS: Chamber opera, *Jezdci* (1955); Trio for 2 Violins and Viola (1957); *3 Serious Compositions* for Flute and Piano (1958); *Astronauts,* overture (1959); *Exercises* for Flute, Oboe, and Clarinet (1959); *Tempi* for String Quartet (1959); 2 wind quintets (1959, 1960); *Variabilité* for String Trio (1960); *Metamorphoses I–VII* for Variable Ensemble (1961–63); *Metra symmetrica* for Wind Quintet (1961); *Rondo* for 8 Winds (1961); *Smích (Laughter)* for Voice, Tape, Flute, Piano, and Percussion (1962); *Spectrum I–III,* musical theater (1963–65); *Die Grube,* solo pantomime, with Bass Clarinet, Guitar, and Percussion (1963); *Kobaltová květina (The Cobalt Flower),* television play for Soprano, Alto, Female Chorus, and Orch. (1964); *Kaleidoscope* for String Trio (1965); *Anticomposizione* for String Trio (1966); *Bericht über eine Katastrophe* for Chamber Ensemble (1966); *Anderer Bericht über eine Katastrophe* for Nonet (1969).

Srebotnjak, Alojz, Slovenian composer; b. Postojni, April 27, 1931. He studied composition with Škerjanc at the Ljubljana Music Academy (1953–58); also studied in Siena (1954–57), in Rome (1958–59), and in London (1960–61). He taught at the Pedagogical Academy of Ljubljana (1964–70), and later at the Ljubljana Academy of Music.

WORKS: *Fantasia notturna* for 3 Violins, Clarinet, and Harp (1956); *Music* for Strings (1956); *Vojne slike (Army Scenes)* for Voice, Viola, Piano, and Percussion (1956); *Pisma (Letters)* for Voice and Harp (1956); 3 violin sonatinas (1956, 1966, 1967); *Mati (Mother)*, cycle for Voice and Strings (1958); Sinfonietta (1958); *Preludes* for Harp (1960); *Invenzione variata* for Piano (1961); *Serenata* for Flute, Clarinet, and Bassoon (1961); *Ekstaza smrti (Ecstasy of Death)*, cantata (1961); *Monologues* for Flute, Oboe, Horn, Timpani, and Strings (1962); *6 Pieces* for Bassoon and Piano (1963); *Kraška suita* for Orch. (1964); *Micro-songs* for Soprano and 13 Instruments (1964); *Antifona* for Orch. (1964); *Episodes* for Orch. (1965); Harp Concerto (1970); choruses.

Srnka, Jiří, Czech composer; b. Písek, Aug. 19, 1907; d. Prague, Jan. 31, 1982. He took violin lessons at the Prague Cons. under A. Mařák and J. Feld (1922–24); then studied composition there with Otaker Šín (1924–28) and V. Novák (1928–32); had instruction in quarter-tone music with Alois Hába (1927–28, 1934–37). He was an assistant conductor and violinist with J. Ježek's Liberated Theater in Prague (1929–35); then became interested in film music; produced over 120 film scores. From 1950 to 1953 he taught classes in film music at the Academy of Musical Arts in Prague.
WORKS: For orch.: *Symphonic Fantasy* (1932); Violin Concerto (1957; Olomouc, Sept. 23, 1958); *Historical Pictures from the Písek Region* for Amateur String Orch. (1961); *Partita* for Violin and Chamber Orch. (1962); Piano Concerto (1968); Concerto for Flute, String Orch., and Piano (1974; Prague, March 8, 1975); *Nocturne* for Strings (1975); *Echo of Songs of the Prácheň Region* (1976); Sinfonietta (1977); *Mater Dolorosa* for Flute, Harp, and String Orch. (1977); *Lyrical Symphony* (1979). Chamber music: 2 string quartets (1928, 1936); Wind Quartet (1928); *Suite* for Violin and Piano (1929); String Quintet (1930); *3 Pieces* for Violin and Piano (1961); *Léto budiž pochváleno (Summer Be Thou Praised)* for String Quartet (1980); *Byl tichý letní večer (There Was a Quiet Summer Evening)* for String Quartet (1980); Nonet (1981). For piano: *Suite* (1933); *Fantasy* (1934); *2 Quarter-Tone Pieces* (1936); *3 Pieces* (1936); songs.

Šrom, Karel, Czech composer; b. Pilsen, Sept. 14, 1904. He studied composition with Jan Zelinka and Karel Hába (1919–25); from 1928 to 1945 wrote music criticism in Prague; then headed the music dept. of Czech Radio (1945–50).
WORKS: 2 symphs. (1930, 1951); *Plivník (The Gnome)*, scherzo for Orch. (1953); *Vzdech na bruslích (A Sigh on Skates)*, symph. allegretto (1957); *Hayaya*, orch. suite for adults and children (1961); Piano Concerto (1961); *Etudes* for Orch. (1970); Violin Sonata (1920); 3 string quartets (1923, 1941, 1966); *Scherzo Trio* for String Trio (1943); *Vynajitka (Fairytale)* for Nonet (1952); *Etudes* for Nonet (1959); Concertino for 2 Flutes, and String Quintet or String Orch. (1971); *Whiles,* piano trifles (1942); *7 Pieces* for Piano (1942); *Black Hour,* cycle for Piano (1965). He wrote a biography of Karel Ančerl

(Prague, 1968).

Stabile, Mariano, Italian baritone; b. Palermo, May 12, 1888; d. Milan, Jan. 11, 1968. He studied voice at the Santa Cecilia Academy in Rome, and made his debut in Palermo in 1909. For a number of seasons he sang in provincial opera houses in Italy. The turning point in his career came when he was engaged by Toscanini to sing Falstaff in Verdi's opera at La Scala (Dec. 26, 1921). He triumphed and the role became his major success; he sang it more than 1,000 times. He was also noted as an interpreter of the part of Rigoletto. He retired from the stage in 1960.

Stäblein, Bruno, German musicologist; b. Munich, May 5, 1895. He studied music theory with Beer-Walbrunn at the Munich Academy of Music and musicology with Adolf Sandberger and Theodor Kroyer at the Univ. of Munich; his Ph.D. dissertation of 1918 was *Musicque de Joye: Studien zur Instrumentalmusik des 16. Jahrhunderts.* He then was a theater conductor in Innsbruck, Coburg, and Regensburg, where he was also active as an adviser in musical studies. He was a prof. and chairman of the seminars in musicology at the Univ. of Erlangen (1956–63); in 1967 he was appointed director of the Society for Bavarian Music History; he edited the important collection *Monumenta Monodica Medii Aevi* (Kassel, 1956–70); contributed a number of informative articles on the music of the Middle Ages and the Renaissance; edited reprints of documentary materials pertaining to these epochs. A Festschrift in his honor, issued for his 70th birthday, contains a complete list of his publications (Kassel, 1967).

Stachowski, Marek, Polish composer; b. Piekary Śląskie, March 21, 1936. He studied piano composition with Penderecki at the State College of Music in Cracow (1963–66); then taught there and at the Jagiellonian Univ. in Cracow. His music is both constructivistically impressionistic and sonoristically coloristic.
WORKS: *Pieć zmysłów i rósa (5 Senses and the Rose)* for Voice, Flute, Horn, Trombone, and Marimbaphone (1964); *Chamber Music* for Flute, Harp, and Percussion (1965); 2 string quartets (1965, 1972); *Musica con una battuta del tam-tam (Music with One Stroke of Tam-tam)* for String Orch. and Tam-tam (1968); *Lines of Dylan Thomas* for 2 Choruses and Orch. (1967); *Sequenze concertanti* for Orch. (1968); *Neusis II* for 2 Choral Groups, Percussion, Cello, and Double Bass (1968); *Chant de l'espoir (Song of Hope)*, after Eluard, for Narrator, Soprano, Baritone, Mixed Chorus, Boys' Chorus, and Orch. (1969); *Irisation* for Orch. (1969–70; Graz, Austria, Oct. 23, 1970); *Audition* for Flute, Cello, and Piano (1970); *Words* for Soprano, Bass, Chorus, and Orch. (1971); *Solemn Music* for Orch. (1973; Warsaw, Sept. 27, 1974); *Extensions,* 3 pieces in sequence for One, 2, or 3 Performers on Piano (1971–74); *Thakurian Songs* for Chorus and Orch. (1974); *Poème sonore* for Orch. (1975; Mönchengladbach, Germany, June 24,

1976).

Stacy, Thomas, American English-horn player; b. Little Rock, Ark., Aug. 18, 1938. He studied at the Eastman School of Music in Rochester, N.Y., graduating in 1960; made his solo debut with the Minneapolis Symph. Orch. (now the Minnesota Orch.), with which he served as solo English-horn player; since 1972, has served the same role with the N.Y. Phil. He premiered 2 of the principal works for the instrument, the concertos by Skrowaczewski (Minneapolis, 1970) and Persichetti (N.Y., 1977).

Stade, Frederica. See **Von Stade, Frederica.**

Stade, Friedrich, German organist and writer on music; b. Arnstadt, Jan. 8, 1844; d. Leipzig, June 12, 1928. He studied in Leipzig with Riedel and Richter; served as church organist (1885–95); edited works by Bach; publ. *Vom Musikalisch-Schönen* (1870; 2nd ed., 1904), using the title of the celebrated treatise by Hanslick, but directed against Hanslick's ideas.

Stade, Heinrich Bernhard, German organist and composer; b. Ettischleben, near Arnstadt, May 2, 1816; d. Arnstadt, May 29, 1882. He was organist and town cantor at Arnstadt; restored the organ of St. Bonifaziuskirche, on which Bach had played (1703–7). He publ. *Der wohlvorbereitete Organist, Ein Präludien-, Choral- und Postludienbuch,* in 2 parts; other organ music.

Stade, Wilhelm, German organist and composer; b. Halle, Aug. 25, 1817; d. Altenburg, March 24, 1902. He studied with Fr. Schneider in Dessau; was court organist and conductor at Altenburg (1860–91). With Liliencron he edited *Die Lieder und Sprüche aus der letzten Zeit des Minnesangs* (1854). He composed the celebrated *Vor Jena,* which became a favorite student song; also wrote 2 symphs.; a Violin Sonata; 7 books of organ pieces; an attractive and unique *Kindersonate* for Piano, 4-hands; many sacred and secular choral works.

Staden, Johann, German organist and composer; b. Nuremberg, (baptized, July 2) 1581; d. there, of the plague, (buried, Nov. 15) 1634. He served as court organist at Bayreuth (1604), and then at Kulmbach (1605–10); in 1611 he settled in Nuremberg as church organist, first at the Spitalkirche (in 1616), then at S. Lorenz (until 1618), and at St. Sebald (from 1618). He publ. 4 vols. of *Harmoniae sacrae* (1616, 1621, 1628, 1632); 2 vols. of church music (1625-26; the 2nd vol. contains a brief treatise on the basso continuo); 4 vols. of *Haus-Musik* (1623–28; posthumous collected ed., 1648, containing sacred songs with instrumental accompaniment); *Musicalischer Freuden- und Andachtswecker* (1630); *Herzentrost-Musica* (1630); *Geistlicher Musik-Klang* (1633); 3 books of dance pieces (1618, 1625, and a posthumous ed., 1643); etc. Selected works by Staden were edited by E. Schmitz for the Denkmäler der Tonkunst in Bayern and by K. Sannwald for Nagel's *Musik-Archiv* (1936).

BIBLIOGRAPHY: R. Eitner, "Johann Staden: Eine Bio- und Bibliographie," *Monatshefte für Musikgeschichte,* XV (1883); W. Nagel, "Zur Biographie Johann Stadens und seiner Söhne," *Monatshefte für Musikgeschichte,* XXIX (1897).

Staden, Sigmund Theophilus, German organist and composer, son of **Johann Staden;** b. Kulmbach (baptized, Nov. 6), 1607; d. there (buried, July 30), 1655. As a youth he studied in Augsburg with the organist Jacob Paumann, and later in Berlin with the resident English player on the viola da gamba, Walter Rowe. In 1627 he went to Nuremberg, where he obtained the position of town piper; in 1634 succeeded his father as organist at the St. Lorenz Church. Staden wrote the earliest extant German opera, *Seelewig,* in an Italian manner; it was produced in Nuremberg in 1644. The text, and separately the music, for voices and thoroughbass, was publ. in Harsdörffer's *Frauenzimmer Gesprächspiele* (vol. IV, 1644); reprinted by Eitner in vol. XIII of *Monatshefte für Musik-Geschichte.* R. Schulz-Dornburg arranged the score for a production at Cologne in 1912. Staden edited Hans Leo Hassler's *Kirchengesänge* (1637), adding 11 songs by his father and 5 songs of his own.

BIBLIOGRAPHY: E. Schmitz, "Zur Bedeutung der Harsdörfferschen *Frauenzimmer-Gesprächspiele,*" in the "Liliencron-Festschrift" (Leipzig, 1910); P. Keller, *Stadens Oper "Seelewig"* (Diss., Univ. of Zürich, 1970).

Stader, Maria, Hungarian-born Swiss soprano; b. Budapest, Nov. 5, 1911. She studied voice with Keller in Karlsruhe, Durigo in Zürich, Lombardi in Milan, and T. Schnabel in N.Y. After a brief career as an opera singer, she settled in Zürich as a vioce teacher; also gave periodic master classes in the U.S. She publ. an instructive manual, *Wie Meister Üben* (Zürich, 1967; in Eng., *Learning with the Masters,* 1968).

Stadler, Anton, famous Austrian clarinet player; b. Bruck an der Leitha, June 28, 1753; d. Vienna, June 15, 1812. He is remembered chiefly for his friendship with Mozart; his name is attached to Mozart's so-called Stadler Quintet (K. 581); he was also helpful to Mozart in the composition of the Clarinet Concerto (K. 622). Stadler himself was a competent composer for clarinet and for the basset horn, on which he was a virtuoso. His brother, **Johann Stadler** (b. Vienna, May 6, 1775; d. there, May 2, 1804), was also a proficient clarinet player.

Stadler, Maximilian, Austrian organist and composer; b. Melk, Aug. 4, 1748; d. Vienna, Nov. 8, 1833. He was ordained a priest in the Benedictine Order in 1772; was abbot at Lilienfeld (1786–89), then at Kremsmünster (1789–91); was consistorial adviser to the bishop of Linz in 1791–96; settled in Vienna in 1796. He was a friend of Mozart, and took care of Mozart's MS of the Requiem, which he copied at Mozart's death. When the authenticity of the work was called into question by Gottfried Weber and others, Stadler publ. a pamphlet in its defense, *Verteidigung der Echtheit des Mozartschen Requiems* (Vienna, 1825; supplement, 1826). He was also a composer; publ. a cantata, *Die Frühlingsfeier;* much church music; sonatas for organ; songs. His oratorio *Die Befreiung von Jerusalem* (Vienna, 1811) enjoyed considerable success.

BIBLIOGRAPHY: H. Sabel, *Maximilian Stadlers weltliche Werke* (Cologne, 1940); H. Sabel, "Maximilian Stadler und W.A. Mozart," *Neues Mozart-Jahrbuch,* 3 (1943); K. Wagner, *Abbé Maximilian Stadler* (Kassel, 1974).

Stadlmair, Hans, Austrian conductor and composer; b. Neuhofen an der Krems, May 3, 1929. He received his musical training in Linz and Vienna; eventually settled in Munich. In 1956 he founded the Munich Chamber Orch., with which he traveled on numerous tours in Europe, the U.S., South America, Africa, and Asia. As a composer, he wrote mostly instrumental works, in a neo-Baroque manner, among them a Toccata for Strings and Harpsichord (1966), a Trumpet Concerto with Strings (1967), and *Sinfonia serena* for Strings (1970); he also wrote some choral pieces.

Stadtfeld, Alexandre, composer; b. Wiesbaden, April 27, 1826; d. Brussels, Nov. 4, 1853. He studied with Fétis at the Brussels Cons., winning the Belgian Prix de Rome in 1849. He composed the operas *Hamlet* (Darmstadt, 1857), *Abu Hassan, L'Illusion,* and *La Pedrina;* 4 symphs.; overtures; 2 concertinos for Piano and Orch.; String Quartet; Piano Trio; a Mass; a Te Deum; etc.

BIBLIOGRAPHY: M. Weber, *Alexandre Stadtfeld, Leben und Werk* (Bonn, 1969).

Staempfli, Edward, Swiss composer; b. Bern, Feb. 1, 1908. He studied composition with Jarnach in Cologne and Paul Dukas in Paris. He returned to Switzerland at the outbreak of war; in 1954 he went to Berlin. In his music he was influenced chiefly by the French School of composition; later he adopted the Schoenbergian method of composition with 12 tones.

WORKS: Operas: *Ein Traumspiel* (1943) and *Medea* (1954); 3 symphs. (1938, 1942, 1945); 4 concertante symphs.; ballets: *Choreographisches divertimento* (1945); *Prinzessin und der Schweinehirt* (1944); *Spannungen* (1962); oratorio, *Der Spiegel der Welt* (1950); cantata, *Nimmermehr* (*Nevermore;* 1955); 4 piano concertos (1932–63); 3 violin concertos (1936–66); *Ornamente* for 2 Flutes, Celesta, and Percussion (1960); 6 string quartets (1926–62); Quartet for Clarinet, Violin, Cello, and Harp (1965); Duo for Clarinet and Piano (1970); several choral works.

Stagno, Roberto (real name, **Vincenzo Andriolo**), Italian tenor; b. Palermo, Oct. 11, 1840; d. Genoa, April 26, 1897. He studied with Giuseppe Lamperti; sang all over Europe, and was a member of the staff of the Metropolitan Opera Co. in N.Y. during its first season (1883–84). His 2nd wife was the singer **Gemma Bellincioni,** whom he married in 1881; their daughter **Bianca Stagno-Bellincioni** (b. Budapest, Jan. 23, 1888) was also a singer.

Stahl, Richard, German-American composer; b. Elbing, Prussia, Oct. 19, 1858; d. New York, July 5, 1899. He emigrated to America in 1880; wrote an opera, *The Salem Witch,* which was publ. in Boston in 1883.

Stahl, Wilhelm, German organist and writer on music; b. Gross Schenkenberg (Lauenburg), April 10, 1872; d. Lübeck, July 5, 1953. He studied with Stiehl in Lübeck; was organist there at St. Matthew's Church (1896–1922) and at the Lübeck Cathedral (1922–39).

WRITINGS: *Die Lübecker Abendmusiken* (Lübeck, 1937); *Franz Tunder und Dietrich Buxtehude* (Leipzig, 1926); *Geschichte der Kirchenmusik in Lübeck* (Lübeck, 1931); *Dietrich Buxtehude* (Kassel, 1937); *Musikgeschichte Lübecks* (with J. Hennings, Kassel, 1951–52).

Stahlbeg, Fritz, German violinist and composer; b. Ketzin, June 7, 1877; d. Los Angeles, July 23, 1937. He studied in Stuttgart; emigrated to America in 1899, joining the Pittsburgh Symph. Orch. as a violinist; from 1908 was a member of the N.Y. Phil., and in 1912 was also assistant conductor. He went to Hollywood in 1929, and was in charge of the music dept. for Metro-Goldwyn-Mayer Pictures. He wrote 2 symphs.; a symph. suite, *Im Hochland;* violin pieces; songs.

Stählin, Jakob von, German music historian; b. Memmingen, May 10, 1709; d. St. Petersburg, July 6, 1785. He went to Russia in 1735 and remained there until his death. He publ. an important account, *Nachrichten von der Musik in Russland* (Leipzig, 1769–70), which is the prime source of information on Russian music of the 18th century.

Stahlman, Sylvia, American soprano; b. Nashville, March 5, 1933. She studied voice at the Juilliard School of Music in N.Y.; then went to Europe and pursued her budding career under a suitably Italianate pseudonym, **Giulia Bardi;** made her debut in Brussels in 1951. In 1956, under her own name, she joined the N.Y. City Opera; then sang at San Francisco (1958) and Chicago (1960). From 1954 until 1972 she was engaged as a guest artist with the municipal theaters in Frankfurt, West Germany.

Stainer, Jakob, Austrian manufacturer of violins; b. Absam, July 14, 1621; d. there, 1683. The son of poor peasants, he was a shepherd boy; as a youth he began making "Schwegelpfeifen" and other woodwind instruments; then was apprenticed to a lute maker in Innsbruck. He sold his instruments in his native Tyrol, but soon attracted the attention of the Vienna court, and from 1648 was in the service of Archduke Ferdinand Carl. In 1658 he was given the title of violin maker to the court. His fortunes suffered an adverse turn when, in 1669, he was accused of Lutheran leanings, and spent several months in prison; his mind became unbalanced and he died insane. His brother, **Markus Stainer,** made excellent violins and violas. The Stainer violins are highly prized, and differed greatly from Italian models (the oft-repeated assertions that Jakob Stainer worked in Italian shops are not substantiated); their shape created flute-like tones of great subtlety.

BIBLIOGRAPHY: S. Ruf, *Der Geigenmacher Jacobus Stainer von Absam im Tirol* (Innsbruck, 1872; 2nd ed., 1892); F. Lentner, *Jacob Stainers Lebenslauf im Lichte archivarischer Forschung* (Leipzig, 1898); E. Heron-Allen, "A Pilgrimage to the House of Jacob Stainer," *Musical Times* (Aug. 1900); Princesse A. de la Tour et Taxis, *Le Violon de Jakob Stainer* (Paris, 1910); W. Senn, *Jakob Stainer, der Geigenmacher zu Absam* (Innsbruck, 1951).

Stainer, Sir John, English organist and composer; b. London, June 6, 1840; d. Verona, March 31, 1901. He was a chorister at St. Paul's Cathedral in London (1847–56); played organ there and in other churches as a youth; studied theory with Charles Steggall; filled various positions as a church organist and teacher, and in 1872 was appointed organist of St. Paul's; failing eyesight compelled him to resign in 1888, in which year he was knighted. In 1889 he became a prof. at Oxford Univ., retaining this position until his death.

WORKS: Oratorios: *Gideon* (Oxford, 1865) and *The Crucifixion* (London, Feb. 24, 1887); cantatas: *The Daughter of Jairus* (Worcester, 1878) and *St. Mary Magdalene* (Gloucester, 1882); 4 church services; canticles, anthems, songs; publ. a treatise on harmony, another on the organ, *Dictionary of Musical Terms* (with W.A. Barrett; 1876; 4th ed., 1898), etc.; edited (with his daughter, **Cecile Stainer**) *Dufay and his Contemporaries* (1898; 50 selected compositions) and *Early Bodleian Music from about* A.D. *1185 to about* A.D. *1505* (3 vols., 1901); *The Music of the Bible* (London, 1879; revised by Francis W. Galpin, London, 1914; reprint, N.Y., 1970).

BIBLIOGRAPHY: F.G. Edwards, "John Stainer," *Musical Times* (1901); P. Carlton, *The Life and Influence of Sir John Stainer* (Diss., Univ. of East Anglia, 1976); idem, *John Stainer and the Musical Life of Victorian Britain* (Newton Abbot, 1984).

Stainlein, Comte Louis Charles Georges Corneille de, cellist and composer; b. Hungary, July 3, 1819; d. Angleur-lez-Liège, Belgium, Nov. 22, 1867. A talented cellist, he appeared with success in Germany and France; with Sivori, Ney, and others he gave concerts of chamber music in Paris.

WORKS: Violin Sonata; Piano Trio; 2 string quartets; String Quintet; String Sextet; pieces for cello and piano; male choruses; songs.

Stainov, Petko, Bulgarian composer; b. Kazanluk, Dec. 1, 1896; d. Sofia, June 25, 1977. Despite an almost complete loss of sight in infancy, he learned to play piano by ear; later took music theory lessons with Ernst Münch at the Dresden Cons. (1920–24); returned to Bulgaria in 1926 and taught piano at the State Inst. for the Blind in Sofia (1927–44). In 1967 he became director of the National Council of Amateur Art and Music.

WORKS: *Thracian Dances* for Orch. (1925–26); *Legend,* symph. poem (Sofia, Jan. 1, 1928); *Balkan,* concert overture (1936); 2 symphs. (1945, 1948); *Youth Concert Overture* (1952); a number of choruses.

BIBLIOGRAPHY: V. Krastev, *Petko Stainov* (Sofia, 1957).

Stair, Patty, American organist and composer; b. Cleveland, Nov. 12, 1869; d. there, April 26, 1926. She studied at the Cleveland Cons. (1882–93); filled several positions as organist in Cleveland; from 1902 taught at the Cleveland Cons. She wrote 2 light operas, *The Fair Brigade* and *Sweet Simplicity; Berceuse* for Violin and Piano; songs.

Stalvey, Dorrance, American clarinetist and composer; b. Georgetown, S.C., Aug. 21, 1930. He studied clarinet and general music subjects at the College of Music in Cincinnati (M.M., 1955). In composition he was wholly self-taught, and thanks to that developed an independent style marked by quaquaversal contrapuntal and harmonic techniques vivified by asymmetrical rhythms. He embraced a variegated career of teaching, composing, and management, while engaging in free-lance performances on the clarinet and saxophone. He lectured on music history, off and on, at various schools; was an assistant prof. in composition at the Immaculate Heart College in Los Angeles from 1972–77, and full prof. from 1977–80. In 1971 he assumed the post of artistic director of the Monday Evening Concerts in Los Angeles; also served as a radio commentator. He had numerous conducting engagements; received several awards from ASCAP and other musical organizations. His compositions had surprisingly frequent performances, and astonishingly good reviews from habitually fatigued critics for his special spatial effects in multifarious multimedia productions.

WORKS: Music for Jazz Group and Orch. (1955); String Trio (1960); Movements and Interludes for 7 Instruments (1964); *Celebration-Principium* for 2 Trumpets, 2 Trombones, and Percussion (1967); *Points-Lines-Circles* for Clarinet, Double Bass, Harp, Guitar, and Percussion (1968); *Conflicts* for Multimedia Ensemble (1970); *Togethers:* I for Guitar and Tape (1970); II for Percussion and Tape (1970); III for Clarinet and Tape (1970); *Celebration-Sequents* for Various Instruments: I (1973); II (1976); III (1978); IV (1980); *Agathlon* for Modern Dance and Instruments (1978); theatrical multi-lectures, jazz pieces, piano solos; composite compositions compounded of combinational composts of original numbers.

Stam, Henk, Dutch composer; b. Utrecht, Sept. 26, 1922. He studied instrumentation with Hendrik Andriessen and piano with Jan Wagenaar and André Jurres at the Utrecht Cons.; later studied musicology at Utrecht Univ. and composition with Fortner in Germany. He taught at the music school in Deventer (1948–54); was director at the music schools in Zeeland (1954–61) and Rotterdam (1962–73).

WORKS: 5 piano sonatinas (1943, 1946, 1946, 1947, 1955); *Rispetti* for Baritone and String Orch. (1944); 3 string quartets (1947, 1948, 1949); *Histoire de Barbar,* 8 pieces for Piano (1948); *Cassation, Divertissement satirique* for 2 Speakers, Chorus, Flute, Violin, Cello, and Percussion (1949); Violin Sonata (1950); Sonata for Solo Violin (1952); *Suite* for Violin and Piano (1953); *Ouverture Michiel de Ruyter* (1957); Sonata for Flute, Oboe, Bassoon, and Harpsichord (1959); *Serenade* for Solo Cello (1959); *5 Bagatelles* for Small Orch. (1960); Cello Sonata (1966); *Tropic* for Flute, Oboe, and Piano (1971); Flute Sonata (1972); *Klachte der Prinsesse van Oranjen* for Chorus and 3 Trumpets ad libitum (1973); choruses.

Stamaty, Camille-Marie, pianist; b. Rome, March 23, 1811; d. Paris, April 19, 1870. He was of Greek-French origin; his mother, a Frenchwoman, educated him after the death of his father in 1818, and took him to Paris, where he became a pupil of Kalkbrenner; in 1836 he went to Leipzig, where he studied with Mendelssohn. He returned to Paris the next year and remained there as a teacher; among his students were Saint-Saëns and Gottschalk. He publ. a number of didactic works: *Le Rhythme des doigts, Etudes progressives; Etudes concertantes; Esquisse; Etudes pittoresques; 6 études caractéristiques sur Obéron;* and 12 transcriptions entitled *Souvenir du Conservatoire;* also publ. 3 piano sonatas, a Piano Trio, a Piano Concerto, etc.

Stamitz, Anton (Thadäus Johann Nepomuk), Bohemian composer, son of **Johann Wenzel Anton Stamitz;** b. Deutsch-Brod (baptized, Nov. 27), 1750; place and date of death unknown to any degree of certainty, but probably in Paris, after Oct. 27, 1796. He was a member of the famous musical family of Bohemia; studied violin with his father; with his brother **Carl Stamitz** he went to Strasbourg, and from there to Paris c.1770; made his appearance in Paris playing with his brother at a Concert Spirituel (March 25, 1772). From 1782 to 1789 he was a member of the Royal Chapel Orch. in Versailles. Rodolphe Kreutzer was one of his pupils. He was exceptionally equipped as a composer of instrumental works; he wrote 15 symphs.; 54 quartets, trios, and duets for strings; at least 15 violin concertos; several viola concertos; and 5 piano concertos.

BIBLIOGRAPHY: M. Pincherle, *Feuillets d'histoire du violon* (Paris, 1927; pp. 110–17).

Stamitz, Carl (Philipp), Bohemian violinist and composer, son and pupil of **Johann Wenzel Anton Stamitz;** b. Mannheim (baptized, May 8), 1745; d. Jena, Nov. 9, 1801. He was trained by his father, and after his death received further instruction with Christian Cannabich, Ignaz Holzbauer, and Franz X. Richter. In 1762 he was engaged as violinist in the Electoral Orch. at Mannheim; in 1770, in company with his brother **Anton Stamitz,** he went to Strasbourg, and then to Paris; the brothers made their debut at the Concert Spirituel on March 25, 1772; as soon as Carl arrived in Paris he became concertmaster to the Duc de Noailles; at various times he played in Germany and Austria, and visited Russia. In 1794 he became Kapellmeister at Jena. He left an extraordinary number of works, but a large part of his MSS was lost after his death. The putative number of his symphs. is at least 80, among them 26 *Symphonies concertantes;* he also wrote some 50 concertos for various instruments, and chamber music. Hugo Riemann edited 2 symphs. in Denkmäler der Tonkunst in Bayern, 15 (8.ii), and chamber music in vols. 27 and 28 (15 and 16) of the same series; chamber music was edited by Altmann, C. Meyer, and Klengel; a "symphonie concertante," by K. Geiringer (Vienna, 1935); the Viola Concerto was edited by S. Beck (N.Y. Public Library, 1937).

BIBLIOGRAPHY: Fr. C. Kaiser, *Carl Stamitz* (Marburg, 1962; contains a thematic catalogue of orch. works).

Stamitz, Johann Wenzel Anton, Bohemian violinist and one of the creators of the modern style of instrumental music; b. Deutsch-Brod, June 19, 1717; d. Mannheim, March 27, 1757. He went to a Jesuit school in Iglau (1728–34); in 1741 he entered the service of the Margrave of Pfalz, Carl Philipp, and later of his successor, Carl Theodor (from 1743). His playing at the coronation of the Emperor Charles VII on Feb. 12, 1742, created a sensation, and Prince Carl Theodor, who in 1743 became Elector Palatine, engaged him as a chamber musician; the court journals reported on his virtuosity in extravagant terms, extolling his ability to perform his own concerto on several different instruments—violin, viola d'amore, violoncello, and contra-violon solo. In 1743 the Elector made him "first court violinist" in Mannheim; the next year he married Maria Antonia Lüneborn. So widespread was his fame that Baron Grimm publ. in Paris a satirical pamphlet, *Le Petit Prophète de Boehmisch-Broda,* ridiculing Stamitz's innovations. Stamitz made his mark in Paris, too, when La Poupelinière engaged him in 1754 as leader and composer for his Orch. de Passy. He appeared at the Concerts Spirituels, in which he produced a symph. with clarinets in the score, a bold innovation at the time. His musical reforms reached in several directions; he conducted the Mannheim Orch., making it the finest in Europe, principally because of the introduction of dynamic nuances, in contrast with the prevailing chiaroscuro of the time; Mozart admired its playing. He had numerous pupils who achieved fame, among them his own sons **Carl** and **Anton,** Cannabich, W. Cramer, and I. Fränzl. As an instrumental composer, he virtually created the Classical sonata form through the introduction of the contrasting elements into a single movement, represented in Classical music by the primary and secondary subjects, and with variety governing the development of the themes. This new type of thematic statement and development became the foundation of musical composition after Bach's time, cultivated by Stamitz's pupils, as well as others, among them Johann Christian Bach, Schobert, Boccherini, Dittersdorf, Eichner, and Gossec. His music was publ. in Paris, London, and Amsterdam during his lifetime. His works include 74 symphs.; violin concertos; sonatas for violin solo and for violin, with basso continuo. Of his works, 58 symphs., 10 orch. trios, and 17 violin concertos are extant. A selection from his symphs. was publ. by Hugo Riemann in Denkmäler der Tonkunst in Bayern (with an important introduction); in the same series there are found examples of Stamitz's chamber music. Two symphs. were edited by R. Sondheimer (Berlin, 1933); a symph. edited by H.T. David was publ. by the N.Y. Public Library (1937); 6 duos for Violin and Cello were brought out by W. Altmann and others.

BIBLIOGRAPHY: P. Gradenwitz, *Johann Stamitz: Das Leben* (Brno, 1936); idem, "The Symphonies of Johann Stamitz," *Music Review* (1940); idem, "The Stamitz Family: Some Errors, Omissions and Falsifications Corrected," *Notes* (Dec. 1949); Paul Nettl, *Der kleine "Prophète von Böhmisch-Broda"* (Esslingen, 1953); E.K. Wolf, *The Symphonies of Johann Stamitz: Authenticity, Chronology and Style* (Diss., N.Y. Univ., 1972; 3 vols.).

Standage, Simon, English violinist; b. High Wycombe, Buckinghamshire, Nov. 8, 1941. He studied at Bryanston School and Cambridge Univ.; subsequently took private lessons with Ivan Galamian in N.Y. (1967–69). Upon his return to England, he became an associate member of the London Symph. Orch. and sub-concertmaster of the English Chamber Orch. In 1973 he was appointed principal violin of the English Concert and concertmaster of the Richard Hickox Orch. and City of London Sinfonia. In 1981 he founded the Salomon String Quartet. In 1983 he was appointed teacher of baroque violin at the Royal Academy of Music.

Stanford, Sir Charles Villiers, eminent composer and pedagogue; b. Dublin, Sept. 30, 1852; d. London, March 29, 1924. Brought up in an intellectual atmosphere, he was a diligent student in his early youth; took organ lessons in Dublin with Robert Stewart; in 1862 was sent to London, where he studied piano with Ernst Pauer. In 1870 he entered Queen's College, Cambridge, as an organ student; in 1873 became organist at Trinity College there (resigned, 1892). For 2 years (1875–76) he studied composition with Reinecke in Leipzig, and in 1877 with Kiel in Berlin. He received his M.A. degree at Cambridge in 1877; honorary degrees of Mus.Doc. at Oxford (1883) and at Cambridge (1888). In 1883 he was appointed prof. of composition at the Royal College of Music and conductor of the orch. there; in 1887 he also became a prof. of music at Cambridge, holding both positions until his death; he was conductor of the Leeds Festivals from 1901 to 1910, and appeared as guest conductor of his own works in Paris, Berlin, Amsterdam, Brussels, etc.; was knighted in 1902. He

was an extremely able and industrious composer in a distinctly Romantic style, yet unmistakably national in musical materials, both Irish and English. His music, however, remains virtually unknown outside Great Britain.

WORKS: OPERAS: *The Veiled Prophet of Khorassan* (London, Feb. 6, 1881); *Savonarola* (Hamburg, April 18, 1884); *The Canterbury Pilgrims* (London, April 23, 1884); *Much Ado about Nothing* (London, May 30, 1901); *The Critic, or An Opera Rehearsed* (London, Jan. 14, 1916); *The Traveling Companion* (posthumous; premiere, Liverpool, April 30, 1925, by an amateur group; first professional perf., Bristol, Oct. 25, 1926). FOR ORCH.: 7 symphs.: No. 1 (1876); No. 2, *Elegiac* (1882); No. 3, *Irish* (London, May 17, 1887); No. 4 (Berlin, Jan. 14, 1889); No. 5, inspired by *L'Allegro* and *Il Penseroso* of Milton (1894); No. 6 (1905); No. 7 (1911); *5 Irish Rhapsodies* (1901–14); 2 sets of Irish dances; *Overture in the Style of Tragedy; Suite* for Violin and Orch. (Berlin, Jan. 14, 1889; Joachim, soloist); 2 violin concertos; 3 piano concertos; *Irish Concertino* for Violin, Cello, and Orch. CHAMBER AND PIANO MUSIC: 8 string quartets; Piano Quintet; 2 string quintets; 3 piano trios; 2 violin sonatas; 2 cello sonatas; Piano Sonata; 10 *Dances* for Piano; 24 preludes for Piano; *Ballade* for Piano. CHORAL WORKS: *Eden*, oratorio (1891); Mass (1892); 3 sets of Elizabethan pastorals; *6 Irish Folksongs; Songs of the Sea; Songs of the Fleet* (1910); a number of part-songs; *Ode to Discord,* musical caricature of modern composers (London, June 9, 1909); about 200 songs to Eng. words, and 12 songs to texts by Heine, in German. He ed. and arranged *Moore's Irish Melodies; Songs of Erin* (3 vols., 130 folk songs); *Songs of Old Ireland; Irish Songs and Ballads;* for the Irish Literary Society he ed. *The Complete Petrie Collection* (3 vols., 1902–5; 1,582 Irish airs).

WRITINGS: *Studies and Memories* (1908); *Musical Composition* (1911); *Pages from an Unwritten Diary* (1914); *A History of Music* (with Cecil Forsyth; 1916); *Interludes: Records and Reflections* (1922).

BIBLIOGRAPHY: *Musical Times* (Dec. 1898); R.A. Streatfeild, *Musiciens anglais contemporains* (Paris, 1913); J.F. Porte, *Sir Charles V. Stanford* (London, 1921); J.A. Fuller-Maitland, *The Music of Parry and Stanford* (Cambridge, 1934); H.P. Greene, *Charles Villiers Stanford* (London, 1935). A complete list of works is given by Frederick Hudson in *Music Review,* May 1976.

Stange, Hermann, German organist; b. Kiel, Dec. 19, 1835; d. there, June 22, 1914. He studied at the Leipzig Cons.; subsequently served as organist at Rossal College in England (1860–64); from 1878 was music director, and from 1887 a prof., at Kiel Univ., until his retirement in 1911.

Stange, Max, German singing teacher and composer, nephew of **Hermann Stange;** b. Ottensen, May 10, 1856; d. Berlin, Jan. 25, 1932. He was a prof. of singing at the Hochschule für Musik in Berlin. He composed *Jauchzet dem Herrn, alle Welt* for Baritone Solo, Chorus, and Orch.; *Nachtstück* for Orch.;

An die Heimat, overture; *Adagio* for Cello and Orch.; *Serenade* and *Nachtgebet* for String Orch.; *2 Romanzen* for String Orch.; many male choruses and songs.

Stankovich, Evgeny, Soviet composer; b. Sbaliava, in the Carpathian region of the Ukraine, Sept. 19, 1942. He studied composition at the Kiev Cons. with Liatoshinsky, graduating in 1970. In 1975 he joined the Communist Party. In his music he follows the doctrine of socialist realism, with an emphasis on Ukrainian folk motifs. He wrote 3 symphs.: *Sinfonia larga* for 15 String Instruments (1973); Symph. No. 2 (1975); Symph. No. 3, *I Commit Myself,* with Chorus (1976; his most popular work); Cello Concerto (1970); *Sinfonietta* (1971); Chamber Symph. (1973); cantata, *Lenin* (1980); numerous choruses and songs; chamber music; film scores.

Stanley, Albert Augustus, American organist and composer; b. Manville, R.I., May 25, 1851; d. Ann Arbor, Mich., May 19, 1932. He studied at the Leipzig Cons. with Reinecke, Richter, and others; returning to America in 1876, he served as a church organist in Providence; in 1888 was appointed director of the Univ. Musical Society at Ann Arbor. He classified the valuable collection of musical instruments given to the Univ. by F. Stearns in 1898, and compiled an extensive catalogue of it (publ. 1918 and 1921). He wrote a cantata, *The City of Freedom* (Boston, 1883); the symph. poems *The Awakening of the Soul* (1896) and *Altis* (1898); anthems; part-songs.

Stanley, John, English organist and composer; b. London, Jan. 17, 1712; d. there, May 19, 1786. Blind from early childhood, he studied organ with Maurice Greene, and soon was able to fill church positions; composed theater music, and publ. a number of instrumental works. In 1779 he succeeded Boyce as Master of the King's Band of Music. He enjoyed the friendship and esteem of Handel, after whose death he conducted performances of Handel's oratorios with J.C. Smith.
    WORKS: Oratorios: *Jephtha* (c.1751–52); *Zimri* (Covent Garden, March 12, 1760); *The Fall of Egypt* (Drury Lane, March 23, 1774); dramatic pastoral, *Arcadia* (for George III's wedding; London, Oct. 26, 1761); opera, *Teraminta;* incidental music; songs; etc.; also 8 solos for Flute, Violin, or Harpsichord; 6 concertos for Strings; 30 voluntaries for Organ; etc.
    BIBLIOGRAPHY: G. Finzi, "John Stanley," *Tempo* (Spring 1953); Mollie Sands, "The Problem of *Teraminta," Music & Letters* (1952); G. Williams, *The Life and Works of John Stanley (1712–86)* (Diss., Univ. of Reading, 1977).

Stapp, Olivia, American soprano; b. New York, May 30, 1940. She studied voice in N.Y.; subsequently appeared at the N.Y. City Opera, San Francisco Opera, Chicago Lyric Opera, Hamburg State Opera, and Vienna State Opera. She scored an excellent success in the role of Lady Macbeth in Verdi's opera at the Metropolitan Opera in N.Y. on Dec. 7, 1982. Her other roles were Norma, Tosca, Aida, Elektra,

and Turandot.

Starczewski, Felix, Polish composer; b. Warsaw, May 27, 1868; d. there, Nov. 29, 1945. He studied in Berlin and Paris; returning to Poland, he was engaged in various activities as a teacher, composer, and music critic. He wrote an opera in one act, *Taniec kwatów* (Warsaw, April 28, 1918); a Violin Sonata; songs.

Starer, Robert, American composer; b. Vienna, Jan. 8, 1924. He studied music in Vienna; after the Anschluss in 1938, went to Jerusalem and studied at the Palestine Cons. there (1938–43). After the war he emigrated to the U.S.; took courses at the Juilliard School of Music in N.Y. (1947–49), and in 1949 became a member of its staff; also taught at the N.Y. College of Music (1959–60) and the Jewish Theological Seminary (1962–63); in 1963 he was appointed prof. of music at Brooklyn College.
    WORKS: Operas: *The Intruder* (N.Y., Dec. 4, 1956); *Pantagleize* (N.Y., April 7, 1973); *The Last Lover* (Caramoor Festival, Katonah, N.Y., Aug. 2, 1975); *Apollonia* (1979); ballets: *The Dybbuk* (Berlin, 1960); *Samson Agonistes* (N.Y., 1961); *Phaedra* (N.Y., 1962); *The Lady of the House of Sleep* (N.Y., 1968); *Holy Jungle,* ballet for Martha Graham (N.Y., April 2, 1974); 3 symphs. (1950, 1951, 1969); 3 piano concertos (1947, 1953, 1972); *Concerto à tre* for Piano, Trumpet, Trombone, and Strings (1954); Concerto for Viola, Strings, and Percussion (Geneva, July 3, 1959); Concerto for Violin, Cello, and Orch. (Pittsburgh, Oct. 11, 1968); Violin Concerto (Boston, Oct. 16, 1981); String Quartet (1947); *5 Miniatures* for Woodwinds (1948); Trio for Clarinet, Cello, and Piano (1964); *Variants* for Violin and Piano (1963); *Profiles in Brass* for Brass Quartet (N.Y., May 20, 1974); 2 piano sonatas (1949, 1965); *Sketches in Color* for Piano (1963); *Fantasia concertante* for Piano, 4-hands (1959); *Evanescents* for Piano (1975); several cantatas on biblical subjects; songs. For a list of works see *Composers of the Americas,* vol. 18 (Washington, D.C., 1972).

Stark, Ludwig, German pianist; b. Munich, June 19, 1831; d. Stuttgart, March 22, 1884. He studied with Ignaz and Franz Lachner in Munich; in 1857 was co-founder of the Stuttgart Cons., where he taught singing and theory; with Lebert he edited the *Grosse Klavierschule* (revised by M. Pauer, 1904); brought out a singing method, *Deutsche Liederschule* (1861); also publ. the *Klassischer Hausschatz* (24 transcriptions for piano of movements of classical chamber music works). He wrote a number of sacred and secular choral pieces, piano music, songs, etc.; publ. *Kunst und Welt* (1844).

Stark, Robert, eminent German clarinetist; b. Klingenthal, Sept. 19, 1847; d. Würzburg, Oct. 29, 1922. He studied at the Dresden Cons.; began his career as an orch. player at Chemnitz; from 1873 to 1881 played the clarinet in Wiesbaden; then was a prof. at the Hochschule für Musik in Würzburg. He publ. valuable and practical pieces for his instrument: 3 concertos; *Romanze* for Clarinet and Orch.; also a *Ballade* for Trombone and Orch.; *Quintett concertante* for Flute, Oboe, Clarinet, Horn, and Bassoon; *Serenade* for Oboe and Piano; instructive works: *Die Kunst der Transposition auf der Klarinette, Grosse theoretisch-praktische Klarinett-Schule,* in 2 parts, followed by part III, *Die hohe Schule des Klarinett-Spieles* (24 virtuoso studies).

Starker, Janos, renowned Hungarian-American cellist and pedagogue; b. Budapest, July 5, 1924. He studied cello with Adolf Cziffer at the Budapest Academy of Music; began playing in public when he was 11 years old. After graduating, he served as first cellist of the Budapest Opera (1945–46), but decided to leave Hungary; he emigrated to the U.S. in 1948; then held the positions of first cellist in the Dallas Symph. Orch. (1948–49), the Metropolitan Opera Orch. (1949–53), and the Chicago Symph. Orch. (1953–58); subsequently he embarked upon a solo career. In 1958 he was appointed a prof. of music at the Indiana Univ. School of Music in Bloomington. As a soloist, he achieved renown in authentic performances of Bach's unaccompanied-cello suites; but he also devoted much attention to modern music; he promoted cello works of Kodály and gave first performances of cello compositions by Messiaen, Peter Mennin, Miklós Rozsa, and others. He publ. a book, *An Organized Method of String Playing.*
BIBLIOGRAPHY: David Ewen, *Musicians since 1900* (N.Y., 1978).

Starmer, William Wooding, English organist and expert on bells; b. Wellingborough, Nov. 4, 1866; d. Birmingham, Oct. 27, 1927. He studied at the Royal Academy of Music; in 1924 was appointed lecturer on campanology at Birmingham Univ. He publ. several informative papers on the subject of bells in the *Proceedings of the Musical Association.*

Starokadomsky, Mikhail, Russian composer; b. Brest-Litovsk, June 13, 1901; d. Moscow, April 24, 1954. He studied composition with Miaskovsky at the Moscow Cons., graduating in 1928. He remained in Moscow, where he became a prof. of orchestration. His works follow the traditional line of Russian nationalism, but several of his early orch. scores are purely neo-Classical, and in this respect parallel the European developments.
WORKS: Opera, *Sot* (1933); operettas: *3 Encounters* (1942); *The Gay Rooster* (1944); *The Sun Flower* (1947); Concerto for Orch. (Paris Festival of the International Society for Contemporary Music, June 22, 1937); Violin Concerto (Moscow, March 20, 1939); some chamber music; numerous songs for children, by which he is best known in Russia.

Starr, "Ringo" (real name, **Richard Starkey**), English drummer, member of the celebrated Liverpudlian vocal quartet The Beatles; b. Liverpool, July 7, 1940 (delivered by forceps on account of his enormous puerperal bulk). His nickname, "Ringo," originated from his ostentatious habit of wearing several rings on each of his fingers. As an adolescent he performed menial jobs as a messenger boy for British railways, a barman on a boat, etc. A sickly boy, he spent several years in hospitals to cure an effusion on the lung, but he played drums in ward bands. He spontaneously evolved a rhythmic technique of an overwhelming animal vitality. In 1962 Ringo Starr joined The Beatles; his association with them continued until the dissolution of the group in 1970. His histrionic ability in handling the drums became the most striking visual feature in the beat-lophonic ritual, contributing much to the mass frenzy that attended their shows wherever The Beatles went.
BIBLIOGRAPHY: Hunter Davies, *The Beatles,* "the authorized biography" (N.Y., 1968); Ned Rorem, "The Beatles," *N.Y. Review of Books* (Jan. 18, 1968); G. Geppert, *Songs der Beatles. Texte und Interpretationen* (2nd ed., Munich, 1968); E. Davies, "The Psychological Characteristics of Beatle Mania," *Journal of the History of Ideas* (April–June 1969); P. McCabe and R.D. Schonfeld, *Apple to the Core: The Unmaking of the Beatles* (N.Y., 1972); F. Seloron, *Les Beatles* (Paris, 1972); W. Mellers, *Twilight of the Gods: The Music of the Beatles* (N.Y., 1973).

Staryk, Steven, Canadian-American violinist of Ukrainian parentage; b. Toronto, April 28, 1932. He studied with 15 different teachers before and after enrolling in the Royal Cons. of Music in Toronto; at the age of 24 he became concertmaster of the Royal Phil. Orch. of London; then concertmaster of the Concertgebouw Orch. of Amsterdam (1960) and of the Chicago Symph. (1963–67); also taught at the Amsterdam Cons. As a soloist, he appeared all over Europe, Canada, the U.S., and Japan. In 1968–72 he was a prof. at the Oberlin College Cons. in Ohio; subsequently was active in Canada as a performer and teacher.

Starzer, Josef, Austrian composer; b. Vienna, 1726; d. there, April 22, 1787. He was a violinist in the court chapel at Vienna; from 1760 to 1770 he was court composer in St. Petersburg, where he produced 2 ballets: *Floras Sieg* and *L'Amore medico.* After his return to Vienna, he became very popular as a composer of ballets, of which he produced about 20; also wrote instrumental music. Two divertimentos by Starzer are reprinted in Denkmäler der Tonkunst in Österreich, 61 (31).
BIBLIOGRAPHY: L. Braun, "Die Balletkomposition von J. Starzer," *Studien zur Musikwissenschaft,* 13.

Stasny, Carl Richard, German pianist; b. Mainz, March 16, 1855; d. Boston, April 22, 1920. He studied with Brüll in Vienna, and later was a pupil of Liszt in Weimar (1879–81); while working as a piano teacher at the Hoch Cons. in Frankfurt, he made a special study of Schumann's works with Clara Schumann. In 1891 he settled in Boston, where he taught at the New England Cons. He publ. *Finger Training, Scales, Chords and Arpeggios.*

Stasny, Ludwig, popular Bohemian bandmaster; b. Prague, Feb. 26, 1823; d. Frankfurt, Oct. 30, 1883. He studied at the Prague Cons.; was bandmaster in the Austrian army; settled in Frankfurt in 1871. He produced 2 operas in Mainz: *Liane* (1851) and *Die beiden Grenadiere* (1879). He was noted for his popular dances (211 opus numbers) and for his potpourris from Wagner's music dramas.

Stasov, Vladimir, famous Russian writer on music; b. St. Petersburg, Jan. 14, 1824; d. there, Oct. 23, 1906. He attended a law school until 1843; in 1845 he became connected with the St. Petersburg Public Library; in 1872 was appointed director of the Dept. of Fine Arts, which post he held until his death. He played a very important role in the emergence of the Russian national school, and was to the end of his days an ardent promoter of Russian music. It was Stasov who first launched the expression "Moguchaya Kuchka" ("mighty little company," in an article publ. on May 24, 1867, in a St. Petersburg newspaper); although he did not specifically name the so-called "Five" (Balakirev, Borodin, Cui, Mussorgsky, and Rimsky-Korsakov), these composers became identified with the cause championed by Stasov. When young Glazunov appeared on the scene, Stasov declared him a natural heir to the Five. His numerous writings, including biographies of Glinka, Mussorgsky, and others, have the value of authenticity. Those publ. between 1847 and 1886 were reissued in book form in honor of his 70th birthday (3 vols., St. Petersburg, 1894); a 4th vol. was brought out in 1905, containing essays written between 1886 and 1904; among them, "Russian Music during the Last 25 Years" and "Art in the 19th Century" are particularly important. His collected works, including articles on art and other subjects, were publ. in Moscow in 1952. Some of his *Selected Essays on Music* were publ. in English (London, 1968).
BIBLIOGRAPHY: *To the Memory of Vladimir Stasov* (St. Petersburg, 1910); V.D. Komarova (his niece), *V. V. Stasov* (2 vols., St. Petersburg, 1927); T. Livanova, *Stasov and the Russian Classical Opera* (Moscow, 1957); A. Lebedev and A. Solodovnikov, *Vladimir Stasov* (Moscow, 1966).

Statkowski, Roman, Polish composer; b. Szczpiorna, Jan. 5, 1860; d. Warsaw, Nov. 12, 1925. He studied law at the Univ. of Warsaw, graduating in 1886. In 1886 he entered the St. Petersburg Cons. as a student of Soloviev (composition) and Rimsky-Korsakov (orchestration). In 1904 he returned to Warsaw. He wrote the operas *Filenis* (Warsaw, Sept. 14, 1904; won first prize at the International Opera Contest in London) and *Maria* (Warsaw, March 1, 1906); *Polonaise* for Orch.; *Fantasy* for Orch.; 6 string quartets. His style represents a blend of German and Russian influences.

Staudigl, Josef, Jr., baritone, son of **Josef Staudigl, Sr.;** b. Vienna, March 18, 1850; d. Karlsruhe, April 1916. He studied with Rokitansky at the Vienna Cons.; in 1884–86 was principal baritone at the Metropolitan Opera House, where he created the role of Pogner in the American premiere of *Die Meistersinger* (Jan. 4, 1886); then sang until his retirement in 1905 at various German theaters (Berlin, Hamburg, Bayreuth, etc.), often together with his wife, the contralto **Gisela Koppmayer,** whom he married in 1885. In the spring of 1898 they sang with the Damrosch-Ellis Opera Co. on an American tour.

Staudigl, Josef, Sr., Austrian bass; b. Wöllersdorf, April 14, 1807; d. insane at Michaelbeuerngrund, near Vienna, March 18, 1861. He gave up the study of medicine to join the chorus at the Vienna Court Opera, later becoming leading bass; then was at the Theater an der Wien (1845–48); from 1848 to 1854 was again at the court opera.

Stavenhagen, Bernhard, German pianist; b. Greiz, Nov. 24, 1862; d. Geneva, Dec. 25, 1914. He was one of the last pupils of Liszt, with whom he studied in 1885–86. After a tour as a pianist in Europe and the U.S., he became court conductor at Weimar in 1895; in 1898 he obtained a similar position in Munich. In 1907 he went to Geneva, where he conducted the municipal orch. He wrote 2 piano concertos and other piano works.

Stearns, Theodore, American composer; b. Berea, Ohio, June 10, 1880; d. Los Angeles, Nov. 1, 1935. He studied in Germany; returning to America, he conducted theater performances; in 1932 became a member of the faculty of the Univ. of Calif., Los Angeles. His opera-ballet, *Snowbird,* to his own libretto, was produced by the Chicago Civic Opera Co. on Jan. 13, 1923; he also wrote a lyric drama, *Atlantis* (1926), and a symph. poem, *Tiberio.*
BIBLIOGRAPHY: E.E. Hipsher, *American Opera and Its Composers* (Philadelphia, 1934; pp. 387–91).

Stebbins, George Waring, American organist and composer; b. Albion, N.Y., June 16, 1869; d. New York, Feb. 21, 1930. He received his early education from his father, the well-known evangelist George C. Stebbins (1846–1945); then studied organ with H.R. Shelley in N.Y. and with Guilmant in Paris. He held various posts as a church organist in Brooklyn and N.Y., and publ. a number of playable pieces for organ (*Wedding Song, A Song of Joy, Scherzando,* etc.), as well as anthems and hymns.

Steber, Eleanor, eminent American soprano; b. Wheeling, W.Va., July 17, 1916. She studied singing with her mother; then with William Whitney at the New England Cons. of Music in Boston and with Paul Althouse in N.Y. She won the Metropolitan Opera Auditions of the Air in 1940; made her debut with the Metropolitan Opera as Sophie in *Der Rosenkavalier* on Dec. 7, 1940, and remained with the company until 1962; altogether she appeared 286 times in N.Y. and 118 times on tour; she sang 28 leading roles in the extremely large repertoire. She performed brilliantly in the roles of Donna Anna in *Don Giovanni,* Pamina in *Die Zauberflöte,* and the

Countess in *Le nozze di Figaro,* as well as in other Mozart operas; her other roles were Violetta, Desdemona, Marguerite, Manon, Mimi, and Tosca; in Wagner's operas she sang Eva in *Die Meistersinger* and Elsa in *Lohengrin;* she also performed the challenging part of Marie in Alban Berg's opera *Wozzeck.* She sang the title role in the premiere of Samuel Barber's opera *Vanessa* on Jan. 15, 1958. After several years of absence from the Metropolitan Opera, she took part in the final gala performance in the old opera building on April 16, 1966. Her European engagements included appearances at Edinburgh (1947), Vienna (1953), and the Bayreuth Festival (1953). After partial retirement in 1962, she was head of the voice dept. at the Cleveland Inst. of Music (1963–72); from 1971 she taught at the Juilliard School of Music in N.Y. She established the Eleanor Steber Music Foundation in 1975 to assist young professional singers.

BIBLIOGRAPHY: David Ewen, *Musicians since 1900* (N.Y., 1978).

Stecker, Karel, Czech organist and writer on music; b. Kosmanos, Jan. 22, 1861; d. Mladá Boleslav, March 13, 1918. He studied law and philosophy in Prague; then entered the Organ School of Prague; in 1888 he became a lecturer in music history at Charles Univ., while being employed also as a church organist in Prague. He composed mostly sacred music and organ pieces; also publ. a history of music in the Czech language (2 vols., 1894, 1903), a treatise on musical form (1905), and an interesting essay on nonthematic improvisation (1903).

BIBLIOGRAPHY: C. Sychra, *Karel Stecker* (Prague, 1948).

Štědroň, Bohumír, Czech musicologist, brother of Vladimír Štědroň; b. Vyškov, Oct. 30, 1905; d. Brno, Nov. 24, 1982. He studied at the Univ. of Brno; then taught courses on music education at the Pedagogical Academy there (1931–39); in 1963 he was appointed prof. at the Univ. of Brno. He publ. a fundamental monograph on Janáček, *Dílo L. Janáčka,* in Czech and Eng. (Prague, 1959), and numerous informative articles dealing with various aspects of Czech music. A Festschrift was offered to him on the occasion of his 60th birthday, containing a list of his writings (1965).

Štědroň, Miloš, significant Czech composer; b. Brno, Feb. 9, 1942. He studied composition at the Janáček Academy of Music in Brno (1965–71).

WORKS: Chamber opera, *Aparát (The Apparatus),* after Kafka's *In the Penal Colony* (1967); a ballet, *Justina,* after de Sade (1969); *Meditation* for Solo Bass Clarinet (1963); *Via crucis* for Flute, Bass Clarinet, Piano, Harpsichord, and Percussion (1964); *Dyptich* for Bass Clarinet, Piano, Strings, and Percussion (1967); *Lai* for Bass Clarinet and Timpani (1967); *Utis II* for Bass Clarinet and Tape (1967); *Util II* for Bass Clarinet, Piano, and Tape (1968); *Moto balladico* for Orch. (1968); *O, Sancta Caecilia* for Double Bass and Tape (1968); *Musica ficta* for Wind Quintet (1968); *Duplum* for Bass

Clarinet and Double Bass (1968); *Free Landino Jazz* for Bass Clarinet and Piano (1968); *Agrafon* for Madrigal Choir, Renaissance Instruments, and Jazz Ensemble (1968); *Affeti graziosi* for Violin and Piano (1969); *Saluti musicali* for Bass Clarinet and Piano (1969); *4 Together (Everyman for Himself)* for Bass Clarinet, Piano, and Jazz Combo (1969); *Mourning Ceremony,* cantata for Chorus, Trumpet, Oboe, and Church Bell (1969; Czech Radio, Feb. 21, 1969); *Quiet Platform* for Orch. (1969); Vocal Symph. for Soprano, Bass-baritone, and Orch. (1969); *Verba,* cantata for Chorus and 2 Trumpets (1969); String Quartet (1970); Concerto for Double Bass and Strings (1971); *Jazz Moments* for Piano (1971); *To the Memory of Gershwin* for Piano and Jazz Orch. (1971); *Diagram* for Piano and Jazz Orch. (1971); *Affetti banalissimi* for Piano (1971); *Music for Ballet* for Chamber Orch. (1972); *Kolo (Wheel),* symph. in memory of Yugoslav partisans of World War II (1971–72); *Jazz trium vocum,* free jazz for Chorus and Jazz Ensemble (1972).

Štědroň, Vladimír, Czech composer, brother of Bohumír Štědroň; b. Vyškov, March 30, 1900; d. Brno, Dec. 12, 1982. He studied law in Prague; simultaneously took lessons in composition with Foerster, Novák, and Suk at the Prague Cons. (1919–23). He served for many years as a judge, but found time to compose. His music is couched in an unassuming style inspired by native folk songs.

WORKS: *Fidlovačka,* overture (1916); *Fantastic Scherzo* for Orch. (1920); 2 string quartets (1920, 1940–45); *Variation Fantasy* for String Quartet (1923); *Illusions,* symph. poem (1936); *Little Domestic Suite* for 2 Violins and Viola (1937); *Janka,* polka for Orch. (1962); *Moto balladico* for Orch. (1967); *Monologe* for Solo Flute (1967); *Monologe* for Solo Horn (1969).

Stefan, Paul (full name, **Paul Stefan Grünfeldt**), Czech writer on music; b. Brno, Nov. 25, 1879; d. New York, Nov. 12, 1943. He was educated at the Univ. of Vienna, where he studied music theory with Hermann Grädener. He was employed as a municipal functionary, and at the same time became associated with the modern group of musicians in Vienna; edited the progressive music periodical *Musikblätter des Anbruch,* and was a co-founder of the International Society for Contemporary Music in 1922. After the Anschluss he went to Switzerland, and later to Lisbon, eventually emigrating to the U.S. in 1941.

WRITINGS: *Gustav Mahler* (Munich, 1910; 7th ed., 1921; in Eng., N.Y., 1913); *Die Feindschaft gegen Wagner* (Regensburg, 1918); *Das neue Haus,* a history of the Vienna Opera (Vienna, 1919); *Neue Musik und Wien* (Vienna, 1921; also in Eng.); *Arnold Schönberg* (Vienna, 1924); *Franz Schubert* (Berlin, 1928); *Geschichte der Wiener Oper* (Vienna, 1932); *Arturo Toscanini* (Vienna, 1936; in Eng., N.Y., 1936; in Italian, Milan, 1937); *Bruno Walter* (Vienna, 1936). He brought out an abridged German trans. of Šourek's biography of Dvořák (Vienna, 1935; in Eng., N.Y., 1941); also various essays on specific works by composers.

Stefani, Jan, Bohemian-Polish composer and conductor; b. Prague, c.1746; d. Warsaw, Feb. 24, 1829. He was Kapellmeister to Count Kinsky and violinist in the orch. of the Vienna Opera. In Feb. 1779 he entered the service of Stanislaus Poniatowski in Warsaw, and was appointed conductor at the Warsaw Opera. He wrote several Polish operas, of which *Krakowiacy i Górale (The Cracovites and the Mountaineers)*, produced in Warsaw on March 1, 1794, was very successful, remaining in the repertoire for 65 years. Other operas (all produced in Warsaw) are *Król w kraju rozkoszy* (Feb. 3, 1787); *Wdzieczni paddani panu* (July 24, 1796); *Frozyna* (Feb. 21, 1806); *Rotmistrz Gorecki* (April 3, 1807). He also wrote a great number of polonaises.

Stefani, Józef, Polish composer and conductor, son of **Jan Stefani;** b. Warsaw, April 16, 1800; d. there, March 19, 1867. He was a pupil of his father and of Chopin's teacher, Elsner; conducted ballet at the Warsaw Opera, and wrote a number of light operas, which enjoyed a modicum of success during his lifetime: *Dawne czasy* (April 26, 1826); *Lekcja botaniki* (March 15, 1829); *Figle panien* (Aug. 6, 1832); *Talizman* (Dec. 7, 1849); *Zyd wieczny tulacz* (Jan. 1, 1850); *Piorun* (May 21, 1856); *Trwoga wieczorna* (posthumous, July 25, 1872). He also wrote church music, which was often performed in religious services in Poland.

Stefánsson, Fjölnir, Icelandic composer; b. Reykjavik, Oct. 9, 1930. He studied cello and took theory lessons with Jón Thórarinsson at the Reykjavik Music School, graduating in 1954; then went to England, where he studied composition with Mátyás Seiber (1954–58). Returning to Iceland, he taught at his alma mater (1958–68); in 1968 was appointed a member of the board of the Icelandic Music Information Center. He composed a Trio for Flute, Clarinet, and Bassoon (1951); Violin Sonata (1954); Duo for Oboe and Clarinet (1974); numerous arrangements of Icelandic folk songs for chorus.

Steffan, Joseph Anton, Austrian composer; b. Kopidlno, Bohemia, March 14, 1726; d. Vienna, April 12, 1797. A pupil of Wagenseil, he settled in Vienna, where he was a renowned teacher; among his pupils were the princesses Marie Antoinette (later Queen of France) and Caroline (later Queen of Naples). He wrote some church music and numerous works for piano (divertimentos, concertos, and sonatas). Steffan is historically important for his songs, *Sammlung deutscher Lieder* (4 books), which are among the best of that time. Specimens were publ. by M. Friedlaender in *Das deutsche Lied im 18. Jahrhundert* (1902); see also Denkmäler der Tonkunst in Österreich, 79 (42.ii).

Steffani, Abbate Agostino, Italian composer; b. Castelfranco Veneto, July 25, 1654; d. Frankfurt, Feb. 12, 1728. He began his musical career as a choirboy at Padua, where his beautiful soprano voice so charmed Count Tattenbach that the latter obtained permission to take him to the Electoral Court at Munich, where he was trained by Kerll in 1668–71; in 1672–74 he studied at Rome with E. Bernabei at the Elector's expense, and in 1674 was appointed court organist at Munich. In 1678–79 he visited Paris, where he made an advantageous study of Lully's music. He took Holy Orders in 1680 and was made titular Abbot of Lepsing in 1682. In 1681 he became director of the Elector's chamber music (together with G.A. Bernabei, his former teacher's son); in 1688 he became court Kapellmeister at Hannover. His services as a diplomat were also in demand; in 1696 he brought to a triumphant conclusion the delicate negotiations for the creation of a 9th Elector of Braunschweig, and was rewarded by an appointment as Bishop of Spiga (*in partibus*); from 1698 he was privy councillor and papal protonotary at Düsseldorf, though still holding his position as Kapellmeister at Hannover until 1711, when he joyfully relinquished it to Handel. Some works of the later epoch were produced under the name of his copyist, **Gregorio Piva.**
WORKS: Operas: Performed in Munich: *Marco Aurelio* (1680); *Solone* (1685); *Audacia e rispetto* (1685); *Servio Tullio* (1686); *Alarico* (1687); *Niobe* (1688); at Hannover: *Enrico detto il Leone* (Jan. 30, 1689); *La lotta d'Ercole con Acheloo* (1689); *La superbia d'Alessandro* (1690; revised in 1691 as *Il zelo di Leonato*); *Orlando generoso* (1691); *Le Rivali concordi, o Atlanta* (1693); *La Libertà contenta* (1693); *I Baccanali* (1695); *Il trionfo del fato, o Le glorie d' Enea* (1695; given at Braunschweig in 1716 as *Enea in Italia, o Didone*); *Briseide* (1696); at Düsseldorf: *Arminio* (1707); *Tassilone* (1709); *Amor vien dal destino ossia Il turno Aricino* (1709). Other works: *Psalmodia vespertina a 8* (1674); *Sacer Janus Quadrifrons* (1685; motets *a* 3, with Continuo; any voice may be omitted at pleasure); *Sonate da camera a 2 violini, alto e continuo* (1679); *Duetti da camera a soprano e contralto con il basso continuo* (1683; historically important and intrinsically valuable); and the pamphlet *Quanta certezza habbia da' suoi principii la musica* (Amsterdam, 1695; German by Werckmeister, 1699, and Albrecht, 1760). In MS he left 85 chamber duets, with continuo (16 of these, along with 2 scherzi for one voice, with instruments, and 2 church cantatas, were publ. by A. Einstein and A. Sandberger in Denkmäler der Tonkunst in Bayern, 11 [6.ii]); a chamber cantata for Soprano and Continuo (publ. by T.W. Werner in *Zeitschrift für Musikwissenschaft,* I/8); a famous Stabat Mater for 6 Voices and 2 Violins, 3 Violas, Cello, and Continuo (Organ); also 4 vols. of short cantatas and arias. H. Riemann publ. *Alarico* (complete score; also a full bibliography of all Steffani's operas) in Denkmäler der Tonkunst in Bayern, 21 (11.ii); selections from other operas in vol. 23 (12.ii).
BIBLIOGRAPHY: *Memoirs of the Life of A. S.* (authorship attributed to John Hawkins; London, 18th century); F.M. Rudhart, *Geschichte der Oper am Hofe zu München* (Freising, 1865); G. Fischer, *Musik in Hannover* (2nd ed., Hannover, 1902); A. Neisser, *Servio Tullio von A. S.* (Diss., Univ. of Leip-

zig, 1902); A. Untersteiner, "A. S.," *Rivista Musicale Italiana,* 14 (1907); P. Hiltebrandt, *Preussen und die römische Kurie* (Berlin, 1910; vol. I contains material concerning S.); H. Riemann, "A. S. als Opernkomponist," in Denkmäler der Tonkunst in Bayern, 23 (12.ii; 1912); R. de Rensis, "A. S.," *Musica d'Oggi* (1921); T.W. Werner, "A. S.s Operntheater in Hannover," *Archive für Musikforschung* (1938); A. Einstein, in *Kirchenmusikalisches Jahrbuch,* 23 (1910), in *Neue Musik-Zeitung* (1928), and in *Zeitschrift der Internationalen Musik-Gesellschaft,* X/6; J. Loschelder, "Aus Düsseldorfs italienischer Zeit," in K.G. Fellerer, ed., *Beiträge zur Musikgeschichte der Stadt Düsseldorf* (Cologne, 1952); P. Keppler, "Agostino Steffani's Hannover Operas and a Rediscovered Catalogue," in H.S. Powers, *Studies in Music History* (Princeton, N.J., 1968).

Steffek, Hanny, Austrian soprano; b. Biala, Galicia, Dec. 12, 1927. She studied at the Vienna Academy of Music and at the Salzburg Mozarteum made her operatic debut in Wiesbaden in 1951; then sang in Graz, Frankfurt, and Munich; made guest appearances with the Vienna State Opera, the Salzburg Festival, and Covent Garden in London, etc. A fine interpreter of roles in Mozart's operas, she also excelled in Viennese operetta.

Steffen, Wolfgang, German composer; b. Neuhaldensleben, April 28, 1923. He studied at the Cons. in Berlin (1946–49) and with Tiessen at the Hochschule für Musik there (1949–53); after graduation, he devoted himself principally to the promotion of new music.

WORKS: *Serenade* for Flute and String Orch. (1948); Sinfonietta for String Orch. (1949); *Dance Impressions I* for Piano and Orch. (1950) and *II* for Piano, Percussion, and String Orch. (1970); *Intrada seria* for Orch. (1953); *Méditations de la nuit* for Small Orch. (1954); ballet, *Der göttliche Tänzer* (1954); *Aus dem Lebensbuch eines Tänzers,* ballet suite (1954); Piano Concerto (1955); Violin Concerto (1966); Harpsichord Concerto (1969); *Polychromie* for Piano and 10 Instruments (1970); *Klangsegmente* for Cymbal, Harp, Harpsichord, and Orch. (1973–74); *Sinfonia da camera* (1976); *Nachtwachen,* cantata for Chorus, Harp, Oboe, Clarinet, and String Quintet (1954); *3 Lieder* for Soprano and Orch. (1955); *Hermann-Hesse-Zyklus* for Chorus, Viola, Percussion, Piano, and Organ (1973); *Botschaft,* oratorio (1975); Trio for Oboe, Clarinet, and Bassoon (1947); *Theme with 8 Variations* for String Quartet (1948); Trio for Clarinet, Cello, and Piano (1959); *Diagram* for Viola or Cello, and Piano (1965); Wind Quintet (1966); *Jeu* for Violin and Piano (1967); Trio for Flute, Cello, and Piano (1971); *Triplum 72* for Flute, Piano, and Percussion (1972); *Tetraphonie* for Flute Ensemble (1974); *Trilogie 75* for Bandoneon, Flute, and Percussion (1975); *Music for Piano and 7 Players* (1975); for Piano: *Fantasy* (1947); Sonata (1955); *Reihenproportionen* (1961); *Notturno* for 4-hands (1968); *Les Spirales* (1969); choruses; songs.

Steggall, Charles, English organist and composer; b. London, June 3, 1826; d. there, June 7, 1905. He was a pupil of Sterndale Bennett at the Royal Academy of Music; became a prof. there in 1851. After 52 years of continued service, he resigned his professorship in 1903. He wrote anthems and other religious music; edited *Church Psalmody* (1848), *Hymns Ancient and Modern* (1889), etc. His son **Reginald Steggall** (b. London, April 17, 1867; d. there, Nov. 16, 1938) was also a pupil at the Royal Academy of Music, where he taught organ playing from 1895. He wrote a number of organ pieces; a Mass; a Symph.; orch. variations and overtures.

Steglich, Rudolf, German musicologist; b. Rats-Damnitz, Feb. 18, 1886; d. Scheinfeld, July 8, 1976. He studied musicology with Hugo Riemann in Leipzig (Dr.Phil., 1911). He was in the German army during World War I; then was active as music critic of the Hannover *Anzeiger* (1919–29); in 1929 was appointed to the faculty of the Univ. of Erlangen; retired from there in 1956. He was editor of the *Händel-Jahrbuch* (1928–33) and of the *Archiv für Musikforschung* (1936–40); edited works by Bach's sons, old German song collections, etc.

WRITINGS: *Die "Quaestiones in musica": Ein Choraltraktat des zentralen Mittelalters* (Leipzig, 1911); *Die elementare Dynamik des musikalischen Rhythmus* (Leipzig, 1930); *J.S. Bach* (Potsdam, 1935); *G.F. Händel: Leben und Werk* (Leipzig, 1939); *Wege zu Bach* (Regensburg, 1949); *Georg Friedrich Händel* (Wilhelmshaven, 1960); *Tanzrhythmus in der Musik J.S. Bachs* (Wolfenbüttel and Zürich, 1962); numerous essays.

Stegmayer, Ferdinand, Austrian conductor and composer; b. Vienna, Aug. 25, 1803; d. there, May 6, 1863. He was the son of **Matthaeus Stegmayer;** studied music with Seyfried; was chorus master at Linz and Vienna; then conductor of a German opera troupe in Paris (1829–30). After filling various engagements as a theater conductor in Leipzig, Bremen, and Prague, he settled in Vienna in 1848; was a teacher of singing at the Vienna Cons.; co-founded, with August Schmidt, the Vienna Singakademie (1858). He wrote church music, piano pieces, and songs.

Stegmayer, Matthaeus, Austrian singer and composer; b. Vienna, April 29, 1771; d. there, May 10, 1820. He was a chorister in the Dominican church in Vienna; then sang in small provincial theatrical companies, returning to Vienna in 1793; made his debut as a singer at Schikaneder's Freihaustheater auf der Wieden in 1796; in 1804 became chorus master at the new Theater an der Wien. He was the first to use the term "quodlibet" for theatrical light pieces; arranged Mozart's *Schauspieldirektor* (1814); composed an operetta, *Der Salzburger Hans und sein Sohn, der Hansl* (Vienna, Nov. 14, 1800), and contributed separate numbers to many others (mainly with Ignaz von Seyfried). He wrote the text for the quodlibet *Rochus Pumpernickel,* produced at the Theater an der Wien on Jan. 28, 1809, with music assembled by Seyfried from various works, including pieces by Haydn and Mozart. It was so successful that he followed it with a sequel, *Die Familie Pumpernickel* (Feb. 13, 1810). A complete list of his works as composer, joint composer, and librettist is found in Anton Bauer, *Opern und Operetten in Wien* (Vienna, 1955).

Stehle, Adelina, outstanding Austrian soprano; b. Graz, 1860; d. Milan, Dec. 24, 1945. She studied in Milan; made her debut in Broni in 1881 as Amina; then sang in Bologna, Florence, and Venice; in 1890 she joined La Scala in Milan, where she created soprano roles in *Falstaff* as Nanetta, in *Guglielmo Ratcliff* as Maria, and others; also sang in Berlin, Vienna, St. Petersburg, South America, and the U.S. After her marriage to the Italian tenor **Edoardo Garbin,** she appeared under the name of **Stehle Garbin.**

Stehle, J. Gustav Eduard, German organist and composer; b. Steinhausen, Feb. 17, 1839; d. St. Gall, Switzerland, June 21, 1915. He was organist in Rorschach (1869–74); in 1874 he settled in Switzerland as music director at the St. Gall Cathedral. His Cathedral choir of 140 voices was regarded as one of the finest in Europe. For 25 years he also was editor of the *Chorwächter.* He wrote a great deal of religious music: an oratorio, *Legende von der heiligen Cäcilia;* a cantata, *Lumen de Coelo* (to words by Pope Leo XIII); *Die Nonnen von Compiègne* for Double Chorus; *Frithjofs Heimkehr* for Solo, Male Quartet, and Mixed Chorus; *Die Heinzelmännchen,* humorous choral ballad for Double Chorus a cappella; a symph. poem for Organ, *Saul;* 438 preludes in the church modes; etc.
BIBLIOGRAPHY: A. Locher, *J.-G.-E. Stehlé* (Strasbourg, 1928).

Stehle, Sophie, German soprano; b. Hohenzollern-Sigmaringen, May 15, 1838; d. Schloss Harterode, near Hannover, Oct. 4, 1921. She was a prominent member of the Munich Opera, where she created the roles of Fricka in *Das Rheingold* (Sept. 22, 1869) and Brünnhilde in *Die Walküre* (June 26, 1870). She also distinguished herself in other Wagnerian parts (Elisabeth, Elsa, Eva).

Stehman, Jacques, Belgian composer; b. Brussels, July 8, 1912; d. Heist-aan-Zee, May 20, 1975. He studied piano with Del Pueyo, composition with Jean Absil, and orchestration with Paul Gilson at the Brussels Cons.; then taught harmony there. His music is cautiously modernistic, with engaging touches of obsolescent jazz.
WORKS: *Symphonie de poche* (1950); *Musique de mai* for Strings (1961); *Dialogues* for Harp and Small Orch. (1964); *Melos* for Mezzo-soprano, Flute, and Strings (1968); *Escapades* for Piano and String Orch. (1968); *Piano Concerto* (1965–72); *Lamento* for Cello and Piano (1947); *Burlesques en 6 formes* for Piano (1934); *Colloque* for 2 Pianos (1943); *3 rythmes* for 2 Pianos (1955); *Montmartre* for 2 Pianos (1975); songs.

Steibelt, Daniel, renowned German pianist and composer; b. Berlin, Oct. 22, 1765; d. St. Petersburg, Oct. 2, 1823. He studied with Kirnberger (piano and theory); publ. sonatas for Piano and Violin, as opp. 1 and 2 (Munich, 1788); then gave concerts in Germany, proceeding to Paris in 1790. There he found himself in strong competition with Ignaz Pleyel, but won out, and became a favorite piano teacher in Paris. His opera *Roméo et Juliette* was produced at the Théâtre Feydeau on Sept. 10, 1793, and, despite the revolutionary turmoil of the time, achieved excellent success. He left Paris in 1796, going to the Netherlands and then to London; became a soloist at Salomon's Concerts; played the solo part of his 3rd Piano Concerto (March 19, 1798), with its rousing finale *L'Orage, précédé d'un rondeau pastoral,* which as a piano solo became as popular as Koczwara's *Battle of Prague.* In London he produced an opera, *Albert and Adelaide* (Covent Garden, Dec. 11, 1798); returned to Germany in 1799; then proceeded to Vienna, where he challenged Beethoven to a contest of skill, but was easily bested. His next destination was Paris, where he produced Haydn's *Creation* (Dec. 24, 1800), with an orch. of 156 players, in an arrangement by Steibelt himself; Napoleon was present at that performance. A ballet by Steibelt, *Le Retour de Zéphire,* was produced at the Paris Opéra on March 3, 1802; he then went to London, where he staged 2 ballets, *Le Jugement du berger Paris* (May 24, 1804) and *La Belle Laitère* (Jan. 26, 1805). Returning once more to Paris, he wrote a festive intermezzo, *La Fête de Mars,* to celebrate Napoleon's victory at Austerlitz; it was produced at the Opéra on March 4, 1806. In the autumn of 1808 he gave concerts in Frankfurt and Dresden; in the spring of 1809 he went to Russia by way of Warsaw, Vilna, and Riga. In St. Petersburg he produced a new opera, *Cendrillon,* to a French libretto (Oct. 26, 1810), and 2 ballets. Although he held the position of chapel master at the court of Czar Alexander I, he did not prosper, and at his death a public subscription was undertaken to help his family. He publ. 5 piano concertos, 37 sonatas with Violin, 29 sonatas and sonatinas for Piano Solo, 15 rondos, 18 fantasias, etc. His *Méthode de Piano* had considerable vogue.
BIBLIOGRAPHY: G. Müller, *Daniel Steibelt, Sein Leben und seine Klavierwerke* (Strasbourg, 1933); K. Hagberg, *Daniel Steibelt's Cendrillon: A Critical Edition with Notes on Steibelt's Life and Works* (Diss., Eastman School of Music, 1975).

Steigleder, Johann Ulrich, German organist and composer; b. Schwäbisch-Hall, March 22, 1593; d. Stuttgart, Oct. 10, 1635. He was organist at Lindau (1613) and then at Stuttgart abbey church (1617), serving also as musician to the court of Württemberg (1627). Two of his publications survive: *Ricercar tabulatura, organis et organoedis* (1624) and *Tabulatur-Buch,* containing 40 variations for organ and other instruments upon the Lord's Prayer (Strasbourg, 1627); 2 variations are to be found in Ritter's *Geschichte des Orgelspiels im 14.–18. Jahrhundert* (1884; new ed. by Frotscher, 1933).

BIBLIOGRAPHY: E. Emsheimer, *J.U. Steigleder* (Diss., Univ. of Kassel, 1928).

Stein, Erwin, Austrian conductor and editor; b. Vienna, Nov. 7, 1885; d. London, July 19, 1958. He studied composition with Schoenberg in Vienna (1905–10) and became Schoenberg's early champion. From 1910 to 1914 he conducted various theater orchs. in Austria and Germany; returning to Vienna, he was a member, with Schoenberg, Berg, and Anton von Webern, of the famous Society for Musical Private Performances, which excluded music critics from attendance (1920–23). He then became an editor for Univeral Edition in Vienna, where he was instrumental in bringing out works by the composers of the modern Vienna School. He also conducted a tour with a Vienna group named Pierrot Lunaire Ensemble. After the Anschluss in 1938 he went to London and joined the music publishing firm of Boosey & Hawkes. He contributed a fundamental paper on Schoenberg's method of composition with 12 tones, "Neue Formprinzipien," publ. in *Anbruch* (1924). He publ. a selective collection of Schoenberg's letters (Mainz, 1958; in Eng., London, 1964); a collection of essays, *Orpheus in New Guises* (London, 1953); his theoretical monograph *Musik, Form und Darstellung* was publ. posthumously, first in Eng. as *Form and Performance* (London, 1962) and later in German (Munich, 1964).

Stein, Fritz, eminent German musicologist; b. Gerlachsheim, Baden, Dec. 17, 1879; d. Berlin, Nov. 14, 1961. He studied theology in Karlsruhe, then took courses in musicology with P. Wolfrum in Heidelberg; subsequently went to Leipzig, where he studied organ with Straube; also attended Riemann's lectures at the Univ. of Leipzig; obtained his Dr.Phil. from the Univ. of Heidelberg in 1910 with the dissertation *Zur Geschichte der Musik in Heidelberg* (publ. 1912; new ed., 1921, as *Geschichte des Musikwesens in Heidelberg bis zum Ende des 18. Jahrhunderts*). In 1913 he was appointed prof. of musicology at the Univ. of Jena; was in the German army during World War I and directed a male chorus for the troops at the front. He became a reader in musicology at Kiel Univ. in 1920, then a prof. from 1928–33; in 1933 he became director of the Hochschule für Musik in Berlin, holding this position to the end of the war in 1945. He achieved notoriety when he discovered in the library of the Univ. of Jena the parts of a symph. marked by an unknown copyist as a work by Beethoven. The symph. became famous as the "Jena Symphony" and was hailed by many as a genuine discovery; the score was publ. by Breitkopf & Härtel in 1911, and performances followed all over the world; Stein publ. his own exegesis of it as "Eine unbekannte Jugendsymphonie Beethovens?" in the *Sammelbände der Internationalen Musik-Gesellschaft* (1911). Doubts of its authenticity were raised, but it was not until 1957 that the American musicologist H.C. Robbins Landon succeeded in locating the original MS, proving that the "Jena Symphony" was in reality the work of Friedrich Witt (1770–1837). Stein publ. a

monograph on Max Reger (Potsdam, 1939) and *Max Reger: Sein Leben in Bildern* (a pictorial biography; Leipzig, 1941; 2nd ed., 1956); brought out a thematic catalogue of Reger's works (Leipzig, 1934; definitive ed., 1953); edited works by Johann Christian Bach, Telemann, Handel, Beethoven, etc.; contributed essays to numerous learned publications. A Festschrift was publ. in his honor on his 60th birthday (1939).

Stein, Horst, German conductor; b. Elberfeld, May 2, 1928. He studied at the Hochschule für Musik in Cologne, and at age 23 was engaged as a conductor at the Hamburg State Opera (1951–55); then was on the staff of the State Opera in Berlin (1955–61) and again at the Hamburg Opera (1961–63). From 1963 to 1970 he was music director and conductor at the National Theater in Mannheim; from 1972 to 1977 he was music director at the Hamburg State Opera; concurrently was Generalmusikdirektor of the Hamburg Phil. (1973–76). He also conducted at the Bayreuth Festival, and appeared as a guest conductor at the major European opera houses, in South America, and in the U.S.; in 1978 became chief conductor of the Orch. de la Suisse Romande in Geneva. He is regarded as one of the most efficient and competent opera conductors of his generation.

Stein, Johann Andreas, German inventor of the "German" (Viennese) piano action; b. Heidelsheim, Palatinate, May 6, 1728; d. Augsburg, Feb. 29, 1792. He was trained in the Strasbourg workshop of J.A. Silbermann (1748–49). In 1750 he settled in Augsburg, where he built the organ of the Barfüsserkirche; was appointed organist there in 1757. He spent a few months in Paris in 1758 before returning to Augsburg. He experimented with various types of keyboard instruments; invented a "polytoni-clavichordium" (1769), a "melodika" (1772), a "vis-à-vis Flügel" (1777), and a "Saitenharmonika" (1789). The business was carried on by his son, **Andreas Stein,** and his daughter, **Nanette Stein Streicher** (wife of the Austrian piano maker J.A. Streicher), who moved it to Vienna in 1802.

BIBLIOGRAPHY: F. Luib, *Biographische Skizze des J.A. Stein* (1886); T. Bolte, *Die Musikerfamilien Stein und Streicher* (Vienna, 1917); K.A. Fischer, *J.A. Stein* (Augsburg, 1932); Eva Hertz, *J.A. Stein: Ein Beitrag zur Geschichte des Klavierbaues* (Würzburg, 1937); Donald Boalch, *Makers of the Harpsichord and Clavichord, 1440 to 1840* (London, 1956; pp. 117–18).

Stein, Leon, American composer and conductor; b. Chicago, Sept. 18, 1910. He studied violin at the American Cons. in Chicago (1922–27), and theory at Crane Junior College in Chicago (1927–29); took private lessons in composition with Leo Sowerby, in orchestration with Eric DeLamarter, and in conducting under Frederick Stock and Hans Lange (1937–40); received his M.M. in 1935 and a Ph.D. in 1949 from De Paul School of Music. In 1931 he was appointed to the faculty of the De Paul School, and taught there for 45 years; served as director of its graduate division and chairman of the dept. of theory and composition (1948–66), and dean of the School of Music (1966–76); was head of the Inst. of Music of the College of Jewish Studies in Chicago (1952–57); also conducted the De Paul Univ. Community Orch. His music is academic, but not devoid of occasional modernities.

WORKS: 2 operas: *The Fisherman's Wife* (1954; St. Joseph, Mich., Jan. 10, 1955) and *Deirdre*, after Yeats (1956; perf. with a piano reduction, Chicago, May 18, 1957); 2 ballets for Piano: *Exodus* (1939; Chicago, Jan. 29, 1939) and *Doubt* (1940; Chicago, Jan. 21, 1940); *Prelude and Fugue* for Orch. (1935); *Passacaglia* for Orch. (1936); *Sinfonietta* for String Orch. (1938); Violin Concerto (1938–39; Chicago, Dec. 3, 1948); 4 symphs.: No. 1 (1940); No. 2 (1942); No. 3 (1950–51); No. 4 (1974); *3 Hassidic Dances* for Orch. (1940–41; Chicago, April 13, 1942); *Triptych on 3 Poems of Walt Whitman* for Orch. (1943; Chicago, March 29, 1949); *Great Lakes Suite* for Small Orch. (1943–44); *Rhapsody* for Solo Flute, Harp, and String Orch. (1954; Chicago, Nov. 8, 1955); *Adagio and Rondo Ebraico* for Orch. (1957); *Then Shall the Dust Return* for Orch. (1971); *Adagio and Dance* for Piano Trio (1931); Sonatina for 2 Violins (1931); Violin Sonata (1932); 5 string quartets (1933, 1962, 1964, 1965, 1967); *Adagio and Hassidic Dance* for Solo Flute (1935); Wind Quintet (1936); *12 Preludes* for Violin and Piano (1942–49); Trio for 3 Trumpets (1953); Quintet for Saxophone and String Quartet (1957); Sextet for Saxophone and Wind Quintet (1958); Quartet for Trombones (1960); 12 solo sonatas: one each for Violin (1960), for Flute (1968), and for Oboe, Clarinet, Bassoon, Horn, Trumpet, Trombone, Tuba, Viola, Cello, and Double Bass (1969–70); Trio for Violin, Saxophone or Viola, and Piano (1961); *Suite* for Saxophone Quartet (1962); Saxophone Sonata (1967); Trio for Clarinet, Saxophone, and Piano (1969); *Phantasy* for Solo Saxophone (1970); *Suite* for Wind Quintet (1970); Brass Quintet (1975); Quintet for Harp and String Quartet (1976–77). He publ. *Structure and Style* (Evanston, Ill., 1962) and *Anthology of Musical Forms* (Evanston, 1962).

Stein, Leonard, eminent American music scholar; b. Los Angeles, Dec. 1, 1916. He attended the Los Angeles City College (1933–36) and studied piano privately with Richard Buhlig (1936–39); enrolled in the class of composition and musical analysis with Arnold Schoenberg at the Univ. of Southern Calif. (1935–36) and at the Univ. of Calif. at Los Angeles (1936–42); in 1939–42 was Schoenberg's teaching assistant; received the degrees of B.A. (1939) and M.M. (1941) from the Univ. of Calif. at Los Angeles, and his D.M.A. from the Univ. of Southern Calif. (1965); was the recipient of a Guggenheim fellowship (1965–66). He held several teaching positions: at Occidental College (1946–48); Los Angeles City College (1948–60); Pomona College (1961–62); Univ. of Calif. at Los Angeles (1962–64); Claremont Graduate School (1963–67); Univ. of Calif. at San Diego (1966); Calif. State College at Dominguez Hills (1967–70); in 1970 was appointed member of the music faculty of the Calif. Inst. of the Arts; in 1975 became adjunct prof. in the School of Music at the Univ. of Southern Calif. In 1975 he was elected director of the Arnold Schoenberg Inst. of the Univ. of Southern Calif., Los Angeles, and editorial director of the *Journal of the Arnold Schoenberg Institute,* I/1 (Oct. 1976). He contributed a number of articles on the proper performance of piano works by Schoenberg; was a member of the editorial board of *Sämtliche Werke* (Mainz and Vienna, vol. 1, 1966); edited Schoenberg's *Nachtwandler* (1969); Piano Concerto (1972); *Ode to Napoleon Bonaparte* (1973); *Brettl-Lieder* (1974); edited and completed Schoenberg's pedagogical works: *Preliminary Exercises in Counterpoint* (1963); *Models for Beginners in Composition* (revision of the text, 1972); *Structural Functions of Harmony* (revision, 1969); *Style and Idea. Selected Writings of Arnold Schoenberg* (London, 1975; received the 1976 ASCAP award).

Stein, Richard Heinrich, German music theorist and composer; b. Halle, Feb. 28, 1882; d. Santa Brigida, Canary Islands, Aug. 11, 1942. He studied law and music; received his Dr.Phil. from the Univ. of Erlangen in 1911 with the thesis *Die psychologischen Grundlagen der Wundtschen Ethik.* From 1914 to 1919 he lived in Spain; from 1920 to 1932 taught musical subjects in Berlin. In 1933 he left Germany and went to the Canary Islands, where he remained until his death. He was a composer of experimental tendencies; his *2 Konzertstücke* for Cello and Piano, op. 26 (1906), was the first composition containing quarter-tones to be publ. In 1909 he wrote a brochure giving a detailed exposition of his quarter-tone system, and in 1914 he built a quarter-tone clarinet. He composed about 100 piano pieces and about 50 songs; *Scherzo fantastico* for Orch.; publ. the books *La música moderna* (Barcelona, 1918; in Spanish and German), *Grieg* (1921), and *Tschaikowsky* (1927).

Steinbach, Fritz, German conductor; b. Grünsfeld, June 17, 1855; d. Munich, Aug. 13, 1916. He studied in Leipzig, Vienna, and Karlsruhe. In 1880 he was appointed 2nd Kapellmeister in Mainz, where his interpretations of Beethoven and Brahms won praise; Brahms recommended him as successor to Hans von Bülow at Meiningen (1886); in 1902 he went to Cologne as director of the Cons. there; resigned in 1914 and settled in Munich.

BIBLIOGRAPHY: I. Fellinger, "Fritz Steinbach," in *Rheinischer Musiker,* IV (Cologne, 1966).

Steinbauer, Othmar, Austrian violinist and composer; b. Vienna, Nov. 6, 1895; d. Altenburg, Sept. 5, 1962. He studied violin at the Vienna Academy of Music; founded the Chamber Concert Society of Vienna, playing and conducting works of the modern Viennese School. He publ. a theoretical treatise, *Das Wesen der Tonalität* (Munich, 1928). In 1938 he founded the Musikschule der Stadt Wien. After 1945 he devoted himself mainly to manufacturing new instruments; constructed a violin specially adapted for easy performance by amateurs. His own music is quite conservative.

Steinberg, Maximilian, significant Russian composer and pedagogue; b. Vilna, July 4, 1883; d. Leningrad, Dec. 6, 1946. He studied at the St. Petersburg Cons. with Glazunov and Rimsky-Korsakov (whose daughter he married on June 17, 1908). In 1908 he was appointed teacher of theory and composition there. His early compositions reflected the influence of his teachers, but gradually he evolved a more personal style distinguished by rhapsodic eloquence and somewhat touched with procedures of French Impressionism. In 1934 he was appointed director of the Leningrad Cons., and maintained the high standards established before him by Rimsky-Korsakov and Glazunov. Among his pupils were Shostakovich, Shaporin, and other prominent composers of the Soviet period.

WORKS: Symph. No. 1 (1907); Symph. No. 2 (St. Petersburg, Nov. 27, 1909); *Metamorphoses,* ballet (2nd part perf. by Diaghilev, Paris, June 2, 1914); *La Princesse Maleine,* after Maeterlinck, for Orch. and Women's Chorus (1916); *Heaven and Earth,* dramatic poem for 6 Soloists and Orch. (1918); Symph. No. 3 (Leningrad, March 3, 1929, composer conducting); Symph. No. 4, subtitled *Turksib,* to celebrate the opening of the Turkestan-Siberian railroad (Leningrad, Dec. 2, 1933); *In Armenia,* symph. picture (Leningrad, Dec. 24, 1940); Violin Concerto (1946); 2 string quartets; etc. He also wrote a number of lyric songs and piano pieces; made several arrangements of Turkmenian songs for voice and orch.; also arranged for orch. a Concerto in D by C.P.E. Bach (1911) and a Cello Sonata by Gaillard (1924); ed. Rimsky-Korsakov's *Foundations of Orchestration* (2 vols., St. Petersburg, 1913).

BIBLIOGRAPHY: A.N. Rimsky-Korsakov, *Maximilian Steinberg* (Moscow, 1928; in Russian and German).

Steinberg, Michael, American music critic; b. Breslau, Oct. 4, 1928. He went to England in 1939 and to the U.S. in 1943; studied music at Princeton Univ. (A.B., 1949; M.F.A., 1951); then was in Italy (1952–54). Returning to America, he taught music courses at Princeton Univ., Hunter College, Manhattan School of Music, Univ. of Saskatchewan, Smith College, Brandeis Univ., Boston Univ., and (from 1968) the New England Cons. of Music. In 1964 he was appointed music critic of the Boston *Globe.* His criticisms, utterly disrespectful of the most sacrosanct musical personalities, aroused periodic outbursts of indignation among outraged artists, aggrieved managers, and chagrined promoters. In 1969 several Boston Symph. Orch. players petitioned the management to banish him from their concerts. Then, in a spectacular peripeteia, he left the Boston *Globe* in 1976 and was appointed director of publications for the Boston Symph.; remained there until 1979, when he assumed the position of artistic adviser and publications director to the San Francisco Symph.

Steinberg, William (Hans Wilhelm), eminent German-American conductor; b. Cologne, Aug. 1, 1899; d. New York, May 16, 1978. He studied piano and violin at home; conducted his own setting for chorus and orch. of a poem from Ovid's *Metamorphoses* in school at the age of 13; then took lessons in conducting with Hermann Abendroth, and studied piano with Lazzaro Uzielli and music theory with Franz Bölsche at the Cons. of Cologne, graduating in 1920, with the Wüllner Prize for conducting; subsequently became assistant to Otto Klemperer at the Cologne Opera, and in 1924 became principal conductor. In 1925 he was engaged as conductor of the German Theater in Prague; in 1929 he was appointed Generalmusikdirektor at the Frankfurt Opera, where he brought out several modern operas, including Alban Berg's *Wozzeck.* With the advent of the Nazi regime in 1933, he was removed from his position and became orch. conductor for the Jewish Culture League, restricted to Jewish audiences. In 1936 he left Germany and became one of the conductors of the Palestine Orch., which he rehearsed and prepared for Toscanini, who subsequently engaged him as an assistant conductor of the NBC Symph. in N.Y. in 1938. His career as an orch. conductor was then connected with major American orchs. He became an American citizen in 1944. He was conductor and music director of the Buffalo Phil. (1945–52); in 1952 he was appointed principal conductor of the Pittsburgh Symph. Orch.; concurrently, he served as music director (for 2 seasons) of the London Phil. (1958–60); then was music director and conductor of the Boston Symph. (1969–72), while continuing at his post with the Pittsburgh Symph., retiring in 1976. Also conducted numerous guest appearances with major American and European orchs., acquiring a reputation as one of the most competent modern conductors; his performances were marked by impeccable taste and fidelity to the music; in this respect he was a follower of the Toscanini tradition.

BIBLIOGRAPHY: Hope Stoddard, *Symphony Conductors of the U.S.A.* (N.Y., 1957; pp. 207–14).

Steinberg, Zeev, German-born Israeli violinist and composer; b. Düsseldorf, Nov. 27, 1918. In 1934 he emigrated to Palestine, where he studied viola and composition with Partos. In 1942 he joined the viola section of the Palestine Phil. in Tel Aviv; in 1957 became the violinist in the New Israeli String Quartet; in 1969–72 was a lecturer at the Tel Aviv Academy of Music. His own compositions present an agreeable blend of oriental melos, asymmetrical rhythms, and sharp atonal progressions in dissonant counterpoint.

WORKS: Sonata for 2 Violas (1955–56); 2 string quartets (1959, 1969); *6 Miniatures* for Cello and Piano (1961); *4 Bagatelles* for 2 Recorders (1962); 2 *concerti da camera:* No. 1 for Viola and String Orch. (1962) and No. 2 for Violin and 8 Instruments (1966); *Purim Variations* on a nursery song for Horn and String Trio (1963); *The Story of Rahab and the Spies,* biblical cantata (1969); *Festive Prologue* for Flute, Oboe, and String Trio (1969); *2 Songs without*

Words for Viola, String Quartet, and String Orch. (1970); *a little suite for a big flute* for Solo Bass Flute in C (1972); arrangements of works by Vivaldi, Bach, Schubert, and others.

Steiner, Emma, American composer and conductor; b. 1850; d. New York, Feb. 27, 1928. Her grandfather led the Maryland 16th Brigade, which won the battle of North Point (near Fort McHenry, Baltimore) on Sept. 13, 1814, enabling Francis Scott Key to finish the last stanza of *The Star-Spangled Banner.* She was a prolific composer, having written 7 light operas, plus ballets, overtures, and songs; purportedly she was also the first woman ever to receive payment for conducting. Conried, the manager of the Metropolitan Opera House, is said to have declared that he would have let her conduct a performance had he dared to put a woman armed with a baton in front of a totally male orch. According to unverifiable accounts, she conducted 6,000 performances of 50 different operas. She also organized an Emma R. Steiner Home for the Aged and Infirm Musicians at Bay Shore, Long Island. On Feb. 28, 1925, she conducted a concert at the Metropolitan Opera to commemorate the 50th anniversary of her first appearance as conductor. Her works, of different genres and light consistency, aggregate more than 200 opus numbers, most of them publ. by an *ad hoc* firm, MacDonald-Steiner.

Steiner, Max(imilian Raoul Walter), American composer of film music; b. Vienna, May 10, 1888; d. Hollywood, Dec. 28, 1971. He studied at the Vienna Cons. with Fuchs and Grädener, and also had some advice from Mahler. At the age of 14 he wrote an operetta. In 1904 he went to England; in 1911 proceeded to Paris. In 1914 he settled in the U.S.; after conducting musical shows in N.Y., he moved in 1929 to Hollywood, where he became one of the most successful film composers. His music offers a fulsome blend of lush harmonies artfully derived from both Tchaikovsky and Wagner, arranged in a manner marvelously suitable for the portrayal of psychological drama on the screen. Among his film scores, of which he wrote more than 150, are *King Kong* (1933), *The Charge of the Light Brigade* (1936), *Gone with the Wind* (1939), and *Treasure of Sierra Madre* (1948).

Steinert, Alexander Lang, American composer, conductor, and arranger; b. Boston, Sept. 21, 1900; d. New York, July 7, 1982. He was the son of a piano manufacturer; studied at Harvard Univ., graduating in 1922; then took private lessons in composition with Loeffler in Boston, and with Koechlin and Vincent d'Indy in Paris. He lived much of his time in Europe; was active as a conductor and arranger in Hollywood; for several years was a pianist with the Boston Symph. Orch. His music bears the imprint of the French modern school.
WORKS: For Orch.: *Nuit méridionale* (Boston, Oct. 15, 1926); *Leggenda sinfonica* (Rome, 1930); *Concerto sinfonico* for Piano and Orch. (Boston, Feb. 8, 1935, composer soloist); *Rhapsody* for Clari-

net and Orch. (1945); *The Nightingale and the Rose,* after Oscar Wilde, for Speaker and Orch. (Philadelphia, March 31, 1950); Violin Sonata; Piano Trio; piano pieces; songs.

Steingräber, Johann Georg, German piano maker, son of **Theodor Steingräber;** b. Berlin, Jan. 1, 1858; d. there, March 16, 1932. For several years he was in the U.S. and worked for Steinway & Sons in N.Y.; in 1907 he returned to Berlin. He made excellent harpsichords as well as pianos.

Steingräber, Theodor, German music publisher; b. Neustadt an der Orla, Jan. 25, 1830; d. Leipzig, April 5, 1904. He was the son of a piano manufacturer, and founded a music publishing firm bearing his name in Hannover in 1878; in 1890 it was moved to Leipzig. Under the pseudonym **Gustav Damm,** Steingräber publ. a piano method (1868). From 1903 to 1916 the firm was managed by Walter Friedel, and from 1916 to 1926 by Friedel's son-in-law Georg Heinrich. The firm was moved to Frankfurt in 1953, and to Offenbach in 1956.

Steingruber, Ilona, Austrian soprano; b. Vienna, Feb. 8, 1912; d. there, Dec. 10, 1962. She studied piano and voice; was on the staff of the Vienna Opera from 1948 to 1951. In 1946 she married the composer **Friedrich Wildgans.**

Steinhard, Erich, German-Bohemian musicologist; b. Prague, May 26, 1886; d. in a concentration camp in Lodz, Poland, c.1942 (was transported there on Oct. 26, 1941). He was a pupil of Knittl and Novák; studied musicology with J. Wolf, H. Kretzschmar, and M. Friedlaender in Berlin (Dr.Phil., Univ. of Prague, 1911, with a thesis on organum). He became librarian of the Univ. of Prague; from 1921 was editor of *Der Auftakt,* and from 1929, music critic for the *Prager Tageblatt.*
WRITINGS: *Andreas Hammerschmidt* (Prague, 1914); *Zur deutschen Musik in der Tschechoslowakischen Republik* (2nd part of V. Helfert's *Geschichte der Musik in der Tschechoslowakischen Republik;* Prague, 1936); *Musikgeschichte von der Urzeit zur Gegenwart* (with G. Černušák; Prague, 1936).

Steinhardt, Milton, American musicologist; b. Miami, Okla., Nov. 13, 1909. After preliminary study at the Univ. of Kansas he went to Europe; took courses at the Akademie der Tonkunst in Munich, and had violin lessons with Maurice Hewitt in Paris. Returning to the U.S., he enrolled in the Eastman School of Music in Rochester, N.Y. (B.M., 1936; M.M., 1937); then attended courses of Otto Kinkeldey at Cornell Univ. and Curt Sachs and Gustave Reese at N.Y. Univ. (Ph.D., 1950). He was a lecturer at Michigan State Univ. (1948–50), Ohio Univ. (1950–51), and the Univ. of Kansas (1951–75). He edited the works of Jacobus Vaet for Denkmäler der Tonkunst in Österreich (vols. 98, 100, 103/104, 108/109, 113/114, 116); publ. the dissertation *Jacobus Vaet and His*

Motets (East Lansing, Mich., 1951); also edited *P. de Monte: New Complete Edition,* which began publication in Louvain in 1975.

Steinitz, Paul, English organist and conductor; b. Chichester, Aug. 25, 1909. He studied at the Royal Academy of Music in London, and also privately. He then served as church organist in Ashford, Kent (1933–42). In 1947 he organized the South London Bach Society; this choral group later became noteworthy under the name of the London Bach Society. He also served as organist and choirmaster at the Church of St. Bartholomew-the-Great in London (1949–61). In 1969 he founded the Steinitz Bach Players, which he conducted on tours. In 1945 he became a prof. at the Royal Academy of Music in London; also taught at Goldsmiths' College, Univ. of London (1948–76). He publ. *Bach's Passions* (London, 1979).

Steinitzer, Max, German writer on music; b. Innsbruck, Jan. 20, 1864; d. Leipzig, June 21, 1936. He was a pupil of A. Kirchner (piano) and J. Hüttner (theory) in Munich; received his Dr.Phil. from the Univ. of Munich in 1885 with the dissertation *Über die psychologischen Wirkungen der musikalischen Formen.* He subsequently conducted theater orchs. in Germany; in 1903–11 was a prof. at the Cons. in Freiburg im Breisgau; in 1911–30, music critic of the *Leipziger Neueste Nachrichten.* An intimate friend of Richard Strauss from boyhood, Steinitzer wrote a comprehensive and authoritative biography of him.
WRITINGS: *Die menschlichen und tierischen Gemütsbewegungen* (Munich, 1889); *Musikalische Strafpredigten* (Berlin, 1901; 12th ed., 1926); *Musikgeschichtlicher Atlas. Eine Beispielsammlung zu jeder Musikgeschichte* (1908); *Merkbüchlein für Mitglieder von Männerchoren* (1908); *Richard Strauss* (Berlin, 1911; 2nd ed., 1914; 3rd revised ed., 1927); *Richard Strauss in seiner Zeit* (Leipzig, 1914; 2nd ed., 1922); *Zur Entwicklungsgeschichte des Melodrams und Mimodrams* (Leipzig, 1919); *Meister des Gesanges* (Berlin, 1920); *Das Leipziger Gewandhaus im neuen Heim unter Carl Reinecke* (Leipzig, 1924); *Tschaikowsky* (Leipzig, 1925); *Beethoven* (Leipzig, 1927); *Pädagogik der Musik* (Leipzig, 1929).

Steinpress, Boris, erudite Soviet musicologist and encyclopedist; b. Berdyansk, Aug. 13, 1908. He studied piano with Igumnov at the Moscow Cons., graduating in 1931, and took a course in music history with Ivanov-Boretsky, completing it in 1936; concurrently he gave lectures on foreign music. In 1938 he received the title of candidate of fine arts for his dissertation on Mozart's *Le nozze di Figaro.* In 1938–40 and 1943–59 he was chief contributor to the music section of the *Great Soviet Encyclopedia.* In 1942 he joined the Communist Party of the Soviet Union. In 1942–43 he taught at the Cons. of Sverdlovsk in the Urals. Although engaged primarily in musical encyclopedic work, Steinpress also composed; his patriotic songs were popular in the U.S.S.R. during World War II. His publications are particularly important in musical biography; he decisively refuted the legend of Salieri's poisoning Mozart. His biography of Aliabiev clarifies the story of Aliabiev's life and his internal exile on the false charge of murder in a duel. With I. Yampolsky he edited the extremely valuable and accurate one-vol. *Encyclopedic Musical Dictionary* (Moscow, 1959; 2nd ed., 1966); also with Yampolsky he compiled a useful *Brief Dictionary for Music Lovers* (Moscow, 1961; 2nd ed., 1967). In 1963 he publ. a partial vol. of a monumental work on opera premieres covering the period 1900–40, giving exact dates and names of theaters for all opera productions worldwide.
WRITINGS: *Problems of Material Culture in Music* (Moscow, 1931); *A History of So-Called Gypsy Songs in Russia* (Moscow, 1934; a critical dissection of spurious Gypsy songs); *Pages from the Life of Aliabiev* (Moscow, 1956); *Aliabiev in Exile* (Moscow, 1959); *Classicism and Romanticism* (Moscow, 1968); *Sketches and Studies* (Moscow, 1980).

Steinway & Sons, piano manufacturers of New York and Hamburg. The founder of the firm was **Heinrich Engelhard Steinweg** (b. Wolfshagen, Germany, Feb. 15, 1797; d. New York, Feb. 7, 1871; in 1864 he Anglicized his name to Henry E. Steinway). He learned cabinetmaking and organ building at Goslar, and in 1818 entered the shop of an organ maker in Seesen, also becoming church organist there. From about 1820 he became interested in piano making and worked hard to establish a business of his own. He married in 1825, and his first piano was probably finished at that time. In 1839 he exhibited one grand and 2 square pianos at the Braunschweig State Fair, winning the gold medal. The Revolution of 1848 caused him to emigrate to America with his wife, 2 daughters, and 4 of his 5 sons: **Charles (Christian Karl Gottlieb;** b. Seesen, Jan. 4, 1829; d. there, March 31, 1865); **Henry (Johann Heinrich Engelhard;** b. Seesen, Oct. 29, 1830; d. N.Y., March 11, 1865); **William (Johann Heinrich Wilhelm;** b. Seesen, March 5, 1835; d. N.Y., Nov. 30, 1896); and **(Georg August) Albert** (b. Seesen, June 10, 1840; d. N.Y., May 14, 1877). The management of the German business at Seesen was left in charge of the eldest son, **(Christian Friedrich) Theodore** (b. Seesen, Nov. 6, 1825; d. Braunschweig, March 26, 1889). The family arrived in N.Y. on June 29, 1850, and for about 2 years father and sons worked in various piano factories there. On March 5, 1853, they established a factory of their own under the above firm name, with premises in Varick St. In 1854 they won a gold medal for a square piano at the Metropolitan Fair in Washington, D.C. Their remarkable prosperity dates from 1855, when they took first prize for a square over-strung piano with cast-iron frame (an innovation then) at the N.Y. Industrial Exhibition. In 1856 they made their first grand, and in 1862 their first upright. Among the numerous honors subsequently received may be mentioned first prize at London, 1862; first grand gold medal of honor for all styles at Paris, 1867 (by unanimous verdict); diplomas for "highest degree of excellence in all styles" at Philadelphia, 1876. In 1854 the family name (Steinweg) was legally changed to Steinway. In 1865, upon the death of his brothers Charles and Henry, Theodore gave up the Braunschweig business and became a full partner in the N.Y. firm; he built Steinway Hall on 14th St., which, in addition to the offices and retail warerooms, housed a concert hall that became a leading center of N.Y. musical life. In 1925 headquarters were established in the Steinway Building on 57th St. Theodore was especially interested in the scientific aspects of piano construction and made a study of the acoustical theories of Helmholtz and Tyndall, which enabled him to introduce important improvements. He returned to Germany in 1870. On May 17, 1876, the firm was incorporated and William was elected president; he opened a London branch in 1876, and established a European factory at Hamburg in 1880. In the latter year he also bought 400 acres of land on Long Island Sound and established there the village of Steinway (now part of Long Island City), where since 1910 the entire manufacturing plant has been located. William was for 14 years president of the N.Y. Deutsche Liedertafel. Control and active management of the business, now the largest of its kind in the world, has remained in the hands of the founder's descendants. **Theodore E. Steinway** (d. N.Y., April 8, 1957), grandson of Henry E. Steinway, was president from 1927; also a stamp collector, he was honored by Liechtenstein with his portrait on a postage stamp on Sept. 7, 1972; in 1955 he was succeeded by his son, **Henry Steinway.**

BIBLIOGRAPHY: O. Floersheim, *W. S.* (Breslau, 1894); E. Hubbard, *The Story of the Steinways* (East Aurora, N.Y., 1911); A. Dolge, *Pianos and Their Makers,* vol. I (1911); Theodore E. Steinway, *People and Pianos* (N.Y., 1953; 2nd ed., 1961); C. Ehrlich, *The Piano: A History* (London, 1976).

Steinweg, original name of the Steinway family. **(Christian Friedrich) Theodore Steinway** continued the piano-making business established by his father at Seesen until 1852, when he transferred it to Wolfenbüttel; in 1859 he moved it to Braunschweig, carrying it on there until 1865, when he left for America. The business was then taken over by his partners, Grotrian, Helfferich, and Schulz, under the name "Theodore Steinweg Nachfolger." In 1886 Grotrian became sole owner, and the business was carried on by his sons Willi and Kurt, the firm name being "Grotrian-Steinweg."

Stekke, Léon, Belgian composer; b. Soignies, Oct. 12, 1904; d. Anderlecht, near Brussels, Jan. 24, 1970. He studied with Joseph Jongen and Paul Gilson in Brussels; from 1942 until his death he taught at the Royal Cons. in Brussels.

WORKS: Opera, *Les Cornes du Croissant* (Brussels, 1952); 2 cantatas: *Héro et Léandre* (1931) and *La Légende de St.-Hubert* (1933); *Fantaisie-rapsodie* for Orch.; *Burlesco* for Oboe and Orch.; Trumpet Concerto (Brussels, 1948); *Fantaisie élégiaque* for English Horn and Orch.; *Poème sylvestre* for French Horn and Orch.; *Impression de cinéma* for Bassoon and Orch.; *Variations* for Trombone and Orch.;

songs; piano pieces.

Stella, Antonietta, Italian soprano; b. Perugia, March 15, 1929. She studied voice with Aldo Zeetti in Perugia; made her operatic debut in Rome as Leonore in *La forza del destino* in 1951; in 1953 she sang at La Scala in Milan; further engagements were at Covent Garden in London (1955) and at the Vienna Opera. She made her American debut at the Metropolitan Opera in N.Y. on Nov. 13, 1956, in *Aida;* after several seasons on its roster, she returned to Europe to continue her career.

Stellfeld, Jean-Auguste, Belgian musicologist; b. Antwerp, Feb. 17, 1881; d. there, Sept. 14, 1952. He was a practicing lawyer, and a judge; at the same time he became associated with various musical organizations in Belgium; accumulated an enormously rich library of music from the 16th, 17th, and 18th centuries. After his death, the library was purchased by the Univ. of Michigan, Ann Arbor (cf. the article by L.E. Cuyler, G.A. Sutherland, and H.T. David in *Notes,* Dec. 1954). He publ. *Bronnen tot de geschiedenis der antwerpsche clavecimbel- en orgelbouwers in de XVIe en XVIIe eeuwen* (Antwerp, 1942); *Andries Pevernage* (Louvain, 1943); *Bibliographie des éditions musicales plantiniennes* (Brussels, 1949).

Stenberg, Jordan, American avant-garde composer of Swedish and Spanish extraction; b. Fresno, Calif., May 31, 1947. He studied music theory with Robert Moran at the San Francisco Cons. and worked on electronic problems with Robert Ashley at Mills College. In his compositions he aims at creating an organic expression of cosmic philosophy as formalized by his deep reading of Russian theosophists and Indian psychologists. His zodiacal parameters are sun in Gemini, moon in Scorpio, with Libra rising.

WORKS: *88 Fog-Horn Seconds,* a recording of actual Foghorns on Electronic Tape (1967); *A Snail's Progress in a Goldfish Bowl* for Strings glissandi within a definite integral of white noise (1968); *Music for 4 Horse-Drawn Carriages,* a literal equestrian exercise (1968); *Mind over Matter,* film opera for Voices and Instruments (1969); *Extension Chords,* to be perf. by nomadic bands on the desert floor during a lunar eclipse or at the winter solstice (1970); *A Stitch in Time* for 11 Acoustical Sources (1970); *The Clock Struck One,* opera-play for Voices, Instruments, and Dervish Dancers (1970); *Circles, Lines, Planes,* a choreographed acoustical dance notated in the form of an enneagram, to be produced in a canyon by 9 Bagpipers and 9 × 9 Buglers (1970). He has also written music for flower conservatories to stimulate the growth of timid plants.

Stenborg, Carl, Swedish composer; b. Stockholm, Sept. 25, 1752; d. Djurgarden, Aug. 1, 1813. He studied at the Univ. of Uppsala; from 1773 to 1806 was a singer at the Swedish Opera in Stockholm. His opera *Konung Gustaf Adolphs Jagt* (Stockholm, June 25, 1777) is of significance as the first opera based on a Swedish historical subject.

Stendhal, famous French writer (real name, **Marie-Henri Beyle**); b. Grenoble, Jan. 23, 1783; d. Paris, March 23, 1842. He was a military official under Napoleon, taking part in the German and Russian campaigns; from 1815 he lived in Milan, Paris, and Rome; in 1830 became French consul at Trieste, and from 1831 in Civitavecchia. He is best known as a novelist (*Le Rouge et le noir, La Chartreuse de Parme,* etc.), but also wrote on music; under the pseudonym **Louis Alexandre Bombet** he publ. *Lettres écrites de Vienne, en Autriche, sur le célèbre compositeur Joseph Haydn, suivies d'une vie de Mozart, et de considérations sur Métastase et l'état présent de la musique en France et en Italie* (Paris, 1814; in Eng., London, 1817; new ed. in 1817 as *Vies de Haydn, Mozart et Métastase,* by Stendhal; republ. in 1914 with an introduction by R. Rolland, "Stendhal et la musique"; German trans., Vienna, 1921). The life of Haydn is in part trans. from Carpani's *Le Haydine;* the first 4 chapters of the life of Mozart are taken from Schlichtegroll's Necrology (1791), the last 3 from Cramer's *Anecdotes sur Mozart.* In Jan. 1824 Stendhal's life of Rossini was publ. in London as *Memoirs of Rossini,* in a trans. made from the original MS (republ. as *The Life of Rossini,* London, 1956); the French version, considerably expanded, was publ. in Paris later the same year (2 vols.; German trans., Leipzig, 1824; republ. in a complete ed. of Stendhal's works, Paris, 1922, with an introduction by Henry Prunières, "Stendhal et Rossini," which was also publ. in the *Musical Quarterly,* Jan. 1921). The oft-repeated assertion that this work was plagiarized from Carpani's *Le Rossiniane* is without foundation.

BIBLIOGRAPHY: A. Paupe, *Histoire des œuvres de Stendhal* (Paris, 1903); H. Prunières, "Stendhal et la musique," *Revue Hebdomadaire* (1921); A.E.A. Beau, *Das Verhältnis Stendhals zur Musik* (Diss., Univ. of Hamburg, 1930); D. Maurice, *Stendhal* (Paris, 1931); P. Jourda, *Stendhal, L'Homme et l'œuvre* (Paris, 1934); F.C. Green, *Stendhal* (Cambridge, 1939); H. Imbert, "Stendhal critique musical," in *Symphonie* (Paris, 1891; pp. 87–124); J.W. Klein, "Stendhal as a Music Critic," *Musical Quarterly* (Jan. 1943).

Stenhammar, Per Ulrik, Swedish composer; b. Törnvalla, Feb. 20, 1828; d. Stockholm, Feb. 8, 1875. He received his primary musical education from A.F. Lindblad; became interested in sacred music, and wrote choral works in Mendelssohn's style; many solo songs. His oratorio, *Saul och David* (1869), was orchestrated by his son, **Wilhelm Stenhammar.**

Stenhammar, Wilhelm, significant Swedish composer, conductor, and pianist, son of **Per Ulrik Stenhammar;** b. Stockholm, Feb. 7, 1871; d. there, Nov. 20, 1927. He studied organ with Heintze and Lagergren; passed the organists' examination privately in 1890; studied theory with Joseph Dente (1888–89); in 1892–93 went to Berlin for further piano study with Karl Heinrich Barth; toured Scandinavia and Germany as a concert pianist. In his own music he followed Wagnerian formulas, but his merit as a national composer resides in his ability to absorb and transmute authentic folk melodies. His hymnal tune *Sverige (Sweden),* which is the 2nd song in his cycle of 5 songs for Baritone, Chorus, and Orch., entitled *Ett Folk (The People),* enjoys the status of an unofficial national anthem of Sweden. His first large work for Solo Voices, Chorus, and Orch., *I Rosengård (In a Rose Garden;* 1888–89; after K.A. Melin's collection of fairy tales, *Prinsessan och svennen),* was performed in Stockholm on Feb. 16, 1892, attracting considerable attention; on Dec. 9, 1898, he brought out his music drama *Tirfing* (1897–98) at the Stockholm Opera; this was followed by a German opera, written earlier, *Das Fest auf Solhaug (The Feast at Solhaug;* 1892–93), after Ibsen, which was heard first at Stuttgart on April 12, 1899, and 3 years later in Swedish (Swedish title, *Gildet på Solhaug),* in Stockholm on Oct. 31, 1902. These works are music dramas of a Wagnerian type, but their redeeming value lies in an ingratiating use of folk-song materials. From 1897 to 1900 Stenhammar was conductor of the Phil. Society in Stockholm; later also led orch. and choral groups in Göteborg (1906–22); then conducted at the Royal Opera in Stockholm (1924–25); the Univ. of Göteborg conferred on him the degree of Mus.Doc. in 1916, in appreciation of his services to the city. His other works are *Snöfrid (Snow Peace;* 1891) and *Midvinter* (1907) for Chorus and Orch.; cantata, *Sången (The Song;* 1921); 2 symphs. (1902–3, 1911–15); 2 piano concertos: No. 1 (1893; rescored by Kurt Atterberg, 1945–46) and No. 2 (1904–7); overture, *Excelsior* (1896); *2 Sentimental Romances* for Violin and Orch. (1910); *Serenade* for Orch. (1911–13; revised 1919); incidental music to Strindberg's drama *Drömspelet (A Dreamplay;* 1916; rescored for concert perf. by Hilding Rosenberg, 1968–69); 6 string quartets (1894; 1896; 1897–1900; 1904–9; *Serenade,* 1910; 1916); Violin Sonata (1899–1900); 2 piano sonatas (1890, 1895); *3 Fantasies* for Piano (1895); *Nights of Late Summer,* 5 piano pieces (1914); a cappella choral works; solo songs.

BIBLIOGRAPHY: Sten Broman, "Wilhelm Stenhammar: A Survey," *Music Review* (May 1947); special issue of *Musikrevy,* XXVI/6 (1971); H. Connor, "Wilhelm Stenhammar," *Svensk musik* (Stockholm, 1974).

Štěpán, Václav, Czech pianist and writer on music; b. Pečky, near Kolín, Dec. 12, 1889; d. Prague, Nov. 24, 1944. He studied musicology at the Univ. of Prague (Dr.Phil., 1913); from 1919 he was a prof. of esthetics at the Prague Cons.; appeared as a pianist in Czechoslovakia and in France; contributed valuable articles on Czech musicians to foreign encyclopedias and music dictionaries; publ. 2 vols. of Bohemian folk songs (1917) and 2 vols. of Slovak folk songs (1925); also *Das Symbol in der Programm-Musik* (1914). He wrote some chamber music and other works, but did not pursue a composer's career.

Stepanian, Aro, Armenian composer; b. Elizavet-pol, April 24, 1897; d. Erevan, Jan. 9, 1966. He studied at the Leningrad Cons. with Vladimir Shcherba-chev. He moved to Erevan, capital of Soviet Armenia, in 1930 and remained there for the rest of his life. He wrote 5 operas on Armenian subjects: *Brave Nazar* (Erevan, . Nov. 29, 1935); *David of Sasun* (1937); *Lusabatsin* (*At the Dawn;* 1938); *Nune* (1947); *Heroine* (1950); he further wrote 3 symphs. (1943, 1945, 1953); 2 piano concertos (1947, 1955); Viola Concerto (1955); *Rhapsody* for Piano and Orch. (1962); 4 string quartets; 2 violin sonatas; Cello Sonata; numerous choruses and songs.
BIBLIOGRAPHY: M. Kazakhian, *Aro Stepanian* (Erevan, 1962).

Stepanov, Lev, Russian composer; b. Tomsk, Siberia, Dec. 26, 1908. He studied with Miaskovsky at the Moscow Cons., graduating in 1938. He wrote several operas on Russian subjects, among them *Dunia's Happiness* (1937); *The Guards* (Tashkent, Nov. 8, 1947); *Ivan Bolotnikov* (Perm, Dec. 17, 1950); a ballet, *The Native Shore* (1941); 2 piano concertos (1947, 1955); Viola Concerto (1955); chamber music; choruses; many songs.

Stephan, Rudi, German composer; b. Worms, July 29, 1887; d. near Tarnopol, Galicia, Sept. 29, 1915. He studied with Sekles in Frankfurt and with R. Louis in Munich; developed a fine talent for lyric songs, combining German Romantic traits with Impressionism in instrumental coloring. His death in battle was lamented by German musicians.
WORKS: *Music für 7 Saiteninstrumente* for String Quintet, Piano, and Harp (1912); *Music für Orchester* (1913); *Music für Violine und Orchester* (1914); *Liebeszauber,* ballad for Baritone and Orch.; piano pieces. His opera, *Die ersten Menschen,* was produced posthumously in Frankfurt on July 1, 1920.
BIBLIOGRAPHY: K. Holl, *Rudi Stephan* (1920); A. Machner, *Rudi Stephans Werk* (Diss., Univ. of Breslau, 1942).

Stephanescu, George, Rumanian composer; b. Bucharest, Dec. 13, 1843; d. there, April 24, 1925. He studied in Bucharest, and at the Paris Cons. with Ambroise Thomas and Auber (1867–71). From 1872 to 1909 he taught voice at the Bucharest Cons. He was the composer of the first Rumanian symph. work based on national themes, *Uvertura na-tionala* (1876), and of the first symph. written by a Rumanian (1869). He also wrote many choruses and solo songs to Rumanian texts.

Stephani, Hermann, German musicologist and composer; b. Grimma, June 23, 1877; d. Marburg, Dec. 3, 1960. He studied at the Leipzig Cons. with Jadassohn and Reinecke, and at the Univ. of Munich with Lipps and Sandberger; obtained his Dr.Phil. from the Univ. of Leipzig in 1902 with the dissertation *Das Erhabene, insonderheit in der Tonkunst, und das Problem der Form* (publ. in Leipzig, 1903; 2nd ed., 1907). In 1921 he was appoint-ed to the faculty of the Univ. of Marburg; taught musicology there until 1946. His scholarly publica-tions include: *Der Charakter der Tonarten* (Habili-tationsschrift, Univ. of Marburg, 1921; publ. in Regensburg, 1923); *Grundfragen des Musikhörens* (Leipzig, 1925); *Das Vierteltonproblem* (Leipzig, 1925); *Polare Harmonik bei Beethoven* (Leipzig, 1927); *Das Problem des Orgelstils* (Essen, 1942). He advocated a reform in score notation through the exclusive use of the G clef with octave indications ("Einheitspartitur") and edited Schumann's *Man-fred* overture using this system (1905). He was a prolific composer; wrote about 100 opus numbers, mostly vocal works; also contrapuntal pieces for various combinations of instruments; edited works by Handel, Weber, etc. A Festschrift was presented to him on his 70th birthday (Regensburg, 1947).

Stephens, Charles Edward, English organist and teacher; b. London, March 18, 1821; d. there, July 13, 1892. He studied piano with Cipriani Potter; in 1843 he was appointed to his first church position as or-ganist, and was active in that capacity in various churches in London until 1875. From 1850 he was associated with the Phil. Society, as treasurer and director. He composed a Piano Trio, several orch. overtures, a String Quartet, and a Symph.; all these works were performed in London.

Sterkel, Abbé Johann Franz Xaver, German ec-clesiastic and composer; b. Würzburg, Dec. 3, 1750; d. there, Oct. 12, 1817. He studied theology and became a priest; was self-taught in music, but ac-quired sufficient proficiency as an organist to occu-py various positions as music director. In 1778 he became chaplain and organist in the Elector's court at Mainz; in 1782 he was in Italy, where he produced his opera *Farnace* (Naples, Jan. 12, 1782). Beethoven heard Sterkel play in 1791, in Aschaffenburg, and was greatly impressed by his style as both a compos-er and a pianist. When the French expelled the Elector in 1794, Sterkel left Mainz and returned to his native city. From 1810 he was again court musi-cian to the Elector of Mainz, until 1814, when the military campaign forced him to go back to Würz-burg once more. He was a prolific composer; publ. 10 symphs., 2 overtures, a Piano Quartet, a String Quartet, 6 string trios, 6 piano concertos, a consider-able amount of piano music. His *Rondo comique* for Piano was very popular.
BIBLIOGRAPHY: A. Scharnagl, *J.F.X. Sterkel: Ein Beitrag zur Musikgeschichte Mainfrankens* (Würzburg, 1943).

Sterling, Antoinette, American contralto; b. Ster-lingville, N.Y., Jan. 23, 1850; d. London, Jan. 9, 1904. She studied with Abella in N.Y., Mathilde Marchesi in Cologne, and Pauline Viardot-Garcia in Baden; also took lessons with Manuel García in London. Returning to America, she sang in Henry Ward Beecher's church in Brooklyn; then went to London, where she made her debut at a Covent Garden Promenade Concert (Nov. 5, 1873). She introduced many favorite songs (most of which were composed especially for her), such as Arthur Sullivan's *Lost Chord* (Jan. 31, 1877) and Barnby's *When the Tide Comes In.* In 1875 she toured the U.S.; her permanent home was in London.

BIBLIOGRAPHY: Malcolm S. MacKinlay (her son), *Antoinette Sterling and Other Celebrities* (London, 1906).

Sterling, Winthrop Smith, American organist and teacher; b. Cincinnati, Nov. 28, 1859; d. there, Nov. 16, 1943. He studied in Leipzig, and later in London, where he remained for several years as an organist. From 1887 to 1903 he was head of the organ dept. and teacher of singing at the Cincinnati College of Music; later taught organ at the Univ. of Miami. He composed a number of organ pieces and songs.

Stern, Adolf, German writer on music; b. Leipzig, June 14, 1835; d. Dresden, April 15, 1907. He publ. several books dealing with music: *Wanderbuch* (1877; about the Bayreuth Festivals); *Die Musik in der deutschen Dichtung* (1888); *Gluck in Versailles* (1904); edited the poems of Peter Cornelius (1890) and *Liszts Briefe an K. Gille* (1903). In 1881 he married the pianist **Margarete Herr** (b. Dresden, Nov. 25, 1857; d. there, Oct. 4, 1899), who was a pupil of Liszt, and after her death he publ. her biography (Leipzig, 1901).

Stern, Isaac, outstanding American violinist; b. Kremenetz, Russia, July 21, 1920. He was taken to the U.S. as an infant and was trained in music by his mother, who was a professional singer. He studied the violin at the San Francisco Cons. (1928–31), then with Louis Persinger; also studied with Naoum Blinder (1932–37). He made his professional debut with the San Francisco Symph. Orch. at the age of 11, and played in N.Y. on Oct. 11, 1937, eliciting praise from the critics. In 1947 he toured Australia; made his European debut at the Lucerne Festival in 1948; subsequently appeared regularly with American and European orchs.; in 1956 he made a spectacularly successful tour of Russia. In 1961 he organized a trio with the pianist Istomin and the cellist Leonard Rose. Isaac Stern belongs to the galaxy of virtuoso performers to whom fame is a natural adjunct to talent and industry; he is also active in general cultural undertakings, and is an energetic worker for the cause of human rights.

Stern, Julius, eminent German music pedagogue; b. Breslau, Aug. 8, 1820; d. Berlin, Feb. 27, 1883. He studied violin with Lüstner, and later took courses with Rungenhagen in Berlin; in 1847 he founded the famous Sternscher Gesangverein in Berlin, conducting it until 1874. In 1850 he founded the Berlin Cons. with Kullak and Marx; Kullak withdrew in 1855, and Marx in 1857; thenceforth Stern became the sole head of the institution, now known as the Stern Cons.; it prospered and acquired the reputation of one of the greatest music schools in Europe. Stern conducted the Berlin Sinfonie-Kapelle from 1869 to 1871, and later led the "Reichshalle" concerts (1873–75). He was also a composer, and re-

ceived commendation from Mendelssohn for his songs; publ. *Barcarolle* for Voice, Cello, and Piano; *Les Adieux* for Violin and Piano; male choruses; songs. His opera, *Ismene,* was not produced.

BIBLIOGRAPHY: Richard Stern, *Erinnerungsblätter an Julius Stern* (Berlin, 1886).

Stern, Leo, English cellist; b. Brighton, April 5, 1862; d. London, Sept. 10, 1904. He studied cello at the Royal Academy of Music in London with Piatti, and later with Julius Klengel in Leipzig. He was an assistant artist on Adelina Patti's concert tour in 1888; made a tour in America in 1897–98. He composed pieces for cello and songs. His 2nd wife was **Suzanne Adams,** the opera singer.

Sternberg, Constantin, Russian-American pianist and composer; b. St. Petersburg, July 9, 1852; d. Philadelphia, March 31, 1924. He studied piano with Moscheles at the Leipzig Cons., and later had lessons with Theodor Kullak; also visited Liszt at Weimar. He toured Russia as a concert pianist; in 1880 emigrated to the U.S. In 1890 he established the Sternberg School of Music in Philadelphia, and was its director until his death. He was greatly esteemed as a piano teacher. He wrote some 200 salon pieces for piano, and *Danses cosaques* for Violin; publ. *Ethics and Esthetics of Piano Playing* (N.Y., 1917) and *Tempo Rubato and Other Essays* (N.Y., 1920).

Sternberg, Erich Walter, German-born Israeli composer; b. Berlin, May 31, 1891; d. Tel Aviv, Dec. 15, 1974. He studied composition with Hugo Leichtentritt in Berlin; emigrated to Palestine, and taught at the Tel Aviv Cons. He was co-founder of the Palestine Symph. Orch. (now the Israel Phil.). As a composer, he was inspired by biblical subjects.

WORKS: Children's opera, *Dr. Dolittle* (Jerusalem, 1939); opera "for children and others," *Pacifica, the Friendly Island* (1972–74); 2 string quartets (1924, 1926); *The Story of David and Goliath* for Baritone and Orch. (1927); *Joseph and His Brothers,* suite for String Orch. (1938); *12 Tribes of Israel,* variations for Orch. (1941; Tel Aviv, May 3, 1942); *My People,* 5 songs for Soprano or Tenor, and Orch. (1945); *Amcha-Suite* for Orch., from incidental music to a play; *Höre Israel* for Orch. (1948); *Toccata* for Piano (1950); *The Raven,* after Poe, for Baritone and Orch. (1953); Violin Sonata (1955); *Contrapuntal Study* for Orch. (1955); *Sichot Haruach (Conversations with the Wind)* for Contralto and Orch. (1956); *The Distant Flute,* 3 songs for Voice and Flute (1958); oratorio, *Techiat Israel (The Resurrection of Israel,* 1959); *Tewat Noah (Noah's Ark),* 4 movements for Orch. in the form of a symph. (1960); *Tefilot (Prayers of Humility)* for Contralto and Chamber Orch. (1962); *The Sacrifice of Isaac* for Soprano and Orch. (1965); *Love Songs* for Chorus and Orch. (1968); *The Wretched* for Baritone and String Orch. (1969); *My Brother Jonathan* for Chorus and String Orch. (1969); Piano Trio; Wind Quintet; songs.

Sternefeld, Daniel, Belgian conductor and composer; b. Antwerp, Nov. 27, 1905. He studied composition with Paul Gilson; took lessons in conducting from Paumgartner, Krauss, and Karajan at the Mozarteum in Salzburg. He was a flutist in the orch. of the Royal Flemish Opera in Antwerp from 1929; was appointed 2nd conductor in 1938; was principal conductor in 1944–48; then was principal conductor of the Belgian Radio and Television Orch. (1948–72); also appeared as a guest conductor in Europe and South America. He taught conducting at the Antwerp Cons. (1949–71). His few compositions include an opera influenced by Strauss, *Mater Dolorosa* (1934; Antwerp, 1935); a ballet, *Pierlala* (1938); *Variations symphoniques* (1928); *Elégie* for Orch. (1931); *Suite de vieilles chansons flamandes et wallonnes* for Chamber Orch. (1934); Symph. (1943); *Frère Jacques*, variations for Brass and Percussion (1955).

Sternfeld, Frederick William, Austrian-American musicologist; b. Vienna, Sept. 25, 1914. He studied at the Univ. of Vienna (1933–37); then went to the U.S., and enrolled at Yale Univ. (1940–43), obtaining his Ph.D. there. He taught at Wesleyan Univ. in Conn. (1940–46) and at Dartmouth College (1946–56); since 1956 has been a lecturer at Oxford Univ. He was editor of *Renaissance News* (1946–54); publ. a number of informative studies in the *Musical Quarterly* and other American and British publications. His Ph.D. dissertation of 1943, *Goethe and Music*, served as the basis for his *Goethe and Music: A List of Parodies* and *Goethe's Relationship to Music: A List of References* (N.Y., 1954). He also wrote *Music in Shakespearean Tragedy* (London, 1963; 2nd ed., 1967) and *Songs from Shakespeare's Tragedies* (London, 1964).

Sternfeld, Richard, German writer on music; b. Königsberg, Oct. 15, 1858; d. Berlin, June 21, 1926. A thoroughly trained musician, he publ. valuable books concerning music.

WRITINGS: *Beethoven und Wagner* (1885); *Hans von Bülow* (1898); *Beethovens Missa Solemnis* (1900); *Albert Niemann* (1904); *Schiller und Wagner* (1905); *Richard Wagner und die Bayreuther Bühnenfestspiele* (2 vols., 1906); *Aus Richard Wagners Pariser Zeit* (1906); *Musikalische Skizzen und Humoresken* (1919); *Berühmte Musiker und ihre Werke* (1922).

Steuerlein, Johann, German composer; b. Schmalkalden, July 5, 1546; d. Meiningen, May 5, 1613. He studied in Magdeburg; occupied various positions as a clerk; became a notary public in Meiningen in 1589; in 1604 he was given the rank of poet laureate by the Emperor. At the same time he was active as a song composer, and brought out *21 Geistliche Lieder* for 4 Voices (1575); *24 Weltliche Gesänge* (1575); *23 Geistliche Gesänge* for 4–6 Voices (1576); *27 Geistliche Gesänge* for 4 Voices (1588); *8 Geistliche Gesänge* for 5 Voices (1589). He was the composer of the celebrated New Year song *Das alte Jahr vergangen ist.*

BIBLIOGRAPHY: G. Kraft, "Johann Steuerlein,"

Zeitschrift für Musikwissenschaft (May 1931).

Steuermann, Edward, eminent Polish-American pianist and composer; b. Sambor, near Lwow, June 18, 1892; d. New York, Nov. 11, 1964. He studied piano with Ferruccio Busoni in Berlin (1911–12), and theory with Schoenberg (1912–14); also took some composition lessons with Engelbert Humperdinck. Returning to Poland, he taught at the Paderewski School in Lwow, and concurrently at the Jewish Cons. in Cracow (1932–36). In 1936 he emigrated to the U.S.; taught piano at the Juilliard School of Music in N.Y. (1952–64); also was on the faculty of the Philadelphia Cons. (1948–63); gave summer classes at the Mozarteum in Salzburg (1953–63) and Darmstadt (1954, 1957, 1958, 1960); conducted a chamber music seminar in Israel in the summer of 1958. As a concert pianist and soloist with major orchs., Steuermann was an ardent champion of new music, particularly of Schoenberg; gave the first performance of Schoenberg's Piano Concerto (1944); made excellent arrangements for piano of Schoenberg's operatic and symph. works, among them *Erwartung, Die glückliche Hand, Kammersymphonie* No. 1, and Piano Concerto; in 1952 he received the Schoenberg Medal from the International Society for Contemporary Music (1952); recorded the complete piano works of Schoenberg; was also curator of the Arnold Schoenberg Inst. at the Univ. of Southern Calif. Steuermann was also a composer; although he did not follow Schoenberg's method of composition with 12 tones with any degree of consistency, his music possesses an expressionistic tension that is characteristic of the modern Vienna School.

WORKS: *Variations* for Orch. (1958); *Music for Instruments* (1959–60); *Suite* for Chamber Orch. (1964); *7 Waltzes* for String Quartet (1946); Piano Trio (1954); *Improvisation and Allegro* for Violin and Piano (1955); String Quartet, subtitled *Diary* (1960–61); *Dialogues* for Unaccompanied Violin (1963); Piano Sonata (1926); *Piano Suite* (1952); *3 Choirs* (1956); *Cantata*, after Franz Kafka, for Chorus and Orch. (1964); *Brecht-Lieder* for Contralto (1945); a number of other songs to Polish and German texts.

Stevens, Bernard, English composer; b. London, March 2, 1916; d. there, Jan. 2, 1983. He studied at Cambridge Univ.; also at the Royal College of Music in London; was appointed to its faculty in 1948. He wrote a number of works for various instrumental combinations; his music adheres to traditional concepts of harmony, while the programmatic content is often colored by his radical political beliefs.

WORKS: *Symphony of Liberation* (1946); Violin Concerto (1946); Cello Concerto (1952); Piano Concerto (1955); cantatas: *The Harvest of Peace* (1952) and *The Pilgrims of Hope* (1956); Symph. No. 2 (1964); Trio for Violin, Horn, and Piano (1966); *Choriamb* for Orch. (1968); *The Turning World* for Baritone, Chorus, and Orch. (1971); *The Bramble Briar* for Guitar (1974).

Stevens, Denis (William), distinguished English violinist, musicologist, and conductor; b. High Wycombe, Buckinghamshire, March 2, 1922. He studied music with R.O. Morris, Egon Wellesz, and Hugh Allen at Jesus College, Oxford (M.A., 1947); played violin and viola in the Philharmonia Orch. of London (1946–49); then was a program planner in the music dept. of the BBC (1949–54). He served as a visiting prof. of music at Cornell Univ. (1955) and Columbia Univ. (1956), and taught at the Royal Academy of Music in London (1956–61). He subsequently was a visiting prof. at the Univ. of Calif. at Berkeley (1962) and at Pa. State Univ. (1963–64). In 1965 he became a prof. of musicology at Columbia Univ. He was further a visiting prof. at the Univ. of Calif. at Santa Barbara (1974) and at the Univ. of Washington at Seattle (1976–77). As a conductor, he was co-founder of the Ambrosian Singers and served as president and artistic director of the Accademia Monteverdiana; in his programs he emphasized early polyphonic works. He edited several important collections, including *The Mulliner Book,* vol. I in the Musica Brittanica series (1951; 3rd ed., revised, 1962), *Early Tudor Organ Music,* in the Early English Church Music series (1969), and works by Monteverdi.

WRITINGS: *The Mulliner Book: A Commentary* (London, 1952); *Tudor Church Music* (N.Y., 1955; 3rd ed., 1966); *Thomas Tomkins 1572–1656* (London, 1957; 2nd ed., 1967); edited *A History of Song* (London, 1960; 2nd ed., 1970); co-edited, with A. Robertson, *The Pelican History of Music* (3 vols., Harmondsworth, 1960–68); *Plainsong Hymns and Sequences* (London, 1965); *Claudio Monteverdi: Sacred, Secular and Occasional Music* (N.Y., 1977); edited and was translator for *The Letters of Claudio Monteverdi* (London, 1980); also edited *Ten Renaissance Dialogues* (Seven Oaks, 1981).

Stevens, Halsey, significant American composer, conductor, and educator; b. Scott, N.Y., Dec. 3, 1908. He studied theory and composition with William Berwald at Syracuse Univ. (B.A., 1931); then served as an instructor of music there (1935–37). From 1937 to 1941 he was on the music faculty of Dakota Wesleyan Univ. at Mitchell, S.Dak.; from 1941 to 1943 taught at the College of Music of Bradley Polytechnic Inst. in Peoria, Ill.; in 1943–46 served in the U.S. Naval Reserve; while in the service, he took composition lessons with Ernest Bloch at the Univ. of Calif. in Berkeley. In 1948 he was appointed to the music faculty of the Univ. of Southern Calif., Los Angeles, remaining on the staff until 1976, when he became prof. emeritus. He was also a visiting prof. at Yale Univ. (1960–61), and guest lecturer at several other univs. in the U.S. His own music is above all a monument of sonorous equilibrium; melodies and rhythms are coordinated in a fine melorhythmic polyphony; dissonances are emancipated and become natural consorts of triadic harmony. Tonality remains paramount, while a stream of coloristic passages contributes to the brilliance of the instrumental texture. Stevens wrote only "absolute" music, without resort to the stage; there are no operas or ballets in his creative catalogue. He does not apply conventional modernistic devices in his music, designed at its culmination to please the aural sense. Apart from composition, Stevens took great interest in the autochthonous music of the peoples of the earth; he was particularly fascinated by the fieldwork that Béla Bartók undertook in gathering authentic folk songs of southeastern Europe. He mastered the Hungarian language, retraced Bartók's travels, and assembled materials on Bartók's life; the result was his exemplary biography, *The Life and Music of Béla Bartók* (N.Y., 1953; revised ed., 1964). Stevens has received numerous grants and honors; he held 2 Guggenheim fellowships (1964 and 1971), a grant from the National Endowment for the Arts (1976), and the Abraham Lincoln Award of the American Hungarian Foundation (1978).

WORKS: FOR ORCH.: Symph. No. 1 (San Francisco, March 7, 1946, composer conducting; revised version, Los Angeles, March 3, 1950); Symph. No. 2 (1945; N.Y., May 17, 1947); *A Green Mountain Overture* (Burlington, Vt., Aug. 7, 1948); *Triskelion* (figure with 3 branches; Louisville, Feb. 27, 1954); *Sinfonia breve* (Louisville, Nov. 20, 1957); *Symphonic Dances* (San Francisco, Dec. 10, 1958); Cello Concerto (1964; Los Angeles, May 12, 1968); *Threnos: In Memoriam Quincy Porter* (1968); Concerto for Clarinet and String Orch. (Denton, Texas, March 20, 1969); Double Concerto for Violin, Cello, and String Orch. (Los Angeles, Nov. 4, 1973); Viola Concerto (1976). CHAMBER MUSIC: Quintet for Flute, Violin, Viola, Cello, and Piano (Middlebury, Vt., Aug. 30, 1946); *Suite* for Clarinet and Piano (1946); Bassoon Sonata (1949); String Quartet No. 3 (1949); *3 Hungarian Folk Songs* for Viola and Piano (1950); Viola Sonata (1950); Horn Sonata (1953); Trumpet Sonata (1956); Piano Trio No. 3 (1954); *Sonatine piacevole* for Flute and Harpsichord (1956); Septet for Clarinet, Bassoon, Horn, 2 Violas, and 2 Cellos (Urbana, Ill., March 3, 1957); *Divertimento* for 2 Violins (1958–66); Suite for Viola and Piano (1959); Sonatina for Bass Tuba and Piano (1960); *12 Slovakian Folk Songs* for 2 Violins (1962); Cello Sonata (1965); *8 Canons* for 2 Violins (1969); Oboe Sonata (1971); *Quintetto "Serbelloni"* for Woodwinds (1972). FOR SINGLE INSTRUMENTS: Sonatina for Solo Harp (1954); *Suite* for Solo Violin (1954); Sonata for Solo Cello (1956–58); *6 Slovakian Folk Songs* for Harp (1966). FOR PIANO: 3 sonatas (1945–48); 6 preludes (1951–56); *Partita* (1954); *Ritratti* (1960); *Fantasia* (1961); various minor pieces. VOCAL WORKS: *The Ballad of William Sycamore* for Chorus and Orch. (Los Angeles, Oct. 6, 1955); *2 Shakespeare Songs* for Voice, Flute, and Clarinet (1959); *A Testament of Life* for Tenor, Bass, Chorus, and Orch. (1959); *4 Canciones* for Voice and Piano (1961); *Magnificat* for Chorus and String Orch. (1962); *7 Canciones* for Voice and Piano (1964); *Campion Suite* for Chorus (1967); *Te Deum* for Chorus, Brass Septet, Organ, and Timpani (1967); *Chansons courtoises* for Chorus (1967); *Songs from the Paiute* for Chorus, 4 Flutes, and Timpani (1976).

BIBLIOGRAPHY: David Ewen, *American Composers* (N.Y., 1982).

Stevens, Richard John Samuel, English composer of glees; b. London, March 27, 1757; d. there, Sept. 23, 1837. He was a chorister at St. Paul's Cathedral in London; from 1786 to 1810 he served as organist at the Inner Temple; from 1801 was a prof. of music at Gresham College. He received numerous prizes for his glees, of which the most famous were *Sigh no more, Ladies; Ye spotted snakes; The cloud-pact towers; Crabbed Age and Youth;* and *From Oberon in Airy Land.* He also brought out 3 sonatas for Harpsichord, and edited a 3-vol. collection of vocal music by Italian and English composers.

BIBLIOGRAPHY: J.B. Trend, "R.J.S. Stevens," *Music & Letters,* 14.

Stevens, Risë, American mezzo-soprano; b. New York, June 11, 1913. Her original family surname was **Steenberg,** and she was the child of a mixed marriage: Her father was a Lutheran from Oslo, Norway; her mother was Jewish-American. She studied voice with Orry Prado; she made excellent progress, and appeared on a Sunday morning radio broadcast, "The Children's Hour." After graduating from high school, she sang minor roles with the N.Y. Opera-Comique Co. The enterprise soon went bankrupt, and for a while she had to earn her living by dress modeling, before she was offered free singing lessons by Anna Schoen-René at the Juilliard School of Music. She was subsequently sent to Salzburg to study with Marie Gutheil-Schoder at the Mozarteum, and later entered classes in stage direction with Herbert Graf. In 1936 she was engaged by George Szell, who was then conductor at the Prague Opera, to sing contralto there; she prepared several roles from standard operas, coaching with George Schick. She went on a tour to Cairo, Egypt, with a Vienna opera group, and then sang at the Teatro Colón in Buenos Aires. She made her American debut as Octavian in *Der Rosenkavalier* with the Metropolitan Opera in Philadelphia on Nov. 22, 1938. She greatly extended her repertoire, and added Wagnerian roles to her appearances with the Metropolitan. On Jan 9, 1939, she married in N.Y. the Czech actor Walter Surovy, who became her business manager. In the summer of 1939 she sang at the Glyndebourne Festival in England; on Oct. 12, 1940, she appeared with the San Francisco Opera as Cherubino; in 1941 she joined Nelson Eddy in a motion picture production of the operetta *The Chocolate Soldier,* and in 1944 acted in the movie *Going My Way,* in which she sang the Habanera from *Carmen;* on Dec. 28, 1945, she appeared as Carmen at the Metropolitan Opera, scoring a fine success. Carmen became her most celebrated role; she sang it 75 times with the Metropolitan. She remained with the Metropolitan until 1961. On March 24, 1954, she appeared for the first time at La Scala in Milan. In 1975 she joined the teaching staff at the Juilliard School of Music in N.Y. She also served as president of the Mannes College of Music in N.Y. (1975-78).

BIBLIOGRAPHY: K. Crichton, *Subway to the Met: Risë Steven's Story* (N.Y., 1959); David Ewen, *Musicians since 1900* (N.Y., 1978).

Stevenson, Robert (Murrell), erudite and brilliant American musicologist, educator, composer, and pianist; b. Melrose, N.Mex., July 3, 1916. He studied at the Univ. of Texas, El Paso (A.B., 1936); then went to N.Y. to study piano with Ernest Hutcheson at the Juilliard School of Music; subsequently entered Yale Univ., studying composition with David Stanley Smith and musicology with Leo Schrade (M.Mus., 1939). In 1939 he had 23 private lessons in composition (at $25 a session) with Stravinsky at Cambridge, Mass., and in 1940 he took private piano lessons (at $40 a lesson) with Artur Schnabel in N.Y.; then attended classes in composition with Howard Hanson at the Eastman School of Music in Rochester, N.Y. (Ph.D., 1942); he later had regular music courses at Harvard Univ. (S.T.B., 1943). He also took graduate degrees in theology from the Harvard Divinity School and the Theological Seminary at Princeton Univ. (Th.M., 1949). He served as chaplain with the U.S. Army (1942–46); received the Army Commendation Ribbon; remained in service as a reserve officer until 1953. He then went to Oxford Univ. in England, where he took courses in musicology with Sir Jack Allan Westrup (B.Litt., 1954). While thus occupied, he pursued an active career as a concert pianist; gave his first N.Y. recital on Jan 5, 1942; gave another recital there on March 20, 1947; in both he included his own compositions; he played in London on Oct 7, 1953. He taught music at the Univ. of Texas at El Paso in 1941–43 and 1949; lectured on church music at Westminster Choir College in Princeton, N.J., from 1946 to 1949. In 1949 he was appointed to the music faculty at the Univ. of Calif., Los Angeles; was made a prof. of music in 1961; was named faculty research lecturer in 1981. In 1955–56 he was a visiting assistant prof. at Columbia Univ.; also was a visiting prof. at Indiana Univ. in Bloomington (1959–60) and at the Univ. of Chile in Santiago (1965–66). A widely informed musical scientist, he gave courses at the Univ. of Calif. on music appreciation, special seminars on individual composers, and a highly popular course in 1983 on rock-'n'-roll music. He also presented piano recitals as part of the curriculum. A master of European languages, he concentrated his scholarly energy mainly on Latin-American, Spanish, and Portuguese music, both sacred and secular, and his publications on these subjects are of inestimable value; he is also an investigative explorer of Italian Renaissance music. He contributed more than 400 articles to *The New Grove Dictionary of Music and Musicians,* and numerous articles on the Baroque period and on American composers to *Die Musik in Geschichte und Gegenwart;* was its American editor from 1967 to the completion of the last fascicle of its supplement. He held numerous grants, fellowships, and awards from learned societies; was the recipient of Fulbright research awards (1958–59, 1964, and 1970–71); of a Carnegie Foundation Teaching Award (1955–56); Gulbenkian Foundation fellowship (1953–54); Guggenheim fellowship (1962); Ford Foundation fellowship (1966 and 1981); National Endowment for Humanities fellowship (1974); as well as one from the American Philosophical Society. He was a contributor, beginning in

1976, to the *Handbook of Latin American Studies* at the Library of Congress; from 1978 was editor and principal contributor to *Inter-American Music Review.* His avowed mission in his work is "to rescue the musical past of the Americas." Stevenson's own compositions are marked by kinetic energy and set in vigorous and often acrid dissonant counterpoint. His symph. *2 Peruvian Preludes* were performed by Stokowski with the Philadelphia Orch. on June 28, 1962; the score was later expanded into *3 preludias peruanos* and first performed in Mexico City, on July 20, 1963, with Luis Herrera de la Fuente conducting. Other works include *Nocturne in Ebony* and *A Texas Suite* for Orch.; Sonata for Clarinet and Piano; 3 piano sonatas: *A Cambridge Sonata, A Manhattan Sonata,* and *A New Haven Sonata.* He also wrote *Coronation Concerto* for Solo Organ and *A Sandburg Cantata* for Mixed Chorus.

WRITINGS: *Music In Mexico. A Historical Survey* (N.Y., 1952); *Patterns of Protestant Church Music* (Durham, N.C., 1953); *La musica en la catedral de Sevilla, 1478–1606; Documentos para su estudio* (Los Angeles, 1954); *Music before the Classic Era* (London, 1955; 2nd. ed., 1958; reprint. Westport, Conn., 1973); *Cathedral Music in Colonial Peru* (Lima, 1959); *The Music of Peru: Aboriginal and Viceroyal Epochs* (Washington, D.C., 1960); *Juan Bermudo* (The Hague, 1960); *Spanish Music in the Age of Columbus* (The Hague, 1960); *Music Instruction in Inca Land* (Baltimore, 1960); *Spanish Cathedral Music in the Golden Age* (Berkeley, Calif., 1961); *Mexico City Cathedral Music, 1600–1750* (Washington, 1964); *Protestant Church Music in America* (N.Y., 1966); *Music in Aztec and Inca Territory* (Berkeley, 1968); *Renaissance and Baroque Musical Sources in the Americas* (Washington, 1970); *Foundations of New World Opera, with a Transcription of the Earliest Extant American Opera, 1701* (Lima, 1973); *Christmas Music from Baroque Mexico* (Berkeley, 1974); *Latin American Colonial Music Anthology,* (Washington, 1975); *A Guide to Caribbean Music History* (Lima, 1975). He edited, transcribed, and annotated *Vilancicos portugueses* for *Portugaliae Musica XXIX* (Lisbon, 1976); contributed informative articles dealing with early American composers, South American operas, sources of Indian music, and studies on Latin-American composers to the *Musical Quarterly, Revista Musical Chilena, Journal of the American Musicological Society, Ethnomusicology,* and *Inter-American Music Review.*

Stevenson, Ronald, Brythonic composer; b. Blackburn, Lancashire, March 6, 1928, of Scottish and Welsh ancestry. He studied piano as a child; began to compose at 14; took courses in composition at the Royal Manchester College at 17. In 1955 he went to Italy on a scholarship granted by the Italian government; studied at the Santa Cecilia Academy in Rome. Returning to England, he was appointed lecturer at Edinburgh Univ. (in the Extra-Mural Dept.) in 1962; was on the music staff at the Univ. of Cape Town (South Africa) in 1963–65. A fervent intellectual, he contributed cultured articles to the *Listener*

and other publications; engaged in a thoroughgoing bio-musical tome on Busoni, with whose art he felt a particular kinship; publ. a book, *Western Music: An Introduction* (London, 1971).

WORKS: He adheres to neo-Baroque polyphony; a formidable exemplar is his *Passacaglia on DSCH* for Piano, a Brobdingnagian set of variations in 3 parts, 80 minutes long, derived from the initial D of the first name and the first 3 letters of the last name of Dmitri Shostakovich, in German notation (D; S = Es = E-flat; C; H = B), first perf. by Stevenson himself in Cape Town, Dec. 10, 1963. Other works include: *Anger Dance* for Guitar (1965); *Triptych,* on themes from Busoni's opera *Doktor Faust,* for Piano and Orch. (Piano Concerto No. 1; Edinburgh, Jan. 6, 1966, composer soloist); *Scots Dance Toccata* for Orch. (Glasgow, July 4, 1970); *Peter Grimes Fantasy* for Piano, on themes from Britten's opera (1971); *Duo-Sonata* for Harp and Piano (1971); Piano Concerto No. 2 (1972); numerous settings for voice and piano and for chorus of Scottish folk songs; transcriptions of works of Purcell, Bach, Chopin, Berlioz, Busoni, Paderewski, Delius, Britten, Alban Berg, Pizzetti, Percy Grainger, and many others.

Stewart, Humphrey John, organist and composer; b. London, May 22, 1856; d. San Diego, Calif., Dec. 28, 1932. He studied privately in England; in 1886 emigrated to the U.S. and settled in San Francisco as a church organist; he was one of the founders of the American Guild of Organists. His 3 operas were produced in San Francisco: *His Majesty* (1890); *The Conspirators* (1900); *King Hal* (1911); the scores of the first 2 were lost in the San Francisco earthquake and fire of 1906. His most successful work was the sacred music drama *The Hound of Heaven* (San Francisco, April 24, 1924); he further wrote the orch. suites *Montezuma* and *Scenes in California;* a Mass; organ pieces; songs.

BIBLIOGRAPHY: E.E. Hipsher, *American Opera and Its Composers* (Philadelphia, 1934; pp. 391–94).

Stewart, Reginald, Scottish-American pianist and conductor; b. Edinburgh, April 20, 1900; d. Montecito, near Santa Barbara, Calif., July 8, 1984. He was a boy soprano in a church choir; then took piano lessons with Mark Hambourg and Arthur Friedheim in London and with Isidor Philipp in Paris, where he also studied composition with Nadia Boulanger. He made his London debut as a concert pianist in 1924; in 1933 he went to Canada, where he organized the Toronto Phil. and inaugurated a series of Promenade Symph. Concerts which proved an auspicious opening of his career as a conductor. In 1941 he moved to the U.S.; became head of the Peabody Cons. in Baltimore, occupying this post until 1958; concurrently, he was conductor of the Baltimore Symph. Orch. (1942–52). In 1962 he went to California, where he was named head of the piano dept. and artist-in-residence at the Music Academy of the West in Santa Barbara.

Stewart, Sir Robert Prescott, Irish organist and

composer; b. Dublin, Dec. 16, 1825; d. there, March 24, 1894. He was a chorister of Christ Church Cathedral in Dublin, and at the age of 18 was appointed organist there. In 1852 he became vicar-choral at St. Patrick's Cathedral in Dublin; in 1861 was appointed to the faculty of Dublin Univ. as a teacher of harmony. He was engaged as conductor of the Dublin Phil. in 1873. He gave concerts as an organist in England; wrote several cantatas and odes for various occasions; also anthems, glees, and miscellaneous songs.

BIBLIOGRAPHY: O. Vignoles, *Memoir of Sir Robert P. Stewart* (London, 1899); J.C. Culwick, *The Works of Sir Robert Stewart* (Dublin, 1902).

Stewart, Thomas, distinguished American baritone; b. San Saba, Texas, Aug. 29, 1928. He studied electrical engineering in Waco; later went to N.Y., where he became a student of Mack Harrell at the Juilliard School of Music; made his debut there in 1954 as La Roche in *Capriccio* by Richard Strauss; then sang in the N.Y. City Opera and the Chicago Opera in bass roles. In 1957 he received a Fulbright grant and went to Berlin; was engaged as a baritone with the Städtische Oper; made his debut there as Minister in *Fidelio* (1957); remained on its roster as ensemble singer until 1964. In 1965 he sang at the Bayreuth Festival and in 1967 appeared at the Salzburg Festival. He made his Metropolitan Opera debut in N.Y. on March 9, 1966, as Ford in Verdi's *Falstaff;* in 1981 he sang the role of Lear in the American premiere of Reimann's *King Lear* with the San Francisco Opera. His other roles were Don Giovanni, Count di Luna in *Il Trovatore,* Escamillo in *Carmen,* Iago in *Otello,* and Wotan. In 1955 he married the American soprano **Evelyn Lear.**

Stibilj, Milan, Slovenian composer; b. Ljubljana, Nov. 2, 1929. He studied composition with Karol Pahor at the Ljubljana Academy of Music (1956–61) and with Kelemen at the Zagreb Academy of Music (1962–64); took courses in electronic music at the Univ. of Utrecht (1966–67). He composes in an advanced idiom, exploring the techniques of integral serial organization of musical parameters.

WORKS: *Anekdote* for Piano (1957); *Koncertantna glasba (Concertante Music)* for Horn and Orch. (1959); *Skladbe (Composition)* for Horn and Strings (1959); *Sarabanda* for 4 Clarinets (1960); *Slavček in vrtnica (The Nightingale and the Rose),* symph. poem (1961); *Skladja (Congruences)* for Piano and Orch. (1963); *Impressions* for Flute, Harp, and String Quintet or String Orch. (1963); *Epervier de ta faiblesse, Domine* for Narrator and 5 Percussionists (1964); *Verz* for Orch. (1964); *Assimilation* for Solo Violin (1965); *Contemplation* for Oboe and String Quintet (1966); *Apokatastasis,* Slovenian Requiem for Tenor, Chorus, and Orch. (1967); *Condensation* for Trombone, 2 Pianos, and Percussion (1967); *Zoom* for Clarinet and Bongos (1970); *Indian Summer* for Chamber Orch. (1974).

Stich, Jan Václav (Johann Wenzel; he Italianized his German name, Johann Stich, as **Giovanni**

Punto), famous Czech horn player; b. Žehušice, near Čáslav, Sept. 28, 1746; d. Prague, Feb. 16, 1803. He studied in Prague, Munich, and Dresden; traveled in Germany and Hungary; visited England; then entered the service of the Elector at Mainz (1769–74); subsequently served at the court of the Prince-Bishop of Würzburg, and in 1782 became chamber musician to the Comte d'Artois (later Charles X) in Paris; in Paris he met Mozart, who wrote the *Symphonie concertante* (K. Anhang 9) for him, the flutist Wendling, the oboist Ramm, and the bassoonist Ritter. During the French Revolution (1789–99) Stich was in charge of the music at the Théâtre des Variétés Amusantes; returned to Germany in 1799; proceeded to Vienna in 1800; made the acquaintance of Beethoven, who was enchanted by his playing and wrote for him a Sonata for Horn and Piano (op. 17), and played it with him at a concert on April 18, 1800. He went to Prague in 1801. His works comprise 14 horn concertos, much chamber music with horn, a method for horn (1798; a revision of one by his Dresden teacher Hampel); he also publ. a book of exercises for the horn (Paris, 1795).

BIBLIOGRAPHY: H.A. Fitzpatrick, *The Horn & Horn-Playing and the Austro-Bohemian Tradition 1680–1830* (London, 1970); R. Morley-Pegge, *The French Horn* (London, 1960; 2nd ed., London, 1973).

Stich-Randall, Teresa, American soprano; b. West Hartford, Conn., Dec. 24, 1927. She studied voice at the Hartford School of Music and Columbia Univ.; then sang in N.Y., where she appeared with Toscanini and the NBC Symph. Orch. In 1951 she won the singing competition held in Lausanne; in 1952 she made her Vienna State Opera debut; in 1962 she was made a Kammersängerin. On Oct. 24, 1961, she made her debut at the Metropolitan Opera in N.Y. as Fiordiligi in *Così fan tutte;* also appeared as a soloist with European and American orchs.

Stiedry, Fritz, eminent Austrian conductor; b. Vienna, Oct. 11, 1883; d. Zürich, Aug. 9, 1968. He studied jurisprudence in Vienna and took a course in composition with Eusebius Mandyczewski. Mahler recommended him to Ernst von Schuch in Dresden, and he became his assistant conductor (1907–8); he subsequently was active as a theater conductor in the German provinces, and in Prague. He conducted at the Berlin Opera (1916–23); then led the Vienna Volksoper (1923–25). After traveling as a guest conductor in Italy, Spain, and Scandinavia (1925–28), he returned to Berlin and was music director of the Berlin Municipal Opera (1929–33). With the advent of the Nazi regime in 1933, he went to Russia, where he conducted the Leningrad Phil. (1933–37). In 1938 he emigrated to the U.S.; conducted the New Friends of Music Orch. in N.Y. In 1946 he joined the staff of the Metropolitan Opera. As a conductor, he championed the modern Vienna School of composition. He was a close friend of Schoenberg; conducted first performances of his opera *Die glückliche Hand* in Vienna (1924) and his 2nd Chamber Symph. in N.Y. (1940). But he also gave fine performances of the operas of Wagner and Verdi. In 1958 he left the U.S., and lived mostly in Zürich thereafter.

Stiehl, Carl Johann Christian, German organist and music historian; b. Lübeck, July 12, 1826; d. there, Dec. 1, 1911. He was a pupil of his father, **Johann Dietrich Stiehl;** served as church organist in Jever (1848–58) and at Eutin (1858–77); in 1878 returned to Lübeck, where he conducted the Musikverein and Singakademie (until 1897); also wrote music criticism, and was in charge of the music section in the Lübeck Library.
WRITINGS: *Zur Geschichte der Instrumentalmusik in Lübeck* (1885); *Lübeckisches Tonkünstler-Lexikon* (1887); *Musikgeschichte der Stadt Lübeck* (1891); *Geschichte des Theaters in Lübeck* (1902); ed. Buxtehude's sonatas *a* 3 and 4 (vol. 11 of Denkmäler Deutscher Tonkunst).

Stiehl, Heinrich (Franz Daniel), German organist, choral conductor, and composer, son of **Johann Dietrich Stiehl;** b. Lübeck, Aug. 5, 1829; d. Reval, May 1, 1886. He studied with Moscheles, Gade, and Hauptmann at the Leipzig Cons.; in 1853 he went to St. Petersburg, where he remained for 13 years as organist at the Lutheran Church and conductor of a German choral society. He was subsequently active in Vienna (1867–69), Italy (1869–72), London (1872–73), and Belfast (1874–77). In 1880 he was engaged as organist and conductor in Reval, Estonia, where he remained to the end of his life, with occasional appearances in St. Petersburg. He wrote in all 172 opus numbers, including 2 light operas: *Der Schatzgräber* and *Jery und Bätely; Die Vision* for Orch.; 2 piano quartets; 3 piano trios; Violin Sonata; Cello Sonata; numerous piano pieces of programmatic content, such as *Spaziergänge im Schwarzwald, Italienische Reisebilder, Hexentanz, Musikalische Portraits,* etc.

Stiehl, Johann Dietrich, German organist; b. Lübeck, July 9, 1800; d. there, June 27, 1873. He lived virtually all his life in Lübeck, where he was organist at St. Jacobi; his sons, **Heinrich** and **Carl Johann Christian,** were also organists.

Stierlin, Adolf, German composer, singer, and pedagogue; b. Adenau, Oct. 14, 1859; d. Münster, April 26, 1930. He studied singing and was engaged as a bass at various theaters in Germany; in 1897 he opened his own music school in Münster. He wrote the operas *Scapina* (Münster, 1887) and *Zamora* (Halle, 1893); a ballet, *Die sieben Todsünden;* choruses.

Stigelli, Giorgio (real name, **Georg Stiegele**), celebrated German tenor; b. 1815; d. in his villa, Boschetti, near Monza, Italy, July 3, 1868. He made extensive concert tours in Europe, and appeared in America in 1864–65. He composed many songs, among them the popular *Die schönsten Augen.*

Stignani, Ebe, Italian mezzo-soprano; b. Naples,

July 11, 1903; d. Imola, Oct. 6, 1974. She studied voice in Naples; made her debut there at the Teatro San Carlo. In 1926 Toscanini invited her to join him at La Scala in Milan, where she remained until 1956. She also made appearances in London, Paris, San Francisco, and Chicago. She excelled in the Italian repertoire.

Still, Robert, English composer; b. London, June 10, 1910; d. Bucklebury, Reading, Jan. 13, 1971. He was educated at Eton College (1923–28) and Oxford Univ. (1929–32); later took courses in musicology at the Royal College of Music in London (1932–33). He served with the Royal Artillery during World War II; began to compose in earnest only after the war. He was also interested in psychoanalysis and publ. an essay on Mahler from the Freudian point of view. His works include 4 symphs. (1954, 1956, 1960, 1964); Violin Concerto (1969); Piano Concerto (1970); 5 string quartets; minor pieces.

Still, William Grant, eminent American composer, called "The Dean of Afro-American Composers"; b. Woodville, Miss., May 11, 1895; d. Los Angeles, Dec. 3, 1978. His father was a musician, but he died when Still was in infancy. His mother, a graduate of Atlanta Univ., moved the family to Little Rock, Ark., where she became a high school teacher. He grew up in a home with cultured, middle-class values, and his stepfather encouraged his interest in music by taking him to see operettas and buying him operatic recordings. He attended Wilberforce Univ. as a science student, but became active in musical activities on campus and abandoned science. After leaving the univ., he worked with various dance bands and wrote arrangements for W.C. Handy; he then attended the Oberlin Cons. During World War I he played violin in the U.S. Army; afterward returned to work with Handy, and became oboist in the Shuffle Along orch. (1921); then studied composition with Varèse, and at the New England Cons. with Chadwick; held a Guggenheim fellowship in 1934–35; was awarded honorary doctorates by Howard Univ. (1941), Oberlin College (1947), and Bates College (1954). Determined to develop a symph. type of Negro music, he wrote an *Afro-American Symphony* (1930). In his music he occasionally made use of actual Negro folk songs, but mostly he invented his thematic materials. He married the writer Verna Arvey, who collaborated with him as librettist in his stage works.
WORKS: FOR ORCH.: *From the Black Belt* (1926); *Darker America* (Rochester, N.Y., Nov. 21, 1927); *From the Journal of a Wanderer* (Rochester, May 8, 1929); *Africa,* symph. poem (1930); Symph No. 1, *Afro-American Symphony* (1930; Rochester, Oct. 29, 1931); *3 Dances,* from the ballet *La Guiablesse* (Rochester, May 5, 1933); *Kaintuck (Kentucky)* for Piano and Orch. (Rochester, Jan. 16, 1936); *Dismal Swamp* (Rochester, Oct. 30, 1936); *Ebon Chronicle* (Fort Worth, Nov. 3, 1936); Symph. No. 2, in G minor (Philadelphia, Dec. 19, 1937); *And They Lynched Him on a Tree* for Narrator, Contralto, Chorus, and Orch. (N.Y., June 25, 1940); *Plain Chant for Ameri-*

cans for Baritone and Orch. (N.Y., Oct. 23, 1941); *Old California* (1941); *Pages from Negro History* (1943); *In Memoriam: The Colored Soldiers Who Died for Democracy* (N.Y., Jan. 5, 1944); *Poem* (Cleveland, Dec. 7, 1944); *Festive Overture* (Cincinnati, Jan. 19, 1945); Symph. No. 3 (1945; discarded); *Archaic Ritual* (1946); *Wood Notes* (Chicago, April 22, 1948); Symph. No. 4, *Autochthonous* (1949; Oklahoma City, March 18, 1951); new Symph. No. 3, *The Sunday Symphony* (1958); Symph. No. 5, *Western Hemisphere* (Oberlin College, Ohio, Nov. 9, 1970; revision of original Symph. No. 3). FOR SYMPH. BAND: *From the Delta* (1945); *To You, America* (1952); etc. VOCAL WORKS: *Caribbean Melodies* for Chorus, Piano, and Percussion (1941); *Wailing Woman* for Soprano and Chorus (1946); etc. STAGE WORKS: *La Guiablesse,* ballet (1927); *Sahdji,* ballet (1930); *Blue Steel,* opera in 3 acts (1935); *Lenox Avenue,* ballet (1937); *Troubled Island,* opera in 4 acts (1938); *A Bayou Legend,* opera in 3 acts (1940); *Miss Sally's Party* (1940); *A Southern Interlude,* opera in 2 acts (1942); *Costaso,* opera in 3 acts (1949); *Highway No. 1, U.S.A.,* one-act opera (Miami, May 13, 1963). Also, *Pastorela* for Violin and Piano (1946).

BIBLIOGRAPHY: M. Cuney-Hare, *Negro Musicians and Their Music* (Washington, D.C., 1936); A. Locke, *The Negro and His Music* (Washington, D.C., 1936); Verna Arvey, *William Grant Still* (N.Y., 1939); R.B. Haas, ed., *William Grant Still and the Fusion of Cultures in American Music* (Los Angeles, 1972); F.H. Douglass, "A Tribute to William Grant Still," *Black Perspective in Music* (Spring 1974); "A Birthday Offering to William Grant Still upon the Occasion of His 80th Anniversary," special issue of *Black Perspective in Music* (May 1975). See also *Modern Music ... Analytic Index,* compiled by Wayne Shirley, ed. by W. and C. Lichtenwanger (N.Y., 1976; pp. 207–8).

Stillman, Mitya, Russian-American viola player and composer; b. Ilyintza, near Kiev, Jan. 27, 1892; d. New York, April 12, 1936. He studied violin; then was a pupil of Glière in composition at the Kiev Cons.; after the Russian Revolution he emigrated to the U.S.; played the viola in the Detroit Symph. Orch. and in the CBS Radio Orch. As a composer, Stillman developed a strong individual style in a peculiarly compact contrapuntal technique. He wrote 8 string quartets, of which No. 7 received a posthumous first-prize award from the NBC Guild as the best chamber music work for 1936. He also wrote some programmatic orch. pieces, among them *Dnieprostroy* (1933); *Yalta Suite* for String Trio; *Cyprus* for Strings, Woodwinds, and Percussion; etc.

Stillman-Kelley, Edgar. See **Kelley, Edgar Stillman.**

Stilwell, Richard, American baritone; b. St. Louis, May 6, 1942. He studied at the Indiana Univ. School of Music with Frank St. Leger and then in N.Y. with Daniel Ferro. In 1970 he made his operatic debut as Pelléas at the N.Y. City Opera; also sang in England at the Glyndebourne Festival (1973) and London's Covent Garden (1974). On Oct. 15, 1975, he made his Metropolitan Opera debut as Guglielmo in *Così fan tutte.*

Stirling, Elizabeth, English organist and composer; b. Greenwich, Feb. 26, 1819; d. London, March 25, 1895. She studied organ and piano with Edward Holmes, and harmony with G.A. Macfarren. She was appointed organist of All Saints', Poplar, at the age of 20, and retained this position for nearly 20 years, when she competed for one at St. Andrew's, Undershaft. She won the contest, and was organist there until 1880. In 1856 she passed the examination for the degree of Mus.Bac. at Oxford (her work was *Psalm 130* for 5 Voices, with Orch.), but, ironically, her earned degree could not be granted to a woman. In 1863 she married F.A. Bridge. She made many organ transcriptions from classical works; publ. *6 Pedal-Fugues* and other organ pieces; also partsongs, of which *All among the Barley* won great popularity.

Stitt, "Sonny" (Edward Stitt), black American jazz tenor and alto saxophonist; b. Boston, Feb. 2, 1924; d. Washington, D.C., July 22, 1982. He took up the clarinet and alto saxophone; made his way to N.Y., where he played with Dizzy Gillespie (1945–46); then led his own band and combo for several years. He became one of the leading tenor and alto saxophonists of his generation.

Stobaeus, Johann, German composer; b. Graudenz, July 6, 1580; d. Königsberg, Sept. 11, 1646. In 1595 he went to Königsberg, where from 1599 to 1608 he was a pupil of J. Eccard; in 1601 he entered the Electoral chapel as a bass, and in 1602 was cantor at the Cathedral. He succeeded Krocker as Kapellmeister to the Elector of Brandenburg in 1626. He publ. *Cantiones sacrae 5–6, 7, 8 et 10 vocibus item aliquot Magnificat 5 et 6 vocibus adornatae* (Frankfurt, 1624); a new edition of *Geistliche Lieder auf ... Kirchen-Melodeyen* for 5 Voices, with some additional songs of his own (1634); Eccard's *Preussische Festlieder* (2 vols., 1642, 1644; modern ed. by Teschner, 1858).

BIBLIOGRAPHY: R. Eitner, *Monatshefte für Musikgeschichte* (1883); A. Mayer-Reinach, "Zur Geschichte der Königsberger Hofkapelle," *Sammelbände der Internationalen Musik-Gesellschaft,* VI/1 (1904); L. Kamieński, *Johann Stobaeus z Grudziadz* (Posen, 1928).

Stock, David F., American composer; b. Pittsburgh, June 3, 1939. He studied trumpet; then enrolled at the Carnegie Inst. of Technology in Pittsburgh, where he took courses in composition with Nicolai Lopatnikoff and musicology with Frederick Dorian. He subsequently obtained his M.F.A. (1963) at Brandeis Univ., studying advanced composition with Arthur Berger and Harold Shapero; played trumpet in various orchs. His works include *Divertimento* for Orch. (1957); *Capriccio* for Small Orch. (1963); *Symphony in One Movement* (1963);

Quintet for Clarinet and Strings (1966); *Flashback for Chamber Ensemble* (1968).

Stock, Frederick A., German-American conductor; b. Jülich, Nov. 11, 1872; d. Chicago, Oct. 20, 1942. He was trained in music by his father, a bandmaster; then studied violin with G. Japha and composition with Wüllner, Zöllner, and Humperdinck at the Cologne Cons. (1886–91); subsequently played the violin in the Municipal Orch. in Cologne (1891–95). In 1895 he was engaged by Theodore Thomas as first viola in the newly organized Thomas Symph. Orch. in Chicago (the future Chicago Symph. Orch.); he was then delegated to conduct the orch. at concerts outside of Chicago proper; after Thomas died in 1905, Stock inherited the orch., now renamed the Theodore Thomas Orch. He became a naturalized U.S. citizen in 1919. As a conductor, Stock was extremely competent, even though he totally lacked that ineffable quality of making orch. music a vivid experience in sound; but he had the merit of giving adequate performances of the classics, of Wagner, and of the German Romantic school. He also programmed several American works, as long as they followed the Germanic tradition. The flowering of the Chicago Symph. Orch. was to be accomplished by his successors Fritz Reiner and Georg Solti. Stock was also a composer; his Violin Concerto was performed under his direction by Efrem Zimbalist at the Norfolk Festival on June 3, 1915.
BIBLIOGRAPHY: P.A. Otis, *The Chicago Symphony Orchestra* (Chicago, 1925).

Stock, Larry, American pianist and composer of popular music; b. New York, Dec. 4, 1896; d. Lakehurst, N.J., May 4, 1984. He studied at Manhattan's Inst. of Musical Art (later, the Juilliard School of Music) with Percy Goetschius. He started his career as a concert pianist; then joined dance bands, and wrote songs in the jazz manner, later switching to swing and rock music. Among the lyricists who wrote words to his tunes were Al Lewis and Vincent Rose. Many famous men and women of the era performed and recorded his songs, among them Louis Armstrong, Elvis Presley, Frank Sinatra, Perry Como, Ella Fitzgerald, Nat (King) Cole, Bing Crosby, and Guy Lombardo. His hit songs included *Raindrop Serenade, Adoration Waltz, Song of Devotion,* and *I Sent a Letter to Santa.*

Stockhausen, Franz, Jr., German conductor and educator, son of **Franz Stockhausen, Sr.,** and brother of **Julius Stockhausen;** b. Gebweiler, Alsace, Jan. 30, 1839; d. Strasbourg, Jan. 4, 1926. He received his early training from his father; then was a student of Alkan in Paris; subsequently studied at the Leipzig Cons., where his teachers were Moscheles, Richter, and Hauptmann (1860–62). He subsequently occupied various posts as a choral conductor and educator. In 1871 he was appointed director of the Strasbourg Cons.; he retired in 1907.

Stockhausen, Franz, Sr., German singer and harpist; b. Cologne, Sept. 1, 1789; d. Colmar, Sept. 10, 1868.

In 1822 he organized in Paris the Académie de Chant, and gave concerts as a harpist.

Stockhausen, Julius, German baritone and teacher, son of the harpist and singer **Franz Stockhausen, Sr.;** b. Paris, July 22, 1826; d. Frankfurt, Sept. 22, 1906. He studied at the Paris Cons. and in London, where he was a pupil of Manuel García. He began his career as a concert singer and a choral conductor; conducted the Phil. concerts and the Singakademie in Hamburg (1862–67), and the Sternscher Gesangverein in Berlin (1874–78). Subsequently he was engaged as a singing teacher at the Frankfurt Hochschen Konservatorium. He was a personal friend of Brahms and was regarded as one of the finest interpreters of his lieder. He publ. *Gesangsmethode,* a standard work on singing (2 vols., 1886, 1887; also in Eng.).
BIBLIOGRAPHY: Julia Wirth-Stockhausen, *Julius Stockhausen der Sänger des deutschen Liedes* (Frankfurt, 1927) and *Unverlierbare Kindheit* (Stuttgart, 1949); A.H. Fox Strangways, "Julius Stockhausen," *Monthly Musical Record* (March–April 1949).

Stockhausen, Karlheinz, German composer, leader of the cosmopolitan avant-garde; b. Mödrath, near Cologne, Aug. 22, 1928. He studied piano at the Hochschule für Musik in Cologne (1947–50) and took a course in composition with Frank Martin during the latter's residence there (1950–51); then went to Paris, where he studied privately with Olivier Messiaen and Darius Milhaud (1951–53); also investigated the potentialities of *musique concrète* and partly incorporated its techniques into his own empiric method of composition, which from the very first included highly complex contrapuntal conglomerates with uninhibited applications of non-euphonious dissonance as well as recourse to the primal procedures of obdurate iteration of single tones; all this set in the freest of rhythmic patterns and diversified by constantly changing instrumental colors with obsessive percussive effects. He further perfected a system of constructivist composition, in which the subjective choice of the performer determines the succession of given thematic ingredients and their polyphonic simultaneities, ultimately leading to a totality of aleatory procedures in which the ostensible application of a composer's commanding function is paradoxically reasserted by the inclusion of prerecorded materials and recombinant uses of electronically altered thematic ingredients. He further evolved energetic missionary activities in behalf of new music as a lecturer and master of ceremonies at avant-garde meetings all over the world; conducted summer seminars for the Ferienkurse für Musik in Darmstadt, which attracted auditors and musical cultists from the 5 continents of the globe; having mastered the intricacies of the English language, he made a lecture tour of Canadian and American univs. in 1958; was a visiting prof. at the Univ. of Calif., Davis, in 1966–67; in 1969 gave highly successful public lectures in England which were attended by hordes of musical and unmusical novitiates; publ. numerous misleading guidelines for the benefit of a growing contingent of his apostles, disciples, and acolytes. Stockhausen is a pioneer of "time-space" music, marked by a controlled improvisation, and adding the vectorial (i.e., directional) parameter to the 4 traditional aspects of serial music (pitch, duration, timbre, and dynamics), with performers and electronic apparatuses placed in different parts of the concert hall; such performances, directed by himself, are often accompanied by screen projections and audience participation; he also specifies the architectural aspects of the auditoriums in which he gives his demonstrations; thus, at the world's fair in Osaka, Japan, in 1970, he supervised the construction of a circular auditorium in the German pavilion; these demonstrations continued for 183 days, with 20 soloists and 5 lantern projections in live performances of his own works, each session lasting 5½ hours; the estimated live, radio, and television audience was 1,000,000 listeners. In 1963 he inaugurated courses of new music in Cologne; in 1971 he was appointed prof. of composition at the Hochschule für Musik there.

WORKS: *Kreuzspiel* for Orch. (1952); *Kontra-Punkte* for 10 Instruments (Cologne, May 26, 1953); *Klavierstück XI* (one of a series of constructivist pieces); *Zeitmasse* for Oboe, Flute, English Horn, Clarinet, and Bassoon (1956); *Der Gesang der Jünglinge*, to a text composed of disjected verbal particles from the Book of Daniel, dealing with the ordeal of 3 monotheistic Hebrew youths in the Babylonian fiery furnace, scored for 5 groups of loudspeakers surrounding the audience (first perf. at the Radio Studio in Cologne, May 30, 1956); *Gruppen*, spatial work for 3 Chamber Orchs. and 3 Conductors beating 3 different tempi (Cologne, March 24, 1959); *Kontakte* for Electronic Instruments, Piano, and Percussion (Cologne, June 11, 1960); *Carré* for 4 Orchs., 4 Choruses, and 4 Conductors (Hamburg, Oct. 28, 1960); *Zyklus* for One Percussionist (1961); *Momente* for Soprano, 4 Choruses (singing, speaking, whispering, screaming, laughing, stamping, clapping, etc.), 13 Instrumentalists, and Percussion (Cologne, May 21, 1962; extended and revised, 1965); *Mikrophonie I* and *II* for Flexible Ensembles (1964, 1965); *Stimmung* for 6 Singers (1967); *X* for Dancers autogenetically producing sounds by activating eggshells placed on the floor or piano wires strung across the stage (1967); *Hymnen*, electronic piece (Cologne, Nov. 30, 1967); *Aus den Sieben Tagen* for Optional Instruments, written out in graphic notation with verbal instructions, such as "play a tone in the certainty that you have plenty of time and space" (1968); *Telemusik* for an Instrumental Ensemble and Electronic Instruments (Warsaw, Sept. 23, 1968); *Plus-Minus* for Clarinet, Trombone, Cello, and 3 Pianos (Warsaw, Sept. 25, 1968); *Kurzwellen* for 5 Performers (1969); *Prozession* for Tam-tam, Viola, Electronium, Piano, and Microphone (1969); *Für kommende Zeiten* for "17 texts of intuitive music" (1968–70); *Beethausen, opus 1970, von Stockhoven*, bicentennial homage to Beethoven for Multimedia, using fragments from Beethoven's works and including a reading of the

Heiligenstadt Testament (1970); *Mantra* for 2 Pianos (Donaueschingen, Oct. 18, 1970); *Sternklang*, "park music" for 5 Groups (1971); *Musik im Bauch (Music in the Belly)* for Percussion and Musical Clocks (1975); *Inori (Adorations)* for Soloists and Orch. (Donaueschingen, Oct. 20, 1974); *Atmen gibt das Leben* for Chorus (1974; Hamburg, May 16, 1975; revised as a choral opera, 1977); *Harlekin* for Clarinet (1975); *Tierkreis (Zodiac)* for Chamber Orch. (1975–77); *Sirius*, multimedia work for Vocalists, Trumpet, Bass Clarinet, and Electronic Sound, dedicated to American pioneers on earth and in space (first demonstrated at the National Air and Space Museum at the Smithsonian Institution, Washington, D.C., July 18, 1976); *Amour*, 5 pieces for Clarinet (1976); *In Freundschaft* for various Solo Instruments (1977); also the grand spectacle *Light: The 7 Days of the Week* for Solo Voices, Solo Instruments, Solo Dancers, Chorus, Orch., Dancers, Electronic and Concrete Music; each day is its own opera; *Tuesday*, in one scene, entitled *Der Jahreslauf (In the Course of the Year)*, for Dancers and Orch. (1977); *Thursday*, in 3 acts: *Michaels Jugend (Michael's Youth)* for Soprano, Bass, Tenor, Trumpet, Basset Horn, Trombone, Modulated Piano, 3 Dancers, and Tape (1978–79), *Michaels Reise um die Erde (Michael's Journey around the Earth)* for Trumpet and Orch. (1978), and *Michaels Heimkehr (Michael's Return)* for Soprano, Tenor, Bass, Trumpet, Basset Horn, Trombone, 3 Dancers, Chorus, and Orch. (1979); *Saturday*, including *Lucifer's Dream* (1981–83); *Jubilee* for Orch. (N.Y., Sept. 10, 1981).

BIBLIOGRAPHY: Karl H. Wörner, *Karlheinz Stockhausen, Werk und Wollen 1950–62* (Rodenkirchen, 1963; augmented Eng. trans., 1973); J. Cott, *Stockhausen: Conversations with the Composer* (London, 1973); Cornelius Cardew, *Stockhausen Serves Imperialism*, a rambling diatribe by a disenchanted follower who became a militant Maoist (London, 1974); J. Harvey, *The Music of Stockhausen: An Introduction* (London, 1975); Robin Maconie, *The Works of Karlheinz Stockhausen* (London, 1976). His annotations to his own works were publ. in 3 vols. under the title *Texte zur elektronischen und instrumentalen Musik* (Cologne, 1963, 1964, 1966); he also publ. *Ein Schlüssel für Momente* (Kassel, 1971).

Stockhoff, Walter William, American composer; b. St. Louis, Nov. 12, 1876 (of German parentage); d. there, April 1, 1968. He was largely autodidact, and began to compose early in life. In his music he was influenced mainly by German Romantic composers, but his thematic material is distinctly American. In some of his early piano music he made use of modernistic devices, such as the whole-tone scale, cadential triads with the added sixth, etc. Busoni wrote an enthusiastic article about Stockhoff (1915) in which he described him as one of America's most original composers. The orch. version of Stockhoff's piano suite *To the Mountains* was performed for the first time, under the title *American Symphonic Suite*, in Frankfurt, Germany, on Dec. 10, 1924. Several of his piano works and some chamber music were publ. by Breitkopf & Härtel. Other works include *5 Dramatic Poems* for Orch. (1943); Piano Sonata; *Metamorphoses* for Piano; etc.

Stoeckel, Carl, American patron of music, son of **Gustav Jakob Stoeckel;** b. New Haven, Conn., Dec. 7, 1858; d. Norfolk, Conn., Nov. 1, 1925. His contribution to American musical culture was the establishment in 1902 of the summer festivals on his estate in Norfolk. He offered cash prizes to composers who appeared at the festival in performances of their own works. Sibelius composed his tone poem *Aallottaret* especially for the Norfolk Festival, and conducted its world premiere there in 1914. Among other composers represented were J.A. Carpenter, G.W. Chadwick, S. Coleridge-Taylor, H.F. Gilbert, P. Grainger, H.K. Hadley, E.S. Kelly, C.M. Loeffler, H. Parker, D.S. Smith, C.V. Stanford, and Deems Taylor.

Stoeckel, Gustav Jakob, German-American musician; b. Maikammer, Bavarian Palatinate, Nov. 9, 1819; d. Norfolk, Conn., May 14, 1907. He emigrated to America in 1847; served as chapel organist at Yale Univ. and was a prof. of music there until 1896. He composed some vocal and instrumental pieces, arranged college songs, and assisted in editing the *College Hymn Book* for men's voices.
BIBLIOGRAPHY: D.S. Smith, *G.J. Stoeckel, Yale Pioneer in Music* (New Haven, 1939).

Stoessel, Albert, American conductor and composer; b. St. Louis, Oct. 11, 1894; d. New York, May 12, 1943. He went to Germany as a youth; studied violin with Willy Hess and theory with Kretzschmar in Berlin, and appeared as a violin soloist there in 1914. Returning to the U.S., he turned to conducting; succeeded Walter Damrosch as conductor of the N.Y. Oratorio Society; in 1930 was appointed director of the opera dept. of the Juilliard Graduate School of Music in N.Y. He was stricken fatally while conducting the first performance of the symph. sketch *Dunkirk,* by Walter Damrosch. His *Suite Antique* for 2 Violins and Piano (1922) enjoyed a few performances. His opera *Garrick* was produced under his direction at Juilliard on Feb. 24, 1937. He publ. *The Technic of the Baton* (N.Y., 1920; new ed., 1928).

Stoeving, (Carl Heinrich) Paul, German-American violinist and composer; b. Leipzig, May 7, 1861; d. New York, Dec. 24, 1948. He studied violin in Leipzig and in Paris; toured as a soloist in Russia and Scandinavia; in 1896 went to London, where he taught at the Guildhall School of Music. At the outbreak of World War I he emigrated to the U.S. and was employed as a violin teacher in New Haven and N.Y. He wrote the "song-play" *Gaston and Jolivette* and some violin music of considerable insignificance, but his publications on violin technique have a certain pragmatic value; among them are *The Art of Violin Bowing* (London, 1902); *The Story of the Violin* (London, 1904); *The Mastery of the Bow and*

Bowing Subtleties (N.Y., 1920); *The Violin, Cello and String Quartet* (N.Y., 1927); *The Violin: Its Famous Makers and Players* (Boston, 1928).

Stöhr, Richard, Austrian music theorist and composer; b. Vienna, June 11, 1874; d. Montpelier, Vt., Dec. 11, 1967. He studied medicine (M.D., 1898), but then turned to music and studied with Robert Fuchs and others at the Vienna Cons. In 1903 he was appointed instructor in theory there, and during his long tenure he had many pupils who later became celebrated (Artur Rodzinski, Erich Leinsdorf, etc.). In 1938 he was compelled to leave Vienna; settled in the U.S., where he taught at the Curtis Inst. of Music in Philadelphia (1939–42); then taught music and German at St. Michael's College in Winooski, Vt. (1943–50). A concert of his works was given by the Vermont State Symph. Orch. on Oct. 31, 1954, including the world premiere of his *Vermont Suite,* an early symph., and songs accompanied by the composer. He further wrote 4 symphs.; much chamber music; piano pieces. He publ. a popular manual, *Praktischer Leitfaden der Harmonielehre* (Vienna, 1909; 21st ed., 1963); also *Praktischer Leitfaden des Kontrapunkts* (Hamburg, 1911); *Modulationslehre* (1932).
BIBLIOGRAPHY: R. Felber, "Richard Stöhr," in *Cobbett's Cyclopedic Survey of Chamber Music* (London, 1929; vol. 2); H. Sittner, *Richard Stöhr, Mensch, Musiker, Lehrer* (Vienna, 1965).

Stojanović, Peter Lazar, violinist and composer; b. Budapest, Sept. 6, 1877; d. Belgrade, Sept. 12, 1957. He studied violin with Hubay at the Budapest Cons. and with J. Grün at the Vienna Cons.; in 1913 established his own school for advanced violin playing in Vienna. In 1925 he settled in Belgrade and became a prof. at the Stankovic Music School; was its director from 1925 to 1928; in 1937–45 he was a prof. of violin at the Belgrade Academy of Music. His works include the operas *A Tigris (The Tiger;* Budapest, Nov. 14, 1905); *Das Liebchen am Dache* (Vienna, May 19, 1917); *Der Herzog von Reichsstadt* (Vienna, Feb. 11, 1921); an operetta, *Orlić;* 2 ballets; a symph. poem, *Heldentod;* 7 violin concertos, 2 viola concertos, a Flute Concerto, a Horn Concerto; several pieces of chamber music, including a Piano Trio, a Piano Quartet, and a Piano Quintet. He publ. *Schule der Skalentechnik* for Violin.

Stojowski, Sigismund, Polish pianist; b. Strzelce, May 14, 1869; d. New York, Nov. 5, 1946. He was a pupil of Zelenski at Cracow and of Diémer (piano) and Delibes (composition) at the Paris Cons. (1887–89), winning first prize for piano playing and composition; later he took a course with Paderewski. At an orch. concert of his own works given in Paris in 1891, he played his Piano Concerto; he remained in Paris until 1906, when he emigrated to the U.S. as head of the piano dept. at the Inst. of Musical Art in N.Y.; later held a similar position at the Von Ende School of Music in N.Y.; taught at the Juilliard Summer School for several years. He became a naturalized American citizen in 1938. In his prime he was extremely successful as a concert pianist, and in his later years was greatly esteemed as a pedagogue. His works include, besides his Piano Concerto, *Prologue, Scherzo and Variations* for Piano and Orch., performed by him (as Piano Concerto No. 2) in London, June 23, 1913, under the direction of Nikisch; many solo piano pieces; *Prayer for Poland* for Chorus and Orch. (1915); 2 violin sonatas; a Cello Sonata.

Stoker, Richard, English composer; b. Castleford, Yorkshire, Nov. 8, 1938. He studied composition with Eric Fenby and later with Lennox Berkeley at the Royal Academy of Music in London, and with Nadia Boulanger in Paris. In his music he cultivates the 12-tone technique, but derives it tonally from the quintal cycle of scales. As a believer in the universality of the arts, he writes utilitarian music for dilettantes, amateurs, musicasters, and children.

WORKS: Trio for Flute, Oboe, and Clarinet (1960); *Festival Suite* for Trumpet and Piano (1961); Clarinet Sonata (1961); Wind Quintet (1962); *Miniature String Trio* (1963); Sextet for Wind and Strings (1963); Violin Sonata (1964); Piano Trio (1965); *3 Miniature Quartets* (1966); an opera, *Johnson Preserv'd* (London, July 4, 1967).

Stokowski, Leopold, celebrated, spectacularly endowed, and magically communicative English-American conductor; b. (of a Polish father and an Irish mother) London, April 18, 1882; d. Nether Wallop, Hampshire, Sept. 13, 1977. He attended Queen's College, Oxford, and the Royal College of Music in London, where he studied organ with Stevenson Hoyte, music theory with Walford Davies, and composition with Sir Charles Stanford. At the age of 18 he obtained the post of organist at St. James, Piccadilly. In 1905 he went to America and served as organist and choirmaster at St. Bartholomew's in N.Y.; became a U.S. citizen in 1915. In 1909 he was engaged to conduct the Cincinnati Symph. Orch.; although his contract was for 5 years, he obtained a release after 3 years of tenure in order to accept an offer from the Philadelphia Orch. This was the beginning of a long and spectacular career as a symph. conductor; he led the Philadelphia Orch. for 23 years, bringing it to a degree of brilliance that rivaled the greatest orchs. in the world. In 1931 he was officially designated by the board of directors of the Philadelphia Orch. as music director, which gave him control over the choice of guest conductors and soloists. He conducted most of the repertoire by heart, an impressive accomplishment at the time; he changed the seating of the orch., placing violins to the left and cellos to the right. After some years of leading the orch. with a baton, he finally dispensed with it and shaped the music with the 10 fingers of his hands. He emphasized the colorful elements in the music; he was the creator of the famous "Philadelphia sound" in the strings, achieving a well-nigh *bel canto* quality. Tall and slender, with an aureole of blond hair, his figure presented a striking contrast with his stocky, mustachioed German predecessors; he was the first conductor to attain the status of a star comparable to that of a motion picture actor. Abandoning the proverbial ivory tower in which most conductors dwelt, he actually made an appearance as a movie actor in the film *One Hundred Men and a Girl*. In 1940 he agreed to participate in the production of Walt Disney's celebrated film *Fantasia*, which featured both live performers and animated characters; Stokowski conducted the music and in one sequence engaged in a bantering colloquy with Mickey Mouse. He was lionized by the Philadelphians; in 1922 he received the Edward Bok Award of $10,000 as "the person who has done the most for Philadelphia." He was praised in superlative terms in the press, but not all music critics approved of his cavalier treatment of sacrosanct masterpieces, for he allowed himself to alter the orchestration; he doubled some solo passages in the brass, and occasionally introduced percussion instruments not provided in the score; he even cut out individual bars that seemed to him devoid of musical action. Furthermore, Stokowski's own orch. arrangements of Bach raised the pedantic eyebrows of professional musicologists; yet there is no denying the effectiveness of the sonority and the subtlety of color that he succeeded in creating by such means. Many great musicians hailed Stokowski's new orch. sound; Rachmaninoff regarded the Philadelphia Orch. under Stokowski, and later under Ormandy, as the greatest with which he had performed. Stokowski boldly risked his popularity with the Philadelphia audiences by introducing modern works. He conducted Schoenberg's music, culminating in the introduction of his formidable score *Gurrelieder* on April 8, 1932. An even greater gesture of defiance of popular tastes was his world premiere of *Amériques* by Varèse on April 9, 1926, a score that opens with a siren and thrives on dissonance. Stokowski made history by joining the forces of the Philadelphia Orch. with the Philadelphia Grand Opera Co. in the first American performance of Alban Berg's modern masterpiece *Wozzeck* (March 31, 1931). The opposition of some listeners was now vocal; when the audible commotion in the audience erupted during Stokowski's performance of Anton von Webern's Symph., he abruptly stopped conducting, walked off the stage, then returned only to begin the work all over again. From his earliest years with the Philadelphia Orch., Stokowski adopted the habit of addressing the audience, to caution them to keep their peace during the performance of a modernistic score, or reprimanding them for their lack of progressive views; once he even took to task the prim Philadelphia ladies for bringing their knitting to the concert. In 1933 the board of directors took an unusual step in announcing that there would be no more "debatable music" performed by the orch.; Stokowski refused to heed this proclamation. Another eruption of discontent ensued when Stokowski programmed some Soviet music at a youth concert and trained the children to sing the Internationale. Stokowski was always interested in new electronic sound; he was the first to make use of the Theremin in the orch. in order to enhance the sonorities of the bass section. He was instrumental in introducing electrical recordings. In 1936 he resigned as music director of the Philadelphia Orch.; he was succeeded by Eugene Ormandy but continued to conduct occasional concerts as co-conductor of the orch. In 1940–42 he took a newly organized All-American Youth Orch. on a tour in the U.S. and in South America. During the season 1942–43 he was associate conductor, with Toscanini, of the NBC Symph. Orch.; he shared the season of 1949–50 with Mitropoulos as conductor of the N.Y. Phil.; from 1955 to 1960 he conducted the Houston Symph. In 1962 he organized in N.Y. the American Symph. Orch. and led it until 1972; on April 26, 1965, at the age of 83, he conducted the orch. in the first complete performance of the 4th Symph. of Charles Ives. In 1973 he went to London, where he continued to make recordings and conduct occasional concerts; he also appeared in television interviews. He died in his sleep at the age of 95; rumor had it that he had a contract signed for a gala performance on his 100th birthday in 1982. Stokowski was married 3 times: his first wife was the pianist **Olga Samaroff,** whom he married in 1911; they were divorced in 1923; his 2nd wife was Evangeline Brewster Johnson, heiress to the Johnson and Johnson drug fortune; they were married in 1926 and divorced in 1937; his 3rd marriage, to Gloria Vanderbilt, produced a ripple of prurient newspaper publicity because of the disparity in their ages; he was 63, she was 21; they were married in 1945 and divorced in 1955. Stokowski publ. a popular book, *Music for All of Us* (N.Y., 1943), which was translated into the Russian, Italian, and Czech languages.

BIBLIOGRAPHY: Hope Stoddard, *Symphony Conductors of the U.S.A.* (N.Y., 1957; pp. 215–27); Harold Schonberg, *The Great Conductors* (N.Y., 1967); Herbert Kupferberg, *Those Fabulous Philadelphians* (N.Y., 1969; pp. 30–111); E. Johnson, ed., *Stokowski: Essays in Analysis of His Art* (London, 1973); Abram Chasins, *Stoki, the Ageless Apollo* (N.Y., 1979); Oliver Daniel, *Stokowski. A Counterpoint of View* (N.Y., 1982); P. Opperby, *Leopold Stokowski* (Tunbridge Wells, 1982).

Stoltz, Rosine (real name, **Victoire Noël**), French mezzo-soprano; b. Paris, Feb. 13, 1815; d. there, July 28, 1903. She was the daughter of a janitor; was sent by Duchess de Berri to a convent, and in 1826 to the Choron School, which she entered under the name of Rosa Nina. She first appeared in public under the assumed name of **Mlle. Ternaux,** later as **Mlle. Héloise Stoltz** (the latter being derived from her mother's maiden name, Stoll). Her first important engagement was in Brussels on June 3, 1836, when she sang Rachel in Halévy's *La Juive,* with Adolphe Nourrit, who recommended her to the administration of the Paris Opéra; made her debut there as Rachel on Aug. 25, 1837. She became intimate with Leon Pillet, manager of the Opéra from 1844, and through him wielded considerable influence on appointments of new singers; after a series of attacks in the press, accusing her of unworthy intrigues, she resigned in March 1847; fought for vindication through 3 obviously inspired pamphlets (C. Cantin-

jou, *Les Adieux de Madame Stoltz;* E. Pérignon, *Rosine Stoltz;* and J. Lemer, *Madame Rosine Stoltz*), all publ. in 1847. At the invitation of the Brazilian Emperor Don Pedro (who was romantically attached to her) she made 4 tours of Brazil between 1850 and 1859, at a salary of 400,000 francs a season. She was married to A. Lescuyer (March 2, 1837, legitimizing a son born Sept. 21, 1836); was subsequently married to the Duke Carlo Lesignano (May 18, 1872); assumed the title of Baroness von Ketschendorf, from the castle given her by Ernest Ketschendorf, Duke of Saxe-Coburg-Gotha. She publ. 6 songs (not composed by her, in all probability), and her name (as Princesse de Lesignano) was used as author of a learned vol., *Les Constitutions de tous les pays civilisés* (1880), which was written in her behalf. The mystifying aspects of her private life and public career are recounted by G. Bord in *Rosine Stoltz* (Paris, 1909) and by A. Pougin in "La Vérité sur Madame Stoltz," *Le Ménestrel* (Aug. 28, 1909, *et seq.*).

Stoltzer, Thomas, German composer of sacred music; b. Schweidnitz, Silesia, c.1475; d. as chaplain of the Hungarian King Louis in the battle of Mohács, Aug. 29, 1526. He entered the service of Hungary in 1522. His Latin Psalms were publ. in 1538, 1545, and 1569; German songs were included in collections of 1536, 1539, and 1544. His *Octo tonorum melodiae,* containing instrumental fantasies for 5 voices, is a collection of pieces in all 8 church modes. Modern reprints are in Denkmäler Deutscher Tonkunst, 34 and 65; *Das Chorwerk,* 6; and *Das Erbe deutscher Musik,* 22 and 66.

BIBLIOGRAPHY: K.L. Hampe, *Die deutschen Psalmen des Thomas Stoltzer* (Halle, 1943); G. Reese, *Music in the Renaissance* (N.Y., 1954).

Stoltzman, Richard, American clarinet virtuoso; b. Omaha, July 12, 1942. He earned a B.Mus. degree from Ohio State Univ. and a M.Mus. degree from Yale Univ.; spent summers at the Marlboro Music School and Festival; became a founding member of TASHI, the chamber music ensemble; subsequently toured the U.S., South America, Europe, and Japan with it. His repertoire is extensive, and includes the standard literature as well as contemporary works.

Stolz, Robert, Austrian operetta composer; b. Graz, Aug. 25, 1880; d. West Berlin, June 27, 1975. He studied music with his father; then took lessons with Robert Fuchs in Vienna and with Humperdinck in Berlin. He conducted performances at the Theater an der Wien for 12 years, and also filled guest engagements in Europe. In 1938 he went to Paris, and in 1940 proceeded to the U.S.; he returned to Vienna in 1946. He possessed an extraordinary facility for stage music and composed 27 operettas in a typical Viennese manner; of these the most famous is *2 Herzen im 3/4 Takt* (Zürich, Sept. 30, 1933). Other operettas are: *Die lustigen Weiber von Wien* (Munich, 1909); *Das Glücksmädel* (1910); *Das Lumperl* (Graz, 1915); *Lang, lang, ist's her* (Vienna, March 28, 1917); *Der Tanz ins Glück* (Vienna, Oct. 18, 1921);

Die Tanzgräfin (Vienna, May 13, 1921); *Mädi* (Vienna, Oct. 5, 1923); *Ein Ballroman oder Der Kavalier von zehn bis vier* (Vienna, Feb. 29, 1924); *Eine einzige Nacht* (Vienna, Dec. 23, 1927); *Peppina* (1931); *Wild Violets* (1932); *Venus in Seide* (1932); *Frühling im Prater* (Vienna, Dec. 22, 1949); *Karneval in Wien* (1950); *Trauminsel* (Bregenz, July 21, 1962); *Frühjahrs-Parade* (Vienna, March 25, 1964). He wrote a number of film scores and nearly 2,000 lieder. After he was forced to leave Austria, he composed a funeral march for Hitler (at a time when Hitler was, unfortunately, very much alive).
BIBLIOGRAPHY: G. Holm, *Im 3/4 Takt durch die Welt,* a biography (Linz, 1948); W.-D. Brümmel and Fr. van Booth, *Robert Stolz, Melodie eines Lebens* (Hamburg, 1967); contains a chronology of his productions); O. Herbrich, *Robert Stolz, König der Melodie* (Vienna and Munich, 1975).

Stolz, Teresa (Teresina), soprano; b. Kosteletz, Bohemia, June 2, 1834; d. Milan, Aug. 23, 1902. She studied at the Cons. of Prague, and later with Luigi Ricci in Trieste; began her operatic career in Russia; her debut was in Tiflis in 1857; from 1863 to 1879 she appeared with brilliant success at the principal Italian opera houses. She was greatly admired by Verdi, and was famous in the roles of Aida, and of Leonora in *La forza del destino.* Her farewell appearance was in Verdi's *Requiem* at La Scala in Milan on June 30, 1879.
BIBLIOGRAPHY: U. Zoppi, *Mariani, Verdi e Stolz* (Milan, 1947); F. Walker, *The Man Verdi* (London, 1962).

Stolze, Gerhard, German tenor; b. Dessau, Oct. 1, 1926; d. Garmisch-Partenkirchen, March 11, 1979. He studied voice in Dresden; made his debut at the Dresden State Opera in 1949. From 1951 he made regular appearances at the Bayreuth Festivals; also sang at the Vienna State Opera, and from 1953, at the Berlin Staatsoper. He established his reputation as a Wagnerian singer, but also sang leading parts in German contemporary operas.

Stölzel (Stölz), Gottfried Heinrich, German composer; b. Grünstädtl, Jan. 13, 1690; d. Gotha, Nov. 27, 1749. He studied with the cantor Umlaufft at Schneeberg, and with Melchior Hofmann at Leipzig; became a music teacher in Breslau (1710–12), where his opera *Narcissus* was performed in 1711; this was followed by productions of his operas *Valeria, Artemisia,* and *Orion* (all in 1712). After a journey to Italy, he was in Prague, where he brought out the operas *Venus und Adonis* (1714), *Acis und Galathea* (1715), and *Das durch die Liebe besiegte Glück* (1716). He subsequently went to Bayreuth, where he produced the opera *Diomedes* (1717); to Gera; and to Gotha, where he produced *Der Musenberg* (1723). Altogether he wrote 22 operas, the pastoral *Rosen und Dornen,* 14 oratorios, 8 double sets of cantatas and motets for the church year, other religious works, symphs., serenades, concertos, etc.; a Concerto Grosso edited by Schering is found in Denkmäler Deutscher Tonkunst, 29–30; a Solo Cantata for Contralto was edited by J. Bachmair (1926). Stölzel's autobiography was reprinted in *Selbstbiographien deutscher Musiker,* edited by Willi Kahl (Cologne, 1948).
BIBLIOGRAPHY: W. Schmidt-Weiss, *G.H. Stölzel als Instrumentalkomponist* (Würzburg, 1939); F. Hennenberg, *Das Kantatenschaffen von Gottfried Heinrich Stölzel* (Diss., Univ. of Leipzig, 1976).

Stone, Kurt, German-American musicologist; b. Hamburg, Nov. 14, 1911. He studied music in Hamburg and Copenhagen; came to N.Y. in 1938 and entered the field of music publishing; held editorial positions with the Associated Music Publishers and G. Schirmer, Inc.; contributed knowledgeable articles on modern music and composers to various periodicals. He also edited reprints of old music, among them *Parthenia* (N.Y., 1951); trans. from the German (with his wife, Else Stone) the *Handbook of Percussion Instruments* by Karl Peinkofer and Fritz Tannigel (N.Y., 1977); also with his wife, edited and annotated *The Writings of Elliott Carter* (Bloomington, Ind., 1977).

Stöpel, Franz (David Christoph), German writer on music; b. Oberheldrungen, Nov. 14, 1794; d. Paris, Dec. 19, 1836. He introduced Logier's method of piano teaching in Berlin in 1822; later taught it in other cities, finally in Paris, but nowhere with striking success.
WRITINGS: *Grundzüge der Geschichte der modernen Musik* (1821); *Beiträge zur Würdigung der neuen Methode des gleichzeitigen Unterrichts einer Mehrzahl Schüler im Pianofortespiel und der Theorie der Harmonie* (1823); *System der Harmonielehre* (after Logier; 1825); *Über J.B. Logiers System der Musikwissenschaft* (1827); etc.

Stör, Carl, German violinist and composer; b. Stolberg, June 29, 1814; d. Weimar, Jan. 17, 1889. He was a pupil of Götze and Lobe at Weimar; was appointed court conductor in 1857, but in a few years failing eyesight compelled him to resign. He composed the opera *Die Flucht* (Weimar, 1843); *Tonbilder zu Schillers "Lied von der Glocke"* for Orch.; Violin Concerto; several ballets; a *Ständchen* for Cello, with Orch.; songs.

Storace, (Anna Selina) Nancy, celebrated English soprano; b. London, Oct. 27, 1765; d. there, Aug. 24, 1817. She was of Italian origin; her father, **Stefano Storace,** was a player on the double bass; her brother **Stephen Storace** was a composer. She was a pupil of Rauzzini and of Sacchini in Venice; sang in Florence (1780), Parma (1781), and Milan (1782); then went to Vienna (1783), where she was engaged at the court opera. She created the role of Susanna in Mozart's *Nozze di Figaro* (May 1, 1786). Returning to England in 1787, she became popular as a singer in comic operas. She retired from the stage in 1808.
BIBLIOGRAPHY: M.K. Ward, "Nancy Storace," *Musical Times* (Nov. 1949); B. Matthews, "The Childhood of Nancy Storace," *Musical Times*

(1969).

Storace, Stephen, English composer; b. London, April 4, 1762; d. there, March 19, 1796. He was a brother of **Nancy Storace,** and son of **Stefano Storace,** an excellent double-bass player of Italian descent; the original family name was Sorace, but upon moving to England it was found that the pronunciation "sore-ass" was offensive. He studied violin at the Cons. di S. Onofrio in Naples; then followed his sister to Vienna, and became acquainted with Mozart there. Two of his operas to Italian librettos were produced in Vienna, with satisfying success: *Gli Sposi malcontenti* (June 1, 1785) and *Gli equivoci* (Dec. 27, 1786). Back in London he produced another Italian opera, *La Cameriera astuta* (March 4, 1788), and a number of English operas, among which *The Haunted Tower,* produced on Nov. 24, 1789, became extremely successful, and was revived in performance in London as late as 1922. His other operas were *No Song, No Supper* (April 16, 1790); *The Siege of Belgrade* (Jan. 1, 1791); *The Pirates* (Nov. 21, 1792); *The Prize* (March 11, 1793); *My Grandmother* (Dec. 16, 1793); *The Cherokee* (Dec. 20, 1794); *The 3 and the Deuce* (Sept. 2, 1795). A grand opera, *Mahmoud, or The Prince of Persia,* left unfinished at his death, was completed by Michael Kelly and performed posthumously on April 30, 1796. Storace wrote several other pieces for the theater, some of them adaptations, admitted or concealed, of operas by other composers, e.g., Dittersdorf's *Doktor und Apotheker* and Salieri's *Grotta di Trofonio.*
BIBLIOGRAPHY: R. Graves, "The Comic Operas of Stephen Storace," *Musical Times* (Oct. 1954).

Storch, M. Anton, Austrian conductor and composer; b. Vienna, Dec. 22, 1813; d. there, Dec. 31, 1888. He was conductor at the Carl and Josephstadt theaters in Vienna, and produced several of his operettas and opera-burlesques there: *Romeo und Julie* (Oct. 31, 1863); *Das Festkleid* (April 1, 1865); *Löwen im Dorfe* (Sept. 27, 1866); *Wiener Zugstücke* (April 26, 1868); *Prinz Taugenichts* (March 8, 1870; successful); wrote many favorite male quartets (*Letzte Treue, Grün,* etc.).

Storchio, Rosina, Italian soprano; b. Venice, May 19, 1876; d. Milan, July 24, 1945. She studied at the Milan Cons.; then made her debut at Milan's Teatro del Verme as Micaela in *Carmen* in 1892. On Feb. 17, 1904, she created the title role in the world premiere of *Madama Butterfly* at La Scala in Milan. After a series of tours in South America and in Europe, she was briefly engaged at the Chicago Opera (1920–21); then retired from the stage. She was paralyzed during the last years of her life as a result of an apoplectic stroke.

Storck, Karl, Alsatian writer on music; b. Dürmenach, April 23, 1873; d. Olsberg, May 9, 1920. He studied at the univs. of Strasbourg and Berlin (Dr.Phil., 1895); wrote music criticism for the *Deutsche Zeitung* (Berlin). He publ. a unique edition,

Musik und Musiker in Karikatur und Satire (Oldenburg, 1911), richly illustrated by numerous reproductions of caricatures on musical subjects; other publications include: *Der Tanz* (1903); *Geschichte der Musik* (1904; 6th ed., 1926); *Das Opernbuch* (1905; 44th printing, 1946); *Die Kulturelle Bedeutung der Musik* (1907); *Mozart* (1908; 2nd ed., 1923); *Musik-Politik* (1911); *Emil Jaques-Dalcroze* (1912). He edited selections from the letters of Beethoven (1905; 3rd ed., 1922), Mozart (1906; 3rd ed., 1927), and Schumann (1906).

Storer, John, English organist and composer; b. Hulland, near Derby, May 18, 1858; d. Berwick-on-Tweed, May 1, 1930. He was a chorister at various churches before entering Oxford Univ. (Mus.Bac., 1878). In 1891 he became music director of the old Globe Theatre in London, and later filled similar positions in London; settled in Waterford, Ireland, as organist of the Roman Catholic Cathedral, and prof. of plainchant at St. John's Ecclesiastical College; left Waterford in 1916 and lived in Sheffield and Reading, England. He composed the operas *The Punchbowl* (London, 1887) and *Gretna Green* (London, 1889); an oratorio, *Deborah and Barak* (1881); 2 symphs.: *The Holiday* (1909) and *Vita* (1914); several masses; church services; songs; organ pieces.

Stout, Alan, significant American composer; b. Baltimore, Nov. 26, 1932. He studied composition with Henry Cowell at the Peabody Cons. in Baltimore; sporadically had composition lessons with Riegger in N.Y. (1951–56); then went to Denmark and took a course with Holmboe (1954–55); returning to the U.S., he had lessons with John Verrall at the Univ. of Washington (1958–59), acquiring an M.A. in music and in Swedish language; from 1959 to 1962 was employed in the music dept. of the Seattle Public Library; in 1963 he was appointed to the music faculty of Northwestern Univ.; in 1973 was a visiting lecturer at the State College of Music in Stockholm. Besides his primary activities as a composer and a teacher, he also performed valuable service in editing (with some conjectural reconstruction) fragmentary pieces by Ives, to prepare them for practical performance.
WORKS: FOR ORCH.: 4 symphs.: No. 1 (1959); No. 2 (1951–66; Ravinia Festival, Chicago Symph., Aug. 4, 1968); No. 3 for Soprano, Male Chorus, and Orch. (1959–62); No. 4 (1962–71; Chicago, April 15, 1971); *3 Hymns* for Orch. (1953–54); *Intermezzo* for English Horn, Percussion, and Strings (1954); *Pietà* for String or Brass Orch. (1957); *Serenity* for Solo Cello or Bassoon, Percussion, and Strings (1959); *Ricercare and Aria* for Strings (1959); *Movements* for Violin and Orch. (1962; Fish Creek, Wis., Aug. 17, 1966); *Fanfare for Charles Seeger* for Orch. (1972); *Pulsar* for 3 Brass Choirs and Timpani (1972); *Nimbus* for 18 Strings (1979); *Pilvia* (1983). VOCAL WORKS: *2 Hymns* for Tenor and Orch. (1953); *Die Engel* for Soprano, Flute, Piano, Percussion, and Brass (1957); *2 Ariel Songs* for Soprano and Chamber Ensemble (1957); *Laudi* for Soprano, Baritone, and Small Orch. (1961); *Elegiac Suite* for Soprano

and Strings (1959–61); *Canticum canticorum* for Soprano and Chamber Ensemble (1962); *George Lieder* for High Baritone and Orch. (1962; revised 1965 and 1970; Chicago, Dec. 14, 1972); *Christmas Poem* for Soprano and Chamber Ensemble (1962); *Prologue*, oratorio (1963–64); *Nattstycken (Nocturnes)* for Narrator, Contralto, and Chamber Ensemble (1969–70; Chicago, Nov. 10, 1970); *Dialogo per la Pascua* for Soloists, Chorus, and 8 Instruments (1973); *O Altitudo* for Soprano, Women's Chorus, Solo Flute, and Instrumental Ensemble (1974); *Passion,* oratorio (1953–75; Chicago, April 15, 1976); *5 visages de Laforgue* for Voice and Chamber Orch. (1978); *Triptych* for Soloists, Children's Chorus, and Orch. (1981); choruses, including *The Great Day of the Lord* (with Organ, 1956). CHAMBER MUSIC: 10 string quartets (1952–53, 1952, 1954, 1954, 1957, 1959, 1960, 1960, 1962, 1962); *Solemn Prelude* for Trombone and Organ (1953); Quintet for Clarinet and String Quartet (1958); *Triptych* for Horn and Organ (1961); *Suite* for Flute and Percussion (1962); *Toccata* for Saxophone and Percussion (1965); Cello Sonata (1966); *Music* for Oboe and Piano (1966); *Music* for Flute and Harpsichord (1967); *2 Movements* for Clarinet and String Quartet (1968); *Recitative, Capriccio and Aria* for Oboe, Harp, and Percussion (1970); *Suite* for Saxophone and Organ (1973); Concertino for Clarinet and Chamber Ensemble (1978); *Meditation* for Tenor Saxophone and Organ (1982); Brass Quintet (1984). FOR PIANO: *Varianti* (1962); *Fantasia* (1962); *Suite* (1964–67); 2-piano Sonata (1975); *Waltz* (1977). FOR ORGAN: A set of 8 *Chorales* (1960); set of 3 *Chorales* (1967); *Study in Densities and Durations* (1966–67); *Study in Timbres and Interferences* (1977); *Study in Timbres and Interferences* for Fully Mechanical Organ (1978).

Stoutz, Edmond de, Swiss conductor; b. Zürich, Dec. 18, 1920. He studied law at the Univ. of Zürich; then entered the Zürich Musikhochschule to study music theory; he had instruction in conducting in Lausanne, Salzburg, and Vienna. He began his career as a cellist in various ensembles in Zürich; then founded the Zürich Chamber Orch., which in time achieved considerable renown. In his programs he invariably included works by contemporary composers.

Stöwe, Gustav, German pianist and pedagogue; b. Potsdam, July 4, 1835; d. there, April 13, 1891. He studied at the Stern Cons. in Berlin; in 1875 founded the Potsdam Musikschule, and was its director until he died. He publ. *Die Klaviertechnik, dargestellt als musikalisch-physiologische Bewegungslehre* (1886; thorough analysis of the elements of piano touch); wrote piano pieces.

Stoyanov, Pancho, Bulgarian composer, son of **Veselin Stoyanov;** b. Sofia, Feb. 9, 1931. He studied composition with Vladigerov at the Bulgarian State Cons. in Sofia, graduating in 1954, then took courses at the Moscow Cons.; returning to Bulgaria, he taught at the Cons. in Sofia.

WORKS: 4 symphs. (1958, 1971, 1971, 1975); *Divertimento* for String Orch. (1959); 2 violin concertinos (1961, 1965); 2 *Rhapsodies* for Orch. (1963, 1969); 2 violin sonatas (1953, 1970); 3 string quartets (1953, 1959, 1977); Concertino for Flute, Clarinet, and Bassoon (1969); Piano Quintet (1975); Piano Sonata (1965). He has publ. 9 theoretical texts, including *Interaction between the Musical Forms* (Sofia, 1975).

Stoyanov, Veselin, Bulgarian composer; b. Shumen, April 20, 1902; d. Sofia, June 29, 1969. He studied piano with his brother **Andrei Stoyanov** at the Bulgarian State Cons. in Sofia, graduating in 1926; then went to Vienna, where he studied with Joseph Marx and Franz Schmidt. In 1937 he was appointed prof. of musical subjects at the Cons. in Sofia; was director of the Cons. in 1943–44 and 1956–62.

WORKS: 3 operas: *Zhensko tsarstvo* (*Kingdom of Women;* Sofia, April 5, 1935); *Salambo* (Sofia, May 22, 1940); *Hitar Petar* (*The Wise Peter;* 1952; Sofia, 1958); ballet, *Popess Joan* (1966; Sofia, Oct. 22, 1968); cantata, *Da bade den* (*Let There Be Day;* 1952); *Capriccio* for Orch. (1934); *Bai Ganyu* (*Uncle Ganyu*), grotesque suite for Orch. (1941); 2 piano concertos (1942, 1953); *Kravava pesen* (*Song of the Blood*), symph. poem (1947); Violin Concerto (1948); Cello Concerto (1960); 2 symphs. (1962, 1968); 3 string quartets (1933, 1934, 1935); Violin Sonata (1934); Piano Sonata (1930); *Suite* for Piano (1931); *3 Pieces* for Piano (1956).

Stracciari, Riccardo, Italian baritone; b. Casalecchio, near Bologna, June 26, 1875; d. Rome, Oct. 10, 1955. He studied in Bologna; then made his debut there as Marcello in 1898; was a member of La Scala in Milan (1904–6); also sang at Covent Garden in London (1905). He made his debut at the Metropolitan Opera in N.Y. on Dec. 1, 1906, as Germont *père;* remained on the roster until 1908; then returned to Europe, continuing his career there and in South America. He returned to the U.S. to sing with the Chicago Opera (1917–19) and in San Francisco (1925); continued to make appearances in Italy until 1944. He was noted for his performances of Italian operas; was a famous Figaro. His most eminent student was Boris Christoff.

Stradal, August, Bohemian pianist; b. Teplitz, May 17, 1860; d. Schönlinde, Germany, March 13, 1930. He studied composition with Bruckner at the Vienna Cons. and piano with Door; was a pupil of Liszt in 1884, and became an ardent propagandist for Liszt's piano music; gave concerts in Germany, Austria, France, and England; made arrangements of Liszt's orch. works; also of works by Bach, Frescobaldi, etc. His original compositions consist of piano pieces (*Ungarische Rhapsodie,* etc.) and songs. He wrote *Erinnerungen an Franz Liszt* (Bern, 1929).

BIBLIOGRAPHY: Hildegard Stradal, *August Stradals Lebensbild* (Bern, 1934).

Stradella, Alessandro, important Italian composer; b. Nepi, near Viterbo, 1644; d. (murdered) Genoa,

Feb. 25, 1682. He was a scion of nobility; received his early training in Bologna. In 1667 he went to Rome, where he composed oratorios, prologues, intermezzos for opera, etc. He led a tempestuous life, replete with illicit liaisons, flights from personal vendettas, and some criminal acts. In Rome he attempted to embezzle funds from the Roman Catholic Church, and in 1669 fled the city to avoid exposure. He returned to Rome after the affair calmed down, but again got in trouble when he aroused the enmity of Cardinal Alderon Cibo. In 1677 he was forced to flee Rome again, and he went to Venice, where he became involved in a torrid affair with the fiancée of the Venetian nobleman Alvise Contarini; he persuaded the lady to accompany him to Turin, and the outraged bridegroom and a band of assassins followed in hot pursuit. Stradella escaped and fled to Genoa. There he became entangled with a married woman, a sister of the Lomellini brothers, who had a high social standing in the town. This time Stradella failed to evade the vengeful brothers, who hired an experienced murderer to kill him; the bloody deed was done on Feb. 25, 1682. A rather successful opera, *Alessandro Stradella* by Flotow (Hamburg, 1844), dramatized his stormy life and death; other operas on Stradella were composed by Niedermeyer (Paris, 1837) and Sinico (Lugo, 1863).

As a composer, Stradella left an important legacy, both in opera and in instrumental writing. His operas *La forza dell'amor paterno, Le gare dell'amore eroico,* and *Il Trespole tutore* were staged in Genoa (1678–79); he also composed the oratorio *La Susanna* and a wedding serenade, *Il barcheggio,* for Duke Francesco d'Este of Modena (1681). Other operas were *Il moro per amore, Il Corispero,* and *Doriclea.* His oratorios include *S. Giovanni Battista* and *S. Giovanni Crisostomo;* another oratorio, *S. Editta, vergine e monaca, regina d'Inghilterra,* remained unfinished. He wrote about 25 sinfonias (sonatas), most of them for violin, with basso ostinato; motets; arias; and canzonettas. An edition of Stradella's oratorios was begun in 1969, under the editorship of L. Bianchi.
BIBLIOGRAPHY: P. Bourdelot and P. Bonnet-Bourdelot, *Histoire de la musique et de ses effets depuis son origine jusqu'à présent* (Paris, 1715); A. Catelani, *Delle opere di A. S. esistenti nell'archivio musicale della R. Biblioteca Palatina di Modena* (Modena, 1866); P. Richard, "S. et les Contarini," *Le Ménestrel,* XXXII/51–52 (1865) and XXXIII/1–5 (1866); H. Hess, *Die Opern A. S.'s,* in *Publicationen der Internationalen Musik-Gesellschaft,* Supplement, II/3 (1906); F. Crawford, *S.* (London, 1911); A. Einstein, "Ein Bericht über den Turiner Mordanfall auf A. S.," in *Festschrift zum 50. Geburtstag Adolf Sandberger* (Munich, 1918); E. Dufflocq, "A. S.," *Bollettino Bibliografico Musicale,* IV (1929); A. Gentili, *A. S.* (Turin, 1936); G. Roncaglia, "Le composizioni strumentali di A. S. esistenti presso la R. Biblioteca Estense di Modena," *Revista Musicale Italiana,* XLIV (1940) and XLV (1941); idem, *Il genio novatore di A. S.* (Modena, 1941); idem, "Le composizioni vocali di A. S.," *Rivista Musicale Italiana,* XLV (1941) and XLVI (1942); E. Allam, "A. S.," *Proceedings of the Royal Musical Association,* LXXX (1953–

54); E. Krohn, "Some Solo Cantatas of A. S.," *Manuscripta,* II (1958); O. Jander, *A Catalogue of the Manuscripts of Compositions by A. S. found in European and American Libraries* (Wellesley, Mass., 1960; 2nd ed., revised, 1962); R. Giazotto, *Vita di A. S.* (2 vols., Milan, 1962); O. Jander, *A. S. and His Minor Dramatic Works* (Diss., Harvard Univ., 1962); L. Bianchi, *Carissimi, S., Scarlatti e l'oratorio musicale* (Rome, 1969); O. Jander, "The Prologues and Intermezzos of A. S.," *Analecta musicologica,* no. 7 (1969); H. Dietz, "Musikalische Struktur und Architektur im Werke A. S.s," *Analecta musicologica,* no. 9 (1970); C. Gianturco, *The Operas of A. S. (1644–1682)* (Diss., Oxford Univ., 1970); E. McCrickard, *A. S.'s Instrumental Music* (Diss., Univ. of North Carolina, 1971); C. Gianturco, "Caratteri stilistici delle opere teatrali di S.," *Rivista Italiana di Musicologia,* VI (1972); idem, "Corelli e A. S.," *Studi corelliani: 2° congresso internazionale: Fusignano 1974;* K. Chaikin, *The Solo Soprano Cantatas of A. S.* (Diss., Stanford Univ., 1975); C. Gianturco, "The Oratorios of A. S.," *Proceedings of the Royal Musical Association,* CI (1974–75); E. McCrickard, "Temporal and Tonal Aspects of A. S.'s Instrumental Music," *Analecta musicologica,* no. 19 (1979); N. O'Loughlin, "Stradella's 'Santa Pelagia,'" *Musical Times* (May 1981); C. Gianturco, "A. S.: A True Biography," *Musical Times* (Nov. 1982); valuable articles may be found in *Atti del convegno internazionale A. S.: Siena 1982.*

Stradivari (Stradivarius), Antonio, the most celebrated of all violin makers; b. Cremona, 1644 (according to Bacchetta, end of 1648 or beginning of 1649); d. there, Dec. 18, 1737. He was a pupil of Niccolò Amati and worked for him from about 1666 to 1679. He purchased the house in which, for half a century, his workshop was situated, in 1680. His finest instruments were made in the period from 1700 to 1725, but he still worked up to the year of his death; he made his last instrument at the age of 92. His label reads: "Antonius Stradivarius Cremonensis. Fecit Anno ... (A × S)." His cellos command even higher prices than the violins, and violas the highest of all, for he made very few of them. Stradivari had 11 children; of them **Francesco** (b. Feb. 1, 1671; d. May 11, 1743) and **Omobono** (b. Nov. 14, 1679; d. July 8, 1742) were his co-workers. Stradivari also made viols of early types, guitars, lutes, mandolins, etc.
BIBLIOGRAPHY: F.J. Fétis, *A. S., Luthier célèbre* (Paris, 1856; Eng. trans., London, 1864); P. Lombardini, *Cenni sulla celebre scuola Cremonense degli stromenti ad arco e sulla famiglia del sommo A. S.* (Cremona, 1872; with genealogical table from the 13th century to date of publication); A. Reichers, *The Violin and the Art of Its Construction; A Treatise on S.* (1895); H. Petherick, *A. S.* (London, 1900); W.H., A.F., and A.E. Hill, *A. S. His Life and Work* (London, 1902; the standard work); A. Mandelli, *Nuove indagini su A. S.* (Milan, 1903); H. Herrmann, *Geschichte und Beschreibung von zwei Meisterwerken des A. S.* (N.Y., 1929); R. Bacchetta, *S.* (1937); G. Hoffmann, *S. l'enchanteur* (Paris, 1938);

W.D. Orcutt, *The S. Memorial at Washington, D.C.* (Washington, 1938); M. Boger, *Das Geheimnis des S.* (Berlin, 1944); D.J. Balfoort, *A. S.* (Amsterdam, 1945; also in Eng.); E.N. Doring, *How Many Strads? . . . A tabulation of works believed to survive, produced in Cremona by A. S. between 1666 and 1737* (Chicago, 1945); G. Ottani, *S.* (Milan, 1945); H. Goodkind, *Violin Iconography of A. S.* (Larchmont, N.Y., 1972); S. Sacconi, *I "segreti" di S.* (Cremona, 1972); H. Goodkind, *Violin Iconography of A. S. 1644–1737* (Larchmont, N.Y., 1973).

Straesser, Joep, Dutch composer; b. Amsterdam, March 11, 1934. He studied at the Municipal Univ. of Amsterdam (1952–55); then took organ lessons with Van der Horst (1956–59) and composition with Ton de Leeuw (1960–65) at the Amsterdam Cons.; was a church organist (1953–61); in 1962 was appointed to the faculty of the Utrecht Cons.

WORKS: *5 Close-ups* for Piano (1960–61; revised 1973); *Music* for Oboe Quartet (1962); *Psalmus* for Male Chorus, Winds, and Percussion (1963); *22 Pages,* after a text of John Cage essays, for Wind Orch., Percussion, and 3 Male Voices (Hilversum, Sept. 14, 1965); String Quartet No. 2 (1966); *Chorai* for 48 String Instruments and Percussion (1966; Hilversum, Sept. 14, 1967; re-composed in 1974 for Full Orch. and retitled *Chorai Revisited*); *Duet* for 2 Cellos (1967); *Seismograms* for 2 Percussionists (1967); *Adastra,* music for ballet (1967); *Summer Concerto* for Oboe and Chamber Orch. (1967; Styrian Autumn Festival, Graz, Austria, Oct. 24, 1969); *Ramasasiri (Traveling Song),* on texts in the Papuan language, for Soprano, Flute, Vibraphone, Piano, and 2 Percussionists (1967–68); *Musique pour l'homme* for Soprano, Alto, Tenor, Bass, and Orch. (1968; Amsterdam, Dec. 9, 1968); *Missa* for Chorus and Wind Instruments (1969); *Intersections I* for Wind Quintet and 5 Instrumental Groups spatially positioned (1969); *II* for 100 or More Musicians (1970; Amsterdam, April 3, 1971; except for Percussionists, all orch. members improvise freely); *III* for Piano (1971); *IV* for Oboe, Violin, Viola, and Cello (1972); *V (A Saxophone's World)* for 4 Saxophones (1974) and *V-2* for Bass Clarinet and Piano (1975); *Sight-Seeing I, II, III* for Flute and Prepared Piano (1969); *IV* for Solo Double Bass (1970); *V (Spring Quartet)* for String Quartet (1971); *Emergency Case* for Flute, Piano, and Percussion (1970); *Enclosures* for Winds and Percussion (1970; perf. as a ballet, Rotterdam, Oct. 3, 1971); *Eichenstadt und Abendstern,* 6 songs for Soprano and Piano (1972); *Encounters* for Bass Clarinet and 6 Percussionists (1973); *Intervals* for Chamber Chorus, Flute, Cello, and Harp (1975–76); *3 Psalms* for Chorus and Organ (1976).

Straeten, Edmund. See **Van der Straeten.**

Strakosch, Maurice, Bohemian impresario; b. Gross-Seelowitz, 1825; d. Paris, Oct. 9, 1887. He studied with Sechter at the Vienna Cons.; traveled as a pianist in Europe; came to America in 1848, settling in N.Y. as a teacher; from 1856 he was active mainly as an impresario. He was the brother-in-law of Adelina Patti, and managed her concerts. He gave his first season of Italian opera in N.Y. in 1857, and in 1859 took his company to Chicago; then went to Europe. His opera *Giovanna di Napoli* was brought out in N.Y.; he also wrote salon pieces for piano; publ. *Ten Commandments of Music for the Perfection of the Voice* (posthumous; 1896) and *Souvenirs d'un Impresario* (Paris, 2nd ed., 1887). After his departure from America, his brother, Max Strakosch (1834–92), carried on the management of his enterprises.

Strang, Gerald, inventive American composer; b. Claresholm, Canada, Feb. 13, 1908; d. Loma Linda, Calif., during open-heart surgery, Oct. 2, 1983. He joined the ranks of the early California modernists, headed by Henry Cowell. He studied at Stanford Univ., at the Univ. of Calif., Los Angeles, and at the Univ. of Southern Calif., where he received his doctorate. He also took private lessons in composition with Ernst Toch and Arnold Schoenberg, and served as Schoenberg's assistant at the Univ. of Calif. from 1936–38. He interrupted his musical pursuits during the war years, when he was employed as an engineer at Douglas Aircraft Co. After the war he resumed his teaching at Long Beach City College (1938–43 and 1945–58); in 1958 he founded the music dept. at Calif. State Univ. at Northridge (formerly, San Fernando Valley State College). From 1965–69 he was chairman of the music dept. at Calif. State Univ. at Long Beach; later taught electronic music composition at the Univ. of Calif., Los Angeles, retiring in 1974. His music is strongly formal, with a unifying technical idea determining the content. An intelligent, energetic, and astute musical technician, he experimented successfully with the new resources available in the fields of acoustics, electronics, and computers; he was also active as an editor of modern works and was for many years an associate of Henry Cowell in editing Cowell's *New Music Quarterly.* The titles of his compositions give clues to their formative semiotics; thus his piano piece *Mirrorrorrim* is an obvious palindrome or cancrizans. His series of 4 *Synclavions* is an electronic synthesis of keyboard variations. Similarly suggestive are his various pieces bearing such titles as *Compusitions* (= computerized compositions) and *Synthions* (= synthetic ions). Strang was also active in the field of acoustics, and served as a consultant on some 25 newly built auditoriums in California and elsewhere.

Stransky, Josef, Bohemian conductor; b. Humpoletz, near Deutschbrod, Bohemia, Sept. 9, 1872; d. New York, March 6, 1936. While studying medicine (M.D., Univ. of Prague, 1896), he also studied music, in Leipzig with Jadassohn and in Vienna with R. Fuchs, Bruckner, and Dvořák. In 1898 he was engaged by A. Neumann as first Kapellmeister at the Landestheater in Prague; in 1903 he went in a similar capacity to the Stadttheater in Hamburg; in 1910 he resigned from the Hamburg opera to devote himself to concert work; in the autumn of 1911 became Mahler's successor as conductor of the N.Y. Phil.

Society, a position he held until 1923. A bequest of $1,000,000 to the society (by Joseph Pulitzer, 1912) enabled Stransky to carry out successfully the sweeping reforms instituted by his illustrious predecessor (chief of which was a system of daily rehearsals during the season of 23 weeks). He wrote an operetta, *Der General,* which was produced in Hamburg.

BIBLIOGRAPHY: Howard Shanet, *Philharmonic. A History of New York's Orchestra* (Garden City, N.Y., 1975).

Straram, Walther, French conductor; b. London (of French parents), July 9, 1876; d. Paris, Nov. 24, 1933. He was educated in Paris; played violin in Paris orchs.; then was choirmaster at the Opéra-Comique; later traveled to America as assistant to André Caplet at the Boston Opera Co. Returning to Paris, he established the Concerts Straram, which enjoyed a fine reputation. He conducted the first performance of Ravel's *Boléro* for Ida Rubinstein (dance recital, Nov. 22, 1928).

Strassburg, Robert, American music educator and composer; b. New York, Aug. 30, 1915. He studied composition with Marion Bauer at N.Y. Univ.; then enrolled in Harvard Univ. (M.A., 1950). He subsequently lived in Miami; was conductor and founder of the All-Miami Youth Symph. (1957–60). In 1961 he joined the faculty of the Univ. of Judaism in Los Angeles; from 1966 he was on the faculty of Calif. State College. His works include *4 Biblical Statements* for String Orch. (1946); *Fantasy and Allegro* for Violin and Orch. (1947); *Torah Sonata* for Piano (1950); folk opera, *Chelm* (1956); *Tropal Suite* for String Orch. (1967). He is the author of a monograph, *Ernest Bloch, Voice in the Wilderness* (Los Angeles, 1977).

Strässer, Ewald, German composer; b. Burscheid, June 27, 1867; d. Stuttgart, April 4, 1933. He studied with Wüllner at the Cologne Cons.; taught theory there until 1921; from 1922 to his death was a prof. at the Stuttgart Hochschule für Musik. He wrote 6 symphs., 5 string quartets, piano pieces, and songs.

BIBLIOGRAPHY: A. Strässer, *Ewald Strässer* (Stuttgart, 1936).

Stratas, Teresa (real name, **Anastasia Stratakis**), outstanding Canadian soprano of Greek extraction; b. Toronto, May 26, 1938. Her father owned a restaurant in a town near Toronto, and she was allowed from her earliest childhood to sing for customers. She also sang in concert with her brother, a violinist, and her sister, a pianist. In 1954 she entered the Royal Cons. of Music of Toronto, where she studied voice with Irene Jessner; she graduated with an Artist Diploma in 1959. She made her professional operatic debut with the Toronto Opera Festival as Mimi on Oct. 13, 1958. In 1959 she was a co-winner of the Metropolitan Opera Auditions, which led to her formal debut with the company in N.Y. on Oct. 28, 1959, as Poussette in *Manon.* She soon established herself as a singer of great versatility. She

sang virtually all the standard soprano parts, and she demonstrated her particular mettle and fettle in the complete version of Alban Berg's opera *Lulu,* which was given for the first time in Paris on May 28, 1979. She won international acclaim for her dramatic portrayal of Violetta in Zeffirelli's film version of *La Traviata* (1983). She also sang at the Bolshoi Theater in Moscow and at La Scala in Milan. In 1972 she was made an Officer of the Order of Canada.

BIBLIOGRAPHY: David Ewen, *Musicians since 1900* (N.Y., 1978).

Strategier, Herman, Dutch composer; b. Arnhem, Aug. 10, 1912. He studied music with his father, a church organist, and with H. Andriessen; succeeded his father at St. Walpurgis at Arnhem in 1935, but the church was destroyed in war action in 1944. He taught at the Inst. for Catholic Church Music in Utrecht (1939–63); then was appointed to the faculty of music science at Utrecht Univ. He is notable mainly as a composer of liturgical music of the Roman Catholic rite.

WORKS: FOR VOICE: *Stabat Mater* for Chorus and Small Orch. (1939); *Septem cantica* for Mezzo-soprano and Piano (1941); *4 Drinkliederen* for Baritone and Orch. (1945); *Van der mollenfeeste,* an old ballad for Chorus and Small Orch. (1947–48); *Henric van Veldeke* for Narrator, Baritone, and Orch. (1952); *5 Minneliederen* for Middle Voice, Flute, and Small String Orch. (1952); *Koning Swentibold,* oratorio (1955); *Arnhemsche Psalm* for Narrator, Soloists, Chorus, and Orch. (1955); *Rembrandt Cantata* (1956); *Requiem* for Chorus, Wind Quintet, and Strings (1961); *Ballade van de Maagd van Wognum* for Chorus and Orch. (1965); *Plaisanterie* for Chorus and Orch. (1966); *Te Deum* for Soprano, Alto, Chorus, and Orch. (1967); *Colloquia familiaria* for Soprano, Chorus, and String Orch. (1969); *Zoo, Buddingh'zoo* for Baritone, Chorus, and Small Orch. (1970); *Ligeia or The Shadow Out of Time* for Chorus, Flute, 6 Percussionists, Organ, and Harp (1973). FOR ORCH.: *Divertimento* for String Orch. and 4 Winds (1937); Flute Concerto (1943); *Haarlemsuite* (1945–47); *Ramiro-suite* (1946); Piano Concerto (1947–48); Symph. No. 1 (1949); Clarinet Concertino (1950); *Musique pour faire plaisir* for Strings (1950); *Intrada sinfonica* (1954); *Rondo giocoso* (1955); *Rapsodia elegiaca* (1956); *Turandot-suite* (1956); *Kadullen Varieties* for Flute, Bassoon, and Strings (1958); *Triptych* for Piano and Wind Orch. (1960); Accordion Concerto (1969); *Concertante Speelmuziek* for Flute, Bassoon, and Orch. (1970). CHAMBER MUSIC: 3 string quartets (1935, 1936, 1937); *3 pièces* for Oboe and String Quartet (1937); Sextet for Piano and Wind Quintet (1951); *Suite* for Solo Harp (1961); Quartet for Flute, Violin, Viola, and Cello (1968); *Curven* for Accordion and String Quartet (1970); *Divertissement* for Oboe, Clarinet, and Bassoon (1970); Piano Trio (1974). FOR PIANO: *Suite* for 4-hands (1945); Sonata (1948); Sonatina (1951); *Tema con variazioni* for 4-hands (1952); *Elégie* (1954); *4 pièces brèves* for 4-hands (1973); *Suite* for Piano and Harpsichord (1973); *3 Speelmuziekjes*

(1974); *6 études* (1974). FOR ORGAN: *Preludium, Intermezzo and Theme with Variations* (1939); *Ritornello capriccioso* (1944); *Toccatina* (1951); *Chaconne* (1955); *Voluntary* (1975); songs and choruses.

Stratton, George (Robert), English violinist and pedagogue; b. London, July 18, 1897; d. there, Sept. 4, 1954. He studied in London; was concertmaster of the London Symph. Orch. (1933–52); also organized the Stratton String Quartet (1925–42). He publ. (in collaboration with Alan Frank) a practical book, *The Playing of Chamber Music* (London, 1935; reprinted 1951).

Stratton, Stephen Samuel, English organist; b. London, Dec. 19, 1840; d. Birmingham, June 25, 1906. He was a pupil of C. Gardner (organ) and C. Lucas (composition); settled in 1866 in Birmingham, where he held various posts as organist, the last being at the Church of the Saviour (1878–82). He was the author (with J.D. Brown) of a valuable work, *British Musical Biography* (1897); also publ. *Mendelssohn* (1901; revised ed., 1934) and *Nicolo Paganini: His Life and Work* (1907). His compositions include chamber music, piano pieces, partsongs, and songs.

Straube, Karl, prominent German organist; b. Berlin, Jan. 6, 1873; d. Leipzig, April 27, 1950. He was a scion of an ancient ecclesiastical family; his father was an organist and instrument maker in Berlin; his mother was an Englishwoman who was a piano student of Sir Julius Benedict. He studied organ with Dienel; then took organ lessons with Reimann in Berlin. From 1897 to 1902 he was organist at the Cathedral of Wesel; in 1902 he became organist at the famous Thomaskirche in Leipzig; in 1903 he was appointed conductor of the Bachverein there, and in 1907 became a prof. at the Leipzig Cons. and organist *ex officio* at Gewandhaus. In 1918 he became cantor at the Thomaskirche. At his suggestion the Gewandhaus Chorus and the Bachverein were united in 1919, and he conducted the combined choir. He conducted the Handel Festival in 1925, leading to the formation of the Handel Society. In his teaching he followed the great tradition of Leipzig organists, traceable to Bach. A Festschrift was publ. for him on his 70th birthday (Leipzig, 1943). Among Straube's numerous collections of organ and choral pieces are *Alte Orgelmeister* (1904); *45 Choralvorspiele alter Meister* (1907); *Alte Meister des Orgelspiels* (2 vols., 1929); *Ausgewählte Gesänge des Thomanerchors* (1930); he brought out editions of several works of Bach, Handel, and Liszt. His *Briefe eines Thomaskantors* was publ. posthumously (Stuttgart, 1952).

Straus, Oscar, Austrian operetta composer; b. Vienna, March 6, 1870; d. Bad Ischl, Jan. 11, 1954. (His name was spelled "Strauss" on his birth certificate; he cut off the 2nd "s" to segregate himself from the multitudinous musical Strausses.) He studied privately in Vienna with A. Prosnitz and H. Grädener, and with Max Bruch in Berlin. From 1893 to 1900 he conducted at various theaters in Austria and Germany; in 1901 he became conductor of the artistic cabaret Überbrettl, managed by Ernst von Wolzogen in Berlin, and wrote a number of musical farces for it. He remained in Berlin until 1927; then lived in Vienna and Paris; on Sept. 3, 1939, he became a French citizen. In 1940 he went to America; lived in N.Y. and Hollywood until 1948, when he returned to Europe. He was one of the most successful composers of Viennese operettas.

WORKS: His most celebrated production was *Der tapfere Soldat,* based on G.B. Shaw's play *Arms and the Man* (Vienna, Nov. 14, 1908; in N.Y. as *The Chocolate Soldier,* Nov. 13, 1909; London, Sept. 10, 1910; numerous perfs. all over the world). Other operettas are: *Die lustigen Nibelungen* (Vienna, Nov. 12, 1904); *Hugdietrichs Brautfahrt* (Vienna, March 10, 1906); *Ein Walzertraum* (Vienna, March 2, 1907; revised 1951); *Didi* (Vienna, Oct. 23, 1909); *Das Tal der Liebe* (Berlin and Vienna, simultaneously, Dec. 23, 1909); *Mein junger Herr* (Vienna, Dec. 23, 1910); *Die kleine Freundin* (Vienna, Oct. 20, 1911); *Love and Laughter* (London, 1913); *Rund um die Liebe* (Vienna, Nov. 9, 1914; in N.Y. as *All around Love,* 1917); *Die himmelblaue Zeit* (Vienna, Feb. 21, 1914); *Die schöne Unbekannte* (Vienna, Jan. 15, 1915; in N.Y. as *My Lady's Glove,* 1917); *3 Walzer* (Zürich, Oct. 5, 1935); *Ihr erster Walzer* (Munich, May 16, 1952). He further wrote a *Serenade* for String Orch.; *Alt-Wiener Reigen* for String Orch.; *Suite in Tanzform* for Violin, Cello, and Piano; *Der Traum ein Leben,* overture; many piano pieces; an album, *Bilderbuch ohne Bilder,* for 4-hands.

BIBLIOGRAPHY: B. Grun, *Prince of Vienna: The Life, the Times, and the Melodies of Oscar Straus* (London, 1955; N.Y., 1957).

Strauss, Eduard, Austrian conductor, brother of **Johann Strauss, Jr.;** b. Vienna, March 15, 1835; d. there, Dec. 28, 1916. A pupil of G. Preyer in composition, he made a successful debut with his own orch. at the Dianasaal in 1862; acted as Johann's substitute during the latter's tour of Russia (1865); succeeded him as conductor of the court balls (1872–78). For many years he gave concerts in the Volksgarten (summer) and in the hall of the Musikverein (winter); also made extended tours, visiting the U.S. in 1890 and from Oct. 1900 to early 1901. In 1901 he dissolved his orch. (founded by his father in 1826), which, after three-quarters of a century of uninterrupted success, had become almost a historical institution. His publ. dances comprise 318 opus numbers, but could not rival his brother's in popularity. In 1906 he publ. *Erinnerungen.*

Strauss, Franz, German horn virtuoso, father of **Richard Strauss;** b. Parkstein, Feb. 26, 1822; d. Munich, May 31, 1905. Until his retirement in 1889 he was solo hornist at the Hofoper in Munich; although a violent opponent of Wagner, the master valued him highly, and entrusted to him at the premieres of *Tristan, Meistersinger,* and *Parsifal* the important solo passages; until 1896 he was a prof. of his instrument at the Akademie der Tonkunst, and in

1875–96 conducted an excellent amateur orch., the Wilde Gungl, in Munich. He wrote a Horn Concerto in C minor (op. 8); *Nocturne* (op. 7) and *Empfindungen am Meere* (op. 12) for Horn and Piano; 17 *Konzertetüden* and *Übungen für Naturhorn* (2 books).

BIBLIOGRAPHY: F. Trenner, "Der Vater: Franz Strauss," *Zeitschrift für Musik* (June 1955).

Strauss, Johann (III), Austrian waltz composer; son of **Eduard Strauss;** b. Vienna, Feb. 16, 1866; d. Berlin, Jan. 9, 1939. He was active as a ballroom music director in Vienna and later led popular concerts in Berlin. He was the last musician of the great Strauss family of waltz composers. His *Dichterliebe* waltz became popular.

Strauss, Johann, Jr., greatly celebrated Austrian composer of light music, called "The Waltz King"; b. Vienna, Oct. 25, 1825; d. there, June 3, 1899. His father intended all 3 of his sons for business; but the mother privately procured instruction on the violin (from Kohlmann) and in composition (Hofmann and Drechsler) for Johann, who threw off paternal control, tender though it was, and appeared as conductor of his own ensemble of 15 players at Dommayer's Restaurant in Hietzing (Oct. 15, 1844). His success was instantaneous, and his new waltzes won wide popularity. Despite his father's objections to this rivalry in the family, Johann Strauss continued his concerts with increasing success; after his father's death in 1849 he united his father's band with his own; made a tour through Austria, Germany, Poland, and Russia. From 1863 to Jan. 1871 he was conductor of the court balls in Vienna, resigning in favor of his brother **Eduard** to obtain more leisure for composition. Turning from dance music, in which he had won supreme artistic and popular success, he then concentrated on operetta. In 1872 he accepted an invitation to visit the U.S., and directed 14 "monster-concerts" in Boston and 4 in N.Y. He contracted 3 marriages: to the singer Henriette Treffz, the actress Angelika Dittrich, and Adele Deutsch. He wrote almost 500 pieces of dance music (498 opus numbers); of his waltzes the greatest popularity was achieved by *An der schönen blauen Donau (The Blue Danube Waltz),* op. 314 (1867), whose main tune became one of the best known in all music. Brahms wrote on a lady's fan the opening measures of it, and underneath: "Leider nicht von Brahms" ("Alas, not by Brahms"); Wagner, too, voiced his appreciation of the music of Strauss. Other well-known waltzes are *Geschichten aus dem Wiener Wald* (1868); *Wein, Weib, Gesang* (1869); *Wiener Blut* (1870); *Rosen aus dem Süden* (1878); *Frühlingsstimmen* (1881); *Tausend und eine Nacht, Künstlerleben;* etc.; also numerous quadrilles, polkas, polka-mazurkas, marches, galops, etc. His finest operetta is *Die Fledermaus,* an epitome of the Viennese spirit that continues to hold the stage as one of the masterpieces of its genre. It was first staged at the Theater an der Wien on April 5, 1874, and was given within a few months in N.Y. (Dec. 29, 1874); productions followed all over

the world. It was performed in Paris with a new libretto as *La Tzigane* (Oct. 30, 1877); the original version was presented there as *La Chauve-souris* on April 22, 1904. Also very successful was the operetta *Der Zigeunerbaron* (Vienna, Oct. 24, 1885). All his operettas were first produced in Vienna, with the exception of *Eine Nacht in Venedig* (Berlin, Oct. 3, 1883). A complete list of Vienna productions includes: *Indigo und die vierzig Räuber* (Feb. 10, 1871); *Der Karneval in Rom* (March 1, 1873); *Cagliostro in Wien* (Feb. 27, 1875); *Prinz Methusalem* (Jan. 3, 1877); *Blindekuh* (Dec. 18, 1878); *Das Spitzentuch der Königin* (Oct. 1, 1880); *Der lustige Krieg* (Nov. 25, 1881); *Simplizius* (Dec. 17, 1887); *Ritter Pázmán* (Jan. 1, 1892); *Fürstin Ninetta* (Jan. 10, 1893); *Jabuka, oder Das Apfelfest* (Oct. 12, 1894); *Waldmeister* (Dec. 4, 1895); *Die Göttin der Vernunft* (March 13, 1897).

BIBLIOGRAPHY: L. Eisenberg, *J. S.* (Leipzig, 1894); R. von Procházka, *J. S.* (Berlin, 1900); R. Specht, *J. S.* (Berlin, 1909); F. Lange, *J. S.* (Leipzig, 1912); J. Schnitzer, *Meister Johann* (2 vols., Vienna, 1920); E. Decsey, *J. S.* (Berlin, 1922; reprinted Vienna, 1948); K. Kobald, *J. S.* (Vienna, 1925); S. Loewy, *Rund um J. S.* (Vienna, 1925); H. Sündermann, *J. S., Ein Vollender* (Brixlegg, 1937); Ada B. Teetgen, *The Waltz Kings of Old Vienna* (London, 1939); A. Witeschnik, *Die Dynastie Strauss* (Vienna, 1939); H.E. Jacob, *J. S. und das 19. Jahrhundert* . . . (Amsterdam, 1937; Eng. trans. as *J. S., Father and Son, A Century of Light Music,* N.Y., 1940); W. Jaspert, *J. S.* (Berlin, 1939); Erich Schenk, *J. S.* (Potsdam, 1940); David Ewen, *Tales from the Vienna Woods: The Story of J. S.* (N.Y., 1944); J. Andriessen, *J. S., De koning van de wals* (Amsterdam, 1950); J. Pastene, *Three-Quarter Time: The Life and Music of the Strauss Family* (N.Y., 1951); P. Kuringer, *J. S.* (Haarlem, 1952); J. Wechsberg, *The Waltz Emperors* (1973); Egon Gartenberg, *J. S.; The End of an Era* (1974). See also *J. S. schreibt Briefe,* ed. by his 3rd wife, Adele Strauss (Vienna, 1926). A complete catalogue of works is found in C. Flamme, ed., *Verzeichnis der sämtlichen im Drucke erschienenen Kompositionen von J. S. (Vater), J. S. (Sohn), Josef Strauss, und Eduard Strauss* (Leipzig, 1898), and in A. Weinmann, *Verzeichnis sämtlicher Werke von J. S., Vater und Sohn* (Vienna, 1956). An ed. of collected works of Johann Strauss, Jr., was begun in 1967 by the Johann Strauss Gesellschaft in Vienna, under the direction of F. Racek.

Strauss, Johann, Sr., "The Father of the Waltz"; b. Vienna, March 14, 1804; d. there, Sept. 25, 1849. His father, who kept a beer house and dance hall, apprenticed him to a bookbinder; after Strauss had run away, his parents consented to his becoming a musician. He studied the violin under Polyschansky, and harmony under Seyfried; at 15 joined Pamer's orch. in the Sperl dance hall, and the Lanner Quartet in 1823, later acting as deputy conductor of Lanner's orch.; organized an independent orch. of 14 in 1825, playing at various resorts, and producing his first waltzes (op. 1 is the *Täuberl-Walzer,* for the garden concerts at the Zwei Tau-ben). His renown spread, and his orch. increased rapidly in size and efficiency; from 1833 he undertook concert tours in Austria, and in 1834 was appointed bandmaster of the first Vienna militia regiment. His tours extended to Berlin in 1834, and to the Netherlands and Belgium in 1836; in 1837–38 he invaded Paris with a picked corps of 28, and had immense success both there and in London. In 1845 he was made conductor of the court balls at Vienna.

WORKS: Among 152 publ. waltzes, the *Lorelei-, Gabrielen-, Taglioni-, Cäcilien-, Victoria-, Kettenbrücken-,* and *Bajaderen-Walzer;* the *Elektrische Funken, Mephistos Höllenrufe,* and the *Donau-Lieder;* are prime favorites. He also wrote 24 galops, 13 polkas, 32 quadrilles, 6 cotillons and contredances, 18 marches, and 6 potpourris. His complete works (251 opus numbers), edited by his son **Johann,** were publ. by Breitkopf & Härtel in 1889: vols. I–V, Waltzes; vol. VI, Polkas, Galops, Marches; vol. VII, Quadrilles (piano scores only; full scores in Denkmäler der Tonkunst in Österreich, 63, 68, and 74 [32.ii, 35.ii, and 38.ii]).

BIBLIOGRAPHY: L. Scheyrer, *J. S.s musikalische Wanderung durch das Leben* (Vienna, 1851); R. Kleinecke, *J. S.* (Leipzig, 1894); F. Lange, *Josef Lanner und J. S.* (Vienna, 1904; 2nd ed., 1919); M. Farga, *Lanner und S.* (Vienna, 1948); M. Schönherr and K. Reinöhl, *J. S. Vater* (Vienna, 1953); H. Jacob, *J. S., Vater und Sohn: Die Geschichte einer musikalischen Weltherrschaft* (Bremen, 1960).

Strauss, Josef, Austrian composer of waltzes, brother of **Johann Strauss, Jr.;** b. Vienna, Aug. 22, 1827; d. there, July 21, 1870. He was versatile and gifted, and at various times wrote poetry, painted, and patented inventions. He first appeared in public conducting in Vienna a set of his waltzes (July 23, 1853); was often asked by his brother to replace him as conductor, and accompanied him on tours to Germany, Russia, etc. He wrote 283 opus numbers, of which some are well worthy of his family's renown. His op. 173, *Dynamiden,* was used by Richard Strauss for a theme in *Der Rosenkavalier.*

BIBLIOGRAPHY: A. Witeschnik, *Die Dynastie Strauss* (Vienna, 1939).

Strauss, Paul, American conductor; b. Chicago, June 29, 1922. He began taking violin lessons as a child and then turned to piano and viola. He studied musical subjects at Northwestern Univ.; subsequently went to Europe, and in 1967 was appointed music director of the Orch. de Liège, a post he held for 10 years.

Strauss, Richard, great German composer; b. Munich, June 11, 1864; d. Garmisch-Partenkirchen, Sept. 8, 1949. His father, the well-known horn player **Franz Strauss,** supervised his son's education. At the age of 4, Richard received regular instruction from A. Tombo, the harpist of the court orch.; at 8 he began to study the violin with Benno Walter, the concertmaster of the court orch.; from 1875 to 1880 he studied composition with the court conductor, F.W. Meyer. His first attempt at writing music (a

Polka in C) dates from the year 1870, when he was 6, and he wrote piano pieces, songs, and even orch. overtures as a child; his op. 1, a *Festmarsch* for Orch., written at the age of 12, was publ. in 1880. In the meantime, he completed an academic course of study at the Gymnasium, graduating in 1882; then attended lectures on philosophy at the Univ. of Munich (1882–83). On March 30, 1881, Strauss's first major work, the Symph. in D minor, was performed in Munich by Hermann Levi; also in Munich, on Feb. 8, 1883, Benno Walter, Strauss's teacher, played his Violin Concerto. These works, written in the forms of the classic masters, revealed an astonishing degree of technical mastery and won for Strauss immediate recognition; he was only 20 when he could boast the distinction of an American premiere, for on Dec. 13, 1884, Theodore Thomas, then conductor of the N.Y. Phil., gave the first U.S. performance of the Symph. in F minor. Strauss spent the winter of 1883–84 in Berlin, where Hans von Bülow became interested in him and engaged him as assistant conductor with Bülow's orch. in Meiningen. When Bülow left Meiningen in 1885, Strauss became his successor. Although he remained in Meiningen for only one season (1885–86), this sojourn proved to be a turning point in his career, for in that short time he became intimately associated with the poet and musician Alexander Ritter, who revealed to Strauss the meaning of the revolution in esthetics produced by Wagner and Liszt. Ritter urged on Strauss the concept of "music as expression," and thenceforward Strauss became convinced of the artistic importance of music with a literary or philosophical outline. After a journey to Italy in the spring of 1886, he became one of the conductors of the court opera in Munich (1886–89); his duties were not onerous, and he had ample time for composition; in Munich he wrote the symph. fantasy *Aus Italien,* and his first significant works in the new style, the tone poems *Don Juan* and *Tod und Verklärung.* In the autumn of 1889 he was appointed first conductor of the Weimar Court Orch.; there he remained until the spring of 1894. In Weimar he brought out *Don Juan* on Nov. 11, 1889, and another tone poem, *Macbeth,* on Oct. 13, 1890; on June 21, 1890, he conducted the first performance of *Tod und Verklärung,* at the meeting of the Allgemeiner Deutscher Musik-Verein in Eisenach. These works were revelations of a talent of striking originality and boldness, and made Strauss one of the greatest figures of the nascent era of musical modernism; he was praised extravagantly by admirers, and damned violently by traditionalists. Hans von Bülow called him "Richard the 2nd," as a legitimate heir to Wagner's mantle. Indeed, Strauss extended Wagner's system of leading motifs to the domain of symph. music; his tone poems are interwoven with motifs, each representing some relevant programmatic element. Analytical brochures, compiled especially by German commentators, illustrate the complex involvements of thematic allusions in these works. Strauss spent the winter of 1892 in Greece, Egypt, and Sicily, writing the text and music of his first stage work, the opera *Guntram,* which he conducted in Weimar on May 12,

1894. **Pauline de Ahna** sang the leading part; she married Strauss on Sept. 10, 1894, and remained with him throughout his life, dying a few months after he did. Strauss was appointed successor to Bülow as conductor of the Berlin Phil. in the autumn of 1894, and led it during the season of 1894–95. In 1896 he conducted his own works in Brussels, Liège, and Moscow, and also in many German cities; in 1897 he visited Amsterdam, Paris, London, and Barcelona. In the meantime, he continued unremittingly to write music; in quick succession, he brought out his masterpieces of musical characterization: *Till Eulenspiegels lustige Streiche* (Cologne, Nov. 5, 1895, Wüllner conducting); *Also sprach Zarathustra,* philosophical poem after Nietzsche (Frankfurt, Nov. 27, 1896, composer conducting); and *Don Quixote,* variations with a cello solo, after Cervantes (Cologne, March 8, 1898, Wüllner conducting). The series of his great tone poems was concluded with the autobiographical work *Ein Heldenleben* (Frankfurt, March 3, 1899, composer conducting). For his first visit to America in the early months of 1904, Strauss wrote a new work of considerable dimensions, *Symphonia domestica,* which he conducted at Carnegie Hall in N.Y. on March 21, 1904. The score was so naturalistic, and so frankly autobiographical, that it amused and shocked the public; but the music itself fell distinctly below the poetically charged inspiration of the preceding tone poems. Even more literal was his last symph. work *Eine Alpensinfonie,* which calls for a wind machine and a thunder machine to portray a storm in the Alps; it was first performed by the composer himself in Berlin, on Oct. 28, 1915. But while his symph. production lagged, he turned vigorously to the field of the opera, producing works of exceptional merit. After *Guntram,* he wrote *Feuersnot* (Dresden, Nov. 21, 1901), which attracted little attention. Then on Dec. 9, 1905, the Dresden Opera staged the opera *Salome,* after Oscar Wilde's French play, trans. into German. In this score Strauss went far beyond the limits of Wagnerian music drama, and created a psychological tragedy of shattering impact; the erotic subject was illustrated by sensuous music. The opera made the rounds of European theaters in quick succession, but when the Metropolitan Opera Co. produced *Salome* in N.Y. (Jan. 22, 1907) there were violent protests, and it was taken out of the repertoire, not to be revived until many years later. Scarcely less forceful was the impression produced by the next opera, *Elektra* (Dresden, Jan. 25, 1909), in which the horrors of matricide were pictured with extraordinary strength. Then, as if to make a graceful concession to public taste, Strauss produced *Der Rosenkavalier* (Dresden, Jan. 26, 1911), a charming comedy, which quickly became famous. With *Elektra* and *Der Rosenkavalier,* Strauss established his fruitful collaboration with the poet Hugo von Hofmannsthal, who wrote the librettos for these works, and also for the subsequent operas *Ariadne auf Naxos* (Stuttgart, Oct. 25, 1912); *Die Frau ohne Schatten* (Vienna, Oct. 10, 1919); *Die ägyptische Helena* (Dresden, June 6, 1928); and *Arabella* (Dresden, July 1, 1933). After Hofmannsthal's death in 1929, Strauss turned to

Stefan Zweig for the libretto of *Die schweigsame Frau* (Dresden, June 24, 1935), and to Josef Gregor for *Friedenstag* (Munich, July 24, 1938), *Daphne* (Dresden, Oct. 15, 1938), and *Die Liebe der Danae* (written in 1938–40; produced posthumously, Salzburg, Aug. 14, 1952). The last opera by Strauss was *Capriccio,* to a libretto by the conductor Clemens Krauss (Munich, Oct. 28, 1942). The operas after *Der Rosenkavalier* were received with deference and interest, but were not retained in the permanent repertoire. It may be said, therefore, that the great creative period of Strauss ended for his stage works in 1911, with *Der Rosenkavalier,* and for his symph. compositions in 1899, with *Ein Heldenleben.* From 1898 to 1918 Strauss was on the staff of the Berlin Opera; in 1919 he became co-director (with Franz Schalk) of the Vienna State Opera, holding this position until 1924, although not on a permanent basis, so that he had time for extended tours, one of which took him again to America in 1921. He also spent much time at his villa in Garmisch, Bavaria. On Nov. 15, 1933, Strauss was appointed president of the Reichsmusikkammer under the Nazi regime, but resigned in June 1935. He visited London as conductor of his own works in 1937, and received there the gold medal of the Phil. Society. He was the recipient of numerous other honors and decorations. In 1902 the Univ. of Heidelberg made him Dr.Phil., *honoris causa.* He remained in his home at Garmisch during World War II, and wrote the mournful *Metamorphosen* (with a symbolic quotation from Beethoven's funeral march from the *Eroica*) in the last months of the war; then lived for some time in Switzerland. He was strong enough to travel to England for a series of concerts in 1947; returning to Germany, he had to face the special court at Munich, investigating collaborators with the Nazis, but was officially exonerated (June 8, 1948).

WORKS: OPERAS: *Guntram* (Weimar, May 10, 1894; new version, Weimar, Oct. 22, 1940); *Feuersnot* (Dresden, Nov. 21, 1901); *Salome* (Dresden, Dec. 9, 1905); *Elektra* (Dresden, Jan. 25, 1909); *Der Rosenkavalier* (Dresden, Jan. 26, 1911); *Ariadne auf Naxos* (Stuttgart, Oct. 25, 1912); *Die Frau ohne Schatten* (Vienna, Oct. 10, 1919); *Intermezzo* (Dresden, Nov. 4, 1924); *Die ägyptische Helena* (Dresden, June 6, 1928); *Arabella* (Dresden, July 1, 1933); *Die schweigsame Frau* (Dresden, June 24, 1935); *Friedenstag* (Munich, July 24, 1938); *Daphne* (Dresden, Oct. 15, 1938); *Die Liebe der Danae* (1938–40; Salzburg, Aug. 14, 1952); *Capriccio* (Munich, Oct. 28, 1942).

BALLETS: *Josephslegende* (Paris, May 14, 1914); *Schlagobers* (Vienna, May 9, 1924).

FOR ORCH.: *Festmarsch* (1876); Symph. in D minor (Munich, March 30, 1881); Violin Concerto (Munich, Feb. 8, 1883, with Piano; full orch. version, Leipzig, Feb. 17, 1896); Symph. in F minor (N.Y., Dec. 13, 1884); Horn Concerto No. 1 (Meiningen, March 4, 1885); *Aus Italien,* symph. fantasy (Munich, March 2, 1887); *Don Juan,* tone poem, after Lenau (Weimar, Nov. 11, 1889); *Tod und Verklärung,* tone poem (Eisenach, June 21, 1890); *Burleske* for Piano and Orch. (Eisenach, June 21, 1890, composer conducting; Eugen d'Albert, soloist); *Macbeth,* after Shakespeare (Weimar, Oct. 13, 1890); *Till Eulenspiegels lustige Streiche,* tone poem (Cologne, Nov. 5, 1895); *Also sprach Zarathustra,* tone poem, after Nietzsche (Frankfurt, Nov. 27, 1896); *Don Quixote,* variations based on Cervantes (Cologne, March 8, 1898); *Ein Heldenleben,* tone poem (Frankfurt, March 3, 1899); *Symphonia domestica* (N.Y., March 21, 1904); *Festliches Praeludium* (Vienna, Oct. 19, 1913); *Eine Alpensinfonie* (Berlin, Oct. 28, 1915); *Parergon zur Symphonia domestica* for Piano, left-hand, and Orch. (Dresden, Oct. 16, 1925; Paul Wittgenstein, soloist); *München Walzer* (originally written for film, 1939; new version, 1945; perf. posthumously, Vienna, March 31, 1951); *Festmusik* on the 2,600th anniversary of the Japanese Empire (Tokyo, Oct. 27, 1940); *Divertimento* on pieces by Couperin (Vienna, Jan. 31, 1943); Horn Concerto No. 2 (Salzburg, Aug. 11, 1943); *Metamorphosen* for 23 String Instruments (Zürich, Jan. 25, 1946); Oboe Concerto (Zürich, Feb. 26, 1946); Duet Concertino for Clarinet, Bassoon, Strings, and Harp (Radio Svizzera Italiana, April 5, 1948).

CHAMBER MUSIC: String Quartet (1879–80); Cello Sonata (1882–83); *Serenade* for 13 Wind Instruments (1881); Piano Quartet (1884); Violin Sonata (1887); Sonatina No. 1 for 16 Wind Instruments (1943); Sonatina No. 2 for 16 Wind Instruments (1944–45).

CHORAL WORKS: Chorus for Sophocles' *Electra* (1880); *Wanderers Sturmlied* for Chorus and Orch. (1884); *Eine deutsche Motette* for Solo Voices and 16-part Chorus (1923); *Die Tageszeiten,* cycle for Men's Chorus and Orch. (1928); many unpubl. choral pieces.

FOR VOICE AND ORCH.: 4 songs (1896–97); 4 hymns for Soprano (1921); *3 Gesänge* for High Voice (1948); *Im Abendrot* for High Voice (1948).

FOR VOICE AND PIANO: 26 albums to words in German; of these songs the earliest are the most famous: *Zueignung* (1882); *Die Nacht* (1882); *Allerseelen* (1883); *Ständchen* (1885); *Barcarole* (1886); *Breit über mein Haupt* (1886); *Cäcilie, Heimliche Aufforderung,* and *Morgen* (1893–94); *Traum durch die Dämmerung* (1894); *Ich trage meine Minne* (1896).

FOR RECITATION AND PIANO: *Enoch Arden,* after Tennyson (1890), and *Das Schloss am Meer,* after Uhland (1899). A collected edition of the songs, in 4 vols., was ed. by F. Trenner and publ. in 1964–65.

FOR PIANO: 5 pieces (1881); Sonata (1881); *4 Stimmungsbilder* (1883).

ARRANGEMENTS AND EDITIONS: Strauss arranged Gluck's *Iphigénie en Tauride* for production at Weimar; his version was used for the American premiere at the Metropolitan Opera House in N.Y., Nov. 25, 1916; trans., revised, and enlarged the *Traité d'Instrumentation* of Berlioz (1905); made a new arrangement of Beethoven's *The Ruins of Athens* (Vienna, 1927); ed. Mozart's *Idomeneo* (1930); harmonized a number of folk songs for Peters's *Volksliederbuch für Männerchor;* ed. and publ. his father's posthumous works for horn. He publ. his memoirs, *Betrachtungen und Erinnerungen* (Zürich, 1949; ed. by W. Schuh; in Eng., N.Y., 1953).

THEMATIC CATALOGUES: R. Specht, *Vollständiges Verzeichnis der im Druck erschienenen Werke von R. S.* (Vienna, 1910; also contains valuable biographical data); Erich Hermann Mueller von Asow, *R. S., Thematisches Verzeichnis* (3 vols., 1955–74).

BIBLIOGRAPHY: BIOGRAPHY: A. Seidl and W. Klatte, *R. S. Eine Charakterskizze* (Prague, 1896); G. Brecher, *R. S. Eine monographische Skizze* (Leipzig, 1900); E. Urban, *R. S.* (Berlin, 1901); Ernest Newman, *R. S.* (London, 1908); M. Steinitzer, *R. S.* (Berlin, 1911; 17th ed., 1928); H.T. Finck, *R. S. The Man and His Works* (Boston, 1917); R. Specht, *R. S. und sein Werk* (2 vols., Leipzig, 1921); H.W. von Waltershausen, *R. S.* (Munich, 1921); R.C. Muschler, *R. S.* (Hildesheim, 1924); W. Hutschenruyter, *R. S.* (in Dutch; The Hague, 1929); E. Gehring, ed., *R. S. und seine Vaterstadt* (Munich, 1934); F. Gysi, *R. S.* (Potsdam, 1934); R. Tenschert, *Anekdoten um R. S.* (Vienna, 1945); idem, *R. S. und Wien* (Vienna, 1949); W. Brandl, *R. S., Leben und Werk* (Wiesbaden, 1949); K. Pfister, *R. S., Weg, Gestalt, Denkmal* (Vienna, 1949); C. Rostand, *R. S.* (Paris, 1949); O. Erhardt, *R. S. Leben, Wirken, Schaffen* (Olten, 1953); F. Trenner, *R. S. Dokumente seines Lebens und Schaffens* (Munich, 1954); E. Krause, *R. S., Gestalt und Werk* (Leipzig, 1955); I. Fabian, *R. S.* (Budapest, 1962); G. Marek, *R. S.: The Life of a Non-Hero* (N.Y., 1967); Han Jefferson, *The Life of R. S.* (London, 1973); A. Kennedy, *R. S.* (London, 1976; 2nd ed., revised, 1983); W. Schuh, *R. S.: Jugend und Meisterjahre; Lebenschronik 1864–1898* (Zürich, 1976; Eng. trans. as *R. S.: A Chronicle of the Early Years 1864–1898,* Cambridge, 1982).

CRITICISM, APPRECIATION: Analyses of the instrumental works are found in H. Kretzschmar's *Führer durch den Konzertsaal* (Leipzig, 1887; 4th ed., 1913) and in Schlesinger's *Musikführer* and *Meisterführer* (Berlin); guides to the dramatic works in Schlesinger's *Opernführer* (Berlin), Wossidlo's *Opernbibliothek* (Leipzig), and the numerous handbooks of Kufferath, Taubmann, Chop, Roese, Gilman, Schanzer, etc. See also G. Jorisienne, *R. S. Essai critique et biologique* (Brussels, 1898); J. Huneker, *Mezzotints in Modern Music* (N.Y., 1899); E. Urban, *S. contra Wagner* (Berlin, 1902); J. Huneker, *Overtones* (N.Y., 1904); L. Gilman, *Phases of Modern Music* (N.Y., 1904); E. Newman, "R. S. and the Music of the Future," in *Musical Studies* (London, 1905); O. Bie, *Die Moderne Musik und R. S.* (Berlin, 1906); F. Draeseke, *Die Konfusion in der Musik* (Stuttgart, 1906); F. Niecks, *Program Musik in the Last Four Centuries* (London, 1907); E. Schmitz, *R. S. als Musikdramatiker* (Munich, 1907); E. Zeigler, *R. S. in seinen dramatischen Dichtungen* (Munich, 1907); J.C. Manifarges, *R. S. als Dirigent* (Amsterdam, 1907); R. Rolland, *Musiciens d'aujourd'hui* (Paris, 1908; in Eng., 1914); L. Gilman, *Aspects of Modern Opera* (N.Y., 1908); L.A. Coerne, *The Evolution of Modern Orchestration* (N.Y., 1908); P. Bekker, *Das Musikdrama der Gegenwart* (Stuttgart, 1909); R. Louis, *Die deutsche Musik der Gegenwart* (Munich, 1909); L. Schmidt, *Aus dem Musikleben der Gegenwart* (Berlin, 1909; with preface by Strauss); F. Santoliquido, *Il Dopo-Wagner: C. Debussy e R. S.* (Rome, 1909); G. Tebaldini, *Telepatia musicale e proposito dell'Elektra di R. S.* (Turin,

1909); M. Steinitzer, *Straussiana und Anderes* (Stuttgart, 1910); O. Hübner, *R. S. und das Musikdrama* (Leipzig, 1910); R. Mayrhofer, *Zur Theorie des Schönen* (Leipzig, 1911); H. Rutters, *R. S. en de S.-feesten* (Amsterdam, 1911); *Modern Music and Drama* (2 vols., Boston, 1911, 1915; gives a list of several hundred titles of articles publ. about Strauss in British and American journals); H. Daffner, *Salome: Ihre Gestalt in Geschichte und Kunst* (Munich, 1912); A. Seidl, *Straussiana* (Regensburg, 1913); M. Steinitzer, *R. S. in seiner Zeit* (Leipzig, 1914; 2nd ed., 1922); P. Rosenfeld, *Musical Portraits* (N.Y., 1920); W. Schrenk, *R. S. und die neue Musik* (Berlin, 1924); J. Subirá, *R. S., Su hispanismo* (in Spanish; 1925); C. Gray, *Survey of Contemporary Music* (London, 1927); E. Blom, *The Rose Cavalier* (London, 1930); T. Armstrong, *S.'s Tonepoems* (London, 1931); K.J. Krüger, *Hugo von Hofmannsthal und R. S.* (Berlin, 1935); H. Rüttger, *Das Formproblem bei R. S.* (Berlin, 1937); J. Gregor, *R. S. Der Meister der Oper* (Munich, 1939); R. Tenschert, *3 × 7 Variationen über das Thema R. S.* (Vienna, 1944); W. Schuh, *Über Opern von R. S.* (Zürich, 1947); F. von Schuch, *R. S., Ernst von Schuch und Dresdens Oper* (2nd ed., Leipzig, 1953); G. Hausswald, *R. S., Ein Beitrag zur Dresdner Operngeschichte seit 1945* (Dresden, 1953); Strauss issues of the *Allgemeine Musikzeitung* (1939) and *Die Musik*, IV/8 and XIII/17; N. Del Mar, *R. S.: A Critical Commentary on His Life and Works* (2 vols.: I, London, 1962; II, Philadelphia, 1969); A. Jefferson, *The Operas of R. S. in Britain, 1910–1963* (London, 1963); W. Mann, *R. S.: A Critical Study of the Operas* (London, 1964); Lotte Lehmann, *Five Operas and R. S.* (N.Y., 1964); W. Schuh, *Der Rosenkavalier* (Frankfurt, 1971); K. Forsyth, *Ariadne auf Naxos by Hugo von Hofmannsthal and R. S.: Its Genesis and Meaning* (Oxford, 1982); R. Hartmann, *R. S.: The Staging of His Operas and Ballets* (Oxford, 1982).

CORRESPONDENCE: *R. S. Briefwechsel mit Hugo von Hofmannsthal,* ed. by Franz Strauss (S.'s son; Vienna, 1926; in Eng., N.Y., 1927); *R. S. und Hugo von Hofmannsthal: Briefwechsel* (complete ed., by Franz and Alice Strauss; Zürich, 1952; in Eng., under the title *A Working Friendship: The Correspondence between R. S. and Hugo von Hofmannsthal,* London, 1961); *R. S. et Romain Rolland; Correspondance* (Paris, 1951); *Briefe an die Eltern: 1882–1906* (Zürich, 1954); *Correspondence: Hans von Bülow and R. S.* (London, 1955); *R. S. und Josef Gregor: Briefwechsel, 1934–1949* (Salzburg, 1955); *Briefwechsel zwischen R. S. und Stefan Zweig* (Frankfurt, 1957); *Briefwechsel mit Clemens Krauss* (Berlin, 1963–64); *R. S. und Ludwig Thuille, Briefe der Freundschaft 1877–1907* (Munich, 1969).

Stravinsky, Feodor, distinguished Russian bass, father of **Igor Stravinsky;** b. near Rechitza, in the district of Minsk, June 20, 1843; d. St. Petersburg, Dec. 4, 1902. He made his debut in Kiev, Sept. 3, 1873, as Count Rodolpho in *La Sonnambula.* He became a member of the Russian Imperial Opera at St. Petersburg in 1876 and established himself as one of the greatest Russian basses before Chaliapin; his interpretation of heroic and comical characters in Russian operas evoked unbounded praise from the critics. He was famous as Méphistophélès in Gounod's *Faust,* and was distinguished not only for the power of his voice, but also for his dramatic talent on the stage. Altogether, he made 1,235 appearances in 64 operatic roles.

Stravinsky, Igor, Russian composer, one of the greatest masters of modern music, whose works exercised the most profound influence on the evolution of music, in its emancipation of rhythm, melody, and harmony; b. Oranienbaum, near St. Petersburg, June 17, 1882; d. New York, April 6, 1971 (his body was flown to Venice and buried in the Russian corner of the cemetery island of San Michele). He was the son of a famous opera singer, the bass at the Russian Imperial Opera **Feodor Stravinsky,** and was brought up in an artistic atmosphere; he often went to opera rehearsals when his father sang, and acquired an early love for the musical theater. He took piano lessons with one Alexandra Snetkova, and later with Leokadia Kashperova, who was a pupil of Anton Rubinstein; but it was not until much later that he began to study music theory, first with Akimenko and then with Kalafati (1900–3). His progress in composition was remarkably slow; he never entered a music school or a cons., and never earned an academic degree in music. In 1901 he enrolled in the faculty of jurisprudence at St. Petersburg Univ., and took courses there for 8 semesters, without graduating; a fellow student was Vladimir Rimsky-Korsakov, a son of the composer. In the summer of 1902 Stravinsky traveled in Germany, where he met another son of Rimsky-Korsakov, Andrei, who was a student at the Univ. of Heidelberg at the time; Stravinsky became his friend. He was introduced to Rimsky-Korsakov, and became a regular guest at Rimsky-Korsakov's periodic gatherings in St. Petersburg. In 1903–4 Stravinsky wrote a piano sonata for the Russian pianist Nicolai Richter, who performed it at Rimsky-Korsakov's home. In 1905 Stravinsky began taking regular lessons in orchestration with Rimsky-Korsakov, who taught him free of charge, and under his tutelage composed a Symph. in E-flat major; the 2nd and 3rd movements from it were performed on April 27, 1907, by the court orch. in St. Petersburg, and a complete performance of it was given by the same orch. on Feb. 4, 1908. The work, dedicated to Rimsky-Korsakov, had some singularities and angularities that showed a deficiency of technique; there was little in this work that presaged Stravinsky's ultimate development as a master of form and orchestration. At the same concert, Stravinsky's *Le Faune et la bergère* for voice and orch. had its first performance; this score revealed a certain influence of French Impressionism. To celebrate the marriage of Rimsky-Korsakov's daughter Nadezhda to the composer Maximilian Steinberg on June 17, 1908, Stravinsky wrote an orch. fantasy entitled *Fireworks.* Rimsky-Korsakov died a few days after the wedding; Stravinsky deeply mourned his ier and wrote a funeral song for wind in his memory; it was first performed sburg on Jan. 30, 1909. There followed a *antastique* for orch., inspired by Maeterook *La Vie des abeilles.* As revealed in his ondence with Rimsky-Korsakov, Stravinsky first planned a literal program of composition, illustrating events in the life of a beehive by a series of descriptive sections; some years later, however, Stravinsky gratuitously denied all connection of the work with Maeterlinck's book.

A signal change in Stravinsky's fortunes came when the famous impresario Diaghilev commissioned Stravinsky to write a work for the Paris season of his company, the Ballets Russes. The result was the production of Stravinsky's first ballet masterpiece, *The Firebird,* staged by Diaghilev in Paris on June 25, 1910. Here Stravinsky created music of extraordinary brilliance, steeped in the colors of Russian fairy tales. There are numerous striking effects in the score, such as a glissando of harmonics in the string instruments; the rhythmic drive is exhilarating, and the use of asymmetrical time signatures is extremely effective; the harmonies are opulent; the orchestration is coruscating. Stravinsky drew 2 orch. suites from the work; in 1919 he reorchestrated the music to conform to his new beliefs in musical economy; in effect he plucked the luminous feathers off the magical firebird, but the original scoring remained a favorite with conductors and orchs. Stravinsky's association with Diaghilev demanded his presence in Paris, which he made his home beginning in 1911, with frequent travels to Switzerland. His 2nd ballet for Diaghilev was *Pétrouchka,* produced in Paris on June 13, 1911, with triumphant success. Not only was the ballet remarkably effective on the stage, but the score itself, arranged in 2 orch. suites, was so new and original that it marked a turning point in 20th-century music; the spasmodically explosive rhythms, the novel instrumental sonorities, with the use of the piano as an integral part of the orch., the bold harmonic innovations in employing 2 different keys simultaneously (C major and F-sharp major, the "Pétrouchka Chord") became a potent influence on modern European composers. Debussy voiced his enchantment with the score, and young Stravinsky, still in his 20s, became a Paris celebrity. Two years later, Stravinsky brought out a work of an even greater revolutionary import, the ballet *Le Sacre du printemps (Rite of Spring;* Russian title, *Vesna sviashchennaya,* literally *Spring the Sacred*); its subtitle was "Scenes of Pagan Russia." It was produced by Diaghilev with his Ballets Russes in Paris on May 29, 1913, with the choreography by Nijinsky. The score marked a departure from all conventions of musical composition; while in *Pétrouchka* the harmonies, though innovative and dissonant, could still be placed in the context of modern music, the score of *Le Sacre du printemps* contained such corrosive dissonances as scales played at the intervals of major sevenths and superpositions of minor upon major triads with the common tonic, chords treated as unified blocks of sound, and rapid metrical changes that seemingly defied performance.

The score still stands as one of the most daring creations of the modern musical mind; its impact was tremendous; to some of the audience at its first performance in Paris, Stravinsky's "barbaric" music was beyond endurance; the Paris critics exercised their verbal ingenuity in indignant vituperation; one of them proposed that *Le Sacre du printemps* should be more appropriately described as *Le Massacre du printemps.* On May 26, 1914, Diaghilev produced Stravinsky's lyric fairy tale *Le Rossignol,* after Hans Christian Andersen. It too abounded in corrosive discords, but here it could be explained as "Chinese" music illustrative of the exotic subject. In 1914–18 Stravinsky worked on his ballet *Les Noces* (Russian title, *Svadebka;* literally, *Little Wedding*), evoking Russian peasant folk modalities; it was scored for an unusual ensemble of chorus, soloists, 4 pianos, and 17 percussion instruments.

The devastation of the war led Stravinsky to conclude that the era of grandiose Romantic music had become obsolete, and that a new spirit of musical economy was imperative in an impoverished world. As an illustration of such economy, he wrote the musical stage play *L'Histoire du soldat,* scored for only 7 players, with a narrator. About the same time he wrote a work for 11 instruments entitled *Ragtime,* inspired by the new American dance music. He continued his association with Diaghilev's Ballets Russes in writing the ballet *Pulcinella,* based on themes by Pergolesi and other 18th-century Italian composers. He also wrote for Diaghilev 2 short operas, *Mavra,* after Pushkin, and *Renard,* to a Russian fairy tale (both produced by the Ballets Russes in Paris on May 18, 1922). These 2 works were the last in which Stravinsky used Russian subjects, with the sole exception of an orch. *Scherzo à la russe,* written in 1944. Stravinsky had now entered the period usually designated as neo-Classical. The most significant works of this stage of Stravinsky's development were his Octet for wind instruments and the Piano Concerto commissioned by Koussevitzky. In these works, Stravinsky abandoned the luxuriant instrumentation of his ballets and their aggressively dissonant harmonies; instead, he used pandiatonic structures, firmly tonal but starkly dissonant in their superposition of tonalities within the same principal key. His reversion to old forms, however, was not an act of ascetic renunciation but, rather, a grand experiment in reviving Baroque practices, which had fallen into desuetude. The Piano Concerto provided him with an opportunity to appear as soloist; Stravinsky was never a virtuoso pianist, but he was able to acquit himself satisfactorily in such works as the Piano Concerto; he played it with Koussevitzky in Paris on May 22, 1924, and during his first American tour with the Boston Symph. Orch., also under Koussevitzky, on Jan. 23, 1925. The Elizabeth Sprague Coolidge Foundation commissioned Stravinsky to write a pantomime for string orch.; the result was *Apollon Musagète,* given at the Library of Congress in Washington, D.C., on April 27, 1927. This score, serene and emotionally restrained, evokes the manner of Lully's court ballets. Stravinsky continued to explore the resources of neo-Baroque writing in his *Capriccio* for piano and orch., which he performed as soloist, with Ernest Ansermet conducting, in Paris, on Dec. 6, 1929; this score is impressed by a spirit of hedonistic entertainment, harking back to the *style galant* of the 18th century; yet it is unmistakably modern in its polyrhythmic collisions of pandiatonic harmonies. Stravinsky's growing disillusionment with the external brilliance of modern music led him to seek eternal verities of music in ancient modalities. His well-nigh monastic renunciation of the grandiose edifice of glorious sound to which he himself had so abundantly contributed found expression in his opera-oratorio *Oedipus Rex;* in order to emphasize its detachment from temporal aspects, he commissioned a Latin text for the work, even though the subject was derived from a Greek play; its music is deliberately hollow and its dramatic points are emphasized by ominous repetitive passages. Yet this very austerity of idiom makes *Oedipus Rex* a profoundly moving play. It had its first performance on May 30, 1927; its stage premiere took place in Vienna on Feb. 23, 1928. A turn to religious writing found its utterance in Stravinsky's Symph. of Psalms, written for the 50th anniversary of the Boston Symph. and dedicated "to the glory of God." The work is scored for chorus and orch., omitting the violins and violas, thus emphasizing the lower instrumental registers and creating an austere sonority suitable to its solemn subject. Owing to a delay of the Boston performance, the world premiere of the Symph. of Psalms took place in Brussels on Dec. 13, 1930. In 1931 Stravinsky wrote a Violin Concerto commissioned by the violinist Samuel Dushkin, and performed by him in Berlin on Oct. 23, 1931. On a commission from the ballerina Ida Rubinstein, Stravinsky composed the ballet *Perséphone;* here again Stravinsky exercised his mastery of simplicity in formal design, melodic patterns, and contrapuntal structure. For his American tour Stravinsky wrote *Jeu de cartes,* a "ballet in three deals" to his own scenario depicting an imaginary poker game (of which Stravinsky was a devotee). He conducted its first performance at the Metropolitan Opera House in N.Y. on April 27, 1937. His concerto for 16 instruments entitled *Dumbarton Oaks,* named after the Washington, D.C., estate of Mr. and Mrs. Robert Woods Bliss, who commissioned the work, was first performed in Washington, on May 8, 1938; in Europe it was played under the noncommittal title *Concerto in E-flat;* its style is hermetically neo-Baroque. It is germane to note that in his neo-Classical works Stravinsky began to indicate the key in the title, e.g., Concerto in D for Violin and Orch. (1931), Concerto in E-flat (*Dumbarton Oaks,* 1938), Symph. in C (1938), Concerto in D for String Orch. (1946), and Serenade in A for Piano (1925).

With the war engulfing Europe, Stravinsky decided to seek permanent residence in America. He had acquired French citizenship on June 10, 1934; in 1939 he applied for American citizenship; he became an American citizen on Dec. 28, 1945. To celebrate this event he made an arrangement of the *Star-Spangled Banner,* which contained a curious modulation into the subdominant in the coda. He conducted it with the Boston Symph. on Jan. 14, 1944, but because of legal injunctions existing in the state of Massachusetts against intentional alteration, or any mutilation, of the national anthem, Stravinsky was advised not to conduct his version at the 2nd pair of concerts, and the standard version was substituted. In 1939–40 Stravinsky was named Charles Eliot Norton lecturer at Harvard Univ.; about the same time he accepted several private students, a pedagogical role he had never exercised before. His American years form a curious panoply of subjects and manners of composition. He accepted a commission from the Ringling Bros. to write a *Circus Polka* "for a young elephant." In 1946 he wrote *Ebony Concerto* for a swing band. In 1951 he completed his opera *The Rake's Progress,* inspired by Hogarth's famous series of engravings, to a libretto by W.H. Auden and C. Kallman. He conducted its world premiere in Venice, on Sept. 11, 1951, as part of the International Festival of Contemporary Music there. The opera is a striking example of Stravinsky's protean capacity for adopting different styles and idioms of composition to serve his artistic purposes; *The Rake's Progress* is an ingenious conglomeration of disparate elements, ranging from 18th-century British ballads to cosmopolitan burlesque. But whatever transmutations Stravinsky's music underwent during his long and productive career, he remained a man of the theater at heart. In America he became associated with the brilliant Russian choreographer George Balanchine, who produced a number of ballets to Stravinsky's music, among them his *Apollon Musagète,* Violin Concerto, Symph. in 3 movements, *Scherzo à la russe, Pulcinella,* and *Agon.* It was in his score of *Agon* that Stravinsky essayed for the first time to adopt the method of composition with 12 tones as promulgated by Schoenberg; *Agon* (the word means "competition" in Greek) bears the subtitle "ballet for 12 tones," perhaps in allusion to the dodecaphonic technique used in the score. Yet the 12-tone method had been the very antithesis of Stravinsky's previous tenets. In fact, an irreconcilable polarity existed between Stravinsky and Schoenberg even in personal relations. Although both resided in Los Angeles for several years, they never met socially; Schoenberg once wrote a canon in which he ridiculed Stravinsky as Herr Modernsky, who put on a wig to look like "Papa Bach." After Schoenberg's death, Stravinsky became interested in examining the essence of the method of composition with 12 tones, which was introduced to him by his faithful musical factotum Robert Craft; Stravinsky adopted dodecaphonic writing in its aspect of canonic counterpoint as developed by Anton von Webern. In this manner he wrote his *Canticum sacrum ad honorem Sancti Marci nominis,* which he conducted at San Marco in Venice on Sept. 11, 1956. Other works of the period were also written in a modified 12-tone technique, among them *The Flood,* for narrator, mime, singers, and dancers, presented in a CBS Television broadcast in N.Y. on June 14, 1962; its first stage performance was given in Hamburg on April 30, 1963.

Stravinsky was married twice; his first wife, Catherine Nosenko, whom he married on Jan. 24, 1906, and who bore him 3 children, died in 1939; on March 9, 1940, Stravinsky married his longtime mistress, Vera, who was formerly married to the Russian painter Serge Sudeikin. She was born Vera de Bosset in St. Petersburg, on Dec. 25, 1888, and died in N.Y. on Sept. 17, 1982, at the age of 93. An ugly litigation for the rights to the Stravinsky estate continued for several years between his children and their stepmother; after Vera Stravinsky's death, it was finally settled in a compromise, according to which $^2/_9$ of the estate went to each of his 3 children and a grandchild and $^1/_9$ to Robert Craft. The value of the Stravinsky legacy was spectacularly demonstrated on Nov. 11, 1982, when his working draft of *Le Sacre du printemps* was sold at an auction in London for the fantastic sum of $548,000, higher than any MS by any composer. The purchaser was Paul Sacher, a Swiss conductor and philanthropist whose fortune derived from his wife's holdings of the shares of the international pharmaceutical company that manufactures the sedative drugs Valium and Librium. Even more fantastic was the subsequent sale of the entire Stravinsky archive, consisting of 116 boxes of personal letters and 225 drawers containing MSS, some of them unpubl. Enormous bids were made for it by the N.Y. Public Library and the Morgan Library, but they were all outbid by Paul Sacher, who offered the overwhelming purse of $5,250,000, which removed all competition. The materials were to be assembled in a specially constructed 7-story Sacher Foundation building in Basel, to be eventually opened to scholars for study.

In tribute to Stravinsky as a naturalized American citizen, the U.S. Postal Service issued a 2-cent stamp bearing his image to mark his centennial in 1982, an honor theretofore never granted to a foreign-born composer (the possible exception being Victor Herbert, but his entire career was made in America).

Few composers escaped the powerful impact of Stravinsky's music; ironically, it was his own country that had rejected him, partly because of the opposition of Soviet ideologues to modern music in general, and partly because of Stravinsky's open criticism of Soviet ways in art. But in 1962 Stravinsky returned to Russia for a visit, and was welcomed as a prodigal son; as if by magic, his works began to appear on Russian concert programs, and Soviet music critics issued a number of laudatory studies of his works. Yet it is Stravinsky's early masterpieces, set in an attractive colorful style, that continue to enjoy favor with audiences and performers, while his more abstract and recursive scores are appreciated mainly by specialists.

WORKS: FOR THE STAGE: *L'Oiseau de feu (The Firebird),* ballet (1909–10; Paris Opéra, June 25, 1910; 3 suite versions: 1911, 1919, and 1945; 2 sections arranged for Violin and Piano, 1926); *Pétrouchka,* ballet (1910–11; Paris, June 13, 1911, Pierre Monteux conducting; revised 1946; excerpts officially designated as a "suite" in 1946); *Le Sacre du printemps,* ballet, "scenes of pagan Russia" (1911–13; Paris, May 29, 1913, Pierre Monteux conducting; first concert perf., Moscow, Feb. 18, 1914, Serge Koussevitzky conducting; first Paris concert perf., April 5, 1914, Monteux conducting); *Le Rossignol,* "lyric tale" in 3 acts, after Hans Christian Andersen (1908–14; Paris Opéra, May 26, 1914, Monteux conducting; in 1917 the 2nd and 3rd acts were scored as both a symph. poem and a ballet, *Le Chant du rossignol;* ballet version, Paris Opéra, Feb. 2, 1920; complete opera revised 1962); *Renard,* burlesque chamber opera (1915–16; Paris, May 18, 1922; revised 1962); *L'Histoire du soldat,* ballet with Narrator and 7 Instrumentalists (1918; Lausanne, Sept. 28, 1918; concert suite with original instrumentation, 1920; also *Petite suite* for Violin, Clarinet, and Piano extracted from the score, 1919); *Pulcinella,* ballet "after Pergolesi" (1919–20; Paris Opéra, May 15, 1920; revised 1965; an orch. suite was extracted from it in 1922, and first perf. in Boston, Dec. 22, 1922, revised, 1947; 2 chamber pieces, *Suite italienne*); *Mavra,* comic opera, after Pushkin (1922; first public perf., Paris Opéra, June 3, 1922); *Les Noces (The Wedding),* ballet-cantata, subtitled "choreographic Russian scenes," revision for Soloists, Chorus, 4 Pianos, and 17 Percussion Instruments (1921–23; Paris, June 13, 1923; originally scored with Full Orch., 1914–17); *Oedipus Rex,* opera-oratorio, after Sophocles (1926–27; concert perf., Paris, May 30, 1927; first stage perf., Vienna, Feb. 23, 1928; revised 1948); *Apollon Musagète,* classic ballet for String Orch. (1927–28; Washington, D.C., April 27, 1928; revised 1947); *Le Baiser de la fée,* ballet on themes of Tchaikovsky (1928; Paris Opéra, Nov. 27, 1928; in 1934 several sections were collected for an independent symph. piece called *Divertimento;* entire ballet revised 1950); *Perséphone,* melodrama in 3 parts for Female Narrator, Tenor, Chorus, and Orch., to a text by André Gide (1933; Paris Opéra, April 30, 1934; revised 1949); *Jeu de cartes (Card Game),* "ballet in 3 deals" (1935–37; N.Y., April 27, 1937); *Orpheus,* ballet (1946–47; N.Y., April 28, 1948); *The Rake's Progress,* opera after Hogarth's engravings, with libretto by W.H. Auden and C. Kallman (1948–51; Venice, Sept. 11, 1951, Stravinsky conducting); *Agon,* ballet for 12 Dancers (1954–57; Los Angeles, June 17, 1957); *Noah and the Flood,* also called just *The Flood,* biblical spectacle narrated, mimed, sung, and danced (1961–62; CBS Television broadcast, N.Y., June 14, 1962; first stage perf., Hamburg, April 30, 1963).

FOR ORCH.: Symph. in E-flat major, op. 1 (1905–7; first partial perf., 2nd and 3rd movements only, St. Petersburg, April 27, 1907; first complete perf. St. Petersburg, Feb. 4, 1908; revision, Montreux, Switzerland, April 2, 1914); *Scherzo fantastique,* op. 3 (1907; St. Petersburg, Feb. 6, 1909); *Fireworks,* op. 4 (1908; St. Petersburg, June 17, 1908; reorchestrated and first perf. in St. Petersburg, Jan. 22, 1910); *Chant funèbre* for Wind Instruments, on the death of Rimsky-Korsakov (1908; St. Petersburg, Jan. 30, 1909; score lost); *Le Chant du rossignol,* symph. poem (from the opera *Le Rossignol;* Geneva, Dec. 6, 1919); *Symphonies of Wind Instruments,* in memory of Debussy (1920; London, June 10, 1921; revised 1945–47); Suite No. 1 for Small Orch. (1917–25; orch.

arrangement of Nos. 1–4 of the *5 pièces faciles* for Piano, 4-hands: Andante, Napolitana, Española, Balalaika); Suite No. 2 for Small Orch. (1921; orch. arrangement of *3 pièces faciles* and No. 5 of *5 pièces faciles* for Piano, 4-hands: March, Waltz, Polka, Galop); Concerto for Piano, with Wind Instruments, Double Basses, and Percussion (1923–24; Paris, May 22, 1924; revised 1950); Capriccio for Piano and Orch. (1928–29; Paris, Dec. 6, 1929; revised 1949); 4 études for Orch.: Danse, Excentrique, Cantique, Madrid (1928; orch. arrangement of 3 pieces for String Quartet, and Etude for Pianola; Berlin, Nov. 7, 1930; revised 1952); Concerto in D for Violin and Orch. (1931; Berlin, Oct. 23, 1931; adapted in 1940 for Balanchine's ballet *Balustrade*); Divertimento (sections of the ballet *Le Baiser de la fée*, combined in 1934); Praeludium for Jazz Ensemble (1936–37; revised 1953; Los Angeles, Oct. 19, 1953); Concerto in E-flat, *Dumbarton Oaks*, for Chamber Orch. (1937–38; Washington, D.C., May 8, 1938); Symph. in C (1938–40; Chicago, Nov. 7, 1940); Tango, arrangement by Felix Günther of the piano piece (Philadelphia, July 10, 1941, Benny Goodman conducting; Stravinsky's own orchestration, 1953; Los Angeles, Oct. 19, 1953); *Danses concertantes* for Chamber Orch. (1941–42; Los Angeles, Feb. 8, 1942); *Circus Polka* for Piano (commissioned by the Ringling Bros. Circus, to accompany the elephant numbers; arranged for band by David Raksin, 1942; arranged by Stravinsky for a symph. orch. and conducted by him with the Boston Symph. Orch., in Cambridge, on Jan. 13, 1944); 4 *Norwegian Moods* (1942; Cambridge, Mass., Jan. 13, 1944, Stravinsky conducting); *Ode*, in 3 parts (1943; Boston, Oct. 8, 1943); *Scènes de ballet* (originally composed for Billy Rose's Broadway show *The Seven Lively Arts*, which opened in Philadelphia, Nov. 24, 1944; revised for concert performance and first perf. in N.Y., Feb. 3, 1945); *Scherzo à la russe* (1944; San Francisco, March 22, 1946; originally for big jazz band); Symph. in 3 movements (1942–45; N.Y., Jan. 24, 1946); *Ebony Concerto* for Clarinet and Swing Band (1945; N.Y., March 25, 1946); Concerto in D for String Orch., *Basler* (1946; Basel, Jan. 21, 1947); *Greeting Prelude* ("Happy Birthday," written for Monteux's 80th birthday; Boston, April 4, 1955); Movements for Piano and Orch. (1958–59; N.Y., Jan. 10, 1960); *Variations: Aldous Huxley, In Memoriam* (1963–64; Chicago, April 17, 1965; as a ballet, N.Y., March 31, 1966); Canon, from finale of *The Firebird*, in memory of Monteux (Toronto, Dec. 16, 1965).

CHAMBER MUSIC: 3 pieces for String Quartet (1914); *Ragtime* for 11 Instruments (1918; London, April 27, 1920); *Petite suite* for Violin, Clarinet, and Piano (1919; arranged from *L'Histoire du soldat*); 3 pieces for Clarinet Solo (1919); Concertino for String Quartet (1920; revised for 12 Instruments, 1952); Octet for Wind Instruments (1922–23; Paris, Oct. 18, 1923); *Duo concertant* for Violin and Piano (1931–32; Berlin, Oct. 28, 1932); *Russian Dance* for Violin and Piano, from *Pétrouchka* (1932); *Suite italienne* No. 1 for Cello and Piano, and No. 2 for Violin and Piano (both from *Pulcinella*; 1932, 1934); *Pastorale* for Violin, Oboe, English Horn, Clarinet, and Bassoon (1933; arrangement of vocal *Pastorale*); Diverti-

mento for Violin and Piano, based on material from *Le Baiser de la fée* (1934); *Elégie* for Unaccompanied Violin and Viola (1944); Septet for Piano, and String and Wind Instruments (1952; Washington, D.C., Jan. 24, 1954); *Epitaphium for Prince Max of Fürstenberg* for Flute, Clarinet, and Harp (1959; Donaueschingen, Oct. 17, 1959); Double Canon for String Quartet (1959); *Monumentum pro Gesualdo di Venosa ad CD Annum*, an instrumental surrealization of 3 madrigals by Gesualdo (1960; Venice, Sept. 27, 1960); 8 instrumental miniatures for 15 Players (1962; instrumentation of *Les Cinq Doigts* for Piano); *Fanfare for a New Theater* for 2 Trumpets (1964).

VOCAL WORKS: *Le Faune et la bergère* for Mezzo-soprano and Orch. (1906; St. Petersburg, Feb. 4, 1908); *Pastorale*, "song without words" for Soprano and Piano (1908; version for Soprano, Oboe, English Horn, Clarinet, and Bassoon, 1923); *Le Roi des étoiles (Zvezdoliki)*, cantata for Male Chorus and Orch. (1912; first perf., Brussels Radio, April 19, 1939); 3 poems from the Japanese for Soprano, 2 Flutes, 2 Clarinets, Piano, and String Quartet (1912–13); *Pribaoutki (Peasant Songs)* for Voice and 8 Instruments (1914; Vienna, June 6, 1919); *The Saucer*, 4 Russian songs for Women's Voices (1914–17; as *4 Russian Peasant Songs*, with 4 Horns added, 1954); *Berceuses du chat*, suite of 4 songs for Female Voice and 3 Clarinets (1915–16; Vienna, June 6, 1919); *Les Noces (The Wedding)*, ballet-cantata for Soloists, Chorus, 4 Pianos, and 17 Percussion Instruments (1921–23; Paris, June 13, 1923); *Paternoster* for Mixed Chorus a cappella (1926); *Symphony of Psalms* for Chorus and Orch. (1930; Brussels, Dec. 13, 1930; Boston, Dec. 19, 1930); *Credo* for Mixed Chorus a cappella (1932); *Ave Maria* for Mixed Chorus a cappella (1934); Tango for Wordless Voice and Piano (1940); *Babel* for Male Narrator, Male Chorus, and Orch. (1944; 7th and final movement of *Genesis Suite*, a collaborative effort, with Schoenberg, Shilkret, Tansman, Milhaud, Castelnuovo-Tedesco, and Toch, each contributing a movement); Mass for Men's and Boys' Voices and 10 Wind Instruments (1944–48; Milan, Oct. 27, 1948); Cantata on 4 poems by anonymous English poets of the 15th and 16th centuries, for Soprano, Tenor, Female Chorus, and 5 Instruments (1951–52; Los Angeles, Nov. 11, 1952); 3 songs from William Shakespeare for Mezzo-soprano, Flute, Clarinet, and Viola (1953; Los Angeles, March 8, 1954); *In Memoriam Dylan Thomas* for Tenor, String Quartet, and 4 Trombones (1954; Hollywood, Sept. 20, 1954); *4 Russian Songs* for Soprano, Flute, Guitar, and Harp (1954); *Canticum sacrum ad honorem Sancti Marci nominis* for Tenor, Baritone, Chorus, and Orch. (1955–56; Venice, Sept. 13, 1956, Stravinsky conducting); arrangement for Chorus and Orch. of J.S. Bach's *Choral-Variationen über das Weihnachtslied "Vom Himmel hoch da komm' ich her"* (1956); *Threni*, on Lamentations of Jeremiah from the Vulgate, for 6 Solo Voices, Chorus, and Orch. (1957–58; International Festival for Contemporary Music, Venice, Sept. 23, 1958); *A Sermon, a Narrative and a Prayer*, cantata for Speaker, Alto, Tenor, Chorus, and Orch. (1960–62; Basel, Feb. 23, 1962); anthem, *A Dove Descending*

Stravinsky

Breaks the Air, after T.S. Eliot (1962); *Elegy for J.F.K.* for Baritone, 2 Clarinets, and Corno di Bassetto (1964; Los Angeles, April 6, 1964); *Abraham and Isaac,* sacred ballad for Baritone and Chamber Orch., to Hebrew texts (1962–64; Jerusalem, Aug. 23, 1964); *Introitus (T.S. Eliot in Memoriam)* for 6 Male Voices, Harp, Piano, Timpani, Tam-tams, Solo Viola, and Double Bass (1965; Chicago, April 17, 1965); *Requiem Canticles* for 4 Vocal Soloists, Chorus, and Orch. (1965–66; Princeton, N.J., Oct. 8, 1966); *The Owl and the Pussycat,* after Lear, for Voice and Piano (1966).

PIANO MUSIC: Sonata in F-sharp minor (1903–4; recovered from Leningrad library, 1962; publ. in Russia, 1973); 4 Etudes, op. 7 (1908); *Le Sacre du printemps* for Piano, 4-hands (1912); *3 pièces faciles* for Piano, 4-hands (1915); *5 pièces faciles* for Piano, 4-hands (1917); Etude for Pianola (1917); Piano-Rag-Music (1919); 3 movements from *Pétrouchka* (1921); *Les Cinq Doigts* (1920–21); Sonata (1924); Serenade in A (1925); Concerto for 2 Solo Pianos (1931–35; Paris, Nov. 21, 1935); Tango (1940); Circus Polka (1942); Sonata for 2 Pianos (1943–44; first public perf., Edgewood College of the Dominican Sisters, Madison, Wis., Aug. 2, 1944).

NONDESCRIPT: *Do Not Throw Paper Towels in Toilet* for Treble Voice Unaccompanied, to text from poster in men's room at Harvard Univ. (dated Dec. 16, 1939).

WRITINGS: *Chroniques de ma vie* (2 vols., Paris, 1935; in Eng. as *Chronicles of My Life,* London, 1936); *Poétique musicale,* the Charles Eliot Norton Lectures at Harvard Univ. (Paris, 1946; in Eng. as *Poetics of Music,* Cambridge, Mass., 1948); with Robert Craft, 6 vols. of revelatory autobiographical publications: *Conversations with Igor Stravinsky* (N.Y., 1958); *Memories and Commentaries* (N.Y., 1959); *Expositions and Developments* (N.Y., 1962); *Dialogues and a Diary* (N.Y., 1963); *Themes and Episodes* (N.Y., 1967); and *Retrospections and Conclusions* (N.Y., 1969); *Themes and Conclusions,* amalgamated and ed. from *Themes and Episodes* and *Retrospections and Conclusions* (1972); also R. Craft, ed., *S.: Selected Correspondence* (vol. 1, N.Y., 1982).

A sharp debate raged, at times to the point of vitriolic polemical exchange, among Stravinsky's associates as to the degree of credibility of Craft's reports in his dialogues, or even of the factual accounts of events during Stravinsky's last years of life. Stravinsky was never a master of the English language; yet Craft quotes him at length as delivering literary paragraphs of impeccable English prose. Craft admitted that he enhanced Stravinsky's actual words and sentences (which were never recorded on tape), articulating the inner, and at times subliminal, sense of his utterances. Craft's role was made clear beyond dispute by Stravinsky himself, who, in a letter to his publishing agent dated March 15, 1958, urged that the title of the book be changed to *Conversations with Igor Stravinsky by Robert Craft,* and emphatically asserted that the text was in Craft's language, and that in effect Craft "created" him.

BIBLIOGRAPHY: C.S. Wise, "Impressions of I. S.," *Musical Quarterly* (April 1916); R.D. Chennevière, "The Two Trends of Modern Music in S.'s Works," *Musical Quarterly* (April 1919); Boris de Schloezer, *I. S.* (Paris, 1926); A. Casella, *S.* (Rome, 1926); J. Vainkop, *I. S.* (in Russian, Leningrad, 1927); V. Belaiev, *I. S.'s Les Noces: An Outline* (London, 1928); Igor Glebov, *S.* (Leningrad, 1929); C.F. Ramuz, *Souvenirs sur I. S.* (Paris, 1929; revised ed., Lausanne, 1946); P. Collaer, *S.* (Brussels, 1930); E.W. White, *S.'s Sacrifice to Apollo* (London, 1930); H. Fleischer, *S.* (Berlin, 1931); A. Schaeffner, *I. S.* (Paris, 1931); J. Handschin, *I. S.* (Zürich, 1933); E. Evans, *The Firebird and Pétrouchka* (London, 1933); D. de Paoli, *I. S.* (Turin, 1934); M. Blitzstein, "The Phenomenon of S.," *Musical Quarterly* (July 1935); M. Armitage, ed., *S.,* a compendium of articles (N.Y., 1936); *S.,* special issue of *La Revue Musicale* (May–June, 1939); A. Kall, "S. in the Chair of Poetry," *Musical Quarterly* (July 1940); S. Babitz, "S.'s Symphony in C," *Musical Quarterly* (Jan. 1941); M.D. Fardell, *S. et les Ballets Russes* (Nice, 1941); G.F. Malipiero, *S.* (Venice, 1945); A. Casella, *S.* (Brescia, 1947, a different work from his book publ. in 1926); E.W. White, *S.: A Critical Survey* (London, 1947; N.Y., 1948); A. Tansman, *I. S.* (Paris, 1948; in Eng., N.Y., 1949); Th. Stravinsky, *Le Message d'I. S.* (Lausanne, 1948; in Eng. as *The Message of I. S.,* London, 1953); M. Lederman, ed., *S. in the Theater* (N.Y., 1949); E. Corle, ed., *I. S.* (N.Y., 1949, a compendium of articles, some of them reprinted from M. Armitage's collection of 1936); F. Onnen, *S.* (Stockholm, 1949, in Eng.); J.E. Cirlot, *I. S.* (Barcelona, 1949); R.H. Myers, *Introduction to the Music of S.* (London, 1950); W.H. Auden et al., *I. S.* (Bonn, 1952); H. Strobel, *I. S.* (Zürich, 1956; in Eng. as *S.: Classic Humanist,* N.Y., 1956); special issue of *Score* for Stravinsky's 75th birthday (London, 1957); *I. S.: A Complete Catalogue of His Published Works* (London, 1957); H. Kirchmeyer, *I. S.: Zeitgeschichte im Persönlichkeitsbild* (Regensburg, 1958); R. Vlad, *S.* (Rome, 1958; in Eng., London, 1960); R. Siohan, *S.* (Paris, 1959; in Eng., London, 1966); F. Herzfeld, *I. S.* (Berlin, 1961); special issue of the *Musical Quarterly* on S.'s 80th birthday (July 1962); *S. and the Dance: A Survey of Ballet Productions, 1910–1962* (N.Y. Public Library, 1962); E.W. White, *S.: The Composer and His Works* (Berkeley, Calif., 1966); P.H. Lang, *S.: The Composer and His Works* (London, 1966); special S. issue of *Tempo* (Summer 1967); A. Boucourechliev, ed., *S.* (Paris, 1968); *The Rite of Spring: Sketches, 1911–1913* (London, 1969); V. Smirnov, *Tvorcheskoye formirovanye I. S.* (Leningrad, 1970); A. Dobrin, *I. S.: His Life and Time* (London, 1970); B. Boretz and E.T. Cone, eds., *Perspectives on Schoenberg and S.* (N.Y., 1972); P. Horgan, *Encounters with S.* (N.Y., 1972); L. Libman, *And Music at the Close: S.'s Last Years, A Personal Memoir* (N.Y., 1972); D.R. De Lerma, *I. S., 1882–1971, A Practical Guide to Publications of His Music* (N.Y., 1974); Th. Stravinsky, *Catherine and I. S.: A Family Album* (N.Y., 1973); B. Yarustovsky, ed., *I. S.: Articles and Materials* (Moscow, 1973); Vera Stravinsky and R. Craft, *S.* (N.Y., 1975); idem, *S. in Pictures and Documents* (N.Y., 1976); L. Morton, "Footnotes to S.'s Studies: *Le Sacre du printemps,*" *Tempo* (1979); R. Taruskin,

"Russian Folk Melodies in *The Rite of Spring*," *Journal of the American Musicological Society* (1980); A. Schouvaloff and V. Borovsky, *S. on Stage* (London, 1982); S. Karlinsky, "S. and Russian Pre-Literate Theater," *19th Century Music* (Spring 1983); M. Ruskin, *I. S.: His Personality, Works and Views* (Cambridge, 1983); P.C. van den Toorn, *The Music of I. S.* (London, 1983).

Stravinsky, Soulima, pianist, son of **Igor Stravinsky;** b. Lausanne, Sept. 23, 1910. He studied in Paris with Isidor Philipp and Nadia Boulanger; then gave piano recitals in Europe and America; appeared frequently with his father, playing his works for 2 pianos.

Strayhorn, William (Billy), black American jazz pianist and composer; b. Dayton, Ohio, Nov. 29, 1915; d. New York, May 31, 1967. He studied music in Pittsburgh; joined Duke Ellington's band as lyricist and arranger in 1939. Many songs credited to Ellington (*Chelsea Bridge, Perfume Suite, Such Sweet Thunder, A Drum Is a Woman,* etc.) are in fact products of a mutually beneficial musical symbiosis, with Ellington suggesting the initial idea, mood, and character and Strayhorn doing the actual writing, often using Ellington's quasi-impressionistic techniques (e.g., modal harmonies, whole-tone scales, etc.). Strayhorn's own acknowledged songs, *Lush Life, Take the "A" Train,* and others, are jazz standards.

Streatfeild, Richard Alexander, English writer on music; b. Edenbridge, June 22, 1866; d. London, Feb. 6, 1919. He studied at Pembroke College, Cambridge; in 1889 became an assistant in the Dept. of Printed Books in the British Museum; was music critic of the *Daily Graphic* (1898–1912). He publ. the following books: *Masters of Italian Music* (1895); *The Opera* (1897; 5th ed., enlarged, 1925); *Modern Music and Musicians* (1906); *Handel* (1909); *Life Stories of Great Composers* (Philadelphia, 1910); *Musiciens anglais contemporains* (French trans., 1913; Eng. original not publ.); *Handel, Canons and the Duke of Chandos* (London, 1916); contributed many articles to English publications.

Street, Tison, American composer; b. Boston, May 20, 1943. He studied composition with Kirchner and Del Tredici at Harvard Univ.; received his B.A. (1965) and M.A. (1971) there; had studied violin with Einar Hansen of the Boston Symph. (1951–59); was a composer-in-residence at the Marlboro Music Festival during 4 summers (1964, 1965, 1966, 1972) and a visiting lecturer at the Univ. of Calif., Berkeley (1971–72); in 1979 he joined the staff at Harvard Univ. He was the recipient of awards from the National Inst. of the American Academy of Arts and Letters (1973), Rome Prize Fellowship (1973), and Mass. Arts and Humanities Foundation (1977). WORKS: String Trio (1963); *Variations* for Flute, Guitar, and Cello (1964); *6 Odds and Ends from "So Much Depends"* for Voices and Diverse Instruments (1964–73); String Quartet (1972); String Quin-

tet (1974; revised 1976); *Piano Phantasy* (1975); *3 Pieces* for consort of Viols and Harpsichord (1977); *John Major's Medley* for Solo Guitar (1977); *Adagio in E-flat* for Oboe and Strings (1977).

Streich, Rita, soprano; b. Barnaul, Russia, Dec. 18, 1920 (of Russian-German parentage). She studied voice with Erna Berger, Maria Ivogün, and Willi Domgraf-Fassbänder; made her debut in Aussig in 1943; from 1946 she sang with the Berlin State Opera; in 1951 she joined the Berlin Städtische Oper. She also appeared in Vienna, Bayreuth, Salzburg, and Glyndebourne; made her U.S. debut with the San Francisco Opera in 1957. In 1974 she became a prof. at the Folkwang-Hochschule in Essen. She was a leading interpreter of soprano parts in Mozart operas.

Streicher, Johann Andreas, German piano maker; b. Stuttgart, Dec. 13, 1761; d. Vienna, May 25, 1833. During a stay at Augsburg in 1793 he married Nanette Stein (b. Augsburg, Jan. 2, 1769; d. Vienna, Jan. 16, 1835), daughter of the piano manufacturer Johann Andreas Stein; in 1802 succeeded Stein in the business and moved it to Vienna. He invented the piano action in which the hammer strikes from above. He was on friendly terms with Beethoven.
BIBLIOGRAPHY: T. Bolte, *Die Musiker-Familien Stein und Streicher* (Vienna, 1917); T. von Frimmel, "Beethoven und das Ehepaar Streicher," *Alt-Wiener Kalender* (1925); W. Lütge, "Andreas und Annette Streicher," *Der Bär* (1927).

Streicher, Theodor, Austrian song composer, great-grandson of **Johann Andreas Streicher;** b. Vienna, June 7, 1874; d. Wetzelsdorf, near Graz, May 28, 1940. He studied singing with F. Jäger in Vienna and J. Kniese in Bayreuth; piano with F. Löwe in Vienna; composition with H. Schulz-Beuthen in Dresden. He lived most of his life in Vienna; wrote numerous songs in a Romantic manner, reminiscent of Hugo Wolf. He set to music 36 poems from *Des Knaben Wunderhorn;* wrote *Wanderers Nachtlied,* after Goethe, for Chorus a cappella; a Sextet for Strings; etc. He also orchestrated the accompaniments of Carl Loewe's ballades. In 1934 a "Theodor Streicher Gemeinde" was founded in Vienna to propagate his music.
BIBLIOGRAPHY: R. Wursten, *Theodor Streicher: His Life and Music* (Diss., Univ. of Wisconsin, 1977).

Streisand, Barbra (Barbara Joan Streisand), popular American singer and actress; b. New York, April 24, 1942. She studied acting for a short time in N.Y.; also learned to sing in Greenwich Village. In 1962 she made her Broadway debut in *I Can Get It for You Wholesale;* then made a hit in *Funny Girl* in 1964, a musical she filmed in 1968, and for which she received an Academy Award. Her other films include *On a Clear Day You Can See Forever* (1970), *A Star Is Born* (1976), and *Yentl* (1983). As a recording artist, she received Gold Record Awards for her albums *People* (1965), *My Name Is Barbra* (1965),

Color Me Barbra (1966), *Stony End* (1971), *Barbra Joan Streisand* (1972), *The Way We Were* (1974), *A Star Is Born* (1976), *Superman* (1977), and others. While not at all educated, her natural talent prevailed over a lack of general culture.

Strelezki, Anton, English pianist and composer; b. Croydon, Dec. 5, 1859; d. 1907. According to some sources, his real name was **Burnand.** He studied with Clara Schumann; settled in London, where he was very popular; place and exact date of his death are unknown. He publ. a great deal of piano music (more than 225 opus numbers), some of which was widely used: *Valse-Souvenir; Jagdstück; Valsette; Sérénade espagnole; Menuet à l'antique; Barcarolle;* also songs; publ. *Personal Recollections of Chats with Liszt* (1895).

Strelnikov, Nicolai, Russian composer; b. St. Petersburg, May 14, 1888; d. there (Leningrad), April 12, 1939. He studied composition with Liadov in St. Petersburg; in 1922 he became music director of the Young People's Theater in Leningrad. He wrote 2 operas, *A Fugitive* (Leningrad, May 26, 1933) and *Count Nulin,* after Pushkin (1935); but he is chiefly remembered for his operettas: *The Black Amulet* (Leningrad, 1927); *Luna-Park* (Moscow, 1928); *The Heart of a Poet* (Leningrad, 1934); *Presidents and Bananas* (1939). Other works include a Piano Concerto, choruses, and chamber music. He also publ. monographs on several Russian composers.

Strens, Jules, Belgian composer; b. Ixelles, near Brussels, Dec. 5, 1892; d. there, March 19, 1971. He studied with Paul Gilson; in 1925 was one of 8 founders of the Group des Synthétistes (all Gilson pupils), endeavoring to establish a modern style of composition within the formal categories of old music. Professionally, he was active mainly as an organist.
WORKS: 2 operas: *Le Chanteur de Naples* (1937) and *La Tragédie d'Agamemnon* (1941); *Gil Blas,* symph. variations (1921); symph. poem, *Les Elfes* (1923); *Danse funambulesque* for Orch. (1925); *Rapsodie tzigane* for Orch. (1927); *Fantaise concertante* for Piano and Orch. (1938); *Symphonie Sylvestre* for Soli, Chorus, and Orch. (1939); Violin Concerto (1951); Concerto for Organ and String Orch. (1958); Piano Trio (1920); 4 string quartets (1925, 1929, 1933, 1935); Cello Sonata (1926); String Sextet (1935); Wind Quintet (1943); Quartet for 4 Horns (1950); *Suite* for 4 Horns (1951); Viola Sonata (1954); Trio for Oboe, Clarinet, and Bassoon (1954); Piano Quartet (1955); piano pieces; organ pieces; songs.

Strepponi, Giuseppina, Italian soprano, wife of **Giuseppe Verdi;** b. Lodi, Sept. 8, 1815; d. Sant' Agata, near Busseto, Nov. 14, 1897. She was the daughter of the opera conductor in Trieste, **Feliciano Strepponi;** having completed her studies at the Milan Cons. (1830–34), she made a successful debut in Adria in Dec. 1834, and was engaged at the Italian Opera in Vienna and in Trieste in 1835. Her appearances in Rome, Florence, Venice, and other Italian cities es-

tablished her reputation as a foremost interpreter of dramatic roles. She created a sensation by her performance of Abigaile in Verdi's *Nabucco* (Milan, March 9, 1842). Verdi admired her greatly, and after many years of intimacy they were married (1859).
BIBLIOGRAPHY: M. Mundula, *La Moglie di Verdi: Giuseppina Strepponi* (Milan, 1938).

Stresemann, Wolfgang, German conductor and orchestral Intendant; b. Dresden, July 20, 1904. His father, Gustav Stresemann, was the distinguished chancellor and foreign minister of the Weimar Republic. Wolfgang Stresemann was educated in Berlin, Heidelberg, and Erlangen (Dr.Jur., 1928); also studied music in Berlin. After the Nazis came to power, he left Germany and eventually settled in the U.S. He served as assistant conductor of the National Orch. Assoc. in N.Y. (1939–45); then conducted the Toledo (Ohio) Orch. (1949–55). He then returned to Germany and held the post of Intendant of the Berlin Radio Symph. Orch. (1956–59). In 1959 he assumed the prestigious post of Intendant of the Berlin Phil. Orch., with Herbert von Karajan as its artistic director. He retired in 1978. He wrote an informative history of the Berlin Phil., *The Berlin Philharmonic from Bülow to Karajan: Home and History of a World-Famous Orchestra* (in German and Eng.; Berlin, 1979). He also composed some orch. music and songs.

Strickland, Lily Teresa, American composer; b. Anderson, S.C., Jan. 28, 1887; d. Hendersonville, N.C., June 6, 1958. She studied at Converse College in Spartanburg, S.C.; later in N.Y. with A.J. Goodrich and W.H. Humiston. She married J. Courtney Anderson of N.Y. in 1912; traveled in the Orient between 1920 and 1930, and spent several years in India; then returned to the U.S. She publ. a number of successful songs, such as *Mah Lindy Lou, Dreamin' Time, Songs of India, Song from High Hills;* piano suites (*Moroccan Mosaics, Egyptian Scenes, Himalayan Idylls,* etc.); *Oasis* for Orch. (1942); compiled (with Helen Frost) *Oriental and Character Dances* (N.Y., 1930).

Strickland, William, American conductor; b. Defiance, Ohio, Jan. 25, 1914. He studied organ and singing; then devoted himself to conducting; entered the U.S. Army in 1941; was appointed Warrant Officer and Instructor at the Army Music School at Fort Myer, Va., in 1942; organized the Army Music School Choir, which he conducted in Washington, D.C., including a performance at the White House. After discharge from the Army, he founded the Nashville Symph. Orch. and led it from 1946 to 1951. In 1953 he conducted in Austria; returning to the U.S., he was music director of the Oratorio Society of N.Y. (1955–59); also made guest appearances as a radio conductor. In 1958 he went on a tour of Asia; conducted in Manila, Tokyo, and Seoul; in 1962 he went on a European trip; conducted guest engagements in Scandinavia, in Poland, and in Germany (until 1969). He received numerous awards from educational institutions for his service to American music.

Striegler, Kurt, German composer and conductor; b. Dresden, Jan. 7, 1886; d. Wildthurn, near Landau, Aug. 4, 1958. He studied with Draeseke at the Dresden Cons. He became répétiteur at the Dresden Opera in 1905, and then conductor there in 1912; was associated with the company for half a century, and for 40 years (1905–45) taught at the Dresden Hochschule für Musik. In 1945 he became director of the Cons. of Coburg. He went to Munich in 1950. He wrote 4 symphs.; Violin Concerto; Cello Concerto; *Scherzo* for 7 Kettledrums, with Orch.; much chamber music; numerous choruses; songs and piano pieces; also the operas *Der Thomaskantor* and *Hand und Herz* (Dresden, 1924).

Striggio, Alessandro, Italian lutenist, organist, and composer; b. Mantua, c.1535; d. there, Feb. 29, 1592. By the 1560s he lived at the court of Cosimo de' Medici in Florence, and by 1584 at Mantua as court composer. In 1567 he was in Paris and London, and in 1574 at the court of the Emperor Maximilian. He composed 3 musical intermezzi for *Psiche ed Amore* and other festival music. He publ. several books of madrigals and *Il cicalamento delle donne* (1567; descriptive songs in the manner of Janequin); many compositions by Striggio are found in collections of the period (1559–1634); 5 madrigals were reprinted by Torchi in *L'Arte Musicale in Italia,* I. His son, **Alessandro** (called **Alessandrino**), was a poet, and a notable player of the violin and lyra. He was active at the court of Mantua (still there in 1628), and in 1607 wrote the libretto of Monteverdi's *La favola d'Orfeo.* In 1596–97 he publ. 3 books of his father's madrigals for 5 voices.
BIBLIOGRAPHY: Letters of Striggio (the father) were publ. by Gandolfi in *Rivista Musicale Italiana,* XX, pp. 527ff.; see also A. Solerti, *Gli albori del melodramma* (Milan, 1904); O.G. Sonneck, "A Description of A.S. and F. Corteccia's Intermedi *Psyche and Amor,* 1565," in *Miscellaneous Studies in the History of Music* (N.Y., 1921); R. Tadlock, "Alessandro Striggio, Madrigalist," *Journal of the American Musicological Society,* XI (1958).

Strimer, Joseph, Russian-American pianist and composer; b. Rostov-on-the-Don, Oct. 21, 1881; d. New York, Jan. 1962. He studied with Rimsky-Korsakov, Liadov, Steinberg, Tcherepnin, and Glazunov at the St. Petersburg Cons.; after graduation, went to Germany, where he studied conducting with Arthur Nikisch. He lived mostly in Paris after 1920; came to N.Y. in 1941 and established himself as a teacher of piano and composition. He publ. a number of piano pieces; paraphrases of works by Rimsky-Korsakov, Borodin, Liadov, etc.; arrangements of folk songs.

Stringfield, Lamar, American composer and conductor; b. Raleigh, N.C., Oct. 10, 1897; d. Asheville, N.C., Jan. 21, 1959. He served in the U.S. Army during World War I; after the Armistice he studied mu-

sic theory with Goetschius and flute with Georges Barrère at the Inst. of Musical Art in N.Y.; also took lessons in conducting with Chalmers Clifton. In 1930 he organized the Inst. of Folk Music at the Univ. of North Carolina, and conducted its orch.; for a season was conductor of the Knoxville Symph. Orch. (1946–47), then of the Charlotte Symph. Orch. (1948–49). The source material of his own compositions is largely derived from the folk songs of the U.S. South. He learned the trade of printing and was able to publ. his own works.
WORKS: A musical folk-drama, *Carolina Charcoal* (1952); for Orch.: *Indian Legend* (1923); suite, *From the Southern Mountains* (1928; contains his best-known piece, *Cripple Creek*); *A Negro Parade* (1931); *Moods of a Moonshiner* (1934); *Mountain Dawn* (1945); *About Dixie* (1950); chamber music: *Chipmunks* for Flute, Clarinet, and Bassoon; *From a Negro Melody* for 12 Instruments; *Indian Sketches* for Flute and String Quartet; *Virginia Dare Dance* for Wind Quintet; sacred cantata, *Peace,* for Chorus a cappella; etc. He publ. *America and Her Music* (Chapel Hill, N.C., 1931).
BIBLIOGRAPHY: D. Nelson, *The Life and Works of Lamar Stringfield (1897–1959)* (Diss., Univ. of North Carolina, 1971).

Stringham, Edwin John, American music educator and composer; b. Kenosha, Wis., July 11, 1890; d. Chapel Hill, N.C., July 1, 1974. He studied at Northwestern Univ. and at the Cincinnati Cons.; in 1920 went to Italy, where he took lessons in composition with Respighi. Returning to the U.S., he occupied teaching posts at the Denver College of Music (1920–29), Teachers College of Columbia Univ. (1930–38), Juilliard School of Music in N.Y. (1930–45), and Queens College of the City Univ. of N.Y. (1938–46). In 1948 he settled in Chapel Hill.
WORKS: For Orch.: *Visions,* symph. poem (1924); *The Ancient Mariner,* after Coleridge (Denver, March 16, 1928); Symph. No. 1 (Minneapolis, Nov. 15, 1929); *Fantasy on American Folk Tunes* for Violin and Orch. (1942); chamber music; songs. He publ. the books *Listening to Music Creatively* (N.Y., 1943; revised ed., 1959); *Creative Harmony and Musicianship* (with H.A. Murphy, N.Y., 1951).

Strobel, Heinrich, eminent German musicologist; b. Regensburg, May 31, 1898; d. Baden-Baden, Aug. 18, 1970. He studied musicology with Sandberger and Kroyer in Munich, obtaining his Dr.Phil. degree in 1922. He was music critic of the *Börsenkurier* in Berlin (1927–1933) and the *Tageblatt* (1934–38); in 1939 he went to Paris; after the war he settled in Baden-Baden, where he was active as music critic and music director at the radio station; was editor of the progressive magazine *Melos* until his death. He devoted himself energetically to the cause of modern music; wrote numerous articles on the subject; promoted programs of avant-garde composers on the radio and at the various festivals in Germany. He was the author of a basic biography of Hindemith (Mainz, 1928; new enlarged ed., 1948) and of a monograph on Debussy (Zürich, 1940; 5th German ed., 1961; French ed., Paris, 1942; Spanish ed., Madrid, 1966); also publ. *Igor Stravinsky* (Zürich, 1956; Eng. version as *Stravinsky: Classic Humanist,* N.Y., 1955).

Strobel, Otto, German musicologist; b. Munich, Aug. 20, 1895; d. Bayreuth, Feb. 23, 1953. He studied at the Univ. of Munich (Dr.Phil., 1924). After working as an archivist at Bayreuth, he was appointed in 1938 director of the newly created Richard Wagner Inst. there. He publ. *Genie am Werk: Richard Wagners Schaffen und Wirken im Spiegel eigenhandschriftlicher Urkunden* (Bayreuth, 1934); *Richard Wagner* (Bayreuth, 1952); edited *König Ludwig II. und Richard Wagner: Briefwechsel* (4 vols., Karlsruhe, 1936–37) and a supplement to this, *Neue Urkunden zur Lebensgeschichte Richard Wagners* (Karlsruhe, 1939); *Neue Wagner-Forschungen,* vol. 1 (Karlsruhe, 1943).

Stroe, Aurel, Rumanian composer; b. Bucharest, May 5, 1932. He studied composition with Negrea, Rogalski, I. Dumitrescu, and Chirescu at the Bucharest Cons. (1951–56); had a course in electronic music in Munich (1966) and attended the annual summer courses in new music given in Darmstadt (1966–69) by Kagel, Ligeti, and Stockhausen; in 1962 he joined the faculty of the Bucharest Cons.; then worked at the Bucharest Computing Center (1966–69). His early music is rooted in folklore, but in his later period he experimented with sonoristic constructions, some of which were put together by computerized calculations.

WORKS: 3 operas: *Nu va Primi premiul Nobel* (*Ça n'aura pas le Prix Nobel;* 1965–69; Kassel, Nov. 28, 1971); *De Ptolemaeo,* mini-opera for Tape (1970); *La Paix,* after Aristophanes (1973); Concerto for String Orch. (1950); Trio for Oboe, Clarinet, and Bassoon (1953); *Pastorale* for Orch. (1959); Piano Sonata (1955); *Chipul păcii,* chamber cantata, after Eluard, for Mezzo-soprano, Chorus, and Chamber Orch. (1959); *Monumentum* for Male Chorus and Orch. (1961); *Uvertura burlesque* (1961); *Arcade* for 11 Instrumental Groups (1962); incidental music to *Oedipus in Colonne,* after Sophocles, for Mezzo-soprano, Male Chorus, and Orch. (1963; Bucharest, June 16, 1964); *Signum* for Winds (1963); *Muzica da concert* for Piano, Brasses, and Percussion (1964; Cluj, April 2, 1974); *Numai prin timp poate fi timpul cucerit (Only through Time, Time Is Conquered),* after T.S. Eliot, for Baritone, Organ, and 4 Gongs (1965); *Laudes I* for 28 Strings (1966); *Laudes II* for 12 Instrumental Formations, including 2 Ondes Martenots (1968); *Canto I* and *II* for 12 Instrumental Formations (1967, 1971); *Son et echo* for Tape (1969); *Rêver c'est desengrener les temps superposés* for Clarinet, Cello, and Harpsichord (1970); String Quartet (1972); *De profundis* for Harpsichord, Piano, Organ, and Tape (1973); *Il giardino delle Strutture + Rime de Michelangelo* for Baritone, Trombone, Violin, Viola, Cello, Harpsichord, and Tape (1975); songs.

Strong, George Templeton, American composer; b. New York, May 26, 1856; d. Geneva, June 27, 1948. He was the son of the N.Y. lawyer G.T. Strong, who was also a music-lover, and whose diary, expressing his dislike of Liszt and Wagner, was publ. in 1952. From him, and from his mother, who was an amateur pianist, Strong received his first training. In 1879 he went to Leipzig, where he studied with Jadassohn. He entered the Liszt circle at Weimar, and became an adherent of program music; from 1886 to 1889 he lived in Wiesbaden, where he became friendly with MacDowell; he returned briefly to America, and taught theory at the New England Cons. in Boston (1891–92); then went back to Europe and settled in Switzerland. He expressed his indignation at the lack of recognition of American composers in their own country; most performances of his works took place in Switzerland. In 1930 he donated many of his original MSS to the Library of Congress in Washington, D.C. Toscanini performed his orch. suite *Die Nacht* with the NBC Symph. Orch. in N.Y. on Oct. 21, 1939; his other symph. suite, *Une Vie d'artiste* for Violin and Orch., was presented at the 20th festival of the Assoc. des Musiciens Suisses at Zürich in June 1920; he also wrote 3 symphs.: No. 1, *In den Bergen;* No. 2, *Sintram;* No. 3, *An der See;* and the symph. poems *Undine* and *Le Roi Arthur.*

BIBLIOGRAPHY: J. Matthey, *Inventaire du fonds musical George Templeton Strong* (Lausanne, 1973).

Strouse, Charles, American composer of popular music; b. New York, June 7, 1928. He studied at the Eastman School of Music in Rochester, N.Y., and later took private lessons in composition with Aaron Copland and Nadia Boulanger, under whose guidance he wrote some ambitious instrumental music. Among his successful musicals are *Bye Bye, Birdie* (1960) and *Golden Boy,* after a play by Clifford Odets (1964).

Strozzi, Pietro, Florentine composer who flourished in the last quarter of the 16th century. He was a member of the Bardi circle in Florence, and one of the creators of the "stile rappresentativo," leading to the development of opera. With Caccini, Merulo, and Striggio he wrote the festival music for the wedding of Francesco de' Medici in 1579; in 1595 he set to music Rinuccini's libretto *La mascherata degli accecati;* 2 madrigals by Strozzi are in Luca Bati's *Secondo libro di madrigali* (Venice, 1598).

Strube, Gustav, German-American composer and music educator; b. Ballenstedt, March 3, 1867; d. Baltimore, Feb. 2, 1953. He was taught the violin by his father, and later by Brodsky at the Leipzig Cons.; was a member of the Gewandhaus Orch. there until 1891, when he emigrated to America; was a violinist in the Boston Symph. from 1891 to 1913; then he became head of the theory dept. of the Peabody Cons. in Baltimore. In 1916 he was appointed conductor of the newly organized Baltimore Symph. Orch., which he led until 1930; was director of the Peabody Cons. from 1916 to 1946. He publ. a use-

ful manual, *The Theory and Use of Chords: A Text-book of Harmony* (Boston, 1928).
WORKS: Symph., subtitled "Lanier" (after Sidney Lanier, poet and musician; Washington, D.C., March 17, 1925, composer conducting); *Sinfonietta* (1922); *Symphonic Prologue* (Baltimore, April 24, 1927, composer conducting); 2 violin concertos (1924, 1930); *Americana* for Orch. (1930); *Harz Mountains,* symph. poem (1940); *Peace Overture* (1945); 2 string quartets (1923, 1936); 2 violin sonatas (1923); *Viola Sonata* (1924); *Cello Sonata* (1925); *Piano Trio* (1925); Quintet for Wind Instruments (1930); opera, *Ramona* (1916).
BIBLIOGRAPHY: G. Klemm, "Gustav Strube: The Man and the Musician," *Musical Quarterly* (July 1942).

Strungk, Nicolaus Adam, German violinist, organist, and composer; b. Braunschweig (baptized, Nov. 15), 1640; d. Dresden, Sept. 23, 1700. He studied with his father, Delphin Strungk (1601–94), whose assistant he became at the age of 12 at the Church of St. Magnus in Braunschweig; studied violin at Lübeck under Schnittelbach while attending Helmstedt Univ. At 20 he became first violinist in the Braunschweig orch., later holding similar positions at Celle and Hannover. In 1678 Strungk became music director at Hamburg's Cathedral and of the city; wrote and produced operas in German (in keeping with the nationalist trend of the time), among them *Der glückselig-steigende Sejanus* and its sequel, *Der unglücklich-fallende Sejanus* (1678), with German librettos by Christoph Richter adapted from the Italian; *Die Liebreiche, durch Tugend und Schönheit erhöhete Esther* and *Doris* (both in 1680); *Semiramis* (1681); *Theseus* and *Floreeto* (both in 1683); etc. (The opera *Die drey Töchter Cecrops',* formerly attributed to Strungk, was written by Johann Wolfgang Franck.) Strungk was subsequently chamber organist to the Elector Ernst August of Hannover, where he won the admiration of Corelli. On Jan. 26, 1688, Strungk was appointed vice Kapellmeister in Dresden, succeeding Carlo Pallavicino, whose unfinished opera *Antiope* Strungk completed. In this post he was beset with difficulties arising from friction with Italian musicians, and only managed to maintain his authority through the intervention of his patron, the Elector Johann Georg III; when Bernhard, Kapellmeister in Dresden, died in 1692, Strungk was appointed to succeed him. In 1693 he organized an opera company in Leipzig; between 1693 and 1700 he wrote 16 operas for it, among them *Alceste* (perf. at the inauguration of the Leipzig opera house, May 18, 1693) and *Agrippina* (1699). Financially, the enterprise was a failure, but Strungk continued to receive his salary from Dresden until his retirement on a pension in 1697. He publ. the important manual *Musicalische Übung auf der Violine oder Viola da Gamba in etlichen Sonaten über die Festgesänge, ingleichen etlichen Ciaconen mit 2 Violinen bestehend* (1691). A selection of airs from his operas was publ. in Hamburg under the title *Ein hundert auserlesenen Arien zweyer Hamburgischen Operen, Semira-*

mis und Esther. Mit beigefügten Ritornellen (1684). Among his instrumental works, a Sonata for 2 Violins and Viola da Gamba, and several other sonatas are extant; MS No. 5056 of the Yale Univ. Music Library (Lowell Mason Collection) contains capriccios and ricercari by Strungk, among them the *Ricercar sopra la Morte della mia carissima Madre Catherina Maria Stubenrauen* (Venice, 1685). Six capriccios and a Ricercare by Strungk, included in Denkmäler der Tonkunst in Österreich, 17 (13.ii), are wrongly ascribed to Georg Reutter (Senior).
BIBLIOGRAPHY: F. Zelle, *J. Theile und N.A. Strungk* (Berlin, 1891); F. Berend, *Nicolaus Adam Strungk: Sein Leben und seine Werke* (Hannover, 1915); G. Frotscher, *Geschichte des Orgelspiels* (Berlin, 1934–35, vol. I).

Strunk, (William) Oliver, distinguished American musicologist; b. Ithaca, N.Y., March 22, 1901; d. Grottaferrata, Italy, March 12, 1980. He studied at Cornell Univ. (1917–19); in 1927 took a course in musicology with Otto Kinkeldey there; then entered the Univ. of Berlin to study musicology with J. Wolf (1927–28). Returning to America, he served as a member of the staff of the Music Division at the Library of Congress in Washington, D.C. (1928–37). In 1937 he was appointed to the faculty of Princeton Univ.; after retirement in 1966 lived mostly in Italy. A Festschrift in his honor was publ. at Princeton under the title *Studies in Music History. Essays for Oliver Strunk* (1968). He publ. *State and Resources of Musicology in the U.S.* (Washington, D.C., 1932) and the extremely valuable documentary *Source Readings in Music History* (N.Y., 1950). He was editor of *Monumenta musicae Byzantinae* (Copenhagen, 1961–71).

Stryja, Karol, Polish conductor; b. Cleszyn, Feb. 2, 1915. He was educated at the State Academy of Music in Katowice; in 1953 he became chief conductor of the Katowice Phil. In 1968 he was appointed chief conductor of the Odense Symph. Orch. in Denmark; also appeared as conductor with the Danish Radio Symph. Orch. and the Royal Danish Orch. in Copenhagen.

Stuart, Leslie (real name, **Thomas A. Barrett**), English operetta composer; b. Southport, March 15, 1864; d. Richmond, Surrey, March 27, 1928. He was a church organist in various provincial towns in England; settled in London in 1895, where he soon became known as a composer of popular songs. He achieved enormous success with his operetta *Floradora,* produced in London on Nov. 11, 1899, and subsequently performed in England and America for many seasons, but failed to duplicate this success in any of his later works, which included *The Silver Slipper* (1901); *The School Girl* (1903); *The Belle of Mayfair* (1906); *Havana* (1908); *Captain Kidd* and *The Slim Princess* (1910); *Peggy* (1911).

Stuck, Jean Baptiste, French-Italian composer of operas; b. Livorno, c.1680; d. Paris, Dec. 8, 1755. He played the cello in theater orchs. in Italy and in Paris, and also wrote incidental music for various plays; lived most of his life in Paris, except for a brief sojourn in Bavaria (1714). He wrote 3 operas to French texts: *Méléagre* (Paris, May 24, 1709); *Manto la fée* (1709; Paris, Jan. 29, 1711); *Polidore* (Paris, Feb. 15, 1720); ballets for the Versailles court; publ. 4 books of cantatas (1706, 1708, 1711, 1714) and a collection of airs (1709).

Stucken, Frank Van Der. See **Van Der Stucken, Frank.**

Stuckenschmidt, Hans Heinz, eminent German music critic and writer; b. Strasbourg, Nov. 1, 1901. He studied piano and composition; from 1929 to 1933 he was music critic of the Berlin daily *B. Z. am Mittag,* and was active as a lecturer and writer on modern music. In 1934 he was forbidden to continue journalism in Germany, and went to Prague, where he wrote music criticism until 1941, when his activities were stopped once more by the occupation authorities; was drafted into the Germany army; after the war, became director of the dept. for new music of the radio station RIAS in Berlin; also was a lecturer (1948), reader (1949), and prof. of music history (1953) at the Technical Univ. there; he retired in 1967. He publ. *Arnold Schönberg* (Zürich, 1951; 2nd ed., 1957; Eng. trans., 1960); *Neue Musik* (as vol. 2 of the series Zwischen den beiden Kriegen, Berlin, 1951; in French, Paris, 1956); *Schöpfer der neuen Musik: Portraits und Studien* (Frankfurt, 1958); *J.N. David* (Wiesbaden, 1965); *Maurice Ravel: Variationen über Person und Werk* (Frankfurt, 1966; Eng. trans., 1968); *Ferruccio Busoni. Zeittafel eines Europäers* (Zürich, 1967; in Eng., *Ferruccio Busoni. Chronicle of a European,* London, 1970); *Twentieth Century Music* (in Eng., N.Y., 1969); *Germany and Central Europe,* as part of the series Twentieth Century Composers (London, 1970); *Arnold Schönberg, Leben, Umwelt, Werk* (Zürich, 1974; in Eng. as *Schoenberg: His Life, World and Work,* N.Y., 1978). Along with Josef Rufer he founded and edited the monthly music magazine *Stimmen* (Berlin, 1947–49). The Festschrift *Aspekte der neuen Musik* was presented to him on his 65th birthday (Kassel, 1968).

Stückgold, Grete (née **Schneidt**), soprano; b. London, June 6, 1895; d. Falls Village, Conn., Sept. 13, 1977. Her mother was English, her father German. She studied voice with **Jacques Stückgold,** whom she married (divorced in 1928). She was a member of the Berlin State Opera before coming to America in 1927. On Nov. 2, 1927, she made her debut at the Metropolitan Opera as Eva in *Die Meistersinger,* and remained on its roster, with interruptions, until 1939. In 1953 she opened an opera school in N.Y. Her 2nd husband was the baritone **Gustav Schützendorf.**

Stückgold, Jacques, singing teacher and writer; b. Warsaw, Jan. 29, 1877; d. New York, May 4, 1953. He studied in Venice; in 1899 settled in Germany as a singing teacher; in 1933 came to the U.S., and lived in N.Y. He publ. *Der Bankrott der deutschen Gesangskunst* and *Über Stimmbildungskunst.*

Stumpf, Carl, eminent German musicologist; b. Wiesentheid, Lower Franconia, April 21, 1848; d. Berlin, Dec. 25, 1936. He studied philosophy, theology, and the natural sciences at Würzburg and Göttingen (Dr.Phil., 1870), and in 1873 became a full prof. at Würzburg; he was then a pedagogue in Prague (1879–84), in Halle (1884–89), and in Munich (1889–93). In 1893 he went to Berlin, where he founded the prestigious Psychological Inst.; its purpose was a scientific analysis of tonal psychology as it affected musical perception; but, realizing the utterly speculative and arbitrary premises of his theories, he revised them, and proposed the concepts of Konkordanz and Diskordanz to describe the relative euphony of triads and chords of several different notes. He retired in 1928. Stumpf publ. *Beiträge zur Akustik und Musikwissenschaft* (1898–1924), which incorporated his evolving theories, and, with Hornbostel, issued the *Sammelbände für vergleichende Musikwissenschaft* (1922–23). WRITINGS: *Tonpsychologie,* his most important publication (2 vols., 1883, 1890; reprint, Hilversum, 1965); *Geschichte des Konsonanzbegriffs* (Munich, 1901); *Die Anfänge der Musik* (Leipzig, 1911); *Die Sprachlaute. Experimentell-phonetische Untersuchungen nebst einem Anhang über Instrumentalklänge* (Berlin, 1926); numerous articles in scholarly publications. BIBLIOGRAPHY: E. Schumann, "Die Förderung der Musikwissenschaft durch die akustisch-psychologische Forschung C. Stumpfs," *Archiv für Musikwissenschaft* (1923); C. Sachs, "Zu Carl Stumpfs achtzigstem Geburtstag," *Zeitschrift für Musikwissenschaft,* 10 (1927–28).

Stuntz, Joseph Hartmann, German conductor and composer; b. Arlesheim, near Basel, July 23, 1793; d. Munich, June 18, 1859. He studied in Munich with Peter Winter; succeeded him as conductor in 1825; wrote several operas produced at Munich; publ. 2 overtures; a String Quartet; men's choruses. BIBLIOGRAPHY: K. Gross, *Joseph Hartmann Stuntz als Opernkomponist* (Diss., Univ. of Munich, 1934).

Stupka, František, Czech conductor; b. Tedrazice, Jan. 18, 1879; d. Prague, Nov. 24, 1965. He studied violin with Sevčik at the Prague Cons., graduating in 1901; then went to Russia, where he became a violin teacher at the Odessa Cons. He left Russia after the Revolution; served as 2nd conductor of the Czech Phil. in Prague (1919–39); also was a guest conductor with various European orchs. He specialized in the repertoire of Czech composers.

Sturgeon, Nicholas, English divine and composer; date and place of birth unknown; d. London, May 31, 1454. In 1442 he became precentor of St. Paul's Cathedral in London. He was the owner, and possibly the scribe, of the MSS found in Old Hall, near Ware; 7 works by Sturgeon (2 not complete) are part of the Old Hall MS collection, including a curious isorhythmic motet, *Salve mater Domini,* for 3 Voices, which was probably written for the journey of Henry V to France (1416), on which Sturgeon accompanied him. A. Hughes and M. Bent, eds., publ. *The Old Hall Manuscript,* in Corpus Mensurabilis Musicae, XLVI (1969–72).

Stürmer, Bruno, German composer; b. Freiburg im Breisgau, Sept. 9, 1892; d. Bad Homburg, May 19, 1958. He studied piano at the Cons. of Karlsruhe; then organ and composition with Philipp Wolfrum at the Univ. of Heidelberg, and musicology with Sandberger and Kroyer at the Univ. of Munich. After service in the German army during World War I, he taught piano in Karlsruhe (1917–22); was theater conductor in Remscheid, Essen, and Duisburg (1922–27); in 1927 founded a music school in Homburg; then was a conductor of choral societies in Kassel and elsewhere (until 1945); after 1945, lived in Darmstadt and Frankfurt. He was a prolific composer (about 150 opus numbers) in a distinctly modern manner; was particularly adept at choral writing.
WORKS: *Die Messe des Maschinenmenschen* for Baritone, Male Chorus, and Orch. (1932); dance drama, *Die Maske der Katze;* cantatas with Orch.: *Von der Vergänglichkeit, Vom Tod zum Leben, Aus Liebe, Gott in der Natur;* for Voice, with Chamber Groups: *Erlösungen, Marienlieder, Lieder der Geischa, Lieder aus den Lüften, Musikantenleben, Das Lied vom Kinde,* etc.; *Der Zug des Todes* for 8-part Chorus and Percussion; *Der Rattenfänger von Hameln* for Baritone, Children's Chorus, and Chamber Orch.; Requiem; many choruses a cappella; several instrumental concertos; much chamber music.

Sturzenegger, (Hans) Richard, Swiss composer and cellist; b. Zürich, Dec. 18, 1905; d. Bern, Oct. 24, 1976. He studied cello with F. Reitz at the Zürich Cons. and later had lessons with Pablo Casals; took a course in composition with Nadia Boulanger at the Ecole Normale de Musique in Paris (1924–27); then went to Germany and studied cello with Emanuel Feuermann and composition with Ernst Toch in Berlin (1929–33); returning to Switzerland, he was a member of the Bern String Quartet (1935–49); taught cello at the Bern Cons. (1935–63) and chamber music at the Zürich Cons. (1954–63). In 1963 he became director of the Bern Cons.
WORKS: Opera, *Atalante* (1963–68); 4 cello concertos (1933, 1937, 1947, 1974); *Triptychon* for Orch. (1951); *3 Gesänge Davids* for Violin and Orch. (1963); *Fresco* for String Orch. (1965); *Chorale Fantasy* for Contralto, Strings, Trumpet, and Drums (1941); *Cantico di San Francesco* for Chorus, Strings, and Harp (1945); *Richardis,* festival music for Chorus, Wind Orch., and Organ (1949); Sonata for Solo Cello (1934); String Trio (1937); 2 string quartets (1940, 1974); Cello Sonata (1950); *Elegie* for Cello, Oboe, Harp, Viola, Cello, and Double Bass (1950); Piano Trio (1964).
BIBLIOGRAPHY: *Richard Sturzenegger, Werk-*verzeichnis (Zürich, 1970); E. Hochuli, ed., *Variationen: Festgabe für Richard Sturzenegger zum siebzigsten Geburtstag* (Bern, 1975).

Stutschewsky, Joachim, Ukrainian-born Israeli cellist, composer, and pedagogue; b. Romny, Feb. 7, 1892; d. Tel Aviv, Nov. 14, 1982. He received his early education at a music school in Kherson; as a youth, played in various orchs. in southern Russia; in 1909 went to Leipzig, where he studied cello with Julius Klengel and orch. playing with Hans Sitt; in 1913–14 he was an orch. cellist in Jena; at the outbreak of war in 1914 he settled in Zürich, where he was active as a performer and teacher. In 1924 he went to Vienna, where he entered the circle of Schoenberg, Berg, and Webern. Together with the violinist Rudolf Kolisch, he formed the Wiener Streichquartet (later known as the Kolisch String Quartet). With the usurpation of Austria by the Nazi hordes in 1938, Stutschewsky emigrated to Palestine, and eventually became an Israeli citizen. From 1939–48 he served as inspector of music in the cultural section of the Jewish National Council. In 1977 he was given the honorary title of Distinguished Citizen of Tel Aviv. In his early compositions he followed the median modern techniques; then began a study of Jewish folklore in diaspora, and wrote music of profound racial feeling, set in the framework of advanced harmonies. He also contributed to the study of cello techniques; publ. the voluminous methods *Studien zu einer neuen Spieltechnik auf dem Violoncell* (3 vols., Mainz, 1927) and *Das Violoncellspiel* (4 vols., Mainz, 1932), and also *Etudes* (4 vols., Mainz, 1931). He further publ. an essay, *Mein Weg zur jüdischen Musik* (Vienna, 1935), detailing his approach to national Jewish music. His compositions are set mostly for chamber music groups.
WORKS: *Dreykut* for Cello and Piano (1924); *Palestinian Sketches* for Piano (1931); Duo for Violin and Cello (1940); *Hassidic Suite* for Cello and Piano (1946); *Israeli Landscapes* for Piano (1949); *Legend* for Cello and Piano (1952); *Israeli Dances* for Flute, Cello, and Piano (1953); *Verschollene Klänge* for Flute, String Quartet, and Percussion (1955); *Hassidic Fantasy* for Clarinet, Cello, and Piano (1956); Piano Trio (1956); *5 Pieces* for Flute Solo (1956); String Quartet (1956); *Songs of Radiant Sadness,* cantata for Soloists, Chorus, Speaking Chorus, and Orch. (1958); Concertino for Clarinet and Strings (1958); *Terzetto* for Oboe, Clarinet, and Bassoon (1959); *Fantasy* for Oboe, Harp, and Strings (1959); String Trio (1960); Wind Sextet (1960); symph. poem, *Safed* (1960); chamber cantata, *Jemama baschimscha (24 Hours in the Looking Glass)* for Narrator, 2 Sopranos, and 6 Instruments (1960); *Israeli Suite* for Cello and Piano (1962); *Monologue* for Clarinet Solo (1962); *3 Pieces* for Bassoon Solo (1963); *Moods* for Oboe Solo (1963); *Impressions* for Clarinet and Bassoon (1963); *Soliloquy* for Viola Solo (1964); *3 Miniatures* for 2 Flutes (1964); symph. suite, *Israel* (1964; Tel Aviv, May 7, 1973); *Kol Kore (Calling Voice)* for Horn Solo (1965); *Fragments* for 2 Clarinets (1966); *4 Movements* for Wind Quintet (1967); *3 for 3,* 3 pieces for 3 Cellos (1967); *4 Inatten-*

dus for Piano (1967); Woodwind Quintet (1967); *Visions* for Flute Solo (1968); *Thoughts and Feelings* for Violin Solo (1969); *Prelude and Fugue* for 2 Trumpets and 2 Trombones (1969); *Monologue* for Trombone Solo (1970); *Dialogues variés* for 2 Trumpets (1970); *Imaginations* for Flute, Violin, Cello, and Piano (1971); *Kol Nidrei* for Cello and Piano (1972); *The Rabbi's Nigun* for Cello and Piano (1974); *Sine nomine* for Cello Solo (1975); *Splinters* for Piano (1975); *2 Pieces* for Double-bass Solo (1975); numerous arrangements for Cello of works by Mozart, Tartini, and Boccherini.

BIBLIOGRAPHY: *Joachim Stutschewsky's 70th Anniversary: Catalogue of Works* (Tel Aviv, 1971).

Styne, Jule (real name, **Jules Stein**), American composer of popular music; b. London, Dec. 31, 1905. He was taught piano by his parents; was taken to the U.S. at the age of 8; appeared with the Chicago Symph. Orch. as a child pianist, but did not pursue a concert career; in 1942 he went to Hollywood and rapidly established himself as a successful composer of musical comedies; wrote the scores of *High Button Shoes* (1947); *Gentlemen Prefer Blondes* (1949); *Bells Are Ringing* (1956); *Gypsy*, to the life story of the striptease artist Gypsy Rose Lee (1959); and *Funny Girl*, a musical biography of the singer Fanny Brice (1965); he also wrote music for the films.

Subirá (Puig), José, eminent Spanish musicologist; b. Barcelona, Aug. 20, 1882; d. Madrid, Jan. 5, 1980. He studied at the Madrid Cons. and simultaneously qualified for the practice of law (Dr.Jur., 1923). He specialized in the study of old Spanish theater music, and publ. a number of valuable monographs on the subject. In 1953 he was elected member of the Royal Academy of Fine Arts in Madrid. Apart from his scholarly pursuits he publ. a novel, *Su virginal pureze* (1916), and a historical account, *Los Españoles en la guerra de 1914–1918* (4 vols.).

WRITINGS: *La Tonadilla escénica* (3 vols., Madrid, 1928–30); *La participación musical en el antiguo teatro español* (Barcelona, 1930); *Tonadillas teatrales inéditas* (Madrid, 1932); *Celos aun del aire matan, Opera del siglo XVII* (Barcelona, 1933); *La opera en los teatros de Barcelona* (2 vols., Barcelona, 1946); *Historia de la música teatral en España* (Barcelona, 1945); *Historia y ancedotario del Teatro Real* (Madrid, 1949); *El Compositor Iriarte y el cultivo español del melólogo* (2 vols., Barcelona, 1949–50); *El Teatro del Real Palacio* (Madrid, 1950). Other publications: *Enrique Granados* (Madrid, 1926); *La música en la Casa de Alba* (Madrid, 1927); *Manuscritos de Barbieri existentes en la Biblioteca Nacional* (Madrid, 1936); *Historia de la música* (2 vols., Madrid, 1947; revised ed., 1951); *La música, etapas y aspectos* (Barcelona, 1949); *Historia de la música española y hispano-americana* (Barcelona, 1953); *Sinfonismos madrileños del siglo XIX* (Madrid, 1954); *Temario de crítica musical* (Madrid, 1955). With H. Anglés he publ. *Catálogo musical de la Biblioteca Nacional de Madrid* (vol. 1, Barcelona, 1946).

Subotnick, Morton, American avant-garde composer; b. Los Angeles, April 14, 1933. He studied music at the Univ. of Denver; then at Mills College with Darius Milhaud. He subsequently taught at Mills College; was in charge of the Intermedia Program at the School of Arts at N.Y. Univ.; also directed exhibits at the Electric Circus in Greenwich Village in N.Y. In 1969 he was appointed associate dean and director of electronic music at the School of Music at the Calif. Inst. of the Arts in Los Angeles. He is at his best in multimedia theatrical presentations, with emphasis on electronic devices. His works include 4 pieces for mixed media under the all-embracing title *Play!*; *The Tarot* for 10 Instruments and Tape; *Concert* for Woodwind Quintet, 2 Film Projectors, Electronic Sounds, and 12 Spotlights; *Music for 12 Elevators; Lamination* for Orch. and Electronic Sounds; *The Wild Bull* for Electronic Music Synthesizer; *Before the Butterfly* for Orch. (Los Angeles, Feb. 26, 1976); *The Double Life of Amphibians,* music drama in 3 parts: *Ascent into Air* for 10 Instruments and Computer-generated Sound (1981), *The Last Dream,* and *Fluttering of Wings* (also titled *Angels*) for String Quartet and an electronic "ghost" score (1981); the work was premiered in its entirety in Los Angeles, June 20, 1984. He also wrote incidental music for the plays *Galileo, The Balcony,* and *The Caucasian Chalk Circle.*

Such, Percy Frederick, English-American cellist; b. London, June 27, 1878; d. New York, Feb. 16, 1959. He studied cello in Germany (1892–98); went to the U.S. in 1928; became a prof. of cello at Rutgers Univ.; subsequently was on the faculty of the N.Y. College of Music (1938–49). With Sir Donald Tovey he edited the cello sonatas of Beethoven; publ. cello arrangements of classical works, and editions of old cello music.

Sucher, Joseph, Hungarian conductor; b. Döbör, Nov. 23, 1843; d. Berlin, April 4, 1908. He studied in Vienna with Sechter; in 1876 was conductor of the Leipzig City Theater; in 1877 he married the soprano **Rosa Hasselbeck;** they were at the Hamburg Stadttheater from 1878 to 1888; Sucher then became conductor of the Berlin Opera, his wife being engaged there as prima donna; he left the Berlin post in 1899. He was especially distinguished as an interpreter of the Wagnerian repertoire. He composed several vocal works: *Aus alten Märchen* for Women's Voices, with Orch.; *Waldfräulein* for Soprano Solo, Mixed Chorus, and Orch.; *Seeschlacht bei Lepanto* for Male Chorus and Orch.; songs.

Sucher, Rosa (née **Hasselbeck**), German operatic soprano, wife of **Joseph Sucher;** b. Velburg, Feb. 23, 1849; d. Eschweiler, April 16, 1927. She received her early musical training from her father, a chorus master; sang in provincial operas, then in Leipzig, where she married the conductor Joseph Sucher in 1877; they were both engaged by the Hamburg Opera (1878–88). She became noted for her performances of Wagner's roles; sang at the Bayreuth Festivals (1886–99); on Feb. 25, 1895, she made her American debut as Isolde at the Metropolitan Opera House in N.Y., under the sponsorship of the Damrosch Opera Co. She publ. her memoirs, *Aus meinem Leben* (Leipzig, 1914).

Suchoff, Benjamin, distinguished American music educator and musicologist; b. New York, Jan. 19, 1918. He studied at Cornell Univ. (B.S., 1940); then took courses in composition with Vittorio Giannini at the Juilliard School of Music in N.Y. (1940–41). After serving in the U.S. Army in Europe and Asia in World War II, he resumed his studies, first at Juilliard (1946–47) and then at N.Y. Univ. (M.A., 1949; Ph.D., 1956, with the dissertation *Guide to Bartók's Mikrokosmos;* publ. in London, 1957; 3rd ed., N.Y., 1982). From 1950 to 1978 he was administrator of music at Hewlett-Woodmere Union Free School on Long Island, where he also taught electronic music. In 1973 he became adjunct prof. of arts and letters at the State Univ. of N.Y. at Stony Brook; also was director of its special collections and of the Center for Contemporary Arts and Letters, where he guided the fortunes of the COMMPUTE Program, a consortium of institutions active in research and development of computer-oriented music studies. In 1953 he became curator of the N.Y. Bartók Archive; in 1968 was made successor-trustee of the Bartók estate. He is the editor of the N.Y. Bartók Archive edition of Bartók's writings in English translations in its Studies in Musicology series; also is editor of its edition of Bartók's compositions, known as *The Archive Edition.*

Suchoň, Eugen, significant Slovak composer; b. Pezinok, Sept. 25, 1908. He studied piano and composition with Kafenda at the Bratislava School of Music (1920–28); then took a course in advanced composition with Vítězslav Novák at the Master School of the Prague Cons. (1931–33). Subsequently he taught composition at the Bratislava Academy (1933–48) and music education at the Pedagogical Faculty of the Bratislava Univ. (1949–60); was a prof. of music theory there from 1959 to 1974; in 1971 he was appointed prof. at the College of Music and Dramatic Art in Bratislava. In 1958 he was named National Artist of the Republic of Czechoslovakia. He is one of the creators of the modern Slovak style of composition, based on authentic folk motifs and couched in appropriately congenial harmonies. WORKS: *Krútňava (The Whirlpool;* 1941–49; Bratislava, Dec. 10, 1949; the most important national Slovak opera of modern times); opera, *Svätopluk* (1952–59; Bratislava, March 10, 1960); *Fantasy and Burlesque* for Violin and Orch. (originally a *Burlesque,* 1933; the *Fantasy* was added in 1948); *Balladic Suite* for Orch. or Piano (1935); *Metamorphoses,* symph. variations (1951–52); *Sinfonietta rustica* (1956); *6 Pieces* for String Ensemble or String Quartet (1955–63); *Rhapsodic Suite* for Piano and Orch. (1965); *Kaleidoscope,* 6 cycles for String Orch., Percussion, and Piano (1967–68); *Symphonic Fantasy on B-A-C-H* for Organ, Strings, and Percus-

sion (1971); Clarinet Concertino (1975); *Prielom Symphony* (1976); *Nox et solitudo* for Soprano, and Small Orch. or Piano (1933); *Carpathian Psalm,* cantata (1937–38); *Ad astra,* 5 songs for Soprano and Small Orch. (1961); *Contemplations* for Narrator and Piano (1964); Violin Sonata (1930); String Quartet (1931; revised 1939); *Serenade* for Wind Quintet (1931); Piano Quartet (1932–33); Violin Sonatina (1937); *Poème macabre* for Violin and Piano (1963); piano pieces, including a *Toccata* (1973).

Suckling, Norman, English composer and writer on music; b. London, Oct. 24, 1904. He received his academic education at Queen's College, Oxford, specializing in French literature; was assistant master at Liverpool Collegiate School (1925–43); then was a lecturer in French language and literature at King's College, Newcastle upon Tyne, in the Federal Univ. of Durham (1943–70). While thus occupied, he developed sufficient mastery of the piano to give concerts, at which he presented programs of modern French music. He publ. a monograph on Gabriel Fauré (London, 1946) and several books on French literature; also contributed articles on English and French composers to the *Listener* and other literary publications. His compositions are mostly in small forms; his songs are particularly fine. WORKS: *Introduction and Scherzo* for String Quartet (1923); *Ode* for Violin and Piano (1925); *A Vision of Avalon,* chamber opera (1928); *A Cycle of Shakespeare Sonnets* for Tenor, Violin, and Piano (1928); Violin Sonata (1928); *Man in the Beginning,* ballet (1934); *Berceuse élégiaque* for Clarinet and Piano, to commemorate a pet kitten, and written for the composer's first wife (1943); *Pastorale saugrenue* for Flute and Bassoon (1944); *Variations on a Theme of Rameau* for Flute and Piano (1947); many songs to words by English poets.

Suda, Stanislav, blind Czech flutist and composer; b. Starý Plzenec, April 30, 1865; d. Plzen, Sept. 2, 1931. He was brought up at the Prague Inst. for the Blind, and developed his innate musical abilities to the point where he could give concerts and compose operas, 3 of which were produced at Plzen: *U Božich Muk* (March 22, 1897); *Lešetínský Kovář* (April 4, 1903); *Il divino Boemo* (Dec. 30, 1927). He also wrote an autobiographical symph. poem, *Život ve tmách (The Life in Darkness).*

Sudds, William, English-American composer; b. London, March 5, 1843; d. Gouverneur, N.Y., Sept. 25, 1920. He was taken to America as a child; was a bandmaster during the Civil War; studied violin with Eichberg in Boston; wrote over 100 piano pieces, about 75 pieces of church music, many songs, etc. He publ. 2 albums of organ music, *Organ Gems* and *50 Organ Voluntaries;* also guides to violin playing.

Suesse, Dana, American composer of popular music; b. Kansas City, Dec. 3, 1911. She took piano lessons with Siloti and composition with Rubin Goldmark in N.Y.; traveled to Paris for lessons with Nadia Boulanger. A precocious musician, she won 2 prizes as a composer from the National Federation of Music, at the ages of 9 and 10; played piano in Paul Whiteman's band; wrote *Symphonic Waltzes* and *Jazz Concerto* for him. Her most famous popular song was *You Oughta Be in Pictures.*

Sugár, Rezsö, Hungarian composer; b. Budapest, Oct. 9, 1919. He was a pupil of Kodály at the Budapest Academy of Music (1937–42); taught in Budapest at the Béla Bartók Cons. (1949–68); from 1968 taught at the Academy.
WORKS: Ballet, *Acisz és Galatea (Acis and Galatea;* 1957; revised in 1961 as *A tenger lánya [The Daughter of the Sea]);* patriotic oratorio, *Hunyadi-Hösi ènek (Heroic Song;* 1951); cantata, *Kömüves Kelemen (Kelemen, the Mason;* 1958); *Divertimento* for String Orch. (1948); *Rondo* for Piano and String Orch. (1952); *Concerto in Memoriam Béla Bartók* for Orch. (1962); *Metamorfosi* for Orch. (1966); *Partita* for String Orch. (1967); *Variation Symphony* (1970); *Serenade* for 2 Violins and Viola (1943); Violin Sonata (1946); 3 string quartets (1947, 1950, 1969); *Frammenti musicali,* sextet for Piano and Wind Quintet (1958); *Rhapsody* for Cello and Piano (1959); *Baroque Sonatina* for Piano (1943–46); songs.

Suggia, Guilhermina, Portuguese cellist; b. Oporto, June 27, 1888; d. there, July 31, 1950. She was a child prodigy and played first cello in the Oporto Orch. at the age of 12. Under the patronage of the Queen of Portugal she was sent to Leipzig in 1904 to study with Julius Klengel; made her debut with the Gewandhaus Orch. under Nikisch at the age of 17. In 1906 she married **Pablo Casals** (divorced, 1912). Shortly afterward she settled in London, where she continued to appear in concerts until 1949, when she went back to Portugal. She was greatly appreciated for her fine musicianship as well as virtuosity. In 1923 Augustus John painted her portrait, which became famous.

Suitner, Otmar, Austrian conductor; b. Innsbruck, May 16, 1922. He studied piano at the Innsbruck Cons. and conducting with Clemens Krauss at the Salzburg Mozarteum. In 1945 he conducted at the Innsbruck Landestheater; was then music director in Remscheid (1952–57) and Generalmusikdirektor in Ludwigshafen (1957–60). From 1960 to 1964 he served as Generalmusikdirektor of the Dresden State Opera and Dresden State Orch.; from 1964 to 1971 conducted at the East Berlin State Opera, and in 1974 was appointed its Generalmusikdirektor. He also conducted in America; was a guest conductor with the San Francisco Opera.

Suk, Josef, Czech violinist and composer; b. Křečovice, Jan. 4, 1874; d. Benešov, near Prague, May 29, 1935. He studied with his father, a chorus master, and at the Prague Cons.; after graduation he took a course in composition with Dvořák, whose daughter Otilie he married in 1898. In 1892 he became 2nd

violinist in the celebrated Bohemian String Quartet, continuing with it until 1933. He was a devoted follower of Dvořák in his style of composition; his works are cast in a characteristically Romantic vein, with the rhythmic elements drawn from Bohemian folk music. When his wife died in 1905, he was disconsolate; he expressed his sorrow in his 2nd Symph., *Asrael,* dedicated to her memory and to the memory of Dvořák. He continued to compose, developing an individual manner marked by deep expressiveness and religious feeling.
WORKS: Operatic fairy tale, *Radúz and Mahulena* (Prague, April 6, 1898); dramatic legend, *Pod jabloní (Under the Apple Trees;* 1902; Prague, Jan. 31, 1934); *Dramatic Overture* (Prague, July 9, 1892); *Serenade* in E-flat for String Orch. (1892); *Winter's Tale,* overture after Shakespeare (1894); 2 symphs.: No. 1, in E (1897–99; Prague, Nov. 25, 1899), and No. 2, *Asrael* (1905–6; Prague, Feb. 3, 1907); *Fantasia* for Violin and Orch. (1902; Prague, Jan. 9, 1904); *Scherzo fantastique* for Orch. (1903; Prague, April 18, 1905); 3 symph. poems: *Praga* (1904); *Pohádka léta (A Summer Fairytale;* 1907–9; Prague, Jan. 26, 1909); *Zrání (Maturity;* 1912–17; Prague, Oct. 30, 1918); *Meditations on the Chorale "St. Venceslas"* for String Orch. or String Quartet (1914); *Legend about Dead Victors* for Orch. (1919); symph. march, *Forward to a New Life* (1919–20); *Epilogue,* for Soli, Chorus, and Orch. (1920–32); 2 string quartets (1896, 1910–11); Piano Quartet (1891); Piano Trio (1892); Piano Quintet; *Allegro giocoso* for String Quartet; other chamber music; several sets of choruses; a number of piano pieces.
BIBLIOGRAPHY: *Josef Suk,* a collection of articles, ed. by Jan M. Květ (Prague, 1935); V. Štěpan, *Novák a Suk* (Prague, 1945); Jiří Berkovec, *Josef Suk* (Prague, 1956); Jan M. Květ, *Josef Suk v obrazech* (Prague, 1964); Ratibor Budis, ed., *Josef Suk* (Prague, 1965); Jiří Berkovec, *Josef Suk* (Prague, 1968).

Suk, Josef, outstanding Czech violinist, grandson of the composer **Josef Suk** and great-grandson of **Dvořák;** b. Prague, Aug. 8, 1929. He studied the violin with Jaroslav Kocian; made his professional debut in 1940. From 1951–53 he took courses at the Prague Academy. In 1952 he founded the Suk Trio with the pianist Jan Panenka and the cellist Josef Chuchro, and toured widely with it; his interest in chamber music led him to form a duo with Zuzana Růžičková in 1963; from 1967–69 he was also a member of a trio with Julius Katchen and Janos Starker. In 1959 he made a grand tour as soloist to three continents with the Czech Phil. On Jan. 23, 1964, he made his U.S. debut with the Cleveland Orch., and subsequently appeared as soloist with other American orchs. In 1964 he received a Czech State Prize; in 1970 he was made an Artist of Merit and in 1977 was named a National Artist of Czechoslovakia.

Suk, Váša, Czech conductor and composer; b. Kladno, Nov. 16, 1861; d. Moscow, Jan. 12, 1933. He studied with Fibich at the Prague Cons.; then played the violin in the Warsaw Symph. (1879–81); conducted opera in Kiev and Moscow (1881–84); in 1906 joined the staff of the Moscow Opera. He was appreciated in Russia for his thoroughness in drilling the singers and the orch.; achieved a fine reputation as an operatic conductor. He wrote an opera, *The Forest King*, which he conducted at Kharkov on Feb. 16, 1900; a symph. poem, *Jan Huss;* a Serenade for String Orch.; a number of piano pieces and songs.

BIBLIOGRAPHY: I. Remezov, *V. Suk* (Moscow, 1933).

Sukegawa, Toshiya, Japanese composer; b. Sapporo, July 15, 1930. He studied with Ikenouchi from 1951; graduated in composition from the Univ. of Arts in Tokyo in 1957.

WORKS: Television opera, *Pôra no Hiroba* (1959); *Passacaglia* for Orch. (1954); String Quartet (1956); *Music* for Flute, Clarinet, Violin, Cello, Percussion, and Piano (1958); Piano Sonata (1958); *Divertimento* for 2 Pianos (1958); *Partita* for Orch. (1960); Wind Quintet (1962); *Legend* for Orch. (1965); *5 Metamorphoses* for Viola and Piano (1966); *3 Parts for 5 Flute Players* (1967); *Tapestry* for Piano (1966–68); *3 Scenes* for Jushichigen, 3 Violins, and Viola (1969); *A Projection* for Solo Marimba, Piccolo, Trombone, Piano, and Percussion (1969); *The White World* for Chorus and Piano (1971); *Eika* for Chorus and Japanese Percussion (1972); *5 Symbolic Pictures* for Piano (1972); *5 Pieces after Paul Klee* for Solo Marimba (1973).

Šulek, Stjepan, Croatian violinist and composer; b. Zagreb, Aug. 5, 1914. He studied violin with Huml, and was largely self-taught in composition; yet he succeeded in becoming a composer of considerable merit. In 1954 he was appointed prof. of composition at the Music Academy in Zagreb.

WORKS: Operas: *Coriolan,* after Shakespeare (Zagreb, Oct. 12, 1958); *Oluja (The Tempest),* after Shakespeare (Zagreb, 1969); 6 symphs. (1944, 1946, 1948, 1954, 1963, 1966); festive prologue, *Scientiae et arti,* for Orch. (1966); 4 piano concertos (1949, 1951, 1963, 1970); Cello Concerto (1950); Violin Concerto (1951); Bassoon Concerto (1958); Violin Concerto (1959); Clarinet Concerto (1967); cantata, *Zadnji Adam (The Last Adam;* 1964); other vocal works; piano pieces; songs.

BIBLIOGRAPHY: K. Kovačević, *Hrvatski Kompozitori i Njihova Djela* (Zagreb, 1960); K. Šipuš, *Stjepan Šulek* (Zagreb, 1961).

Sullivan, Sir Arthur Seymour, famous English composer; b. London, May 13, 1842; d. there, Nov. 22, 1900. In 1854 he entered the Chapel Royal as a chorister, under Helmore; publ. an anthem in 1855; was elected (the first) Mendelssohn Scholar in 1856, studying at the Royal Academy of Music from 1857 under Bennett, Goss, and O'Leary, and at the Leipzig Cons. in 1858–61 under Moscheles, Hauptmann, Richter, Plaidy, etc., conducting a performance of his overture to *Lalla Rookh* (Leipzig, May 25, 1860), and writing string quartets and music to *The Tempest* (Leipzig, April 6, 1861; revised version, Crystal Palace, April 5, 1862). His cantata *Kenilworth* (Birmingham Festival, Sept. 8, 1864) stamped him as a composer of high rank. In 1864 he visited Ireland and there composed his "Irish Symphony" (London, March 10, 1866). In 1866 he was appointed prof. of composition at the Royal Academy of Music. About this time he formed a lifelong friendship with Sir George Grove, whom he accompanied in 1867 on a memorable journey to Vienna in search of Schubert MSS, leading to the discovery of the score of *Rosamunde.* The year 1867 was also notable for the production of the first of those comic operas upon which Sullivan's fame chiefly rests. This was *Cox and Box* (libretto by F.C. Burnand), composed in 2 weeks and performed on April 27 at the home of Arthur Lewis; later it had a long public run. Less successful were *The Contrabandista* (London, Dec. 18, 1867) and *Thespis* (London, Dec. 23, 1871); but the latter is significant as inaugurating Sullivan's collaboration with Sir W.S. Gilbert, the celebrated humorist, who became the librettist of all Sullivan's most successful comic operas, beginning with *Trial by Jury* (March 25, 1875). This was produced by Richard D'Oyly Carte, who in 1876 formed a company expressly for the production of the "Gilbert and Sullivan" operas. The first big success obtained by the famous team was with *H.M.S. Pinafore* (May 25, 1878), which had 700 consecutive performances in London, and enjoyed an enormous vogue in "pirated" productions throughout the U.S. In an endeavor to protect their interests, Gilbert and Sullivan went to N.Y. in 1879 to give an authorized performance of *Pinafore,* and while there they also produced *The Pirates of Penzance* (Dec. 31, 1879). On April 23, 1881, came *Patience,* a satire on exaggerated esthetic poses exemplified by Oscar Wilde, whose American lecture tour was conceived as a "publicity stunt" for this work. On Nov. 25, 1882, *Iolanthe, or The Peer and the Peri* began a run that lasted more than a year. This was followed by the comparatively unsuccessful *Princess Ida* (Jan. 5, 1884), but then came the universal favorite of all the Gilbert and Sullivan operas, *The Mikado* (March 14, 1885). The list of these popular works is completed by *Ruddigore* (Jan. 22, 1887), *The Yeomen of the Guard* (Oct. 3, 1888), and *The Gondoliers* (Dec. 7, 1889). After a quarrel and a reconciliation, the pair collaborated in 2 further works, of less popularity: *Utopia Limited* (Oct. 7, 1893) and *The Grand Duke* (March 7, 1896). Sullivan's melodic inspiration and technical resourcefulness, united with the delicious humor of Gilbert's verses, raised the light opera to a new height of artistic achievement, and his works in this field continue to delight countless hearers. Sullivan was also active in other branches of musical life. He conducted numerous series of concerts, more especially those of the London Phil. Society (1885–87) and the Leeds Festivals (1880–98). He was principal of, and a prof. of composition at, the National Training School for Music from 1876 to his resignation in 1881. Sullivan received the degree of Mus.Doc. *honoris causa* from Cambridge (1876) and Oxford (1879); was named Chevalier of the Legion of Honor (1878); was grand organist to the Freemasons (1887); etc. He was knighted by Queen Victoria in 1883. Parallel with his comic creations, he composed many "serious" works, including the grand opera *Ivanhoe* (Jan. 31, 1891), which enjoyed a momentary vogue. Among his cantatas the most successful was *The Golden Legend*, after Longfellow (Leeds Festival, Oct. 16, 1886); he also wrote the famous hymn *Onward, Christian Soldiers*, to words by Rev. Sabine Baring-Gould (1871). His songs were highly popular in their day, and *The Lost Chord*, to words by Adelaide A. Proctor (publ. 1877), is still a favorite. Among his oratorios, *The Light of the World* (Birmingham Festival, Aug. 27, 1873) may be mentioned. Other stage works: *The Zoo* (June 5, 1875); *The Sorcerer* (Nov. 17, 1877); *Haddon Hall* (Sept. 24, 1892); *The Chieftain* (revision of *The Contrabandista;* Dec. 12, 1894); *The Martyr of Antioch* (Edinburgh, Feb. 15, 1898; a stage arrangement of the cantata); *The Beauty-Stone* (with Pinero; May 28, 1898); romantic opera, *The Rose of Persia* (Nov. 29, 1899); *The Emerald Isle* (completed by E. German, April 27, 1901); 2 ballets: *L'Ile enchanté* (1864) and *Victoria and Merrie England* (1897).

BIBLIOGRAPHY: A. Lawrence, *Sir A. S.: Life-Story, Letters and Reminiscences* (with complete list of works; Chicago, 1900); W.J. Wells, *Souvenir of Sir A. S.* (London, 1901) B.W. Findon, *Sir A. S.: His Life and Music* (London, 1904); idem, *Sir A. S. and His Operas* (London, 1908); F. Cellier and C. Bridgeman, *Gilbert, S., and D'Oyly Carte* (London, 1914); H.M. Walbrook, *Gilbert and S.: A History and a Comment* (1922); S.J.A. Fitz-Gerald, *The Story of the Savoy Opera* (London, 1924); A.H. Godwin, *Gilbert and S.* (1926); H. Sawara Wyndham, *A.S. S.* (1926); N. Flower and H. Sullivan, *A. S.* (1927); T.F. Dunhill, *S.'s Comic Operas* (1928); L. Bradstock, *S.* (1928); I. Goldberg, *The Story of Gilbert and S.* (1928); F.J. Halton, *The Gilbert and S. Operas: A Concordance* (N.Y., 1935); H. Pearson, *Gilbert and S.* (N.Y., 1935); G.E. Dunn, *A Gilbert and S. Dictionary* (N.Y., 1936); C.L. Purdy, *Gilbert and S.: Masters of Mirth and Melody* (N.Y., 1947); W.A. Darlington, *The World of Gilbert and S.* (N.Y., 1950); A. Jacobs, *Gilbert and S.* (London, 1951); L. Bailey, *The Gilbert and S. Book* (N.Y., 1952; new ed., 1957); A. Williamson, *Gilbert and S. Operas: A New Assessment* (N.Y., 1953); A. Powers-Waters, *The Melody Maker. The Life of Sir A. S.* (N.Y., 1959); M. Green, *Treasury of Gilbert and S.* (London, 1961); R. Mander and J. Mitcheson, *A Picture History of Gilbert and S.* (London, 1962); N.G. Wymer, *Gilbert and S.* (London, 1962); C.R. Bulla, *Stories of Gilbert and S. Operas* (N.Y., 1968); J. Helyar, *Gilbert & S., Papers Presented at the International Conference. . . , 1970* (Lawrence, Kans., 1971); P.M. Young, *Sir Arthur S.* (London, 1971); P. Kline, *Gilbert and S. Production* (N.Y., 1972); L. Ayre, *The Gilbert and S. Companion* (N.Y., 1972); J.M.D. Hardwick, *The Drake Guide to Gilbert and S.* (N.Y., 1973); L.W.A. Baily, *Gilbert and S. and Their World* (London, 1973); Reginald Allen, *Sir Arthur S.: Composer & Personage* (N.Y., 1975); I. Bradley, ed., *The Annotated Gilbert and S.* (London, 1982); A. Williamson, *Gilbert & S. Opera* (London, 1983).

Sulzer, Julius Salomon, Austrian violinist, son of

Salomon Sulzer; b. Vienna, 1834; d. there, Feb. 13, 1891. He was a professional violinist and conductor; served as music director of the Hofburgtheater in Vienna from 1875.

Sulzer, Salomon, important Austrian-Jewish composer, reformer of synagogal songs; b. Hohenems, Vorarlberg, March 30, 1804; d. Vienna, Jan. 17, 1890. He was only 16 when he was appointed cantor at the chief synagogue in his hometown. He studied music with Seyfried in Vienna; from 1825 to 1881 was cantor of the new Vienna synagogue. He undertook a bold reform of liturgical music by the introduction of musical form and actual compositions from the Classical period, setting Schubert's songs as a model. By so doing, he succeeded in bringing traditional Jewish cantillation together with Western modes. He brought out an anthology, *Schir Zion* (*The Heart of Zion;* publ. in 1839–65), and *Denkschrift an die Wiener israelitische Cultus-Gemeinde* (Vienna, 1876).

BIBLIOGRAPHY: M. Steiner, *Salomon Sulzer* (Vienna, 1904); P. Minkowski, *Der Sulzerismus* (Vienna, 1905); E. Mandell, "Salomon Sulzer, 1804–1890," *Journal of Synagogue Music*, 1 (1968).

Sumac, Yma, Peruvian singer of a phenomenal diapason, whose origin is veiled in mystical mist; b. Ichocan, Sept. 10, 1927. Her family name was **Chavarri;** the probability is that she was really a child of the Andean highlands; it is credible that she developed her phenomenal voice of 5 octaves in range because her lungs were inflated by the necessity of breathing enough oxygen at the high altitude. However that might be, she married one **Moises Vivanco,** who was an arranger for Capitol Records and who launched her on a flamboyant career as a concert singer. She was billed by unscrupulous promoters as an Inca princess, a direct descendant of Atahualpa, the last emperor of the Incas, a Golden Virgin of the Sun God worshiped by the Quechua Indians. On the other hand, some columnists spread the scurrilous rumor that she was in actuality a Jewish girl from Brooklyn whose real name was Amy (retrograde of Yma) Camus (retrograde of Sumac). But Yma Sumac never spoke with a Brooklyn accent. She exercised a mesmeric appeal to her audiences, from South America to Russia, from California to Central Europe; expressions such as "miraculous" and "amazing" were used by Soviet reviewers during her tour of Russia in 1962; "supersonic vocal skill" was a term applied by an American critic. Her capacity did not diminish with age; during her California appearances in 1984 she still impressed her audiences with the expressive power of her voice.

Sundelius, Marie, Swedish-American singer and vocal teacher; b. Karlsbad, Feb. 4, 1884; d. Boston, June 26, 1958. She was taken to America at the age of 8, and studied singing in Boston; made her debut as an opera singer with the Metropolitan Opera in N.Y. on Nov. 25, 1916; was on its roster, with interruptions, until 1928; made a tour of Sweden in 1924;

then returned to Boston.

Sundgrén-Schnéevoigt, Sigrid Ingeborg, Finnish pianist; b. Helsinki, June 17, 1878; d. Stockholm, Sept. 14, 1953. She studied at the Helsinki Cons., and then with Busoni in Berlin (1894–97). In 1907 she married the conductor **Georg Schnéevoigt,** with whom she made several tours of Scandinavia and Germany; from 1910 was for many years a piano teacher at the Helsinki Cons.; later lived in Paris.

Suñol y Baulenas, Dom Gregorio María, learned Spanish ecclesiastic and authority on Gregorian chant; b. Barcelona, Sept. 7, 1879; d. Rome, Oct. 26, 1946. He studied at Montserrat and at the Abbey of Solesmes; became prior of the Monastery of Montserrat and president of the Asociación Gregoriana of Barcelona. During his last years he was president of the Pontificio Instituto di Musica Sacra in Rome. He publ. the valuable editions *Método completo de canto gregoriano* (6 Spanish eds.; also in Eng., French, and German); *Introducció a la paleografía musical gregoriana* (Montserrat, 1925; also in French, 1935); "Els Cants dels Romeus," in *Analecta Montserratensia* (with examples of folk music from the 14th century); brought out *Antiphonale missarum juxta ritum sanctae ecclesiae medilolanensis* (1935).

Suolahti, Heikki, Finnish composer; b. Helsinki, Feb. 2, 1920; d. there, Dec. 27, 1936. He studied at the Helsinki Cons. and conducted children's orchs. at festivals. His tragically premature death at 16 moved Sibelius to say that "Finland lost one of her greatest musical talents." Suolahti composed a few fine pieces of music, among them a Violin Concerto, written at the age of 14, and a *Sinfonia piccola,* which he composed at 15 and which was performed in Helsinki after his death; he also left some songs.

Supervia, Conchita, famous Spanish mezzo-soprano; b. Barcelona, Dec. 9, 1895; d. London, March 30, 1936. She studied at the Colegio de las Damas Negras in Barcelona; made her debut with a visiting opera company at the Teatro Colón in Buenos Aires on Oct. 1, 1910, in Stiattesi's opera *Blanca de Beaulieu.* She then traveled to Italy; sang the role of Octavian in the first Italian production of *Der Rosenkavalier* in Rome. In 1912 she sang Carmen in Bologna; in 1914 she sang at the Havana Opera. She then appeared in Chicago (1915–16); in 1924 she sang at La Scala in Milan. She endeared herself to the Italian public by reviving Rossini's operas *L'Italiana in Algeri* and *La Cenerentola;* she also attracted favorable critical attention by performing the part of Rosina in *Il Barbiere di Siviglia* in its original version as a coloratura contralto. In addition, she filled guest engagements in Paris and London. In 1931 she married the British industrialist Sir Ben Rubenstein. She died at the age of 40, as a result of complications following the birth of a child.

Suppé, Franz von, famous operetta composer; b. Spalato, Dalmatia, April 18, 1819; d. Vienna, May 21, 1895. He was of Belgian descent, and his real name was **Francesco Ezechiele Ermenegildo Cavaliere Suppe-Demelli.** At the age of 11 he played the flute, and at 15 wrote a Mass. He was then sent by his father to study philosophy at Padua, where he also took music courses with Cigala and Ferrari; on his father's death he went with his mother to Vienna, where he continued serious study at the Vienna Cons. with Sechter and Seyfried. He became a conductor in the theaters of Pressburg and Baden, and then was on the staff at the Theater an der Wien (1845–62); then was at the Kaitheater in 1862–65; subsequently at the Carl theater in 1865–82. All the while, he wrote light operas and other theater music of all degrees of levity, obtaining increasing success rivaling that of Offenbach. His music possesses the charm and gaiety of the Viennese genre, but also contains elements of more vigorous popular rhythms.

WORKS: His most celebrated single work is the overture to *Dichter und Bauer (Poet and Peasant),* which still retains a firm place in the light repertoire. His total output comprises about 30 comic operas and operettas and 180 other stage pieces, most of which were brought out in Vienna; of these the following obtained considerable success: *Dichter und Bauer* (Aug. 24, 1846); *Das Mädchen vom Lande* (Aug. 7, 1847); *Der Bandit* (1848; in Italy as *Cartouche); Paragraph 3* (Jan. 8, 1858); *Das Pensionat* (Nov. 24, 1860); *Die Kartenaufschlägerin* (April 26, 1862); *Zehn Mädchen und kein Mann* (Oct. 25, 1862); *Flotte Bursche* (April 18, 1863); *Franz Schubert* (Sept. 10, 1864); *Die schöne Galatea* (Berlin, June 30, 1865); *Leichte Cavallerie* (March 24, 1866; enormously popular); *Freigeister* (Oct. 23, 1866); *Banditenstreiche* (April 27, 1867); *Die Frau Meisterin* (Jan. 20, 1868); *Tantalusqualen* (Oct. 3, 1868); *Isabella* (Nov. 5, 1869); *Cannebas* (Nov. 2, 1872); *Fatinitza* (Jan. 5, 1876; extremely popular); *Der Teufel auf Erden* (Jan. 5, 1878); *Boccaccio* (Feb. 1, 1879; very popular); *Donna Juanita* (Feb. 21, 1880); *Der Gascogner* (March 22, 1881); *Herzblättchen* (Feb. 4, 1882); *Die Afrikareise* (March 17, 1883); *Bellmann* (Feb. 26, 1887); *Die Jagd nach dem Glücke* (Oct. 27, 1888); *Das Modell* (posthumous; Oct. 4, 1895); *Die Pariserin* (posthumous; Jan. 26, 1898); several other operettas were produced in Prague, Berlin, and Hamburg. In addition to his theater works, he wrote a Symph.; several string quartets; songs; also *Missa dalmatica* (1867).

BIBLIOGRAPHY: G. Sabalich, *F. Suppé e l'operetta* (Zara, 1888); O. Keller, *Franz von Suppé, der Schöpfer der deutschen Operette* (Leipzig, 1905); E. Rieger, *Offenbach und seine Wiener Schule* (Vienna, 1920).

Surdin, Morris, Canadian composer; b. Toronto, May 8, 1914; d. there, Aug. 19, 1979. He learned to play piano, violin, cello, horn, and trombone; studied composition with Gesensway in Philadelphia (1937) and with Henry Brant in N.Y. (1950); worked as a music arranger for the Canadian Broadcasting Corp. (1939–41) and with the Columbia Broadcasting System in N.Y. (1949–54). Returning to Canada, he became engaged primarily in scoring for musicals, radio, television, and films.

WORKS: FOR THE STAGE: Opera-musical, *Wild Rose* (1967); musical comedy, *Look Ahead* (1962); ballet, *The Remarkable Rocket,* after Oscar Wilde (1960–61). FOR ORCH.: *4 X Strings* for Strings (1947); *Credo* (1950); *Inheritance* for Wind Quartet and Strings (1951); *Concert Ballet* (1955); *Incident I* for Strings (1961); Concerto for Mandolin and Strings (1961–66); *5 Shades of Brass* for Trumpet and Orch. (1961); 2 concertos for Free-bass Accordion: No. 1 (1966; Toronto, Jan. 29, 1967) and No. 2, with Strings, Electric Guitar, and Percussion (1977); *2 Solitudes* for Horn or English Horn, and Strings (1967); *Formula I* and *II* for Concert Band (1968–69); *Horizon* for String Orch. (1968); *Short!* (No. 1) for Piano and Strings (1969) and *Short!* (No. 2) for Piano, Wind Quartet, and Strings (1969); *Alteration I* for Piccolo and Strings (1970) and *II* for Strings (1970); *Terminus* for Oboe, Bassoon, and Strings (1972); *B'rasheet (In the Beginning)* for Solo Mandolin, Solo Clarinet, and String Orch. (1974; Toronto, June 15, 1974); *Eine kleine "Hammer-Klapper" Musik* for Chamber Orch. (1976); *Berceuse* for Horn and Chamber Orch. (1977); *A Group of 6* for Strings in first position (1977); *5 for 4* for Strings in first position (1977); *Who's on Bass?* for Strings (1977); *6 Pieces in Search of a Sequence* for Solo Instruments and String Orch. (1969–78); Violin Concerto (1978). FOR VOICE: *A Spanish Tragedy* for Soprano and Orch. (1955); *Suite canadienne* for Chorus and Orch. (1970); *Feast of Thunder* for Soloists, Male Chorus, and Orch. (1972); *Music Fair* for Soprano, Cello, and Harp (1975); *Quartet for Trio* for Low Voice, Cello, and Harp (1976); *Pegleg's Fiddle* for Male Chorus, Solo Violin, Mandolin Orch., Piano, and Percussion (1977); *Leave It Be* for Solo Bass, Chorus, and Orch. (1977; based on the musical comedy *Look Ahead*). CHAMBER MUSIC: *Suite* for Viola and Piano (1954); *Carol Fantasia* for Brass (1955); *Incident II* for Woodwinds, Horns, and Harp (1961); *Elements* for 2 Violins, Double Bass, and Harpsichord (1965); *Matin* for Wind Quartet (1965); *Arioso* for 4 Cellos (1966); String Quartet (1966); Trio for Saxophones (1968); *Piece* for Wind Quintet (1969); *Serious I–XVI* for Solo Accordion (1969–73); *Trinitas in Morte* for 3 Oboes, Bassoon, 3 Horns, Timpani, 8 Cellos, and 2 Double Basses (1973); *Heritage I–IV* for varying Brass Quartets (1975–79); *Sly'd Trombones I* & *II* for Trombone and Bass Trombone, or Trombone Ensemble (1975); *Landscapes,* sonatina for Solo Harp (1978); *2 fabliaux* for Solo Cello (1979). FOR PIANO: *Naiveté,* 6 pieces (1962); *Poco Giocoso Variations* (1966); *In Search of Form I* and *II* (1970); *Fragmentations I–III* (1972).

BIBLIOGRAPHY: Michael Schulman, "At Last, Recognition for Morris Surdin's Music," *Canadian Composer* (March 1978).

Surette, Thomas Whitney, eminent American music educator; b. Concord, Mass., Sept. 7, 1861; d. there, May 19, 1941. He studied piano with Arthur Foote and composition with J.K. Paine at Harvard Univ., graduating in 1891; then was active mainly as a church organist. Deeply interested in making musical education accessible and effective in the U.S., he founded in 1914 the Concord Summer School of Music; with A.T. Davison he edited The Concord Series of educational music, which found a tremendously favorable acceptance on the part of many schools, particularly in New England; the series provided an excellent selection of good music which could be understood by most music teachers and performed by pupils. Surette was also largely responsible for the vogue of music appreciation courses that swept the country and spilled over into the British Isles. He publ. *The Appreciation of Music* (with D.G. Mason; 5 vols., of which vols. 2 and 5 were by Mason alone; N.Y., 1907; innumerable subsequent printings), and, on a more elevated plane, *Course of Study on the Development of Symphonic Music* (Chicago, 1915) and *Music and Life* (Boston, 1917); he also publ. popular articles on music and musicians, notable for their lack of discrimination and absence of verification of data. He was also a composer of sorts; wrote a light opera, *Priscilla, or The Pilgrim's Proxy,* after Longfellow (Concord, March 6, 1889; had more than 1,000 subsequent perfs. in the U.S.), and a romantic opera, *Cascabel, or The Broken Tryst* (Pittsburgh, May 15, 1899).

Suriano (or **Soriano**), **Francesco,** a composer of the Roman school; b. Soriano, 1549; d. there, July 19, 1621. He was a chorister at St. John Lateran; later a pupil of Nanino and Palestrina; in 1580, choirmaster at S. Ludivico de' Francesi; from 1581 to 1586, in Mantua; in 1587, at S. Maria Maggiore; in 1588, again at S. Ludovico, returning to S. Maria Maggiore in 1595; in 1599, at St. John Lateran; and from 1600, once more at S. Maria Maggiore (pensioned, June 23, 1620). He collaborated with F. Anerio in the revision of the *Editio Medicaea* of the Gradual (cf. Palestrina). Suriano publ. 2 books of madrigals *a 5* (1581, 1592); one book of madrigals *a 4* (1601); motets *a 8* (1597); masses *a 4–8* (1609; includes an arrangement of Palestrina's *Missa Papae Marcelli* for 8 Voices); *Canoni . . . sopra l'Ave Maris Stella a 3–8 voci* (1610); 2 books of Psalms and motets (1614, 1616); *Villanelle a 3* (1617); a Passion and several Magnificats (1619).

BIBLIOGRAPHY: F.X. Haberl, in *Kirchenmusikalisches Jahrbuch* (1895); R. Molitor, *Die nachtridentiniche Choralreform* (1901–2); S.P. Kniseley, *The Masses of Francesco Suriano* (Gainesville, Fla., 1967).

Surinach, Carlos, Spanish-American composer and conductor; b. Barcelona, March 4, 1915. He studied in Barcelona with Morera (1936–39) and later with Max Trapp in Berlin (1939–43). Returning to Spain in 1943, he was active mainly as a conductor. In 1951 he went to the U.S.; became an American citizen in 1959; was a visiting prof. of music at Carnegie-Mellon Inst. in Pittsburgh in 1966–67.

WORKS: *El Mozo que casó con mujer brava,* one-act opera (Barcelona, Jan. 10, 1948); ballet, *Monte*

Carlo (Barcelona, May 2, 1945); 3 symphs.: No. 1, *Passacaglia-Symphony* (Barcelona, April 8, 1945, composer conducting); No. 2 (Paris Radio, Jan. 26, 1950, composer conducting); No. 3, *Sinfonía chica* (1957); *Sinfonietta flamenca* (Louisville, Ky., Jan. 9, 1954); *Feria mágica*, overture (Louisville, March 14, 1956); *3 cantos berberes* for Flute, Oboe, Clarinet, Viola, Cello, and Harp (1952); *Flamenquerías* for 2 Pianos (1952); *Ritmo Jondo* for Clarinet, Trumpet, Xylophone, and Percussion (N.Y., May 5, 1952; extended version in ballet form, *Deep Rhythm*, was perf. in N.Y., April 15, 1953); *Tientos* for English Horn, Harpsichord, and Timpani (1953); *A Place in the Desert* (1960); *Symphonic Variations* (1963); *Drama Jondo*, overture (1964); *Melorhythmic Dramas* for Orch. (1966); *The Missions of San Antonio*, symph. canticles (1968); chamber music of various descriptions; songs.

Surzyński, Józef, Polish music scholar; b. Szrem, near Poznan, March 15, 1851; d. Koscian, March 5, 1919. He studied at Regensburg and Leipzig, then theology in Rome. In 1882 he returned to Poznan, dedicating himself to the codification of Polish sacred music; also was conductor of the cathedral chorus there. Beginning in 1885, he brought out the valuable series Monumenta Musices Sacrae in Polonia, containing works by Polish composers of the 16th and 17th centuries; also publ. several manuals for use in Polish churches; wrote many choral compositions, using Gregorian modes. His 2 brothers, **Stefan** and **Mieczyslaw,** were also musicians.

Susa, Conrad, American composer; b. Springdale, Pa., April 26, 1935. He studied piano, organ, flute, oboe, clarinet, and French horn. Upon receiving a scholarship from Carnegie-Mellon Univ. in Pittsburgh, he took composition courses with Nicolai Lopatnikoff; after graduation he entered the Juilliard School of Music in N.Y., where his composition teachers were William Bergsma and Vincent Persichetti. He subsequently engaged in theater conducting. He excels in choral writing. Among his works are 5 serenades for various groups of voices and instruments, a *Pastorale* for Strings, and numerous accompanied and unaccompanied choruses. He has achieved his greatest acclaim with his opera *Transformations*, to the text from poems by Anne Sexton, produced by the Minnesota Opera Co. in Minneapolis on May 5, 1973; another opera, *Black River*, was produced in Minneapolis on Nov. 1, 1975.

Susato, Johannes (real name, **Johannes Steinwert von Soest**), German composer and singing master; b. Unna, 1448; d. Frankfurt, May 2, 1506. He was a chorister at Soest, then was in Cleve and Bruges, where he studied with English musicians; was subsequently active as a singing master in Cologne, Kassel, and (from 1472) Heidelberg; Virdung was one of his pupils there. He was also a physician, and c.1500 went to Frankfurt as a municipal doctor.

Susato, Tielman, German publisher and composer, son of **Johannes Susato;** b. probably in Cologne,

c.1500; d. possibly Antwerp, c.1561. In 1529 he moved from Cologne to Antwerp, where he was a town trumpeter; then established a music printing shop (1543) and issued 13 books of chansons, 4 vols. of masses, 4 vols. of motets, 4 books of various songs, etc.; several of these miscellaneous works were of his own composition.

BIBLIOGRAPHY: P. Bergmans, "Un Imprimeur musicien: Tilman Susato," *Bulletin de la Société Bibliophile Anversoise* (Antwerp, 1923); A. Goovaerts, *Histoire et bibliographie de la typographie musicale dans les Pays-Bas* (Antwerp, 1881); Ute Meissner, *Der Antwerpener Notendrucker Tylman Susato* (Berlin, 1967); L. Bernstein, "The Cantus-Firmus Chansons of Tylman Susato," *Journal of the American Musicological Society* (Summer 1969).

Süss, Christian, German conductor; b. Leipzig, Oct. 8, 1937. He was educated at the Hochschule für Musik in Leipzig; also studied in Berlin. He was a conductor at the Mannheim National Theater (1964–67); then was first conductor at the City Theater in Saarbrücken (1967–70) and Düsseldorf (1970–73). In 1973 he became Generalmusikdirektor of Heidelberg. He appeared several times as a guest conductor of the Hamburg State Opera.

Susskind, (Jan) Walter, Czech-born English conductor; b. Prague, May 1, 1913; d. Berkeley, Calif., March 25, 1980. He studied theory with Josef Suk and advanced composition with Alois Hába at the Prague Cons. (1928–33); took conducting lessons with George Szell and was Szell's assistant conductor at the German Opera House in Prague (1933–38). He then toured Europe as a conductor and pianist; went to England, where he was the pianist-member of the London Czech Trio (1939–42) and conducted the Carl Rosa Opera Co. (1942–45); was subsequently conductor of the Scottish National Orch. in Glasgow (1946–52), having become a British citizen in 1946. He then conducted the Victorian Symph. Orch. in Melbourne (1953–55); from 1956 to 1965 he was conductor of the Toronto Symph. Orch. and was music director of the Aspen (Colo.) Music Festival (1961–68), the St. Louis Symph. Orch. (1968–75), and the Mississippi River Festival in Edwardsville, Ill. (1969–75). His last position was that of music adviser and principal guest conductor of the Cincinnati Symph. Orch., from 1978 until his death. Susskind was also a composer; among his works are 4 songs for Voice and String Quartet (Prague Festival of the International Society for Contemporary Music, Sept. 2, 1935); *9 Slovak Sketches* for Orch.; *Passacaglia* for Timpani and Chamber Orch. (St. Louis, Feb. 24, 1977).

BIBLIOGRAPHY: Donald Brook, *International Gallery of Conductors* (N.Y., 1951; pp. 200–6); Roland Turner, ed., *The Annual Obituary 1980* (N.Y., 1981; pp. 197–99).

Süssmayr, Franz Xaver, Austrian composer; b. Schwanenstadt, 1766; d. Vienna, Sept. 17, 1803. He was a pupil of Salieri, and also of Mozart, of whom he became an intimate friend; after Mozart's death his widow entrusted the completion of his Requiem to Süssmayr; he was clever in emulating Mozart's style of composition, and his handwriting was so much like Mozart's that it is difficult to distinguish between them. He was conductor at the National Theater in Vienna from 1792, and 2nd conductor at the Vienna Court Opera from 1794.

WORKS: Süssmayr wrote a number of operas and operettas, which he produced in Vienna, among them: *Moses* (May 4, 1792); *L'Incanto superato* (July 8, 1793); *Der Spiegel von Arkadien* (Nov. 14, 1794); *Idris und Zenide* (May 9, 1795); *Die edle Rache* (Aug. 27, 1795); *Die Freiwilligen* (Sept. 27, 1796); *Der Wildfang* (Oct. 4, 1797); *Der Marktschreier* (July 6, 1799); *Soliman der Zweite, oder Die drei Sultaninnen* (Oct. 1, 1799); *Gülnare* (*Gonora;* July 5, 1800); *Phasma* (July 25, 1801). He wrote *secco* recitatives for Mozart's opera *La clemenza di Tito* (Prague, Sept. 6, 1791); composed several numbers for the Vienna production of Grétry's *La Double Epreuve,* given there under the title *Die doppelte Erkenntlichkeit* (Feb. 28, 1796). Other works include a Clarinet Concerto and pieces for the English horn, for guitar, and for other instruments. Most of his works are in MS.

BIBLIOGRAPHY: G.L.P. Sievers, *Mozart und Süssmayr* (1829); W. Pole, *Mozart's Requiem* (1879); W. Lehner, "F.X. Süssmayr als Opernkomponist," *Studien zur Musikwissenschaft,* 18 (1931); H.H. Hausner, *Franz Xaver Süssmayr* (Vienna, 1964); F. Beyer, "Mozarts Komposition zum Requiem. Zur Frage der Ergänzung," *Acta Mozartiana,* XVIII/2 (1971).

Suter, Hermann, Swiss composer and conductor; b. Kaiserstuhl, April 28, 1870; d. Basel, June 22, 1926. He was a pupil of his father, an organist and cantor; then studied with Hans Huber in Basel; also took courses in Stuttgart with Faisst and in Leipzig with Reinecke (1888–91). From 1892 to 1902 he conducted choral societies in various Swiss communities; in 1896 was appointed to the faculty of the Zürich Cons.; in 1902, settled in Basel, where he was active as a conductor and a teacher; was director of the Basel Cons. from 1918 to 1921. His best-known work is the oratorio *Le Laudi di S. Francesco d'Assisi* (1924); he also wrote a number of other vocal works, a Symph., a Violin Concerto, 3 string quartets, a String Sextet, and 3 song cycles.

BIBLIOGRAPHY: W. Merian, *Hermann Suter* (Basel, 1936).

Suter, Robert, Swiss composer; b. St. Gallen, Jan. 30, 1919. He studied theory, piano, and composition with W. Geiser at the Basel Cons. (1937–43), and privately with Wladimir Vogel in 1956; then devoted himself primarily to educational work; taught at the Musik-Akademie in Basel; in 1968 was appointed to the editorial board of Basel Radio.

WORKS: *Lyrical Suite* for Chamber Orch. (1959); *Fantasia* for Clarinet, Harp, and String Orch. (1964–65); *Sonata* for Orch. (1967; Basel, Feb. 22, 1968); *Epitaffio* for Winds, Strings, and Percussion (1968; Lucerne, Aug. 7, 1968); *3 Nocturnes* for Viola and Orch. (1968–69; Basel, March 19, 1970); *Airs et Ritournelles* for Percussion and Instrumental Group (1973); *Musik* for Orch. (1975–76; Basel, May 25, 1977); *Musikalisches Tagebuch Nr. 1* and *Nr. 2* for Voice and 7 Instruments (1946, 1950); *Die Ballade von des Cortez Leuten* for Narrator, Chorus, Speaking Chorus, and Orch. (1960); *Heilige Leier, sprich, sei meine Stimme* for Soprano, Flute, and Guitar (1960); *. . . aber auch lobet den Himmel,* after Brecht, for Solo Voices, Male Chorus, Boys' Speaking Chorus, and Instrumental Ensemble (1976; Basel, June 3, 1977); String Quartet (1952); *Divertimento* for Flute, Oboe, and Bassoon (1955); *Estampida* for 7 Instruments and Percussion (1960); *4 Movements* for String Trio (1961); *4 Etudes* for Wind Quintet (1962); *Serenata* for 7 Instruments (1963–64); *Fanfares et Pastorales* for 2 Horns, Trumpet, and Trombone (1965); *Duetti* for Flute and Oboe (1967); *Elégie* for Solo Cello (1969); *Pastorales d'hiver* for Horn, Violin, Viola, Cello, and Piano (1972); *Jeux à quatre* for 4 Saxophones (1976); *Contrapunti,* études for Violin and Piano (1977); Piano Sonata (1966–67).

Sutermeister, Heinrich, important Swiss composer; b. Feuerthalen, Aug. 12, 1910. He studied philology at the Sorbonne Univ. in Paris (1930–31) and composition with Carl Orff and Walter Courvoisier at the Munich Academy of Music (1931–34). Subsequently he devoted himself mainly to composition, until 1963, when he was appointed to the faculty of the Hochschule für Musik in Hannover, Germany; he retired from there in 1975. His main endeavor is to create a type of modern opera that is dramatically effective and melodically pleasing; in his musical philosophy he follows the organic line of thought, with the natural impulses of the human body determining the rhythmic course of a composition; discordant combinations of sounds are legitimate parts of modern harmony in Sutermeister's works, but he rejects artificial doctrines such as orthodox dodecaphony.

WORKS: Operas: *Die schwarze Spinne,* radio opera (1935; Bern Radio, Oct. 15, 1936; revised for the stage and produced in St. Gall, March 2, 1949); *Romeo und Julia,* after Shakespeare (1938–40; Dresden, April 13, 1940; his first and greatest success); *Die Zauberinsel,* after Shakespeare's *The Tempest* (1941–42; Dresden, Oct. 31, 1942); *Niobe* (1943–45; Zürich, June 22, 1946); *Raskolnikoff,* after Dostoyevsky's *Crime and Punishment* (1946–48; Stockholm, Oct. 14, 1948); *Der rote Stiefel* (1949–51; Stockholm, Nov. 22, 1951); *Titus Feuerfuchs,* burlesque opera (1956–58; Basel, April 14, 1958); *Seraphine,* opera-buffa after Rabelais (Zürich Radio, June 10, 1959; stage premiere, Munich, Feb. 25, 1960); *Das Gespenst von Canterville,* television opera after Oscar Wilde (1962–63; German television, Sept. 6, 1964); *Madame Bovary,* after Flaubert (1967; Zürich, May 26, 1967); *La Croisade des Enfants,* television opera (1969); *Der Flaschenteufel (The Bottle Imp),* television opera after R.L. Stevenson (1969–70; German television, 1971); a radio ballad, *Füsse im Feuer* (also arranged for an operatic pro-

duction, staged at the Berlin City Opera, Feb. 12, 1950); a radio melodrama, *Fingerhütchen* (produced in operatic form at St. Gall, April 26, 1950); 2 ballets: *Das Dorf unter dem Gletscher* (1936; Karlsruhe, May 2, 1937) and *Max und Moritz* (1951; first stage perf., St. Gall, 1963); 8 numbered cantatas: No. 1, *Andreas Gryphius,* for Chorus a cappella (1935–36); No. 2 for Contralto, Chorus, and 2 Pianos (1943–44); No. 3, *Dem Allgegenwärtigen,* for Soloists, Chorus, and Orch. (1957–58); No. 4, *Das Hohelied,* for Soloists, Chorus, and Orch. (1960); No. 5, *Der Papagei aus Kuba,* for Chorus and Chamber Orch. (1961); No. 6, *Erkennen und Schaffen* (in French, *Croire et créer*), for Soloists, Chorus, and Orch. (1963); No. 7, *Sonnenhymne des Echnaton,* for Male Chorus, 2 Horns, 3 Trumpets, 2 Trombones, Tuba, Piano, and Percussion (1965); No. 8, *Omnia ad Unum,* for Baritone, Chorus, and Orch. (1965–66); *Missa da Requiem* for Soloists, Chorus, and Orch. (1952; Basel, June 11, 1954); *Ecclesia* for Soloists, Chorus, and Orch. (1972–73; Lausanne, Oct. 18, 1975); *Te Deum* for Soprano, Chorus, and Orch. (1974); *Divertimento No. 1* for String Orch. (1936) and *No. 2* for Orch. (1959–60); 3 piano concertos (1943, 1953, 1961–62); 2 cellos concertos (1954–55, 1971); *Sérénade pour Montreux* for 2 Oboes, 2 Horns, and String Orch. (1970); Clarinet Concerto (1974); chamber pieces.
BIBLIOGRAPHY: D. Larese, *Heinrich Sutermeister* (Amristwil, 1972).

Suthaus, Ludwig, eminent German tenor; b. Cologne, Dec. 12, 1906; d. Berlin, Sept. 7, 1971. He studied voice in Cologne; made his operatic debut in Aachen in 1928 as Walther von Stolzing in *Die Meistersinger von Nürnberg;* sang in Essen (1931–33) and Stuttgart (1933–41); in 1941 he joined the Berlin State Opera, where he made many appearances until 1948; then sang with the Berlin Städtische Oper until 1965. He made his U.S. debut with the San Francisco Opera in 1953. He was one of the outstanding Heldentenors of his time and was engaged at several Bayreuth Festivals in Wagnerian roles.

Sutherland, Dame Joan, celebrated Australian soprano; b. Sydney, Nov. 7, 1926. She received her early vocal training in Sydney; made her debut as Dido in a concert performance of *Dido and Aeneas* in Sydney in 1947; made her stage debut in Sydney in 1951; then went to London, where she studied voice with Clive Carey at the Royal College of Music. After an appearance at Covent Garden in a minor role in 1952, she rapidly asserted herself as an important artist; obtained a signal success at Covent Garden as Lucia, on Feb. 17, 1959. She made her first American appearance with the Dallas Opera in 1960; on Nov. 26, 1961, she made her Metropolitan Opera debut as Lucia, to great acclaim. She married the Australian conductor **Richard Bonynge;** was made a Dame Commander of the Order of the British Empire in 1978.
BIBLIOGRAPHY: R. Braddon, *Joan Sutherland* (London, 1962); E. Greenfield, *Joan Sutherland* (London, 1972).

Sutherland, Margaret, Australian composer; b. Adelaide, Nov. 20, 1897. She studied piano with Edward Goll and composition with Fritz Hart at the Marshall Hall Cons. (1914); then taught at the Melbourne Cons. In 1923–25 she traveled in Europe. In 1970 she was made an Officer of the Order of the British Empire for her services to Australian music. Her own compositions are marked by classical restraint; most of them follow Baroque forms.
WORKS: Violin Sonata (1925); Trio for Clarinet, Viola, and Piano (1934); *Suite on a Theme of Purcell* for Orch. (1935); *House Quartet* for Clarinet or Violin, Viola, Horn or Cello, and Piano (1936); *Pavane* for Orch. (1938); *The Soldier* for Chorus and Strings (1938); 2 string quartets (1939, 1967); *Prelude and Jig* for Strings (1939); ballet, *Dithyramb* (1941); Sonata for Clarinet and Piano (1944); Concerto for Strings (1945); *Adagio* for 2 Solo Violins and Orch. (1946); Trio for Oboe and 2 Violins (1951); *Contrasts* for 2 Violins (1953); tone poem, *Haunted Hills* (1953); Violin Concerto (1954); *4 Symphonic Studies* (1954); Concerto Grosso for Orch. (1955); Quartet for English Horn and String Trio (1955); *6 Bagatelles* for Violin and Viola (1956); Piano Sonatina (1958); *Divertimento* for String Trio (1958); Sonatina for Oboe and Piano (1958); *3 Temperaments* for Orch. (1958); *Fantasy* for Violin and Orch. (1960); *Concertante* for Oboe, Percussion, and String Orch. (1962); one-act chamber opera, *The Young Kabbarli* (1964); Quartet for Clarinet and Strings (1967); *Extension* for Piano (1967); *Chiaroscuro 1* and *2* for Piano (1968); *Voices 1* and *2* for Piano (1968).

Sutro, Florence Edith (née **Clinton**), American music educator; b. New York, May 1, 1865; d. there, April 29, 1906. A graduate of the N.Y. Cons. of Music, she was the first woman in the U.S. to receive a degree of Mus.Doc. In 1898 she organized the National Federation of Musical Clubs, and was its first president; for her efforts in behalf of women composers and executants she was awarded a gold medal at the Atlanta Exposition in 1895. On Oct. 1, 1884, she married Theodore Sutro of N.Y., a prominent lawyer. She wrote *Women in Music and Law* (N.Y., 1895).

Sutro, Rose Laura (b. Baltimore, Sept. 15, 1870; d. there, Jan. 11, 1957) and **Ottilie** (b. Baltimore, Jan. 4, 1872; d. there, Sept. 12, 1970), American duo-pianists; daughters of Otto Sutro, a patron of art and founder of the Baltimore Oratorio Society. Both began piano lessons with their mother, and in 1889 were sent to Berlin, where they continued their studies. They made a spectacular debut in London on July 13, 1894; their first American appearance took place in Brooklyn on Nov. 13, 1894, followed by a tour of the U.S. Returning to Europe, they won fresh laurels, and were invited to play before Queen Victoria. Max Bruch wrote his Concerto for 2 Pianos and Orch. expressly for them, and they gave its premiere with the Philadelphia Orch. on Dec. 29, 1916. In 1953 the sisters established the Sutro Club Room at the Maryland Historical Society in memory of their father.

Suzuki, Shin'ichi, influential Japanese educator and violin teacher; founder of the Suzuki method of violin instruction; b. Nagoya, Oct. 18, 1898. He was the son of **Masakichi Suzuki** (1859–1944), a maker of string instruments and the founder of the Suzuki Violin Seizo Co. He studied violin with Ko Ando in Tokyo and with Karl Klinger in Berlin (1921–28); upon his return to Japan, he formed the Suzuki Quartet with 3 of his brothers; also made appearances as a conductor with his own Tokyo String Orch. He became president of the Teikoku Music School in 1930. He subsequently devoted most of his time to education, especially the teaching of children. He maintained that any child, given the right stimuli under proper conditions in a group environment, could achieve a high level of competence as a performer. In 1950 he organized the Saino Kyoiku Kenkyu-kai in Matsumoto, where he taught his method most successfully. In subsequent years his method was adopted for instruction on other instruments as well. He made many tours of the U.S. and Europe, where he lectured and demonstrated his method.

BIBLIOGRAPHY: C. Cook, *Suzuki Education in Action* (N.Y., 1970); E. Mills and T. Murthy, eds., *The Suzuki Conception: An Introduction to a Successful Method for Early Music Education* (Berkeley, 1973).

Svanholm, Set, noted Swedish tenor; b. Västeras, Sept. 2, 1904; d. Saltsjö-Duvnäs, Oct. 4, 1964. He served as a church organist in Tillberga and Säby; studied voice with John Forsell at the Opera School of the Stockholm Cons. He made his operatic debut as a baritone at the Royal Theater in Stockholm in 1930; in 1936 he began singing tenor roles. In addition to his appearances at the Royal Theater in Stockholm, he also sang at the Salzburg Festival and the Vienna State Opera (1938), the Berlin State Opera, La Scala in Milan (1941–42), and the Bayreuth Festival (1942). In 1946 he appeared as Tristan in Rio de Janeiro and as Lohengrin in San Francisco; on Nov. 15, 1946, he made his Metropolitan Opera debut in N.Y. as Siegfried; remained on its roster until his farewell appearance as Parsifal on March 24, 1956. From 1948–57 he sang at London's Covent Garden. From 1956–63 he was director of the Royal Theater in Stockholm. Among his best roles were Radames, Tannhäuser, Otello, and Siegmund; he was equally successful in operas of Wagner and Verdi.

Svečenski, Louis, Croatian-American violinist; b. Osijek, Nov. 6, 1862; d. New York, June 18, 1926. He studied violin with J. Grün and J. Hellmesberger at the Vienna Cons.; emigrated to America in 1885 and became a member of the Boston Symph. Orch. (1885–1903); he was also the violist throughout the entire career of the Kneisel Quartet (1885–1917); in 1917 went to live in N.Y. He publ. *25 Technical Exercises for Viola.*

Sved, Alexander, Hungarian baritone; b. Budapest, May 28, 1906; d. Vienna, June 9, 1979. He stud-ied violin at the Cons. in Budapest; then went to Milan for vocal studies with Sammarco and Stracciari. He made his operatic debut as Count Luna in Budapest in 1928; was a member of the Vienna State Opera (1936–39); also sang at Covent Garden in London and the Salzburg Festival. On Dec. 2, 1940, he made his debut at the Metropolitan Opera in N.Y. as Renato in *Un ballo in maschera;* he remained on its roster until 1948, and then returned for the 1949–50 season. He subsequently sang in Rome, in Paris, and at the Bayreuth Festival; also made appearances with the Budapest Opera, and later toured as a concert singer.

Sveinsson, Atli Heimir, Icelandic composer; b. Reykjavik, Sept. 21, 1938. He studied at the Reykjavik School of Music; then in Cologne with Raphael, B.A. Zimmermann, and Petzold at the Hochschule für Musik (1959–62), and with Stockhausen and Pousseur at the School for New Music (1963); attended seminars in electronic music with Koenig in Bilthoven, the Netherlands (1964). Returning to Iceland, he devoted himself to teaching.

WORKS: *Hljómi (Sonant)* for Chamber Orch. (1963); *Fönsun I–III* for Singers, Actors, Tape, and Chamber Ensemble; *Klif (Tautology)* for Flute, Cello, and Piano (1968); *Seimur (Soundings)* for One or 2 Pianos, and any number of Instruments (1968); *Spectacles* for Percussion and Tape (1969); *Tengsl (Connections)* for Orch. (1970); *Bizzarreries I* for Flute, Piano, and Tape (1970); *Könnun,* Viola Concerto (1971); Flute Concerto (1973); *Flower Shower* for Orch. (1974); *I Call It* for Contralto, Piano, Cello, and 2 Percussionists (1974); a chamber opera, *The Silken Drum* (Reykjavik, June 6, 1982); *Infinitesimal Fragments of Eternity* for Chamber Orch. (St. Paul, Oct. 7, 1982); *Kurt Weill, in memoriam* for Chamber Orch. (Reykjavik, Feb. 26, 1983); incidental music.

Svendsen, Johan (Severin), eminent Norwegian composer; b. Christiania, Sept. 30, 1840; d. Copenhagen, June 14, 1911. He acquired practical experience in music from his father, a bandmaster, and played several instruments; then conducted a band himself. It was not before he was 23 that he began serious study at the Leipzig Cons. with F. David, Reinecke, and others; then played violin in theater orchs. in Paris; wrote incidental music for Coppée's play *Le Passant* (Paris, Jan. 14, 1869), a Violin Concerto, and other violin works. In 1870 he went back to Leipzig; then traveled to America, and married an American lady, Sarah Levett. Returning to Norway, he became conductor of the Christiania Musical Assoc. (1872–77 and again in 1880–83). In 1883 he was appointed court conductor in Copenhagen as well as conductor of the Royal Theater there. He retired in 1908. His most popular works are the *4 Norwegian Rhapsodies* for Orch. and the *Carnaval des artistes norvégiens* (also for Orch.), based on genuine folk melodies; he further wrote 2 symphs.; String Quartet; String Quintet; String Octet; Cello Concerto; 2 albums of songs to German, French, and Norwegian words; a *Romance* for Violin and Orch.

(very popular); arrangements of Scandinavian melodies for String Quartet; etc.

BIBLIOGRAPHY: A. Grönwold, *Norske musikere* (1883); G. Schjelderup, in *Norges Musikhistorie.* Letters of Svendsen were publ. by G. Hauch in *Tilskueren* (Copenhagen, 1913); Bjarne Kortsen, *Chamber Music Works by Johan Svendsen* (Bergen, 1971).

Svetlanov, Evgeny, Russian conductor and composer; b. Moscow, Sept. 6, 1928. He studied composition with Gnessin and Shaporin, and conducting with Gauck. After graduation in 1955 he joined the staff of the Bolshoi Theater in Moscow; was its principal conductor from 1962 to 1964. In 1965 he was appointed music director of the State Orch. of the U.S.S.R.; in 1979 became a principal guest conductor of the London Symph. Orch. He wrote a Symph. (1956); *Siberian Fantasy* for Orch. (1953); Piano Concerto (1951); incidental music for plays; film scores.

Sviridov, Georgi, significant Soviet Russian composer; b. Fatezh, near Kursk, Dec. 16, 1915. He studied at the Leningrad Cons. with Shostakovich. In his music, Sviridov adheres to the ideals of socialist realism, seeking inspiration in Russian folk songs; the texts of his vocal works are usually taken from Russian literature. His *Oratorio pathétique* (1959), to words by Mayakovsky, composed in a grandly songful "optimistic" style, became one of the most successful scores by a Soviet composer.

WORKS: Music for Shakespeare's *Othello* (1944); *Twinkling Lights,* operetta (1951); music for films: *Blizzard* (1964) and *Time Forge Ahead!* (1966); Symph. for String Orch. (1940); *Little Triptych* (1964); Piano Quintet (1945); Piano Trio (1945); String Quartet (1945); *Music for Chamber Orchestra* (1964); choral works: *The Decembrists,* oratorio (1955); *Poem to the Memory of Sergei Essenin* (1956); *Poem about Lenin* for Bass, Chorus, and Orch. (1960); *5 Songs about Our Fatherland* for Voices, Chorus, and Orch. (1967); numerous piano pieces and songs.

BIBLIOGRAPHY: D. Frishman, ed., *Georgy Sviridov* (a collection of articles; Moscow, 1971).

Svoboda, Tomáš, Czech composer; b. Paris, Dec. 6, 1939, of Czech parents (his father was a renowned mathematician, Antonín Svoboda). The family went to Prague in 1946; he studied piano privately and composition with Hlobil, Kabeláč, and Dobiáš at the Prague Cons., graduating in 1959. In 1964 he left Czechoslovakia and settled in the U.S. In 1970 he was appointed member of the faculty at Portland (Oreg.) State Univ.; in 1979 he settled on Treasure Island, Fla. His music is marked by broad melodic lines in economically disposed harmonies; there are elements of serialism in chromatic episodes.

WORKS: Symph. No. 1 (Prague, Sept. 7, 1957); Symph. No. 2 (1964–65); Symph. No. 3 (1965); Trio for Piano, Oboe, and Bassoon (1962); *Rezanička,* dance for String Orch. (1962); *Classical Sonatina* for Oboe and Piano (1962); *Etude* for Chamber Orch. (1963);

Ballade for Bassoon and Piano (1963); Viola Sonata (1963); Suite for Bassoon, Strings, and Harpsichord (1963); *Ballet Etudes* for 7 Instruments (1963); *Chamber Concertino* for Harp and Chamber Orch. (1964); *Suite* for Mezzo-soprano and Orch. (1964); *Parabola* for Clarinet, Piano, Violin, Viola, and Cello (1971); 2 string quartets (1960, 1967); *Child's Dream* for Children's Chorus and Orch. (1973); Duo for Flute and Oboe (1974); Symph. No. 4 (1974); Symph. No. 5 (1978).

Swan, Alfred (Julius), Russian-born English-American musicologist and educator; b. St. Petersburg (of English parents), Oct. 9, 1890; d. Haverford, Pa., Oct. 2, 1970. After attending a German-language school in St. Petersburg, he studied at Oxford Univ., receiving the degree of B.A. (1911), and later his M.A. (1934). Returning to Russia in 1911, he took courses in composition at the St. Petersburg Cons. During the Civil War in Russia, he served with the American Red Cross in Siberia (1918–19); then emigrated to the U.S.; taught at the Univ. of Virginia (1921–23); in 1926 he was appointed head of the music depts. at Swarthmore College and Haverford College in Pennsylvania, retiring from these posts in 1958. His specialty was Russian music. Swan was also a composer; he wrote a Trio for Flute, Clarinet, and Piano (1932); 2 violin sonatas (1913, 1948); 4 piano sonatas (1932-46); several albums of songs.

WRITINGS: *Scriabin* (London, 1923; reprint, N.Y., 1969); *Music 1900–1930* (N.Y., 1930); "Znamenny Chant of the Russian Church," *Musical Quarterly* (April, July, Oct. 1940); many other articles on Russian music and Russian composers in various publications. He also brought out a useful brochure, *The Music Director's Guide to Musical Literature* (N.Y., 1941). His *Russian Music and Its Sources in Chant and Folksong* was publ. posthumously (N.Y., 1973). He ed. *Songs from Many Lands* (1923) and *Recueil de chansons russes* (1936).

Swan, Timothy, American hymn-tune writer; b. Worcester, Mass., July 23, 1758; d. Northfield, Mass., July 23, 1842. His only musical training consisted of 3 weeks at a singing school, and while serving in the Continental Army he also learned to play the flute. From 1783 he lived in Suffield, Conn., and in 1807 moved to Northfield, Mass. He composed the hymn tunes *Poland, China, Ocean,* and *Pownal;* publ. *The Songster's Assistant* (c.1800); *New England Harmony* (1801); and also probably was the author of *The Songsters' Museum* (1803).

BIBLIOGRAPHY: F.J. Metcalf, *American Writers and Compilers of Sacred Music* (N.Y., 1925; pp. 103ff.); G.B. Webb, *Timothy Swan: Yankee Tunesmith* (Univ. of Illinois at Urbana-Champaign, 1972).

Swann, Frederick, American organist; b. Lewisburg, W.Va., July 30, 1931. He studied at the Northwestern Univ. School of Music in Evanston, Ill. (Mus.B., 1952) and at the School of Sacred Music of the Union Theological Seminary (M. of Sacred Mus., 1954). In 1958 he became organist of the Riverside Church in N.Y.; also served as director of music there from 1966. He made numerous recital appearances in the U.S., Canada, and Europe; from 1972 he also held the position of chairman of the organ dept. of the Manhattan School of Music in N.Y.

Swanson, Howard, black American composer; b. Atlanta, Aug. 18, 1907; d. New York, Nov. 12, 1978. As a youth he earned a living by manual labor on the railroad and as a postal clerk. He entered the Cleveland Inst. of Music at the age of 20, enrolling in evening courses with Herbert Elwell; obtained a stipend to go to Paris, where he studied composition with Nadia Boulanger (1938–40). Returning to the U.S., he took a job with the Internal Revenue Service (1941–45). In 1952 he received a Guggenheim fellowship that enabled him to go back to Paris, where he lived until 1966 before settling permanently in N.Y. Swanson's songs attracted the attention of such notable singers as Marian Anderson and William Warfield, who sang them on tours. He achieved signal success with his *Short Symphony* (Symph. No. 2, 1948), a work of simple melodic inspiration, which received considerable acclaim at its first performance by the N.Y. Phil., conducted by Mitropoulos (Nov. 23, 1950). In 1952 it won the Music Critics' Circle Award for the best orch. work performed in N.Y. during the 1950–51 season.

WORKS: Symph. No. 1 (1945); *Night Music* for a Chamber Orch. of Wind Quintet and Strings (1950); *Music* for Strings (1952); *Songs for Patricia* for Voice, and Orch. or Piano (1952); Concerto for Orch. (1956; Louisville, Ky., Jan. 9, 1957); *Fantasy Piece* for Soprano Saxophone or Clarinet, and Strings (1969); Symph. No. 3 (1969–70; N.Y., March 1, 1970); *Nocturne* for Violin and Piano (1948); *Suite* for Cello and Piano (1949); *Soundpiece* for Brass Quintet (1952); *Vista No. 2* for String Octet (1969); Cello Sonata (1973; N.Y., May 13, 1973); Trio for Flute, Oboe, and Piano (1975); 3 piano sonatas (1948, 1976, 1976); *2 Nocturnes* for Piano (1967); songs, including *Ghosts in Love, Junk Man, Night Song, Pierrot, Snowdunes, Still Life, The Negro Speaks of Rivers.*

BIBLIOGRAPHY: M. Yestadt, "Song Literature for the 70's: A Socio-Musical Approach," *NATS Bulletin* (May/June 1973); David N. Baker, ed., *The Black Composer Speaks* (Metuchen, N.J., 1978; pp. 337–55, including a complete list of works).

Swarowsky, Hans, Austrian conductor; b. Budapest, Sept. 16, 1899; d. Salzburg, Sept. 10, 1975. He studied in Vienna with Schoenberg and Anton von Webern, with whom he formed a friendly association; he also was in close relationship with Richard Strauss. He devoted himself mainly to conducting; occupied posts as opera conductor in Hamburg (1932) and in Berlin (1934). From 1937 to 1940 he was conductor of the Zürich Opera; during the season 1944–45 led the Polish Phil. in Cracow. After the war he was principal conductor of the Vienna Symph. (1945–47) and of the Graz Opera (1947–50); in 1957–59 he was conductor of the Scottish National Orch. in Glasgow; from 1959 appeared occasionally as guest conductor of the Vienna State Opera; in 1965

became a regular staff conductor there. In his programs he gave prominent place to the works of the Vienna School; his performances of Mahler were particularly fine. Swarowsky was an excellent instructor in conducting; he led a special seminar at the Vienna Academy of Music; among his students were Claudio Abbado and Zubin Mehta. He was a highly competent editor of music by various composers; also trans. a number of Italian librettos into German; publ. *Wahrung der Gestalt* (Vienna, 1979).

Swarthout, Gladys, American mezzo-soprano; b. Deepwater, Mo., Dec. 25, 1900; d. Florence, July 7, 1969. She studied at the Bush Cons. in Chicago, also opera with L. Mugnone; made her debut in a minor part with the Chicago Civic Opera in 1924; and then made regular appearances with the Ravinia Opera Co. in Chicago. On Nov. 15, 1929, she sang the part of La Cieca in *La Gioconda* at the Metropolitan Opera; she remained on its roster, with several interruptions, until 1945. She married the singer **Frank Chapman** in 1932; publ. an autobiography, *Come Soon, Tomorrow* (N.Y., 1945).

Swayne, Giles, British composer; b. Stevenage, June 30, 1946. He studied with Nicholas Maw; in 1968 entered the Royal Academy, where he took courses in composition and piano; served as répétiteur at the Wexford Festival (1972–73) and at Glyndebourne (1973–74); also attended Messiaen's classes in composition in Paris (1976–77). In 1982 he visited West Africa to study the music of the Jola people of Senegal and The Gambia. In common with many other British composers of his generation, he resolutely eschewed musical gourmandise to become a convinced populist. He wrote music for the general public.

WORKS: *4 Lyrical Pieces* for Cello and Piano (1970; Aldeburgh, June 16, 1971); String Quartet No. 1 (1971); String Quartet No. 2 (1977; Manchester, Oct. 30, 1978); *The Good Morrow,* cycle of 5 settings of John Donne for Mezzo-soprano and Piano (1971); *Paraphrase on a Theme of Tallis* for Organ (1971); *Canto* for Guitar (1972); *Canto* for Piano (1973); *Canto* for Violin (1973); *Synthesis* for 2 Pianos (1974); *Orlando's Music* for Orch. (1974; Liverpool, Feb. 3, 1976); *Canto* for Clarinet (1975); *Duo* for Violin and Piano (1975); Suite for Guitar (1976); *Pentecost-Music* for Orch. (1977; Manchester, April 8, 1981); *Cry* for 28 amplified Solo Voices depicting the creation of the world (1979; London, July 23, 1980); *A World Within,* tape composition for ballet, consisting of multitrack recordings of Horn, based on the life of the Brontë sisters (1978; Stoke-on-Trent, June 2, 1978); *Freewheeling* for Viola, Baryton, and Cello (1980; Kuhmo Festival, Finland, July 25, 1980); *Canto* for Cello (1981); *Count-Down* for 16-part Choir and 2 Percussion Players (1981; Merton Festival, Yorkshire, May 23, 1982); *Morgan* for Organ (1982); Symph. (1982); *Song for Hadi* for Drums and Instruments (1983; Bath Festival, June 4, 1983).

Sweelinck, Jan Pieterszoon, great Dutch organist and composer; b. Deventer (or Amsterdam), May

1562; d. Amsterdam, Oct. 16, 1621. Contrary to repeated assertions that Sweelinck was a pupil of Zarlino in Venice, documentary evidence proves that he remained in Amsterdam virtually all his life; this also refutes the theory that Sweelinck was the carrier of Venetian ideas and techniques in Northern Europe. About 1580 he became organist of the Old Church in Amsterdam, a position previously held by his father, Pieter Sweelinck (d. 1573). As a player and teacher, he was celebrated far and wide; most of the leading organists in northern Germany, of the next generation, were his pupils. Sweelinck was the first to employ the pedal in a real fugal part, and originated the organ fugue built up on one theme with the gradual addition of counter-themes leading up to a highly involved and ingenious finale—a form perfected by Bach. In rhythmic and melodic freedom, his vocal compositions show an advance over the earlier polyphonic style, though replete with intricate contrapuntal devices. A complete edition of Sweelinck's works, in 12 vols., edited by Max Seiffert for the Vereeniging voor Nederlandsche Muziekgeschiedenis, was publ. by Breitkopf & Härtel (1894–1901): vol. I, works for organ and clavier; vol. II, first half of the First Book of Psalms (1604); vol. III, 2nd half of the same; vol. IV, first half of the 2nd Book of Psalms (1613); vol. V, 2nd half of the same; vol. VI, 3rd Book of Psalms (1614); vol. VII, 4th Book of Psalms (1621); vol. VIII, *Cantiones sacrae a* 5; vol. IX, *Chansons a* 5; vol. X, *Rimes françaises et italiennes a* 2–4; vol. XI, processional compositions; vol. XII, rules for composition, edited by H. Gehrmann. Vols. II–VII comprise the 150 Psalms of David in the rhymed French version by Marot and Beza. A new edition, *Opera Omnia, editio altera,* was begun by the same series in 1957.

BIBLIOGRAPHY: F.H.J. Tiedeman: *J.P. S., Een bio-bibliografische Schets* (Amsterdam, 1876; 2nd ed., 1892); M. Seiffert, "J.P. S. und seine direkten deutschen Schüller," *Vierteljahrsschrift für Musikwissenschaft* (1891); idem, "J.P. S.," *Tijdschrift van de Vereeniging voor Nederlandsche Muziekgeschiedenis* (1900); D.F. Scheurleer, "Sweelinckiana," ibid. (1914); C. Van den Borren, *Les Origines de la musique de clavier dans les Pays-Bas jusque vers 1630* (Brussels, 1912); O. Gombosi, "Ein neuer S.-Fund," *Tijdschrift* ... (1932); E.R. Sollitt, *From Dufay to S.* (N.Y., 1933); B. van den Sigtenhorst Meyer, *J.P. S. en zijn instrumentale muziek* (The Hague, 1934; 2nd ed., 1946); idem, *De vocale Muziek van J.P. S.* (The Hague, 1948); R.L. Tusler, *The Organ Music of J.P. S.* (2 vols., Bilthoven, 1958; in Eng.); R.H. Tollefsen, "J.P. Sweelinck. A Bio-Bibliography, 1604–1842," *Tijdschrift* ... XXII/2 (1971).

Swert, Jules de. See **Deswert, Jules.**

Swift, Richard, American composer; b. Middlepoint, Ohio, Sept. 24, 1927. He studied at the Univ. of Chicago (M.A., 1956); then became a member of the faculty of the Univ. of Calif., Davis; was appointed chairman of the music dept. there in 1963. In his compositions he applies a variety of functional seri-

al techniques, including electronic and aleatory devices, while preserving the external forms of Baroque music.

WORKS: *A Coronal* for Orch. (Louisville, Ky., April 14, 1956); *Serenade concertante* for Piano and Wind Quintet (1956); Sonata for Clarinet and Piano (1957); Trio for Clarinet, Cello, and Piano (1957); Concerto for Piano and Chamber Ensemble (1961); *Extravaganza* for Orch. (1962); *The Trial of Tender O'Shea,* one-act opera (Univ. of Calif., Davis, Aug. 12, 1964); *Thrones* for Alto Flute and Double Bass (1966); *Tristia* for Orch. (Oakland, Calif., April 20, 1968); Violin Concerto (Oakland, May 28, 1968); Symph. (1970); 3 string quartets (1955, 1958, 1964); *Music for a While,* 2 works for 3 instruments; 8 works for different instrumental groups, or solos, entitled *Stravaganza,* and 3 works under the generic title *Domains* for Voice, Instruments, and Percussion; 25 sets of incidental music for the theater, including *musique concrète* and electronic sounds.

Swoboda, Adalbert (Viktor), Czech-German writer on music; b. Prague, Jan. 26, 1828; d. Munich, May 19, 1902. He founded (in 1880) and edited until his death the *Neue Musikzeitung* in Stuttgart; was the author of *Illustrierte Musikgeschichte* (2 vols., 1893).

Swoboda, Henry, Czech-American conductor; b. Prague, Oct. 29, 1897. He studied music with Zemlinsky and Talich; received his Ph.D. at the German Univ. in Prague. From 1931 to 1938 he was conductor with Prague Radio. In 1938 he settled in the U.S.; conducted occasional concerts in the U.S. and in Europe; served as music director of recording companies; wrote articles on American music. In 1964 he was appointed conductor of the Univ. Orch. and director of the Opera Workshop at the Univ. of Texas, Austin, which he left in 1968.

Sychra, Antonín, Czech musicologist; b. Boskovice, June 9, 1918; d. Prague, Oct. 21, 1969. He studied music in Brno and Prague; received his Ph.D. from the Univ. of Prague in 1946; settling in Prague, he publ. a number of scholarly monographs on esthetics; also taught music history at the Charles Univ. in Prague. He publ. *Leoš Janáček* (Prague, 1956); *Estetika Dvořákovy symfonické tvorby* (Prague, 1959); "The Method of Psychoacoustic Transformation Applied to the Investigation of Expression in Speech and Music," *Kybernetica* (1969; in Eng.); several other papers on the application of cybernetics to musical analysis.

Sydeman, William, American composer; b. New York, May 8, 1928. He studied at Mannes College with Felix Salzer; later had a session with Sessions at Tanglewood. In 1958 he joined the faculty of Mannes College in N.Y. He retired in 1969. His style of composition stems primarily from Mahler and Berg, and tends toward atonal Expressionism invigorated by spasmodic percussive rhythms in asymmetrically arranged meters.

WORKS: *Orchestral Abstractions* (1958; N.Y.,

Sygiètynski – Szabó

Jan. 10, 1962); *Study for Orchestra* (1959); Concertino for Oboe, Piano, and String Orch. (1956); Divertimento for 8 Instruments (1957); *Concerto da camera No. 1* for Violin and Chamber Orch. (1959) and *No. 2* for Violin and Chamber Orch. (1960); *Chamber Concerto* for Piano, 2 Flutes, and String Quartet (1961); *7 Movements* for Septet (1960); 2 woodwind quintets (1955, 1959); Westbrook Quintet for Clarinet, Horn, Double Bass, Piano, and Percussion (1959); String Quartet (1955); Quartet for Clarinet, Violin, Trumpet, and Double Bass (1955); Quartet for Oboe and Strings (1961); *The Affections,* suite for Trumpet and Piano (1965); *Malediction* for Tenor, Speaking Actor, String Quartet, and Electronic Tape, to words from Laurence Sterne's *Tristram Shandy* (N.Y., Feb. 5, 1971); numerous other works for various instrumental ensembles. N. Reich ed. *A Catalog of the Works of William Sydeman* (N.Y., 1968).

Sygiètynski, Tadeusz, Polish conductor and arranger; b. Warsaw, Sept. 24, 1896; d. there, May 19, 1955. He studied music in Lwow with Roman Statkowski and Henryk Melcer; later took courses with Max Reger in Leipzig and with Schoenberg in Vienna. In 1949 he organized in Poland the Mazowsze State Song and Dance Ensemble for the purpose of popularizing Polish folk music; toured with it in the Far East and in Western Europe with considerable acclaim. He made numerous arrangements of Polish folk songs for this group; in 1951 he received a state prize, and later was awarded the Banner of Labor by the State Council of Poland.

Sykes, James Andrews, American pianist; b. Atlantic City, N.J., July 10, 1908. He studied at Princeton (A.B., 1930) and at the Univ. of Rochester (A.M., 1933); subsequently held teaching positions at Colorado College (1935–46) and Colgate Univ. (1947–53); in 1953 was appointed a prof. at Dartmouth College. He toured West Germany (1954); South America (1960); Greece, Turkey, Malaysia, Vietnam, Pakistan, Iran, Lebanon, and Japan, as an American Specialist for the State Dept. (1965). He specializes in modern American piano music.

Sykora, Bogumil, Russian cellist; b. Glinsk, Jan. 15, 1890; d. New York, Jan. 19, 1953. He studied with Julius Klengel at the Leipzig Cons. (1909) and made his professional debut there on Jan. 20, 1911; toured Russia (1913–15); then came to America; gave his first recital in N.Y. on Dec. 12, 1916. He composed a Concerto and a number of pieces for cello.

Symonds, Norman, Canadian composer; b. Nelson, British Columbia, Dec. 23, 1920. He studied clarinet and piano at the Royal Cons. in Toronto (1945–47); took lessons in composition privately with Gordon Delamont in Toronto (1947–50). In 1953 he organized his own jazz octet, which continued in action until 1957. Most of his compositions are in the "third stream" idiom, combining jazz and symph. styles. WORKS: One-act opera, *The Spirit of Fundy* (1972); jazz opera, *Opera for 6 Voices* (1961); televi-

sion ballet, *Tensions,* with Jazz Quintet and Orch. (1962); *Concerto grosso* for Jazz Quintet and Orch. (1957); *Autumn Nocturne* for Tenor Saxophone and Strings (1960); *Pastel* for String Orch. (1963); *The Nameless Hour* for Improvising Soloist and String Ensemble (1966); *The Democratic Concerto* for Jazz Quintet and Orch. (Winnipeg, Dec. 14, 1967); *Impulse* for Orch. (Toronto, March 18, 1969); *3 Atmospheres* for Orch. (1970); *The Story of the Wind* for Narrator, Singer, and Jazz Ensemble (1970); *Concerto for Flute and Others* (1971); *The Land* for Narrator, Singer, and Jazz Ensemble (1972–73); *Maya* for Small Orch. (1973); *Circles* for Saxophone and 4 Synthesizers (1977); 2 concertos for Jazz Octet (1955, 1956); *Forest and Sky* for Orch. (1977); electronic pieces.

Szabados, Béla Antal, Hungarian composer; b. Budapest, June 3, 1867; d. there, Sept. 15, 1936. He studied with Erkel and Volkmann at the Budapest Academy of Music; later joined its staff as a piano teacher and vocal coach. He wrote 2 operas: *Maria* (Budapest, Feb. 28, 1905; in collaboration with Arpád Szendy) and *Fanny* (Budapest, Feb. 16, 1927); 11 musical comedies; 4 string quartets; a Psalm; several song cycles; also publ. several vocal manuals.

Szabelski, Boleslaw, Polish organist and composer; b. Radoryż, near Lublin, Dec. 3, 1896; d. Katowice, Aug. 27, 1979. He was an organist; studied composition with Szymanowski and Statkowski at the Warsaw Cons.; then became a teacher of organ and composition at the State College of Music in Katowice (1929–39, 1945–74). WORKS: 5 symphs. (1926; 1934, with Soprano and Chorus; 1951; 1956; 1968, with Chorus and Organ); *Suite* for Orch. (1938); Organ Sonata (1943); Sinfonietta for String Orch. and Percussion (1946); *Poemat bohaterski (Heroic Poem)* for Chorus and Orch. (1952); *Solemn Overture* (1953); *Concerto grosso* for Orch. (1954); Piano Concertino (1955); 2 string quartets (1935, 1956); *3 Sonnets* for Orch. (1958); *Improvisations* for Chorus and Chamber Orch. (1959); *Wiersze (Verses)* for Piano and Orch. (1961); *Aphorisms "9"* for Chamber Ensemble (1962); *Preludes* for Chamber Orch. (1963); Flute Concerto (1964); *Nicolaus Copernicus,* oratorio (1976; Poznan, April 2, 1976); *The Wola Redoubt* for 3 Vocal Soloists and Orch. (1976; Warsaw, Nov. 5, 1976); Piano Concerto (1978).

Szabó, Ferenc, distinguished Hungarian composer; b. Budapest, Dec. 27, 1902; d. there, Nov. 4, 1969. He studied with Kodály, Siklós, and Leo Weiner at the Budapest Academy of Music (1922–26); in 1926 he became aligned with the labor movement in Hungary; in 1932 went to Russia, where he became closely associated with the ideological work of the Union of Soviet Composers. In 1945 he returned to Hungary and was appointed prof. at the Budapest Academy; served as its director in 1958–67. He was awarded the Kossuth Prize in 1951 and 1954. His music initially followed the trends of Central European modernism, with strong undertones of Hungarian melorhythms, but later he wrote music in the manner of socialist realism; his choruses are permeated with the militant spirit of the revolutionary movement.

WORKS: 3-act opera, *Légy jó mindhalálig (Be Faithful until Death;* 1968–69; posthumous, Budapest, Dec. 5, 1975; score completed by his pupil András Borgulya); ballet, *Lúdas Matyi* (1960; Budapest, May 16, 1960); oratorio, *Föltámadott a tenger (In Fury Rose the Ocean;* 1955; Budapest, June 15, 1955); cantata, *Meghalt Lenin (Lenin Is Dead;* 1933); *Suite* for Chamber Orch. (1926; revised as *Sérénade oubliée,* 1964); *Class Struggle,* symph. poem (Moscow, April 27, 1933); *Sinfonietta* for an ensemble of Russian National Instruments (1935); *Lyrical Suite* for String Orch. (1936); *Moldavian Rhapsody* for Orch. (1940); Concerto for Orch., subtitled *Hazatérés (Homecoming;* 1948); *Számadás (Summary),* symph. poem (1949); *Emlékeztetö (Memento),* symph. (1952); 2 string quartets (1926, 1962); Trio for 2 Violins and Viola (1927); Sonata for Solo Cello (1929); 2 sonatas for Solo Violin (1930); *Sonata alla rapsodia* for Clarinet and Piano (1964); *Toccata* for Piano (1928); *8 Easy Piano Pieces* (1933); 3 piano sonatas (1940, 1947, 1957–61); *Felszabadult melódiák (Melodies of Liberation),* cycle of piano pieces (1949); a cappella choruses: *Song of the Wolves* (1929); *Work and Bread* (1930); *Liberty Be the Watchword* (1932); *November 7th* (1932); *Song at Dawn* (1953); *Vallomás (Declaration)* for Chorus, Brass, and Percussion (1967).

Szabolcsi, Bence, eminent Hungarian music scholar; b. Budapest, Aug. 2, 1899; d. there, Jan. 21, 1973. He studied jurisprudence at the Univ. of Budapest; concurrently took music courses with Kodály at the Budapest Academy and with Abert at the Univ. of Leipzig, where he received his Ph.D. in 1923. He was a prof. of music history at the Budapest Academy of Music from 1945 until his death. He was editor of the Hungarian music periodical *Zenei Szemle* (with Bartha) from 1926 (except for the war years, when it suspended publication). With Aladár Tóth he brought out a music dictionary in the Hungarian language (1930–31); publ. a history of music (Budapest, 1940), a monograph on Beethoven (Budapest, 1948), and a number of valuable papers in various European magazines. But his most abiding concern was the publication of documents on Béla Bartók. On his 70th birthday he was presented a Festschrift, edited by Bartha, *Bence Szabolcsi septuagenario* (Budapest, 1969). Of his writings on Bartók, the most important are *Bartók—Sa vie et son œuvre* (Budapest, 1956; 2nd ed., 1968); *Béla Bartók* (Leipzig, 1968); *Béla Bartók, Musiksprachen* (Leipzig, 1972). Two of his books were publ. in Eng.: *The Twilight of Ferenc Liszt* (Budapest, 1959) and *A Concise History of Hungarian Music* (Budapest, 1964).

Szalonek, Witold, Polish composer; b. Katowice, March 2, 1927. He studied composition with Woytowicz at the State College of Music in Katowice (1949–56); attended summer courses in new music at Darmstadt (1960) and had a course in musical analysis with Nadia Boulanger in Paris (1962–63). Returning to Poland, he taught at the Katowice State College, and became its director in 1972. In 1974 he became a prof. of composition at the Hochschule für Musik in West Berlin.

WORKS: *Pastorale* for Oboe, and Orch. or Piano (1952); Trio for Flute, Clarinet, and Bassoon (1952); *Toccata polyphonica* for String Orch. (1954); *Suite kurpienne* for Solo Contralto and 9 Instruments (1955); *Symphonic Satire* (1956); Cello Sonata (1958); *Wyznania (Confessions),* triptych for Narrator, Chorus, and Chamber Orch. (1959); Flute Concertino (1962); *Arabesques* for Violin and Piano (1964); *Les Sons* for Orch., without Violins and Cellos (1965); *4 Monologues* for Solo Oboe (1966); *Mutations* for Chamber Orch. (1966); *Proporzioni* for Flute, Viola, and Harp (1967); *Improvisations sonoristiques* for Clarinet, Trombone, Cello, and Piano (1968); *Mutanza* for Piano (1968); *1 + 1 + 1 + 1* for One, 2, 3, or 4 String Instruments (1969); cantata, *Ziemio mila (O, Pleasant Earth)* for Voice and Orch. (1969); *Proporzioni II* for Flute, Cello, and Piano or Harp (1967–70); *Aarhus Music* for Wind Quintet (1970; Aarhus is a city in Denmark where Szalonek lectured in 1970); *3 Sketches* for Harp (1972); *Connections* for Wind Quintet, 4 Strings, and Piano (1972).

Szalowski, Antoni, Polish-French composer; b. Warsaw, April 21, 1907; d. Paris, March 21, 1973. He studied composition (with K. Sikorski) and conducting at the Warsaw Cons., graduating in 1930; continued studies with Nadia Boulanger in Paris (1936), where he then lived until his death, becoming a French citizen in 1968. His music follows the Parisian manner of modern Baroque.

WORKS: 4 string quartets (1928, 1934, 1936, 1956); *Symphonic Variations* (1928); Piano Concerto (1930); Piano Sonata (1933); *Overture* (1936); Clarinet Sonatina (1936); Symph. (1939); Sinfonietta (1940); Concerto for Strings (1942); a ballet, *Zaczarowana oberza (The Enchanted Inn;* 1943–46; Warsaw, Feb. 7, 1962); Oboe Sonatina (1946); *Tryptyk* for Orch. (1950); Concertino for Flute and String Orch. (1951); Suite for Orch. (1952); Wind Quintet (1954); Violin Concerto (1949–54); Partita for String Orch. (1954); Divertimento for Oboe, Clarinet, and Bassoon (1955); *La Danse* for Orch. (1957); a television ballet, *La Femme têtue (The Obstinate Woman;* Paris, 1958); *Moto perpetuo* for Orch. (1958); Concerto for Oboe, Clarinet, Bassoon, and Orch. (1958); *The Resurrection of Lazarus,* symph. poem (1960); *Intermezzo* for Orch. (1961); *Allegretto* for Bassoon and Orch. (1962); *Berceuse pour Clemantine* for Orch. (1964); *2 Pieces* for Ondes Martenot (1967); *Music* for Strings (1970); numerous piano pieces and songs; *6 Sketches* for Orch. (1972).

Szántó, Theodor, Hungarian pianist and composer; b. Vienna, June 3, 1877; d. Budapest, Jan. 7, 1934. He studied with Dachs (piano) and Fuchs (composition) at the Vienna Cons., and later with Busoni in Berlin (1898–1901). In 1905 he settled in Paris; from

1914 to 1921 lived in Switzerland; then divided his time between Paris and Budapest. His opera on a Japanese story, *Typhoon,* was produced in Mannheim on Nov. 29, 1924, and there were a few subsequent performances in other cities. He also wrote a *Japanese Suite* for Orch. (1926); several symph. works based on Hungarian folk songs; chamber music; many piano pieces (of which *Variations on a Hungarian Folksong* became fairly well known).

Sze, Yi-Kwei, Chinese bass-baritone; b. Shanghai, June 1, 1919. He received his musical training at the Cons. in Shanghai; then emigrated to the U.S., where he studied with Alexander Kipnis. He toured widely in Europe, South America, and Asia.

Székely, Endre, Hungarian composer; b. Budapest, April 6, 1912. He studied with Siklós at the Budapest Academy of Music (1933–37). After the war, in 1945, he became active as a conductor of workers' choral groups; edited the periodicals *Éneklö munkás (The Singing Worker)* and *Éneklö nép (The People Sing).* In 1960 he was appointed to the faculty of the Budapest Training College for Teachers.
WORKS: Opera, *Vizirózsa* (*Water Rose;* 1959; Budapest Radio, 1962); operetta, *Aranycsillag* (*The Golden Star;* Budapest, 1951); *Meditations* for Tenor and Orch. (1961–62); *Maqamat* for Soprano and Chamber Ensemble (1970); 3 suites: No. 1 for Small Orch. (1947); No. 2 for String Orch. (1961); No. 3 for Full Orch. (1965); Symph. (1956); *Rhapsody* for Violin and Orch. (1956); *Partita* for Strings (1957); Concerto for Piano, Percussion, and Strings (1958); *Sinfonia concertante* for Violin, Piano, and Chamber Orch. (1960–61); Concerto for 8 Solo Instruments and Orch. (1964); *Partita* for Orch. (1965); *Fantasma* for Orch. (1969); Trumpet Concerto (1971); *Riflessioni,* concerto for Cello and Orch. (1973); *Humanisation* for Chamber Ensemble and Tape (1974); String Trio (1943); 3 wind quintets (1952, 1961, 1966); 4 string quartets (1953, 1958, 1962, 1972); *Rhapsody* for Viola and Piano (1956); 2 wind trios (1958, 1959); *Capriccio* for Flute and Piano (1961); *Chamber Music for 8* (1963); *Chamber Music for 3* (1965); *Musica notturna* for Piano, Wind Quintet, and String Quintet (1967); *Trio* for Percussion, Piano, and Cello (1968–69); 3 piano sonatas (1952, 1962, 1972); choruses; songs.

Székely, Mihály, Hungarian bass; b. Jászberény, May 8, 1901; d. Budapest, March 22, 1963. He studied in Budapest; made his debut as Fernando in *Il Trovatore* in 1920 at the Budapest Opera, where he established himself as a principal member of the company, remaining on its roster until his death; also made guest appearances throughout Europe. On Jan. 17, 1947, he sang the role of Hunding in *Die Walküre* at his Metropolitan Opera debut in N.Y.; continued on the roster until 1948, and then returned for the 1949–50 season. He subsequently sang in Europe, appearing at the Glyndebourne Festival, the Holland Festival, the Bavarian State Opera in Munich, etc. He was renowned for his Wagnerian roles.

Szelényi, István, Hungarian composer; b. Zólyom, Aug. 8, 1904; d. Budapest, Jan. 31, 1972. He studied at the Budapest Academy of Music with Kodály; toured as a concert pianist (1928–30); was a prof. at the State Music High School in Budapest (1945–49), at the Bartók Cons. (1950–66), and at the Liszt Academy (1966–72). In 1951–56 he edited the periodical *Új Zenei Szemle (New Music Review).*
WORKS: 2 pantomimes: *A tékozló fiú* (*The Prodigal Son;* 1931) and *Babiloni vásár* (*The Fair at Babylon;* 1931); operetta, *Hidavatás* (1936); oratorios: *Virata* (1935); *Spartacus* (1960); *10 Days That Shook the World* (1964); *Pro Pace* (1968); etc.; Symph. No. 1 (1926); Violin Concerto (1930); *Ouverture activiste* (1931); Triple Concerto for Violin, Cello, Piano, and Wind Orch. (1933); *Géptánc—Munkatánc (Machine Dance—Work Dance)* for Orch. (1942); *Az ösök nyomában (In the Footsteps of the Ancestors),* symph. for String Orch. (1946); *Egy gyár szimfóniája (Symphony for a Factory;* 1946–47); *Hommage à Bartók* for Orch. (1947); Violin Concertino (1947–48); *Suite* for String Orch. (1952); *Summa vitae* for Piano and Orch. (1956); *Concerto da camera* for Orch. (1963); *Dance Suite* for String Orch. (1964); Piano Concertino (1964); *Variations concertants* for Piano and Orch. (1965); Piano Concerto (1969); 2 solo violin sonatas (1925, 1934); Flute Sonata (1926); 4 string quartets (1927, 1928, 1929, 1964); 2 piano trios (1934, 1962); Sonata for 4 Violins (1946); 2-violin Sonatina (1963); *Sinfonietta a tre* for 3 Violins (1964); *3 Dialogues* for Violin and Cello (1965); *Chamber Music* for 2 Trumpets, 2 Horns, and 2 Trombones (1966); 7 piano sonatas (1924–69); Piano Sonatina (1960); *Toccata* for Piano (1964); *Musical Picture Book* for Piano (1967); choral works; songs. He also publ. books on music history, on Hungarian music, and on principles of folk-song harmonization.

Szeligowski, Tadeusz, notable Polish composer and pedagogue; b. Lwow, Sept. 12, 1896; d. Poznan, Jan. 10, 1963. He studied composition with Jachimecki in Cracow (1918–23) and with Nadia Boulanger in Paris (1929–31); returning to Poland, he taught classes in Poznan (1932–39, 1947–62) and in Warsaw (1951–62).
WORKS: 3 operas: *Bunt Żaków* (*Rebellion of Clerks;* 1951; Wroclaw, July 14, 1951); *Krakatuk,* after E.T.A. Hoffmann (1955; Gdansk, Dec. 30, 1956); *Theodor gentleman* (1960; Wroclaw, 1963); 2 ballets: *Paw i dziewczyna* (*The Peacock and the Maiden;* 1948; Wroclaw, Aug. 2, 1949) and *Mazeppa* (1957; Warsaw, 1959); *Kaziuki,* suite for Orch. (1928); Concerto for Orch. (1932); Clarinet Concerto (1932); *Epitaph for Karol Szymanowski* for String Orch. (1937); Piano Concerto (1941; Cracow, May 17, 1946); *Suita lubelska* for Small Orch. (1945); *Nocturne* for Orch. (1947); *Burlesque Overture* (1952); *Triptych* for Soprano and Orch. (1946); *Kantata o sporcie* for Voice, Chorus, and Orch. (1947); *Wesele lubelskie (Lublin Wedding),* suite for Soprano, Chorus, and Small Orch. (1948); *Rapsod* for Soprano and Orch. (1949); *Panicz i dziewczyna (The Young Squire and the Country Girl),* musical dialogue for Soprano,

Baritone, Chorus, and Orch. (1949); cantata, *Karta serc* (*The Charter of Hearts;* 1952); *Renegade,* ballad for Bass and Orch. (1953); songs; 2 string quartets (1929, 1934); *Nocturne* for Cello and Piano (1945); *Orientale* for Cello and Piano (1945); Wind Quintet (1950); Flute Sonata (1953); *Air grave et air gai* for English Horn and Piano (1954); Piano Trio (1956); Piano Sonatina (1940); Piano Sonata (1949).

Szell, George, greatly distinguished Hungarian-American conductor; b. Budapest, June 7, 1897; d. Cleveland, July 30, 1970. His family moved to Vienna when he was a small child. He studied piano with Richard Robert and composition with Mandyczewski; also in Prague with J.B. Foerster. He played a Mozart piano concerto with the Vienna Symph. Orch. when he was 10 years old, and the orch. also performed an overture of his composition. At the age of 17 he led the Berlin Phil. in an ambitious program which included a symph. work of his own. In 1915 he was engaged as an assistant conductor at the Royal Opera of Berlin; in 1917 he was conductor of the Strasbourg Municipal Theater. His next appointments as an opera conductor were in Prague (1919), Düsseldorf (1922–24), and the State Opera House in Berlin (1924–29). From 1929 to 1937 he filled conducting engagements in Prague and Vienna. He made his U.S. debut as guest conductor of the St. Louis Symph. Orch. in 1930. In 1937 he was appointed conductor of the Scottish Orch. in Glasgow; he was also a regular conductor with the Residentie Orkest in The Hague (1937–39). He then conducted in Australia. At the outbreak of war in Europe in 1939 he was in America, which was to become his adoptive country. His American conducting engagements included appearances with the Los Angeles Phil., NBC Symph. Orch., Chicago Symph., Detroit Symph., and Boston Symph. In 1942 he was appointed conductor of the Metropolitan Opera House in N.Y., where he received the highest praise for his interpretation of Wagner's music dramas; remained on its roster until 1946. He also conducted performances with the N.Y. Phil. in 1944–45. In 1946 he was appointed conductor of the Cleveland Orch., a post which he held for 24 years; he was also music adviser and senior guest conductor of the N.Y. Phil. from 1969 until his death. He was a stern disciplinarian, demanding the utmost exertions from his musicians to achieve tonal perfection, but he was also willing to labor tirelessly at his task. Under his guidance, the Cleveland Orch. rose to the heights of symphonic excellence, taking its place in the foremost rank of American orchs.
BIBLIOGRAPHY: R. Marsh, *The Cleveland Orchestra* (Cleveland and N.Y., 1967); H. Schonberg, *The Great Conductors* (N.Y., 1967; pp. 337–39).

Szeluto, Apolinary, fecund Russian-Polish composer; b. St. Petersburg, July 23, 1884; d. Chodziez, Aug. 22, 1966. He studied with Noskowski at the Warsaw Cons. and with Godowsky in Berlin. In association with Szymanowski, Fitelberg, and Rözycki he formed a progressive musical group, Young Poland. He also studied law at Dorpat (Tar-

tu) Univ.; then went to Ufa, where he worked as a lawyer. He wrote a number of symphs. in piano score; only 10 were orchestrated. His music is ultra-Romantic in its essence; most of his works bear descriptive titles. Several of them are inspired by contemporary political and military events.
WORKS: 28 symphs., of which 18 exist without complete orchestration: No. 1, *Academic* (1920); No. 2, *Spontaneous* (1938); No. 3, *Impressionistic* (1942); No. 4, *Romantic* (1942); No. 5, *Majestic Room* (1942); No. 6, *Birth of Stalingrad* (1943); No. 7, *Revolutionary* (1943); No. 8, *Resurrection* (1942); No. 9, *Elegiac* (1943); No. 10, *Oriental* (1944); No. 11, *Iberian* (1944); No. 12, *Nordic* (1944); No. 13, *Samurai* (1943–46); No. 14, *Neapolitan* (1943); No. 15, *Los Angeles American* (1944); No. 16, *Fate* (1946); No. 17, *Kujawska Region* (1946); No. 18, *Litewska;* No. 19, *Slaska;* No. 20, *Kupiowska;* No. 21, *Podhalanska;* No. 22, *To the Building of a Communist People's Union;* Nos. 23–28 without titles; 5 piano concertos (1937, 1939, 1940, 1943, 1948); Violin Concerto (1942–48); Cello Concerto (1942); some 32 other orch. works; 9 ballets; 14 chamber music pieces; 18 choral works; an utterly unbelievable number (purportedly 78) of operas; conservatively counting, 205 piano pieces and maybe 165 songs.
BIBLIOGRAPHY: J. Kanski, "Apolinary Szeluto: 1884–1966," *Ruch muzyczny* (1967); Janusz Dobrowoski, "Katalog utworow fortepianowych Apolinarego Szeluty," *Muzyka* (1973).

Szendrei, Aladár (in the U.S. he changed his name to **Alfred Sendrey**), Hungarian-American conductor and composer; b. Budapest, Feb. 29, 1884; d. Los Angeles, March 3, 1976. He studied with Hans Koessler at the Budapest Academy of Music (1901–5); after serving as a theater conductor in Germany, he went to the U.S., where he conducted opera in Chicago (1911–12) and N.Y. (1913–14). He returned to Europe in 1914; served in the Austrian army during World War I; after the Armistice, conducted opera in Leipzig (1918–24) and also symph. concerts there (1924–32). In 1933 he left Germany and went to Paris, where he conducted at Radiodiffusion Française; he also taught conducting; Charles Munch took private lessons in conducting with him in Paris (1933–40); after the fall of Paris Szendrei emigrated to the U.S. and settled in Los Angeles. He was prof. of Jewish music at the Univ. of Judaism in Los Angeles (1962–73).
WORKS: One-act opera, *Der türkisenblaue Garten* (Leipzig, Feb. 7, 1920); ballet, *Danse d'odalisque; Hungarian Overture* for Orch. (1904); Symph. in B-flat major (1923); Piano Quintet (1925); *Stabat Mater* for 8 Solo Voices and a cappella Chorus (1905).
WRITINGS: *Rundfunk und Musikpflege* (Leipzig, 1931); *Dirigierkunde* (Leipzig, 1932; 2nd ed., 1952); *Bibliography of Jewish Music* (N.Y., 1951); and in Eng., under the naturalized American name Sendrey, *David's Harp: A Popular History of the Music in Biblical Times* (N.Y., 1964); *Music in Ancient Israel* (1969); *The Music of the Jews in the Diaspora* (1969); *Music in the Social and Religious*

Life of Antiquity (1974).

Szendy, Arpád, Hungarian pianist and composer; b. Szarvas, Aug. 11, 1863; d. Budapest, Sept. 10, 1922. He studied at the Budapest Cons. and at the Academy of Music there; then became a student of Liszt (1881). In 1890 he was appointed to the faculty of the Academy of Music; enjoyed great esteem in Hungary as a piano teacher. He publ. numerous editions of piano classics; wrote an opera, *Mária* (with Béla Szabados; Budapest, Feb. 28, 1905); a String Quartet; much piano music; songs.

Szenkar, Eugen, Hungarian conductor; b. Budapest, April 9, 1891; d. Düsseldorf, March 28, 1977. He studied music with his father, a prominent organist; later attended classes at the Academy of Music in Budapest. He began his career as an assistant choral conductor at the Budapest Opera; then was successively conductor at the German Opera in Prague (1911–13), the Popular Opera in Budapest (1913–15), the Mozarteum at Salzburg (1915–16), Altenburg (1916–20), the Frankfurt Opera (1920–23), the Volksoper in Berlin (1923–24), and the Cologne Opera (1924–33). With the advent of the Nazi regime, as a Jew he was forced to interrupt his activities, and went to Moscow, where he remained from 1933 to 1937. In 1939 he went to Brazil and was conductor of the Brazilian Symph. Orch. in Rio de Janeiro; in 1941, in response to Brazilian social and governmental conventions, he accepted Brazilian citizenship. In 1950 he went back to Germany; from 1952 to 1960 was music director of the Düsseldorf Opera and of the Düsseldorf Symph. Orch.; also filled in guest engagements in Germany.

Szervánszky, Endre, Hungarian composer; b. Kistétény, Dec. 27, 1911; d. Budapest, June 25, 1977. Of a musical family, he learned to play the clarinet as a child; studied composition with Siklós and clarinet with F. Förster at the Liszt Academy of Music in Budapest (1923–28, 1931–36); taught at the National Cons. (1942–48), and after 1948 at the Liszt Academy. His music follows the modern Hungarian school of composition of Kodály and Bartók; he was the recipient of the Kossuth Prize in 1951 and 1955 and of the Erkel Prize in 1953 and 1954; in 1972 was awarded the title Merited Artist of the Hungarian People's Republic.

WORKS: *Napkeleti mese (Oriental Tale),* dance play (1948–49); cantatas: *Három körösztény játék* (*3 Christian Plays;* 1940); *Honvéd cantata* (*Home Guard Cantata;* 1949); *Tavasi szél* (*Spring Breeze;* 1950); a Requiem, *Sötét mennyország* (*Dark Heaven;* 1963); *Divertimento I* for Strings (1939), *II* for Small Orch. (1942), and *III* for Strings (1942–43); 2 suites for Orch. (1944–45, 1946); Symph. No. 1 (1946–48); *Serenade* for Strings (1947–48); *Rhapsody* for Orch. (1950); *Serenade* for Clarinet and Orch. (1950–51); Flute Concerto (1953); *Variations* for Orch. (1964); Clarinet Concerto (1965); 2 string quartets (1936–37, 1956–57); *20 Little Duets* for 2 Violins (1942); Violin Sonata (1945); *25 Duos* for 2 Violins (1946); Clarinet Quintet (1948); Trio for Oboe, Clarinet, and Bassoon (1950); Trio for Flute, Violin, and Viola (1951); Flute Sonatina (1951); 2 wind quintets (1953, 1957); *5 Concert Etudes* for Solo Flute (1956); *Suite* for 2 Flutes (1956); *2 Duos* for 2 Flutes (1972); Piano Sonatina (1940); Sonatina for Piano Duet (1950); songs; choruses; incidental music to films and plays.

Szeryng, Henryk, celebrated violinist and pedagogue of Polish birth; b. Zelazowa Wola, Sept. 22, 1918. He was the son of a wealthy Jewish industrialist. He learned to play piano from his mother; then turned to the violin, and had lessons with Maurice Frenkel, a teacher at the St. Petersburg Cons., who inculcated in Szeryng the Russian tradition of violin playing. In 1929 he went to Berlin, where he studied with Carl Flesch; in 1932 he moved to Paris, and studied with Jacques Thibaud and Gabriel Bouillon at the Paris Cons., graduating in 1937; he also took private lessons in composition with Nadia Boulanger. On Jan. 6, 1933, he made his debut in the Brahms Concerto with the Warsaw Phil. At the outbreak of war in 1939 he went to London and served as official translator for the Polish government-in-exile in England. In 1942 he settled in Mexico, becoming a Mexican citizen in 1946. He continued his concert career, traveling around the globe. In 1983 he made a grand tour of Europe and America to mark the 50th anniversary of his career.

Szidon, Roberto, Brazilian pianist; b. Porto Alegre, Sept. 21, 1941. He gave a concert in his native city at the age of 9; later studied in N.Y. with Claudio Arrau; then toured in the U.S., South America, and Europe as soloist with the leading orchs. and in recitals.

Szigeti, Joseph, great Hungarian violinist; b. Budapest, Sept. 5, 1892; d. Lucerne, Feb. 19, 1973. He studied violin with Hubay in Budapest; from 1906 to 1913 he lived in England; from 1917 to 1925 he gave master courses in violin at the Geneva Cons.; subsequently devoted himself mainly to concert appearances. In 1940 he went to the U.S., becoming an American citizen in 1951; eventually returned to Europe. Szigeti was particularly noted as an intellectual violinist; he may have lacked flashy virtuosity, but he was greatly admired by musicians. He was a champion of 20th-century music; played works of Stravinsky, Prokofiev, Béla Bartók, and Ernest Bloch. He publ. several semi-autobiographical books: *With Strings Attached* (N.Y., 1947); *A Violinist's Notebook* (London, 1965); *Szigeti on the Violin: Improvisations on a Violinist's Themes* (N.Y., 1969). He also annotated new editions of Beethoven's Violin Concerto and the Violin Concerto of Brahms.

BIBLIOGRAPHY: R. Gelatt, *Music Makers* (N.Y., 1953; pp. 135–48); Y.L. Soroker, *Joseph Szigeti* (Moscow, 1968).

Szokolay, Sándor, Hungarian composer; b. Kunágota, March 30, 1931. He studied at the Budapest Academy of Music with Szabó and Farkas (1950–57);

worked in the music dept. of Hungarian Radio (1957–61); in 1966 was appointed to the faculty of the Budapest Academy of Music. He was awarded the Erkel Prize in 1960 and 1965 and the Kossuth Prize in 1966.

WORKS: 3 operas: *Vérnász,* after García Lorca (*Blood Wedding;* 1962–64; Budapest, Oct. 30, 1964); *Hamlet,* after Shakespeare (1966–68; Budapest, Oct. 19, 1968); *Sámson* (1973; Budapest, Oct. 23, 1973); 3 ballets: *Orbán és az ördög* (*Urban and the Devil;* 1958); *Az iszonyat balladája* (*The Ballad of Horror;* 1960); *Tetemrehivás* (*Ordeal of the Bier;* 1961–62; Pécs, 1962); oratorios: *A tüz marciusa* (*The Fire of March;* 1958) and *Isthar's Descent to Hell* (1960); *Cantata nigra* (*Negro Cantata;* 1962); *Déploration,* Requiem in memory of Poulenc (1964); *A zene hatalma* (*The Power of Music),* choral fantasy, with Orch. (1969); *Musza Dag,* oratorical incidental music for Chorus and Orch. (1969); *Concert Rondo* for Piano and String Orch. (1955); Violin Concerto (1956); Piano Concerto (1958); Trumpet Concerto (1969); Sonata for Solo Violin (1956); String Quartet (1973); Piano Sonatina (1955); songs.

Szöllösy, András, Hungarian composer; b. Szászváros, Transylvania, Feb. 27, 1921. He studied with Kodály and Viski at the Budapest Academy of Music (1939–44); then took a course in composition with Goffredo Petrassi at the Santa Cecilia Academy in Rome (1947–48). In 1950 he was appointed to the faculty of his alma mater. His music draws upon all modern resources, often building up massive sound blocks.

WORKS: 2 ballets: *Oly korban éltem* (*Improvisations on the Fear;* 1963) and *Pantomime* (1965); *Nyugtalan ösz* (*Restless Autumn),* cantata for Baritone and Piano (1955); *Kolzsvári éjjel* (*Night at Kolozsvár),* elegy for Voice and Wind Quintet (1955); Concerto for Strings, Brass, Piano, and Percussion (1957); *3 pezzi* for Flute and Piano (1964); Concerto for 16 Strings (1968); Concerto for Chamber Orch. (1970); *Transfigurazioni* for Orch. (1972; Budapest, June 1, 1973); *Musica per Orchestra* (1972; Vienna, Sept. 26, 1973); *Musica concertante* for Small Orch. (1972–73); *Preludio, Adagio e Fuga* for Orch. (1973); songs; choruses. He publ. books and collections: *Kodály's Art* (1943); *Selected Musical Writings of Béla Bartók* (1948); *Arthur Honegger* (1960); *Collected Writings of Bartók,* I (1967).

Szönyi, Erzsébet (Elisabeth), Hungarian composer; b. Budapest, April 25, 1924. She studied piano and composition at the Budapest Academy of Music, graduating in 1947; then went to Paris, where she took courses at the Paris Cons. with Tony Aubin and Messiaen; also took private lessons in composition with Nadia Boulanger. Returning to Budapest, she joined the faculty of the Academy of Music in 1948. In 1959 she was awarded the Erkel Prize.

WORKS: 3 operas: *Dalma* (1952); a children's opera, *The Stubborn Princess* (1955); *Florentine Tragedy,* after Oscar Wilde (1957); 2 musical comedies: *The Hypochondriac* (1961) and *The Small Ragged One* (1962); 2 divertimentos for Orch. (1948,

1951); Organ Concerto (1958); *Musica festiva* for Orch. (1964); 2 piano sonatinas (1944, 1946); Piano Sonata (1953); choral works. She publ. *Methods of Musical Reading and Writing I, II & III* (Budapest, 1953; Eng. ed., 1972) and *Kodály's Principles in Practice* (Budapest, 1973).

Szulc, Jósef Zygmunt, Polish operetta composer; b. Warsaw, April 4, 1875; d. Paris, April 10, 1956. He studied at the Warsaw Cons. with Noskowski; then took piano lessons in Paris with Moszkowski. He remained in Paris as a piano teacher; then turned to composition of light operas. His first work in this genre, *Flup* (Brussels, Dec. 19, 1913), was surprisingly successful and had numerous performances in Europe; he continued to produce operettas at regular intervals; the last one was *Pantoufle* (Paris, Feb. 24, 1945). He also wrote a ballet, *Une Nuit d'Ispahan* (Brussels, Nov. 19, 1909).

Szumowska, Antoinette, Polish pianist and teacher; b. Lublin, Feb. 22, 1868; d. Rumson, N.J., Aug. 18, 1938. She studied at the Warsaw Cons. with Michalowski, and later took lessons with Paderewski in Paris (1890–95). In 1895 she emigrated to the U.S., settling in Boston, where she taught at the New England Cons. for many years. In 1896 she married the cellist **Josef Adamowski,** and with him and his brother Timothée, a violinist, formed the Adamowski Trio, which presented numerous concerts in New England.

Szymanowska, Maria (née **Wolowska**), Polish pianist and composer; b. Warsaw, Dec. 14, 1789; d. St. Petersburg, July 24, 1831. She studied piano with local teachers in Warsaw, and began to play in public as a child. In 1810 she married a Polish landowner, Theophilus Joseph Szymanowski (divorced, 1820). In 1822 she toured in Russia, and was appointed court pianist; in 1823, played in Germany; in 1824, in France; then in England, the Netherlands, and Italy (1824–25), returning to Warsaw in 1826. In 1828 she settled in St. Petersburg as a pianist and teacher, and remained there until her death (of cholera). She was admired by Goethe, whom she met in Germany; his poem *Aussöhnung (Trilogie der Leidenschaft)* alludes to her (cf. Goethe's correspondence with Zelter). She publ. 24 mazurkas and several character pieces for piano, of which *Le Murmure* became popular. Her piano studies were commended by Schumann.

BIBLIOGRAPHY: I. Boelza, *Maria Szymanowska* (Moscow, 1956).

Szymanowski, Karol, eminent Polish composer; b. Timoshovka, Ukraine, Oct. 6, 1882; d. Lausanne, March 28, 1937. The son of a cultured landowner, he grew up in a musical environment. He began to play the piano and compose very early in life. His first teacher was Gustav Neuhaus in Elizavetgrad; in 1901 he went to Warsaw, where he studied with Noskowski. His first work, *9 Preludes* for Piano, op. 1, was publ. in 1906 in Berlin by the Assoc. of Young Polish Composers (later known as Young Poland in

Szymanowski

Music). Szymanowski lived in Berlin from 1906 to 1908, writing symph. and other music, much influenced by Richard Strauss. He returned to Warsaw in 1909, and his First Symph. was performed there on March 26, 1909; however, he was dissatisfied with the score, and withdrew it from further performance. In 1911 he completed his 2nd Symph., which demonstrated a stylistic change from German dominance to Russian influences, paralleling the harmonic evolution of Scriabin; it was played for the first time in Warsaw, on April 7, 1911. From 1912 to 1914 Szymanowski lived in Vienna, where he wrote his one-act opera, *Hagith;* the years of World War I (1914–18) he spent in Timoshovka, where he wrote his 3rd Symph.; he appeared in concert with the violinist Paul Kochanski in Moscow and St. Petersburg, giving first performances of his violin works; it was for Kochanski that he composed his violin triptych, *Mythes* (*La Fontaine d'Aréthuse* in this cycle is one of his best-known compositions). About this time, his music underwent a new change in style, veering toward French Impressionism. During the Russian Revolution of 1917 the family estate at Timoshovka was ruined, and Szymanowski lost most of his possessions. From 1917 to 1919 he lived in Elizavetgrad, where he continued to compose industriously, despite the turmoil of the Civil War. Early in 1920 he settled in Warsaw; he traveled to other Polish cities, and soon established his reputation as the most important modern composer of Poland.

His international renown also was considerable; his works were often performed in Europe, and figured at festivals of the International Society for Contemporary Music. He visited Paris, London, and N.Y. (1921). He was director of the Warsaw Cons. (1927–29) and reorganized the system of teaching along more liberal lines; was rector there in 1930–31. His *Stabat Mater* (1926) produced a profound impression, and his ballet *Harnasie* (1923–31), based on the life and music of the Tatra mountain dwellers, demonstrated his ability to treat national subjects in an original and highly effective manner. In 1932 he appeared as soloist in the first performance of his 4th Symph., *Symphonie concertante* for Piano and Orch., at Poznan, and repeated his performances in Paris, London, and Brussels. In April 1936, greatly weakened in health by chronic tuberculosis, he attended a performance of his ballet *Harnasie* at the Paris Opéra. Through successive influences, Szymanowski developed into a national composer whose music acquired universal significance. Of particular interest is his treatment of the mazurka; though he was a lifelong admirer of Chopin, he found a way to treat this dance form in an original manner.

WORKS: FOR THE STAGE: Operetta, *Loteria na mężów* (*Lottery for a Husband;* 1909; unfinished); 2 full operas: *Hagith* (1912–13; Warsaw, May 13, 1922) and *Król Roger* (*King Roger;* 1918–24; Warsaw, June 19, 1926); a "grotesque ballet," *Mandragora* (Warsaw, June 15, 1920); ballet-pantomime, *Harnasie* (1923–31; Prague, May 11, 1935); incidental music for *Kniaź Patiomkin* (*Prince Potemkin;* Warsaw, March 6, 1925).

FOR ORCH.: *Concert Overture* (1904–5; Warsaw, Feb. 6, 1906; revised 1913); 4 symphs.: No. 1 (1906–7; Warsaw, March 26, 1909); No. 2 (1909–10; Warsaw, April 7, 1911; revised 1934; further revision was made by Stanislaw Skrowaczewski, who conducted this version with the Minnesota Orch. on Oct. 14, 1967); No. 3, *Pieśń o nocy* (*Song of the Night*), for Tenor, Chorus, and Orch. (1914–16; London, Nov. 26, 1921, without Tenor or Chorus); No. 4, *Symphonie concertante,* for Piano and Orch. (1932; Poznan, Oct. 9, 1932, composer soloist); 2 violin concertos: No. 1 (1915–16; Warsaw, Nov. 1, 1922) and No. 2 (1932–33; Warsaw, Oct. 6, 1933).

FOR VOICE: *Salome* for Soprano and Orch. (1906); *Penthesilea* for Soprano and Orch. (1908); *8 Love Songs of Hafiz,* cycle 1 for Voice and Piano (1911) and cycle 2 for Voice and Orch. (1914); *Demeter* for Alto, Women's Chorus, and Orch. (1917; revised 1924); *Agave* for Alto, Female Chorus, and Orch. (1917); *Stabat Mater* for 3 Solo Voices, Chorus, and Orch. (1926; Warsaw, Jan. 11, 1929); *Veni Creator* for Soprano, Chorus, and Orch. (1929); *Litany of the Virgin Mary,* 2 fragments to J. Liebert's text, for Soprano, Female Chorus, and Orch. (1930–33); *6 Kurpian Songs* for Mixed Chorus a cappella (1928–29); about 100 songs.

CHAMBER MUSIC: 2 string quartets: No. 1, in 3 movements (1917; a projected fugal final movement never materialized), and No. 2, in 3 movements (1927); Piano Trio (1907; discarded); Violin Sonata (1904); *Romance* for Violin and Piano (1909); *Notturno e tarantella* for Violin and Piano (1914; orchestrated by G. Fitelberg); *Mythes,* 3 poems for Violin and Piano: *La Fontaine d'Aréthuse, Narcisse,* and *Dryades et Pan* (1915); *La Berceuse d'Aitacho Enia* for Violin and Piano (1925).

FOR PIANO: 3 sonatas (1904, 1910, 1917); *9 Preludes* (1900); *Variations in B-flat minor* (1901–3); *4 Etudes* (1900–2); *Variations on a Polish Theme* (1900–4); *Fantasy* (1905); *Prelude and Fugue* (1905); *Métopes,* 3 poems: *L'Ile des sirènes, Calypso,* and *Nausicaa* (1915); *12 Etudes* (1917); *Masques,* 3 poems: *Shéhérazade, Tantris le bouffon,* and *Sérénade de Don Juan* (1917); *Valse romantique* (1925; regarded as lost but discovered in 1967); *4 Polish Dances* (1926); *20 Mazurkas* (1924–26); *2 Mazurkas* (1933–34).

A complete edition of Szymanowski's works, in 26 vols., was begun in Cracow in 1965.

BIBLIOGRAPHY: Z. Jachimecki, "Karol Szymanowski," *Musical Quarterly* (Jan. 1922); A. Tansman, "Karol Szymanowski," *Revue Musicale* (May 1922); G. Pannain in *Modern Composers* (trans. from the Italian, N.Y., 1932); Z. Jachimecki, "Karol Szymanowski," *Slavonic and East European Review* (July 1938); Szymanowski issue of *Muzyka Polska* (Warsaw, 1937); S. Lobaczewska, *Karol Szymanowski* (Cracow, 1950; exhaustive biography and musical analysis); S. Golachowski, *Karol Szymanowski* (Cracow, 1956; T. Chylińska, *Szymanowski* (Cracow, 1962; 3rd ed., 1973; Eng. trans., 1973); J.M. Chomiński, *Studia nad twórczościa Karola Szymanowskiego* (Cracow, 1969); A. Wightman, *The Music of Karol Szymanowski* (Diss., Univ. of York, 1972); J. Samson, *The Music of*

Szymanowski (London, 1980); A. Wightman, "Szymanowski and Joyce," *Musical Times* (Oct. 1982); T. Chylińska edited Szymanowski's correspondence (vol. 1; Warsaw, 1982).

T

Tabachnik, Michel, Swiss conductor and composer of Russian extraction; b. Geneva, Nov. 10, 1942. He studied at the Geneva Cons.; attended the courses in modern music given by Boulez, Pousseur, and Stockhausen at the Darmstadt summer series. In 1973–75 he was principal conductor for the Gulbenkian Foundation in Lisbon; became principal conductor of the Lorraine Phil. Orch. in Nancy in 1975; also conducted guest engagements in Europe. He composed *Mondes* for Orch. (1972); *Movimenti,* electronic score (1973); *Les Imaginaires* for Orch. (1974).

Tabourot, Jehan. See **Arbeau, Thoinot.**

Tabuteau, Marcel, outstanding French oboist and pedagogue; b. Compiègne, July 2, 1887; d. Nice, Jan. 4, 1966. He studied oboe with Georges Gillet at the Paris Cons.; won a premier prix at the age of 17; in 1905 he went to the U.S., where he played in the N.Y. Symph. Orch.; also was a member of the orch. of the Metropolitan Opera. In 1915 Stokowski engaged him in the Philadelphia Orch., where he remained until 1954; he was also on the faculty of the Curtis Inst. of Music in Philadelphia.

Tacchinardi, Nicola, Italian tenor; b. Livorno, Sept. 3, 1772; d. Florence, March 14, 1859. After singing on Italian stages (La Scala, Milan, 1805), he was engaged at the Théâtre des Italiens in Paris (1811–14), with Crivelli; in 1822–31, was "primo cantante" in the Grand Ducal chapel at Florence, also appearing repeatedly on the stage; then lived in Florence as a teacher, one of his pupils being his daughter, **Fanny Tacchinardi-Persiani.** He publ. vocalises and exercises; also *Dell'opera in musica sul teatro italiano e de' suoi difetti.* His son, **Guido Tacchinardi** (b. Florence, March 10, 1840; d. there, Dec. 6, 1917), was a composer and theorist; from 1891 was director of the Istituto Musicale at Florence.

Tacchino, Gabriel, French pianist; b. Cannes, Aug. 4, 1934. He studied at the Paris Cons. and made his concert debut in 1953. After winning first prizes in competitions held in Vercelli (1953), Geneva (1955), and Naples (1956), he launched an international career; he particularly distinguished himself in refined interpretations of the Classical and Romantic repertoire.

Tachezi, Herbert, Austrian organist and harpsichordist; b. Wiener Neustadt, Feb. 12, 1930. He studied organ with Alois Forer, composition with Alfred Uhl, and musicology with Otto Siegl at the Vienna

Academy of Music; also attended the Univ. of Vienna. In 1958 he joined the faculty of the Vienna Academy of Music, where he taught organ and composition; in 1972 he was made a prof. there (it became the Hochschule für Musik in 1970). He appeared regularly as an organist and harpsichordist with the Concentus Musicus in Vienna; was named organist of Vienna's Hofmusikkapelle in 1974.

Taddei, Giuseppe, Italian baritone; b. Genoa, June 26, 1916. He received his musical training in Genoa and Rome; made his debut in Rome in 1936; then sang with many of the leading Italian opera houses; became a regular member of La Scala in Milan. In 1951 he appeared with the Metropolitan Opera in N.Y. He was renowned for both his lyrico-dramatic and buffo parts; among his best roles were Figaro in *The Barber of Seville,* Papageno in *Die Zauberflöte,* and Rigoletto.

Tadolini, Giovanni, Italian composer; b. Bologna, 1785; d. there, Nov. 29, 1872. He studied composition with Mattei and singing with Babini; from 1811 to 1814 he was on the staff of the Théâtre des Italiens in Paris; then went to Italy, where he produced a succession of operas: *Le Bestie in uomini* (Venice, 1815); *La Principessa di Navarra* (Bologna, 1816); *Il Credulo deluso* (Rome, 1817); *Tamerlano* (Bologna, 1818); *Moctar* (Milan, 1824); *Mitridate* (Venice, 1826); *Almansor* (Trieste, 1827); from 1829 to 1839 he was again at his post at the Théâtre des Italiens. He also wrote many canzonets and romances; one of them, *Eco di Scozia,* was popular in his time.

Taffanel, (Claude-) Paul, French flutist and conductor; b. Bordeaux, Sept. 16, 1844; d. Paris, Nov. 22, 1908. He was a pupil of Dorus (flute) and Reber (composition). From 1864 to 1890 he was a flutist in the Paris Opéra orch.; in 1867–90, flutist of the Cons. concerts, which he conducted from 1890 to 1903; from 1892 till his death he was one of the "chefs d'orchestre" at the Opéra; in 1893 he succeeded Altès as prof. of flute playing at the Cons. In 1879 he founded the Société des Quintettes pour Instruments à Vent. With Gaubert he wrote *Méthode complète de flûte.*

Tag, Christian Gotthilf, German composer; b. Bayerfeld, Saxony, April 2, 1735; d. Niederzwonitz, near Zwickau, June 19, 1811. From 1749 to 1755 he studied at the Kreuzschule in Dresden; in 1755–1808 was cantor at Hohenstein.
WORKS: 6 chorale preludes (1783); 12 preludes and a Symph. for Organ (1795); songs (1783, 1785, 1793, 1798); 70 variations for Piano on an Andantino (1785); *Der Glaube,* melody with Organ (1793); *Urians Reise um die Welt* and *Urians Nachricht von der Aufklärung* (1797); *Naumann, ein Todtenopfer* (1803; Voice with Piano); *Melodie zum Vaterunser und den Einsetzungsworten* (1803; with Organ); *Wörlitz,* an ode (1803; Voice with Piano); many sacred and instrumental works are in MS.
BIBLIOGRAPHY: J.F. Rochlitz, *Für Freunde der Tonkunst,* vol. III (1830); H.J. Vieweg, *Christian Gotthilf Tag* (Leipzig, 1933).

Tagliabue, Carlo, Italian baritone; b. Mariano Comense, Jan. 12, 1898; d. Monza, April 6, 1978. He studied with Gennai and Guidotti; then made his debut as Amonasro in 1922 in Lodi. After singing in Italian provincial opera houses, he joined La Scala in Milan in 1930; continued to appear there regularly for 25 years; also sang in Florence and Rome, at the Teatro Colón in Buenos Aires, and at Covent Garden in London (1938, 1946). On Dec. 2, 1937, he made his Metropolitan Opera debut in N.Y. as Amonasro; continued on its roster until 1939. He retired in 1958. He was a distinguished interpreter of the baritone roles in Verdi's operas; also had a fine reputation in Italy as a Wagnerian singer.

Tagliaferro, Magda, Brazilian pianist; b. Petropolis, Jan. 19, 1893. She studied at the Paris Cons., and privately with Cortot. She began her concert career in 1908, and continued her appearances for 70 years, without showing signs of lassitude; she made numerous appearances in solo recitals in the U.S., the last one in 1980 at the age of 87. From 1937 she was on the faculty of the Paris Cons.

Tagliafico, (Dieudonné) Joseph, French bassbaritone; b. Toulon, Jan. 1, 1821; d. Nice, Jan. 27, 1900. He studied with Piermarini and Lablache in Paris; made his debut there in 1844; in 1847 he joined the new Royal Italian Opera company at Covent Garden in London, remaining on its roster until 1876; then was its stage manager until 1882. He appeared as a guest artist in France, Russia, and the U.S. He was best known for his French and Italian roles.

Tagliapietra, Gino, Italian pianist and composer; b. (of Italian parentage) Ljubljana, May 30, 1887; d. Venice, Aug. 8, 1954. He studied piano with Julius Epstein in Vienna and with Busoni in Berlin; in 1906 was appointed to the faculty of the Liceo Benedetto Marcello in Venice; retired in 1940. His compositions include a ballet, *La Bella dormente nel bosco* (Venice, March 11, 1926); Piano Concerto; numerous studies for piano. He edited for Ricordi an important anthology of keyboard music from Willaert to modern times, *Antologia di musica antica e moderna* (18 vols., 1931–32; containing 519 works by 157 composers).
BIBLIOGRAPHY: F. Vadalá, *Gino Tagliapietra* (Diss., Univ. of Messina, 1976).

Tagliapietra, Giovanni, Italian baritone; b. Venice, Dec. 24, 1846; d. New York, April 11, 1921. He studied naval architecture and graduated from the Univ. of Padua. After a study of singing with Giovanni Corsi, he appeared in various Italian opera houses; made a tour of South America; in 1874 was engaged as member of Max Strakosch's company and sang in the U.S. In 1876 he married the famous pianist **Teresa Carreño,** but they were divorced; his brother Arturo was married to her in 1902.

Tagliavini, Ferruccio, prominent Italian tenor; b. Reggio Emilia, Aug. 14, 1913. After studying at the Cons. of Parma, he won first prize for singing at the May Festival in Florence (1938); made his opera debut there as Rodolfo in *La Bohème* (Oct. 1938); later sang at La Scala, Milan, and other opera houses in Italy; in 1946 toured South America; on Jan. 10, 1947, made a very successful first appearance, as Rodolfo, at the Metropolitan Opera, N.Y.; remained on its roster until 1954; again in 1961–62; has also given recitals in the major American cities; subsequently traveled widely in both hemispheres. In 1941 he married the soprano **Pia Tassinari.**

BIBLIOGRAPHY: C. Tedeschi, *Ferruccio Tagliavini* (Rome, 1942).

Tagliavini, Luigi, Italian organist, harpsichordist, and musicologist; b. Bologna, Oct. 7, 1929. He studied organ at the Bologna Cons. and with Marcel Dupré at the Paris Cons.; then entered the Univ. of Padua, receiving his Ph.D. there in 1951 with the dissertation *Studi sui testi delle cantate sacre J.S. Bach* (publ. in Padua, 1956); he then taught organ at the Bologna Cons. (1952–54); also was its librarian (1953 –60); concurrently he served as a prof. of organ at the Monteverdi Cons. in Bolzano (1954–64); from 1964 he was on the faculty of the Cons. of Parma. In 1959 he joined the staff of the Univ. of Bologna; from 1965 he taught music history at the Univ. of Fribourg. He toured widely as an organist and harpsichordist while pursuing his academic activities; he was also an authority on organ restoration.

Tagore, Sir Surindro Mohun (Rajah Saurindramohana Thakura), Hindu musicologist; b. Calcutta, 1840; d. there, June 5, 1914. At the age of 17 he began to study Hindu music under Luchmi Prasad and Kshetra Mohun Gosvami, and European music under a German teacher in Calcutta; he founded and endowed from his personal fortune the Bengal Music School (1871) and the Bengal Academy of Music (1882), continuing to preside over both until his death. A connoisseur of Eastern instrumentation, he was at various times commissioned by the principal museums of Europe to procure for them instruments of Asiatic nations; perhaps the finest collection is that in the Metropolitan Museum of Art in N.Y. He wrote nearly 60 books on an amazing variety of subjects; those concerning music (publ. in Calcutta, in Bengali, and some in Eng.) include: *Yantra Kosha, or A Treasury of the Musical Instruments of Ancient and Modern India* (1875); *Hindu Music, from Various Authors* (1875; 2nd ed., in 2 vols., 1882); *Short Notices of Hindu Musical Instruments* (1877); *6 Principal Ragas* (1876; 3rd ed., 1884); *The 8 Principal Ragas of the Hindus* (1880); *The Five Principal Musicians of the Hindus, or A Brief Exposition of the Essential Elements of Hindu Music* (1881); *The Musical Scales of the Hindus with Remarks on the Applicability of Harmony to Hindu Music* (1884); *The 22 Musical Srutis of the Hindus* (1886); *Universal History of Music* (1896).

BIBLIOGRAPHY: F. Chrysander, "Über Tagores *Hindu Music*," *Allgemeine Musikalische Zeitung* (1879; pp. 540ff.); idem, "Über altindische Opfermusik," *Vierteljahrsschrift für Musikwissenschaft* (1885; pp. 21ff.).

Tailleferre, Germaine (original name, **Taillefesse,** altered to dispel the unwanted anatomical association in the second syllable), fine French composer; b. Parc-St.-Maur, near Paris, April 19, 1892; d. Paris, Nov. 7, 1983. She studied at the Paris Cons., and also had some informal lessons with Ravel. She received recognition as the only feminine member of the group of French composers known as Les Six (the other members were Honegger, Milhaud, Poulenc, Auric, and Durey). Her style of composition was pleasingly, teasingly modernistic and feministic (Jean Cocteau invoked a comparision with a young French woman painter, Marie Laurencin, saying that Tailleferre's music was to the ear what the painter's pastels were to the eye). Indeed, most of her works possess a fragile charm of unaffected *joie de jouer la musique*. She was married to an American author, Ralph Barton, in 1926, but soon divorced him and married a French lawyer, Jean Lageat. She visited the U.S. in 1927 and again in 1942. In 1974 she publ. an autobiographical book, *Mémoires à l'emporte pièce.*

WORKS: *Image* for Piano, Flute, Clarinet, String Quartet, and Celesta (1918); *Jeux de plein air* for 2 Pianos (1918); String Quartet (1918); Piano Concerto (1919); 2 violin sonatas (1921, 1951); *Pastorale* for Violin and Piano (1921); ballet, *Le Marchand d'oiseaux* (Paris, May 25, 1923); Concertino for Harp and Orch. (1926; Boston Symph. Orch., Cambridge, Mass., March 3, 1927); *Chansons françaises* for Voice and Instruments (Liège Festival of the International Society for Contemporary Music, Sept. 2, 1930); Overture for Orch. (Paris, Dec. 25, 1932); Concerto for 2 Pianos, Voice, and Orch. (Paris, May 3, 1934); *Cantate du Narcisse* for Voice and Orch. (1937); *Pastorale* for Flute and Piano (1939); ballet, *Paris-Magie* (Paris, June 3, 1949); *Dolores,* operetta (Paris, 1950); lyric satire, *Il était un petit navire* (Paris, March 1951); musical comedy, *Parfums* (Monte Carlo, 1951); *La Guirlande de Campra* for Orch. (1952); comic opera, *Parisiana* (Copenhagen, 1955); *Concerto des vaines paroles* for Baritone and Orch. (1956); opera, *La Petite Sirène* (1958); opera-buffa, *Mémoires d'une bergère* (1959); chamber opera, *Le Maître* (1959).

Tajčević, Marko, Serbian composer; b. Osijek, Jan. 29, 1900. He studied in Zagreb, Prague, and Vienna; in 1945 was appointed a prof. at the Belgrade Music Academy, retiring in 1966. He is primarily a folklore composer and is at his best in choral works derived from regional folk songs. His *7 Balkan Dances* for Piano are brilliant stylizations of Serbian melorhythms.

BIBLIOGRAPHY: D. Despić, *Marko Tajčevič* (Belgrade, 1972).

Tajo, Italo, Italian bass; b. Pinerolo, April 25, 1915. He studied voice in Turin; made his debut there in 1935; then sang at the Rome Opera and at La Scala in Milan. He made his U.S. debut in Chicago in 1946. On Dec. 28, 1948, he appeared at the Metropolitan Opera in N.Y. as Don Basilio in *The Barber of Seville;* remained on its roster until 1950. In 1966 he was appointed prof. at the Univ. of Cincinnati College-Cons. of Music as "basso-in-residence." In 1980, after an absence of 30 years, he returned to the Metropolitan Opera for a couple of seasons. He was equally adept in dramatic roles and buffo bass parts, and he also proved himself an intelligent interpreter of difficult parts in modern operas by Milhaud, Malipiero, Pizzetti, and even Luigo Nono.

Takács, Jenö, Hungarian composer; b. Siegendorf, Sept. 25, 1902. He studied composition with Joseph Marx and Hans Gál at the Vienna Cons.; in 1927 he was engaged as a teacher at the Cons. of Cairo, Egypt; then traveled to Manila, in the Philippine Islands, returning to Cairo in 1934. During his travels, he collected much material on oriental music; his research in this field is reflected in some of his own works. From 1940 to 1942 he taught at the Music School at Szombathely, Hungary; then was director of the Cons. of Pécs in Hungary (1942–48) and later visiting prof. at the conservatories of Lausanne and Geneva (1949); in 1952 he was engaged as a prof. of piano at the Cincinnati Cons.; he retired in 1971 and went back to his birthplace, Siegendorf. In 1962 he was awarded the State Prize of Austria. Reflecting his background of travel and residence in many different countries, his music contains elements of Hungarian, oriental, American, and cosmopolitan idioms.
WORKS: Ballet, *The Nile Legend* (Budapest, May 8, 1940); *Philippine Suite* for Orch. (1934); *Antiqua Hungarica* for Orch. (1941); 2 piano concertos (1932, 1937); *Partita* for Guitar and Orch. (1950); *Gumbry,* oriental rhapsody for Violin and Piano (1930); Sonata for Trombone and Piano (1957); *Homage to Pan* for 4 Pianos (1968); *Essays in Sound* for Clarinet (1968); *2 Fantastics* for Alto Saxophone (1969); *Musica reservata* for Double Bass (1970); *Tagebuch-Fragmente* for 2 Pianos (1973). He publ. several short essays on the music of the countries in which he lived, among them *Music of the Philippines* (Manila, 1933) and *Tune and Chant in Egypt* (Johannesburg, South Africa, 1935).

Takagi, Tôroku, Japanese composer and pianist; b. Okayama, July 7, 1904. He graduated from the Tokyo Academy of Music in 1928; later studied in Paris. His opera *Shunko-Den* was produced in Tokyo on Nov. 20, 1948. His other works include a ballet, *Crane* (1939); *Korean Dance,* suite for Orch. (1940); 2 piano concertos (1942, 1944); Cello Concerto (1943); *Japanese Dance Music* for 2 Pianos (1941, 1943); songs.

Takahashi, Yuji, Japanese composer and pianist; b. Tokyo, Sept. 21, 1938. He studied composition with Shibata and Ogura at the Toho School of Music in Tokyo (1954–58); then went to Berlin and was trained in electronics as a student of Xenakis; also studied computer music in N.Y. (1966–68) and was a member of the Center for Creative and Performing Arts at the State Univ. of N.Y. in Buffalo (1968–69). In his own music he follows the stochastic procedures as practiced by Xenakis. He also has acquired considerable renown as a pianist in programs of avant-garde music.
WORKS: *Phonogène* for 2 Instruments and Tape (1962); *Chromamorphe I* for Violin, Double Bass, Flute, Trumpet, Horn, Trombone, and Vibraphone (1963); *Chromamorphe II* for Piano (1964); *6 Stoicheia (Elements in Succession)* for 4 Violins (1965); *Bridges I* for Electric Harpsichord or Piano, Amplified Cello, Bass Drum, and Castanets (1967); *Bridges II* for 2 Oboes, 2 Clarinets, 2 Trumpets, and 3 Violas (1968); *Rosace I* for Amplified Violin (1967); *Rosace II* for Piano (1967); *Operation Euler* for 2 or 3 Oboes (1967); *Metathèse* for Piano (1968); *Prajna Paramita* for 4 Voices, each in one of 4 Instrumental Ensembles (1969); *Orphika* for Orch. (Tokyo, May 28, 1969); *Yé Guèn* for Tape (1969); *Nikité* for Oboe, Clarinet, Trumpet, Trombone, Cello, and Double Bass (1971); *Kagahi* for Piano and 30 Instruments (Ojai, Calif., May 30, 1971); *Michi-Yuki* for Chorus, 2 Percussionists, and Electric Cello (1971); *Corona Borealis* for Piccolo, Oboe, Clarinet, Bassoon, and Horn (1971); *Tadori* for Tape (1972).

Takata, Saburô, Japanese composer; b. Nagoya, Dec. 18, 1913. He studied composition with Klaus Pringsheim at the Tokyo Academy of Music; in 1953 was appointed a prof. at the Kunitachi Music College in Tokyo.
WORKS: Opera, *The Dark-Blue Wolf* (1970–72; Tokyo, Oct. 15, 1972); cantata, *Wordless Tears,* for Narrator, Soprano, Baritone, Chorus, and Orch. (Tokyo, March 27, 1964); *Ballade Based on a Folk Song from Yamagata (Fantasy and Fugue)* for Orch. (Tokyo, Nov. 15, 1941; revised 1965); *Seasons,* suite for Orch. (1942); *Ballade* for Violin and Orch. (1943; Tokyo, Jan. 13, 1945); *The New Earth and Man* for Orch. (1944); *2 Rhapsodies* for Orch. (both 1945); Octet for Clarinet, Bassoon, Horn, Trumpet, and String Quartet (1939); *Prelude and Fugue* for String Quartet (1940); Violin Sonata (1948–49); Cello Sonatina (1949–50); *Suite* for Flute, Oboe, 2 Clarinets, and Bassoon (1951); *Marionette,* suite for String Quartet (1954); *Fantasy* for String Quartet (1968); 2 piano sonatas (1935, 1941); *5 Preludes* for Piano (1947); organ pieces; choruses; songs.

Takata, Shin-ichi, Japanese composer; b. Tokyo, Jan. 24, 1920. He studied at the Tokyo Academy of Music; has written a symph. poem, *In Praise of Peace* (Tokyo, Nov. 25, 1948), of which a full score has been publ. The style of this work reveals the influence of Richard Strauss.

Takeda, Yoshima, Japanese conductor; b. Yokohama, Feb. 3, 1933. He was educated at the Tokyo Univ. of the Arts; then went to the U.S. on a fellowship to work with George Szell and the Cleveland Orch. In 1964 he became associate conductor of the Honolulu Symph.; in 1970 was appointed music director of the Albuquerque Symph. Orch., now called the New

Mexico Symph.; in addition, he was named music director of the Kalamazoo Symph. in 1974. He had guest engagements off and on in Detroit, Phoenix, San Diego, and Chicago.

Takemitsu, Toru, prominent Japanese composer; b. Tokyo, Oct. 8, 1930. He studied composition privately with Yasuji Kiyose. In 1951, jointly with Yuasa and others, he organized in Tokyo an "Experimental Laboratory," with the aim of creating new music that would combine traditional Japanese modalities with modernistic procedures. In 1970 he designed the "Space Theater" for Expo '70 in Osaka, Japan. In 1975 he visited the U.S. and gave a seminar in composition at Yale Univ. His music belies Kipling's famous asseveration that East is East and West is West, and never the twain shall meet, for Takemitsu performed through music just this kind of interpenetration; in an oriental way, it is often formed from short motifs played out as floating dramas, subtle and exotic, through which Takemitsu seeks "to achieve a sound as intense as silence"; and on the Western side, he employs every conceivable technique developed by the European and American modernists.
WORKS: FOR ORCH.: *Requiem* for String Orch. (1957; Tokyo, June 20, 1958); *Solitude sonore* (1958); *Ki No Kyoku (Music of Trees;* 1961); *Arc,* Part I (1963, in 3 movements) and Part II (1964–66, in 3 movements) for Piano and Orch.; *Arc* for Strings (1963; from the 3rd movement of *Arc,* Part I); *Textures* for Piano and Orch. (1964; first movement of *Arc,* Part II); *The Dorain Horizon* for 17 Strings in 2 groups (1966; San Francisco, Feb. 1967, Aaron Copland conducting; *November Steps* for Biwa, Shakuhachi, and Orch. (N.Y. Phil., Nov. 9, 1967); *Green (November Steps II;* Tokyo, Nov. 3, 1967); *Asterism* for Piano and Orch. (1968; Toronto, Jan. 14, 1969); *Eucalypts I* for Flute, Oboe, Harp, and Strings (Tokyo, Nov. 16, 1970); *Winter* (Paris, Oct. 29, 1971); *Corona* for 22 Strings (1971); *Cassiopeia* for Solo Percussion and Orch. (1970–71; Chicago Symph., Ravinia Festival, Highland Park, Ill., July 8, 1971); *Gemeaux* for Oboe, Trombone, and 2 Orchs. with separate conductors (1971–72); *Autumn* for Biwa, Shakuhachi, and Orch. (1973); *Gitimalya (Bouquet of Songs)* for Marimba and Orch. (Rotterdam, Nov. 1975); *Quatrain* for Violin, Cello, Clarinet, Piano, and Orch. (Tokyo, Sept. 1, 1975); *Marginalia* (Tokyo, Oct. 20, 1976); *A Flock Descends into the Pentagonal Garden* (San Francisco, Nov. 30, 1977); *In an Autumn Garden* for Gagaku Orch. (1979); *Far Calls. Coming Far!* for Violin and Orch. (Tokyo, May 24, 1980); *Dreamtime* (1981; ballet version, The Hague, May 5, 1983); *Toward the Sea II* for Alto Flute, Harp, and String Orch. (1981); *Star-Isle* (1982); *Rain Coming* for Chamber Orch. (1982); *To the Edge of Dream* for Guitar and Orch. (1982–83; Liège, March 12, 1983). FOR VOICE: *Tableau noir* for Narrator and Orch. (1958); *Coral Island* for Soprano and Orch. (1962); *Wind Horse* for a cappella Female Chorus (1962); *Crossing* for 12 Female Voices, Guitar, Harp, Piano, Vibraphone, and 2 Orchs. (1969); *Grass* for a cappella Male Chorus (1982). CHAMBER MUSIC: *Son

calligraphie I–III for Double String Quartet (1958, 1958, 1963); *Mask* for 2 Flutes (1959); *Landscape* for String Quartet (1960); *Ring* for Flute, Terz-guitar, and Lute (1961); *Sacrifice* for Flute, Lute, and Vibraphone (1962); *Valeria* for Violin, Cello, Guitar, Electric Organ, and 2 Piccolos obbligato (1962); *Hika* for Violin and Piano (1966); *Cross Talk* for 2 Bandoneons and Tape (1968); *Stanza I* for Piano, Guitar, Harp, Vibraphone, and Female Voice (1968); *Stanza II* for Solo Harp (1971); *Stanza III* for Solo Oboe, or Oboe and Shō (1971); *Eucalypts II* for Flute, Oboe, and Harp (1970); *Seasons* in versions for One or 4 Percussionists (1970); *Voice* for Solo Flute (1971); *Munari by Munari* for Percussion (1972); *Distance* for Solo Oboe, or Oboe and Shō (1972); *Voyage* for 3 Biwas (1973); *Folios* for Guitar (1973); *Garden Rain* for 4 Trumpets, 3 Trombones, Bass Trombone, Horn, and Tuba, separated into 2 groups (1974); *Waves* for Solo Clarinet, Horn, 2 Trumpets, and Percussion (1976); *Bryce* for Flute, 2 Harps, Marimba, and Percussion (1976); *Quatrain I* for Clarinet, Violin, Cello, and Piano (1976); *Waterways* for Piano, Clarinet, Violin, Cello, 2 Harps, and 2 Vibraphones (1978); String Quartet No. 1, subtitled *A Way a lone* (1981). FOR PIANO: *2 Lentos* (1950); *Undisturbed Rest* (1952–59); *Piano Distance* (1961); *Corona* for Pianist(s) (1962); *For Away* (1973); *Les Yeux clos* (1979); *Rain Tree Sketch* (1981). FOR TAPE ALONE: *Sky, Horse and Death* (1954); *Static Relief* (1955); *Vocalism A-1* (1956); *Water Music* (1960); *Quiet Design* (1960); *Kwaidan* (1966; revision of music from the film); *Toward* (1970); also music for a number of films including *Hara-Kiri* (1962); *Woman in the Dunes* (1964); *Kwaidan* (1964); *Empire of Passion* (1978).

Taktakishvili, Otar, Soviet Georgian composer; b. Tiflis, July 27, 1924. He studied at the Tiflis Cons., graduating in 1947; in 1949 was appointed prof. of composition there. In 1982 he was awarded the Lenin Prize. His music is imbued with the characteristic melorhythms of the Caucasus; he has a natural knack for instrumental color.
WORKS: Opera, *Mindia* (Tiflis, July 23, 1961); 2 symphs. (1949, 1953); 3 overtures (1950, 1951, 1955); symph. poems: *Samgori* (1950) and *Mtsyri* (1956); Cello Concerto (1947); Piano Concerto (his most successful work, written in a virtuoso manner; Tiflis, Nov. 15, 1951); Trumpet Concerto (1954); Piano Trio (1947); several cantatas and choruses; solo songs; many piano pieces.
BIBLIOGRAPHY: L. Polyakova, *Otar Taktakishvili* (Moscow, 1956; 2nd ed., 1979).

Taktakishvili, Shalva, Soviet Georgian composer; b. Kvemo-Khviti, Aug. 27, 1900; d. Tiflis, July 18, 1965. He studied at the Tiflis Cons.; then taught music theory at the Batumi Music School, of which he was a co-founder; then served as conductor at Tiflis Radio; and from 1952 to the time of his death, conducted the Georgian State Orch.
WORKS: Operas: *Sunrise* (Tiflis, 1926) and *The Delegate* (Tiflis, 1939); 2 overtures (1944, 1949); symph. poem, *The Year 1905* (1931); Cello Concerto (1932); 2 string quartets (1930, 1933); Violin Sonata

(1952); numerous piano pieces, choruses and songs.

BIBLIOGRAPHY: P.V. Hukua, *Shalva Taktakish-vili* (Tiflis, 1962).

Taku, Koji, Japanese composer; b. Sakai-City (Osaka), March 10, 1904. He studied piano with Alfred Cortot and composition with Nadia Boulanger at the Ecole Normale de Musique in Paris; upon his return to Japan he taught at the Tokyo Music Academy. He composed 2 ballets: *White Flower* (1942) and *Journey* (1954); String Quartet (1933); Piano Sonata (1942); *Variations on a Theme of Poulenc* for Piano (1952); *Suite* for Harpsichord and Chamber Ensemble (1953); several albums of piano pieces for children.

Tal (real name, **Gruenthal**), **Josef (Joseph),** Polish-born Israeli composer and pianist; b. Pinne, near Poznan, Sept. 18, 1910. He studied composition with Tiessen and piano with Trapp at the Staatlich Akademische Hochschule für Musik in Berlin (1928–30); emigrated to Palestine in 1934 and taught composition and piano at the Jerusalem Academy of Music; served as its director in 1948–52. He was later on the music faculty of the Hebrew Univ. in Jerusalem, and headed its musicology dept. (1965–71). In 1957 he received a munificent UNESCO grant to study electronic music; in 1961 he was appointed director of the Israel Center for Electronic Music; in 1971 was named a Fellow of the West Berlin Academy of the Arts. A true musical intellectual, he applies in his music a variety of techniques, being free of doctrinal introversion and open to novel potentialities without fear of public revulsion. Patriotic Hebrew themes often appear in his productions.

WORKS: *Saul at Ein Dor,* opera concertante (1957); *Amnon and Tamar,* short opera (1961); *Ashmedai,* opera in 2 acts, with Electronic Sound (1968–70; Hamburg, Nov. 9, 1971; an electronic overture from the opera represents an independent concert number); *Masada 967,* opera in 15 scenes (1971–72; Jerusalem, June 17, 1973); *Die Versuchung (The Temptation),* opera in 2 acts (1973–75; Munich Festival, July 26, 1976); *The Death of Moses,* requiem-oratorio for Soloists, Chorus, and Tape (1967); *The Mother Rejoices,* symph. cantata for Chorus, Piano, and Orch. (1949); *Succoth Cantata* (1955); *Misdar Hanoflim (Parade of the Fallen),* cantata (1968); 3 electronic scores for ballet: *Ranges of Energy* (1963); *From the Depth of the Soul* (1964); *Variations* (1970); *Exodus,* choreographic poem for Baritone and Orch. (1946; Tel Aviv, Dec. 14, 1947); 6 piano concertos: No. 1, with Orch. (1944); No. 2, with Orch. (1953); No. 3, with Solo Tenor and Chamber Orch. (1956); Nos. 4–6 solely for Piano and Electronics (1962, 1964, 1970); *Reflections* for String Orch. (1950); Viola Concerto (1954; Mount Carmel Festival of the International Society for Contemporary Music, June 3, 1954); *Festive Vision* for Orch. (1959); Concerto for Cello and String Orch. (1961); *Double Concerto* for Violin, Cello, and Chamber Orch. (1970); *The Wooden Horse* for Soloists, Chorus, and Electronics (1973); Concerto for Harpsichord and

Electronics (1964); Concerto for Harp and Electronics (1971); *Lament* for Cello and Harp (1950); Violin Sonata (1952); Oboe Sonata (1952); 2 string quartets (1959, 1964); *Intrada* for Harp (1959); Viola Sonata (1960); *Structure* for Harp (1962); *Duo* for Viola and Piano (1965); Wind Quintet (1966); *Songs on Texts by Heine* for Baritone or Alto, Flute, Horn, Piano, and Tam-tams (1971); *Treatise* for Solo Cello (1973); Piano Trio (1973); Piano Sonata No. 1 (1950); *Inventions* for Piano (1956); *Dodecaphonic Episodes* for Piano (1962); electronic pieces: *Min Hameitzar Karati Yah (I Called Upon the Lord in Distress;* 1971); *Frequencies 440–462 (Homage to Blacher;* 1972); *Overture for Opera* (1973); *3 Songs* for Chorus a cappella (1953).

Talbot, Howard (real name, **Munkittrick**), English operetta composer; b. Yonkers, N.Y., March 9, 1865; d. London, Sept. 12, 1928. He was taken to England at the age of 4, and studied music at the Royal College of Music under Parry, Bridge, and Gladstone; from 1900, was active as a conductor in various London theaters. He was a prolific composer of light operas, all produced in London; his greatest success was *A Chinese Honeymoon* (1899); his last work was *The Daughter of the Gods* (posthumous, 1929). Other operettas: *Monte Carlo* (1896); *3 Little Maids* (1902); *The Blue Moon* (1905); *The White Chrysanthemum* (1905); *The Girl behind the Counter* (1906); *The 3 Kisses* (1907); *The Belle of Brittany* (1908); *The Arcadians* (1909); *The Pearl Girl* (1913); *A Narrow Squeak* (1913); *A Mixed Grill* (1914); *A Lucky Miss* (1914); *The Light Blues* (1915); etc.

Talich, Václav, eminent Czech conductor; b. Kroměříž, May 28, 1883; d. Beroun, March 16, 1961. He received his early musical training from his father, Jan Talich; then studied violin with Ševčik at the Prague Cons. (1897–1903). He was concertmaster of the Odessa Orch. in Russia, and then taught violin in Tiflis. He returned to Prague in 1907; conducted the Phil. Orch. of Ljubljana; in 1910 went to Leipzig, where he took lessons in composition with Max Reger and Hans Sitt and in conducting with Arthur Nikisch. He was then opera conductor at Pilsen (1912–15) and chief conductor of the Czech Phil. (1919–31); in 1931–33 was conductor of the Konsertforeningen in Stockholm; then in 1933 returned as chief conductor of the Czech Phil. (until 1941), which he brought to a high degree of excellence; toured with it in Italy, Germany, France, and England. Subsequently he was conductor as well as administrator of the National Opera in Prague (1935–44); from 1947 to 1948 was its artistic leader; then moved to Bratislava, where he conducted the Slovak Phil. Orch. (1949–52); returned as guest conductor of the Czech Phil. (1952–54); retired from concert appearances in 1954. He also taught conducting in Prague and Bratislava; among his pupils were Ančerl and I. Krejčí.

BIBLIOGRAPHY: M. Kuna, *Václav Talich* (Prague, 1980; in Czech, with abridged trans. included, in Russian, German, and Eng.).

Talley, Marion, American soprano; b. Nevada, Mo., Dec. 20, 1906; d. Los Angeles, Jan. 3, 1983. She sang in churches in Kansas City, and at the age of 16 appeared in a performance of *Mignon* there, producing such an explosion of local pride that the community raised funds to send her to N.Y. to study voice with Frank La Forge; later she went to Italy in quest of further musical enlightenment. She was then given a chance to appear at the Metropolitan Opera in N.Y. on Feb. 17, 1926, as Gilda in *Rigoletto.* She was only 19 years old at the time, and she became an instant *rara avis,* a genuine American warbler, an authentic, native thrush, and newspapers went wild over her. She sang the part of the nightingale in Stravinsky's opera *Le Rossignol* at the Metropolitan on March 6, 1926, and performed the role of the Queen of the Night in *The Magic Flute* there on Nov. 6, 1926. In 1928 she made a U.S. tour as a concert singer; in 1933 she sang Gilda at the Chicago Opera, with meager success; she was no longer a young American nightingale. From then on she made little music before sinking into impenetrable oblivion in darkest Hollywood; even her death went unrecorded in the daily journals.

Tallis (or **Tallys, Talys**), **Thomas,** English organist and composer; b. c.1505; d. Greenwich, Nov. 23, 1585. He was "joculator organorum" at the Dover Priory (1532), at St. Mary-at-Hill in London (1537), and at the Augustine Abbey Holy Cross in Waltham, Essex (1538–1540); from about 1543 served as Gentleman of the Chapel Royal during the reigns of Henry VIII, Edward VI, Mary, and Elizabeth, and as joint organist with Byrd. With Byrd, he obtained in 1575 letters patent for the exclusive privilege of printing music and ruled music paper, the first work issued by them being 34 *Cantiones quae ab argumento sacrae vocantur, 5 et 6 partium,* in 1575 (16 motets by Tallis and 18 by Byrd). Tallis's most famous work is *Spem in alium non habui,* a "song of 40 parts" for 8 5-part choirs (specimen page in first ed. of *Grove's Dictionary,* vol. III, p. 274). A composer of great contrapuntal skill, he was among the first to set Eng. words to music for the rites of the Church of England. Surviving are 3 masses, 2 Magnificats, 2 Lamentations, 52 motets and other pieces with Latin text, over 20 Eng. anthems, 3 sets of Psalms, etc., as well as some keyboard music. In Barnard's *First Book of Selected Church Music* (1641) is a First Service, or Short Service (*a* 4), Preces, Responses, etc., often republ. (by Rimbault, Novello, Jebb, Davison & Apel, etc.); J. Day's *Morning and Evening Prayer* (1560), Boyce's *Cathedral Music,* and the histories by Hawkins and Burney contain specimens of his music. Rimbault republ. the *Order of Daily Service, with the Musical Notation,* R. Terry edited a Mass *a* 4 in 1908 (Breitkopf & Härtel), and most of Tallis's church music is in vol. VI of *Tudor Church Music* (1928). There are many works in MS at Oxford, Cambridge, and in the British Library. Additional modern editions include D. Stevens, ed., *T. Tallis: Complete Keyboard Works* (London, 1953); L. Ellinwood, ed., *T. Tallis: English Sacred Music,* I, *Anthems;* II, *Service Music,* in *Early English Church Music,* XII and XIII (revised by P. Doe, 1974).

BIBLIOGRAPHY: H.B. Collins, "T. T.," *Music & Letters* (1929); B. Schofield, "The Manuscripts of T.'s Forty-Part Motet," *Musical Quarterly* (April 1951); D. Stevens, "The Keyboard Music of T. T.," *Musical Times* (July 1952); R. Illing, *T.'s Psalm Tunes* (Adelaide, 1968); P. Doe, *Tallis* (London, 1968; 2nd ed., 1976); J. Milsom, "A New Tallis Contrafactum," *Musical Times* (June 1982).

Talma, Louise, American composer; b. Arcachon, France, Oct. 31, 1906. She studied at N.Y. Univ. (B.M., 1931) and at Columbia Univ. (M.A., 1933); took piano lessons with Isidor Philipp and composition with Nadia Boulanger at the Fontainebleau School of Music in France. In 1946 she received a Guggenheim fellowship; received a 2nd Guggenheim in 1947; joined the faculty at Hunter College in N.Y. She became the first woman composer to be elected to the National Inst. of Arts and Letters, in 1974. In her music she adopts a strongly impressionistic style.

WORKS: *Toccata* for Orch. (1944); *Introduction and Rondo Giocoso* (1946); *3 Madrigals* for Women's Voices and String Quartet (1929); *La Belle Dame sans merci* for Baritone Solo (1929); *Terre de France,* song cycle (1925); *5 Sonnets from the Portuguese,* song cycle (1934); *Piano Sonata* (1943); *The Divine Flame,* oratorio (1948); *Let's Touch the Sky,* cycle of poems, after e.e. cummings, for Chorus and Woodwind Instruments (1952); *The Alcestiad,* opera (Frankfurt, Germany, March 1, 1962); *All the Days of My Life* for Tenor, Clarinet, Cello, Piano, and Percussion (1965); *Voices of Peace* for Chorus and Strings (1973); *Summer Sounds* for Clarinet and String Quartet (1973); *Textures* for Piano (1978); other piano pieces.

BIBLIOGRAPHY: Madeleine Goss, *Modern Music-Makers* (N.Y., 1952).

Talmi, Yoav, Israeli conductor; b. Kibbutz Merhavia, April 28, 1943. He studied at the Rubin Academy of Music in Tel Aviv and at the Juilliard School of Music in N.Y. In 1969 he won the Koussevitzky Memorial Conducting Prize. He then served as associate conductor of the Louisville Orch. (1968–70), music director of the Kentucky Chamber Orch. (1969–71), and conductor of the Israel Chamber Orch. (1970–72). In 1974 he became artistic director of the Het Gelders Orch. in Arnhem, the Netherlands. In 1979 he was appointed principal guest conductor of the Munich Phil. Orch.

Taltabull, Cristòfor, Catalan composer and pedagogue; b. Barcelona, July 28, 1888; d. there, May 1, 1964. He studied piano with Granados and composition with Felipe Pedrell. In 1908 he went to Germany, where he took lessons with Max Reger. In 1912 he went to Paris, where he engaged in various occupations: as an accompanist to singers, as proofreader for the publisher Durand, and as a music copyist; he also composed popular songs for vaudeville and wrote film music. After the outbreak of World War II in 1939, he returned to Barcelona, where he became a teacher of composition. Many important Spanish composers of the younger generation were his pupils. As a composer, he was particularly successful in songs to French and Catalan texts. His style of composition is impressionistic, mainly derived from Debussy, and he had a delicate sense of color and rhythm; thematically, most of his music retains Spanish, or Catalan, melorhythmic characteristics.

Talvela, Martti, remarkable Finnish bass; b. Hiitola, Karelia, Feb. 4, 1935, of a family of musically gifted children (he was No. 8 of the total of 10 offspring). He studied voice with Martin Oehman; made his operatic debut as the Commendatore in *Don Giovanni* at the Royal Stockholm Opera in 1961; subsequently sang at the Berlin Deutsche Oper and the Bayreuth Festival. He made his American debut in Verdi's Requiem in Cleveland in 1968; then appeared at the Metropolitan Opera in N.Y. on Oct. 7, 1968, in the role of the Grand Inquisitor in Verdi's *Don Carlos.* On Dec. 16, 1974, he appeared at the Metropolitan in his greatest role, that of Boris Godunov in the original version of Mussorgsky's opera; he also sang Boris Godunov in Russian during his appearances in the U.S.S.R. On May 13, 1977, he sang Sarastro in a new production at the Paris Opéra of *Die Zauberflöte.* Other important roles in his repertoire were Gurnemanz in *Parsifal,* King Henry in *Lohengrin,* and Hagen in *Götterdämmerung.* Despite his international tours, Talvela kept close to musical life in his native land; in 1972 he assumed the post of artistic director of the summer Savonlinna Opera Festival in Finland. He also sang the chief role in the Helsinki production of the Finnish opera *Viimeiset Kiusaukset* by Kokkonen, on Sept. 2, 1975. A man of enormous hulk, rising erect to 6 feet 7 inches, and weighing up to 300 pounds, Talvela can command bass parts in opera with an almost awesome effect; a true Finn, he continues to engage in such manly pursuits as hunting, boating, and logging in the woods and lakes of central Finland. In 1973 Talvela received the Pro Finlandia Prize from the Finnish government.
BIBLIOGRAPHY: David Ewen, *Musicians since 1900* (N.Y., 1978).

Tamagno, Francesco, famous Italian tenor; b. Turin, Dec. 28, 1850; d. Varese, near Turin, Aug. 31, 1905. He was at first apprenticed to a baker, and later to a locksmith; entered the Turin Cons. as a pupil of Pedrotti, and in 1873 made his debut as 2nd tenor at the Teatro Regio there, his powerful voice immediately attracting attention. Following his appearance in *Un ballo in maschera* at Palermo on Jan. 17, 1874, his success was rapid. In 1876–77 he sang at the Liceo of Barcelona, and from 1877 at La Scala, Milan, where in 1887 he created the role of Otello in Verdi's opera. He sang at the Metropolitan Opera, N.Y., during the 1894–95 season (debut, Nov. 21, 1894, as Arnold in Rossini's *Guillaume Tell*). Other engagements included performances in South America, Lisbon, Madrid, Paris, and London. In 1902, having made a fortune, he retired from the stage.
BIBLIOGRAPHY: E. de Amicis, *Francesco Tamagno* (Palermo, 1902); M. Corsi, *Tamagno* (Milan, 1937); E. Gara, "Francesco Tamagno," *La Scala* (Jan. 1954).

Tamberg, Eino, Estonian composer; b. Tallinn, May 27, 1930. He studied composition with E. Kapp at the Cons. in Tallinn (1950–53); served as a sound engineer at Estonian Radio; in 1967 joined the staff of the Cons. of Tallinn.
WORKS: Operas: *Raudne kodu* (*The House of Iron,* Tallinn, July 15, 1965), glorifying the revolutionary spirit of Estonian proletarian patriots; *Cyrano de Bergerac* (1974); 2 ballets: *Poiss ja liblik* (*The Boy and the Butterfly,* 1963) and *Joanna tentata* (1970); 2 oratorios: *Rahva vabaduse eest* (*For the Freedom of the People,* 1953) and *Kuupaiste-oratorium* (*Moonlight Oratorio,* 1962); *Symphonic Suite* (1955); *Concerto grosso* for Orch. (1956); *Symphonic Dances* (1957); *Ballet-Symphony* (1959); *Oedipus Rex,* suite for Chorus and Orch. (1959); *Toccata* for Orch. (1967); Trumpet Concerto (1972); cantata, *Fanfare des Sièges* (1975); String Quartet (1958); *Rondo* for Violin and Piano (1961); *Song for Africa* for Male Chorus and Percussion (1961); *Music* for Solo Oboe (1970); Wind Quintet (1976); choruses; songs.

Tamberlik, Enrico, celebrated Italian tenor; b. Rome, March 16, 1820; d. Paris, March 13, 1889. He studied singing with Zirilli in Rome and with Guglielmi in Naples, where he made his stage debut in 1841, as Tybalt in *I Capuleti e i Montecchi.* On April 4, 1850, he made his first London appearance, as Masaniello in Auber's *La Muette de Portici,* at the Royal Italian Opera, Covent Garden, and sang annually in London until 1864, with the exception of 1857, when he undertook an extensive European tour, including Spain and Russia. In 1860 he settled in Paris, and lived there most of his life. Verdi admired him, and wrote the part of Don Alvaro in *La forza del destino* for him; Tamberlik sang in its world premiere at St. Petersburg, Russia, on Oct. 30, 1862, and this role became one of his most famous interpretations. He appeared at the Academy of Music in N.Y., on Sept. 18, 1873, but his American season was a brief one. He was famous for his rich high notes, and his ability to sustain the high C was legendary.
BIBLIOGRAPHY: H. Brody, "La Carrière d'un ténor italien," *Revue Musicale* (April 15, 1904, et seq.).

Tamburini, Antonio, Italian baritone; b. Faenza, March 28, 1800; d. Nice, Nov. 8, 1876. He first learned to play the horn as a pupil of his father; then studied singing with A. Rossi and B. Asioli; made his debut at Cento in 1818; thereafter sang on the chief stages of Italy, being engaged by Barbaja from 1824 to 1832. During 1832–41 he sang at the Théâtre Italien in Paris, as part of a brilliant company that included Grisi, Persiani, Viardot, Rubini, and Lablache, appearing in London in alternate seasons; after a short stay in Italy, he remained for 10 years in Russia. In 1855 he retired to his estate at Sèvres, near Paris. His greatest triumph was in Bellini's *La Straniera*, in which he created a frenzy of enthusiasm by his singing of the aria *Meco tu vieni, o misera*. In 1822 he married the singer **Marietta Goja**.

BIBLIOGRAPHY: J. de Biez, *Tamburini et la musique italienne* (Paris, 1877); H. Gelli-Ferraris, *Antonio Tamburini nel ricordo d'una nipote* (Livorno, 1934).

Tamkin, David, American composer; b. Chernigov, Russia, Aug. 28, 1906; d. Los Angeles, June 21, 1975. He was taken to the U.S. as an infant; the family settled in Portland, Oreg., where he studied violin with Henry Bettman, a pupil of Ysaÿe; he took lessons in composition with Ernest Bloch. In 1937 he settled in Los Angeles; from 1945 to 1966 he was principal composer at Universal Pictures in Hollywood. His music is deeply permeated with the melodic and rhythmic elements of the Hassidic Jewish cantillation. His magnum opus is the opera *The Dybbuk*, to a libretto by his brother Alex Tamkin, from S. Ansky's Jewish classic of that title; he composed the work in 1928–31 but it was not produced until Oct. 4, 1951, by the N.Y. City Opera. In 1962 he wrote another opera, *The Blue Plum Tree of Esau* (also to his brother's libretto); among his other works are 2 string quartets, a Woodwind Sextet, and several choruses.

Tanaka, Toshimitsu, Japanese composer; b. Aomori, July 17, 1930. He studied music at the Kunitani Music College in Tokyo; after graduation in 1951, he joined its staff. His music is based on the melorhythmic patterns of Japanese folk songs.

WORKS: 2 dance suites: *Tamanna* for 2 Pianos and Percussion (1967) and *Magic Festival in the Mountain Crease* for Chorus, Ryûteki, and various types of Wadaiko (1968); *Epic "Wolf Boy" for Shamisen* for Solo Soprano, Shamisen, Shakuhachi, Wadaiko, and Strings (Tokyo, Nov. 27, 1968); requiem, *The Grave*, for Chorus and Orch. (Radio Tokyo, Nov. 5, 1972); Violin Sonata (1957); String Quartet (1962); *Suite* for Marimba, 7 Strings, and 2 Percussionists (1971); choruses; songs.

Tanev, Alexander, Hungarian-born Bulgarian composer; b. Budapest, Oct. 23, 1928. He studied composition with Veselin Stoyanov at the Bulgarian State Cons. in Sofia, graduating in 1957. His works include a Sinfonietta (1959); *Youth Concerto* for Violin and String Orch. (1969); *Rondo Scherzando* for Trombone and Orch. (1971); Concerto for Winds and Percussion (1972); *Builder's Music* for 2 Pianos and Percussion, or Orch. (1974); choruses; songs.

Taneyev, Alexander, Russian composer; b. St. Petersburg, Jan. 17, 1850; d. there, Feb. 7, 1918; a distant relative of **Sergei Taneyev**. He studied composition with F. Reichel in Dresden; upon his return to St. Petersburg, he took lessons with Rimsky-Korsakov.

Music was his avocation; he followed a government career, advancing to the post of head of the Imperial Chancellery. The style of his music is Romantic, lapsing into sentimentalism; the main influence is that of Tchaikovsky.

WORKS: Operas: *Cupid's Revenge* (concert perf., St. Petersburg, May 19, 1899) and *Buran (The Snow Storm); Festival March* for Orch.; 3 symphs. (1890; 1903; 1908); 2 orch. mazurkas; *Hamlet Overture;* 2 suites for Orch.; *Ballade,* after a poem (*Alyosha Popovich*) by Alexei Tolstoy, for Orch.; 3 string quartets; *Arabesque* for Clarinet and Piano; piano pieces; songs.

Taneyev, Sergei, greatly significant Russian composer and pedagogue; b. Vladimir district, Nov. 25, 1856; d. Dyudkovo, Zvenigorodsk district, June 19, 1915. He began taking piano lessons at the age of 10 at the Moscow Cons.; after attending academic school for a year, he re-entered the Cons. and studied piano with Nicolai Rubinstein and composition with Tchaikovsky, forming a lifelong friendship with the latter. He made a very successful debut in Moscow as a pianist, playing the D-minor Concerto of Brahms (Jan. 31, 1875); after a tour of Russia with Leopold Auer, he visited Turkey, Greece, and Italy; spent the winter of 1877–78 in Paris; in the autumn of 1878 he succeeded Tchaikovsky as prof. of harmony and orchestration at the Moscow Cons.; after the death of Nicolai Rubinstein in 1881, he took over the latter's piano classes there; from 1885 to 1889 he was director; from 1889 to 1906 he taught composition. Taneyev was a first-class pianist; Tchaikovsky regarded him as one of the finest interpreters of his music; but Taneyev was not interested in a virtuoso career, and gradually confined himself to composition and pedagogy. His position as a composer is anomalous: he is one of the most respected figures of Russian music history, and there is a growing literature about him; his correspondence and all documents, however trivial, concerning his life are treasured as part of the Russian cultural heritage; yet outside Russia his works are rarely heard. He wrote a treatise on counterpoint, *Podvizhnoi kontrapunkt strogavo pisma* (1909; in Eng. as *Convertible Counterpoint in the Strict Style;* Boston, 1962). The style of his compositions presents a compromise between Russian melos and Germanic contrapuntal writing; the mastery revealed in his symphs. and quartets is unquestionable. His most ambitious work was the trilogy *Oresteia,* after Aeschylus, in 3 divisions: *Agamemnon, Choëphorai,* and *Eumenides,* first performed in St. Petersburg on Oct. 29, 1895. Other works are *John of Damascus,* cantata, after Alexei Tolstoy (1884); *At the Reading of the Psalm,* cantata (1914); 4 symphs., including Symph. in C minor (1896–97; first perf. under the direction of Glazunov, St. Petersburg, April 2, 1898); 3 string quintets; 9 string quartets; Piano Quartet; 2 string trios; Piano Trio (1914); about 50 songs, most of them of a very high quality. After his death an almost completed *Treatise on Canon and Fugue* was found among his papers and publ. in 1929.

BIBLIOGRAPHY: K.A. Kuznetsov, ed., *Memorial*

and Bibliography of S.I. Taneyev (Moscow, 1925); V. Yakovlev, *S.I. Taneyev: His Musical Life* (Moscow, 1927); V. Karatygin, "To the Memory of S.I. Taneyev," *Musical Quarterly* (Oct. 1927); V. Protopopov, ed., *Memorial of S. Taneyev* (Moscow, 1947); G. Bernandt, *S. Taneyev* (Moscow, 1950); a symposium, *S. Taneyev; Materials and Documents* (vol. I, 1952); Jacob Weinberg, "S. Taneyev," *Musical Quarterly* (Jan. 1958); T. Khoprova, *S.I. Taneyev* (Leningrad, 1968); F.G. Arzamonov, *S.I. Taneyev* (Moscow, 1963); N. D. Bazhanov, *Taneyev* (Moscow, 1971); L.Z. Korabelnikova, *S.I. Taneyev at the Moscow Conservatory* (Moscow, 1974).

Tango, Egisto, Italian conductor; b. Rome, Nov. 13, 1873; d. Copenhagen, Oct. 5, 1951. He first studied engineering; then entered the Naples Cons.; made his debut as an opera conductor in Venice (1893); conducted at La Scala in Milan (1895); then at Berlin (1903–8). He conducted at the Metropolitan Opera in N.Y., in 1909–10; in Italy (1911–12); and in Budapest (1913–19), where he gave the earliest performances of stage works by Béla Bartók. From 1920 to 1926 he was active in Germany and Austria. In 1927 he settled in Copenhagen. He was distinguished for the technical precision and interpretative clarity of his performances.

Tannenberg, David, German-American organ builder; b. Berthelsdorf, Upper Lusatia, March 21, 1728; d. York, Pa., May 19, 1804. Tannenberg came to America in 1749 and became a member of the Moravian Church settlement at Bethlehem, Pa. Following the death of his teacher and colleague Johann Gottlob Clemm (1762), he established himself in Lititz, Pa. (1765); made 32 organs for churches in Pennsylvania, N.Y., Maryland, Virginia, and North Carolina; he also made a few pianos.
BIBLIOGRAPHY: P.E. Beck, "David Tannenberg, Organ Builder," *Papers Read before the Lancaster, Pa. Historical Society* (Jan. 1926); D.M. McCorkle, "The Moravian Contribution to American Music," *Notes* (Sept. 1956; reprinted as Moravian Music Foundation Publication No. 1, Winston-Salem, N.C., 1956); idem, "Musical Instruments of the Moravians of North Carolina," *American German Review* (Feb.–March 1955).

Tannhäuser, lyric poet and minnesinger; b. c.1200, probably in Oberpfalz; d. after 1266. He led a wandering life typical of his calling; for a time was at the court of Friedrich II, Duke of Austria; then with Otto II of Bavaria. His name became legendary through the tale of the Venusberg, pagan intimacy with Venus, penitence, pilgrimage to Rome, and the miracle of the flowering of his pilgrim's staff. Wagner's *Tannhäuser* is based on this legend, which is unconnected with the life of the real Tannhäuser. A complete|edition of his works has been edited by H. Lomnitzer and U. Müller, *Tannhäuser* (Göppingen, 1973).
BIBLIOGRAPHY: F. Zander, *Die Tannhäusersage und der Minnesinger Tannhäuser* (1858); J. Siebert, *Tannhäuser* (1894); R. Taylor, *The Art of the Minnesinger* (Cardiff, 1968).

Tansman, Alexandre, Polish composer; b. Lodz, June 12, 1897. He studied with Piotr Rytel in Warsaw, and piano with Lütschg. After a brief service in the Polish army, he went to Paris, which became his permanent home. He first appeared in public, playing his piano works, in Paris on Feb. 17, 1920; performances of his symph. and chamber music followed in rapid succession; his *Danse de la sorcière* for Chamber Orch. was presented at the Zürich Festival of the International Society for Contemporary Music (June 22, 1926). He made an extensive tour of the U.S. in 1927–28 as pianist in his own works. In 1933 he toured the Far East. After the occupation of Paris by the Germans in 1940, he made his way to the U.S.; lived in Hollywood, where he wrote music for films; returned to Paris in 1946. His music is distinguished by a considerable melodic gift and a vivacious rhythm; his harmony is often bitonal; there are some impressionistic traits that reflect his Parisian tastes.
WORKS: OPERAS: *La Nuit kurde* (1925–27; Paris Radio, 1927); *Le Serment* (Brussels, March 11, 1955); *Sabbatat Lévi, le faux Messie,* lyric fresco (Paris, 1961); *Le Rossignol de Boboli* (Nice, 1965); ballets: *Sextuor* (Paris, May 17, 1924; also in Chicago, as *The Tragedy of the Cello,* Dec. 26, 1926); *La Grande Ville* (1932); *Bric-à-Brac* (1937); *Train de nuit* for 2 Pianos (London, 1950); *Les Habits neufs du roi,* after H.C. Andersen (Venice, 1959); *Resurrection,* after Tolstoy (Nice, 1962). FOR ORCH.: 7 symphs.: No. 1 (1925; Boston, March 18, 1927); No. 2 (1926); No. 3, *Symphonie concertante* (1931); No. 4 (1939); No. 5 (1942; Baltimore, Feb. 2, 1943); No. 6, *In memoriam* (1943); No. 7 (1944; St. Louis, Oct. 24, 1947); *Danse de la sorcière* (Brussels, May 5, 1924); *Sinfonietta* (Paris, March 23, 1925); *Ouverture symphonique* (Paris, Feb. 3, 1927); Piano Concerto No. 1 (Paris, May 27, 1926, composer soloist); Piano Concerto No. 2 (Boston, Dec. 28, 1927, composer soloist); *Suite* for 2 Pianos and Orch. (Paris, Nov. 16, 1930); Viola Concerto (1936); *Fantaisie* for Violin and Orch. (1937); *Fantaisie* for Cello and Orch. (1937); *Rapsodie polonaise* (St. Louis, Nov. 14, 1941); *Études symphoniques* (1943); Concertino for Guitar and Orch. (1945); *Ricercari* (St. Louis, Dec. 22, 1949); *Capriccio* (Louisville, March 6, 1955). CHAMBER MUSIC: 8 string quartets (1917–56); *Suite baroque* (1958); *Symphonie de chambre* (1960); *Stèle: In memoriam Igor Stravinsky* (1972); *Dyptique* for Chamber Orch. (1969); Cello Concerto (1962); Flute Concerto (1968); *Danse de la sorcière* for Woodwind Quintet and Piano (a version of the ballet; 1925); String Sextet (1940); *Divertimento* for Oboe, Clarinet, Trumpet, Cello, and Piano (1944); Violin Sonata (1919); Flute Sonata (1925); Cello Sonata (1930); etc. FOR PIANO: *20 pièces faciles polonaises* (1924); 5 sonatas; mazurkas, and other Polish dances; *Sonatine transatlantique* (1930; very popular; contains imitations of jazz; also for Orch., Paris, Feb. 28, 1931; used by Kurt Jooss in his ballet *Impressions of a Big City,* Cologne, Nov. 21, 1932); *Pour les enfants,* 4 albums for Piano. He publ. a monograph on Stravinsky (Paris,

Tans'ur – Tăranu

1948; in Eng., *Igor Stravinsky: The Man and His Music,* N.Y., 1949).
BIBLIOGRAPHY: Irving Schwerké, *Alexandre Tansman, Compositeur polonais* (Paris, 1931); R. Petit, "Alexandre Tansman," *Revue Musicale* (Feb. 1929).

Tans'ur (real name, **Tanzer**), **William,** English organist, composer, and lexicographer; b. Dunchurch, 1700 (baptized, Nov. 6, 1706); d. St. Neots, Oct. 7, 1783. He was a church organist and taught music in various provincial towns in England. His publications include: *The Royal Melody Compleat, or the New Harmony of Sion* (2nd ed., 1760; 3rd ed., in 3 parts, 1764, 1765, 1766; at least 11 American eds. are known, publ. as *The American Harmony, or Royal Melody Complete,* or under similar, slightly varying, titles); *Heaven on Earth, or the Beauty of Holiness* (1738); *Sacred Mirth, or the Pious Soul's Daily Delight* (1739); *The Universal Harmony* (1743, etc.); *The Psalm-Singer's Jewel* (1760, etc.); *Melodia sacra* (1771, 1772); *New Musical Grammar* (1746; 7th ed., 1829); an epitome of this last, *The Elements of Musick Displayed* (1772). For details on various eds. see I. Lowens and Allen P. Britton, in *Papers of the Bibliographical Society of America,* 4 (1955; pp. 340-54).

Tapper, Thomas, American music educator; b. Canton, Mass., Jan. 28, 1864; d. White Plains, N.Y., Feb. 24, 1958. He studied music in Europe; from 1897 to 1905 was editor of the *Musician;* then taught at N.Y. Univ. (1908–12); was lecturer at the Inst. of Musical Art (1905–24); also filled other editorial and educational positions. He publ. *The Music Life* (1891); *The Education of the Music Teacher* (1914); *Essentials in Music History* (1914; with Percy Goetschius); *The Melodic Music Course* (28 vols.; with F.H. Ripley); *Harmonic Music Course* (7 vols.); *The Modern Graded Piano Course* (19 vols.); *Music Theory and Composition* (6 vols.); *From Palestrina to Grieg* (Boston, 1929; 2nd ed., 1946). His wife, **Bertha Feiring Tapper** (b. Christiania, Norway, Jan. 25, 1859; d. New York, Sept. 2, 1915), was a good pianist; she studied with Agathe Backer-Gröndahl in Norway and with Leschetizky in Vienna; came to America in 1881; taught piano at the New England Cons., Boston (1889–97) and at the Inst. of Musical Art, N.Y. (1905–10); she edited 2 vols. of Grieg's piano works; publ. piano pieces and songs. She married Thomas Tapper on Sept. 22, 1895.

Tappert, Wilhelm, German music scholar and writer; b. Ober-Thomaswaldau, Silesia, Feb. 19, 1830; d. Berlin, Oct. 27, 1907. He was trained as a schoolmaster till 1856, when he entered Kullak's Academy of Music in Berlin; studied theory privately with Dehn; settled in Berlin. He was editor of the *Allgemeine Deutsche Musikzeitung* (1876–80); collected a large assemblage of old tablatures, including unique specimens; after his death this collection and his entire valuable library were acquired by the Royal Library of Berlin. An ardent admirer of Wagner, he publ. a curious vol., *Ein Wagner-Lex-*

ikon: Wörterbuch der Unhöflichkeit, enthaltend grobe, höhnende, gehässige und verläumderische Ausdrücke welche gegen den Meister Richard Wagner, seine Werke und seine Anhänger von den Feinden und Spöttern gebraucht worden sind. Zur Gemütsergötzung in müssigen Stunden gesammelt, a collection of anti-Wagner reviews (Leipzig, 1877); a 2nd, enlarged edition was publ. under the title *Richard Wagner im Spiegel der Kritik* (Leipzig, 1903). Other publications: *Musik und musikalische Erziehung* (1867); *Musikalische Studien* (1868); *Das Verbot der Quintenparallelen* (1869); *Wandernde Melodien* (2nd ed., 1889); *54 Erlkönig-Kompositionen* (1898; 2nd ed., 1906); *Sang und Klang aus alter Zeit* (1906); also arrangements of old German songs. He composed 50 left-hand studies for piano; other piano pieces.

Tappolet, Willy, Swiss writer on music; b. Lindau, near Zürich, Aug. 6, 1890; d. Chêne-Bongeries, Feb. 24, 1981. He studied philology and musicology in Berlin, Zürich, and Geneva; was on the faculty of the Univ. of Geneva from 1950–60. He obtained his Ph.D. from the Univ. of Zürich in 1918 and an additional degree from the Univ. of Geneva in 1938 for his dissertation *La Notation musicale et son influence sur la pratique de la musique* (Neuchâtel, 1947). He further publ. monographs on Honegger (in German, Zürich and Leipzig, 1933; in French, Neuchâtel, 1939; revised ed., in German, 1954; in French, 1957) and on Ravel (Olten, 1950). In 1955–60 he was a prof. of music at the Univ. of Geneva.

Tăranu, Cornel, Rumanian composer; b. Cluj, June 20, 1934. He studied with Toduţă and Muresianu at the Cons. in Cluj (1951–57); in 1957 he was named senior lecturer at the Cluj Cons.; traveled to Paris and took lessons with Nadia Boulanger and Messiaen (1966–67); attended the seminars of Ligeti and Maderna at Darmstadt (1968–72); then returned to Cluj. His music is austerely formal, with atonal sound structures related through continuous variation, with permissible aleatory interludes from performers.
WORKS: Opera, *Secretul lui Don Giovanni* (*The Secret of Don Juan;* 1969–70); cantatas: *Cîntare unui ev aprins* (*Hymn for a Fiery Age,* 1962) and *Stejarul lui Horia* (*The Oak of Horia,* 1963); Symph. for String Orch. (1957); *Secvenţe* (*Sequences*) for String Orch. (1960); *Sinfonia brevia* (1962); *Simetrii* (*Symmetries*) for Orch. (1964; Cluj, May 14, 1965); *Incantaţii* (*Incantations*) for Orch. (1965; Cluj, Jan. 15, 1966); Piano Concerto (1966; Cluj, May 29, 1967); *Intercalări* (*Intercalations*) for Piano and Orch. (1967–69; Cluj, Dec. 13, 1969); *Sinfonietta giocosa* for String Orch. (1968); *Alternanţe* (*Alternations*) for Orch. (1968; Bucharest, May 29, 1969); *Racorduri* (*Transitions*) for Chamber Orch. (1971); String Trio (1952); *Poem-Sonata* for Clarinet and Piano (1954); Cello Sonata (1960); Flute Sonata (1961); Oboe Sonata (1963); *3 Pieces* for Clarinet and Piano (1964); *Dialogues for 6* for Flute, Clarinet, Trumpet, Vibraphone, Percussion, and Piano (1966); *Ebauche* for Voice, Clarinet, Violin, Viola, Cello,

and Piano (1966–68); *Le Lit de Procruste (The Bed of Procrustes)* for Baritone, Clarinet, Viola, and Piano (1968–70); *Odă în metru antic (Ode in Ancient Meter)*, cantata for Baritone, Clarinet, Piano, and Percussion (1975); piano pieces; songs.

Tarchi, Angelo, Italian composer; b. Naples, c.1755; d. Paris, Aug. 19, 1814. He studied at the Cons. dei Turchini in Naples with Fago and Sala; was music director and composer at the King's Theatre in London in 1787–88 and again in 1789; subsequently was active in Italy until settling in Paris in 1797. He wrote about 45 operas in Italian, and 6 in French; of these the following were produced at La Scala in Milan: *Ademira* (Dec. 27, 1783); *Ariarte* (Jan., 1786); *Il Conte di Saldagna* (June 10, 1787); *Adrasto* (Feb. 8, 1792); *Le Danaidi* (Dec. 26, 1794); *L'impostura poco dura* (Oct. 10, 1795). In Paris he produced the French version of *Il Conte di Saldagna* as *Bouffons de la foire St. Germain* (1790); *D'Auberge en auberge* (Opéra-Comique, April 26, 1800); etc. He acquired a certain notoriety by his attempt to rewrite the 3rd and 4th acts of Mozart's *Le nozze di Figaro* (1787); regarding this episode, see A. Einstein, "Mozart e Tarchi," *Rassegna Musicale* (July 1935); also C. Sartori, "Lo *Zeffiretto* di Angelo Tarchi," *Rivista Musicale Italiana* (July 1954).

Tarditi, Giovanni, Italian bandleader and composer; b. Acqui, March 10, 1857; d. Rome, Sept. 19, 1935. He traveled as a bandleader in Europe and America; publ. manuals for band playing such as *Segnalofono* for trumpet calls; wrote the operettas *Monte Carlo* (Genoa, March 1, 1897) and *L'isola degli antropofagi* (Rome, June 1, 1925), military marches, etc.

Tardos, Béla, Hungarian composer; b. Budapest, June 21, 1910; d. there, Nov. 18, 1966. He studied with Kodály at the Budapest Academy of Music (1934–36); upon graduation was active as a concert manager and music publisher. He composed much choral music for mass singing employing the modalities of Hungarian folk songs.
WORKS: Comic opera, *Laura* (1958, revised 1964; posthumous, Debrecen, Dec. 11, 1966); 3 cantatas: *May Cantata* (1950); *A város peremén (Upon the City's Outskirts,* 1958); *Az új Isten (The New Gold,* 1966); *Overture* (1949); *Suite* for Orch. (1950); Piano Concerto (1954); *Overture to a Fairy Tale* (1955); Symph., in memory of the victims of fascism (1960); *Fantasy* for Piano and Orch. (1961); Violin Concerto (1962); *Evocatio* for Orch. (1964); Wind Octet (1935); Piano Quartet (1941); 3 string quartets (1947, 1949, 1963); *Improvisations* for Clarinet and Piano (1960); *Prelude and Rondo* for Flute and Piano (1962); *Quartettino-Divertimento* for 4 Wind Instruments (1963); *Cassazione* for Harp Trio (1963); Violin Sonata (1965); *5 Bagatelles* for Piano (1955); *6 Small Studies* for Piano (1963); songs.

Tariol-Baugé, Anne, French singer; b. Clermont-Ferrand, Aug. 28, 1872; d. Asnières, near Paris, Dec. 1, 1944. She made her opera debut in Bordeaux; then

went to Russia; returning to France, she sang in Toulouse and Nantes; then settled in Paris, where she appeared mainly in light opera; she sang the title role at the premiere of Messager's opera *Véronique* at the Bouffes-Parisiens (Dec. 10, 1898); distinguished herself especially in Offenbach's operettas. She was married to the baritone **Alphonse Baugé.**

Tarisio, Luigi, Italian violin maker and trader; b. Fontanetto, near Milan, c.1795; d. Milan, Oct. 1854. He was a carpenter by trade, and in his leisure hours acquired sufficient skill to play the violin at country fairs. He also began collecting old violins, which he repaired and sold at a profit. In 1827 he made his first trip to Paris, and in 1851 visited London; soon he became known as a reliable trader, and obtained many rich clients. He left a collection of about 200 violins, which were later purchased by Vuillaume in Paris.
BIBLIOGRAPHY: G. Hart, *The Violin: Famous Makers and Their Imitators* (London, 1875; many subsequent printings); H.R. Haweis, *Old Violins* (London, 1898); W.A. Silverman, *The Violin Hunter* (N.Y., 1957; mostly anecdotal).

Tarp, Svend Erik, Danish composer; b. Thisted, Jutland, Aug. 6, 1908. He studied theory with Knud Jeppesen and piano with Rudolf Simonsen at the Copenhagen Cons. (1929–31); then was appointed to its faculty (1934–42); concurrently lectured at the Univ. of Copenhagen (1935–42) and the Royal Opera Academy (1935–40); occupied various administrative and editorial posts in music organizations in Denmark; was chairman of the board of directors of the Society for Publishing of Danish Music (1935–58 and again after 1976); was editor of *Edition Dania* (1941–60).
WORKS: 2 operas: *Princessen i det Fjerne (The Princess at a Distance,* 1952; Copenhagen, May 18, 1953) and *9,90,* burlesque television opera (Copenhagen, Aug. 12, 1962); 2 ballets: *Skyggen (The Shadow,* after Hans Christian Andersen, 1941–44; Copenhagen, April 1, 1960) and *Den detroniserede dyretoemmer (The Dethroned Tamer,* 1943–44; Copenhagen, Feb. 5, 1944); Sinfonietta for Chamber Orch. (1931); Violin Concertino (1931); Flute Concertino (1937); *Orania,* suite for Orch. (1937); *Mosaique,* miniature suite for Orch. (1937); *Comedy Overture No. 1* (1939); *Comedy Overture No. 2* (1950); Piano Concerto (1943); 7 symphs.: No. 1, *Sinfonia devertente* (1945); No. 2 (1948); No. 3, *Sinfonia quasi una fantasia* (1958); No. 4 (1975); No. 5 (1975); No. 6 (1976); No. 7 (1977); *Pro defunctis,* overture (1945); *Partita* for Orch. (1947); *The Battle of Jericho,* symph. poem (1949); *Preludio patetico* for Orch. (1952); *Divertimento* for Orch. (1954); *Scandinavian Design* for Orch. (1955); *Lyrical Suite* for Orch. (1956); *Little Dance Suite* for Orch. (1964); *Little Festival Overture* (1969); *Te Deum* for Chorus and Orch. (1938); *Christmas Cantata* for Narrator, Baritone, Chorus, Organ, and Orch. (1946); *Serenade* for Flute, Clarinet, and String Trio (1930); *Serenade* for Flute and String Trio (1936); Duet for Flute and Vi-

ola (1941); String Quartet (1973); Piano Sonata (1950); other piano pieces; music for about 40 films and 15 radio and television dramas; songs.

Tarr, Edward H(ankins), American trumpeter and musicologist; b. Norwich, Conn., June 15, 1936. He studied the trumpet in Boston with Roger Voisin (1953) and in Chicago with Adolph Herseth (1958–59); then studied musicology with Schrade in Basel (1959–64). He subsequently was active both as a trumpet virtuoso and a musicologist; in 1967 he organized the Edward H. Tarr Brass Ensemble, with which he performed Renaissance and Baroque music on original instruments and on modern replicas. From 1968–70 he taught at the Rheinische Musikschule in Cologne; in 1972 was appointed to the faculty of the Schola Cantorum Basiliensis in Basel. He contributed numerous articles on trumpet playing to various publications, and publ. the book *Die Trompete* (Bern, 1977; 2nd ed., 1978). He also edited a number of trumpet works, including a complete edition of the trumpet music of Torelli.

Tárrega, Francisco, Spanish guitar virtuoso; b. Villarreal, Castellón, Nov. 21, 1852; d. Barcelona, Dec. 15, 1909. He studied at the Madrid Cons.; composed many pieces for his instrument, also made many transcriptions of classical and modern works.
BIBLIOGRAPHY: E. Pujol, *Tárrega, ensayo biográfico* (Lisbon, 1960).

Tartini, Giuseppe, important Italian violinist, composer, and theorist; b. Pirano, Istria, April 8, 1692; d. Padua, Feb. 26, 1770. The story of Tartini's early years abounds in unverifiable reports. In 1709 he enrolled at the Univ. of Padua as a law student, and at the age of 19 contracted a secret marriage to the 21-year-old Elisabetta Premazore, a protégée of the powerful Cardinal Cornaro, who, according to some biographies, vengefully brought a charge of abduction against him. Tartini had to take refuge from prosecution in the Franciscan monastery at Assisi; there he is said to have taken music lessons with the organist Czernohorsky, known as "il padre bohemo." According to further accounts, the cardinal dropped action against Tartini, who then returned to Padua; later he went to Ancona to study violin. In 1721 he was appointed solo violinist at S. Antonio in Padua. In 1723–26 he served as chamber musician to Count Kinsky in Prague; then resumed his residence in Padua, where he organized a music school in 1728; among his students there were Nardini and Pugnani. He subsequently developed a brilliant career as a violinist, making numerous concert tours in Italy. His style of playing, and in particular his bowing, became a model for other concert violinists. Tartini was a prolific composer of violin music, including concertos, sonatas, and chamber combinations. An edition of his collected works was initiated in Milan in 1971 under the editorship of E. Farina and G. Scimone, as *Le opere di Giuseppe Tartini.* A thematic catalogue of his violin sonatas was printed in Milan in 1975.
Although Tartini lacked scientific training, he made several acoustical discoveries, the most important of which were the summation and differential tones; Tartini observed these effects in 1714 and summarized his findings in his *Trattato di Musica,* publ. in 1754; the differential tone became known also as Tartini's tone, or "terzo suono." Tartini's tones were actually described in an earlier German publication, *Vorgemach der musicalischen Composition* by G.A. Sorge, publ. in 1745–47. These tones were also known, rather misleadingly, as "beat tones." They are in fact produced by the interference of frequencies of higher overtones. The "wolf tones" of string instruments are different in origin, and are produced by vibrations of the body of the instrument. Violinists are usually aware of interferences from differential tones and also from the less audible summation tones resulting from added frequencies; they correct them experimentally by a slight alteration of tuning. Among Tartini's compositions the most famous is his violin sonata known under the sobriquet *Trillo del Diavolo,* supposedly inspired by Tartini's dream in which the Devil played it for him; the eponymous diabolical trill appears in the last movement of the sonata.
WORKS: Uncounted violin concertos, possibly as many as 150; about 100 violin sonatas, of which *Trillo del Diavolo* was publ. posthumously in Cartier's *L'Art du violon;* other works include 6 concertos, op. 1 (1734), 3 of which were republished in Paris, and 3 others printed with 2 viola parts added by Blainville and publ. as *Concerti grossi;* 12 Violin Sonatas with Cello and Cembalo, also publ. as op. 1; 6 Violin Sonatas, op. 2; 12 Sonatas, including op. 2, for Violin and Bass, as op. 3; *6 Concerti a Violino solo, 2 Violini, Viola e Violoncello o Cembalo di concerto,* op. 4; 6 Sonatas for Violin with Continuo (also as op. 4); opp. 5, 6, and 7, each comprising 6 Sonatas for Violin and Continuo; *6 Sonate a 3,* op. 8; *L'arte dell'arco* (reprinted in French by Choron as *L'Art du violon*); *Trillo del Diavolo* (numerous eds.).
WRITINGS: *Regole per arrivare a saper ben suonar il violino,* a violin method (1752–56; partially trans. into French as *Traité des agréments de la musique* (1771); *Trattato di musica secondo la vera sienza dell'armonia* (1754); *Risposta alla critica del di lui Trattato di musica di Msgr. Le Serre di Ginevra* (1767); *De' principi dell'armonia musicale contenuta nel diatonico genere* (1767); *Lettera alla signora Maddalena Lombardini inserviente ad una importante lezione per i suonatori di violino* (1770; Eng. trans. by Burney, London, 1771).
BIBLIOGRAPHY: F. Fanzago, *Orazione delle lodi di G. T.* (Padua, 1770); J.A. Hiller, *Lebensbeschreibungen berühmter Musikgelehrten und Tonkünstler* (Leipzig, 1784); F. Fanzago, *Elogi* (Padua, 1792); C. Ugoni (1802; in *Della letteratura italiana,* vol. I, pp. 1–28); F. Fayolle, *Notices sur Corelli, Tartini, etc.* (Paris, 1810); G. Benedetti, *Brevi cenni su G. T.* (Trieste, 1897); M. Tamaro, *G. T.* (Parenzo, 1897; in *Atti e menorie della Società istriana,* vol. XII); A. Bachmann, *Les Grands Violinistes du passé* (Paris, 1913); C. Bouvert, *Une Leçon de T.* (Paris, 1918); M. Dounias, Die *Violinkonzerte G. T.s* (Munich, 1935); H.P. Schökel, *G. T.* (Berlin,

1936); A. Capri, *G. T.* (Milan, 1945; includes a thematic index of the Tartini MSS at Padua); A. Spalding, *A Fiddle, a Sword, and a Lady* (N.Y., 1953; a fictionalized account of Tartini's life). A thematic index of Tartini's concertos was publ. by G. Tebaldini, in *L'archivio musicale* (Padua, 1895).

Taskin, (Emile-) Alexandre, French baritone, grandson of **Henri-Joseph Taskin;** b. Paris, March 8, 1853; d. there, Oct. 5, 1897. He was a pupil of Ponchard and Bussine at the Paris Cons.; made his debut at Amiens in 1875. He sang in Lille and Geneva; returned to Paris in 1878; was engaged at the Opéra-Comique in 1879, and created important parts in many new operas. He retired in 1894, and from then until his death was prof. of lyrical declamation at the Cons. On the night of the terrible catastrophe of the burning of the Opéra-Comique (May 25, 1887) he was singing in *Mignon;* through his calmness and bravery many lives were saved, and the government decorated him with a medal.

Taskin, Pascal, French manufacturer of keyboard instruments; b. Theux, near Liège, 1723; d. Paris, Feb. 9, 1793. He went to Paris at an early age and entered Blanchet's atelier, later succeeding to the business and becoming highly celebrated as an instrument maker. He invented the leather plectra for the harpsichord (1768), replacing the crow quills previously in use. He built his first piano in 1776. His nephew **Pascal-Joseph Taskin** (b. Theux, Nov. 20, 1750; d. Versailles, Feb. 5, 1829) was Keeper of the King's Instruments from 1772 until the Revolution; his son **Henri-Joseph Taskin** (b. Versailles, Aug. 24, 1779; d. Paris, May 4, 1852) was an organist and composer.
BIBLIOGRAPHY: D.H. Boalch, *Makers of the Harpsichord and Clavichord, 1440–1840* (London, 1956; 2nd ed., revised, 1974).

Tassinari, Pia, Italian mezzo-soprano; b. Modigliana, Sept. 15, 1909. She received her musical training in Bologna and Milan; made her debut at Castel Monferrato in 1929; then sang at La Scala in Milan (1931–37) and at the Rome Opera (1933–44). She made her American debut at the Metropolitan Opera in N.Y. on Dec. 26, 1947, as Tosca. Although she began her career as a soprano, in later years she preferred to sing mezzo-soprano parts. Her repertoire included both soprano and mezzo-soprano roles, e.g., Mimi, Tosca, Manon, and Marguerite, and also Amneris and Carmen. She married the noted tenor **Ferruccio Tagliavini.**

Tate, Phyllis (Margaret Duncan), English composer; b. Gerrards Cross, Buckinghamshire, April 6, 1911. She studied composition with Harry Farjeon at the Royal Academy of Music in London; composed a Symph., a Cello Concerto, and several other works, but withdrew them as immature. In her music she follows the zeitgeist of the modern era; her music bristles with abrasive dissonances and asymmetrical rhythms, while the form retains its Classical purity. She married the musical scholar and

publishing official **Alan Frank** in 1935.
WORKS: Cello Concerto (1933); *Valse lointaine* for Small Orch. (1941); *Prelude, Interlude and Postlude,* for Chamber Orch. (1942); Saxophone Concerto (1944); Sonata for Clarinet and Cello (1947; perf. at the Salzburg Festival of the International Society for Contemporary Music, June 23, 1951); String Quartet (1952); *Occasional Overture* (1955); *The Lady of Shalott,* after Tennyson, cantata for Tenor, Viola, Percussion, 2 Pianos, and Celesta (1956); *The Lodger,* opera (London, July 14, 1960); television opera, *Dark Pilgrimage* (1963); *A Victorian Garland,* after Matthew Arnold, for Soprano, Contralto, Horn, and Piano (1965); *Secular Requiem* for Chorus and Orch. (1967); *Christmas Ale* for Soloists, Chorus, and Orch. (1967); *Apparitions,* ballad sequence for Tenor, Harmonica, String Quartet, and Piano (1968); *Illustrations* for Brass Band (1969); *Variegations* for Solo Viola (1971); music for schools and amateur musicians: *Twice in a Blue Moon,* fantasy operetta (1968); *Serenade to Christmas* for Mezzo-soprano, Chorus, and Orch. (1972); *Lyric Suite* for 2 Pianos (1973); *The Rainbow and the Cuckoo* for Oboe, Violin, Viola, and Cello (1974); *Sonatina Pastorale* for Harmonica and Harpsichord (1974); *St. Martha and the Dragon* for Narrator, Soloists, Chorus, and Orch. (1976); *Seasonal Sequence* for Viola and Piano (1977); *Panorama* for Strings (1977); *All the World's a Stage* for Chorus and Orch. (1977).
BIBLIOGRAPHY: M. Carner, "The Music of Phyllis Tate," *Music & Letters* (April 1954); H. Searle, "Phyllis Tate," *Musical Times* (May 1955).

Tatum, Art(hur), black American jazz pianist; b. Toledo, Ohio, Oct. 13, 1910; d. Los Angeles, Nov. 5, 1956. He was blind in one eye and had limited vision in the other; he attended a school for the blind in Columbus, Ohio, and learned to read Braille music notation; at the age of 16 began to play in nightclubs. In 1932 he went to N.Y. and became successful on the radio. In 1938 he made a spectacular tour of England; then was again in N.Y. for many years; eventually went to California, where he died of uremia. He brought "stride" piano playing to a point of perfection, scorning such academic niceties as proper fingering, but achieving small miracles in the melody while throwing effortless cascades of notes across the keyboard; he also had a knack of improvising variations on popular pieces by defenseless deceased classical composers; his audiences adored Art's art, while professional musicians knitted their brows in wild surmise.
BIBLIOGRAPHY: Arnold Laubich and Ray Spencer, *Art Tatum: A Guide to His Recorded Music* (N.Y., 1982).

Tauber, Richard (real name, **Ernst Seiffert**), eminent Austrian tenor; b. Linz, May 16, 1892; d. London, Jan. 8, 1948. He studied music at the Hoch Cons. in Frankfurt; made his debut at Chemnitz as Tamino in *Die Zauberflöte* (March 2, 1913) with such success that he was engaged in the same year at the

Dresden Opera; in 1915 he appeared with the Berlin Royal Opera at Salzburg. Later he sang mostly in light opera; was particularly successful in the leading parts of Lehár's operettas. He made his American debut on Oct. 28, 1931, in a N.Y. recital; was noted for his performance of Mozart as well as for being a fine recitalist. In 1938 he went to England; became a British subject in 1940. In London he wrote an operetta, *Old Chelsea,* and took the leading role at its production there (Feb. 17, 1943). He made his last American appearance at Carnegie Hall, N.Y., on March 30, 1947.

BIBLIOGRAPHY: H. Ludwigg, ed., *Richard Tauber* (Berlin, 1938); Diana Napier-Tauber (his 2nd wife), *Richard Tauber* (Glasgow, 1949); W. Korb, *Richard Tauber* (Vienna, 1966); C. Castle and Diana Napier-Tauber, *This Was Richard Tauber* (London, 1971).

Taubert, Ernst Eduard, German composer and music critic; b. Regenwalde, Sept. 25, 1838; d. Berlin, July 14, 1934. He studied theology in Bonn, and music there with Albert Dietrich; later with Friedrich Kiel in Berlin, where he became a teacher at the Stern Cons. and music critic for the *Berliner Post;* he also contributed to various German music magazines. His works include a Piano Quintet; Wind Quintet; Piano Quartet; 5 string quartets; Piano Trio; *Ballade* for Orch.; piano pieces for 2- and 4-hands; songs.

Taubert, (Carl Gottfried) Wilhelm, German composer; b. Berlin, March 23, 1811; d. there, Jan. 7, 1891. He was a piano pupil of Neithardt, later of L. Berger, and for composition, of Bernhard Klein. He appeared early as a concert player; taught music in Berlin; became assistant conductor of the court orch. in 1831; was Generalmusikdirektor of the Royal Opera, Berlin, in 1845–48; also court Kapellmeister from 1845 to 1869; continued to conduct the court orch. until 1883. He conducted his First Symph. in Berlin at the age of 20 (March 31, 1831). His operas (all produced in Berlin) include: *Die Kirmes* (Jan. 23, 1832); *Marquis und Dieb* (Feb. 1, 1842); *Der Zigeuner* (Sept. 19, 1834); *Joggeli* (Oct. 9, 1853); *Macbeth* (Nov. 16, 1857); *Cesario,* after Shakespeare's *Twelfth Night* (Nov. 13, 1874). He composed much instrumental music, but is best remembered for his *Kinderlieder* (opp. 145, 160), the favorites among his 300 songs.

BIBLIOGRAPHY: W. Neumann, *Wilhelm Taubert und Ferdinand Hiller* (Kassel, 1857).

Taubman, Howard, American music critic; b. New York, July 4, 1907. He studied at Cornell Univ.; joined the staff of the *N.Y. Times* in 1930; in 1955 succeeded Olin Downes as chief music critic there, and in 1960 succeeded Brooks Atkinson as drama critic; was succeeded as senior music critic by Harold C. Schonberg in 1960; retired in 1972; then became music adviser for television productions sponsored by the Exxon Corp.

WRITINGS: *Opera: Front and Back* (N.Y., 1938); *Music as a Profession* (N.Y., 1939); *Music on My Beat* (N.Y., 1943); *The Maestro: The Life of Arturo Toscanini* (N.Y., 1951); *How to Build a Record Library* (N.Y., 1953; new ed., 1955); *How to Bring Up Your Child to Enjoy Music* (Garden City, N.Y., 1958).

Taubmann, Otto, German conductor and composer; b. Hamburg, March 8, 1859; d. Berlin, July 4, 1929. After graduation from school he followed a commercial career for 3 years; then studied music under Wüllner, Rischbieter, Nicodé, and Blassmann at the Dresden Cons.; traveled a year for further study, and began his career as a theater conductor; in 1886–89 he was director of the Wiesbaden Cons.; in 1891–92, theater conductor in St. Petersburg; in 1892–95, conductor of the Cäcilienverein in Ludwigshafen; then settled in Berlin, where from 1898 he was music critic of the *Börsen-Courier.* He composed chiefly choral works, of which the most successful was *Eine deutsche Messe* for Soli, Double Chorus, Organ, and Orch. (1896).

Taucher, Curt, German tenor; b. Nuremberg, Oct. 25, 1885; d. Munich, Aug. 7, 1954. He studied with Heinrich Hermann in Munich; made his debut as Faust in Augsburg in 1908; then sang in Chemnitz (1911–14) and Hannover (1915–20). In 1920 he joined the Dresden State Opera, remaining there until 1934; during his tenure there he created the role of Menelaus in Strauss's opera *Die Aegyptische Helena.* On Nov. 23, 1922, he sang the role of Siegmund in *Die Walküre* at his Metropolitan Opera debut in N.Y.; continued on its roster until 1927. He made guest appearances at Covent Garden in London (1932), at the Berlin State Opera, and at the Bavarian State Opera in Munich. He was noted for his roles in Wagner's operas.

Taudou, Antoine (-Antonin-Barthélemy), French violinist and composer; b. Perpignan, Aug. 24, 1846; d. St.-Germain-en-Laye, July 6, 1925. He studied at the Paris Cons., winning the Grand Prix de Rome in 1869 with the cantata *Francesca da Rimini;* in 1883, became prof. of harmony at the Cons. He publ. *Marche-Ballet, Chant d'automne,* and *Marche nocturne* for Orch.; Violin Concerto; String Quartet; Piano Trio; Trio for Flute, Viola, and Cello; etc.

Tauriello, Antonio, Argentine composer; b. Buenos Aires, March 20, 1931. He studied piano with Walter Gieseking and composition with Alberto Ginastera; while still a youth, he was engaged to conduct opera and ballet at the Teatro Colón, Buenos Aires. His music is neo-Classical in its general mold.

WORKS: *Serenade* for Orch. (1957); *Ricercare* for orch. (1963); *Transparencies* for 6 Instrumental Groups (Washington, D.C., 3rd Inter-American Music Festival, May 12, 1965); Piano Concerto (Washington, 4th Inter-American Music Festival, June 29, 1968; Hilde Somer, soloist); *Mansión de Tlaloc* for Piano, Percussion, and Strings (1969); *Signos de los tiempos* for Flute, Clarinet, Violin, Cello, and Piano

(1969).

Tausch, Franz, celebrated German clarinetist; b. Heidelberg, Dec. 26, 1762; d. Berlin, Feb. 9, 1817. At the age of 8 he played in the Electoral orch. at Mannheim; was engaged at Munich (1777–89), and then in the court orch. at Berlin, where he founded a school for wind instruments in 1805; Heinrich Bärmann was his pupil. He publ. 2 clarinet concertos, 3 concertantes for 2 Clarinets, Andante and Polonaise for Clarinet, clarinet duos, trios for 2 Clarinets with Bassoon, 6 quartets for 2 Basset Horns and 2 Bassoons (with 2 Horns ad libitum), 6 military marches, etc.

Tausch, Julius, German conductor and composer; b. Dessau, April 15, 1827; d. Bonn, Nov. 11, 1895. He studied with Friedrich Schneider, and at the Leipzig Cons. (1844–46); then settled in Düsseldorf; there he became conductor of the Künstlerliedertafel; was Schumann's deputy from 1853, and in 1855 his successor as conductor of the Music Society and Subscription Concerts in Düsseldorf, retiring in 1890. He composed the cantatas *Der Blumen Klage auf den Tod des Sängers; Dein Leben schied, dein Ruhm begann; Germanenzug; Rheinfahrt;* piano pieces; male choruses.

Tausig, Carl, celebrated piano virtuoso; b. Warsaw, Nov. 4, 1841; d. Leipzig, July 17, 1871. He was trained by his father, **Aloys Tausig** (1820–85), who was a pupil of Thalberg and wrote brilliant piano music. Carl Tausig studied with Liszt, and emulated his bravura style; he made his debut in 1858, at an orch. concert conducted by Hans von Bülow at Berlin. During the next 2 years he gave concerts in German cities, making Dresden his headquarters; then went to Vienna in 1862, giving orch. concerts with "advanced" programs similar to Bülow's at Berlin. He settled in Berlin in 1865, and opened the Schule des Höheren Klavierspiels. He gave concerts in the principal towns of Germany, and at St. Petersburg and other Russian centers. He died of typhoid fever at the age of 29.
WORKS: For Piano: 2 études de concert; *Ungarische Zigeunerweisen; Nouvelles soirées de Vienna; Valses-Caprices* on themes from Strauss; *Tägliche Studien* (transposing chromatic exercises; ed. by Ehrlich); also transcriptions and arrangements.
BIBLIOGRAPHY: K.F. Weitzmann, *Der Letzte der Virtuosen* (Leipzig, 1868); W. von Lenz, *Die grossen Pianoforte-Virtuosen unserer Zeit* (Berlin, 1872; in Eng., N.Y., 1899).

Tausinger, Jan, Rumanian-born Czech composer; b. Piatra Neamt, Nov. 1, 1921; d. Prague, July 29, 1980. He studied composition with Cuclin, Jora, and Mendelsohn at the Bucharest Cons., graduating in 1947; then went to Prague, where he had lessons in conducting with Ančerl; concurrently took courses in advanced harmony with Alois Hába and Bořkovec at the Prague Academy (1948–52). From 1952 to 1958 he was director of the State Cons. in Ostrava; subsequently occupied other posts in the musical organizations of the area. His music is greatly diversified in style, idiom, and technique, ranging from neo-Classical modalities to integral dodecaphony; he made use of optical representational notation when justified by the structure of a particular piece.
WORKS: FOR THE STAGE: Opera, *Ugly Nature,* after Dostoyevsky (1971); ballet, *Dlouhá noc (The Long Night;* 1966). FOR ORCH.: *Suite in the Old Style* (1946–47); Symph. No. 1, *Liberation* (1952); Violin Concerto (1962–63); *Confrontazione I* and *II* (1964); *Concertino meditazione* for Viola and Chamber Ensemble (1965); *A Prayer* for Soprano and Chamber Orch. (1965); *Praeludium, Sarabande and Postludium* for Winds, Harp, Piano, and Percussion (1967); *Noc (The Night),* musical collage, after a poem by Pushkin, for Soprano, Chorus, Orch., and Guitar (1967); *Správná věc (The Right Thing),* symph. picture to words of Mayakovsky, for Tenor, Baritone, Chorus, and Orch. (1967); *Musica evolutiva* for Chamber Orch. (1967; Zagreb, Nov. 24, 1971); *Improvisations,* in honor of Bach, for Piano and Orch. (1970); *Ave Maria* for Narrator, Soprano, and Orch. (Prague, Oct. 17, 1972); *Sinfonia bohemica* for Bass, Male Chorus, Trumpet, Harpsichord, and Orch. (1973–75); *Sinfonia slovacca* (1979). CHAMBER MUSIC: Violin Sonata (1954); *Partita* for Viola and Piano (1957–58); 2 string trios (1960, 1965); 4 string quartets (1961; 1966; 1970; *Structures,* 1972); *Colloquium* for 4 Wind Instruments (1964); Trio for Violin, Viola, and Guitar (1965); *Le avventure* for Flute and Harp (1965); *Canto di speranza* for Piano Quartet (1965); *Happening* for Piano Trio, based on proclamation of J. Shweik (1966); *De rebus musicalibus* for Flute, Bass Clarinet, Vibraphone, Piano, and Percussion (1967); *Čmáranice po nebi (Scrawling in the Sky),* to a poem by an early Russian futurist, Khlebnikov, for Soprano, Flute, Bass Clarinet, Piano, and Percussion (1967); *Sonatina emancipata* for Trumpet and Piano (1967); Brass Quintet (1968); *Hommage à Ladislav Černý* for Viola and Piano (1971); *"On revient toujours ...,"* suite for Violin and Piano (1974); *"Comme il faut,"* sonatina for Oboe and Piano (1974); *Hukvaldy Nonet* (1974); *"Au dernier amour...,"* suite-sonata for Cello and Piano (1974–75); *Non-isosceles* for Flute, Cello, and Piano (1975); Clarinet Sonata (1975); *4 Evocations* for Flute, Viola, Cello, and Piano (1976); *Sketches,* 2nd nonet (1976); *Reminiscences,* 3rd nonet (1976); Sextet for Wind Quintet and Piano (1976); *7 Microchromophonies* for Clarinet, Viola, and Piano (1977); *4 Nuances* for Flute, Harp, Violin, Viola, and Cello (1978); Piano Sonata (1948–50); *10 Dodecaphonic Studies* for Piano (1972); songs; including *Duetti compatibili (Zero Point)* for Soprano and Viola (1971) and *Starting Point* for Soprano and 2 Violins (1979–80); choruses.

Tauwitz, Eduard, German conductor and composer; b. Glatz, Silesia, Jan. 21, 1812; d. Prague, July 25, 1894. He was Kapellmeister at theaters in Vilna (1837), Riga (1840), Breslau (1843), and Prague (1846; was pensioned in 1863). He wrote more than 1,000 compositions, including 3 operas: *Trilby* (Vilna, 1836); *Bradamante* (Riga, 1844); *Schmolke und Bakel* (Breslau, 1846); also church music; songs; part-songs.

Tavares, Hekel, Brazilian composer; b. Rio de Janeiro, Sept. 16, 1896; d. there, Aug. 8, 1969. He was the son of a wealthy plantation owner and, working in the fields, acquired intimate knowledge of native folk songs. Without benefit of formal education, Tavares wrote instrumental and vocal music in large forms; his works include a Piano Concerto which bears the advanced opus number 105; it is based on urban and rural dance forms; another significant work on Brazilian themes is a Violin Concerto. But the bulk of his compositions consists of popular songs.

Tavener, John, British composer; b. London, Jan. 28, 1944. He studied with Lennox Berkeley at the Royal Academy of Music; also took a course with the Australian composer David Lumsdaine. Among the formative influences of his creative evolution were medieval hymnology and Indian transcendentalism; his technical equipment is, by contrast, ultramodern, including combinatorial serialism and electronic generation of sound.

WORKS: Piano Concerto (1962–63; London, Dec. 6, 1963); *3 Holy Sonnets* for Baritone and Chamber Orch., to poems by John Donne (1962; London, July 1964); *3 Sections from T.S. Eliot's Four Quartets* for Tenor and Piano (1964); *The Cappemakers,* dramatic cantata (1964; revised for stage, 1965; Charleston Manor, Sussex, June 14, 1964); *Cain and Abel,* dramatic cantata for Soloists and Chamber Orch. (1965; London, Oct. 22, 1966); Chamber Concerto (1965; revised 1968; London, June 12, 1968); *The Whale,* dramatic cantata for Narrator, Soloists, Chorus, and Orch. (1966; London, Jan. 24, 1968); *Grandma's Footsteps* for Chamber Group (London, March 14, 1968); *Introit for the Feast of St. John Damascene* for Soprano, Contralto, Chorus, and Orch. (London, March 27, 1968); Concerto for Orch. (1968); *3 Surrealist Songs* for Mezzo-soprano, Piano, Bongos, and Tape (BBC, March 21, 1968); *In Alium* for Soprano, Orch., and Tape (London, Aug. 12, 1968); *A Celtic Requiem,* dramatic cantata for Soloists, Children's Choir, Chorus, and Orch. (London, July 16, 1969); *Ultimos ritos* for Soloists, 5 Choruses, Brass Ensemble, and Orch. (1972; Haarlem, June 22, 1974); *Coplas* for Soloists, Chorus, and Tape (Cheltenham, July 9, 1970); *Nomine Jesu* for 5 Male Speaking Voices, Mezzo-soprano, Chorus, 2 Alto Flutes, Organ, and Harpsichord (Dartington, South Devon, Aug. 14, 1970); *Canciones españolas* for 2 Countertenors or Sopranos, 2 Flutes, Organ, and Harpsichord (London, June 8, 1972); *In memoriam Igor Stravinsky* for 2 Alto Flutes, Organ, and Bells (1971); *Ma fin est mon commencement* for Tenor Chorus, 4 Trombones, Piano, and 4 Cellos (London, April 23, 1972); *Little Requiem for Father Malachy Lynch* (Winchester Cathedral, July 29, 1972); *Variations on 3 Blind Mice* for Chamber Orch. (1972); *Requiem for Father Malachy* for 6 Soloists and Chamber Orch. (London, June 10, 1973); *Thérèse,* op-

era (1973–76; Covent Garden, London, Oct. 1, 1979); *Canticle of the Mother of God* for Soprano and Chorus (1976); *A Gentle Spirit,* chamber opera after the story by Dostoyevsky (Bath, June 6, 1977); *Kyklike Kinesis* for Soprano, Cello, Chorus, and Orch. (1977; London, March 8, 1978); *Lamentation, Last Prayer and Exaltation* for Soprano and Handbells (1977); *Palintropos* for Piano and Orch. (1977; Birmingham, March 1, 1979); *The Last Prayer of Mary Queen of Scots* for Soprano and Handbells (1977); *6 Russian Folk Songs* for Soprano and Ensemble (1978); *The Liturgy of St. John Chrysostom* for Chorus a cappella (London, May 6, 1978); *The Immurement of Antigone,* monodrama for Soprano and Orch. (1978; London, March 30, 1979); *6 Abbasid Songs* for Tenor and 3 Flutes (1979); *Akhmatova: Requiem* for Soprano, Baritone, and Ensemble (1980; Edinburgh, Aug. 20, 1981); *Sappho, Lyric Fragments* for 2 Sopranos and Strings (1980); *Risen!* for Chorus and Ensemble (1980); *Prayer for the World* for 16 Solo Voices (1981); *Funeral Ikos* for Chorus (1981); *Towards the Son: Ritual Procession* for Orch. (London, Nov. 15, 1983).

Taverner, John, important English composer; b. c.1490; d. Boston, Lincolnshire, Oct. 18, 1545. In 1526 he was appointed master of the choristers at Cardinals' College in Oxford. In 1530 he became lay clerk of the choir of the parish church St. Botolph, in Boston, Lincolnshire. In 1537 he was elected a member of the Guild Corpus Christi there; then became treasurer. In 1545 he was appointed a town alderman, but died soon afterward. The widely circulated stories of his imprisonment for heresy and of his serving as an agent for Cromwell are totally unfounded. Taverner was a prolific composer of church music; among his works are 8 masses, 3 Magnificats, a Te Deum, and 28 motets. He also wrote 3 secular vocal compositions for W. de Worde's *Song-book* (1530). His church music is found in vols. I and III of *Tudor Church Music* (1923–24).

BIBLIOGRAPHY: H.B. Collins, "John Taverner's Masses," *Music & Letters* (1924); F. Harrison, "John Taverner," in *The New Oxford History of Music,* vol. III (Oxford, 1960); H. Benham, *The Music of John Taverner: A Study and Assessment* (Diss., Univ. of Southampton, 1970); C. Hand, *John Taverner: His Life and Music* (London, 1978); D. Josephson, *John Taverner, Tudor Composer* (Ann Arbor, Mich., 1979).

Taylor, Billy (William), black American jazz pianist; b. Greenville, N.C., July 24, 1921. He studied piano with Henry Grant; then enrolled at Virginia State College in Petersburg (B.Mus., 1942); in 1975 received his D.Ed. degree from the Univ. of Mass. In 1951 he formed the Billy Taylor Trio; served as a radio disc jockey and program director; was host of the "Jazz Alive" radio series. He was also active as a teacher; was on the staff of the Manhattan School of Music and Howard Univ. His image became an intaglio of jazz, so that he was popularly dubbed "Mr. Jazz."

Taylor, Cecil, black American jazz pianist; b. New York, March 15, 1933. He studied at the New England Cons.; gained experience as a jazz pianist in Boston; subsequently led his own combos and made many tours of the U.S. and Europe. He was also active as a teacher at the Univ. of Wisconsin, Antioch College, and Glassboro State College. A digitally agile pianist, he was instrumental in developing the "free" jazz style of the 1960s.

Taylor, Clifford, American composer; b. Avalon, Pa., Oct. 20, 1923. He studied composition with Lopatnikoff at the Carnegie-Mellon Univ. in Pittsburgh, and with Irving Fine, Hindemith, Piston, and Thompson at Harvard Univ. (M.A., 1950). He taught at Chatham College in Pittsburgh (1950–63); in 1963 joined the faculty of Temple Univ., in Philadelphia.
WORKS: Opera, *The Freak Show* (1975); *Theme and Variations* for Orch. (1951); *Concerto Grosso* for String Orch. (1957); 2 symphs.: No. 1 (1958) and No. 2 (1965; Philadelphia Orch., Dec. 16, 1970); Concerto for Organ and Chamber Orch. (1963); *Sinfonia Seria* for Concert Band, Flute, and Baritone Horn (1965); Piano Concerto (1974); Violin Sonata (1952); String Quartet for Amateurs (1959); Trio for Clarinet, Cello, and Piano (1959–60); String Quartet No. 1 (1960); *Concert Duo* for Violin and Cello (1961); Duo for Saxophone and Trombone (1965); *Serenade* for Percussion Ensemble (1967); *Movement for 3* for Violin, Cello, and Piano (1967); *5 Poems* for Oboe and 5 Brasses (1971); *Fantasia and Fugue* for Piano (1959); *30 Ideas* for Piano (1972); *36 More Ideas* for Piano (1976); numerous a cappella choruses, including choral settings of Western Pennsylvania folk songs (1958) and *A Pageant of Characters from William Shakespeare* for Chorus and Soloists (1964); songs.

Taylor, David Clark, American singing teacher; b. New York, Nov. 11, 1871; d. there, Dec. 6, 1918. A graduate of the College of the City of N.Y. (B.A., 1890), he studied piano with O.W. Wilkinson (1888–94), theory with A. Remy (1893–97), and singing (1890–96) with several teachers in N.Y. He was long connected with the Macmillan Co. He wrote *The Psychology of Singing* (N.Y., 1908); *Self Help for Singers* (N.Y., 1914); *New Light on the Old Italian Method* (N.Y., 1916); *The Melodic Method in School Music* (N.Y., 1918).

Taylor, (Joseph) Deems, greatly popular American composer and writer; b. New York, Dec. 22, 1885; d. there, July 3, 1966. He graduated from N.Y. Univ. (B.A., 1906); studied theory with O. Coon (1908–11). After doing editorial work for various publications and serving as war correspondent for the *N.Y. Tribune* in France (1916–17), he became music critic for the *N.Y. World* (1921–25), editor of *Musical America* (1927–29), and critic for the *N.Y. American* (1931–32). He was a member of the National Inst. of Arts and Letters; received a Mus.Doc. *(honoris causa)* from N.Y. Univ. (1927); a Litt.D. from Juniata College (1931). Following the success of his orch. suite *Through the Looking-Glass*, after Lewis Carroll's tale (1923), he was commissioned by Walter Damrosch to compose a symph. poem, *Jurgen* (1925). Meanwhile, 2 widely performed cantatas, *The Chambered Nautilus* and *The Highwayman*, had added to his growing reputation, which received a strong impetus when his opera *The King's Henchman* (libretto by Edna St. Vincent Millay), commissioned by the Metropolitan Opera, was produced in that house on Feb. 17, 1927. Receiving 14 performances in 3 seasons, it established a record for American opera at the Metropolitan Opera House, but it was surpassed by Taylor's next opera, *Peter Ibbetson* (Feb. 7, 1931); this attained 16 performances in 4 seasons. These successes, however, proved ephemeral, and the operas were allowed to lapse into unmerited desuetude. From 1942 to 1948 he was president of the American Society for Composers, Authors and Publishers.
WORKS: *The Echo,* musical comedy (N.Y., 1909); *The King's Henchman,* opera (N.Y., Feb. 17, 1927); *Peter Ibbetson,* opera (N.Y., Feb. 7, 1931); *Ramuntcho,* opera (Philadelphia, Feb. 10, 1942); *The Dragon,* opera (N.Y. Univ., Feb. 6, 1958); *The Siren Songs,* symph. poem (1912; N.Y., July 18, 1922); *Through the Looking-Glass,* suite for Chamber Orch. (1917–19; N.Y., Feb. 18, 1919; rescored for Full Orch., 1921–22; N.Y., March 10, 1923); *The Portrait of a Lady* for 11 Instruments (1918); *Jurgen,* symph. poem (N.Y., Nov. 19, 1925); *Circus Day,* suite for Jazz Orch. (1925; for Symph. Orch., 1933); ballet music from *Casanova* for Orch. (N.Y., April 18, 1937); *Marco Takes a Walk,* variations for Orch. (N.Y., Nov. 14, 1942); *A Christmas Overture* (N.Y., Dec. 23, 1943, composer conducting); *Elégie* for Orch. (Los Angeles, Jan. 4, 1945); *Restoration Suite* for Orch. (Indianapolis, Nov. 18, 1950); *The Chambered Nautilus,* cantata for Mixed Voices and Orch. (1914); *The Highwayman,* cantata for Baritone, Women's Voices, and Orch. (1914); *Lucrece,* suite for String Quartet; *A Kiss in Xanadu,* pantomime for Piano or 2 Pianos; part-songs; songs; piano pieces.
WRITINGS: *Of Men and Music* (N.Y., 1937); *The Well Tempered Listener* (N.Y., 1940); *Walt Disney's Fantasia* (N.Y., 1940); *Music to My Ears* (N.Y., 1949); *Some Enchanted Evenings: The Story of Rodgers and Hammerstein* (N.Y., 1953). With R. Kerr he revised Rupert Hughes's *Biographical Dictionary of Musicians* (N.Y., 1940).
BIBLIOGRAPHY: J.T. Howard, *Deems Taylor* (N.Y., 1927); W. and C. Lichtenwanger, eds., *Modern Music... Analytic Index,* compiled by Wayne Shirley (N.Y., 1976, pp. 219–20).

Taylor, Franklin, English pianist and teacher; b. Birmingham, Feb. 5, 1843; d. London, March 19, 1919. He was a pupil of C. Flavell (piano) and T. Bedsmore (organ); also studied (1859–61) at the Leipzig Cons. Returning to London, he settled there as a highly successful concert pianist and teacher; in 1876–82, was a prof. at the National Training School, and from 1883, at the Royal College of Music. He publ. *Primer of Pianoforte Playing* (1877); *Pianoforte Tutor; Technique and Expression in Pianoforte Playing* (1897).

Taylor, Raynor, English-American composer; b. in England, c.1747; d. Philadelphia, Aug. 17, 1825. He received his early training as a chorister in the Chapel Royal, and in 1765 became organist of a church in Chelmsford; that same year he was also appointed music director at Sadler's Wells Theatre, London. In 1792 he emigrated to the U.S., going first to Baltimore and then to Annapolis, where he was organist of St. Anne's Church. Moving to Philadelphia in 1793, he became organist of St. Peter's there, and in 1820 was one of the founders of the Musical Fund Society. A gifted singer, he gave humorous musical entertainments which he called "olios," and in 1796 conducted an orch. concert that included several of his own compositions. In collaboration with A. Reinagle, who had been his pupil in London, he composed a monody on the death of Washington (1799), and a ballad opera, *Pizarro, or the Spaniards in Peru* (1800); some of his song MSS are in the N.Y. Public Library.

BIBLIOGRAPHY: L.C. Madeira, *Annals of Music in Philadelphia* (1896); O.G. Sonneck, *Early Concert-Life in America* (1905); J.T. Howard, *A Program of Early American Piano Music* (1931).

Tchaikovsky, Boris, Russian composer; b. Moscow, Sept. 10, 1925. He studied at the Moscow Cons. with Shostakovich, Shebalin, and Miaskovsky. He publ. his earliest piano works at the age of 13; wrote an opera, *The Star* (1949); Symph. No. 1 (1947); *Fantasy on Russian Themes* for Orch. (1950); *Slavic Rhapsody* for Orch. (1951); *Symphonietta* (1953); Symph. No. 2 (1967); Piano Concerto (1969); Violin Concerto (1970); 4 string quartets; Piano Trio; Violin Sonata; piano pieces. He is not related to Piotr Ilyich Tchaikovsky.

Tchaikovsky, Modest, Russian playwright and librettist; brother of **Piotr Ilyich Tchaikovsky;** b. Alapaevsk, Perm district, May 13, 1850; d. Moscow, Jan. 15, 1916. He was the closest intimate of Tchaikovsky, and the author of the basic biography. His plays had only a passing success, but he was an excellent librettist; he wrote the librettos of Tchaikovsky's last 2 operas, *The Queen of Spades* and *Iolanthe.*

Tchaikovsky, Piotr Ilyich, famous Russian composer; b. Votkinsk, Viatka district, May 7, 1840; d. St. Petersburg, Nov. 6, 1893. The son of a mining inspector at a plant in the Urals, he was given a good education; had a French governess and a music teacher. When he was 10, the family moved to St. Petersburg and he was sent to a school of jurisprudence, from which he graduated at 19, becoming a government clerk; while at school he studied music with Lomakin, but did not display conspicuous talent as either a pianist or composer. At the age of 21 he was accepted in a musical inst., newly established by Anton Rubinstein, which was to become the St. Petersburg Cons. He studied with Zaremba (harmony and counterpoint) and Rubinstein (composition); graduated in 1865, winning a silver medal for his cantata to Schiller's *Hymn to Joy.* In 1866 he

became prof. of harmony at the Moscow Cons. under the directorship of Nicolai Rubinstein. As if to compensate for a late beginning in his profession, he began to compose with great application. His early works (a programmatic symph. subtitled *Winter Dreams,* some overtures and small pieces for string quartet) reveal little individuality. With his symph. poem *Fatum* (1869) came the first formulation of his style, highly subjective, preferring minor modes, permeated with nostalgic longing and alive with keen rhythms. In 1869 he undertook the composition of his overture-fantasy *Romeo and Juliet;* not content with what he had written, he profited by the advice of Balakirev, whom he met in St. Petersburg, and revised the work in 1870; but this version proved equally unsatisfactory; Tchaikovsky laid the composition aside, and did not complete it until 1879; in its final form it became one of his most successful works. A Belgian soprano, Désirée Artôt, a member of an opera troupe visiting St. Petersburg in 1868, took great interest in Tchaikovsky, and he was moved by her attentions; for a few months he seriously contemplated marriage, and so notified his father (his mother had died of cholera when he was 14 years old). But this proved to be a passing infatuation on her part, for soon she married the Spanish singer Padilla; Tchaikovsky reacted to this event with a casual philosophical remark about the inconstancy of human attachments. Throughout his career Tchaikovsky never allowed his psychological turmoil to interfere with his work. Besides teaching and composing, he contributed music criticism to Moscow newspapers for several years (1868–74), made altogether 26 trips abroad (to Paris, Berlin, Vienna, N.Y.), and visited the first Bayreuth Festival in 1876, reporting his impressions for the Moscow daily *Russkyie Vedomosti.* His closest friends were members of his own family, his brothers (particularly **Modest,** his future biographer), and his married sister Alexandra Davidov, at whose estate, Kamenka, he spent most of his summers. The correspondence with them, all of which was preserved and eventually publ., throws a true light on Tchaikovsky's character and his life. His other intimate friends were his publisher, Jurgenson, Nicolai Rubinstein, and several other musicians. The most extraordinary of his friendships was the epistolary intimacy with Nadezhda von Meck, a wealthy widow whom he never met but who was to play an important role in his life. Through the violinist Kotek she learned about Tchaikovsky's financial difficulties, and commissioned him to write some compositions, at large fees; then arranged to pay him an annuity of 6,000 rubles. For more than 13 years they corresponded voluminously, even when they lived in the same city (Moscow, Florence); on several occasions Madame von Meck hinted that she would not be averse to a personal meeting, but Tchaikovsky invariably declined such a suggestion, under the pretext that one should not see one's guardian angel in the flesh. On Tchaikovsky's part, this correspondence had to remain within the circumscribed domain of art, personal philosophy, and reporting of daily events, without touching on the basic problems of his existence. On

July 18, 1877, Tchaikovsky contracted marriage with a conservatory student named Antonina Milyukova, who had declared her love for him. This was an act of defiance of his own nature; Tchaikovsky was a deviate, and made no secret of it in the correspondence with his brother Modest (who was also abnormal in this respect). He thought that by flaunting a wife he could prevent the already rife rumors about his abnormality from spreading further. The result was disastrous, and Tchaikovsky fled from his wife in horror. He attempted suicide by walking into the Moskva River in order to catch pneumonia, but suffered nothing more severe than simple discomfort. He then went to St. Petersburg to seek the advice of his brother Anatol, a lawyer, who made suitable arrangements with Tchaikovsky's wife for a separation. (They were never divorced; she died in an insane asylum in 1917.) Madame von Meck, to whom Tchaikovsky wrote candidly of the hopeless failure of his marriage (without revealing the true cause of that failure), made at once an offer of further financial assistance, which Tchaikovsky gratefully accepted. He spent several months during 1877–78 in Italy, Switzerland, Paris, and Vienna. During these months he completed one of his greatest works, the 4th Symph., dedicated to Mme. von Meck. It was performed for the first time in Moscow on Feb. 22, 1878, but Tchaikovsky did not cut short his sojourn abroad to attend the performance. He resigned from the Moscow Cons. in the autumn of 1878, and from that time dedicated himself entirely to composition. The continued subsidy from Mme. von Meck allowed him to forget money matters. Early in 1879 he completed his most successful opera, *Eugene Onegin* ("lyric scenes," after Pushkin); it was first produced in Moscow by a cons. ensemble, on March 29, 1879, and gained success only gradually; the first performance at the Imperial Opera in St. Petersburg did not take place until 5 years later (Oct. 31, 1884). A morbid depression was still Tchaikovsky's natural state of mind, but every new work sustained his faith in his destiny as a composer, despite many disheartening reversals. His Piano Concerto No. 1, rejected by Nicolai Rubinstein as unplayable, was given its world premiere (somewhat incongruously) in Boston, on Oct. 25, 1875, played by Hans von Bülow, and afterward was performed all over the world by famous pianists, including Nicolai Rubinstein himself. The Violin Concerto, criticized by Leopold Auer (to whom the score was originally dedicated) and attacked by Hanslick with sarcasm and virulence at its world premiere by Brodsky in Vienna (1881), survived all its detractors to become one of the most celebrated pieces in the violin repertoire. The 5th Symph. (1888) was successful from the very first. Early in 1890 Tchaikovsky wrote his 2nd important opera, *The Queen of Spades,* which was produced at the Imperial Opera in St. Petersburg in that year. His ballets *Swan Lake* (1876) and *The Sleeping Beauty* (1889) became famous on Russian stages. But at the peak of his career, Tchaikovsky suffered a severe psychological blow; Mme. von Meck notified him of the discontinuance of her subsidy, and with this announcement she abruptly terminated their correspondence. Tchaikovsky could now well afford the loss of the money, but his pride was deeply hurt by the manner in which Mme. von Meck had acted. It is indicative of Tchaikovsky's inner strength that even this desertion of one whom he regarded as his staunchest friend did not affect his ability to work. In 1891 he undertook his first and only voyage to America. He was received with honors as a celebrated composer; he led 4 concerts of his works in N.Y. and one each in Baltimore and Philadelphia. He did not linger in the U.S., however, and returned to St. Petersburg in a few weeks. Early in 1892 he made a concert tour as a conductor in Russia, and then proceeded to Warsaw and Germany. In the meantime he had purchased a house in the town of Klin, not far from Moscow, where he wrote his last symph., the *Pathétique*. Despite the perfection of his technique, he did not arrive at the desired form and substance of this work at once, and discarded his original sketch. The title *Pathétique* was suggested to him by his brother Modest; the score was dedicated to his nephew, Vladimir Davidov. Its music is the final testament of Tchaikovsky's life, and an epitome of his philosophy of fatalism. In the first movement, the trombones are given the theme of the Russian service for the dead. Remarkably, the score of one of his gayest works, the ballet *The Nutcracker,* was composed simultaneously with the early sketches for the *Pathétique*. Tchaikovsky was in good spirits when he went to St. Petersburg to conduct the premiere of the *Pathétique,* on Oct. 28, 1893 (which was but moderately successful). A cholera epidemic was then raging in St. Petersburg, and the population was specifically warned against drinking unboiled water, but apparently Tchaikovsky carelessly did exactly that. He showed the symptoms of cholera soon afterward, and nothing could be done to save him. The melodramatic hypothesis that the fatal drink of water was a defiance of death, in perfect knowledge of the danger, since he must have remembered his mother's death of the same dread infection, is untenable in the light of publ. private letters between the attendant physician and Modest Tchaikovsky at the time. Tchaikovsky's fatalism alone would amply account for his lack of precaution. Almost immediately after Tchaikovsky's death a rumor spread that he had committed suicide, and reports to that effect were publ. in respectable European newspapers (but not in Russian publications), and repeated even in some biographical dictionaries (particularly in Britain). After the grim fantasy seemed definitely refuted, a ludicrous paper by an émigré Russian woman was publ., claiming private knowledge of a homosexual scandal involving a Russian nobleman's nephew (in another version a member of the Romanov imperial family) which led to a "trial" of Tchaikovsky by a jury of his former school classmates, who offered Tchaikovsky a choice between honorable suicide or disgrace and possible exile to Siberia; a family council, with Tchaikovsky's own participation, advised the former solution, and Tchaikovsky was supplied with arsenic; the family doctor was supposed to be a part of the conspiracy, as were Tchaikovsky's own brothers. Amazingly enough, this outrageous fabrication was accepted as historical fact by some biographers, and even found its way into the pages of *The New Grove*. In Russia, the truth of Tchaikovsky's homosexuality was totally suppressed, and any references to it in his diary and letters were carefully expunged.

As a composer, Tchaikovsky stands apart from the militant national movement of the "Mighty Five." The Russian element is, of course, very strong in his music, and upon occasion he made use of Russian folk songs in his works, but this national spirit is instinctive rather than consciously cultivated. His personal relationship with the St. Petersburg group of nationalists was friendly without being intimate; his correspondence with Rimsky-Korsakov, Balakirev, and others was mostly concerned with professional matters. Tchaikovsky's music was frankly sentimental; his supreme gift of melody, which none of his Russian contemporaries could match, secured for him a lasting popularity among performers and audiences. His influence was profound on the Moscow group of musicians, of whom Arensky and Rachmaninoff were the most talented. He wrote in every genre, and was successful in each; besides his stage works, symphs., chamber music, and piano compositions, he composed a great number of lyric songs that are the most poignant creations of his genius. By a historical paradox, Tchaikovsky became the most popular Russian composer under the Soviet regime. His subjectivism, his fatalism, his emphasis on melancholy moods, even his reactionary political views (which included a brand of amateurish anti-Semitism), failed to detract from his stature in the new society. In fact, official spokesmen of Soviet Russia repeatedly urged Soviet composers to follow in the path of Tchaikovsky's esthetics. Tchaikovsky's popularity is also very strong in Anglo-Saxon countries, particularly in America; much less so in France and Italy; in Germany his influence is insignificant.

WORKS: OPERAS: *The Voyevode* (1867–68; Moscow, Feb. 11, 1869); *Undine* (1869); *The Oprichnik* (1870–72; St. Petersburg, April 24, 1874); *Vakula the Smith* (1874; St. Petersburg, Dec. 6, 1876); *Eugene Onegin* (1877–78; Moscow, March, 29, 1879); *The Maid of Orleans* (1878–79; St. Petersburg, Feb. 25, 1881); *Mazeppa* (1881–83; Moscow, Feb. 15, 1884); *Tcherevichki* (*The Little Shoes;* revised version of *Vakula the Smith;* 1885; Moscow, Jan. 31, 1887); *The Sorceress* (1888–87; St. Petersburg, Nov. 1, 1887); *The Queen of Spades* (1890; St. Petersburg, Dec. 19, 1890); *Iolanta* (1891; St. Petersburg, Dec. 18, 1892).

BALLETS: *Swan Lake* (1875–76; Moscow, March 4, 1877); *The Sleeping Beauty* (1888–89; St. Petersburg, Jan. 15, 1890); *The Nutcracker* (1891–92; St. Petersburg, Dec. 18, 1892).

FOR ORCH.: 6 symphs.: No. 1 (*Winter Dreams;* 1868; revised 1874; Moscow, Feb. 15, 1868); No. 2 *(Little Russian* or *Ukrainian Symph.;* 1872; Moscow, Feb. 7, 1873); No. 3 (1875; Moscow, Nov. 19, 1875); No. 4 (1877; Moscow, Feb. 22, 1878); No. 5 (1888; St. Petersburg, Nov. 17, 1888); No. 6 (*Pathétique;* 1893; St. Petersburg, Oct. 28, 1893); overture to Ostrovsky's play *The Storm* (1864); symph. poem, *Fatum* (1868; Moscow, Feb. 27, 1869); overture, *Romeo and Juliet* (1869; Moscow, March 16, 1870; final version, 1879); symph. fantasy, *The Tempest,* after Shakespeare (1873; Moscow, Dec. 19, 1873); First Piano Concerto (1874–75; Boston, Oct. 25, 1875); *Sérénade mélancolique* for Violin with Orch. (1875; Moscow, Jan. 28, 1876); *Slavonic March* (1876; Moscow, Nov. 17, 1876); symph. fantasy, *Francesca da Rimini,* after Dante (1876; Moscow, March 9, 1877); suite from the ballet *Swan Lake* (1876); *Variations on a Rococo Theme* for Cello and Orch. (1876; Moscow, Nov. 30, 1877); *Valse-Scherzo* for Violin and Orch. (1877; Paris, Oct. 21, 1878); *Suite* No. 1 (1878–79; Moscow, Nov. 23, 1879); Violin Concerto (1878; Vienna, Dec. 4, 1881); Piano Concerto No. 2 (1879–80; Moscow, May 30, 1882); *Capriccio italien* (1880; Moscow, Dec. 18, 1880); *1812 Overture* (1880; Moscow, Aug. 20, 1882); *Serenade* for String Orch. (1880; Moscow, Jan. 28, 1882); *Suite* No. 2 (1883; Moscow, Feb. 16, 1884); *Suite* No. 3 (1884; St. Petersburg, Jan. 28, 1885); *Concert Fantasy* for Piano with Orch. (1884; Moscow, March 6, 1885); symph., *Manfred,* after Byron (1885; Moscow, March 23, 1886); *Suite* No. 4, *Mozartiana* (1887; Moscow, Nov. 26, 1887); overture-fantasy, *Hamlet* (1888; St. Petersburg, Nov. 24, 1888); *Pezzo capriccioso* for Cello with Orch. (1887; Moscow, Dec. 7, 1889); suite from the ballet *The Sleeping Beauty* (1889); symph. ballad, *The Voyevode,* after Pushkin's trans. of Mickiewicz's ballad (1890–91; Moscow, Nov. 18, 1891); suite from the ballet *Nutcracker* (1892; St. Petersburg, March 19, 1892); 3rd Piano Concerto (one movement only; posthumous; St. Petersburg, Jan. 19, 1895); *Andante and Finale* for Piano with Orch. (1893; actually 2nd and 3rd movements of the 3rd Piano Concerto; posthumous; St. Petersburg, Feb. 20, 1896).

CHAMBER MUSIC: 3 string quartets (1871, 1874, 1876); Piano Trio, in memory of Nicolai Rubinstein (Moscow, Oct. 30, 1882); *Souvenir de Florence* for String Sextet (1887; St. Petersburg, Dec. 7, 1892); also *Souvenir d'un lieu cher* for Violin and Piano (1878); several fragments of early works.

FOR PIANO: *Scherzo à la russe* (1867); *Souvenir de Hapsal,* 3 pieces (No. 3 is the famous *Chant sans paroles;* 1867); *Valse-Caprice* (1868); *Romance* in F minor (1868); *Valse-Scherzo* (1870); *Capriccio* (1870); *3 morceaux: Rêverie, Polka de salon, Mazurka de salon* (1870); *2 morceaux: Nocturne* and *Humoresque* (1871); *6 morceaux: Rêverie du soir, Scherzo humoristique, Feuillet d'album, Nocturne, Capriccioso, Thème original et variations* (1872); *6 morceaux sur un seul thème: Prelude, Fugue, Impromptu, Marche funèbre, Mazurka, Scherzo* (1873); *Grande sonate,* in G major (1879); *Les Quatre Saisons,* 12 characteristic pieces for each month of the year (1875–76; of these the most famous are No. 6, *Barcarole;* No. 10, *Chant d'automne;* No. 11, *En traineau;* No. 12, *Noël;* *12 morceaux* (1876–78; among them *Chanson triste* and *Danse russe);* *Album pour enfants,* 24 pieces (1878); *6 pièces* (1882); *Dumka* (1886); *18 morceaux* (1893); Sonata in C-sharp minor (1865; posthumous).

VOCAL WORKS: Cantata, *An die Freude* (Schiller) for Chorus and Orch. (1865); *Liturgy of St. John Chrysostom* for Mixed Chorus in 4 parts (1878); Vesper Service for Mixed Chorus (1882); *Moskva,* coronation cantata for Solo Voices, Chorus, and Orch. (1883); *3 Cherubic Hymns* for Mixed Chorus (1884); 6 church songs (1885); other sacred and secular vocal pieces; about 100 songs, among them such favorites as *Nur wer die Sehnsucht kennt* (after Goethe), *Berceuse,* etc.; 6 duets.

He publ. *Manual of Harmony* (Moscow, 1870; many eds.; Eng. trans. as *Guide to the Practical Study of Harmony,* 1900). The collected criticisms and reminiscences were publ. in 1898; new ed., revised and enlarged, Moscow, 1953; diaries, comprising 11 separate fragments, covering the years between 1873 and 1891, were publ. in Moscow in 1923 (Eng. trans., N.Y., 1945). A centennial ed. of the complete works, in as many as 120 vols., was begun in 1940, interrupted during the war years, and resumed in 1946. Most of the MSS, correspondence, etc. are preserved in Tchaikovsky's house in Klin (now the Tchaikovsky Museum). A thematic catalogue was issued by B. Jurgenson (Moscow, 1897; reprinted N.Y., 1941). More recently the Tschaikowsky-Studio Inst. International issued the *Systematisches Verzeichnis der Werke von P. I. Tschaikowsky* (Hamburg, 1973).

BIBLIOGRAPHY: The basic source is the 3-vol. biography by Modest Tchaikovsky, *The Life of P.I. T.* (Moscow, 1900–1902), but in it the author was compelled to withhold essential facts of Tchaikovsky's life; translations were made, into German by Paul Juon (2 vols.; Leipzig, 1900, 1902) and into Eng. by Rosa Newmarch (abridged) as *The Life and Letters of P.I. T.* (London, 1906). Chapters on Tchaikovsky are included in all music histories and books dealing specifically with Russian music. Books and articles in various languages that should be noted include: V. Tcheshikhin, *P. T.: Attempt at a Characterization* (Riga, 1893); H. Laroche and N. Kashkin, *In Memory of T.* (Moscow, 1894); N. Kashkin, *Reminiscenses of T.* (Moscow, 1897); E. Markham Lee, *T.* (Music of the Masters series; N.Y., 1904); Edwin Evans, Sr., *T.* (London, 1906; revised ed., 1935); *P.I. T.,* a symposium, in the series The Past of Russian Music (Petrograd, 1920), containing documents relating mainly to the Tchaikovsky Museum in Klin; Igor Glebov, *T.: An Essay of Characterization* (Petrograd, 1922); idem, *P.I. T.: His Life and Works* (Petrograd, 1922; a different book from the preceding); H. Laroche, *Collected Musico-Critical Articles,* vol. 2 (Moscow, 1922); M. Steinitzer, *T.* (Leipzig, 1925); R.H. Stein, *T.* (Stuttgart, 1927); Eric Blom, *T.; Orchestral Works* (Musical Pilgrim series; London, 1927); M.D. Calvocoressi and Gerald Abraham, *Masters of Russian Music* (London, 1936); pp. 249–334; this essay publ. separately, 1949); Nikolai von Pals, *P. T.* (Potsdam, 1939); H. Weinstock, *T.* (N.Y., 1943); Gerald Abraham, *T.: A Short Biography* (London, 1944); H. Célis and W.-P. Right, *T.* (Brussels, 1945); Gerald Abraham, *T.: A Symposium* (London, 1945; in the U.S. as *The Music of T.;* N.Y., 1946); D. Brook, *6 Great Russian Composers* (London, 1946); D. Shostakovich and others, *Russian Symphony; Thoughts about T.* (N.Y., 1947); R. Hofmann, *T.* (Paris, 1947); A. Alshvang, *Analytic Essay on T.'s Creative Work* (Moscow, 1951); J.A. Kremlev,

Symphonies of P.I. Tchaikovsky (Moscow, 1955); G. Dombayev, *Creative Work of T.* (Moscow, 1958); B.I. Rabinovich, *P.I. Tchaikovsky and Songs of the People* (Moscow, 1963); *House-Museum of P.I. Tchaikovsky in Klin,* a guide (2nd revised ed., Moscow, 1967); A.A. Alshvang, *P.I. Tchaikovsky* (Moscow, 1970); B.V. Asafiev, *On the Music of Tchaikovsky: Selections* (Leningrad, 1972); J. Warrack, *Tchaikovsky* (1973); L.M. Konisskaya, *Tchaikovsky in St. Petersburg* (Leningrad, 1974); D. Brown, *T.: A Biographical and Critical Study, Vol. I: The Early Years (1840–1874)* (London, 1978) and *Vol. II: The Crisis Years (1874–1878)* (London, 1982). Numerous pamphlets dealing with Tchaikovsky's operas, ballets, orch. works, etc. have been issued in Russia; of these, the most valuable are: N. Findeisen, *T.'s Chamber Music* (Moscow, 1930), A. Budiakovsky, *P.I. T., Symphonic Music* (Leningrad, 1935), V. Bogdanov-Berezovsky, *Operatic and Choreographic Works of T.* (Moscow, 1940), B.M. Yarustovsky, *Operatic Dramaturgy of T.* (Moscow, 1947), and N. Nikolayeva, *Symphonies of T.* (Moscow, 1958). V. Yakovlev compiled a most detailed chronology (often day by day) of Tchaikovsky's life, *Days and Years of T.* (Moscow, 1940). Of the greatest importance is the publication of the complete extant correspondence between Tchaikovsky and Mme. von Meck, in 3 vols. (Moscow, 1933, 1934, 1936). Other correspondence includes *Letters to Relatives* (vol. 1, Moscow, 1940); *Correspondence with P.I. Jurgenson* (2 vols., Moscow, 1939, 1952); letters to and from S. Taneyev (Moscow, 1951); selected letters to intimates (Moscow, 1955); also, G. von Meck, *P.I. T.: Letters to His Family: An Autobiography* (London, 1981). Magazine articles on Tchaikovsky include the following, publ. in the *Musical Quarterly:* Olga Bennigsen, "A Bizarre Friendship: T. and Mme. von Meck" (Oct. 1936); N. Slonimsky, "Further Light on T." (April 1938); S. Bertenson, "The T. Museum at Klin" (July 1944); also, I. Berlin, "T., Pushkin and Onegin," *Musical Times* (March 1980). There are several fictional biographies of Tchaikovsky, among them one by Catherine D. Bowen and Barbara von Meck, *Beloved Friend* (N.Y., 1937); also Klaus Mann, *Symphonie pathétique* (Amsterdam, 1938, in German; in Eng., N.Y., 1948).

Tchaikowsky, André, Polish composer and pianist (not by any genetic interplay related to the great Tchaikovsky); b. Warsaw, Nov. 1, 1935; d. Oxford, England, June 26, 1982. His parents fell victim to the Nazis in Warsaw, but he was spirited away to France. After the war, he returned to Poland and studied piano with Stefan Askenase. In 1955 he won the Chopin Prize at the Warsaw Academy; then went to Paris to study with Nadia Boulanger. In 1957 he settled in London, where he acquired a reputation as an eccentric who played Mozart's concertos with grotesque embellishments of his own. He also composed; among his works were a Clarinet Sonata (1959); 2 string quartets (1967, 1970); Piano Concerto (1966–71); *Trio notturno* for Violin, Cello, and Piano; and a nearly completed opera, *The Merchant of Venice,* on which he worked half of his life

(1960–82). He was a Shakespeare enthusiast; he bequeathed his skull to the Royal Shakespeare Co. for use in the graveside scene in *Hamlet* ("Alas, poor André, A fellow of infinite jest"); in this postmortem fashion he hoped to satisfy his craving to act in a Shakespeare play. The skull was deposited, still in its box, in the store at the Royal Shakespeare Co.'s headquarters in Stratford-upon-Avon for possible use in an eventual production of *Hamlet*.

Tchakarov, Emil, Bulgarian conductor; b. Burgas, June 29, 1948. He studied at the State Cons. in Sofia, where he conducted the youth orch. (1965–72); then directed the Bulgarian Television Chamber Orch. (1968–70). In 1971 he won 3rd prize at the International Conductors' Competition of the Herbert von Karajan Foundation; in 1972 he studied conducting with Franco Ferrara and in 1974 with Eugen Jochum. While still in his 20s he filled engagements as a guest conductor all over the world: with the Berlin Phil., the Vienna Radio Orch., San Francisco Symph. Orch., Holland Radio Orch., and various symph. groups in France, England, Canada, Australia, Japan, and Russia. In 1974 he was appointed permanent conductor of the State Phil. in Plovdiv, Bulgaria. He made his debut at the Metropolitan Opera in N.Y. on Sept. 27, 1979.

Tcherepnin, Alexander, greatly significant Russian composer and pianist; son of **Nicolas Tcherepnin;** b. St. Petersburg, Jan. 20, 1899; d. Paris, Sept. 29, 1977. (The name is pronounced with the stress on the last syllable.) He studied piano as a child with his mother; was encouraged by his father in his first steps in composition, but did not take formal lessons with him. He began to compose in his early youth; wrote a short comic opera at the age of 12, and a ballet when he was 13; then produced a number of piano works; composed 14 piano sonatas before he was 19 years old. In 1917 he entered the Petrograd Cons., where he studied music theory with Sokolov, and piano with Kobiliansky, but remained there only one school year; then joined his parents in a difficult journey to Tiflis, in the Caucasus, during a gradually expanding civil war; in Tiflis, he took lessons in composition with Thomas de Hartmann. In 1921 the family went to Paris, where he continued his studies, taking piano lessons with Isidor Philipp and composition with Paul Vidal. In 1922 he played a concert of his own music in London; in 1923 he was commissioned by Anna Pavlova to write a ballet, *Ajanta's Frescoes*, which she produced in London with her troupe. Tcherepnin progressed rapidly in his career as a pianist and a composer; he played in Germany and Austria; made his first American tour in 1926. Between 1934 and 1937 he made two journeys to the Far East; gave concerts in China and Japan; numerous Chinese and Japanese composers studied with him; he organized a publishing enterprise in Tokyo for the publication of serious works by young Japanese and Chinese composers. He married a Chinese pianist, **Lee Hsien-Ming.** Despite his wide travels, he maintained his principal residence in Paris, and re-

mained there during the war. He resumed his international career in 1947; gave concerts in Scandinavia and elsewhere in Europe. In 1949 he and his wife joined the faculty of De Paul Univ. in Chicago, and taught there for 15 years. In the meantime his music began to be well known; he had 34 publishers; his symph. works were conducted by Koussevitzky, Stokowski, Monteux, Munch, Mitropoulos, Fritz Reiner, Kubelik, William Steinberg, Skrowaczewski, and other famous conductors; he was also a frequent soloist in his piano concertos, which he performed with the major symph. orchs. in America and Europe. He became an American citizen in 1958. In May 1967, Tcherepnin made his first visit to Russia after nearly half a century abroad. In his early works he followed the traditions of Russian Romantic music; characteristically, his Piano Sonata No. 13, which he wrote as a youth, is entitled *Sonatine romantique*. But as he progressed in his career, he evolved a musical language all his own; he derived his melodic patterns from a symmetrically formed scale of 9 degrees, subdivided into 3 equal sections (e.g. C, D, E-flat, E, F-sharp, G, G-sharp, A-sharp, B, C); the harmonic idiom follows a similar intertonal formation; Tcherepnin's consistent use of such thematic groupings anticipated the serial method of composition. Furthermore, he developed a type of rhythmic polyphony, based on thematic rhythmic units, which he termed "interpunctus." However, he did not limit himself to these melodic and rhythmic constructions; he also explored the latent resources of folk music, both oriental and European; he was particularly sensitive to the melorhythms of Russian national songs. A composer of remarkable inventive power, he understood the necessity of creating a communicative musical language, and was primarily concerned with enhancing the lyric and dramatic qualities of his music. At the same time he showed great interest in new musical resources, including electronic sound. His sons **Serge** and **Ivan** are both engaged in experimental musical production.

WORKS: OPERAS: *Ol-Ol,* after Leonid Andreyev (Weimar, Jan. 31, 1928); *Die Hochzeit der Sobeide,* after Hugo von Hofmannsthal (Vienna, March 17, 1933); *The Farmer and the Fairy* (Aspen Festival, Colorado, Aug. 13, 1952); completed Mussorgsky's opera *The Marriage* (Essen, Sept. 14, 1937). BALLETS: *Ajanta's Frescoes* (Anna Pavlova's production, London, Sept. 10, 1923); *Training* (Vienna, June 19, 1935); *Der fahrend Schüler mit dem Teufelsbannen* (1937; score lost during the war; reconstructed, 1965); *Trepak* (Mordkin's Russian Ballet, Richmond, Va., Oct. 10, 1938); *La Légende de Razin* (1941); *Déjeuner sur l'herbe* (Paris, Oct. 14, 1945); *L'Homme à la peau de léopard* (with Arthur Honegger and Tibor Harsányi; Monte Carlo, May 5, 1946); *La Colline des fantômes* (1946); *Jardin persan* (1946); *Nuit kurde* (Paris, 1946); *La Femme et son ombre,* after Paul Claudel (Paris, June 14, 1948); *Aux temps des tartares* (Buenos Aires, 1949). CANTATAS: *Vivre d'amour* (1942); *Pan Kéou* (Paris, Oct. 9, 1945); *Le Jeu de la Nativité* (Paris, Dec. 30, 1945); *Les Douze,* poem by Alexander Blok for Narrator, Strings, Harp, Piano, and Percussion (Paris, Nov. 9,

1947); *Vom Spass und Ernst,* folk-song cantata for Voice and Strings (1964); *The Story of Ivan the Fool,* cantata with Narrator (London, Dec. 24, 1968). FOR ORCH.: Overture (1921); Symph. No. 1 (Paris, Oct. 29, 1927); Symph. No. 2 (Chicago, March 20, 1952); Symph. No. 3 (Indianapolis, Jan. 15, 1955); Symph. No. 4 (Boston, Dec. 5, 1958); *Symphony-Prayer* (Chicago, Aug. 19, 1960); *Magna Mater* (Munich, Oct. 30, 1930); *Russian Dances* (Omaha, Feb. 15, 1934); *Mystère* for Cello and Chamber Orch. (Monte Carlo, Dec. 8, 1926); *Concerto da camera* for Flute, Violin, and Chamber Orch. (1924); *Concertino* for Violin, Cello, Piano, and Strings (1931); *Suite georgienne* (Paris, April 17, 1940); 6 piano concertos: No. 1 (Monte Carlo, 1923); No. 2 (Paris, Jan. 26, 1924, 2-piano version, composer soloist; Nadia Boulanger accompanist); No. 3 (Paris, Feb. 5, 1933, composer soloist); No. 4 (retitled *Fantasia;* 1947); No. 5 (West Berlin, Oct. 13, 1963, composer soloist); No. 6 (Lucerne, Sept. 5, 1972); *Serenade* for String Orch. (1964); *Musica sacra* for String Orch. (Lourdes, April 28, 1973); *Evocation* (1948); *Suite* (Louisville, May 1, 1954); *Concerto* for Harmonica and Orch. (Venice, Sept. 11, 1956); *Divertimento* (Chicago, Nov. 14, 1957). CHAMBER MUSIC: Piano Trio (1925); 2 string quartets (1922, 1926); Piano Quintet (1927); *Ode* for Cello and Piano (1919); 3 cello sonatas (1924, 1925, 1926); Violin Sonata (1922); *Elegy* for Violin and Piano (1927); *Le Violoncelle bien temperé,* 12 preludes for Cello with Piano, 2 of them with a Drum (Berlin, March 23, 1927); *Suite* for Cello Solo (1946); *Mouvement perpétuel* for Violin and Piano (1935); Sonatina for Kettledrums and Piano (1939); *Sonatine sportive,* for Bassoon or Saxophone, and Piano (1939); *Andante* for Tuba and Piano (1939); Trio for Flutes (1939); Quartet for Flutes (1939); *Marche* for 3 Trumpets (1939); *Sonata da chiesa* for Viola da Gamba and Organ (1966). FOR PIANO: *Scherzo* (1917); *10 bagatelles* (1913–18); *Sonatine romantique* (1918); 2 sonatas (1918, 1961); *Toccata* (1921); *Feuilles libres* (1920–24); *5 arabesques* (1921); *9 inventions* (1921); *2 novelettes* (1922); *4 préludes nostalgiques* (1922); *6 études de travail* (1923); *Message* (1926); *Entretiens* (1930); *Etudes de piano sur la gamme pentatonique* (1935); *Autour des montagnes russes* (1937); *Badinage* (1942); *Le Monde en vitrine* (1946); 12 Preludes (1952); 8 Piano Pieces (1954); *Suite* for Harpsichord (1966). VOCAL WORKS: *Lost Flute,* 7 songs on poems trans. from the Chinese, for Narrator and Piano (1954); several albums of songs to poems in Russian, French, and Chinese. He compiled an *Anthology of Russian Music* (with Eng. and German texts, Bonn, 1966).

BIBLIOGRAPHY: Willi Reich, *Alexander Tcherepnin* (Bonn, 1959; 2nd revised ed., 1970; in German; French trans., Paris, 1962); N. Slonimsky, "Alexander Tcherepnin, Septuagenarian," *Tempo* (Jan. 1969); P. Ramey, "Alexander Tcherepnin," *Ovation* (May 1984).

Tcherepnin, Ivan, American composer, son of **Alexander Tcherepnin;** b. Paris, Feb. 5, 1943. He received his early musical training at home in Paris; then followed his father to the U.S., where he entered Harvard Univ., graduating in 1964; also attended courses with Karlheinz Stockhausen and Henri Pousseur in Cologne, and with Pierre Boulez in Darmstadt; studied electronic techniques in Toronto in 1966; returned to Harvard for graduate studies as a pupil of Randall Thompson and Leon Kirchner, obtaining his M.A. degree in 1969. He was an instructor at the San Francisco Cons. of Music (1969–72); in 1972 was appointed to the faculty of Harvard Univ. to teach courses in electronic composition.

WORKS: *Suite progressive pentatonique* for Flute, Cello, and Timpani (1959); *2 entourages sur un thème russe* for Ondes Martenot, Percussion, and Piano (1961); *Mozartean Suite* for Flute, Clarinet, and Bassoon (1962); *Reciprocals* for Flute, Clarinet, and Bassoon (1962); *Work Music* for Electric Guitar, French Horn, Clarinet, and Cello (1965); *Sombres lumières* for Flute, Guitar, and Cello (1965); *Wheelwinds* for 9 Wind Instruments (1966); *Rings* for String Quartet and Ring Modulators (1968); *Summer Music* for Brass Sextet (1970); *Light Music with Water* for 4 Instrumental Groups, 4 Sound-activated Strobe Lights, Electronic Accessories, and Prepared Tape (1970); *set, hold, squelch and clear* for Oboe and Synthesizer (Merce Cunningham dance perf., N.Y., Feb. 21, 1976); *Le va et le vient* for Orch. (1978); *Flores musicales* for Violin, Oboe, Cello, and Psaltery electronically manipulated (Boston, Nov. 29, 1979); Concerto for Oboe, Brass, Woodwind, Harp, and Percussion (1980).

Tcherepnin, Nicolas, noted Russian composer, conductor, and eminent pedagogue; b. St. Petersburg, May 14, 1873; d. Issy-les-Moulineaux, near Paris, June 26, 1945. He was a student of Rimsky-Korsakov at the St. Petersburg Cons. (1895–98); in 1905 was appointed to its faculty; taught orchestration and conducting; Prokofiev was among his many students. He conducted at the festival of Russian music in Paris in 1908; until 1912 toured with the Diaghilev Ballets Russes in Europe. He then returned to Russia; after the Revolution of 1917, he proceeded to the Caucasus, and was director of the Tiflis Cons. (1918–21); then went to Paris, accompanied by his son **Alexander,** and remained there until his death; served as director of the Russian Cons. in Paris (1925–29 and 1938–45). His music embodies the best elements of the Russian national school; it is melodious and harmonious; lyrical and gently dynamic; in some of his works there is a coloristic quality suggesting French impressionistic influence.

WORKS: OPERAS: *Vanka* (Belgrade, 1935); *Svat,* after Ostrovsky. Ballets: *Pavillon d'Armide* (St. Petersburg, Nov. 25, 1907); *Narcisse et Echo* (Monte Carlo, April 26, 1911, composer conducting); *Masque de la Mort Rouge,* after Poe (Petrograd, Jan. 29, 1916, composer conducting); realization and completion of Mussorgsky's opera *The Fair at Sorochinsk* (Monte Carlo, March 17, 1923; Metropolitan Opera, N.Y., Nov. 29, 1930). FOR ORCH.: *Prelude* to Rostand's play *La Princesse lointaine* (1897); *Fantaisie dramatique* (1903); *Le Royaume enchanté,* symph. tableau (1904); Piano Concerto (1907). CHAMBER MUSIC: *Poème lyrique; Cadence fantastique; Un Air ancien* for Flute and Piano; *Pièce calme* for Oboe and Piano; *Pièce insouciante* for Clarinet and Piano; *Variations simples* for Bassoon and Piano; *Fanfare* for Trumpet and Piano; String Quartet; Quartet for Horns; *Divertissement* for Flute, Oboe, and Bassoon. FOR PIANO: *14 esquisses sur les images d'un alphabet russe* (an orch. version of 8 of these was perf. by the Boston Symph. Orch., Nov. 27, 1931); *Primitifs; Pièces de bonne humeur; Pièces sentimentals.* VOCAL WORKS: Liturgical music of the Russian Orthodox rite, including masses a cappella; *Pilgrimage and Passions of the Virgin Mary* (Paris, Feb. 12, 1938); over 200 songs, some of them perennial favorites in Russia.

Tcherepnin, Serge, American composer; son of **Alexander Tcherepnin;** b. Paris, Feb. 2, 1941. He studied violin as a child; was taken to the U.S. in 1949; received his training in theory with his father; then took courses in composition with Karlheinz Stockhausen, in conducting with Pierre Boulez in Darmstadt, and in electronic music with Herbert Eimert. He pursued his regular academic education at Harvard Univ., where he studied with Walter Piston, Leon Kirchner, and Billy Jim Layton, obtaining his B.A. in 1964. In 1966 he went to Milan to study electronic techniques. Returning to the U.S., he became in 1970 an instructor in electronic music at the School of Music in Valencia, Calif. He is the inventor of a portable music synthesizer, patented as the Serge Modular Music System.
WORKS: String Trio (1960); String Quartet (1961); *Kaddish* for Speaker, Clarinet, Violin, Oboe, Flute, Piano, and Percussion, to a poem by Allan Ginsberg (1962); *Figures—Ground* for an Optional Ensemble of 7 to 77 Instruments (1964); several multimedia pieces for theater and films.

Tchesnokov, Pavel, Russian composer; b. near Voskresensk, Oct. 24, 1877; d. Moscow, March 14, 1944. He studied at the Moscow Cons. with Vasilenko, graduating in 1917; also took courses with Sergei Taneyev and Ippolitov-Ivanov. He devoted himself exclusively to choral composition, both secular and sacred; from 1920 was prof. of choral conducting at the Moscow Cons. He publ. a manual for choral singing (Moscow, 1940).

Teagarden, Weldon Leo ("Jack"), American jazz trombonist; b. Vernon, Texas, Aug. 29, 1905; d. New Orleans, Jan. 15, 1964. He began to play the piano as a child; took up the trombone at 10; after playing with bands in Texas, he appeared in N.Y., Chicago, and other cities; was a member of Paul Whiteman's Orch. (1933–38). He led his own big bands (1939–46); played in Louis Armstrong's All Stars (1947–51); then formed his own All Stars, which he led until his death. One of the great jazz trombonists, he also doubled as a singer.

Tear, Robert, Welsh tenor; b. Barry, March 8, 1939. He was educated at King's College, Cambridge;

served as a chorister at St. Paul's Cathedral; made his debut with the English Opera Group in London in 1963; subsequently appeared with the Welsh National Opera. In 1970 he joined the staff at Covent Garden in London; he also toured as a concert singer in the U.S., Canada, Japan, and Russia. In 1984 he was made a Commander of the Order of the British Empire.

Tebaldi, Renata, celebrated Italian soprano; b. Pesaro, Feb. 1, 1922. Her mother, a nurse, took her to Langhirano after the breakup of her marriage to a philandering cellist. There she began to study piano with Giuseppina Passani; at the age of 16 she entered the singing class of Ettore Campogalliani at the Parma Cons.; later she took a course of vocal instruction with the soprano Carmen Melis at the Pesaro Cons. She made her operatic debut in Rovigo as Elena in Boito's *Mefistofele* in 1944. In 1946 Toscanini chose her as one of his artists for the reopening concert at La Scala in Milan, and she subsequently became one of its leading sopranos. She made her first appearance in England in 1950 with the visiting La Scala company at London's Covent Garden; also in 1950 she sang Aida with the San Francisco Opera. On Jan. 31, 1955, she made her Metropolitan Opera debut in N.Y. as Desdemona in Verdi's *Otello;* she continued to appear regularly there until 1973. She toured Russia in 1975 and 1976. Her repertoire was almost exclusively Italian; she excelled in both lyric and dramatic roles; was particularly successful as Violetta, Tosca, Mimi, and Madame Butterfly. She also sang the role of Eva in *Die Meistersinger.* On Nov. 3, 1958, she was the subject of a cover story in *Time* magazine.
BIBLIOGRAPHY: K. Harris, *Renata Tebaldi: An Authorized Biography* (N.Y., 1974); David Ewen, *Musicians since 1900* (N.Y., 1978).

Tebaldini, Giovanni, Italian music scholar; b. Brescia, Sept. 7, 1864; d. San Benedetto del Tronto, May 11, 1952. He studied with Ponchielli and Amelli at the Cons. of Milan; served as maestro di cappella at San Marco in Venice (1889–94), at the Padua Cathedral (1894–97), and at the Santa Casa of Loreto (1902–24); was director of the Cons. of Parma (1897–1902); taught at the Cons. di San Pietro in Naples (1925–30); then went to Genoa, where he was appointed director of the Ateneo Musicale (1931). His specialty was Italian sacred music, but his name suddenly sprang into sensational prominence when he publ. an article provocatively entitled "Telepatia musicale" (*Rivista Musicale Italiana,* March 1909), in which he cited thematic similarities between the opera *Cassandra,* by the relatively obscure Italian composer Vittorio Gnecchi, which was produced in 1905, and *Elektra* by Richard Strauss, written considerably later, implying a "telepathic" plagiarism on the part of Strauss. However, the juxtaposition of musical examples from both operas proved specious and failed to support Tebaldini's contention.
WRITINGS: *La musica sacra in Italia* (Milan, 1894); *Gasparo Spontini* (Recanati, 1924); *Ildebrando Pizzetti* (Parma, 1931); also *Metodo teorico*

pratico per organo (with Enrico Bossi; Milan, 1897).

Tedesco, Ignaz (Amadeus), Bohemian pianist, called the "Hannibal of octaves"; b. Prague, 1817; d. Odessa, Nov. 13, 1882. He studied with Triebensee and Tomaschek; made successful concert tours, especially in southern Russia; settled in Odessa. He composed for piano in a salon style; made transcriptions.

Teed, Roy, English pianist and composer; b. Herne Bay, Kent, May 18, 1928. He studied composition with Lennox Berkeley at the Royal Academy in London; also obtained a diploma in piano. He composed a Piano Concerto (1952); *Festival Suite* for Cello and String Orch. (1958); *Introduction and Scherzo* for Flute, Oboe, and Piano (1960); *So Blest a Day,* Christmas cantata (1960); *The Pied Piper* for Soloists, Chorus, and Orch. (1961); Quartet for Flute and Strings (1961); *Around the Town,* comedy march (1962); *The Jackdaw of Rheims,* narrative cantata (1964); numerous choruses and carols.

Teichmüller, Robert, German pianist and teacher; b. Braunschweig, May 4, 1863; d. Leipzig, May 6, 1939. He studied piano with his father and with Reinecke at the Leipzig Cons., where from 1897 until his death he taught piano; was made a prof. in 1908. With K. Hermann he publ. a valuable guide, *Internationale moderne Klaviermusik* (Leipzig, 1927).
BIBLIOGRAPHY: A. Baresel, *R. T. als Mensch und Künstler* (Leipzig, 1922); idem, *R. T. und die Leipziger Klaviertradition* (Leipzig, 1934).

Teike, Carl (Albert Hermann), German composer of band music; b. Altdamm, Feb. 5, 1864; d. Landsberg, May 22, 1922. He studied French horn in his early youth; at 19 joined the band of the 123rd König Karl Regiment, stationed at Ulm on the Danube. He soon began writing marches that were to become perennial favorites with German bands; at 25 he composed *Alte Kameraden (Old Comrades),* one of the best known of German military marches, marked by a typically stolid square rhythm, with heavily accented downbeats. Teike resigned from the regiment as a result of disagreement with the bandmaster and joined the Royal German Police at Potsdam (1895–1908); then served with the postal service at Landsberg; he continued, however, to compose marches; during World War I he wrote the march *Graf Zeppelin* (known in English editions as *Conqueror*) which, despite its narrow militaristic nature, enjoyed international fame.

Te Kanawa, Dame Kiri, brilliant New Zealand soprano; b. Gisborne, March 6, 1944. Her father was an indigenous Maori who traced his ancestry to the legendary warrior Te Kanawa; her mother was Irish. She attended the Catholic schools in Auckland, and was coached in singing by a nun. She was sent to Melbourne to compete in a radio show; she won the first prize in the Melbourne *Sun* contest, and remained in Melbourne, earning her living by singing at various social functions. In 1966 she received a grant for study in London; there she took private vocal lessons with Vera Rozsa. In 1967 she married Desmond Stephen Park, a mining engineer. In 1970 she made her debut at Covent Garden in London, where she sang the role of the Countess in *The Marriage of Figaro.* In the summer of 1971 she sang the same role in her American debut with the Santa Fe Opera; it became one of her most remarkable interpretations. She sang it again with the San Francisco Opera in 1972. A proverbial *coup de théâtre* in her career came on Feb. 9, 1974, when she was called upon to substitute at a few hours' notice for the ailing Teresa Stratas in the part of Desdemona in Verdi's *Otello* at the Metropolitan Opera in N.Y. It was a triumphant achievement against desperate odds (she suffered a cramp in the groin in the 3rd act), winning for her unanimous critical praise. On Jan. 11, 1975, she sang Donna Elvira in *Don Giovanni* at the Metropolitan. She also acted in the film production of *The Marriage of Figaro.* She sang Pamina in *Die Zauberflöte* at the Paris Opéra on May 13, 1977. On Dec. 31, 1977, she took the role of Rosalinde in a Covent Garden production of *Die Fledermaus,* which was televised to the U.S. She excelled equally as a subtle and artistic interpreter of lyric roles in Mozart's operas and in dramatic representations of grand operas by Verdi. Critics were unanimous in awarding her the status of *prima donna assoluta.* She was the soloist in "Let the Bright Seraphim" from Handel's oratorio *Samson* at the wedding of Prince Charles and Lady Diana Spencer in 1981. In 1982 she was named a Dame Commander of the Order of the British Empire.
BIBLIOGRAPHY: David Ewen, *Musicians since 1900* (N.Y., 1978); David Fingleton, *Kiri Te Kanawa* (N.Y., 1983).

Tekeliev, Alexander, Bulgarian composer; b. Svilengrad, June 3, 1942. He studied composition with Veselin Stoyanov at the Bulgarian State Cons. in Sofia, graduating in 1968; then became head of the music dept. of the Committee for Television and Radio in Sofia; also assumed music teaching duties at the Inst. for Musical and Choreographical Training.
WORKS: Oratorio-requiem, *The Year 1923* (1971); Clarinet Concerto (1968); *Ode to the USSR* for Narrator, Chorus, and Orch. (1970); *Adagio and Scherzo* for String Orch. (1972); *Poem* for Viola and Orch. (1973); 2 chamber symphs. (1974, 1976); choral music and songs.

Telemann, Georg Philipp, greatly significant German composer; b. Magdeburg, March 14, 1681; d. Hamburg, June 25, 1767. He received his academic training at a local school; also learned to play keyboard instruments and the violin; he acquired knowledge of music theory from the cantor Benedikt Christiani. He subsequently attended the Gymnasium Andreanum in Hildesheim, where he became active in student performances of German cantatas. In 1701 he entered the Univ. of Leipzig as a student of jurisprudence; in 1702 organized a collegium musicum there; later was appointed music director of the Leipzig Opera, where he used the services of his student singers and instrumentalists. In 1705 he went to Sorau as Kapellmeister to the court of Count Erdmann II of Promnitz. In 1708 he was appointed Konzertmeister to the court orch. in Eisenach; later he was named Kapellmeister there. In 1709 he married Louise Eberlin, a musician's daughter, but she died in 1711 in childbirth. In 1712 Telemann was appointed music director of the city of Frankfurt; there he wrote a quantity of sacred music as well as secular works for the public concerts given by the Frauenstein Society, of which he served as director. In 1714 he married Maria Katharina Textor, the daughter of a local town clerk. They had 8 sons and 2 daughters, of whom only a few survived infancy. His wife later abandoned him for a Swedish army officer. In 1721 he received the post of music director of 5 churches in Hamburg, which became the center of his important activities as composer and music administrator. In 1722 Telemann was appointed music director of the Hamburg Opera, a post he held until 1738. During his tenure he wrote a number of operas for production there, and also staged several works by Handel and Keiser. In 1737–38 he visited France. His eyesight began to fail as he grew older; his great contemporaries Bach and Handel suffered from the same infirmity. An extraordinarily prolific composer, Telemann mastered both the German and the Italian styles of composition prevalent in his day. While he never approached the greatness of genius of Bach and Handel, Telemann nevertheless became an exemplar of the German Baroque at its grandest development. According to Telemann's own account, he composed about 20 operas for Leipzig; wrote about 4 for Weissenfels, 2 for Bayreuth, and 3 operettas for Eisenach. He lists 35 operas for Hamburg, but included in this list are preludes, intermezzi, and postludes.

WORKS: OPERAS (all produced in Hamburg): *Der gedultige Socrates* (Jan. 28, 1721); *Ulysses* (1721; with Vogler); *Sieg der Schönheit* (1722; later performed as *Gensericus*); *Belsazar* (July 19, 1723; 2nd version, Sept. 30, 1723); *Der Beschluss des Carnevals* (1724; with Campara and Conti); *Omphale* (1724); *Der neu-modische Liebhaber Damon* (June 1724); *Cimbriens allgemeines Frolocken* (Feb. 17, 1725); *Pimpinone oder Die ungleiche Heyrath,* intermezzo (Sept. 27, 1725); *La Capricciosa e il Credula,* intermezzo (1725); *Adelheid* (Feb. 17, 1727); *Buffonet und Alga,* intermezzo (May 14, 1727); *Calypso* (1727); *Sancio* (1727); *Die verkehrte Welt* (1728); *Miriways* (May 26, 1728); *Emma und Eginhard* (1728); *Aesopus* (Feb. 28, 1729); *Flavius Bertaridus, König der Langobarden* (Nov. 23, 1729); *Margaretha, Königin in Castilien* (Aug. 10, 1730); *Die Flucht des Aeneas* (Nov. 19, 1731); *Judith, Gemahlin Kayser Ludewig des Frommen* (Nov. 27, 1732; with Chelleri); *Orasia oder Die rachgierige Liebe* (Oct. 1736).

SACRED MUSIC: Oratorios: *Der königliche Prophete David als ein Fürbild unseres Heilands Jesu* (1718; not extant); *Freundschaft geget über Liebe* (1720; not extant); *Donnerode* (1756–60); *Sing, unsterbliche Seele, an Mirjam und deine Wehmut,* from Klopstock's *Der Messias* (1759); *Das befreite Israel* (1759); *Die Hirten bei der Krippe zu Bethlehem* (1759); *Die Auferstehung und Himmelfahrt Jesu* (1760); *Der Tag des Gerichts* (1762). Cantatas: He publ. the following sets of cantatas, each set containing 72 works: *Harmonischer Gottes-Dienst, oder Geistliche Cantaten zum allgemeinen Gebrauche* (Hamburg, 1725–26); *Auszug derjenigen musicalischen und auf die gewöhnlichen Evangelien gerichteten Arien* (Hamburg, 1727); *Fortsetzung des Harmonischen Gottesdienstes* (Hamburg, 1731–32); *Musicalisches Lob Gottes in der Gemeine des Herrn* (Nuremberg, 1744); more than a thousand cantatas; 46 Passions; masses; Psalms; motets; wedding music; pieces for special church occasions.

INSTRUMENTAL MUSIC: One of his most important collections was his *Musique de table* (Hamburg, 1733); it contained 3 orch. suites, 3 concertos, 3 quartets, 3 trios, and 3 sonatas. His orch. output was prodigious, comprising numerous overtures, concertos, sonatas, quartets, quintets, etc. A complete edition of his works, *Georg Philipp Telemann: Musikalische Werke,* began publ. in Kassel and Basel in 1950.

BIBLIOGRAPHY: Telemann's autobiography of 1718 was publ. in J. Mattheson, *Grosse Generalbass-schule* (Hamburg, 1731); his autobiography of 1739 was publ. in J. Mattheson, *Grundlage einer Ehren-Pforte* (Hamburg, 1740; new ed. by M. Schneider, Berlin, 1910); both of these, plus his autobiographical letter to Walther of 1729, have been republ. in W. Kahl, *Selbstbiographien deutscher Musiker des XVIII. Jahrhunderts* (Cologne, 1948). See also the following: B. Schmid, ed., *Herr G.Ph. Telemann: Lebenslauf* (Nuremberg, c.1745; in German and French); J.D. Winckler, "G.Ph. Telemann," *Nachrichten von niedersächsischen berühmten Leuten und Familien,* I (Hamburg, 1768); R. Rolland, *Voyage musical au pays du passé* (Paris, 1919; Eng. trans., 1922); M. Frey, *Georg Philipp Telemanns Singe-, Spiel- und Generalbass-Übungen* (Zürich, 1922); H. Graeser, *Georg Philipp Telemanns Instrumental-Kammermusik* (Diss., Univ. of Munich, 1924); E. Valentin, *Georg Philipp Telemann* (Burg, 1931; 3rd ed., 1952); H. Hörner, *Georg Philipp Telemanns Passionsmusiken* (Leipzig, 1933); K. Schäfer-Schmuck, *Georg Philipp Telemann als Klavierkomponist* (Diss., Univ. of Kiel, 1934); H. Büttner, *Das Konzert in den Orchestersuiten Georg Philipp Telemanns* (Wolfenbüttel and Berlin, 1935); W. Menke, *Das Vokalwerk Georg Philipp Telemanns* (Kassel, 1942); F. Funk, *The Trio Sonatas of Georg Philipp Telemann* (Diss., George Peabody College for Teachers, 1954); C. Rhea, *The Sacred Oratorios of Georg Philipp Telemann* (Diss., Florida State Univ., 1958); E. Valentin, *Telemann in seiner Zeit* (Hamburg, 1960); R. Petzoldt, *Telemann und seine Zeitgenossen* (Magdeburg, 1966); W. Bergmann, "Telemann in Paris," *Musical Times,* CVIII (1967); C. Gilbertson, *The Methodical Sonatas of Georg Philipp Telemann* (Diss., Univ. of Kentucky, 1967); R. Petzoldt, *Georg Philipp Telemann: Leben und Werk* (Leipzig, 1967; in Eng., 1974); K. Zauft, *Tele-*

manns Liedschaffen und seine Bedeutung für die Entwicklung des deutschen Liedes in der 1. Hälfte des 18. Jahrhunderts (Magdeburg, 1967); *G.Ph. Telemann, Leben und Werk: Beiträge zur gleichnamigen Ausstellung* (Magdeburg, 1967); A. Hoffmann, *Die Orchestersuiten Georg Philipp Telemanns* (Wolfenbüttel and Zürich, 1969); S. Kross, *Das Instrumentalkonzert bei Georg Philipp Telemann* (Tutzing, 1969); M. Peckham, *The Operas of Georg Philipp Telemann* (Diss., Columbia Univ., 1969); K. Grebe, *Georg Philipp Telemann in Selbstzeugnissen und Bilddokumenten* (Reinbeck bei Hamburg, 1970); I. Allihn, *G.Ph. Telemann und J.J. Quantz* (Magdeburg, 1971); H. Grosse and H. Jung, eds., *Georg Philipp Telemann, Briefwechsel* (Leipzig, 1972); *Telemann-Renaissance: Werk- und Wiedergabe* (Magdeburg, 1973); W. Maertens, *Telemanns Kapitänsmusiken* (Diss., Univ. of Halle, 1975); J. Wenzel, *Geschichte der Hamburger Oper, 1678–1978* (Hamburg, 1978); *George Philipp Telemann: Leben—Werk—Wirkung* (Berlin, 1980); E. Klessmann, *Telemann in Hamburg* (Hamburg, 1980).

Telemann, Georg Michael, German theorist and composer; grandson of **Georg Philipp Telemann;** b. Plön, Holstein, April 20, 1748; d. Riga, March 4, 1831. In 1773 he went to Riga and became cantor there (was pensioned in 1828). He publ. *Unterricht im Generalbass-Spielen, auf der Orgel oder sonst einem Clavier-Instrumente* (1773); *Beytrag zur Kirchenmusik* (1785; organ pieces); *Sammlung alter und neuer Kirchenmelodien* (1812); *Über die Wahl der Melodie eines Kirchenliedes* (1821); composed a book of trio sonatas, 6 violin sonatas; organ works.

Tellefsen, Thomas Dyke, Norwegian pianist and composer; b. Trondheim, Nov. 26, 1823; d. Paris, Oct. 6, 1874. In 1842 he went to Paris, where he studied with Kalkbrenner; in 1844 he became a pupil of Chopin, and accompanied him to England and Scotland in 1848. He publ. an edition of Chopin's works, and played Chopin's music at recitals in Paris and in Scandinavia. His own compositions were imitative of Chopin; he wrote nocturnes, waltzes, and mazurkas, but also made use of Norwegian folk songs in many of his works, and thus became an early proponent of national music in Norway.

Telmányi, Emil, Hungarian violinist; b. Arad, June 22, 1892. He studied with Hubay at the Academy of Music in Budapest. In 1911 he began an active career as a concert player; in 1918 he married a daughter of Carl Nielsen; his 2nd wife, whom he married in 1936, is the pianist **Annette Schiöler.** In 1940 he settled in Denmark and taught at the Cons. of Aarhus, retiring in 1969; then lived in Holte, near Copenhagen. He toured the U.S. in 1950. He made a number of arrangements for violin of works by Chopin, Schumann, Brahms, and others; supervised the devising of a curved bow for the playing of Bach's unaccompanied sonatas and partitas.

Telva, Marian, American contralto; b. St. Louis,

December 26, 1897; d. Norwalk, Conn., Oct. 23, 1962. Her real name was **Marian Toucke,** but she changed it to Telva for the sake of euphony. She sang in church in her hometown; then went to N.Y. for further study, and soon was engaged at the Metropolitan Opera, where she sang minor roles between 1920 and 1933 (the 1931–32 season excepted). In the meantime she married a wealthy banker and afterward made only sporadic appearances as a concert singer.

Temianka, Henri, American violinist and conductor; b. Greenock, Scotland, Nov. 19, 1906, of Polish-Jewish parentage. He was taken to the Netherlands as a child; took violin lessons with Willy Hess in Berlin and Jules Boucherit in Paris. In 1926 he emigrated to America and studied at the Curtis Inst. of Music in Philadelphia with Carl Flesch (violin) and Artur Rodzinski (conducting). In 1946 he became the founder and leader of the Paganini Quartet; appeared as soloist with major orchs. in Europe and America. He settled in Los Angeles, where he organized the California Chamber Symph. (1960), with which he toured in the U.S. and Canada. He publ. a book of reminiscences, *Facing the Music* (N.Y., 1973).

Temirkanov, Yuri, noted Russian conductor; b. Nalchik, in the Caucasus, Dec. 10, 1938. He studied at the Leningrad Cons.; made his conducting debut with the Leningrad Opera in 1965. In 1966 he won first prize in the U.S.S.R. All-Union Conductors' Competition, which energized his career. From 1968 to 1976 he conducted the Leningrad Symph. Orch.; also served as chief conductor of the Kirov Opera and Ballet in Leningrad. He then went on an American tour; conducted in Philadelphia, Cincinnati, San Francisco, and Minneapolis. In 1979 he became principal guest conductor of the Royal Phil. Orch. in London. As is to be expected, he shines most glitteringly in the Russian repertoire, and he invariably places Soviet works on his programs.

Temperley, Nicholas, English musicologist; b. Beaconsfield, Aug. 7, 1932. He was educated at Eton College; also studied at the Royal College of Music in London and at King's College, Cambridge (B.A., 1955; Mus.B., 1956; Ph.D., 1959, with the dissertation *Instrumental Music in England, 1800–1850*). In addition to numerous articles and reviews for music periodicals, he publ. *The Music of the English Parish Church* (Cambridge, 1979).

Templeton, Alec, blind pianist and composer; b. Cardiff, Wales, July 4, 1909; d. Greenwich, Conn., March 28, 1963. He studied at the Royal College of Music in London until 1923 and at the Royal Academy of Music until 1931. He settled in the U.S. in 1935, becoming a citizen in 1941; was extremely successful as a radio pianist, especially with his humorous musical sketches, parodies, etc., such as *Bach Goes to Town, Mozart Matriculates,* etc. He also wrote some more ambitious works, including *Concertino lirico* (1942) and *Gothic Concerto* for

Piano and Orch (N.Y., Dec. 19, 1954, composer soloist).
BIBLIOGRAPHY: *Alec Templeton's Music Boxes, as told to R.B. Baumel* (N.Y., 1958).

Templeton, John, Scottish tenor; b. Riccarton, near Kilmarnock, July 30, 1802; d. New Hampton, July 2, 1886. He sang in various churches in Edinburgh; then went to London, where he took lessons in singing with Tom Cooke; also studied theory with Blewitt. On Oct. 13, 1831, he made his debut at Drury Lane Theatre; subsequently became a regular member of Drury Lane. Maria Malibran selected him as tenor for her operatic appearances in London (1833–35). In 1842 he was in Paris; during the season of 1845–46 he made an American tour announced as "Templeton Entertainment," singing folk songs of Great Britain; his commentaries and reminiscences were publ. as *A Musical Entertainment* (Boston, 1845). He retired in 1852.
BIBLIOGRAPHY: W.H. Husk, ed., *Templeton and Malibran. Reminiscences* (London, 1880).

Tenducci, Giusto Ferdinando, celebrated Italian castrato; b. Siena, c.1736; d. Genoa, Jan. 25, 1790. He went to England in 1758 and was received with enthusiasm; led the Handel Festivals from 1784 until his departure for Italy in 1789. He was nicknamed "Triorchis" (triple-testicled), on account of the singular plurality of his reproductive organs that enabled him to marry; indeed, he eloped in 1767 with one of his pupils, 16-year old Dorothy Maunsell, but the marriage was annulled in 1775. She publ. an account of the affair under the title *A True and Genuine Narrative of Mr. and Mrs. Tenducci* (London, 1785). He wrote a treatise on singing, *Instruction of Mr. Tenducci to his Scholars* (London, 1785); also composed music for a comic opera, *The Campaign,* produced in London in 1784, and a group of *Ranelagh Songs.*
BIBLIOGRAPHY: A. Heriot, *The Castrati in Opera* (London, 1956; pp. 185–89; provides an account of Tenducci's extraordinary marriage).

Tennstedt, Klaus, brilliant German conductor; b. Merseburg, June 6, 1926. He studied piano and violin at the Leipzig Cons.; in 1948 was appointed concertmaster at the municipal theater in Halle, and in 1952 became principal conductor there. He subsequently occupied conducting posts at the Dresden Opera (1958–62) and at the State Theater in Schwerin (1962–71); also conducted concerts with the Gewandhaus Orch. in Leipzig, and filled conducting engagements in Czechoslovakia and Russia. In 1971 he went to Sweden, where he conducted at the State Theater in Göteborg and led the Swedish Radio Symph. in Stockholm. He subsequently was engaged as an opera conductor in Kiel, Germany; in 1974 he was invited to conduct the Toronto Symph. Orch.; this was followed by a highly successful debut with the Boston Symph. Orch.; on Feb. 24, 1977, he began a 2-week engagement with the N.Y. Phil.; from 1979 to 1983 he was guest conductor of the Minnesota Orch. in Minneapolis; concurrently

he held the post of chief conductor of the North German Radio Symph. Orch. of Hamburg (1979–82); in 1983 he was engaged to succeed Solti as principal conductor of the London Phil. On Dec. 14, 1983, he made his debut at the Metropolitan Opera in N.Y., in an impressive performance of *Fidelio.* His concerts in Western Europe and in America were received with exceptional acclaim; even his idiosyncrasies (such as bending the knees in anticipation of a powerful crescendo, and other graphic body motions, which caused one critic to liken him to "a demented stork") did not seem to lessen the enthusiasm of both the players and the audiences.

Tenschert, Roland, Austrian musicologist; b. Podersam, Bohemia, April 5, 1894; d. Vienna, April 3, 1970. He studied at the Leipzig Cons. and in Vienna (Dr.Phil., 1921); from 1926 to 1931 he was librarian and teacher at the Mozarteum in Salzburg; in 1945, became prof. of music history at the Vienna Academy of Music.
WRITINGS: *Die Ouvertüren Mozarts* (Diss., Univ. of Vienna, 1921; publ. in the *Mozart Jahrbuch,* 1924); *Mozart: Ein Künstlerleben in Bildern und Dokumenten* (Leipzig, 1931); *Mozart* (Leipzig, 1931); *J. Haydn* (Berlin, 1932); *Musikerbrevier* (Vienna, 1940); *Mozart: Ein Leben für die Oper* (Vienna, 1941); *Dreimal sieben Variationen über das Thema Richard Strauss* (Vienna, 2nd ed., 1945); *Frauen um Haydn* (Vienna, 1946); *Salzburg und seine Festspiele* (Vienna, 1947); *Richard Strauss und Wien, Eine Wahlverwandtschaft* (Vienna, 1949); *C.W. Gluck* (Olten, 1951); *W.A. Mozart* (Salzburg, 1951; in Eng., 1952); *Franz Schubert* (Vienna, 1971).
BIBLIOGRAPHY: E. Tenschert, *Musik als Lebensinhalt* (Vienna, 1971; contains a list of writings).

Teodorini, Helena, Rumanian soprano; b. Craiova, March 25, 1857; d. Bucharest, Feb. 27, 1926. She studied piano with Fumagalli and singing with Sangiovanni at the Cons. Verdi in Milan; made her debut as a contralto at the Teatro Municipale in Cuneo in 1879; gradually her voice changed to a mezzo-soprano of wide range. She made her first appearance in La Scala, Milan, on March 20, 1880; then sang in Warsaw (1881), and in Madrid (1884–86); subsequently she toured in South America. In 1905 she established herself as a vocal teacher in Paris; eventually returned to Rumania. In 1964 the Rumanian government issued a postage stamp in her honor bearing her stage portrait.
BIBLIOGRAPHY: Viorel Cosma, *Elena Teodorini* (Bucharest, 1962).

Terényi, Eduard, Rumanian composer; b. Tîrgu-Mureş, March 12, 1935. He studied with Jodál and Demian at the Cons. of Cluj (1952–58); in 1960 became an instructor on its faculty. In his own compositions he applies a variety of modernistic resources.
WORKS: *Pasărea măiastră (The Wonderful Bird),* variations for Orch., dedicated to the Ru-

manian sculptor Brancusi (1965); Piano Concerto (1969); Violin Sonatina (1955, revised 1965); *3 Pieces for Prepared Piano* (1968); *Prelude, Toccata, Fantasy and Fugue* for Organ (1968); *Cantată lirică,* cycle for Voice and Flute (1966); other songs.

Terhune, Anice (née **Potter**), American pianist and composer; b. Hampden, Mass., Oct. 27, 1873; d. Pompton Lakes, N.J., Nov. 9, 1964. She studied in Cleveland, in Rotterdam (with Louis Coenen), and in N.Y. (with E.M. Bowman). In 1901 she married Albert Payson Terhune, the author. She publ. several books of songs for children *(Dutch Ditties, Chinese Child's Day, Colonial Carols, Our Very Own Book,* etc.) and a number of separate songs; also many piano pieces for children; the operas *Hero Nero* (1904) and *The Woodland Princess* (1911); a book, *Music-Study for Children* (1922), and an autobiography, *Across the Line* (N.Y., 1945).

Ternina, Milka, Croatian soprano; b. Vezisče, near Zagreb, Dec. 19, 1863; d. Zagreb, May 18, 1941. She studied voice at the Vienna Cons. with Gänsbacher; made her operatic debut as Amelia in *Un ballo in maschera* in Zagreb (1882); then sang in Leipzig (1883–84) and Graz (1884–86). She subsequently was a member of the Bremen Opera (1886–89), and of the Munich Opera (1890–99), where she distinguished herself as a Wagnerian singer. She was engaged by Walter Damrosch for his German Opera Co. in N.Y., and made her American debut as Elsa in *Lohengrin* in Boston on March 4, 1896; also appeared at Covent Garden, London, as Isolde (June 3, 1898); after a series of successes at the Bayreuth Festivals, she was engaged by the Metropolitan Opera Co., making her debut there on Jan. 27, 1900, and sang there until 1904 (the 1902–3 season excepted); she sang Tosca at the American premiere (Feb. 4, 1901) and Kundry in *Parsifal* (Dec. 24, 1903). She retired from the stage in 1906 and settled in Zagreb, where she remained until her death.

Terrabugio, Giuseppe, Italian composer; b. Fiera di Primiero, May 13, 1842; d. there, Jan. 8, 1933. He studied in Padua, and then in Munich under Rheinberger. In 1883 he settled in Milan, where, as editor of *Musica Sacra,* he exerted a strong influence in reforming Italian church music. His publ. works (about 100 opus numbers) are almost exclusively for the church (12 masses, a Requiem, litanies, motets, etc.); he also publ. *L'organista pratico* (3 vols.).

Terradellas, Domingo (Italianized as **Domenico Terradeglias**), Spanish composer; b. Barcelona (baptized, Feb. 13), 1713; d. Rome, May 20, 1751. He studied with Durante at the Cons. dei Poveri di Gesù Cristo in Naples (1732–36); began his career as a composer with the oratorio *Giuseppe riconosciuto* (1736); then came the opera *Astarto* (Rome, Jan. 3, 1739); from 1743 to 1745, he was at the Spanish church of Santiago y S. Ildefonso, Rome; in 1746 he went to London, where he produced his operas *Mitridate* (Dec. 2, 1746) and *Bellerofonte* (March 24, 1747); he returned to Italy in 1750, after traveling through Belgium and France (1748–49). There is no foundation for the story that he drowned himself in the Tiber owing to the failure of his opera *Sesostri* (Rome, 1751). Twelve arias and 2 duets were publ. in 1747 by J. Walsh of London, who also publ. "the favourite songs" from the operas *Mitridate* and *Bellerofonte.*

BIBLIOGRAPHY: J.R. Carreras y Bulbena, *Domingo Terradellas* (Barcelona, 1908); H. Volkmann, "Domingo Terradellas," *Zeitschrift der Internationalen Musik-Gesellschaft,* XIII (1911–12; p. 306).

Terrasse, Claude, French composer; b. Grand-Lemps, near Grenoble, Jan. 27, 1867; d. Paris, June 30, 1923. He studied at the Lyons Cons. and at the Ecole Niedermeyer in Paris; from 1888 to 1895 was church organist in Arcachon; then in Paris until 1899, when he began to write for the stage, producing a series of successful operettas; the best known are *Les Travaux d'Hercule* (March 7, 1901); *Le Sire de Vergy* (April 16, 1903); *Monsieur de la Palisse* (Nov. 2, 1904); *La Marquise et le marmiton* (Dec. 11, 1907); *Le Coq d'Inde* (April 6, 1909); *Le Mariage de Télémaque* (May 4, 1910); *Les Transatlantiques* (May 20, 1911); *Cartouche* (March 9, 1912).

Terry, Charles Sanford, eminent English music scholar; b. Newport Pagnell, Buckinghamshire, Oct. 24, 1864; d. Westerton of Pitfodels, near Aberdeen, Nov. 5, 1936. He read history at Clare College, Cambridge, 1883–86; in 1890 became a lecturer in history at Durham College of Science, Newcastle upon Tyne; joined the faculty of the Univ. of Aberdeen, 1898; in 1903–30 held the Burnett-Fletcher chair of history there, and occupied himself with historical research; at the same time he devoted much of his energy to the study of Bach and his period. His biography of Bach (1928; revised ed., 1933; 6th ed., 1967; German trans., Leipzig, 1934) places Bach's life within historical perspective with a fine discernment; it has become a standard in the literature on Bach in English. Other books and editions dealing with Bach include: *Bach's Chorals* (3 vols., 1915–21); *J.S. Bach's Original Hymn-Tunes for Congregational Use* (1922); *J.S. Bach, Cantata Texts, Sacred and Secular* (1926); *The Four-Part Chorals of J.S. Bach* (5 vols., 1929; 2nd ed., 1964); *The Origin of the Family of Bach Musicians* (1929); *Bach: The Historical Approach* (1930); *Bach's Orchestra* (1932; 4th ed., 1966); *The Music of Bach: An Introduction* (1933). To the Musical Pilgrim series he contributed analyses of the B-minor Mass (1924), the cantatas and oratorios (1925), the Passions (1926), and the Magnificat, Lutheran masses, and motets (1929). He arranged and publ. a stage version of the "Coffee Cantata" as *Coffee and Cupid* (1924); also trans. into Eng. Forkel's life of J.S. Bach (1920), and wrote a biography of Johann Christian Bach (1929; 2nd ed., revised, 1967, prepared by H.C. Landons Robbin).

Terry, Sir Richard Runciman, English music editor; b. Ellington, Northumberland, Jan. 3, 1865; d. London, April 18, 1938. In 1890 he was appointed organist and music master at Elstow School; in

1892–96, was organist and choirmaster at St. John's Cathedral, Antigua, West Indies; in 1896–1901, was at Downside Abbey. There he attracted attention by his revival of the Catholic church music of early English masters (Byrd, Tallis, Tye, Morley, Mundy, White, Fayrfax, etc.); in 1901–24, he was organist and director of music at Westminster Cathedral. He was chairman of the committee appointed to prepare the Eng. supplement of the Vatican Antiphonary, and music editor of the *Westminster Hymnal*, the official Roman Catholic hymnal for England. He was knighted in 1922. Besides masses, motets, and other church music, he composed 48 *Old Rhymes with New Tunes* (1934). He edited *The Shanty Book* (2 vols.; 1921; 1926); *Old Christmas Carols* (1923); *Hymns of Western Europe* (with Davies and Hadow; 1927); *Salt Sea Ballads* (1931); *A Medieval Carol Book* (1932); *200 Folk Carols* (1933); *Calvin's First Psalter* [1539], harmonized (1932); also the collections of 16th-century music *Downside Masses* and *Downside Motets, Motets Ancient and Modern,* and many separate works by early Eng. composers. He wrote the books *Catholic Church Music* (1907; 2nd ed., enlarged, entitled *The Music of the Roman Rite,* 1931), *On Music's Borders* (1927), *A Forgotten Psalter and Other Essays* (1929), *The Music of the Roman Rite* (1931), *Voodooism in Music and Other Essays* (1934).

BIBLIOGRAPHY: H. Andrews, *Westminster Retrospect: A Memoir of Sir Richard Terry* (London, 1948).

Terschak, Adolf, Hungarian flutist and composer; b. Hermannstadt, Transylvania, April 6, 1832; d. Breslau, Oct. 3, 1901. He studied at the Vienna Cons.; made long tours, as far west as London, and as far east as Siberia. He wrote numerous pieces for the flute with orch. or piano; also character pieces for orch.; publ. *Ecole de mécanisme* for the flute.

Tertis, Lionel, eminent English viola player; b. West Hartlepool, Dec. 29, 1876; d. London, Feb. 22, 1975. He studied violin at the Leipzig Cons. and at the Royal Academy of Music in London; played the viola in various quartets, and decided to make it his chief instrument. He eventually became one of the most renowned viola players in Europe; traveled also in America. He was named in 1950 a Commander of the Order of the British Empire. He wrote *Beauty of Tone in String Playing* (London, 1938); a 2-vol. autobiography, *Cinderella No More* (1953) and *My Viola and I: A Complete Autobiography* (1974). He designed and publ. specifications of a very large viola: see *Music & Letters* (July 1947).

Tervani, Irma, Finnish mezzo-soprano; b. Helsinki, June 4, 1887; d. Berlin, Oct. 29, 1936. She received her primary training with her mother, the soprano **Emmy Strömer-Askté;** then studied voice in Paris and Dresden; made her debut with the Dresden Court Opera in 1908 as Dalila, remaining on its roster until 1932. She gained renown through her appearance in the role of Carmen opposite Caruso in Frankfurt in 1910.

Terzakis, Dimitris, Greek composer; b. Athens, March 12, 1938. He studied composition with Y. Papaioannou at the Athens Cons. (1960–65); went to Germany and took courses with B.A. Zimmermann and Herbert Eimert at the Hochschule für Musik in Cologne (1965–67); attended summer courses of new music at Darmstadt; subsequently joined the staff of the Hochschule für Musik in Düsseldorf (1974). In his music he steers a resolute course in the cosmopolitan avant-garde, leaving no tonal stone unturned; yet ancestral Grecian ethos is present both in the titles and in the modalities of his output.

WORKS: *8 Aphorisms* for Piano (1964); Septet for 7 Flutes (1965); *Medea* for Voice, Percussion, and Cello (1965–66); *Echochronos I* for Tape (1967), *II* for 8 Instruments and Percussion (1968; revised 1973), and *III* for 7 Amplified Instruments and Tape (1969–70); *Oceanids* for Women's Voices and Orch. (1967); Trio for Cello, Guitar, and Percussion (1967); *Chronika* for Flute and Guitar (1968); *Oikos* for 8-part a cappella Chorus (1969); String Quartet (1969); *Stixis* for Solo Oboe (1969–70); *Chorai* for Orch. (1970); *Achos* for Guitar, Voice, and Percussion (1970); *Nuances* for Mezzo-soprano, Viola, Percussion, and Tape (1970); *Hommage à Morse* for Strings and Wind Octet (1970); *Transcriptions télégraphiques* for Orch. (1971; Baden-Baden, June 12, 1974); *X* for Chorus, Instrumental Ensemble, and Tape (1971); *Katavassia (Retreat),* cantata for 6 Solo Voices (1971–72); *3 Pieces* for Solo Violin (1972); *Ethos A* for Oboe, Cello, and Tape (1972) and *B* for Mezzo-soprano, Flute, and Cello (1972); *Sticheron* for Chorus and 6 Instruments (1972); Duo for Cello and Percussion (1973); *To Allithoro Psari (The Squinty Fish)* for Tape (1973); *Kosmogramm* for Orch. (1974; Kassel, Germany, Nov. 1, 1974); *Eroticon* for Soprano, Clarinet, Violin, and Cello (Cologne, April 19, 1980).

Terziani, Eugenio, Italian composer; b. Rome, July 29, 1824; d. there, June 30, 1889. He studied with Mercadante at the Naples Cons.; at the age of 19 produced an oratorio, *La caduta di Gerico* (Rome, March 31, 1844), followed by the operas *Giovanna regina di Napoli* (Ferrara, 1844) and *Alfredo* (Rome, Feb. 21, 1852); was conductor in Rome at the Teatro Apollo from 1847 to 1869, at La Scala, Milan (1867–71), then in Rome again in 1871–75, and finally (from 1875) prof. of composition at the Santa Cecilia Academy in Rome. His last opera, *L'assedio di Firenze,* was produced in Rome on Feb. 24, 1883. He was also the composer of a ballet, *Una Silfide a Pechino* (Rome, Dec. 26, 1859), and of much sacred music.

Teschner, Gustav Wilhelm, German music editor and teacher of singing; b. Magdeburg, Dec. 26, 1800; d. Dresden, May 7, 1883. He was a pupil of Zelter in Berlin and of Crescentini in Italy; mastered Italian teaching methods thoroughly, specializing in the Italian repertoire. He publ. elementary vocal exercises of his own, and edited many works by Italian masters (Clari, 8 books; Crescentini, 5 books; Zingarelli, 10 books; etc.); also brought out early choral church music.

Tesi (Tesi-Tramontini), Vittoria, famous Italian contralto; b. Florence, Feb. 13, 1700; d. Vienna, May 9, 1775. She received her instruction in Florence and Bologna; appeared on the stage at the age of 16 in Parma; then was engaged in Venice (1718) and Dresden (1719). She sang in Italy every year, and also appeared in Madrid (1739) and Vienna (1747-48). She was married to one Tramontini, a barber by trade, and adopted the professional name Tesi-Tramontini. She was remarkably free in her morals, and many stories, in which it is impossible to separate truth from invention, were circulated about her life. Her letters to a priest were publ. by Benedetto Croce in his book *Un Prelato e una cantante del secolo XVIII* (Bari, 1946).

Tess (original name, **Tesscorolo**), **Giulia,** noted Italian soprano; b. Verona, Feb. 9, 1889; d. Milan, March 17, 1976. She made her debut as a mezzo-soprano in 1904 in Prato; later sang soprano roles after being encouraged by Battistini. In 1922 she was invited by Toscanini to sing at La Scala in Milan, where she created the role of Jaele in Pizzetti's *Debora e Jaele.* From 1940 she taught voice in Florence, and then in Milan at the La Scala Opera School (from 1946); her students included Tagliavini and Barbieri; she also produced opera at La Scala and other Italian opera houses. In addition to the Italian repertoire, she gained distinction as an interpreter of roles by Richard Strauss, excelling as Salome and Elektra.

Tessarini, Carlo, Italian violinist and composer; b. Rimini, c.1690; d. after 1766. He was a follower, if not actually a pupil, of Corelli; in 1729 he was a violinist at the San Marco in Venice, and later served at the Cathedral of Urbino; he then went to Rome and to Fano (1743); and finally entered the service of Cardinal Hannibal in Brünn, Moravia. His violin sonatas, generally in 3 movements, contributed to the establishment of a 3-movement sonata as a norm. He publ. several trio sonatas, duets, concertinos, concerti grossi, and a violin method, *Grammatica di musica* (Rome, 1741; also in French and Eng. trans.).
BIBLIOGRAPHY: A. Schering, *Geschichte des Instrumentalkonzerts* (Leipzig, 1905; pp. 107ff.); A. Dunning, "Some Notes on the Biography of Carlo Tessarini and His Musical Grammar," *Studien zur Musikwissenschaft,* XXV (1962).

Tessier, André, French musicologist; b. Paris, March 8, 1886; d. there, July 2, 1931. He studied law, history of art, and other subjects; then devoted himself to musicology; took his diploma at the Ecole du Louvre, 1921; was archivist in the Ministry of Fine Arts; also editor of the *Revue de Musicologie,* in which his catalogue of the Versailles Library was publ. (nos. 38–39). He edited the complete works of Chambonnières (with P. Brunold; 1925), and Denis Gaultier's *Rhétorique des Dieux* (facsimile, 1932; transcription, 1933). He was the author of a book on Couperin (Paris, 1926); prepared materials for the complete edition of Couperin's works, but died before his work was finished. A complete list of his writings was publ. by A. Schaeffner in *Revue de Musicologie* (Dec. 1953).
BIBLIOGRAPHY: P. Brunold, "Quelques souvenirs sur André Tessier," *Revue de Musicologie* (Aug. 1931).

Tessier, Charles, French lutenist and composer; b. Pézanas (Hérault), c.1550; date and place of death unknown. He was chamber musician to Henri IV; traveled in England; his book *Chansons et airs de cour* for 4 and 5 voices, was publ. in London (1597), dedicated to Lady Penelope Riche (Sir Philip Sidney's "Stella"); his *Airs et villanelles* for 3, 4, and 5 voices was publ. in Paris (1604).
BIBLIOGRAPHY: *Musical Antiquary,* 1 (1901; p. 53); G. Ungerer, "The French Lutenist Charles Tessier and the Essex Circle," *Renaissance Quarterly,* XXVIII (1975); J. Ward, "Tessier and the Essex Circle," *Renaissance Quarterly,* XXIX (1976); N. McBride, *The Chansons of Charles Tessier: A Transcription and Commentary* (Diss., Queen's Univ., Belfast, 1977); F. Dobbins, "The Lute Airs of Charles Tessier," *Lute Society Journal,* XX (1978).

Tessier, Roger, French composer; b. Nantes, Jan. 14, 1939. He received his education in Nantes and Paris. His works, mostly for small instrumental groups, include a String Trio (1964), *Concerto da camera* (1965), *5 etudes* for Wind Instruments, Piano, Percussion, and Harp (1965), and *Suite concertante* for Flute, Piano, and Strings (1969).

Tessmer, Hans, German writer on music; b. Berlin, Jan. 19, 1895; d. there (killed in an air raid), March 1, 1943. He studied music in Berlin, becoming music critic of the *Tägliche Rundschau* in 1921; also was engaged as stage director at the opera houses in Dresden (1923–27), Berlin (1928–30), Stuttgart (1934–35), and Görlitz (from 1935).
WRITINGS: *Profile und Fantasien* (1921); *Anton Bruckner* (1922); *Richard Wagner* (1930); *Robert Schumann* (1930); also a fictionalized story of Schumann, *Der klingende Weg* (1923). He revised Cherubini's opera *Lo Sposo di tre, marito di nessuna* and produced it under the title *Don Pistacchio, Der dreifach Verlobte* (Dresden, Nov. 27, 1926).

Testore, Carlo Giuseppe, Italian instrument maker; b. Novara, c.1660; d. c.1720. He was a pupil of Grancino and worked in Milan (1690–1715); made mostly cellos and double basses, and only a few violins. His son, **Paolo Antonio** (1690–1760), made violins on the model of Guarneri.
BIBLIOGRAPHY: O.A. Mansfield, "Carlo Giuseppe Testore," *British Musician* (1927; p. 38).

Testori, Carlo Giovanni, Italian music theorist; b. Vercelli, March 24, 1714; d. there, May 20, 1782. He publ. *La musica raggionata* (Vercelli, 1767), a theoretical treatise based on the system of Rameau; it was followed by 3 supplements (1771, 1773, 1782).

BIBLIOGRAPHY: C. Negri, *Brevi considerazioni sull'evoluzione storica ed estetica della musica: Biografie di musicisti vercellesi* (Vercelli, 1909); R. Allorto, *"La musica raggionata* di Carlo Giovanni Testori," *Rivista Musicale Italiana* (July–Sept. 1951).

Tetrazzini, Eva, Italian soprano; sister of **Luisa Tetrazzini;** b. Milan, March, 1862; d. Salsomaggiore, Oct. 27, 1938. She studied with Ceccherini in Florence, and made her debut there in 1882, as Marguerite in *Faust.* She sang Desdemona in Verdi's *Otello* at its first American production (N.Y., April 16, 1888). On May 15, 1887, she married the conductor **Cleofonte Campanini.** She sang with the Manhattan Opera in N.Y. in 1908; then returned to Italy.

Tetrazzini, Luisa (real Christian name, **Luigia**), celebrated Italian coloratura soprano; b. Florence, June 28, 1871; d. Milan, April 28, 1940. She learned the words and music of several operas by listening to her elder sister **Eva;** then studied at the Liceo Musicale in Florence with Ceccherini, who was also her sister's teacher. She made her opera debut as Inez in *L'Africaine* in Florence (1890); then traveled with various opera companies to South America. In 1904 she reached the U.S. and made her American debut at the Tivoli Opera House in San Francisco. She made her London debut at Covent Garden as Violetta on Nov. 2, 1907. She was then engaged by Hammerstein to sing with his Manhattan Opera House in N.Y., where she sang Violetta on Jan. 15, 1908; she remained with the Manhattan Opera until its closing in 1910; subsequently appeared for a single season at the Metropolitan Opera (1911–12), making her debut there on Dec. 27, 1911, as Lucia. She made the first broadcast on the British radio in 1925; her last American appearance was in N.Y. in 1931. She then returned to Italy and taught singing in Milan. Her fame was worldwide, and her name became a household word, glorified even in food, as in Turkey Tetrazzini. She publ. *My Life of Song* (London, 1921) and *How to Sing* (N.Y., 1923). She acquired a great fortune, only to die in poverty.

Teyber, Anton, Austrian composer; b. Vienna, Sept. 8, 1754; d. there, Nov. 18, 1822. He studied with Padre Martini at Bologna; from 1792 was cembalist at the Imperial Opera in Vienna and assistant of Salieri; from 1793 was court composer and music master to the Imperial children. He wrote an opera, 2 oratorios, a Passion, a melodrama, many masses, symphs., string quartets, minuets, etc. Some of his songs are printed in Denkmäler der Tonkunst in Österreich, 79 (42.ii).

Teyber, Franz, Austrian composer; brother of **Anton Teyber;** b. Vienna, Nov. 15, 1756; d. there, Oct. 22, 1810. He studied with Wagenseil; after a concert tour in southern Germany and Switzerland, he conducted Schikaneder's itinerant opera troupe; was then Konzertmeister at Karlsruhe and Bern, and from 1801 to 1807, composer for Schikaneder's Theater an der Wien; he then went to the Leopoldstadt

Theater. In 1809 he became organist at St. Stephen's Cathedral; in 1810, court organist. He produced a number of operas and singspiels: *Die Dorfdeputierten* (Dec. 18, 1785); *Fernando und Jariko, oder Die Indianer* (Sept. 5, 1789); *Alexander* (June 13, 1801); *Der Schlaftrunk* (Nov. 12, 1801); *Die Neuigkeitskrämer* May 12, 1802); *Pfändung und Personalarrest* (Dec. 7, 1803); *Scheredin und Almanzor* (Aug. 9, 1804); *Der Zerstreute* (Jan. 29, 1805); *Ruthards Abentheuer* (July 26, 1808); *Pumphia und Kulikan* (Oct. 8, 1808); *Das Spinner-Kreutz am Wienerberge* (posthumous; Aug. 24, 1811).

Teyte (real name, **Tate**), **Maggie,** English soprano; b. Wolverhampton, April 17, 1888; d. London, May 26, 1976. She studied in London; then was a pupil of Jean de Reszke in Paris (1903–7). In order to ensure correct pronunciation of her name in France, she changed the original spelling *Tate* to *Teyte.* She made her operatic debut as Zerlina at Monte Carlo (1907); was very successful as a concert singer in Paris, and appeared with Debussy at the piano; Debussy also selected her as successor to Mary Garden in the role of Mélisande (1908). She sang at the Opéra-Comique (1908–10), with Beecham's Opera Co. in London (1910–11), with the Chicago Opera Co. (1911–14), and with the Boston Grand Opera Co. (1915–17). She continued her recitals of French music in London during World War II. In 1958 she was named a Dame of the British Empire. She had 2 indifferent husbands and 2 prominent lovers: Sir Thomas Beecham in London and Georges Enesco in Paris. She publ. a book of memoirs, *Star on the Door* (London, 1958).

BIBLIOGRAPHY: C. Wallis, "Maggie Teyte," *Opera* (London, April 1952); Garry O'Connor, *The Pursuit of Perfection, A Life of Maggie Teyte* (N.Y., 1979).

Thadewaldt, Hermann, German conductor and composer; b. Bodenhagen, April 8, 1827; d. Berlin, Feb. 11, 1909. He was bandmaster at Düsseldorf (1850–51) and Dieppe (1853–55); from 1857 to 1869, was conductor of his own orch. in Berlin, and in 1871 of the concerts at the Zoölogical Gardens there. In 1872 he founded the Allgemeiner Deutscher Musikerverband, of which he was the first president, and to whose interests he devoted his entire time until his death. He publ. a symph. poem, *Das Rätsel der Sphinx; Im Walde* for Orch.; *Meermusik* for String Orch.; *Herbstlied* for String Quintet; etc.

Thalberg, Sigismond, celebrated piano virtuoso and composer; b. Geneva, Jan. 8, 1812; d. Posilipo, near Naples, April 27, 1871. His parents were Joseph Thalberg of Frankfurt and Fortunée Stein, also of Frankfurt, but resident in Geneva. Thalberg, however, pretended to be the natural son of Prince Moritz Dietrichstein, who took charge of his education. His first instructor was Mittag, the bassoonist of the Vienna Court Opera; he subsequently studied piano with Hummel and composition with Sechter. He played as a precocious pianist in the aristocratic salons of Vienna, and began to compose piano mu-

sic. In 1830 he made a successful concert tour through Germany; in 1834 he was appointed court pianist in Vienna; in 1835 he went to Paris, where he perfected his playing under Kalkbrenner; from that time he became one of the most admired piano virtuosos of Paris, and soon extended his triumphs through most of Europe, including Russia. In 1843 he married the widow of the painter Boucher. In 1855 he set out on a concert tour through Brazil and the U.S. (1856); made a 2nd Brazilian tour in 1863, and in 1864 retired to Naples. Thalberg was unexcelled as a performer of fashionable salon music and virtuoso studies. He possessed a wonderful legato, eliciting from Liszt the remark, "Thalberg is the only artist who can play the violin on the keyboard." His technical specialty was to play a central melody with the thumb of either hand, surrounding it with brilliant arpeggios and arabesques. To present this technique graphically in notation, he made use of the method initiated by Francesco Pollini of writing piano music on 3 staves. He wrote 2 operas, *Florinda* (London, July 3, 1851) and *Cristina di Suezia* (Vienna, June 3, 1855), which were not successful; but his brilliant piano pieces were the rage of his day, easily eclipsing in popular favor those of Chopin, his close contemporary. Among them are a group of nocturnes; several *Caprices;* 2 *Romances sans paroles; Grandes valses brillantes; Le Départ, varié en forme d'étude; Marche funèbre variée; Barcarole; Valse mélodique; Les Capricieuses; Tarentelle; Souvenir de Pest; La Cadence* (very popular); *Les Soirées de Pausilippe* (6 albums); *Célèbre Ballade; La Napolitaine;* several sonatas, many pianistic studies; fantasies on operas by Rossini, Bellini, Meyerbeer, Weber, Verdi, and others.
BIBLIOGRAPHY: H.C. Schonberg, *The Great Pianists* (N.Y., 1963); G. Puchelt, *Verlorene Klänge. Studien zur deutschen Klaviermusik 1830–1880* (Berlin, 1969); V. Vitale, "Sigismond Thalberg a Posillipo," *Nuova Rivista Musicale Italiana* (Oct.–Dec. 1972).

Thallon, Robert, organist and composer; b. Liverpool, March 18, 1852; d. Brooklyn, March 13, 1910. He was taken to N.Y. as a small child; studied in Germany, in Paris, and in Florence (1864–76); upon his return to the U.S., he settled in Brooklyn as an organist and music teacher; publ. a number of songs and piano pieces, and some orch. arrangements.

Thayer, Alexander Wheelock, American writer and authority on Beethoven; b. South Natick, Mass., Oct. 22, 1817; d. Trieste, July 15, 1897. After graduation from Harvard Univ. in 1843, he became assistant librarian there; during 6 years' work in the library, he matured a plan for writing a detailed and trustworthy biography of Beethoven. For preliminary study, and to collect material, he first spent 2 years (1849–51) in Germany, also writing letters for newspapers; in 1852 he joined the staff of the *N.Y. Tribune,* and returned to Europe in 1854, where, excepting 2 years (1856–58) spent in Boston, he remained. Dr. Lowell Mason and Mrs. Mehetable Adams (of Cambridge, Mass.) gave generous and disinterested aid at this juncture. In 1862 Thayer was attached to the American embassy at Vienna; in 1865 Abraham Lincoln appointed him consul at Trieste, a post held until 1882. He then publ. a *Chronologisches Verzeichniss der Werke Ludwig van Beethoven* (Berlin, 1865); in 1866, vol. I of his life-work, *Ludwig van Beethovens Leben,* appeared in German, trans. from the Eng. MS by Deiters; vol. II was publ. in 1872; vol. III, in 1879. In 1877 he publ. *Ein kritischer Beitrag zur Beethoven-Litteratur.* Unhappily, his wonderful capacity for work was overtaxed, and vol. IV of his nobly conceived work, executed with a painstaking thoroughness and scrupulous fidelity beyond praise, was left unfinished. Though he lived for years in straitened circumstances, he resolutely refused offers from firms like Novello & Co. and G. Schirmer, hoping to recast entirely the Eng. version of his *Beethoven,* which was publ. in 3 vols. by Krehbiel in 1921. A redaction, titled *Thayer's Life of Beethoven,* prepared by Elliot Forbes, was publ. in 1964 (2nd ed., revised, 1967).
BIBLIOGRAPHY: H.E. Krehbiel, "A.W. Thayer and His *Life of Beethoven," Musical Quarterly* (Oct. 1917); Christopher Hatch, "The Education of A.W. Thayer," ibid. (July 1956).

Thayer, Arthur Wilder, American music educator and choral conductor; d. Dedham, Mass., Aug. 26, 1857; d. there, Nov. 17, 1934. He first studied singing; then took lessons in music theory with Chadwick and in conducting with Zerrahn. He led various choral societies in New England and was music director of schools around Boston. He publ. a number of songs and some pieces of sacred choral music.

Thayer, (Whitney) Eugene, American organist; b. Mendon, Mass., Dec. 11, 1838; d. Burlington, Vt., June 27, 1889. He began to study the organ at 14; in 1862 assisted at the opening of the great organ in the Music Hall, Boston, where he became regular organist after study (1865–66) under Haupt, Wieprecht, etc., in Germany; was also conductor of the Boston Choral Union, etc. For a Festival Cantata he received the degree of Mus.Doc. from Oxford Univ. He publ. a Mass; 4 organ sonatas; part-songs; also *The Art of Organ Playing* (5 parts).

Thayer, William Armour, American organist and song composer; b. Brooklyn, Oct. 5, 1874; d. there, Dec. 9, 1933. He was a pupil of J.H. Brewer (organ), D. Buck (theory), and J.D. Mehan (voice); in 1893–1914, was organist of St. James' Protestant Episcopal Church, Brooklyn; from 1914, of St. Mark's Methodist Episcopal Church; from 1907 was also prof. of music at Adelphi College, Brooklyn. He publ. many songs, of which the best known is *My Laddie.*

Thebom, Blanche, American mezzo-soprano; b. Monessen, Pa., Sept. 19, 1918, of Swedish parents. She studied singing with Margaret Matzenauer and Edyth Walker; made her concert debut in N.Y. on Jan. 12, 1944, and her operatic debut at the Metropolitan Opera, N.Y., as Fricka, Dec. 14, 1944; remained on its roster until 1959, and again from 1960 to 1967; also sang in various opera houses in America and Europe, with increasing success. In 1958 she appeared as a guest artist in Russia. In 1967 she was appointed head of the Southern Regional Opera Co. in Atlanta; it folded in 1968; in 1980 she was appointed director of the opera workshop of San Francisco State Univ. Among her best roles are Ortrud in *Lohengrin,* Azucena in *Il Trovatore,* Amneris in *Aida,* Laura in *La Gioconda,* and Carmen.

Theile, Johann, German composer; b. Naumburg, July 29, 1646; d. there (buried, June 24), 1724. He was a pupil of H. Schütz at Weissenfels; in 1673, became Kapellmeister to the Duke of Holstein at Gottorf; went to Hamburg and wrote (for the opening of the Hamburg Opera House in 1678) the singspiels *Adam und Eva* (Jan. 12, 1678) and *Orontos;* he also produced a Christmas Oratorio in 1681. In 1685, he became Kapellmeister to the Braunschweig court at Wolfenbüttel; then became Kapellmeister at Merseburg (1691). He eventually settled in Naumburg c.1718. He was called by contemporaries "the father of counterpoint." Among his numerous pupils were Buxtehude and Zachau.
WORKS: German Passion (publ. in Lübeck, 1675; reprinted by Zelle in Denkmäler Deutscher Tonkunst, 17); *Noviter inventum opus musicalis compositionis 4 et 5 vocum, pro pleno choro* (20 masses); *Opus secundum, novae sonatae rarissimae artis et suavitatis musicae* (a collection of instrumental sonatas, preludes, courantes, airs, and sarabands *a* 2–5, in single, double, triple, and quadruple counterpoint).
BIBLIOGRAPHY: F. Zelle, *Johann Theile und N.A. Strungk* (Berlin, 1891); W. Maxton, *Johann Theile* (Diss., Univ. of Tübingen, 1926); J. Mackay, *The Sacred Music of Johann Theile* (Diss., Univ. of Michigan, 1968).

Theodorakis, Mikis (Michael George), Greek composer; b. Chios, July 29, 1925. He studied at the Athens Cons.; composed melodies in the authentic spirit of modern Greek folk songs; wrote music for productions of ancient Greek tragedies, among them *Œdipus Tyrannos.* He achieved international success with the musical score for the film *Zorba the Greek.* At the same time he was actively engaged in politics. In 1963 he was chosen chairman of the Greek United Democratic Left Party; in 1964 he was elected a member of the Greek Parliament and joined the Communist Party. After the military coup of 1967 he was arrested and held on a farm near Corinth; later was sent to Zatouna, in the central Peloponnesus; there he wrote the music for the film *Z,* dealing with the police murder of the Socialist politician Gregory Lambrakis in Salonika in 1963. The film and the music were greatly acclaimed in Europe and America, and the fate of Theodorakis became a cause célèbre. Yielding to pressure from the international public opinion, the military Greek government freed Theodorakis in 1970, and he went to Paris; in July 1970 he was a participant in the Congress at the United Nations World Youth Assembly in N.Y.
WORKS: Piano Trio (1945); 2 violin sonatinas (1945, 1958); *Œdipus Tyrannus* for Orch. (1946; version for Strings, 1955); *Preludio-Penia-Choros* for Percussion, Celesta, and Strings (1948); Symph. No. 1 (1948–52; Athens, 1954); Suite No. 1 for Piano and Orch. (1954; Athens, Feb. 24, 1957); Suite No. 2 for Chorus and Orch. (Paris, 1956); Suite No. 3, *The Insane Mother,* for Soprano, Chorus, and Orch. (1956); *Antigone,* ballet (1958-59); *Axion Esti,* pop oratorio (1960); *Epiphania Averoff,* oratorio (perf. at the Averoff prison, 1968); *Raven,* cantata (1970).
BIBLIOGRAPHY: J. Coubard, *Mikis Theodorakis* (Paris, 1969); Gail Host, *Theodorakis: Myth and Politics in Modern Greek Music* (Amsterdam, 1981).

Theremin, Leon (real name, **Termen;** pronounced in Russian with the accent on the last syllable; gallicized as Thérémin; Anglicized as Theremin, with the accent on the first syllable), Russian inventor of the space-controlled electronic instrument that bears his name; b. St. Petersburg, Aug. 15, 1896. He studied physics and astronomy at the Univ. there; also cello and theory. He continued his studies in physics at the Leningrad Physico-Technical Inst., where in 1919 he became director of the Laboratory of Electrical Oscillators. On Aug. 5, 1920, he gave a demonstration at the Physico-Technical Inst. in Petrograd of his Aetherophone, which was the prototype of the Thereminovox, later known simply as Theremin. He also gave a special demonstration of it for Lenin, who was interested in artistic uses of electricity. In 1927 he demonstrated his new instruments in Germany, France, and the U.S., where on Feb. 28, 1928, he obtained a patent for the Thereminovox. On April 29, 1930, at Carnegie Hall, he presented a concert with an ensemble of 10 of his instruments, also introducing a space-controlled synthesis of color and music. On April 1, 1932, in the same hall, he introduced the first electrical symph. orch., conducted by Stoessel, including Theremin fingerboard and keyboard instruments. He also invented the Rhythmicon, for playing different rhythms simultaneously or separately (introduced by Henry Cowell), and an automatic musical instrument for playing directly from specially written musical scores (constructed for Percy Grainger). Until 1938 Theremin was director of his own research laboratory in N.Y.; he then returned to Russia. In 1964 he was appointed a prof. of acoustics at the Moscow Univ.; was still active in 1977.

Thibaud, Jacques, celebrated French violinist; b. Bordeaux, Sept. 27, 1880; d. (in an airplane crash near Mt. Cemet, in the French Alps) Sept. 1, 1953, en route to French Indo-China. He was taught by his father, and then entered the class of Martin Marsick at the Paris Cons., winning first prize in 1896. Obliged to earn his living, he played the violin at the Café Rouge, where he was heard by the conductor Colonne, who offered him a position in his orch.; in 1898 he made his debut as a soloist (with Colonne) with such success that he was engaged for 54 con-

certs in Paris in the same season. Subsequently he appeared in all the musical centers of Europe, and from 1903 visited America numerous times. With his 2 brothers, a pianist and a cellist, he formed a trio, which had some success; but this was discontinued when he joined Alfred Cortot and Pablo Casals in a famous trio. His playing was notable for its warmth of expressive tone and fine dynamics; his interpretations of Beethoven ranked very high, but he was particularly authoritative in French music.
BIBLIOGRAPHY: J.-P. Dorian, ed., *Un Violon parle; Souvenirs de Jacques Thibaud* (Paris, 1947).

Thibault, Geneviève (Comtesse de Chambure), French musicologist; b. Neuilly-sur-Seine, May 20, 1902; d. Strasbourg, Aug. 31, 1975. She studied at the Sorbonne in Paris, under André Pirro; then became engaged in business, but continued her great interest in musical research; assembled a fine private library, containing rare editions of Renaissance music, which she opened to research scholars; initiated the Société de Musique d'Autrefois, for the purpose of presenting concerts of old music performed on old instruments; from 1955 she lectured at the Sorbonne. Her own contributions to musicology (usually in collaboration with other scholars) include: *Poètes et musiciens du XVe siècle* (Paris, 1924; with E. Droz); *Trois chansonniers français du XVe siècle* (Paris, 1927; with A. Pirro, E. Droz, and Y. Rokseth); *Bibliographie des poésies de P. de Ronsard mises en musique au XVIe siècle* (Paris, 1941; with L. Perceau); *Bibliographie des éditions d'Adrien Le Roy et Robert Ballard* (Paris, 1955; with F. Lesure); *Eighteenth-Century Musical Instruments in France and Britain* (London, 1973). She also compiled an inventory of musical-instrument collections, completed after her death by Jean Jenkins (Amsterdam, 1978).

Thibaut, Anton Friedrich Justus, German music scholar and learned collector; b. Hameln, Jan. 4, 1772; d. Heidelberg, March 28, 1840. He studied law, and from 1806 was a prof. of jurisprudence in Heidelberg; was also director of a singing club there; wrote *Über Reinheit der Tonkunst* (1825; often republ.; new ed., with biography of Thibaut by R. Heuler, 1907; in Eng. as *On Purity in Musical Art,* 1877). His valuable music library (catalogue publ. in 1842) was acquired by the Hofbibliothek in Munich.
BIBLIOGRAPHY: E. Baumstark, *A.F.J. Thibaut* (Leipzig, 1841).

Thibaut IV, King of Navarre and **Count of Champagne,** one of the most notable of the trouvères; b. Troyes, May 30, 1201; d. Pamplona, July 7, 1253. Sixty-three of his songs were publ. by Bishop La Ravallière in 1742 as *Poésies du Roi de Navarre;* the transcription of the melodies is very faulty. In Pierre Aubry's ed. of the *Chansonnier de l'Arsenal* (Paris, 1909), there are 59 melodies by Thibaut transcribed in modern notation; see also the examples in J. Beck's transcription of the *Chansonnier Cangé (Les Chansonniers des troubadours et des trouvères),* 4 vols. (Philadelphia, 1927–38), and A. Schering, *Ge-*

schichte der Musik in Beispielen (1931, p. 7).
BIBLIOGRAPHY: P. Aubry, *Trouvères and Troubadours* (Eng. trans., N.Y., 1914, p. 122).

Thiel, Carl, German editor and pedagogue; b. Klein-Öls, Silesia, July 9, 1862; d. Bad Wildungen, July 23, 1939. He was a pupil at the Königliche Inst. für Kirchenmusik, and in Bargiel's master class at the Akademie der Künste. On a government stipend he traveled in Italy; won the Mendelssohn Prize in 1894, and became organist at the Sebastiankirche in Berlin; later was a teacher at the Inst. für Kirchenmusik. In 1930 he became director of the Kirchenmusikschule in Regensburg. He edited old a cappella music; composed masses, motets, cantatas.
BIBLIOGRAPHY: C.A. Preising, *Carl Thiel* (Regensburg, 1951).

Thiele, (Johann Friedrich) Louis, German organist; b. Quedlinburg, Nov. 18, 1816; d. Berlin, Sept. 17, 1848. He studied with A.W. Bach at the Royal Inst. for Church Music at Berlin; from 1839 was organist of the Parochialkirche. He publ. concert pieces, variations, preludes, etc., for organ.

Thiemé, Frédéric, French music pedagogue; b. Rheims, June 3, 1750; d. Rouen, March 29, 1802. He taught general music courses in Paris from 1780 until 1792; in the wake of the French Revolution he went to Germany and settled in Bonn, where he was known under the German name **Friedrich Thieme;** eventually moved to Rouen. He publ. *Eléments de musique pratique* (Paris, 1783); *Principes abrégés de musique;* several books of violin duos; papers on acoustics.

Thienen, Marcel van, French composer; b. Paris, Oct. 3, 1922. He studied at the Paris Cons., graduating as a violinist in 1941. In 1953 he went to Haiti, where he organized the Cons. National de Musique. In 1956 he returned to Paris and established a studio for electronic music. His music aims to achieve an immediate effect by using topical subjects, much in the manner of Erik Satie.
WORKS: Opera-farce, *Le Ferroviaire* (1951); *Petite symphonie sur le temps* (1944); *Petite suite digestive* (1951); several pieces for various instruments under the generic title *Amusette; Le Damné* for Soprano, Baritone, Men's Chorus, Electronic Music, and Orch. (1964); songs with orch. accompaniment.

Thierfelder, Albert (Wilhelm), German composer and writer on music; b. Mülhausen, Thuringia, April 30, 1846; d. Rostock, Jan. 6, 1924. He studied at Leipzig Univ. (1865–69) and at the same time with Hauptmann, Richter, and Paul. In 1870–87, he was a singing teacher and cantor at Brandenburg; from 1887, was music director and prof. at Rostock Univ., succeeding Kretzschmar; he received the title of prof. in 1898. He publ. *Altgriechische Musik: Sammlung von Gesängen aus dem klassischen Alterthume vom 5. bis 1. Jahrhundert vor Christus nach* den überlieferten Melodien mit Altgriechischem und deutschem Texte nebst einleitenden Vorbemerkungen herausgegeben und für den Konzertvortrag eingerichtet (3 vols.; Leipzig, 1899, 1900, 1919), a collection of the remains of ancient Greek music; also *System der altgriechischen Instrumentalnotenschrift* (1897).

Thiman, Eric Harding, English music educator, organist, and composer; b. Ashford, Kent, Sept. 12, 1900; d. London, Feb. 13, 1975. He studied at the Royal Academy of Music; was a prof. there from 1930, having obtained the degree of D.Mus. from London Univ. in 1927. In 1952 he was appointed examiner to the faculty of music at London Univ.; became organist and director of music at City Temple, London, in 1957. He publ. *A Guide to Elementary Harmony* (London, 1941); *Practical Free Counterpoint* (London, 1947); *Musical Form for Examination Students* (1951); wrote a number of organ and choral works and some light orch. music (*Dance for a Children's Party, Stirling Castle March,* etc.).

Thimus, Albert, Freiherr von, German writer on music; b. Aachen, May 23, 1806; d. Cologne, Nov. 6, 1878. He publ. *Die harmonikale Symbolik des Altertums* (2 vols., 1868–76). As an introduction to this work, R. Hasenclever wrote *Die Grundzüge der esoterischen Harmonik des Altertums* (1870).
BIBLIOGRAPHY: R. Haase, "Der Aachener Albert von Thimus als Musiktheoretiker," in C.M. Brand, ed., *Beiträge zur Musikgeschichte der Stadt Aachen* (Cologne, 1954); L. Spitzer, *Die harmonikale Symbolik des Albert von Thimus* (Vienna, 1977).

Thiriet, Maurice, French composer; b. Meulan, May 2, 1906; d. Puys, near Dieppe, Sept. 28, 1972. He studied with Charles Koechlin and Roland-Manuel; then became engaged in radio work in Paris. His music reflects his preoccupation with the theater.
WORKS: Opera-bouffe, *Le Bourgeois de Falaise* (Paris, June 21, 1937); *Rapsodie sur des thèmes incas* for Orch. (Lyons, Jan. 20, 1936); *Afriques* for Orch. (1949); ballets: *La Nuit vénitienne* (Paris Opéra, March 17, 1938); *La Précaution inutile,* on themes by Rossini (1946); *Bonaparte à Nice* (Nice, 1960); *Le More de Venise* (Monte Carlo, 1960); *Les Amants de Mayerling* (Nice, 1961); *La Chambre noire* (Toulouse, 1969); *Blues de l'horloge* for Violin and Piano; songs; piano pieces.
BIBLIOGRAPHY: Jean Solar, *Maurice Thiriet* (Paris, 1958).

Thoinan, Ernest, French writer on music (pen name of **Antoine-Ernest Roquet**); b. Nantes, Jan. 23, 1827; d. Paris, May 26, 1894. He was a merchant by trade, but also an ardent student of music; during his extensive travels in Italy, England, and Russia, he collected a fine music library.
WRITINGS: *La Musique à Paris en 1862* (1863); *L'Opéra "Les Troyens" au "Père Lachaise"* (1863; a satire); *Les Origines de la chapelle-musique des souverains de France* (1864); *Les Origines de l'opéra français* (1886; with Ch. Nuitter); *Déploration de Guillaume Crétin sur le trépas de Jean Ockeghem* (1864); *Maugars, célèbre joueur de viole* (1865); *Antoine de Cousu et les singulières destinées de son livre rarissime "La Musique universelle"* (1866); *Curiosités musicales et autres trouvées dans les œuvres de Michel Coyssard* (1866); *Un Bisaïeul de Molière; Recherches sur les Mazuel, musiciens des XVIᵉ et XVIIᵉ siècles* (1878); *Louis Constantin, roi des violons* (1878); *Notes bibliographiques sur la guerre musicale des Gluckistes et Picinistes* (1878); *Les Hotteterre et les Chédeville* (1894); also an annotated ed. of *Entretien des Musiciens* [1643] by Annibal Gantez (1878).

Thomán, István, Hungarian pianist and pedagogue; b. Homonna, Nov. 4, 1862; d. Budapest, Sept. 22, 1940. He studied with Erkel and Volkmann, and was a piano student of Liszt. In 1888 he was appointed a prof. at the Royal Music Academy in Budapest; retired from teaching in 1906. He was greatly esteemed as a teacher; among his students were Dohnányi and Béla Bartók. He publ. a collection of technical piano studies in 6 vols., and also composed songs and piano pieces. His wife, **Valerie Thomán** (b. Budapest, Aug. 16, 1878; d. there, Sept. 8, 1948), was a renowned concert singer, who gave early performances of works by Kodály and Bartók; their daughter **Maria Thomán** (b. Budapest, July 12, 1899; d. there, Feb. 25, 1948) was an excellent violinist.

Thomas, (Charles Louis) Ambroise, French composer; one of the finest representatives of Romantic French opera; b. Metz, Aug. 5, 1811; d. Paris, Feb. 12, 1896. He entered the Paris Cons. in 1828; his teachers there were Zimmermann (piano) and Dourlen (harmony and accompaniment); he studied privately with Kalkbrenner (piano) and Barbereau (harmony); later with Lesueur (composition); in 1829 he won the first prize for piano playing, in 1830 for harmony, and in 1832 the Grand Prix de Rome, with the dramatic cantata *Hermann et Ketty.* After 3 years in Italy, and a visit to Vienna, he returned to Paris and applied himself with great energy to the composition of operas. In 1851 he was elected to the Académie; in 1856 he became a prof. of composition at the Paris Cons.; in 1871 he became director there, as successor to Auber (disregarding the brief incumbency of Salvador Daniel, adherent of the Paris Commune, who was killed in battle on May 23, 1871). As a composer of melodious operas in the French style, he was second only to Gounod; his masterpiece was *Mignon,* based on Goethe's *Wilhelm Meister* (Opéra-Comique, Nov. 17, 1866); this opera became a mainstay of the repertoire all over the world; it had nearly 2,000 performances in less then 100 years at the Opéra-Comique alone. Equally successful was his Shakespearean opera *Hamlet,* produced shortly after *Mignon* (Paris Opéra, March 9, 1868).
WORKS: The complete list of his operas (all produced in Paris) includes: *La Double Echelle* (Aug. 23, 1837); *Le Perruquier de la régence* (March 30, 1838); *Le Panier fleuri* (May 6, 1839); *Carline* (Feb.

24, 1840); *Le Comte de Carmagnola* (April 19, 1841); *Le Guerillero* (June 22, 1842); *Angélique et Médor* (May 10, 1843); *Mina, ou Le Ménage à trois* (Oct. 10, 1843); *Le Caïd* (Jan. 3, 1849); *Le Songe d'une nuit d'été* (April 20, 1850); *Raymond, ou Le Secret de la reine* (June 5, 1851); *La Tonelli* (March 30, 1853); *La Cour de Célimène* (April 11, 1855); *Psyché* (Jan. 26, 1857); *Le Carnaval de Venise* (Dec. 9, 1857); *Le Roman d'Elvire* (Feb. 4, 1860); *Mignon* (Nov. 17, 1866); *Hamlet* (March 9, 1868); *Gille et Gillotin* (April 22, 1874); *Françoise de Rimini* (April 14, 1882). He contributed an act to a ballet, *La Gipsy* (Paris, Jan. 28, 1839), and wrote the ballets *Betty* (Paris, July 10, 1846) and *La Tempête* (Paris, June 26, 1889); *Messe solennelle* (1857); other sacred works; some chamber music; songs.

BIBLIOGRAPHY: A. Hervey, *Masters of French Music* (London, 1894); J. Simon, "Ambroise Thomas," *Revue de Paris* (March–April 1896); H. Delaborde, *Notice sur la vie et les œuvres d'Ambroise Thomas* (Paris, 1896); C. Bellaigue, *Etudes musicales et nouvelles silhouettes des musiciens* (Paris, 1898; in Eng., 1899); E. Destranges, "Ambroise Thomas," *Revue Musicale de Lyon* (1911, p. 97); H. de Curzon, *Ambroise Thomas* (Paris, 1921); M. Cooper, "Charles Louis Ambroise Thomas," in *The Music Masters* (vol. II, London, 1950).

Thomas Aquinas (Saint), b. Roccasecca, near Aquino, Italy, 1227; d. Fossa Nuova, near Terracina, March 7, 1274. This famed theologian and scholastic philosopher entered the Dominican order in 1245. In 1263 Pope Urban IV commissioned him to compose a communion service, which contains the memorable numbers *Lauda Sion* (Corpus Christi sequence) and *Pange lingua, Sacra solemnis, Verbum supernum,* and *Adoro te* (hymns). An extended chapter on music is contained in his *Summa Theologica* (II, *quaestio XLI*).

BIBLIOGRAPHY: *D. Thomas Aquinatis de arte musica nunc primum ex codice bibl. univ. Ticinensis ed. illustr. Sac. Guarinus Amelli* (1880); G. Amelli, *S. Tomaso e la musica* (1876); C.F. Bellet, *St. Th. d'Aquin* (Paris, 1902); J.L. Callahan, *A Theory of Esthetics According to the Principles of St. Th. Aquinas* (Diss., Catholic Univ., Washington, D.C., 1927).

Thomas, Arthur Goring, English composer; b. Ratton Park, Sussex, Nov. 20, 1850; d. London, March 20, 1892. He was a pupil of Emile Durand in Paris (1874–77), and of Arthur Sullivan and Ebenezer Prout at the Royal Academy of Music in London; later studied orchestration in Berlin with Max Bruch. He was mainly interested in creating English operas in the best German tradition; his operas were performed in England and Germany, and he had many important supporters for his art in England, but his music totally lacked vitality, and became of only antiquarian interest after his death. In the last year of his life he suffered from a mental illness.

WORKS: Operas: *The Light of the Harem* (partial perf., London, Nov. 7, 1879); *Esmeralda* (London, March 26, 1883; also in German, produced in Berlin, Hamburg, and Cologne); *Nadezhda* (London, April 16, 1885); *The Golden Web* (posthumous; Liverpool, Feb. 15, 1893). He further wrote a choral ode, *The Sun Worshippers* (Norwich Festival, 1881); cantata, *The Swan and the Skylark* (posthumous; Birmingham Festival, 1894; orchestrated by C.V. Stanford); vocal scene, *Hero and Leander* (1880); *Out of the Deep,* anthem for Soprano Solo, Chorus, and Orch. (1878); some chamber music; songs.

BIBLIOGRAPHY: J. Klein, "Tragic, Forgotten Pioneer: Arthur Goring Thomas," *Music Review,* XXXVI (1975).

Thomas, Christian Gottfried, German composer and writer on music; b. Wehrsdorf, near Bautzen, Feb. 2, 1748; d. Leipzig, Sept. 12, 1806. He publ. *Praktische Beiträge zur Geschichte der Musik* (1778); chiefly for the music trade); *Unparteiische Kritik der vorzüglichsten seit 3 Jahren in Leipzig aufgeführten Kirchenmusiken, Concerte und Opern* (1798, 1799); *Musikalische kritische Zeitschrift* (1805; 2 vols.). His compositions include a *Gloria* for 3 Choirs, with Instruments; a cantata; quartets.

Thomas, Eugen, Dutch conductor; b. Surabaya, Java, Jan. 30, 1863; d. Schloss Orth, near Gmunden, Aug. 1922. In 1878 he went to Delft, the Netherlands, where he studied engineering, and at the same time music; he completed his music studies at the Vienna Cons.; was founder (1902) and conductor of the Wiener a cappella Chor. He publ. *Die Instrumentation der "Meistersinger" von R. Wagner* (2 vols., 1899; 2nd ed., 1907); and the *Wiener Chorschule* (1907).

Thomas, Gustav Adolf, German organist and composer; b. Reichenau, near Zittau, Oct. 13, 1842; d. St. Petersburg, May 27, 1870. He studied at the Leipzig Cons.; was organist at the Reformed Church in Leipzig; then succeeded H. Stiehl as organist at St. Peter's in St. Petersburg. He wrote excellent works for organ: *Konzert-Fantasie; Sechs Trios über bekannte Choralmelodien; Fuga eroica;* études; piano pieces; ed. Bach's *Kunst der Fuge* and Handel's organ concertos.

Thomas, Jess, American tenor; b. Hot Springs, S.Dak., Aug. 4, 1927. After studying psychology at the Univ. of Nebraska and at Stanford Univ., he turned to singing; went to Europe and in 1958 was accepted as a member of the Karlsruhe Opera; in 1962 he sang at the Württemberg State Opera in Stuttgart; and in 1963 joined the Bavarian State Opera in Munich, where he was named Kammersänger, an uncommon distinction for an American. He then sang at the Vienna Opera in 1965 and at the Berlin Opera in 1969; in 1973 he was engaged by the Zürich Opera. On Dec. 11, 1962, he made his debut at the Metropolitan Opera in N.Y. as Walter in *Die Meistersinger.*

Thomas, John, celebrated Welsh harpist; b. Bridgend, Glamorganshire, March 1, 1826; d. London, March 19, 1913. He also used the names **Aptommas** (or **Apthomas;** i.e., son of Thomas) and **Pencerdd Gwalia** (Chief of Minstrels, bardic name bestowed on him at the Aberdare Eisteddfod in 1861). He entered the Royal Academy at 14; studied harp with Chatterton, and upon the latter's death in 1872, succeeded him as Harpist to the Queen. He gave in London a series of annual concerts of Welsh music; the first took place at St. James's Hall, July 4, 1862, with a chorus of 400, and 20 harps. He was also a leader of the Eisteddfod festivals. He wrote 2 harp concertos; the dramatic cantata *Llewelyn* (1863) and *The Bride of Neath Valley,* a Welsh scene (1866); publ. a collection of Welsh melodies (1862) and a *History of the Harp* (London, 1859); made transcriptions for harp of many classical pieces. His brother, **Thomas Thomas** (1829–1913), also a harpist, went to America in 1895, eventually settling in Ottawa.

Thomas, John Charles, American baritone; b. Meyersdale, Pa., Sept. 6, 1891; d. Apple Valley, Calif., Dec. 13, 1960. He studied at the Peabody Cons. in Baltimore; from 1913 sang in musical comedy in N.Y.; then entered the concert field, in which he achieved outstanding success. He also sang in opera; was a member of the Théâtre de la Monnaie in Brussels (1925–28); later at Covent Garden, London (made his debut on June 28, 1928, as Valentin in *Faust*). In 1930 he appeared with the Chicago Opera Co.; on Feb. 2, 1934, he sang the role of the elder Germont in *La Traviata,* at his first appearance with the Metropolitan Opera; he continued to be on its roster until 1943; then settled in California.

Thomas, John Rogers, American baritone and composer of songs; b. Newport, Wales, March 26, 1829; d. New York, April 5, 1896. He was a lawyer's clerk in London; came to America in 1849, and acquired considerable success as an oratorio singer. A number of his songs enjoyed tremendous popularity in their day (*The Mother's Prayer, The Cottage by the Sea, Beautiful Isle of the Sea, Must we then meet as strangers,* etc.). He publ. an operetta, *Diamond Cut Diamond;* a children's cantata, *The Picnic;* and much sacred music.

Thomas, Kurt, German choral conductor; b. Tönning, Schleswig-Holstein, May 25, 1904; d. Bad Oeynhausen, West Germany, March 31, 1973. He studied organ with Karl Straube, piano with Teichmüller, and composition with Grabner at the Leipzig Cons.; then taught music theory there (1925–34); from 1934 to 1939 he was a prof. at the Berlin Hochschule für Musik; held various teaching appointments in Frankfurt, Detmold, and Leipzig. He was subsequently conductor of the choral concerts of the Bach-Verein in Cologne (1960–65); in 1969 was appointed instructor in choral conducting at the Music Academy in Lübeck. On the occasion of his 65th birthday he was honored with a Festschrift, *Chorerziehung und Neue Musik* (Wiesbaden, 1969). He publ. a useful manual, *Lehrbuch der Chorleitung,*

in 3 vols. (Leipzig, 1935; many reprints; also in Eng. as *The Choral Conductor,* N.Y., 1971).

Thomas, Michael Tilson, greatly talented American conductor; b. Los Angeles, Dec. 21, 1944. A grandson of Boris and Bessie Thomashefsky, founders of the Yiddish Theater in N.Y., he was brought up in a cultural atmosphere; he studied at the Univ. of Southern Calif., where he received instruction in composition with Ingolf Dahl; he also studied with the pianist John Crown and the harpsichordist Alice Ehlers; concurrently he took courses in chemistry. He acquired his conductorial skill by practical work with the Young Musicians Foundation Debut Orch., which he began to conduct at the age of 19, in 1963; he held this post for 4 years. He served as pianist in the master classes of Heifetz and Piatigorsky at the Univ. of Southern Calif. in Los Angeles; also conducted at the Monday Evening Concerts, where he presented first performances of works by Stravinsky, Copland, Boulez, and Stockhausen. In 1966 he attended master classes at the Bayreuth Festival; in 1967 he was assistant conductor to Boulez at the Ojai Festival; he conducted there also in 1968, 1969, and 1973. As a conducting fellow at the Berkshire Music Center at Tanglewood in 1968, he won the Koussevitzky Prize. The crowning point of his career was his appointment in 1969 as assistant conductor of the Boston Symph. Orch.; he was the youngest to receive such a distinction with that great ensemble. He was spectacularly catapulted into public notice on Oct. 22, 1969, when he was called upon to conduct the 2nd part of the N.Y. concert of the Boston Symph. Orch., substituting for its music director, William Steinberg, who was taken suddenly ill. In 1970 he was appointed associate conductor of the Boston Symph. Orch., and then was a principal guest conductor there with Colin Davis from 1972 to 1974. From 1971 to 1979 he was music director of the Buffalo Phil. Orch.; served as music director of the N.Y. Phil. Young People's Concerts (1971–76). In 1981 he became a principal guest conductor of the Los Angeles Phil. Orch., sharing the post with Simon Rattle. He also conducted guest engagements in Germany, Spain, Israel, and Japan. Among his avocations is dancing, in which he excels astonishingly well. He is also an excellent pianist. Above all, he is a modern musician, energetic, pragmatically proficient, and able to extract the maximum value of the music on hand.
BIBLIOGRAPHY: David Ewen, *Musicians since 1900* (N.Y., 1978).

Thomas, Theodore, renowned German-American conductor; b. Esens, East Friesland, Oct. 11, 1835; d. Chicago, Jan. 4, 1905. Taught by his father, a violinist, he played in public at the age of 6. In 1845 the family went to N.Y., where Thomas soon began to play for dances, weddings, and in theaters, helping to support the family; in 1851 he made a concert tour as a soloist, and in 1853 he joined Jullien's orch. on its visit to N.Y., later touring the country with Jenny Lind, Grisi, Sontag, Mario, etc. He became a member of the N.Y. Phil. Society in 1854. In 1862 he organized an orch. for "Symphony Soirées" at Irving Hall in N.Y., which were continued until 1878 (after 1872, in Steinway Hall); in 1866 he began a series of summer concerts in Terrace Garden, relocating these in 1868 to Central Park Garden. The influence of these enterprises on musical culture in N.Y. was enormous; Thomas's programs attained European celebrity. The first concert tour with the orch. was made in 1869, with 54 players, and for 9 consecutive years he made annual tours of the East and Midwest. In 1873 he established the famous Cincinnati Biennial Festival, which he conducted till his death. He also founded the Cincinnati College of Music, of which he was president and director in 1878–80, having given up his own orch. in N.Y. and the conductorship of the N.Y. Phil. Society (1877–78) to accept this post. After his resignation he returned to N.Y., where he immediately reorganized his own orch. and was reelected conductor of the Phil. Society Orch. and the Brooklyn Phil. Orch. (having been conductor of the latter in 1862–63, 1866–68, and 1873–78). Besides conducting these orch. bodies, he was at different times director of several choruses; in 1885–87 he was conductor and artistic director of the American Opera Co. In 1891 he settled permanently in Chicago as conductor of the Chicago Orch. In recognition of Thomas's distinguished services, a permanent home, Orch. Hall, was built by popular subscription, and formally opened in Dec. 1904, with a series of festival concerts, which were the last directed by him. After his death the name of the orch. was changed to the Theodore Thomas Orch.; in 1912 the final title, Chicago Orch., was officially reinstated.

The influence of Thomas upon the musical development of the U.S. has been strong and lasting. An ardent apostle of Wagner, Liszt, and Brahms, he also played for the first time in America works of Tchaikovsky, Dvořák, Rubinstein, Bruckner, Goldmark, Saint-Saëns, Cowen, Stanford, Raff, and Richard Strauss.

BIBLIOGRAPHY: *T. T.: A Musical Autobiography,* ed. by G.P. Upton (2 vols.; Chicago, 1905); R.F. Thomas (his wife), *Memoirs of T. T.* (N.Y., 1911); P.A. Otis, *The Chicago Symphony Orchestra* (Chicago, 1925); C.E. Russell, *The American Orchestra and T. T.* (N.Y., 1927); T. T. and F.A. Stock, *Talks about Beethoven's Symphonies* (N.Y., 1930); E.T. Rice, "T. and Central Park Garden," *Musical Quarterly* (April 1940); A. Loft, "Richard Wagner, T. T., and the American Centennial," ibid. (April 1951); T. Russell, *T. T.: His Role in the Development of Musical Culture in the U.S., 1835–1905* (Diss., Univ. of Minnesota, 1969).

Thomas (Thomas-San-Galli), Wolfgang Alexander,

German writer on music; b. Badenweiler, Sept. 18, 1874; d. Baden-Baden, June 14, 1918. He studied philosophy, history and law in Freiburg, Bonn, Munich, and Marburg (Dr. Jur., 1898); in 1899–1908, was the viola player of the Süddeutsches Streich-Quartett in Freiburg; in 1908–11, editor of the *Rheinische Musik- und Theaterzeitung* in Co-

logne; he then lived in Berlin as a writer. In 1898 he married the pianist **Helene San Galli.** WRITINGS: *Sein oder Nichtsein? Aphorismen über Ethisches und Ästhetisches* (1905); *Joh. Brahms. Eine musikpsychologische Studie* (1905); *Musik und Kultur* (1908); *Musikalische Essays* (1908); *Die "unsterbliche Geliebte" Beethovens, Amalie Sebald* (1909; an attempt to prove that the famous letter was addressed to Amalie Sebald); *Beethoven und die unsterbliche Geliebte. Amalie Sebald, Goethe, Therese Brunswick, und Anderes* (1910); *Mozart-Schatzkästlein* (1911); *Joh. Brahms* (1912; biography); *L. van Beethoven* (1913; biography). He edited *Beethovens Briefe* (1910; selection with commentary) and *Beethovens Briefe an geliebte Frauen* (1913).

Thomé, Francis

(baptismal names, **Joseph-François-Luc**), French composer; b. Port Louis, Island of Mauritius, Oct. 18, 1850; d. Paris, Nov. 16, 1909. He went to Paris as a youth, and studied at the Cons. with Marmontel (piano) and Duprato (theory). He became a successful teacher; wrote the operas *Le Caprice de la Reine* (Cannes, April 1892) and *Le Château de Königsberg* (Paris, April 22, 1896); the ballets *Djemmah* (1886), *La Folie parisienne* (1900), etc.; the religious mystery play *L'Enfant Jésus* (1891); 2 symph. odes, *Hymne à la nuit* and *Vénus et Adonis;* etc. But he is remembered chiefly for his piano pieces, of which *Simple aveu* and *Les Lutins* became very popular.

Thommessen, Olav Anton,

imaginative Norwegian composer; b. Oslo, May 16, 1946. From 1958 to 1969 he was in America, where he studied piano, cello, and composition with Heiden and Xenakis at Indiana Univ. (1965–69); in 1970–71 he was in Warsaw; then went to the Netherlands and attended courses at the Inst. for Sonology in Utrecht (1972–73). Returning to Norway in 1973, he taught at the Norwegian State Academy of Music in Oslo. As a composer, he devoted himself to practical composition of what he liked to call "commercial-industrial gold music," with reference to film scores. On a loftier plane he professed adhesion to the ideals of Varèse and Messiaen.

WORKS: Chamber opera, *Hermaphroditen (The Hermaphrodite;* 1975); theater song, *Blasphemy,* for Soloists, Chorus, and Ensemble (1978). For ORCH.: *Vørlesning (Thaw)* for Solo String Quartet, Flute, 5 Horns, Percussion, and Strings (1969); *As Many As* for Piano and School Orch. (1971); *Opp-Ned (Upside-Down;* 1972; revised 1973); *Barbaresk* (1974; arranged for Orch. in 1977 by his student Arnt Bukkevold from Thommessen's original piece for Brass and Percussion entitled *Stabsarabesk); Spring-Night Variations* for Piano and Ensemble (1975); *Overture Trivialis* for Small Orch. (1975–76); *Macro-Fantasy on Grieg's Piano Concerto* (1980); *Beyond Neon: Post-Commercial Sound Sculptures* for Horn and Orch. (1981; Minneapolis, Sept. 22, 1982). For VOICE: *Litt Lyd (Some Sound)* for Chorus and Orch. (1971); *Chamber Concert* for Soprano and Ensemble (1971) *Gjensidig (Mutually)* for 2 Sopranos, 2 Flutes, 2 Clarinets, and Percussion (1973); *The Overtone* for Soprano and Ensemble (1977; based on a D.H. Lawrence short story); *Stabat Mater Speciosa* for Chorus a cappella (1977); *Et Glassperlespill (A Game of Marbles)* for Narrator, Chorus, and Orch. (1979–80). CHAMBER MUSIC: Violin Sonata (1966); Duo-Sonata for Cello and Piano (1968); 2 string quartets (1969, 1970); *Kvadratspill I* and *II* for 4 Percussionists (1972, 1974); *Stanza* for Solo Clarinet (1975); *Stances* for 6 Clarinets (1975); *S-15* for Vihuela, Renaissance Lute, and Percussion (1976; the title refers to Shostakovich's 15th Symph.); *Nok en Til (Yet Another)* for Wind Quintet (1977); *3 Miniatures* for Piccolo and Percussion (1977); *Disco-Info-Fanfare* for Flute and Horn (1979); *Please Accept My Ears* for Violin and Piano (1981); *Scherzophonia/Scherzofrenia*, Piano Trio (1982). FOR PIANO: Sonatina (1965); *2-KA: An Attack on a Grand Piano* (1980).

Thompson, John Sylvanus, American pianist and teacher; b. Williamstown, Pa., March 8, 1889; d. Tucson, Ariz., March 1, 1963. He was educated at the Leefson-Hille Cons. in Philadelphia, and at the Univ. of Pa. He traveled through the U.S. as a concert pianist; also appeared in London and Berlin. In 1917 he settled in Kansas City. He publ. much teaching material, including the very successful *Modern Course for Piano (Something New Every Lesson)* (Cincinnati, 1936; 6 vols.); *The Adult Preparatory Piano Book* (Cincinnati, 1943); *Melody All the Way* (7 vols., Cincinnati, 1949–51; the last 2 vols. are subtitled *Supplementary Piano Course*).

Thompson, John Winter, American organist and composer; b. Leland, Mich., Dec. 21, 1867; d. St. Charles, Ill., March 8, 1951. After graduating from the Oberlin Cons. (1890) he went to Germany, where he studied at the Leipzig Cons. with Schreck. Returning to the U.S., he became a teacher of organ at Knox College, Galesburg, Ill. He publ. organ works, motets, and anthems; also *A Course in Harmony* (Boston, 1923).

Thompson, Oscar, American music critic and editor; b. Crawfordsville, Ind., Oct. 10, 1887; d. New York, July 3, 1945. He was educated at the Univ. of Washington, Seattle; studied music with G. Campanari and others; took up journalism and in 1919 joined the staff of *Musical America,* later becoming associate editor and finally editor (1936–43). He was music critic for the *N.Y. Evening Post* (1928–34); from 1937 to his death was music critic for the *N.Y. Sun* (succeeding W.J. Henderson). In 1928 he established the first class in music criticism in the U.S., at the Curtis Inst. in Philadelphia; he also gave courses at the N.Y. College of Music. In 1939 he brought out *The International Cyclopedia of Music and Musicians* in one vol. of more than 2,000 pages, with feature articles by eminent authorities; it went through 10 editions and reprints. He wrote the books *Practical Musical Criticism* (1934); *How to Understand Music* (1935); *Tabulated Biographical History of Music* (1936); *The American Singer* (1937); *Debussy, Man and Artist* (1937); ed. *Plots of the Operas* (1940) and *Great Modern Composers* (1941), both vols. being extracts from the *Cyclopedia.*

BIBLIOGRAPHY: Article by I. Lowens in *Dictionary of American Biography,* Supplement III.

Thompson, Randall, eminent American composer and pedagogue; b. New York, April 21, 1899; d. Boston, July 9, 1984. He was a member of an intellectual New England family; studied at Lawrenceville School in New Jersey, where his father was an English teacher; he began taking singing lessons and received his rudimentary music training as page turner for a local organist named Francis Cuyler Van Dyck, who played Bach. When he died, Thompson took over his organ duties in the school. Upon graduation, he went to Harvard Univ., where he studied academic music subjects with Walter Spalding, Edward Burlingame Hill, and Archibald T. Davison. He obtained his B.A. degree in 1920 and his M.A. in 1922. In 1920–21 he had some private lessons in N.Y. with Ernest Bloch. In 1922 he submitted his orch. prelude *Pierrot and Cothurnus,* inspired by the poetical drama *Aria da Capo* by Edna St. Vincent Millay, for the American Prix de Rome, and received a grant for residence in Rome; he conducted it there at the Santa Cecilia Academy on May 17, 1923. Encouraged by its reception, he proceeded to compose industriously, for piano, for voices, and for orch. He returned to the U.S. in 1925. From 1927 to 1929 he taught at Wellesley College; in 1929 he was appointed a lecturer in music at Harvard Univ.; in 1929–30 he held a Guggenheim fellowship. On Feb. 20, 1930, his First Symph. had its premiere in Rochester, N.Y., with Howard Hanson conducting, and on March 24, 1932, Hanson conducted in Rochester the first performance of Thompson's 2nd Symph., which was destined to become one of the most successful symph. works by an American composer; it enjoyed repeated performances in the U.S. and also in Europe. Audiences found the work distinctly American in substance; the unusual element was the inclusion of jazz rhythms in the score. Equally American and equally appealing, although for entirely different reasons, was his choral work *Americana,* to texts from Mencken's satirical column in his journal, the *American Mercury.* There followed another piece of Americana, the nostalgic a cappella choral work *The Peaceable Kingdom,* written in 1936, and inspired by the painting of that name by the naturalistic fantasist Edward Hicks; for it, Thompson used biblical texts from the Prophets. Another piece for a cappella chorus, deeply religious in its nature, was *Alleluia* (1940), which became a perennial favorite in the choral literature; it was first performed at Tanglewood, Mass., at the inaugural session of the Berkshire Music Center, on July 8, 1940. In 1942 Thompson composed his most celebrated piece of choral writing, *The Testament of Freedom,* to words of Thomas Jefferson; it was first performed with piano accompaniment at the Univ. of Virginia on April 13, 1943. A version with orch. was presented by the Boston Symph. Orch. on April 6, 1945. With this work Thompson firmly established his reputation as one of the finest composers of choral music in America. But he did not limit himself to choral music. His First String Quartet in D minor (1941) was praised, as was his only opera, *Solomon and Balkis,* after Kipling's *The Butterfly That Stamped,* a parody on Baroque usages, broadcast over CBS on March 29, 1942. In 1949 Thompson wrote his 3rd Symph., which was presented at the Festival of Contemporary American Music at Columbia Univ. in N.Y., on May 15, 1949. Thompson's subsequent works were an orch. piece, *A Trip to Nahant* (1954), a *Requiem* (1958), *The Nativity According to St. Luke* (1961), *The Passion According to St. Luke* (1965), *The Place of the Blest,* a cantata (1969), and *A Concord Cantata* (1975). During all this time he did not neglect his educational activities; he taught at Wellesley College (1936–37); the Univ. of Calif. at Berkeley (1937–39); the Curtis Inst. of Music in Philadelphia, where he served as director from 1939 to 1941; the School of Fine Arts at the Univ. of Virginia (1941–46); Princeton Univ. (1946–48); and Harvard Univ. (1949–65), where he retired as prof. emeritus in 1965. He also publ. a book, *College Music* (N.Y., 1935). In his compositions Thompson preserved and cultivated the melodious poetry of American speech, set in crystalline tonal harmonies judiciously seasoned with euphonious discords, while keeping resolutely clear of any modernistic abstractions.

WORKS: For the stage: *Solomon and Balkis,* one-act opera after Kipling's *The Butterfly That Stamped* (CBS Radio, March 29, 1942; stage production, Cambridge, Mass., April 14, 1942); incidental music to *The Grand Street Follies* (N.Y., June 25, 1926); incidental music to *The Straw Hat* (N.Y., Oct. 14, 1926). For orch.: *Pierrot and Cothurnus* (Rome, May 17, 1923, composer conducting); *The Piper at the Gates of Dawn,* symph. prelude (Rome, May 27, 1924, composer conducting); *Jazz Poem* for Piano and Orch. (Rochester, N.Y., Nov. 27, 1928, composer at the piano); Symph. No. 1 (Rochester, Feb. 20, 1930); Symph. No. 2 (Rochester, March 24, 1932); Symph. No. 3 (N.Y., May 15, 1949); *A Trip to Nahant,* fantasy for Orch. (Philadelphia, March 18, 1955). Chamber music: *Scherzino* for Flageolet, Violin, and Viola (1920); Quintet for Flute, Clarinet, Viola, Cello, and Piano (1920); *Septette* for Flute, Clarinet, String Quartet, and Piano (1927); Suite for Oboe, Clarinet, and Viola (1940); Trio for 3 Double Basses, a dinner-piece in honor of Koussevitzky (1949); 2 string quartets (1941, 1967). For chorus: *5 Odes of Horace* for Male Voices and Orch. (1924); *Pueri hebraeorum* for Chorus a cappella (1927); *Rosemary* for Female Chorus a cappella (1929); *Americana* for Chorus and Piano, to texts from Mencken's journal, the *American Mercury* (N.Y., April 3, 1932); *The Peaceable Kingdom* for Chorus a cappella, inspired by a painting of Edmund Hicks (Cambridge, Mass., March 3, 1936); *Tarantella* for Male Voices and Piano (1937); *The Lark in the Moon* for Chorus a cappella (1938); *Alleluia* for Chorus a cappella, to the single word "Alleluia" of the text (Berkshire Music Center, Tanglewood,

Mass., July 8, 1940); *The Testament of Freedom* for Male Voices with Piano or Orch., to words culled from the writings of Thomas Jefferson (broadcast over CBS, April 13, 1943, from the Univ. of Virginia; orch. version, Boston Symph., April 6, 1945); *The Last Words of David* for Chorus and Orch. (Berkshire Music Center, Tanglewood, Aug. 12, 1949); *Mass of the Holy Spirit* for Chorus a cappella (1955–56); *Ode to the Virginian Voyage* for Chorus and Orch. (Jamestown, Va., April 1, 1957); *Requiem,* dramatic dialogue in 5 parts for Double Chorus and String Ensemble (Berkeley, Calif., May 22, 1958); *Frostiana,* to words by Robert Frost, for Chorus with Piano Accompaniment (1959); *The Nativity According to St. Luke,* sacred drama for 12 Voices, Mixed Chorus, Children's Chorus, Chamber Orch., Organ, and Church Bells (Christ Church, Cambridge, Mass., Dec. 12, 1961); *A Feast of Praise* for Chorus and Instrumental Ensemble (1963); *The Best of Rooms* for Chorus a cappella (1963); *The Passion According to St. Luke,* oratorio (Boston, March 28, 1965); *A Psalm of Thanksgiving* for Mixed Chorus, Children's Chorus, and Orch. (Boston, Nov. 15, 1967, composer conducting); *The Place of the Blest,* cantata (N.Y., March 2, 1929); *Bitter-Sweet* for Chorus a cappella (1970); *Antiphon* for Chorus a cappella (1971); *A Hymn for Scholars and Pupils* for Chorus and Chamber Orch. (1973); *A Concord Cantata,* written for the bicentennial of Concord, Mass. (Concord, May 2, 1975); *The Morning Stars* for Chorus and Orch. (Lexington, Ky., March 18, 1976); *5 Love Songs* for Baritone Solo, Chorus, and String Quintet (Rocky Ridge Music Center, Estes Park, Colo., Aug. 6, 1978). Songs for voice and piano: *Spring* (1920); *The Ship Starting* (1922); *Tapestry* (1925); *The Heavens Declare* (1926); *Discipleship* (1926); *Southwind* (1926); *Velvet Shoes* (1927); *The Wild Home Pussy* (1927); *The Echo Child* (1927); *My Master Hath a Garden* (1927); *Doubts* (1929); *Prairie Home* (1951); *Veritas* (1954). For piano: *The Boats Were Talking* (1925); *Little Prelude* (1935); *Jabberwocky* (1951).

BIBLIOGRAPHY: Elliot Forbes, "The Music of Randall Thompson," *Musical Quarterly* (Jan. 1949); David Ewen, *American Composers* (N.Y., 1982); *The Boston Composers Project* (Cambridge, Mass., 1983).

Thompson, Will Lamartine, American hymn-tune writer; b. East Liverpool, Ohio, Nov. 7, 1847; d. there, Sept. 20, 1909. He studied music at the Boston Cons.; wrote a number of religious and patriotic songs. His best known hymn is *Softly and Tenderly Jesus Is Calling.*

BIBLIOGRAPHY: R.G. McCutchan, *Our Hymnody* (N.Y., 1937).

Thomson, César, eminent Belgian violinist; b. Liège, March 17, 1857; d. Lugano, Aug. 21, 1931. He entered the Liège Cons. at the age of 7, winning the Gold Medal at 11; he subsequently studied with Vieuxtemps, Léonard, Wieniawski, and Massart. For several years he was household musician to a wealthy Russian patron of arts, Baron Paul von Derwies, at Lugano; in 1879 he became concertmaster of Bilse's orch. in Berlin; in 1882 he became prof. of violin at the Liège Cons.; he left Liège for Brussels in 1898, when he succeeded Ysaÿe as prof. of violin at the Brussels Cons.; there he founded a celebrated string quartet (with Lamoureux, Vanhout, and Jacobs). In 1914 he settled in Paris as a prof. at the Cons. In 1924 he visited America; taught at the Cons. of Ithaca, N.Y., and at the Juilliard School of Music, N.Y., returning to Europe in 1927. He was a famous violin teacher, emphasizing perfection of technical and expressive performance, rather than bravura. He made arrangements for the violin of various works by early Italian composers.

Thomson, George, Scottish collector of folk songs; b. Limekilns, Dunfermline, March 4, 1757; d. Leith, Feb. 18, 1851. For 59 years (1780–1839) he was secretary to the Board of Trustees for the Encouragement of Arts and Manufactures in Scotland. An ardent collector of Scotch, Welsh, and Irish melodies, he issued a series of vols. containing authentic melodies, with piano accompaniments and instrumental arrangements by the most celebrated musicians of his time, including Beethoven, Haydn, Pleyel, and Koželuh. Each song had, in accordance with his plan, a prelude, coda, and ad libitum parts throughout (for violin, or flute, or cello). The collections are: *A Select Collection of Original Scottish Airs* (6 vols., London; vol. I, 1793; vol. II, 1798; vol. III, 1799; vol. IV, 1802; vol. V, 1818–26; vol. VI, 1841); *Collection of the Songs of R. Burns, Sir W. Scott, etc.* (6 vols., London, 1822); *Select Collection of Original Welsh Airs* (3 vols., London, 1809); *Select Collection of Original Irish Airs* (2 vols., London, 1814–16); *20 Scottish Melodies* (Edinburgh, 1839).
BIBLIOGRAPHY: J.C. Hadden, *George Thomson, the Friend of Burns. His Life and Correspondence* (London, 1898; contains full and interesting details, notably Beethoven's letters); R. Aldrich, "Beethoven and George Thomson," *Music & Letters* (April 1927); Karl Geiringer, "Haydn and the Folksong of the British Isles," *Musical Quarterly* (April 1949); C.B. Oldman, "Beethoven's Variations on National Themes," *Music Review* (Feb. 1951); Cecil Hopkinson and C.B. Oldman, *Thomson's Collections of National Song* (Edinburgh Bibliographical Society Transactions, 1940 and 1954).

Thomson, John, Scottish composer and writer on music; b. Sprouston, Roxburgh, Oct. 28, 1805; d. Edinburgh, May 6, 1841. He studied in Leipzig with Schnyder von Wartensee, and became an intimate of Mendelssohn, Schumann, and Moscheles. In 1839 he was appointed the first Reid Prof. of Music at Edinburgh Univ. At the 3rd concert given by the Edinburgh Professional Society (Feb. 1837), an analytical program was issued by Thomson, then conductor; this is the first recorded instance of the use of such programs. He composed the opera *Hermann, or The Broken Spear* (London, Oct. 27, 1834) and the musical play *The Shadow on the Wall* (London, April 20, 1835); also wrote incidental music to Walter Scott's drama *The House of Aspen* (Edinburgh, Dec. 19, 1829).

Thomson, Virgil, many-faceted American composer of great originality and a music critic of singular brilliance; b. Kansas City, Mo., Nov. 25, 1896. He studied at Harvard Univ.; took piano lessons with Heinrich Gebhard, and organ with Wallace Goodrich in Boston; then went to Paris, where he had a course with Nadia Boulanger (1921–22); returning to America, he studied composition with Rosario Scalero in N.Y. He then was organist at King's Chapel in Boston (1923–24). In 1925 he went to Paris for a prolonged stay; there he established friendly contacts with cosmopolitan groups of musicians, writers, and painters; his association with Gertrude Stein was particularly significant in the development of his esthetic ideas. In his music he refused to follow any set of modernistic doctrines; rather, he embraced the notion of popular universality, which allowed him to use the techniques of all ages and all degrees of simplicity or complexity, from simple triadic harmonies to dodecaphonic intricacies; in so doing he achieved an eclectic illumination of astonishing power of direct communication, expressed in his dictum "jamais de banalité, toujours le lieu commun." Beneath the characteristic Parisian persiflage in some of his music there is a profoundly earnest intent. His most famous composition is the opera *Four Saints in Three Acts*, to the libretto by Gertrude Stein, in which the deliberate confusion wrought by the author of the play (there are actually 4 acts and more than a dozen saints, some of them in duplicate) and the composer's almost solemn, hymn-like treatment, create a hilarious modern opera-buffa. It was first introduced at Hartford, Conn., on Feb. 8, 1934, characteristically announced as being under the auspices of the "Society of Friends and Enemies of Modern Music," of which Thomson was director (1934–37); the work became an American classic, with constant revivals staged in America and Europe. In 1940 Thomson was appointed music critic of the *N.Y. Herald-Tribune;* he received the Pulitzer Prize in 1948 for his score to the motion picture *Louisiana Story*. Far from being routine journalism, Thomson's music reviews are minor masterpieces of literary brilliance and critical acumen. He resigned in 1954 to devote himself to composition and conducting. In 1982 he received an honorary degree of D.Mus. from Harvard Univ. In 1983 he was awarded the 6th Annual Kennedy Center Honor for lifetime achievement.
WORKS: OPERAS: *4 Saints in 3 Acts* (Hartford, Conn., Feb. 8, 1934); *The Mother of Us All*, libretto by Gertrude Stein on the life of the American suffragist Susan B. Anthony (N.Y., May 7, 1947); *Byron* (N.Y., April 13, 1972). FOR ORCH.: *Symphony on a Hymn Tune* (1928; N.Y., Feb. 22, 1945, composer conducting); Symph. No. 2 (Seattle, Nov. 17, 1941); *The Seine at Night* (Kansas City, Feb. 24, 1948); *Wheatfield at Noon* (Louisville, Dec. 7, 1948); Cello Concerto (Philadelphia, March 24, 1950); *5 Songs for Voice and Orch.*, after William Blake (Louisville, Feb. 6, 1952); *Sea Piece with Birds* (Dallas, Dec. 10, 1952; grouped with *The Seine at Night* and *Wheatfield at Noon* as *3 Pictures for Orchestra*); Concerto for Flute, Strings, and Percussion (Venice, Sept. 18,

1954); *A Solemn Music* for Band (1949); *Missa pro defunctis* for Chorus and Orch. (State Univ. College of Education, Potsdam, N.Y., May 14, 1960); *The Feast of Love* for Baritone and Orch. (Washington, Nov. 1, 1964); Symph. No. 3 (1972; orchestration of his String Quartet No. 2). CHAMBER MUSIC: *Sonata da chiesa* for 5 Instruments (1926); Violin Sonata (1930); String Quartet No. 1 (1932); String Quartet No. 2 (1932); 4 piano sonatas; 2 sets of études for piano; organ pieces; sacred choral works; *Hymns from the Old South* for Mixed Chorus a cappella; songs to French and Eng. texts; Mass for Solo Voice (Unison Chorus, 1960); a number of *Portraits* for various instruments, among them more than 50 for piano, 8 for violin solo, 5 for 4 clarinets, 4 for violin and piano, etc., each "portrait" being a musical characterization of a definite person. FILM MUSIC: *The Plough that Broke the Plains* (1936; an orch. suite was drawn from it); *Louisiana Story* (1948; 2 orch. suites were drawn from it, including *Acadian Songs and Dances*); *The Goddess* (1957); *Power among Men* (1958); *Journey to America* for the American Pavilion at the N.Y. World's Fair (1964). WRITINGS: *The State Of Music* (N.Y., 1939; 2nd ed., 1961); *The Musical Scene* (N.Y., 1945); *The Art of Judging Music* (N.Y., 1948); *Music, Right and Left* (N.Y., 1951); an autobiography, disarmingly titled *Virgil Thomson* (N.Y., 1966); *Music Reviewed 1940–54*, a collection of criticisms (N.Y., 1967); *American Music since 1910* (N.Y., 1971).

BIBLIOGRAPHY: K.O. Hoover and John Cage, *Virgil Thomson: His Life and Music* (N.Y., 1959); *A Virgil Thomson Reader* (Boston, 1981); *Modern Music ... Analytic Index*, compiled by W. Shirley and ed. by W. and C. Lichtenwanger (N.Y., 1976; pp. 222–24).

Thooft, Willem Frans, Dutch composer; b. Amsterdam, July 10, 1829; d. Rotterdam, Aug. 27, 1900. He studied with A. Dupont in Brussels and with Hauptmann at the Leipzig Cons.; then went to Rotterdam, where he organized the German Opera.

WORKS: Opera, *Aleida von Holland* (Rotterdam, 1866); *Gevonden* for Baritone Solo, Male Chorus, and Orch.; 3 symphs. (including one with Chorus, surnamed *Kaiser Karl V*); *In Leid und Freud,* fantasy for Orch.; *Die Jungfrau von Orleans,* overture; Psalms; piano pieces; songs.

Thórarinsson, Leifur, Icelandic composer; b. Reykjavik, Aug. 13, 1934. He studied with Jón Thórarinsson at the Reykjavik School of Music; then in Vienna with Hanns Jelinek (1954); and with both Wallingford Riegger and Gunther Schuller in N.Y. Returning to Iceland, he became a music critic and member of the modern group Musica Nova; later moved to Denmark.

WORKS: *Child's Play* for Piano (1954); Piano Sonata (1957); *Mosaic* for Violin and Piano (1960); Piano Trio (1961); *Epitaph (Wallingford Riegger in Memoriam)* for Orch. (1961); *Kadensar* for Harp, Oboe, Clarinet, Bass Clarinet, and Bassoon (1962); Symph. No. 1 (1963); musical comedy, *Hornakórallinn* (1966); String Quartet (1969); Violin Concerto (1970; revised 1976); *Óró* for 7 Instruments; *Variations* for Clarinet, Cello, and Piano.

Thorborg, Kerstin, Swedish contralto; b. Venjan, May 19, 1896; d. Hedemora, Sweden, April 12, 1970. She studied at the Stockholm Opera School; made her debut in 1924 at the Stockholm Royal Opera, and remained as a regular member there until 1930; then sang in Berlin and Vienna. On Dec. 21, 1936, she made her American debut as Fricka at the Metropolitan Opera House, N.Y.; remained with the Metropolitan until 1950 (the 1946–47 season excepted); gave concerts throughout the U.S. and Canada; then returned to Sweden and became a voice teacher in Stockholm.

Thorne, Edward Henry, English organist and composer; b. Cranbourne, Dorset, May 9, 1834; d. London, Dec. 26, 1916. He was a chorister at St. George's Chapel; served as a church organist in London; gave organ and piano recitals in London and elsewhere; was especially noted for his Bach programs. He was made a Mus.Doc. by the Archbishop of Canterbury in 1913. He wrote a number of sacred choral works; an overture, *Peveril of the Peak* (after Walter Scott); 2 piano trios; violin sonatas; cello sonatas; publ. 7 books of organ pieces.

Thorne, Francis, American composer; b. Bay Shore, Long Island, N.Y., June 23, 1922. Of a cultural heritage (his maternal grandfather was the opera expert **Gustav Kobbé**), he absorbed musical impressions crouching under the grand piano while his father, a banker, played ragtime; at puberty, he sang in a school chorus; entering Yale Univ., he was a member of the varsity rowing team, as a prelude to service in the U.S. Navy during World War II. Returning from the war, he joined the stockbrokerage firm of Harris, Upham & Co. as a customers' man, but soon defected and joined various N.Y. jazz groups as a pianist; then went to Italy; took lessons in advanced composition with David Diamond in Florence. Impressed, depressed, and distressed by the inhumanly impecunious condition of middle-aged atonal composers, he established the eleemosynary Thorne Music Fund, drawing on the hereditary wealth of his family, and disbursed munificent grants to those who qualified, among them Stefan Wolpe, Ben Weber, Lou Harrison, Lester Trimble, John Cage, and David Diamond. In 1976 he founded the American Composers' Orch.; has been executive director of the American Composers' Alliance since 1975. Thorne's own music shares with that of his beneficiaries the venturesome spirit of the cosmopolitan avant-garde, with a prudently dissonant technique serving the conceptual abstractions and titular paronomasia of many modern compositions.

WORKS: Symph. No. 1 (1961); *Elegy* for Orch. (1963); *Burlesque Overture* (1964); Symph. No. 2 (1964); *Rhapsodic Variations* for Piano and Orch. (1964); Piano Concerto No. 1 (1965); *Gemini Variations* for Viola, Double Bass, and Orch. (1968); *Sonar Plexus* for Electric Guitar and Orch. (1968); *Chamber Deviation I* for Clarinet, Double Bass, and Percussion (1968); Symph. No. 3 for Percussion and Strings (1969); *Liebesrock* for 3 Electric Guitars and Orch. (1969); *Contra Band Music* for Band (1970); *Antiphonies* for Wind Instruments and Percussion (1970); *Chamber Deviation II* for Brass Quintet, Guitar, and Percussion (1971); Piano Sonata (1972); *Fanfare, Fugue and Funk* for Orch. (1972); Piano Concerto No. 2 (1973); *Cantata Sauce* (1973); Cello Concerto (1974); Violin Concerto (1976); Symph. No. 4, subtitled *Waterloo Bridge* (1977); *Divertimento No. 1* for Flute, String Orch., and Percussion (1979); *Pop Partita* for Piano and Chamber Orch. (1979); *Divertimento No. 2* for Solo Bassoon, Harp, Guitar, and Strings (1980); *The Eternal Light* for Voice and Orch. (1980); *Gems from Spoon River* for Instruments (1980); *Lyric Variations* for Orch. (1981); 4 string quartets; *Duo Sonatina* for 2 Solo Bassoons; *5 Set Pieces* for Saxophone Quartet; *Grand Duo* for Oboe and Harpsichord; *Love's Variations* for Flute, Soprano, and Piano; Sonatina for 2 Solo Violins.

Thornhill, Claude, American pianist and bandleader; b. Terre Haute, Ind., Aug. 10, 1909; d. Caldwell, N.J., July 1, 1965. He received regular academic training at the Cincinnati Cons. and at the Curtis Inst. of Music in Philadelphia; was an arranger for Benny Goodman and others; in 1940 organized a band of his own. Because of his uncommon musical literacy, he was able to make use of plausible novelties in his arrangements.

Thouret, Georg, German writer on music; b. Berlin, Aug. 25, 1855; d. there, Jan. 17, 1924. He studied philology and history in Tübingen, Berlin, and Leipzig. The discovery of forgotten military music in the castles of Berlin, Charlottenburg, and Potsdam led him to make a special study of the subject; for the Vienna Exposition (1892), he arranged an exhibition of German military music; publ. the collections *Altpreussische Militärmärsche* and *Musik am preussischen Hofe.*
WRITINGS: *Führer durch die Fachausstellung der deutschen Militärmusik* (1892; official catalogue of the Vienna Exposition); *Katalog der Musiksammlung auf der königlichen Hausbibliothek im Schlosse zu Berlin* (1895); *Friedrich der Grosse als Musikfreund und Musiker* (1898).

Thrane, Waldemar, Norwegian composer; b. Christiania, Oct. 8, 1790; d. there, Dec. 30, 1828. He studied violin with K. Schall in Copenhagen; then went to Paris, where he was a pupil of Baillot (violin) and of Reicha and Habeneck (composition). Returning to Christiania, he conducted theater music and also directed a music school. He is historically important as the composer of the first Norwegian opera, *Fjeldeventyret (A Mountain Adventure);* the score was publ. in 1824; the first concert perf. took place at the Musical Lyceum in Christiania, on Feb. 9, 1825; the first stage production was given posthumously (Christiania, April 9, 1850).
BIBLIOGRAPHY: J.G. Conradi, *Musikkens Udvikling i Norge* (Christiania, 1878); F. Benestad, *Waldemar Thrane: En pioner i norsk musikk*

(Oslo, 1961).

Thuille, Ludwig (Wilhelm Andreas Maria), renowned German composer and pedagogue; b. Bozen, Tyrol, Nov. 30, 1861; d. Munich, Feb. 5, 1907. He studied with Pembaur at Innsbruck (piano and theory); then went to Munich, where he was a pupil of Karl Bärmann (piano) and Rheinberger (composition) at the Hochschule für Musik there; in 1883 he became a prof. there. Encouraged by Alexander Ritter, he began to compose music in the grand Wagnerian manner; wrote 3 operas, chamber music, song cycles, and choral works. But he made his mark chiefly as a fine pedagogue; with Rudolf Louis he publ. the well-known manual *Harmonielehre* (1907; abridged ed. as *Grundriss der Harmonielehre,* 1908; new revised ed., by Courvoisier and others, 1933).
WORKS: Operas: *Theuerdank* (Munich, Feb. 12, 1897), *Lobetanz* (Karlsruhe, Feb. 6, 1898); *Gugeline* (Bremen, March 4, 1901); *Romantische Ouvertüre* (introduction to the opera *Theuerdank*); Symph. (1886); Sextet for Piano and Wind Instruments; Piano Quintet; Cello Sonata.
BIBLIOGRAPHY: F. Munter, *Ludwig Thuille* (Munich, 1923); E. Istel, "Ludwig Thuille," *Musical Quarterly* (July 1932).

Thuren, Hjalmar Lauritz, Danish musical folklorist; b. Copenhagen, Sept. 10, 1873; d. there, Jan. 13, 1912. From 1899 to 1907 he taught at the Fredericksberg Folk-School and was secretary of the Danish Folklore Society. He made valuable studies of folk music in Denmark, in the Faroe Islands, and among the Eskimos.
WRITINGS: *Dans og Kvaddigtning paa Färöerne* (1901); *Folkesangen paa Färöerne* (1908); *Eskimo Music* (with W. Thalbitzer; Copenhagen, 1911; in French as *La Musique chez les Eskimos,* Publications de la Revue S. I. M., 1912); *Melodies from East Greenland* (1914).

Thürlings, Adolf, German writer on music; b. Kaldenkirchen, July 1, 1844; d. Bern, Feb. 15, 1915. He took the Dr.Phil. degree in Munich with the dissertation *Die beiden Tongeschlechter und die neuere musikalische Theorie* (Berlin, 1877); publ. *Die schweizerischen Tonmeister im Zeitalter der Reformation* (1903); also edited works by Senfl in *Denkmäler der Tonkunst in Bayern,* 5 (3.ii).

Thurner, Frédéric Eugène de, French oboe virtuoso; b. Montbéliard, Dec. 9, 1785; d. Amsterdam, March 21, 1827. He wrote 3 symphs., an overture, 4 oboe concertos, 4 quartets for oboe and strings, rondos and divertissements for oboe with string quartet, Trio for Oboe with 2 Horns, duos for oboe and piano, piano music, etc.

Thursby, Emma, American soprano; b. Brooklyn, Feb. 21, 1845; d. New York, July 4, 1931. She studied with Achille Errani in N.Y.; in 1873 went to Italy, where she studied with Lamperti and Sangiovanni in Milan. Upon her return to America in 1875, she was engaged by the bandleader Gilmore for his summer concerts, and toured the country with him; subsequently appeared in the European music centers; in 1903 she sang in China and Japan; then returned to the U.S., living in retirement in N.Y.

BIBLIOGRAPHY: R.M. Gipson, *The Life of Emma Thursby, 1845–1931* (N.Y., 1940); article by V.L. Scott in *Notable American Women* (Cambridge, Mass., 1971), III.

Thybo, Leif, Danish composer and organist; b. Holstebro, June 12, 1922. He studied at the Cons. in Copenhagen, 1940–44; then at the Univ. of Copenhagen, 1945–48. He taught harmony and counterpoint at the Univ. of Copenhagen, 1949–65; taught theory (from 1952) and organ (from 1960) at the Cons. of Copenhagen; was also active as a church organist.

WORKS: Chamber opera, *Den odödliga berättelsen (The Immortal Story;* Vadstena, Sweden, July 8, 1971); Concerto for Chamber Orch. (1947); 2 organ concertos (1954, 1956); Concerto for Strings (1957); *Philharmonic Variations* for Orch. (1958); Concertino for Organ, Chamber Orch., and Mezzo-soprano (Copenhagen, Oct. 19, 1960); Cello Concerto (1961); Piano Concerto (1961–63); Concerto for Flute and Chamber Orch. (1966); Violin Concerto (1969); Viola Concerto (1972); *Markus-passionen (Passion According to St. Mark)* for Soloists, Chorus, and Orch. (Copenhagen, March 19, 1964); *Te Deum* for Chorus and Winds (Copenhagen, Nov. 18, 1965); *Prophetia* for Soprano, Bass, Chorus, and Orch. (Copenhagen, Feb. 28, 1965); *In dieser Zeit* for Solo Voice, Vocal Quartet, and Instruments (1967); *Dialogue* for Soloists, Chorus, and Instruments (Copenhagen, May 27, 1968); *The Ecstacy* for Soprano, Narrator, Recorder, Oboe, Viola da Gamba, and Spinet (1972); Cello Sonata (1950); 2 violin sonatas (1953, 1960); Sonata for Violin and Organ (1955); Trio for Clarinet, Cello, and Piano (1963); String Quartet (1963); Flute Quintet (1965); *Concerto breve* for Piano, Flute, Violin, Viola, and Cello (1966); *Hommage à Benjamin Britten* for Flute Quartet (1968); Trio for Oboe, Horn, and Bassoon (1970); 2 piano sonatas (1947, 1956); other piano works; organ pieces; songs.

Tibaldi Chiesa, Maria, Italian writer on music; b. Milan, April 28, 1896. She studied at the Univ. of Rome; wrote opera librettos, and publ. books of verse. Her musical publications include: *Schubert* (1932; 2nd ed., 1936); *Ernest Bloch* (1933); *Mussorgsky* (1935); *Vita romantica di Liszt* (1937); *Cimarosa e il suo tempo* (1939); *Paganini* (3rd ed., 1944); *Ciaikovsky* (1943).

Tibbett, Lawrence, outstanding American baritone; b. Bakersfield, Calif., Nov. 16, 1896; d. New York, July 15, 1960. His real name was **Tibbet,** but it was accidentally misspelled when he appeared in opera, and he retained the final extra letter. His ancestry was connected with the California Gold Rush of 1849; his great-uncle was reputed to be a pioneer in the navel orange industry; Tibbett's fa-

ther was a sheriff of Bakersfield who was shot dead by one of the outlaws he had hunted. His mother ran a hotel in Long Beach. Tibbett led a typical cowboy life, but dreamed of a stage career; he played parts in Shakespearian productions. During World War I he served in the U.S. Navy; after the Armistice he earned a living by singing at weddings and funerals in a male quartet. He also took vocal lessons with Joseph Dupuy, Basil Ruysdael, Frank La Forge, and Ignaz Zitmorsky. He made his operatic debut in N.Y. with the Metropolitan Opera on Nov. 24, 1923, in the minor role of Lovitsky in *Boris Godunov;* then sang Valentin in *Faust* (Nov. 30, 1923); achieved a striking success as Ford in Verdi's *Falstaff* (Jan. 2, 1925). He gave his farewell at the Metropolitan as Ivan in *Khovanshchina* on March 24, 1950. Altogether he sang 396 times with the Metropolitan Opera in N.Y., and 163 times on tour. His repertoire grew with experience and success on the stage. Among his roles were Tonio in *Pagliacci,* Wolfram in *Tannhäuser,* Tetramund in *Lohengrin,* Marcello in *La Bohème,* Scarpia in *Tosca,* Iago in *Otello,* and the title roles in *Rigoletto* and *Falstaff.* He also sang important parts in modern American operas, such as Colonel Ibbetson in Deems Taylor's *Peter Ibbetson,* Brutus Jones in Gruenberg's *The Emperor Jones,* and Wrestling Bradford in Howard Hanson's *Merry Mount.* During his first European tour in 1937 he sang the title role in the world premiere of *Don Juan de Mañara* by Eugene Goossens (Covent Garden, London, June 24, 1937); he also sang in Paris, Vienna, and Stockholm. A sincere believer in musical democracy, he did not disdain the lower arts; he even took part in such a mundane entertainment as the radio show "Your Hit Parade," undisturbed by interruptions from cigarette sponsors extolling the manly virtues of Lucky Strike smokers. He also appeared in talking pictures, among them *The Rogue Song, The Southerner,* and *Cuban Love Song.* During World War II he sang in army camps. He was a featured singer at the inaugurations of Calvin Coolidge, Herbert Hoover, and Franklin D. Roosevelt. He received all kinds of honors, including the Swedish medal Litteris et Artibus; a gold medal given by the American Academy of Arts and Letters; and several honorary doctorates from American univs. His life's progress is summarized in his autobiography, proudly entitled *The Glory Road* (Brattleboro, 1933).

BIBLIOGRAPHY: David Ewen, *Musicians since 1900* (N.Y., 1978).

Tibbits, George, Australian composer and architect; b. Boulder, Western Australia, Nov. 7, 1933. He studied architecture and urban planning at the Univ. of Melbourne; music was his avocation, which he plied off and on at leisure hours. His compositions often follow pictorial and literary images; a number of his instrumental pieces bear titles related to passages from the writings of James Joyce; their technical idiom oscillates quaquaversally from a Dorian columnar manner to lapidary dodecaphony. In 1968 he was appointed lecturer in architectural history at the Univ. of Melbourne.

WORKS: FOR ORCH.: *Neuronis Nephronicus and His Lowly Queen* (1968); *Fanfare for the Great Hall* (1968); *I thought you were all glittering with the noblest of carriage,* after James Joyce (1969); *Serenade* (1969); *Beside the rivering waters of,* after Joyce (1970); *Where oranges have been laid to rest upon the green,* after Joyce (1971); *Antediluvia* for String Orch. (1971). FOR VOICE: *5 Songs* for Contralto and Piano (1969); *Golden Builders* for Soprano, Small Chorus, and Chamber Ensemble (1972); *5 Bells,* after Kenneth Slesson, for Soprano and String Quartet (1972); *Shadows,* after Slesson, for Soprano, Harpsichord, and Small String Orch. (1974); *The Ice Fisherman—Lake Erie,* after Andrew Taylor, for Soprano and Orch. (1974). CHAMBER MUSIC: *Silop* for Flute and Celesta (1963); Quintet for Flute, Clarinet, Viola, Cello, and Piano (1964); String Sextet (1964); Trio for Flute, Viola, and Harpsichord (1964); *Ziz, King of Birds* for Flute, Clarinet, English Horn, French Horn, Violin, and Piano (1966); *Quashq* for Flute, Clarinet, Horn, and Piano (1966); *Pili* for 13 Instruments (1966); String Quartet (1968); *Macrame* for Flute, Bassoon, and Guitar (1974); *Gâteau* for Wind Quintet (1975). FOR PIANO: *Variations,* 4-hands (1969); *Stasis,* 12 pieces (1970). FOR ORGAN: *Fantasy on the ABC* (1975).

Tiby, Ottavio, Italian musicologist; b. Palermo, May 19, 1891; d. there, Dec. 4, 1955. He studied at the Cons. of Palermo, graduating in composition in 1921; later studied in Rome. Returning to Palermo, he devoted himself to collecting Sicilian music; was also an authority on Byzantine music.
WRITINGS: *Acustica musicale e organologia degli strumenti musicali* (Palermo, 1933); *La musica bizantina: Teoria e storia* (Milan, 1938); *La musica in Grecia e a Roma* (Florence, 1942); ed. *Antichi musicisti italiani* (1934).

Tichatschek, Joseph Aloys, Bohemian tenor; b. Blasewitz, near Dresden, July 11, 1807; d. Dresden, Jan. 18, 1886. He was the son of a poor weaver; in 1827 went to Vienna as a medical student, but then joined the chorus at the Kärnthnertor Theater, and had vocal instruction from Ciccimara; was soon engaged at Graz for 2 years; then sang in Vienna. His career received a new impetus after his highly successful appearance at the Dresden Opera (Aug. 11, 1837); he remained there for 33 years, retiring in 1870. He created the roles of Rienzi (Oct. 20, 1842) and Tannhäuser (Oct. 19, 1845) in Wagner's operas. Wagner mentions him often and with great praise in his autobiography.
BIBLIOGRAPHY: M. Fürstenau, *Joseph Tichatschek* (Dresden, 1868); E. Kloss, "Joseph Tichatschek," *Neue Zeitschrift für Musik,* LXXIV (1907).

Tieffenbrucker. See **Duiffopruggar.**

Tiehsen, Otto, German composer; b. Danzig, Oct. 13, 1817; d. Berlin, May 15, 1849. He studied at the Royal Academy in Berlin, where he settled as a teacher. He wrote the comic opera *Annette* (Berlin, 1847); *Christmas Cantata; Kyrie* and *Gloria a 6;* songs of high merit.

Tiensuu, Jukka, Finnish composer; b. Helsinki, Aug. 30, 1948. He studied piano and composition under Paavo Heininen at the Sibelius Academy in Helsinki; later traveled in America. He composed *Preludio and Fuga* for String Quartet (1970); *Largo* for String Orch. (1971); *Concerto da camera* for Flute, English Horn, Clarinet, Bassoon, and Cello (1972); *Overture* for Flute and Harpsichord (1972); *Fiato* for Wind Orch. (1974); *Threnos* for Orch. (Helsinki, Feb. 26, 1975).

Tierney, Harry, American composer of popular music; b. Perth Amboy, N.J., May 21, 1890; d. New York, March 22, 1965. He studied piano and planned a concert career; then turned to composition of popular songs; wrote many numbers for the Ziegfeld Follies. His musical shows *Irene* (N.Y., Nov. 18, 1919), *Up She Goes* (N.Y., Nov. 6, 1922), and *Kid Boots* (N.Y., Dec. 31, 1923) were quite successful, but were eclipsed by the fame of his *Rio Rita* (N.Y., Feb. 2, 1927). His early song *M-i-s-s-i-s-s-i-p-p-i* (1916) flooded the nation.

Tiersch, Otto, German music theorist; b. Kalbsrieth, Sept. 1, 1838; d. Berlin, Nov. 1, 1892. He studied with J.G. Töpfer at Weimar and with Bellermann at Berlin; taught singing at the Stern Cons. in Berlin. As a theorist he was a disciple of Hauptmann.
WRITINGS: *System und Methode der Harmonielehre* (1868); *Elementarbuch der musikalischen Harmonie- und Modulationslehre* (1874); *Kurze praktische Generalbass-, Harmonie- und Modulationslehre* (1876); *Kurzes praktisches Lehrbuch für Contrapunkt und Nachahmung* (1879); *Kurzes praktisches Lehrbuch für Klaviersatz und Accompagnement* (1881); *Notenfibel* (1882); *Die Unzulänglichkeit des heutigen Musikstudiums an Conservatorien,* etc. (1883); *Allgemeine Musiklehre* (1885; with Erk); *Rhythmik, Dynamik und Phrasierungslehre der homophonischen Musik* (1886).

Tiersot, (Jean-Baptiste-Elisée-) Julien, French musicologist; b. Bourg-en-Bresse, July 5, 1857; d. Paris, Aug. 10, 1936. He was a pupil of Savard, Massenet, and César Franck at the Paris Cons.; in 1883 was appointed assistant librarian at the Cons., and in 1909, chief librarian, retiring in 1921. He dedicated himself to musical ethnography, and contributed greatly to the documentation on French folk music. He was a prof. at the Ecole des Hautes Etudes Sociales and president of the Société Française de Musicologie. His compositions include a Mass on the tercentenary of the death of Roland de Lassus (1894); *Danses populaires françaises* for Orch. (1900); *Hellas* (after Shelley) for Chorus and Orch.; etc.
WRITINGS: *Histoire de la chanson populaire en France* (1889); *Musiques pittoresques* (1889); *Rouget de Lisle, Son œuvre, sa vie* (1892); *Les Types mélodiques dans la chanson populaire française* (1894); *Etude sur les Maîtres-Chanteurs de Richard Wagner* (1899); *Ronsard et la musique de son temps*

(1903); *Index musical pour le Romancero populaire de la France par G. Doncieux* (1904); *Hector Berlioz et la société de son temps* (1904); *Notes d'ethnographie musicale* (Part I, 1905; Part II is *La Musique chez les peuples indigènes de l'Amérique du Nord,* 1910); *Les Fêtes et les chants de la Révolution française* (1908); *Gluck* (1910); *Beethoven, musicien de la Révolution* (1910); *J.-J. Rousseau* (1912); *Histoire de la Marseillaise* (1915); *Un Demi-siècle de musique française 1870–1917* (1918; 2nd ed., 1924); *La Musique dans la comédie de Molière* (1921); *La Damnation de Faust de Berlioz* (1924); *Lettres de musiciens écrites en français du XVe au XXe siècle* (2 vols.; 1924, 1936); *Smetana* (1926); *Les Couperin* (1926); *La Musique aux temps romantiques* (1930); *La Chanson populaire et les écrivains romantiques* (1931); *Don Juan de Mozart* (1933); *J.-S. Bach* (1934). Collections of music: *Chansons populaires recueillies dans les Alpes françaises* (1903); *Noëls français* (1901); *Chants populaires, pour les écoles* (3 vols., 1907–29); *44 French Folksongs and Variants from Canada, Normandy, and Brittany* (N.Y., 1910); *60 Folksongs of France* (Boston, 1915); *Chansons de Ronsard* (1924); *Chansons populaires françaises* (1921); *Mélodies populaires des provinces de France* 1928); *Chansons nègres* (1933).
BIBLIOGRAPHY: L. de La Laurencie, *Un Musicien bressan: J. Tiersot* (Bourg, 1932).

Tiessen, Heinz, German composer and conductor; b. Königsberg, April 10, 1887; d. Berlin, Nov. 29, 1971. He studied music with Rüfer and Klatte in Berlin; was music critic of the *Allgemeine Musikzeitung* (1911–17); led Der Junge Chor for children of workers (1922–32). In 1925 he was appointed to the faculty of the Hochschule für Musik in Berlin; from 1946 to 1949 was director of the Municipal Cons. of Berlin, returning in 1949 to the Hochschule. He left the Hochschule in 1955 to become music director at the West Berlin Academy of the Arts. His style of composition is influenced by Richard Strauss, with whom he was friendly; he publ. a guide to Strauss's *Josephslegende* (1914); *Zur Geschichte der jüngsten Musik, 1913–28* (Mainz, 1928); and *Musik der Natur,* a study of bird songs (1953). His compositions include 2 symphs.; Piano Concerto; *Naturtrilogie* for Piano Solo; Septet for Flute, Clarinet, Horn, and String Quartet; String Quintet; about 60 songs; incidental music to plays.
BIBLIOGRAPHY: Autobiography, "Selbstzeugnis des Künstlers," *Musica* (Kassel, April 1948).

Tietjen, Heinz, noted German conductor and opera producer; b. Tangier, June 24, 1881; d. Baden-Baden, Nov. 30, 1967. He studied conducting with Nikisch; was then active as an opera producer in Trier (1904–22); later was administrator of the Berlin City Opera (1925–27); from 1931 to 1944 was artistic director of the Bayreuth Festivals, where he also conducted. He was again administrator of the Berlin City Opera (1948–55) and also of the Hamburg State Opera (1956–59); then retired in Baden-Baden.

Tietjens, Therese Johanne Alexandra, famous German soprano; b. Hamburg, July 17, 1831; d. London, Oct. 3, 1877. She was trained in Hamburg and made a successful debut there in 1849; sang at Frankfurt, and was engaged for the Vienna Court Opera in 1856; went to London in 1858, and remained there until her death, for long years the reigning favorite, singing at Her Majesty's Theatre, Drury Lane, Covent Garden, and the Haymarket. She visited Paris in 1863, and America in 1874 and 1876, appearing at the Academy of Music in N.Y. under Strakosch's management.

Tigranian, Armen, Armenian composer; b. Alexandropol, Dec. 26, 1879; d. Tiflis, Feb. 10, 1950. He studied flute and theory in Tiflis; returned to Alexandropol in 1902 and organized a choral society, specializing in Armenian music; in 1913 settled in Tiflis, where he became an esteemed music pedagogue; received the Order of Lenin in 1939. He composed the operas *Anush* (Alexandropol, Aug. 17, 1912) and *David-bek* (Erevan, Dec. 3, 1950); *Dance Suite* for Orch. (1946); cantata, *The Bloody Night* (1936); *Suite of Armenian Dances* for Piano; numerous other piano pieces; songs; theater music.
BIBLIOGRAPHY: K. Melik-Wrtanessian, *Armen Tigranian* (Moscow, 1939); R. Atanian and M. Muradian, *Armen Tigranian* (Moscow, 1966).

Tijardović, Ivo, Croatian composer; b. Split, Sept. 18, 1895. He studied in Zagreb; began his professional career by conducting theater orchs.; wrote operettas of the Viennese type; of these, *Little Floramy* (1924) became successful in Yugoslavia. His opera *Dimnjiaci uz Jadran (The Chimneys of the Adriatic Coast),* produced in Zagreb on Jan. 20, 1951, depicts the patriotic uprising of Yugoslav partisans during World War II; he also wrote the opera *Marco Polo* (Zagreb, Dec. 3, 1960).
BIBLIOGRAPHY: I. Plamenac, *Ivo Tijardović* (Split, 1954).

Tikka, Kari, Finnish conductor and composer; b. Siilinjärvi, April 13, 1946. He studied composition with Joonas Kokkonen and oboe at the Sibelius Academy in Helsinki and later in Berlin. He learned the practical side of the art in conducting at the Finnish National Opera. In 1975 he was appointed a conductor of the Royal Swedish Opera in Stockholm.
WORKS: *3 Fantasiestücke* for Flute, Clarinet, Bassoon, Trumpet, Horn, Viola, and Cello (1969); *2 Days à la Vam* for Orch. (1970); *2 Aphorisms* for 2 Violas and Cello (1971); *2 pezzi* for Flute, Clarinet, Bassoon, Piano, and 4 Percussionists (1973).

Tikotsky, Evgeni, Russian composer; b. St. Petersburg, Dec. 25, 1893; d. Minsk, Nov. 24, 1970. He studied composition with Deshevov; in 1944 became music director of the Phil. Concerts in Minsk.
WORKS: Operas: *Mihas Podhorny* (Minsk, March 10, 1939) and *Alesya* (Minsk, Dec. 24, 1944); 6 symphs. (1927, 1940, 1949, 1955, 1958, 1963); *The Stormy Petrel,* after Maxim Gorky, for Bass,

Chorus, and Orch. (1944); Trombone Concerto (1944); Piano Concerto (1953); piano pieces; songs.

Till, Johann Christian, American Moravian teacher, organist, and composer; b. Gnadenthal, near Nazareth, Pa., May 18, 1762; d. Bethlehem, Pa., Nov. 19, 1844. From 1793 till 1808 he was a teacher and organist at Hope, N.J.; from 1813 to 1844, was organist of the Bethlehem congregation. In his later years he also made pianos. His compositions are listed in A.G. Rau and H.T. David, *A Catalogue of Music by American Moravians* (Bethlehem, 1938).

Tillis, Mel, American country-music singer and songwriter; b. Pahokee, Fla., Aug. 8, 1932. He began writing songs while still in school; eventually settled in Nashville, Tenn., where he became one of the leading songwriters of country music. His popular songs include *Ruby, Don't Take Your Love to Town; One More Time; Heart over Mind;* and *Take Time.*

Tillyard, Henry Julius Wetenhall, English musicologist; b. Cambridge, Nov. 18, 1881; d. Safbron Walden, Jan. 2, 1968. He studied at Gonville and Caius College, Cambridge (1900–4), and at the English schools in Rome and Athens (1904–7), specializing in ancient and medieval music; studied Greek church music with J.T. Sakellarides in Athens. From 1908–17 he taught Greek at the Univ. of Edinburgh; in 1919–21 was a prof. of classics at the Univ. of Johannesburg, South Africa; prof. of Russian at the Univ. of Birmingham, 1921–26; prof. of Greek, Univ. of Cardiff, 1926–44; and lecturer in classics, Grahamstown, South Africa, 1946–49. He publ. *Byzantine Music and Hymnology* (London, 1923) and *Handbook of the Middle Byzantine Musical Notation* (Copenhagen, 1935; vol. 1 of *Monumenta musicae byzantinae. Subsidia).*

Tilman, Alfred, Belgian composer; b. Brussels, Feb. 3, 1848; d. Schaerbeck, near Brussels, Feb. 20, 1895. He studied at the Brussels Cons. (1866–71); wrote the cantata *La Sirène;* also 24 vocal fugues for 2 and 3 voices.

Tilmant, Théophile, French conductor; b. Valenciennes, July 8, 1799; d. Asnières, May 7, 1878. From 1834–38 he served as 2nd maître de chapelle, at the Théâtre Italien; then first maître de chapelle, 1838–49; then conductor of the Opéra-Comique, until his retirement in 1868; was also conductor of the Cons. Concerts from 1860–63.

Tilney, Colin, English harpsichordist; b. London, Oct. 31, 1933. He studied modern languages and music at King's College, Cambridge; then took lessons in harpsichord with Mary Potts and with Gustav Leonhardt in Amsterdam; subsequently became engaged as a soloist and ensemble player in England and on the Continent; made his first tour of the U.S. in 1971. His extensive repertoire covers the harpsichord literature of the 16th, 17th, and 18th centuries; it is his preference to use historical instruments or modern replicas of harpsichords, clavichords, and fortepianos in his concerts.

Timm, Henry Christian, German-American pianist, organist, and composer; b. Hamburg, July 11, 1811; d. Hoboken, N.J., Sept. 5, 1892. After study in Germany, he settled in the U.S. in 1835; was employed as a church organist in N.Y., Boston, etc. He was president of the N.Y. Phil. from 1848–63. He wrote choral works, organ pieces, and some piano music; made numerous transcriptions for 2 pianos of various classical works.

Timmermans, Ferdinand, Dutch organist and carillonneur; b. Rotterdam, Sept. 7, 1891. He studied organ with J.H. Besselaar and H. de Vries. In 1924 he became the municipal carillonneur at Rotterdam, and in 1926, at Schiedam. He subsequently gave exhibitions in Belgium, France, and England; soon he won the reputation of being one of the world's greatest carillonneurs. On May 5, 1954 he gave a concert in Washington, D.C., playing on the 50-bell carillon presented to the U.S. by the people of the Netherlands. He publ. *Luidklokken en beiaarden in Nederland* (Amsterdam, 1944).

Tinayre, Yves (Jean), French singer and music scholar; b. Paris, April 25, 1891; d. New York, July 12, 1972. He studied voice in London and Milan; gave recitals in France, England, Austria, etc., specializing in old songs; also revived some medieval French, German, and Italian sacred songs.

Tinctoris, Johannes, renowned Franco-Flemish music theorist and early musical lexicographer; b. Braine l'Alleud, near Nivelles, c.1435; d. before Oct. 12, 1511. He matriculated at the German Nation of Orleans Univ. (April 1, 1463). About 1472 he became tutor to the daughter of King Ferdinand I of Naples. In 1487 Ferdinand dispatched him to the courts of Charles VIII of France and Maximilian of Rome to recruit singers for his chapel. At the time of his death, Tinctoris was a canon and prebendary in Nivelles. About 1472 he compiled a dictionary of musical terms, *Terminorum musicae diffinitorium* (Treviso, 1495), which was the first of its kind. The only other work known to have been publ. in his lifetime was *De inventione et usu musicae* (Naples, c.1487). Tinctoris also wrote poetry, and served as a cleric. For editions of his writings, see C.E.H. de Coussemaker, ed., *Johannes Tinctoris tractatus de musica* (Lille, 1875) and A. Seay, *Johannes Tinctoris: Opera theoretica,* in *Corpus scriptorum de musica,* XXII (1975).
WRITINGS: *Terminorum musicae diffinitorium* (Treviso, 1495; German trans. in *Jahrbuch für Musikwissenschaft,* I, 1863; French trans., Paris, 1951; Eng. trans., London, 1964); *Complexus effectuum musices* (written c.1473–74; Italian trans., Bologna, 1979); *Proportionale musices* (written c.1473–74; Eng. trans. in *Journal of Music Theory,* I, 1957); *Liber imperfectionum notarum musicalium* (written c.1474–75); *Tractatus de regulari valore*

notarum (written c.1474–75); *Tractatus de notis et pausis* (written c.1474–75); *Liber de natura et proprietate tonorum* (dated Nov. 6, 1476; Eng. trans., Colorado Springs, 1967; 2nd ed., revised, 1976); *Liber de arte contrapuncti* (dated Oct. 11, 1477; Eng. trans. in *Musicological Studies and Documents,* V, 1961); *Tractatus alterationum* (written after 1477); *Scriptum super punctis musicalibus* (written after 1477); *Expositio manus* (written after 1477); *De inventione et usu musicae* (Naples, c.1487).

WORKS: Sacred: *Missa "Cunctorum plasmator summus"* for 4 Voices; *Missa "Nos amis"* for 3 Voices; *Missa sine nomine* (2 for 3 Voices; one for 4 Voices); *Alleluia* for 2 Voices; *Fecit potentiam* for 2 Voices; *Lamentationes Jeremie* for 4 Voices; *O virgo miserere mei* for 3 Voices; *Virgo Dei throno digna* for 3 Voices. Secular: Various chansons. For a modern edition of his works, see W. Melin, ed., *Johannes Tinctoris: Opera omnia,* in Corpus Mensurabilis musicae, XVIII (1976).

BIBLIOGRAPHY: U. Kornmüller, "Die alten Musiktheoretiker: Johannes Tinctoris," *Kirchenmusikalisches Jahrbuch,* XVIII (1903); K. Weinmann, "Ein unbekannter Traktat des Johannes Tinctoris," in the *Riemann-Festschrift* (Leipzig, 1909); G. Pannain, *La teoria musicale di Giovanni Tinctoris* (Naples, 1913); K. Weinmann, *Johannes Tinctoris und sein unbekannter Traktat "De inventione et usu musicae"* (Regensburg, 1917); C. van den Borren, "Tinctoris, Johannes," in *Biographie nationale (belge)* (Brussels, 1931); L. Balmer, *Tonsystem und Kirchentöne bei Johannes Tinctoris* (Diss., Univ. of Bern, 1935); E. Krenek, *A Discussion of the Treatment of Dissonances in Ockeghem's Masses as Compared with the Contrapuntal Theory of Johannes Tinctoris* (St. Paul, Minn., 1947); G. Reese, *Music in the Renaissance* (N.Y., 1954; 2nd ed., revised, 1959); E. Ferand, "What is Res facta?," *Journal of the American Musicological Society,* X (1957); W. Melin, *The Music of Johannes Tinctoris (c.1435–1511): A Comparative Study of Theory and Practice* (Diss., Ohio State Univ., 1973); G. Gerritzen, *Untersuchungen zur Kontrapunktlehre des Johannes Tinctoris* (Diss., Univ. of Cologne, 1974); R. Strohm, "Die Missa super 'Nos amis' von Johannes Tinctoris," *Die Musikforschung,* XXXII (1979).

Tinel, Edgar, Belgian composer; b. Sinay, March 27, 1854; d. Brussels, Oct. 28, 1912. He was taught at first by his father, a schoolmaster and organist; entered the Brussels Cons. in 1863 as a pupil of Brassin, Dupont, Gevaert, Kufferath, and Mailly; in 1873 took first prize for piano playing; won the Belgian Prix de Rome in 1877 with the cantata *De Klokke Roeland.* In 1882 he became director of the Inst. for Sacred Music at Mechlin; was appointed to the staff of the Brussels Cons. in 1896, and in 1909 (after Gevaert's death) became its director.

WORKS: *Franciscus,* oratorio (Mechlin, 1888; N.Y., 1893); *Godoleva,* music drama (Brussels, July 22, 1897); *Katharina,* sacred opera (Brussels, Feb. 27, 1909); many German and Flemish songs; Te Deum for Mixed Chorus and Organ; *Missa in honorem beatae Mariae Virginis de Lourdes* for 5-part Chorus a cappella; Psalms; motets; sacred songs. He publ. *Le Chant grégorien, Théorie sommaire de son exécution* (1890).

BIBLIOGRAPHY: A. van der Elst, *Edgar Tinel* (Ghent, 1901); Paul Tinel (his son), *Edgar Tinel: Le récit de sa vie et l'exégèse de son œuvre de 1854 à 1886* (Brussels, 1922); idem, *Edgar Tinel* (Brussels, 1946).

Tinsley, Pauline, English soprano; b. Wigan, Nov. 23, 1928. She studied at the Northern School of Music in Manchester; then with Joan Cross at the National School of Opera in London; made her operatic debut in London in 1951 as Desdemona in Rossini's *Otello;* then sang with the Welsh National Opera and the Handel Opera Society. She joined the Sadler's Wells Opera in 1963; sang at Covent Garden from 1965. She also appeared with the N.Y. City Opera, Houston Opera, Santa Fe Opera, Hamburg State Opera, and others.

Tiomkin, Dimitri, Russian-American composer of film music; b. St. Petersburg, May 10, 1894; d. London, Nov. 11, 1979. He studied piano with Isabelle Vengerova at the St. Petersburg Cons.; left Russia in 1921; lived in Berlin. He began his career as a concert pianist in Europe; emigrated to America in 1925, and was naturalized in 1937. After a few years in N.Y., he settled in Hollywood, where he became a highly successful composer of movie music; wrote scores for more than 100 motion picture films, including *The Bridge of San Luis Rey, Duel in the Sun, Lost Horizon,* and *Dial M for Murder.* He received an Academy Award for *The High and Mighty* (1954) and *The Old Man and the Sea* (1958). His most popular score was that for *High Noon* (1952), which received the Academy Award for best score and best theme song; he also was the recipient of numerous awards of merit, scrolls of appreciation, plaques of recognition, and a Golden Globe. He publ. a dictated autobiography under the title *Please Don't Hate Me* (N.Y., 1959).

Tippett, Sir Michael (Kemp), greatly renowned English composer; b. London, Jan. 2, 1905. He studied in London at the Royal College of Music (1923–28), where his teachers in composition were Charles Wood and C.H. Kitson; took piano lessons there with Aubin Raymar and attended courses in conducting under the direction of Sir Adrian Boult and Sir Malcolm Sargent. Later he studied counterpoint and fugue with R.O. Morris (1930–32). He subsequently held several positions as a teacher and conductor; from 1933 to 1940 he led the South London Orch. at Morley College; then served as director of music there (1940–51). Tippett was acutely sensitive to social events; his oratorio *A Child of Our Time* was inspired by the case of Henschel Grynsban, a Jewish boy who assassinated a member of the German embassy in Paris in 1938. As a conscientious objector, Tippett entertained extreme pacifist convictions; he refused to serve even in a non-combatant capacity in the British military forces; for this intransigent attitude he was sentenced to prison for 3 months; he served his term in a Surrey County gaol with the suggestive name Wormwood Scrubs (June 21–Aug. 21, 1943). He regained the respect of the community after the end of the war. In 1951 he initiated a series of broadcasts for the BBC; in 1969–74 he directed the Bath Festival. He received high honors from the British government; in 1959 he was named a Commander of the Order of the British Empire, and in 1966 he was knighted. He visited the U.S. in 1965, and thereafter was a frequent guest in America; his symph. works were often performed by major American orchs. Tippett's music has a grandeur of Romantic inspiration that sets it apart from the prevalent type of contemporary music; it is infused with rhapsodic eloquence and further enhanced by a pervading lyric sentiment free from facile sentimentality. He excelled in large-scale vocal and instrumental forms; he was a consummate master of the modern idioms, attaining heights of dissonant counterpoint without losing the teleological sense of inherent tonality. Yet he did not shun special effects; three times in his 4th Symph. he injects episodes of heavy glottal aspiration, suggested to him by viewing a film depicting the dissection of fetuses of pigs. A man of great general culture, Tippett possesses a fine literary gift; he writes his own librettos for his operas and oratorios.

WORKS: OPERAS: *The Midsummer Marriage* (1946–52; London, Jan. 27, 1955); *King Priam* (1958–61; Coventry, May 29, 1962); *The Knot Garden* (1966–69; London, Dec. 2, 1970); *The Ice Break* (1973–76; London, July 7, 1977). FOR ORCH.: Concerto for Double String Orch. (1938–39; London, April 21, 1940, composer conducting); *Fantasia on a Theme by Handel* for Piano and Orch. (1939–41; London, March 7, 1942); Symph. No. 1 (Liverpool, Nov. 10, 1945); *Little Music* for String Orch. (London, Nov. 9, 1946); Suite in D major, for the birthday of Prince Charles (BBC, London, Nov. 15, 1948); *Ritual Dances,* from *The Midsummer Marriage* (Basel, Feb. 13, 1953); *Fantasia Concertante on a Theme by Corelli* for String Orch. (Edinburgh, Aug. 29, 1953, composer conducting); *Divertimento on Sellinger's Round* for Chamber Orch. (Zürich, Nov. 5, 1954); Concerto for Piano and Orch. (1953–55; Birmingham, Oct. 30, 1956); Symph. No. 2 (1956–57; London, Feb. 5, 1958); *Praeludium* for Brass, Bells, and Percussion (London, Nov. 14, 1962); Concerto for Orch. (Edinburgh, Aug. 28, 1963); Symph. No. 3 for Soprano and Orch. (1970–72; London, June 22, 1972); Symph. No. 4 (Chicago, Oct. 6, 1977); Triple Concerto for Violin, Viola, Cello, and Orch. (1979; London, Aug. 22, 1980). VOCAL MUSIC: *A Child of Our Time,* oratorio with text by the composer, inspired by the case of the Jewish boy Henschel Grynsban, who assassinated in 1938 a Nazi member of the German embassy in Paris (1939–41; London, March 19, 1944); *Boyhood's End,* cantata to a text by W.H. Hudson, for Tenor and Piano (London, June 5, 1943); *The Heart's Assurance,* song cycle to poems by Sidney Keyes and Alun Lewis, for High Voice and Piano (London, May 7, 1951); *Dance, Clarion Air,* madrigal for 5 Voices, with text by Christopher Fry (1952;

June 1, 1953); *Crown of the Year,* cantata for Chorus and Instrumental Ensemble, with text by Christopher Fry (Bristol, July 25, 1958); *Music for Words Perhaps* for Speaking Voices and Chamber Ensemble, to love poems by W.B. Yeats (BBC, London, June 8, 1960); *Music,* unison song to the poem by Shelley, for Voices, Strings, and Piano (April 1960); *Magnificat and Nunc Dimittis* for Chorus and Organ (1961; Cambridge, March 13, 1962); *Songs for Ariel* for Medium Voice and Instrumental Ensemble (1962); *The Vision of Saint Augustine* for Baritone, Chorus, and Orch. (1963–65; London, Jan. 19, 1966; Dietrich Fischer-Dieskau, soloist; composer conducting); *The Shires Suite* for Chorus and Orch. (1965–70; Cheltenham, July 8, 1970, composer conducting); *The Mask of Time* for Chorus and Orch. (1981–84; Boston, April 5, 1984). CHAMBER MUSIC: 4 string quartets (1935, revised 1944; 1943; 1946; 1979); *4 Inventions* for Descant and Treble Recorders (1954); Sonata for 4 Horns (1955); *Wolf Trap Fanfare* for 3 Trumpets, 2 Trombones, and Tuba (1980); *The Blue Guitar* for Guitar (1983). FOR PIANO: 4 Sonatas: No. 1 (1938; revised 1942 and 1954); No. 2 (1962); No. 3 (1973); No. 4 (1979); also *Preludio al Vespro di Monteverdi* for Organ (1946).

BIBLIOGRAPHY: I. Kemp, ed., *Michael Tippett: A Symposium on His 60th Birthday* (London, 1965); A. Milner, "The Music of Michael Tippett," *Musical Quarterly* (Oct. 1974); M. Hurd, *Tippett* (London, 1978); E. White, *Tippett and His Operas* (London, 1979); D. Matthews, *Michael Tippett: An Introductory Study* (London, 1980); M. Bowen, *Michael Tippett* (London, 1982); A. Whittall, *The Music of Britten and Tippett: Studies in Themes and Techniques* (Cambridge, 1982).

Tirabassi, Antonio, Italian-born Belgian musicologist; b. Amalfi, July 10, 1882; d. Brussels, Feb. 5, 1947. He began his career as a church organist; in 1910 went to Belgium, where he founded the Inst. Belge de Musicologie (1920); brought out editions of works by Monteverdi, Corelli, and other composers. He wrote the books *Ecole flamande (1450 à 1600). La Mesure dans la notation proportionelle et sa transcription moderne* (Brussels, 1927); *Grammaire de la notation proportionnelle et sa transcription moderne* (Brussels, 1930).

BIBLIOGRAPHY: M. Schiavo, *Antonio Tirabassi* (Salerno, 1970).

Tircuit, Heuwell (Andrew), American composer, percussion player, and music critic; b. Plaquemine, La., Oct. 18, 1931. He played drums at the age of 9; served in U.S. Army bands (1954–56). In 1956 he went to Japan; played percussion in Japanese orchs. and wrote music criticism for the *Japan Times;* returned to the U.S. in 1963; was music critic of the *San Francisco Chronicle.* In his compositions, he cultivates a disestablishmentarian latitudinarianism uncircumscribed by doctrinaire precepts; as a professional drummer he makes liberal use in his music of a broad variety of percussionable objects.

WORKS: 2 string quartets (1953, 1957); Trumpet Sonata (1954); Cello Concerto (1960); Violin Sonata

(1960); Viola Sonata (1961); *Knell* for 27 Flutes and Percussion (1962); *Symphony Concertante* (1976).

Tirindelli, Pier Adolfo, Italian violinist and composer; b. Conegliano, May 5, 1858; d. Rome, Feb. 6, 1937. He studied violin at the Milan Cons., then in Vienna with Grün and in Paris with Massart. From 1885 to 1895 he taught violin at the Liceo Benedetto Marcello in Venice. He then went to the U.S.; taught violin at the Cincinnati Cons. (1896–1920). He wrote an Italian opera, *Atenaide* (Venice, Nov. 19, 1892) and a French opera, *Blanc et noir* (Cincinnati, Dec. 15, 1897); also composed some attractive songs to Italian and French words, among them *Mistica, Vaticinio, Je ne t'aime plus, Une Existence,* etc.
BIBLIOGRAPHY: E. Montanaro, *P.A. Tirindelli e la sua musica* (Rome, 1933).

Tischer, Gerhard, German music publisher; b. Lübnitz, Nov. 10, 1877; d. Starnberg, Dec. 1, 1959. He studied music theory in Berlin; obtained his Dr.Phil. with the dissertation *De aristotelischen Musikprobleme* (1903); lectured on music theory at the Handelhochschule in Cologne (1904–19) and at the Univ. of Cologne (1919–21). In 1910 he founded in Cologne the music publishing firm of Tischer & Jagenberg, and in 1923 bought the Wunderhorn Verlag of Munich. In 1943 the firm moved to Starnberg; it was liquidated in 1969.

Tischhauser, Franz, Swiss composer; b. Bern, March 28, 1921. He studied at the Zürich Cons.; in 1951 joined the staff of Zürich Radio and in 1971 was appointed director of its music dept.
WORKS: Ballet, *Birthday of the Infanta* (1941); Concertino for Piano and Small Orch. (1945); *Divertimento* for 2 Horns and String Orch. (1948); *Punctus contra punctum* for Tenor, Baritone, and Small Orch. (1962); *Omaggi a Mälzel* for 12 Stringed Instruments (1963); *Mattinata* for 23 Wind Instruments (1965); *Antiphonarium profanum* for 2 Men's Choruses a capella (1967); *Kontertänze* for 2 Orchs. (1968); *Eve's Meditation on Love* for Soprano, Tuba, and String Orch. (1972); *The Beggar's Concerto* for Clarinet and String Orch. (1975–76).

Tischler, Hans, distinguished Austrian-American musicologist; b. Vienna, Jan. 18, 1915. He studied piano with Paul Wittgenstein and Bertha Jahn-Beer, composition with Richard Stöhr and Franz Schmidt, and musicology with Robert Lach, Robert Haas, and Egon Wellesz at the Univ. of Vienna (Ph.D., 1937, with the dissertation *Die Harmonik in den Werken Gustav Mahlers*). He left Austria in 1938, settling in the U.S.; continued his musicological studies with Leo Schrade at Yale Univ. (Ph.D., 1942, with the dissertation *The Motet in 13th-Century France*). He taught music history at West Virginia Wesleyan College (1945–47) and at Roosevelt Univ. in Chicago (1947–65). In 1965 he was appointed prof. of musicology at Indiana Univ. in Bloomington.
WRITINGS: *The Perceptive Music Listener* (N.Y., 1955); *Practical Harmony* (Boston, 1964); *A*

Structural Analysis of Mozart's Piano Concertos (Brooklyn, N.Y., 1966); the Eng. ed. of Willi Apel's *History of Keyboard Music to 1700* (Bloomington, Ind., 1973); *A Medieval Motet Book* (N.Y., 1973); *The Montpellier Codex* (3 vols., Madison, Wis., 1978); *Chanter m'estuet: Songs of the Trouvères* (with S. Rosenberg; Bloomington, 1981); *The Earliest Motets: A Complete Comparative Edition* (New Haven, Conn., 1981); *The Earliest Motets: Their Style and Evolution* (Henryville, Pa., 1983); *The Parisian Two-Part Organa: A Complete Comparative Edition* (N.Y., 1983).

Tishchenko, Boris, Soviet composer; b. Leningrad, March 23, 1939. He studied composition at the Leningrad Cons. with Salmanov, Voloshinov, and Evlakhov, graduating in 1962; later took lessons with Shostakovich. In his works he demonstrates a strong rhythmic power and polyphonic mastery; his musical idiom is greatly advanced without overstepping the bounds of tonality.
WORKS: One-act opera, *The Stolen Sun* (1968); ballets: *The 12,* after the poem of Alexander Blok (Leningrad, Dec. 31, 1964); *Yaroslavna* (1974); *Lenin Lives,* cantata (1959); 5 symphs. (1960, 1964, 1966, 1970, 1974); Violin Concerto (1958); 2 cello concertos (1963, 1969); Piano Concerto (1962); Flute Concerto (1972); Harp Concerto (1977); *Palekh,* homage to Russian folk painters, for Chamber Orch. (1965); 4 string quartets (1957, 1959, 1969, 1980); 2 sonatas for Solo Violin (1957, 1976); 2 sonatas for Solo Cello (1960, 1979); *Capriccio* for Violin and Piano (1965); 6 piano sonatas (1957, 1960, 1965, 1972, 1973, 1975); *Sad Songs* for Soprano and Piano (1962); *Suzdal,* to folk texts from the Suzdal region, for Soprano, Tenor, and Chamber Orch. (1964); *Hard Frost,* aria for Mezzo-soprano and Orch. (1975).

Tisne, Antoine, French composer; b. Lourdes, Nov. 29, 1932. He studied with Darius Milhaud and Jean Rivier at the Paris Cons., obtaining the Premier Second Grand Prix de Rome in 1962.
WORKS: Symph. No. 1 (1960); 3 piano concertos (1958, 1961, 1963); *A une ombre* for 22 Players (1963); Violin Sonata (1963); String Quartet (1963); Cello Sonata (1964); *Visions des temps immémoriaux* for Ondes Martenot, Piano, and Percussion (1965); *Caractères* for 10 Wind Instruments (1965); Flute Concerto (1965); Cello Concerto (1965); Symph. No. 2 (1966); *Cosmogonies* for 3 Orchs. (Paris, Dec. 10, 1968); *Disparates* for Wind Quintet (1968); *Elégie* for Double Bass and Piano (1969); *Séquences pour un rituel* for String Orch. (1969); *Hommage à Calder* for Clavecin (1969).

Titelouze, Jean (or Jehan), French organist and composer; b. St.-Omer, c.1563; d. Rouen, Oct. 24, 1633. In 1588 he became organist at the Cathedral in Rouen, a position he held until his death; he also served as a canon there in 1610. He publ. 2 collections of organ works, *Hymnes de l'église* (1623) and *Le Magnificat* (1626); these sets of versets are in actuality keyboard fantasias. He also wrote poetry, which gained him prizes at the Puy de Rouen in 1613 and 1630. A complete edition of his organ works was brought out by Pirro and Guilmant in the *Archives des maîtres de l'orgue* (vol. 1, Paris, 1898). BIBLIOGRAPHY: A. Pirro, *Les Organistes français du XVIIᵉ siècle: Jean Titelouze* (Paris, 1898); M. Vanmackelberg, "Autor de Jehan Titelouze," *Recherches sur la musique française classique,* IV (1964); E. Higginbottom, "Jehan Titelouze, 1563–1633," *Musical Times* (Sept. 1983).

Titl, Anton Emil, Bohemian conductor and composer; b. Pernstein, Oct. 2, 1809; d. Vienna, Jan. 21, 1882. In 1840 he went to Vienna as conductor of the Theater in der Josefstadt; from 1850 to 1870 was conductor at the Burgtheater there; wrote 2 operas: *Die Burgfrau* (Brünn, 1832) and *Das Wolkenkind* (Vienna, March 14, 1845); a Mass for 8 Voices; overtures; violin pieces. His *Serenade* for Violin was very popular in numerous arrangements.

Titov, Alexei, Russian composer; b. St. Petersburg, June 24, 1769; d. there, Nov. 20, 1827. He served in the cavalry, reaching the rank of major general at his retirement; was an amateur violinist, and wrote operas in the traditional Italian style; of these, the following were produced in St. Petersburg: *Andromeda and Perseus* (1802); *The Judgment of Solomon* (1803); *Nurzadakh* (June 7, 1807); *The Wedding of Filatka* (April 25, 1808); *Errant Moment* (July 10, 1812); *Emmerich Tekkely* (Dec. 13, 1812); *Intrigue in the Basket* (May 12, 1817); *Valor of the People of Kiev, or These Are the Russians* (May 12, 1817); *The Feast of the Mogul* (Sept. 15, 1823); *The Brewer, or The Hidden Ghost of Evil* (Moscow, 1788); a ballet-pantomime, *Le Nouveau Werther,* was first given in St. Petersburg, on Jan. 30, 1799. His brother **Sergei Titov** (1770–1825) was a cellist who wrote the operas (all produced in St. Petersburg) *The Forced Wedding* (Sept. 4, 1789), *Credulous Folk* (July 10, 1812), and *Old-Fashioned Christmas* (Jan. 25, 1813).

Titov, Nicolai, Russian songwriter, son and pupil of **Alexei Titov;** b. St. Petersburg, May 10, 1800; d. there, Dec. 22, 1875. He received a military upbringing; like his father, he reached the rank of major general. He had no formal musical education; took some singing lessons, and studied a manual of thoroughbass; he was a typical dilettante, but possessed a gift of melodic invention; he knew Glinka and Dargomyzhsky, who helped him to develop his ability. He wrote about 60 songs, which were extremely popular in his time; his early song *The Pine Tree,* publ. in 1820, is erroneously believed to be the first Russian art song, but it had precursors; other of his songs that were popular include *Perfidious Friend, The Blue Scarf,* and *A Tree Branch.* He wrote a curious *Quadrille* for Piano, 3-hands, the treble part to be played by a beginner; another interesting project was a "musical romance in 12 waltzes" (under the general title *When I Was Young*), which remained incomplete. A waltz entitled *Past Happiness,* the *Quadrille,* and 4 songs were reproduced in *History*

of Russian Music in Examples, ed. by S. Ginsburg (Moscow, 1942; vol. 2, pp. 381–93).

Titta Ruffo. See **Ruffo, Titta.**

Titus, Alan, American baritone; b. New York, Oct. 28, 1945. He studied at the Juilliard School of Music in N.Y.; made his debut in Washington, D.C., in *La Bohème* in 1969; then sang with the N.Y. City Opera; subsequently, appeared in Amsterdam, Aix-en-Provence, Strasbourg, and other European cities. He made his debut with the Metropolitan Opera as Harlekin in *Ariadne auf Naxos* in N.Y. on March 20, 1976; also sang in San Francisco and Chicago.

Tizon, Juan, Afro-American jazz trombonist; b. San Juan, Puerto Rico, Jan. 22, 1900; d. Inglewood, Calif., April 23, 1984. He studied trombone playing with his uncle, Manual Tizol, a member of the Municipal Band in San Juan; he used a valve trombone, which was generally adopted in Puerto Rico. He went to America in 1920 and joined Duke Ellington's orch. in 1929, remaining with it until 1944, when he became a member of the orch. led by Henry James, alternating with repeat engagements with Duke Ellington; he also appeared on television with Frank Sinatra and Nat King Cole. He was instrumental in introducing the Cuban type of jazz, of which his song *Caravan* became a popular specimen.

Tobani, Theodore Moses, German-American composer and arranger of a multitude of marches, gavottes, waltzes, and other popular forms; b. Hamburg, May 2, 1855; d. Queens, N.Y., Dec. 12, 1933. His family emigrated to the U.S. c.1870; Tobani earned his living as a youth playing violin at theaters and drinking emporia; then became associated with the music publ. firm of Carl Fischer in N.Y.; he is said to have composed or arranged over 5,000 pieces for piano or organ that enjoyed gratifying commercial success; the best known of these works, and one epitomizing the sentimental popular tastes of the time, was *Hearts and Flowers* (op. 245), which Tobani claimed to have tossed off in an hour in the late summer of 1893. Since he publ. so much music, he used a number of pseudonyms, among which **Florence Reed** and **Andrew Herman** were his favorites.

Tobias, Rudolf, Estonian composer; b. Käina, May 29, 1873; d. Berlin, Oct. 29, 1918. He studied organ with L. Homilius, and composition with Rimsky-Korsakov at the St. Petersburg Cons., graduating in 1897. He worked as an organist in St. Petersburg (1898–1904) and Tartu (1905–8). In 1909 he went to Leipzig, and in 1910 settled in Berlin. In several of his compositions he made use of national Estonian subjects. WORKS: Oratorio, *Des Jonah Sendung* (1909); *Black Raven, Harbinger of War* for Voices and Orch. (1909); *The Virgin of Light,* after an Estonian epic, for Soprano and Orch. (1911); 2 melodramas for Narrator and Orch.: *Kalevipoeg's Dream* (1906) and *Kalevipoeg at the Gate of the Kingdom of Death* (1912); choruses; chamber music; songs.

BIBLIOGRAPHY: *Rudolf Tobias,* centennial monograph (Tallinn, 1973).

Tocchi, Gian-Luca, Italian composer; b. Perugia, Jan. 10, 1901. He studied in Rome with Respighi; his early works were written in a Romantic and impressionist manner: a symph. poem, *Il Destino,* after Maeterlinck; *Rapsodia romantica* (1929); *3 canzoni alla maniera popolare italiana* (1931); he then changed to contemporary subjects, exemplified by such works as *Record* (1933), *Film* (1936), and a Concerto for Jazz Band.

Tocco, James, American pianist; b. Detroit, Sept. 21, 1943. He won a scholarship to study at the summer academy of the Salzburg Mozarteum; also studied in Paris. In 1973 he won first prize in the Munich Competition; subsequently made extensive tours of Europe, Russia, South America, and the Middle East. In 1977 he joined the faculty of the Indiana Univ. School of Music.

Toch, Ernst, eminent Austrian-American composer; b. Vienna, Dec. 7, 1887; d. Los Angeles, Oct. 1, 1964. His father was a Jewish dealer in unprocessed leather, and there was no musical strain in the family; Toch began playing piano without a teacher in his grandmother's pawnshop; he learned musical notation from a local violinist, and then copied Mozart's string quartets for practice; using them as a model, he began to compose string quartets and other pieces of chamber music; at the age of 17 he had one of them, his 6th String Quartet, op. 12 (1905), performed by the famous Rose Quartet in Vienna. From 1906 to 1909 he studied medicine at the Univ. of Vienna. In 1909 he won the prestigious Mozart Prize and a scholarship to study at the Frankfurt Cons., where he studied piano with Willy Rehberg and composition with Iwan Knorr. In 1910 he was awarded the Mendelssohn Prize; also won 4 times in succession the Austrian State Prize. In 1913 he was appointed instructor in piano at Zuschneid's Hochschule für Musik in Mannheim. In 1914–18 he served in the Austrian army; during a furlough in Vienna in 1916 he married Lilly Zwack. After the Armistice he returned to Mannheim, resumed his musical career, and became active in the modern movement, soon attaining, along with Hindemith, Krenek, and others, a prominent position in the new German school of composition. In the meantime he continued his academic studies; earned his Dr.Phil. degree in 1921 with the dissertation *Beiträge zur Stilkunde der Melodie* (publ. in Berlin under the title *Melodielehre*). In 1929 he went to live in Berlin, where he established himself as a piano teacher. In 1932 he made an American tour as a pianist playing his own works; he returned to Berlin, but with the advent of the Nazi regime was forced to leave Germany in 1933. He went to Paris, then to London, and in 1935 emigrated to the U.S.; gave lectures on music at The New School for Social Research in N.Y.; in 1936 moved to Hollywood, where he wrote music for films. He became an American citizen on July 26, 1940; in 1940–41 he taught composition at the Univ. of Southern Calif., Los Angeles; subsequently taught privately; among his students were many, who, like André Previn, became well-known composers in their own right. From 1950 until his death, Toch traveled frequently and lived in Vienna, Zürich, the MacDowell Colony in New Hampshire, and Santa Monica, Calif.

Toch's music is rooted in the tradition of the German and Austrian Romantic movement of the 19th century, but his study of the classics made him aware of the paramount importance of formal logic in the development of thematic ideas. His early works consist mostly of chamber music and pieces for piano solo; following the zeitgeist during his German period, he wrote several pieces for the stage in the light manner of sophisticated entertainment; he also composed effective piano works of a virtuoso quality, which enjoyed considerable popularity among pianists of the time. Toch possessed a fine wit and a sense of exploration; his *Geographical Fugue* for speaking chorus, articulating in syllabic counterpoint the names of exotic places on earth, became a classic of its genre.

It was not until 1950 that Toch wrote his first full-fledged symph., but from that time on, until he died of stomach cancer, he composed fully 7 symphs., plus sinfoniettas for Wind and String Orch. He was greatly interested in new techniques; the theme of his last String Quartet (No. 13, 1953) is based on a 12-tone row. In the score of his 3rd Symph. he introduced an optional instrument, the Hisser, a tank of carbon dioxide that produced a hissing sound through a valve.

Among the several honors Toch received were the Pulitzer Prize for his 3rd Symph. (1956), membership in the National Inst. of Arts and Letters (1957), and the Cross of Honor for Sciences and Art from the Austrian government (1963). An Ernst Toch Archive was founded at the Univ. of Calif., Los Angeles, in 1966, serving as a depository for his MSS, publ. and unpubl.

WORKS: FOR THE STAGE: Unfinished opera, *Wegwende* (1925; sketches destroyed); musical fairy tale, *Die Prinzessin auf der Erbse* (*The Princess and the Pea;* 1927; Baden-Baden, July 17, 1927); *Egon und Emilie,* "not a family drama" (1928; Mannheim, Oct. 21, 1928); opera-capriccio, *Der Fächer* (*The Fan;* 1930; Königsberg, June 8, 1930); a Sheherazade opera, *The Last Tale* (1960–62; unperf.).

FOR ORCH.: *Scherzo* (1904); *Kammersymphonie* for 10 Instruments (1906); *Phantastische Nachtmusik* (1920; Mannheim, March 22, 1921); *5 Pieces* for Chamber Orch. (1924); Concerto for Cello and Small Orch. (1925; Kiel, June 17, 1925); Piano Concerto (1926; Düsseldorf, Oct. 8, 1926; Gieseking, soloist); *Spiel für Blasorchester* (*Divertimento for Orchestra;* 1926; Donaueschingen, July 24, 1926); *Komödie für Orchester* (1927; Berlin, Nov. 13, 1927); *Vorspiel zu einem Märchen* (*Overture to a Fairy Tale;* 1927; overture from the opera *Princess and the Pea*); *Bunte Suite* (*Motley Suite;* 1928; Frankfurt, Feb. 22, 1929); *Fanal* (*Beacon*) for Orch. and Organ (1928); *Kleine Theater-Suite* (1931; Berlin,

Feb. 9, 1931); Symph. for Piano and Orch. (Piano Concerto No. 2, 1932; London, Aug. 20, 1934); *Miniature Overture* for Winds (1932); *Big Ben,* variation fantasy on the Westminster Chimes (1934; Boston Symph., Cambridge, Mass., Dec. 20, 1934; revised 1955); *Pinocchio,* "a merry overture" (1936; Los Angeles, Dec. 10, 1936); *The Idle Stroller,* suite (1938); "The Covenant," 6th movement of 7-movement, collaborative *Genesis Suite,* commissioned by Nathaniel Shilkret (Los Angeles, Nov. 18, 1945; score lost); *Hyperion,* dramatic prelude after Keats (1947; Cleveland, Jan. 8, 1948); 7 symphs.: No. 1 (1949–50; Vienna, Dec. 20, 1950); No. 2, dedicated to Albert Schweitzer (1950–51; Vienna, Jan. 11, 1952); No. 3 (1954–55; Pittsburgh, Dec. 2, 1955; won Pulitzer Prize, 1956); No. 4 (1957; Minneapolis, Nov. 22, 1957); No. 5, subtitled *Jephta, Rhapsodic Poem* (1961–62; Boston, March 13, 1964); No. 6 (1963; posthumous, Zürich Radio, Jan. 22, 1967); No. 7 (1964; posthumous, Bavarian Radio, 1967); *Notturno* (1953; Louisville, Ky., Jan. 2, 1954); *Circus Overture* (1954; Ravinia Festival, Highland Park, Ill., July 8, 1954); *Peter Pan,* fairy tale in 3 parts (1955–56; Seattle, Feb. 13, 1956); 3 Pieces for "Doctor's" Orch.: *Short Story* (1960), *Intermezzo* (1960), and *Epilogue* (1961); *3 Pantomimes: Puppet Show, Capriccio,* and *The Enamoured Harlequin* (all 1963–64); Sinfonietta for String Orch. (1964; posthumous, Philadelphia, Feb. 13, 1967); Sinfonietta for Winds and Percussion (1964; posthumous, Zürich Radio, Nov. 11, 1967).

CHAMBER MUSIC: 13 string quartets: Nos. 1–5 (1902–3; lost); No. 6 in A minor (1905); No. 7 (1908); No. 8 (1911); No. 9 (1919); No. 10, on the name "Bass" (1920); No. 11 (1924); No. 12 (1946); No. 13 (1953); duos for Violins (1909; for open strings only in the pupil's part); Serenade for 3 Violins (1912); Violin Sonata (1912); *"Spitzweg" Serenade* for 2 Violins and Viola (1917); *Tanz Suite* for Flute, Clarinet, Violin, Viola, Bass, and Percussion (1923; excerpts choreographed as *Der Wald,* Mannheim, Nov. 19, 1923; first complete perf., Münster, Oct. 29, 1924); *2 Divertimenti* for String Duos (1926); Violin Sonata (1928); Cello Sonata (1929); *2 Etudes* for Cello Solo (1930); String Trio (1936); Piano Quintet (1938); *Dedication* for String Quartet or String Orch. (1948); *Adagio elegiaco* for Clarinet and Piano (1950); *5 Pieces* for Flute, Oboe, Clarinet, Bassoon, 2 Horns, and Percussion (1959); *Sonatinetta* for Flute, Clarinet, and Bassoon (1959); *3 Impromptus* for Solo Violin, Solo Viola, and Solo Cello (1963); Quartet for Oboe, Clarinet, Bassoon, and Viola (1964).

FOR PIANO: *Melodische Skizzen* (1903); *3 Preludes* (1903); *Capriccio* (1905; lost); Sonata in C-sharp minor (1905; lost); Sonata in D major (1905; lost); *Stammbuchverse (Album Verses;* 1905); *Begegnung (Meeting;* 1908); *Reminiszenzen* (1909); *4 Klavierstücke* (1914; lost); *Canon* (1915); *3 Burlesken* (1923; includes the popular *Der Jongleur,* publ. separately); *3 Klavierstücke* (1925); *5 Capriccetti* (1925); *Tanz- und Spielstücke (Pieces for Dancing and Playing;* 1927); *Studie* for Mechanical Piano (1927); Sonata, op. 17 (1928); *Kleinstadtbilder (Echoes from a Small Town),* 14 easy pieces (1929); *Fünfmal Zehn Etüden,* 50 études (1931); *Profiles* (1946); *Ideas*

(1946); *Diversions* (1956); *Sonatinetta* (1956); *3 Little Dances* (1961); *Reflections,* 5 pieces (1961); Sonata for Piano, 4-hands (1962).

FOR VOICE: *An mein Vaterland (To My Homeland),* symph. for Soprano, Mixed and Boys' Choruses, Orch., and Organ (1913); *Die chinesische Flöte (The Chinese Flute),* chamber symph. for Soprano and 14 Solo Instruments (1922; Frankfurt, June 24, 1923; revised 1949); 9 songs for Soprano and Piano (1926); *Der Tierkreis (The Zodiac)* for 2-part Women's Chorus (1930); *Das Wasser (Water),* cantata for Tenor, Baritone, Narrator, Chorus, Flute, Trumpet, Percussion, and Strings (1930; Berlin Festival of New Music, June 18, 1930); *Gesprochene Musik (Music for Speaking Chorus;* 1930; Berlin Festival of New Music, June 17, 1930; includes the famous *Fuge aus der Geographie [Geographical Fugue],* publ. separately in Eng. and German eds.); *Music for Orchestra and Baritone Solo on Poems by Rilke* for Baritone and Orch. (1932); *Cantata of the Bitter Herbs* for Soloists, Narrator, Chorus, and Orch. (1938); *Poems to Martha,* quintet for Voice and Strings (1942); *The Inner Circle,* 6 a cappella choruses (1953); *There Is a Season for Everything* for Mezzo-soprano, Flute, Clarinet, Violin, and Cello, to words from Ecclesiastes (1953); *Vanity of Vanities, All Is Vanity* for Soprano, Tenor, Clarinet, Violin, Viola, and Cello, to words from Ecclesiastes (1954); *Phantoms* for Narrator, Women's Speaking Chorus, and Chamber Orch. (1957); *Lange schon haben meine Freunde versucht (For a Long Time Now My Friends Have Tried),* duet for Soprano and Baritone (1958); *Song of Myself,* after Whitman, for Mixed Chorus a cappella (1961); *Valse* for Speaking Chorus and Percussion (1961; in separate Eng. and German eds.); folk-song arrangements.

FILM SCORES: *Peter Ibbetson* (1935); *Outcast* (1937); *The Cat and the Canary* (1939); *Dr. Cyclops* (1940); *The Ghost Breakers* (1940); *Ladies in Retirement* (1941); *First Comes Courage* (1943); *None Shall Escape* (1944); *Address Unknown* (1944); *The Unseen* (1945). He also wrote incidental music for stage and radio plays.

PUBLICATIONS: *Die Melodielehre* (Berlin, 1923); *The Shaping Forces in Music* (N.Y., 1948; new ed., with a valuable introduction by Toch's grandson, Lawrence Weschler, and an 18-page complete list of Toch's works, with publishers, N.Y., 1977).

BIBLIOGRAPHY: E. Beninger, "Pianistische Probleme, im Anschluss an die Klavierwerke von Ernst Toch," *Melos* (1928); Paul Pisk, "Ernst Toch," *Musical Quarterly* (Oct. 1938); *Composers of the Americas,* vol. 7 (Washington, D.C., 1961; pp. 83–95); Arthur Cohn, *Twentieth-Century Music in Western Europe* (Philadelphia and N.Y., 1965; pp. 286–93); Lawrence Weschler, *Ernst Toch, 1887–1964: A Biographical Essay Ten Years after His Passing,* a publ. of the Ernst Toch Archive of The Music Library of the Univ. of Calif., Los Angeles (1974).

Toda, Kunio, Japanese composer; b. Tokyo, Aug. 11, 1915. He studied law at Tokyo Univ., graduating in 1938; concurrently studied music; then entered the

Japanese diplomatic service; served as cultural attaché in the Japanese embassies in Germany and Russia; at the outbreak of the war he returned to Japan, where he resumed his musical studies with Saburo Moroi; in 1955 he was appointed a lecturer at the Toho Junior College of Music; taught also at the Toho Gakuen School of Music.

WORKS: 2 operas: *Akemi* (1956; Tokyo, 1956) and *Kyara Monogatari* (*The Story of Kyara City;* Tokyo, 1973); 5 ballets: *Salome in Studio* (Tokyo, Nov. 23, 1951); *Le Cirque rouge* (Tokyo, Nov. 4, 1953); *The Cave* (Tokyo, Nov. 7, 1954); *Dance of the Red Death*, after Edgar Allan Poe (Osaka, 1956); *Miranda* (Tokyo, Oct. 26, 1968); scenic oratorio-mystery, *Santo Paulo*, for 4 Soloists, Chorus, and Orch. (1961–64; concert version, Tokyo, Feb. 15, 1973); *Symphonic Overture* (1943); *Légende,* symph. fantasy (1944); 2 piano concertos (1944, 1955); *Passacaglia and Fugue* for Orch. (1949); *Overtura buffa* (1950); Symph. in G (1956); *Concerto grosso* for 6 Solo Instruments and Orch. (Tokyo, Jan. 25, 1968); Piano Trio (1948); *Amoroso* for Violin and Piano (1951); Violin Sonata (1957); *Message* for Soprano, Clarinet, and Harp (1961); *Bassoon Sonata* (1966); *Triptychon* for Solo Baritone, Recorder, and Guitar (1967, revised 1972); *3 intermezzi* for Piano (1942); *Fantaisie sur les sons de koto* for Piano (1961); Piano Sonatina (1966); *4 pezzi deformati* for Piano (1968); choruses; songs.

Todi, Luiza Rosa de Aguilar, Portuguese mezzo-soprano; b. Setubal, Jan. 9, 1753; d. Lisbon, Oct. 1, 1833. She made her debut as a comic actress at age 14; married the violinist **Francisco Todi** at 16; studied singing with David Perez. She made her opera debut in 1770 in Scolari's *Il Viaggiatore ridicolo;* made appearances in London (1772 and 1777–78), Madrid (1777), Paris (1778–79 and 1781–82), and Berlin (1782). In 1783 her rivalry with Elisabeth Mara became a sensation in musical Paris, 2 hostile factions being formed, the Todistes and the Maratistes. In 1784 she went to Russia, where she obtained considerable success at the court of Catherine the Great; in 1787 Friedrich Wilhelm II engaged her at a high salary in Berlin; in 1789 she sang again in Paris; in 1793 she returned to Portugal; during the last years of her life she was completely blind.

BIBLIOGRAPHY: J. Vasconcellos, *Luiza Todi* (Oporto, 1873; 2nd ed., 1929); R.-Aloys Mooser, *Annales de la Musique et des Musiciens en Russie au XVIIIe siècle* (Geneva, 1948–51; vol. 2, pp. 509–13).

Toduţă, Sigismund, Rumanian composer; b. Simeria, May 30, 1908. He studied with Negrea at the Cons. in Cluj (1931–33), and later at the Santa Cecilia Academy in Rome (1936–38) with Pizzetti (composition) and Casella (piano). In 1946 he was appointed to the faculty of the Cluj Cons. (he was its director from 1962–64); in 1971 he became managing director of the Cluj State Phil. His music is distinguished by a flowing Romantic melody in large rhapsodic sonorities.

WORKS: Opera, *Mesterul Manole* (1943–47); oratorio, *Miorita* (1958); *Balada Steagului* for Soprano, Chorus, and Orch. (1961); *Eglogă* for Orch. (1933);

Symphonic Variations (1940); Piano Concerto (1943); 3 concertos for String Orch. (1951, 1971, 1973); *Divertissement* for String Orch. (1951); 5 symphs.: No. 1 (1954); No. 2, in memory of Enesco, with Organ (1956); No. 3, *Ovidiu* (1957); No. 4 for Strings (1961); No. 5 (1963); *Uvertură festivă* (1959); Sinfonietta (1971); Concerto for Winds and Percussion (1976); Cello Sonata (1952); Flute Sonata (1952); Violin Sonata (1953); *Adagio* for Cello and Piano (1954); Oboe Sonata (1956); *Passacaglia* for Piano (1943); Piano Sonatina (1950); *Prelude, Chorale and Toccata* for Piano (1975); choruses; songs.

Toebosch, Louis, Dutch composer and organist; b. Maastricht, March 18, 1916. He studied at the School of Church Music in Utrecht, the Music Lyceum in Maastricht, and then the Royal Cons. in Liège, Belgium (1934–39); was active as a church organist in Breda (1940–65); conducted the Tilburg Symph. Orch. (1946–52); taught at the conservatories of Tilburg and Maastricht (1944–65); was director of the Brabant Cons. (1965–74). His music combines the polyphonic style of the Renaissance with modern techniques; he applies the 12-tone method of compostion in both secular and sacred music.

WORKS: 2 suites for Orch. (1939, 1948); *Allegro* for Organ and Orch. (1941); *Tema con variazioni* for Orch. (1945); *Breda Suite* for Orch. (1948); *Het Lied van Hertog Jan* for Orch. (1949); oratorio, *St. Vincentius* (1954); *Carnavalsige Ouverture* (1955); *Concertante Ouverture* (1956); *Variations* for Orch. (1957); Sinfonietta No. 1 for Male Chorus and Orch. (1957); Sinfonietta No. 2 for Orch. (1961); *Kerstcantate (Christmas Cantata)* for Soprano, Male Chorus, and Orch. (1959); *Feestelijke Ouverture* (1960); *Philippica moderata*, written for the 50th anniversary of scientific research of Philips Co., for Contralto, Baritone, Chorus, and Orch. (1963; winner of the 1966 Sem Dresden Prize); *Agena,* divertimento for Small Orch. (1966); *Changements* for Organ and Orch. (Rotterdam, March 28, 1968); Piano Sonata (1947); organ pieces: *Praeludium et Fuga super Te Deum laudamus* (1954), *Toccana* (1973), and *Orgelspiegel* (*Organ Mirror,* 1975); *Sarabande and Allegro* for Wind Quintet (1959); *Suite polyphonica* for 2 Pianos (1962); *The King's Quartet* for String Quartet (1968); *Aria and Finale* for Solo Viola (1969); *Pasticcio di Rofena* for Piano, 4-hands (1973).

Toëschi, Carlo Giuseppe (Toesca della Castella-Monte), Italian violinist and composer; b. Ludwigsburg (baptized, Nov. 11), 1731; d. Munich, April 12, 1788. He was the son of **Alessandro Toëschi,** a member of the Mannheim Orch., who had moved to Germany. He studied with Johann Stamitz in Mannheim and entered its orch. in 1752 as a violinist; in 1759 he became concertmaster of the Mannheim Orch. He followed the court to Munich in 1778, and was appointed court musician in 1780. A highly productive composer, he wrote about 25 ballet scores and at least 66 known symphs.; 19 flute concertos and 11 violin concertos; also a number of quartets, quintets, sextets, trio sonatas, violin sonatas and other pieces of chamber music. Riemann

publ. his Symph. *a* 8 in Denkmäler der Tonkunst in Bayern, 13 (7.ii); in the same series are reprinted a Flute Quartet and Flute Quintet (vol. 27 [15]) and a Trio (vol. 28 [16]); it also contains a thematic catalogue, listing 60 chamber works. A Symph. in D was arranged by A. Carse, and publ. in London (1936).
BIBLIOGRAPHY: R. Münster, *Die Sinfonien Toeschis* (Diss., Univ. of Munich, 1956).

Toëschi, Johann Baptist (Giovanni Battista), Italian-German violinist and composer, brother of **Carlo Giuseppe Toëschi;** b. Stuttgart (baptized, Oct. 1), 1735; d. Munich (buried, April 3), 1800. Like his brother, he was a violinist in the Mannheim Orch. (from 1755); followed the court to Munich in 1778, and became music director in Munich in 1793. He produced a ballet, *Arlechin, Kaiser in China* (Mannheim, April 26, 1778); composed a great number of chamber music pieces. A thematic catalogue of his works appears in Denkmäler der Tonkunst in Bayern, 28 (16).

Tofft, Alfred, Danish composer; b. Copenhagen, Jan. 2, 1865; d. there, Jan. 30, 1931. Abandoning a commercial career, he studied music with J. Nebelong (organ) and G. Bohlmann (theory); was music critic for the *Berlinske Tidende* in Copenhagen, and president of the Danish Composers' Society. He was a fine organist and a talented composer of songs (op. 2, *Heine-Album;* op. 4, *Jacobsen-Album;* etc.). Two operas were produced in Copenhagen: *Vifandaka* (Jan. 1, 1898) and *Anathema* (May 10, 1928).

Togni, Camillo, Italian composer; b. Gussago, Oct. 18, 1922. He studied with Alfredo Casella in Rome (1939–43); took courses in philosophy at the Univ. of Pavia; then devoted himself entirely to music. His early works follow the neo-Classical style of the Italian Baroque; later he adopted the 12-tone method of composition.
WORKS: *Variations* for Piano and Orch. (1946); *Psalmus CXXVII* for Solo Voices, Violin, Viola, and Cello (Brussels Festival of the International Society for Contemporary Music, June 24, 1950); *Ricercar* for Baritone and 5 Instruments, to a text from *La Nausée* by Sartre (1953); *Fantasia concertante* for Flute and String Orch. (Cologne, March 25, 1958); *Recitativo* for Electronic Sound (1961); *Gesang zur Nacht* for Contralto and Chamber Orch. (1962); *3 rondeaux per dieci* for Soprano and 9 Instruments (1964); *Aubade* for 6 Instruments (1965); 4 capriccios for Piano (1954, 1956, 1957, 1969); *3 Pieces* for Chorus and Orch. (Venice, Sept. 17, 1972).

Tokatyan, Armand, Bulgarian operatic tenor of Armenian descent; b. Plovdiv, Feb. 12, 1896; d. Pasadena, Calif., June 12, 1960. He was educated in Alexandria, Egypt; then studied voice with Cairone in Milan and Wolf in Vienna. He made his operatic debut in Milan, in 1921; then went to the U.S., where he toured with the Scotti Opera Co. He made his debut at the Metropolitan Opera House, N.Y., on Nov. 19, 1922, as Turiddu in a concert performance of *Cavalleria rusticana,* and remained a member of the staff of the Metropolitan, with interruptions, until 1946. He also made appearances in London, Berlin, and Vienna.

Tolbecque, Auguste, French cellist; b. Paris, March 30, 1830; d. Niort, March 8, 1919. He won first prize for cello at the Paris Cons. in 1849; taught at the Marseilles Cons. (1865–71); later was cellist at the Paris Cons. concerts. He publ. *La Gymnastique du violoncelle* (op. 14; excellent exercises and mechanical studies), a *Konzertstück* for Cello and Orch., and pieces for cello and piano; produced a one-act comic opera, *Après la valse* (Niort, 1894). He also wrote *Souvenirs d'un musicien en province* (1896), *Notice historique sur les instruments à cordes et à archet* (1898), and *L'Art du luthier* (1903).

Tolbecque, Jean-Baptiste-Joseph, Belgian violinist; b. Hanzinne, April 17, 1797; d. Paris, Oct. 23, 1869. He was a pupil of Kreutzer and Reicha at the Paris Cons.; played violin at the Théâtre Italien and then became a successful conductor at court balls, for which he wrote waltzes, galops, quadrilles, and other fashionable dances, which enjoyed tremendous success. In 1851 he staged his ballet, *Vert-Vert* (in collaboration with Deldevez), at the Paris Opéra. His 3 brothers, **Isidore-Joseph** (1794–1871), **Auguste-Joseph** (1801–69), and **Charles-Joseph** (1806–35), were professional violinists and theater conductors.

Toldrá, Eduardo, Catalan conductor; b. Villanueva y Geltrú, Catalonia, April 7, 1895; d. Barcelona, May 31, 1962. He studied the violin, and was a member of a string quartet, with which he toured in Europe. In 1921 he became a prof. of violin at the Barcelona Municipal School of Music; in 1943, was appointed conductor of the Municipal Orch. He publ. an album of pieces in the form of Catalan folk dances.
BIBLIOGRAPHY: M. Capdevila Massana, *Eduardo Toldrá* (Barcelona, 1964; new augmented ed., 1972).

Tollefsen, Carl H., American violinist; b. Hull, England, Aug. 15, 1882; d. Brooklyn, N.Y., Dec. 10, 1963. He emigrated to America as a youth, and studied at the National Cons. in N.Y. (1898–1902) and later at the Inst. of Musical Art (1906–8), where his teachers were Franz Kneisel (violin), and Goetschius and Rubin Goldmark (composition); was a violinist in various orchs. in N.Y. On Aug. 7, 1907, he married the pianist **Augusta Schnabel** (b. Boise, Idaho, Jan. 5, 1885; d. Brooklyn, April 9, 1955), and formed the Tollefsen Trio with her and with Paul Kéfer; this trio toured the U.S. for more than 30 years (succeeding cellists were M. Penha, P. Gruppe, R. Thrane, and W. Durieux). In 1939 he founded the Brooklyn Chamber Music Society. He formed a large collection of autographs of famous musicians and MS biographies (including the biographical archives gathered by Alfred Rémy, editor of the 3rd ed. of *Baker's Biographical Dictionary of Musicians*). In

1947 the cellist Yuri Bilstin bequeathed to him a collection of old instruments. After Tollefsen's death his entire collection was turned over to the Southern Illinois Univ. Lovejoy Library at Edwardsville.

Tolonen, Jouko, Finnish composer; b. Porvoo, Nov. 2, 1912. He studied piano with Linko and composition with Krohn, Madetoja, and Fougestedt at the Univ. of Helsinki; was executive director of the Finnish National Opera in 1956–60; taught at the Sibelius Academy in Helsinki in 1960–66 and at the Univ. of Turku (Åbo) in 1965–72; was a prof. of musicology in 1972–77. He composed *Andante and Rondo alla burla* for Orch. (1948); *Andante* for Piano and Strings (1950); Symph. (1952); *3 Arabesques* for Orch. (1953); *Les Fanfares* for Brass (1970).

Tolstoy, Dmitri, Soviet composer, son of the writer Alexei Tolstoy; b. Berlin, Jan. 20, 1923. He went to Russia with his father after the latter's temporary emigration; studied at the Leningrad Cons., graduating in 1947; took courses in composition with Shebalin in Moscow and Shostakovich in Leningrad.
WORKS: *Poem about Leningrad* for Orch. (1953); *Spring Victory,* cantata (1946); *Masquerade,* opera (Moscow, Jan. 17, 1956); *Mariuta,* opera (Perm, Dec. 30, 1960); 3 piano sonatas; 12 preludes for Piano; many songs.

Tomaschek, Wenzel Johann (Bohemian spelling, **Václav Jan Křitite Tomášek**), important Bohemian composer and pedagogue; b. Skutsch, April 17, 1774; d. Prague, April 3, 1850. He was the youngest of 13 children; learned the rudiments of singing and violin playing from P.J. Wolf and studied organ with Donat Schuberth. In 1787 he became an alto chorister at the Minorite monastery in Iglau; in 1790 he went to Prague, supporting himself by playing piano in public places; also took law courses at the Univ. of Prague. From 1806–22 he was attached to the family of Count Georg Bucquoy de Longeval as music tutor. In 1824 he established his own music school in Prague. Among his many pupils were J.H. Woržischek (Vořišek), Dreyschock, Hanslick, and Schulhoff. Tomaschek was the first to use the instrumental form of the rhapsody systematically in a number of his piano pieces, although it was anticipated by W.R. Gallenberg in a single composition a few years earlier; he also adopted the ancient Greek terms "eclogue" and "dithyramb" for short character pieces. He wrote an autobiography, publ. in installments in the Prague journal *Libussa* (1845–50); a modern edition was prepared by Z. Němec (Prague, 1941); excerpts appeared in the *Musical Quarterly* (April 1946).
WORKS: Operas: *Seraphine, oder Grossmut und Liebe* (Prague, Dec. 15, 1811) and *Alvaro* (unfinished). Choral music: Requiem (1820); *Krönungsmesse* (1836); Te Deum. Instrumental music: 3 symphs. (1801, 1805, 1807); 2 piano concertos (1805, 1806); 3 string quartets (1792–93); Piano Trio (1800); Piano Quartet (1805). For Solo Piano: 7 sonatas

(1800–6); 42 eclogues (1807–23); 15 rhapsodies (1810); 6 *allegri capricciosi* (1815, 1818); 6 dithyrambs (1818–23).
BIBLIOGRAPHY: M. Tarantová, *Václav Jan Tomášek* (Prague, 1946); P. Nettl, *Forgotten Musicians* (N.Y., 1951; pp. 91–109); M. Postler, *V.J. Tomášek: Bibliografie* (Prague, 1960); T. Straková, "V.J. Tomášek a jeho klavírní eklogy," *Časopis Moravského musea,* XLV (1960); A. Simpson and S. Horsfall, "A Czech Composer Views His Contemporaries," *Musical Times,* CXV (1974); T. Volek and S. Jareš, "Portréty V.J. Tomáška," *Hudebni veda,* XII (1975).

Tomášek, Jaroslav, Czech composer; b. Koryčany, Moravia, April 10, 1896; d. Prague, Nov. 26, 1970. He studied music with Vítězslav Novák; also attended a course in musicology at the Univ. of Prague. He composed mostly in small forms; wrote 2 song cycles: *To Woman* for High Voice (1919–20; with Orch., 1944–46) and *Grief* for Tenor, Soprano, Bass, and Orch. (1958–59); *Rondo* for Piano, left hand (1924); Piano Sonata for left hand (1925); 2 string quartets; *Symphonic Rondo* for Piano and Orch. (1962); songs. His wife, **Jaromíra Tomášková-Nováková** (b. Jaroměř, May 23, 1892; d. Prague, April 25, 1957), was a concert soprano; she taught singing at the Prague Cons. from 1920 on.

Tomasi, Henri, French composer; b. Marseilles, Aug. 17, 1901; d. Paris, Jan. 13, 1971. He studied with Paul Vidal at the Paris Cons.; won the 2nd Grand Prix de Rome for his cantata *Coriolan* (1927). He served in the French army (1939–40); was awarded the Grand Prix de Musique Française in 1952. His music is marked by impressionistic colors; he was particularly attracted to exotic subjects, depicting in fine instrumental colors scenes in Corsica, Cambodia, Laos, Sahara, Tahiti, etc. He also wrote music inspired by Gregorian chant and medieval religious songs. During his last period he was motivated in his music by political events, and wrote pieces in homage to the Third World and Vietnam.
WORKS: OPERAS: *Don Juan de Mañara* (Munich, March 29, 1956); *Altantide* (Mulhouse, Feb. 26, 1954); *Sampiero Corso* (Bordeaux, May, 1956); *Il Poverello* (1957); opera-bouffe, *Princesse Pauline* (1960); chamber opera-bouffe, *L'Elixir du R.P. Gaucher,* after *Les Lettres de mon moulin* by Alphonse Daudet (1962); *Le Triomphe de Jeanne* (Rouen, 1956). BALLETS: *La Grisi* (Paris, Oct. 7, 1935); *La Rosière de village* (Paris, May 26, 1936); *Les Santons* (Paris, Nov. 18, 1938); *La Féerie cambodgienne* (Marseilles, Jan. 31, 1952); *Les Folies mazarguaises* (Marseilles, Oct. 5, 1953); *Noces de cendre* (Strasbourg, Jan. 19, 1954); choreographic poem, *Dassine, sultane du Hoggar,* for 2 Speakers, Chorus, and Orch. (1959); *Les Barbaresques* (Nice, 1960); *Nana,* after Emile Zola (1962). FOR ORCH.: *Chants de Cyrnos,* symph. poem (Paris, Nov. 30, 1929); *Mélodies corses* (1931); *Vocero,* symph. poem (Paris, Feb. 5, 1933); *Scènes municipales* (1933); *Tam-Tam,* symph. poem (Paris, June 13, 1933); *Chants laotiens* (1934); *2 danses cambodgiennes* (1934); *Chant des*

geishas (1936); *Impressions sahariennes* (1938); Symph. (Paris, May 4, 1943); *Concert asiatique* for Percussion and Orch. (1939); Flute Concerto (1947); Trumpet Concerto (1949); Viola Concerto (1951); Saxophone Concerto (1951); Horn Concerto (1955); Clarinet Concerto (1956); Trombone Concerto (1956); Bassoon Concerto (1958); Oboe Concerto (1958); Violin Concerto (1962); Cello Concerto (1970); *Jabadao,* symph. poem (Paris, Jan. 10, 1960); *Taïtienne de Gauguin* (1963); *Symphonie du tiers monde* (Paris, Feb. 18, 1968); *Chant pour le Vietnam,* symph. poem for Wind Band and Percussion (Paris, Dec. 7, 1969). CHAMBER MUSIC: *Concerto champêtre* for Oboe, Clarinet, and Bassoon (1939); String Trio (1943); *Divertimento Corsica* for Woodwind Trio (1952); Wind Quintet (1952); *Concerto de printemps* for Flute, Strings, and Percussion (1965); *La Moresca* for 8 Wind Instruments (1965); *Danseuses de Degas* for Harp and String Quartet (1964); *Sonatine attique* for Clarinet (1966); many piano pieces; song cycles.

Tomasini, Luigi (Aloysius), Italian violinist and composer; b. Pesaro, June 22, 1741; d. Esterház, April 25, 1808. From 1756 he was a violinist at Prince Paul Anton Esterházy's residence in Eisenstadt, and was a friend of Haydn there; in 1761 he became concertmaster in Haydn's orch.; remained in the household of Prince Nicholas, successor to Paul Anton Esterházy, and was pensioned in 1790. Several of Haydn's concertos were dedicated to Tomasini, who was a composer of considerable merit himself; he wrote 24 divertimentos for Baryton, Viola, and Cello, string quartets; etc. His son **Anton Tomasini** (b. Eisenstadt, Feb. 17, 1775; d. there, June 12, 1824) was a viola player; another son, **Luigi Tomasini,** was an excellent violinist in Haydn's orch., highly commended by Haydn; he went to Vienna in 1796 and to Berlin in 1808.

Tómasson, Jónas, Icelandic composer; b. Isafjordur, Nov. 21, 1946. He studied composition with Sigurbjörnsson in Reykjavik and with Ton de Leeuw in Amsterdam; then taught at the Isafjordur Music School.
WORKS: Wind Quintet (1970); *1,41* for Orch. (1970); 13 compositions entitled Sonatas, among them one for Flute, Oboe, Clarinet, and Bassoon; one for Organ and Cello; and one for String Quartet (1975); Viola Concerto (1971); *4 Quartets* for Flute, Clarinet, Bass Clarinet, and Horn; *Invention and Coda* for Chamber Ensemble; *Cantata I* for 5 Voices and Chamber Ensemble; *Cantata II* for Soprano, Flute, Bassoon, Clarinet, Horn, and Cello (1973); *Play, Play* for Orch.; *11 Thoughts about the Settlement* for Orch. (1974); *Orgia* for Orch. (1977).

Tombelle, Fernand de la. See **La Tombelle, Fernand de.**

Tomilin, Victor, Russian composer; b. Berdichev, May 15, 1908; killed in combat near Leningrad, Dec. 9, 1941. He was a pupil of Vladimir Shcherbachev at the Leningrad Cons., graduating in 1932. He wrote 2 symph. suites, *Episodes of Civil War* (1936) and *Crimean Suite* (1939); a number of songs and piano pieces.

Tomkins, Thomas, English organist and composer; b. St. David's, 1572; d. Martin Hussingtree, near Worcester, June (buried, June 9) 1656. He came from a family of musicians, of whom many members flourished in the 16th and 17th centuries. He was a pupil of William Byrd; was appointed organist of the Worcester Cathedral about 1596, holding this position for half a century, until 1646. In 1607 he received the degree of Mus.B. at Oxford, and in 1621 was appointed an organist of the Chapel Royal. He was one of the most inspired of the English madrigalists; his ballets, keyboard pieces, and sacred works are also of a high quality. His publ. works include *Songs of 3, 4, 5 and 6 parts* (reprinted in the *English Madrigal School,* vol. 18) and *Musica Deo Sacra* (posthumous, 1668), containing 5 services and 95 anthems (services reprinted in *Tudor Church Music,* vol. 7). Other church music is in MS. His keyboard music was publ. by Stephen D. Tuttle in *Musica Britannica,* vol. 5; 2 pieces are in Davison and Apel, *Historical Anthology of Music,* vol. 1 (Cambridge, Mass., 1946).
BIBLIOGRAPHY: S. de B. Taylor, *Thomas Tomkins* (London, 1933); G. Reese, *Music in the Renaissance* (N.Y., 1954); Denis Stevens, *Thomas Tomkins* (London, 1957; 2nd ed., 1967).

Tomlins, William Lawrence, British-American music educator and choral leader; b. London, Feb. 4, 1844; d. Delafield, Wis., Sept. 26, 1930. He was a pupil of G.A. Macfarren and E. Silas; in 1869 he emigrated to the U.S.; in 1875–98, conducted the Apollo Glee Club, Chicago; having made a specialty of training children's choruses and teachers, he established in 1903 the National Training School for Music Teachers, in Chicago. He publ. *Children's Songs, and How to Sing Them* (1885).

Tommasini, Vincenzo, Italian composer; b. Rome, Sept. 17, 1878; d. there, Dec. 23, 1950. He studied violin with Pinelli; theory with Falchi at the Santa Cecilia Academy in Rome; then went to Berlin, where he took lessons with Max Bruch; after sojourns in Paris, London, and N.Y., he returned to Rome. He wrote music in the poetic tradition of Italian Romanticism; his operas, symph. works, and chamber music obtained immediate performances and favorable receptions; however, his most successful piece, *Le Donne di buon umore (The Good-humored Ladies),* was not an original work but a comedy-ballet written on music from sonatas by Domenico Scarlatti, arranged in a series of tableaux and brilliantly orchestrated; this was a commission for the Ballets Russes of Diaghilev, who staged it at Rome in April 1917, and kept it in the repertoire during his tours all over the world. Other works by Tommasini include the operas *Medea,* to the composer's own libretto (Trieste, April 8, 1906), and *Uguale fortuna* (Rome, 1913); for Orch.: *La vita è un sogno* (1901); *Poema erotico* (1909); *Inno alla*

beltà (1911); *Ciari di luna* (Rome, 1916); *Il beato regno* (Rome, 1922); *Paesaggi toscani* (Rome, 1923); *Il Carnevale di Venezia* (N.Y., Oct. 10, 1929, Toscanini conducting); *Nápule (Naples),* fantasy (Freiburg, Dec. 7, 1931); Violin Concerto (1932); *4 pezzi* (1934); *Le Diable s'amuse,* ballet suite on themes by Paganini (1936); Concerto for String Quartet and Orch. (1939); *La tempesta* (1941); *Tiepolesco,* ballet suite (1945); *Duo concertante* for Piano and Orch. (1948); 3 string quartets; Violin Sonata; Harp Sonata; *Due Macchiette* for Cello and Piano (1940); piano pieces; *La luce invisibile* (1929) and *Saggio di estetica sperimentale* (1942).
BIBLIOGRAPHY: G. Gatti, "Some Italian Composers of Today: Tommasini," *Musical Times* (Nov. 1921); M. Zanotti-Bianco, "Vincenzo Tommasini," *Chesterian* (Feb. 1923); A. Casella, "Vincenzo Tommasini," *Revue Musicale* (1927); M. Rinaldi, "Vincenzo Tommasini," *Rivista Musicale Italiana* (Oct.–Dec. 1951).

Tomowa-Sintow, Anna, Bulgarian soprano; b. Stara Zagora, Sept. 22, 1941. She studied at the State Cons. in Sofia. In 1967 she joined the Leipzig Opera; in 1971 she won the international singers' competition held in Rio de Janeiro. In 1973 Herbert von Karajan chose her for the world premiere of Carl Orff's *De temporum fine comedia,* which was given at the Salzburg Festival. In subsequent seasons she sang in Munich (1974), in San Francisco (1974), at Covent Garden in London (1975), and in Vienna (1977). On April 3, 1978, she sang Donna Anna in Mozart's *Don Giovanni* in her debut at the Metropolitan Opera in N.Y.

Toni, Alceo, Italian musicologist and composer; b. Lugo, May 22, 1884; d. Milan, Dec. 4, 1969. He was a pupil of L. Torchi and E. Bossi in Bologna; then lived in Milan. He edited numerous works by Corelli, Locatelli, Torelli, Monteverdi, Carissimi, and other old Italian composers. His own compositions include a Requiem Mass, chamber music, and songs. Some of his many articles were collected in a book, *Studi critici di interpretazione* (Milan, 1923). With Tullio Serafin, he compiled a 2-vol. edition, *Stile, tradizioni e convenzioni del melo dramma italiano del Settecento e dell'Ottocento* (Milan, 1958–64).

Tonning, Gerard, American choral conductor and composer; b. Stavanger, Norway, May 25, 1860; d. New York, June 10, 1940. He studied in Munich with Rheinberger and others; in 1887 he emigrated to America, settling in Duluth, Minn., where he organized several choral societies; in 1905 he moved to Seattle, where he remained until 1917; then went to N.Y.
WORKS: Historical opera, to a Norwegian libretto, *Leif Erikson* (Seattle, Dec. 10, 1910; Brooklyn Academy of Music, Oct. 4, 1924; both perfs. in Norwegian); one-act romantic opera, *All in a Garden Fair* (Seattle, Nov. 1, 1913); pantomime, *Woman's Wiles, or Love Triumphant;* Piano Trio; *Suite moderne* for Violin and Piano; *Rapsodie nor-*

végienne for Violin and Piano; piano pieces (*Norwegian Dances,* 3 nocturnes, etc.); songs (*Arabian Love Songs* for 4 Solo Voices); etc.
BIBLIOGRAPHY: E.E. Hipsher, *American Opera and Its Composers* (Philadelphia, 1934, pp. 404–7).

Töpfer, Johann Gottlob, famous German organist and writer on organ building; b. Niederrossla, Dec. 4, 1791; d. Weimar, June 8, 1870. He studied with the cantor Schlömilch; then at Weimar with Destouches and A.E. Müller; also attended the Weimar Seminary, where he became a teacher of music in 1817; from 1830 was town organist of Weimar. An expert on organ construction, he wrote *Die Orgelbaukunst* (1833); *Die Scheibler'sche Stimm-Methode* (1842); *Die Orgel; Zweck und Beschaffenheit ihrer Theile* (1843); *Lehrbuch der Orgelbaukunst* (a fundamental work, 1855; 4 vols.; 2nd ed. by M. Allihn, 1888; 3rd ed. by P. Smets, 1934–39); *Theoretisch-praktische Organistenschule* (1845); *Allgemeines und vollständiges Choralbuch* (a 4, with organ interludes); a cantata, *Die Orgelweihe; Konzertstück* for Organ; sonatas, fantasias, preludes, fugues, etc., for organ; piano pieces.
BIBLIOGRAPHY: A.W. Gottschalg, *Johann Gottlob Töpfer* (Berlin, 1870).

Töpper, Hertha, Austrian mezzo-soprano; b. Graz, April 19, 1924. She was educated at the Graz Cons.; made her debut at the Graz Opera in 1945; in 1952 she became a member of the Bavarian State Opera in Munich; also sang at Bayreuth, at Covent Garden in London, at La Scala in Milan, etc. She made her American debut at the Metropolitan Opera in N.Y. as Octavian in *Der Rosenkavalier* on Nov. 19, 1962. She also toured as a concert singer, giving successful recitals in Switzerland, Italy, Russia, Finland, the U.S., and Japan.

Toradze, David, Soviet Georgian composer; b. Tiflis, April 14, 1922; d. there, Nov. 7, 1983. He studied at the Tiflis Cons.; then at the Moscow Cons. with Glière; in 1952 became a teacher at the Tiflis Cons.; a reader in 1966; a prof. in 1973. He wrote the operas *The Call of the Mountains* (Tiflis, Nov. 20, 1947) and *The Bride of the North* (1958); a ballet, *For Peace* (Tiflis, June 17, 1953); Symph. (1946); chamber music; choruses; songs.

Torchi, Luigi, eminent Italian musicologist; b. Mondano, near Bologna, Nov. 7, 1858; d. Bologna, Sept. 18, 1920. He studied at the Liceo Musicale of Bologna, the Naples Cons. (composition with Serrao), and the Leipzig Cons. (Jadassohn and Reinecke); from 1885–91, was prof. of music history and esthetics, also librarian, at the Liceo Musicale Rossini in Pesaro; from 1895 to 1916 he held similar positions at the Bologna Cons., also teaching composition there. From its foundation (1894) until 1904 he was editor of the *Rivista Musicale Italiana,* for which he wrote many valuable essays. In 1890 he publ. *R. Wagner: Studio critico* (1890; 2nd ed., 1913). Besides a collection of *Eleganti canzoni ed arie italiane* of the 17th century (Milan, 1894) and *A Collection of*

Pieces for the Violin Composed by Italian Masters of the 17th and 18th Centuries (London; both with piano accompaniment by Torchi), in 1897 he began publishing the important anthology *L'arte musicale in Italia.*

BIBLIOGRAPHY: F. Vatielli, "Necrologia di Luigi Torchi," *Rivista Musicale Italiana* (1920).

Torelli (Torrelli), Gasparo, Italian composer; b. Borgo San Sepolcro, near Lucca; d. some time after 1613. He publ. *Brevi concetti d'amore* (madrigals *a* 5; 1598); 4 books of *Canzonette a 3* (1593–1608); and *I fidi amanti,* "favola pastorale" (in madrigal style, 4 voices; 1600; reprinted in Torchi's *L'arte musicale in Italia,* vol. 4).

Torelli, Giuseppe, Italian violinist and composer, probable originator of the solo concerto for violin; b. Verona, April 22, 1658; d. Bologna, Feb. 8, 1709. He studied in Bologna, where he was a member of the Accademia Filarmonica and viola player at the church of S. Petronio (1684–95). He became Kapellmeister to the Margrave of Brandenburg at Ansbach (1698–99). From 1699 he was in Vienna, where he produced an oratorio; returned to Bologna in 1701. He had generally been regarded as the originator of the concerto grosso until Arnold Schering, in 1903, showed that Stradella, who died in 1682, had written such works. But Torelli's *Concerti grossi,* op. 8 (1709), were the first to be publ. (Corelli's op. 6 was not publ. until 1712, though composed earlier).

WORKS: *Balletti da camera a 3 violini e basso continuo,* op. 1 (Bologna, 1686); *Concerto da camera a 2 violini e basso,* op. 2 (1686); *Sinfonie a 2–4 stromenti,* op. 3 (1687); *Concertino per camera a violino e violoncello,* op. 4 (Bologna, 1688); *6 sinfonie a 3, e 6 concerti a 4,* op. 5 (1692); *Concerti musicali a 4,* op. 6 (with organ; Augsburg, 1698); *Capricci musicali per camera a violino e viola ovvero arciliuto,* op. 7; *Concerti grossi con una pastorale per il Santissimo Natale,* op. 8 (Bologna, 1709), written for 2 Violini Concertanti, 2 Violini di Ripieno, Viola, and Continuo. The so-called Christmas Eve Concerto (op. 8, no. 6) and other works from op. 8 and op. 6 have been reprinted in modern editions.

BIBLIOGRAPHY: A. Schering, *Geschichte des Instrumentalkonzerts* (Leipzig, 1905; 2nd ed., 1927); F. Vatielli, *Arte e vita musicale a Bologna* (Bologna, 1927); R. Brenzoni, "Giuseppe Torelli, musicista veronese," *Note d'Archivio per la Storia Musicale* (1936); F. Giegling, *Giuseppe Torelli, Ein Beitrag zur Entwicklungsgeschichte des italienischen Konzerts* (Kassel, 1949); R. Norton, *The Chamber Music of Giuseppe Torelli* (Diss., Northwestern Univ., 1967); E. Enrico, *Giuseppe Torelli's Music for Instrumental Ensemble with Trumpet* (Diss., Univ. of Michigan, 1970).

Torjussen, Trygve, Norwegian composer and music teacher; b. Drammen, Nov. 14, 1885; d. Oslo, Feb. 12, 1977. He studied in Oslo, Rome, and Stuttgart; was on the staff of the Oslo Cons. (1911–17) and the Barratt-Due Music Inst. (1931–41). Among his works are various suites for small orch.; *Kark* for Tenor, Bass, Female Chorus, and Orch. (Oslo, 1939); *A Musical Bridge-Evening* for String Quartet (Oslo, 1935); over 70 piano pieces, including a sonata; 30 songs.

Torkanowsky, Werner, German-American conductor; b. Berlin, March 30, 1926. He studied music with his mother; went to Palestine after 1933; emigrated to the U.S. in 1948. He began his musical career as a violinist; was a member of the Pittsburgh Symph. Orch. In 1955 he joined the master class of Pierre Monteux in Maine; subsequently conducted at the Spoleto Festivals. From 1963 to 1977 he was conductor of the New Orleans Phil. Symph. Orch.

Torme, Mel (Melvin Howard), American singer and composer; b. Chicago, Sept. 13, 1925. He began his career as a nightclub singer, performing his own songs, some of which attained popularity, among them *Stranger in Town, Lament to Love, Welcome to the Club, Reminiscing in Tempo,* and *The Jet Set.* He also wrote an account of the life of Judy Garland under the title *The Other Side of the Rainbow* (N.Y., 1970).

Törne, Bengt von, Finnish composer; b. Helsinki, Nov. 22, 1891; d. Turku, May 4, 1967. He studied composition with Furuhjelm at the Helsinki Inst. of Music and, during the winter of 1916–17, took a course in orchestration with Sibelius. He wrote 6 symphs. (1935, 1939, 1948, 1954, 1964, 1966); 3 sinfoniettas; *Sinfonia da camera* for Strings (1951); Piano Concerto; Piano Quintet; 2 string quartets; 2 violin sonatas; Piano Trio; publ. a monograph on Sibelius (London, 1937; in Italian, Florence, 1943; in Finnish, Helsinki, 1945; in Swedish, Stockholm, 1945).

Torner, Eduardo Martínez, Spanish folklore specialist; b. Oviedo, April 8, 1888; d. London, Feb. 17, 1955. He was a pupil of Vincent d'Indy at the Schola Cantorum in Paris; returned to Spain in 1914 and settled in Madrid. He publ. the folk song collections *Cancionero musical de la lírica popular asturiana* (Madrid, 1920), *40 canciones españolas* (1924), and *Cancionero musical* (1928); also the essay *Temas folklóricos; Música y poesía* (1935); edited and arranged for piano selected pieces from tablature books of the 16th century, and publ. them under the title *Colección de vihuelistas españoles del siglo XVI* (Madrid, 1923).

BIBLIOGRAPHY: A. Muñiz Toca, *Vida y obra de E.M. Torner* (Oviedo, 1961).

Torrance, Rev. George William, Irish clergyman and composer; b. Rathmines, near Dublin, 1835; d. Kilkenny, Aug. 20, 1907. He was a chorister at Christ Church Cathedral, Dublin; was organist at St. Andrew's and St. Anne's; studied music at Leipzig in 1856–57; was ordained as a priest in 1865; in 1869 he emigrated to Melbourne, Australia, where he remained till 1897. He was appointed chaplain to the bishop of Ossory in 1897; in 1900 was made Prebendary of Killamery, canon of St. Canice's Cathedral, and librarian of St. Canice's Library, Kilkenny. Torrance's madrigal *Dry be that tear* won the medal of the Madrigal Society in 1903.

Torrefranca, Fausto, eminent Italian musicologist; b. Monteleone Calabro, Feb. 1, 1883; d. Rome, Nov. 26, 1955. Trained as an engineer, he took up music under E. Lena in Turin (harmony and counterpoint) and also studied by himself. It was through his initiative that the first chair of musicology was established in Italy; in 1913, he became a lecturer at the Univ. of Rome; in 1914–24, was a prof. of music history at the Cons. di S. Pietro in Naples, and from 1915, also librarian there; from 1924 to 1938 was librarian of the Milan Cons. From 1907 he was editor for several years of the *Rivista Musicale Italiana.* In 1941 he was appointed a prof. of music history at the Univ. of Florence.
WRITINGS: *La vita musicale dello spirito* (Turin, 1910); *L'intuizione musicale quale sintesi a priori estetica* (1911); *Giacomo Puccini e l'opera internazionale* (1912); *Le sinfonie dell'Imbrattacarte, G.B. Sanmartini* (1915); *Le origine italiane del romanticismo musicale* (1930); *Il segreto del quattrocento* (1939).

Torri, Pietro, Italian composer; b. Peschiera, c.1650; d. Munich, July 6, 1737. He served as court organist and later Kapellmeister at the court in Bayreuth (until 1684); in 1689 he became an organist at Munich; in 1696 he was conductor for the carnival season at Hannover; in 1701 he was appointed chamber music director at Munich, following the Elector to Brussels upon the latter's exile in 1704; he fled Brussels with the Elector (1706). In Brussels he produced the oratorio *Les Vanités du monde* (1706); from 1715 he was again in Munich, where he was made Hofkapell-Direktor; later he was named Hofkapellmeister (1732). He composed 26 operas; produced at the Munich court the operas *Lucio Vero* (Oct. 12, 1720) and *Griselda* (Oct. 12, 1723); also some chamber duets. Selections from the operas were publ. in Denkmäler der Tonkunst in Bayern, 31 (19/20).
BIBLIOGRAPHY: H. Junker, "Zwei Griselda Opern," in the *Sandberger-Festschrift* (1928); K. Kremer, *Pietro Torri und seine Kammermusikwerke* (Diss., Univ. of Munich, 1956).

Torrington, Frederick Herbert, English organist; b. Dudley, Worcestershire, Oct. 20, 1837; d. Toronto, Canada, Nov. 19, 1917. He went to Canada in 1856; served as a church organist in Montreal (1857–69); then was music director at King's Chapel, Boston; in 1873 was appointed organist at the Metropolitan Church, Toronto, and conductor of the Toronto Phil. Society (until 1894). He composed organ music and hymn tunes.

Tort, César, Mexican composer; b. Puebla, Sept. 4, 1929. He studied piano with Ramón Serratos in 1946; composition with Conrado del Campo at the Cons. in Madrid (1950–53). Returning to Mexico, he dedicated himself to a reform of children's musical edu-

cation. He wrote mostly for piano: *Impresiones* (1954), *El orador* (1955), *El piano mágico* (1972), etc.; also a symph. poem, *Estirpes* (1958), and a cantata, *La espada* (1966).

Tortelier, Paul, noted French cellist; b. Paris, March 21, 1914. He studied cello with Gérard Hekking at the Paris Cons., and won first prize at the age of 16; he made his debut with the Lamoureux Orch. at the age of 17; from 1935–37 he was first cellist of the orch. in Monte Carlo; from 1937–39 was a member of the Boston Symph. Orch. He was subsequently first cellist of the Paris Cons. Orch. (1946–47). In 1947 he was a soloist at the Festival of Richard Strauss in London. He lived in Israel in 1955–56; then returned to France and joined the faculty of the Paris Cons. He also made occasional appearances as a conductor. He composed several cello concertos, *Israel Symphony,* and a Cello Sonata; also publ. the vol. *How I Play, How I Teach* (London, 1975).

Tosar Errecart, Héctor, Uruguayan composer; b. Montevideo, July 18, 1923. He studied piano and composition in his native city; taught at the Montevideo Cons. (1951–54). In 1974 he was made chairman of the composition dept. of the Puerto Rico Cons. His music is neo-Classical in facture, with a considerable influx of Latin American melorhythms.
WORKS: 3 symphs. (1945, 1950, 1973); Concertino for Piano and Orch. (1941); *Sinfonia concertante* for Piano and Orch. (1957); Violin Sonata (1947); Clarinet Sonata (1957); *Oda a amigas* for Speaker and Orch. (1951); *Naves Errantes* for Baritone and 11 Instruments (1964); madrigals; sacred choruses; songs; many piano pieces; *Stray Birds,* triptych for Baritone and 11 Instruments, to text by Rabindranath Tagore (Washington, D.C., May 11, 1965).

Tosatti, Vieri, Italian composer; b. Rome, Nov. 2, 1920. He studied piano and composition with Pizzetti in Rome. In his compositions he often exploits sensational or morbid subjects, setting them to pungent music, with a liberal application of special effects.
WORKS: *Il concerto della demenza* for Narrator, 2 Pianos, and Chamber Orch. (1946); music drama, *Dionisio* (1947); "paradoxical drama," *Il sistema della dolcezza* (1949); "boxing opera," *La partita a pugni* (*Fist Fight;* Venice Festival of Contemporary Music, Sept. 8, 1953); operas: *Il giudizio universale* (Milan, 1955); *L'isola del tesoro* (Bologna, 1958); *La fiera della Meraviglie* (Rome, 1963); Piano Concerto (1945); Viola Concerto (1966); *Concerto iperciclico* for Clarinet and Orch. (1970); Concerto for Wind Quintet and Piano (1945); *Introduzione fiabesca* for Piano Trio (1943); *Piccola sonata* for Violin and Piano (1945); *Sinfonia corale* for Chorus and Orch. (1944); *Requiem* (1963); *2 coretti* for 3 Women's Voices (1970); songs; a variety of whimsical piano pieces.

Toscanini, Arturo, one of the greatest conductors

of modern times; b. Parma, Italy, March 25, 1867; d. New York, Jan. 16, 1957. He entered the Parma Cons. at the age of 9, studying the cello with Carini and composition with Dacci; graduated in 1885 as winner of the first prize for cello; received the Barbacini Prize as the outstanding graduate of his class. In 1886 he was engaged as cellist for the Italian opera in Rio de Janeiro; on the 3rd night of the spring season (June 20, 1886) he was unexpectedly called upon to substitute for the regular conductor, when the latter left the podium at the end of the introduction after the public hissed him; the opera was *Aida,* and Toscanini led it without difficulty; he was rewarded by an ovation and was engaged to lead the rest of the season. Returning to Italy, he was engaged to conduct the opera at the Teatro Carignano in Turin, making his debut there on Nov. 4, 1886, and later conducted the Municipal Orch. there. Although still very young, he quickly established a fine reputation. For 10 seasons, between 1887 and 1898, he conducted opera and symph. orchs. in major Italian cities. On May 21, 1892, he led the world premiere of *Pagliacci* in Milan, and on Feb. 1, 1896, the premiere of Puccini's *La Bohème* in Turin. He also conducted the first performance by an Italian opera company, sung in Italian, of *Götterdämmerung* (Turin, Dec. 22, 1895) and *Siegfried* (Milan, 1899); he made his debut as a symph. conductor on March 20, 1896, with the orch. of the Teatro Regio in Turin. In 1898 the impresario Gatti-Casazza engaged him as chief conductor for La Scala, Milan, where he remained until 1903, and again from 1906 to 1908. In the interim, he conducted opera in Buenos Aires (1903–4 and 1906). When Gatti-Casazza became general manager of the Metropolitan Opera Co. (1908), he invited Toscanini to be principal conductor; Toscanini's debut in N.Y. was in *Aida* (Nov. 16, 1908). While at the Metropolitan, Toscanini conducted Verdi's *Requiem* (Feb. 21, 1909), as well as 2 world premieres, Puccini's *The Girl of the Golden West* (Dec. 10, 1910) and Giordano's *Madame Sans-Gêne* (Jan. 25, 1915); he also brought out for the first time in America Gluck's *Armide* (Nov. 14, 1910), Wolf-Ferrari's *Le Donne curiose* (Jan. 3, 1912), and Mussorgsky's *Boris Godunov* (March 19, 1913). On April 13, 1913, he gave his first concert in N.Y. as a symph. conductor, leading Beethoven's 9th Symph. In 1915 he returned to Italy; during the season of 1920–21 he brought the La Scala Orch. on a tour of the U.S. and Canada. From 1921 to 1929 he was artistic director of La Scala; there he conducted the posthumous premiere of Boito's opera *Nerone,* which he himself completed for performance (May 1, 1924). In 1926–27 he was guest conductor of the N.Y. Phil. Orch., returning in subsequent seasons and in 1929–30 as associate conductor with Mengelberg. After the fusion of the N.Y. Phil. and the N.Y. Symph. in 1928, Toscanini was engaged as permanent conductor of the newly organized ensemble; in the spring of 1930 he took the orch. on a tour of Europe; he resigned this position in 1936; conducted in Bayreuth in 1930 and 1931, the first non-German to conduct opera there. Deeply touched by the plight of the Jews in Germany, he acceded to the request of the violinist Hubermann,

founder of the Palestine Symph. Orch., to conduct the inaugural concert of that orch. at Tel Aviv (Dec. 26, 1936). During this period he also filled summer engagements at the Salzburg Festivals (1934, 1935, 1936, 1937), and conducted in London (1937, 1938, 1939). Returning to the U.S., he became music director of the NBC Symph. Orch., a radio orch. that had been organized especially for him, giving his opening concert on Dec. 25, 1937; in 1940 he took it on a tour of South America, and on another major tour in 1950. He continued to lead the NBC Symph. until the end of his active career; he conducted his last concert from Carnegie Hall, N.Y., on April 4, 1954 (10 days after his 87th birthday), and then sent a doleful letter of resignation to NBC, explaining the impossibility of further appearances. He died in his sleep, a few weeks before his 90th birthday.

Toscanini was a unique figure among conductors; undemonstrative in his handling of the orch., he possessed an amazing energy and power of command. He demanded absolute perfection, and he erupted in violence when he could not obtain from the orch. what he wanted (a lawsuit was brought against him in Milan when he accidentally injured the concertmaster with a broken violin bow). Despite the vituperation he at times poured on his musicians, he was affectionately known to them as "The Maestro" who could do no wrong. His ability to communicate his desires to singers and players was extraordinary, and even the most celebrated opera stars or instrumental soloists never dared to question his authority. Owing to extreme nearsightedness, Toscanini committed all scores to memory; his repertoire embraced virtually the entire field of Classical and Romantic music; his performances of Italian operas, of Wagner's music dramas, of Beethoven's symphs., and of modern Italian works were especially inspiring. Among the moderns, he conducted works by Richard Strauss, Debussy, Ravel, Prokofiev, and Stravinsky, and among Americans, Samuel Barber, whose *Adagio for Strings* he made famous; he also had his favorite Italian composers (Catalani, Martucci), whose music he fondly fostered. In his social philosophy, he was intransigently democratic; he refused to conduct in Germany under the Nazi regime. He militantly opposed Fascism in Italy, but never abandoned his Italian citizenship, despite his long years of residence in America.

BIBLIOGRAPHY: G.M. Ciampelli, *Arturo Toscanini* (Milan, 1923); E. Cozzani, *Arturo Toscanini* (Milan, 1927); T. Nicotra, *Arturo Toscanini* (trans. from the Italian, N.Y., 1929); D. Bonardi, *Toscanini* (Milan, 1929); Paul Stefan, *Arturo Toscanini* (Vienna, 1936; in Eng., N.Y., 1936); L. Gilman, *Toscanini and Great Music* (N.Y., 1938); S.W. Hoeller, *Arturo Toscanini* (pictorial biography; N.Y., 1943); A. Della Corte, *Toscanini* (Vicenza, 1946); G.M. Ciampelli, *Toscanini* (Milan, 1946); D. Nives, *Arturo Toscanini* (Milan, 1946); A. Segre, "Toscanini: The First Forty Years," and H. Taubman, "Toscanini in America," *Musical Quarterly* (April 1947); F. Sacchi, *Toscanini* (Milan, 1951; publ. in Eng. under the title *The Magic Baton: Toscanini's Life for Music,* N.Y., 1957, with supplementary data); David Ewen,

The Story of Arturo Toscanini (N.Y., 1951); H. Taubman, *The Maestro: The Life of Arturo Toscanini* (N.Y., 1951); S. Chotzinoff, *Toscanini: An Intimate Portrait* (N.Y., 1956); R.C. Marsh, *Toscanini and the Art of Orchestral Performance* (Philadelphia, 1956); Patrick Cairns (Spike) Hughes, *The Toscanini Legacy: A Critical Study of Arturo Toscanini's Performances of Beethoven, Verdi, and Other Composers* (London, 1959); B.H. Haggin, *Conversations with Toscanini* (N.Y., 1959; 2nd ed., enlarged, 1979); Luciana Frassati, *Il Maestro Arturo Toscanini e il suo mondo* (Turin, 1967); H. Schonberg, *The Great Conductors* (N.Y., 1967; pp. 252–64); Arturo F. Armani, ed., *Toscanini e La Scala* (Milan, 1972); G. Marek, *Toscanini* (N.Y., 1975); H. Sachs, *Toscanini* (Philadelphia, 1978); Denis Matthews, *Arturo Toscanini* (Tunbridge Wells and N.Y., 1982).

Toselli, Enrico, Italian pianist and composer; b. Florence, March 13, 1883; d. there, Jan. 15, 1926. He studied with Sgambati and Martucci; gave concerts in Italy as a pianist, and composed a number of songs; of these, *Serenata* because enormously popular; also wrote the symph. poem *Fuoco* (after d'Annunzio) and an opera, *La Principessa bizzarra* (Milan, 1913). In 1907 he married the former Crown Princess Luise of Saxony, creating an international furor; wrote an account of this affair, *Il mio matrimonio con Luisa di Sassonia* (Milan, 1918).

Tosi, Pier Francesco, Italian contralto (castrato) and singing teacher; b. Bologna, 1654; d. Faenza, April 1732. He studied with his father, Giuseppe Felice Tosi; sang successfully in Italy; in 1692 settled in London, where he gave regular concerts, and was highly esteemed as a vocal teacher. He served as chapel master at the Austrian court in Vienna from 1705 to 1711; was again in London (about 1723); c.1727 went to Bologna and was ordained a priest. He owes his fame chiefly to the work *Opinioni de' cantori antichi e moderni o sieno osservazioni sopra il canto figurato* (Bologna, 1723; in Eng., 1742, as *Observations on the Florid Song;* in German as *Anleitung zur Singkunst,* 1757; in French as *L'Art du chant,* 1774; the Eng. ed. was republ. in London in 1967).

Tosti, Sir Francesco Paolo, Italian singing master and vocal composer; b. Ortona, Abruzzi, April 9, 1846; d. Rome, Dec. 2, 1916. He was a pupil, from 1858, of the Collegio di S. Pietro a Majella, Naples, and was appointed sub-teacher (maestrino) by Mercadante. He visited London in 1875; had great success in concerts and settled there as a teacher, becoming singing master to the Royal Family in 1880, and prof. of singing at the Royal Academy of Music in 1894; was knighted in 1908. In 1913 he returned to Italy, taking up his residence in Rome. Besides many original songs, in both English and Italian, he publ. a collection of *Canti popolari abruzzesi.* His songs were highly popular; some of the best known are *Goodbye Forever and Forever, Mattinata,* and *Vorrei morire.*
BIBLIOGRAPHY: E.A. Mario, *Francesco Paolo Tosti* (Siena, 1947); A. Piovano, *Ommagio a F.P. Tosti* (Ortona, 1972).

Totenberg, Roman, Polish violinist; b. Lodz, Jan. 1, 1911. He studied violin with Michalowicz in Warsaw, Carl Flesch in Berlin, and Georges Enesco in Paris. In 1932 he won the Mendelssohn Prize in Berlin. In 1935–36 he toured Europe with Karol Szymanowski, giving violin-piano recitals; then emigrated to the U.S.; became an American citizen in 1943. From 1950 to 1960 he was in charge of the violin dept. at the Aspen (Colo.) Inst.; in 1961–78 was a prof. of music at Boston Univ.; he settled in Newton, Mass.; in 1978 became director of the Longy School of Music in Cambridge, Mass.

Tottmann, Albert (Karl), German violinist and writer on music; b. Zittau, July 31, 1837; d. Leipzig, Feb. 26, 1917. He studied in Dresden and Leipzig; was a violinist in the Gewandhaus Orch.
WRITINGS: *Kritisches Repertorium der gesammten Violin- und Bratschen-Litteratur* (1873; 3rd ed., 1900, as *Führer durch die Violin-Literatur;* a compendious and valuable work); *Abriss der Musikgeschichte* (1883); *Der Schulgesang und seine Bedeutung für die Verstandes und Herzensbildung der Jungend* (1887; 2nd ed., 1904); *Das Büchlein von der Geige* (1890; 2nd, augmented ed., 1904); *Mozarts Zauberflöte* (1908). He composed a melodrama, *Dornröschen;* sacred and secular choruses; songs.

Tough, Dave, American jazz drummer; b. Oak Park, Ill., April 26, 1908; d. Newark, N.J., Dec. 6, 1948. He began his career in Chicago; then played with Bud Freeman, Eddie Condon, and Red Nichols. In 1936 he joined Tommy Dorsey's orch.; subsequently worked with Benny Goodman, Jack Teagarden, Artie Shaw, and Charlie Spivak. He gained renown as a jazz drummer during his stint with Woody Herman's band in 1944–45; however, his career was cut short by a chronic illness.

Toulmouche, Frédéric (Michel), French composer; b. Nantes, Aug. 3, 1850; d. Paris, Feb. 20, 1909. He studied with Victor Massé in Paris; in 1894 became director of the Menus-Plaisirs theater. He composed several opéras-comique: *Le Moûtier de St.-Guignolet* (Brussels, 1885); *La Veillée des noces* (Paris, 1888; in London, 1892, as *The Wedding Eve*); *L'Ame de la patrie* (St. Brieuc, 1892); *La Perle du Cantal* (Paris, 1895); *La St.-Valentin* (Paris, 1895); about a dozen operettas and some ballets.

Tourangeau, Huguette, Canadian mezzo-soprano; b. Montreal, Aug. 12, 1938. She studied voice at the Montreal Cons. and made her debut as Cherubino in *The Marriage of Figaro* in Montreal in 1964; in 1968 she sang with the N.Y. City Opera, and in 1969 was engaged as a guest artist at the Hamburg State Opera. In 1973 she appeared in a minor role at the Metropolitan Opera in N.Y.

Tourel, Jennie (real name, **Jennie Davidson**), American mezzo-soprano of Russian-Jewish parentage; b. St. Petersburg, June 22, 1900; d. New York, Nov. 23, 1973. She played flute; then studied piano. After the Revolution, her family left Russia and settled temporarily near Danzig; they later moved to Paris, where Jennie Tourel continued to study piano and contemplated a concert career; she then began to take voice lessons with Anna El-Tour, and decided to devote herself to professional singing; she changed her last name to Tourel by transposing the syllables of her teacher's name. She made her opera debut at the Opéra Russe in Paris in 1931; at the Metropolitan Opera in N.Y. on May 15, 1937, as Mignon. In 1940, just before the occupation of Paris by Nazi troops, she went to Lisbon, Portugal, and eventually emigrated to the U.S.; appeared on the Metropolitan Opera roster in 1943–45 and 1946–47; became a naturalized citizen in 1946. She continued to appear in concert and occasionally in opera; also taught singing at Juilliard in N.Y.

Tourjée, Eben, American music educator; b. Warwick, R.I., June 1, 1834; d. Boston, April 12, 1891. While working in a cotton factory in Harrisville, R.I., he played the organ in church; then went to Germany and studied with Carl August Haupt in Berlin. Returning to America, he settled in Boston, and in 1867 founded there (with R. Goldbeck) the New England Cons. of Music, which he directed till his death. He assisted Patrick S. Gilmore in organizing the 2 great "peace jubilees" in Boston (1869, 1872); was the first president of the Music Teachers National Assoc. (1876), and dean of the College of Music of Boston Univ.
BIBLIOGRAPHY: *Dictionary of American Biography,* 18.

Tournemire, Charles, French organist and composer; b. Bordeaux, Jan. 22, 1870; d. Arcachon, Nov. 3, 1939. He was a pupil of César Franck at the Paris Cons., winning the first prize for organ in 1890; also studied composition with Vincent d'Indy at the Schola Cantorum. In 1898 he succeeded Pierné as organist at Ste. Clotilde, remaining until 1939. As an organ virtuoso, he toured throughout Europe. He was prof. of ensemble playing at the Paris Cons. (1919–38).
WORKS: Operas: *Nitletis* (1905–7); *Les Dieux sont morts* (1910–12; first stage perf., Paris Opéra, March 19, 1924); *Il Poverello di Assisi* (1937–38); a dramatic cantata, *Le Sang de la Sirène* (1902–3; Paris, Nov. 17, 1904; won the Prize of the City of Paris); *La Queste du Saint-Graal* for Soli, Chorus, and Orch. (1926–27; Lyons, Jan. 1930); an oratorio, *La Douloureuse Passion du Christ* (1936–37); 8 symphs.: No. 1 (1900); No. 2 (1908–9; Paris, April 4, 1909); No. 3, *Moscou* (1912; Amsterdam, Oct. 19, 1913); No. 4 (1912; Paris, 1914); No. 5, *Dans les Alpes* (1914; The Hague, March 10, 1920); No. 6 for Soloist, Chorus, Organ, and Orch. (1915–18); No. 7 (1915–19); No. 8, *Le Triomphe de la mort* (1921–24); symph. poems; *Rhapsodie* for Piano and Orch., or Solo Piano (1907); *Poème* for Organ and Orch. (1909–10);

Violin Sonata (1892–93); Cello Sonata (1895); Piano Quartet (1899); Piano Trio (1901); *Musique orante,* string quartet (1899); *Sonate-poème* for Violin and Piano (1935); Piano Sonata (1899); many piano pieces; several Psalms for a cappella Choruses; for Organ: *L'Orgue mystique (51 offices de l'année liturgique,* 253 pieces, 1927–32); *Pièces symphoniques, Fantaisie symphonique* (1933), *Symphonie-Choral* (1935), *Symphonie sacrée* (1936), etc. Also, a monograph, *César Franck* (Paris, 1931).
BIBLIOGRAPHY: F. Peeters, "L'Œuvre d'orgue de Charles Tournemire," *Musica Sacra* (Bruges, 1940). A complete list of his works, with dates, is found in *Le Courrier Musical de France,* no. 66 (1979).

Tours, Berthold, Belgian violinist, composer, and music editor; b. Rotterdam, Dec. 17, 1838; d. London, March 11, 1897. He received his musical training from his father, Barthélemy Tours (1797–1864); went to London in 1861; in 1878 became musical adviser to Novello & Co., and editor of their publications. He publ. a *Primer of the Violin* and wrote many anthems for Anglican services.

Tours, Frank E., English-American composer, son of **Berthold Tours;** b. London, Sept. 1, 1877; d. Santa Monica, Calif., Feb. 2, 1963. He studied with Stanford, Parratt, and Bridge at the Royal College of Music; came to N.Y. in 1904 and conducted light opera productions. Later he entered the motion picture field. He wrote many successful songs, among them *Mother o' Mine, Beyond the Sunset, Red Rose,* and *In Flanders Fields.*

Tourte, François, French violin-bow maker; b. Paris, 1747; d. there, April 26, 1835. He was the creator of the modern bow: the shape of the wood and inward curve of the stick, the selection and preparation of the wood (Pernambuco), the length of the bow and all its modern appurtenances, are the product of his skill.

Tovey, Sir Donald Francis, eminent English musical scholar; b. Eton, July 17, 1875; d. Edinburgh, July 10, 1940. He studied privately with Sophie Weisse (piano), Sir W. Parratt (counterpoint), and James Higgs (composition) until 1894, when he won the Nettleship scholarship at Balliol College, Oxford; graduated with Classical Honors (B.A., 1898). In 1900–1901 he gave a series of chamber music concerts in London, at which he performed several of his own works; in 1901–2 he gave similar concerts in Berlin and Vienna; played his Piano Concerto in 1903 under Henry Wood and in 1906 under Hans Richter; from 1906 to 1912 he gave in London regular series of chamber music concerts, known as The Chelsea Concerts. In 1914 he succeeded Niecks as Reid Prof. of music at Edinburgh Univ. (named after John Reid); there he established the Reid Symph. Concerts, for which he organized in 1917 the Reid Symph. Orch. of 50 musicians. He made his American debut as a pianist in 1925, and in 1927–28 made a tour of the U.S. He was knighted in 1935.

Though highly esteemed as a composer, he was most widely known as a writer and lecturer on music, his analytical essays being models of their kind. Besides much chamber music and several piano pieces (a sonata, *Balliol Dances* for 4-hands, etc.), he composed an opera, *The Bride of Dionysus* (Edinburgh, April 25, 1932); a Symph. (1913); Cello Concerto (premiere by Pablo Casals, composer conducting, Edinburgh, Nov. 22, 1934); etc. He publ. a collection of 16th-century church music, *Laudate pueri* (Part I of *Northlands Singing Book*), and edited Bach's *Kunst der Fuge.* He wrote many of the music articles for the *Encyclopædia Britannica* (beginning with the 11th ed.).

WRITINGS: *A Companion to Bach's Art of the Fugue* (1931); *A Companion to Beethoven's Pianoforte Sonatas* (1931); *Musical Form and Matter* (1934); *Normality and Freedom in Music* (1936); *Essays in Musical Analysis* (6 vols., 1935–39: I and II, orch. works; III, concertos; IV, polyphony and illustrative music; V, vocal music; VI, supplement, index, and glossary). Posthumous publications: *Walter Parratt: The Master of Music* (with G. Parratt; London, 1941); *A Musician Talks* (London, 1941); *Musical Articles from the Encyclopædia Britannica* (London, 1944); *Beethoven* (London, 1944); *Essays in Musical Analysis: Chamber Music* (London, 1944); *Essays and Lectures on Music* (London, 1949; U.S. ed. as *The Main Stream of Music*).

BIBLIOGRAPHY: M. Grierson, *Donald Francis Tovey* (London, 1952).

Tower, Joan, American composer; b. New Rochelle, N.Y., Sept. 6, 1938. She played piano as a child; studied composition with 12 teachers, among whom were Henry Brant at Bennington College (B.A.); Otto Luening, Vladimir Ussachevsky, and Wen-Chung Chou at Columbia Univ. (M.A.); and Wallingford Riegger and Darius Milhaud afield. Her music reflects these dodecuple didacticisms, but adds a lot more. A blithe spirit, Joan Tower engages in quaquaversal activities, including lecturing in schools and other public places. In 1979 she organized a chamber group in N.Y. called the Da Capo Players, for which she acts as pianist. In 1977 she was awarded a Guggenheim fellowship.

WORKS: Percussion Quartet (1963); *Brimset* for Flute and Percussion (1965); *Prelude* for 5 Players (1971); *Movements* for Flute and Piano (1974); *Breakfast Rhythms* for Clarinet and 5 Instruments (N.Y., Feb. 23, 1974); *Hexachords* for Flute Solo (1976); *Amazon I* for Quintet (1978); also in a version for Chamber Orch., as *Amazon II* (1980); *Platinum Spirals* for Violin (1980); *Red Garnet Waltz* for Piano (1980); *Petroushskates* for Piano, with a dual allegiance to Stravinsky's ballet and Olympic skaters (N.Y., March 23, 1980, composer soloist); *Black Topaz* for Piano and 6 Instruments (1981); *Wings* for Clarinet (1981); *Sequoia* for Orch. including 54 Percussion Players (1981; N.Y. Phil., Zubin Mehta conducting, Sept. 23, 1982; also given at a gala perf. at the United Nations, Oct. 24, 1982).

Townsend, Douglas, American composer and musicologist; b. New York, Nov. 8, 1921. He studied composition with Tibor Serly, Stefan Wolpe, Felix Greissle, and Otto Luening; became active in N.Y. as a music editor; arranged for performance and publication works by Pergolesi, Süssmayr, Danzi, Tommaso Giordani, Rosetti, etc. He writes for, and is an official of, the Musical Heritage Society (recordings).

WORKS: Septet for Brass (1947); *Sinfonietta* (1949); *Fantasy* for Chamber Orch. (1951); *The Infinite,* ballet (N.Y., Feb. 13, 1952); *Canzona* for Flute, Viola, and Bassoon (1954); *Lima Beans,* chamber opera (N.Y., Jan. 7, 1956); *Ballet Suite* for 3 Clarinets (1956); Duo for Violas (1957); *Tower Music* for Brass Quintet (1957); *4 Fantasies on American Songs* for Orch. (1957); Symph. for Strings (N.Y., Nov. 29, 1958); 3 chamber concertos: No. 1 for Violin and Strings; No. 2 for Trombone and Strings; No. 3 for Piano, Horn, and Flute, with Strings.

Townshend, Pete, seeded British rock artist; b. Chiswick, May 19, 1945. He began playing banjo in a Dixieland jazz group, in which another British musician, John Entwhistle (b. Chiswick, Oct. 9, 1946), blew the trumpet. They teamed with the guitarist and vocalist Roger Daltrey (b. Hammersmith, March 1, 1944) and organized a group to which they gave the mysterious-sounding pronominal moniker The Who. The drummer Keith Moon (b. Wembley, Aug. 23, 1947; found dead in his London flat of a sedative overdose, Sept. 7, 1978) joined the group in 1964. Anxious to project a mod image in an alien world, they sported odd clothes, cultivated bizarre behavior, and indulged in maniacal conduct on the stage, which included physical destruction of their instruments in front of the public in the manner of punk rock. Their habit of flaunting loud obscenities and invitations to mayhem aroused the destructive instincts of their audiences. A murderous climax of their career was reached in Cincinnati at their concert of Dec. 3, 1979, when 11 young people were trampled to death in a mad rush for seats. Professing deep sorrow at the loss of life, The Who and their managers did not overlook the commercial advantages of wide publicity attending the incident. In the meantime, Townshend turned to fashionable oriental philosophy, worshiping at the feet of a transient guru, and producing a devotional album, *Who Came First,* with the rock hymns *Pure and Easy* and *Nothing Is Everything.* The Who took part in such media extravaganzas as the outrageous movies *Tommy* and *Quadrophenia;* Roger Daltrey also acted in *Lisztomania,* a film that depicted Liszt as a human attachment to an immense penis used as a seesaw by a bevy of naked females; and Keith Moon tripped around in Frank Zappa's video-movie *200 Motels.* Other influential works by The Who included the song *My Generation,* the psychedelic *I Can See for Miles,* and their album *Who's Next.*

Toyama, Yuzo, Japanese composer; b. Tokyo, May 10, 1931. He graduated from the Tokyo Music Academy in 1952; studied in Vienna (1958–60); in 1953 organized (with Mamiya and Hayashi) the group Yagi no Kai with the purpose of promoting Japanese music.

WORKS: Chamber opera, *Such a Long Absence* (Osaka, April 3, 1972); musical, *Gion Festival,* for Soloists, Chorus, and Orch. (1966); ballet, *Yugen* (1965); *Little Symphony* (1953); *Rhapsody* for Orch. (1960); *Divertimento* for Orch. (1961; Prague, Jan. 2, 1962); 2 piano concertos (1962, 1963); 2 violin concertos (1963, 1966); *Fantasy* for Clarinet and String Orch. (1963); *Rhapsody on an Okinawan Melody* for Orch. (1961); *Toki (War Cry) No. 1* and *Toki No. 2* for Orch. (1965, 1966); symph., *Homeward* (1966); Cello Concerto (1967); *Kaleidoscope* for Orch. (1968); *Ofukuro* for Chorus and Strings (1968); *Response,* suite for Chorus and String Orch. (1968–69); symph., *Song of Flame,* for Chorus and Orch. (1970); cantata, *Kyoto,* for Soprano, Chorus, Harp, and Orch. (1970); Trio for Flute, Cello, and Piano (1958); *Chamber Concerto* for Wind Quintet, Piano, Double Bass, Vibraphone, and Percussion (1958); Violin Sonata (1964); *Divertimento* for String Ensemble (1965); *Guzai* for String Quartet (1965); *Meditation* for Violin and Piano (1970); choruses.

Toye, (John) Francis, English music critic; b. Winchester, Jan. 27, 1883; d. Florence, Oct. 31, 1964. He was a pupil of S.P. Waddington and E.J. Dent; became a critic for various papers in London; in 1923 he lectured on modern music in the U.S.; in 1939–46 lived in Rio de Janeiro; from 1946, in Florence. He wrote *The Well-Tempered Musician* (1925); *Giuseppe Verdi: His Life and Works* (1931; new ed., London, 1962); *Rossini: A Study in Tragicomedy* (1934; 2nd ed., 1954); *For What We Have Received: An Autobiography* (Melbourne, 1950); *Italian Opera* (London, 1952); *Truly Thankful? A Sequel to an Autobiography* (London, 1957).

Toye, Geoffrey, English conductor and composer; brother of **Francis Toye;** b. Winchester, Feb. 17, 1889; d. London, June 11, 1942. He studied at the Royal College of Music in London; became a conductor at various theaters there; was manager of opera productions at Sadler's Wells. He wrote an opera, *The Red Pen* (broadcast from London, Feb. 7, 1927); a ballet; and some other works.

Tozzi, Giorgio (real first name, **George**), gifted American bass of Italian descent; b. Chicago, Jan. 8, 1923. His father was a day laborer. He studied biology at De Paul Univ.; also took vocal lessons in Chicago with Rosa Raisa, Giacomo Rimini, and John Daggett Howell. He made his professional debut in N.Y. in the American premiere of Britten's *The Rape of Lucretia* as the rapist Tarquinius (Dec. 29, 1948). In 1949 he went to Europe, and sang in a musical comedy, *Tough at the Top,* in London. With the earnings obtained through this employment, he financed a trip to Italy, where he took lessons with Giulio Lorandi in Milan. He sang at the Teatro Nuovo in Milan, and in Dec. 1953 appeared at La Scala. He then returned to the U.S.; on March 9, 1955, he made his Metropolitan debut in N.Y. as Alvise in *La Gioconda;* continued to sing at the Met-

ropolitan in a variety of parts, among them Don Giovanni in Mozart's opera; Figaro in *Le nozze di Figaro,* Don Basilio in *Il barbiere di Siviglia,* Méphistophélès in Gounod's *Faust,* Hans Sachs in *Die Meistersinger,* King Mark in *Tristan und Isolde,* and the title role in *Boris Godunov.* He also made regular appearances with the San Francisco Opera, where he sang for the first time on Sept. 15, 1955. He was a guest artist at the Salzburg Festival, and sang at Munich, Hamburg, and other European music centers. A true modern man, he did not spurn the world of musical commerce, and even sang a commercial for the Fiat automobile company, putting on an ancestral Italian accent, albeit of dubious authenticity in his generation.

BIBLIOGRAPHY: David Ewen, *Musicians since 1900* (N.Y., 1978).

Trabaci, Giovanni Maria, Italian composer; b. Montepeloso, c.1575; d. Naples, Dec. 31, 1647. He studied with Giovanni Macque; became organist at the Viceregal Chapel in Naples in 1601; after Macque's death (1614) he succeeded him as choir director there. During the rebellion of the Neapolitan populace against the fruit tax of 1647, Trabaci fled to the monastery of the Trinità degli Spagnuoli, where he died. The bulk of his music consists of Psalms, masses, motets, and madrigals. Two keyboard publications are extant: *Ricercare, canzone francese, capricci, canti fermi, gagliarde, partite diverse, etc., Libro primo* (Naples, 1603) and *Il secondo libro di ricercate ed altri varii capricci* (Naples, 1615). Some of his vocal works were publ. by Pannain in *Istituzioni e monumenti dell'arte musicale italiana* (vol. 5); these include 12 motets *a* 5, 4 *a* 6, and 4 *a* 8; also 2 masses for Double Chorus. Keyboard works are reprinted in L. Torchi, *L'arte musicale in Italia* (vol. 3), in Tagliapietra, *Antologia di musica antica e moderna* (vol. 5), and in Davison and Apel, *Historical Anthology of Music.* Trabaci's canzonas include examples of rhythmic variants of a single theme ("variation canzonas"), anticipating Frescobaldi in this respect.

BIBLIOGRAPHY: W. Apel, "Neapolitan Links between Cabezón and Frescobaldi," *Musical Quarterly* (Oct. 1938); R. Jackson, *The Keyboard Music of Giovanni Maria Trabaci* (Diss., Univ. of Calif., Berkeley, 1964).

Traetta, Filippo, Italian musician; son of **Tommaso Traetta;** b. Venice, Jan. 8, 1777; d. Philadelphia, Jan. 9, 1854. He was a pupil of Fenaroli and Perillo at Venice, later of Piccinni at Naples. Becoming a soldier in the patriot ranks, he was captured and cast into prison; he escaped 6 months afterward, and sailed to Boston, arriving there in 1799. There he wrote his *Vocal Exercises* and *Washington's Dead March.* Proceeding to N.Y., he wrote the cantatas *The Christian's Joy* and *Prophecy;* also an opera, *The Venetian Masker.* He managed a traveling theatrical troupe; lived in Virginia for some years, and settled in Philadelphia, c.1828, founding the American Cons. with his pupil U.K. Hill. He produced 2 oratorios, *Jerusalem in Affliction* (1828) and

Daughter of Zion (1829); later 2 cantatas, *The Nativity* and *The Day of Rest;* also instrumental and vocal quartets, trios, and duets; songs; etc.; publ. *Rudiments of the Art of Singing* (2 vols.; 1841–43) and *An Introduction to the Art and Science of Music* (1829) for his Cons. He was active as a singing teacher until his death.

BIBLIOGRAPHY: F.L. Ritter, *Music in America* (1883); *Dictionary of American Biography*, 18 (1936).

Traetta, Tommaso (Michele Francesco Saverio), Italian composer; b. Bitonto, Naples, March 30, 1727; d. Venice, April 6, 1779. He entered the Cons. di Loreto in Naples at the age of 11, and was there a pupil of Durante. His first opera, *Il Farnace,* was produced at the Teatro San Carlo with fine success, on Nov. 4, 1751; there followed several more operas in Naples, and later in other Italian cities: *Buovo d'Antona* (Venice, Dec. 27, 1758), *Ippolito ed Aricia* (Parma, May 9, 1759), etc. In 1758 he was appointed maestro di cappella to the Duke of Parma; his *Armida* was staged in Vienna (Jan. 3, 1761) with excellent success, and he was commisioned to write another opera for Vienna, *Ifigenia in Tauride,* which was produced there on Oct. 4, 1763. He settled in Venice in 1765, and was director of the Cons. dell'Ospedaletto S. Giovanni there for 3 years. In 1768 he was engaged for the court of Catherine the Great as successor to Galuppi, and arrived in St. Petersburg in the autumn of that year. He staged several of his operas there (mostly versions of works previously performed in Italy); also arranged music for various occasions (anniversary of the coronation of Catherine the Great; celebration of a victory over the Turkish fleet; etc.). He left Russia in 1775 and went to London, where he produced the operas *Germondo* (Jan. 21, 1776), *Telemacco* (March 15, 1777), and *I capricci del sesso* (1777), without much success; returned to Italy, and produced 3 more operas in Venice. In many respects, he was an admirable composer, possessing a sense of drama and a fine melodic gift. In musical realism, he adopted certain procedures that Gluck was to employ successfully later on; he was highly regarded by his contemporaries. Besides operas, he wrote an oratorio, *Salomone* (Venice, 1766), a Stabat Mater, and other church music. Excerpts from Traetta's operas, edited by H. Goldschmidt, are in Denkmäler der Tonkunst in Bayern, 25 and 29 (14.i and 17).

BIBLIOGRAPHY: V. Capruzzi, *Traetta e la musica* (Naples, 1878); C.H. Bitter, *Die Reform der Oper durch Gluck und Wagner* (Braunschweig, 1884); H. Kretzschmar, *Geschichte der Oper* (1919); A. Nuovo, *Tommaso Traetta* (Rome, 1922); A. Damerini, "Un precursore italiano di Gluck: Tommaso Traetta," *Il Pianoforte* (July 1927); idem, "Tommaso Traetta," *Bollettino Bibliografico Musicale* (July 1927); V. Raeli, "Tommaso Traetta," *Rivista Nazionale di Musica* (March 1927); A. Bonaventura, "Tommaso Traetta," *Pensiero Musicale* (April–May 1927); V. Raeli, "The Bicentenary of Tommaso Traetta," *Chesterian* (1927); A. Mooser, *Annales de la musique et des musiciens en Russie au XVIIIᵉ siècle* (Geneva, 1949–51; vol. II, pp. 87–132); F. Schlitzer, ed., *Tommaso Traetta, Leonardo Leo, Vincenzo Bellini: Notizie e documenti* (Siena, 1952); E. Saracino, *Tommaso Traetta* (Bitonto, 1954); F. Casavola, *Tommaso Traetta di Bitonto* (Bari, 1957); D. Binetti, *Tommaso Traetta nella vita e nell'arte* (1972).

Tragó, José, Spanish pianist and pedagogue; b. Madrid, Sept. 25, 1856; d. there, Jan. 3, 1934. He studied at the conservatories of Madrid and Paris, winning first prizes for piano at both; was for many years a prof. at the Madrid Cons. He was the teacher of Manuel de Falla and Joaquín Turina.

Trambitsky, Victor, Russian composer; b. Brest-Litovsk, Feb. 12, 1895; d. Leningrad, Aug. 13, 1970. He studied with Kalafati at the St. Petersburg Cons. In 1930 he moved to Sverdlovsk, as prof. at the Cons. there. He composed the operas *Gadfly* (Sverdlovsk, 1929), *Orlena* (Sverdlovsk, 1935), *Storm* (Sverdlovsk, 1942), and *The Laceworker Nastia* (Leningrad, 1963); a Symph. (1945); *Symphonic Pictures* (1955); Violin Concerto (1921); arrangements of Russian folk songs.

Trampler, Walter, eminent German-American violist and pedagogue; b. Munich, Aug. 25, 1915. He received his early musical training from his father; later enrolled at the Munich State Academy of Music; made his debut in Munich as a violinist in 1933; then played mostly the viola; from 1935–38 served as first violist in the orch. of Radio Deutschlandsender; then emigrated to America. From 1947 to 1955 he was a member of the New Music String Quartet; also made appearances with the Yale, Emerson, Budapest, Juilliard, and Guarneri quartets and with the Beaux Arts Trio. In 1962 he was appointed prof. of viola and chamber music at the Juilliard School of Music in N.Y.; in 1971 was named prof. at the Yale School of Music; in 1972 became a member of the faculty at Boston Univ.

Tranchell, Peter (Andrew), British composer; b. Cuddalore, British India, July 14, 1922. He studied at King's College, Cambridge (Mus.Bac., 1949). Most of his works are evocative of old English balladry; yet he has also experimented with modern techniques, as in his 6 piano pieces entitled *Dodecafonia*. His opera *The Mayor of Casterbridge* was produced in Cambridge, on July 30, 1951. Other works include the ballets *Falstaff* (1950), *Fate's Revenge* (1951), *Euridice* (1952), *Spring Legend* (1957), and *Images of Love* (1964); *Scherzetto* for Orch. (1960); *Festive Overture* (1966); Concerto Grosso (1972); Trio for Violin, Horn, and Piano; *Triolet* for Flute, Clarinet, and Piano; songs from Chinese poets with instrumental accompaniment; organ pieces; piano pieces; solo songs.

Trapp, Max, German composer; b. Berlin, Nov. 1, 1887; d. there, May 31, 1971. He studied piano with

Ernst von Dohnányi and composition with Paul Juon; then taught at the Berlin Hochschule für Musik and also at the Cons. of Dortmund; in 1929 became a member of the Berlin Academy of Arts, where he taught a master class in composition (1934–45); from 1951 to 1953 he was on the staff of the Municipal Cons. in Berlin. His style is neo-Classical with a strong polyphonic texture, in the tradition of Max Reger. He was also active as a landscape painter.

WORKS: 6 symphs.: No. 1, *Sinfonia giocosa* (1915); No. 2 (1918); No. 3 (1924); No. 4 (1931); No. 5 (1936); No. 6 (1946); 3 concertos for Orch. (1934, 1940, 1946); Violin Concerto (1922); Piano Concerto (1930); Cello Concerto (1935); Piano Quintet (1910); 3 piano quartets; 2 string quartets; piano pieces; songs; a cantata, *Vom ewigen Licht* (1942).

BIBLIOGRAPHY: W. Matthes, "Max Trapp," *Zeitschrift für Musik* (Oct. 1937).

Traubel, Helen, American soprano; b. St. Louis, June 20, 1899; d. Santa Monica, Calif., July 28, 1972. She made her concert debut at St. Louis in 1925, and appeared for the first time at the Metropolitan Opera in N.Y. on May 12, 1937, as Mary Rutledge in *The Man without a Country.* She made several transcontinental tours; sang in Buenos Aires in 1943; also gave numerous concerts in Europe. She was married to Louis Carpenter in 1922; they were divorced the same year; and in 1938 she married William L. Bass. In 1953 she made appearances in N.Y. nightclubs; this prompted objections from the Metropolitan Opera management, and as a result she resigned from the Metropolitan. She publ. the mystery novels *The Ptomaine Canary* and *The Metropolitan Opera Murders* (N.Y., 1951), and an autobiography, *St. Louis Woman* (N.Y., 1959).

Trautwein, Friedrich, German electrical engineer; b. Würzburg, Aug. 11, 1888; d. Düsseldorf, Dec. 21, 1956. He was trained in engineering; was an instructor in musical acoustics at the Berlin Hochschule für Musik. In 1930 he constructed an electronic musical instrument which became known, after the first syllable of his name, as the Trautonium. Hindemith wrote a concerto for it. Trautwein contributed numerous articles on electronic music to German periodicals.

Travers, John, English organist and composer; b. c.1703; d. London, June 1758. He was a chorister of St. George's Chapel, Windsor; was a pupil of M. Greene and Dr. Pepusch; from 1737, was organist of the Chapel Royal. He publ. *The Whole Book of Psalms for 1, 2, 3, 4, and 5 voices, with a thorough bass for the harpsichord* (2 vols., 1750) and *18 Canzonets for 2 and 3 voices, the words chiefly by Matthew Prior* (1745); 12 voluntaries for organ or harpsichord were publ. posthumously.

Travis, Merle, American country–music singer, guitarist, and songwriter; b. Rosewood, Ky., Nov. 29, 1917; d. Tahlequah, Okla., Oct. 20, 1983. He sang at various clubs and hotels; eventually became a regu-

lar performer on the radio station WLW in Cincinnati. After serving in the Marine Corps during World War II, he went on tour, gaining success with his popular songs *Old Mountain Dew, Dark as a Dungeon, Double Talking Baby,* and *16 Tons.* In 1974 he received the Pioneer of Country Music Award, and in 1977 he was inducted into the Country Music Hall of Fame. He also appeared in several Western movies, among them *Honky Tonk Man* (1982).

Travis, Roy, American composer; b. New York, June 24, 1922. He studied composition with Bernard Wagenaar at the Juilliard School of Music in N.Y. (1947–50); then took a course with Otto Luening at Columbia Univ.; in 1950 he went to Paris and had instruction with Darius Milhaud. Returning to the U.S., he taught at Columbia Univ. and at the Mannes College of Music in N.Y. In 1957 he was appointed to the faculty of the Univ. of Calif. at Los Angeles; apart from composition, he began a thorough investigation of electronic music and also worked at the Inst. of Ethnomusicology there. His most outstanding work is the 2-act opera *The Passion of Oedipus,* composed in 1965 and produced at the Opera Workshop at the Univ. of Calif. in Los Angeles on Nov. 8, 1968; its music, rooted in Greek homophony, is enhanced by an acridly dramatic idiom. His other important works include *African Sonata* for Piano (1966), based on tribal African modes; Concerto for Flute with recorded African Instruments metamorphosed by a Synthesizer (1970 –71); *Songs and Epilogues,* a song cycle with Piano interludes, to texts from Sappho (1965); *Collage* for Orch. (1967–68); Septet for Flute, Clarinet, Violin, Cello, Double Bass, Piano, and Percussion (1968); Piano Concerto (1969).

Traxel, Josef, German tenor; b. Mainz, Sept. 29, 1916; d. Stuttgart, Oct. 8, 1975. He studied at the Hochschule für Musik in Darmstadt; then made his debut in Mainz in 1942; in 1946 he joined the Opera in Nuremberg; from 1952 he was a member of the Württemberg State Theater in Stuttgart; later taught at the Hochschule für Musik there. He also sang at Salzburg, Bayreuth, Berlin, Vienna, and Munich; toured North America as well. His opera repertoire ranged from Mozart to Wagner; he was also renowned as a concert singer.

Trebelli, Zelia (real name, **Zelia Gilbert**), French mezzo-soprano; b. Paris, 1838; d. Etretat, Aug. 18, 1892. She studied with Wartel; made her debut in 1859 as Rosina in *Il Barbiere di Siviglia,* followed by appearances in England (1862). She was long a favorite in London; also toured the U.S. (1878 and 1884).

BIBLIOGRAPHY: M. de Mensiaux, *Trebelli: A Biographical Sketch* (London, 1890).

Tregian, Francis, English musician; b. 1574; d. London, 1619. He was a recusant, and fled England to escape persecution; was attached to Catholic dignitaries in Douai and in Rome. Returning to England to settle his father's estate, he was convicted in 1609, remaining in prison until his death. His significance for English music lies in the fact that he was the scribe of the *Fitzwilliam Virginal Book* and of 2 MSS containing more than 2,000 motets, madrigals, etc., some of them possibly of his own composition.

BIBLIOGRAPHY: Elizabeth Cole, "In Search of Francis Tregian," *Music & Letters* (Jan. 1952).

Treharne, Bryceson, English-American music editor and composer; b. Merthyr Tydfil, Wales, May 30, 1879; d. New York, Feb. 4, 1948. He studied at the Royal College of Music in London, under Parry, Stanford, and Davies. In 1901 he went to Australia; was a prof. at the Univ. of Adelaide; returning to Europe in 1911, he lived in Paris, Milan, Vienna, and Munich; at the outbreak of World War I, he was interned in Germany, at Ruhleben. There he wrote nearly 200 songs and other works; an exchange of prisoners of war enabled him to return to England. In 1917 he settled in America; was music editor for the Boston Music Co. and Willis Music Co. (1928–47). Among his songs are *Ozymandias, The Fair Circassian, A Lover's Prayer, The Night, Dreams, Love's Tribute,* and *Renunciation.*

Treigle, Norman, remarkable American bass-baritone; b. New Orleans, March 6, 1927; d. there, Feb. 16, 1975. He sang in a church choir as a child; upon graduation from high school in 1943 he served in the navy. After two years in service he returned to New Orleans and studied voice with Elizabeth Wood; made his debut in 1947 with the New Orleans Opera as Lodovico in Verdi's *Otello.* In 1952 he went to N.Y. and joined the N.Y. City Opera, making his debut there on March 28, 1953, as Colline in *La Bohème;* he remained with the company for 20 years, establishing himself as a favorite with the public. Among his most successful roles were Figaro in Mozart's *Le nozze di Figaro,* Don Giovanni, Méphistophélès, and Boris Godunov; he also sang in modern operas, including the leading parts in the world premieres of 3 operas by Carlisle Floyd: *The Passion of Jonathan Wade* (N.Y., Oct. 11, 1962), *The Sojourner and Mollie Sinclair* (Raleigh, N.C., Dec. 2, 1963), and *Markheim* (New Orleans, March 31, 1966). Treigle's other parts in contemporary operas were the title role in Dallapiccola's *The Prisoner* and that of the grandfather in Copland's *The Tender Land.* He also made a successful appearance at Covent Garden in London, as Méphistophélès in *Faust* on Nov. 13, 1973. His untimely death, from an overdose of sleeping pills at his home in New Orleans, deprived the American musical theater of one of its finest talents.

BIBLIOGRAPHY: David Ewen, *Musicians since 1900* (N.Y., 1978).

Tremblay, George, Canadian-American composer; b. Ottawa, Jan. 14, 1911; d. Tijuana, Mexico, July 14, 1982. He studied music with his father, a church organist; in 1919 he was taken to the U.S.; eventually settled in Los Angeles; there he met Schoenberg and became his ardent disciple and friend. He adopted the method of composition with 12-tones, which he diversified considerably, expounding his theoretical ideas in a book, *The Definitive Cycle of the 12-Tone Row,* publ. in 1974. In Hollywood, he became an esteemed teacher; among his students were André Previn, Quincy Jones, and Johnny Mandel, as well as numerous successful composers for television and motion pictures.

WORKS: 3 symphs. (1949, 1952, 1970); Wind Sextet (1968); 2 wind quintets (1940, 1950); 4 string quartets (1936–63); Piano Quartet (1958); Quartet for Oboe, Clarinet, Bassoon, and Viola (1964); Piano Trio (1959); String Trio (1964); Duo for Viola and Piano (1966); Double-bass Sonata (1967); 3 piano sonatas; other piano works.

Tremblay, Gilles, Canadian composer; b. Arvida, Quebec, Sept. 6, 1932. He had private lessons with Papineau-Couture; studied piano with Germaine Malépart and composition with Claude Champagne at the Montreal Cons. (1949–54). In 1954 he went to Paris, where he took courses with Messiaen (analysis), Yvonne Loriod (piano), Andrée Vaurabourg-Honegger (counterpoint), and Maurice Martenot (Ondes Martenot); subsequently worked with the Groupe de Recherches Musicales at Paris Radio (1960–61). He returned to Canada in 1961; in 1962 was appointed a prof. at the Montreal Cons. He follows the modern French method of composition and uses graphic notation in his scores.

WORKS: *Scherzo* for Piano (1950); *Double Quintet* for Winds (1950); *Mouvement* for 2 Pianos (1954); *2 pièces (Phases* and *Réseaux)* for Piano (1956–58); *Cantiques de durées* for Orch. (1960; Paris, March 24, 1963); *Mobile* for Violin and Piano (1962); *Champs I* for Piano and 2 Percussionists (1965); *Sonorisation du Pavillon de Québec* at Expo '67 in Montreal, for an icositetrastereophonic electro-acoustical system of 24 Channels (1967); *Souffles (Champs II)* for 2 Flutes, Oboe, Clarinet, Horn, 2 Trumpets, 2 Trombones, 2 Percussionists, Double Bass, and Piano (1968; Montreal, March 21, 1968); *Vers (Champs III)* for 2 Flutes, Clarinet, Trumpet, Horn, 3 Violins, Double Bass, and 3 Percussionists (Stratford Festival, Ontario, Aug. 2, 1969); *Solstices (ou Les Jours et les saisons tournent)* for Flute, Clarinet, Horn, Double Bass, and 2 Percussionists (Montreal, May 17, 1972); *Jeux de solstices* for 4 Instrumental Soloists (Violin, Flute, Clarinet, and Trumpet) and Small Orch. (Ottawa, April 23, 1974); *Oralléluiante* for Soprano, Bass Clarinet, Horn, 3 Double Basses, and 2 Percussionists (1975); *Fleuves* for Orch. (1975–76; Montreal, May 3, 1977).

Trend, John Brande, English music scholar; b. Southampton, Dec. 17, 1887; d. Cambridge, April 20, 1958. He received his education at Cambridge Univ.; spent several years in Spain; in 1933 was appointed prof. of Spanish at Cambridge Univ. He wrote the books *A Picture of Modern Spain: Men and Music* (London, 1921); *Luis Milán and the Vihuelistas* (London, 1925); *The Music of Spanish History to 1600* (London, 1926); *Manuel de Falla and Spanish*

Music (N.Y., 1929).

Trento, Vittorio, Italian composer; b. Venice, 1761; d. Lisbon, 1833. He was a pupil of Bertoni; produced several ballets at Venice, followed by a number of cantatas, farces, and comic operas. He was cembalist at the Teatro S. Samuele, Venice, and then at La Fenice; was music director of the Italian opera at Amsterdam (1806), and some years later at Lisbon. His most popular stage work was the opera buffa *Quanti casi in un sol giorno, ossia Gli assassini* (Venice, Dec., 1801), which was also given in London, as *Roberto l'assassino* (Feb. 3, 1807). Other operas are: *Teresa vedova* (Venice, Jan. 13, 1802), *Ines de Castro* (Livorno, Nov. 9, 1803), *Ifigenia in Aulide* (Naples, Nov. 4, 1804), *Andromeda* (Naples, May 30, 1805), and *Le Gelosie villane* (Florence, Nov. 2, 1825).

Treptow, Günther, German tenor; b. Berlin, Oct. 22, 1907; d. there, March 28, 1981. He studied at the Berlin Hochschule für Musik; made his debut in 1936 at the Deutsches Opernhaus in Berlin as the Steerman in *Der fliegende Holländer;* then sang at Berlin's Städtische Oper (1936–42, 1945–50) and at the Vienna State Opera (1947–55). He made his Metropolitan Opera debut in N.Y. as Siegmund in *Die Walküre* on Feb. 1, 1951; remained on its roster until the close of that season; continued to sing in Europe until his retirement in 1961. He was noted for his performances of the roles of Siegmund, Tristan, and Siegfried in Wagner's operas.

Tretyakov, Viktor, Russian violinist; b. Krasnoyarsk, Oct. 17, 1946. He studied at the Irkutsk Music School as a child, stoutly braving the Siberian cold; then moved to a more temperate climate in Moscow, where he enrolled in the Central Music School. In 1966 he won the International Tchaikovsky Competition, which automatically lifted him to the upper layers of the violinistic firmament, with applause-rich tours in Russia and later the enviable European and American engagements. A typical product of the unmatched Russian school of violin playing, Tretyakov combined the expected virtuosity in technical resources with a diffuse lyricism touched with melancholy in the Romantic repertoire.

Treu (Italianized as **Fedele**), **Daniel Gottlieb,** German composer; b. Stuttgart, 1695; d. Breslau, Aug. 7, 1749. He studied violin with Kusser, and with Vivaldi at Venice. After bringing out 12 operas at Venice, he took an Italian opera troupe to Breslau, where he produced his operas *Astarte, Coriolano, Ulisse e Telemacco,* and *Don Chisciotte,* with much success. In 1727 he became Kapellmeister at Prague; then was again in Breslau.

Tréville, Yvonne de (real name, **Edyth La Gierse**), American coloratura soprano; b. (of a French father and an American mother) Galveston, Texas, Aug. 25, 1881; d. New York, Jan. 25, 1954. She made her debut in N.Y. as Marguérite (1898); then went to Paris, where she studied with Madame Marchesi; appeared at the Opéra-Comique as Lakmé (June 20, 1902); sang in Madrid, Brussels, Vienna, Budapest, Cairo, and in Russia; from 1913, gave concert tours in the U.S. and sang in light operas. Her voice had a compass of 3 full octaves, reaching high G.

Trial, Jean-Claude, French composer; b. Avignon, Dec. 13, 1732; d. Paris, June 23, 1771. He studied violin in his native city, then went to Paris, where he became associated with Rameau; was conductor at the Paris Opéra. He wrote several operas: *Silvie* (Fontainebleau, Oct. 17, 1765), *Théonis ou Le Toucher* (Paris, Oct. 11, 1767), *La Fête de Flore* (Paris, June 18, 1770); also instrumental pieces.

Trifunović, Vitomir, Serbian composer; b. Bukovica, Nov. 4, 1916. He studied composition with Slavenski and Živković at the Belgrade Academy of Music; became an editor for new music at Radio Belgrade in 1959. His early music is Romantic, but later he acquired a thoroughly modern sound. WORKS: Piano Sonatina (1956); Violin Sonata (1958); 2 string quartets (1959, 1973); *Sumadija,* suite for Chamber Orch. (1960); *Lamentoso* for String Orch. (1961); *Heroic Overture* (1962); *Toccata* for Orch. (1963); *Simfonijska slika (Symphonic Picture,* 1964); *Folklorni triptih (Folklore Triptychon)* for Orch. (1961); *Symphonic Dance* (1968); *Synthesen 4* for Orch. (1969); cantata, *Vidici (The Horizons,* 1971); *Antinomije* for Orch. (1972); *Asocijacije (Associations)* for Orch. (1973); arrangements of folk music.

Trimble, Lester, American composer; b. Bangor, Wis., Aug. 29, 1923. He studied composition with Nikolai Lopatnikoff at the Carnegie Inst. of Technology in Pittsburgh and later took private lessons in Paris with Darius Milhaud and Arthur Honegger; subsequently taught at the Juilliard School of Music. WORKS: 2 string quartets (1950, 1955); Symph. No. 1 (1951); Sextet for Woodwinds, Horn, and Piano (1952); Violin Concerto (1955); *Closing Piece* for Orch. (1957); *5 Episodes* for Orch. (1961); *Kennedy Concerto* for Chamber Orch. (1964); *In Praise of Diplomacy and Common Sense* for Baritone, Percussion, Male Speaking Chorus, and 2 Speaking Soloists (1965); Symph. No. 2 (1968); *Solo for a Virtuoso* for Solo Violin (1971); *Panels I* for Chamber Ensemble (Tanglewood Festival, Berkshire, Mass. Aug. 6, 1973); several other pieces entitled *Panels.*

Tristano, "Lennie" (Leonard Joseph Tristano), American jazz pianist; b. Chicago, March 19, 1919; d. New York, Nov. 18, 1978. He became blind in childhood but did not allow this handicap to deflect him from a study of music; he attended the American Cons. of Music in Chicago, and then settled in N.Y. He was remarkable in his piano improvisations; several jazz musicians, including Lee Konitz and Bud Freeman, took lessons with him.

Tritto, Giacomo, Italian composer; b. Altamura, April 2, 1733; d. Naples, Sept. 16, 1824. He studied with Cafaro at the Cons. della Pietà de' Turchini; became subteacher (primo maestrino) and Cafaro's assistant in teaching harmony, also succeeded him as concertmaster at the Teatro San Carlo. From 1799 to 1807 he was principal teacher (primo maestro) at the Cons.; followed Paisiello in 1816 as maestro di cappella of the Royal Chapel. Bellini, Spontini, Mercadante, Meyerbeer, and Conti were his pupils. His first opera, *La fedeltà in amore,* was performed at Naples in 1764; some 50 others were produced subsequently in Naples, Rome, Venice, Milan, etc.; of these, *Le vicende amorose* (Rome, 1788) and *Gli Americani* (Naples, Nov. 4, 1802) were fairly successful. Other works included 3 cantatas, a Mass for Double Chorus with 2 Orchs., 7 other masses (3 of them with Orch.), 2 Passions with Orch., a Te Deum, motets, etc. (none printed). He publ. *Partimenti e regole generali per conoscere qual numerica dar si deve ai vari movimenti del basso* (1821), and *Scuola di contrappunto, ossia Teoria musicale* (1823).
BIBLIOGRAPHY: F. Florimo, *La scuola musicale di Napoli,* vol. III (Naples, 1880); J.A. de la Fage, in *Miscellanées musicales* (Paris, 1844); G. de Napoli, "Giacomo Tritto," *La Lettura* (Oct. 1924); idem, *La triade melodrammatica altamurana: G. Tritto, V. Lavigna, S. Mercandante* (Milan, 1931).

Trneček, Hanuš, Czech harpist and composer; b. Prague, May 16, 1858; d. there, March 28, 1914. He studied at the Prague Cons.; was harpist in the Hoftheater in Schwerin (1882–88); then taught harp and piano at the Prague Cons.
WORKS: Operas: *Der Geigenmacher von Cremona* (Schwerin, April 16, 1886); *Amaranta* (Prague, Nov. 16, 1890; in Czech); *Andrea Crini* (Prague, Feb. 2, 1900); Symph.; Piano Concerto; Violin Concerto; piano pieces.

Trojan, Manfred, German composer; b. Cremlingen, near Braunschweig, Oct. 22, 1949. He studied flute in Braunschweig (1966–70); then enrolled in the Hochschule für Musik in Hamburg (1970–78); also took private lessons in composition with Diether de la Motte (1970–73). His music is neo-Baroque in form and programmatic in content; his songs are expressionistic in their chromatic Angst.
WORKS: FOR ORCH.: 3 symphs.: No. 1, *Makramee* (1973); No. 2 (1978; Donaueschingen, Oct. 22, 1978); No. 3 (1982–83); *Notturni trasognati* for Alto Flute and Orch. (1977; London, June 13, 1977); *Conduct,* 2nd version, for Strings and Perscussion (1978; Gelsenkirchen, May 14, 1979; first version is for Organ Solo); *Abschied,* fragment (1978; Düsseldorf, Oct. 18, 1979); Flute Concerto (1977–83; Berlin, Sept. 14, 1983); *Berceuse* (1980); *Erstes See-Bild* (1979–80; U.S. premiere, N.Y., Feb. 24, 1983). VOCAL MUSIC: *Risse des Himmels,* 4 songs for Soprano, Flute, and Guitar (1968–74); *Architectura Caelestis* for 8 Female Voices and Orch. (1974–76); *... stiller Gefährt der Nacht,* chamber music after a poem by Klopstock, for Soprano, Flute, Cello, Percussion, and Celesta

(1978); *Elegía del tiempo final* for Tenor and 7 Instruments (1981–82); *Zweites See-Bild,* subtitled *Schatten von Kähnen,* after a poem by Georg Haym, for Mezzo-soprano and Orch. (1981). CHAMBER MUSIC: *Les Couleurs de la pluie* for 5 Flutes and Alto Flute (1972); *Kammerkonzert* for 8 Instruments (1973); *2 Brief Pieces* for String Quartet (1973); 3 string quartets: No. 1 (1976); No. 2, with Clarinet and Mezzo-soprano (1979–80); No. 3 (1983); *Fantasia* for Solo Guitar (1979); Violin Sonata (1982); Cello Sonata (1983).

Trojan, Václav, Czech composer; b. Pilsen, April 24, 1907; d. Prague, July 5, 1983. He studied composition with Křička and Alois Hába, and conducting with Ostrčil and Dědeček at the Prague Cons., graduating in 1928. He dedicated himself mainly to light music for the theater; many of his pieces are humorous in intent.
WORKS: 2 string quintets (1928, 1929); Wind Quintet on folk themes (1935); children's opera, *Kolotoč (The Merry-go-round;* 1936–40; Ostrava, 1960); *Pohádky (Fairy Tales)* for Accordion and Orch. (1959); *Sinfonietta armoniosa* for Chamber Orch. (1971); *Capricious Variations* for Trombone, Saxophone, and Orch. (1971); "stage poem" with dance, *The Golden Gate* (1973; Prague, Feb. 17, 1974); *4 Caricatures (and One Extra)* for Wind Orch., Percussion, and Piano (1974); Concertino for Trumpet and Chamber Orch. (1977); *Divertimento* for Wind Quintet (1977); *Noneto Favoloso* for Wind Quintet and String Quartet (1977); *Sen noci svatojanski (A Midsummer Night's Dream),* ballet-pantomime after Shakespeare (1982); film music.

Tromlitz, Johann Georg, German flutist and flute maker; b. Reinsdorf über Artern (Halle), Nov. 8, 1725; d. Leipzig, Feb. 4, 1805. He publ. *Kurze Abhandlung von Flötenspielen* (1786); *Ausführlicher und gründlicher Unterricht die Flöte zu spielen* (1791); *Über di Flöte mit mehreren Klappen* (1800); articles in the *Allgemeine Musik-Zeitung* (1799); also 3 concertos for Flute and Strings; 2 books of sonatas for Piano and Flute; 6 *Partien* for Flute; songs.

Trommer, Wolfgang, German conductor; b. Wuppertal, July 10, 1927. He was educated at the Hochschule für Musik in Cologne and the Northwest German Music Academy in Detmold. He conducted at the Opera in Hannover (1955–61); then joined the Aachen Opera, becoming Generalmusikdirektor (1962–74). In 1973 he also made appearances as guest conductor at the Hamburg State Opera. In addition, he taught conducting classes at the Cons. of Maastricht in the Netherlands.

Trotère, Henry (real name, **Trotter**), English song composer; b. London, Dec. 14, 1855; d. there, April 10, 1912. Some of his songs that enjoyed success were *Once for All, Léonore, Ever dear, Asthore, The Deathless Army, Love can wait.*

Trotter, Thomas Henry Yorke, English musical

educator; b. London, Nov. 6, 1854; d. there, March 11, 1934. He studied at New College, Oxford (M.A., 1887; Mus.Doc., 1892); also took music lessons with Frank Bridge; was principal of the London Academy of Music from 1915, developing there a new system for teaching music, based on ear-training and cultivation of the rhythmic sense; he came to the U.S. and introduced his system at the Eastman School of Music in Rochester, N.Y. He wrote *Constructive Harmony* (1911); *Rhythmic Gradus; Ear-training and Sight-reading Gradus; The Making of Musicians* (1914); *Music and Mind* (1924).

Troutbeck, Rev. John, English compiler of hymnals; b. Blencowe, Cumberland, Nov. 12, 1832; d. London, Oct. 11, 1899 He studied at Oxford (B.A., 1856; M.A., 1858); in 1865–69, served as precentor of Manchester Cathedral; in 1869, became canon of Westminster. He publ. *The Manchester Psalter* (1868); *Manchester Chant Book* (1871); *Cathedral Paragraph Psalter; Hymn Book for Use in Westminster Abbey; Music Primer for Schools,* with R.F. Dale (1873; often reprinted); *Church Choir Training* (1879). He made translations of German, French, and Italian opera librettos publ. by Novello.

Troyanos, Tatiana, brilliant American mezzo-soprano; b. New York, Sept. 12, 1938. She received her musical training at the Juilliard School of Music; made her debut with the N.Y. City Opera in 1963; in 1964 she went to Europe; made appearances with the Hamburg State Opera. In 1969 she sang at Covent Garden in London; in 1971 she was engaged at the Paris Opéra. On March 8, 1976, she made a memorable Metropolitan Opera debut in N.Y. as Octavian in *Der Rosenkavalier;* in subsequent seasons she became one of the company's leading members.

Trudić, Božidar, Serbian composer; b. Smederevska Palanka, March 24, 1911. He studied with Slavenski; became a teacher in Sarajevo. His music is inspired by Serbian folk songs, but the harmonic treatment is often modernistic. Among his works are a cantata, *1804* (Sarajevo, Dec. 26, 1956); Violin Concerto (1951); Cello Concerto (1952); 2 symphs. (1946, 1957); choruses and songs.

Truhn, Friedrich Hieronymus, German composer and writer on music; b. Elbing, Nov. 14, 1811; d. Berlin, April 30, 1886. He studied with Dehn, Klein, and Mendelssohn; wrote for the Leipzig *Neue Zeitschrift für Musik* during Schumann's editorship; lived chiefly at Berlin, where he founded and conducted the Neue Liedertafel; made a concert tour with Hans von Bülow in 1854.
WORKS: Marionette opera, *Der baierische Hiesel* (Berlin, 1832); operetta, *Der vierjährige Posten* (1833); comic opera, *Trilby* (Berlin, May 22, 1835); melodrama, *Kleopatra* (Berlin, 1853); he also wrote *Über Gesangskunst* (1885).

Truinet. See **Nuitter.**

Trunk, Richard, German music critic, composer, and choral conductor; b. Tauberbischopsheim, Baden, Feb. 10, 1879; d. Herrsching-am-Ammersee, June 2, 1968. He studied music with Iwan Knorr at the Hoch Cons. in Frankfurt (1894–95) and later took courses at the Akademie der Tonkunst in Munich. He was then active as a choral instructor and music critic in Munich, Bayreuth, and Cologne; in 1934 was appointed director of the Akademie der Tonkunst in Munich; after 1945 lived in retirement at Ammersee. He was a prolific composer of choral music and also wrote a singspiel, *Herzdame,* which was produced in 1917 in Munich.
BIBLIOGRAPHY: A. Ott, *Richard Turner: Leben und Werk* (Munich, 1964).

Trutovsky, Vasili, Russian composer and collector of folk songs; b. Ivanovskaya Sloboda, c.1740; d. St. Petersburg, 1810. He was the son of an Orthodox priest; was a court singer and player on the *gusli* during the reigns of Elizabeth, Peter III, and Catherine II. His historic achievement was the compilation of the first comprehensive collection of Russian folk songs, in 4 fascicles (1776, 1778, 1779, 1795). He also was the first in Russia to publ. piano pieces; the earlier publications of Russian piano music were anonymous. His *Chanson russe variée* for Harpsichord or Piano (St. Petersburg, 1780) was republ. in *Old Russian Piano Music,* ed. by A. Drozdov and T. Trofimov (Moscow, 1946).

Tschaikowsky. See **Tchaikovsky.**

Tschirch, (Friedrich) Wilhelm, German choral conductor and composer; b. Lichtenau, June 8, 1818; d. Gera, Jan. 6, 1892. He was a pupil at the Royal Inst. for Church Music, Berlin; music director at Liegnitz in 1843–52; then court conductor at Gera. By invitation of German-American choral societies he visited the U.S. in 1869, and produced many of his celebrated men's choruses at N.Y., Philadelphia, Baltimore, Washington, D.C., and Chicago. He publ. salon pieces for piano under the pseudonym **Alexander Czersky.**

Tschudi. See **Broadwood.**

Tsfasman, Alexander, foremost Russian conductor of jazz; b. Alexandrovsk, Ukraine, Dec. 14, 1906; d. Moscow, Feb. 20, 1971. He studied piano with Felix Blumenfeld at the Moscow Cons. In 1926 he organized a jazz band in Moscow, and from 1939 to 1946 was music director of the All-Union Radio Jazz Band; he toured with it all over Russia. He also composed a Concerto for Piano and Jazz Band, and numerous popular songs.

Tsindsadze, Sulkhan, Soviet Georgian composer and cellist; b. Gori, Aug. 23, 1925. He studied cello and composition at the Moscow Cons.; in 1963 joined the faculty of the Tiflis Cons. In his music he emphasizes ethnic elements, presenting them in congenial modal harmonies. In 1966 he joined the Communist party.

WORKS: For the stage: *The Golden Fleece* (1953) and *Pautina* (*The Spider's Web*, 1964); 2 ballets: *The Treasure of the Blue Mountain* (1956); *The Demon*, after Lermontov's poem (1961). For Orch.: *Georgian Rhapsody* for Violin and Orch. (1955); 2 violin concertos (1947, 1968); 2 cello concertos (1947, 1964); 2 piano concertos (1949, 1968); 3 suites for String Orch. (1948, 1950, 1955); 4 symphs. (1952, 1963, 1969, 1979); oratorio, *Immortality*, for the centenary of Lenin's birth (1970). Chamber music: 9 string quartets (1947, 1948, 1955, 1956, 1962, 1966, 1970, 1973, 1978). For Piano: *24 Preludes* (1980).

Tsouyopoulos, Georges, Greek composer; b. Athens, Oct. 11, 1930. He received his early training in Athens and Milan; then went to Zürich to study with Hindemith. In 1962 he settled in Munich. His early compositions are neo-Classical in style; later he adopted serial methods, determinedly pursuing the goal of structural indeterminacy.

WORKS: *Sinfonietta da camera* for 8 Instruments (1955); *Serenata* for Soprano, Flute, Guitar, and Viola (1957); *2 madrigali* for Soprano and Orch. (1957); *3 frammenti* for Chorus and Orch. (1958); 3 toccatas for Piano (1958, 1959, 1965); *Music for Percussion* (1959); 2 string quartets; vocal pieces.

Tsukatani, Akihirô, Japanese composer; b. Tokyo, March 16, 1919. He graduated in law from Tokyo Univ. in 1941 and became a prof. in the history of economics there; concurrently he took lessons in music theory from Saburo Moroi. In 1949, with Yoritsuné Matsudaira, he organized the Shin Sakkyokuka Kyokai (New Composers' Association); taught music at Tokyo Univ.

WORKS: 3 operas: *Pongo*, based on a Japanese Noh drama (1965); *Ajatasatru* (1966); *Kakitsubata* (Tokyo, May 24, 1967); a musical, *Fairy's Cap*, for Chorus, Piano, and Percussion (Tokyo, Dec. 9, 1968); *Saiten (Festival)*, symph. suite (1950); *Mythology of Today*, ballet suite (1956); *Suite* for Percussion and String Orch. (1960); Piano Concerto (1961); *Japan Festival Dance Music* for Chamber Orch. (1969); Sonata for Flute, Cello, and Piano (1949); Clarinet Sonata (1952); *Suite* for Horn, Trumpet, Trombone, and Timpani (1959); *Fu 1* and *Fu 2* for Solo Flute (1970); *3 Worlds* for Solo Flute (1971–72); *2 Movements* for Solo Cello (1972); *Fantasia* for Violin, Piano, and Tam-tam (1973); choruses; songs.

Tua, Teresina (real name, **Maria Felicità**), Italian violinist; b. Turin, May 22, 1867; d. Rome, Oct. 29, 1955. She studied with Massart at the Paris Cons., where she took the first prize in 1880; toured the Continent with brilliant success; made her English debut at the Crystal Palace in London, May 5, 1883; also appeared in America (1887). In 1889 she married Count Franchi-Verney della Valetta, and withdrew from the concert stage till the autumn of 1895, when she set out on a successful European tour, including Russia, where her accompanist and joint artist was Rachmaninoff. Franchi died in 1911; in 1913 she married Emilio Quadrio. She taught at the Milan Cons. from 1915 to 1924, and then at the Santa Cecilia Academy in Rome; subsequently abandoned her career, and entered the Convento dell'Adorazione in Rome as Sister Maria di Gesù.

Tubb, Carrie (Caroline Elizabeth), English soprano; b. London, May 17, 1876; d. there, Sept. 20, 1976, at the age of 100. She studied at the Guildhall School of Music; began her career singing minor roles in productions by the Beecham Opera Co.; then abandoned the stage and devoted herself to the oratorio and solo recitals. She excelled both in Mozart arias and in concert excerpts from Wagner and Verdi. At the zenith of her career, her singing was described in glowing superlatives by such otherwise sober auditors as Eric Blom. As her voice betrayed the inexorable signs of senescence, she applied herself to teaching, following G.B. Shaw's dictum, "Who can, do; who cannot, teach."

Tubb, Ernest (Dale), American country-music singer; b. near Crisp, Texas, Feb. 9, 1914; d. Nashville, Tenn., Sept. 6, 1984. Following in the path of Jimmie Rodgers, he became a leading figure in the development of the "western swing" or "honkytonk" style of country-western music; his recording of *Walking the Floor over You* in 1941 established his reputation; from 1942 he made regular appearances on the "Grand Ole Opry" radio program in Nashville. In 1965 he was elected to the Country Music Hall of Fame.

Tubin, Eduard, Estonian-born Swedish composer; b. Kallaste, near Tartu (Dorpat), June 18, 1905; d. Stockholm, Nov. 17, 1982. He studied with A. Kapp at the Cons. of Tartu and later with Kodály in Budapest. From 1931 to 1944 he conducted the Tartu Symph. Orch.; in 1944 he settled in Stockholm. In 1961 he became a Swedish citizen; in 1982 was elected to the Royal Swedish Academy of Music. He was at work on his 11th Symph. at the time of his death.

WORKS: Operas: *Barbara von Tisenhusen* (Tallinn, Estonia, Dec. 4, 1969) and *Prosten från Reigi* (*The Priest from Reigi*, 1971); ballet, *Skratten* (*Laughter;* 1939–41); 10 symphs.: No. 1 (1934); No. 2, *Legendary* (1937); No. 3 (1942; Tallinn, Feb. 26, 1943); No. 4, *Lyrical* (1943; Tallinn, April 16, 1944; revised 1978; Bergen, Nov. 5, 1981); No. 5 (1946); No. 6 (1954); No. 7 (1958); No. 8 (1966); No. 9, *Sinfonia semplice* (1969); No. 10 (1973); *Estonian Dance Suite* for Orch. (1938); 2 violin concertos (1942, 1945); *Concertino* for Piano and Orch. (1944–46); Double-bass Concerto (1948); Balalaika Concerto (1964); 2 violin sonatas (1936, 1949); Saxophone Sonata (1951); Solo Violin Sonata (1962); Viola Sonata (1965); *Capriccio* for Violin and Piano (1971); *5 Kosjalaulud* for Baritone and Orch. (1975); 10 preludes for Piano (1928–76); *Ylermi*, ballad for Baritone and Orch. (1935; revised 1977); *Requiem for Fallen Soldiers* for Alto, Male Chorus, Solo Trumpet, Percussion, and Organ (1979); Flute Sonata (1979); *Suite on Estonian Dance Tunes* for Solo Violin (1979); *Quartet on Estonian Motifs* for String Quartet (1979).

Tucci, Gabriella, Italian soprano; b. Rome, Aug. 4, 1929. She studied at the Santa Cecilia Academy in Rome, and then with Leonardo Filoni. In 1951 she won the international singing competition in Spoleto; after appearances in provincial Italian opera houses, she sang at La Scala in Milan and at the Rome Opera. On Sept. 25, 1959, she made her American debut as Madeleine in *Andrea Chénier* at the San Francisco Opera; her Metropolitan Opera debut followed in N.Y. on Oct. 29, 1960, as Cio-Cio-San in *Madama Butterfly.* She continued to sing at the Metropolitan with increasing success; especially noted were her appearances as Desdemona (March 10, 1963), Marguerite in Gounod's *Faust* (Sept. 27, 1965), and Mimi in *La Bohème* (April 16, 1966). Her other roles were Violetta, Aida, Tosca, Gilda in *Rigoletto,* and Liù in *Turandot.* Her European career was equally successful; she sang at Covent Garden in London, at San Carlo in Naples, at the Vienna State Opera, at the Deutsche Oper in Berlin, at the Munich Opera, at the Bolshoi Theatre in Moscow, at the Teatro Colón in Buenos Aires, and in Japan.
BIBLIOGRAPHY: David Ewen, *Musicians since 1900* (N.Y., 1978).

Tucher, Gottlieb, Freiherr von, German writer on music; b. Nuremberg, May 14, 1798; d. Munich, Feb. 17, 1877. He was in the judicial service in Bavaria; from 1856 to 1868 was judge of the Supreme Court of Munich. His musical publications include: *Kirchengesänge der berühmesten älteren italienischen Meister* (1827; dedicated to Beethoven) and *Schatz des evangelischen Kirchengesangs* (1848; 2 vols.); he also wrote *Über den Gemeindegesang der evangelischen Kirche* (1867).

Tucker, Richard (real name, **Reuben Ticker**), brilliant American tenor; b. Brooklyn, Aug. 28, 1913; d. Kalamazoo, Mich., Jan. 8, 1975. He sang in a synagogue choir in N.Y. as a child; studied voice with Paul Althouse; subsequently sang on the radio. His first public appearance in opera was as Alfredo in *La Traviata* in 1943 with the Salmaggi Co. in N.Y. On Jan. 25, 1945, he made his Metropolitan Opera debut in N.Y. as Enzo in *La Gioconda;* he remained on its roster until his death, specializing in the Italian repertoire. In 1947 he made his European debut at the Verona Arena as Enzo (Maria Callas made her Italian debut as Gioconda in the same performance); he also sang at Covent Garden in London, at La Scala in Milan, in Vienna, and in other major music centers abroad. He died suddenly while on a concert tour. He was the brother-in-law of the American tenor **Jan Peerce.**

Tuckerman, Samuel Parkman, American organist and composer; b. Boston, Feb. 11, 1819; d. Newport, R.I., June 30, 1890. He was a pupil of Carl Zeuner in Boston; from 1856 to 1864 he lived in England. He wrote much church music; edited *The Episcopal Harp* (Boston, 1844), *The National Lyre* (Boston, 1848) *Cathedral Chants* (1858), and *Trinity Collection of Church Music* (Boston, 1864).

Tuckey, William, English singing master; b. Somersetshire, 1708; d. Philadelphia, Sept. 14, 1781. He claimed to have been a vicar-choral at Bristol Cathedral before going to America, where he was active from 1754; established himself as a singing teacher in N.Y. On Jan. 16, 1770, he conducted what was probably the first performance in America of Handel's *Messiah* (overture and 16 numbers). He composed a *Thanksgiving Anthem* (1760), a setting of the 97th Psalm.
BIBLIOGRAPHY: O.G. Sonneck, *Early Concert-Life in America* (1907).

Tuckwell, Barry, Australian virtuoso horn player; b. Melbourne, March 5, 1931, in a musical family. He was taught piano by his father and violin by his older brother; was a chorister at St. Andrew's Cathedral in Sydney, and also acted as an organist there. At age 13 he began studying the French horn with Alan Mann at the Cons. of Sydney; making rapid progress, he joined the Sydney Symph., then conducted by Eugene Goossens (1947–50). In 1950 he went to England, where he met Dennis Brain, the virtuoso horn player, who gave him valuable suggestions on horn technique; he also gathered some ideas about horn sound from listening to recordings by Tommy Dorsey. He filled positions as assistant first horn with the Hallé Orch. in Manchester (1951–53), with the Scottish National Orch. (1953–54), and, as first horn, with the Bournemouth Symph. Orch. (1954–55); then served for 13 years (1955–68) as first horn player with the London Symph. Orch. After leaving this orch. he launched a career as a soloist, achieving recognition as one of the foremost virtuosos on the instrument. In the academic field, he compiled a horn method and edited horn literature. Several modern composers wrote special works for him: Thea Musgrave (a Concerto that requires the horn to play quartertones); Richard Rodney Bennett (*Actaeon* for Horn and Orch.); Iain Hamilton (*Voyage* for Horn and Orch.); Alun Hoddinott (Concerto); and Don Banks (Concerto). In 1978 he made his first appearance as a conductor in the U.S., in a program of Baroque music.
BIBLIOGRAPHY: Winthrop Sargeant, "Profiles: Something I Could Do," *New Yorker* (March 14, 1977).

Tudor, David, American avant-garde pianist and aleatory composer; b. Philadelphia, Jan. 20, 1926. He studied organ with William Hawke, piano with Irma Wolpe, and composition with Stefan Wolpe. He played the organ in St. Mark's Church in Philadelphia (1938–43) and at Swarthmore College (1944–48); these ecclesiastical services to the contrary notwithstanding, he simultaneously plunged into uninhibited experimentation; developed a hypermodern virtuoso technique as a quaquaversal hyperdactyl pianist; earned an awesome reputation by performing the insurmountable, impregnable, and inscrutable 2nd Piano Sonata of Pierre Boulez (N.Y., Dec. 17, 1950) from memory. He became the unique collaborator, animator, and divinator of the recondite practices of John Cage, and was the first to unplay John Cage's monumental tacit piece *4' 33*S'(Woodstock, N.Y., Aug. 29, 1952); was also unheard in it in Cologne, Germany, and elsewhere, obtaining vociferous acclaim. In audible performance he often applies special piano techniques; in playing *5 Piano Pieces for David Tudor* by Sylvano Bussotti, he is apt to put on thick leather gloves for tone-clusters. As a composer, he has the following works to his credit: *Fluorescent Sound* (Stockholm, Sept. 13, 1964); *Bandoneon—!* (factorial bandoneon, idempotentially multiplied ad infinitum); *Reunion* (in collaboration with the painter Marcel Duchamp and others); *Rainforest* for Dancers; and, in collaboration with John Cage, *Talk I* (Ann Arbor, Mich., Sept. 19, 1965) and *Fontana Mix* for Bass Drum and Electronic Circuits (Brandeis Univ., Waltham, Mass., April Fools' Day, 1967). Some of his biographers claim for him a direct descent, through a morganatic line, from Henry Tudor (Henry VII), and/or from one of the decapitated lovers of the beheaded Queen Anne Boleyn. Since Henry VIII himself dabbled in "aleatorick musick," David Tudor's own preoccupation with tonal indeterminacy may be a recessive royal trait.

Tudoran, Ionel, Rumanian tenor; b. Baragtii de Vede, June 24, 1913. He studied at the Cons. in Jassy; made his debut there as Roland in Ziehrer's *Landstreicher* in 1936; then sang with the Cluj Opera (1937–48); subsequently joined the Bucharest Opera (1948–63); also made guest appearances in Prague, Leipzig, Berlin, Dresden, Moscow, and other music centers. He retired in 1963 and taught voice at the Bucharest Cons. His finest roles were Don José, Faust, and Cavaradossi.

Tudway, Thomas, English composer; b. 1650; d. Cambridge, Nov. 23, 1726. From 1660 he was a chorister in the Chapel Royal, under Dr. Blow; he became lay-vicar at St. George's Chapel, Windsor, in 1664; was organist of King's College, Cambridge, from 1670 to 1680; became teacher of choristers there in 1679; became a prof. of music at Cambridge Univ. in 1705; was suspended 1706–7, retired 1726. From Cambridge Univ. he received the degrees of Mus.Bac. (1681) and Mus.Doc. (1705). He composed services, motets, and anthems; his *Collection of Services and Anthems used in the Church of England from the Reformation to the Restoration of King Charles II,* in 6 MS vols., is in the British Library.
BIBLIOGRAPHY: E. Turnbull, "Thomas Tudway and the Harleian Collection," *Journal of the American Musicological Society,* VII (1955).

Tufts, John, American minister and pioneer compiler of church music; b. Medford, Mass., Feb. 26, 1689; d. Amesbury, Mass., Aug. 17, 1750. He graduated from Harvard Univ. in 1708; was ordained a minister at Newbury, Mass., in 1714; upon retirement in 1738 he moved to Amesbury, where he settled as a shopkeeper. About 1721 he publ. *A Very Plain and Easy Introduction to the Art of Singing Psalm Tunes* (no copy previous to the 1721 ed. is known to exist); in this book, letters instead of notes were used on the staff; it was very popular (at least 11 eds. publ. up to 1774; reprint, Philadelphia, 1954).
BIBLIOGRAPHY: N.D. Gould, *Church Music in America* (1853); F.J. Metcalf, *American Writers and Compilers of Sacred Music* (1925); E.H. Pierce, "The Rise and Fall of the 'Fugue-Tune' in America," *Musical Quarterly* (April 1930); *Dictionary of American Biography,* 19 (1936); C.K. Shipton, *Sibley's Harvard Graduates* (Boston, 1937; pp. 457–61); I. Lowens, "John Tufts' Introduction to the Singing of Psalm-Tunes (1721–1744): The First American Music Textbook," *Journal of Research in Music Education,* 2 (1954).

Tufts, John Wheeler, American organist and teacher; b. Dover, N.H., May 12, 1825; d. Camden, Maine, March 18, 1908. He went to Germany in 1846; studied in Leipzig, where his teachers were Moscheles in piano and Hauptmann in theory. He returned to America in 1848 and organized in Bangor, Maine, a choral society which he conducted for several years; he then served as church organist in Portland, Maine, and in Boston. He wrote many songs and hymn tunes, and brought out a series of school-music works, notably the *Normal Music Course* and the *Cecilian Series of Study and Song.*

Tulindberg, Erik, Finnish composer; b. Lillkyro, Feb. 22, 1761; d. Åbo (Turku), Sept. 1, 1814. He studied academic disciplines at the Åbo Academy, obtaining the degree of Magister Philosophiae in 1782; was subsequently a municipal functionary. Music was his avocation; he learned to play the violin; owned a large library, including works of Mozart, Haydn, and Boccherini; in 1797 he was elected member of the Swedish Academy of Music. He wrote a Violin Concerto and 6 string quartets in the traditional style of the Viennese School.

Tully, Alice, American singer and music patroness; b. Corning, N.Y., Sept. 11, 1902. A scion of a family of wealth, she studied voice in Paris, where she made her concert debut with the Pasdeloup Orch. in 1927. Returning to the U.S., she gave a song recital in N.Y. in 1936, and received critical praise for her interpretation of French songs. She eventually gave up her artistic ambition and devoted herself to various philanthropic endeavors. Her major gift was to Lincoln Center in N.Y., for the construction of a chamber music hall; it was dedicated as Alice Tully Hall in 1969. She also helped to organize the Chamber Music Society of Lincoln Center.

Tulou, Jean-Louis, French flutist; b. Paris, Sept. 12, 1786; d. Nantes, July 23, 1865. He was a pupil of Wunderlich at the Paris Cons.; in 1813 succeeded him at the Paris Opéra, resigning in 1822, but resumed the position in 1826 (with the title of "première flûte solo"); in 1829 was appointed prof. of flute at the Cons.; retired from both positions in 1856. He performed on the old-fashioned flute, and obstinately opposed the introduction of Böhm's improved instrument into the Cons. He wrote 5 flute concertos; *airs variés* for flute with orch.; a Trio for 3 Flutes; flute duos; many solo pieces for flute.

Tuma, Franz, Bohemian virtuoso on the viola da gamba and composer; b. Kostelecz, Oct. 2, 1704; d. Vienna, Jan 30, 1774. He was a pupil of Czernohorsky at Prague and Fux at Vienna; from 1741, was chamber composer to the dowager Empress Elisabeth. He composed 65 masses, a Miserere, responses, etc.; also instrumental pieces. A selection of Tuma's works was publ. by O. Schmid (choruses, Passion music, piano pieces); a Symph. was edited by Paul Pisk.
BIBLIOGRAPHY: O. Schmid, in *Sammelbände der Internationalen Musik-Gesellschaft,* II; O. Ball, *Franz Tuma* (Diss., Univ. of Vienna, 1901); A. Peschek, *Die Messen von Franz Tuma* (Diss., Univ. of Vienna, 1956).

Tunder, Franz, celebrated German organist and composer; b. Bannesdorf, near Burg, Fehmarn, 1614; d. Lübeck, Nov. 5, 1667. In 1632–41 he was court organist at Gottorp, where he studied with J. Heckelauer, a pupil of Frescobaldi; in 1641, he became organist of the Marienkirche in Lübeck, being succeeded at his death by his son-in-law, **Dietrich Buxtehude.** Seven chorale fantasias for organ by Tunder were discovered in 1903 in the Lüneburg tablature books (one was publ. by Straube, in Alte Meister des Orgelspiels, new series). Solo and choral cantatas were edited by M. Seiffert in Denkmäler Deutscher Tonkunst, 3; 2 preludes and fugues for organ were edited by R. Buchmayer (1927); 4 organ, preludes, etc. are in *Organum.* A complete edition of Tunder's organ chorale arrangements was begun in 1958, edited by Rudolf Walter; *Collected Organ Works,* edited by Klaus Beckmann, was publ. in Wiesbaden (1974). Two works by Tunder from the Pelplin MS in Poland were publ. in vol. X, part 2, of *Corpus of Early Keyboard Music,* under the auspices of the American Inst. of Musicology (1967).
BIBLIOGRAPHY: W. Stahl, *F. T. und D. Buxtehude* (Leipzig, 1926) and "F. T.," *Archiv für Musikwissenschaft,* 8; J. Hennings, "Tunderiana," *Lübeckische Blätter,* 75, no. 53 (1934); K. Gudewill, *Franz Tunder und die nordelbingische Musikkultur seiner Zeit* (Lübeck, 1967); G. Sharp, "Franz Tunder: 1614–1667," *Musical Times,* CVIII (1967).

Tupkov, Dimiter, Bulgarian composer; b. Sofia, July 12, 1929. He studied with Goleminov at the Bulgarian State Cons. in Sofia, graduating in 1956; then joined its faculty.
WORKS: Flute Concerto (1955); *The Story of Belassitsa Mountain,* overture (1956); 3 *Children's Sinfoniettas* (1961, 1968, 1975); Concerto for Orch. (1969); *Rhapsodic Divertimento* for Orch. (1970); Harp Concerto (1971); *6 Bagatelles* for Orch. (1972); *September Overture* (1974); *Peace Cantata* (1975); 2 string quartets (1956, 1958); choral songs; folk-song arrangements.

Turchaninov, Piotr, Russian composer of sacred music; b. Kiev, Dec. 1, 1779; d. St. Petersburg, March 28, 1856. He studied music with Sarti when the latter was at the St. Petersburg court; was ordained a priest in 1803; taught singing at the imperial court chapel; from 1831 to 1841 was archpriest at various churches. His masterly arrangements and harmonizations of old liturgical melodies of the Russian Church were publ. in 5 vols., edited by Kastalsky (Moscow, 1906). His autobiography was publ. in St. Petersburg in 1863.
BIBLIOGRAPHY: A. Preobrazhensky, *The Archpriest P.I. Turchaninov* (St. Petersburg, 1910); V. Lebedev, *P.I. Turchaninov* (Tambov, 1910).

Turchi, Guido, Italian composer; b. Rome, Nov. 10, 1916. He studied composition with Ildebrando Pizzetti, and in his early music followed Pizzetti's style of Italian Baroque, with Romantic and impressionistic extensions; he then changed his idiom toward a more robust and accentuated type of music-making, influenced mainly by a study of the works of Béla Bartók. Turchi's Concerto for String Orch. is dedicated to Bartók's memory. From 1960 to 1967 he taught at the Cons. of Rome; in 1967 was appointed director of the Cons. of Parma.
WORKS: Trio for Flute, Clarinet, and Viola (1945); *Invettiva* for Small Chorus and 2 Pianos (1946); Concerto for String Orch. (Venice, Sept. 8, 1948); *Piccolo concerto notturno* for Orch. (1950); opera, *Il buon soldato Svaik* (Milan, April 6, 1962); *3 metamorfosi* for Orch. (1970).
BIBLIOGRAPHY: F. d'Amico, "Guido Turchi," *Tempo* (Autumn 1951).

Tureck, Rosalyn, eminent American pianist and harpsichordist; b. Chicago, Dec. 14, 1914, in a musical family of Russian and Turkish background. She studied piano in Chicago with Sophia Brilliant-Liven (1925–29), Jan Chiapusso (1929–31), and Gavin Williamson (1931–32); then went to N.Y., where she studied with Olga Samaroff at the Juilliard School of Music, graduating in 1935. In her concert career she dedicated herself mainly to Bach. In 1947 she made her first European tour; subsequently gave concerts in South America, South Africa, and Israel. In 1971 she made a world tour, including India and the Orient. She held teaching posts at the Philadelphia Cons. of Music (1935–42), Juilliard School of Music (1943–55), and Univ. of Calif., San Diego (1966–72). In 1977 she received the honorary degree of Mus.D. from Oxford Univ. In order to demonstrate the universal applicability of Bach's keyboard techniques, she played Bach on the Moog synthesizer; in 1971 she gave a concert announced as "Bach and Rock." She publ. *An Introduction to the Performance of Bach* (3 vols., London, 1959–60; also publ. in Japanese, 1966, and Spanish, 1972).

Turina, Joaquín, prominent Spanish composer; b. Seville, Dec. 9, 1882; d. Madrid, Jan. 14, 1949. He studied with local teachers; then entered the Madrid Cons. as a pupil of Tragó (piano). In 1905 he went to Paris, where he studied composition with

Vincent d'Indy at the Schola Cantorum, and piano with Moszkowski. In Paris a meeting with Albéniz and Manuel de Falla proved a turning point in his career; he determined to write national Spanish music; returning to Madrid in 1913, he produced 2 symph. works in a characteristic Spanish style: *La procesión del rocío* and *Sinfonía sevillana*, combining Romantic and impressionist elements in an individual manner; the same effective combination is found in his chamber music of Spanish inspiration (*Escena andaluza, La oración del torero,* etc.) and his piano music (*Sonata romántica, Mujeres españolas,* etc.); he also wrote operas and incidental music for the theater. In 1930 he was appointed a prof. of music at the Cons. of Madrid.

WORKS: OPERAS: *Margot* (Madrid, Oct. 10, 1914) and *Jardín de oriente* (Madrid, March 6, 1923). INCIDENTAL MUSIC: *Navidad* (Madrid, 1916); *La adúltera penitente* (Barcelona, 1917); *La Anunciación* (Madrid, 1924). ORCH. MUSIC: *La procesión del rocío,* symph. poem (Madrid, March 30, 1913); *Evangelio,* symph. poem (Madrid, April 8, 1915); *3 danzas fantásticas* (1920); *Sinfonía sevillana* (San Sebastian, Sept. 11, 1920); *Rítmos,* choreographic fantasy (Barcelona, Oct. 25, 1928); *Rapsodia sinfónica* for Piano and String Orch. (Madrid, March 11, 1933). CHAMBER MUSIC: Piano Quintet (1907); String Quartet (1911); *Escena andaluza* for Viola, String Quartet, and Piano (1912); *La oración del torero* for String Quartet (1925); 2 piano trios (1926, 1933); 2 violin sonatas (1929, 1934); Piano Quartet (1931); *Serenata* for String Quartet (1935); *Círculo* for Violin, Cello, and Piano (1936); *Las nueve Musas* (9 pieces for Various Instruments; 1945). PIANO MUSIC: *Sevilla, suite pintoresca* (1909); *Sonata romántica* (1909); *Coins de Séville,* suite (1911); *3 danzas andaluzas* (1912); *Album de viaje* (1916); *Mujeres españolas* (2 sets; 1917, 1932); *Cuentos de España,* 2 sets of 7 pieces each (1918, 1928); *Niñerías,* 2 sets of children's pieces (1919, 1931); *Sanlúcar de Barrameda* (1922); *El Cristo de la Calavera* (1924); *Jardines de Andalucía,* suite (1924); *La venta de los gatos* (1925); *El Barrio de Santa Cruz* (1925); *La leyenda de la Giralda,* suite (1927); *2 danzas sobre temas populares españoles* (1927); *Verbena madrileña,* 5 pieces (1927); *Mallorca,* suite (1928); *Evocaciones,* 3 pieces (1929); *Recuerdos de la antigua España,* 4 pieces (1929); *Viaje marítimo,* suite (1930); *Ciclo pianístico: Tocata y fuga, Partita, Pieza romántica, El castillo de Almodóvar* (1930–31); *Miniaturas,* 8 pieces (1930); *Danzas gitanas,* 2 sets of 5 pieces each (1930, 1934); *Tarjetas postales* (1931); *Sonata fantasía* (1930); *Radio Madrid,* suite (1931); *Jardín de niños,* 8 pieces (1931); *El circo,* 6 pieces (1932); *Silhuetas,* 5 pieces (1932); *En la zapatería,* 7 pieces (1933); *Fantasía italiana* (1933); *Trilogía: El poema infinito* (1933); *Ofrenda* (1934); *Hipócrates* (1934); *Rincones de Sanlúcar* (1933); *Bailete, suite de danzas del siglo XIX* (1933); *Preludios* (1933); *Fantasía sobre cinco notas* (1934); *Concierto sin orquesta* (1935); *En el cortijo,* 4 pieces (1936–40); *Prelude* for Organ (1914); *Musette* for Organ (1915). GUITAR MUSIC: *Sevillana* (1923); *Fandanguillo* (1926); *Ráfaga* (1930); *Sonata* (1932); *Homenaje a Tárrega,* 2 pieces (1935). SONGS: *Rima* (1911); *Poema en forma de canciones* (1918); 3 arias (1923); *Canto a Sevilla,* cycle (1927); *2 canciones* (1927); *Corazón de mujer* (1927); *Tríptico* (1929); *3 sonetos* (1930); *3 poemas* (1933); *Homenaje a Lope de Vega* (1935).

WRITINGS: *Enciclopedia abreviada de la música* (Madrid, 1917).

BIBLIOGRAPHY: C. Bosch, *Impresiones estéticas* (Madrid, 1918); H. Collet, *L'Essor de la musique espagnole au XXᵉ siècle* (Paris, 1929); A. Salazar, *La música contemporánea en España* (Madrid, 1930); F. Sopeña, *Joaquín Turina* (Madrid, 1943; 2nd ed., revised, 1956); W. Dean, "Joaquín Turina," *Chesterian* (April 1949); L. Powell, *The Piano Music of Joaquín Turina* (Diss., Univ. of North Carolina, 1974).

Turini, Ronald, Canadian pianist; b. Montreal, Sept. 30, 1934. He studied at the Quebec Cons.; subsequently took private lesseons with Isabelle Vengerova and Vladimir Horowitz. He toured Europe as a soloist with the Montreal Symph. Orch. in 1962; also gave recitals in the major music centers.

Türk, Daniel Gottlob, German organist and teacher; b. Clausnitz, Saxony, Aug. 10, 1756; d. Halle, Aug. 26, 1813. He was a pupil in harmony and counterpoint of Homilius while studying at the Kreuzschule in Dresden; he had learned to play the violin at home and after he entered Leipzig Univ. J.A. Hiller continued his instruction, and engaged him as violinist at the theater and the Grosses Concert. In 1776 he was cantor of the Ulrichskirche, Halle, and music teacher at the Gymnasium; in 1779, he became music director of the Univ.; on becoming organist at the Liebfrauenkirche in 1787, he resigned his positions as cantor and teacher. He publ. an important clavier method (1789; 2nd ed., 1802) and instructive pieces for piano; 18 sonatas and sonatinas for piano; songs; theoretical works. An opera, church music, symphs., and organ pieces are in MS. Some piano pieces for 4-hands were edited by Doflein (1933).

BIBLIOGRAPHY: H. Glenewinkel, *D.G. T.* (Diss., Univ. of Halle, 1909); G.E. Hedler, *D.G. T.* (Diss., Univ. of Leipzig, 1936); *Daniel Gottlob Türk,* Festschrift publ. on the 125th anniversary of his death (Halle, 1938).

Turle, James, English organist and composer; b. Somerton, Somerset, March 5, 1802; d. London, June 28, 1882. He was assistant organist to Greatorex at Westminster Abbey till 1831; then succeeded him as organist and master of the choristers, resigning in 1875. He conducted the Antient Concerts, 1840–43; was music master at the School for the Indigent Blind, 1829–56. He composed services, anthems, chants, and hymn tunes; edited several collections of church music (e.g., *The Westminster Abbey Chant Book,* with Dr. Bridge).

Turner, Alfred Dudley, American pianist and composer; b. St. Albans, Maine, Aug. 24, 1854; d. there, May 7, 1888. He studied at the New England Cons. of Music in Boston, and later was on its faculty. He publ. a *Sonate dramatique* for Piano, and various other perishable piano pieces; also 2 violin sonatas and the useless *3 morceaux* for Cello and Piano.

Turner, Charles, American composer; b. Baltimore, Nov. 25, 1921. He studied composition with Samuel Barber; later took courses with Nadia Boulanger. He served as a naval officer during World War II; played concerts in Europe; in 1954 received a fellowship awarded by the Italian government, and took up residence in Rome. Among his works are the ballet *Pastorale* (N.Y., Jan. 14, 1957); *The Marriage of Orpheus* for Orch. (1965); chamber music.

Turner, Godfrey, English composer; b. Manchester, March 27, 1913; d. (suicide) N.Y., Dec. 7, 1948. He studied with E.J. Dent at Cambridge Univ. (musicology) and with Nadia Boulanger in Paris. He came to the U.S. in 1936; taught at the San Francisco Cons. (1938–43); was music editor for Boosey & Hawkes, N.Y. (1944–46); then secretary of the American Music Center, N.Y. (1946–48).
WORKS: *Trinity Concerto* for Chamber Orch.; Viola Concerto; *Sonata concertante* for Piano and String Orch.; *Fanfare, Chorale and Finale* for Brass; *Saraband and Tango; Gregorian Overture* (Columbus, Ohio, Dec. 2, 1947; winner of the Broadcast Music, Inc., contest).

Turner, Ike, American soul-rock musician; b. Clarksdale, Miss., Nov. 5, 1931. He played piano and guitar as a child; while still in school he formed a group called The Rhythm Kings and in 1951 recorded with a vocalist the rhythm-and-blues number *Rocket 88,* with the allusion to the 88 keys of the piano keyboard; the record was one of the first in the rock'n'roll manner. In 1954 he went to St. Louis, where he started a revue; there he met Tina Bullock of Tennessee, and married her in 1958. They scored several hits and expanded their activities by recruiting a female trio known as The Ikettes. Among their hits were *River Deep—Mountain High, Proud Mary, Souled Out,* and *Feel Good.* Their marriage lasted until 1977.

Turner, Joe, black American jazz pianist; b. Baltimore, Nov. 3, 1907. As a child, he studied piano with his mother; later took lessons with Frank Johnson and cultivated a method that became known as "stride" pianism. He worked with several bands, including those of Benny Carter and Louis Armstrong.

Turner, Joseph Vernon ("Big Joe"), black American blues singer; b. Kansas City, Mo., May 18, 1911. He first worked as a singing bartender in local nightclubs; then became associated with the pianist Pete Johnson; in 1938 they appeared at Carnegie Hall in N.Y. After moving to California, he sang with Duke Ellington's band; in 1945 he and Pete Johnson began appearing at their own club in Los Angeles; he later made tours in the U.S. and Europe.

Turner, Robert Comrie, Canadian composer; b. Montreal, June 6, 1920. He studied with Champagne at McGill Univ. in Montreal, graduating in 1943; with Herbert Howells and Gordon Jacob at the Royal College of Music in London (1947–48), with Messiaen at the Berkshire Music Center in Tanglewood, Mass. (summer 1949), and with Roy Harris at Nashville (1949–50); received his Mus.Doc. degree from McGill Univ. in 1953. From 1952 to 1967 he was a music producer for the Canadian Broadcasting Corp. in Vancouver; taught at the Univ. of British Columbia (1955–57) and at Acadia Univ. in Wolfville, Nova Scotia (1968–69); in 1969 was appointed to the music faculty of the Univ. of Manitoba.
WORKS: Opera, *The Brideship* (Vancouver, Dec. 12, 1967); *Canzona* for Orch. (1950); Concerto for Chamber Orch. (1950); *Sinfonia* for Small Orch. (1953); *Opening Night,* overture (1955); *Lyric Interlude* for Orch. (1956); *A Children's Overture* (1958); *The Pemberton Valley,* suite for Orch. from a film score (1958); Symph. for String Orch. (Montreal, March 27, 1961); *3 Episodes* for Orch. (Toronto, Feb. 27, 1966); 2-piano Concerto (1971); *Eidolons,* 12 images for Chamber Orch. (Vancouver, Sept. 12, 1972); Chamber Concerto for Bassoon and 17 Instruments (1973); *Capriccio concertante* for Cello, Piano, and Orch. (1975); *From a Different Country (Homage to Gabrieli)* for Solo Brass Quintet and Chamber Orch. (1976); 3 string quartets (1949, 1954, 1975); Oboe Sonatina (1956); *Robbins Round,* concertino for Jazz Band (1959); *Variations and Toccata* for Wind and String Quintets (1959); *Mobile* for Chorus and 7 Percussionists (1960); *Serenade* for Wind Quintet (1960); *4 Fragments* for Brass Quintet (1961); *Fantasia* for Organ, Brass Quintet, and Timpani (1962); *The Phoenix and the Turtle* for Mezzo-soprano and 8 Instruments (Vancouver, Aug. 23, 1964); *Suite in Homage to Melville* for Soprano, Alto, and Piano (1966); *Diversities* for Violin, Bassoon, and Piano (1967); Piano Trio (1969); *Nostalgia* for Saxophone and Piano (1972); *Sonata lyrica* for Piano (1955, revised 1963); *Nocturne* for Piano (1956; orchestrated 1965); *6 Voluntaries* for Organ (1959).

Turner, Tina, seeded American songstress and soul thrush; b. Brownsville, Tenn., Nov. 26, 1938, as Annie Mae "Tina" Bullock. She joined Ike Turner's revue in Knoxville, and married him in 1958. Together, they produced a mingled squash of Midwestern blues seasoned with raunchy sex, and toured the "chitlin" circuit. They produced such albums as *The Soul of Ike and Tina Turner* and *The Gospel According to Ike and Tina Turner* to signalize their return to cleanliness and godliness. In 1969, they toured with The Rolling Stones, gaining popular exposure that led to the money temples of Las Vegas and the sultry cabarets of San Francisco. Tina Turner also performed the part of the Acid Queen in Ken Russell's gaudy psychedelic version of The Who's *Tommy.* Gradually, she became distanced from Ike, and they were divorced in 1977.

Turner, Walter James, English poet and writer on music; b. Shanghai, China, Oct. 13, 1889; d. London,

Nov. 18, 1946. He studied with his father (who was organist of St. Paul's Cathedral, Melbourne, Australia) and privately in Dresden, Munich, and Vienna. He settled in London, where he became music critic for the *New Statesman.*

WRITINGS: *Music and Life* (1922); *Variations on the Theme of Music* (1924); *Orpheus, or The Music of the Future* (1926); *Beethoven: The Search for Reality* (1927; new ed., 1933); *Musical Meanderings* (1928); *Music: A Short History* (1932; 2nd ed., 1949); *Facing the Music* (1933); *Wagner* (1933); *Berlioz: The Man and His Work* (1934); *Music: An Introduction to Its Nature and Appreciation* (1936); *Mozart: The Man and His Work* (1938); *English Music* (1941); *English Ballet* (1944).

Turner, William, English composer; b. Oxford, 1651; d. London, Jan. 13, 1740. He was a chorister at Christ Church, Oxford, under E. Lowe, and later at the Chapel Royal under H. Cooke; in 1669 he was made a Gentleman of the Chapel Royal; received the degree of Mus.Doc. from Cambridge Univ. in 1696. He composed church music, anthems, songs, and catches.

Turnhout, Gérard de (real name, **Gheert Jacques**), Netherlandish composer; b. Turnhout, c.1520; d. Madrid, Sept. 15, 1580. In 1545, he was a choir singer at Antwerp Cathedral; was appointed Kapellmeister there in 1563; in 1572, Philip II of Spain called him to Madrid as maestro of the Royal Chapel. He publ. a book of motets a 4–5 (1568), a book of motets and chansons a 4–6 (1569), and a Mass in *Praestantissimorum divinae musices auctorum Missae X* (1570). His son **Jean de Turnhout** was Kapellmeister to the Archduke Alexander Farnese, governor of the Netherlands, at Brussels from 1586; from 1611, he served as Kapellmeister of the Royal Chapel there. He publ. 2 books of madrigals and one of motets. L. Wagner edited *Gérard de Turnhout, Sacred and Secular Songs for Three Voices* (Madison, Wis., 1970).

Turnovský, Martin, Czech conductor; b. Prague, Sept. 29, 1928. He studied conducting with Karel Ančerl at the Prague Academy of Music, and later with Szell. In 1958 he won first prize at the Besançon competition; then became chief conductor of the Brno Phil. Orch. (1959–63). He subsequently served as Generalmusikdirektor of the Dresden State Opera and Orch. (1966–68). After the period of political turmoil in Czechoslovakia in 1968, he went to Vienna; in 1975–80 he served as music director of the Norwegian Opera in Oslo; in 1979 became chief conductor of the City Theater in Bonn; also shared the chief conductorship of the Beethoven Hall Orch. there with Jan Krenz. In 1968 he made his American debut as guest conductor with the Cleveland Orch.

Turok, Paul, American composer; b. New York, Dec. 3, 1929. He studied composition at Queens College with Karol Rathaus (B.A., 1950); then at the Univ. of Calif., Berkeley, with Roger Sessions (M.A., 1951) and at the Juilliard School of Music with Bernard Wagenaar (1951–53). He subsequently held several teaching posts, among them at the City College of N.Y. (1959–63) and at Williams College (1963–64). As a composer, he follows the principle of stylistic freedom and technical precision, without doctrinaire adherence to any circumscribed modernistic modus operandi.

WORKS: *Richard III,* opera (1975); *Scene: Domestic,* chamber opera (Aspen, Colo., Aug. 2, 1973); *Youngest Brother,* ballet (N.Y., Jan. 23, 1953); for Orch.: Violin Concerto (1953); *Symphony in 2 Movements* (1955); *Lyric Variations* for Oboe and Strings (Louisville, March 9, 1973); *Scott Joplin Overture* (Cleveland, June 19, 1973); *Sousa Overture* (Philadelphia, May 13, 1976); *Ragtime Caprice* for Piano and Orch. (1976); chamber music: *Variations on a Theme by Schoenberg* for String Quartet (1952); 3 string quartets (1956–70); String Trio (1974); Wind Quintet (1960); Brass Quintet (1971); Clarinet Trio (1974); sonatas for unaccompanied viola (1975); solo pieces for cello, oboe, bassoon, horn, trumpet, trombone; music for 9 horns; music for 5 horns; a piece for violin and percussion; vocal works; 3 songs for soprano and flute; *Chorus of the Frogs; Transcendental Etudes,* and other works for piano.

Turpin, Edmund Hart, English organist and composer; b. Nottingham, May 4, 1835; d. London, Oct. 25, 1907. He was a pupil of Hullah and Pauer in London, where he settled in 1857; he served as organist of various churches; publ. a collection for organ, *Student's Edition of Classical Authors;* wrote the oratorios *St. John the Baptist* and *Hezekiah;* hymn tunes; many works for organ. He was editor of the *Musical Standard* (from 1880) and for a time also of the *Musical World.*

BIBLIOGRAPHY: C.W. Pearce, *A Biographical Sketch of E.H. Turpin* (London, 1911).

Turski, Zbigniew, Polish composer; b. Konstancin, near Warsaw, July 28, 1908; d. Warsaw, Jan. 7, 1979. He studied composition with Rytel at the State Cons. in Warsaw; was music producer of Polish Radio (1936–39); after World War II he conducted the Baltic Phil. in Gdansk (1945–46); in 1957 established himself in Warsaw. He writes in an advanced harmonic idiom, influenced by French modernism. All of his early music MSS were lost during World War II.

WORKS: Micro-opera, *Causettes* (*Chats,* 1966; Warsaw, 1967); ballet, *Medalion Gdański* (1964); *Sinfonia da camera* (1947); Symph. No. 2, *Sinfonia Olimpica* (1948; awarded a prize by the music jury of the 14th Olympiad, London); 2 violin concertos (1951, 1959); Symph. No. 3 (1953); *Little Overture* (1955); 2 cantatas, *Ziemia* (1952) and *Vistula River* (1953); *L'Ombre (Shade),* nocturne for Tenor, Chorus, and Percussion (1967); *Canti de nativitate patriae* for Tenor, Bass, Chorus, and Orch. (1969); *Regno Ejukori,* triptych for Bass and Orch. (Wroclaw, Sept. 2, 1974); String Quartet No. 2 (1951); miscellaneous piano pieces; songs; music for the theater, films, and radio.

Tusler, Robert Leon, American musicologist; b. Stoughton, Wis., April 1, 1920. He studied piano and organ at Friends' Univ., Wichita, Kans. (B.M., 1947); musicology at the Univ. of Calif., Los Angeles (M.A., 1952); then at the Univ. of Utrecht, the Netherlands (1956–58). In 1958 he joined the music faculty of the Univ. of Calif., Los Angeles; retired in 1983. He wrote *The Style of J.S. Bach's Chorale Preludes* (Berkeley, Calif., 1956); *The Organ Music of Jan Pieterszoon Sweelinck* (Bilthoven, 1958).

Tuthill, Burnet Corwin, American composer and conductor; b. New York, Nov. 16, 1888; d. Knoxville, Tenn., Jan. 18, 1982. His father, William Burnet Tuthill, was the architect of Carnegie Hall. He studied at Columbia Univ. (M.A., 1910); conducted the Columbia Univ. Orch. (1909–13). In 1919 he organized the Society for Publication of American Music, which continued to function for nearly half a century, and which publ. about 85 works by American composers. He then devoted himself to administrative jobs in music; was executive secretary of the National Assoc. of Schools of Music in Cincinnati (1924–59); concurrently he served as director of music at Southwestern College in Memphis. He began to compose rather late in life, but compensated for this delay by increasing productivity in the subsequent years.
WORKS: *Bethlehem,* pastorale for Orch. (Interlochen, Mich., July 22, 1934); *Laurentia,* symph. poem (Rochester, N.Y., Oct. 30, 1936); *Come 7,* rhapsody for Orch. (1935; St. Louis, Feb. 19, 1944); several instrumental concertos: for Clarinet (1949); for Double Bass (1962); for Saxophone (1965); for Trombone (1967); for Tuba (1975); numerous pieces with a multiplicity of clarinets; Flute Sonata; Oboe Sonata; Trumpet Sonata; Saxophone Sonata; a plethora of sacred choruses.

Tuukkanen, Kalervo, Finnish conductor and composer; b. Mikkeli, Oct. 14, 1909; d. Helsinki, July 12, 1979. He studied composition with Leevi Madetoja and with Krohn in Helsinki; subsequently conducted local orchs. and choirs; in 1967–69 was a visiting prof. of music at the Chinese Univ. of Hong Kong. He wrote 6 symphs. (1944, 1949, 1952, 1958, 1961, 1978); 2 violin concertos (1943, 1956); a Cello Concerto (1946); a Sinfonietta (1948); *Man and the Elements* for Soprano, Chorus, and Orch. (1949); an opera, *Indumati* (1962); *Youth Cantata* (1963); and *A Chorale Echo* for Flute and Piano (1967). He also publ. a monograph on the life and works of his teacher Leevi Madetoja (Helsinki, 1947).

Tuxen, Erik, German-Danish conductor; b. Mannheim (of Danish parents) July 4, 1902; d. Copenhagen, Aug. 28, 1957. In 1916 he moved to Denmark; studied architecture and music in Copenhagen; conducted the Danish State Radio Orch. (1936–41); made guest appearances in the U.S. (1950–51), presenting a concert of Scandinavian music at Carnegie Hall (April 2, 1951); in the summer of 1954 he conducted in South America.

Tveitt, Geirr, Norwegian composer and pianist; b. Hardanger, Oct. 19, 1908; d. Oslo, Feb. 1, 1981. He studied in Leipzig, Vienna, and Paris, where he took private lessons with Florent Schmitt and Honegger. He toured Europe as a pianist; upon his return to Norway he was given a life pension by the government that enabled him to carry on his work. He made a profound study of Norwegian folk instruments, which he employed in his own compositions.
WORKS: 5 operas: *Nordvest—Sud—Nordaust—Nord* (1939); *Dragaredokko* (1940); *Roald Amundsen; Stevleik,* chamber opera; *Jeppe* (1964; Bergen, June 10, 1966; revised 1968); 3 ballets: *Baldurs draumar (Dreams of Baldur;* Berlin, 1935); *Birgingu* (Oslo, 1939); *Husguden (The Household Deity;* Bergen, 1956); 6 piano concertos: No. 1 (1930); No. 2 (Vienna, 1933); No. 3, *Hommage à Brahms* (Bergen, 1947); No. 4, *Northern Lights* (Paris, 1947); No. 5 (Paris, 1954); No. 6 (1960); Concerto for String Quartet and Orch. (Oslo, 1933); *Variations* for 2 Pianos and Orch. (Oslo, 1937); *8 Dances* for Orch. (Paris, 1939); Violin Concerto (Oslo, 1939); 2 harp concertos; 2 concertos for Hardanger Fiddle (Bergen, 1956; Brussels, 1965; the only concertos written for this, the Norwegian national instrument); *100 Folk Tunes from Hardanger,* originally for Piano, then arranged in 5 orch. suites; 4 symphs.; *Skaldaspillirs kvad: Håkonarmål* for Soloists, Chorus, and Orch. (Bergen, 1962); incidental music to the play *Jonsoknatt,* for Small Orch. (Oslo, 1936); Quartet for 4 Violins (Oslo, 1935); 2 string quartets; 3 string sextets (No. 3, Oslo, 1934); *8 Arabian Melodies* for Flute, Celesta, and Percussion (Oslo, 1962); fully 29 piano sonatas. He publ. *Tonalitätstheorie des parallelen Leittonsystems* (Oslo, 1937; traces the origin of church modes back to old Norwegian scale forms).

Twardowski, Romuald, Polish composer; b. Vilna, June 17, 1930. He studied composition and piano in Vilna (1952–57), and with Woytowicz at the State College of Music in Warsaw (1957–60); studied medieval polyphony with Nadia Boulanger in Paris (1963).
WORKS: 3 operas: *Cyrano de Bergerac* (1962; Bytom, 1963); a "morality," *Tragedyja albo rzecz o Janie i Herodzie (Tragedy, or Story of John and Herod,* 1965; Lodz, 1969); *Lord Jim,* after Joseph Conrad (1972–73); radio opera, *Upadek ojca Suryna (The Fall of Father Surin,* 1968; scenic version, Cracow, 1969); 2 ballets: *The Naked Prince* (1960; Warsaw, 1964) and *The Magician's Statues* (1963; Wroclaw, 1971); *3 Sketches* for Strings (1955); Piano Concerto (1956); Concerto for Orch. (1957); *Suita w dawnym stylu (Suite in Old Style)* for Orch. (1957); *Mala symfonia koncertująca (Little Symphony Concertante)* for Piano, Strings, and Percussion (1958); *Antifone* for 3 Orch. Groups (1961); *Nomopedia,* 5 movements for Orch. (1962); *Ode 64* for Orch. (1964); *The St. Mary Triptych,* 3 scenes and dances for String Orch. (1973); *Prelude, Toccata and Chorale* for Orch. (1973); *Study in A* for Orch. (1974; Warsaw, Sept. 21, 1976); *2 Landscapes* for Orch. (1975); cantata, *Pieśń o Białym Domu (Song about the White House)* for Tenor, Chorus, 2 Pianos, and

Percussion (1959); *Cantus antiqui* for Soprano, Harpsichord, Piano, and Percussion (1962); *Trittico fiorentino: I, 3 studi secondo Giotto* for Chamber Orch. (1966), *II, Sonetti di Petrarca* for Tenor Solo and 2 Choruses a cappella (1965), and *III, Impressioni fiorentini* for 4 Instrumental Choruses (1967); *Mala liturgia prawoslawna (Little Orthodox Liturgy)* for Vocal Ensemble and 3 Instrumental Groups (1969); *Oda do mlodości (Ode to Youth)* for Narrator, Chorus, and Orch. (1969); *3 sonnets d'adieux* for Bass-baritone, Piano, Strings, and Percussion (1971); *Polish Landscape*, 3 songs for Bass-baritone and Orch. (1975); *Little Sonata* for Piano (1958); *Toccata* for 2 Pianos (1974); *Improvisations and Toccata* for 2 Pianos (1974).

Tweedy, Donald, American composer; b. Danbury, Conn., April 23, 1890; d. there, July 21, 1948. He was educated at Harvard Univ. (B.A., 1912; M.A., 1917), where his teachers were Walter Spalding and E.B. Hill. He taught at Vassar College (1914–16), the Eastman School of Music (1923–27), Hamilton College (1937–38), and Texas Christian Univ. (1945–46). He publ. a *Manual of Harmonic Technic Based on the Practice of J.S. Bach* (1928).
WORKS: Ballet, *Alice in Wonderland* (1935); *L'Allegro*, symph. study (Rochester, May 1, 1925); *3 Dances* for Orch. (1925); *Williamsburg*, suite for Orch. (1941); Viola Sonata (1916); Violin Sonata (1920); Cello Sonata (1930); piano pieces.

Twitty, Conway (real name, **Harold Jenkins**), American rock and country–music entertainer; b. Friars Point, Miss., Sept. 1, 1933. After completing his army service, he launched his career as a rock musician, appearing with his own group in nightclubs. By 1958 he attained a high position on the blues, rock, and country charts, and maintained his high scoring with a succession of hits.

Tye, Christopher, English organist and composer; b. c.1500; d. c.1572. In 1536 he received his Mus.B. from Cambridge; on Sept. 10, 1541, he was appointed organist of Ely Cathedral (resigned in 1561); became magister choristarum there in 1543; Mus. Doc. at Cambridge in 1545; was ordained a priest in 1560 at Doddington. He described himself as a gentleman of the King's Chapel on the title page of his only publ. work, *The Actes of the Apostles, translated into Englyshe metre to synge and also to play upon the Lute* (London, 1553; it includes the first 14 chapters of the Acts). The hymn tunes *Windsor* and *Winchester Old* are adaptations from this collection. Tye was an important composer of English church music; he left masses, services, motets, and anthems. The *Euge Bone* mass was edited by Arkwright in *The Old English Edition* (no. 10); other examples are found in *The Oxford History of Music* (vol. II) and in Walker's *History of Music in England.* The following editions of his works have been publ.: R. Weidner, *Christopher Tye: The Instrumental Music* (New Haven, Conn., 1967); J. Satterfield, *Christopher Tye: The Latin Church Music* (Madison, Wis., 1972); J. Morehen, *Christopher Tye:*

The English Sacred Music in *Early English Church Music,* XIX (1977).
BIBLIOGRAPHY: G. Reese, *Music in the Renaissance* (N.Y., 1954; 2nd ed., revised, 1959); R. Weidner, "The Instrumental Music of Christopher Tye," *Journal of the American Musicological Society,* XVII (1964); J. Langdon, "Tye and His Church Music," *Musical Times,* CXIII (1972); N. Davison, "Tye's Mass 'Euge bone,'" *Musical Times* (Nov. 1980).

Tyes, John, English organist and composer who flourished early in the 15th century. A Gloria for 2 Voices and One Instrument and a Sanctus for 4 Voices are among the works included in the *Old Hall Manuscripts.*

Tyler, James, American lutenist, and cittern and viol player; b. Hartford, Conn., Aug. 3, 1940. He studied at the Hartt School of Music in Hartford; also took lessons with Joseph Ladone. He made his debut in 1962 with the N.Y. Pro Musica; later went to Germany, where he specialized in performances on early Renaissance instruments; was a member of the Studio der frühen Musik in Munich. He went to England in 1969, where he joined the Early Music Consort of London and Musica Reservata; also served as co-director of the Consort of Musicke with Anthony Rooley. In 1974 he became a member of the Julian Bream Consort. In 1976 he organized The London Early Music Group, devoted principally to performing works of the 16th and 17th centuries. A versatile musician, he also gave concerts of ragtime music with his own quintet, the New Excelsior Speaking Machine. He wrote *The Early Guitar* (London, 1980).

Tyndall, John, eminent physicist and acoustician; b. Leighlin Bridge, Ireland, Aug. 2, 1820; d. Hindhead, Surrey, England, Dec. 4, 1893. His 2 works in the domain of acoustics are *Sound* (1867; many subsequent eds.), a lucid and scholarly explanation of acoustical phenomena, and *On the Transmission of Sound by the Atmosphere* (1874). He was a prof. of natural philosophy at the Royal Inst. from 1853.
BIBLIOGRAPHY: *Dictionary of National Biography* (vol. 19, pp. 1358–63).

Tyner, (Alfred) McCoy, American jazz pianist and composer; b. Philadelphia, Dec. 11, 1938. He studied piano; in 1961 he joined John Coltrane's jazz group; in 1966 he formed his own trio, with which he toured in the U.S., in Europe, and in Japan.

Typp, W., English singer and composer who was active in the early decades of the 15th century. An Agnus Dei, 2 Credos, and 4 Sanctus settings by him are found among the *Old Hall Manuscripts.*

Tyrwhitt, Gerald. See **Berners, Lord.**

Tyson, Alan, English musicologist; b. Glasgow, Oct. 27, 1926. He was educated at Magdalen College,

Oxford; later joined its faculty (1947–51); in 1952 was elected a fellow of All Souls College, Oxford; in 1971 became a senior research fellow there. He has made extensive textual and bibliographical studies of the period 1770–1850; particularly noteworthy are his contributions to the study of Beethoven.

WRITINGS: *The Authentic English Editions of Beethoven* (London, 1963); with O. Neighbour, *English Music Publishers' Plate Numbers in the First Half of the Nineteenth Century* (London, 1965); *Thematic Catalogue of the Works of Muzio Clementi* (Tutzing, 1967); ed., *Beethoven Studies* (N.Y., 1974), *Beethoven Studies 2* (London, 1977), *Beethoven Studies 3* (London, 1982).

Tzarth (Czarth, Zarth), Georg, Bohemian violinist; b. April 8, 1708; d. probably in Mannheim, 1778. He was a friend of Franz Benda, whom he accompanied to Warsaw; in 1734 he entered the chapel of Crown Prince Frederick at Rheinsberg; in 1758 joined the court orch. at Mannheim. He wrote symphs., concertos, string trios, violin sonatas, etc., in the "Mannheim School" style; examples of his works, ed. by Riemann, are in Denkmäler der Tonkunst in Bayern, 27/28 (15/16).

Tzipine, Georges, French conductor; b. Paris, June 22, 1907. He studied violin at the Paris Cons.; also took courses in harmony, counterpoint, and conducting; was then active as a conductor for the Paris Radio; then served as music director of the Cannes Casino (1945–49); also conducted in Australia. In 1966 he joined the faculty of the Paris Cons.

Tzvetanov, Tzvetan, Bulgarian composer; b. Sofia, Nov. 6, 1931. He studied composition with Khadjiev and Vladigerov at the Bulgarian State Cons. in Sofia, graduating in 1956; then joined its faculty. His works include a Sinfonietta (1956); ballet, *Orpheus and Rhodopa* (1960); *The Great Beginning,* symph. poem (1962); 4 symphs.: No. 1 (1964); No. 2 for Strings, Piano, Harp, Xylophone, Vibraphone, Kettledrums, and Triangle (1968); No. 3, *1923* (1972; Sofia, Feb. 27, 1973); No. 4 (1975); *The Ladder,* ballad for Solo Alto, Male Chorus, and Orch. (1965); Concertino for Piano and Chamber Orch. (1971); *Festive Concerto* (1974); Violin Sonata (1954); *Variations for String Quartet.*

Tzybin, Vladimir, Russian flutist and composer; b. Ivanovo-Voznesensk, 1877; d. Moscow, May 31, 1949. He played the flute in the orch. of the Bolshoi Theater in Moscow from 1896 to 1907 and from 1921 to 1929. From 1907 to 1920 he was first flutist at the Imperial Opera of St. Petersburg. He composed 2 operas: *Flengo* (1918) and *Tale of the Dead Princess and 7 Heroes* (1947); publ. several collections of flute pieces. He was esteemed as a pedagogue.

U

Uber, Christian Friedrich Hermann, German composer; b. Breslau, April 22, 1781; d. Dresden, March 2, 1822. He was a law student at Halle, but also studied music under Türk, and became chamber musician to Prince Louis Ferdinand of Prussia. After holding various positions as violinist and conductor, he settled in Dresden. He wrote the operas *Der falsche Werber* (Kassel, 1808) and *Der frohe Tag* (Mainz, 1815); incidental music to various plays; some violin works; songs to texts in German and French.

Uberti (Hubert), Antonio, male soprano; b. (of German parents) Verona, 1697; d. Berlin, Jan. 20, 1783. He was one of the most brilliant pupils of Porpora, and was known as "il Porporino" (little Porpora). In 1741 he entered the service of Frederick the Great in Berlin. He was greatly renowned in Germany for his singing of Italian operas.

Uccellini, Marco, Italian composer; b. Forlimpopoli, c.1603; d. there, Sept. 10, 1680. He became head of instrumental music at the Este court of Modena in 1641, and was maestro di cappella at the Cathedral there in 1647–65. He was then at the Farnese court in Parma as maestro di cappella until his death. From 1639 to 1667 he publ. a variety of chamber music (sonatas, arias, canzonas, etc.); his advanced violin technique calls for use of the 6th position. He also wrote an opera, *Li eventi di Filandro ed Edessa,* which was presented in Parma in 1675 (the music is not extant); 2 ballet pieces: *Le navi d'Enea* (1673) and *Il Giove d'Elide fulminato* (1677). Riemann publ. a sonata by Uccellini in *Alte Kammermusik;* some pieces were publ. by Wasielewski; others by Torchi in *L'arte musicale in Italia* (vol. VII).

Udbye, Martin Andreas, Norwegian composer; b. Trondheim, June 18, 1820; d. there, Jan. 10, 1889. He studied in Leipzig with Hauptmann; returning to Trondheim, he was organist at various churches. He wrote 2 operettas, *Hjemvé* (Oslo, April 8, 1864) and *Junkeren og Flubergrosen* (Oslo, Jan. 7, 1870); several cantatas; 3 string quartets; military marches; organ pieces; piano works; songs.

d'Udine, Jean (real name, **Albert Cozanet**), French writer on music; b. Landivisiau, Finistère, July 1, 1870; d. Paris, May 9, 1938. He was a practicing lawyer, but also wrote music criticism. In 1909 he founded in Paris the Ecole Française de Gymnastique Rythmique for teaching the methods of Jaques-Dalcroze.

WRITINGS: *La Corrélation des sons et des couleurs en art* (1897); *Lettres paradoxales sur la musique* (Paris, 1900); *L'Orchestration des couleurs* (1903); *Paraphrases musicales* (Paris, 1904); *Gluck* (1906); *L'Art et le geste* (1912); *Les Transmutations rythmiques* (1921); *Qu'est-ce que la musique?* (1925); *Traité de géométrie rythmique* (1926). He also wrote songs: *Les Chants de la jungle* (1905), *Rondels pour après* (1924), etc.

Ugalde, Delphine (née **Beaucé**), French soprano; b. Paris, Dec. 3, 1829; d. there, July 19, 1910. She received her first instruction in singing from her mother, an actress; subsequently studied with Moreau-Sainti; made her debut in Paris in 1848 as Angèle in Auber's *Domino noir;* in 1866 assumed the management of the Bouffes-Parisiens, taking leading roles in Offenbach's operettas; in 1867 she appeared in her own operetta, *La Halte au moulin.* She retired in 1871, and settled down as a successful vocal teacher.

Ugarte, Floro M., Argentine composer; b. Buenos Aires, Sept. 15, 1884; d. there, June 11, 1975. He studied in Buenos Aires, and at the Paris Cons. under Fourdrain, with whom he collaborated in writing the ballet *Sigolene.* He returned to Argentina in 1913; in 1924 became a prof. at the National Cons. there; was also for several years music director of the Teatro Colón; in that capacity he visited N.Y. in 1940, to engage singers.
WORKS: Operatic fairy tale, *Saika* (Buenos Aires, July 21, 1920); *Entre las montañas,* symph. suite (conducted in Buenos Aires by Richard Strauss in 1923 during his guest appearances there); *La rebelión del agua,* symph. poem (Buenos Aires, Oct. 16, 1935); *De mi tierra,* symph. suite (1927); *Piri,* choreographic poem (1944); Symph. in A (1946; Buenos Aires, May 13, 1952); *Tango* for Orch. (Buenos Aires, Sept. 5, 1951); Violin Concerto (1963); chamber music; songs; piano pieces.

Ugolini, Vincenzo, Italian composer; b. Perugia, c.1570; d. Rome, May 6, 1638. He was a pupil of G.B. Nanino from 1592 to 1594 at the choir school of S. Luigi dei Francesi, Rome; was a bass there from 1600; from 1603 to 1609 he was choirmaster at the Church of S. Maria Maggiore; from 1610 to 1614, was at the Cathedral of Benevento; then returned to Rome; was director of music to Cardinal Arrigoni; in 1616 became choirmaster of S. Luigi dei Francesi; in 1620 he succeeded Suriano as maestro of the Cappella Giulia of St. Peter's (until 1626); in 1631 he resumed his former post at S. Luigi dei Francesi, retaining it till his death. He was the teacher of Benevoli. A notable representative of Palestrina's school, he publ. 4 books of motets for 1, 2, 3, and 4 Voices with Continuo (1616–19); 2 books of Psalms for 8 Voices (1620); 2 books of masses and motets for 8 and 12 Voices (1623); 1 book of songs and motets *a* 12 (1624); 2 books of madrigals *a* 5 (1615).

Ugolino de Orvieto, Italian musical theorist; b. Forli, c.1380; d. Ferrara, c.1457. He was archpriest at the Cathedral of Ferrara between c.1435 and 1440; remained there until 1448; his treatise *De musica mensurata* (MS) is in the Biblioteca Casanatense in Rome. Publication of his *Declaratio musicae disciplinae* was undertaken by A. Seay in the *Corpus Scriptorum Musicae* (Rome, American Inst. of Musicology), in 3 vols., 1959–62.
BIBLIOGRAPHY: U. Kornmüller, "Die Musiklehre des Ugolino de Orvieto," *Kirchenmusikalisches Jahrbuch* (1895); A. Seay, "Ugolino of Orvieto, Theorist and Composer," *Musica Disciplina,* IX (1955).

Uhde, Hermann, noted German bass-baritone; b. Bremen, July 20, 1914; d. (during a performance) Copenhagen, Oct. 10, 1965. He studied in Bremen; made his debut there in 1936; then sang with the Bavarian State Opera in Munich (1940–43) and with the German Opera at The Hague (1943–44). He subsequently was engaged at Hannover (1947–48), Hamburg (1948–50), Vienna (1950–51), Munich (1951–56), Stuttgart (1956–57), and again in Vienna (1957–61). He made his American debut at the Metropolitan Opera in N.Y. as Telramund in *Lohengrin* on Nov. 18, 1955; was on its roster until 1957, then again in 1958–61 and 1963–64. He was particularly acclaimed for his performances in Wagnerian roles.

Uhl, Alfred, Austrian composer; b. Vienna, June 5, 1909. He was a pupil of Franz Schmidt; was in the Austrian army (1940–43), and was severely wounded. In 1945 he was appointed a teacher of composition at the Vienna Academy of Music. His music is patterned after Classical forms, with particular emphasis on contrapuntal clarity.
WORKS: *Kleines Konzert* for Viola, Clarinet, and Piano (1936; version for Piano Trio, 1972); *Eine vergnügliche Musik* for 8 Wind Instruments (1943); *4 Capriccios* for Orch. (1944); *Konzertante Sinfonie* for Clarinet and Orch. (1944); String Quartet (1945–46); *Sonata graziosa* for Orch. (1947); Concertino for Violin and 22 Wind Instruments (1950); *Gilgamesch,* oratorio (1954–56; revised 1968–69); *Wer einsam ist der hat es gut,* cantata (1960); *Jubiläumsquartett* for Strings (1961); opera, *Der mysteriöse Herr X* (1962–65; Vienna, 1966); *Concerto a ballo* for Orch. (1967); *Festlicher Auftakt* for Chorus, Organ, and Orch. (1970).
BIBLIOGRAPHY: A. Witeschnik, *Alfred Uhl: Eine biographische Studie* (Vienna, 1966).

Uhl, Fritz, Austrian tenor; b. Vienna, April 2, 1928. He studied at the Academy of Music in Vienna. He then sang in Graz (1952–53), Oberhausen (1954–56), and Wuppertal; in 1958 he joined the Bavarian State Opera in Munich; in 1961 became a member of the Vienna State Opera; also made regular appearances at Bayreuth, Salzburg, Covent Garden in London, and the San Francisco Opera. He distinguished himself primarily in Wagnerian roles.

Uhlig, Theodor, German violinist and writer on music; b. Wurzen, near Leipzig, Feb. 15, 1822; d.

Dresden, Jan. 3, 1853. He studied violin with Schneider in Dessau, and in 1841 became a violinist in the Dresden Orch. He was one of the most devoted friends and admirers of Wagner; prepared the vocal score of *Lohengrin;* Wagner's letters to him were publ. in 1888 (Eng. trans., 1890). His death at the age of 30 was lamented. Of his 84 works (symphs., chamber music, theater pieces, etc.) only a Violin Concerto and some piano pieces and songs were publ. His articles are of some importance; they were publ. as *Musikalische Schriften* by L. Frankenstein (Regensburg, 1913).

BIBLIOGRAPHY: M. Ahrend, *Theodor Uhlig, Der früh verstorbene Wagnerianer* (Bayreuth, 1904).

Ujj, Béla, Hungarian composer of operettas; b. Vienna, July 2, 1873; d. there, Feb. 1, 1942. He lost his sight in childhood, but studied music and composed a number of successful operettas which were produced in Vienna. They include the following: *Der Herr Professor* (Dec. 4, 1903); *Kaisermanöver* (March 4, 1905); *Die kleine Prinzessin* (May 5, 1907); *Drei Stunden Leben* (Nov. 1, 1909); *Chanteclee* (Oct. 25, 1910); *Der Türmer von St. Stephan* (Sept. 13, 1912); *Teresita* (June 27, 1914); *Der Müller und sein Kind* (Oct. 30, 1917).

Ulbrich, Maximilian, Austrian composer; b. Vienna, c.1752; d. there, Sept. 14, 1814. He studied with Wagenseil; was a government clerk and pursued music as an avocation. His singspiel *Der blaue Schmetterling* was produced in Vienna on April 2, 1782; he also wrote an oratorio; several symphs.; church music.

Ulfrstad, Marius Moaritz, Norwegian composer; b. Borgund, Sept. 11, 1890; d. Oslo, Oct. 29, 1968. He played organ as a youth; graduated in organ and music theory from the Cons. in Oslo (1910); then studied in Berlin with Humperdinck and others, and with Pizzetti in Florence; also had some informal sessions with Ravel in Paris. Returning to Oslo, he founded his own music school there (1921); was music critic of the *Morgenposten* (1922–40) and the *Aftenposten* (1945–47).

WORKS: Cantatas: *Arnljot Gjelline* (Oslo, 1932); *Eternal Spring* (Oslo, 1932); *Saint Olav* (Oslo, 1933); *The Spark* (Trondheim, 1935); 5 symphs. (1921–44); 2 violin concertos (1923, 1935); Piano Concerto (1935); several suites for Orch., most of them inspired by the geography of Norway, Iceland, and Greenland (*Stavern og Sörlands, Islandia, Arctic, Norvegia, Grönlandia, Svalbardia, Möre og Romsdal, Oslo, Norwegian Middleage,* etc.); some chamber music; incidental music; about 250 choral pieces; nearly 1,000 songs, including arrangements of folk songs.

Ulfung, Ragnar, Norwegian tenor; b. Oslo, Feb. 28, 1927. He studied in Oslo and Milan; began his career in Oslo; then sang in Bergen and Göteborg; in 1958 he joined the Royal Opera in Stockholm. In America, he made appearances in San Francisco and Santa Fe, and also appeared at the Metropolitan Opera in N.Y.

Ullmann, Viktor, Austrian composer; b. Teschen, Jan. 1, 1898; d. in Auschwitz in all probability, Oct. 1944. He studied composition with Schoenberg; then went to Prague. He wrote music in the expressionistic manner, without renouncing latent tonality. His works include the operas *Peer Gynt* and *Der Sturz des Antichrist.* As an homage to Schoenberg, he wrote an orch. work, *5 Variations and Double Fugue,* based on the themes of a Schoenberg *Klavierstück.* After the seizure of Czechoslovakia by the Nazis, he was sent to the concentration camp in Theresienstadt; there he composed a one-act opera, *Der Kaiser von Atlantis,* depicting a tyrannical monarch who outlaws death but later begs for its return to relieve humanity from the horrors of life. The MS was preserved, and the work was performed for the first time in Amsterdam on Dec. 16, 1975.

Ulrich, Homer, American musicologist; b. Chicago, March 27, 1906. He studied bassoon and cello at the Chicago Musical College, and played these instruments in various orchs.; was bassoonist with the Chicago Symph. Orch. (1929–35); received his M.A. at the Univ. of Chicago with the thesis *The Penitential Psalms of Lasso* (1939). He was head of the music dept. of Monticello College (1935–38); then taught at the Univ. of Texas (associate prof., 1939; prof., 1951); also played bassoon with the San Antonio Symph. In 1953 he was appointed head of the music dept. of the Univ. of Maryland; retired in 1972. He publ. *Chamber Music* (a valuable survey; N.Y., 1948; 2nd ed., 1966); *Education of a Concert-Goer* (N.Y., 1949); *Symphonic Music* (N.Y., 1952); *Famous Women Singers* (N.Y., 1953); *Music: A Design for Listening* (N.Y., 1957; 3rd ed., 1970); *A History of Music and Musical Style* (with Paul Pisk; N.Y., 1963); *A Survey of Choral Music* (N.Y., 1973).

Ulrich, Hugo, German composer; b. Oppeln, Silesia, Nov. 26, 1827; d. Berlin, May 23, 1872. After studying in Breslau, he went to Berlin in 1846 and took lessons from Dehn. For a few years he taught at the Stern Cons. (1859–63); otherwise earned his living by working for publishers. He wrote 3 symphs., of which the 2nd, *Symphonie triomphale,* won a prize of 1,500 francs offered by the Brussels Academy in 1853. Other works include a Piano Trio, Cello Sonata, String Quartet, piano pieces, and songs. He made excellent arrangements of Beethoven's symphs. for piano, 4-hands.

Ulybyshev, Alexander. See **Oulibishev, Alexander.**

Um Kalthoum (Fatma el-Zahraa Ibrahim), Egyptian singer; b. Tamay az-Zahirah, 1898; d. Cairo, Feb. 3, 1975. During a career of more than 50 years, she became one of the most famous singers in the Arab world; she was particularly renowned for her renditions of nationalistic, religious, and sentimental songs, which resulted in her being dubbed the "Star of the East" and the "Nightingale of the Nile." Her death precipitated widespread mourning in Egypt and other Arab countries.

Umlauf, Ignaz, Austrian composer; b. Vienna, 1746; d. Meidling, June 8, 1796. In 1772 he became a violinist in the court theater, and in 1778, conductor of the German Opera in Vienna; in 1789 he was appointed sub-conductor (under Salieri) of the Imperial Chapel in Vienna. He was a highly popular composer of singspiels; inaugurated the season of the German singspiels at the Burg Theater (Feb. 17, 1778) with his piece *Bergknappen;* there followed a number of others: *Die Apotheke* (June 20, 1778); *Die pucefarbenen Schuhe, oder Die schöne Schusterin* (June 22, 1779); *Das Irrlicht, oder Endlich fand er sie* (Jan. 17, 1782); *Der Oberamtmann und die Soldaten* (1782); *Der Ring der Liebe* (Dec. 3, 1786). *Zu Steffan sprach im Traume,* an aria from *Das Irrlicht,* enjoyed great popularity; Eberl wrote a set of variations on it which was misattributed to Mozart. The score of Umlauf's first singspiel, *Die Bergknappen,* was edited by R. Haas in Denkmäler der Tonkunst in Österreich, 36 (18.i).

Umlauf, Michael, Austrian violinist and composer, son of **Ignaz Umlauf;** b. Vienna, Aug. 9, 1781; d. Baden, near Vienna, June 20, 1842. He played the violin at the Vienna Opera; conducted at court theaters; wrote piano music; brought out a singspiel, *Der Grenadier* (Vienna, July 8, 1812). He assisted Beethoven in conducting the 9th Symph. and other works (actually led the performances, with Beethoven indicating the initial tempos).

Underwood, James, American composer; b. Richmond, Calif., March 4, 1951. He played the trumpet as a youth; then studied composition with Robert Basart at Calif. State Univ. in Hayward (1969–75; M.A., 1975) and with Frederick Fox at Indiana Univ. (1978–82; D.A., 1982). His music is prudently modernistic, with atonal and polytonal divagations from modal harmonic structures within a general Baroque framework; there is an element of neo-Handelian humor in some of his compositions.
WORKS: *Variations on B-A-C-H* (Hayward, Calif., June 8, 1973); *The Orchestral Noises of October Nights* (1980–81; Bloomington, Ind., March 31, 1982). For Voice: *The Road* for Chorus and Orch. (Richmond, Calif., June 11, 1969); *Requiem* for Male Voice and Orch. (1970); *Dynamisms* for Soprano and Orch. (1975; Hayward, May 2, 1975); *Arms and the Boy* for Soprano, Narrator, Flute, Bass Clarinet, Trumpet, 2 Violins, Viola, Piano, and 5 Percussionists (1979); *To Eros* for Soprano, Violin, Viola, Piano, and Percussion (1980); *After Dinner with Al Capone* for Soprano and Trumpet (1981); *Remembrance* for Soprano, Flute, Clarinet, Violin, Cello, Piano, and Percussion (1982). Chamber music: *Lament* for Solo Clarinet (1970); *Textures I* for 5 Instruments (1971); *Textures II* for Solo Flute (1979); *Textures III* for 2 Cellos (1972); *Loomings* for Double String Quartet and Bass (1979); *4 Jurassic Scenes*

for Trombone, Bass Trombone, and 3 Percussionists (1980); *Then* for 2 Violins (1980); *Cornucopias* for Horn and Piano (1980); *Nightwork* for 8 Instruments (1981); *Brave New Zoos* for String Quartet (1982); *Reactions* for Solo Piccolo (1982); *Green County Purple* for Solo Bassoon (1983); *Cadenzas* for Alto Trombone, String Quartet, Piano, and Percussion (1983); *Deluge* for Brass Quintet (1983).

Unger (Ungher), Caroline, famous Hungarian contralto; b. Stuhlweissenburg, Oct. 28, 1803; d. at her villa near Florence, March 23, 1877. She studied voice in Milan with D. Ronconi, and in Vienna with Aloysia Lange (Mozart's sister-in-law) and with Johann Michael Vogl. Beethoven chose her to sing the contralto parts in the first performances of his *Missa Solemnis* and 9th Symph. (May 7, 1824); long afterward she recounted that she turned Beethoven's head around that he might see the applause, which he could no longer hear. She went to Italy, where she changed the spelling of her name to Ungher, to secure proper pronunciation in Italian. Several Italian composers (Donizetti, Bellini, Mercadante) wrote operas especially for her. In 1833 she appeared in Paris. In 1839 she was engaged to be married to the poet Lenau; but the engagement soon was broken; in 1841 she married the French writer François Sabatier (1818–91) and retired from the stage. She publ. an album of 46 songs, under the title *Lieder, Mélodies et Stornelli.*
BIBLIOGRAPHY: O. Hartwig, "Fr. Sabatier und Karoline Sabatier-Unger," *Deutsche Rundschau* (May 1897); F. Margit Polgár, *Unger-Sabatier* (Budapest, 1941).

Unger, Georg, German tenor; b. Leipzig, March 6, 1837; d. there, Feb. 2, 1887. He was originally a student of theology; made his operatic debut in Leipzig at the age of 30. Hans Richter heard him in Mannheim and recommended him to Wagner for the role of Siegfried. He studied the part with Hey, and his interpretation of it made him famous.

Unger, Gerhard, German tenor; b. Bad Salzungen, Nov. 26, 1916. He received his musical education at the Berlin Hochschule für Musik; began his career as a concert singer. In 1947 he sang opera in Weimar; from 1949 to 1961 was a member of the East Berlin State Opera; then sang in Stuttgart (1961–63), at the Hamburg State Opera (1963–66), and at the Vienna State Opera (1966–70); also made guest appearances at the Bayreuth Festival, at La Scala in Milan, and at the Chicago Lyric Opera.

Unger, Heinz, German-Canadian conductor; b. Berlin, Dec. 14, 1895; d. Toronto, Feb. 25, 1965. He studied in Berlin and Munich; was active as a choral conductor in Berlin until the advent of the Nazi regime in 1933. He then went to Russia; was conductor of the Leningrad Radio Orch. (1934–36). After a sojourn in England, he settled in Canada in 1948 and acquired a great renown as conductor of the Toronto Symph. Orch. He publ. an account of his conducting experiences in Russia under the title *Hammer,*

Sickle and Baton (London, 1939).

Unger, Hermann, German composer and writer on music; b. Kamenz, Oct. 26, 1886; d. Cologne, Dec. 31, 1958. He studied philology in Leipzig and Munich; received his Dr.Phil. in 1910 with a dissertation on Greek poetry; then took a course in musicology in Munich with Edgar Istel and Joseph Haas; subsequently went to Meiningen, where he took lessons with Max Reger (1910–13). He served in the German army in World War I; then was a lecturer at the Cons. of Cologne (1919–25) and at the Cologne Hochschule für Musik (1925–46).
WORKS: Operas: *Der Zauberhandschuh* (1927) and *Richmodis von Aducht* (1928); Christmas fairy tale, *Die Geschichten vom Weihnachtsbaum* (1943); 2 symphs.; several symph. poems; much chamber music; choral works; song cycles; piano suites.
WRITINGS: *Musikalisches Laienbrevier* (Munich, 1921); *Max Reger* (Munich, 1921); *Musiktheoretische Laienfibel* (Stuttgart, 1922); *Musikgeschichte in Selbstzeugnissen* (Munich, 1928); *Musikanten gestern und heute* (Siegen, 1935); *Anton Bruckner und seine 7. Sinfonie* (Bonn, 1944); *Harmonielehre* (Frankfurt, 1946); *Die musikalische Widmung* (Munich, 1958).

Unger, Max, German musicologist; b. Taura, May 28, 1883; d. Zürich, Dec. 1, 1959. He studied at the Leipzig Cons., and also attended Riemann's lectures at the Univ. of Leipzig; obtained his Dr.Phil. in 1911 with the dissertation *Muzio Clementis Leben* (publ. in Langensalza, 1914). He was active as a music critic, but was compelled to leave Germany in 1933 after the advent of the Nazi regime; lived mostly in Zürich. He devoted his research mainly to Beethoven; publ. about 150 papers dealing with various aspects of Beethoven's life and works; of these the most important are *Auf Spuren von Beethovens unsterblicher Geliebten* (Langensalza, 1911); *Ludwig van Beethoven und seine Verleger S.A. Steiner und Tobias Haslinger in Wien, A.M. Schlesinger in Berlin* (Berlin, 1921); *Beethovens Handschrift* (Bonn, 1926); *Ein Faustopernplan Beethovens und Goethes* (Regensburg, 1952); he also edited the catalogue of the Bodmer Beethoven collection in Zürich, under the title *Eine schweizer Beethovensammlung: Katalog* (Zurich, 1939).

Uninsky, Alexander, Russian-American pianist; b. Kiev, Feb. 2, 1910; d. Dallas, Texas, Dec. 19, 1972. He studied at the Kiev Cons.; in 1932 he won the first prize at the International Chopin Contest in Warsaw; after a concert tour in Europe, he went to the U.S. in 1943, and gave recitals; he excelled as a performer of Chopin's music. In 1955 he was appointed prof. of piano at the Cons. of Toronto, Canada; then held a similar position at the Southern Methodist Univ. in Dallas.

Untersteiner, Alfredo, Italian musicologist; b. Rovereto, April 28, 1859; d. Merano, Jan., 1918. He studied with Pembaur in Innsbruck; lived in Merano; was interned there as an enemy alien by the Austrians during World War I, and died in a concentration camp. He publ. *Storia della musica* (2 vols.; 1900; many reprints; in Eng. as *A Short History of Music*, N.Y., 1902) and *Storia del violino, dei violinisti e della musica per violino* (1904).

Uppman, Theodor, American baritone; b. San Jose, Calif., Jan. 12, 1920. He studied at the Curtis Inst. of Music in Philadelphia (1939–41); also attended the opera workshops at Stanford Univ. and the Univ. of Southern Calif. In 1948 he sang with the N.Y. City Center Opera; in 1951 he created the title role in Benjamin Britten's opera *Billy Budd* at Covent Garden in London. On Nov. 27, 1953, he made his Metropolitan Opera debut in N.Y. as Pelléas in Debussy's *Pelléas et Mélisande*, and in 1955 joined the company's membership. In 1977 he was appointed to the vocal faculty of the Mannes College of Music in N.Y.

Upton, George Putnam, American writer on music; b. Roxbury, Mass., Oct. 25, 1834; d. Chicago, May 19, 1919. He studied at Brown Univ., graduating in 1854; then went to Chicago, where he joined the editorial staff of the *Chicago Tribune* and wrote music criticism. He publ. a number of worthwhile books of reference, of which *The Standard Operas* was the most successful.
WRITINGS: *Letters of Peregrine Pickle* (1870); *Woman in Music* (1880); *The Standard Operas* (1886; new ed., 1928; enlarged by Felix Borowski, 1936; reprint, 1947); *The Standard Oratorios* (1887; 12th ed., 1909); *The Standard Cantatas* (1888; 7th ed., 1899); *The Standard Symphonies* (1889); *Musical Pastels* (1902); *The Standard Light Operas* (1902); edited the autobiography of Theodore Thomas (1905); wrote *E. Reményi. Musician, Littérateur and Man* (with G.D. Kelley; 1906); *Musical Memories* (an autobiography; 1908); *The Standard Concert Guide* (1908; new eds., 1930, 1947); *Standard Concert Repertory* (1909); *Standard Musical Biographies* (1910); *The Song* (1915); *In Music's Land* (1920).

Upton, William Treat, American musicologist; b. Tallmadge, Ohio, Dec. 17, 1870; d. Adelphi, Md., Jan. 19, 1961. He was educated at Oberlin College and its Cons. of Music; later studied piano with Leschetizky in Vienna (1896–98) and with Josef Lhévinne in Berlin (1913–14). From 1898 he taught piano at the Oberlin Cons.; also was a church organist in Cleveland (until 1918).
WRITINGS: *Art-Song in America* (Boston, 1930; supplement, 1938); *Anthony Philip Heinrich: A 19th-Century Composer in America* (N.Y., 1939); *William Henry Fry, American Journalist and Composer-Critic* (N.Y., 1954); a new ed. of O.G. Sonneck's *Bibliography of Early Secular American Music* (Washington, D.C., 1945, greatly augmented; 2nd ed., 1964).

Urbach, Otto, German pianist and composer; b. Eisenach, Feb. 6, 1871; d. Dresden, Dec. 14, 1927. He studied with Iwan Knorr and Humperdinck in Frankfurt, with Draeseke in Dresden, and with Klindworth in Berlin. In 1898 he was appointed a prof. of piano at the Dresden Cons. He wrote an opera, *Der Müller von Sans-Souci* (Frankfurt, 1896); an overture, *Bergfahrt;* String Quartet; Septet for Wind Instruments; piano pieces; many songs.

Urban, Friedrich Julius, German singing teacher and composer; brother of **Heinrich Urban;** b. Berlin, Dec. 23, 1838; d. there, July 17, 1918. He studied with Ries (violin) and Elsler (singing); was a successful singing teacher in Berlin; publ. a manual, *Die Kunst des Gesangs,* and some songs and choruses.

Urban, Heinrich, noted German music pedagogue; brother of **Friedrich Julius Urban;** b. Berlin, Aug. 27, 1837; d. there, Nov. 24, 1901. He studied with Ries (violin), Laub, and others in Berlin; was a professional violinist; wrote much symph. and chamber music; in 1881 became a prof. at Kullak's Academy in Berlin. He acquired fame as a theory teacher; among his pupils was Paderewski. His works include a concert overture, *Scheherazade;* a symph., *Frühling;* Violin Concerto; many violin pieces; songs.

Urbánek, Mojmir, Czech music publisher; b. Prague, May 6, 1873; d. there, Sept. 29, 1919. He was a son of the music publisher **Franz Urbánek** (1842–1919); left his father's firm and founded his own business in 1901, developing it into the largest of its kind in Czechoslovakia; it included a music shop, printing plant, concert agency, and concert hall ("Mozarteum"); it publ. works by Suk, Novák, Foerster, and other Czechoslovak composers, and the musical monthly *Dalibor.*

Urbanner, Erich, Austrian composer; b. Innsbruck, March 26, 1936. He studied composition with Karl Schiske and Hanns Jelinek at the Vienna Academy of Music (1955–61); then engaged in teaching score reading and composition.
WORKS: *Intrada* for Orch. (1957); Piano Concerto (1958); Symph. (1963); *Serenade* for String Orch. (1964); *Dialogue* for Piano and Orch. (1965); *Theme, 19 Variations and Night Piece* for Orch. (1968); *Kontraste* for Orch. (1970); Violin Concerto (1971); *Concerto "Wolfgang Amadeus"* for 2 Orchs., 3 Trombones, and Celesta (1972; Salzburg, Jan. 1, 1973); Double-bass Concerto (1973); 3 string quartets (1956, 1957, 1972); *8 Pieces* for Flute and Piano (1957); *8 Aphorisms* for Flute, Clarinet, and Bassoon (1966); *Improvisation III* for Chamber Ensemble, and *IV* for Wind Quintet (both 1969); *Solo* for Violin (1971); *Lyrica* for Chamber Ensemble (1971); *Kammermusik* for Flute, Oboe, Bassoon, Violin, Cello, and Harpsichord (1972); 2 piano sonatinas (1956, 1957); *Improvisation II* for 2 Pianos (1966).

Urfey, Thomas d' (known as **Tom Durfey**), English playwright and poet; b. Exeter, 1653; d. London, Feb. 26, 1723. He produced about 30 plays, the songs in some of which were set to music by Purcell (e.g. *The Comical History of Don Quixote,* in 3 parts, 1694–96). He ingratiated himself into the intimate circle of Charles II by his talent for singing his poems, adapted to popular airs of his time. Between 1683 and 1710 he publ. several collections of airs with music, and in 1719 he edited *Songs Compleat, Pleasant and Divertive* (5 vols., his own songs assembled in vols. 1 and 2); this was reissued the same year under the better-known title *Wit and Mirth: or Pills to Purge Melancholy* (a 6th vol. was added in 1720), and the whole was reprinted and edited by C.L. Day (N.Y., 1959).
BIBLIOGRAPHY: C.L. Day, *The Songs of Thomas D'Urfey* (Cambridge, Mass., 1933).

Urhan, Chrétien, French violinist; b. Montjoie, near Aix-la-Chapelle, Feb. 16, 1790; d. Paris, Nov. 2, 1845. He was a pupil of Le Sueur in composition; revived the viole d'amour, playing in Baillot's Quartet; from 1814 he was a violinist (later soloist) in the Opéra orch. In the Cons. Concerts he employed a 5-stringed violin (*violon-alto,* with the tuning *c-g-d¹-a¹-e²*), producing charming effects. He composed some chamber music.
BIBLIOGRAPHY: P.D. Förster, *Chrétien Urhan* (Raigern, 1907); P. Garnault, "Chrétien Urhan," *Revue de Musicologie* (1930).

Uriarte, Father Eustaquio de, Spanish musicologist; b. Durango, Nov. 2, 1863; d. Motrico, Sept. 17, 1900. In 1878 he entered the Augustinian Order at Valladolid and in 1888 went to the monastery of Silos, near Burgos, devoting himself to the study and restoration of Gregorian chant; was a promoter of the Asociación Isidoriana, for the reform of religious music in Spain. His fundamental work was the *Tratado teórico-prático de canto gregoriano, según la verdadera tradición* (Madrid, 1891). His shorter studies were publ., with a biographical sketch, by L. Villalba: *Estética y crítica musical del padre Uriarte* (Barcelona, 1904).

Uribe-Holguín, Guillermo, foremost composer of Colombia; b. Bogotá, March 17, 1880; d. there, June 26, 1971. He studied violin with Narciso Garay; in 1907 went to Paris, where he studied with Vincent d'Indy at the Schola Cantorum; then took violin lessons with César Thomson and Emile Chaumont in Brussels. He returned to Colombia in 1910 and became director of the newly reorganized National Cons. in Bogotá; resigned in 1935 and devoted his time to the family coffee plantation. He continued to compose and conduct, and was again director of the Cons. in 1942–47. In 1910 he married the pianist **Lucía Gutiérrez.** His music bears the imprint of the modern French style, but his thematic material is related to native musical resources; particularly remarkable are his *Trozos en el sentimiento popular* for Piano, of which he wrote about 350; they are stylizations of Colombian melorhythms in a brilliant pianistic setting. He publ. an autobiography, *Vida de un músico colombiano* (Bogotá, 1941).
WORKS: For Orch. (all perf. by the composer in

Bogotá): *Sinfonía del terruño* (Oct. 20, 1924); *3 danzas* (May 27, 1927); *Marcha festiva* (Aug. 20, 1928); *Serenata* (Oct. 29, 1928); *Carnavalesca* (July 8, 1929); *Cantares* (Sept. 2, 1929); *Villanesca* (Sept. 1, 1930); *Bajo su ventana* (Oct. 20, 1930); *Suite típica* (Nov. 21, 1932); *Concierto a la manera antigua* for Piano and Orch. (Oct. 15, 1939); *Bochica* (April 12, 1940); 11 symphs. (1910–1950); *Conquistadores* (Bogotá, April 3, 1959); 2 violin concertos; Viola Concerto; 10 string quartets; 2 piano trios; 7 violin sonatas; Cello Sonata; Viola Sonata; Piano Quartet; 2 piano quintets; choruses; sacred works; numerous song cycles.

BIBLIOGRAPHY: F.C. Lange, "Guillermo Uribe-Holguín," *Boletín Latino-Americano de Música* (Bogotá, 1938).

Urich, Jean, composer and publisher; b. on the island of Trinidad, Sept. 9, 1849; d. London, Dec. 14, 1939. He studied in Paris with Lenepveu (1868), and in London with Gounod during the latter's sojourn there (1871–74). In 1890 he founded the Edition Paul Dupont in Paris, and edited *Le Figaro Musical.*

WORKS: Operas: *L'Orage* (Brussels, 1879); *Flora Macdonald* (Bologna, 1885); *Le Pilote* (Monte Carlo, 1890); *Le Carillon* (Aix-les-Bains, 1895); *Hermann und Dorothea* (Berlin, 1899); *La Cigale et la fourmi* (in Eng. as *The Cicada,* London, 1912); *Tsing-Tau* (London, 1914).

Urio, Francesco Antonio, Italian church composer; b. Milan, c.1660; d. there after 1700. He became a Franciscan monk; in 1690 was maestro at the Church of the 12 Apostles in Rome. He publ. *Motetti di concerto a 2, 3, e 4 voci con violini e senza,* op. 1 (Rome, 1690); *Salmi concertati a 3 voci con violini,* op. 2 (Bologna, 1697); also composed a Te Deum, from which Handel "borrowed" numerous themes, chiefly for his *Dettingen Te Deum,* and also for his *Saul* and *Israel in Egypt.* Urio's Te Deum was publ. by Chrysander in vol. 5 of his collection *Denkmäler der Tonkunst* (later publ. as Supplement 2 of Handel's complete works).

BIBLIOGRAPHY: E. Prout, "Urio's Te Deum and Handel's Use Thereof," *Monthly Musical Record* (Nov. 1871); S. Taylor, *The Indebtedness of Handel to Works by Other Composers* (Cambridge, 1906); P. Robinson, *Handel and His Orbit* (London, 1908).

Urlus, Jacques, noted German tenor; b. Hergenrath, near Aachen, Jan. 9, 1867; d. Noordwijk, June 6, 1935. When he was 10, his parents moved to Tilburg, the Netherlands, and there he received his first instruction from an uncle, who was a choral conductor; then he studied engineering in Utrecht; subsequently studied singing with Cornelia van Zanten. He made his operatic debut as Beppo in *Pagliacci* at Amsterdam (Sept. 20, 1894); then was engaged at the Stadtheater in Leipzig (1900–15). He made his American debut in Boston as Tristan (Feb. 12, 1912); sang this role at his first appearance with the Metropolitan Opera (Feb. 8, 1913); was on its staff until 1917.

BIBLIOGRAPHY: Otto Spengler, *Jacques Urlus* (N.Y., 1917; in German and Eng.).

Urreta, Alicia, Mexican pianist and composer; b. Veracruz, Oct. 12, 1935. She studied piano with Joaquín Amparán and harmony with Rodolfo Halffter in Mexico City (1948–54); then engaged in teaching. Among her works are a radio opera, *Romance de Doña Balada* (Mexico City, 1972); *De natura mortis* for Voice, Instruments, and Tape (1972); several scores of *musique concrète.*

Urrutia-Blondel, Jorge, Chilean composer; b. La Serena, Sept. 17, 1905. He studied with Humberto Allende and Domingo Santa Cruz; in 1928 traveled to Europe, where he took lessons with Charles Koechlin, Paul Dukas, and Nadia Boulanger in Paris, and with Hindemith and Hans Mersmann in Berlin. Returning to Chile, he was appointed prof. of harmony at the Cons. in Santiago. His major work is the ballet *La guitarra del diablo* (1942), based on Chilean folk songs (Santiago, Nov. 27, 1942), from which he extracted 2 symph. suites. Other works: *Música para un Cuento de Antaño* for Orch. (1948); Piano Concerto (1950); Piano Trio (1933); Concertino for Harp and Guitar (1943); String Quartet (1944); Violin Sonata (1954); several choruses; song cycles on Chilean motifs; piano pieces.

BIBLIOGRAPHY: Vincente Salas Viú, *La creación musical en Chile 1900–1951* (Santiago, 1952; pp. 459–67).

Urso, Camilla, French-American violinist; b. Nantes, June 13, 1842; d. New York, Jan. 20, 1902. Her father was an Italian musician, and her mother a Portuguese singer. Her father took her on an American tour when she was 10 years old; she appeared as a child wonder with various enterprises including P.S. Gilmore's band; also toured Australia and South Africa; eventually ceased public appearances and earned a living as a violin teacher.

BIBLIOGRAPHY: C. Barnard, *Camilla: A Tale of a Violin, Being the Artist Life of Camilla Urso* (Boston, 1874); A.R. Coolidge in *Notable American Women* (Cambridge, Mass., 1971), III.

Urspruch, Anton, German pianist and composer; b. Frankfurt, Feb. 17, 1850; d. there, Jan. 7, 1907. He had lessons with Raff and Liszt; subsequently taught at the Raff Cons. in Frankfurt. He wrote a comic opera, *Das Unmöglichste von Allem,* after Lope de Vega's comedy *El mayor imposible* (Karlsruhe, Nov. 5, 1897). Other works: Symph.; Piano Concerto; Piano Quintet; Piano Trio; Violin Sonata; Cello Sonata; many piano pieces.

Ursprung, Otto, German musicologist; b. Günzlhofen, Jan. 16, 1879; d. Schöndorf-am-Ammersee, Sept. 14, 1960. He studied philosophy and theology at the Univ. of Munich (1899–1904) and was ordained as a Catholic priest. From 1932 to 1949 he taught at the Univ. of Munich. He wrote the books *Restauration und Palestrina-Renaissance in der katholischen Kirchenmusik* (Augsburg, 1924); *Münchens musikalische Vergangenheit* (Munich, 1927); *Die katholische Kirchenmusik* (Potsdam, 1931).

Ursuleac, Viorica, noted Rumanian soprano; b. Cernăuți, March 26, 1894. She studied in Vienna with Franz Steiner and Philip Forstén; made her debut as Charlotte in Massenet's *Werther* in Agram in 1922; then sang in Cernăuți (1923–24) and with the Vienna Volksoper (1924–26). In 1926 she joined the Frankfurt Opera, and then began a distinguished career as a member of the Vienna State Opera (1930–34), the Berlin State Opera (1935–37), and the Bavarian State Opera in Munich (1937–44). Richard Strauss held her in the highest esteem; in his operas she created the roles of Arabella (1933), Maria in *Der Friedenstag* (1938), the Countess in *Capriccio* (1942), and Danae in *Die Liebe der Danae* (public dress rehearsal, 1944). She was also highly successful in the operas of Wagner and Verdi. She was married to the eminent Austrian conductor **Clemens Krauss.**

Usandizaga, José María, Basque composer; b. San Sebastián, March 31, 1887; d. Yanti, Oct. 5, 1915. He studied piano with Planté and composition with Vincent d'Indy at the Schola Cantorum in Paris; upon his return to Spain he associated himself with the Basque musical movement, to which he gave a great impetus with the production of his opera *Mendy-Mendiyan* (Bilbao, 1910); his 2nd opera, *Las golondrinas (The Swallows),* obtained excellent success at its production in Madrid on Feb. 5, 1914. His last opera, *La llama (The Flame),* was produced in Madrid in 1915. He also wrote several symph. overtures; 2 string quartets; many piano pieces on Basque themes. His death from tuberculosis at the age of 28 was deeply lamented by Spanish musicians.
BIBLIOGRAPHY: L. Villalba, *J.M. Usandizaga* (Madrid, 1918); J.M. de Arozamena, *José María Usandizaga y la bella época donostiarra* (San Sebastian, 1969).

Usiglio, Emilio, Italian conductor and composer; b. Parma, Jan. 8, 1841; d. Milan, July 7, 1910. He studied with Mabellini; was a successful opera conductor; gave the first Italian performance of *Carmen.* He was married to the singer **Clementina Brusa.**
WORKS: Operas: *La Locandiera* (Turin, Sept. 5, 1861); *L'eredità in Corsica* (Milan, June 17, 1864); *Le Educande di Sorrento* (Florence, May 1, 1868); *La scommessa* (Florence, July 6, 1870); *Le Donne curiose* (Madrid, Feb. 11, 1879); *Le nozze in prigione* (Milan, March 23, 1881); several ballets.

Usmanbaş, Ilhan, Turkish composer; b. Istanbul, Sept. 28, 1921. He studied cello as a child; then studied harmony and counterpoint with Saygun at the Ankara Cons.; in 1948 he was appointed to its faculty. In 1952 he traveled to the U.S. His early compositions followed the ethnic patterns of Turkish folk songs, but after his travels in the U.S. he gradually adopted serial techniques, with occasional aleatory episodes.
WORKS: Violin Concerto (1946); Symph. (Ankara, April 20, 1950); *Music* for String Orch., Percussion, Piano, and Narrator (1950); *Mortuary* for Narrator, Chorus, and Orch. (1952–53); Clarinet Quintet (1949); Oboe Sonata (1949); Trumpet Sonata (1949); *3 Pictures of Salvador Dali* for Strings (1953); *Un Coup de dés* for Chorus and Orch. (1959); *Shadows* for Orch. (1964); *Immortal Sea Stones* for Piano (1965); *Questionnaire* for Piano (1965); *A Jump into Space* for Violin and 4 Instruments (1966); *Bursting Sinfonietta* for Orch. (1968); *Open Forms* for Different Groups (1968); *Music for a Ballet* for Orch. (1969); *String Quartet '70* (1970); *Senilikname* for Voice, Percussion, Harp, and Women's Chorus (1970).

Uspensky, Victor, Russian composer; b. Kaluga, Aug. 31, 1879; d. Tashkent, Oct. 9, 1949. He was brought up in Central Asia, where his father held a government post; attended the composition classes of Liadov at the St. Petersburg Cons.; graduated in 1913. In 1918 he went to Tashkent; from 1932 to 1948 was in charge of the Musical Folklore Division of Uzbekistan, and did valuable research work in native folklore; he also worked on the restoration of Uzbek musical instruments; from these authentic materials he fashioned an Uzbek opera, *Farhad and Shirin,* produced in Tashkent on Feb. 26, 1936. Other works include *Turkmenian Capriccio* for Orch. (1945); *Uzbek Rhapsody* for Orch. (1946); several choral works; piano pieces; songs. He collaborated with Victor Belaiev on a scholarly treatise, *Turkmenian Music* (Moscow, 1928).

Ussachevsky, Vladimir (Alexis), American composer of Russian parentage; b. Hailar, Manchuria, Nov. 3, 1911. His parents settled in Manchuria shortly after the Russo-Japanese War of 1905, at the time when Russian culture was still a powerful social factor there. His father was an officer of the Russian army, and his mother was a professional pianist. In 1930 he went to the U.S. and settled in California, where he took private piano lessons with Clarence Mader; from 1931–33 he attended Pasadena Junior College; in 1933 he received a scholarship to study at Pomona College (B.A., 1935). He then enrolled in the Eastman School of Music in Rochester, N.Y., in the classes of Howard Hanson, Bernard Rogers, and Edward Royce in composition (M.M., 1936; Ph.D., 1939); he also had some instruction with Burrill Phillips. In 1942, as an American citizen, Ussachevsky was drafted into the U.S. Army; thanks to his fluency in Russian, his knowledge of English and French, and a certain ability to communicate in rudimentary Chinese, he was engaged in the Intelligence Division; subsequently he served as a research analyst at the War Dept. in Washington, D.C. In 1947 he was appointed to the music faculty of Columbia Univ. in N.Y.; became a full prof. in 1964; retired in 1980. At various times he taught at other institutions, including several years as composer-in-residence at the Univ. of Utah (1975–80). His early works were influenced by Russian church music, in the tradition of Tchaikovsky and Rachmaninoff. A distinct change in his career as a composer came in 1951, when he became interested in the resources of electronic music; to this period belong his works

Transposition, Reverberation, and *Underwater Valse,* which make use of electronic sound. On Oct. 28, 1952, Stokowski conducted in N.Y. the first performance of Ussachevsky's *Sonic Contours,* in which a piano part was metamorphosed with the aid of various sonorific devices, superimposed on each other. About that time he began a fruitful partnership with Otto Luening; with him he composed *Incantation for Tape Recorder,* which was broadcast in 1953. Luening and Ussachevsky then conceived the idea of combining electronic tape sounds with conventional instruments played by human musicians; the result was *Rhapsodic Variations,* first performed in Louisville, Ky., on March 20, 1954. The work anticipated by a few months the composition of the important score *Déserts* by Varèse, which effectively combined electronic sound with other instruments. The next work by Ussachevsky and Luening was *A Poem in Cycles and Bells* for Tape Recorder and Orch., first performed by the Los Angeles Phil. on Nov. 22, 1954. On March 31, 1960, Leonard Bernstein conducted the N.Y. Phil. in the commissioned work by Ussachevsky and Luening entitled *Concerted Piece for Tape Recorder and Orchestra.* On Jan. 12, 1956, Ussachevsky and Luening provided taped background for Shakespeare's *King Lear,* produced by Orson Welles, at the N.Y. City Center, and later for Margaret Webster's production of *Back to Methuselah* for the N.Y. Theater Guild. They also provided the electronic score for the documentary *The Incredible Voyage,* broadcast over the CBS Television network on Oct. 13, 1965. Among works that Ussachevsky wrote for electronic sound without partnership were *A Piece for Tape Recorder* (1955), *Studies in Sound Plus* (1958), and *The Creation* (1961). In 1968 Ussachevsky began experimenting with the synthesizer, with the aid of a computer. One of the works resulting from these experiments was *Conflict* (1971); it is intended to represent the mystical struggle between 2 ancient deities. In 1959 Ussachevsky was one of the founders of the Columbia-Princeton Electronic Music Center; was active as a lecturer at various exhibitions of electronic sounds; traveled also to Russia and in China to present his music. He held 2 Guggenheim fellowships, in 1957 and in 1960. In 1973 Ussachevsky was elected to membership in the National Inst. of Arts and Letters.

WORKS: *Jubilee Cantata* for Baritone, Narrator, Chorus, and Orch. (1938); *Transposition, Reverberation, Composition* for Tape Recorder (1951); *Sonic Contours* for Piano and Voices on Tape (N.Y., Oct. 28, 1952, Stokowski conducting); *Incantations* for Tape Recorder (with Otto Luening; 1953); *Rhapsodic Variations* for Tape Recorder and Orch. (with Otto Luening; Louisville, March 20, 1954); *A Poem of Cycles and Bells* for Tape Recorder and Orch. (with Otto Luening; Los Angeles, Nov. 22, 1954); *Concerted Piece for Tape Recorder and Orch.* (with Otto Luening; N.Y. Phil., March 31, 1960, Leonard Bernstein conducting); *The Creation* for 4 Choruses, Soloists, and Tape (1961); *Epilogue: Spell of Creation* for Mixed Chorus and Electronic Sounds (1971); *Conflict* for Computerized Sound (Salt Lake City, May 10, 1971); *Missa Brevis* for Soprano, Chorus,

and Brass Ensemble (1972); *Colloquy for Orchestra and Tape Recorder* (1976); *Celebration* for String Orch. and Electronic Valve Instruments (1980).

BIBLIOGRAPHY: David Ewen, *American Composers* (N.Y., 1982).

Ustvolskaya, Galina, Soviet composer; b. Petrograd, July 17, 1919. She was a student of Shostakovich at the Leningrad Cons., graduating in 1947. Her early music was marked by a Romantic Russian manner; later she progressed toward greater melodic diversity and harmonic complexity; in some of her chamber music she boldly applies serial procedures.

WORKS: *Stepan Razin's Dream* for Bass and Orch. (Leningrad, Feb. 10, 1949); *A Man from the Tall Mountain* for Voices and Orch. (Leningrad, May 22, 1952); Sinfonietta (1951); 2 symphs.: No. 1 for 2 Boy Sopranos and Orch. (1955); No. 2 for Voice, Wind Instruments, and Piano (1964); symph. poems: *Heroic Deed* (1957); *Fire in the Steppes* (1958); Piano Concerto (1947); Octet for 4 Violins, 2 Oboes, Piano, and Kettledrums (1951); *Composition* for Piccolo, Tuba, and Piano (1970); *Composition* for Double Bass and Piano (1971); Violin Sonata; Cello Sonata; 3 piano sonatas (1948, 1951, 1952).

Utendal, Alexander, Flemish composer; b. in the Netherlands, c.1530; d. Innsbruck, May 7, 1581. He was court musician to the Archduke Ferdinand of Austria at Innsbruck. He publ. *7 Penitential Psalms* (1570); 3 books of motets (1570–77); masses and Magnificats (1573); *Fröliche neue teutsche und französische Lieder* for 4–8 Voices (1574).

Uttini, Francesco Antonio Baltassare, Italian composer; b. Bologna, 1723; d. Stockholm, Oct. 25, 1795. He studied with Perti; in 1743 became a member of the Accademia dei Filarmonici in Bologna. He first appeared as a singer; in 1755 went to Stockholm as conductor of an Italian opera company, and remained there until his death, except for a visit to London in 1768. He was court conductor at the Stockholm Opera from 1767 to 1787, and wrote 7 Italian and 5 French operas. Historically he is important as the composer of the earliest operas on Swedish texts; the first, *Thetis och Pelée,* was written for the inauguration of the new opera house in Stockholm (Jan. 18, 1773); another opera to a Swedish libretto, trans. from the French, was *Aline Drotning uti Golconda (Aline Queen of Golconda),* produced at the Stockholm Opera on Jan. 11, 1776. Of Uttini's Italian operas the best is *Il Re pastore* (Stockholm, July 24, 1755). A great admirer of Gluck, he brought out many of that composer's works in Stockholm. He also wrote 2 oratorios, 3 symphs. (for 4, 6, and 8 instruments), 12 sonatas, 9 trios for 2 Violins with Continuo; 6 of his sonatas were publ. at London in 1768.

BIBLIOGRAPHY: E. Sundström, "F.A. Uttini och Adolf Fredriks italienska operatrupp," *Svensk Tidskrift för Musikforskning,* 13 (1931).

Utyosov, Leonid, Soviet composer of jazz music; b.

Utyosov

Odessa, March 21, 1895; d. Moscow, March 10, 1982. He played violin as a child; after the Revolution, he performed as an actor and entertainer in various cabarets, often combining different functions, including acrobatics. In 1920 he organized the first Soviet jazz group, which he named Tea Jazz, with allusion to the song *Tea for Two* by Youmans, which was immensely popular in Russia at the time; subsequently he created various brief musical comedies such as *Jazz on the Turning Point* (1930). He also performed numerous popular Russian songs and revived old army and navy ballads. He publ. a brief biographical book, *Thanks, Heart* (Moscow, 1976).

V

Vaccai, Nicola, Italian composer and singing teacher; b. Tolentino, March 15, 1790; d. Pesaro, Aug. 5, 1848. He went to Rome as a youth and took lessons in counterpoint with Jannaconi; then studied with Paisiello in Naples (from 1812). He became a singing teacher in Venice (1818–21), Trieste (1821–23), Vienna (1823), Paris (1829–31), and London (1832), with an ever-growing reputation; was a prof. of composition at the Milan Cons. (1838–44); in 1844 he retired to Pesaro, where he remained until his death.

WORKS: Operas: *Pietro il Grande* (Parma, Jan. 17, 1824); *La Pastorella feudataria* (Turin, Sept. 18, 1824); *Giulietta e Romeo,* after Shakespeare (Milan, Oct. 31, 1825; the last scene was often used in perfs. of Bellini's *I Capuletti e i Montecchi*); his subsequent 10 operas were failures. He publ. *Metodo pratico di canto italiano per camera* and *12 ariette per camera, per l'insegnamento del belcanto italiano.*

BIBLIOGRAPHY: G. Vaccai, *Vita di N. Vaccai* (Bologna, 1882).

Vacek, Miloš, Czech composer; b. Horní Roveň, June 20, 1928. He studied organ at the Prague Cons. (1943–47); then took a course in composition with Řikdý and Pícha at the Prague Academy of Arts and Music (1947–51); wrote music scores for the Prague Puppet Theater which became popular.

WORKS: Opera, *Jan Želivský* (1953–56; revised 1974); 6 ballets: *The Comedian's Fairytale* (1957); *Wind in the Hair* (1960–61); *The Last Dandelion* (1964); *Meteor* (1966); *The Mistress of 7 Robbers* (1966); *Lucky Sevens* (1966); blues drama, *The Night Is My Day,* inspired by the life of Bessie Smith, the American blues singer (Frankfurt, March 15, 1964); musicals: *The Emperor's New Clothes* (1962); *Madame Sans-Gêne* (1968); *Wind from Alabama* (1970); Sinfonietta (1951); *The Brigand's Rhapsody* for Orch. (1952); *Spring Suite* for Flute, Horn or English Horn, Clarinet, and String Orch. (1963); *Serenade* for Strings (1965); *Fairytale Suite* for Orch. (1966); *Festive Day,* symph. march (1971); *Amoroso of My Country* for Orch. (1973); *Majova (May),* sinfonia (1974); *Poema o padlých hrdinech (Poem of Fallen Heroes)* for Orch. and Vocalizing Soprano (1974); *The Olympic Flame,* symph. poem (1975); cantata, *The Landscape of My Youth* (1976); *Sonnets of Early Spring,* lyrical cycle for Soprano and Orch. (1972–73); *Suite* for Cello and Piano (1947); Violin Sonatina (1949); String Quartet (1949); *Divertimento* for Violin, Cello, Guitar, and Bass Clarinet (1965); *Sumava Metamorphoses* for Flute, Oboe, Violin, Viola, and Cello (1971); *Hunting Suite* for 4 Horns (1973); *Sonata drammatica* for Piano (1972); *Dramatic Prelude* for Organ (1958); *Organum Pragense* for Organ (1966).

Vach, Ferdinand, Moravian choral leader; b. Jažlovice, Feb. 25, 1860; d. Brno, Feb. 16, 1939. He studied at the Organ School in Prague; in 1886 was appointed conductor of the "Moravian" choir at Kroměříž; also taught singing at the Pedagogium there, and from among his pupils formed in 1903 the Moravian Teachers' Choir, with which he toured in Germany, Russia, and England (1919). In 1905 he became a prof. at the Teachers' School in Brno; he composed choruses, cantatas, and church music.

Vachon, Pierre, violinist and composer; b. Arles, June 1731; d. Berlin, Oct. 7, 1803. He was a pupil of Chiabrano in Paris from 1751; first appeared at the Concert Spirituel on Dec. 24, 1756; from 1761, was solo violinist to the Prince de Conti; from 1786, at the Royal Chapel in Berlin; he was pensioned in 1798. Besides stage works, he composed violin concertos, string quartets, trios, sonatas, etc. (publ. in Paris, London, and Berlin). A Quartet for Strings and Continuo (op. 5, no. 3) was edited by Sidney Beck for the N.Y. Public Library (1937).

Vačkář, Dalibor, Czech violinist, composer, and writer; b. Korčula, Yugoslavia, Sept. 19, 1906. He was the son of **Václav Vačkář** (1881–1954), composer of popular music. He studied violin with Reissiga and composition with O. Šin at the Prague Cons. (1923–29); also attended master classes of K. Hoffman and J. Suk (1929–31). From 1934–45 he played violin in the Prague Radio Orch.; then joined the film studio in Prague and composed film music under various pseudonyms. Under the nom de plume **Dalibor C. Faltis,** he publ. 4 books of poems, a book of short stories, 12 plays, and 3 opera librettos. His son, **Tomáš Vačkář,** was a talented composer who committed suicide at the age of 17. He left a sketchbook of melodies and themes; after his death, his father composed pieces based solely on these materials. WORKS: BALLETS: *Svanda dudák (Svanda the Bagpiper;* 1950–53; Prague Radio, April 7, 1954) and *Sen noci svatojanské, (A Midsummer Night's Dream),* after Shakespeare (1955–57).
FOR ORCH.: *Overture* (1929); 2 violin concertos (1931, 1958); 5 symphs.: No. 1, *Optimistická (Optimistic;* 1941); No. 2, *Země vyvolená (The Chosen Land),* with Contralto and Chorus (1947); No. 3, *Smoking Symphony* (1947–48; orchestration of his *Smoking Sonata* for Piano; the curious subtitle, symbolizing fire and smoke in the life of men from antiquity to the present day, is in Eng. only); No. 4, *O Míru (Of Peace;* 1949–50); No. 5, *Pro juventute* (1978–82); *Symphonic Scherzo* (1945); Sinfonietta for Strings, Horn, Timpani, and Piano (1947); *Czech Concerto* for Piano and Orch. (1952); *Prelude and Metamorphoses* (1953); *Furiant-Fantasie* for Chamber Orch. (1960); *Concerto da camera* for Bassoon and Chamber String Orch. (1962); *Charakteristikon,* concerto for Trombone and Orch. (1965); *Legenda o člověku (Legend of Men),* concerto for

Harpsichord, Winds, and Percussion (1966); Clarinet Concerto (1966); *Prelude* for Chamber String Orch. (1966); *Concerto Grosso* for Soprano Saxophone, Accordion, Guitar, and Orch. (1967); *In Fide, Spe et Caritate,* concerto for Organ, Winds, and Percussion (1969); *Appellatio,* with Female Chorus (1970; Prague, Oct. 20, 1977); *Příběh o pěti kapitolách (5-Chapter Story),* music for Clarinet, Strings, and Percussion (1971); *Musica Concertante* (1973).
CHAMBER MUSIC: *Trio giocoso* for Piano Trio (1929); Violin Sonata (1930); String Quartet (1931–32); *Jaro 38,* Piano Trio (1938); *Monolog* for Solo Violin (1940); Quartet for Piano, Oboe, Clarinet, and Bassoon (1948); *Quintetto giocoso* for Wind Instruments (1950; music from the ballet *Svanda dudák*); *Suite giocoso* for Piano Trio (1960); *Dialogue* for Solo Violin (1961); *3 Studies* for Harpsichord (1961); *Dedication,* sonata for Violin and Piano (1961; each movement is dedicated to a different teacher of Vačkář's: Reissiga, Šin, Hoffmann, and Suk); Concerto for String Quartet (1962); Concerto for Trumpet, Piano, and Percussion (1963); *Pianoforte cantante,* 5 lyric reminiscences for Solo Piano, Double Bass, and Percussion (1968); *Partita* for Solo Trumpet (1968); *Listy z deníku (Pages from a Diary),* 4 movements for Bassoon and Piano (1968); *Milieu d'enfant* for 5 Percussion Groups (1970); *Intimní hudba (Private Music)* for Violin and Piano (1972); *Furiant-fantasie* for Piano Trio (1974); *Verses* for Flute and Guitar (1975); *Capriccio* for Cello and Guitar (1976); *Symposium* for Brass Quintet (1976); *Oboe concertante* for Solo Oboe, Clarinet, Bass Clarinet, Horn, String Quartet, Percussion, and Piano (1977); *Monograms,* 4 poems for String Quartet (1979; transcribed from the piano work); *Portraits* for Wind Quintet (1980; transcribed from the piano work); *Juniores,* 4 movements for String Quartet (1981; transcribed from the piano work).
FOR PIANO: *Smoking Sonata* (1936); *Extempore,* 6 pieces (1937); *Piano Fantasy,* on a theme from Schubert's *The Arch* (1962); *Perspektivy* (1971); *3 Etudes* (1977); *Monograms* (1978); *Portraits* (1980); *Juniores* (1981).
WRITINGS: *Instrumentation for Symphonic Orchestra and Brass Band* (with his father; Prague, 1954).

Vačkář, Tomáš, Czech composer, son of **Dalibor Vačkář;** b. Prague, July 31, 1945; d. (suicide) there, May 2, 1963. He came from a well-known Czech family of musicians; his grandfather, **Václav Vačkář,** was a composer of light music, and his father, **Dalibor Vačkář,** an eminent composer, dramatist, and poet. Young Tomáš was a gifted composer, but chose to end his life shortly after his graduation from the Prague Cons. at the age of 18. His works, all written between July 1960 and April 1963, include *Sonatina furore* for Piano; *Concerto Recitativo* for Flute, String Orch., and Piano; *Tři dopisy dívkam (3 Letters to a Girl),* after a poem by an anonymous Czech student, for Voice, and Piano or Winds and Percussion; *Teen-agers,* piano sonata; *Metamorfózy na tema japonske ukolebavky (Metamorphoses on the Theme of a Japanese Lullaby)* for

Orch.; *Scherzo melancolico* for Orch.; *Skicář Tomáše Vačkáře (Tomáš Vačkář's Sketchbook),* 10 pieces for Piano; a *Requiem* remained unfinished.

Vaet, Jacobus, Flemish composer; b. 1529; birthplace is not certain; it may be Courtrai or Harlebeke; d. Vienna, Jan. 8, 1567. He was a choirboy in the Church of Notre Dame at Courtrai (1543–46); after his voice changed, he received a subsidy for 2 years of further study; in 1550 he was a tenor in the Flemish Chapel of Charles V; on Jan. 1, 1554, he was listed as Kapellmeister of the chapel of Maximilian, then the nominal King of Bohemia. His position was enhanced when his patron became Emperor Maximilian II. Vaet's music exhibits a great variety of techniques, ranging in style from those of Josquin des Prez to those of Lassus. The formative influence, however, is mainly that of Nicolas Gombert, with a characteristic florid imitation in contrapuntal parts. The extant works of Vaet comprise 82 motets and hymns, 10 masses, 8 Magnificats, and 3 chansons; a relatively large number of his motets (at least 11) are ceremonial, written to celebrate state or court occasions. Two vols. of his motets, *Modulationes 5 vocum* and *Modulationes 5 et 6 vocum,* were publ. in 1562 by Gardano in Venice; a 6-voice motet, *Qui operatus est Petro,* was printed in luxurious format on a large single parchment sheet by Hofhalter of Vienna in 1560 (facsimile in Haas, *Aufführungspraxis der Musik,* Potsdam, 1931, p. 129). Zacconi printed a hymn in his *Prattica di musica,* Libro I, folio 50. Vaet is represented also in the publications of Berg and Neuber (30 motets), Giovanelli (24 motets), Susato (7 motets), Gerlach (3 motets), Phalèse (3 motets, 2 chansons), Stephani (2 motets, one chanson), Waelrant and Laet (one chanson), Nicolas du Chemin (one chanson), and Rühling (one motet in organ tablature). Reprints appear in Commer's *Collectio operum musicorum Batavorum* (20 motets) and his *Musica sacra* (one Mass), and in Maldeghem, *Trésor musical* (one motet). E.H. Meyer edited *Jacobus Vaet, Sechs Motetten* as vol. 2 of *Das Chorwerk* (1929), and Milton Steinhardt edited *Jacobus Vaet, Zwei Hymnen* as vol. 8 of *Musik alter Meister* (1958). A complete edition of his work was undertaken by M. Steinhardt in Denkmäler der Tonkunst in Österreich, vols. 98, 100, 103/104, 108/109, 113/114, 116, 118.

BIBLIOGRAPHY: Milton Steinhardt, *Jacobus Vaet and His Motets* (Michigan State College Press, 1951; thematic index and 3 complete works included); idem, "The Hymns of Jacobus Vaet," *Journal of the American Musicological Society* (Fall 1956); G. Reese, *Music in the Renaissance* (N.Y., 1954; 2nd ed., revised, 1959); M. Steinhardt, "Addenda to the Biography of Jacobus Vaet," in *The Commonwealth of Music* (N.Y., 1965); idem, "The *Missa Di me tenes:* A Problem of Authorship," in *Aspects of Medieval and Renaissance Music* (N.Y., 1966).

Vainberg, Moisei, Soviet composer; b. Warsaw, Dec. 8, 1919. He studied piano with Turczynski at the Warsaw Cons., graduating in 1939; then went to Minsk, where he studied composition with Zolotarev at the Minsk Cons.; in 1943 he settled in Moscow. In his music he follows the precepts of socialist realism in its ethnic aspects; according to the subject, he makes use of Jewish, Polish, Moldavian, or Armenian folk melos, in tasteful harmonic arrangements devoid of abrasive dissonances.

WORKS: Operas: *The Sword of Uzbekistan* (1942); *The Woman Passenger* (1968); *Love of D'Artagnan,* after Alexandre Dumas (1972); ballets: *Battle for the Fatherland* (1942); *The Golden Key* (1955); *The White Chrysanthemum* (1958); *Requiem* (1967); cantatas: *On This Day Lenin Was Born* for Chorus and Orch. (1970); *Hiroshima Haikus* (1966); *The Diary of Love* (1965). For Orch.: 16 symphs.: No. 1 (1942); No. 2 for String Orch. (1946); No. 3 (1949); No. 4 (1957); No. 5 (1962); No. 6, with Boys' Chorus (1963); No. 7 for Strings and Harpsichord (1964); No. 8, subtitled *The Flowers of Poland,* for Tenor, Chorus, and Orch. (1964); No. 9, subtitled *Surviving Pages,* for Reader, Chorus, and Orch. (1967); No. 10 for String Orch. (1968); No. 11, *Triumphant Symphony,* for Chorus and Orch., dedicated to Lenin's centennial (1969); No. 12 (1976; Moscow, Oct. 13, 1979); No. 13 (1976); No. 14 (1977; Moscow, Oct. 8, 1980); No. 15, with Chorus, "I have faith in this earth" (1977; Moscow, April 12, 1979); No. 16 (1981; Moscow, Oct. 19, 1982); 2 sinfoniettas (1948, 1960); *Moldavian Rhapsody* for Orch. (Moscow, Nov. 30, 1949); *Slavic Rhapsody* for Orch. (1950); Cello Concerto (1956); Violin Concerto (1960); Flute Concerto (1961); Trumpet Concerto (1967); Clarinet Concerto (1970); 12 string quartets (1937–70); Piano Quintet (1944); Piano Trio (1945); String Trio (1951); 20 sonatas and 2 sonatinas for various instruments, with piano; 24 preludes for cello solo; 23 preludes for piano; songs.

Valabrega, Cesare, Italian pianist and writer on music; b. Novara, Dec. 27, 1898; d. Munich, Feb. 4, 1965. He studied piano at the Cons. of Pesaro and literature at the Univ. of Bologna; taught music history in Naples and Perugia; then settled in Rome as a lecturer and critic. He wrote *Schumann: Arte e natura; arte e vita; arte e fede* (1934; 3rd ed., 1956); *Domenico Scarlatti: Il suo secolo, la sua opera* (1937; 2nd ed., 1955); *Il piccolo dizionario musicale per tutti* (1929; 2nd ed., 1952); *Johann Sebastian Bach* (1950); *La lirica di camera di Vincenzo Davico* (1953).

Valcárcel, Edgar, Peruvian composer and pianist, nephew of **Teodoro Valcárcel;** b. Puno, Dec. 4, 1932. He studied composition with Andrés Sas at the Lima Cons.; then went to N.Y., where he studied with Donald Lybbert at Hunter College; subsequently traveled to Buenos Aires, where he took composition lessons with Alberto Ginastera; also had sessions with Olivier Messiaen in Paris, and with Riccardo Malipiero, Bruno Maderna, and Luigi Dallapiccola in Italy; furthermore, he joined the Electronic Music Center of Columbia-Princeton Univs. and worked with Vladimir Ussachevsky; held 2 Guggenheim Foundation grants (1966 and 1968). In

Peru he became a teacher of piano and harmony at the Cons. of Lima. In his compositions he adopted an extremely advanced idiom that combined serial and aleatory principles, leaving to the performer the choice to use or not to use given thematic materials.

WORKS: FOR ORCH.: Concerto for Clarinet and Strings (Lima, March 6, 1966); *Quenua* (Lima, Aug. 18, 1965); *Aleaciones* (Lima, May 5, 1967); Piano Concerto (Lima, Aug. 8, 1968); *Checán II* (Lima, June 5, 1970); *Ma'karabotasaq hachana* (1971); *Sajra* (1974). CHAMBER MUSIC: 2 string quartets (1962, 1963); *Espectros I* for Flute, Viola, and Piano (1964); *Espectros II* for French Horn, Violoncello, and Piano (1968); *Dicotomías III* for 12 Instruments (Mexico City, Nov. 20, 1966); *Fisiones* for 10 Instruments (1967); *Hiwana uru* for 11 Instruments (1967); Trio for Amplified Violin, Trombone, and Clarinet (1968); *Poema* for Amplified Violin, Voice, Piano, and Percussion (1969); *Chacán I* for 6 Instruments (1969); *Checán III* for 19 Instruments (1971); *Montage 59* for String Quartet, Clarinet, Piano, and Lights (1971); *Espectros III* for Oboe, Violin, and Piano (1974); *Checán V* for Strings (1974). FOR PIANO: *Dicotomías I* and *II* (1966); 2 sonatas (1963, 1972). ELECTRONIC WORKS: *Antaras* for Flute, Percussion, and Electronic Sounds (1968); various multimedia pieces with chorus, electronic sounds, and lights; also several choruses a cappella.

Valcárcel, Teodoro, Peruvian composer; b. Puno, Oct. 17, 1900; d. Lima, March 20, 1942. He studied at the Cons. of Milan and with Felipe Pedrell in Barcelona. Returning to Peru in 1920, he settled in Lima; in 1928 he won the National Prize for Peruvian composers, and was awarded a gold medal from the municipality of Lima for his studies in Peruvian folk music. In 1929 he went to Europe once more; presented a concert of his works in Paris (April 12, 1930). He was of pure Indian origin; as a native of the highlands, he was able to collect Indian songs unpolluted by urban influences. He publ. *30 cantos de alma vernacular; 4 canciones incaicas; 25 romances de costa y sierra peruana; 180 melodias del folklore.* Among his original works are the ballets (with singing) *Suray-Surita* and *Ckori Kancha;* a symph. poem, *En las ruinas del Templo del Sol* (1940); a violin concerto, entitled *Concierto indio* (1939); *3 ensayos* for an ensemble of Native Instruments; *Fiestas andinas* for Piano; *Suite autóctona* for Violin and Piano; songs. A catalogue of his works was publ. by R. Holzmann in *Boletín Bibliográfico* (Lima, Dec. 1942).

Valdengo, Giuseppe, Italian baritone; b. Turin, May 24, 1914. He studied cello at the Turin Cons., and also played the oboe; then decided to cultivate his voice, and took singing lessons with Michele Accoriutti. In 1936 he sang Figaro in *Il Barbiere di Siviglia* in Parma; in 1939 was engaged to sing at La Scala in Milan. In 1946 he went to the U.S. and sang with the N.Y. City Opera. On Dec. 19, 1947, he made his Metropolitan Opera debut in N.Y. as Tonio; continued on the company's roster until 1954; was also chosen by Toscanini to sing the roles of Amonasro, Renato, Iago, and Falstaff with the NBC Symph. Orch. He made guest appearances in London, Paris, Vienna, and South America. He also acted the part of Antonio Scotti in the film *The Great Caruso.*

Valderrábano, Enrique Enriquez de. See **Enriquez de Valderrábano, Enrique.**

Valderrama, Carlos, Peruvian composer; b. Trujillo, Sept. 4, 1887; d. Lima, Aug. 1, 1950. He studied engineering at Cornell Univ., then decided to devote himself to music; made his debut as a pianist at Carnegie Hall in N.Y. (Feb. 22, 1920). He wrote many piano pieces on old Inca themes, in a salon style (several of them publ.), and some ballet music.

Valdrighi, Luigi Francesco, Italian music scholar; b. Modena, July 30, 1827; d. there, April 20, 1899. He was notable for his excellent collection of early musical instruments, which he bequeathed to the Museum of Modena. He publ. numerous valuable monographs on the music and musicians of Modena; among his theoretical writings the most important was *Nomocheliurgografia antica e moderna* (1884; with 2 supplements, 1888 and 1894). With G. Ferrari-Moreni he completed a chronicle of theater life in Modena, *Cronistoria dei teatri di Modena* (1873).

BIBLIOGRAPHY: E. Zoccoli, *Il Conte Luigi Francesco Valdrighi* (Modena, 1899).

Válek, Jiří, remarkable Czech composer; b. Prague, May 28, 1923. He studied composition at the Prague Cons. and at the Master's School with Řídký (1946–48); received a doctorate of philosophy from Charles Univ. (1951). He was secretary of the Guild of Czech Composers (1949–51) and editor in chief of children's musical programming at Czech Radio in Prague (1951–53), of the editorial division of the Central House of the Czech Army (1953–58), and of Panton, the publishing house of the Guild (1959–63); then was an instructor in music theory at the Prague Cons.

WORKS: 12 programmatic symphs.: No. 1, *Rok 1948 (The Year 1948),* for Trumpet, Piano, and Orch. (1948); No. 2, *Klasická (Classic),* for 2 Flutes, 2 Clarinets, Chamber String Orch., and Piano (1957); No. 3, *Romantická,* for Soprano Saxophone, Tenor Saxophone, and Orch. (1962); No. 4, *Dialogy s vnitřním hlasem (Dialogues with an Inner Voice),* to Shakespearean texts, for Contralto, Baritone, Large Wind Orch., Percussion, and Piano (1967); No. 5, *Guernica,* after the Picasso painting (1968); No. 6, *Ekpyrosis,* reflecting philosophical ideals of Heraclitus, for Flute, String Orch., Percussion, and Piano (1968–69); No. 7, *Pompejské fresky (Pompeian Frescoes),* for Chamber Orch., Piano, and Percussion (1969–70); No. 8, *Hic sunt homines!,* on the theme of a novella by Stefan Zweig, for Soprano and Orch. (1970–71); No. 9, *Renesanční (Renaissance),* triple concerto for Violin, Viola, Cello, and String Orch. (1971); No. 10, *Barokní (Baroque),* to commemorate the 300th anniversary of the death of the Czech Baroque painter Karel Škréta and the 150th anniversary of the birth of Smetana, a double concerto for Violin, Piano, and Orch. (1973); No. 11, *Revoluční (Revolutionary),* to commemorate the 30th anniversary of Czech liberation, for Piano Trio, Wind Quintet, and Orch. (1974); No. 12, *Shakespearean,* a double concerto for Violin, Viola, and Chamber String Orch. (1976); Sinfonietta (1944); *The Dam,* symph. poem (1959); *Reflections on a Summer Lake,* dance suite for Orch. (1972); *Beyond the Bounds of Tomorrow,* ceremonial march for Orch. (1972); *La portenza della Primavera,* 5 dithyrambs for Soprano and Orch. (1972); *Hymnus slunce (Hymn to the Sun),* violin concerto (1975); 4 string quartets (1943; 1945; *The Rumburk Uprising,* 1960; *Quattrocento,* 1972–73); 2 violin sonatas (1944, 1960); 2 viola sonatas (1948, 1961); *Serenade* for 9 Winds and Piano (1959); *Eroica,* sonata for Trumpet or Clarinet, and Piano (1960); *Suite dramatica* for Double Bass and Piano (1967); *Concerto-notturno* for Violin, Viola, and Cello (1967); *Shakespeare Variations* for Nonet (1967); Flute Sonata (1969); *Nenie* for Solo Violin or Cello (1969); Concerto for Flute, Oboe, Violin, Viola, Cello, and Harpsichord (1970); *Villa dei Misteri,* 11 fresques for Violin and Piano (1971); *Aesop* for Children's Choir, Narrator, Ballet, Flute, 2 Clarinets, Bassoon, and Percussion (1972); 3 piano sonatas (*The Year 1942,* 1942; 1961; 1970); songs.

Valen, Fartein, Norwegian composer noted for his originality, both in thematic invention and in the use of audacious modern techniques; b. Stavanger, Aug. 25, 1887; d. Haugesund, Dec. 14, 1952. His father was a missionary in Madagascar, and Valen spent his childhood there. Upon returning to Norway, he studied philology at the Univ. of Oslo (1906–9), and music theory and organ with Elling at the Oslo Cons.; subsequently went to Berlin and enrolled in the Hochschule für Musik in the class of composition of Max Bruch (1909–11). From 1916 to 1924 he stayed on his family's farm in Valevåg; from 1924 to 1938 he was in Oslo; then retired on the family farm. In 1935 he received the Norwegian State Salary of Art (a government life pension). His early music reflects the influence of Brahms, but later he developed a sui generis method of composition which he termed "atonal polyphony," completely free from traditional tonal relationships but strongly cohesive in contrapuntal fabric and greatly varied in rhythm; his first work in which he made use of this technique was a Piano Trio written in 1924. He never adopted an explicit 12-tone method of composition, but a parallelism with Schoenberg's music is observable. Valen stood apart from all nationalist developments in Oslo, yet his music attracted attention in modern circles; a Valen Society was formed in Norway in 1949, and in England in 1952, shortly before his death. WORKS: FOR ORCH.: 5 symphs.: No. 1 (1937–39; Bergen, Feb. 2, 1956); No. 2 (1941–44; Oslo, March 28, 1957); No. 3 (1944–46; Oslo, April 13, 1951); No. 4 (1947–49; Malmö, Sweden, Oct. 16, 1956); No. 5 (1951–52; unfinished); *Pastorale* (1929–30); *Sonetto di Mi-*

chelangelo (1932); *Nenia* (1932); *Cantico di ringraziamento (Song of Thanksgiving;* 1932–33); *An die Hoffnung (To Hope,* after Keats's poem; 1933); *Epithalamion* (1933); *Le Cimetière marin (Graveyard by the Sea;* 1933–34); *La isla de las calmas (The Silent Island;* 1934); *Ode til Ensomheten (Ode to Solitude;* 1939); Violin Concerto (1940; Oslo, Oct. 24, 1947; also perf. at the Amsterdam Festival, June 12, 1948); Concerto for Piano and Chamber Orch. (1949–51; Oslo, Jan. 15, 1953). FOR SOPRANO AND ORCH.: *Ave Maria* (1917–21); *3 Gedichte von Goethe* (1925–27); *Mignon,* 2 songs after Goethe (1920–27); *2 chinesische Gedichte* (1925–27); *Dearest Thou Now, O Soul,* after Whitman (1920–28); *La noche oscura del alma (The Dark Night of the Soul),* after St. John of the Cross (1939). CHAMBER MUSIC: Violin Sonata (1916); Piano Trio (1917–24); 2 string quartets (1928–29, 1930–31); *Serenade* for Wind Quintet (1946–47). FOR PIANO: *Legend* (1907); 2 sonatas: No. 1 (1912) and No. 2, *The Hound of Heaven,* after the poem by Francis Thompson (1940–41); *4 Pieces* (1934–35); *Variations* (1935–36); *Gavotte and Musette* (1936); *Prelude and Fugue* (1937); *2 Preludes* (1937); *Intermezzo* (1939–40). FOR ORGAN: *Prelude and Fugue* (1939) and *Pastoral* (1939). He also wrote songs and motets.

BIBLIOGRAPHY: O. Gurvin, *Fartein Valen, En banebryter i nyere norsk musikk (Fartein Valen, a Pioneer in Norwegian Music;* Oslo, 1962); B. Kortsen, *Studies of Form in Fartein Valen's Music* (Oslo, 1962); idem, *Melodic Structure and Thematic Unity in Fartein Valen's Music* (2 vols., Glasgow, 1963); idem, *Fartein Valen, Life and Music* (3 vols., Oslo, 1965); Anonymous, *Komponisten Fartein Valen 1887–1952* (Oslo, 1976); P. Rapoport, *Opus Est: Six Composers from Northern Europe* (London, 1978; pp. 135–59); N. Grinde, *Contemporary Norwegian Music 1920–1980* (Oslo, 1980; pp. 19–25).

Valencia, Antonio María, Colombian pianist and composer; b. Cali, Nov. 10, 1902; d. there, July 22, 1952. He studied at the Schola Cantorum in Paris (from 1923) with Vincent d'Indy and Paul Le Flem; returning to Colombia in 1930, he founded the Cali Cons., and was its director until his death. WORKS: *Chirimía y bambuco sotareño* for Orch. (1942); *Egloga incaica* for Flute, Oboe, Clarinet, and Bassoon (1935); *Emociones caucanas* for Piano, Violin, and Cello (1938); numerous pieces for piano solo, inspired by native melorhythms (*8 ritmos y cantos suramericanos, Sonatina boyacense,* etc.); Requiem (1943); other church music; choruses and songs.

Valente, Antonio (known as "il Cieco," "the blind man"), Italian organist and composer; b. Naples, c.1520. Blind from infancy, he played the organ; was organist at Sant'Angelo a Nido in Naples. His first publication, *Intavolatura de cimbalo: Recercate, fantasie et canzoni francese desminuite con alcuni tenori balli et varie sorti de contraponti...* (Naples, 1575), is in Spanish keyboard tablature and contains early keyboard fantasias, written out in detail; his 2nd book, *Versi spirituali sopra tutte le note, con diversi canoni spartiti per suonar negli* *organi, messe, vespere et altri offici divini* (Naples, 1580), represents an early type of keyboard partitura; 3 numbers were reprinted by L. Torchi in *L'arte musicale in Italia,* 3. A modern edition was brought out by I. Fuser, editor, *Antonio Valente: Versi spirituali per organo* (Padua, 1958).

BIBLIOGRAPHY: N. Caravaglios, "Una nuova *Intavolatura de Cimbalo* di Antonio Valente Cieco," *Rivista Musicale Italiana,* 23 (p. 491); Willi Apel, "Neapolitan Links between Cabezón and Frescobaldi," *Musical Quarterly* (Oct. 1938).

Valente, Benita, American soprano; b. Delano, Calif., Oct. 19, 1939. She studied voice with Lotte Lehmann at the Music Academy of the West at Santa Barbara; also took lessons with Martial Singher there. Later she enrolled at the Curtis Inst. of Music in Philadelphia, graduating in 1960. She sang at the Marlboro Festival in Vermont; there she met the bassoon player **Anthony Checchia,** whom she married in 1959; they settled in Philadelphia. In 1962 she went to Germany and appeared at the Freiburg Opera; upon returning to the U.S., she made an auspicious debut at the Metropolitan Opera in N.Y. as Pamina in *Die Zauberflöte* (Sept. 22, 1973) and became a regular member of the Metropolitan; made an appearance as Almirena in Handel's opera *Rinaldo* there in 1982; her other roles were Violetta and Gilda. She further showed her mettle in modern works, such as Penderecki's *Te Deum.*

BIBLIOGRAPHY: Bridget Paolucci, "Benita Valente," *Ovation* (Jan. 1984).

Valente, Giorgio. See **Vitalis, George.**

Valente, Vincenzo, Italian operetta composer; b. Corigliano Calabro, Feb. 21, 1855; d. Naples, Sept. 6, 1921. At the age of 15 he wrote a song, *Ntuniella,* which became popular; he continued writing Neapolitan songs of great appeal (*Basta ca po', Comme te voglio amà!, Canzone Cafona, Mugliera comme fa, Ninuccia, Tiempe felice, L'Acqua,* etc.), about 400 songs in all. He also brought out numerous operettas: *I Granatieri* (Turin, Oct. 26, 1889); *La Sposa di Charolles* (Rome, March 3, 1894); *Rolandino* (Turin, Oct. 15, 1897); *L'usignuolo* (Naples, May 10, 1899); *Lena* (Foggia, Jan. 1, 1918); *L'Avvocato Trafichetti* (Naples, May 24, 1919); *Nèmesi* (posthumous, Naples, July 23, 1923). His son, **Nicola Valente** (b. Naples, Aug. 28, 1881), was also a composer of Neapolitan songs and light operas.

Valenti, Fernando, noted American harpsichordist; b. New York, Dec. 4, 1926. He studied piano with José Iturbi; then attended Yale Univ., where he took instruction in harpsichord with Ralph Kirkpatrick. He made his N.Y. recital debut in 1950. In 1951 he was appointed prof. of harpsichord playing at the Juilliard School of Music in N.Y. He was especially renowned for his authentic interpretation of keyboard works by Scarlatti.

Valentin, Erich, distinguished German musicologist; b. Strasbourg, Nov. 27, 1906. He studied music with Courvoisier and Röhr in Munich; took courses in musicology with Sandberger at the Univ. of Munich, where he received his Ph.D. in 1928 with the dissertation *Die Entwicklung der Tokkata im 17. und 18. Jahrhundert* (publ. in Munich, 1930). From 1929–35 he taught at the Staatliches Privatmusiklehrer-Seminar in Magdeburg; from 1939–45 he was director of the Zentralinstitut für Mozartforschung. He taught at the Nordwestdeutsche Hochschule für Musik in Munich in 1953; was its director from 1964–72. From 1950–55 he was editor in chief of the *Zeitschrift für Musik,* and from 1955–59 co-editor of the *Neue Zeitschrift für Musik.* He became editor in chief of *Acta Mozartiana* in 1954. In addition to his many articles for music journals, he also prepared editions of works by Mozart, Telemann, and others.

WRITINGS: *Georg Philipp Telemann* (Burg, 1931; 3rd ed., 1952); *Richard Wagner* (Regensburg, 1937); *Dichtung und Oper: Eine Untersuchung zum Stilproblem der Oper* (Leipzig, 1938); *Hans Pfitzner* (Regensburg, 1939); *Wege zu Mozart* (Regensburg, 1941; 4th ed., 1950); *Beethoven* (Salzburg, 1942; Eng. ed., N.Y., 1958); *W.A. Mozart: Wesen und Wandlung* (Hamelin, 1948); *Kleine Bilder grosser Meister* (Mainz, 1952); *Handbuch der Chormusik* (Regensburg, 1953–74); *Handbuch der Instrumentenkunde* (Regensburg, 1954; 6th ed., 1974); *Der früheste Mozart* (Munich, 1956); *Beethoven* (pictorial bibliography; Munich, 1957); *Die Tokkata,* in *Das Musikwerk,* XVII (1958); *Mozart* (pictorial bibliography; Munich, 1959); *Musica domestica: Über Wesen und Geschichte der Hausmusik* (Trossingen, 1959); *Telemann in seiner Zeit* (Hamburg, 1960); *Handbuch der Schulmusik* (Regensburg, 1962); *Die goldene Spur: Mozart in der Dichtung Hermann Hesses* (Augsburg, 1965); *Die evangelische Kirchenmusik* (with F. Hofmann; Regensburg, 1967); *Handbuch des Musikunterrichts* (with W. Gebhardt and W. Vetter; Regensburg, 1970); *Die schönsten Beethoven-Briefe* (Munich, 1973).

BIBLIOGRAPHY: G. Weiss, ed., *Erich Valentin zum 70. Geburtstag* (Regensburg, 1976).

Valentini, Giovanni, Italian composer; b. Venice, 1582; d. Vienna, April 29, 1649. He was a pupil of Giovanni Gabrieli; from 1614, was organist to the Archduke Ferdinand at Graz, becoming court organist at Vienna when Ferdinand ascended the throne in 1619; by 1626 succeeded Prioli as Imperial Kapellmeister. He was a renowned teacher of organ. He publ. *Motetti a 6 voci* (1611); 5 books of madrigals for 3 to 11 Voices, with Instruments; *Musiche a 2 voci,* with Bass, for Organ (1622); *Canzoni per sonar* for 4–8 Voices; in MS, masses, Magnificats, a Stabat Mater, and sonatas. Riemann publ. an "Enharmonische Sonate" in *Alte Kammermusik,* but its authenticity is disputed.

Valentini, Giuseppe, Italian violinist and composer; b. Florence, c.1680; d. after 1759. He was at Rome in 1700; was in the service of Prince Francesco Maria Ruspoli as a violinist, c.1708–13; may then have been at Bologna in the service of the Prince di Caserta; and from 1735 was at the grand-ducal court of Florence. His violin technique was highly developed (some compositions call for the 6th position). He publ. 12 *Sinfonie* for 2 Violins and Continuo (Organ); 7 *Bizarrerie* for 2 Violins and Cello; 12 *Fantasie* for 2 Violins and Continuo; 12 *Sonate* for the same; *Idee per camera* for Violin Solo and Cello (or Cembalo); 12 *Concerti grossi* for Strings and Continuo; 12 *Sonate o Alletamenti* for Violin and Continuo.

Valentini, Pier Francesco, Italian theorist and composer of the Roman School; b. Rome, c.1570; d. there, 1654. He was a pupil of G.B. Nanino.
WORKS: *Canone sopra le parole del Salve Regina, "Illos tuos misericordes oculos ad nos converte," con le resolutioni a 2, 3, 4 e 5 voci* (1629; a canon with over 2000 possible resolutions; the theme is in Kircher's *Musurgia,* I, p. 402); *Canone nel nodo di Salomone a 96 voci* (1631; also in *Musurgia,* I, p. 104); *Canone a 6, 10, 20 voci* (1645); 2 books of madrigals *a* 5, with Continuo ad libitum, and 2 books of motets, with Instruments (1654); 6 books of *Canzonetti spirituali* for One to 4 Voices (1655–56); 2 books of *Musiche spirituali* for One and 2 Voices, *Canzoni, sonetti ed arie a voce sola,* 4 books of *Canzonette ed arie a 1, 2 voci* (all 1657); 2 books of litanies and motets for 2 to 4 Voices. Also 2 stage works *(favole), La mitra* and *La trasformazione di Dafne* (both 1654), and several theoretical works (in MS).
BIBLIOGRAPHY: L. Kurz, *Die Tonartenlehre des römischen Theoretikers und Komponisten P.F. Valentini* (Diss., Univ. of Kassel, 1937).

Valentino,   Henri-Justin-Armand-Joseph, French conductor; b. Lille, Oct. 14, 1785; d. Versailles, Jan. 20, 1865. In 1820 he was 2nd conductor, and in 1824 became first conductor, at the Opéra in Paris; from 1831 to 1836 was conductor at the Opéra-Comique; then founded a society of popular concerts of classical music, as a rival enterprise to the Cons. Concerts, at the Salle St.-Honoré (since called the Salle Valentino); he discontinued them in 1841.

Valerius, Adrianus (Adriaan), Dutch musician; b. Middelburg, 1575; d. Veer, Jan. 27, 1625. From 1606 he lived in Veer as a notary; publ. an important lute tablature book, *Neder-Landtsche Gedenck-Clanck* (Haarlem, 1626); it was reprinted in Utrecht in 1871, in The Hague in 1893, again in Utrecht in 1931, and, in a new edition, in Amsterdam in 1942. It was publ. in a facsimile edition in N.Y. in 1968. A selection was brought out by E. Kremser, with an Eng. text by T. Baker, in N.Y. in 1894.
BIBLIOGRAPHY: J.W. Enschedé, "De Wilhelmus-melodie in de Gedenck-Clanck van Valerius," *Tijdschrift van de Vereeniging voor Nederlandsche Muziekgeschiedenis,* 5 (1897).

Valkare, Gunnar, Swedish composer of the extreme avant-garde; b. Norrköping, April 25, 1943. He studied composition with Lidholm at the Royal Cons. of Stockholm (1963–70). His music is militantly aggressive in its tonal, atonal, and polytonal assault on the most cherished notions of harmonious sweetness.
WORKS: *4 Cardiograms* for Solo Singers, Chorus, and Instruments in varying combinations (1965–66); *A Study in the Story of Human Stupidity* for Orch. (Aarhus, Denmark, Feb. 5, 1968); *Nomo* for 7 Narrators, 6 Winds, and Tape (1967); church drama, *Eld för ett altare (Fire from an Altar;* 1968); *Kanske en pastoral om det får tina upp (Perhaps a Pastorale If It Will Thaw)* for Percussion, Piano, and Strings (1968); musical-dramatic dance, *A Play about the Medieval Värend and the Dacke Feud,* for Winds, Violin, Nickelharp, and Xylophone (1971); *Från mitt rosa badkar (From My Rosy Bathtub)* for Orch., Pop Group, and Chorus (1971); *Det ringer i mitt öra (There Is a Ringing in My Ears)* for Voices and Instruments (1972); *Tahuantisuyos ekonomi* for Chorus, Winds, and Strings (1974); *Mellan berg och hav, mellan himmel och jard (Between the Mountains and the Ocean, Between the Sky and the Earth),* a play on Chinese history, for Singer, Actor, and Instrumental Ensemble (1975).

Vallas, Léon, French writer on music; b. Roanne (Loire), May 17, 1879; d. Lyons, May 9, 1956. After studying medicine in Lyons, he took up music; in 1903 founded the *Revue Musicale de Lyon* (from 1912 to 1914 this was known as the *Revue de Musique Française,* and from 1920 to 1929, as the *Nouvelle Revue Musicale);* from 1908 to 1911 he was engaged as a lecturer on music history at the Univ. of Lyons; also at the Cons. there, in 1912; and at the Sorbonne in Paris, in 1928–30.
WRITINGS: *La Musique à l'Académie de Lyon au XVIIIe siècle* (part of his doctoral thesis, Univ. of Lyons, 1908; the complete work was publ. as *Un Siècle de musique et de théâtre à Lyon, 1688–1789,* Lyons, 1932); *Le Théâtre et la ville, 1694–1712* (1919); *Les Idées de Claude Debussy, musicien français* (Paris, 1927; Eng. trans. as *The Theories of Claude Debussy,* London, 1929); *Georges Migot* (Paris, n.d.); *Claude Debussy et son temps* (Paris, 1932; Eng. trans. as *Claude Debussy, His Life and Works,* London, 1933); *Achille-Claude Debussy,* a brief biography (Paris, 1944); a 2-vol. biography of Vincent d'Indy: vol. 1, *La Jeunesse (1851–1886),* and vol. 2, *La Maturité, la vieillesse (1886–1931),* publ. in Paris (1946; 1950); *La Véritable Histoire de César Franck* (Paris, 1955; reprint, 1972; an Eng. ed. appeared in 1951, earlier than the Paris printing; reprint, Westport, Conn., 1973).

Valle de Paz. See **Del Valle de Paz.**

Valle-Riestra, José María, Peruvian composer; b. Lima, Nov. 9, 1859; d. there, Jan. 25, 1925. He studied as a child in London; after his return to Lima, he continued his musical education without a teacher; as a mature musician, he went to Paris for further studies with André Gédalge (1895–97). When the Academia Nacional de Música was organized in Lima, he was appointed a prof. there. In his compositions, it was his aim to contribute toward the establishment of a national school by the employment of old Inca melodies. His opera *Ollanta* (Lima, Dec. 26, 1900) was a successful dramatization of an Inca subject. His other 2 operas on Inca themes were *Las rosas de Jamaica* (one act) and *Atahualpa* (3 acts). He also wrote *Misa de Requiem* for Chorus and Orch.; *En Oriente* for Orch.; *Elegía* for String Orch.; choruses a cappella; songs.

Vallerand, Jean, Canadian composer; b. Montreal, Dec. 24, 1915. He studied violin at an early age; then took lessons in composition from Champagne (1935–42); served as director of music programs for the French Radio Network of the Canadian Broadcasting Corp. (1960–66). As a composer, he wrote music in a neo-Romantic manner; in his later compositions he experimented with serial techniques. WORKS: *Le Magicien*, chamber opera; *Le Diable dans le beffroi* for Orch. (1939); Violin Sonata (1950; orchestrated as a Violin Concerto, 1951); String Quartet (1958); *Réverbérations contractoires* for Orch. (Montreal, March 6, 1961); *Cordes en mouvements (Strings in Motion)* for String Orch. (1961; Montreal, March 27, 1961); *Etude concertante* for Violin and Orch. (1969).

Valleria (real name, **Schoening**), **Alwina,** American soprano; b. Baltimore, Oct. 12, 1848; d. Nice, Feb. 17, 1925. She studied singing in London with Luigi Arditi; made her first appearance in London (June 2, 1871); was engaged to sing Italian opera at St. Petersburg; returning to England, she became very successful in opera, including the Wagnerian repertoire. She made her American debut as Marguérite (N.Y., Oct. 22, 1879); sang Leonora in *Il Trovatore* at the Metropolitan Opera House (Oct. 26, 1883), but retired from the stage after that season.

Vallet, Nicolas, French lutenist; b. Corbéni, 1583; d. Amsterdam, after 1633. In 1615 he publ. at Amsterdam a book of French, German, and English songs, also preludes, fantasias, etc., in lute tablature: *Secretum musarum* (2nd ed., 1618, with the title *Paradisus musicus testudinis*); he also publ. *Le Second Livre de tabulature de luth* (1618) and *21 Psaumes de David* (in lute tablature; 1619). A modern edition, *Œuvres de Nicolas Vallet pour luth seul: Le Secret des Muses, livres I, II*, edited by A. Souris, appeared in 1970.

Valletti, Cesare, Italian tenor; b. Rome, Dec. 18, 1922. He studied with Tito Schipa; made his debut in Bari in 1947; then sang in Rome and at La Scala in Milan. On Dec. 10, 1953, he made his Metropolitan Opera debut in N.Y.; remained on the company's roster until 1960. He also sang at Covent Garden in London. His repertoire ranges from Mozart to the Italian bel canto roles.

Vallotti, Francesco Antonio, Italian theorist and composer; b. Vercelli, June 11, 1697; d. Padua, Jan. 10, 1780. A Franciscan monk, he was a pupil of Calegari at Padua; was 3rd organist at the basilica, 1723; on Feb. 21, 1730, was elected maestro at the church of S. Antonio, remaining in that post for 50 years. He was one of the foremost organists of his time. WRITINGS: *Responsoria in parasceve, Responsoria in Sabbato Sancto,* and *Responsoria in Coena Domini,* all *a* 4 (masses, motets, etc., in MS at Padua); *Della scienza teorica e pratica della moderna musica,* Book 1 (Padua, 1779; republ. by Bernandino Rizzi, Padua, 1950; other 3 books unpubl.), a learned work agreeing in its main principles with Rameau and Tartini, and correcting some of their errors; Vallotti's system is explained in *La vera idea delle musicali numeriche signature* of L.A. Sabbatini, who, like Abbé Vogler, was Vallotti's pupil. BIBLIOGRAPHY: L.A. Sabbatini, *Notizie sopra la vita e le opere di F.A. Vallotti* (Padua, 1780).

Valvasensi, Lazaro, Italian organist and composer; b. Valvasone, Udine, (baptized, June 20), 1585; d. there, June 26, 1661. In 1622 he was an organist at Murano (Venice); in 1626, choirmaster at Tolmezzo (Udine); from 1634 to 1640 was an organist at Valvasone. He publ. *Letanie della B. V. a 5 voci, con un Mottetto nell'ultimo concertato per sonar nell'Organo* (Venice, 1622); *Compieta concertata a 4 voci,* with Continuo (Venice, 1626); *Secondo giardino d'amorosi fiori* (23 solo airs and one duet, with Instrumental Accompaniment; Venice, 1634; unique copy at Christ Church, Oxford). BIBLIOGRAPHY: V. Formentini and L. Stella, "Lazaro Valvasensi: Musicista di Valvasone," *Itinerari* (1974).

Valverde, Joaquín, Spanish composer of light opera; b. Badajoz, Feb. 27, 1846; d. Madrid, March 17, 1910. He played the flute in bands from the age of 13; then studied at the Cons. of Madrid; received a prize for his orch. work, *Batylo* (1871). From 1871 to 1889 he conducted theater orchs. in Madrid; taught flute at the Madrid Cons., and wrote melodic studies for his instrument. In collaboration with Chueca he wrote a number of zarzuelas, of which the most celebrated was *La gran vía* (Madrid, July 2, 1886; produced in London on April 18, 1906, as *Castles in Spain*); it contains the march *Cádiz,* which became immensely popular. His son, **Joaquín Valverde y San Juan,** known under his diminutive given name, **Quinito** (b. Madrid, Jan. 2, 1875; d. Mexico City, Nov. 4, 1918), was also a composer; he wrote some 250 light pieces for the theater; his zarzuela *El gran capitán* was especially successful. He died during an American tour which he undertook as conductor of a light opera company.

Van Aerde, Raymond (Joseph Justin), Belgian musicologist; b. Mechlin, June 4, 1876; d. there, March 16, 1944. He was a librarian and a lecturer on music history at the Cons. of Mechlin. WORKS (all publ. in Mechlin): A life of Cipriano de Rore (1909); *Les Tuerlinckx, luthiers à Malines* (1914); *Ménestrels communaux et instrumentistes* *à Malines de 1311 à 1790* (1911); *Musicalia; Documents pour servir à l'histoire de la musique à Malines* (2 vols., 1925–30); *Les Ancêtres flamands de Beethoven* (1928).

Van Allan, Richard, English bass; b. Nottingham, May 28, 1935. He received his musical training at the Birmingham School of Music; then sang in the Glyndebourne Festival Chorus; made his operatic debut there in 1966. From 1969 he sang at the Sadler's Wells Opera, and from 1971, at Covent Garden.

Van Beinum, Eduard. See **Beinum, Eduard van.**

Van Bree, Joannes. See **Bree, Jean Bernard van.**

Vancea, Zeno, outstanding Rumanian composer and musicologist; b. Bosca-Vasiovei (Banat), Oct. 21, 1900. He studied at the Cluj Cons. (1919–21); then took lessons in composition with Ernst Kanitz in Vienna. Returning to Rumania, he taught at conservatories in Tîrgu-Mures (1926–40; director, 1946–48), Timisoara (1940–45), and Bucharest (1949–73). He was the editor of the important Rumanian monthly *Muzica* (1953–64). Vancea belongs to the national school of Rumanian composers; in his music he makes use of folk-song patterns without direct quotations. Harmonically, he adopts many procedures of cosmopolitan modern music while cautiously avoiding abrasive sonorities. WORKS: Ballet, *Priculiciul (The Werewolf;* 1932–33; Bucharest, 1942; revised 1957); *Requiem* (1941); cantata, *Cîntecul păcii (Song of Peace;* 1961); 2 *Rapsodia bănăteana* for Orch. (1926, 1950); *Scoarte,* suite for Chamber Orch. (1928); 2 *Grotesque Dances* for Orch. (1937); 2 sinfoniettas (1948, 1967); *O zi de vară (On a Summer Day),* suite for Orch. (1951); *Symphonic Triptych* (1958; also known as *Preambule, Intermezzo and March); Burlesca* for Orch. (1959); Concerto for Small Orch. (1960); 5 *Pieces* for String Orch. (1964); *Symphonic Prologue* (1973); *Cvartet bizantin,* string quartet in the Byzantine style (1931); 6 string quartets (1934, 1953, 1957, 1965, 1969–70, 1975); choruses; solo songs. He publ. a valuable book on Rumanian music of the 19th and 20th centuries, *Creatia muzicală românească Sec. XIX–XX* (Bucharest, 1968).

Van Cleve, John Smith, American pianist and composer; b. Maysville, Ky., Oct. 30, 1851; d. New York, Dec. 28, 1917. He became totally blind at the age of 9; studied with Apthorp in Boston; was active in Cincinnati as a piano teacher and music critic (1879–97); then lived in Chicago; in 1913 moved to N.Y. He publ. a *Gavotte humoresque* for Piano, and some other pieces.
BIBLIOGRAPHY: L.C. Elson, *The History of American Music* (N.Y., 1904; p. 331).

Van Dam, José (real name, **Joseph Van Damme**), bass-baritone; b. Brussels, Aug. 25, 1940. He studied at the Royal Cons. of Music in Brussels; made his operatic debut at the Paris Opéra in 1961. Herbert von Karajan engaged him as a soloist with the Berlin Phil. during its American tour in 1976. He greatly distinguished himself in assuming the title role in the world premiere of Messiaen's opera *Saint François d'Assise* (Paris Opéra, Nov. 28, 1983).

Van Delden, Lex. See **Delden, Lex van.**

Van de Moortel, Arie, Belgian composer and violist; b. Laeken, July 17, 1918; d. Brussels, May 1, 1976. He studied at the Royal Cons. in Brussels and in Ghent; made his debut as a violist in 1938 in the "Trio of the Court of Belgium"; taught chamber music at the Brussels Cons. (1946–76) and was director of the music academy at Anderlecht (1957–76). WORKS: *Silly Symphony;* Trio for Oboe, Clarinet, and Bassoon (1939; revised 1954); Concerto for Orch.; *Toccata* for Piano; Viola Sonata; *Nocturne* for Clarinet, Saxophone, Cello, and Piano; Sonata for Solo Harp (1955); *Capriccio* for Carillon (1957); *Danse d'Espagne* for Solo Harp; *Improvisation on a Choral Theme* for Flute and Piano (1967); Sonata for Flute Solo (1968); Violin Sonatina (1969); *Rondo-pastorale,* in memoriam E. Ysaÿe, for Violin and Piano (1970); *Sonata ostinato* for Violin and Organ (1974).

Van den Boorn-Coclet, Henriette, Belgian composer; b. Liège, Jan. 15, 1866; d. there, March 6, 1945. She studied with Radoux and Dupuis at the Liège Cons., and subsequently taught harmony there. Her compositions attracted considerable attention. She wrote a Symph.; a symph. poem, *Le Renouveau; Sérénade* for Cello and Piano; various piano pieces (*Mazurka, Caprice,* etc.); songs.

Van den Borren, Charles (-Jean-Eugène), eminent Belgian musicologist; b. Ixelles, near Brussels, Nov. 17, 1874; d. Brussels, Jan. 14, 1966. He studied theory with E. Closson; after receiving the degree of Dr.Juris, he practiced law until 1905; then devoted himself to historical research in music. He became one of the greatest authorities on the music of the Renaissance; was a lecturer at the Univ. of Liège (1927–44); from 1926, was a prof. of music history at the Univ. Libre of Brussels; he held many positions in learned societies. WRITINGS: *L'Œuvre dramatique de César Franck* (1907); *Les Origines de la musique de clavecin en Angleterre* (1912; Eng. trans. as *The Sources of Keyboard Music in England,* 1914); *Les Musiciens belges en Angleterre à l'époque de la Renaissance* (1913); *Les Origines de la musique de clavecin dans les Pays-Bas (Nord et Sud) jusque vers 1630* (1914); *Les Débuts de la musique à Venise* (1914); *Orlande de Lassus* (1920); *Le Manuscrit musical M.222 C.22 de la Bibliothèque de Strasbourg* (Antwerp, 1924); *Guillaume Dufay* (1926); *Etudes sur le quinzième siècle musical* (Antwerp, 1941); *Peter Benoît* (Brussels, 1942); *Roland de Lassus* (Brussels, 1944); *Geschiedenis van de muziek in de Nederlanden* (2 vols., Antwerp, 1948–51); etc. He ed. *Polyphonia sacra* (15th-century pieces; publ. in London, 1932); *Pièces polyphoniques profanes de prove-*

Van den Eeden – Van der Velden

nance liégeoise (XVᵉ siècle) (Brussels, 1950); was co-editor of the collected works of Philippe de Monte (1927–39).

BIBLIOGRAPHY: A compendium, *Hommage à Charles Van den Borren* (Antwerp, 1945), with a list of his works; another Hommage was publ. to honor his 80th birthday (Brussels, 1954), and another to commemorate the centenary of his birth (Brussels, 1974).

Van den Eeden, Jean-Baptiste. See **Eeden, Jean-Baptiste van den.**

Van der Horst, Anthon. See **Horst, Anthon van der.**

Van der Linden, Cornelis, Dutch conductor and composer; b. Dordrecht, Aug. 24, 1839; d. Amsterdam, May 29, 1918. He studied with Kwast (piano) and F. Böhme (theory); after sojourns in Belgium, Paris, and Germany, he conducted various choral organizations; from 1875 also led symph. concerts; he was conductor of the newly established Nederlandsche Oper in Amsterdam (1888–94); produced 2 of his own operas there: *Catharina en Lambert* (Nov. 24, 1888) and *Leiden ontzet (The Relief of Leiden;* April 1, 1893); he also wrote 7 overtures and many choral works.

Vandermaesbrugge, Max, Belgian composer; b. Couillet, June 14, 1933. He studied with Moulaert, Souris, Stehman, Louel, and Absil at the Royal Cons. in Brussels (1951–60); taught piano and solfeggio at the music academies in Anderlecht (1955–62), Josseten-Noode (1958–62), and de Forest (1959–62), and at Etterbeek (1963–66). In 1966 he was appointed to the faculty of the Brussels Cons.; in 1972 he succeeded Defossez as inspector of Belgian music schools.

WORKS: *Drum follies,* variations for 10 Percussionists (1961); *Caprice* for Violin and Piano (1961); *4 fables de Florian* for Soprano, Contralto, and Baritone (1961); *Miniature Variations* for Guitar Solo (1962); Duo for Flute and Viola (1962); *En petits caractères* for 2 Trumpets and Piano obbligato (1963); Quartet for 4 Clarinets (1965); *Tema e Variazioni* for Carillon (1967); *Divertimento* for Flute and Strings (1969); *Hiver,* symph. poem (1970); *4 instantanés* for Flute and Guitar (1972); *Sinfonia* for Strings (1972); *Saxofolies* for Saxophone Septet (1974).

Vandernoot, André, Belgian conductor; b. Brussels, June 2, 1927. He studied at the Brussels Cons.; later took courses at the Vienna Academy of Music. In 1958 he was appointed first conductor of the Royal Flemish Opera in Antwerp; from 1959 to 1973 he served as music director of the Théâtre Royal de la Monnaie in Brussels. In 1974–75 he was music director of the Orch. National de Belgique in Brussels; in 1976 was named first guest conductor of the Antwerp Phil. He also made guest appearances as a conductor in Europe, Japan, the U.S., and South America.

Van der Straeten, Edmond, Belgian music historian; b. Audenarde, Dec. 3, 1826; d. there, Nov. 26, 1895. He studied philosophy in Ghent; went to Brussels in 1857 as secretary to Fétis, with whom he studied counterpoint. He held a lifelong position at the Royal Library, and rarely left Belgium; was active as a music critic (1859–72); wrote an opera, *Le Proscrit.* His reputation rests upon his scholarly publications, dealing with music in the Low Countries.

WRITINGS: He publ. a monumental work of reference, *La Musique au Pays-Bas avant le XIXᵉ siècle* (8 vols., 1867–88); other writings are: *Coup d'œil sur la musique actuelle à Audenarde* (1851); *Notice sur Charles-Félix de Hollande* (1854); *Notice sur les carillons d'Audenarde* (1855); *Recherches sur la musique à Audenarde avant le XIXᵉ siècle* (1856); *Examen des chants populaires des Flamands de France, publiés par E. de Coussemaker* (1858); *J.-F.-J. Janssens* (1866); *Wagner; Verslag aan den heer minister van binnenlandsche Zaaken* (1871); *Le Théâtre villageois en Flandre* (2 vols., 1874, 1880); *Les Musiciens belges en Italie* (1875); *Voltaire musicien* (1878); *Les Ballets des rois en Flandre; Xylographie, musique, coutumes, etc.* (1892); *Charles V musicien* (1894); *Les Willems, luthiers gantois du XVIIᵉ siècle* (1896; with C. Snoeck).

Van der Straeten, Edmund Sebastian Joseph, German cellist; b. Düsseldorf, April 29, 1855; d. London, Sept. 17, 1934. He studied cello in Cologne and London; also played the viola da gamba, and organized a trio with his son Ludwig and N. Greiffenhagen, which gave performances of music for viols by composers of the Baroque. He wrote *The Technics of Violoncello Playing* (1898; 2nd ed., 1905); *The Romance of the Fiddle* (1911); *History of the Violoncello, the Viol da Gamba, Their Precursors and Collateral Instruments* (1915); *The History of the Violin* (2 vols., 1933).

Van der Stucken, Frank (Valentin), American conductor; b. Fredericksburg, Texas, Oct. 15, 1858; d. Hamburg, Aug. 16, 1929. He was taken by his parents to Antwerp as a child, and studied music with Peter Benoit; then became associated with Reinecke in Leipzig; he also met Liszt. In 1884 he returned to the U.S., and became a choral conductor. He was the first to conduct a concert of American music in Europe, when at the Paris Exposition (July 12, 1889) he gave the first European performances of works by MacDowell, Foote, Chadwick, and Huss; he also gave similar programs in Germany. From 1895 to 1903 he was director of the Cincinnati College of Music; concurrently, he conducted concerts of the Cincinnati Symph. Orch. (1895–1907). In 1898 he was called upon to lead the remaining concerts of the season of the N.Y. Phil., following the death of Anton Seidl. In 1907 he went to Germany, and remained there for the rest of his life. He composed a few orch. pieces and choruses.

Van der Velden, Renier, Belgian composer; b. Antwerp, Jan. 14, 1910. He studied in Brussels with

Jan Broeckx, Karel Candael, and Joseph Jongen; in 1945 was appointed program director of the French services of Belgian Radio in Antwerp. In 1970 he became a member of the Royal Flemish Academy of Arts, Letters, and Sciences.

WORKS: 12 ballets: *Indruk aan Zee* for Small Orch. (1930); *Provinciestad 1900* (1937); *L'Enlèvement de Proserpine* (1947); *Les Amours de torero* (1948); *De zakdoekjes* (1947); *Dulle Griet* (1949; revised 1967); *Les Ancêtres* (1949); *Arlequinade* (1950); *Judith* for 2 Pianos and Percussion (1951; orch. version, 1953); *De Triomf van de dood* (1963); *Oostendse maskers* (1965); *Ballet Music* for 20 Winds and Piano (1972); *Impression maritime* for Small Orch. (1930); *Divertimento* for String Orch. (1938); *Hommage à Ravel,* symph. suite (1938; the 2nd part, *Habanera,* is often played separately); Trumpet Concerto (1940); Oboe Concerto (1941); Sinfonietta for String Orch. (1942); 2 suites for Orch. (1945, 1955); Concertino for Clarinet, Bassoon, Piano, and String Orch. (1949); *Kamermuziek* for Viola and Chamber Ensemble (1956); Violin Concerto (1958); Concertino for Viola and Chamber Orch. (1964); Concertino for Flute and Strings (1965); *Beweging (Movement)* for Orch. (1968); *Etude* for 11 Instruments (1969); Sinfonietta (1969); Concertino for Piano and Strings (1971); *Hulde aan Janáček (Homage to Janáček),* 3 short pieces for Flute, Oboe, and String Orch. (1973); 2 concertos for Wind Quintet (1939, 1955); *Adagio and Finale* for String Trio (1940); Trio for Oboe, Clarinet, and Bassoon (1943); Sextet for Wind Quintet and Piano (1948); *Divertimento* for Oboe, Clarinet, and Bassoon (1957); Concertino for Brass Quintet and 2 Pianos (1965); *Fantaisie* for 4 Clarinets (1967); *2 Dialogues* for Clarinet and Piano (1971); 2 suites for Piano (1937, 1944); *Beweging* for 2 Pianos (1965); songs, among them *8 poèmes de Karel van de Woestijne* for High Voice and Piano (1946; orchestrated 1951).

Van de Woestijne, David, Belgian composer; b. Llanidloes, Wales, Feb. 18, 1915; d. Brussels, May 18, 1979. He was the son of the painter Gustav van de Woestijne and the nephew of the Flemish poet Karel van de Woestijne. After studies in harmony and counterpoint with Désiré Defauw and Paul Gilson, he took lessons with the Spanish composer Oscar Esplá during Esplá's stay in Belgium. Van de Woestijne's music reflects the trends of cosmopolitan modernism, gravitating toward neo-Baroque techniques.

WORKS: Opera, *Graal 68 ou L'Impromptu de Gand* (Ghent, 1968); opera-ballet, *Le Débat de la folie et de l'amour* (1959); television opera, *De zoemende musikant* (1967); Double Concerto for Piano, Cello, and Orch. (1935); *Fantasia* for Oboe and Orch. (1936); Piano Concerto (1938); *Ballade* for Piano and Orch. (1940); Concerto for Violin and 12 Solo Instruments (1945); *Sérénades* for Piano, 12 Wind Instruments, Double Bass, and Percussion (1946; International Society for Contemporary Music Festival, Copenhagen, June 2, 1947); 2 cantatas: *La Belle Cordière* for Soprano and Orch. (1954) and *Les Aéronauts* for Soli, Chorus, Speaking Chorus,

and Orch. (1963); Symph. (1958); Symph. in One Movement (1965); *Concertino da camera* for Flute, Oboe, and Strings (1967); *Aswoendag (Ash Wednesday)* for Narrator, Soli, Chorus, and Orch. (1971); Concerto for 2 Pianos (1972); Concerto for String Quartet, 14 Wind Instruments, and Double Bass (1974); *Hommage à Purcell* for Harpsichord and Strings (1974); *Fénentwintig* for Piano, 19 Winds, and Double Bass (1976); *Divertimento* for Oboe, Clarinet, and Bassoon (1942); Quintet for Flute, Oboe, Violin, Viola, and Cello (1953); Violin Sonata (1956); Variations for 7 Instruments (1965); *Sarabande* for 2 Guitars (1965); String Quartet (1970); *Devant une sculpture* for 12 Instruments (1969); *Notturno* for Flute and Piano (1976); *Music* for Tuba or Saxhorn, and Piano (1976); *Minuetto capriccioso* for Trumpet and Piano (1976); *Toccata* for Piano (1935); Piano Sonatina (1945); 2-Piano Sonata (1955); songs.

Van Dieren, Bernard. See **Dieren, Bernard van.**

Van Doorslaer, Georges, Belgian musicologist; b. Mechlin, Sept. 27, 1864; d. there, Jan. 16, 1940. He was a physician by profession, but studied music as an avocation; wrote several valuable treatises dealing with Belgian musicians: *Herry Bredemers, 1472–1522* (Antwerp, 1915); *De Toonkunstenaars der familie Vredeman* (Antwerp, 1920); *La Vie et les œuvres de Philippe de Monte* (Brussels, 1921); *Rinaldo del Mel* (Antwerp, 1922). He also edited 8 vols. in the collected edition of works by Philippe de Monte.

Van Dresser, Marcia, American soprano; b. Memphis, Tenn., Dec. 4, 1877; d. London, July 11, 1937. She studied in Chicago and N.Y.; sang minor parts at the Metropolitan Opera (1903–4); then, after further study in Germany, she made her European debut in Dresden (1907); was a member of the Dessau Opera (1908–10) and the Frankfurt Opera (1911–14). Returning to the U.S. in 1915, she gave a recital in N.Y. (March 22, 1915), and joined the Chicago Opera (1915–17).

Van Durme, Jef, Belgian composer; b. Kemzeke-Waas, May 7, 1907; d. Brussels, Jan. 28, 1965. He studied at the Royal Flemish Cons. in Antwerp with Flor Alpaerts; in 1931 he went to Vienna, where he took lessons in advanced composition with Alban Berg.

WORKS: Operas: *Remous,* after Weterings (Brussels, 1936); *The Death of a Salesman,* after Arthur Miller (1954–55); also *King Lear* (1955–57), *Anthony and Cleopatra* (1957–59), and *Richard III* (1960–61), all after Shakespeare; 2 ballets: *De dageraad* (1932–33; Antwerp, 1934) and *Orestes* (1934–35; suite for Orch., 1936–40); 2 symph. poems: *Hamlet* (1929) and *Beatrice* (1930); oratorio, *De 14 stonden* (1931); 6 symphs.: No. 1 (1934); No. 2 (1938–39); No. 3 (1945–46); No. 4 (1950–51); No. 5 (1952); No. 6 (1953); 2 *Elegies* for Orch. (1933, 1938); *Poème héroïque* (1935); *Breughel Symphony* (1935–42); 2 *Sinfonie da camera* (1937, 1949); 3 *Ballads* for Orch.: No. 1, *In memoriam Alban Berg* (1938); No. 2 (1947–48); No.

3 (1961); 2 piano concertos (1943, 1946); *Symphonic Prologue* (1944–45); Violin Concerto (1946–47); 3 suites for Orch. (1947, 1948–60, 1962); *Van Gogh Suite* for Orch. (1954); Sinfonietta for Strings (1962); 3 violin sonatas (1928, 1938, 1947); Sextet for Piano and Wind Quintet (1930); 5 string quartets (1932–33, 1937, 1945–48, 1948–53, 1953); Piano Quartet (1934); 2 piano sonatas (1946, 1952–53); 4 piano trios (1928, 1929, 1942, 1949); Cello Sonata (1952); Wind Quintet (1951–52); piano pieces; 21 songs, 2 with orch.

Van Duyze, Florimond, Belgian music scholar and composer; b. Ghent, Aug. 4, 1843; d. there, May 18, 1910. He studied at the Ghent Cons.; publ. some valuable collections of old Netherlandish vocal music, among them *Het oude nederlandsche lied* (4 vols., 1903–8).
BIBLIOGRAPHY: P. Bergmans, "Florimond van Duyze," *Annuaire de l'Académie royale des sciences* (Brussels, 1919).

Van Dyck, Ernest (Marie Hubert), Belgian tenor; b. Antwerp, April 2, 1861; d. Berlaer-lez-Lierre, Aug. 31, 1923. He studied law; was a journalist in Paris; sang in the 9th Symph. of Beethoven at a Lamoureux concert (Dec. 2, 1883); made his operatic debut as Lohengrin in the memorable French premiere, on May 3, 1887; from 1888 to 1898 he was a member of the Vienna Opera; from 1898 to 1902 he sang Wagnerian roles at the Metropolitan Opera (debut as Tannhäuser, Nov. 29, 1898). After his return to Europe he continued to appear as a Wagnerian tenor until 1906, when he settled down as a singing teacher in Brussels and Antwerp. In 1886 he married Augusta Servais, a sister of the famous cellist.

Van Gilse, Jan. See **Gilse, Jan van.**

Van Hagen, Peter Albrecht, Dutch musician active in America; b. in the Netherlands, 1750; d. Boston, 1803. After his arrival in America from the Netherlands in 1774, he settled in Charleston, S.C., as a music teacher; from 1789 to 1796 was in N.Y., giving concerts with his wife and son; in 1796 the family moved to Boston. He composed a *Federal Overture* (1797; not to be confused with *The Federal Overture* by B. Carr); *Funeral Dirge for George Washington* (1800); much theater music. His son, **Peter Albrecht, Jr.** (1781–1837), born in Charleston, was also a musician; he wrote songs and composed an overture.
BIBLIOGRAPHY: O.G. Sonneck and W.T. Upton, *Early Concert-Life in America* (1907; revised 1945).

Van Hal, Johann Baptist. See **Wanhal, Johann Baptist.**

Van Hoogstraten, Willem. See **Hoogstraten, Willem van.**

Van Hoose, Ellison, American tenor; b. Murfreesboro, Tenn., Aug. 18, 1868; d. Houston, Texas, March 24, 1936. He studied with Luckstone in N.Y., Jean de Reszke in Paris, and also in Rome and London. He made his operatic debut with the Damrosch Opera Co. in Philadelphia as Tannhäuser (Dec. 11, 1897); toured with Mme. Melba in the U.S. (1903–5) and with Mme. Sembrich (1906–7); toured in Europe (1908–10); was a member of the Chicago Opera Co. (1911–12); then devoted himself mainly to oratorio singing.

Van Katwijk, Paul. See **Katwijk, Paul van.**

Van Lier, Bertus, Dutch composer; b. Utrecht, Sept. 10, 1906; d. Roden, Feb. 14, 1972. He studied composition with Willem Pijper in Amsterdam and conducting with Scherchen in Strasbourg; settled in Utrecht as a conductor, composer, and music critic. He taught at the Rotterdam Cons. (1945–60) and thereafter worked in the dept. of art history at the Univ. of Groningen. His early compositions are modeled on Pijper's "germ-cell" theory, to which he imparted a literary symbolism.
WORKS: Ballet, *Katharsis* (1945; concert version, Utrecht, Nov. 29, 1950); 3 symphs. (1928; 1930–31, revised 1946; 1938–39); Concertino for Cello and Chamber Orch. (1933); *De Dijk (The Dike)* for Narrator and Chamber Orch. (1937); *Canticum* for Female Chorus; 2 Flutes; Piano, 4-hands; and Strings (1939); *O Netherlands, Pay Attention,* cantata for Chorus, Timpani, and Strings (1945); *Het Hooglied (The Song of Songs)* for Soloists, Chorus, and Small Orch. (1949; in Dutch and Eng.); Bassoon Concerto (1950); *Symfonia* for 2 String Orchs., Double Wind Quintet, and Timpani (1954); *Cantate voor Kerstmis (Christmas Cantata)* for Chorus and Orch. (1955); *Divertimento facile* for Orch. (1957); *Concertante Music* for Violin, Oboe, and Orch. (1959); *5 Mei: Zij (5th of May: They),* oratorio (Radio Hilversum, May 5, 1963, 18th anniversary of the liberation of the Netherlands); *Intrada reale e Sinfonia festiva* for Orch. (1964); *Variaties en thema* for Orch. (1967; Bergen, Norway, Jan. 17, 1968); String Quartet (1929); Solo Violin Sonata (1931); *Small Suite* for Violin and Piano (1935); *3 Old Persian Quatrains* for Soprano, Bass Flute, Oboe d'Amore, and Piano (1956); incidental music for Sophocles' *Ajax* (1932) and *Antigone* (1952); piano pieces; choruses. He publ. a number of essays on music under the title *Buiten de maastreep (Beyond the Bar Line;* Amsterdam, 1948) and *Rhythme en metrum* (Groningen, 1967).

Van Lier, Jacques, Dutch cellist; b. The Hague, April 24, 1875; d. Worthing, England, Feb. 25, 1951. He studied cello with Hartog in The Hague and with Eberle in Rotterdam; joined the Berlin Phil. in 1897; from 1899 to 1915 was an instructor of cello at the Klindworth-Scharwenka Cons. in Berlin. He was cellist in the Holländisches Trio, with J. van Veen (violin) and Coenraad Bos (piano); the trio enjoyed a European reputation (1900–1907); in 1915 he settled in The Hague; after 1939 he went to England. He publ. *Violoncellbogentechnik* and *Moderne Violoncelltechnik der linken und der rechten Hand;*

also edited about 400 classical pieces for cello.
BIBLIOGRAPHY: *Musical Opinion* (Oct. 1931).

Van Maldeghem, Robert Julien. See **Maldeghem, Robert Julien van.**

Van Maldere, Pierre. See **Maldere, Pierre van.**

Vanni-Marcoux. See **Marcoux, Vanni.**

Vannuccini, Luigi, noted Italian singing master; b. Fojano, Dec. 4, 1828; d. Montecatini, Aug. 14, 1911. He studied at the Cons. in Florence, where he became an opera conductor (1848); then turned to the study of the piano, and appeared as a concert pianist with excellent success; finally settled in Florence, devoted himself exclusively to vocal training, and acquired fame as a singing master. He publ. some songs and piano pieces.
BIBLIOGRAPHY: L. Neretti, "Luigi Vannuccini," *Musica d'Oggi* (1931).

Van Otterloo, Willem. See **Otterloo, Willem van.**

Van Raalte, Albert. See **Raalte, Albert van.**

Van Rooy, Anton (Antonius Maria Josephus), Dutch baritone; b. Rotterdam, Jan. 1, 1870; d. Munich, Nov. 28, 1932. He was a church chorister; studied voice with Stockhausen at Frankfurt. In 1897 he was engaged to sing at Bayreuth, and performed there the 3 Wotans with excellent success. On Dec. 14, 1898, he made his American debut as Wotan in *Die Walküre* at the Metropolitan Opera, where he appeared each season (except 1900–1901) until 1908, singing during the summers at Covent Garden in London and at Bayreuth. In 1908 he was engaged as a regular member of the Frankfurt Opera. He retired from the stage in 1913. He was particularly distinguished in Wagnerian roles, but also was noted for his interpretations of Escamillo in *Carmen* and Valentin in *Faust.*

Van Rossum, Frédéric, Belgian composer; b. Ixelles, near Brussels, Dec. 5, 1939. He studied with Marcel Quinet at the Brussels Cons. (1956–62); then taught piano there (1965–68); later was an instructor in music analysis. He won a Premier Grand Prix de Rome in 1965 for his *Cantate de la Haute Mer.*
WORKS: *Petite piece* for Clarinet and Piano (1961); Piano Sonata (1963); *Capriccio* for Wind Quintet (1963); Sinfonietta (1964); *Cantata sacrée* for Chorus, Strings, and Harpsichord (1966); *12 Miniatures* for Piano or Orch. (1967); String Quartet (1967); *Divertimento* for String Orch. (1967); *Sinfonie concertante* for Horn, Piano, Percussion, and Orch. (1968); *Graffiti* for Violin and Piano (1968); *Duetto* for Cello and Piano (1968); *Pyrogravures* for Wind Quintet (1968); *Threni* for Mezzosoprano and Orch. (1969); *Der Blaue Reiter*, in homage to German expressionistic painters, for Orch. (1971); *Epitaph* for String Orch. (1972); Piano Quintet (1972); *Rétrospection* for Soprano, Contralto, Chorus, 2 Pianos, and Percussion (1973); *Réquisitoire* for Brass and Percussion (1973); Piano Concerto (1975).

Van Slyck, Nicholas, American composer, conductor, pianist, and music educator; b. Philadelphia, Oct. 25, 1922; d. Boston, July 3, 1983. He studied piano with George Reeves, conducting with Henry Swoboda, and composition with Walter Piston at Harvard Univ., where he obtained his M.A. He was founder and conductor of the Dedham (Mass.) Chorus in 1954 and also led the Quincy (Mass.) Orch. (1962–67); served as director of the South End Music Center of Boston (1950–62) and of the Longy School of Music (1962–76). In 1976 he organized the New School of Music in Cambridge, Mass. His music is pragmatic in its form and destination, while the technical structure is catholic, ranging from triadic to dodecaphonic. He compiled a piano anthology, *Looking Forward* (1981).
WORKS: *Variations* for Piano and Orch. (1947); 2 clarinet sonatas (1947, 1958); 2 divertimenti for Chamber Orch. (1947, 1948); Sonatina for Clarinet and String Orch. (1948); *Concert Music* for Piano and Orch. (1954); Piano Concerto No. 2 (1957); 2 cello sonatas (1954, 1968); 4 violin sonatas (1956–65); Flute Sonata (1957); Quartet for Clarinet, Violin, Cello, and Piano (1959); *2 Symphonic Paraphrases* (1960, 1966); Octet for Flute, Clarinet, Horn, Violin, Viola, Cello, Timpani, and Piano (1962); *Legend of Sleepy Hollow* for Chamber Orch. (1963); 6 piano sonatas (1947–59); 6 piano sonatinas (1956–68); numerous piano pieces, choruses, and songs.

Van Vactor, David, American composer and conductor; b. Plymouth, Ind., May 8, 1906. He enrolled in the premedical classes at Northwestern Univ. (1924 –27); then changed to the music school there, studying flute with Arthur Kitti and theory of composition with Arne Oldberg, Felix Borowski, and Albert Noelte. He obtained his B.A. degree there in 1928, and went to Vienna, where he studied composition with the venerable composer Franz Schmidt. In the summer of 1931 he went to Paris, where he took a course in composition with Paul Dukas at the Ecole Normale de Musique and also studied flute with Marcel Moyse at the Paris Cons. Returning to the U.S., he was engaged as a flutist in the Chicago Symph. Orch., holding this post for 12 years (1931– 43). He also began to conduct; in 1943–45 he was assistant conductor of the Kansas City Phil., and also played flute in the orch. In 1947 he was engaged as conductor of the Knoxville Symph. Orch., and held this position until 1972; joined the faculty at the Univ. of Tennessee, where he was prof. of composition from 1947 to 1977. In 1957 he received a Guggenheim fellowship. He made 3 tours of South America under the auspices of the State Dept. In his own music, Van Vactor adheres mainly to basic tonalities, but he enhances them with ingeniously contrived melodic gargoyles, creating a simulation of atonality. The rhythmic vivacity of his inventive writing creates a cheerful, hedonistic atmosphere.
WORKS: FOR ORCH.: *Chaconne* for String Orch.

(Rochester, N.Y., May 17, 1928); *5 Small Pieces for Large Orchestra* (Ravinia Park, Ill., July 5, 1931); *The Masque of the Red Death,* after Edgar Allan Poe (1932); Flute Concerto (Chicago, Feb. 26, 1933); *Passacaglia and Fugue* (Chicago, Jan. 28, 1934); *Concerto Grosso* for 3 Flutes, Harp, and Orch. (Chicago, April 4, 1935); *Overture to a Comedy* No. 1 (Chicago, June 20, 1937); *Overture to a Comedy* No. 2 (Indianapolis, March 14, 1941); *Symphonic Suite* (Ravinia Park, Ill., July 21, 1938); 8 symphs.: No. 1 in D (1936–37; N.Y., Jan. 19, 1939, composer conducting; awarded prize of $1,000 in the American Composers Contest sponsored by the N.Y. Phil.); No. 2, *Music for the Marines* (1943; Indianapolis, March 27, 1943; programmed as a suite, not a symph.); No. 3 (1958; Pittsburgh, April 3, 1959; perf. and recorded as No. 2); No. 4, *Walden,* for Chorus and Orch., to texts from Thoreau's *Walden* (1970–71; first complete perf., Maryville, Tenn., May 9, 1971; listed as Symph. No. 3 at its premiere); No. 5 (1976; Knoxville, Tenn., March 11, 1976); No. 6 for Orch. or Band (1980; for Orch., Knoxville, Nov. 19, 1981; for Band, Ball State Univ., April 13, 1983); No. 7 (1983); No. 8 (1984); *5 Bagatelles* for Strings (Chicago, Feb. 7, 1938); Viola Concerto (Ravinia Park, July 13, 1940); *Variazioni Solenne* (1941; first perf. under the title *Gothic Impressions* by the Chicago Symph. Orch., Feb. 26, 1942); *Pastorale and Dance* for Flute and Strings (1947); Violin Concerto (Knoxville, April 10, 1951); *Fantasia, Chaconne and Allegro* (1957; Louisville, Ky., Feb. 20, 1957); *Suite* for Trumpet and Small Orch. (1962); *Suite on Chilean Folk Tunes* (1963); *Passacaglia, Chorale and Scamper* for Band (1964); *Sinfonia Breve* (1964; Santiago, Chile, Sept. 3, 1965; American premiere, Indianapolis, Oct. 30, 1966); *Sarabande and Variations* for Brass Quintet and Strings (1968; Knoxville, May 4, 1969); *Requiescat* for Strings (Knoxville, Oct. 17, 1970); *Andante and Allegro* for Saxophone and Strings (1972); *Set of 5* for Wind Instruments and Percussion (1973); *Nostalgia* for Band (1975); *Prelude and Fugue* for Strings (1975); *Fanfare and Chorale* for Band (1977); *The Elements* for Band (Univ. of Tennessee, May 22, 1979).

FOR VOICE: *Credo* for Chorus and Orch (1941); Cantata for 3 Treble Voices and Orch. (1947); *The New Light,* Christmas cantata (1954); *Christmas Songs for Young People* for Chorus and Orch. (1961); *A Song of Mankind,* first part of a 7-part cantata (1971; Indianapolis, Sept. 26, 1971); *Processional "Veni Immanuel"* for Chorus and Orch. (1974); *Brethren We Have Met to Worship* for Chorus and Orch. (1975); *Episodes—Jesus Christ* for Chorus and Orch. (1977; Knoxville, May 2, 1977); *Processional* for Chorus, Wind Instruments, and Percussion (1979; Univ. of Tennessee, Dec. 1, 1979).

CHAMBER MUSIC: Quintet for 2 Violins, Viola, Cello, and Flute (1932); *Suite* for 2 Flutes (1934); *Divertimento* for Wind Quintet (1936); 2 string quartets (1940, 1949); Piano Trio (1942); Flute Sonatina (1949); *Duettino* for Violin and Cello (1952); Wind Quintet (1959); *Children of the Stars,* 6 pieces for Violin and Piano (1960); *5 Etudes* for Trumpet Solo (1963); Octet for Brass (1963); *Economy Band* No. 1 for Trumpet, Trombone, and Percussion (1966);

Economy Band No. 2 for Horn, Tuba, and Percussion (1969); *Music for Woodwinds* (1966–67); *4 Etudes* for Wind Instruments and Percussion (1968); Tuba Quartet (1971); Suite for 12 Solo Trombones (1972); *5 Songs* for Flute and Guitar (1974).
BIBLIOGRAPHY: David Ewen, *American Composers* (N.Y., 1982).

Van Vechten, Carl, American novelist and writer on music; b. Cedar Rapids, Iowa, June 17, 1880; d. New York, Dec. 21, 1964. He graduated from the Univ. of Chicago (1903); was music critic of the *N.Y. Times* (1906–7 and 1910–13); was its Paris correspondent in 1908–9. In 1931 he occupied himself with photography, and took a great number of pictures of musicians; his collection of photographs is at Fiske Univ. in Nashville. He publ. *5 Old English Ditties* (1904). His books on music are: *Music after the Great War* (1915); *Music and Bad Manners* (1916); *Interpreters and Interpretations* (1917); *The Music of Spain* (1918); *Red: Papers on Musical Subjects* (1925).
BIBLIOGRAPHY: E.G. Lueders, *Carl Van Vechten and the Twenties* (Albuquerque, 1955).

Van Vleck, Jacob, Moravian minister, violinist, and organist; b. New York, 1751; d. Bethlehem, Pa., July 3, 1831. He was director of the Young Ladies' Seminary at Bethlehem from 1790 to 1800; was consecrated a bishop in 1815. He was the first American-born Moravian to be active as a composer.
BIBLIOGRAPHY: A.G. Rau and H.T. David, *A Catalogue of Music by American Moravians* (Bethlehem, 1938); H.T. David, "Background for Bethlehem: Moravian Music in Pennsylvania," *Magazine of Art* (April 1939); idem, "Musical Life in the Pennsylvania Settlements of the *Unitas Fratrum,*" *Transactions of the Moravian Historical Society* (1942; reprinted as Moravian Music Foundation Publication No. 6, Winston-Salem, N.C., 1959); J.O. Falconer, "The Second Berlin Song School in America," *Musical Quarterly* (July 1973).

Van Vliet, Cornelius, Dutch cellist; b. Rotterdam, Sept. 1, 1886; d. Morelia, Mexico, Jan. 1973. He began to study cello at 9; in 1903 went to Leipzig, where he appeared as a soloist; then joined the Czech Phil. and traveled with it in Poland and Russia; in 1908 was engaged by Mahler as first cellist with the Vienna Phil.; in 1911 settled in the U.S. He was first cellist of the Minneapolis Symph. Orch. (1912–19); of the N.Y. Phil. (1919–29); of the Pittsburgh Symph. Orch. (1938–41); was a prof. of cello at the Univ. of Colorado (1948–53). In 1954 he settled in Mexico.

Van Westerhout, Niccolò, Italian composer; b. (of Dutch parentage) Mola di Bari, Dec. 17, 1857; d. Naples, Aug. 21, 1898. He was a pupil of Nicola d'Arienzo at the Naples Cons.; then became a prof. of harmony there. He wrote 3 operas: *Cimbelino* (Rome, April 7, 1892); *Fortunio* (Milan, May 16, 1895); *Dona Flor* (Mola di Bari, April 18, 1896, on the opening of the Teatro Van Westerhout, named after him); another opera, *Colomba,* was produced posthumously (Naples, March 27, 1923). He also wrote 2 symphs. and a Violin Concerto; publ. many piano pieces of considerable merit, as well as songs.

Van Wyk, Arnold. See **Wyk, Arnold van.**

Van Zandt, Marie, American coloratura soprano; b. New York, Oct. 8, 1861; d. Cannes, Dec. 31, 1919. She studied with her mother, the well-known American soprano **Jennie van Zandt,** and with Lamperti; made her debut in Turin (1879); was engaged at the Opéra-Comique in Paris (1880–85); sang at the Metropolitan Opera in N.Y. during the season of 1891–92; in 1896 she rejoined the Opéra-Comique. Delibes wrote the role of Lakmé for her, and she created it at the Opéra-Comique on April 14, 1883.

Van Zanten, Cornelia, famous Dutch soprano and pedagogue; b. Dordrecht, Aug. 2, 1855; d. The Hague, Jan. 10, 1946. She studied with K. Schneider at the Cologne Cons., and in Milan with Lamperti, who developed her original contralto into a coloratura soprano voice. She made her debut in Turin; then sang in Germany; toured in America in 1886–87 as a member of the National Opera Co. under the directorship of Theodore Thomas; then returned to Europe; appeared in special performances of *Der Ring des Nibelungen* in Russia; finally became a member of the Nederlandsche Oper in Amsterdam; also taught at the Amsterdam Cons. (1895–1903); subsequently lived in Berlin, highly esteemed as a singing teacher; eventually settled in The Hague. She publ. songs to German and Dutch texts; with C.E. Poser, brought out *Leitfaden zum Kunstgesang* (Berlin, 1903).
BIBLIOGRAPHY: J.W. Hofstra, "C. van Zanten," *Mens en Melodie,* 1 (1946).

Varady, Julia, Rumanian soprano; b. Oradea, Sept. 1, 1941. She was educated at the Cons. in Cluj and at the Burcharest Cons. She sang at the Cluj Opera and later at the Bucharest Opera and the Budapest Opera; expanded her operatic career by appearances in Frankfurt, Hamburg, Vienna, Berlin, and Paris. She married the German baritone **Dietrich Fischer-Dieskau.**

Vardi, Emanuel, outstanding Jewish-American violist; b. Jerusalem, April 21, 1917. He began to study the viola in his youth; also studied painting at the Florence Academy of Fine Arts. In 1940 he came to the U.S., and soon established a hegemony in the limited field of viola literature. He arranged works by Bach, Frescobaldi, Tartini, Paganini, and Chopin for viola; also commissioned works for the viola to Michael Colgrass, Alan Hovhaness, Alan Shulman, and others. For variety's sake he made an incursion into the conducting arena; was music director of the South Dakota Symph. Orch. (1978–82). In his leisure time he painted. In 1951 he won the International Prize of Rapallo, and had one-man exhibits in N.Y., South Dakota, and Italy.

Varèse, Edgar, one of the most remarkable composers of his century, who introduced a totally original principle of organizing the materials and forms of sound, profoundly influencing the direction of new music; b. Paris, Dec. 22, 1883; d. New York, Nov. 6, 1965. The original spelling of his first Christian name was **Edgard,** but most of his works were first publ. under the name Edgar; about 1940 he chose to return to the legal spelling, Edgard. He spent his early childhood in Burgundy, and began to compose early in life. In 1892 his parents went to Turin; his paternal grandfather was Italian; his other grandparents were French. In Turin he took private lessons in composition with Giovanni Bolzoni, who taught him gratis. Varèse gained some performing experience by playing percussion in the school orch. He stayed in Turin until 1903; then went to Paris. In 1904 he entered the Schola Cantorum, where he studied with Vincent d'Indy, Albert Roussel, and Charles Bordes; in 1906 he attended the classes of Widor at the Paris Cons. In 1907 he received the "bourse artistique" offered by the City of Paris; at that time he founded and conducted the chorus of the Université Populaire and organized concerts at the Château du Peuple. In Paris he became associated with musicians and artists of the avant-garde; he also met Debussy, who showed interest in his career. In 1907 he married a young actress, Suzanne Bing; they had a daughter. Together they went to Berlin, at that time the center of new music that offered opportunities to Varèse. The marriage was not successful, and they separated in 1913. Romain Rolland gave to Varèse a letter of recommendation for Richard Strauss, who in turn showed interest in Varèse's music. He was also instrumental in arranging a performance of Varèse's symph. poem *Bourgogne,* which was performed in Berlin on Dec. 15, 1910. In Berlin he also met Karl Muck. But the greatest experience for Varèse in Berlin was his meeting and friendship with Busoni. Varèse greatly admired Busoni's book on new music esthetics, and was profoundly influenced by Busoni's views. He composed industriously, mostly for orch.; the most ambitious of these works was a symph. poem, *Gargantua,* but it was never completed. Other works were *Souvenirs, Prélude à la fin d'un jour, Cycles du Nord,* and an incomplete opera, *Oedipus und die Sphinx,* to the text by Hofmannsthal. All these works, in manuscript, were lost under somewhat mysterious circumstances, and Varèse himself destroyed the score of *Bourgogne* later in life. A hostile reception that he encountered from Berlin critics for *Bourgogne* upset Varèse, who expressed his unhappiness in a letter to Debussy. However, Debussy responded with a friendly letter of encouragement, advising Varèse not to pay too much attention to critics. As early as 1913, Varèse began an earnest quest for new musical resources; upon his return to Paris he worked on related problems with the Italian musical futurist Luigi Russolo, although he disapproved of the attempt to find a way to new music through the medium of instrumental noises. He was briefly called to the French army at the outbreak of the First World War, but was discharged because of a chronic lung

Varèse

ailment. In 1915 he went to N.Y. There he met the young American writer Louise Norton; they set up a household together; in 1921, when she obtained her own divorce from a previous marriage, they were married. As in Paris and Berlin, Varèse had chronic financial difficulties in America; the royalties from his few publ. works were minimal; in order to supplement his earnings he accepted a job as a piano salesman, which was repulsive to him. He also appeared in a minor role in a John Barrymore silent film in 1918. Some welcome aid came from the wealthy artist Gertrude Vanderbilt, who sent him monthly allowances for a certain length of time. Varèse also had an opportunity to appear as a conductor. As the U.S. neared the entrance into war against Germany, there was a demand for French conductors to replace the German music directors who had held the monopoly on American orchs. On April 1, 1917, Varèse conducted in N.Y. the Requiem Mass of Berlioz. On March 17, 1918, he conducted a concert of the Cincinnati Symph. Orch. in a program of French and Russian music; he also included an excerpt from *Lohengrin,* thus defying the general ban on German music. However, he apparently lacked that indefinable quality that makes a conductor, and he was forced to cancel further concerts with the Cincinnati Symph. Eager to promote the cause of modern music, he organized a symph. orch. in N.Y. with the specific purpose of giving performances of new and unusual music; it presented its first concert on April 11, 1919. In 1922, he organized with Carlos Salzedo the International Composers' Guild, which gave its inaugural concert in N.Y. on Dec. 17, 1922. In 1926 he founded, in association with a few progressive musicians, the Pan American Society, dedicated to the promotion of music of the Americas. He intensified his study of the nature of sound, working with the acoustician Harvey Fletcher (1926–36), and with the Russian electrical engineer Leo Theremin, then resident in the U.S. These studies led him to the formulation of the concept of "organized sound," in which the sonorous elements in themselves determined the progress of composition; this process eliminated conventional thematic development; yet the firm cohesion of musical ideas made Varèse's music all the more solid, while the distinction between consonances and dissonances became no longer of basic validity. The resulting product was unique in modern music; characteristically, Varèse attached to his works titles from the field of mathematics or physics, such as *Intégrales, Hyperprism* (a projection of a prism into the 4th dimension), *Ionisation* (atomic fission), *Density 21.5* (the specific weight of platinum), etc., while the score of his large orch. work *Arcana* derived its inspiration from the cosmology of Paracelsus. An important development was Varèse's application of electronic music in his *Déserts* and, much more extensively, in his *Poème électronique,* commissioned for the Brussels World Exposition in 1958. Varsèse wrote relatively few works in small forms, and none for piano solo. The unfamiliarity of Varèse's idiom and the tremendous difficulty of his orch. works militated against frequent performances. Among conductors only

Leopold Stokowski was bold enough to put Varèse's formidable scores *Amériques* and *Arcana* on his programs with the Philadelphia Orch.; they evoked yelps of derision and outbursts of righteous indignation from the public and the press. Ironically, it was left to a mere beginner, Nicolas Slonimsky, to be the first to perform and record Varèse's unique masterpiece, *Ionisation.* An extraordinary reversal of attitudes toward Varèse's music, owing perhaps to the general advance of musical intelligence and the emergence of young music critics, took place within Varèse's lifetime, resulting in a spectacular increase of interest in his works and the number of their performances; also, musicians themselves learned to overcome the rhythmic difficulties presented in Varèse's scores. Thus Varèse lived to witness this long-delayed recognition of his music as a major stimulus of modern art; his name joined those of Stravinsky, Ives, Schoenberg, and Anton von Webern among the great masters of 20th-century music. Recognition came also from an unexpected field when scientists working on the atom bomb at Oak Ridge in 1940 played Slonimsky's recording of *Ionisation* for relaxation and stimulation in their work. Like Schoenberg, Varèse refused to regard himself as a revolutionary in music; indeed, he professed great admiration for his remote predecessors, particularly those of the Notre Dame school, representing the flowering of the Ars Antiqua. On the centennial of his birth in 1983, festivals of his music were staged in Strasbourg, Paris, Rome, Washington, D.C., N.Y., and Los Angeles. A number of monographs on Varèse were publ. in Europe and America. In 1981, Frank Zappa, the leader of the modern school of rock-and-roll music and a sincere admirer of Varèse's music, staged in N.Y. at his own expense a concert of Varèse's works; he presented a similar concert in San Francisco in 1982.

WORKS: *Offrandes* for Voice and Chamber Orch. (originally titled *Dedications;* N.Y., April 23, 1922, Carlos Salzedo conducting); *Hyperprism* for 9 Wind Instruments and 18 Percussion Devices (N.Y., March 4, 1923, composer conducting); *Octandre* for Flute, Oboe, Clarinet, Bassoon, Horn, Trombone, and Double Bass (N.Y., Jan. 13, 1924); *Integrales* for Small Orch. and Percussion (N.Y., March 1, 1925, Leopold Stokowski conducting); *Amériques* for Large Orch. (Philadelphia, April 9, 1926, Stokowski conducting); *Arcana* for Large Orch. (1925–27; Philadelphia, April 8, 1927, Stokowski conducting); *Ionisation* for 13 Percussion Players (using percussion instruments of indefinite pitch), Piano, and 2 Sirens (1931; N.Y., March 6, 1933, Nicolas Slonimsky conducting); *Ecuatorial* for Bass Voice, 4 Trumpets, 4 Trombones, Piano, Organ, Percussion, and Thereminovox (1933–34; N.Y., April 15, 1934, Slonimsky conducting; another version was scored for Male Chorus, 2 Ondes Martenot, and Orch.); *Density 21.5* for Solo Flute (N.Y., Feb. 16, 1936; George Barrere, soloist, on his platinum flute of specific gravity 21.5; hence the title); *Etude pour espace* for Mixed Chorus, 2 Pianos, and Percussion (N.Y., Feb. 23, 1947); *Déserts* for Wind Instruments, Percussion, and 3 interpolations of Electronic Sound (Paris,

Dec. 2, 1954); *Poème électronique* (Philips Pavilion at the Brussels World Exposition, spatially distributed over 400 Loudspeakers, 1958); *Nocturnal for Soprano, Bass, 12 Wind Instruments, Strings, Piano, and Percussion* (unfinished; completed by Chou Wen-Chung from sketches). Varèse publ. several seminal papers, among them "Les Instruments de musique et la machine électronique," in *L'Age nouveau* (1955) and "The Liberation of Sound," in *Perspectives of New Music* (Fall–Winter 1966); a vol. of Varèse's writings, *Ecrits,* compiled by Louise Hirbour, was publ. in Paris in 1983.

BIBLIOGRAPHY: Paul Rosenfeld, *An Hour with American Music* (Philadelphia, 1929; pp. 160–79); Henry Cowell, "The Music of Edgar Varèse," in *American Composers on American Music* (Stanford, 1933); M. Wilkinson, "An Introduction to the Music of Edgar Varèse," *Score* (March 1957); several articles, in memoriam, *Perspectives of New Music* (Spring–Summer 1966); Chou Wen-Chung, "Open Rather than Unbounded," *Perspectives of New Music* (Fall–Winter 1966); Fernand Ouellette, *Edgard Varèse* (Paris, 1966); George Charbonnier, *Entretiens avec Edgar Varèse* (Paris, 1970); Louise Varèse, *A Looking Glass Diary,* vol. I: 1883–1928 (N.Y., 1972); Odile Vivier, *Varèse* (Paris, 1973); Hilda Jolivet, *Varèse* (Paris, 1973); Grete Wehmeyer, *Edgard Varèse* (Regensburg, 1977); S. Van Solkema, ed., *The New Worlds of Edgard Varèse: A Symposium* (Brooklyn, 1979); Alejo Carpentier, *Varèse vivant* (Paris, 1982).

Varesi, Felice, noted French-Italian baritone; b. Calais, 1813; d. Milan, March 13, 1889. He made his debut in Donizetti's *Furioso all' isola di San Domingo* in Varese in 1834; then sang throughout Italy; created the title roles in Verdi's *Macbeth* in Florence in 1847, and *Rigoletto* in Venice in 1851; he also sang the role of Germont *père* at the premiere of *La Traviata* in Venice in 1853.

Varga, Ovidiu, Rumanian composer; b. Pascani, Oct. 5, 1913. He studied violin and composition in Jassy; subsequently became a prof. at the Bucharest Cons. He excels in vocal music; has written several cantatas on patriotic subjects; a Concerto for String Orch. and Percussion (1957); many mass songs and instrumental pieces.

Varga, Tibor, Hungarian violinist; b. Györ, July 4, 1921. He studied violin with Hubay at the Budapest Music Academy; subsequently took lessons with Carl Flesch in Berlin; gave concerts as a child; then went to London, where he became active mainly as a teacher. In 1964 he organized a series of summer concerts in Sion, Wallis, where he took up residence, and also conducted classes in interpretation; both as a performer and instructor, he devoted his efforts mainly to the promotion of modern music.

Varlamov, Alexander, Russian composer of songs; b. Moscow, Nov. 27, 1801; d. St. Petersburg, Oct. 27, 1848. At the age of 10 he entered the Imperial Chapel at St. Petersburg, where his fine voice

attracted the attention of Bortniansky, the director, who then became his teacher. As a young man he was attached to the Russian embassy at The Hague as leader of the Russian church choir there (1819–23); he then returned to Moscow, where he taught singing and violin (1823–29); later went to St. Petersburg as a singing teacher. He wrote 223 songs (publ. in 12 vols. by Stellovsky) in the Russian folk style; one of them, *Krasny sarafan (The Red Dress),* achieved tremendous popularity; Wieniawski made use of it in his violin piece *Souvenir de Moscou.* Varlamov was the author of the first Russian singing method, *Shkola penya* (Moscow, 1840).

BIBLIOGRAPHY: Natalya Listova, *Alexander Varlamov* (Moscow, 1968).

Varnay, Astrid, soprano; b. Stockholm, April 25, 1918, of Hungarian parents, both professional singers. She was taken to America as a child, and studied first with her mother, then with Hermann Weigert (1890–1955), whom she married in 1944. She made her debut as Sieglinde at the Metropolitan Opera (Dec. 6, 1941), substituting for Lotte Lehmann without rehearsal; appeared at the Metropolitan until 1956, and again from 1974 to 1976; her last performance there was in 1979, in Weill's *Aufstieg und Fall der Stadt Mahagonny;* she then lived mostly in Munich.

BIBLIOGRAPHY: B. Wessling, *Astrid Varnay* (1965).

Varney, Louis, French composer; b. New Orleans, La., May 30, 1844; d. Cauterets, France, Aug. 20, 1908. His father, **Pierre Joseph Alphonse Varney,** was director of a French opera company in New Orleans (1840–50). Louis Varney was taken to Paris at the age of 7 and remained there for the rest of his life. From 1876 he produced about 40 light theater works, including the comic opera *Les Mousquetaires au couvent* (Paris, March 16, 1880), which remained a standard item in the French light opera repertoire.

Varney, Pierre Joseph Alphonse, French composer; b. Paris, Dec. 1, 1811; d. there, Feb. 7, 1879. He studied with Reicha at the Paris Cons.; was active as a theater conductor in Belgium, the Netherlands, and France. From 1840 to 1850 he was director of the French Opera Co. in New Orleans, where he married Jeanne Aimée Andry; their son **Louis Varney** was born there. The family returned to Paris in 1851. Varney set to music a poem by Rouget de Lisle, *Mourir pour la patrie,* which became popular during the Paris revolution of 1848.

Varro, Marie-Aimée, French pianist; b. Brunoy, Feb. 18, 1915; d. Neuchâtel, Sept. 14, 1971. She studied piano at the Paris Cons., obtaining the Premier Prix; subsequently worked with Robert Casadesus and Alfred Cortot; she completed her advanced studies with Emil von Sauer in Vienna, who gave her indications for authentic interpretation of Liszt's piano works, which he had received from Liszt himself. In her own career, she specialized in the works of the great Romantic composers, particularly Schumann, Chopin, Liszt, and Brahms. She gave recitals in Europe and America; also appeared as a soloist with major orchs.

Varviso, Silvio, Swiss conductor; b. Zürich, Feb. 26, 1924. He studied piano at the Zürich Cons. and conducting in Vienna with Clemens Krauss. In 1944 he made his debut at St. Gallen, conducting *Die Zauberflöte,* and remained at the theater there until 1950; then conducted at the Basel Stadttheater, where he later served as its music director (1956–62); also made guest appearances with the Berlin State Opera, San Francisco Opera, Paris Opéra, and Metropolitan Opera in N.Y. From 1965–72 he was chief conductor of the Royal Opera in Stockholm; from 1972–80 served as Generalmusikdirektor of the Württemberg State Theater in Stuttgart. In 1980 he was appointed chief conductor of the Paris Opéra.

Varvoglis, Mario, Greek composer; b. Athens, Dec. 22, 1885; d. there, July 30, 1967. He studied at the Paris Cons. with Leroux, and later at the Schola Cantorum with Vincent d'Indy. Returning to Greece in 1922, he was appointed a prof. of music history at the Athens Cons. His early music was influenced by Massenet; later he evolved a more independent style, using some Greek melodic patterns. His symph. prelude, *Sainte-Barbara* (1912), was publ. by the French Inst. of Athens in 1948. He also wrote the one-act opera *An Afternoon of Love* (1935); incidental music to the classical Greek tragedies *Agamemnon* (1932) and *Medea* (1942); *Suite pastorale* for Strings (1910); *Caprice grec* for Cello Solo and Orch. (1914); a symph. poem, *Behind the Wire Fence* (1945); a "study in symph. contrasts," *Lauriers et cyprès* (1950). In 1937 he received the Grand Prize for Music of the Athens Academy of Arts.

Vàsàry, Tamàs, noted Hungarian pianist and conductor; b. Debrecen, Aug. 11, 1933. He studied piano at the Franz Liszt Academy of Music in Budapest; in 1947 won first prize in the Liszt Competition, and later garnered several more prizes. He made his London debut in 1961, and played in N.Y. in 1962. Soon, however, he abandoned his career as a pianist and sought engagements as a symph. conductor. In 1979 he was appointed artistic director of the Northern Sinfonia Orch. in Newcastle upon Tyne. In America he was a guest conductor in Washington, D.C., Denver, San Diego, Dallas, and Cleveland.

Vasconcellos, Joaquim de, Portuguese lexicographer; b. Oporto, Feb. 10, 1849; d. there, March 1, 1936. From 1865 to 1869 he studied at the Univ. of Coïmbra; in 1871–75, traveled in Germany, France, England, and Spain; from 1883 was a prof. of German at the Lyceum of Oporto, and from 1886, also director of the Museum for Industries and Commerce. He publ. the biographical dictionary *Os musicos portuguezes* (1870), containing much new matter and many emendations of old; a monograph on *Luiza Todi* (1873; 2nd ed., 1929); *Ensajo critico sobre o catalogo del rey Don Joño IV* (1873); a facsimile edition of the catalogue of the Royal Library of Lisbon, destroyed by the earthquake of 1755 (1874–76; with index and commentary, 1905); he also contributed to Pougin's supplement to Fétis's *Biographie universelle.*

Vasconcelos, Jorge Croner de, Portuguese composer; b. Lisbon, April 11, 1910. He took piano lessons with Aroldo Silva in Lisbon (1927–31); studied composition with Luís de Freitas Branco at the National Cons. there (1927–34); then went to Paris and had courses with Paul Dukas, Nadia Boulanger, and Roger-Ducasse (1934–37). Returning to Portugal in 1939, he taught composition at the Lisbon Cons.
WORKS: Ballets: *A Faina do mar* (1940) and *Coimbra* (1959); *Melodias sobre antigos textos portugueses* for Voice, Flute, and String Quartet (1937); Piano Quartet (1938); *Partita* for Piano (1961); *A vela vermelha* for Orch. (1962); *Vilancico para a Festa de Santa Cecilia* for Chorus and Orch. (1967).

Vasilenko, Sergei, noted Russian composer; b. Moscow, March 30, 1872; d. there, March 11, 1956. He studied jurisprudence at Moscow Univ., graduating in 1895; concurrently took private music lessons with Gretchaninov and G. Conus; in 1895 entered the Moscow Cons. in the classes of Taneyev, Ippolitov-Ivanov, and Safonov, graduating in 1901; while still a student, he served as assistant in Safonov's opera class. He also studied ancient Russian chants under the direction of Smolensky. In 1906 he joined the faculty of the Moscow Cons.; subsequently was prof. of orchestration there (1932–41 and 1943–56). From 1907 to 1917 he conducted in Moscow a series of popular symph. concerts in programs of music arranged in a historical sequence; in 1909 and 1912 he conducted concerts in Berlin. In 1938 he went to Tashkent, Uzbekistan, to help native musicians develop a national school of composition. His music is inspired primarily by the pattern of Russian folk song, but he was also attracted by exotic subjects, particularly those of the East; in his harmonic settings there is a distinct influence of French Impressionism.
WORKS: Operas: *The Legend of the Great City of Kitezh and the Calm Lake Svetoyar,* dramatic cantata (Moscow, March 1, 1902; operatic version, Moscow, March 3, 1903; composed several years before Rimsky-Korsakov's famous opera on the same subject); *Son of the Sun* (Moscow, May 23, 1929; deals with the Boxer Rebellion in China); *Christopher Columbus* (1933); *Buran,* written with the Uzbek composer Ashrafi (Tashkent, June 12, 1939); *The Grand Canal* (Tashkent, Jan. 12, 1941); *Suvorov* (Moscow, Feb. 23, 1942). Ballets, etc.: *Noya* (1923); *Joseph the Handsome* (Moscow, March 3, 1925); *Lola* (1926; revised, and produced in Moscow, June 25, 1943); *The Gypsies,* after Pushkin (Leningrad, Nov. 18, 1937); *Akbilyak* (Tashkent, Nov. 7, 1943); *Mirandolina* (Moscow, Jan. 16, 1949). For orch.: 5 symphs.: No. 1 (Moscow, Feb. 17, 1907); No. 2 (Moscow, Jan. 7, 1913); No. 3, *Italian,* for Wind Instruments and Russian Folk Instruments (1925); No. 4, *Arctic* (Moscow, April 5, 1933); No. 5 (1938); *Vir* for

Bass and Orch. (Kislovodsk, July 6, 1896); *3 Combats,* symph. poem (1900); *Poème épique,* symph. poem (Moscow, March 14, 1903); *The Garden of Death,* symph. poem after Oscar Wilde (Moscow, May 4, 1908); *Hircus nocturnus* (Moscow, Feb. 3, 1909; his most popular work; frequently perf. abroad; N.Y., Nov. 20, 1918, by the Russian Symph. Orch.); *Incantation* for Voice and Orch. (1910); Violin Concerto (1910–13); *Au Soleil,* suite for Orch. (Moscow, 1911); *Valse fantastique* (Moscow, Jan. 16, 1915); *Zodiac,* suite on old French melodies (1914); *Exotic Suite* for Tenor and 12 Instruments (1916); *Chinese Suite* (Leningrad, Oct. 30, 1927); *Hindu Suite* (Moscow, 1927); *Turkmenian Suite* (Moscow, 1931); *Soviet East* (1932); *Uzbek Suite* (1942); Cello Concerto (1944); *Ukraine* (1945); Trumpet Concerto (1945); several works for folk instruments; Concerto for Balalaika and Orch. (1931). CHAMBER MUSIC: 3 string quartets; Piano Trio; Viola Sonata; *Serenade* for Cello and Piano; *Oriental Dance* for Clarinet and Piano (1923); *Japanese Suite* for Wind Instruments, Xylophone, and Piano (1938); *Chinese Sketches* for Woodwind Instruments (1938); Woodwind Quartet on American themes (1938); Suite for Balalaika and Accordion (1945). SONGS: He wrote a number of songs, of which *A Maiden Sang in a Church Choir* (1908) is the best; *10 Russian Folk Songs* for Voice, Oboe, Balalaika, Accordion, and Piano (1929). Vasilenko publ. a book of memoirs, *Pages of Reminiscences* (Moscow, 1948), and vol. I of a manual of orchestration (1952).

BIBLIOGRAPHY: Victor Belaiev, *S.N. Vasilenko* (Moscow, 1927; in Russian and German); G. Polianovsky, *Sergei Vasilenko* (Moscow, 1964).

Vasiliev-Buglay, Dmitri, Soviet composer of popular songs; b. Moscow, Aug. 9, 1888; d. there, Oct. 15, 1956. He studied with Kastalsky at the Moscow Synod Seminary (1898–1906); after the Revolution he became an active member of RAPM (Russian Assoc. of Proletarian Musicians), postulating the necessity of creating music for the needs of the class-conscious, socialist proletariat, and also joined the Union of Revolutionary Composers and Musical Workers. He was one of the pioneers of mass Soviet songs; wrote patriotic ballads and many choruses to revolutionary texts. He also composed the opera *Fatherland's Call,* to promote self-discipline on collective farms.

BIBLIOGRAPHY: D. Lokshin, *Dmitri Vasiliev-Buglay* (Moscow, 1958).

Vásquez, Juan, Spanish composer; b. Badajoz, c.1510; d. c.1560. He composed many excellent villancicos, for 3, 4, and 5 voices, often using folk songs for the chief melodic part. Many of these are found in Spanish tablature books of the period (e.g., those of Milán, Fuenllana, Enriquez de Valderrábano, Pisador, and Daza, from 1535 to 1576), arranged as solo songs with instrumental accompaniment. He publ. *Villancicos y canciones a 3 y a 4* (Osuna, 1551); *Recopilación de sonetos y villancicos a 4 y a 5* (Seville, 1560; modern ed. by H. Anglès in *Monumentos de la música española,* Barcelona, 1946).

Vasseur, Léon (-Félix-Augustin-Joseph), French composer; b. Bapaume, Pas-de-Calais, May 28, 1844; d. Paris, July 25, 1917. He studied at the Ecole Niedermeyer in Paris; in 1870 became organist of the Versailles Cathedral; after a few years he turned to composing light music; also conducted theater orchs. He wrote about 30 operettas, but his most successful one was his first production, *La Timbale d'argent* (Paris, April 9, 1872). He also publ. sacred music: *L'Office divin* (a collection of masses, offertories, antiphons, etc.); *20 motets des grands maîtres;* a method for organ or harmonium; transcriptions for harmonium and piano.

Vatielli, Francesco, Italian musicologist; b. Pesaro, Dec. 31, 1876; d. Portogruaro, Dec. 12, 1946. He studied philology in Bologna and Florence; music at the Liceo Musicale Rossini in Pesaro; from 1905 to 1906 was an instructor of music history at the Liceo Musicale in Bologna; then was its librarian until 1945; was co-founder of the Associazione dei Musicologisti Italiani; also edited various music journals. He wrote incidental music for several plays; also piano pieces and songs; publ. a number of important papers dealing mainly with music in Bologna: *Vita ed arte musicale a Bologna* (1922; reprinted in 1927 as *Arte e vita musicale a Bologna;* 2 vols.); also books on other subjects: *La "Lyra Barberina" di G.B. Doni* (1908); *Primordi dell'arte del violoncello* (1918); *Materia e forme della musica* (1922; 2nd ed., 1928); *Il Principe di Venosa e Leonore d'Este* (on Gesualdo; Milan, 1941); edited a collection of 17th-century airs, *Antiche cantate d'amore* (3 vols., 1916–20); also *Antiche cantate spirituali, Antichi maestri bolognesi,* etc.

BIBLIOGRAPHY: A. Della Corte, "Francesco Vatielli," *Rivista Musicale Italiana* (April–Sept. 1947).

Vaucorbeil, Auguste-Emmanuel, French composer; b. Rouen, Dec. 15, 1821; d. Paris, Nov. 2, 1884. He studied with Marmontel and Cherubini at the Paris Cons.; produced a comic opera, *La Bataille d'amour* (Paris, April 13, 1863); another opera, *Mahomet,* remained unperformed. His lyric scene *La Mort de Diane,* for Solo, Chorus, and Orch., had some success. In 1872 he became government commissioner for the Paris theaters; from 1879, was director of the Opéra.

Vaughan, Denis, Australian conductor; b. Melbourne, June 6, 1926. He studied in London with George Thalben Ball and in Paris with André Marchal; also took double-bass lessons in London and Vienna. He served in the multiple, but apparently not mutually exclusive, capacities of bass player, organist, harpsichordist, and pianist, with the Royal Phil. Orch. of London, beginning with its American tour in 1950. In 1953 he became assistant conductor to Sir Thomas Beecham; then was assistant to Vittorio Gui at Glyndebourne (1951) and to Hans Knappertsbusch in Bayreuth (1957). While thus engaged, he discovered myriad discrepancies in the printed scores of operas by Verdi and Puccini, and proceeded to agitate for publishing corrected editions of these works. Expanding his multifarious activities, he served as consultant for the design of the organ in Alice Tully Hall at Lincoln Center in N.Y. He also gave organ recitals. His main endeavor, however, remained conducting. He formed an orch. in Naples, with which he toured in Europe. In 1972 he joined the permanent staff of the Munich Opera; in 1977 he made a tour of Australia, conducting the symph. orchs. in Sydney, Melbourne, Brisbane, etc.; in 1980 was appointed music director of the South Australian Opera. The press everywhere sang his praises, and deservedly so.

Vaughan, Sarah (Lois), black American jazz singer and pianist; b. Newark, N.J., March 27, 1924. She began to study music as a child; after winning an amateur singing contest at Harlem's Apollo Theater in N.Y. in 1942, she joined the Earl Hines band in the dual role of singer and pianist; also played and sang with the bands of Billy Eckstine and John Kirby. A versatile musician, she also ventured to appear as a soloist with bona fide symph. orchs.

Vaughan Williams, Ralph (the original surname of the family was **Williams**), great English composer who created the gloriously self-consistent British style of composition, deeply rooted in native folk songs, yet unmistakably participant of modern ways in harmony, counterpoint, and instrumentation; b. Down Ampney, Gloucestershire, Oct. 12, 1872; d. London, Aug. 26, 1958. His father, a clergyman, died when Vaughan Williams was a child; the family then moved to the residence of his maternal grandfather at Leith Hill Place, Surrey. There he began to study piano and violin; in 1887 he entered Charterhouse School in London and played violin and viola in the school orch. In 1890–92 he studied harmony with F.E. Gladstone, theory of composition with Parry, and organ with Parratt at the Royal College of Music in London; then enrolled at Trinity College, Cambridge, where he took courses in composition with Charles Wood and in organ playing with Alan Gray, obtaining his Mus.B. in 1894 and his B.A. in 1895; he subsequently returned to the Royal College of Music, studying with Stanford. In 1897 he went to Berlin for further instruction with Max Bruch; in 1901 he took his Mus.D. at Cambridge. Dissatisfied with his academic studies, he decided, in 1909, to seek advice in Paris from Ravel in order to acquire the technique of modern orchestration that emphasized color. In the meantime, he became active as a collector of British folk songs; in 1904 he joined the Folk Song Society; in 1905 he became conductor of the Leith Hill Festival in Dorking, a position that he held, off and on, until his old age. In 1906 he composed his *3 Norfolk Rhapsodies,* which reveal the ultimate techniques and manners of his national style; he discarded the 2nd and 3rd of the set as not satisfactory in reflecting the subject. In 1903 he began work on a choral symph. inspired by Walt Whitman's poetry and entitled *A Sea Symphony;* he completed it in 1909; there followed in 1910 *Fantasia on a Theme of Thomas Tallis,* scored for

string quartet and double string orch.; in it Vaughan Williams evoked the song style of an early British composer. After this brief work, Vaughan Williams engaged in a grandiose score, entitled *A London Symphony* and intended as a musical glorification of the great capital city. However, he emphatically denied that the score was to be a representation of London life. He even suggested that it might be more aptly entitled *Symphony by a Londoner,* which would explain the immediately recognizable quotations of the street song *Sweet Lavender* and of the Westminster chimes in the score; indeed, Vaughan Williams declared that the work must be judged as a piece of absolute or abstract music. Yet prosaically minded commentators insisted that *A London Symphony* realistically depicted in its 4 movements the scenes of London at twilight, the hubbub of Bloomsbury, a Saturday-evening reverie, and, in conclusion, the serene flow of the Thames River. Concurrently with *A London Symphony,* Vaughan Williams wrote the ballad opera *Hugh the Drover,* set in England in the year 1812, and reflecting the solitary struggle of the British against Napoleon.

At the outbreak of World War I in 1914 Vaughan Williams enlisted in the British army, and served in Salonika and in France as an officer in the artillery. After the Armistice, he was from 1919 to 1938 a prof. of composition at the Royal College of Music in London; from 1920 to 1928 he also conducted the London Bach Choir. In 1921 he completed his major work, *A Pastoral Symphony,* the music of which reflects the contemplative aspect of his inspiration; an interesting innovation in this score is the use of a wordless vocal solo in the last movement. In 1922 he visited the U.S. and conducted the *Pastoral Symphony* at the Norfolk (Conn.) Festival; in 1932 he returned to the U.S. to lecture at Bryn Mawr College. In 1930 he was awarded the Gold Medal of the Royal Phil. Society of London; in 1935 he received the Order of Merit from King George V. In 1930 he wrote a masque, *Job,* based on Blake's *Illustrations of the Book of Job,* which was first performed in concert version in 1930 and was then presented on the stage in London on July 5, 1931. His 4th Symph., in F minor, written between 1931 and 1935 and first performed by the BBC Symph. Orch. in London on April 10, 1935, presents an extraordinary deviation from his accustomed solid style of composition. Here he experimented with dissonant harmonies in conflicting tonalities, bristling with angular rhythms. A peripheral work was *Fantasia on Greensleeves,* arranged for harp, strings, and optional flutes; this was the composer's tribute to his fascination with English folk songs; he had used it in his opera *Sir John in Love,* after Shakespeare's *The Merry Wives of Windsor,* performed in London in 1929. He always professed great admiration for Sibelius; indeed, there was a harmonious kinship between the 2 great contemporary nationalist composers; there was also the peculiar circumstance that in his 4th Symph. Sibelius ventured into the domain of modernism, as did Vaughan Williams in his own 4th Symph., and both were taken to task by astounded critics for such musical philandering. Vaughan Williams dedicated his 5th Symph., in D major, composed between 1938 and 1943, to Sibelius as a token of his admiration. In the 6th Symph., in E minor, written during the years 1944 and 1947, Vaughan Williams returned to the erstwhile serenity of his inspiration, but the symph. has its turbulent moments and an episode of folksy dancing exhilaration. Vaughan Williams was 80 years old when he completed his challenging *Sinfonia antartica,* scored for soprano, women's chorus, and orch.; the music was an expansion of the background score he wrote for a motion picture on the expedition of Sir Robert Scott to the South Pole in 1912. Here the music is almost geographic in its literal representation of the regions that Scott had explored; it may well be compared in its realism with the *Alpine Symphony* of Richard Strauss. In *Sinfonia antartica* Vaughan Williams inserted, in addition to a large orch., several keyboard instruments and a wind machine. To make the reference clear, he used in the epilogue of the work the actual quotations from Scott's journal. Numerically, *Sinfonia antartica* was his 7th; it was first performed in Manchester on Jan. 14, 1953. In the 8th Symph., he once more returned to the ideal of absolute music; the work is conceived in the form of a neo-Classical suite, but, faithful to the spirit of the times, he included in the score the modern instruments, such as vibraphone and xylophone, as well as the sempiternal gongs and bells. His last symph. bore the fateful number 9, which had for many composers the sense of the ultimate, since it was the numeral of Beethoven's last symph. In this work Vaughan Williams, at the ancient age of 85, still asserted himself as a composer of the modern age; for the first time, he used a trio of saxophones, with a pointed caveat that they should not behave "like demented cats," but rather remain their romantic selves. Anticipating the inevitable, he added after the last bar of the score the Italian word "niente." The 9th Symph. was first performed in London on April 2, 1958; Vaughan Williams died later in the same year. It should be mentioned as a testimony to his extraordinary vitality that after the death of his first wife, he married, on Feb. 7, 1953 (at the age of 80), the poet and writer Ursula Wood, and in the following year he once more paid a visit to the U.S. on a lecture tour to several American univs.

Summarizing the esthetic and technical aspects of the style of composition of Vaughan Williams, there is a distinctly modern treatment of harmonic writing, with massive agglomeration of chordal sonorities; parallel triadic progressions are especially favored. There seems to be no intention of adopting any particular method of composition; rather, there is a great variety of procedures integrated into a distinctly personal and thoroughly English style, nationalistic but not isolationist. Vaughan Williams was particularly adept at exploring the modern ways of modal counterpoint, with tonality freely shifting between major and minor triadic entities; this procedure astutely evokes sweetly archaic usages in modern applications; thus Vaughan Williams combines the modalities of the Tudor era with the sparkling polytonalities of the modern age.

WORKS: OPERAS: *Hugh the Drover,* ballad opera (1911–14; London, July 14, 1924); *The Shepherds of the Delectable Mountains,* a "pastorale episode" after Bunyan's *The Pilgrim's Progress* (1921–22; London, July 11, 1922); *Sir John in Love,* after Shakespeare's *The Merry Wives of Windsor* (1925–29; London, March 21, 1929); *Riders to the Sea,* after the drama by John Millington Synge (1925–32; London, Dec. 1, 1937); *The Poisoned Kiss,* a "romantic extravaganza" (1927–29; Cambridge, May 12, 1936; revised 1934–37 and 1956–57); *The Pilgrim's Progress,* a "morality" (includes material from the earlier opera *The Shepherds of the Delectable Mountains;* 1925–36, 1944–51; Covent Garden, London, April 26, 1951).

BALLETS: *Old King Cole* (1923; Cambridge, June 5, 1923); *On Christmas Night,* masque (1925–26; Chicago, Dec. 26, 1926); *Job, a Masque for Dancing* (1927–30; concert perf., Norwich, Oct. 23, 1930; stage perf., London, July 5, 1931).

INCIDENTAL MUSIC: To Ben Jonson's *Pan's Anniversary* (1905; Stratford-upon-Avon, April 24, 1905); to Aristophanes' *The Wasps* (1909; Cambridge, Nov. 26, 1909); film music: *49th Parallel* (1940–41); *The People's Land* (1941–42); *Coastal Command* (1942); *The Story of a Flemish Farm* (1943; suite for Orch. from it, London, July 31, 1945); *Stricken Peninsula* (1944); *The Loves of Joanna Godden* (1946); *Scott of the Antarctic* (1947–48; material taken from it incorporated in the *Sinfonia antartica*); *Dim Little Island* (1949); *Bitter Springs* (1950); *The England of Elizabeth* (1955); *The Vision of William Blake* (1957); also unpubl. music for a radio serial, *The Mayor of Casterbridge,* after Thomas Hardy (1950).

VOCAL WORKS: *Willow Wood* for Baritone, Women's Chorus, and Orch., after Dante Gabriel Rossetti (1903; Liverpool Festival, Sept. 25, 1909); *Songs of Travel* for Voice and Piano, to texts by Robert Louis Stevenson (1904; London, Dec. 2, 1904); *Toward the Unknown Region* for Chorus and Orch., after Walt Whitman (1905–7; Leeds Festival, Oct. 10, 1907; revised 1918); *A Sea Symphony* (Symph. No. 1) for Soprano, Baritone, Chorus, and Orch., after Walt Whitman (1906–9; Leeds Festival, Oct. 12, 1910, composer conducting); *On Wenlock Edge,* song cycle for Tenor, Piano, and String Quartet ad libitum, to poems from A.E. Housman's *A Shropshire Lad* (1909; London, Nov. 15, 1909); *5 Mystical Songs* for Baritone, Optional Chorus, and Orch. (1911; Worcester Cathedral, Sept. 14, 1911); *Fantasia on Christmas Carols* for Baritone, Chorus, and Orch. (1912; Hereford Festival, Sept. 12, 1912); *4 Hymns* for Tenor and Piano, with Viola obbligato (1914; Cardiff, May 26, 1920); Mass in G minor (1920–21; Birmingham, Dec. 6, 1922); *Flos Campi,* suite for Viola, wordless Mixed Chorus, and Small Orch. (1925; London, Oct. 19, 1925); *Sancta civitas* for Tenor, Baritone, Chorus, and Orch. (1923–25; Oxford, May 7, 1926); *Te Deum* for Mixed Chorus and Organ (1928; Canterbury Cathedral, Dec. 4, 1928); *Benedicite* for Soprano, Chorus, and Orch. (1929; Dorking, May 2, 1930); *The Hundredth Psalm* for Mixed Chorus and Orch. (1929; Dorking, April 29, 1930); *3 Choral Hymns* for Baritone, Mixed Chorus, and Orch. (1930; Dorking,

April 30, 1930); *In Windsor Forest,* cantata for Mixed Chorus and Orch., adapted from the opera *Sir John in Love* (1931; Windsor, Nov. 9, 1931); *Magnificat* for Contralto, Women's Chorus, and Orch. (1932; Worcester Cathedral, Sept. 8, 1932); *5 Tudor Portraits* for Mezzo-soprano, Baritone, Chorus, and Orch. (1935; Norwich Festival, Sept. 25, 1936); *Dona nobis pacem* for Soprano, Baritone, Chorus, and Orch. (1936; Huddersfield, Oct. 2, 1936); *Festival Te Deum* (1937); *Flourish for a Coronation* (1937; London, April 1, 1937); *Serenade to Music* for 16 Solo Voices and Orch. (1938; London, Oct. 5, 1938); *The Bridal Day,* masque based on Edmund Spenser's *Epithalamion,* (1938–39; revised 1952–53; BBC television, London, June 5, 1953, in celebration of the coronation of Elizabeth II; revised as the cantata *Epithalamion,* London, Sept. 30, 1957); *Thanksgiving for Victory* for Soprano, Speaker, Chorus, and Orch. (1944; BBC broadcast, London, May 13, 1945); *An Oxford Elegy* for Speaker, Chorus, and Orch., to words by Matthew Arnold (1949; Dorking, Nov. 20, 1949); *Folk Songs of the 4 Seasons,* cantata on traditional folk songs, for Women's Voices and Orch. (1949; London, June 15, 1950); *The Sons of Light* for Children's Chorus (1951; London, May 6, 1951); *Hodie (This Day),* Christmas cantata for Soprano, Tenor, Baritone, Chorus, and Orch. (1953–54; Worcester, Sept. 8, 1954); *A Vision of Aeroplanes,* motet for Chorus and Organ, on a text from Ezekiel, Chapter 1 (1955; St. Michael's, Cornhill, London, June 4, 1956); *10 Blake Songs* for Tenor and Oboe (1958; BBC, London, Oct. 8, 1958); other songs to words by English poets; arrangements of English folk songs; hymn tunes; carols.

FOR ORCH.: *Serenade* for Small Orch. (1898); *Bucolic Suite* (1902; Bournemouth, March 10, 1902); *2 Impressions: Harnham Down* and *Boldrewood* (1902; London, Nov. 12, 1907); *3 Norfolk Rhapsodies* (1906; No. 1, in E minor, London, Aug. 23, 1906; No. 2, Cardiff Festival, Sept. 27, 1907; No. 3, not perf.; Nos. 2 and 3 withdrawn by the composer); *In the Fen Country,* symph. impression for Orch. (1904 and subsequent revisions; London, Feb. 22, 1909, Beecham conducting); *The Wasps,* Aristophanic suite (1909; London, July 23, 1912, composer conducting); *Fantasia on a Theme by Thomas Tallis* for String Quartet and Double String Orch. (1910; Gloucester Festival, Sept. 6, 1910, composer conducting; revised 1923); *A London Symphony* (Symph. No. 2; 1911–14; London, March 27, 1914; revised version, London, May 4, 1920); *The Lark Ascending,* romance for Violin and Orch. (1914–20; London, June 14, 1921); *A Pastoral Symphony* (Symph. No. 3; 1916–21; London, Jan. 26, 1922); Concerto in D minor for Violin and Strings, *Concerto accademico* (1924–25; London, Nov. 6, 1925); Piano Concerto in C major (1926–31; London, Feb. 1, 1933; also revised for 2 Pianos and Orch., 1946); *Fantasia on Sussex Folk-Tunes* for Cello and Orch. (1930; London, March 13, 1930; Casals, soloist; Barbirolli conducting); Prelude and Fugue in C minor for Orch. (1930; Hereford, Sept. 12, 1930); Suite for Viola and Small Orch. (1934; London, Nov. 12, 1934); *Fantasia on Greensleeves* (arranged from the opera *Sir John in Love* by Greaves, 1934); Symph. No. 4, in F

minor (1931–35; London, April 10, 1935, Boult conducting); *5 Variants of "Dives and Lazarus"* for String Orch. and Harp, commissioned by the British Council for the N.Y. World's Fair (1939; N.Y., June 10, 1939); *Serenade to Music* (orch. version of 1938 original, 1940; London, Feb. 10, 1940); Symph. No. 5, in D major (1938–43; London, June 24, 1943, composer conducting); Concerto in A minor for Oboe and Strings (1943–44; Liverpool, Sept. 30, 1944); Symph. No. 6, in E minor (1944–47; London, April 21, 1948, Boult conducting); Partita for Double String Orch. (orch. version of Double Trio for String Sextet, 1946–48; BBC, London, March 20, 1948); Concerto Grosso for String Orch. (1950; London, Nov. 18, 1950, Boult conducting); *Romance* in D-flat major for Harmonica, Strings, and Piano (1951; N.Y., May 3, 1952); *Sinfonia antartica* (Symph. No. 7; 1949–52; Manchester, Jan. 14, 1953, Barbirolli conducting); Concerto in F minor for Tuba and Orch. (1954; London, June 14, 1954); Symph. No. 8, in D minor (1953–55; Manchester, May 2, 1956, Barbirolli conducting); *Flourish for Glorious John* (for Sir John Barbirolli; 1957; Manchester, Oct. 16, 1957, Barbirolli conducting); Symph. No. 9, in E minor (1956–58; London, April 2, 1958, Sargent conducting).

CHAMBER MUSIC: String Quartet in C minor (1898; June 30, 1904); Quintet in D major for Clarinet, Horn, Violin, Cello, and Piano (June 5, 1900); Piano Quintet in C minor for Piano, Violin, Viola, Cello, and Double Bass (London, Dec. 14, 1905); String Quartet in G minor (No. 1; London, Nov. 8, 1909); Phantasy Quintet for 2 Violins, 2 Violas, and Cello (1912; London, March 23, 1914); 6 studies in English folk song for Cello and Piano (London, June 4, 1926); Double Trio for String Sextet (London, Jan. 21, 1939); String Quartet No. 2, in A minor (1942–44; London, Oct. 12, 1944); Violin Sonata in A minor (BBC, London, Oct. 12, 1954); also some short piano pieces; Introduction and Fugue for 2 Pianos (1946); organ pieces.

WRITINGS: *The English Hymnal* (1906; 2nd ed., 1933); *Songs of Praise* (with M. Shaw; 1925; 2nd ed., 1931); *The Oxford Book of Carols* (with P. Dearmer and M. Shaw; 1928); lectures and articles, reprinted in *National Music and Other Essays* (London, 1963). R. Palmer edited *Folk Songs Collected by Ralph Vaughan Williams* (London, 1983).

BIBLIOGRAPHY: A.H. Fox Strangways, "R. V. W.," *Music & Letters,* I (1920); H. Colles, "The Music of V. W.," *Chesterian,* XXI (1922); H. Howells, "V. W.'s 'Pastoral Symphony,' " *Music & Letters,* III (1922); A. Dickinson, *An Introduction to the Music of R. V. W.* (London, 1928); H. Ould, "The Songs of R. V. W.," *English Review,* XLVI (1928); F. Toye, "Studies in English Music: V. W. and the Folk Music Movement," *Listener,* V (1931); E. Rubbra, "V. W., Some Technical Characteristics," *Monthly Musical Record,* LXIV (1934); idem, "The Later V. W.," *Music & Letters,* XVIII (1937); S. Goddard, "The Operas of V. W.," *Listener,* XX (1938); W. Kimmel, "V. W.'s Choice of Words," *Music & Letters,* XIX (1938); idem, "V. W.'s Melodic Style," *Musical Quarterly* (Oct. 1941); H. Foss, "V. W.'s Symphonic Manner," *Listener,* XXVII (1942); idem, *R. V. W.* (London, 1950); A. Hutchings, "V. W. and the Tudor Tradition," *Listener,* XLV (1951); E. Payne, *The Folksong Element in the Music of V. W.* (Diss., Univ. of Liverpool, 1953); R. Taylor, "V. W. and English National Music," *Cambridge Journal,* VI (1953); P. Young, *V. W.* (London, 1953); F. Howes, *The Music of R. V. W.* (London, 1954); E. Payne, "V. W. and Folksong," *Music Review,* XV (1954); J. Bergsagel, *The National Aspects of the Music of R. V. W.* (Diss., Cornell Univ., 1957); S. Pakenham, *R. V. W.: A Discovery of His Music* (London, 1957); J. Warrack, "V. W. and Opera," *Opera,* IX (1958); D. Brown, "V. W.'s Symphonies: Some Judgments Reviewed," *Monthly Musical Record,* XC (1960); J. Day, *V. W.* (London, 1961; 2nd ed., revised, 1975); P. Willetts, "The R. V. W. Collection," *British Museum Quarterly,* XXIV (1961); A. Dickinson, "The V. W. Manuscripts," *Music Review,* XXIII (1962); idem, *V. W.* (London, 1963); M. Kennedy, *The Works of R. V. W.* (London, 1964; 2nd ed., revised, 1980); H. Ottaway, "VW5—A New Analysis," *Musical Times,* CV (1964); E. Schwartz, *The Symphonies of R. V. W.* (Amherst, 1964); U. Vaughan Williams, *R. V. W.: A Biography* (London, 1964); H. Ottaway, *V. W.* (London, 1966); P. Starbuck, *R. V. W., O.M., 1872–1958: A Bibliography of His Literary Writings and Criticism of His Musical Works* (Diss., Library Assoc., 1967); M. Hurd, *V. W.* (London, 1970); J. Lunn and U. Vaughan Williams, *R. V. W.: A Pictorial Biography* (London, 1971); U. Vaughan Williams, "V. W. and Opera," *Composer,* XLI (1971); R. Douglas, *Working with R. V. W.* (London, 1972); H. Ottaway, *V. W. Symphonies* (London, 1972); U. Vaughan Williams, "The VW Centenary," *Musical Times,* CXIII (1972); M. Kennedy, "The Unknown V. W.," *Proceedings of the Royal Musical Association,* XCIX (1972–73).

Vautor, Thomas, English composer; b. c.1590; date and place of death unknown. In 1616 he received the degree of B.Mus. at Lincoln College, and in 1619 publ. a collection of madrigals, *The First Set: Beeing Songs of divers Ayres and Natures, of 5 and 6 parts* (reprinted by Fellowes in *The English Madrigal School,* 34). Another work by Vautor is *An Elegie in the Death of his right worshipful Master, Sir Thomas Beaumont* (1614).
　　BIBLIOGRAPHY: E.H. Fellowes, *The English Madrigal Composers* (1921).

Vázsonyi, Bálint, distinguished pianist; b. Budapest, March 7, 1936. He entered the Franz Liszt Academy of Music in Budapest; made his debut as a pianist at 12. He left Hungary in the midst of political turmoil in 1956; eventually came to America, where he continued his studies with Ernst von Dohnányi. In 1977 he made a transcontinental tour of the U.S.; in 1978 he joined the faculty at the Indiana Univ. School of Music. One of his signal feats of pianofortitude was his performance, on 2 consecutive days, of all 32 piano sonatas of Beethoven in chronological order (N.Y., Oct. 31 and Nov. 1, 1976); he repeated this cycle in Boston and London shortly afterward. He is the author of the standard biography of Dohnányi (Budapest, 1971; Eng. version in progress). His pianism is marked by a tran-

scendental virtuosity of technique coupled with the mellow lyricism typical of traditional Hungarian pianism, and particularly effective in the music of Liszt.

Vazzana, Anthony, American composer and educator; b. Troy, N.Y., Nov. 4, 1922. He was of a musical family; his father played the mandolin. He studied piano with George H. Pickering; attended the State Univ. of N.Y. College at Potsdam; in 1943 he was inducted into the U.S. Air Force, where he arranged and conducted suitable music in concert bands. He resumed his musical studies after his discharge, and in 1946 enrolled at the Berkshire Summer Music School in Tanglewood, Mass., where his instructors were Irving Fine, Robert Shaw, Stanley Chapple, Leonard Bernstein, and Hugh Ross. In 1948 he enrolled at the Univ. of Southern Calif. in the classes of Halsey Stevens, Ingolf Dahl, and Ernest Kanitz; received his M.M. in 1948. Subsequently he divided his time between composing and teaching; was successively on the faculty of Calif. State Univ. at Long Beach and at Los Angeles, Champlain College, and Danbury (Conn.) State College. In 1959 he received the degree of doctor in composition at the Univ. of Southern Calif., and in 1959 joined the faculty of its School of Music. In his teaching he resolutely promoted advanced techniques in composition; wrote a set of books on music theory, *Projects in Musicianship* (4 vols., 1965–68). In his own compositions, he pursued a logical evolutionary line, beginning with neo-Classical formations and continuing with progressive harmonic and contrapuntal complications, in which dissonances are ultimately emancipated and rhythms become increasingly asymmetrical, all this aided and abetted by eloquent pregnant pauses separating brief melodic ejaculations. Special effects, such as whipping and scourging the bodies of musical instruments with taps and kicks, soundlessly blowing through the embouchure of a wind instrument, such as a French horn, and the like, add to the quaquaversal quality of sonorism in his works. Vazzana's students admire him.
　　WORKS: Sonata for Clarinet, Horn, and Piano (1947); String Quartet (1948); Woodwind Quintet (1948); Suite for Viola and Piano (1948); Quartet for Violin, Viola, Cello, and Piano (1949); *Andante and Allegro* for Orch. (1949); Sonata for Violin and Piano (1958); *Symphonic Allegro* for Orch. (1958); *Harlequin Suite* for Orch. (1959); Sonata for Piano (1962); *Songs of Life and Nature* for Voice and Piano (1962); *Music for 2 Flutes* (1962); Suite for Strings (1963); Symph. No. 1 (1963); *Spectra* for Band (1965); *Fantasia Concertante* for Cello and Piano (1970); *Incontri* for Violin and Piano (1971); *Partite sopra victimae paschali laudes* for Wind Orch. (1976); *Tre Monodie* for Solo Trombone (1976); *Cambi* for Solo Tuba and Solo Percussion (1977); *Trinakie* for Orch. (1977); *Disegni* for Piano (1978); *Montaggi* for 4 Tubas (1978); *Studi* for Solo Saxophone (1979); *Buccina* for Horn and Piano (1979); *Partita* for Euphonium, Piano, and Percussion (1980); *Concerto a Tre* for Clarinet, Double Bass, and Instrumental En-

semble (1981); *Varianti* for Orch. (1982); *Corivolano* for Viola and French Horn (1982).

Veasey, Josephine, English mezzo-soprano; b. London, July 10, 1930. She studied voice with Audrey Langford in London; was then a member of the chorus at Covent Garden, and made her operatic debut there as Cherubino; she then sang in Vienna, Munich, Milan, Berlin, and Salzburg. She made her Metropolitan Opera debut in N.Y. on Nov. 22, 1968, as Fricka in *Das Rheingold.*

Veazie, George Augustus, American music educator; b. Boston, Dec. 18, 1835; d. Chelsea, Mass., Nov. 20, 1915. From 1869 to 1903 he was supervisor of music in the public schools of Chelsea; during many years of cooperation with Luther W. Mason, he brought about important reforms and improvements in the system of primary instruction. He composed several light operas and numerous part-songs, and edited collections of school songs.

Vecchi, Orazio (Horatio), Italian composer; b. Modena (baptized, Dec. 6), 1550; d. there, Feb. 19, 1605. He was a pupil of Salvatore Essenga in Modena; was maestro di cappella in Salò (1581–84) and at the Cathedral of Modena (1584–86); in 1586 he took Holy Orders; then went to Correggio, where he obtained a canonry. In 1593 he returned to Modena and was appointed maestro at the Cathedral; was promoted to *mansionario* there on Oct. 14, 1596; 2 years later he was also maestro at the ducal court there, and music master to the young princes. On Oct. 7, 1604, he was deprived of his post as choirmaster at the Cathedral, probably through the intrigues of a former pupil, Geminiano Capilupi; this circumstance is believed to have hastened his death. Vecchi was highly regarded as a composer in his day; his works (masses, motets, madrigals, canzonette, etc.) were printed chiefly in Venice, but editions also appeared in Germany and elsewhere. He was invited to the court of Emperor Rudolf II at Vienna, and in 1600 went to Rome in the suite of Cardinal Alessandro d'Este. His lasting fame is due above all to his "commedia harmonica" *L'Amfiparnasso,* performed at Modena in 1594 and printed at Venice in 1597; this is a kind of musical farce written not in the monodic style of Peri's *Dafne,* but in madrigal style, with all the text sung by several voices (i.e., a chorus *a* 4–5); it has been called a "madrigal opera," but it was not intended for the theater and it stood entirely apart from the path that opera was to take. Modern editions of *L'Amfiparnasso* have been publ. by Eitner in vol. 26 of *Publikationen der Gesellschaft der Musikforschung* and by Torchi in *L'arte musicale in Italia,* 4. Of special interest among Vecchi's other compositions is the *Veglie di Siena ovvero I varii humori della musica moderna a 3–6 voci* (1604; also Nuremburg, 1605, as *Noctes ludicrae;* modern ed. by B. Somma), which uses colorful devices to express a wide variety of moods and feelings. Examples of Vecchi's music are in Schering's *Beispielen* (no. 164); Chilesotti's *Biblioteca di rarità musicali,* vol. 5; Torchi's *L'arte musicale in Italia,* 2; Einstein's *Golden Age of the Madrigal;* etc.

BIBLIOGRAPHY: A. Catellani, *Della vita e delle opere di O. V.* (Milan, 1858); E.J. Dent, "The *Amfiparnasso* of O. V.," *Monthly Musical Record* (1906); idem, "Notes on the *Amfiparnasso* of O. V.," *Sammelbände der Internationalen Musik-Gesellschaft* (1910–11); L. Frati, "Un capitolo autobiografico di O. V.," *Rivista Musicale Italiana* (1915); J.C. Hol, *H. V. als weltlicher Komponist* (Diss., Univ. of Basel, 1917); idem, "H. V. et l'évolution créatrice," in "Scheurleer-Festschrift" (1925); idem, "H. V.," *Rivista Musicale Italiana* (1930); idem, *H. V.s weltliche Werke* (Strasbourg, 1934); G. Roncalgia, "Il luogo e la data di nascità di O. V.," *Rassegna Musicale* (April 1929); C. Perinello, "*L'Amfiparnasso,* commedia harmonica d'H. V.," *Rivista Musicale Italiana* (1937); G. Roncaglia, "O.V.," ibid. (1949); *O. V., Precursore del melodramma,* a symposium on the 400th anniversary of Vecchi's birth (Modena, 1950); A. Lualdi, "O. V.," *Rivista Musicale Italiana* (1950); G. Camillucci, "*L'Amfiparnasso,* commedia harmonica," ibid. (1951); G. Roncaglia, "Gli elementi precursori del melodramma nell'opera di O. V.," ibid. (1953); L. Ronga, "Lettura storica dell' *Amfiparnasso* di O. V.," *Rassegna Musicale* (1953); J. Rodgers, *The Madrigals of Orazio Vecchi* (Diss., Univ. of Calif., Los Angeles, 1954); *Commemorazione di Orazio Vecchi nel 350° anniversario della morte* (Modena, 1955); W. Martin, *The Convito musicale of Orazio Vecchi* (Diss., Oxford Univ., 1964); R. Ruegge, *Orazio Vecchis geistliche Werke* (Bern, 1967).

Vecchi, Orfeo, Italian composer of sacred music; b. Milan, 1550; d. there, 1604. He was maestro di cappella at Santa Maria della Scala in Milan; most of his MSS are preserved there. His extant publ. works include 3 collections of masses for 5 voices (1588, 1598, 1602); 2 Magnificats; 7 Penitential Psalms for 6 Voices (1601); *Cantiones sacrae* for 6 Voices (1603) and for 5 (1608); etc.

BIBLIOGRAPHY: F.X. Haberl, "Orfeo Vecchi," *Kirchenmusikalisches Jahrbuch* (1907); A. Einstein, "Un libro di canzoni spirituali di Orfeo Vecchi," *Bibliofilia* (Florence, 1938).

Vecsei, Desider Josef, Hungarian pianist; b. Budapest, Sept. 25, 1882; d. Hollywood, March 1, 1966. He studied in Budapest, and then with Emil Sauer at the Vienna Cons. He made concert appearances as a child; toured in Europe until 1915; then went to the U.S., and settled in Hollywood as a piano teacher. He wrote songs and piano pieces.

Vecsey, Franz von, Hungarian violinist; b. Budapest, March 23, 1893; d. Rome, April 6, 1935. He received his first instruction from his father, Ludwig Vecsey, a good violinist; at the age of 8 he became a pupil of Hubay, and made such rapid progress that his parents decided to send him on a European tour as a child prodigy; he appeared in Berlin (Oct. 17, 1903), London (May 2, 1904), and N.Y. (Jan. 10, 1905); toured Italy, Scandinavia, and Russia; then lived in Germany and Italy. He composed some violin pieces.

Vécsey, Jenö, Hungarian musicologist and composer; b. Felsöcéce, July 19, 1909; d. Budapest, Sept. 18, 1966. He studied at the Univ. of Sciences and took a course in composition with Kodály at the Budapest Academy of Music (1930–35). He joined the staff of the National Széchényi Library in 1942; was appointed to the Music Dept. and made valuable contributions to the historical and bibliographical music literature preserved there. He initiated and directed editorial work on the Musica Rinata series (1963–66); did preparatory work on the new Haydn Collected Edition.
WORKS: Ballet, *Scholar Kele* (1943); *Divertimento* for Orch. (1939–40); *Intermezzi* for Strings (1942); *Rhapsody* for Orch. (1940–41); *2 Symphonic Dances* (1945); symph. poem, *Castle Boldogkö* (1951; revised and retitled *Prelude, Notturno and Scherzo*, 1958); Piano Concertino (1953–56); Double-bass Concertino (1954); *Rhapsody* for Harp and Orch. (1954); String Quartet (1942); String Sextet (1956); *Bagatelles* for 2 Pianos (1962); songs.

Vedernikov, Alexander, Russian bass; b. Mokino, Dec. 23, 1927. He studied voice at the Moscow Cons., graduating in 1955; won first prize at the International Schumann Competition in Berlin in 1956 and, in the same year, first prize at the Soviet competition for performing songs by Soviet composers. In 1957 he made his debut at the Bolshoi Theater in Moscow. In 1961 he went to Italy and entered the La Scala Opera School of Milan as an aspirant; subsequently toured as a concert singer in France, Italy, England, Austria, and Canada. He was particularly noted for his performances of the Russian repertoire; his portrayal of Boris Godunov in Mussorgsky's opera approached Chaliapin's in its grandeur. He also distinguished himself in the Italian buffo roles, such as Don Basilio in Rossini's *Barber of Seville.* In 1964 he joined the Communist Party of the U.S.S.R.

Veerhoff, Carlos, Argentine-German composer; b. Buenos Aires, June 3, 1926. He studied in Berlin with Grabner (1943–44); returned to Argentina and taught in Tucumán. He moved permanently to Germany in 1951; was an assistant to Fricsay in Berlin (1951–52) and studied with Boris Blacher at the Hochschule für Musik there (1952); then settled in Munich.
WORKS: 2 operas: *Targusis* (1958) and *Die goldene Maske* (1968); chamber opera, *Der Grune* (1972); mini-opera, *Es gibt doch Zebrastreifen* (Ulm, West Germany, Jan. 20, 1972); 2 ballets: *Pavane royale* (1953) and *El porquerizo del ray* (Buenos Aires, Teatro Colón, 1963); *Prólogo sinfónico* (1951); *Symphonic Movement* (1952); 4 symphs.: No. 1, *Panta rhei* (*Everything Flows;* the philosophic apothegm of Heraclitus; 1953); No. 2, in one movement (1956); No. 3, *Spirales* (1966; revised 1969); No. 4 (1974); *Mirages* for Orch. (1961); *Akróasis* for 24 Winds and Percussion (1966); *Textur* for String Orch. (1969; revised 1971); *Torso* for Orch.

(Lübeck, Jan. 14, 1974); *Sinotrauc* for Orch. (Munich, Jan. 19, 1973); *Gesänge auf dem Wege* for Baritone and Orch. (1964); *Ut omnes unum sint,* chamber cantata (1967); 2 string quartets (1951, 1974); 2 wind quintets (1958, 1969); Solo Violin Sonata (1954); *Dialogues* for Saxophone and Piano (1967).

Vega, Aurelio de la, Cuban-American composer; b. Havana, Nov. 28, 1925. He studied law at the Univ. of Havana (1945–47) and music with Frederick Kramer (1942–46). In 1947 he went to the U.S., and served as cultural attaché at the Cuban Consulate in Los Angeles; there he took composition lessons with Ernst Toch. Returning to Cuba, he was dean of the Music School at the Univ. of Oriente in Santiago de Cuba (1953–59); in 1959 he settled in California, and taught at the San Fernando Valley State College (Calif. State Univ., Northridge). In his early works he cultivated Cuban melorhythms, but later adopted increasingly radical modernistic methods of composition with fantastically reticulated, circumvoluted, and in some instances palindromic, contrapuntal schemes, graphically notated in optically proportioned note values, so that the linear extant of a bar is invariant in relation to the aggregate of rhythmic units contained therein, reaching its heroic ultima ratio in a work entitled *Olep ed Arudamot* (backward reading of a Spanish idiom meaning "pulling your leg"); the visual impression of the score itself is that of an abstract expressionist painting. Sonorifically, he avails himself of a great variety of acoustical materials, electronic and humanoid, including the whirring sound of shuffling feet by string players.
WORKS: Piano Trio (1949); *Soliloquio* for Viola and Piano (1950); *Obertura a una Farsa seria* (Havana, April 28, 1951); *Leyenda del Ariel Criollo* for Cello and Piano (1953); *Elegía* for Strings (London, Nov. 16, 1954); String Quartet (1957); Wind Quintet (1959); Trio for Flute, Oboe, and Clarinet (1960); *Sinfonía en 4 partes* (Inter-American Music Festival, Washington, D.C., April 30, 1961); *Structures* for Piano and String Quartet (1962); *Coordinates* for Magnetic Tape (1963); *Analigus* for Orch. (1966); *Intrata* for Orch. (Los Angeles, May 12, 1972); *Olep ed Arudamot* (available in several versions; 1974); *Septicilium* for Solo Clarinet and Instrumental Ensemble (1975); *Inflorescence* for Soprano, Bass Clarinet, and Tape, to a text by the composer (Los Angeles, Oct. 25, 1976); *The Infinite Square* for any combination of any Instruments and/or Voices (Los Angeles, Sept. 24, 1977); *Adiós* for Orch., to bid farewell to the departing conductor of the Los Angeles Phil., Zubin Mehta (conducted by Mehta, Los Angeles, April 20, 1978); *Undici colori* for Solo Bassoon, Stamping Right Foot, and Slide Projections (1981; Los Angeles, Jan. 25, 1982); *Galandiacoa* for Clarinet and Guitar (1982); piano music; songs.

Vega, Carlos, Argentine writer on music; b. Cañuelas, near Buenos Aires, April 14, 1898; d. Buenos Aires, Feb. 10, 1966. He studied at the Univ. of Buenos Aires (philosophy and literature); subsequently devoted himself mainly to folklore research in music. In 1933 he was placed in charge of the folklore division of the literature faculty at the Univ. of Buenos Aires. He traveled throughout the rural regions of Argentina and other South American countries to collect materials on folk songs and folk dances, using a phonograph to record them; devised a special choreographic notation. His many books are basic sources for the study of Argentine folk music.

WRITINGS: *Danzas y canciones argentinas* (Buenos Aires, 1936); *La música popular argentina: Canciones y danzas criollas* (1941); *Panorama de la música popular argentina* (Buenos Aires, 1944); a series of monographs on Argentine dances (with choreographic ideograms): *La Chacarera, El Cuando, El Gato, El Triunfo, El Carnavalito, La Condición* (Buenos Aires, 1944–45); *Los instrumentos musicales de la Argentina* (Buenos Aires, 1946).

Veinus, Abraham, American musicologist; b. New York, Feb. 12, 1916. He studied at the City College of N.Y., Cornell Univ. (M.A., 1937), and Columbia Univ. (1946–48). In 1948 he joined the faculty of the Dept. of Fine Arts at Syracuse Univ. He wrote *The Concerto* (1944; 2nd ed., revised, 1964); *The Victor Book of Concertos* (1948); *The Pocket Book of Great Operas* (with Henry Simon, 1949); *Understanding Music* (with W. Fleming, N.Y., 1958).

Veit, Wenzel Heinrich, Bohemian composer; b. Leitmeritz, Jan. 19, 1806; d. there, Feb. 16, 1864. He was a member of the judiciary, but applied himself earnestly to the study of music; was music director at Aachen. He wrote a number of works in various genres; he is remembered chiefly for his effective choruses and solo songs.

WORKS: *Festmesse* in D, for Soli, Chorus, and Orch.; overtures; Symph.; 5 string quintets; 4 string quartets; Piano Trio; male choruses in Czech and German; songs.

BIBLIOGRAPHY: A. John, *W.H. Veit. Lebensbild eines deutschen Tondichters* (Eger, 1903); H. Ankert, *W.H. Veit als Musikdirektor in Aachen* (Leitmeritz, 1906); K. Fiala, *W.H. Veit* (Liberec, 1964).

Velasco-Llanos, Santiago, Colombian composer; b. Cali, Jan. 28, 1915. He studied in Cali with Antonio María Valencia, and later with Domingo Santa Cruz and Pedro Humberto Allende in Santiago, Chile. Returning to Colombia, he was appointed director of the Cali Cons.

WORKS: *Sinfonia breve* (1947); *Sinfonietta* (1966); *Bambuco jocoso* for Orch. (1967); 2 string quartets; piano pieces; choruses; songs.

Velasco Maidana, José María, Bolivian composer and conductor; b. Sucre, July 4, 1899. He studied violin in Buenos Aires; subsequently taught music history at the National Cons. of La Paz. In 1937 he conducted some of his works in Buenos Aires, and in 1938, in Berlin; in 1943 he toured in South America and Mexico. His ballet *Amerindia*, on a subject from pre-Columbian history, was produced in Berlin (Dec. 6, 1938), and later in La Paz (May 27, 1940). He conducted the first performance of his symph. works with the La Paz Symph. Orch., of which he was the regular conductor: *Cory Wara* (Oct. 6, 1941); *Los hijos del Sol* (Feb. 6, 1942); *Vida de Cóndores* (March 14, 1942); *Los Huacos* (April 22, 1942); *Los Khusillos* and *Cuento brujo* (April 11, 1943).

Velázquez, Higinio, Mexican composer; b. Guadalajara, Jan. 11, 1926. He studied composition with Bernal Jiménez and Rodolfo Halffter; was a violinist in the National Symph. Orch.; in 1969 became violinist in the string quartet of the National Inst. of Fine Arts.

WORKS: *Vivencias* for Orch. (1958); *Cacique*, overture (1958); "sinfonia breve," *Juárez* (1961); *Revolución*, symph. poem (1963); *Elegía* for Oboe and Piano (1969); *Estructuas* for Piano (1969); Sonatina for Cello Solo (1970); String Quartet (1970); *Andante atonal* for Strings (1971).

Velimirović, Miloš, eminent Serbian-American music scholar; b. Belgrade, Dec. 10, 1922. He studied violin and piano at the Music Academy in Belgrade with Petar Stojanovic; in 1943 was sent to a forced labor camp by the German occupation authorities; after the war he studied Byzantine art at the Univ. of Belgrade, graduating in 1951; simultaneously took composition lessons with Mihovil Logar at the Belgrade Music Academy; in 1952 he emigrated to the U.S.; studied at Harvard Univ., obtaining his M.A. in 1953 and his Ph.D. in 1957; also took a course in Byzantine music with Egon Wellesz at Dumbarton Oaks in Washington, D.C. (1954). He subsequently devoted himself to teaching; was on the faculty of Yale Univ. (1957–69) and the Univ. of Wisconsin (1969–73); in 1973 was appointed a prof. of music at the Univ. of Virginia in Charlottesville; served as chairman of the music dept. there (1974–77). A linguist, he has contributed a number of scholarly articles to various publications, mainly on subjects connected with liturgical music in Byzantium and in the Slavic countries. He publ. *Byzantine Elements in Early Slavic Chant* (2 vols., Copenhagen, 1960); was associate editor (jointly with Egon Wellesz) of *Studies in Eastern Chant* (4 vols., London, 1966–78); wrote "Liturgical Drama in Byzantium and Russia," *Dumbarton Oaks Papers* (1962); articles on Russian and Slavic church music for the 6th edition of *The New Grove Dictionary of Music and Musicians* (1980).

Venatorini. See **Mysliveczek, Joseph.**

Venegas de Henestrosa, Luis, Spanish organist and composer; b. Henestrosa, Burgon, c.1500; d. Toledo, after 1557. He was in the service of Cardinal Juan Tavera in Toledo; publ. the oldest known Spanish book of organ music, *Libro de cifra nueva para tecla, harpa y vihuela* (Alcalà de Henares, 1557; modern ed. by H. Anglès, Barcelona, 1944); it contains organ pieces by Palero, P. Vila, Soto, Venegas himself, etc.; also pieces for vihuela, transcriptions of sacred works by Morales, Josquin, Soto, etc., and solo songs with instrumental accompaniment. The book is written in Spanish organ tablature.

BIBLIOGRAPHY: G. Morphy, *Les Luthistes espagnols du XVIᵉ siècle* (Leipzig, 1902); J.B. Trend, *Luis Milan and the Vihuelistas* (London, 1925); H. Anglès, "Orgelmusik der Schola Hispanica vom XV.–XVII. Jahrhundert," in "Peter Wagner–Festschrift" (Leipzig, 1926); J. Ward, "The Editorial Methods of Venegas de Henestrosa," *Musica Disciplina* (1952).

Vengerova, Isabelle, distinguished piano pedagogue; b. Minsk, Russia, March 1, 1877; d. New York, Feb. 7, 1956. She studied at the Vienna Cons. with Joseph Dachs, and privately with Leschetizky; then with Anna Essipoff in St. Petersburg. In 1906 she was appointed an instructor at the St. Petersburg Cons.; in 1910 she became a prof. there. She toured Russia as a pianist; in 1923 came to the U.S.; made her American debut with the Detroit Symph. Orch. (Feb. 8, 1925) in Schumann's Piano Concerto. She became a prof. at the Curtis Inst. of Music in Philadelphia when it was founded in 1924; in 1950 she received an honorary doctor's degree there. Among her piano pupils at the Curtis Inst. were Leonard Bernstein, Samuel Barber, and Lukas Foss. She also taught privately in N.Y.

BIBLIOGRAPHY: Robert D. Schick, *The Vengerova System of Piano Playing* (Pa. State Univ., 1982).

Vennard, William D., American voice teacher; b. Bloomington, Ill., Jan. 31, 1909; d. Los Angeles, Jan. 10, 1971. He was a graduate of Northwestern Univ. and the American Cons. of Music in Chicago. In 1946 he joined the faculty of the Univ. of Southern Calif. in Los Angeles. He was a prolific writer of articles for professional journals, including *American Music Teacher, Journal of Speech and Hearing,* and *Folia Phoniatrica.* He publ. the manuals *Singing: The Mechanism and the Technique* and *Developing Voices;* also appeared as a singer at various functions in California.

Venth, Carl, German-American violinist, conductor, and composer; b. Cologne, Feb. 16, 1860; d. San Antonio, Texas, Jan. 29, 1938. His father was a German, his mother Croatian. He studied violin with his father, and composition with Ferdinand Hiller at the Cologne Cons. In 1880 he emigrated to the U.S.; was concertmaster of the Metropolitan Opera Orch. (1884–88) and of the St. Paul Symph. Orch. (1907–12); conducted the Brooklyn Symph. Orch. (1889–1902) and the Dallas Symph. Orch. (1911–13). In 1913 he organized the Fort Worth Symph. Orch., which he conducted for several years. In 1932 he joined the faculty of San Antonio Univ., remaining there until his death. In his own compositions he cultivated exotic subjects for the theater.

WORKS: *Pan in America,* "lyric dance drama" (won the prize of the National Federation of Music Clubs; produced at its Biennial Convention, Asheville, N.C., June 13, 1923); *The Rebel,* fairy opera with dance (Fort Worth, May 29, 1926); *La vida de la misión* (San Antonio, Oct. 28, 1959); also *Lima Beans,* short opera; *Alexander's Horse,* musical play; *The Juggler* for Voices and Instruments; *Dolls,* "musical extravaganza"; *The Sun God,* "oriental" opera; *Cathal,* short music drama; *Jack,* music drama; several symph. works (*Forest Scenes, Norse Dance, Indian Prologue,* etc.); Mass in D; 2 string quartets; Piano Trio; numerous piano compositions (*Sonata appassionata,* 2 rhapsodies, etc.); songs. His autobiography, *My Memories,* was publ. posthumously (1939).

BIBLIOGRAPHY: E.E. Hipsher, *American Opera and Its Composers* (Philadelphia, 1934; pp. 416–18).

Ventura, Ray(mond), French jazz bandleader; b. Paris, April 16, 1908; d. Palma, Majorca, Spain, March 29, 1979. He founded the Collegiate Five in 1925, which later was expanded to additional musicians to form the Collegians; after the jazz violinist Stéphane Grapelli joined the band, it became popular in France. During World War II, he led it on tours in South America. After the war, he returned to France; then became director of a film company. The renditions by the Collegians of Paul Misraki's *Fantastique* (1932) and *Tout va très bien, Madame la marquise* (1935) were famous.

Venuti, "Joe" (Giuseppe Venuti), Italian-born American jazz violinist; b. Lecco, April 4, 1898; d. Seattle, Aug. 14, 1978. He was brought to the U.S. as a child and reared in Philadelphia. There he received a thorough classical training on the violin, but after meeting the jazz guitarist Eddie Lang, he turned to popular music. After playing with Paul Whiteman, he formed his own band in 1935 and led it until 1943; then went to the West Coast, where he became a studio musician in Hollywood. His great merit was to make the theretofore-suspect violin a respectable instrument among the plebs of California.

Venzano, Luigi, Italian composer; b. Genoa, 1814; d. there, Jan. 26, 1878. He played cello at the Carlo Felice Theater in Genoa, and taught at the Cons. there; publ. many songs, including *Valzer cantabile,* which is often sung in the lesson scene of *The Barber of Seville;* also composed an operetta, *La notte dei schiaffi* (Genoa, April 25, 1873), and a ballet, *Benvenuto Cellini* (Milan, Aug. 24, 1861); publ. piano pieces and singing exercises.

Veprik, Alexander, Soviet composer; b. Balta, near Odessa, June 23, 1899; d. Moscow, Oct. 13, 1958. While still a young boy he went to Leipzig, where he took piano lessons with Karl Wendling; returning to Russia, he entered the Moscow Cons., where he took a course in composition with Miaskovsky (1921–23); from 1923 to 1943 he taught orchestration there. He was associated with the Jewish cultural movement in Russia, and composed several works in the traditional ethnic manner of Jewish cantillations. In his harmonic and formal treatment he followed the "orientalistic" tradition of the Russian national school.

WORKS: Opera, *Toktogul,* on Kirghiz motifs (Frunze, Kirghizia, 1940); for Chorus and Orch.: *Fascism Be Cursed!* (1944) and *The People Hero* (1955); for Orch.: 2 symphs. (1931, 1938); *Dances and Songs of the Ghetto* (1927); *Kaddish* for Voice, with Instruments (1925); *The Song of Jubilation* (Moscow, March 17, 1937); *Pastorale* (1946); chamber music: *Rhapsody* for Viola and Piano (1926); 3 piano sonatas (1922, 1924, 1928); film music; also *Jewish Communist Youth Song* (1926).

WRITINGS: *The Problem of Class Aspects of Orchestration* (Moscow, 1931); *Treatment of Orchestral Instruments* (posthumous, Moscow, 1961).

BIBLIOGRAPHY: A. Bogdanov-Berezovsky, *Alexandr Veprik* (Moscow, 1964).

Veracini, Francesco Maria, noted Italian violinist and composer; b. Florence, Feb. 1, 1690; d. there, Oct. 31, 1768. He studied violin with his uncle, Antonio Veracini, a prominent musician in Florence; subsequently took courses with Giovanni Maria Casini, and with Francesco Feroci. In 1711 Veracini went to Venice; in 1714 he visited London, where he played in a series of benefit concerts. In 1716 he returned to Venice. In 1717 he was called to Dresden, where he entered the service of the Prince Elector Friedrich August of Saxony. Mattheson states that Veracini attempted suicide in 1722; indeed, other contemporary writers noted his erratic behavior. In 1723 he returned to Florence; in 1733 he again went to London, where he became associated with the Opera of the Nobility, in opposition to Handel's opera company. He spent about 12 years in England. In 1745 he returned to Italy. In 1755 he became maestro di cappella for the Vallambrosian fathers in the Church of S. Pancrazio in Florence; in 1758 he assumed the same position for the Teatini fathers in the Church of S. Michele agl' Antinori.

WORKS: Operas: *Adriano in Siria* (London, Nov. 26, 1735); *La clemenza di Tito* (London, April 12, 1737); *Partenio* (London, March 14, 1738); *Rosalinda* (London, Jan. 31, 1744); oratorios, motets, masses, a Te Deum, cantatas, and songs. Instrumental music: 2 vols. of sonatas, 12 as op. 1 (Dresden, 1721; modern ed. by W. Kolneder, Leipzig, 1958–59) and 12 as op. 2 (London, 1744; modern ed. by F. Bär, Kassel, beginning in 1959); 12 early sonatas (1716; modern ed. by W. Kolneder, Leipzig, 1959–61); 12 *Dissertazioni . . . sopra l'opera quinta del Corelli* (modern ed. by W. Kolneder, Mainz, 1961).

BIBLIOGRAPHY: J. Mattheson, *Critica musica,* I (Hamburg, 1722); A. Naldo, "Un trattato inedito e ignoto di F.M. Veracini," *Rivista Musicale Italiana,* XLII (1938); A. Damerini, "Elogio dell' asino e monte di Stradella in un trattato di F.M. Veracini," *La Scala* (March 1956); M. Fabbri, "Gli ultimi anni di vita di Francesco Maria Veracini," *Collectanea historiae musicae,* III (1963); H. Smith, *F.M. Veracini's Il trionfo della pratica musicale* (Diss., Indiana Univ., 1963); M. Clarke, *The Violin Sonatas of F.M. Veracini: Some Aspects of Italian Late Baroque Instrumental Style Exemplified* (Diss., Univ. of N.C., 1967); F. Ricci, "Appunti per una biografia di Francesco Maria Veracini nel bicentenario della morte (1690–1768)," *Annuario dell' Accademia nazionale di Santa Cecilia* (1968); J. Hill, *The Life and Works of Francesco Maria Veracini* (Diss., Harvard Univ., 1972; revised, Ann Arbor, 1979); M. White, "The Life of Francesco Maria Veracini," *Music & Letters,* LIII (1972); J. Hill, "Veracini in Italy," *Music & Letters,* LVI (1975); J. Hill, "The Anti-galant Attitude of F.M. Veracini," in *Studies in Musicology in Honor of Otto E. Albrecht* (Kassel, 1977, and Clifton, N.J., 1980).

Verbesselt, August, Belgian flutist and composer; b. Klein-Willebroek, Oct. 22, 1919. He studied at the Antwerp Cons.; from 1942 was flute soloist at the Antwerp Opera. His works include a Flute Concerto (1952); *Hexatone-Synthèse* for Flute, Oboe, Clarinet, Cello, and Harp (1964); *Diagrams* for Chamber Orch. (1972); *Universum* for 2 Orchs. and Tape (1975). He also wrote ballet music.

Verbrugghen, Henri, Belgian violinist and conductor; b. Brussels, Aug. 1, 1873; d. Northfield, Minn., Nov. 12, 1934. He studied with Hubay and Ysaÿe at the Brussels Cons.; in 1893 was engaged as a violinist in the Scottish Orch. in Glasgow; then was concertmaster in various orchs. in Wales; also conducted summer concerts there while retaining his position in Glasgow. In 1915 he went to Australia, and established the National Cons. in Sidney. In 1922–23 he was a guest conductor of the Minneapolis Symph. Orch.; then became its regular conductor (until 1932).

Verdelot, Philippe, noted French composer; b. Verdelot, Les Loges, Seine-et-Marne, c.1470–80; d. before 1552. He made his way to northern Italy; in 1522 he was in Florence, where he served as maestro di cappella at the Baptisterium S. Giovanni (1523–27); from 1529 to 1533 he was active in Rome; in 1533–35 was in Venice in a secular capacity. Verdelot's madrigals and motets were publ. in collections in the 16th century, although several works attributed to him are of doubtful authenticity. He composed 2 masses, one entitled *Philomena* (1544); also wrote a Magnificat and several chansons. The *Opera omnia,* edited by A.-M. Bragard in Corpus Mensurabilis Musicae, began publication in 1966.

BIBLIOGRAPHY: A.-M. Bragard, "Verdelot en Italie," *Revue Belge de Musicologie,* XI (1957); D. Hersh, *Philippe Verdelot and the Early Madrigal* (Diss., Univ. of Calif., Berkeley, 1963); A.-M. Bragard, *Etude bio-bibliographique sur Philippe Verdelot, musicien français de la Renaissance* (Brussels, 1964); N. Böker-Heil, *Die Motetten von Philippe Verdelot* (Cologne, 1967).

Verdi, Giuseppe (Fortunino Francesco), great Italian opera composer whose genius for dramatic, lyric, and tragic stage music has made him the perennial favorite of a multitude of opera enthusiasts; b. Le Roncole, near Busseto, Duchy of Parma, Oct. 9, 1813; d. Milan, Jan. 27, 1901. His father kept a tavern, and street singing gave Verdi his early appreciation of music produced by natural means. A *magister parvulorum,* one Pietro Bai-strocchi, a church organist, noticed Verdi's love of musical sound and took him on as a pupil. When Baistrocchi died, Verdi, still a small child, took over some of his duties at the keyboard. His father sent him to Busseto for further musical training; there he began his academic studies and also took music lessons with Ferdinando Provesi, the director of the municipal music school. At the age of 18 Verdi became a resident in the home of Antonio Barezzi, a local merchant and patron of music; Barezzi sup-plied him with enough funds so that he could go to Milan for serious study. Surprisingly enough, in view of Verdi's future greatness, he failed to pass an entrance examination to the Milan Cons.; the registrar, Francesco Basili, reported that Verdi's piano technique was inadequate and that in compo-sition he lacked technical knowledge. Verdi then turned to Vincenzo Lavigna, an excellent musician, for private lessons, and worked industriously to master counterpoint, canon, and fugue. In 1834 Ver-di applied for the post of *maestro di musica* in Bus-seto, and after passing his examination received the desired appointment. On May 4, 1836, he mar-ried a daughter of his patron Barezzi; it was a love marriage, but tragedy intervened when their 2 in-fant children died, and Verdi's wife herself suc-cumbed on June 18, 1840. Verdi deeply mourned his bereavement, but he found solace in music. In 1838 he completed his first opera, *Oberto, conte di San Bonifacio.* In 1839 he moved to Milan. He submitted the score of *Oberto* to the directorship of La Scala; it was accepted for a performance, which took place on Nov. 17, 1839, with satisfactory success. Verdi was now under contract to write more operas for that renowned theater. His comic opera *Un gior-no di regno* was performed at La Scala in 1840, but it did not succeed at pleasing the public. Somewhat downhearted at this reverse, Verdi began composi-tion of an opera, *Nabucodonosor,* on the biblical subject (the title was later abbreviated to *Nabucco*). It was staged at La Scala on March 9, 1842, scoring considerable success. Giuseppina Strepponi created the leading female role of Abigaille. *Nabucco* was followed by another successful opera on a historic subject, *I Lombardi alla prima Crociata,* produced at La Scala on Feb. 11, 1843. The next opera was *Ernani,* after Victor Hugo's drama on the life of a revolutionary outlaw; the subject suited the rise of national spirit, and its production in Venice on March 9, 1844, won great acclaim. Not so popular were Verdi's succeeding operas, *I due Foscari* (1844), *Giovanna d'Arco* (1845), *Alzira* (1945), and *Attila* (1946). On March 14, 1847, Verdi produced in Florence his first Shakespearean opera, *Macbeth.* In the same year he received a commission to write an opera for London; the result was *I Masnadieri,* based on Schiller's drama *Die Räuber.* It was pro-duced at Her Majesty's Theatre in London on July 22, 1847, with Jenny Lind taking the leading female role. A commission from Paris followed; for it Verdi revised his opera *I Lombardi alla prima Crociata* in a French version, renamed *Jérusalem;* it was pro-duced at the Paris Opéra on Nov. 26, 1847; the Ital-ian production followed at La Scala on Dec. 26, 1850.

This was one of the several operas by Verdi and other Italian composers where mistaken identity was the chief dramatic device propelling the ac-tion. During his stay in Paris for the performance of *Jérusalem,* he renewed his acquaintance with Giuseppina Strepponi; after several years of cohabitation, their union was legalized in a private ceremony in Savoy on Aug. 29, 1859. In 1848 Verdi produced his opera *Il Corsaro,* after Byron's poem *The Corsair.* There followed *La battaglia di Legna-no,* celebrating the defeat of the armies of Bar-barossa by the Lombards in 1176. Its premiere took place in Rome on Jan. 27, 1849, but Verdi was forced to change names and places so as not to offend the central European powers that dominated Italy. The subsequent operas *Luisa Miller* (1849), after Schil-ler's drama *Kabale und Liebe,* and *Stiffelio* (1850) were not successful. Verdi's great triumph came in 1851 with the production of *Rigoletto,* fashioned af-ter Victor Hugo's drama *Le Roi s'amuse;* it was per-formed for the first time at the Teatro La Fenice in Venice on March 11, 1851, and brought Verdi lasting fame; it entered the repertoire of every opera house around the globe. The aria of the libidinous Duke, "La donna è mobile," became one of the most popu-lar operatic tunes sung, or ground on the barrel or-gan, throughout Europe. This success was followed by an even greater acclaim with the production in 1853 of *Il Trovatore* (Rome, Jan. 19, 1853) and *La Traviata* (Venice, March 6, 1853); both captivated world audiences without diminution of their melo-dramatic effect on succeeding generations in Europe and America, and this despite the absurdity of the action represented on the stage. *Il Trovatore* resorts to the common device of unrecognized iden-tities of close relatives, while *La Traviata* strains credulity when the eponymous soprano sings en-chantingly and long despite her struggle with ter-minal consumption. The character of Traviata was based on the story of a real person, as depicted in the drama *La Dame aux camélias* by Alexandre Dumas *fils.* The Italian title is untranslatable, *Traviata* being the feminine passive voice of the verb meaning "to lead astray," and it would have to be rendered, in English, by the construction "a woman who has been led astray." Another commis-sion coming from Paris resulted in Verdi's first French opera, *Les Vêpres siciliennes,* after a libret-to by Scribe to Donizetti's unfinished opera *Le Duc d'Albe;* the action deals with the medieval slaugh-ter of the French occupation army in Sicily by local patriots. Despite the offensiveness of the subject to French patriots, the opera was given successfully in Paris on June 13, 1855. His next opera, *Simone Boc-canegra,* was produced at the Teatro La Fenice in Venice on March 12, 1857. This was followed by *Un ballo in maschera,* which made history. The origi-nal libretto was written by Scribe for Auber's opera *Gustave III,* dealing with the assassination of King Gustave III of Sweden in 1792. But the censors would not have any regicide shown on the stage, and Verdi was compelled to transfer the scene of action from Sweden to Massachusetts. Ridiculous as it was, Gustave III became Governor Riccardo of Boston; the opera was produced in this politically

Verdi

sterilized version in Rome on Feb. 17, 1859. Attempts were made later to restore the original libretto and to return the action to Sweden, but audiences resented the change of the familiar version. Unexpectedly, Verdi became a factor in the political struggle for the independence of Italy; the symbol of the nationalist movement was the name of Vittorio Emanuele, the future king of Italy. Demonstrators painted the name of Verdi in capital letters, separated by punctuation, on fences and walls of Italian towns (V.E.R.D.I., the initials of Vittorio Emanuele, Re D'Italia), and the cry "Viva Verdi!" became "Viva Vittorio Emanuele Re D'Italia!" In 1861 Verdi received a commission to write an opera for the Imperial Opera of St. Petersburg, Russia; he selected the mystic subject *La forza del destino.* The premiere took place in St. Petersburg on Nov. 10, 1862, and Verdi made a special trip to attend. He then wrote an opera to a French text, *Don Carlos,* after Schiller's famous drama. It was first heard at the Paris Opéra on March 11, 1867, with numerous cuts; they were not restored in the score until a century had elapsed after the initial production. In June 1870 Verdi received a contract to write a new work for the opera in Cairo, Egypt, where *Rigoletto* had already been performed a year before. The terms were most advantageous, with a guarantee of 150,000 francs for the Egyptian rights alone. The opera, based on life in ancient Egypt, was *Aida;* the original libretto was in French; Antonio Ghislanzoni prepared the Italian text. It had its premiere in Cairo on Christmas Eve of 1871, with great éclat. A special boat was equipped to carry officials and journalists from Italy to Cairo for the occasion, but Verdi stubbornly refused to join the caravan despite persuasion by a number of influential Italian musicians and statesmen; he declared that a composer's job was to supply the music, not to attend performances. The success of *Aida* exceeded all expectations; the production was hailed as a world event, and the work itself became one of the most famous in opera history.

After Rossini's death, in 1868, Verdi conceived the idea of honoring his memory by a collective composition of a Requiem, to which several Italian composers would contribute a movement each, Verdi reserving the last section, *Libera me,* for himself. He completed the score in 1869, but it was never performed in its original form. The death of the famous Italian poet Alessandro Manzoni in 1873 led Verdi to write his great *Messa da Requiem,* which became known simply as the "Manzoni" Requiem, and he incorporated in it the section originally composed for Rossini. The *Messa da Requiem* received its premiere on the first anniversary of Manzoni's death, on May 22, 1874, in Milan. There was some criticism of the Requiem as being too operatic for a religious work, but it remained in musical annals as a masterpiece. After a lapse of some 13 years of rural retirement, Verdi turned once more to Shakespeare; the result this time was *Otello;* the libretto was by Arrigo Boito, a master poet who rendered Shakespeare's lines into Italian with extraordinary felicity. It received its premiere at La Scala on Feb. 5, 1887. Verdi was 79 years old when he wrote yet another Shakespearean opera, *Falstaff,* also to a libretto by Boito; in his libretto Boito used materials from *The Merry Wives of Windsor* and *Henry IV. Falstaff* was performed for the first time at La Scala on Feb. 9, 1893. The score reveals Verdi's genius for subtle comedy coupled with melodic invention of the highest order. Verdi's last composition was a group of sacred choruses, an *Ave Maria, Laudi alla Vergine Maria, Stabat Mater,* and *Te Deum,* publ. in 1898 as *4 pezzi sacri;* in the *Ave Maria,* Verdi made use of the so-called "scala enigmatica" (C, D-flat, E, F-sharp, G-sharp, A-sharp, B, and C).

Innumerable honors were bestowed upon Verdi. In 1864 he was elected to membership in the Académie des Beaux Arts in Paris, where he filled the vacancy made by the death of Meyerbeer. In 1875 he was nominated a senator to the Italian Parliament. Following the premiere of *Falstaff,* the King of Italy wished to make him "Marchese di Busseto," but Verdi declined the honor. After the death of his 2nd wife, on Nov. 14, 1897, Verdi founded in Milan the Casa di Riposo per Musicisti, a home for aged musicians; for its maintenance, he set aside 2,500,000 lire. On Jan. 21, 1901, Verdi suffered an apoplectic attack; he died 6 days later at the age of 87.

Historic evaluation of Verdi's music changed several times after his death. The musical atmosphere was heavily Wagnerian; admiration for Wagner produced a denigration of Verdi as a purveyor of "barrel-organ" music. Then the winds of musical opinion reversed their direction; sophisticated modern composers, music historians, and academic theoreticians discovered unexpected attractions in the flowing Verdian melodies, easily modulating harmonies, and stimulating symmetric rhythms; a theory was even advanced that the appeal of Verdi's music lies in its adaptability to modernistic elaboration and contrapuntal variegations. By natural transvaluation of opposites, Wagnerianism went into eclipse after it reached the limit of complexity. The slogan "Viva Verdi!" assumed, paradoxically, an esthetic meaning. Scholarly research into Verdi's biography greatly increased. The Istituto di Studi Verdiani was founded in Parma in 1959. An American Inst. for Verdi Studies was founded in 1976 with its archive at N.Y. Univ.; it publ. a newsletter.

WORKS: OPERAS: In the literature on Verdi, mention is sometimes made of 2 early operatic attempts, *Lord Hamilton* and *Rocester;* however, nothing definitive has ever been established concerning these 2 works. The accepted list of his operas is as follows: *Oberto, conte di San Bonifacio* (1837–38; La Scala, Milan, Nov. 17, 1839; libretto revised by Graffigna and given as *I Bonifazi ed i Salinguerra* in Venice in 1842); *Un giorno di regno* (later known as *Il finto Stanislao*), melodramma giocoso (1840; La Scala, Milan, Sept. 5, 1840); *Nabucodonosor* (later known as *Nabucco*), dramma lirico (1841; La Scala, Milan, March 9, 1842); *I Lombardi alla prima Crociata,* dramma lirico (1842; La Scala, Milan, Feb. 11, 1843; revised version, with a French libretto by Royer and Vaëz, given as *Jérusalem* at the Paris Opéra, Nov. 26, 1847); *Ernani,* dramma lirico (1843; Teatro La Fenice, Venice, March 9, 1844); *I due Foscari,* tragedia lirica (1844; Teatro Argentina, Rome, Nov. 3, 1844); *Giovanna d'Arco,* dramma lirico (1844; La Scala, Milan, Feb. 15, 1845); *Alzira,* tragedia lirica (1845; Teatro San Carlo, Naples, Aug. 12, 1845); *Attila,* dramma lirico (1845–46; Teatro La Fenice, Venice, March 17, 1846); *Macbeth* (1846–47; Teatro alla Pergola, Florence, March 14, 1847; revised version, with a French trans. by Nuittier and Beaumont of the Italian libretto, Théâtre-Lyrique, Paris, April 21, 1865); *I Masnadieri* (1846–47; Her Majesty's Theatre, London, July 22, 1847); *Il Corsaro* (1847–48; Teatro Grande, Trieste, Oct. 25, 1848); *La battaglia di Legnano,* tragedia lirica (1848; Teatro Argentina, Rome, Jan. 27, 1849); *Luisa Miller,* melodramma tragico (1849; Teatro San Carlo, Naples, Dec. 8, 1849); *Stiffelio* (1850; Teatro Grande, Trieste, Nov. 16, 1850; later revised as *Aroldo*); *Rigoletto,* melodramma (1850–51; Teatro La Fenice, Venice, March 11, 1851); *Il Trovatore,* dramma (1851–52; Teatro Apollo, Rome, Jan. 19, 1853; revised 1857); *La Traviata* (1853; Teatro La Fenice, Venice, March 6, 1853); *Les Vêpres siciliennes* (1854; Opéra, Paris, June 13, 1855); *Simone Boccanegra* (1856–57; Teatro La Fenice, Venice, March 12, 1857; revised 1880–81; La Scala, Milan, March 24, 1881); *Aroldo* (revision of *Stiffelio;* 1856–57; Teatro Nuovo, Rimini, Aug. 16, 1857); *Un ballo in maschera,* melodramma (1857–58; Teatro Apollo, Rome, Feb. 17, 1859); *La forza del destino* (1861; Imperial Theater, St. Petersburg, Nov. 10, 1862; revised version, La Scala, Milan, Feb. 27, 1869); *Don Carlos* (1866; Opéra, Paris, March 11, 1867; revised version, 1883–84, with Italian libretto by Lauzières and Zanardini, La Scala, Milan, Jan. 10, 1884); *Aida* (1870–71; Opera House, Cairo, Dec. 24, 1871); *Otello,* dramma lirico (1884–86; La Scala, Milan, Feb. 5, 1887); *Falstaff,* commedia lirica (1889–93; La Scala, Milan, Feb. 9, 1893).

OTHER WORKS: *Inno popolare* for Men's Voices and Piano (1848); *Inno delle Nazioni* for Solo Voice, Mixed Chorus, and Orch. (1862; London, May 24, 1862; composed for the London Exhibition); *Libera me* for Soprano, Mixed Chorus, and Orch. (1868–69; composed for the *Rossini Requiem* and later incorporated in the *Messa da Requiem*); String Quartet in E minor (1873); *Messa da Requiem* for Soprano, Alto, Tenor, Bass, Mixed Chorus, and Orch., the "Manzoni" Requiem (1873–74; San Marco, Milan, May 22, 1874); *Ave Maria* for Soprano and Strings (1880); *Pater noster* for 5-part Chorus a cappella (1880); *4 pezzi sacri: Ave Maria* for Chorus a cappella (1888–89), *Stabat Mater* for Chorus and Orch. (1895–97), *Laudi alla Vergine Maria* for Female Chorus a cappella (1888–89), and *Te Deum* for Soprano, Double Mixed Chorus, and Orch. (1895–97). —Songs: 6 *Romanze* (1838; *Non t'accostare all'urna; More, Elisa, lo stanco poeta; In solitaria stanza; Nell'orro di notte oscura; Perduta ho la pace; Deh, pietoso, oh Addolorata*); *Notturno* for Soprano, Tenor, Bass, and Piano, with Flute obbligato (1839); *L'Esule* (1839); *La seduzione* (1839); *Chi i bei di m'adduce ancora* (1842); 6 *Romanze* (1845; *Il tramonto* [2 versions]; *La Zingara; Ad una stella; Lo Spazzacamino; Il mistero; Brindisi*); *Il Poveretto* (1847); *Suona la tromba* (1848); *L'Aban-*

donnée (1849); *Barcarola* (1850); *La preghiera del poeta* (1858); *Il brigidino* (1863); *Tu dici che non m'ami* (1869); *Cupo è il sepolcro mutolo* (1873); *Pietà, Signor* (1894).—Also a *Tantum ergo* for Tenor and Orch. (1836?); *Romanza senza parole* for Piano (1865); Waltz for Piano.

BIBLIOGRAPHY: COLLECTED WORKS, SOURCE MATERIAL: There is still no complete critical ed. of Verdi's works, but Ricordi and the Univ. of Chicago Press are preparing a definitive ed.

Important sources include the following: C. Vanbianchi, *Nel I° centenario di G. V., 1813–1913: Saggio di bibliografia verdiana* (Milan, 1913); C. Hopkinson, "Bibliographical Problems Concerned with V. and His Publishers," *I° congresso internazionale di studi verdiani: Venezia 1966;* D. Lawton, "Per una bibliografia ragionata verdiana," ibid.; M. Pavarani, "Per una bibliografia e documentazione verdiana," ibid.; O. Strunk, "Verdiana alla Biblioteca del Congresso," ibid.; G. Tintori, "Bibliografia verdiana in Russia," ibid.; D. Kämpfer, "Das deutsche V.-Schriften: Hauptlinien der Interpretation," *Analecta Musicologica,* no. 11 (1972); D. Lawton and D. Rosen, "V.'s Non-Definitive Revisions: The Early Operas," *3° congresso internazionale di studi verdiani: Milano 1972;* C. Hopkinson, *A Bibliography of the Works of G. V., 1813–1901* (2 vols., N.Y., 1973 and 1978); M. Chusid, *A Catalog of V.'s Operas* (Hackensack, N.J., 1974); M. Mila, *La giovinezza di V.* (Turin, 1974); E. Surian, "Lo stato attuale degli studi verdiani: Appunti e bibliografia ragionata," *Rivista Italiana di Musicologia,* XII (1977).

BIOGRAPHICAL: G. Monaldi, *V. e le sue opere* (Florence, 1878); A. Pougin, *G. V.: Vita aneddotica* (Milan, 1881; in French, Paris, 1886; in Eng., N.Y., 1887); E. Hanslick, "G. V. Zur Geschichte seines Lebens, inbesondere seiner Jugendzeit," in *Suite* (Vienna, 1884); L. Parodi, *G. V.* (Genoa, 1895); Prince de Valori, *V. et son œuvre* (Paris, 1895); F. Crowest, *V.: Man and Musician* (London, 1897); G. Cavarretta, *V.: Il genio, la vita, le opere* (Palermo, 1899); G. Monaldi, *V.* (Turin, 1899; German trans. as *G. V. und seine Werke,* Stuttgart, 1898, publ. before the Italian original; 4th Italian ed., 1951); C. Perinello, *G. V.* (Berlin, 1900); M. Basso, *G. V.: La sua vita, le sue opere, la sua morte* (Milan, 1901); O. Boni, *L'Uomo, le opere, l'artista* (Parma, 1901; 2nd ed., 1913); E. Checchi, *G. V.* (Florence, 1901); N. Marini, *G. V.* (Rome, 1901); E. Colonna, *G. V. nella vita e nelle opere* (Palermo, 1902); F. Garibaldi, *G. V. nella vita e nell'arte* (Florence, 1904); L. Sorge, *G. V.: Uomo, artista, patriota* (Lanciano, 1904); P. Voss, *G. V.: Ein Lebensbild* (Diessen, 1904); G. Bragagnolo and E. Bettazzi, *La vita di G. V. narrata al popolo* (Milan, 1905); A. Visetti, *V.* (London, 1905); A. d'Angeli, *G. V.* (Bologna, 1910; 2nd ed., 1912); C. Bellaigue, *V.: Biographie critique* (Paris, 1912; Italian trans., Milan, 1913); M. Chop, *V.* (Leipzig, 1913); M. Lottici, *Bio-bibliografia di G. V.* (Parma, 1913); A. Mackenzie, *V.* (N.Y., 1913); G. Monaldi, *Il Maestro della rivoluzione italiana* (Milan, 1913); A. Righetti, *G. V.: Vita aneddotica* (Rome, 1913); A. Neisser, *G. V.* (Leipzig, 1914); G. Roncaglia, *G. V.* (Naples, 1914); A. Weissmann, *V.* (Berlin, 1922); A. Bonaventura, *G. V.* (Paris, 1923); F. Werfel, *V., Roman der Oper* (a biographical novel; Berlin, 1924; Eng. trans., N.Y., 1925); G. Monaldi, *V. anedottico* (Turin, 1926); E. Gascó Contell, *V., Su vida y sus obras* (Paris, 1927); F. Ridella, *V.* (Genoa, 1928); F. Bonavia, *V.* (London, 1930; 2nd ed., 1947); C. Gatti, *V.* (Milan, 1931; 2nd ed., 1951; Eng. trans. as *V.: The Man and His Music,* N.Y., 1955); F. Toye, *G. V.: His Life and Works* (London, 1931); H. Gerigk, *G. V.* (Potsdam, 1932); R. de Rensis, *Franco Faccio e V.* (Milan, 1934); R. Manganella, *V.* (Milan, 1936); L. d'Ambra, *G. V.* (Milan, 1937); D. Hussey, *V.* (London, 1940; 5th ed., 1973); F. Botti, *G. V.* (Rome, 1941); G. Roncaglia, *G. V.* (Florence, 1941); K. Holl, *V.* (Vienna, 1942); U. Zoppi, *Angelo Mariani, G. V. e Teresa Stolz* (Milan, 1947); D. Humphreys, *V., Force of Destiny* (N.Y., 1948); F. Törnblom, *V.* (Stockholm, 1948); G. Cenzato, *Itinerari verdiani* (Parma, 1949; 2nd ed., Milan, 1955); A. Cherbuliez, *G. V.* (Zürich, 1949); A. Oberdorfer, *G. V.* (Verona, 1949); L. Orsini, *G. V.* (Turin, 1949); F. Abbiati, ed., *G. V.* (Milan, 1951); L. Gianoli, *V.* (Brescia, 1951); G. Monaldi, *V., La vita, le opere* (Milan, 1951); E. Radius, *V. vivo* (Milan, 1951); G. Stefani, *V. e Trieste* (Trieste, 1951); idem, *G. V.* (a collection of articles; Siena, 1951); F. Botti, *V. e l'ospedale di Villanova d'Arda* (Parma, 1952); G. Mondini, *Nel cinquantennio della morte di G. V.* (Cremona, 1952); T. Ybarra, *V., Miracle Man of Opera* (N.Y., 1955); M. Mila, *G. V.* (Bari, 1958); P. Petit, *V.* (Paris, 1958); V. Sheean, *Orpheus at Eighty* (N.Y., 1958); F. Abbiati, *G. V.* (the standard biography; 4 vols., Milan, 1959); F. Walker, *The Man V.* (contains new material on Verdi; N.Y., 1962); G. Martin, *V.: His Music, Life and Times* (N.Y., 1963; 2nd ed., revised, 1964); M. Matz, "The V. Family of Sant'Agata and Roncole: Legend and Truth," *1° congresso internazionale di studi verdiani: Venezia 1966;* idem, "V.: The Roots of the Tree," *Verdi: Bollettino dell'Istituto di studi verdiani,* III (1969–73); J. Wechsberg, *V.* (N.Y., 1974); W. Weaver, ed., *V.: A Documentary Study* (N.Y. and London, 1977); M. Conati, ed., and R. Stokes, trans., *Interviews and Encounters with V.* (London, 1984).

CRITICAL, ANALYTICAL: A. Basevi, *Studio sulle opere di G. V.* (Florence, 1859); G. Bertrand, *Les Nationalités musicales étudiées dans le drame lyrique. Verdisme et Wagnérisme* (Paris, 1872); E. Hanslick, *V., in Die moderne Oper* (Berlin, 1875; several subsequent eds.); B. Roosevelt, *V., Milan and Otello* (Milan, 1887); V. Maurel, *A propos de la mise-en-scène du drame lyrique "Otello"* (Rome, 1888); E. Destranges, *L'Evolution musicale chez V.: Aïda, Otello, Falstaff* (Paris, 1895); C. Abate, *Wagner e V. Studio critico-musicale* (Mistretta, 1896); P. Bellezza, *Manzoni e V., i due grandi* (Rome, 1901); A. Soffredini, *Le opere di G. V.: Studio critico-analitico* (Milan, 1901); G. Tebaldini, *Da Rossini a V.* (Naples, 1901); J. Huneker, *Overtones* (N.Y., 1904); F. Flamini, *Pagine di critica e d'arte* (contains a study on the operas of Verdi; Livorno, 1905); J. Hadden, *The Operas of V.* (London, 1910); K. Regensburger, *Über den "Trovador" des García Gutiérrez, die Quelle von V.s "Il Trovatore"* (Berlin, 1911); C. Vanbianchi, *Saggio di bibliografia verdiana* (Milan, 1913); G. Roncaglia, *G. V.: L'ascensione dell'arte sua* (Naples, 1914); E. Istel, "The 'Othello' of V. and Shakespeare," *Musical Quarter-*

ly (July 1916); A. St. John-Brenon, "G. V.," ibid. (Jan. 1916); E. Istel, "A Genetic Study of the Aïda Libretto," ibid. (Jan. 1917); P. Berl, *Die Opern V.s in ihrer Instrumentation* (Diss., Univ. of Vienna, 1931); A. Maecklenburg, "V. and Manzoni," *Musical Quarterly* (April 1931); G. Menghini, *G. V. e il melodramma italiano* (Rimini, 1931); M. Mila, *Il melodramma di V.* (Bari, 1933); A. Parente, *Il problema della critica verdiana* (Turin, 1933); L. Unterholzner, *G. V.s Operntypus* (Hannover, 1933); R. Gallusser, *V.s Frauengestalten* (Diss., Univ. of Zürich, 1936); G. Engler, *V.s Anschauung vom Wesen der Oper* (Diss., Univ. of Breslau, 1938); J. Loschelder, *Das Todesproblem in V.s Opernschaffen* (Cologne, 1938); G. Roncaglia, *L'ascensione creatrice di G. V.* (Florence, 1940); G. Mule and G. Nataletti, *V., Studi e memorie* (Rome, 1941); M. Rinaldi, *V. critico* (Rome, 1951); C. Gatti, *Revisioni e rivalutazioni verdiane* (Turin, 1952); E. Cone, "The Stature of Falstaff: Technique and Content in V.'s Last Opera," *Center,* I (1954); F. Travis, *V.'s Orchestration* (Zürich, 1956); G. Roncaglia, *Galleria verdiana: Studi e figure* (Milan, 1959); M. Mila, *Il melodramma di V.* (Milan, 1960); W. Herrmann, Jr., *Religion in the Operas of G. V.* (Diss., Columbia Univ., 1963); P. Pingagli, *Romanticismo di V.* (Florence, 1967); W. Dean, "V.'s *Otello:* A Shakespearian Masterpiece," *Shakespeare Survey,* XXI (1968); S. Hughes, *Famous V. Operas* (London, 1968); C. Osborne, *The Complete Operas of V.* (London, 1969); G. Baldini, *Abitare la battaglia: La storia di G. V.* (Milan, 1970); A. Porter, "The Making of Don Carlos," *Proceedings of the Royal Musical Association,* XCVIII (1971–72); W. Osthoff, "Die beiden Fassungen von V.s *Macbeth,*" *Archiv für Musikwissenschaft,* XXIX (1972); J. Budden, "The Two *Traviatas,*" *Proceedings of the Royal Musical Association,* XCIX (1972–73); idem, *The Operas of V.* (a valuable study; London, 1973—); A. Geck, *"Aïda," Die Oper: Schriftenreiche über musikalische Bühnenwerke* (Berlin, 1973); D. Lawton, *Tonality and Drama in V.'s Early Operas* (Diss., Univ. of Calif., Berkeley, 1973); V. Godefroy, *The Dramatic Genius of V.: Studies of Selected Operas* (2 vols., London, 1975 and 1977); D. Rosen, *The Genesis of V.'s Requiem* (Diss., Univ. of Calif., Berkeley, 1976); F. Noske, *The Signifier and the Signified: Studies in the Operas of Mozart and V.* (The Hague, 1977); H. Busch, *V.'s Aida: The History of an Opera in Letters and Documents* (Minneapolis, 1978); W. Weaver and M. Chusid, eds., *The V. Companion* (N.Y., 1979); D. Kimbell, *V. in the Age of Italian Romanticism* (Cambridge, 1981).

CORRESPONDENCE, ICONOGRAPHY: I. Pizzi, *Ricordi verdiani inediti* (Turin, 1901); T. Costantini, *Sei lettere di V. a Giovanni Bottesini* (relating to the production of *Aïda* in Cairo; Trieste, 1908); G. Cesari and A. Luzio, *G. V.: I copialettere pubblicati e illustrati* (Leipzig, 1913; Eng. trans. in an abridged ed. by C. Osborne as *Letters of G. V.,* 1971); G. Monaldi, *Saggio di iconografia verdiana* (Bergamo, 1913); J.-G. Prod'homme, "Unpublished Letters from V. to Camille Du Locle (1866–76)," *Musical Quarterly* (Jan. 1921); A. Martinelli, *G. V.: Raggi e Penombre. Le ultime lettere* (Trieste, 1926); F. Werfel and P. Stefan, *Das Bildnis G. V.s* (Vienna, 1926; Eng. trans.

in an enlarged ed. as *V., The Man in His Letters,* N.Y., 1942); G. Morazzoni, *Lettere inedite di G. V.* (Milan, 1929); A. Alberti, *V. intimo: Carteggio di G. V. con il conte Opprandino Arrivabene (1861–1866)* (Verona, 1931); L. Garibaldi, *G. V. nelle lettere di Emanuele Muzio ad Antonio Barezzi* (Milan, 1931); A. Luzio, *Carteggi verdiani* (Rome; vols. I–II, 1935; vols. III–IV, 1947); H. Schultz, *G. V., 1813–1901: Sein Leben in Bildern* (Leipzig, 1938); C. Gatti, *V. nelle immagini* (Milan, 1941); C. Graziani, *G. V.: Autobiografia dalle lettere* (a censored ed.; Milan, 1941; complete ed., 1951, under Graziani's real name, Aldo Oberdorfer); F. Walker, "Verdian Forgeries," *Music Review,* XIX (1958) and XX (1959); J. Klein, "Verdian Forgeries: A Summing-up," ibid., XX (1959); H. Kuehner, *G. V. in Selbstzeugnissen und Bilddokumenten* (Reinbek bei Hamburg, 1961); R. Petzoldt, *G. V., 1813–1901: Sein Leben in Bildern* (Leipzig, 1961).

Vere, Clémentine Duchene de (real name, **Wood de Vere**), French soprano; b. Paris, Dec. 12, 1864; d. Mount Vernon, N.Y., Jan. 19, 1954. Her father was a Belgian nobleman; her mother, an English lady. Her musical education was completed under the instruction of Mme. Albertini-Baucardé in Florence, where she made her début at the age of 16 as Marguerite de Valois in *Les Huguenots.* On Feb. 2, 1896, she made her American debut at the Metropolitan Opera, N.Y., as Marguerite in Gounod's *Faust;* she remained on its roster until 1897; was again at the Metropolitan in 1898–1900; her other roles with it were Violetta, Gilda, and Lucia. In 1892 she married the conductor **Romualdo Sapio;** after 1914 she lived mostly in N.Y., as a private teacher. Her voice was a brilliant high soprano; she excelled in coloratura.

Vered, Ilana, Israeli pianist; b. Tel Aviv, Dec. 6, 1939. Her mother was a concert pianist and her father was a violinist; she took piano lessons as a child with her mother; at 13 won an Israeli government grant to continue her studies at the Paris Cons.; subsequently took lessons with Rosina Lhévinne and Nadia Reisenberg at the Juilliard School of Music in N.Y. In 1969 she received a grant from the Martha Baird Rockefeller Foundation for a major tour of Europe; subsequently continued her concert career in America.

Vereen, Ben(jamin Augustus), black American entertainer; b. Miami, Oct. 10, 1946. He studied at the High School of Performing Arts in N.Y., the Dance Theater of Harlem, and the Pentacostal Theological Seminary. He began his career as a singer with the Brooklyn group Sensational Twilights; made his professional debut in 1965 in Langston Hughes's play *The Prodigal Son;* subsequently he was active mainly as a nightclub singer.

BIBLIOGRAPHY: *Current Biography* (April 1978).

Veremans, Renaat, Belgian composer; b. Lierre, March 2, 1894; d. Antwerp, June 5, 1969. He studied at the Lemmens Inst. in Mechlin and at the Antwerp Cons. with Auguste De Boeck; was awarded the Premier Prix in organ and piano in 1914; from 1921 to 1944 he served as director of the Flemish Opera in Antwerp; for 31 years, taught at the Antwerp Cons. In his music he follows the Romantic tradition of the Belgian-Flemish school of composition.

WORKS: 4 operas: *Beatrijs* (1928); *Anna-Marie* (Antwerp, Feb. 22, 1938); *Bietje* (1954); *Lanceloot en Sanderien* (Antwerp, Sept. 13, 1968); 2 operettas: *The Strange Adventure* and *The Mill of Sans Souci;* 2 oratorios: *The XIV Stations of the Cross* and *The 5 Joyful Mysteries; Groenendal Cantata;* 3 symphs. (1959, 1961, 1968); Trumpet Concerto (1960); Concerto for Flute and Chamber Orch. (1962); Concerto for Oboe and Small Orch. (1964); Horn Concerto (1965); symph. poems: *Morgendeschemer (Dawn); Night and the Awakening of Day beside the River Nete; Sylvan Scenes;* chamber music; choruses; many songs.

Veress, Sándor, Hungarian-Swiss composer; b. Kolozsvár, Feb. 1, 1907. He studied piano with his mother, and later with Béla Bartók; studied composition with Zoltán Kodály at the Royal Academy of Music in Budapest (1923–27); obtained his teacher's diploma (1932); also took lessons with László Lajtha at the Hungarian Ethnographical Museum (1929–33). He worked with Bartók on the folklore collection at the Academy of Sciences in Budapest (1937–40); subsequently taught courses at the State Academy of Music in Budapest (1943–48). In 1949 he went to Switzerland, where he received an appointment as guest prof. on folk music at Bern Univ.; taught composition, harmony, and counterpoint at Bern Cons. from 1950. In 1965–67 he was a visiting prof. at the Peabody Cons. in Baltimore; then was a lecturer at the Univ. of Adelaide in Australia (1967); from 1968 he taught musicology at Bern Univ.; then taught at the Univ. of Oregon in Portland (1972); returned to Switzerland and resumed his teaching position at Bern Univ.; became a Swiss citizen in 1975.

WORKS: 2 ballets: *Die Wunderschalmei* (1937) and *Térszili Katicza* (1942–43; Stockholm, Feb. 16, 1949); *Divertimento* for Orch. (1935); *Partita* for Orch. (1936); Violin Concerto (1937–39; Zürich, Jan. 9, 1951); 2 symphs.: No. 1 (1940) and No. 2, *Sinfonia Minneapolitana* (1953; Minneapolis, March 12, 1954); *4 Transylvanian Dances* for String Orch. (1944–49); *Threnos, in memoriam Béla Bartók* for Orch. (1945); *Hommage à Paul Klee,* fantasia for 2 Pianos and String Orch. (1951; Bern, Jan. 22, 1952); Concerto for Piano, Strings, and Percussion (1952; Baden-Baden, Jan. 19, 1954, composer soloist); Sonata for Orch. (1952; Brussels, July 8, 1952); Concerto for String Quartet and Orch. (1960–61; Basel, Jan. 25, 1962); *Passacaglia concertante* for Oboe and Strings (1961; Lucerne, Aug. 31, 1961); *Variations on a Theme of Kodály* for Orch. (1962); *Elegie* for Baritone, String Orch., and Harp (1964); *Expovare* for Flute, Oboe, and Strings (1964); *Musica concertante* for Strings (1965–66); Sonatina for Oboe, Clarinet, and Bassoon (1931); 2 string quartets (1931, 1936–37);

Veretti – Vermeulen

Violin Sonatina (1932); Cello Sonatina (1933); Sonata for Solo Violin (1935); Sonata No. 2 for Violin and Piano (1939); String Trio (1954); Piano Trio (1962); Sonata for Solo Cello (1967); Trio for Clarinet, Violin, and Cello (1972); piano pieces, including a Sonatina (1932); songs.

Veretti, Antonio, Italian composer; b. Verona, Feb. 20, 1900; d. Rome, July 13, 1978. He studied composition with Alfano at the Liceo Musicale of Bologna, graduating in 1921. He founded his own Cons. Musicale della Gioventù Italiana in Rome, teaching there until 1943; was director of the Cons. G. Rossini in Pesaro (1950–52) and of the Cons. of Cagliari in Sardinia (1953–55); in 1956–70 he was director of the L. Cherubini Cons. His music follows the traditional lines of Italian modernism, but in some of his later works he experimented with serial techniques.
WORKS: 2 operas: *Il Medico volante* (1928; won a prize of the newspaper *Il Secolo,* but was never perf.) and *Il Favorito del re* (La Scala, Milan, March 17, 1932; a condensed version, titled *Burlesca,* was perf. in Rome, Jan. 29, 1955); 2 ballets: *Il galante tiratore* (*The Gallant Killer;* San Remo, Feb. 11, 1933) and *Una favola di Andersen* (*A Fable by Andersen;* Venice, Sept. 15, 1934); choreographic musical mystery, *I sette peccati* (La Scala, April 24, 1956); 2 oratorios: *Il Cantico dei Cantici* (Bologna, 1922) and *Il Figliuol prodigo* (Rome, Nov. 21, 1942); *Sinfonia italiana* (Liège Festival of the International Society for Contemporary Music, Sept. 4, 1930); *Suite* for Orch. (1934); *Morte e deificazione di Dafni* for Voice and 11 Instruments (Venice Festival, Sept. 8, 1937); *Sinfonia epica* (1938); *Divertimento* for Harpsichord and 6 Instruments (1939); *Sinfonia sacra* for Male Voices and Orch. (1946; Rome, April 1947); Piano Concerto (Venice International Festival, Sept. 9, 1950); *4 poesie di Giorgio Vigolo* for Voice, and Orch. or Piano (1950; orch. version, Torino, Feb. 17, 1956); *Ouverture della campana* (RAI Radio, Nov. 10, 1951); *Fantasie* for Clarinet, and Orch. or Piano (1959); Concertino for Flute, and Chamber Orch. or Piano (1959); *Duo strumentale* for Violin and Piano (1925); Cello Sonata (1926); Piano Trio (1927); Violin Sonata (1952); *Elegie in Friulano* for Voice, Violin, Clarinet, and Guitar (1963); music for films.
BIBLIOGRAPHY: N. Costarelli, "Antonio Veretti," *Rassegna Musicale* (Jan.–March 1955).

Verevka, Grigori, Ukrainian composer; b. Bereznia, Chernigov district, Dec. 25, 1895; d. Kiev, Oct. 21, 1964. He was a boy chorister in Chernigov; then studied at the Kiev Inst. of Music and Drama; became engaged in choral conducting. He wrote a number of choruses which entered the general repertoire; made choral arrangements of nearly 100 revolutionary songs.

Vergnet, Edmond-Alphonse-Jean, French tenor; b. Montpellier, July 4, 1850; d. Nice, Feb. 25, 1904. He first played violin in the orch. of the Théâtre-Lyrique in Paris; then studied voice in Paris; made his debut at the Paris Opéra in 1874, continuing as a member there until 1893; also made guest appearances at La Scala in Milan, Covent Garden in London (1881–82), and in the U.S. (1885–86). Among the roles he created were Jean in Massenet's *Hérodiade* and Admeto in Catalani's *Dejanice;* his other roles were Faust, Radames, and Lohengrin.

Verheyden, Edward, Belgian composer; b. Antwerp, Oct. 8, 1878; d. there, April 10, 1959. He studied violin in Antwerp and Brussels; then turned to composition. He wrote the operas *Heibieke* (1908) and *De Geest* (1924); symph. works; lieder and choruses.

Verhulst, Johannes (Josephus Herman), Dutch conductor and composer; b. The Hague, March 19, 1816; d. there, Jan. 17, 1891. He studied violin at The Hague and Cologne; in 1838 went to Leipzig, where he became friendly with Mendelssohn; was engaged as conductor of the Euterpe concerts (until 1842); then returned to The Hague. He was conductor of the renowned Diligentia concerts at The Hague from 1860 until 1886; also conducted in Amsterdam and Rotterdam. He wrote a number of symph. works; chamber music; sacred songs; choruses to Dutch words.

Vermeulen, Matthijs, remarkable Dutch composer and music critic; b. Helmond, Feb. 8, 1888; d. Laren, July 26, 1967. Principally self-taught, he traveled in 1905 to Amsterdam, where he received musical guidance from Daniël le Lange and Alphons Diepenbrock; in 1908 he began to write music criticism for Dutch and French publications, and continued his journalistic activities until 1956. In 1921 Vermeulen went to France; returned to the Netherlands in 1947, when he became music editor of *De Groene Amsterdammer.* He entertained a strong belief in the mystical powers of music; in order to enhance the universality of melodic, rhythmic, and contrapuntal elements, he introduced in his compositions a unifying set of *cantus firmi* against a diversified network of interdependent melodies of an atonal character; it was not until the last years of his life that his works began to attract serious attention for their originality and purely musical qualities.
WORKS: FOR ORCH.: 7 symphs.: No. 1, *Symphonia Carminum* (1912–14; Arnhem, March 12, 1919; first professional perf., Amsterdam, May 5, 1964); No. 2, *Prélude à la nouvelle journée* (1919–20; first perf. as an identified work, Amsterdam, July 5, 1956; had won fifth prize at the Queen Elisabeth Composition Competition in Brussels in 1953 and was performed anonymously on Dec. 9); No. 3, *Thrène et Péan* (1921–22; Amsterdam, May 24, 1939); No. 4, *Les Victoires* (1940–41; Rotterdam, Sept. 30, 1949); No. 5, *Les Lendemains Chantants* (1941–45; Amsterdam, Oct. 12, 1949); No. 6, *Les Minutes heureuses* (1956–58; Utrecht, Nov. 25, 1959); No. 7, *Dithyrambes pour les temps à venir* (1963–65; Amsterdam, April 2, 1967); *Passacaille et Cortège* (1930; concert fragments from his music for the open-air play *The Flying Dutchman*); *Symphonic Prolog* (1930). OTHER WORKS: Songs: *The Soldier,* after Rupert Brooke

(1916); *On ne passe pas* (1917); *Les Filles du roi d'Espagne* (1917); *La Veille* (1917; orchestrated 1929); *3 Salutations à Notre-Dame* (1942); *Le Balcon* (1943); *3 Chants d'amour* (1962); 2 cello sonatas (1918, 1938); String Trio (1924); Violin Sonata (1925); String Quartet (1960–61).

WRITINGS: *De twee muzieken* (*The Two Musics;* 2 vols., Leyden, 1918); *Klankbord* (*Sound Board*) and *De eene grondtoon* (*The One Key Note*) in *De vrije bladen* (Amsterdam, 1929 and 1932); *Het avontuur van den geest* (*The Adventure of the Spirit;* Amsterdam, 1947); *Princiepen der Europese Muziek* (*Principles of European Music;* Amsterdam, 1948); *De Muziek, Dat Wonder* (*Music, A Miracle;* The Hague, 1958).

BIBLIOGRAPHY: W. Paap, "De Componist Matthijs Vermeulen," *Mens en Melodie* (Nov. 1949); E. Vermeulen, "Matthijs Vermeulen," *Sonorum Speculum,* 28 (1966); W. Paap, "In Memoriam Matthijs Vermeulen," *Mens en Melodie* (Sept. 1967); R. de Leeuw, "Matthijs Vermeulen," *Sonorum Speculum,* 52 (1973); J. Bernlef, " 'I've Never Felt the Need of a System,' " and O. Ketting, "Prelude as Postlude," *Key Notes,* 3 (1976; 35–45); P. Rapoport, *Opus Est: Six Composers from Northern Europe* (London, 1978).

Verne sisters, **Mathilde, Alice,** and **Adela,** English pianists, also sisters of **Marie Wurm.** Their real name was Wurm, but they adopted the name Verne in 1893. **Mathilde Verne** (b. Southampton, May 25, 1865; d. London, June 4, 1936) studied with her parents, and then became a pupil of Clara Schumann in Frankfurt; was very successful in England; from 1907 to 1936 gave concerts of chamber music in London; was a renowned teacher. **Alice Verne Bredt** (b. Southampton, Aug. 9, 1868; d. London, April 12, 1958) was best known as a piano teacher; she also composed pedagogical works. **Adela Verne** (b. Southampton, Feb. 27, 1877; d. London, Feb. 5, 1952) studied with her sisters, and later took lessons from Paderewski in Switzerland; returning to London, she developed a successful career, and became extremely popular as a concert player in England; also made tours in the U.S.

BIBLIOGRAPHY: Mathilde Verne, *Chords of Remembrance* (London, 1936).

Verneuil, Raoul de, Peruvian composer; b. Lima, April 9, 1899. He studied in Paris with André Bloch, and lived there for many years; returned to Lima in 1940, after a brief sojourn in N.Y. On Nov. 21, 1940, he gave a concert of his chamber music in Lima. His works include *Danza Peruana* for Orch.; *Inca Legend* for Voice and 8 Instruments; *Rítmos del Sol* for 12-part Chorus; piano pieces.

Verrall, John, American composer; b. Britt, Iowa, June 17, 1908. He studied piano and composition with Donald Ferguson; then went to Europe, where he attended classes at the Royal College of Music in London and took lessons with Kodály in Budapest. Returning to the U.S., he entered the Univ. of Minnesota (B.A., 1934). He held teaching positions at

Hamline Univ. (1934–42), at Mount Holyoke College (1942–46), and at the Univ. of Washington in Seattle (1948–73).

WORKS: Operas: *The Cowherd and the Sky Maiden,* after a Chinese legend (Seattle, Jan. 17, 1952); *The Wedding Knell,* after Hawthorne (Seattle, Dec. 5, 1952); *3 Blind Mice* (Seattle, May 22, 1955); Symph. No. 1 (Minneapolis, Jan. 16, 1940); Symph. No. 2 (1943); Violin Concerto (1946); *Symphony for Young Orchestras* (1948); *The Dark Night of St. John* for Chamber Orch. (1949); *Sinfonia festiva* for Band (1954); Piano Concerto (1960); Chamber Symph. (1967); Viola Concerto (1968); *Nonet* for String Quartet and Wind Quartet (1970); *Appalachian Folk Song* for Cello and Piano (1953); *Suite* for 3 Clarinets (1957); *Nocturne* for Bass Clarinet and Piano (1958); string quartets (1940, 1943, 1948, 1949, 1952, 1956, 1971); Horn Sonata (1942); 2 viola sonatas (1939, 1963); Flute Sonata (1972); numerous piano works and choruses. He publ. the teaching manuals *Elements of Harmony* (1937), *Form and Meaning in the Arts* (1958), *Fugue and Invention in Theory and Practice* (1966), and *Basic Theory of Scales, Modes and Interludes* (1969).

Verrett, Shirley, black American mezzo-soprano; b. New Orleans, May 31, 1931. Her father, a choirmaster at the Seventh-Day Adventist church in New Orleans, gave her rudimentary instruction in singing. Later she moved to California and took voice lessons with John Charles Thomas and Lotte Lehmann. In 1955 she won the Marian Anderson Award and a scholarship at the Juilliard School of Music, where she became a student of Marion Székely-Frescki. She made her N.Y. debut on Nov. 4, 1958. In July 1962 she sang Carmen at the Festival of Two Worlds at Spoleto, Italy, in a production by Gian Carlo Menotti. In 1963 she made a tour of the Soviet Union, and sang Carmen at the Bolshoi Theater in Moscow. Further engagements followed, at Covent Garden in London and in Israel. On Sept. 21, 1968, she made her debut at the Metropolitan Opera in N.Y., again as Carmen. On Oct. 22, 1973, she undertook 2 parts, those of Dido and Cassandra, in *Les Troyens* of Berlioz, produced at the Metropolitan. She was equally at ease in soprano and mezzo-soprano roles; thus she sang the title in Bellini's *Norma,* a soprano, and also the role of mezzo-soprano Adalgisa in the same opera. Her other roles included Tosca, Azucena, Amneris, and Dalila. She also showed her ability to cope with difficult parts in modern operas, such as Britten's *The Rape of Lucretia* and Bartók's *Bluebeard's Castle.* Her voice is of a remarkably flexible quality, encompassing lyric and dramatic parts with equal expressiveness and technical proficiency.

Verstovsky, Alexei, important Russian opera composer; b. on the family estate in Tambov district, March 1, 1799; d. Moscow, Nov. 17, 1862. He was taken as a child to the town of Ufa in the Urals; at the age of 17 was sent to St. Petersburg, where he entered the Inst. of Transport Engineers; at the same time he studied music privately with several excellent European teachers who were resident in Russia; took piano lessons with Johann Heinrich Miller, Daniel Steibelt, and the famous pianist and composer John Field; studied violin with Ludwig Maurer and voice with Tarquini. He became a member of the flourishing literary and artistic milieu in St. Petersburg; among his friends was Pushkin. In 1823 he went to Moscow. Almost all of his compositions for the stage followed the French model, with long scenes of speech accompanied on the keyboard; his first production was a vaudeville, *The Sentimental Landlord in the Country* (1817); he also composed popular songs and couplets for various plays. He contributed a great deal to the progress of operatic art in Russia, but his music lacked distinction and inventive power; with the advent of Glinka and Dargomyzhsky on the Russian operatic scene, Verstovsky's productions receded into insignificance.

WORKS: Light operas (all produced in St. Petersburg): *Grandmother's Parrot* (Aug. 10, 1819); *Quarantine* (Aug. 7, 1820); *New Mischief* (Feb. 24, 1822); *The Madhouse* (Oct. 28, 1822); *A Charade in Action* (Jan. 15, 1823); with Maurer, a long series of vaudevilles (all produced in Moscow): *Who Is Brother, Who Is Sister?* (Feb. 5, 1824); *Teacher and Pupil* (May 6, 1824); *The Petitioner* (June 10, 1824); *30,000 Men* (Feb. 10, 1825); *The Caliph's Amusements* (April 21, 1825); *The Miraculous Nose* (Oct. 20, 1825); *Itinerant Doctors* (Feb. 16, 1827); *5 Years in 2 Hours* (Feb. 1, 1828); *15 Years in Paris* (Feb. 8, 1828); *Man and Wife* (June 4, 1830); *The Old Hussar* (June 17, 1831); serious operas (all produced in Moscow): *Pan Tvardovsky* (June 5, 1828); *Vadim, or 1?; Sleeping Maidens* (Dec. 7, 1832); *Askold's Grave* (Sept. 27, 1835; his most important work; still in the repertoire of Russian opera houses); *Homesickness* (Sept. 2, 1839); *Gromoboy* (Feb. 5, 1858). A modern ed. of Verstovsky's songs and couplets from his music to theatrical plays was brought out in Moscow in 1971.

BIBLIOGRAPHY: V. Cheshikhin, *History of Russian Opera* (St. Petersburg, 1905, pp. 98–108); B. Dobrohotov, *Verstovsky* (Moscow, 1949).

Vesque von Püttlingen, Johann, Austrian composer; b. Opole, Poland, July 23, 1803; d. Vienna, Oct. 29, 1883. He studied law in Vienna and became a councillor of state; at the same time he studied music with Moscheles (piano) and Sechter (theory), and made his mark as a composer of operas, under the pseudonym **J. Hoyen.** The following operas by him were produced in Vienna: *Turandot* (Oct. 3, 1838); *Johanna d'Arc* (Dec. 30, 1840); *Abenteuer Carls des Zweiten* (Jan. 12, 1850). His opera *Der lustige Rat* was produced in Weimar on April 12, 1852. He publ. a useful book, *Das musikalische Autorrecht* (1865).

BIBLIOGRAPHY: E. Hanslick, "Vesque von Püttlingen," *Musikalisches Skizzenbuch* (Berlin, 1888); H. Schultz, *Johann Vesque von Püttlingen* (Regensburg, 1930).

Vetter, Walther, distinguished German musicologist; b. Berlin, May 10, 1891; d. there, April 1, 1967. He studied at the Leipzig Cons.; subsequently took a course in musicology with Hermann Abert at the Univ. of Halle, where he received his Ph.D. in 1920 with the dissertation *Die Arie bei Gluck;* he completed his Habilitation at the Univ. of Breslau with his *Das frühdeutsche Lied* in 1927 (publ. in Münster, 1928). He taught at the universities of Halle, Hamburg, Breslau, and Greifswald before joining the Univ. of Poznan (Posen) in 1941; from 1946–58 he was a prof. at Humboldt Univ. in Berlin, and also served as director of its Inst. of Musicology. From 1948–61 he was co-editor of *Die Musikforschung;* from 1956–66 he was editor of the *Deutsches Jahrbuch für Musikwissenschaft.*

WRITINGS: *Der humanistische Bildungsgedanke in Musik und Musikwissenschaft* (Langensalza, 1928); *Franz Schubert* (Potsdam, 1934); *Antike Musik* (Munich, 1935); *J.S. Bach: Leben und Werk* (Leipzig, 1938); *Beethoven und die militärpolitische Ereignisse seiner Zeit* (Poznan, 1943); *Der Kapellmeister Bach: Versuch einer Deutung Bachs auf Grund seines Wirkens als Kapellmeister in Köthen* (Potsdam, 1950); *Der Klassiker Schubert* (2 vols., Leipzig, 1953); *Mythos—Melos—Musica: Ausgewählte Aufsätze zur Musikgeschichte* (a collection of articles; 2 vols., Leipzig, 1957 and 1961); *Christoph Willibald Gluck* (Leipzig, 1964).

BIBLIOGRAPHY: *Musa—mens—musici: Im Gedenken an Walther Vetter* (Leipzig, 1969).

Veyron-Lacroix, Robert, noted French pianist and harpsichordist; b. Paris, Dec. 13, 1922. He studied piano at the Paris Cons. with Yves Nat and Samuel-Rousseau. After a series of successful recitals as pianist and harpsichordist, he toured as accompanist to the famous flutist Jean-Pierre Rampal. He also was a noted teacher; conducted seminars at the Schola Cantorum in Paris (1956); then was appointed to the piano faculty at the Paris Cons. (1967). He publ. *Recherches de musique ancienne* (Paris, 1955).

Viadana, Lodovico da, Italian composer; b. Viadana, near Mantua, 1560; d. Gualtieri, May 2, 1627. His family name was **Grossi,** but he is generally known by the name of his birthplace. In 1596 he became a Franciscan monk; from 1594 till c.1597, was maestro di cappella at the Mantua Cathedral; was in Rome at the end of the century; in 1602 became maestro di cappella at the convent of S. Luca in Cremona; then at the Cathedral of Concordia, near Venice, in 1608–9; from 1610 to 1612, was chorus master at Fano (Papal States), then in Venice, and finally in Mantua again. He was formerly accredited with the invention of the basso continuo (thoroughbass), but Peri's *Euridice* (publ. 1600) has a figured bass in certain numbers, as does Banchieri's *Concerti ecclesiastici* (publ. 1595), whereas Viadana's *Cento concerti con il basso continuo* did not appear till 1602 (Venice). However, he was the first to write church concertos with so few parts that the organ continuo was employed as a necessary harmonic support. A very prolific composer, he publ. numerous masses, Psalms, Magnificats, Lamentations, motets, etc. C. Gallico brought out *Opere di Lodovico Viadana* in Monumenti Musicali Mantovani (Kassel, 1964—).

BIBLIOGRAPHY: A. Parazzi, *Della vita e delle opere musicali di L. Grossi-Viadana* (Milan, 1876); F.X. Haberl, in *Kirchenmusikalisches Jahrbuch* (1881) and *Musica Sacra* (1897); M. Schneider, *Die Anfänge des Basso Continuo* (with 11 numbers from the *Cento concerti* of 1602; 1918); F.T. Arnold, *The Art of Accompaniment from a Thorough-Bass* (London, 1931); F.B. Pratella, "Viadana e la sinfonia," *Il Pensiero Musicale* (Sept.–Nov. 1922); G. Reese, *Music in the Renaissance* (N.Y., 1954; 2nd ed., revised, 1959).

Vianesi, Auguste - Charles - Léonard - François, Italian conductor; b. Livorno, Nov. 2, 1837; d. New York, Nov. 4, 1908. After studying in Italy, he went to Paris in 1857; then became conductor at Drury Lane in London; in 1858–59 he was in N.Y.; in 1870–80 he conducted Italian opera at Covent Garden in London; in 1887 became principal conductor at the Grand Opéra in Paris. He conducted the performance of *Faust* at the opening night of the Metropolitan Opera House in N.Y. (Oct. 22, 1883), and was on its staff throughout its first season; also conducted during the season of 1891–92; then remained in N.Y. as a vocal teacher.

Vianna (Viana), Fructuoso (Frutuoso), Brazilian composer; b. Itajubá, Oct. 6, 1896; d. Rio de Janeiro, April 22, 1976. He studied music with his father, a municipal judge, who composed polkas and waltzes. In 1912 he began to study piano with Henrique Oswald and harmony with Arnaud Gouveia. In 1923 he went to Paris, where he studied the Dalcroze method of eurhythmics. Returning to Brazil, he taught at the Cons. of São Paulo. In 1941 he settled in Rio de Janeiro. His works are based on native Brazilian melorhythms pleasurably seasoned with acrid dissonances, achieving a certain *trompe-l'oreille* euphony. His musical output consists mainly of piano pieces and songs of such nature; among them are numerous "valsas" (European waltzes in a Brazilian dressing), "toadas" (melodious romances), and "tanguinhos" (little tangos *à la brésilienne).* They are all perfumed with impressionistic overtones.

Vianna da Motta, José. See **Da Motta, José Vianna.**

Viardot-García, Pauline, celebrated singer, daughter of **Manuel del Popolo García;** b. Paris, July 18, 1821; d. there, May 18, 1910. She was taken by her parents to England and America; on returning to Paris in 1828, she had piano lessons with Liszt. Her father and mother both gave her vocal instruction; Reicha was her teacher in harmony. Her concert debut was at Brussels in 1837; her stage debut was in London, May 9, 1839, as Desdemona in Rossini's *Otello;* later she was engaged by Viardot, the direc-

tor of the Théâtre Italien in Paris; sang there until her marriage to Viardot in 1840; he then accompanied her on long tours throughout Europe. She created the role of Fides in Meyerbeer's *Le Prophète* at the Paris Opéra in 1849, and that of Sapho in Gounod's opera in 1851; after another succession of tours, she took the role of Orphée in Berlioz's revival of Gluck's opera at the Théâtre Lyrique (1859), singing the part for 150 nights to crowded houses. She retired in 1863. Her voice was a mezzo-soprano of extraordinary compass. For some years she taught at the Paris Cons.; among her pupils were Désirée Artôt and Antoinette Sterling. A thoroughly trained musician, she also composed operas, one of which, *La Dernière Sorcière,* was performed (in a German version) at Weimar (April 8, 1869). In Paris she maintained a long Platonic friendship with the Russian novelist Turgenev. She owned the holograph of Mozart's *Don Giovanni,* which she left to the library of the Cons. in Paris.

BIBLIOGRAPHY: La Mara, *P. Viardot-Garcia* (Leipzig, 1882); L.H. Torrigi, *P. Viardot-Garcia. Sa biographie, ses compositions, son enseignement* (Geneva, 1901); C.H. Kaminski, *Lettres à Mlle. Viardot d'Ivan Tourgéneff* (Paris, 1907); the memoirs of her daughter, Louise Héritte-Viardot, *Memories and Adventures* (London, 1913; trans. from original German MS; also in French, Paris, 1923); "P. Viardot-Garcia to J. Rietz. Letters of Friendship," *Musical Quarterly* (July 1915–Jan. 1916); T. Marix-Spire, "Gounod and His Interpreter, Pauline Viardot," *Musical Quarterly* (April, July 1945); A. Rachmanowa (pseud.), *Die Liebe eines Lebens: Iwan Turgenjew und Pauline Viardot* (Frauenfeld, 1952); April FitzLyon, *The Price of Genius: A Life of Pauline Viardot* (London, 1964).

Vicentino, Nicola, Italian music theorist; b. Vicenza, 1511; d. Rome, 1572. He was a pupil of Willaert at Venice; then became maestro and music master to Cardinal Ippolito d'Este in Ferrara and in Rome. There his book of madrigals for 5 voices, an attempt to revive the chromatic and enharmonic genera of the Greeks, led to an academic controversy with the learned Portuguese musician Lusitano; defeated, Vicentino publ. a theoretical treatise, *L'antica musica ridotta alla moderna prattica* (1555), which contains a description of his invention, an instrument called the archicembalo (having 6 keyboards, with separate strings and keys for distinguishing the ancient genera—diatonic, chromatic, and enharmonic). He also invented and described (1561) an "archiorgano." In chromatic composition he was followed by Cipriano de Rore and Gesualdo. His work paved the way for the monodic style, and the eventual disuse of the church modes. H. Kaufmann brought out the modern edition *Nicola Vicentino: Opera omnia* in Corpus Mensurabilis Musicae, XXVI (1963).

BIBLIOGRAPHY: H. Riemann, *Geschichte der Musiktheorie* (Leipzig, 1898); T. Kroyer, "Die Anfänge der Chromatik im italienischen Madrigal des XVI. Jahrhunderts," *Beihefte der Internationalen Musik-Gesellschaft;* G. Reese, *Music in the Renais-*

sance (N.Y., 1954; 2nd ed., 1959).

Vickers, Jon(athan Stewart), eminent Canadian tenor; b. Prince Albert, Saskatchewan, Oct. 29, 1926. He sang in church choirs as a boy; engaged in a mercantile career to earn a living and served as a manager in Canadian Woolworth stores; then was employed as a purchasing agent for the Hudson's Bay Co. and moved to Winnipeg. He won a scholarship at the Royal Cons. of Music of Toronto, where he studied voice with George Lambert; made his opera debut in 1952 at the Toronto Opera Festival as the Duke in *Rigoletto*. In 1957 he was invited to Covent Garden in London; in 1958 he appeared as Siegmund in *Die Walküre* at the Bayreuth Festival; in 1959 he sang at the Vienna State Opera; on Jan. 17, 1960, he made his debut at the Metropolitan Opera in N.Y. as Canio in *Pagliacci*. He is particularly renowned as the Heldentenor in Wagner's operas. In 1969 he was made a Companion of Honour of the Order of Canada.

BIBLIOGRAPHY: David Ewen, *Musicians since 1900* (N.Y., 1978).

Victoria, Tomás Luis de (Italianized form, **Tommaso Luigi da Vittoria**), one of the greatest Spanish Renaissance composers; b. Avila, 1548; d. Madrid, Aug. 20, 1611. He received his first musical training as a choirboy at the Cathedral in Avila. In 1565 he went to Rome, and to prepare himself for the priesthood entered the Collegium Germanicum, a seminary founded by St. Ignatius Loyola in 1552. In Rome his teacher may have been Palestrina, who from 1566 to 1571 was music master at the Roman Seminary, at this time amalgamated with the Collegium Germanicum. Victoria was about the same age as Palestrina's 2 sons, Rodolfo and Angelo, who were students at the Roman Seminary; the Italian master is known to have befriended his young Spanish colleague, and when Palestrina left the Seminary in 1571, it was Victoria who succeeded him as maestro there. In 1569 Victoria had left the Collegium Germanicum to become choirmaster and organist in the Church of Sta. Maria di Montserrato; from this time on he also officiated frequently at musical ceremonies in the Church of S. Giacomo degli Spagnuoli. In June 1573, he returned to the Collegium Germanicum as maestro di cappella; 2 years later the Collegium moved to new quarters in the Palazzo S. Apollinare, and Victoria thereby became choirmaster of the adjoining Church of S. Apollinare. In Aug. 1575, he was ordained a priest; in Jan. of that year he had received a benefice at León from the Pope, and in 1579 he was granted another benefice at Zamora, neither requiring residence. In 1578 he resigned his post at the Collegium Germanicum and was admitted as a priest to the Church of S. Girolamo della Carità, where he lived until 1585; this was the church where St. Philip Neri held his famous religious meetings, which led to the founding of the Congregation of the Oratory in 1575. Though Victoria was not a member of the Oratory, he must have taken some part in its important musical activities, living as he did for 5 years under the same roof with its founder (St. Philip left S. Girolamo in 1583); he is known to have been on terms of the closest friendship with Juvenal Ancina, a priest of the Oratory who wrote texts for many of the "Laudi spirituali" sung at the meetings of the Congregation. In 1583, dedicating a vol. of masses to Philip II, Victoria expressed a desire to return to his native land. He probably returned to Spain by 1587; in the dedication of his 2nd book of masses (1592) he mentions for the first time his appointment as chaplain to the widowed Empress-Mother Maria, sister of Philip II, who in 1581 had taken up her residence in the Convent of the Descalzas Reales in Madrid. After his return to Spain, Victoria became organist and choirmaster at this convent, and when the Empress Maria died in 1603, he continued to act as chaplain to her daughter, the Princess Margaret, who was a nun in the Descalzas Reales. His last work, a Requiem Mass for the Empress Maria, regarded as his masterpiece, was publ. in 1605.

Beginning with a vol. of motets in 1572, dedicated to his chief patron, Cardinal Otto Truchsess, Bishop of Augsburg, most of Victoria's works were printed in Italy, in sumptuous editions, showing that he had the backing of wealthy patrons. A vol. of masses, Magnificats, motets, and other church music publ. at Madrid in 1600 is of special interest because it makes provision for an organ accompaniment.

A man of deep religious sentiment, Victoria expresses in his music all the ardor and exaltation of Spanish mysticism. He is generally regarded as a leading representative of the Roman School, but it should be remembered that, before the appearance of Palestrina, this school was already profoundly marked by Hispanic influences through the work of Morales, Guerrero, Escobedo, and other Spanish composers resident in Rome. Thus Victoria inherited at least as much from his own countrymen as from Palestrina, and in its dramatic intensity, its rhythmic variety, its tragic grandeur and spiritual fervor, his music is thoroughly personal and thoroughly Spanish.

WORKS: Motets for 4, 5, 6, and 8 Voices (Venice, 1572; contains the well-known motets *O quam gloriosum* and *O vos omnes*); *Liber primus qui Missas, Psalmos, Magnificat, ad Virginem Dei Matrem Salutationes, aliaque complectitur* (Venice, 1576); *Cantica B. Virginis per annum* (Rome, 1581); *Hymni totius anni* (Rome, 1581; new ed., Venice, 1600); motets for 4, 5, 6, 8, and 12 Voices (Rome, 1583); *Missarum libri duo* for 4–6 Voices (Rome, 1583); *Officium Hebdomadae Sanctae* (Rome, 1585); *Motecta Festorum totius anni* for 4, 5, 6, and 8 Voices (Rome, 1585; new eds. printed at Milan and Dillingen in 1589); *Missae Liber secundus* for 4–8 Voices (Rome, 1592); *Missae, Magnificat, Motecta, Psalmi* for 8, 9, and 12 Voices (Madrid, 1600; contains both old and new works); *Officium defunctorum* for 6 Voices (Madrid, 1605). Pedrell brought out a complete modern ed. of Victoria's works in 8 vols. (Breitkopf & Härtel, 1902–13); a corrected ed., edited by H. Anglès, was publ. in 1965–68.

BIBLIOGRAPHY: L. Cellar, *La Semaine Sainte au Vatican* (Paris, 1867); H. Collet, *Le Mysticisme musical espagnol au XVIᵉ siècle* (Paris, 1913) and *T.L. de Victoria* (Paris, 1914); F. Pedrell, *T.L. de Victoria* (Valencia, 1918); R. Mitjana, *Estudios sobre algunos músicos españoles del siglo XVI* (Madrid, 1918); R. Casimiri, *"Il Vittoria"* (Rome, 1934); Hans von May, *Die Kompositionstechnik T.L. de Victorias* (Bern, 1943); P. Wagner, *Geschichte der Messe*, I, pp. 421ff.; Hugo Leichtentritt, *Geschichte der Motett*, pp. 373ff.; G. Reese, *Music in the Renaissance* (N.Y., 1954); T.N. Rive, "Victoria's *Lamentationes Geremiae*," *Anuario Musical* (1967); H. Anglès, "Problemas que presenta la nueva edición de las obras de Morales y de Victoria," in J. Robijns et al., *Renaissance-muziek* (Leuven, 1969).

Victory, Gerard, Irish composer; b. Dublin, Dec. 24, 1921. He studied modern languages at Univ. College in Dublin and music at Trinity College; in 1967 was appointed music director of Dublin Radio. His compositions are imbued with the broad pentatonic melos of Irish folk music; but in some of his instrumental works of a later period he began to apply serial structures.
WORKS: Operas: *An fear a phós balbhin (The Silent Wife),* to a libretto in Gaelic (Dublin, April 6, 1953); *Music Hath Mischief* (Dublin, Dec. 2, 1968); *Chatterton* (1967); operettas: *Nita* (1944) and *Once upon a Moon* (1949); ballet, *The Enchanted Garden* (1950); *The Midnight Court* for Orch. (1959); 2 symphs.: No. 1, *Short Symphony* (1961), and No. 2, *Il Ricorso* (1977); *5 Mantras* for Orch. (1963); 2 piano concertos (1954, 1972); Wind Quintet (1957); *Rodomontade* for 5 Woodwind Instruments (1964); String Quartet (1963); *Voyelles* for Soprano, Flute, Percussion, and String Orch., to the text of Arthur Rimbaud (1966); *Jonathan Swift,* symph. portrait (1970); *Tetragon* for Oboe and Orch. (1971); Harp Concerto (1971; London, Oct. 1, 1975); *Capriccio* for Violin and Orch. (1975); *Barocco Suite* for Orch. (1978); *9 Variations on the Cravate* for Orch. (1978); Cello Concerto (1978); *3 Irish Pictures* for Orch. (1979–80); *6 Epiphanies on the Author,* in memory of Joyce, for Orch. (Dublin, Feb. 5, 1982); film music.

Vidal, Louis-Antoine, French writer on music; b. Rouen, July 10, 1820; d. Paris, Jan. 7, 1891. He studied cello with Franchomme; made a specialty of research on string instruments; publ. a valuable survey, *Les Instruments à archet, les faiseurs, les joueurs d'instruments, leur histoire sur le continent européen, suivie d'un calalogue général de la musique de chambre* (3 vols., Paris, 1876–78; with 120 illustrative plates); sections of this work were publ. separately as *Les Vieilles Corporations de Paris* (1878) and *La Lutherie et les luthiers* (1889).

Vidal, Paul, noted French composer and pedagogue; b. Toulouse, June 16, 1863; d. Paris, April 9, 1931. He studied at the Paris Cons., and in 1883 won the Prix de Rome with his cantata *Le Gladiateur;* in 1889 he joined the staff of the Paris Opéra as assistant choral director; later became chief conductor there (1906). He taught elementary courses at the Paris Cons. from 1894 until 1910, when he was ap-

pointed a prof. of composition. He was music director of the Opéra-Comique in 1914–19.
WORKS: Ballet, *La Maladetta* (Paris Opéra, Feb. 24, 1893); opera, *Guernica* (Opéra-Comique, June 7, 1895); mystery play, *Noël, ou Le Mystère de la Nativité* (Galerie Vivienne, Paris, Nov. 25, 1890); operetta, *Eros* (Bouffes-Parisiens, April 22, 1892); several instructive manuals, much used in France: *Manuel pratique d'harmonie; Notes et observations sur la compositions et exécution;* he compiled *52 leçons d'harmonie de Luigi Cherubini* (3 vols.); *Solfège* (2 vols., Paris, 1922).

Vidu, Ion, Rumanian composer; b. Minerau (Banat), Dec. 14, 1863; d. Lugoj (Banat), Feb. 7, 1931. He studied in Jassy; became a choral conductor in Lugoj. He wrote a great number of choruses in a distinct native style, but harmonized his melodies according to German models; many of his arrangements have become repertoire pieces in Rumania.

Vieira, Ernesto, Portuguese music historian; b. Lisbon, May 24, 1848; d. there, April 26, 1915. His main achievement was the publication of the *Diccionario biografico de musicos portuguezes* (Lisbon, 1900), which supplemented the earlier dictionary by Vasconcellos (1870).

Vierdanck, Johann, German organist and composer; b. 1605; d. (buried) Stralsund, April 1, 1646. He was a chorister in Dresden, where he was a pupil of Schütz; was sent to Vienna in 1628 for further study; was church organist at the Marienkirche in Stralsund (1635–46). He publ. *Ballette und Corrente* for Violin, with Continuo (1637; 1641); spiritual "concertos" for 2–9 voices; of these, several were brought out in modern editions by Hans Engel (Kassel, 1932 and 1934) and Hans Erdmann (Kassel, 1950).
BIBLIOGRAPHY: G. Weiss, *Johann Vierdanck (c.1605–1646): Sein Leben und sein Werk* (Diss., Univ. of Marburg, 1956).

Vierling, Georg, German organist and composer; b. Frankenthal, Bavaria, Sept. 5, 1820; d. Wiesbaden, May 1, 1901. He was a pupil of his father, the organist Jacob Vierling (1796–1867); then studied composition with A.B. Marx in Berlin. He occupied various posts as an organist and choral conductor in the German provinces; settled in Berlin, where he founded and conducted the Bach-Verein. A catalogue of his works was issued in 1897; they include the secular cantatas *Der Raub der Sabinerinne, Alarichs Tod,* and *Constantin;* the choral works (with Orch.) *Hero und Leander* and *Zur Weinlese;* a Symph.; several overtures (*Maria Stuart, Die Hexe, Im Frühling,* etc.); *Capriccio* for Piano and Orch.; *Phantasiestück* for Cello and Piano; 2 string quartets; Piano Trio; a number of piano pieces (*Valse-Caprice,* 2 impromptus, etc.); songs.

Vierling, Johann Gottfried, German organist and composer; b. Metzels, near Meiningen, Jan. 25, 1750;

d. Schmalkalden, Nov. 22, 1813. His teachers were C.P.E. Bach in Hamburg and Kirnberger in Berlin, from whom he acquired contrapuntal skill in composition in the Baroque style. He publ. several collections of organ pieces; a Piano Quartet; 2 piano trios; 8 piano sonatas; brought out the theoretical manuals *Versuch einer Anleitung zum Präludieren* (1794) and *Allgemein fasslicher Unterricht im Generalbass* (1805).

BIBLIOGRAPHY: K. Paulke, "J.G. Vierling," *Archiv für Musikwissenschaft* (1922).

Vierne, Louis, blind French organist and composer; b. Poitiers, Oct. 8, 1870; d. Paris, June 2, 1937. He was a pupil of César Franck and Widor at the Paris Cons., winning first prize for organ playing; in 1892 he became Widor's assistant at St. Sulpice, and in 1900 was appointed organist at Notre Dame, holding this position until his death (he died suddenly while playing the organ at a service there). From 1912 he taught organ at the Schola Cantorum; gave many concerts in Europe; in 1927 played in the U.S. His organ works include 6 organ symphs., one orchestral symph., and many smaller pieces. Among his pupils were Nadia Boulanger, Marcel Dupré, and Joseph Bonnet.

BIBLIOGRAPHY: *In Memoriam Louis Vierne* (Paris, 1939); B. Gavoty, *Louis Vierne, La Vie et l'œuvre* (Paris, 1943).

Vieru, Anatol, outstanding Rumanian composer; b. Iasi (Jassy), June 8, 1926. He studied harmony with Paul Constantinescu, orchestration with Theodore Rogalski, and conducting with Constantin Silvestri at the Bucharest Cons.; in 1951 he went to Russia, where he studied composition at the Moscow Cons. with Khachaturian (1951–54). In 1954 he was appointed to the faculty of the Bucharest Cons. In 1968 he visited the U.S. as a member of the Composers' Forum at the Juilliard School of Music in N.Y. In 1982 and 1983 he gave summer courses at the Rubin Academy for Music and Dance in Jerusalem. In 1980 he publ. in Bucharest *The Book of Modes.* From his earliest years he composed music in a relatively advanced idiom, without losing contact with the characteristic melorhythmic patterns of Rumanian folk songs. Interesting in this respect is his oratorio *Miorița* (1957), after a Rumanian folk tale, in which he applies serial procedures to folklike materials. His Concerto for Cello and Orch. (1962), written in an original manner combining neo-Baroque and impressionistic traits, brought him international attention when it received first prize in a 1962 Geneva competition.

WORKS: FOR THE STAGE: *Jonah (Iona),* opera after the tragedy by Marin Sorescu (1971–75; Bucharest, Oct. 31, 1976); *The Punishment,* opera after the "tragic farce" of M. Sorbul (1979–80); *Telegram, Theme and Variations,* and *Pedagogue of the New School,* operatic triptych (1982–83). FOR ORCH.: *Suite in Ancient Style* for String Orch. (1945); 4 symphs.: No. 1, *Ode to Silence* (1966); No. 2 (1973; West Berlin, March 21, 1974); No. 3, *Et la terre trembla* (1977); No. 4 (1982); Concerto for Orch. (1954–55); *Clepsydra*

I (Water Clock) for Trumpet obbligato and Orch. (1968); *Ecran* (1969; Royan Festival, April 9, 1971); *Scoica* for 15 String Instruments (1982); Flute Concerto (1958); Cello Concerto (1962); Violin Concerto (1963); Clarinet Concerto (1975); Double Concerto for Violin, Cello, and Orch. (1963); *Jocuri (Games)* for Piano and Orch. (1963); *Museum Music* for Electronically Amplified Harpsichord and 12 String Instruments (1968). CHAMBER MUSIC: 5 string quartets: No. 1 (1955; also arranged as Concerto for Orch.); No. 2 (1956); No. 3, with Soprano obbligato (1973); No. 4 (1980); No. 5 (1982); *2 Pieces* for Trumpet and Piano (1953); Quintet for Clarinet and String Quartet (1958); Sonata for Cello Solo (1962); *Trepte ale taceri (Steps of Silence)* for String Quartet and 6 Percussion Instruments (1966; Library of Congress, Washington, D.C., Jan. 12, 1968; also as a ballet, N.Y., Nov. 13, 1968); *Sita lui Eratostene (Eratosthenes' Sieve)* for Violin, Viola, Cello, Clarinet, and Piano (1969); *Inscripto* for Flute, 2 Trombones, and 2 Amplified Guitars (1978); *Joseph et ses frères* for 11 Instruments and Tape (1979); *Double Duos* for Saxophone or Bass Clarinet, and Vibraphone or Marimbaphone (1983). FOR VOICES: *Miorița,* oratorio (1956–57; Bucharest, Feb. 27, 1958); *Cantata anilor lumină (Cantata of Luminous Years;* Bucharest, June 18, 1960); *Musica pentru Bacovia și Labis* (1956–63), to words by Bacovia and Labis, for various combinations of Voices and Instruments, consisting of 3 separate works: *Lupta cu inerția (Struggle against Inertia)* for Tenor, Mezzo-soprano, Piano, Clarinet, and Violin; *Nocturne și Rezonanțe Bacovia (Nocturne and Resonance of Bacovia)* for Flute, Soprano, and Piano; and *Catrene* for Mezzo-soprano and Piano; *Clepsydra II* for Orch., Chorus, Panpipes, and Cimbalom (1971); *Scène nocturne,* suite of 7 pieces, to poems by García Lorca, for Double Chorus a cappella (1972); *Quatre angles pour regarder Florence* for Soprano, Piano, and Percussion (1973). FOR PIANO: *Children's World,* 20 miniatures (1958); *Nautilos* for Piano and Tape (1968); Sonata (1976).

Vietinghoff-Scheel, Boris, Baron, Russian composer; b. in Latvia, 1829; d. St. Petersburg, Sept. 25, 1901. He was a student of Henselt and Dargomyzhsky in St. Petersburg. Three of his operas were produced in St. Petersburg: *Mazeppa* (May 17, 1859), *Tamara* (May 2, 1886), and *Don Juan de Tenorio* (Nov. 2, 1888); 2 other operas, *Mary Stuart* and *Heliodora,* were not produced. He also wrote a *Fantastic Overture* (1859; Liszt commented with interest on the use of the whole-tone scale in the finale; see *Letters of Franz Liszt,* London, 1894; vol. 1). Vietinghoff publ. a book of memoirs, *World Celebrities* (St. Petersburg, 1899).

Vieuille, Felix, French bass; b. Saugeon, Oct. 15, 1872; d. there, Feb. 28, 1953. He was a member of the Opéra-Comique from 1898; created the role of Arkel at the premiere of Debussy's *Pelléas et Mélisande* (1902).

Vieuxtemps, Henri, celebrated Belgian violinist

and composer; b. Verviers, Feb. 17, 1820; d. Mustapha, Algiers, June 6, 1881. His first teacher was his father, a piano tuner, who soon turned him over to Lecloux, with whom he made a concert tour at the age of 8. He then continued his studies with Bériot in Brussels (1829–30); took harmony lessons from Sechter in Vienna (1833) and Reicha in Paris (1835). In 1834 he visited London, where he appeared with the Phil. (June 2, 1834). In 1837 he revisited Vienna; in 1838–39 he gave concerts in Russia. During his constant travels, he composed violin concertos and other violin works which became part of the standard repertoire, and which he performed in Europe to the greatest acclaim. He made his first American tour in 1843–44. In 1846 he was engaged as a prof. at the St. Petersburg Cons., and remained in Russia for 5 seasons; his influence on Russian concert life and violin composition was considerable. In 1853 he recommenced his concert tours in Europe; paid 2 more visits to America, in 1857 (with Thalberg) and in 1870 (with Christine Nilsson). He was a prof. of violin playing at the Brussels Cons. (1871–73); a stroke of paralysis, affecting his left side, forced him to end all his concert activities, but he continued to teach privately. He went to Algiers for rest, and died there; one of his most prominent pupils, Jenö Hubay, was with him at his death. In 1844, Vieuxtemps married the pianist **Josephine Eder** (b. Vienna, Dec. 15, 1815; d. Celle-St. Cloud, June 29, 1868). With Bériot, Vieuxtemps stood at the head of the modern French school of violin playing; contemporary accounts speak of the extraordinary precision of his technique and of his perfect ability to sustain a flowing melody; the expression "le roi du violon" was often applied to him in the press. Besides his 7 violin concertos (the last one being posthumous), he wrote for violin and orch.: *Fantasie-Caprice; Souvenirs de Russie; Fantasia appassionata; Ballade et polonaise;* and *Old England,* a caprice on English airs of the 16th and 17th centuries. For violin and piano he composed *Hommage à Paganini; Grosse Fantasie über slavische Volksmelodien; Andante and Rondo; Suite* in B minor; *Marche funèbre; Danse Négro-Créole* (1844); etc.; numerous brilliant transcriptions of operatic airs.
BIBLIOGRAPHY: L. Escudier, *Mes Souvenirs: Les Virtuoses* (Paris, 1868); M. Kufferath, *Henri Vieuxtemps* (Brussels, 1882); J.T. Radoux, *Vieuxtemps, Sa vie, ses œuvres* (Liège, 1891); P. Bergmans, *Henri Vieuxtemps* (Turnhout, 1920).

Viganò, Salvatore, Italian composer and choreographer; b. Naples, March 25, 1769; d. Milan, Aug. 10, 1821. He was the son and pupil of a dancer; studied music with **Luigi Boccherini,** who was his uncle; began his career as a dancer at Rome in 1783, and also produced there an opera buffa, *La Vedova scoperta;* then went to Madrid, where he married the celebrated ballerina María Medina; in 1791 he returned to Italy; in 1793 was at Vienna; then made a tour of the principal European cities. He is remembered chiefly because Beethoven wrote the music for Viganò's "heroic ballet" *Die Geschöpfe des Prometheus* (Vienna, March 28, 1801), in which Viganò

danced the leading male role.
BIBLIOGRAPHY: C. Ritorni, *Commentarii della vita e delle opere coreodrammatiche di Salvatore Viganò* (Milan, 1838); H. Prunières, "Salvatore Viganò," *Revue Musicale* (1921); Thayer's *Life of Beethoven.*

Viglone-Borghese, Domenico, Italian baritone; b. Mondovì, July 13, 1877; d. Milan, Oct. 26, 1957. He studied in Pesaro and Milan; made his debut as the Herald in *Lohengrin* in Lodi in 1899, and continued to sing in provincial Italian opera companies; then gave up singing and went to the U.S., where he earned his living as a railroad worker in San Francisco. There he met Caruso, who recommended him to an impresario who engaged him in a traveling opera troupe in Mexico and Venezuela. He returned to Italy in 1907 and sang in a number of opera houses there; among his roles one of the most brilliant was that of the sheriff Jack Rance in Puccini's "American" opera *La Fanciulla del West,* of which he gave the first Italian production.

Vignas, Francisco, noted Spanish tenor; b. Moya, near Barcelona, March 27, 1863; d. Barcelona, July 14, 1933. He studied at the Barcelona Cons., and later in Paris. He made his debut in Barcelona in 1888 as Lohengrin; then sang in Italian opera houses; made his first appearance in London in 1893 at the Shaftesbury Theatre. On Nov. 29, 1893, he made his Metropolitan Opera debut as Turiddu; after only one season there, he returned to Europe.

Vila, Pedro Alberto, Spanish composer; b. 1517; d. Barcelona, Nov. 16, 1582. He was organist and canon of the Cathedral at Barcelona; was one of the few Spanish composers who cultivated the madrigal; publ. *Odarum quas vulgo Madrigales appellamus* (Barcelona, 1561) with texts in Spanish, Catalan, Italian, and French; some of his organ works are found in the tablature book of Venegas de Henestrosa. His nephew **Luis Ferrán Vila** succeeded him as organist at the Barcelona Cathedral.
BIBLIOGRAPHY: F. Pedrell, *Catàlech de la Biblioteca Musical de la Diputació de Barcelona* (1908–9); S. Kastner, *Contribución al estudio de la música española y portuguesa* (Lisbon, 1941).

Vilback, Renaud de, French organist and composer; b. Montpellier, June 3, 1829; d. Paris, March 19, 1884. He studied piano, organ, and composition at the Paris Cons. under Lemoine and Halévy, winning the Grand Prix de Rome at the age of 15. In 1856 he became organist at St.-Eugène, Paris; remained there until 1871. He wrote 2 operas: *Au clair de lune* (1857) and *Almanzor* (1858); publ. a method for piano; *3 morceaux de salon, Les Amazones,* etc.; also transcriptions from operas.

Vilboa (Villebois), Konstantin, Russian composer of French origin; b. St. Petersburg, May 29, 1817; d. Warsaw, July 16, 1882. He studied in a military school, and was sent by the government to collect folk songs in the country; also directed various choirs in military establishments. In 1876 he went to Warsaw as a functionary in the ministry of war, and remained there until his death. His opera *Natasha, or The Volga Brigands* was produced in Moscow on Nov. 12, 1861, and in St. Petersburg in 1863. Two other operas, *Taras Bulba* (after Gogol) and *Tziganka (The Gypsy),* remain unperformed.

Vilhar, Franz, Croatian composer; b. Senožeče, Jan. 5, 1852; d. Zagreb, March 4, 1928. He studied music with Skuherský in Prague; after serving as an organist in various churches, he settled in Zagreb, in 1891, as choirmaster at St. Mark's. He composed a Croatian opera, *Smiljana* (Zagreb, Jan. 31, 1897); *Croatian Dances* for Orch.; and a number of choruses that were popular for a time.

Villa, Ricardo, Spanish composer and conductor; b. Madrid, Oct. 23, 1873; d. there, April 10, 1935. He studied at the Cons. of Madrid, and conducted the municipal band there, which he organized in 1909; wrote the operas *El Cristo de la Vega* and *Raimundo Lulio,* and a number of pieces for band in the Spanish vein: *La visión de Fray Martín, Impresiones sinfónicas,* and also *Cantos regionales asturianos; Rapsodía asturiana* for Violin and Orch. (played by Sarasate); *Fantasía española* for Piano and Orch.; also light music.

Villa-Lobos, Heitor, remarkable Brazilian composer of great originality and unique ability to recreate native melodic and rhythmic elements in large instrumental and choral forms; b. Rio de Janeiro, March 5, 1887; d. there, Nov. 17, 1959. He studied music with his father, a writer and amateur cello player; after his father's death in 1899, Villa-Lobos earned a living by playing the cello in cafés and restaurants. In 1905 he traveled to the northern states of Brazil in order to collect authentic folk songs. In 1907 he entered the National Inst. of Music in Rio de Janeiro, where he studied with Frederico Nascimento, Angelo França, and Francisco Braga. In 1912 he undertook an expedition into the interior of Brazil, where he gathered a rich collection of Indian songs. On Nov. 13, 1915, he presented in Rio de Janeiro a concert of his compositions, creating a sensation by the exuberance of his music and the radical character of his technical idiom. He met the pianist Artur Rubinstein, who became his ardent admirer; for him Villa-Lobos composed a transcendentally difficult *Rudepoema.* In 1923 Villa-Lobos went to Paris on a Brazilian government grant; upon returning to Brazil in 1930, he was appointed director of music education in Rio de Janeiro. He introduced bold innovations into the national program of music education, with an emphasis on the cultural resources of Brazil; compiled a *Guia pratico,* containing choral arrangements of folk songs of Brazil and other nations; organized the "orpheonic concentrations" of schoolchildren, whom he trained to sing according to his own cheironomic method of solfeggio. In 1944 he made his first tour of the U.S., and conducted his works in Los Angeles,

Boston, and N.Y. In 1945 he established in Rio de Janeiro the Brazilian Academy of Music; in 1947 he made his 2nd visit to the U.S.; in 1949 he was in Europe, but retained his permanent home in Rio de Janeiro.

Villa-Lobos was one of the most original composers of the 20th century. He lacked formal academic training, but far from hampering his development, this deficiency liberated him from pedantic restrictions, so that he evolved an idiosyncratic technique of composition, curiously eclectic, but all the better suited to his musical esthetics. An ardent Brazilian nationalist, he resolved from his earliest attempts in composition to use authentic Brazilian song materials as the source of his inspiration; yet he avoided using actual quotations from popular songs; rather, he wrote melodies which are authentic in their melodic and rhythmic content. In his desire to relate Brazilian folk resources to universal values, he composed a series of extraordinary works, *Bachianas brasileiras,* in which Brazilian melorhythms are treated in Bachian counterpoint. He also composed a number of works under the generic title *Chôros,* a popular Brazilian dance form, marked by incisive rhythm and a ballad-like melody. An experimenter by nature, Villa-Lobos devised a graphic method of composition, using geometrical contours of drawings and photographs as outlines for the melody; in this manner he wrote *The New York Skyline,* using a photograph for guidance. Villa-Lobos wrote operas, ballets, symphs., chamber music, choruses, piano pieces, songs; the total number of his compositions is in excess of 2,000.

WORKS: OPERAS (several left uncompleted): Most notably, *Izaht* (1914; revised 1932; premiere, in concert form, Rio de Janeiro, April 6, 1940); *Magdalena,* light opera (Los Angeles, July 26, 1948); *Yerma,* after Federico García Lorca (1955; posthumous, in Spanish, at Santa Fe, Aug. 12, 1971); a children's opera, *Daughter of the Clouds* (1957–58).

BALLETS (many converted from symph. poems): *Uirapuru* (1917; Buenos Aires, May 25, 1935; revised 1948); *Dança da terra* (1939; Rio de Janeiro, Sept. 7, 1943); *Rudá* (1951); *Genesis* (1954; as a symph. poem, posthumous, Rio de Janeiro, 1969); *Emperor Jones* (1955; N.Y., July 12, 1956).

9 BACHIANAS BRASILEIRAS: No. 1 for 8 Cellos (Rio de Janeiro, Sept. 12, 1932); No. 2 for Chamber Orch. (1933); No. 3 for Piano and Orch. (1934); No. 4 for Piano (1930–40; orchestration, N.Y., June 6, 1942); No. 5 for Voice and 8 Cellos (1938; Rio de Janeiro, March 25, 1939); No. 6 for Flute and Bassoon (1938); No. 7 for Orch. (1942; Rio de Janeiro, March 13, 1944); No. 8 for Orch. (1944; Rome, Aug. 6, 1947); No. 9 for Chorus a cappella or String Orch. (1944).

15 CHOROS: No. 1 for Guitar (1920); No. 2 for Flute and Clarinet (1921); No. 3 for Male Chorus and 7 Wind Instruments (1925); No. 4 for 3 Horns and Trombone (1926); No. 5, *Alma Brasileira,* for Piano (1926); No. 6 for Orch. (1926; Rio de Janeiro, July 15, 1942); No. 7 for Flute, Oboe, Clarinet, Saxophone, Bassoon, Violin, and Cello (1924); No. 8 for Large Orch. and 2 Pianos (1925; Paris, Oct. 24, 1927); No. 9 for Orch. (1929; Rio de Janeiro, July 15, 1942, com-

poser conducting); No. 10, *Rasga o Coração,* for Chorus and Orch. (1925; Rio de Janeiro, Dec. 15, 1926); No. 11 for Piano and Orch. (1928; Rio de Janeiro, July 15, 1942); No. 12 for Orch. (1929; Cambridge, Mass., Feb. 21, 1945, composer conducting the Boston Symph. Orch.); No. 13 for 2 Orch. and Band (1929); No. 14 for Orch., Band, and Chorus (1928); also a supernumerary *Chôros bis* for Violin and Cello (1928).

OTHER ORCH. WORKS: 12 symphs.: No. 1, *Imprevisto* (1916; Rio de Janeiro, Aug. 30, 1920); No. 2, *Ascenção* (1917); No. 3, *Guerra* (Rio de Janeiro, July 30, 1919); No. 4, *Vitória* (1920); No. 5, *Paz* (1921); No. 6, *Montanhas do Brasil* (1944); No. 7, *Odisséia da Paz* (1945; London, March 27, 1949); No. 8 (1950; Philadelphia, Jan. 14, 1955); No. 9 (1951; posthumous, Philadelphia Orch. at the Caracas Festival, May 16, 1966); No. 10, *Sume Pater Patrium,* for Soloists, Chorus, and Orch. (1952; Paris, April 4, 1957); No. 11 (1955; Boston, March 2, 1956, composer conducting); No. 12 (1957; First Inter-American Music Festival, Washington, D.C., April 20, 1958). Also, *Dansas africanas* (1914; Paris, April 5, 1928); 2 cello concertos: No. 1, *Grand Concerto* (1915), and No. 2 (1953; N.Y., Feb. 5, 1955); 2 sinfoniettas (1916, 1947); *Amazonas* (1917; Paris, May 30, 1929); *Fantasy of Mixed Movements* for Violin and Orch. (Rio de Janeiro, Dec. 15, 1922); *Momoprecoce* for Piano and Orch. (Amsterdam, 1929); *Caixinha de Boãs Festas* (Rio de Janeiro, Dec. 8, 1932); *Ciranda das sete notes* for Bassoon and String Orch. (1933); 3 of 4 suites titled *Descobrimento do Brasil* (1937; No. 4 is an oratorio); *The New York Skyline* (1939); *Rudepoema* (orch. version of the piano work of that name; Rio de Janeiro, July 15, 1942, composer conducting); *Madona,* tone poem (1945; Rio de Janeiro, Oct. 8, 1946, composer conducting); 5 piano concertos (1945, 1948, 1952–57, 1952, 1954); *Fantasia* for Cello and Orch. (1945); *Fantasia* for Soprano Saxophone, String Orch., and 2 Horns (1948); *Erosion, or The Origin of the Amazon River* (Louisville, Ky., Nov. 7, 1951); Guitar Concerto (1951); Harp Concerto (1953; Philadelphia, Jan. 14, 1955); *Odyssey of a Race,* symph. poem written for Israel (1953; Mount Carmel Festival of the International Society for Contemporary Music, Haifa, May 30, 1954); *Dawn in a Tropical Forest* (1953; Louisville, Jan. 23, 1954); Harmonica Concerto (1955; Jerusalem, Oct. 27, 1959); *Izi,* symph. poem (1957).

OTHER CHAMBER MUSIC: 17 string quartets (1915, 1916, 1917, 1931, 1938, 1942, 1944, 1945, 1946, 1948, 1950, 1952, 1953, 1954, 1955, 1958); 3 piano trios (1911, 1916, 1918); *Quinteto duplo de cordas* (1912); 4 *Sonatas-Fantasia* for Violin and Piano (1912, 1914, 1915, 1918); 2 cello sonatas (1915, 1916); Piano Quintet (1916); *Mystic Sextet* for Flute, Clarinet, Saxophone, Celesta, Harp, and Guitar (1917); Trio for Oboe, Clarinet, and Bassoon (1921); Woodwind Quartet (1928); *Quintet in the Form of a Chôros* for Flute, Oboe, Clarinet, Bassoon, and English Horn (1928; revised 1953, replacing English Horn with French Horn); String Trio (1946); *Duo* for Violin and Viola (1946); *Fantasia concertante* for Piano, Clarinet, and Bassoon (1953); *Duo* for Oboe and Bassoon (1957); Quintet for Flute, Harp, Violin, Viola, and

Cello (1957); *Fantasia concertante* for Cello Ensemble (N.Y., Dec. 10, 1958).

OTHER VOCAL MUSIC: For Chorus: *Crianças* (1908); *Vidapura,* oratorio for Chorus, Orch., and Organ (1918; Rio de Janeiro, Nov. 11, 1922); *Hinos aos artistas* for Chorus and Orch. (1919); Quartet for Harp, Celesta, Flute, Saxophone, and Women's Voices (1921); Nonetto for Flute, Oboe, Clarinet, Saxophone, Bassoon, Harp, Celesta, Percussion, and Chorus (1923); *Cantiga da Roda* for Women's Chorus and Orch. (1925); *Na Bah a tem* (1925); *Canção da Terra* (1925); *Missa São Sebastião* (1937); Suite No. 4 of *Descobrimento do Brasil* for Orch. and Chorus (1937); *Mandu-Cararã,* cantata profana for Chorus and Orch. (1940; N.Y., Jan. 23, 1948; also a ballet); *Bendita sabedoria (Blessed Wisdom;* 1958); *Magnificat-Alleluia* for Boy Contralto, Chorus, Organ, and Orch. (1958; Rio de Janeiro, Nov. 8, 1958; by request of Pope Pius XII); etc. Songs: *Confidencia* (1908); *Noite de Luar* (1912); *Mal secreto* (1913); *Fleur fanée* (1913); *Il nome di Maria* (1915); *Sertão no Estio* (1919); *Canções típicas brasileiras* (10 numbers; 1919); *Historiettes* (6 numbers; 1920); *Epigrammes ironiques et sentimentales* (8 numbers; 1921); *Suite* for Voice and Violin (1923); *Poème de l'Enfant et de sa Mère* for Voice, Flute, Clarinet, and Cello (1923); *Serestas* (suite of 14 numbers; one of his best song cycles; 1925); *3 poemas indígenas* (1926); *Suite sugestiva* for Voice and Orch. (1929); *Modinhas e canções* (2 albums; 1933, 1943); *Poem of Itabira* for Alto and Orch. (1941; Rio de Janeiro, Dec. 30, 1946); *Canção das aguas claras* for Voice and Orch. (1956).

OTHER WORKS FOR PIANO: *Valsa romantica* (1908); *Brinquedo de Roda* (6 pieces; 1912); *Primeira suite infantil* (5 pieces; 1912); *Segunda suite infantil* (4 pieces; 1913); *Danças africanas* (1915); *Prole do Bebé,* Suite No. 1 (8 pieces, including the popular *Polichinello;* 1918); *Fábulas características* (3 pieces; 1914–18); *Historia da Carochinha* (4 pieces; 1919); *Carnaval das crianças brasileiras* (8 pieces; 1919); *Lenda do Caboclo* (1920); *Dança infernal* (1920); *Prole do Bebé,* Suite No. 2 (9 pieces; 1921); *Sul América* (1925); *Cirandinhas* (12 pieces; 1925); *Rudepoema* (1921–26); *Cirandas* (16 pieces; 1926); *Alma brasileira (Chôros* No. 5; 1926); *Prole do Bebé,* Suite No. 3 (9 pieces; 1929); *Lembrança do Sertão* (1930); *Caixinha de música quebrada* (1931); *Ciclo brasileiro* (4 pieces; 1936); *As Três Marías* (3 pieces; 1939; very popular); *Poema Singelo* (1942); *Homenagem a Chopin* (1949).

BIBLIOGRAPHY: F.C. Lange, "Villa-Lobos, Pedagogo Criador," *Boletín Latino-Americano de Música* (Montevideo, 1935; pp. 189ff.); Burle Marx, "Brazilian Portrait," *Modern Music* (Oct.–Nov. 1939); special issue of *Musica Viva* (Rio de Janeiro, 1941); N. Slonimsky, *Music of Latin America* (N.Y., 1945; pp. 142–50); O.L. Fernandez, "A Contribuição Harmonica de Villa-Lobos para a Música Brasiliera," *Boletín Latino-Americano de Música* (Rio de Janeiro, 1946, pp. 183–300); O. Meyer-Serra, *Música y Músicos de Latino-América* (Mexico, 1947; vol. 2, pp. 1,059–85); L.M. Peppercorn, "The History of Villa-Lobos' Birth-Date," *Monthly Musical Record* (July–Aug. 1948); Vasco Mariz, *Heitor Villa-Lobos,*

Compositor brasileiro (Rio de Janeiro, 1948; 5th ed., revised and augmented, 1977); C.M. de Paula Barros, *O Romance de Villa-Lobos* (Rio de Janeiro, 1951); C. Maul, *A gloria escandaloso de Heiter Villa-Lobos* (Rio de Janeiro, 1960; a scurrilous "exposé," unconvincingly accusing Villa-Lobos of plagiarism); M. Beaufils, *Villa-Lobos, Musicien et poete du Brésil* (Rio de Janeiro, 1967); L. Guimares, *Villa-Lobos* (Rio de Janeiro, 1972); F. Pereira da Silva, *Villa-Lobos* (Rio de Janeiro, 1974).

Villalba Muñoz, Padre Luis, Spanish musicologist and composer; b. Valladolid, Sept. 22, 1872; d. Madrid, Jan. 8, 1921. He entered the Augustinian order at the age of 14; was chorus master at the monastery of the Escorial (1898–1916); also taught history and other subjects; later lived in Madrid; edited the review *La Ciudad de Dios,* to which he contributed valuable essays on Spanish music; also edited the *Biblioteca Sacro-Musical.* He publ. the valuable *Antología de organistas clásicos españoles,* 10 *Canciones españolas de los siglos XV y XVI;* wrote monographs on Pedrell, Granados, and Usandizaga, and *Últimos músicos españoles del siglo XIX* (Madrid, 1914); composed organ works; sacred choruses; chamber music.

Villanis, Luigi Alberto, Italian writer on music; b. San Mauro, near Turin, June 20, 1863; d. Pesaro, Sept. 27, 1906. He studied law; later devoted himself to musical journalism; publ. numerous pamphlets dealing with musical esthetics. He publ. *Il Leitmotiv nella musica moderna* (1891); *Estetica del libretto nella musica* (1892); *Lo spirito moderno nella musica* (1902); *Saggio di psicologia musicale* (1904); *Piccola guida alla bibliografia musicale* (1906); *L'arte del pianoforte in Italia* (1907).

Villar, Rogelio, Spanish composer and music critic; b. León, Nov. 13, 1875; d. Madrid, Nov. 4, 1937. He studied at the Madrid Cons., and later taught ensemble there; was editor of the *Revista Musical Hispano-Americana* (ceased publication in 1917). He composed some symph. pieces, 2 string quartets, violin sonatas, and piano works; publ. *Músicos españoles,* 2 series (biographical sketches of contemporary Spanish musicians); *La armonía en la música contemporánea* (Madrid, 1927); *Soliloquios de un músico español* (Madrid, 1928); etc.

Villoing, Alexander, notable Russian pianist; b. Moscow, March 12, 1804; d. there, Sept. 2, 1878. He was born of a French émigré family; studied piano with the famous Irish pianist and composer John Field, who was then resident in Moscow. Villoing established himself in Moscow as a piano teacher (1830–62); enjoyed a reputation as one of the best pedagogues in Russia. Anton and Nicolai Rubinstein were among his pupils; he traveled with them in Europe. His *Ecole pratique du piano* (St. Petersburg, 1863) was accepted by the St. Petersburg Cons. as a teaching guide. He publ. a book of piano exercises, which he called *Exercises for the Rubinstein Brothers.*

Villoing, Vasili, Russian violinist, pianist, composer, conductor, and music teacher; b. Moscow, Oct. 28, 1850; d. Nizhny-Novgorod, Sept. 15, 1922. He studied piano with his uncle, the Russian pianist **Alexander Villoing,** and violin with Ferdinand Laub at the Moscow Cons. He then moved to Nizhny-Novgorod, where he organized a music school and conducted a local orch. founded by him. Among his piano students were Dobrowen and Liapunov. He composed 3 operas, 4 string quartets, and a number of piano pieces and songs.

Villoteau, Guillaume-André, French music scholar; b. Bellême, Orne, Sept. 6, 1759; d. Tours, April 27, 1839. He was a chorister at the Cathedral of Le Mans, and later at Notre-Dame in Paris. Having studied philosophy at the Sorbonne, he was qualified for election as a member of the scientific commission that accompanied Napoleon to Egypt, and he made a special study of oriental music. He contributed 4 essays to the 20-vol. edition *La Description de l'Egypte* (Paris, 1809–26): "Mémoire sur la musique de l'antique Egypte," "Dissertation sur les diverses espèces d'instruments de musique que l'on remarque parmi les sculptures qui décorent les antiques monuments de l'Egypte," "De l'état actuel de l'art musical en Egypte," and "Description historique, technique et littéraire des instruments de musique des Orientaux"; he also publ. *Mémoire sur la possibilité et l'utilité d'une théorie exacte des principes naturels de la musique* (1807), an introduction to his *Recherches sur l'analogie de la musique avec les arts qui ont pour object l'imitation du langage* (2 vols., 1807).

Viña (Manteola), Facundo de la, Spanish composer; b. Gijon, Feb. 21, 1876; d. Madrid, Nov. 19, 1952. He studied at the Madrid Cons. and later in Paris; his music reflects the character of Asturian regional folklore. He composed the operas *Almas muertas; La Princesa flor de roble; La Espigadora* (Barcelona, 1927); the symph. poems *Canto de trilla; Sierra de Gredos; Covadonga; Por tierras de Castilla.*

Vinay, Ramón, Chilean tenor; b. Chillan, Aug. 31, 1912. He studied voice in Mexico City; made his debut there as a baritone; then began singing tenor roles and became especially noted for his Otello. In 1946 he joined the Metropolitan Opera; continued to sing there until 1961; also sang at Bayreuth. During the last years of his career, he returned to baritone roles. From 1969 to 1971 he served as artistic director of the Santiago Opera.

Vincent, Alexandre-Joseph Hydulphe, French music theorist; b. Hesdin, Pas-de-Calais, Nov. 20, 1797; d. Paris, Nov. 26, 1868. An investigator of ancient Greek and Latin music, he advanced the idea that the Greeks used chorus (harmony); he similarly sought to revive the employment of the intervals smaller than a half-tone that were described in Greek theory. On these subjects he publ. a great number of essays, some of which were reprinted in pamphlet form. Especially important is his *Notice sur divers manuscrits grecs relatifs à la musique* (1847).

Vincent, Charles John, English organist; b. Houghton-le-Spring, Durham, Sept. 19, 1852; d. Monte Carlo, Feb. 28, 1934. He was a chorister at the Cathedral of Durham; studied at the Leipzig Cons. (1876–78); then was a church organist in England; received from Oxford Univ. the degrees of Mus.Bac. (1878) and Mus.Doc. (1885). He publ. a number of useful textbooks: *A Year's Study at the Piano, First Principles of Music, Choral Instructor for Treble Voices,* etc.; composed an oratorio, *Ruth;* several church cantatas; operettas; vocal duets; more than 100 songs.

Vincent, Heinrich Joseph (real name, **Winzenhörlein**), German singer, composer, and theorist; b. Teilheim, near Würzburg, Feb. 23, 1819; d. Vienna, May 19, 1901. He studied law, and also sang tenor parts in theaters in Vienna (1847), Halle, and Würzburg; eventually settled in Vienna as a singing teacher. He composed 2 operas, *Die Bettlerin* (Halle, 1864) and *König Murat* (Würzburg, 1870); also operettas and popular songs. He followed the tenets of the Chroma Society in championing the harmonic system based on the functional equality of the 12 notes of the chromatic scale; publ. the studies *Kein Generalbass mehr* (1860), *Die Einheit in der Tonwelt* (1862), *Die Neuklaviatur* (1874), *Die Zwölfzahl in der Tonwelt* (1885), and *Eine neue Tonschrift* (1900), and articles on the chromatic keyboard and notation.

Vincent, Henry Bethuel, American organist and composer; b. Denver, Dec. 28, 1872; d. Erie, Pa., Jan. 7, 1941. He studied organ with W.H. Sherwood in Oberlin and with Widor in Paris; settled in Erie as an organist and choirmaster. He wrote an oratorio, *The Prodigal Son* (Erie, 1901); an opera, *Esperanza* (Washington, D.C., 1906); an operetta, *Indian Days;* anthems; organ pieces; songs, including a cycle, *The Garden of Kama.*

Vincent, John, American composer and teacher; b. Birmingham, Ala., May 17, 1902; d. Santa Monica, Calif., Jan. 21, 1977. He studied flute with Georges Laurent at the New England Cons. in Boston (1922–26), and composition there with Converse and Chadwick (1926–27); then took courses at the George Peabody College in Nashville (M.A., 1933) and at Harvard Univ., where his principal teacher was Walter Piston (1933–35); then went to Paris, where he studied at the Ecole Normale de Musique (1935–37) and took private lessons with Nadia Boulanger. He received his Ph.D. from Cornell Univ. in 1942. He subsequently occupied various teaching positions: was in charge of music in the El Paso (Texas) public schools (1927–30); then taught at George Peabody College in Nashville (1930–33), at Western Kentucky Teachers College (1937–46), and at the Univ. of Calif., Los Angeles (1946–69). After his death, the John Vincent Archive was estab-

lished at UCLA. In his music he evolved a tonal idiom which he termed "paratonality"; fugal elements are particularly strong in his instrumental compositions.
WORKS: Opera, *Primeval Void,* to his own libretto (1969); ballet, *3 Jacks* (1942); Symph. in D (Louisville, Ky., Feb. 5, 1952; revised version, Philadelphia, April 12, 1957); *Consort* for Piano and Strings (Seattle, April 9, 1962; later amplified for full string orch., and renamed Symph. No. 2); *Symphonic Poem after Descartes* (Philadelphia, March 20, 1959; his most significant work, with the motto of Descartes, "Cogito ergo sum," suggested by the thematic rhythm on the kettledrums); *La Jolla Concerto* for Chamber Orch. (La Jolla, Calif., July 19, 1959); *Benjamin Franklin Suite* for Orch. and Glass Harmonica (based on the string quartet attributed to Benjamin Franklin; Philadelphia, March 24, 1963); *Rondo-Rhapsody* (Washington, D.C., May 9, 1965); *The Phoenix, Fabulous Bird,* symph. poem (Phoenix, Ariz., Feb. 21, 1966); 2 string quartets (1936, 1967); *Nude Descending a Staircase* for String Orch., after Marcel Duchamp's painting (1948); *Stabat Mater* for Male Chorus and Soprano Solo (1969); *Mary at Calvary* for Chorus and Organ (1972); *Percussion Suite* (1973); *Nacre,* tone poem for Band (1973); choruses (*O God, Our Help in Ages Past; Cindy Gal; Glory to God; Behold the Star;* etc.); *Baroque Album,* 16 Baroque works transcribed for String Orch., with Piano (1972). He publ. the books *Music for Sight Reading* (N.Y., 1940); *More Music for Sight Reading* (N.Y., 1941); *The Diatonic Modes in Modern Music* (N.Y., 1951; completely revised, Hollywood, 1974).

Vinci, Leonardo, Italian composer; b. Strongoli, 1690; d. Naples, May 27, 1730. He studied at the Cons. dei Poveri di Gesù Cristo in Naples, where he was a pupil of Gaetano Greco. In 1725 he received the post of vice-maestro at the Royal Chapel in Naples, and remained there until his death 5 years later. He produced about 40 operas for various Italian cities (25 for Naples, 11 for Rome), of which the most important are: *Silla dittatore* (Naples, Oct. 1, 1723); *Astianatte* (Naples, Dec. 2, 1725); *La caduta dei Decemviri* (Naples, Oct. 1, 1727); *Artaserse* (libretto by Metastasio; Rome, Feb. 4, 1730).
BIBLIOGRAPHY: E.J. Dent, "Notes on Leonardo Vinci," *Musical Antiquary* (July 1913); A. Della Corte, *L'opera comica italiana nel 1700,* vol. I (Bari, 1923); A. Cametti, "Leonardo Vinci e i suoi drammi in musica al Teatro delle Dame," *Musica d'Oggi* (Oct. 1924); U. Prota-Giurleo, *Nicola Logroscino* (Naples, 1927; appendix, "La morte di Vinci," pp. 61–63); K. Geiringer, "Ein Geburtstagkantate von P. Metastasio und L. Vinci," *Archiv für Musikwissenschaft,* 9 (1926); G. Silvestri Silva, *Illustri musici calabresi: Leonardo Vinci* (Genoa, 1935).

Vinci, Pietro, Italian composer; b. Nicosia, Sicily, 1540; d. there, 1584. He was maestro di cappella at Santa Maria Maggiore in Bergamo (1568–80); returned to Nicosia in 1580. He publ. 10 books of madrigals; motets; *Sonetti spirituali;* etc.

BIBLIOGRAPHY: F. Mompellio, *Pietro Vinci, madrigalista siciliano* (Milan, 1937).

Vincze, Imre, Hungarian composer; b. Kocs, Sept. 26, 1926; d. Budapest, May 3, 1969. He studied with Szabó at the Budapest Academy of Music; later taught there; won the Erkel Prize in 1952 and 1956. He wrote 3 symphs. (1951, 1953, 1963); *Felicitation,* overture (1954); *Movimento sinfonico* (1957); *Aforismo* for Orch. (1959); Concertino for Orch. (1961); *Rapsodia concertante* for Piano and Orch. (1966); 4 string quartets (1954, 1958, 1961, 1965); Violin Sonata (1956); *Divertimento* for Wind Quintet (1962); Bassoon Sonata (1964); *Fantasy and Fugue* for Organ (1960); choral works; film music.

Viñes, Ricardo, Spanish pianist; b. Lérida, Feb. 5, 1875; d. Barcelona, April 29, 1943. He studied in Barcelona with Juan Pujol, and with Godard at the Paris Cons., winning the first prize for piano in 1894. In 1895 he gave his first concert in Paris, and established himself in later years as an ardent propagandist of new French and Spanish music; he possessed particular affinity with the composers of the modern French school and performed their works in a colorful and imaginative manner. He gave concerts in London, Berlin, and other music centers, but lived most of his life in Paris; contributed articles on Spanish music to publications in France and Spain.

Vinogradsky, Alexander, Russian conductor; b. Kiev, Aug. 5, 1855; d. there, Oct. 17, 1912. He studied at the St. Petersburg Cons.; in 1888 became conductor of the symph. concerts of the Imperial Russian Music Society in Kiev; also conducted in Paris, Vienna, and Berlin. He wrote 2 symphs.; a symph. fantasy, *En Bourgogne;* a symph. poem, *La Nonne;* a number of minor pieces.

Vinton, John, American writer on music; b. Cleveland, Jan. 24, 1937. He studied at Ohio State Univ. (1954–58) and N.Y. Univ. (1958–63); his principal teachers in musicology were Jan LaRue and Gustave Reese. From 1964–67 he was on the staff of the *Washington Evening Star.* He edited the useful *Dictionary of Contemporary Music* (N.Y., 1974); also publ. *Essays after a Dictionary* (Lewisburg, Pa., 1977).

Viola, Alfonso della, Italian composer; b. Ferrara, 1508; d. there, 1570. He was maestro di cappella to Duke Ercole II d'Este at Ferrara. He is noteworthy as an early composer of pastorals and incidental music for the court of Ferrara: *L'Orbecche* (1541), *Il Sacrifizio* (1554), *Lo Sfortunato* (1557), and *Aretusa* (1563), all in madrigal style, the dialogue sung by a chorus. He publ. 2 books of madrigals *a* 4 (1539, 1540).

Viola, Francesco, Italian 16th-century madrigalist. He was a pupil of Adrian Willaert; was for some time in the service of Alfonso d'Este, Duke of Ferrara, whom he accompanied to Venice in 1562; publ. a book of madrigals *a* 4 at Venice in 1550; other madrigals in various collections; he also edited the collection *Musica nova,* containing motets and madrigals by Willaert.

Viola, P. Anselm, Catalan composer; b. Teruel, July 1738; d. Montserrat, Jan. 25, 1798. He was a monk at Montserrat; wrote much instrumental music of surprising excellence in a fine Baroque style. His Concerto for 2 Oboes, 2 Horns, Violins, and Cellos obbligato is included in vol. II of *Música instrumental,* publ. by the Monastery of Montserrat in 1936, edited by Dom David Pujol.

Viole, Rudolf, German pianist and composer; b. Schochwitz, Mansfeld, May 10, 1825; d. Berlin, Dec. 7, 1867. He was a pupil of Liszt, who recommended his compositions and edited his 100 études. Viole wrote mostly for piano, including 11 sonatas, a *Caprice héroïque,* a Ballade, a Polonaise, etc.

Viotta, Henri (Henricus Anastasius), Dutch conductor and music scholar, son of **Johannes Josephus Viotta;** b. Amsterdam, July 16, 1848; d. Montreux, Feb. 17, 1933. He studied with his father and with R. Hol in Amsterdam; was a student of jurisprudence at the Univ. of Leyden; received a Dr.Juris (1877) with the dissertation *Het auteursrecht van den componist,* but gave up legal practice; he became a conductor of various musical groups in Amsterdam, including the Wagner Society. In 1896 he was appointed director of the Cons. at The Hague, retaining this position until 1917; he founded the Residentie Orch. there (1904), and conducted it until he retired in 1917. He publ. the valuable *Lexicon der toonkunst* (3 vols., 1881–85) and the *Handboek der muziekgeschiedenis* (1916). In 1920 he went to live in Switzerland.

Viotta, Johannes Josephus, Dutch composer; b. Amsterdam, Jan. 14, 1814; d. there, Feb. 6, 1859. He was of Italian descent; studied medicine; music was his avocation. He wrote mainly for the voice, and some of his songs in the popular vein (*De zilveren vloot, Een scheepje in de haven lag,* etc.) became exceedingly well known. In the Netherlands he played a very important role, especially in spreading the cult of Mendelssohn and other German composers.

Viotti, Giovanni Battista, famous Italian violinist and composer; b. Fontanetto da Po, May 12, 1755; d. London, March 3, 1824. His father, a blacksmith, was an amateur musician; taught him music, and bought a small violin for him to practice on. At the age of 11 Viotti was sent to Turin, where he gained the favor of Alfonso del Pozzo, Prince della Cisterna, who paid for his lessons with Pugnani. Viotti soon acquired a virtuoso technique, and also began to compose violin music. In 1780 he made a grand tour of Germany, Poland, and Russia with Pugnani, and was welcomed at the court of Catherine the

Great. On March 17, 1782, he made his first appearance in Paris at the Concert Spirituel. He became a court musician to Marie Antoinette, and in 1788 was appointed manager of the Théâtre de Monsieur, jointly with the Queen's hairdresser, Léonard; he reorganized the enterprise, and invited famous singers to participate in operatic productions. He was also successful as a teacher; among his pupils were Baillot and Rode. He was intimate with Cherubini, and lodged with him in 1785; often played in private, but shunned public appearances, being satisfied with the generous emolument from the court. He remained in Paris for 3 years after the Revolution, but in 1792, when the situation became extremely dangerous for friends of the Queen, he went to London, where he was employed as a conductor of Italian operas; also was soloist in his own concertos at the celebrated Salomon concerts (1794–95). In 1798 he was obliged to leave England on suspicion of political intrigue; he lived for some years at Schönfeld, near Hamburg, devoting himself to composition. In 1801 he returned to London and engaged in a wine business, but sustained financial losses. After the restoration of the French monarchy, he returned to Paris; was appointed director of the Italian Opera (1819–21), but suffered repeated reverses, and in 1823 returned to London, broken in spirit and health, and heavily in debt. He died 2 years later.

Viotti's role in the history of instrumental music, in both performance and composition, was very important. He elevated performing standards from mere entertainment to artistic presentation, and may be regarded as one of the chief creators of modern violin playing. He was the first to write violin concertos in a consciously formulated sonata form, with the solo part and the orch. accompaniment utilizing the full resources of instrumental sonority more abundantly than ever before in violin concertos. He publ. 29 violin concertos (of which No. 22, in A minor, is a great favorite); 10 piano concertos (some of which are transcriptions of violin concertos); 2 *symphonies concertantes* for 2 Violins, Strings, Oboes, and Horns; 21 string quartets; 36 string trios; 54 duets for 2 Violins; 6 serenades for 2 Violins; several duos for 2 Cellos; 3 divertissements for Violin Unaccompanied; 12 sonatas for Violin and Piano; 9 piano sonatas. His song known as "La polacca de Viotti" (used in Paisiello's *La Serva padrona*, 1794) acquired great popularity. For the rectification of Viotti's birth date (heretofore given as May 23, 1753), see *Stampa di Torino* of Sept. 29, 1935, which publ. for the first time the text of his birth certificate; an infant brother of Viotti was born in 1753; their Christian names were identical (the brother having died before the birth of the future musician), which led to confusion; the bicentennial of Viotti was widely celebrated in the wrong year (1953). BIBLIOGRAPHY: A.M. d'Eymar, *Anecdotes sur Viotti, précédées de quelques réflexions sur l'expression en musique* (Paris, 1792); F. Fayolle, *Notices sur Corelli et Viotti* (Paris, 1810); P.M. Baillot, *Notice sur J.B. Viotti* (Paris, 1825); E.F. Miel, *Notice historique sur J.B. Viotti* (Paris, 1827); A. Pougin,

Viotti et l'école moderne de violon (Paris, 1888); H. de Curzon, "Quelques souvenirs de Viotti," *Le Ménestrel* (April 1924); L. de La Laurencie, "Les Débuts de Viotti comme directeur de l'Opéra en 1819," *Revue de Musicologie* (Aug. 1924); idem, *L'École française de violon de Lully à Viotti* (Paris, 1922–25); M. Pincherle, *Les Violinistes compositeurs et virtuoses* (Paris, 1922); W.H. Riehl, *Viotti und das Geigenduett*, in *Musikalische Charakterköpfe* (vol. II); A. Moser, *Geschichte des Violinspiels* (Berlin, 1923); A. Della Corte, *L'interpretazione musicale e gli interpreti* (Turin, 1951); R. Giazotto, *G.B. Viotti* (Milan, 1956); C. White, "Did Viotti Write Any Original Piano Concertos?" *Journal of the American Musicological Society*, XXII (1969).

Virdung, Sebastian, German theorist; b. Amberg, 1465. He was at first a priest in Eichstätt, and from 1500 a member of the court chapel in Heidelberg; wrote a work of importance for the history of musical instruments: *Musica getutscht und auszgezogen durch Sebastianum Virdung, Priesters von Amberg, und alles Gesang ausz den Noten in die Tabulaturen diser benannten dryer Instrumenten, der Orgeln, der Lauten und der Flöten transferieren zu lernen kurtzlich gemacht* (Basel, 1511; facsimile reprint in Eitner's *Publikationen älterer praktischer und theoretischer Musikwerke*, vol. 11, 1882; also by L. Schrade, Kassel, 1931, and by K.W. Niemöller, Kassel, 1970). Virdung's method was violently attacked by Arnolt Schlick in his *Tabulatur etlicher Lobgesänge* (1512). Four of Virdung's songs are in Schöffer's *Teutsche Lieder mit 4 Stimmen* (1513). BIBLIOGRAPHY: B.A. Wallner, "Sebastian Virdung von Amberg," *Kirchenmusikalisches Jahrbuch* (1911); H.H. Lenneberg, "The Critic Criticized: Sebastian Virdung and His Controversy with Arnold Schlick," *Journal of the American Musicological Society* (Spring 1957).

Viscarra Monje, Humberto, Bolivian composer; b. Sorata, March 30, 1898; d. La Paz, Sept. 2, 1971. He studied at the National Cons. of Bolivia in La Paz; then went to Europe, and studied piano and composition in Italy and France. Returning to Bolivia, he served as director of the Cons. of La Paz (1930–32 and 1950–68). He composed some attractive piano pieces based on Bolivian motifs.

Visconti, Luchino, Italian film, theater, and opera director; b. Milan, Nov. 2, 1906; d. Rome, March 17, 1976. After World War II, he assumed a leading position among film directors, producing motion pictures notable for their realism. In 1954 he enlarged the scope of his work to include opera; was highly successful in his productions with Maria Callas at La Scala in Milan; also produced opera at Covent Garden in London. His opera productions were impressive, particularly for his ability to complement the dramatic qualities of the music with the action on stage to effect a total theatrical experience.

Visée, Robert de, French guitar player, lutenist,

and composer; b. c.1650; d. c.1725. He was a court musician from about 1686 to 1721; publ. 2 books of guitar pieces (1682, 1686) and *Pièces de théorbe et de luth, mises en partition* (1716). The guitar works have been edited by R. Strizich (Paris, 1971).

Visetti, Alberto Antonio, Italian singing teacher; b. Salona, May 13, 1846; d. London, July 10, 1928. He studied at the Milan Cons.; first appeared as a pianist; went to Paris, where he was appointed a chamber musician to Empress Eugénie. After the fall of the Empire in France, he settled in London, where he taught singing; also conducted the Bath Phil. Society (1878–90). He publ. *History of the Art of Singing* and *Verdi* (1905); the score of his opera *Les Trois Mousquetaires* was lost during the siege of Paris (1871). He also wrote a cantata, *The Desert and the Praise of Song;* and a waltz-song for Adelina Patti, *La Diva.*

Vishnevskaya, Galina, Russian soprano; b. Leningrad, Oct. 25, 1926. After vocal studies in Leningrad she sang in operetta; in 1952 she joined the operatic staff of the Bolshoi Theater in Moscow; there her roles were Violetta, Tosca, Madama Butterfly, and an entire repertoire of soprano parts in Russian operas. She made her debut at the Metropolitan Opera in N.Y. on Nov. 6, 1961, as Aida. She is married to the famous cellist **Mstislav Rostropovich.** Owing to the recurrent differences that developed between Rostropovich and the cultural authorities of the Soviet Union (Rostropovich had sheltered the dissident writer Solzhenitsyn in his summer house), they left Russia in 1974; eventually settled in the U.S., when Rostropovich was appointed conductor of the National Symph. Orch. in Washington, D.C. In March 1978, both he and Vishnevskaya, as "ideological renegades," were stripped of their Soviet citizenship by a decree of the Soviet government.

Viski, János, Hungarian composer; b. Kolozsvár, June 10, 1906; d. Budapest, Jan. 16, 1961. He studied violin at an early age; then took lessons in composition from Kodály at the Budapest Academy of Music (1927–32). From 1942 until his death he was a prof. of composition at the Budapest Academy of Music; won the Erkel Prize in 1954 and the Kossuth Prize in 1956. Most of his music is permeated with Hungarian melorhythms, and is set in classical forms. WORKS: *Symphonic Suite* (1935); *2 Hungarian Dances* for Orch. (1938); *Enigma,* symph. poem (1939–40); Violin Concerto (1947); Piano Concerto (1953); Cello Concerto (1955); *Az irisórai szarvas (The Deer of Irisóra)* for Baritone and Orch. (1958); String Trio (1930, lost); *Epitaph for Anton Webern* for Piano (1960); choral works; songs.

Vitali, Filippo, Italian composer; b. Florence, c.1590; d. 1653. In 1631 he became a singer in the Pontifical Choir in Rome; was also chamber virtuoso to Cardinal Barberini; in 1642 he returned to Florence and succeeded Gagliano as maestro di cappella of the ducal chapel and of the Cathedral of S. Lorenzo; in 1648–49, was maestro at Sta. Maria Maggiore in Bergamo. His "favola in musica" *L'Aretusa,* performed on Feb. 8, 1620, at the home of Monsignor Corsini, is regarded as the first attempt at opera in Rome (publ. there, 1620). In 1622 he composed 6 intermedi for the comedy *La finta mora* by J. Cicognini, performed at the palace of Cardinal de' Medici in Florence (publ. there, 1623). He also publ. several books of madrigals, arias with instrumental accompaniment, Psalms, hymns, and motets. Vitali was outstanding among composers in the monodic style.

Vitali, Giovanni Battista, Italian composer; b. Bologna, Feb. 18, 1632; d. Modena, Oct. 12, 1692. He was a pupil of M. Cazzati in Bologna; from about 1667 he played the viola da braccio in the Church of S. Petronio there; from 1674 he was 2nd, and from 1684, first, maestro di cappella at the ducal court of Modena; in 1686 he was demoted to vice-maestro. WORKS: *Correnti e Balletti da camera* for 2 Violins and Continuo (1666 and other eds.); *Sonate a 2 violini col basso cont. per l'organo* (1667, etc.); *Balletti, Correnti e Sinfonie da camera a 4 stromenti* (1667, etc.); *Balletti, Correnti, etc., a violino e violone o spinetta, con il secondo violino a beneplacito* (1668, etc.); *Sonate da chiesa a 2, 3, 4 e 5 stromenti* (1669); *Salmi concertati da 2 a 5 voci con stromenti* (1677); *Sonate a 2 violini e basso cont.; Varie sonate alla francese ed all'italiana a 6 stromenti* (1684); *Balli in stile francese a 5 stromenti* (1690); *Sonate da camera a 3 stromenti* (1692); etc. Eighteen pieces are in Torchi's *L'arte musicale in Italia* (vol. 7), and his *Artifici musicali* of 1689 was publ. as vol. 14 of the Smith College Music Archives (1959), ed. by L. Rood and G.P. Smith.

Vitalini, Alberico, Italian composer; b. Rome, July 18, 1921. He studied at the Santa Cecilia Cons. in Rome, obtaining diplomas in violin (1940), viola (1942), composition (1944), and conducting (1945). He subsequently became active mainly as a conductor; in 1950 was appointed director of musical programs of Radio Vaticana; in 1973 was nominated a member of the Accademia Internazionale de Propaganda Culturale. He specializes in sacred choral music. WORKS: *Fantasia* for Piano and Orch. (1949; Rome, 1969); *Assisi* for Chorus and Orch. (1949; Rome, 1967); *Le sette parole di Cristo* for Baritone and String Orch. (Rome, 1952); *Magnificat* for Soprano, Chorus, and Orch. (1954; Rome, 1957); *Tiberiade* for Small Orch. (1955); *Canti in italiano,* for a new liturgy in the Italian language (1965–71).

Vitalis, George, Greek composer and conductor; b. Athens, Jan. 9, 1895; d. there, April 27, 1959. He studied with Armani in Milan; conducted light opera in Athens (1923–36); came to the U.S. in 1945; settled in N.Y. He composed the operas *Perseus and Andromeda, The Return of the Gods,* and *Golfo* (N.Y., Jan. 1, 1949, in concert form, composer conducting); *Greek Fantasy* for Orch. (Athens, Nov. 11, 1945); light orch. pieces under the pseudonym **Giorgio Valente.**

Vitry, Philippe de (Philippus de Vitriaco), famous churchman and musician; b. Vitry, Champagne, Oct. 31, 1291; d. Meaux, June 9, 1361. There are 6 towns in Champagne named Vitry, and it is not known in which of these Vitry was born; he was ordained a deacon early in life and from 1323 held several benefices; he was canon of Soissons and archbishop of Brie. He became a clerk of the royal household in Paris, and about 1346 was made counselor of the court of requests ("maître des requêtes"); from 1346–50 he was also in the service of Duke Jean of Normandy (heir to the throne), with whom he took part in the siege of Aiguillon (1346); when Duke Jean became king in 1350, he sent Vitry to Avignon on a mission to Pope Clement VI, who on Jan. 3, 1351, appointed him bishop of Meaux. Vitry was known as a poet and a composer, but his enduring fame rests on his *Ars nova,* a treatise expounding a new theory of mensural notation, particularly important for its development of the principle of binary rhythm; it also gives the most complete account of the various uses to which colored notes were put. Of the 4 treatises attributed to Vitry in Coussemaker's *Scriptores,* III, only the last 10 of the 24 chapters of *Ars nova* (also publ., with corrections, in *Musica disciplina,* 1956) are now considered authentic. Most of Vitry's works are lost; the extant pieces were publ. by L. Schrade in vol. I of his *Polyphonic Music of the 14th Century* (Monaco, 1956). Separate pieces were brought out in Denkmäler der Tonkunst in Österreich, 76 (40).
BIBLIOGRAPHY: Hugo Riemann, *Geschichte der Musiktheorie im 9.–19. Jahrhundert* (1898); Joh. Wolf, *Geschichte der Mensuralnotation* (1904); J. Combarieu, *Histoire de la musique,* vol. I (1913); A. Coville, "Philippe de Vitry, Notes biographiques," *Romania* (Oct. 1933); G. Reese, *Music in the Middle Ages* (N.Y., 1940); L. Schrade, "Philippe de Vitry: Some New Discoveries," *Musical Quarterly* (July 1956).

Vittadini, Franco, Italian composer; b. Pavia, April 9, 1884; d. there, Nov. 30, 1948. He studied at the Milan Cons.; settled in Pavia, where he headed a music school.
WORKS: Operas: *Anima allegra* (Rome, April 15, 1921; Metropolitan Opera, N.Y., Feb. 14, 1923); *Nazareth* (Pavia, May 28, 1925); *La Sagredo* (Milan, La Scala, April 26, 1930); *Caracciolo* (Rome, Feb. 7, 1938); pastoral triptych, *Il natale di Gesù* (Bari, Dec. 20, 1933); *Fiordisole,* ballet (Milan, Feb. 14, 1935); *Le sette parole di Cristo,* oratorio; 10 masses; symph. poem, *Armonie della notte* (1925); organ pieces.
BIBLIOGRAPHY: A. Baratti, *Vita del musicista F. Vittadini* (Milan, 1955).

Vittoria, Tommaso Luigi da. See **Victoria, Tomás Luis de.**

Vivaldi, Antonio, greatly renowned Italian composer; b. Venice, March 4, 1678; d. Vienna (buried, July 28), 1741. He was the son of **Giovanni Battista Vivaldi,** a violinist at San Marco in Venice, and he studied violin with him; also took theory lessons with Giovanni Legrenzi. He entered the priesthood, taking the tonsure in 1693, and Holy Orders 10 years later. Because of his red hair he was called "il prete rosso" ("the red priest"). In 1703 he became a violin teacher at the Ospedale della Pietà in Venice; in 1718–20 he was music director at the court of Prince Philip, landgrave of Hesse Darmstadt at Mantua; in 1725 he traveled to Amsterdam, where he arranged for publication of several of his works; among them was a collection of 12 violin concertos under the title *La cetra* (1727), which he dedicated to Emperor Charles VI, who then invited him to come to his court in Vienna. Vivaldi accepted the offer, and remained in Vienna to the end of his life, except for visits to Prague and Dresden. Vivaldi devoted the early years of his career as a composer mainly to operatic productions, which were successfully staged in Florence, Milan, Rome, Verona, and other Italian cities, as well as in Vienna; however, his greatness lies mainly in his superb instrumental works, particularly concerti grossi and solo concertos. Despite the difference in treatment and function between his operas and instrumental music, Vivaldi often used material from his operas in his concertos, and vice versa; thus, some of his operatic arias are constructed in the form of a Baroque air in a suite, while the slow movements of instrumental works often find their analogous structures in the operatic "laments." The importance of Vivaldi was enhanced in music history through Bach's use of Vivaldi's concertos as models for his own keyboard concertos; however, of the 16 "Concertos after Vivaldi" for clavier publ. in the *Bach Gesellschaft* edition, only 6 are transcriptions of Vivaldi. Until about the middle of the 20th century Vivaldi was regarded by most music historians as merely an estimable composer who dwelt in the shadow of Bach; not even the basic biographical data (exact date of birth, place and date of death) were established with accuracy until the middle of the 20th century. But comparisons with Bach are misguided. Vivaldi's music possesses neither the surpassing genius nor the conceptual grandeur of Bach's works; his contrapuntal skill was minimal compared to Bach's epic achievements in fugal writing. Furthermore, the uniformity of Vivaldi's structures and the extraordinary repetitiousness of thematic statements in his instrumental works tend to blur the individuality of each particular piece; it has been said that Vivaldi did not write 400 concertos known under his name, but only one concerto which he copied 399 times. Proper taxonomy of Vivaldi's works is further complicated by the profuse cross-pollination of his operatic and instrumental fragments and even of complete sections of various compositions, as well as the abundance of arrangements of pieces by other composers. Under such circumstances, duplication of individual items becomes a rule rather than an exception. Vivaldi's catalogue of works must therefore be subject to periodic verifications and rectifications; 770 works can be assumed to exist, among them 46 operas, of which 21 are extant (Vivaldi himself listed in 1739 the number of his operas as 94, but he included numerous separate arias and instrumental intermezzi); 344 solo concertos; 81 concertos for 2 or more solo instruments; 61 sinfonias; 23 chamber concertos; 93 sonatas and trios; 3 oratorios; 8 serenades; 38 secular solo cantatas; 12 motets; 37 liturgical works; many of these exist in several versions.

WORKS: 21 extant operas: *Ottone in villa* (Vicenza, 1713); *Orlando finto pazzo* (Venice, 1714); *L'incoronazione di Dario* (Venice, 1716); *Arsilda regina di Ponto* (Venice, 1716); *Armida al campo D'Egitto* (Mantua, 1718); *Il teuzzone* (Mantua, 1719); *Tito Manlio* (Mantua, 1719); *La verità in cimento* (Venice, 1720); *Ercole sul Termodonte* (Rome, 1723); *Giustino* (Rome, 1724); *Dorilla in Tempo* (Venice, 1726); *Farnace* (Venice, 1727); *Orlando furioso* (Venice, 1727); *L'Atenaide* (Florence, 1729); *La fida ninfa* (Verona, 1732); *L'Olimpiade* (Venice, 1734); *Griselda* (Venice, 1735); *Catone in Utica* (Verona, 1737). The following are probably by Vivaldi, but only the librettos are extant: *Scanderbeg* (Florence, 1711); *Ipermestra* (Florence, 1727); *Semiramide* (Mantua, 1732); *Montezuma* (Venice, 1733); *Feraspe* (1739); 2 oratorios: *Moyses Deus Pharaonis* (Venice, 1714) and *Juditha triumphans devicta Holofernis barbarie* (Venice, 1716); 38 solo secular cantatas; 12 motets; 37 liturgical works. Instrumental works: *12 sonate da camera* for 2 Violins and Continuo, op. 1; 18 violin sonatas, with Continuo, opp. 2 and 5; *L'estro armonico*, 12 concertos for One, 2, or 4 Solo Violins, Solo Cello, Strings, and Continuo, op. 3; *La stravaganza*, 12 concertos for Solo Violin, Strings, and Continuo, op. 4; 18 concertos for 3 Violins, Viola, and Continuo, opp. 6 and 7; *Il cimento dell'Armonia e dell'Invenzione*, including *Le quattro stagione (The 4 Seasons)*, 12 concertos for Solo Violin, Strings, and Continuo, op. 8; *La cetra*, 12 concertos for Solo Violin, Strings, and Continuo, op. 9; 6 concertos for Flute, Strings, and Organ, op. 10; 12 concertos for Solo Violin, Strings, and Organ, opp. 11 and 12. A complete ed. of Vivaldi's instrumental works, under the general editorship of Gian Francesco Malipiero, was brought out in 1947-72, in 16 series comprising 530 compositions; numerous individual works were publ. separately. An all-encompassing catalogue is by Peter Ryom, *Les Manuscrits de Vivaldi* (Paris, 1977); other catalogues are: M. Rinaldi, *Catalogo numerico tematico delle composizioni di Antonio Vivaldi* (Rome, 1945); A. Fanna, *Antonio Vivaldi, Catalogo numerico-tematico delle opere strumentali* (Milan, 1968); L. Coral, *A Concordance of the Thematic Indexes to the Instrumental Works of Antonio Vivaldi* (2nd ed., Ann Arbor, Mich., 1972); Peter Ryom, *Antonio Vivaldi, Table de concordances des œuvres* (Copenhagen, 1973); P. Damilano, *Inventario delle composizioni musicali manuscripti di Antonio Vivaldi* (Turin, 1968).

BIBLIOGRAPHY: A. Schering, *Geschichte des Instrumental-Konzerts* (Leipzig, 1905; reprint, Wiesbaden, 1972); Alfredo Casella et al., *Antonio Vivaldi: Note e documenti* (Siena, 1939); M. Rinaldi, *Antonio Vivaldi* (Milan, 1943); S.A. Luciani, *Vivaldi: Concerti e Sonate* (Milan, 1946); M. Pincherle, *Antonio Vivaldi et la musique instrumentale* (2 vols., Paris, 1948); G. Guerrini, *Antonio Vivaldi: La vita e l'opera* (Florence, 1951); M. Pincherle, *Vivaldi* (Paris, 1955; in Eng., *Vivaldi, Genius of the Baroque*, N.Y., 1962); Walter Kolneder, *Antonio Vivaldi: Leben und Werk* (Wiesbaden, 1964; also in Eng., London, 1970); idem, "Die Vivaldi-Forschung: Geschichte, Probleme, Aufgaben," *Österreichische Musikzeitschrift* (June 1967); F. Degrada and M.T. Muraro, *Antonio Vivaldi: Da Venezia all'Europa* (Milan, 1978); M. Talbot, *Vivaldi* (London, 1979); Eric Cross, *The Late Operas of Antonio Vivaldi* (1980); A. Bellini, B. Brizi, and M. Pensa, *I libretti Vivaldiana: Recensione e collazione dei testimoni a stampa* (Florence, 1982).

Vivell, Cölestin, German ecclesiastic, writer on Gregorian chant; b. Wolfach, Oct. 21, 1846; d. Seckau (Styria), March 10, 1923. Having completed his univ. studies, he joined the order of Benedictines at Beuron; from 1883 lived in the monastery at Seckau.

WRITINGS: *Der gregorianische Gesang. Eine Studie über die Echtheit seiner Tradition* (Graz, 1904); *Die liturgisch gesangliche Reform Gregors des Grossen* (Seckau, 1904); *Erklärung der vatikanischen Choralschrift* (Graz, 1906); *Vom Musiktraktate Gregors des Grossen* (Leipzig, 1911); *Initia tractatuum musices ex codicibus* (Graz, 1912; alphabetical list of beginnings of treatises in Gerbert's and Coussemaker's *Scriptores*); *Fritolfi Breviarum de musica* (Vienna, 1919).

Vives, Amadeo, Spanish composer; b. Collbató, near Barcelona, Nov. 18, 1871; d. Madrid, Dec. 1, 1932. He was a pupil of Felipe Pedrell in Barcelona; with L. Millet, founded the famous choral society Orfeó Català (1891). In his first opera, *Artus* (Barcelona, 1895), he made use of Catalonian folk songs. Subsequently he moved to Madrid, where he produced his comic opera *Don Lucas del Cigarral* (Feb. 18, 1899); his opera *Euda d'Uriach*, originally to a Catalan libretto, was brought out in Italian at Barcelona (Oct. 24, 1900). Then followed his most popular opera, *Maruxa* (Madrid, May 28, 1914); other operas are *Balada de Carnaval* (Madrid, July 5, 1919) and *Doña Francisquita* (Madrid, Oct. 17, 1923). The style of his stage productions shared qualities of the French light opera and the Spanish zarzuela; he wrote nearly 100 of these; also composed songs and piano pieces; publ. a book of essays, *Sofía* (Madrid, 1923).

Vivier, Albert-Joseph, Belgian music theorist; b. Huy, Dec. 15, 1816; d. Brussels, Jan. 3, 1903. He studied with Fétis at the Brussels Cons.; wrote an interesting *Traité complet d'harmonie* (1862; many later eds.), in which he explained secondary chords as accidental formations through incorporation of auxiliary notes; he also wrote essays on acoustics (*Des vrais rapports des sons musicaux, Eléments d'acoustique musicale*, etc.). His opera *Spadillo le tavernier* was produced in Brussels on May 22, 1857.

Vivier, Claude, Canadian composer; b. Montreal, April 14, 1948; d. Paris (found strangled to death, by parties unknown, in his apartment, March 7, 1983). He studied music with Tremblay at the Montreal

Cons. (1967–70); then went to the Netherlands and took courses in electronic music with Koening at the Inst. of Sonology in Utrecht; also attended classes in electronic composition given by Stockhausen in Cologne. In 1976 he traveled in the Orient to study non-European musical cultures. He was in Paris on a Canada Council Grant to compose an opera on the death of Tchaikovsky, to be titled *Crois-tu en l'immortalité de l'âme?*, at the time of his murder.

WORKS: Chamber opera, *Copernicus (Rituel de mort)* for Soloists, Instruments, and Tape (1979; Montreal, May 8, 1980); String Quartet (1969); *Proliferation* for Ondes Martenot, Piano, and Percussion (1969; revised 1975); *Hiérophanie* for Soprano and Chamber Ensemble (1970); *Deva et Asura* for Chamber Ensemble (1972); *Désintégration* for 2 Pianos, 4 Violins, and 2 Violas (1972); *O! Kosmos* for a cappella Chorus (1974); *Lettura di Dante* for Soprano and Ensemble (1974); *Liebesgedichte* for Vocal Quartet and Instruments (1975); *Piece* for Bassoon and Piano (1975); *Pour violon et clarinette* (1975); *Siddhartha* for Orch. (1976); *Orion* for Orch. (1979); *Zipangu* for String Orch. (1980); *Bouchara (Chanson d'amour)* for Soprano and 11 Instruments (1982).

Vivier, Eugène-Léon, French-horn virtuoso; b. Brioude, Haute-Loire, Dec. 4, 1817; d. Nice, Feb. 24, 1900. He learned to play violin, then took up the French horn. He moved to Paris, where he became successful through his connections at the French court. An eccentric, he prided himself on his ability to play 2 notes simultaneously on his instrument, through clever overblowing. He publ. a number of pamphlets on music and the theater, and also an autobiography (largely fictitious), *La Vie et les aventures d'un corniste* (Paris, 1900).

Vix, Geneviève, French soprano; b. Nantes, Dec. 31, 1879; d. Paris, Aug. 25, 1939. She studied at the Paris Cons.; won first prize for opera (1908); sang at the Paris Opéra, in Madrid, and in Buenos Aires; made her American debut with the Chicago Opera Co. as Manon in Massenet's opera (Dec. 1, 1917); married Prince Cyril Naryshkin in N.Y. (Feb. 9, 1918). She possessed a fine lyric voice and was also adept as an actress.

Vlad, Roman, Italian composer and writer on music; b. Cernauti, Rumania, Dec. 29, 1919. He was a pupil at the Cernauti Cons.; in 1938 went to Rome, where he studied piano and composition with Casella; in 1943 he adopted the 12-tone method of composition.

WORKS: *La strada sul caffé,* ballet (Rome, June 9, 1945); *La Dama delle camelie,* ballet in the form of 5 waltzes (Rome, Nov. 20, 1945); *Sinfonia* (Venice Festival, Sept. 8, 1948); *Divertimento* for 11 Instruments (Capri, Sept. 15, 1948); *De profundis* for Soprano, Mixed Chorus, and Orch. (Paris, June 2, 1949); *Storia d'una mamma,* musical fable (Venice Festival, Oct. 5, 1951); 5 elegies for Voice and String Orch. (1952); *Le Ciel est vide* for Chorus and Orch.

(Turin, Oct. 29, 1954); *Variazioni concertanti* for Piano and Orch., based on a series of 12 notes in Mozart's *Don Giovanni* (Venice Festival, Sept. 18, 1955); *Studi dodecafonici* for Piano (1943–57); *Colinde transilvane* for Chorus (1957); *Musica concertata* for Harp and Orch. (Turin, April 24, 1958); *3 invocazioni* for Voice and Orch. (Rome, June 6, 1958); *Masques ostendais,* ballet (Spoleto Festival, June 12, 1959); *Il Dottore di vetro,* radiophonic opera (Turin, Feb. 23, 1959); *Il ritorno,* ballet (Cologne, 1962); *Ode super "Chrysea Phorminx"* for Guitar and Orch. (1964); *La fontana,* television opera (1967); *Divertimento sinfonieo* for Orch. (1968); *Il magico flauto di Severino* for Flute and Piano (1971). He publ. the books *Modernità e tradizione nella musica contemporanea* (Turin, 1955) and *Storia della dodecafonia* (Milan, 1958), and a monograph on Stravinsky (Turin, 1958; in Eng., London, 1960; 3rd ed., revised, 1979).

Vladigerov, Alexander, Bulgarian conductor and composer, son of **Pantcho Vladigerov;** b. Sofia, Aug. 4, 1933. He studied composition with his father and conducting with Simeonov at the Bulgarian State Cons. in Sofia, graduating in 1956; also took conducting courses in Kiev with Rakhlin. He was conductor of the orch. in Ruse; then was engaged as conductor for Bulgarian Radio and Television.

WORKS: Children's operetta, *Little Red Riding Hood* (1969); 2 musicals: *The Jolly Town Musicians* (1971) and *The Wolf and the 7 Kids* (1973); *Youth March* for Orch. (1948); *Rondo concertante* for Violin and Orch. (1955); *Rumanian Dance* for Orch. (1960); piano pieces.

Vladigerov, Pantcho, prominent Bulgarian composer; b. Zürich, March 13, 1899, in a geminal parturition; d. Sofia, Sept. 8, 1978. Distrustful of Bulgarian puerperal skill, his mother sped from Shumen to Zürich as soon as she learned that she was going to have a plural birth. Pantcho's non-identical twin brother, **Luben,** a violinist, was born 16 hours earlier than Pantcho, on the previous day, March 12, 1899. Vladigerov studied piano and theory with local teachers in Sofia; then went to Berlin, where he took lessons in composition with Paul Juon and Georg Schumann, and piano with Leonid Kreutzer at the Akademie der Künste in Berlin. He remained in Berlin, where he served as conductor and composer of the Max Reinhardt Theater. In 1932 he returned to Bulgaria, and was appointed a prof. at the Music Academy in Sofia; he retired from there in 1972. His music is rooted in Bulgarian folk songs, artfully combining the peculiar melodic and rhythmic patterns of native material with stark modern harmonies; the method is similar to that of Béla Bartók.

WORKS: Opera, *Tsar Kaloyan* (1935–36; Sofia, April 20, 1936); ballet, *Legenda za ezeroto (Legend of the Lake;* 1946; Sofia, Nov. 11, 1962; 2 orch. suites were drawn from it, in 1947 and 1953); 5 piano concertos (1918, 1930, 1937, 1953, 1963); *Legend* for Orch. (1919); *3 Impressions* for Orch. (1920; orchestration of 3 of his *10 Impressions* for Piano); 2 violin concertos (1921, 1968); *Burlesk Suite* for Violin and

Orch. (1922); *Scandinavian Suite* for Orch. (1924); *Bulgarian Suite* for Orch. (1927); *Vardar,* Bulgarian rhapsody for Orch. (1927; orchestration of his earlier violin and piano piece); *7 Bulgarian Symphonic Dances* (1931); 2 overtures: *Zemja* (1933) and *The 9th of September* (1949); 2 symphs.: No. 1 (1939) and No. 2, *Majska (May),* for String Orch. (1949); *Concert Fantasy* for Cello and Orch. (1941); *4 Rumanian Symphonic Dances* (1942) *Improvisation and Toccata* for Orch. (1942; orchestration of the final 2 pieces of his piano cycle *Episodes*); *2 Rumanian Symphonic Sketches* (1943); *Prelude and Balkan Dance* for Orch. (1950); *Evreyska poema (Jewish Poem)* for Orch. (1951); *Song of Peace,* dramatic poem for Orch. (1956); *7 Pieces* for String Orch. (1969–70; orchestration of pieces taken from 3 different piano cycles); Violin Sonata (1914); Piano Trio (1916); works for Violin and Piano: *2 Improvisations* (1919); *4 Pieces* (1920); *Vardar* (1922); *2 Bulgarian Paraphrases* (1925); *2 Pieces* (1926); String Quartet (1940); several piano cycles, many of which are also scored for chamber orch.: *4 Pieces* (1915); *11 Variations* (1916); *10 Impressions* (1920); *4 Pieces* (1920); *3 Pieces* (1922); *6 Exotic Preludes* (1924); *Classical and Romantic,* 7 pieces (1931); *Bulgarian Songs and Dances* (1932); *Sonatina concertante* (1934); *Shumen,* 6 miniatures (1934); *5 Episodes* (1941); *Aquarelles* (1942); *3 Pictures* (1950); *Suite,* 5 pieces (1954); *3 Pieces* (1957); *3 Concert Pieces* (1959); *5 Novelettes* (1965); *5 Pieces* (1965); orchestration of Dinicu's *Hora staccato.*
BIBLIOGRAPHY: E. Pavlov, *Pantcho Vladigerov: A Monograph* (Sofia, 1961).

Vlasov, Vladimir, Russian composer and ethnomusicologist; b. Moscow, Jan. 7, 1903. He studied violin at the Moscow Cons.; was active as a teacher. In 1936 he traveled to Frunze, Kirghizia, where he diligently went about collecting authentic songs of the natives. In collaboration with Vladimir Fere, similarly intentioned, he wrote a number of operas based on Kirghiz national melorhythms supplied by local musicians. These operas were subsequently produced in Frunze and at ethnic festivals in Moscow. They include: *Golden Girl* (Frunze, May 1, 1937); *Moon Beauty* (Frunze, April 15, 1939); *For People's Happiness* (Frunze, May 1, 1941); *Patriots* (Frunze, Nov. 6, 1941); *Son of the People* (Frunze, Nov. 8, 1947); *On the Shores of Issyk-Kul* (Frunze, Feb. 1, 1951); *The Witch,* radio opera (1961); *The Golden Maiden* (1972). He also wrote a Cello Concerto (1963); 3 string quartets; a variety of minor pieces and songs.

Vlijmen, Jan van, Dutch composer; b. Rotterdam, Oct. 11, 1935. He studied composition with Kees van Baaren. Upon completion of his musical education at the Utrecht Cons., he was director of the Amersfoort Music School (1961–65); taught theoretical subjects at the Utrecht Cons. (1965–68); became deputy director of The Hague Cons. in 1967, and, upon Baaren's death, became its director in 1971. WORKS: 2 operas, in collaboration with fellow Dutch composers: *Reconstructie,* an anti-U.S. op-

era, composed with Louis Andriessen, Misha Mengelberg, Reinbert de Leeuw, and Peter Schat (1968–69; Holland Festival, June 29, 1969), and *Axel,* with Reinbert de Leeuw (1975–77; Holland Festival, Scheveningen, June 10, 1977); String Quartet (1955); *Morgensternlieder* for Mezzo-soprano and Piano (1958); 2 wind quintets (1958, 1972); *Construzione* for 2 Pianos (1959); *Serie* for 6 Instruments (1960); *Gruppi* for 20 Instruments in 4 groups, and Percussion (1961–62); *Mythos* for Mezzo-soprano and 9 Instruments (1962); *Spostamenti* for Orch. (1963); *Serenata I* for 12 Instruments and Percussion (1963–64; revised 1967); *Serenata II* for Flute and 4 Instrumental Groups (Amsterdam, Sept. 10, 1965); *Sonata* for Piano and 3 Instrumental Groups (1966); *Dialogue* for Clarinet and Piano (1966); *Per diciasette* for 17 Winds (1967); *Interpolations* for Orch. and Electronic Sound (Rotterdam, Nov. 24, 1968); *Ommagio a Gesualdo* for Violin and 6 Instrumental Groups (Amsterdam, April 9, 1971); *4 Songs* for Mezzo-soprano and Orch. (1975).

Vockerodt, Gottfried, German writer; b. Mühlhausen, Thuringia, Sept. 24, 1665; d. Gotha, Oct. 10, 1727. It was his opinion that excessive enjoyment of music injures the intellect, and that Nero and Caligula became totally depraved through their passion for music. He advocated these ideas in *Consultatio de cavenda falsa mentium intemperatarum medicina* (1696); *Missbrauch der freien Künste, insonderheit der Musik* (1697); and *Wiederholtes Zeugnis der Wahrheit gegen die verderbte Musik und Schauspiele, Opern, etc.* (1698).

Vockner, Josef, Austrian organist, composer, and teacher; b. Ebensee, March 18, 1842; d. Vienna, Sept. 11, 1906. He was a pupil of Bruckner; became a prof. of organ at the Vienna Cons. He composed an oratorio, *Das jüngste Gericht;* Cello Sonata; Piano Quartet; fugues and other pieces for organ; songs.

Vogel, Adolf, German bass-baritone; b. Munich, Aug. 18, 1897; d. Vienna, Dec. 20, 1969. He studied voice with Anna Bahr-Mildenburg and J. Kiechle; was a member of the Munich Opera from 1933 to 1937; made his American debut at the Metropolitan Opera as Alberich (Dec. 3, 1937); remained on its roster for 2 seasons.

Vogel, Charles Louis Adolphe, French violinist and composer; b. Lille, May 17, 1808; d. Paris, Sept. 11, 1892. He was a grandson of **Johann Christoph Vogel**; studied at the Paris Cons. with A. Kreutzer (violin) and Reicha (theory). After winning popularity with his song *Les Trois Couleurs* during the July Revolution (1830), he brought out a series of successful operas: *Le Podestat* (Paris, Dec. 16, 1831); *Le Siège de Leyde* (The Hague, March 14, 1847); *La Moissonneuse* (Paris, Sept. 3, 1853); *Rompons* (Paris, Sept. 21, 1857); *Le Nid de Cigognes* (Baden-Baden, Sept. 1858); *Gredin de Pigoche* (Paris, Oct. 19, 1866); *La Filleule du roi* (Brussels, April 1875). He also wrote symphs., chamber music, sacred works, songs, and piano pieces.

Vogel, Emil, German musicologist; b. Wriezen-on-Oder, Jan. 21, 1859; d. Nikolassee, near Berlin, June 18, 1908. He studied at Greifswald and Berlin; in 1893 he organized the Peters Music Library in Leipzig and was its librarian till 1901; at the same time he edited the *Peters Jahrbuch.* He publ. the catalogue *Die Handschriften nebst den älteren Druckwerken der Musikabteilung der herzoglichen Bibliothek zu Wolfenbüttel* (1890) and *Bibliothek der gedruckten weltlichen Vokalmusik Italiens aus den Jahren 1500–1700* (1892; new ed., completely revised by Alfred Einstein, publ. in *Notes,* June 1945–Sept. 1948; another ed. by F. Lesure and C. Sartoi, eds., *Il nuovo Vogel: Bibliografia della musica italiana vocale profana pubblicata dal 1500–1700,* Geneva, 1977).

Vogel, Friedrich Wilhelm Ferdinand, German organist and composer; b. Havelberg, Prussia, Sept. 9, 1807; d. Bergen, Norway, July 20, 1892. He studied with Birnbach in Berlin; made tours as an organ virtuoso; taught at Hamburg (1838–41) and Copenhagen (1845–52); then settled in Bergen, where he founded an organ school. He publ. a number of works for organ, including 60 chorale-preludes, 10 postludes, and 2 preludes and fugues; also chamber music; overtures; choruses.

Vogel, Johann Christoph, German composer; b. Nuremberg (baptized, March 18), 1758; d. Paris, June 27, 1788. He was a pupil of Riepel at Regensburg; went to Paris in 1776, and wrote 2 operas in Gluck's style: *La Toison d'or* (Paris, Sept. 5, 1786) and *Démophon,* which he completed shortly before his untimely death at the age of 32, and which was produced posthumously (Paris, Sept. 22, 1789). He also composed a great deal of instrumental music: 3 symphs.; a Bassoon Concerto; 3 clarinet concertos; 6 string quartets; 6 quartets for horn and strings; 3 quartets for bassoon and strings; 6 trios for 2 violins and bass; 6 duos for 2 clarinets; 6 duos for 2 bassoons; etc.

Vogel, Wilhelm Moritz, German pianist and composer; b. Sorgau, Silesia, July 9, 1846; d. Leipzig, Oct. 30, 1922. He studied in Leipzig, and settled there as a teacher; also conducted choral societies and wrote music criticism. He publ. a series of instructive piano pieces, and a method (in 12 parts); also songs and organ works; edited *Deutsches Schulliederbuch* (a collection of 200 part-songs); brought out a *Geschichte der Musik* (1900) and several didactic books.

Vogel, Wladimir, significant Russian-German composer; b. Moscow, Feb. 29, 1896; d. Zürich, June 19, 1984. His father was German, his mother Russian. At the outbreak of World War I he was interned in Russia as an enemy alien; after the Armistice in 1918 he went to Berlin, where he studied with Heinz Tiessen and later (1920–24) with Busoni, who exercised a profound influence on him. From 1929 to 1933 Vogel taught at the Klindworth-Scharwenka Cons. in Berlin; with the advent to power of the Nazi government, Vogel, although not a Jew, chose to leave Germany. He worked in Strasbourg and Brussels with Hermann Scherchen on various problems of musical techniques; then went to Switzerland, and in 1954 became a Swiss citizen. Vogel's idiom of composition underwent several changes throughout the years. A convinced believer in the mystical power of music, he felt great affinity with Scriabin's mystical ideas and techniques; he built his melodies along the upper overtones of the harmonic series, and his harmonies on a massive superimposition of perfect fourths and tritones. Gradually he approached the method of composition in 12 tones as promulgated by Schoenberg, while Busoni's precepts of neo-Classical structures governed Vogel's own works as far as formal design was concerned; many of his polyphonic compositions adhered to the Classical harmonic structures in 4 parts, which he maintained even in choral pieces using the *Sprechstimme.* Serialist procedures are adumbrated in Vogel's music through the astute organization of melodic and rhythmic elements.

WORKS: FOR ORCH.: *Sinfonia fugata* (1930–32); *2 Studies* (London, July 28, 1931); *Tripartita* (Geneva, Nov. 21, 1935); Violin Concerto (1937); *Passacaglia* for Chamber Orch. (1946); *Sept aspects d'une série de douze sons* (1949–50); *Spiegelungen* (Frankfurt, June 26, 1953); Cello Concerto (Zürich, Nov. 27, 1956); *Cantique en forme d'un canon à quatre voix* (1969); *Aus der Einheit: Die Vielfalt, in der Vielfalt, die Einheit,* "Hörformen" ("Listening Forms") for Piano and String Orch. (1973); *Abschied* for String Orch. (1973); *Meloformen* for String Orch. (1974); *Hommage* for String Orch. (1974). CHAMBER MUSIC: *La Ticinella* for Flute, Oboe, Clarinet, Saxophone, and Bassoon (1941); *12 variétudes* for Flute, Clarinet, Violin, and Cello (1942); *Inspiré par Jean Arp* for Violin, Flute, Clarinet, and Cello (1965); *Analogien,* "Hörformen" for String Quartet (1973); *Monophonie* for Solo Violin (1974); *Für Flöte, Oboe, Klarinette, und Fagott* (1974); *Poème* for Solo Cello (1974); *Terzett* for Flute, Clarinet, and Bassoon (1975). FOR PIANO: *Nature vivante,* 6 expressionistic pieces (1917–21); *Einsames Getröpfel und Gewuchsel* (1921; revised 1968); *Dai tempi più remoti,* 3 pieces (1922–31; revised 1968); *Etude-Toccata* (1926); *Epitaffio per Alban Berg* (1936); *Klavier-eigene Interpretationsstudie einer varierten Zwölftonfolge* (1972); *4 Versionen einer Zwölftonfolge* (1972); *Musik* for Wind Quartet and Strings (1975). FOR VOICE: Oratorio, *Thyl Claes (Till Eulenspiegel)* in 2 parts: *Oppression* (1938; Geneva, 1943) and *Liberation* (1943–45; Geneva, 1947; an orch. suite from the oratorio was given at the Palermo Festival of the International Society for Contemporary Music, April 26, 1949); *Wagadus Untergang durch die Eitelkeit,* cantata for 3 Soloists, Mixed Chorus, Speaking Chorus, and 5 Saxophones (1930); *An die Jugend der Welt* for Chorus and Chamber Orch. (1954); *Goethe-Aphorismen* for Soprano and Strings (Venice International Festival, Sept. 1955); *Eine Gotthardkantate* for Baritone and Strings (1956); *Jona ging doch nach Ninive* for Baritone, Speaking Soloists and Chorus, Mixed Chorus, and Orch. (1958); *Meditazione su Amadeo Modigliani* for 4 Soloists,

Narrator, Chorus, and Orch. (Lugano, March 31, 1962); *Die Flucht,* dramatic oratorio (1963–64; Zürich, Nov. 8, 1966); *Schritte* for Alto and Orch. (1968); *Gli Spaziali* for Speakers, Vocalists, and Orch., to words from the writings of Leonardo da Vinci, *Autour de la lune* by Jules Verne, and utterances of the American astronauts (1969–71).

BIBLIOGRAPHY: Hans Oesch, *Wladimir Vogel; Sein Weg zu einer neuen musikalischen Wirklichkeit* (Bern, 1967).

Vogeleis, Martin, Alsatian music scholar; b. Erstein, June 5, 1861; d. Sélestat, Aug. 11, 1930. He studied for the priesthood, and was ordained in 1885; taught music at the Episcopalian Seminary in Zillesheim (1886–91); then was chaplain and choirmaster in Grafenstaden (1891–96); was pastor in Behlenheim (1896–1906); from 1908 was pastor in Schlettstadt (Sélestat). He made a special study of music in Alsace; publ. *Quellen und Bausteine zu einer Geschichte der Musik und des Theaters im Elsass 500–1800* (1911).

Vogelweide, Walther von der, famous German minnesinger and lyric poet; b. probably in Tyrol, c.1170; d. Würzburg, c.1230. In Wagner's *Tannhäuser* he appears as one of the rival singers at the Wartburg. He led a wandering life; was in Worms in 1198, in Frankfurt in 1212, then in Würzburg. Very few of his melodies are extant; 3 of these were found in the Münster "Bruchstücke" (MS collection of musical fragments from the Middle Ages), including the so-called "Palestine Song" (1228); 5 others are contained in the Colmar Codex and in the "Singebuch" of Adam Puschmann.

BIBLIOGRAPHY: R. Kralik, in the supplement to Mantuani's *Geschichte der Musik in Wien,* vol. 1 (1904); R. Wustmann, "Die Hofweise Walthers von der Vogelweide," in the "Liliencron-Festschrift" (1910); idem, *Walther von der Vogelweide* (1912); R. Molitor, "Die Lieder des Münsterischen Fragmentes," *Sammelbände der Internationalen Musik-Gesellschaft,* 12 (with facsimiles); R. Wustmann, "Walthers Palästinalied," ibid., 13; F. Ludwig, in Adler's *Handbuch der Musikgeschichte* (Frankfurt, 1924); F. Gennrich, "7 Melodien zu mittelhochdeutschen Minneliedern," *Zeitschrift für Musikwissenschaft* (1924–25); H.J. Moser, *Geschichte der deutschen Musik,* vol. 1 (5th ed., 1928); idem, *Gedenkblatt auf Walther von der Vogelweide* (1929); H. Rietsch, in Denkmäler der Tonkunst in Österreich, 41 (20.ii); C. Bützler, *Untersuchungen zu den Melodien Walthers von der Vogelweide* (Jena, 1940); H. Böhm, *Walther von der Vogelweide* (Stuttgart, 1949); J.A. Huisman, *Neue Wege zur dichterischen und musikalischen Technik Walthers von der Vogelweide* (Diss., Univ. of Utrecht, 1950); K.K. Klein, *Zur Spruchdichtung und Heimatfrage Walthers von der Vogelweide* (Innsbruck, 1952); D. Kralik, *Die Elegie Walthers von der Vogelweide* (Vienna, 1952); F. Maurer, ed., *Die Lieder Walthers von der Vogelweide unter Beifügung erhaltener und erschlossener Melodien,* vol. 1 (Tübingen, 1955).

Vogl, Heinrich, famous German tenor; b. Au, near Munich, Jan. 15, 1845; d. Munich, April 21, 1900. He studied music with Franz Lachner; made a successful debut as Max in *Der Freischütz* at the Munich Court Opera (Nov. 5, 1865) and remained on its roster until his death. He succeeded Schnorr von Carolsfeld as the model Tristan in Wagner's opera, and was for years considered the greatest interpreter of that role. He frequently sang at Bayreuth; created the role of Loge in *Das Rheingold* (1869) and of Siegmund in *Die Walküre* (1870). He made his debut at the Metropolitan Opera in N.Y. on Jan. 1, 1890, as Lohengrin; sang Wagner during the rest of that season. He was also a composer; wrote an opera, *Der Fremdling,* in which he sang the leading role (Munich, May 7, 1899). In 1868 he married the German soprano **Therese Thoma** (b. Tutzing, Nov. 12, 1845; d. Munich, Sept. 29, 1921), who sang the part of Isolde with him; she also created the role of Sieglinde.

BIBLIOGRAPHY: H. von der Pfordten, *Heinrich Vogl. Zur Erinnerung und zum Vermächtnis* (Munich, 1900); K. Pottgiesser, "Heinrich Vogl," *Allgemeine Musikzeitung* (May 4, 1900).

Vogl, Johann Michael, Austrian baritone; b. Ennsdorf, near Steyr, Aug. 10, 1768; d. Vienna, Nov. 19, 1840. He studied law in Vienna; Süssmayr, then conductor of the Vienna Court Theater, discovered his voice, and persuaded him to join his opera company; Vogl remained on its roster from 1794 until 1822 (his debut there was on May 1, 1795). He was the first professional singer to perform Schubert's songs at concerts.

BIBLIOGRAPHY: A. Liess, *J.M. Vogl, Hofoperist und Schubertsänger* (Graz, 1954).

Vogler, Georg Joseph, Abbé or **Abt,** noted German composer and theorist; b. Pleichach, near Würzburg, June 15, 1749; d. Darmstadt, May 6, 1814. The son of a violin maker, he mastered the organ at an early age; studied theology and law at Würzburg and Bamberg. In 1771 he went to Mannheim; there he wrote music for a ballet and gained the favor of the Elector, who provided him with funds for study in Italy. After a brief course in Bologna with Padre Martini, he proceeded to Padua, where he studied composition with Vallotti; but he soon left for Rome, and took Holy Orders in 1773; was made Apostolic Protonotary, Chamberlain to the Pope, and Knight of the Golden Spur; also joined the Academy of the Arcadians. In 1775 he returned to Mannheim as court chaplain and 2nd Kapellmeister; founded there the Mannheimer Tonschule for teaching his own method of composition. In 1780 he was in Paris, where he submitted a paper to the Académie Royale des Sciences, *Essai de diriger le goût des amateurs de musique,* an explanation of his system of teaching (publ. in Paris, 1782); in Paris he also produced his opera *La Kermesse* (1783), which was a fiasco. From France he traveled to Spain, Portugal, England, and Denmark. In 1784 he was called to the Electoral Court in Munich (it had moved from Mannheim in 1778), and became first

Kapellmeister. In 1786 he was engaged as court conductor in Stockholm, where he founded a music school; in 1788 he spent some time in St. Petersburg; in 1790 he was in London as an organist; after traveling in Poland and Germany, he again was Kapellmeister in Stockholm (1793–94). In 1794 he went to Paris, and subsequently traveled to Greece and the Near East. From 1796 to 1799 he was again in Sweden, and afterward visited Copenhagen. In 1800 he went to Berlin; was then in Vienna and Prague. Wherever he went, he solicited interest for his system of organ construction, and exhibited a portable organ called the "orchestrion," but was unsuccessful. After spending 2 years in Vienna, where he produced his opera *Samori* (1804), and brief sojourns in various German towns, he finally settled in Darmstadt; from 1807 until his death was Hofkapellmeister to the Grand Duke of Hessen-Darmstadt; established a Tonschule; Carl Maria von Weber and Meyerbeer became his pupils there. Vogler found his most congenial work in teaching; his pedagogical and acoustic writings were also of importance.

WORKS: OPERAS: *Der Kaufmann von Smyrna* (Mannheim, 1771); *Albert III von Bayern* (Munich, 1781); *Erwin und Elmire*, after Goethe (Darmstadt, 1781); *La Kermesse* (Paris, Nov. 15, 1783); *Castore e Polluce* (Munich, Jan. 12, 1787); *Gustav Adolph och Ebba Brahe* (Stockholm, Jan. 24, 1788); *Samori* (Vienna, May 17, 1804). BALLETS: *Rendez-vous de chasse* (Darmstadt, 1772) and *Le Forgeron villageois;* other stage music. SACRED WORKS: Many, including masses and a Requiem (his masterpiece); 3 Misereres, motets, Te Deum, Stabat Mater (with Orch.), about 50 hymns. INSTRUMENTAL MUSIC: 6 trios for Piano, Violin, and Bass, op. 1; 6 easy sonatas for Piano, op. 2; 6 easy sonatas for Violin and Piano, op. 3; 6 sonatas for 2, 3, and 4 Instruments, op. 4; 6 concertos for Piano, op. 5; 6 piano trios, op. 6; 6 piano trios, op. 7; 12 divertissements for Piano, op. 8; a Piano Concerto; Nocturne for Piano and Strings; *Quatuor concertante* for Piano, Violin, Viola, and Bass; 6 sonatas for 2 Pianos; Sonata for Piano, 4-hands; Sonata for Piano and Strings, called *Der eheliche Zwist; Polymelos, ou Caractères de musique des différentes nations* for Piano and Strings; other variations on national airs; a set of variations on *Ah que vous dirai-je Maman* for Piano, with Orch.; several symphs. and overtures; 32 preludes for organ in every key (a didactic work).

WRITINGS: *Tonwissenschaft und Tonsetzkunst* (Mannheim, 1776), *Stimmbildungskunst* (Mannheim, 1776), and *Churpfälzische Tonschule* (Mannheim, 1778), all 3 republ. together as *Mannheimer Tonschule;* a monthly paper, *Betrachtungen der Mannheimer Tonschule* (1778–81); *Inledning til harmoniens kännedom* (*Introduction to the Theory of Harmony;* Stockholm, 1795); Swedish methods for piano, organ, and thoroughbass (Stockholm, 1797); *Choralsystem* (Copenhagen, 1800); *Data zur Akustik* (Offenbach, 1801); *Gründliche Anleitung zum Clavierstimmen* (Stuttgart, 1807); *System für den Fugenbau* (Offenbach, 1811); *Über Choral und Kirchengesänge* (Munich, 1814).

BIBLIOGRAPHY: J. Fröhlich, *Biographie des grossen Tonkünstlers Abt Vogler* (Würzburg, 1845); H. Künzel, *Abt Vogler* (Darmstadt, 1867); E. Pasqué, *Abt Vogler als Tonkünstler, Lehrer und Priester* (Darmstadt, 1884); K.E. von Schafhäutl, *Abt G.J. Vogler, Sein Leben, sein Charakter und musikalisches System* (Augsburg, 1888; with a list of works); M. Brenet, "L'Abbé Vogler à Paris," *Archives Historiques Artistiques et Littéraires* (Feb. 1891); J. Simon, *Abt Voglers kompositorisches Wirken* (Berlin, 1904); E. Rupp, *Abbé Vogler als Mensch, Musiker, und Orgelbautheoretiker* (Ludwigsburg, 1922); P. Vretblad, *Abbé Vogler in Stockholm* (Würzburg, 1924); idem, *Abbé Vogler* (1933); H. Kelletat, *Zur Geschichte der deutschen Orgelmusik in der Frühklassik* (Kassel, 1933); H. Schweiger, *Abbé G.J. Voglers Orgellehre* (Diss., Univ. of Vienna, 1938); idem, "Abt Vogler," *Musical Quarterly* (April 1939); H. Kreitz, *Abbe Georg Joseph Vogler als Musiktheoretiker* (Diss., Univ. of Saarbrücken, 1957); D. Britton, *Abbe Georg Joseph Vogler: His Life and His Theories on Organ Design* (Diss., Univ. of Rochester, 1973).

Vogrich, Max (Wilhelm Karl), pianist and composer; b. Szeben (Hermannstadt), Transylvania, Jan. 24, 1852; d. New York, June 10, 1916. He gave a piano concert at the age of 7; then studied at the Leipzig Cons. with Reinecke and Moscheles; traveled as a pianist in Europe, South America, and the U.S.; also toured Australia. In 1886 he settled in N.Y.; then lived in Weimar (1902–8), and in London until 1914, returning to N.Y. at the outbreak of World War I. He wrote several operas to his own librettos: *Vanda* (Florence, 1875); *King Arthur* (Leipzig, Nov. 26, 1893); *Der Buddha* (Weimar, 1904); etc.; an oratorio, *The Captivity* (1884); 2 symphs.; Piano Concerto; several pieces for violin, including a Violin Concerto subtitled *E pur si muove* (1913); 12 concert studies for Piano; *Album of Ancient and Modern Dances* for Piano (20 dances, 2 books); anthems; songs. He edited the complete piano works of Schumann, Clementi's *Gradus ad Parnassum* (in progressive order), and other collections.

Vogt, Augustus Stephen, Canadian choral conductor; b. Elmira, Ontario, Aug. 14, 1861; d. Toronto, Sept. 17, 1926. He studied at the New England Cons., and then at the Leipzig Cons. In 1888 he settled in Toronto; founded and conducted the Mendelssohn Choir there (1894–97 and 1900–1917); toured with it in the U.S.; was principal of the Toronto Cons. (1913–26). He was an important figure in music education in Canada; publ. choral works: *The Sea, Crossing the Bar, An Indian Lullaby, The Lord's Prayer,* etc.; *Standard Anthem Book* (1894); *Modern Pianoforte Technique* (1900).

BIBLIOGRAPHY: A. Bridle, "Vogt, A Great Chorus Master," *Year Book of Canadian Art* (1913).

Vogt, Gustav, French oboe player and composer; b. Strasbourg, March 18, 1781; d. Paris, May 30, 1870. He studied at the Paris Cons.; was first oboist at the Opéra-Comique, and then at the Opéra (1812–34). He taught at the Paris Cons. (1816–53); wrote 4 oboe concertos; duos for 2 oboes; potpourris and marches for military band.

Vogt, Johann (Jean), German pianist and composer; b. Gross-Tinz, near Liegnitz, Jan. 17, 1823; d. Eberswalde, July 31, 1888. He studied in Berlin and Breslau; taught piano playing in St. Petersburg (1850–55); subsequently lived in Dresden and in Berlin; visited N.Y. (1871–73). He wrote a Piano Trio, String Quintet, many salon pieces for piano (in all, over 150 opus numbers).

Voicu, Ion, Rumanian violinist; b. Bucharest, Oct. 8, 1925. He studied in Bucharest with Enesco; also in Moscow with David Oistrakh. He made his debut in Bucharest in 1940; then played violin in the Bucharest Phil. In 1969 he founded a chamber orch. in Bucharest; toured widely with this ensemble in succeeding years.

Voigt, Henriette (née **Kunze**), German pianist; b. Leipzig, Nov. 24, 1808; d. there, Oct. 15, 1839. She studied with Ludwig Berger; married the merchant Karl Voigt, whose house was the rendezvous of the most eminent musicians of the time. Schumann dedicated to her the Piano Sonata in G minor (op. 22).
BIBLIOGRAPHY: "Acht Briefe und ein Faksimile von F. Mendelssohn-Bartholdy" (Leipzig, 1871); Eng. trans. in *Macmillan's Magazine*, June 1871); J. Gensel, *Schumanns Briefwechsel mit Henriette Voigt* (Leipzig, 1892); idem, *Aus Rochlitzens Briefen an Henriette Voigt* (Leipzig, 1906).

Voigt, Johann Georg Hermann, German organist and composer; b. Osterwieck, May 14, 1769; d. Leipzig, Feb. 24, 1811. He served for many years as organist at the Thomaskirche in Leipzig; publ. chamber music and piano pieces.

Voisin, Roger, distinguished French-born American trumpeter and teacher; b. Angers, June 26, 1918. He was taken to Boston as a child by his family; studied initially with his father, a member of the Boston Symph. Orch.; subsequently he took lessons with Georges Mager and Marcel LaFosse. In 1935 he became 3rd trumpeter in the Boston Symph. Orch., until his retirement in 1973. He taught at the Berkshire Music Center, the New England Cons. of Music, and Boston Univ.

Volbach, Fritz, German choral conductor and composer; b. Wipperfürth, near Cologne, Dec. 17, 1861; d. Wiesbaden, Nov. 30, 1940. He studied at the Cologne Cons. with Hiller, Jensen, and Seiss, and in Berlin with Taubert and Löschhorn. In 1891 he was appointed conductor of the Liedertafel and the Damengesangverein in Mainz; brought out many choral works by modern German composers; received a Dr.Phil. from the Univ. of Bonn with the dissertation *Die Praxis der Händel-Aufführung* (publ. in 1900). A versatile musician, he had command of almost every orch. instrument.
WORKS: Symph. poems: *Ostern* and *Es waren zwei Königskinder;* Symph.; Piano Quintet; numerous choral works, among them a *Festkantate* for the 5th centenary of the birth of Gutenberg (1900). He publ. the valuable books *Lehrbuch der Begleitung des gregorianischen Gesangs* (1888); *Händel* (1898; in Riemann's *Berühmte Musiker*); *Die Zeit des Klassizismus: Beethoven* (1905; 2nd ed., 1929); *Die deutsche Musik im 19. Jahrhundert* (1909); *Das moderne Orchester in seiner Entwicklung* (1910; 2nd ed., 1919; *Die Instrumente des Orchesters* (1913; 2nd ed., 1921); *Handbuch der Musikwissenschaften* (2 vols., 1926, 1930); *Die Kunst der Sprache* (1929); *Der Chormeister* (1931). A vol. of memoirs, *Erlebtes und Erstrebtes,* was publ. posthumously (Mainz, 1956).
BIBLIOGRAPHY: J. Hagemann, "Fritz Volbach," in *Monographien moderner Musiker* (Leipzig, 1909); G. Schwake, *Fritz Volbachs Werke* (Münster, 1921).

Volckmar, Wilhelm Valentin, German organist and composer; b. Hersfeld, Dec. 26, 1812; d. Homberg, near Kassel, Aug. 27, 1887. In 1835 he settled at Homberg, where he taught music and played organ. He wrote several organ concertos, 20 organ sonatas, an Organ Symph.; publ. *Orgelschule, Schule der Geläufigkeit* for Organ; pieces for piano and for violin; hymns; songs.

Völker, Franz, gifted German tenor; b. Neu-Isenburg, March 31, 1899; d. Darmstadt, Dec. 5, 1965. He made his debut at the Frankfurt Opera as Florestan in 1926 without the benefit of formal vocal studies; continued on its roster until 1935; also sang at the Vienna State Opera (1931–36, 1939–40, 1949–50), the Berlin State Opera (1933–43), and the Bavarian State Opera in Munich (1936–37, 1945–52); he subsequently made guest appearances at Covent Garden, and in Salzburg and Bayreuth; after his retirement in 1952, he taught voice in Neu-Isenburg; was a prof. at the Stuttgart Hochschule für Musik from 1958. Among his finest roles were Parsifal, Lohengrin, and Siegmund in Wagner's operas.

Volkert, Franz, organist and composer, b. Heimersdorf, Bohemia, Feb. 2, 1767; d. Vienna, March 22, 1845. He was active as an organist; was (from 1814) conductor at the Leopoldstadt Theater in Vienna; produced over 100 comic operas, singspiels, melodramas, farces, etc., many of which were popular; also church music, chamber music, and organ pieces.

Volkmann, Hans, German musicologist, grandnephew of **Robert Volkmann;** b. Bischofswerda, April 29, 1875; d. Dresden, Dec. 26, 1946. He studied German philology and music in Munich and Berlin; undertook research in Italy and France; in 1921 settled in Dresden, where he taught music history; in 1946 became a prof. at the Dresden Cons.
WRITINGS: *Neues über Beethoven* (1904); *Emanuel d'Astorga* (2 vols., 1911, 1919; fundamental and important biography; establishes the verifiable facts of d'Astorga's life); *Beethoven in seinen*

Beziehungen zu Dresden (Dresden, 1942). He publ. the standard biography of Robert Volkmann (Leipzig, 1903; abridged ed., 1915); ed. *Briefe von Robert Volkmann* (1917); compiled a *Thematisches Verzeichnis der Werke von Robert Volkmann* (Dresden, 1937).

Volkmann, Robert (complete name, **Friedrich Robert Volkmann**), significant German composer; b. Lommatzsch, April 6, 1815; d. Budapest, Oct. 29, 1883. He studied with his father, a cantor (organ and piano); with Friebel (violin and cello) and Anacker (composition); then in Leipzig with K.F. Becker; was greatly encouraged by Schumann. After teaching music in Prague (1839–41), he settled in Budapest, where he spent the rest of his life, except for 4 years (1854–58) in Vienna. In 1875 he was appointed a prof. at the National Academy of Music in Budapest. His music was regarded very highly in his lifetime, but after his death it faded into oblivion; however, several publications dealing with his works, including a thematic index, were brought out by his grandnephew, **Hans Volkmann.**
WORKS: 2 symphs.; 3 serenades for Strings; 2 overtures; Cello Concerto; 6 string quartets; 2 piano trios; *Konzertstück* for Piano and Orch.; *Chant du Troubadour* for Violin and Piano; *Allegretto capriccioso* for Violin and Piano; 2 violin sonatinas; *Romanze* for Cello and Piano; *Capriccio* for Cello and Piano; *Schlummerlied* for Harp, Clarinet, and Horn (also arranged for Piano, Viola, and Cello; his last completed work). For Piano Solo: *Phantasiebilder; Dithyrambe und Toccate; Souvenir de Maróth; Nocturne;* Sonata in C minor; *Buch der Lieder; Deutsche Tanzweisen; Cavatine und Barcarole; Visegrád;* 4 marches; *Wanderskizzen; Fantasie; Intermezzo; Variations* on a theme of Handel; *Lieder der Grossmutter; 3 Improvisations; Am Grab des Grafen Széchenyi; Ballade und Scherzetto;* transcriptions of songs by Mozart and Schubert; etc. For Piano, 4-hands: *Musikalisches Bilderbuch; Ungarische Skizzen; Die Tageszeiten;* 3 marches; *Rondino und Marsch-Caprice;* transcriptions of his other works. Vocal works: 2 masses for male chorus; 5 sacred songs for mixed chorus; offertories; Christmas carol of the 12th century; old German hymn for double male chorus; 6 duets on old German poems; *An die Nacht* for Alto Solo, with Orch.; dramatic scene for Soprano and Orch., *Sappho; Kirchenarie* for Bass, Flute, and Strings; *Weihnacht* for Female Chorus; *Im Wiesengrün* for Mixed Chorus; etc.
BIBLIOGRAPHY: B. Vogel, *Robert Volkmann* (Leipzig, 1875); H. Volkmann, *Robert Volkmann. Sein Leben und seine Werke* (Leipzig, 1903; standard biography; abridged ed., 1915); C. Preiss, *Robert Volkmann. Kritische Beiträge zu seinem Schaffen* (Graz, 1912); V. von Herzfeld, "Robert Volkmann," *Musical Quarterly* (July 1915); T. Brawley, *The Instrumental Works of Robert Volkmann* (Diss., Northwestern Univ., 1975).

Volkonsky, Andrei, Russian composer; b. Geneva, of Russian parents of princely nobility, Feb. 14, 1933. He studied piano with Dinu Lipatti in Geneva and composition with Nadia Boulanger in Paris. In 1947 he went to Russia, where he studied music theory with Shaporin at the Moscow Cons. (1950–54). In 1955 he was a co-founder, with Barshai, of the Moscow Chamber Orch.; then devoted himself to harpsichord playing; in 1964 he organized in Moscow the concert group Madrigal, with which he gave annual series of highly successful concerts in the Soviet Union, East Germany, and Czechoslovakia. His early works were set in evocative impressionistic colors, in the manner of the French modern school, but soon he deployed a serial technique of composition analogous to Schoenberg's method of composition with 12 tones outside traditional tonality. He was outspoken in his criticism of the direction that Soviet music was taking, and he entirely rejected the official tenets of socialist realism. This attitude, and the nature of his own music, resulted in the cancellation of performances of his works; he was expelled from the Union of Soviet Composers, and could no longer give concerts. In 1973 he left Russia, and returned to Switzerland.
WORKS: Cantatas: *Rus* (Russia), after Gogol (1952), and *The Image of the World* (Moscow, May 8, 1953); Concerto for Orch. (Moscow, June 10, 1954); *Capriccio* for Orch.; Piano Quintet (1954); String Quartet (1955); Piano Sonata (1956); *Musica stricta* for Piano (1956); *2 Japanese Songs* for Chorus, Electronic Sound, and Percussion (1957); *Music* for 12 Instruments (1957); *Serenade to an Insect* for Chamber Orch. (1959); *Suite des miroirs* for Soprano, Organ, Guitar, Violin, Flute, and Percussion (1960); Viola Sonata (1960); *The Lament of Shaza* for Soprano and Small Orch. (1961; Moscow, May 12, 1965); *Jeux à trois* for Flute, Violin, and Harpsichord (1962); *Concerto itinérant* for Soprano, Violin, Percussion, and 26 Instruments (1967); *Réplique* for Small Orch. (1969); *Les Mailles du temps* for 3 Instrumental Groups (1969); some music for plays.

Volkov, Feodor, Russian musician; b. Kostroma, Feb. 19, 1729; d. St. Petersburg, April 14, 1763. He was educated in Yaroslavl, where he organized a theatrical group which presented performances of plays with music. In 1754 he entered a military school in St. Petersburg; in 1759 he was sent to Moscow, where he was in charge of the spectacles accompanying the coronation of Catherine II (1763). Volkov was an able practical musician, even though he totally lacked professional training. His supposed authorship of the comic opera *Taniusha, or A Happy Encounter* (1756) is extremely doubtful; in fact, the existence of such an opera has never been proved. Volkov's role in the early history of the Russian musical stage is confined to his activities as an organizer.
BIBLIOGRAPHY: V. Tcheshikhin, *History of Russian Opera from 1674 to 1903* (St. Petersburg, 1905; pp. 57–60); M. Luchansky, *Fyodor Volkov* (Moscow, 1937).

Vollerthun, Georg, German composer and conductor; b. Fürstenau, Sept. 29, 1876; d. Strausberg (near Berlin), Sept. 15, 1945. He studied with Tappert, Radecke, and Gernsheim; was a theater conductor in Prague, Berlin, Barmen, and Mainz (1899–1905); spent 3 years in Paris (1908–10); then settled in Berlin as a music critic and teacher; from 1922 lived mostly in Strausberg.

WORKS: Operas: *Veeda* (Kassel, 1916); *Island-Saga* (Munich, Jan. 17, 1925); *Der Freikorporal* (Hannover, Nov. 10, 1931; his most successful opera; also given in Berlin, June 10, 1933); *Das königliche Opfer* (Hannover, 1942); *Alt-Danzig Suite* for Orch. (1938); cantatas and other vocal works; many German songs.

BIBLIOGRAPHY: E. Krieger, *Georg Vollerthun* (Berlin, 1942).

Voloshinov, Victor, Soviet composer; b. Kiev, Oct. 17, 1905; d. Leningrad, Oct. 22, 1960. He studied composition with Scherbatchev at the Leningrad Cons.; later became a prof. there. He wrote the operas *Glory* (1939) and *Stronger Than Death* (1942); several symph. suites on Central Asian themes; chamber music; songs; incidental music for the theater. He enjoyed great renown as a pedagogue; many Soviet composers were his students.

Volpe, Arnold, Russian-American conductor; b. Kovno, Lithuania, July 9, 1869; d. Miami, Fla., Feb. 2, 1940. He studied with Leopold Auer at the St. Petersburg Cons. (1887–91), and composition there with Soloviev (1893–97). In 1898 he emigrated to America, settling in N.Y.; in 1902 founded the Young Men's Symph. Orch. of N.Y., which he conducted until 1919; also conducted a group called the Volpe Symph. Orch. (1904–14). In 1918 he organized the summer concerts at the Lewisohn Stadium in N.Y., and conducted for a few seasons there; then moved to Washington, D.C., where he was music director of the Washington, D.C., Opera Co. (1919–22); subsequently was director of the Kansas City Cons. (1922–25); in 1926 he went to Florida, where he organized the Univ. of Miami Symph. Orch. He composed some chamber music and many songs to Eng. words.

BIBLIOGRAPHY: Marie Volpe (his widow), *Arnold Volpe. Bridge between Two Musical Worlds* (Coral Gables, Fla., 1950).

Vomáčka, Boleslav, Czech composer; b. Mladá Boleslav, June 28, 1887; d. Prague, March 1, 1965. He studied law at the Charles Univ. in Prague (LL.D., 1913); took music courses with Vítězslav Novák (1909–10); was in the service of the Labor Ministry in Prague (1919–50); wrote music criticism in several newspapers there; was editor of *Listy Hudební Matice* (1922–35). He began to compose early in life; developed a strong national style of composition.

WORKS: Operas: *Vodník* (*The Water Spirit;* 1934–37; Prague, Dec. 17, 1937); *Boleslav I* (1955; Prague, March 8, 1957); *Čekanky* (*Waiting for a Husband;* 1956); oratorio, *Živi mrtvým* (*The Living to the Dead;* 1927–28; Prague, Feb. 24, 1929); cantatas: *Romance Svatojirská* (*Romance of St. George;* 1922–43); *Strážce majáku* (*The Keeper of the Lighthouse;* 1931–33); *The Partisan Bojka*

(1952); *Under the Banner of Communism* (1959); *Vlastenecké zpěvy* (*Patriotic Hymns*) for Chorus and Orch. (1939); *1914,* cycle of 5 songs with Orch. (1919–20); *Cesta z bojiště* (*The Return from the Battlefield*), cycle of 5 songs with Orch. (1922–28); *Mladí* (*Youth*), symph. poem with Chorus (1914–16); *Czech Eroica,* symph. (1944–46); *Dukla,* overture (1948); *Fanfáry míru* (*Fanfares of Peace*), 3 pieces for Trumpet and Orch. (1960); Violin Sonata (1912); *Quartettino* for Strings (1941); Nonet for Wind Instruments (1957); String Quartet (1959); 2 piano sonatas (1917; *Sonata quasi fantasia,* 1942); piano pieces; *S.O.S.* for Male Chorus (1927); *Balada o snu* (*Ballad of a Dream*) for Mixed Chorus (1933); many part-songs.

BIBLIOGRAPHY: H. Doležil, *Boleslav Vomáčka* (Prague, 1941).

Von Blon, Franz, German composer and conductor; b. Berlin, July 16, 1861; d. there, Oct. 21, 1945. He studied in Berlin at the Stern Cons.; was active as a conductor in Warsaw and Berlin; wrote several operettas (*Sub rosa, Die Amazone, Die tolle Prinzess,* etc.) and much light music for piano; also a number of military marches, of which one, *Unter dem Siegesbanner,* became extremely popular.

Von der Hoya, Amadeo, American violinist; b. New York, March 13, 1874; d. Linz, Austria, April 4, 1922. He studied violin in Berlin; was concertmaster of the Vienna Opera (1894–96); in 1901 was appointed concertmaster of the Musikverein in Linz. He publ. *Grundlagen der Violintechnik,* a valuable method; also *Moderne Lagenstudien für Violine* and *Studienbrevier.*

Vonk, Hans, Dutch conductor; b. Amsterdam, June 18, 1942. He studied law at the Univ. of Amsterdam; also took courses at the Amsterdam Cons. In 1966 he became conductor of the Netherlands National Ballet. In 1969 he was named associate conductor of the Concertgebouw Orch. He then became permanent conductor of the Netherlands Radio Phil. Orch. In 1976 he assumed the post of music director of the Netherlands Opera. He served as associate conductor of the Royal Phil. Orch. of London (1976–79); in 1980 he became chief conductor of the Residentie Orch. at The Hague. He made his American debut with the San Francisco Symph. Orch. in 1974.

Von Stade, Frederica, remarkable American mezzo-soprano; b. Somerville, N.J., June 1, 1945. She was a scion of a German-American colonial family. The nobiliary particle of her name derives from the German locative indicating the connection with the town of Stade, near Hamburg, in which one of her paternal ancestors served as burgomaster. Her father, Charles von Stade, a lieutenant in the U.S. Army, was killed during the final weeks of World War II, shortly before she was born. She went to Paris and studied piano at the Ecole Mozart. Returning to the U.S., she earned a living as a saleswoman at Tiffany's jewelry store in N.Y.; then enrolled at the Mannes College of Music in N.Y., where she studied voice with Sebastian Engleberg. She auditioned successfully for the Metropolitan Opera and, on Jan. 11, 1970, made her debut there in the inconspicuous part of one of the 3 spirits in *Die Zauberflöte.* She progressed gradually toward greater but still minor roles at the Metropolitan, such as Siebel in Gounod's *Faust.* She also sang with the San Francisco Opera. In 1972 she went to Europe, where she advanced rapidly, gathering encomiums for her performances at the Glyndebourne and Salzburg festivals. Her career now in full swing, she enlarged her repertoire, singing Octavian in *Der Rosenkavalier* in 1975 in Houston and Rosina in *The Barber of Seville* at Covent Garden in London. During the 1976–77 season she sang Mélisande in Paris and Geneva. She subsequently was a guest artist at La Scala in Milan. In 1973 she married the photographer Peter Elkus.

Voormolen, Alexander Nicolas, Netherlandish composer; b. Rotterdam, March 3, 1895; d. The Hague, Nov. 12, 1980. He was a scion of a family of municipal functionaries in the Netherlands, and on his mother's side was a descendant of Claude Rameau, a brother of Jean-Philippe Rameau. He entered the Utrecht School of Music, where he studied with Johan Wagenaar; he began to compose as a very young man; from his earliest steps he experienced a strong influence of French Impressionism; he went to Paris, where he was befriended by Ravel, whose influence became decisive in Voormolen's own compositions. In his idiom Voormolen affected richly extended harmonies, and followed Ravel's example in writing works in neo-Baroque forms, marked by gentle symmetric melodies. His music was played frequently in the Netherlands, but as the general trend in modern music moved away from impressionistic mannerisms, it fell into desuetude. His last years of life were unhappy. WORKS: 4 ballets: *Le Roi Grenouille* (1916; withdrawn); *Baron Hop,* in 2 suites (1923–24, 1931); *Diana* (1935–36); *Spiegel-Suite* for Small Orch., to Langendijk's play (1943); *De drei ruitertjes (The 3 Little Horsemen),* variations on a Dutch song, for Orch. (1927); *Een Zomerlied* for Orch. (1928); Oboe Concerto (1938); *Sinfonia* (1939); *Kleine Haagsche Suite* for Small Orch. (1939); *Pastorale* for Oboe and String Orch. (1940); Cello Concerto (1941); *Arethuza,* symph. myth after the Dutch novelist L. Couperus (1947; Amsterdam, Nov. 11, 1948); *La Sirène* for Solo Saxophone and Orch. (1949); Concerto for 2 Harpsichords or Pianos, and Orch. (1950); *Sinfonia concertante* for Clarinet, Horn, and String Orch. (1951); *Eline,* nocturne for Orch. (1957; orchestrated and enlarged version of the 1951 piano piece); *Chaconne en Fuga* for Orch. (1958); 2 violin sonatas (1917, 1934); *Suite* for Cello and Piano (1917); Piano Trio (1918); *Suite* for Harpsichord (1921); *Divertissement* for Cello and Piano (1922); 2 string quartets (1939, 1942); Viola Sonata (1935); for Piano: *Valse triste* (1914); *Suite* No. 1 (1914–16); *Falbalas* (1915); *Eléphants* (1919); *Tableaux des Pays Bas,* in 2 series (1919–20, 1924); *Scène et danse érotique* (1920); *Le Souper clandestin* (1921); *Sonnet*

(1922); *Livre des enfants,* in 2 series (1923, 1925); *Berceuse* (1924); *Sonata* (1944); *Eline,* nocturne (1951); for Voice: *Beatrijs,* melodrama for Narrator and Piano (1921); *3 Gedichten* for Voice and Orch. (1932); *Een nieuwe Lente op Holland's erf* for Voice and Orch. (1936); *Herinneringen aan Holland (Memories of Holland)* for Baritone, Bass Clarinet, and Strings (1966); *Stanzas of Charles II* for Baritone, Flute, English Horn, Celesta, Percussion, and Strings (1966); cantata; *Amsterdam* (1967); *From: The Recollection* for Medium Voice, String Orch., and Celesta (1970); *Ex minimis patet ipse Deus,* hymn for Middle Voice, Strings, and Celesta (1971; exists in many alternate versions); *Ave Maria* for Chorus, Harp, and String Orch. (1973; exists in many alternate versions); songs and choruses to Dutch, German, and French texts.
BIBLIOGRAPHY: Cor Backers, *Nederlandse Componisten van 1400 tot op onze Tijd* (The Hague, 1949; pp. 141–47); Eduard Reeser, "Alexander Voormolen," *Sonorum Speculum,* 22–23 (1965); Peter-Jan Wagemans, "Alexander Voormolen," in *Key Notes* (1982/1).

Voorn, Joop (Josephus Hermanus Maria), Dutch composer; b. The Hague, Oct. 16, 1932. He studied at the Brabant Cons., and since 1969 has taught there. He composed *Cyclus* for Organ (1967); *Psalm CXIV—In Exitu* for Soprano, Children's Chorus, and Orch. (1968); *Ludi ed Interludi* for Piano (1969); 2 string quartets (No. 2, 1970); *Nakupenda,* trio for Flute, Violin, and Viola (1971); *Soft Music for Angela* for Solo Flute (1973); *Immobile: Music for Tutankhamun* for Orch. (Brabant, Dec. 2, 1975); *Sucevita chorals* for 2 Oboes, 2 Clarinets, Bass Clarinet, and Bassoon (1974); Trio for Oboe, Clarinet, and Bassoon (1974); *Petit concert de printemps* for Flute and Strings (1975; Brabant, April 25, 1976); *Prelude and Fugue,* Quintet for Piano, Oboe, Clarinet, Horn, and Bassoon (1975–76).

Vopelius, Gottfried, German composer; b. Herwigsdorf, near Zittau, Jan. 28, 1635; d. Leipzig, Feb. 3, 1715. He studied at the Univ. of Leipzig; was cantor of St. Nicholas at Leipzig from Dec. 12, 1676; harmonized old German hymns and publ. *Neu Leipziger Gesangbuch* (1682), containing 100 hymns originally brought out in Schein's *Cantional oder Gesangbuch* (1627).

Voříšek, Jan Hugo. See **Worzischek, Johann Hugo.**

Vorlová, Sláva, Czech composer; b. Náchod, March 15, 1894; d. Prague, Aug. 24, 1973. She studied piano with her mother and composition with Vítězslav Novák in Prague. The war interrupted her musical studies; she resumed composition after the end of the Nazi occupation of Czechslovakia. She became interested in writing music for instruments rarely used for solo performances; wrote one of the few concertos for bass clarinet. Her music is tinted with impressionistic colors. WORKS: 4 operas: *Zlaté ptáče (The Golden Bird;*

1949–50); *Rozmarýnka* (*Rosemary;* 1952; Kladno, 1955); *Náchodská kasace* (*The Náchod Cassation;* 1955); *Dva světy* (*2 Worlds;* 1958); *Fantasy* for Cello and Orch. (1940); *Symphony JM,* dedicated to Jan Masaryk (1947–48); *Songs of Gondwana,* symph. epos with Soloists and Chorus (1948–49); *Božena Němcová,* suite in 8 parts (1950–51); Oboe Concerto (1952); Trumpet Concerto (1953); Viola Concerto (1954); Clarinet Concerto (1957); Flute Concerto (1959); Concerto for Bass Clarinet and Strings (1961); Concerto for Oboe and Harp (1963); Concerto for Double Bass and Strings (1968); *3 Bohemian Dances* for Orch. (1952–53); *The Gamekeeper's Wife,* melodramatic triptych (1960); *Memento* for Orch. (1957); *Thuringian Dances* for Orch. (1957); *Kybernetic Studies* for Orch. (1962); *Dedications* for Orch. (1965); *Bhukhar (Fever Birds)* for Orch. (1965); *Model Kinetic,* ballet music (1966); *Correlations* for Bass Clarinet, Piano, and Strings (1968); *Polarization* for Harp, Wind Orch., and Percussion (1970); *Emergence* for Violin and Orch. (1973; posthumous, Prague, March 24, 1974); String Quartet (1939); Nonet (1944); *Melodious Variations* for String Quartet (1950); *Puzzles* for 2 Pianos (1953); *Miniatures* for Bass Clarinet and Piano (1962); *Dessins tetraharpes* for 4 Harps (1963); *2 African Fables* for Narrator, Alto Flute, and Percussion (1964); *Variations on a Theme by Handel* for Bass Clarinet and Piano (1965); *6 pro 5* for Brass Quintet (1967); *Immanence* for Bass Clarinet, Piano, and Percussion (1970); *Brief Considerations* for Soprano, Alto, and Piano (1971); songs.

Voss, Charles, German pianist; b. Schmarsow, Sept. 20, 1815; d. Verona, Aug. 29, 1882. He studied in Berlin, but made his career in Paris, where he went in 1846; enjoyed great success in Paris society as a pianist and composer; publ. a great number of salon pieces, transcriptions, paraphrases, etc.; also wrote piano concertos and études. His First Piano Concerto, in F minor, was praised by Mendelssohn.

Voss (Vossius), Isaac, music theorist; b. Leyden, the Netherlands, 1618; d. Windsor, England, Feb. 21, 1689. He was the son of the German scholar Gerhard Johann Voss (1577–1649), who lived in the Netherlands. After his father's death, he went to Stockholm, where he was at the court of Queen Christina (1649–54); subsequently he went to England (1670), where he remained till his death. He publ. an important treatise in Latin, *De poematum cantu et viribus rythmi* (1673).

Vostřák, Zbyněk, Czech composer and conductor; b. Prague, June 10, 1920. He studied composition privately with Rudolf Karel (1938–43); attended the conducting classes of Pavel Dědeček at the Prague Cons. In 1963 he became conductor of the Prague chamber ensemble Musica Viva Pragensis; worked in an electronic music studio in Prague. His music evolved from the Central European type of modernism; later he annexed serial techniques, electronic sound, and aleatory practices.
WORKS: Operas: *Rohovín čtverrohý* (*The 4-*

horned *Rohovín;* 1947–48; Olomouc, 1949); *Kutnohorští havíři* (*The King's Master of the Mint;* 1951–53; Prague, 1955); *Pražské nokturno* (*A Prague Nocturne;* 1957–58; Ústí-on-the-Elbe, 1960); *Rozbitý džbán* (*The Broken Jug;* 1960–61; Prague, 1963); 4 ballets: *The Primrose* (1944–45); *Filosofská historie* (*A Story of Students of Philosophy;* 1949); *Viktorka* (*Little Victoria;* 1950); *Sněhurka* (*Snow White;* 1955); *Serenade* for Small Orch. (1940); *Prague Overture* (1941); *Zrození měsíce* (*The Birth of the Moon*) for Chamber Orch. (Prague, March 8, 1967); *Kyvadlo času* (*The Pendulum of Time*) for Cello, 4 Instrumental Groups, and Electric Organ (1966–67; Donaueschingen, Oct. 19, 1968); *Metahudba* (*Metamusic*) for Orch. (1968; Prague, March 2, 1970); *Tajemství elipsy* (*The Secret of Ellipsis*) for Orch. (1970; Prague, March 5, 1971); *3 Sonnets after Shakespeare* for Bass and Chamber Orch. (1963); *Cantata,* to words by Kafka, for Chorus, Winds, and Percussion (1964); *Burlesque* for Clarinet and Piano (1945); *Contrasts* for String Quartet (1961); *Crystallizations* for 12 Winds (1962); *Recollection* for Solo Violin (1962); *Affects* for 7 Instruments (1963); *Elements* for String Quartet (1964); *Synchronia* for 6 Instruments (1965); *Trigonum* for Violin, Oboe, and Piano (1965); *Tao,* cards for 9 Players (1967); *Kosmogonia* for String Quartet (1968); *Sextant* for Wind Quintet (1969); *Concomitances* for Percussionist and Tape (1971); *3 Essays* for Piano (1962); tape pieces: *2 Foci* (1969); *Telepathy* (1969); *7 Thresholds* (1970); *The Net of Silence* (1971); String Quartet (1980); *Das Opfer der Kerze* for Instrumental and Electronic Ensemble (Baden-Baden, May 20, 1981).

Votapek, Ralph, American pianist; b. Milwaukee, March 20, 1939. He studied at the Wisconsin Cons. in his hometown; then took piano lessons at the Manhattan School of Music and the Juilliard School of Music in N.Y., where his principal teachers were Rosina Lhévinne and Robert Goldsand. He won the Van Cliburn International Competition for pianists in 1962, and then embarked on a successful career as a soloist, in recital, and with orchs.; played in major cities of the U.S.; made 7 tours of South America; in 1975 played engagements in Russia. He settled in East Lansing, Mich., as artist-in-residence at Michigan State Univ., and continued his concert career.

Votto, Antonino, Italian pianist and conductor; b. Piacenza, Oct. 30, 1896. He studied piano with Longo and composition with De Nardis at the Cons. di Musica S. Pietro a Majella in Naples; made his debut as a concert pianist in Trieste in 1919. In 1919–21 he taught piano at the Cons. di Musica G. Verdi in Trieste. Toscanini chose him as maestro sostituto at La Scala in Milan; later he became a regular conductor there and led numerous performances for Maria Callas and other prima donnas. His other engagements included a stint at the Teatro Colón in Buenos Aires, and guest appearances at Covent Garden in London and at the Chicago Lyric Opera.

Vranken, Jaap, Dutch organist and composer; b. Utrecht, April 16, 1897; d. The Hague, April 20, 1956. He was the son of the organist **Joseph Vranken** (1870–1948), with whom he studied organ and theory. In 1916–18 he was in the U.S., studying with Percy Goetschius. He returned to the Netherlands in 1920, and was appointed organist at the church of St. Anthonius in The Hague; acquired a fine reputation as a teacher. He composed mostly sacred music; also instrumental music in Classical style; publ. a manual on counterpoint (1948). His last work was *Missa polyphonica* (1953).

Vredenburg, Max, Belgian-born Dutch composer; b. Brussels, Jan. 16, 1904, of Dutch parents; d. Laren, the Netherlands, Aug. 9, 1976. He was taken to the Netherlands as a child and received an elementary musical education there; in 1926 went to Paris and studied at the Ecole Normale with Paul Dukas; was a music correspondent for a Rotterdam newspaper; at the outbreak of World War II, he was sent by the Dutch government to Java, where he was interned by the Japanese (1942–45); but he was allowed to organize concerts in Indonesia with a fellow internee, the violinist Szymon Goldberg; he returned to the Netherlands after the war and settled in Amsterdam; in 1953 succeeded Sem Dresden as director of the Dutch section of Jeunesses Musicales. In 1957 he established the National Youth Orch., which he led until his death.
WORKS: *Au Pays des Vendanges,* wind quintet (1951); Oboe Concerto (1951); *Akiba* for Mezzo-soprano and Chamber Orch. (1951); *Du printemps* for Mezzo-soprano and Chamber Orch. (1952); *Lamento* for Viola and Piano (1953); *Suite dansante* for Youth Orch. (1956); *Horizons hollandaises* for Orch. (1959); Trio for Oboe, Clarinet, and Bassoon (1965). He publ. a book, *Langs de vijf Lijnen* (1947).

Vretblad, Viktor Patrik, Swedish organist and musicologist; b. Svartnäs, April 5, 1876; d. Stockholm, Jan. 15, 1953. He studied at the Stockholm Cons. (1895–1900) and later in Berlin; wrote music criticism; acted as a church organist; was an official in the Ministry of Postal Services for 40 years (1900–1940). He devoted his research mainly to early Swedish music; publ. basic biographies of J.H. Roman (Stockholm, 1914, 1945); *Konsertlivet i Stockholm under 1700-talet* (1918); *A. Hallén* (1918); *Abbé Vogler* (1933).

Vreuls, Victor, Belgian composer; b. Verviers, Feb. 4, 1876; d. Brussels, July 27, 1944. He studied at the Cons. in Verviers; later took harmony lessons with Sylvain Dupuis and counterpoint with J.T. Radoux at the Cons. in Liège. He then went to Paris, where he took a course with d'Indy at the Schola Cantorum; from 1906 to 1926 was director of the Luxembourg Cons.
WORKS: 2 operas: *Olivier le simple* (1909–11; Brussels, March 9, 1922) and *Un Songe d'une nuit d'été,* after Shakespeare (1923–24; Brussels, Dec. 17, 1925); ballet, *Le Loup-garou (The Werewolf;* 1935; Ghent, 1937); 3 symph. poems: *Cortège héroïque*

(1894); *Jour de fête* (1904); *Werther* (1907); Symph., with Solo Violin (1899); 2 *Poèmes* for Cello and Orch. (1900, 1930); *Elégie* for Flute and Chamber Orch. (1917); *Morceau de concert* for Trumpet and Orch. (1917); *Fantaisie* for Horn and Orch. (1918); *Romance* and *Caprice* for Violin and Chamber Orch. (both 1924); *Suite de danses* for Orch. (1939); *Ouverture pour un drame* (1940); Piano Quartet (1894); Piano Trio (1896); 2 violin sonatas (1899, 1919); String Quartet (1918); Cello Sonata (1922); choruses; songs.

Vriend, Jan, Dutch composer; b. Sijbekarspel, Nov. 10, 1938. He studied piano and music theory with Ton de Leeuw at the Amsterdam Cons.; attended a course in electronic music given by G.M. Koenig at the Inst. of Sonology at Utrecht Univ. (1966–67) and a series of lectures on "formalization in music" given by Xenakis at the Schola Cantorum in Paris (1968). He taught theory and conducted ensembles for contemporary music at the Utrecht Cons. (1968–69). He builds his musical thematics on the theories of Xenakis, involving probabilities and stochastic teleologies.
WORKS: *4 12-Tone Studies* for Piano (1960); *Pour le flûte* for Solo Flute (1961); String Quartet (1962–63); *Paroesie for* 10 Instruments (1963); *Mater-Muziek* for 65 Performers and Electronic Sound (1966); *Diamant,* subtitled "a symphony for the Earth," for Orch. (1964–67); *Transformation (on the way to Halleluja)* for Chorus and Orch. (1965–67); *Huantan* for Organ and 28 Wind Instruments in 4 Groups (1967–68); *Introitus (Hommage to Ton de Leeuw)* for Chorus, 6 Clarinets, 2 Bass Clarinets, and 4 Trombones (1969); *Bau* for Small Orch. (1970); *Elements of Logic* for Wind Orch. (in collaboration with Jos Kunst, 1972; Scheveningen, Feb. 25, 1973); *Kri* for Chorus and Chamber Ensemble (1975).

Vrieslander, Otto, German composer and writer on music; b. Münster, July 18, 1880; d. Tegna, Switzerland, Dec. 16, 1950. After attending the Cologne Cons., he went to Munich in 1904; in 1911–12 he was in Vienna, where he studied with Heinrich Schenker, becoming one of his disciples. From 1912 he lived in Ebertsberg, near Munich; in 1929 settled in Switzerland. He wrote some highly expressive song cycles (*Lieder aus des Knaben Wunderhorn, Pierrot lunaire,* etc.); edited works by C.P.E. Bach, 6 of whose symphs. he arranged for piano, 4-hands; publ. various studies on him: *Ph.E. Bachs Klavierstücke für Anfänger mit kompositionstechnischer Analyse* (1914); *Lieder und Gesänge von Ph.E. Bach nebst Einleitung* (1922); "Ph.E. Bach als Klavierkomponist," in *Ganymed* (Dresden, 1922); *Ph.E. Bach* (1923); "Ph.E. Bach als Theoretiker," in *Von neuer Musik* (1925).

Vrionides, Christos, conductor; b. Khania, Crete, Jan. 12, 1894; d. Yaphank, Long Island, N.Y., Dec. 31, 1961. He studied in Athens at the Odeon, and taught theory and double bass there (1920–22); then came to the U.S.; studied at the Inst. of Musical Art in N.Y. (graduated in 1929); conducted the Vrionides Sinfonietta in N.Y. (1929–35); also led the Byzantine Vocal Ensemble (1924–38); taught Greek liturgy in N.Y. and Boston. His musical settings of the liturgy of the Greek Orthodox Church have been accepted in Greek churches in the U.S. and South America.

Vronsky, Vitya (real name, **Victoria Vronsky**), pianist; b. Evpatoria, Crimea, Aug. 22, 1909. She studied at the Kiev Cons.; then with Petri and Schnabel in Berlin, and with Cortot in Paris. She married the pianist **Victor Babin** on Aug. 31, 1933; came to America in 1937; toured widely with Babin in duo-piano recitals.

Vroons, Frans, Dutch tenor; b. Amsterdam, April 28, 1911. He studied in Amsterdam; made his debut there as Don Curzio in *Le nozze di Figaro* in 1938; was then a principal member of the Netherlands Opera in Amsterdam (1941–71); was also active in an administrative capacity there, serving as director of its opera school (1956–71). He made guest appearances as a singer at Covent Garden in London (1948–50), in N.Y., and in San Francisco. After his retirement in 1971, he taught voice in Amsterdam.

Vroye, Théodore-Joseph de, Belgian music scholar; b. Villers-la-Ville, Aug. 19, 1804; d. Liège, July 19, 1873. He entered the priesthood in 1828, and in 1835 became canon of the Liège Cathedral. He made a profound study of Gregorian chant; publ. *Vesperal* (1829); *Graduel* (1831); *Traité du plainchant à l'usage des séminaires* (1839); *Manuale cantorum* (1849); *Processionale* (1849); *Rituale Romanum* (1862); *De la musique religieuse* (1866; with Elewyck).

Vuataz, Roger, Swiss composer and organist; b. Geneva, Jan. 4, 1898. He studied with Otto Barblan and Jaques-Dalcroze at the Geneva Cons.; was a church organist for over 50 years in Geneva (1917–73) and a music critic there (1940–60); was director of music programming at Radio Geneva (1961–71); taught at the Geneva Cons. (1962–69); conducted choruses. WORKS: Opera-buffa, *Monsieur Jabot* (Geneva, Nov. 28, 1958); 3 ballets: *Le Rhône* for Chorus and Orch. (1929); *Poème méditerranéen pour un ballet* for Orch. (1938–50); *Solitude* for Orch. (1962); radiophonic pieces; *Genève ouverte au ciel,* "évocation lyrique" in 5 pictures for Tenor, Narrator, 3 Choruses, Orch., and Organ (1941); 2 oratorios: *Abraham* (1927; revised 1936) and *Jésus* (1949); *Suite symphonique* (1925); *8 poèmes d'Orient* for Soprano and Orch. (1925); *Petit concert* for Orch. (1932); *Triptych* for Orch. (1929–42); *Images de Grèce,* symph. (1938–39); *Nocturne and Dance* for Trumpet and Orch. (1940); *4 rondeaux de Charles d'Orléans* for Soprano and Orch. (1946–61); Violin Concerto (1948); *Epopée antique,* 2 suites for Orch. (1947–51); *Estampes genévoises,* suite for Orch. (1959); Piano Concerto (1964); *Fantaisies I–III,* concerto for Harp and Orch. (1973); *Images poétiques et pathétiques* for Cello and Orch. (1977); Cello Sonata (1928); 2 suites for Solo Ondes Martenot (1930); Vio-

lin Sonatina (1933–34); *Musique* for Wind Quintet (1937–61); *Frivolités,* suite for Sextet (1952); *Destin,* "symphonie à trois" for Saxophone, Harp, and Percussion (1954); Flute Sonata (1948–54); *Thrène* for Horn and Piano (1960); String Quartet (1970); *Nocturnes* for Solo Cello (1974); piano pieces.

Vučković, Vojislav, Serbian composer; b. Pirot, Oct. 18, 1910; d. Belgrade (killed by German police), Dec. 25, 1942. He studied in Prague with J. Suk and Zdeněk Nejedlý. Returning to Belgrade in 1934, he displayed energetic activity as a composer, conductor, publicist, and writer on economic subjects; publ. pamphlets on the materialistic interpretation of music in the light of Marxist dialectics. He was in the resistance movement during the German occupation, and was killed on the street by Nazis. WORKS: 2 symphs.; symph. poem, *Burevesnik* (*Stormy Petrel;* 1942; Belgrade, Dec. 25, 1944); *Heroic Oratorio* (1942; Cetinje, Sept. 5, 1951); chamber music; choruses. After a period of composition in the expressionistic manner (including the application of quarter-tones), out of ideological considerations he abruptly changed his style to programmatic realism.
    BIBLIOGRAPHY: V. Peričić, ed., *Vojislav Vučković, Umetnik i borac* (2 vols., Belgrade, 1968).

Vuillaume, Jean-Baptiste, celebrated French violin maker; b. Mirecourt, Oct. 7, 1798; d. Paris, March 19, 1875. He came from a family of violin makers, and learned the trade from his father, **Claude Vuillaume** (1772–1834). At 19 he went to Paris and worked with Chanot till 1821, and in 1821–25 for Lété, with whom he then entered into partnership. After Lété's retirement in 1828, Vuillaume worked alone, and put his own name on several instruments which he had constructed with the greatest care and fine craftsmanship; but he was unable to overcome the general distrust of the native product, and began manufacturing imitations of Italian instruments. After long and patient labor he placed a "Stradivarius" violin on the market for 300 francs; it bore the master's label and possessed a full, sonorous tone; he also built a cello priced at 500 francs. The sight of a Duiffoprugcar viola da gamba inspired him with the idea of further imitations, hence the hundreds of "Duiffoprugcar" violins and cellos with their quaint shape, carved scrolls, inlays, and the motto "viva fui in sylvis, etc." By dint of indefatigable research and experiments, Vuillaume carried the construction of these various instruments to the highest perfection. His own inventions were numerous: in 1849 the huge "Octobasse," a double bass 4 meters in length, 3-stringed (CC–GG–C), with a special lever-mechanism to aid the left hand (an "octobasse" is in the Museum of the Paris Cons.); in 1855 a viola, which he called the "contre-alto," with greater strength of tone, but clumsy to play; in 1867 a kind of mute, the "pédale sourdine"; also a machine for manufacturing gut strings of perfectly equal thickness. He also formulated the laws governing the tapering of the stick of the Tourte bow.

BIBLIOGRAPHY: R. Millant, *Jean-Baptiste Vuillaume, Sa vie et son œuvre* (London, 1972; in French, Eng., and German).

Vuillermoz, Emile, French music critic; b. Lyons, May 23, 1878; d. Paris, March 2, 1960. He studied organ and piano in Lyons, and composition at the Paris Cons. with Fauré. He was one of the organizers of the Société Musicale Indépendante (1911) and edited the *Revue Musicale S. I. M.;* eventually became music critic of the daily *L'Excelsior,* and also contributed articles to *Le Temps.* He publ. *Musiques d'aujourd'hui* (1923), *La Vie amoureuse de Chopin* (1927), and *Histoire de la musique* (Paris, 1949; revised and completed by Jacques Lonchampt, 1973); *Gabriel Faure* (Paris, 1960; in Eng., Philadelphia, 1969); *Claude Debussy* (Geneva, 1957; 2nd ed., 1962).

Vuillermoz, Jean, French composer; b. Monte Carlo, Dec. 29, 1906; d. Lobsonn, Alsace, June 21, 1940 (killed while on patrol duty in the last hours before the Franco-German armistice). He studied with Busser and Rabaud at the Paris Cons.; received the 2nd Prix de Rome for his cantata *Le Pardon* (1932).
WORKS: *Triptique* for Orch. (Paris, May 31, 1932); Concerto for French Horn and Orch. (Paris, March 11, 1934); ballet, *Veglione* (1937); Cello Concerto; *Promenade zoologique* for Chamber Orch.; Piano Trio; String Trio.

Vukdragović, Mihailo, Serbian composer; b. Okučani, Nov. 8, 1900. He studied in Prague; in 1927 returned to Belgrade and was active as a conductor and pedagogue. He wrote several works in an impressionistic style before embracing the esthetics of socialist realism.
WORKS: Symph. poem, *Put u pobedu* (*Road to Victory;* Belgrade, Oct. 19, 1945); cantata, *Vezilja slobode* (*Champion of Freedom;* Belgrade, Jan. 5, 1948); cantata for Bass, Speaker, Chorus, and Orch., *Srbija* (*Serbia;* Niš, July 6, 1961); 2 string quartets (1925, 1944).
BIBLIOGRAPHY: V. Peričić, *Muzički Stvaraoci u Srbiji* (Belgrade, 1969; pp. 582–90).

Vulpius (Latinized form of real name, **Fuchs**), **Melchior,** German composer; b. Wasungen, c.1570; d. Weimar, 1615 (buried, Aug. 7). From 1596 to his death, he was cantor in Weimar.
WORKS: 2 books of *Cantiones sacrae* (1602; 2nd ed., 1603; and 1604; 2nd ed., 1611); *Kirchengesänge und geistliche Lieder* for 4 and 5 Voices (1604); *Canticum beatissimae Virginis Mariae* for 4–8 Voices (1605); *Lateinische Hochzeitstücke* (1608); *Opusculum cantionum sacrarum* for 4–6 Voices (1610); *Das Leiden und Sterben unseres Herrn* (Passion after Matthew; 1613); 3 books of *Sonntägliche Evangelische Sprüche* for 4 Voices (1619, 1620, 1621); also a new ed. of Heinrich Faber's *Compendiolum musicae* (1610) with a German trans. and a supplementary chapter. Modern eds. are: the Matthew-Passion by Ziebler (1934); hymns by Heyden (1932); Christmas choruses by Twittenhoff and Heyden (1932).
BIBLIOGRAPHY: C. von Winterfeld, *Zur Geschichte heiliger Tonkunst,* I (1850); H.H. Eggebrecht, *Melchior Vulpius* (Diss., Univ. of Jena, 1949); idem, "Das Leben des Melchior Vulpius," in *Max Schneider Festschrift* (1955).

Vycpálek, Ladislav, Czech composer; b. Prague, Feb. 23, 1882; d. there, Jan. 9, 1969. He studied philosophy at the Charles Univ. in Prague, obtaining his doctorate in 1906; then took private lessons in composition with Vítězslav Novák (1908–12). From 1907 to 1942 he worked as a music librarian.
WORKS: 3 cantatas: *Kantáta o posledních věcech člověka* (*Cantata on the Last Things of Man,* 1920–22); *Blahoslavený ten člověk* (*Blessed Is the Man,* 1933); *České requiem/Smrt a spasení* (*Czech Requiem/Death and Salvation,* 1940); String Quartet (1909); *Cestou* (*The Way*), 6 pieces for Piano (1901–14); *Chvála houslí* (*In Praise of the Violin*), sonata for Violin, Piano, and Mezzo-soprano, to the poem by S. Hanuš "The Violin of an Old German Master" (1927–28); Duo for Violin and Viola (1929); *Suite* for Solo Viola (1929); *Suite* for Solo Violin (1930); *Vzhůru srdce* (*Courage, My Heart!*), 2 variation fantasies to songs from the Huss period, for Orch. (1950); *Doma* (*At Home*), suite for Piano (1959); choruses; many songs.
BIBLIOGRAPHY: J. Smolka, *Ladislav Vycpálek* (Prague, 1960).

Vyshnegradsky, Ivan. See **Wyschnegradsky, Ivan.**

Vyvyan, Jennifer, English soprano; b. Broadstairs, Kent, March 13, 1925; d. London, March 28, 1974. She studied with Roy Henderson at the Royal Academy of Music in London; made her debut as Jenny Diver in *The Beggar's Opera* with the English Opera Group in 1947; then sang with the Sadler's Wells Opera and the Covent Garden Opera, and at the Glyndebourne Festivals; also made guest appearances in Milan, Rome, Vienna, and Paris. She appeared in many contemporary operas, particularly those by Benjamin Britten; was equally distinguished as a concert singer.

Waack, Karl, German conductor; b. Lübeck, March 6, 1861; d. Neumünster, March 7, 1922. He was a pupil of the grand-ducal Musikschule in Weimar; settled in Riga as a teacher and conductor of the Wagnerverein. After the outbreak of the war in 1914, he went to Lübeck, where he conducted the Verein der Musikfreunde. He edited *Tristan und Isolde* (1904) and *Lohengrin* (1907) for Breitkopf & Härtel's *Textbibliothek* (with leading motifs in notation, and references to the full and piano scores); also wrote historical introductions and prepared tables of motifs for all the Wagner operas in the new editions brought out by Breitkopf & Härtel (1913). He publ. *Richard Wagner, Ein Erfüller und Vollender deutscher Kunst* (1918).

Waart, Edo de, noted Dutch conductor; b. Amsterdam, June 1, 1941. He was a member of a musical family; his father sang in the chorus of the Netherlands Opera. He first studied the piano; at 13 he took up the oboe; at 16 he entered the Muzieklyceum, where he studied oboe and later cello; during the summer of 1960 he attended the conducting classes in Salzburg given by Dean Dixon; after graduating from the Muzieklyceum in 1962, he played oboe in the Amsterdam Phil.; in 1963 he joined the Concertgebouw Orch.; he also studied conducting with Franco Ferrara in Hilversum; then made his debut as a conductor with the Netherlands Radio Phil. in 1964. He went to the U.S. in 1964 and was one of the winners in the Mitropoulos Competition in N.Y.; in 1965–66 he was assistant conductor with the N.Y. Phil. Upon his return to Amsterdam in 1966 he was appointed assistant conductor of the Concertgebouw Orch., and accompanied it on a tour of the U.S. in 1967. He also organized the Netherlands Wind Ensemble and traveled with it in Japan and Pakistan as an oboe player. In 1967 he became a guest conductor of the Rotterdam Phil.; from 1973 to 1979 served as its chief conductor. He toured with it in England in 1970 and 1974; in the U.S. in 1971, 1975, and 1977; and in Germany and Austria in 1976. In 1971, 1972, and 1975 he was a guest conductor of the Santa Fe Opera in New Mexico; in 1975 he also conducted opera in Houston. In 1976 he conducted at Covent Garden in London. On Feb. 27, 1974, he made a successful debut with the San Francisco Symph.; this success led to his permanent engagement with it, first as its principal guest conductor in 1975, and then as music director in 1977. In 1980 he inaugurated the Louise M. Davies Hall in a gala concert with the San Francisco Symph. Orch. Edo de Waart represents the modern generation of symph. conductors, free from egotistical projections and attending to his duties *sine ira et studio*. He is tall, athletic-looking, and boasts a rich crown of hair; these attributes, topologically speaking, help him dominate the orch.

BIBLIOGRAPHY: David Ewen, *Musicians since 1900* (N.Y., 1978); P. Hart, *Conductors: A New Generation* (N.Y., 1979; pp. 197–219).

Waart, Hendrikus Aloysius Petrus de, Dutch composer and organist; b. Amsterdam, June 28, 1863; d. Voorburg, near The Hague, April 2, 1931. He studied in The Hague; then taught piano and organ at the Cons. there; wrote 3 symphs., numerous choral works, a String Trio, piano works, and songs.

Wachs, Paul Etienne Victor, French pianist and composer; b. Paris, Sept. 19, 1851; d. St. Mandé, July 6, 1915. He studied with César Franck and Victor Massé at the Paris Cons., and won first prize for organ playing; subsequently was engaged as a church organist in Paris. He wrote works for organ, chamber music, etc., but achieved his most signal success as a composer of attractive salon pieces for piano (*Pluie d'étoiles, Le Collier de perles, Les Doigts,* etc.); also well known are his *Pastorale* and *Hosanna* for Organ.

Wachtel, Theodor, German tenor; b. Hamburg, March 10, 1823; d. Frankfurt, Nov. 14, 1893. The son of a livery-stable keeper, he carried on the business from the age of 17, after his father's death. When his voice was discovered, he was sent to Hamburg for study, and soon appeared in opera. After further study in Vienna, he sang at the Berlin Opera (1865–68); in 1869 he appeared in Paris; made 2 American tours (1871, 1875); accumulated a considerable fortune. His voice was a powerful and brilliant lyric tenor; the role in which he made himself famous was that of the postillion in Adam's *Postillon de Longjumeau,* which he sang more than 1,000 times; also was successful as Raoul in *Les Huguenots.* His sole attempt as a Wagner singer, in *Lohengrin* (Leipzig, 1876), was a dismal failure.

Wachtmeister, Axel Raoul, Count, composer; b. London (son of the Swedish ambassador there), April 2, 1865; d. Paris, Dec. 12, 1947. He studied music with Gédalge and Vincent d'Indy. He lived mostly in Paris, going to Sweden in the summers; spent some time in the U.S.; his cantata *Sappho* was performed in N.Y. in 1917. He also wrote 2 symphs.; a symph. poem, *Le Récit de l'horloge; Hymne à la lune* for Baritone, Chorus, and Orch. (Cincinnati, 1933); *Suite romantique* for Piano; songs.

Wackernagel, Philipp, German music historian; b. Berlin, June 28, 1800; d. Dresden, June 20, 1877. He publ. several books dealing with music: *Das deutsche Kirchenlied, von Luther bis auf N. Hermann* (2 vols., 1841); *Bibliographie zur Geschichte des deutschen Kirchenliedes im 16. Jahrhundert* (1855); *Das deutsche Kirchenlied von der ältesten Zeit bis zum Anfang des 17. Jahrhunderts* (5 vols., 1864–77).

Waddington, Sidney Peine, English composer and pedagogue; b. Lincoln, July 23, 1869; d. Uplyme, Devon, June 2, 1953. He studied in London, Frankfurt, and Vienna; returning to England, he was engaged as chorus master at St. Mary of the Angels, Bayswater, London (1894–1905); in 1905 joined the staff of the Royal College of Music as a harmony teacher. He wrote an operetta for children, *Whimland; Ode to Music* for Soli, Chorus, and Orch.; Piano Concerto; Piano Quintet; String Quartet; String Trio; *Suite de pièces* for Piano, 4-hands; Violin Sonata; Cello Sonata; etc.

Wade, Joseph Augustine, Irish composer; b. Dublin, 1796; d. London, July 15, 1845. He went to London in 1821, and established himself as a highly successful composer of popular ballads; his song *Meet me by moonlight alone* (1826) enjoyed great vogue, as did his vocal duet *I've wandered in dreams.* He also wrote an opera, *The 2 Houses of Granada* (London, Oct. 31, 1826), and an operetta, *The Pupil of Da Vinci* (London, Nov. 30, 1839).

Wadsworth, Charles, American pianist and harpsichordist; b. Barnesville, Ga., May 21, 1929. He studied piano with Rosalyn Tureck and conducting with Jean Morel at the Juilliard School of Music in N.Y.; also studied the French song repertoire with Pierre Bernac in Paris and German lieder with Meinhard von Zallinger in Munich. In 1960 Gian Carlo Menotti invited him to organize the Chamber Music Concerts at the Festival of Two Worlds in Spoleto, Italy; he was its director and pianist for 20 years. In 1969 he helped to found the Chamber Music Society of Lincoln Center in N.Y., and was made its artistic director; in 1977 he also created the chamber music series for the Charleston, South Carolina, Spoleto Festival U.S.A. In addition to numerous appearances as a pianist and harpsichordist with various ensembles, he also appeared in performances with such noted musicians as Dietrich Fischer-Dieskau, Beverly Sills, Hermann Prey, and Shirley Verrett.

Waechter, Eberhard, Austrian baritone; b. Vienna, July 9, 1929. He studied piano and music theory at the Univ. of Vienna and at the Academy of Music there (1950–53); took private voice lessons; in 1953 he sang at the Vienna Volksoper; in 1955 he became a member of the Vienna State Opera; subsequently made guest appearances at Bayreuth, Salzburg, Covent Garden in London, and La Scala in Milan. On Jan. 25, 1961, he made his debut at the Metropolitan Opera in N.Y. as Wolfram in *Tannhäuser.* In 1963 he was named Austrian Kammersänger. He was particularly distinguished in lyric baritone parts, among them Count Almaviva, Don Giovanni, and Wolfram; he also sang the role of Orest in *Elektra* by Richard Strauss.

Waefelghem, Louis van, Belgian violinist and composer; b. Bruges, Jan. 13, 1840; d. Paris, June 19,

1908. He studied violin at the Brussels Cons. with Meerts; went to Germany in 1860; played violin in the orch. of the Budapest Opera; settled in Paris in 1863; often visited London as a chamber music player. With Grillet, Diémer, and Delsart he founded the Société des Instruments Anciens in Paris (1895), where he played the viola d'amore; composed and arranged a number of pieces for that instrument.

Waelput, Hendrik, Flemish composer; b. Ghent, Oct. 26, 1845; d. there, July 8, 1885. He studied at the Brussels Cons.; won the Prix de Rome for his cantata *Het Woud (The Forest)*. He was assistant director of the Bruges Cons. (1869–71); conducted theater orchs. at The Hague, Dijon, Douai, Fécamp, and Lille (1872–76). From 1876 to 1879 he was active in Ghent; in 1879 was appointed prof. of harmony at the Antwerp Cons.; became director of the Ghent Opera in 1884. He wrote 2 operas: *La Ferme du diable* (Ghent, 1865) and *Stella* (in Flemish; Brussels, March 14, 1881); 5 symphs.; cantatas; other works.
BIBLIOGRAPHY: E. Callaert, *Levensschets van Hendrik Waelput* (1886); P. Bergmans, *Notice biographique sur Henry Waelput* (1886); E. de Vynck, *Henry Waelput* (Brussels, 1935).

Waelrant, Hubert, Flemish composer and theorist; b. Tongerloo, Brabant, c.1517; d. Antwerp, Nov. 19, 1595. He matriculated at the Univ. of Louvain in 1534; in 1544 became a tenor at Notre Dame in Antwerp, where he founded a music school in 1547. In 1554 he established a music publishing business in partnership with Jean Laet, retiring in 1558. As a teacher, he abandoned the old system of solmization by hexachords and introduced a new system of the 7 tone-names, *bo ce di ga lo ma ni* (hence called "Bocedization"; also "Voces belgicae"). His compositions include a book of chansons, publ. by Phalèse in Louvain (1553–54), and a book of madrigals for 5 Voices (Antwerp, 1558); as a publisher, he brought out several sacred works by various composers; edited a collection, *Symphonia angelica,* containing madrigals of his own (1585).
BIBLIOGRAPHY: G. Becker, *Hubert Waelrant et ses psaumes. Notice biographique et bibliographique* (Paris, 1881); G. Reese, *Music in the Renaissance* (N.Y., 1954).

Waesberghe, Joseph Smits van, Dutch musicologist; b. Breda, April 18, 1901. He studied philosophy; joined the Jesuit Order; then took courses in music with C. Huygens (church music) and Marius Monnikendam (theory); taught at the Cons. of Rotterdam (1928–43) and in 1943 was appointed to the staff of the Amsterdam Cons.
WRITINGS: *Muziekgeschiedenis der middeleeuwen,* a voluminous survey of medieval music history in 2 parts (Tilburg, 1935–39, 1939–47); *Klokken en klokkegieten in de Middeleeuwen* (1937); *Muziek en drama in de Middeleeuwen* (Amsterdam, 1942; in Eng. as *Music and Drama in the Middle Ages,* Stockholm, 1947); *De Gregoriaansche zang* (Amsterdam, 1943; in Eng. as *Gregorian Chant and Its Place in the Catholic Liturgy,* Stockholm, 1947);

School en muziek in de Middeleeuwen (Amsterdam, 1949); *Melodieleer* (Amsterdam, 1950; in Eng. as *A Textbook of Melody,* Dallas, American Inst. of Musicology, 1955). A Festschrift, *Organicae voces,* was presented him on his 60th birthday (Amsterdam, 1963).

Wagemans, Peter Jan, Dutch composer; b. The Hague, Sept. 7, 1952. He studied organ, composition (with Vlijmen), and music theory; often performs 2-piano pieces on radio. He composed a Symph. (1972); *Overture* (1972); Wind Quintet (1973); Saxophone Quartet (1975); *Music I* for Winds and Timpani (1975); *Music II* for Strings, 3 Trumpets, 3 Trombones, and Percussion (1976; Baden-Baden, Oct. 20, 1979); *From "De zangen van Maldoror"* for Orch. (1976); *Alla marcia* for Tuba and 12 Instrumentalists (1977).

Wagenaar, Bernard, American composer and teacher, son of **Johan Wagenaar;** b. Arnhem, the Netherlands, July 18, 1894; d. York, Maine, May 19, 1971. He studied music with his father; violin with Gerard Veerman in Utrecht. In 1920 he came to the U.S.; was a violinist in the N.Y. Phil. (1921–23). He joined the Inst. of Musical Art in 1925, and remained with it when it became the Juilliard School of Music, teaching composition and orchestration.
WORKS: *Pieces of 8,* operatic comedy (1943; N.Y., 1944); Symph. No. 1 (N.Y., Oct. 7, 1928); *Divertimento* (Detroit, Nov. 28, 1929); *Sinfonietta* (N.Y., Jan. 16, 1930); Symph. No. 2 (N.Y., Nov. 10, 1932, Toscanini conducting); Symph. No. 3 (N.Y., Jan. 23, 1937, composer conducting); Violin Concerto (1940); Triple Concerto for Flute, Harp, Cello, and Orch. (N.Y., May 20, 1941, composer conducting); Symph. No. 4 (Boston, Dec. 16, 1949); *5 Tableaux* for Cello and Orch. (Amsterdam, Jan. 9, 1955); *3 Songs from the Chinese* (1921); Violin Sonata (1925); 3 string quartets; Piano Sonata; Sonatina for Cello and Piano; Concertino for 8 Instruments.
BIBLIOGRAPHY: D. Fuller, "Bernard Wagenaar," *Modern Music* (May 1944); *Modern Music . . . Analytic Index,* compiled by Wayne Shirley, ed. by W. and C. Lichtenwanger (N.Y., 1976; p. 223).

Wagenaar, Johan, Dutch organist and composer; b. Utrecht, Nov. 1, 1862; d. The Hague, June 17, 1941. He studied with Richard Hol in Utrecht (1875–85) and with H. von Herzogenberg in Berlin (1889); established himself as an organist at the Utrecht Cathedral; from 1887 to 1904 he was director of the Utrecht Music School; from 1919 to 1937, director of the Royal Cons. at The Hague.
WORKS: Operas: *De Doge van Venetie* (Utrecht, 1904) and *De Cid* (Utrecht, 1916); burlesque opera, *Jupiter Amans* (Scheveningen, 1925); symph. poems: *Levenszomer* (1901); *Saul and David* (1906); *Elverhöt* (1940); overtures: *Koning Jan* (1889); *Cyrano de Bergerac* (1905); *De getemde feeks* (1906); *Driekoningenavond* (1927); *De philosofische prinses* (1931); numerous choral works; songs; organ pieces.
BIBLIOGRAPHY: C. Backers, *Nederlandse Com-*

ponisten van 1400 tot op onze Tijd (The Hague, 1941; pp. 96–99).

Wagenmann, Josef Hermann, German singing teacher and writer; b. Engingen, May 11, 1876; d. Berlin, July 30, 1940. He studied jurisprudence in Heidelberg and Leipzig; then studied singing with various teachers in Italy; became a renowned singing teacher in Berlin; in 1934 was appointed prof. at the Academy for Church and School Music there. He publ. *Neue Ära der Stimmbildung für Singen und Sprechen* (1903); *Umsturz in der Stimmbildung* (1904; 2nd ed., 1922); *Lilli Lehmanns Geheimnis der Stimmbänder* (1905; 2nd ed., 1926); *Ein automatischer Stimmbildner* (1906); *Enrico Caruso und das Problem der Stimmbildung* (1911; 3rd ed., 1924); *Heinrich Knote* (1931).

Wagenseil, Georg Christoph, Austrian composer and theorist; b. Vienna, Jan. 29, 1715; d. there, March 1, 1777. He studied with J.J. Fux; was the music teacher of the Empress Maria Theresa and her children; in 1739 was appointed court composer; remained in the Imperial service until his death. He wrote many operas in Italian.
WORKS: Operas (all produced in Vienna): *La generosità trionfante* (1745); *Ariodante* (May 14, 1746); *La clemenza di Tito* (Oct. 15, 1746); *Alexander der Grosse in Indien* (July 7, 1748); *Il Siroe* (Oct. 4, 1748); *L'Olimpiade* (May 13, 1749); *Andromeda* (March 30, 1750); *Antigone* (May 13, 1750); *Armida placato* (August 28, 1750); *Euridice* (July 26, 1750); *Le Cacciatrici amanti* (Laxenburg, June 1755); *Demetrio* (1760); 3 oratorios; 30 symphs.; 27 harpsichord concertos; organ works. Two symphs. and a Trio Sonata are in Denkmäler der Tonkunst in Österreich, 31 (15.ii); a Divertimento was ed. by Blume. Wagenseil publ. the following: *Suavis, artificiose elaboratus concentus musicus, continens: 6 selectas parthias ad clavicembalum compositas* (1740); *18 Divertimenti di cembalo,* opp. 1–3; Divertimento for 2 Harpsichords; 2 divertimentos for Harpsichord, 2 Violins, and Cello, op. 5; 10 symphs. for Harpsichord, 2 Violins, and Cello, opp. 4, 7, 8; 6 violin sonatas, with Harpsichord, op. 6.
BIBLIOGRAPHY: K. Horwitz, *Wagenseil als Symphoniker* (Diss., Univ. of Vienna, 1906); W. Vetter, "G.C. Wagenseil, Ein Vorläufer Glucks," *Zeitschrift für Musikwissenschaft,* 8 (1926); idem, "Der Opernkomponist G.C. Wagenseil und sein Verhältnis zu Mozart und Gluck," in the "Hermann Abert-Gedenkschrift" (Halle, 1928); J. Pelikant, *Die Klavier-Werke Wagenseils* (Vienna, 1926); G. Hausswald, "Der Divertimento-Begriff bei G.C. Wagenseil," *Archiv für Musikwissenschaft* (1952); L. Kucaba, *The Symphonies of G.C. Wagenseil* (Diss., Boston Univ., 1967); H. Scholz-Michelitsch, *G.C. Wagenseil als Klavierkomponist: Eine Studie zu seinen zyklischen Soloklavierwerken* (Diss., Univ. of Vienna, 1967).

Wagenseil, Johann Christoph, German historian and librarian; b. Nuremberg, Nov. 26, 1633; d. Altdorf, Oct. 9, 1708. He publ. an important book, *De Sacri Rom. Imperii Libera Civitate Noribergensi Commentatio* (Altdorf, 1697), with a 140-page supplement (in German), *Buch von der Meister-Singer holdseligen Kunst: Anfang, Fortübung, Nutzbarkeiten und Lehr-Sätz,* containing poems and melodies by Frauenlob, Mügling, Marner, and Regenbogen; this section was the main literary source that Wagner used in *Die Meistersinger von Nürnberg.*
BIBLIOGRAPHY: K. Mey, *Der Meistergesang in Geschichte und Kunst* (2nd ed., 1901); H. Thompson, *Wagner & Wagenseil. A Source of Wagner's Opera "Die Meistersinger"* (London, 1927).

Waghalter, Ignatz, conductor and composer, b. Warsaw, March 15, 1882; d. New York, April 7, 1949. He studied in Berlin, where he became conductor of the Komische Oper (1907–11); then conducted in Essen (1911–12), and at the Deutsches Opernhaus in Berlin-Charlottenburg. In 1925 he succeeded Stransky as conductor of the State Symph. Orch. in N.Y. (for one season only); then returned to Berlin; in 1933 he went to Prague, and in 1934 to Vienna. He then went to America, settling in N.Y. in 1938.
WORKS: Operas: *Der Teufelsweg* (Berlin, 1911); *Mandragola* (Berlin, Jan. 23, 1914; N.Y., March 4, 1925); *Jugend* (Berlin, 1917); *Der späte Gast* (Berlin, 1922); *Sataniel* (Berlin, 1923); operettas: *Der Weiberkrieg* and *Wem gehört Helena?;* Violin Concerto; Violin Sonata; String Quartet; piano pieces.
BIBLIOGRAPHY: Hugo Leichtentritt, *Ignatz Waghalter* (N.Y., 1924).

Wagner, Cosima, wife of **Richard Wagner,** daughter of **Franz Liszt** and the Countess Marie d'Agoult; b. Bellaggio, on Lake Como, Dec. 24, 1837; d. Bayreuth, April 1, 1930. She received an excellent education in Paris; married **Hans von Bülow** on Aug. 18, 1857; there were 2 daughters of this marriage, Blandine and Daniela; the 3rd daughter, Isolde, was Wagner's child, as was the 4th, Eva, and the son, Siegfried. A divorce followed on July 18, 1870; the marriage to Wagner took place in a few weeks, on Aug. 25, 1870. A woman of high intelligence, practical sense, and imperious character, Cosima Wagner emerged after Wagner's death as a powerful personage in all affairs regarding the continuation of the Bayreuth Festivals, as well as the complex matters pertaining to the rights of performance of Wagner's works all over the world. She publ. her reminiscences of Liszt: *Franz Liszt, Ein Gedenkblatt von seiner Tochter* (Munich, 2nd ed., 1911).
BIBLIOGRAPHY: M. Strauss, *Wie ich Frau Cosima Wagner sehe* (Magdeburg, 1912); E. Schuré, *Femmes inspiratrices* (Paris, 1930); W. Siegfried, *Frau Cosima Wagner* (Stuttgart, 1930); F. Blei, *Gefährtinnen* (Berlin, 1931); R. Du Moulin-Eckart, *Cosima Wagner* (Munich, 1929; Eng. trans., in 2 vols., N.Y., 1930); M. von Waldberg, *Cosima Wagners Briefe an ihre Tochter Daniela von Bülow, 1866–85* (Stuttgart, 1933); L. Scalero, *Cosima Wagner* (Zürich, 1934); P. Pretzsch, *Cosima Wagner und H.S. Chamberlain im Briefwechsel, 1888–1908* (Leipzig, 1934); *Briefwechsel zwischen Cosima Wagner und Fürst Ernst zu Hohenlohe-Langenburg* (Stuttgart,

1937); M. von Millenkovich (M. Morold), *Cosima Wagner, Ein Lebensbild* (Leipzig, 1937); E. Thierbach, ed., *Die Briefe Cosima Wagners an Friedrich Nietzsche* (Weimar, 1938–40); Alice Hunt Sokoloff, *Cosima Wagner, Extraordinary Daughter of Franz Liszt* (N.Y., 1969).

Wagner, Georg Gottfried, German violinist; b. Mühlberg, April 5, 1698; d. Plauen, March 23, 1756. He studied with Kuhnau at the Thomasschule in Leipzig (1712–18); studied at the Univ. of Leipzig (1718–26); was a violinist in Bach's orch., and was recommended by Bach for the post of cantor at Plauen, which he held from 1726 to his death. He wrote numerous sacred works and instrumental compositions; his motet *Lob und Ehre* was misattributed to Bach by Breitkopf & Härtel (publ. 1819).
BIBLIOGRAPHY: B. Hammerschmidt, *G.G. Wagner* (Chemnitz, 1912).

Wagner, Gerrit Anthonie Alexander, Dutch conductor and composer; b. Amsterdam, March 8, 1862; d. Antwerp, Nov. 24, 1892. He studied with Brandts-Buys in Amsterdam and with Benoit and Blockx in Antwerp; became a choral conductor there. He wrote an oratorio, *Babylonische gevangenschap;* a symph. poem, *Zusterengelen;* much choral music; his promising career was terminated by an early death.

Wagner, Johanna, German soprano; b. Lohnde, near Hannover, Oct. 13, 1826; d. Würzburg, Oct. 16, 1894. She was a natural daughter of Lieutenant Bock von Wülfingen of Hannover, and was adopted by Richard Wagner's brother, Albert; was thus regarded as Wagner's niece. Of a precocious talent, she acted on the stage as a small child; through Wagner she obtained a position at the Dresden Opera when she was 17; produced an excellent impression as Agathe in *Der Freischütz,* and was engaged as a regular member. She studied the part of Elisabeth in *Tannhäuser* with Wagner, and sang it in the premiere of the opera on Oct. 19, 1845, when she was barely 19 years old. In 1846 she went to Paris for further study, with Mme. Viardot-Garcia (1846–48); then was engaged at the Hamburg Opera (1849) and finally at the court opera in Berlin (1850–61). In 1859 she married the district judge Jachmann. After 1862 she acted mainly on the dramatic stage, reappearing in opera at the Bayreuth Festival in 1876 in the parts of Schwertleite and the First Norn. In 1882 she settled in Munich as a singing teacher.
BIBLIOGRAPHY: J. Kapp and H. Jachmann, *Richard Wagner und seine erste "Elisabeth," Johanna Jachmann-Wagner* (Berlin, 1927; in Eng. as *Wagner and His First Elisabeth,* London, 1944).

Wagner, Josef Franz, Austrian composer of light music; b. Vienna, March 20, 1856; d. there, June 5, 1908. He was a popular leader of military bands in Vienna; produced the operetta *Der Herzbub* (Vienna, Feb. 7, 1895), which had little success, but achieved fame as the composer of the Austrian march *Under the Double Eagle,* which became a semi-official march of the Austro-Hungarian Empire.

Wagner, Joseph Frederick, American composer and conductor; b. Springfield, Mass., Jan. 9, 1900; d. Los Angeles, Oct. 12, 1974. He was educated at the Technical High School in Providence and studied piano and organ privately; then entered the New England Cons., where he studied composition with Frederick Converse; later took lessons in composition with Alfredo Casella in Boston in 1927, and with Nadia Boulanger in Paris in 1935; studied conducting with Pierre Monteux in Paris and Felix Weingartner in Basel, Switzerland. He was assistant director of music in Boston public schools (1923–44); taught at Boston Univ. (1929–40), Hunter College in N.Y. (1945–56), and Brooklyn College (1945–47). In 1925 he organized the Boston Civic Symph. Orch., which he conducted until 1944; subsequently was conductor of the Duluth Symph. Orch. (1947–50) and of the Orquesta Sinfónica Nacional de Costa Rica in San José (1950–54); was also a guest conductor in Helsinki, Stockholm, Washington, D.C., and Buffalo. In 1960 he settled in Hollywood; in 1961 was appointed a prof. at Pepperdine College in Los Angeles. His music is distinguished by excellent craftsmanship; it is set in a fairly advanced idiom, with bitonality as a frequent resource in his later works. Shortly before his death he completed the score of *Tribute to America* (Symph. No. 4) for Chorus, Soprano Solo, Narrator, and Orch., planned for the bicentennial year 1976, but never performed. Indeed, most performances of Joseph Wagner's orch. works were conducted by himself. Wistfully, he kept a file of rejection slips from conductors, arranged in alphabet cal order, from A to Z (from Abravanel to Zipper). A memorial brochure, *Joseph Wagner: A Retrospective of a Composer-Conductor,* edited by Lance Bowling, with an introductory article, "Joseph Wagner: The Most Undiscovered among American Composers," by Nicolas Slonimsky, was publ. in Lomita, Calif., in 1976.
WORKS: Opera, *New England Sampler* (Los Angeles, Feb. 26, 1965); ballets: *The Birthday of the Infanta,* after Oscar Wilde (1935) and *Hudson River Legend* (1941; Boston, March 1, 1944); *Miniature Concerto* for Piano and Orch. (1919; Providence, June 11, 1920; revised as *Concerto in G Minor;* New Brunswick, N.J., Aug. 3, 1930); *Rhapsody* for Piano, Clarinet, and Strings (1925); Symph. No. 1 (Rochester, N.Y., Oct. 19, 1944); Symph. No. 2 (1945; Wilmington, March 1, 1960); Symph. No. 3 (1951); Violin Concerto (1955); Sinfonietta No. 1 (1931); Sinfonietta No. 2 for String Orch. (1941); *Pastoral Costarricense* (1958); *Merlin and Sir Boss,* symph. tale for Concert Band, after Mark Twain's *A Connecticut Yankee* (1963); Concerto for Organ, Brass, and Percussion (1963); Harp Concerto (1964); Violin Sonata (1941); *Introduction and Scherzo* for Bassoon and Piano (1951); *Patterns of Contrast* for Wind Quartet (1959); *Fantasy Sonata* for Harp Solo (1963); *Preludes and Toccata* for Harp, Violin, and Cello (1964); *Fantasy and Fugue* for Woodwind Quartet

(1968); *Sonata of Sonnets* for Voice and Piano (1961); *12 Concert Preludes* for Organ (1974); for Piano: *Radio City Snapshots* (1945) and *Sonata with Differences* (1952); *David Jazz* for Men's Chorus, with Piano (1934); for Chorus: *Under Freedom's Flag* (1940) and *Ballad of Brotherhood* (1947); *Missa sacra* for Chorus, Mezzo-soprano, and Orch. (1952); *American Ballad* for Chorus a cappella (1963). He publ. 2 useful books: *Orchestration: A Practical Handbook* (N.Y., 1958) and *Band Scoring* (N.Y., 1960).

Wagner, Karl Jakob, German composer; b. Darmstadt, Feb. 22, 1772; d. there, Nov. 24, 1822. He was a French-horn player and conductor in the Darmstadt Orch.; studied theory with Abbé Vogler. He wrote 4 operas, all produced in Darmstadt: *Pygmalion* (1809); *Der Zahnarzt* (1810); *Siaph und Nitetis* (1811); *Chimene* (1821). He also wrote 2 symphs.; 4 overtures; trios for Violin, Flute, and Cello; duos for Flute and Violin; 40 horn duos; 3 violin sonatas; piano pieces.

Wagner, Peter (Joseph), eminent German musicologist; b. Kürenz, near Trier, Aug. 19, 1865; d. Freiburg, Switzerland, Oct. 17, 1931. He studied at the Univ. of Strasbourg; received his degree of Dr.Phil. with the dissertation *Palestrina als weltlicher Komponist* (1890); studied further in Berlin under Bellermann and Spitta; in 1893 he was appointed instructor of church music at the Univ. of Freiburg, Switzerland. In 1901 he established at the Univ. the Gregorianische Akademie for theoretical and practical study of plainsong, in which field he was an eminent authority. He was a member of the Papal Commission for the *Editio Vaticana* of the Roman Gradual, and was made a Papal Chamberlain. In the course of numerous visits to Spain he did valuable research on the Mozarabic liturgical chant.

WRITINGS: *Einführung in die gregorianischen Melodien* (1895); 2nd ed. in 3 parts: I. *Ursprung und Entwicklung der liturgischen Gesangsformen bis zum Ausgang des Mittelalters* (1901; 3rd ed., 1911; Eng. trans., 1907), II. *Neumenkunde* (1905; reprint, 1912), III. *Gregorianische Formenlehre; Eine choralische Stilkunde* (1921); *Das Freiburger Dreikönigspiel* (1903); *Über traditionellen Choral und traditionellen Choralvortrag* (1905); *Elemente des gregorianischen Gesanges* (1909; 2nd ed., 1916); *Geschichte der Messe* (vol. I [to 1600], 1913); *Einführung in die katholische Kirchenmusik* (1919). A Festschrift for him, ed. by K. Weinmann, was publ. in 1926.

Wagner, (Wilhelm) Richard, great German composer whose operas, written to his own librettos, have radically transformed the concept of stage music, postulating the inherent equality of drama and symph. accompaniment, and establishing the uninterrupted continuity of the action; b. Leipzig, May 22, 1813; d. Venice, Feb. 13, 1883. The antecedents of his family, and his own origin, are open to controversy. His father was a police registrar in Leipzig who died when Wagner was only 6 months old; his mother, Johanna (Rosine), née Pätz, was the daughter of a baker in Weissenfels; it is possible also that she was an illegitimate offspring of Prince Friedrich Ferdinand Constantin of Weimar. Eight months after her husband's death, Johanna Wagner married, on Aug. 28, 1814, the actor Ludwig Geyer. This hasty marriage generated speculation that Geyer may have been Wagner's real father; Wagner himself entertained this possibility, pointing out the similarity of his and Geyer's prominent noses; in the end he abandoned this surmise. The problem of Wagner's origin arose with renewed force after the triumph of the Nazi party in Germany, as Hitler's adoration of Wagner was put in jeopardy by suspicions that Geyer might have been Jewish and that if Wagner was indeed his natural son then he himself was tainted by Semitic blood. The phantom of Wagner's possible contamination with Jewish hemoglobins struck horror into the hearts of good Nazi biologists and archivists; they delved anxiously into Geyer's own ancestry, and much to the relief of Dr. Goebbels and other Nazi intellectuals, it was found that Geyer, like Wagner's nominal father, was the purest of Aryans; Wagner's possible illegitimate birth was of no concern to the racial tenets of the Nazi Weltanschauung.

Geyer was a member of the court theater in Dresden, and the family moved there in 1814. Geyer died on Sept. 30, 1821; in 1822 Wagner entered the Dresden Kreuzschule, where he remained a pupil until 1827. Carl Maria von Weber often visited the Geyer home; these visits exercised a beneficial influence on Wagner in his formative years. In 1825 he began to take piano lessons from a local musician named Humann, and also studied violin with Robert Sipp. Wagner showed strong literary inclinations, and under the spell of Shakespeare, wrote a tragedy, *Leubald.* In 1827 he moved with his mother back to Leipzig, where his uncle Adolf Wagner gave him guidance in his classical reading. In 1828 Wagner was enrolled in the Nikolaischule; while in school, he had lessons in harmony with Christian Gottlieb Müller, a violinist in the theater orch. In June 1830 Wagner entered the Thomasschule, where he began to compose; he wrote a String Quartet and some piano music; his *Overtüre* in B-flat major was performed at the Leipzig Theater on Dec. 24, 1830, under the direction of the famous musician Heinrich Dorn. Now determined to dedicate himself entirely to music, Wagner became a student of Theodor Weinlig, cantor of the Thomaskirche, from whom he received a thorough training in counterpoint and composition. Wagner's first publ. work was a Piano Sonata in B-flat major, to which he assigned the opus number 1; it was brought out by the prestigious publishing house of Breitkopf & Härtel in 1832. He then wrote an overture to *König Enzio,* which was performed at the Leipzig Theater on Feb. 19, 1832; it was followed by an Overture in C major, which was presented at a Gewandhaus concert on April 30, 1832. Wagner's first major orch. work, a Symph. in C major, was performed at a Prague Cons. concert in Nov. 1832; on Jan. 10, 1833, it was played by the Gewandhaus Orch. in Leipzig; he was 19 years old at the time. In 1832 he wrote an opera, *Die Hochzeit,* after J.G. Büsching's *Ritterzeit und Ritterwesen;* an introduction, a septet, and a chorus from this work are extant. Early in 1833 he began work on *Die Feen,* to a libretto after Carlo Gozzi's *La Donna serpente.* Upon completion of *Die Feen* in Jan. 1834, he offered the score to the Leipzig Theater, but it was rejected. In June 1834 he began to sketch out a new opera, *Das Liebesverbot,* after Shakespeare's play *Measure for Measure.* In July 1834 Wagner obtained the position of music director with Heinrich Bethmann's theater company, based in Magdeburg; he made his debut in Bad Lauchstadt, conducting Mozart's *Don Giovanni.* On March 29, 1836, he led in Magdeburg the premiere of his opera *Das Liebesverbot,* presented under the title *Die Novize von Palermo.* Bethmann's company soon went out of business; Wagner, who was by that time deeply involved with Christine Wilhelmine ("Minna") Planer, an actress with the company, followed her to Königsberg, where they were married on Nov. 24, 1836. In Königsberg he composed the overture *Rule Britannia;* on April 1, 1837, he was appointed music director of the Königsberg town theater. His marital affairs suffered a setback when Minna left him for a rich businessman by the name of Dietrich. In Aug. 1837 Wagner went to Riga as music director of the theater there; coincidentally, Minna's sister was engaged as a singer at the same theater; Minna soon joined her, and became reconciled with Wagner. In Riga Wagner worked on his new opera, *Rienzi, der letzte der Tribunen,* after a popular novel by Bulwer-Lytton.

In March 1839 he lost his position in Riga; he and Minna, burdened by debts, left town to seek their fortune elsewhere. In their passage by sea from Pillau they encountered a fierce storm, and the ship was forced to drop anchor in the Norwegian fjord of Sandwike. They made their way to London, and then set out for Boulogne; there Wagner met Meyerbeer, who gave him a letter of recommendation to the director of the Paris Opéra. He arrived in Paris with Minna in Sept. 1839, and remained there until 1842. He was forced to eke out a meager subsistence by making piano arrangements of operas and writing occasional articles for the *Gazette Musicale.* In Jan. 1840 he completed his Overture to *Faust* (later revised as *Eine Faust-Ouvertüre*). Soon he found himself in dire financial straits; he owed money which he could not repay, and on Oct. 28, 1840, he was confined in debtors' prison; he was released on Nov. 17, 1840. The conditions of his containment were light, and he was able to leave prison on certain days. In the meantime he had completed the libretto for *Der fliegende Holländer;* he submitted it to the director of the Paris Opéra, but the director had already commissioned another composer to write an opera on the same subject; he was willing, however, to buy the libretto, and offered to pay 500 French francs for it; Wagner accepted the offer. The libretto was later trans. into French and was used by Pierre-Louis Dietsch for his own opera under the title *Le Vaisseau fantôme,* which was produced at the Paris Opéra on Nov. 9, 1842.

In 1842 Wagner received the welcome news from Dresden that his opera *Rienzi* had been accepted for production; it was staged there on Oct. 20, 1842, with considerable success. *Der fliegende Holländer* was also accepted by Dresden, and Wagner conducted its first performance there on Jan. 2, 1843. On Feb. 2 of that year, Wagner was named 2nd Hofkapellmeister in Dresden, where he conducted a large repertoire of Classical operas, among them *Don Giovanni, Le nozze di Figaro, Die Zauberflöte, Fidelio,* and *Der Freischütz.* In 1846 he conducted a memorable performance in Dresden of Beethoven's 9th Symph. In Dresden he led the prestigious choral society Liedertafel, for which he wrote several works, including the "biblical scene" *Das Liebesmahl der Apostel.* He was also preoccupied during those years in working on the score and music for *Tannhäuser,* completing it on April 13, 1845. He conducted its first performance in Dresden on Oct. 19, 1845. He subsequently revised the score, which was staged to better advantage there on Aug. 1, 1847. Concurrently, he began work on *Lohengrin,* which he completed on April 28, 1848. Wagner's efforts to have his works publ. failed, leaving him again in debt. Without waiting for further performances of his operas which had already been presented to the public, he drew up the first prose outline of *Der Nibelungen-Mythus als Entwurf zu einem Drama,* the prototype of the epic *Ring* cycle; in Nov. 1848 he began work on the poem for *Siegfrieds Tod.* At that time he joined the revolutionary Vaterlandsverein, and was drawn into active participation in the movement, culminating in an open uprising in May 1849. An order was issued for his arrest, and he had to leave Dresden; he made his way to Weimar, where he found a cordial reception from Liszt; he then proceeded to Vienna, where a Prof. Widmann lent him his own passport so that Wagner could cross the border of Saxony on his way to Zürich; there he made his home in July 1849; Minna joined him there a few months later. Shortly before leaving Dresden Wagner had sketched 2 dramas, *Jesus von Nazareth* and *Achilleus;* both remained unfinished. In Zürich he wrote a number of essays expounding his philosophy of art: *Die Kunst und die Revolution* (1849), *Das Kunstwerk der Zukunft* (1849), *Kunst und Klima* (1850), *Oper und Drama* (1851; revised 1868), and *Eine Mitteilung an meine Freunde* (1851). The ideas expressed in *Das Kunstwerk der Zukunft* gave rise to the description of Wagner's operas as "music of the future" by his opponents; they were also described as Gesamtkunstwerk, "total artwork," by his admirers. Wagner rejected both descriptions as distortions of his real views. He was equally opposed to the term "music drama," which nevertheless became an accepted definition for all of his operas.

In Feb. 1850 Wagner was again in Paris; there he fell in love with a Jessie Laussot, the wife of a wine merchant; however, she eventually left Wagner, and he returned to Minna in Zürich. On Aug. 28, 1850, Liszt conducted the successful premiere of *Lohengrin* in Weimar. In 1851 Wagner wrote the verse text of *Der junge Siegfried,* and prose sketches for *Das Rheingold* and *Die Walküre.* In June 1852 he finished the text of *Die Walküre* and of *Das Rhein-*

gold; he completed the entire libretto of *Der Ring des Nibelungen* on Dec. 15, 1852, and it was privately printed in 1853. In Nov. 1853 Wagner began composition of the music for *Das Rheingold,* completing the full score on Sept. 26, 1854. In June 1854 he commenced work on the music of *Die Walküre,* which he finished on March 20, 1856. In 1854 he became friendly with a wealthy Zürich merchant, Otto Wesendonck, and his wife, Mathilde. Wesendonck was willing to give Wagner a substantial loan, to be repaid out of his performance rights. The situation became complicated when Wagner developed an affection for Mathilde, which in all probability remained Platonic. But he set to music 5 lyric poems written by Mathilde herself; the album was publ. as the *Wesendonk-Lieder* in 1857. In 1855 Wagner conducted a series of 8 concerts with the Phil. Society of London (March 12–June 25). His performances were greatly praised by English musicians, and he had the honor of meeting Queen Victoria, who invited him to her lodge at the intermission of his 7th concert. In June 1856 Wagner made substantial revisions in the last dramas of *Der Ring des Nibelungen,* changing their titles to *Siegfried* and *Götterdämmerung.* Throughout these years he was preoccupied with writing a new opera, *Tristan und Isolde,* permeated with the dual feelings of love and death. In April 1857 he prepared the first sketch of *Parzival* (later titled *Parsifal*). In 1858 Wagner moved to Venice, where he completed the full score of the 2nd act of *Tristan und Isolde.* The Dresden authorities, acting through their Austrian confederates and still determined to bring Wagner to trial as a revolutionary, pressured Venice to expel Wagner from its territory. Once more Wagner took refuge in Switzerland; he decided to stay in Lucerne; while there he completed the score of *Tristan und Isolde,* on Aug. 6, 1859.

In Sept. 1859 he moved to Paris, where Minna joined him. In 1860 he conducted 3 concerts of his music at the Théâtre-Italien. Napoleon III became interested in his work, and in March 1860 ordered the director of the Paris Opéra to produce Wagner's opera *Tannhäuser;* after considerable work, revisions, and a trans. into French, it was given at the Opéra on March 13, 1861. It proved to be a fiasco, and Wagner withdrew the opera after 3 performances. For some reason the Jockey Club of Paris led a vehement protest against Wagner; the critics also joined in this opposition, mainly because the French audiences were not accustomed to the mystically romantic, heavily Germanic operatic music. Invectives hurled against Wagner by the Paris press make extraordinary reading; the comparison of Wagner's music with the sound produced by a domestic cat walking down the keyboard of the piano was one of the favorite critical devices. The French caricaturists exercised their wit by picturing Wagner in the act of hammering a poor listener's ear. A Wagner "Schimpflexikon" was compiled by Wilhelm Tappert and publ. in 1877 in the hope of putting Wagner's detractors to shame, but they would not be pacified; the amount of black bile poured on Wagner even after he had attained the stature of celebrity is incredible for its grossness

and vulgarity. Hanslick used his great literary gift and a flair for a striking simile to damn Wagner as a purveyor of cacophony. Oscar Wilde added his measure of wit. "I like Wagner's music better than anybody's," he remarked in *The Picture of Dorian Gray.* "It is so loud that one can talk the whole time without people hearing what one says." In an amazing turnabout, Nietzsche, a worshipful admirer of Wagner, publ. a venomous denunciation of his erstwhile idol in *Der Fall Wagner,* in which he vesuviated in a sulfuric eruption of righteous wrath; Wagner made music itself sick, he proclaimed; but at the time Nietzsche himself was already on the borderline of madness.

Politically, Wagner's prospects began to improve; on July 22, 1860, he was informed of a partial amnesty by the Saxon authorities. In Aug. 1860 he visited Baden-Baden, in his first visit to Germany in 11 years. Finally, on March 18, 1862, he was granted a total amnesty, which allowed him access to Saxony. In Nov. 1861 Wesendonck had invited Wagner to Venice; free from political persecution, he could now go there without fear. While in Venice he returned to a scenario he had prepared in Marienbad in 1845 for a comic opera, *Die Meistersinger von Nürnberg.* In Feb. 1862 he moved to Biebrich, where he began composing the score for *Die Meistersinger.* Minna, after a brief period of reconciliation with Wagner, left him, settling in Dresden, where she died in 1866. In order to repair his financial situation, Wagner accepted a number of concert appearances, traveling as an orch. conductor to Vienna, Prague, St. Petersburg, Moscow, and other cities (1862–63). In 1862 he gave in Vienna a private reading of *Die Meistersinger.* It is said that the formidable Vienna critic Hanslick was angered when he found out that Wagner had caricatured him in the part of Beckmesser in *Die Meistersinger* (the original name of the character was Hans Lick), and he let out his discomfiture in further attacks on Wagner.

Wagner's fortunes changed spectacularly in 1864 when young King Ludwig II of Bavaria ascended the throne and invited Wagner to Munich with the promise of unlimited help in carrying out his various projects. In return, Wagner composed the *Huldigungsmarsch,* which he dedicated to his royal patron. The publ. correspondence between Wagner and the King is extraordinary in its display of mutual admiration, gratitude, and affection; still, difficulties soon developed when the Bavarian Cabinet told Ludwig that his lavish support of Wagner's projects threatened the Bavarian economy. Ludwig was forced to advise Wagner to leave Munich. Wagner took this advice as an order, and late in 1865 he went to Switzerland. A very serious difficulty arose also in Wagner's emotional life, when he became intimately involved with Liszt's daughter Cosima, wife of Hans von Bülow, the famous conductor and an impassioned proponent of Wagner's music. On April 10, 1865, Cosima Bülow gave birth to Wagner's daughter, whom he named Isolde after the heroine of his opera which Hans von Bülow was preparing for performance in Munich. Its premiere took place with great acclaim on June 10, 1865, 2 months after the birth of Isolde, with Bülow conducting. During the summer of 1865 Wagner prepared the prose sketch of *Parzival,* and began to dictate his autobiography, *Mein Leben,* to Cosima. In Jan. 1866 he resumed the composition of *Die Meistersinger;* he settled in a villa in Tribschen, on Lake Lucerne, where Cosima joined him permanently in Nov. 1868. Wagner completed the full score of *Die Meistersinger* on Oct. 24, 1867. On June 21, 1868, Hans von Bülow conducted its premiere in Munich in the presence of King Ludwig, who sat in the royal box with Wagner. A son, significantly named Siegfried, was born to Cosima and Wagner on June 6, 1869. On Sept. 22, 1869, *Das Rheingold* was produced in Munich. On June 26, 1870, *Die Walküre* was staged there. On July 18, 1870, Cosima and Hans von Bülow were divorced, and on Aug. 25, 1870, Wagner and Cosima were married in Lucerne. In Dec. 1870 Wagner wrote the *Siegfried Idyll,* based on the themes from his opera; it was performed in their villa in Bayreuth on Christmas morning, the day after Cosima's birthday, as a surprise for her. In 1871 Wagner wrote the *Kaisermarsch* to mark the victorious conclusion of the Franco-German War; he conducted it in the presence of Kaiser Wilhelm I at a concert in the Royal Opera House in Berlin on May 5, 1871.

On May 12 of that year, while in Leipzig, Wagner made public his plans for realizing his cherished dream of building his own theater in Bayreuth for the production of the entire cycle of *Der Ring des Nibelungen.* In Dec. 1871 the Bayreuth town council offered him a site for a proposed Festspielhaus; on May 22, 1872, the cornerstone was laid; Wagner commemorated the event by conducting a performance of Beethoven's 9th Symph. (this was Wagner's 59th birthday). In 1873 Wagner began to build his own home in Bayreuth, which he called "Wahnfried," i.e., "Free from Delusion." In order to complete the building of the Festspielhaus, Wagner appealed to King Ludwig for additional funds. Ludwig gave him 100,000 talers for this purpose. Now the dream of Wagner's life was realized. Between June and Aug. 1876 *Der Ring des Nibelungen* went through 3 rehearsals; King Ludwig attended the final dress rehearsals; the official premiere of the cycle took place on Aug. 13, 14, 16, and 17, 1876, under the direction of Hans Richter. Kaiser Wilhelm I made a special journey from Berlin to attend the performances of *Das Rheingold* and *Die Walküre.* In all, 3 complete productions of the *Ring* cycle were given between Aug. 13 and Aug. 30, 1876. Ludwig was faithful to the end to Wagner, whom he called "my divine friend." In his castle Neuschwanstein he installed architectural representations of scenes from Wagner's operas. Soon Ludwig's mental deterioration became obvious to everyone, and he was committed to an asylum. There, on June 13, 1883, he overpowered the psychiatrist escorting him on a walk and dragged him to his death in the Starnberg Lake, drowning himself as well. Ludwig survived Wagner by 4 months.

The spectacles in Bayreuth attracted music-lovers and notables from all over the world. Even those who were not partial to Wagner's ideas or appreciative of his music went to Bayreuth out of curiosity.

Tchaikovsky was one such skeptical visitor. Despite world success and fame, Wagner still labored under financial difficulties. He even addressed a letter to an American dentist practicing in Dresden (who also treated Wagner's teeth) in which he tried to interest him in arranging Wagner's permanent transfer to the U.S. He voiced disillusionment in his future prospects in Germany, and said he would be willing to settle in America provided a sum of $1 million would be guaranteed to him by American bankers, and a comfortable estate for him and his family could be found in a climatically clement part of the country. Nothing came of this particular proposal. He did establish an American connection when he wrote, for a fee of $5,000, a *Grosser Festmarsch* for the observance of the U.S. centennial in 1876, dedicated to the "beautiful young ladies of America." In the middle of all this, Wagner became infatuated with Judith Gautier; their affair lasted for about 2 years (1876–78). Wagner completed the full score of *Parsifal* (as it was now called) on Jan. 13, 1882, in Palermo. It was performed for the first time at the Bayreuth Festival on July 26, 1882, followed by 15 subsequent performances. At the final performance, on Aug. 29, 1882, Wagner stepped to the podium in the last act and conducted the work to its close; this was his last appearance as a conductor. He went to Venice in Sept. 1882 for a period of rest (he had angina pectoris). Early in the afternoon of Feb. 13, 1883, he suffered a massive heart attack, and died in Cosima's presence. His body was interred in a vault in the garden of his Wahnfried villa in Bayreuth.

Wagner's role in music history is immense. Not only did he create works of great beauty and tremendous brilliance, but he generated an entirely new concept of the art of music, exercising an influence on generations of composers all over the globe. Richard Strauss extended Wagner's grandiose vision to symph. music, fashioning the form of a tone poem that uses leading motifs and vivid programmatic description of the scenes portrayed in his music. Even Rimsky-Korsakov, far as he stood from Wagner's ideas of musical composition, reflected the spirit of *Parsifal* in his own religious opera, *The Legend of the City of Kitezh.* Schoenberg's first significant work, *Die verklärte Nacht,* is Wagnerian in its color. Lesser composers, unable to escape Wagner's magic domination, attempted to follow Wagner literally by writing trilogies and tetralogies on a parallel plan with Wagner's *Ring;* a pathetic example is the career of August Bungert, who wrote 2 operatic cycles using Homer's epics as the source of his libretti. Wagner's reform of opera was incomparably more far-reaching in aim, import, and effect than that of Gluck, whose main purpose was to counteract the arbitrary predominance of the singers; this goal Wagner accomplished through insistence upon the dramatic truth of his music. When he rejected traditional opera, he did so in the conviction that such an artificial form could not serve as a basis for true dramatic expression. In its place he gave the world a new form and new techniques. So revolutionary was Wagner's art that conductors and singers had to undergo special training in the new style of interpretation in order to perform his works. Thus Wagner became the founder of interpretative conducting and of a new school of dramatic singing, so that such terms as "Wagnerian tenor" and "Wagnerian soprano" became a part of the musical vocabulary.

In his many essays and declarations Wagner condemns the illogical plan of Italian opera and French grand opera. To quote his own words, "The mistake in the art-form of the opera consists in this, that a means of expression (music) was made the end, and the end to be expressed (the drama) was made a means." The choice of subjects assumes utmost importance in Wagner's esthetics. He wrote: "The subject treated by the word-tone poet [*Worttondichter*] is entirely human, freed from all convention and from everything historically formal." The new artwork creates its own artistic form; continuous thematic development of basic motifs becomes a fundamental procedure for the logical cohesion of the drama; these highly individualized generating motifs, appearing singly, in bold relief, or subtly varied and intertwined with other motifs, present the ever-changing soul states of the characters of the drama, and form the connecting links for the dramatic situations of the total artwork, in a form of musical declamation which Wagner described as "Sprechsingen." Characters in Wagner's stage works become themselves symbols of such soul states, so that even mythical gods, magic-workers, heroic horses, and speaking birds become expressions of eternal verities, illuminating the human behavior. It is for this reason that Wagner selected in most of his operas figures that reflect philosophical ideas. Yet, this very solemnity of Wagner's great images on the stage bore the seeds of their own destruction in a world governed by different esthetic principles. Thus it came to pass that the Wagnerian domination of the musical stage suddenly lost its power with changes in human society and esthetic codes. Spectators and listeners were no longer interested in solving artistic puzzles on the stage. A demand for human simplicity arose against Wagnerian heroic complexity. The public at large found greater enjoyment in the realistic nonsense of Verdi's romantic operas than in the unreality of symbolic truth in Wagner's operas. By the 2nd quarter of the 20th century, few if any composers tried to imitate Wagner; all at once his grandeur and animation became an unnatural and asphyxiating constraint.

In the domain of melody, harmony, and orchestration, Wagner's art was as revolutionary as was his total artwork on the stage. He introduced the idea of an endless melody, a continuous flow of diatonic and chromatic tones; the tonality became fluid and uncertain, producing an impression of unattainability, so that the listener accustomed to Classical modulatory schemes could not easily feel the direction toward the tonic; the Prelude to *Tristan und Isolde* is a classic example of such fluidity of harmonic elements. The use of long unresolved dominant-ninth-chords and the dramatic tremolos of diminished-seventh-chords contributed to this state of musical uncertainty, which disturbed the

critics and the audiences alike. But Wagnerian harmony also became the foundation of the new method of composition that adopted a free flow of modulatory progressions. Without Wagner the chromatic idioms of the 20th century could not exist. In orchestration, too, Wagner introduced great innovations; he created new instruments, such as the so-called "Wagner tuba," and he increased his demands on the virtuosity of individual orch. players. The vertiginous flight of the bassoon to the high E in the Overture to *Tannhäuser* could not have been attempted before the advent of Wagner.

An 1869 cartoon issued by G. Schirmer in N.Y., captioned "The Music of the Future," depicts a conductor leading an orch. of desperate musicians, goats, cats, and other animals; a discarded score at the conductor's feet proclaims, "Wagner not to be played much till 1995." The prophecy may well come true, not because of the incomprehensibility of Wagner's music but, to the contrary, because of its lack of interest to listeners. But will Wagner's music be returned to favor even in 1995? The *Ride of the Walküre*, the *Rienzi Overture*, the *Tannhäuser Bacchanale*, which were the pabulum of concertgoers early in the century, have practically disappeared from orch. programs.

Wagner became the target of political contention during World War I when audiences in the Allied countries associated his sonorous works with German imperialism. An even greater obstacle to further performances of Wagner's music arose with the rise of Hitler. Hitler ordered the slaughter of millions of Jews; he was an enthusiastic admirer of Wagner, who himself entertained anti-Semitic notions; *ergo*, Wagner was guilty by association of mass murder. Can art be separated from politics, particularly when politics become murderous? Jewish musicians in Tel Aviv refused to play the Prelude to *Tristan und Isolde* when it was put on the program of a symph. concert under the direction of an American conductor, and booed him for his intention to inflict Wagner on Wagner's philosophical victims.

Several periodicals dealing with Wagner were publ. in Germany and elsewhere; Wagner himself began issuing *Bayreuther Blätter* in 1878 as an aid to understanding his operas; this journal continued publication until 1938. Remarkably enough, a French periodical, *Revue Wagnérienne*, began appearing in 1885, at a time when French composers realized the tremendous power of Wagnerian esthetics; it was publ. sporadically for a number of years. A Wagner Society in London publ., from 1888 to 1895, a quarterly journal entitled, significantly, *The Meister*.

WORKS: OPERAS AND MUSIC DRAMAS: *Die Hochzeit* (1832–33; partly destroyed; introduction, septet, and chorus perf. at the Neues Theater, Leipzig, Feb. 13, 1938); *Die Feen,* romantische Oper (1833–34; Königliches Hof- und Nationaltheater, Munich, June 29, 1888, Fischer conducting); *Das Liebesverbot, oder Die Novize von Palermo,* grosse komische Oper (1834–35; Magdeburg, March 29, 1836, composer conducting); *Rienzi, der Letzte der Tribunen,* grosse tragische Oper (1837–40; Königliches Hoftheater,

Dresden, Oct. 20, 1842, Reissiger conducting; revised 1843); *Der fliegende Holländer,* romantische Oper (1841; Königliches Hoftheater, Dresden, Jan. 2, 1843, composer conducting; reorchestrated in 1846, then revised in 1852 and 1860); *Tannhäuser und der Sängerkrieg auf Wartburg,* grosse romantische Oper (first titled *Der Venusberg;* "Dresden" version, 1842–45; Königliches Hoftheater, Dresden, Oct. 19, 1845, composer conducting; revised 1845–47; "Paris" version, a revision with additions and a French trans., 1860–61; Opéra, Paris, March 13, 1861, Dietsch conducting; final version, with a German trans. of the French revision and additions, 1865; Königliches Hof- und Nationaltheater, Munich, March 5, 1865); *Lohengrin,* romantische Oper (1845–48; Hoftheater, Weimar, Aug. 28, 1850, Liszt conducting); *Tristan und Isolde* (1856–59; Königliches Hof- und Nationaltheater, Munich, June 10, 1865, Bülow conducting); *Die Meistersinger von Nürnberg* (first sketch, 1845; 1861–67; Königliches Hof- und Nationaltheater, Munich, June 21, 1868, Bülow conducting); *Der Ring des Nibelungen,* Bühnenfestspiel für drei Tage und einen Vorabend (first prose outline as *Der Nibelungen-Mythus als Entwurf zu einem Drama,* 1848; Vorabend: *Das Rheingold,* 1851–54; Königliches Hof- und Nationaltheater, Munich, Sept. 22, 1869, Wüllner conducting; erster Tag: *Die Walküre,* 1851–56; Königliches Hof- und Nationaltheater, Munich, June 26, 1870, Wüllner conducting; zweiter Tag: *Siegfried,* first titled *Der junge Siegfried;* 1851–52, 1857, 1864–65, and 1869; Festspielhaus, Bayreuth, Aug. 16, 1876, Richter conducting; dritter Tag: *Götterdämmerung,* first titled *Siegfrieds Tod;* 1848–52 and 1869–74; Festspielhaus, Bayreuth, Aug. 17, 1876, Richter conducting; first complete perf. of the *Ring* cycle, Festspielhaus, Bayreuth, Aug. 13, 14, 16, and 17, 1876, Richter conducting); *Parsifal,* Bühnenweihfestspiel (first titled *Parzival;* first sketch, 1857; 1865 and 1877–82; Festspielhaus, Bayreuth, July 26, 1882, Levi conducting).

FOR ORCH.: Overture in B-flat major, the *Paukenschlag-Ouvertüre* (Leipzig, Dec. 24, 1830; not extant); Overture to Schiller's *Die Braut von Messina* (1830; not extant); Overture in C major (1830; not extant); Overture in D minor (Leipzig, Dec. 25, 1831); Overture in E-flat major (1831; not extant); Overture to Raupach's *König Enzio,* in E minor (Leipzig, Feb. 17, 1832); Overture in C major (Leipzig, April 30, 1832); Symph. in C major (Prague, Nov. 1832); Symph. in E major (1834; fragment); Overture to Apel's *Columbus,* in E-flat major (Magdeburg, Feb. 16, 1835); Overture *Polonia,* in C major (begun 1832, finished 1836); Overture *Rule Britannia,* in D major (1837); music for Singer's *Die letzte Heidenverschwörung in Preussen* (1837; fragment); Overture to Goethe's *Faust* (1840; reorchestrated 1843–44; Dresden, July 22, 1844; revised and reorchestrated as *Eine Faust-Ouvertüre,* 1855; Zürich, Jan. 23, 1855); *Trauermusik* for Wind Instruments, after motifs from Weber's *Euryanthe* (Dresden, Dec. 14, 1844, for the reburial ceremony of Weber's remains); *Träume* for Violin and Small Orch. (Zürich, Dec. 23, 1857); *Huldigungsmarsch* (first version, for Military Band, Munich, Oct. 5,

1864; 2nd version, for Large Orch., completed by Raff); *Siegfried Idyll* for Small Orch. (Tribschen, Dec. 25, 1870); *Kaisermarsch* (Berlin, May 5, 1871); *Grosser Festmarsch zur Eröffnung der hundertjährigen Gedenkfeier der Unabhängigkeitserklärung der vereinigten Staaten von Nord-Amerika* (also known as *The American Centennial March;* Philadelphia, May 10, 1876).—Also a projected orch. work in E minor (1830?; fragment); a scene for a pastoral play after Goethe's *Laune der Verliebten* (1830?); *Entreacte tragique* No. 1, in D major (1832?; fragment); *Entreacte tragique* No. 2, in C minor (1832?; sketch).

CHORAL WORKS: *Neujahrs-Kantate* for Mixed Chorus, and Orch. (Magdeburg, Dec. 31, 1834; arranged with a new text by Peter Cornelius as *Künstlerweihe,* and produced at Bayreuth on Wagner's 60th birthday, May 22, 1873; *Nicolai Volkshymne* for Tenor or Soprano, Mixed Chorus, and Orch. (Riga, Nov. 21, 1837); *Descendons, descendons* for Mixed Chorus, for *La Descente de la courtille* (1840); *Weihegruss zur feierlichen Enthüllung des Denkmals Königs Friedrich August I ("des Gerechten") von Sachsen (Der Tag erscheint)* for Men's Chorus a cappella (1843; *Gesang zur Enthüllung des Denkmals Sr. Mag. des hochseligen Königs Friedrich August des Gerechten am 7. Juni 1843* for Men's Chorus and Brass; for the unveiling of the statue of King Friedrich August of Saxony, Dresden, June 7, 1843); *Das Liebesmahl der Apostel,* biblical scene for Men's Chorus and Orch. (Dresden, July 6, 1843); *Gruss seiner Treuen an Friedrich August den Geliebten (Im treuen Sachsenland)* for Men's Chorus a cappella (Dresden, Aug. 12, 1843; for the return from England of King Friedrich August of Saxony); *Hebt an den Sang (An Webers Grabe)* for Men's Chorus a cappella (Dresden, Dec. 15, 1844; for the reburial ceremony of Weber's remains); *Wahlspruch für die deutsche Feuerwehr (Treue sei unsre Zier)* (1869); *Kinderkatechismus zu Kosels Geburtstag* for 4 High Voices (1873; orchestrated 1874).—Also a scene and aria for Soprano and Orch. (1832; not extant); "Doch jetzt wohin ich blicke," aria for Tenor and Orch. for Marschner's opera *Der Vampyr* (1833); aria for Bass and Orch. for Weigl's opera *Die Schweizerfamilie* (1837; not extant); "Sanfte Wehmut will sich regen," aria for Bass and Orch. for Blum's singspiel *Marie, Max und Michel* (Riga, Sept. 1, 1837); "Norma il prédesse," aria for Bass, Male Chorus, and Orch. for Bellini's opera *Norma* (1839).

FOR PIANO: Sonata in D minor (1829; not extant); Sonata in F minor (1829; not extant); *Doppelfuge* (1831?; 103 bars, with corrections in Weinlig's hand); Sonata in B-flat major, for 4-hands (1831; not extant); Sonata in B-flat major, op. 1 (1831); *Fantasie* in F-sharp minor, op. 3 (1831); *Polonaise* in D major (1831–32); *Polonaise* in D major, for 4-hands, op. 2 (1832?); Sonata in A major, op. 4 (1832); *Albumblatt (Lied ohne Worte)* in E major (1840); Polka in G major (1853); *Eine Sonate für das Album von Frau M*[athilde]. *W*[esendonck]. in A-flat major (1853); *Züricher Vielliebchen: Walzer, Polka oder sonst was* in E-flat major (1854); *Albumblatt, In das Album der Fürstin M*[etternich]. in C major (1861);

Ankunft bei den schwarzen Schwänen (Albumblatt for Countess Pourtalès) in A-flat major (1861); *Albumblatt für Frau Betty Schott* in E-flat major (1875).

SONGS: *Sieben Kompositionen zu Goethes Faust,* op. 5: 1, *Lied der Soldaten (Burgen mit hohen Mauern);* 2, *Bauer unter der Linde (Der Schäfter putzte sich zum Tanz);* 3, *Branders Lied (Es war eine Ratt im Kellernest);* 4, *Lied des Mephistopheles (Es war einmal ein König);* 5, *Lied Des Mephistopheles (Was machst du mir vor Liebchens Tür);* 6, *Gretchen am Spinnrade (Meine Ruh ist hin);* 7, *Melodram Gretchens (Ach neige, du Schmerzenreiche)* (1831; revised 1832); *Glockentöne* (1832; not extant); *Carnevalslied* from *Das Liebesverbot* (1835–36); *Der Tannenbaum* (1838); *Tout n'est qu'images fugitives* (1839); *3 mélodies:* 1, *Dors, mon enfant;* 2, *Mignonne;* 3, *L'Attente* (1839); *Adieux de Marie Stuart* (1840); *Les Deux Grenadiers,* to the poem by Heine (1840); *Gruss seiner Treuen an Friedrich August den Geliebten (Im treuen Sachsenland)* (a version for Baritone; 1844); *5 Gedichte für eine Frauenstimme (Wesendonk-Lieder):* 1, *Der Engel* (1857); 2, *Stehe still* (1858); 3, *Im Treibhaus* (1858); 4, *Schmerzen* (1857); 5, *Träume* (1857); *Scherzlied für Louis Kraft* (1871); also *Extase* (1839; fragment) and *La Tombe dit à la rose* (1839; fragment).

ARRANGEMENTS AND EDITIONS: Piano score of Beethoven's 9th Symph. (1830; unpubl.); Piano score of J. Haydn's Symph. No. 103, in E-flat major (1831–32; not extant); Aria from Bellini's *Il Pirata,* as orchestrated from the piano score for use in *La Straniera* (1833); arrangement of vocal score for Donizetti's *La Favorite* (1840) and *L'elisir d'amore* (1840); arrangement of vocal score for Halévy's *La Reine de Chypre* (1841) and *Le Guitarrero* (1841); new trans. and new close to the overture of Gluck's *Iphigénie en Aulide* (1846–47; Dresden, Feb. 22, 1847); Palestrina's *Stabat Mater,* with indications for performance (Dresden, March 8, 1848); Mozart's *Don Giovanni,* version of dialogues and recitatives and, in parts, new trans. (Zürich, Nov. 8, 1850; not extant).

WRITINGS: Wagner devoted a large amount of his enormous productive activity to writing. Besides the dramatic works he set to music, he also wrote the following: *Leubald. Ein Trauerspiel* (1826–28); *Die hohe Braut, oder Bianca und Giuseppe,* 4-act tragic opera (prose scenario, 1836 and 1842; music composed by Johann Kittl and produced as *Bianca und Giuseppe, oder Die Franzosen vor Nizza* in Prague, 1848); *Männerlist grösser als Frauenlist, oder Die glückliche Bärenfamilie,* 2-act comic opera (libretto, 1837; some music completed); *Eine Pilgerfahrt zu Beethoven,* novella (1840); *Ein Ende in Paris,* novella (1841); *Ein glücklicher Abend,* novella (1841); *Die Sarazenin,* 3-act opera (prose scenario, 1841–42; verse text, 1843); *Die Bergwerke zu Falun,* 3-act opera (prose scenario for an unwritten libretto, 1841–42); *Friedrich I.,* play (prose scenario, 1846 and 1848); *Alexander der Grosse,* sketch for a play (184?; not extant); *Jesus von Nazareth,* play (prose scenario, 1849); *Achilleus,* sketch for a play (1849–50; fragments only); *Wieland der Schmied,* 3-act opera (prose scenario, 1850); *Die Sieger,* opera (prose sketch, 1856); *Luther* or *Luthers Hochzeit,* sketch for a play (1868); *Lustspiel in 1 Akt* (draft, 1868); *Eine Kapitulation: Lustspiel in antiker Manier,* poem (1870).

Wagner expounded his theories on music, politics, philosophy, religion, etc., in numerous essays; among the most important are *Über deutsches Musikwesen* (1840); *Die Kunst und die Revolution* (1849); *Das Kunstwerk der Zukunft* (1849); *Kunst und Klima* (1850); *Oper und Drama* (1851; revised 1868); *Eine Mitteilung an meine Freunde* (1851); *Über Staat und Religion* (1864); *Über das Dirigieren* (1869); *Beethoven* (1870); *Über die Anwendung der Musik auf das Drama* (1879); and *Religion und Kunst* (1880). The first ed. of his collected writings, *R. Wagner: Gesammelte Schriften und Dichtungen* (9 vols., Leipzig, 1871–73; vol. 10, 1883), was prepared by Wagner himself; W.A. Ellis ed. and trans. it into Eng. as *Richard Wagner's Prose Works* (8 vols., London, 1892–99). H. von Wolzogen and R. Sternfeld ed. the 5th ed. of the German original as *Sämtliche Schriften und Dichtungen,* adding vols. XI and XII (Leipzig, 1911); they also prepared the 6th ed., adding vols. XIII–XVI (Leipzig, 1914).

Wagner's important autobiography, *Mein Leben,* in 4 parts, was privately publ.; parts 1–3, bringing the narrative down to Aug. 1861, were publ. between 1870 and 1875; part 4, covering the years from 1861 to 1864, was publ. in 1881; these were limited eds., being distributed only among his friends; the entire work was finally publ. in an abridged ed. in Munich in 1911 (Eng. trans. as *My Life,* London and N.Y., 1911); the suppressed passages were first publ. in *Die Musik,* XXII (1929–30), and then were trans. into Eng. in E. Newman's *Fact and Fiction about Wagner* (London, 1931); a definitive ed., based on the original MS, was publ. in Munich in 1963, ed. by M. Gregor-Dellin.

Another important source is Wagner's diary-notebook, the so-called *Brown Book,* in which he made entries between 1865 and 1882; it was ed. by J. Bergfeld as *Richard Wagner: Das Braune Buch: Tagebuchaufzeichnungen, 1865–1882* (Zürich, 1975; Eng. trans. by G. Bird as *The Diary of Richard Wagner, 1865–1882; The Brown Book,* London, 1980). See also the diaries of Cosima Wagner; they have been ed. by M. Gregor-Dellin and D. Mack as *Cosima Wagner: Die Tagebücher, 1869–1877* (2 vols., Munich, 1976–77; Eng. trans. by G. Skelton as *Cosima Wagner's Diaries,* 2 vols., N.Y., 1977 and 1980).

BIBLIOGRAPHY: COLLECTED EDITIONS, SOURCE MATERIAL: The first collected ed. of his works, *Richard Wagners Werke,* was ed. by M. Balling (10 vols., Leipzig, 1912–29); the Bayerischen Akademie der Schönen Künste of Munich is now publishing a new critical ed., the *Gesamtausgabe der Richard Wagners,* under the editorship of C. Dahlhaus (Mainz, 1970—).

E. Kastner prepared a *Wagner-Catalog: Chronologisches Verzeichniss der von und über Richard Wagner erschienen Schriften, Musikwerke* (Offenbach, 1878). J. Deathridge, M. Geck, and E. Voss have ed. an exhaustive *Verzeichnis der musikalischen Werke Richard Wagners und ihrer Quellen* (Mainz, 1983).

Other sources include the following: N. Oester-

Wagner

lein, *Katalog einer R. W.—Bibliothek: Nach den vorliegenden Originalien zu einem authentischen Nachschlagebuch durch die gesammte insbesondere deutsche W.-Litteratur bearbeitet und veröffentlicht* (describes the treasures of the W.-Museum and contains an extensive bibliography of books and articles publ. about the composer during his life [10,181 titles]; 4 vols., Leipzig, 1882, 1886, 1891, and 1895); C. Glasenapp and H. von Stein, *W.-Lexikon. Hauptbegriffe der Kunst und Weltanschauung W.s in wörtlichen Ausführungen aus seinen Schriften zusammengestellt* (Stuttgart, 1883); C. Glasenapp, *W.-Enzyklopädie. Haupterscheinungen der Kunst- und Kulturgeschichte im Lichte der Anschauung W.s in wörtlichen Ausführungen aus seinen Schriften dargestellt* (2 vols., Leipzig, 1891); E. Kastner, *Verzeichnis der ersten Aufführungen von R. W.s dramatischen Werken* (Vienna, 1896; 2nd ed., Leipzig, 1899); H. Silège, *Bibliographie wagnérienne française* (Paris, 1902); P. Pabst, *Verzeichnis von R. W.s Werken, Schriften und Dichtungen, deren hauptächlichsten Bearbeitungen, sowie von besonders interessanter Litteratur, Abbildungen, Büsten und Kunstblättern, den Meister und seine Schöpfungen betreffend* (Leipzig, 1905); L. Frankenstein, *Biliographie der auf R. W. bezüglichen. Literatur für die Jahre 1907–11* (Berlin, 1912); M. Burrell, *Catalogue of the Burrell Collection of W. Documents, Letters and Other Biographical Material* (London, 1929); O. Strobel, *Genie am Werk: R. W.s Schaffen und Wirken im Spiegel eigenhandschriftlicher Urkunden: Führer durch die einmalige Ausstellung einer umfassenden Auswahl von Schätzen aus dem Archiv des Hauses Wahnfried* (Bayreuth, 1933; revised ed., 1934); E. Terry, *A R. W. Dictionary* (N.Y., 1939); O. Strobel, "R.-W.-Forschungsstätte und Archiv des Hauses Wahnfried," *Das Bayerland,* LII (1942); H. Barth, ed., *Internationale W.-Bibliographie: 1945–55* (Bayreuth, 1956; also for 1956–60, publ. 1961, and for 1961–66, publ. 1968); C. von Westernhagen, *R. W.s Dresdener Bibliothek, 1842–1849: Neue Dokumente zur Geschichte seines Schaffens* (Wiesbaden, 1966); H. Kirchmeyer, *Das zeitgenössische W.-Bild* (3 vols., Regensburg; vol. I, *W. in Dresden,* publ. 1972; vol. II, *Dokumente, 1842–45,* publ. 1967; vol. III, *Dokumente, 1846–50,* publ. 1968; H.-M. Plesske, *R. W. in der Dichtung: Bibliographie deutschsprachiger Veröffentlichungen* (Bayreuth, 1971); W. Schuler, *Der Bayreuther Kreis von seiner Entstehung bis zum Ausgang der wilhelminischen Ära: Wagnerkult und Kulturreform im Geiste völkischer Weltanschauung* (Münster, 1971); H. Klein, *Erst- und Frühdrucke der Textbücher von R. W.: Bibliographie* (Tutzing, 1979); J. Deathridge, "Cataloguing W.," *Musical Times* (Feb. 1983).

YEARBOOKS AND OTHER PUBLICATIONS: *Bayreuther Blätter* (founded by Wagner; Chemnitz, later Bayreuth, 1878–1938); *La Revue Wagnérienne* (Paris, 1885–88); *R.-W.-Jahrbuch* (Stuttgart, 1886); *The Meister* (quarterly journal of the British Wagner Society, London, 1888–95); *Bayreuth. Handbuch für Festspielbesucher* (Bayreuth, 1894–1930); *Bayreuther Festspielführer* (also issued under other titles; Bayreuth, 1901–39); L. Frankenstein, ed., *R.-W.-*

Jahrbuch (5 vols., Berlin, 1906, 1907, 1908, 1912, and 1913); O. Strobel, ed., *Neue W.-Forschungen. Veröffentlichungen der R.-W.-Forschungsstätte Bayreuth* (Karlsruhe, 1943); *Das Bayreuther Festspielbuch* (Bayreuth, 1950–51); *"Bayreuth"—Jahreshefte* (Bayreuth, 1954—); *Tribschener Blätter* (publ. by the Zeitschrift der Schweizerischen Richard-Wagner-Gesellschaft of Lucerne, 1956—); *W.* (publ. by the Wagner Society of London, 1971—).

CORRESPONDENCE: F. Hueffer, ed., *Briefwechsel zwischen W. und Liszt* (2 vols., Leipzig, 1887; Eng. trans., London, 1888; 3rd German ed., revised and enlarged, by E. Kloss, 1910); E. Wille, *Fünfzehn Briefe des Meisters, nebst Erinnerungen und Erläuterungen* (Leipzig, 1887; 3rd ed., revised, by C. Meyer, 1935); H. von Wolzogen, ed., *R. W.'s Briefe an Theodor Uhlig, Wilhelm Fischer, Ferdinand Heine* (Leipzig, 1888; Eng. trans., London, 1890); H.S. Chamberlain, ed., *R. W.s echt Briefe an Ferdinand Praeger* (Bayreuth, 1894; 2nd ed., revised, Berlin, 1908); La Mara, ed., *R. W.s Briefe an August Röckel* (Leipzig, 1894; Eng. trans., London, 1897; 2nd German ed., 1903); E. Kastner, ed., *Briefe von R. W. an seine Zeitgenossen (1830–83)* (Berlin, 1897); A. Heintz, ed., *Briefe R. W.'s an Otto Wesendonck* (Charlottenburg, 1898; 2nd ed., enlarged, by W. Golther, 1905; Eng. trans., 1911); K. Heckel, ed., *Briefe R. W.s an Emil Heckel: Zur Entstehungsgeschichte der Bühnenfestspiele in Bayreuth* (Berlin, 1899; Eng. trans., London, 1899; 3rd German ed., 1911); W. Golther, ed., *R. W. an Mathilde Wesendonck: Tagebuchblätter und Briefe, 1853–1871* (Berlin and Leipzig, 1904; Eng. trans., London, 1905; numerous reprints of the German ed.); W. Altmann, *R. W.s Briefe nach Zeitfolge und Inhalt: Ein Beitrag zur Lebensgeschichte des Meisters* (synopses of 3,143 letters; Leipzig, 1905); W. Golther, ed., *Briefe R. W.s an Otto Wesendonck* (Berlin, 1905; Eng. trans., London, 1911); C. Glasenapp, ed., *Familienbriefe von R. W., 1832–1874* (Berlin, 1906; Eng. trans., London, 1911); D. Spitzer, ed., *Briefe R. W.s an eine Putzmacherin* (Vienna, 1906; in Eng. as *R. W. and the Seamstress,* N.Y., 1941; enlarged German ed., by L. Kusche, 1967); C. Glasenapp, ed., *Bayreuther Briefe von R. W. (1871–1883)* (Berlin, 1907; 2nd ed., 1912; Eng. trans., 1912); E. Kloss, ed., *R. W. an seine Künstler* (Berlin, 1908); H. von Wolzogen, ed., *R. W. an Minna Wagner* (2 vols., Berlin, 1908; Eng. trans., London, 1909); E. Kloss, ed., *R. W. an Freunde und Zeitgenossen* (Berlin, 1909); T. Apel, Jr., ed., *R. W. an Theodor Apel* (Leipzig, 1910); W. Altmann, ed., *Briefwechsel mit B. Schott's Söhne* (Mainz, 1911); idem, *R. W.s Briefwechsel mit seinen Verlegern: Briefwechsel mit Breitkopf & Härtel* (3 vols., Leipzig, 1911). Almost all of the above collections were republ. by Breitkopf & Härtel as *R. W.s Briefe in Originalausgaben* (17 vols., Leipzig, 1912); a number of the letters appear in mutilated form (portions expressing political and religious views being suppressed); an early attempt to bring out an unmutilated ed. was begun by J. Kapp and E. Kastner, *R. W.s Gesammelte Briefe (1830–50)* (2 vols., Leipzig, 1914); however, this ed. was never completed; J.-G. Prod'homme, "W. and the Paris Opéra: Unpublished Letters (February–March, 1861)," *Musical*

Quarterly (April 1915); E. Kloss, *Briefe an Hans von Bülow* (Jena, 1916); S. von Hausegger, ed., *R. W.s Briefe an Frau Julie Ritter* (Munich, 1920); L. Karpath, ed., *R. W.: Briefe an Hans Richter* (Berlin, 1924); W. Altmann, *R. W.s Briefe, ausgewählt und erläutert* (2 vols., Leipzig, 1925; Eng. trans., London, 1927); W. Lippert, *R. W.s Verbannung und Rückkehr, 1849–62* (Dresden, 1927; Eng. trans. as *W. in Exile*, London, 1930); R. Sternfeld, *R. W. Aufsätze und Briefe des Meisters aus Paris* (Grossenwörden, 1927); H. Scholz, ed., *R. W. an Mathilde Maier (1862–1878)* (Leipzig, 1930); E. Lenrow, ed. and trans., *The Letters of R. W. to Anton Pusinelli* (N.Y., 1932); J. Tiersot, *Lettres françaises de R. W.* (Paris, 1935); K. Geiringer, "W. and Brahms, with Unpublished Letters," *Musical Quarterly* (April 1936); W. Schuh, ed. and trans., *Die Briefe R. W.s an Judith Gautier* (Zürich, 1936; enlarged ed., with French original, as *R. et Cosima W.: Lettres à Judith Gautier,* ed. by L. Guichard, 1964); O. Strobel, ed., *König Ludwig II. und R. W.: Briefwechsel, mit vielen anderen Urkunden* (5 vols., Karlsruhe, 1936–39); A. Holde, "Four Unknown Letters of R. W.," *Musical Quarterly* (April 1941); J. Burk, ed., *Letters of R. W. The Burrell Collection* (N.Y., 1950; German ed., Frankfurt, 1953); G. Strobel and W. Wolf, eds., *R. W.: Sämtliche Briefe* (a projected complete ed. in 15 vols.; Leipzig, 1967—).

BIOGRAPHICAL: C. Cabrol, *R. W.* (Paris, 1861); A. de Gasperini, *La Nouvelle Allemagne musicale: R. W.* (Paris, 1866); F. Hueffer, *R. W.* (London, 1872; 3rd ed., 1912); F. Filippi, *R. W.* (Leipzig, 1876); C. Glasenapp, *R. W.s Leben und Wirken* (2 vols., Leipzig, 1876–77; 3rd ed., revised and enlarged, as *Das Leben R. W.s,* 6 vols., Leipzig, 1894–1911; Eng. trans. by W. Ellis as *Life of R. W.,* 6 vols., London, 1900–8; vols. I–III based on Glasenapp; reprinted N.Y., 1977, with new introduction by George Buelow; 5th German ed., revised, 1910–23); P. Lindau, *R. W.* (Paris, 1885); A. Jullien, *R. W.: Sa vie et ses œuvres* (Paris, 1886; Eng. trans., Boston, 1892); G. Kobbé, *W.'s Life and Works* (2 vols., N.Y., 1890); H. Finck, *W. and His Works* (2 vols., N.Y., 1893; 5th ed., 1898); H. Chamberlain, *R. W.* (Munich, 1896; Eng. trans., London, 1897; 9th German ed., 1936); M. Burrell, compiler, *R. W.: Life and Works from 1813 to 1834* (London, 1898); W.J. Henderson, *R. W., His Life and His Dramas* (N.Y., 1901; revised ed., 1923); R. Bürkner, *R. W.: Sein Leben und seine Werke* (Jena, 1906; 6th ed., 1911); M. Koch, *R. W.* (3 vols., Berlin, 1907, 1913, and 1918); J. Kapp, *R. W.* (Berlin, 1910; numerous reprints); F. Pfohl, *R. W.: Sein Leben und Schaffen* (Berlin, 1911; 4th ed., Bielefeld, 1924); E. Newman, *W. as Man and Artist* (London, 1914; 2nd ed., revised, 1924); L. Barthou, *La Vie amoureuse de R. W.* (Paris, 1925; in Eng. as *The Prodigious Lover,* N.Y., 1927); H. Lichtenberger, *W.* (Paris, 1925); W. Wallace, *W. as He Lived* (London, 1925; new ed., 1933); V. d'Indy, *R. W. et son influence sur l'art musical français* (Paris, 1930); M. Morold (pen name of Max von Millenkovitch), *W.s Kampf und Sieg, dargestellt in seinen Beziehungen zu Wien* (Zürich, 1930; 2nd ed., 1950); H. Reisiger, *Unruhiges Gestirn; Die Jugend R. W.s* (Leipzig, 1930; in Eng. as *Restless Star,* N.Y., 1932); G. de Pourtalès, *W.: Histoire d'un*

artiste (Paris, 1932; Eng. trans., N.Y., 1932; 2nd French ed., enlarged, 1942); P. Lalo, *R. W.* (Paris, 1933); E. Newman, *The Life of R. W.* (an exhaustive study; it should be supplemented by consulting the more recent 2-vol. biography by C. von Westernhagen listed below; 4 vols., N.Y., 1933, 1937, 1941, and 1946); A. Spring, *R. W.s Weg und Wirken* (Stuttgart, 1933); W. Turner, *W.* (London, 1933); M. Fehr, *R. W.s Schweizer Zeit* (2 vols., Aarau, 1934–53); W. Hadow, *R. W.* (London, 1934); R. Jacobs, *R. W.* (London, 1935; 3rd ed., 1947); H. Malherbe, *R. W. Révolutionnaire* (Paris, 1938); E. Kretzschmar, *R. W.: Sein Leben in Selbstzeugnissen, Briefen und Berichten* (Berlin, 1939); O. Strobel, *Neue Urkunden zur Lebensgeschichte R. W.s, 1864–1882* (a supplement to his ed. of *König Ludwig II. und R. W.: Briefwechsel;* Karlsruhe, 1939; see CORRESPONDENCE); M. von Millenkovitch, *Dreigestirn: W., Liszt, Bülow* (Leipzig, 1941); W. Reich, *R. W., Leben, Fühlen, Schaffen* (Olten, 1948); K. Ipser, *R. W. in Italien* (Salzburg, 1951); L. Strecker, *R. W. als Verlagsgefährte: Eine Darstellung mit Briefen und Dokumenten* (Mainz, 1951); T. Adorno, *Versuch über W.* (Berlin, 1952); P. Loos, *R. W., Vollendung und Tragik der deutschen Romantik* (Munich, 1952); O. Strobel, *R. W.: Leben und Schaffen: Eine Zeittafel* (Bayreuth, 1952); Z. von Kraft, *R. W.: Ein dramatisches Leben* (Munich, 1953); R. Dumesnil, *R. W.* (Paris, 1954); H. Mayer, *R. W.s geistige Entwicklung* (Düsseldorf and Hamburg, 1954); C. von Westernhagen, *R. W.: Sein Werk, sein Wesen, seine Welt* (Zürich, 1956); W. Vordtriede, "R. W.s 'Tod in Venedig,'" *Euphorion,* LII (1958–59); H. Mayer, *R. W. in Selbstzeugnissen und Bilddokumenten* (Reinbek bei Hamburg, 1959; Eng. trans., 1972); O. Daube, *R. W.: "Ich schreibe keine Symphonien mehr": R. W.s Lehrjahre nach den erhaltenen Dokumenten* (Cologne, 1960); H. Schonberg, *The Great Conductors* (N.Y., 1967; pp. 128–43); R. Gutman, *R. W.: The Man, His Mind and His Music* (London, 1968); C. von Westernhagen, *W.* (an extensive and well-balanced study of the man and his music; based upon material not available to Newman; 2 vols., Zürich, 1968; 2nd ed., revised and enlarged, 1978; Eng. trans., Cambridge, 1978); M. Gregor-Martin, *W.-Chronik: Daten zu Leben* (Munich, 1972; 2nd revised ed., 1983); H. Barth, D. Mack, and E. Voss, eds., *W.: Sein Leben und seine Welt in zeitgenössischen Bildern und Texten* (Vienna, 1975; Eng. trans. as *W.: A Documentary Study,* London, 1975); R. Taylor, *R. W.: His Life, Art and Thought* (London, 1979); D. Watson, *R. W.: A Biography* (N.Y. and London, 1979); M. Gregor-Dellin, *R. W.: Sein Leben, sein Werk, sein Jahrhundert* (Munich, 1980; in Eng. as *R. W.: His Life, His Work, His Century,* London, 1983); Derek Watson, *R. W.* (N.Y., 1981); G. Skelton, *R. and Cosima W.: A Biography of a Marriage* (London, 1982); M. van Amerongen, *W.: A Case History* (London, 1983).

PERSONAL REMINISCENCES: H. von Wolzogen, *Erinnerungen an R. W.* (Leipzig, 1883; Eng. trans., Bayreuth, 1894); A. Schilling, *Aus R. W.s Jugendzeit* (Berlin, 1898; reminiscences of Wagner's stepsister Cäcilie Avenarius); E. Schuré, *Souvenirs sur R. W.* (Paris, 1900; German trans., Leipzig, 1900); E. von Possart, *Die Separat-Vorstellungen vor König Lud-*

wig II. Erinnerungen (Munich, 1901); L. Schemann, *Meine Erinnerungen an R. W.* (Stuttgart, 1902); G.A. Kietz, *R. W. in den Jahren 1842–49 und 1873–75* (Dresden, 1905); A. Kohut, *Der Meister von Bayreuth* (Berlin, 1905); E. Michotte, *Souvenirs: La Visite de R. W. à Rossini (Paris, 1860): Détails inédites et commentaires* (Paris, 1906; Eng. trans. by H. Weinstock, Chicago, 1968); A. Gobineau, *Ein Erinnerungsbild aus Wahnfried* (Stuttgart, 1907); A. Neumann, *Erinnerungen an R. W.* (Leipzig, 1907; Eng. trans., N.Y., 1908); H. Schmidt and U. Hartmann, *R. W. in Bayreuth. Erinnerungen* (Leipzig, 1910); Siegfried Wagner, *Erinnerungen* (Stuttgart, 1923; extended ed., privately printed, 1935); Judith Gautier, *Auprès de R. W.; Souvenirs (1861–1883)* (Paris, 1943).

RELATIONS WITH CONTEMPORARIES: J.L. Craemer, *König Ludwig II. und R. W.* (Munich, 1901); F. Gerard, *Romance of King Ludwig II of Bavaria. His Relation with R. W.* (London, 1901); S. Röckel, *Ludwig II. und R. W. in den Jahren 1864–65* (Munich, 1903; 2nd ed., 1913); J. Kapp, *R. W. und Franz Liszt. Eine Freundschaft* (Berlin, 1908); H. Bélart, *Friedrich Nietzsches Freundschaftstragödie mit R. W.* (Dresden, 1912) and *R. W.s Liebestragödie mit Mathilde Wesendonck* (Dresden, 1912); J. Kapp, *R. W. und die Frauen* (Berlin, 1912; new revised ed., 1951; in Eng. as *The Women in W.'s Life*, N.Y., 1931); E. Förster-Nietzsche, *W. und Nietzsche zur Zeit ihrer Freundschaft* (Munich, 1915; Eng. trans. as *The Nietzsche-Wagner Correspondence*, N.Y., 1921); C. Sarti, *W. and Nietzsche* (N.Y., 1915); E. Schuré, *Femmes inspiratrices* (Paris, 1930); M. Herwegh, *Au banquet des dieux: F. Liszt, R. W. et ses amis* (Paris, 1931); L. Barthou, "R. W. et Judith Gautier," *Revue de Paris* (1932); P.G. Dippel, *Nietzsche und W.* (Berne, 1934); D. Fischer-Dieskau, *W. und Nietzsche* (Stuttgart, 1974; Eng. trans., N.Y., 1976).

CRITICAL, ANALYTICAL: Liszt's essays on *Tannhäuser* (1849), *Lohengrin* (1850), *Der fliegende Holländer* (1854), and *Das Rheingold* (1855) are in vol. III, 2, of his *Gesammelte Schriften* (Leipzig, 1899); F. Hinrichs, *R. W. und die neuere Musik: Eine kritische Skizze* (Halle, 1854); F. Müller, *R. W. und das Musik-Drama* (Leipzig, 1861); L. Nohl, *Gluck und W. über die Entwicklung des Musikdramas* (Munich, 1870); F. Nietzsche, *Die Geburt der Tragödie aus dem Geiste der Musik* (Leipzig, 1872; Eng. trans. by W. Kaufmann as *The Birth of Tragedy out of the Spirit of Music* in *The Basic Writings of Nietzsche*, N.Y., 1968); E. Dannreuther, *R. W. His Tendencies and Theories* (London, 1873); F. Hueffer, *R. W. and the Music of the Future* (London, 1874); E. Schuré, *Le Drame musical: I. La Musique et la Poésie dans leur développement historique. II. W. Son œuvre et son idée* (Paris, 1875; 3rd ed., augmented, 1894); L. Nohl, *Das moderne Musikdrama* (Vienna, 1884); G. Kobbé, *R. W.s "Tristan und Isolde"* (N.Y., 1886); W. Ellis, *R. W. as Poet, Musician and Mystic* (London, 1887); F. Nietzsche, *Der Fall W.* (Leipzig, 1888; Eng. trans. by W. Kaufmann as *The Case of W.* in *The Basic Writings of Nietzsche*, N.Y., 1968); idem, *Nietzsche contra W.* (Leipzig, 1888; Eng. trans. by W. Kaufmann in *The Portable Nietzsche*, N.Y., 1954); H. von Wolzogen, *Wagneriana: Gesammelte*

Aufsätze über R. W.s Werke vom Ring bis zum Gral (Bayreuth, 1888); M. Kufferath, *Parsifal de R. W.: Légende, drame, partition* (Paris, 1890; Eng. trans., 1904); L. Torchi, *Riccardo W.: Studio critico* (Bologna, 1890); H. Krehbiel, *Studies in the Wagnerian Drama* (N.Y., 1891); M. Kufferath, *Le Théâtre de W. de Tannhäuser à Parsifal. Essais de critique littéraire, esthétique et musicale* (6 vols., Paris, 1891–98); A. Smolian, *The Themes of "Tannhäuser"* (London, 1891); H. Chamberlain, *Das Drama R. W.s: Eine Anregung* (Leipzig, 1892; 5th ed., 1913; Eng. trans., London, 1915); M. Kufferath, *Guide thématique et analyse de Tristan et Iseult* (Paris, 1894); A. Lavignac, *Le Voyage artistique à Bayreuth* (Paris, 1897; many subsequent printings; Eng. trans. as *The Music-Dramas of R. W.*, N.Y., 1898; new ed., 1932); G. Servières, *R. W. jugé en France* (Paris, 1897); G.B. Shaw, *The Perfect Wagnerite* (London, 1898; 4th ed., 1923; also in vol. 17 of the complete works, 1932); J. Tiersot, *Etudes sur les Maîtres-Chanteurs de Nuremberg, de R. W.* (Paris, 1899); A. Smolian, *R. W.'s Bühnenfestspiel Der Ring des Nibelungen: Ein Vademecum* (Berlin, 1901); F. Muncker, "R. W.s Operntext 'Die Hochzeit,'" *Die Musik*, I (1901–2); A. Seidl, *Wagneriana* (2 vols., Berlin, 1901–2); G. Adler, *R. W.: Vorlesungen gehalten an der Universität zu Wien* (Vienna and Munich, 1904; 2nd ed., 1922); G. Kobbé, *W.'s Music Dramas Analyzed* (N.Y., 1904); H. Abert, "Gedanken zu R. W.s 'Die Meistersinger von Nürnberg,'" *Die Musik*, IV (1904–5); W. Golther, "Zur Entstehung von R. W.s Tristan," ibid., V (1905–6); K. Mey, "Über R. W.s Huldigungschor an König Friedrich August II. von Sachsen 1844," ibid.; W. Dry, *Erläuterungen zur R. W.s Tondramen* (2 vols., Leipzig, 1906–7); K. Mey, "R. W.s Webertrauermarsch," *Die Musik*, VI (1906–7); W. Golther, *Tristan und Isolde in den Dichtungen des Mittelalters und der neuen Zeit* (Leipzig, 1907); S. Hamer, *The Story of "The Ring"* (N.Y., 1907); M. Burckhardt, *Führer durch R. W.s Musikdramen* (Berlin, 1909); E. Istel, *Das Kunstwerk R. W.s* (Leipzig, 1910; 2nd ed., 1919); E. Kloss, *R. W. über die "Meistersinger von Nürnberg": Aussprüche des Meisters über sein Werk* (Leipzig, 1910); W. Krienetz, *R. W.s "Feen"* (Munich, 1910); A. Altmann, "Zur Geschichte der Entstehung und Veröffentlichung von W.s 'Der Ring des Nibelungen,'" *Allgemeine Musik-Zeitung*, XXXVIII (1911); A. Heuss, "Die Grundlagen der Parsifal-Dichtung," *Die Musik*, XII (1912–13); E. Lindner, *R. W. über "Parsifal": Aussprüche des Meisters über sein Werk* (Leipzig, 1913); idem., *R. W. über "Tannhäuser": Aussprüche des Meisters über sein Werk* (Leipzig, 1914); A. Seidl, *Neue Wagneriana: Gesammelte Aufsätze und Studien* (Regensburg, 1914); H. von Wolzogen, *R. W. über den "Fliegenden Holländer": Die Entstehung, Gestaltung und Darstellung des Werkes aus den Schriften und Briefen des Meisters zusammengestellt* (Leipzig, 1914); A. Halm, *Von Grenzen und Ländern der Musik* (Munich, 1916); E. Kurth, *Romantische Harmonik und ihre Krise in W.s "Tristan"* (Berlin, 1920; 2nd ed., 1923); H. von Waltershausen, *Das Siegfried-Idyll, oder Die Rückkehr zur Natur* (Munich, 1920); L. Windsperger, *Das Buch der Motive und Themen aus sämtlichen Opern und Musikdramen*

R. W.s (for piano, with explanatory text; Mainz, 1921); F. Zademack, *Die Meistersinger von Nürnberg: R. W.s Dichtung und ihre Quellen* (Berlin, 1921); W. Wilmshurst, *Parsifal* (London, 1922); R. Sternfeld, "Die erste Fassung von W.s Faust-Ouvertüre," *Die Musik*, XV (1922–23); P. Bekker, *R. W.: Das Leben im Werke* (Stuttgart, 1924; Eng. trans., London, 1931); A. Cœuroy, *La Walkyrie de R. W.* (Paris, 1924); O. Strobel, *R. W. über sein Schaffen: Ein Beitrag zur "Künstlerästhetik"* (Munich, 1924); H. Wiessner, *Der Stabreimvers in R. W.s "Ring des Nibelungen"* (Berlin, 1924); A. Himonet, *Lohengrin de R. W.* (Paris, 1925); L. Leroy, *W.'s Music Drama of the Ring* (London, 1925); C. Winn, *The Mastersingers of W.* (London, 1925); A. Dickinson, *The Musical Design of "The Ring"* (London, 1926); W. Hapke, *Die musikalische Darstellung der Gebärde in R. W.s Ring des Nibelungen* (Leipzig, 1927); A. Buesst, *R. W., The Nibelung's Ring* (London, 1932; 2nd ed., 1952); O. Strobel, "Zur Entstehungsgeschichte der Götterdämmerung: Unbekannte Dokumente," *Die Musik*, XXV (1932–33); H. Engelsmann, *W.s klingendes Universum* (Potsdam, 1933); J. Kapp, *Das Liebesverbot, Entstehung und Schicksale des Werkes von R. W.* (Berlin, 1933); idem, *W. und die Berliner Oper* (Berlin, 1933); T. Mann, "Leiden und Grösse R. W.s," *Neue Rundschau*, XLIV (1933; Eng. trans. by H. Lowe-Porter in *Thomas Mann: Past Masters and Other Papers*, N.Y., 1933); R. Grisson, *Beiträge zur Auslegung von R. W.'s "Ring des Nibelungen"* (Leipzig, 1934); H. Nathan, *Das Rezitativ der Frühopern R. W.s: Ein Beitrag zur Stilistik des Opernrezitativs in der ersten Hälfte des 19. Jahrhunderts* (Diss., Univ. of Berlin, 1934); A. Bahr-Mildenburg, *Tristan und Isolde: Darstellung der Werke R. W.s aus dem Geiste der Dichtung und Musik: Vollständige Regiebearbeitung sämtlicher Partien mit Notenbeispielen* (Leipzig, 1936); L. Gilman, *W.'s Operas* (N.Y., 1937); V. d'Indy, *Introduction à l'étude de Parsifal de W.* (Paris, 1937); T. Mann, "R. W. and the Ring" (lecture, Univ. of Zürich, 1937; publ. in *Essays of Three Decades*, N.Y., 1947); R. Schuster, *R. W. und die Welt der Oper* (Munich, 1937); E. Borrelli, *Estetica wagneriana* (Florence, 1940); A. Hutcheson, *A Musical Guide to the R. W. Ring of the Nibelung* (N.Y., 1940); J. Barzun, *Darwin, Marx, W.; Critique of a Heritage* (Boston, 1941; revised ed., 1958); S. Luciani, *Il Tristano e Isolda di R. W.* (Florence, 1942); G. Gavazzeni, *Il Siegfried di R. W.* (Florence, 1944); M. Doisy, *L'Œuvre de R. W. du Vaisseau fantôme à Parsifal* (Brussels, 1945); K. Beaufils, *W. et le wagnérisme* (Paris, 1947); K. Overhoff, *R. W.s Tristan Partitur; Eine musikalisch-philosophische Deutung* (Bayreuth, 1948); E. Newman, *W. Nights* (London, 1949; American ed. as *The W. Operas*, N.Y., 1949); K. Overhoff, *R. W.s Parsifal* (Lindau im Bodensee, 1951); T. Adorno, *Versuch über W.* (Berlin and Frankfurt, 1952); W. Hess, " 'Die Meistersinger von Nürnberg': Ihr dichterisch-musikalische Gesamtform," *Zeitschrift für Musik*, 113 (1952); P. Jacob, *Taten der Musik; R. W. und sein Werk* (Regensburg, 1952); P. Loos, *R. W.: Vollendung und Tragik der deutschen Romantik* (Bern and Munich, 1952); H. Engel, "Versuche einer Sinn-

deutung von R. W.s 'Ring des Nibelungen,' " *Die Musikforschung*, X (1957); H. Blümer, *Über den Tonarten-Charakter bei R. W.* (Diss., Univ. of Munich, 1958); V. Levi, *Tristano e Isotta di Riccardo W.* (Venice, 1958); E. Lippman, "The Aesthetic Theories of R. W.," *Musical Quarterly* (April 1958); W. Serauky, "Die Todesverkündigungsszene in R. W.s Walküre als musikalisch-geistige Achse des Werkes," *Die Musikforschung*, XII (1959); J. Stein, *R. W. and the Synthesis of the Arts* (Detroit, 1960); H. von Stein, *Dichtung und Musik im Werk R. W.s* (Berlin, 1962); M. Vogel, *Der Tristan-Akkord und die Krise der modernen Harmonie-Lehre* (Düsseldorf, 1962); C. von Westernhagen, *Vom Holländer zum Parsifal: Neue W. Studien* (Freiburg, 1962); J. Bergfeld, *W.s Werk und unsere Zeit* (Berlin and Wunsiedel, 1963); R. Donington, *W.s "Ring" and Its Symbols: The Music and the Myth* (London, 1963; 3rd ed., revised and enlarged, 1974); H. Engel, "Über R. W.s Oper *Das Liebesverbot*," in *Festschrift Friedrich Blume* (Kassel, 1963); H. Gál, *R. W.: Versuch einer Würdigung* (Frankfurt, 1963; Eng. trans., 1976); G. Knepler, "R. W.s musikalische Gestaltungsprinzipien," *Beiträge zur Musikwissenschaft*, V (1963); J. Mainka," "Sonatenform, Leitmotiv und Charakterbegleitung," ibid.; H. Scharschuch, *Gesamtanalyse der Harmonik von R. W.s Musikdrama "Tristan und Isolde": Unter spezifischer Berücksichtigung der Sequenztechnik des Tristanstiles* (Regensburg, 1963); H. Truscott, "W.'s Tristan and the Twentieth Century," *Music Review*, XXIV (1963); C. von Westernhagen, "Die Kompositions-Skizze zu 'Siegfrieds Tod' aus dem Jahre 1850," *Neue Zeitschrift für Musik*, 124 (1963); E. Zuckerman, *The First Hundred Years of W.'s "Tristan"* (N.Y. and London, 1964); H. Mayer, *Anmerkungen zu W.* (Frankfurt, 1966); W. Mitchell, "The Tristan Prelude: Techniques and Structure," *Music Forum*, I (1967); W. White, *An Introduction to the Life and Works of R. W.* (Englewood Cliffs, N.J., 1967); K. Overhoff, *Die Musikdramen R. W.s: Eine thematisch-musikalische Interpretation* (Salzburg, 1968); R. Bailey, *The Genesis of Tristan und Isolde, and a Study of W.'s Sketches and Drafts for the First Act* (Diss., Princeton Univ., 1969); R. Raphael, *R. W.* (N.Y., 1969); C. Dahlhaus, ed., *Das Drama R. W.s als musikalisches Kunstwerk* (Regensburg, 1970); C. Dahlhaus, *Die Bedeutung des Gestischen in W.s Musikdramen* (Munich, 1970); E. Voss, *Studien zur Instrumentation R. W.s* (Regensburg, 1970); D. Coren, *A Study of R. W.s "Siegfried"* (Diss., Univ. of Calif., Berkeley, 1971); C. Dahlhaus, *Die Musikdramen R. W.s* (Velber, 1971; Eng. trans. as *R. W.'s Music Dramas*, Cambridge, 1979); idem, *W.s Konzeption des musikalischen Dramas* (Regensburg, 1971); A. Sommer, *Die Komplikationen des musikalischen Rhythmus in den Bühnenwerken R. W.s* (Giebing, 1971); R. Bailey, "The Evolution of W.'s Compositional Procedure after Lohengrin," *International Musicological Society Congress Report*, XI (Copenhagen, 1972); W. Breig, *Studien zur Entstehungsgeschichte von W.s "Ring des Nibelungen"* (Diss., Univ. of Freiburg, 1973); C. von Westernhagen, *Die Entstehung des "Ring," dargestellt an den Kompositionsskizzen R. W.s* (Zürich, 1973;

Wagner

Eng. trans. as *The Forging of the "Ring,"* Cambridge, 1976); J. Deathridge, "The Nomenclature of W.'s Sketches," *Proceedings of the Royal Musical Association,* CI (1974–75); R. Jackson, *"Leitmotive and Form in the Tristan Prelude," Music Review,* XXXVI (1975); K. Kropfinger, *W. und Beethoven: Untersuchungen zur Beethoven-Rezeption R. W.s* (Regensburg, 1975); J. Culshaw, *Reflections on W.'s Ring* (N.Y., 1976); P. Machlin, *The Flying Dutchman: Sketches, Revisions and Analysis* (Diss., Univ. of Calif., Berkeley, 1976); H.-J. Bauer, *W.s Parsifal: Kriterien der Kompositionstechnik* (Munich, 1977); J. Deathridge, *W.'s Rienzi: A Reappraisal Based on a Study of the Sketches and Drafts* (Oxford, 1977); E. Voss, *R. W. und die Instrumentalmusik: W.s symphonischer Ehrgeiz* (Wilhelmshaven, 1977); J. Di Gaetani, *Penetrating W.'s Ring: An Anthology* (Cranbury, N.J., 1978); P. Oberkogler, *R. W.: Vom Ring zum Gral; Wiedergewinnung seines Werkes aus Musik und Mythos* (Stuttgart, 1978); P. Wapnewski, *Der traurige Gott: R. W. in seinen Helden* (Munich, 1978); P. Burbridge and R. Sutton, eds., *The W. Companion* (N.Y., 1979); D. Cooke, *I Saw the World End: A Study of W.'s Ring* (London, 1979); L. Rather, *The Dream of Self-Destruction: W.'s Ring and the Modern World* (Baton Rouge, La., 1979); A. Blyth, *W's Ring: An Introduction* (London, 1980); L. Beckett, *R. W.: Parsifal* (Cambridge, 1981); M. Ewans, *W. and Aeschylus: The Ring and the Oresteia* (London, 1982); C. Dahlhaus, "W.'s 'A Communication to My Friends': Reminiscence and Adaptation," *Musical Times* (Feb. 1983); N. Benvenga, *Kingdom on the Rhine: History, Myth and Legend on W.'s Ring* (Harwich, 1983); J. Deathridge, "Rienzi . . . a few of the facts," *Musical Times* (Sept. 1983).

WAGNER'S ART IN RELATION TO ESTHETICS, PHILOSOPHY, AND RELIGION: F. von Hausegger, *R. W. und Schopenhauer* (Leipzig, 1878; 2nd ed., 1897); J. Freson, *Essais de philosophie et de l'art: L'Esthétique de R. W.* (2 vols., Paris, 1893); M. Hébert, *Le Sentiment religieux dans l'œuvre de R. W.* (Paris, 1894); R. Louis, *Die Weltanschauung R. W.s* (Leipzig, 1898); D. Irvine, *Parsifal and W.'s Christianity* (London, 1899); M. Kufferath, *Musiciens et philosophes: Tolstoy, Schopenhauer, Nietzsche, W.* (Paris, 1899); P. Moos, *R. W. als Ästhetiker* (Berlin, 1906); R. Richter, *Kunst und Philosophie bei R. W.* (Leipzig, 1906); H. Bélart, *F. Nietzsche und R. W.: Ihre persönlichen Beziehungen, Kunst- und Weltanschauungen* (Berlin, 1907); G. Robert, *Philosophie et drame. Essai d'une explication des drames wagnériens* (Paris, 1907); O. Schmiedel, *R. W.s religiöse Weltanschauung* (Tübingen, 1907); W. Vollert, *R. W.s Stellung zur christlichen Religion* (Wismar, 1907); L. Dauriac, *Le Musicien-poète R. W. Etude de psychologie musicale* (Paris, 1908); G. Braschowanoff, *Von Olympia nach Bayreuth* (2 vols., Leipzig, 1911–12); F. Gross, *Die Wiedergeburt des Sehers* (Zürich, 1927); A. Drews, *Ideengehalt von W.s dramatischen Dichtungen* (Leipzig, 1931); G. Wooley, *R. W. et le symbolisme français* (Paris, 1931); F. Gross, *Der Mythos W.s* (Vienna, 1932); G. Frommel, *Der Geist des Antike bei R. W.* (Berlin, 1933); I. Wyzewska, *La Revue Wagnérienne; Essai sur l'in-*terprétation esthétique de W. en France (Paris, 1934); K.R. Karzer, *R. W. der Revolutionär gegen das 19. Jahrhundert* (1934); W. Engelsmann, *Erlösung dem Erlöser: R. W.s religiöse Weltgestalt* (Leipzig, 1936); M. Boucher, *Les Idées politiques de R. W.* (Paris, 1948; in Eng., N.Y., 1950); K. Overhoff, *R. W.s germanisch-christlicher Mythos* (Dinkelsbühl, 1955); B. Magee, *Aspects of W.* (London, 1968; revised ed., 1972); M. Gregor-Dellin, *R. W.: Die Revolution als Oper* (Munich, 1973); R. Hollinrake, *Nietzsche, W. and the Philosophy of Pessimism* (London, 1982).

WAGNER'S ART IN RELATION TO THEORY AND TECHNIQUE: C. Kistler, *Harmonielehre* (Heilbronn, 1879; 2nd ed., greatly augmented, 1903; based on Wagner's harmonic innovations); K. Mayrberger, *Die Harmonik R. W.s* (Chemnitz, 1883); S. Jadassohn, *Melodik und Harmonik bei R. W.* (Berlin, 1899); E. Thomas, *Die Instrumentation der "Meistersinger" von R. W.* (2 vols., Mannheim, 1899; 2nd ed., Leipzig, 1907); G. Capellen, *Ist das System Simon Sechters ein geeigneter Ausgangspunkt für die theoretische Wagnerforschung?* (Leipzig, 1902); E. Poirée, *Le Discours musical, son principe, ses formes expressives, spécialement d'après la partition des "Maîtres-Chanteurs" de R. W.* (Paris, 1902); E. Ergo, *Über R. W.s Harmonik und Melodik* (Leipzig, 1914); E. Kurth, *Romantische Harmonik und ihre Krise in W.s "Tristan"* (Bern and Leipzig, 1920; 2nd ed., Berlin, 1923; valuable); A. Lorenze, *Das Geheimnis der Form bei R. W.* (4 vols., Berlin: I, *Der Ring,* 1924; II, *Tristan,* 1926; III, *Meistersinger,* 1930; IV, *Parsifal,* 1933; valuable).

WAGNER AND BAYREUTH: F. Nietzsche, *W. in Bayreuth* (Chemnitz, 1876; in vol. I of *Nietzsches Werke,* Leipzig, 1895; new ed., 1931; Eng. trans. in complete works, Edinburgh, 1910–14); H. von Wolzogen, *Grundlage und Aufgabe des Allgem. Patronalvereins zur Pflege und Erhaltung der Bühnenfestspiele in Bayreuth* (Chemnitz, 1877); K. Heckel, *Die Bühnenfestspiele in Bayreuth* (Leipzig, 1891); H. Porges, *Die Bühnenproben zu den Festspielen des Jahren 1876* (Leipzig, 1896); F. Weingartner, *Bayreuth, 1876–96* (Berlin, 1896; 2nd ed., 1904); H.S. Chamberlain, *Die ersten 20 Jahre der Bayreuth Bühnenfestspiele* (Bayreuth, 1896); E. Kloss, *Zwanzig Jahre Bayreuth* (Berlin, 1896; Eng. trans., London, 1896); F. Hofmann, *Bayreuth und seine Kunstdenkmale* (Munich, 1902); W. Golther, *Bayreuth* (Berlin, 1904); R. Sternfeld, *R. W. und die Bayreuth Bühnenfestspiele* (2 vols., Berlin, 1906; new ed., 1927); M.G. Conrad, *W.s Geist und Kunst in Bayreuth* (Munich, 1906); K.F. Glazenapp, *Bayreuther Briefe von R. W.* (Berlin, 1907; abridged Eng. trans. as *The Story of Bayreuth as Told in the Bayreuth Letters of R. W.,* Boston, 1912); A. Prüfer, *Das Werk von Bayreuth* (Leipzig, 1909); idem, *R. W. in Bayreuth* (Leipzig, 1910); H. von Wolzogen, *Heinrich von Steins Briefwechsel mit H. von Wolzogen. Ein Beitrag zur Geschichte des Bayreuther Gedankens* (Leipzig, 1910); H. Bahr and A. Bahr-Mildenburg, *Bayreuth und das W.-Theater* (Leipzig, 1910; 2nd ed., 1912; Eng. trans., London, 1921); R. Du Moulin-Eckart, *Wahnfried* (Leipzig, 1925); P. Bülow, *R. W. und sein Werk von Bayreuth* (Frankfurt, 1927); F.

Klose, *Bayreuth. Eindrücke und Erlebnisse* (Regensburg, 1929); O. Bie, *R. W. und Bayreuth* (Leipzig, 1931); J. Kneise, *Der Kampf zweier Welten um das Bayreuther Erbe* (Kassel, 1931); L. Reichwein, *Bayreuth* (Bielefeld and Leipzig, 1934); H.B. Brand, *Aus R. W.s Leben in Bayreuth* (Munich, 1935); S. Rützow, *R. W. und Bayreuth* (Munich, 1943; 2nd ed., 1953); J. Bertram, *Der Seher von Bayreuth* (Berlin, 1943); E. Ebermayer, *Magisches Bayreuth, Legende und Wirklichkeit* (Stuttgart, 1951); W. Wagner, ed., *R. W. und das neue Bayreuth* (Munich, 1962); G. Skelton, *W. at Bayreuth: Experiment and Tradition* (London, 1965; revised ed., 1976); P. Turing, *New Bayreuth* (London, 1969; revised ed., 1971); H. Barth, ed., *Der Festspielhügel: 100 Jahre Bayreuther Festspiele in einer repräsentativen Dokumentation* (Bayreuth, 1973; 2nd ed., 1976); L. Lucas, *Die Festspiel-Idee R. W.s* (Regensburg, 1973); M. Karbaum, *Studien zur Geschichte der Bayreuther Festspiele: 1876–1976* (Regensburg, 1976); R. Hartford, ed., *Bayreuth: The Early Years* (London, 1980). WAGNER'S LITERARY SOURCES: F. Schultz, *Das neue Deutschland. Seine alten Heldensagen und R. W.* (Leipzig, 1888); E. Meinck, *Die sagenwissenschaftlichen Grundlagen der Nibelungendichtung W.s* (Berlin, 1892); J.L. Weston, *The Legends of the Wagnerian Drama* (London, 1896; new ed., 1903); A.M. Bowen, *The Sources and Text of W.'s "Die Meistersinger von Nürnberg"* (Munich, 1897); J. Nover, *Die Tannhäuserage und ihre poetische Gestaltung* (Hamburg, 1897); E. Wechsler, *Die Sage vom hl. Gral in ihrer Entwickelung bis auf R. W.s "Parsifal"* (Halle, 1898); J. Nover, *Die Lohengrinsage und ihre poetische Gestaltung* (Hamburg, 1899); Hermann von der Pfordten, *Handlung und Dichtung der Bühnenwerke R. W.s nach ihren Grundlagen in Sage und Geschichte* (Berlin, 1900; 4th ed., 1908); W. Golther, *Die sagengeschichtlichen Grundlagen der Ringdichtung R. W.s* (Berlin, 1902); S. Valot, *Les Héros de R. W. Etudes sur les origines indo-européennes des légendes wagnériennes* (Paris, 1903); W.C. Sawyer, *Teutonic Legends in the Nibelungenlied and the Nibelungen Ring* (Philadelphia, 1904); W. Golther, *Tristan und Isolde in den Dichtungen des Mittelalters und der neuen Zeit* (Leipzig, 1907); R. von Kralik, *Die Gralssage* (Ravensburg, 1907); E. Elster, *Tannhäuser in Geschichte, Sage und Dichtung* (Bromberg, 1908); L. von Schroeder, *Die Wurzeln der Sage vom hl. Gral* (Vienna, 1910); F. Strich, *Die Mythologie in der deutschen Litteratur von Klopstock bis W.* (2 vols., Halle, 1910); W. Golther, *Zur deutschen Sage und Dichtung* (Leipzig, 1911); O. Rank, *Die Lohengrinsage* (Vienna, 1911); W. Golther, *Parsifal und der Gral in deutscher Sage des Mittelalters und der Neuzeit* (Leipzig, 1913); A. Bonilla y San Martin, *Las leyendas de W. en la literatura española* (Madrid, 1913); G. Brownell, *The Wagnerian Romances* (N.Y., 1925); H. Thompson, *W. and Wagenseil: A Source of W.'s Opera "Die Meistersinger"* (London, 1927); M. Unger, "The Cradle of the Parsifal Legend," *Musical Quarterly* (July 1932); A. Salazar, "Parsifal in Romantic Lands," ibid. (Jan. 1939); R.M. Rayner, *Wagner and "Die Meistersinger"* (Oxford, 1940); H. Hirsch, *R. W. und das deutsche Mittelalter*

(Vienna, 1944). CHARACTERS: C. Maude, *W.'s Heroes* (London, 1896) and *W.'s Heroines* (London, 1896); H. von Wolzogen, *R. W.s Heldengestalten erläutert* (Hannover, 1896); A. Höfler, *Wotan, Eine Studie zum "Ring des Nibelungen"* (Vienna, 1897); H. Bélart, *Taschenbuch der Wagnerkünstlerin. W.s Frauengestalten in gesangdramatischer Beziehung* (Leipzig, 1898); E. Destranges, *Les Femmes dans l'œuvre de R. W.* (Paris, 1899); F. Schwabe, *Die Frauengestalten W.s als Typen des "Ewig-weiblichen"* (Munich, 1902); H. Materna, *R. W.s Frauengestalten* (Leipzig, 1904); W. Broesel, *Evchen Pogner* (Berlin, 1906); H. Güntert, *Kundry* (Heidelberg, 1928). WAGNER AS WRITER: H. von Wolzogen, *Die Sprache in R. W.s Dichtungen* (Leipzig, 1878); J. Gautier, *R. W. et son œuvre poétique* (Paris, 1882); B. Vogel, *W. als Dichter. Ein Überblick seines poetischen Schaffens* (Leipzig, 1889); A. Ernst, *L'Art de W.: L'Œuvre poétique* (Paris, 1893); H. Lichtenberger, *R. W., poète et penseur* (Paris, 1898; new ed., 1931; German trans., Dresden, 1899 [augmented ed., 1913]); O. Lüning, *R. W. als Dichter und Denker* (Zürich, 1900); W. Golther, *R. W. als Dichter* (Berlin, 1904; Eng. trans., London, 1905); R. Weltrich, *R. W.s "Tristan und Isolde" als Dichtung. Nebst einigen allgemeinen Bemerkungen über W.s Kunst* (Berlin, 1904); E. Meinck, *Fr. Hebbels und R. W.s Nibelungen-Trilogien* (Leipzig, 1905); J. Schuler, *The Language of R. W.'s "Ring des Nibelungen"* (Lancaster, Pa., 1910); K. Reichelt, *R. W. und die englische Litteratur* (Leipzig, 1912); E. von Schrenck, *R. W. als Dichter* (Munich, 1913); P. Bülow, *Die Jugendschriften R. W.s* (Leipzig, 1917); W. Ramann, *Der dichterische Stil R. W.s* (Leipzig, 1929); O. Strobel, *Skizzen und Entwürfe zur Ring-Dichtung* (Munich, 1930); H. Galli, *W. und die deutsche Klassik* (Berne, 1936); H. Garten, *W. the Dramatist* (London, 1977). ICONOGRAPHY: J. Grand-Carteret, *R. W. en caricatures* (Paris, 1892); E. Fuchs and E. Kreowski, *R. W. in der Karikatur* (Berlin, 1907; 6th ed., 1913); A. Vanselow, *R. W.s photographische Bildnisse* (Munich, 1908); E. Engel, *W.s Leben und Werke im Bilde* (2 vols., Vienna, 1913; new ed., Leipzig, 1922); J. Kapp, *R. W. Sein Leben, sein Werk, seine Welt in 260 Bildern* (Berlin, 1933); P. Bülow, *R. W. Sein Leben in Bildern* (Leipzig, 1936); R. Bory, *R. W. Sein Leben und sein Werk in Bildern* (Leipzig, 1938); M. Geck, *Die Bildnesse R. W.s* (Munich, 1970); W.-S. Wagner, *Die Geschichte unserer Familie in Bildern* (Munich, 1976; Eng. trans. as *The W. Family Albums,* London, 1976). MISCELLANEOUS: C. Baudelaire, *R. W. et Tannhäuser à Paris* (Paris, 1861); W. Tappert, *Wagner-Lexikon. Wörterbuch der Unhöflichkeit* (Leipzig, 1877; new augmented ed. as *R. W. im Spiegel der Kritik,* 1903; an interesting collection of adverse and abusive comments); *Über Schicksale und Bestimmung des W.-Museums* (Leipzig, 1892); E. Kloss, *Das W.-Museum in Eisenach,* in *Ein W.-Lesebuch* (Leipzig, 1904); K. Grunsky, *R. W. und die Juden* (Munich, 1921); W. Lange, *W. und seine Vaterstadt, Leipzig* (Leipzig, 1921); J. Marnold, *Le Cas W.: La Musique pendant la guerre* (Paris, 1920);

W. et la France, special issue of the *Revue Musicale* (Oct. 1923; reprinted N.Y., 1977); P. Stefan, *Die Feindschaft gegen W.* (Regensburg, 1918); E. Newman, *Fact and Fiction about W.* (N.Y., 1931); E. Stemplinger, *W. in Munich* (Munich, 1933); W. Golther, *R. W. Leben und Werke in urkundlichen Zeugnissen, Briefen, Schriften, Berichten* (Ebenhausen, near Munich, 1936); W. Lange, *R. W.s Sippe,* with genealogical table (Leipzig, 1938); L. Weinhold, *Handschriften von R. W. in Leipzig* (Leipzig, 1938); O. Daube, *Humor bei R. W.* (Gütersloh, 1944); L. Stein, *The Racial Thinking of R. W.* (N.Y., 1950); L. Strecker, *R. W. als Verlagsgefährte* (Mainz, 1951); R. Holloway, *Debussy and W.* (London, 1979); F. Glass, *The Fertilizing Seed: W.'s Concept of the Poetic Intent* (Ann Arbor, Mich., 1983); Philip Winters, "W.: Writing the Wrongs," *New Criterion* (Feb. 1983).

Wagner, Robert, Austrian conductor and educator; b. Vienna, April 20, 1915. He studied piano, composition, and conducting at the Vienna Academy of Music; also attended the Univ. of Vienna (Ph.D., 1938). He conducted in Graz (1938–45) and at the Salzburg Mozarteum (1945–51); taught at the International Summer Academy. From 1951 to 1961 he was Generalmusikdirektor in Münster; then was appointed chief conductor of the Innsbruck Symph. (1960–66).

Wagner, Roger, French-born American choral conductor; b. Le Puy, Jan. 16, 1914. He was brought to the U.S. as a child; after studying for the priesthood in Santa Barbara, he returned to France to study organ with Marcel Dupré; he settled in Los Angeles in 1937 and became organist and choirmaster at St. Joseph's; also took courses in philosophy and French literature at the Univ. of Calif. in Los Angeles, and at the Univ. of Southern Calif. He studied conducting with Otto Klemperer and Bruno Walter, and orchestration with Lucien Caillet. In 1946 he founded the Roger Wagner Chorale, and toured extensively with it in the U.S., Canada, and Latin America. In 1965 he organized the Los Angeles Master Chorale and Sinfonia Orch., which opened its inaugural season on Jan. 27, 1965; he took his Master Chorale on a tour of the Soviet Union in 1974. He was head of the dept. of music at Marymount College in Los Angeles (1951–66); also taught at the Univ. of Calif. from 1959. He was knighted by Pope Paul VI in 1966.

Wagner, Sieglinde, Austrian contralto; b. Linz, April 21, 1921. She received her musical training in Linz; then took vocal lessons in Munich with Luise Willer and Carl Hartmann. After making her debut in Linz in 1943, she sang at the Vienna Opera (1947–52); in 1952 she joined the Berlin City Opera; also sang in Rome, Milan, Amsterdam, Salzburg, and Bayreuth; made many concert appearances as well.

Wagner, Siegfried, son of **Richard** and **Cosima Wagner;** b. Triebschen, June 6, 1869; d. Bayreuth, Aug. 4, 1930. His parents were married on Aug. 25, 1870, and Siegfried was thus legitimated. Wagner named the *Siegfried Idyll* for him, and it was performed in Wagner's house in Triebschen in 1870 on Christmas Day (Cosima Wagner's birthday). He attended a polytechnic school, but the lure of music proved overwhelming, and he took up studies under Julius Kniese and Humperdinck; began to compose; also embarked on a conductorial career; appeared as a symph. conductor in Germany, Austria, Italy, and England. In 1894 he was appointed assistant conductor in Bayreuth, and in 1896 became one of the regular conductors. He conducted from memory, and left-handed. In 1908 he succeeded his mother as general superviser of the Bayreuth Festivals. On Sept. 21, 1915, he married Winifred Williams, an adopted daughter of Karl Klindworth. In 1923–24 he visited the U.S. in order to raise funds for the reopening of the Bayreuth Festspielhaus, which had been closed in the course of World War I. In his career as a composer, he was greatly handicapped by the inevitable comparisons with his father. He wrote a symph. poem, *Sehnsucht,* after Schiller (1895); *Fahnenschwur* for Men's Chorus and Orch. (1914); a Violin Concerto (1915); chamber music and vocal works. But his main interest was in music drama; like his father, he wrote his own librettos.
WORKS: Operas: *Der Bärenhäuter* (Munich, Jan. 22, 1899); *Herzog Wildfang* (Munich, March 14, 1901); *Der Kobold* (Hamburg, Jan. 29, 1904); *Bruder Lustig* (Hamburg, Oct. 13, 1905); *Sternengebot* (Hamburg, Jan. 21, 1908); *Banadietrich* (Karlsruhe, Jan. 15, 1910); *An Allem ist Hütchen Schuld* (Stuttgart, Dec. 6, 1917); *Schwarzschwanenreich* (Karlsruhe, Nov. 5, 1918); *Sonnenflammen* (Karlsruhe, 1926); *Der Heidenkönig* (Cologne, Dec. 16, 1933); *Der Schmied von Marienburg* (Rostock, Dec. 16, 1923). His reminiscences, *Erinnerungen,* were publ. at Stuttgart in 1923.
BIBLIOGRAPHY: L. Karpath, *Siegfried Wagner als Mensch und Künstler* (Leipzig, 1902); K.F. Glasenapp, *Siegfried Wagner und seine Kunst* (Leipzig, 1911; 3rd ed., 1919); P. Pretzsch, *Die Kunst Siegfried Wagners* (1919); O. Daube, *Siegfried Wagner und sein Werk* (Bayreuth, 1925); R. Du Moulin-Eckart, *Wahnfried* (Leipzig, 1925); H. Rebois, *Lettres de Siegfried Wagner* (Paris, 1933); O. Daube, *Siegfried Wagner und die Märchenoper* (Leipzig, 1936); Zdenko von Kraft, *Der Sohn: Siegfried Wagners Leben und Umwelt* (1969).

Wagner, Wieland, grandson of **Richard Wagner,** great-grandson of **Franz Liszt;** b. Bayreuth, Jan. 5, 1917; d. Munich, Oct. 16, 1966. He received his general education in Munich, and devoted himself to the problem of modernizing the productions of Wagner's operas. When the Bayreuth Festivals were resumed in 1951, after World War II, Wieland Wagner assumed the tasks of its scenic director. Abandoning the luxuriant scenery of 19th-century opera, he emphasized the symbolic meaning of Wagner's music dramas, eschewing realistic effects, such as machinery propelling the Rhine maidens through the wavy gauze of the river, or the bright paper flames of the burning Valhalla. He even introduced

Freudian sexual overtones, as in his production of *Tristan und Isolde,* where a phallic pillar was conspicuously placed on the stage.

Wagner, Winifred, British-born daughter-in-law of **Richard Wagner;** b. Hastings, England, 1897; d. Überlingen, on Lake Constance, March 5, 1980. Her father was a British journalist, her mother a Swedish actress; both her parents died when she was an infant, and she was adopted by the German musician Karl Klindworth. In 1915 she married Wagner's son **Siegfried,** and she became totally Germanized, Wagnerized, and Nazified. Adolf Hitler was a frequent guest at her house after she became a widow; her outspoken admiration for his person became public knowledge, so that newspapers openly speculated that the 2 might decide to get married in some barbarous Nordic ceremony. Her politics created a serious rift between her and her 2 sons, Wieland and Wolfgang, who, though loyal to the greatness of their grandfather, took a jaundiced view of Hitler's appropriation of Wagner's music as a Nazi symbol. Her daughter Friedekin was also militantly opposed to her idealization of Hitler. Winifred Wagner emigrated to the U.S. in 1939, and spent her last years of life with her daughter Verena, whose politics were neutral.

Wagner, Wolfgang, son of **Siegfried Wagner,** grandson of **Richard Wagner,** great-grandson of **Franz Liszt,** German opera producer, designer, and administrator; b. Bayreuth, Aug. 30, 1919. He studied music privately; then worked in various capacities at the Bayreuth Festivals and the Berlin State Opera. When the Bayreuth Festival was resumed in 1951, he directed its administration and participated in its productions as stage designer and director. After the death of his brother **Wieland** in 1966, he assumed the total direction of the Bayreuth Festivals and, for the first time since the early 1950s, invited other designers and directors to work at the festival. Like his brother, he departed radically from the traditional staging of the Wagner operas, and introduced a psychoanalytic and surrealist mise-en-scène, often with suggestive phallic and other sexual symbols in the décor.

Wagner-Régeny, Rudolf, Hungarian-German composer; b. Régen, Transylvania, Aug. 28, 1903; d. Berlin, Sept. 18, 1969. He studied piano with Robert Teichmüller at the Leipzig Cons., conducting and theory at the Hochschule für Musik in Berlin. He occupied various posts as theater and cinema conductor; was in the German army during World War II; director of the Hochschule für Musik in Rostock (1947–50); in 1950 was appointed director of the State Cons. in East Berlin.
WORKS: In 1934 he was commissioned (together with J. Weismann) by the Ministry of Culture to write new musical settings for *A Midsummer Night's Dream,* to replace Mendelssohn's score; his music was produced at Düsseldorf on June 6, 1935. Other works: operas: *Moschopulus* (Gera, 1928); *Der nackte König* (Gera, 1928); *Sganarelle* (Essen, 1929);

Die heilige Courtisane (1932); *Der Günstling* (Dresden, Feb. 20, 1935); *Die Bürger von Calais* (Berlin, Jan. 28, 1939); *Johanna Balk* (Vienna, April 4, 1941); *Das Opfer* (1942); *Der Darmenwäscher* (1950); *Prometheus* (Kassel, Sept. 12, 1959); *Das Bergwerk zu Falun* (Salzburg, Aug. 16, 1961); several ballets, among them *Der zerbrochene Krug* (1937); *Mythologische Figurinen* for Orch. (Salzburg Festival of the International Society for Contemporary Music, June 21, 1952); *3 Movements* for Orch. (1952); *Einleitung und Ode* for Orch. (1967); String Quartet (1948); *Divertimento* for 3 Woodwinds and Timpani (1954); various pieces of chamber music.
BIBLIOGRAPHY: A. Burgartz, *Rudolf Wagner-Régeny* (Berlin, 1935); T. Müller-Medek, ed., *Rudolf Wagner-Régeny: Begegnungen, Biographische Aufzeichnungen, Tagebücher und sein Briefwechsel mit Caspar Neher* (Berlin, 1968).

Wagoner, Porter, American country-music singer and guitarist; b. West Plains, Mo., Aug. 12, 1927. He was forced to drop out of grade school to help his father on the family farm; at the same time he took up the guitar, and soon secured a spot singing and playing on a local radio station; subsequently he toured as a country-music entertainer, and scored major hits with his renditions of such country staples as *Satisfied Mind, The Green Grass of Home, Julie,* and *The Cold Hard Facts of Life.*

Wahlberg, Rune, Swedish conductor and composer; b. Gävle, March 15, 1910. He studied in Stockholm (1928–35), Leipzig (1936–37), and Göteborg (1943–51); has been active as a conductor and a concert pianist.
WORKS: Piano Concerto (1938); *Meditation* for Violin and Orch. (1941); 4 symphs.: No. 1 (1941); No. 2 (1945); No. 3 (1951; Toronto, March 6, 1961); No. 4 (1959; Hofors, March 13, 1960); *Nordic Suite* for Orch. (1943); *Afrodite,* suite for Orch. (1944); *Preludium, Larghetto and Fugue* for Orch. (1952); *Nordland* for Male Chorus and Orch. (1957); Violin Concerto (1958); Violin Sonata (1959); *Concerto barocco* for Violin and String Orch. (1960); Cello Concerto (1961); Bass-clarinet Concerto (1961); *Concert Suite* for Strings (1961); *Prisma,* saxophone quartet (1961); Violin Concertino (1963); *Florez och blanzeflor* for Male Chorus and Orch. (1963); *Concert Fantasy* for Piano and Orch. (1967); *Havsfyren* for Male Chorus and Orch. (1971); *Helgdagsvisa* for 4 Violins (1971); String Quartet (1972); *Concerto fantastico* for Percussion (1973); *Lyric Fantasy* for Violin and Piano (1975); *En Saga,* an opera (1952).

Wailly, (Louis Auguste) Paul (Warnier) de, French composer; b. Amiens, May 16, 1854; d. Paris, June 18, 1933. He was a pupil of César Franck, and in his works showed himself a follower of Franck's precepts. He wrote 3 symphs.; a dramatic oratorio, *L'Apôtre* (1924); *26 pièces* for Harmonium; publ. *La Vie et l'âme de César Franck* (Paris, 1922).
BIBLIOGRAPHY: A. Laurent, *Paul de Wailly: L'Artiste, l'œuvre* (Paris, 1933); idem, *Paul de Wailly: Le Compositeur, l'artiste* (Eu, 1940).

Waisselius, Matthäus, German composer and lute player; b. c.1540; d. probably in Königsberg, 1602. He was a schoolmaster in the vicinity of Königsberg; publ. several books, in tablature notation, of music for the lute, among them *Cantiones 4, 5, et 6 vocum* (Frankfurt, 1573) and *Lautenbuch,* comprising instruction for the lute and a selection of dance tunes (1592).

Wakasugi, Hiroshi, Japanese conductor; b. Tokyo, May 31, 1935. He studied conducting with Hideo Saito and Nobori Kaneko; in 1967 he was awarded a prize by the Japanese Ministry of Culture. In 1975 he became conductor of the Kyoto Symph. Orch. In 1977 he assumed the post of chief conductor of the Cologne Radio Symph. Orch. In 1981 he became Generalmusikdirektor of the Deutsche Oper am Rhein in Düsseldorf. He was a guest conductor with the Berlin Phil., Vienna Symph., Dresden State Orch., and radio orchs. in Hamburg, Munich, Copenhagen, and other cities; was also a regular conductor with the Dresden State Opera. In 1981 he made his U.S. debut as a guest conductor of the Boston Symph.

Walaciński, Adam, Polish composer; b. Cracow, Sept. 18, 1928. He studied violin with E. Umińska at the State College of Music in Cracow (1947–52); had private composition lessons with S. Kisielewski (1953–55) and with Bogusław Schäffer; was a violinist in the Cracow Radio Orch. (1948–56). In 1972 he was appointed instructor at the Cracow College of Music. He is a member of the avant-garde Grupa Krakowska.
WORKS: *Composition "Alfa"* for Orch. (1958); String Quartet (1959); *Modifications* for Viola and Piano (1960); *Rotazioni* for Piano (1961); *Intrada* for 7 Players (1962); *Canto tricolore* for Flute, Violin, and Vibraphone (1962); *Horizons* for Chamber Orch. (1962); *Sekwencje* for Concertante Flute and Orch. (1963); *Liryka sprzed zaśniecia (A Lyric before Falling Asleep)* for Soprano, Flute, and 2 Pianos (1963); *Concerto da camera* for Violin and String Orch. (1964; revised 1967); *Fogli volanti,* optically notated composition for String Trio (1965); *Canzona* for Cello, Piano, and Tape (1966); *Epigrams* for Chamber Ensemble (1967); *Dichromia* for Flute and Piano (1967); *Refrains et réflexions* for Orch. (1969); *Notturno 70* for 24 Strings, 3 Flutes, and Percussion (1970); *Allaloa,* optically notated composition for electronically transformed Piano (1970); *Torso* for Orch. (1971; Cracow, Jan. 21, 1972); *On peut écouter* for Flute, Oboe, and Bassoon (1971); *Divertimento interrotto* for 13 Players (1974); *Mirophonies* for Soprano, Actor, Clarinet, Viola, Cello, Harp, and Percussion (1974).

Walcha, Helmut, noted German organist; b. Leipzig, Oct. 27, 1907. He lost his eyesight in his youth, but courageously persevered in his musical studies; took organ lessons with Ramin in Leipzig; then served as assistant organist at the Thomaskirche there (1926–29). In 1929 he settled in Frankfurt as a church organist; in 1933 he joined the faculty of the Frankfurt Cons.; in 1938 was named prof. at the Hochschule für Musik there. He retired in 1972. He was honored with a Festschrift for his 70th birthday (Frankfurt, 1978).

Walcker, Eberhard Friedrich, German organ builder; b. Cannstadt, near Stuttgart, July 3, 1794; d. Ludwigsburg, Oct. 2, 1872. Trained in the workshops of his father, a skilled organ builder, he set up for himself in Ludwigsburg in 1820 and won great renown by his excellent work and numerous inventions. After his death the business passed to his 5 sons: **Heinrich** (b. Oct. 10, 1828; d. Kirchheim, Nov. 24, 1903), **Friedrich** (b. Sept. 17, 1829; d. Dec. 6, 1895), **Karl** (b. March 6, 1845; d. Stuttgart, May 19, 1908), **Paul** (b. May 31, 1846; d. 1928), and **Eberhard** (b. April 8, 1850; d. 1927). In 1916 **Oscar Walcker** (son of Friedrich; b. Jan. 1, 1869; d. Nov. 4, 1948) became head of the firm; in 1932 he effected a merger with the firm Ziegler of Steinsfurt (in 1910 a merger with the firm of W. Sauer of Frankfurt had taken place). His reminiscences, *Erinnerungen eines Orgelbauers,* were publ. in Kassel, 1948. The firm has built more than 2,500 organs; some of the largest are those in the Ulm Cathedral (1856; 95 speaking stops; rebuilt and enlarged in 1914 to 171); the Music Hall in Boston (now removed; 1863; 86 stops); the Paulskirche in Frankfurt (1833; 74 stops); St. Peter's in St. Petersburg (1840; 65 stops); the Reval Cathedral (1842; 65 stops); the Votivkirche in Vienna (1878; 61 stops); the Riga Cathedral (1885; 124 stops); St. Stephen's Cathedral in Vienna (1886; 90 stops); St. Michael's in Hamburg (1912; 154 stops, 5 manuals, and pedal).
BIBLIOGRAPHY: J. Fischer, *Das Orgelbauergeschlecht Walcker* (Kassel, 1949).

Wald, Max, American composer and teacher; b. Litchfield, Ill., July 14, 1889; d. Dowagiac, Mich., Aug. 14, 1954. After studying in Chicago, he was active as a theater conductor; went to Paris in 1922 to study with Vincent d'Indy, and remained in Europe until 1936; then returned to Chicago and became chairman of the theory dept. of the Chicago Musical College.
WORKS: His symph. poem *The Dancer Dead* won 2nd prize in the National Broadcasting Co. competition in 1932, and was broadcast from N.Y. on May 1, 1932. His other works include *Retrospectives* for Orch. (Chicago, Jan. 15, 1926); *Comedy Overture* (1937); *In Praise of Pageantry* for Orch. (Chicago, Oct. 31, 1946); *October Moonlight,* song cycle for Soprano, String Quartet, Flute, Clarinet, and Piano (1937); 2 piano sonatas; other piano music; also an opera, *Mirandolina* (1936), and a light opera, *Gay Little World* (1942).

Waldersee, Paul, Graf von, German music editor; b. Potsdam, Sept. 3, 1831; d. Königsberg, June 14, 1906. He was a Prussian officer (1848–71), but became absorbed in musical studies; was co-editor of Breitkopf & Härtel's collected editions of Mozart and Beethoven; edited the valuable *Sammlung musikalischer Vorträge* (1879–84) and the 2nd edition of Köchel's catalogue of Mozart's works (Leipzig, 1905).

Waldman, Frederic, Austrian-born American conductor; b. Vienna, April 17, 1903. He studied conducting with Szell; made his way to N.Y. in 1941; taught at the Juilliard School of Music, where he served as director of its Opera Theater. In 1961 he organized the Musica Aeterna Orch. and Chorus, with which he gave many concerts of rarely performed music.

Waldmann, Maria, Austrian mezzo-soprano; b. Vienna, 1842; d. Ferrara, Nov. 6, 1920. She studied in Vienna with Passy-Cornet and in Milan with Lamperti; made her debut as Pierotto in *Linda di Chamounix* in Pressburg in 1865; then sang in Wiesbaden, Amsterdam, Trieste, and Moscow (with the Italian Opera, 1869–70), at La Scala in Milan (1871–72), and in Cairo (1873–76). She retired in 1876. Verdi admired her singing, and he chose her for the premiere of his Requiem.

Waldrop, Gid, American composer; b. on a ranch in Haskell County, Texas, Sept. 2, 1918. He studied at the Eastman School of Music in Rochester, N.Y. (Ph.D., 1952). He was editor of the *Musical Courier* (1954–58). In 1961 he was appointed assistant to the president of the Juilliard School of Music; in 1963 became dean. He wrote a Trio for Viola, Clarinet, and Harp (1939); *Lydian Trumpeter* for Trumpet and Piano (1946); Symph. (1952); choruses.

Waldstein, Ferdinand Ernst Gabriel, Graf von, amateur musician, friend of Beethoven; b. Dux, Bohemia, March 24, 1762; d. Vienna, Aug. 29, 1823. While serving his novitiate in the Deutscher Orden at Bonn (1787–88), he became acquainted with Beethoven, and on several occasions aided him materially, pretending that the sums were extra allowances from the Elector; after Beethoven's departure for Vienna, Waldstein introduced him in the circles of the aristocracy there; in later life their friendship seems to have cooled. Beethoven wrote a set of variations in C for piano, 4-hands, on a theme of Waldstein (publ. 1794), and later (1805) dedicated to him the great Sonata in C, op. 53. Waldstein also planned the *Ritter-Ballet* (1791), to which Beethoven wrote the music (score publ. 1872).
BIBLIOGRAPHY: J. Heer, *Der Graf von Waldstein und sein Verhältnis zu Beethoven* (Bonn, 1933).

Waldteufel, (Charles-) Emile (the original surname of the family was **Lévy**), famous French composer of waltzes; b. Strasbourg, Dec. 9, 1837; d. Paris, Feb. 12, 1915. His parents ran a music school in Strasbourg; his father also directed a small dance band. Waldteufel took piano lessons at home with his mother; then began to study in earnest with Joseph Heyberger. In 1853 he entered the Paris Cons. in the classes of Louis-Antoine Marmontel and Adolphe Laurent, but left without completing his courses and took a job with the piano manufacturer Scholtus; when he had time, he composed dance music for Paris salons. His first waltz, *Joies et peines,* which he publ. at his own expense in 1859, was an immediate success, and he became known in Paris high society. In 1865 he was appointed director of the court balls and chamber musician to the Empress Eugénie. In 1867 he publ. another successful waltz, with the German title *Vergissmeinnicht (Forget Me Not).* Then followed a series of waltzes that established his fame as a French counterpart to Johann Strauss, Jr.: *Manolo* (1873), *Mon rêve* (1877), *Pomone, Toujours ou jamais* (1877), *Les Sirènes* (1878), *Très jolie* (1878), *Pluie de diamants* (1879), *Dolores* (1880), and the most famous of them, *Les Patineurs* (1882). His dance music symbolized the "gai Paris" of his time as fittingly as the music of Johann Strauss reflected the gaiety of old Vienna. Waldteufel lived most of his life in Paris, but he also filled conducting engagements abroad, visiting London in 1885 and Berlin in 1889.

Waley, Simon, English pianist and composer; b. London, Aug. 23, 1827; d. there, Dec. 30, 1875. He studied in London with Moscheles and Bennett (piano); later with Molique (theory); began to compose as a child, and developed rapidly; wrote a Piano Concerto, 2 piano trios, and many solo pieces; 2 Psalms for the synagogue service, which were publ. in vol. 1 of *Musical Services of the West London Synagogue.* Eventually he abandoned composition, and turned to a mercantile career; became a member of the London Stock Exchange.

Walker, Edyth, American mezzo-soprano; b. Hopewell, N.Y., March 27, 1867; d. New York, Feb. 19, 1950. She studied singing with Aglaja Orgeni at the Dresden Cons.; made her debut as Fides in *Le Prophète* at the Berlin Opera on Nov. 11, 1894. She then became a member of the Vienna Court Opera, where she was engaged until 1903. She made her American operatic debut with the Metropolitan Opera as Amneris (N.Y., Nov. 30, 1903); remained with the company until 1906; then sang in Germany, particularly excelling in Wagnerian roles. In 1936 she returned to N.Y.
BIBLIOGRAPHY: F.D. Perkins, in *Notable American Women,* III (Cambridge, Mass., 1971).

Walker, Ernest, English writer on music; b. Bombay, India, July 15, 1870; d. Oxford, Feb. 21, 1949. He was educated at Balliol College, Oxford (D.Mus., 1898); became director of music there (1901–25); also examiner and member of the Board of Studies for music at Oxford Univ. He publ. the valuable compendium *A History of Music in England* (Oxford, 1907; 2nd ed., 1924; 3rd ed., revised by J.A. Westrup, 1952); a monograph on Beethoven in the Music of the Masters series (1905). His collection of essays, *Free Thought and the Musician,* was publ. in 1946. He was also a composer; wrote a number of choral works; 2 piano quartets; Piano Quintet; Horn Quintet; Cello Sonata; piano pieces; songs to German and Eng. words.
BIBLIOGRAPHY: M. Deneke, *Ernest Walker* (London, 1951).

Walker, Frank, English musicologist; b. Gosport, Hampshire, June 10, 1907; d. (suicide) Tring, England, March 4, 1962. He studied telegraphy; in 1926 went to Rio de Janeiro as a representative of the Western Telegraph Co. From 1931 to 1943 he was in London; in 1944–45 he was in Naples, and later in Vienna, before returning to London. He contributed valuable articles on the composers of the Neapolitan School; wrote the books *Hugo Wolf* (London, 1951; 2nd ed., 1968) and *The Man Verdi* (London, 1962).

Walker, George, black American composer and pianist; b. Washington, D.C., June 27, 1922. He studied at Oberlin College (M.B., 1941); then entered the Curtis Inst. of Music in Philadelphia, where he studied piano with Rudolf Serkin, composition with Rosario Scalero and Gian Carlo Menotti, and chamber music with Piatigorsky and Primrose (Artist Diploma, 1945); also took piano lessons with Robert Casadesus in Fontainebleau in France (diploma, 1947); obtained his D.M.A. from the Eastman School of Music in Rochester, N.Y., in 1957. In 1957 he received a Fulbright fellowship for travel to Paris, where he took courses in composition with Nadia Boulanger. Returning to the U.S., he was also active as a teacher; held appointments at Dillard Univ. in New Orleans (1953), The New School for Social Research in N.Y., the Dalcroze School of Music (1961), Smith College (1961–68), and the Univ. of Colorado (1968). In 1969 he was appointed a prof. at Rutgers Univ.; was chairman of the composition dept. there in 1974; in 1975 was named Distinguished Prof. at the Univ. of Delaware and adjunct prof. at the Peabody Inst. in Baltimore. In 1969 he received a Guggenheim fellowship; also held 2 Rockefeller fellowships for study in Italy (1971, 1975). In his music he maintains a median modern line without necessarily emphasizing the racial element.
WORKS: For Orch.: Trombone Concerto (1957); *Address* (1959; Mons, Belgium, Oct. 22, 1971); Symph. (1961); *Antiphonies* for Chamber Orch. (1968); *Variations* (1971); *Spirituals* (1974); Piano Concerto (1975); *Dialogues* for Cello and Orch. (1975–76); *Mass* for Soloists, Chorus, and Orch. (1976); *Overture: In Praise of Folly* (1980); Cello Concerto (N.Y., Jan. 14, 1982); *An Eastman Overture* (Washington, D.C., Jan. 15, 1983); *Serenata* for Chamber Orch. (1983); Violin Concerto (1984); *Sinfonia* (1984). Chamber music: 2 string quartets (1946, 1967); Cello Sonata (1957); Violin Sonata (1958); *Perimeters* for Clarinet and Piano (1966); *Music for 3* for Violin, Cello, and Piano (1970); *5 Fancies* for Clarinet and Piano, 4-hands (1974); *Music (Sacred and Profane)* for Brass (1975); 3 piano sonatas (1953, 1957, 1975); numerous vocal works, including *3 Lyrics* for Chorus (1958) and *3 Spirituals* for Medium Voice and Piano (1975).
BIBLIOGRAPHY: David Ewen, *American Composers* (N.Y., 1982).

Walker, John, English voice teacher; b. Colney Hatch, Middlesex, March 18, 1732; d. London, Aug. 1, 1807. He wrote *The Melody of Speaking Delineated* (1787; often republ.) with an original notation for representing the musical inflections of the speaking voice.

Walker, Joseph Cooper, Irish writer; b. Dublin, Nov. 1760; d. St.-Valéry, France, April 12, 1810. He publ. the valuable books *Historical Memoirs on the Irish Bards,* with notes on Irish music (London, 1786), and *An Historical Account and Critical Essay on the Opera* (1805).

Wallace, (William) Vincent, Irish composer; b. Waterford, March 11, 1812; d. Château de Bagen (Haute-Garonne), France, Oct. 12, 1865. The son of a bandmaster, Wallace was brought up in a musical atmosphere. He was 15 when the family moved to Dublin, and soon entered a professional career, playing violin in theater orchs. and organ in churches. One of his earliest compositions was *The Harp in the Air,* which later became famous when he incorporated it into his opera *Maritana.* In 1831 he married Isabella Kelly. He applied himself to the study of violin, and subsequently was able to give successful concerts. With his wife he traveled in Australia, South America, Mexico, and the U.S. Returning to Europe in 1844, he toured Germany; in 1845 he was in London, where he produced his opera *Maritana* (Drury Lane, Nov. 15, 1845), which obtained excellent success; it was followed by another opera, *Matilda of Hungary* (Drury Lane, Feb. 2, 1847), which was a failure. In 1850 he resumed his wanderings and revisited the U.S.; he declared his first marriage invalid, and married an American pianist, **Helen Stoepel.** Back in England, he produced several operas, of which *Lurline* (Covent Garden, Feb. 23, 1860) had tremendous acclaim; his other operas were *The Amber Witch* (Haymarket, Feb. 28, 1861), *Love's Triumph* (Covent Garden, Nov. 3, 1862), and *The Desert Flower* (Covent Garden, Oct. 12, 1863); several operas remain unfinished. His piano music enjoyed great vogue during his lifetime; some noted numbers are *La Gondola; 2 Nocturnes; Chant d'amour; Nocturne mélodique; Mélodie irlandaise; Music Murmuring in the Trees; Valse brillante de salon; Tarentelle,* etc.
BIBLIOGRAPHY: A. Pougin, *W.V. Wallace, Etude biographique et critique* (Paris, 1866); W.H.G. Flood, *W.V. Wallace: A Memoir* (Waterford, 1912).

Wallace, William, Scottish composer and music educator; b. Greenock, July 3, 1860; d. Malmesbury, Wiltshire, Dec. 16, 1940. The son of a surgeon, he studied medicine at Glasgow Univ. (M.D., 1888); specialized in ophthalmology in Vienna, and was employed in the Royal Army Medical Corps during World War I. He was self-taught in music; devoted much of his energy to the protection of the rights of British composers; served on the Composers' Copyright Committee of the Society of British Authors; also taught at the Royal Academy of Music.
WORKS: Symph. poems: *The Passing of Beatrice* (1892); *Amboss oder Hammer,* after Goethe (1896); *Sister Helen* (1899); *To the New Century* (1901);

William Wallace (for the 6th centenary of the death of the national hero of Scotland, and namesake of the composer; 1905); *François Villon* (1909); a symph., *The Creation* (1899); suites for Orch.: *The Lady from the Sea*, after Ibsen (1892), and *Pelléas and Mélisande*, after Maeterlinck (1900); overture, *In Praise of Scottish Poesie* (1894); *The Massacre of the Macpherson*, burlesque cantata; song cycles: *Freebooter Songs* (with Orch.; his most famous work); *Lords of the Sea; Jacobite Songs*.

WRITINGS: *The Threshold of Music: An Inquiry into the Development of the Musical Sense* (1908); *The Musical Faculty: Its Origins and Processes* (1914); *Richard Wagner as He Lived* (1925); *Liszt, Wagner and the Princess* (1927).

Wallaschek, Richard, Austrian music theorist; b. Brünn, Nov. 16, 1860; d. Vienna, April 24, 1917. He studied law and philosophy in Vienna, Heidelberg, and Tübingen; from 1890 to 1895 was in London, engaged in research work; in 1896 joined the faculty of the Univ. of Vienna; wrote music criticism. He wrote a number of essays on esthetics, primitive music, and psychology of musical perception. His publications include *Asthetik der Tonkunst* (1886) and several books publ. in London, in Eng.: *On the Origin of Music* (1891); *Natural Selection and Music* (1892); *On the Difference of Time and Rhythm in Music* (1893); *Primitive Music: An Inquiry into the Origin and Development of Music, Song, Instruments, Dances and Pantomimes of Savage Races* (1893; German ed., enlarged, as *Anfänge der Tonkunst*, 1903; reprint, N.Y., 1970); *Das k. k. Hofopentheater* (Vienna, 1909).

BIBLIOGRAPHY: R. Lach, *Zur Erinnerung an Richard Wallaschek* (Vienna, 1917).

Wallat, Hans, German conductor; b. Berlin, Oct. 18, 1929. He was educated at the Schwerin Cons.; then conducted in several provincial music centers. In 1956 he became music director in Cottbus; from 1958-61 was first conductor of the Leipzig Opera; then conducted in Stuttgart (1961-64) and at the Deutsche Oper in West Berlin (1964-65). He was Generalmusikdirektor of the Mannheim National Theater (1965-70); also served in the same capacity at the Bremen Opera (1965-70). He further conducted at the Vienna State Opera (from 1968). In 1970 he was guest conductor at the Bayreuth Festival. In 1971 he made his American debut, conducting *Fidelio* at the Metropolitan Opera in N.Y.

Wallberg, Heinz, German conductor; b. Herringen-Hamm, March 16, 1923. He studied violin and a trumpet in Dortmund and Cologne; later served as both a violinist and a trumpet player in Cologne and Darmstadt; subsequently devoted himself to conducting; led orchs. in Münster, Augsburg, Bremen, and Hamburg. Concurrently he served as Generalmusikdirektor of the Wiesbaden Municipal Theater; from 1964 to 1975 he also conducted the Vienna Tonkünstler Orch. In 1975 he was named Generalmusikdirektor at Essen and acted as principal conductor of the Munich Radio Orch.

Wallenstein, Alfred, American cellist and conductor; b. Chicago, Oct. 7, 1898; d. New York, Feb. 8, 1983. His parents were of German and Austrian extraction; Wallenstein believed that he was a direct descendant of Albrecht von Wallenstein, the illustrious leader during the Thirty Years' War. The family moved to Los Angeles in 1905; Wallenstein took cello lessons with the mother of Ferde Grofé; as a young boy he began to be professionally engaged, playing in hotels and movie theaters; also gave public recitals advertised as "the wonder-boy cellist." He toured with a vaudeville circuit; then joined the San Francisco Symph. Orch. (1916-17); subsequently toured in South America with the troupe of Anna Pavlova, being featured as cello soloist to accompany her famous portrayal of the dying swan. In 1919 he became a member of the Los Angeles Phil.; in 1920 he went to Germany and took cello lessons with Julius Klengel in Leipzig; he also took some courses in medicine at the Univ. of Leipzig. On returning to the U.S., he was engaged in the cello section of the Chicago Symph. (1922–29), and also appeared with it as a soloist; from 1927–29 he served as head of the cello dept. of the Chicago Musical College. In 1929 Toscanini engaged him as first cellist with the N.Y. Phil.; it was Toscanini who urged Wallenstein to try his hand at conducting; he began his conducting career by leading classical programs over the radio. In 1933 he formed the Wallenstein Sinfonietta, giving regular Sunday broadcasts; an important feature was a series of performances of Bach's cantatas. He also programmed numerous premieres of works by contemporary composers; in appreciation of his work in this direction, he received several awards from various cultural organizations. After Toscanini resigned as music director of the N.Y. Phil. in 1936, Wallenstein also left his job as first cellist of the orch., and devoted himself exclusively to radio performances and guest conducting. In 1943 he was named conductor of the Los Angeles Phil., the first American to head a major symph. orch. From 1952–56 he also served as the music director at the Hollywood Bowl. In 1956 he made a tour of the Orient with the Los Angeles Phil. under the auspices of the State Dept.; after this tour he resigned as conductor of the Los Angeles Phil., but continued to give guest appearances with radio orchs. In 1968 he joined the faculty of the Juilliard School of Music in N.Y. as instructor in conducting. In 1979, at the age of 81, he made his last public appearance as a conductor, leading the Juilliard School Orch. in N.Y. Wallenstein never pretended to be a glamorous virtuoso of the baton, but he was a master builder of orchestral. organizations; more in praise than in dispraise, he was described as a "vertical" conductor who offered dispassionate rather than impassionate interpretations; but no one doubted his selfless devotion to music and musicians.

BIBLIOGRAPHY: David Ewen, *Musicians since 1900* (N.Y., 1978).

Wallenstein, Martin, German pianist and composer; b. Frankfurt, July 22, 1843; d. there, Nov. 29,

1896. He studied with Dreyschock in Prague, and with Hauptmann and Rietz in Leipzig; made many successful tours as a pianist. His opera, *Das Testament,* was produced at Frankfurt in 1870; he also wrote a Piano Concerto; many piano studies and characteristic pieces.

Waller, "Fats" (real first name, **Thomas**), black American jazz pianist and composer; b. New York, May 21, 1904; d. Kansas City, Dec. 15, 1943. As a child he had private piano instruction and studied violin and double bass in school, but his most significant early lessons came from the player piano and nickelodeon pianists whom he studiously imitated; at 14 he was playing organ professionally in a Harlem theater; at 16 he resumed formal study with ragtime pianist James P. Johnson; George Gershwin advised him to make a study of classical piano, and he took lessons with Leopold Godowsky. Soon Waller began making piano rolls and recordings; he also composed music for Broadway revues; obtained an excellent success with *Hot Chocolates* (1929), which includes the song *Ain't Misbehavin';* in the 1930s he made many radio appearances; also had small roles in Hollywood movie vignettes. As a jazz pianist, he was considered a leading exponent of "stride piano," playing with a delicacy and lightness of touch that belied his considerable bulk of almost 300 pounds. But much of his popularity was due to his skills as an entertainer; he was especially effective in improvising lyrics to deflate the sentimentality of popular songs. A musical tribute to Fats Waller, the revue *Ain't Misbehavin',* was one of the great successes of the N.Y. theater season in 1978.

BIBLIOGRAPHY: J.R.T. Davies, *The Music of Fats Waller* (London, 1953); W.I. Kirkeby, *Ain't Misbehavin'. The Story of Fats Waller* (N.Y., 1966); Morroe Berger, "Fats Waller—The Outsider Insider," *Journal of Jazz Studies* (Oct. 1973); J. Vance, *Fats Waller. His Life and Times* (N.Y., 1977); Maurice Waller (his son) and A. Calabrese, *Fats Waller* (N.Y., 1977).

Wallerstein, Anton, German violinist and composer; b. Dresden, Sept. 28, 1813; d. Geneva, March 26, 1892. He played in public as a child; joined the Dresden court orch. (1829–32) and later was a member of the Hannover Orch. (1832–41). He wrote a number of popular dance compositions, of which about 300 were publ.; also violin pieces and songs.

Wallerstein, Lothar, Bohemian pianist and conductor; b. Prague, Nov. 6, 1882; d. New Orleans, Nov. 13, 1949. He studied art and music in Prague and Munich; also attended the Geneva Cons., where he later taught piano; after a brief engagement as accompanist at the Dresden Opera (1909), he held the posts of conductor and stage director in Poznan (1910–14), in Breslau (1918–22), in Duisberg (1922–24), and in Frankfurt (1924–26); was producer at the Vienna State Opera (1927–29); then conducted at La Scala in Milan (1929). He came to the U.S. in 1941; was a producer at the Metropolitan Opera in N.Y.;

eventually settled in New Orleans.

BIBLIOGRAPHY: A. Berger, *Über die Spielleitung der Oper. Betrachtungen zur musikalischen Dramaturgie Dr. Lothar Wallensteins* (Graz, 1928).

Wallnöfer, Adolf, Austrian tenor and composer; b. Vienna, April 26, 1854; d. Munich, June 9, 1946. He studied singing with Rokitansky; composition with Krenn and Dessoff. He began his career as a baritone, but developed his voice into a tenor in 1880; joined Neumann's Wagner troupe in 1881; then sang in Bremen and at the German Opera in Prague (1885–95); in 1896–98, appeared in the U.S.; then toured in Russia (1899); in 1906 he was engaged at the Vienna Opera; in 1908 he went to Munich, where he remained until his death. He composed an opera, *Eddystone* (Prague, 1889); several works for solo voice, chorus, and orch. (*Die Grenzen der Menschheit, Gersprenz, Hymne an die Erde,* etc.); piano pieces; numerous songs and ballads, a selection of which was publ. in 5 vols. He publ. *Resonanztonlehre* (1911).

Walmisley, Thomas (Attwood), English organist and composer, son of **Thomas Forbes Walmisley;** b. London, Jan. 21, 1814; d. Hastings, Jan. 17, 1856. His father placed him under the guidance of Thomas Attwood, his own teacher. He showed remarkable progress, and became organist at Trinity and St. John's colleges at Cambridge at the age of 19. In 1836 he became a prof. of music; continued to study nonetheless; received his B.A. degree in 1838, M.A. in 1841, and Mus.D. in 1848. He wrote several odes and anthems for Trinity College. He enjoyed the reputation of being one of the best organists in England of his day. His anthems and church services were brought out by his father, who survived him by 10 years; they were included in the vol. *Cathedral Music* (1857).

Walmisley, Thomas Forbes, English organist and composer; b. London, May 22, 1783; d. there, July 23, 1866. He was a chorister at Westminster Abbey; studied organ with Thomas Attwood; then was organist at the Female Orphan Asylum (1810–14) and at St. Martin-in-the-Fields (1814–54). He was a popular composer of glees; publ. 3 sets containing 6 glees each; also *A Collection of Glees, Trios, Rounds and Canons* (1826); several single glees and songs.

Walsh, John, English music publisher; b. c.1666; d. London, March 13, 1736. From about 1690 he had his business at the sign of the "Golden Harp and Hoboy" in the Strand in London; in 1692 he was appointed "musical instrument maker in ordinary to His Majesty." He developed a flourishing trade, and achieved great renown; in England he was unquestionably the foremost publisher of music in his time. In 1711 he publ. Handel's *Rinaldo,* and remained Handel's principal publisher. He was succeeded by his son, also named **John Walsh** (b. London, Dec. 23, 1709; d. there, Jan. 15, 1766), who maintained the firm's high standards.

BIBLIOGRAPHY: F. Kidson, "Handel's Publisher, John Walsh, His Successors and Contemporaries," *Musical Quarterly* (July 1920); W.C. Smith, "Handel's *Rinaldo;* An Outline of the Early Editions," *Musical Times* (Aug. 1935); idem, *A Bibliography of the Musical Works Published by J. Walsh during the Years 1695–1720* (London, 1948); W.C. Smith and C. Humphries, *A Bibliography of the Musical Works Published by the Firm of John Walsh during the Years 1721–1766* (London, 1968).

Walter, Arnold, Moravian-born Canadian composer; b. Hannsdorf, Aug. 30, 1902; d. Toronto, Oct. 6, 1973. He received a doctorate in law from Prague Univ. in 1926; then studied music in Berlin with H. Albert, Joh. Wolf, and Curt Sachs; emigrated to Canada in 1937 and taught at the Upper Canada College in Toronto; was director of the Royal Cons. Senior School (1945–52) and director of the music faculty of the Univ. of Toronto (1952–68); among his numerous honors is the Companion of the Order of Canada (1971). He turned to composition rather late in life; most of his music is Romantic in its sources of inspiration.

WORKS: Cello Sonatina (1940); Violin Sonata (1940); Piano Trio (1940); *Sacred Songs* for Soprano and String Trio (1941); Symph. in G minor (1942; Toronto, Feb. 1, 1944); *Toccata* for Piano (1947); *For the Fallen,* cantata (1949); Piano Sonata (1950); Concerto for Orch. (1958); *Legend* for Piano (1962); electronic pieces.

Walter, Bruno (real name, **B.W. Schlesinger**), eminent German conductor; b. Berlin, Sept. 15, 1876; d. Beverly Hills, Calif., Feb. 17, 1962. He studied at the Stern Cons. in Berlin with H. Ehrlich, L. Bussler, and R. Radecke. At the age of 17 he became opera coach at the Municipal Opera of Cologne; also did occasional conducting there; in the following year he was engaged as assistant conductor at the Hamburg Stadttheater, under Gustav Mahler; this contact was decisive in his career, and he became in subsequent years an ardent champion of Mahler's music; conducted the premieres of the posthumous Symph. No. 9 and *Das Lied von der Erde.* During the 1896–97 season Walter was engaged as 2nd conductor at the Stadttheater in Breslau; then became principal conductor in Pressburg, and in 1898 at Riga, where he conducted for 2 seasons. In 1900 he received the important engagement of conductor at the Berlin Opera under a 5-year contract; however, he left this post in 1901 when he received an offer from Mahler to become his assistant at the Vienna Opera. He established himself as an efficient opera conductor; also conducted in England (first appearance, March 3, 1909, with the Royal Phil. Society in London). He remained at the Vienna Opera after the death of Mahler; on Jan. 1, 1913, he became court conductor and music director in Munich; under his guidance, the Munich Opera enjoyed brilliant performances, particularly of Mozart's works. Seeking greater freedom for his artistic activities, he left Munich in 1922, and gave numerous performances as a guest conductor with European orchs.;

conducted the series "Bruno Walter Concerts" with the Berlin Phil. from 1921 to 1933; from 1925 he also conducted summer concerts of the Salzburg Festival; his performances of Mozart's music there set a standard. He also appeared as pianist in Mozart's chamber works. On Feb. 15, 1923, he made his American debut with the N.Y. Symph. Society, and appeared with it again in 1924 and 1925. From 1925 to 1929 he was conductor of the Städtische Oper in Berlin-Charlottenburg; in 1929 he succeeded Furtwängler as conductor of the Gewandhaus Orch. in Leipzig, but continued to give special concerts in Berlin. On Jan. 14, 1932, he was guest conductor of the N.Y. Phil., acting also as soloist in a Mozart piano concerto; was reengaged during the next 3 seasons as associate conductor with Toscanini. He was also a guest conductor in Philadelphia, Washington, D.C., and Baltimore. With the advent of the Nazi regime in Germany his engagement with the Gewandhaus Orch. was canceled, and he was also prevented from continuing his orch. concerts in Berlin. He filled several engagements with the Concertgebouw in Amsterdam, and also conducted in Salzburg. In 1936 he was engaged as music director of the Vienna Opera; this was terminated with the annexation of Austria in 1938. Walter with his family then went to France, where he was granted French citizenship. After the outbreak of World War II he sailed for America, establishing his residence in California, and eventually becoming an American citizen. He was guest conductor with the NBC Symph. Orch. (1939); also conducted many performances of the Metropolitan Opera in N.Y. (debut in *Fidelio* on Feb. 14, 1941). From Feb. 1947 to 1949 he was conductor and musical adviser of the N.Y. Phil.; returned regularly as guest conductor until 1960; also conducted in Europe (1949–60), giving a farewell performance in Vienna with the Vienna Phil. in 1960. He subsequently lived in Beverly Hills.

Walter achieved the reputation of a perfect classicist among contemporary conductors; his interpretations of the masterpieces of the Vienna School are particularly notable. He is acknowledged to have been a foremost conductor of Mahler's symphs. His own compositions include 2 symphs.; *Siegesfahrt* for Solo Voices, Chorus, and Orch.; String Quartet; Piano Quintet; Piano Trio; several albums of songs. He publ. the books *Von den moralischen Kräften der Musik* (Vienna, 1935); *Gustav Mahler* (Vienna, 1936; Eng. trans., London, 1937; new trans. with additions, N.Y., 1958); *Theme and Variations,* an autobiography (N.Y., 1946); *Von der Musik und vom Musizieren* (Frankfurt, 1957; in Eng., N.Y., 1961).

BIBLIOGRAPHY: M. Komorn-Rebhan, *Was wir von Bruno Walter lernten* (Vienna, 1913); Paul Stefan, *Bruno Walter* (Vienna, 1936); Thomas Mann, "To Bruno Walter on His 70th Birthday," *Musical Quarterly* (Oct. 1946); Donald Brook, *International Gallery of Conductors* (Bristol, 1951; pp. 207–20); B. Gavoty, *Bruno Walter* (Geneva, 1956); H. Schonberg, *The Great Conductors* (N.Y., 1967; pp. 281–88); *Briefe 1894–1962,* ed. by Lotte Walter-Lindt (1969).

Walter, David Edgar, American composer and

bass-baritine; b. Boston, Feb. 2, 1953. He studied composition at the Juilliard School of Music in N.Y. with David Diamond, Otto Luening, and Vincent Persichetti (B.M. in composition, 1975); continued study with Edward Richer and Calvin Hampton (1976–78) and at Boston Univ. with David del Tredici, Joyce Mekeel, and John Thow (1978–81). He also studied voice at Rutgers Univ. with John Powell (1970–75) and at Trenton State College with Oren Brown, Lois Bove, and Shirley Meier (M.A., 1978); finally enrolled in the Boston Cons. and the New England Cons., where he took voice lessons with Janet Wheeler. In subsequent years he appeared as a bass-baritone at Trinity Church in Boston and Resurrection and Calvary Church in N.Y. He also wrote vocal music for church performances for which he himself took part as soloist. In his compositions he follows the ideal of unmitigated accessibility to the public and practical convenience for the performer.
WORKS: *Passion According to St. Mark* for 13 Soloists, Chorus, Flute, and Organ; *A Lavender Requiem* for Soprano, Chorus, Strings, and Timpani; *Scrooge, The Great Liberator,* ballet; *Scaramouche et Pulcinella,* ballet; *The Balcony,* opera for 3 Singers and Pianos; *Five Choral Preludes* for Organ; *The Book of the Hanging Fruit Flies* for Piano, 5-Fingers; *Antithesis of Kevin* for String Quartet; Harpsichord Sonata; Flute Octet; numerous organ pieces and choruses.

Walter, Fried, German composer; b. Ottendorf-Okrilla, near Dresden, Dec. 19, 1907. He studied in Dresden; filled various posts as opera coach and conductor in Germany; in 1949 became a chief of the light music dept. at Berlin Radio.
WORKS: Operas: *Königin Elizabeth* (Stockholm, Nov. 24, 1939); *Andreas Wolfius* (Berlin, Dec. 19, 1940); *Dorfmusik* (Wiesbaden, Nov. 1, 1943); dance drama, *Kleopatra* (Prague, 1943); dance fairy tale, *Der Pfeil* (Berlin, Dec. 22, 1946); *Kleine Sinfonie* (1942); numerous dramatic ballads; chamber music; songs.

Walter, Friedrich Wilhelm, German writer on music; b. Mannheim, Sept. 3, 1870; d. Heidelberg, Nov. 4, 1956. He studied in Heidelberg (Dr.Phil., 1892); lived most of his life in Mannheim, and publ. a number of valuable monographs dealing with musical life there: *Die Entwickelung des Mannheimer Musik- und Theaterlebens* (1897); *Geschichte des Theaters und der Musik am kurpfälzischen Hofe* (1898); *Archiv und Bibliothek des Grossherzoglichen Hof- und National-Theaters in Mannheim* (2 vols., 1899).

Walter, Georg A., German composer and teacher; b. Hoboken, N.J., Nov. 13, 1875 (of German parents); d. Berlin, Sept. 13, 1952. He studied singing in Berlin, Milan, and London; composition with Wilhelm Berger in Berlin; made a career as a singer, particularly distinguishing himself in the works of Bach and Handel. He was a prof. at the Stuttgart Hochschule für Musik (1925–34); then taught in Berlin

until 1945. He wrote a number of songs; brought out new editions of works by the sons of Bach, Schütz, etc.

Walter, George William, American organist; b. New York, Dec. 16, 1851; d. Washington, D.C., March 11, 1911. At the age of 5 he played the organ at Trinity Chapel; studied with J.K. Paine in Boston and with S.P. Warren in N.Y.; settled in Washington in 1869. He enjoyed a high reputation as an improviser; accumulated a musical library which was one of the finest in America.

Walter (Walther; real name, Blanckenmüller), Johann (Johannes), one of the earliest composers for the Lutheran church; b. Kahler, Thuringia, 1496; d. Torgau, March 25, 1570. He studied at the Univ. of Leipzig from 1521–25; during this time he entered the chapel of the Elector Friedrich the Wise of Saxony as a bass (the Elector divided his residence between Altenburg and Torgau). In 1524, at Wittenberg, he publ. the *Geystlich Gesangk-Buchleyn* for 3–5 Voices, the first Protestant singing book. In 1525 he was summoned to Wittenburg by Luther to assist in the composition and regulation of the German Mass. Shortly after the death of the Elector Friedrich (1525) his chapel was disbanded, and Walter became cantor of the Municipal Latin-School in Torgau and director of the Stadtkantorei (community choir) there (1526–48). In 1548 he was called upon by the new Elector of Saxony, Moritz, to organize the court chapel in Dresden, and remained there as Kapellmeister until 1554, when he retired to Torgau on a pension. He publ. *Cantio septem vocum in laudem Dei omnipotentis et Evangelii ejus* (1544); *Magnificat 8 tonorum* (1557); *Ein newes christliches Lied* (1561); *Ein gar schöner geistlicher und christlicher Bergkreyen* (1561); *Lob und Preis der himmlischen Kunst Musica* (1564); *Das christlich Kinderlied Dr. Martin Luthers, "Erhalt uns Herr bei deinem Wort"* (1566); etc. The *Geystlich Gesangk-Buchleyn* was reprinted in vol. VII of the *Publikationen der Gesellschaft für Musikforschung* (1878); a list of other reprints is found in W. Ehmann's article "Johann Walter, Der erste Kantor der protestantischen Kirche," in *Musik und Kirche,* 6 (1934). Instrumental works by Walter were discovered in the library of the Thomasschule in Leipzig by B. Engelke in 1912 (examples in A. Schering's *Geschichte der Musik in Beispielen,* nos. 80 and 81). A complete edition of Walter's works was edited by Otto Schröder and Max Schneider in 6 vols. (Kassel, 1953–70).
BIBLIOGRAPHY: O. Kade, *Johann Walthers Wittenbergisch geistlig Gesangbuch von 1524* (1878); H. Holstein, "Der Lieder- und Tondichter Johann Walther," *Archiv für Literaturgeschichte* (1884); A. Aber, *Die Pflege der Musik unter den Wettinern* (1921); R. Haas, "Zu Walthers Choralpassion nach Matthäus," *Archiv für Musikwissenschaft,* 4 (1922); A. Schmitz in "Siebs-Festschrift" (1933); W. Gurlitt, "Johannes Walter und die Musik der Reformationzeit," *Luther-Jahrbuch* (1933); O. Michaelis, *Johann Walther, der Musiker-Dichter in Luthers*

Gefolgschaft (Leipzig, 1939); C. Gerhardt, *Die Torgauer Walter-Handschriften; Eine Studie zur Quellenkunde der Musikgeschichte der deutschen Reformationzeit* (Kassel, 1949); G. Reese, *Music in the Renaissance* (N.Y., 1954; 2nd ed., revised, 1959); J. Stahlmann, *Johann Walters Cantiones latinae* (Diss., Univ. of Tübingen, 1960).

Walter, Karl, German organist and campanologist; b. Cransberg, Oct. 27, 1862; d. Montabaur, Dec. 4, 1929. He studied at the Seminary in Montabaur, where he became an instructor in 1893; in 1899 was appointed diocesan inspector for the building of organs and bells; in 1903 became an instructor of church music at the Limburg Seminary. He wrote organ music and sacred works; publ. several manuals on organ building, and on the construction of bells, a field in which he was an authority. His publications are *Kleine Orgelbaulehre* (1904); *Orgelbegleitung zu den Melodien des Gesangbuchs für das Bistum Limburg* (1907; 2nd ed., 1911); *Glockenkunde* (1913); *Kleine Glockenkunde* (1916).

Walter, Thomas, American clergyman and author of singing books; b. Roxbury, Mass., Dec. 13, 1696; d. there, Jan. 10, 1725. He was the son of a clergyman, and a nephew of Cotton Mather; educated at Harvard College (M.A., 1713); on Oct. 29, 1718, he was ordained; was assistant pastor to his father at Roxbury. With the aim of correcting what he described as "an horrid medley of confused and disorderly sounds" prevailing in the singing in New England churches, he publ. *The Grounds and Rules of Musick Explained; or, an Introduction to the Art of Singing by Note; Fitted to the meanest capacities* (Boston, 1721; several other eds. up to 1764). It was the 2nd singing book to be publ. in America, following that of John Tufts. He also publ. *The Sweet Psalmist of Israel* (1722).
BIBLIOGRAPHY: F.J. Metcalf, *American Writers and Compilers of Sacred Music* (1925); E.H. Pierce, "The Rise and Fall of the 'Fugue-Tune' in America," *Musical Quarterly* (April 1930); M.B. Jones, "Bibliographical Notes on Thomas Walter's 'Grounds and Rules,'" *Proceedings of the American Antiquarian Society* (Oct. 1932; also reprinted separately, Worcester, Mass., 1933).

Waltershausen, (Hermann) Wolfgang von, German composer and writer on music; b. Göttingen, Oct. 12, 1882; d. Munich, Aug. 13, 1954. He was a pupil of M.J. Erb in Strasbourg and of Ludwig Thuille in Munich, where he settled. In 1917 he established there a seminar for operatic dramaturgy; was a prof. and assistant director at the Akademie der Tonkunst (1920–23), then director (1923–33). After 1933 he remained in Munich as a private teacher; in 1948 established a seminar for all musical subjects in Munich. In his own music he adopted a neo-Romantic style, rather advanced in harmonic treatment.
WORKS: Operas: *Oberst Chabert,* to his own libretto after Balzac (Frankfurt, Jan. 18, 1912; also several productions in other German cities; his

most successful work); *Else Klapperzehen* (Dresden, May 15, 1909); *Richardis,* a dramatic mystery (Karlsruhe, Nov. 14, 1915); *Die Rauensteiner Hochzeit* (Karlsruhe, 1919); *Die Gräfin von Tolosa* (1934); other works: *Apokalyptische Symphonie* (1924); symph. poem, *Hero und Leander* (1925); *Krippenmusik* for Chamber Orch., with Harpsichord (1926); an orch. partita (1928); piano pieces; songs. Having lost his right arm in a childhood accident, he developed a piano technique for the left hand alone, and publ. studies and transcriptions for left hand which he performed in public. He also publ. a number of valuable writings on music: *Musikalische Stillehre in Einzeldarstellungen* (1920–23); *Richard Strauss* (1921); *Musik, Dramaturgie, Erziehung* (1926); *Dirigenten-Erziehung* (1929); "Der stilistische Dualismus in der Musik des 19. Jahrhunderts," in the "Adler-Festschrift" (Vienna, 1930); *Die Kunst des Dirigierens* (1943; 2nd ed., 1954); also publ. a book of poetry (1952).

Walther, Johann Gottfried, noted German composer and musicographer; b. Erfurt, Sept. 18, 1684; d. Weimar, March 23, 1748. He was a pupil of J. Bernhard Bach at Erfurt, where he was made organist of the Thomaskirche in 1702; in 1707 he was town organist at Weimar, and music master to the children of the ducal family; from 1721, court musician. He stands next to Bach as a master of chorale-variations for organ. His greatest work is the *Musikalisches Lexikon oder Musikalische Bibliothek,* the first music encyclopedia of biography, bibliography, and terms (Leipzig, 1732; facsimile ed., Kassel, 1953, by R. Schaal, with bibliographical notes); he had previously publ. the 64-page *Alte und neue musikalische Bibliothek, oder Musikalisches Lexikon* (1728; only entries under letter A printed, as a preliminary to the main work). His publ. musical compositions include: *Clavierconcert* (unaccompanied; 1741); Prelude and Fugue (1741); 4 chorale-variations (*Jesu meine Freude, Meinen Jesum lass' ich nicht, Allein Gott in der Höh' sei Ehr', Wie soll ich dich empfangen*); many chorale-variations, preludes, fugues, and toccatas, in MS; also 5 collections of "Choralbearbeitungen" by other composers. His organ works were edited by M. Seiffert in vols. 26 and 27 of Denkmäler Deutscher Tonkunst (with biographical sketch). His *Praecepta der musikalischen Composition* was publ. at Leipzig in 1955, edited by Peter Benary.
BIBLIOGRAPHY: H. Gehrmann, "J.G. Walther als Theoretiker," *Vierteljahrsschrift für Musikwissenschaft* (1891); G. Schünemann, "J.G. Walther und H. Bokemeyer," *Bach-Jahrbuch* (1933); O. Brodde, *J.G. Walther. Leben und Werk* (1937).

Walther, Johann Jakob, notable German violinist and composer; b. Witterda, near Erfurt, 1650; d. Mainz, Nov. 2, 1717. He was concertmaster at the Electoral Court of Saxony in Dresden (from 1674), and Italian secretary, in charge of the correspondence with Rome, to the Elector of Mainz (from 1681); in 1693 he was designated as *Doctor.* He publ. *Scherzi da violino solo,* with Continuo (1676; reprinted in *Das Erbe deutscher Musik,* 17); *Hortulus Chelicus, uni violino, duabus, tribus et quatuor subinde chordis simul sonantibus* (1688; 2nd ed. as *Wohlgepflanzter violinischer Lustgarten,* 1694).

BIBLIOGRAPHY: J.W. von Wasielewski, *Die Violine und ihre Meister* (7th ed., 1927); G. Beckmann, *Das Violinspiel in Deutschland vor 1700* (1918); A. Moser, *Geschichte des Violinspiels* (1923; 2nd ed., revised, 1966–67).

Walther von der Vogelweide. See **Vogelweide, Walther von der.**

Walthew, Richard Henry, English composer and pedagogue; b. London, Nov. 4, 1872; d. East Preston, Sussex, Nov. 14, 1951. He studied with Parry at the Royal College of Music (1890–94); after a directorship of the Passmore Edwards Settlement Place (1900–1904), he was appointed instructor of the opera class at the Guildhall School of Music; in 1907 became a prof. of music at Queen's College; also conducted provincial orchs. His works include 2 operettas: *The Enchanted Island* (London, May 8, 1900) and *The Gardeners* (London, Feb. 12, 1906); cantatas: *Ode to a Nightingale* and *The Pied Piper of Hamelin;* Piano Concerto; Piano Quintet; Piano Quartet; 2 piano trios; Violin Sonata; vocal quartets, with piano; songs. He was the author of *The Development of Chamber Music* (1909).

BIBLIOGRAPHY: *Cobbett's Cyclopedic Survey of Chamber Music* (London, 1929); K.H. Leech, "R.H. Walthew," *Musical Opinion* (Jan. 1952).

Walton, Sir William (Turner), eminent British composer; b. Oldham, Lancashire, March 29, 1902; d. Ischia, Italy, March 8, 1983. Both his parents were professional singers, and Walton himself had a fine singing voice as a youth; he entered the Cathedral Choir School at Christ Church, Oxford, and began to compose choral pieces for performance. Sir Hugh Allen, organist of New College, advised him to develop his interest in composition, and sponsored his admission to Christ Church at an early age; however, he never graduated, and instead began to write unconventional music in the manner that was fashionable in the 1920s. His talent manifested itself in a string quartet he wrote at the age of 17, which was accepted for performance for the first festival of the International Society for Contemporary Music in 1923. In London he formed a congenial association with the Sitwell family of quintessential cognoscenti and literati who combined a patrician sense of artistic superiority with a benign attitude toward the social plebs; they also provided Walton with residence at their manor in Chelsea, where he lived off and on for some 15 years. Fascinated by Edith Sitwell's oxymoronic verse, Walton set it to music bristling with novel jazzy effects in brisk, irregular rhythms and modern harmonies; Walton was only 19 when he wrote it. Under the title *Façade,* it was first performed in London in 1923, with Edith Sitwell herself delivering her doggerel with a megaphone; as expected, the show provoked an outburst of feigned indignation in the press and undisguised delight among the young in spirit. But Walton did not pursue the path of facile hedonism so fashionable at the time; he soon demonstrated his ability to write music in a Classical manner in his fetching concert overture *Portsmouth Point,* first performed at the Zürich Festival in 1926, and later in the comedy-overture *Scapino.* His biblical oratorio *Belshazzar's Feast,* written in 1931, reveals a deep emotional stream and nobility of design that places Walton directly in line from Handel and Elgar among English masters. His symph. works show him as an inheritor of the grand Romantic tradition; his concertos for violin, for viola, and for cello demonstrate an adroitness in effective instrumental writing. Walton was a modernist in his acceptance of the new musical resources, but he never deviated from fundamental tonality and formal clarity of design. Above all, his music was profoundly national, unmistakably British in its inspiration and content. Quite appropriately, he was asked to contribute to two royal occasions: he wrote *Crown Imperial March* for the coronation of King George VI in 1937 and *Orb and Sceptre* for that of Queen Elizabeth II in 1953. He received an honorary doctorate from Oxford Univ. in 1942; was knighted in 1951. He spent the last years of his life on the island of Ischia off Naples with his Argentinian-born wife, Susana Gil Passo.

WORKS: FOR THE STAGE: Opera, *Troilus and Cressida,* after Chaucer (London, Dec. 3, 1954); *The Bear,* "an extravaganza" in one act, after a comedy by Chekhov (Aldeburgh Festival, June 3, 1967); *Façade,* "an entertainment" for Declamation, Flute, Clarinet, Saxophone, Trumpet, Cello, and Percussion, to texts in blank verse by Edith Sitwell (first perf. privately at the Sitwell home in London, Jan. 24, 1922; it had its first public hearing in London, on June 12, 1923; it was revised in 1942, scored for an augmented ensemble); *The Wise Virgins,* ballet arranged from 6 pieces by Bach (London, April 24, 1940); *The Quest,* ballet (1943).

FOR ORCH.: *Portsmouth Point,* concert overture (Zürich Festival of the International Society for Contemporary Music, June 22, 1926); *Siesta* (1926); *Sinfonia concertante* for Piano and Orch. (London, Jan. 5, 1928); Viola Concerto (London, Oct. 3, 1929, Paul Hindemith, soloist; revised for a reduced orch. accompaniment, and first perf. in this new version in London, Jan. 18, 1962); Symph. No. 1 (London, Nov. 6, 1935); *Crown Imperial,* coronation march for King George VI (Westminster Abbey, London, May 12, 1937); 2 orch. suites from *Façade:* No. 1 (Siena Festival of the International Society for Contemporary Music, Sept. 14, 1928) and No. 2 (N.Y., March 30, 1938); Violin Concerto (Cleveland, Dec. 7, 1939; Jascha Heifetz, soloist); *Scapino,* comedy-overture (Chicago, April 3, 1941); *Spitfire: Prelude and Fugue,* glorifying the famous British combat plane (1942); *Orb and Sceptre,* coronation march for Elizabeth II (Westminster Abbey, London, June 2, 1953); *Johannesburg Festival Overture* (Johannesburg, South Africa, Sept. 25, 1956); Cello Concerto (Boston, Jan. 25, 1957; Piatigorsky, soloist); *Partita* (Cleveland, Jan. 30, 1958); *Fanfare* for the Queen's entrance at the NATO Parliamentary Conference

(London, June 5, 1959); Symph. No. 2 (Edinburgh, Sept. 2, 1960); *Variations on a Theme by Hindemith* (London, March 8, 1963); *Capriccio Burlesco* (N.Y., Dec. 7, 1968); *Improvisations on an Impromptu of Britten* (San Francisco, Jan. 14, 1970); Sonata for String Orch. (1972; orchestration of the 1947 String Quartet); *Varii Capricci* (London, May 4, 1976; orchestration of the *5 Bagatelles* for Guitar); *Prologo e Fantasia* (London, Feb. 20, 1982).

VOCAL WORKS: *Belshazzar's Feast*, oratorio for Baritone, Chorus, and Orch. (Leeds Festival, Oct. 8, 1931); *In Honour of the City of London* for Chorus and Orch. (Leeds Festival, 1937); *Te Deum* for the coronation of Queen Elizabeth II (London, June 2, 1953); *Gloria* for Vocal Soloists, Mixed Chorus, and Orch. (Liverpool, Nov. 24, 1961); *A Song for the Lord Mayor's Table* for Soprano and Piano (London, July 18, 1962); *The Twelve* for Chorus and Organ (Oxford, May 16, 1965); *Missa Brevis* for Double Mixed Chorus and Organ (Coventry, April 10, 1966); *Cantico del Sole* for Chorus a cappella (1974).

CHAMBER MUSIC: Piano Quartet (1918; revised 1974); String Quartet (1922; Salzburg Festival of the International Society for Contemporary Music, Aug. 4, 1923); *Toccata* for Violin and Piano (1923); String Quartet (1947); Violin Sonata (1949); *5 Bagatelles* for Solo Guitar (1972).

FILM MUSIC: *Escape Me Never* (1934); *As You Like It* (1936); *Stolen Life* (1939); *Major Barbara* (1941); *Henry V* (1944); *Hamlet* (1947); *Richard III* (1954); etc.; several suites have been drawn from these scores.

BIBLIOGRAPHY: H.J. Foss, "William Walton," *Musical Quarterly* (Oct. 1940); F.S. Howes, *The Music of William Walton*, 2 vols. (London, 1942 and 1943; new amplified edition, 1965); E. Evans, "William Walton," *Musical Times* (1944); K. Avery, "William Walton," *Music & Letters* (Jan. 1947); S. Craggs, *William Walton: A Thematic Catalogue of His Musical Works* (London, 1977); A. Poulton, *Sir William Walton: A Discography* (London, 1980); B. Northcott, *"In Search of Walton," Musical Times* (March 1982).

Waltz, Gustavus, German bass; place and date of birth unknown; d. London, c.1759; was a member of Handel's household in London, serving as a major-domo. He appeared on the London stage in 1732 in Handel's *Acis and Galatea* and subsequently sang in Handel's oratorios. He is chiefly celebrated because of the reported acrid comment of Handel on Gluck: "He knows no more of counterpoint than my cook, Waltz."
BIBLIOGRAPHY: W.C. Smith, "Gustavus Waltz: Was He Handel's Cook?" in *Concerning Handel* (London, 1948).

Walzel, Leopold Matthias, Austrian composer; b. Vienna, Nov. 29, 1902; d. there, June 9, 1970. A lawyer by profession, he also studied music at the Univ. of Vienna; composed 5 symphs.; an opera, *Salamis;* Piano Quartet; Octet; 2 quintets; several song cycles.

Wambach, Emile, Belgian composer; b. Arlon, Luxembourg, Nov. 26, 1854; d. Antwerp, May 6, 1924. He studied with Benoit, Mertens, and Callaerts at the Antwerp Cons.; in 1913 became its director. He wrote music in the National Flemish style, following the model of Benoit. He wrote the Flemish opera *Nathans Parabel;* 4 oratorios: *Mozes op den Nijl* (1881); *Yolande* (1884); *Blancefloer* (1889); *Jeanne d'Arc* (1909); choral works; piano pieces; songs.
BIBLIOGRAPHY: L. Vocht, "Levensbericht over Emile Wambach," *Annuaire* of the Académie Royale de Belgique, 118 (1952; with a list of works).

Wand, Günter, German conductor; b. Elberfeld, Jan. 7, 1912. He studied at the Cologne Cons. and at the Munich Academy of Music. In 1944–45 he conducted the Mozarteum Orch. in Salzburg. In 1947 he became Generalmusikdirektor of the Gürzenich Orch. of Cologne, a position he held until 1974. He also headed the conducting classes at the Cologne Cons. He eventually settled in Bern, Switzerland, where he led the local orch. society and toured widely with it; in 1968 he took it on a concert tour in Japan.
BIBLIOGRAPHY: F. Berger, *Günter Wand. Gürzenichkapellmeister 1947–74* (Cologne, 1974).

Wangemann, Otto, German music scholar; b. Loitz-on-the-Peene, Jan. 9, 1848; d. Berlin, Feb. 25, 1914. He studied with F. Kiel in Berlin; in 1886 settled there as a church organist and singing teacher. He publ. *Grundriss der Musik-Geschichte* (1878); *Geschichte der Orgel* (1897; 3rd ed., 1887); *Geschichte des Oratoriums* (1880); also singing manuals for schools; *Weihnachtsmusik* for Solo Voices, Chorus, and Orch.; school songs; piano pieces.

Wangenheim, Volker, German conductor; b. Berlin, July 1, 1928. He studied piano, oboe, violin, composition, and conducting at the Hochschule für Musik in Berlin; later played oboe with several Berlin ensembles. In 1957 he became chief conductor of the Beethovenhalle Orch. in Bonn; then served as Generalmusikdirektor of the city of Bonn (1963–76). In 1971 he was appointed instructor of the conducting class at the Musikhochschule in Cologne; was named prof. there in 1973. In 1980 he was engaged as music director of the Bournemouth Sinfonietta in England; also had numerous engagements as guest conductor, in South America, the U.S., and Japan. He was also a composer; among his works are *Concerto per archi* (1963); *Sinfonia notturna* (1964); *Klangspiel I* for Strings (1971); *Klangspiel II* for Chamber Ensemble (1972); also a certain number of sacred choral compositions.

Wanhal (Vanhall), Johann Baptist, Bohemian composer; b. Nechanicz, Bohemia, May 12, 1739; d. Vienna, Aug. 20, 1813. His musical ability brought him the patronage of Countess Schaffgotsch, who enabled him to study in Vienna with Dittersdorf; another patron, Baron Riesch, sent him to Italy for further study. He settled in Vienna. An extremely prolific composer, he wrote a great number of piano pieces, which enjoyed considerable popularity among amateurs. He also composed an enormous amount of instrumental music (about 73 authenticated symphs. and numerous string quartets); about 60 masses; 2 Requiems; over 60 offertories. Among his publ. works are 12 symphs. for strings, 2 oboes, and 2 horns; 12 string quartets; 12 trios for 2 violins and cello; quartets (concerti) for piano and strings; quartets for piano, flute, violin, and cello; piano trios; 5 piano sonatas for 4-hands, and 6 for 2-hands; violin duos; 6 violin sonatas, with piano; characteristic sonatas (*Militaire, The Battle of Würzburg, The Battle of Trafalgar*); many piano sonatinas; 70 books of piano variations; fantasias, dances, and other piano pieces; fugues, preludes, etc., for organ; etc.

BIBLIOGRAPHY: M. von Dewitz, *J.B. Vanhall, Leben und Klavierwerke* (Diss., Univ. of Munich, 1933); G. Wolters, *J. Wanhal als Sinfoniker* (Diss., Univ. of Cologne, 1933); P.R. Bryan, *The Symphonies of Johann Vanhall* (Diss., 2 vols., Univ. of Michigan, 1955).

Wanless, John, English organist and composer; d. York (buried, Feb. 2), 1712. He was organist at the Lincoln Cathedral between 1616 and 1625; only a few of his church works are extant, among them an anthem, *Plead thou my cause.* His son, **Thomas Wanless** (d. 1721), was organist of York Minster from 1691 to 1695. He publ. a psalter, *The Metre Psalm-tunes,* in 4 parts (London, 1702); composed *York Litany.*

Wannenmacher (Latinized as **Vannius**), **Johannes,** German composer; b. Neuenburg am Rhein, c.1485; d. Interlaken, 1551. He was cantor at Bern, Switzerland, in 1510, and at Freiburg im Breisgau in 1513; because of his inclinations toward Lutheranism, he was obliged to leave Germany; settled in Interlaken in 1531 as town clerk, and remained there until his death. He was greatly esteemed in his time as a fine polyphonist; Glareanus cites a motet for 4 voices in the *Dodecachordon.* Wannenmacher's *An Wasserflüssen Babylon* for 3–6 Voices was publ. in Ott's *Liederbuch* (1544); some German songs by him were publ. posthumously.

BIBLIOGRAPHY: A. Geering, *Die Vokalmusik in der Schweiz zur Zeit der Reformation: Leben und Werke von Bartholomäus Frank, Johannes Wannenmacher, Cosmas Alder* (Aarau, 1933).

Warburg, Felix Moritz, patron of music; b. Hamburg, Jan. 14, 1871; d. New York, Oct. 20, 1937. He came to the U.S. in 1894, and became associated with the banking firm of Kuhn, Loeb & Co.; became a U.S. citizen in 1900. He participated in many musical activities as a sponsor; was a member of the board of the Inst. of Musical Art. He owned a quartet of Stradivarius instruments, and sponsored the concerts of the Stradivarius String Quartet.

Ward, David, Scottish bass; b. Dumbarton, July 3, 1922; d. Dunedin, July 16, 1983. He studied at the Royal College of Music in London; later had voice

training with Hans Hotter in Munich. In 1953 he made his operatic debut at the Sadler's Wells Opera in London; in 1960 he joined the Royal Opera, Covent Garden. He was equally proficient in dramatic, heroic, and buffo roles. In 1972 he was made a Commander of the Order of the British Empire.

Ward, Frank Edwin, American organist and composer; b. Wysox, Pa., Oct. 7, 1872; d. Wolfeboro, N.H., Sept. 15, 1953. He studied at the N.Y. College of Music with J.P. Lawrence (organ) and S.A. Pearce (theory); was a student of MacDowell at Columbia Univ. (1898–1903); later became associate prof. of music there (1909–19); for 40 years (1906–46) was organist and choirmaster at the Church of the Holy Trinity in N.Y. His works include a Lenten cantata, *The Saviour of the World;* a Christmas cantata, *The Divine Birth; Ocean Rhapsody* for Orch.; services; anthems; organ pieces; part-songs; also 2 string quartets and other chamber music.

Ward, John, English composer; b. Canterbury (baptized, Sept. 8) 1571; d. c.1638. He was in the service of Sir Henry Fanshawe, to whom he dedicated *The First Set of English Madrigals* (London, 1613); wrote services and anthems, and pieces for the virginal. His madrigals were reprinted in vol. XIX of *The English Madrigal School.*

BIBLIOGRAPHY: E.H. Fellowes, *The English Madrigal Composers* (1921); M. Forster, *The Sacred Music of John Ward* (Diss., Univ. of Durham, 1971).

Ward, John Milton, American musicologist; b. Oakland, Calif., July 6, 1917. He studied at the Univ. of Washington (M.M., 1942); obtained his Ph.D. at N.Y. Univ. (1953); then was an instructor in the Dept. of Fine Arts of Michigan State Univ. (1947–53); was on the faculty of the Univ. of Illinois (1953–55), and after 1955 at Harvard Univ. He brought out *The Dublin Virginal MS* (Wellesley, Mass., 1954; 2nd revised ed., 1964); contributed numerous essays and specialized articles to various scholarly music magazines.

Ward, Robert, American composer; b. Cleveland, Sept. 13, 1917. He studied at the Eastman School of Music in Rochester, N.Y., with Howard Hanson and Bernard Rogers (B.Mus., 1939) and at the Juilliard School of Music in N.Y. with Frederick Jacobi (composition) and Albert Stoessel (conducting); obtained his M.A. in 1946; subsequently he taught at the Juilliard School (1946–56); served as vice-president and managing editor of the Galaxy Music Corp.; then was a prof. of music at the North Carolina School of the Arts. As a composer, he has evolved an effective idiom, modern but not aggressively so; he particularly excels in dramatic and compact stage works on American subjects.

WORKS: Operas: *Pantaloon,* after Leonid Andreyev's play *He Who Gets Slapped* (Juilliard School of Music, N.Y., May 17, 1956); *The Crucible* (N.Y., Oct. 26, 1961; received the Pulitzer Prize); *The Lady from Colorado* (Central City, Colo., July 3, 1964); *Claudia Legare,* after Ibsen's *Hedda Gabler*

(Minneapolis, April 14, 1978); *Minutes till Midnight,* on the subject of the super bomb, "Cosmic Bomb" (Miami, June 4, 1982); for Orch.: Symph. No. 1 (N.Y., May 10, 1941); *Jubilation Overture* (Los Angeles, Nov. 21, 1946); Symph. No. 2 (Washington, D.C., Jan. 25, 1948); Symph. No. 3 (Washington, March 31. 1950); Symph. No. 4 (1958); Symph. No. 5, *Canticles for America* (1976); *Jonathon and the Gingery Snare* for Narrator, Small Orch., and Percussion (Young People's Concert, N.Y. Phil., Feb. 4, 1950); *Euphony* for Orch. (1954); *Divertimento* (1961); *Festive Ode* (1966); *Antiphony* for Wind Instruments (1967); Piano Concerto (1968); String Quartet (1965); other chamber music; choruses and songs.
BIBLIOGRAPHY: *Composers of the Americas,* vol. 9 (Washington, D.C., 1963).

Ward, Samuel Augustus, American composer of hymns and dealer in musical instruments; b. Newark, N.J., Dec. 28, 1848; d. there, Sept. 28, 1903. He was the author of the famous hymn *Materna,* first publ. in the *Parish Choir* (Boston, 1888) to the words of "O Mother dear, Jerusalem." Eventually, Ward's hymn tune was combined with the words of the poem *America, the Beautiful,* written by Katherine Lee Bates, a prof. of English at Wellesley College, in 1893, and became one of the most widely sung patriotic American anthems.

Ware, Harriet, American pianist and composer; b. Waupun, Wis., Aug. 26, 1877; d. New York, Feb. 9, 1962. She received her musical instruction from her father, who was a professional musician and choral conductor; she studied piano with Dr. William Mason in N.Y. and Sigismund Stojowski in Paris, composition with Hugo Kaun in Berlin; in 1906 she returned to the United States. Her *Women's Triumphal March* was made the national song of the Federation of Women's Clubs in 1927; her symph. poem *The Artisan* was given by the N.Y. Symph. Orch. in 1929. Some of her songs (*Boat Song, Joy of the Morning, The Call of Radha, Stars, Sunlight Waltz Song,* etc.) have achieved considerable popularity. She also wrote the choral cycles *Trees* and *Undine;* an operetta, *Waltz for 3;* piano pieces (*Mountain Pictures, Midnight Waltz,* etc.).

Wareing, Herbert Walter, English composer; b. Birmingham, April 5, 1857; d. Malvern, March 29, 1918. He studied at the Leipzig Cons. with Reinecke, Jadassohn, and Papperitz; upon his return to England he filled various positions as an organist; in 1909 became a prof. of piano at Malvern College, where he remained until his death. He wrote several operettas for children: *Princess Snowflake, The Court of Queen Summergold, A Garden of Japan, A Day in Roseland;* cantatas: *The Wreck of the Hesperus, The Angel Reapers, The Nativity, The Good Shepherd, New Year's Eve;* numerous choruses and solo songs; church services; piano pieces.

Warfield, Sandra, American mezzo-soprano; b. Kansas City, Mo., Aug. 6, 1929. She studied voice in Kansas City, and later in Milan; returning to the U.S., she won first prize in the Metropolitan Opera Auditions of the Air, which led to her debut in N.Y. on Nov. 20, 1953, in a minor role in *Le nozze di Figaro;* later she sang more important roles at the Metropolitan, and also appeared with other American opera houses, and in Europe. Married to the noted American tenor **James McCracken,** she sang numerous concert duos with him. Among her most successful operatic roles are Dalila in *Samson et Dalila,* Amneris in *Aida,* and Carmen.

Warfield, William, black American baritone; b. Helena, Ark., Jan. 22, 1920. He studied at the Eastman School of Music in Rochester, N.Y., graduating in 1946; sang in opera and musical comedy; gave his first N.Y. song recital on March 19, 1950, with excellent critical acclaim. He subsequently toured Europe in the role of Porgy in the production of Gershwin's *Porgy and Bess.* He married the soprano **Leontyne Price** in 1952 (divorced in 1972). In 1974 he was appointed a prof. of music at the Univ. of Illinois.

Waring, Fred, famous American conductor of popular music, and an inventor of sundry kitchen appliances; b. Tyrone, Pa., June 9, 1900; d. Danville, Pa., July 29, 1984. He learned music at his mother's knee, and a sense of moral rectitude was inculcated in him by his father, a banker who gave speeches at spiritual revivals and temperance meetings. Fred Waring attended Pa. State Univ., where he studied engineering and architecture; he retained his love for gadgets throughout his musical career, and in 1937 patented the Waring Blendor, for whipping food or drinks to a foam; another invention was a traveling iron. He took up banjo playing at 16, and organized a quartet which he called The Banjazzatra. He also played in the Boy Scouts Drum Corps and sang at Prohibition rallies. He acquired fame with his own band, The Pennsylvanians, which played on national tours at concert halls, hotels, and college campuses; the group was particularly successful on radio programs sponsored by tobacco companies and the Ford Motor Co. His repertoire consisted of wholesome American songs, many of them composed by himself. Among his soloists on special programs were Bing Crosby, Hoagy Carmichael, Irving Berlin, and Frank Sinatra. Waring had a natural streak for publicity; he once bet that he could lead a bull into a Fifth Avenue china shop, and succeeded, without breaking a single piece of crockery. He was a friend of President Dwight Eisenhower. In Dec. 1983 President Ronald Reagan awarded Waring the Congressional Gold Medal. He continued to lead youth choral groups, giving a concert at Pa. State Univ. a day before he suffered a stroke, and 2 days before his death.

Warlich, Reinhold von, baritone; b. St. Petersburg, May 24, 1877; d. New York, Nov. 10, 1939. His father, a German musician resident in Russia, was an opera conductor in St. Petersburg, and Warlich received his training at home; then studied at the

Hamburg Cons., in Florence, and in Cologne. He toured in Europe as a singer of German lieder, and was especially distinguished as an interpreter of Schubert, whose song cycles he gave in their entirety. He lived for some time in Canada; later was a singing teacher in Paris and London; made concert tours in the U.S. from 1909, eventually settling in N.Y.

Warlock, Peter. See **Heseltine, Philip.**

Warnecke, (Johann Heinrich) Friedrich, German double-bass player and pedagogue; b. Bodenteich, Nov. 19, 1856; d. Hamburg, March 1, 1931. He studied with Bontemps in Ülzen and with Walther in Hannover; was a member of various military bands (1874–89); then settled in Hamburg; from 1893 to 1924 he was a member of the Hamburg Phil. and a prof. at the Hamburg Cons. He publ. *Das Studium des Kontrabass-Spiels* (2 parts; with German and Eng. text); piano pieces and songs; was the author of *"Ad infinitum." Der Kontrabass, seine Geschichte und seine Zukunft. Probleme und deren Lösung zur Hebung des Kontrabass-Spiels* (1909) and *Der Kontrabass* (1929).

Warner, Harry Waldo, English viola player and composer; b. Northampton, Jan. 4, 1874; d. London, June 1, 1945. He studied violin with Alfred Gibson and theory with R. Orlando Morgan at the Guildhall School of Music; was engaged as viola player in the London String Quartet (1907–28). In 1921 he received the Elizabeth Sprague Coolidge prize for a piano trio, and a Cobbett prize for another piano trio. He also wrote several other attractive pieces for string quartet; one of them, arranged for string orch., was performed in London on Sept. 22, 1928, under the title *Suite in the Olden Style.*
BIBLIOGRAPHY: *Cobbett's Cyclopedic Survey of Chamber Music* (London, 1929).

Warner, Sylvia Townsend, English novelist and writer on music; b. London, Dec. 6, 1893; d. Maiden Newton, Dorset, May 1, 1978. Apart from her well-known novels and books of poetry, she publ. valuable papers in music history, among them *The Point of Perfection in 16th Century Notation* (1919); was one of the editors of the collection *Tudor Church Music.* She also composed a rhapsody for Voice and String Quartet, *Memorial;* and a song cycle, *Children of the Earth.*

Warnots, Henri, Belgian tenor and composer; b. Brussels, July 11, 1832; d. Saint-Josse-ten-Noode, Feb. 27, 1893. He studied at the Brussels Cons.; then sang in Paris and Strasbourg. In 1867, he became a prof. at the Brussels Cons.; in 1870, established a music school in Saint-Josse-ten-Noode, where he remained until his death. His operetta, *Une Heure de mariage,* was produced in Strasbourg on Jan. 24, 1865.

Warrack, John, English writer on music; b. London, Feb. 9, 1928. He studied at Winchester College; then took up oboe and composition at the Royal College of Music; subsequently played oboe in several ensembles. In 1953 he became music editor of the Oxford Univ. Press; in 1954 he joined the staff of the *Daily Telegraph,* where he was a music critic; then was chief music critic of the *Sunday Telegraph* (1961–72). In 1977 he became director of the Leeds Festival. He contributed numerous articles and reviews to *Opera* and *Gramophone.* His biography of Weber is the standard modern source.
WRITINGS: *Six Great Composers* (London, 1958); co-ed. (with H. Rosenthal), *The Concise Oxford Dictionary of Opera* (London, 1964; 2nd ed., revised, 1979); *Carl Maria von Weber* (London, 1968; also in German, 1972; 2nd ed., revised, London, 1976); *Tchaikovsky: Symphonies and Concertos* (London, 1969; 2nd ed., revised, 1974); *Tchaikovsky* (London, 1973); *Tchaikovsky: Ballet Music* (London, 1978).

Warren, Elinor Remick, American pianist and composer of songs; b. Los Angeles, Feb. 23, 1905. She was educated at the Westlake School for Girls and at Mills College; publ. her first composition while still in high school; later studied in N.Y. with Frank La Forge, Paolo Gallico, and Clarence Dickinson; appeared as a pianist.
WORKS: *The Harp Weaver* for Women's Chorus, Baritone, Harp, and Orch.; *The Passing of King Arthur* for Orch.; *Singing Earth,* song cycle for Voice, and Piano or Orch.; *Abram in Egypt,* cantata (1961); *Good Morning America!* for Narrator, Chorus, and Orch. (Calif. State Univ., Fullerton, Nov. 21, 1976); Symph. (1970); many songs (*White Horses of the Seas, Children of the Moon, My Lady Lo Fu, We Two, Christmas Candle,* etc.).

Warren, George William, American organist and composer of sacred music; b. Albany, N.Y., Aug. 17, 1828; d. New York, March 17, 1902. He was self-taught; held positions as a church organist in Albany (1846–60), in Brooklyn (1860–70), and at St. Thomas's in N.Y. (from 1870 until his death). He publ. *Warren's Hymns and Tunes, as Sung at St. Thomas Church* (1888); also wrote salon piano music; his "Marche di Bravura," *The Andes,* was the rage of the salons in 1862–63, especially in a 2-piano arrangement made by Louis Moreau Gottschalk. He is remembered chiefly for his tune *National Hymn,* to which *God of Our Fathers* is sung.

Warren, Harry, American composer of popular songs; b. Brooklyn, Dec. 24, 1893; d. Los Angeles, Sept. 22, 1981. His real name was **Salvatore Guaragna;** he was the 11th child in a proliferating but impoverished Italian family; his father was a boot maker who, like most Brooklyn-born Italians, also loved music. Harry Warren dropped out of high school to play drums with a touring carnival company; with the money earned, he bought himself a ramshackle old piano and became engaged as a movie pianist for the silent screen. Endowed with a God-given gift of melody, he turned out, without benefit of academic training, a slew of irresistible tunes, some of which became perennial favorites. His early hits were *Rose of the Rio Grande, Back Home in Pasadena,* and *So This Is Venice* (Venice, Calif., that is). In 1932 Salvatore Guaragna, now advantageously transfigured into Harry Warren, moved to the center of musical glamour, Hollywood, and unleashed an avalanche of hits for films. Among his greatest songs were *42nd Street, Wonder Bar, Night in Rio, Weekend in Havana, Springtime in the Rockies, Sweet Rosie O'Grady, Lullaby of Broadway, Chattanooga Choo-Choo, Topeka and the Sante Fe, You Must Have Been a Beautiful Baby, Jeepers Creepers, I Found a Million Dollar Baby in a 5 & 10 Cent Store, Shuffle Off to Buffalo, We're in the Money,* and *Cheerful Little Earful.*

Warren, Leonard, outstanding American baritone; b. New York, April 21, 1911; d. there, March 4, 1960, on the stage of the Metropolitan Opera House while singing the role of Don Carlo during a performance of *La forza del destino.* The original family name was Warenoff; it was Americanized as Warren when his father came from Russia to the U.S. His father was in the fur business in N.Y., and Leonard Warren helped him in his work; in 1935 he joined the chorus of the Radio City Music Hall; he also studied voice with Sidney Dietch and Guiseppe De Luca. In 1938 he won the Metropolitan Opera Auditions of the Air and was granted a stipend to study in Italy, where he took voice lessons with Pais and Piccozi. Returning to America, he made his debut at the Metropolitan Opera in excerpts from *La Traviata* and *Pagliacci* during a concert in N.Y. on Nov. 27, 1938; his formal operatic debut took place there on Jan. 13, 1939, when he sang Paolo in *Simon Boccanegra.* He quickly advanced in the favor of the public, eventually assuming a leading place among the noted baritones of his time. He also sang in San Francisco, Chicago, Canada, and South America. He appeared at La Scala in Milan in 1953; in 1958 he made a highly successful tour of the Soviet Union. His last complete performance at the Metropolitan Opera was as Simon Boccanegra on March 1, 1960, 3 days before his tragic death. He was particularly acclaimed as one of the foremost interpreters of the great Verdi baritone roles; he also sang the parts of Tonio in *Pagliacci,* Escamillo in *Carmen,* and Scarpia in *Tosca.* During his stay at the Metropolitan, he gave altogether 416 performances in N.Y. and 206 on tour, singing 26 different roles. He collapsed while singing the aria "Urna fatale dal mio destino," underlining the tragic irony of the words, and died of a cerebral hemorrhage backstage. Of Jewish parentage, he converted to Catholicism upon his marriage to an Italian woman. He was reputed to be a person of an intractable character, who always tried to impose his will on stage designers, managers, and even conductors, in the matters of production, direction, and the tempi. He caused pain, a colleague said, but he had a great voice.

BIBLIOGRAPHY: David Ewen, *Musicians since 1900* (N.Y., 1978).

Warren, Raymond, English composer; b. Weston-Super-Mare, Nov. 7, 1928. He studied with Robin Orr at Cambridge Univ. (1949–52) and later took lessons with Michael Tippett and Lennox Berkeley; received his Mus.B. at Cambridge Univ. (1952); taught at the Univ. of Belfast (1955–72); in 1972 was appointed prof. of music at Bristol Univ.

WORKS: *The Lady of Ephesus,* one-act chamber opera (Belfast, Feb. 16, 1959); *Finn and the Black Hag,* children's opera after an Irish folk tale (Belfast, Dec. 11, 1959); *The Passion,* oratorio (Belfast, Feb. 19, 1962); *Graduation Ode,* comic opera (Belfast, Nov. 17, 1963); Symph. No. 1 (1965); Violin Concerto (1966); *Songs of Old Age* for Baritone and Piano (1968); 2 string quartets (1966, 1975); Symph. No. 2 (1971); *Duo concertante* for Cello and Piano (1973); songs.

Warren, Richard Henry, American organist and composer, son of **G.W. Warren;** b. Albany, N.Y., Sept. 17, 1859; d. South Chatham, Mass., Dec. 3, 1933. He was organist and choirmaster in various churches in N.Y.; in 1886 founded the Church Choral Society, which he conducted until 1895 and again from 1903 to 1907, producing many important works, including the American premieres of choral compositions by Dvořák, Liszt, Gounod, Saint-Saëns, etc. Horatio Parker wrote his *Hora Novissima* for this society, and Warren brought it out on May 3, 1893. Among Warren's own compositions are operettas: *Igala* (1880); *All on a Summer's Day* (1882); *Magnolia* (1886); *The Rightful Heir* (1899); a "romantic opera," *Phyllis* (N.Y., May 7, 1900); a cantata, *Ticonderoga* (1894); services; anthems; songs.

Warren, Samuel Prowse, American organist; b. Montreal, Feb. 18, 1841; d. New York, Oct. 7, 1915. He studied organ with Haupt in Berlin, piano with Gustav Schumann, and theory with Wieprecht. After filling various positions in N.Y. churches, he inaugurated a series of organ recitals, which were greatly appreciated and created for him a reputation as one of the foremost concert organists in the U.S. He publ. many organ pieces and songs; also made excellent transcriptions for organ of works by Weber, Beethoven, Schumann, and Wagner.

Wartel, Pierre-François, noted French singer and teacher; b. Versailles, April 3, 1806; d. Paris, Aug. 3, 1882. He studied at the Paris Cons. with Nourrit; was engaged as a tenor at the Paris Opéra (1831–46), but became known chiefly as an experienced singing teacher; Christine Nilsson was one of his many famous pupils. He also gave song recitals, in which he performed songs by Schubert for the first time in France. His wife, **Atale Thérèse Annette Wartel** (née **Adrien;** b. Paris, July 2, 1814; d. there, Nov. 6, 1865), was a talented pianist; she also composed piano studies and other pieces.

Warwick, (Marie) Dionne, black American singer of popular music; b. Orange, N.J., Dec. 12, 1940. She made her first appearance as a singer with the Drinkard Singers, a gospel group managed by her mother; toured with the Gospelaires, a group formed by her and her sister; in her free time attended the Hartt College of Music of the Univ. of Hartford, where she took lessons in piano playing and voice training. She soon quit an unnecessary college education and plunged into her natural environment as a born singer of popular songs. Her decision was wise, for she made a hit with audiences. Her most engaging songs were *I'll Never Fall in Love Again, Raindrops Keep Falling on My Head, What the World Needs Now,* and *Do You Know the Way to San Jose.*

Washburn, Robert, American composer; b. Bouckville, N.Y., July 11, 1928. He attended the State College of Potsdam, N.Y., where he received his M.S. He served in the U.S. Air Force (1950–54) and later studied composition at the Eastman School of Music in Rochester, N.Y., with Bernard Rogers. In 1954 he was appointed prof. of music at the State College of Education at Potsdam, N.Y.
WORKS: Symph. No. 1 (1959); *Synthesis* for Orch. (1960); *St. Lawrence Overture* (1962); Sinfonietta for String Orch. (1964); *Serenade* for Strings (1966); *Symphonic Essay* (1967); *North Country Overture* (1969); *Blue Lake Overture* (1970); *Excursion* for Orch. (1970); *Elegy* for Orch. (1974); *Sinfonia* for Voices and Instruments (1977); chamber music.

Washington, Dinah, black American singer of blues and popular music; b. Tuscaloosa, Ala., Aug. 8, 1924; d. (as a result of an overdose of drugs) Detroit, Dec. 14, 1963. She went to Chicago; won an amateur singing contest at the age of 15; made local appearances before joining Lionel Hampton's band (1942–46); she soon established herself as a major rhythm and blues artist with such songs as *Blow Top Blues* and *Evil Gal Blues.* She was best known for her renditions of *What a Difference a Day Makes, Homeward Bound, Stormy Weather,* and *September in the Rain.*

Wasielewski, Wilhelm Joseph von, eminent German music scholar; b. Gross-Leesen, near Danzig, June 17, 1822; d. Sondershausen, Dec. 13, 1896. He studied violin as a private pupil of Ferdinand David in Leipzig, and also had lessons with Mendelssohn (1843–46). He joined the Gewandhaus Orch. (until 1850); went to Düsseldorf, where he was concertmaster under Schumann (1850–52); then was choral conductor in Bonn (1852–55); in 1855 he settled in Dresden as a writer, in which capacity he greatly distinguished himself. In 1869 he became town music director in Bonn, remaining in that position until 1884, when he went to Sondershausen.
WRITINGS: *Robert Schumann* (1858; 4th ed., 1906; Eng. trans., 1871), with important supplementary matter in *Schumanniana* (1883); *Die Violine und ihre Meister* (1869; 2nd augmented ed., 1883; 7th ed., 1927); *Die Violine im 17. Jahrhundert und die Anfänge ser Instrumentalkomposition* (1874; 2nd ed., 1905); *Geschichte der Instrumentalmusik im 16. Jahrhundert* (1878); *Beethoven* (2 vols., 1888);

Das Violoncell und seine Geschichte (1889; 3rd ed. by his son Waldemar, 1925; in Eng., 1894); *Carl Reinecke, Sein Leben, Wirken und Schaffen* (Leipzig, 1892); *Aus 70 Jahren,* memoirs (Stuttgart, 1897).

Wassermann, Heinrich Joseph, German conductor and composer; b. Schwarzbach, near Fulda, April 3, 1791; d. Riehen, near Basel, Sept. 3, 1838. He was a pupil of Spohr; became an orch. conductor in Switzerland. He wrote a *Thème original varié* for String Quartet; Quartet for Flute, Violin, Viola, and Cello; *Air varié* for Bassoon and String Orch.; *Divertissement* (on the Tyrolian "Alma Lied") for Violin and Orch.; a number of orch. dances; pieces for guitar.

Watanabe, Akeo, Japanese conductor; b. Tokyo, June 5, 1919. He studied conducting with Joseph Rosenstock, who was then resident in Japan; in 1950 went to the U.S. and took a course in conducting with Jean Morel at the Juilliard School of Music in N.Y.; returning to Japan, he founded in 1956 the Nippon Phil. Orch., which he led until 1968; he also made guest appearances as a conductor in the U.S. and in Europe. In 1972 he was appointed music director of the Tokyo Metropolitan Orch.

Waters, Edward N(eighbor), eminent American musicologist; b. Leavenworth, Kans., July 23, 1906. He studied piano and theory at the Eastman School of Music in Rochester, N.Y. (B.M., 1927; M.M. in musicology, 1928). In 1931 he joined the staff of the Music Division of the Library of Congress in Washington, D.C.; from 1972 to 1976 served as chief of the Music Division; was president of the Music Library Assoc. (1941–46); was program annotator for the concerts of the National Symph. Orch. in Washington (1934–43); was editor of *Notes,* publ. by the Music Library Assoc. (1963–66); also wrote many articles and book reviews for professional journals. The Cleveland Inst. of Music conferred upon him the honorary degree of D.Mus. (1973). He is the author of a definitive biography of Victor Herbert (N.Y., 1955).

Waters, Ethel, American jazz and blues singer; b. Chester, Pa., Oct. 31, 1896 (the fruit of a knife-point rape, when her mother was 12½ years old); d. New York, Sept. 1, 1977. After a disastrous marriage at the age of 13, she worked as a laundress in Philadelphia. When her ability as a natural singer was discovered, she appeared in vaudeville, singing the *St. Louis Blues* and jazz songs. Later she joined a traveling show. She became the first black singer to be featured by all-white bands when she appeared with Benny Goodman and the Dorsey Brothers in 1929. Her memoirs, *To Me It's Wonderful,* were publ. in N.Y. in 1972.
BIBLIOGRAPHY: David Ewen, *All the Years of American Popular Music* (Englewood Cliffs, N.J., 1977; pp. 333–35).

Waters, Muddy (real name, **McKinley Morgan-**

field), black American blues singer, top exponent of the Mississippi Delta Blues style; b. Rolling Fork, Miss., April 4, 1915; d. Westmont, suburb of Chicago, April 30, 1983. His parents were separated, and he was reared by his maternal grandmother on a plantation near Clarksdale, Miss.; she called him "Muddy" because of his childhood habit of playing in the mud; his playmates called him "Waters," and he accepted the nickname "Muddy Waters" when he began to sing and play the guitar. In 1941, Alan Lomax and John Work recorded his singing for the Library of Congress; this encouraged him to try his luck in commercial recording. In 1943 he moved to Chicago, where he made his first successes; indeed, he soon earned the sobriquet "King of Chicago Blues." Fortunately for him, for his followers, and for the jazz historians, he totally lacked any vocal training and was forced to develop his own unrestricted lexicon of sounds, ranging from soft trembling moans to a ferocious animal-like roar. To make his mode of delivery even more physically stunning, he used electric amplification on his guitar, and soon assembled a band that hit an all-time decibel record. He played electric blues in England in 1958, which struck holy terror into the ears and hearts of sissified British folk-song experts, but he recruited to his cause the young enthusiasts, among them Mick Jagger; in fact, Jagger and his friends named their famous band The Rolling Stones after an early hit song, *Rollin' Stone,* of Muddy Waters; the rock journal *Rolling Stone* also owed its name to Muddy's song; Bob Dylan created his own rock tune *Like a Rolling Stone* as an unconscious tribute to Muddy Waters. He died peacefully, in his sleep.
BIBLIOGRAPHY: J. Rooney, *Bossmen: Bill Monroe and Muddy Waters* (N.Y., 1971).

Watson, Claire, American soprano; b. New York, Feb. 3, 1927. She studied voice in N.Y. with Elisabeth Schumann and Sergius Kagen; received further training in Vienna. She made her operatic debut in Graz in 1951; was a member of the Frankfurt Opera (1956–58) and the Bavarian State Opera in Munich (from 1958); made guest appearances at the Salzburg Festival and with the opera houses of London, Vienna, Milan, Rome, Chicago, and San Francisco. She retired in 1976.

Watson, Henry, English composer; b. Burnley, Lancashire, April 30, 1846; d. Salford, Jan. 8, 1911. He studied with private teachers; then was organist in various churches. In 1867 he founded (with Henry Wilson) the Manchester Vocal Union, becoming its conductor in 1885 (after Wilson's death); also taught the choral class at the Royal College of Music, Manchester. In 1899 he presented his valuable library (some 30,000 vols.) to the Corp. of Manchester. He composed an opera, *Fair Rosine* (Manchester, 1882); *A Shakespearian Cantata; The Deliverance of Israel,* oratorio for Solo Voices, Chorus, and Orch.; many part-songs.

Watson, William Michael, English composer and poet; b. Newcastle upon Tyne, July 31, 1840; d. London, Oct. 3, 1889. He established the West End School of Music in London in 1883; composed a cantata, *Aladdin* (1885); part-songs; piano pieces; etc.

Watts, André, brilliant American pianist; b. in a U.S. Army camp in Nuremberg, June 20, 1946, of a Hungarian mother, Maria Alexandra Gusmits, and a black American soldier, Sergeant Herman Watts, stationed in Germany. The family moved to Ulm, where André's father was transferred. His mother could play piano, and she gave him his early lessons. The family returned to the U.S., making their home in Philadelphia. There André Watts was enrolled in the Philadelphia Musical Academy as a pupil of Genia Robiner, Doris Bawden, and Clement Petrillo; at the age of 9 he made his first public appearance playing the Haydn Concerto in D major at a children's concert of the Philadelphia Orch. His parents were divorced in 1962, and his mother continued to guide his studies. At 14 he played César Franck's *Symphonic Variations* with the Philadelphia Orch.; at 16 he became an instant celebrity when he played Liszt's First Piano Concerto at one of the televised Young People's Concerts with the N.Y. Phil., conducted by Leonard Bernstein, on Jan. 15, 1963. His youth and the fact that he was partly black contributed to his success, but it was the grand and poetic manner of his virtuosity that conquered the usually skeptical press. Still, he insisted on completing his academic education. In 1969 he joined the class of Leon Fleisher at the Peabody Cons. of Music in Baltimore, obtaining his Artist's Diploma in 1972. In the meantime he developed an international career. He made his European debut as soloist with the London Symph. Orch. on June 12, 1966; then played with the Concertgebouw Orch. in Amsterdam. On Oct. 26, 1966, he played his first solo recital in N.Y., inviting comparisons in the press with the great piano virtuosos of the past. In 1967 he was soloist with the Los Angeles Phil. under Zubin Mehta on a tour of Europe and Asia. On his 21st birthday he played the 2nd Piano Concerto of Brahms with the Berlin Phil. On Aug. 14, 1970, he revisited his place of birth and played a solo recital with a success that was made all the more sensational because he was a native son, albeit not of the native race. He also became a favorite at important political occasions; he played at Richard Nixon's inaugural concert at Constitution Hall in 1969, at the coronation of the Shah of Iran, and at a festive celebration of the President of the Congo. In 1973 he toured Russia. On Nov. 28, 1976, he played a solo recital on network television, the first to be accorded such an appearance. He was also the subject of a film documentary. In 1973 he received an honorary doctorate from Yale Univ.; in 1975 he was given another honorary doctorate, by Albright College.
BIBLIOGRAPHY: David Ewen, *Musicians since 1900* (N.Y., 1978).

Watts, Helen, Welsh contralto; b. Milford Haven, Dec. 7, 1927. She was educated at the Royal Academy of Music in London; made her debut in a Promenade Concert in London in 1955; in 1958 sang with the Handel Opera Society at the Camden Festival; later appeared with the English Opera Group in London and with the Welsh National Opera. She made her U.S. debut in a concert with the N.Y. Phil. in 1966. In 1978 she was made a Commander of the Order of the British Empire.

Watts, Wintter, American composer; b. Cincinnati, March 14, 1884; d. Brooklyn, Nov. 1, 1962. He studied at the Inst. of Musical Art in N.Y. He received the American Prix de Rome, which enabled him to study at the American Academy in Rome (1923–25). He lived for some time in Europe, returning to N.Y. in 1931. Among his larger works are a *Bridal Overture* (1916) and an orch. suite, *Etchings* (1921), but he is chiefly known as a composer of fine songs: *Wings of Night, Joy, With the Tide, Wild Tears, Alone;* a cycle of 9 songs to poems by Sara Teasdale, *Vignettes of Italy;* etc.
BIBLIOGRAPHY: W.T. Upton, *Art-Song in America* (N.Y., 1930; pp. 182–97).

Watzke, Rudolf, German bass; b. Niemes, April 5, 1892; d. Wuppertal, Dec. 18, 1972. He studied voice in Reichenberg, Bayreuth, and Berlin; from 1924 to 1928 was a member of the Berlin State Opera. After 1928 he devoted himself mainly to oratorio performances; also taught at the Dortmund Cons. (1956–69).

Waxman, Franz, German-American composer; b. Königshütte, Dec. 24, 1906; d. Los Angeles, Feb. 24, 1967. He studied in Dresden and Berlin; went to the U.S. in 1934 and settled in Hollywood, where he took lessons with Arnold Schoenberg; became a successful composer for films; his musical score for *Sunset Boulevard* won the Academy Award for 1950; other works include a Sinfonietta for String Orch. and Timpani (1955); oratorio, *Joshua* (Dallas, May 23, 1959); a fantasy on *Carmen* for Violin and Orch.; etc.

Wayditch, Gabriel (real name, **Baron Gabriel Wajditsch Verbovac von Dönhoff**), Hungarian-American composer; b. Budapest, Dec. 28, 1888; d. New York, July 28, 1969. He studied piano with Emil Sauer and composition with Hans Koessler at the Budapest Academy of Music. In 1907 he emigrated to the U.S.; lived mostly in N.Y. He wrote 14 lengthy operas to his own libretti in Hungarian, dealing mostly with oriental or religious subjects; of these only one, *Horus,* was performed in his lifetime, at his own expense (Philadelphia, Jan. 5, 1939). His longest opera, *The Heretics,* takes 8 hours to perform; the shortest, *The Caliph's Magician,* in one act, takes 2 hours. The other operas are: *Opium Dreams, Buddha, Jesus before Herod, Maria Magdalena, Maria Tesztver, Nereida, Sahara, The Catacombs, Anthony of Padua, The Venus Dwellers, Neptune's Daughter.*

Weatherford, Teddy, black American jazz pianist and bandleader; b. Bluefield, W.Va., Oct. 11, 1903; d. Calcutta, India, April 25, 1945. He learned to play the piano in New Orleans; then worked in Chicago; in 1926 he became a member of Jack Carter's Orch. and accompanied it on a tour to the Orient; he decided to remain there, and led his own bands in Singapore, Manila, and Shanghai; eventually settled in Calcutta, where he led his own band at the city's Grand Hotel.

Weathers, Felicia, black American soprano; b. St. Louis, Aug. 13, 1937. She took vocal lessons at the Indiana Univ. School of Music in Bloomington, with Dorothée Manski; then went to Europe; made her operatic debut in Kiel in 1961. In 1963 she sang at the Hamburg State Opera and subsequently became a regular member (1966–70). In 1965 she made her Metropolitan Opera debut in N.Y.; also sang at Covent Garden in London in 1970.

Weaver, Powell, American pianist and composer; b. Clearfield, Pa., June 10, 1890; d. Kansas City, Dec. 22, 1951. He studied organ with Pietro Yon in N.Y., and composition with Respighi in Rome. Returning to the U.S., he was engaged as accompanist to prominent singers; also gave organ recitals.
WORKS: For Orch.: *Plantation Overture* (1925); *The Little Faun* (1925; Boston Women's Symph. Orch., April 14, 1929); *The Vagabond,* symph. poem (Minneapolis, March 6, 1931); *Dance of the Sand-Dune Cranes* for Piano and Orch. (1941); choral works: *Boating, Song, Spirit of God, Moon-Marketing, The Humming-Bird,* also a *Sabbath Evening Service; An Ode* for Piano and Strings; Violin Sonata; etc.

Webb, Charles H., American pianist, conductor, and educator; b. Dallas, Feb. 14, 1933. He was educated at Southern Methodist Univ. (A.B. and M.M., 1955) and Indiana Univ. (D.Mus., 1964); later joined the faculty of Indiana Univ. as an instructor in piano (1958); became an assistant prof. of music in 1964 and an associate prof. in 1967. He was named assistant dean of the School of Music in 1964, associate dean in 1969, and dean in 1973. He toured the U.S. with the pianist Wallace Hornibrook in duo-recitals. In 1967 he was appointed conductor of the Indianapolis Symph. Choir.

Webb, Daniel, English writer on music; b. Ireland, c.1718; d. Bath, Aug. 2, 1798. He publ. the important paper *Observations on the Correspondence between Poetry and Music* (London, 1769; reprinted in his *Miscellanies,* 1803).

Webb, Frank Rush, American organist and bandmaster; b. Covington, Ind., Oct. 8, 1851; d. Baltimore, Oct. 20, 1934. He studied at the New England Cons. in Boston; then was a church organist in Indianapolis and a piano teacher in Ohio; from 1883 to 1910 he was director of the School of Music in the Virginia Female Inst. in Staunton, Va.; from 1883 to 1892, bandmaster of the Stonewell Brigade Band. He publ. nearly 200 pieces for military band; also much salon music for piano, amounting to 108 opus numbers; church music; songs.

BIBLIOGRAPHY: M.M. Brice, *The Stonewall Brigade Band* (Verona, Va., 1967).

Webb, George James, American organist and magazine editor; b. Rushmore Lodge, near Salisbury, England, June 24, 1803; d. Orange, N.J., Oct. 7, 1887. He settled in Boston in 1830; served as organist of the Old South Church; was a founder of the Boston Academy of Music in 1836, and president of the Handel and Haydn Society in 1840. In 1870 he settled in Orange, N.J., but continued musical activities in N.Y. as a teacher. He edited 2 periodicals: *The Musical Library* (1835–36), with L. Mason, and *The Musical Cabinet* (1841–42), with T.B. Hayward; also brought out the *Young Ladies' Vocal Class Book* (Boston, 1853), *The Glee Hive* and *The New Odeon* (both with L. Mason), and *Cantica laudis* (N.Y., 1850; also with Mason); publ. *Vocal Technics* and *Voice Culture* (with C.G. Allen). His hymn tune, known simply as *Webb,* became popular.

Webb, William ("Chick"), black American jazz drummer and bandleader; b. Baltimore, Feb. 10, 1909; d. there, June 16, 1939. He took up the drums as a youngster; then played in the Jazzola Orch.; moving to N.Y., he led his own band there, scoring a success at the Savoy Ballroom. In 1935 he introduced Ella Fitzgerald, and she subsequently toured with his group.

Webbe, Samuel, Jr., English composer, son of **Samuel Webbe, Sr.;** b. London, 1770; d. there, Nov. 25, 1843. He was a pupil of his father, and also received instruction from Clementi. He wrote many glees and catches, obtaining several prizes from the Catch Club; also produced his musical comedy, *The Speechless Wife* (Covent Garden, May 22, 1794). He lived in Liverpool from 1798 until 1817; returned to London, where he taught at Logier's School of Music and served as organist at the Spanish Embassy. Besides glees, duets, hymn tunes, organ voluntaries, sonatas for harpsichord, etc., he wrote *L'Amico del principiante* (28 short solfeggi) and *Harmony Epitomised, or Elements of the Thorough-bass;* also edited *Convito armonico* (4 vols.; a collection of madrigals, glees, catches, canons, etc., by prominent composers).

Webbe, Samuel, Sr., famous English composer of catches and glees; b. London, 1740; d. there, May 25, 1816. He began his career as a copyist for the London publisher Welcker, who enabled him to study music with the organist Barbandt; was appointed organist and choirmaster at the Chapel of the Portuguese Embassy in 1776, and later obtained a similar appointment at the Sardinian Embassy (holding both positions concurrently); from 1794 until his death he was secretary of the Catch Club, also librarian of the Glee Club (from 1787). In 1766 his canon *O that I had wings* won the prize of the Catch Club, and subsequently he carried off 26 other prizes with various catches and glees (reprinted later with 3 additional vols.), *Cecilian Ode* for 6 Voices, Con-

certo for Harpsichord, *Divertissement* for Wind Band, and several collections of masses and motets. His glee *Glorious Apollo* was the opening work sung at every meeting of the Glee Club throughout its history.

Webber, Amherst, English composer; b. Cannes, France, Oct. 25, 1867; d. London, July 25, 1946. He studied in Oxford, Dresden, and Paris. His first professional occupation was that of an opera coach at Covent Garden in London and at the Metropolitan Opera in N.Y. He wrote a comic opera, *Fiorella* (London, June 7, 1905), and many songs to French and English words. His Symph. had several performances in Europe and America.

Weber, Alain, French composer; b. Château-Thierry, Dec. 8, 1930. He studied at the Paris Cons. with Tony Aubin and Messiaen; received the Premier Grand Prix de Rome in 1952. His music is hedonistic in its lucid harmony and kinetic rhythmic dash.

WORKS: Ballet, *Le Petit Jeu* (Paris, 1953); chamber opera, *La Voie unique* (1958); *Suite pour une pièce vue* for Orch. (1954); *Symphonie* (1957); symph. poem, *Midjaay* (1963); Horn Concerto (1954); Trumpet Concerto (1965); *Strophes* for Trumpet, Strings, and Percussion (1966); *Solipsisme* for String Quartet, Piano, and Percussion (1968); Wind Quintet (1954); Woodwind Trio (1959); Sonata for Oboe and Harp (1960); *Variants* for 2 Pianos and Percussion (1964); *Strophes* for Trumpet and Orch. (1966); *Commentaires concertantes* for Flute and Orch. (1967); *Palindromes* for Bassoon and Piano (1967); Violin Sonata (1968); *Synecdoque* for Oboe Solo (1968); *Syllepse* for Chamber Orch. (1970).

Weber, Ben, American composer; b. St. Louis, July 23, 1916; d. New York, May 9, 1979. He studied medicine at the Univ. of Illinois; then entered De Paul Univ. in Chicago, where he studied voice, piano, and music theory. In composition he was practically self-taught, but he was attracted to the method of composition with 12 tones after meeting Schoenberg; paradoxically, he retained the firm tonal foundation of his melodic and contrapuntal structures. He moved to N.Y., where he held various positions in the recording industry; also taught composition privately. He received 2 Guggenheim grants (1950, 1953), the Thorne music award (1965), and the Koussevitzky grant (1967).

WORKS: *Symphony on Poems of William Blake* for Baritone and Chamber Orch. (N.Y., Oct. 28, 1952); Violin Concerto (1954); *Prelude and Passacaglia* (Louisville, Ky., Jan. 1, 1955); *Rapsodie concertante* for Viola and Orch. (1957); *Chamber Fantasy* for Small Orch. (1959); Piano Concerto (1961); 2 string quartets (1942, 1952); 2 string trios (1943, 1946); *The Pool of Darkness* for Flute, Violin, Trumpet, Bassoon, Cello, and Piano (1950); *Aubade* for Flute, Harp, and Cello (1950); Concerto for Piano, Cello, and Woodwind Quintet (1950); *Colloquy* for Brass Septet (1953); Serenade for Harpsichord,

Flute, Oboe, and Cello (1953); Concertino for Flute, Oboe, Clarinet, and String Quartet (1955); Serenade for String Quintet (1955); Nocturne for Flute, Celesta, and Cello (1962); *Dolmen: An Elegy* for Winds and Strings (1964); *Concert Poem* for Violin and Orch. (1970); *Sinfonia Clarion* for Orch. (N.Y., Feb. 26, 1974); Consort of Winds for Wind Quintet (1974); Capriccio for Cello and Piano (1975); 2 violin sonatas; 2 dances for Cello and Piano; songs.

BIBLIOGRAPHY: *Composers of the Americas,* vol. 9 (Washington, D.C., 1963).

Weber, Bernhard Anselm, German pianist and composer; b. Mannheim, April 18, 1764; d. Berlin, March 23, 1821. He studied with Abbé Vogler and Holzbauer; also took courses in theology and law at the Univ. of Heidelberg; then traveled as a performer on the Xänorphica, a keyboard instrument invented by Röllig. In 1787 he became music director of Grossmann's opera troupe; went to Stockholm in 1790; in 1792 was appointed conductor of the Königstadt Theater in Berlin, remaining in this capacity after its union with the Italian Opera. A great admirer of Gluck, he was the first to introduce Gluck's operas in Berlin, and his own works closely followed Gluck's style. He produced in Berlin 2 of his operas: *Mudarra* (March 10, 1800) and *Die Wette* (Jan. 21, 1805). Some of his songs were popular for a time.

BIBLIOGRAPHY: H. Fischer, *B.A. Weber* (Diss., Univ. of Berlin, 1923).

Weber, Bernhard Christian, German organist and composer; b. Wolferschwenda, Dec. 1, 1712; d. Tennstedt, Feb. 5, 1758. He settled in Tennstedt as town organist in 1732. Inspired by Bach's example, and at the instigation of Bach's pupil G.H. Noah, Weber composed for organ a work containing 24 preludes and fugues in all keys, and entitled it *Das wohltemperierte Klavier.*

Weber, Carl Maria (Friedrich Ernst), Freiherr von, celebrated German composer, founder of the German Romantic school; b. Eutin, Oldenburg, Nov. 18, 1786; d. London, June 5, 1826. His father, Franz Anton von Weber (1734–1812), was an army officer and a good musical amateur who played the violin and served as town musician in Eutin. It was his fondest wish to see one of his children become a great musician; Constanze Weber, Mozart's wife, was his niece (so that Carl Maria Weber was Mozart's first cousin by marriage), and Mozart was constantly the family's ideal to follow. Carl Maria's mother was a singer of some ability; she died when he was 12 years old. Franz Anton von Weber led a wandering life as music director of a traveling theatrical troupe, and he took his family with him. Although this mode of life interfered with Weber's regular education, it gave him practical knowledge of the stage, and stimulated his imagination as a dramatic composer. Weber's first teacher was his stepbrother Fritz, a pupil of Haydn; at Hildburghausen, where he found himself with his father's company in 1796, he received piano instruction from J.P. Heuschkel. The next year he was in Salzburg, where he attracted the attention of Michael Haydn, who taught him counterpoint. As his peregrinations continued, he was taught singing by Valesi (J.B. Wallishauser), and composition by J.N. Kalcher, in Munich (1798–1800); by that time he had already publ. his first work, 6 fughettas for Piano (1798). At the age of 13, he wrote an opera, *Die Macht der Liebe und des Weins;* it was never performed, and the score is lost. Through a meeting with Aloys Senefelder, the inventor of lithography, he became greatly interested in engraving; while a mere boy, he acquired considerable skill in the process, and even worked out some improvements; engraved his *Variations* for Piano, op. 2, himself, in 1800. His father, too, became interested in the business possibilities of lithography, and set up a workshop with him in Freiberg, Saxony; the venture did not succeed, and Carl Maria turned again to music; wrote a 2-act opera, *Das Waldmädchen,* which was produced in Freiberg 6 days after his 14th birthday, on Nov. 24, 1800; performances followed in Chemnitz (Dec. 5, 1800) and, 4 years later, in Vienna. In 1801 the family was once more in Salzburg, where Weber studied further with Michael Haydn, and wrote another opera, *Peter Schmoll und seine Nachbarn;* after a stay in Hamburg (1802), they proceeded to Augsburg (1803) and finally to Vienna. There, Weber made a serious study of the works of the great masters under the guidance of Abbé Vogler, at whose recommendation he secured the post of conductor of the Breslau City Theater (1804); in 1806 he became Musik-Intendant to Duke Eugen of Württemberg at Schloss Carlsruhe in Silesia; in Sept. 1807 he was engaged as private secretary to Duke Ludwig at Stuttgart, and music master to his children. This employment was abruptly terminated when Weber became innocently involved in a scheme of securing a ducal appointment for a rich man's son in order to exempt him from military service, and accepted a loan of money; as a result of the disclosure of this affair, Weber was arrested and kept in prison for 2 weeks, after which he was expelled from Stuttgart. He went to Darmstadt, where he rejoined his old teacher Abbé Vogler, for whom he did some editorial and analytic work in publishing an edition of Bach's chorales. On Sept. 16, 1810, Weber's opera *Silvana* was successfully presented in Frankfurt; on June 4, 1811, he brought out in Munich a new opera, *Abu Hassan.* In the meantime, he appeared as a pianist, giving concerts in Frankfurt, Würzburg, Nuremberg, Bamberg, Weimar, Gotha, and other German towns. In 1813 he received his first important appointment, that of conductor of the German Opera in Prague; there he presented a distinguished repertoire, which included Beethoven's *Fidelio;* traveled to Vienna to engage a company of singers; among them was **Caroline Brandt,** his future wife. His reputation as a music director and composer rose considerably, and the King of Saxony called him to Dresden to take charge of the German Opera Theater there. He opened his Dresden season on Jan. 30, 1817; became friendly with Friedrich Kind, a Dresden lawyer and writer, and suggested to him the idea of writing a libretto on a typically German subject. They agreed on *Der Freischütz,* a fairy tale from J.A. Apel and F. Laun's collection of ghost stories, *Gespensterbuch.* The composition of this work, which was to prove his masterpiece, occupied him fully 3 years; the overture was finished in May 1820; interrupting his work, he wrote (in 3 weeks) several musical numbers to *Preciosa,* a play in 4 acts with spoken dialogue; it was produced in Berlin on March 14, 1821; another stage work, *Die drei Pintos,* which Weber started at about the same time, was left unfinished. Finally, *Der Freischütz* was completed, and accepted for performance at the new Berlin Opera Theater. There existed an undercurrent of rivalry with Spontini, director of the Berlin Opera and an almost absolute master of operatic policy in Berlin; the challenge was that of rising German nationalism against the Italian-French tradition. Weber conducted the premiere on June 18, 1821; the work's success surpassed all expectations; the cause of new Romantic art was won; *Der Freischütz* was soon staged by all the major opera houses of Europe. In English, it was given first in London, on July 22, 1824; translations into other languages followed. Weber's next opera was *Euryanthe,* produced in Vienna on Oct. 25, 1823, with only moderate success. Meanwhile, Weber's health was affected by incipient tuberculosis and he was compelled to go to Marienbad for a cure (1824). He recovered sufficiently to begin the composition of *Oberon,* commissioned from him by Covent Garden in London; the English libretto was by J.R. Planché, based on a translation of C.M. Wieland's *Oberon.* Once more illness interrupted Weber's progress on his work; he spent some time in Ems to recuperate, then embarked on the voyage to England early in 1826. He rehearsed the opera thoroughly, and conducted the premiere at Covent Garden on April 12, 1826, obtaining tremendous success with the London audience. Despite his greatly weakened condition, he conducted 11 more performances of *Oberon,* and participated also in various London concerts, playing for the last time a week before his death. He was buried in London; his remains were removed to Dresden on Dec. 15, 1844; on that occasion Richard Wagner delivered an oration and conducted a funeral march on motifs from *Euryanthe,* as well as a funeral ode for double chorus expressly written for the service.

Weber's role in music history is epoch-making; in his operas, particulary in *Der Freischütz,* he opened the era of musical Romanticism, in decisive opposition to the established Italianate style. The highly dramatic and poetic portrayal of a German fairy tale, with its aura of supernatural mystery, appealed to the public, whose imagination had been stirred by the emergent Romantic literature of the period. Weber's melodic genius and his mastery of the craft of composition made it possible for him to break with tradition and to start on a new path, at a critical time when individualism and nationalism began to emerge as sources of creative artistry. His instrumental works, too, possess a new quality which signalizes the transition from Classical to Romantic music. For piano he wrote pieces of extraordinary brilliance, introducing some novel ele-

ments in chord writing and passage work. He was himself an excellent pianist; his large hands gave him an unusual command of the keyboard—he could stretch the interval of a twelfth. Weber's influence on the development of German music was very great. The evolutionary link to Wagner's music drama is evident in the coloring of the orch. parts in Weber's operas and in the adumbration of the principle of leading motifs.

WORKS: OPERAS: *Das Waldmädchen* (Freiberg, Nov. 24, 1800); *Peter Schmoll und seine Nachbarn* (Augsburg, March, 1803); *Rübezahl* (1805; unfinished); *Abu Hassan* (Munich, June 4, 1811); *Preciosa* (Berlin, March 14, 1821); *Der Freischütz* (Berlin, June 18, 1821); *Die drei Pintos* (1821; unfinished; completed by Gustav Mahler after Weber's sketches and produced in Leipzig, Jan. 20, 1888); *Euryanthe* (Vienna, Oct. 25, 1823); *Oberon, or The Elf King's Oath* (London, April 12, 1826).

INCIDENTAL MUSIC: To Gozzi's *Turandot* (1809), Moreto's *Donna Diana* (1817), Adolf Müllner's *König Yngurd* (1817), Theodor Hell's *Das Haus Anglade* (1818), Grillparzer's *Sappho* (1818), Gehe's *Heinrich IV* (1818), Rublack's *Leib' um Liebe* (1818), Houwald's *Der Leuchtturm* (1820), Ludwig Robert's *Den Sachsensohn vermählet heute* (1822).

VOCAL WORKS: *Der erste Ton,* cantata for Declamation, Chorus, and Orch. (1808); op. 36, *In seiner Ordnung schafft der Herr* for Soli, Chorus, and Orch. (1812); op. 44, *Kampf und Sieg,* cantata on the battle of Waterloo (1815); *L'Accoglianza* for 6 Solo Voices, Chorus, and Orch. (1817); op. 58, *Jubel-Kantate* for Soli, Chorus, and Orch. (1818); op. 61, *Natur und Liebe,* cantata for 2 Sopranos, 2 Tenors, and 2 Basses, with Piano (1818); other occasional cantatas; 2 masses (E-flat, G); 2 offertories for Soli, Chorus, and Orch.; op. 42, 6 part-songs for Men's Voices (to T. Körner's *Leyer und Schwert;* achieved great popularity with students); op. 53b, 5 part-songs for Men's Chorus; op. 68, 6 part-songs for Men's Chorus; 5 scenes for Soprano, with Orch. (op. 16, "Il Momento s'avvicina," and op. 50, "Misera me" for *Atalia,* 1811; op. 51, "Non paventar, mia vita" for *Ines de Castro,* 1816; op. 52, "Ah, se Edmondo fosse l'uccisor" for Méhul's *Hélène,* 1815; op. 56, "Was sag' ich? Schaudern macht mich der Gedanke" for Cherubini's *Lodoiska*); op. 53, scena for Tenor, Double Chorus, and Orch., "Signor, se padre sei," for *Ines de Castro;* scena and aria for Tenor, Men's Chorus, and Orch., "Qual altro attendi"; recitative, "Doch welche Töne steigen jetzt hernieder," for Spontini's *Olympie;* many songs (opp. 13, 15, 23, 25, 29, 30, 41, 43, 46, 47, 54, 64, 66, 71, 80); 8 part-songs for Mixed Voices, with and without accompaniment; 6 canons for 3 and 4 Voices; duets (op. 31); 10 Scottish folk songs arranged with accompaniment of Flute, Violin, Cello, and Piano.

FOR ORCH.: Op. 27, *Der Beherrscher der Geister,* overture (to the unfinished opera *Rübezahl*); op. 59, *Jubel-Ouvertüre;* 2 symphs., both in C major; March for Wind Instruments; Waltz for Wind Instruments; 2 piano concertos (op. 11, C; op. 32, E-flat) and *Konzertstück* in F minor (op. 79); Concertino for Clarinet and Orch. in E-flat major (op. 26) and 2 clarinet

Weber

concertos (op. 73, F minor; op. 74, E-flat); *Andante und Rondo* in C minor for Bassoon and Orch. (op. 35); Concerto in F for Bassoon and Orch. (op. 75); Concertino in E minor for Horn and Orch. (op. 45); *Romanza siciliana* for Flute and Orch.; *6 Variations on a German Folksong* for Cello and Orch.; *Andante and Variations* in D minor for Cello and Orch.; *Adagio and Rondo* for "Harmonichord" and Orch.

CHAMBER MUSIC: Op. 8, Piano Quartet in B-flat; op. 13, 6 sonatas for Violin and Piano (F, G, D minor, E-flat, A, C); op. 22, *Variations on a Norwegian Theme* for Violin and Piano, in D minor; op. 33, Variations for Clarinet and Piano in B-flat; op. 34, Clarinet Quintet in B-flat; op. 48, *Duo concertant* in E-flat for Clarinet and Piano; op. 63, Piano Trio in G minor.

FOR PIANO: 4 sonatas (op. 24, C; op. 39, A-flat; op. 49, D minor; op. 70, E minor); op. 1, *6 Fughetten;* op. 2, *Variations* on an original theme; op. 3, *12 Allemandes;* op. 5, *Variations on an Air de ballet* from Vogler's *Castor et Pollux;* op. 6, *Variations on an Air* from Vogler's *Samori;* op. 7, *Variations* on an original theme; op. 12, *Momento capriccioso;* op. 21, *Grande polonaise* in E-flat; op. 28, *Variations* on a theme from Méhul's *Joseph;* op. 40, *Variations* on a Russian theme; op. 50, *Polonaise brillante* in E; op. 53, *Caprice and Variations* on a theme from *Preciosa;* op. 55, *Variations* on a Gypsy theme; op. 62, *Rondo brillant* in E-flat major; op. 65, *Aufforderung zum Tanz (Invitation to the Dance;* in 2 orch. versions, by Berlioz and Weingartner, and in innumerable arrangements for various instruments); op. 72, *Polacca brillante* (arranged for Piano and Orch. by Liszt); op. 81, *Les Adieux,* fantasy; 6 *Ecossaises; 18 valses favorites de l'Impératrice de France;* for Piano, 4-hands: op. 3, *Sechs leichte Stücke;* op. 10, *6 sonates progressives et agréables;* op. 60, *Acht leichte Stücke.* A popular piece publ. under the title *Weber's Last Waltz* (or *Weber's Last Thought*) is a composition of K.G. Reissiger, not Weber.

A complete edition of Weber's works was undertaken in 1926 under the general editorship of H.J. Moser; only the following vols. were publ.: vols. I–II, early operas, ed. by A. Lorenz and W. Kaehler; vol. III, the Salzburg Mass, ed. by C. Schneider; *Preciosa,* ed. by L.K. Mayer. Previously unpubl. works are found in L. Hirschberg's *Reliquienschrein des Meisters C.M. von Weber* (Berlin, 1827). A complete thematic catalogue of Weber's works was publ. by F.W. Jähns, *C.M. von Weber in seinen Werken* (Berlin, 1871).

WRITINGS: An unfinished novel, criticisms, explanatory remarks on new works produced by him in Dresden, poems, etc., were publ. by T. Hell as *Hinterlassene Schriften von C.M. von Weber* (3 vols., Dresden, 1828; 2nd ed., 1850). A more complete and better edition is that of G. Kaiser, *Sämtliche Schriften von C.M. von Weber* (Berlin, 1908). R. Kleinecke publ. *Ausgewählte Schriften von K.M. von Weber* (Leipzig, 1892); a more recent collection was publ. by W. Altmann, *Webers Ausgewählte Schriften* (Regensburg, 1928). *Ein Brevier* was edited by H. Dünnebeil (Berlin, 1949.)

BIBLIOGRAPHY: BIOGRAPHY: Weber's "Autobiographische Skizze," in Kaiser's edition of Weber's *Sämtliche Schriften* (pp. 3–8); W. Neumann, *Weber. Eine Biographie* (Kassel, 1855); Max M. von Weber (son of the composer), *C.M. von Weber. Ein Lebensbild* (3 vols., Leipzig, 1864–66; Eng. adaptation by J.P. Simpson as *Weber: The Life of an Artist,* 2 vols., London, 1865; abridged ed. by R. Pechel, Berlin, 1912; still the standard biography); F.W. Jähns, *Weber. Eine Lebensskizze nach authentischen Quellen* (Leipzig, 1873); J. Benedict, *Weber* (London and N.Y., 1881; 5th ed., 1899; in the series Great Musicians); L. Nohl, *Weber* (Leipzig, 1883); A. Reissmann, *Weber, Sein Leben und seine Werke* (Berlin, 1886); H. Gehrmann, *Weber* (Berlin, 1899); G. Servières, *Weber* (Paris, 1906; new ed., 1925; in the series Musiciens Célèbres); H. von der Pfordten, *Weber* (Leipzig, 1919); A. Cœuroy, *Weber* (Paris, 1925; in the series Les Maîtres de la Musique; new ed., 1953); J. Kapp, *Weber. Eine Biographie* (Berlin, 1922; 5th revised ed., 1931); E. Kroll, *Weber* (Potsdam, 1934); L.P. and R.P. Stebbins, *Enchanted Wanderer: The Life of C.M. von Weber* (N.Y., 1940); W. Saunders, *Weber* (London and N.Y., 1940); H.J. Moser, *C.M. von Weber. Leben und Werk* (Leipzig, 1941; 2nd ed., 1955); P. Raabe, *Wege zu Weber* (Regensburg, 1942); W. Zentner, *C.M. von Weber. Sein Leben und sein Schaffen* (Olten, 1952); H. Schnoor, *Weber: Gestalt und Schöpfung* (Dresden, 1953); H. Dünnebeil, *Webers Leben und Wirken in chronologischen Tafeln* (Berlin, 1953); F. Grüniger, *C.M. von Weber: Leben und Werk* (Freiburg im Breisgau, 1954); J. Warrack, *Carl Maria von Weber* (N.Y., 1968).

CRITICISM, APPRECIATION: A. Jullien, *Weber à Paris en 1826* (Paris, 1877); Wagner's articles on Weber are found in vol. VII of his complete works (Eng. trans., London, 1898); also in C.F. Glasenapp's *Wagner-Encyklopädie,* II (Leipzig, 1891; pp. 259–80); G.F. Kaiser, *Beiträge zu einer Charakteristik Webers als Musikschriftsteller* (Leipzig, 1910); G. Servières, *Le "Freischütz" de Weber* (Paris, 1913); W. Georgii, *Weber als Klavierkomponist* (Diss., Univ. of Halle, 1914); H.W. von Waltershausen, *Der Freischütz. Ein Versuch über die musikalische Romantik* (Munich, 1920); H. Allekotte, *Webers Messen* (Bonn, 1913); E.J. Dent, "A Weber Centenary," *Music & Letters* (July 1921); F. Hasselberg, *Der Freischütz. Friedrich Kinds Operndichtung und ihre Quellen* (Berlin, 1921); M. Degen, *Die Lieder von Weber* (Basel, 1923); A. Cœuroy, "Le Problème *d'Euryanthe,*" *Le Correspondent* (Oct. 25, 1923); idem, "Weber as Writer," *Musical Quarterly* (Jan. 1925); E. Reiter, *Webers künstlerische Persönlichkeit aus seinen Schriften* (Leipzig, 1926); H. Abert, "Weber und sein Freischütz," *Jahrbuch der Musikbibliothek Peters* (1927; reprinted in Abert's *Gesammelte Schriften,* Halle, 1929); J.G. Prod'homme, "The Works of Weber in France," *Musical Quarterly* (July 1928); A. Sandt, *Webers Opern in ihrer Instrumentation* (Frankfurt, 1932); G. Kinsky, "Was Mendelssohn Indebted to Weber?" *Musical Quarterly* (April 1933); G. Abraham, "Weber as Novelist and Critic," *Musical Quarterly* (Jan. 1934); P. Listl, *C.M. von Weber als Ouvertürenkomponist* (Diss., Univ. of Würzburg, 1936); A. Einstein, "C.M. Weber," *Music & Letters* (Jan. 1937); H. Schnoor, *W. auf dem Welttheater; Ein Freischützbuch* (Dresden, 1942); P.R. Kirby, "Weber's Operas in London," *Musical Quarterly* (July 1946).

CORRESPONDENCE: L. Nohl, *Musiker-Briefe* (Leipzig, 1867; 2nd ed., 1873; Eng. trans. by Lady Wallace as *Letters of Distinguished Musicians*, London, 1867); L. Nohl, *Mosaik für musikalisch-gebildete* (Leipzig, 1882); A. von Weber (grandson of the composer), *Reise-Briefe von Weber an seine Gattin Caroline* (Leipzig, 1886); E. Rudorff, *Briefe von Weber an Heinrich Lichtenstein* (Braunschweig, 1900); G. Kaiser, *Webers Briefe an den Grafen Karl von Brühl* (Leipzig, 1911); L. Hirschberg, *77 bisher ungedruckte Briefe Webers* (Hildburghausen, 1926); G. Kinsky, "Ungedruckte Briefe Webers," *Zeitschrift für Musik* (1926).

WEBER AND HIS CONTEMPORARIES: J.C. Lobe, "Gespräche mit Weber," in his *Fliegende Blätter für Musik* (Leipzig, 1853; reprinted in his *Consonanzen und Dissonanzen*, 1869); M. Runze, "Loewe und Weber," in his *Loewe Redivivus* (Berlin, 1888); H.A. Krüger, *Pseudoromantik, Friedrich Kind und der Dresdener Liederkreis* (Leipzig, 1904); H.B. and C.O.E. Cox, *Leaves from the Journal of Sir G. Smart* (London, 1907); K. Huschke, "Webers Beziehungen zu Ludwig von Beethoven und Franz Schubert," *Deutsche Revue* (May–June 1919); E. Kroll, "E.T.A. Hoffmann und Weber," *Neue Musik-Zeitung* (1921); K. Huschke, "Spohr und Weber," *Allgemeine Musik Zeitung* (1934); E. Kroll, "Beethoven und Weber," *Neues Beethoven-Jahrbuch* (Augsburg, 1935); O. Kroll, "Weber und Bärmann," *Neue Zeitschrift für Musik* (1936).

MISCELLANEOUS: R. Haas, "Ein Notizen-Buch C.M. von Webers aus Prag," *Der Merker* (1916); A. Maecklenburg, "Der Fall Spontini-Weber," *Zeitschrift für Musikwissenschaft* (1923–24); O. Hellinghaus, *Weber. Sein Persönlichkeit in seinen Briefen und Tagebüchern und in Aufzeichnungen seiner Zeitgenossen* (Freiburg im Breisgau, 1924); E. Kroll, *Weber. Sein Leben in Bildern* (Leipzig, 1936); F. Rapp, *Ein unbekanntes Bildnis Webers* (Stuttgart, 1937); G. Hausswald, ed., *Weber: Eine Gedenkschrift* (Dresden, 1951).

Weber, Franz, German organist and conductor; b. Cologne, Aug. 26, 1805; d. there, Sept. 18, 1876. He studied with Bernhard Klein in Berlin; in 1838 was appointed organist of the Cologne Cathedral. He wrote a *Kriegsgesang der Rheinpreussen* for Male Chorus and Orch.; publ. several songbooks (*Kommersbuch, Turner-Liederbuch, Des deutschen Soldaten Liederbuch,* etc.).

Weber, Friedrich August, German physician and composer; b. Heilbronn, Jan. 24, 1753; d. there, Jan. 21, 1806. He wrote numerous oratorios and cantatas with orch.; also symphs., chamber music, piano sonatas for 4-hands; contributed articles on music to various journals.

Weber, Friedrich Dionys, Bohemian composer and writer on music; b. Velichov, Oct. 9, 1766; d. Prague, Dec. 25, 1842. He studied with Abbé Vogler; in 1811 was one of the founders of the Prague Cons., and its first director; among his pupils were Moscheles and Kalliwoda. He wrote several operas, 18 cantatas, a number of military marches, a Sextet for 6 Trombones, a Sextet for 6 Cornets, quartets for 4 cornets, variations for violin and cello, numerous popular quadrilles, *Ländler,* etc., for piano. He publ. *Das Konservatorium der Musik zu Prag* (1817); *Allgemeine theoretisch-praktische Vorschule der Musik* (1828); *Theoretisch-prakitisches Lehrbuch der Harmonie und des Generalbasses* (4 parts; 1830–41).

Weber, Georg Viktor, German ecclesiastic and choral conductor; b. Ober-Erlenbach, Feb. 25, 1838; d. Mainz, Sept. 24, 1911. He took Holy Orders in 1863; in 1866 was appointed music director and organist at the Mainz Cathedral, where he presented fine concerts of a cappella music of the 15th and 16th centuries with his excellent choir. He was also an expert on organ building.

WRITINGS: *Manuale cantus ecclesiastici juxta ritum S. Rom. ecclesiae* (1878; 2nd ed., 1897); *Orgelbuch zum Mainzer Diocesan-Gesangbuch* (1880; 3rd ed., 1896); *Über Oregeldispositionen* (1890); *Die Verbesserung der "Medicaea"* (1901).

Weber, Gottfried, eminent German theorist and composer; b. Freinsheim, near Mannheim, March 1, 1779; d. Kreuznach, Sept. 21, 1839. He studied law at Heidelberg and Göttingen, and filled positions as judge in Mannheim (1802), Mainz (1814), and Darmstadt (1818); was appointed public prosecutor for the state of Hesse in 1832. He was an excellent amateur pianist and also played the flute and the cello; in 1806 founded a musical society called "Conservatorium" in Mannheim; in 1824 began the magazine *Caecilia,* and edited it until his death. He made a thorough study of the theoretical works of Marpurg, Kirnberger, Abbé Vogler, and others, and then brought out his important treatise *Versuch einer geordneten Theorie der Tonsetzkunst* (3 vols., 1817–21; 2nd ed. in 4 vols., 1824; 3rd ed. in 4 vols., 1830–32), in which he introduced the now widely accepted symbols for designating the major keys with capital letters and minor keys with small letters, Roman figures for degrees of the scale, etc. It was publ. in Eng. in Boston (1846) and London (1851). His other theoretical publications include *Über chronometrische Tempobezeichnung* (1817); *Beschreibung und Tonleiter der G. Weber'schen Doppelposaune* (1817); "Versuch einer praktischen Akustik der Blasinstrumente," in Ersch and Gruber's *Encyclopädie; Allgemeine Musiklehre zum Selbstunterrichte* (1822; 3rd ed., 1831; in Eng., Boston, 1824); "Über Saiteninstrumente mit Bünden," *Berliner Musikzeitung* (1825); *Die Generalbasslehre zum Selbstunterrichte* (1833); many essays for the *Allgemeine Musikalische Zeitung* and for his own paper, *Caecilia.* He questioned the authenticity of Mozart's Requiem (in *Caecilia,* 1826). As a composer, he wrote 3 masses, a Requiem, and a Te Deum

Weber – Webern

(all with orch.); variations for guitar and cello; some chamber music; part-songs.

Weber, Gustav, Swiss composer; b. München-buchsee, Oct. 30, 1845; d. Zürich, June 12, 1887. He studied at the Leipzig Cons. and with Tausig in Berlin; his symph. poem *Zur Iliade* was presented by Liszt at the Beethoven Centennial Festival in 1870. In 1872 he settled in Zürich as a church organist, teacher at the Cons., and choral conductor. He publ. a group of waltzes for piano, 4-hands; Piano Quartet; Piano Trio; Violin Sonata; *Prinz Carneval,* an album of children's pieces; many choruses; choral arrangements of old German songs. For several years he was editor of the *Schweizerische Musikzeitung.*
BIBLIOGRAPHY: A. Schneider, *G. Weber* (Zürich, 1888); A. Steiner, *Gustav Weber* (Zürich, 1910).

Weber, Josef Miroslaw, Czech violinist and composer; b. Prague, Nov. 9, 1854; d. Munich, Jan. 1, 1906. He was taught by his father, and played violin in public as a child; then studied at the Prague Cons. He subsequently occupied posts as concertmaster in Sondershausen (1873–75), Darmstadt (1873–75), and Wiesbaden (1883–93); joined the court opera in Munich in 1894 and became its concertmaster in 1901; he remained there until his death. He wrote the operas *Der selige Herr Vetter* (Wiesbaden, 1894) and *Die neue Mamsell* (Munich, 1896); a ballet, *Die Rheinnixe* (Wiesbaden, 1884); Violin Concerto; Septet for Violin, Viola, Cello, Clarinet, Bassoon, and 2 Horns; String Quintet; etc.

Weber, Ludwig, eminent Austrian bass; b. Vienna, July 29, 1899; d. there, Dec. 9, 1974. He studied in Vienna with Alfred Boruttau; made his debut at the Vienna Volksoper in 1920; then sang in Düsseldorf, Cologne, and Munich; from 1945 to 1960 he was one of the principal singers at the Vienna State Opera; also sang regularly at the Bayreuth Festivals (from 1951). In 1961 he became a prof. at the Salzburg Mozarteum. He was regarded as one of the foremost Wagnerian bass singers of his time.

Weber, Margrit, Swiss pianist; b. Ebnat-Kappel, Feb. 24, 1924. She studied organ in Zürich; was employed as an organist at the age of 15; then devoted herself chiefly to the piano. She toured Europe in concert recitals, presenting many new works; in 1956 and in 1965 she played in the U.S. and Canada. She was the soloist in the first performances of piano concertos by Martinů and Alexander Tcherepnin, and of Stravinsky's *Movements* for Piano and Orch., which she performed under Stravinsky's own direction in N.Y., on Jan. 10, 1960.
BIBLIOGRAPHY: *Modern Music... Analytic Index,* compiled by Wayne Shirley; ed. by W. and C. Lichtenwanger (N.Y., 1976; pp. 236–37).

Weber, Wilhelm, German choral conductor and composer; b. Bruchsal, Nov. 16, 1859; d. Augsburg, Oct. 14, 1918. After studying at the Stuttgart Cons., he went to Augsburg, where he taught at the Hochschule für Musik from 1884, becoming its director in 1905. From 1892 he was conductor of the Oratorienverein, notable for its numerous German premieres of works by foreign composers; he also conducted at various festivals in Germany. He publ. 2 books of *Landsknechtslieder* and other songs; choruses; piano pieces. He was the author of *Beethovens Missa solemnis* (1897; 2nd ed., 1903) and *Händels Oratorien, übersetzt und bearbeitet von F. Chrysander* (3 vols., 1898, 1900, 1902).

Webern, Anton (Friedrich Wilhelm) von, remarkable Austrian composer (he removed the nobiliary particle "von" in 1918 when such distinctions were outlawed in Austria); b. Vienna, Dec. 3, 1883; d. (accidentally shot and killed by an American soldier) Mittersill, Sept. 15, 1945. He received his first instruction in music from his mother, an amateur pianist; then studied piano, cello, and theory with Edwin Komauer in Klagenfurt; also played cello in the local orch. there. In 1902 he entered the Univ. of Vienna, where he studied harmony with Graedener and counterpoint with Navratil; also attended classes in musicology with Guido Adler; received his Ph.D. in 1906 with a dissertation on Heinrich Isaac's *Choralis Constantinus II.* In 1904 he began private studies in composition with Arnold Schoenberg, whose ardent disciple he became; Alban Berg also studied with Schoenberg; together, Schoenberg, Berg, and Webern laid the foundations of what became known as the 2nd Viennese School of composition. The unifying element was the adoption of Schoenberg's method of composition with 12 tones related only to one another. Malevolent opponents referred to Schoenberg, Berg, and Webern as a Vienna Trinity, with Schoenberg as God the Father, Berg as God the Son, and Webern as the Holy Ghost; the last appellation was supposed to describe the phantomlike substance of some of Webern's works. From 1908 to 1914 Webern was active as a conductor in Vienna and in Germany; in 1915–16 he served in the army; in 1917–18 was conductor at the Deutsches Theater in Prague. In 1918 he settled in Mödling, near Vienna, where he taught composition privately; in 1918–22 he supervised the programs of the Verein für Musikalische Privataufführungen (Society for Private Musical Performances), organized in Vienna by Schoenberg with the intention of promoting modern music without being exposed to reactionary opposition (music critics were not admitted to these performances). Webern was conductor of the Schubertbund (1921–22) and the Mödling Male Chorus (1921–26); he also led the Vienna Workers' Symph. concerts (1922–34) and the Vienna Workers' Chorus (1923–34), both sponsored by the Social Democratic Party. From 1927 to 1938 he was a conductor on the Austrian Radio; furthermore, he conducted guest engagements in Germany, Switzerland, and Spain; from 1929 made several visits to England, where he was a guest conductor with the BBC Symph. Orch. For the most part, however, he devoted himself to composition, private teaching, and lecturing. After Hitler came to power in Germany in 1933, Webern's music was banned as a manifestation of "cultural Bolshevism" and "degenerate art." His position became more difficult after the Anschluss in 1938, for his works could no longer be publ.; he eked out an existence by teaching a few private pupils and making piano arrangements of musical scores by others for Universal Edition. After his son was killed in an air bombardment of a train in Feb. 1945, he and his wife fled from Vienna to Mittersill, near Salzburg, to stay with his married daughters and grandchildren. His life ended tragically on the evening of Sept. 15, 1945, when he was shot and killed by an American soldier after stepping outside his son-in-law's residence (for a full account, see H. Moldenhauer, *The Death of Anton Webern: A Drama in Documents,* N.Y., 1961).

Webern left relatively few works, and most of them are of short duration (the 4th of his 5 Pieces for Orch., op. 10, scored for clarinet, trumpet, trombone, mandolin, celesta, harp, drum, violin, and viola, takes only 19 seconds to play), but in his music he achieves the utmost subtilization of expressive means. He adopted the 12-tone method of composition almost immediately after its definitive formulation by Schoenberg (1924), and extended the principle of nonrepetition of notes to tone colors, so that in some of his works (e.g., Symph., op. 21) solo instruments are rarely allowed to play 2 successive thematic notes. Dynamic marks are similarly diversified. Typically, each 12-tone row is divided into symmetric sections of 2, 4, or 6 members, which enter mutually into intricate but invariably logical canonic imitations. Inversions and augmentations are inherent features; melodically and harmonically, the intervals of the major seventh and minor ninth are stressed; single motifs are brief, and stand out as individual particles or lyric ejaculations. The impact of these works on the general public and on the critics was disconcerting; and upon occasion led to violent demonstrations; however, the extraordinary skill and novelty of technique made this music endure beyond the fashions of the times; performances of Webern's works multiplied after his death, and began to influence increasingly larger groups of modern musicians; Stravinsky acknowledged the use of Webern's methods in his latest works; jazz composers have professed to follow Webern's ideas of tone color; analytical treatises have been publ. in several languages. The International Webern Festival celebrated the centennial of his birth in Dec. 1983 in Vienna.

WORKS: FOR ORCH.: *Im Sommerwind,* idyll for Large Orch. (1904; Seattle, May 25, 1962, Ormandy conducting); *Passacaglia,* op. 1 (1908; Vienna, Nov. 4, 1908, composer conducting); *6 Orchestral Pieces,* op. 6 (1909; Vienna, March 31, 1913, Schoenberg conducting; revised 1928; Berlin, Jan. 27, 1929); *5 Orchestral Pieces,* op. 10 (1911–13; Zürich Festival of the International Society for Contemporary Music, June 22, 1926, composer conducting); *5 Orchestral Pieces,* op. posthumous (1913; Cologne, Jan. 13, 1969); Symph. for Chamber Ensemble, op. 21 (1928; N.Y., League of Composers, Dec. 18, 1929); 5 Movements for String Quartet, op. 5, arranged for String

Orch. (1928–29; Philadelphia, March 26, 1930); *Variations,* op. 30 (1940; Winterthur, March 3, 1943). VOCAL MUSIC: *Entflieht auf leichten Kähnen,* op. 2, for Unaccompanied Chorus (1908; Furstenfeld, April 10, 1927); 2 songs to words by Goethe, op. 19, for Chorus, Celesta, Guitar, Violin, Clarinet, and Bass Clarinet (1926); *Das Augenlicht,* op. 26, for Chorus and Orch. (1935; London, BBC concert, June 17, 1938); *First Cantata* for Soprano, Mixed Chorus, and Orch. (1938–39; London, BBC concert, July 12, 1946); *2nd Cantata* for Soprano, Bass, Mixed Chorus, and Orch. (1941–43; Brussels, June 23, 1950); 2 sets of 5 songs for Voice and Piano, to poems by Stefan George, opp. 3 and 4 (1908–9); 2 songs for Voice and Instrumental Ensemble, on poems by Rilke, op. 8 (1910; revised 1921 and 1925); 4 songs for Voice and Piano, op. 12 (1915–17); 4 songs for Voice and Orch., op. 13 (1914–18); 6 songs for Voice and Instruments, on poems by Georg Trakl, op. 14 (1919–21; Donaueschingen, July 20, 1924); *5 Sacred Songs* for Voice and Instruments, op. 15 (1917–22; Vienna, Oct. 9, 1924, composer conducting); *5 Canons* on Latin texts for Voice, Clarinet, and Bass Clarinet, op. 16 (1923–24; N.Y., May 8, 1951); *3 Traditional Rhymes* for Voice and Instruments, op. 17 (1924–25; N.Y., March 16, 1952); 3 songs for Voice, Clarinet, and Guitar, op. 18 (1925; Los Angeles, Feb. 8, 1954); 3 songs for Voice and Piano, op. 23 (1933–34); 3 songs for Voice and Piano, op. 25 (1934). CHAMBER MUSIC: String Quartet, in one movement (1905; posthumous, Seattle, May 26, 1962); Piano Quintet, in one movement (Vienna, Nov. 7, 1907); 5 Movements for String Quartet (1909; Vienna, Feb. 8, 1910); 4 pieces for Violin and Piano, op. 7 (1910; revised 1914); 6 bagatelles for String Quartet, op. 9 (1911–13; Donaueschingen, July 19, 1924); *3 Little Pieces* for Cello and Piano, op. 11 (1914; Mainz, Dec. 2, 1924); String Trio, op. 20 (1926–27; Vienna, Jan. 16, 1928); Quartet for Violin, Clarinet, Tenor Saxophone, and Piano, op. 22 (1930; Vienna, April 13, 1931); Concerto for 9 Instruments, op. 24 (1934; Prague, Sept. 4, 1935); String Quartet, op. 28 (1936–38; Pittsfield, Mass., Sept. 22, 1938); Variations for Piano Solo (1936; Vienna, Oct. 26, 1937); arrangements for Chamber Orch. of Schoenberg's Chamber Symph., op. 9 (1923), Schubert's *Deutsche Tanze* (1931), and Bach's Ricercare *a* 6 from *Das musikalische Opfer* (London, April 25, 1935, Webern conducting).

WRITINGS: W. Reich has edited *Der Weg zur neuen Musik* (first publ. in Vienna, 1933; new ed., 1960; Eng. trans., 1963) and *Anton Webern: Weg und Gestalt: Selbstzeugnisse und Worte der Freunde* (Zürich, 1961).

BIBLIOGRAPHY: "W. zum 50. Geburtstag," special issue of the magazine *23,* no. 14 (Vienna, 1934); R. Leibowitz, *Schoenberg et son école* (Paris, 1947; Eng. trans., 1949); L. Rognoni, *Espressionismo e dodecafonia* (Turin, 1954; 2nd ed., revised, 1966, as *La scuola musicale di Vienna*); "A. W.: Dokumente, Bekenntnis, Erkenntnisse, Analysen," *Die Reihe,* no. 2 (1955; Eng. trans. in *Die Reihe,* 1958); W. Kolneder, *A. W.: Einführung in Werk und Stil* (Rodenkirchen, 1961; Eng. trans., 1968); H. Moldenhauer, *The Death of A. W.: A Drama in Documents* (N.Y., 1961); G. Perle, *Serial Composition and Aton-*

ality: An Introduction to the Music of Schoenberg, Berg and W. (Berkeley, 1962; 5th ed., revised, 1982); H. Moldenhauer and D. Irvine, eds., *A. von W.: Perspectives* (Seattle, 1966); F. Wildgans, *A. W.* (London, 1966); *A. von W.: Sketches (1926–1945)* (facsimile reproductions from W.'s sketchbooks, with commentary by E. Krenek and foreword by H. Moldenhauer; N.Y., 1968); R. Ringger, *A. W.s Klavierlieder* (Zürich, 1968); L. Somfai, *A. W.* (Budapest, 1968); C. Rostand, *A. W.: L'Homme et son œuvre* (Paris, 1969); H. Deppert, *Studien zur Kompositionstechnik im instrumentalen Spätwerk A. W.s* (Darmstadt, 1972); W. Stroh, *A. von W.; Historische Legimation* (Göppingen, 1973); F. Döhl, *W.s Beitrag zur Stilwende der neuen Musik* (Munich, 1976); H. and R. Moldenhauer, *A. von W.: Chronicle of His Life and Work* (N.Y., 1978); A. Whittall, "Webern and Atonality: The Path from the Old Aesthetic," *Musical Times* (Dec. 1983); Z. Roman, *A. von W.: An Annotated Bibliography* (Detroit, 1983).

Webster, Beveridge, American pianist; b. Pittsburgh, May 30, 1908. He studied music with his father, who was director of the Pittsburgh Cons. of Music; at the age of 13 he was sent to Paris to study with Isidor Philipp at the Paris Cons.; graduated in 1926, winning the Grand Prix for piano playing. He gave concerts in Europe; returned to the U.S. in 1934, and developed a successful concert career, appearing with major symph. orchs.; also continued to give concerts in Europe. In 1946 he was appointed prof. of piano at the Juilliard School of Music in N.Y.; gave a piano recital at the Juilliard Theater on his 70th birthday, in May 1978.

Webster, Sir David, English operatic administrator; b. Dundee, Scotland, July 3, 1903; d. London, May 11, 1971. He was educated at Liverpool Univ.; then commenced a commercial career while pursuing his various interests in the arts; from 1940–45 was chairman of the Liverpool Phil. Society. In 1945 he became general administrator of the Covent Garden Opera Trust; in this capacity he helped to launch the careers of many famous singers, among them Jon Vickers and Dame Joan Sutherland. He was knighted in 1961 and was made a Knight Commander of the Royal Victorian Order in 1970. An account of his career by M. Haltrecht, under the title *The Reluctant Showman,* was publ. in 1975.

Wecker, Georg Kaspar, German organist and composer; b. Nuremberg (baptized, April 2), 1632; d. there, April 20, 1695. He studied organ with Erasmus Kindermann, and soon obtained a position as church organist in Nuremberg; his last appointment was at the Sebaldkirche there (1686–95). He also was a respected teacher; Johann Krieger and Pachelbel were among his pupils. Several of his sacred songs were publ. in hymnbooks in Nuremberg; 3 sacred choral works are reproduced in Denkmäler der Tonkunst in Bayern, 10 (6.i).

Weckerlin, Jean-Baptiste-Théodore, eminent French music scholar and composer; b. Gebweiler, Alsace, Nov. 9, 1821; d. Buhl, May 20, 1910. He was trained for his father's business of cotton-dyeing; but went over to music in 1844, studying under Ponchard (singing) and Halévy (composition) at the Paris Cons., producing a heroic symph., *Roland,* for Soli, Chorus, and Orch., in 1847; on leaving the Cons. in 1849, he gave music lessons; took part with Seghers in the direction of the Société Sainte-Cécile, which brought out some of his works; and achieved success in 1853 with a one-act comic opera, *L'Organiste dans l'embarras* (100 perfs. at the Théâtre-Lyrique). This was followed by 2 comic operas in Alsatian dialect, *Die drifach Hochzitt im Bäsethal* (Colmar, 1863) and *D'r verhäxt' Herbst* (Colmar, 1879), and the one-act opera *Après Fontenoy* (Théâtre-Lyrique, 1877). Meantime he had become an assistant librarian at the Paris Cons. (1869); in 1876 succeeded Félicien David as librarian, and in 1885 publ. a bibliographical catalogue; was also chosen librarian of the Société des Compositeurs, for whose bulletins he wrote important articles. He retired in 1909. He won distinction as a composer of grand choral works; also wrote choruses a cappella, songs, and a grand *Symphonie de la forêt* for Orch.; but his greatest achievement was the compilation of old French songs. His *Echos du temps passé* (1853–55) and *Souvenirs du temps passé* (1864) are collections of chansons, noëls, madrigals, etc., from the 12th–18th centuries; the *Musiciana* (3 vols., 1877, 1890, 1899) is a collection of rare and curious works on music, with anecdotes, etc.; other collections are *Les Echos d'Angleterre* (1877; folk songs, with Piano); *Chansons et rondes populaires* (children's songs, with Piano); *Les Poètes français mis en musique* (1868); *Chansons populaires des provinces de la France; L'Ancienne Chanson populaire en France* (1886); *Chansons populaires du Pays de France* (2 vols., 1903). A catalogue of his private library was publ. at Leipzig in 1910.

Weckmann, Matthias, German organist and composer; b. Niederdorla, near Mühlhausen, Thuringia, c.1619; d. Hamburg, Feb. 24, 1674. He was the son of a schoolmaster; was a chorister in the Dresden court chapel, where he was a pupil of Heinrich Schütz. In 1633 he was sent to Hamburg for further study with Reinken, Jakob Praetorius, and H. Scheidemann, by whom he was trained in the organ method of Sweelinck. In 1637 he became organist for the crown prince in Dresden, and in 1642 was appointed to a similar post in Copenhagen; he returned in 1647 to Dresden, where he became a friend of J.J. Froberger; in 1655 he went to Hamburg as organist at the Jacobikirche, and there founded, with Christoph Bernhard, the Collegium Musicum, a concert society for the performance of new works (it was discontinued after Weckmann's death). Weckmann's solo cantatas and choral works with instrumental accompaniment were publ. by Max Seiffert in Denkmäler Deutscher Tonkunst, 6; instrumental pieces and songs in Erbe Deutscher Musik (series 2, vol. 4); 2 numbers are reproduced in A. Schering's *Geschichte der Musik in Beispielen* (nos. 212 and 213); etc.

BIBLIOGRAPHY: M. Seiffert, "Matthias Weck-mann und das Collegium Musicum in Hamburg," *Sammelbände der Internationalen Musik-Gesell-schaft,* 2 (1900); G. Ilgner, *Matthias Weckmann. Sein Leben und seine Werke* (Wolfenbüttel, 1939); G. Sharp, "Matthias Weckmann, 1619–74," *Musical Times,* CXV (1974).

Wedge, George (Anson), American organist and educator; b. Danbury, Conn., Jan. 15, 1890; d. Barbados, Oct. 31, 1964. He studied organ, piano, and composition at the Inst. of Musical Art in N.Y.; subsequently occupied various teaching positions: at N.Y. Univ. (1920–27); at the Curtis Inst. of Music in Philadelphia (1924–26); was dean of the Inst. of Musical Art and of the Juilliard School of Music (1938–46); director of the Juilliard Summer School (1932–47). He publ. *Ear-training and Sight-singing* (1921); *Advanced Ear-training and Sight-singing* (1922); *Keyboard Harmony* (1924); *Rhythm in Music* (1927); *Applied Harmony* (2 vols., 1930–31); *The Gist of Music* (1936).

Weelkes, Thomas, English composer; b. c.1575; d. London, Nov. 30, 1623. In 1597 he publ. a book of madrigals for 3–6 voices; in 1598 he publ. *Balletts and Madrigals* for 5 voices, dedicated to Edward Darcey, Groom of the Privy Chamber; in 1600 he brought out 2 more books, containing madrigals for 5 and 6 voices; served as organist at the College of Winchester (1600–2). He was a friend of Morley, to whose collection *The Triumphes of Oriana* (1601–3) he contributed a fine madrigal for 6 voices, *As Vesta was from Latmos Hill Descending.* In 1602 he was granted the degree of B.Mus. at the New College, Oxford, and was appointed organist of Chichester Cathedral. A subsequent publication was *Ayres; or, Phantasticke Spirits for 3 voices* (1608; reprinted by Arkwright in the *Old English Edition*). Weelkes was one of the greatest English madrigalists, possessing remarkable power in melodic characterization of the text; he occasionally used chromatic progressions in harmony that were well in advance of his time. He wrote a considerable amount of church music (services and anthems); also instrumental works (2 pavanes and other pieces, for 5 viols). His madrigals and other vocal works are reprinted in *The English Madrigal School,* edited by E.H. Fellowes (vols. 9–13); anthems in the series Tudor Church Music and in *Musica Britannica,* 23.
BIBLIOGRAPHY: E.H. Fellowes, *The English Madrigal Composers* (London, 1921; 2nd ed., 1948); D.M. Arnold, "Thomas Weelkes and the Madrigal," *Music & Letters* (Jan. 1950); David Brown, *Thomas Weelkes: A Biographical and Critical Study* (London, 1969).

Weerbecke (Weerbeke, Werbecke), Gaspar van, Flemish composer; b. Audenarde, c.1445. He was a pupil of Ockeghem; in 1472 he was organizer of the ducal court chapel at Milan; his singers including Josquin des Prez. From 1481 to 1489 he was a singer in the papal chapel at Rome, a post he resumed from 1500 to 1509 after sojourns in Milan and Flanders; there is no trace of him after 1517. Masses, motets, and Lamentations by Weerbecke were publ. by Petrucci (1505–9).
BIBLIOGRAPHY: G. Cesari, in the *Rivista Musicale Italiana* (1922); G. Croll, "Gaspar van Weerbeke," *Musica Disciplina,* 6 (1952; with a list of works); idem, *Das Motettenwerk Gaspar van Weerbecke* (Diss., Univ. of Göttingen, 1954); G. Reese, *Music in the Renaissance* (N.Y., 1954; 2nd ed., revised, 1959).

Wegeler, Franz Gerhard, German physician and music amateur; b. Bonn, Aug. 22, 1765; d. Coblenz, May 7, 1848. He was a practicing physician in Bonn and Coblenz, and knew Beethoven as a youth. With Ries, he publ. *Biographische Notizen über Ludwig van Beethoven* (1838; supplement, 1845; reprinted by A. Kalischer, 1906).
BIBLIOGRAPHY: S. Ley, ed., *Beethoven als Freund der Familie Wegeler* (Bonn, 1927).

Wegelius, Martin, eminent Finnish composer and pedagogue; b. Helsinki, Nov. 10, 1846; d. there, March 22, 1906. He studied philosophy, taking his master's degree in 1869; studied music with Rudolf Bibl in Vienna (1870–71), and with Richter and Paul in Leipzig (1871–73); he went to Leipzig for further study in 1877–78. Returning to Finland, he became operatic coach at the Helsinki National Theater. In 1882 he was appointed director of the newly founded Helsinki Cons., holding this post until his death. Under his guidance, the institution became one of the finest schools in Europe, with excellent teachers. Sibelius was one of the pupils of Wegelius; others were Järnefelt, Melartin, and Palmgren. Wegelius emphasized the cultivation of national Finnish music, and thus was mainly responsible for the magnificent development of Finland as a musical nation.

WORKS: Overture, *Daniel Hjort* (1872); *Divertissement à la hongroise* (1880); *Rondo quasi fantasia* for Piano and Orch. (1872); *Mignon,* 6 songs with Orch., after Goethe's *Westöstlicher Diwan* (1875); Christmas Cantata (1877); festival cantata, *The 6th of May* (1878); Violin Sonata; piano pieces; songs. He publ. (in Swedish) a number of manuals and books on music history: *Lärobok i allmän musiklära och analys* (2 vols., 1888–89); *Hufvuddragen af den västerländska musikens historia* (3 vols., 1891–93); *Kurs i tonträffning* (3 vols., 1893–95); *Kurs i homofon sats* (2 vols., 1897–1905); etc.
BIBLIOGRAPHY: K.T. Flodin, *Martin Wegelius* (in Swedish, Stockholm, 1916; in Finnish, Helsinki, 1922); *Martin Wegelius* (letters; 2 vols., Helsinki, 1918–19); Arvi Karvonen, "Martin Wegelius," in *Suomen Säveltäjiä,* ed. by Sulho Ranta (Helsinki, 1945; pp. 169–83).

Wehle, Gerhard Fürchtegott, German musicologist and composer; b. Paramaribo, Dutch Guiana, Oct. 11, 1884; d. Berlin, Oct. 15, 1973. He studied in Germany, and settled in Berlin (1907); he was active primarily as a music critic and pedagogue; taught improvisation and other subjects; publ. *Die Kunst der Improvisation* (2 vols., Münster, 1925–26); *Die Orgel-Improvisation* (Leipzig, 1932; both titles reissued in 3 vols., Hamburg, 1950–53); *Neue Wege im Kompositions-Unterricht* (2 vols., Hamburg, 1955); *Die höhere Kompositionstechnik* (2 vols., Hamburg, n.d.). Among his musical works are 26 symph. cantatas; 3 symphs.; much chamber music. He was also a successful novelist.

Wehle, Karl, Bohemian pianist; b. Prague, March 17, 1825; d. Paris, June 3, 1883. Trained for a mercantile career, he abandoned it for music; studied piano with Moscheles at Leipzig and Kullak in Berlin; made extended tours to Asia, Africa, America, and Australia, but resided chiefly in Paris. He publ. a number of brilliant compositions for piano, among them *Sérénade napolitaine, Allegro à la hongroise, 3 tarentelles, 2 impromptus, Berceuse javanaise, Marche cosaque, Fête bohémienne, Un Songe à Vaucluse.*

Wehrli, Werner, Swiss composer; b. Aarau, Jan. 8, 1892; d. Lucerne, June 27, 1944. He studied at the Zürich Cons. with Hegar and in Frankfurt with Knorr; wrote a number of "festival operas" in a Romantic vein; cantatas; chamber music. His oratorio *Wallfahrt* (1939) enjoyed a modicum of success. His opera *Das heiss Eisen,* after Hans Sachs, was produced in Bern on Dec. 11, 1918.
BIBLIOGRAPHY: G.H. Leuenberger, "Werner Wehrli," *Schweizerische Musikzeitung* (May 1952).

Weidemann, Friedrich, German baritone; b. Ratzeburg, Jan. 1, 1871; d. Vienna, Jan. 30, 1919. He studied with Vilmar in Hamburg and Muschler in Berlin; made his debut in 1896 in Brieg; then sang in Essen (1897–98), Hamburg (1898–1901), and Riga (1901–3). In 1903 he joined the Vienna Court Opera, where he remained until his death. He was highly regarded for his performances in operas by Wagner and Richard Strauss.

Weidig, Adolf, American music teacher and composer; b. Hamburg, Nov. 28, 1867; d. Hinsdale, Ill., Sept. 23, 1931. He studied at the Hamburg Cons. with Bargheer (violin) and later with Hugo Riemann (theory); then in Munich with Rheinberger (composition). In 1892 he settled in Chicago; played the violin in the Chicago Orch. (1892–96); in 1898 he joined the faculty of the American Cons. of Music; conducted his own works in Chicago, Minneapolis, and also in Germany. He was greatly esteemed as a teacher; publ. *Harmonic Material and Its Uses* (1923); composed 2 symphs.; a symph. poem, *Semiramis; 3 Episoden* for Orch.; String Quintet; 3 string quartets; Piano Trio; songs.
BIBLIOGRAPHY: *Dictionary of American Biography.*

Weidt, Lucy, German soprano; b. Troppau, Silesia, 1880; d. Vienna, July 28, 1940. She studied piano and singing with her father, and then with Rosa Papier in Vienna, where she made her debut in 1904; sang with the Vienna Opera until 1927. She sang in Germany, appearing at the Wagner festival in 1908–10. On Nov. 18, 1910, she made her first American appearance, as Brünnhilde in *Die Walküre* at the Metropolitan Opera in N.Y.; after a season there, she sang in Italy. In 1909 she married Baron Joseph von Urmenyi. Her voice was of unusual attractiveness and power, enabling her to perform Wagnerian parts with distinction.

Weigel, Eugene Herbert, American composer; b. Cleveland, Oct. 11, 1910. He studied violin with Maurice Hewitt and composition with Arthur Shepherd in Cleveland; after holding various teaching positions, he was appointed in 1956 to the music faculty of the Univ. of Montana in Missoula. Among his works are an opera, *The Mountain Child* (Missoula, July 27, 1958); *Prairie Symphony* (1953); Quintet for Clarinet and Strings (1946); other chamber music; piano pieces; songs.

Weigl, Bruno, Czech writer on music and composer; b. Brno, June 16, 1881; d. there, Sept. 25, 1938. He publ. several useful teaching manuals in German: *Die Geschichte des Walzers, nebst einem Anhang über die moderne Operette* (Langensalza, 1910); *Handbuch der Violoncell-Literatur* (Vienna, 1911; revised ed., 1929); *Harmonielehre* (2 vols., Mainz, 1925); composed a comic opera, *Mandragola* (Brno, 1912); song cycles; organ works.

Weigl, Joseph, Austrian composer; b. Eisenstadt, March 28, 1766; d. Vienna, Feb. 3, 1846. His father, **Joseph Franz Weigl** (1740–1820), was a cellist in the service of Prince Esterházy with Haydn; his mother was a singer; he was a godson of Haydn. Brought up in a musical environment, he wrote an operetta, *Die unnützige Vorsicht* (Vienna, Feb. 23, 1783), at the age of 16 for a puppet show; Salieri accepted him as a pupil; he also studied with Albrechtsberger. He was assistant conductor to Salieri at the Vienna Court Theater from 1790 until 1823. Altogether, Weigl wrote 14 operas in Italian and 19 in German. The most successful were *La Principessa d'Amalfi* (Vienna, Jan. 10, 1794; Haydn described it as a masterpiece in a letter to Weigl after the perf.) and *Die Schweizerfamilie* (Vienna, March 14, 1809; produced in Paris, Feb. 6, 1827, as *Emmeline, ou La Famille suisse;* also staged in opera houses all over Europe until about 1900, when it disappeared from the repertoire). The following operas by Weigl were produced in Vienna with varying success: *Il Pazzo per forza* (Nov. 14, 1788); *La caffettiera bizzarra* (Sept. 15, 1790); *L'Amor marinaro* (Oct. 15, 1797); *Das Dorf im Gebürge* (April 17, 1798); *Die Uniform* (Feb. 15, 1805); *Vestas Feuer* (Aug. 7, 1805); *Kaiser Hadrian* (May 21, 1807); *Adrian von Ostade* (July 3, 1807); *Das Waisenhaus* (Oct. 4, 1808); *Nachtigall und Rabe* (April 20, 1818); *Baals Sturz* (April 13, 1820); *König Waldemar* (May 11, 1821); *Edmund und Caroline* (Sept. 21, 1821); *Die eiserne Pforte* (Feb. 27, 1823); 4 operas were produced at La Scala in Milan: *Cleopatra* (Dec. 19, 1807); *Il Rivale di se* *stesso* (April 18, 1808); *L'Imboscata* (Nov. 8, 1815); *Margarethe von Anjou* (July 26, 1816). Weigl also wrote 18 ballets; 2 oratorios; 22 cantatas; 11 masses; other church music.

BIBLIOGRAPHY: W. Neumann, *Joseph Weigl* (Kassel, 1855); A. Eisner-Eisenhof, "Joseph Weigl," *Rivista Musicale Italiana* (1904); W. Bollert, "Joseph Weigl und das deutsche Singspiel," in his *Aufsätze zur Musikgeschichte* (Bottrop, 1938); for details of productions of Weigl's operas, see A. Loewenberg's *Annals of Opera* (Cambridge, 1943; 2nd ed., Geneva, 1955).

Weigl, Karl, Austrian composer; b. Vienna, Feb. 6, 1881; d. New York, Aug. 11, 1949. He studied piano with Door and music theory with Fuchs at the Cons. of the Gesellschaft der Musikfreunde in Vienna; also took composition lessons with Zemlinsky; attended courses in musicology at the Univ. of Vienna (Ph.D., 1903); subsequently was an opera coach under Mahler. In 1918 he was appointed to the faculty of the New Vienna Cons.; from 1930 to 1938 taught music theory at the Univ. of Vienna. After the Anschluss in 1938, he emigrated to N.Y. He was respected both in Austria and in America as a composer, and a concerted effort was made to promote his music, but with little success. His 5th Symph., subtitled *Apocalyptic,* was performed posthumously by Leopold Stokowski with the American Symph. Orch. (N.Y., Oct. 27, 1968). He wrote 6 symphs.: No. 1 (1908); No. 2 (1912); No. 3 (1931); No. 4 (1936); No. 5 (1945); No. 6 (1947); several overtures; Violin Concerto (1928); 8 string quartets; String Sextet; 2 violin sonatas; numerous choruses; piano pieces; songs.

Weigl, Thaddäus, Austrian composer and publisher, brother of **Joseph Weigl;** b. Vienna, April 8, 1776; d. there, Feb. 29, 1844. He wrote the singspiels *Die Marionettenbude* (Vienna, March 17, 1795) and *Idoli* (Vienna, March 12, 1796); also 13 ballets. In 1801 he established in Vienna a publishing firm, which issued several works by Schubert.

Weigl, Vally (Valery), Austrian composer and music therapist; b. Vienna, Sept. 11, 1894; d. New York, Dec. 25, 1982. She studied music in Vienna with **Karl Weigl,** whom she married. She taught music in Vienna and Salzburg (1921–38); after the Anschluss she and her husband went to America, where she obtained employment as music adviser with the American Theater Wing (1947–58); from 1954 to 1964 she gave courses in music therapy at the N.Y. Medical College and wrote therapy programs for UNESCO. She was an energetic peace activist, and served as a co-founder of the Friends' Arts for World Unity Committee. With equal energy she promoted her husband's compositions, which were little appreciated and seldom played. WORKS: *New England Suite* for Clarinet, Cello, and Piano (1955); *Nature Moods* for Soprano, Clarinet, and Violin (1960); *Mood Sketches* for Wind Quintet (1964); *Peace Is a Shelter* for Chorus, Soloist, and Piano (1970); cantata, *The People Yes* (1976).

Weikert, Ralf, Austrian conductor; b. St. Florian, Nov. 10, 1940. He studied at the Bruckner Cons. in Linz; then took a course in conducting with Hans Swarowsky at the Vienna Academy of Music. In 1965 he won first prize in the Nicolai Malko Conducting Competition in Copenhagen. In 1966 he became conductor of the City Theater in Bonn; then was chief conductor there (1968–77). In 1977 he was appointed deputy Generalmusikdirektor of the Frankfurt Opera; also conducted opera with the Hamburg State Opera, the Deutsche Oper in Berlin, the Vienna State Opera, and the Zürich Opera. In 1981 he was named chief conductor of the Salzburg Mozarteum Orch. and music director of the Landestheater in Salzburg.

Weikl, Bernd, Austrian baritone; b. Vienna, July 29, 1942. He studied at the Mainz Cons. (1962–65) and at the Hochschule für Musik in Hannover (1965–67). In 1968 he sang at the Opera in Hannover. In 1973 he became a member of the Hamburg State opera. He also was a guest artist at the Bayreuth Festivals (1973–75). His finest roles were Figaro in *The Barber of Seville* and Don Giovanni in Mozart's opera. He also gave excellent renditions of the parts of Wolfram in *Tannhäuser* and Mandryka in *Arabella* at the Metropolitan Opera in N.Y.

Weil, Hermann, German baritone; b. Karlsruhe, May 29, 1877; d. (of a heart attack, while fishing in Blue Mountain Lake, N.Y.) July 6, 1949. He studied voice with Adolf Dippel in Frankfurt; made his debut as Wolfram in *Tannhäuser* at Freiburg, Baden, on Sept. 6, 1901; then sang in Vienna, Brussels, Amsterdam, Milan, and London; participated in the Bayreuth Festivals during the summers of 1909–12. On Nov. 17, 1911, he made a successful American debut as Kurvenal in *Tristan und Isolde,* at the Metropolitan Opera in N.Y. under Toscanini. In 1917 he returned to Germany. The extensive range of his voice, spanning 3 full octaves, enabled him to undertake bass parts as well as those in the baritone compass. He had about 100 roles in his repertoire, excelling in Wagnerian operas.

Weill, Kurt, remarkable German composer of modern operas; b. Dessau, March 2, 1900; d. New York, April 3, 1950. He was a private pupil of Albert Bing in Dessau (1914–18); in 1918 he studied for one semester at the Berlin Hochschule für Musik with Humperdinck and Krasselt. He was then engaged as an opera coach in Dessau and was also theater conductor at Lüdenscheid. In 1921 he moved to Berlin and became a private student of Busoni; it was then that he completed his first major work, which became designated as the Berlin Symph. (*Berliner Symphonie*); its MS could not be located until many years after Weill's death, and the work was performed posthumously by the Hamburg Radio Orch. in 1958. Under the impact of new trends in the musical theater, Weill proceeded to write short satirical operas in a sharp modernistic manner: *Der Protagonist* (1925) and *Royal Palace* (1926). There followed a striking "songspiel" (a hybrid term of English and

German words), *Mahagonny,* to a libretto by Bertolt Brecht, savagely satirizing the American primacy of money (1927); it was subsequently remodeled and was presented as a 3-act opera under the title *Aufstieg und Fall der Stadt Mahagonny* (*Rise and Fall of the City of Mahagonny;* 1929). Weill's greatest hit in this genre came with a modernistic version of *The Beggar's Opera,* to a pungent libretto by Brecht; under the title *Die Dreigroschenoper* (1928), it was staged all over Germany, and was also produced in translation in Poland, the Netherlands, Denmark, Hungary, France, Russia, and England. Marc Blitzstein made a new libretto of the opera, versified in a modern American style, and produced as *The Threepenny Opera,* the exact translation of the German title. Its hit number, *Mack the Knife,* became tremendously successful.

After the Nazi ascent to power in Germany, Weill and his wife, the actress and singer Lotte Lenya, who appeared in many of his musical plays, went to Paris, and then to London. In 1935 they settled in the U.S.; Weill became a citizen in 1943. Quickly absorbing the modes and fashions of American popular music, Weill re-created, with astonishing facility, and felicity, the typical form and content of American musicals; this stylistic transition was facilitated by the fact that in his European productions he had already absorbed elements of American popular songs and jazz rhythms. His highly developed assimilative faculty enabled him to combine this Americanized idiom with the advanced techniques of modern music (atonality, polytonality, polyrhythms) and present the product in a pleasing, and yet sophisticated and challenging, manner. But for all his success in American-produced scores, the great majority of his European works remained to be produced in America only posthumously.

WORKS: FOR THE STAGE: *Der Protagonist* (1925; Dresden, March 27, 1926); *Royal Palace* (1925; Berlin, March 2, 1927; the original orchestration was lost; Gunther Schuller and Noam Sheriff reconstructed the work in the form of a ballet, produced in San Francisco, Oct. 5, 1968); *Mahagonny,* a satire on life in America, to a libretto by Bertolt Brecht (1927; Baden-Baden, July 17, 1927; subsequently remodeled as a 3-act opera, under the title *Aufstieg und Fall der Stadt Mahagonny,* produced in Leipzig, March 9, 1930; a U.S. production did not take place until April 28, 1970, in N.Y.); *Der Zar lässt sich photographieren* (1927; Leipzig, Feb. 18, 1928; U.S. production under the title *The Shah Has Himself Photographed,* N.Y., Oct. 27, 1949); *Die Dreigroschenoper* (Berlin, Aug. 31, 1928; in the U.S. as *The Threepenny Opera,* N.Y., April 13, 1933; subsequently, with a new libretto by Marc Blitzstein, produced in concert version at Brandeis Univ., Waltham, Mass., June 14, 1952; in stage form, N.Y., March 10, 1954); *Die Zaubernacht,* children's ballet (Berlin, Nov. 18, 1922); musical comedy, *Happy End* (Berlin, Sept. 2, 1922; professional U.S. premiere, New Haven, Conn., April 6, 1972); school opera, *Der Jasager* (Berlin, June 23, 1930; N.Y., April 25, 1933, under the title *The One Who Says Yes*); opera, *Die Bürgschaft* (*The Pledge;* 1931; Berlin, March 10, 1932); musical play, *Der Silbersee* (1932; Leipzig, Er

furt, and Magdeburg simultaneously, Feb. 18, 1933; U.S. premiere, as *Silverlake,* slightly abridged and with the addition of Weill's 1927 incidental music to Strindberg's play *Gustav III,* N.Y., March 20, 1980). In Paris: ballet with songs, *Die sieben Todsünden der Kleinbürger* (*The 7 Deadly Sins of the Petty-Bourgeois;* Paris, June 7, 1933; produced in London as *Anna Anna;* in the U.S. in N.Y., Dec. 4, 1958); opera, *Marie galante* (Paris, Dec. 22, 1934). In London: musical play, *A Kingdom for a Cow* (London, June 28, 1935). In the U.S.: operas: *Street Scene* (to a play by Elmer Rice; N.Y., Jan. 9, 1947) and *Lost in the Stars* (text by Maxwell Anderson after Alan Paton's *Cry, the Beloved Country;* N.Y., Oct. 20, 1949); a pageant of Jewish history, *The Eternal Road* (after Franz Werfel; 1934–35; N.Y., Jan. 7, 1937); musical fable, *Johnny Johnson* (text by Paul Green; N.Y., Nov. 19, 1936); musical comedies: *Knickerbocker Holiday* (book and lyrics by Maxwell Anderson; Hartford, Conn., Sept. 26, 1938; contains the popular "September Song"); *Lady in the Dark* (text by Moss Hart and lyrics by Ira Gershwin; N.Y., Jan. 23, 1941); *One Touch of Venus* (text by S.J. Perelman and Ogden Nash; N.Y., Oct. 7, 1943); *The Firebrand of Florence* (text by E.J. Mayer and Ira Gershwin; N.Y., March 22, 1945); musical plays: *A Flag Is Born* (text by Ben Hecht; N.Y., Sept. 5, 1946) and *Love Life* (text by Alan Jay Lerner; N.Y., Oct. 7, 1948); background music for the stage spectacle *Railroads on Parade* (N.Y. World's Fair, 1939); folk opera, *Down in the Valley* (1945–48; Indiana Univ., Bloomington, July 15, 1948).

FOR ORCH.: Symph. No. 1 (*Berliner Sinfonie;* 1921; score recovered in 1955, and perf. by the Hamburg Radio Orch., Jan. 17, 1958; U.S. premiere, Greenwich, Conn., Oct. 21, 1978); Symph. No. 2 (*Pariser Symphonie;* 1933; Amsterdam, Oct. 11, 1934, Bruno Walter conducting; perf. in the U.S. under the title *3 Night Scenes* by the N.Y. Phil., Dec. 13, 1934, Bruno Walter conducting); *Fantasia, Passacaglia, und Hymnus* (1922); *Quodlibet* (1924; Coburg, Feb. 6, 1926; N.Y., Feb. 24, 1963; material drawn from *Zaubernacht*); Concerto for Violin, Woodwinds, Double Bass, and Percussion (1924; Paris, June 11, 1925; Cincinnati, March 28, 1930); *Kleine Dreigroschenmusik* for Winds (1929; concert suite from *The Threepenny Opera*).

VOCAL WORKS: Radio cantata, *Der Lindberghflug,* in collaboration with Brecht and Hindemith, commemorating Lindbergh's transatlantic flight of 1927 (Baden-Baden Festival, July 28, 1929; rescored solely by Weill, and with Hindemith's name eliminated, Berlin, Dec. 5, 1929; revised in 1930 as *Der Flug des Lindberghs* and in 1950 retitled *Der Ozeanflug,* without Lindbergh's name, as a gesture of protest against Lindbergh's militant neutrality toward Nazi Germany); *The Ballad of Magna Carta,* modern historical drama for Soloists, Chorus, and Orch., with text by Maxwell Anderson (Columbia Network broadcast, Feb. 4, 1940); *Divertimento* for Small Orch., with Male Chorus (1922; reconstructed by David Drew in 1971); *Rilke-Lieder* for Voice and Orch. (1925); *Der neue Orpheus,* cantata for Soprano, Violin, and Orch. (1925; Berlin, March 2, 1927; New Haven, Oct. 5, 1972); *Von Tod im Wald* for Bass

Voice and 10 Wind Instruments (Berlin, Nov. 23, 1927; N.Y., March 7, 1977); *Das Berliner Requiem* for Tenor, Baritone, Male Chorus, and Wind Orch. (1927; Frankfurt Radio, May 22, 1929; Cincinnati, April 3, 1970); *3 Walt Whitman Songs* for Baritone, and Small Orch. or Piano (1940); *Recordare* for Mixed Chorus and Boys' Chorus a cappella (1923; Utrecht, July 2, 1971; N.Y., Jan. 4, 1980); *Frauentanz* for Soprano, Viola, Flute, Clarinet, Horn, and Bassoon (Berlin, Feb. 1924; Salzburg Festival, Aug. 6, 1924); *The Legend of the Dead Soldier* for Chorus a cappella (1929); songs.

CHAMBER MUSIC: 2 movements for String Quartet: *Allegro deciso* and *Andantino* (N.Y., March 7, 1977); String Quartet in B minor (1919); Cello Sonata (1920; U.S. premiere, Philadelphia, May 4, 1979); String Quartet No. 1, op. 8 (1923; U.S. premiere, Yale Univ., May 13, 1971).

BIBLIOGRAPHY: P. Bekker, *Briefe an zeitgenössische Musiker* (1932); Virgil Thomson, "Most Melodious Tears," *Modern Music* (Nov.–Dec. 1933); *Current Biography* (1941; pp. 905–7); H.W. Heinsheimer, "Kurt Weill," *Tomorrow* (March 1948); H. Strobel, "Erinnerung an Kurt Weill," *Melos* (May 1950); D. Drew, "Topicality and the Universal: The Strange Case of Weill's *Die Bürgschaft*," *Music & Letters* (July 1958); H. Kotschenreuther, *Kurt Weill* (Berlin, 1962); J.C.G. Waterhouse, "Weill's Debt to Busoni," *Musical Times* (1964; pp. 897–99); special issue of *Opera News* (Dec. 1, 1979) devoted to *Mahagonny*; K. Kowalke, *Kurt Weill in Europe* (Ann Arbor, Mich., 1979; contains the most complete catalogue of Weill's compositions up to 1935); R. Sanders, *The Days Grow Short* (N.Y., 1980). For details on performances of Weill's operas: A. Loewenberg, *Annals of Opera* (Cambridge, 1943; 2nd ed., Geneva, 1955).

Weinberg, Jacob, pianist and composer; b. Odessa, July 5, 1879; d. New York, Nov. 2, 1956. He studied at the Moscow Cons. with Igumnov (piano) and with Taneyev and Ippolitov-Ivanov (composition); was a private pupil of Leschetizky in Vienna (1910–11); taught piano at the Odessa Cons. (1915–21); then went to Palestine, where he stayed for 5 years (1921–26). In 1926 he came to the U.S.; taught piano at Hunter College and the N.Y. College of Music. He composed an opera on a modern Hebrew subject, *Hechalutz (The Pioneers);* fragments were performed in Jerusalem, in Hebrew, on April 4, 1925; the complete opera was performed in N.Y. on Nov. 25, 1934, under the title *The Pioneers of Israel,* in English; he also wrote the oratorios *Isaiah* (1948) and *The Life of Moses* (1952); *The Gettysburg Address,* ode for Chorus and Orch. (N.Y., 1936); *Sabbath Liturgy* for Baritone, Chorus, and Organ; Piano Concerto; Piano Trio; String Quartet; Violin Sonata; contributed essays on Russian music to the *Musical Quarterly* and other periodicals.

Weinberger, Jaromir, notable Czech composer; b. Prague, Jan. 8, 1896; d. (suicide by overdose of sedative drugs) St. Petersburg, Fla., Aug. 8, 1967. He studied with Křička and Hofmeister at the Prague Cons., then briefly with Max Reger in Leipzig. In 1922 he visited the U.S., and taught for a semester at the Ithaca Cons. in N.Y. Returning to Europe, he was active as a teacher in Bratislava, Prague, and Vienna; lived mostly in Prague until 1937; in 1939 he settled permanently in the U.S., living in St. Petersburg. He achieved sudden fame with the production of his opera in a popular Bohemian style, *Švanda dudák (Schwanda the Bagpiper),* at the National Theater in Prague on April 27, 1927. Its success was immediate, and performances followed all over Europe in several languages; it was produced in German (as *Schwanda der Dudelsackpfeifer)* at the Metropolitan Opera in N.Y. on Nov. 7, 1931; the *Polka and Fugue* from this opera has become a popular number in the orch. repertoire. His other operas include *Die geliebte Stimme* (Munich, Feb. 28, 1931); *Lidé z Pokerflatu (The Outcasts of Poker Flat,* after Bret Harte; Brno, Nov. 19, 1932); *A Bed of Roses,* light opera (Prague, 1934); *Wallenstein,* lyric tragedy after Schiller (Vienna, Nov. 18, 1937); for Orch.: *Marionette Overture* (1913); 6 Bohemian songs and dances (1929); *Under the Spreading Chestnut Tree,* variations and fugue (N.Y., Oct. 12, 1939); *Song of the High Seas* (N.Y., Nov. 9, 1940); *Lincoln Symphony* (Cincinnati, Oct. 17, 1941); *Czech Rhapsody* (Washington, D.C., Nov. 5, 1941); *A Bird's Opera* (Detroit, Nov. 13, 1941); *Préludes religieuses et profanes* (1953); *Ecclesiastes* for Soprano, Baritone, Mixed Chorus, and Organ (1945); other choral works; violin pieces; piano pieces; etc.

Weiner, Lazar, Russian-born American composer; b. Cherkassy, near Kiev, Oct. 27, 1897; d. New York, Jan. 10, 1982. He emigrated to America in 1914, and became associated with numerous Jewish artistic activities in N.Y.; also took private lessons in composition with Robert Russell Bennett, Frederick Jacobi, and Joseph Schillinger. From 1929 to 1975 he led the choir of the Central Synagogue in N.Y.; conducted classes in the Yiddish art song at Hebrew Union College and at the Jewish Theological Seminary in America; directed the Workmen's Circle Chorus; and served as host of the weekly radio broadcast "The Message of America." He wrote a number of songs to Yiddish words; also composed several Sabbath services; the cantatas *Legend of Toil* (1933), *Man of the World* (1939), *Fight for Freedom* (1943), *To Thee, America* (1944), and *The Last Judgement* (1966); and an opera, *The Golem,* produced in White Plains, N.Y., on Jan. 13, 1957. His son, **Yehudi Weiner,** a composer, changed his surname to **Wyner** in order to approximate phonetically the right pronunciation.

Weiner, Léo, outstanding Hungarian composer; b. Budapest, April 16, 1885; d. there, Sept. 13, 1960. He was a pupil of Hans Koessler at the Budapest Academy of Music (1901–6), winning several prizes for excellence; in 1906 he won the Franz-Josef-Jubiläumspreis, which enabled him to study further in Austria, Germany, and France. Returning to Budapest, he became a prof. at the Academy (1908); was pensioned in 1949. He won the Coolidge Prize in

Weingartner

1922 for his 2nd String Quartet, the Kossuth Prize in 1950, and became an Eminent Artist of the Hungarian People's Republic in 1953. In his works he adopted a characteristic Hungarian style within the framework of Romantic forms.

WORKS: *Scherzo* for Orch. (1905); *Serenade* for Orch. (1906; Budapest, Oct. 22, 1906; his most successful work); *Farsang (Carnival-Time)*, humoresque for Small Orch. (1907); incidental music for Vörösmarty's play *Csongor and Tünde* (1913; also an orch. suite); Piano Concertino (1923); 5 divertimenti: Nos. 1 and 2, on old Hungarian tunes, for Strings (1923, 1938) and Nos. 3–5 for Orch. (1948, 1951, 1951); *Katonásdi (Playing at Soldiers)* for Orch. (1924); *Suite (Hungarian Folk Dances)* for Orch. (1931); *Pastorale, Fantasy and Fugue* for String Orch. (1938); *Ballad* for Clarinet and Orch. (1949); *Romance* for Cello, Harp, and Orch. (1949); *Variations on a Hungarian Folk Song* for Orch. (1950); 2 violin concertos (1950, 1957; transcriptions of violin sonatas of 1911 and 1918); *Prelude, Nocturne et Scherzo diabolico* for Orch. (1950); *Festive Music*, overture (1951); *Toldi*, symph. poem (1952; 2 suites, 1954–55); *Passacaglia* for Orch. (1955); 3 string quartets (1906; 1921); *Pastorale, Fantasy and Fugue*, 1938); String Trio (1908); 2 violin sonatas (1911, 1918); *Ballad* for Clarinet and Piano (1911); *Romance* for Cello and Piano (1921); *Recruiting Dance from Pereg* for Violin or Viola or Clarinet, and Piano (1951); a number of piano pieces; cadenzas for Beethoven's piano concertos Nos. 1–4 (1949); orch. transcriptions of works by Bach, Beethoven, Liszt, Schubert, and Bartók; didactic vols. on musical form (1911), on harmony (1911 and 1917), on analytical harmony (1943), and on forms of instrumental music (1954).

Weingartner, (Paul) Felix, Edler von Münzberg, illustrious German conductor; b. Zara, Dalmatia, June 2, 1863; d. Winterthur, Switzerland, May 7, 1942. After his father's death in 1868, his mother took him to Graz, where he studied music with W.A. Remy. He publ. some piano pieces when he was 16 years old; Brahms recommended him for a stipend which enabled him to go to take music courses with Reinecke, Jadassohn, and Paul at the Leipzig Cons. (1881–83). He received the Mozart Prize at his graduation; he was introduced to Liszt, who recommended Weingartner's opera *Sakuntala* for production in Weimar (March 23, 1884), a signal honor for a young man not yet 21 years old. While progressing rapidly as a composer, Weingartner launched a brilliant career as a conductor, which was to become his prime vocation. He conducted in Königsberg (1884), Danzig (1885–87), Hamburg (1887–89), and Mannheim (1889–91). In 1891 he was engaged as conductor at the Berlin Royal Opera; from 1898 to 1905 he led the Kaim Orch. in Munich; simultaneously he was conductor of the symph. concerts of the Royal Orch. in Berlin (1891–1907). His reputation as a fine musician was enhanced by his appearances as an ensemble player in the Weingartner Trio, with himself as pianist, Rettich as violinist, and Warnke as cellist. In 1908 he succeeded Mahler as music director of the Vienna Court Opera, and conducted there until 1911. From 1912 to 1914 he conducted the Municipal Opera in Hamburg; from 1914 to 1918 was in charge of the Darmstadt Orch. He was subsequently music director at the Vienna Volksoper (1919–24), and conducted the Vienna Phil. (1908–27); in 1927 he was appointed director of the Basel (Switzerland) Cons.; was guest conductor at the Vienna State Opera during the season 1934–35; served as director in 1935–36, and continued guest appearances until 1938. In the interim he had engagements as guest conductor with major European orchs.; made his American debut with the N.Y. Phil. on Feb. 12, 1904, and later conducted the N.Y. Symph. Society (Jan.–March 1906). He appeared as opera conductor with the Boston Opera Co. on Feb. 12, 1912, conducting *Tristan und Isolde;* he and his 3rd wife, the mezzo-soprano **Lucille Marcel,** were engaged for a season with the Boston Opera Co. in 1913. (His first wife was Marie Juillerat, whom he married in 1891; his 2nd wife was the Baroness Feodora von Dreifus, whom he married in 1903). He made his debut at Covent Garden in London in 1939, conducting *Parsifal.* He eventually settled in Interlaken, Switzerland, where he established a summer conducting school. Weingartner was a competent music editor; he was on the editorial board for the complete works of Berlioz (1899) and of Haydn (1907). Despite the pressure of his activities as a conductor, he found time for composition. After his early opera *Sakuntala,* he produced several others: *Genesius* (Berlin, Nov. 15, 1892); *Orestes,* a trilogy (Leipzig, Feb. 15, 1902); *Kain und Abel* (Darmstadt, May 17, 1914); *Dame Kobold* (Darmstadt, Feb. 23, 1916); *Die Dorfschule* (Vienna, May 13, 1920); *Meister Andrea* (Vienna, May 13, 1920); wrote his own librettos, and conducted the first performances. He also composed 7 symphs. and a great deal of chamber music; made arrangements of Beethoven's "Hammerklavier" Sonata, op. 106, and of Weber's *Aufforderung zum Tanz.* He was an excellent writer on musical subjects. Among his publications are: *Die Lehre von der Wiedergeburt und das musikalische Drama* (1895); *Über das Dirigieren* (1896; 5th ed., 1913; a fundamental essay on conducting); *Bayreuth 1876–1896* (1897; 2nd ed., 1904); *Die Symphonie nach Beethoven* (1897; 4th ed., 1901; in Eng., 1904; new trans. as *The Symphony since Beethoven,* 1926); *Ratschläge für Aufführung der Sinfonien Beethoven* (1906; 3rd ed., 1928; in Eng., London, 1907); a polemical pamphlet, *Erlebnisse eines kgl. Kapellmeisters in Berlin* (1912; an attack upon the Berlin intendancy; a rebuttal was publ. by A. Wolff in *Der Fall Weingartner,* 1912); *Ratschläge für Aufführung der Sinfonien Schuberts und Schumanns* (1918); *Ratschläge für Aufführung der Sinfonien Mozarts* (1923); *Musikalische Walpurgisnacht* (1907; a satirical comedy); *Akkorde* (1912; collected essays); *Bo Yin Ra* (1927); *Lebenserinnerungen* (vol. I, 1923; vol. II, 1929; Eng. version as *Buffets and Rewards: A Musician's Reminiscences,* London, 1937); *Unwirkliches und Wirkliches* (1936).

BIBLIOGRAPHY: E. Krause, *Felix Weingartner als schaffender Künstler* (Berlin, 1904); P. Riesenfeld, *Felix Weingartner. Ein kritischer Versuch* (Breslau, 1906); W. Hutschenruyter, *Levensschets en portret van Felix Weingartner* (Haarlem, 1906); Paul Stefan, *Gustav Mahlers Erbe* (Munich, 1908); J.C. Lustig, *Felix Weingartner. Persönlichkeiten* (Berlin, 1908); P. Raabe, "Felix Weingartner," *Die Musik* (Jan. 1908); F. Günther, *Felix Weingartner* (1917); W. Jacob, *Felix Weingartner* (Wiesbaden, 1933); *Festschrift für Dr. Felix Weingartner* (for his 70th birthday; Basel, 1933); Harold Schonberg, *The Great Conductors* (N.Y., 1967; pp. 244–50); C. Dyment, *Felix Weingartner: Recollections and Recordings* (London, 1975).

Weinlig, Christian Ehregott, German organist and composer; b. Dresden, Sept. 30, 1743; d. there, March 14, 1813. He studied with Homilius at the Kreuzschule; in 1767 he was organist at the Evangelical Church in Leipzig; in 1773, at Thorn; in 1780, accompanist at the Italian Opera in Dresden, and organist at the Frauenkirche; in 1785, succeeded his teacher, Homilius, as cantor of the Kreuzschule. He publ. sonatas for piano, with flute and cello; brought out several oratorios; also light theater pieces.

Weinlig, (Christian) Theodor, noted German music theorist and teacher, nephew and pupil of **Christian Ehregott Weinlig;** b. Dresden, July 25, 1780; d. Leipzig, March 7, 1842. After a period of study under his uncle, he became a pupil of Stanislao Mattei in Bologna; returning to Dresden, he was cantor at the Kreuzschule (1814–17); in 1823 he succeeded Schicht as cantor of the Thomasschule in Leipzig. He enjoyed high repute as a teacher of theory and composition; Richard Wagner was his pupil. His own works include a *Deutsches Magnificat* for Soli, Chorus, and Orch.; vocalises; he publ. a practical manual, *Theoretisch-praktische Anleitung zur Fuge, für den Selbstunterricht* (1845; 2nd ed., 1852).
BIBLIOGRAPHY: A. Kurz, *Geschichte der Familie Weinlig von 1580–1850* (Bonn, 1912); R. Roch, *Theodor Weinlig* (Leipzig, 1917).

Weinmann, Karl, German musicologist, authority on church music; b. Vohenstrauss, Upper Palatinate, Dec. 22, 1873; d. Pielenhofen, near Regensburg, Sept. 26, 1929. He was a pupil of Haberl and Haller at the Kirchenmusikschule in Regensburg; after further study under Peter Wagner in Freiburg, Switzerland, he obtained the degree of Dr.Phil. with the dissertation *Das Hymnarium Parisiense* (1905). After his ordination to the priesthood, he became a prof. at the Kirchenmusikschule in Regensburg; in 1910 succeeded Haberl as its director; in 1917 he was made Dr.Theol. He was editor of the *Kirchenmusikalisches Jahrbuch* (1909–11), of *Musica Sacra* (from 1911), and of the *Cäcilienvereinsorgan* (from 1926). He edited for Pustet (after the *Editio vaticana*) *Römisches Gradualbuch* (1909; 4th ed., 1928); *Graduale* (1910); *Kyriale* (1911); *Totenoffizium* (1912; 2nd ed., 1928); *Graduale parvum* (1913); *Römisches Vesperbuch mit Psalmenbuch* (1915); *Karwochenbuch* (1924); *Feier der heiligen Karwoche* (1925); *Sonntagsvesper und Komplet* (2nd

ed., 1928). Was also editor of the collection *Kirchenmusik,* for which he wrote *Geschichte der Kirchenmusik* (1906; 4th ed., 1925; Eng. trans., 1910; also trans. into French, Italian, Polish, and Hungarian), and monographs on Leonhard Paminger (1907) and Carl Proske (1909). Other writings include *Palestrinas Geburtsjahr* (Regensburg, 1915); *Stille Nacht, heilige Nacht: Die Geschichte des Liedes zu seinem 100. Geburtstag* (1918; 2nd ed., 1920); *Das Konzil von Trient und die Kirchenmusik* (1919).

Weinrich, Carl, eminent American organist; b. Paterson, N.J., July 2, 1904. After graduation from N.Y. Univ. (B.A., 1927), he studied at the Curtis Inst. of Music in Philadelphia (1927–30); also studied organ privately with Lynnwood Farnam and Marcel Dupré, and piano with Abram Chasins. In 1930 he became the successor of Lynnwood Farnam as organist at the Holy Communion Church in N.Y.; taught organ at the Westminster Choir School in Princeton, N.J. (1934–40), and at Columbia Univ. (1942–52); in 1943 was appointed director of music at the Princeton Univ. Chapel; he retired from there in 1973.

Weinstock, Herbert, American writer on music; b. Milwaukee, Nov. 16, 1905; d. New York, Oct. 21, 1971. He was educated in his native town; later took courses at the Univ. of Chicago. He publ. the following books: *Tchaikovsky* (1943; also publ. in French, Portuguese, Spanish, and German); *Handel* (1946; 2nd ed., 1959; also in German); *Chopin: The Man and His Music* (1949; 2nd ed., 1959); *Music As an Art* (1953; 2nd ed., 1966, under the title *What Music Is*); co-author, with Wallace Brockway, of *Men of Music* (1939; revised and enlarged, 1950) and *The Opera: A History of Its Creation and Performance* (1941; 2nd ed., 1962, entitled *The World of Opera*); *Donizetti and the World of Opera in Italy, Paris and Vienna in the First Half of the 19th Century* (N.Y., 1963); *Rossini* (N.Y., 1968); *Vincenzo Bellini: His Life and Operas* (N.Y., 1971). For some years before his death he was music editor for the book publishing firm of Alfred A. Knopf in N.Y.

Weinwurm, Rudolf, Austrian choral conductor; b. Schaidldorf-on-the-Thaja, April 3, 1835; d. Vienna, May 26, 1911. He was trained musically as a chorister in the Imperial Chapel in Vienna; conducted the Vienna Singakademie (from 1864) and the Männergesangverein (from 1866); in 1880 he became music director of Vienna Univ. He publ. the manuals *Allgemeine Musiklehre* (1870); *Musikalische Lehrmittel* (1873); *Methodik des Gesangunterrichts* (1876); composed a *Deutsches Requiem* for Male Chorus a cappella, and one for Female Chorus, with Organ; also other church music.

Weinzierl, Max, Ritter von, Austrian conductor and composer; b. Bergstadtl, Bohemia, Sept. 16, 1841; d. Mödling, near Vienna, July 10, 1898. He served as conductor at various theaters in Vienna; from 1882 he was chorus master of the Männergesangverein. He wrote the operas *Don Quixote* (Vienna, Feb. 15,

1879; with L. Roth); *Die weiblichen Jäger* (Vienna, May 5, 1880); *Moclemos* (Vienna, June 5, 1880); *Fioretta* (Prague, 1886); *Page Fritz* (Prague, 1889); *Der Schwiegerpapa* (Berlin, 1893); oratorio, *Hiob* (Vienna, 1870); choral works, with Orch.: *Nachtgruss, Liedesweihe, Gesang der Nixen, Die Sphinx, Der Zigeuner, Donausage, Hubertus,* etc.; many male choruses a cappella.

Weinzweig, John, prominent Canadian composer; b. Toronto, March 11, 1913. He learned to play piano, tuba, and saxophone; then took lessons in orchestration with MacMillan, in counterpoint with Willan, and in harmony with Leo Smith at the Univ. of Toronto (1934–37); continued his study in composition with Bernard Rogers at the Eastman School of Music in Rochester, N.Y. (1937–38). In 1939 he was appointed to the faculty of the Toronto Cons.; in 1952 joined the music staff at the Univ. of Toronto. On Feb. 3, 1951, he organized the Canadian League of Composers and was its first president.
WORKS: Ballet, *Red Ear of Corn* (Toronto, March 2, 1949); *Legend* for Orch. (1937); *The Enchanted Hill* for Orch. (1938); *Suite* for Orch. (1938); *Spectre* for String Orch. and Timpani (1938); *A Tale of Tamotu* for Bassoon and Orch. (1939); Symph. (1940); *Rhapsody* for Orch. (1941); *Interlude in an Artist's Life* for String Orch. (1943); *Our Canada* for Orch. (1943); *Divertimento No. 1* for Flute and String Orch. (Vancouver, Dec. 29, 1946); *Divertimento No. 2* for Oboe and String Orch. (Toronto, April 30, 1948); *Divertimento No. 3* for Bassoon and String Orch. (Toronto, May 5, 1961); *Divertimento No. 5* for Solo Trumpet, Trombone, and Wind Ensemble (Pittsburgh, June 9, 1961; numbered out of chronological order); *Divertimento No. 4* for Clarinet, and String Orch. or String Quintet (Vancouver, Sept. 19, 1968); *Divertimento No. 6* for Saxophone and String Orch. (Toronto, Aug. 21, 1972); *Edge of the World,* symph. poem (1946); *Round Dance* for Small Orch. (1950; version for Full Orch., 1977); Violin Concerto (Toronto, May 30, 1955); *Wine of Peace,* 3 songs for Soprano and Orch. (1957); *Symphonic Ode* (1958); Piano Concerto (Toronto, Dec. 15, 1966); Concerto for Harp and Chamber Orch. (Toronto, April 30, 1967); *Dummiyah (Silence)* for Orch. (Toronto, July 4, 1969); 3 string quartets (1937, 1946, 1962); Violin Sonata (1941); cello sonata, *Israel* (1949); Wind Quintet (1964); Clarinet Quartet (1965); *Around the Stage in 25 Minutes during Which a Variety of Instruments Are Struck* for Solo Percussionist (1970); *Trialogue* for Soprano, Flute, and Piano (1971); *Riffs* for Solo Flute (1974); *Pieces of 5,* brass quintet (1976); *Contrast* for Solo Guitar (1976); *Refrains* for Double Bass and Piano (1977); 2 suites for Piano (1939, 1950); Piano Sonata (1950); *Impromptus* for Piano (1973); *Improvisation on an Indian Tune* for Organ (1942); choruses; *Private Collection,* 8 songs for Soprano and Piano (1975).

Weir, Gillian, organist and harpsichordist; b. Martinborough, New Zealand, Jan. 17, 1941. She studied at the Royal Academy of Music in London (1962–65);

won the St. Albans International Organ Competition in 1964; in 1965 she made her debut at London's Royal Festival Hall; in 1967 toured Canada and the U.S.; later continued to give recitals in Europe and America as an organist and harpsichordist.

Weis, (Carl) Flemming, Danish composer and organist; b. Copenhagen, April 15, 1898; d. there, Sept. 30, 1981. He studied composition with Carl Nielsen and Gustav Helsted at the Royal Danish Cons. in Copenhagen (1917–20); then took lessons in composition with Paul Graener and organ with Karl Straube at the Hochschule für Musik in Leipzig (1921–23). He served as organist of the St. Anna Church in Copenhagen (1929–68); was a member of the board of the Society for Contemporary Music (1926–56; president, 1942–56) and a member of the board of the Danish Society of Composers (president, 1963–75). His music follows the traditions of the Danish School; under the influence of his teacher Carl Nielsen he wrote a number of symph. pieces imbued with Romantic fervor and gentle humor.
WORKS: *Praeludium og Intermezzo* for Oboe and Strings (1933); Concertino for Clarinet and Strings (1935); *Symphonic Overture* (1938); *In temporis vernalis* for Orch. (1945; Copenhagen, Jan. 14, 1948); *Introduction grave* for Piano and Orch. (1941); 2 symphs. (1942, 1948); *Det forjoettede land (The Promised Land)* for Chorus and Orch. (Copenhagen, Nov. 8, 1949); *Musikantiski ouverture* (1949); *Sinfonia proverbiorum* for Chorus and Orch. (Copenhagen, June 21, 1959); Concertino for Strings (1960); *Femdelt form III (Quintuple Form)* for Orch. (Randers, Feb. 5, 1963); *Sine nomine* for Orch. (Copenhagen, March 18, 1973); *Chaconne* for Orch. (1974); 4 string quartets (1922, 1925, 1937, 1977); *Music* for 3 Woodwinds (1928); Clarinet Sonata (1931); Violin Sonata (1932–41); *Serenade uden reelle hensigter (Serenade without Serious Intentions)* for Wind Quintet (1938); Sonatina for Flute, Violin, and Cello (1942); *Diverterende musik (Diverting Music)* for Flute, Violin, Viola, and Cello (1943); Oboe Sonata (1946); *Variations* for Wind Quintet (1946); Flute Sonata (1956); *Fantasia seria* for String Quartet (1956); *5 Epigrams* for String Quartet (1960); *Femdelt form II* for String Quintet (1962); *Rhapsodic Suite* for Solo Violin (1966); *Static Situations* for String Quartet (1970); *3 søstre (3 Sisters)* for Solo Cello (1973); *3 Mobiles* for Flute, Violin, Viola, and Cello (1974); *3 Aspects* for Guitar (1975); *3 Japanese Bird Cries* for Soprano, Viola, and Guitar (1976); *Dialogues* for Flute and Guitar (1977). For Piano: *Suite* in B (1945–46); Sonatina (1949); *12 Monologues* (1958); *Femdelt Form I* (1961); *Limitations I* (1965); *Limitations II* (1968). For Organ: Concertino (1957); *Coeli enarrant* for Soprano and Organ (1955–56); choruses; songs; anthems.

Weis, Karel, Czech conductor and composer; b. Prague, Feb. 13, 1862; d. there, April 4, 1944. He studied violin at the Prague Cons.; also organ with Skuhersky and composition with Fibich at the Organ School in Prague; subsequently filled various posts as organist and conductor in Prague and other towns in Bohemia. He devoted much of his time to collecting Bohemian folk songs, and publ. them in 15 vols. (1928–41).

WORKS: Operas: *Viola*, after Shakespeare's *Twelfth Night* (Prague, Jan. 17, 1892); *Der polnische Jude* (Prague, March 3, 1901; very successful; produced in Eng. at the Metropolitan Opera House, N.Y., March 9, 1921); *Die Dorfmusikanten* (Prague, Jan. 1, 1905); *Der Revisor*, after Gogol (1907); *Utok na mlýn*, after Zola's *L'Attaque su Moulin* (Prague, March 29, 1912); *Lešetínský kovář* (*The Blacksmith of Lešetín;* Prague, June 6, 1920); Symph.; String Quartet; piano pieces; songs.

BIBLIOGRAPHY: L. Firkušný, *Karel Weis* (Prague, 1949).

Weisbach, Hans, German conductor; b. Glogau, July 19, 1885; d. Wuppertal, April 23, 1961. He studied at the Hochschule für Musik in Berlin; then became an opera coach in Munich; subsequently conducted in various provincial towns in Germany; held the post of music director and conductor at Düsseldorf (1926–33); then conducted the Leipzig Radio Orch. (1933–39) and the Municipal Orch. of Vienna (1938–45); in 1947 he was appointed music director at Wuppertal. He made several appearances in London; also conducted in Russia.

BIBLIOGRAPHY: C. Heinzen, "Hans Weisbach," *Die Musik* (Feb. 1931).

Weisberg, Arthur, American bassoonist and conductor; b. New York, April 4, 1931. He attended the Juilliard School of Music in N.Y., where he studied bassoon with Simon Kovar and conducting with Jean Morel. He played bassoon with the Houston, Baltimore, and Cleveland orchs.; from 1956 to 1972 was bassoonist with the N.Y. Woodwind Quintet. In 1960 he formed the Contemporary Chamber Ensemble, with which he travels widely in Europe and America. He held teaching posts at the Juilliard School of Music (1962–69), at the State Univ. of N.Y. (from 1965), and at Yale Univ. (from 1974).

Weisgall, Hugo, American composer; b. Ivančice, Moravia, Oct. 13, 1912. His family emigrated to the U.S. in 1920, and settled in Baltimore; he studied music theory with Louis Cheslock at the Peabody Cons. there; later had private sessions with Sessions in N.Y.; also took composition lessons with Rosario Scalero at the Curtis Inst. in Philadelphia. In 1952 he was appointed chairman of the faculty at the Seminary College of Jewish Music in N.Y.; from 1957 to 1968 was on the staff of the Juilliard School of Music; also taught at Queens College. His music constitutes the paragon of enlightened but inoffensive modernism; he is a master of all musical idioms, and a bungler of none. His intentions in each of his works never fail in the execution; for this reason his music enjoys numerous performances, which are usually accepted with pleasure by the audiences, if not by the majority of important music critics.

WORKS: Operas: *Night* (1932); *Lillith* (1934); *The Tenor* (Baltimore, Feb. 11, 1952); *The Stronger*, after

Strindberg (Lutherville, Md., Aug. 9, 1952); *6 Characters in Search of an Author* (N.Y., April 26, 1959); *Purgatory,* in one act to the text of W.B. Yeats (Library of Congress, Washington, D.C., Feb. 17, 1961); *Athaliah* (N.Y., Feb. 17, 1964); *9 Rivers from Jordan* (N.Y., Oct. 9, 1968); *The Hundred Nights* (N.Y., April 22, 1976); *The Gardens of Adonis* (1980); ballets: *Quest* (Baltimore, May 17, 1938); *One Thing Is Certain* (Baltimore, Feb. 25, 1939); *Overture in F* (London, July 29, 1943); *A Garden Eastward,* cantata for High Voice and Orch. (Baltimore, Jan. 31, 1953); *Soldier Songs* for Baritone and Orch. (1946); 2 choral études (1937, 1953); a number of songs.

BIBLIOGRAPHY: G. Rochberg, "Hugo Weisgall," *Bulletin of American Composers Alliance* (1958); B. Saylor, "The Music of Hugo Weisgall," *Musical Quarterly* (1973).

Weisgarber, Elliot, American composer; b. Pittsfield, Mass., Dec. 5, 1919. He studied with Bernard Rogers and Howard Hanson at the Eastman School of Music in Rochester, N.Y. (1939–43); then had lessons with Nadia Boulanger in Paris (1952–53) and with Halsey Stevens in Los Angeles (1958–59). From 1966 to 1969 he was in Japan, where he studied koto and other indigenous instruments. Returning to America, he taught at the Women's College of the Univ. of North Carolina (1944–60); in 1960 was appointed instructor in composition and Asian music at the Univ. of British Columbia.

WORKS: Sonata for Flute, Clarinet, and Piano (1953); *Divertimento* for String Trio (1956); *Divertimento* for Horn, Viola, and Piano (1959); *Sinfonia pastorale* (1961); *Sinfonia concertante* for Oboe, 2 Horns, and Strings (1962); Flute Sonata (1963); *Suite* for Viola and Piano (1964); Sonata for Solo Cello (1965); *Kyōto Landscapes,* lyrical evocations for Voice and Orch. (1970); *Illahee Chanties* for Chamber Orch. (1971); Bassoon Sonata (1973); *Epigrams* for Flute and Piano (1973); *Night* for Solo Baritone, Chorus, and String Quartet (1973); *Autumnal Music* for English Horn and String Orch. (1973); *Musica serena* for Orch. (1974); *Netori: A Fantasia* for Saxophone and Orch. (1974); *A Pacific Trilogy* for Orch. (1974); Violin Concerto (1974); String Quartet (1975); *Fantasia a 3* for Horn, Violin, and Piano (1975); several works for Japanese instruments.

Weismann, Julius, German composer; b. Freiburg im Breisgau, Dec. 26, 1879; d. Singen (Bodensee), Dec. 22, 1950. He studied in Munich with Rheinberger and Thuille; devoted himself mainly to the composition of operas, the most important of which was *Leonce und Lena* (Freiburg im Breisgau, June 21, 1925). Other operas: *Schwanenweiss,* after Strindberg (Duisburg, Sept. 29, 1923); *Ein Traumspiel* (Duisburg, 1925); *Regina del Lago* (Karlsruhe, 1928); *Die Gespenstersonate,* after Strindberg (Munich, Dec. 19, 1930); *Landsknechte* (Essen, 1936); *Die pfiffige Magd,* after Holberg (Leipzig, Feb. 11, 1939); a symph., *Über einem Grabe,* for Chorus and Orch.; *Fingerhütchen,* fairy ballad for Baritone Solo, Female Chorus, and Orch.; *Macht hoch die Tür,* cantata; *Tanzfantasie* for Orch.; Piano Concerto;

Violin Concerto; much chamber music, including 2 piano trios, 2 violin sonatas, etc.

BIBLIOGRAPHY: W. Thomas-San Galli, "Julius Weismann," in vol. 2 of *Monographien moderner Musiker* (Leipzig, 1907); F. Doldinger, "Julius Weismann," *Neue Musikzeitschrift* (Dec. 1947); H.J. Moser, "Julius Weismann," *Musica* (June 1955).

Weismann, Wilhelm, German composer; b. Alfdorf, Sept. 20, 1900. He studied at the Stuttgart Cons. with Karg-Elert, and in Leipzig with M. Ludwig. From 1946 to 1955 he was on the faculty of the Hochschule für Musik in Leipzig; served as editor for the C.F. Peters Publishing firm in Leipzig (1929–65), while continuing his teaching at the Hochschule für Musik (rejoined in 1961). He wrote a number of choral works, both secular and sacred; also composed several collections of madrigals, as well as solo cantatas. He supervised a complete edition of madrigals by Gesualdo.

Weiss, Adolph, American composer and bassoonist; b. Baltimore, Sept. 12, 1891 (of German parents); d. Van Nuys, Calif., Feb. 21, 1971. He studied piano, violin, and the bassoon; at the age of 16, was engaged as first bassoonist of the Russian Symph. Orch. of N.Y.; then played in the N.Y. Phil. under Mahler; for many years was with the N.Y. Symph. under Walter Damrosch. In the meantime, he studied composition with Cornelius Rybner at Columbia Univ. In 1916 he joined the Chicago Symph. Orch. as bassoonist; studied theory with Adolf Weidig and Theodore Otterstrom there; then was bassoonist with the Rochester (N.Y.) Orch. In 1925 he went to Europe to study with Arnold Schoenberg, whose influence was decisive in the formation of his musical style, which is in the 12-tone idiom. Returning to the U.S., he played in the San Francisco Symph. Orch.; then moved to Hollywood, where he settled.

WORKS: *Fantasie* for Piano (1918); *I Segreti* for Orch. (1922; Rochester, May 1, 1925); 3 string quartets (1925, 1926, 1932); Chamber Symph. for 10 Instruments (1927); *12 Preludes* for Piano (1927); *American Life,* "Scherzoso Jazzoso" for Large Orch. (N.Y., Feb. 21, 1930); *Sonata da camera* for Flute and Viola (1929); *7 Songs* for Soprano and String Quartet (1928); *The Libation Bearers,* choreographic cantata for Soloists, Chorus, and Orch. (1930); Quintet for Flute, Oboe, Clarinet, Bassoon, and Horn (1931); Piano Sonata (1932); *Theme and Variations* for Large Orch. (1933); *Suite* for Orch. (1938); *Petite suite* for Flute, Clarinet, and Bassoon (1939); Violin Sonata (1941); *Passacaglia* for Horn and Viola (1942); *10 Pieces* for Low Instrument and Orch. (1943); *Ode to the West Wind* for Baritone, Viola, and Piano (1945); *Protest* for 2 Pianos (1945); Sextet for Flute, Oboe, Clarinet, Bassoon, Horn, and Piano (1947); Trio for Clarinet, Viola, and Cello (1948); Concerto for Bassoon and String Quartet (1949); *Pulse of the Sea,* étude for Piano (1950); Concerto for Trumpet and Orch. (1952); Trio for Flute, Violin, and Piano (1955); *5 Fantasies* for Violin and Piano (1956); *Tone Poem* for Brass and Percussion (1957); *Rhapsody* for 4 French Horns (1957); *Vade mecum* for a group of Wind Instruments (1958).

BIBLIOGRAPHY: W. Riegger, "Adolph Weiss and Colin McPhee," in H. Cowell, ed., *American Composers on American Music* (Stanford, Calif., 1933); *Bulletin of American Composers Alliance* (1958, No. 3).

Weiss, Amalie. See **Joachim, Amalie.**

Weiss, Franz, viola player; b. Silesia, Jan. 18, 1778; d. Vienna, Jan. 25, 1830. When Prince Razumovsky formed his string quartet in Vienna (1808), Franz Weiss was engaged as viola player, with Schuppanzigh as first violin, Prince Razumovsky as 2nd violin, and Linke as cellist. Weiss composed some chamber music; *Variations brillantes* for Violin and Orch.; several piano sonatas; Symph. for Flute, Bassoon, and Trumpet; etc.

Weiss, Johann, Austrian hymnologist; b. St. Ruprecht-on-Raab, Styria, Nov. 20, 1850; d. there, Sept. 7, 1919. He studied theology; in 1881 was appointed teacher of hymnology at the Graz Seminary; was organist at the Graz Cathedral (1884–91). He publ. *Die musikalischen Instrumente in den heiligen Schriften des Alten Testaments* (1895).

Weiss, Julius, German violinist; b. Berlin, July 19, 1814; d. there, June 30, 1898. He studied with Henning; wrote music criticism; publ. instructive works for violin; was also active in music publishing.

Weiss, Sylvius Leopold, German lute player and composer; b. Breslau, Oct. 12, 1686; d. Dresden, Oct. 16, 1750. He learned to play the lute from his father; served as lutenist at the court of Düsseldorf (1706); then with Alexander Sobieski, Prince of Poland, in Rome (1708–14); and at Hesse-Kassel (1715–16). In 1717 he went to Dresden, where he remained for the rest of his life, with the exception of a few months in Berlin (1728). He was regarded as one of the greatest lute players of his time; in 1728, publ. a treatise on the lute. Six of his suites are reprinted in vol. 12 of the *Reichsdenkmale (Das Erbe deutscher Musik).*

BIBLIOGRAPHY: H. Neemann, "Die Lautenhandschriften von S.L. Weiss in der Bibiliothek Dr. Werner Wolffheim, Berlin," *Zeitschrift für Musikwissenschaft,* 10 (1928); H. Neemann, "Die Lautenistenfamilie Weiss," *Archiv für Musikforschung,* 4 (1939).

Weissberg, Yulia, Russian composer; b. Orenburg, Jan. 6, 1879; d. Leningrad, March 1, 1942. She studied at the St. Petersburg Cons. with Rimsky-Korsakov, and married his son **Andrei;** in 1907 took a course with Max Reger in Germany; was a co-editor of the periodical *Muzykalny Sovremennik* (1915–17).

WORKS: Operas: *Mermaid,* after Andersen (1923); *Gülnara* (1935); *The Dead Princess* (1937); 2 children's operas: *Little Rabbit's House* (1935) and *Geese and Swans* (1937); *The 12,* to the poem of Alexander Blok, for Chorus and Orch. (Leningrad,

May 12, 1926); symph. poem, *In the Night* (1929); *Sailor's Dance* for Orch. (1936); several song cycles for Voice, with Instruments; children's choruses; a number of solo songs; transcriptions of folk songs.

Weisse, Hans, Austrian music theorist and composer; b. Vienna, March 31, 1892; d. New York, Feb. 10, 1940. He studied with Schenker and became an exponent of his theory. In 1931 he came to the U.S. and gave courses in theory at the Mannes Music School in N.Y. He wrote mostly chamber music: 3 string quartets (1920–36); String Sextet (1924); Quintet for Clarinet and Strings (1928); Octet for Strings and Winds (1929); Concerto for Flute, Oboe, and Harpsichord (1937); *Choral Partita* for Strings and Winds (1938).

Weissenbäck, (Franz) Andreas, Austrian choral conductor and composer; b. St. Lorenzen, Styria, Nov. 26, 1880; d. Vienna, March 14, 1960. He studied in Graz; in 1899, entered the monastery at Klosterneuburg, near Vienna; became a Catholic priest in 1904; then took up musicology under Guido Adler at the Univ. of Vienna (Dr.Phil., 1912); was for many years choirmaster at Klosterneuburg. He publ. *Sacra musica,* a lexicon of Catholic church music (1937); contributed valuable papers to various publications, particularly on Gregorian chant; also was an expert on church bells. He composed a German Mass for Male Chorus; publ. many sacred works; also a Mass for Mixed Chorus and 7 Wind Instruments, including 2 Saxophones.

Weissenberg, Alexis, pianist; b. Sofia, July 26, 1929. He studied in Sofia with Pantcho Vladigerov; during the German occupation of Bulgaria, he and his mother were confined in a concentration camp, but managed to flee to Palestine. In 1946 he went to N.Y.; studied with Artur Schnabel, Olga Samaroff, and Wanda Landowska. In 1947 he won the youth competition sponsored by the Philadelphia Orch.; in 1948 he won the Leventritt Competition and appeared with the N.Y. Phil. He then toured widely as a concert pianist, visiting Italy, Germany, Russia, and Japan.

Weissenborn, Günther, German pianist and conductor; b. Coburg, June 2, 1911. He studied at the Hochschule für Musik in Berlin; was an organist and choir director there (1934–37). He was then a conductor at the Municipal Theater in Halle (1937–42) and in Hannover (1944). Later he conducted in Göttingen (1945–47); then returned to Hannover as conductor of the Hausegger Chamber Orch. Apart from his activities as a conductor, Weissenborn earned a fine reputation as a piano accompanist in lieder recitals.

Weissheimer, Wendelin, conductor and composer; b. Osthofen, Alsace, Feb. 26, 1838; d. Nuremberg, June 16, 1910. He studied at the Leipzig Cons., and later took lessons in composition with Liszt at Weimar. He was opera conductor at Würzburg, at

Mainz, and at Strasbourg; then lived in various towns on the Rhine and in Bavaria. As a composer, he followed the Wagnerian vogue; wrote 2 dramas, *Theodor Körner* (Munich, May 28, 1872) and *Meister Martin und seine Gesellen* (Karlsruhe, April 14, 1879); also 18 songs to words by Goethe; *5 geistliche Sonette* for Voice, Flute, Oboe, Clarinet, and Harmonium. His book of reminiscences, *Erlebnisse mit Richard Wagner, Franz Liszt und vielen anderen Zeitgenossen, nebst deren Briefen* (Stuttgart, 1898), quotes many letters from Wagner, with whom he maintained an intimate friendship.

Weissmann, Adolf, German writer on music; b. Rosenberg, Silesia, Aug. 15, 1873; d. Saïda, near Haifa, April 23, 1929. He studied in Berlin, Breslau, Florence, etc.; obtained his Dr.Phil. in 1914. He was critic for the *Berliner Tageblatt* (1900–15), and from 1916 for the *Berliner Zeitung am Mittag;* also wrote for German musiche *Berliner Tageblatt* (1900–15), and from 1916 for the *Berliner Zeitung am Mittag;* also wrote for German music magazines; went on a lecture tour in Palestine and died there.

WRITINGS: *Berlin als Musikstadt (1740–1911)* (1911); *G. Bizet* (1907; in the collection *Die Musik,* ed. by Richard Strauss); *Chopin* (1912; 3rd ed., 1919); *Der Virtuose* (1918); *Die Primadonna* (1920); *Der klingende Garten. Impressionen über das Erotische in der Musik* (1920); the 3 preceding titles together as *Die Musik der Sinne* (1925); *Giacomo Puccini* (1922); *Die Musik in der Weltkrise* (1922; Eng. trans. as *The Problems of Modern Music,* London, 1925); *Verdi* (1922); *Der Dirigent in 20. Jahrhundert* (1925); *Die Entgötterung der Musik* (1928; Eng. trans. as *Music Come to Earth,* London, 1930).

BIBLIOGRAPHY: E. Preussner, "Adolf Weissmann," *Die Musik,* 21 (1929).

Weissmann, John, Hungarian musicologist; b. Budapest, July 10, 1910; d. London, March 23, 1980. He studied at the Budapest Cons.; was opera coach at the Municipal Theater (1932–34); then assistant conductor there (1935–37). In 1937 he settled in London, where he attended classes of conducting at the Royal Academy of Music. Subsequently he devoted his attention mainly to musicology; contributed numerous valuable essays to various periodicals.

WRITINGS: *Gottfredo Petrassi* (Milan, 1957); *Bartok and His String Quartets* (Hamburg, 1962).

Weitzmann, Carl Friedrich, noted German theorist and composer; b. Berlin, Aug. 10, 1808; d. there, Nov. 7, 1880. He studied violin with Henning and theory with Klein; later, at Kassel, was a pupil of Spohr and Hauptmann. He then held the post of concertmaster in Riga (1832–34), Reval (1834–36), and St. Petersburg (1836–46). After sojourns in Paris and London (1846–48), he settled in Berlin as a teacher of composition. He was an ardent disciple and friend of Wagner and Liszt; among his posthumous papers was found the original MS of a double fugue for piano by Wagner, with corrections in the handwriting of Weinlig (Wagner's teacher). The piece was publ. by E. Istel in *Die Musik* (July 1912).

Weitzmann was an original thinker in his harmonic theories; made an investigation of the modulatory functions of the whole-tone scale, and interested Liszt in its use. He composed a 4th variation to Liszt's *Todtentanz.* A full exposition of his theories is found in a book by his American pupil E.M. Bowman, *K.F. Weitzmann's Manual of Musical Theory* (N.Y., 1877). Weitzmann's theoretical works in German include *Der übermässige Dreiklang* (1853); *Der verminderte Septimenakkord* (1854); *Geschichte der Septimen-Akkordes* (1854); *Harmoniesystem* (1860); *Die neue Harmonielehre im Streit mit der alten* (1861); *Geschichte des Klavierspiels ind der Klavierlitteratur* (1863, as Part III of the Lebert-Stark piano method; 2nd ed., 1879, printed separately, with an added *Geschichte des Klaviers;* in Eng., N.Y., 1894, with a biographical sketch by Otto Lessmann; 3rd German ed., Leipzig, 1899, as *Geschichte der Klaviermusik,* ed. by Max Seiffert, with a supplement, *Geschichte des Klaviers,* by Otto Fleischer); *Der letzte der Virtuosen* (on Tausig; 1868); many essays in various musical periodicals. As a composer, he followed the fashionable Romantic trends; wrote the operas *Räuberliebe* (1834), *Walpurgisnacht* (1835), and *Lorbeer und Bettelstab* (1836), which he brought out in Reval; 3 books of *Valses nobles* for Piano; *Preludes and Modulations* for Piano, 2 parts, "Classic" and "Romantic"; also wrote 2 books of ingenious canonic *Rätsel* for piano, 4-hands, and 2 books of *Kontrapunkt-Studien* for piano.

Welch, Roy Dickinson, American pianist and music educator; b. Dansville, N.Y., Jan. 19, 1885; d. Princeton, N.J., Jan. 8, 1951. He studied at the Univ. of Michigan (B.A., 1909); then went to Berlin, where he took piano lessons from Josef Lhévinne (1910–12). From 1914 to 1935 he was chairman of the music dept. of Smith College in Northampton, Mass.; went to Europe on a Guggenheim fellowship (1930–32); in 1935 was appointed chairman of the music dept. of Princeton Univ. He publ. *The Study of Music in the American College* (Northampton, 1925) and *The Appreciation of Music* (N.Y., 1927; revised ed., 1945).

Weld, Arthur Cyril Gordon, American conductor; b. Boston, March 4, 1862; d. near West Point, N.Y., Oct. 11, 1914 (of apoplexy, while driving an automobile). He studied in Dresden, in Berlin, and in Munich. Upon returning to America, he became general director of the H.W. Savage Opera Co., and conducted the first performance of the famous musical comedy *Floradora* (N.Y., 1900). Some of his songs were publ.

Weldon, George, English conductor; b. Chichester, June 5, 1906; d. Cape Town, South Africa, Aug. 16, 1963. He studied at the Royal College of Music with Malcolm Sargent; conducted various provincial orchs.; traveled as a guest conductor in North Africa, Turkey, and Yugoslavia. He was conductor of the Birmingham City Orch. from 1943 to 1950.
BIBLIOGRAPHY: Donald Brook, *International*

Gallery of Conductors (London, 1951; pp. 221–23).

Weldon, Georgina (née **Thomas**), English soprano; b. London, May 24, 1837; d. Brighton, Jan. 11, 1914. She took up singing after her marriage to Capt. Weldon in 1860, and did not appear in public until 1870. She organized an orphan asylum for the purpose of musical education, and also dabbled in music publishing. Special interest attaches to her because of her romantic friendship with Gounod, who during his London sojourn (1870–75) lived at her residence, and whom she assisted in training the Gounod Choir. She trans. his autobiography (which goes only as far as 1859) into Eng. (1875). Their relationship deteriorated, leading to a legal entanglement in connection with her claims regarding the copyright of Gounod's choral works; she wrote acrimonious letters to the press, defending her stand. She also publ. some songs of her own (to French texts) and the didactic manuals *Hints for Pronunciation in Singing* (1872) and *Musical Reform* (1875).

Welin, Karl-Erik, Swedish organist, pianist, and composer of the extreme avant-garde; b. Genarp, May 31, 1934. He studied organ with Alf Linden at the Royal College of Music in Stockholm (1956–61); took composition lessons with Gunnar Bucht (1958–60) and Lidholm (1960–64); then attended summer seminars in new music at Darmstadt (1960–62), working with the American pianist David Tudor on avant-garde techniques. In 1958 he joined the experimental group "Fylkingen" in Stockholm. As a composer, he followed in his youthful works the fashionable impressionistic trends, mostly in miniature forms, in colorful and unusual instrumental groupings. He created a sensation at his piano recital at the Stockholm High School of Music on March 6, 1964, when he exploded a pyrotechnical device lodged in the frame of the piano and then proceeded to saw off the piano legs with an electrically powered handsaw, accidentally cutting himself so seriously that he had to undergo surgery.
WORKS: *4 Chinese Poems* for Chorus (1956); *Sermo modulatus* for Flute and Clarinet (1959); *Renovations* for Soprano, Flute, Violin, Mandolin, Celesta, and Percussion (1960); *Cantata* for Children's Chorus, Violin, Flute, and Harpsichord (1960); *Manzit* for Clarinet, Trombone, Violin, Piano, and Percussion (1962); *Esservecchia* for Electric Guitar, Horn, Trombone, and Piano (1963); *Warum nicht?* for Flute, Violin, Cello, Xylophone, Vibraphone, and Tam-tam (1964); *Pereo* for 36 Strings (1964); *Kazimir* for 4 Flutes (1965); *Visoka 12* for 2 Flutes, 2 Violins, and 2 Cellos (1965); *Etwas für . . .* for Wind Quintet (1966); a children's television opera, *Dummerjöns (Tom Fool),* after H.C. Andersen (1966–67); *Eigentlich nicht,* 2nd string quartet (1967); *Copelius,* ballet of concrete music (1968); *Ondine,* theater music (1968); *Vindarnas grotta (Cave of the Winds),* television ballet (Stockholm Television, March 30, 1969); *Glazba* for 3 Flutes, Bassoon, and Soprano (1968); *Ben fatto* for a Solo Instrument or an infinite number of Instruments (1968); *Improvisiation* for Organ (1969); *PC-132* for String

Quartet (1970); *A New Map of Hell* for Chorus (1971); *Recidivans,* 3rd string quartet (1972); *Aver la forza di . . .* for Chorus and String Orch. (1972); opera, *Drottning Jag* (*Queen Ego;* 1972; Stockholm, Feb. 17, 1973); *Harmonies* for Clarinet, Trombone, Cello, and Piano (1972); *Pagabile* for Chamber Ensemble (1972); *Residuo,* 4th string quartet (1974).

Welitsch, Ljuba (real name, **Velitchkova**), Bulgarian soprano; b. Borisovo, near Varna, July 10, 1913. She played the violin as a child; then entered high school; subsequently took courses in philosophy at the Univ. of Sofia; then went to Vienna, where she studied voice with Lierhammer. She made her operatic debut as Nedda in *Pagliacci* at the Graz Opera (1936); from 1941 to 1943 she sang in Hamburg and Berlin; in 1943–46 was in Munich. On June 11, 1944, she made her first appearance as Salome (later to become her most famous role) in Vienna, under the direction of Richard Strauss himself, on his 80th birthday. She made her debut in London with the Vienna State Opera as Donna Anna in *Don Giovanni* on Sept. 20, 1947. Her American debut, at the Metropolitan Opera House in N.Y., in *Salome* (Feb. 4, 1949) was greatly acclaimed. She remained a member of the Metropolitan until 1952.

Welk, Lawrence, popular American conductor of entertainment music; b. Strasburg, N.Dak., March 11, 1903. He received his training in California; in 1955 he began a series of television concerts which became increasingly popular, thanks to his skillful selection of programs containing a varied mixture of semi-classical pieces, western American ballads, and Slavic folk-dance tunes. His use of an accordion section in his arrangements, steadfast rhythmic beat, and sentimentalized tempi impart to his renditions a rudimentary sound quality that makes him a favorite with undiscriminating audiences. He publ. (with some outside help) an autobiography, *Wunnerful, Wunnerful!*(N.Y., 1971), radiating euphoria, and a sequel: *Ah-one, ah-two: Life with My Musical Family* (N.Y., 1974).

Wellek, Albert, Austrian musicologist; b. Vienna, Oct. 16, 1904; d. Mainz, Aug. 27, 1972. He studied philosophy at the univs. of Prague, Vienna, and Leipzig; also took music courses at the Prague Cons.; received his Ph.D. in 1928 from the Univ. of Vienna. In 1929 he became especially interested in the problems of musical psychology; served as assistant to Felix Krueger in his dept. of psychology at the Univ. of Leipzig; in 1943 he was appointed prof. of psychology at Breslau, and from 1946 taught at the Univ. of Mainz, where he remained until his death. He wrote *Das absolute Gehör und seine Typen* (Leipzig, 1938); *Typologie der Musikbegabung im deutschen Volke* (Munich, 1939; 2nd ed., 1970); also numerous articles dealing with the development of new musical resources, including quartertones and dodecaphony.

Weller, Walter, Austrian conductor; b. Vienna, Nov. 30, 1939. He was educated at the Vienna Academy of Music, where he studied violin and attended classes in conducting held by Karl Böhm. In 1958 he founded the noted Weller Quartet; also in 1958 he joined the Vienna Phil., and in 1962 became its concertmaster, a post he held, alternating with others, until 1969. He then embarked upon a conducting career. He conducted both the Vienna State Opera and Volksoper; was Generalmusikdirektor in Duisburg (1971–72); also conducted the Vienna Tonkünstler Orch. (1975–78). In 1977 he was named principal conductor and musical adviser of the Royal Liverpool Phil. In 1980 he became principal conductor of the Royal Phil. Orch. of London.

Wellesz, Egon, eminent Austrian composer and musicologist; b. Vienna, Oct. 21, 1885; d. Oxford, Nov. 9, 1974. He studied harmony with Carl Frühling, musicology with Guido Adler, and counterpoint and composition with Schoenberg in Vienna (1904–6); obtained the degree of Dr.Phil. in 1908 with a thesis on Giuseppe Bonno, publ. in the *Sammelbände der Internationalen Musik-Gesellschaft,* 11 (1910). From 1911 to 1915 he taught music history at the Neues Cons. in Vienna; in 1913 he was engaged as a lecturer on musicology at the Univ. of Vienna, and was a prof. there from 1930 to 1938, when the annexation of Austria by Nazi Germany compelled him to leave. He went to England in 1938; joined the music dept. of Oxford Univ., which in 1932 had conferred upon him the degree of Mus.Doc. *(honoris causa).* In 1940 he became a lecturer in music history at Oxford Univ.; in 1946 he was appointed to the editorial board of the *New Oxford History of Music,* to which he then contributed, and was Univ. Reader in Byzantine music at Oxford (1948–56); received the Prize of the City of Vienna in 1953; was president of the Oxford Univ. Byzantine Society (1955–66); in 1957 was made a Commander of the Order of the British Empire and was awarded the Grande Medaille d'Argent of the City of Paris. In 1956–57 he gave lectures in the U.S. A scholar and a musician of extraordinary capacities, Wellesz distinguished himself as a composer of highly complex musical scores, and as an authority on Byzantine music. WORKS: OPERAS: *Die Prinzessin Girnara* (1919–20; Hannover, May 15, 1921; revised version, Mannheim, Sept. 2, 1928); *Alkestis* (1922–23; Mannheim, March 20, 1924); *Opferung des Gefangenen* (1924–25; Cologne, April 10, 1926); *Scherz, List und Rache* (1926–27; Stuttgart, March 1, 1928); *Die Bakchantinnen* (1929–30; Vienna, June 20, 1931); *Incognita* (Oxford, Dec. 5, 1950). BALLETS: *Das Wunder der Diana* (1915; Mannheim, March 20, 1924); *Persisches Ballet* (1920; Donaueschingen, 1924); *Achilles auf Skyros* (1921; Stuttgart, March 4, 1927); *Die Nächtlichen* (1923; Berlin, Nov. 20, 1924). FOR ORCH.: 9 symphs.: No. 1, in C (1945); No. 2, in E-flat (1948); No. 3, in A (1951); No. 4, *Symphonia Austriaca,* in G (1953); No. 5 (1956; Düsseldorf, Feb. 20, 1958); No. 6 (1965; Nuremberg, June 1, 1966); No. 7 (1968); No. 8 (1971); No. 9 (1971; Vienna, Nov. 22, 1972); *Vorfrühling,* symph. poem (1912); *Suite* for Violin and Chamber Orch. (1924); Piano Concerto (1934); *Pros-*

peros Beschwörungen, after Shakespeare's *The Tempest* (1936–38; Vienna, Feb. 19, 1938); Violin Concerto (1961; Vienna, Jan. 19, 1962); *Music* for String Orch. (1964); *Divertimento* for Chamber Orch. (1969); *Symphonischer Epilog* (1969). FOR VOICE: *Gebete der Mädchen zur Maria* for Soprano, Chorus, and Orch. (1909); *Mitte des Lebens,* cantata (1932); *Amor timido,* cantata for Soprano and Orch. (1935); *5 Sonnets by Elizabeth Barrett Browning* for Soprano and String Quartet (1935); *Lied der Welt* for Soprano and Orch. (1937); *Leben, Traum und Tod* for Contralto and Orch. (1937); *Short Mass* for Chorus and Small Orch. (1937); *The Leaden Echo and the Golden Echo,* after Hopkins, for Soprano, Violin, Clarinet, Cello, and Piano (1944); *4 Songs of Return* for Soprano and Small Orch. (1961); *Duineser Elegie* for Soprano, Chorus, and Chamber Ensemble (1963); *Ode to Music* for Baritone and Chamber Orch. (1964); *Vision* for Soprano and Orch. (1966); *Mirabile Mysterium,* Christmas cantata (1967); *Canticum Sapientiae* for Baritone, Chorus, and Orch. (1968; Graz, Austria, Oct. 25, 1969). CHAMBER MUSIC: 9 string quartets (1912, 1917, 1918, 1920, 1944, 1947, 1948, 1957, 1966); *Geistiges Lied* for Piano Trio (1918); Sonata for Solo Cello (1921); *2 Pieces* for Clarinet and Piano (1922); Sonata for Solo Violin (1924); *Suite* for Violin and Piano (1937); *Little Suite* for Solo Flute (1937); Octet for Clarinet, Horn, Bassoon, and String Quintet (1948–49); *Suite* for Wind Quintet (1954); *Suite* in 3 movements for Solo Bassoon (1956); Clarinet Quintet (1959); 2 string trios (1962, 1969); *5 Miniatures* for Violin and Piano (1965); *Music* for String Quartet (1968); String Quintet (1970). FOR PIANO: *3 Piano Pieces* (1912); *Epigramme* (1913); *5 Dance Pieces* (1927); *Triptych* (1966); *Studies in Grey* (1969). FOR ORGAN: *Partita* (1966).

WRITINGS: *Arnold Schönberg* (Vienna, 1921; Eng. trans., London, 1924); *Der Beginn des musikalischen Barock und Die Anfänge der Oper in Wien,* in *Wiener literarische Anstalt* (Vienna, 1922); *Byzantinische Kirchenmusik* (Breslau, 1927); *Eastern Elements in Western Chant* (Oxford, 1947; 2nd ed., 1967); *A History of Byzantine Music and Hymnography* (Oxford, 1949; 3rd ed., revised, 1963); *Essays on Opera* (London, 1950); *The Origin of Schoenberg's Twelve-Tone System* (Washington, D.C., 1958); numerous essays on a variety of subjects in German and English periodicals. He edited Fux's *Costanza e Fortezza,* in Denkmäler der Tonkunst in Österreich, 34/35 (17); *Trésor de Musique Byzantine,* vol. I (Paris, 1934); *Die Hymnen des Sticherarium für September* (1936; vol. I of *Monumenta musicae byzantinae, Transcripta*); vol. I of the *New Oxford History of Music,* "Ancient and Oriental Music" (1957); *Die Hymnen der Ostkirche* (Kassel, 1962); *J.J. Fux* (London, 1965).

BIBLIOGRAPHY: O.F. Beer, "Egon Wellesz und die Oper," *Die Musik* (Sept. 1931); H.F. Redlich, "Egon Wellesz," *Musical Quarterly* (Jan. 1940); R. Reti, "Egon Wellesz, Musician and Scholar," *Musical Quarterly* (Jan. 1956); R. Schollum, *Egon Wellesz* (Vienna, 1964).

Wells, Kitty (Muriel Deason Wright), American

singer of country music; b. Nashville, Tenn., Aug. 30, 1919. She sang gospel tunes in local churches while a child; then appeared with John and Jack and the Tennessee Mountain Boys; in 1952 she joined the "Grand Ole Opry" radio program; also made many recordings.

Wels, Charles, American pianist and composer; b. Prague, Aug. 24, 1825; d. New York, May 12, 1906. After studying in Prague, he went to America in 1849 and settled in N.Y.; filled various positions as church organist and teacher; retired in 1901. He composed about 170 opus numbers, including 5 masses; a Piano Concerto; fantasias, other pieces, transcriptions, and arrangements for piano, 2- or 4-hands; several male quartets; songs.

Welsh, Thomas, English singer and composer; b. Wells, c.1780; d. Brighton, Jan. 24, 1848. He was a chorister at Wells Cathedral, and a pupil of J.B. Cramer and Baumgarten. He made his opera debut in London at the age of 12; after his voice changed, he became a bass, and sang in oratorio. He was particularly distinguished as a vocal teacher; publ. *Vocal Instructor, or the Art of Singing Exemplified in 15 Lessons leading to 40 Progressive Exercises* (1825); piano sonatas; glees, duets, and part-songs; also wrote several musical pieces for the theater. His wife and pupil, **Mary Anne** (née **Wilson;** 1802–67), was a noted soprano who made her debut at Drury Lane on Jan. 18, 1821, in Arne's *Artaxerxes.*

Welte, Michael, German manufacturer of musical instruments; b. Unterkirnach, Black Forest, Sept. 29, 1807; d. Freiburg im Breisgau, Jan. 17, 1880. Having served an apprenticeship with Josef Blessing, a maker of musical clocks, he established himself at Voehrenbach (1832); exhibited his first "orchestrion" at Karlsruhe in 1849; later took his sons (**Emil, Berthold,** and **Michael, Jr.**) into partnership. His instruments obtained first prizes at London (1862), Paris (1867), Munich (1885), Vienna (1892), Chicago (1893), St. Louis (1904), Leipzig (1909), and Turin (1911); in 1872 the factory was removed to Freiburg im Breisgau. His oldest son, **Emil Welte** (b. Voehrenbach, April 20, 1841; d. Norwich, Conn., Oct. 25, 1923), established a branch in N.Y. (1865); he improved the then newly invented paper roll (taking the place of the earlier wooden cylinders), and was the first to use it, in connection with a pneumatic action, in a large orchestrion built for Theiss's Alhambra Court (N.Y.). A son of Berthold Welte, **Edwin** (b. Freiburg, 1875; d. there, Jan. 4, 1958), applied the paper roll to the piano, creating in 1904 the "Welte-Mignon Reproducing Piano," which could control pedaling and gradations of touch, a definite improvement on the ordinary player-piano, which could produce only pitches. Josef Hoffmann, Paderewski, and Wanda Landowska made rolls for it. The application of the same principle to the organ resulted in the invention of the "Philharmonic Organ" (1912). The firm ceased to exist in 1954.

Welting, Ruth, American soprano; b. Memphis,

Tenn., May 11, 1949. She studied voice in N.Y. with Daniel Ferro, in Rome with Luigi Ricci, and in Paris with Jeanne Reiss; made her operatic debut at the N.Y. City Opera in 1970 as Blondchen in Mozart's *Die Entführung aus dem Serail;* also sang with opera companies in Houston, San Antonio, Dallas, Santa Fe, and San Francisco. She made her Metropolitan Opera debut in N.Y. on March 20, 1976, as Zerbinetta in *Ariadne auf Naxos.*

Wen-Chung, Chou. See **Chou, Wen-Chung.**

Wendel, Ernst, German violinist and conductor; b. Breslau, March 26, 1876; d. Jena, May 20, 1938. He studied violin with Joachim in Berlin; theory with Bargiel. In 1896 he went to America and was a member of the Chicago Symph. Orch. for 2 seasons; returning to Germany, he was conductor of the Musikverein in Königsberg (1898–1909); then conductor in Bremen, Berlin, Frankfurt, and Nuremberg. He composed *Das Grab im Busento* and *Das deutsche Lied,* both for Men's Chorus, with Orch.; also men's choruses a cappella and songs.

Wendel, Eugen, Rumanian composer; b. Valea-Rea, Dec. 18, 1934. He studied with Vancea, Olah, and Stroe at the Bucharest Cons. (1959–65); worked as a sound engineer with the Rumanian recording firm Electrecord.
WORKS: Concerto for Orch. (1964); *Symphonic Meditations* (1965); *Gravitations* for Orch. (1968); *Transmutations* for Orch. (1969); *Resonances* for Orch. (1972); Violin Sonata (1963); String Quartet (1964); *Interferences* for Violin, Viola, Cello, Clarinet, and Piano (1966); *Fusion* for Clarinet, Piano, and Tape (1968); *Rêve,* music for 8 Instrumentalists (1969; also a version for Clarinet, Violin, Viola, Cello, and Piano); *Genèse* for Piano Quartet (1972); *Verso* for Solo Oboe (1973); Piano Sonata (1966); choruses; songs.

Wendland, Waldemar, German composer; b. Liegnitz, May 10, 1873; d. Zeitz, Aug. 15, 1947. He studied for a short time with Humperdinck while acting as an assistant conductor at the Frankfurt Opera; then settled in Berlin. He wrote the operas *Das kluge Felleisen* (Madgeburg, 1909); *Das vergessene Ich* (Berlin, 1911); *Der Schneider von Malta* (Leipzig, 1818); *Peter Sukoff* (Basel, 1921); *Die vier Temperamente* (Freiburg, 1927); *Koreanisches Märchen* (Altenburg, May 11, 1946); several ballets; orch. works; chamber music; about 200 songs.

Wendling, Johann Baptist, Alsatian flutist; b. Rappoltsweiler, June 17, 1723; d. Munich, Nov. 27, 1797. He was an excellent flute player; was active in Mannheim; accompanied Mozart on his journey to Paris in 1778; then lived in Mannheim and in Munich. He wrote a number of flute concertos. His wife, **Dorothea Wendling** (1736–1811), was an opera singer; Mozart wrote an aria for her.

Wendling, Karl, German pianist; b. Frankenthal,

Nov. 14, 1857; d. Leipzig, June 20, 1918. He studied at the Leipzig Cons.; made a specialty of the Jankó keyboard, on which he became highly proficient; also taught piano at the Leipzig Cons.; publ. *Meisterwerke aus der Etüden-Literatur* (4 books, in progressive order).

Wendt, Ernst Adolf, German pianist and composer; b. Schwiebus, Prussia, Jan. 6, 1806; d. Neuwied, Feb. 5, 1850. He was a pupil of Zelter in Berlin; then became an instructor at the Teacher's Seminary there. He publ. variations for piano and orch.; Piano Trio; 4-hand Piano Sonata; a collection of his organ pieces was publ. by Karl Becker as *Wendt Album.*

Wenkel, Ortrun, German mezzo-soprano; b. Buttstädt, Oct. 25, 1942. She studied at the Franz Liszt Hochschule für Musik in Weimar, and at the Frankfurt Hochschule für Musik with Paul Lohmann and Elsa Cavelti; made her operatic debut in Gluck's *Orpheus* in Heidelberg in 1971; then sang in Stuttgart, Munich, Cologne, Bayreuth, Geneva, and in the U.S.

Wenkoff, Spas, Bulgarian tenor; b. Tirnovo, Sept. 23, 1928. He received his musical training in Sofia and Dresden. After an operatic debut in his native town of Tirnovo in 1954, he undertook a number of guest engagements, in Russia (1962–65), Dobeln (1965–68), Magdeburg (1968–71), and Halle (1971–75). In 1976 he joined the Berlin State Opera. He distinguished himself mainly in lyric tenor parts.

Wennerberg, Gunnar, Swedish writer and composer; b. Lidköping, Oct. 2, 1817; d. Läckö, Aug. 22, 1901. He studied at the Univ. of Uppsala, and entered the Swedish Parliament. He learned music by himself; began to write songs for male voices, which became very successful in Sweden; publ. the collections *Frihetssånger* (1847) and *Gluntarne* (1849–51; reprinted, Uppsala, 1949); also composed a Christmas oratorio, and settings of the Psalms of David for solo voices, chorus, and piano. His literary works were publ. in 4 vols. (1881–85).
BIBLIOGRAPHY: S. Almquist, *Om Gunnar Wennerberg: Hans tid och hans gärning* (Stockholm, 1917); C.F. Hennerberg, *Förteckning över G. Wennerbergs Tonverk* (Stockholm, 1918); G. Jeanson, *G. Wennerberg som Musiker* (Stockholm, 1929).

Wenzel, Ernst Ferdinand, German pianist and teacher; b. Walddorf, near Löbau, Jan. 25, 1808; d. Bad Kösen, Aug. 16, 1880. A student of philosophy at Leipzig Univ., he also had private piano lessons with Friedrich Wieck, became a friend of his fellow-pupil Schumann, and was a frequent contributor to the *Neue Zeitschrift für Musik* during Schumann's editorship (until 1844). He was also an intimate friend of Mendelssohn; taught piano at the Leipzig Cons. from its foundation in 1843 until his death; the majority of the English-speaking students there were in his classes, or had private instruction from him.

Wenzel, Leopold, Italian violinist, conductor, and composer; b. Naples, Jan. 23, 1847; d. Asnières, near Paris, Aug. 21, 1925. He studied at the Cons. S. Pietro a Majella in Naples, but left it at the age of 13, traveling as a violinist in Greece, Turkey, and Egypt, eventually going to Paris as a theater conductor. From 1889 to 1914 he was in London, conducting at the Empire Theatre and the Gaiety Theatre. He wrote about 20 ballets, the most successful being *Dream of Wealth, Katrina,* and *The Girl I Left Behind Me;* operettas: *Le Chevalier Mignon* (Paris, 1884) and *L'Elève du Conservatoire* (Paris, 1894); also many songs.

Wenzinger, August, Swiss cellist and music editor; b. Basel, Nov. 14, 1905. He received his basic training at the Basel Cons.; then went to Germany and studied cello with Paul Grümmer and music theory with Philipp Jarnach at the Hochschule für Musik in Cologne; also took private cello lessons with Emanuel Feuermann in Berlin. He subsequently served as first cellist at the City Orch. in Bremen (1929–34). He became interested in reviving the classical Baroque repertoire on original instruments, and acquired facility on the viola da gamba; conducted Baroque music with the West German Radio Orch. in Cologne (1954–58) and later led performances of Baroque operas in Hannover (1958–66). He then taught at the Schola Cantorum Basiliensis (until 1970); eventually settled in Bottmingen, near Basel. He edited Bach's unaccompanied cello suites and several Baroque operas; publ. exercises for the viola da gamba, *Gambenübung* (2 vols., 1935, 1938) and *Gambenfibel* (with Marianne Majer, 1943).

Werba, Erik, eminent Austrian pianist, composer, and writer on music; b. Baden, near Vienna, May 23, 1918. He studied piano with Oskar Dachs and composition with Joseph Marx at the Vienna Academy of Music; musicology with Lach, Wellesz, and Schenk; received his Dr.Phil. in 1940 at the Univ. of Vienna. In 1948 he was appointed a prof. at the Vienna Academy of Music; from 1964 to 1971 he was also a visiting prof. at the Academy of Music in Graz. He was engaged mainly as a piano accompanist to famous singers, with whom he traveled in Europe and Japan; returning to Vienna, he devoted himself primarily to musical journalism; in 1953 he became editor of the *Österreichische Musikalische Zeitung;* publ. a number of informative and reliable monographs on Austrian composers: Joseph Marx (Vienna, 1964), Hugo Wolf (Vienna, 1971), and Erich Marckhl (Vienna, 1972). He composed a singspiel, *Trauben für die Kaiserin* (Vienna, 1949); several song cycles and chamber music pieces, among them *Sonata notturna* for Bassoon and Piano (1972).

Werckmeister, Andreas, German organist and theorist; b. Benneckenstein, Nov. 30, 1645; d. Halberstadt, Oct. 26, 1706. He studied organ with his uncles, Christian and Victor; was organist at Hasselfelde (1664–74), at Quedlinburg (1675–96), and finally at Halberstadt, from 1696 to his death. He publ. the important treatise *Orgelprobe* (1681; 2nd ed., 1698; 3rd ed., 1716; 4th ed., 1764; Eng. trans. in *Organ Institute Quarterly,* 6, 1956); *Musicae mathematicae Hodegus curiosus, oder Richtiger musikalisher Weg-Weiser* (1686; 2nd ed., 1698); *Der edlen Music-Kunst Würde, Gebrauch und Missbrauch* (1691); *Musikalische Temperatur* (1691; the earliest treatise on equal temperament); *Hypomnemata musica, oder Musikalisches Memorial* (1697); *Die nothwendigsten Anmerckungen und Regeln wie der Bassus continuus könne tractiret werden* (1698); *Harmonologia musica, oder Kurtze Anleitung zur musikalischen Composition* (1702); *Organum Gruningense redivivum, oder Kurtze Beschreibung des in der grüningischen Schloss-Kirchen berühmten Orgel-Wercks* (1705); *Musikalische Paradoxal-Discourse* (posthumous; 1707). A facsimile reprint of the *Orgelprobe* (ed. of 1698) was publ. in Kassel in 1927; the *Organum Gruningense* was republ. in Mainz in 1932.

BIBLIOGRAPHY: W. Serauky, "Andreas Werckmeister als Musiktheoretiker," in the *Max Schneider Festschrift* (Halle, 1935); R. Dammann, "Zur Musiklehre des Andreas Werckmeister," in *Archiv für Musikwissenschaft,* 11 (1954).

Werder, Felix, German-born Australian composer; b. Berlin, Feb. 22, 1922. He acquired early music training from his father, a cantor and composer of liturgical music; also learned to play piano, viola, and clarinet. His family emigrated to England in 1934 to escape Nazi persecution; then went to Australia. Werder taught music at high schools in Melbourne, and was a music critic for the Melbourne newspaper the *Age* (1960–77). He wrote 500 works, but discarded about 60% of them; his musical idiom was determined by the cross-currents of European modernism, with a gradual increase in the forcefulness of his resources; these include electronics.

WORKS: FOR THE STAGE: 6 operas: *Kisses for a Quid* (1961); *The General* (1966); *Agamemnon* (1967); *The Affair* (1969); *Private,* television opera (1969); *The Vicious Square* (1971); ballet, *En passant* (1964). FOR ORCH: 5 symphs.: No. 1 (1951; withdrawn); No. 2 (1959); No. 3, *The Laocoön* (1965); No. 4 (1970); No. 5 (1971); Flute Concerto (1954); Piano Concerto (1955); 2 violin concertos (1956, 1966); *Brand,* symph. poem (1956); *Sinfonia in Italian Style* (1957); *La Primavera,* symph. poem (1957); *Abstraction* (1958); *Hexastrophe* (1961); *Monostrophe* (1961); Clarinet Concerto (1962); Viola Concerto (1963); *Konzert Musik* for 10 Solo Instruments and Orch. (1964); *Dramaturgie* (1966); *Morgen Rot* for Violin and Chamber Orch. (1968); *Strettophone* (1968); *Tower Concerto* (1968); *After Watteau* for Violin and Orch. (1968); *Sound Canvas* (1969); *Klang Bilder* (1969); *Triple Measure* (1970); *Don Giovanni Retired,* epilogue (1971); *Prom Gothic* for Organ and Orch. (1972). FOR VOICE: Oratorio, *Francis Bacon Essays* (1971); an anti-Vietnam War cantata, *Radics Piece* (1967); songs. CHAMBER MUSIC: 9 string quartets (Nos. 1–3, withdrawn; Nos. 4–9: 1955, 1956, 1962, 1965, 1966, 1968); 3 violin sonatas (1947, 1958, 1963); Piano Quartet (1954); *3-Part Fantasias* for String Trio (1955); Cello Sonata (1956); 3 piano trios (1958, 1963, 1969); Quintet for Clarinet, Horn, and String Trio (1959); Flute Sonata (1960); Clarinet Sonata (1960); Horn Sonata (1960); Sonata for Wind Quintet (1961); Septet for Flute, Clarinet, Horn, and Strings (1963); Piano Quintet (1963); Solo Violin Sonata (1965); *Apostrophe* for Wind Quintet (1965); Quintet for Clarinet and String Quartet (1965); *Satyricon* for 6 Horns (1967); Sonata for Cello Solo (1968); *Strophe* for Solo Violin (1968); Trio for Harp, Bass Clarinet, and Percussion (1969); *Activity* for Piano and Percussion (1969); *Triphony* for Flute, Guitar, and Bongos (1969); *Faggotiana* for Bassoon and String Trio (1970); *Tetract* for Viola, Oboe, and 2 Percussionists (1970); *Divertimento* for Guitar and String Quartet (1971); Wind Quartet (1971); *Percussion Play* for Solo Percussion (1971); *Banker,* music theater for 2 Synthesizers, Percussion, Guitar, and Piano (1973). FOR KEYBOARD: 4 piano sonatas (1942, 1953, 1968, 1970); 2-piano Sonata (1960); Harpsichord Sonata (1963); *Toccata* for Organ (1971).

Werder, Richard, American composer and pianist; b. Williamsburg, Iowa, Dec. 21, 1919. He studied at the Juilliard School of Music in N.Y., and at Columbia Univ.; later taught at the Catholic Univ. in Washington, D.C. Among his works, mostly for piano, are *Black on White, The Drum, Procession of the Pachyderms, Resting Time,* and *Down, Up.*

Werle, Lars Johan, Swedish composer; b. Gävle, June 23, 1926. He studied with Sven-Erik Bäck (composition) and Carl-Allan Moberg (musicology) at Uppsala Univ. (1948–51); held positions at the Swedish Broadcasting Corp., and as an instructor at the National School of Music Drama in Stockholm. In his music he employs an amiably modern idiom, stimulating to the untutored ear while retaining the specific gravity of triadic tonal constructions. His 3 theater operas have been received with smiling approbation.

WORKS: *Drömmen om Thérèse (The Dream of Thérèse),* with Electronic Sound, after Zola's short story *Pour une nuit d'amour* (Stockholm, May 26, 1964); *Resan (The Voyage),* after a novel by J.P. Jersild, containing film-projection (Hamburg, March 2, 1969); *Tintomara,* after C.J.L. Almquist's novel *The Queen's Jewels* (Stockholm, Jan. 18, 1973); television opera, *En saga om sinnen* (Swedish Television, June 21, 1971); *Pentagram* for String Quartet (1959); *Sinfonia da camera* (1960); *Summer Music 1965* for Strings and Piano (1965); *Attitudes* for Piano (1965); *Zodiak,* ballet (Stockholm, Feb. 12, 1967); *Canzona 126 di Francesco Petrarca* for Chorus (1967); *Nautical Preludes* for Chorus (1970); *Variété* for String Quartet (1971); 2 "run-and-sing" stage works: *Fabel* for 5 Singers, Percussion, and Piano (1974) and *Flower Power* for 6 Singers and 6 Instrumentalists (1974).

Wermann, Friedrich Oskar, German organist and composer; b. Neichen, near Trebsen, April 30, 1840; d. Oberloschwitz, near Dresden, Nov. 22, 1906. He was a pupil of Friedrich Wieck (piano); later of Rei-

necke, Hauptmann, and Richter at the Leipzig Cons. He occupied various positions as an organist in Alsace, before settling in Dresden (1868) as a teacher and church organist; also conducted the Lehrergesangverein there. He composed a Christmas fairy tale, *Die Wunderglocke;* a symph. poem, *König Witichis;* several overtures; a *Reformationskantate;* a *Passionskantate;* 2 masses; several Psalms for double chorus a cappella; numerous organ works; études for piano; part-songs.

Werner, Arno, German organist and musicologist; b. Prittitz, Weissenfels, Nov. 22, 1865; d. Bitterfeld, Feb. 15, 1955. He studied at the Royal Inst. for Church-Music in Berlin (1889–90); in 1890 became municipal organist at Bitterfeld; in 1894 was appointed music teacher at the Gymnasium there, retiring in 1931; he continued his activities as a musicologist until his death; contributed articles to *Die Musik in Geschichte und Gegenwart* (1953).

WRITINGS: *Samuel und Gottfried Scheidt* (1900); *Geschichte der Kantorei-Gesellschaften im Gebiete des Kurfürstentums Sachsen* (1902); *Die Kantorei zu Bitterfeld* (1903); *Städtische und fürstliche Musikpflege in Weissenfels* (1911); *Städtische und fürstliche Musikpflege in Zeitz* (1922); *Zur Geschichte der Kantorei in Zörbig* (1927); *Musikpflege in Stadt und Kreis Bitterfeld* (1931); *Vier Jahrhunderte im Dienste der Kirchenmusik. Geschichte der Kantoren, Organisten und Stadtpfeifer seit der Reformation* (1932); *Der deutsche Kantor* (1933); *Freie Musikgemeinschaften im mitteldeutschen Raum* (1940).

Werner, Eric, musicologist; b. Lundenberg, near Vienna, Aug. 1, 1901. He studied composition with Kornauth in Vienna, and with Schrecker and Busoni in Berlin; also took courses at the univs. of Graz, Vienna, Prague, Berlin, Göttingen, and Strasbourg; received his Ph.D. in 1928 from the Univ. of Strasbourg; held teaching positions in Saarbrücken (1926–33) and Breslau (1935–38). In 1938 he settled in the U.S. He is an authority on Jewish and early Christian music; publ. *In the Choir Loft* (N.Y., 1957); *The Sacred Bridge* (London, 1958); *Mendelssohn: A New Image of the Composer and His Age* (N.Y., 1963); *A Voice Still Heard: the Sacred Songs of the Ashkenazic Jews* (Philadelphia, 1976); composed a *Symphony-Requiem;* chamber music; various other pieces.

Werner, Gregor Joseph, Austrian music scholar and composer; b. Ybbs, Lower Austria (baptized, Jan. 29), 1693; d. Eisenstadt, March 3, 1766. In 1728 he was appointed Kapellmeister to Prince Esterházy at Eisenstadt; in 1761 Haydn was named Vice-Kapellmeister, and succeeded him after his death. Werner wrote a number of works, including 40 masses, 18 oratorios, and many instrumental pieces. Haydn had great respect for him, and arranged his fugues for string quartet. Among modern reprints are his *Hirtenkantate, Hirtenmusik, Kleine Hirtenmusik,* etc., edited by E.F. Schmid; other pieces appeared in *Das Erbe deutscher Musik* (vol. 31).

Werner, Heinrich, German composer; b. Kirch-ohmfeld, Oct. 2, 1800; d. Braunschweig, May 3, 1833. His song *Haidenröslein* became a perennial favorite in Germany; he also publ. male quartets and light piano music.

BIBLIOGRAPHY: Fr. Mecke, *Heinrich Werner* (Diss., Univ. of Bonn, 1913); P. Egert, *Festschrift zur Einweihung des Denkmals für den Komponisten Heinrich Werner in Kirchohmfeld* (1910).

Werner, Johann Gottlob, German organist and teacher; b. Grossenhain, 1777; d. Chemnitz, July 19, 1822. After holding minor positions as an organist in provincial towns, he was appointed cathedral organist and music director at Merseburg, but died 3 years later. He publ. organ methods which were much in use: *Orgelschule* (1805; Part II as *Lehrbuch, das Orgelwerk ... kennen ... zu lernen,* 1823; both often republ.); *Musikalisches ABC* for beginners on the piano (1806; often republ.); *Choralbuch zum holländischen Psalm- und Gesangbuch* (1814); *Choralbuch zu den neuern sächsischen Gesangbüchern* (Leipzig); *Versuch einer kurzen und deutlichen Darstellung der Harmonielehre* (2 parts, 1818, 1819); many chorale preludes; 40 organ pieces for beginners; etc.

Werner, Josef, German cellist; b. Würzburg, June 25, 1837; d. Munich, Nov. 14, 1922. He studied at the Würzburg Cons.; became a teacher at the Munich Musikschule; publ. *Praktische Violoncell-Schule* (with 7 supplements); *Der erste Anfang im Violoncellspiel;* several books of *Übungen für Violoncell;* numerous pieces for cello with piano; a Quartet for 4 Cellos.

Werner, Theodor Wilhelm, German writer on music; b. Hannover, June 8, 1874; d. Salzburg, Dec. 6, 1957. He studied philology; then music with Draeseke and Noren in Dresden; musicology with Johannes Wolf in Berlin and with Sandberger and Kroyer in Munich; received a Dr.Phil. in 1917. He became an instructor at Hannover; also wrote music criticism; from 1945 lived in Salzburg. He publ. *Musik in Frankreich* (1927); edited works by G. Benda (Denkmäler Deutscher Tonkunst, 64), Telemann (*Das Erbe deutscher Musik,* 6), and others; composed 2 symphs.; 2 string quartets; choruses.

Wernick, Richard, American composer; b. Boston, Jan. 16, 1934. He studied composition with Irving Fine, Harold Shapero, and Arthur Berger at Brandeis Univ. (B.A., 1955) and with Leon Kirchner at Mills College in Oakland, Calif. (M.A., 1957); also took lessons in composition with Ernst Toch, Boris Blacher, and Aaron Copland and in conducting with Leonard Bernstein and Seymour Lipkin at the Berkshire Music Center in Tanglewood (1954, 1955). He composed much music for the theater, films, and television between 1953 and 1962; was for a season music director and composer-in-residence of the Royal Winnipeg Ballet of Canada (1957–58). He taught at the State Univ. of N.Y. at Buffalo (1964–65) and at the Univ. of Chicago (1965–68). In 1968 he joined the faculty of the Univ. of Pa.; was made a prof. of music there in 1977. In 1976 he received a Guggenheim fellowship. He was awarded the Pulitzer Prize in Music in 1977 for his *Visions of Terror and Wonder.* In his early compositions he integrated the techniques of all his teachers, but ultimately fashioned an individual style of his own.

WORKS: Duo Concertante for Cello and Piano (1960); Trio for Violin, Clarinet, and Cello (1961); *Hexagrams* for Chamber Orch. (1962); String Quartet No. 1 (1963); *Music* for Viola d'Amore (1964); *Stretti* for Clarinet, Violin, Viola, and Guitar (1965); *Lyrics from IXI* for Soprano, Vibraphone-Marimba, and Contrabass, after e.e. cummings (1966); *Aevia* for Orch. (1966); *Haiku of Bashō* for Soprano, Flute, Clarinet, Violin, Contrabass, 2 Percussion Instruments, Piano, and Tape (1968); *Moonsongs from the Japanese* for Soprano and 2 prerecorded tracks of Soprano Voice (1969); *Cadenzas and Variations II* for Violin (1970); *A Prayer for Jerusalem* for Mezzo-soprano and Percussion (1971); *Kaddish Requiem,* a "secular service for the victims of Indo-China" for Mezzo-soprano, Chamber Ensemble, and Tape (1971); *Cadenzas and Variations III* for Cello (1972); String Quartet No. 2 (1972–73); *Songs of Remembrance* for Shawm, English Horn, Oboe, and Mezzo-soprano (1973); *Visions of Terror and Wonder* for Mezzo-soprano and Orch., to texts from the Bible and the Koran, in Hebrew, Arabic, and Greek (Aspen Music Festival, July 19, 1976); *Contemplations of the Tenth Muse, Books I–II* for Soprano (1977, 1979); *Introits and Canons* for Chamber Ensemble (1977); Partita for Violin (1978); "And on the Seventh Day—," sacred service for Cantor and Percussion Players (1979); *A Poison Tree* for Flute, Clarinet, Violin, Cello, Piano, and Soprano (1979); Concerto for Cello and 10 Players (1979); *Formula: P--- ----m* for Chamber Ensemble (1981); Piano Sonata (1982); Sonata for Cello and Piano, *Portraits of Antiquity* (1982); *The Oracle of Shimon Bar Yochai* for Cello, Piano, and Soprano (1982); Concerto for Violin and Orch. (1984).

Werrekoren (Verecoren, Werrecore), Hermann Mathias, 16th-century German composer. He was maestro di cappella in Milan (1522–57); his principal work is a descriptive composition for 4 Voices a cappella entitled *Die Schlacht vor Pavia (The Battle of Pavia),* publ. in Schmeltzl's collection *Guter seltzamer ... teutscher Gesang* (Nuremberg, 1544) and reprinted by Gardano in Venice in 1549 as *La battaglia taliana;* he also publ. a book of motets for 4 Voices (1555); various other motets were publ. in the collections of the period. Werrekoren was mistakenly identified with Matthäus Le Maistre by Fétis and Kade; research by Haberl, Elsa Bienenfeld, and Cecie Stainer demonstrated the fallacy of this assumption.

BIBLIOGRAPHY: Haberl's articles in *Kirchenmusikalisches Jahrbuch* (1871 and 1873); Elsa Bienenfeld in *Sammelbände der Internationalen*

Musik-Gesellschaft (1904–5).

Werrenrath, Reinald, American baritone; b. Brooklyn, Aug. 7, 1883; d. Plattsburg, N.Y., Sept. 12, 1953. He was a pupil of his father, a tenor; then studied with David Bispham and Herbert Witherspoon. He began his career as a concert singer; also in oratorio; made his operatic debut on Feb. 19, 1919, at the Metropolitan Opera House in N.Y., as Silvio in *Pagliacci*, and remained with the company until 1921; then devoted himself to teaching and concert singing; appeared in public for the last time at Carnegie Hall in N.Y., on Oct. 23, 1952. He edited *Modern Scandinavian Songs* (2 vols.; Boston, 1925–26). He was married 3 times: to Ada Peterson (1909; divorced, 1927), to Verna True Nidig (1928; divorced, 1941), and to Frances M. Aston (1942).

Wert, Giaches de (Jakob van Wert), Flemish contrapuntist; b. Weert, between May 6 and Aug. 18, 1535; d. Mantua, May 6, 1596. He was a boy chorister in the retinue of Maria di Cardona, Marchesa della Padulla, and followed the household to Italy. At the age of 9 he entered the ducal choir at Novellara; in 1549 he went to Ferrara to study with Cyprian de Rore. In 1558 he was appointed maestro di cappella at the court at Novellara; then joined the court chapel of the Duke of Mantua, who appointed him maestro di cappella in 1565. He held this position until his death, with an interval as vice-maestro at Novellara (1567–74); from 1565 to 1583 was also choirmaster of the Church of Santa Barbara in Mantua. He was greatly esteemed by contemporary musicians; Palestrina praised him, and he was also mentioned favorably by Thomas Morley, Artusi, G.B. Doni, and Monteverdi. His compositions were included in many collections of sacred and secular music, beginning in 1558. He publ. 11 books of madrigals for 5 voices, one for 4 voices, and one for 5 and 6 voices; one book of canzonets, and 3 of motets for 5 and 6 voices. 16 vols. of his collected works were publ. in Rome, 1961—.
BIBLIOGRAPHY: A.-M. Bautier-Regnier, "Jacques de Wert," *Revue Belge de Musicologie* (1950); G. Reese, *Music in the Renaissance* (N.Y., 1954; 2nd ed., revised, 1959); C. MacClintock, "Some Notes on the Secular Music of Giaches de Wert," *Musica Disciplina*, 10 (1956); idem, *Giaches de Wert (1535–1596): Life and Works*, in *Musicological Studies and Documents*, XVII (1966); idem, "New Light on Giaches de Wert," in *Aspects of Medieval and Renaissance Music: A Birthday Offering to Gustave Reese* (N.Y., 1966).

Wesembeek. See **Burbure de Wesembeek.**

Wesendonck, Mathilde (née **Luckemeyer**), German poetess, friend of Wagner; b. Elberfeld, Dec. 23, 1828; d. at her villa, Traunblick, near Altmünster on the Traunsee, Austria, Aug. 31, 1902. Her first meeting with Wagner took place in Zürich, early in 1852, and soon developed into a deep friendship. She wrote the famous *Fünf Gedichte (Der Engel, Stehe still, Träume, Schmerzen, Im Treibhaus)*, which Wagner set to music as studies for *Tristan und Isolde*. On May 19, 1848, she married **Otto Wesendonck** (b. March 16, 1815; d. Berlin, Nov. 18, 1896); in 1857 he gave Wagner the use of a beautiful house on his estate on Lake Zürich, where the first act of *Tristan und Isolde* was written, and the 2nd act sketched.
BIBLIOGRAPHY: A. Heintz, "Meine Erinnerungen" (reminiscences of Mathilde Wesendonck), in *Allgemeine Musikzeitung* (Feb. 14, 1896); W. Golther, ed., *Richard Wagner an Mathilde Wesendonck. Tagebuchblätter und Briefe* (Berlin, 1904; many subsequent eds.; Eng. trans., London, 1905); W. Golther, ed., *Briefe Richard Wagners an Otto Wesendonck* (Berlin, 8th printing, 1905; in Eng., London, 1911); H. Bélart, *Richard Wagners Liebestragödie mit Mathilde Wesendonck* (Dresden, 1912); E.H. Müller von Asow, ed., *Johannes Brahms und Mathilde Wesendonck; Ein Briefwechsel* (Vienna, 1943).

Wesley, Charles, English organist and harpsichord player; nephew of **John Wesley;** b. Bristol, Dec. 11, 1757; d. London, May 23, 1834. He was a pupil of Kelway and Boyce in London; then held various positions as a church organist; publ. *6 Concertos for the Organ or Harpsichord*, op. 1; anthems; hymns; etc.; 6 string quartets. He was the brother and teacher of **Samuel Wesley.**
BIBLIOGRAPHY: R. Green, *Works of John and Charles Wesley* (London, 1896); R.S. Stevenson, in *Notes* (March 1970, pp. 515–17).

Wesley, John, founder of the Wesleyan Methodist Church; b. Epworth, June 17, 1703; d. London, March 2, 1791. He was educated at Christ Church, Oxford; in 1735 he came to America with his brother Charles to do missionary work, and 2 years later publ. his first *Collection of Psalms and Hymns* (Charlestown, 1737). Returning to England, he spread the doctrine of Methodism and became famous as a preacher and writer. He has been called "the father of Methodist hymnology."
BIBLIOGRAPHY: R. Green, *Works of John and Charles Wesley* (London, 1896); J.T. Lightwood, *Methodist Music in the 18th Century* (London, 1927); J.L. Nuelsen, *John Wesley und das deutsche Kirchenlied* (Bremen, 1938).

Wesley, Samuel, English organist and composer; brother of **Charles Wesley;** nephew of **John Wesley;** b. Bristol, Feb. 24, 1766; d. London, Oct. 11, 1837. He studied with his brother, and began to compose at the age of 8; learned to play the violin as well as the organ. He publ. *Eight Lessons for the Harpsichord* when he was 11 (1777). Subsequently he developed his fine talent as an organist and was generally regarded as the greatest performer and improviser of his time. Although he suffered from a skull injury as a result of a fall, which seriously interfered with his activities, he continued to give public concerts till the year of his death.
WORKS: 11 organ concertos; voluntaries, preludes, and fugues for organ; 4 symphs.; 4 overtures;

2 string quartets; String Quintet; Trio for Oboe, Violin, and Cello; Trio for 2 Flutes and Piano; much church music, including 4 masses, motets, several services, anthems, and psalm-tunes; choral pieces; songs; vocal duets; a number of rondos for piano, based on popular songs and on operatic arias; also numerous glees, for 3 and 4 voices.

BIBLIOGRAPHY: W. Winters, *An Account of the Remarkable Musical Talents of Several Members of the Wesley Family* (London, 1874); E. Wesley (his daughter), *Letters of Samuel Wesley to Mr. Jacobs relating to the Introduction into this Country of the Works of Bach* (London, 1875; 2nd ed., 1878); G.J. Stevenson, *Memorials of the Wesley Family* (London, 1876); J.T. Lightwood, *Samuel Wesley, Musician: The Story of His Life* (London, 1937); E. Douthey, *The Musical Wesleys* (London, 1968).

Wesley, Samuel Sebastian, English organist and composer; natural son of **Samuel Wesley;** b. London, Aug. 14, 1810; d. Gloucester, April 19, 1876. He was a boy chorister at the Chapel Royal; from the age of 16 held appointments as an organist in London churches; in 1832, he became organist of Hereford Cathedral; in 1835, at Exeter Cathedral; in 1842, at Leeds Parish Church; in 1849, at Winchester Cathedral; in 1865, at Gloucester Cathedral. He received the degrees of B.Mus. and D.Mus. at Oxford (1839). His works include 4 church services; 2 Psalms; 27 anthems; several glees; an *Ode to Labour* (1864); pieces for organ; songs. He publ. *A Few Words on Cathedral Music and the Musical System of the Church, with a Plan of Reform* (1849).

BIBLIOGRAPHY: G.J. Stevenson, *Memorials of the Wesley Family* (London, 1876); E. Douthey, *The Musical Wesleys* (London, 1968).

Wessel, Mark, American composer; b. Goldwater, Mich., March 26, 1894; d. Beverly Hills, Mich., May 2, 1973. He studied at Northwestern Univ. (M.M., 1918); then went to Europe and had instruction with Schoenberg in Vienna (1922). Returning to America, he was active primarily as a teacher. He wrote a Symph. (1932); 2 piano concertos; *Plains and Mountains* for Piano and String Quartet (1937); Sextet for Piano and 5 Wind Instruments; 2 cello sonatas; piano pieces.

West, Dottie, American country-music singer; b. McMinnville, Tenn., Oct. 11, 1932. After receiving an A.B. degree from Tennessee Tech., she launched her career as a singer and songwriter; with her first husband, **Bill West,** she wrote the hit *Here Comes My Baby,* and soon after, she became a regular performer at the Grand Ole Opry in Nashville; she also toured widely and made recordings.

West, John Ebenezer, English organist and composer; b. London, Dec. 7, 1863; d. there, Feb. 28, 1929. He was a nephew of **Ebenezer Prout,** and studied with him at the Royal Academy of Music; was organist and choirmaster at various London churches; in 1884 was appointed to the editorial staff of Novello & Co. He wrote 2 cantatas, *The*

Healing of the Canaanite's Daughter (1882) and *Seed-time and Harvest* (1892); several church services and anthems; an orch. march, *Victoria, Our Queen;* organ music; publ. an important book, *Cathedral Organists* (London, 1899; new ed., 1921).

Westbrook, William Joseph, English organist and composer; b. London, Jan. 1, 1831; d. Sydenham, March 24, 1894. He was an organist at several churches in London; in 1851 was appointed to St. Bartholomew's, Sydenham, and held this post until his death. In 1862 he founded the periodical *Musical Standard* (with Hammond and Crowdy). He wrote an oratorio, *Jesus;* a cantata, *The Lord Is My Shepherd;* services; anthems; part-songs; sonatas and voluntaries for organ; several textbooks on the organ; etc.

Westenburg, Richard, American conductor; b. Minneapolis, April 26, 1932. He studied at Lawrence Univ. (B.Mus., 1954) and at the Univ. of Minnesota (M.A., 1956); then went to Paris, where he studied with Nadia Boulanger and Pierre Cochereau (1959–60); subsequently did postgraduate work at the Theological Seminary School of Sacred Music in N.Y. (1960–66). From 1956–60 he taught music at the Univ. of Montana; then served as director of music at the First Unitarian Church in Worcester, Mass. (1960–62). In 1964 he went to N.Y., where he was engaged as organist and choirmaster of the Central Presbyterian Church, holding this position until 1974. In 1968 he became music director of Musica Sacra; also served as music director of the Collegiate Chorale (1973–79). He became music director of the Cathedral Church of St. John the Divine in 1974. In 1977 he was appointed head of the choral dept. of the Juilliard School of Music.

Westerberg, Stig, Swedish conductor; b. Malmö, Nov. 26, 1918. He was educated at the Royal College of Music in Stockholm; made his conducting debut in Stockholm in 1945; was appointed conductor of the Gävleborg Symph. (1949–53); then conducted at the Royal Opera in Stockholm (1953–57). In 1957 he was named a conductor with the Swedish Radio Symph. in Stockholm, with which he presented many contemporary scores; also appeared as a guest conductor throughout Europe. In 1978 he became chief conductor of the Malmö Symph. Orch.

Westergaard, Peter, American composer and pedagogue; b. Champaign, Ill., May 28, 1931. He studied composition at Harvard Univ. with Walter Piston (A.B., 1953); then had fruitful sessions with Sessions at Princeton Univ. (M.F.A., 1956). In 1956 he went to Germany, where he studied with Fortner in Detmold. Returning to the U.S., he joined the music faculty of Columbia Univ., N.Y. (1958–66); then was at Amherst (1967–68); in 1968 became associate prof. at Princeton Univ.; prof. in 1971; was chairman of the music dept., 1974–78. He publ. *An Introduction to Tonal Theory* (N.Y., 1974). In his music he explores the possibility of total organization of tones, rhythms, and other elements of composition.

WORKS: Chamber operas: *Charivari* (1953) and *Mr. and Mrs. Discobbolos* (N.Y., 1966); *Symphonic Movement* (1954); *5 Movements* for Small Orch. (1958); *Invention* for Flute and Piano (1955); Quartet for Violin, Vibraphone, Clarinet, and Cello (1961); Trio for Flute, Cello, and Piano (1962); *Variations* for 6 Instruments (1964); *Divertimento on Discobolic Fragments* for Flute and Piano (1967); *Noises, Sounds and Sweet Airs* for Flute, Clarinet, Horn, Trumpet, Celesta, Harpsichord, Percussion, and Strings (1968); cantatas: *The Plot Against the Giant*, to words by Wallace Stevens (1956); *A Refusal to Mourn the Death, by Fire, of a Child in London* for Bass and 10 Instruments, to words by Dylan Thomas (1958); *Leda and the Swan* for Mezzo-soprano, Clarinet, Viola, Vibraphone, and Marimba (1961); *Spring and Fall: To a Young Child* for Voice and Piano (1960); *Moto perpetuo* for 6 Wind Instruments (1976).

Westergaard, Svend, Danish composer; b. Copenhagen, Oct. 8, 1922. He studied composition with Høffding, Hjelmborg, and Jersild at the Royal Danish Cons. in Copenhagen, graduating in 1947; began teaching there in 1951; was a prof. of theory from 1967; also its director (1967–71).

WORKS: *Elegy* for Strings (1949); *Pezzo sinfonico* (1950); Oboe Concerto (1950); 2 symphs.: No. 1, *Sinfonia* (1955), and No. 2, *Sinfonia da camera* (1968); *L'Homme armé*, canzona for 16 Instruments (1959); *Capriccio* for Violin and String Orch. (1960); *Variazioni sinfoniche* (Danish Radio, June 12, 1961); Cello Concerto (Aarhus, Oct. 22, 1962); *Pezzo concertante* for Orch. (Danish Radio, Aug. 19, 1965); *Sinfonia da camera* (Copenhagen, March 24, 1969); *Varianti sinfoniche* for Winds and Percussion (1972); 2 wind quintets (1948, 1949); *Tema con variazioni* for Clarinet Quintet (1949); String Quartet (1968); Sonata for Solo Flute (1971).

Westerhout, Niccolò van. See **Van Westerhout, Niccolò.**

Westlake, Frederick, English pianist and composer; b. Romsey, Hampshire, Feb. 25, 1840; d. London, Feb. 12, 1898. He studied at the Royal Academy of Music with W. Macfarren (piano) and G.A. Macfarren (harmony); in 1862 was appointed to the faculty as a piano teacher. He wrote several masses, hymns, piano pieces, and a collection of part-songs, *Lyra Studentium.*

Westmorland, John Fane, Earl of (Lord Burghersh), English composer; b. London, Feb. 3, 1784; d. Apthorpe House, Northants, Oct. 16, 1859. He was in the British army, fought in the Spanish campaign and in Egypt, attaining the rank of general in 1854; also occupied various diplomatic posts between wars. He studied music in Lisbon with Marcos Portugal (1809–12); was a founder of the Royal Academy of Music in London (1822). He wrote 7 Italian operas; the following were performed at his own palace in Florence (where he served as British Resi-

dent): *Fedra* (Nov. 17, 1824); *L'Eroe di Lancastro* (June 13, 1829); *Lo scompiglio teatrale* (1830). Other works include several church services; some piano music; also *Sinfonia in D* for Orch. A list of his works is in W.W. Cazelet's *The History of the Royal Academy of Music* (London, 1854).

Westphal, Rudolf (Georg Hermann), notable German music scholar; b. Oberkirchen, July 3, 1826; d. Stadthagen, July 10, 1892. He was a student of classical philology in Marburg; taught at the Univ. of Breslau (1858–62); then went to Moscow as a teacher at a lyceum (1875–80); subsequently lived in Leipzig, Bückeburg, and Stadthagen. He wrote numerous learned papers on Greek music, and maintained that the Greeks employed polyphony, a theory that he himself eventually abandoned as untenable.

WRITINGS: *Metrik der griechischen Dramatiker und Lyriker* (with Rossbach; 3 vols., 1854–63; 3rd ed. as *Theorie der musischen Künste der Hellenen*, 1885–89); *Die Fragmente und Lehrsätze der griechischen Rhythmiker* (1861); *System der antiken Rhythmik* (1865); *Geschichte der alten und mittelalterlichen Musik* (1865; unfinished; includes *Plutarch über die Musik*, 1864); *Theorie der neuhochdeutschen Metrik* (1870; 2nd ed., 1877); *Elemente des musikalischen Rhythmus mit besonderer Rücksicht auf unsre Opernmusik* (1872); *Allgemeine Theorie der musikalischen Rhythmik seit J.S. Bach* (1880); *Die Musik des griechischen Altertums* (1883); *Allgemeine Metrik der indo-germanischen und semitischen Völker auf Grundlage der vergleichenden Sprachwissenschaft* (1892; with addendum by R. Kruse, *Der griechische Hexameter in der deutschen Nachdichtung*); *Metrik und Rhythmik des klassischen Hallenentums* (2 vols., 1883–93).

Westrup, Sir Jack Allan, eminent English musicologist; b. London, July 26, 1904; d. Headley, Hampshire, April 21, 1975. He received his education at Dulwich College, London, and at Balliol College, Oxford (B.Mus., 1926; M.A., 1929). He was an assistant classics master at Dulwich College (1928–34); then was a music critic for the *Daily Telegraph* (1934–39); also was editor of the *Monthly Musical Record* (1933–45). He was actively engaged in musical education. He gave classes at the Royal Academy of Music (1938–40); then was lecturer in music at King's College, Newcastle upon Tyne (1941–44), the Univ. of Birmingham (1944–47), and Wadham College (1947–71). In 1946 he received an honorary degree of D.Mus. at Oxford Univ. In 1947 he was named chairman of the editorial board of *The New Oxford History of Music*. In 1959 he succeeded Eric Blom as editor of *Music & Letters*. From 1958–63 he was president of the Royal Musical Assoc. He was also active as a conductor; he conducted the Oxford Opera Club (1947–62), the Oxford Univ. Orch. (1954–63), and the Oxford Bach Choir and Oxford Orch. Society (1970–71). He was knighted in 1961.

PUBLICATIONS: He prepared major revisions of Walker's *A History of Music in England* (Oxford,

3rd ed., 1952) and of Fellowes's *English Cathedral Music* (London, 5th ed., 1969); he also supervised revised eds. of Blom's *Everyman's Dictionary of Music* (4th ed., 1962; 5th ed., 1971). He was co-editor, with F. Harrison, of the *Collins Music Encyclopedia* (London, 1959; American ed. as *The New College Encyclopedia of Music*, N.Y., 1960). His other publications include *Purcell* (London, 1940); *Sharps and Flats* (a vol. of selected articles; London, 1940); *British Music* (London, 1943; 3rd ed., 1949); *The Meaning of Musical History* (London, 1946); *An Introduction to Musical History* (London, 1955); *Music: Its Past and Its Present* (Washington, D.C., 1964); *Bach Cantatas* (London, 1966); *Schubert Chamber Music* (London, 1969); *Musical Interpretation* (London, 1971).
BIBLIOGRAPHY: F. Sternfeld and others, eds., *Essays on Opera and English Music in Honour of Sir Jack Westrup* (Oxford, 1975).

Wettergren, Gertrud (née **Palson**), Swedish contralto; b. Eslöv, Feb. 17, 1897. She studied at the Stockholm Cons., and later in London; made her operatic debut at the Royal Opera in Stockholm in 1922, and remained on its roster for 27 years. On Dec. 20, 1935, she appeared at the Metropolitan Opera House, as Amneris in *Aida;* sang there until 1938; also sang with the Chicago City Opera (1936–38); then returned to Sweden. In 1925 she married Erik Wettergren (director of the National Museum of Stockholm).

Wetz, Richard, German composer and teacher; b. Gleiwitz, Feb. 26, 1875; d. Erfurt, Jan. 16, 1935. He studied with R. Hofmann in Leipzig and Thuille in Munich; in 1906 went to Erfurt as a choral conductor and teacher; also taught in Weimar.
WORKS: Opera, *Das ewige Feuer* (Düsseldorf, March 19, 1907); *Kleist-Ouvertüre; Traumsommernacht* for Women's Chorus and Orch.; *Gesang des Lebens* for Male Chorus and Orch.; *Nicht geboren ist das Beste* for Mixed Chorus and Orch.; *Hyperion* for Baritone Solo, Chorus, and Orch.; about 100 songs. He publ. monographs on Bruckner (1922), Liszt (1925), and Beethoven (1927; 2nd ed., 1933). A Richard Wetz Society was founded in Gleiwitz in 1943.
BIBLIOGRAPHY: G. Armin, *Die Lieder von Richard Wetz* (Leipzig, 1911); E.L. Schellenberg, *Richard Wetz* (Leipzig, 1911; 2nd ed., 1914); H. Polack, *Richard Wetz. Sein Werk* (Leipzig, 1935).

Wetzel, Justus Hermann, German composer and musicologist; b. Kyritz, March 11, 1879; d. Überlingen (Bodensee), Dec. 6, 1973. He studied natural sciences, philosophy, and art history (Dr.Phil., 1901); then took up music, and was a teacher at the Riemann Cons. in Stettin (1905–7); settled in Berlin in 1910; taught at the Academy for Church and School Music (from 1925; became a prof. in 1935). He composed about 400 songs; choral works; chamber music; piano pieces; edited and arranged several collections of German songs.
BIBLIOGRAPHY: F. Welter, *Justus Hermann*

Wetzel (Berlin, 1931; with list of works).

Wetzler, Hermann Hans, German-American conductor and composer; b. Frankfurt, Sept. 8, 1870; d. New York, May 29, 1943. He was brought to the U.S. as a child, but in 1882 returned to Germany, where he studied at Hoch's Cons. in Frankfurt with Clara Schumann (piano), Iwan Knorr (counterpoint), and Humperdinck (instrumentation). In 1892 he went to N.Y.; was a church organist for several years; in 1903 he established the Wetzler Symph. Concerts, which had considerable success; Richard Strauss conducted a series of 4 concerts of his own works with the Wetzler group (Feb.–March, 1904), including the world premiere of the *Sinfonia domestica.* In 1905 Wetzler went to Europe again; conducted opera in various German cities and in Basel. In 1940 he returned to the U.S. He composed an opera, *Die baskische Venus* (Leipzig, Nov. 18, 1928); *Assisi,* legend for Orch. written in commemoration of the 700th anniversary of the death of St. Francis of Assisi (1925); *Symphonic Dance in Basque Style* (1927); *Symphonie concertante,* for Violin and Orch. (1932); chamber music; choral works; songs.

Weweler, August, German composer; b. Reike, Oct. 20, 1868; d. Detmold, Dec. 8, 1952. He studied at the Leipzig Cons. with Jadassohn and others; in 1898 settled in Detmold as a teacher. He composed the operas *Dornröschen* (Kassel, 1903) and *Der grobe Märker* (Detmold, 1908); the oratorio *Die Sintflut* (Detmold, 1914); a ballet, *Des Malers Traumbild;* male choruses and piano pieces. He publ. *Ave Musica! Das Wesen der Tonkunst und die modernen Bestrebungen* (1913; 2nd ed., 1919).

Weymarn, Pavel, Russian writer on music and composer; b. St. Petersburg, 1857; d. Narva, Sept. 22, 1905. He studied piano and theory at the St. Petersburg Cons.; in 1888–90 edited the music periodical *Bayan;* publ. monographs on Napravnik (1889) and Cui (1897); was music critic for several Russian newspapers. He composed a String Quartet and some piano pieces and songs.

Weyrauch, August Heinrich von, German song composer; b. Riga, April 30, 1788; date of death unknown. In 1824 he publ. (under his own name) a song, *Nach Osten* (words by Wetzel). About 1840 an anonymous Paris publisher reprinted it, with Schubert's name on the title page, as *Adieu* (French words by Bélanger); a piano transcription of it, also crediting the authorship to Schubert, was publ. by Döhler in Germany (1843); Schlesinger of Berlin reprinted the song, with a German trans. of the French text, as Schubert's in 1845; since then it has been reprinted many times as Schubert's by European and American publishers.
BIBLIOGRAPHY: O.E. Deutsch, *Schubert: Thematic Catalogue of All His Works in Chronological Order* (London, 1951, p. 491).

Weyse, Christoph Ernst Friedrich, German-Danish composer; b. Altona, March 5, 1774; d. Copenhagen, Oct. 8, 1842. He was a pupil of his grandfather, a cantor at Altona; in 1789 he went to Copenhagen, where he studied with J.A.P. Schulz. In 1794 he was appointed organist at the Reformed Church; in 1805 became organist at the Fruekirke; in 1819 he was appointed court composer. Through the court conductor Kunzen he became interested in a movement for the establishment of a national school of Danish opera, for which his works (together with those of Kuhlau) effectively prepared the way.

WORKS: Operas (all perf. in Copenhagen): *Sovedrikken* (*The Sleeping-Potion;* April 21, 1809); *Faruk* (Jan. 30, 1812); *Ludlams hule* (*Ludlam's Cave;* Jan. 30, 1816); *Floribella* (Jan. 29, 1825); *Eventyr i Rosenborg have* (*Adventure in Rosenborg Gardens;* May 26, 1827); *Balders død* (*The Death of Baldur;* Nov. 23, 1832); *Festen paa Kenilworth* (after Walter Scott; Jan. 6, 1836); about 30 cantatas; *Miserere* for Double Chorus and Orch.; *Te Deum* for Chorus and Orch.; 4 symphs.; preludes and fugues for organ; piano pieces (including sonatas and études); songs. He collected 100 Danish folk songs, of which he harmonized 59; they were publ. by his pupil A.P. Berggreen as *100 gamle kæmpevisemelodier (Old Ballad Melodies).* A thematic and bibliographic catalogue of his works was publ. in Copenhagen (1979).

BIBLIOGRAPHY: A.P. Berggreen, *C.E.F. Weyses biographie* (in Danish; Copenhagen, 1876); R. von Liliencron, "Weyse und die dänische Musik seit dem vorigen Jahrhundert," in Raumer-Riehl, *Historisches Taschenbuch* (Leipzig, 1878); W. Behrend, "Weyse und Kuhlau," *Die Musik*, III/22 (1904); J.P. Larsen, *Weyses romancer og sange* (Copenhagen, 1944).

Whear, Paul William, American composer; b. Auburn, Ind., Nov. 13, 1925. He studied engineering at Marquette Univ. (B.N.S.), DePauw Univ. (B.A.), and Case Western Reserve Univ. (Ph.D.); then made a 180° turn toward the art of music; attended classes of Gardner Read at Boston Univ. and of Wayne Barlow at the Eastman School of Music in Rochester, N.Y. From 1960 to 1969 Whear served as chairman of the music dept. at Doane College; in 1969 was appointed a prof. of music and chairman of the theory and composition dept. at Marshall Univ. He wrote 4 symphs.; Symph. No. 2 (1971) is subtitled *The Bridge;* Symph. No. 3 (1975), *The Galleries;* Symph. No. 4 is for Band (1979). He also wrote overtures, chamber music, and choral works.

White, Clarence Cameron, black American violinist and composer; b. Clarksville, Tenn., Aug. 10, 1880; d. New York, June 30, 1960. He studied at Howard Univ. and the Oberlin Cons.; in London with Samuel Coleridge-Taylor, and in Paris with Laparra; held various positions as a violinist and teacher in Boston, at West Virginia State College, and at the Hampton Inst. He won the Harmon Foundation Award and the Rosenwald Foundation Fellowship for composition; also the David Bispham Medal, for his opera *Ouanga,* to a libretto by John F. Matheus

from a Haitian historic episode (concert perf., Chicago, Nov. 1932; stage perf., South Bend, Ind., June 10, 1949). His *Elegy* for Orch. won the 1954 Benjamin Award for "tranquil music" (New Orleans, March 16, 1954); he also composed, for violin, *Bandana Sketches* (1920), *Cabin Memories* (1921), and *From the Cotton Fields* (1921); for Orch.: Symph. in D minor, *Piece for Strings and Timpani,* and *Kutamba;* ballet, *A Night in Sans Souci;* he arranged for voice and piano *40 Negro Spirituals* (1927) and *Traditional Negro Spirituals* (1940); also wrote exercises for violin.

White, Donald H(oward), American composer and pedagogue; b. Narberth, Pa., Feb. 28, 1921. He studied with Bernard Rogers and Howard Hanson at the Eastman School of Music in Rochester, N.Y. After graduation he was appointed to the music faculty of DePauw Univ. in Greencastle, Ind., in 1947; was named a full prof. in 1951; in 1981 became a prof. and chairman of the music dept. at Central Washington State College in Ellensburg.

WORKS: *Andante* for Oboe, Harp, and Strings (1951); Cello Concerto (1952); *3 for 5* for Woodwind Quintet (1958); *Serenade* for Orch. (1962); *Divertissement No. 1* for Clarinet Choir (1965); Sonata for Trombone and Piano (1966); *Divertissement No. 2* for String Orch. (1968); *Lyric Suite* for Euphonium and Piano (1970); *Tetra Ergon* for Bass Trombone and Piano (1972); band pieces; choruses.

White, Eric Walter, English writer on music; b. Bristol, Sept. 10, 1905. He studied at Oxford Univ.: was a member of the Secretariat of the League of Nations (1929–33), subsequently of the National Council of Social Service, London (1935–42) and of the Council for the Encouragement of the Arts Council of Great Britain (from 1946). He publ. a fundamental biography of Stravinsky (London, 1947) and a highly valuable annotated catalogue of Stravinsky's works (Berkeley and Los Angeles, 1966); a monograph, *Benjamin Britten* (London, 1948; new ed., 1954); *The Rise of English Opera* (London, 1951); *A History of English Opera* (London, 1983); *A Register of First Performances of English Operas and Semi-Operas from the 16th Century to 1980* (London, 1983); numerous informative essays on modern composers.

White, Felix Harold, English composer; b. London, April 27, 1884; d. there, Jan. 31, 1945. He was born into a Jewish family originally named Weiss. He was mostly self-taught, except for some piano lessons from his mother. He was a keyboard player in the London Phil. Orch. (1933–35); concurrently was on the staff at Covent Garden. He devoted himself mainly to composition; also was active as a writer on music; publ. a *Dictionary of Musical Terms;* wrote short biographical monographs on noted musicians; edited the piano works of Scriabin.

WORKS: For Orch.: *Shylock,* overture (London, 1907); *Polonaise in B minor* (1908); *Astarte Syriaca,* tone poem after D.G. Rossetti (1909; London, 1911); *Meditation* (1911; Bournemouth, 1923); Suite (1913);

Impressions of England, suite (London, 1918); *The Deserted Village,* tone poem (1923); Nocturne (1936); Overture in F major (1937). Chamber music: Romance in D major for Cello and Piano (London, 1907); Cello Sonata (1910); *Dawn,* study for 12 Cellos (1922); Trio for Oboe or Violin, Viola, and Piano, a setting of Andrew Marvell's *The Nymph's Complaint for the Death of Her Fawn* (1922; Carnegie Award); *4 Proverbs* for Flute, Oboe, Violin, Viola, and Cello (1925; Carnegie Award); *Orison* for 4 Cellos (1937); choral works; 60 part-songs; about 250 songs; 80 piano pieces.

BIBLIOGRAPHY: S. Craggs, "Felix White: A Centenary Note," *Musical Times* (April 1984).

White, John, American organist and composer; b. West Springfield, Mass., March 12, 1855; d. Bad Nauheim, Germany, July 18, 1902. He studied organ with Dudley Buck in N.Y. and August Haupt in Berlin; composition with Rheinberger in Munich. He was organist of the Church of the Ascension in N.Y. from 1887 to 1896; then went back to Germany. He publ. *Missa solemnis; Requiem; Te Deum;* many Latin hymns for mixed chorus a cappella; an oratorio, *Alpha and Omega.*

White, John Reeves, American musicologist and conductor; b. Houston, Miss., May 2, 1924; d. New York, July 12, 1984. He studied at the Cincinnati Cons. (1941–43); also took courses at the Cons. National de Musique in Paris (1945); obtained his M.A. at Colorado College in 1948, and his Ph.D. at Indiana Univ. in 1952; also received the degree of Dr. of Natural Philosophy at the Inst. of Neuro-phenomenology in Amherst, Mass. (1975). He held teaching posts at Colorado College (1947–52), the Univ. of Richmond (1953–61), and Indiana Univ. (1961–66 and 1970–71); in 1971 was appointed to the faculty of Hunter College. From 1966 to 1970 he conducted concerts of the N.Y. Pro Musica; produced reconstructions of several medieval and Renaissance dramatic works, among them *An Entertainment for Elizabeth,* a 16th-century court masque; *The Play of the Risen Christ,* a 13th-century liturgical drama; *The Play of Mary,* a 14th-century liturgical drama; etc.; served as a specialist on cetacean vocalization at the N.Y. Zoological Society and was a member of the N.Y. Inst. for Comparative Neuro-phenomenology; edited *The Keyboard Tablature of Johannes of Lublin* (6 vols., Corpus of Early Keyboard Music No. 6, American Inst. of Musicology, 1964–67); *François Dandrieu, Harpsichord Music* (Pa. State Univ., 1965); *Michelangelo Rossi, Complete Keyboard Works* (Corpus of Early Keyboard Music No. 16, 1967); *The Arts between the Wars. A Symposium* (with John Dos Passos and Harriet Fitzgerald, 1964).

White, José, Cuban violinist and composer; b. Matanzas, Jan. 17, 1836; d. Paris, March 15, 1918. He went to Paris as a youth; studied violin with Alard at the Paris Cons., obtaining first prize in 1856. He served as court musician for the Emperor Pedro II of Brazil until 1889, then returned to Paris. He composed a Violin Concerto, a String Quartet, and some church music.

White, Maude Valérie, English composer; b. Dieppe, France (of English parents), June 23, 1855; d. London, Nov. 2, 1937. She studied with W.S. Rockstro; entered the Royal Academy of Music in 1876; was elected a Mendelssohn Scholar in 1879 (the first woman to win this honor); then continued her studies under Sir G. Macfarren, and later with R. Fuchs in Vienna. She traveled extensively through Europe and South America; lived in London, and for some years in Florence. She wrote a number of attractive songs to English, German, French, and Italian texts; a vocal quintet to Heine's poem *Du bist wie eine Blume;* an album of piano pieces, *Pictures from Abroad; Naissance d'amour* for Cello and Piano; etc. She publ. her memoirs, *Friends and Memories* (London, 1914), and *My Indian Summer* (London, 1932).

White, Michael, American composer; b. Chicago, March 6, 1931. He studied at the Chicago Musical College and at the Juilliard School of Music in N.Y., with Peter Mennin. In 1963 he received a Guggenheim fellowship and lived in Italy.

WORKS: *Fantasy* for Orch. (1957); *Suite* for Orch. (1959); *Gloria* for Chorus and Orch. (1960); *The Diary of Anne Frank* for Soprano and Orch. (1960); *Prelude and Ostinato* for String Orch. (1960); *The Dybbuk,* opera (1960–62); *Sleep, Little Lord* for Children's Chorus and Strings (1961); opera, *Through the Looking Glass,* after Lewis Carroll (1965); choruses; songs.

White, Paul, American violinist, composer, and conductor; b. Bangor, Maine, Aug. 22, 1895; d. Henrietta, near Rochester, N.Y., May 31, 1973. He studied theory at the New England Cons. of Music in Boston; then took violin lessons with Eugène Ysaÿe in Cincinnati; also studied conducting with Eugene Goossens in Rochester, N.Y. In 1929 he was appointed associate conductor of the Rochester Civic Orch. He composed *Pagan Festival Overture* (Rochester, April 28, 1936); *Andante and Rondo* for Cello and Orch. (1945); *5 Miniatures* for Piano, including the popular *Mosquito Dance;* various pieces of chamber music.

White, Robert, one of the most important English composers of the 16th century; b. c.1535; d. London, Nov. 1574. He studied music for several years, obtaining the degree of Mus.Bac. at Cambridge Univ. on Dec. 13, 1560; was appointed master of the choristers at Ely Cathedral in 1562, retaining this post until 1566; was then master of the choristers at Westminster Abbey, from 1570. He died of the plague. He composed Latin services and motets, English anthems, etc. Some of his works are reprinted in *Tudor Church Music,* 5 (1926). His instrumental music has been edited by I. Spector in the Recent Researches in the Music of the Renaissance series, XII (1972).

White, William, English composer of the 17th century; d. c.1660. He wrote fantasies, pavans, and other court dance tunes for viols. Apparently he was held in some esteem, for his name is mentioned by Simpson in *Principles of Practicle Musick* (1665) and by Thomas Mace in *Musick's Monument* (1676).

White, William C., American bandleader and march composer; b. Centerville, Utah, Sept. 29, 1881; d. Tenafly, N.J., Sept. 30, 1964. He studied violin at the New England Cons. in Boston and later at the Inst. of Musical Arts in N.Y., graduating in 1914. He was a member of the 10th U.S. Coast Artillery Band (1907–12) and later led the Mecca Temple Band (1919–20) and the Almes Temple Band in Washington, D.C. (1921–28). He then served for many years as principal of the Army Music School on Governors Island. He composed several marches, among them the popular *American Doughboy;* publ. *A History of Military Music in America* (1943); *Military Band Arranging; Tone Building and Intonation Studies for Military Bands.*

Whitehill, Clarence Eugene, American bass; b. on a farm near Parnell, Iowa, Nov. 5, 1871; d. New York, Dec. 18, 1932. He studied with L.A. Phelps in Chicago; earned his living as a clerk in an express office, and also sang in churches; then went to Paris in 1896, where he studied with Giraudet and Sbriglia; made his operatic debut on Oct. 31, 1898, at the Théâtre de la Monnaie in Brussels; was the first American male singer to be engaged at the Opéra-Comique (1899); then was a member of Henry Savage's Grand English Opera Co. at the Metropolitan Opera House in the autumn of 1900; went for further study to Stockhausen in Frankfurt, and from there to Bayreuth, where he studied the entire Wagnerian repertoire with Cosima Wagner; after engagements in Germany, he became a member of the Cologne Opera (1903–8), the Metropolitan Opera (1909–10), the Chicago Opera (1911–14 and 1915–17), and again at the Metropolitan (1914–32).

Whitehouse, William Edward, English cellist; b. London, May 20, 1859; d. there, Jan. 12, 1935. He studied at the Royal Academy of Music in London; joined its faculty after graduation. From 1889 until 1904 he was cellist in the London Trio, with Achille Simonetti (violin) and Amina Goodwin (piano), with whom he toured all over Europe. He was greatly esteemed as a teacher; among his pupils were Felix Salmond and Beatrice Harrison. He wrote a number of attractive cello pieces (*Allegro perpetuo, Remembrance, Serenade,* etc.) and edited several cello works of the 18th century. He publ. a memoir, *Recollections of a Violoncellist* (London, 1930).

Whiteman, Paul, celebrated American conductor of popular music; b. Denver, Colo., March 28, 1890; d. Doylestown, Pa., Dec. 29, 1967. He played viola in the Denver Symph. Orch. and later in the San Francisco People's Symph. Orch.; in 1917–18 was conductor of a 40-piece band in the U.S. Navy. He then formed a hotel orch. in Santa Barbara, Calif., and

began to develop a style of playing known as "symphonic jazz," which soon made him famous. On Feb. 12, 1924, he gave a concert in Aeolian Hall in N.Y., at which he introduced Gershwin's *Rhapsody in Blue,* written for his orch., with Gershwin himself as soloist. In 1926 he made a tour in Europe. While not himself a jazz musician, he was popularly known as the "King of Jazz," and frequently featured at his concerts such notables of the jazz world as Bix Beiderbecke, Frank Trumbauer, and Benny Goodman; Bing Crosby achieved his early fame as a member of Paul Whiteman's Rhythm Boys. Whiteman established the Whiteman Awards, made annually for "symphonic jazz" compositions written by Americans. He publ. the books *Jazz* (with M.M. McBride; N.Y., 1926), *How to Be a Bandleader* (with L. Lieber; N.Y., 1941), and *Records for the Millions* (N.Y., 1948).

Whithorne, Emerson, American composer; b. Cleveland, Sept. 6, 1884; d. Lyme, Conn., March 25, 1958. His name was **Whittern;** he had it legally changed in 1918 to Whithorne (the original family name of his paternal grandfather). He studied in Cleveland with J.H. Rogers; embarked on a musical career at the age of 15, and appeared as a pianist on the Chautauqua circuit for 2 seasons. In 1904 he went to Vienna and took piano lessons with Leschetizky and composition with Robert Fuchs; in 1905–7 he was a pupil of Artur Schnabel. In 1907 he married the pianist-composer **Ethel Leginska,** acting as her impresario in Germany until 1909; they were separated in 1912, and divorced in 1916. Between 1907 and 1915, Whithorne lived mainly in London; he studied Chinese and Japanese music from materials in the British Museum, and wrote several pieces based on oriental tunes (*Adventures of a Samurai;* settings for *The Yellow Jacket; The Typhoon*). Returning to America, he became editor for the Art Publication Society of St. Louis (1915–20); then settled in N.Y. and devoted himself entirely to composition; was an active member of the League of Composers in N.Y. In his music he assumed a militantly modernistic attitude; wrote several pieces in the fashionable "machine music" style. WORKS: For Orch.: *The Rain* (Detroit, Feb. 22, 1913); *The Aeroplane* (Birmingham, England, Jan. 30, 1926; orch. version of the piano piece written in 1920, one of the earliest examples of "machine music"); *Saturday's Child,* to poems by Countee Cullen, for Mezzo-soprano, Tenor, and Small Orch. (N.Y., March 13, 1926); *New York Days and Nights* (Philadelphia, July 30, 1926; originally for Piano); *Poem* for Piano and Orch. (Chicago, Feb. 4, 1927); *Fata Morgana,* symph. poem (N.Y., Oct. 11, 1928); incidental music to Eugene O'Neill's *Marco Millions* (1928); Symph. No. 1 (1929; Cincinnati, Jan. 12, 1934); *The Dream Pedlar,* symph. poem (Los Angeles, Jan. 15, 1931); Violin Concerto (Chicago, Nov. 12, 1931); *Fandango* (N.Y., April 19, 1932); *Moon Trail,* symph. poem (Boston, Dec. 15, 1933); Symph. No. 2 (Cincinnati, March 19, 1937); *Sierra Morena* (N.Y., May 7, 1938); Piano Quintet (N.Y., Dec. 19, 1926); other chamber music; also piano pieces; songs.

BIBLIOGRAPHY: J.T. Howard, *Emerson Whithorne* (N.Y., 1929); R. Hammond, "Emerson Whithorne," *Modern Music* (Jan.–Feb. 1931).

Whiting, Arthur Battelle, American composer and pianist; nephew of **George E. Whiting;** b. Cambridge, Mass., June 20, 1861; d. Beverly, Mass., July 20, 1936. He studied in Boston with Sherwood (piano), Maas (harmony), and Chadwick (composition). In 1883 he went to Munich and took courses at the Cons. there with Rheinberger. Returning to the U.S., he stayed in Boston until 1895, when he settled in N.Y.; from 1907, gave educational chamber music concerts at Yale, Harvard, Princeton, and Columbia; in 1911 he inaugurated a series of concerts of early music, playing the harpsichord, other artists being Constance Edson (violin), Georges Barrère (flute), and Paul Kéfer (viola da gamba). WORKS: *Concert Overture* (Boston, Feb. 5, 1886); Piano Concerto (Boston, Nov. 16, 1888, composer soloist); *Fantasie* for Piano and Orch. (Boston, March 5, 1897, composer soloist); *Suite* for Strings and 4 Horns (Boston, March 13, 1891); Piano Quintet; String Quartet; Piano Trio; Violin Sonata; a number of piano pieces: *6 Bagatelles; Suite moderne; 3 Characteristic Waltzes;* also *Melodious Technical Studies; Pianoforte Pedal Studies* (with text in Eng. and German); musical settings from the *Rubáiyát of Omar Khayyám* for Baritone; anthems; etc.
BIBLIOGRAPHY: R. Hughes, *Contemporary American Composers* (Boston, 1900; pp. 283–91); D.G. Mason, "Arthur Whiting," *Musical Quarterly* (Jan. 1937); idem, *Music in My Time* (N.Y., 1938, pp. 65–80); *National Cyclopedia of American Biography* (vol. 27, pp. 46–47).

Whiting, George Elbridge, American organist and composer; b. Holliston, Mass., Sept. 14, 1840; d. Cambridge, Mass., Oct. 14, 1923. He began to study with his brother Amos, a church organist, and played in public at the age of 13; at 17 he became organist of the North Congregational Church at Hartford; studied with George W. Morgan in N.Y.; then went to England, where he became a pupil of W.T. Best of Liverpool (1863). Returning to America, he became organist at St. Joseph's in Albany, N.Y., where the famous soprano Emma Albani sang in his choir. He then moved to Boston, where he was organist at King's Chapel; in 1874 he went to Berlin and studied harmony with Haupt and orchestration with Radecke. Settling finally in Boston, he taught the organ at the New England Cons. (until 1879, and again from 1883 to 1897). In the interim he was a teacher at the Cincinnati College of Music (1880–83). He was renowned as a teacher and composer of organ music; publ. *The Organist* (Boston, 1870) and *The First 6 Months on the Organ* (1871). He also wrote many sacred works: 2 masses; Vesper Services; a *Te Deum;* the secular cantatas *The Tale of the Viking; Dream Pictures; March of the Monks of Bangor; Midnight; Henry of Navarre;* the one-act opera *Lenora,* to an Italian libretto (1893); Symph.; an overture to Tennyson's *The Princess;* Piano Concerto; Suite for Cello and Orch.; piano pieces; songs.

BIBLIOGRAPHY: L.C. Elson, *The History of American Music* (N.Y., 1904; pp. 265–67).

Whitmer, Thomas Carl, American organist and composer; b. Altoona, Pa., June 24, 1873; d. Poughkeepsie, N.Y., May 30, 1959. He studied piano with C. Jarvis, organ with S.P. Warren, and composition with W.W. Gilchrist. He was director of the School of Music, Stephens College, Columbia, Mo. (1899–1909); director of music at the Pa. College for Women in Pittsburgh (1909–16); organist and choirmaster of the Sixth Presbyterian Church in Pittsburgh (1916–32); then taught privately in N.Y. WORKS: *Poem of Life* for Piano and Orch. (1914); *A Syrian Night,* ballet suite for Orch. (Philadelphia Orch., Pittsburgh, Feb. 17, 1919); *When God Laughed* for Chorus a cappella (1932); *Radiations over a 13th Century Theme* for String Orch. (1935); *Supper at Emmaus,* choral suite (Pittsburgh, Feb. 21, 1939); cantata, *Chant Me the Poem That Comes from the Soul of America,* after Walt Whitman (Pittsburgh, Feb. 19, 1942); one-act opera, *Oh, Isabel* (1951); chamber music; piano pieces; songs. He also publ. the books *The Way of My Heart and Mind* (Pittsburgh, 1920) and *The Art of Improvisation: A Handbook of Principles and Methods* (N.Y., 1934; revised ed., 1941).

Whitney, Myron William, American bass; b. Ashby, Mass., Sept. 5, 1836; d. Sandwich, Mass., Sept. 19, 1910. He was a pupil of E.H. Frost in Boston, Randegger in London, and Vannucini in Florence. He sang in concerts and oratorios in America and Great Britain; was a member of the Boston Ideal Opera Co. (1879) and the American Opera Co. (1885–86); retired in 1900. His son, **Myron Whitney, Jr.** (1872–1954), a baritone, traveled as joint artist with Melba and Nordica; for many years taught singing at the New England Cons. in Boston.
BIBLIOGRAPHY: H.C. Lahee, *Famous Singers of Today and Yesterday* (Boston, 1898; pp. 322–23).

Whitney, Robert, American conductor; b. Newcastle upon Tyne, England (of an American father and an English mother), July 9, 1904. He studied with Leo Sowerby in Chicago; took lessons in conducting with Eric De Lamarter. In 1937 he was engaged as conductor of the Louisville Phil. (later renamed the Louisville Orch.) A munificent grant from the Rockefeller Foundation enabled the Louisville Orch. to commission works from American and foreign composers, each to be paid a set fee of $1,000; the project proved highly successful, and the orch. was able to give first performances of works by Honegger, Milhaud, Malipiero, Petrassi, Krenek, Dallapiccola, Toch, Chávez, Villa-Lobos, Ginastera, Schuman, Virgil Thomson, Cowell, Piston, Sessions, Antheil, Creston, Mennin, and others; it recorded 189 contemporary symphonic works on Louisville Orch. Records. After completing his tenure as conductor in 1967, Whitney was in charge of various special projects at the School of Music at the Univ. of Louisville. Among his own compositions are: *Concerto Grosso* (1934); Symph. in E minor (1936);

Sospiri di Roma for Chorus and Orch. (1941); Concertino (1960).

BIBLIOGRAPHY: Hope Stoddard, *Symphony Conductors of the U.S.A.* (N.Y., 1957; pp. 248–56).

Whittaker, Howard, American composer; b. Lakewood, Ohio, Dec. 19, 1922. He studied with Herbert Elwell in Cleveland; in 1948 was appointed director of the Cleveland Music School Settlement. He has written a Piano Concerto, 2 string quartets, Piano Sonata, works for organ, and songs. His *2 Murals for Orchestra,* inspired by paintings of Orozco, was performed for the first time by the Cleveland Orch., on March 31, 1960. In most of his works he applies modified serial procedures, but refuses to abandon tonality.

Whittaker, William Gillies, English choral conductor and composer; b. Newcastle upon Tyne, July 23, 1876; d. Orkney Islands, July 5, 1944. He studied organ and singing; conducted various choral societies in Newcastle and London; in 1929 he was appointed a prof. at the Univ. of Glasgow; he left in 1938. He edited *North Country Folk Tunes* for voice and piano (2 vols.); *Oxford Choral Songs;* sonatas of John Blow; church cantatas of Bach; etc.; was the author of *Fugitive Notes on Certain Cantatas and the Motets of J.S. Bach* (London, 1924), *Class Singing* (London, 1925), and *Collected Essays* (London, 1940); publ. *Time Exercises* for Piano; received Carnegie Publication awards for his piano quintet, *Among the Northumbrian Hills,* and for his *A Lyke Wake Dirge* for Chorus and Orch. (1924); he also composed piano pieces and songs.

Whittall, Gertrude Clarke, American patron of music and literature; b. Bellevue, Nebr., Oct. 7, 1867; d. Washington, D.C., June 29, 1965. Her maiden name was **Clarke;** she married Matthew John Whittall on June 4, 1906. In 1935 she donated to the Library of Congress in Washington, D.C., a quartet of Stradivari instruments—2 violins (including the famous "Betts"), a viola, and a cello—together with 4 Tourte bows; she added another Stradivari violin (the "Ward") and another Tourte bow in 1937. In 1936 she established an endowment fund in the Library of Congress to provide public concerts at which these instruments would be used, and in 1938 the Whittall Pavilion was built in the library to house them and to serve other purposes in the musical life of the library. In subsequent years, she continued to add to her gifts to the library on behalf of both music and literature; one series enabled the Whittall Foundation to acquire many valuable autograph MSS of composers from Bach to Schoenberg, and in particular the finest single group of Brahms MSS gathered anywhere in the world.

BIBLIOGRAPHY: W.D. Orcutt, *The Stradivari Memorial at Washington* (Washington, 1938); E.N. Waters, *Autograph Musical Scores in the Whittall Foundation Collection* (Washington, 1951).

Whittenberg, Charles, American composer; b. St. Louis, July 6, 1927; d. Hartford, Conn., Aug. 22, 1984.

He studied with Burrill Phillips and Bernard Rogers at the Eastman School of Music in Rochester, N.Y. (1944–48); in 1962 became affiliated with the Columbia-Princeton Electronic Music Center; in 1967 he was appointed associate prof. of music at the Univ. of Connecticut in Storrs, where he became director of Contemporary Music Projects. He received Guggenheim fellowships in 1963 and 1964, and the prize of the American Academy in Rome (1965–66).

WORKS: *Dialogue and Aria* for Flute and Piano (1956); *Electronic Study* for Cello and Tape (1960); *Structures* for 2 Pianos (1961); *Fantasy* for Wind Quintet (1961); *Electronic Study II* for Double Bass and Tape (1962); *Triptych* for Brass Quintet (1962); *Event* for Chamber Orch. (1963; N.Y., April 28, 1964); *Identities and Variations* for Piano (1963); Chamber Concerto for Violin and 7 Instrumentalists (1963); *Duo-Divertimento* for Flute and Double Bass (1963); *Composition* for Cello and Piano (1963); *3 Pieces* for Solo Cello (1963); Variations for 9 Players (1964–65); String Quartet in one movement (1965); *Polyphony* for Solo Trumpet (1965); *3 Compositions* for Piano (1967; revised 1969); *Conversations* for Solo Double Bass (1967); Sextet (1967); *Games of 5* for Wind Quintet (1968); *Iambi* for 2 Oboes (1968); Concerto for Brass Quintet (1968–69); *A due* for Flutes and Percussion (1969); *Correlations* for Orch. (1969); *From John Donne: A Sacred Triptych* for 8 Solo Voices (1970–71).

Whittlesey, Walter Rose, American music librarian; b. Hartford, Conn., Jan. 5, 1861; d. Washington, D.C., April 9, 1936. Upon the opening of the new building of the Library of Congress (Sept. 1, 1897), he took charge of the musical copyright deposits which formed the basis of the present music collection; when O.G. Sonneck was appointed first chief of the Music Division, Whittlesey became his assistant; after Sonneck's resignation (1917) he was acting chief (until 1921); retired in 1932. He publ. *Catalogue of First Editions of Stephen C. Foster* (1915; with O.G. Sonneck).

Whythorne, Thomas, English song composer; b. c.1528; d. Aug. 1595. He studied at Oxford Univ.; about 1553 he traveled through Europe and collected German, Austrian, and Neapolitan songs. Upon his return to London he publ. a collection of 76 original songs under the title *Songes, for three, fower and five voyces* (London, 1571); these were among the earliest sets of secular vocal pieces publ. in England. In 1590 Whythorne brought out another collection, comprising 52 vocal duos. His autobiography, discovered in 1955, was publ. in Oxford in 1961 in his original phonetic spelling, and reprinted in modern spelling in 1963, edited by J.M. Osborn.

BIBLIOGRAPHY: Peter Warlock, *Thomas Whythorne: An Unknown Elizabethan Composer* (Oxford, 1927).

Wich, Günther, German conductor; b. Bamberg, May 23, 1928. He was educated at the Freiburg Hochschule für Musik; then served as a conductor at Graz (1959–61); later was Generalmusikdirektor in Hannover (1961–65) and at the Düsseldorf-Duisburg Opera (1965–80).

Wichmann, Hermann, German composer; b. Berlin, Oct. 24, 1824; d. Rome, Sept., 1905. He was a pupil of Taubert, Mendelssohn, and Spohr; lived most of his life in Berlin. He composed 7 string quartets; a String Quintet; Piano Trio; Violin Sonata; several piano sonatas; publ. a collection of essays, *Gesammelte Aufsätze* (2 vols.; 1884, 1887), and *Frohes und Ernstes aus meinem Leben* (Leipzig, 1898).

Wichtl, Georg, German violinist and composer; b. Trostberg, Feb. 2, 1805; d. Bunzlau, June 3, 1877. He studied in Munich; was a violinist and conductor in various orchs. in Silesia; wrote an opera, *Almaïda;* an oratorio, *Die Auferstehung und Himmelfahrt Jesu;* symphs. and overtures; a String Quartet; 6 trios for 2 violins and cello; 3 trios for 3 violins; 6 duets for violin and cello; many instructive pieces for violin.

Wickede, Friedrich von, German composer; b. Dömitz-on-Elbe, July 28, 1834; d. Schwerin, Sept. 11, 1904. He studied with J. Vieth; held various government posts; composition was his avocation. He wrote 2 operas, *Ingo* and *Per aspera ad astra;* piano pieces; songs (which were praised by the critics).

Wickenhauser, Richard, Austrian composer; b. Brünn, Feb. 7, 1867; d. Vienna, July 1, 1936. He studied at the Leipzig Cons. with Jadassohn and Paul; won a state stipend in 1894 (awarded by Brahms and Hanslick); conducted choral societies in Brünn, Graz, and Vienna; from 1907 was conductor of the Vienna Singakademie. He publ. *Sang fahrender Schüler* for Male Chorus and Orch.; *Suite* for String Orch.; Violin Sonata; Cello Sonata; *10 Choralvorspiele* for Organ; numerous male choruses a cappella; songs; also *Anton Bruckners Symphonien* (Leipzig, 1927).

Wickham, Florence, American contralto singer; b. Beaver, Pa., 1880; d. New York, Oct. 20, 1962. She studied in Philadelphia; then went to Germany, where she was a pupil of Franz Emerich in Berlin. After making appearances in Wiesbaden and Munich, she sang the role of Kundry in *Parsifal* in Henry W. Savage's touring opera troupe in America (1904–5). She was a member of the Metropolitan Opera Co. from 1909 to 1912. Subsequently she retired from the stage and took up composition; wrote an operetta, *Rosalynd,* after Shakespeare's *As You Like It* (1938); also songs; lived mostly in N.Y.

Widmann, Benedikt, German music pedagogue; b. Bräunlingen, near Donaueschingen, March 5, 1820; d. Frankfurt, March 4, 1910. He was active in music instruction in Frankfurt; publ. several manuals: *Formenlehre der Instrumentalmusik* (1862); *Katechismus der allgemeinen Musiklehre* (2nd ed., 1879); *Grundzüge der musikalischen Klanglehre* (1868); *Praktischer Lehrgang für einen rationellen Gesangunterricht; Handbüchlein der Harmonie-, Melodie- und Formenlehre* (5th ed., 1889); *Generalbass-Übungen* (1859; 5th ed., 1893); *Die kunsthistorische Entwicklung des Männerchors* (1884); *Alberich Zwyssig als Komponist* (1905); etc.

Widmann, Erasmus, German composer and theorist; b. Hall, Württemberg (baptized, Schwäbisch Hall, Sept. 15), 1572; d. Rothenburg, Oct. 31, 1634. After serving as cantor in Graz and Weickersheim, he became a schoolmaster at Rothenburg (1613). He wrote church music and some instrumental dance suites; publ. a treatise, *Praecepta musicae Latino-Germanica* (Nuremberg, 1615). A complete edition of his works was publ. by G. Reichert in *Das Erbe deutscher Musik,* III (1955).
BIBLIOGRAPHY: G. Reichert, *Erasmus Widmann: Leben und Werk* (Tübingen, 1940).

Widmann, Joseph Viktor, Swiss writer and journalist; b. Nennowitz, Moravia, Feb. 20, 1842; d. Bern, Nov. 6, 1911. He was brought to Switzerland as a child; became engaged in the literary profession; was well known as a dramatist; from 1880 he was literary editor of the *Berner Bund;* he also wrote librettos. He was a friend of Brahms, and publ. *Johannes Brahms in Erinnerungen* (Berlin, 1898; new ed., Basel, 1947).
BIBLIOGRAPHY: E. and M. Widmann, *Joseph Viktor Widmann* (2 vols.; 1922, 1924); M. Waser, *Josef Viktor Widmann* (Leipzig, 1927).

Widor, Charles-Marie (-Jean-Albert), distinguished French organist, pedagogue, and composer; b. Lyons, Feb. 21, 1844; d. Paris, March 12, 1937. His father, an Alsatian of Hungarian descent, was organist at the church of St.-François in Lyons; as a boy, Widor was a skillful improviser on the organ; he studied later in Brussels under Lemmens (organ) and Fétis (composition). While still a youth, he was appointed organist at his father's church in Lyons (1860), and gained high repute in concerts in provincial French cities. In 1870 he obtained the important post of organist at St.-Sulpice in Paris, holding it for more than 60 years; he retired in 1934. On April 19, 1934, he played at St.-Sulpice his *Pièce mystique,* composed at the age of 90. In 1890 he succeeded César Franck as prof. of organ at the Paris Cons.; in 1896 became prof. of counterpoint, fugue, and composition. He was active also as a music critic for *L'Estafette,* under the pen name *Aulétès;* also conducted the oratorio society Concordia. In 1910 he was elected a member of the Académie des Beaux-Arts, of which he became permanent secretary in 1913. He had many distinguished pupils, including Albert Schweitzer, with whom he collaborated in editing the first 5 vols. of a definitive 8-vol. ed. of J.S. Bach's organ works (brought out by G. Schirmer, N.Y.); he also edited the collection *L'Orgue moderne.* As a composer he wrote copiously in many forms, but is best known for his organ music, especially his 8 "symphonies" (suites); also the *Sympho-*

nie gothique (op. 70) and the *Symphonie romaine* (op. 73).

WORKS: Operas (all produced in Paris): *Maître Ambrose* (Opéra-Comique, May 6, 1886); *Les Pêcheurs de Saint-Jean* (Opéra-Comique, Dec. 26, 1905; his most successful opera); *Nerto* (Paris Opéra, Oct. 27, 1924); incidental music to *Conte d'avril*, after Shakespeare's *Twelfth Night* (Odéon, Sept. 22, 1885); *Les Jacobites* (Nov. 21, 1885); etc.; ballet, *La Korrigane* (Paris Opéra, Dec. 1, 1880); symph. poem, *Une Nuit de Valpurgis* (London, April 19, 1888, composer conducting); 3 symphs.; *Symphonie antique* (with Organ and Final Chorus); *Sinfonia sacra* (with Organ); *Ouverture espagnole;* 2 piano concertos; Cello Concerto; *Fantaisie* for Piano and Orch.; *Choral et variations* for Harp and Orch.; chamber music: 2 piano quintets; String Quartet; Piano Trio; *Soirs d'Alsace* for Piano Trio; 2 violin sonatas; *Suite* for Cello and Piano; Cello Sonata; *3 valses* for Violin and Piano; *3 pièces* for Cello and Piano; for Piano: *Airs de ballet; La Prière; Caprice; 3 valses; Impromptu; 6 morceaux; Prélude, andante et finale; Scènes de bal; 6 valses caractéristiques; 12 feuillets d'album; Dans les bois; Romance; Suite polonaise;* Suite in B minor; *Suite écossaise;* vocal music: Mass for 2 Choirs and 2 Organs; *Psalm 83* for Chorus and String Quintet; *Psalm 112* for 2 Choirs, 2 Organs, and Orch.; *Tu es Petrus* for Double Chorus and Organ; *Sacerdos et Pontifex* for Chorus and Organ; other church music; *Chant séculaire* for Soprano, Chorus, and Orch.; several song cycles; duets; choruses a cappella. He edited Berlioz's *Traité de l'instrumentation et d'orchestration modernes,* and wrote a supplement, *Technique de l'orchestre moderne* (1904; 2nd ed., 1906; in Eng., London, 1906, 1946); publ. *Initiation musicale* (1923); *L'Orgue moderne* (1929); etc.

BIBLIOGRAPHY: H. Reynaud, *L'Œuvre de Charles-Marie Widor* (Lyons, 1900); J.F.E. Rupp, *Charles-Marie Widor und sein Werk* (Bremen, 1912); Isidor Philipp, "Charles-Marie Widor," *Musical Quarterly* (April 1944); A. Thomas, "C.M. Widor: A Revaluation," *Musical Times* (March 1984).

Wiechowicz, Stanislaw, Polish composer; b. Kroszyce, Nov. 27, 1893; d. Cracow, May 12, 1963. He studied successively in Cracow, Dresden, St. Petersburg and Paris; taught at the Poznan Cons. (1921–39); from 1945 to his death, taught at the State College of Music in Cracow.

WORKS: *Babie lato,* symph. poem (1922); *Chmiel (The Hopvine),* symph. scherzo (1926); *Ulegalki* for Orch. (1944); *Kasia (Kitty),* folk suite for 2 Clarinets and String Orch. (1946); *Koncert staromiejski (Old Town Concerto)* for String Orch. (1954); *Pastoralki,* recitation for Chorus and Orch. (1927); *Kantata romantyczna* (1930); *Kantata zniwna* (1948); *A czemuześ nie przyjechal? (Why Did You Not Come?),* rustic scene for Chorus and Orch. (1948); *List do Marc Chagalla (Letter to Marc Chagall),* dramatic rhapsody for Soprano, Mezzo-soprano, 2 Narrators, Chorus, and Orch. (1961); *Zstap, golebico (O Dove, Descend),* Cantata (1962–63); choruses.

Wieck, Alwin, German pianist; brother of **Clara Schumann**; b. Leipzig, Aug. 27, 1821; d. Dresden, Oct. 21, 1885. He studied piano with his father, and violin with David; was a member of the Italian Opera orch. at St. Petersburg; then taught piano in Dresden. He publ. *Materialien zu F. Wiecks Pianoforte-Methodik* and *Vademecum perpetuum für den ersten Pianoforte-Unterricht nach F. Wiecks Methode;* also piano pieces.

Wieck, Friedrich, German pianist; father of **Clara Schumann**; b. Pretzsch, near Torgau, Aug. 18, 1785; d. Loschwitz, near Dresden, Oct. 6, 1873. He studied theology at Wittenberg, and at the same time pursued musical studies in private; established a piano factory and a circulating music library in Leipzig, but gave up both in order to devote himself to teaching the piano, in which profession he had extraordinary success. Among his pupils were his daughters **Clara** and **Marie,** his son **Alwin,** Hans von Bülow, Fritz Spindler, Isidor Seiss, and Gustav Merkel. He was also Robert Schumann's teacher, but bitterly opposed Schumann's marriage to Clara. He settled in Dresden in 1840. In 1843 Mendelssohn offered him a professorship at the newly established Leipzig Cons., but Wieck declined. Wieck's first wife (née Tromlitz) was the mother of Clara Schumann and Alwin; after her divorce she married Bargiel, the father of Woldemar Bargiel; Marie Wieck was Wieck's daughter by his 2nd wife, Clementine Fechner. He publ. 2 books of piano studies, and also *Clavier und Gesang* (1853; 3rd ed., 1878; also in Eng.) and *Musikalische Bauernsprüche* (2nd ed., 1875, by Marie Wieck).

BIBLIOGRAPHY: A. von Meichsner, *Friedrich Wieck und seine beiden Töchter Clara und Marie* (Leipzig, 1875); A. Kohut, *Friedrich Wieck* (Dresden, 1887); V. Joss, *Friedrich Wieck und sein Verhältnis zu Robert Schumann* (Dresden, 1900); idem, *Der Musikpädagoge Friedrich Wieck und seine Familie* (Dresden, 1902); Marie Wieck, *Aus dem Kreise Weick-Schumann* (Dresden, 1912; 2nd augmented ed., 1914).

Wieck, Marie, German pianist, daughter of **Friedrich Wieck;** b. Leipzig, Jan. 17, 1832; d. Dresden, Nov. 2, 1916. She studied with her father; at the age of 11 made her debut at a concert of her half sister, **Clara Schumann;** was appointed court pianist to the Prince of Hohenzollern in 1858; after tours of Germany, England, and Scandinavia, she settled in Dresden as a teacher of piano and singing. Her last public appearance was with the Dresden Phil. Orch. in Nov. 1915, playing the Schumann Concerto. She publ. piano pieces and songs; edited her father's *Pianoforte-Studien;* wrote *Aus dem Kreise Wieck-Schumann* (1912; 2nd augmented ed., 1914).

Wiedebein, Gottlob, German organist and conductor; b. Eilenstadt, July 27, 1779; d. Braunschweig, April 17, 1854. After studying in Magdeburg, he settled in Braunschweig as an organist. He enjoyed a great reputation; Schumann sought his advice. He wrote some excellent lieder; was in correspondence with Beethoven, Schumann, and other composers; part of this correspondence was publ. in various German sources: *Die Musik* (1911); *Zeitschrift für Bücherfreunde* (1913); etc.

Wiedemann, Ernst Johann, German composer and teacher; b. Hohengiersdorf, Silesia, March 28, 1797; d. Potsdam, Dec. 7, 1873. From 1818 to 1852 he was organist of the Roman Catholic Church in Berlin; founded and conducted 2 singing societies there; composed a Te Deum for Soli, Chorus, and Orch.; masses; motets; hymns.

Wiederkehr, Jacob Christian Michael, Alsatian composer; b. Strasbourg, April 28, 1739; d. Paris, April 1823. From 1783 he was in Paris; played cello at the Concert Spirituel; bassoon at the Théâtre-Lyrique; trombone at the Opéra; taught singing at the Cons. (1795–1802). He composed 12 *concertantes* for wind instruments; 2 quintets and 10 quartets for strings; 6 quintets for piano and wind instruments; 6 piano trios; 6 violin sonatas; etc.

Wiegand, (Josef Anton) Heinrich, German bass; b. Fränkisch-Crumbach in the Odenwald, Sept. 9, 1842; d. Frankfurt, May 28, 1899. He studied voice privately in Paris; became a member of the opera at Zürich in 1870; then sang in Cologne, and from 1873 to 1877 was the leading bass at the Frankfurt Opera. In 1877 he toured America with the Adams-Pappenheim troupe; then was in Leipzig (1878–82); sang at the Vienna Court Opera (1882–84); then was engaged at Hamburg. He also appeared in the *Nibelung* cycle in Berlin (1881) and London (1882).

Wiehmayer, (Johann) Theodor, German pianist; b. Marienfeld, Jan. 7, 1870; d. Starnberg, March 15, 1947. He studied at the Leipzig Cons. under Jadassohn (composition) and Reinecke (piano). After his debut in Leipzig (1890) he undertook a successful tour in Sweden; then settled in Leipzig as a teacher, also giving concerts in other towns; from 1902–6, was a teacher of piano in the Leipzig Cons.; from 1908 to 1925, was at the Stuttgart Cons. He was the author of *Muskialische Rhythmik und Metrik* (1917) and *Musikalische Foremenlehre in Analysen* (1927); publ. technical studies for piano.

Wiel, Taddeo, Italian musicologist and composer; b. Oderzo, Treviso, Sept. 24, 1849; d. Venice, Feb. 17, 1920. He studied in Venice; became assistant librarian at San Marco; publ. valuable papers on Venetian music history: *I codici contariniani nella R. Biblioteca di San Marco in Venezia* (1888); *I teatri musicali veneziani del settecento* (1897); *Francesco Cavalli Musical* (Venice, 1914).

Wielhorsky, Count Mikhail, Russian patron of the arts; b. Volynia, Nov. 11, 1788; d. Moscow, Sept. 9, 1856. His home in St. Petersburg was the gathering place of the most eminent musicians of the time. He wrote a String Quartet and some songs, one of which, *Autrefois,* was arranged for piano by Liszt (1843). His brother, **Matvei Wielhorsky** (1794–1866), was a cellist; a distant relative, **Joseph Wielhorsky** (1817–92), wrote piano pieces and songs (48 opus numbers).

Wiéner, Jean, French pianist and composer of Austrian parentage; b. Paris, March 19, 1896; d. there, June 8, 1982. He studied with Gédalge at the Paris Cons. From 1920 to 1924 he organized in Paris a series of Concerts Jean Wiéner, devoted to the energetic propaganda of new music; he presented several world premieres of works by modern French composers; also performed pieces by Schoenberg, Berg, and Anton von Webern. He was the first Frenchman to proclaim jazz as a legitimate art form; from 1925 to 1939 he teamed with Clément Doucet in duo-piano recitals, in programs stretching from Mozart to jazz. His own compositions reflect his ecumenical convictions, as exemplified in such works as *Concerto franco-américain* for Clarinet and Strings (1923) and a desegregationist operetta, *Olive chez les nègres* (1926). He also wrote an Accordion Concerto (1957) and a Concerto for 2 Guitars (1966), but he became famous mainly for his idiosyncratic film music.

Wiener, Otto, Austrian baritone; b. Vienna, Feb. 13, 1913. He was educated in Vienna; made his concert debut in 1939; in 1953 he sang opera in Graz; later appeared in Düsseldorf, Frankfurt, Stuttgart, and Berlin. In 1957 he became a member of the Vienna State Opera; from 1960 to 1970 he sang at the Bavarian State Opera in Munich; later filled engagements as a guest solo artist at Covent Garden in London, at La Scala in Milan, and at several Bayreuth Festivals. In 1963 he sang at the Metropolitan Opera in N.Y.

Wieniawski, Adam Tadeusz, Polish composer, nephew of **Henri** and **Joseph Wieniawski**; b. Warsaw, Nov. 27, 1879; d. Bydgoszcz, April 21, 1950. He studied in Warsaw with Melcer and Noskowski; then in Berlin with Bargiel, and in Paris with Vincent d'Indy, Fauré, and Gédalge. He fought in the French army during World War I; returned to Warsaw in 1923; was appointed director of the Chopin School of Music in 1928.
  WORKS: Operas: *Megae* (Warsaw, Dec. 28, 1912); *Wyzwolony* (Warsaw, 1928); *Król Kochanek* (Warsaw, March 19, 1931); ballets: *Lalita* and *Le Festin chez Hérode* (1927); symph. poems: *Kamaralmazan* (Paris, 1910) and *Princesse Baudour; Suite Polonaise* for Orch. (1913); *Obrazki,* Piano Suite (also for Orch.); arrangements of folk songs.

Wieniawski, Henryk (Henri), famous Polish violinist; b. Lublin, July 10, 1835; d. Moscow, March 31, 1880. His mother, Regina Wolff-Wieniawska, was a talented pianist; on the advice of her brother, **Eduard Wolff,** a pianist and composer who lived in France, she took Henryk to Paris, where he entered the Cons. at the age of 8, first in Clavel's class, and the following year, in the advanced class of Massart. At the age of 11 he graduated with first prize

in violin, an unprecedented event in the annals of the Paris Cons. He made his debut in Paris on Jan. 30, 1848; gave his first concert in St. Petersburg on March 31, 1848, and played 4 more concerts there; then played in Finland and the Baltic provinces; after several successful appearances in Warsaw, he returned in 1849 to Paris, where he studied composition with Hippolyte Collet at the Cons., graduating (again with first prize) in 1850. He then traveled with his brother, **Joseph,** in Russia (1851–53); went to Paris (1858) and London (1859); in 1860, was appointed solo violinist to the Czar; taught at the newly founded St. Petersburg Cons. (1862–68); played the viola in the Ernst String Quartet. In 1872 he went on a tour of the U.S. with Anton Rubinstein; one of the featured works was Beethoven's *Kreutzer Sonata,* which they performed about 70 times. When Rubinstein returned to Europe, Wieniawski continued his American tour, which included California. He returned to Europe in 1874, gave several concerts with Rubinstein in Paris, and in the same year succeeded Vieuxtemps as prof. of violin at the Brussels Cons., resigning in 1877 owing to an increasingly grave heart condition; he suffered a heart attack during a concert in Berlin in 1878, but still agreed to play several concerts in Moscow, where he remained until his death at the age of 44. He was married to Isobel Hampton, an Englishwoman; their youngest daughter, Irene, wrote music under the pen name **Poldowski.** Wieniawski was undoubtedly one of the greatest violinists of the 19th century; he possessed a virtuoso technique and an extraordinary range of dynamics. He was equally distinguished as a chamber music player. Many of his compositions are in the repertoire of every violinist; of these the most famous are his Concerto in D minor; *Légende* for Violin and Orch.; *Souvenir de Moscou,* on Russian themes, for Violin and Orch.; and *Le Carnaval russe* for Violin and Piano. He also wrote, for Violin and Orch.: Concerto in F-sharp minor; *Polonaise; Scherzo-Tarentelle; Fantaisie brillante* (on themes from Gounod's *Faust*); *Polonaise brillante;* for Violin and Piano: *Caprice fantastique; Souvenir der Posen; Adagio élégiaque; Capriccio-Valse; Romance sans paroles et Rondo élégant;* 2 mazurkas; *Gigue; Etudes-Caprices* for 2 Violins; etc. With his brother, Joseph, he wrote *Allegro de sonate* and *Grand duo polonais.*
BIBLIOGRAPHY: A. Desfossez, *Henri Wieniawski: Esquisse* (The Hague, 1856); J. Reiss, *Henryk Wieniawski* (Warsaw, 1931); I. Yampolski, *Henryk Wieniawski* (Moscow, 1955); W. Reiss, *H. Wieniawski* (Cracow, 1962; 2nd ed., 1970).

Wieniawski, Joseph, Polish pianist and composer, brother of **Henryk Wieniawski;** b. Lublin, May 23, 1837; d. Brussels, Nov. 11, 1912. He studied at the Paris Cons. with Zimmermann, Marmontel, and Alkan (piano), and with LeCouppey (composition); in 1851 he went on tour with his brother, Henryk; studied with Liszt at Weimar (1855–56), and returned to Paris in 1858. In 1866 he settled in Moscow as a teacher at the Cons., but soon established a piano school of his own, which flourished. In 1875–76 he

was director of the Warsaw Music Society; then settled in Brussels, teaching at the Cons. He also made numerous concert tours throughout Europe.
WORKS: *Suite romantique* for Orch.; *Guillaume le Taciturne,* overture; Piano Concerto; String Quartet; Piano Trio; *Grand duo polonais* for Piano and Violin (with his brother); Cello Sonata; *Fantasia* for 2 Pianos; for Piano Solo: 4 polonaises; 5 waltzes; Sonata in B minor; mazurkas; *Fantaisie et fugue; Sur l'Océan; Barcarole; Ballade; Notturno; Barcarole-Caprice; Romanze-Etüde,* etc.; also *24 études de mécanisme et de style.*
BIBLIOGRAPHY: L. Delcroix, *Joseph Wieniawski. Notices biographiques et anecdotiques* (Brussels, 1908).

Wieprecht, Friedrich Wilhelm, German trombonist and inventor; b. Aschersleben, Aug. 8, 1802; d. Berlin, Aug. 4, 1872. He studied in Dresden and Leipzig, where he was already famous as a trombonist. He invented the bass tuba (1835, with the instrument maker Moritz); the bathyphon, a sort of bass clarinet (1839, with Skorra); the "piangendo" on brass instruments with pistons; and an improved contrabass bassoon; his claim of priority over Sax, in the invention of the saxhorns, was not upheld by the courts.
BIBLIOGRAPHY: A. Kalkbrenner, *F.W. Wieprecht* (1888).

Wier, Albert Ernest, American music editor; b. Chelsea, Mass., July 22, 1879; d. Brooklyn, Sept. 8, 1945. He studied music at the New England Cons. and at Harvard Univ.; from 1900 was music editor for various publ. firms in N.Y.; brought out a large number of collections and arrangements: *Whole World Music Series, The Pianist's Music Shelf, The Violinist's Music Shelf, Young Folks' Music Library, Radio Music Library,* etc.; devised the "arrow signal" system, in which arrows and other markings are added to orch. scores to identify the main themes; using this system, he issued numerous collections: *Classic Violin Concertos, The 9 Symphonies of Beethoven, The Symphonies of Brahms and Tschaikowsky, The Valkyrie,* etc.; he also edited *The Macmillan Encyclopedia of Music and Musicians* (1938; withdrawn from circulation owing to an excessive number of demonstrable errors) and other reference works of questionable scholarship.

Wiesengrund-Adorno, Theodor. See **Adorno, Theodor.**

Wieslander, (Axel Otto) Ingvar, Swedish composer; b. Jönköping, May 19, 1917; d. Malmö, April 29, 1963. He studied at the Royal Academy of Music in Stockholm; also took lessons in composition from S.-E. Svensson in Uppsala. He was music director of the Sundbyberg Orch. Society (1944–47); later served as music director at the Malmö Municipal Theater (1949–60) and as its choirmaster (1960–63). His own music followed the eclectic modalities of Scandinavian Romanticism; but he was not averse to circumspect experimentation in modernistic modalities, including a mitigated dodecaphonic scheme, while steadfastly maintaining the framework of Baroque forms.

WORKS: 2 chamber operas: *Fröknarna i parken* (1953) and *Skälknallen* (1958; Malmö, Feb. 7, 1959); 2 ballets: *Nordisk saga* (1950) and *Skymningslekar* (1954); 6 symphs.: Symph. in D (1951); *Sinfonia piccola* (1953); *Sinfonia notturna* (1954); *Sinfonia seria* (1956); *Sinfonia da camera* (1962); *Sinfonia ecloga,* with Solo Soprano (1962); *Overtura giocosa* (1957); Concerto for String Orch. (1961); *Förspel (Intrada seria)* for Orch. (1961); *Mutazioni* for 2 Pianos and Orch. (Malmö, Nov. 27, 1962); 5 string quartets (1948; 1949, revised 1954; 1957; 1958; 1961); choruses; songs.

Wigglesworth, Frank, American composer; b. Boston, March 3, 1918. He studied at Columbia Univ. and at Converse College in Spartanburg, S.C.; also took lessons in N.Y. with Henry Cowell and Otto Luening. He was in the U.S. Army Air Force during World War II; then taught at Columbia Univ. (1947–51) and Queens College (1954–55). He is a great-nephew of Mrs. Elizabeth Sprague Coolidge.

WORKS: 3 symphs. (1955; 1958; 1967–69); *Creation* for Chorus and Small Orch. (1940); *New England Concerto* for Violin and Strings (1941); *The Plunger* for Soprano, Flute, Viola, Cello, and Piano (1941); Trio for Flute, Banjo, and Harp (1942); *Jeremiah* for Baritone, Chorus, and Orch. (1942); *Sleep Becalmed* for Chorus and Orch., after Dylan Thomas (1948); *3 Movements* for String Orch. (1949); *Telesis* for Chamber Orch. and Percussion (1949); *Serenade* for Flute, Viola, and Guitar (1952); Brass Quintet (1957).

Wihan, Hans (Hanuš), Czech cellist; b. Politz, near Braunau, Bohemia, June 5, 1855; d. Prague, May 1, 1920. He studied at the Prague Cons.; as a young man, became instructor of cello at the Mozarteum in Salzburg; then was chamber musician in various courts in Germany; in 1880 he became a member of the private string quartet of King Ludwig of Bavaria, and frequently played at Wagner's soirées at Wahnfried; from 1888 he was a prof. of cello at the Prague Cons. In 1891 he formed the Bohemian String Quartet, selecting his four most talented pupils (Karel Hoffmann, Josef Suk, Oscar Nedbal, and Otto Berger); after Berger's retirement in 1897, owing to ill health, Wihan himself took his place as cellist (until 1914); the Bohemian String Quartet for years enjoyed the highest reputation.

Wihtol (Vitols), Joseph, foremost Latvian composer and pedagogue; b. Volmar, July 26, 1863; d. Lübeck, April 24, 1948. He studied at the St. Petersburg Cons. (1880–86) with Rimsky-Korsakov; after graduation, was engaged as an instructor there; succeeded Rimsky-Korsakov in 1908 as prof. of composition; among his students were Prokofiev and Miaskovsky. He was also music critic for the German daily *St. Petersburger Zeitung.* In 1918 he left St. Petersburg; was for a season director of the Latvian

Opera in Riga; in 1919 founded the National Cons. there; many Latvian composers were his students. As the Soviet armies approached Riga (1944), Wihtol went to Germany, remaining there until his death. In his music he followed the harmonic practices of the Russian school, but often employed Latvian folk-song patterns. Most of his works were publ. by Belaieff.

WORKS: Symph. (St. Petersburg, Dec. 17, 1887); *La Fête Ligho,* symph. tableau (1890); *Beverinas dziedonis (The Bard of Beverin)* for Chorus and Orch. (1891); *Ouverture dramatique* (1895); *Gaismas pils (The Castle of Light)* for Chorus and Orch. (1899); *Upe un cilvēka dzive (River and Human Life)* for Chorus (1903); *Spriditis,* Latvian fairy tale for Orch. (1908); cantatas: *Song* (1908) and *Aurora Borealis* (1914); arrangements of 200 Latvian songs for voice and piano and for piano solo (2 books; 1906, 1919); many Latvian choral ballads; String Quartet; *10 chants populaires lettons,* "miniature paraphrases" for piano; songs.

BIBLIOGRAPHY: O. Gravitis, *Latvian Composers* (Riga, 1955; in Russian; pp. 30-39); a vol. of reminiscences, articles, and letters of Wihtol were publ. in Russian in Leningrad (1969).

Wijdeveld, Wolfgang, Dutch composer and pianist; b. The Hague, May 9, 1910. He is the son of the noted Dutch architect Hendricus Wijdeveld. He studied piano with Willem Andriessen, theory with Sem Dresden, and violin with Kint at the Amsterdam Cons.; also took private lessons in composition with Willem Pijper. He was director of the Cons. at Zwolle (1940–46); taught piano at the Utrecht Cons. (1946–76); was music critic for the Amsterdam newspaper *Het Vrije Volk* (1956–68). He toured the U.S. in 1939 with the Yvonne Georgi Ballet as a pianist and composer; gave concerts and seminars at 15 North American univs. (1962–63).

WORKS: *Psalm 150* for Chorus and Orch. (1950); *Concertstük* for Wind Quintet and Strings (1952); *Matrooslied* for Chorus and Small Orch. (1966); Wind Quintet (1934); Trio for Flute, Oboe, and Bassoon (1958); Concerto for Guitar and String Trio (1960); Sonata for 2 Violins and Piano (1952); Violin Sonata (1948); *Sonatine Simple* for Violin and Piano (1952); *Introduction and Caprice* for Violin and Piano (1956); Flute Sonatina (1948); *Snarenspel* for Guitar and Piano (1958); Sonatina for Solo Accordion (1963); 3 piano sonatas: No. 1 (1940), No. 2 (1956), and No. 3, *For Americans* (1963); 2 piano sonatinas (1946, 1953); *Escapades* for Piano (1944–45); *Kermesse,* ballet music for 2 Pianos (1935); *Notebooks I, II, III, IV* for Piano (1968–69); *Notebook V* for Harpsichord (1968); *Introduction and Gigue* for Organ (1949); *3 Songs,* after Walt Whitman, for 2 Voices, Violin, Viola, Clarinet, and Piano (1949); other songs.

Wijk, Arnold. See **Wyk, Arnold van.**

Wiklund, Adolf, Swedish composer and conductor; b. Langserud, June 5, 1879; d. Stockholm, April 2, 1950. He studied with J. Lindegren (composition)

and R. Andersson (piano) at the Stockholm Cons.; was granted a state fellowship for study abroad; took lessons with James Kwast in Berlin (piano); was engaged as an opera coach in Berlin; returning to Sweden in 1911, he became 2nd conductor of the Stockholm Opera; then led the Stockholm Court Orch. (1911–24) and the Concert Society (1925–38); was also guest conductor in London and Jena. He composed a Symph. (1922); 2 piano concertos (1906, 1916); *Konzertstück* for Piano and Orch. (1902); symph. poem, *Sommarnatt och soluppgang* (1918); *Little Suite* for Orch. (1928); *3 Pieces* for String Orch. (1924); Violin Sonata (1906); several albums of lyric pieces for piano; songs.

Wikmanson, Johan, Swedish organist and composer; b. Stockholm, Dec. 28, 1753; d. there, Jan. 10, 1800. He was trained as an engineer, but also studied music; played organ in Stockholm churches; took composition lessons with J.M. Kraus. He wrote 5 string quartets; 2 piano sonatas; songs. His style closely approximates that of Haydn.
BIBLIOGRAPHY: G.S. Möner, *Johan Wikmanson* (Stockholm, 1952).

Wilbye, John, one of the greatest English madrigalists; b. Diss, Norfolk (baptized, March 7), 1574; d. Colchester, Sept. 1638. From 1595 until 1628 he was resident musician at Hengrave Hall, the home of Sir Thomas Kytson, near Bury St. Edmunds. After the death of Lady Kytson (1628), Wilbye settled in Colchester. He made frequent visits to London, where the Kytsons had a town house. His first book of madrigals (for 3, 4, 5, and 6 voices) appeared in 1598 (reprinted London, 1841); it contains 30 compositions; his 2nd book, containing 34 madrigals (also for 3 to 6 voices), came out in 1609 (reprinted London, 1846). To Leighton's *Teares or Lamentations* (1614) he contributed 2 hymns, and for *The Triumphes of Oriana* he wrote a 6-part madrigal, *The Lady Oriana.* His madrigals were reprinted in vols. 6/7 of *The English Madrigal School.*
BIBLIOGRAPHY: E.H. Fellowes, *The English Madrigal Composers* (1921; 2nd ed., 1948); H. Heurich, *John Wilbye in seinen Madrigalen* (Augsburg, 1931); P. Johnson, *Form and Transformation in the Music and Poetry of the English Renaissance* (New Haven, 1972); D. Brown, *Wilbye* (Oxford Studies of Composers, 11; London, 1974).

Wilckens, Friedrich, Austrian pianist and composer; b. Liezen, April 13, 1899. He studied piano with Lalewicz in Vienna and composition with Franz Schreker there and in Berlin (1916–20); in 1933 he settled in Seefeld. As a ballet pianist, he made 17 tours in the U.S. and 3 tours in South America. He wrote several ballets (*Himmel und Erde, Schwingender Tempel,* etc.), film music; piano pieces. He retired in 1960 and lived in Tyrol.

Wild, Earl, greatly talented American piano virtuoso; b. Pittsburgh, Nov. 26, 1915. He was educated at the Carnegie Inst. in Pittsburgh; among his piano teachers were Selmar Jansen, Egon Petri, and Paul Doguereau. In 1942 Toscanini invited him to appear with the NBC Symph. Orch.; thus, he became the first and youngest American artist to play under Toscanini. Subsequently, he made extensive tours of the U.S., Europe, and the Orient; was a soloist with the Boston Symph., the Chicago Symph., the Cleveland Orch., and the N.Y. Phil. He commissioned several concertos, among them one by Paul Creston and one by Marvin David Levy. A phenomenal technician of the keyboard, he was greatly acclaimed for his brilliant performances of works of the Romantic era of pianism. He also made transcendentally resonant piano transcriptions of various vocal and orch. works.

Wildberger, Jacques, Swiss composer; b. Basel, Jan. 3, 1922. He studied piano at the Basel Cons., and took lessons in composition with Wladimir Vogel (1948–52); then went to Germany, where he was active as a music teacher in Karlsruhe (1956–66); in 1967 he was appointed a lecturer in harmony and instrumentation at the Basel Musical Academy. In his music he observes the formal traditions of the Baroque, but develops a highly intricate system of interrelated tones, intervals, and rhythms, resulting in a sui generis serial system, with a total emancipation of dissonances.
WORKS: Quartet for Flute, Clarinet, Violin, and Cello (1952); *Tre mutazioni* for Chamber Orch. (1953); Trio for Oboe, Clarinet, and Bassoon (1953); *Vom Kommen und Gehen des Menschen,* cantata (1954); *Concertrum* for Harpsichord (1956); *Ihr meint, das Leben sei kurz,* cantata for Chorus and 10 Instruments (1957); *Intensio—Centrum—Remissio* for Orch. (1958); *Zeitebenen* for 8 Instruments (1958); *Musik* for Cello and Piano (1960); *Musik* for 22 Solo Strings (1960); *Rondeau* for Solo Oboe (1962); *Epitaphe pour Evariste Galois,* "documented action" commemorating a mathematical genius killed in a duel at the age of 20, scored for Narrator, Soprano, Baritone, Speaking Chorus, Tape, and Orch. (1962; Basel, May 20, 1964); Oboe Concerto (1963); *In My End Is My Beginning,* cantata after T.S. Eliot, for Soprano, Tenor, and Chamber Orch. (1964); *Mouvements* for Orch. (1964); Quartet for Flute, Oboe, Harp, and Piano (1967); *Rencontres* for Flute and Piano (1967); *La notte,* trittico for Tape, Mezzo-soprano, and 5 Instruments (1967); *Contratempi* for Solo Flute and 4 Orch. Groups (1970); *Double Refrain* for Flute, English Horn, Guitar, and Tape (1972); *Pour les 9 doigts* for Solo Oboe (1973); *Vision fugitive* for Piano (1973); *Die Stimme, die alte, schwächer werdende Stimme* for Soprano, Cello, Tape, and Orch. (1974); *Diario* for Solo Clarinet (1975); *Prismes* for Solo Saxophone (1975); *Schattenwerk* for Organ (1976).

Wildbrunn (original name, **Wehrenpfennig**), **Helen,** Austrian soprano; b. Vienna, April 8, 1882; d. there, April 11, 1972. She studied with Rosa Papier in Vienna; made her debut as a contralto at the Vienna Volksoper in 1906; then sang in Dortmund (1907–14), she began singing soprano roles in 1914, when she joined the Stuttgart Opera, where she remained until 1918; also sang with the Berlin State Opera (1916–25) and the Deutsche Oper there (1926–29); was a principal member of the Vienna State Opera (1919–32); made guest appearances at Covent Garden in London, La Scala in Milan, and the Teatro Colón in Buenos Aires. After her retirement in 1932, she taught voice at the Vienna Academy of Music (until 1950). Among her finest roles were Kundry and Brünnhilde.

Wilder, Alec (Alexander), remarkably gifted American composer, distinguished in both popular and serious music; b. Rochester, N.Y., Feb. 16, 1907; d. Gainesville, Fla., Dec. 22, 1980. He studied composition at the Eastman School of Music in Rochester with Herbert Inch and Edward Royce; then moved to N.Y., where he entered the world of popular music; he also wrote excellent prose. His popular songs were performed by Frank Sinatra, Judy Garland, and other celebrated singers; his band pieces were in the repertoire of Benny Goodman and Jimmy Dorsey. He excelled in the genre of short operas scored for a limited ensemble of singers and instruments and suitable for performance in schools, while most of his serious compositions, especially his chamber music, are set in an affably melodious, hedonistic, and altogether ingratiating manner. He publ. a useful critical compilation, *American Popular Song: The Great Innovators* (N.Y., 1972), which included analyses of the songs of Jerome Kern, Vincent Youmans, George Gershwin, Cole Porter, and others.

WORKS: FOR THE STAGE: *The Lowland Sea,* folk drama (Montclair, N.J., May 8, 1952); *Cumberland Fair,* a jamboree (Montclair, May 22, 1953); *Sunday Excursion,* musical comedy (Interlochen, Mich., July 18, 1953); *Miss Chicken Little* (Columbia Broadcasting System, Television, Dec. 27, 1953; stage production, Piermont, N.Y., Aug. 29, 1958); 3 operas: *Kittiwake Island* (Interlochen, Aug. 7, 1954); *The Long Way* (Nyack, N.Y., June 3, 1955); *The Impossible Forest* (Westport, Conn., July 13, 1958); *The Truth about Windmills,* chamber opera (Rochester, N.Y., Oct. 14, 1973); *The Tattooed Countess,* chamber opera (1974); *The Opening,* comic opera (1975); 3 children's operas: *The Churkendoose; Rachetty Pachetty House; Herman Ermine in Rabbit Town;* ballet, *Juke Box* (1942). FOR ORCH.: *8 Songs* for Voice and Orch. (Rochester, June 8, 1928); *Symphonic Piece* (Rochester, June 3, 1929); *Suite* for Clarinet and Strings (1947); Concerto for Oboe and Strings (1950); *Beginner's Luck* for Wind Ensemble (1953); 2 concertos for Horn and Chamber Orch. (1954, 1960); 4 works entitled *An Entertainment* (1961–71): No. 1 for Wind Ensemble; No. 2 for Orch.; No. 3 for Wind Ensemble; No. 4 for Horn and Chamber Orch.; 2 concertos for Trumpet and Wind Ensemble; Concerto for Tuba and Wind Ensemble; *Suite* for Horn and Strings (1965); Suite for Saxophone and Strings (1965); Concerto for Saxophone and Chamber Orch. (1967); *Air* for Horn and Wind Ensemble (1968); Concerto for Euphonium and Wind Ensemble (1971). CHAMBER MUSIC: Nonet for Brass (1969); 10 wind quintets (1953–72); 4 brass

quintets; quintets, quartets, trios, duets (many called *Suites*) for numerous wind and brass instruments; 2 flute sonatas (1958, 1962); Clarinet Sonata (1963); 3 bassoon sonatas (1964, 1968, 1973); Saxophone Sonata (1960); 3 horn sonatas (1954, 1957, 1965); sonatas for Viola, Cello, String Bass, Oboe, English Horn, Trumpet, Trombone, Bass Trombone, Euphonium, and Tuba; piano pieces (Sonata; *12 Mosaics; A Debutante's Diary; Neurotic Goldfish; Walking Home in the Spring;* etc.). FOR VOICE: Many songs, of which the most popular were *The Sounds around the House, Blackberry Winter, I'll Be Around, While We're Young, It's So Peaceful a Country,* and *Who Can I Turn To.* He also composed a choral work, *Children's Plea for Peace,* for Narrator, Chorus, and Orch. (1969), and a series of vocal ensembles with satirical words, such as *The House Detective Registers.*

Wilder, (Jérôme Albert) Victor (van), Belgian writer on music; b. Wetteren, near Ghent, Aug. 21, 1835; d. Paris, Sept. 8, 1892. He was a journalist; contributed articles to various publications in Paris, where he settled; wrote librettos; translated Wagner's texts into French, including *Der Ring des Nibelungen;* wrote *Mozart, L'Homme et l'artiste* (Paris, 1880; Eng. trans., 1908) and *Beethoven, Sa vie et ses œuvres* (Paris, 1883).

Wilderer, Johann Hugo von, German composer; b. in Bavaria, c.1670; d. Mannheim (buried, June 7), 1724. He studied with Legrenzi in Venice; was court organist in Düsseldorf and Mannheim. He wrote operas to Italian libretti; of these, *La forza del giusto* had a modicum of success. He also composed sacred music.

BIBLIOGRAPHY: G. Steffen, "Wilderer, Johann Hugo von," in *Rheinische Musiker,* II (Cologne, 1962).

Wildgans, Friedrich, Austrian composer; b. Vienna, June 5, 1913; d. Mödling, near Vienna, Nov. 7, 1965. He studied with J. Marx; taught at the Salzburg Mozarteum (1934–36); then played clarinet at the Vienna Opera; from 1945–47 and from 1950–65, was a prof. at the Vienna State Academy of Music. He has written music in all genres, in an ultramodern style, eventually adopting the 12-tone technique. In 1946 he married the Austrian soprano **Ilona Steingruber.**

WORKS: Opera, *Der Baum der Erkenntniss* (1935); choral symph., *Mayakovsky* (1946); *Sinfonia Austriaca;* 2 clarinet concertos; 3 piano sonatas; chamber music and choruses; he was also the author of *Entwicklung der Musik in Österreich im 20. Jahrhundert* (Vienna, 1950).

Wilding-White, Raymond, American composer; b. Caterham, Surrey, England, Oct. 9, 1922. He studied at the Juilliard School of Music in N.Y. (1947–49) and at the New England Cons. (1949–51); spent the summers of 1949, 1950, and 1951 at Tanglewood studying with Ibert, Dallapiccola, and Copland. He was a producer-director of radio and television in

Boston (1951–56); held the Kulas Chair of Music at the Case Inst. of Technology in Cleveland (1961–67); in 1967 was appointed to the faculty of De Paul Univ. in Chicago, where he founded a multimedia ensemble, The Loop Group.

WORKS: Ballet, *The Trees,* for Wind Quartet, Brass, Percussion, and Piano (1949); chamber opera, *The Tub,* for Soloists and Piano (1952); *The Selfish Giant,* fable for television (1952; Cleveland, 1965); *The Lonesome Valley,* ballet for Organ and Percussion (1960); opera, *Yerma* (1962); *Monday Morning at the Gargoyle Works,* "action-piece" for 5 Performers (1968); Piano Concerto (1949); *Even Now,* variations for Baritone and Orch. (1954); Concertante for Violin, Horn, and Strings (1963); *Bandmusic* for Concert Band (1966); *Haiku* for Soprano, Tenor, and Instruments (1967); *Whatzit* No. 4 (for Louis Lane) for Orch. and Tape (1969); 10 other *Whatzits,* mostly for a particular solo performer, usually accompanied by tape (1967–75); String Quartet (1948); Piano Sonata (1950); Violin Sonata (1956); *Variations* for Chamber Organ and String Trio (1959); *Paraphernalia,* regalia of madrigalia from Pound, for Chorus, Trumpet, Oboe, Clarinet, Violin, and Harpsichord (1959); *For Mallets* for Percussion Ensemble (1962); *5 Fragments* for Jazz Ensemble (1966); *Movement* for String Quartet (1973); songs; a cappella works; electronic pieces.

Wilhelm, Carl Friedrich, German choral composer; b. Schmalkalden, Sept. 5, 1815; d. there, Aug. 26, 1873. From 1839 to 1864 he was director of the Crefeld Liedertafel, for which he composed many men's choruses, among them *Die Wacht am Rhein,* which became a national song of the Germans; it was first performed by the Liedertafel on June 11, 1854, and first publ. in the *Chorliedersammlung* of Erk and Greef (Essen, 1854). In 1860 he received the title of Royal Prussian Music Director; in 1870 he was granted a pension of 3,000 marks.

BIBLIOGRAPHY: K. Gollmick, *C.F. Wilhelm* (Frankfurt, 1848); W. Buchner, *C.F. Wilhelm* (Leipzig, 1874); G. Rogati, *Carl Wilhelm* (Diss., Univ. of Bonn, 1927).

Wilhelmj, August (Emil Daniel Ferdinand Viktor), famous violin virtuoso; b. Usingen, Germany, Sept. 21, 1845; d. London, Jan. 22, 1908. He received his earliest instruction in music from his mother, who was an amateur pianist; then studied violin with Konrad Fischer, court musician at Wiesbaden; made his first appearance there as a child prodigy, on Jan. 8, 1854. In 1861, at the recommendation of Liszt, he was sent to the Leipzig Cons., where he studied with Ferdinand David (violin) and with Hauptmann and Richter (theory); in 1864 he went to Frankfurt for an additional course with Raff; in 1865 he began his concert career, touring Switzerland; then played in the Netherlands and England (1866); France and Italy (1867); Russia, Switzerland, France, and Belgium (1869); England, Scotland, and Ireland (1869–70); then traveled through the Netherlands, Scandinavia, Germany, and Austria (1871–74); to England (1875–77) and to America (1878);

made a 4-year tour of the world to South America, Australia, and Asia (1878–82). In 1876 he was concertmaster of the Bayreuth orch. at the production of *Der Ring des Nibelungen.* For several years he lived chiefly at Biebrich-am-Rhine, where he established (with R. Niemann) a master school for violin playing. In 1886 he moved to Blasewitz, near Dresden; in 1894 he was appointed prof. of violin playing in the Guildhall School of Music in London. His first wife, whom he married in 1866, was Baroness Liphardt, a niece of Ferdinand David; in 1895 he married the pianist **Mariella Mausch.** He made a famous arrangement of Bach's air from the orch. *Suite* in D major which became known as the *Air on the G String* (Bach's original bore no such specification); also arranged Wagner's *Träume* for violin and orch.; wrote a cadenza to Beethoven's Violin Concerto; further composed, for Violin and Orch., 2 *Konzertstücke* (No. 2, *In memoriam*), *Alla polacca,* and Theme and Variations (after 2 caprices of Paganini); *Romanze* for Piano; songs. With James Brown he publ. *A Modern School for the Violin* (6 parts).

BIBLIOGRAPHY: E. Frassinesi, *August Wilhelmj Violinista. Memorie* (Mirandola, 1913); E. Wagner, *Der Geigerkönig August Wilhelmj* (Homburg, 1928).

Wilhem (real name, **Bocquillon**), **Guillaume-Louis,** French music educator; b. Paris, Dec. 18, 1781; d. there, April 26, 1842. The son of an army officer, he himself entered active service at the age of 12; but from 1795–1801 studied at the school of Liancourt, and then for 2 years in the Paris Cons. He taught music in the military school of Saint-Cyr, and in 1810 was appointed a teacher of music at the Lycée Napoléon (later the Collège Henri IV), occupying this position until his death. The system of *enseignement mutuel* (mutual instruction), which had been introduced into the popular schools of France, attracted Wilhem's attention; in 1815 he began to apply it in music teaching, and met with such marked success that in 1819 he was chosen to organize a system of music instruction for the primary schools in Paris; he was appointed singing teacher to the Polytechnique in 1820, and director of the Normal School of Music. In 1833 he conceived the idea of instituting regular reunions of the pupils in one grand chorus, to which he gave the name of Orphéon. In 1835 he was made director-general of music instruction in all the primary schools of Paris, and was created a Chevalier of the Legion of Honor. Besides his school classes, he formed classes of adults, chiefly workingmen, in which the success of his system was equally conspicuous, and which later, under the name of Orphéons, included several popular singing societies. He publ. numerous songs and choruses; also a collection of a cappella choruses, *Orphéon,* in 5 (later 10) vols.; and 4 textbooks.

BIBLIOGRAPHY: E. Niboyet, *Notice historique sur la vie et les ouvrages de G.L.B. Wilhem* (Paris, 1843); J.A. La Fage, *Notice sur Bocquillon-Wilhem* (Paris, 1845).

Wilke, Christian Friedrich Gottlieb, German organist and organ builder; b. Spandau, March 13, 1769; d. Treuenbrietzen, Aug. 1, 1848. He was an organist in Spandau from 1791; in 1821 was named government commissioner for organ building. He publ. *Beiträge zur Geschichte der neuen Orgelbaukunst* (1846); *Über Wichtigkeit und Unentbehrlichkeit der Orgelmixturen* (1839).

Wilkes, Josué Teófilo, Argentine composer and musicologist; b. Buenos Aires, Jan. 8, 1883; d. there, Jan. 10, 1968. He studied with Alberto Williams; in 1908 went to Europe for further study; took some lessons from Liapunov in St. Petersburg, and also at the Schola Cantorum in Paris; returned to Argentina in 1914; for many years taught music in primary schools in Buenos Aires. He made a special study of Gregorian chant; also transcribed and harmonized old colonial songs; composed 3 operas: *Nuite persane* (1916–20), *Por el cetro y la corona,* Byzantine tragedy after *Bajazet* of Racine (1924), *El horoscopo* (after Calderón; 1926–27); secular oratorio, *La cautiva;* symph. trilogy, *Humahuaca* (1911–14); String Octet; other chamber music; songs; *50 canciones populares cuyanas* (arranged and harmonized); *Cancionero musical rioplatense* (Argentine dances). With I. Guerrero Cárpena he publ. *Formas musicales rioplatenses* (Buenos Aires, 1946).

Wilkomirska, Maria, Polish pianist, daughter of **Alfred Wilkomirski;** b. Moscow, April 3, 1904. She studied at the Moscow Cons. with Briusova and Yavorsky; in 1920 she went to Warsaw and continued her studies with Turczyński. She subsequently taught piano in Kalisz, Gdansk, and Lodz; in 1951 she became a prof. at the Warsaw Music School. With her brother, the cellist **Kazimierz Wilkomirski,** and her sister, the violinist **Wanda Wilkomirska,** she organized a trio which gave successful concerts in Europe, China, and Japan.

Wilkomirska, Wanda, Polish violinist, daughter of **Alfred Wilkomirski;** b. Warsaw, Jan. 11, 1929. She studied violin with her father, and later with Irene Dubiska in Warsaw and with Zathureczky in Budapest. She won a prize at the international violin competition in Geneva in 1946 and similar prizes in Budapest in 1948 and in Poznan in 1953. In 1960 she went to Paris and took lessons with Henryk Szeryng. With her brother, the cellist **Kazimierz Wilkomirski,** and her sister, the pianist **Maria Wilkomirska,** she formed a trio which gave successful concerts in Europe and the Orient.

Wilkomirski, Alfred, Polish violinist and pedagogue; b. Asov, Russia, Jan. 3, 1873; d. Lodz, July 31, 1950. He studied with Hřimaly at the Moscow Cons.; in 1920 went to Poland and taught violin in Kalisz (1920–26) and in Lodz (1929–39, 1945–50). His son, **Kazimierz,** the cellist, and his daughters, **Maria,** the pianist, and **Wanda,** the violinist, were all accomplished musicians who formed a successful trio.

Wilkomirski, Kazimierz, Polish cellist, conductor, composer, and pedagogue, son of **Alfred Wilkomirski;** b. Moscow, Sept. 1, 1900. He studied cello and composition at the Moscow Cons.; then went to Warsaw and took courses in composition with Mlynarski at the Warsaw Cons. (1919–23); later traveled to Switzerland and attended classes in conducting with Scherchen in Winterthur. In 1926 he was appointed conductor of the Warsaw Phil.; from 1935 until 1939 he served as director of the Cons. of Gdansk and also conducted the Gdansk Opera. The Nazi assault on Poland forced Wilkomirski to interrupt his musical activities. After the war, he was appointed rector of the Lodz Cons. (1945–47), and later served as a pedagogue at the conservatories of Zoppport (1952–57), Wroclaw (1958–65), and Warsaw (from 1963). His own works are attractively eclectic and Romantically imitative; the best of them are his cello pieces, including several concertos, a method of cello playing, and 12 études. His autobiography, *Wspomnenia,* was publ. in 1971. With his sisters, the pianist **Maria** and the violinist **Wanda,** he formed a trio that achieved notable success in tours in Europe and the Orient.

Willaert, Adrian, important Flemish composer and pedagogue; b. Bruges or Roulaers, c.1490; d. Venice, Dec. 7, 1562. He enrolled as a law student at the Univ. of Paris; then devoted himself to music; studied composition with Jean Mouton, a musician in the Royal Chapel. In 1515 he entered the service of Cardinal Ippolito I d'Este of Ferrara; he accompanied the cardinal, who was Archbishop of Esztergom, to Hungary in 1517; the cardinal died in 1520, and Willaert entered the service of Duke Alfonso I d'Este of Ferrara (1522); subsequently was in the service of Cardinal Ippolito II d'Este, the Archbishop of Milan (1525–27). On Dec. 12, 1527, he was appointed maestro di cappella of St. Mark's in Venice; with the exception of 2 visits to Flanders (1542 and 1556–57), he remained in Venice for the rest of his life, as a composer and teacher. Among his famous pupils were Zarlino, Cipriaro de Rore, Andrea Gabrieli, and Costanzo Porta. Willaert was justly regarded as a founder of the great Venetian school of composition; the style of writing for 2 antiphonal choirs (prompted by the twin opposed organs of St. Mark's Cathedral) was principally initiated by him. He was one of the greatest masters of the madrigal and of the instrumental ricercare; he also wrote motets, chansons, Psalms, and masses.

WORKS: *Liber quinque missarum* (Venice, 1536); *Hymnorum musica* (Venice, 1542); *I sacri e santi salmi che si cantano a Vespro e Compieta...* for 4 Voices (Venice, 1555; augmented ed., 1571); *Motecta... liber primus* for 4 Voices (Venice, 1539; augmented ed., 1545); *Mottetti... libro secundo* for 4 Voices (Venice, 1539; augmented ed., 1545); *Motecta... liber primus* for 5 Voices (Venice, 1539; *Il primo libro di motetti* for 6 Voices (Venice, 1542); *Musica nova* (Venice, 1559); *Livre de meslanges... 26 chansons* (Paris, 1560); *Cincquiesme livre de chansons* for 3 Voices (Paris, 1560); *Musica nova* (Venice, 1559); *Madrigali* for 4 Voices (Venice,

1563); *9 ricercares a 3* (1551; ed. by H. Zenck, Mainz and Leipzig, 1933). For the complete works, see H. Zenck and W. Gerstenberg, eds., *Adrian Willaert: Opera omnia,* in the Corpus Mensurabilis Musicae series, iii/1— (Rome, 1950—).

BIBLIOGRAPHY: E. Gregoir, *Adrien Willaert* (Brussels, 1869); E. Hertzmann, *Adrian Willaert in der weltlichen Vokalmusik seiner Zeit* (Leipzig, 1931); R.B. Lenaerts, "Notes sur Adrien Willaert," *Bulletin de l'Institut Historique Belge de Rome,* XV (1935); R.B. Lenaerts, "La Chapelle de Saint-Marc à Venise sous Adrien Willaert," *Bulletin de l'Institut Historique Belge de Rome,* XIX (1938); J.S. Levitan, "Adrian Willaert's Famous *Duo Quidnam ebrietas,*" *Tijdschrift van de Vereniging voor Nederlandse Muziekgeschiedenis,* XV/3 (1938) and XV/4 (1939); R.B. Lenaerts, "Voor de biographie van Adrian Willaert," in *Hommage à Charles van den Borren: Mélanges* (Antwerp, 1945); A. Carapetyan, "The Musica Nova of Adrian Willaert," *Journal of Renaissance and Baroque Music,* I (1946–47); A. Einstein, *The Italian Madrigal* (Princeton, 1949); G. Reese, *Music in the Renaissance* (N.Y., 1954; 2nd ed., revised, 1959); E. Lowinsky, "Adrian Willaert's Chromatic Duo Re-examined," *Tijdschrift van de Vereniging voor Nederlandse Muziekgeschiedenis,* XVIII/1 (1956); H. Beck, "Adrian Willaerts Messen," *Archiv für Musikwissenschaft,* XVII (1960); A. Carver, "The Psalms of Willaert and His North Italian Contemporaries," *Acta Musicologica,* XLVII (1975).

Willan, Healey, eminent English-born Canadian composer, organist, and music educator; b. Balham, Surrey, Oct. 12, 1880; d. Toronto, Feb. 16, 1968. He received his musical training at St. Saviour's Choir School in Eastbourne (1888–1895); was a church organist in London until 1913, when he went to Canada as head of the theory dept. at the Royal Cons. in Toronto; was vice-principal there (1920–36). In 1914 he was appointed a lecturer and examiner at the Univ. of Toronto; in 1937, a prof. of music; he retired in 1950; was also the Univ. organist (1932–64) and organist of St. Mary Magdalene Church in Toronto from 1921 until his death; was founder and conductor of the Tudor Singers (1934–39). In 1956 he was awarded the historic Lambeth Doctorate by the Archbishop of Canterbury, and in 1967 was the first musician to become a Companion of the Order of Canada. He was greatly esteemed as a pedagogue.

WORKS: 2 radio operas, *Transit through Fire* (1941–42; Canadian Radio, March 8, 1942) and *Deirdre* (1943–45; Canadian Radio, April 20, 1946; revised 1962 and 1965; first stage perf., Toronto, 1965); historical pageant, *Brébeuf and His Brethren* (CBC Radio, Sept. 26, 1943); several ballad-operas; 2 symphs.: No. 1 (Toronto, Oct. 8, 1936) and No. 2 (1941; revised 1948; Toronto, May 18, 1950); Piano Concerto (Montreal, Aug. 24, 1944; revised 1949); *Agincourt Song* for Chorus and Small Orch. (1929); *Overture to an Unwritten Comedy* (1951); several ceremonial pieces, including *Coronation March* for Orch. (1937), *Te Deum Laudamus* for Chorus and Small Orch. (1937), *Coronation Suite* for Chorus and Orch. (1952), *Royal Salute* for Orch. (1959), and *Centennial March* for Orch. (1967); *Royce Hall Suite* for Symph. Band (1949); 2 violin sonatas (1920, 1923); several character pieces for piano; organ works; carols and hymn tunes; church services; motets a cappella; anthems with organ accompaniment; many other choral works; songs; arrangements of Canadian and British songs; school manuals. A catalogue of Willan's works was publ. by G. Bryant (Ottawa, 1972).

BIBLIOGRAPHY: F. Clarke, *Healy Willan: Life and Music* (Toronto, 1983).

Willcocks, Sir David, English organist, conductor, and educator; b. Newquay, Dec. 30, 1919. He was educated at Clifton College and King's College, Cambridge; served in the British army; after the war he was organist at Salisbury Cathedral (1947–50) and Worcester Cathedral (1950–57); then at King's College, Cambridge (1957–73); also held the posts of univ. lecturer (1957–74) and univ. organist (1958–74) at Cambridge; concurrently he led the City of Birmingham Choir (1950–57) and was conductor of the Cambridge Univ. Musical Society (1958–73). In 1960 he became music director of the Bach Choir; in 1974 he also assumed the post of director of the Royal College of Music in London. He was awarded the Order of the British Empire in 1971; was knighted in 1977. He served as general editor of the Church Music series of the Oxford Univ. Press.

Willeke, Willem, Dutch-American cellist; b. The Hague, Sept. 29, 1879; d. Pittsfield, Mass., Nov. 26, 1950. He studied cello in the Netherlands; then was a cellist in various German orchs.; also at the Vienna Opera (under Mahler). In 1908 he came to the U.S. and joined the Kneisel Quartet, with which he remained until its disbandment in 1917; taught at the Inst. of Musical Art in N.Y.; then was appointed director of the Berkshire Music Colony, in Pittsfield, Mass., where he remained until his death.

Willent-Bordogni, Jean-Baptiste-Joseph, French bassoon virtuoso; b. Douai, Dec. 8, 1809; d. Paris, May 11, 1852. He studied with Delcambre at the Paris Cons.; played the bassoon in the orch. of the Théâtre Italien in Paris; married the daughter of the singing teacher Bordogni (1834) and added her name to his; taught at the Brussels Cons.; in 1848 was appointed to the faculty of the Paris Cons. He wrote a number of works for the bassoon, and publ. a method for it; also brought out 2 operas in Brussels: *Le Moine* (1844) and *Van Dyck* (1845).

Williams, Alberto, prolific Argentine composer; b. Buenos Aires, Nov. 23, 1862; d. there, June 17, 1952. He was the grandson of an Englishman; his maternal grandfather, **Amancio Alcorta,** was one of Argentina's early composers. Williams studied composition at the Paris Cons. with Guiraud, Durand, and Godard, piano with Mathias (a pupil of Chopin), and organ and counterpoint with César Franck. He returned to Argentina in 1889; founded the Alberto

Williams Cons. in 1893; also organized branches of the Cons. in provincial towns of Argentina, numbering more than 100; founded a music publ. firm La Quena (also a music magazine of that name). He was the most prolific composer of Argentina; 112 opus numbers were publ. by La Quena. The greatest influence in his music was that of Franck, but modernistic usages are found in Williams's application of whole-tone scales, parallel chord progressions, etc. In many of his works he used characteristic melorhythms of Argentina; composed a number of piano pieces in Argentinian song and dance forms (milongas, gatos, cielitos, etc.).

WORKS: 9 symphs., all perf. for the first time in Buenos Aires: No. 1 (Nov. 25, 1907); No. 2, *La bruja de las montañas* (Sept. 9, 1910); No. 3, *La Selva sagrada* (Dec. 8, 1934); No. 4, *El Ataja-Caminos* (Dec. 15, 1935); No. 5, *El corazón de la muñeca* (Nov. 29, 1936); No. 6, *La muerte del cometa* (Nov. 26, 1937); No. 7, *Eterno reposo* (Nov. 26, 1937); several suites of Argentine dances; 3 violin sonatas; Cello Sonata; Piano Trio; a great number of piano albums, the last of which was *En el parque* (1952). He composed 136 opus numbers in all. He also publ. numerous didactic works and several books of poetry. A complete catalogue of his works is found in vol. 2 of *Composers of the Americas,* publ. by the Pan-American Union, Washington, D.C. (1956; pp. 138–55).

BIBLIOGRAPHY: Z.R. Lacoigne, *Alberto Williams; Músico argentino* (Buenos Aires, 1942); *Homenajes a Alberto Williams,* containing messages and opinions of musicians on the occasion of his 80th birthday (Buenos Aires, 1942); N. Slonimsky, "Alberto Williams: Father of Argentinian Music," *Musical America* (Jan. 10, 1942); V.A. Risolía, *Alberto Williams, Curriculum vitae* (Buenos Aires, 1944).

Williams, Andy (Andrew), American singer of popular music; b. Wall Lake, Iowa, Dec. 3, 1930. With 3 of his brothers, he formed the Williams Brothers Quartet and sang on the radio in Des Moines, Chicago, Cincinnati, and Los Angeles; Kay Thompson later joined the group; they toured together until 1953; he then began a solo career as a vocalist; made numerous concert appearances, as well as films, television stints, and recordings.

Williams, Charles Francis Abdy, English writer on music; b. Dawlish, Devonshire, July 16, 1855; d. Milford, near Lymington, Feb. 27, 1923. While pursuing his studies at Trinity College, Cambridge, he played violin and viola in the orch. of the Cambridge Univ. Musical Society; then went to New Zealand, where he was a church organist in Auckland; returning to England in 1881, he took the degree of Mus.Bac. at Oxford (1889) and Cambridge (1891); from 1895–1901, was director of music at the Greek Theatre at Bradfield College, where he wrote choruses in ancient Greek modes for the productions of Greek tragedies. Retiring from teaching in 1901, he devoted himself to scholarly work; in 1904 he introduced the Solesmes system of performing plainchant at the priests' seminary in Capri, which won him recognition from the Pope.

WRITINGS: *A Short Historical Account of the Degrees in Music at Oxford and Cambridge* (1893); *Bach* (1900; new ed., 1934) and *Handel* (1901; new ed., 1935; in the series The Master Musicians); *The Story of the Organ* (1903); *The Story of Notation* (1903); *The Story of Organ Music* (1905); *The Rhythm of Modern Music* (1909); *The Aristoxenian Theory of Musical Rhythm* (1911); essays on Greek music and plainchant in various journals.

Williams, Charles Lee, English organist and composer; b. Winchester, May 1, 1853; d. Gloucester, Aug. 29, 1935. He was a pupil of Dr. Arnold at the Cathedral of Winchester; from 1872 filled various posts as an organist and choirmaster in Ireland and England; conducted several of the Three Choirs Festivals held at Gloucester; after 1898 became active in the educational field. He composed the cantatas *Gethsemane, Bethany, A Harvest Song, A Dedication,* etc.; much church music; brought out (with H.G. Chance) a continuation (1895, covering the years 1864–94) of D. Lysons's *Origin and Progress of the Meeting of the Three Choirs of Gloucester, Worcester, and Hereford* (1812, covering the years 1724–1811; supplemental vol. by John Amott in 1865, covering the years 1812–64); in 1931 brought out, with H.G. Chance and T. Hannan-Clark, a further continuation (covering the years 1895–1930) of the work, under the title *Annals of the Three Choirs.*

Williams, Charles Melvin, a.k.a. **"Cootie,"** black American jazz trumpeter; b. Mobil, Ala., July 24, 1910. He took trumpet lessons with Charles Lipskin; made his way to N.Y., and joined groups led by Chick Webb and Fletcher Henderson. From 1929 to 1940 he was a member of Duke Ellington's band; led his own groups for a time, but returned to Ellington's band in 1962.

Williams, Christopher à Becket, English composer and writer on music; b. Dorchester, July 2, 1890; d. London, Nov. 3, 1956. He studied at Keble College, Oxford; was in the British army during World War I; subsequently traveled in Europe, Asia, and America; wrote 2 travel books, 3 novels, etc.; also contributed to musical periodicals. He composed several orch. suites: *5 Impressions, Pepperpot Suite, Welsh Suite, Theme and Derivations* for Strings, etc.; 3 violin sonatas; Cello Sonata; 2 piano sonatas; several piano suites.

Williams, Clifton, American bandmaster; b. Traskwood, Ark., March 26, 1923; d. South Miami, Fla., Feb. 12, 1976. He studied at Louisiana State Univ. (B.M., 1947) and with Bernard Rogers and Howard Hanson at the Eastman School of Music in Rochester, N.Y. (M.M., 1948). He played French horn with the symph. orchs. of San Antonio and New Orleans; was on the staff of the music dept. at the Univ. of Texas in Austin (1949–66); then at the Univ. of Miami (1966–76). He composed band music, including the phenomenally popular *Sinfonians.* His other band pieces include *Trail Scenes; Trilogy Suite; Concertino* for Percussion and Band; 3 symph. dances; *Fanfare and Allegro; Dedicatory Overture; Dramatic Essay: The Ramparts; The Patriots* (commissioned by NORAD); *Songs of Heritage; Academic Procession; Castle Gap March; Strategic Air Command.*

Williams, David Christmas, Welsh conductor and composer; b. Llanwrtyd, Sept. 12, 1871; d. there, March 21, 1926. He studied with J. Parry at the South Wales School of Music; conducted various music societies in Wales; wrote a cantata, *The Sands of Lavan,* which received a prize at Cardiff (1893); *The Battle of the Severn* for Chorus and Orch.; *Psalms of Praise;* men's choruses; songs; piano pieces.

Williams, Frederic Arthur, American pianist, composer, and pedagogue; b. Oberlin, Ohio, March 3, 1869; d. Cleveland, July 31, 1942. He studied piano and composition with W.G. Smith and others in Cleveland; subsequently occupied various teaching posts in Ohio. He wrote about 250 pieces for piano; also some songs. His technical publications for piano include *Wrist and Forearm Studies* and *Octave and Chord Studies.*

Williams, Grace, Welsh composer; b. Barry, Glamorganshire, Feb. 19, 1906; d. there, Feb. 10, 1977. Her father led the local boys' chorus and played the piano in a home trio, with Grace Williams on the violin and her brother on the cello. In 1923 she entered the music dept. of the Univ. of Wales in Cardiff, in the composition class of David Evans. Upon graduation in 1926 she enrolled at the Royal College of Music in London. There she was accepted as a student of Vaughan Williams, who had the greatest influence on her career as a composer, both in idiom and form; she also took classes with Gordon Jacob. She subsequently received the Octavia Traveling Scholarship and went to Vienna to take lessons with Egon Wellesz (1930–31). She did not espouse the atonal technique of the 2nd Viennese School, but her distinctly diatonic harmony with strong tertian underpinning was artfully embroidered with nicely hung deciduous chromatics of a decidedly nontonal origin. She marked May 10, 1951, in her diary as a "day of destruction," when she burned all her MSS unworthy of preservation. Among her practical occupations was teaching school and writing educational scripts for the BBC. She was particularly active in her advancement of Welsh music.
WORKS: For the stage: *Theseus and Ariadne,* ballet (1935); *The Parlour,* opera (1961). For Orch.: 2 symphs. (1943; 1956, revised 1975); *Sinfonia concertante* for Piano and Orch. (1941); *Sea Sketches* (1944); *The Dark Island Suite* (1950); *Castell Caernarfon,* for the investiture of the Prince of Wales (1962); Violin Concerto (1950); Trumpet Concerto (1963). Chamber music: Sextet for Oboe, Trumpet, Violin, Viola, Cello, and Piano (1931); *Suite* for 9 Instruments (1934); numerous choruses and songs.
BIBLIOGRAPHY: Malcolm Boyd, *Grace Williams* (Cardiff, 1980).

Williams, Hank, seeded American country-western singer; b. Georgiana, Ala., Sept. 17, 1923; d. in his automobile en route to a performance in Canton, Ohio, Jan. 1, 1953. He sang church hymns and learned to play the organ at a very early age; then took guitar lessons from a black street singer. At 12 he won a prize in an amateur contest in Montgomery singing his own song, *W.P.A. Blues.* At 14 he formed his own band, Hank Williams and His Drifting Cowboys. In 1946 he went to Nashville; in 1949 he joined the famous "Grand Ole Opry" there, and made an instant success with his rendition of *Lovesick Blues;* its disk sold over a million copies. In 1950 he put out several recordings of his own songs, *Long Gone Lonesome Blues, I Just Don't Like This Kind of Livin', Why Don't You Love Me?,* and *Moanin' the Blues,* which sold prodigiously. His subsequent releases, also magically successful, were *Hey, Good Lookin'; Your Cheatin' Heart; Move It On Over; Cold, Cold Heart;* and *Jambalaya (On the Bayou);* but the nemesis of so many country singers—drugs, alcohol, women in excess—and a cardiac disorder killed him before he reached the age of 30. His son, **Hank Williams, Jr.,** was also a successful country singer, and was also beset by alcohol and drug problems, but after a horrible automobile accident, he became rehabilitated. A television show on his life, *Living Proof,* was produced in 1983.

Williams, Harry Evan, American tenor; b. Mineral Ridge, Ohio, Sept. 7, 1867; d. Akron, Ohio, May 24, 1918. Originally he worked in a mine and steel mill; then studied singing in Cleveland and N.Y.; made his debut at the Worchester (Mass.) Festival of 1896, and then sang in oratorio at many other festivals; gave nearly 1,000 recitals.

Williams, John, enormously successful American composer and conductor; b. Flushing, N.Y., Feb. 8, 1932. He grew up in a musical atmosphere; his father was a film studio musician. He began to take piano lessons; later he learned to play trombone, trumpet, and clarinet. In 1948 the family moved to Los Angeles, where he studied orchestration with Robert van Epps at Los Angeles City College and composition privately with Mario Castelnuovo-Tedesco; he also took piano lessons with Rosina Lhévinne at the Juilliard School of Music in N.Y. He began his career as a composer, arranger, and conductor for films and television; wrote the film scores, rich in sounding brass and tinkling cymbals, for *Close Encounters of the Third Kind, Superman, The Empire Strikes Back, Raiders of the Lost Ark, E.T., The Extraterrestrial,* and *Return of the Jedi.* He won Academy Awards for *Fiddler on the Roof* (1971), *Jaws* (1975), and *Star Wars* (1977). The record albums for these background scores sold into the millions. He also wrote 2 symphs., a Violin Concerto, a Flute Concerto, an *Essay for Strings,* and a number of chamber music pieces. In 1980 he was chosen conductor of the Boston Pops Orch., succeeding the late Arthur Fiedler, who had held that post for almost 50 years; Williams declared openly that no one could hope to equal Fiedler in charisma and showmanship, not to mention Fiedler's splendiferous aureole of white hair (as contrasted with his successor's alopecia), but he said he would try his darndest to bridge the gap. He largely succeeded, and diversified his appeal to Boston Pops audiences by playing selections from his own sparkling film scores.

BIBLIOGRAPHY: R. Dyer, "John Williams," *Ovation* (June 1983).

Williams, John, remarkable guitarist; b. Melbourne, Australia, April 24, 1941. He first studied with his father, a noted guitar teacher; then took guitar lessons with Segovia in Siena; also attended courses in music theory at the Royal College of Music in London. In 1958 he made a successful debut in London; in 1962 made a tour of the Soviet Union; also played in America and Japan. In addition to classical music, he includes in his programs pieces of pop music and jazz; this egalitarian versatility makes him a favorite with untutored youth in England and America.

Williams, John Gerrard, English composer; b. London, Dec. 10, 1888; d. Oxted, Surrey, March 7, 1947. He was an architect by profession, but took some lessons in music from Richard Walthew, and soon began to compose; presented a concert of his works (chamber music, piano pieces, and songs) in London on March 27, 1922. He wrote a ballad opera, *Kate, the Cabin-Boy* (London, 1924); 2 operettas; a ballet, *The Wings of Horus* (1928); *3 Miniatures* and *Elegiac Rhapsody* for Orch.; 2 string quartets; many songs and part-songs.

Williams, John M., American pianist and pedagogue; b. on a plantation in Washington County, Texas, Jan. 1, 1884; d. Los Angeles, Dec. 6, 1974. He studied in N.Y. and Chicago; from 1913 lectured on musical pedagogy to music teachers in the major cities of the U.S., Canada, England, and Scotland. His teaching material has had worldwide distribution, having been publ. in Great Britain, Australia, Cuba, and South America (Spanish eds.). Some 10 million copies of his various piano books have been sold. Among his teaching publications are the *Grade by Grade* and *Year by Year* books; *A Child's First Music Book; Nothing Easier or Adventures of Ten Little Fingers in Mother Goose Land: First Book for the Adult Beginner.*

Williams, Joseph, English music publisher. He was the son of Lucy Williams, who established a printing shop in London in 1808. Joseph Williams continued the business; was succeeded in 1883 by his son, **Joseph Benjamin Williams** (who publ. some of his own pieces under the nom de plume of **Florian Pascal**); the business was incorporated as Joseph Williams, Ltd., in 1900. Upon the death of J.B. Williams, his son, **Florian Williams,** became head of the company. Joseph Williams, Ltd. specialized in publishing contemporary English music; also brought out Elizabethan works.

BIBLIOGRAPHY: Florian Williams, "After Forty Years. Recollections of a Music Publisher," *Musical Opinion* (Feb.–Dec. 1940).

Williams, Mary Lou (Mary Elfrieda Scruggs), black American jazz pianist, composer, and arranger; b. Atlanta, May 8, 1910; d. Durham, N.C., May 28, 1981. She began her career as a pianist in Kansas City with Andy Kirk's band; in 1931 she became pianist and arranger for Kirk's Twelve Clouds of Joy band, and provided him with such songs as *Walkin' & Swingin', Twinklin', Cloudy,* and *Little Joe from Chicago;* she then worked with Duke Ellington, Benny Goodman, and others. In 1945 she composed the bebop hit *In the Land of Oo-Bla-Dee* for Dizzy Gillespie; she also wrote *The Zodiac Suite,* which was performed by the N.Y. Phil. After becoming a Roman Catholic, she composed a number of religious works, including *St. Martin de Porres* and 3 masses; her mass *Music for Peace* became popularly known as "Mary Lou's Mass." In 1977 she was named artist-in-residence at Duke Univ. in Durham. She was one of the leading figures in the jazz field for almost 60 years.

Williams, Ralph Vaughan. See **Vaughan Williams, Ralph.**

Williams, Spencer, American composer of popular music; b. New Orleans, Oct. 14, 1889; d. New York, July 14, 1965. He played piano in nightclubs in New Orleans, Chicago and N.Y.; wrote songs in the slow rhythmic manner of the New Orleans blues. In 1932 he went to Europe for a prolonged stay; lived in Paris (where he was accompanist for Josephine Baker), London, and Stockholm; returned to the U.S. in 1957. His most famous song is *Basin Street Blues* (1928); he wrote many blues and other songs: *Tishomingo Blues* (1917), *Arkansas Blues, Mississippi Blues, Royal Garden Blues;* his *Mahogany Hall Stomp* became a perennial favorite.

Williamson, John Finley, American choral conductor; b. Canton, Ohio, June 23, 1887; d. Toledo, Ohio, May 28, 1964. He studied singing with Witherspoon and Bispham in N.Y.; organ with Karl Straube in Leipzig. In 1921 he founded the Westminster Choir, and in 1926, the Westminster Choir School (later College) at Princeton, N.J.; was its president until 1958, when he resigned. With his choir he gave 1,000 concerts in America; also made 2 European tours; edited the Westminster Series of choral music.

Williamson, Malcolm, Australian composer; b. Sydney, Nov. 21, 1931. He studied composition with Eugene Goossens at the Sydney Cons. (1944–50); in 1953 went to London, where he took lessons with Elisabeth Lutyens and Erwin Stein (1953–57); learned to play the organ and was employed as a church organist in England (1955–60); visited the U.S. in 1970, and was composer-in-residence at

Westminster Choir College in Princeton, N.J. for an academic season; then returned to England. In 1975 he became Master of the Queen's Musick; in 1976 was made a Commander of the Order of the British Empire; in 1977 was elected president of the Royal Phil. Orch.

WORKS: OPERAS: *Our Man in Havana,* after Graham Greene's novel (London, July 2, 1963); *The English Eccentrics,* chamber opera (Aldeburgh Festival, June 11, 1964); *The Happy Prince,* children's opera after Oscar Wilde (Farnham, May 22, 1965); *Julius Caesar Jones,* children's opera for Children's Voices and 3 Adults (London, Jan. 4, 1966); *The Violins of St. Jacques,* in 3 acts (London, Nov. 29, 1966); *Dunstan and the Devil,* chamber opera (Cookham, May 19, 1967); *The Growing Castle,* chamber opera for 4 Singers, Piano, Harpsichord, Tubular Chimes, and Drums, after Strindberg's *Dream Play* (Dynevor Festival, Aug. 13, 1968, with the composer alternately at the piano and the harpsichord); *Lucky-Peter's Journey,* after Strindberg's fairy-tale play (1969); *The Stone Wall* (London, Sept. 18, 1971); *Genesis* (1971; London, April 23, 1973); *The Red Sea* (1972); *The Death of Cuchulain* (1972); *The Winter Star* (1972); choral operatic sequence *The Brilliant and the Dark,* for Women's Voices and Orch. (1969); 3 cassations for Audience, and Orch. or Piano: *The Moonrakers* (1967; Brighton, April 22, 1967); *Knights in Shining Armour* (1968; Brighton, April 19, 1968); *The Snow Wolf* (Brighton, April 30, 1968). BALLETS: *The Display,* dance symph. in 4 movements (Adelaide Festival, March 14, 1964); *Sun into Darkness* (London, April 13, 1966). FOR ORCH.: *Elevamini,* Symph. No. 1 (1956–57); *Santiago de Espada,* overture (1958); 3 piano concertos (1958; with String Orch., 1960; 1961); Organ Concerto (1961); *Sinfonietta concertante* for 3 Trumpets, Piano, and Strings (1959–61); Violin Concerto (Bath, England, June 15, 1965; Yehudi Menuhin, soloist); Sinfonietta (1965); *Concerto Grosso* for Orch. (London, Aug. 28, 1965); *Symphonic Variations* (Edinburgh, Sept. 9, 1965); Symph. No. 2 (Bristol, Oct. 29, 1969); *Epitaphs for Edith Sitwell* for Strings (1969; originally for Organ, 1965); Concerto for 2 Pianos and Strings (1972); *The Icy Mirror* for Soloists, Chorus, and Orch. (Cheltenham Festival, July 9, 1972); *Ode to Music* for Chorus, Echo Chorus, and Orch. (London, Feb. 3, 1973); *Hammerskjöld Portrait* for Soprano and Strings (London, July 30, 1974). CHAMBER MUSIC: *Variations* for Cello and Piano (1964); Concerto for 2 Pianos (8-hands) and Wind Quintet (1965); *Serenade* for Flute, Piano, and String Trio (1967). FOR KEYBOARD: 2 piano sonatas (1958; revised 1971–72); *5 Preludes* for Piano (1966); 2-piano Sonata (1967); Piano Quintet (1968); Symph. for Organ (1960). FOR VOICE: Choruses, including *Symphony for Voices* a cappella (1960) and *The Musicians of Bremen* (1972).

BIBLIOGRAPHY: James Murdoch, *Australian Contemporary Composers* (Melbourne, 1972; pp. 205–209).

Willis, Henry, English organ builder; b. London, April 27, 1821; d. there, Feb. 11, 1901. As a youth he worked for John Gray (later Gray & Davidson), and while yet an apprentice, invented the special manual and pedal couplers which he later used in his own instruments; from 1842 to 1845 he worked for Evans at Cheltenham, and in 1845 established his own business in London. He rebuilt the organ in the Gloucester Cathedral; exhibited a large organ at the Crystal Palace in 1851, which won the Council Medal and was installed in the Winchester Cathedral; he subsequently was commissioned to build the great organ in St. George's Hall in Liverpool (1855). In 1878 he took his sons **Vincent** and **Henry** into partnership, adopting the firm name of Henry Willis & Sons; he became generally known as "Father Willis." Willis himself regarded the organ in St. Paul's, which he built in 1891, as his masterpiece (77 speaking stops, 19 couplers). After the founder's death in 1901, his son Henry Willis became the head of the business, and soon took his son, also named **Henry Willis,** into partnership. They built the organ in the Liverpool Cathedral (167 speaking stops, 48 couplers) in 1912–14; this organ was the largest in the world at the time.

Willis Music Co., American music publishers. The business was founded by **Charles H. Willis** at Cincinnati in 1899, in association with his son **William H. Willis.** The firm became known as W.H. Willis & Co.; after the absorption of G.B. Jennings & Co. in 1910 it was incorporated as the Willis Music Co. On July 1, 1919, the business was acquired by Gustave Schirmer of N.Y. The company specialized in educational publications.

Willis, Richard Storrs, American composer and writer on music; b. Boston, Feb. 10, 1819; d. Detroit, May 7, 1900. He was a brother of the poet Nathaniel Parker Willis; studied at Yale Univ., where he was president of the Beethoven Society (1837), for which he wrote choruses and instrumental pieces. He then went to Germany, and studied theory with Schnyder von Wartensee in Frankfurt and with Hauptmann in Leipzig. Returning to N.Y., he edited the periodical *Musical World* (1852–60); brought out the collections *Church Chorals and Choir Studies* (N.Y., 1850) and *Our Church Music* (N.Y., 1856); also composed student songs and patriotic hymns, later collected as *Waif of Song* and publ. in Paris (1876).

Willman, Allan, American composer and pianist; b. Hinckley, Ill., May 11, 1909. He studied at the Chicago Musical College (M.M., 1930); then took lessons with Nadia Boulanger in Paris (1935). In 1936 he joined the faculty of the Univ. of Wyoming. His works include *Idyl* for Orch. (1930); *Solitude* for Orch. (1930; Boston, Symph., April 20, 1936); *A Ballade of the Night* for Voice and String Quartet (1936); numerous piano pieces and songs.

Willmers, Rudolf, pianist and composer; b. Copenhagen, Oct. 31, 1821; d. Vienna, Aug. 24, 1878. His father, a Danish agriculturist, sent him to Germany at the age of 13 to study science, but Willmers turned to music; took lessons with Hummel for 2 years and with Friedrich Schneider for a year; became a concert pianist and toured successfully in Germany and Austria; was much acclaimed in Paris and London (1846–47); in 1866 settled in Vienna. His technical specialty was the performance of "chains of trills," for which he was famous. He wrote a number of brilliant piano solos: *6 études; Sérénade érotique* (for the left hand); *Sehnsucht am Meere; Un Jour d'été en Norvège; 2 études de concert (La pompa di festa* and *La danza delle Baccanti); Sonata héroïque; Tarantella giocosa; La Sylphide; Trillerketten; Aus der Geisterwelt,* tremolo-caprice; *Allegro symphonique;* he also composed some chamber music.

BIBLIOGRAPHY: T. de L***, "Notice sur la vie et les travaux artistiques de R. Willmers," *Archives des Hommes du Jour* (April 1847; also separately).

Willner, Arthur, pianist and composer; b. Teplice, Czechoslovakia, March 5, 1881; d. London, April 7, 1959. He studied at the Leipzig Cons. and in Munich. From 1904 to 1924 he taught at the Stern Cons. in Berlin; from 1924 to 1938 he lived in Vienna; in 1938 settled in London. His list of works includes more than 100 opus numbers: a Symph.; Cello Concerto; Piano Concerto; 5 string quartets; 4 violin sonatas; 3 sonatas for violin and piano; 4 piano sonatas and several character pieces; choral works; organ works; songs.

Wills, Bob (James Robert Wills), American country-music singer, bandleader, and songwriter; b. near Kosse, Texas, March 6, 1905; d. Fort Worth, May 13, 1975. He first took up the mandolin, then began to play the fiddle; through his association with local black musicians, he learned blues and jazz as well. In 1929 he organized his own group, the Wills Fiddle Band; subsequently he appeared on radio and made many recordings. After settling in Tulsa, Okla., he became a fixture on station KVOO with his Texas Playboys band. He gained popularity with his composition *San Antonio Rose;* he was elected to the Country Music Hall of Fame in 1968.

Willson, Meredith, American composer of coruscating Americanistic musicals, and a fine flutist; b. Mason City, Iowa, May 18, 1902; d. Santa Monica, Calif., June 15, 1984. He learned to play the flute as a child, and played in a school orch. at the age of 11. In 1916 he was sent to N.Y., where he took flute lessons with Georges Barrère. In 1919 he joined Sousa's band as a flute player and traveled with it until 1922. From 1923 to 1928 he was a flutist in the N.Y. Phil. He then entered the field of radio as a conductor and composer. For the 30th anniversary of the San Francisco earthquake he wrote a symph., which he conducted in its first performance, in San Francisco on April 19, 1936. His 2nd Symph. was first played by the Los Angeles Phil. on April 4, 1940. His other symph. works include *The Jervis Bay; Symphonic Variations on an American Theme;* and *O.O. McIntyre Suite.* He also wrote many band pieces and a choral work, *Anthem of the Atomic Age.* Then he devoted himself to the composition of popular music, in which he revealed a triple talent as a performer, writer, and composer. He appeared as a comedian on a radio program, "The Big Show," in which he engaged in a comic colloquy with Tallulah Bankhead, closing with an inspirational hymn, *May the Good Lord Bless and Keep You,* which became very popular as an anthem. Willson achieved his triumph with his musical revue *The Music Man,* for which he wrote the book, the lyrics, and the music. It opened on Broadway on Dec. 19, 1957, and became an immediate success, thanks to the satirical and yet somehow patriotic subject, dealing with a traveling salesman of band uniforms and instruments who sells them to hick-town suckers; and to the sparkling score, containing the hit chorus *76 Trombones.* His subsequent musicals were *The Unsinkable Molly Brown,* produced on Broadway in 1960, for which he wrote the musical score, and *Here's Love,* produced on Broadway in 1963, an adaptation of the film *Miracle on 34th Street. The Music Man* and *The Unsinkable Molly Brown* were made into films. Willson was also active as an arranger and orchestrator in Hollywood; he helped Charlie Chaplin in arranging the score for his anti-Hitler, anti-Mussolini film, *The Great Dictator.* He publ. several autobiographical books: *And There I Stood with My Piccolo* (N.Y., 1948), *Eggs I Have Laid* (N.Y., 1955), and *But He Doesn't Know the Territory* (descriptive of the origin of *The Music Man;* N.Y., 1959).

Willy. Pen name of **Gauthier-Villars, Henri.**

Wilm, Nicolai von, German pianist and composer; b. Riga, March 4, 1834; d. Wiesbaden, Feb. 20, 1911. He studied with Plaidy, Hauptmann, and Richter at the Leipzig Cons.; then in 1857 went to Riga as a theater conductor, and in 1860 proceeded to St. Petersburg, where he became an instructor at the Imperial Nicolayevsky Inst.; returned to Germany in 1875 and lived mostly in Dresden and Wiesbaden.

WORKS: A highly prolific composer (243 opus numbers), he is best known through his chamber music; wrote a String Sextet, String Quartet, Piano Trio, Cello Sonata, 2 violin sonatas, Sonata for Violin and Harp; numerous pieces for piano solo: *Kleine Suite; Herbstfrüchte; Im russischen Dorf; Stimmungen; Dorf- und Waldidyllen; Musikalisches Dekameron;* etc.; for Piano, 4-hands: *Eine Nordlandfahrt; Reisebilder aus Schlesien; Musikalische Federzeichnungen; Kalendarium;* etc.; also variations and other pieces for 2 pianos; men's choruses; songs.

Wilms, Jan Willem, Dutch composer of German birth; b. Witzhelden, Schwarzburg-Sondershausen, March 30, 1772; d. Amsterdam, July 19, 1847. He received his early musical training from his father. In 1791 he went to Amsterdam, where he appeared as a pianist and harpist. He composed 2 piano concertos, 2 flute concertos, 2 string quartets, 2 piano trios, 3 violin sonatas, 2 flute sonatas, a Clarinet Concerto; also 3 symphs. He was the author of the Dutch national song *Wien Neerlandsch bloed door d'ader-*

en vloeit (1815).

BIBLIOGRAPHY: E. Klusen, *Johann Wilhelm Wilms und das Amsterdamer Musikleben (1772–1847)* (Buren, 1975).

Wilsing, Daniel Friedrich Eduard, German composer; b. Hörde, near Dortmund, Oct. 21, 1809; d. Berlin, May 2, 1893. He was an organist in Wesel from 1829 to 1834; then moved to Berlin. He composed an oratorio in 2 parts, *Jesus Christus* (produced in Bonn in 1889, by Wilsing's pupil Arnold Mendelssohn); a *De profundis a* 16, which won the gold medal for art at Berlin; piano sonatas; songs.

Wilson, Brian, American balladeer; b. Hawthorne, Calif., June 20, 1942. He twanged the string bass and banged the keyboard. In 1961 he got together with his similarly endowed brothers, **Dennis Wilson,** who beat the drums (b. Hawthorne, Dec. 4, 1944; drowned while surfing at Marina del Rey, Dec. 28, 1983), and **Carl Wilson** (b. Hawthorne, Dec. 21, 1946) and, in company with their first cousin, **Mike Love** (b. Los Angeles, March 15, 1941), and their mutual friend Al Jardin (b. Los Angeles, Sept. 3, 1942), organized a band named The Beach Boys, devoted to the celebration of surfing, fast cars, and long-legged California girls. Their adoration of these ingredients of California's life-style was reflected in their songs with such fetching titles as *Surfin' USA, Surfer Girl, Little Deuce Coupe, Surfin' Safari, Be True to Your School, Help Me Rhonda* and such reiterative chants as *Fun, Fun, Fun,* and *Dance, Dance, Dance.* Overdoing things, Brian Wilson suffered a nervous breakdown and a serious attack of aphasia, ailments which he commemorated in something called *Death Sounds.* Without waiting for Brian Wilson to come back to reality, The Beach Boys issued a monumental single recording called *Good Vibrations,* which hit the ears of teeny-boppers with a multidecibel roar and, figuratively speaking, drove them into the sea like a horde of mythical lemmings. A physiological reaction to this frenzy turned The Beach Boys toward the mystical world of Transcendental Meditation, as Mike Love led them to worship at the feet of a luxuriantly bearded Indian guru; but they soon returned to their commercially profitable recording work (75 million of their records were estimated to have been sold) and once more deployed their contented large bodies on the white sand beaches of California until tragedy struck on Dec. 28, 1983, when Dennis Wilson dived off their boat and never surfaced alive. By special dispensation (which involved an intercession from President Ronald Reagan, an admirer of The Beach Boys), Dennis Wilson was allowed at his widow's request to be buried bodily at sea, without preliminary cremation, circumventing the California law banning such burials, but it was specified that this should take place at more than 3 miles from the shore and at no less than 100 fathoms below the surface of the sea.

Wilson, Charles M., Canadian composer; b. Toronto, May 8, 1931. He attended the Univ. of Toronto (D.Mus., 1954); during 2 successive summers studied composition with Lukas Foss (1950) and Carlos Chávez (1951) at the Berkshire Music School at Tanglewood; also studied conducting there with Leonard Bernstein. From 1962 to 1970 he was head of the music dept. at Guelph Collegiate Vocational Inst. His music is contrapuntally dense and dissonant, but the formal element is preserved in Baroque structures.

WORKS: 2 operas: *Heloïse and Abelard* (Toronto, Sept. 8, 1973) and *Kamouraska* (1975); church opera, *The Summoning of Everyman* (Halifax, April 6, 1973); children's opera, *The Selfish Giant* (Toronto, Dec. 20, 1973); 3 string quartets (1950, 1968, 1975); Symph. in A (1954); *Sonata da chiesa* for Oboe and Strings (1960); String Trio (1963); *The Angels of the Earth,* oratorio (1966; Guelph, June 19, 1967); *En Guise d'Orphée* for Baritone and String Orch. (1968); *Phrases from Orpheus,* mixed-media score for Chorus and Dancers (Guelph Spring, Ontario, May 10, 1971); *Concerto 5x4x3* for String Quintet, Woodwind Quartet, and Brass Trio (1970); *Sinfonia* for Double Orch. (Toronto, March 3, 1973); *Image out of Season* for Chorus and Brass Quintet (1973); *Cristo paremus canticam* for Chorus and Orch. (Hamilton, Dec. 2, 1973); *Symphonic Perspectives,* subtitled *Kingsmere* (Ottawa, Oct. 4, 1974); *Missa brevis* for Chorus and Organ (1975).

Wilson, Domingo Santa Cruz. See **Santa Cruz Wilson, Domingo.**

Wilson, Grenville Dean, American composer; b. Plymouth, Conn., Jan. 26, 1833; d. Nyack, N.Y., Sept. 20, 1897. He was taught piano by his mother; then studied theory with A.W. Johnson in Boston; some of his piano pieces were publ. before he was 10 years old. In 1871 he was head of the music dept. of the Rockland Inst. in Nyack; in 1877 he organized the Nyack Symph. Society. He publ. 178 pieces, chiefly for piano, some of which were popular (*The Shepherd-boy, Wayside Chapel, Chapel in the Mountains, Moonlight on the Hudson, Voix du matin,* etc.).

Wilson, Jackie, top-seeded black American rock-and-roll singer; b. Detroit, June 9, 1934; d. Mount Holly, N.J., Jan. 21, 1984. He was trained as a boxer but, yielding to his mother's pleas, he turned to the relatively less hazardous pursuit of rock singing. In 1953 he joined the Dominoes, a rhythm-and-blues group, as its lead singer. He made discs for the Motown Record Co. in Detroit; his recording of *Lonely Teardrops* topped the popularity charts in its category in 1959, selling more than a million copies. Among his other hits were *Am I the Man* and *Higher and Higher.* A bit of scandal touched him in 1961 when he was shot in a N.Y. hotel by a scorned female groupie; he was not badly hurt. As a performer, Jackie Wilson exercised a mesmeric force over his audience; his voice was almost operatic in its range; he emulated coloratura effects with his explosions of blues chromatics. All this was abruptly ended when he suffered a massive heart attack onstage on Sept. 29, 1975, resulting in an irreversible coma. He lingered for several years while a court battle for his estate raged between his estranged wife and a son by a previous marriage. The wife won the litigation.

BIBLIOGRAPHY: *Rolling Stone* (March 15, 1984).

Wilson, John, English lutenist and song writer; b. (probably in Faversham, Kent) April 5, 1595; d. London, Feb. 22, 1674. He was musically gifted; at the age of 19, wrote music for *The Maske of Flowers.* According to some indications, he participated as a singer in a production of Shakespeare's *Much Ado about Nothing* (as Jacke Wilson). In 1635 he was made one of the King's Musicians; was in favor with Charles I, whom he followed to Oxford during the civil war in 1644, and was made a D.Mus. by Oxford Univ. on March 10, 1644; he was "Musick Professor" there from 1656 until 1661. Upon the Restoration he resumed his post at court, and on Oct. 22, 1662, became the successor of Henry Lawes as a Gentleman of the Chapel Royal. He publ. *Psalterium Carolinum* (London, 1657), *Cheerfull Ayres or Ballads* (Oxford, 1660); wrote several songs to Shakespeare's words. Some of his songs were included in Playford's *Select Musicall Ayres and Dialogues* (1652, 1653), *Select Ayres and Dialogues* (1659), *Catch that catch can: or the Musical Companion* (1667), and *The Treasury of Musick* (1669).

BIBLIOGRAPHY: E.R. Rimbault, *Who was "Jacke Wilson," the Singer of Shakespeare's Stage?* (London, 1846); E.F. Hart, "Caroline Lyrics and Contemporary Song-Books," *Library* (June 1953); V.H. Duckles, "The 'Curious' Art of John Wilson," *Journal of the American Musicological Society* (Summer 1954); H. Henderson, *The Vocal Music of John Wilson* (Diss., Univ. of North Carolina, 1962).

Wilson, Mortimer, American organist and composer; b. Chariton, Iowa, Aug. 6, 1876; d. New York, Jan. 27, 1932. He studied organ with Middelschulte in Chicago; composition with F.G. Gleason; in 1907 he went to Leipzig to study with Max Reger. Returning to America in 1911, he became conductor of the Atlanta Phil. Orch. (until 1915); then taught at various music schools; settled in N.Y. He wrote 5 symphs.; an overture, *New Orleans; Concerto Grosso* for Strings; 2 piano trios; 3 violin sonatas; *Echoes from Childhood* and *Romance* for Violin and Piano; etc. He was the author of *The Rhetoric of Music* (Lincoln, Nebr., 1907) and *Harmonic and Melodic Technical Studies;* publ. *A series of work tables prepared for students of harmony* (1921).

Wilson, Nancy, black American singer of popular music; b. Chillicothe, Ohio, Feb. 20, 1937. She sang in a church choir; commenced a professional career at 16 with appearances in local nightclubs; in 1959 she met Cannonball Adderley, who was instrumental in launching her on a career as a vocalist; she made numerous tours, singing jazz, soul, pop, and blues numbers, and even received an honorary doctorate in music from an Ohio college.

Wilson, Olly, black American composer; b. St. Louis, Sept. 7, 1937. He was educated at Washington Univ. in St. Louis (B.M., 1959), at the Univ. of Illinois (Mus.M., 1960), and at the Univ. of Iowa, where his teachers were Robert Sykes, Robert Kelley, and Phillip Bezanson (Ph.D., 1964). In 1971–72 he traveled in West Africa to study indigenous music; then devoted himself to teaching and composition; was on the faculty of Florida A. & M. Univ. (1960–62 and 1964–65); at the Oberlin Cons. of Music (1965–70), and later at the Univ. of Calif., Berkeley.

WORKS: *Prelude and Line Study* for Woodwind Quartet (1959); Trio for Flute, Cello, and Piano (1959); String Quartet (1960); *Wry Fragments* for Tenor and Percussion (1961); Violin Sonata (1961); *Dance Suite* for Wind Ensemble (1962); *Soliloquy* for Bass Viol (1962); Sextet (1963); *3 Movements* for Orch. (1964); *Piece for 4* for Flute, Trumpet, Double Bass, and Piano (1966); *In Memoriam Martin Luther King, Jr.,* for Chorus and Electronic Sound (1968); *Voices* for Orch. (1970); *The 18 Hands of Jerome Harris,* electronic ballet (1971); *Akwan* for Piano, Electronic Piano, and Orch. (1972); *Black Martyrs,* electronic composition (1972); *Spirit Song* for Soprano, Chorus, and Orch. (1973); *Sometimes* for Tenor and Tape (1976); Piano Trio (1977).

Wilson, Philip, English singer and music editor; b. Hove, Sussex, Nov. 29, 1886; d. London, July 26, 1924. After studying singing in London, he went to Australia in 1913 as a vocal teacher at the Sydney Cons.; returning to England in 1920, he gave historical recitals, especially of Elizabethan songs. With Peter Warlock (Philip Heseltine) he edited *English Ayres, Elizabethan and Jacobean* and *Chromatic Tunes of 1606;* also edited *The Musical Proverbs* (London, 1924), from the "Lekingfelde" MS.

Wilson, Ransom, outstanding American flutist; b. Tuscaloosa, Ala., Oct. 25, 1951. He studied with Philip Dunigan at the North Carolina School of the Arts; also profited from advice given by Jean-Pierre Rampal. He made a European tour with the Juilliard Chamber Orch. under Peter Maag, and soon established himself as a brilliant virtuoso. In 1980 he founded and served as conductor-soloist with his own ensemble, Solisti New York; also appeared as guest conductor with other ensembles. His repertoire is catholic, covering all periods and styles; he also commissioned special works for the flute, and arranged music for use in his concerts.

Wilson, Richard, American composer and pianist; b. Cleveland, May 15, 1941. He studied cello and theory in Cleveland; in 1959 entered Harvard Univ., where he took courses in music with Randall Thompson, G. Wallace Woodworth, and Robert Moevs (A.B., 1963, magna cum laude); he subsequently attended classes at Rutgers Univ. (M.A., 1966); also studied piano with Leonard Shure in N.Y. (1960) and with Friedrich Wuhrer in Munich (1963). In 1966 he joined the faculty of Vassar College; was made a prof. in 1976; from 1979 to 1982 served as chairman of the music dept. there.

WORKS: *Suite for 5 Players* (1963); Trio for Oboe, Violin, and Cello (1964); *Fantasy and Variations* for Chamber Ensemble (1965); *A Dissolve* for Women's Chorus (1968); String Quartet No. 1 (1968); *Music* for Violin and Cello (1969); Quartet for 2 Flutes, Double Bass, and Harpsichord (1969); *Initiation* for Orch. (1970); *Music* for Solo Cello (1971); *Music* for Solo Flute (1972); Wind Quintet (1974); *Eclogue* for Solo Piano (1974); String Quartet No. 2 (1977); *Serenade: Variations on a Simple March* for Clarinet, Viola, and Double Bass (1978); *Sour Flowers: 8 Piano Pieces for the Form of an Herbal* (1979); *Deux pas de trois: Pavane and Tango* for Flute, Oboe, and Harpsichord (1979); Concerto for Violin and Chamber Orch. (1979); *Profound Utterances* for Solo Bassoon (1980); *Figurations* for Clarinet and Cello (1981); *Gnomics* for Flute, Oboe, and Clarinet (1981); String Quartet No. 3 (1982); *Dithyramb* for Oboe and Clarinet (1982); Suite for Wind Instruments (1983); Concerto for Bassoon and Chamber Orch. (1983).

Wilson, Theodore ("Teddy"), black American jazz pianist; b. Austin, Texas, Nov. 24, 1912. He studied piano and violin; attended Talladega College in Alabama for a year as a music student. After working in Detroit, he moved to Chicago, where he played with Louis Armstrong and Jimmie Noone; then went to N.Y. and made recordings with Billie Holiday; later worked with Benny Goodman, and led his own band; also taught jazz piano at the Juilliard School of Music in N.Y.

Wiltberger, August, German composer; brother of **Heinrich Wiltberger;** b. Sobernheim, April 17, 1850; d. Stuttgart, Dec. 2, 1928. He was engaged as a music teacher in various towns in Alsace; wrote a number of sacred works; a secular cantata, *Barbarossas Erwachen;* chamber music; organ pieces; was the author of *Harmonielehre; Zum Gebrauch in Lehrerbildungsanstalten* (1906; 3rd ed., 1912).

Wiltberger, Heinrich, German composer and teacher; brother of **August Wiltberger;** b. Sobernheim, Aug. 17, 1841; d. Colmar, May 26, 1916. He studied with his father, an organist; taught in various music schools in Alsace; his setting of Alsatian folk songs for male chorus were very popular. He also wrote *Märchen* for String Orch.; Requiem; several masses; brought out collections of Latin and German hymns; publ. *Der Gesangsunterricht in der Volksschule* (1907).

Wimberger, Gerhard, Austrian composer; b. Vienna, Aug. 30, 1923. He studied in Salzburg; took courses at the Mozarteum there. He wrote several comic operas: *Schaubundengeschichte* (Mannheim, 1954); *Der Handschuh* (Frankfurt, 1955); *La battaglia* (Schwetzingen, 1960); also *Kantate vom Sport* (1953); Concerto for Piano and 15 String Instruments (1955); *Divertimento* for String Orch. (1956); *Loga-Rhythmen* for Orch. (1956); *Figuren und Phantasien* for Orch. (1957); *Risonanze* for 3 Orch. Groups (Berlin, Jan. 31, 1968); *Ars Amatoria,* to texts from Ovid, for Voices, Chorus, Jazz Combo, and Orch. (Vienna, Feb. 7, 1969); *Lebensregeln,* "catechism with music" (Munich, Aug. 27, 1972); *Multiplay* for 23 Players (1974).

Winderstein, Hans (Wilhelm Gustav), German conductor; b. Lüneburg, Oct. 29, 1856; d. Giessen, June 23, 1925. He studied at the Leipzig Cons. with H. Schradieck (violin) and Richter (theory); also played in the Gewandhaus Orch. He conducted the concerts of the phil. societies of Nuremberg and Fürth (1890–93). In 1896 he organized the Winderstein Orch. in Leipzig, which he conducted until 1919; from 1920 he conducted summer concerts in Bad Nauheim. He composed *Trauermarsch, Valse-Caprice,* and *Ständchen* for Orch.; violin pieces; piano pieces.

Windgassen, Wolfgang, distinguished German tenor; b. Annemasse, Haute Savoie, June 26, 1914; d. Stuttgart, Sept. 8, 1974. He received his early vocal training from his father, **Fritz Windgassen** (b. Hamburg, Feb. 9, 1883; d. Murnau, April 17, 1963), who was a leading tenor at the Stuttgart Opera; then continued his studies at the Stuttgart Cons. with Maria Ranzow and Alfons Fischer. He made his operatic debut in Pforzheim in 1941 as Alvaro in *La forza del destino;* after military service in the German army, he joined the Stuttgart Opera in 1945, remaining on its roster until 1972. From 1951–70 he appeared at the Bayreuth Festivals, where he was a leading Heldentenor. He made his Metropolitan Opera debut in N.Y. on Jan. 22, 1957, as Siegmund. He sang regularly at Convent Garden from 1955–66. He was especially successful in Wagnerian roles, as Tannhäuser, Tristan, Parsifal, Siegfried, and Lohengrin; he also appeared as Radames in *Aida* and Don José in *Carmen.*

BIBLIOGRAPHY: B.W. Wessling, *Wolfgang Windgassen* (Bremen, 1967).

Winding, August (Henrik), Danish pianist and composer; b. Taaro, March 24, 1835; d. Copenhagen, June 16, 1899. He studied with Gade; was appointed a prof. at the Copenhagen Cons. in 1867; from 1891 till his death was its director. He composed a Symph.; *Nordische Ouvertüre;* Piano Concerto; cadenzas to Beethoven's piano concertos and to many of Mozart's; String Sextet; Piano Quartet; 2 violin sonatas; many piano pieces (*3 Fantasiestücke, Reisebilder, Ländliche Szenen, Studien und Stimmungen, Idyllen und Legenden, Albumblätter,* etc.); songs.

Winding, Kai (Chresten), Danish-born American jazz trombonist and composer; b. Aarhus, May 18, 1922; d. Yonkers, N.Y., May 6, 1983. He was brought to the U.S. in 1934; took up the trombone while in high school; then served in the U.S. Coast Guard. Following his discharge, he played with Benny Goodman (1945–46) and Stan Kenton (1947); was a member of J.J. Johnson's quintet (1954–56); then led his own septet. As a trombone player, he excelled in bop.

Windingstad, Ole, Norwegian-American conductor; b. Sandefjord, May 18, 1886; d. Kingston, N.Y., June 3, 1959. He graduated from the Oslo Cons. in 1902; then studied at the Leipzig Cons.; settled in America in 1913, and established the Scandinavian Symph. Orch., which he conducted until 1929; also conducted the Brooklyn Symph. Orch. (1930–32), the Knickerbocker Symph. Orch. in Albany, N.Y. (1937–39), the New Orleans Symph. Orch. (1940–44), and the Albany Symph. Orch. (1945–48). In 1929 he was decorated with the Norwegian Order of Saint Olaf. He composed a Symph. (1913); a cantata, *The Skald of Norway* (1929); *The Tides* for Orch. (Albany, Feb. 13, 1938, composer conducting); many minor pieces.

Windsperger, Lothar, German composer; b. Ampfing, Oct. 22, 1885; d. Frankfurt, May 30, 1935. He studied with R. Louis and others in Munich; from 1913, was in Mainz as artistic adviser to the music publisher B. Schott's Söhne. Among his works are a Symph.; *Lumen amoris,* symph. fantasy; Piano Concerto; Violin Concerto; *Missa symphonica;* Requiem; chamber music; piano pieces; organ pieces; songs.

Windt, Herbert, German composer; b. Senftenberg, Sept. 15, 1894; d. Deisenhofen, Nov. 22, 1965. He studied piano as a child; then took courses in music theory with Klatte and Schreker in Berlin. In 1923 he obtained the Mendelssohn Prize; in 1936 was awarded the Olympic Prize for his work *Marathon 1936.*
WORKS: *Andromache,* opera, to his own libretto (Berlin, March 16, 1932); cantata, *Flug zum Niederwald* (1935); chamber symph., *Andante religioso,* for Voice and 35 Instruments (1921); numerous film scores.

Wingham, Thomas, English piano teacher and composer; b. London, Jan. 5, 1846; d. there, March 24, 1893. He studied with Sterndale Bennett at the Royal Academy of Music; became a prof. of piano playing there in 1871; also served as a church organist. He composed 2 masses, motets, offertories, and other church music; also 4 symphs.; 6 overtures; *Concert-Capriccio* for Piano and Orch.; 2 string quartets; Septet for Piano, Strings, and Wind Instruments; songs.

Winham, Godfrey, British-American composer and computer specialist; b. London, Dec. 11, 1934; d. Princeton, N.J., April 26, 1975. He studied composition and piano at the Royal Academy of Music in London; in 1954 went to the U.S., where he took courses at Princeton Univ. (A.B., 1956; M.F.A., 1958); received his Ph.D. degree there with the thesis *Composition with Arrays* (1965); then joined the staff as a lecturer on electronic music and computer composition. In 1969 he worked on the computerized synthesis of music and speech. Apart from his programmed compositions on a computer, he wrote 2 string quartets, *The Habit of Perfection* for Voice and String Quartet, and several piano pieces. He was married to the American singer **Bethany**

Beardslee.

Winkelmann, Hermann, German tenor; b. Braunschweig, March 8, 1849; d. Vienna, Jan. 18, 1912. He started out as a piano maker, but became interested in singing; made a successful debut at Sondershausen (1875), and then sang at Altenburg, Darmstadt, and Hamburg. His interpretations of Tannhäuser and Lohengrin (in special engagements at Vienna) induced Richter to recommend him to Wagner, who chose him to create the role of Parsifal at Bayreuth (July 26, 1882). From 1883 to 1906, when he retired on a pension, he was one of the brightest stars of the Vienna Opera, where one of his most brilliant achievements was the performance of the role of Tristan (with Materna as Isolde) in the Vienna premiere (Oct. 4, 1883). In 1884 he sang in the U.S. at the Wagner festivals given by Theodore Thomas in N.Y., Boston, Philadelphia, Cincinnati, and Chicago.

Winkler, Alexander, Russian composer and pianist; b. Kharkov, March 3, 1865; d. Besançon, France, Aug. 6, 1935. He studied with Duvernoy in Paris, and with Leschetizky (piano) and Navrátil (composition) in Vienna. Returning to Russia, he became a piano teacher in his native city (1890–96); then was a prof. at the St. Petersburg Cons. (1907–24); among his students was Prokofiev. In 1924 he emigrated to France and became director of the Besançon Cons. He composed an overture, *En Bretagne;* orch. variations on a Russian folk song and on a Finnish folk song; String Quintet; 3 string quartets; Piano Quartet; Piano Trio; Viola Sonata; several albums of piano pieces; songs.

Winkler, Peter K., American composer; b. Los Angeles, Jan. 26, 1943. He studied at the Univ. of Calif. at Berkeley (A.B., 1964) and at Princeton Univ. (M.A., 1966). His works include *Etude* for 2 Horns (1964); String Quartet (1967); *Praise of Silence* for Soprano, Chorus, Instruments, and Tape (1969); incidental music for plays, radio, and television.

Winner, Septimus, American composer of popular music; b. Philadelphia, May 11, 1827; d. there, Nov. 22, 1902. He learned to play the violin; married at the age of 20 and opened a music store in Philadelphia, where he began giving lessons on the violin, guitar, and banjo. In 1854 he wrote his best-known song, *Listen to the Mocking Bird* (based on a melody originated by his black errand boy, "Whistling Dick" Milburn), selling the copyright for $5; in his lifetime the song sold 20 million copies. In 1862 he wrote *Give Us Back Our Old Commander: Little Mac, the People's Pride,* voicing a widespread sentiment for the return of General McClellan; the song was regarded as subversive and Winner was arraigned, but soon released; later the song, slightly altered, was used for Grant's presidential campaign. Winner also wrote the song *Whispering Hope,* which became extremely popular. He was a pioneer in bringing music to the masses; wrote over 200 vols. of music, including many instructive

works, for 23 different instruments, and made about 2,000 arrangements for violin and piano. He used the pen name **Alice Hawthorne** (in honor of his mother, Mary Ann Hawthorne) for many of his songs, including *Listen to the Mocking Bird.*
BIBLIOGRAPHY: C.E. Claghorn, *The Mocking Bird: The Life and Diary of Its Author, Sep. Winner* (Philadelphia, 1937).

Winograd, Arthur, American cellist and conductor; b. New York, April 22, 1920. He studied at the New England Cons. (1937–40) and at the Curtis Inst. (1940–41); played the cello in the Boston Symph. (1940–41) and in the NBC Symph. Orch. (1942–43); then was a member of the Juilliard String Quartet; joined the faculty of the Juilliard School of Music (1946–55) and later began to conduct. He was the conductor of the Birmingham (Ala.) Symph. Orch. (1960–64); in 1964 was appointed conductor and music director of the Hartford (Conn.) Symph. Orch.

Winogron, Blanche, American pianist; b. New York, May 8, 1911. She studied at Hunter College and later took composition lessons with Henry Holden Huss, Stefan Wolpe, and Felix Salzer. In 1968 she was appointed to the faculty of the New England Cons. of Music in Boston. She publ. a number of teaching pieces for piano.

Winter, Peter, German composer; b. Mannheim (baptized, Aug. 28), 1754; d. Munich, Oct. 17, 1825. He was a violinist in the Electoral orch. at the age of 10; was given permanent employment there in 1776; studied with Abbé Vogler; went with the court to Munich in 1778 and became music director of its theater; was appointed court conductor in 1798 and held this post until his death. In Munich he brought out a number of operas, of which the most important were *Helena und Paris* (Feb. 5, 1782), *Der Bettelstudent* (Feb. 2, 1785), *Marie von Montalban* (Jan. 28, 1800), and *Colmal* (Sept. 15, 1809). Frequent leaves of absence from Munich enabled him to travel; in Venice he produced his operas *Catone in Utica* (1791), *I sacrifizi di Creta* (Feb. 13, 1792), *I Fratelli rivali* (Nov. 1793), and *Belisa* (Feb. 5, 1794). In Vienna he brought out *Das unterbrochene Opferfest* (June 14, 1796; his most successful opera; produced all over Europe), *Babylons Pyramiden* (Oct. 25, 1797), and *Das Labirint* (June 12, 1798); in Paris he produced his only French opera, *Tamerlan* (Sept. 14, 1802); in London, the Italian operas *La grotta di Calipso* (May 31, 1803), *Il trionfo dell'amor fraterno* (March 22, 1804), *Il ratto di Proserpina* (May 3, 1804), and *Zaira* (Jan. 29, 1805); in Milan, *Maometto II* (Jan. 28, 1817), *I due Valdomiri* (Dec. 26, 1817), and *Etelinda* (March 23, 1818). He also wrote several ballets; 3 oratorios and 17 sacred cantatas for the Munich court chapel; 26 masses and a vast amount of other church music; 9 symphs. (including the grand choral symph. *Die Schlacht*); overtures; 2 septets; 6 string quartets; 2 string quintets; concertos for clarinet, for bassoon, and other instruments with orch.; and *Vollständige Singschule* in 3 parts. Some of his chamber music was

republ. by Riemann in Denkmäler der Tonkunst in Bayern, 27 and 28 (15 and 16; with a thematic catalogue).
BIBLIOGRAPHY: V. Frensdorf, *Peter Winter als Opernkomponist* (Diss., Univ. of Erlangen, 1908); E. Löffler, *Die Messen Peter Winters* (Frankfurt, 1928).

Winter-Hjelm, Otto, Norwegian organist and composer; b. Christiania, Oct. 8, 1837; d. Oslo, May 3, 1931. He studied with H. Kjerulf in Christiania, and with Kullak and Wüerst in Berlin. He was organist in the Trefoldighetskirke in Christiania from 1874 till 1921; wrote music criticism in the *Aftenposten* (1887–1913).
WORKS: Symph. No. 1 (Christiania, Sept. 27, 1862); Symph. No. 2 (1862; first perf., Christiania, March 18, 1916); many choruses for men's voices; edited *50 Melodier til Hauges og Landstads Salmebøger* and *50 Salmemelodier* for Piano; also church music. He publ. *Af Kristiania teaterliv i den seneste tid* (essays; Christiania, 1875).

Winterberger, Alexander, German pianist and composer; b. Weimar, Aug. 14, 1834; d. Leipzig, Sept. 23, 1914. He studied at the Leipzig Cons. (1848) and with Liszt. In 1861 he went to Vienna; in 1869, became piano prof. at the St. Petersburg Cons.; he returned to Leipzig in 1872 and remained there as a teacher and music critic. He publ. some piano pieces: *Alinen-Tänze* (waltzes, mazurkas, minuets, etc.), *Concert-Etude, Valse-Caprice, Concert-Adagio;* songs; German and Slavonic duets.
BIBLIOGRAPHY: O. Foerster, *Alexander Winterberger. Seine Werke, sein Leben* (Hannover, 1905; with a list of works).

Winterfeld, Carl von, German writer on music; b. Berlin, Jan. 28, 1784; d. there, Feb. 19, 1852. He studied law at the Univ. of Halle; then occupied juridical positions in Breslau and Berlin. He collected a valuable library of old music, which he donated to the Library of Berlin.
WRITINGS: *Palestrina* (1832); *J. Gabrieli und sein Zeitalter* (1834; 3 vols.); *Über K. Fr. Chr. Faschs geistliche Gesangswerke* (1839); *Dr. Martin Luthers deutsche geistliche Lieder* (1840); *Der evangelische Kirchengesang und sein Verhältnis zur Kunst des Tonsatzes* (1843–47; 3 vols.); *Über Herstellung des Gemeinde- und Chorgesangs in der evangelischen Kirche* (1848); *Zur Geschichte heiliger Tonkunst* (2 parts; 1850, 1852); *Musiktreiben und Musikempfindungen im 16. und 17. Jahrhundert* (1851); *Alceste von Lulli, Händel und Gluck* (1851); *Allegorisch-poetische Festopern am Kaiserlichen Hofe zu Wien in der letzten Hälfte des 17. Jahrhunderts* (1852).
BIBLIOGRAPHY: A. Prüfer, *Briefwechsel zwischen Carl von Winterfeld und Eduard Krüger* (Leipzig, 1898).

Winternitz, Emanuel, Austrian-American musicologist and museum curator; b. Vienna, Aug. 4, 1898; d. New York, Aug. 22, 1983. He served in the Austrian army in World War I; after the Armistice, studied jurisprudence at the Univ. of Vienna (LL.D., 1922); then was engaged as a corporate lawyer in Vienna (1929–38). After the Anschluss he emigrated to the U.S., where he devoted himself mainly to lecturing on art; served as Peripatetic Professor for the Carnegie Foundation. In 1942 he was appointed keeper of musical instruments at the Metropolitan Museum in N.Y.; in 1949 was named curator of the Crosby Brown Collection of Musical Instruments of All Nations at the Metropolitan. He also administered the André Mertens Galleries for Musical Instruments (1971–73). In 1973 he became curator emeritus of the Metropolitan. Among his principal endeavors was musical iconography; he publ. a valuable reference work, *Musical Autographs from Monteverdi to Hindemith* (2 vols., Princeton, 1955); other editions were *Die schönsten Musikinstrumente das Abendlandes* (Munich, 1966; in Eng. as *Musical Instruments of the Western World*, N.Y., 1967); *Leonardo da Vinci as a Musician* (New Haven, 1982).

Wintzer, Richard, German composer; b. Nauendorf, near Halle, March 9, 1866; d. Berlin, Aug. 14, 1952. He studied painting, and also music (with Bargiel); lived mostly in Berlin, and was active as a painter, composer, and music critic. He wrote 2 operas, *Die Willis* (1895) and *Marienkind* (1905); *Auf hohen Bergen* for Baritone Solo, Chorus, and Orch.; some fine songs *(Ernste Gesänge, Kinderlieder, Sturmlieder);* piano pieces. He also publ. *Menschen von anderem Schlage* (1912) and an autobiography.
BIBLIOGRAPHY: H. Killer, "Richard Wintzer, Ein Leben zwischen den Künsten," *Musik* (March 1941).

Winwood, Stevie, British pop singer and songwriter; b. Birmingham, May 12, 1948. He learned to play guitar, keyboard instruments, and string bass; joined The Spencer Davis Group and composed, in part, its hits *Gimme Some Lovin'* and *I'm a Man.* He soon formed his own band, called Traffic, with which he toured America in 1968. The personnel of Traffic changed with eponymous rapidity, with the titles of their record albums reflecting their loss of direction: *Last Exit, Traffic, Heavy Traffic,* and *On the Road.* Winwood found the right turn on his rocking freeway with his solo album *Arc of a Diver,* which received a platinum award.

Wiora, Walter, renowned German musicologist; b. Katowice, Dec. 30, 1906. He studied musicology in Berlin with Abert, Blume, Gurlitt, Hornbostel, H.J. Moser, Schering, Schünemann, and J. Wolf; received his Ph.D. in 1937 from the Univ. of Freiburg. He served in the German army during World War II; after 1945 he was in charge of the German Folk Music Archives in Freiburg im Breisgau. In 1958 he succeeded Friedrich Blume as a prof. at Kiel Univ. In 1962–63 he was a visiting prof. at Columbia Univ. in N.Y.; from 1964 to 1972 was a prof. of musicology at the Univ. of Saarland in Saarbrücken; since 1955 he has been a member of the International Folk Music Council. A Festschrift in his honor was publ.

in 1967, in Kassel, containing a list of his publications. A 2nd Festschrift was publ. in his honor in Tutzing in 1979. His principal achievement is research in the field of German folk music.
WRITINGS: *Zur Frühgeschichte der Musik in den Alpenländern* (Basel, 1949); *Das echte Volkslied* (Heidelberg, 1950); *Europäischer Volksgesang: Gemeinsame Formen in charakteristischen Abwandlungen* (Cologne, 1952); a biography of Bruckner (Freiburg, 1952); *Die rheinisch-bergischen Melodien bei Zuccalmaglio und Brahms* (Bad Godesberg, 1953); *Europäische Volksmusik und abendländische Tonkunst,* vol. 1 in the series Die Musik im Alten und Neuen Europa (Kassel, 1957; a work of fundamental significance); *Die vier Weltalter der Musik* (Stuttgart, 1961; in Eng., *The Four Ages of Music,* N.Y., 1965); *Das deutsche Lied. Zur Geschichte und Ästhetik einer musikalischen Gattung* (Wolfenbüttel, 1971); with M. Gosebruch and C. Wolters, *Methoden der Kunst- und Musikwissenschaft* (Munich, 1970).

Wirén, Dag Ivar, prominent Swedish composer; b. Noraberg, Örebro, Oct. 15, 1905. He studied at the Stockholm Cons. with Oskar Lindberg and Ernest Ellberg (1926–31); then in Paris with Leonid Sabaneyev (1932–34). He returned to Sweden in 1934, and was music critic for the *Svenka Morgonbladet* (1938–46); was vice-president of the Society of Swedish Composers (1947–63). His early music was influenced by Scandinavian Romanticism; later he adopted a more sober and more cosmopolitan neo-Classicism, stressing the symmetry of formal structure; in his thematic procedures he adopts the method of systematic intervallic metamorphosis rather than development and variation.
WORKS: *Serenade* for Strings (1937); ballet, *Oscarbalen (Oscarian Ball,* 1949); television ballet, *Den elaka drottningen (The Wicked Queen,* 1960; Swedish television perf., Nov. 22, 1961); 2 radio operettas, *Blätt, gult, rött* (1940; inspired by Churchill's famous speech containing the phrase "Blood, sweat, tears") and *Den glada patiensen* (1941); 2 concert overtures (1931, 1940); 5 symphs.: No. 1 (1932); No. 2 (1939); No. 3 (1943–44); No. 4 (1951–52); No. 5 (1964; Stockholm, Dec. 5, 1964); *Sinfonietta* for Orch. (1933–34); Cello Concerto (1936); *Little Suite* for Orch. (1941); *Romantic Suite* for Orch. (1945); Violin Concerto (1945–46); Piano Concerto (1947–50); *Divertimento* for Orch. (1954–57); *Triptyk* for Orch. (1958); *Music* for Strings (1966–67; Stockholm, Jan. 12, 1968); Flute Concertino (1972); 5 string quartets (1930, 1935, 1941–45, 1952–53, 1969–70); *Theme and Variations* for Piano (1933); 2 piano trios (1933, 1961); Violin Sonatina (1939); *5 Ironic Miniatures* for Piano (1942–45); Piano Sonatina (1950); Quartet for Flute, Oboe, Clarinet, and Cello (1956); *5 Improvisations* for Piano (1959); *Little Serenade* for Guitar (1964); Wind Quintet (1971); *Little Piano Suite* (1971); incidental music for many plays and films; songs.
BIBLIOGRAPHY: M. Pergament, "Dag Wirén," *Svenska Tonsättare* (Stockholm, 1943, pp. 154–59).

Wirth, Emanuel, Bohemian violinist; b. Luditz, Bohemia, Oct. 18, 1842; d. Berlin, Jan. 5, 1923. He was a pupil of Kittl at the Prague Cons.; then taught at the Cons. of Rotterdam, and was concertmaster of the local orch.; succeeded Rappoldi as viola player in the Joachim String Quartet, in Berlin; subsequently formed his own trio, with R. Hausmann (cello) and H. Barth (piano), presenting numerous concerts in Germany.

Wirth, Friedrich Moritz, German writer on music; b. Euba, near Chemnitz, Sept. 14, 1849; d. Leipzig, April 26, 1917. He studied classical philology and philosophy at the Univ. of Leipzig, where he lived. His writings include *Drohender Untergang Bayreuths* (1887); *Wagner-Museum und Zukunft des Wagnertums* (1894); *Der Ring des Nibelungen als Wotandrama* (1912); *Parsifal in neuem Lichte* (1914).

Wirth, Helmut, German musicologist and composer; b. Kiel, Oct. 10, 1912. He studied composition with R. Oppel, and musicology with Fritz Stein and Blume; received a Dr.Phil. (1937) at Kiel Univ. with the dissertation *Joseph Haydn als Dramatiker* (Wolfenbüttel, 1940); from 1936 was active on Hamburg Radio. He composed *Goldoni Suite* for Chamber Orch. (1939); Oboe Sonata (1940); Harpsichord Sonata (1946); many songs.

Wirth, Herman Felix, Dutch music scholar; b. Utrecht, May 6, 1885. He studied at the Cons. of Utrecht, and later with Hugo Riemann in Leipzig (1906–07). After teaching at the Brussels Cons. he taught at the Univ. of Berlin (1933–38); in 1955 he went to Marburg, where he became absorbed in the study of Christian religions; publ. *Um den Ursinn des Menschseins* (Vienna, 1960), dealing with subjects of primordial beliefs. He edited works by Dutch masters of the 17th century.

Wise, Michael, English singer and composer; b. Wiltshire, c.1648; d. Salisbury, Aug. 24, 1687. After an apprenticeship under Cooke at the Chapel Royal in London, he was appointed, at the age of 20, organist of Salisbury Cathedral; in 1676 he became Gentleman of the Chapel Royal; in 1687 he was appointed master of the choristers of St. Paul's Cathedral. He was killed by a watchman during a street dispute. He wrote anthems, church services, and catches; 6 of his anthems are included in Boyce's *Cathedral Music;* other pieces are found in various collections of the 17th century.

Wiske, Charles Mortimer, American choral conductor; b. Bennington, Vt., Jan. 12, 1853; d. Lewiston, Maine, July 9, 1934. He studied piano and organ; was engaged by Theodore Thomas to drill the mass chorus (3,000 voices) for the N.Y. May Festival of 1882, and was also chorusmaster during a series of Wagner festivals given by Thomas in the U.S. in 1884; subsequently conducted the N.Y. Chorus Society and various choruses in Paterson and Newark, N.J.

Wislocki, Stanislaw, Polish conductor and composer; b. Rzeszów, July 7, 1921. He studied music in Lwow and then in Rumania; conducted the Poznan Phil. (1947–58); conducted the National Phil. in Warsaw (1961–67); also taught conducting at the State College of Music in Warsaw. In 1977 he was appointed artistic director of the Great Symph. Orch. of Polish Radio and Television in Katowice. He composed a Symph. (1944); *4 Poems* for Tenor and Chamber Orch. (1944); *Symphonic Nocturne* (1947); Piano Concerto (1948–49); *Symphonic Ballad* (1950); *Symfonia tańcu (Symphony on Dancing,* 1952).

Wissmer, Pierre, Swiss composer; b. Geneva, Oct. 30, 1915. He studied with Roger-Ducasse at the Paris Cons. and with Daniel-Lesur at the Schola Cantorum; in 1963 was appointed honorary director of the Schola Cantorum. He writes affable and pleasingly dissonant music in a natural contrapuntal idiom which is never congested by polyphonic superfluities.
WORKS: Radio opera, *Marion ou La Belle au tricorne* (Geneva, Radio Suisse Romande, April 16, 1947); comic opera, *Capitaine Bruno* (Geneva, Nov. 9, 1952); opéra bouffe, *Léonidas ou La Cruauté mentale* (Paris, Sept. 12, 1958); ballet, *Le Beau Dimanche* (1939; Geneva, March 20, 1944); *Alerte, puits 21* (Geneva, 1964); *Christina et les chimères* (French Television, 1967); *Naïades* for Narrator, Soli, Chorus, and Orch. (Geneva, Jan. 21, 1942); *Le Quatrième Mage,* oratorio (Paris, Oct. 14, 1969); 5 symphs. (1938, 1951, 1955, 1962, 1969); *Divertissement sur un choral* for 11 Instruments (Geneva, Dec. 8, 1939); *Mouvement* for String Orch. (Geneva, Feb. 1, 1940); symph. suite, *Antoine et Cléopâtre* (Geneva, Oct. 2, 1946); overture, *La Mandrellina* (Geneva, April 16, 1952); 2 string quartets (1937, 1949); *Sérénade* for Oboe, Clarinet, and Bassoon (1938); Sonatina for Clarinet and Piano (1941); Sonatina for Violin and Piano (1946); Piano Sonata (1949); *Concerto valcrosiano* for Orch. (1966); 2 piano concertos (1937, 1948); 2 violin concertos (1944, 1954); Guitar Concerto (1957); Clarinet Concerto (1960); Trumpet Concerto (1961); Oboe Concerto (1963); *Concertino-Crosière* for Flute, String Orch., and Piano (1966); Wind Quintet (1966); *Quadrige* for Flute, Violin, Cello, and Piano (1961); *Cantique en l'ounour dou grand santlouis, rei de franco et patroun de vaucros de cuers* for Chorus, with Piano or Organ (1971); songs; choruses.

Wiszniewski, Zbigniew, Polish composer; b. Lwow, July 30, 1922. He studied composition with Sikorski at the Cons. in Lodz (1948–52); taught at the Warsaw Cons. (1954); in 1957 was appointed director of Polish Radio in Warsaw.
WORKS: 3 radio operas: *Neffru* (1958–59; Warsaw, 1959); *Tak jakby (As If,* 1968–70; Warsaw, 1970) and *Paternoster* (1972; Warsaw, 1972); 2 ballets: *Obywatel walc* (1955) and *Ad hominem* (1962); 2 oratorios: *Genesis* (1967–68) and *Brothers* (1970–72);

2 cantatas: *Aubade* (1960) and *Sichel versäumter Stunden* (1971); *3 pezzi della tradizione* for 3-part Chorus and Orch. (1964); Oboe Concerto (1951); Symph. (1954); Concerto for Clarinet and String Orch. (1968–70); 2 string quartets (1954, 1957); Trio for Oboe, Harp, and Viola (1963); Solo Violin Sonata (1963); *Kammermusik I* for Oboe, Oboe d'Amore, English Horn, and Bassoon (1965), *II* (1966), and *IV, Little Symphony,* for 10 Instruments (1972–73); Duo for Flute and Viola (1966); *Cadenza* for Percussion (1969); Quartet for Flute, Horn, Piano, and Double Bass (1972); *Pezzo concertante* for Flute and 3 Percussionists (1975); piano pieces.

Wit, Paul de, Dutch cellist; b. Maastricht, Jan. 4, 1852; d. Leipzig, Dec. 10, 1925. In 1880 he founded (with O. Laffert) the *Zeitschrift für Instrumentenbau;* opened a museum of musical instruments at Leipzig in 1886, but sold his collections to the Berlin Hochschule für Musik in 1888 and 1891; he then made a 3rd collection, which he sold in 1906 to Heyer of Cologne. Wit was a fine player on the viola da gamba, as well as a cellist. He published *Geigenzettel alter Meister vom 16. bis zur Mitte des 19. Jahrhunderts* (1902; 2nd ed., 1910); *Weltadressbuch der gesammten Musikinstrumenten-Industrie* (1903; 8th ed., 1912); *Katalog des musikhistorischen Museums von P. de Wie* (1903).

Witek, Anton, Bohemian violinist; b. Saaz, Bohemia, Jan. 7, 1872; d. Winchester, Mass., Aug. 19, 1933. He studied violin with his father and with A. Bennewitz at the Prague Cons. From 1894 to 1910 he was concertmaster of the Berlin Phil.; in 1895 he formed a duo with the Danish pianist **Vita Gerhardt** (1868–1925), whom he later married (1910). In 1910 he was engaged as concertmaster of the Boston Symph. Orch. (until 1918); from 1920 to 1925 he was in Germany; then returned to America. After the death of his first wife (1925), he married the American violinist **Alma Rosengrein.** He publ. *Fingered Octaves* (1919).

Witherspoon, Herbert, American bass; b. Buffalo, N.Y., July 21, 1873; d. New York, May 10, 1935. He studied with Horatio Parker at Yale Univ., and also took lessons with MacDowell in N.Y. He then studied singing with Bouhy in Paris, Henry Wood in London, and G.B. Lamperti in Berlin. Returning to America, he made his concert debut at New Haven (Oct. 21, 1895); made 5 tours of England as an oratorio singer; he made his American opera debut at the Metropolitan Opera House as Titurel in *Parsifal* (Nov. 26, 1908); remained on its roster until 1916; then devoted himself to teaching; in 1925 became president of the Chicago Musical College; in 1931, president of the Cincinnati Cons. of Music; in 1933 he returned to N.Y., and in May 1935, was chosen to succeed Gatti-Casazza as general manager of the Metropolitan Opera Co., but he died suddenly of a heart attack. He publ. *Singing: A Treatise for Teachers and Students* (N.Y., 1925), and *36 Lessons in Singing for Teacher and Student* (Chicago, 1930).

Witkowski, Georges-Martin, French composer; b. Mostaganem, Algeria, Jan. 6, 1867 (of a French father and a Polish mother); d. Lyons, Aug. 12, 1943. He was educated at the military school of St.-Cyr; began music study with Vincent d'Indy at the Schola Cantorum; later left for the army and settled in Lyons, where he founded the Société des Grands Concerts in 1905 for the production of oratorios. In 1924 he was appointed director of the Lyons Cons.; he retired from there in 1941.

WORKS: Opera, *La Princesse lointaine,* after Rostand (Paris, March 26, 1934); 2 symphs. (1900, 1910); *Poème de la maison* for Solo Voices, Chorus, and Orch. (Lyons, Jan. 25, 1919); *Mon lac* for Piano and Orch. (Lyons, Nov. 20, 1921); for Voice and Orch.: *4 poèmes de Cœur Innombrable* (1925), *3 poèmes de Ronsard* (1935), *Paysage rêvé* (1937); *Introduction et Danse* for Violin and Orch. (Paris, Oct. 10, 1937); Piano Quintet (1897); String Quartet (1902); Violin Sonata (1907).

BIBLIOGRAPHY: M. Boucher, "G.-M. Witkowski," *Revue Musicale* (March 1926).

Witt, Franz Xaver, German composer of church music; b. Walderbach, Feb. 9, 1834; d. Schatzhofen, Dec. 2, 1888. He studied with Proske and Schrems in Regensburg; took Holy Orders in 1856. In 1866 he established and edited *Fliegende Blätter für katholische Kirchenmusik* and *Musica Sacra;* in 1868 he founded the Allgemeiner Deutscher Cäcilienverein for the improvement of Catholic church music, which, while opposing the introduction of orch. instruments into the church, helped to arouse interest in the great masterpieces of church music. In his own early masses, Witt employed the orch. Besides numerous masses, he publ. 2 Requiems, many litanies, offertories, motets, and hymns (55 opus numbers); also some secular men's choruses; was the author of *Der Zustand der katholischen Kirchenmusik* (1865), *Über das Dirigieren der katholischen Kirchenmusik,* and *Das bayerische Kultusministerium* (1886); his articles are collected in a centennial vol., *Ausgewählte Anfsätze zur Kirchenmusik* (Cologne, 1934).

BIBLIOGRAPHY: A. Walter, *Dr. Franz Witt. Ein Lebensbild* (Regensburg, 1889; 2nd ed., 1906; includes a full list of works).

Witt, Friedrich, German violinist and composer; b. Hallenbergstetten, Württemberg, Nov. 8, 1770; d. Würzburg, Jan. 3, 1836. At the age of 19, he was engaged as violinist in the orch. of Prince von Oettingen; from 1802 he was Kapellmeister at Würzburg, at first to the Prince-Bishop, then to the Grand Duke, finally to the city. It was Witt who composed the so-called Jena Symphony, misattributed to Beethoven (see H.C. Robbins Landon's article in the *Music Review* for May 1957). Other works by Witt include the historical opera *Palma* (Frankfurt, 1804); the comic opera *Das Fischerweib* (Würzburg, 1806); the oratorios *Der leidende Heiland* (Würzburg, 1802) and *Die Auferstehung Jesu;* masses and cantatas; 9 symphs.; music for wind band; Septet for Clarinet, Horn, Bassoon, and Strings; Quintet for

Piano and Winds; Flute Concerto; etc.

Witt, Theodor de, German music editor and composer; b. Wesel, May 9, 1823; d. Rome, Dec. 1, 1855. He studied organ with his father. When Liszt visited Witt's native town he became interested in the talented boy, and gave a concert for his benefit to enable him to study in Berlin (under Dehn). At 22 Witt developed tuberculosis and was sent to Italy; there he made a detailed study of church music; edited the first 4 vols. of Breitkopf & Härtel's complete edition of Palestrina's works. His own works include a Piano Sonata and some vocal pieces.

Wittassek, Johann Nepomuk August, Bohemian pianist and composer; b. Hořín, March 23, 1770; d. Prague, Dec. 7, 1839. The son of a schoolmaster, he received a good education; took music lessons with F.X. Dušek and J.A. Koželuch in Prague; succeeded Koželuch in 1814 as music director at the Prague Cathedral; was appointed director of the School for Organists in Prague in 1830. He wrote an opera, *David,* brought out in Prague; 4 piano concertos; concertos for violin, for clarinet, and for bassoon; 6 string quartets; 4 violin sonatas; much church music.

Witte, Georg Hendrik, Dutch organist and composer; b. Utrecht, Nov. 16, 1843; d. Essen, Feb. 1, 1929. He studied at The Hague; then at the Leipzig Cons., with Moscheles and Plaidy (piano), Hauptmann and Reinecke (composition). In 1871 he was appointed conductor of the Musikverein at Essen, which post he held for 40 years, retiring in 1911. He wrote *Der Essener Musikverein 1838 bis 1913* (1913). His works include a Cello Concerto; a choral work, *An die Sonne;* Piano Quartet; numerous piano pieces; also songs.

Wittgenstein, Count Friedrich Ernst. See **Sayn-Wittgenstein-Berleburg, Count Friedrich Ernst.**

Wittgenstein, Paul, Austrian pianist; b. Vienna, Nov. 5, 1887; d. Manhasset, Long Island, N.Y., March 3, 1961. He was of a musical family; studied piano with Josef Labor and Leschetizky; made his first public appearance as a pianist in 1913, in Vienna. He lost his right arm in World War I, at the Russian front; was a prisoner of war in Omsk, Siberia; was repatriated in 1916. He then developed an extraordinary technique for left hand alone, and performed a concerto specially composed for him by his teacher, Josef Labor. He subsequently commissioned left-hand piano concertos from Richard Strauss, Ravel, Prokofiev, Korngold, Benjamin Britten, and other composers, of which he gave the world premieres (except the Prokofiev concerto, which he found unsuitable). He appeared in the major musical centers in Europe; toured America in 1934; in 1939 settled in N.Y.; became a U.S. citizen in 1946. He was a brother of the famous philosopher Ludwig Wittgenstein.

Wittich, Marie, German soprano; b. Giessen, May 27, 1868; d. Dresden, Aug. 4, 1931. She studied in Würzburg; made her debut as Azucena at the age of 14 in Magdeburg in 1882; then sang in Düsseldorf, Basel, and Schwerin; in 1889 became a member of the Dresden Court Opera, remaining on its roster until 1914; while there, she was chosen by Richard Strauss to create the role of Salome in 1905; she also made guest appearances at Covent Garden in London (1905–6) and in Bayreuth (1901–10).

Witting, Karl, German violinist and composer; b. Jülich, Sept. 8, 1823; d. Dresden, June 28, 1907. He studied in Paris under A. Reichel; returned to Germany in 1855, living in Berlin, Hamburg, and Glogau, and finally settling in Dresden in 1861 as a teacher. He publ. a Cello Sonata, instructive pieces for violin and piano, *Violinschule;* edited a collection, *Die Kunst des Violinspiels* (8 books), and a collection of duets for 2 violins (4 books); wrote *Musikalisches Wörterbuch* (1887); *Geschichte des Violinspiels* (1900); analyses for Breitkopf and Härtel's *Konzertführer.*

Wittinger, Robert, Austrian-born German composer; b. Knittelfeld, April 10, 1945. He grew up in Hungary, and studied there with Zsolt Durkó; then went to West Germany to live. His technique of composition is sonoristic, with sound blocks forming thematic groups, while the continuity is achieved by Baroque formulas; the titles of his pieces are indicative of their construction (Dissociations, Concentrations, Compensations, Irreversibilities, Divergences, Montage, Tendencies, Tensions, Symmetrical Structures, etc.).

WORKS: *Dissoziazioni* for Orch. (1964); *Consonante* for English Horn and Orch. (1965); *Espressioni,* ballet music (1966); *Concentrazione* for Orch. (1966); *Compensazioni* for Small Orch. (1967); *Irreversibilitazione* for Cello and Orch. (1967); *Om* for Orch. (1968); *Divergenti* for Orch. (West Berlin, Oct. 4, 1970); *Sinfonia* for String Orch. (1970); *Costellazioni* for Orch. (Stuttgart, Sept. 25, 1971); *Montaggio,* concerto No. 1 for Small Orch. (1972); *Relazioni* for 7 Soloists and Orch. (West Berlin, April 11, 1972); Concerto for Oboe, Harp, and String Orch. (1972); *Concerto Lirico* for Orch. (1977); *Concerto Entusiastico* for Orch. (1977); *Sinfonia II* for Orch. (1977–78); 4 string quartets (1964, 1966, 1970, 1977); *Concentrazioni,* wind quintet (1965); *Itrospezioni* for Solo Bassoon (1967); *Tendenze* for Piano, Cello, and Percussion (1970); *Tensioni,* wind quintet (1970); *Tolleranza* for Oboe, Celesta, and Percussion (1970); 6 *Strutture simmetriche,* each for a different Solo Instrument (1970); *Catalizzazioni* for 24 Vocalists and 7 Instrumentalists (1972); *Sillogismo* for Violin and Percussion (1974).

Wittrisch, Marcel, German tenor; b. Antwerp, Oct. 1, 1901; d. Stuttgart, June 3, 1955. He studied at the Munich and Leipzig conservatories; made his debut as Konrad in *Hans Heiling* in Halle in 1925; then sang in Braunschweig (1927–29); in 1929 he became a member of the Berlin State Opera, where he sang leading roles until 1943; also made guest appearances at Covent Garden in London (1931) and at Bayreuth (1937); in 1950 he joined the Stuttgart Opera, where he remained until his death. In addition to his operatic career, he gained wide renown as a concert singer.

Wixell, Ingvar, Swedish baritone; b. Lulea, May 7, 1931. He was educated at the Stockholm Cons.; made his concert debut in 1952 in Gävle. In 1956 he joined the Royal Opera in Stockholm; also sang regularly with the Deutsche Oper in West Berlin. He then launched an international career, which took him to London, Salzburg, Bayreuth, Chicago, and San Francisco. On Jan. 29, 1973, he made his debut at the Metropolitan Opera in N.Y. as Rigoletto.

Wodell, Frederick William, British-American choral conductor and composer; b. London, Dec. 17, 1859; d. St. Petersburg, Fla., Feb. 13, 1938. He studied piano, voice, and composition with various teachers in London; settling in the U.S., he was for many years conductor of the People's Choral Union in Boston; also taught singing there. He composed a cantata, *The American Flag,* for Tenor, Baritone, Men's Chorus, and Orch.; many anthems, songs, etc.; publ. *Choir and Chorus Conducting* (Philadelphia, 1901; 12th ed., 1931), and *How to Sing by Note* (1915).

Woehl, Waldemar, German music editor and educator; b. Lipine, near Bethuen, Prussia, Aug. 31, 1902. He studied with his father, and later in Berlin at the Akademie für Kirchen- und Schulmusik with Max Seiffert, Thiel, and Jöde; taught at the Folkwangschule in Essen; during World War II, led the Musikschule für Jugend und Volk in Villach, Austria; eventually settled in Soyen, Bavaria, as a teacher and flute maker; started a movement for the restoration of vertical flutes (recorders). He publ. *Melodielehre* (Leipzig, 1929); *Klavierbuch für den Anfang* (Berlin, 1932); *Das Bach-Buch für Klavierspieler* (Berlin, 1932); *Musik für Blockflöten* (4 vols.; Hannover, 1930–34); a method, *Blockflötenschule* (1930); *Kurze Spielanweisung für das Scheitholz* (1951); composed numerous pieces for the recorder and for ensembles of recorders; edited much 18th-century chamber music.

Wohl, Yehuda, German-born Israeli composer; b. Berlin, 1904. He came to Palestine in 1933 and had private studies with Ben-Haim in Tel Aviv; taught in Israel until 1972. Under the pseudonym **Yehuda Bentow,** he wrote popular songs in the ethnic style. WORKS: 2 radio operas: *Hagadér* (1947) and *The Circle* (1976); 3 symphs. (1944, 1946, 1954); *Rondo patetico* for String Orch. (1950); *Miriam-Danze* for Orch. (1955); *Discussione* for Piano and Orch. (1956); *An Arch Smile* for Narrator and Orch. (1959); *Fata morgana* for Orch. (1960); *Canto capricioso* for Orch. (1967); *With Mixed Feelings* for Piano, Percussion, and String Orch. (1970); *Light and Shadow* for Orch. (1972); *Those Were the Days* for Orch. (1973); *Quartetto appassionato* for String Quartet (1949); *Duo sensible* for Violin and Piano

(1951); *Tagore-Songs* for 2 Voices, Piano, and Flute (1955); *Diary* for Flute, Oboe, Clarinet, and Bassoon (1961); *Associations* for Chamber Ensemble (1966); *Hagashot (Encounters)* for Chamber Ensemble (1968); *Atmosphere* for Organ and Tape (1970); *Trigon* for Piano Trio (1971); *Faces* for Brass Ensemble and Percussion (1973).

Wohlfahrt, Franz, German piano pedagogue; son of **Heinrich Wohlfahrt;** b. Frauenpriesnitz, March 7, 1833; d. Gohlis, Feb. 14, 1884. He taught at Leipzig; publ. many piano studies, some of which have become standard exercises.

Wohlfahrt, Heinrich, German piano pedagogue; b. Kössnitz, near Apolda, Dec. 16, 1797; d. Connewitz, near Leipzig, May 9, 1883. He studied with Häser at Weimar; was a cantor and tutor in Thuringian towns; taught at Jena and (from 1867) Leipzig. WRITINGS: *Kinder-Klavierschule* (24 eds.); *Der erste Klavierunterricht; Der Klavierfreund* (36 children's studies); *Klavierübungen; Grössere und rein praktische Elementar-Klavierschule; Schule der Fingermechanik; Anthologische Klavierschule; Theoretischpraktische Modulationsschule* (Eng. trans., Boston, 1878); *Vorschule der Harmonielehre; Wegweiser zum Componiren für Musik-Dilettanten* (Eng. trans., Boston, 1859); also 3 children's sonatas; *Kleine Leute;* etc.

Wohlgemuth, Gustav, German composer and choral conductor; b. Leipzig, Dec. 2, 1863; d. there, March 2, 1937. He studied at the Leipzig Cons.; in 1891 founded the Leipziger Männerchor, which he conducted for many years; later also conducted other choral societies in Leipzig; was editor (1907–26) of the *Deutsche Sängerbundeszeitung;* publ. some 100 male choruses (some with orch.). BIBLIOGRAPHY: *Gustav Wohlgemuth, Sein Leben und Wirken* (Leipzig, 1934), a collection of articles.

Woikowski-Biedau, Viktor Hugo von, German composer; b. Nieder-Arnsdorf, near Schweidnitz, Sept. 2, 1866; d. Berlin, Jan. 1, 1935. He studied music with Wilhelm Berger in Berlin; was employed in the government statistics bureau. WORKS: Operas: *Helga* (Wiesbaden, 1904); *Der lange Kerl* (Berlin, 1906); *Das Nothemd* (Dessau, 1913); 3 melodramas: *Jung Olaf; Der Todspieler; Die Mette von Marienburg;* 4 ballads for Baritone and Orch.: *Die Jüdin von Worms; Der Triumph des Lebens; Rahab, die Jerichonitin; Jan van Jühren; Aus einem Menschenleben* for Violin and Piano; several song cycles (*Frühlingslieder; Lebensträume; Schiffslieder; Königslieder; Pagen-Balladen; Osterzauber; Des Sultans Gesetz;* etc.).

Woldemar, Michel, French violinist and composer; b. Orléans, June 17, 1750; d. Clermont-Ferrand, Dec. 19, 1815. He studied with Lolli; for some years was a conductor for a traveling theatrical troupe. By adding a 5th string *(c)* to the violin, he obtained an instrument that he called "violon-alto," because it included the viola range, and for which he wrote a concerto. He also publ. 3 violin concertos, a String Quartet, duos for 2 violins and for violin and viola; *Sonates fantomagiques* for Violin (*L'Ombre de Lolli, de Mestrino, de Pugnani, de Tartini*); 12 grand solos; *6 rêves ou Caprices; Caprices ou Etudes; Le Nouveau Labyrinth pour violon,* followed by studies in double stops; *Le Nouvel Art de l'archet; Etude élémentaire de l'archet moderne;* variations on *Les Folies d'Espagne,* etc.; methods for violin, viola, and clarinet; also a system of musical stenography *(Tableau mélotachigraphique)* and a method of musical correspondence *(Notographie).*

Wöldike, Mogens, Danish organist and conductor; b. Copenhagen, July 5, 1897. He studied with Carl Nielsen; was organist and choirmaster in several Copenhagen churches; in 1937 he became conductor of the Madrigal Chorus of Danish Radio; toured with it in Scandinavia, England, and Italy; was also director for the series of records Masterpieces of Music before 1750, in collaboration with W.W. Norton & Co. and the Haydn Society of Vienna and Copenhagen. From 1959 to 1972 he was organist of the Copenhagen Cathedral.

Wolf, Ernst Wilhelm, German composer; b. Grossenbehringen, near Gotha (baptized, Feb. 25), 1735; d. Weimar, (buried, Dec. 1) 1792. In 1772 he became Kapellmeister to the music-loving Duchess of Saxe-Weimar, Anna Amalia.
WORKS: About 20 operas, of which the most successful were *Das Rosenfest* (Weimar, 1770) and *Die Dorfdeputierten* (Berlin, June 15, 1772); other works include Passion oratorios and Easter cantatas; 6 piano concertos; 4 quintets for Piano, Flute, Violin, Viola, and Cello; 6 string quartets; 7 books of piano sonatas, each containing 6 numbers; in MS are 15 symphs., 17 partitas, 12 piano concertos, and much chamber music. He also wrote *Kleine musikalische Reise* (1782) and *Musikalischer Unterricht* (1788; 2nd ed., 1804).
BIBLIOGRAPHY: J. Brockt, *Ernst Wilhelm Wolf* (Diss., Univ. of Striegau, 1927).

Wolf, Ferdinand, Austrian writer on literature and music; b. Vienna, Dec. 8, 1796; d. there, Feb. 18, 1866, as librarian of the Imperial Library. His book *Über die Lais, Sequenzen und Leiche, Ein Beitrag zur Geschichte der rhythmischen Formen und Singweisen der Volkslieder und der volksmässigen Kirchen- und Kunstlieder im Mittelalter* (Heidelberg, 1841) is a valuable compendium.

Wolf, Hugo, Austrian composer, one of the greatest masters of the German lied; b. Windisch-Gräz, March 13, 1860; d. Vienna, Feb. 22, 1903. He studied piano and violin with his father, an amateur musician; then took lessons from Sebastian Weixler, a schoolmaster. In 1870 he was sent to Graz, where he entered a primary school, but left after a single semester and was enrolled in the seminary at the Benedictine monastery of St. Paul in Carinthia; in 1873 he went to a Gymnasium in Marburg; in 1875 he moved to Vienna, where he became a pupil at the Cons., studying piano with Wilhelm Schenner and harmony with Robert Fuchs. When Wagner visited Vienna in 1875, Wolf went to see him, bringing along some of his compositions; the fact that Wagner received him at all, and even said a few words of encouragement, gave Wolf great impetus toward further composition. But he was incapable of submitting himself to academic discipline, and soon difficulties arose between him and the Cons. authorities. He openly expressed his dissatisfaction with the teaching of Franz Krenn (who was also the teacher of Mahler), and was so impertinent to the director, Josef Hellmesberger, that he was expelled. In March 1877, he returned to his native town, but after a few months at home decided to go to Vienna again; there he managed to support himself by giving music lessons to children in the homes of friends. By that time he was composing diligently, writing songs to texts by his favorite poets—Goethe, Lenau, Heine. An unhappy encounter with Brahms, who advised him to study counterpoint before attempting to compose, embittered him, and he became determined to follow his own musical inclinations without seeking further advice. After a brief (and unsuccessful) employment as chorusmaster in Salzburg (1881), he secured in 1883 the position of music critic of the weekly *Wiener Salonblatt*. He took this opportunity to indulge his professional frustration by attacking those not sympathetic to new trends in music; he poured invective of extraordinary virulence on Brahms, thus antagonizing the influential Hanslick and other admirers of Brahms. But he also formed a coterie of staunch friends, who had faith in his ability. Yet he was singularly unsuccessful in his repeated attempts to secure performances for his works. He submitted a string quartet to the celebrated Rosé Quartet, but it was rejected. Finally, Hans Richter accepted for the Vienna Phil. Wolf's symph. poem *Penthesilea,* but the public performance was a fiasco, and Wolf even accused Richter of deliberately sabotaging the work; later he reorchestrated the score, eliminating certain crudities of the early version. In 1887 he resigned as music critic of the *Wiener Salonblatt* and devoted himself entirely to composition. He became convinced that he was creating the greatest masterpieces of song since Schubert and Schumann, and stated his conviction in plain terms in his letters. In historical perspective, his self-appraisal has proved remarkably accurate, but psychologists may well wonder whether Wolf was not consciously trying to give himself the needed encouragement by what must have seemed to him a wild exaggeration. However, a favorable turn in his fortunes came in 1889, when his 27 songs to words by Mörike and 10 songs to words by Eichendorff appeared in print. There followed 25 Goethe songs in 1890, and the album of exquisite songs after Heyse and Geibel, *Spanisches Liederbuch,* in 1891, as well as 6 songs to poems of Keller, *Alte Weisen.* The singer Ferdinand Jäger became a champion of Wolf's music, and gave repeated performances of his songs at the meetings of the Vienna Wagner-

Verein. Soon Wolf's name became known in Germany; he presented concerts of his own works in Berlin, Darmstadt, Mannheim, and other musical centers. He completed the first part of his great cycle of 22 songs, *Italienisches Liederbuch,* in 1891, and composed the 2nd part (24 songs) in 5 weeks, in the spring of 1896. In 1897 he wrote the *3 Gedichte von Michelangelo.* While Wolf could compose songs with a facility and degree of excellence that were truly astounding, he labored painfully on his orch. works. His early symph. was never completed, nor was a violin concerto; the work on *Penthesilea* took him a disproportionately long time. In 1895 he undertook the composition of his opera, *Der Corregidor,* to the famous tale by Alarcón, *El sombrero de tres picos,* and, working feverishly, completed the vocal score with piano accompaniment in a few months. The orchestration took him a much longer time. *Der Corregidor* had its premiere in Mannheim on June 7, 1896, but it proved a disappointment. The opera was ineffective dramatically, and the orchestration was weak. Wolf subsequently revised the score, and in its new version *Der Corregidor* was brought out in Strasbourg on April 29, 1898. He never completed his 2nd opera, *Manuel Venegas* (also after Alarcón); fragments were presented in concert form on March 1, 1903. In the meantime, his fame grew. A Hugo Wolf-Verein was organized at Berlin in 1896, and did excellent work in furthering performances of Wolf's songs in Germany. Even more effective was the Hugo Wolf-Verein in Vienna, founded by Michel Haberlandt on April 22, 1897 (disbanded in 1906). Amid these encouraging signs of recognition, tragedy struck. A supposed rebuke administered to Wolf by Mahler, at that time the newly appointed director of the Vienna Opera, who had been considering a performance of *Der Corregidor,* precipitated in him a mental breakdown. He declared to friends that Mahler had been relieved of his post, and that he, Wolf, was appointed director of the Vienna Opera in Mahler's stead. On Sept. 20, 1897, he was placed in a private mental institution; after a favorable remission, he was discharged (Jan. 24, 1898), and traveled in Italy and Austria. After his return to Vienna, symptoms of mental derangement manifested themselves in even greater degree. He attempted suicide by throwing himself into a lake, and then was committed to a state asylum at his own request. (A parallel with Schumann's case forcibly suggests itself.) He remained in confinement, gradually lapsing into complete irrationality. He died at the age of 42, and was buried near the graves of Schubert and Beethoven; a monument was unveiled on Oct. 20, 1904.

Wolf's significance in music history rests on his songs, about 300 in number, many of them publ. posthumously. The sobriquet "the Wagner of the lied" may well be justified in regard to involved contrapuntal texture and chromatic harmony, for Wolf accepted the Wagnerian idiom through natural affinity as well as by clear choice. The elaboration of the accompaniment, and the incorporation of the vocal line into the contrapuntal scheme of the whole, are Wagnerian traits. But with these external similarities, Wolf's dependence on Wagner's models ceases. In his intimate penetration of the poetic spirit of the text, Wolf appears a legitimate successor to Schubert and Schumann. Wolf's songs are symph. poems in miniature, artistically designed and admirably arranged for voice and piano, the combination in which he was a master.

WORKS: FOR THE STAGE: Incidental music to Ibsen's *Das Fest auf Solhaug* (Vienna, Nov. 21, 1891); *Der Corregidor,* 4-act comedy opera, after Alarcón's *El sombrero de tres picos* (Mannheim, June 7, 1896; revised version, Strasbourg, April 29, 1898); *Manuel Venegas,* 3-act tragic opera, text after Alarcón's *El niño de la bola* (fragments perf. in concert form, Mannheim, March 1, 1903).

CHORAL WORKS: *6 geistliche a cappella Chöre* (1881; ed. by E. Thomas; arranged for men's voices by Max Reger); *Christnacht* for Solo Voices, Chorus, and Orch. (1886–89); *Elfenlied* for Soprano Solo, Chorus, and Orch. (1889–91); *Dem Vaterland* for Male Chorus and Orch. (1890; many revisions).

INSTRUMENTAL WORKS: String Quartet in D minor (1878–84); *Penthesilea,* symph. poem after Kleist (1883–85); *Italienische Serenade* (1892; a transcription of the *Serenade* in G major for String Quartet, 1887); fragments from an early Symph. in D minor and from a Violin Concerto.

SONGS: *12 Lieder aus der Jugendzeit* (1888); *Lieder nach verschiedenen Dichtern,* 31 songs (1877–97); *Gedichte von Mörike,* 53 songs (1888); *Gedichte von Eichendorff,* 20 songs (1886–88); *Gedichte von Goethe,* 51 songs (1888–89); *Spanisches Liederbuch,* 44 songs after Geibel and Heyse (1889–90); *Italienisches Liederbuch,* 46 songs after Heyse, in 2 parts: 22 songs (1890–91), 24 songs (1896). 20 of the songs were orchestrated by Wolf; others by Max Reger. 40 previously unpubl. songs, mostly of the earliest period, were publ. in Leipzig in 1936, in 4 vols., as *Nachgelassene Werke,* ed. by R. Haas and H. Schultz. Wolf's collected writings were brought out by R. Batka and H. Werner as *Hugo Wolfs musikalische Kritiken* (Leipzig, 1911). A complete ed. of the songs was publ. by Peters (Leipzig, 1935). A complete works ed. was begun by the Internationalen Hugo Wolf–Gesellschaft, under the direction of H. Janick, in 1960, reaching 18 vols. by 1978. For an index of his works, see P. Müller, *H.W. Verzeichnis seiner Werke* (Leipzig, 1908). An Eng. trans. of the texts of all of Wolf's solo songs was publ. by Henry S. Drinker (N.Y., 1949).

BIBLIOGRAPHY: P. Müller, "Erinnerungen an Hugo Wolf," *Die Musik* (March–April 1903); M. Haberlandt, *Hugo Wolf. Erinnerungen und Gedanken* (Leipzig, 1903; 2nd ed., Darmstadt, 1911); E. Decsey, *Hugo Wolf* (4 vols., Berlin, 1903–6; new ed. in one vol., 1919; the standard work for facts and sources); P. Müller, *Hugo Wolf* (Berlin, 1904); E. Schmitz, *Hugo Wolf* (Leipzig, 1906); E. Newman, *Hugo Wolf* (London, 1907); M. Morold, *Hugo Wolf* (Leipzig, 1912; 2nd ed., 1920); H. Werner, *Hugo Wolf in Maierling* (Leipzig, 1913) and *Der Hugo Wolf-Verein in Wien* (Regensburg, 1922); G. Shur, *Erinnerungen an Hugo Wolf* (Regensburg, 1922); H. Werner, *Hugo Wolf in Perchtoldsdorf* (Regensburg, 1925) and *Hugo Wolf und der wiener akademische Wagner-Verein* (Regensburg, 1926); K. Grunsky,

Hugo Wolf (Leipzig, 1928); B.B. Viterbi, *Hugo Wolf* (in Italian; Rome, 1931); H. Schouten, *Hugo Wolf: Mensch en Componist* (in Dutch; Amsterdam, 1935); A. von Ehrmann, *Hugo Wolf. Sein Leben in Bildern* (Leipzig, 1937); R. Litterscheid, *Hugo Wolf* (Potsdam, 1939); M. von Graedener-Hattingberg, *Hugo Wolf: Vom Wesen und Werk des grössten Liedschöpfers* (Vienna and Leipzig, 1941; revised 1953); A. von Ehrmann, "Johannes Brahms and Hugo Wolf: A Biographical Parallel," *Musical Quarterly* (Oct. 1943); A. Orel, *Hugo Wolf* (Vienna, 1947); W. Reich, *Hugo Wolf-Rhapsodie* (Zürich, 1947); F. Walker, *Hugo Wolf: A Biography* (London, 1951; 2nd ed., 1968); N. Loeser, *Wolf* (Haarlem, 1955); D. Lindner, *Hugo Wolf* (Vienna, 1960); E. Werba, *Hugo Wolf oder Der zornige Romantiker* (Vienna, 1971).

CRITICISM, APPRECIATION: *Gesammelte Aufsätze über Hugo Wolf* (2 vols.; Vienna, 1898, 1899); E. von Hellmer, *Der Corregidor. Kritische und biographische Beiträge zu seiner Würdigung* (Vienna, 1900); K. Heckel, *Hugo Wolf in seinem Verhältnis zu Richard Wagner* (Munich, 1905); K. Grunsky, *Hugo Wolf-Fest in Stuttgart* (Stuttgart, 1906); *Hugo Wolf-Programme für alle Stimmlagen* (Leipzig, 1907); R. Rolland, *Musiciens d'aujourd'hui* (1908; in Eng., N.Y., 1914); O. Bie, *Das deutsche Lied* (Berlin, 1926; pp. 199–246); K. Varges, *Der Musikkritiker, Hugo Wolf* (Magdeburg, 1934); V.O. Ludwig, *Mörike in der Lyrik von Hugo Wolf* (Bern and Leipzig, 1935); G. Bieri, *Die Lieder von Hugo Wolf* (Bern, 1935); A. Maecklenburg, "Hugo Wolf and Anton Bruckner," *Musical Quarterly* (July 1938); R. Hernried, "Hugo Wolf's *Corregidor* at Mannheim," *Musical Quarterly* (Jan. 1940); F. Walker, "The History of Wolf's *Italian Serenade*," *Music Review* (Aug. 1947); E. Sams, *The Songs of Hugo Wolf* (N.Y., 1962); Rita Egger, *Die Deklamationsrhythmik Hugo Wolfs in historischer Sicht* (Tutzing, 1963); M. Carner, *Hugo Wolf Songs* (London, 1982).

CORRESPONDENCE: E. von Hellmer, *Hugo Wolfs Briefe an Emil Kauffman* (Berlin, 1903); M. Haberlandt, *Hugo Wolfs Briefe an Hugo Faisst* (Stuttgart, 1904); P. Müller, "Ungedruckte Briefe von Hugo Wolf an Paul Müller," *Jahrbuch Peters* (1904); H. Werner, *H. Wolfs Briefe an Oskar Grohe* (Berlin, 1905); E. von Hellmer, *Hugo Wolf. Eine Persönlichkeit in Briefen* (Leipzig, 1912; family letters); *Wolfs Briefe an Rosa Mayreder* (Vienna, 1921); H. Nonveiller, *Wolfs Briefe an Heinrich Potpeschnigg* (Stuttgart, 1923); H. Werner, *Wolfs Briefe an Henriette Lang* (Regensburg, 1923); H. Werner, "Some Unpublished Letters of Hugo Wolf," *Monthly Musical Record* (1927).

Wolf, Johannes, eminent German musicologist; b. Berlin, April 17, 1869; d. Munich, May 25, 1947. He studied at the Hochschule für Musik in Berlin; took courses in musicology at the Univ. of Berlin with Philipp Spitta and Heinrich Bellermann, and then with Riemann at the Univ. of Leipzig, where he received his Ph.D. in 1893 with the dissertation *Ein anonymer Musiktraktat des 11. bis 12. Jahrhunderts;* he completed his Habilitation at the Univ. of Berlin with his *Florenz in der Musikgeschichte des 14. Jahrhunderts* in 1902, and then taught the history of early music and church music there; also was on the faculty of the Berlin Akademie für Kirchen- und Schulmusik from 1908 to 1927. He was appointed director of the early music collection of the Prussian State Library in Berlin in 1915; from 1927 to 1934 he was director of its entire music collection. He was a leading authority on medieval and Renaissance music; his writings on the history of notation are especially important. He edited a complete edition of the works of Obrecht (Leipzig, 1908–21); for Denkmäler Deutscher Tonkunst he selected vocal works of J.R. Ahle (vol. V, 1901) and G. Rhau's *Newe deudsche geistliche Gesenge für die gemeinen Schulen* (vol. XXXIV, 1908); for Denkmäler der Tonkunst in Österreich he edited H. Isaac's secular works (vols. XXVIII, Jg. XIV/1, 1907, and XXXIII, Jg. XVI/1, 1909); also edited *Der Squarcialupi-Codex aus dem Nachlass herausgegeben von H. Albrecht* (Lippstadt, 1955).

WRITINGS: *Geschichte der Mensuralnotation von 1250 bis 1460 nach den theoretischen und praktischen Quellen* (very important; Leipzig, 1904); *Handbuch der Notationskunde* (very valuable; 2 parts, Leipzig, 1913 and 1919); *Musikalische Schrifttafeln* (Leipzig, 1922–23; 2nd ed., 1927); *Die Tonschriften* (Breslau, 1924); *Geschichte der Musik in allgemeinverständlicher Form* (3 vols., Leipzig, 1925–29).

BIBLIOGRAPHY: W. Lott, H. Osthoff, and W. Wolffheim, eds., *Musikwissenschaftliche Beiträge: Festschrift für Johannes Wolf zu seinem 60. Geburtstag* (Berlin, 1929); O. Gombosi, "Johannes Wolf," *Musical Quarterly* (April 1948); O. Kinkeldey, "Johannes Wolf," *Journal of the American Musicological Society* (Spring 1948).

Wolf, Ludwig, German pianist and composer; b. Frankfurt, 1804; d. Vienna, Aug. 6, 1859. He studied composition with Seyfried; was skillful both as a pianist and violinist; composed 3 string quartets; a Piano Quartet; 4 string trios; many other works in MS.

Wolf, Wilhelm, German pianist; b. Breslau, April 22, 1838; d. Berlin, Jan. 8, 1913. He studied with Theodor Kullak; in 1881 established himself in Berlin as a teacher; contributed to musical periodicals; wrote *Musik-Ästhetik in kurzer und gemeinfasslicher Darstellung* (2 vols., 1895, 1906); a collection of essays appeared as *Gesammelte musikästhetische Aufsätze* (1894).

Wolf-Ferrari, Ermanno, famous Italian opera composer; b. Venice, Jan. 12, 1876; d. there, Jan. 21, 1948. His mother was Italian; his father was a well-known German painter. Wolf-Ferrari was sent to Rome to study art, but became interested in opera and decided to devote himself to music; accordingly, he was sent to Munich, where he studied with Rheinberger (1893–95). In 1899 he returned to Venice, where his oratorio *La Sulamite* was successfully performed. This was followed by the production of his first opera, *Cenerentola* (1900). From 1902 to 1907 he was director of the Liceo Benedetto Marcello in Venice; then taught at the Salzburg Mozarteum; lived mostly in Neu-Biberg, near Munich; obtained his first success with the production of the comic opera *Le Donne curiose* (Munich, 1903); the next opera, *I quattro rusteghi* (Munich, 1906), was also well received; there followed his little masterpiece, *Il segreto di Susanna*, a one-act opera buffa in the style of the Italian *verismo* (Susanna's secret being not infidelity, as her husband suspected, but indulgence in surreptitious smoking). Turning toward grand opera, he wrote *I gioielli della Madonna (The Jewels of the Madonna);* it was brought out at Berlin in 1911, and soon became a repertoire piece everywhere; he continued to compose, but his later operas failed to match the appeal of his early creations.

WORKS: OPERAS: *Cenerentola* (Venice, Feb. 22, 1900; in Bremen as *Aschenbrödel,* Jan. 31, 1902); *Le Donne curiose* (Munich, Nov. 27, 1903; in German as *Die neugierigen Frauen;* in Italian, N.Y., Jan. 3, 1912); *I quattro rusteghi* (Munich, March 19, 1906; in German as *Die vier Grobiane); Il segreto di Susanna* (Munich, Dec. 4, 1909; in German as *Susannens Geheimnis;* in Italian, N.Y., March 14, 1911); *I gioielli della Madonna* (Berlin, Dec. 23, 1911; in German as *Der Schmuck der Madonna;* in Italian, Chicago, Jan. 16, 1912; in Eng. as *The Jewels of the Madonna,* N.Y., Oct. 14, 1913); *L'Amore medico,* after Molière (Dresden, Dec. 4, 1913; in German as *Der Liebhaber als Arzt;* in Italian, N.Y., Metropolitan Opera, March 25, 1914); *Gli Amanti sposi* (Venice, Feb. 19, 1925; *Veste di cielo* (Munich, April 21, 1927); in German as *Das Himmelsklied); Sly,* after the prologue to Shakespeare's *The Taming of the Shrew* (Milan, La Scala, Dec. 29, 1927; in Italian as *La leggenda del dormiente risvegliato); La Vedova scaltra,* after Goldoni (Rome, March 5, 1931); *Il Campiello,* after Goldoni (Milan, Feb. 1, 1936); *La Dama boba,* after Lope de Vega (Milan, Feb. 1, 1939); *Gli dei a Tebe* (Hannover, June 5, 1943; in German as *Der Kuckuck in Theben);* also a revision of Mozart's *Idomeneo* (Munich, June 15, 1931).

OTHER WORKS: *La Sulamite,* biblical cantata (1889); *Talitha kumi,* mystery for Solo Voices, Chorus, and Orch. (1900); *La Vita nuova,* after Dante, oratorio (Munich, Feb. 21, 1903; N.Y., Dec. 4, 1907); *Serenade* for String Orch.; *Kammersymphonie* (1901); *Idillio-concertino* for Oboe, String Orch., and 2 Horns (Venice Festival, 1932); *Suite-concertino* for Bassoon, String Orch., and 2 Horns (Rome, March 26, 1933); *Suite veneziana* for Orch. (1936); *Arabeschi* for Orch. (1937); *Divertimento* for Orch. (1938); *Kleines Konzert* for English Horn and Orch. (posthumous; Salzburg, Jan. 18, 1955); 2 violin sonatas; 2 piano trios; String Quartet; Piano Quintet; piano pieces; songs.

BIBLIOGRAPHY: H. Teibler, *Ermanno Wolf-Ferrari* (Leipzig, 1906); E.L. Stahl, *Ermanno Wolf-Ferrari* (Salzburg, 1936); R. de Rensis, *Ermanno Wolf-Ferrari, La sua vita d'artista* (Milan, 1937); A.C. Grisson, *Ermanno Wolf-Ferrari: Lebensbeschreibung* (Regensburg, 1941).

Wolfe, Jacques, American composer and teacher; b. Botoshan, Rumania, April 29, 1896; d. Bradenton, Fla., June 22, 1973. He was brought to the U.S. as a child; studied music in N.Y. at the Inst. of Musical Art with Goetschius, Robinson, and Friskin (graduated in 1915). During World War I he was a clarinetist in the 50th Infantry Band; then was sent to North Carolina, where he studied Negro spirituals. Many of his songs are in the manner of spirituals; some of them acquired popularity (*De Glory Road, Gwine to Hebb'n, Halleluja Rhythm, Short'nin' Bread,* etc.); he also wrote *Betsy's Boy, The Hand-Organ Man, Sailormen, British Children's Prayer;* numerous choral works; piano pieces.

Wolfe, Stanley, American music educator and composer; b. Brooklyn, Feb. 7, 1924. After service in the U.S. Army during World War II, he enrolled at the Juilliard School of Music in N.Y., studying composition with William Bergsma, Vincent Persichetti, and Peter Mennin (B.S., 1952; M.S., 1955); then joined its faculty; in 1963 was appointed director of the Juilliard Extension Division.

WORKS: *Adagio* for Woodwind Quintet (1948); Symph. No. 1 (1954); Symph. No. 2 (1955); *3 Profiles* for Piano (1955); *Lincoln Square Overture* (1957); Symph. No. 3 (Albuquerque, Nov. 18, 1959); Symph. No. 4 (Albuquerque, Dec. 7, 1966); *Variations* for Orch. (1967); Symph. No. 5 (N.Y., April 2, 1971).

Wolfes, Felix, German-American pianist and conductor; b. Hannover, Sept. 2, 1892; d. Boston, March 28, 1971. He studied at the Leipzig Cons. with Max Reger (theory) and R. Teichmüller (piano); later in Strasbourg with Pfitzner (composition); made his conducting debut in Breslau in 1923; conducted opera at Breslau, Essen (1924–31), and Dortmund (until 1933); then went to France; in 1938 came to the U.S., and was appointed assistant conductor at the Metropolitan Opera House; subsequently joined the faculty of the New England Cons. in Boston as vocal teacher.

Wolff, Albert (Louis), noted French conductor; b. Paris (of Dutch parents), Jan. 19, 1884; d. there, Feb. 20, 1970. He studied with Leroux, Gédalge, and Vidal at the Paris Cons.; began his career as a pianist in Parisian cabarets; from 1906 to 1910 was organist at St. Thomas Aquinas. In 1908 he became a member of the staff of the Opéra-Comique; after serving as its chorus master, he made his conducting debut there, leading the premiere of Laparra's *La Jota,* on April 26, 1911. From 1919 to 1921 he was conductor of the French repertoire at the Metropolitan Opera in N.Y.; conducted the world premiere of his opera *L'Oiseau bleu* there on Dec. 27, 1919. Upon his return to Paris in 1921, he was appointed Messager's successor as music director of the Opéra-Comique until 1924; in 1925 he became 2nd conductor of the Concerts Pasdeloup, and then was principal conductor from 1934 to 1940; also was conductor of the Concerts Lamoureux from 1928 to 1934. He toured South America from 1940 to 1945; then returned to Paris, where he was director-general of the Opéra-

Comique in 1945–46; thereafter he continued to conduct occasionally there; also at the Paris Opéra from 1949; in addition, he made appearances as a symph. conductor. He particularly distinguished himself as a champion of French music of his era; he conducted the premieres of Debussy's *La Boîte à joujoux,* Ravel's *L'Enfant et les sortilèges,* Roussel's Symph. No. 4, and Poulenc's *Les Mamelles de Tirésias.*

BIBLIOGRAPHY: S. Wolff, "Albert Wolff, doyen de l'Opéra-Comique," *Guide du Concert et du Disque* (Oct. 3, 1958).

Wolff, Auguste (Désiré Bernard), French pianist and piano manufacturer; b. Paris, May 3, 1821; d. there, Feb. 3, 1887. He studied piano with Zimmerman at the Paris Cons. and composition with Halévy; after a few years of teaching, he joined the firm of the piano maker Camille Pleyel in 1852, succeeding him as head in 1855; the firm then became known as Pleyel-Wolff & Cie.

Wolff, Christian, American composer of the avantgarde; b. Nice, France, March 8, 1934. He came to the U.S. in 1941; studied piano in N.Y.; took lessons in composition with John Cage. He studied classical languages at Harvard Univ.; received his Ph.D. in comparative literature in 1963. In 1962 he was appointed an instructor in Greek and Latin at Harvard, and in 1976 joined the faculty at Dartmouth College to teach classics and music. He evolved a curiously static method of composition, using drastically restricted numbers of pitches. His only structural resources became arithmetical progressions of rhythmic values and the expressive use of rests. He used 3 different pitches in his Duo for Violin and Piano; 4 different pitches in the Trio for Flute, Cello, and Trumpet (1951); 9 in a piano piece called *For Piano I.* Beginning in 1957 he introduced into his works various degrees of free choice; sometimes the players are required to react to the musical activities of their partners according to unforeseen cues.

WORKS: Trio for Flute, Cello, and Trumpet (1951); *9* for 9 Instruments (1951); *For 6 or 7 Players* (1959); *Summer* for String Quartet (1961); *Duo for Violinist and Pianist* (1961); *For 5 or 10 Players* (1962); *In between Pieces* for 3 Players (1963); *For 1, 2 or 3 People* (1964); Septet for any Instruments (1964); piano pieces, entitled *For Pianist; For Piano I; For Piano II; Duo for Pianists I and II* for 2 Pianos, 4-hands; *Duet I* for Piano, 4-hands; *Duet II* for Piano and Horn; *Snowdrop* for Harpsichord (1970); *You Blew It* for Chorus (1971).

Wolff, Christoph, eminent German musicologist; b. Solingen, May 24, 1940. He studied church music at the Berlin Hochschule für Musik and in Freiburg im Breisgau; took courses in musicology at the univs. of Berlin and Erlangen; obtained his Ph.D. in 1966 from the latter (Diss., *Der stile antico in der Musik Johann Sebastian Bachs: Studien zu Bachs Spätwerk,* publ. in Wiesbaden, 1968). He taught at the Univ. of Erlangen (1965–69); also at the Univ. of

Toronto in Canada (1968–70); then at Columbia Univ. (1970–76). In 1976 he became a prof. of music at Harvard Univ. He has written extensively on the history of music from the 15th to the 20th century, particularly on Bach and Mozart. He has distinguished himself by innovative research into formative elements in Bach's works. He became editor of the *Bach-Jahrbuch* in 1974; edited vols. of the *Neue Bach-Ausgabe* (V/2, *Goldberg Variations;* 14 Canons; VIII/1, *Musical Offering;* Canons); the *Neue Mozart-Ausgabe* (V/15, 2–3, Piano Concertos), and the *Hindemith-Gesamtausgabe* (opera *Cardillac,* op. 39). He wrote the major portion of the article on the Bach family for *The New Grove Dictionary of Music and Musicians* (London, 1980); also edited *The String Quartets of Haydn, Mozart, and Beethoven: Studies of the Autograph Manuscripts* (Cambridge, Mass., 1980). In 1978 he was awarded the Dent Medal of the Royal Musical Association of London. In 1982 he was elected a Fellow of the American Academy of Arts and Sciences.

Wolff, Edouard, Polish pianist and composer; b. Warsaw, Sept. 15, 1816; d. Paris, Oct. 16, 1880. He studied in Warsaw with Zawadski (piano) and Elsner (composition); then was a piano pupil of Würfel in Vienna. In 1835 he settled in Paris, and became an esteemed teacher; he was a friend of Chopin, and imitated him in his piano music. He publ. 350 opus numbers for piano, among them several albums of études; a waltz, *La Favorite; Chansons polonaises originales; Tarentelle; Chansons bacchiques;* a Piano Concerto; also 30 celebrated duos for piano and violin with de Beriot, and 8 more with Vieuxtemps. His sister, **Regina Wolff,** a pianist, was the mother of the violinist **Henryk Wieniawski.**

Wolff, Erich, Austrian pianist; b. Vienna, Dec. 3, 1874; d. New York, March 20, 1913 (while on a concert tour). He studied in Vienna with Anton Door (piano); lived in Vienna, and (from 1906) in Berlin; became well known as an excellent accompanist of singers. A vol. of 60 of his German songs was publ. posthumously, eliciting great praise. He also wrote a Violin Concerto and some chamber music.

Wolff, Ernst Victor, German pianist and harpsichordist; b. Berlin, Aug. 6, 1889; d. East Lansing, Mich., Aug. 21, 1960. He studied piano with Philipp Scharwenka in Berlin; musicology at the Univ. of Berlin; received a Dr.Phil. there with the dissertation *Robert Schumanns Lieder in ersten und späteren Fassungen* (Leipzig, 1914); was active in Germany as a harpsichord player; lived mostly in Berlin until 1933; then went to London, and in 1936 settled in N.Y.; in 1947 joined the faculty of Michigan State Univ. He publ. *With Reason and Rhyme* (New Haven, 1957).

Wolff, Fritz, German tenor; b. Munich, Oct. 28, 1894; d. there, Jan. 18, 1957. He studied with Heinrich König in Würzburg; made his debut as Loge in 1925 at the Bayreuth Festival, where he continued to make appearances until 1941; also sang in Hagen and Chemnitz. In 1930 he joined the Berlin State Opera, remaining on its roster until 1943; also made guest appearances at Covent Garden in London, and in Vienna, Paris, Chicago, and Cleveland. From 1950 he was a prof. at the Hochschule für Musik in Munich. His finest roles included Parsifal and Lohengrin.

Wolff, Hellmuth Christian, Swiss musicologist and composer; b. Zürich, May 23, 1906. He studied musicology in Berlin with Abert, Schering, Blume, and Sachs; received his Dr.Phil. with the dissertation *Die venezianische Oper in der 2. Hälfte des 17. Jahrhunderts* (Univ. of Berlin, 1932; publ. in Berlin, 1937). He completed his Habilitation at the Univ. of Kiel in 1942 with *Die Barockoper in Hamburg 1678–1738* (publ. in Wolfenbüttel, 1957); in 1954–71 he was a prof. of musicology at the Univ. of Leipzig; beginning in 1956 he devoted a great deal of his time to painting, and exhibited in Leipzig and other German cities.
WORKS: Oboe Concerto (1933); *Inferno 1944,* symph. poem (1946); Piano Concerto (1948); Violin Concerto (1948); several scenic oratorios; chamber music; choruses.
WRITINGS: *Die Musik der alten Niederländer* (Leipzig, 1956); *Die Händel-Oper auf der modernen Bühne* (Leipzig, 1957); *Die Oper* (3 vols.; Cologne, 1971–72; also in Eng.); *Originale Gesangsimprovisationen des 16. bis 18. Jahrhundert* (Cologne, 1972; also in Eng.).

Wolff, Hermann, German concert manager; b. Cologne, Sept. 4, 1845; d. Berlin, Feb. 3, 1902. He was a pupil of Franz Kroll and Wüerst; was editor of the *Neue Berliner Musikzeitung* (1878–79); also co-editor of the *Musikwelt.* In 1881 he founded the Hermann Wolff Concert Management, which became famous; it was later styled H. Wolf & J. Sachs (until 1935). He also composed piano pieces and songs.
BIBLIOGRAPHY: E. Stargardt-Wolff, *Wegbereiter grosser Musiker* (Berlin, 1954).

Wolff, Max, Austrian operetta composer; b. Moravia, Feb. 1840; d. Vienna, March 23, 1886. He studied music with Marx and Dessoff; became a successful composer of operettas, of which the following were produced in Vienna: *Die Pilger* (Sept. 6, 1872); *Die Porträt-Dame* (March 1, 1877); *Césarine* (Dec. 13, 1878).

Wolff, Werner, German conductor and writer on music; b. Berlin, Oct. 2, 1894; d. Rüschlikon, Switzerland, Nov. 23, 1961. He was the son of the concert manager **Hermann Wolff.** He studied music with Klatte; conducted opera in Vienna, Prague, Danzig, and Düsseldorf; from 1917 to 1932 was a conductor of the Hamburg State Opera. In 1938 he emigrated to the U.S.; taught at Wesleyan College, Tennessee; was conductor of the Chattanooga Opera Assoc. (1943–59). He composed symph. and chamber music; piano pieces and songs. He publ., in Eng., *Anton Bruckner: Rustic Genius* (N.Y., 1942; revised German ed. as *Anton Bruckner: Genie und Einfall,*

Zürich, 1948).

Wolffheim, Werner (Joachim), German musicologist; b. Berlin, Aug. 1, 1877; d. there, Oct. 26, 1930. While studying jurisprudence in Munich and Berlin (1895–98), he took courses in musicology with Sandberger and Fleischer; later studied with Kretzschmar and Johannes Wolf. With H. Springer and Max Schneider, he was co-editor of *Miscellanea bio-bibliographica* (supplement to Eitner's *Quellen-Lexikon*); edited the piano concertos for Breitkopf & Härtel's complete ed. of Haydn's works, and prepared (with Kretzschmar) a new ed. of Spitta's life of Bach. He formed a valuable music library (catalogue in 2 vols.), which he sold in 1928–29.

Wölfl (Woelfl, Wölffl), Joseph, Austrian pianist and composer; b. Salzburg, Dec. 24, 1773; d. London, May 21, 1812. He was a pupil of Leopold Mozart and Michael Haydn; served as a chorister at the Salzburg Cathedral (1783–86); was then in Vienna (1790–92) and Warsaw (1793); again in Vienna from 1795; was considered Beethoven's rival as a pianist; in 1798 he married the actress Therese Klemm. Traveling through Germany, he gave numerous concerts as a pianist, reaching Paris in 1801; he settled there for several years; produced 2 French operas and was acclaimed as a piano virtuoso. In 1805 he went to London, and almost immediately established himself in the public's favor as a pianist and teacher. He was, however, of an eccentric disposition, and became involved in all sorts of trouble. He died in obscurity at the age of 38. In his professional life, he emphasized the sensational element; gave fanciful titles to his works; named one of his piano sonatas *Ne plus ultra,* and claimed that it was the most difficult piece ever written.
WORKS: Operas: *Der Höllenberg* (Vienna, Nov. 21, 1795), *Der Kopf ohne Mann* (Vienna, Dec. 3, 1798), *Das schöne Milchmädchen* (Vienna, Jan. 5, 1797), *Das trojanische Pferd* (Vienna, 1797), *L'Amour romanesque* (Paris, 1804), *Fernando, ou Les Maures* (Paris, 1805); ballets: *La Surprise de Diane* (London, Dec. 21, 1805) and *Alzire* (London, Jan. 27, 1807); 7 piano concertos, including *Le Calme* and *Concerto militaire;* other publ. compositions are 2 symphs.; 9 string quartets; 12 piano trios; 2 trios for 2 Clarinets and Bassoon; 42 violin sonatas; 58 piano sonatas; 24 sets of variations for Piano; a *Méthode de piano* (with 100 studies); sonatas for 4-hands; waltzes; polonaises, rondos, fantasias, etc.; also songs. Some of his piano pieces were publ. in monthly issues, under the title *The Harmonic Budget* (London, 1810).
BIBLIOGRAPHY: R. Duval, "Un Rival de Beethoven: Joseph Woelfl," *Rivista Musicale Italiana* (1898; also separately, Turin, 1898); R. Baum, *Joseph Wölfl. Leben, Klavierwerke, Klavierkammermusik und Klavierkonzerte* (Kassel, 1928).

Wolfram, Joseph Maria, Bohemian composer; b. Dobrzan, July 21, 1789; d. Teplitz, Sept. 30, 1839. He studied with J.A. Koželuch in Prague; moved to Vienna as a music teacher; then became a government official at Theusing, and mayor of Teplitz (1824). He brought out several successful operas: *Maja und Alpino* (Prague, May 24, 1826); *Der Bergmönch* (Dresden, March 14, 1830); *Das Schloss Candra* (Dresden, Dec. 1, 1832); a *Missa nuptialis* and some piano pieces and songs by him were publ.

Wolfrum, Philipp, German musicologist and composer; b. Schwarzenbach-am-Wald, Dec. 17, 1854; d. Samaden, May 8, 1919. He was a pupil of Rheinberger and Wüllner in Munich; received his Dr.Phil. at Leipzig Univ. in 1890 with the dissertation *Die Entstehung und erste Entwickelung des deutschen evangelischen Kirchenliedes in musikalischer Beziehung.* He publ. *Joh. Seb. Bach* (2 vols., 1906; 2nd ed. of vol. 1, 1910); *Die evangelische Kirchenmusik: Ihr Stand und ihre Weiterentwicklung* (1914); *Luther und Bach* (1917); *Luther und die Musik* (1918). WORKS: *Ein Weihnachtsmysterium,* Christmas play, for Chorus and Orch. (1899); *Das grosse Hallelujah* for Male Chorus and Orch.; Piano Quartet; String Quartet; Piano Trio; Cello Sonata; 3 organ sonatas; he also edited *Der evangelische Kirchenchor* (collection of 44 hymns) and *Pfälzisches Melodienbuch.* BIBLIOGRAPHY: K. Hasse, "Philipp Wolfrum," *Zeitschrift für Musikwissenschaft* (1919).

Wolfurt, Kurt von, German composer; b. Lettin, Sept. 7, 1880; d. Munich, Feb. 25, 1957. He studied science at the univs. of Dorpat, Leipzig, and Munich; then took lessons in composition with Max Reger in Munich, where he settled. He composed the opera *Dame Kobold* (Kassel, March 14, 1940); *Faust,* after Goethe, for Soprano, Chorus, and Orch.; *Gesang des Meeres,* symph. poem; *Concerto grosso;* Piano Concerto; chamber music; etc. He publ. monographs on Mussorgsky (Stuttgart, 1927) and Tchaikovsky (Zürich, 1951). BIBLIOGRAPHY: Special issue of *Zeitschrift für Musik* (Oct. 1940).

Wolgast, Johannes, German musicologist; b. Kiel, July 2, 1891; d. Leipzig, Oct. 24, 1932. He studied with Riemann, Straube, and Pembaur in Leipzig; was in the German army during World War I; after the Armistice, continued his studies with Schering and Abert in Berlin; received a Dr.Phil. in 1923, with the dissertation *Georg Böhm;* then taught at the Kirchenmusik-Inst. in Leipzig and at the Leipzig Cons.; edited the collected works of Georg Böhm (2 vols.; 1927, 1932); compiled various useful catalogues; contributed articles to German musical magazines.

Wolkenstein, Oswald von, one of the last of the Minnesänger; b. Burg Wolkenstein, Grödener Tal (Tyrol), 1377; d. Meran, Aug. 2, 1445. He led an adventurous life, traveling through Russia, Persia, Greece, Spain, France, Italy (with King Ruprecht in 1401), etc. For several years (from 1415) he was in the service of King (later Emperor) Sigismund, whom he accompanied to the Council of Constance. The musical settings that he devised for his poems

are notable for their genuine melodic quality; some of them are in 2-part and 3-part counterpoint; there are also examples of canonic imitation. His works were edited by Schatz and Koller for Denkmäler der Tonkunst in Österreich, 18 (9.i). BIBLIOGRAPHY: J. Beyrich, *Untersuchungen über des Stil Oswalds von Wolkenstein* (Leipzig, 1910); W. Türler, *Stilistische Studien zu Oswald von Wolkenstein* (Heidelberg, 1920); J. Schatz, *Sprache und Wortschatz Oswalds von Wolkenstein* (Vienna, 1930); A. Wolkenstein-Rodenegg, *Oswald von Wolkenstein* (Innsbruck, 1930); W. Salmen, "Werdegang und Lebensfülle des Oswald Wolkenstein," *Musica Disciplina* (1953).

Wollanck, (Johann Ernst) Friedrich, German composer; b. Berlin, Nov. 3, 1781; d. there, Sept. 6, 1831. He was a lawyer and held a government position as counselor of the city court in Berlin. His works include an opera, *Der Alpenhirt* (Berlin, 1811); a "Liederspiel," *Thibaut von Lowis;* 2 masses; a Requiem and other church music; more than 100 songs; 33 part-songs; 3 string quartets; 2 string sextets; other chamber music; piano sonatas.

Wolle, John Frederick, American choral conductor and organist; b. Bethlehem, Pa., April 4, 1863; d. there, Jan. 12, 1933. He went to Germany to study with Rheinberger in Munich (1884–85); upon his return to the U.S. served as organist at the Moravian Church in Bethlehem (1885–1905); in 1900 he inaugurated the Bach Choir in Bethlehem, which became famous for its fine performances. BIBLIOGRAPHY: R. Walters, *The Bethlehem Bach Choir* (Boston, 1918); M.A. DeWolfe Howe, "Venite in Bethlehem," *Musical Quarterly* (April 1942).

Wolle, Peter, Moravian minister, bishop, and composer; b. New Herrnhut, St. Thomas, West Indies, Jan. 5, 1792; d. Bethlehem, Pa., Nov. 14, 1871. He was consecrated to the episcopacy on Sept. 26, 1845. He left several compositions; edited the *Moravian Tune Book* (1836). One of his anthems, for Double Chorus with Strings and Organ, is included in the series Music of the Moravians in America, publ. by the N.Y. Public Library (1939). BIBLIOGRAPHY: A.G. Rau and H.T. David, *A Catalogue of Music by American Moravians* (Bethlehem, 1938).

Wollenhaupt, Hermann Adolf, German pianist and composer; b. Schkeuditz, near Leipzig, Sept. 27, 1827; d. New York, Sept. 18, 1863. He studied in Leipzig with Julius Knorr (piano) and Moritz Hauptmann (composition). In 1845 he settled in N.Y.; made a reputation as a concert pianist and teacher. He wrote about 100 brilliant piano pieces, among them *Galop di bravura, Valses styriennes, Improvisation, Nocturne,* and *Scherzo brillante;* he also made numerous transcriptions and arrangements.

Wollgandt, Edgar, German violinist and teacher;

b. Wiesbaden, July 18, 1880; d. Halle, Dec. 25, 1949. He studied violin with H. Heermann in Frankfurt; in 1903 became concertmaster of the Gewandhaus Orch. in Leipzig; also was first violin of the Gewandhaus Quartet. He taught for many years in Leipzig, and in 1947 became a prof. of the Hochschule für Musik in Halle.

Wolpe, Stefan, significant modern composer; b. Berlin, Aug. 25, 1902; d. New York, April 4, 1972. He studied music theory with Paul Juon and Franz Schreker at the Berlin Hochschule für Musik (1919–24). After graduation, he became associated with choral and theatrical groups in Berlin, promoting social causes; composed songs on revolutionary themes. With the advent of the anti-Semitic Nazi regime, he went to Vienna, where he took lessons with Anton von Webern; then traveled to Palestine; taught music theory at the Jerusalem Cons. In 1938 he emigrated to the U.S., where he devoted himself mainly to teaching; was on the faculty of the Settlement Music School in Philadelphia (1946–48); at the Philadelphia Academy of Music (1949–52); at Black Mountain College, North Carolina (1952–56); and at Long Island Univ. (1957–68). He also taught privately. Among his students were Elmer Bernstein, Ezra Laderman, Ralph Shapey, David Tudor, and Morton Feldman. He was married successively to Ola Okuniewska, a painter, in 1927, to **Irma Schoenberg** (b. 1902; d. 1984), a Rumanian pianist, in 1934, and to Hilda Morley, a poetess, in 1948. In his style of composition, he attempted to reconcile the contradictions of triadic tonality (which he cultivated during his early period of writing "proletarian" music), atonality without procrustean dodecaphony, and serialism of contrasts obtained by intervallic contraction and expansion, metrical alteration, and dynamic variegation; superadded to these were explorations of Jewish cantillation and infatuation with jazz. Remarkably enough, the very copiousness of these resources contributed to a clearly identifiable idiom.
WORKS: Operas: *Schöne Geschichten* (1927–29); *Zeus und Elida* (1928); *Cantata about Sport* (1952); *Street Music* for Baritone, Speaker, and 5 Instruments, to Wolpe's own text (1963–68); Cantata to texts by Hölderlin, Herodotus, and Robert Creeley (1963–68); incidental music: *Da liegt Hund begraben* (1932); *The Good Woman of Setzuan,* to a play by Bertolt Brecht (1953); *The Exception and the Rule,* to a play by Bertolt Brecht (1960); for Orch.: *Passacaglia* (1957); *The Man from Midian,* ballet suite (1942); Symph. (1955–56; revised 1964); *Chamber Piece No. 1* for 14 Players (1964); *Chamber Piece No. 2* for 14 Players (1965–66); chamber music: *Duo in Hexachord* for Oboe and Clarinet (1936); Oboe Sonata (1941); Violin Sonata (1949); Quartet for Trumpet, Saxophone, Percussion, and Piano (1950); Oboe Quartet (1955); Quintet with Voice for Baritone, Clarinet, Horn, Cello, Harp, and Piano (1956–57); Trio for Flute, Cello, and Piano (1964); *From Here on Farther* for Clarinet, Bass Clarinet, Violin, and Piano (1969); String Quartet (1969); *Piece for Trumpet and 7 Instruments* (1971); for Piano:

March and Variations for 2 Pianos (1933); *4 Studies on Basic Rows* (1935–36); *Toccata* (1941); *Enactments* for 3 Pianos (1950–53); *Broken Sequences* (1969). He contributed numerous articles to German and American music magazines.
BIBLIOGRAPHY: Marion Bauer, "Stefan Wolpe," *Modern Music* (1940); Herbert Sucoff, *Catalogue and Evaluation of the Work of Stefan Wolpe* (N.Y., 1969).

Wolpert, Franz Alfons, German composer and theorist; b. Wiesentheid, Oct. 11, 1917; d. there, Aug. 7, 1978. He sang in the Cathedral choir in Regensburg, and studied there at a church seminary; took lessons in composition with Wolf-Ferrari in Salzburg (1939–41). He taught music at the Mozarteum (1941–50); then was engaged as a music teacher in Überlingen, where he settled.
WORKS: Song cycles to words by Uhland, Lenau, and Goethe; 2 violin sonatas; 2 viola sonatas; 2 cello sonatas; Clarinet Trio; 2 piano sonatas; *Das Göttliche* for Soprano Chorus and Orch.; cantata after Goethe (1961); 15 Shakespeare sonnets for Bass and Piano (1949–68). He publ. *Neue Harmonik* (Regensburg, 1952; new enlarged ed., Wilhelmshaven, 1972).

Wolstenholme, William, blind English organist and composer; b. Blackburn, Lancashire, Feb. 24, 1865; d. London, July 23, 1931. He entered the College for Blind Sons of Gentlemen in Worcester at the age of 9; studied with Dr. Done, the Cathedral organist there; received a Mus.Bac. from Oxford in 1887; subsequently filled various posts as a church organist in Blackburn, and (from 1902) in London. In 1908 he visited the U.S.
WORKS: *Lord Ullin's Daughter,* cantata; *Sir Humphrey Gilbert,* ballad for Women's Voices; *To Take the Air,* madrigal; *Suite* in F for String Orch.; about 100 compositions for organ; Wind Quintet; Piano Quartet; 2 string quartets; Piano Trio; Violin Sonata; piano pieces: *Impromptu-Polonaise, Marche humoresque, Fantasy-Intermezzo,* etc.; songs and part-songs.
BIBLIOGRAPHY: F.H. Wood, "William Wolstenholme," *Musical Times* (1931).

Wolzogen, Alfred, Freiherr von, German writer on music; b. Frankfurt, May 27, 1823; d. San Remo, Jan. 14, 1883. From 1868 he was Intendant of the court theater at Schwerin. He was the author of *Über Theater und Musik* (Breslau, 1860); *Über die szenische Darstellung von Mozarts "Don Giovanni"* (1860); *Wilhelmine Schröder-Devrient* (Leipzig, 1863); new German versions of Mozart's *Don Giovanni* and *Schauspieldirektor;* also articles in periodicals.

Wolzogen, Ernst, Freiherr von, German poet and musical journalist; son of **Alfred von Wolzogen** and half brother of **Hans von Wolzogen;** b. Breslau, April 23, 1855; d. Munich, July 30, 1934. He studied at the univs. of Strasbourg and Leipzig. In 1901 he established in Berlin (with O.J. Bierbaum and F. Wedekind) the Überbrettl, a kind of artistic cabaret

for the production of dramatic pieces, pantomimes, poems with recitation and music, etc., most of them reflecting or satirizing contemporary German life; Oskar Straus provided most of the music, and Schoenberg contributed some of the numbers; 2 journals, *Das moderne Brettl* and *Bühne und Brettl,* were publ. for a year or so to promote the ideas of the enterprise, but the cabaret closed after 2 sensationally successful seasons. Wolzogen publ. 2 books dealing with music: *Der Kraftmayr* (1897; humorous novel with Liszt as the central figure; Eng. trans. as *Florian Mayr,* 1914) and *Ansichten und Aussichten* (1908; essays). His wife, **Elsa Laura** (née **Seeman von Mangern**), became known as a singer, making a specialty of songs with lute accompaniment; with her husband she made a tour of the U.S. (1910–11); publ. 7 vols. of folk songs with lute accompaniment *(Meine Lieder zur Laute).*
BIBLIOGRAPHY: A. Hertwig, *Ernst von Wolzogens "Überbrettl" in Wort und Bild* (Berlin, 1901).

Wolzogen, Hans, Freiherr von, German writer on music and authority on Wagner; b. Potsdam, Nov. 13, 1848; d. Bayreuth, June 2, 1938. He studied mythology and comparative philology in Berlin (1868–71); then devoted himself to literature; in 1878, at Wagner's invitation, he became editor of the *Bayreuther Blätter* and lived in Bayreuth most of his life. He popularized the term "leitmotif," first used by F.W. Jähns, in his "Motive in Wagners *Götterdämmerung,*" publ. in the *Musikalisches Wochenblatt* in 1887 (Wagner's preferred term was "Grundthema").
WRITINGS: *Der Nibelungenmythos in Sage und Literatur* (1876); *Thematischer Lietfaden durch die Musik von R. Wagners Festspiel "Der Ring des Nibelungen"* (1876; 4th ed. as *Erläuterungen zu R. Wagners Nibelungendrama,* 1878); *Die Tragödie in Bayreuth und ihr Satyrspiel* (1876; 5th ed., 1881); *Poetische Lautsymbolik. Psychische Wirkungen der Sprachlaute aus R. Wagners "Ring des Nibelungen"* (1876; 3rd ed., 1897); *Grundlage und Aufgabe des allgemeinen Patronatvereins zur Pflege und Erhaltung der Bühnenfestspiele in Bayreuth* (1877); *Die Sprache in Wagners Dichtungen* (1877; 2nd ed., 1881); *R. Wagners Tristan und Isolde* (1880); *Unsre Zeit und unsre Kunst* (1881); *Was ist Stil? was will Wagner?* (1881); *Die Religion des Mitleidens* (1882); *Parsifal. Ein thematischer Leitfaden* (1882; 21st printing, 1914); *R. Wagners Heldengestalten erläutert* (2nd ed., 1886); *Wagneriana* (1888); *R. Wagner und die Tierwelt; auch eine Biographie* (1890; 3rd ed., 1910); *Wagners Lebensbericht* (1884; the original work of "The Work and Mission of My Life," publ. 1879 in the *North American Review,* under Wagner's name); *Erinnerungen an R. Wagner* (1883); *Die Idealisierung des Theaters* (1885); *Grossmeister deutscher Musik* (1897); "Wagner-Brevier," *Die Musik* (1904); *R. Wagner* (1905; in Remer's series Die Dichtung); *Musikalisch-dramatische Parallelen* (1906); *E.T.A. Hoffmann und R. Wagner* (1906); *Aus R. Wagners Geisteswelt* (1908); *Kunst und Kirche* (1913); *E.T.A. Hoffmann, Der deutsche Geisterseher* (1922); *Le-* *bensbilder* (autobiographical; 1923); *Wagner und seine Werke* (1924); *Wohltäterin Musik* (1925); *Musik und Theater* (1929); edited Wagner's *Ausgewählte Schriften über Staat und Kunst und Religion* (1902; 3rd ed., 1914) and *Entwürfe zu "Die Meistersinger," "Tristan und Isolde" und "Parsifal"* (1907).

Wonder, Stevie, black American rock singer (real name, **Steveland Judkins Hardaway**); b. Saginaw, Mich., May 13, 1950. He was blind from birth; learned to play the drums and piano; improvised his first song, *Lonely Boy,* at the age of 10, and at 12 composed *Fingertips,* which became a hit. Possessed by that indefinable gift of song, he rapidly advanced in the rosters of popular success; the shows at which he sings, accompanying himself at the piano, have become great money-makers. Among his pop hits are *Living for the City, You Are the Sunshine of My Life, My Cherie Amour, I Was Made to Love Her,* and *Uptight.*

Wood, Charles, Irish organist and composer; b. Armagh, June 15, 1866; d. Cambridge, England, July 12, 1926. He studied at the Royal College of Music in London, and subsequently taught harmony there; received his Mus.Doc. degree from Cambridge in 1894. In 1924 he succeeded Stanford as prof. of music at Cambridge Univ. He wrote 6 string quartets (mostly in an Irish manner); vocal works with Orch.: *Ode on Time* (1898), *Dirge for 2 Veterans* (1901), *Song of the Tempest* (1902), *Ballad of Dundee* (1904); church music; edited a collection of Irish folk songs (1897).

Wood, David Duffie, blind American organist; b. Pittsburgh, March 2, 1838; d. Philadelphia, March 27, 1910. Having lost his eyesight in an accident at the age of 3, he was educated at the Pa. Inst. for the Blind; from 1858 till his death he was an instructor of music there. He was a fine organist; wrote anthems and songs. He publ. *A Dictionary of Musical Terms, for the Use of the Blind* (Philadelphia, 1869).

Wood, Haydn, English violinist and composer; b. Slaithwaite, March 25, 1882; d. London, March 11, 1959. He entered the Royal College of Music in London at 15; studied there with Fernández Arbós (violin) and Stanford (composition); later studied with César Thomson in Brussels. His works include 8 overtures, 8 rhapsodies for band, 18 orch. studies, 31 entr'actes for orch., 12 violin solos, 2 flute pieces, 3 accordion solos, and about 200 songs.

Wood, Sir Henry J(oseph), eminent English conductor; b. London, March 3, 1869; d. Hitchin, Hertfordshire, Aug. 19, 1944. Of musical parentage, he was taught to play the piano by his mother; he participated in family musicales from the age of 6; was equally precocious on the organ; at the age of 10 he often acted as a deputy organist, and gave organ recitals at the Fisheries Exhibition (1883) and at the Inventions Exhibition (1885). In 1886 he entered the

Royal Academy of Music, where his teachers were Prout, Steggall, Macfarren, and Garcia; he won 4 medals. In 1888 he brought out some of his songs; then composed light operas and cantatas. But soon his ambition crystallized in the direction of conducting; he traveled with an opera company in 1889; then became assistant conductor at the Savoy Theatre (1890); was engaged as a conductor for various other operatic enterprises. On Aug. 10, 1895, he began his first series of Promenade Concerts (the famous "Proms") in Queen's Hall, London, with an orch. of about 80 members. Their success was so conspicuous that a new series of concerts was inaugurated on Jan. 30, 1897, under Wood's direction, and flourished from the beginning. In 1899 he founded the Nottingham Orch.; also was appointed conductor of the Wolverhampton Festival Choral Society (1900), the Sheffield Festival (1902–11), and the Norwich Festival (1908). In 1904 he conducted in N.Y. He was married to Olga Urusova, a Russian noblewoman, and became greatly interested in Russian music, which he performed frequently at his concerts. He adopted a Russian pseudonym, **Paul Klenovsky,** for his compositions and arrangements, and supplied an imaginary biography of his alter ego for use in program notes. His wife died in 1909, and Wood married Muriel Greatorex in 1911. He was knighted in 1911. In 1918 he was offered the conductorship of the Boston Symph. Orch. as successor to Muck, but declined. In 1923 he was appointed prof. of conducting and orch. playing at the Royal Academy of Music. In 1925 he conducted in California; in 1926 received the degree of Mus.Doc. (*honoris causa*) from Oxford Univ. Wood continued to conduct the Promenade Concerts almost to the end of his life, presenting the last concert on July 28, 1944. Among his popular arrangements are Chopin's *Marche Funèbre,* some works by Bach, and the *Trumpet Voluntary* (mistakenly attributed to Purcell, but actually by Jeremiah Clarke). He publ. *The Gentle Art of Singing* (4 vols.; 1927–28) and *About Conducting* (London, 1945), and edited the *Handbook of Miniature Orchestral and Chamber Music Scores* for J.W. Chester & Co. (1937); wrote an autobiography, *My Life and Music* (London, 1938). A commemorative postage stamp with his portrait was issued by the Post Office of Great Britain on Sept. 1, 1980.

BIBLIOGRAPHY: Rosa Newmarch, *Henry J. Wood,* in the Living Masters of Music series (London, 1904); R. Hill and others, *Sir Henry Wood: Fifty Years of the "Proms"* (London, 1944); J. Wood, *The Last Years of Henry J. Wood* (London, 1954; with a foreword by Sir Malcolm Sargent); Reginald Pound, *Sir Henry Wood: A Biography* (London, 1969); A. Orga, *The Proms* (London, 1974); D. Cox, *The Henry Wood Proms* (London, 1980).

Wood, Hugh, English composer; b. Parbold, near Wigan, Lancashire, June 27, 1932. He studied theory and composition with Anthony Milner, Iain Hamilton, and Mátyás Seiber in London (1957–60); taught at Morley College in London (1958–67) and at the Royal Academy of Music (1962–65); was composer-in-residence at the Univ. of Glasgow (1966–70); from 1971–73 he was a lecturer at the Univ. of Liverpool; in 1976 was appointed a lecturer at Cambridge.

WORKS: *Variations* for Viola and Piano (1957–59); *4 Songs* for Mezzo-soprano, Clarinet, Violin, and Cello (1959–61); Trio for Flute, Viola, and Piano (1961); 3 string quartets (1962, 1970, 1978); *3 Pieces* for Piano (1960–63); *Scenes from "Comus,"* after Milton, for Soprano, Tenor, and Orch. (1962–65; London, Aug. 2, 1965); Quintet for Clarinet, Horn, Violin, Cello, and Piano (1967); Cello Concerto (1965–69; London, Aug. 26, 1969); Chamber Concerto (1970–71; London, Nov. 27, 1971); Violin Concerto (1970–72; Liverpool, Sept. 19, 1972); *Song Cycle to Poems of Neruda* for High Voice and Chamber Orch. (1973; London, Feb. 18, 1974).

Wood, Joseph, American composer; b. Pittsburgh, May 12, 1915. He studied with Bernard Wagenaar at the Juilliard School in N.Y., graduating in 1949, and with Otto Luening at Columbia Univ. (M.A., 1950). In 1950 he was appointed prof. in composition at the Oberlin Cons. of Music in Ohio. His music is couched in a modern Romantic vein; upon occasion he applies serial techniques.

WORKS: Opera, *The Mother* (1945); 3 symphs. (1939, 1952, 1958); Piano Trio (1937); Viola Sonata (1938); String Quartet (1942); Violin Sonata (1947); Piano Quintet (1956); *Divertimento* for Piano and Chamber Orch. (1959); choruses; incidental music for theatrical plays; piano pieces; songs.

Wood, Mary Knight, American pianist and composer; b. Easthampton, Mass., April 7, 1857; d. Florence, Dec. 20, 1944. She studied in Boston with B.J. Lang and in N.Y. with Huss; married A.B. Mason and went to live in Florence, where she remained for many years until her death. She publ. about 30 songs, among them *Ashes of Roses, In Harbor,* and *Poppies.*

Wood, Thomas, English composer and author; b. Chorley, Lancashire, Nov. 28, 1892; d. Bures, Essex, Nov. 19, 1950. He was educated at Exeter College, Oxford; then studied at the Royal Academy of Music with Stanford; was music director at Tonbridge School (1920–24); lecturer and precentor at Exeter College (1924–28). His extensive travels took him to the Far East and the Arctic; his familiarity with the sea was reflected in many of his compositions (for Chorus and Orch.), such as *40 Singing Seamen* (1925), *Master Mariners* (1927), *Merchantmen* (1934), and in *A Seaman's Overture* (for Orch., 1927). He edited vol. II of the *Oxford Song Book* (1928; 3rd ed., 1937). His books include *Music and Boyhood* (1925) and the autobiographical *True Thomas* (1936); he also publ. *Cobbers* (on his Australian tour of 1930–32), which became highly popular in England, and a sequel to it, *Cobbers Campaigning* (1940).

BIBLIOGRAPHY: N. Coghill, "Thomas Wood," *Music & Letters* (April 1951).

Wood, William G., Irish organist; brother of

Charles Wood; b. Armagh, Jan. 16, 1859; d. London, Sept. 25, 1895. He studied at the Royal Academy of Music in London; from 1886 till his death he was organist and music master at the Highgate Grammar School. He composed some fine organ music (3 canons, a Sonata, *Fantasia and Fugue, Introduction and Allegro, Minuet and Trio,* etc.).

Wood-Hill, Mabel, American composer; b. Brooklyn, March 12, 1870; d. Stamford, Conn., March 1, 1954. She was educated at Smith College and at Columbia Univ., where she studied composition with Rybner. She wrote songs and choruses; orchestrated pieces by Couperin *(Louis XIV Suite)* and Bach. Her pantomime, *The Adventures of Pinocchio,* was performed for the first time in N.Y., on April 13, 1931.

Woodbury, Arthur, American composer; b. Kimball, Nebr., June 20, 1930. He studied at the Univ. of Idaho (B.S., 1951; M.M., 1955); also attended the Univ. of California, Berkeley (1957–58). A bassoon player by profession, he was a member of various orchs.; also played the saxophone. In 1963 he joined the staff of the Univ. of Calif. at Davis; remained there until 1972, when he joined the faculty at the Univ. of Southern Florida. His early works are written in a traditional modern idiom; later he branched out as a composer of experimental music, cultivating electronic and aleatory techniques.
WORKS: Woodwind Quartet (1955); Symph. (1958); *Autobiography: Patricia Belle* for Soprano, Electronic Instruments, and an amplified Chamber Ensemble (1968); *Remembrances* for Violin, Saxophone, and Vibraphone (1968); *Recall,* theater piece (1969); *An Evening of the Music of Neil Jansen, A Put-on* for Tape, utilizing the Moog Synthesizer (1969); *Werner Vonbrawnasaurus Rex* for Tape, Slide Guitar, Electric Piano, and Music Synthesizer (1970).

Woodbury, (original name, **Woodberry**), **Isaac Baker,** American composer of songs; b. Beverly, Mass., Oct. 23, 1819; d. Columbia, S.C., Oct. 26, 1858. Originally a blacksmith, he took up music, going to Europe in 1838 for study in Paris and London; upon his return he settled in Boston. From 1850 to his death he was an editor of a N.Y. music magazine publ. successively as *American Monthly Musical Review, Musical Pioneer,* etc. His collection of sacred songs, *The Dulcimer,* enjoyed great popularity; he also compiled a *Collection of Church Music* for the Boston Music Educational Society (1842) and *The Choral* (1845); publ. *Woodbury's Self-Instructor in Musical Composition and Thorough-Bass,* and many secular songs.
BIBLIOGRAPHY: F.J. Metcalf, *American Writers and Compilers of Sacred Music* (1925); *Dictionary of American Biography;* R. Copeland, *The Life and Works of Isaac Baker Woodbury (1819–1858)* (Diss., Univ. of Cincinnati, 1974).

Woodhouse, George, English pianist; b. Cradley Heath, near Birmingham, Dec. 16, 1877; d. Southsea, Jan. 4, 1954. He studied in Birmingham and later took piano lessons with Leschetizky in Vienna. He established his own piano school in London; publ. *The Artist at the Piano* (London, 1910), *Creative Technique* (London, 1922), *From Keyboard to Music* (London, 1949), and *A Realistic Approach to Piano Playing* (London, 1953).

Woodman, Raymond Huntington, American organist and composer; b. Brooklyn, Jan. 18, 1861; d. there, Dec. 25, 1943. He studied piano with his father; theory with Dudley Buck; then went to Paris, where he took lessons in organ playing from César Franck (1888). He filled various posts as a church organist and teacher in N.Y.; also taught theory and conducted a choral society in Brooklyn. He publ. about 150 compositions, among them anthems, organ pieces, piano pieces *(Romance, The Brook, Spring Song, 3 Album-Leaves,* etc.), and songs, of which *A Birthday* was especially successful.

Woods, Francis Cunningham, English organist and composer; b. London, Aug. 29, 1862; d. there, Sept. 21, 1929. He studied at the National Training School for Music under Sullivan, Prout, Stainer, and Cowen; after serving as organist at Brasenose College and Exeter College, was private organist to the Duke of Marlborough (1891–94); then prof. of organ and lecturer at Oxford Univ. (1890–95); in 1896 he succeeded William G. Wood as organist and music master at the Highgate Grammar School in London. He composed *King Harold,* "historical cantata"; *Greyport Legend,* ballad for Baritone, Men's Chorus, and Orch.; *Old May-Day,* cantata for Women's Voices and Piano; *The Lords of Labor,* ode; some orch. pieces; songs.

Woodward, Roger, Australian pianist; b. Sydney, Dec. 20, 1942. He studied piano with Alexander Sverjensky in Sydney; then obtained a Polish government scholarship and went to Warsaw, where he took lessons with Zbigniew Drzwiecki. He won the Chopin Competition Prize in 1968, an auspicious award that propelled him on an international career. In 1971 he settled in London, where he gained renown among international avant-garde composers by repeatedly performing works by such uncompromising celebrants of quaquaversal modern idioms as Takemitsu, Barraqué, Stockhausen, and Birtwistle; faithful to his antecedents, he also placed on his programs works of Australian composers such as Boyd, Meale, and Sculthorpe. He participated in several American concerts of contemporary music, including a marathon series presented in Los Angeles. In 1980 he received for his musical valor the Order of the British Empire.

Woodworth, G(eorge) Wallace, American choral conductor and music educator; b. Boston, Nov. 6, 1902; d. Cambridge, Mass., July 18, 1969. He was educated at Harvard Univ. (B.A., 1924; M.A., 1926); also studied at the Royal College of Music in London (1927–28). In 1924 he joined the staff of the music dept. at Harvard, and was engaged as conductor of the Radcliffe Choral Society; also led the Pierian

Sodality Orch. of Harvard Univ. (1928–32) and the Harvard Glee Club (1933–38). In 1940 he was appointed organist and choirmaster for the Harvard Univ. Chapel. He was made James Edward Ditson Professor of Music at Harvard in 1954. He conducted the Harvard-Radcliffe Chorus on its transcontinental U.S. tour in 1954, and took the Harvard Glee Club on its European tour in 1956. He retired in 1969. He publ. *The World of Music* (Cambridge, Mass., 1964).

BIBLIOGRAPHY: L. Berman, ed., *Words and Music: The Composer's View: A Medley of Problems and Solutions in Honor of G. Wallace Woodworth* (Cambridge, 1972).

Wooldridge, David, English composer, conductor, and writer on music; b. Deal, Kent, Aug. 24, 1927. He is a grandson of the English musicologist **Harry Ellis Wooldridge** and godson of Rachmaninoff, from whom he received some friendly piano lessons at the age of 4. He began studying the violin at 6; at 16 made his conducting debut; in 1952 he graduated from the Univ. of London, summa cum laude; was then apprenticed to Clemens Krauss at the Vienna State Opera; in 1954 he became junior conductor at the Bavarian State Opera. In 1956–58 he was in the U.S. as a guest conductor in Minneapolis, Cincinnati, Cleveland, and Rochester; from 1961 to 1965 conducted the Lebanese National Orch. in Beirut; then was conductor of the Cape Town Symph. in South Africa (1965–67); subsequently was a visiting prof. at Indiana Univ. (1968–69); Grinnell College, Iowa (1971); the Univ. of Calif. at Santa Cruz (1972); Wabash College, Indiana (1976); and the Univ. of Calif. at Riverside (1977); concurrently was music director of the Bridgewater (Conn.) Concert Assoc. (1973–78).

WORKS: Viola Concerto (1949); ballet, *Les Parapluies* (1956); Cello Concerto (1957); ballet, *Octet* (1958); *Suite Libanaise* (1962); *4 Armenian Dances* (1964); *Partita* for Small Orch. (1967); *Partita* for Large Orch. (1968); ballet, *Movements* (1970); symph. poem, *The Legend of Lillanonah* (1975); opera, *The Duchess of Amalfi* (1978); incidental music; film scores. He publ. the books *Conductor's World* (N.Y., 1970) and *From the Steeples and Mountains,* a biography of Charles Ives (N.Y., 1974).

Wooldridge, Harry Ellis, English musicologist; b. Winchester, March 28, 1845; d. London, Feb. 13, 1917. While studying at Trinity College, Oxford (1860–64), he became deeply interested in painting and music; entered the Royal Academy of Fine Arts in 1865, at the same time beginning his research regarding early music in the libraries of Oxford and London; from 1895 till his death he was Slade Prof. of Fine Arts at Oxford Univ.

WRITINGS: *The English Metrical Psalter* (1890); *The Polyphonic Period,* being vols. I and II of the *Oxford History of Music* (1901, 1905; 2nd ed., revised by P.C. Buck, 1929–32); he radically revised Chappell's *Popular Music of the Olden Times,* and publ. it under the title *Old English Popular Music* (2 vols., 1893); also edited *Early English Harmony* (2

vols., 1897, 1913; pieces from the 10th to 15th centuries); *The Yattendon Hymnal* (1899; with R. Bridges); Purcell's sacred compositions (vols. 13, 14, and 18 of Novello's ed. of Purcell's complete works).

Wooler, Alfred, American music teacher and composer; b. Shipley, Yorkshire, May 11, 1867; d. Lake Winola, Pa., Aug. 7, 1937. He settled in the U.S. as a youth, and studied at the Univ. of Pa.; taught harmony at Scranton, Buffalo, and N.Y.; also conducted choral societies. He composed about 250 anthems, songs, and part-songs; also piano pieces.

Woolf, Benjamin Edward, American composer and music critic; b. London, Feb. 16, 1836; d. Boston, Feb. 7, 1901. He was taken to America as a child; studied organ with W.R Bristow in N.Y.; in 1870 settled in Boston, where he wrote on music and drama in the Boston *Globe* and the Boston *Herald.* He composed the "operatic comedietta" *Lawn Tennis, or Djakh and Djill* (Boston, 1880); comic opera, *Pounce & Co.* (Boston, 1883); operetta, *Westward Ho!* (Boston, Dec. 31, 1894); also some chamber music and piano pieces.

Woolhouse, Wesley S.B., English mathematician and writer on musical subjects; b. North Shields, May 6, 1809; d. London, Aug. 12, 1893. He was head assistant at the Nautical Almanach Establishment. He publ. *Essay on Musical Intervals, Harmonics, and the Temperament of the Musical Scale* (1835; new ed., 1888); *A Catechism of Music* (1843); *Treatise on Singing.* He owned a fine collection of violins.

Woollen, Russell, American composer; b. Hartford, Conn., Jan. 7, 1923. He studied for the priesthood; attended the Pius X School of Liturgical Music in N.Y.; in 1948 studied Gregorian chant at the Benedictine Abbey at Solesmes. He was ordained a priest of the Hartford Diocese, in 1947; was released by his bishop in 1964, and was married twice (1971, 1977). He received his B.A. from St. Mary's Univ. in Baltimore (1944); an M.A. in Romance languages from the Catholic Univ. of America in Washington, D.C. (1948); he had private lessons in piano and organ; studied composition with Franz Wasner of the Trapp Family Singers, with Nicolas Nabokov at the Peabody Cons. in Baltimore (1949–51), with Nadia Boulanger in Paris (1951), and with Walter Piston at Harvard Univ. (1953–55). He was a member of the music faculty of the Catholic Univ. (1948–62) and of Howard Univ. (1969–74); in 1956 was appointed staff keyboard artist of the National Symph. in Washington, D.C.

WORKS: Opera, *The Decorator* (N.Y., Catholic Univ., May 24, 1959); Symph. No. 1 (1957–58); Symph. No. 2 (1978); Piano Quartet (1952); Quartet for Flute and Strings (1953); Woodwind Quintet (1955); Piano Trio (1957); *Suite* for Flute and Strings (1966); Trio for Flute, Oboe, and Harpsichord (1967); *Fantasy* for Flute and Harpsichord (1968); Sonata for Trombone and Piano (1972); Quartet for Woodwinds (1975); *2 Pieces* for Piano and Orch. (1962–76); 16

masses; numerous choral works; 40 duets on *Au clair de la lune* for Recorders.

Woollett, Henri (Henry) Edouard, French composer; b. (of English parentage) Le Havre, Aug. 13, 1864; d. there, Oct. 9, 1936. He studied in Paris with Pugno (piano) and Massenet (composition); returning to Le Havre, he established himself as a teacher; among his students were André Caplet and Honegger. His music is of a lyrical nature, in the manner of his teacher Massenet.
WORKS: *La Rose de Sharon,* "poème lyrique" for Orch. (1895); *Konzertstück* for Cello and Orch. (1911); String Quartet (1929); 2 violin sonatas (1908, 1922); Viola Sonata; Flute Sonata; Cello Sonata; many piano pieces in a Romantic vein *(Nocturnes et pastorales, Pièces intimes, A travers la vie, Au jardin de France, Préludes et valses);* many attractive songs. He publ. *Petit traité de prosodie* (Paris, 1903) and *Histoire de la musique depuis l'antiquité jusqu'à nos jours* (4 vols., Paris, 1909–25).

Wordsworth, William, English composer; b. London, Dec. 17, 1908. He studied with his father; then with Sir Donald Tovey in Edinburgh. He began to compose rather late in life; his music is marked by a certain austerity in the deployment of thematic materials.
WORKS: *Sinfonia* for Strings (1936); *3 Pastoral Sketches* for Orch. (1937); *Theme and Variations* for Orch. (1941); 5 symphs. (1944, 1947–48, 1951, 1953, 1959–60); Piano Concerto (1946); *Divertimento* for Orch. (1954); Violin Concerto (1955); Sinfonietta for Small Orch. (1957); *Variations on a Scottish Theme* for Small Orch. (1962); Cello Concerto (1963); *A Highland Overture* (1964); *Jubilation* for Orch. (1965); *Conflict,* overture (1968); *Sinfonia semplice* for Amateur String Orch. (1969); *Valediction* for Orch. (1969); *A Pattern of Love* for Low Voice and String Orch. (1969–70); *Spring Festival Overture* (1970); *Symposium* for Solo Violin, Strings, and Percussion (1972); *The Houseless Dead,* after D.H. Lawrence, for Baritone, Chorus, and Orch. (1939); oratorio, *Dies Domini* (1942–44); *Lucifer Yields* for Soloists, Chorus, and Orch. (1949); *A Vision* for Women's Chorus and Strings (1950); *A Song of Praise* for Chorus and Orch. (1956); dramatic cantata, *The Two Brigs* (1971); *The Solitary Reaper* for Soprano, Piano, and Clarinet (1973); 6 string quartets (1943, 1946, 1948, 1950, 1955, 1964); 2 cello sonatas (1937, 1959); 2 violin sonatas (1944, 1967); String Trio (1945); Piano Quartet (1948); Piano Trio (1949); Oboe Quartet (1949); Clarinet Quintet (1952); Wind Trio (1953); Piano Quintet (1959); Sonata for Solo Cello (1961); Violin Sonatina (1961); *Dialogue* for Horn and Piano (1965); piano pieces, including a Sonata (1939); songs.

Work, Henry Clay, American composer of popular songs; b. Middletown, Conn., Oct. 1, 1832; d. Hartford, June 8, 1884. He was a printer by trade; was entirely self-taught in music; his first success was *We Are coming, Sister Mary;* other well-known songs are *Grandfather's Clock; Father, Come Home; Shadows on the Floor;* his Civil War song *Marching through Georgia* became celebrated; other songs of the Civil War were *Drafted into the Army; God Save the Nation; Song of a Thousand Years; Wake, Nicodemus; Kingdom Coming,* etc.
BIBLIOGRAPHY: R.S. Hill, "The Mysterious Chord of Henry Clay Work," *Notes* (March–June 1953).

Workman, William, American baritone; b. Valdosta, Ga., Feb. 4, 1940. He studied with Martial Singher at the Curtis Inst. of Music in Philadelphia and at the Music Academy of the West in Santa Barbara; then went to Europe and took voice lessons with Hedwig Schilling in Hamburg; made his operatic debut with the Hamburg State Opera in 1965. In 1972 he became a member of the Frankfurt Opera; also made guest appearances in Stuttgart, Strasbourg, Paris, and Vienna.

Wormser, André (Alphonse-Toussaint), French composer; b. Paris, Nov. 1, 1851; d. there, Nov. 4, 1926. He studied at the Paris Cons. with Marmontel (piano) and Bazin (theory); won first prize for piano in 1872, and the Grand Prix de Rome in 1875 with the cantata *Clytemnestre.* His most successful work was the pantomime, or "wordless opera," *L'Enfant prodigue* (Paris, June 14, 1890); he also composed other stage works; orch. works; men's choruses; songs; piano pieces.

Wörner, Karl(heinz) H(einrich), German musicologist; b. Waldorf, near Heidelberg, Jan. 6, 1910; d. Heiligenkirchen, near Detmold, Aug. 11, 1969. He studied musicology in Berlin with Schünemann and Schering, and conducting with Julius Prüwer; received the degree of Dr.Phil. at Berlin Univ. with the dissertation *Beiträge zur Geschichte des Leitmotivs in der Oper,* publ. in *Zeitschrift für Musikwissenschaft* (Dec. 1931); was a critic for the *B.Z. am Mittag* (1933–34); then (1935–40) opera conductor at Stettin, Magdeburg, and Frankfurt. He was in the German army during World War II; in 1944 was taken prisoner of war by the U.S. Army and spent 2 years in an American internment camp. Returning to Germany in 1946, he was active as a lecturer. From 1954–58 he was on the staff of B. Schott's Söhne (Mainz); in 1958 was on the faculty of the Folkwangschule in Essen; from 1961 taught at the North-West Germany Academy of Music in Detmold.
WORKS: *Mendelssohn-Bartholdy* (Wiesbaden, 1947); *Musik der Gegenwart* (Mainz, 1949); *Robert Schumann* (Zürich, 1949); *Musiker-Worte* (Baden-Baden, 1949); *Geschichte der Musik* (Göttingen, 1954; 6th ed., augmented, 1975; in Eng., 1973); *Neue Musik in der Entscheidung* (Mainz, 1954); *Gotteswort und Magie: Die Oper "Moses und Aron" von Arnold Schönberg* (Heidelberg, 1959; augmented Eng. trans., 1963); *Karlheinz Stockhausen: Werk und Wollen 1950–62* (Rodenkirchen, 1963; augmented Eng. trans., 1973); *Das Zeitalter der thematischen Prozesse in der Geschichte der Musik* (Regensburg, 1969); *Die Musik in der Geistesgeschichte*

(Bonn, 1970).

Woronoff, Wladimir, Russian-born Belgian composer; b. St. Petersburg, Jan. 5, 1903. He studied violin as a child; left Russia after the Revolution and settled in Belgium in 1922; took lessons in composition with André Souris in Brussels. In 1954 he destroyed most of his early works, including the ballet *Le Masque de la mort rouge, Suite de Bruxelles* for Orch., and *Concert lyrique* for Piano and Orch.; he revised most of his remaining scores. His catalogue of extant works after this self-auto-da-fé can boast of the following: *La Foule* for Bass, Chorus, and Orch. (1934; revised 1965); *Annas et le Lépreux* for Low Voice and Piano (1946); *Les 12,* 3 fragments from the poem by Alexander Blok, for Low Voice, and Orch. or Piano (1921–63); *Strophes concertantes* for Piano and Orch. (1964); *Lueur tournante* for Narrator and Orch. (1967); *Tripartita* for Viola and Chamber Orch. (1970); *Vallées* for 2 Pianos (1971).

Worp, Johannes, Netherlandish organist, composer, and arranger; b. Broek, Dec. 24, 1821; d. Groningen, April 21, 1891. He studied in Amsterdam, where he was active as a church organist; then went to Leipzig, where he took a course with Moscheles; returning to the Netherlands, he became organist at Groningen. He publ. valuable organ works and methods, which have gone through numerous editions: *De melodieën der evangelische gezangen* for Organ, Piano, and Chorus; *De melodieën der Psalmen en lof- en bedezangen* for Organ, Piano, and Chorus (20th printing, 1947); the manual *Algemeene muziekleer* (13th printing, 1932; revised by Sem Dresden); *Kleine muziekleer* for schools; *Eerste en tweede zangboekje* for schools; *De zingende kinderwereld* (songs for children; many eds.); *Volksliedjes uit het land der liefde;* etc.

Woržischek (Voříšek), Johann Hugo, Bohemian composer; b. Wamberg, Bohemia, May 11, 1791; d. Vienna, Nov. 19, 1825. He studied with his father and with Tomaschek in Prague, where he lived from 1801; in 1813 he went to Vienna and became known as a pianist; in 1818 he was appointed conductor of the Gesellschaft der Musikfreunde. Having studied law, he obtained a post in the civil service in 1822, but abandoned it after a year, when he was made court organist. He composed a Symph.; choral works with Orch.; a Piano Concerto; etc.; of more interest are his piano pieces, especially the *Rhapsodies* (1818) and *Impromptus* (1822), because Schubert was strongly influenced by them. A Piano Sonata in B minor (1820) shows kinship with Beethoven, whom Woržischek knew intimately.

Wöss, Josef Venantius von, Austrian musicologist; b. Cattaro, Dalmatia, June 13, 1863; d. Vienna, Oct. 22, 1943. He received his first musical instruction from his mother and an uncle; studied composition at the Vienna Cons. with Franz Krenn; wrote music criticism for *Musica Divina;* was later in the editorial dept. of Universal Edition, for which he edited the collection *Deutsche Meisterlieder.*

WORKS: Operas: *Lenzlüge* (Elberfeld, 1905) and *Flaviennes Abenteuer* (Breslau, 1910); *Heiliges Lied* for Male Chorus and Orch.; *Serenade* for Orch.; *Sakuntala,* overture; Piano Sextet; sacred music (a Te Deum and 2 masses); motets with Orch.; songs (*Sulamith, 4 slawische Lieder, 4 orientalische Gesänge,* etc.). He made the piano scores of Mahler's *Das klagende Lied, Lied von der Erde,* and symphs. Nos. 3, 4, 8, and 9; edited Bruckner's symphs.; publ. *Die Modulation* (Vienna, 1921).

Wöss, Kurt, Austrian conductor; b. Linz, May 2, 1914. He studied conducting with Felix Weingartner in Vienna, and also pursued musicological studies at the Univ. of Vienna with Haas, Lach, Orel, and Wellesz; taught an orch. class at the Vienna Academy (1938–40); after the war, he conducted the Tonkünstler-Orch. in Vienna (1948–51); subsequently went to Japan, where he conducted the Nippon Phil. Orch. in Tokyo (1951–54). From 1956 to 1960 he was principal conductor of the Victorian Symph. Orch. in Melbourne and of the Australian National Opera; in 1961 he returned to Linz, where he became music director of the Bruckner Orch. (1966–74). In 1974 he went again to Japan, where he was appointed music director of the Fumiwara Opera in Tokyo; also was conductor of the Tokyo Phil. He publ. *Ratschläge zur Aufführung der Symphonien Anton Bruckners* (Linz, 1974).

Wotquenne (-Plattel), Alfred, Belgian musicologist; b. Lobbes, Jan. 25, 1867; d. Antibes, France, Sept. 25, 1939. He studied at the Brussels Cons. with Mailly (organ), and Joseph Dupont and Gevaert (theory); from 1894 to 1918 was librarian, secretary, and inspector of studies at the Brussels Cons.; then moved to Antibes in southern France, where in 1921 he became maître de chapelle.

WRITINGS: *Catalogue de la bibliothèque du Cons. Royal de Musique de Bruxelles* (vol. I, 1894; with a supplement, *Libretti d'opéras et d'oratorios italiens du XVIIe siècle,* 1901; II, 1902; III, 1908; IV, 1912; V, 1914); *Baldassare Galuppi* (1899; 2nd augmented ed., 1902, as *Baldassare Galuppi. Etude bibliographique sur ses œuvres dramatiques*); *Thematisches Verzeichnis der Werke von Chr. W. v. Gluck* (1904); *Catalogue thématique des œuvres de C.Ph.E. Bach* (1905); *Table alphabétique des morceaux mesurés contenus dans les œuvres dramatiques de Zeno, Metastasio et Goldoni* (1905); *Etude bibliographique sur le compositeur napolitain Luigi Rossi* (1909; with thematic catalogue). He prepared a card catalogue of 18,000 Italian "cantate da camera" of the 18th century; edited *Chansons italiennes de la fin du XVIe siècle* (canzonette *a* 4); continued the collections begun by Gevaert, *Répertoire classique du chant français* and *Répertoire français de l'ancien chant classique;* and ed. a new collection, *Répertoire Wotquenne* (4 vols. publ.); also ed. violin sonatas of Tartini, Veracini, and others; composed much sacred music. The MSS. of several important bibliographies in his collection were bought out by the Library of Congress in 1929; these comprise *Répertoire des textes publiés par les édi-*

teurs parisiens Ballard; *Histoire musicale et chronologique du Théâtre de la Foire depuis 1680 jusqu'à 1762; Histoire du nouveau Théâtre-Italien à Paris (1718–1762);* etc. A large part of his private music library was also bought by the Library of Congress.

Wouters, (François) Adolphe, Belgian organist and composer; b. Brussels, May 28, 1849; d. there, April 16, 1924. He studied at the Brussels Cons.; then taught piano there (1871–1920); from 1868 he was also organist at Notre-Dame-de-Finistère and maître de chapelle at Saint-Nicolas. He composed church music, men's choruses, technical studies and transcriptions for piano, etc.

Woyrsch, Felix von, composer and conductor; b. Troppau, Silesia, Oct. 8, 1860; d. Altona-Hamburg, March 20, 1944. He studied with A. Chevallier in Hamburg, but was chiefly self-taught. In 1887 he settled in Altona as conductor of the Allgemeine Liedertafel; from 1893 led the Kirchenchor, the Singakademie (from 1895), and the municipal symph. concerts and Volkskonzerte (from 1903); from 1895 to 1903 he was organist of the Friedenskirche; then of the Johanniskirche until 1926; retired from public life in 1937.
WORKS: Operas: *Der Pfarrer von Meudon* (Hamburg, 1886); *Der Weiberkrieg* (Hamburg, 1890); *Wikingerfahrt* (Nuremberg, 1896). For Orch.: symph. prologue to the *Divina commedia; Skaldische Rhapsodie* for Violin and Orch.; 2 symphs.; *3 Böcklin-Phantasien (Die Toteninsel, Der Eremit, Im Spiel der Wellen); Hamlet,* overture. Vocal works with Orch.: *Da Jesus auf Erden ging,* a mystery play (Hamburg, Jan. 29, 1917; one of his best works); *Geburt Jesu; Deutscher Heerbann; Der Vandalen; Auszug; Passions-Oratorium; Sapphische Ode an Aphrodite; Totentanz; Da lachte schön Sigrid; Wollt' er nur fragen; Edward.* Chamber music: Piano Quintet; String Quartet. For Piano: *3 Notturnos; 2 Walzer; Walzer* (4-hands); *Theme and Variations; 4 Impromptus; Improvisationen; Metamorphosen.* He also composed song cycles (*Persische Lieder; Spanisches Liederbuch; 10 Rattenfängerlieder);* edited *Deutsche Volkslieder* (14th–16th centuries), and choral works of Heinrich Schütz for practical use (3 vols.).

Woytowicz, Boleslaw, Polish pianist and composer; b. Dunajowce, Podolia, Dec. 5, 1899; d. Katowice, July 11, 1980. He studied piano with Michalowski; composition with Statkowski and Maliszewski; obtained a diploma at the Chopin College of Music in Warsaw as a concert pianist; then went to Paris, where he took lessons in composition with Nadia Boulanger (1930–32). In 1945 he was appointed a prof. of piano and composition at the State College of Music in Katowice.
WORKS: *Kolysanka (Cradle Song)* for Soprano, Flute, Clarinet, Bassoon, and Harp (1931); 2 string quartets (1932, 1953); Piano Concerto (1932); *Zalobny poema (Funeral Poem)* for Orch. (1935); ballet, *Powrót* (1937); 3 symphs.: No. 1 (1938), No. 2 (1945;

Cracow, Sept. 27, 1946), and No. 3, *Concertante,* for Piano and Orch. (1963); *Kantata na pochwale pracy (Cantata in Praise of Labor,* 1948); *12 Etudes* for Piano (1948); *Symphonic Sketches* for Orch. (1949); cantata, *Prorok (The Prophet,* 1950); Flute Sonata (1952); *Lamento* for Soprano, Piano, and Clarinet (1960); *10 Etudes* for Piano (1960); *Little Piano Sonata* (1974).

Wrangel, Vasili, Baron, Russian composer; b. St. Petersburg, June 25, 1862; d. there, March 10, 1901. A functionary at the Ministry of Home Affairs, he was a musician by avocation; took several courses at the St. Petersburg Cons. His songs, many of which were publ., attracted singers by their artless melodic quality, and enjoyed some popularity for a time; he also wrote a ballet, *The Mikado's Daughter* (St. Petersburg, Dec. 1, 1897).

Wranitzky, Anton, Bohemian violinist and composer; b. Neureisch, Moravia, June 13, 1761; d. Vienna, Aug. 6, 1820. He studied with his older brother **Paul Wranitzky;** also had lessons in Vienna with Albrechtsberger, Haydn, and Mozart. In 1797 he was appointed Kapellmeister to Prince Lobkowitz at his castle in Bohemia, and later (1808) in Vienna. He wrote 15 violin concertos; much chamber music; marches; dances.

Wranitzky, Paul, Bohemian violinist and composer; brother of **Anton Wranitzky;** b. Neureisch, Moravia, Dec. 30, 1756; d. Vienna, Sept. 26, 1808. After studying in various provincial towns of Moravia, he went in 1776 to Vienna, where he was a pupil of Joseph Martin Kraus. In 1780 he became a member of Prince Esterházy's orch. at Eisenstadt; in 1790 became concertmaster of the Vienna Opera, and retained this position until his death. His opera *Oberon, König der Elfen* was given with excellent success in Vienna on Nov. 7, 1789; other operas and singspiels produced by him in Vienna were *Rudolf von Felseck* (Oct. 6, 1792); *Merkur, der Heurat-Stifter* (Feb. 21, 1793); *Das Fest der Lazzaroni* (Feb. 4, 1794); *Die gute Mutter* (May 11, 1795); *Johanna von Montfaucon* (Jan. 25, 1799); *Der Schreiner* (July 18, 1799); *Mitgefühl* (April 21, 1804); *Die Erkenntlichkeit* (July 22, 1805). He also produced numerous ballets; wrote incidental music to several plays; composed a great deal of instrumental music, including 51 symphs.; 5 concertos for various instruments with orch.; 6 quintets; over 80 string quartets; 12 quartets for flute and strings; 3 piano quartets, and string trios.

Wrede, Ferdinand, German pianist and composer; b. Brökel, Hannover, July 28, 1827; d. Frankfurt an der Oder, Jan. 20, 1899. He studied with Marschner and Litolff; then was active as a singing teacher and choral conductor; wrote men's choruses and songs.

Wrightson, Herbert James, English-American composer and teacher; b. Sunderland, England, Dec. 20, 1869; d. West Lebanon, N.Y., Dec. 24, 1949. He studied at the Leipzig Cons. with Jadassohn and Reinecke. In 1897 he settled in the U.S.; taught in Philadelphia, Chicago, etc. His works include a Symph.; 15 organ pieces; 29 piano pieces; 2 melodramas for Speaker with Music; 144 songs, of which nearly 100 were publ. His hymns are included in various hymnals. He publ. *Elements of the Theory of Music* (Boston, 1921).

Wuensch, Gerhard, Austrian-born Canadian composer; b. Vienna, Dec. 23, 1925. He received a Dr.Phil. degree from the Univ. of Vienna in 1950, and an artist's diploma in composition and piano from the State Academy of Music in Vienna in 1952; studied music theory with Paul Pisk at the Univ. of Texas (1954–56). He then occupied teaching positions at Butler Univ. in Indianapolis (1956–62), the Univ. of Toronto (1963–69), and the Univ. of Calgary (1969–73); in 1973 was appointed to the faculty of the Univ. of Western Ontario in London, Ontario. He writes in an affable modernistic vein in neo-Classical forms.
WORKS: Ballet, *Labyrinth* (1957); musical comedy, *Il pomo d'oro* (1958); *Nocturne* for Orch. (1956); *Variations on a Dorian Hexachord* for Orch. (1959); *Caribbean Rhapsody* for Symph. Band (1959); Symph. No. 1 (1959); Piano Concerto (1961); *Ballad* for Trumpet and Orch. (1962); *Symphonia sacra* for Soloists, Chorus, Brass, and Percussion (1965); Symph. for Brass and Percussion (1967); Concerto for Piano and Chamber Orch. (1971); *Scherzo* for Piano and Wind Ensemble (1971); *6 Guises* for Narrator, Winds, and Percussion (1972); Bassoon Concerto (1976); Organ Concerto (1979); Trio for Clarinet, Bassoon, and Piano (1948); 2 string quartets (1955, 1963); *Mosaic* for Brass Quartet (1959); *Partita* for Horn and Piano (1961); *Viola Sonatina* (1963); *Ricercare* for 8 Horns and Organ (1963); 2 wind quintets (1963, 1967); Horn Sonata (1964); *Music* for 7 Brasses (1966); Trumpet Sonata (1966); Sextet for Horns (1966); *Suite* for Trumpet and Organ (1970); *Music in 4 Dimensions* for Brass, Harp, and Percussion (1970); Piano Trio (1971); *Variations* for Clarinet and Piano (1971); *Prelude, Aria and Fugue* for Accordion and String Quartet (1971); *Saxophone Sonata* (1971); *Aria and Fugue* for Oboe and Organ (1975); *Musica giocosa* for Flute and Piano (1977); *Concerto grosso* for Accordion and Strings (1978); *Cameos II* for Oboe and Piano (1979); *6 Songs* for Voice, Flute, and Accordion (1970); *Laus sapientiae,* cantata (1978); piano pieces: *Esquisse* (1950); *Canzona and Toccata* (1963); 2 sonatinas (1969); *Mini Suite* No. 2 (1977); Sonata for 4-hands (1978); organ pieces: *Toccata piccola* (1963); *Sonata breve* (1963); *Toccata nuptialis* (1976); solo accordion pieces: *4 Mini-Suites* (1968); *Sonata da camera* (1970); *Monologue* (1972); *Diversions* (1972); choruses.

Wüerst, Richard (Ferdinand), German composer; b. Berlin, Feb. 22, 1824; d. there, Oct. 9, 1881. He studied violin with Ferdinand David at the Leipzig Cons., where he also took lessons with Mendelssohn. He then taught at Kullak's Neue Akademie der Tonkunst in Berlin. As music critic for the *Ber-*

liner Fremdenblatt he exercised considerable influence; publ. *Leitfaden der Elementartheorie der Musik* (1867; Eng. trans. as *Elementary Theory of Music and Treatment of Chords,* Boston, 1893). As a composer he was a follower of Mendelssohn.
WORKS: Operas: *Der Rotmantel* (Berlin, 1848); *Vineta* (Bratislava, Dec. 21, 1862); *Eine Künstlerreise* (with Winterfeld; Berlin, 1868); *Faublas* (Berlin, 1873); *A-ing-fo-hi* (Berlin, Jan. 28, 1878); *Die Offiziere der Kaiserin* (Berlin, 1878); cantata, *Der Wasserneck;* 3 symphs.; *Ein Märchen,* symph. fantasy; *Variations sur une chanson nègre de Kentucky* for Orch. (on Stephen Foster's *My Old Kentucky Home*); *Sous le balcon,* serenade for String Orch. with Cello Obbligato; *Russische Suite* for String Orch. with Violin Obbligato; *Tanz der Mücken, Fliegen und Käfer,* orch. scherzo; Piano Trio; Cello Sonata; 3 string quartets; various violin pieces; songs; vocal duets and terzets.

Wührer, Friedrich, distinguished Austrian pianist and pedagogue; b. Vienna, June 29, 1900. He studied piano with Franz Schmidt at the Vienna Academy of Music (1915–20); concurrently took a course in jurisprudence at the Univ. of Vienna; then engaged on a far-flung tour that took him through all of Europe, and also to Asia and Africa. At his concerts he never failed to include works by modern composers, among them Bartók, Hindemith, Prokofiev, Stravinsky, and his teacher Franz Schmidt. He held numerous teaching positions, at the Vienna Academy of Music (1922–32), at the Hochschule für Musik in Mannheim (1934–36), in Kiel (1936–39), in Vienna (1939–45), at the Salzburg Mozarteum (1948–51), in Mannheim (1952–57), and in Munich (1957–68). He publ. *Meisterwerke der Klaviermusik* (Wilhelmshaven, 1966).

Wüllner, Franz, important German pianist, conductor, and composer; b. Münster, Jan. 28, 1832; d. Braunfels-on-the-Lahn, Sept. 7, 1902. He studied with Schindler in Münster and Frankfurt. In 1854 he went to Munich; was a teacher at the Munich Cons. (1856–58); then municipal music director at Aachen (1858–64). He returned to Munich in 1864; succeeded Hans von Bülow as conductor of the Munich Court Theater in 1869. Under unfavorable conditions (against Wagner's wishes), he prepared and conducted the first performance of *Das Rheingold* (Sept. 22, 1869) and *Die Walküre* (June 26, 1870). In 1877 he became court conductor at Dresden; in 1882 Schuch was promoted to take his place; thereafter Wüllner was one of the conductors of the Berlin Phil. for the 1882–85 seasons; became conductor of the Gurzenich Concerts in Cologne in 1884, and on Oct. 1, 1884, succeeded Hiller as director of the Cologne Cons., later becoming also municipal music director, posts he held until his death. He was highly regarded as a choral composer; publ. the valuable book of vocal exercises *Chorübungen der Münchener Musikschule* (1867; new ed. by E. Schwickerath, Munich, 1931). He was a friend of Brahms.
WORKS: Vocal with Orch.: *Die Flucht der heiligen Familie; Heinrich der Finkler; Deutscher Sie-*

gesgesang; Lied und Leben; Psalm 98; Psalm 127; church music; songs.

BIBLIOGRAPHY: O. Klauwell, *Studien und Erinnerungen* (Langensalza, 1906); E. Wolff, ed., *Johannes Brahms im Briefwechsel mit Franz Wüllner* (Berlin, 1922; with a list of works); J. Wüllner, "Johannes Brahms in seiner Lebensfreundschaft mit Franz Wüllner," *Die Musik* (March 1942).

Wüllner, Ludwig, distinguished German singer; son of **Franz Wüllner;** b. Münster, Aug. 19, 1858; d. Kiel, March 19, 1938. He studied Germanic philology at the univs. of Munich, Berlin, and Strasbourg; taught Germanic philology at the Akademie in Münster (1884–87), and sang occasionally in concert; his musical training began only in 1887, when he took a course of study at the Cologne Cons. A second change of vocation brought him to the Meiningen court theater, where he appeared as an actor of heroic parts in the spoken drama (1889–95); he became friendly with Brahms, who commended his singing of German folk songs. In 1895 he gave song recitals in Berlin with such acclaim that he decided to devote himself mainly to lieder. He then made tours of all Europe, arousing tremendous enthusiasm; his first recital in N.Y. (Nov. 15, 1908) was a sensational success, and he followed it by an extensive tour of the U.S. and then another (1909–10). His peculiar distinction was his ability to give an actor's impersonation of the character of each song, introducing an element of drama on the concert stage.

BIBLIOGRAPHY: F. Ludwig, *L. Wüllner. Sein Leben und seine Kunst* (Leipzig, 1931).

Wunderer, Alexander, Austrian oboist, composer, and teacher; b. Vienna, April 11, 1877; d. Zinkenbach, near St. Gilgen (Salzkammergut), Dec. 29, 1955. He taught the oboe and other wind instruments at the State Academy of Music in Vienna (1919–37); wrote chamber music; was co-author of a book on orchestration. After 1945 he taught oboe classes at the Salzburg Mozarteum.

Wunderlich, Fritz, noted German tenor; b. Kusel, Sept. 26 1930; d. Heidelberg, Sept. 17, 1966. He received his musical education at the Freiburg Hochschule für Musik; then sang opera in Stuttgart (1955–58), Frankfurt (1958–60), and Munich (from 1960). While still a young man, he gained a fine reputation as a lyric tenor; his performances of Mozart roles were especially acclaimed for their expressive power. His untimely death (in a domestic accident) deprived the opera stage of one of its finest artists.

Wunsch, Hermann, German composer; b. Neuss, Aug. 9, 1884; d. Berlin, Dec. 21, 1954. He studied in Düsseldorf and Cologne, and later at the Hochschule für Musik in Berlin, where he subsequently taught, becoming a prof. in 1945. He composed 6 symphs., of which the 5th won the Schubert Memorial Prize (German section) of the Columbia Phonograph Co. contest (Schubert Centennial, 1928). Other works include the chamber operas *Bianca* (Weimar, May 22, 1927), *Don Juans Sohn* (Weimar, 1928), and *Franzosenzeit* (Schwerin, 1933); 2 masses; *Südpolkantate* for Chorus and Orch.; *Helden* for Chorus and Orch. (Berlin, 1941); 3 violin concertos; Concerto for Piano and Small Orch.; *Kleine Lustspielsuite* for Orch.; *Fest auf Monbijou,* suite for Chamber Orch.; *Erntelied,* symph. with a concluding chorus.

Wünsch, Walther, Austrian ethnomusicologist; b. Gablonz, July 23, 1908. He studied the theory of folk music with Becking in Prague; received his doctorate with the dissertation *Die Geigentechnik der jugoslawischen Guslaren* (Brno, 1934); subsequently worked in the Inst. of Acoustics in Berlin; in 1943 he completed graduate studies at the Univ. of Vienna, despite the difficult war conditions. After the war he was active mainly as a chamber music player. In 1960 he joined the faculty of the Univ. of Graz, and later was appointed a prof. at the Inst. of Ethnomusicology at the Hochschule für Musik in Graz. He publ. several important studies on ethnomusicology, including *Heldensänger in Südosteuropa* (Leipzig, 1937).

Wuorinen, Charles, American composer; b. New York, June 9, 1938. His family roots originated in Finland; his father was a prof. of history at Columbia Univ.; the environment at home was highly intellectual. Wuorinen received a fine academic training; he began to plan piano and to compose, so they say, at the incredible age of 5. He then took lessons in music theory with Beeson and Ussachevsky. He received the Young Composers Award from the N.Y. Phil. when he was 16 years old. At 18 he wrote his earliest orch. work, *Into the Organ Pipes and Steeples.* At the age of 21 he composed, in quick succession, 3 full-fledged symphs. In 1956 he entered Columbia Univ. as a student of Otto Luening; received his B.A. in 1961 and his M.A. in 1963. In 1964 he was appointed an instructor in music at Columbia, and taught there until 1971, when he resigned in a flurry of angry controversy, vesuviating in sulfuric wrath and ire about the refusal of the faculty to grant him tenure. He then taught at the Manhattan School of Music (1972–79). In 1968 and 1972 he held Guggenheim fellowships. In 1969 he received a commission from Nonesuch Records for a work using synthesized sound, titled *Time's Encomium;* it was awarded the Pulitzer Prize in 1970, an unprecedented honor for a work written expressly for a recording; later he rearranged it for a regular orch. From his very first essays in free composition, Wuorinen asserted himself as a true representative of the modernistic 2nd half of the 20th century. His techniques derived from Stravinsky's early period, when stark primitivism gave way to austere linear counterpoint; an even greater affinity in Wuorinen's music is with the agglutinative formations of unrelated thematic statements as practiced by Varèse; a more literal dependence connects Wuorinen's works with the dodecaphonic method of composition as promulgated by Schoenberg. These modalities and relationships coalesce in Wuorinen's writing into a sui generis complex subdivided into melodic, harmonic, and contrapuntal units that build a definitive formal structure. The foundation of his method of composition is serialism, in which pitch, time, and rhythmic divisions relate to one another in a "time point system," which lends itself to unlimited tonal and temporal arrangements, combinations, and permutations. Enormously prolific, Wuorinen finds it possible to explore the entire vocabulary of serial composition. Most of his works are instrumental, but he also wrote an opera entitled *The W. of Babylon* (alluding to the apocalyptic Babylonian whore), a work he prefers to describe as a "baroque burlesque." Its *dramatis personae* include a libidinous assortment of lascivious French nobel and ignoble men and women of the immoral 17th century, spouting lewd declarations and performing lecherous acts. As a helpful glossary to his music, Wuorinen publ. a manual, *Simple Composition* (N.Y., 1979).

WORKS: FOR THE STAGE: Masque, *The Politics of Harmony* (1967); opera, *The W. of Babylon* (partial perf. given by the Group for Contemporary Music in N.Y. on Dec. 15, 1975). FOR ORCH.: 3 symphs. (1958, 1959, 1959); 4 *concertante* for Solo Instruments and Orch. (1957–59); *Concertone* for Brass Quintet and Orch. (1960); *Evolutio transcripta* (1961); *Orchestral and Electronic Exchanges* for Orch. and Tape (1965); Piano Concerto No. 1 (1966); *Contrafactum* (1969); Concerto for Amplified Violin and Orch. (Tanglewood, Boston Symph., Aug. 4, 1972; Paul Zukofsky, soloist; Michael Tilson Thomas conducting); Piano Concerto No. 2 for Amplified Piano and Orch. (N.Y. Phil., Dec. 6, 1974, composer soloist); *A Reliquary for Igor Stravinsky* (Ojai [Calif.] Festival, May 30, 1975); *Tashi Concerto* for 4 Instruments and Orch. (Tashi Chamber Music Ensemble, Cleveland, Oct. 13, 1976, composer conducting); *Percussion Symphony* (1976; Somerset, N.J., Jan. 26, 1978); *Two-Part Symphony* (N.Y., Dec. 11, 1978); *"ng. c."* (1980); *Bamboula Squared* (N.Y., June 4, 1984). CHAMBER MUSIC: *Triptych* for Flute, Viola, and Percussion (1957); *Alternating Currents* for Chamber Ensemble (1957); *Dr. Faustus Lights the Lights* for Narrator and Instruments (1957); *3 Pieces* for String Quartet (1958); *Spectrum* for Violin, Brass Quintet, and Piano (1958); *Trio concertante* (1959); *Musica duarum partum ecclesiastica* for Brass Quintet, Piano, Organ, and Timpani (1959); Flute Sonata (1960); *Turetzky Pieces* for Flute, Clarinet, and Double Bass (1960); *Tiento sobre cabeza* for 7 Instruments (1961); Octet for Flute, Clarinet, Horn, Trombone, Violin, Cello, Double Bass, and Piano (1962); Chamber Concerto for Cello and 10 Players (1963); *Composition* for Violin and 10 Instruments (1964); Chamber Concerto for Flute and 10 Players (1964); *Janissary Music* for Percussion (1966); *Harpsichord Division* for Harpsichord (1966); *John Bull: Salve Regina Versus Septem* for Chamber Ensemble (1966); Duo for Violin and Piano (1966–67); String Trio (1968); *Ringing Changes* for Percussion Ensemble (1970); Chamber Concerto for Tuba, 12 Wind Instruments, and 12 Drums (1970); *Canzona* for 12 Instruments (1971); Harp Variations for Harp, Violin, Viola, and Cello

(1972); Bassoon Variations for Bassoon, Harp, and Timpani (1972); Violin Variations (1972); *On Alligators* for 8 Instruments (1972); *Speculum speculi* for Flute, Oboe, Bass Clarinet, Double Bass, Piano, and Percussion (1972); *Grand Union* for Cello and Drums (1973); *Arabia felix* for Flute, Bassoon, Violin, Electric Guitar, Vibraphone, and Piano (1973); Fantasia for Violin and Piano (1974); *Hyperion* for 12 Instruments (1976); *The Winds* for 8 Instruments (1977); *Fast Fantasy* for Solo Cello (1977); *Archangel* for Bass Trombone and String Quartet (1977); Wind Quintet (1977); 6 Pieces for Violin and Piano (1977); *Ancestors* for Chamber Ensemble (1978); *Joan's* for Chamber Ensemble (1980); *Archaeopteryx* for Bass Trombone (1980); Trio for Double Bass, Bass Trombone, and Tuba (1981); Horn Trio (1981). FOR VOICE: *Madrigali spirituale* for Tenor, Baritone, 2 Oboes, 2 Violins, Cello, and Double Bass (1960); *Symphonia sacra* for Tenor, Baritone, Bass, 2 Oboes, 2 Violins, Double Bass, and Organ (1961); *The Prayer of Jonah* for Voices and String Quintet (1962); *Super Salutem* for Male Voices and Instruments (1964); *A Message to Denmark Hill* for Baritone, Flute, Cello, and Piano (1970); *A Song to the Lute in Musicke* for Soprano and Piano (1970); *Mannheim, 87.87.87* for Unison Chorus and Organ (1973); *An Anthem for Epiphany* for Chorus, Organ, and Trumpet (1974); *6 Songs* for 2 Voices, Violin, and Piano (1977); *The Celestial Sphere*, sacred oratorio for Chorus and Orch. (1979; Augustana College, April 25, 1981). ELECTRONIC MUSIC: *Consort from Instruments and Voices* for Magnetic Tape (1961); *Time's Encomium* for synthesized sound and processed synthesized sound (1969; received the Pulitzer Prize in 1970).

BIBLIOGRAPHY: David Ewen, *American Composers* (N.Y., 1982).

Würfel, Wilhelm, Bohemian pianist and composer; b. Plánany, near Kolín, May 6, 1790; d. Vienna, March 23, 1832. He taught at the Warsaw Cons., where Chopin was one of his students in organ playing; in 1824–26 he became assistant conductor at the Kärthnertor Theater in Vienna. His opera *Rübezahl* was first performed in Prague on Oct. 7, 1824, with excellent success, and enjoyed popularity for some years; he also wrote many piano pieces in a bravura style.

Wurlitzer, Rudolph H., American instrument dealer; b. Cincinnati, Dec. 30, 1873; d. there, May 27, 1948. He was the son of the founder of the Wurlitzer Co. (established 1856); studied violin at the Cincinnati College of Music and later in Berlin with Emanuel Wirth. He became secretary-treasurer of the Wurlitzer Co. in 1899; later vice-president, and finally president. In 1929 the company purchased 64 string instruments from the Rodman Wanamaker Collection, including some fine specimens. Several richly illustrated catalogues of string instruments in the Wurlitzer Collection have been issued: *Old Master Violins, Violas, Violoncellos* (Cincinnati, 1915); *Masterpieces of the Great Violin Makers* (N.Y., 1917; 2nd ed., 1918); *Rare Violins, Violas, Violoncellos of the 17th, 18th, and 19th Centuries*

(N.Y., 1931); *Rare Bows for Violin, Viola, Violoncello, by Makers of the 18th and 19th Centuries* (N.Y., 1931); *Rare Violas by Celebrated Makers of the 16th–19th Centuries* (N.Y., 1940).

Wurm, Marie, noted English pianist; b. Southampton, May 18, 1860; d. Munich, Jan. 21, 1938. She studied piano with Raff and Clara Schumann in Germany; returning to England, she took theory lessons with Stanford and Arthur Sullivan. She was quite successful as a concert pianist in England and Germany; in 1925 she settled in Munich. Her avocation was conducting; she organized a women's orch. in Berlin, and conducted its inaugural concert on Oct. 10, 1899, arousing considerable curiosity. She also was an ambitious composer.
WORKS: Opera, *Die Mitschuldigen* (Leipzig, 1923); Piano Concerto; String Quartet; Violin Sonata; Cello Sonata; Piano Sonata; numerous piano pieces (*Valse de concert, Barcarolle, Sylph Dance, Suite,* gavottes, mazurkas, etc.); she publ. *Das ABC der Musik* and *Praktische Vorschule zur Caland-Lehre.* Her sisters, **Adela Wurm** and **Mathilda Wurm,** who made their careers in England, changed their last name to **Verne** in order to exorcise the vermicular sound of the original German family name, as pronounced in English.

Würz, Anton, German composer and musicologist; b. Munich, July 14, 1903. He studied with Sandberger at Munich Univ.; was music critic of the *Münchner Telegraph-Zeitung* (1927–45). His works include several song cycles, to words by Rilke, Eichendorff, etc.; a String Quintet; 4 string quartets; String Trio; Violin Sonata; Viola Sonata; he publ. numerous opera and operetta guidebooks.

Würz, Richard, German music critic and pedagogue; b. Munich, Feb. 15, 1885; d. there, Feb. 2, 1965. He took private lessons with Max Reger (1903–6); in 1907 he became music critic of the *Münchner Neueste Nachrichte,* holding this position until 1945; he was also active as a music teacher in Munich. He composed a number of choruses and piano pieces; publ. a monograph on Max Reger (Munich, 1920).
BIBLIOGRAPHY: W. Zentner, "Richard Würz," *Neue Musikzeitschrift* (Jan. 1950).

Wüst, Philipp, German conductor; b. Oppau, May 3, 1894; d. Saarbrücken, Nov. 1, 1975. He took private lessons in piano and composition with Ernst Toch in Berlin; beginning in 1928 he filled engagements as an opera conductor in Saarbrücken, Bremerhaven, and Oldenburg. From 1936 to 1943 he was music director in Breslau, and later in Stuttgart. In 1946 he moved to Saarbrücken, where he taught at the Hochschule für Musik, and also conducted at the opera theater there; in 1969 he was named its honorary member.

Wustmann, Rudolf, German musicologist; b. Leipzig, Jan. 5, 1872; d. Bühlau, near Dresden, Aug. 15, 1916. He was the son of the bibliographer Gustav Wustmann; studied philology, history, and musicology (with Kretzschmar) at the univs. of Munich and Leipzig; was a teacher of academic subjects in Leipzig (1895–1900); later lived in Bolzano, Italy, and finally in Bühlau, devoting himself to philological and historical research. He publ. *Musikalische Bilder* (Leipzig, 1907); *Musikgeschichte Leipzigs* (Leipzig, 1909; vol. I only, up to the mid-17th century; vols. II and III were written by Schering); *J.S. Bachs Kantatentexte* (Leipzig, 1913); *Die Hofweise Walthers von der Vogelweide* (Strasbourg, 1913); numerous articles in German musical periodicals.

Wyk, Arnold van, South African composer; b. Calvinia, Cape Province, April 26, 1916; d. Cape Town, May 27, 1983. He studied at Stellenbosch Univ., near Cape Town (1936–38); then went to London, where he attended the Royal Academy of Music (1938–43). From 1939 to 1944 he worked with the British Broadcasting Corp.; went back to South Africa in 1946; taught there at the Univ. of Cape Town (1949–61); in 1961 joined the faculty of Stellenbosch Univ.; retired in 1978.
WORKS: *Southern Cross* for Orch. (1943); Symph. No. 1 (1944); *Christmas Oratorio* (1949); *Rhapsody* for Orch. (Cape Town Festival, March 4, 1952); Symph. No. 2 (Cape Town Festival, March 13, 1952); *5 Elegies* for String Quartet (1941); song cycle, *Liefde en Verlatenheid* (Festival of the International Society for Contemporary Music, Haifa, May 31, 1954); String Quartet No. 1 (1957); symph. suite, *Primavera* (1960); symph. variations, *Masquerade,* on a South African folk song (1964); choruses; songs; piano pieces.
BIBLIOGRAPHY: H. Ferguson, "Arnold van Wyk: Recently Published Works," *Tempo* (Summer 1958).

Wykes, Robert, American flutist and composer; b. Aliquippa, Pa., May 19, 1926. He studied at the Eastman School of Music (M.M., 1950) and at the Univ. of Illinois (D.M.A., 1955). Trained as a flute player, he was a member of the St. Louis Symph. Orch. (1963–65). In 1965 he was appointed a prof. of music at Washington Univ. in St. Louis.
WORKS: *The Prankster,* chamber opera (Bowling Green, Ohio, Jan. 12, 1952); String Sextet (1958); Piano Quintet (1959); *Horizons* for Orch. (1964); *Wave Forms and Pulses* for Orch. (1964); *The Shape of Time* for Orch. (1965); *Man against Machine* for Chamber Group (1966); *In Common Cause* for Strings, Trumpet, English Horn, and Percussion (1966); *Towards Time's Receding* for Orch. (St. Louis, April 7, 1972); *4 American Indian Lyrics* for Chorus (1957); also music for documentary films.

Wylde, Henry, English conductor, composer, and educator; b. Bushey, Herts, May 22, 1822; d. London, March 13, 1890. He was the son of **Henry Wylde,** a London organist and composer of glees. He studied piano with Moscheles and Cipriani Potter at the Royal Academy of Music in London. In 1852 he founded in London the New Phil. Society, and conducted its concerts in cooperation with Spohr until

1858, when he took complete charge of its concerts (until 1879). In 1861 he founded the London Academy of Music; supervised the building of St. George's Hall (1867) to house it. In 1863 he became a prof. of music there, retaining this post until his death.

WORKS: *Paradise Lost,* oratorio after Milton (London, May 11, 1853); Piano Concerto (London, April 14, 1852); songs; piano pieces; he also publ. the books *The Science of Music* (1865); *Music in Its Art-Mysteries* (1867); *Modern Counterpoint in Major Keys* (1873); *Occult Principles of Music* (1881); *Music as an Educator* (1882); *The Evolution of the Beautiful in Sound* (1888).

Wyman, Addison P., American violinist and composer; b. Cornish, N.Y., June 23, 1832; d. Washington, Pa., April 15, 1872. He was active as a violin teacher, and founded a music school at Claremont, N.Y., in 1869. He also publ. a number of popular piano pieces, with romantic titles (*Silvery Waves, Woodland Echoes, Moonlight Musings, Music among the Pines,* etc.).

Wyner, Susan Davenny, American soprano; b. New Haven, Conn., Oct. 17, 1943. She was educated at Cornell Univ. graduating summa cum laude in music and English literature. She then received a Fulbright scholarship and a grant from the Ford Foundation; also won the Walter W. Naumberg Prize. An exceptionally intelligent singer, she became equally successful as a performer of music in all historic idioms, from early Renaissance works to the most intransigent ultramodern scores.

Wyner, Yehudi, American composer, son of the composer **Lazar Weiner** (whose name he phonetically changed to Wyner); b. Calgary, Canada, June 1, 1929. He followed his parents to the U.S.; enrolled in the Juilliard School of Music in N.Y., graduating in 1946; then entered Yale Univ., where his principal teacher was Richard Donovan (A.B., 1950; B.Mus., 1951; M.Mus., 1953); he also acquired an M.A. degree from Harvard Univ. After occupying several temporary teaching posts, he joined the staff of Yale Univ. in 1963; was chairman of the music dept. there, 1969–73. In 1976 he joined the faculty of the Berkshire Music Center in Tanglewood; in 1978 became dean of music at the State Univ. of N.Y. at Purchase. His music is expressively vigesimosecular in its structural sobriety and melorhythmic aggressiveness; his serial techniques, anchored in tritones and major sevenths, are mitigated by a certain combinatorial harmoniousness; formally, he follows neo-Baroque practices.

WORKS: *Dance Variations* for Wind Octet (1953); Piano Sonata (1954); *Concerto Duo* for Violin and Piano (1957); *3 Informal Pieces* for Violin and Piano (1961); *Friday Evening Service* for Cantor, Chorus, and Organ (1963); *Torah Service* (1966); *Da camera* for Piano and Orch. (1967); *Cadenza* for Clarinet and Harpsichord (1969); *De novo* for Cello and Small Ensemble (1971); *Canto cantabile* for Soprano and Concert Band (1972); *Intermedio* for Soprano and String Orch. (1974); *Dances of Atone-ment* for Violin and Piano (1976).

Wynette, Tammy (real name, **Wynette Pugh**), American country-music singer; b. Red Bay, Ala., May 5, 1942. She taught herself to play the piano and guitar; after holding various jobs, including a position as a beauty operator, she decided to seek fame and fortune in Nashville as a singer of country music; in 1969 she joined the "Grand Ole Opry." She struck a responsive chord with such songs as *Your Good Girl's Gonna Go Bad, Bedtime Story,* and *Let's Get Together;* her hit recording of *Stand by Your Man* also served as the title of her autobiography (written with J. Dew; N.Y., 1979). She was for a time married to the country-music star **George Jones.**

Wyschnegradsky, Ivan, foremost composer of microtonal music; b. St. Petersburg, May 16, 1893; d. Paris, Sept. 29, 1979. He studied composition with Nicolas Sokoloff at the St. Petersburg Cons.; emigrated after the Russian Revolution, and in 1920 settled in Paris, where he remained until his death. He devoted virtually his entire musical career to the exploration and creative realization of music in quarter-tones and other microtonal intervals; had a quarter-tone piano constructed for him; also publ. a guide, *Manuel d'harmonie à quarts de ton* (Paris, 1932). On Nov. 10, 1945, he presented in Paris a concert of his music, at which he conducted the first performance of his *Cosmos* for 4 Pianos, with each pair tuned at quarter-tones. The Canadian composer and pianist Bruce Mather took interest in Wyschnegradsky's music and gave a concert of his works at McGill Univ. in Montreal that included 3 world premieres (Feb. 10, 1977). But with the exception of these rare concerts, Wyschnegradsky remains a figure of legend; few performances of his music are ever given in Europe or North America. He regarded his *La Journée de l'existence (The Day of Existence)* for Narrator, ad lib. Chorus, and Orch. (to his own text; 1916–17; revised 1927 and 1940) as his germinal work, opening the path to microtonal harmony; he dated this "awakening to ultrachromaticism" as having occurred on Nov. 7, 1918. At his death he left sketches for a short opera in 5 scenes, *L'Eternel Etranger,* begun in 1939 but never completed. Also unfinished was the ambitious *Polyphonie spatiale.*

OTHER WORKS (all in quarter-tones unless otherwise shown): *Chant douloureux et étude* for Violin and Piano (1918); *7 Variations on the Note C* for 2 Pianos (1918–20; perf. in 1945 as *5 Variations;* then 2 more were added); *Chant funèbre* for Strings and 2 Harps (1922); *Chant nocturne* for Violin and 2 Pianos (1923; revised 1972); 2 string quartets (1924, 1931–32); *2 Choruses* for Voices and 4 Pianos (1926); *Prélude et fugue sur un chant de l'Evangile rouge* for String Quartet (1927); *Prélude et Danse* for 2 Pianos (1928); *Ainsi parlait Zarathoustra (Thus Spake Zarathoustra)* for Orch. (1929–30; arranged for 4 Pianos, 1936); *2 études de concert* for Piano (1931; arranged for 2 Pianos, 1936); *Etude en forme de scherzo* for 2 Pianos (1932); *Prélude et Fugue* for 2 Pianos (1933); *24 préludes* for 2 Pianos (1934; revised 1958–60); 4 *Fragments symphoniques* for 4 Pianos (1934, final version, 1968; 1937; 1946; 1956); *Le Mot* for Soprano and Piano (1935; half-tones); *Linnite*, pantomime for 3 Female Voices and 4 Pianos (1937); *Acte chorégraphique* for Bass-baritone, Chorus, and 4 Pianos (1938–40; revised 1958–59); *Cosmos* for 4 Pianos (1940; suppressed); *Prélude et Fugue* for 3 Pianos (1945); *2 Fugues* for 2 Pianos (1951); *5 variations sans thème et conclusion* for Orch. (1951–52); *Sonate en un mouvement* for Viola and 2 Pianos (1956; suppressed); *Transparences I and II* for Ondes Martenot and 2 Pianos (1956, 1963); *Arc-en-ciel* for 6 Pianos (1956); *Etude sur le carré magique sonore* for Piano (1956; based on the "magic square" principle of cyclical structure, written in a tempered scale without quarter-tones); *Etude tricesimoprimal* for Fokker-organ (1959; for the Dutch physicist Adriaan Fokker's 31-tone organ); *Composition* for String Quartet (1960); *2 pièces* for Microtonal Piano (1960); *Etude sur les mouvements rotatoires* for 4 Pianos (1961; orchestrated 1964); *2 Compositions:* No. 1 for 3 Pianos and No. 2 for 2 Pianos (1962); *Prélude et étude* for Microtonal Piano (1966); *Intégrations* for 2 Pianos (1967); *Symphonie en un mouvement* for Orch. (1969); *Dialogues à trois* for 3 Pianos (1973–74; sixth-tones).

BIBLIOGRAPHY: Claude Ballif, ed., "Ivan Wyschnegradsky, L'Ultrachromatisme, et les espaces non octaviants," special issue of *La Revue Musicale* (no. 290–291, 1972–73).

Wyss, Niklaus, Swiss conductor; b. Zürich, Nov. 5, 1936. He studied piano and violin in Zürich; conducting in Brussels and Rome. He is active mainly in Italy, Switzerland, and the Netherlands.

Wyttenbach, Jürg, Swiss pianist and composer; b. Bern, Dec. 2, 1935. He studied composition at the Bern Cons.; later in Paris with Lefébure and Calvet (1955–57). He taught piano at the Biel Cons. (1959–67); was a prof. of piano at the Bern Cons. (1962–66); was at the Basel Academy from 1967. His music pursues the median line of European modernism, marked by a strong rhythmic pulse, dissonant counterpoint, and atonal diversions, without falling into the bottomless pit of dodecaphony.

WORKS: 4 works of "instrumental theater": *Execution ajournee I–III* (1969–70) and *Kunststücke, die Zeit totzuschlagen* (*Tricks to Kill Time*, 1972); Piano Concerto (1959; revised 1973); Sonata for Solo Oboe (1961); *3 Movements* for Oboe, Harp, and Piano (1962); ballet, *Der Gefesselte* (Heidelberg, 1962); *Divisions* for Piano and 9 Solo Strings (1964); *De Metalli* for Baritone and Orch. (1964–65); *Anrufungen und Ausbruch* for 28 Woodwinds and Brass (1966); *Nachspiel* for 2 Pianos (1966); *Paraphrase* for a Narrator, a Flutist, and a Pianist (1967–68); *Conteste* for Chamber Orch. (1969); *3 Pieces* for Piano (1969); *Ad libitum* for one or 2 Flutes (1969).

Wyzewa, Théodore de (real name, **Wyzewski**), noted musicologist; b. Kalushin, Russian Poland, Sept. 12, 1862; d. Paris, April 7, 1917. In 1869 his parents settled in Châtelleraut, France, where he received his education; in 1884 he founded in Paris, with Edouard Dujardin, the *Revue Wagnérienne*, which, until it ceased publication in 1888, did much to advance the cause of Wagner in France. Wyzewa's importance as a musicologist rests upon his research concerning the life and work of Mozart, about whom he publ. new facts in "Recherches sur la jeunesse de Mozart," in the *Revue des Deux Mondes* (1904–5), and in *W.A. Mozart. Sa vie musicale et son œuvre de l'enfance à la pleine maturité* (with G. de Saint-Foix; 2 vols., Paris, 1912; 3 more vols. added by Saint-Foix in 1937, 1940, and 1946). Wyzewa also wrote *Beethoven et Wagner* (Paris, 1898; new ed., 1914); edited 20 piano sonatas of Clementi with a biographical notice (vol. I, Paris, 1917; vol. II, posthumous, brought out by Henry Expert).

Xanrof, Léon, French composer of popular music; b. Paris, Dec. 9, 1867; d. there, May 17, 1953. His real name was **Léon Fourneau;** Xanrof is an anagram of its Latin equivalent *(fornax).* He was a lawyer by profession; from 1890 produced light stage pieces in the Paris theaters; the chansonette *Le Fiacre,* which he wrote for Yvette Guilbert, achieved great popularity. He also contributed music criticism to various Paris papers.

Xenakis, Iannis, eminent avant-garde theorist and composer of Greek descent; b. Brăila, Rumania, May 29, 1922. At the age of 10 he was taken by his family to Greece, where he began to study engineering, but he became involved in the Greek resistance movement against the Nazi occupation forces; was wounded in a skirmish. In 1947 he went to France; studied architecture with Le Corbusier and became his assistant (1948–60); during the same period he took lessons in composition with Honegger and Milhaud at the Ecole Normale de Musique in Paris and with Messiaen at the Paris Cons. (1950–53). He aided Le Corbusier in the design of the Philips Pavillion at the 1958 World's Fair in Brussels; met Varèse, who was then working on his *Poème électronique* for the exhibit, and received from him some stimulating advice on the creative potentialities of the electronic medium. During his entire career, Xenakis strove to connect mathematical concepts with the organization of a musical composition, using the theory of sets, symbolic logic, and probabilistic calculus; he promulgated the stochastic method, which is teleologically directed and deterministic, as distinct from a purely aleatory handling of data. He publ. a comprehensive vol. dealing with these procedures, *Musiques formelles* (Paris, 1963; in Eng., N.Y., 1971). He was founder and director of the Centre d'Etudes Mathématiques et Automatiques Musicales in Paris, and founder and director of the Center for Mathematical and Automated Music at Indiana Univ. in the U.S., where he served on the faculty from 1967 to 1972. His influence on the development of advanced composition in Europe and America is considerable; several composers adopted his theories and imitated the scientific-sounding titles of some of his compositions. Xenakis uses Greek words for the titles of virtually all of his works to stress the philosophical derivation of modern science and modern arts from classical Greek concepts; in some cases he uses computer symbols for titles.

WORKS: *Metastasis* for 61 Instruments (1953–54; Donaueschingen, Oct. 15, 1955); *Pithoprakta* for 50 Instruments (1955–56; Munich, March 8, 1957);

Achorripsis for 21 Instruments (1956–57; Brussels, July 20, 1958); *Diamorphoses* for Tape (1957); *Concret PH* for Tape (1957); *Analogiques A & B* for 9 Strings and Tape (1959); *Syrmos (Chain of Events)* for 18 Strings (1959); *Duel,* musical game for 2 "antagonistic" Conductors and 2 Orchs. playing different material, mathematically based on game theory, with the audience determining the winning orch. (1959; Radio Hilversum, Oct., 1971); *Orient-Occident* for Tape (1960); *Herma (Foundation)* for Piano (1960–61); *ST/48—1,240162* (1956–62; ST = stochastic; 48 = number of players; 1 = first work for this contingent; 240162 = 24 January 1962, date on which the work, derived from earlier sketches, was finally calculated by the IBM 7090 electronic computer in Paris as programmed probabilistically by Xenakis); *ST/10—1,080262* (1956–62; ST = stochastic; 10 = number of players; 1 = first work of this contingent; 080262 = 8 February 1962, date on which this work was finally electronically calculated; a version of this work for String Quartet is entitled *ST/4*); *Morsima-Amorsima* (Morsima = that which comes by Fate; Amorsima = that which does not come by Fate) for Violin, Cello, Double Bass, and Piano (1956–62); *Atrées (Law of Necessity)* for 10 Players (1956–62; written in homage to Blaise Pascal and calculated by the 7090 computer, with some license); *Stratégie,* musical game for 2 Conductors and 2 Orchs. (1959–62; Venice Festival, April 23, 1963; Bruno Maderna's orch. won over that of Konstantin Simonovic); *Bohor I* and *II* for Tape (1962, 1975); *Polla ta dhina (Many Are the Wonders)* for Children's Choir and Small Orch., to a text from Sophocles' *Antigone* (1962); *Eonta* (neuter plural of the present participle of the verb "to be" in the Ionian dialect, the title being in Cypriot syllabic characters of Creto-Mycenean origin) for Piano, 2 Trumpets, and 3 Tenor Trombones (1963–64); *Hiketides (The Suppliants),* stage music for 50 Women's Voices, 10 Instruments, and Percussion, after Aeschylus (1964); *Akrata (Pure)* for 16 Wind Instruments (1964–65; Oxford, June 28, 1966); *Terretektorh (Action of Construction)* for 88 Players scattered among the audience (1965–66; Royan Festival of Contemporary Music, April 3, 1966); *Oresteia,* incidental music for Aeschylus' tragedy, for Chorus and Chamber Orch. (1965–66; also a concert suite); *Nomos Alpha (Law Alpha)* for Solo Cello (1966); *Polytope de Montréal,* light-and-sound spectacle for the Montreal EXPO '67, for 4 Small, Identical Orchs. (1967); *Nuits* for 12 Mixed Voices a cappella (1967); *Medea,* stage music for Male Chorus and Instrumental Ensemble (1967); *Nomos* *Gamma* for 98 Players scattered among the audience (1967–68; Royan Festival, April 3, 1969); *Kraanerg (Perfection of Energy),* ballet music for Tape and Orch. (1968–69; Ottawa, June 2, 1969); *Anaktoria* for 8 Instruments (1969); *Persephassa* for 6 Percussionists scattered among the audience (1969); *Synaphai* for One or 2 Pianos, and Orch. (1969); *Hibiki-Hana-Ma,* 12-channel electroacoustic music distributed kinematically over 800 loudspeakers, for the Osaka EXPO '70 (1969–70; also a 4-channel version); *Charisma* for Clarinet and Cello (1971); *Aroura* for 12 Strings (1971); *Persepolis,* light-and-sound spectacle with 8- or 4-channel electroacoustic music (1971); *Antikhthon,* ballet music for Orch. (1971; Bonn, Sept. 21, 1974); *Linaia-Agon* for Horn, Tenor Trombone, and Tuba (1972); *Mikka* for Solo Violin (1972); *Polytope de Cluny,* version of *Polytope de Montréal,* for 4-channel Tape (1972); *Eridanos* for 8 Brasses and 10 String Instruments or their multiples (1973; La Rochelle Festival, 1973); *Evryali* for Piano (1973); *Cendrées* for Chorus and Orch. (1974; Lisbon, June 18, 1974); *Erikhthon* for Piano and Orch. (1974; Paris, May 1974); *Gmeeoorh* for Organ (1974); *Noomena* for Orch. (1974; Paris, Oct. 16, 1974); *Empreintes* for Orch. (1975; La Rochelle Festival, June 29, 1975); *Phlegra* for 11 Instruments (1975; London, Jan. 28, 1976); *Psappha* for Solo Percussion (1975); *N'shima* for 2 Horns, 2 Trombones, Cello, and 2 Mezzo-sopranos (1975); *Theraps* for Solo Double Bass (1975–76); *Khoaï* for Solo Harpsichord (1976); *Retours—Windungen* for 12 Cellists (1976; Bonn, Dec. 20, 1976); *Dmaathen* for Oboe and Percussion (1976); *Epeï* for English Horn, Clarinet, Trumpet, 2 Tenor Trombones, and Double Bass (1976); *Mikka S* for Solo Violin (1976); *Akanthos* for 9 Players (1977); *Kottos* for Solo Cello (1977); *Hélène* for Mezzo-soprano, Female Chorus, and 2 Clarinets (1977); *Diatope* for 4- or 8-track Tapes (1977); *Ais* for Baritone, Solo Percussion, and Orch.; *Palimpsest* for Piano and Percussion (1979); *Embellie* for Solo Viola (1981).

BIBLIOGRAPHY: N. Matossian, *Iannis Xenakis* (Paris, 1981).

Xyndas, Spyridon, Greek composer; b. Corfu, June 8, 1812; d. Athens, Nov. 12, 1896. He studied in Italy; composed many attractive popular Greek songs; several operas to Italian librettos (*Il Conte Giuliano, I due pretendenti,* etc.); also *The Parliamentary Candidate* (Athens, March 1888), which was probably the first opera with a Greek text. He became blind toward the end of his life.

Y

Yamada, Kôsçak, eminent Japanese composer and conductor; b. Tokyo, June 9, 1886; d. there, Dec. 29, 1965. He studied at the Imperial Academy of Music in Tokyo; then in Berlin with Max Bruch (1908–13). Returning to Japan in 1914, he organized the Tokyo Phil. Orch., which gave its first concert in 1915. On Oct. 16, 1918, he conducted a program of Japanese music in Carnegie Hall, N.Y., including some of his own works (*Festival of Autumn, The Dark Gate, Flower of Madara,* and *Oriental Suite*); appeared as a guest conductor in the U.S. until 1921; in 1930, and again in 1933, he conducted in Russia; in 1937 he toured Europe. Most of his MSS were destroyed during the air raid on Tokyo of May 25, 1945; several scores have been restored from the extant orch. parts.

WORKS: Operas: *Alladine et Palomides,* after Maeterlinck (1913); *The Depraved Heavenly Maiden* (1908; Tokyo, Dec. 3, 1929); *Ayame (The Sweet Flag;* Tokyo, Feb. 24, 1935); *The Black Ships* (Tokyo, 1940); *Yoake (The Dawn;* Nov. 28, 1940); *Hsiang Fei* (1946); cantatas: *Bonno-Koru* (Tokyo, Oct. 9, 1931) and *The Dawn of the Orient* (Tokyo, July 7, 1941); Symph. (Tokyo, Dec. 6, 1914); *Ode to Meiji* for Chorus and Orch. (Tokyo, April 26, 1925); *Homage to Showa,* symph. poem (Tokyo, May 13, 1939); *Kamikaze,* symph. suite (1944); chamber music; nearly 1,000 choral pieces and songs.

Yamash'ta, Stomu (really **Tsutomu Yamashita**), Japanese virtuoso percussionist and composer; b. Kyoto, March 10, 1947. He was trained in music by his father; played piano in his infancy, and drums at puberty; in early adolescence became a timpanist for the Kyoto Phil. and Osaka Phil.; also worked in several film studios in Tokyo; at the same time he was active in sports; won the speed skating championship of Japan for his age group. At 16 he went to London for further study; later went to the U.S. as a scholarship student at the Interlochen Arts Academy; continued his musical education in Boston, N.Y., and Chicago. Returning to Japan, he gave solo performances as a percussionist; developed a phenomenal degree of equilibristic prestidigitation, synchronously manipulating a plethora of drums and a congregation of oriental bells and gongs while rotating 360° from the center of a circle to reach the prescribed percussionable objects. As a composer, he cultivates a manner of controlled improvisation marked by constantly shifting meters. In 1970 he formed the Red Buddha Theater (an ensemble of 36 actors, musicians, and dancers), for which he composed 2 musical pageants, *Man from the East* (1971) and *Rain Mountain* (1973). Other works: a ballet,

Fox (1968); *Hito* for any 3 Instruments (1970); *Prisms* for Solo Percussion (1970); *Red Buddha* for Chamber Ensemble (1971); percussion scores for some 77 Japanese films, as well as for Ken Russell's *The Devils* (with Peter Maxwell Davies, 1971) and Robert Altman's *Images* (1972).

Yampolsky, Izrail, Russian musicologist and lexicographer; b. Kiev, Nov. 21, 1905; d. Moscow, Sept. 20, 1976. He studied violin; then entered the Moscow Cons., where he took courses in advanced music theory with Miaskovsky and Glière; he subsequently taught violin at the Music Academy in Moscow (1931–58); gave lectures in music history there; also taught at the Cons. (1934–49). A fine and diligent research scholar, he publ. a number of excellent monographs dealing mainly with violin and violinists: *Foundations of Violin Fingering* (Moscow, 1933; 3rd expanded ed., 1955; in Eng., London, 1967); *Henryk Wieniawski* (Moscow, 1955); *Enescu* (Moscow, 1956; also in Rumanian, Bucharest, 1959); *Music of Yugoslavia* (Moscow, 1958); *Paganini* (Moscow, 1961; 2nd ed., 1968); *David Oistrakh* (Moscow, 1964); *Fritz Kreisler* (1975). He was co-editor, with Boris Steinpress, of the one-vol. reference work *Encyclopedic Music Dictionary* (Moscow, 1959; revised 1966). He was acting editor in chief of the first 3 vols. of the 5-vol. *Musical Encyclopedia* (Moscow, 1973, 1974, 1976).

Yancey, "Jimmy" (James Edward Yancey), black American jazz pianist; b. Chicago, c.1894; d. there, Sept. 17, 1951. He was a singer and dancer in a vaudeville act as a child; then taught himself to play the piano and appeared in Chicago clubs. In 1925 he gave up his stage career and worked as a groundskeeper at Comiskey Park. With the revival of boogie-woogie, he returned to playing jazz piano, and became quite a figure in jazz circles.

Yannay, Yehuda, Rumanian-born Israeli-American composer of hypermodern tendencies; b. Timisoara, May 26, 1937. He went to Israel in 1951, and studied composition with Boscovich (1959–64); received a Fulbright travel grant and went to the U.S., where he studied composition with Arthur Berger and Harold Shapero at Brandeis Univ. (M.F.A., 1966); attended summer classes of Gunther Schuller at the Berkshire Music Center in Tanglewood (1965); later studied composition at the Univ. of Illinois, Urbana (1968–70). In 1970 he joined the faculty of the Univ. of Wisconsin at Milwaukee; organized there a group called the Music from Almost Yesterday Ensemble with the intention of producing music of the problematic future and that of the tenable yesteryear. He received his Ph.D. in 1974 from the Univ. of Illinois at Urbana. In his own composition he liberates himself from all prejudices of the past, present, and future. He invented an elastic nylon string monochord, which he named, with a commendable eschewment of obsolescent modesty, "Yannaychord." Most of his creations are public exhibitions of a theatrical nature, in which all arts and human actions are united

and all social conventions scorned, spurned, or both; the pugnacious determination to "épater les bourgeois" motivates his productions in the deluded hopes that the bourgeois will be epatated beyond endurance and precipitate a physical encounter of the kind that animated the fabled exhibitions of the futurists of yore.
WORKS: *Variations* for 2 Flutes (1970); *The Chain of Proverbs* for Choir, Recorders, and Percussion (1962); *Sefiroth (Spheres)* for Soprano, Flute, Clarinet, Bass Clarinet, Harp, Prepared Piano, and Percussion (1963); *Incantations* for Voices, Keyboard, and the Piano Interior (1964); *Interconnections* for 14 Instruments (1965); *Mirkamim,* textures of sound for Orch. of 84 Solo Instruments (1967); *Per se,* chamber concerto (1968; Chicago, Nov. 10, 1970); *Coloring Book for the Harpist,* playing with Combs (1969); *Wraphap* for Amplified Actress lying upon a large aluminum sheet, and strumming the Yannaychord (1969); *Houdini's 9th* for Double Bass and Escape Artist (straitjacketed to his instrument), while a recording plays the "Hymn to Joy" from Beethoven's 9th Symph. and 2 hospital orderlies supervise the soloist (1969); Concerto for Audience, Orch., and 29 Red, Yellow, and Green Slides monitoring the involuntary participants (1971); *3 Events: The Urbana (Illinois) Crystal Lake Park Gathering, Piano without Pianist,* and *The Vestibule Peep-In-Pipe-Out* (1968–71); *Bug Piece* for any irritants capable of bugging the captive audience, the bugging being symbolized by the projection on a screen of a centipede, a millipede, or fornicating ants, or any other terrestrial arthropods (1972); *A Noiseless Patient Spider* for Women's Chorus a cappella (1975); *American Sonorama,* ballet score derived from sounds of the more obnoxious speeches by singularly illiterate politicians (1975–76); *The Decline and Fall of the Sonata in B-flat,* symbolic theater sketch (1970–76).

Yansons, Arvid, conductor; b. Leipaja, Latvia, Oct. 24, 1914. He studied violin in Riga; then played in the Opera orch. there. In 1944 he was engaged as a conductor at the Riga Opera; in 1952 he became a regular conductor of the Leningrad Phil. Orch.; was a guest conductor in Eastern Europe. He also made successful appearances in England, most notably with the Hallé Orch. of Manchester.

Yardumian, Richard, American composer; b. (of Armenian parents) Philadelphia, April 5, 1917. He was self-taught in music. His compositions reflect the spirit of Armenian folk songs and religious melodies. His *Armenian Suite* for Orch. was performed for the first time by the Philadelphia Orch. on March 5, 1954. Other symph. works (also brought out by the Philadelphia Orch.) are *Desolate City* (April 6, 1945); Violin Concerto (March 30, 1950); Piano Concerto (Philadelphia, Jan. 3, 1958); Symph. No. 1 (Philadelphia, Dec. 1, 1961); Symph. No. 2 (*Psalms*) for Orch. and Contralto (Philadelphia, Nov. 13, 1964); *Come Creator Spirit,* mass for Contralto, Chorus, and Orch. (1966); oratorio, *The Story of Abraham* (1971; May 4, 1972); *2 Chorales:* No. 1 for

Organ Solo (1976) and No. 2 for Orch. (1978).

Yarrow, Peter, American folksinger, of the singing trio Peter, Paul and Mary; b. New York, May 31, 1938. A serious musician, he went to Cornell Univ. to study psychology. He sang at the Newport Folk Festival in 1960; then got together with two other folk singers, Paul Stookey (b. Birmingham, Mich., Nov. 30, 1937) and Mary Travers (b. Louisville, Ky., Nov. 7, 1937), and launched a trio using only their first names and specializing in folksy and unambiguously wholesome songs dedicated to the improvement of humanity and of America by non-violent means. They aligned themselves with such social singers as Pete Seeger and Bob Dylan. By himself, Yarrow recorded the solipsistic songs *Peter* and *That's Enough for Me.* Together they sang Pete Seeger's nostalgic numbers *Where Have All the Flowers Gone, Puff, the Magic Dragon,* and *Song Will Rise.* They were most successful singing other people's songs in folk style, among them *Blowin' in the Wind, I Dig Rock-and-Roll Music,* and *Leaving on a Jet Plane.*

Yarustovsky, Boris, Russian musicologist; b. Moscow, May 14, 1911; d. there, July 12, 1978. He studied music history and theory at the Moscow Cons., graduating in 1941; also obtained the degree of Doctor of Arts in 1953 with the dissertation *Some Problems of the Dramaturgy of Classical Russian Operas.* He publ. *Tchaikovsky, Life and Works* (Moscow, 1940); *Operatic Dramaturgy of Tchaikovsky* (Moscow, 1947); *Stravinsky, Life and Works* (Moscow, 1963); *Music of the New World* (Moscow, 1964).

Yashirō, Akio, Japanese composer; b. Tokyo, Sept. 10, 1929; d. Yokohama, April 9, 1976. He studied piano in Tokyo with Leonid Kreutzer and composition with Moroi and Ifukube at the National Univ. of Tokyo, graduating in 1951; then went to Paris, where he studied composition with Noël Gallon at the Paris Cons. (1951–54), and took private lessons with Nadia Boulanger and Messiaen. Returning to Japan, he joined the music faculty of the Univ. of Tokyo.
WORKS: String Quartet (1954–55); Sonata for 2 Flutes and Piano (1957–58); Symph. (Tokyo, June 9, 1958); Cello Concerto (Tokyo, June 24, 1960); Piano Sonata (1960); Piano Concerto (Tokyo, Nov. 5, 1967); *Ouverture de fête* for Brass Ensemble (perf. at the opening ceremony of the 14th Winter Olympic Games in Sapporo, Feb. 3, 1972).

Yasser, Joseph, Russian-American organist and musicologist; b. Lodz, Poland, April 16, 1893. He studied at the Moscow Cons., graduating in 1917 as an organist; after several years of teaching organ in Moscow and Siberia, he reached Shanghai in 1922, and conducted a choral society there; subsequently emigrated to the U.S. (1923); served as organist at Temple Rodeph Sholom in N.Y. (1929–60); held various positions in American musicological groups. His most important contribution to music theory was *A Theory of Evolving Tonality* (N.Y., 1932), in which he proffered an ingenious hypothesis as to the origin of the pentatonic and heptatonic scales, and, operating by inductive reasoning, suggested that the ultimate Western scale would contain 19 degrees. He contributed several articles to the *Musical Quarterly* (April and July 1937 and July 1938) dealing with quartal harmony, which were publ. in a separate edition (N.Y., 1938).
BIBLIOGRAPHY: Albert Weisser, compiler, *Joseph Yasser: An Annotated Bibliography of His Selected Writings and Lectures* (N.Y., 1970).

Yates, Peter B., Canadian-American writer on music; b. Toronto, Nov. 30, 1909; d. New York, Feb. 25, 1976. He studied at Princeton Univ. (B.A., 1931); married the pianist **Frances Mullen** in 1933. From 1937 to 1962 he was a functionary at the Calif. Dept. of Employment in Los Angeles, but this bureaucratic occupation did not preclude his activities as a musical catalyst. In 1939 he inaugurated on the rooftop of his house in the Silver Lake district of Los Angeles a chamber concert series which was to become an important cultural enterprise in subcultural California, under the name Evenings on the Roof; he served as coordinator of these concerts from 1939 to 1954, when they were moved to a larger auditorium in downtown Los Angeles and became known as the Monday Evening Concerts. In 1968 he was appointed chairman of the music dept. at the State Univ. of N.Y. at Buffalo. He publ. *An Amateur at the Keyboard, Twentieth-Century Music,* and a collection of poems.

Yavorsky, Boleslav, Russian pianist and music theorist; b. Kharkov, June 22, 1877; d. Saratov, Nov. 26, 1942. He studied piano and composition with Taneyev in Moscow; in 1906 founded a People's Cons. there. From 1916 to 1921 he taught at the Kiev Cons.; then went to Moscow. His theory of aural gravitation as the determining factor of the formation of modes is embodied in his publications *Structure of Musical Speech* (Moscow, 1908) and *Exercises in Schematic Formation of Modal Rhythm* (Moscow, 1915), and in several monographs. He was also active in the field of general musical education, and his methods influenced Soviet practice in pedagogy. Vol. 1 of the collected edition of his articles and letters was publ. in Moscow in 1964.

Yepes, Narciso, Spanish guitarist; b. Lorca, Nov. 14, 1927. He was educated at the Valencia Cons.; made his debut with the Orquesta Nacional in Madrid in 1947; then launched an international career, appearing in the U.S., South America, and Japan. He also wrote music for films.

Yo-Yo Ma. See **Ma, Yo-Yo.**

Yoffe, Shlomo, Polish-born Israeli composer; b. Warsaw, May 19, 1909. He studied in Poland and Czechoslovakia; went to Palestine in 1930; studied with Partos and Boscovich at the music academies of Jerusalem and Tel Aviv; was director of the Studio for Music Education for Gilboa and Bet-Shean (1953–73).

WORKS: *Ruth,* symph. suite (1954); 3 symphs. (1955, 1957, 1958); Violin Concerto (1956); *Views of the Emek,* symph. suite (1958); *Symphonic Poem on Jewish Themes* (1959); *Divertimento* for Orch. (1959); Cello Concertino (1959); Oboe Concerto (1960); Concerto for Strings (1961); *3 Pieces* for Horn and Strings (1966); *Fantasia concertante* for Brass Quartet and Orch. (1968); *Beit-Alfa,* symph. poem (1972); *Introduction, Dance and Finale* for Chamber Orch. (1972); *Sobu Zion,* overture (1973); *5 Sketches of Old Jerusalem* for Chamber Orch. (1973); *Fantasy* for Oboe and Chamber Orch. (1975); 6 cantatas: *Alilot Hagilboa* (1954); *Erez Hanegev* (1955); *Alu* (1958); *Shaalu Shelom Yerushalayim* (1967); *Religious Cantata* (1969); *Psalm CXX* (1974); Quartet for 2 Flutes, Cello, and Piano (1957); 2 string quartets (1961, 1969); *Fantasy* for String Quartet (1966); *Chamber Concerto* for Violin and 10 Players (1966); *Affettuoso* for 2 Flutes (1966); Brass Quartet (1967); *Musica concertante* for Clarinet and 3 Percussionists (1973); *4 Miniatures* for Wind Quintet (1973); *Etude* for 13 Players (1974); *Serenata* for Wind Quintet (1975); *5 Songs* for Soprano and 13 Players (1975); *Nonetto,* fantasy for Strings (1976); choruses.

Yon, Pietro Alessandro, Italian-American organist and composer; b. Settimo Vittone, Aug. 8, 1886; d. Huntington, Long Island, N.Y., Nov. 22, 1943. He studied with Fumagalli at the Milan Cons.; then at the Turin Cons. (1901–4), and at the Santa Cecilia in Rome with Remigio Renzi (organ) and Sgambati (piano), graduating in 1905; subsequently served as organist at St. Peter's in Rome (1905–7). In 1907 he emigrated to the U.S.; from 1907 to 1919, and again from 1921 to 1926, was organist at St. Francis-Xavier's in N.Y.; then was appointed organist of St. Patrick's Cathedral in N.Y., a post he held until his death. He became a naturalized U.S. citizen in 1921. He was greatly esteemed as an organist and teacher; composed numerous organ pieces, of which *Gesù Bambino* (1917) became popular and was publ. in various instrumental and vocal arrangements; he also wrote an oratorio, *The Triumph of St. Patrick* (N.Y., April 29, 1934); several masses and other religious services. A novel based on his life, *The Heavens Heard Him,* written by V.B. Hammann and M.C. Yon, was publ. in N.Y. in 1963.

Yonge (Young), Nicholas, English musician; b. Lewes; d. London (buried, Oct. 23), 1619. He was a chorister at St. Paul's Cathedral. He trans. and arranged a number of Italian madrigals, which he publ. in 2 books under the general title *Musica transalpina* (1588, 1597).

BIBLIOGRAPHY: A. Obertello, *Madrigali italiani in Inghilterra* (Milan, 1949).

York, Francis Lodowick, American organist and teacher; b. Ontonagon, Mich., March 9, 1861; d. there, Jan. 13, 1955. He studied piano in Boston and Detroit; in 1892 went to Paris to study with Guil-

mant; upon returning to the U.S., he devoted himself to teaching. He publ. the manuals *Harmony Simplified* (1897) and *Counterpoint Simplified* (1907).

Yossifov, Alexander, Bulgarian composer; b. Sofia, Aug. 12, 1940. He studied composition with Vladigerov and conducting with Iliev at the Bulgarian State Cons. in Sofia, graduating in 1966.

WORKS: Opera, *Back to the Beginning;* 3 ballets: *Wings of Friendship* (1969); *The Woman Partisan* (1969); *Student's Farewell Ball* (1969); 2 oratorios: *Homeland* (1966) and *The Great White Road* (1969); 5 nationalistic cantatas; *Revolution,* overture (1964); 2 symph. tales: *The Wolf and the 7 Kids* (1966) and *Little Red Riding Hood* (1969); 4 symphs.: No. 1, *Sinfonietta* (1966); No. 2 (1970); No. 3, *Bulgarian Blood,* for Bass and Orch. (1975); No. 4 (1974); Concerto for 2 Pianos, String Orch., and Percussion (1970); Piano Concerto (1971–72); *Festive Overture* (1974).

Yost, Gaylord, American violinist and composer; b. Fayette, Ohio, Jan. 28, 1888; d. Wauseon, Ohio, Oct. 10, 1958. After studying music in Toledo and Detroit, he went to Berlin, where he took violin lessons with Issaye Barmas. Upon returning to the U.S., he organized the Yost String Quartet (1925). He taught at the Indiana College of Music in Indianapolis (1915–21), and at the Pittsburgh Music Inst. (1921–43). In 1951 he turned to politics and journalism; became editor and publisher of the *Fayette Review,* founded by his father. In 1954 he was elected mayor of Fayette, serving until 1957. He publ. *The Yost System,* in 8 vols. (1932; abridged ed. as *The Yost Violin Method,* in 3 vols.); also *Basic Principles of Violin Playing* (1940).

Yost, Michel, famous French clarinetist; b. Paris, 1754; d. there, July 5, 1786. He studied with Beer; wrote 14 clarinet concertos; 30 quartets for Clarinet and Strings; 8 books of duos for clarinets; *Airs variés* for Clarinet, with Viola and Bass.

Youdin, Mikhail, Russian composer; b. St. Petersburg, Sept. 29, 1893; d. Kazan, Feb. 8, 1948. He studied at the St. Petersburg Cons., graduating in 1923; joined its staff as an instructor in 1926. He went to Kazan in 1942, and taught at the Cons. there until his death.

WORKS: Opera, *Farida* (1943); cantata, *Song of Spring and Joy* (Leningrad, Nov. 25, 1936); *Heroic Oratorio* (1937); *Poem 1926* for Orch. (Leningrad, March 30, 1927); other symph. pieces; 2 string quartets; Piano Sonata; Organ Toccata; choruses; songs; arrangements of folk songs.

Youll, Henry, English composer; flourished c.1600. He publ. *Canzonets to three voyces* (1608), a collection of 24 vocal pieces (*Slow, slow, fresh fount,* to Ben Jonson's words; *Pipe, shepherds, pipe;* etc.). It was republ. in *The English Madrigal School* (vol. 28).

Youmans, Vincent, American composer of popular music; b. New York, Sept. 27, 1898; d. Denver, April 5, 1946. He took piano lessons as a child, but was apprenticed by his father to enter the business world; he served as a messenger in a Wall Street bank; then enlisted in the U.S. Navy; also played the piano in a Navy band; wrote a song, *Hallelujah,* which was picked up by John Philip Sousa, who performed it with his own bands; later it was incorporated by Youmans in his musical *Hit the Deck.* After World War I, Youmans earned a living as a song plugger for publishers in N.Y. He produced 2 musical comedies, *2 Little Girls in Blue* (May 3, 1921) and *Wildflower* (1923); both were moderately successful, but he achieved fame with his next production, *No No Nanette;* it opened in Detroit on April 21, 1924; was next staged in Chicago on May 5, 1924, and after a 49-week run there, moved to London, where it was produced on March 11, 1925; it finally reached Broadway on Sept. 16, 1925, and proved to be one of the most beguiling and enduring American musicals; its hit song, *Tea for Two,* became a perennial favorite all over the world (Shostakovich arranged it in 1927 for a salon orch. under the title *Tahiti Trot*). There followed several other successful musicals: *A Night Out* (1925), *Oh! Please* (1926), *Hit the Deck* (1927), *Rainbow* (1928), *Great Day* (1929), and *Through the Years* (1932). In 1933 Youmans went to Hollywood to complete his score for the film *Flying Down to Rio.* Because of an increasingly aggravated tubercular condition, he retired to Denver in the hope of recuperation in its then-unpolluted environment, and remained there until his death. Among his songs the following were hits: *Bambalina; I Want to Be Happy; Hallelujah; Sometimes I'm Happy; Great Day; Without a Song; Time on My Hands; Through the Years; Oh, Me, Oh, My, Oh, You; Carioca; Orchids in the Moonlight; Drums in My Heart; More Than You Know; Rise 'n' Shine.*

Young, Alexander, English tenor; b. London, Oct. 18, 1920. He studied at the Royal College of Music in London; made his debut at the Edinburgh Festival in 1950; then sang opera at Glyndebourne and Covent Garden; in America, appeared at the San Francisco Opera. He enjoyed a fine reputation as a concert singer in wide-ranging programs of classical and modern music.

Young, Angus, 1970's AC&DC.

Young, Anthony, English organist and composer; b. c.1685; d. after 1720. He was an organist at various churches in London; wrote numerous songs; he is chiefly known as one of the composers falsely credited with the authorship of the tune of *God Save the Queen.*

Young, Cecilia, English singer; b. London, c.1710; d. there, Oct. 6, 1789. She made her appearance at the Drury Lane Theatre on March 4, 1730; in 1735 was engaged by Handel for his opera company; married **T.A. Arne** on March 15, 1737; went with him to Dublin in 1742, and sang soprano parts in his works presented there (*Comus, Judgment of Paris, Alfred,*

etc.).

Young, Douglas, English composer; b. London, June 18, 1947. He studied at the Royal College of Music with Anthony Milner (composition) and Anthony Hopkins (piano) in 1966. He composes mostly instrumental music. Among his works are Sonata for Horn and Piano (1965); *Sonnet* for Orch. (1967); Sonata for Violin, Viola, and Cello (1968); *The Listeners,* ballet (London, Dec. 13, 1969); piano pieces for children.

Young, Faron, American singer of country and popular music; b. Shreveport, La., Feb. 25, 1932. He took up the guitar; after attending Centenary College for a time, he began his career as a singer of country music on the "Louisiana Hayride" program. He served in the Korean War; after his discharge he joined the Grand Ole Opry in Nashville; also appeared in films and on television. His hits included *Hello Walls* (1957) and *It's Four in the Morning* (1971).

Young, La Monte, American composer of the extreme avant-garde; b. Bern, Idaho, Oct. 14, 1935. He studied clarinet and saxophone with William Green in Los Angeles; then took courses in composition with John Vincent and Leonard Stein at the Univ. of Calif., Los Angeles (1956–57), and later at Berkeley (1957–60); subsequently worked with Richard Maxfield at the New School for Social Research in N.Y. (1960–61). In 1963 he married the artist and illustrator Marian Zazeela, and gave a number of audiovisual performances with her in a series of "Sound/Light Environments" in Europe and America. In 1970 he visited India to study Eastern philosophy and train himself physically, mentally, and vocally for cosmic awareness, gradually arriving at the realization that any human, subhuman, or inhuman activity constitutes art; in his *Composition 1990* he starts a fire on the stage while releasing captive butterflies in the hall. In his attempt to overcome terrestrial limitations he has decreed for himself a circadian period of 26 hours. He achieves timelessness by declaring, "This piece of music may play without stopping for thousands of years." Several of his works consist solely of imperious commands: "Push the piano to the wall; push it through the wall; keep pushing," or, more succinctly, "Urinate." He edited *An Anthology of Chance Operations, Concept Art, Anti-Art,* etc. (N.Y., 1963); his own contribution to it was a line drawn in India ink on a 3 × 5 filing card.
ASCERTAINABLE WORKS: *5 Little Pieces* for String Quartet (1956); *For Guitar* (1958); String Trio (1958); *Poem for Tables, Chairs, and Benches* (moving furniture about; Univ. of Calif., Berkeley, Jan. 5, 1960); *Arabic Numeral (any Integer)* for Gong or Piano (1960); *Studies in the Bowed Disc* for Gong (1963); *The Well-Tuned Piano* (1964); *The Tortoise Droning Selected Pitches from the Holy Numbers of the 2 Black Tigers, the Green Tiger, and the Hermit* (N.Y., Oct. 30, 1964) and *The Tortoise Recalling the Drone of the Holy Numbers as They Were Re-*

vealed in the Dreams of the Whirlwind and the Obsidian Gong, Illuminated by the Sawmill, the Green Sawtooth Ocelot, and the High-Tension Line Stepdown Transformer (N.Y., Dec. 12, 1964); an arbitrary number of pieces of "conceptual" music and tape recordings of his own monophonous vocalizing achieved by both inspiration and expiration so that the vocal line is maintained indefinitely; various physical exercises with or without audible sounds. His Selected Writings were publ. in Munich in 1969.

Young, Lester Willis ("Prez"), black American jazz tenor saxophonist; b. Woodville, Miss., Aug. 27, 1909; d. New York, March 15, 1959. He studied trumpet, alto sax, violin, and drums with his father; then played in his family's band; turning to the tenor saxophone, he began a highly successful career playing in the bands of Bennie Moten, Fletcher Henderson, Count Basie, and others; also made recordings with Billie Holiday, who dubbed him "Prez" (a contraction of "The President") for his outstanding abilities. One of the great jazz saxophonists, he influenced numerous successors through his sinuous tone quality and improvised solos.

Young, Neil, Canadian-born folk-rock singer, instrumentalist, and composer; b. Toronto, Nov. 12, 1945. He learned to play the banjo and guitar in his youth; moving to Los Angeles in 1966, he formed the Buffalo Springfield band, which produced Young's hits Broken Arrow and I Am a Child. In 1969 he joined with David Crosby, Stephen Stills, and Graham Nash at the Woodstock Festival, later scoring a hit with their album Déjà Vu. Eventually he espoused a solo career, making the albums Everybody Knows This Is Nowhere and After the Goldrush, with the backup group Crazy Horse. In his songs he created an effective conglomeration of folk, country music, and hard rock; among his best songs were Southern Man, Cowgirl in the Sand, Heart of Gold, Country Girl, Helpless, and the surrealistic Vampire Blues.

Young, Percy Marshall, English writer on music; b. Northwich, Cheshire, May 17, 1912. He studied organ at Selwyn College, Cambridge (B.A., 1934); then went to Dublin, where he graduated from Trinity College (Mus.D., 1937); upon his return to England he took courses with C.B. Rootham and E.J. Dent in Cambridge; subsequently occupied various teaching posts; from 1944 to 1966 was director of music at the College of Technology in Wolverhampton. He publ. a number of arrangements of old English songs, and also composed some vocal pieces; but he is known principally for his scholarly biographical studies and essays.
    WRITINGS (all publ. in London): Handel (1947; 3rd ed., revised, 1979); The Oratorios of Handel (1953); A Critical Dictionary of Composers and Their Music (1954; in America as Biographical Dictionary of Composers); Elgar, O.M.: A Study of a Musician (1955; revised ed., 1972); The Story of Song

(1955); Instrumental Music (1955); In Search of Music (1956); Concerto (1957); Tragic Muse. The Life and Works of Robert Schumann (1961; revised 1967); Symphony (1957); Music Makers of Today (1958); The Choral Tradition: An Historical and Analytical Survey from the 16th Century to the Present Day (1962); Zoltán Kodály (1964); Britten (1966); A History of British Music (1967); Great Ideas in Music (1967); Keyboard Musicians of the World (1967); Debussy (1969); The Bachs, 1500–1850 (1970); Sir Arthur Sullivan (1971); A Concise History of Music (1974); Alice Elgar: Enigma of a Victorian Lady (1977). He ed. Sir Edward Elgar. Letters and Other Writings (1956).

Young, Polly (Mary), English singer; b. London, c.1745; d. there, Sept. 20, 1799. She lived in Dublin with her aunt, the singer Cecilia Young (Mrs. T.A. Arne), and made her debut as a singer upon her return to London in 1762. In 1766 she married the composer **François-Hippolyte Barthélémon;** their daughter, **Cecilia Maria** (Mrs. Henslowe), was a talented musician.

Young, Victor, American pianist and composer; b. Bristol, Tenn., April 9, 1889; d. Ossining, N.Y., Sept. 2, 1968. He studied piano with Isidor Philipp in Paris; toured in England and the U.S. as accompanist to prominent singers; held various teaching positions; was music director in Thomas A. Edison's Experimental Laboratory in West Orange, N.J., conducting tonal tests and making piano recordings under Edison's personal supervision (1919–27). He wrote the musical score for one of the earliest sound motion pictures, In Old California; composed some 300 film scores altogether; also wrote, for orch., Scherzetto, Jeep, In the Great Smokies, Charm Assembly Line Ballet, etc.; piano pieces (including Under a Spanish Moon); songs (Gossip, Cuckoo Clock, etc.).

Young, Victor, American composer of popular music; b. Chicago, Aug. 8, 1900; d. Palm Springs, Calif., Nov. 10, 1956. As a youth he was sent to Poland, where he studied violin at the Warsaw Cons., and made his debut with the Warsaw Phil. He returned to Chicago in 1914 and, after further study, became active on the radio. In 1935 he went to Hollywood, where he wrote film music. Some of his songs became famous (Sweet Sue, Street of Dreams, Can't We Talk It Over, My Romance, Ghost of a Chance, Love Letters, Golden Earrings, Stella by Starlight, My Foolish Heart, Song of Delilah, etc.). Shortly before his death, he completed the musical score for the motion picture Around the World in 80 Days (1956).

Young, William, English violinist, flutist, and composer; date of birth unknown; d. London, Dec. 21, 1671. He was attached to the court of the Archduke Ferdinand Karl in Innsbruck, where he publ. a book of 30 Sonate a 3, 4, 5 voci con allemande, corranti (1653). In 1660 he was a flutist in the private orch. of Charles II in London. The following year he also played the violin. Other pieces by Young include

Ayre, Almain and 2 Sarabands, in Playford's *Musick's Recreation on the Lyra Viola* (1652), and *Fantasies for 3 viols,* in Playford's *Treasury of Musick* (1669); numerous MSS are in the Bodleian Library, Oxford; Gresham College, London; Corporation Music Library, Manchester; and in some private collections.

BIBLIOGRAPHY: W. Gillies Whittaker, *The Concerted Music of William Young* (Oxford, 1931).

Young-Uck Kim. See **Kim, Young-Uck.**

Youssoupoff, Prince Nicolas Russian musical dilettante and writer on musical subjects; b. St. Petersburg, 1827; d. Baden-Baden, Aug. 3, 1891. He studied violin with Vieuxtemps, and was an eager collector of violin literature; had a private orch. in his palace in St. Petersburg, but lived abroad for many years. He composed a programmatic symph., *Gonzalvo de Córdova,* with Violin obbligato; *Concerto symphonique* for Violin and Orch.; several pieces for violin and piano (*Féeries de la scène, Hallucination, Chant d'amour, Plainte, Saltimbanques,* etc.); publ. an interesting book on violin making, *Luthomonographie, historique et raisonnée* (Frankfurt, 1856; printed in French in Munich), and *Musique sacrée suivie d'un choix de morceaux de chants d'église* (Paris, 1862, as vol. I of a projected *Histoire de la musique en Russie;* contains a valuable study of Russian neumes and examples of traditional chants). Themes from Youssoupoff's *Ballet d'Espagne* were used by Bériot for a group of 6 violin duets.

Yradier (Iradier), Sebastián de, Spanish song composer; b. Lanciego, Álava, Jan. 20, 1809; d. Vitoria, Dec. 6, 1865. He composed theater music; after 1851 became singing master to the Empress Eugénie in Paris; for some time lived in Cuba. He publ. a number of melodious songs in a Spanish manner; one of them, *El arreglito,* subtitled *Chanson havanaise,* was used by Bizet for the famous Habanera in *Carmen;* Bizet retained the key and the pattern of the accompaniment, making minor changes in the melody to adjust it to French words. Yradier's other songs that became famous are *La paloma* and *Ay Chiquita!* In Paris he publ. 2 collections, *Echo d'Espagne* (8 songs) and *Fleurs d'Espagne* (25 songs).

BIBLIOGRAPHY: E. Istel, *Bizet und "Carmen"* (Stuttgart, 1927); J. Tiersot, "Bizet and Spanish Music," *Musical Quarterly* (Oct. 1927).

Yriarte, Tomás de, Spanish poet and musician; b. Orotava, Tenerife, Canary Islands, Sept. 18, 1750; d. Santa María, near Cádiz, Sept. 17, 1791. He was secretary at the Chancellery of State in Madrid and chief archivist at the Ministry of War. His literary works include a long didactic poem, *La música* (Madrid, 1779; Eng. trans., 1807). He composed tonadillas and some vocal and instrumental music.

BIBLIOGRAPHY: E. Cotarelo y Mori, *Yriarte y su época* (Madrid, 1897); J. Subirá, *El compositor Yriarte y el cultivo español del melólogo* (2 vols.,

Madrid, 1949–50).

Ysaÿe, Eugène, famous Belgian violinist, conductor, and composer; b. Liège, July 16, 1858; d. Brussels, May 12, 1931. At the age of 4 he began to study violin with his father, a theater conductor; at the age of 7 he was enrolled at the Cons. of Liège as a pupil of Désiré Heynberg; he then studied with Rodolphe Massart there; in 1867 he obtained 2nd prize for violin playing (sharing it with Ovide Musin); in 1868, he obtained first prize for violin and chamber music; and the silver medal in 1874. While still a very young boy, he played in his father's orchs.; in 1876 he was sent to Brussels to study with Henryk Wieniawski, and later was also a pupil of Vieuxtemps. After a sojourn in Bordeaux, he became concertmaster of Bilse's orch. in Berlin; appeared as a soloist at Pauline Lucca's concerts in Cologne and Aachen; in Germany he met Anton Rubinstein, who took him to Russia, where he spent 2 winters; he also toured in Norway. In 1883 he settled in Paris, where he met César Franck, Vincent d'Indy, etc., and gave successful concerts; he formed a duo with the pianist Raoul Pugno, and started a long series of concerts with him, establishing a new standard of excellence. On Sept. 26, 1886, he married Louise Bourdeau; César Franck dedicated his Violin Sonata to them as a wedding present; Ysaÿe's interpretation of this work made it famous. In 1886 he was named a prof. at the Cons. of Brussels (resigned in 1898); in 1886 he also organized the Ysaÿe Quartet (with Crickboom, Léon Van Hout, and Joseph Jacob); Debussy dedicated his String Quartet to Ysaÿe's group, which gave it its first performance at the Société Nationale in Paris, on Dec. 29, 1893. In 1889 Ysaÿe made successful appearances in England; on Nov. 16, 1894, he made his American debut, playing the Beethoven Violin Concerto with the N.Y. Phil., and created a sensation by his virtuosity. He revisited America many times, with undiminished acclaim. He began his career as a conductor in 1894, and established in Brussels his own orch., the Société des Concerts Ysaÿe. When the Germans invaded Belgium in 1914 he fled to London, where he remained during World War I. On April 5, 1918, he made his American debut as a conductor with the Cincinnati Symph. Orch., and also led the Cincinnati May Festival in that year. His success was so great that he was offered a permanent position as conductor of the Cincinnati Symph. Orch., which he held from 1918 to 1922. He then returned to Belgium and resumed leadership of the Société des Concerts Ysaÿe. After the death of his first wife, he married, on July 9, 1927, an American pupil, Jeannette Dincin (b. Brooklyn, Aug. 26, 1902).

Ysaÿe's style of playing is best described as heroic; but his art was equally convincing in the expression of moods of exquisite delicacy and tenderness; his frequent employment of "tempo rubato" produced an effect of elasticity without distorting the melodic line. Ysaÿe was also a composer. His works include 8 violin concertos; 6 violin sonatas; *Poème nocturne* for Violin, Cello, and Strings; *Les Harmonies du soir* for String Quartet and String

Orch.; *Divertimento* for Violin and Orch.; *Médita-tion* for Cello and String Orch.; *Chant d'hiver* for Violin and Chamber Orch.; *Trio de concert* for 2 Violins, Viola, and Orch.; *Amitié* for 2 Violins and Orch. At the age of 70 he began the composition of an opera in the Walloon language, *Piér li Houïeu (Peter the Miner),* which was produced in Liège on March 4, 1931, in the presence of the composer, who was brought to the theater in an invalid's chair, suffering from the extreme ravages of diabetes, which had necessitated the amputation of his left foot. He began the composition of a 2nd Walloon opera, *L'Avierge di Piér (La Vierge de Pierre),* but had no time to complete it. In 1937 Queen Elisabeth of Belgium inaugurated the annual Prix International Eugène Ysaÿe in Brussels; the first winner was the famous Russian violinist David Oistrakh.

BIBLIOGRAPHY: M. Pincherle, *Feuillets d'his-toire du violon* (Paris, 1927); J. Quitin, *Eugène Ysaÿe: Etude biographique et critique* (Brussels, 1938); E. Christen, *Ysaÿe* (Geneva, 1946; 2nd ed., 1947); Antoine Ysaÿe and B. Ratcliffe, *Ysaÿe: His Life, Work and Influence* (London, 1947); Antoine Ysaÿe, *Eugène Ysaÿe: Sa vie d'après les documents receuillis par son fils* (Brussels, 1948; a considerably altered version of the preceding; in Eng. trans. as *Ysaÿe, By His Son Antoine,* Buckinghamshire, 1980).

Ysaÿe, Théophile, Belgian pianist and composer, brother of **Eugène Ysaÿe;** b. Verviers, March 22, 1865; d. Nice, March 24, 1918. He was a pupil at the Liège Cons.; then studied at the Kullak Academy in Berlin, and also took lessons from César Franck in Paris; returning to Belgium, he became director of the Académie de Musique in Brussels; was noted as a fine ensemble player, and gave sonata recitals with his brother; during the latter's absence on tours, he also conducted the Société des Concerts Ysaÿe in Brussels. After the invasion of Belgium in 1914, he went with his brother to London; fearful of the Zeppelin air raids on London, he went to Nice, where he remained until his death. He was a prolific composer; his brother conducted a concert of Théophile's works in Brussels, on Nov. 6, 1904, including the premieres of his Symph. in F major and the symph. poem *Le Cygne.* Other works are: Piano Concerto; symph. poems (*Les Abeilles, La Forêt et l'oiseau*); *Fantaisie sur un thème populaire wallon* for Orch.; Piano Quintet; piano pieces; a Requiem.

Yttrehus, Rolv, American composer; b. Duluth, March 12, 1926. He studied at the Univ. of Minnesota (1946–50); then enrolled in the Univ. of Michigan 1950–53), obtaining his M.M.; went to Europe, where he took lessons with Brustad in Oslo (1953–54) and with Nadia Boulanger in Paris (1954–55); upon his return home he had satisfying sessions with Sessions (1957–60) at Princeton Univ.; then went to Rome and had instruction in advanced composition with Petrassi at the Santa Cecilia Academy (1960–62). Back in the U.S., he held several teaching positions: at the Univ. of Missouri (1963–68), Purdue Univ. (1968–69), the Univ. of Wisconsin in Oshkosh

(1969–77), and, from 1977, Rutgers Univ. He ditched the scores written in the first 35 years of his life as deciduous juvenilia; in his later works he cultivated distributive serialism, in which each note, each interval, and each rhythmic unit stands in an esoteric but surmisable relationship with other individual note groups.

WORKS: *Music* for Winds, Percussion, and Viola (1961); *Espressioni* for Orch. (1962); *Music* for Winds, Percussion, Cello, and Voices (1969); Sextet for Trumpet, Horn, Violin, Double Bass, Piano, and Percussion (1969–70; revised 1974); *Angstwagen* for Soprano and Percussion (1971); Quintet for Violin, Cello, Flute, Clarinet, and Piano (1973); *Gradus ad Parnassum,* on texts by Nietzsche and J.J. Fux, for Soprano, Chamber Ensemble, and Tape (1974–77).

Yuasa, Joji, Japanese composer; b. Koriyama, Aug. 12, 1929. He was a medical student at Keio Univ.; studied composition in the "experimental workshop" in Tokyo (1951–57). In 1968 he received a Japan Society Fellowship for a lecture tour throughout the U.S. and Europe. In 1969 he was one of the organizers of the Crosstalk Festival of Japanese and American multimedia works in Tokyo and Osaka; was a member of the "tranSonic" composers' group, in association with Ichiyanagi, Matsudaira, Takemitsu, and others. In his productions he adopts the most advanced multimedia techniques.

WORKS: *Projection* for 7 Players (1955); *Cosmos Haptic* for Piano (1957); *Projection Topologic* for Piano (1959); *Aoi no Ue,* musique concrète (1961); *Interpenetration* for 2 Flutes (1963); *Projection Esemplastic* for Electronic Media (1964); *Kansoku* for Voices (1965); *Projection* for Cello and Piano (1967); *Projection* for several Kotos and Orch. (1967); *Projection* for Electric Guitars (1968); *Projection* for String Quartet (1970); *Triplicity* for Double Bass (1970); *Questions* for Chorus (1971); *On the Keyboard* for Piano (1971); *Interposiplaytion I* for Flute, Piano, and Percussion (1972) and *II* for Flute, Harp, and Percussion (1973); *Chronoplastic* for Orch. (1972; Tokyo, Nov. 15, 1972); *Territory* for Marimba, Flute, Clarinet, Percussion, and Double Bass (1974); *Time of Orchestral Time* for Orch. (1976).

Yudina, Maria, eminent Russian pianist and pedagogue; b. Nevel, near Vitebsk, Sept. 9, 1899; d. Moscow, Nov. 19, 1970. She took piano lessons in Vitebsk with Frieda Teitelbaum-Levinson, a pupil of Anton Rubinstein. Then she enrolled at the Petrograd Cons., where studied piano with Anna Essipoff, Vladimir Drozdov, and Leonid Nikolayev; music theory with Maximilian Steinberg and J. Wihtol; and score reading with N. Tcherepnin and Emil Cooper. In 1921 she joined the piano faculty of the Petrograd Cons., holding this position until 1930. In 1932–34 she taught at the Cons. of Tiflis, Georgia. From 1936–51 she was a prof. at the Moscow Cons., and from 1944–60 taught piano and chamber music performance at the Gnessin Inst. in Moscow. Among her students was Andrei Balanchivadze (brother of George Balanchine). Yudina began her career as a pianist in 1921; gave her last concert in Moscow on May 18, 1969. She also was a guest artist in East Germany (1950) and in Poland (1954). She further publ. memoirs and reminiscences of famous composers she had met in Russia. Yudina enjoyed great renown as an intellectual musician capable of presenting the works she performed with a grand line, both didactic and inspired. But rather than accepting the traditional interpretation of classical music, she introduced a strong personal element differing from accepted norms, so that her performances of works by Bach, Mozart, Beethoven, and Brahms were revelations to some listeners, and abominations to the old school of pianism. Yudina was also an ardent champion of modern music, placing on her programs compositions by such masters of new techniques as Stravinsky, Schoenberg, Berg, Webern, and Bartók at a time when their works were not acceptable in Russia. She also played piano pieces by Soviet composers, particularly Prokofiev and Shostakovich. She gave numerous concerts of chamber music.

BIBLIOGRAPHY: *Maria Yudina: Articles, Reminiscences, Materials,* an anthology (Moscow, 1978).

Yun, Isang, important Korean composer; b. Tongyong, Sept. 17, 1917. He studied Western music in Korea (1935–37) and in Japan (1941–43). After the war he taught music in South Korean schools; in 1956 he went to Berlin, where he took lessons in composition with Boris Blacher and Josef Rufer at the Berlin Hochschule für Musik. He settled permanently in Berlin, where he produced several successful theatrical works, marked by a fine expressionistic and coloristic quality, and written in an idiom of euphonious dissonance. His career was dramatically interrupted when, on June 17, 1967, he and his wife were brutally abducted from West Berlin by secret police agents of South Korea, and forced to board a plane for Seoul, where they were brought to trial for sedition; he was sentenced to life imprisonment; his wife was given 3 years in jail. This act of lawlessness perpetrated on the territory of another country prompted an indignant protest by the government of West Germany, which threatened to cut off its substantial economic aid to South Korea; 23 celebrated musicians, including Igor Stravinsky, issued a vigorous letter of protest. As a result of this moral and material pressure, South Korea released Yun and his wife after nearly 2 years of detention, and they returned to Germany. In 1970 he was appointed a prof. at the Hochschule für Musik in Berlin.

WORKS: Operas: *Der Traum des Liu-Tung* (Berlin, Sept. 25, 1965); *Die Witwe des Schmetterlings* (completed by him in his Seoul prison cell and produced in absentia in Bonn on Dec. 9, 1967; Eng. version as *Butterfly Widow,* Northwestern Univ., Evanston, Ill., Feb. 27, 1970); *Träume* (an amalgam of the previous 2 operas, Nuremberg, Feb. 23, 1969); *Geisterliebe* (1969–70; Kiel, Germany, June 20, 1971); *Sim Tjong* (1971–72; Munich, Aug. 1, 1972); *Symphonische Szene* (1960); *Bara* for Orch. (1960); *Colloides sonores* for String Orch. (1961); *Fluktuationen* for Orch. (1964; Berlin, Feb. 10, 1965); *Réak* for Orch. (Donaueschingen, Oct. 23, 1966); *Dimensionen* for Orch. (Nuremberg, Oct. 22, 1971); *Konzertante Figuren* for Small Orch. (1972; Hamburg, Nov. 30, 1973); *Ouvertüre* (1973–74); Cello Concerto (Royan, March 25, 1976); Concerto for Flute and Small Orch. (1977); Double Concerto for Oboe, Harp, and Small Orch. (1977); *Om mani padme hum,* cycle for Soprano, Baritone, Chorus, and Orch. (1964; Hannover, Jan. 30, 1965); *Namo* for 3 Sopranos and Orch. (Berlin, May 4, 1971); *Der weise Mann,* cantata after P. Salomo, for Baritone, Chorus, and Small Orch. (1977); *Musik* for 7 Instruments (1959); String Quartet No. 3 (1959; Nos. 1 and 2 were withdrawn); *Loyang* for Chamber Ensemble (1962); *Gasa* for Violin and Piano (1963); *Garak* for Flute and Piano (1963); *Nore* for Cello and Piano (1964); *Riul* for Clarinet and Piano (1968); *Images* for Flute, Oboe, Violin, and Cello (1968); *Glissées* for Solo Cello (1970); *Piri* for Solo Oboe (1971); *Gagok* for Guitar, Percussion, and Voice (1972); Trio for Flute, Oboe, and Violin (1972–73); *Memory* for Mezzo-soprano, Baritone, Narrator, and Percussion (1974); *Etüden* for Solo Flute (1974); *Harmonia* for 13 or 16 Winds, Harp, and Percussion (1974); *An der Schwelle,* 2 sonnets for Baritone, Female Chorus, Organ, and Instruments (1975); *Rondell* for Oboe, Clarinet, and Bassoon (1975); Piano Trio (1972–75); *Pièce concertante* for Chamber Ensemble (1976); Duo for Viola and Piano (1976); *Königliches Thema* for Solo Violin (1976); *5 Pieces* for Piano (1959); *Shao Yang Yin* for Harpsichord (1966); *Tuyaux sonores* for Organ (1967); *Fragment* for Organ (1975).

Yuon, Paul. See **Juon, Paul.**

Yurgenson, Peter. See **Jurgenson, Pyotr.**

Yussupov, Prince Nicolas. See **Youssoupoff, Prince Nicolas.**

Yvain, Maurice, French composer of musical comedies; b. Paris, Feb. 12, 1891; d. there, July 28, 1965. Among his successful productions are *Ta bouche* (1922), *Pas sur la bouche* (1925), *Bouche à bouche* (1936), and film scores (*Rien qu'un baiser; J'ai tant d'amour;* etc.). He also produced a ballet, *Blanche neige* (Paris Opéra, Nov. 14, 1951).

Yzac, Heinrich. See **Isaac, Heinrich.**

Z

Zabaleta, Nicanor, Spanish harpist; b. San Sebastian, Jan. 7, 1907. He went to Paris to study with Marcel Tournier; toured in Europe, South America, and the U.S. He is noted for his efforts to increase the number of works available for the harp, both by bringing to light neglected compositions of old composers, and by prompting modern composers to write music for the harp. In 1958 he made a long European tour as soloist with leading orchs.

Zabalza y Olaso, Don Dámaso, Spanish composer and pianist; b. Irurita, Navarra, Dec. 11, 1833; d. Madrid, Feb. 25, 1894. He studied with Mariano García; in 1858 settled in Madrid as a piano teacher at the National Cons. He publ. a number of piano pieces, many of which became very popular; also piano studies that were used at the Paris Cons., in Italy, and in Spain.

Zabel, Albert Heinrich, German harpist; b. Berlin, Feb. 22, 1834; d. St. Petersburg, Feb. 16, 1910. He studied at the Inst. für Kirchenmusik in Berlin; toured Germany, Russia, England, and America with Gungl's orch. In 1862 he joined the staff of the newly founded St. Petersburg Cons., and held that post until his death. He composed a Harp Concerto and numerous short pieces for the harp (*Elégie fan-*

tastique, Légende, Marguérite au rouet, Am Springbrunnen, Chanson du pêcheur, Warum?, Murmure de cascade, etc.); publ. a harp method (in German, French, and Eng.) and a pamphlet, *A Word to Composers about the Practical Employment of the Harp in the Orchestra* (St. Petersburg, 1899; in Russian and German).

Zabrack, Harold, American pianist and composer; b. St. Louis, June 30, 1928. He studied piano with Rudolph Ganz at the Chicago Musical College (M.M., 1951); composition with Nadia Boulanger at Fontainebleau. In 1955–57 he held a Fulbright grant for travel in Europe; gave concerts in West Germany. Returning to St. Louis, he became active as a concert pianist and teacher; in 1974 he left St. Louis to teach at Westminster Choir College. He publ. *Creative Musical Encounters* (N.Y., 1978).

WORKS: *Piano Variations* (1959); 2 duets for Viola and Oboe (1961); Piano Sonata (1964); Piano Concerto No. 1 (St. Louis, April 5, 1964, composer soloist); Piano Concerto No. 2 (1965); *Symphonic Variations* for Piano and Orch.

Zaccaria, Nicola, Greek bass; b. Piraeus, March 9, 1923. He was educated at the Royal Cons. in Athens; made his debut at the Athens Opera in 1949. In 1953 he sang at La Scala in Milan; also made appearances in Rome, Verona, and Florence; subsequently he had engagements at the Vienna State Opera; in Berlin, Cologne, and London; and at the Edinburgh and Salzburg festivals. In addition to opera, he was successful in solo recitals.

Zacconi, Lodovico, Italian music theorist; b. Pesaro, June 11, 1555; d. Fiorenzuola, near Pesaro, March 23, 1627. He was a pupil of Baccusi and A. Gabrieli in Venice; studied theology in Padua; entered the Order of St. Augustine, and became maestro di cappella at the monastery of his order in Venice; was a tenor in the court chapel at Graz (1585), and at Munich (1590–96); then returned to Venice. His chief work, *Prattica di musica,* in 2 parts (Venice, 1592, 1619), contains treatises on mensural theory and counterpoint, detailed descriptions of contemporary musical instruments, and explanations for executing the ornaments in vocal polyphonic music. He also wrote 4 books of *Canoni musicali,* with comments and solutions (publ. by F. Vatielli, Pesaro, 1905); *Ricercari* for Organ, and 2 collections of examples of counterpoint, are still in MSS. His MS autobiography (written in 1626) is in the library of the Liceo Musicale, Bologna.
BIBLIOGRAPHY: F. Chrysander, "L. Zacconi als Lehrer des Kunstgesanges," *Vierteljahrsschrift für Musikwissenschaft* (vols. 7, 9, 10; 1891–94; with an epitome of the autobiography); F. Vatielli, *Un musicista pesarese nel secolo XVI* (Pesaro, 1904); H. Kretzschmar, "L. Zacconis Leben auf Grund seiner Autobiographie," *Jahrbuch der Musikbibliothek Peters* (1910); F. Vatielli, *Notizie su la vita e le opere di L. Zacconi* (Pesaro, 1912); G. Gruber, *Lodovico Zacconi als Musiktheoretiker* (Habilitationsschrift, Univ. of Vienna, 1972).

Zach, Jan, Czech composer; b. Czellakowitz, Nov. 13, 1699; d. Ellwangen, May 24, 1773. He studied with Czernohorsky in Prague; held the appointment of court Kapellmeister in Mainz (1745–56). He wrote church music; also concertos and orch. works in a style resembling that of the Mannheim School.
BIBLIOGRAPHY: K.M. Komma, *Johann Zach und die tschechischen Musiker im deutschen Umbruch des 18. Jahrhunderts* (Diss., Univ. of Kassel, 1938).

Zach, Max (Wilhelm), Austrian conductor and viola player; b. Lwow, Aug. 31, 1864; d. St. Louis, Feb. 3, 1921. He studied violin with Grün, harmony with Fuchs, and composition with Krenn at the Vienna Cons. In 1886 he emigrated to the U.S., and played first viola in the Boston Symph. Orch.; also was the violist in the Adamowski Quartet; for 10 seasons conducted the Boston Pops (1887–97). In 1907 he was appointed conductor of the St. Louis Symph. Orch., and held this post until his death.

Zacharewitsch, Michael, Russian-English violinist; b. Ostrov, Aug. 26, 1879; d. London, Dec. 20, 1953. He studied with Ševčik in Prague, and later with Ysaÿe in Brussels. He went to London in 1903, and became a British subject in 1915; toured Australia, New Zealand, and South Africa. He wrote *The New Art of Violin Playing* (1934), and composed *Dunkirk* (1945) for Violin and Orch., as well as violin exercises.

Zachau (Zachow), Friedrich Wilhelm, German organist and composer; b. Leipzig (baptized, Nov. 14), 1663; d. Halle, Aug. 7, 1712. He studied with his father, who was a town musician in Leipzig, and learned to play the organ, violin, oboe, and harpsichord. From 1684 to his death he was organist of the Liebfrauenkirche in Halle, where Handel studied with him as a boy. Max Seiffert publ. Zachau's works in Denkmäler Deutscher Tonkunst (vols. 21, 22); organ pieces, chorale settings, etc., were publ. in Breitkopf & Härtel's *Sammlung von Präludien, Fugen . . .* and in *Organum.*

Zádor, Dezsö, Hungarian baritone; b. Horna Krupa, March 8, 1873; d. Berlin, April 24, 1931. He studied in Budapest and Vienna; made his debut as Almaviva in 1898 in Czernowitz; then sang in Elberfeld (1898–1901) and Prague (1901–6); was subsequently a member of the Komische Oper in Berlin (1906–11). In 1911 he joined the Dresden Court Opera, singing there until 1916; then went to the Budapest Opera (1916–19); was later a member of the Berlin Städtische Oper (1920–24). He made guest appearances at Covent Garden in London and in Paris, Milan, and Chicago. During the last years of his career he sang bass roles.

Zádor, Eugen, Hungarian-American composer; b. Bátaszék, Nov. 5, 1894; d. Hollywood, April 4, 1977. (In the U.S. he Americanized his name to **Eugene Zador.**) He studied music with a local teacher; in 1911 enrolled in the Vienna Cons.; studied composition with Richard Heuberger. In 1913 he went to Leipzig, where he took a course with Max Reger; also attended classes in musicology with Hermann Abert and Arnold Schering; continued musicological studies with Fritz Volbach at the Univ. of Münster; in 1921 he obtained his degree of Dr.Phil. with the dissertation *Wesen und Form der symphonischen Dichtung von Liszt bis Strauss.* He settled in Vienna and taught at the Neues Konservatorium there. Following the Anschluss of Austria by the Nazi regime in 1938, Zádor emigrated to the U.S.; he settled in Hollywood, where he became successful and prosperous as an orchestrator of film scores; made some 120 orchestrations in all; at the same time he continued to compose music in every conceivable genre. Zádor was a master of musical sciences, excelling in euphonious modern harmonies, and an expert weaver of contrapuntal voices; his colorful writing for instruments was exemplary. He possessed a special skill in handling Hungarian folk motifs in variation form; in this, he followed the tradition of Liszt. During his European period he composed some fashionable "machine music," as demonstrated with particular effect in his *Sinfonia tecnica.*
WORKS: OPERAS: *Diana* (Budapest, Dec. 22, 1923);

A holtak szigete (The Island of the Dead; Budapest, March 29, 1928); *X-mal Rembrandt* (referring to the multiple copies of Rembrandt's self-portraits; Gera, May 24, 1930); *Asra* (Budapest, Feb. 15, 1936); *Christoph Columbus* (N.Y., Oct. 8, 1939); *Revisor (Inspector General),* after Gogol (1928; revised, reorchestrated, and finally brought to perf. for the first time in Los Angeles, June 11, 1971); *The Virgin and the Fawn* (Los Angeles, Oct. 24, 1964); *The Magic Chair* (Baton Rouge, La., May 14, 1966); *The Scarlet Mill* (Brooklyn, Oct. 26, 1968).

FOR ORCH.: Symph. poem, *Bánk bán* (1918); 4 symphs.: No. 1, *Romantische Symphonie* (1922); No. 2, *Sinfonia tecnica* (Paris, May 26, 1932); No. 3, *Tanzsymphonie* (Budapest, Feb. 8, 1937); No. 4, *Children's Symphony* (1941); *Variations on a Hungarian Folk Song* (Vienna, Feb. 9, 1927; his most successful work of this type); *Rondo* (Vienna, 1934); *Hungarian Caprice* (Budapest, Feb. 1, 1935, followed by numerous perfs. in Europe and America); *Pastorale and Tarantella* (Chicago, Feb. 5, 1942); *Biblical Triptych* (Chicago, Dec. 9, 1943); *Elegie and Dance* (Philadelphia, March 12, 1954); *Divertimento* for Strings (1955); *Fugue-Fantasia* (1958); *Rhapsody* (Los Angeles, Feb. 5, 1961); *Christmas Overture* (1961); *The Remarkable Adventure of Henry Bold* for Narrator and Orch. (Beverly Hills, Calif., Oct. 24, 1963); *Variations on a Merry Theme* (1963; Birmingham, Ala., Jan. 12, 1965); *5 Contrasts for Orchestra* (Philadelphia, Jan. 8, 1965); Trombone Concerto (Rochester, Mich., July 20, 1967); *Rhapsody* for Cimbalom and Orch. (Los Angeles, Nov. 2, 1969); *Studies for Orchestra* (Detroit, Nov. 12, 1970); *Fantasia hungarica* for Double Bass and Orch. (1970); *Hungarian Scherzo* for Orch. (1975).

CHAMBER MUSIC: *Chamber Concerto* for Strings, 2 Horns, and Piano (1930); Piano Quintet (1933); *Suite for Brass* (1961); *Suite for 8 Celli* (1966); *Suite* for Woodwind Quintet (1972); Brass Quintet (1973).

FOR CHORUS: *Cantata tecnica* (1961); *Scherzo domestico* (1961); *Triptych* (1964). He also wrote songs; piano pieces; a ballet, *Maschinenmensch* (1934).

BIBLIOGRAPHY: Donald Tovey, *Essays in Musical Analysis* (vol. VI; London, 1939); Leslie Zador, *Eugene Zador. A Catalogue of His Works* (San Diego, Calif., 1978).

Zadora, Michael, American pianist and composer; b. New York (of Polish parents), June 14, 1882; d. there, June 30, 1946. He studied with his father; then at the Paris Cons. (1899), and later with Leschetizky and Busoni. He taught a master class at the Lwow Cons. (1911–12); then at the Inst. of Musical Art in N.Y. (1913–14). He transcribed for piano several organ and violin works by Buxtehude and Bach; also composed piano pieces, songs, etc.

Zafred, Mario, Italian composer and conductor; b. Trieste, Feb. 21, 1922. He studied with Pizzetti at the Santa Cecilia Academy in Rome; was music critic of *Unità* (1949–56) and *Giustizia* (1956–63); then conducted opera in Trieste and in Rome. In conformity with his political philosophy of Communism, he renounced the modernistic trends of his musical environment and wrote music in an idiom accessible to the common people.

WORKS: Operas: *Amleto* (Rome, 1961) and *Wallenstein* (Rome, 1965); 7 symphs. (1943, 1944, 1949, 1950, 1954, 1958, 1970); *Sinfonia breve* for String Orch. (1955); Flute Concerto (1951); Violin Concerto (1953); Triple Concerto for Violin, Cello, Piano, and Orch. (1954); Harp Concerto (1956); Viola Concerto (1957); Cello Concerto (1958); Piano Concerto (1960); Concerto for 2 Pianos and Orch. (1961); *Metamorfosi* for Orch. (1964); Concerto for Strings (1969); String Sextet (1967); Wind Quintet (1952); 4 string quartets (1941, 1947, 1948, 1953); 3 piano trios (1942, 1945, 1954); 4 piano sonatas (1941, 1943, 1950, 1960); numerous choruses and solo songs.

Zagiba, Franz, Slovak music scholar; b. Rosenau, Oct. 20, 1912; d. Vienna, Aug. 12, 1977. He studied music and philology at the Univ. of Vienna; received his Ph.D. in 1937 from the Univ. of Bratislava; joined the staff of the Univ. of Vienna in 1944; in 1972 was named a full prof. there. He publ. *Die Musikdenkmäler der Franziskanerklöster in der Ostslowakei* (Prague, 1940); *Geschichte der slowakischen Musik* (vol. I, Bratislava, 1943; in Czech, with German summary); *Opernführer* (Bratislava, 1947); *Chopin und Wien* (Vienna, 1951); *Tschaikovskij, Leben und Werk* (Zürich, 1953); *Johann L. Bella (1843–1936) und das wiener Musikleben* (Vienna, 1955); *Zur Errichtung einer Chopin-Gedächtnisstätte in Wien* (Vienna, 1970); numerous valuable articles dealing with music in Slovakia and historical developments in Slavic music.

Zagortsev, Vladimir, Soviet composer; b. Kiev, Oct. 27, 1944. He studied composition with Boris Lyatoshinsky and Andrei Shtogarenko at the Kiev Cons. Upon graduation, he joined a group of Soviet avant-garde composers who were active in Kiev and who followed the Western techniques. Zagortsev set for himself the task of organizing the elements of pitch, rhythm, dynamics, and tone color in a total serial procedure, but he never abandoned the ethnic resources of Ukrainian folk songs, which remain the thematic source of many of his works, even those written in an extreme modern style.

WORKS: *Priskazki,* vocal cycle on Ukrainian folk texts (1963); Violin Sonata (1964); String Quartet (1964); *Obyomi (Sizes)* for 5 Instruments (1965); *Gradations* for Chamber Group (1966); *Games* for Chamber Orch. (1967–68); Symph. No. 1 (1968); *Music for 4 Strings* No. 1 (1968); Sonata for Strings, Piano, and Percussion (1969); *Rhythms* for Piano (1969–70); Symph. No. 2 for Soprano, Tenor, and Orch., on Ukrainian folk texts (1976–78); Oboe Sonata (1978); *Music for 4 Strings* No. 2 (1978); *A Day in Pereyaslavl* for Soloists, Chorus, and Orch., on Ukrainian folk texts (1978–79); *In the Children's Room,* cantata on Russian folk texts (1978–79).

Zagwijn, Henri, Dutch composer; b. Nieuwer-Amstel, July 17, 1878; d. The Hague, Oct. 23, 1954. He had no formal education in music, but followed the trends of Impressionism and wrote music in the modern French style. In 1916 he was appointed a teacher at the Rotterdam School of Music; in 1918, founded (with Sem Dresden) the Society of Modern Composers in the Netherlands; he later settled in The Hague. From 1931 he was a teacher at the Rotterdam Cons. He was a follower of Rudolf Steiner's anthroposophic movement, and publ. *De muziek in het licht der anthroposophie* (1925); also publ. a biography of Debussy (The Hague, 1940).

WORKS: *Auferstehung,* overture (1918); 2 *concertantes* for Piano and Orch. (1939, 1946); Harp Concerto (1948); String Sextet (1932); Quintet for Flute, Violin, Viola, Cello, and Harp (1937); Trio for Flute, Oboe, and Clarinet (1944); Trio for Violin, Viola, and Cello (1946); Quintet for Flute, Oboe, Clarinet, Horn, and Bassoon (1948); Trio for Flute, Oboe, and Clarinet (1949); 2 string quartets; several albums of piano pieces; choral works; a number of songs; *Musik zur Eurhythmie* (6 books of piano pieces for eurhythmic exercises).

BIBLIOGRAPHY: W. Paap, "Henri Zagwijn," *Mens en Melodie* (Sept. 1948; Nov. 1954).

Zahn, Johannes, German composer and music scholar; b. Eschenbach, Aug. 1, 1817; d. Neudettelsau, Feb. 17, 1895. He was a student of theology at Munich and Berlin; was director of the teachers' seminary at Altdorf (1854–88). In 1875 he founded the periodical *Siona,* devoted to liturgy and church music. He publ. a valuable work, *Die Melodien der deutschen evangelischen Kirchenlieder, aus den Quellen geschöpft und mitgetheilt* (6 vols., 1889–93); *Sonntagsschulbuch für die lutherischen Gemeinden Nordamerikas* (1894); and various other scholarly and didactic works on church music.

Zajc, Ivan. See **Zaytz, Giovanni von.**

Zajic, Florian, Bohemian violinist; b. Unhoscht, May 4, 1853; d. Berlin, May 17, 1926. He studied at the Prague Cons.; then was a theater violinist in various German cities; in 1891 he became a violin teacher at the Stern Cons. in Berlin; gave sonata recitals; publ. 30 études for violin.

Zajiček, Jeronym, Czech-American composer; b. Krásné Březno, Nov. 10, 1926. He studied musicology at the Charles Univ. in Prague (1946–49); then left Czechoslovakia and served as program director of the Czech section of Radio Free Europe in Munich (1950–52). He emigrated to the U.S. in 1952; studied composition with K. Jirák at Roosevelt Univ. in Chicago (1955–58) and later with Paul Pisk (1959–60). In 1964 he was appointed an instructor in composition and conducting at the Chicago City College in the Loop. He became an American citizen in 1957. His music mirrors the lyrical traditions of his Czech heritage.

WORKS: Variations for Piano (1956–57); Piano Trio (1957); Clarinet Sonata (1957); Sinfonietta (1958); Violin Sonata (1961); String Quartet (1962–63); Concertino for Flute and String Orch. (1963–64;

Chicago, Feb. 26, 1967); *Intrada and Processionale* for Brass, Timpani, and Organ (1970); Cello Sonata (1975); songs.

Zak, Yakov, Soviet pianist; b. Odessa, Nov. 20, 1913; d. Moscow, June 28, 1976. He was a student of Neuhaus at the Moscow Cons., graduating in 1935. At the International Competition for pianists in Warsaw in 1937 he received first prize and a special award of a posthumous mask of Chopin for his performance of a Chopin mazurka. He joined the faculty of the Moscow Cons. in 1935; became head of the piano dept. there in 1965. As a concert pianist, Zak toured all over Europe. He played in the U.S. in 1965 and 1967, and was acclaimed for his Soviet-like virtuosity.

Zakharov, Vladimir, Soviet composer of songs; b. Bogodukhov, on the Don Basin, Oct. 18, 1901; d. Moscow, July 13, 1956. He studied at the Rostov Cons.; after 1932, devoted himself mainly to the composition of mass songs, derived from the polyphonic essence of Russian folk music and employing asymmetric meters. Of these songs, *2 Falcons* and *Who can tell?* attained immense popularity in Russia. He received several prizes and was awarded the Order of Lenin.

Zallinger, Meinhard von, Austrian conductor; b. Vienna, Feb. 25, 1897. He studied piano and conducting at the Salzburg Mozarteum; also took music courses at the Univ. of Innsbruck. He conducted at the Mozarteum (1920–22); then was on the staff of the Bavarian State Opera in Munich (1926–29) and the Cologne Opera (1929–35). He returned to the Bavarian State Opera in 1935, conducting there until 1944; was then made Generalmusikdirektor in Duisburg. In 1947 he became director of the Mozarteum Orch.; also held the same office at the Salzburg Landestheater. He was music director in Graz (1949–50) and of the Vienna Volksoper (1950–53) and the Komische Oper in East Berlin (1953–56). He served again as a conductor at the Bavarian State Opera (1956–73); was concurrently director of the summer academy at the Mozarteum (1956–68).

Zamara, Antonio, Italian harpist; b. Milan, June 13, 1829; d. Hietzing, near Vienna, Nov. 11, 1901. He studied with Sechter in Vienna; for nearly 50 years was first harpist at the Kärnthnertor Theater; for many years also was a prof. at the Vienna Cons. He publ. *Harfenschule* (4 books); a number of pieces for Harp Solo (*Barcarolle, La Rêveuse, Chant du berceau, L'Absence, Marche des Croates,* etc.); also pieces for Harp and Cello (*Elégie, L'addio,* etc.) and transcriptions of operatic airs for 2 harps.

Zamboni, Luigi, noted Italian bass; b. Bologna, 1767; d. Florence, Feb. 28, 1837. He made his debut in 1791 in Ravenna in *Fanatico in Berlin* by Cimarosa; then sang throughout Italy, establishing himself as one of the finest interpreters of buffo roles of his time; 1816 he created the role of Figaro in Rossini's *Il Barbiere di Siviglia*. He retired from the stage in 1825.

Zampieri, Giusto, Italian writer on music; b. Trieste, Nov. 6, 1879; d. Pavia, June 8, 1950. He was a prof. of music history at the Cons. of Milan (1908–23), then at the Univ. of Pavia. He publ. *Il pianoforte* (Milan, 1912), *F. Gafurio* (Pavia, 1925), and other books.

Zandonai, Riccardo, Italian composer; b. Sacco, Trentino, May 30, 1883; d. Pesaro, June 5, 1944. He was a pupil of Gianferrari at Rovereto (1893–98); then studied with Mascagni at the Liceo Rossini in Pesaro. He graduated in 1902; for his final examination he composed a symph. poem for Solo Voices, Chorus, and Orch., *Il ritorno di Odisseo*. He then turned to opera, which remained his favored genre throughout his career. His first opera was *Il grillo del focolare*, based on *The Cricket on the Hearth* of Dickens and produced in Turin on Nov. 28, 1908, with excellent success. With his next opera, *Conchita*, after the novel *La Femme et le pantin* by Pierre Louÿs (Milan, Oct. 14, 1911), he established himself as an important Italian composer; the title role was created by the soprano **Tarquinia Tarquini,** whom Zandonai married in 1917. *Conchita* received its American premiere in San Francisco on Sept. 28, 1912; as *La Femme et le pantin* it was given at the Opéra-Comique in Paris on March 11, 1929. Zandonai's reputation was enhanced by subsequent works, notably *Francesca da Rimini*, after Gabriele d'Annunzio (Turin, Feb. 19, 1914; Metropolitan Opera, N.Y., Dec. 22, 1916), but a previous opera, *Melenis* (Milan, Nov. 13, 1912), was unsuccessful. During World War I Zandonai participated in the political agitation for the return of former Italian provinces; he wrote a student hymn calling for the redemption of Trieste (1915). His other operas were: *La via della finestra* (Pesaro, July 27, 1919; revised version, Trieste, Jan. 18, 1923); *Giulietta e Romeo* (Rome, Feb. 14, 1922); *I Cavalieri di Ekebù* (Milan, March 7, 1925); *Giuliano* (Naples, Feb. 4, 1928); *Una partita* (Milan, Jan. 19, 1933); and *La farsa amorosa*, after Alarcón's *El sombrero de tres picos* (Rome, Feb. 22, 1933). He further wrote the symph. poems *Primavera in Val di Sole* (1908), *Patria lontana* (1918), *Fra gli alberghi delle Dolomiti* (1932); *Concerto romantico* for Violin and Orch. (1921); *Concerto andaloso* for Cello and Small Orch. (1937); *Rapsodia trentina* for Orch. (1937); *Messa da Requiem;* some chamber music. In 1939 he was appointed director of the Liceo Rossini in Pesaro, remaining there for the rest of his life.

BIBLIOGRAPHY: "Bibliografia delle opere musicali di Riccardo Zandonai," *Bollettino Bibliografico Musicale* (Dec. 1931); V. Bonajuti Tarquini, *Riccardo Zandonai, nel ricordo dei suoi intimi* (Milan, 1951).

Zandt, Marie Van. See **Van Zandt, Marie.**

Zanella, Amilcare, Italian composer; b. Monticelli d'Ongina, Piacenza, Sept. 26, 1873; d. Pesaro, Jan. 9, 1949. He studied with Andreotti in Cremona, then with Bottesini at the Parma Cons., graduating in 1891. In 1892 he went to South America as a pianist and opera conductor; returning to Italy in 1901, he organized his own orch., giving symph. concerts in the principal Italian cities and introducing his own works. He then was director of the Parma Cons. (1903–5); succeeded Mascagni as director of the Liceo Rossini in Pesaro in 1905, and held this post until 1939, when he was succeeded by Zandonai.

WORKS: Operas: *Aura* (Pesaro, Aug. 27, 1910); *La Sulamita* (Piacenza, Feb. 11, 1926); *Il Revisore*, after Gogol (Trieste, Feb. 20, 1940); Symph.; 2 symph. poems *Fede* and *Vita and Festa campestre; Danza paesana* for Orch.; *Fantasia e Fugato* for Piano and Orch.; Nonet for Strings, Woodwind Instruments, and Piano; Piano Trio; a number of piano pieces (*Due leggende, Passero solitario, Canto d'anima, Ansia,* etc.).

BIBLIOGRAPHY: *Amilcare Zanella, artista, uomo, educatore*, a compendium (Ferrara, 1932); A. Dioli and M.F. Nobili, *La vita e l'arte di Amilcare Zanella* (Bergamo, 1941).

Zanelli (original name, **Morales**), **Renato,** Chilean tenor; b. Valparaiso, April 1, 1892; d. Santiago, March 25, 1935. He studied in Santiago; made his debut as a baritone there as Valentine in 1916. On Nov. 19, 1919, he appeared for the first time with the Metropolitan Opera in N.Y. as Amonasro; he remained on its roster until 1923; then went to Milan, where he resumed vocal studies; made his debut as a tenor in the role of Raoul at the Teatro San Carlo in Naples in 1924; subsequently appeared in Rome, in London (Covent Garden, 1928–30), at La Scala in Milan (1920–32), and at the Teatro Colón in Buenos Aires.

Zanettini, Antonio. See **Gianettini, Antonio.**

Zang, Johann Heinrich, German organist and composer; b. Zella St. Blasii, near Gotha, April 13, 1733; d. Würzburg, Aug. 18, 1811. As a youth he was trained by Bach in Leipzig (for 2 years); composed and engraved *Die singende Muse am Main* (1776); wrote *Kunst- und Handwerksbuch*, Part II of which is *Der vollkommene Orgelmacher, oder Lehre von der Orgel und Windprobe* (1804). In MS are church cantatas; organ trios; piano sonatas; etc.

Zanger (Zangerus), Johannes, Austrian theologian and musician; b. Innsbruck, 1517; d. Braunschweig, April 5, 1587. He was a pupil of Heinrich Finck, Arnold von Bruck, and others in Vienna; then studied law in Prague and in Cologne. In 1542 he joined the Protestant Church, and occupied positions as cantor, rector, and pastor in Braunschweig. He publ. *Musicae practicae praecepta* (Leipzig, 1554).

BIBLIOGRAPHY: H.J. Moser, "Johannes Zanger's *Praecepta*," *Musica Disciplina*, 5 (1951).

Zangius, Nikolaus, German organist and composer; b. c.1570; d. Berlin, c.1618. He was a chamber musician in Braunschweig (1597); went to Danzig as deputy Kapellmeister (1599) and soon became Kapellmeister at the Marienkirche; left at the outbreak of the plague in 1602; was active in the imperial court in Prague until 1605; returned to Danzig in 1607, but soon went to Stettin; finally returned to his court post in Prague in 1610. He was active in Berlin as Kapellmeister to the Elector of Brandenburg from 1612. He composed a cappella works: choruses, motets, and a number of quodlibets. His *Cantiones sacrae* and 3-part German songs are reprinted in Denkmäler der Tonkunst in Österreich, 87.

BIBLIOGRAPHY: Joh. Sachs, *N. Zangius weltliche Lieder* (Diss., Univ. of Vienna, 1934).

Zanotelli, Hans, German conductor of Italian descent; b. Wuppertal, Aug. 23, 1927. He received his musical training at the Cologne Cons.; then conducted concerts in Düsseldorf, Bonn, and Hamburg. From 1963 to 1972 he was Generalmusikdirektor of Darmstadt. In 1972 he assumed the post of chief conductor of the Stuttgart Phil.

Zanten, Cornelia Van. See **Van Zanten, Cornelia.**

Zappa, Frank, seeded American rock artist; b. Baltimore, Dec. 21, 1940, of Italian descent (Zappa means "hoe" in Italian). His full name was **Francis Vincent Zappa.** The family moved to California. From his school days he played guitar and organized groups with weird names such as The Omens and Captain Glasspack and His Magic Mufflers. In 1960 he composed the sound track for the film *The World's Greatest Sinner,* and in 1963 he wrote another sound track, *Run Home Slow.* In 1965 he joined the rhythm-and-blues band The Soul Giants; he soon took it under his own aegis and thought up for it the surrealist logo *The Mothers of Invention.* His recording of it, and another album, *Freak Out!,* became underground hits; along with *We're Only in It for the Money* and *Cruising with Ruben and The Jets,* these works constituted the earliest "concept" albums, touching every nerve in a gradually decivilized California life-style—rebellious, anarchistic, incomprehensible, and yet tantalizing. The band became a mixed-media celebration of total artistic, political, and social opposition to the Establishment, the ingredients of their final album, *Mothermania.* Moving farther afield, Zappa produced a video-movie, *200 Motels,* glorifying itinerant sex activities. He became a cult figure, and as such suffered the penalty of violent adulation. Playing in London in 1971, he was painfully injured when a besotted fan pushed him off the stage. Similar assaults forced Zappa to hire an athletic bodyguard for protection. In 1982 his planned appearance in Palermo, Sicily, the birthplace of his parents, had to be cancelled because the mob rioted in anticipation of the event. He deliberately confronted the most cherished social and emotional sentiments by putting on such songs as *Broken Hearts Are for Assholes,* and his release *Jewish Princess* offended,

mistakenly, the sensitivity of American Jews. His production *Joe's Garage* contained Zappa's favorite scatological materials, and he went on analyzing and ridiculing urinary functions in such numbers as *Why Does It Hurt When I Pee.* He managed to upset the members of his own faith in the number titled *Catholic Girls.* His *Hot Rats,* a jazz-rock release, included the famous *Willie the Pimp,* and exploited the natural revulsion to unclean animals. In 1980 he produced the film *Baby Snakes,* which shocked even the most impervious senses. He declared in an interview that classical music is only "for old ladies and faggots." But he astounded the musical community when he proclaimed his total adoration of the music of Edgar Varèse and gave a lecture on Varèse in N.Y. Somehow, without formal study, he managed to absorb the essence of Varèse's difficult music. This process led Zappa to produce truly astonishing full orch. scores reveling in artful dissonant counterpoint, *Bob in Dacron and Sad Jane* and *Mo' 'n Herb's Vacation,* and the cataclysmic *Penis Dimension* for chorus, soloists, and orch., with a text so anatomically precise that it could not be performed for any English-speaking audience. An accounting of Zappa's scatological and sexological proclivities stands in remarkable contrast to his unimpeachable private life and total abstention from alcohol and narcotic drugs. An unexpected reflection of Zappa's own popularity was the emergence of his adolescent daughter, curiously named Moon Unit, as a voice-over speaker on his hit *Valley Girls,* in which she used the vocabulary of growing womanhood of the San Fernando Valley near Los Angeles, with such locutions as "Grody to the Max" (repellent) and "Barfs Me Out" (disgusting).

BIBLIOGRAPHY: Norbert Obermanns, *Zappalog* (Los Angeles, 1981).

Zarate, Eliodoro Ortíz de, Chilean composer; b. Valparaiso, Dec. 29, 1865; d. Santiago, June 27, 1953. He studied in his native city, and at the Milan Cons., graduating in 1888. Returning to Chile, he brought out his opera (to his own libretto in Italian), *La Fioraia di Lugano* (Santiago, Nov. 1, 1895), which was one of the earliest operas, if not the first, by a Chilean composer to be produced in Santiago.

Zarębski (Zarembski), Juliusz, Polish pianist and composer; b. Zhitomir, Feb. 28, 1854; d. there, Sept. 15, 1885. He studied piano with Dachs at the Vienna Cons., and later enrolled in the St. Petersburg Cons. (1872–74). In 1874 he joined Liszt in Rome; from 1880 to 1885 he taught piano at the Brussels Cons. As a composer, he is known primarily for his effective salon pieces in the manner of Chopin, among them *Suite polonaise, Ballade, Sérénade burlesque, Berceuse, A travers Pologne, Sérénade espagnole.*

BIBLIOGRAPHY: T. Strumillo, *Juliusz Zarębski* (Cracow, 1954).

Zaremba, Nicolai, Russian composer and pedagogue; b. near Vitebsk, June 15, 1821; d. St. Petersburg, April 8, 1879. He studied piano and cello; then went to Berlin, where he took lessons with Adolf

Marx. When the St. Petersburg Cons. was founded in 1862, he was engaged as a teacher of composition; from 1867 to 1871 he was its director. He was the first to teach music theory using Russian terminology rather than the prevalent German nomenclature; among his students was Tchaikovsky. In his musical views Zaremba was extremely conservative; he was also apt to connect harmony rules with religious notions (such as piety being expressed by major keys, and sin and corruption by minor keys). Mussorgsky ridiculed Zaremba in his satirical piece *Rayok,* in which he illustrated Zaremba's Classical tastes by a mock quotation from Handel.

Zarinš, Margeris, Latvian composer; b. Jaunpiebalga, May 24, 1910. He studied composition in Riga with Wihtol; also took lessons in piano and organ. From 1956 to 1968 he was secretary-general of the Union of Latvian Composers. In his works he stylizes the elements of Latvian folk songs; he is particularly successful in his operas on contemporary subjects, often with a satirical tilt. In his *Opera uz lankuma* (*Opera in the Town Square;* 1970), he attempted to revive the early Soviet attempts to bring theatrical spectacles into the streets.
WORKS: Operas: *Kungs un spēlmanitis* (*The King and the Little Musician;* 1939); *Uz jauno krastu* (*To New Shores;* 1955); *Zaļas dzirnavas* (*The Green Mill;* 1958); *Nabaqu opera* (*Beggar's Opera;* 1964); *Sveta Mauricija brinumdarbs* (*Miracle of St. Mauritius;* 1964); *Opera uz lankuma* (*Opera in the Town Square;* 1970); oratorios: *Valmieras varoni* (*The Heroes of Valmiera;* 1950); *Mahagoni* (*Mahagonny*), a propaganda work denouncing the Western colonial policies in Africa (1965); Piano Concerto (1937); *Greek Vases* for Piano and Orch. (1946; revised 1960); numerous choruses based on Latvian folk songs; film music.
BIBLIOGRAPHY: L. Krasinska, *Margeris Zarinš* (Riga, 1960).

Zarlino, Gioseffo (Zarlinus Clodiensis), important Italian music theorist and composer; b. Chioggia, probably in Jan. 1517; d. Venice, Feb. 4, 1590. He entered the Franciscan order in 1539, and in 1541 went to Venice, where he became a pupil of Willaert. In 1565 he succeeded his fellow pupil Cipriano de Rore as maestro di cappella at San Marco, holding this position until his death; also held the office of chaplain at San Severo. He was greatly esteemed not only as a teacher but also as a composer; indeed, Foscarini describes him as "the famous regenerator of music in all Italy." Most of Zarlino's MSS are lost; his extant works comprise *21 modulationes 6 vocum* (Venice, 1566; ed. by Zarlino's pupil Usberti), *3 lectiones pro mortuis* (part of a collection of motets *a* 4 by Cipriano de Rore and others; publ. by Scotto, Venice, 1563), and a Mass (MS in the library of the Liceo Filarmonico in Bologna). Two motets *a* 5 were publ. by L. Torchi in *L'arte musicale in Italia* (vol. I).
Zarlino's lasting significance lies in his theoretical works, particularly the *Istituzioni armoniche* (in 4 sections; Venice, 1558; republ. 1562, 1573), in

which Zarlino treats the major and minor thirds as inversions within a fifth, and consequently, the major and minor triads as mutual mirror reflections of component intervals, thus anticipating the modern dualism of Rameau, Tartini, Hauptmann, and Riemann; he also gives lucid and practical demonstrations of double counterpoint and canon, illustrated by numerous musical examples; while adhering to the system of 12 modes, he places the Ionian rather than the Dorian mode at the head of the list, thus pointing toward the emergence of the major scale as the preponderant mode; he gives 10 rules for proper syllabification of the text in musical settings; suggests equal temperament for the tuning of the lute. In 1571 he publ. *Dimostrationi armoniche,* in the form of 5 dialogues between Willaert and his disciples and friends. Zarlino's theories were attacked, with a violence uncommon even for the polemical spirit of the age, by Vincenzo Galilei, one of his former pupils, in *Dialogo della musica antica e della moderna* (Florence, 1581) and *Discorso intorno alle opere di Gioseffo Zarlino* (Florence, 1589). In reply to the first of Galilei's books, Zarlino publ. *Sopplimenti musicali* (Venice, 1588). Collected works of Zarlino (4 vols.), publ. in Venice in 1589, included, in addition to his former books, a theological tract, *Trattato della pazienza.* Books III and IV of the *Istituzioni armoniche* are publ. in Eng. trans. in O. Strunk, *Source Readings in Music History* (N.Y., 1950).
BIBLIOGRAPHY: G. Ravagnan, *Elogio di G. Zarlino* (Venice, 1819); G. Caffi, *Narrazione della vita e delle opere del prete Gioseffo Zarlino* (Venice, 1836); G. Caffi, *Storia della musica sacra nella già cappella di San Marco in Venezia* (Venice, 1854; vol. I); H. Riemann, *Geschichte der Musiktheorie* (2nd ed., 1921); V. Bellenio, *Gioseffo Zarlino* (Chioggia, 1884); F. Högler, "Bemerkungen zu Zarlinos Theorie," *Zeitschrift für Musikwissenschaft,* 9 (1926); H. Zenck, "Zarlinos *Istituzioni armoniche,*"ibid., 13 (1930); G. Reese, *Music in the Renaissance* (N.Y., 1954); R. Flury, *Gioseffo Zarlino als Komponist* (Winterthur, 1962).

Zarotus, Antonio, Italian music printer, active in Milan. He printed a *Missale Romanum* dated April 26, 1476, in which he used for the first time movable type for the music (the type is in Gothic style). This incunabulum was publ. 6 months earlier than the Missale of Ulrich Han, at one time considered the earliest specimen of music printed from movable type.
BIBLIOGRAPHY: Otto Kinkeldey, "Music and Music Printing in Incunabula," *Papers of the Bibliographic Society of America* (1932).

Zarzycki, Alexander, Polish pianist and composer; b. Lwow, Feb. 21, 1834; d. Warsaw, Nov. 1, 1895. He studied in Lwow and later in Paris (1856–61) with Reber; gave brilliant concerts in France, Germany, Austria, and Poland; was director of the Warsaw Music Society (1871–75). From 1879 to 1888 he was director of the Warsaw Music Inst. He wrote effective piano pieces (nocturnes, mazurkas, waltzes, etc.); also a Piano Concerto; *Grande Polonaise* for Piano, with Orch.; *Introduction et Cracovienne* for Violin and Orch.; *Suite polonaise* for Orch.; *Mazourka* in G major for Violin, with Orch. (very popular); also 2 albums of songs.

Zaslaw, Neal, American musicologist; b. New York, June 28, 1939. He studied at Harvard Univ. (B.A., 1961); then took flute lessons at the Juilliard School of Music (M.S., 1963); subsequently studied musicology with Paul Henry Lang at Columbia Univ. (M.A., 1965; Ph.D., 1970, with the dissertation *Materials for the Life and Works of Jean-Marie Leclair l'Aîné*). He taught at City College of the City Univ. of N.Y. (1968–70); in 1970 he joined the faculty of Cornell Univ. He was editor in chief of *Current Musicology* (1967–70); publ. the vol. *Edward A. MacDowell* (N.Y., 1964). iv. He was editor in chief of *Current Musicology* (1967–70); publ. the vol. *Edward A. MacDowell* (N.Y., 1964).

Zaslawsky, Georges, Russian-American conductor; b. Kiev, Feb. 15, 1880; d. New York, Jan. 28, 1953. He studied violin with Leopold Auer, and composition with Liadov, at the St. Petersburg Cons. In 1922 he emigrated to the U.S.; made his debut as a conductor at a special concert in Carnegie Hall, N.Y., on April 12, 1926; in 1927 founded and conducted a Beethoven Symph. Orch. in N.Y., which was discontinued after a few concerts. He also conducted in South America.

Zaun, Fritz, German conductor; b. Cologne, June 19, 1893; d. Düsseldorf, Jan. 17, 1966. He was educated at the Cologne Cons. and the univs. of Bonn and Cologne; was conductor at the Düren Stadttheater (1919–20); then conducted the Volksorchester in Cologne (1920–26) and served as director of the Volksoper there (1921–22). In 1924 he became director of the Opera in Mönchen-Gladbach; then in Zürich in 1927. In 1929 he was appointed Generalmusikdirektor of the Cologne Opera; in 1939 he became chief conductor of the Städtischen Orchester in Berlin. After World War II he conducted in Zagreb; in 1951 became director of the Graz Opera, and in 1956 first conductor of the Deutsche Oper am Rhein in Düsseldorf, continuing as a regular conductor there from 1960.

Zavertal, Ladislao, Italian bandmaster (of Bohemian extraction); b. Milan, Sept. 29, 1849; d. Cadenabbia, Jan. 29, 1942. He was the son of the clarinetist **Wenceslas Hugo Zavertal** (1821–99). After studying at home, he went to Treviso (where he produced an opera) and then to Milan (1869). In 1871 he went to Glasgow, where he conducted various orch. groups; in 1881 he became bandmaster of the Royal Artillery Band at Woolwich; from 1895 to 1905 he conducted Sunday band concerts at Albert Hall in London, which enjoyed considerable popularity. He returned to Italy in 1906. He was a voluminous composer; wrote operas, symphs., and band pieces; received various honors from the governments of England, Italy, Greece, Serbia, and Turkey.

BIBLIOGRAPHY: A. Faraone, *Il Commendatore Ladislao Zavertal* (Treviso, 1929); H.G. Farmer, *Ladislao Zavertal: His Life and Work* (London, 1949); idem, *Cavaliere Zavertal and the Royal Artillery Band* (London, 1951).

Zay, (William) Henri, American singing teacher and composer; b. Findlay, Ohio, March 20, 1869; d. New York, Nov. 2, 1927. He studied at the Cleveland Cons. and at the Royal Academy of Music in London. Returning to the U.S., he established himself as a voice specialist, gradually evolving and perfecting his own method, publ. as *Practical Psychology of Voice and of Life* (N.Y., 1917; reprinted 1945); composed *Cosmic Conception* for Orch., and several song cycles.

Zaytz, Giovanni von (real name, **Ivan Zajc**), Croatian composer; b. Fiume, Aug. 3, 1831; d. Zagreb, Dec. 16, 1914. He was trained by his father, a bandmaster in the Austrian army; then in Milan by Lauro Rossi. Returning to Fiume, he conducted the municipal band; then was a theater conductor in Vienna (1862–70). Upon entering professional life, he changed his name to Giovanni von Zaytz. In 1870 he settled in Zagreb; was conductor of the Zagreb Opera (1870–89) and director of the Cons. there (until 1908). He composed about 1,200 works of all descriptions (among them 20 operas), and was the author of the first Croatian national opera, *Nikola Šubrič Zrinski* (Zagreb, Nov. 4, 1876). He also wrote several Italian operas, of which *Amelia, ossia Il Bandito* (Fiume, April 14, 1860) enjoyed considerable popularity. Other operas and operettas (all produced by him in Vienna) are: *Mannschaft an Bord* (Dec. 15, 1863); *Fitzliputzli* (Nov. 5, 1864); *Die Lazzaroni vom Stanzel* (May 4, 1865); *Die Hexe von Boissy* (April 24, 1866); *Nachtschwärmer* (Nov. 10, 1866); *Das Rendezvous in der Schweiz* (April 3, 1867); *Das Gaugericht* (Sept. 14, 1867); *Nach Mekka* (Jan. 11, 1868); *Somnambula* (Jan. 25, 1868); *Schützen von Einst und Jetzt* (July 25, 1868); *Meister Puff* (May 22, 1869); *Der gefangene Amor* (Sept. 12, 1874). In addition, he wrote incidental music for 23 plays; 60 cantatas; 250 choral works, sacred and secular; 40 overtures; symph. poems; more than 200 songs.

Zbar, Michel, French composer; b. Clermont-Ferrand, April 24, 1942. He studied at the Paris Cons. with Olivier Messiaen and Tony Aubin, graduating in 1967; also worked with Pierre Schaeffer at the Groupe de Recherches Musicales of Paris Radio. In 1968 he won the competition for the Prix de Rome with his *Tragédie d'Hamlet*. Other works include *Tropismes* for Violin and Orch. (1969); *Incandescences* for Soprano, Speaker, and Orch. (1970); *Swingle Novae* for the Swingle Singers, Chorus, and 5 Instrumental Groups (1970); *Apex II* for Chamber Orch. (1971); *Negative—Positive* for Ondes Martenot, Electric Guitar, and Percussion (Orléans, France, March 23, 1973).

Zbinden, Julien-François, Swiss composer; b. Rolle, Nov. 11, 1917. He studied at the Cons. of Lausanne; then was a pupil of Marie Panthès (piano) and René Gerber (composition). After playing in jazz orchs., he became a pianist and assistant director of Radio Lausanne in 1947; in 1956 he joined the Service Musical of Radio-Television Suisse Romande; in 1973 he became president of the Assoc. of Swiss Musicians.

WORKS: Opera, *Fait divers* (1960); farce-ballet, *La Pantoufle,* for 5 Soloists and 2 Pianos (1958); 4 "pièces radiophoniques": *Microbus 666* (1955), *Le Petit Garçon de l'autobus* (1958), *Esperanto* (1961), and *Ethiopiques* (1971–72); Piano Concerto (1944); Concertino for Trumpet, String, and Timpani (1946); *Divertissement* for Double Bass and Orch. (1948); *Concerto da camera* for Piano and String Orch. (1950–51); 2 symphs. (1953, 1951–57); *Fantaisie* for Flute and Chamber Orch. (1954); *Suite française* for String Orch. (1954); *Rhapsodie* for Violin and Orch. (1956); *Jazzific 59–16* for Jazz Group and Strings (1958); *Ballade* for Bassoon and Orch. (1961); *Concerto breve* for Cello and Orch. (1962); Violin Concerto (1962–64); *Orchalau-Concerto* for Orch. (1962); *Lémanic 70,* overture (1970); Concerto for Orch. (1977); *Terra Dei,* oratorio (1966–67); *Monophrases* for Chorus, 2 Pianos, and 6 Percussionists (1970); *Jardins,* suite for Baritone, Soprano, and Orch. (1974); Septet (1947); String Trio (1949); Trio for Trumpet, Horn, and Trombone (1949); Violin Sonata (1950); *3 Pieces* for 4 Horns (1953); *Partita* for Violin and Cello (1954); *Prelude, Fugue and Postlude* for Trumpet and Piano (1963); Capriccio for Flute, English Horn, Bassoon, Violin, and Harpsichord (1968); *Sonate en Trio* for 2 Viole da Gamba and Harpsichord (1969); *Dialogue* for Trumpet and Organ (1972–73); *Introduction and Scherzo-Valse* for Flute and Harp (1974).

BIBLIOGRAPHY: H. Jaccard, *Initiation à la musique contemporaine. Trois compositeurs vaudois: Raffaele d'Alessandro, Constantin Regamey, Julien-François Zbinden* (Lausanne, 1955).

Zdravković, Živojin, Serbian conductor; b. Belgrade, Nov. 24, 1914. He studied music theory at the Belgrade Music Academy and conducting with Talich in Prague. He conducted the Belgrade Radio Orch. (1948–51); was assistant conductor of the Belgrade Phil. (1951–61); in 1961 became its music director. In the 1960s he toured as guest conductor in the Near East, South America, Brazil, and the U.S.

Zeani (original name, **Zahan**), **Virginia,** Rumanian soprano; b. Solovastru, Oct. 21, 1928. She studied in Bucharest and Milan; made her debut as Violetta in Bologna in 1948; then sang in London (1953), in Rome, at La Scala in Milan (1956), and at Covent Garden in London (1959). She made her Metropolitan Opera debut in N.Y. as Violetta on Nov. 12, 1966. In 1980 she joined the faculty of the Indiana Univ. School of Music in Bloomington. She married the bass **Nicola Rossi-Lemeni.**

Zecchi, Adone, Italian composer and conductor; b. Bologna, July 23, 1904. He studied composition with Franco Alfano at the Liceo Musicale in Bologna, graduating in 1926; in 1930 he established the Orch. Bolognese de Camera, and also organized the choral group Corale Euridice, which he led from 1927 to 1943; in 1942 he was appointed to the faculty of the Bologna Cons.; he became its director in 1961. In his compositions he follows the path of Italian neo-Classicism, but applies dodecaphonic formulas in some of his music.

WORKS: *Partita* for Orch. (1933); *Toccata, Ricercare e Finale* for Orch. (1941); *2 astrazioni in forma di fuga* for Small Ensemble (Copenhagen, Festival of the International Society for Contemporary Music, June 2, 1947); *Requiem* for Chorus and Orch. (1946); *Caleidofonia* for Violin, Piano, and Orch. (1963); *Trattenimento musicale* for 11 groups of String Instruments (1969). He publ. a number of manuals on choral conducting, including the reference work *Il coro nella storia e dizionario dei nomi e dei termini* (Bologna, 1960) and *Il direttore di coro* (Milan, 1965). In collaboration with R. Allorto he brought out *Educazione musicale* (Milan, 1962); *Canti natalizi di altri paesi* (Milan, 1965); *Canti natalizi italiani* (Milan, 1965); *Canti della vecchia America* (Milan, 1966); and *Il mondo della musica* (Milan, 1969).

Zecchi, Carlo, Italian pianist and conductor; b. Rome, July 8, 1903. He studied piano with Artur Schnabel and Busoni in Berlin; began his concert career as a pianist at the age of 17, and in 1931 made a tour of the U.S. In 1938 he became interested in conducting and made excellent progress in his new career; appeared as a guest conductor in Vienna, Amsterdam, London, and Leningrad; also made tours as a conductor in the U.S., South America, and Japan.

Zech, Frederick, American pianist and composer; b. Philadelphia, May 10, 1858; d. San Francisco, Oct. 25, 1926. After preliminary training as a pianist in San Francisco he went to Berlin, where he studied at Kullak's Music School; returning to San Francisco, he held classes in advanced piano playing; also tried to conduct symph. concerts there. He composed 4 symphs. and 4 symph. poems (*The Eve of St. Agnes; Lamia; The Raven,* after Poe; *The Wreck of the Hesperus,* after Longfellow; 4 piano concertos; Violin Concerto; Cello Concerto; Piano Quintet; 2 string quartets; Piano Trio; 3 violin sonatas; Cello Sonata; Flute Sonata; 2 clarinet sonatas; also composed the light operas *La Paloma* and *Wa-Kin-Yon, or The Passing of the Red Man.*

Zechlin, Ruth, East German composer and harpsichordist; b. Grosshartmannsdorf, near Freiberg, June 22, 1926. She studied composition with Johann Nepomuk David and Wilhelm Weismann at the Hochschule für Musik in Leipzig, and keyboard playing with Karl Straube, Günther Ramin, and Rudolf Fischer (1943–49). In 1950 she became a lecturer in composition at the Hochschule für Musik in East Berlin; in 1975 she was appointed to the faculty of the Akademie der Künste in East Berlin. She gave concerts as a harpsichord player; concurrently composed music in all genres; her style of composition follows linear principles with a contrapuntal ornamentation in a quasi-impressionistic vein. WORKS: FOR THE STAGE: Opera for actors, *Reineke Fuchs* (1967); *Aphrodite*, scenic chamber music for Alto, Baritone, 2 Pantomimists, and 7 Instrumentalists (1976). FOR ORCH.: *Music for Orchestra* No. 1 (1957); *Music for Chamber Orchestra* (1961); Violin Concerto (1963); Suite for Strings (1963); 3 symphs. (1965, 1966, 1971); *Amor und Psyche* for Harpsichord and Chamber Orch. (1966); 2 chamber symphs. (1967, 1974); *Lineare Meditationen* for String Orch. (1968); *Polyphone Meditationen* for String Orch. (1968); Oboe Concertino (1969); *Thema mit 5 Veränderungen* for Orch. (1969); *Dynamische Studien* for Chamber Ensemble (1971); *Emotionen* (1971); Piano Concerto (1974); Organ Concerto No. 1 (1974); Organ Concerto No. 2 (1975); *Kristalle* for Harpsichord and Strings (1975); *Dionysos und Apollo* for Flute, Strings, and Percussion (1976); *Farbspiele*, after Paul Dessau (1977); *Vita Nova, Briefe* (1978); *Szenen*, homage to Shakespeare, for Flute, Oboe, English Horn, Trumpet, and Strings (1978); *Prager Orgelkonzert* (Prague Spring Festival, 1981); *Situationen* (1980); *Music for Orchestra* No. 2 (1980). CHAMBER MUSIC: Flute Sonatina (1955); Trio for Oboe, Viola, and Cello (1957); 6 string quartets (1959, 1965, 1970, 1971, 1971, 1977); *Gedanken über ein Klavierstück von Prokofiev (Thoughts on a Piano Piece by Prokofiev)* for Piano and 10 Instruments (1967); *Stationen* for Wind Quintet and Keyboard Instruments (1972); *17 Kommentare*, inspired by Van Gogh, for String Quartet (1973); *Exercitien* for Flute and Harpsichord (1973); *Hommage à PHL* for String Quintet and Percussion (1973); *Kammermusik zu Kleists "Marquise von O"* for Oboe, Cello, and Percussion (1974); *Harfentrio* for Flute, Viola, and Harp (1978); *Reflexionen* for 14 Solo Strings (1979). FOR VOICE: *Lidice Kantate* for Baritone, Chorus, and Chamber Orch. (1958); *Wenn der Wacholder blüht*, oratorio (1961); *Ode an die Luft*, to texts by Neruda, for Mezzo-soprano and Orch. (1962); *Keuner Geschichten*, after Brecht, for Voice and Chamber Ensemble (1966); *Gedanken der Liebe* for Chorus and Orch. (1970); *Canzoni alla Notte*, after Quasimodo, for Baritone and Orch. (1974; Leipzig, Oct. 14, 1976); *Das Hohelied* for Tenor and Orch. (1979); choruses; songs. FOR PIANO: *Suite* (1953); Sonatina (1955); *Kleine Klaviermusik* (1959); *4 Inventionen* (1968); *Konstellationen* (1974); *Stücke für Palucca* (1976). FOR HARPSICHORD: *Toccata und Passacaglia* (1969); *Kontrapunkte* (1970); *Epitaph* (1973). FOR ORGAN: *5 Visionen* (1969); *Wandlungen* (1972); *Spektrum* (1973); *Orpheus* (1975). BIBLIOGRAPHY: Ursula Stürzbecher, *Komponisten in der DDR: 17 Gespräche* (Hildesheim, 1979).

Zeckwer, Camille, American pianist and composer; b. Philadelphia, June 26, 1875; d. Southampton, N.Y., Aug. 7, 1924. He was educated by his father, **Richard Zeckwer,** and had the good fortune to take composition lessons in N.Y. with Dvořák during the

latter's stay in America; then went to Berlin in quest of more musical education and studied with Philipp Scharwenka; returning to Philadelphia, he began teaching young Americans what he was taught by old Germans. Like his father, he composed a number of unnecessary orch. and other pieces; his symph. poem *Sohrab and Rustum* was performed in Philadelphia on Feb. 4, 1916; he performed his Piano Concerto thrice with the Philadelphia Orch. (1899, 1904, and 1914); wrote an opera, *Jane and Janetta,* but could not secure a production for it.

Zeckwer, Richard, German-American pianist and composer; b. Stendal, April 30, 1850; d. Philadelphia, Dec. 30, 1922. He studied piano with Moscheles, and theory with Hauptmann, Richter, and Reinecke at the Leipzig Cons. In 1870 he emigrated to the U.S., and settled in Philadelphia as a piano teacher and church organist. He composed a couple of unnecessary concert overtures and a number of perishable songs; publ. a purported guide, *A Scientific Investigation of Piano-Touch* (1902).

Zedda, Alberto, Italian conductor and musicologist; b. Milan, Jan. 2, 1928. He studied conducting at the Milan Cons. with Votto and Giulini; in 1956 made his debut as a conductor in Milan. He subsequently went to the U.S., where he taught at the Cincinnati College of Music (1957–59). Returning to Europe, he conducted at the Deutsche Oper in West Berlin (1961–63); then conducted at the N.Y. City Opera. With Philip Gossett, he served as co-editor of the complete works of Rossini.

Zednik, Heinz, Austrian tenor; b. Vienna, Feb. 21, 1940. He studied voice in Vienna; made his operatic debut in Graz in 1963. He then joined the Vienna State Opera in 1965, and also appeared in Munich, Paris, Nice, and Moscow. In 1976 he sang the parts of Loge and Mime in the centennial production of the *Ring* cycle at the Bayreuth Festival.

Zeerleder, Niklaus, Swiss cleric and theorist; b. Bern, July 5, 1628; d. Kirchberg, July 5, 1691. He was a cantor in Bern, and later in Kirchberg. He publ. a singing instruction book, *Musica figuralis oder Kurtze Gründliche Underweysung der Sing Kunst* (Bern, 1658).

Zehnder, Max, Swiss composer; b. Turgi, Canton Aargau, Nov. 17, 1901; d. St. Gallen, July 16, 1972. He studied at the Zürich Cons. and later became active in various capacities as a conductor, singing teacher, and instructor in church music. He wrote much religious music; also composed some instrumental pieces in the traditional vein, including a Concerto for Flute, Oboe, and Strings (1945); String Quartet (1928); String Trio (1933); vocal solos with orch. accompaniment.

Zeidman, Boris, Soviet composer and pedagogue; b. St. Petersburg, Feb. 10, 1908. He studied composition at the Leningrad Cons. with Maximilian Steinberg, graduating in 1931; then taught music in various schools in Russia, Azerbaijan, and Uzbekistan. He performed an important educational service in these regions, formerly deficient in music culture, as teacher and adviser.

WORKS: Operas: *The People's Wrath* (Baku, Dec. 28, 1941); *Son of the Regiment* (Baku, Feb. 23, 1955); *Zainab and Omon* (1958); *The Russians* (1970); ballets: *The Gold Key* (1955); *The Dragon and the Sun* (1964); for Orch.: *Songs of Struggle* (1966); *Days of Spring* (1971); 2 piano concertos (1931, 1935); Violin Concerto (1968); Viola Concerto (1938); Cello Concerto (1948); Bassoon Concerto (1938); several pieces of chamber music; songs; an album of 24 children's pieces for Piano; teaching collections.

Zeinally, Assaf, Azerbaijani composer; b. Derbent, April 5, 1909; d. Baku, Oct. 27, 1932. He studied cello and trumpet at the Baku Cons., graduating in 1931, but died a year later, at the age of 23. He was a highly promising musician; his particular merit was the attempt to compose music in classical forms on folk themes; in this manner he wrote several violin pieces, a Children's Suite for Piano, and many songs to words by native poets.

BIBLIOGRAPHY: Kh. Melikov, *Assaf Zeinally* (Baku, 1956; 2nd ed., 1969).

Zeisl, Eric, Austrian-American composer; b. Vienna, May 18, 1905; d. Los Angeles, Feb. 18, 1959. A son of prosperous parents who owned a coffeehouse, he entered the Vienna State Academy of Music at 14; publ. his first songs at 16. In 1934 he won the Austrian State Prize for his *Requiem concertante*. After the seizure of Austria by the Nazis in 1938, he fled to Paris, and at the outbreak of World War II in 1939, went to the U.S.: in 1941 he settled in Los Angeles; in 1945 he became an American citizen. He taught at the Southern Calif. School of Music; from 1949 until his death he was on the staff at Los Angeles City College. Increasingly conscious in exile of his Jewish heritage, he selected biblical themes for his stage works; death interrupted the composition of his major work, the music drama *Job;* Hebraic cantillation is basic to this period. His style of composition reflects the late Romantic school of Vienna, imbued with poetic melancholy, with relief provided by eruptions of dancing optimism. He was at his best in his song cycles.

WORKS: Children's opera, *Die Fahrt ins Wunderland* (Vienna, 1934); *Leonce und Lena* (1937; Los Angeles, 1952); ballets: *Pierrot in der Flasche* (Vienna Radio, 1935); *Uranium 235* (1946); *Naboth's Vineyard* (1953); *Jacob und Rachel* (1954); for Orch.: *Kleine Symphonie* (Vienna Radio, May 30, 1937); *Passacaglia-Fantasie* (Vienna, Nov. 4, 1937); *November,* suite for Chamber Orch. (N.Y., Jan. 25, 1941); *Cossack Dance* (from the unfinished music drama *Job,* Hollywood, Aug. 18, 1946); *Return of Ulysses,* suite for Chamber Orch. (Chicago, Nov. 17, 1948); *Variations and Fugue on Christmas Carols* (1950); Piano Concerto (1951); *Concerto grosso* for Cello and Orch. (1956); chamber music: Trio for

Flute, Viola, and Harp (1956); Violin Sonata (1950); Viola Sonata (1950); Cello Sonata (1951); vocal works: *Requiem ebraico* (1945); *Mondbilder* for Baritone and Orch. (1928); choruses; the song cycles *Kinderlieder* for Soprano; *6 Lieder* for Baritone.

BIBLIOGRAPHY: Malcolm S. Cole, "Eric Zeisl: The Rediscovery of an Emigré Composer," *Musical Quarterly* (April 1978).

Zeisler, Fannie (Bloomfield), noted pianist; b. Bielitz, Austrian Silesia, July 16, 1863; d. Chicago, Aug. 20, 1927. Her original name was **Blumenfeld**; it was changed to Bloomfield when the family settled in Chicago in 1868. Her first teachers there were Carl Wolfsohn and Bernhard Ziehn. She made her concert debut in Chicago on Feb. 26, 1875; in 1878 she went to Vienna, where she studied with Leschetizky (1878–83). From 1883 until 1893 she played annually in the U.S.; in 1893 she made a tour of Germany and Austria, which established her reputation as one of the best women pianists; other European tours followed in 1894–95, 1898, 1902–3, 1911–12, and the spring of 1914. She then returned to Chicago; made her farewell appearance there on Feb. 25, 1925, in a special concert to mark her golden jubilee. On Oct. 18, 1885, she married Sigmund Zeisler, a Chicago lawyer.

BIBLIOGRAPHY: *Dictionary of American Biography.*

Zeitlin, Zvi, violinist; b. Dubrovnik, Yugoslavia, Feb. 21, 1923. He was educated at the Juilliard School of Music in N.Y.; then began his career as a soloist with leading orchs. in America and Europe; also gave many recitals. In 1967 he joined the faculty of the Eastman School of Music in Rochester, N.Y. He appeared as a soloist in the U.S., South America, Europe, and Israel; was particularly noted for his intelligent performances of modern violin concertos.

Zelenka, Istvan, Hungarian composer; b. Budapest, July 30, 1936. He studied music in Budapest and later took a course with Hanns Jelinek in Vienna; in 1962 he went to Geneva, where he became an acoustical engineer. His works, all in an experimental style, with the application of serial and electronic techniques, include a chamber opera, *Ein Zwischenspiel* (1960); *Conversionen* for 3 String Quartets, Piano, Harmonium, and Harpsichord (1961); *Décors* for Chamber Orch. (1962); *Biais* for Chamber Orch., spatially and serially divided into 3 autochthonic groups (1963); *Hommage à Joan Miró* for Orch. (1965).

Zelenka, Jan Dismas, Bohemian composer; b. Louňovice, Oct. 16, 1679; d. Dresden, Dec. 22, 1745. He received his general education in Prague; in 1710 he joined the court orch. in Dresden, playing the double bass; then studied with Lotti in Italy (1716) and with Fux in Vienna (1717–19). In 1719 he returned to Dresden, where he became assistant to Heinichen. In 1735 he was given the title of Kirchen-Compositeur. He was a prolific composer; wrote much church music, including 21 masses, 3 Requiems, and many motets; 3 Italian oratorios, etc.; a melodrama, *De Sancto Venceslao;* also an interesting overture, *Hypocondria.*

BIBLIOGRAPHY: M. Fürstenau, *Zur Geschichte der Musik und des Theaters am Hofe zu Dresden,* vol. II (Dresden, 1862); N. Schulz, *Jan Dismas Zelenka* (Diss., Univ. of Berlin, 1944).

Zeleński, Wladislaw, Polish composer and pedagogue; b. Grodkowice, near Cracow, July 6, 1837; d. Cracow, Jan. 23, 1921. He studied with Mirecki in Cracow, Krejči in Prague, and Reber in Paris. He returned to Poland in 1871; was a teacher of theory at the Warsaw Cons. (1872–81). In 1881 he organized the Cracow Cons., and remained its director until his death; he also taught piano and theory there. As a pedagogue, he enjoyed a very high reputation; among his pupils were Stojowski, Opienski, and Szopski.

WORKS: Operas: *Konrad Wallenrod* (Lwow, Feb. 26, 1885); *Goplana* (Cracow, July 23, 1896); *Janek* (Lwow, Oct. 4, 1900); *Stara baśń* (Lwow, March 14, 1907); 2 symphs.; 2 overtures; Piano Concerto; 7 cantatas; 2 masses; motets for men's voices; 2 violin sonatas; Piano Trio; 2 string quartets; String Sextet; Piano Quartet; 3 piano sonatas; about 80 songs to Polish words; a number of piano pieces (*Valse-caprice, Humoreske und Gavotte, Grand scherzo de concert, Grosse Polonaise, Moments d'un carnaval,* etc.); 25 preludes for Organ.

BIBLIOGRAPHY: F. Szopski, *W. Zeleński* (Warsaw, 1928); Z. Jachimecki, *Wladislaw Zeleński; Zycie i twórczość, 1837–1921* (Cracow, 1952).

Železný, Lubomír, Czech composer; b. Ostrava, March 16, 1925; d. Prague, Sept. 27, 1979. He studied composition with Karel Janeček at the Prague Cons. (1945–48) and with Bořkovec at the Prague Academy of Musical Arts (1948–50). He worked in the music dept. of Prague Radio before 1951; arranged songs for the Vít Nejedlý Army Artistic Ensemble (1951–56); was chairman of the Union of Czech Composers and Concert Artists (1972–79).

WORKS: 2 *Gavottes* for Orch. (1954); 2 violin concertos (1958–59, 1974–75); 2 symphs.: No. 1 for Large Orch. (1961–62) and No. 2 for Small Orch. (1970); Concerto for Flute, Strings, and Piano (1966); Cello Concerto (1968); *Concertant Music* for Viola, Strings, and Piano (1969); *Festive March* for Orch. (1971); *Brigand Songs* for Tenor and Orch. (1958); Flute Sonata (1943); Trio for Flute, Viola, and Cello (1946); 2 violin sonatas (1948, 1971); Quartet for Flute, Violin, Viola, and Cello (1948); 2 string quartets (1959–60, 1968); Piano Trio (1966); Quintet for 2 Violins, Clarinet, Viola, and Cello (1969); Wind Quintet (1970); choruses; songs.

Zelinka, Jan Evangelista, Czech composer; b. Prague, Jan. 13, 1893; d. there, June 30, 1969. He studied music with his father, an organist, and later with J.B. Foerster, Suk, Novák, and Ostrčil.

WORKS: Operas: *Dceruška hostinského* (*The Tavernkeeper's Little Daughter;* Prague, Feb. 24,

1925); *Devátá louka* (*The 9th Meadow;* Prague, Sept. 19, 1931); *Odchod dona Quijota* (*Departure of Don Quixote;* 1936); *Paličatý švec* (*The Stubborn Cobbler;* Prague, March 28, 1944); *Meluzína* (*The Wailing Wind;* Pilsen, April 15, 1950); radio opera, *Námluvy bez konce* (*Endless Wooing;* Czech Radio, Jan. 27, 1950); *Masopustní noc* (*Shrovetide Night;* 1956); *Lásky žal i smích,* after Goldoni (*Love's Woe and Laughter;* 1958); *Škola pro ženy,* after Molière (*School for Wives;* 1959); *Blouznivé jaro* (*A Fanciful Spring;* 1960); satirical opera, *Dřevěný kůň* (*The Wooden Horse;* 1962–63); ballet pantomime, *Skleněná panna* (*The Glass Doll;* 1927; Prague, July 2, 1928); scenic melodrama, *Srdce na prázdninách* (*Heart on a Fishhook;* 1932; Brno, Jan. 28, 1938); for Orch.: *Overture to a Renaissance Comedy* (1919); *Pariz—Glotton,* overture burlesque (1931); *Weekend,* suite (1939); *Sinfonia rustica* (1956); *A Slovak Summer* (1959); *Musichetta primaverale* for Chamber Orch. (1962); *Satiricon,* suite (1964); numerous cantatas; much chamber music, including 2 nonets: *Capriccio* (1937) and *Cassation* (1943); *Late Summer,* piano trio (1949); *Sonata leggera* for Saxophone and Piano (1962); Piano Sonata (1926); organ pieces; songs and incidental music.

Zeljenka, Ilja, Slovak composer; b. Bratislava, Dec. 21, 1932. He studied composition with Cikker, piano with Macudzinski, and esthetics with Ferenczy at the Bratislava Academy of Music and Dramatic Arts (1951–56). He was dramaturge of the Slovak Phil. in Bratislava (1957–61) and lecturer for Bratislava Radio (1961–68); in 1961 he and Ivan Statdrucker established at Czech Radio in Bratislava the first electronic music studio in Czechoslovakia. After a period of infatuation with hedonistic simplicity laced with permissible discords, he turned toward modern sonorism, including electronics.

WORKS: *Suite* for Small Orch. (1952); 2 piano quintets (1953, 1959); 3 symphs. (1954; for String Orch., 1960; 1975); *Dramatic Overture* (1955); *Bagatelles* for Piano (1955); *Ballad* for Chorus and Orch. (1957); 2 piano sonatas (1958, 1975); *Oswieczym,* melodrama on the tragedy of the infamous Nazi concentration camp, for 2 Narrators, 2 Choruses, and Orch. (1960; Bratislava, April 29, 1965); *7 Compositional Studies* for Chamber Ensemble (1962); ballet, *Cosmos* (1962–63); 2 string quartets (1963, 1976); *Štruktúry* (*Structures*) for Orch. (1964); *Metamorphoses XV,* after Ovid, for Speaker and 9 Instruments (1964); *Polymetric Quartet* for 4 Piano Parts (1965); *Hudba* (*Music*) for Chorus and Orch. (1965); Piano Concerto (1966); *Zaklínadlá* (*Incantations*) for Chorus and Orch. (1967); *Hry* (*Games*), musical dada for 13 Singers playing Bells and Drums (1968); *Musica polymetrica* for 4 String Quartets (1970); *Meditation* for Orch. (1971); Violin Concerto (1974); Piano Trio (1975); *Elegy* for Chamber Orch. (1975).

Zelle, Friedrich, German musicologist; b. Berlin, Jan. 24, 1845; d. there, Sept. 10, 1927. He studied piano with Kullak, composition with Geyer and Bellermann; taught at the Humboldt Akademie in Berlin (1875–92) and later was director of the Berlin

Realschule (1893–1915). He edited Hassler's *Lustgarten* (1887), J.W. Franck's *Choral-kantate* (1890), and Keiser's opera *Jodelet* (1892); also Passions by Sebastiani and Theile for Denkmäler Deutscher Tonkunst, 17.

WRITINGS: *Beiträge zur Geschichte der ältesten deutschen Oper: I, J.W. Franck* (1889), II, *Joh. Theile und N.A. Strungk* (1891), III, *J.Ph. Förtsch* (1893); *Die Singweisen der ältesten evangelischen Lieder* (1899, 1900); *Theorie der Musik* (1880); *Das erste evangelische Choralbuch* [Osiander, 1586] (1913); *Das älteste lutherische Hausgesangbuch* [the so-called *Färbefass-Enchiridion* of 1524] (1903); *Ballettstücke aus Keiserschen Opern* (1890).

Zeller, Karl, Austrian composer of operettas; b. St. Peter-in-der-Au, June 19, 1842; d. Baden, near Vienna, Aug. 17, 1898. He was an official in the Austrian Ministry of Education. Although following music only as an avocation, he became one of the most popular operetta composers of the day, winning extraordinary success with his *Der Vogelhändler* (Vienna, Jan. 10, 1891) and *Der Obersteiger* (Vienna, Jan. 5, 1894). Other successful operettas (all produced in Vienna) were *Joconda* (March 18, 1876), *Die Carbonari* (Nov. 27, 1880), *Der Vagabund* (Oct. 30, 1886), and *Der Kellermeister* (Dec. 21, 1901).

BIBLIOGRAPHY: C.W. Zeller, *Mein Vater Karl Zeller* (St. Pölten, 1942).

Zellner, Julius, Austrian pianist and composer; b. Vienna, May 18, 1832; d. Mürzzuschlag, July 28, 1900. He was first engaged in a mercantile career, but abandoned it for music; became successful in Vienna as a teacher and composer.

WORKS: 2 symphs.; *Melusine,* symph. suite; Piano Concerto; Piano Quartet; 3 piano trios; 2 cello sonatas; 2 violin sonatas; a number of piano pieces (*Adagio und Allegro appassionato; 2 kleine Suiten; 2 Sonatinen;* etc.); piano pieces, 4-hands (*3 deutsche Tänze,* etc.); also a puppet play, *Wasserkaspar.*

Zellner, Leopold Alexander, Austrian organist and music editor; b. Agram, Sept. 23, 1823; d. Vienna, Nov. 24, 1894. He studied with his father, organist of the Agram Cathedral; at 15 became a church organist; taught music in Vienna; founded and edited the *Blätter für Theater, Musik und bildende Kunst* (1855–68). In 1868 he became a prof. of harmony at the Vienna Cons.; wrote a method for the harmonium, and made improvements in its mechanism; publ. instructive pieces; also composed choruses and chamber music; edited violin sonatas by Nardini and Vivaldi with additional piano parts. His lectures were publ. as *Vorträge über Akustik* (2 vols., 1892) and *Vorträge über Orgelbau* (1893).

Zelter, Carl Friedrich, eminent German composer and teacher; b. Berlin, Dec. 11, 1758; d. there, May 15, 1832. The son of a mason, he was brought up in the same trade, but his musical inclinations soon asserted themselves; he studied organ, and at the age of 18 had a cantata of his composition performed in a church; then he became a pupil of C.F.C. Fasch and Kirnberger; was engaged as music director in Rellstab's Liebhaber-Konzerte; in 1786 he brought out a funeral cantata on the death of Frederick the Great; in 1791 he joined the Singverein (later Singakademie) conducted by Fasch, often acting as his deputy, and succeeding him in 1800. He was elected associate ("Assessor") of the Akademie in 1806; became a prof. in 1809. In 1807 he organized a Ripienschule for orch. practice; and in 1809 he founded in Berlin the Liedertafel, a pioneer men's choral society which became famous; similar organizations were subsequently formed throughout Germany, and later in America. Zelter composed about 100 men's choruses for the Liedertafel. In 1822 he founded the Royal Inst. for Church Music, of which he was director until his death (the Inst. was later reorganized as the Akademie für Kirchen- und Schulmusik). Goethe greatly admired Zelter's musical settings of his poems, preferring them to Schubert's and Beethoven's; this predilection led to their friendship, which was reflected in a voluminous correspondence, *Briefwechsel zwischen Goethe und Zelter* (ed. in 6 vols. by F.W. Riemer, Berlin, 1833–34; ed. in 3 vols. by L. Geiger, Leipzig, 1906; ed. in 4 vols. by M. Hecker, Leipzig, 1913; Eng. trans. by A.D. Coleridge, London, 1887). His songs are historically important, since they form a link between old ballad types and the new art of the lied, which found its flowering in Schubert and Schumann. Zelter's settings of Goethe's *König von Thule* and of *Es ist ein Schuss gefallen* became extremely popular. Other songs were publ. in collections of 12 each (1796 and 1801), followed by other albums: *Sämtliche Lieder, Balladen, Romanzen* (1810 et seq.), *Neue Sammlung* (1821), and *6 deutsche Lieder* (1827). New editions were brought out by Jöde (1930), Landshoff (1932), etc.; the cantatas *Johanna Sebus* and *Die Gunst des Augenblicks* were publ. by Müller-Blattau. He publ. a biography of Fasch (Berlin, 1801). Zelter's autobiography was first publ. under the title *C.F. Zelter. Eine Lebensbeschreibung nach autobiographischen Manuscripten,* ed. by W. Rintel; then as *C.F. Zelter. Darstellungen seines Lebens* (Weimar, 1931).

BIBLIOGRAPHY: W. Bornemann, *Die Zeltersche Liedertafel in Berlin* (Berlin, 1851); L. Sieber, *C.F. Zelter und der deutsche Männergesang* (Basel, 1862); H. Kuhlo, *Geschichte der Zelterschen Liedertafel von 1809–1909* (Berlin, 1909); G.R. Kruse, *Zelter* (Leipzig, 1915); J.W. Schottländer, "Zelters Beziehungen zu den Komponisten seiner Zeit," *Zeitschrift für Musikwissenschaft,* 15; H.J. Moser, "Goethes Dichtung in der neueren Musik," *Goethe-Jahrbuch* (1931); J. Müller-Blattau, "Goethe und die Kantate," *Jahrbuch Peters* (1931); G. Schünemann, *C.F. Zelter, der Begründer der preussischen Musikpflege* (Berlin, 1932); G. Wittmann, *Das klavierbegleitete Sololied C.F. Zelters* (Diss., Univ. of Giessen, 1936); G. Schünemann, *C.F. Zelter: Der Mensch und sein Werk* (Berlin, 1937); S. Holtzmann, ed., *C.F. Zelter im Spiegel seines Briefwechsel mit Goethe* (Weimar, 1957); W. Reich, ed., *C.F. Zelter, Selbstdarstellung,* a collection of documents (Zürich, 1958); K.H. Taubert, *Carl Friedrich Zelter. Ein Leben durch das Handwerk für die Musik* (Berlin, 1958).

Zeltser, Mark, talented Russian-born American pianist; b. Kishinev, April 8, 1947. He began piano lessons with his mother as a small child, and at the age of 9 was a soloist with the Kishinev Phil.; then studied with Flier at the Moscow Cons., graduating in 1971; he won a prize at the Marguerite Long-Jacques Thibaud Competition in Paris, and at the Busoni Competition in Italy; in 1976 he emigrated to the U.S., making his home in N.Y.; in 1977 played at the Salzburg Festival; subsequently was soloist in a series of concerts with Karajan and the Berlin Phil.; also played with the N.Y. Phil., Boston Symph., Cleveland Orch., Chicago Symph., and Philadelphia Orch., and made tours in recitals in Asia, Africa, and Australia.

Zemlinsky, Alexander von, important Austrian composer and conductor of partly Jewish parentage (he removed the nobiliary particle "von" in 1918, in accordance with a general rescission of aristocratic name references in republican society); b. Vienna, Oct. 14, 1871; d. Larchmont, N.Y., March 15, 1942. At the Vienna Cons. he studied piano with Door (1887–90) and composition with Krenn, Robert Fuchs, and J.N. Fuchs (1890–92). In 1893 he joined the Vienna Tonkünstlerverein; in 1895 he became connected with the orch. society Polyhymnia, and met Schoenberg, whom he advised on the technical aspects of chamber music; Schoenberg always had the highest regard for Zemlinsky as a composer and lamented the lack of appreciation for Zemlinsky's music. There was also a personal bond between them; in 1901 Schoenberg married Zemlinsky's sister Mathilde. Zemlinsky's first opera, *Sarema,* to a libretto by his own father, was produced in Munich on Oct. 10, 1897; Schoenberg made a Klavierauszug of it. Zemlinsky also entered into contact with Mahler, then conductor and music director of the Vienna court opera, who accepted Zemlinsky's opera *Es war einmal* for performance; Mahler conducted its premiere at the court opera on Jan. 22, 1900, and it became Zemlinsky's most popular production. From 1900–6 Zemlinsky served as conductor of the Karlstheater in Vienna; in 1903 he conducted at the Theater an der Wien; in 1904 he was named chief conductor of the Volksoper; in 1910 he orchestrated and conducted the ballet *Der Schneemann* by the greatly talented 11-year-old *wunderkind* Erich Korngold. About that time, Zemlinsky and Schoenberg organized in Vienna the Union of Creative Musicians, which performed Zemlinsky's tone poem *Seejungfrau.* In 1911 Zemlinsky moved to Prague, where he became conductor at the German Opera, and also taught conducting and composition at the Prague College of Music. In 1927 he moved to Berlin, where he obtained the appointment of assistant conductor at the Kroll Opera, with Otto Klemperer as chief conductor and music director. When the Nazis came to power in Germany in 1933, he returned to Vienna, and also filled engagements as guest conductor in Russia and elsewhere. After the Anschluss of 1938 he emigrated to America, where

he died a few years afterward. As a composer, Zemlinsky followed the post-Romantic trends of Mahler and Richard Strauss. He was greatly admired but his works were seldom performed, despite the efforts of Schoenberg and his associates to revive his music. How strongly he influenced his younger contemporaries is illustrated by the fact that Alban Berg quoted some of Zemlinsky's music from the *Lyric Symphony* in his own *Lyrische Suite.*

WORKS: FOR THE STAGE: Operas: *Sarema* (1894–95; Munich, Oct. 10, 1897); *Es war einmal* (1897–99; Vienna, Jan. 22, 1900); *Der Traumgörge* (1903–6; not produced until Oct. 11, 1980, when it was perf. in Nuremberg); *Kleider machen Leute* (1908; Vienna, Dec. 2, 1910; revised 1921); *Eine florentinische Tragödie,* after Oscar Wilde (1915–16; Stuttgart, Jan. 30, 1917); *Der Zwerg,* after Oscar Wilde's *The Birthday of the Infanta* (1920–21; Cologne, May 28, 1922); *Der Kreidekreis* (1930–32; Zürich, Oct. 14, 1933); *König Kandaules* (1935–36; unfinished; completed only in short score); 5 other unfinished operas: *Malwa,* based on Maxim Gorki's short story (1902/1912–13); *Herrn Arnes Schatz* (1917); *Raphael,* based on Balzac's *La Peau de chagrin* (1918); *Vitalis* (1926); *Circe* (1939–41). Ballets: *Das gläserde Herz,* after Hofmannsthal (1901) and *Cymbeline,* incidental music to Shakespeare's play (1914). Also a "mimodrama," *Ein Lichtstrahl* (1903). FOR ORCH.: Symph. No. 1 (1892); Symph. No. 2 (1897; Vienna, March 5, 1899); *Die Seejungfrau,* tone poem after Andersen (1903); *Lyrische Symphonie* in 7 sections, after Rabindranath Tagore, for Soprano, Baritone, and Orch. (1922–23; Prague, June 4, 1924); Sinfonietta (1934); overture, *Der Ring des Ofterdingen* (1894–95). CHAMBER MUSIC: *Ländliche Tänze* for Piano (1891); Serenade in A (1892); Suite in A for Violin and Piano (1892); String Quartet (1895); Trio for Clarinet (or Viola), Cello, and Piano (1895); *Fantasien über Gedichte von Richard Dehmel* for Piano (1898); 4 string quartets: No. 1 (1895; Vienna, Dec. 2, 1896); No. 2 (1913–15); No. 3 (1924); No. 4 (1936). VOCAL MUSIC: *Waldgespräch* for Soprano, 2 Horns, Harp, and Strings (1895–96); *Der alte Garten* and *Die Reisen,* to poems by Eichendorff, for Voice and Orch. (1895) *Früglingsbegräbnis* for Chorus, Soloists, and Orch. (1896; Vienna, Feb. 11, 1900); *Frühlingsglaube* for Chorus and Strings (1896); 3 Psalms for Chorus and Orch.: No. 83 (1900); No. 23 (1910); No. 13 (1935); *Symphonische Gesänge* for Voice and Orch. (1929); 4 vols. of lieder to texts by Heyse and Liliencron (1894–97); also songs to words by Dehmel, Jacobsen, Bierbaum, Morgenstern, Ammann, Heine, George, Kalidasa, Maeterlinck, Goethe, Beer-Hofmann, Baudelaire, and Hofmannsthal (1898–1913; 1929–36).

BIBLIOGRAPHY: Special issue of *Der Auftakt,* 1 (Prague, 1921); Lawrence A. Ongley, "The Works of Alexander Zemlinsky: A Chronological List," *Notes* (Dec. 1977); Horst Weber, *Alexander Zemlinsky: Eine Studie* (Vienna, 1977); A. Clayton, "Zemlinsky's One-act Operas," *Musical Times* (Aug. 1983).

Zenatello, Giovanni, Italian tenor; b. Verona, Feb. 22, 1876; d. New York, Feb. 11, 1949. He was originally trained as a baritone; made his official debut as such in Belluno in 1898 as Silvio in *Pagliacci;* sang in minor opera companies in Italy; then went to Milan, where he took lessons from Moretti and changed his voice to tenor; made his debut in Naples as Canio in *Pagliacci* in 1901; sang the role of Pinkerton in the first performance of Puccini's *Madama Butterfly* (La Scala, Milan, Feb. 17, 1904); in 1905 he sang at Covent Garden, London; on Nov. 4, 1907, made his American debut in N.Y. as Enzo Grimaldo in Ponchielli's *La Gioconda.* From 1909 to 1912, and again in 1913–14, he was the leading tenor of the Boston Opera Co.; during the season of 1912–13 he sang with the Chicago Opera Co; also traveled with various touring opera companies in South America, Spain, and Russia. He eventually settled in N.Y. as a singing teacher, maintaining a studio with his wife, the contralto **Maria Gay,** whom he married in 1913. Together, they trained many famous singers, among them Lily Pons and Nino Martini. He retired from the stage in 1928.

Zenck, Hermann, German musicologist; b. Karlsruhe, March 19, 1898; d. Freiburg im Breisgau, Dec. 2, 1950. He studied with Ordenstein at the Karlsruhe Cons.; later in Heidelberg (with Kroyer) and in Munich and Leipzig (Dr.Phil., 1924); then became assistant at the Inst. for Musicology in Leipzig, where he also taught at the Cons. In 1932 he joined the faculty of the Univ. of Göttingen; in 1943, went to Freiburg im Breisgau as a prof. at the Univ. there. He edited the periodical *Musik und Volk;* was editor of works by Willaert (2 vols. publ. in 1937; vol. 3, in 1950) and Sixtus Dietrich (1942); also edited the *Megalynodia* of Praetorius (1934); Johann Schultz's *Musikalischer Lustgarten* (1937); Handel's Italian cantatas, etc. He publ. *Marienklage und Osterspiel des Wolfenbüttler Codex* (Hamburg, 1927) and *Sixtus Dietrich* (Leipzig, 1928).

Zender, Hans, German conductor and composer; b. Wiesbaden, Nov. 22, 1936. He was educated at the Freiburg Cons.; then conducted opera there (1959–63); subsequently served as chief conductor of the City Theater in Bonn (1964–68) and as Generalmusikdirektor in Kiel (1969–71). In 1971 he became chief conductor of the Saarland Radio Symph. in Saarbrücken. In 1977 he was engaged as conductor at the Hamburg State Opera. His compositions reveal a humorous quirk of mind, as evidenced by such pieces as *Schachspiel (Chess Game)* for 2 Pianos (1967), the cantata *Der Mann von La Mancha* for Voices and a Moog Synthesizer (1969), and the surrealist choral work *Continuum and Fragments* (1973).

Zenger, Max, German composer and conductor; b. Munich, Feb. 2, 1837; d. there, Nov. 18, 1911. He studied in Munich and Leipzig; in 1860 became a theater conductor in Regensburg; in 1869, music director of the Munich Court Opera; then was court conductor at Karlsruhe (1872–78); conductor of the Munich Oratorio Society (1878–85) and other choral societies in Munich.

WORKS: Operas: *Die Foscari* (Munich, 1863); *Ruy Blas* (Mannheim, 1868); *Wieland der Schmied* (Munich, 1880; revised 1894); *Eros und Psyche* (Munich, 1901); oratorio, *Kain,* after Byron (Munich, 1867; often perf. elsewhere in Germany); secular cantata, *Die Heinzelmännchen;* 2 ballets for King Ludwig II of Bavaria, *Venus und Adonis* and *Les Plaisirs de l'île enchantée* (1881); 2 Gretchen scenes from *Faust* for Soprano and Small Orch.; *2 Konzertstücke* for Mixed Chorus and String Orch.; *Altgriechisches Liederspiel* for Soprano Solo, Chorus, and Orch.; *Die Kraniche des Ibikus,* melodrama with Orch.; *Die deutsche Flotte* for Men's Chorus and Orch.; Symph.; *Tragische Ouvertüre; Adagio concertante* for Cello and Orch.; Piano Trio; Cello Sonata; choruses; piano pieces; songs. He wrote the valuable *Entstehung und Entwicklung der Instrumentalmusik* (Langensalza, 1906) and *Geschichte der Münchener Oper* (posthumous; ed. by Th. Kroyer, 1923).

Zeno, Apostolo, famous Italian opera librettist; b. Venice, Dec. 11, 1668; d. there, Nov. 11, 1750. In 1710 he founded the *Giornale dei Letterati d'Italia;* in 1718 was appointed court poet at Vienna; returned to Venice in 1729. The total number of librettos written by him (some in collaboration with Pietro Pariati) is 71; they were collected and edited by Gasparo Gozzi as *Poesie drammatiche di Apostolo Zeno* (10 vols., Venice, 1744; reprinted in 11 vols. at Orléans, 1785–86). A man of great knowledge and culture, he was also an ardent numismatist; his large collection of coins was exhibited at Vienna in 1955.

BIBLIOGRAPHY: A. Wotquenne, *Libretti d'opéras et d'oratorios italiens du XVIIe siècle* (Brussels, 1901); idem, *Table alphabétique des morceaux mesurés contenus dans les œuvres dramatiques de Zeno, Metastasio et Goldoni* (Leipzig, 1905; also in German); M. Fehr, *Apostolo Zeno und seine Reform des Operntexts* (Diss., Univ. of Zürich, 1912); O.G. Sonneck, *Catalogue of Opera Librettos Printed before 1800* (2 vols., Washington, D.C., 1914); R. Giazotto, "Apostolo Zeno, Pietro Metastasio e la critica del settecento," *Rivista Musicale Italiana* (1946); M.F. Robinson, *Naples and Neapolitan Opera* (London, 1972).

Zepler, Bogumil, German composer; b. Breslau, May 6, 1858; d. Krummhübel im Riesengebirge, Aug. 17, 1918. He studied architecture in Berlin, then medicine at the Univ. of Breslau (M.D., 1884); later began the study of music with H. Urban in Berlin; he attracted attention in 1891 with *Cavalleria Berolina,* a parody on Mascagni's *Cavalleria rusticana;* wrote stage music for Ernst von Wolzogen's artistic cabaret, "Überbrettl" (1901–2); also wrote a parody on Strauss's *Salome.* He further composed the comic operas *Der Brautmarkt zu Hira* (Berlin, 1892), *Der Vicomte von Letorières* (Hamburg, 1899), *Die Bäder von Lucca* (Berlin, 1905), *Monsieur Bonaparte* (Leipzig, 1911); several operettas (*Diogenes, Pick und Pocket, Die Liebesfestung,* etc.); a serious one-act opera, *Nacht* (Bern, 1901); 2 pantomimes: *Die Galgenfrist* and *Die Geisterbraut;* songs

(*Rokokolieder,* etc.).

Zerrahn, Carl, German-American conductor; b. Malchow, Mecklenburg, July 28, 1826; d. Milton, Mass., Dec. 29, 1909. He studied in Rostock, Hannover, and Berlin; after the revolutionary events of 1848, he emigrated to the U.S. and settled in Boston, then a center of German musical culture in America. He played the flute in the Germania Orch.; then became a professional conductor. For 42 years (1854–96) he led the concerts of the Handel and Haydn Society in Boston, and also conducted the Boston Phil. (1855–63) and the Harvard Musical Assoc. (1865–82). He was music director, from 1866 to 1897, of the prestigious music festivals in Worcester, Mass., and choral director for the famous Peace Jubilee Concerts in Boston in 1869 and 1872, leading the huge choruses assembled on these occasions. For many years he also taught harmony and singing at the New England Cons. (until 1898).

BIBLIOGRAPHY: *Dictionary of American Biography.*

Zeuner, Charles (real name, **Heinrich Christoph**), German-American organist; b. Eisleben, Saxony, Sept. 20, 1795; d. (suicide) Philadelphia, Nov. 7, 1857. He studied in Erfurt. About 1830 he settled in Boston, where he became organist at the Park St. Church; was also organist of the Handel and Haydn Society (1830–37), and briefly its president (1838–39). He then went to Philadelphia, where he served as a church organist. He composed one of the earliest American oratorios, *The Feast of Tabernacles* (Boston, May 3, 1837); publ. *Church Music, Consisting of New and Original Anthems, Motets and Chants* (1831); *The American Harp* (1832); *The Ancient Lyre,* a book of hymn tunes (1834 and several later eds.); *Organ Voluntaries* (1840); contributed to Lowell Mason's *Lyra Sacra* (1832); some of his compositions are also included in *The Psaltery,* edited by Mason and Webb (1845).

BIBLIOGRAPHY: F.J. Metcalf, *American Writers and Compilers of Sacred Music* (1925); *Dictionary of American Biography;* an account of his suicide is in the *N.Y. Musical Review and Gazette* for Nov. 14, 1857.

Zeuner, Karl Traugott, German pianist and composer; b. Dresden, April 28, 1775; d. Paris, Jan. 24, 1841. He studied with Türk in Halle and Clementi in Russia; gave concerts and taught in Paris, Vienna, St. Petersburg, and Dresden. He composed 2 piano concertos; 3 string quartets; *Variations on a Russian Theme* for Piano, Violin, and Cello; polonaises, fantasias, etc., for piano; these pieces were much in vogue in his time.

Zganec, Vinko, Croatian enthnomusicologist; b. Vratišinci, Jan. 22, 1890; d. Zagreb, Dec. 12, 1976. He studied law at the Univ. of Zagreb; then became interested in song collecting; traveled in the countryside gathering native melodies; publ. several albums of harmonizations of these songs and numerous articles in Croatian, German, and American music journals dealing with specific aspects of Croatian songs; in his analyses of their structure he applied modern methods of ethnomusicology.

Zhelobinsky, Valeri, Russian composer; b. Tambov, Jan. 27, 1913; d. Leningrad, Aug. 13, 1946. He received elementary musical training in Tambov; then entered the Leningrad Cons. as a student of Vladimir Shcherbachev (1928–32). He gave piano recitals, playing his own compositions; taught at the Tambov Music School; then returned to Leningrad. During his brief span of life, he composed several operas in a fine Romantic manner, as well as symphs. and chamber music.

WORKS: Operas: *Kamarinsky muzhik* (Leningrad, Sept. 15, 1933); *Her Saint's Day* (Leningrad, Feb. 22, 1935); *Mother,* after Maxim Gorky (Leningrad, Dec. 30, 1938); operetta, *The Last Ball* (Leningrad, March 30, 1939); 6 symphs.: No. 1 (1930); No. 2, *To the Memory of Revolutionary Victims* (1932); No. 3, *Dramatic Symphony* (Moscow, Dec. 17, 1939); No. 4 (Moscow, May 30, 1943); No. 5 (1944); No. 6 (1946); 3 piano concertos (1933, 1934, 1939); Violin Concerto (1934); *Romantic Poem* for Violin and Orch. (1939); *24 Preludes* for Piano; 2 children's albums for piano; film music.

Zhiganov, Nazib, Russian composer of Tatar heritage; b. Uralsk, Jan. 15, 1911. He was brought up in an orphan asylum; was educated in a music school in Kazan; went to Moscow, where he studied in a technological school; then took courses with Litinsky at the Moscow Cons., graduating in 1938. In 1945 he was appointed director and prof. of the newly founded Cons. of Kazan. In his music he set for himself the task of creating a new national Tatar school of composition, following the harmonic and instrumental precepts of the Russian national school; wrote several successful operas, symphs. and symph. suites on Tatar themes.

WORKS: Operas (all first perf. in Kazan): *Katchkyn* (June 17, 1939); *Irek* (*Liberty;* Feb. 24, 1940); *Altyntchetch* (*The Golden-haired;* July 12, 1941); *Ildar* (Nov. 7, 1942); *Tulyak* (July 27, 1945); *Namus* (*Honor;* June 25, 1950); ballet, *Zugra* (Kazan, May 17, 1946); *2 Legends* (1970); cantata, *My Republic* (1960); operatic monologue, *Dzhalil* (1950); 4 symphs. (1937, 1968, 1971, 1973); several suites on Tatar themes; chamber music; piano pieces; songs.

BIBLIOGRAPHY: Y. Girshman, *Nazib Zhiganov* (Moscow, 1957).

Zhitomirsky, Alexander, Russian composer and pedagogue; b. Kherson, May 23, 1881; d. Leningrad, Dec. 16, 1937. He took violin lessons in Odessa and in Vienna; also studied piano. Returning to Russia, he entered the St. Petersburg Cons. as a student of Rimsky-Korsakov, Liadov, and Glazunov, graduating in 1910; from 1915 to 1937 he was on its faculty, as an instructor in composition and orchestration. Among his pupils were the Soviet conductors Melik-Pashayev and Gauck, and the composers Veprik, Tchishko, and others. In his own compositions, he followed the style and manner of the Russian national school; he wrote a Violin Concerto (1937); String Quartet (1923); a number of songs and choruses.

Zhivotov, Alexei, Russian composer; b. Kazan, Nov. 14, 1904; d. Leningrad, Aug. 27, 1964. He studied at the Leningrad Cons. with Vladimir Shcherbachev, graduating in 1930. During the siege of Leningrad by the Nazis (1941–42), he remained in the city and was awarded a medal for valor. Most of his music is set in a lyrical-dramatic vein; he also wrote patriotic songs and choruses.

WORKS: For Orch.: *Dance Suite* (1935); *Romantic Poem* (1940); *Heroic Poem* (1946); *Theater Suite* (1949); vocal works: *The West*, song cycle with Orch. Accompaniment (1932); *Lyric Etudes* (1934); *Spring* (1942); *Happiness* (1943); *Songs of Leningrad* (1944); film music.

Zhukovsky, Herman, Ukrainian composer; b. Radzivilovo, Volynya, Nov. 13, 1913; d. Kiev, March 15, 1976. He studied piano and composition at the Kiev Cons., graduating in 1941; from 1951 to 1958 he taught music theory there. He wrote operas, ballets, symph. music, and other works in the approved style of socialist realism, using authentic Ukrainian song patterns for his materials, but a crisis supervened in his steady progress when his opera *From the Bottom of My Heart* (Moscow, Jan. 16, 1951) was viciously attacked by the cultural authorities of the Soviet government for alleged ideological and musical aberrations; he revised the score, and the new version was approved. His other operas are *Marina* (Kiev, March 12, 1939); *The First Spring* (1960); *Contrasts of Centuries,* operatic trilogy (1967); monodrama for Baritone, *A Soldier's Wife* (1968); ballets: *Rostislava* (1955); *Forest Song* (Moscow, May 1, 1961); several political cantatas: *Oath of the World Youth* (1951); *My Fatherland* (1949); several orch. suites; chamber music; film scores.

Ziani, Marco Antonio, Italian composer, nephew of **Pietro Andrea Ziani;** b. Venice, c.1653; d. Vienna, Jan. 22, 1715. In 1700 he became vice-Kapellmeister at the Vienna court; in 1712, Kapellmeister. He composed 45 operas and serenades, of which the following were produced in Vienna: *Il Giordano pio* (July 26, 1700); *Gli ossequi della notte* (July 22, 1701); *Temistocle* (June 9, 1701); *La fuga dell'invidia* (Nov. 15, 1701); *Il Romolo* (June 9, 1702); *Cajo Popilio* (June 9, 1704); *L'Ercole vincitore dell'invidia* (March 19, 1706); *Meleagro* (Aug. 16, 1706); *Chilonida* (April 21, 1709); *Il Campidoglio ricuperato* (July 26, 1709); *L'Atenaide* (with Negri and Caldara; Nov. 19, 1714). He also composed church music.

Ziani, Pietro Andrea, Italian organist and composer, uncle of **Marco Antonio Ziani;** b. Venice, c.1620; d. Naples, Feb. 12, 1684. In 1669 he succeeded Cavalli as first organist at San Marco in Venice; went to Naples in 1677; was maestro di cappella at the Cons. S. Onofrio from 1680; was pensioned in 1684. He wrote 23 operas, including *Le fortune di Rodope, e di Damira* (Venice, Carnival of 1657), *L'Antigona delusa da Alceste* (Venice, Jan. 15, 1660), *La congiura del vizio contra la virtù* (Vienna, Nov. 15, 1663), and *La Circe* (Vienna, June 9, 1665); an oratorio, *Le lagrime della Vergine* (Venice, 1662); *Sacrae laudes a 5* (1659); sonatas for 3, 4, 5, or 6 instruments (1691); church music; etc.

BIBLIOGRAPHY: H. Kretzschmar, "Weitere Beiträge zur Geschichte der venezianischen Oper," *Jahrbuch der Bibliothek Peters* (1910).

Zich, Jaroslav, Czech musicologist and composer, son of **Otakar Zich;** b. Prague, Jan. 17, 1912. He studied with his father and with J.B. Foerster (1928–31); went to the Charles Univ. in Prague, obtaining a Ph.D. in 1936; then devoted himself to administrative work and program directing at Prague Radio; in 1952 was appointed to the faculty at the Academy of Musical Arts in Prague.

WORKS: *Letmý host (The Temporary Guest),* cycle of songs with Orch. (1932); Duo for Violin and Cello (1932); String Quartet (1932); *Romance helgolandská,* melodrama with Orch. (1934); *U muziky (At the Dance),* 9 dances on folk motifs for Octet (1940); *Rhapsody* for Cello and Orch. (1956); Wind Quintet (1965). He publ. the manuals *Instrumentation in Groups* (Prague, 1957) and *Chapters of Musical Esthetics* (Prague, 1974).

Zich, Otakar, Czech composer and musicologist, father of **Jaroslav Zich;** b: Králové Městec, March 25, 1879; d. Ouběnice, near Benešov, July 9, 1934. He was educated at the Charles Univ. in Prague (1897–1901; Ph.D., 1902); was appointed lecturer there in 1911; in 1920 became a prof. of esthetics at Masaryk Univ. in Brno; in 1924 he again became a member of the faculty of the Charles Univ., where he remained until his death.

WORKS: Operas: *Marlířský nápad (Painter's Whim;* Prague, March 11, 1910); *Vina (Guilt;* Prague, March 14, 1922); *Preciézky,* after Molière's *Les Précieuses ridicules* (Prague, May 11, 1926); also cantatas, song cycles, part-songs, etc. He compiled *Vojenský spěvník československý* (unaccompanied melodies; Prague, 1922).

BIBLIOGRAPHY: J. Hutter, *Otakar Zich a jeho "Vina"* (Prague, 1922).

Zichy, Géza, Count Vasony-Keö, Hungarian left-hand pianist and composer; b. Sztára Castle, July 22, 1849; d. Budapest, Jan. 14, 1924. He studied with Volkmann and Liszt. At the age of 14 he lost his right arm in a hunting accident, and, refusing to give up music, developed his left-hand technique to the point of virtuosity; also made arrangements for left hand. On several occasions he played in public with Liszt an arrangement of the *Rákóczy March* for 3 hands. From 1875 to 1918 he was president of the National Cons. in Budapest; was also Intendant of the National Theater and Opera there (1890–94). He composed operas, produced at Budapest: *A vár története (Castle Story;* May 16, 1888); *Alár* (April 11, 1896); *Roland mester* (Jan. 10, 1899); a dramatic trilogy on the life of Rákóczi: *Nemo* (March 30,

1905), *Rákóczi Ferenz* (Jan. 30, 1909), and *Rodostó* (March 20, 1912); ballet, *Gemma* (Prague, 1903); cantata, *Dolores* (1889); Piano Concerto (1902); Piano Sonata; studies and piano pieces for the left hand alone; songs; etc. He publ. an autobiography, *Aus meinem Leben* (German ed., 3 vols., 1911–20).

Ziehn, Bernhard, noted German-American music theorist and teacher; b. Erfurt, Jan. 20, 1845; d. Chicago, Sept. 8, 1912. He studied in Erfurt; was a schoolteacher in Mühlhausen; in 1868 he emigrated to the U.S.; taught German, mathematics, and music theory at the German Lutheran School in Chicago (1868–71); subsequently became a private music teacher and established himself as a theorist. His "enharmonic law," built on the principle of functional equality of chords, is an original contribution to the theory of harmony.
WRITINGS: *System der Übungen für Clavierspieler* (1881); *Ein Lehrgang für den ersten Clavierunterricht* (1881); *Harmonie- und Modulationslehre* (1887; 2nd ed., 1909; completely recast and publ. in Eng. as *Manual of Harmony: Theoretical and Practical,* 1907; valuable for the choice and range of the examples); *Five- and Six-Part Harmonies* (1911); *Canonical Studies; A New Technic in Composition* (1912; in both Eng. and German); a collection of his articles was publ. by the German-American Historical Society of Illinois, as *Gesammelte Aufsätze zur Geschichte und Theorie der Musik* (Chicago, 1927).
BIBLIOGRAPHY: W. Sargeant, "Bernhard Ziehn, Precursor," *Musical Quarterly* (April 1933); H.J. Moser, *Bernhard Ziehn: Der deutsch-amerikanische Musiktheoretiker* (Bayreuth, 1950); *Dictionary of American Biography.*

Ziehrer, Karl Michael, Austrian bandleader and composer of operettas; b. Vienna, May 2, 1843; d. there, Nov. 14, 1922. Entirely self-taught in music, he organized in 1863 a dance orch., with which he made tours of Austria and Germany, introducing his own pieces; with an enlarged orch. (50 players), he established a regular series of popular concerts in Vienna, which met with great success; in 1908 he was appointed music director of the court balls. He wrote nearly 600 marches and dances for orch. (some very popular: *Meeresleuchten, Evatöchter, Donauwalzer, Alt-Wien, Ziehrereien,* etc.) and produced in Vienna a number of operettas: *Wiener Kinder* (Feb. 19, 1881); *Mahomeds Paradies* (Feb. 26, 1866); *König Jerôme* (Nov. 28, 1878); *Ein Deutschmeister* (Nov. 30, 1888); *Der schöne Rigo* (May 24, 1898); *Die Landstreicher,* his best work (July 29, 1899); *Die drei Wünsche* (March 9, 1901); *Der Fremdenführer* (Oct. 11, 1902); *Der Schätzmeister* (Dec. 10, 1904); *Fesche Geister* (July 7, 1905); *Am Lido* (Aug. 31, 1907); *Ein tolles Mädel* (Nov. 8, 1907); *Der Liebeswalzer* (Oct. 24, 1908); *Die Gaukler* (Sept. 6, 1909); *Herr und Frau Biedermeier* (Oct. 5, 1910); *In 50 Jahren* (Jan. 7, 1911); *Fürst Casimir* (Sept. 13, 1913); *Der Husarengeneral* (Oct. 3, 1913); *Das dumme Herz* (Feb. 27, 1914); *Die verliebte Eskadron* (July 11, 1920).

BIBLIOGRAPHY: M. Schönherr, *Carl Michael Ziehrer* (Vienna, 1973); idem, *Carl Michael Ziehrer: Sein Werk, sein Leben, seine Zeit* (Vienna, 1975).

Zielinski, Jaroslaw de, Polish-American pianist; b. Lubycza Królewska, Galicia, March 31, 1844; d. Santa Barbara, Calif., July 25, 1922. He studied piano with Mikuli in Lwow and Schulhoff in Vienna; took part in the Polish uprising against Russia in 1863; was severely wounded; went to the U.S. in 1864, enlisted in a Massachusetts regiment, and served to the end of the Civil War; subsequently was active as a pianist and teacher in N.Y., Detroit, and Buffalo; eventually settled in California, where he founded the Zielinski Trio Club. He publ. some graceful piano music (*Prelude, At the Spring, Gavotte, Minuet, Bourrée, Dreams,* mazurkas, etc.).

Zika, Richard, Czech violinist and composer; b. Vsetín, Moravia, Jan. 9, 1897; d. Prague, Nov. 10, 1947. He studied with his father, and later took courses at the Prague Cons.; was first violinist in the Prague Quartet (1920–32), and then (1932–46) in the Ondříček Quartet; in 1946 became a prof. at the Prague Academy of Musical Arts. He composed some quartet music.

Zilcher, Hermann, German composer; b. Frankfurt, Aug. 18, 1881; d. Würzburg, Jan. 1, 1948. He studied piano with his father, Paul Zilcher, a music teacher; later at the Hoch Cons. in Frankfurt, with Kwast (piano), Knorr and B. Scholz (composition). In 1901–5 he was in Berlin as a concert pianist and teacher; in 1905–8, taught piano at the Hoch Cons.; in 1908–20, was a prof. at the Akademie der Tonkunst in Munich; from 1920, was director of the Würzburg Cons. and conductor of the symph. concerts there; retired from the Cons. in 1944. He toured as a pianist; also in the U.S. (1905, with Franz von Vecsey).
WORKS: Incidental music for several Shakespearean plays: *As You Like It* (1917), *The Winter's Tale* (1919), *The Taming of the Shrew* (1926), and *A Comedy of Errors* (1934); comic opera, *Doktor Eisenbart* (Mannheim, 1922); *Liebesmesser,* oratorio (Strasbourg, 1913); 5 symphs. (No. 5, 1947; perf. posthumously, Hamburg, Feb. 11, 1948); Double Concerto for 2 Violins and Orch.; Violin Concerto; Piano Concerto; chamber music; many piano pieces; about 150 songs; etc.
BIBLIOGRAPHY: W. Altmann, *Hermann Zilcher* (Leipzig, 1907); H. Oppenheim, *Hermann Zilcher* (Munich, 1921).

Zillig, Winfried, German conductor and composer; b. Würzburg, April 1, 1905; d. Hamburg, Dec. 17, 1963. He studied with Schoenberg in Vienna and Berlin; from 1928 to 1943 conducted opera in Oldenburg, Düsseldorf, Essen; in 1947–51, was conductor at Hesse Radio. He was director of the music division of North German Radio in Hamburg in 1959–63.
WORKS: Operas: *Rossknecht* (Düsseldorf, Feb. 11, 1933); *Das Opfer* (Hamburg, Nov. 12, 1937); *Die Windsbraut* (Leipzig, May 12, 1941); (Linz, Nov. 23,

1963); *Troilus und Cressida* (Düsseldorf, Feb. 3, 1951); *Das Verlöbnis Chorfantasie* for Chorus and Orch. (Frankfurt, May 30, 1952); Cello Concerto; several string quartets and other chamber music; songs; piano pieces. He publ. *Variationen über neue Musik* (Munich, 1959); *Die neue Musik: Linien und Porträts* (Munich, 1963).

Ziloti, Alexander. See **Siloti, Alexander.**

Zimbalist, Efrem, eminent Russian-American violinist and pedagogue; b. Rostov-on-the-Don, April 21, 1889. He studied violin with his father, an orch. musician; from 1901 to 1907 he was a pupil of Leopold Auer at the St. Petersburg Cons., graduating with the gold medal. He made a highly successful European appearance as a soloist in Berlin, Nov. 7, 1907. In 1911 he emigrated to the U.S.; made his American debut with the Boston Symph. Orch. on Oct. 27, 1911, playing the first American performance of Glazunov's Violin Concerto. In 1914 he married the singer **Alma Gluck,** who died in 1938; his 2nd wife, whom he married in 1943, was Mary Louise Curtis Bok, founder of the Curtis Inst. of Music in Philadelphia; he was director of the Curtis Inst. from 1941 to 1968. After Mrs. Zimbalist's death in 1970, he moved to Reno, Nev., to live with his daughter. His son, Efrem Zimbalist, Jr., is a well-known actor. Zimbalist was also a composer. He wrote the opera *Landara* (Philadelphia, April 6, 1956); a musical comedy, *Honeydew* (N.Y., 1920); *Slavonic Dances* for Violin and Orch. (1911); *American Rhapsody* for Orch. (Chicago, March 3, 1936; revised version, Philadelphia, Feb. 5, 1943); *Portrait of an Artist,* symph. poem (Philadelphia, Dec. 7, 1945); Violin Concerto (1947); Cello Concerto (1969); String Quartet; Violin Sonata; *Concert Phantasy on Le Coq d'or* for Violin and Piano; *Sarasateana* for Violin and Piano; songs; etc. He publ. *One Hour's Daily Exercise* for the violin.

Zimerman, Krystian, Polish pianist; b. Zabrze, Dec. 5, 1956. He studied with Andrzej Jasiński at the Academy of Music in Katowice. In 1975 he won first prize in the Chopin Competition in Warsaw; then played with great success in Munich, Paris, London, and Vienna. In 1976 he was a soloist with the Berlin Phil. He made his first American appearance in 1979, as a soloist with the N.Y. Phil.

Zimmer, Friedrich, German composer of church music, son of **Friedrich August Zimmer;** b. Gardelegen, Sept. 22, 1855; d. Giessen, Dec. 5, 1919. He studied theology; publ. several collections of Lutheran hymns; composed choruses and songs for children. He was greatly esteemed as an educator.
BIBLIOGRAPHY: W. Stölten, *Friedrich Zimmer, Ein deutscher Volkserzieher* (Berlin, 1933).

Zimmer, Friedrich August, German organist and music educator; b. Herrengosserstädt, Thuringia, Feb. 26, 1826; d. Berlin, Feb. 8, 1899. He studied in Weissenfels; then devoted himself principally to teaching. He publ. the manuals *Elementarmusiklehre, Violin-Schule,* and *Die Orgel.*

Zimmer, Ján, significant Czech composer; b. Ružomberok, May 16, 1926. He studied piano at the Bratislava Cons. and composition with Ferenc Farkas at the Liszt Musical Academy in Budapest. An accomplished pianist, he limits himself to the performance of his own compositions, either at solo concerts or with orchs.
WORKS: 4 piano sonatas (1948, 1961, 1965, 1971); *2 Tatras Suites* for Piano (1951–52, 1956); Concerto for Solo Piano (1956); *2 Pieces* for 2 Pianos, 8-hands (1969); *2 by Piano* for Piano, 4-hands (1973); 6 piano concertos: No. 1 (1949, Bratislava, March 14, 1950); No. 2 (1952); No. 3 (1958; Bratislava, Jan. 14, 1960); No. 4 (1960; Bratislava, Oct. 11, 1962); No. 5, for left hand alone (1964; Bratislava, June 3, 1965); No. 6 (1972); Concerto for 2 Pianos and Orch. (1967; Bratislava, Nov. 3, 1968); *Concerto grosso* for 2 Pianos, 2 String Orchs., and Percussion (1950–51); *Rhapsody* for Piano and Orch. (1954); Concertino for Piano and Strings (1955; Prague, Feb. 17, 1957); *Small Fantasy* for Piano and Orch. (1960); 9 symphs.: No. 1 (1955; Bratislava, Dec. 2, 1956); No. 2 (1957–58); No. 3 (1959); No. 4, for Soprano, Tenor, Mixed Chorus, and Orch. (1959; Bratislava, Feb. 2, 1961); No. 5 (1961; Bratislava, March 3, 1963); No. 6, *Improvisata* (1964–65); No. 7 (1966; Bratislava, March 4, 1967); No. 8 (1971); No. 9 (1973); Piano Quintet (1949–50); *Magnificat,* cantata (1951); *The Peace* for Male Choir and Orch. (1954); Violin Concerto (1953; Bratislava, May 4, 1956); *Insurrection,* cantata (1954); Concerto for Organ, Strings, and Percussion (1957; Bratislava, Dec. 5, 1957); *Ahasver,* opera (1957—; unfinished); *Suite* for Violin and Piano (1957); Solo Violin Sonata (1958); *Fantasy and Toccata* for Organ (1958); *Strečno,* symph. poem (1958); String Quartet (1960); *The Dove of Peace,* small cantata (1960); Concerto for Solo Organ (1960); *Concerto da camera* for Oboe and Strings (1962); *Oedipus Rex,* opera (1963–64); *The Dead Do Not Return,* oratorio (1968); *French Suite* for Chamber Orch. (1968); Organ Sonata (1970); *Héraklès,* opera (1972); songs; music for films.

Zimmerman, Pierre-Joseph-Guillaume, famous French piano teacher and composer; b. Paris, March 19, 1785; d. there, Oct. 29, 1853. The son of a Paris piano maker, he entered the Paris Cons. in 1798, studying under Boieldieu, Rey, Catel, and Cherubini; won first prize for piano in 1800, and for harmony in 1802; became a prof. of piano at the Cons. in 1816, and was pensioned in 1848. Among his many pupils were Alkan, Marmontel, Lacombe, Ambroise Thomas, and César Franck.
WORKS: Opera, *L'Enlèvement* (Paris, Oct. 26, 1830); 2 piano concertos; Piano Sonata; 24 études; etc. His chief work is the *Encyclopédie du pianiste,* a complete method for piano, part III of which is a treatise on harmony and counterpoint.
BIBLIOGRAPHY: J.B. Labat, *Zimmerman et l'Ecole française de piano* (Paris, 1865).

Zimmermann, Agnes, German-English pianist and composer; b. Cologne, July 5, 1845; d. London, Nov. 14, 1925. As a young girl she went to England, and studied at the Royal Academy of Music in London with Ernst Pauer (piano) and G. Macfarren (composition). She made her debut at the Crystal Palace on Dec. 5, 1863; toured England with excellent success; was praised for her fine renditions of classical works. She edited the sonatas of Mozart and Beethoven and the complete piano works of Schumann (for Novello). She was also a competent composer; wrote a Piano Trio; 3 violin sonatas; a Cello Sonata; and many playable piano pieces.

BIBLIOGRAPHY: Lady Arbuthnot, "In Memoriam Agnes Zimmermann," *Musical Times* (1926).

Zimmermann, Anton, Austrian composer; b. Pressburg, 1741; d. there, Oct. 16, 1781. He served for many years as organist at the Pressburg Cathedral; wrote a singspiel, *Andromeda und Perseus* (produced in Vienna on April 23, 1781); publ. 9 violin sonatas and a programmatic piece, *Die Belagerung von Valenciennes* for Violin and Piano; 6 string quartets; 6 violin duos; other pieces.

Zimmermann, Bernd Alois, important German composer; b. Bliesheim, near Cologne, March 20, 1918; d. (suicide) Königsdorf, Aug. 10, 1970. He studied philology at the univs. of Bonn, Cologne, and Berlin, and earned his living by playing in dance bands. He then took courses in composition in Cologne with Philipp Jarnach; attended lectures of Wolfgang Fortner and René Leibowitz at the summer courses of new music in Darmstadt. He subsequently worked in radio; in 1958 was appointed a lecturer in composition at the Hochschule für Musik at Cologne. Plagued by failing eyesight and obsessed with notions of death, he reflected these moods in his own music of the final period; his *Requiem für einen jungen Dichter* was written to texts by various poets, all of whom committed suicide; he killed himself shortly after the completion of this morbid score. His own idiom of composition is mainly expressionistic, with a melodic line of anguished chromaticism which does not preclude the observance of strict formal structures in his instrumental works. While in his lifetime he was primarily known to limited music circles in Germany, the significance of his music began to be realized after his death.

WORKS: *Alagoana (Caprichos brasileiros),* ballet (1940–43, 1947–50; Essen, Dec. 17, 1955; ballet suite, Hamburg, Nov. 21, 1953); *Lob der Torheit (In Praise of Folly),* burlesque cantata after Goethe (1948; Cologne, May 25, 1948); Concerto for String Orch. (1948; rescoring of a discarded string trio of 1942–43); Violin Sonata (1949); Violin Concerto (1949–50; Baden-Baden, Dec. 10, 1950); an orchestration and revision of the Violin Sonata); *Rheinische Kirmestänze* for 13 Winds (1950; revised 1962); Solo Violin Sonata (1951); Symph. in one movement (1947–52; revised 1953; Brussels, Nov. 20, 1953); *Enchiridion,* small piece for Piano (1949–52); Concerto for Oboe and Small Orch. (1952; Donaueschingen

Festival, Oct. 1952); *Kontraste,* music for an imaginary ballet, for Orch. (1953; orch. suite, Hamburg, 1953; ballet, Bielefeld, April 24, 1954); *Nobody Knows de Trouble I See,* concerto for Trumpet and Orch. (1954; Hamburg, Oct. 11, 1955); Solo Viola Sonata (1955); *Konfigurationen,* 8 pieces for Piano (1954–56); *Perspektiven,* music for an imaginary ballet, for 2 Pianos (1955; ballet version, Düsseldorf, June 2, 1957); *Canto di speranza,* cantata for Cello and Small Orch. (1952–57; Baden-Baden Radio, July 28, 1958); *Omnia tempus habent,* cantata for Soprano and 17 Instruments (1957); *Impromptu* for Orch. (1958); *Vocal Symphony* for 5 Soloists and Orch. (1959; scenes from the opera *Die Soldaten*); *Die Soldaten (The Soldiers),* opera in 4 acts after J.M.R. Lenz (1958–60; revised 1963–64; Cologne, Feb. 15, 1965); Solo Cello Sonata (1959–60); *Dialoge,* Concerto for 2 Pianos and Orch., in homage to Debussy (1960; revised 1965; original version, Cologne Radio, Dec. 5, 1960); *Présence,* "ballet blanc" in 5 scenes for Piano Trio (1961; Darmstadt, Sept. 8, 1961); *Antophonen* for Viola and 25 Instrumentalists, some of whom speak a text drawn from Joyce, Dante, Dostoyevsky, Camus, and Novalis (1961; Zürich, 1966); *5 capricci di G. Frescobaldi, "La Frescobalda,"* for 3 Recorders, Oboe d'Amore, 3 Viole da Gamba, Lute, 3 Trumpets, and 3 Trombones (1962); *Tempus loquendi,* "pezzi ellittici" for Flauto Grande, Flute in G, and Bass Flute Solo, for One Performer (1963); *Monologe* for 2 Pianos (1960–64; version of *Dialoge*); Concerto for Cello and Orch., in the form of a "pas de trois" (1965–66; concert version, Strasbourg, April 8, 1968; ballet version, Wuppertal, May 12, 1968); *Tratto I* and *II* for Tape (in the form of a choreographic study, 1966; 1968); *Musique pour les soupers du Roi Ubu,* "ballet noir" in 7 parts and an entrée, for Orch. (1966; Düsseldorf, 1968); *Intercomunicazione* for Cello and Piano (1967); *Ode to Eleutheria* in the form of death dances from music for the radio play *Die Befristeten (The Numbered),* for Jazz Quintet (1967); *Photoptosis,* prelude for Orch. (1968; Gelsenkirchen, Feb. 19, 1969); *Requiem für einen jungen Dichter (Requiem for a Young Poet),* "lingual" for Narrator, Soprano, and Baritone Soloists, 3 Choruses, Tape, Orch., Jazz Combo, and Organ, to texts drawn from various poems, articles, and news reports (1967–69; Düsseldorf, Dec. 11, 1969); 4 short *Studies* for Solo Cello (1970); *Stille und Umkehr (Stillness and Return),* sketch for Orch. (1970; Nuremberg, March 19, 1971); *Ich wandte mich und sah an alles Unrecht das geschah unter der Sonne (I Come Again to Contemplate All the Oppression That Is Committed under the Sun),* "ecclesiastical action" for 2 Narrators, Solo Bass, and Orch. (1970; Kiel, Sept. 2, 1972).

Zimmermann, Gerhardt, American conductor; b. Van Wert, Ohio, June 22, 1945. He played trumpet in school; then entered Bowling Green (Ohio) State Univ. (B.M., 1967) and the Univ. of Iowa (M.F.A. in orch. conducting, 1971). He served as director of orchs. at Western Illinois Univ. in Macomb (1972–74); in 1974 he became assistant conductor of the St. Louis Symph. Orch., and later its associate conductor (1978–82). In 1980 he also held the post of music director of the Canton (Ohio) Symph. Orch.; in 1982 he was named music director of the North Carolina Symph. Orch. in Raleigh.

Zimmermann, Louis, Netherlandish violinist and composer; b. Groningen, July 19, 1873; d. Amsterdam, March 6, 1954. He studied at the Leipzig Cons. with Hans Sitt and Carl Reinecke; also with Eugène Ysaÿe in Brussels. He was a member of the Concertgebouw Orch. in Amsterdam (1899–1904); taught violin at the Royal College of Music in London (1904–9); then rejoined the Concertgebouw as its concertmaster, retiring in 1940. He wrote numerous violin pieces; also cadenzas for the violin concertos by Beethoven and Brahms.

Zimmermann, Udo, East German composer; b. Dresden, Oct. 6, 1943. He studied composition with J.P. Thilman at the Hochschule für Musik in Dresden (1962–68); from 1968 to 1970 attended the master classes in composition of Günter Kochan at the Akademie der Künste in East Berlin. In 1970 he was appointed composer and producer at the Dresden Opera; in 1974 he founded the Studio of New Music in Dresden. In 1978 he became a prof. of composition at the Dresden Hochschule für Musik, and in 1982 was appointed prof. of the experimental music theater there. His music follows the median course of restrained ultramodernism, with a democratically equal treatment of formerly disallowed dissonances.
WORKS: OPERAS: *Die weisse Rose* (Dresden, 1967); *Die zweite Entscheidung* (Magdeburg, 1970); *Levins Mühle* (1972–73; Dresden, March 27, 1973); *Der Schuhu und die fliegende Prinzessin* (1975); *Die wundersame Schustersfrau* (1978–82). FOR ORCH.: *Dramatische Impression auf den Tod von J.F. Kennedy* for Cello and Orch. (1966; originally written immediately after Kennedy's assassination in 1963, for Cello and Piano); *Musik für Streicher* (1967); *Sieh, meine Augen,* reflections for Chamber Orch. (1970); *Mutazioni* (1972; Dresden, Oct. 26, 1973); *Sinfonia come un grande lamento,* in memory of Federico García Lorca (1977). VOCAL MUSIC: *5 Songs,* after Borchert, for Baritone and Orch. (1964); *L'Homme,* cantata (1969; Dresden, Sept. 22, 1972); *Der Mensch,* cantata for Soprano and 13 Instrumentalists (1969); *Ein Zeuge der Liebe besingt den Tod* for Soprano and Chamber Orch. (1971; Frankfurt, March 11, 1973); *Psalm der Nacht,* after Sachs, for 17-voice Female Choir, Percussion, and Organ (1973); *Ode an das Leben,* to texts by Neruda and Carus, for Mezzo-soprano, 3 Choruses, and Orch. (1974); *Hymnus an die Sonne,* after Kleist, for Soprano, Flute, and Harpsichord (1976); *Pax questuosa* for 5 Soloists, 3 Choirs, and Orch. (1980). CHAMBER MUSIC: *Movimenti caratteristici* for Solo Cello (1965); *Sonetti amorosi* for Contralto, Flute, and String Quartet (1967); *Choreographien nach Edgar Degas* for 21 Instrumentalists (1974).
BIBLIOGRAPHY: Ursula Stürzbecher, *Komponisten in der DDR: 17 Gespräche* (Hildesheim, 1979).

Zinck, Benedikt Friedrich, German composer; b. Husum, Holstein (baptized, March 8), 1743; d. Ludwigslust, Mecklenburg, June 23, 1801. He was a church organist; was a violinist at the Hofkapelle from 1767; in 1783 became court musician at Ludwigslust. Among his works are several symphs.; harpsichord sonatas; chamber music.

Zinck, Harnack Otto Conrad, German composer, brother of **Benedikt Friedrich Zinck;** b. Husum, Holstein, July 2, 1746; d. Copenhagen, Feb. 15, 1832. He was an organist in Hamburg; then joined his brother at Ludwigslust, but left in 1787 for Copenhagen, where he was a church organist and teacher; there he produced an opera to a Danish text, *Selim og Mirza* (Copenhagen, Feb. 1, 1790); also composed several oratorios, instrumental music, etc.; publ. *Die nördliche Harfe* (Copenhagen, 1801; on Scandinavian music) and *Vorlesungen über Musik und ihre nützlichste Anwendung* (Copenhagen, 1813).

Zingarelli, Nicola Antonio, Italian composer; b. Naples, April 4, 1752; d. Torre del Greco, near Naples, May 5, 1837. He studied at the Cons. di Loreto in Naples with Fenaroli and Speranza (composition); also studied violin. His first stage work, *I quattro pazzi,* was performed at the Cons. in 1768. After finishing school in 1772, he earned his living as a violin teacher. He spent much time traveling throughout Italy, supervising the production of his operas. In 1793 he was appointed maestro di cappella at the Cathedral of Milan; in 1794, at the Santa Casa in Loreto; in 1804, at the Sistine Chapel in the Vatican. In 1811, for refusing to conduct a Te Deum to celebrate the birthday of Napoleon's son, the "King of Rome," he was imprisoned at Civitavecchia, and later transported to Paris by order of Napoleon, who set him at liberty and liberally paid him for a Mass written in Paris. As Fioravanti had meanwhile become maestro di cappella at St. Peter's, Zingarelli went to Naples, and in 1813 became director of the royal Collegio di Musica; in 1816 he succeeded Paisiello as maestro di cappella at the Naples Cathedral. He was renowned as a teacher; Bellini, Mercadante, Carlo Conti, Lauro Rossi, Morlacchi, and Sir Michael Costa were his students. His operas, interpreted by the finest singers of the time (Catalani, Crescentini, Grassini, Marchesi, and Rubinelli), were highly successful. His facility was such that he was able to write an opera in a week. He wrote 37 operas in all.
WORKS: Operas (produced at La Scala in Milan): *Alsinda* (Feb. 22, 1785); *Ifigenia in Aulide* (Jan. 27, 1787); *La morte de Cesare* (Dec. 26, 1790); *Pirro, re d'Epiro* (Dec. 26, 1791); *Il mercato di Monfregoso* (Sept. 22, 1792); *La secchia rapita* (Sept. 7, 1793); *Artaserse* (Dec. 26, 1793); *Giulietta e Romeo,* after Shakespeare (Jan. 30, 1796; his best-known work; staged all over Europe, and also in N.Y., with considerable success, but disappeared from the repertoire after Zingarelli's death); *Meleagro* (Jan. 1798); *Il ritratto* (Oct. 12, 1799); *Clitennestra* (Dec. 26, 1800); other operas: *Antigono* (Mantua, April 13, 1786); *Alzira* (Florence, Sept. 7, 1794); *Il Conte di*

Saldagna (Venice, Dec. 26, 1794); *Orazi e Curiazi* (Naples, Nov. 4, 1795); *La morte di Mitridate* (Venice, May 27, 1797); *Il ratto delle Sabine* (Venice, Dec. 26, 1799); *Edipo a Colono* (Venice, Dec. 26, 1802); *La distruzione di Gerusalemme* (Florence, Nov. 27, 1803); *L'Oracolo sannita* (Naples, Oct. 11, 1806); *Il ritorno di Serse* (Modena, July 16, 1808); *Baldovino* (Rome, Feb. 11, 1811); *Berenice, regina d'Armenia* (Rome, Nov. 12, 1811). Oratorios: *Pimmalione* (Naples, 1779); *Ero* (Milan, 1786); *Telemaco* (Milan, 1787); *Il trionfo di David* (Naples, 1788); *Francesca da Rimini* (Rome, 1804); *Tancredi al sepolcro di Clorinda* (Naples, 1805); *La fuga in Egitto* (Naples, 1837); a vast amount of church music; the Cons. di Loreto contains 541 MSS by Zingarelli, in a collection known as "Annuale di Zingarelli" (or "Annuale di Loreto"), including a series of masses for every day in the year; a 4-part Miserere "alla Palestrina" (1827); 73 Magnificats, 28 Stabat Maters, 21 Credos, many Te Deums, motets, hymns, etc.; also solfeggi, arias, organ sonatas, some chamber music.

BIBLIOGRAPHY: R. Liberatore, *Necrologia di N. Zingarelli* (Naples, 1837); A. Schmid, *Joseph Haydn und N. Zingarelli* (Vienna, 1847); F. Florimo, in vol. II of *La scuola musicale de Napoli* (Naples, 1880); S. di Giacomo, "Il fiero Zingarelli," *Musica d'Oggi* (June 1923); P. Dotto, "N. Zingarelli," ibid. (July 1941).

Zingel, Rudolf Ewald, German organist and composer; b. Liegnitz, Sept. 5, 1876; d. there, Feb. 20, 1944. He studied at the Hochschule für Musik in Berlin; then was active as a church organist and choral conductor in Berlin and in Frankfurt an der Oder. He wrote 2 operas, *Margot* (Frankfurt an der Oder, 1902) and *Persepolis* (Rostock, 1909); an operetta, *Liebeszauber* (Stralsund, 1908); symph. poem, *Freudvoll und liedvoll;* secular oratorio, *Der wilde Jäger;* several sacred cantatas for men's chorus and string orch.; numerous piano pieces and songs.

Zinkeisen, Konrad Ludwig Dietrich, German violinist and composer; b. Hannover, June 3, 1779; d. Braunschweig, Nov. 28, 1838. He was trained by his father, and by Rode at Wolfenbüttel; played first violin under Forkel at the Academic Concerts in Göttingen; in 1819 he was appointed a chamber musician in the Braunschweig court orch. He wrote 6 violin concertos, 4 orch. overtures, 3 string quartets; concertos for oboe, for clarinet, for basset horn, and for bassoon; and various other pieces for solo instruments with orch.; music for military band; choral works.

Zinman, David, talented American conductor; b. New York, July 9, 1936. He studied at the Oberlin Cons. (B.M., 1958) and at the Univ. of Minnesota (M.A., 1963); took lessons in conducting at the Berkshire Music Center at Tanglewood, and with Pierre Monteux at his summer school in Maine; from 1961–64 he was Monteux's assistant. After a successful engagement as guest conductor with the Nederlands Kamerorkest, he served as its conductor from 1965–77. In 1972 he was appointed music adviser to the Rochester (N.Y.) Phil.; in 1974 he became its music director. From 1977–82 he served as chief conductor of the Rotterdam Phil. In 1983 he was engaged as principal guest conductor of the Baltimore Symph. Orch. He also appeared as guest conductor with the Philadelphia Orch., Chicago Symph., Los Angeles Phil., Boston Symph., and N.Y. Phil.

Zinnen, Jean-Antoine, Luxembourg composer; b. Neuenbourg, April 25, 1827; d. Neuilly-sur-Seine, May 16, 1898. He was the composer of the National Hymn of Luxembourg (1864); wrote several operettas. In 1881 he went to Paris. After his death, his remains were brought to Luxembourg. A postage stamp in his honor was issued in 1950.

Zipoli, Domenico, Italian composer and organist; b. Prato, Oct. 16, 1688; d. Córdoba, Argentina, Jan. 2, 1726. He went to Rome as a young man; was organist at the Jesuit church there. His oratorios *Sant' Antonio di Padova* (1712) and *Santa Caterina, vergine e martire* (1714) were presented in Rome. In 1716 he publ. *Sonate d'intavolatura per organo e cimbalo.* He joined the Jesuit order at Seville in 1716; in 1717 went to South America, where he became organist of the Jesuit church in Córdoba, Argentina. Walsh of London reprinted parts of the *Sonate d'intavolatura* under the titles *Six Suits of Italian Lessons for the Harpsichord* and *Third Collection of Toccatas, Vollentarys and Fugues.*

BIBLIOGRAPHY: L. Ayestarán, *Domenico Zipoli, el gran compositor y organista romano del 1700 en el Rio de La Plata* (Montevideo, 1941; radically revised and amplified, Montevideo, 1962; basic study establishing biographical facts); A. Salazar, "El Caso de Domenico Zipoli," *Nuestra Musica* (Mexico, May 1946; arguing against the identification of the immigrant organist Zipoli with the composer); V. de Rubertis, "Dove e quando nacque e morì Domenico Zipoli," *Rivista Musicale Italiana* (April–June 1951).

Zipp, Friedrich, German composer and pedagogue; b. Frankfurt, June 20, 1914. He studied at the Hoch Cons. in Frankfurt and with Armin Knab in Berlin; in 1947 was appointed to the faculty of the Hochschule für Musik in Frankfurt; also served as organist there. He composed *Musik* for Orch. (1936); *Sinfonietta* for Youth Orch. (1958); *Kirchensuite* for String Orch. (1962); *Au clair de la lune* for Oboe and Piano (1963); numerous choral pieces and songs. He publ. *Vom Wesen der Musik* (Heidelberg, 1974).

Zítek, Otakar, Czech music critic and composer; b. Prague, Nov. 5, 1892; d. Bratislava, April 28, 1955. He studied composition with Novák at the Vienna Cons. and musicology with Guido Adler and Grädener at the Univ. of Vienna. Upon graduation he wrote music criticism for the *Hudební Revue* and the *Lidové Noviny* in Prague; gave lectures on opera at the Prague Cons.; then was administrator at the National Theater in Brno (1921–29); taught at the Brno Cons. (1931–39). In 1939–41 he was in the

Buchenwald concentration camp, but was released, and worked as a theater director in Pilsen (1941–43); supervised opera theaters in Prague and Brno (1946–49). He composed the operas *Vznesene srdce* (*The Exalted Heart;* 1918) and *Pád Petra Králence* (*The Downfall of Peter Králence;* Brno, March 23, 1923); a ballet after Wilde's *Birthday of the Infanta* (Pilsen, 1942); *Město,* symph. poem (1925); songs; etc. He publ. *O novou zpevohru* (*On New Opera;* Prague, 1920).

Ziv, Mikhail, Soviet composer; b. Moscow, May 25, 1921. He studied at the Moscow Cons. with Kabalevsky; graduated in 1947. As a composer, Ziv devoted himself mainly to the musical theater; wrote the comic operas *Son of a King's Minister* (1973) and *Gentlemen Artists* (1980); several fairy tales for children; 3 symphs. (1946, 1960, 1968); 2 sinfoniettas (1958, 1962); 2 string quartets (1945, 1955); Piano Quintet (1947); many choruses, piano pieces, and songs; film music.

Živković, Milenko, Serbian composer; b. Belgrade, May 25, 1901; d. there, June 29, 1964. He studied law in Belgrade and music at the Leipzig Cons. with Grabner and at the Schola Cantorum in Paris with Vincent d'Indy. Returning to Belgrade, he became director of the Stankovic Music School (1937–47); taught at the Academy of Music (1945–64); was rector and prof. of composition there (1952–60). A follower of the national school of composition, he wrote music permeated with ethnic Balkan melorhythms. His works include: *Symphonic Prologue* (Belgrade, April 16, 1935); *Zelena godina* (*Green Year),* folk ballet scenes for Orch. (Belgrade, April 27, 1937); several suites of Yugoslav dances for piano, and numerous choruses.

Zmeskall, Nikolaus, Baron von Domanovecz, Hungarian diplomat and musical amateur; b. Lestine (baptized, Nov. 20), 1759; d. Vienna, June 23, 1833. He served as secretary of the Hungarian Chancellery in Vienna, and was an intimate friend of Beethoven, who dedicated to him the String Quartet, op. 95. Zmeskall was also a composer in his own right; he wrote 14 string quartets and other instrumental music.
BIBLIOGRAPHY: A. Sandberger, *Beethovens Freund Zmeskall als Komponist* (Munich, 1924); C. Pidoll, *Verklungenes Spiel: Erinnerungen des Herrn Nikolaus Zmeskall* (Innsbruck, 1949).

Znosko-Borovsky, Alexander, Russian composer; b. Kiev, Feb. 27, 1908. He studied violin and composition at the Kiev Cons.; then was active as a composer for films (1931–41). In 1941 he left Kiev, threatened by the Nazi invasion, and went to Ashkhabad, Turkmenia; was instrumental in promoting indigenous music culture there; several of his works are based on Turkmenian themes.
WORKS: Ballet, *Akpamyk* (Ashkhabad, April 14, 1945); cantata, *Our Victory* (Kiev, May 8, 1946); 3 symphs. (1958, 1960, 1967); symph. poem, *Kiev* (Kiev, March 9, 1949); Violin Concerto (Kiev, Dec. 17, 1955);

symph. poem, *At the Mausoleum* (1960); String Quartet on Ukrainian themes (1937); String Quartet on Turkmenian themes (1942); Sonata for Unaccompanied Violin (1950); *Scherzo* for 3 Trombones (1938); various pieces for different instruments.

Zoeller, Carl, German-British composer; b. Berlin, March 28, 1840; d. London, July 13, 1889. He studied violin with Hubert Ries in Berlin; after traveling in Germany with various opera troupes as a violinist, he went to London, settling there in 1873; in 1879, he became bandmaster of the 7th (Queen's Own) Hussars. In England he often performed on the viola d'amore; publ. *The Viola d'Amour, Its Origin and History, and Art of Playing It.* He composed an operetta, *The Missing Heir,* and a serious music drama, *Mary Stuart of Fotheringay;* a Violin Concerto; songs.

Zoellner, Joseph, Sr., American violinist; b. Brooklyn, Feb. 2, 1862; d. Los Angeles, Jan. 24, 1950. He studied violin; traveled to Europe, with a prolonged stay in Brussels (1907–12), where he organized, with his 2 sons and a daughter, the Zoellner Quartet. From 1912 to 1922, they lived in N.Y.; in 1922 Zoellner founded with his children the Zoellner Cons. of Music in Los Angeles.

Zoghby, Linda, American soprano; b. Mobile, Ala., Aug. 17, 1949. She studied voice with Elena Nikolaidi at Florida State Univ.; made her professional debut at the Grant Park Festival in Chicago in 1973; subsequently sang opera in N.Y., Washington, Dallas, Santa Fe, Houston, and New Orleans. She received a critical accolade on Jan. 19, 1982, when she substituted on short notice for Teresa Stratas and sang the role of Mimi in the Zeffirelli production of *La Bohème* at the Metropolitan Opera in N.Y. Her other roles inlcude Pamina, Donna Elvira, and Marguerite in *Faust.*

Zoilo, Annibale, Italian composer; b. Rome, c.1537; d. Loreto, 1592. He was maestro di cappella at San Luigi dei Francesi from 1561 to 1566; at San Giovanni in Laterano from Jan. 1568 to June 1570. In 1570 he became a singer in the Papal Choir in Rome (until 1577, due to ill health); then was at the Cathedral of Todi; returning to Rome, he entered the service of Cardinal Sirleto (until 1584); subsequently became maestro di cappella at the Santa Casa in Loreto (till June 30, 1592). In 1577 he and Palestrina were entrusted with the revision of the Roman Gradual (*Editio Medicaea*). He publ. *Madrigali a 4 e 5 voci* (Rome, 1563); *Salve Regina* for 12 Voices is in Constantini's *Selectae cantiones excellentissimorum auctorum* (Rome, 1614); various compositions in other collections, publ. between 1567 and 1616.
BIBLIOGRAPHY: R. Casimiri, "Annibale Zoilo e la sua famiglia: Nuovi documenti biografici," *Note d'Archivio* (Jan.–April 1940); H. Lincoln, *Annibale Zoilo: The Life and Works of a Sixteenth-Century Italian Composer* (Diss., Northwestern Univ., 1951).

Zöller, Karlheinz, German flutist; b. Höhr-Grenzhausen, Aug. 24, 1928. He was educated at the Northwest German Music Academy in Detmold; subsequently was first flutist with the Berlin Phil. (1960–69). After a series of concert appearances in Europe and America, he rejoined the Berlin Phil. in 1977.

Zöllner, Carl Friedrich, German choral conductor and composer; b. Mittelhausen, March 17, 1800; d. Leipzig, Sept. 25, 1860. He studied at the Thomasschule in Leipzig; became a vocal instructor and began writing male choruses; in 1833 he founded in Leipzig a "Liedertafel" known as the Zöllner-Verein, a male choral society modeled after Zelter's Berlin organization; after Zöllner's death, several choral societies were united to form the Zöllner-Bund. Zöllner was one of the most successful German composers of part-songs for male choruses; he also wrote for mixed chorus, and songs with piano accompaniment.
BIBLIOGRAPHY: R. Hänsch, *Der Liedermeister Carl Friedrich Zöllner* (Dresden, 1927).

Zöllner, Heinrich, German composer; b. Öls, Silesia, May 5, 1792; d. Wandsbeck, near Hamburg, July 2, 1836. He toured Germany as an organist; for a while lived in Vienna; in 1833 settled in Hamburg. He wrote an opera, *Kunz von Kauffungen* (Vienna, March 27, 1826); a melodrama, *Ein Uhr;* publ. masses, motets, Psalms, part-songs, organ pieces, a Piano Sonata, piano pieces, etc.

Zöllner, Heinrich, German composer, son of **Carl Friedrich Zöllner;** b. Leipzig, July 4, 1854; d. Freiburg im Breisgau, May 4, 1941. He studied at the Leipzig Cons., where his teachers were Reinecke, Jadassohn, Richter, and Wenzel (1875–77); then went to Dorpat, Russia, where he was music director at the local univ.; in 1885 he went to Cologne, where he taught at the Cologne Cons. and conducted choruses. In 1890 he was engaged to lead the Deutscher Liederkranz in N.Y.; in 1898 he returned to Germany; from 1902 to 1907 he taught composition at the Leipzig Cons.; from 1907 to 1914 he was conductor at the Flemish Opera in Antwerp; subsequently settled in Freiburg.
WORKS: He wrote 10 operas, of which the following were produced: *Frithjof* (Cologne, 1884); *Die lustigen Chinesinnen* (Cologne, 1886); *Faust* (Munich, Oct. 19, 1887); *Matteo Falcone* (N.Y., 1894); *Der Überfall* (Dresden, Sept. 7, 1895); *Die versunkene Glocke* (Berlin, July 8, 1899; his best opera); *Der Schützenkönig* (Leipzig, 1903); *Zigeuner* (Stuttgart, 1912); the musical comedy *Das hölzerne Schwert* (Kassel, 1897); a great number of choral works with orch.; also 3 symphs. and some chamber music. He publ. a poem, *Beethoven in Bonn. Ein Sang vom Rhein* (1898).
BIBLIOGRAPHY: E. Segnitz, *Heinrich Zöllner* (Leipzig, 1907).

Zolotarev, Vasili, eminent Russian composer and pedagogue; b. Taganrog, March 7, 1872; d. Moscow, May 25, 1964. (His name is pronounced Zolotaryóv.) He studied violin and music theory at the Imperial Court Chapel in St. Petersburg; from 1893 to 1897 he took composition lessons with Balakirev; then entered the St. Petersburg Cons. in the class of Rimsky-Korsakov, graduating in 1900; received the Rubinstein Prize for his cantata *Paradise and Peri.* He subsequently held various teaching positions: was instructor of violin at the Court Chapel (1897–1900); teacher of composition at the Rostov Music School (1906–8), the Moscow Cons. (1908–18), the Ekaterinodar Cons. (1918–24), the Odessa Cons. (1924–26), the Kiev Musico-Dramatic Inst. (1926–31), the Sverdlovsk Music School (1931–33), and the Minsk Cons. (1933–41); after 1945 he lived in Moscow. In 1955 he was awarded the Order of Lenin. Several well-known Soviet composers were his pupils, among them Polovinkin, Dankevich, and Vainberg. In his music Zolotarev continued the line of the Russian national school of composition, based on broad diatonic melos, mellifluous euphonious harmonies, and, in his operas, a resonant flow of choral singing.
WORKS: Operas: *The Decembrists* (Moscow, Dec. 27, 1925) and *Ak-Gul,* on Uzbek themes (1942); ballet, *Lake Prince* (Minsk, Jan. 15, 1949); 7 symphs.: No. 1 (1902); No. 2 (1905); No. 3 (1935); No. 4 (1936); No. 5 (1942); No. 6 (1943); No. 7 (1962); overture, *Fête villageoise; Rhapsodie hébraïque* for Orch.; symph. suites: *Moldavian Suite* (1926); *Uzbek Suite* (1931); *Tadzhik Suite* (1932); *Belorussian Suite* (1936); Cello Concerto (1943); 6 string quartets (1899, 1902, 1907, 1912, 1916, 1945); Piano Quintet (1904); String Quintet (1904); Piano Trio (1905); Violin Sonata (1922); 2 piano sonatas (1903, 1919); many songs. He publ. a manual on the fugue (Moscow, 1932).
BIBLIOGRAPHY: V. Zolotarev, *Reminiscences About My Great Pupils, Friends and Colleagues* (Moscow, 1957); S. Nisievich, *V. Zolotarev* (Moscow, 1964).

Zoltán, Aladár, Rumanian composer; b. Mǎrtinis-Harghita, May 31, 1929; d. Tîrgu-Mures, July 9, 1978. He studied with Jodál and Demian at the Cluj Cons. (1946–53); in 1960 he was appointed secretary of the Tîrgu-Mures branch of the Union of Rumanian Composers, and in 1965 was elected director of the Tîrgu-Mures Phil.
WORKS: For the stage: in Hungarian, *Biborkáne Iánya (The Marriage;* 1962); in Rumanian, *Poarta de sur* (1963); in French, *Coutumes d'hiver* (1969) and *Les "Marieurs" de Bihor* (1971); 4 cantatas; *5 Lyrical Songs* for Tenor and Orch. (1963); *Divertissement* for 2 Clarinets and Strings (1952); 2 symphs. (1961, 1971); *Dansuri de pe Mureş* for Orch. (1968); *Suite piccola* for Orch. (1970); *Introduction and Allegro* for Orch. (1974–77); *Nonet* (1953); Bassoon Sonata (1955); String Quartet (1965); *Suite piccola* for Piano (1964–69); choruses; songs.

Zopff, Hermann, German music critic and composer; b. Glogau, June 1, 1826; d. Leipzig, July 12, 1883. He studied agriculture, then music (at the Stern Cons. in Berlin); founded an "Opernakademie" and an "Orchesterverein" in Berlin; in 1864 he settled in Leipzig as co-editor of the *Neue Zeitschrift für Musik*, becoming editor in chief in 1868. He publ. *Ratschläge für angehende Dirigenten* (1861; 3rd ed., 1922) and *Grundzüge einer Theorie der Oper* (Leipzig, 1868). His compositions include a symph. poem, *Wilhelm Tell; 3 Idyllen* for Small Orch.; *Gesangsstück* for Cello and Orch.; *Aströa, oder Das Evangelium der Tat* for Solo Voices, Chorus, and Orch.; piano pieces; male choruses; songs. His 2 operas, *Makkabäus* and *Mohammed*, were publ. but not produced.

Zoras, Leonidas, Greek composer and conductor; b. Sparta, March 8, 1905. He studied law at the Univ. of Athens; at the same time took conducting lessons with Mitropoulos, and studied composition with Kalomiris, Lavrangas, and Riadis. From 1926 to 1938 he taught music theory at the Odeon Music School; from 1938 to 1940 he lived in Berlin, where he took lessons in composition with Grabner and Blacher; in 1940 he returned to Athens and conducted the Athens Opera (1948–58); then took residence in Berlin. He was director of the Athens National Cons. from 1968. He wrote an opera, *Elektra* (1969); the ballet *Violanto* (1931); *Night Song* for Cello Solo and Chamber Orch. (1927); *Legend* for Orch. (1936); Symph. (1947); Concertino for Violin and 11 Woodwind Instruments (1950); String Quartet (1969); Violin Sonata (1950); numerous piano pieces, choruses, and songs.

Zorzor, Ştefan, Rumanian composer; b. Oradea, April 4, 1932. He studied with Chirescu, Negrea, I. Dumitrescu, Ciortea, Andricu, Olah, and Mendelsohn at the Bucharest Cons. (1951–52, 1956–61); then occupied teaching positions in Bucharest.
WORKS: *Ţara mea (My Country)*, cantata for Female Chorus and Small Orch. (1956); Piano Sonata (1959); 3 string quartets (1960, 1962, 1968); Violin Sonata (1963); Concerto for Orch. (1965); *Nocturne* for Orch. (1966); Wind Quintet (1968); *Heteroquintet* for Flute, Violin, Cello, Piano, and Percussion (1969); *Circulara*, experimental music for 5 Different Instruments (1969); *Pièces diverses* for Piano (1967–72); choruses.

Zottmayr, Georg, distinguished German bass; b. Munich, Jan. 24, 1869; d. Dresden, Dec. 11, 1941. He studied in Munich; began his career primarily as a concert singer. In 1906 he made his operatic debut with the Vienna Court Opera; later was a member of the German Theater in Prague (1908–10). In 1910 he joined the Dresden Court (later State) Opera, where he enjoyed a career of great distinction. He was considered one of the outstanding Wagnerians of his time; among his famous roles were King Marke, Hunding, Gurnemanz, Pogner, and Daland.

Zouhar, Zdeněk, Czech composer; b. Kotvrdovice, Feb. 8, 1927. He studied with Jan Kunc (1948–50) and A. Moyzes (1950–51) in Bratislava. He was head of the music dept. of the Brno Univ. library (1953–61); in 1962 was appointed to the faculty of the Janáček

Music Academy in Brno. In his music he makes multifarious use of modern techniques, including a fairly orthodox dodecaphony.
WORKS: *Spring Suite* for 3 Violins (1949); *Prelude and Epilogue* for Solo Cello (1949); *Aulularia*, suite for Chamber Ensemble (1956); *Partita* for Organ (1956); *Prelude* for 2 Pianos (1957); *Midnight Mass* for Soloists, Chorus, Orch., and Organ (1957); *151*, music for Wind Quintet (1958); *Sportovní stránky (Sports Pages)*, suite for Orch. (1959); Trio for Flute, Clarinet, and Bass Clarinet (1961); *3 Studies* for 4 Horns (1963); *Divertimento* for 4 Winds and Percussion (1965); *Variations* for Oboe and Piano (1965); *Music* for Strings (1966); 2 string quartets (1966, 1972); *Symphonic Triptych* (1967; Brno Radio, Nov. 29, 1967); *Music* for Wind Quintet (1968); *Triple Concerto* for Clarinet, Trumpet, Trombone, and Orch. (1970); chamber radio opera, *Metamorphosis* (1971).

Zschocher, Johann, noted German piano pedagogue; b. Leipzig, May 16, 1821. d. there, Jan. 6, 1897. He was a pupil of Iwan Knorr, Th. Kullak, Henselt, and Liszt. In 1846 he founded the Zschocher'sches Musik-Inst. in Leipzig, which became a flourishing music school, still active in the 20th century.

Zsolt, Nándor, Hungarian violinist and composer; b. Esztergom, May 12, 1887; d. Budapest, June 24, 1936. He studied violin with Hubay in Budapest; in 1908 went to London, where he participated in chamber music concerts; returning to Budapest, he became a violin teacher. His Piano Quintet (1914) was awarded a prize. He also wrote a Symph.; many violin pieces (*Valse caprice, Berceuse, Enchaînée, Satyr et Dryade*, etc.).
BIBLIOGRAPHY: Cyril Scott, "Nándor Zsolt," *Monthly Musical Record* (1915).

Zubiaurre (y Urionabarrenechea), Valentí, Spanish composer; b. Villa de Garay, Feb. 13, 1837; d. Madrid, Jan. 13, 1914. He was a chorister at Bilbao; at the age of 16 he undertook a voyage to South America; he returned to Spain in 1866, and took music lessons with Hilarión Eslava. He wrote a considerable number of sacred works; then turned to opera; received first national prize with his opera *Fernando el Emplazado* (Madrid, May 12, 1871). In 1875, he was named 2nd maestro at the Royal Chapel in Madrid, and in 1878 succeeded Eslava as first maestro; in the same year he was appointed a prof. at the Madrid Cons. His 2nd opera, *Ledia*, was produced with considerable success in Madrid, on April 22, 1877. He also composed several zarzuelas; a Symph.; a potpourri of Basque folk songs; choruses.

Zucca, Mana. See **Mana-Zucca.**

Zuccalmaglio, Anton Wilhelm Florentin von, German collector of folk songs and writer on music; b. Waldbröl, April 12, 1803; d. Nachrodt, near Grüna, Westphalia, March 23, 1869. The son of a physician who was a musical amateur, he learned music at

home; contributed to the *Neue Zeitschrift für Musik* during Schumann's editorship, under the pseudonyms **Wilhelm von Waldbrühl** and **Dorfküster Wedel**; publ. 2 collections of folk songs, in 1829 and 1836 (with E. Baumstark); then brought out (with A. Kretzschmer) the important compilation *Deutsche Volkslieder mit ihren Originalweisen* (2 vols., 1838, 1840; reprint, Hildesheim, 1969). However, these songs are only partly authentic; a few melodies were composed by Zuccalmaglio himself; others were combined from various sources; the texts were frequently rearranged. Brahms made use of the collection for his arrangements of German folk songs.
BIBLIOGRAPHY: M. Friedlaender, "Zuccalmaglio und das Volkslied," *Jahrbuch der Bibliothek Peters* (1918); W. Wiora, "Die Herkunft der Melodien in Kretzschmers und Zuccalmaglios Sammlung," *Jahrbuch für Volksliedforschung* (1941), revised and publ. as *Die rheinisch-bergischen Melodien bei Zuccalmaglio und Brahms* (Bad Godesberg, 1953).

Zuchert, Leon, Russian-born Canadian composer; b. Poltava, May 4, 1904. He emigrated to Canada in 1929; played viola in several orchs. in Canada and the U.S.; was principal violinist and assistant conductor of the Halifax Symph. Orch. (1963–65, 1967–69). He is autodidactic as a composer.
WORKS: *My Canadian Travels* for Orch. (1938); 2 symphs. (1948–50, 1959–62); *Quetico,* symph. suite (1957); *Oriental Romance* for Small Orch. (1960); *Dniepr,* cantata (1961); *Song in Brass* for Voice, Solo Viola, and Orch. without Woodwinds (1964); *Divertimento Orientale* for Oboe and String Orch. (1965); *2 Moods in One* for String Orch. (1968); *My Paintings* for String Orch. (1969); *Impressions of Teneriffe,* symph. suite (1970); *Fantasia on Ukrainian Themes* for Orch. (1973); *In the Gleam of Northern Lights,* choreographic oratorio (1974); *2 Spanish Meditations* for Orch. or Piano (1975); 3 string quartets (1965, 1971, 1972); *Little Prince in Montreal* for Wind Quintet (1968); *Psychedelic Suite* for Brass Quintet (1968); *Short Suite* for Trumpet or Clarinet or Viola, and Piano (1974); *Suite* for Solo Bassoon (1975); Concerto for Bassoon and String Orch. (1976); *Elegy* for Orch. (1977).

Zuelli, Guglielmo, Italian composer; b. Reggio Emilia, Oct. 20, 1859; d. Milan, Oct. 8, 1941. He studied with A. Busi and L. Mancinelli in Bologna; after teaching and conducting in various provincial towns, he became director of the Cons. in Palermo (1894–1911), of the Parma Cons. (1911–29), and of the Liceo Musicale of Alessandria, Piedmont (1929–33); then retired.
WORKS: Opera, *La Fata del Nord* (Milan, May 4, 1884; Sonzogno prize); opera-ballet, *Il Profeta di Korassan; Inno alla notte* for Solo Voices, Chorus, and Orch.; 2 symphs.; *Un saluto al mare,* symph. suite (its 3rd movement, *Festa delle sirene,* became extremely popular as a separate piece); *Il canto del Coaro Romagnuolo* for Orch.; String Quartet; minor pieces for strings; fugues for organ; songs; etc.

He publ. *Gioacchino Rossini: Pagine segrete* (Bologna, 1922).

Zukerman, Eugenia, American flutist; b. Cambridge, Mass., Sept. 25, 1944. She studied flute with Julius Baker at the Juilliard School of Music in N.Y.; made her formal recital debut at Town Hall in N.Y. in 1971, and subsequently appeared as a chamber music player throughout the U.S. She married the violinist and conductor **Pinchas Zukerman,** with whom she toured Europe as a soloist with the English Chamber Orch.; she also authored a novel deceptively called *Deceptive Cadence.*

Zukerman, Pinchas, outstanding Israeli violinist, violist, and conductor; b. Tel Aviv, July 16, 1948. He began to study music with his father, taking up the violin at age 6; he then enrolled at the Cons. in Tel Aviv, where he studied with Ilona Feher. With the encouragement of Isaac Stern and Pablo Casals, he became a scholarship student at the Juilliard School of Music in N.Y., where he studied with Ivan Galamian (1961–67). In 1967 he won first prize in the Leventritt Competition in N.Y., and then launched a brilliant career as a soloist with the major American and European orchs. He also appeared as both violinist and violist in recitals with Isaac Stern and Itzhak Perlman. He subsequently devoted part of his time to conducting, appearing as a guest conductor with the N.Y. Phil., Philadelphia Orch., Boston Symph., Los Angeles Phil., and many others. In 1980 he became music director of the St. Paul Chamber Orch. He married the American flutist **Eugenia Zukerman.** His performances as a violinist are distinguished by their innate emotional élan and modern virtuoso technique.

Zukofsky, Paul, remarkable American violinist; b. Brooklyn, Oct. 22, 1943. Reared in an acutely intellectual environment (his father was a poet who experimented in highly complex verbal forms), he began playing the violin at the age of 4 on a quarter-size instrument; was soloist with the New Haven Symph. at the age of 8. At 16 he entered the Juilliard School of Music, where he studied with Ivan Galamian. From his earliest years he was fascinated by ultramodern music and developed maximal celerity, dexterity, and alacrity in manipulating special techniques, in effect transforming the violin into a multimedia instrument beyond its normal capacities. In 1969 he inaugurated in N.Y. a concert series, Music for the Twentieth Century Violin, performing works often requiring acrobatic coordination. His repertoire includes all 4 violin sonatas by Charles Ives, the violin concertos by William Schuman and Roger Sessions, *Capriccio* by Penderecki, etc. As a violin instructor, he held the post of Creative Associate at the Buffalo Center of the Creative and Performing Arts; also taught at the Berkshire Music Center in Tanglewood and at the New England Cons. of Music. In 1970 his father publ. a novel, *Little,* dealing with the trials and triumphs of a violin *wunderkind.*

Zulauf, Ernst, German conductor; b. Kassel, Feb. 15, 1876; d. Wiesbaden, Jan. 28, 1963. He studied with Carl Reinecke at the Leipzig Cons., and with Kretzschmar at the Univ. of Leipzig; after graduation he devoted himself mainly to opera conducting. He was conductor at the State Theater in Kassel (1903–27)· then in a similar engagement at Wiesbaden (1927–46); he then retired. He composed some orch. works, piano pieces, and songs.

Zulauf, Max, Swiss musicologist; b. Bern, May 19, 1898; d. there, Aug. 3, 1980. He studied with Ernst Kurth at the Univ. of Bern, receiving his Ph.D. with the dissertation *Die Harmonik J.S. Bachs* (Bern, 1927); taught there (1933–48). He publ. *Der Musikunterricht in der Geschichte des bernischen Schulwesens von 1528–1798* (Bern, 1934).

Zumbro, Nicholas, American pianist; b. Murfreesboro, Tenn., Sept. 25, 1935. He studied with Johana Harris in Nashville, and later with Rosina Lhévinne at the Juilliard School in N.Y., obtaining his M.A. in 1960. He began his career with a successful American tour in 1963.

Zumpe, Herman, German conductor and composer; b. Oppach, April 9, 1850; d. Munich, Sept. 4, 1903. He studied in Bautzen and Leipzig. In 1873 he joined Wagner at Bayreuth, aiding in the preparation of the performances of *Der Ring des Nibelungen;* then conducted opera in Salzburg, Würzburg, Madgeburg, Frankfurt, and Hamburg. After some years spent in teaching and composing, he was appointed court conductor in Stuttgart in 1891; in 1895 was called to Munich to become conductor of the Kaim Orch.; then was court conductor in Schwerin (1897–1900); returned to Munich in 1900 as Generalmusikdirektor.
WORKS: Opera, *Anahna* (Berlin, 1881); operettas: *Farinelli* (Hamburg, 1886); *Karin* (Hamburg, 1888); *Polnische Wirtschaft* (Hamburg, 1889); overtures; songs. Two operas were perf. posthumously: *Sawitri* (completed by Rössler; Schwerin, Sept. 8, 1907) and *Das Gespenst von Horodin* (Hamburg, 1910).
BIBLIOGRAPHY: *H. Zumpe. Persönliche Erinnerungen nebst Mitteilungen aus seinen Tagebuchblättern und Briefen,* with an introduction by E. von Possart and a list of works (Munich, 1905).

Zumsteeg, Johann Rudolf, German composer; b. Sachsenflur, Odenwald, Jan. 10, 1760; d. Stuttgart, Jan. 27, 1802. As a pupil at the Karlsschule (near Stuttgart), he was a classmate of Schiller. He studied cello and theory with Poli, whom he succeeded in 1791 as director of the Stuttgart Opera. He produced 8 operas at Stuttgart, of which the best was *Die Geisterinsel,* after Shakespeare's *The Tempest* (Nov. 7, 1798); among his other operas were *Elbondokani, Zalaor,* and *Das Pfauenfest;* he also wrote choruses to Schiller's *Die Räuber;* 21 church cantatas; a Cello Concerto; duos for cellos, and other instrumental music. But it is chiefly as the precursor of Loewe and Schubert in the composition of art

songs that he is historically important; he wrote 20 ballades for Solo Voice with Piano Accompaniment, including settings for Schiller's *Maria Stuart,* Bürger's *Lenore,* Goethe's *Colma,* etc.
BIBLIOGRAPHY: T.F.K. Arnold, *J.R. Zumsteeg. Seine kurze Biographie* (Erfurt, 1810; with a list of works); idem, *Gallerie der berühmtesten Tonkünstler* (part I, pp. 44–96; analysis of *Die Geisterinsel);* L. Landshoff, *J.R. Zumsteeg: Ein Beitrag zur Geschichte des Liedes und der Ballade* (Diss., Univ. of Berlin, 1902); A. Sandberger, "Zumsteeg und Schubert," *Münchner Allgemeine Zeitung* (July 15, 1906); H. von Hase, "J.R. Zumsteeg," *Zeitschrift für Musikwissenschaft,* 2 (1920); F. Szymichowski, *J.R. Zumsteeg als Komponist von Balladen und Monodien* (Diss., Univ. of Stuttgart, 1932).

Zundel, John, German-American hymn writer; b. Hochdorf, Germany, Dec. 10, 1815; d. Cannstadt, Germany, July 1882. He was an organist and bandmaster in St. Petersburg, Russia; in 1847 went to America, where he became organist at the Central Methodist Episcopal Church in N.Y. He went back to Germany in 1877. In America he edited the *Monthly Choir and Organ Journal;* was also one of the compilers, in association with Henry Ward Beecher, of the *Plymouth Collection* (1855). He wrote the celebrated hymn *Love Divine,* also known as *Beecher* or *Zundel;* it is included in *Zundel's Christian Heart Songs* (1870).
BIBLIOGRAPHY: R.G. McCutchan, *Our Hymnody* (N.Y., 1937).

Zupko, Ramon, American composer; b. Pittsburgh, Nov. 14, 1932. He studied composition with Persichetti and piano with Gordon Stanley at the Juilliard School of Music (1954–57; M.M.); took a course with Schiske at the Hochschule für Musik in Vienna (1958–59); was director of the Studio for Electronic and Experimental Music at Roosevelt Univ. in Chicago (1967–71), and later was in charge of an experimental studio at Western Michigan Univ. His highly advanced compositions, beginning in 1965, are the only ones for which he encourages performance.
WORKS: *Elegy* for String Orch. (1957); *Ballade* for Orch. (1957); *Introduction and Bagatelle* for 10 Instruments (1957); ballet, *The Lottery* (1957); *Short Sonata* for Violin and Piano (1958); Piano Trio (1958); Piano Sonata (1959–60); *Prologue, Aria and Dance* for Horn and String Orch. (1961); *Variations* for Orch. (1961); *This Is the Garden* for Chorus, Strings, Solo Winds, and Percussion (1962); Violin Concerto (1962; winner of first prize in the 1965 City of Trieste International Composition Contest); ballet, *Gilgamesh* (1963); *Centroids* for Orch. (1963); *Reflexions* for 8 Instruments (1964); *Winter 64* for Piano (1964; revised 1966); *La Guerre* for Soprano, Piano, Vibraphone, Clarinet, and 2 Percussion Groups (1965); *Conversions* for Wind Band and Percussion (1966); *Translucents* for String Orch. (1967); *Tangents* for 18 Brasses (1967); multimedia score, *3rd Planet from the Sun,* for Dancers, Tape, Musicians, Film, and Slides (1969–70); *Emulations* for

Zur Mühlen – Zweig

Piano and Synthesizer (1969); *Radiants* for Orch. (1971); *Trichromes* for Winds, Percussion, and Tape (1973); *Masques* for Piano and Brass Quintet (1973); *Fixations* for Piano, Violin, Cello, and Tape (1974); Bicentennial multimedia musical theater, *Proud Music of the Storm,* for Orch., 2 Bands, Chorus, Dancers, Films, Slides, and Tape, with costumes and sets (1975–76; Western Michigan Univ., Kalamazoo, Dec. 4, 1976); *Fluxus I* for Tape (1977); *Nocturnes* for 2 Pianos (1977); pieces for symph. band; choruses.

Zur Mühlen, Raimund von, tenor; b. Livonia, Nov. 10, 1854; d. Steyning, Sussex, Dec. 9, 1931. He studied singing with Stockhausen in Frankfurt and with Bussine in Paris; then took a special course with Clara Schumann, who instructed him in the interpretation of songs by Schumann and Schubert; this gave him the foundation of his career. He had his greatest success in England, where he lived from 1905 till his death. It was he who introduced into London the "song recital" (*Liederabend;* programs devoted exclusively to songs). He was also a fine teacher.
BIBLIOGRAPHY: D. von Zur Mühlen, *Der Sänger Raimund von Zur Mühlen* (Hannover, 1969).

Zur Nieden, Albrecht, German composer; b. Emmerich, March 6, 1819; d. Duisburg, April 14, 1873. He studied theology in Bonn, and music with Fr. Schneider at Dessau. In 1850 he settled in Duisburg as a choral conductor. He wrote the "lyrico-dramatic song" *Die Sage von der Martinswand* for Solo Voices, Chorus, and Orch., and 2 more works of a similar nature, *Der blinde König* and *Das Grab im Busento;* also a *Deutscher Marsch* for Piano, 4-hands; songs.

Zuschneid, Karl, German choral conductor; b. Oberglogau, Silesia, May 29, 1854; d. Weimar, Aug. 1, 1926. He studied piano and composition at the Stuttgart Cons.; occupied various posts as a choral conductor and teacher in Göttingen (1879–89), Minden (1889–97), and Erfurt (1897–1907); was director of the Hochschule für Musik in Mannheim; retired in 1917.
WORKS: For Chorus and Orch.: *Hermann der Befreier; Lenzfahrt; Sängergebet; Deutschlands Erwachen; Die Zollern und das Reich; Unter den Sternen;* men's choruses; *Konzertstück* for Violin and Orch.; piano pieces; songs. He publ. *Theoretisch-praktische Klavierschule* and *Methodischer Leitfaden für den Klavierunterricht* (2nd ed., Berlin, 1947).

Zuth, Josef, Austrian guitarist and musicologist; b. Fischern, near Karlsbad, Nov. 24, 1879; d. Vienna, Aug. 30, 1932. He began to study music late in life; studied guitar with R. Batka; attended classes in musicology under Adler and Koczirz at the Univ. of Vienna; received his Dr.Phil. degree in 1919 with the dissertation *Simon Molitor und die wiener Gitarristik.* He taught the guitar at the Volksschule Urania in Vienna (from 1919) and edited (from 1921) the *Zeitschrift für die Gitarre* (in 1927 the title was changed to *Musik im Haus*); edited many works for the guitar; publ. several guitar manuals: *R. Batkas Vorschule des Gitarren- und Lautenspiels* (1919); *Das künstlerische Gitarrenspiel* (1920); *Die Gitarre, Spezialstudien auf theoretischer Grundlage* (6 parts; 1920); *F. Carullis Gitarrenschule* (10 parts; 1921); *Volkstümliche Gitarrenschule* (1922); *Handbuch der Laute und Gitarre* (Vienna, 1926–28).

Zverev, Nicolai, Russian pianist and noted pedagogue; b. Volokamsk, 1832; d. Moscow, Oct. 12, 1893. He was a student of Alexander Dubuc in Moscow and Henselt in St. Petersburg; also took harmony lessons with Tchaikovsky. He established in Moscow a music boarding school for young pianists; among these inmates were Rachmaninoff and Siloti. Scriabin also took piano lessons with Zverev, although he did not lodge in his music school. From 1870 to his death, Zverev taught piano at the Moscow Cons. Zverev was highly esteemed as a pedagogue, and was one of the most prominent representatives of the Russian pianistic method, which emphasized songful melody and freedom of hand movement.

Zvonař, Joseph Leopold, Czech organist and theorist; b. Kublov, near Prague, Jan. 22, 1824; d. Prague, Nov. 23, 1865. He studied at the Prague School for Organists, and taught there from 1844; also served as a church organist. He publ. the first treatise on harmony in the Czech language; contributed articles on Czech music to various publications; publ. a valuable collection of choral arrangements of national songs, *Hudební památky české* (4 vols., 1862–64); composed *Der Ritt zum Elfenstein* for Solo Voices, Chorus, and Orch.; a Requiem; piano pieces (*Impromptu, Loreley,* etc.); men's choruses; songs. His opera *Záboj* remains unperformed.

Zweers, Bernard, Netherlandish composer; b. Amsterdam, May 18, 1854; d. there, Dec. 9, 1924. He studied at the Amsterdam Cons., and later in Leipzig with Jadassohn; returning to the Netherlands, he became a prof. of theory at the Amsterdam Cons. (from 1895). He wrote 3 symphs.; *Kroningscantate* for Soprano, Tenor, Chorus, and Orch.; *St. Nicolasfeest,* children's cantata; *Kosmos* (Psalm 104) for Chorus and Orch.; *Ons Hollandsch* for Men's Chorus and Orch.; church music; songs.
BIBLIOGRAPHY: H. Rutters, "Bernard Zweers," *Mens en Melodie* (Dec. 1949).

Zweig, Fritz, Bohemian-born American conductor; b. Olmütz (Olomouc), Sept. 8, 1893; d. Los Angeles, Feb. 28, 1984. He studied theory with Schoenberg in Vienna; in 1913 was appointed choral coach at the Mannheim National Theater; in 1919 became assistant conductor at Barmen-Elberfeld; in 1923 was conductor at the Volksoper in Berlin; and in 1927 was appointed to the conducting staff of the Städtische Oper in Berlin. With the usurpation of power by the Nazis in 1933, Zweig went to Prague, where he conducted at the German Opera from 1934–38. When Prague, too, was captured by the Nazis, he went to Paris; after the fall of France in 1940, he emigrated to America. In 1947 he settled in Hollywood as a private music teacher.

Zwilich, Ellen Taaffe, American composer; b. Miami, Fla., April 30, 1939. She studied at Florida State Univ., graduating in 1960 (M.M., 1962); then moved to N.Y.; took violin lessons with Ivan Galamian; enrolled at the Juilliard School of Music in N.Y., and had semi-weekly sessions with Sessions there; was the first woman to receive a doctorate in composition from that school (1975). In 1983 she received a Pulitzer Prize for her composition, initially entitled *3 Movements for Orchestra,* and later renamed Symph. No. 1, first performed in N.Y. on May 5, 1982. This was the first time that a woman composer received a Pulitzer Prize.
WORKS: *Einsame Nacht,* after Hesse, song cycle for Baritone and Piano (1971); *Im Nebel,* after Hesse, for Contralto and Piano (1972); *Symposium* for Orch. (1972–73; Juilliard Orch., Jan. 31, 1975, Pierre Boulez conducting); *Impromptus* for Solo Harp (1973); Violin Sonata (1973); *Trompeten* for Soprano and Piano (1974); *Allison* for Chamber Ensemble (1974); String Quartet (1974); *Clarino Quartet* for 4 Trumpets (1977); Violin Concerto (1975–77).

Zwintscher, Bruno, German pianist and pedagogue; b. Ziegenhain, May 15, 1838; d. Oberlössnitz, near Dresden, March 4, 1905. He studied piano with Julius Otto in Dresden and with Moscheles in Leipzig; also took lessons with Plaidy. He subsequently taught piano at the Leipzig Cons. (1875–96); then settled in Dresden, where he became a successful piano teacher. He publ. the manual *Klavier-Technik,* which became extremely successful; it was also publ. in Eng. under the title *Technical Exercises Systematically.* He further publ. *Musikalische Verzierungen,* which contains practical exercises and theoretical notations pertaining to the proper performance of ornamentation.

Zwyssig, Alberich, Swiss composer; b. Bauen, Nov. 17, 1808; d. in the Cistercian monastery at Mehrerau, Nov. 18, 1854. He entered the order of the Cistercians in 1826, giving up his real name, **Joseph,** for the monastic name Alberich; he was Kapellmeister in the monasteries of Wettingen, Zug, Wurmbach, and (shortly before his death) Mehrerau. His *Schweizer Psalm* for Men's Chorus a cappella (1841) attained great popularity, and in 1961 it was named as a *pro tempore* national anthem of Switzerland. He further composed many sacred and secular choruses, and church music with organ accompaniment.
BIBLIOGRAPHY: B. Widmann, *Alberich Zwyssig als Komponist* (Bregenz, 1905); H. Meng, *Alberich Zwyssig, 1808–1854; Gedenkschrift* (Wettingen, 1954).

Zykan, Otto M., Austrian pianist and composer; b. Vienna, April 29, 1935. He studied piano and composition at the Vienna Academy of Music; in 1958 won first prize at the Darmstadt Competition for young pianists and started on a successful concert career, specializing in modern music. His own compositions reveal a strong influence of Anton von Webern, but he does not exclude tonal, and even triadic, combinations, and accepts formal periodicity in structure. His compositions include String Quartet (1956); *Loblied der Kreaturen,* cantata (1961); *3 Sätze* for Percussion, Wind Instruments, and Piano (1962).

Zylis-Gara, Teresa, Polish soprano; b. Landvarov, Jan. 23, 1935. She studied voice in Lodz; in 1957 made her debut with the Cracow Opera; then sang in Oberhausen, Dortmund, Düsseldorf, Vienna, and Salzburg. On Dec. 17, 1968, she made her Metropolitan Opera debut in N.Y. as Elvira in *Don Giovanni;* she sang there in subsequent seasons with much success; also made appearances as a concert artist.